CASSELL'S
ENGLISH & GERMAN
DICTIONARY

The New CASSELL'S GERMAN DICTIONARY

GERMAN-ENGLISH ENGLISH-GERMAN

Based on the editions
by KARL BREUL
Completely revised
and re-edited by
HAROLD T. BETTERIDGE
M.A. (BIRMINGHAM); Ph.D. (LONDON)
SENIOR LECTURER IN GERMAN AT THE
UNIVERSITY OF GLASGOW

With a Foreword by
GERHARD CORDES, Dr. phil.
Professor of Niederdeutsche Sprache und Literatur
at the University of Kiel

FUNK & WAGNALLS
NEW YORK

Library of Congress Catalog Card Number: 58-7924

THE NEW CASSELL'S GERMAN DICTIONARY

Printed in the United States of America

ISBN 0-308-10002-6 (Plain)
0-308-10018-2 (Indexed)

19 20 21 22 23 24 25

CONTENTS

FOREWORD

A CORDIAL welcome must be extended to the new edition of the familiar old 'Breul' which had recently shown some signs of advanced age. Completely revised by an English scholar with a thorough knowledge of the German language, this dictionary can now once again take its traditional place among the great dictionaries.

Dictionaries arranged alphabetically will always remain indispensable, notwithstanding the fact that modern linguistics is increasingly concerned with the organic structure of language according to subject and substance. Nor can alphabetical dictionaries ever be superseded as auxiliaries in the task of interpreting one civilization and one nation to another. For the greater part of the German people as well as for a growing number of English-speaking peoples, the English and German languages are, more than ever before, the main pillars of the bridge leading to mutual understanding. This bridge must be kept in constant repair.

To-day many fresh demands are made upon the compiler of a dictionary. It is no longer enough that he should be fully conversant with the present-day standard of the language. He must not merely bring the vocabulary up to date nor must he confine himself to the definition of a word as such, but he has to take into account its meaning within a given context and its idiomatic variations. This aspect of the language as a living organism has particularly been borne in mind in the present dictionary, which should prove a veritable mine of information for English and German readers alike.

Careful notice has also been taken of those subdivisions of speech which of recent years have claimed the attention of philologists, such as the colloquialisms used within certain social groups (family, school, etc.), and the vernacular of professions and trades (nautical speech, printers' jargon, etc.). Serious attention has been given to the extent to which the standard language is continually being enriched by words and idioms assimilated from the various dialects. To all these concerns of modern linguistics Cassell's Dictionary has been responsive. Ample space has been given to regional and vocational terms, familiar turns of speech, and even slang expressions.

But the new 'Betteridge' does not only serve the everyday requirements of ordinary speech; it is equally helpful to the translator grappling with serious literature, the learner and student of the language, the modern-language master, and the scientist. It is to be hoped that this dictionary will find its way to the shelves of all those who in their various ways can be expected to benefit from its riches.

GERHARD CORDES

PREFACE

CASSELL'S German Dictionary has a long history. Whether the *New German Dictionary*, by Elizabeth Weir, published in 1889, was actually a first edition or whether it was based on an older one must remain a mystery, as the publisher's records were destroyed by fire in 1941. Elizabeth Weir made no reference to an earlier version, claiming only that hers was based on now forgotten works like 'the well-known dictionaries of Lucas, Flügel, Hilpert, and Köhler'. This in itself constitutes no proof that she was Cassell's first editor, for subsequently there has always been editorial reticence about one's predecessors.

The aim and the layout of the work have remained virtually unchanged since this, the first edition accessible to me, though its size and usefulness has developed with the passage of years. There were four reissues before 1896, and ten years later it appeared 'revised and considerably enlarged by K. Breul'. In 1909 Professor Breul assumed sole responsibility for it, and between that date and his death in 1932 it was reprinted with revisions sixteen times. He had completed a substantial re-editing of the German–English section when he died, and the task of seeing this through the press and the work on the English–German section was left to J. H. Lepper and R. Kottenhahn. The parts were issued separately in 1936 and 1939, and combined into one volume in 1940, since when it has continued unchanged.

Though the work had tried to keep pace with the changing times by introducing numerous terms from the fields of commerce, science, motoring, aviation, etc., it had become clear that no amount of patching would make it into a comprehensive modern dictionary. Much of the material included still bore the stamp of the sources to which Miss Weir acknowledged her indebtedness, and which must have seen the light of day nearly one hundred years ago. So in 1948 the publishers decided that the time had come for a complete overhaul, and the task was entrusted to me.

The work has to all intents and purposes been rewritten. Each entry has been scrutinized for its relevance to learners and users of German in the post-war world, and it is my hope that for some years to come it will continue to serve them with the same degree of efficiency as Professor Breul's editions have done for the past forty and more years. Miss Weir's and Professor Breul's work was originally designed to appeal particularly to the learners in schools and universities at a time when German was just making its appearance in the curriculum, and as such it had a distinctly literary bias. Those who wish to read the classical works of German literature are of course still catered for, though for such things as Lessing's use of eighteenth-century chess terminology in *Nathan* recourse should properly be had to notes and glossary rather than to a general dictionary. The German language now interests a far wider range of students than it did before the first world war: scientists of various sorts, economists, engineers, lawyers even, and in recent years many who would not call themselves students at all—people who for various reasons are in contact with the Germans. Cassell's Dictionary was in fact described to me as 'the Bible of the Control Commission'. I have tried to do justice to these non-literary and semi-specialist claims, as also to the very different demands of modern colloquial usage. While making no pretensions that the lawyer or the chemist will be able to dispense with the specialized works of reference which are available to him, I hope I have succeeded in presenting a general-purpose dictionary which, within the limits imposed by its size, will be satisfactory to all types of users as the primary tool in their struggles with German.

No individual can be completely catholic in his tastes, and my preferences as well as my blind spots will be readily apparent. I have tried to throw my net as widely as my knowledge of German permits, and have been able to call on the advice of a large circle of German friends too numerous to mention. It is usual to cite the other works of reference to which one is indebted, but they are either so well known or, where not, so numerous that the list would be of little practical value. The four-volume Muret–Sanders published in 1908, though very out of date, remains unsurpassed as a large dictionary, and Duden's *Rechtschreibung* is invaluable as the final court of appeal on all orthographical points. Much more useful than a list of authorities will be a guide to the more specialized lexicographical literature, to which users of this dictionary may refer in case of need.

L. de Vries, *English-German and German-English Technical and Engineering Dictionary*, Brandstetter-Verlag, Wiesbaden, 1950–54, is by far the best in this large field. Supplements published in 1959 contain valuable material.

H. Bucksch, *Wörterbuch für Ingenieurbau und Baumaschinen*, 2nd edit. Bauverlag, Wiesbaden, 1959.

L. de Vries and O. M. Jörgensen, *Fachwörterbuch des Kraftfahrzeugwesens*, Brandstetter-Verlag, Wiesbaden, 1957.

H. Rau, *Wörterbuch der Kernphysik*, Brandstetter-Verlag, Wiesbaden, 1957.

H. Ashby, *German-English and English-German Botanical Terminology*, London, Murby, 1938.

M. K. King, *German-English and English-German Photographic Dictionary*, Bailey Bros., 1957.

A. M. Patterson, *German-English Dictionary for Chemists*, 3rd ed., Chapman, 1955.

C. A. Gunston and C. M. Corner, *Deutsch-Englisches Glossarium finanzieller und wirtschaftlicher Fachausdrücke*, Knapp-Verlag, Frankfurt a. Main, 3rd edit. 1958.

Polanyi, *Dictionary of Textile Terms*, Pergamon Press, 1956.

K. H. Eitzen, *Deutsch-Englisches, Englisch-Deutsches Militär-Wörterbuch*, Revised edit., Verlag WEU, Bonn, 1957.

Medical dictionaries are all poor; perhaps the best, though very incomplete and with many bad errors, *L. de Vries, German-English Medical Dictionary*, 1952, and for English-German, F. Lejeune and W. E. Bunjes, *Wörterbuch für Ärzte*, Stuttgart, 1951, 1954 (the German-English volume, Stuttgart, 1951, is poorer than de Vries).

E. Veillon, *Medizinisches Wörterbuch*, Huber, Berne, 3rd edit. 1960, is good on anatomy.

The only really safe course with medical German is to refer to authoritative German sources, such as Pschyrembel, *Klinisches Wörterbuch*, De Gruyter, Berlin, 1959, or M. Zetkin and H. Schaldach, *Wörterbuch der Medizin*, 1956 (an East German publication, automatically despised in the West, but very scholarly and in some respects still the best available).

Finally the series of Multilingual Technical Dictionaries by the Elsevier Publishing Co., Amsterdam. These deal in separate volumes with: Electronics, Nuclear Science, Radar and Telecommunications, Cinema, Automation, Building Construction, Railways, Brewing, Gas, Textiles, Wood, Rubber, etc. The volumes, which in some fields tend to overlap, are painstakingly prepared by impressive authorities.

A word of warning must be given about the increasing use of foreign loanwords in scientific and technical German. Very rarely are the approved connotations exactly the same as in the source-language, and both German users and foreign translators are all too liable to succumb to facile assumptions. The only precise and scholarly work on the subject is *Fremdwörterbuch*, VEB Leipziger Druckhaus, 1958.

Up-to-date information about multi-language reference works useful to specialists can be found in the Book Review Section of *Babel*, the journal of the "Fédération Internationale des Traducteurs." The reviews (signed by initials) are not equally reliable: R. W. J. is very good; G. H., W. F., and P.S.A.C. are always sound; W. E. B. is consistently self-opinionated, biased and perverse.

I must finally pay tribute to the friendly co-operation and unfailing patience with which the publishers have eased my difficulties. Without this encouragement the years of arduous labour would have seemed much longer.

H. T. B.

Note: Certain works mentioned above are also published in the United States—for details see page xii.

L. de Vries, *English-German and German-English Technical and Engineering Dictionary;* also *German-English Medical Dictionary,* McGraw-Hill Book Co., N. Y.

K. H. Eitzen, *Deutsch-Englisches, Englisch-Deutsches Militär-Wörterbuch,* Frederick A. Praeger, N. Y. (under the title *German-English, English-German Military Dictionary*).

F. Lejeune and W. E. Bunjes, *Wörterbuch für Ärzte,* Grune & Stratton, N. Y. (under the title *Dictionary for Physicians,* 2 volumes).

Muret and Sanders, *Encyclopedic Dictionary, German and English,* 2 volumes, Frederick Ungar, N. Y.

A. M. Patterson, *German-English Dictionary for Chemists,* John Wiley, N. Y.

M. Polanyi, *Dictionary of Textile Terms, German-English,* Pergamon Press, N. Y.

H. Rau, *Wörterbuch der Kernphysik,* Albert Daub, N. Y. (under the title *English-German, German-English Dictionary of Nuclear Physics*).

ADVICE TO THE USER

GROUPING OF WORDS. Alphabetical order sounds as if it should be a simple criterion. Particularly in German, with its many compounds, this produces a mere word-list which is both unsatisfactory and awkward. *Trinkbar* would precede *trinken*, and *Lehramt* precede *lehren* and *Lehrer*, whereas the basic verb contains the obvious root idea round which the extensions should be grouped. It is not always easy to find a satisfactory compromise between alphabetic word-list and a grouping of related words, but with the help of cross-references from the alphabetic position to the group it is hoped that no great difficulty will be experienced in finding any word. No attempt has been made to distinguish between derivative words, i.e. words formed by terminations such as *trinkbar*, *arbeitsam*, &c., and compound words such as *Trinkhalle*, *Arbeitsgemeinschaft*, &c. It is felt that, real though such a distinction is, it is only likely to be apparent to users who have a linguistic training. Within each entry all extensions of the key-word, or of the significant part of the key-word, are dealt with in alphabetical order.

NUMBERING OF IDENTICAL KEY-WORDS. Key-words which are spelt alike, but which differ in meaning and origin, are kept separate. Thus, *Falle* (= trap) is not mixed up with the entry under *Fall* (= fall; case). When there is complete identity in the spelling of different key-words, they are numbered.

PUNCTUATION. In earlier editions the editor claimed that, when several synonyms were given, all answering to one sense of a word, they were separated by commas, while those representing different senses were separated by semicolons. In practice such a clear distinction as that shown by the example cited could be achieved only rarely. Many lists of equivalents show a gradual shift in meaning and usage, and in such cases the use of commas and semicolons becomes practically meaningless. Where clear demarcation in meaning or usage can be established, the semicolon is still used; otherwise a comma is preferred.

GENDER AND FORM OF NOUNS. In the English–German section nouns are preceded by the definite article to denote the gender. In a list of nouns the same definite article is not repeated, so the user must refer back to the article last mentioned. When an adjective precedes a noun, no article is used and the gender is indicated by the adjectival ending. German masculine nouns indicating an agent or doer of the action regularly form the corresponding feminine by the addition of *-in*. As a rule in such cases only the masculine form is given. In fact, in the German–English section even such masculine nouns will often be looked for in vain, as it is presumed that the user will be able to add the suffix *-er* to the verbal root without further guidance. Wherever guidance is needed, the word will be found, e.g. *Bauer*, entailing change of meaning, or *Jäger*, with change of the verbal root. In the case of German masculine nouns whose terminations vary according to the qualifying article or adjective, the word is given as *Beamte*(*r*), *m.*, signifying *der Beamte, ein Beamter*. When the same form of German noun is used for both the masculine and feminine, it is given as *Vertraute*(*r*), *m. & f.*, signifying *der Vertraute, ein Vertrauter, die* and *eine Vertraute.*

ADVERBIAL FORMS. English adverbial forms ending in '-ly' have generally been omitted when they correspond exactly to the adjectival meaning.

USE OF BRACKETS. Brackets are used in various ways.

(1) They enclose words or parts of words which may be omitted or included without changing the sense. Thus, (*Blut*)*Ader* signifies that both *Ader* and *Blutader* may be used with exactly the same meaning (= vein).

(2) They enclose parts of words which, while not altering the sense, do by their inclusion or omission give forms which are used in different contexts. Thus, 'electric(al)' as the equivalent of *elektrisch* means either 'electric' or 'electrical' without implying that these forms are interchangeable, for 'electric bell' and 'electrical engineer' are the only correct forms. Similarly, '(air)screw' for *Flügelschraube* indicates that both 'screw' and 'airscrew' are permissible translations, though a larger dictionary would be able to make clear that 'screw' is correct on a ship and 'airscrew' on an aeroplane. The illustrative examples following the equivalents will commonly place the correct usage beyond doubt.

(3) When a word or phrase enclosed in brackets in one language is followed by a word or phrase in brackets in the other language, the contents of the one bracket are to be understood as translating the contents of the other. Thus, *Gutes* (*Böses*) *tun* = to do good (evil) is merely a space-saving means of giving the alternative readings.

(4) In order to supply information about correct grammatical usage. Thus, (*Acc.*), (*Dat.*), or (*Gen.*) following a word mean that it governs this case; or (*a th. to a p.*, einem etwas) after a word such as *gewähren* indicates that German requires the accusative of the thing granted and dative for the person to whom it is granted, the dative form preceding the accusative.

(5) In order to indicate the range of usage of a word with the help of

the appropriate abbreviation in italics. Thus, (*Av.*) limits the word preceding it to an aeronautical, and (*Arch.*) to an architectural context. See the List of Abbreviations below.

(6) In order to indicate the stratum of language to which a word belongs. Some discussion of what is implied by these designations is perhaps necessary, since there are no hard-and-fast dividing lines.

(i) (*archaic*) is self-explanatory; it may be thought that a modern dictionary need give no place to such forms, but archaic should not be identified with obsolete, and archaic forms have their rightful place in current English, e.g. in legal phraseology, in stock phrases, and other proper contexts.

(ii) (*Poet.*) may often be much the same as (*archaic*). Again their inclusion may be criticized, but whenever the poetry may have been written, as long as it is still read its forms may rightly claim their place in a modern dictionary. The indication should, however, be taken as a warning that the form is no longer part of the living language.

(iii) (*B.*), indicating biblical language, may be viewed as similar to (ii). There is, however, the further consideration that the Bible has had such an enormous influence on the development of modern English, and many of these forms have become deeply embedded in the language in contexts which are not biblical.

(iv) (*coll.*) indicates language that would not be used in dignified prose or formal speech or even in conversation with respected strangers. It would be normal in polite conversation with one's equals.

(v) (*sl.*) marks language which I would only use in an intimate circle. I would not invariably shun it as bad, but would restrict it to circumstances, as in the family or among close friends, where there is no suggestion of wanting to make a good impression.

(vi) (*vulg.*) marks language which it is embarrassing to hear in mixed company or in public generally. The inclusion of these forms may perhaps be criticized, but with the relaxing of standards in recent years it is scarcely possible to open a modern novel without meeting vulgarisms. They even have their proper place in modern speech. I hold it is better to give them, properly indicated, than to pretend that they do not exist or that one does not know of their existence.

In so far as it is possible, I have tried to give a rendering which is from approximately the same layer of language, even though it is sometimes necessary, in order to avoid ambiguity, to give a more conventional equivalent as well.

(vii) (*dial.*) In the German–English section many more dialect forms have been included than earlier editions, which had a distinct North German bias, thought fit to include. Many Germans from the North, and most English learners, who accept North German as standard, may be inclined to criticize this. I make no excuse for it, though some explanation is perhaps necessary. It is characteristic of the Germans that an idea, pursued long and earnestly enough, becomes more real than reality. So it was with the idea that a united Germany ought to have an accepted standard language. Prussia, the dominant partner in the political unification, more or less dictated the linguistic criteria. Nevertheless, what is described as standard German (*Schriftsprache*, *Hochsprache*, *Gemeinsprache*, *Einheitssprache*) remained an unrealized ideal, or at best the lowest common denominator of the various forms of language used by Germans over the wide language-area. In its printed form, to be sure, a superficial standardization was imposed by the Leipzig typographers. However, in Hamburg, Cologne, Stuttgart, Munich, Zürich, Vienna, educated German-speakers continue to use language which in vocabulary and phonology is very different from this standard. In Zürich and Vienna, and in Munich to some extent at least, there is even no willingness to acknowledge the validity of the standard, for the educated classes there are convinced that their language has as much right as that of the Northerners to be considered good German. Such a realistic view of the language is only slowly finding acceptance; anyone who is interested may find a considered discussion of the whole problem in Walter Henzen's *Schriftsprache und Mundarten* (1954). In the dictionary I have attempted to give a broad survey of German as it exists and is used today, and not only in bookish contexts. The addition of (*dial.*) to an entry indicates that the form has merely local validity, and should be taken as a warning by those who wish to impose a criterion. Further specification has only been possible in the case of Austrian and Swiss forms, of which I have some first-hand experience. It may with justice be protested that (*dial.*) is not a fair description of words from Low German, which some hold to be a language in its own right. It is used here solely in the interest of simplicity. In the English–German section little attempt has been made to introduce dialect forms, for dialect in English implies much more clearly a deviation from the accepted norm of standard English. The only exception is in the case of some Scottish words, for the Scots feel about their language much in the same way as do the Austrians or the Swiss. These inclusions will doubtless not satisfy a Scot as being properly representative, but they are those words which are familiar to an Englishman through some years' residence in Scotland.

PRONUNCIATION. The International Phonetic Transcription is, somewhat simplified, used to indicate pronunciation. The stress mark precedes the syllable which carries the stress.

In the German–English section the pronunciation is only given for words which do not conform to the normal rules, i.e. words of French origin which still keep the French pronunciation, or which combine

German sounds with French stress. In the case of the dialect words included, no attempt is made to indicate the characteristic dialectal vocalization. This can be represented at best very inadequately by means of graphic symbols.

In the English–German section pronunciation is given for all key-words and for all derivatives within the entry in so far as shift of stress has caused change of vowel value. This attempt must be viewed as an indication of the basic pronunciation as it is current in the South. The position of the word in the sentence, its emphasis, the general sentence-rhythm—all can introduce subtle variations to the quality of the vowels in the unstressed syllables.

ABBREVIATIONS

abbr.	abbreviation
Acc.	accusative
Acoust.	acoustics
adj.	adjective
adv.	adverb
Agr.	agriculture
Amer.	American
Anat.	anatomy
Arch.	architecture
Archaeol.	archaeology
Arith.	arithmetic
art.	article
Art	(fine) arts
Artil.	artillery
Astr.	astronomy
Astrol.	astrology
attrib.	attributive
Austr.	Austrian
aux. v.	auxiliary verb
Av.	aviation
B.	biblical
Bacter.	bacteriology
Bak.	baking
Bill.	billiards
Biol.	biology
Bookb.	bookbinding
Bot.	botany
Brew.	brewing
Bridgeb.	bridgebuilding
Build.	building
Butch.	butchery
Cal. Print.	calico printing
cap.	capital
Carp.	carpentry
Cav.	cavalry
Chem.	chemistry
Chron.	chronology
C.L.	commercial language
coll.	colloquial
collect.	collective
comp.	comparative degree
Conch.	conchology
Conf.	confectionery
conj.	conjunction
Cook.	cooking
Coop.	cooperage
Crick.	cricket
Cul.	culinary
Cycl.	cycling
Danc.	dancing
Dat.	dative
def.	definite
dem.	demonstrative
dial.	dialect
dim.	diminutive
Draw.	drawing
Dressm.	dressmaking
Dye.	dyeing
Dyn.	dynamics
Eccl.	ecclesiastical
Elec.	electricity
ellipt.	elliptical
Engin.	engineering
Engr.	engraving
Ent.	entomology
esp.	especially
Ethn.	ethnology
f.	feminine
Fenc.	fencing
fig.	figurative

Firew.	fireworks
Footb.	football
For.	forestry
Fort.	fortification
Found.	foundry-work
Freem.	freemasonry
Furr.	furriery
Gard.	gardening
Gen.	genitive
Geog.	geography
Geol.	geology
Geom.	geometry
Glassw.	glassworks
Gram.	grammar
Gun.	gunnery
Gymn.	gymnastics
h.	*haben*
Harn.	harness
Her.	heraldry
Hist.	history
Horol.	horology
Hort.	horticulture
hum.	humorous
Hunt.	hunting
Hydr.	hydraulics
Ichth.	ichthyology
imp.	impersonal
imper.	imperative
imperf.	imperfect
indef.	indefinite
indec.	indeclinable
indic.	indicative
inf.	infinitive
Inf.	infantry
insep.	inseparable
Insur.	insurance
int.	interjection
inter.	interrogative
inv.	invariable
ir.	irregular
iron.	ironical
Jew.	Jewish
Join.	joinery
Law	legal term
lit.	literal
Liter.	literature
Locom.	locomotive
Log.	logic
m.	masculine
Mach.	machinery
Magnet.	magnetism
Manuf.	manufactures
Math.	mathematics
Mech.	mechanics
Med.	medical
Metall.	metallurgy
metaph.	metaphorical
Meteor.	meteorology
Metr.	metrical
Mil.	military
Min.	mining
Mint.	minting
Mollusc.	mollusca
Motor.	motoring
Mount.	mountaineering
Mus.	music
Myth.	mythology
n.	neuter
Nat. Hist.	natural history
Nat. Soc.	National Socialism
Naut.	nautical
Nav.	navy
Navig.	navigation
Nom.	nominative
num.	numeral
opp.	opposite to
Opt.	optics
Org.	organ
orig.	originally
Orn.	ornithology
o.s.	oneself
pej.	pejorative
p.	person
P.	*Person*
pers.	personal
Paint.	painting
Pap.	papermaking
Parl.	parliament
part.	particle
pass.	passive
Path.	pathology
Pharm.	pharmacy
Phil.	philosophy
Philol.	philology
Phonet.	phonetics
Phot.	photography
Phren.	phrenology
Phys.	physics
Physiol.	physiology
pl.	plural
Poet.	poetry
Pol.	politics
poss.	possessive
Pott.	pottery
p.p.	past participle
prep.	preposition
pres.	present

Print.	printing
pron.	pronoun
pros.	prosody
Prot.	Protestant
Prov.	proverb
pr.p	present participle
Psych.	psychology
Rad.	radio
R.C.	Roman Catholic
Railw.	railways
reg.	regular
rel.	relative
Rel.	religion
Rhet.	rhetoric
s.	substantive
s.	*sein*
S.	*Sache*
Saddl.	saddlery
Sculp.	sculpture
Semp.	sewing
sep.	separable
Sew.-mach.	sewing-machine
Shipb.	shipbuilding
Shoem.	shoemaking
sing.	singular
sl.	slang
Smith.	smith's work
s.o.	someone
Soc.	sociology
Spin.	spinning
s.th.	something
Studs. sl.	students' slang
subj.	subjunctive
sup.	superlative
Surg.	surgery
Surv.	surveying
Tail.	tailoring
Tan.	tanning
Tech.	technology
Tele.	telegraphy
Tenn.	lawn tennis
th.	thing
Theat.	theatre
Theol.	theology
Top.	topography
Typ.	typography
Univ.	university
v.a.	transitive verb
v.aux.	auxiliary verb
Vet.	veterinary medicine
v.imp.	impersonal verb
v.n.	intransitive verb
v.r.	reflexive verb
vulg.	vulgar
Weav.	weaving
Zool.	zoology

KEY TO PRONUNCIATION

WHERE examples are given in both languages, it should not be assumed that the pronunciations are identical. In many cases the similarity is no more than approximate. In the case of the letters *l* and *r* no attempt is made to distinguish between the characteristic English and German treatments of the sounds.

Vowels—Vokale

	ENGLISH	GERMAN
[æ]	man	hängen (*South Germ.*)
[ɑ]	—	Antwort, flach
[ɑ:]	half, father, harbour	Ader, Haar, Jahr
[ɑ̃]	—	Chance (*French*, en)
[ɛ]	very, head	Ente, besser
[ɛ:]	fairy	Fähre, Käse
[ɛ̃]	—	Bassin (*French*, vin)
[e:]	—	Ehre, Teer, Ekel
[ə]	perhaps, idea, mother, honour, horror	Ehre, beantworten
[ə:]	sir, her, fur, word, earn, adjourn	—

	ENGLISH	GERMAN
[ɪ]	bit, hymn	ich, nisten
[ɪ:]	be, beat, see, field	ihre, Liebe
[ɔ]	not, want	Rock
[ɔ:]	for, ward	—
[ɔ̃]	—	Bonbon (*French*, bon)
[o]	molest, obey	—
[o:]	—	Hose, Boot, Sohn
[ʌ]	but, son, flood	—
[ʊ]	foot, pull, could	Futter, Pult
[ʊ:]	do, boot, soup	Mut, Kuh
[y]	—	Hütte, füllen
[y:]	—	Hüte, fühlen
[ø]	—	Hölle
[ø:]	—	Höhle
[œ̃]	—	Parfum (*French*, brun)

Diphthongs—Diphthonge

	ENGLISH	GERMAN
[ɑɪ]	my, wife, high	mein, Mai
[ɑɪə]	fire, higher	Feier, Reihe
[ɑj]	—	Email (*French*)
[ɑʊ]	house, how	Haus
[ɑʊə]	hour	Bauer
[ɛə]	bare, bear, hair, their	—
[eɪ]	same, day, they, remain	—
[ɪə]	here, hear, pierce, interior	—

	ENGLISH	GERMAN
[ɔɪ]	boy, noise	neu, Bäume
[ɔɪə]	royal	Feuer
[oʊ]	go, slow	—
[oʊə]	goer, slower	—
[ʊə]	sure, poor, doer	—
[ʊɪ]	—	pfui
[jʊ:]	few, view, duty deuce, suit, beauty, Tuesday	—

Consonants—Konsonanten

The sounds represented by the symbols [b], [d], [f] [g], [h], [k], [m], [n] [p], [t] are more or less identical in English and German.

	ENGLISH	GERMAN
[ç]	—	ich, nicht
[χ]	(*Scots*) loch	Loch
[dʒ]	just, German, ridge	—
[kw]	quite	—
[ŋ]	hanging, thing	Ring
[ŋk]	sink	sinken
[ŋg]	finger	jonglieren
[s]	see, scent, receive	das, daß, Wasser
[ʃ]	shoe, bush, sugar, session, special, lotion	Schuh, Busch
[ts]	hats	trotz, Zaun, Nation

	ENGLISH	GERMAN
[tʃ]	chin, patch, mixture	Patsche
[θ]	thick, path	—
[ð]	that, father, paths	—
[v]	van, vine, of, gravy	wann, Wein, ewig, Vase
[w]	well, doughy, persuade	—
[j]	yes, battalion	ja
[z]	his, zone, faces	Sohn, Sonne, reisen, Sense
[ʒ]	measure, garage	Journal, Garage

GERMAN-ENGLISH DICTIONARY

GERMAN-ENGLISH DICTIONARY

A, *n.* 1. the letter A; 2. the note A; *A dur* (the key of) A major; *A moll* (the key of) A minor; *in A dur*, in A major; *A-Saite*, the A-string (*of a violin*); (*B.*) *ich bin das A und das O*, I am Alpha and Omega (i.e. the beginning and the end); *das A und* (*das*) *O*, in its entirety, all in all; *von A vis Z*, from beginning to end, from first to last, exhaustively, fully; (*Prov.*) *wer A gesagt hat, muß auch B sagen*, he who has begun a thing must go on with it; in for a penny, in for a pound.

a. *abbr. for* am. an; *Frankfurt a. Main, Frankfurt a. d. Oder.* **a.D.** = *außer Dienst*(*en*), retired, pensioned off. **a.a.O.** = *am angeführten Orte*, in the above-mentioned place, *loc. cit.*, see above.

Aal, *m.* (-(e)s, -e, *dim.* **Älchen**) 1. eel; 2. wrong crease, crumple; 3. (*sl.*) torpedo; *Aal blau* (*gekocht*), boiled eel; *er entschlüpft wie ein –, schlüpfrig wie ein –*, he's as slippery as an eel; *den – beim Schwanz fassen*, to begin a thing at the wrong end. **-artig, -förmig,** *adj.* eel-shaped, anguilliform. **-beere,** *f.* black currant. **-butte,** *f.* eel-pout, burbot. **-glatt,** *adj.* slippery as an eel, elusive. **-mutter,** *f.* viviparous blenny. **-puppe,** *f.* **-quaste,** *f.* bundle of bullrushes used for catching eels. **-quappe,** *f.*, **-raupe,** *f.*, *see* **-butte. -reuse,** *f.* eelpot, eel basket. **-streif, -strich,** *m.* black streak on the back of a dun-coloured horse *or* cow, eel-backed.

aalen, 1. *v.a.* & *n.* fish for eels. 2. *v.r.* (*coll.*) rest in a leisurely manner (*without work or worry*), relax.

Aap, *n.* (-s, -en) mizzen-staysail.

Aar, *m.* (-(e)s, -e) (*archaic & poet.*) (*originally*) any large bird of prey; (*usually*) eagle.

Aas, *n.* (-es, Aase *or* Äser) 1. carrion, (rotten) carcass, offal; 2. bait; 3. (*vulg.*) filthy blackguard; *ein – legen*, to lay a bait; (*B. & Prov.*) *wo ein – ist, da sammeln sich die Adler*, wherever the carcass is, there will the eagles be gathered together. **-fliege,** *f.* dung-fly. **-geier,** *m.* carrion-vulture. **-geruch,** *m.* putrid stench. **-jäger,** *m.* unsportsmanlike hunter, pot-hunter.

aas-en, 1. *v.n.* feed on carrion. 2. *v.a.* flesh, curry (*hides*). 3. *v.n.* (*mit etwas*) waste, spoil (*through dirtiness or lavishness*), make a mess of; *sich voll–en* (*vulg.*), get filthy, dirty. 4. cf. **äsen. -ig,** *adj.* ugly; filthy, foul, beastly; (*Sl.*) *er hat –ig viel Geld*, he is stiff with money, rolling in money.

ab, 1. *adv.* off; down; away from; from; exit; *Maria –*, exit Mary (*stage direction*); (*C.L.*) *– heute*, from today; (*C.L.*) *– Bremen, von Bremen –*, from Bremen;*– Werk*, from the factory; ex works; *von hier –*, from here; *von nun –*, henceforth, in the future; *– ersten Oktober*, on and after the first of October; *weit –*, far off; *Hut – !* off with your hat! *Bajonett –!* unfix bayonets ! (*Mil.*); *Gewehr –!* order arms ! (*Mil.*); *hiervon geht –* deduct; *– an Unkosten*, charges to be deducted; *vom Wege – sein*, leave the road, be off the road; *– und an, – und zu*, off and on, now and then; *Strom –* (*also stromab*), down stream; *berg–*, downhill; *auf und –*, up and down, to and fro; *eine Mark auf oder, –* a mark more or less; (*coll.*) *ich bin ganz –*, I am quite exhausted *or* worn out; *kurz –*, abruptly, shortly; *weiter –*, farther off. 2. *sep. prefix. When employed as a prefix* ab *has a variety of meanings, e.g.* departure, separation from (*abreisen*), movement downwards (*abstürzen*), disinclination to (*ablehnen*), deterioration (*abtragen*, clothes), negation (*abstellen*), imitation (*abschreiben*, copy), appropriation (*abschmeicheln*); *in many verbs it denotes* to tire o.s. by the repeated action of the verb, to do a thing thoroughly (*abarbeiten*).

If a compound verb beginning with ab *is not given in the following lists, look under the simple verb, the meaning of which should then be modified by one or other of the above qualifications.*

abänder-n, *v.a.* alter, change; amend; modify. **-lich,** *adj.* alterable. **-ung,** *f.* alteration; variation; modification. **-ungsfähig,** capable of modification. **-ungsantrag,** *m.* amendment (*of a bill*).

abängstigen, 1. *v.a.* alarm, distress. 2. *v.r.* worry; wear o.s. out with anxiety.

abarbeiten, 1. *v.a.* work off (*a debt*); get (*a ship*) afloat *or* off; wear out (*an implement, a horse, etc.*). usually only *p.p.* as *ein abgearbeiteter Gaul*, a worn-out nag. 2. *v.r.* toil, work hard, wear o.s. out; *das Gröbste –*, rough-hew.

abärgen, 1. *v.a.* wear out by worrying, vex. 2. *v.n.* be mortified, vexed.

Abart, *f.* (-en) species, variety, modification, variation (*Nat. Hist.*).

abart-en, *v.n.* (*aux s.*) degenerate; deviate from type. **-ung,** *f.* variation.

abästen, *v.a.* cut off branches of, lop, trim; *abgeästete Weide*, pollard willow.

abätzen, *v.a.* corrode, eat away, cauterize.

abäuge(l)n, *v.a.* obtain by winning glances; *die Richtung einer Mauer –*, gauge the line of a wall with the eye.

abbangen, *v.a.*; *einem etwas –*, extort s.th. from s.o. by intimidation.

Abbau, *m.* 1. demolition, destruction, act of working a mine, old working (*mine*); 2. retrenchment, economy, 'axe' (*e.g.* reduction of staff); 3. analysis, separation, decomposition, disintegration, degeneration, degradation.

abbauen, *v.a.* 1. demolish (*a building*), dismantle; work (*a mine*); 2. retrench, economize; reduce (*prices*), discharge (*employees*); 3. (*Chem.*) analyse, decompose, disintegrate; 4. (*coll.*) withdraw (*from a contest*), weaken, throw in the towel.

abbefehlen, *ir.v.a.* countermand; *die Parade ist abbefohlen*, the parade has been cancelled.

abbefördern, *v.a.* evacuate (*people or stores*).

abbeißen, *ir.v.a.* bite off; *sich die Nägel –*, bite one's nails; (*coll.*) *er hat aller Scham* (or *Schande*) *den Kopf abgebissen*, he is past all shame.

abbeizen, *v.a.* remove by caustics; macerate, dress (*skins*); (*Metall.*) remove oxidized surface, scour, dip, pickle, taw.

abbekommen, *ir.v.a.* 1. remove, get loose *or* off; *er kann den Stiefel nicht –*, he is unable to get his boot off; 2. *etwas davon –*, get a share of, come in for s.th. *or* one's share; *dabei etwas –*, get hurt; *er hat in der Schlacht nichts –*, he has not been hit in the battle.

abberufen, *ir.v.a.* call away, recall.

abbestell-en, *v.a.* & *n.* countermand, cancel. **-ung,** *f.* counter-order; withdrawal (*of an invitation, etc.*), cancellation.

abbetteln, *v.a.*; *einem etwas –*, obtain s.th. from s.o. by wheedling.

abbezahlen, *v.a.* pay off; discharge (*a debt*); liquidate; *er zahlt seine Schulden in jährlichen Raten ab*, he pays his debts in yearly instalments.

abblegen, 1. *ir.v.a.* bend off, turn aside, branch off, deflect, diverge, deviate; take off layers. 2. *v.n.* (*aux, s.*) turn off *or* aside; *sich* (*vom Wege*) –, branch off (from the road).

Abbild, *n.* (-(e)s, -er) likeness, copy, image.

abbild-en, 1. *v.a.* portray, delineate, illustrate; describe. 2. *v.r.* be reflected, form an image. **-ung,** *f.* illustration; picture; drawing, diagram, figure, image.

abbinden, *ir.v.a.* unbind; untie; detach by ligature, tie off (*warts, etc.*); wean (*a calf*); apply a tourniquet to (*arm, vein, etc.*); set (*of cement, concrete, etc.*); hoop (*a cask*). *In Swiss German it is used for* to settle briefly *or* to say briefly; *kurz abgebunden*, in short.

Abbitte, *f.* (-en) apology; *– tun* (or *leisten*), beg forgiveness, apologize.

abbiten, *ir.v.a.* apologize for; beg forgiveness;

einem etwas –, apologize to s.o. for s.th.; obtain by pleading.
abblas-en, *ir.v.a.* 1. blow off *or* away (*as dust from books*); 2. bring to an end; *den Streik -en*, call off the strike; *das Gefecht -en*, stop the attack, sound the retreat, break off combat. 3. (*Mil.*) *Gas -en*, release gas. **-eventil,** *n.* exhaust valve.
abblassen, *v.n.* (*aux.* s.) turn pale, fade; *abgeblaßte Redensart*, hackneyed expression.
abblätter-n, 1. *v.a.* strip off leaves. 2. *v.r.* & *n.* (*aux.* h.) shed leaves; exfoliate; peel off; scale off; desquamate; laminate. **-ung,** *f.* exfoliation, etc.
abbläuen, 1. *v.a.* blue (*of linen*); dye blue; 2. *v.n.* lose its blue colour.
abbleichen, 1. *v.a.* bleach; 2. *ir.v.n.* (*aux.* s.) lose colour, fade, grow pale.
abblenden, 1. *v.a.* dim, screen, turn off (*lights*), black-out. 2. *v.n.* stop-down (*camera*).
abblitzen, *v.n.* (*aux.* s.) (*coll.*) meet with no success (*wishes, applications, etc.*), get a snub, meet with a rebuff; (*coll.*) *sie ließ ihn* –, she snubbed him.
abblühen, *v.n.* (*aux.* s. & h.) cease blooming; droop, fade, fall (*of flowers*); *die Nelken haben* (or *sind*) *abgeblüht*, the carnations are over.
abborgen, *v.a.* (*einem etwas*) borrow from.
abböschen, *v.a.* slope, slant, incline.
Abbrand, *m.* (-es, ⸚e) (*Metall.*) residual metallic oxides in heat processing, loss as result of such processing.
abbrauchen, *v.a.* use up, wear out *or* off.
abbraunen, *v.n.* lose its brown colour.
abbräunen, *v.a.* brown thoroughly.
abbrausen, 1. *v.n* (*aux.* h.) cease fermenting; cease storming; (*coll.*) rush off. 2. *v.a.* & *r.* douche, rinse off.
abbrech-en, *ir.v.a.* & *n.* (*aux.* s. & h.) 1. break off, snap, demolish, dismantle, pull down; pluck, pick (*fruit, flowers, etc.*); 2. interrupt, discontinue, stop short; *einen Streik -en*, call off a strike; *das Gefecht -en*, bring fighting to an end; *Schießen -en!* Cease fire! (*Mil.*); *jede Minute, die ich der Arbeit -en kann*, every moment I can snatch from work; *abgebrochene Worte*, disjointed words, fragmentary utterances; *kurz -en*, cut short, interrupt suddenly; *ein Gerüst -en*, take down a scaffolding; *das Lager -en*, break camp; *Zelte -en*, strike tents; *die Brücke eines Schiffes -en*, cast off the gangway; *einem Pferde die Eisen -en*, unshoe a horse; *den Mast -en*, carry away the mast; *wir können uns nichts -en lassen*, we can allow no discount; *sich* (*Dat.*) *etwas -en*, deny o.s., deprive o.s. of; *er bricht sich nichts ab*, he does not stint himself in anything, he denies himself nothing. 3. (*Mil.*) change from line into column formation; *zu Vieren brecht ab!* form fours! **-ung,** *f.* taking down, demolition, dismantling.
abbremsen, *v.n.* apply the brake, brake.
abbrennen, 1. *ir.v.a.* burn off; burn down; cleanse by fire; temper (*steel, etc.*); calcine; sear; *Feuerwerk* –, let off fireworks. 2. *v.n.* (*aux.* s.) be burnt down; be damaged by fire; cease burning, go out (*fire*); *die Kerzen sind abgebrannt*, the candles have burnt away; *die Leute sind abgebrannt*, the people have been burnt out (= lost everything in the fire); (*coll.*) *ich bin abgebrannt*, I am penniless, cleaned out.
Abbreviatur, *f.* (-en) abbreviation.
abbringen, *ir.v.a.* remove, get off, out, away *or* afloat; divert; dissuade; *vom rechten Wege* –, lead astray; *davon lasse ich mich nicht* –, I will not be dissuaded from it; *nichts soll mich davon* –, nothing shall prevent me from doing it (*or* from going on with it); *es ist eine Grille von ihm, von der man ihn nicht – kann*, it is a whim to which he clings obstinately.
abbröckeln, *v.n.* crumble away; peel off.
Abbruch, *m.* (-(e)s, ⸚e) the act of breaking off, pulling down; damage, injury, loss; detriment; rupture; discontinuance (*of relations*); the th. broken off; deduction, discount; abatement (*in price*); a break (*in type*); – *tun*, damage, be prejudicial to, injure, impair; *sich* (*Dat.*) *selbst – tun*, deprive o.s. of; *auf – verkaufen*, sell for scrap; – *diplomatischer Beziehungen*, breaking off of diplomatic relations. **-arbeit,** *f.* demolition. **-holz,** *n.* scrap wood. **-linie,** *f.* line of cleavage.

abbrüchig, *adj.* brittle; detrimental, derogatory, prejudicial.
abbrühen, *v.a.* scald; parboil; seethe; *abgebrüht* (*coll.*), hard-boiled.
abbüß-en, *v.a.* atone for, expiate; serve (*Law*); *mit Geld -en*, pay a fine. **-ung,** *f.* atonement, expiation.
Abc (Abece), *n.* abc, alphabet; (*fig.*) the first rudiments. **Abc-weise,** *adv.* alphabetically. **-buch,** *n.* spelling-book.
abdach-en, 1. *v.a* make sloping *or* slanting (*like a roof*), incline; unroof, remove the roof; *eine Mauer -en*, cope a wall. 2. *v.r.* incline, slope away, shelve. **-ig,** *adj.* sloping. **-ung,** *f.* slope, declivity; glacis, scarp; unroofing. **-ungswinkel,** *m.* angle of inclination.
abdächig, *adj.* sloping.
abdämmen, *v.a.* dam up *or* off; stem off; embank.
Abdampf, *m.* exhaust steam (*Eng.*). **-en,** *v.n.* (*aux.* s.) evaporate; (*fam.*) clear off, beat it, hop it. **-rückstand,** *m.* residue after evaporation.
abdämpfen, 1. *v.a.* (cause to) evaporate; 2. damp down, check, stifle (*fire, sound, enthusiasm, etc.*).
abdank-en, 1. *v.a.* dismiss from service; discharge; disband; lay up (*a ship*); *der Offizier ist abgedankt*, the officer has been dismissed *or* retired; *zur Strafe -en*, cashier; pay off (*a crew*). 2. *v.n.* (*aux.* h.) resign, retire, quit the service, abdicate; *bei einer Leiche -en*, (*Swiss dial.*) deliver a funeral oration. **-ung,** *f.* resignation, abdication; dismissal, discharge, disbanding; *geistliche -ung*, (*Swiss dial.*) funeral oration.
abdarben, 1. *v.a.* deprive of, stint in. 2. *v.r.* *sich etwas* –, deny o.s. s.th., stint o.s.; *er darbt sich die besten Bissen für sie ab*, he saves the best pieces for her.
abdeck-en, *v.a.* uncover; unroof (*Arch.*); flay; clear (*the table*); cover (*expenses, damage, etc.*). **-er,** *m.* knacker, flayer. **-erei,** *f.* knacker's yard. **-platte,** *f.* cover plate. **-stein,** *m.* coping stone. **-ung,** *f.* coping (*Arch.*).
abdicht-en, *v.a.* make watertight, *etc.*, caulk, seal. **-ung,** *f.* packing, caulking.
abdienen, *v.a.* pay off by service; serve one's time *or* one's period of enlistment in the army.
abdingen, *ir.v.a.* beat down in bargaining; cheapen (*by haggling*); *einem etwas* –, hire s.th. from s.o., obtain s.th. from s.o. by negotiating; bargain a p. out of a th.; *wir haben den Preis zu fünfzehn Mark abgedungen*, we have agreed on the price at 15 marks; *sich* (*Dat.*) *etwas – lassen*, allow a rebate *or* concession; *ich habe mir nichts – lassen*, I have agreed to no reduction.
abdorren, *v.n.* wither, dry up.
abdörren, *v.a.* dry up, parch, desiccate.
Abdraht, *m.* turnings, swarf.
abdrängen, *v.a.* force away; *einem etwas* –, force s.th. from s.o.; *einen vom Wege* –, push a p. off the road.
abdrechseln, *v.a.* turn off, separate by turning; turn (*on a lathe*).
abdreh-en, *v.a.* twist off; turn off (*gas*), switch off (*electric light*); go into a nose-dive (*Av.*). **-maschine,** *f.* lathe. **-nagel,** *m.* chuck. **-späne,** *m.pl.* = **Abdraht. -stahl,** *m.* lathe tool.
abdreschen, *ir.v.a.* thrash; thresh; **abgedroschen,** *p.p.* & *adj.* trite; *abgedroschene Gedanken* or *Phrasen*, hackneyed ideas; commonplace phrases.
Abdrift, *cf.* **Abtrift.**
abdringen, *ir.v.a.* force away; *einem etwas* –, extort *or* wring a th. from s.o.
abdrosseln, *v.a.n.* throttle down, stall (*an engine*).
Abdruck, *m.* 1. (-(e)s, -e) impression; copy; print; reproduction; – *vor der Schrift*, proofs before letters. 2. (-(e)s ⸚e) stamping; mark; impress, act of pulling the trigger; *Gips*–, plaster-cast; *Finger*–, finger-print. **-en,** *v.a.* print, imprint, stamp; print off. **-masse,** *f.* plaster of Paris. **-srecht,** *n.* copyright.
abdrück-en, *v.a.* separate, loosen *or* set free by pressing; mould; pull the trigger; discharge (*a gun*); *es drückt mir das Herz ab*, it breaks my heart. **-vorrichtung,** *f.* firing mechanism.
abdunst-en, *v.n.* (*aux.* s.) evaporate; vaporize.

abdünst-en, *v.a.* cause to evaporate, convert into steam. **-ung,** *f.* evaporation. **-ungshaus,** *n.* drying-house.

Abece, *see* **Abc.**

Abend, *m.* (-s, -e) 1. evening; night; 2. eve; day preceding (= *Vorabend*); 3. the west; Occident (*Biblical and poetic*); *diesen* –, this evening; *eines –s*, one evening; *des –s*, in the evening, at night; *am* –, on the evening; *gegen* –, towards evening, in the west; *es wird* –, it is getting dark, night is drawing in; *zu – essen*, dine in the evening; *guten – sagen*, say good evening; *heute abend*, tonight, this evening; *gestern abend*, last night; *morgen abend*, tomorrow night; *Dienstag abend*, on Tuesday evening; *abends = des –s; von abends bis früh*, from nightfall to sunrise; *von morgens bis abends*, from dawn till dusk; *Dienstag(s) abends*, every Tuesday evening, on Tuesday evenings; *abends spät, spät abends*, late at night; (*um*) 8 *Uhr abends, abends um* 8 *Uhr*, 8 o'clock in the evening; *am Heiligen* –, on Christmas Eve; *der – vor der Schlacht*, the eve of the battle; *– des Lebens*, decline of life; *der Wind weht aus* –, there is a west wind; (*Prov.*) *es ist noch nicht aller Tage* – or *man soll den Tag nicht vor dem – loben*, don't count your chickens before they're hatched. **-andacht,** *f.*, **-gottesdienst,** *m.* evensong, vespers. **-ausgabe,** *f.* evening edition (*of a newspaper*). **-blatt,** *n.* evening (news-)paper. **-brot,** *n.*, **-essen,** *n.* supper. **-dämmerung,** *f.* evening twilight, dusk. **-falter,** *m.* hawk-moth. **-gebet,** *n.* evening-prayers. **-gesellschaft,** *f.* evening party, soirée, rout. **-land,** *n,* the Occident. **-ländisch,** *adj.* occidental. **-lich,** *adj.* evening; western. **-mahl,** *n.* (*dial.*) supper; (*usually*) *das Heilige –mahl*, the Lord's Supper, Holy Communion; *das –mahl nehmen*, partake of the Lord's Supper, communicate; *das –mahl reichen*, administer the sacrament. **-mahlsgänger,** *m.* **-mahlsgast,** *m.* communicant. **-mahlskelch,** *m.* chalice, communion-cup. **-punkt,** *m.* true west, west-point (*Astr.*). **-rot,** *n.*, **-röte,** *f.* sunset. **-sonne,** *f.* setting sun. **-ständchen,** *n.* serenade. **-stern,** *m.* evening star, Venus, Hesperus. **-tau,** *m.* night dew. **-thermik,** *f.* terrestrial radiation. **-wärts,** *adv.* westerly, westwards. **-wind,** *m.* evening wind; west wind, zephyr.

Abenteu-er, *n.* (-s, –) adventure. **-erin,** *f.* adventuress. **-erlich,** *adj.* adventurous; wonderful; strange; odd; fantastic; quixotic, romantic. **-erlichkeit,** *f.* adventurousness; romance, quixotism; strangeness; (*pl.*) strange things. **-erlust,** *f.* love of adventure. **-ern,** *v.n.* seek adventures. **-rer,** *m.* adventurer, knight-errant.

aber, 1. *conj.* but, though; *nein* –, I say (*expression of astonishment*); *nun* –, but now; say; *– Kinder!* now, now, children! –, –, come, come! 2. *adv.* again, once more; *tausend und – tausend*, thousands and thousands (abertausend *is Austrian*). *In some compounds* Aber *denotes* ill, a bad kind of (*cf.* Ab *in* Abgott, Abgunst). 3. *subst. n.* objection; *es ist ein – dabei*, there is a but in the question; *das Wenn und das* –, the conditions and objections, the difficulties in the way. **-glaube,** *m.* superstition. **-gläubisch,** *adj.* superstitious. **-gläubigkeit,** *f.* superstitiousness. **-malig,** *adj.* reiterated, repeated. **-mals,** *adv.* again, once more. (*rare*) **-saat,** *f.* second sowing. **-wahl,** *f.* (*Swiss dial.*) right of appeal. **-witz,** *m.* craziness; absurdity; conceit. **-witzig,** *adj.* crazy, frantic, foolish.

aberkenn-en, *ir.v.a.*; *einem etwas –en*, give a verdict against s.o.; disallow *or* set aside a p.'s plea. **-ung,** *f.* abjudication of rights; dispossession by judicial decree; *–ung der bürgerlichen Ehrenrechte*, deprivation of civil rights.

abessen, 1. *ir.v.a.* eat up, clear (*a plate*), leave nothing on (*the table*); *einen Knochen* –, pick a bone. 2. *v.n.* (*aux.* h.) finish eating; *abgegessen haben*, have done eating.

abfach-en, *v.a.* partition, divide into compartments; classify. **-ung,** *f.* division into compartments; classification.

abfahr-en, 1. *ir.v.n.* (*aux.* s.) set off, depart; start; put to sea; *der Zug fährt um 3 Uhr ab*, the train starts at 3 o'clock; *er fuhr übel ab*, he fared badly, got the worst of it. 2. *ir.v.a.* cart away; make a road *or* a track by driving over; wear out by driving; overdrive; *ein Rad –en*, lose a wheel. 3. *n.* removal, disposal (*rubbish, etc.*) **-t,** *f.* (-ten) departure; starting time; descent (*in skiing*). **-t(s)bahnsteig,** *m.* departure platform. **-tsort,** *m.* place of departure. **-tzeichen,** *n.* starting signal. **-tzeit,** *f.* time of departure.

Abfall, *m.* (-es, ⸚e) 1. (*usually pl.*) waste, refuse, clippings, shreds, cuttings, scraps, slops, offal, by-products, scrap; 2. steep slope, descent; 3. falling off; apostasy, defection, backsliding; secession, revolt; 4. decrease; fall; short weight, loss in weight. *– zwischen zwei Dingen*, contrast between two things; *– des Laubes*, fall of the leaves; *– der Niederlande*, revolt of the Netherlands; **-en,** *ir.v.n.* (*aux.* s.) fall off; slope away; fall away; decrease; decay, degenerate; desert, revolt, become disaffected, secede; lose flesh; go to waste; contrast strongly, be inferior (*gegen*, to); cast, veer; *es fällt dabei nicht viel ab*, there is little to be gained from it *or* by it; (*coll.*) *sie ließ ihn –en*, she snubbed *or* dropped him *or* gave him the cold shoulder; *der Abgefallene*, the apostate, renegade; *das Schiff fiel vom Striche ab*, the ship fell from her course; *mit dem Wind –en*, fall to leeward (*Naut.*); *–ende Qualität*, inferior quality. **-end,** *adj.* sloping; deciduous. **-eisen,** *n.* scrap iron. **-erzeugnis,** *n.* waste product. **-händler,** *m.* seller of offal. **-haufen,** *m.* scrap heap, dump. **-holz,** *n.* dead wood, waste wood. **-sröhre,** *f.* waste-pipe. **-stoff,** *m.* by-products (*from waste*).

abfällig, *adj.* falling off, shelving, precipitous; decaying; disapproving, critical, dissenting; (*archaic*) disloyal, rebellious; *– werden*, revolt; *vom Glauben – werden*, turn apostate; *sich – über einen äußern, einen – beurteilen*, criticize a p. unfavourably; *einen – bescheiden*, give a negative answer to s.o., refuse a request.

abfang-en, *ir.v.a.* catch, snatch from, seize, intercept; level out (*after diving*), regain control (*Av.*); prop, support (*Arch.*); stab, kill (*wounded game, with the hunting-knife*); *Wasser –en*, turn off water; *einen –en*, catch a p. unawares; *Briefe –en*, intercept letters; *Kunden –en*, entice away customers. **-vorrichtung,** *f.* braking device (*Av.*).

abfärben, *v.n.* (*aux.* h.) rub off (*of colour*); lose colour; *– auf* (*Acc.*) influence, colour. **abgefärbt,** *p.p. & adj.* faded, discoloured, *das Tuch hat rot abgefärbt*, the dye of the red cloth has run; *es färbt nicht ab*, the dye is fast *or* does not run.

abfass-en, *v.a.* 1. compose, write; draw up; 2. catch (*in wrongdoing*); seize, arrest; 3. measure off, weigh out (*articles*); put up (*in parcels*); bend; *in bündigen Ausdrücken abgefaßt*, couched in concise terms; *laß dich ja nicht dabei –en!* mind you don't get caught! **-er,** *m.* one who draws up (*a statement, etc.*); **-ung,** *f.* composition, style, wording, formulation, drawing up, penning, writing.

abfaulen, *v.n.* (*aux.* s.) rot and fall off.

abfedern, 1. *v.a.* pluck (*feathers*). **abgefedert,** *p.p. & adj.* cushioned, (well-)sprung. 2. *v.n.* moult.

abfeg-en, *v.a.* sweep off; cleanse; *Staub –en*, dust. **-mittel,** *n.* detergent.

Abfeilicht, *n.* filings.

abfeilschen, *v.a.* cheapen (*by haggling*), beat down; obtain by haggling.

abfertig-en, *v.a.* finish; dispatch; expedite; forward; dismiss without ceremony; *kurz –en*, send about one's business, treat curtly, snub, make short work of. **-er,** *m,* sender. **-ung,** *f.* act of finishing; dispatch; clearance, expedition; smart rejoinder; reproof, snub; dismissal. **-ungsschein,** *m.* customs declaration; permit. **-ungsstelle,** *f.* dispatch office. **-ungszeit,** *f.* hours of clearance.

Abfett, *n.* (-(e)s, -e), fat skimmings. **-en,** *v.a.* skim off the fat; remove grease, scour (*wool*).

abfeuer-n 1. *v.a.* fire off, discharge. 2. *v.n.* cease firing *or* heating (*a boiler*), draw the fire. **-ung,** *f.* discharge, firing. *–ung der Geschütze*, cannonade, salvo; *unter –ung der Kanonen*, guns saluting. **-ungsverbindung,** *f.* remote control firing mechanism (*Mil.*).

abfind-en, 1. *ir.v.a.* satisfy, compound with (*creditors*); pay off; portion, make a settlement (*upon*); *abgefundene Kinder*, portioned children; *abgefundene Prinzen*, apanaged princes. 2. *v.r.* come to terms (*mit einem*, with a p.), be quits (*with s.o.*); *sich gütlich mit einem -en*, settle things amicably with a p.; *sich mit einer Sache -en*, acquiesce in *or* put up with a th. **-ung,** *f.* act of satisfying; settlement; composition, compromise, indemnification. **-ungsgeld,** *n.*, **-ungssumme,** *f.* money paid as indemnity; sum in full settlement of all claims; composition, compensation; apanage.
abfischen, *v.a.* empty (*a pond*) by fishing; *das Beste* –, skim the cream off; *einem etwas* –, cheat a p. out of a th.
abflachen, 1. *v.a.* level off; face (*Mach.*). 2. *v.r.* slope, subside; shoal.
abflauen, *v.n.* abate (*of wind*); give way (*of prices*); slacken, slump (*of trade*); *der Streik flaut ab* or *ist im – begriffen*, the strike begins to collapse.
abflechten, *ir.v.a.* unplait, untwist.
abfleisch-en, *v.a.* flay; pick the flesh (*from the bone*). **-eisen,** *n.*, **-messer,** *n.* fleshing-knife.
abfliegen, *ir.v.n.* (*aux.* s.) fly off; dry and drop off; take off (*of airmen*).
abfließen, *ir.v.n.* (*aux.* s.) run off, flow off *or* down; ebb; drain.
Abflug, *m.* (–s, ⸚e) flight, departure (*of migratory birds*); take-off (*Av.*).
Abfluß, *m.* (-(ss)es, ⸚(ss)e) flowing off; ebb; discharge, defluxion (*Med.*); sewer; sink; drain; – *des Geldes*, drain of money. **-gebiet,** *n.* catchment area. **-graben,** *m.* drain. **-rohr,** *n.*, **-röhre,** *f.* waste-pipe, gutter.
Abfolge, *f.* succession, sequence.
abfoltern, *v.a.* extort by torturing.
abforder-n, *v.a.* (*einem etwas*) demand from, make a claim against; *einem Rechenschaft -n*, call a p. to account. **-ung,** *f.* demand.
Abform, *f.* (–en) mould; cast. **-en,** *v.a.* mould, form from a mould; *einen Schuh -en*, make a shoe off the last. **-masse,** *f.* moulding compound.
abforsten, *v.a.* cut down, clear (*a forest*).
abfragen, *v.a.* inquire of, ascertain by inquiring, bring out by questioning; answer a call at the switchboard, test the time (*Tele.*).
abfressen, *ir.v.n.* (*aux.* s.) eat off, browse; consume; corrode, erode; *der Gram frißt ihm das Herz ab*, grief gnaws at his heart.
abfrieren, *ir.v.n.* (*aux.* s.) be bitten off by the cold, freeze off; *die Zehen sind ihm abgefroren*, his toes are frost-bitten.
Abfuhr, *f.* removal *or* transportation (*of goods*); carting off, disposal; elimination; (*coll.*) rebuff; (*Studs. sl.*) disabling, wound (*in duelling*). **-lohn,** *m.* cartage. **-wagen,** *m.* dust-cart.
abführ-en, *v.a.* lead away; carry off, down *or* away; mislead; purge; snub; discharge, clear *or* pay off; *Geld -en an*, pay over to; *Wärme -en*, dissipate heat; (*Studs. sl.*) disable one's antagonist (*duelling*); *er wurde in Gewahrsam abgeführt*, he was removed into custody; *diese Arznei führt zu stark ab*, this medicine is too strong an aperient; (*coll.*) *den habe ich glänzend abgeführt*, I have beaten him hollow. **-end,** *pr.p.* & *adj.* purgative, aperient. **-mittel,** *n.* aperient, purgative, laxative. **-ung,** *f.* removal, carrying off; evacuation; *-ung einer Schuld*, settlement of a debt.
abfüll-en, *v.a.* draw off (*wine*), decant; *Wein auf Flaschen -en*, bottle wine. **-maschine,** *f.* bottling machine. **-trichter,** *m.* funnel (*for filling*).
abfurch-en, *v.a.* divide by furrows. **-ung,** *f.* segmentation, division.
abfütter-n, *v.a.* feed; line (*cloth*). **-ung,** *f.* feeding; lining.
Abgabe, *f.* (-n) 1. delivery; emission; output, yield; 2. tax, tribute, duty, royalty; 3. draft, bill of exchange; (*pl.*) fees, dues. *Stimm-*, polling, voting; *Gepäck-*, left-luggage office. **-nfrei,** *adj.* duty-free, free of taxes. **-nwesen,** *n.* (system of) imposts and taxes. **-pflichtig,** *adj.* liable to tax, assessable, taxable, **-satz,** *m.* rate of yield, levy.
Abgang, *m.* (-(e)s, ⸚e) 1. departure; exit; leaving (*of school*); 2. sale; 3. deduction; tare; 4. loss, (*pl.*) scrapings, filings; 5. excrement; *guten – haben*, have a ready sale; *es findet keinen* –, there is no sale for it, it is a drug in the market; *nach – der männlichen Linie*, failing male heirs; *in – kommen*, fall into disuse, go out of fashion; decay. **-sdampf,** *m.* exhaust-steam. **-sprüfung,** *f.* final examination. **-srechnung,** *f.* tare-account. **-swinkel,** *m.* angle of departure (*Artil.*). **-szeugnis,** *n.* leaving-certificate.
abgäng-ig, *adj.* 1. going off, departing; missing (*of papers, etc.*); 2. saleable; 3. declining; deteriorating; shabby; 4. excremental; **-ling,** *m.* waste-matter; abortion. **-sel,** *n.* refuse, clippings.
Abgas, *n.* (-es, -e) exhaust gas (*usually pl.*).
abgeben, 1. *ir.v.a.* deliver (up); hand in *or* over; furnish a contingent; give (*an opinion*); pay (*taxes*); draw (*a bill*); be good for; transfer; *einen Wechsel* or *eine Tratte auf einen* –, draw on a p., give a cheque *or* draft on a p.; *dies ist für Sie abgegeben worden*, this has been left for you; *wir können das Buch zu diesem Preise nicht* –, we cannot supply the book on these terms; *er hätte einen guten Arzt abgegeben*, he would have made a good doctor; *er kann einen Zeugen* –, he can bear witness; *ein Gutachen* –, to give expert opinion; *einem eins* –, give a p. a cutting reply; give a p. a blow; *einem etwas* –, share s.th. with a p.; *jetzt gibt es aber etwas ab*, now we (you) are in for it; *einen Narren* –, play the fool; *seine Stimme* –, cast one's vote; *einen Schuß* –, fire a shot. 2. *v.r.*; *sich mit einem* –, frequent a p.'s company; *mit diesem Menschen gebe ich mich nicht ab*, I won't have anything to do with that fellow; *sich mit etwas* –, occupy *or* concern o.s. with a matter; *er gibt sich viel mit den neueren Sprachen ab*, he spends much time on modern languages.
abgebrannt, *p.p.* & *adj.* burnt out; calcined; *-e Metalle* refined metals; (*fam.*) on the rocks. *See* **abbrennen.**
abgebrochen, *p.p.* & *adj.* broken off; abrupt; disjointed. *See* **abbrechen.**
abgebrüht, *p.p.* & *adj.* (*coll.*) hardened, insensible (to); *er ist gegen Schande* –, he has no feeling of shame whatsoever.
abgedacht, *p.p.* & *adj.* sloping.
abgedroschen, *p.p.* & *adj.* trite. *See* **abdreschen.**
abgefeimt, *p.p.* & *adj.* crafty, cunning, knowing; *-er Bösewicht*, out-and-out rascal.
abgegriffen, *see* **abgreifen.**
abgehen, 1. *ir.v.n.* (*aux.* s.) go off, depart, start; make one's exit; swerve, deviate, go astray; come off *or* undone; wear off; pass (*Med.*); be in want; be missing; lose; sell, find purchasers; *Wann geht die Post ab?* when does the post leave? *davon kann ich nicht* –, I must insist on that; *vom Preise* –, lower the price; *geht nichts von dem Preise ab?* is there no reduction? *von seinem Vorhaben nicht* –, persist in one's plan; *der Pfad geht links ab*, the path branches to the left; *er läßt sich nichts* –, he denies himself nothing; *von der Schule* –, leave school; *von einem Amte* –, resign an office; (*coll.*) *er ist abgegangen worden*, he has been dismissed; *mit Tode* –, depart this life; *das Rad ging ab*, the wheel came off; *die Farbe ging ab*, the colour faded, came off *or* ran; *es sind ihm Würmer abgegangen*, he has passed worms (*Med.*); *mir gehen dafür die Kenntnisse ab*, I haven't the necessary knowledge; *geht mir dadurch etwas ab?* am I the worse for it? *es soll ihr nichts* –, she shall want for nothing; *Shylock geht ab*, exit Shylock; *es wird übel* –, it will turn out badly; *das Konzert ging gut ab*, the concert went off well *or* was a great success; *hiervon geht ab*, discount (*in an account*), deduct; *reißend* –, sell like hot cakes; – *lassen*, send off, forward. 2. *v.a.* wear out by walking; measure by steps.
abgeizen, *v.a.* get by avarice; *sich* (*Dat.*) *etwas* –, starve o.s. *or* stint o.s. in s.th.
abgelagert, *see* **ablagern.**
abgelebt, *pp.* & *adj.* decrepit; faded; worn out; blasé. **-heit,** *f.* decrepitude.

Forms of p.p. in **abge-** *not found here should be sought under Inf.*

abgelegen, *p.p. & adj.* remote, distant; out-of-the-way; *-er Wein*, wine long laid down; **-heit,** *f.* remoteness, isolation.
abgeleitet, *p.p. & adj.* derived (*Mus. & Gram.*).
abgemacht, *see* **abmachen.**
abgemessen, 1. *p.p. & adj.* measured; precise; formal. 2. *adv.* with careful adjustment. **-heit,** *f.* regularity, exactness; formality.
abgeneigt, *p.p. & adj.* unwilling; disinclined, averse (*einer S.* to a th.) **-heit,** *f.* disinclination, repugnance.
abgenutzt, *adj.* worn out, used up; stale; threadbare.
Abgeordnet-e(r), *m.* deputy, delegate, political representative; member of parliament. **-enhaus,** *n.* house of representatives, chamber of deputies.
abgerben, *v.a.* tan; (*coll.*) beat soundly.
abgerechnet, *see* **abrechnen.**
abgerissen, *see* **abreißen.**
abgesagt, *see* **absagen.**
Abgesandte(r), *m.* emissary, ambassador.
Abgesang, *m.* (-(e)s, ⸚e) *a technical term in the language of the mastersingers denoting* the latter portion of a stanza, *the former half being called* Aufgesang.
Abgeschäumte(s), *n.* skimmings, scum.
abgeschieden, *p.p. & adj.* 1. separated; 2. solitary, secluded, retired; 3. departed, defunct, dead; *-er Geist* or *-e Seele*, departed spirit. **-heit,** *f.* seclusion, secluded spot; solitude, privacy, retirement. *See* **abscheiden.**
abgeschliffen, *p.p. & adj.* polished; ground; refined, polite. **-heit,** *f.* polish, refinement, elegance. *See* **abschleifen.**
abgeschlossen, *p.p. & adj.* retired, secluded; self-contained; concluded, settled, closed, complete. **-heit,** *f.* seclusion. *See* **abschließen.**
abgeschmackt, *adj.* tasteless, insipid; absurd; in bad taste. **-heit,** *f.* bad taste; insipidity.
abgesehen, *p.p.*; - *von*, without regard to; apart from; neglecting, exclusive of, irrespective of; - *davon, daß*, without mentioning that; - *auf* (*Acc.*), intended for. *See* **absehen.**
abgesessen! Dismount! (*Mil.*).
abgesondert, *p.p. & adj.* separated; separate; distinct; retired; insulated (*Phys.*); *-e Feuchtigkeit* secretion (*Med.*).
abgespannt, *p.p. & adj.* relaxed, debilitated, tired, weary, exhausted, low. **-heit,** *f.* exhaustion; debility; languor.
abgestanden, *p.p. & adj.* stale; decayed, perished, rotten, brittle, sour, flat. *See* **abstehen.**
abgestempelt, *see* **abstempeln.**
abgestorben, *p.p. & adj.* paralysed, dead; *der Gesellschaft* -, lost to society. **-heit,** *f.* apathy; deadness. *See* **absterben.**
abgestumpft, *p.p. & adj.* blunted; truncated; dull; indifferent; neutralized. *See* **abstumpfen.**
abgestutzt, *see* **abstutzen.**
abgetan, *p.p. & adj.* disposed of, settled, over.
abgetragen, *p.p. & adj.* worn out, threadbare.
abgetrieben, *see* **abtreiben.**
abgewinnen, *ir.v.a.* win from; extract; *einem den Vorteil* -, get the better of a p.; *einem den Vorsprung* -, get the start of, steal a march upon a p.; *die Luft, den Wind* -, gain the wind; *einer S. Geschmack* -, acquire a taste for a th.; *sich* (*Dat.*) *mit Mühe etwas* -, prevail upon o.s. after a struggle.
abgewöhnen, 1. *v.a.* (*einem etwas*) disaccustom, wean from, break of. 2. *v.r.* break o.s. of, give up (*a habit, etc.*); *sich* (*Dat.*) *das Rauchen* -, give up smoking.
abgezirkelt, *see* **abzirkeln.**
abgezogen, *p.p. & adj.* far off, remote; (*C.L.*) deducted; drawn off; distilled, extracted; abstract (*Phil.*); *-er Begriff*, abstract idea. *See* **abziehen.**
abgieren, *v.n.* sheer off *or* away (*Naut.*).
abgieß-en, *ir.v.a.* pour off; decant; cast (*in a foundry*). **-er,** *m.* caster, moulder. **-ung,** *f.* decanting; casting.
Abglanz, *m.* reflected splendour, reflection.
abglätten, 1. *v.a.* smooth, polish. 2. *v.r. Menschen glätten sich ab*, men become polished *or* well-mannered.
abgleich-en, *ir.v.a.* equalize; balance; adjust; *Rechnungen -en*, square accounts. **-ung,** *f.* levelling; equalization; adjustment. **-ungswaage,** *f.* *see* **Justierwaage. -zirkel,** *m.* divider.
abgleiten, *ir.v.n.* (*aux.* s.) slip *or* glide off; creep (*Metall.*); *alles gleitet an ihm ab*, he pays no heed to anything.
abglieder-n, *v.a.* remove in segments. **-ung** *f.*, dismemberment, segmentation; offshoot.
abglimmen, *ir.v.n.* (*aux.* s.) cease to glow, fade away.
abglühen, *v.a.* make red-hot; anneal; mull (*wine*).
Abgott, *m.* (-es, ⸚er) idol; *einen zu seinem - machen*, idolize a p. **-schlange,** *f.* boa-constrictor, anaconda.
Abgött-erei, *f.* idolatry. **-isch,** *adj.* idolatrous; *-isch lieben*, idolize.
abgraben, *ir.v.a.* dig away; separate by a ditch; drain; draw off; *einer Behauptung* (*Dat.*) *den Boden* -, cut the ground away beneath a p.'s feet in an argument.
abgrämen, *v.r.* pine away with grief.
abgrasen, *v.a.* graze (*a field*); cut grass.
abgraten, *v.a.* remove the burr, trim.
abgreifen, *ir.v.a.* 1. wear out by constant handling; *abgegriffene Bücher*, well-thumbed volumes. 2. obtain, determine, read off, measure off (*with compasses*).
abgrenz-en, *v.a.* fix the limits of; define; mark off, demarcate, delineate, differentiate, separate; *gegen den Himmel scharf abgegrenzt*, sharply outlined against the sky. **-bar,** *adj.* definable.
Abgrund, *m.* (-(e)s, ⸚e) abyss, precipice, chasm. **-tief,** *adj.* abysmal, unfathomable.
abgründig, *adj.* precipitous.
abgucken, *v.a.* (*coll.*) (*bei einem etwas*) learn by looking at s.o. surreptitiously.
Abgunst, *f.*, *see* **Mißgunst.**
abgünstig, *adj.* ill-disposed; *er ist mir* -, he is not well-disposed towards me.
Abguß, *m.* (-(ss)es, ⸚(ss)e) pouring off; decanting; casting, founding; cast; mould; copy.
abhaaren, 1. *v.a.* remove hair. 2. *v.n.* (*aux.* h.) lose hair; moult.
abhacken, *v.a.* chop off.
abhaken, *v.a.* unhook.
abhalftern, *v.a.* unharness; remove the halter; (*coll.*) put on the shelf; (*coll.*) *er wurde abgehalftert*, he was dismissed.
abhalt-en, 1. *ir.v.a.* hold off *or* back; restrain; check, prevent, debar, deter, ward off; hinder; hold (*the assizes, a sitting, meeting, review*); deliver (*a speech*); keep (*school*); *lassen Sie sich nicht* (*davon*) *-en*, don't be deterred, don't let me hinder you; *Lehrstunden richtig -en*, give lessons regularly. 2. *v.n.* (*aux.* h.) *vom Lande -en*, bear off from the land (*Naut.*). **-ung,** *f.* hindrance, impediment, prevention; holding (*meeting, etc.*); conducting (*classes, etc.*).
abhand-eln, *v.a.* bargain for; beat down in bargaining; treat of, debate, discuss; negotiate, transact; *einem etwas -eln*, purchase s.th. from s.o. **-lung,** *f.* treatise, essay; discussion; (*pl.*) proceedings, transactions; (*archaic*) act (*Theat.*).
abhanden, *adv.* not at hand, mislaid, missing, lost; - *kommen*, get lost; - *gekommen sein*, be missing; *das Buch ist mir - gekommen*, I cannot lay hands on the book, I have lost the book. **-sein,** *n.* absence; loss.
Abhang, *m.* (-(e)s, ⸚e) slope, declivity. **-en,** *ir.v.n.* 1. hang down; be suspended; 2. ((*coll.*) *abhängen*) depend upon; *es hängt von Ihnen ab*, it depends on you.
abhäng-en, *v.a.* unhang; take down; take off the receiver (*Phone*). **-ig,** *adj.* 1. sloping, inclined; 2. dependent on, subject to; *-ige Rede*, oblique (*or* indirect) speech. **-igkeit,** *f.* 1. slope, declivity; 2. dependence; 3. slope function (*Math.*); *in - igkeit von . . . auftragen*, plot as a function of (*Math.*).
abhärmen, *v.r.* languish; pine away (*from grief*); *sich - über eine S.*, grieve about a th.

Forms of p.p. in **abge-** *not found here should be sought under inf.*

abhärten, 1. *v.a.* harden, temper (*Metall.*). 2. *v.r.* inure o.s. (*to fatigue, etc.*).
abhaschen, *v.a.* (*einem etwas*) –, snatch (s.th. from s.o.).
abhaspeln, *v.a.* 1. unwind from a reel; 2. (*Coll.*) reel off (*a piece of music, a poem*).
abhauen, *ir.v.a.* cut off; cut down; (*sl.*) clear out, scram.
abhäuten, 1. *v.a.* skin, peel; 2 *v.n.* (*aux.* h.) cast the skin, excoriate.
abheb-en, 1. *ir.v.a.* lift up *or* off; contrast, bring into relief; uncover, remove; *wer hebt ab?* whose turn is it to cut? (*Cards*); *Geld –en,* draw money (*from the bank*); *Rahm –en,* skim the cream; *den Abstrich –en,* remove the scum. 2. *v.r.* be contrasted, be brought into relief; *die helle Gestalt hebt sich auf* (or *von*) *dem dunkeln Hintergrunde vorteilhaft ab,* the light figure is set off to advantage against the dark background. **–ung,** *f.* withdrawal (*money*).
abhebern, *v.a.* siphon off.
abheilen, *v.n.* (*aux.* s.) heal completely.
abhelfen, *ir.v.n.* (*aux.* h. *Dat.*) help, remedy, obviate; supply (*a want*); *dem ist nicht abzuhelfen,* that cannot be helped; *einer Schwierigkeit* –, remove a difficulty; *einem Fehler* –, correct a fault; *Beschwerden* –, redress grievances.
abherzen, *v.a.* hug to one's heart's content; (*fam.*) smother with kisses.
abhetzen, 1. *v.a.* tire out, harass. 2. *v.r.* tire o.s. out, overwork.
Abhilfe, *f.* remedy, redress, relief.
Abhitze, *f., see* **Abwärme.**
abhobeln, *v.a.* smooth with a plane; plane off.
abhold, *adj.* (*with Dat.*) averse (to *or* from); disinclined (for *or* from), unfavourable (to).
abholen *v.a.* fetch, call for, go to meet; collect; haul *or* get off (*Naut.*); *einen – lassen,* send for a p.; *ich will Sie bei Ihrem Vater* –, I will call for you at your father's; *das Auto wird mich* –, the car will come for me.
Abholz, *n.* chips of wood; dead wood; waste wood. **–en,** *v.a.* cut down the trees, clear of timber (*a wood*). **–ung,** *f.* deforestation.
abhorch-en, *v.a.*; *einem etwas –en,* learn s.th. from s.o. by listening; overhear. **–trichter,** *m.* sound locator (*Mil.*).
abhör-en, *v.a.* learn by hearing; hear s.o. recite; tap the (telephone) wire; intercept, listen in, tune in; *einen Schüler –en,* hear a pupil's lesson; *die Zeugen –en,* question witnesses; *Zeugen gegen einander –en,* confront witnesses. **–ung,** *f.* hearing; trial; examination.
Abhub, *m.* 1. leavings, remains (*of a meal*); waste, scum, dross; 2. cut (*Cards*).
abhülsen, *v.a.* shell; peel; husk, blanch (*almonds*).
äbich, äbicht, *adj.* turned, being the reversed *or* wrong side (*of cloth*); left (*Tech.*).
abirr-en, *v.n.* (*aux.* s.) lose one's way; deviate; err. **–end,** *adj.* aberrant (*Opt.*). **–ung,** *f.* deviation; aberration (*Opt.*).
Abitur, *n.*, school-leaving examination (qualifying for admission to a university). **–ient,** *m.* (–en, –en) candidate for this examination (= sixth-form scholar, school-leaver).
abjagen, 1. *v.a.* override (*a horse*). 2. *v.r.* overexert o.s.
abkälten, *v.a.* cool; *Wein* –, ice wine.
abkämpfen, *v.a.* exhaust with fighting; *abgekämpfte Truppen,* soldiers worn out with fighting; *einem etwas* –, get s.th. from s.o. by fighting.
abkanten, *v.a.* take off the corners; take off the selvedge; chamfer; bevel.
abkanzeln, *v.a.*; (*coll.*) give a good scolding; (*sl.*) dress down.
abkappen, *v.a.* lop, pollard (*trees*).
abkargen, *v.a. einem etwas* –, stint a p. of s.th.
abkarten, *v.a.* prearrange, plan, concert, plot; *abgekartetes Spiel,* prearranged affair, put-up job.
abkauen, *v.a. sich die Nägel* –, bite one's nails.
Abkauf, *m.* (-(e)s, ¨-e), purchase, act of purchasing; act of buying off (*a claim, etc.*). **–en,** *v.a. einem etwas* –, buy s.th. from s.o.; *sich jedes Wort – lassen,* have the words dragged out of one.
Abkäufer, *m.* purchaser.
Abkehr, *f.* (*no pl.*) act of turning away, withdrawing, renunciation; alienation, estrangement; backsliding; *von Gott,* estrangement from God. **–en** *v.a.* 1. turn away, turn off; avert; divert; distract; 2. brush away; *sich von einem –en,* turn one's back upon a p.; withhold one's assistance (from a p.).
abkeltern, *v.a.* press (*wine*).
abkippen, *v.n.* (*sl.*) dive (*of submarine*).
abklär-en, 1. *v.a.* clear up, clarify, filter; decant; *abgeklärter Mensch,* p. of great self-possession. 2. *v.r.* become *or* grow clear. **–ung,** *f.* clarification, filtration, decantation. **–ungsflasche,** *f.* decanting vessel.
Abklatsch, *m.* (-es, -e) cast, impression; stereotype-plate; copy, poor imitation. **–en,** *v.a.* 1. print off (*a proof-sheet, a medal, etc.*); stereotype; 2. plagiarize, copy.
abkleiden, *v.a.* 1. conceal; 2. partition off (*Arch.*).
abklemmen, *v.a.* pinch off.
abklettern, *v.a.* & *n.* climb down.
abklingen, *v.n.* die away (*of sound, etc.*); fade away.
abklopfen, *v.a.* beat (*carpets, dust from clothes, etc.*), knock off; beat up; test (*by knocking, as a wall*); thrash, beat soundly; *einen Probebogen* –, strike off a proof-sheet.
abknabbern, *v.a.* nibble off, pick (*a bone*).
abknallen, 1. *v.n.* (*aux.* s.) explode, go off with a bang. 2. *v.a.* shoot, kill (*a p.*).
abknappen, abknapsen, *v.a.* break off in little bits; stint; be over-meticulous; *einem am Lohne* –, curtail a p's wages.
abkneifen, *ir.v.a.* pinch *or* nip off; *den Wind* –, haul the wind; ply to windward; *einem Schiffe den Wind* –, take the wind out of a ship's sails.
abknöpfen, *v.a.* unbutton; (*coll.*) *einem etwas* –, take s.th. away from s.o., do a p. out of a th.
abknüpfen, *v.a.* loosen; untie; undo.
abkochen, 1. *v.a.* boil down; decoct; extract (*by boiling*); *Milch* –, scald milk; *Früchte langsam* –, stew fruit. 2. *v.n.* (*aux.* h.) cook a meal (*hurriedly, as on a march*).
abkommandieren, *v.a.* order off, detail, detach.
Abkomm-e, *m.* (-n, -n) *see* **Abkömmling. –en.** 1. *ir.v.n.* (*aux.* s.) 1. come away; get away; take off (*Av.*); 2. get off, be spared; 3. swerve; deviate; digress; 4. be descended from; 5. fall into disuse; become obsolete; go out of fashion; 6. fall to leeward; 7. aim (*Artil.*); *vom Wege –en,* lose the way; *können Sie wohl eine Viertelstunde –en?* can you get away (*or* be spared) for a quarter of an hour? *ich bin davon abgekommen,* I have given it up; *ich bin von meiner früheren Ansicht abgekommen,* I have altered my former opinion. 2. *n.* 1. agreement; *ein –en treffen,* come to an agreement; 2. falling into disuse; 3. origin, descent = *die Abkunft, die Herkunft*; *von gutem –en,* of good stock; 4. take-off, start (*Sport*). **–enschaft,** *f.* offspring, posterity. **–rohr,** *n.* sub-calibre barrel, Morris tube (*Mil.*). **–schießen** *n.* practice fire (*with sub-calibre ammunition*).
abkömm-lich, *adj.* dispensable, needless, superfluous. **–ling,** *m.* (-s -e) descendant; derivative (*Chem.*).
abköpfen, *v.a.* decapitate; top, poll (*trees*).
abkoppeln, *v.a.* uncouple, unleash (*dogs*).
abkramen, *v.a.* remove, clear.
abkratz-en, *v.a.* scrape *or* scratch off; *sich die Schuhe* –, scrape one's shoes. **–eisen,** *n.* (foot-) scraper.
abkriegen, *v.a.* (*einem etwas*) obtain (s.th. from s.o.); get; (*coll.*) *etwas* (*dabei*) –, get a wigging; get a beating; *etwas* (*davon*) –, get a share.
abkühl-en, 1. *v.a.* & *n.* (*aux.* s.) cool off *or* down; anneal; 2. *v.r.* cool o.s. down, refresh o.s. **–apparat,** *m.* refrigerator, cooler. **–ung,** *f.* cooling, refrigeration, chilling. **–ungsfläche,** *f.* cooling surface. **–faß,** *n.* cooling vat, annealing vat. **–verlust,** *m.* loss due to cooling.
abkünd-en, *usually* **–igen,** *v.a.* publish from the pulpit; proclaim, announce; notify to. **–igung,** *f.* proclamation, publishing; publishing of the banns; notice, warning.
Abkunft, *f.* (¨-e) descent, origin, parentage; breed, race; blood lineage; *von niedriger* –, of low birth, of base origin.

abkuppeln, *v.a. see* **abkoppeln**; disengage, disconnect, throw out the clutch.

abkürz–en, 1. *v.a.* shorten; abridge; abbreviate; lessen, curtail, condense; reduce to a lower term (*Arith.*). 2. *v.n.* (*& a.*) take a short cut. **–ung,** *f.* abbreviation; abridgement; reduction (*of fractions, etc.*). **–ungszeichen,** *n.* grammalogue (*Sten.*).

abküssen, *v.a.* kiss away (*as tears*); smother with kisses.

ablad–en, *ir.v.a.* unload; discharge (*cargo*); dump. **–er,** *m.* shipper; unloader, lighterman. **–ung,** *f.* unloading, discharging. **–eort,** *m.*, **–eplatz,** *m.* **–estelle,** *f.* place of discharge; port.

Ablag–e, *f.* (-en) laying aside; compensation to children instead of inheritance; assignment to separate use (*Law*); place of deposit; place for lading and shipping goods, yard; depot, dump, warehouse; *Kleider–e,* cloak-room; *Rechnungs–e* rendering of accounts. **–er,** *n.* resting-place; haunt; bed, deposit; privilege of liege lords of resting for refreshment at any tenant's house. **–ern** 1. *v.a.* deposit; remove from a storehouse; store up; *abgelagerte Zigarren,* well-seasoned (*or* matured) cigars. 2. *v.n. & r.* settle. **–erung,** *f.* deposit; deposition, subsidence, sediment, sedimentation (*Geol.*); furrow, storage; seasoning. **–erungsstelle,** *f.* dumping-ground, dump.

Ablaß, *m.* (-(ss)es, ⁻̈(ss)e), letting off, draining, drainage, blow-off; outlet, escapement; drain, sluice; discount; *vollkommener* –, plenary indulgence. **–brief,** *m.* letter of indulgence; dispensation. **–geld,** *n.* shrove-money. **–hahn,** *m.* drain cock. **–handel,** *m.* sale of indulgences. **–jahr,** *n.* (year of) jubilee. **–krämer,** *m.* **–prediger,** *m.* seller of indulgences. **–rohr,** *n.* waste-pipe. **–schraube,** *f.* drain plug. **–woche,** *f.* week of Corpus Christi. **–zettel,** *m.* ticket of indulgence.

ablassen, 1. *ir.v.a.* drain, empty, let off; decant; tap, broach (*a cask*); rack (*wine*); launch (*a vessel*); start (*a train*); blow off (*steam*); reduce (*in price*); deduct; *zum Selbstkostenpreis* –, to sell at cost-price; *auf beiden Seiten etwas* –, make some reduction on both sides, split the difference; *ein Faß* –, broach a cask. 2. *v.n.* (*aux.* h.) leave off, desist, cease.

ablauern, *v.a.* lie in wait for, lurk, watch for; obtain *or* learn by watching; *dem Wilde die Fährte* –, spy out the track of the game.

Ablauf, *m.* (-es) running off; discharge; lapse, expiration (*of time, of a treaty, etc.*); termination, completion; apophyge (*Arch.*), gutter; issue (*of a matter*); launching; ebb; – *eines Wechsels,* maturity of a bill. **–en,** 1. *ir.v.n.* (*aux.* s.) run down (*of clocks*); run off; set off, depart; start (*races*); elapse, expire; become due; *das Wasser läuft ab,* the tide ebbs *or* has turned; *langsam –en,* ooze; *das wird nicht gut –en,* it will lead to trouble; *gut –en,* pass off well; *die Uhr ist abgelaufen,* the clock has run down; (*Poet.*) *deine Uhr ist abgelaufen,* your sand has run out, your hour is come; *–en lassen,* parry a thrust; answer sharply (*a p.*), snub; start (*races*); launch (*a ship*). 2. *v.a.* wear out (*by walking, as shoes*); *sich* (*Dat.*) *die Beine -en* (*nach*), run o.s. off one's legs; *einem den Rang –en,* outdo a p.; *sich die Hörner –en,* sow one's wild oats; *das habe ich* (*mir*) *längst an den Schuhen abgelaufen,* I knew that long ago. **–(s)frist,** *f.* time (*or* term) of payment. **–(s)loch,** *n.* venthole, outlet. **–(s)rinne,** *f.* sink; gutter; channel. **–(s)röhre,** *f.* waste-pipe. **–seite,** *f.* trailing edge (*Av.*).

Abläufer, *m.* (-s, -) that which runs off; spool; misplaced thread (*Weav.*).

ablauschen, *v.a.* pick up (*Rad.*); lurk, lie in wait for, watch for (*a chance*).

Ablaut, *m.* (-es, -e) vowel-gradation, ablaut. **–sreihe,** *f.* series of graded vowels. **–en,** *v.a.* change the root vowel according to the laws of gradation; *-ende Zeitwörter,* strong verbs.

abläuten, *v.a.* ring the bell (for the train) to start; *der Zug wird gleich abgeläutet,* the bell for the train to start will be rung in a minute.

abläutern, *v.a.* purify, clarify; refine (*sugar*); filter, wash (*ore*).

ableben, 1. *v.n.* (*aux.* s.) die; become decrepit. 2. *n.* death, decease, demise.

ablecken, *v.a.* lick off.

ableg–en, 1. *v.a.* put away, take off; lay off, down *or* aside (*garments, arms, a burden, etc.*); slough off (*skin, etc.*); give up (*habits*); file (*letters, documents*); *Rechenschaft über etwas –en,* render an account of, account for; *die Kleider –en,* undress; *Rechnung –en,* submit accounts, give an account, account; *einen Eid –en,* take an oath; *Zeugnis –en,* bear witness; *ein Bekenntnis –en,* make a confession; *Arbeiter –en,* pay off workers; *die Kinderschuhe –en,* not be a child any longer; *Bitte, legen Sie ab,* take off your things, please! *eine Schuld –en,* pay a debt; *eine Prüfung –en,* take an examination; *abgelegte Kleider,* cast-off clothing. 2. *v.n.* (*aux.* h.) put out to sea; shove off (*Naut.*). **–er,** *m.* layer; scion; sprig, shoot laid out for propagation. **–efehler,** *m.* wrong letter, misprint. **–espan,** *m.* distributing rule (*Typ.*). **–ung,** *f.* laying, laying aside; rendering (*of accounts*); taking (*of an oath*).

ablehn–en, *v.a.* decline, refuse; remove, keep off; *einen Vorschlag –en,* reject a proposal. **–ung,** *f.* refusal, rejection.

ableihen, *ir.v.a.*; *einem etwas* –, borrow s.th. from s.o.

ableist–en, 1. *v.a.*; *einen Eid –en,* take an oath; pass, serve; *Wehrdienst –en,* serve in the armed forces. 2. *n.*; *–en der Dienstpflicht,* performance of military service. **–ung,** *f.* serving (*one's time*); swearing (*of an oath*).

ableit–bar, *adj.* deducible, derivable, capable of being turned aside, drainable. **–en,** *v.a.* lead away, divert, deflect; mislead; draw off, drain; trace back; derive; deduce; let off *or* escape. **–er,** *m.* conduit-pipe, channel. **Blitz–er,** lightning-conductor. **–ung,** *f.* leading off; leakage (*of current* (*Elec.*)); diversion (*of a stream, etc.*); derivation, derivative, differential coefficient (*Math.*). **–ungsgraben,** *m.* communication trench (*Mil.*). **–ungsrinne,** *f.* sewer, drain, duct. **–ungssilbe,** *f.* suffix.

ablenk–en, *v.a.* turn away, divert; deflect, refract; avert, parry. **–ung,** *f.* diversion (*also Mil.*), deviation (*Navig. & Av.*), deflexion. **–ungsangriff,** *m.*, **–ungsmanöver,** *n.* diversion attack, feint (*Mil.*). **–ungswinkel,** *m.* angle of deflexion.

ablernen, *v.a.*; *einem etwas* –, learn s.th. from s.o., imitate.

ables–en, *ir.v.a.* read off (*instruments*); read aloud *or* over; pick off, gather; *einen Winkel –en,* read off an angle; *vom Blatt –en,* read at sight. **–bar,** *adj.* readable (*as markings on a dial*). **–emarke,** *f.* reference point, pointer (*on a dial*).

ableugn–en, *v.a.* deny, disown, disclaim. **–er,** *m.* denier. **–ung,** *f.* denial, disclaimer, disavowal.

abliefer–n, *v.a.* deliver (*over, up*); consign. **–ung,** *f.* delivery; issue (*of provisions*); *zahlbar bei* (or *nach*) *–ung,* payable on delivery; *nach erfolgter –ung,* on (*or* after) delivery. **–ungsschein,** *m.* certificate *or* receipt of delivery. **–ungstag,** *m.* day fixed for delivery. **–ungzeit,** *f.* term of delivery; settling day (*of securities*).

abliegen, *ir.v. n.* (*aux.* s.) lie at a distance, be remote; (*aux.* h.) lie until mellow, grow mature; settle, clear.

ablisten, *v.a.*; *einem etwas* –, obtain s.th. by cunning *or* trickery from s.o.

ablocken, *v.a.* entice away; obtain by flattery, lure from; *einem etwas* –, coax a p. out of a th.; *einem Tränen* –, draw tears from a p.

ablockern, *v.a.* loosen (*earth around roots*).

ablohnen, *v.a.* pay off; discharge.

ablöschen, *v.a.* extinguish, quench; slake (*lime*); temper (*iron*); wipe, blot out.

ablös–en, 1. *v.a.* loosen, unloose; cut off, sever, take off, amputate, detach; scale off; commute (*a penalty*); relieve (*guard*); redeem (*annuity, pledge*); pay, settle, discharge (*debts*). 2. *v.r.* be(come) detached; peel *or* drop off; alternate, relieve one another. **–bar, –lich,** *adj.* redeemable (*of debts*). **–ung,** *f.* loosening; amputation; scaling off; relief; relieving guard; ransom; commutation (*of gratuities*); redemption, discharge (*debts*).

ablöten, *v.a.* unsolder.

abluchsen (*coll.*) *einem etwas* –, swindle a p. out of a th.

Abluft, *f.* (⸚e) foul air, spent air.

ablüften, *v.a.* air

abmach–en, 1. *v.a.* undo, loosen; detach; settle, arrange, conclude; *gütlich –en*, settle amicably; *ein Geschäft –en*, settle a business, transact business; *das ist abgemacht!* agreed! it's a bargain! (*C.L.*) **abgemacht,** in order, paid, settled, agreed. **–ung,** *f.* arrangement, settlement, agreement; stipulation; adjustment; contract; *laut –ung*, according to agreement; *eine –ung treffen* come to an agreement.

abmager–n, *v.n.* (*aux.* s.) grow lean; **abgemagert,** *p.p. & adj.* emaciated. **–ungskur,** *f.* slimming, dieting.

abmähen, *v.a.* mow, cut down.

abmahlen, (*p.p.* abgemahlen), *v.a.* grind thoroughly, finish grinding.

abmahn–en, *v.a.* dissuade (*von*, from), warn (*von*, against). **–end,** *pr.p. & adj.* dissuasive. **–ung,** *f.* dissuasion.

abmalen, *v.a.* paint, portray, copy by painting, depict, describe; *sich – lassen*, have one's portrait painted.

abmärgeln, *v.a.* see **abmergeln.**

abmarkten, *v.a.*; *davon läßt sich nichts –*, nothing can be deducted from this.

Abmarsch, *m.* (-es, ⸚e) departure; marching off, march. **–bereit,** *adj.* ready to start. **–ieren,** *v.n.* (*aux.* s.) march off; decamp; *Mann für Mann –ieren*, file off.

abmartern, *v.a.* torture; torment; vex, plague, worry; *einem etwas –*, extort s.th. from s.o. (by tormenting him).

Abmaß, *n.* measure of a th., dimension.

abmatt–en, *v.a.* 1. fatigue, weary; harass; 2. make dull, remove the shine; *ganz abgemattet*, quite knocked up *or* worn out. **–ung,** *f.* weariness, exhaustion.

abmeiern, *v.a.* expel, eject (*a tenant*).

abmeißeln, *v.a.* chisel off *or* out.

abmeld–en, *v.a.* countermand, announce withdrawal (*or* removal); *einen Fremden auf der Polizei –en*, report a visitor's departure to the police; *einen Schüler beim Direktor –en*, give notice to the headmaster of a boy's removal from school. **–ung,** *f.* notice of withdrawal.

abmergeln, *v.a.* waste, emaciate.

abmerken, *v.a.* observe, perceive.

abmess–en, *ir.v.a.* measure off; gauge; fathom; survey; suit, make to suit; compare; *er mißt seine Ausdrücke nicht ab*, he does not weigh his words; *andere nach sich selbst –en*, judge others by o.s.; *die Zeit –en*, apportion time, time; *einen Vers –en*, scan a verse; *das ist nicht abzumessen*, that cannot be gauged, there is no standard for that. **–er,** *m.* measurer, surveyor. **–bar,** *adj.* measurable. **–ung,** *f.* measurement; dimension; assessment; survey.

abmiet–en, *v.a.* hire *or* rent from; farm. **–er,** *m.* hirer; lessee, tenant.

abmildern, *v.a.* moderate.

abminder–n, *v.a.* diminish, lessen. **–ung,** *f.* diminution, lessening; reduction.

abmontieren, *v.a.* take to pieces, strip, dismantle (*machinery, etc.*).

abmüden, *v.a. & r.* tire out, fatigue.

abmühen, *v.r.* make great exertions, exert o.s., labour, toil.

abmurksen, *v.a.*: (*coll.*) *einen –*, kill a p. secretly, make away with a p.; dispatch a p.

abmüßigen, *v.r.* find time *or* leisure; *ich kann mir die Zeit nicht –*, I cannot spare the time.

abmuster–n, *v.a.* pay off (*a crew*). **–ung,** *f.* paying off (*of the crew*).

abnagen, *v.a.* gnaw off; *sein Verlust nagt ihm das Herz ab*, his loss preys upon his mind; *einen Knochen –*, pick a bone.

Abnahme, *f.* (*-n*) diminution, decline; decrease, falling off, shrinkage, depreciation; decay; taking off *or* down; waning (*of the moon*); ebb; subtraction; decrement; loss; amputation; sale; *die – vom Kreuze*, the Descent from the Cross; *– einer Rechnung*, auditing an account; *– eines Eides*, administering of an oath; *– der Tage*, shortening of the days. **–prüfung,** acceptance test (*for fitness to take over*).

abnehm–en, 1. *ir.v.a.* take off *or* away; amputate; remove; cut (*cards*); gather (*fruit*); buy (*goods*); examine, audit (*an account*); skim (*cream*); narrow, take in (*in sewing, knitting, etc.*); *einem sein Geld –en*, fleece a p.; *wollen Sie nicht –en?* won't you take off your things? *den Hut –en vor*, take off one's hat to; *aus etwas –en*, perceive *or* judge from s.th., conclude; *daraus kann ich –en*, from that I can gather; *einem einen Eid –en*, administer an oath to a p.; *einem ein Versprechen –en*, obtain a promise from s.o.; *die Ruderpinne –en*, unship the tiller; *einem etwas –en*, take s.th. from a p.; *einem Geld –en*, win money from a p. 2. *v.n.* (*aux.* h.) wane; decrease, diminish, reduce, subtract, lose weight, decline, fall off, recede; sink, be lowered; fail; shorten; *der Wein nimmt ab*, the wine deteriorates; *der Mond nimmt ab*, the moon is waning; *es nimmt mit ihm schleunig ab*, he is going downhill rapidly. 3. *n. die Preise sind im –en*, prices are falling. **–bar,** *adj.* removable, detachable. **–end,** *pr.p. & adj.* decreasing; waning (*of the moon*); *–ende Reihe*, diminishing series. **–er,** *m.* buyer purchaser, customer.

abneig–en, 1. *v.a.* turn away; bend down; incline, avert; render averse. 2. *v.r.* turn aside from; incline; diverge. **–end,** *pr.p. & adj.* diverging. **–ung,** *f.* turning aside; disinclination, aversion, antipathy; declination; slope; divergence; (*natürliche*) *–ung*, (*gegen einen*), natural antipathy (to s.o.); *eine –ung fassen gegen*, take a dislike to.

abnieten, *v.a.* unrivet.

abnorm, *adj.* abnormal, irregular, exceptional, anomalous; exorbitant.

abnötigen, *v.a.*; *einem etwas –*, force, extort *or* elicit s.th. from s.o.

abnutz–en, (*sometimes* **abnütz–en**) 1. *v.a.* use up; wear out by use. **–ung,** *f.* wear and tear; wasting, exploitation; abrasion, scoring, erosion; detrition; attrition (*Mil.*). **–ungskrieg,** *m.* war of attrition.

Abonn–ement, *n.* (-s, -s) subscription to (*journals*); *aus dem -ement treten*, drop *or* discontinue one's subscription. **–ementskarte,** *f.* subscriber's ticket; season ticket. **–ent,** *m.* (*-en, -en*) subscriber. **–entin,** *f.* lady subscriber. **–ieren,** *v.a. & r.* subscribe (*auf eine S.*, to a th.).

abordn–en, *v.a.* delegate, depute. **–ung,** *f.* delegation, deputation; committee. *See* **Abgeordneter.**

Abort, *m.* (-(e)s, -e) 1. lavatory, toilet, W.C.; 2. abortion (*Med.*). **–ieren,** *v.n.* (*aux.* h.) have an abortion, abort, miscarry. **–us,** *m.* abortion, miscarriage.

abpacht–en, *v.a.* farm; rent a farm. **–er** (*or* **Abpächter**) *m.* tenant farmer, lessee of a farm.

abpassen, *v.a.* 1. wait, watch, stay for; lurk for; 2. fit, measure, adjust, square; time well *or* ill; *eine Gelegenheit –*, wait for an opportunity.

abpeitschen, *v.a.* whip off; whip soundly.

abpfänden, *v.a.* seize by law, distrain.

abpfeifen, *ir.v.a. & n.* (*Sport*) sound (referee's) whistle (*to interrupt or terminate play*).

abpflöcken, *v.a.* mark with pegs; unpeg and take down from the line (*clothes*).

abpflücken, *v.a.* pluck off, gather.

abplacken, *usually* **abplagen,** 1. *v.a.*; *einem etwas –*, extort s.th. from a p.; worry a p. out of a th. 2. *v.r.* tire o.s. out, worry o.s. to death.

abplatt–en, *v.a.* flatten, crush. **–ung,** *f.* flattening, *–ung der Erde*, oblateness of the earth at the poles.

abplätt–en, *v.a.* transfer pattern (*from paper to cloth*) with a hot iron. **–muster,** *n.* (embroidery) transfer.

abprägen, *v.a.* stamp, coin.

abprall–en, 1. *v.n.* (*aux.* s.) rebound; ricochet; recoil; reverberate. 2. *n.*, **–ung,** *f.* recoil, rebound, reflection. **–er,** *m.* ricochet. **–ungswinkel,** *m.* angle of reflection.

abpressen, *v.a.*; squeeze out of; *einem etwas –*, extort s.th. from s.o.

abprotzen, 1. *v.a.* unlimber (*a gun*). 2. *v.n.* (*vulg.*) shit.

Abputz, *m.* rough-cast, plaster. **–en,** *v.a.* 1. cleanse, clean, polish; snuff (*a candle*); rub down (*a horse*); 2. plaster, rough-cast (*a wall*).

abquälen 1. *v.a.* torment; *einem etwas –*, **get s.th.**

from s.o. by pestering. 2. *v.r.* exert o.s., toil hard; wear o.s. out with worry.
abquetschen, *v.a.* crush, squeeze off.
abquick-en, *v.a.* purify, separate, refine (*metals, usually gold or silver, from ore*). **-beutel,** *m.* filter bag.
abquirlen, *v.a.* beat up, mill, froth.
abrackern, *v.r.* work o.s. to death, drudge, slave.
abraffen, *v.a.* snatch away; tie up in sheaves.
abrahmen, *v.a.* take off the cream, skim; *abgerahmte Milch*, skimmed milk.
abrainen, *v.a.* separate fields by ridges (*on which grass is allowed to grow*); balk off.
abranken, *v.a.* prune (*a vine*); thin out.
abraspeln, *v.a.*, smooth off (*with a rasp*).
abraten, *ir.v.a.* dissuade from, advise against; obtain by guessing; *er rät mir von meinem Vorhaben ab*, he dissuades me from my purpose; *ich rate es dir ab, ich rate dir ab, dies zu tun*, I advise you not to do it; *einem seine Gedanken –*, guess *or* divine a p.'s thoughts.
abrauch-en, *v.n.* (*aux.* s.) evaporate, vaporize, fume. **-schale,** *f.* evaporating-dish.
abräuchern, *v.a.* fumigate, smoke.
abraufen, 1. *v.a.* pull off, tear off. 2. *v.r.* come to blows, fight with all one's might.
Abraum, *m.* (*no pl.*). 1. rubbish; dross; rubble; 2. top layer (*of earth or rock*) over a mineral deposit (*Min.*); waste wood, loppings (*For.*). **-kasten,** *m.* dust-bin. **-salze,** *n.pl.* abraum-salts (*a saline deposit*).
abräum-en, *v.a.* clear, remove; *den Tisch –en*, clear the table; *räume* (*den Tisch*) *ab!* (*usually without the Acc.*), clear the table! **-ung,** *f.* removal, clearance; forest clearing.
abrechn-en, *v.a. & n.* 1. settle accounts; (*also fig.* = get one's own back); 2. deduct, subtract; make allowance for; *abgerechnet davon*, setting aside, not to speak of; *sein Vorurteil abgerechnet ist er . . .*, making allowance for his prejudice he is . . .; *einige Stellen abgerechnet*, with the exception of a few passages. **-ung,** *f.* 1. settlement (*of accounts*); revenge; 2. deduction; discount liquidation; *auf –ung*, on account; *–ung halten*, balance accounts. **-ungsstelle,** *f.* clearing house. **-ungstag,** *m.* settling-day, audit day.
Abrecht-e, *f.* wrong side (*of cloth*). **-en,** *v.a.* dress the wrong side of cloth.
Abrede, *f.* (*pl.* -n) 1. agreement; understanding; 2. denial; *– treffen*, concert together, stipulate, agree, make an appointment; *in – stellen*, dispute, deny; *ich stelle das nicht in –*, I do not deny it; *das ist wider die –*, that is against our agreement. **-n,** *v.a.* 1. *eine S. –n*, agree upon a th.; 2. *einem –n von*, dissuade a p. from; *abgeredetermaßen*, according to arrangement; *abgeredete Sache*, settled affair; *ich will dabei weder zureden noch –n*, I will not say anything either for or against it.
abreib-en, *ir.v.a.* rub, rub off; grind (*colours*); wear by friction, scour, abrade; *reiben Sie mich tüchtig ab!* rub me down well! *die Schuhe –en*, scrape *or* wipe one's shoes; *Einband etwas abgerieben*, binding somewhat rubbed *or* worn; *einen Flecken vom Glas –en*, rub a mark off the glass; *ein Glas von Flecken –en*, clean the glass of all marks. **-ung,** *f.* rubbing down; friction (*Med.*).
abreichen, *v.a.* reach down; reach; grasp.
Abreise, *f.* departure. **-n,** *v.n.* (*aux* s.) set out, start depart (*on a journey*); *–n nach* set out for, leave for.
abreiß-en, 1. *ir.v.n.* (*aux.* s.) break away, tear off; rupture; *abgerissene Sätze*, disconnected sentences; (*coll.*) come to an end; *meine Geduld reißt ab*, I lose all patience. 2. *v.a.* tear, break, pull *or* wrench off, pull down, demolish; wear out; draw a plan of, sketch; force (*a lock*); (*coll.*) *das reißt ja gar nicht ab*, there is no end to it; *das Gefecht reißt im Dunkel ab*, the fight comes to an end in the dark; *er sieht sehr abgerissen aus*, he looks very much out at elbows. **-er,** *m.* tracing-machine. **-kalender,** *m.* tear-off calendar, date-block. **-schnur,** *f.* rip cord (*parachute*), fuse cord (*hand grenade*). **-zünder,** *m.* friction igniter (*Mil.*).
abreiten, 1. *ir.v.n.* (*aux.* s.) ride away. 2. *v.a.* ride along *or* past (*a line of troops*); patrol (*on horseback*); wear out by riding; override; lose by riding (*as a shoe*).
abrennen, 1. *ir.v.n.* (*aux.* s.) run away. 2. *v.a. sich* (*Dat.*) *die Beine –*, run one's legs off.
abricht-en, *v.a.* adjust, measure exactly; level; plane; coach; train, drill, teach tricks, break in (*an animal*); *ein Schiff –en*, fit a ship for sea; rig out; *gut abgerichteter Hund*, well-trained dog. **-er,** *m.* trainer, breaker in; **-hammer,** *m.* straightening hammer. **-peitsche,** *f.* schooling whip. **-ung,** *f.* act of training; training, drill, breaking in.
Abrieb, *m.* (-es, -e), abrasion, particle removed by abrasion, dust. **-fest,** *adj.* durable (*not rubbing off*).
abriegel-n, 1. *v.a.* fasten with a bolt; bar, block (*markets*); cut off, shut off, barricade; 2. *v.r.* fasten *or* bolt one's door. **-ung,** *f.* cutting off. **-ungsfeuer,** *n.* box barrage (*Mil.*).
abrieseln, *v.n.* (*aux.* s.) flow down gently; trickle down.
abrinden, *v.a.* peel *or* strip off; bark; decorticate.
abringen, 1. *ir.v.a.*; *einem etwas –*, wrest s.th. from s.o., wring (*concessions, a confession, etc.*) from s.o.; *sich* (*Dat.*) *die Haut von den Händen –*, wring one's hands in despair. 2. *v.r.* wrestle with; *sich im Todeskampfe –*, struggle to the death.
abrinnen, *ir.v.n.* (*aux.* s.) run off, flow down.
Abriß, *m.* (-(ss)es, -(ss)e) 1. synopsis; abstract; summary; 2. hasty sketch; plan; draft; outline.
Abritt, *m.* (-(e)s, -e) departure on horseback; start (*racing*).
abrollen, 1. *v.a.* 1. roll away, off *or* down; 2. transport goods (*from the railway-station*); 3. unroll; uncoil, unwind (*rope, film, etc.*); *ein Tau –*, pay out cable; 4. mangle. 2. *v.n.* (*aux.* s. & h.) roll *or* run down, roll off; start smartly (*of carriages*); *die Zeit rollt ab*, time rolls on.
abrücken, *v.n. & a.* 1. move off, depart; 2. displace, remove; *die Zeilen –*, begin with a new line; *von etwas –*, disavow a th.
abrudern, *v.n.* (*aux.* s.) row off.
Abruf, *m.* recall; calling away; proclamation; *auf –*, on call. **-bar,** *adj.* recallable; within call. **-en,** *ir.v.a.* 1. call away *or* off; recall; 2. repeat verbally, test the line (*Tele.*); *einen –en lassen*, have a p. called away, send for a p.; *einen Zug –en*, announce a train's departure. **-ung,** *f.* proclamation; recall. **-ungsschreiben,** *n.* letter of recall. **-ungsschuß,** *m.* signal gun for recall.
abrühren, *v.a.* beat up, stir.
abrunden, abründen, *v.a.* round off, even up, round (*periods in writing*); *abgerundete Zahlen*, round figures; *abgerundetes Gewicht*, rough weight.
abrupfen, *v.a.* pluck off.
abrüst-en, *v.a.* 1. disarm; demobilize (*troops, an army*); 2. take down a scaffolding; lay up (*a ship*); dismantle. **-ung,** *f.* disarmament; act of taking down. **-ungskonferenz,** *f.* disarmament conference. **-wagen,** *m.* breakdown lorry.
abrutschen, *v.n.* (*aux.* s.) slip off, glide down; sneak off; sideslip (*Av.*); skid; (*coll.*) leave, decamp.
abrütteln, *v.a.* shake off.
absack-en, 1. *v.a.* pack in bags. 2. *v.n.* (*aux.* h.) drop down with the stream *or* tide (*Naut.*); drift; (*coll.*) pancake (*Av.*); sag; 3. become encysted (*Biol.*). **-ung,** *f.* encystment, sacculation (*Biol.*).
Absag-e, *f.* (-n) refusal (*of an invitation*); countermanding, counter-order; disowning; renunciation; decline. **-ebrief,** *m.* letter of refusal. **-en,** 1. *v.a.* refuse, decline; countermand, retract, revoke; *einen Besuch –en lassen*, cancel a visit; *ich ließ ihm die heutige Stunde –en*, I sent word to cancel his lesson today; *falls Sie mir nicht –en*, unless I hear from you to the contrary; *abgesagter Feind*, declared enemy, sworn enemy. 2. *v.n.* (*aux.* h.) renounce; (*coll.*) cry off. **-ung,** *f. see* **-e.**
absägen, *v.a.* saw off; (*coll.*) get rid of, dismiss.
absatteln, 1. *v.a.* unsaddle (*a horse*); unload (*pack-animals*). 2. *v.n.* (*aux.* h.) dismount.
absättigen, *v.a.* saturate, neutralize (*Chem.*).
Absatz, *m.* (-es, ⸗e) 1. paragraph; contrast; 2. heel (*of a shoe*); knot, joint (*Bot.*); 3. sale, market; turnover; 4. pause, stop, intermission; 5. break in an inclined plane; step, ledge; landing (*on a staircase*); terrace (*of a vineyard*); period, break (*Typ.*). *Ein*

Glas ohne – austrinken, empty a glass at one draught; *lesen Sie bis zum nächsten –*, read as far as the next paragraph; *guten – finden*, sell well; *in Absätzen*, at intervals, intermittently, by fits and starts; *der – der Treppe zum zweiten Stock*, the second-floor landing. **–fähig,** *adj.* marketable. **–gebiet,** *n.* market outlet (*for the sale of goods*). **–gestein,** *n.* sedimentary (stratified) rocks. **–leder,** *n.* heel-piece (*of a shoe*). **–manöver,** *n.* landing exercise (*Av.*). (*C.L.*) **–möglichkeit,** *f.* opening for the sale of. (*C.L.*) **–quelle,** *f.* market. **–weise,** *adv.* intermittently, at intervals; in batches.

absätzig, *adj.* having breaks *or* steps; intermissive; faulty (*of a stratum*).

absaug–en, *ir.v.a.* suck off; withdraw by suction; suck dry. **–pumpe,** *f.* vacuum pump.

absäugen, *v.a.* wean, (*Vet.*); inarch (*Hort.*).

abschab–en, 1. *v.a.* scrape off; grind off; wear out *or* threadbare; scrape (*a ship's bottom*). 2. *v.n.* (*fam.*) take to one's heels; *schab ab!* scram! **abgeschabt,** *p.p.* & *adj.* shabby, threadbare. **–sel,** *n.* parings, shavings, shreds, scrapings.

Abschach (*also* **Abzugsschach**), (*archaic*) double check (*a move by which check is given to king and queen at the same time*).

abschachern, *v.a.* (*einem etwas*), barter (s.th. from s.o.), get by haggling.

abschaff–en, *v.a.* 1. abolish, repeal, abrogate, annul; supersede; 2. do away with; give up keeping; dismiss, discharge, disband; remove. **–bar,** *adj.* abolishable, removable; abatable (*Law*). **–ung,** *f.* abolition; doing away with, discharging, giving up; abrogation (*of a law*).

abschäl–en, 1. *v.a.* peel, pare strip; shell; blanch; cut off the crust. 2. *v.n.* & *r.* peel off.

abschalten, *v.a.* disconnect, break contact, cut off (*Elec.*).

abschärfen, *v.a.* sharpen; pare off; make piquant (*Cook.*).

abschatt–en, *v.a.* shadow out; sketch; shade (*a drawing*); adumbrate. **–ieren,** *v.n.* shade off (*of colours*). **–ung,** *f.* gradation of tints.

abschätz–en, *v.a.* estimate, evaluate, appraise, tax; depreciate. **–er,** *m.* appraiser, assessor, valuer. **–ig,** *adj.* contemptible. **–ung,** *f.* evaluation, estimate, assessment.

Abschaum, *m.* scum, refuse, dregs, dross; *– der Gesellschaft*, dregs of society.

abschäumen, *v.a.* skim off.

abscheid–en, 1. *ir.v.a.* separate; disengage; seclude, divide off; precipitate, deposit (*Chem.*); refine (*metals*). 2. *v.n.* (*aux.* s.) depart; *von der Welt –en*, depart this life; *die Abgeschiedenen*, the departed; *von der Welt abgeschieden*, secluded from the world. 3. *n.* death, decease; parting; separation. **–er,** *m.* refiner; separator, extractor. **–ung,** *f.* parting, separation; elimination, secretion; precipitation, deposit, sediment; death. **–ungsmittel,** *n.* precipitant (*Chem.*). **–ungsprodukt,** *n.* secretion.

abscher–en, *ir.v.a.* shear, shave off, cut off; smash landing-gear (*by forced landing, Av.*). **–ungsfestigkeit,** *f.* shearing strength (*Metall.*).

Abscheu, *m.* aversion, abhorrence, abomination, loathing, disgust; object of aversion; *ich habe* (*einen*) *– vor ihm*, I loathe the very sight of him. **–lich,** *adj.* abominable, detestable; horrible; loathsome.

abscheuern, *v.a.* scour off; scrub; erode; wear away.

abschichten, *v.a.* separate into layers; portion, pay off (*Law*).

abschicken, *v.a.* dispatch; send off.

abschieb–en, *ir.v.a.* shove off; send away, deport; remove; *er will es von sich –en und mir zuschieben*, he wants to clear himself and throw the blame on me; *schieb ab!* (*coll.*) push off! scram! **–ung,** *f.* deportation.

Abschied, *m.* (-(e)s, -e) departure; discharge, dismissal; leave; adieu, good-bye, farewell, parting; final decree (*Law*); *– nehmen*, bid farewell, take leave; resign one's commission, quit the service (*Mil.*); *ohne – weggehen*, take French leave; *einem den – geben*, dismiss *or* discharge a p.; *einem Offizier den – geben*, cashier an officer; *seinen – erbitten*, send in one's resignation; *schlichter –*, unceremonious discharge; *der – des Gerichts ist dahin ausgefallen*, the sentence of the court was. **–sauftritt,** *m.* farewell appearance, farewell performance. **–sessen,** *n.* farewell banquet. **–sgeschenk,** *n.* parting gift. **–sgesuch,** *n.* letter of resignation; application for release (*from duties*). **–srede,** *f.* valedictory address. **–strunk,** *m.* stirrup-cup, 'one for the road'. **–szeugnis,** *n.* testimonial.

abschießen, 1. *ir.v.a.* shoot off (*a leg, etc.*); fire off, discharge; shoot (*an arrow*); shoot down, hit; kill (*of game*); 2. *v.n.* (*aux.* s.) slide *or* shoot down (*a slope*); rush away, dart off; 3. (*aux.* h.) fade (*of dyes*).

abschiffen, 1. *v.a.* ship away. 2. *v.n.* (*aux.* s.) set sail.

abschilder–n, *v.a.* (*Poet.*) depict. **–ung,** *f.* description, picture.

abschilfern, *v.n.* & *r.* come off in thin layers; desquamate.

abschinden, *ir.v.r.* exert o.s. to the utmost; work o.s. to death.

abschirmen, *v.a.* screen, shield, block off (*Rad.*).

abschirren, *v.a.* unharness.

abschlachten, *v.a.* slaughter, butcher.

Abschlag, *m.* (-(e)s, ⸚e) 1. fragments, chips; 2. diminution, reduction, deduction; fall in price; 3. repulse, refusal; 4. contrast; 5. rebound; 6. bully (*hockey*). *es ist ein großer –*, it differs widely; *auf –*, in part payment; in instalments; on account; *auf – nehmen*, take on account; *das Brot ist in – gekommen*, bread is down in price; *mit – verkaufen*, sell at a reduced price. **–en, 1.** *ir.v.a.* 1. knock off; chip; strike *or* cast (*a medal, etc.*); 2. refuse, reject; repulse, repel; deny; *einem den Kopf –en*, strike off a man's head; *einen Pferdeschweif –en*, dock a horse's tail; *eine Brücke –en*, break up a bridge; *eine Bettstelle –en*, take down a bed(stead); *die Segel –en*, unfurl *or* unreef the sails; *einen Angriff –en*, repel an attack: *einen Stoß –en*, parry a thrust; *einem etwas rund –en*, give a p. a flat refusal; *Sie dürfen es mir nicht –en*, I will take no refusal. **2.** *v.n.* (*aux.* s.) abate, decline, fall off; fall in price; fly back, rebound; *die Kälte schlägt ab*, the cold weather abates. **–sanleihe,** *f.* loan to be paid back by instalments. **–szahlung,** *f.* part-payment, payment on account, by instalments.

abschläg–ig, *adj.* negative; containing a refusal; brittle; *–ig bescheiden*, refuse, answer in the negative; *–ige Antwort*, refusal. **–lich,** *adj.* in part-payment, on account.

abschlämmen, (abschlammen), *v.a.* clear of mud, wash, decant.

abschlängeln, *v.r.* meander, wind away; leave quietly, (*coll.*) slink away.

abschleichen, *ir.v.n.* & *r.* slink away.

abschleif–en, 1. *ir.v.a.* grind off; wear away; polish; finish, furbish; whet, sharpen. 2. *v.r.* acquire polish, improve one's manners. **–er,** *m.* polisher. **–ung,** *f.* attrition; sharpening.

abschleifen, *v.a.* drag away (*as on a sledge*).

abschlepp–en, *v.a.* tow away, drag off. **–wagen,** *m.* breakdown lorry.

abschleudern, *v.a.* fling *or* hurl off.

abschlichten, *v.a.* smooth, polish off (*with a plane, file, etc.*).

abschließ–en, 1. *ir.v.a.* 1. lock up; 2. separate; seclude; 3. surround, invest (*Mil.*); close, settle (*a bargain, etc.*); 4. wind up, balance (*accounts, etc.*); *einen Vertrag –en*, sign *or* conclude an agreement, come to terms; 5. conclude, terminate, complete; **2.** *v.r.* seclude o.s.; *abgeschlossen leben*, live in seclusion; **3.** *v.n.* (*aux.* h.); *–en über eine S.*, decide upon a th. **–end,** *pr.p.* & *adj.* definitive, final; positive, definite. **–schraube,** *f.* locking screw (*Engin.*). **–ung,** *f.* locking; occlusion; seclusion; settling (*of accounts, etc.*).

Abschluß, *m.* (-(ss)es, ⸚(ss)e) closing; close, conclusion; winding up, settlement; agreement; *nach – unsrer Bücher*, after balancing our books; *vor dem – stehen*, draw to a close. **–blende,** *f.* diaphragm (*in front of camera lens*). **–hahn,** *m.* stopcock. **–prüfung,** *f.* school certificate examination. **–rechnung,** *f.* balance of account. **–schraube,** *f.* plug. **–zettel,** *m.* broker's contract, broker's note.

abschmeck-en, 1. *v.a.* know by tasting. 2. *v.n.* (*aux.* h.) have a bad taste. **-ig,** *adj.* unsavoury.
abschmelz-en, 1. *ir.v.n.* (*aux.* s.) melt off, away, *or* down; fuse. 2. *reg.v.a.* separate by melting; clarify; melt off. **-draht,** *m.* **-sicherung.** *f.* fuse wire.
abschmieren, 1. *v.a.* grease well; copy carelessly. 2. *v.n.* (*aux.* h.) give off grease, make a greasy stain.
abschmirgeln, *v.a.* grind (*or* rub down) with emery.
abschnallen, *v.a.* unbuckle.
abschnappen, 1. *v.n.* (*aux.* s.) (*coll.*) back out; stop suddenly. 2. *v.a.* snap off; lock, bolt.
abschneid-en, 1. *ir.v.a.* cut off; lop, clip, crop; amputate, truncate; deprive of; *sich* (*Dat.*) *ein Stück Brot -en,* cut o.s. a slice of bread; *die Zufuhr -en,* cut off supplies; *einem den Weg -en,* bar a p.'s passage; *einem das Wort -en,* stop a p. short; *einem die Ehre -en,* injure a p.'s reputation; *einem die Kehle -en,* cut a p.'s throat. 2. *v.n.* (*aux.* h.) form a contrast, differ; *gut* (*schlecht*) *-en,* show up (*or* fare) well (badly). **-ung,** *f.* cutting off; nipping; amputation; deprivation; *see* **Abschnitt.**
abschnellen, 1. *v.a.* jerk off 2. *v.n.* (*aux.* s.) fly off with a jerk.
Abschnitt, *m.* (-(e)s, -e) cut; segment, section, intercept; caesura; paragraph; division; epoch, period, era; zone, sector (*Mil.*); coupon; counterfoil (*C.L.*); balance paid in addition. **-weise,** *adv.* by (*or* in) stages. **-swinkel,** *m.* angle of a segment. **-szeichen,** *n.* section sign (§).
Abschnitzel, *n.* (-s, –), chip, shred, clipping, paring. **-n,** *v.a.* chip, whittle away.
abschnüren, *v.a.* measure with a line; constrict; tie off (*Med.*).
abschöpfen, *v.a.* scoop off, skim; ladle off; *Profite –,* skim off excess profits.
Abschoß, *m.* (-(ss)es, ⸚(ss)e) legacy tax (*archaic*).
abschrägen *v.a.* plane off; slope, slant, bevel, chamfer.
abschrammen, *v.n.* scratch off, scar; (*coll.*) slip off *or* away, bolt; (*sl.*) die.
abschrauben, *v.a.* unscrew, screw off.
abschrecken, *v.a.* 1. frighten off, scare away; 2. chill, quench; *einen von . . . –,* deter a p. from; discourage; *er läßt sich leicht –,* he is easily intimidated; *abgeschrecktes Wasser,* lukewarm water. **-d,** *pr.p. & adj.* deterrent; horrible, forbidding; *-des Beispiel,* warning; deterrent; horrible example.
abschreib-en, *ir.v.a.* copy, transcribe; crib (*in school*), plagiarize; revoke, countermand; put off; transfer; write off (*bad debts*); deduct; carry to one's credit. **-egebühr,** *f.* fee for copying. **-er,** *m.* transcriber, copyist; plagiarist. **-erei,** *f.* plagiarism. **-ung,** *f.* copying; transcription; (*C.L.*) amount written off; depreciation, amortization.
abschreien, 1. *ir.v.a.* cry out, proclaim; 2. *v.r.*; *sich* (*Dat.*) *die Kehle –,* scream o.s. hoarse.
abschreiten, 1. *ir.v.a.* measure by steps, pace off; 2. *v.n.* (*aux.* s.) step aside *or* off.
Abschrift, *f.* (-en) copy, transcript; *beglaubigte –* attested copy.
Abschub, *m.* (-s, ⸚e) evacuation, deportation.
abschuppen, 1. *v.a.* scale, remove the scales from (*Med.*). 2. *v.r.* scale off, peel off, laminate. 3. *n.* desquamation (*Med.*).
abschürf-en, *v.* 1. *a.* scrape off; 2. *r.*; *sich die Haut -en,* scratch, graze one's skin. **-ung,** *f.* abrasion.
Abschuß, *m.* (-(ss)es, ⸚(ss)e) rushing down, fall (*of water*); slope, descent; firing (*a shot*), discharge (*of a gun*); shooting down (*Av., etc.*); killing; *der – des Wildes,* killing (off) of game.
abschüssig, *adj.* precipitous, steep. **-keit,** *f.* declivity, steepness.
abschütteln, *v.a.* shake off; shake violently.
abschütt-en, *v.a.* pour off; pour out (*corn, etc., from a sack*); decant.
abschützen, *v.a.* stop by a flood-gate; let off; drain (*ponds, etc.*); shut off (*steam, etc.*); stop (*an engine*).
abschwäch-en, 1. *v.a.* weaken; lessen, reduce, diminish; attenuate, soften down, mitigate. 2. *v.r.* diminish, decrease, fall off. **-er,** *m.* brake. **-ung,** *f.* weakening, reduction; decrease, diminution, mitigation.
abschwärmen, 1. *v.n.* (*aux.* h.) cease swarming (*of bees*); (*aux.* s.) fly off (*in swarms*). 2. *v.r.* (*coll.*) wear o.s. out by riotous living.
abschwarten, *v.a.* remove the bark, decorticate.
abschwefeln, *v.a.* 1. desulphurize; 2. impregnate with sulphur.
Abschweif, *m.* digression, deviation. **-en,** 1. *v.n.* (*aux.* s.) digress; deviate. 2. *v.a.* scallop. **-end,** *pr.p. & adj.*, **-ig,** *adj.* discursive. **-ung,** *f.* digression, deviation; *ohne -ung,* directly, to the point.
abschwemmen, *v.a.* wash away; cleanse by washing *or* rinsing; flush.
abschwenken, 1. *v.a.* cleanse by rinsing. 2. *v.n.* turn aside; swing; wheel. 3. *n.* wheeling movement; *rechts* (*links*) *abgeschwenkt!* right (left) wheel!
abschwindeln, *v.a.*; *einem etwas –,* get a th. from a p. by deception, swindle a p. out of a th.
abschwingen, 1. *ir.v.a.* shake off; clean by shaking; winnow 2. *v.r.* swing o.s. down.
abschwitzen, *v.a.* remove by sweating (*a disease, superabundant flesh, etc.*).
abschwören, *ir.v.a. & n.* deny upon oath; abjure; *seinen Glauben –,* renounce his faith; *dem Branntwein –,* swear off spirits (*coll.*), swear to abstain from spirits.
Abschwung, *m* (⸚e) leaping down, swinging down (*Gymn.*).
absegeln, *v.n.* (*aux.* s.) set sail, sail away; *vom Winde –,* bear off.
abseh-en, *ir.v.a. & n.* look away from; let alone, neglect; perceive; watch an opportunity; see to the end of; conceive; aim at; *davon abgesehen,* apart from, irrespective of *or* disregarding this; *einem etwas an den Augen -en,* anticipate a p.'s wishes, divine a p.'s thoughts; *ich muß von diesem Plan -en,* I must abandon this plan; *es ist schwer abzusehen,* it is hard to foresee *or* to imagine; *da ist gar kein Ende abzusehen,* there is no end in sight; *das war auf mich abgesehen,* that was meant for me *or* was a hit at me; *ist es darauf abgesehen?* is that the object? 2. *n.* looking away from; design, purpose; *sein ganzes -en richtet sich darauf, daß . . .,* his whole aim is directed to . . . **-bar,** *adj.* visible; within sight; conceivable; *in -barer Zeit,* within a measurable *or* reasonable space of time.
Abseide, *f.* floss-silk, silk waste.
abseif-en, *v.a.* clean with soap; soap well. **-ung,** *f.* cleaning with soap.
abseigern, *v.a.* plumb (*with a plummet*); separate (*Metall.*); deepen (*a shaft*).
abseihen, *v.a.* strain off; filter off; decant.
absein, 1. *ir.v.n.* (*aux.* s) be off *or* away; be broken off; be abolished (*Law*); *wir sind noch weit ab,* we still have a long way to go; (*coll.*) *ich bin ganz ab,* I am tired out, quite exhausted *or* knocked up. 2. *n.* absence; separation; exhaustion.
Abseite, *f.* (-n) vault, wing (*of an edifice*); side-aisle (*of a church*); off side, part further off; reverse (*of a coin*).
abseits, 1. *adv.* aside, apart, aloof; offside (*Footb.*); *– vom Wege,* off the beaten track. 2. *prep.*; *– der Straße,* off from the street.
absend-en, *ir.v.a.* send away, dispatch; mail; depute; detach (*Mil.*). **-er,** *m.* sender; shipper; dispatcher, consigner; *an den -er zurück!* return to sender! **-ung,** *f.* forwarding; dispatch; conveyance, shipping.
absengen, *v.a.* singe off, burn slightly.
absenk-en, 1. *v.a.* sink (*a shaft*); set plants; 2. *v.n.* settle, subside. **-er,** *m.* root, shoot (*of a plant*). **-ung,** *f.* lowering, slope, subsidence.
absetz-en, 1. *v.a.* 1. set down; deposit; put down, drop; wean, set up in type; *Waren -en,* dispose of goods, sell goods; *Fallschirmjäger -en,* drop paratroopers; *Kurs -en,* allow for side-wind (*Av.*); **abgesetzt,** in type; 2. remove (*from office*); depose (*a king*); cashier (*an officer*); dismiss, discard, discharge. **2.** *v.n.* (*aux.* h.) put off (from shore); precipitate; settle (*of liquids*); contrast (*of colours*); discontinue, interrupt; begin a new line; be faulty (*Min.*); *sich vom Gegner -en,* disengage (*of combat*).

3. *n.* fault (*in a stratum*); deposition; subsidence (*of waters*); hesitation (*in speaking, etc.*). **-bar,** *adj.* saleable (*of goods*), deposable, removable (*of people*). **-ung,** *f.* deposition (*of sediment*); removal (*from office*); composition (*Mus., Typ.*); withdrawal from circulation. **-tisch,** *m.* side-table.

Absicht, *f.* (-en) intention, design, purpose, end, aim; *ohne* –, unintentionally; *in der besten* –, with the best intention; *es ist der* – *gemäß*, according to the intention; it answers the purpose. **-lich,** 1. *adj.* intentional, deliberate, wilful. 2. *adv.* intentionally, on purpose. **-lichkeit,** *f.* premeditation. **-slos,** 1. *adj.* unpremeditated. 2. *adv.* unintentionally.

absickern, *v.n.* (*aux.* s.) trickle down.

absieben, *v.a.* sieve, riddle, sift off.

absieden, *ir.v.a.* boil; extract by boiling, decoct.

absingen, *ir.v.a.* sing off; chant; recite.

Absinken, *n.* subsidence (*Geol.*).

absitzen, 1. *ir.v.n.* (*aux.* h.) sit away from; (*aux.* s.) dismount (*cavalry*); – *lassen*, allow to settle (*of liquids*). 2. *v.a.*; *eine Strafe* –, serve a sentence.

absolut, *adj.* absolute; unconditional. **-geschwindigkeit,** *f.* ground speed (*Av.*).

Absolution, *f.* absolution; *einem die* – *erteilen*, give absolution to a p.

Absolutismus, *m.* absolutism.

Absolutorium, *n.* acquittal (*Law*); *see* **Reifeprüfung.**

absolvieren, *v.a.* absolve, acquit; finish, complete (*one's studies at college*).

absonder-n, 1. *v.a.* separate, isolate, insulate, segregate, differentiate, divide; detach; secrete (*Med.*); abstract (*ideas*); *ein Kind -n*, portion off a child (*Law*). 2. *v.r.* separate *or* seclude o.s. **-bar,** *adj.* separable. **-lich,** 1. *adj.* peculiar, singular, odd, bizarre. 2. *adv.* chiefly, expressly; especially, particularly. **-lichkeit,** *f.* singularity, peculiarity, oddness, oddity. **-ung,** *f.* separation, division; seclusion, sequestration; abstraction; secretion (*Med.*); individualization; jointed structure (*of rocks*); isolation (*Phys.*). **-ungsdrüse,** *f.* secretory gland. **-ungsvermögen,** *n.* power of abstraction; power of secreting (*Med.*).

absorbieren, *v.a.* absorb. **-d,** *pr.p.* & *adj.* absorbent. *-de Mittel*, *pl.* absorbents.

Absorption, *f.* (-en) absorption.

abspalten, 1. *v.a.* split off, separate. 2. *v.n.* (*aux.* s.) get separated by splitting.

abspann-en, *v.a.* unbend; slacken (*a drum, etc.*); relax, ease (*the mind*), unyoke; unharness; exhaust utterly; *den Hahn -en*, half cock (*a pistol*).

absparen, *v.a.* spare from; *ich will es mir am Munde* –, I will stint myself for it; *sich* (*Dat.*) *das Brot vom Munde* –, take the very bread from one's lips (*e.g. to feed one's children*).

abspeisen, 1. *v.n.* (*aux.* h.) finish a meal. 2. *v.a.*; *einen mit leeren Worten* –, put a p. off with fair words; *einen kurz* –, cut a p. short.

abspenstig, *adj.* alienated, disloyal; – *machen*, entice away, seduce from allegiance; *einem eine P.* – *machen*, alienate the affections of a p. from s.o.; – *werden*, desert; become disaffected.

absperr-en, *v.a.* shut off, barricade; exclude; separate, confine, isolate. **-hahn,** *m.* stopcock. **-posten,** *m.pl.* cordon of sentries (*Mil.*). **-ung,** *f.* separation, isolation; solitary confinement; exclusion; closing, closure; stoppage; cordon; barrage; forbidden ground. **-ungssystem,** *n.* prohibitive system; system of solitary confinement.

abspiegel-n, 1. *v.a.* reflect (*as in a mirror*). 2. *v.r.* be mirrored *or* reflected. **-ung,** *f.* reflection.

abspielen, 1. *v.a.* play (*a tune*); *vom Blatte* –, play at sight (*Mus.*). 2. *v.r.* occur, happen, take place; run its course; *die Szene spielt sich in B. ab*, the scene is laid in B.

abspitzen, 1. *v.a.* take off the point, blunt; 2. make pointed (*as a quill pen, whiskers, etc.*). **abgespitzt,** *adj.* pointed.

absplittern, 1. *v.n.* (*aux.* s.) splinter, come off in splinters. 2. *v.a.* splinter off.

absprech-en, 1. *ir.v.a.* give a sentence against; gainsay, deprive, deny, refuse; dispute; *einem alle Hoffnung -en*, take away all hope from a p.; *einem das Leben -en*, condemn s.o. to death; *die Ärzte haben ihm das Leben abgesprochen*, the doctors have given him up; *Talent kann man ihm nicht -en*, there is no denying that he has talent; *ich spreche es Ihnen nicht ab*, I do not dispute it with you. 2. *v.n.* (*aux.* h.) decide; decide hastily; dogmatize about; *über* (*eine S.*) *-en*, give a decided (*usually* unfavourable) opinion about (*s.th*). **-end,** *pr.p.* & *adj.* positive; peremptory; fault-finding; unfavourable, adverse; *-end urteilen über einen* or *eine S.* pronounce an adverse criticism on s.o. *or* s.th, **-erisch,** *adj.* decisive, magisterial; dogmatic; fault-finding, unfavourable.

abspreizen, *v.a.* spread, splay (*fingers, legs, etc.*); prop up (*wall, etc., with splayed supports*).

absprengen, *v.a.* blow up with explosive; blast; cause to fly off; chip; cut off (*from the others*), drive off (*from the herd*).

absprießen, *v.a.* brace (*a frame*).

abspring-en, *ir.v.n.* (*aux.* s.) 1. leap off *or* down; bail out; 2. jump off; snap off; chip off; crack off; peel off (*as paint*); gape. warp; 3. rebound; desert; change (*one's party*); shift; digress, fly off (*from one subject to another*); *von einem Versprechen -en*, retract a promise. **-end,** *adj.* 1. desultory; 2. in contrast.

abspritzen, *v.a.* wash down (*with a hose*), spray, spatter.

Absprößling, *m.* (-s, -e) offspring, descendant.

Abspruch, *m.* (-(e)s, ⸚e), sentence, verdict, final decision; – *des Lebens*, sentence of death, doom.

Absprung, *m.* (-(e)s, ⸚e), leap; leaping off; snapping (*of a spring, etc.*); digression, deviation; falling off; parachute jump; reflection; offshoot. **-swinkel,** *m.* angle of reflection.

abspulen, *v.a.* uncoil, reel off.

abspül-en, *v.a.* rinse, wash off; wash away (*a cliff*). **-ung,** *f.* rinsing, washing, washing up (*of tea things, etc.*); ablution.

abstählen, *v.a.* steel; harden (*gegen*, against).

abstamm-en, *v.n.* (*aux.* s.) descend *or* be descended from, come of; derive *or* be derived from (*Gram.*); *aus der Stadt Hannover -end*, a native of the town of Hanover. **-ung,** *f.* descent, parentage; derivation; extraction, source; origin; birth, blood; *von guter -ung*, of good family; *von edler -ung*, of noble birth. **-ungslehre,** *f.* origin of species; theory of derivation. **-ungstafel,** *f.* pedigree, genealogical table.

abstampfen, *v.a.* stamp off; wear out by stamping; pound thoroughly.

Abstand, *m.* (-(e)s, ⸚e) 1. distance; interval, space; clearance; difference, disparity; *greller* –, sharp contrast; *in gleichen Abständen von einander*, spaced equidistantly; 2. renunciation, abandonment; *von einer S.* – *nehmen*, renounce a th. **-sgeld,** *n.* claim, indemnification; forfeit money, key-money (*to obtain occupation of a flat*). **-spunkt,** *m.* apsis (*Astr.*).

abständig, *adj.* deteriorated, decayed, dried up, stale, musty, flat.

abstatten, *v.a.* pay (*in a complimentary sense*); give, make, discharge, render; *einen Besuch* –, pay a visit; *einen Gruß* –, pay a compliment; *seine Schuldigkeit* –, pay one's debt; pay one's respects; *Bericht* –, report; *Zeugnis* –, bear witness; *Dank* – render *or* return thanks; *einem seinen Glückwunsch* – congratulate a p.

abstaub-en, abstäub-en, *v.a.* wipe off the dust, dust. **-er,** *m.* duster; feather-broom, dusting-brush, mop.

abstech-en, 1. *ir.v.a.* 1. bring down with a thrust; stab, pierce, stick (*a pig*); defeat (*in a students' duel*); mark out; 2. draw off, tap, run off (*wine*); *see* **ausstechen;** *Heu -en*, pitch down *or* unload hay; *Rasen -en*, cut sods; *ein Muster -en*, prick a pattern on paper; *eine Zeichnung -en*, engrave a drawing. **2.** *v.n.* (*aux.* s.) sheer off (*Naut.*); (*aux.* h.) contrast; *diese Farbe sticht von der andern zu sehr ab*, this colour contrasts too strongly with the other; *er sticht gut gegen dich ab*, he is a good foil to you. **-er,** *m.* digression; little excursion, trip, ramble; one that marks out. **-eisen,** *n.* spud; scuffling hoe; scraper; turf-spade. **-messer,** *n.* butcher's knife. **-pflug,** *m.* breast-plough.

absteck-en, *v.a.* 1. unpin, unpeg; undo, unfasten

(*hair*); 2. mark out; lay out, trace, stake out; *ein Lager –en*, mark out, peg out *or* stake off a camp. **–eisen,** *n.* iron pole, picket. **–kette,** *f.* surveyor's chain. **–leine,** *f.*, **–pfahl,** *m.*, peg, stake, picket, surveying rod. **–schnur,** *f.* measuring line, marking cord.

abstehen, *ir.v.n.* 1. (*aux.* h.) stand off, be distant; stay away from; stand out, stick out. 2. (*aux.* s.) stand too long, grow flat (*as beer*); get stale, decay, decompose; fade, die away; – *lassen*, let stand (*of liquids*); – *von*, desist from, refrain from, relinquish, give up. **–d,** *pr.p. & adj.* distant; spreading (*Bot.*); *–de Ohren*, prominent ears.

abstehlen, *ir.v.a.* steal (*only fig.*); *ich muß mir die Zeit hierzu –*, I must steal a little time (*from my proper work*) for this.

absteif–en, 1. *v.a.* stiffen; support; reinforce; prop; underpin. 2. *v.n.* (*aux.* s.) grow stiff. **–ung,** *f.* struts, reinforcement.

absteig–en, 1. *ir.v.n.* (*aux.* s.) descend; alight, dismount; put up (*at an inn, etc.*). 2. *n. see* **Abstieg;** descending; alighting; descent. **–end,** *pr.p. & adj.* descending; *–ender Rhythmus*, descending (trochaic) rhythm. **–equartier,** *n.* night-lodging, temporary quarters; billet (*Mil.*); **–ezimmer,** *n.* waiting-room.

abstell–en, *v.a.* 1. put away; put down (*a burden, etc.*); 2. stop, throw out of gear; put out of commission; turn *or* shut off (*steam*). 3. abolish; remedy, redress; remove (*nuisances, etc.*). **–bahnhof,** *m.* shunting yards (*Railw.*). **–gleis,** *n.* siding (*Railw.*). **–hahn,** *m.* regulator tap. **–vorrichtung,** *f.* stopping mechanism.

abstempeln, *v.a.* stamp, cancel (*by stamping*); characterize (*als*, as).

absterben, 1. *ir.v.n.* (*aux.* a.) die away *or* out, wither, perish; fade away; become paralysed *or* benumbed *or* opaque; mortify; *der Welt –*, withdraw from the world; *allen Vergnügungen abgestorben sein*, be indifferent to all pleasure. 2. *n.* death, mortification, atrophy; decay; extinction.

Abstich, *m.* (-(e)s, -e) copy, pattern pricked off; what is dug *or* cut off; contrast; running *or* tapping off (*of liquids, molten metal*); contrast.

Abstieg, *m.* (-(e)s, -e) descent, downward climb.

abstimm–en, 1. *v.a.* tune; lower the pitch; adjust; synchronize; tune-in (*auf*, to) (*Rad.*), gear (to); *gut abgestimmte Glocken*, well-tuned bells. 2. *v.n.* (*aux.* h.) record one's vote, vote; *über eine Sache –en lassen*, put a th. to the vote. **–kondensator,** *m.* tuning condenser (*Rad.*). **–spule,** *f.* tuning coil (*Rad.*). **–ung,** *f.* voting, vote; suffrage; division, show of hands; modulation (*Rad.*), tuning; adjustment, reconciliation, harmonizing; *der Antrag wurde zur –ung gebracht*, the motion was put to the vote; *sich der –ung enthalten*, abstain from voting; *geheime –ung*, voting by ballot. **–ungsgebiet,** *n.* area subject to plebiscite. **(–ungs)schärfe,** *f.* selectivity (*Rad.*).

Abstinenzler, *m.* (-s, -) total abstainer.

abstoppen, 1. *v.a.* 1. time, measure the time (*with a stop-watch*); 2. close, stop up; **2.** *v.n.* stop, come to a halt.

abstöpseln, *v.a.* uncork, unstop.

abstoß–en, 1. *ir.v.a.* 1. knock off, thrust off; scrape, plane; rub off; strike short; play staccato; 2. cast off, repel, repulse; get rid of, dispose of (*merchandise*); *es wird ihm das Herz –en*, it will break his heart; *sich* (*Dat.*) *die Hörner –en*, sow one's wild oats; *eine Schuld –en*, pay off a debt; *die Bienen –en*, kill the bees and take their honey; *Zähne –en*, shed one's teeth. **2.** *v.n.* (*aux.* h.) push off, shear off, get clear of the shore, set sail. **–end,** *pr.p. & adj.* repellent, repulsive, repugnant; *sich* or *einander –ende Naturen*, antipathetic *or* repellent natures. **–ung.** *f.* repulsion. **–(ungs)zeichen,** *n.* staccato sign (*Mus.*).

abstottern, *v.a.* (*coll.*) pay by instalments.

abstrafen, *v.a.* punish, chastise.

abstrahieren, *v.a.* abstract.

Abstrahl, *m.* (-s, -en) reflected ray; splendour. **–en,** 1. *v.a.* reflect. 2. *v.n.* (*aux.* h.) be reflected; radiate. **–ung,** *f.* reflection, radiation. (*archaic*) **–ungswinkel,** *m.* angle of reflection.

abstrakt, *adj.* abstract; *–er Begriff*, abstract idea, abstraction.

abstrapazieren, 1. *v.a.* (*eine S.*) wear a th. out. 2 *v.r.* toil hard; work o.s. to death.

abstreb–en, *v.n.* (*aux.* h.) 1. strive to get loose *or* away (from the centre); 2. brace. **–ung,** *f.* buttress. **–ekraft,** *f.* centrifugal force.

abstreich–en, 1. *ir.v.a.* wipe off; scrape off; strike out, cancel (*from books*); strop, whet (*a razor*); beat (*a field*) for game. 2. *v.n.* (*aux.* s.) sneak away; fly away (*Hunt.; usually of large birds only*). **–er,** *m.* scraper (*for boots*).

abstreifen, 1. *v.a.* strip off, skin; slip, draw off; lay aside; do away with; divest of. 2. *v.n.* (*aux.* s.) wander away; digress; glance off.

abstreiten, *ir.v.a.* dispute; contest; deny; *einem etwas –*, deny a p.'s right to a th.; *das lasse ich mir nicht –*, I won't be argued out of that, in this I cannot give in.

abstreuen, *v.a.* scatter, sprinkle, sweep with fire (*Artil.*).

Abstrich, *m.* (-s, -e) act of skimming; cut, reduction, diminution; skimmings, scum, dross; smear *of microscopic preparations*), swab (*Med.*); downstroke (*in writing*).

abstriegeln, *v.a.* curry, rub down (*a horse*).

abströmen, 1. *v.n.* (*aux.* s.) flow off rapidly; drift away; (*fig.*) disperse, become scattered; *ab- und zuströmen*, ebb and flow; 2. *v.a.* float *or* wash away.

abstrus, *adj.* abstruse.

abstückeln, *v.a.* crumble off.

abstuf–en, 1. *v.a.* break off (*of ore*); form into terraces; grade, graduate, shade off. 2. *v.n.* (*aux.* s.) be shaded, be graduated. **–ung,** *f.* gradation; blending; shading.

abstumpf–en, 1. *v.a.* blunt, dull; dock (*a tail*), truncate; neutralize (*Chem.*); stupefy, deaden; *abgestumpfter Kegel*, truncated cone; 2. *v.n.* become dull, deadened, etc. (*fig.; of feelings, etc.*). **–end,** *pr.p. & adj.* blunting, dulling, neutralizing. **–ung,** *f.* stupefaction; blunting, dulling, neutralization; truncation.

Absturz, *m.* (-es, ⸚e) rapid *or* sudden fall; precipice; – *eines Flugzeuges*, aeroplane crash.

abstürzen, 1. *v.a.* precipitate; hurl down, plunge; 2. *v.n.* (*aux.* s.) fall headlong; fall (*Mount.*); crash (*Av.*); slope away suddenly; *brennend –*, crash in flames (*Av.*).

abstutzen, *v.a.* lop, clip, dock, cut short. **abgestutzt,** *p.p. & adj.* truncated, docked, trimmed.

abstützen, *v.a.* prop, shore up (*a ship*), strut, brace, reinforce.

absuchen, *v.a.* search thoroughly; pick off from; scour (*a field*); patrol; search (*with searchlight*).

Absud, *m.* (-(e)s, -e) decoction; extract.

absumpfen, *v.a.* drain (*marshes*).

absurd, *adj.* absurd; inconsistent, irrational. **–ität,** *f.* absurdity.

Abszeß, *m.* (-(ss)es, -(ss)e) abscess.

Abszi–ß, *m.* (-(ss)es, -(ss)e), **–sse,** *f.* (-ssen) abscissa.

Abt, *m.* (-(e)s, ⸚e) abbot. **–ei,** *f.* abbey (*building*); abbacy (*office*). **–eilich,** *adj.* abbatial.

abtakeln, *v.a.* unrig, dismantle; (*coll.*) put out of action.

abtasten, *v.a.* palpate, feel out, investigate by feel, make contact with, search the ether (*Rad.*).

abtauen, *v.a. & n.* (*aux.* s.) thaw off, melt, defrost.

abtaumeln, *v.n.* (*aux.* s.) reel *or* stagger away.

Abteil, (-(e)s, -e) *n.* compartment (*of railway carriage*); – *erster Klasse*, first-class compartment. **–en,** *v.a.* divide, share; classify; partition off; separate into lots; *Kinder –en*, portion off children, give children their due share (*Law*). **–ung,** *f.* separation (*from*); partition; division; section, detachment, unit (*Mil.*); compartment; department; ward. **–ungszeichen,** *n.* hyphen.

abteuf–en, *v.a.* sink, bore *or* deepen (*a shaft or pit*).

Äbt–in, (-innen), **–issin,** *f.* (-issinnen) abbess. **–lich,** *adj.* as an abbot; pertaining to an abbot, abbatial.

abtoben, 1. *v.n.* rage *or* cease raging. 2. *v.r.* cease raging; exhaust o.s. by raging.

abtön–en, *v.a.* shade; tone down. **–ung,** *f.* shading, shade.

abtöt-en, *v.a.* kill, deaden; mortify (*the flesh, B.*). **-ung,** *f.* mortification (*B.*).
abtraben, *v.n.* (*aux.* s.) trot off.
Abtrag, *m.* (-(e)s, ⸚e), compensation; excavation; *einem – tun,* injure a p. **-en,** *ir.v.a.* carry away; pull down; excavate; demolish; level; clear (*the table*); pay (*debts*); wear out (*clothes*). **-end,** *adj.* abrasive. **-ung,** *f.* denudation, demolition; dismantling (*of a fort*); levelling (*of a hill*); payment, liquidation (*of debts*).
abträglich, *adj.* injurious; *-es Urteil,* unfavourable judgement.
Abtransport, *m.* (-(e)s, -e) evacuation, removal. **-ieren,** *v.a.* move.
abträufeln, *v.n.* (*aux.* s.) trickle down.
abtreib-en, 1. *ir.v.a.* drive off; refine (*Metall.*); overdrive, overwork (*horses*); *abgetriebener Gaul,* jade; (*einer Frau*) *ein Kind -en,* procure abortion. 2. *v.n.* (*aux.* s.) drift off; deviate (*from a course*). **-eofen,** *m.* refining furnace. **-er,** *m.* refiner of metals. **-ung,** *f.* miscarriage procured by an unlawful operation. **-ungsmittel,** *n.* abortifacient.
abtrenn-en, *v.a.* separate; disunite. **-bar, -lich,** *adj.* separable. **-ung,** *f.* separation; ripping off.
abtret-en, 1. *ir.v.a.* tread off (*dirt from shoes*), tread down (*snow, etc.*); wear out by constant treading (*as steps, carpet, etc.*); relinquish, resign, abandon, surrender, cede; *er trat seinem Neffen die Regierung ab,* he abdicated in favour of his nephew; (*einem etwas*) *-en,* yield up (*a right*) to (*a p.*); *ein Geschäft -en,* make over a business. 2. *v.n.* (*aux.* s.) retire; withdraw; make one's exit; quit, secede from; *sie hieß ihn -en,* she ordered him to retire; *tritt ab,* exit; *treten ab,* exeunt (*stage direction*) *abgetreten!* dismiss! (*Mil.*); *von einem Amte -en,* resign an office. 3. *v.r. sich -en* or *sich die Schuhe -en,* scrape *or* wipe one's boots. **-er,** *m.* resigner, transferrer; scraper, doormat. **-ung,** *f.* treading off *or* out; cession; abdication, withdrawal; surrender; exit; transfer; *der, an den die -ung geschieht,* assignee. **-ungsschrift,** *f.,* **-ungsurkunde,** *f.* deed of cession, instrument of conveyance *or* assignment.
Abtrieb, *m.* (-(e)s) driving off *or* away; (*dial.*) driving the cattle down from the Alps; cutting down, felling (*For.*); refusal (*Law*). **-sertrag,** *m.* yield of timber. **-srecht,** *n.* right of refusal, prior right of purchase.
abtriefen, *ir.v.n.* (*aux.* s.) trickle down, drip.
Abtrift, *f.* (-en) right of pasturage *or* common; leeway (*Naut.*); drift (*Av.*).
Abtritt, *m.* (-s, -e) lavatory, W.C., latrine; abdication, withdrawal, renunciation; cession, abandonment; exit; death; grass trodden down by deer.
abtrocknen, 1. *v.a.* wipe dry; dry. 2. *v.n.* (*aux.* s.) dry up, wither away. 3. *v.r.* dry o.s., wipe o.s. dry.
abtrollen, *v.n.* & *r.* (*aux.* s.) (*coll.*) vamoose, slip away, pack off.
abtrommeln, 1. *v.a.* drum; hammer out (*fig.*); *ein Stück auf dem Klavier –,* hammer (*or* bang) away on the piano. 2. *v.n.* (*aux.* h.) leave off drumming; beat the tattoo.
abtropf-en, abtröpfeln, *v.n.* (*aux.* s.) trickle down; drip off; *-en lassen,* drain. **-bank,** *f.,* **-brett,** *n.* draining-board.
abtrotzen, *v.a.* (*einem etwas*); bully (*s.th. out of s.o.*).
abtrudeln, *v.n.* go into a (tail) spin (*Av.*).
abtrumpfen, *v.a.* trump; *einem eine Karte –,* trump s.o.'s cards; *einen –,* snap a p. up, silence s.o. with a snub.
abtrünnig, *adj.* faithless, recreant; disloyal, rebellious; *– werden,* revolt; desert; turn apostate; *– machen,* seduce, draw off (*from a cause, etc.*); *von der Religion –,* apostate; *der -e,* deserter, recreant, renegade; apostate; turncoat. **-keit,** *f.* disloyalty; desertion; apostasy.
abtun, *ir.v.a.* take *or* put off, lay aside; abolish; settle, dispose of; kill, execute; *sich seines Glaubens –,* renounce one's faith (*Poet.*); *die Hand von einem –,* abandon a p.; leave a p. in the lurch; *etwas geschwind –,* finish a th. off hurriedly and carelessly, skimp a th.; *die S. ist abgetan,* the matter is closed.
abtünchen, *v.a.* whitewash.
abtupfen, *v.a.* dry up (*spots, etc.*); remove by blotting *or* dabbing.
aburteilen, *v.a.* & *n.* (*aux.* h.) decide finally; decide against; *über eine S. –,* pass judgement upon a matter.
abverdienen, *v.a.* earn by service; *eine Schuld –,* work off a debt.
abvermieten, *v.a.*; *ein Zimmer –,* sublet a room.
abvisieren, *v.a.* measure by eye; sight out, survey, gauge.
abwäg-en, *reg.* & *ir. v.a.* weigh out; weigh (*one's words*), ponder, consider carefully; *gegeneinander -en,* balance, set one point against the other. **-ung,** *f.* weighing; levelling.
abwalzen, *v.a.* make level, smooth with a roller, roll well.
abwälzen, *v.a.* roll off *or* away; shirk (*responsibility*); *die Beschuldigung von sich –,* shift the blame from one's own shoulders, exculpate o.s. (*by throwing the blame upon others*).
abwandel-n, 1. *v.a.* inflect, modify; decline (*nouns*), conjugate (*verbs*). 2. *v.r.* be inflected; *dies Zeitwort wandelt sich regelmäßig ab,* this verb is conjugated regularly. **-bar,** *adj.* declinable, capable of inflexion. **-ung,** *f.* (*usually* **Abwandlung**) modification, variation, inflexion; conjugation (*verbs*); declension (*nouns*).
abwander-n, *v.n.* (*aux.* s.) depart, wander away; turn to somewhere else. **-ung,** *f.*; *-ung vom Lande nach den Städten,* migration from the country to the towns.
abwanken, *v.n.* (*aux.* s.) totter away.
abwart-en, *v.a.* wait for, await; watch for; tend, attend to; *er kann nichts -en,* he is always in a hurry; *seine Zeit -en,* bide one's time; *den Regen -en,* wait till the rain is over. *-ende Haltung,* attitude of reserve. **-ung,** *f.* waiting for; attendance on, nursing.
abwärts, *prep.* & *adv.* downward; downwards; aside; *den Fluß –,* down the river; *strom –,* down stream; *mit ihm geht's –,* he is on the decline, he is breaking up (*health*), his affairs are going from bad to worse. **-bewegung,** *f.* downward motion.
abwasch-en, *ir.v.a.* wash up; cleanse by washing. **-ung,** *f.* washing; ablution. **-becken,** *n.* wash-basin.
Abwasser, *n.* (-s, ⸚) waste water, dirty water, sewage. **-anlage,** *f.* sewage disposal plant. **-n,** *v.n.* take off from the water (*Av.*).
abwässer-n, *v.a.* water, soak; drain. **-ungsanlage,** *f.* drainage system.
abwechs-eln, 1. *v.a.* exchange; vary; modulate (*the voice*). 2. *v.n.* (*aux.* h.) do alternately, alternate; relieve one another. **-elnd,** 1. *pr.p.* & *adj.* changeable; intermittent; alternate. 2. *adv.* by turns, alternately. **-(e)lung,** *f.* exchange; change; vicissitude; alternation; modulation (*Mus.*); variety; *zur -lung,* for a change. **-lungsweise,** *adv.* alternately.
Abweg, *m.* (-(e)s, -e), byway, wrong way; *-e suchen,* make shifts; *auf -e führen,* misguide, seduce; *auf -e geraten,* go astray. **-ig,** *adj.* devious, off the track, misleading, misguided. **-s,** *adv.* out of the way; aside. **-sam,** *adj.* (*rare*) out of the way; devious.
abwehen, 1. *v.a.* blow off *or* away. 2. *v.n.* (*aux.* s.) blow over.
Abwehr, *f.* (*no pl.*) defence, resistance; repulse, guard, parrying, warding off. **-dienst,** *m.* counter-espionage, intelligence service (*Mil.*). **-en,** *v.a.* ward off; avert; repulse, prevent; *er läßt sich nicht -en,* he won't be repulsed. **-ferment,** *n.* defensive enzymes (*Biol.*). **-mittel,** *n.* means of defence, preventative; prophylactic, protection. **-schlacht,** *f.* defensive battle. **-ung,** *f.* parrying, warding off; protection (from); defence (against).
[1]**abweichen,** *v.a.* soften; detach by soaking; macerate.
[2]**abweich-en,** *ir.v.n.* (*aux.* s.) deviate, diverge; digress; depart from; decline, deflect (*as the magnetic needle*); *von der Wahrheit -en,* swerve from the truth; *er weicht keinen Fingerbreit ab,* he will not budge an inch; *wir weichen sehr voneinander ab,* we differ widely. **-end,** *adj.* divergent, varying; deviating; irregular. **-ung,** *f.* deviation, variation,

divergence, deflexion; declination; exception, anomaly, discrepancy, error, aberration; *mittlere -ung*, mean deviation. **-ungswinkel,** *m.* angle of divergence, angle of magnetic variation.
abweiden, *v.a.* feed on, graze (*a meadow*); feed (*a flock*); *die Alp ist abgeweidet*, the mountain pastures are grazed quite bare.
abweinen, *v.r.* cry one's eyes out.
abweis-en, *ir.v.a.* refuse admittance to, send away, reject, refuse; repulse, repel, beat back; dismiss (*a case*) (*Law*); *kurz -en*, send a p. about his business; *er läßt sich nicht -en*, he will take no refusal; *einen Wechsel -en*, dishonour a bill. **-ung,** *f.* refusal, rejection; disavowal; protestation, non-acceptance; non-suit (*Law*).
abwelk-en, 1. *v.a.* wither, cause to shrivel. 2. *v.n.* (*aux.* s.) wither, fade.
abwend-en, 1. *reg.* & *ir.v.a.* avert, prevent; divert, ward off, parry; *das wolle Gott -en*, God forbid! 2. *v.r.* turn away from; desert. **-bar,** *adj.* preventable. **-ig,** *adj.* alienated, estranged, averse; *-ig machen*, alienate, divert from, seduce; *einem etwas -ig machen*, deprive a p. of a th. **-ung,** *f.* averting, prevention; alienation.
abwerfen, *ir.v.a.* throw, cast, fling *or* knock down; drop (*bombs*); throw (*a horseman*); yield (*a profit*); cast, shed (*feathers, skin, etc.*); *Junge* –, bring forth young.
abwesen-d, *adj.* absent; *geistes-d*, absent-minded, lost in thought. **-heit,** *f.* absence, absenteeism; alibi (*Law*); absent-mindedness.
abweiten, *v.a.* win by wager (*einem*, from a p.).
abwetzen, *v.a.* grind off; whet; wear out by grinding.
abwichsen, *v.a.* polish with wax.
abwickel-n, *v.a.* wind off, unroll, disentangle; wind up (*business, an affair*). **-bar,** *adj.* evolvable.
abwiegeln, *v.a.* pacify, appease.
abwiegen, *v.a.* weigh out.
abwimmeln, *v.a. einen* or *etwas von sich* –, shake off s.th. *or* s.o.
Abwind, *m.* (-(e)s, -e) down current, downdraught (*Meteor.*).
abwinden, *ir.v.a.* unwind, untwist; reel off; let down by a pulley.
abwinken, *v.n.* make a warning gesture; decline with a nod.
abwirtschaften, 1. *v.a.* ruin by bad management, mismanage. 2. *v.n.* & *r.* be ruined by bad management.
abwisch-en, 1. *v.a.* wipe off; *den Staub -en*, dust; *sich* (*Dat.*) *die Hände -en*, wipe one's hands. 2. *v.r.* wipe o.s. clean. **-er,** *m.* duster. **-lappen,** *m.*, **-tuch,** *n.* duster; dish-cloth.
abwittern, 1. *v.a.* scent out. 2. *v.n.* (*aux. s.*) disintegrate, become weathered *or* weatherbeaten.
abwracken, *v.a.* break up; *abgewrackte Schiffe*, ships that have been broken up.
Abwurf, *m.* (-s, ⸚e) throwing down, off *or* away; refuse *or* offal; produce, proceeds; last throw (*at dice*). **-meldung,** *f.* dropped message (*Av.*). **-munition,** *f.* bombs (*Av.*). **-vorrichtung,** *f.* bomb-release mechanism (*Av.*).
abwürgen, *v.a.* throttle; wring the neck of (*poultry*).
abwürzen, *v.a.* add seasoning.
abzahl-en, *v.a.* pay off completely; pay in instalments: *einen -en*, pay a p. out. **-ung,** *f.* part payment; instalment; *auf -ung*, by instalment(s), on hire-purchase. **-ungsgeschäft,** *n.* instalment business. **-ungsrate,** *f.* instalment.
abzählen, *v.a.* count out *or* off; tell off; subtract; number, reckon; *ich kann es mir an den Fingern* –, my senses tell me as much, it's as clear as day.
abzapfen, *v.a.* tap; draw off; bottle; *Blut* –, bleed (*s.o.*); let blood; (*coll.*) *einem etwas* –, get s.th. out of a p.
abzäumen, *v.a.* unbridle.
abzäunen, *v.a.* fence in; separate by a fence.
abzausen, *v.a.* pull *or* tug roughly, worry (*as a dog*).
abzehr-en, 1. *v.a.* waste, consume. 2. *v.n.* (*aux.* s.) & *r.* waste away, become emaciated. **-end,** *pr.p.* & *adj.* wasting, consumptive; *-ende Krankheit*, emaciating disease; atrophy. **-ung,** *f.* emaciation; consumption, wasting away.
Abzeich-en, *n.* (-s, -) mark of distinction; badge; stripe; markings (*Av.*); (*pl.*) insignia. **-nen,** 1. *v.a.* sketch, draw; copy a drawing; mark off. 2. *v.r.*; *sich am Horizont -nen*, stand out against the skyline. **-nung,** *f.* copied drawing; sketch; plan.
abzieh-en, 1. *ir.v.a.* draw, pull *or* take off, remove; turn off, divert (*attention*); abstract; subtract, deduct; distil, rectify; drain; clear (*soup, etc.*), skim; rack off (*wine, etc.*); tape, bottle, decant, siphon; smooth, strip, scrape; whet, sharpen; blanch (*almonds*); string (*beans*); straighten; *den Hut -en*, take off one's hat; *einen Druckbogen -en*, take off *or* pull a proof; *sein Gönner zieht die Hand von ihm ab*, his patron withdraws his aid; *vom Lohne -en*, deduct from wages; *einem die Kopfhaut -en*, scalp a p. 2. *v.n.* (*aux.* s.) retire, retreat, escape; depart, leave; go off guard, be relieved (*Mil.*); march off; *aus der Festung -en*, evacuate the stronghold; *von* (*der*) *Wache -en*, come off guard, be relieved; *heimlich -en*, slink away; (*coll.*) *mit einer langen Nase -en*, go off with a flea in one's ear. **-bild,** *n.* (stick-on) transfer. **-blase,** *f.* still, retort. **-eisen,** *n.* scraper; hackle (*for flax, etc.*). **-end,** *pr.p.* & *adj.*; *der -ende*, subtractor; detractor. **-er,** *m.* abductor muscle. **-feile,** *f.* smoothing file. **-flasche,** *f.*, **-kolben,** *m.* retort. **-leder,** *n.* razor-strop. **-mittel,** *n.* stripping agent. **-muskel,** *m.* abductor (*Anat.*). **-stein,** *m.* grindstone, hone. **-ung,** *f.* drawing *or* moving off; distillation; diversion; subtraction, deduction; abstraction. **-zahl,** *f.* number to be subtracted, subtrahend. **-zeug,** *n.* distilling utensils.
abzielen, *v.n.* (*aux.* h.); *auf eine S.* –, aim at s.th., have a th. in view.
abzirkeln, *v.a.* measure with compasses. **abgezirkelt,** *p.p.* & *adj.*; *abgezirkeltes Benehmen*, stiff *or* formal behaviour; punctiliousness.
Abzucht, *f.* (⸚e) breed, race; conduit, sewer; channel (*Found.*).
Abzug, *m.* (-s, ⸚e) 1. departure, retreat; 2. deduction; abatement; allowance, discount, rebate; tare; 3. drain, conduit; outlet; 4. drawing off, discharge, drainage; 5. proof-sheet; print (*Phot.*); trigger; 6. scum; *nach – der Schulden*, debts having been paid, clear of debts; *zum -e blasen*, sound the retreat; *nach – der Kosten*, expenses deducted; *in – bringen*, deduct. **-sbogen,** *m.* proof-sheet. **-sbügel.** *m.* trigger guard (*Mil.*). **-sfeder,** *f.* sear spring (*Mil.*). **-sgraben,** *m.* drain, ditch, sewer. **-shebel,** *m.* firing lever (*Artil.*), **-spapier,** *n.* duplicating paper. **-srohr,** *n.* waste-pipe. **-sschleuse,** *f.* culvert. **-ssicherung,** *f.* safety catch (*Mil.*).
abzüglich, *adv.* deducting, less; – *des Diskonts*, deducting the discount; – *der Kosten*, allowing for expenses; – *der Unkosten*, less charges.
abzupfen, *v.a.* pull off, pluck off.
abzwacken, *v.a.* cf. **abzwicken.**
abswecken, *v.n.* & *a.* (*etwas or auf eine S.*) aim at (*a th.*).
abzweig-en, 1. *v.a.* lop the branches off. 2. *v.n.* branch off. **-ung,** *f.* lopping, pruning; deviation, branch, bifurcation; branching, offshoot, ramification.
abzwicken, *v.a.* pinch off, nip off.
abzwingen, *ir.v.a.* obtain by force; *einem etwas* –, force a th. from a p.
Ac . . . *see under* **Ak-** *or* **Az-.**
Acc . . . *see under* **Akk-** *or* **Akz-.**
ach 1. *int.* alas! ah! – *wo!* – *was!* by no means! certainly not! 2. *n.*; *mit – und Krach*, with the greatest difficulty; by the skin of one's teeth; *mit – und Weh*, with a doleful outcry.
Achat, *m.* (-s, -e) agate. **-en,** *adj.* of agate.
Achs-e, *f.* (-n) 1. axle-tree; shaft; 2. axis (*Math.*). **-enblech,** *n.* axle-guard. **-enkreuz,** *n.* system of coordinates (*Math.*). **-(en)linie,** *f.* axis. **-enfeder,** *f.* axle spring. **-enlarger,** *n.* axle bearing. **-ennagel,** *m.* linch-pin. **-enneigung,** *f.* obliquity of the ecliptic. **-enverschränkbarkeit,** *f.* radius of turning circle (*Carr.*). **-enschnitte,** *m.pl.* axial intercepts (*Math.*). **-enwinkel,** *m.* angle of the axis (*Math.*). **-stand,** *m.* wheel base.
Achsel, *f.* (–n) shoulder; *die -n zucken*, shrug one's shoulders; *einen über die – ansehen*, scorn *or* look

down upon s.o.; *auf die leichte – nehmen*, make light of. **-drüse,** *f.* axillary gland. **-gelenk,** *n.* shoulder-joint. **-höhle,** *f.* armpit, **-hemd,** *n.* sleeveless shirt. **-schnur,** *f.* shoulder-cord. **-streifen,** *m.*, **-stück,** *n.* **-klappe,** *f.* shoulder-piece *or* tab (*on tunic*). **-träger,** *m.* time-server; opportunist. **-troddel,** *f.* epaulette. **-zucken,** *n.* shrug of the shoulders.

acht, *num. adj.* eight (*sometimes* achte *if the numeral stands predicatively; es sind ihrer acht(e)*, there are eight of them). *– Tage*, a week; *heute über – Tage*, this day week *or* today week; *binnen – Tagen*, within a week; *halb –*, half-past seven; *drei Viertel (auf) –*, a quarter to eight; *mit –en fahren*, drive a coach and eight; *der, die or das –e*, the eighth. **-eck,** *n.* octagon. **-eckig,** *adj.* octagonal. **-ehalb,** *num. adj.* seven and a half. **-el,** *n.* (-els, -el) eighth (part); quaver (*Mus.*). **-elkreis,** arc of 45 degrees. **-ender,** *m.* stag having eight branches to his antlers. **-ens,** *adv.* eighthly. **-er,** *m.* (-ers, -er), figure of eight; eight (*Rowing*). **-erlei,** *adv.* of eight kinds. **-fach,** *adj.*, **-fältig,** *adj. & adv.* eightfold. **-flach,** *n.* octahedron. **-jährig,** *adj.* eight years old; lasting eight years. **-kantig,** *adj.* eight-sided. **-mal,** *adj.* eight times. **-seitig,** *adj.* octagonal. **-silbig,** *adj.* octosyllabic. **-spänner,** *m.* carriage with eight horses. **-stundentag,** *m.* eight-hour day. **-tägig,** *adj.* weekly. **-zehn,** *num. adj.* eighteen. **-zehnt,** *num. adj.* eighteenth. **-zeilig,** *adj.* of eight lines; (*Poet.*) octave. **-zig,** *num. adj.* eighty; *ein –ziger*, an octogenarian; *die –ziger Jahre*, the eighties. **-zigst,** *num. adj.* eightieth.

[1]**Acht,** *f.* outlawry, ostracism; *– und Bann*, outlawry and excommunication; *in die – verfallen*, be outlawed; *einen in die – erklären* or *tun*, outlaw a p. **-brief,** *m.* writ of outlawry *or* proscription. **-(s)erklärung,** *f.* declaration of outlawry.

[2]**Acht,** *f.* (*no pl.*) attention, care, heed, consideration. *ganz außer acht lassen*, entirely disregard, neglect; *aus der* (or *aller*) *Acht lassen*, pay no heed to; *in acht nehmen*, take care of, observe, mind; *sich* (*Acc.*) *in acht nehmen*, take care, be on one's guard. **-bar,** *adj.* respectable, honourable. **-barkeit,** *f.* respectability; **-en,** *v.a. & n.* regard, esteem, respect; deem; pay attention to; *dessenungeachtet*, nevertheless, regardless of this. **-enswert,** *adj* worthy of esteem, *see* **-ungswert; -geben** *or* **-haben auf** (*Acc.*), pay attention to, heed; *Gebt acht!* listen carefully! attention!; **-los,** *adj.* negligent, unmindful, inattentive. **-losigkeit,** *f.* negligence, inattention, carelessness. **-sam,** *adj.* attentive. **-samkeit,** *f.* attention, care. **-ung,** *f.* 1. attention; 2. esteem, respect, regard; *–ung!* attention! (*Mil.*); *vor einem* (or *für einen*) *–ung hegen* (or *empfinden*) hold a p. in high esteem; *einem –ung einflößen*, inspire a p. with respect; *seine –ung bezeigen*, pay one's respects; *–ung genießen*, be respected; *sich –ung verschaffen*, make o.s. respected; *–ung geben auf* (*Acc.*), pay attention to. **-ungsbezeigung,** *f.* tribute of respect. **-ungslos,** *adj.* disrespectful. **-ungsvoll,** *adj.* respectful. **-ungswert,** *adj.*, **-ungswürdig,** *adj.* estimable.

ächt-en, *v.a.* outlaw, proscribe; *geächtet und gebannt*, outlawed (*by the state*) and excommunicated (*by the church*). **-ung,** *f.* outlawing, proscription.

achter, achteraus, achtern, *prep., adj. & adv.*, abaft, after, aft (*Naut.*). **-deck,** *n.* quarter-deck. **-steven,** *m.* stern post (*Naut.*).

ächzen, *v.n.* groan, moan.

Acker, *m.* (-s, ⸚), field, arable land; soil; acre (*old German measure of area; local variations between* 2,500 *and* 5,500 *sq. metres; pl.* Acker); *fetter –*, rich soil; *den – bauen* or *bestellen*, till the ground. **-bau,** *m.* agriculture. **-bauschule,** *f.* school of agriculture. **-bestellung,** *f.* tillage. **-gaul,** *m.* farmhorse. **-geld,** *n.* land tax; farm-expenses. **-gesetz,** *n.* agrarian law. **-hof,** *m.* farm; farmyard; farm-house. **-knecht,** *m.* farm labourer. **-land,** *n.* arable land. **-lohn,** *m.* labourer's wages. **-männchen,** *n.* water-wagtail (*Orn.*). **-n,** *v.a.* till, plough. **-rain,** *m.* ridge (between fields). **-smann,** *m.* husbandman. **-vieh,** *n.* draught cattle. **-walze,** *f.* roller. **-winde,** *f.* bindweed (*Bot.*). **-wirtschaft,** *f.* agriculture. **-zeug,** *n.* agricultural implements, (*Before many botanical terms*, **Acker** = field, wild, *or* corn.).

a conto (*Italian*), on account (*C.L.*). *See* **Akonto.**

Ade, 1. *int.* (*obs. & Poet.*) farewell! 2. *n.* (-s, -s) farewell, adieu.

Adel, *m.* (-s, -) nobility; aristocracy; *von –*, titled, of noble birth; *der niedere –*, the gentry. **-ig** (*only Austrian & Bavarian*), **adlig,** *adj.* noble. **-n,** *v.a.* ennoble, raise to the nobility; dignify; exalt. **-sbrief,** *m.* patent of nobility. **-sbuch,** *n.* peerage (*book*). **-stand,** *m.* nobility; *in den –stand erheben*, ennoble, knight, raise to the rank of a peer. **-sucht,** *f.* tuft-hunting. **-süchtig,** *adj.* tuft-hunting. **-stümlich,** *adj.* noble in bearing, seigniorial.

Ader, *f.* (-n) vein, artery (*Med.*); lode; streak, grain (*in wood*); *zur – lassen*, bleed; *dichterische –*, poetical vein; *es ist keine gute – an ihm*, there is no good in him; *er hat keine – von seinem Vater*, he is wholly unlike his father. **-entzündung,** *f.* phlebitis. **-geflecht,** *n.*, **-gewebe,** *n.* vascular plexus. **-gewächs,** *n.* polypus. **-haut,** *f.* choroid membrane. **-holz,** *n.* wood cut along the grain. **-ig, adrig,** (*also* **äd(e)rig**), *adj.* veined, full of veins. **-knoten,** *m.* varicose vein. **-laß,** *n.* blood-letting. **-presse,** *f.* tourniquet. **-rippig,** *adj.* nerved (*Bot.*). **-schlag,** *m.* pulse-beat, pulsation. **-system,** *n.* venous system.

ädern, *v.a.* grain, vein (*wood, etc.*).

Adhäsion, *f.* adhesion.

adieu, 1. *int.* farewell. 2. *n.* farewell.

Adjunkt, *m.* (–en, –en) assistant.

Adler, *m.* (-s, -) eagle; *doppelter –*, two-headed eagle. **-ähnlich,** *adj.* acquiline. **-fittig,** *m.* eagle's pinion. **-holz,** *n.* aloes-wood. **-horst,** *m.* aerie, eyrie. **-nase,** *f.* aquiline nose. **-orden,** *m.* Order of the Eagle; *Ritter des schwarzen* (or *roten*) *Adlerordens*, Knight of the Black (*or* Red) Eagle.

adlig, *see* **Adel. -e(r),** *m.* noble, peer, aristocrat.

Admiral, *m.* (-s, -e) admiral. **-ität,** *f.* admiralty. **-schaft,** *f.* admiralship; *–schaft machen*, sail under convoy. **-sbrief,** *m.* sailing orders. **-srat,** *m.* admiralty. **-sschiff,** *n.* flag-ship. **-stab,** *m.* naval staff.

adopt-ieren, *v.a.* adopt. **-iv,** *adj.* adoptive; (*in compounds, e.g.* **-ivtochter,** *f.* adopted daughter).

adoucieren, *v.a.* anneal, temper, soften (*Metall.*).

Adress-e, *f.* (–en) address; direction; place of residence; (*C.L.*) firm; *an die –e von, per –e*, care of. **-ant,** *m.* (-anten, -anten) writer, sender. **-at,** *m.* (-aten, -aten) addressee; (*C.L.*) consignee. **-(ß)buch,** *n.* directory. **-ieren,** *v.a.* address; consign. **-(ß)zettel,** *m.* label.

adrett, *adj.* adroit, smart.

adrig, cf. *Ader.*

Advent, *m.* (-s) Advent.

adventiv- (*in comps. only*), adventitious, accessory, *e.g.* **-fieder,** *f.* accessory leaflet. **-wurzel,** *f.* adventitious root.

Advokat, *m.* (-en, -en) lawyer, barrister (at law), advocate; solicitor, attorney; (*in Scotland*) writer to the signet. **-ur,** *f.* advocacy; *zur –ur zugelassen werden*, be called to the bar. **-engebüren,** *f.pl.* lawyer's fees. **-enkniff,** *m.* legal quibble.

Aero-, *insep. prefix.* **-dynamik,** *f.* aerodynamics. **-dynamisch,** *adj.* aerodynamic. **-lith,** *m.* aerolite. **-statik,** *f.* aerostatics. **-statisch,** *adj.* aerostatic.

Affäre, *f.* (-n) job; matter, ncident, occurrence; affair; *sich aus der – ziehen*, make the best of a bad job.

Affe, *m.* (-n, -n) 1. ape, monkey; 2. (*soldiers' sl.*) knapsack; *einen –n an einem gefressen haben*, be infatuated with a p.; (*coll.*) *seinem –n Zucker geben*, be excessively merry; (*sl.*) *einen* (*kleinen*) *–n haben*, be tipsy. **-nartig,** *adj.* monkeyish. **-nfratze,** *f.*, **-ngesicht,** *n* monkey face, monkeyish grimace. **-nhaft,** *adj.* apish. **-njung,** *adj.* very young; (*hum.*) *das –njunge Blut*, the young ninny. **-nliebe,** *f.* blind partiality (*for one's children*). (*sl.*) **-nschande,** *f.* great shame, scandal. **-nschwanz,** *m.* (*fig.*) tomfool; *auf den –nschwanz führen*, lead a dance, bamboozle. **-nweibchen,** *n.* she-ape.

Affekt, *m.* (-s, -e) emotional disturbance, emotional

state. **-ieren,** *v.a.* affect. **-iert,** *p.p. & adj.* affected; conceited. **-iertheit,** *f.* affectation. **-ionspreis,** *m.* fancy-price. **-los,** *adj.* dispassionate. **-losigkeit,** *f.* apathy; calmness, coolness.

äff-en, *v.a.* ape, mock, make a fool of, hoax. **-erei,** *f.* chaff; mimicry. **-in,** *f.* she-ape. **-isch,** *adj.* apish.

Affholder, Afholder, *m.* (-s, -) guelder rose.

affig, *adj.* apish, silly, foolish.

affizier-bar, *adj.* sensitive, irritable. **-en,** *v.a.* affect.

Affodill, *m.* (-s, -e) **-ilie,** *f.* asphodel.

After, 1. *m.* (-s, -) anus; hind quarters, backside. 2. *used in compounds with four main meanings: anatomical* = anal, *e.g.* **-schließer,** *m.* anal sphincter; *botanical, biological, &c.* = pseudo–, *e.g.* **-blatt,** *n.* stipule, **-klaue,** *f.* pseudo-claw; *in C.L.* = at second hand, *e.g.* **-bürge,** *m.* second surety, **-mieter,** *m.* sub-tenant; *and in more figurative extensions* = spurious. **-bildung,** *f.* semi-education; malformation; new formation, secondary growth. **-gelehrsamkeit,** *f.* sham erudition. **-kohle,** *f.* coaldust, slack, dross. **-kritik,** *f.* would-be criticism. **-kugel,** *f.* spheroid. **-lehre,** *f.* heterodoxy, false doctrine. **-muse,** *f.* false muse; perversion of poetic ideal. **-rede,** *f.* calumny, slander. **-weisheit,** *f.* sophistry. *See also* **-geburt,** *f.* afterbirth; **-heu,** *n.* aftermath. **-kind,** *n.* posthumous child. **-zins,** *m.* compound interest. 3. *as sep. pref.* **-reden,** *v.n. & v.a.* (*with Dat.*) slander, calumniate.

Agende, *f.* (-n) liturgy, ritual; office-book; memorandum-book.

Agent, *m.* (-en, -en) agent. **-engebühren,** *f.pl.* commission. **-ur,** *f.* agency.

Ägide, *f.* (-n) aegis; shelter, protection.

agieren, *v.a. & n.* (*aux.* h.) act.

Agio [a:ʒiɔ:], *n.* (-s) agio; premium. **-tage** *f.* stock-jobbing. **-teur,** *m.* stock-jobber. **agiotieren,** *v.n.* speculate in stocks. **-konto,** *n.* agio account.

Agnat, *m.* (-en, -en) paternal relation.

Agraffe, *f.* (-n) brooch, clasp.

Agrar- (*in compounds*) agrarian. **-ier,** *m.* landed proprietor. **-isch,** *adj.* agrarian, agricultural. **-staat,** *m.* agrarian state. **-wesen,** *n.* agriculture.

agronomisch, *adj.* agricultural; *-e Schrift,* treatise on farming.

ah, *int.* ah (*denoting pleasure or admiration*); pooh (*denoting contempt or disgust*).

aha, int. (*denoting realization of an expectation*) aha; there, you see.

Ahle, *f.* (-n) awl, pricker, bodkin.

Ahm, *n.* (-s, -e) aam (*liquid measure*); ship's draught. **-ing,** *f.*, **-ung,** *f.* ship's draught.

Ahn, *m.* (-s *or* -en, -en) ancestor; (*archaic*) grandfather; (*pl.*) ancestors, forefathers; *von vierzehn -en,* with fourteen quarterings. **-e,** *f.* ancestress; (*archaic*) grandmother. **-enprobe,** *f.* proof of ancestry. **-enrecht,** *n.* privilege of birth, ancestral right. **-enreihe,** *f.* pedigree. **-enstolz,** 1. *m.* pride of birth. 2. *adj.* proud of one's birth *or* ancestry. **-entafel,** *f.* family tree. **-frau,** *f. see* **-e.** **-herr,** *m. see* **Ahn.** **-herrlich,** *adj.* ancestral.

ahnd-en, *v.a.* revenge, requite (*a wrong*); punish; (*also obs. for* ahnen). **-ung,** *f.* resentment; requital; revenge; (*also obs. for* Ahnung).

ähn-eln, *v.n.* bear a likeness to, look like, resemble; *sie ähnelt ihrer Mutter,* she takes after her mother. **-lich,** *adj.* similar, like, resembling; analogous to; *er sieht seinem Bruder sehr -lich,* he looks very much like his brother; *das sieht ihm -lich,* that is just like him, that's the sort of thing one expects from him; *und-liches,* and so forth. **-lichkeit,** *f.* resemblance, similarity, likeness, analogy. **-lichkeitsbeweis,** *m.* arguments by analogy. **-lichkeitsgesetz,** *n.* law of similitude.

ahn-en, *v.a. & n.* (*aux.* h.) have a presentiment of; suspect, surmise; *es -t mir nichts Gutes,* I have a foreboding of evil; *-en lassen,* foreshadow; *der Knabe ließ den Mann -en,* the boy gave promise of the man. **-ung,** *f.* misgiving, presentiment; (*coll.*) *keine -ung!* don't ask me, I've no idea; *keine blasse -ung von einer S. haben,* have not the faintest notion of a th. *or* how to do a th. **-ungslos,** *adj.* unsuspecting, without misgiving. **-ungschwer,** *adj.* full of presentiment, portentous. **-ungsvoll,** *adj.* ominous, full of misgivings.

Ahorn, *m.* (-s, -e) (*Feld-*) maple; (*Berg-*) sycamore.

Ähr-chen, *n.* spicule (*Bot.*). **-e,** *f.* (-en) ear of corn, head (*of grasses*); *taube -e,* tare; *-en lesen,* glean. **-ig,** *adj.* (*in compounds, e.g.* kurzährig) having (short) ears *or* spikes. **-enleser,** *m.* gleaner. **-enständig,** *adj.* spicate (*Bot.*).

Ais, *n.* A sharp (*Mus.*).

Akadem-ie, *f.* (-ien) 1. educational establishment for a specialized discipline, and with the standing of a university, e.g. *Forst-*, forestry school; 2. learned society. **-iker,** *m.* person with university education. **-isch,** *adj.* academic; *-isches Viertel,* quarter of an hour between lectures (*university lectures in Germany begin at a quarter past the hour*).

Akazie, *f.* (-n) acacia; *unechte -,* locust-tree. **-ngummi,** *n.* gum arabic.

Akelei, *f.* (-en) columbine.

akkomodieren, 1. *v.a.* render damaged goods saleable. 2. *v.r. sich* (*den Verhältnissen*) -, accommodate, reconcile o.s. (*to circumstances*).

Akkord, *m.* (es, -e) 1. (*Mus.*) chord; 2. (*C.L.*) accord, settlement, composition; price agreed upon; contract; *auf -, in -,* by contract. **-arbeit,** *f.* piece-work. **-ieren,** *v.n.* (*aux.* h.) accord (*Mus.*); be correct; *-ieren über,* agree upon, reach a bargain over; *-ieren wegen,* compound for. **-lohn,** *m.* piece-wages.

akkredit-ieren, *v.a.* open a credit account for; accredit. **-iv,** *n.* (-s, -e) letter of credit; credentials.

Akkumulator, *m.* (-s, -en) storage battery (*Elec.*).

akkurat, *adj.* accurate, exact; particular. **-esse,** *f.* exactness, accuracy.

Akkusativ, *m.* (-s, -e) accusative.

Akoluth, *m.* (-s, -en) acolyte.

Akontozahlung, *f.* payment on account, instalment.

Akrostichon, *n.* (-chen *or* -cha) acrostic.

Akt, *m.* (-es, -e) 1. life model, nude model; depiction of the nude (*Sculp., Paint.*); 2. deed, document, legal instrument; 3. act (*of a play*). **-zeichnen,** *n.* life-drawing.

Akte, *f.* (-n) act; deed, bill, document; (*pl.*) public papers, reports, rolls; *etwas zu den -n legen,* pigeonhole *or* shelve a th. **-nhefter,** *m.* document file. **-nklammer,** *f.* paper-clip. **-nmappe,** *f.* portfolio. **-nmäßig,** *adj.* authentic, documentary. **-npapier,** *n.* folio foolscap paper. **-nreiter,** *m.* pettifogging official bound by red tape. **-nstoß,** *m.* pile of documents. **-nstück,** *n.* official document, deed.

Akt-ie, *f.* (-ien) share, stock. **-ionär,** *m.* (ionärs, -ionäre), shareholder, stockholder. **-ienbörse,** *f.* stock-exchange. **-iengesellschaft,** *f.* joint-stock company. **-ienhändler,** *m.* stock-jobber. **-ieninhaber,** *m.* shareholder. **-ienkapital,** *n.* share capital. **-ienkurse,** *m.pl.* quotation of shares. **-ienmakler,** *m.* stockbroker. **-ienschein,** *m.* scrip. **-ienzeichnung,** *f.* subscription to a joint-stock undertaking.

Aktion, *f. this has recently become very popular, and has the vaguest of connotations:* 1. activity, process, *e.g. Schuttaktion,* clearing rubble; 2. undertaking, procedure, *e.g. Bergbauaktion,* supply of extra rations for miners. **-sbereich,** *n. or m.* cruising radius; effective range.

aktiv, *adj.* active; effective; serving with the colours, on the active list. **- werden,** join a students' club; *er ist bei dem Korps Borussia -,* he is a member of the students' club Borussia. **-a, -en,** *n.pl.* assets, outstanding debts. **-ieren,** *v.a.* activate. **-ität,** *f.* activity. **-handel,** *m.* export trade. **-schulden,** *f.pl. see* **-a.** **-stand,** *m.* assets.

Aktuar, *m.* (-s, -e) actuary.

aktuell, *adj.* topical, of pressing importance at the present time.

Aktus, *m.* (-, -) celebration; School Speech Day; public act.

Akust-ik, *f.* acoustics. **-isch,** *adj.* acoustic.

akut, *adj.* acute; (*coll.*) urgent.

Akzent, *m.* (-s, -e) stress, accent; brogue. **-uieren,** *v.a.* accentuate.

Akzept, *n.* (-s, -e) acceptance (*of a bill*); accepted bill *or* draft. **-ant,** *m.* acceptor, drawee. **-ieren,** *v.a.* accept, honour (*a bill of exchange*).
Akzidens, *n.* (-, -enzien) (*usually pl.*) additional profits, casual emoluments, perquisites.
Akzidenz, *f.* (-en), **-arbeit,** *f.* job(bing)-work.
Akzise, *f.* excise; – *nehmen von,* – *legen auf,* levy an excise on. **-neinnehmer,** *m.*, **-nbediente(r),** *m.*, **-nbeamte(r),** *m.* exciseman, inland revenue officer. **-nfrei,** *adj.* free of excise duty. **-nzettel,** *m.* permit, excise bill.
Alabaster, *m.* alabaster. **-n,** *adj.* of alabaster.
Alant, *m.* (-s, -e) chub (*Icht.*); elecampane (*Bot.*) **-beere,** *f.* black-currant.
Alarm, *m.* (-s, -e) alarm; – *blasen* or *schlagen,* sound an alarm; *blinder* –, false alarm. **-bereit,** *adj.* standing by, at alarm stations (*Mil.*). **-bereitschaft,** *f.* stand-by (*Mil.*). **-ieren,** *v.a.* alarm, raise, give the alarm. **-platz,** *m.* alarm station.
Alaun, *n.* alum. **-artig, -haltig, -ig,** *adj.*, aluminous. **-en,** 1. *adj.* of alum. 2. *v.a.* impregnate with alum. **-t,** *p.p.* **-gar,** *adj.* steeped in alum, tawed. **-gerberei,** *f.* tawing.
Alb, 1. *m.* (-(e)s, -en) elf (*Myth.*); 2. *f. Rauhe* –, *Schwäbische* –, *see* [2]**Alp.**
Alber, *f.* (-n) white poplar (*Bot.*).
albern, *adj.* silly foolish, absurd; *-es Zeug,* nonsense; stuff and nonsense. **-heit,** *f.* silliness; absurdity; tomfoolery.
Album, *n.* album; scrapbook.
Albumin, *n.* albumen. **-artig, -ös,** *adj.* albuminous. **-stoff,** *m.* protein.
Alexandriner, *m.* (-s, -) Alexandrine (*verse of twelve syllables*).
Alfa, *f.* esparto grass.
Alfanz, *m.*, **-erei,** *f.* tomfoolery. **-en,** *v.n.*, *-ereien treiben,* play the fool.
Alge, *f.* (-n) sea-weed. **-nartig,** *adj.* algal.
Algebra, *f.* algebra. **-isch,** *adj.* algebraical.
Alibi, *n.* (-s, -s) alibi; *sein* – *nachweisen,* prove one's alibi.
Aliment, *n.* (-s, -e) alimony. **-ation,** *f.* alimentation. **e-engld,** *n.* allowance for alimony. **-ieren,** *v.a.* maintain (*Law*).
Alk, *m.* (-s, -e) auk (*Orn.*).
Alkal-escenz, *f.* alkalinity (*Chem.*). **-i,** *n.* alkali. **-eisch,** *adj.* alkaline, basic (*Chem.*).
Alkohol, *m.* (-s, -e) alcohol. **-frei,** *adj.* non-alcoholic; (*coll.*) soft. **-haltig,** *adj.* alcoholic. **-iker,** *m.* drunkard. **-isch,** *adj.* alcoholic. **-schmuggel,** *m.* boot-legging. **-verbot,** *n.* prohibition (*in America*).
Alkor, *n.* kind of synthetic leather.
Alkoven, *m.* (-s, -) alcove, recess in a room.
All, *n.* (-s) the universe.
all, *adj.* 1. *used collectively,* all, entire, whole: *-e. sie -e,* all of them; *-e Menschen,* all men, everybody; *-e Welt,* the whole world; everybody. 2. *used distributively,* every, each, any, all; *-e beide,* both of them; *auf -e Fälle,* in any case; whatever happens; *auf -e Weise,* by all means, in every possible way; *-e drei Tage,* every third day; *-e Tage,* every day; *ohne -e Ursache,* without any cause, without rhyme or reason; *ohne -en Zweifel,* undoubtedly; *vor -en Dingen, vor -em,* above all, primarily; *in -er Eile,* in a great hurry; *-e und jede Hoffnung,* all and every hope. **-e,** *adv.* all gone, all spent, at an end, exhausted; (*coll.*) *das Geld ist -e,* the money is spent; (*coll.*) *es ist -e mit ihm,* it is all up with him, he is done for; (*coll.*) *ich bin ganz -e* I am all in; *die Dummen werden nicht -e,* there is no end of fools. **-es,** *n. used substantively,* everything; everybody; *-es rannte dahin,* all (the) people flocked to it; *über -es,* above all things; *um -es in der Welt,* for anything in the world; *-es in -em* (*genommen*), all in all, by and large, all things considered; *er ist -en -es,* he is all things to all men; *er kann -es,* he can do anything *or* is good at everything; *-es aufbieten,* strain every nerve; *es ist -es eins* (*ob*), it is all the same, it is a matter of indifference (whether); *-es Mögliche,* all that is possible; *-es durcheinander,* higgledy-piggledy; *Mädchen für -es,* maid-of-all-work. **-heit,** *f.* sum of all, totality, universality; greatest extension (*of a term*).

All- (*in compounds* = universally; all; *prefixed to adverbs it is archaic and hardly affects the meaning*). **-abendlich,** *adj.* & *adv.* every evening. **-bekannt,** *adj.* notorious. **-da,** *adv.*, **-dort,** *adv.* there. **-deutsch,** *adj.* Pan-German. **-deutschtum,** *n.* Pan-Germanism. **-erbarmer,** *m.* the All-merciful. (*dial.*) **-fällig,** *adj.* eventual, possible. **-geber,** *m.* God, Giver of all. **-gefällig,** *adj.* time-serving, politic, pleasing both sides. **-gegenwart,** *f.* omnipresence. **-gegenwärtig,** *adj.* omnipresent. **-gemach,** *adv.* gradually. **-gemein,** *adj.* universal, general; *im -gemeinen,* in general; *man sagt es -gemein,* it is commonly said; *-gemeine Wehrpflicht,* compulsory military service, conscription. **-gemeinbegriff,** *m.* general conception. **-gemeingültig,** *adj.* generally valid. **-gemeinheit,** *f.* general public. **-gott,** *m.* God of the Universe (*pantheistic conception of divinity*). **-götterei,** *f.* pantheism. **-gütig,** *adj.* all-bountiful, infinitely good. **-heil,** *n.*, **-heilmittel,** *n.* panacea, sovereign remedy. **-jährlich,** *adj.* & *adv.* annual, (occurring) every year. **-macht,** *f.* omnipotence. **-mächtig,** *adj.* omnipotent. **-mählich,** *adj.* & *adv.* gradual, by degrees. **-monatlich,** *adj.* & *adv.* monthly, every month. **-nächtlich,** *adj.* & *adv.* nightly, every night. **-seitig,** *adj.* all round, versatile, universal; *-seitig erwägen,* consider from every point of view; *-seitige Bildung,* liberal education. **-tag,** *m.* weekday; **-tägig, täglich,** *adj.* & *adv.* daily; everyday; commonplace, trite; *-tägliches Fieber,* quotidian fever. **-tagskleid,** *n.* workaday dress. **-tagsleben,** *n.* everyday life. **-tagsmensch,** *m.* commonplace fellow. **-tagswelt,** *f.* workaday world. **-tagsworte,** *n.pl.* household words. **-umfassend,** *adj.* all-embracing,. comprehensive. **-vater,** *m.* Father of all, God (*often applied to Wodan*). **-waltend,** *adj,* supreme, sovereign, all-ruling. **-weisheit,** *f.* infinite wisdom. **-wissend,** *adj.* omniscient. **-wissenheit,** *f.* omniscience. **-wisserei,** *f.* encyclopaedic (but superficial) knowledge. **-wöchentlich,** *adj.* & *adv.* weekly, hebdomadal. **-zu,** *adv.* too much, far too. **-zubald,** *adv.* much too soon. **-zugleich,** *adv.* all together. **-zuhoch,** *adj.* much too high. **-zumal,** *adv.* all at once; altogether. **-zuviel,** *adv.* too much, overmuch.
alle- (*in compounds*); *bei* or *trotz -dem,* for all that. nevertheless. **-mal,** *adv.* always; yet, still, of course; *ein für -mal,* once and for all; *-mal wenn,* whenever. **-nfalls,** *adv.* in any event, at all events; if need be, at most, possibly. **-nthalben,** *adv.* everywhere. **-samt,** *adv.* altogether. **-wege,** *adv.* everywhere and always. **-weile,** *adv.* always; just now. **-zeit,** *adv.* always; at all times.
Allee, *f.* (-n) avenue.
Allegor-ie, *f.* (-ien) allegory. **-isch,** *adj.* & *adv.* allegorical.
allein, 1. *indec. adj.* & *adv.* alone, sole, single; solitary, apart, by o.s.; *dies – würde hinreichen,* this alone would suffice. 2. *adv.* only, merely; *nicht* – . . . *sondern,* not only . . . but. 3. *conj.* only, but; *ich wollte es gern tun,* – *ich konnte nicht,* I wished to do it, but I was unable to. **-ig,** *adj.* & *adv.* exclusive, sole; *der -ige Gott,* the one God; *für seinen -igen Gebrauch,* for his personal use. **-besitz,** *m.* exclusive possession, absolute property. **-betrieb,** *m.* monopoly. **-flug,** *m.* solo flight. **-gänger,** *m.* recluse. **-gesang,** *m.* solo. **-gespräch,** *n.* soliloquy. **-handel,** *m. see* **-betrieb.** **-herr,** *m.* autocrat. **-herrschaft,** *f.* undivided sovereignty; absolute power. **-sein,** *n.* solitude; loneliness. **-seligmachend,** *adj.* only saving (*faith*), claiming the monopoly of the means of grace; *der -seligmachende Glaube,* the only true faith. **-spiel,** *n.* solo (*game*). **-stehend,** *adj.* isolated, detached; unmarried.
Allel, *n.* (-s, -e) variation (*Biol.*). **-ie,** *f.* allelomorphic relationship (*Biol.*)
aller- (*in compounds with the sup.* = of all; *with titles* = most; *the accent falls in most cases on the second part of the compound, e.g.* aller'dings); **-art,** *indec. adj.* diverse, sundry; **-best,** *adj.* very best. **-christlichst,** *adj.* most Christian; *Se. Majestät der -christlichste König,* His Most Christian Majesty

(*a title, officially given to the King of France*). **-dings,** 1. *adv.* certainly, to be sure, of course, by all means, indeed. 2. *conj.* though, **-enden,** *adv.* everywhere. **- erst,** *adj.* & *adv.* first of all; *zu -erst,* first and foremost, originally. **- hand,** *indec. adj.* all sorts, all kinds of, diverse, sundry; (*coll.*) *das ist ja -hand* (*excl. of astonishment or admiration*) fine show! that's a bit thick! **- heiligen,** *pl.* All Saints' Day, **-heiligste,** *n.* Holy of Holies. **- höchstens,** *adv.* at the very most. **- ei,** 1. *indec. adj. see* **-hand** (*but emphasizes the variety rather than the novelty; in the coll. phrase, it implies admiration only*). 2. *n.* variety, medley. **- maßen,** 1. *adv.* in every way, entirely. 2. *conj.* (*archaic*) since. **- meist,** 1. *adj.* most of all. 2. *adv.* especially, chiefly. **-nächst,** 1. *adj.* the very next. 2. *adv.* close, hard by; immediately. **-orts, -orten,** *adv.* everywhere. **-seelen,** *pl.* All Souls' Day. **-seits,** *adv.* on all sides; from all parts; to all (of you). **-wärts,** *adv.* everywhere. **-wege, -wegen,** *adv. see* **allewege.** **-weltskerl,** *m.* smart aleck.

Allianz, *f.* (-en) alliance, league.

alliier-en, *v.a.* ally, unite; *die -ten,* the allies; the allied powers.

Allotria, *n.pl.* trivialities; *- treiben,* play the fool.

¹Alm, *f.* (-en) pasture-land on the mountain-side.

²Alm, *n.* aluminium.

Almanach, *m.* (-s, -e) almanac.

Almosen, *n.* (-s, -) alms; *um ein - bitten,* ask for a charity. **-buchse,** *f.* poor-box. **-empfänger,** *m.* beggar, pauper. **-ier,** *m.* (-iers, -iere) almoner. **-spende,** *f.* distribution of alms.

Aloe, *f.* (-, -n) aloe; aloes.

¹Alp, *m.* (-es, -e), *see* **Alb**; nightmare; incubus. **-drücken,** *n.* nightmare. **-männchen,** *n.* hobgoblin.

²Alp, *f.* (-en) mountain pastures; Alps; *Schwäbische* or *Rauhe -,* hilly tract of Württemberg; *jenseites der -en,* transalpine; *diesseits der -en,* cisalpine. **-enjäger,** *m.pl.* chasseurs alpins, mountain troops (*Mil.*). **-enkiefer,** *f.* mountain pine. **-enrose,** *f.* alpine rose; rhododendron. **-enstock,** *m.* alpenstock. **-entrift,** *f.* alpine pasture. **-enveilchen,** *n.* cyclamen. **-in, -inisch,** *adj.* alpine.

Alpaka, *n.* (-s) alpaca (*wool*); plated German silver.

Alphabet, *n.* (-(e)s, -e) alphabet. **-isch,** *adj.* alphabetical.

Älpler, *m.* (-s, -) native of the Alps; Swiss cowherd. **-in,** *f.* dairy-woman (*on the Alps*).

Alraun, *m.* (-es, -e) mandrake. **-e,** *f.* mandrake. **-enwurzel,** *f.* mandrake root (*Atropa mandragora*).

als, *conj.* (*in comparison*) than; *größer - er,* taller than he; (*demonstratively*) as, in the capacity *or* character of; *ich - Vater,* I as father; (*in an explanatory sense*) as, such as, for example; *- Entschuldigung,* by way of excuse; (*after a negative*), but, except, other than; *nichts -,* nothing but; (*denoting past time in subord. clause*) when, as, as soon as; *- er kam,* when he came; *als daß* (*introducing subord. clause: infinitive clause in English*); *zu gut, - daß man es wegwerfen sollte,* too good to be thrown away; *zu klug, - daß er das nicht merken sollte,* too clever not to notice that; *als ob, als wenn,* as if, as though. **-bald,** *adv.* forthwith, immediately; as soon as may be; thereupon. **-dann,** *adv.* then, thereupon.

also, 1. *adv.* so, thus; *die Sache verhält sich -,* the matter stands thus. 2. *conj.* therefore, consequently, hence, so; *ich ging - hin,* I went there accordingly; *Sie wollen - nicht?* You won't, then? **-bald,** *adv.* (*Austrian dial.*) *see* **alsbald.**

¹alt, *adj.* (*comp.* älter, *sup.* ältest) old, aged, ancient, long-established; stale. (*With small letter*) *-e Geschichte,* old story; *-e Sprachen,* (*pl.*) ancient languages, classics; *-e Gewohnheit,* old habit, ancient custom; *er ist so - wie ich,* he is as old as I am; *er ist noch immer der -e,* he is still the same; *es bleibt beim -en,* let bygones be bygones; *das ist etwas -es,* that is nothing new; *-tun,* assume a knowing air; *- werden,* grow old; *ich bleibe beim -en,* I stick to the old way. (*With capitals*) *mein -er,* my old friend; (*coll.*) old chap; my old man (*my father*); *die -en,* the Ancients, the old people; *der -e,* the old man; *das -e,* old time; *-er Herr,* **past member of a student organization,** 'old boy'; *-e Geschichte,* ancient history. **-angesessen,** *adj.* long-established. **-bekannt,** *adj.* long-known. **-bewährt,** *adj.* of long standing, tried, trusty. **-besitz,** *m.* old holding (*pre-inflation shares, etc.*). **-ehrwürdig,** *adj.* time-honoured, venerable. **-eisen,** *n.* scrap iron. **-enteil,** *n.* part of estate reserved by parents for their use; *sich aufs -enteil zurückziehen,* retire; withdraw from actual participation in a business *or* in general affairs. **-flicker,** *m.* job(bing)-cobbler. **-fränkisch,** *adj.* Old Franconian; antiquated, old-fashioned, old-world. **-gedient,** *adj.*; *-gedienter Soldat,* old soldier. **-gläubig,** *adj.* orthodox. **-hergebracht, -herkömmlich,** *adj.* traditional. **-hochdeutsch,** *adj.* Old High German. **-jüngferlich,** *adj.* old-maidish. **-klug,** *adj.* precocious. **-material,** *n., see* **-stoff** **-meister,** *m.* past-master; patriarch. **-modisch,** *adj.* old-fashioned, out of fashion. **-nordisch,** *adj.* Old Norse. **-philolog(e),** *m.* classical scholar. **-stoff,** *m.* scrap, used material (*suitable for reconditioning*). **-vater,** *m.* progenitor, patriarch. **-väterlich,** *adj.* patriarchal, ancestral, dignified. **-väterisch,** *adj.* old-fashioned, antiquated. **-vertraut,** *adj.* of long acquaintance. **-vordern,** *pl.* ancestors. **-warenhändler,** *m.* second-hand dealer. **-weibergeschichte,** *f.*, **-weibermärchen,** *n.* old wives' tale, idle gossip. **-weibersommer,** *m.* 1. gossamer; 2. Indian summer.

²Alt, *m.* (-(e)s, -e), **-ist,** *m.* alto. **-istin,** *f.* contralto singer. **-geige,** *f.* viola. **-schlüssel,** *m.*, **-zeichen,** *n.* alto clef. **-stimme,** *f.* alto.

Altan, *m.* (-s, -e) balcony; platform; gallery.

Altar, *m.* (-s, ¨-e, & *Austr.* -e) altar. **-bild,** *n.*, **-blatt,** *n.* altar-piece, altar-painting. **-diener,** *m.* priest ministering at the altar; acolyte. **-kelch,** *m.* chalice. **-platz,** *m.*, **-raum,** *m.* chancel. **-schranke,** *f.* altar rail. **-tuch,** *n.* altar-cloth.

Alter, *n.* (-s) age, old age; antiquity; epoch, age; *blühendes -,* prime of life; *man sieht ihm sein - nicht an,* he does not look his age; *bis in das späteste -,* to the last, right till his end; *im - von 70 Jahren,* aged 70 years: *vor -s, von -s her,* of old, of yore; *- schützt vor Torheit nicht,* old age is but a second childhood. **-n,** *v.n.* (*aux* h.) grow old, age; decline, decay. **-sentartung,** *f.* senile decay. **-serscheinung,** *f.* symptom of old age. **-sfolge,** *f.* seniority. **-sgenosse,** *m.*, **-sgenossin,** *f.* person of the same age, contemporary. **-sgrenze,** *f.* age limit. **-sheim,** *n.* institution for aged people. **-sklasse,** *f.* age group. **-srente,** *f.* old-age pension. **-sschwach,** *adj.* decrepit. **-sschwäche,** *f.* senility. **-sstufe,** *f.* stage of life. **-sversicherung,** *f.*, **-sversorgung,** *f.* old-age pension scheme. **-tum,** *n.* (-tums, -tümer) antiquity. **-tümelei,** *f.* antiquarianism. **-tümler,** *m.* antiquary; dabbler in antiquities. **-tümlich,** *adj.* antique, archaic, ancient. **-tumsforscher,** *m.* antiquary, archaeologist. **-tumskunde,** *f.* archaeology. **-ung,** *f.* ageing, seasoning.

ält-er, *adj.* (*comp. of* **alt**) older, elder; elderly; senior; *ein -erer Herr,* an elderly gentleman. **-est,** *adj.* (*sup of* **alt**) oldest, most ancient, eldest, senior. **-ester(r),** *m.* & *f.* senior, elder; (*B.*) *die -esten,* the elders. **-estenamt,** *n.*, **-estenwurde,** *f.* eldership. **-estenrecht,** *n.* right of primogeniture. **-lich,** *adj.* elderly, oldish.

Alumn-at, *n.* (-ats, -ate) boarding-school. **-us,** *m.* (-i) boarder.

am (= **an dem**), *see* **an**; *wer ist - Spiel?* whose turn is it to play? *- Ende,* after all, in short; (*abbr. a.,* e.g. *Frankfurt a. M.,* F. on the Main). *It forms the superlative of the adverb*; *- besten,* best; *- ehesten,* soonest; *ich bin - besten daran,* I have the the best of it.

Amalgam, *n.* (-s, -e) amalgam. **-ieren,** *v.a.* amalgamate.

Amarant, *m.* (-e) amaranth. **-en,** *adj.* amaranthine.

Amateur, *m.* (-s, -e) amateur.

Amazone, *f.* (-n) Amazon; virago; horsewoman. **-nhaft,** *adj.* Amazon-like. **-nkleid,** *n.* lady's riding-habit.

Ambe, *f.* (-n) combination of two lucky numbers drawn in lottery.

Amber, *m.* amber (*resinous gum*); ambergris. (*For compounds see* **Ambra.**)
Amboß, *m.* (-sses, -sse) anvil; incus (*Anat.*).
Ambra, *f.* & *m. see* **Amber. -baum,** *m.* sweet-gum tree; amber-tree. **-duft,** *m.* perfume of amber, fragrant odour. **-in,** *n.*, **-fett,** *n.* ambreine.
Ambros-ia, *f.* ambrosia. **-isch,** *adj.* ambrosial; fragrant.
Ameise, *f.* (-n) ant, emmet. **-nbär,** *m.*, **-nfresser,** *m.*, **-njäger,** *m.* ant-eater. **-nei,** *n.* ant's egg. **-nhaufen,** *m.* ant-hill. **-nkriechen,** *n.*, **-nlaufen,** *n.*, **-nschauder,** *m.* formication. **-nsäure,** *f.* formic acid.
Amel-korn, *n.* kind of spelt *or* German wheat. **-mehl,** *n.* starch.
Ammann, *m.* (-s, ⸗er) magistrate; bailiff (*Swiss dial.*)
Amme, *f.* (*pl.* -n) 1. (wet-)nurse; 2. asexual organism (*Biol.*); *zur – tun,* put (out) to nurse. **-nmärchen,** *n.* fairy tale; cock-and-bull story. **-nstube,** *f.* nursery. **-nzeugung,** *f.* asexual reproduction (*Biol.*).
Ammer, *f.* (-n) bunting (*Orn.*); *Gold-*, yellow-hammer (*Orn.*).
Ammoniak, *n.* (-s) ammonia; *salzsaures –*, chloride of ammonium; *schwefelsaures –*, sulphate of ammonia. **-alisch,** *adj.* ammoniacal. **-gas,** *n.* gaseous ammonia.
Ammon-pulver, *n.* ammonal. **-shorn,** *n.* ammonite.
Amnestie, *f.* (-n) amnesty. **-klausel,** *f.* clause of amnesty.
Amöbe, *f.* (-n) amoeba.
Amorette, *f.* (-n) little Cupid; (*pl.*) amoretti.
amorph, *adj.* amorphous.
amort-isieren, *v.a.* liquidate, cancel, declare null and void; redeem, pay off (*debts*); buy up (*annuities*); sink (*a fund*). **-isation,** *f.* legal extinction (*of a bill*), liquidation (*of mortgage, etc.*); redemption (*of capital of a loan*). **-isationsfonds,** *m.* sinking-fund.
Ampel, *f.* (-n) hanging lamp *or* vase.
Amphibie, *f.* (-n) amphibious animal. **-nhaft,** *adj.* amphibious.
Amsel, *f.* (-n) blackbird; *Ring-*, ouzel. **-schlag,** *m.* blackbird's song.
Amt, *n.* (-(e)s, ⸗er) 1. official position, appointment, post, employment; board, court, council; 2. charge, jurisdiction, domain, sphere of duty; concern; 3. ecclesiastical duty, ministry; Mass; 4. office; (telephone) exchange; bureau, ministry. *Ein öffentliches – bekleiden* or *inne haben,* fill a public office; *– antreten,* enter on one's official duties, take office. *einen seines -es entsetzen,* deprive a p. of his office; *kraft meines -es,* by virtue of my office; *von -(e)s wegen,* ex officio, officially; *seines -es walten,* perform the duties of one's office, officiate; *es ist meines -es nicht,* it is not in my province, it is not my business. *Post-*, post-office; *das Auswärtige –*, Foreign Office; *Amt bitte!* calling exchange; *hier Amt,* exchange speaking. **-ieren,** *v.n.* perform the duties of one's office, officiate. **-lich,** *adj.* official, ministerial. **-mann,** *m.* magistrate; bailiff; **-salter,** *n.* seniority in office. **-sbefehl,** *m.* official order. **-sbefugnis,** *f.* competence, authority. **-sbereich,** *m.* jurisdiction. **-sbericht,** *m.* official report. **-sbescheid,** *m.* sentence, decree. **-sbezirk,** *m.* extent of jurisdiction. **-sblatt,** *n.* official gazette. **-sbruder,** *m.* colleague (*especially used by clergymen*). **-sdauer,** *f.* tenure of office. **-sdiener,** *m.* beadle, usher. **-seid,** *m.* oath of office. **-sentsetzung,** *f.* dismissal from office. **-sfolge,** *f.* rotation of office. **-sführung,** *f.* administration. **-sgebühr,** *f.* (*usually in the pl.*) fees due to an official. **-sgeheimnis,** *n.* official secret. **-sgenosse,** *m.* colleague. **-sgericht,** *n.* police (*or* county) court. **-sgeschäft,** *n.*, **-shandlung,** *f.* official function; ministration (*Theol.*). **-skreis,** *m.* administrative district. **-smäßig,** *adj.* official, professional. **-spersonal,** *n.* official staff. **-srat,** *m. see* **-sgerichtsrat. -srichter,** *m.* district-judge. **-sschimmel,** *m.* red tape. **-(s)stube,** *f.* magistrate's office. **-stag,** *m.* court-day. **-sträger,** *m.* (*Nat. Soc.*) party official. **-sverlust,** *m.* loss of official position. **-sverrichtung,** *f.* performing of an official duty; *-sverrichtungen versehen,* officiate. **-svertreter** *m.* deputy in office. **-sverwalter,** *m.* administrator, manager. **-sverwaltung,** *f.* administration. **-sverweser,** *m.* deputy administrator. **-svogt,** *m.* bailiff; justiciary; beadle. **-svorgänger,** *m.* predecessor in office. **-swalter,** *m.* (*Nat. Soc.*) official, local party boss. **von -swegen,** officially.
amüsant, *adj.* amusing.
amüsier-en, *v.a.* & *r.* amuse; enjoy (o.s.); *wir haben uns in Heidelberg vorzüglich -t,* we had a capital time at H.
an, 1. *prep.* at; at *or* to the edge of; by, close by; against; along; to, towards; near, near to, not far from; as far as, up to, till; on, upon, with; (*very often with verbs,* e.g. *glauben – eine S., Freude finden – einer S.*), of; about, by means of, in respect to, in the way of; by reason of. USED WITH DAT. 1. *when signifying rest or motion within a place* (*in answer to the question* wo? *where?*); 2. *when denoting a point of time* (*in answer to* wann? *when?*); 3. *after verbs expressive of delight, want, doubt, recognition, anger, etc.*; 4. *after such adjectives as* arm, *poor*; reich, *rich*; krank, *sick*; ähnlich, *like*; stark, *strong*; schwach, *weak, etc.*; 5. *in answer to* woran? *on, in* or *of what? etc.*; 6. *in answer to* an wem? *whose?*; *– der Wand,* on the wall; *– der Tür,* at the door; *am Wege,* by the wayside, along the road; (*C.L.*) *am Schiff zu liefern,* to be delivered at the ship's side; *am rechten Orte* (or *recht am Ort*), in the right place; *– der Themse,* on the Thames; *– der Grenze,* at *or* on the frontier; *am Leben,* alive; *am Tode sein,* be at the point of death; *Professor – der Universität,* professor at the university; *das liegt – Ihnen,* that is your fault; *es ist nichts – der S.,* there is no truth in it; *diese Bemerkung ist nicht am Platze,* this remark is out of place; *am Morgen,* in the morning; *ich bin – der Arbeit,* I am at work; *– meiner Statt,* in my place; *wäre ich – Ihrer Stelle,* if I were you *or* in your place; *es ist nichts – ihm,* he is a worthless fellow; *– sich* or *– und für sich,* in the abstract, in itself; *das Unternehmen – sich hat wenig Schwierigkeit,* the undertaking in itself presents few difficulties; *so viel – mir ist,* as far as lies in my power; *– der Hand führen,* lead by the hand; *– einer Stadt vorbeikommen,* pass a town; *– der Küste hin,* along the coast; *ich nehme mir ein Beispiel –*, I take . . . as an example; *tue – mir wie ich – dir,* do by me as I do by you; *– seinen Blicken,* by his looks; *– der Nase erkennen,* recognize at a glance; *einem etwas – den Augen absehen,* be able to read a person's thoughts; *einem am Herzen liegen,* dear to s.o.; *er starb – einem Fieber,* he died of a fever; *es ist – der Zeit,* the time has come; *jung – Jahren,* young in years; *die Reihe* (or *es*) *ist – mir,* it is my turn. USED WITH ACC. 1. *signifying progression or motion towards a place or thing* (*in answer to* wohin? *where to?*); 2. *expressing duration of time* (*in answer to* bis wann? *to what time? etc.*); 3. *after verbs of believing and remembering*; 4. *in answer to the question* an wen? an was? *to whom? to what? and many other idiomatic relations, some of which are indicated below. Nun ging es – die Arbeit,* they now set to work; *seine Tochter – einen Kaufmann verheiraten,* marry one's daughter to a merchant; *er gewöhnte sich – eine spärliche Kost,* he accustomed himself to a frugal diet; *ich ging – die Tür,* I went to the door; *– die Gewehre!* to arms! (*Mil.*); *wenn die Reihe – mich kommt,* when my turn comes; *bis – das Ende* (or *bis ans Ende*), to the end; *bis – die Schultern,* up to the shoulders; *– die Tür klopfen,* knock at the door; *ich dachte – Sie,* I was thinking of you; *ich glaube nicht – Gespenster,* I don't believe in ghosts; *ich schreibe – ihn,* I write to him; *ich erinnere mich – den Tag,* I remember the day; *der Brief ist – Sie,* the letter is for you; *vom Morgen bis – den Abend,* from morning till evening; *es kostet – die 14 Mark,* it costs about 14 marks; *es waren – 400 Zuschauer da,* there were about 400 spectators present; *– die Tausend,* approximately a thousand; *es ging – ein Prügeln,* they came to blows. **2.** *adv.* on, onward, along; up *or* close to, adjoining; *von heute –*, from today (on); *von nun –*, henceforth,

in (the) future; *berg–*, uphill; *himmel–*, heavenwards; *neben–*, close by; next door; (*in* bergan, himmelan, nebenan, an *takes the stress*). **3.** *sep. prefix, often meaning* at, to, on. *Many possible compounds, where the prefix has one of these literal meanings, have been omitted from the following list. The meaning of the root verb should be appropriately modified.*

Anachoret, *m.* (-en, -en) anchoret, anchorite.

analog, *adj.* analogous. **–ie,** (-ien) analogy. **–iebildung,** *f.* formation after (the) analogy (of). **–ieschluß,** *m.* conclusion from analogy.

Analphabet, *m.* (-en, -en) illiterate.

Analy–se, *f.* analysis. **–sieren,** *v.a.* analyse; parse (*Gram.*). **–tiker,** *m.* analyst; **–tisch,** *adj.* analytical.

Ananas, *f.* (-) (*Austrian pl.* -se) pineapple. **–bowle,** *f.* light hock flavoured with pineapple slices (*in a large punch-bowl*). (*dial.*) **–erdbeere,** *f.* large *or* pine strawberry.

anarbeiten, 1. *v.a.* join on to. 2. *v.n.*; *gegen einen –*, oppose a p.; counteract.

Anarch–ie, *f.* (-ien) anarchy. **–isch,** *adj.* anarchical. **–ist,** *m.* anarchist.

Anathem, (-s, -e), **–a,** *n.* (-as, -ata) anathema.

Anatom, *m.* (-en, -en) anatomist. **–ie,** *f.* anatomy. **–isch,** *adj.* anatomical. **–iesaal,** *m.* dissecting-room.

anbahnen, *v.a.* open, pave *or* prepare a way, prepare.

anballen, *v.r.* roll itself up; be rolled up.

anbändeln, *v.n.*; *mit einer* or *einem –*, make up to *or* flirt with s.o.

Anbau, *m.* (-s, -ten) cultivation, culture; settlement; wing, addition (*to a building*); outhouse. **–en,** 1 *v.a.* till, cultivate; add to by building. 2. *v.r.* establish o.s.; become settled. **–er,** *m.* cultivator; settler.

anbefehlen, *ir.v.a.* enjoin; command, order.

Anbeginn, *m.* (-(e)s) earliest beginning, origin.

anbei, *adv.* annexed, enclosed; *– folgt* (*C.L.*) herewith you receive; please find enclosed; *Rechnung –*, account enlosed.

anbeißen, 1. *ir.v.a.* bite at; take a bite of. 2. *v.n.* bite, nibble (at); swallow a bait; (*fig.*) *auf eine S. –*, take the bait; fall for a th.

anbelangen, *v.a.* relate to, concern; *was mich anbelangt*, as for me, for my part, so far as I am concerned.

anbequemen, 1. *v.a.* accommodate *or* adapt to. 2. *v.r.* accommodate *or* adapt o.s. to (*Dat.*).

anberaumen, *v.a.* fix, appoint (*eine Frist, einen Termin*, a time, a date).

anberegt, *adj.* aforesaid, above-mentioned (*Law*).

anbet–en, *v.a.* adore, worship, idolize. **–er,** *m.* adorer, worshipper; admirer, lover. **–ung,** *f.* admiration, worship. **–ungswürdig,** *adj.* adorable.

Anbetracht, *m.*; *in – seines Alters*, considering his age.

Anbetreff, *m.*; *in – seines Alters*, *–s seines Alters*, (*C.L.*) with reference to his age. **–en,** *ir.v.a.* concern, refer to; *was mich anbetrifft*, for my part, as for me.

anbieder–n, *v.r.* behave in a familiar manner; (*coll.*) *sich bei einem –*, chum up with a p. **–ung,** *f.* (tactless) familiarity.

anbiegen, *ir.v.a.* annex; enclose; subjoin; *die angebogene Karte*, the enclosed card.

anbiet–en, 1. *ir.v.a.* offer, proffer, tender; *der Herr bot mir seine Dienste an*, the gentleman offered me his services. 2. *v.r.*; *eine Gelegenheit bietet sich an*, an opportunity presents itself. 3. *v.n.* (*aux.* h.) start a price (*at auctions*); (*C.L.*) **–ung,** *f.* offer. **–ungspreis,** *m.* starting price (*at auctions*).

anbinden, 1. *ir.v.a.* tie on *or* to; tie up (*Hort.*); (*sl.*) *einen Bären bei einem –*, contract a debt with s.o.; *am Fuße –*, tether. 2. *v.n.* (*aux.* h.); *mit einem –*, pick a quarrel with s.o.; *kurz angebunden sein* (*mit einem* or *gegen einen*), be curt, brusque *or* abrupt with s.o.

anblasen, *ir.v.a.* blow at *or* upon; blow (*fire*).

Anblick, *m.* (-s) view, sight, look, aspect, appearance; *beim ersten –*, at first sight. **–en,** *v.a.* look at, look in the face, view.

anbohren, *v.a.* bore, pierce; tap (*casks*).

anbrechen, 1. *ir.v.n.* (*aux.* s.) start; break; dawn; *der Tag brach an*, the day dawned; *bei –dem Tage*, at daybreak. 2. *v.a.* broach; open; start on, break into; cut (*a loaf, etc.*).

anbrennen, 1. *ir.v.a.* kindle; set fire to; scorch; *– lassen*, burn (*meat, etc.*). 2. *v.n.* (*aux.* s.) begin to burn, catch fire.

anbring–en, 1. *ir.v.a.* bring about, bring to bear, put in operation; apply, construct, fix, mount; dispose of, invest, place, settle (*children, etc.*), sell, pass off; lodge (*complaint*); *eine Tochter –en*, marry off a daughter; *einen Sohn –en*, settle *or* find a place for a son; *Geld –en*, place money; *Verbesserungen –en*, effect improvements; *vorteilhaft –en*, place to advantage; find a good sale for; *Wechsel –en*, negotiate bills; *ein Wort –en*, put in a word. **angebracht,** *adj.* fitting, suitable; *wohl angebracht*, seasonable, apt; *ein wohl angebrachter Stoß*, a thrust that went home; *schlecht angebracht*, out of place, inappropriate. **–bar,** *adj.* saleable, marketable. **–er,** *m.*, **–erin,** *f.* (*dial.*) informer, telltale.

Anbruch, *m.* (-(e)s, ⁻e) beginning; opening; decay: *– des Tages*, daybreak; *– der Nacht*, nightfall.

anbrüchig, *adj.* decaying, putrescent.

anbrühen, *v.a.* scald, infuse, steep.

anbrummen, *v.a.* growl at; scold.

anbrüten, *v.a.* begin to hatch; *angebrütete Eier*, addled eggs.

Andacht, *f.* (-en) devotion; prayers; *seine – verrichten*, say one's prayers. **–slos,** *adj.* irreverent. **–svoll,** *adj.* devout.

Andächt–elei, *f.* (-en) hypocrisy. **–eln,** *v.n.* affect devotion; be over-pious. **–ler,** *m.*, **–lerin,** *f.* hypocrite. **–ig,** *adj.* & *adv.* devout, pious; attentive; *sie hörte –ig zu*, she listened with close attention.

andauer–n, *v.n.* continue, last. **–nd,** *adj.* lasting, incessant.

Andenken, *n.* (-s, -) memory, remembrance; keepsake, memento, souvenir; *zum – an ihn*, in memory of him; *seligen –s*, of blessed memory; *im – behalten*, keep in mind.

ander, *adj.* & *pron.* other, else, different (*Decline as follows*: der, die *or* das –e, ein –er, eine –e, ein –es *or* ein andrer, eine andre, ein andres, *but* anderm, andern). (*Archaic*) next, second. *kein –er*, no one else; *nichts –es*, nothing else; *ein –es, etwas –es*, something else; *allerlei –es*, all sorts of other things; *unter –m*, among other things. *einen Tag um den –n*, every other day; *einmal über das –e*, repeatedly; *ein ums* or *um das –e Mal*, alternately, by turns; *einer oder der –e*, some one or other; *ein –es Mal, ein –mal*, another time; *–e Kleider anziehen*, change one's clothes; *das –e Ufer*, the opposite shore *or* bank; *die –e Seite* (*der Münze*), the reverse (of a coin); *–en Sinnes werden*, change one's mind; *–er Meinung sein*, be of a different opinion; *zum –n*, for the second time; *am –n Morgen*, the next morning. **–lei,** *indec. adj.* of another kind. **–nfalls,** *adv.* otherwise, else, on the contrary. **–nteils,** *adv.* on the other hand. **–(er)seits,** *adv.* on the other side. **–s,** *see* **anders.** **–wärtig,** *adj.* of *or* in another place. **–wärts,** *adv.* elsewhere. **–weit,** *adv.* otherwise; elsewhere; at another time; in another manner. **–weitig,** *adj.* from another quarter; done in another way *or* at another time; further; *–weitige Hilfe erwarten*, expect help from another quarter.

änder–n, 1. *v.a.* alter, change, rectify, amend; *das läßt sich nicht –n*, that cannot be helped. 2. *v.r.* alter, vary, reform, change. **–bar,** *adj.* changeable. **–ung,** *f.* change, alteration, variation, correction. **–ungsgeschwindigkeit,** *f.* rate of change.

anders, *adv.* otherwise; else; differently; under other circumstances. *– sein als*, be different from; *nicht – als*, nothing but; *irgendwo –* or *wo –*, somewhere else; *wo anders?* where else?; *wer –?* who else?; *– werden*, change; *sich – besinnen*, change one's mind; *ich kann nicht – als lachen*, I cannot help laughing; *nicht –*, exactly so, just so; *wenn – or wo –*, if indeed, provided; *wenn – nicht*, unless. **–artig,** *adj.* alien, foreign, different. **–geartetheit,** *f.* 'otherness', 'foreignness' (*coined by Nat. Soc.*). **–denkend,** *adj.* dissenting. **–gesinnt,** *adj.* differently minded. **–gläubige(r),** *m.* dissenter, heretic. **–wo,** *adv.* elsewhere. **–woher,** *adv.* from some other place. **–wohin,** *adv.* elsewhere, to another place.

anderthalb, *adj.* one and a half, sesqui- (*in compounds*); – *Pfund*, a pound and a half.

andeut-en, *v.a.* point out, indicate; hint, intimate. **-ung,** *f.* indication, hint; intimation. **-ungsweise,** *adv.* by way of suggestion.

andichten, *v.a.*; *einem etwas* –, attribute *or* impute s.th. to s.o.

andonnern, *v.a.* thunder at; *er stand wie angedonnert*, he stood as if thunderstruck.

Andrang, *m.* (-(e)s) crowd, rush; pressure; accumulation (*of business*); competition; congestion (*Med.*); – *auf eine Bank*, run on a bank.

andrängen, *v.a.* crowd, press towards *or* against.

andreh-en, *v.a.* fix on by turning; screw on; turn on (*gas, water, electricity, etc.*); set going; bring about; (*coll.*) *einem etwas -en*, palm s.th. off on s.o. **-kurbel,** *f.* crank-handle; **-vermögen,** *n.* manœuvrability.

andring-en, *ir.v.a. & n.* (*aux.* s.) press forward; rush (*gegen*, upon), charge (*Mil.*).

androh-en, *v.a.*; *einem etwas -en*, menace *or* threaten a p. with s.th. **-ung,** *f.* threat, menace; *-ung nachteiliger Folgen*, threat of dire consequences.

andurch, *adv.* hereby, by this (*Law*).

aneifern, *v.a.* stimulate, rouse.

aneign-en, *v.r.* acquire, appropriate; adopt; assimilate; annex; *sich* (*Dat.*) *Gewohnheiten -en*, contract habits; *sich* (*Dat.*) *die Meinungen anderer -en*, adopt the opinions of others; *sich eine Provinz -en*, annex a province. **-ung,** *f.* acquisition, appropriation, conversion to one's own use; *gewaltsame -ung*, forcible annexation.

aneinander, *adv.* together; to *or* against one another. **-fügen,** *v.a.* join. **-geraten,** *v.n.* come to blows *or* grips. **-kleben,** *v.n. & a.* stick together. **-liegen,** *v.n.* lie against one another. **-schließen,** *v.a.* join.

Anekdote, *f.* (-n) anecdote.

anekeln, *v.a. & imp.* disgust.

anempfehlen, *ir.v.a.* recommend.

anempfind-en, *v.n.* appreciate *or* share the feelings of others. **-ung,** *f.* adoption of the sentiments of others; true appreciation; *feine -ung für die Schönheit fremder Literatur*, fine appreciation of the beauties of foreign literature.

Anerbe, 1. *m.* (-n, -n) heir to entailed property; next heir. 2. *n.* (-s) heritage. **-nrecht,** *n.* law of entail. **-n,** *v.a.* transmit by inheritance; inherit.

anerbiet-en, 1. *ir.v.a.* offer. 2. *n.*, **-ung,** *f.* offer.

anerkannt, *adj.* admitted, recognized. **-ermaßen,** *adv.* admittedly.

anerkenn-en, *ir.v.a.* recognize, acknowledge; appreciate; admit; (*C.L.*) honour (*a bill*); *nicht -en* disown. **-bar,** *adj.* recognizable; that may be acknowledged. **-tnis,** *f. & n.* acknowledgement; clear perception (*of a truth, etc.*). **-ung,** *f.* acknowledgement; recognition; appreciation; *-ung finden*, meet with approval. **-enswert,** *adj.* worthy of recognition, commendable.

anerschaffen, *p.p. & adj.* innate.

anfachen, *v.a.* blow into a flame; fan; stimulate.

anfahr-en, 1. *ir.v.n.* (*aux.* s.) drive up to; drive *or* strike against; collide with; *bei einem -en*, drive up to a p.'s house; *angefahren kommen*, arrive in a vehicle. 2. *v.a.* carry, convey (*goods*), bring up; (*Naut.*) come up to (*land*), put into (*port*); address angrily, (*coll.*) pitch into; *man muß die Leute nicht so -en*, one must not let fly at people like that; *was wollen Sie? fuhr er mich an*, what do you want? he asked me abruptly. **-bar,** *adj.* accessible (*shore*), fit for landing. **-t,** *f.* (-ten) approach, arrival; place of arrival; landing-place; drive.

Anfall, *m.* (-s, ¨e) attack, assault; onset; shock; fit, paroxysm; (*pl.*) yearly returns; revenue; yield; – *eines Gutes*, accession to an inheritance; *künftige Anfälle*, inheritance in reversion; *im Augenblick des -s verbrauchen*, use as supplied. **-en,** 1. *ir.v.a.* fall on, assail, attack, assault; *ein Land -en*, invade a country. 2 *v.n.* fall to (*of property*) (*Law*); (*C.L.*) fall due. **-srecht,** *n.* right of inheritance, reversion.

anfällig, *adj.* reversionary; inherited, susceptible, – *werden*, be made available.

Anfang, *m.* (-s, ¨e) commencement, beginning, start, onset, outset, origin; *am* –, in the beginning; *von – an*, from the very first; *gleich zu* –, at the very beginning; (*Prov.*) *aller – ist schwer*, the first step is the hardest. **-en,** 1. *ir.v.a.* begin, commence; set about, take up; be occupied with, do; *was wollen Sie heute -en?* what are you going to do today?; *was soll ich -en?* what shall I do?; *ein Geschäft -en*, open a shop; *mit ihm ist nichts anzufangen*, there's no doing anything with him; *etwas verkehrt -en*, begin s.th. at the wrong end; *ich weiß nichts damit anzufangen*, I do not know what to make of it; *sagen Sie mir wie Sie das -en*, tell me how you manage that. 2. *v.n.* (*aux.* h.) begin, originate. **-s,** *adv.* in the beginning, at first, originally, initially; *gleich -s*, at the very beginning. **-sbuchstabe,** *m.* initial letter. **-sgeschwindigkeit,** *f.* initial velocity, muzzle velocity (*Artil.*). **-sgründe,** *m.pl.* rudiments, first principles, elements. **-skurs,** *m.* opening price. **-sstadium,** *n.* initial stage. **-szustand,** *m.* original state.

Anfäng-er, *m.* (-ers, -er), **-erin,** *f.* beginner, novice, tyro, tiro. **-lich,** 1. *adj.* initial, incipient, original. 2. *adv.* at first.

anfassen, *v.a.* take hold of, grasp, seize; set about; touch (*a chessman*), handle; *faßt an!* give (*or* lend) a hand! *falsch* –, bungle; *etwas beim rechten Ende* or *Zipfel* –, set about a th. in the right way.

anfauchen, *v.a.* spit at.

anfaulen, 1. *v.n.* (*aux.* s.) begin to rot; 2. *n.* incipient decay.

anfecht-en, *ir.v.a.* attack, assail, combat; contest, impugn, challenge; trouble; tempt; *was ficht dich an?* what is the matter with you?; *was ficht mich das an?* what is that to me? **-bar,** *adj.* contestable, controvertible; vulnerable. **-ung,** *f.* attack; opposition; impeachment; vexation; (*Theol.*) temptation.

anfeind-en, *v.a.* bear ill-will, show enmity. **-ung,** *f.* persecution; enmity, hostility, ill-will.

anfertig-en, *v.a.* make, manufacture; prepare. **-ung,** *f.* making, manufacture; preparation, production.

anfetten, *v.a.* grease, lubricate, baste.

anfeuchten, *v.a.* moisten, wet.

anfeuern, *v.a.* fire, inflame, incite, excite, stimulate, prime.

anfleh-en, *v.a.* implore. **-ung,** *f.* supplication.

anfliegen, 1. *ir.v.n.* (*aux.* s.) fly to; spring up spontaneously; effloresce; *es fliegt ihm alles an*, he succeeds easily in everything, he picks things up quickly; *die Krankheit ist ihm wie angeflogen*, the illness attacked him very suddenly. 2. *v.a.* land at (*an aerodrome*), attack (*from the air*) (*Av.*).

Anflug, *m.* (-s, ¨e) approach flight (*Av.*); sudden approach; tinge, smattering. slight attack; efflorescence, incrustation, film, coating; – *von Röte*, slight blush; – *von Narrheit*, fit of folly. **-platz,** *m.* landing-ground (*Av.*).

Anfluß, *m.* (-(ss)es, ¨(ss)e) onflow, afflux; rise (*of the tide*); alluvial deposit.

anforder-n, *v.a.* demand as due, exact, claim, request; **-ung,** *f.* claim, demand, requirement; pretension. *-ungen stellen*, set a standard; *hohe -ungen stellen*, expect great things from. **-ungsverpflichtungen** (*pl.*), cash liabilities.

Anfrag-e, *f.* (-n) inquiry; demand; question in the House (*Parl.*); *auf -e*, on application. **-en,** *reg.* (*& ir.*) *v.n.* (*aux.* h.) ask, inquire; *bei einem -en*, put a question to a p., ask a p.

Anfraß, *m.* superficial corrosion, pitting (*Metall.*).

anfress-en, *ir.v.a.* gnaw; corrode; *angefressener Zahn*, decayed tooth. **-end,** *pr.p. & adj.* corrosive, corroding. **-ung,** *f.* corrosion, erosion.

anfreunden, *v.r.*; *sich mit einem* –, become friendly with s.o., make friends with s.o.

anfrisch-en, *v.a.* freshen, refresh, revive; animate, stimulate; reduce, refine (*metals*), prime (*a pump*). **-er,** *m.* refiner (*Metall.*). **-herd,** *m.*, **-ofen,** *m.* refining furnace. **-ung,** *f.* freshening, touching up (*a picture*); reduction (*of metals*); stimulation.

anfügen, *v.a.* join, attach, affix.

anfühlen, 1. *v.a.* touch, feel; know by the feel. 2. *v.r.* feel; *es fühlt sich weich an*, it feels soft.

Anfuhr, *f.* (-en) conveying, transporting, transport, carriage (*of goods*).

anführ–en, *v.a.* lead on; bring up; conduct, lead, guide, direct; quote, cite; allege, adduce; train; hoax, dupe, cheat, trick, take in; *am angeführten Orte* (abbr. *a.a.O.*), loc. cit., see above; *angeführt!* caught! taken in! **–bar,** *adj.* adducible, allegeable. **–er,** *m.* leader; ringleader; cheat. **–ung,** *f.* leadership; lead; quotation; allegation; deception; *falsche –ung,* misquotation; **–ungsstrich** *m.*, **–ungszeichen,** *n.* quotation mark.
anfüllen, *v.a.* fill; cram; *neu –*, replenish.
Angabe, *f.* (-n) declaration, statement; assertion, allegation; denunciation; earnest-money, deposit; *nach –*, according to a statement; *nach seiner –*, according to him; *beglaubigte –*, sworn statement; *nähere –n,* particulars, details, data.
Angang, *m.* (-s, ⸚e) advance, approach; *feindlicher –*, hostile approach, attack.
angängig, *adj.* permissible; feasible, practicable, admissible, applicable; *soweit –*, as far as possible *or* practicable.
angeb–en, 1. *ir.v.a.* declare, state, give an account of; mention, indicate, assign (*a reason*); estimate; denounce, inform against; instance, specify; give in advance, give in part-payment; pretend; *den Ton –en,* give the keynote, set *or* lead the fashion; *Gründe –en,* specify reasons; *Waren –en,* declare goods (*at the custom-house*); *Namen –en,* give one's name; *sein Alter –en,* state one's age. 2. *v.n.* (*aux.* h.) play first (*Cards*). **–er,** *m.* informer; talebearer; first player (*Cards*). **–erei,** *f.* (–ereien) talebearing. **–lich,** *adj. & adv.* alleged, pretended, ostensible; *–licher Preis,* price quoted; *–licher Kaufmann,* person calling himself a merchant.
Angebinde, *n.* (-s, -) gift, (birthday) present.
angebogen, *see* **anbiegen.**
angeboren, *adj.* inborn, innate; congenital, hereditary.
Angebot, *n.* (-es, -e) offer; first bid, quotation, tender; *– und Nachfrage,* supply and demand.
angebracht, *see* **anbringen.**
angedeihen, *ir.v.n.*; *einem etwas – lassen,* confer s.th. upon s.o., grant s.th. to s.o., bestow s.th. upon s.o.
Angedenken, *n. see* **andenken.**
angegangen, *p.p. & adj. see* **angehen.**
Angehänge, *n.* (-s, -) appendage; pendant, amulet.
angeheiratet, *adj.* connected by marriage; *–er Vetter,* cousin by marriage.
angeheitert, *adj.* tipsy.
angehen, 1. *ir.v.a.* approach, apply to, solicit; concern, have to do with, be related to; *einen –*, concern s.o.; *was geht das mich an?* what's that to me?; *was mich angeht,* as for me; *das geht mich nichts an,* that's none of my business; *er geht mich nichts an,* he is nothing to me; *mit Bitten –*, approach with entreaties, beseech; *er hat uns um Unterstützung angegangen,* he has applied to us for support. 2. *v.n.* (*aux.* s.) begin, commence; grow; catch fire; fit (*of clothes*); be passable, tolerable *or* feasible; *das geht nicht an* or *so geht's nicht an,* that won't do; *soweit es angeht,* as far as it is possible; *der Verlust wird wohl noch –*, the loss will not be so great after all. **–d,** 1. *pr.p. & adj.* beginning, incipient, prospective; *bei –der Nacht,* at nightfall *or* dusk; *–der Soldat,* young soldier, (raw) recruit; *–de Schönheit,* budding beauty; *–der Dreißiger,* man just turned thirty. 2. *prep.* concerning, as for; *mich –d,* as for me. **–ds,** *adv.* at first; in the beginning. **angegangen,** *p.p. & adj.* slightly decayed, tainted, 'off'.
angehör–en, *v.n.* (*aux.* s.) belong to, appertain to. **–ig,** *adj.* belonging to; related to; **–ige(r),** *m.* relative, relation; *die –igen,* next of kin, family.
Angeklagt–e(r), *m.* (-en, -en) accused, defendant; *see* **anklagen.**
angekränkelt, *adj.*; *von des Gedankens Blässe –*, sicklied o'er with the pale cast of thought (*Hamlet,* III. 1).
[1]**Angel,** *f.* (-n) door-hinge; pivot; axis; *aus den –n heben,* turn upside down, revolutionize; *zwischen Tür und – sprechen,* say just before leaving (*as hurried parting words*) say hurriedly in passing (*without crossing the threshold*); (*rare*) *zwischen Tür und – stecken,* be in a cleft stick. **–punkt,** *m.* pole (*Astr.*); pivot; cardinal point (*on which the whole question turns*). **–stern,** *m.* pole star. **–weit,** *adj.* wide open. **–zapfen,** *m.* hinge pin.
[2]**Angel,** *f.* (-n) fishing tackle. **–förmig,** *adj.* barbed, hooked. **–haken,** *m.* fish-hook. **–n,** *v.a. & n.* fish, angle (*nach,* for). **–rute,** *f.* fishing rod. **–schnur,** *f.* fishing line.
Angeld, *n.* (-es, -er) deposit, earnest-money; first part-payment.
angelegen, *p.p. & adj. see* **anliegen**; adjacent; important; of consequence; *sich* (*Dat.*) *– sein lassen,* make it one's business. **–heit,** *f.* concern, matter, affair, business; *Minister der auswärtigen –heiten,* Minister for Foreign Affairs. **–tlich,** *adj.* pressing, urgent, earnest, of concern, important.
angeloben, *v.a.* vow; promise solemnly.
Angelöbnis, *n.* (-sses, -sse) vow, solemn protestation.
angemessen, *p.p. & adj.* (*with Dat.*) suitable, adapted to, in keeping with; appropriate, adequate, fair, just, acceptable (*in price*). **–heit,** *f.* suitability, fitness, propriety.
angenehm, *adj.* (*with Dat.*) agreeable, pleasant.
angenommen, *p.p. & adj. see* **annehmen.**
Anger, *m.* (village) green; meadow, pasture, mead, lawn.
angesehen, *see* **ansehen.**
angesessen, *adj.* settled; resident.
Angesicht, *n.* (-s, -er) face; countenance; *von –*, by sight; *von – zu –*, face to face; (*B.*) *im Schweiße seines –s,* in the sweat of his brow; *im –e,* in the presence of; *ins –*, to one's face. **–s,** *prep.* (*Gen.*) in view of, in the face of, considering.
angestammt, *adj.* hereditary, innate; ancestral; *angestammtes Bauerngeschlecht,* family settled on the soil for generations.
Angestellte(r), *m.* employee.
angetan, *see* **antun.**
angetrunken, *see* **antrinken.**
angewandt, *see* **anwenden.**
angewiesen, *see* **anweisen.**
angewöhn–en, 1. *v.a.* accustom, inure (*einem etwas,* to a th.). 2. *v.r.* accustom o.s. to, become accustomed to, contract (*habits*). **–ung,** *f.* accustoming *or* inuring to; *–ung übler Sitten,* contraction of bad habits.
Angewohnheit, *f.* (-en) habit; custom; *aus –*, from habit.
angewurzelt, *adj.* rooted to the spot.
angezeigt, *see* **anzeigen.**
angießen, *ir.v.a.* pour on; join by casting; *das Kleid sitzt wie angegossen,* the dress fits like a glove.
angleich–en, *ir.v.a.* assimilate; approximate. **–ung,** *f.* assimilation, approximation.
Angler, *m.* (-s, -) angler, fisherman; *see* **angeln.**
anglieder–n, *v.a.* annex, incorporate, attach to, append. **–ung,** *f.* combination (*an* (*Acc.*), with); annexation, affiliation (*an,* to); articulation.
anglis–ieren, *v.a.* anglicize. **–t,** *m.* (-en, -en) student *or* teacher of English. **–tik,** *f.* study of English language and literature.
Anglizismus, *m.* (-, -men) anglicism.
Angloman–e, *m.* (-en, -en) Anglomaniac. **–ie,** *f.* Anglomania.
anglotzen, *v.a.* stare at, gape on.
anglühen, 1. *v.a.* heat to a glow; mull (*wine*). 2. *v.n.* (*aux.* s.) begin to glow. **angeglüht,** *p.p. & adj.* heated to redness; red-hot.
angreif–en, 1. *ir.v.a.* handle; lay hands on, seize hold of; undertake, set about; attack, assail, charge, assault; dispute, impugn; weaken, exhaust, fatigue, strain, affect, corrode; *etwas verkehrt –en,* set to work the wrong way; *meine Nerven sind sehr angegriffen,* my nerves are in shreds; *meine Augen sind angegriffen,* my eyes are tired; *es hat ihn sehr angegriffen,* it has affected him very much. 2. *v.r.* exert o.s.; *es greift sich weich an,* it feels soft; (*coll.*) *er hat sich sehr angegriffen,* he has been very free with his money; he has been very munificent. **–bar,** *adj.* assailable, vulnerable, open to criticism. **–end,** *pr.p. & adj.* aggressive; tiring, trying, exhausting; *der –ende Teil,* the assailants. **–er,** *m.* aggressor, assailant, attacker.

Forms of p.p. in **ange–** *not found here should be sought under inf. form.*

angrenze-n, *v.n.* (*aux.* s.) border upon; adjoin. **-nd,** *pr.p.* & *adj.* bordering on, adjacent, neighbouring, adjoining. *-nd an* (*Acc.*), contiguous to. **-r,** *m.* neighbour (*Law*).

Angriff, *m.* (-s, -e) attack, assault, invasion; charge, offensive; *hinhaltender* –, holding (*or* secondary) attack; *umfassender* –, enveloping attack; *zum – blasen*, sound the charge; *dem ersten – standhalten*, bear the brunt of the attack; *einen neuen – machen*, return to the charge; *zum – übergehen*, assume the offensive; *einen – vortragen*, push an attack; *in – nehmen*, set about, begin. **-sbündnis,** *n.* offensive alliance. **-sfreudig, -slustig,** *adj.* aggressive. **-skrieg,** *m.* war of aggression. **-zeit,** *f.* zero hour. **-sweise,** *adv.* aggressively, on the offensive. **-sziel,** *n.* target, objective, goal.

Angst, *f.* (¨e) fear; anxiety; anguish; *Todes–*, death agony; *in – geraten*, take alarm; *einem – machen*, alarm a p.; *– haben*, be afraid; *used as adj. or adv., spelt* **angst,** *e.g. mir ist* –, I am afraid (*vor*, of); *mir wird* –, I am getting uneasy; *ihm wurde – und bange*, he was thoroughly frightened. **-geschrei,** *n.*, **-ruf,** *m.* cry of terror *or* anguish. (*coll.*) **-röhre,** *f.* top-hat. **-schweiß,** *m.* cold sweat. **-voll,** *adj.* fearful; anxious.

ängst-igen, 1. *v.a.* frighten, alarm. 2. *v.r.*; *sich -igen vor*, be afraid of; *sich -igen um*, be anxious about. **-lich,** *adj.* anxious, uneasy; nervous, timid; scrupulous. **-lichkeit,** *f.* anxiety, alarm; nervousness, timidity; scrupulousness.

anhaben, *ir.v.a.* wear, have on, be dressed in; *einem etwas* –, hold s.th. against a p.; *sie konnten ihm nichts* –, they couldn't find fault with him in any way; they could find nothing against him.

anhaften, *v.n.* (*aux.* h. *with Dat.*) adhere to, stick to, cling to, be connected with.

anhaken, *v.a.* hook on; mark with a tick, tick off.

Anhalt, *m.* (-(e)s, -e) basis, support; hold; pause; *einen – gewähren*, give a clue to. **-en, 1.** *ir.v.a.* 1. stop, pull up, check; hold, stay, restrain. 2. spur on, urge, encourage; *den Atem -en*, hold one's breath; *mit angehaltenem Atem*, with bated breath; *einen zum Zahlen -en*, urge s.o. to pay, dun a p. **2.** *v.r. sich -en* (*an einer S.*) cling to, hold on to. **3.** *v.n.* 1. (*aux.* h.) stop, halt, draw up. 2. continue, go on; last, persist, persevere; *-en um*, sue for; *er hat um sie* or *ihre Hand angehalten*, he asked for her hand in marriage; *wenn der Streik anhält*, if the strike lasts. **-end,** *pr.p.* & *adj.* continuous, incessant, persistent, lasting. **-epunkt,** *m.* stopping-place; station; fulcrum. (*coll.*) **-er,** *m.*; *per -er reisen*, hitch-hike, thumb a lift. **-spunkt,** *m.* foothold; essential point; deciding factor; criterion; clue; reference point, base, basis; *keine -spunkte für eine Vermutung haben*, make conjecture without anything to go on.

Anhang, *m.* (-(e)s, ¨e) appendix, supplement, codicil; appendage; followers, adherents, hangers-on. **-en,** *ir.v.n.* (*aux.* s.) hang on; adhere to; (*aux.* h.) (*with Dat.*) stick to, hold by, remain faithful to. (*In Pres. Ind. and Imper. the forms of* hängen *have practically replaced the older and more correct forms of* hangen.)

anhäng-en, 1. *v.a.* hang on, fasten to; attach, append, affix; add, subjoin; hang up, ring off (*Tele.*); *der Katze die Schelle -en*, bell the cat; *einem etwas -en*, cast a slur on a p., make insinuations about a p.; (*coll.*) *einem eine Krankheit -en*, infect a p. with a disease. 2. *v.r.* (*with Dat. or* an & *Acc.*), join, follow, become an adherent to, force o.s. on. **-end,** *adj.* adhering, adhesive. **-er,** *m.* 1. partisan, adherent; disciple, supporter; hanger-on. 2. trailer. 3. appendage, tag, locket. **-eschloß,** *n.* padlock. **-ewagen,** *m.* trailer. **-ig,** *adj.* pending (*Law*); *eine Klage* or *einen Prozeß -ig machen*, bring an action against; *und was dem -ig ist*, with its appurtenances. **-lich,** *adj.* attached, devoted. **-lichkeit,** *f.* attachment, devotion, affection. **-sel,** *n.* appendage; appendix; footling addition.

Anhauch, *m.* (-(e)s) breath (*of wind*); afflation; slight tint; touch, trace, tinge. **-en,** *v.a.* breathe upon; (*sl.*) blow up (*scold*). **angehaucht,** *p.p.* & *adj.* tinged with; *künstlerisch angehaucht*, being s.th. of an artist.

anhauen, *ir.v.a.* make the first cut.

anhäuf-en, *v.a.* heap up; pile up; accumulate; hoard up. **-ung,** *f.* accumulation; massing; aggregation (*Chem.*), agglomeration.

anheb-en, 1. *ir.v.a.* hoist, raise, lift; commence. 2. *v.n.* (*aux.* h.) begin. **-er,** *m.* beginner, author, instigator.

anheften, *v.a.* fasten to, attach, affix; sew, paste *or* pin to *or* on; *unten* –, stitch down; *einem etwas* –, cast a slur on a p.

anheilen, *v.n.* (*aux.* s.) heal up; *der Knochen ist gut angeheilt*, the bone has knit well.

anheim-eln, *v.a.* remind a p. of home, make a p. feel at home. **-elnd,** *pr.p.* & *adj.* homely, cosy. **-fallen,** *v.n.* fall to, devolve on. **-geben,** *v.a.*, **-stellen,** *v.a.* suggest, submit, *or* leave to a p.; *dem Urteile eines andern -stellen*, submit to the judgement of another; *stelle das Weitere dem Himmel* –, leave the rest in the hands of God.

anheischig, *adj.* bound; pledged; *sich* (*Acc.*) *– machen*, pledge o.s., promise, undertake.

anheizen, *v.a.* light a fire.

anher, *adv.* (*archaic* & *formal*) hither, to this place; *bis* –, hitherto, up to now.

anherrschen, *v.a.* address imperiously; hector.

anhetz-en, *v.a.* set on (*hounds*); hound, incite, instigate, stir up; *-en gegen*, incite against. **-er,** *m.* inciter, instigator.

Anhieb, *m.* (-(e)s, -e) first stroke (*Fenc.*); (*coll.*) *auf* –, at the first attempt, right away.

Anhöhe, *f.* (-n) high ground, eminence, hillock, knoll, mound.

anhör-en, *v.a.* hear, listen to; *das läßt sich -en*, that is worth listening to *or* is worth considering; *das hört sich schlecht an*, that sounds bad; *man hört ihm den Ausländer an*, one can tell by his accent that he is a foreigner. **-ung,** *f.* audience, hearing; hearing (*of witnesses, etc.*).

Anilin, *n.* (-s) aniline. **-farben,** *f.pl.* aniline (*or* coal-tar) dyes.

animalisch, *adj.* animal; brutish.

animier-en, *v.a.* incite, encourage, urge. **-t,** *adj.* *-te Stimmung*, high spirits. **-kneipe,** *f.* low tavern. **-mädchen,** *n.* girl (barmaid or drinking partner employed for the purpose) who incites the guests to drink.

Animus, *m.* mind, notion.

Anis, *m.* aniseed.

ankämpfen, *v.a.* (*gegen einen* or *eine S.*) struggle against, combat.

Ankauf, *m.* (-s, ¨e) purchase; acquisition (*by purchase*). **-en,** 1. *v.a.* purchase, buy, buy up. 2. *v.r.* buy land, settle (on one's own property).

Anker, *m.* (-s, -) 1. anchor; 2. armature, rotor (*Elec.*); *vor – gehen, – werfen*, cast anchor, anchor; *vor – liegen*, ride at anchor; *dem – Tau ausstechen*, pay out more cable; *der – greift zu*, the anchor holds; *der – ist triftig, der – setzt durch*, the anchor drags; *den – lichten*, weigh anchor. **-boje,** *f.*, **-flott,** *n.* anchor-buoy. **-fliege,** *f.*, **-flügel,** *m.* fluke of an anchor. **-geld,** *n.* harbour-dues. **-grund,** *m.* anchorage. **-kern,** *m.* armature core. **-los,** *adj.* without anchor; adrift. **-n,** *v.a.* anchor; moor. **-spannung,** *f.* armature voltage (*Elec.*). **-strom,** *m.* armature current (*Elec.*). **-tau,** *n.* anchor-cable. **-uhr,** *f.* lever-watch. **-welle,** *f.* armature shaft. **-wicklung,** *f.* armature winding. **-winde,** *f.* windlass, capstan.

anketten, *v.a.* chain; enchain.

ankitten, *v.a.* cement, fasten with putty.

anklag-en, *v.a.* accuse; *öffentlich* –, impeach, indict; **-bar,** *adj.* indictable; accusable. **-e,** *f.* charge, accusation; indictment, impeachment, arraignment. **-eakte,** *f.* bill of indictment. **-ebank,** *f.* (prisoner's) dock. **-eprozeß,** *m.* prosecution. **-eschrift,** *f.* indictment, accusation, complaint.

Ankläger, *m.* (-s, -), **-in,** *f.* accuser; plaintiff. **-isch,** *adj.* prone to accuse. **-ischerseits,** *adv.* on the part of the plaintiff.

anklammer-n, 1. *v.a.* fasten. 2. *v.r.*; *sich an eine Sache -n*, cling to a th. **-ungspunkt,** m. strong point, centre of resistance (*Mil.*).

Anklang, *m.* (-s, ¨e) accord, harmony, concord; approval, approbation; reminiscence (*an*, of); *der*

Vorschlag fand keinen –, the proposal met with no approval.
ankleben, 1. *v.n.* stick to, stick together, adhere. 2. *v.a.* glue *or* paste on. **–d,** *pr.p. & adj.* adhesive; adherent.
ankleid–en, 1. *v.a.* put on clothes, attire. 2. *v.r.* dress. **–ezimmer,** *n.* dressing-room; vestry (*Eccl.*).
anklingeln, 1. *v.a.*; *einen* –, ring a p. up (*on the telephone*). 2. *v.n.* ring the bell; (*coll.*) *bei einem* –, sound a p.
anklingen, 1. *ir.v.n.* (*aux.* h.) remind slightly (*an* (*Acc.*) of). 2. *v.a.* clink (*glasses*).
anklopf–en, *v.n.* knock (at), rap; *bei einem –en,* knock at a p.'s door, call on a p. **–er,** *m.* person knocking.
anknöpfen, *v.a.* button (to *or* on), fasten with a button.
anknüpf–en, *v.a.* tie, join, fasten with a knot; begin, enter into; *Verbindungen –en,* establish relations; *ein Gespräch wieder –en,* resume a conversation; *eine Bekanntschaft wieder –en,* resume an acquaintance. **–ungspunkt,** *m.* point of contact; starting-point.
ankommen, 1. *ir.v.n.* (*aux.* s.) arrive; approach; reach, overtake; get a job, become established; get on, succeed; depend on, be determined by; be of importance, matter; *darauf kommt es an,* that is the main thing, that is what matters, that depends; *es kommt darauf an, zu wissen,* the question is to know; *es kommt nicht darauf an,* no matter, it matters little; *das kommt auf die Umstände an,* that depends on the circumstances; *bei einem wohl* (*übel*) –, be well (ill) received by a p.; (*iron.*) *da kommen Sie schön an,* you will meet with a nice reception!; *bei mir kommt man damit nicht an,* that will not do for me, that cuts no ice with me; *ich lasse es auf das Äußerste* –, I will push the matter to extremities; *wir wollen es darauf – lassen,* we will chance it; *es soll mir nicht auf ein paar Mark* –, a few shillings more or less won't matter; *es kommt ihm auf einen Tag nicht an,* he is not particular to a day. 2. *v.a.* befall, come upon; *es kam mich* (*mir*) *eine Lust an,* I was overcome with the desire; *der Schlaf kam mich an,* I grew drowsy; *es kam mich* (*mir*) *eine Furcht an,* I was seized with fear; *es kommt mich* (*mir*) *schwer an,* I find it hard.
Ankömmling, *m.* (-s, -e) new-comer, arrival.
ankränkeln, *see* **angekränkelt.**
ankreiden, *v.a.* chalk up; (*sl.*) *etwas – lassen,* have it put on the slate; leave without paying; (*sl.*) *das werde ich ihm schön* –, I shall make him jolly well pay for it.
ankünd–en, –igen, *v.a.* announce; declare, proclaim; advertise. **–igung,** *f.* declaration, proclamation, announcement; notification, prospectus. **–igungsbefehl,** *m.* cautionary word of command (*Mil.*).
Ankunft, *f.* (⸗e) arrival, advent.
ankuppeln, *v.a.* couple, engage, connect.
ankurbeln, *v.a.* start (*Motor.; C.L.*); crank up an engine, turn the crank; stimulate, ginger up.
anlachen, *v.a.* laugh in someone's face; (*fig.*) smile on, show favour.
Anlage, *f.* (-n) 1. talent, ability; natural tendency; predisposition; 'anlage' (*Biol.* = hereditary factors); 2. (pleasure-) ground; grounds, park, enclosure; 3. works, plant, installation, establishment; 4. layout, plan, draft, rough sketch, design, outline; 5. appendix, enclosure (*in a letter*); 6. capital, investment. **–kapital,** *n.* funds, stock, business capital. **–kosten,** *f.pl.* cost of construction; original cost. **–typus,** *m.* genotype (*Biol.*).
anlagern, *v.a. & r.* accumulate.
anlangen, 1. *v.n.* (*aux.* s.) arrive at, reach. 2. *v.a.* concern, relate to; *was das anlangt,* as regards this. **–d,** *pr.p. used as prep.* concerning; as for.
Anlaß, *m.* (-(ss)es, ⸗(ss)e) cause, occasion, motive, inducement; *ohne allen* –, for no reason at all; *zu einem Gerüchte – geben,* give rise to a report. **–farbe,** *f.* oxidization tint (*in tempering metals*). **–kurbel,** *f.* crank starter (*Motor.*).
anlasse–n, 1. *ir.v.a.* leave on, leave running (*as an engine*), set going, start (*an engine*), turn on (*water, etc.*); temper (*metals*); *er hat ihn scharf angelassen,* he has given him a sharp rebuke. 2. *v.r.* appear; promise; *ein junger Mensch, der sich gut anläßt,* a promising youth; *die S. läßt sich nicht übel an,* the matter is getting on quite well. **–r,** *m.* starter, self-starter (*Motor.*).
anläßlich, *prep.* (*Gen.*) apropos of; on the occasion of.
Anlauf, *m.* (-(e)s, ⸗e) take-off, run; rise, onset; advance, attack; crowd; *er nahm einen – zum Springen*, he took a run before leaping; *der – des Wassers,* the rising of the water; *in – sein,* be under headway; *beim ersten* –, at the first attempt *or* (*coll.*) shot *or* go. **–en,** *ir.v.n.* (*aux.* s.) run up to, rush against; call at (*or* touch) a port, make land (*Naut.*); begin to run; rise, swell (*Med.*), mount up (*of debts*); get dim, tarnished, rusty *or* mouldy; *die Fläche läuft sanft an,* the plain rises gently; *in diesem Keller läuft alles an,* everything grows mouldy *or* rusty in this cellar; *Stahl blau –en lassen,* temper steel (*till it is blue*).
Anlaut, *m.* initial sound (*Gram.*). **–en,** *v.n.* begin with a sound *or* letters; *das Wort lautet mit E an,* the initial letter of the word is E. **–end,** *adj.* initial, at the beginning of a word (*Gram.*).
anläuten, *v.a.* ring the bell (*as a signal to commence work*), ring up (*Tel.*).
anleg–en, 1. *v.a.* lay *or* put on *or* against; apply; found; lay out, plan; plot (*a curve*), sketch; take aim, lay (*a gun*); invest (*money*); *Holz –en,* put wood (*on the fire*); *einem Ketten –en,* chain a p.; *das Gewehr –en,* take aim at; *Legt an! Feuer!* present! fire! (*Mil.*); *Feuer –en,* set fire to; *Hand –en,* take in hand; *die letzte Hand –en* (*an, Acc.*), give the finishing touch to; *ein Kleid* or *Trauer –en,* put on a dress *or* mourning; *Geld –en,* invest money; *eine Kolonie –en,* found *or* establish a colony; *etwas mit einem –en,* plan s.th. with s.o.; *einem Pferde den Zaum –en,* bridle a horse; *er legte es darauf an,* he made it his object. 2. *v.r.* lean against; adhere to. 3. *v.n.* (*aux.* h.) land; dock; lie to; lie alongside (*Naut.*); *–en auf* (*Acc.*), take aim at. **–emarken,** *f.pl.* markers. **–eschloß,** *n.* padlock. **–estelle,** *f.* landing-place; moorings. **–ung,** *f.* laying out, planning, inception; establishment; disposition; construction; employment, investment (*of capital*). **–ungsperiode,** *f.* formation period.
anlehn–en, *v.a. & r.* lean against; *die Tür –en,* leave the door ajar; *sich –en an* (*Acc.*), lean upon, follow (example of), be modelled on. **angelehnt,** *p.p. & adj.* adjoining; supported by; in touch with. **–ung,** *f.* leaning; *durch –ung an* (*Acc.*), by association (with), in imitation (of); *in –ung an,* depending on, with reference to.
Anleihe, *f.* (-n) loan; *eine – machen,* raise a loan. **–tilgung,** *f.* amortization.
anleimen, *v.a.* glue on.
anleit–en, *v.a.* guide, conduct; instruct, train; introduce (*to a study, etc.*). **–ung,** *f.* guidance; methodical instruction; introduction; primer.
anlern–en, *v.a.* acquire by study; train, teach, instruct, break in. **–eberuf,** *m.* emergency occupation (*as clerks trained to become factory hands in war-time*). **–ling,** *m.* trainee (*under such a scheme*); *angelernter Arbeiter,* worker on completion of such training.
anlieg–en, 1. *ir.v.n.* lie close to, be adjacent to, border on; fit well (*of clothes*); stand to (*Naut.*); concern; *einem –en,* entreat *or* solicit a p. 2. *n.* desire, wish, request; concern. **–ersiedlung,** *f.* settlement adjacent to a factory, factory estate.
anlock–en, *v.a.* allure, attract, entice. **–end,** *pr.p. & adj.* attractive, alluring. **–ung,** *f.* enticement. **–ungsmittel,** *n.* lure, decoy, bait.
anlöten, *v.a.* solder on.
anlügen, *ir.v.a.* lie to a p.'s face, lie brazenly.
anluven, *v.n.* go to windward, luff.
anmachen, *v.a.* fasten, fix, attach; light (*a fire*); mix, adulterate; *einen Salat* –, dress a salad; *mit Gewürz* –, spice; *Kalk* –, slake lime.
anmalen, *v.a.* paint; give a coat of paint.
Anmarsch, *m.* (-es, ⸗e) approach march, advance (*of troops*). **–ieren,** *v.n.* (*aux.* s.) advance, approach.
anmaß–en, *v.r.* presume; claim, pretend to;

assume, usurp, arrogate; *was maßest du dir an?* what presumption! **-end,** *pr.p.* & *adj.*; **-lich,** *adj.* presumptuous, arrogant; *nicht -end,* unassuming. **-ung,** *f.* presumption; arrogance; usurpation; *kühne -ung,* insolence. **-ungsvoll,** *adj.* full of arrogance; very presumptuous.

anmeld-en, *v.a.* announce, notify; report, register, usher in; *sich -en,* report one's arrival; *sich -en lassen.* have o.s. announced; *sich zu etwas -en,* offer o.s. for, apply for. **-ung,** *f.* announcement, notification.

anmerk-en, 1. *v.a.* perceive, observe, remark, notice; note, write down; *man merkte ihm die Freude an,* one could perceive that he was happy. **-ung,** *f.* remark, observation; note, annotation; comment; *Ausgabe mit -ungen,* annotated edition.

anmessen, *ir.v.a.* measure, take the measure for; fit, suit, adapt; *einem einen Rock -,* measure a p. for a coat; *see* **angemessen.**

anmustern, *v.a.* enlist (*soldiers*); enrol, take on (*a crew*).

Anmut, *f.* grace, charm, sweetness, gracefulness. **-ig,** *adj.* charming; graceful; pleasant, gracious. **-svoll,** *adj. see* **-ig.**

anmut-en, *v.a. es mutet mich fremd an,* it seems strange to me. **-ung,** *f. see* **Zumutung.**

annäher-n, 1. *v.a.* approximate, bring near. 2. *v.r.* approach. 3. *v.n.* (*aux.* s.) approach, draw near. **-nd,** 1. *pr.p.* & *adj.* approximative; contiguous. 2. *adv.* approximately, by approximation. **-ung,** *f.* approach, advance; approximation. **-ungsgraben,** *m.* communication trench (*Mil.*). **-ungskraft,** *f.* centripetal force. **-ungspunkt,** *m.* point of approximation. **-ungswert,** *m.* approximate value.

Annahme, *f.* (-n) 1. acceptance, reception; engagement (*of a servant*); adoption (*of opinions, of children*). 2. supposition, assumption, postulation; hypothesis; *Alles spricht für die -,* there is every reason to believe; (*C.L.*) *- eines Wechsels verweigern,* dishonour a bill; *einem Wechsel eine willige - bereiten,* meet *or* duly honour a bill.

Annal-en, *pl.* annals, records.

Annaten, *pl.* annates, first year's revenue of benefice paid to Pope (*R.C.*).

annehm-en, *ir.v.a.* 1. take, receive; accept, admit; take into one's service; retain, employ; undertake (*a commission*); take up (*a challenge*); take (*colour, impression, polish, etc.*); embrace (*a faith, etc.*); honour, accept (*a bill*); agree to (*a condition, etc.*); assume (*a character, a form, etc.*); contract (*habits*); *nicht -en,* reject, dishonour (*a bill*); *an Kindes Statt -en,* adopt; *Vernunft -en,* listen to reason; *sich* (*Dat.*) *etwas -en,* apply to o.s., lay a th. to one's own account; *sich einer S. -en,* take an interest in a th.; *sich einer Person -en,* show interest in, espouse the cause of *or* assist a p. 2. suppose, take for granted; assume; *angenommen (daß),* supposing *or* assuming (that); *angenommene Freundlichkeit,* assumed friendliness. **-bar,** *adj.* acceptable, admissible. **-lich,** *adj.* acceptable; assumable, assumed. **-lichkeit,** *f.* pleasantness; charm; amenity; comforts.

annektier-en, *v.a.* annex. **-ung,** *f.* annexation.

annoch, *adv.* as yet, hitherto (*Law* & *Archaic*).

Annonc-e [aˈnõsə], *f.* (-n) advertisement. **-ˈieren,** *v.a.* & *n.* advertise.

Anode, *f.* anode, plate (*Rad.*).

anöden, *v.a.* (*sl.*) bore, weary.

anomal, *adj.* anomalous. **-ie,** *f.* (-ien) anomaly.

anonym, *adj.* anonymous. **-ität,** *f.* anonymity.

anordn-en, *v.a.* order, command, direct; put in order, arrange, regulate; marshal, dispose, array (*troops for battle*). **-er,** *m.* director; regulator; compiler. **-ung,** *f.* 1. order, disposition, grouping, arrangement. 2. regulation, instruction, directive; *-ungen treffen,* make arrangements; give orders.

anorganisch, *adj.* inorganic.

anormal, *adj.* abnormal.

anpacken, *v.a.* lay hold of, seize, grasp.

anpass-en, 1. *v.n.* (*aux.* s.) fit, suit. 2. *v.a.* make to fit; adapt; adjust, accommodate; *sich* (*Acc.*) *den Verhältnissen -en,* adapt o.s. to the circumstances. **-end,** *pr.p.* & *adj.* well-fitting; fit, suitable, appropriate to. **-ung,** *f.* adaptation, adjustment, accommodation. **-ungsfähig,** *adj.* adaptable. **-ungsfähigkeit,** *f.* adaptability.

anpeilen, *v.n.* take bearings (*Navig.*).

anpflanz-en, *v.a.* plant; form a plantation; cultivate. **-er,** *m.* planter, settler, colonist. **-ung,** *f.* planting, cultivation, plantation; (*pl.*) improvements.

anpflöcken, *v.a.* fasten with pegs; stretch (*a canvas*).

anpinseln, *v.a.* daub.

anpirschen, *v.r.* stalk (*Hunt.*); (*fig.*) approach stealthily.

anpöbeln, *v.a.* abuse, vilify.

anpochen, *v.a.* knock, rap at; *bei einem -,* knock at a p.'s door.

Anprall, *m.* (-s) collision, crash, forcible impact, shock, brunt. **-en,** *v.n.* (*aux.* s.) strike against violently.

anprangern, *v.a.* pillory, denounce.

anpreisen, *ir.v.a.* praise, extol, commend.

Anprob-e, *f.* (-n) fitting. **-en,** *v.a.*, **-ieren,** *v.a.* try on, fit on.

anpumpen, *v.a.* (*sl.*) borrow money from, touch for.

Anputz, *m.* (-es) dress, finery; dressing. **-en,** 1. *v.a.* dress up, decorate. 2. *v.r.* dress up; deck o.s. out.

anquick-en, *v.a.* amalgamate (*metals*). **-silber,** *n.* amalgam of silver. **-ung,** *f.* amalgamation.

anranken, *v.a.* fasten by tendrils, twine round.

anranzen, *v.a.*; (*coll.*) *einen -,* give a p. a severe scolding, pitch into a p.

anraten, 1. *ir.v.a.*; *einem etwas -,* advise s.o. to do s.th., recommend s.th. to s.o. 2. *n.* advice, counsel; *auf sein -,* on his advice.

anrauchen, *v.a.* begin to smoke; smoke for the first time (*a new pipe*); blacken with smoke; *eine Pfeife -,* season a pipe. **angeraucht,** *p.p.* & *adj.* smoke-stained; seasoned (*of a pipe*).

anräuchern, *v.a.* fumigate.

anrechn-en, *v.a.* debit, charge; rate, attribute to, impute; *einem etwas -en,* charge s.th. to a p. *or* a p. with s.th.; *Sie haben mir zuviel angerechnet,* you have overcharged me; *ich rechne ihm diesen Dienst sehr hoch an,* I value his service highly. **-ung,** *f.* charge; *in -ung bringen,* charge, put down to a p.'s account, debit a p. with.

Anrecht, *n.* (-(e)s, -e) claim, title, right; *ein - auf eine S. haben,* be entitled to a th.

Anred-e, *f.* (-n) speech, address, harangue; apostrophe (*Rhet.*). **-en,** *v.a.* speak to; address; accost.

anreg-en, *v.a.* stir up, incite, stimulate; suggest, allude to, make mention of; *eine Frage -en,* broach a question; *angeregte Unterhaltung,* animated conversation. **-end,** *pr.p.* & *adj.* exciting, stimulating, interesting, suggestive. **-ung,** *f.* 1. stimulus, impulse, stimulation. 2. suggestion, allusion, hint, mention; *in -ung bringen,* allude to, touch upon; mention, suggest; *auf -ung von,* at the instigation of; *erste -ung,* first impulse, initiative; *geistige -ung,* intellectual stimulus.

anreiben, *ir.v.a.* rub against.

anreicher-n, *v.a.* enrich, strengthen, concentrate, increase fertility (*of soil*), increase concentration (*of a solution*) (*Chem.*). **-ung,** *f.* concentration (*Chem.*).

anreihen, 1. *v.a.* string (*beads, etc.*); arrange in sequence; add. 2. *v.r.* join; rank with; follow; form a queue, queue up; *sich - lassen,* be placed in the same rank with; *an diesen Satz lassen sich eine Menge Folgerungen -,* numerous deductions may follow from this proposition.

Anreim, *m.* (-(e)s, -e) alliteration (*Metr.*). **-end,** *adj.* alliterative.

anreiß-en, *ir.v.a.* tear off, tear a little; break in, trace, sketch, make a first sketch; (*fig., coll.*) break in upon, cut into, touch (*capital, sum of money*). **-er,** *m.* tout.

Anreiz, *m.* (-es, -e) incitement, impulse, stimulus, motive, incentive. **-en,** *v.a.* incite, induce (*zu,* to); stimulate, instigate, abet (*Law*); *einen zum Bösen -en,* incite a p. to do wrong, abet a p. in doing wrong. **-end,** *pr.p.* & *adj.* attractive, seductive. **-er,** *m.* instigator. **-ung,** *f.* incitement, instigation, provocation, encouragement; abetment (*Law*); incentive.

anrempeln, *v.a.*; (*coll.*) *einen -,* jostle against a p. on purpose, pick a quarrel with a p.

anrennen, 1. *ir.v.a.* rush upon, assail. 2. *v.n.* (*aux.* s.) run against; start with a run; *übel* –, meet with a bad reception, catch a Tartar; *angerannt kommen*, come running, come in great haste; (*sl.*) *da bist du mal schön angerannt*, there you have caught it hot.
Anricht–e, *f.* (-n) dresser, sideboard. **–en,** *v.a.* 1. regulate; produce, cause; 2. prepare; serve up (*a meal*); dish up; *es ist angerichtet*, the meal is served; *was hast du angerichtet?* what have you done?; (*coll.*) *da haben Sie was Schönes angerichtet*, you have put your foot in it nicely. **–er,** *m.* assayer, dresser. **–ung,** *f.* dressing, preparation, *etc.*; detent (*Horol.*). **–elöffel,** *m.* ladle. **–eschüssel,** *f.* tureen, large dish. **–etisch,** *m.* kitchen-table, dresser. **–ezimmer,** *n.* pantry.
anriechen, *ir.v.a.* smell at; *ich habe ihm den Tabak angerochen*, I noticed that he smelt of tobacco.
Anriß, *m.* crack, flaw.
Anritt, *m.* (-es) approach on horseback; cavalry charge.
anrosten, *v.n.* (*aux.* s.) begin to rust.
anrüchig, *adj.* notorious; infamous; disreputable. **–keit,** *f.* notoriety, disrepute.
anrücken, 1. *v.n.* (*aux.* s.) approach (*marching*), advance. 2. *v.a.* move *or* bring near to, aim at.
Anruf, *m.* (-s, -e) call, appeal; challenge (*of a sentry*) (*Mil.*); telephone call; call signal (*Rad.*). **–en,** *ir.v.a.* call to, hail, challenge; call up, ring up (*Phone*); invoke, implore, appeal to; *zum Zeugen –en*, call as a witness. **–er,** *m.* appellant. **–stelle,** *f.* call-box (*Phone*). **–ung,** *f.* appeal; invocation. **–zeichen,** *n.* call signal (*Rad.*).
anrühren, *v.a.* touch; touch upon; mix, stir, beat-up (*culinary ingredients*); *jemandes guten Namen* –, hurt a man's reputation.
ans, *abbr.* of **an das.**
ansäen, *v.a.* sow (*a field*).
Ansag–e, *f.* (-n) notification, announcement. **–en,** 1. *v.a.* announce; notify, bring word to, give notice of, intimate; summon; *Sie sagen an*, it is your call (*Cards*); 2. *v.r.* announce an intended visit; *sich –en lassen*, to send in one's name (*as a visitor*); *er sagte sich bei uns zum Abendessen an*, he said he would come to dinner. **–er,** *m.* announcer (*Rad.*), compère (*Theat.*). **–ung,** *f.* notification.
ansamm–eln, 1. *v.a.* collect, gather, accumulate, assemble. 2. *v.r.* collect, gather (together); accumulate, assemble. **–lung,** *f.* collection, accumulation; heap; gathering, crowd; concentration (*of troops*); aggregation.
ansässig, *adj.* settled in a place, domiciled, resident; *er hat sich hier – gemacht*, he has settled down here, he has made his home here. **–keit,** *f.* domicile.
Ansatz, *m.* (-es, ⸚e) 1. start, beginning, onset, attack; 2. assessment, charge, rate; statement (*Arith.*); estimate; (*pl.*) charges, items; *einem etwas in – bringen*, charge a th. to a p.'s account; 3. deposit, crust, incrustation; 4. disposition, tendency; 5. mouthpiece (*of a wind-instrument*); method of blowing (*a flute, etc.*); touch (*on the piano*); 6. thing inserted (*as leaf of a table*). **–punkt,** *m.* point of application; jumping-off point, point of departure. **–rohr,** *n.* attached tube. **–schraube,** *f.* set-screw. **–stelle,** *f.* place of attachment. **–stück,** *n.* attached part.
ansäuer–n, *v.a.* acidify, leaven. **–ung,** *f.* acidification, acidulation.
ansaug–en, 1. *ir.v.a.* & *n.* suck. 2. *v.r.* attach o.s. by sucking; take (*of leeches*). **–leitung,** *f.* intake, inlet port (*Engin.*).
ansäuseln, *v.a.* breathe gently on, play around (*of wind, etc.*); (*sl.*) *angesäuselt*, slightly tipsy.
[1]**anschaff–en,** *v.a.* procure; provide; purchase; *er hat sich das Buch angeschafft*, he has bought that book. **–ung,** *f.* procuring, *etc.*; provision; remittance. **–ungskosten,** *pl.* initial cost, outlay.
[2]**anschaffen,** *ir.v.a.* create with *or* in; imprint on; *das ist ihm angeschaffen*, that is innate in him.
anschalten, *v.a.* & *n.* switch on, make connexion (*Elec.*).
anschau–en, 1. *v.a.* look at; contemplate. 2. *n.* aspect. **–end,** *pr.p.* & *adj.* intuitive; contemplative; *–ende Erkenntnis*, intuitive knowledge. **–lich,** *adj.* & *adv.* clear, plain, evident, obvious; vivid, graphic; intuitive, perceptual. **–lichkeit,** *f.* clearness, vividness, perspicuity. **–ung,** *f.* mode of viewing; view; perception; observation; contemplation; intuition; *zur –ung bringen*, demonstrate; exhibit; *zu der –ung kommen*, come to the view *or* conclusion. **–ungsbegriff,** *m.* intuitive idea. **–ungserkenntnis,** *f.* intuitive knowledge. **–ungsmaterial,** *n.* illustrative material. **–ungsunterricht,** *m.* pictorial instruction. **–ungsvermögen,** *n.* power of intuition, intuitive faculty. **–ungsweise,** *f.* way of viewing things, point of view.
Anschein, *m.* appearance, look, semblance, impression; likelihood; *dem* or *allem – nach*, apparently; to all appearances; *sich* (*Dat.*) *den – geben*, *den – haben* or *erwecken*, give the impression, appear *or* look as if. **–en,** 1. *ir.v.n.* (*aux.* h.) appear. 2. shine upon. **–end,** *pr.p.* & *adj.* apparent, seeming, to all appearances; *–ende Gefahr*, apparent danger.
anschicken, *v.r.* get ready, prepare; set about; *sich zu etwas* –, prepare o.s. to do a th.
anschieb–en, 1. *ir.v.a.* shove *or* push against. 2. *v.n.* (*aux.* h.) have first bowl (*at skittles*); *angeschobene Rente*, deferred annuity. **–er,** *m.* lengthening piece (*as an additional leaf of a table*). **–sel,** *n.* appendix, supplement.
anschielen, *v.a.* squint at; look askance at; cast a sidelong glance at.
anschieß–en, 1. *ir.v.a.* wound by shooting; test, prove (*a gun*), add (*as a supplement, etc.*); sew in (*sleeves, etc.*); **angeschossen,** *p.p.* & *adj.* wounded; (*sl.*) smitten. 2. *v.n.* (*aux.* s.) rush along; rush against; shoot forth; crystallize; (*aux.* h.) shoot first, begin shooting; *wer schießt an?* who has the first shot? 3. *n.* gun trials, practice shoot (*Artil.*). **–ung,** *f.* crystallization.
anschimmeln, *v.n.* begin to go mouldy.
anschirren, *v.a.* harness.
Anschlag, *m.* (-s, ⸚e) 1. stroke; striking (*of a clock*); 2. attempted assassination, attempt on one's life, assault, attack; 3. placard, poster; 4. stop, stud, lug, boss, block, chock (*Tech.*); rabbet (*of a door*); 5. calculation, computation, estimate, valuation; tariff; 6. touch, attack (*of a player, Mus.* & *Sport*); *in – bringen*, take into account, allow for; *in – kommen*, be taken into account; *seine Kosten in – bringen*, calculate *or* charge one's expenses; *im –e halten*, point (*a gun*), present (*a rifle*). **–brett,** *n.*, **–tafel,** *f.* notice board, hoarding. **–sarten,** *f.pl.* firing positions (viz. *stehend, knieend, liegend*). **–säule,** *f.* pillar for posters. **–spreis,** *m.* reserve price, upset price (*C.L.*). **–swert,** *m.* estimated value. **–zettel,** *m.* placard, poster.
anschlagen, 1. *ir.v.a.* 1. strike against, upon *or* at; 2. sound, ring, toll (*bells*); 3. affix, post up, stick up; nail on; 4. estimate, value; 5. splice (*a rope*), bend (*sails*); *Feuer* –, strike fire; *Stunden* –, strike the hours; – *auf*, rate (at); *den Ton* –, give the keynote; *das Klavier* –, touch the keys (*piano*); *eine Saite* –, strike a chord; *das Gewehr auf etwas* (*Acc.*) –, take aim at, lay the gun on; *zum Verkaufe* –, put up for sale. **2.** *v.n.* 1. strike *or* fall against; 2. begin to strike; take effect, take root; operate, succeed; 3. bark, bay (*of dogs*); sing (*of birds*); *die Nahrung schlägt gut bei ihm an*, the diet agrees with him. *die Arznei schlägt an*, the medicine is taking effect.
Anschläg–er, *m.* s.o. *or* s.th. which strikes; hammer (*in a piano*); projector, designer. **–ig,** *adj.* ingenious, inventive, full of devices; *–iger Kopf*, resourceful person.
anschließen, 1. *ir.v.a.* fasten on, join on; chain to; annex; connect (*Elec.*). 2. *v.r.* join, attach o.s. to; close ranks (*Mil.*); follow, conform to, agree with, fit; *sich völlig* –, be completely at one with; *rechts angeschlossen!* close to the right! (*Mil.*).
Anschluß, *m.* (-(ss)es, ⸚(ss)e) connexion (*Phone, Railw.*, *etc.*); supply (*of gas, etc.*); accession, addition; junction; contact (*of troops* & *Elec.*); union, annexation (*of Austria with Germany*); fit (*of clothes*). *den – erreichen*, get *or* catch one's connexion (*Railw.*); *den – versäumen*, miss one's connexion; have no connexion (*Railw.*); – *suchen*, try and make contact with people; *er findet keinen* –, he can't make any friends. **–dose,** *f.* junction box

(*Elec.*). **-klemme,** *f.* connexion terminal (*Elec.*). **-klinke,** *f.* connecting jack (*Tele.*). **-kompagnie,** *f.* flank company (*Mil.*). **-schnur,** *f.* connecting line, cord, flex (*Tele.*). **-station,** *f.* junction (*Railw.*).

anschmachten, *v.a.*; *einen* –, cast sheep's eyes at a p.

anschmecken, *v.a.* notice by the taste.

anschmelzen, 1. *reg.* & *ir.v.a.* fuse on. 2. *v.n.* (*aux.* s.) begin to melt, become fused on to.

anschmieden, *v.a.* fasten by forging; chain, fetter, put in irons.

anschmiegen, 1. *v.a.* bend *or* press to; adapt. 2. *v.r.* (*Dat.*) cling to; join closely; nestle against; snuggle up to; adapt o.s. to, fit in with, conform to.

anschmieren, *v.a.* besmear; daub; (*coll.*) cheat.

anschnallen, *v.a.* buckle on, strap in.

anschnauz-en, *v.a.* (*coll.*) snarl at; snap at. **-er,** *m.* (*coll.*) dressing-down, blowing-up.

anschneiden, *ir.v.a.* begin to cut; get a bearing on (*Navig.*, *Artil.*); raise (*a question*).

anschnellen, 1. *v.a.* jerk against. 2. *v.n.* (*aux.* s.) fly against.

Anschnitt, *m.* (-(e)s, -e) first cut; notch; shamfer, bevel; bearing (*Navig.*, *Artil.*).

Anschov-e, -is, *f.* (-en) anchovy.

anschrauben, *v.a.* screw on, screw up.

anschreib-en, *ir.v.a.* write down, note down; ascribe to, charge to; put to account, debit, score up; *nichts –en lassen,* buy nothing on credit; *bei einem übel angeschrieben sein,* stand in bad repute with s.o., be in s.o.'s bad books. **-ebuch,** *n.* note-book; household book, account-book. **-er,** *m.* marker; scorer (*in games*). **-etafel,** *f.* 'slate'.

anschreien, *ir.v.a.* scream *or* shout at.

Anschrift, *f.* (-en) address.

Anschrote, *f.* (-n) selvage (*cloth*).

Anschub, *m.* (-s, ¨-e) first shove, push off.

anschuldigen, *v.a.* accuse of; charge with; *einen eines Diebstahls* –, charge a p. with theft.

anschüren, *v.a.* stir up, rake; tend (*a fire*); excite, inflame; foment (*a quarrel*).

Anschuß, *m.* (-(ss)es, ¨-(ss)e) crystallization.

anschütten, *v.a.* pour out against; heap up against; bank up, fill up.

anschwänger-n, *v.a.* saturate, impregnate (*Chem.*). **-ung,** *f.* impregnation.

anschwärmen, *v.a.* adore, idolize.

anschwärz-en, *v.a.* blacken; slander, calumniate. **-er,** *m.* slanderer, calumniator. **-ung,** *f.* slander, calumny; blackening.

anschwatzen, *v.a.*; (*coll.*) *einem etwas* –, talk s.o. into (*doing, taking, buying, etc.*).

anschweißen, *v.a.* weld on, braze on.

anschwell-en, *reg.* & *ir. v.a.* & *n.* (*aux.* s.) swell up, increase. **-end,** *pr.p.* & *adj.* crescendo (*Mus.*). **-ung,** *f.* swelling, tumour (*Med.*).

anschwemm-en, *v.a.* wash ashore, wash up; deposit alluvium. **-ung,** *f.* wash of the sea against the shore; alluvial deposit, alluvium.

ansegeln, *v.a.* make for (*port*); run foul of (*a ship*).

anseh-en, 1. *ir.v.a.* look at; view; regard, consider; *–en für* or *als,* consider, take for; *man sieht es ihm nicht an,* you wouldn't think so by looking at him, he does not look it; *man sieht es ihm gleich an, wes Geistes Kind er ist,* you can read his character in his face; *ich sah ihn für seinen Bruder an,* I took him for his brother; *etwas mit –en,* be a witness of, stand by and watch, look on; *einen über die Achsel –en,* look down on a p. **angesehen,** *p.p.* & *adj.* distinguished, of high repute, esteemed, respected. 2. *n.* appearance, aspect, exterior; esteem, respect, reputation; authority, consequence; *sich ein –en geben,* give o.s. airs; *dem –en nach,* to all appearance; *ich kenne sie von –en,* I know her by sight; *vor Gott gilt kein –en der Person,* God is no respecter of persons. **-nlich,** *adj.* imposing, considerable; stately, fine-looking; handsome; important; eminent, conspicuous. **-nlichkeit,** *f.* importance; eminence; dignity; stateliness. **-ung,** *f.* view, consideration; *in –ung,* seeing that, whereas (*Law*); *in –ung seines Fleißes,* considering his diligence.

anseilen, *v.n.* rope oneself (*Mount.*).

ansetz-en, *v.* **1.** *a.* 1. put to *or* near; join on, fix, affix, add to, attach, fasten; apply; ram (home) (*a shell*). 2. establish; fix (*price, day, etc.*), charge, rate, quote. 3. begin to; initiate, launch, prepare, form, set (*trees, etc.*); *er wollte den Dolch –en,* he was about to stab; *den Becher –en,* put the goblet to the lips; *Rost –en,* gather rust; *die Feder –en,* take up one's pen, put pen to paper; *den Spaten –en,* begin to dig; *zum Verkauf –en,* put up for sale; *Truppen –en,* bring troops into action. **2.** *v.r.* settle down; stick to, be deposited, set on, crystallize, incrustate, **3.** *v.n.* (*aux.* h.) take a run (*before leaping*); make an onset; try; begin; sprout; thrive; put on flesh. **4.** *v.n.* formation (*Bot.*); quotation (*of a price*); appointment (*of time or place*). **-blatt,** *n.* fly-leaf (*Typ.*); point of application. **-er,** *m.* rammer (*gun*). **-ung,** *f.* application; apposition; prothesis (*Surg.*); quotation (*of a price*); crystallization.

Ansicht, *f.* (-en) sight, view, prospect; opinion, notion; inspection; *nach meiner –, meiner – nach,* in my opinion; *bei – dieses,* on receipt of this; *zur –,* on appro(val); *sich einer – anschließen,* agree with an opinion. **-ig,** *adj.*; *–ig werden* (*Gen.*), catch sight of. **-s(post)karte,** *f.* picture postcard. **-ssache,** *f.* matter of opinion. **-ssendung,** *f.* consignment for inspection *or* approval. **-stafel,** *f.* table, summary (*given on a single sheet*).

ansied-eln, 1. *v.a.* settle, colonize; *Arbeiter auf dem Lande –eln,* settle labourers on the land. 2. *v.r.* settle, establish o.s. **-ler,** *m.* settler, colonist. **-lung,** *f.* colonization; colony, settlement.

ansinnen, 1. *ir.v.a.* demand, expect *or* require of; *einem etwas* –, demand s.th. of s.o. 2. *n.* desire, request, demand.

ansintern, *v.n.* (*aux.* s.) form stalactites.

ansitzen, *ir.v.n.* (*aux.* h.) stick, adhere to; be firmly attached.

Anspänner, *m.* peasant owning *or* in charge of team of draught animals.

anspann-en, *v.a.* 1. yoke to, hitch, harness up (*horses to a carriage*); 2. stretch; bend (*sails*); 3. strain; exert; *er ließ –en,* he ordered the carriage to be got ready. **-er,** *m.* tensor muscle. **-ung,** *f.* harnessing, yoking; tension, strain; exertion.

anspeien, *ir.v.a.* spit at *or* upon.

Anspiel, *n.* (-(e)s, -e) innings. **-en,** *v.n.* (*aux.* h.) 1. begin to play; play first; open (*Cards*); 2. allude (*auf,* to); hint at. **-ung,** *f.* allusion, reference, hint, insinuation.

anspießen, *v.a.* pierce with a spear; impale; spit (*meat*).

anspinnen, 1. *ir.v.a.* contrive, plot, hatch (*a plot*). 2. *v.r.* spring up, develop, originate.

anspitzen, *v.a.* point, sharpen (*a pencil, etc.*).

Ansporn, *m.* incitement, spur, stimulus. **-en,** *v.a.* spur, spur on, stimulate, incite.

Ansprache, *f.* (-n) address, speech.

ansprechen, *ir.v.a.* 1. speak to, accost, address. 2. appeal to, interest, please; touch (*the heart, etc.*); take one's fancy. 3. beg for, ask for, claim; *einen um eine S.* –, beg s.th. of s.o., ask s.o. for s.th.; *das spricht mich nicht an,* that does not appeal to me. **-d,** *pr.p.* & *adj.* pleasing, attractive, prepossessing; plausible; *–de Vermutung,* plausible conjecture; *sie hat etwas sehr –des,* there is something very engaging about her.

ansprengen, 1. *v.a.* force to a gallop. 2. *v.n.* (*aux.* s.) gallop up; *angesprengt kommen,* came at full gallop *or* full tilt.

anspringen, 1. *ir.v.n.* (*aux.* s.) begin to crack; (*aux.* h.) begin to run, leap; start (*of an engine*). 2. *v.a.* jump at, leap at; *angesprungen kommen,* come running *or* jumping *or* skipping.

anspritzen, *v.a.* splash, spray, besprinkle.

Anspruch, *m.* (-s, ¨-e) claim, title, demand, pretension. *– haben auf eine S.,* be entitled to a th.; *– machen* (or *erheben*) *auf eine S., eine S. in – nehmen,* claim, demand, put forward a claim to *or* lay claim to a th.; *es nimmt meine Zeit zu sehr in –,* it takes up too much of my time; *Ansprüche stellen an,* make demands on, tax. **-slos,** *adj.* unassuming, unpretentious, modest. **-slosigkeit,** *f.* modesty, unpretentiousness. **-svoll,** *adj.* pretentious, exacting, fastidious.

anspucken, *v.a.* spit at.

anspül-en, 1. *v.n.* (*aux.* h.) flow *or* wash against. 2. *v.a.* wash up on the tide, deposit. **-ung,** *f.* alluvium.
anstacheln, *v.a.* goad on, spur on, incite.
Anstalt, *f.* (-en) preparation, arrangement; institution; institute; establishment, plant; *ich habe -en getroffen,* I have made arrangements; *höhere Lehr-,* secondary school.
Anstand, *m.* (-(e)s, ⸚e) 1. propriety, decorum, pleasing demeanour; good behaviour, good manners, seemliness, decency; 2. delay, hesitation, pause, respite; *- nehmen,* hesitate, doubt, pause; 3. stand, station (*Hunt.*); *ohne -,* without hesitation, readily; *edler -,* noble bearing, dignity. **-sbesuch,** *m.* formal call. (*C.L.*) **-sbrief,** *m.* letter of respite *or* grace. **-sdame,** *f.* chaperon. **-shalber,** *adv.* for propriety's sake. **-slos,** *adj.* unhesitating (*rare*). **-sregeln,** *f.pl.* rules of etiquette. **-swidrig,** *adj.* indecent; improper; indecorous.
anständig, *adj.* proper, decorous, becoming; decent, respectable, presentable; (*coll.*) *es schneit ganz -,* it is snowing pretty heavily; (*coll.*) *-er Kerl,* decent fellow. **-keit,** *f.* decency, propriety; respectability.
anstapeln, *v.a.* pile up, hoard up.
anstarren, *v.a.* stare at, gaze at.
anstatt, 1. *prep* (*Gen.*); 2. *conj.* instead of, in the place of.
anstauen, *v.a.* dam up, dike.
anstaunen, *v.a.* gaze at (*in astonishment*). **-swert, -swürdig,** *adj.* admirable, wonderful.
anstechen, *ir.v.a.* pierce, puncture, prick, broach, tap (*a cask*).
ansteck-en, *v.a.* put on; pin *or* fasten on; light (*a candle, etc.*); set fire to, kindle; infect, contaminate. *angestecktes Obst,* tainted fruit; *er ist von den Masern angesteckt worden,* he has caught the measles; *Lachen steckt an,* laughing is catching. **-ärmel,** *m.pl* sham sleeves. **-end,** *pr.p. & adj.* infectious, contagious, catching. **-ung,** *f.* infection; contagion. **-ungsgift** *n.,* **-ungsstoff,** *m.* contagious matter, virus.
anstehen, *ir.v.n.* (*aux.* h. & s.) stand near *or* next, be contiguous; be fixed; queue up (*nach,* for); hesitate, scruple; be deferred; (*einem*) -, suit *or* fit (a p.), be becoming (to a p.); be to one's taste; *- lassen,* defer, delay, grant a respite; forbear; *eine Schuld - lassen,* defer payment of a debt; *ich habe nicht angestanden ihm zu sagen,* I have not hesitated to tell him; *es steht ihr alles wohl an,* everything she wears suits her. **-d,** *pr.p. & adj.* (*Geol.*) occurring, cropping out; *-des Gestein,* solid rock, rocky outcrop.
ansteigen, 1. *ir.v.n.* (*aux.* s.) rise, mount, ascend, increase; *jäh -,* rocket, soar (*fig.*). 2. *n.* rise, ascent, surge. **-d,** *adj.* rising, ascending, sloping.
anstell-en, 1. *v.a.* 1. place *or* put near; post, assign positions to; arrange; 2. appoint, employ, engage, take on; 3. set in operation; undertake; make (*an experiment*); start (*an engine*); switch on (*radio, etc.*); draw (*a comparison*); do, cause (*mischief, etc.*); contrive; institute; install; arrange, set up; *ich weiß nicht, wie ich es -en soll,* I don't know how I am to set about it; *fest angestellt,* permanently appointed. 2. *v.r.* queue up; act, behave (*in a certain manner*); feign, pretend; make a fuss; *sich zu etwas -en,* set about a th.; *er stellt sich wohl dazu an,* he sets about it in the right way; *sich -en als ob,* pretend to be, act as if; *er stellte sich jämmerlich an,* he cut a miserable figure; *stell' dich nicht an!* do not make a fuss! **-bar,** adj. adjustable. **-ig,** *adj.* handy, able, skilful. **-ung,** *f.* appointment, post, employment; placing, arranging.
anstemmen, *v.a.* stem, push *or* press against.
ansteuer-n, *v.n.* steer towards, shape a course for (*Naut.*). **-ungsleuchtfeuer,** *n.* (homing) beacon (*Av.*).
Anstieg, *m.* ascent, rise.
anstift-en, 1. *v.a.* cause, set on foot, plot; provoke, incite, instigate, stir up, suborn. 2. *n. see* **-ung.** **-er,** *m.* author, instigator, abettor (*Law*); *-er falscher Zeugen,* suborner. **-ung,** *f.* instigation, machination; suborning; contriving, cause (*of a plot*).
anstimm-en, *v.a.* begin to sing; strike up; give the keynote; tune (*string instruments*). **-ung,** *f.* striking up; intonation; tuning.
Anstoß, *m.* (-(ss)es, ⸚(ss)e) shock, collision; impulse; impetus; initiative, incentive; kick-off (*Football*); scandal, offence; *- geben* or *erregen,* give offence; *- nehmen an* (*einer S.*), take offence at, be scandalized by (a. th.); *Stein des -es,* stumbling-block. **-en,** 1. *ir.v.a.* strike, push *or* knock against, impinge upon; nudge, strike; give offence; *angestoßenes Obst,* bruised fruit. 2. *v.n.* (*aux.* h.) bump, stumble against; touch, abut, adjoin, border on; kick off (*Football*); touch *or* clink glasses; *wir stießen auf seine Gesundheit an,* we drank to his health; *mit dem Kopfe -en an* or *wider,* knock one's head against; *mit der Zunge* or *im Reden -en,* stammer, stutter; *-en wider* or *gegen,* offend against; *-en bei,* give offence; shock, scandalize; *nur nicht -en!* beware of giving offence! **-end,** *pr.p. & adj.* contiguous, adjoining; *-endes Zimmer,* adjoining room.
anstößig, *adj.* offensive, unpleasant, shocking, scandalous, indecent, objectionable, obnoxious; bruised, decaying. **-keit,** *f.* impropriety, offensiveness, indelicacy, indecency.
anstreb-en, 1. *v.n.* (*aux.* h.); *gegen eine S. -en,* strive against a th. 2. *v.a.* aspire to, strive for.
anstreich-en, *ir.v.a.* paint; mark *or* underline (*a passage in a book, etc.*); *weiß -en,* whitewash; (*coll.*) *das werde ich ihm gehörig -en,* I shall make him pay for this. **-er,** *m.* (house-)painter.
anstreifen, *v.n.* (*aux.* h. & s.) graze, rub against, touch lightly in passing.
anstreng-en, 1. *v.a.* strain; stretch; *alle Kräfte -en,* strain every nerve; *einen -en,* fatigue a p.; *eine Klage -en,* bring an action (against); *der kleine Druck strengt die Augen sehr an,* small print is very trying for the eyes; *-ende Arbeit,* exacting work. 2. *v.r.* exert o.s., tax one's energies, strive, make every effort; *sich über die Maßen -en,* over-exert o.s. **-ung,** *f.* exertion, effort, strain; struggle.
Anstrich, *m.* (-s, -e), paint, coat of paint; colouring, tinge, shade; air, appearance; *einer S. einen guten - geben,* gloss over a matter; *- von Gelehrsamkeit,* veneer of learning; *- von Schwermut,* air of melancholy; *vorübergehender - Grund -* first coat; *Deck-,* top coat.
anström-en, 1. *v.n.* (*aux.* s.) flow towards; flock together, crowd towards; *-en an* (*ein Ufer*), wash ashore. 2. *v.a.* deposit, wash up on. **-richtung,** *f.* direction of air flow (*Av.*).
anstück-eln, *v.a.* piece together, patch. **-(e)lung,** *f.* patch; piece added.
Ansturm, *m.* (-s, ⸚e) assault, onset, charge, rush; *im ersten - nehmen,* rush (*a position, defences, etc.*).
anstürmen, *v.n.* (*aux.* s.) rush along; (with *auf, an, gegen, wider, usw.*) assault, assail, storm, charge.
Ansturz, *m.* (-es, ⸚e) violent onset, shock, impact.
anstürzen, *v.n.* (*aux.* s.) rush against; charge; fall violently against; *angestürzt kommen,* come on with a rush.
ansuch-en, 1. *v.n.* (*aux.* h.) ask, apply, sue (*um etwas,* for s.th.); solicit, request, petition; make a requisition. 2. *n.* request, petition; application, requisition; *auf -en,* by request; *auf -en von,* at the request of, upon the application of. **-end,** *pr.p. & adj.* supplicatory; *der -ende,* the petitioner. **-er,** *m.* petitioner. **-ung,** *f.* request, application, requisition, suit, instigation. **-(ungs)schreiben,** *n.* letter of application, requisition.
Antarktis, *f.* the Antarctic.
antasten, *v.a.* touch, handle; question, impugn, dispute; attack, hurt, injure (*a p.'s reputation, etc.*); infringe on, violate (*a p.'s rights*); *einen -,* lay hands on s.o.
Anteil, *m.* (-s, -e) portion, part, share; sympathy, interest; dividend; allotment; constituent, fraction; *- haben an einer S.,* participate in a th. *- nehmen an,* take an interest in, sympathize with. **-haber,** *m.,* **-haberin,** *f.* participator, partaker; share-holder. **-los,** *adj.* indifferent, neutral; unsympathetic. **-mäßig,** *adj.* proportionate. **-nahme,** *f.* sympathy. **-schein,** *m.,* **-verschreibung,** *f.* share certificate, scrip. **-zahl,** *f.* percentage, fraction.
antelephonieren, *v.a.* ring up.

Antenne, *f.* (-n) aerial (*Rad.*), antenna (*also Zool.*). **-nkreis,** *m.* aerial circuit (*Rad.*).
anti-christlich, *adj.* antichristian. **-klopfmittel,** *n.* antiknock agent (*Motor.*). **-kritik,** *f.* reply to a criticism. **-pathie,** *f.* antipathy. **-pode,** *m.* antipode. **-these,** *f.* antithesis; (*and many others with prefix corresponding to English* anti-).
antik, *adj.* antique. **-e,** *f.* (-en) (classical) antiquity; an antique (*work of art*). **-enhändler,** *m.* dealer in antiques.
Antimon, *n.* antimony.
Antipathie, *see* **anti-.**
antippen, *v.a.* touch lightly, tap.
Antiqu-a, *f.* Roman type (*Typ.*). **-ar,** *m.* (-s, -e) second-hand bookseller; (*rare*) dealer in antiquities. **-ariat,** *n.* second-hand bookshop. **-arisch,** *adj.* second-hand (*of books*). **-aschrift,** *f.* Roman type. **-ität,** *f.* (-, -en) (*usually pl.*) antique. **-itätenhändler,** *m.* dealer in antiques. **-itätensammler,** *m.* collector of antiques.
Antlitz, *n.* (-es, -e) (*elevated style*) countenance, face.
Antrag, *m.* (-s, ⸚e) offer, proposition, proposal; tender; motion (*Parl.*). *einen – stellen,* propose a motion, move (*Parl.*); file an application; *einen – durchbringen,* carry a motion; *der – ging ohne Schwierigkeit durch,* the motion was carried easily; *einen – unterstützen,* second a motion; *der – wurde abgelehnt,* the motion was lost; (*einer Dame*) *einen – machen,* propose (*to a lady*). **-en,** *ir.v.a.* propose, offer, tender. *es wurde ihm ein Amt angetragen,* an appointment was offered to him; *auf etwas -en,* move *or* propose a motion for, request, desire a th., *es wurde auf die Bildung eines Ausschusses angetragen,* it was proposed that the matter should be referred to a committee. **-sformular,** *n.* application form. **-steller,** *m.* mover, proposer (*of a resolution*).
antrauen, *v.a.* marry to; *eine Frau einem Manne –,* unite a woman in marriage with a man; *mein angetrauter Mann,* my wedded husband.
antreffen, *ir.v.a.* meet with, fall in with; hit upon, come across; *auf frischer Tat –,* catch in the very act, catch red-handed; *ich traf ihn zufällig an,* I met him by chance; *ich traf ihn gesund an,* I found him well.
antreib-en, 1. *ir.v.a.* drive *or* push on, propel; urge on, incite, impel, prompt; force (*plants*); *vom Hunger angetrieben,* impelled by hunger. 2. *v.n.* (*aux.* s.) drift *or* float against *or* ashore.
antreten, 1. *ir.v.a.* enter upon, begin; set out on (*a journey*); take up (*office*); take possession of; tread on *or* down; (*Poet.*) go up to, approach with a request; *ein Amt –,* take up office; *den Dienst –,* start one's military service, report for work; *einen Beweis –,* undertake to prove. 2. *v.n.* (*aux.* s.) step up for; place o.s., station o.s.; *zum Tanze –,* take one's place (*for dancing*); fall in, form up in ranks (*Mil.*); *angetreten!* fall in! (*Mil.*); *– zum Appell!* fall in for roll call!
Antrieb, *m.* (-s, -e) impulse, motive, incentive, inducement, stimulus; instigation; drive; driving wheel; power, propulsion, motive power. *aus natürlichem –,* instinctively; *aus freiem –,* of one's own accord; *aus eigenem –,* spontaneously, on one's own initiative. **-sachse,** *f.* driving axle (*Motor.*). **-skraft,** *f.* propelling power, momentum. **-sscheibe,** *f.* driving pulley. **-swelle,** *f.* driving shaft.
antrinken, *ir.v.n.* (*aux.* h.) drink first, begin to drink. **angetrunken,** *p.p.* & *adj.* worse for drink, tipsy, fuddled.
Antritt, *m.* (-s, -e) amble (*of a horse*); entrance (upon); start, beginning, commencement; accession (to) (*throne*); assumption (of); setting out (on); first step (*of a staircase*); anteroom; daïs; footstep (*Typ.*). **-saudienz,** *f.* first audience *or* reception (*at court*). **-spredigt,** *f.* inaugural sermon. **-srede,** *f.* inaugural address, maiden speech. **-sschmaus,** *m.* installation banquet. **-svorlesung,** *f.* inaugural lecture.
antrocknen, *v.n.* (*aux.* s.) begin to dry; dry on.
antun, *ir.v.a.* put on (*clothes*), don; do to; inflict violence on, injure, insult; *einem Gutes* (*Böses*) *–,* benefit (injure) a p.; *sich* (*Dat.*) *ein Leid* (or *Leids*) *–,* lay violent hands on o.s.; *sich Zwang –,* constrain o.s.; *einem Gewalt –,* offer violence to a p.; *einem einen Schimpf –,* insult a p.; *Strafe –,* inflict punishment; *einem* or *einer S. Ehre –,* do honour to a p. *or* a th.; *einen Hafen –,* make, touch at (*a port*). **angetan,** *p.p.* & *adj.* clad, attired; adapted; *danach angetan sein,* be suitable for, be likely to; *angetan sein von,* be smitten by; *das Mädchen hat es ihm angetan,* the girl has bewitched him.
Antwort, *f.* (-en) answer, reply; *in – auf* (*Acc.*), in answer to; *er ist gleich mit einer – da,* he is never at a loss for an answer; *sie blieb ihm keine – schuldig,* she had an answer to everything he said; *zur – geben,* answer; *Rede und – stehen über,* account for, answer for; *abschlägige –,* refusal, answer in the negative; *spitzige* or *schlagfertige –,* smart reply, repartee; *um – wird gebeten* (*U.A.w.g.*), (the favour of) an answer is requested (R.S.V.P.); (*Prov.*) *keine – ist auch eine –,* silence gives consent. **-en,** *v.a.* & *n.* answer, reply; *einem auf seine Frage -en,* reply to *or* answer a p.'s question. **-er,** *m.* respondent (*Law*); answerer. **-gesang,** *m.* antiphonal chant. **-karte,** *f.* reply (post-)card. (*C.L.*) **-lich,** *adj. -lich Ihres Briefes,* in reply to your letter. **-schein,** *m.* reply-coupon, coupon de réponse international. **-schreiben,** *n.* written reply, answer in writing.
anüben, *v.a.*; *sich* (*Dat.*) *etwas –,* acquire s.th. by practice.
anulken, *v.a.*; (*sl.*) *einen –,* make fun of a p.
anvertrau-en, 1. *v.a.* confide, entrust to. 2. *v.r.*; *sich einem -en,* confide in a p., enbosom o.s. to a p. **-t,** *p.p.* & *adj.* entrusted; *-tes Geld,* trust money.
anverwandt, *adj.* related, akin, allied; *– und zugetan,* related and devoted to; *der -e,* relative, kinsman.
anvisieren, *v.n.* align sights (*Navig.*).
Anwachs, *m.* increase, growth, swelling, accretion, increment. **-en,** *ir.v.n.* grow to *or* together, adhere to; grow up; take root; increase, swell, rise (*of rivers*); accumulate, augment. **-streifen,** *m.pl.* lines of growth.
anwall-en, *v.n.* (*aux.* s.) roll up (*as waves*). **-ung,** *f.* rolling up; crowding near.
Anwalt, *m.* (-s, ⸚e) lawyer, attorney, solicitor; counsel, advocate, barrister (*NB. in German Law there is no difference between barrister and solicitor*); *see also* Rechtsanwalt, Staatsanwalt. *– der Gläubiger,* official assignee. **-schaft,** *f.* agency, attorneyship. **-sgebühren,** *f.pl.* attorney's fees; agent's fees.
anwand-eln, *v.a. imp.* befall, come over, come upon; attack, seize (*of illness, etc.*); *was wandelte dich an?* what has come over you? *es wandelte ihn eine Ahnung an,* a presentiment came over him; *es wandelte mich eine Ohnmacht an,* I was seized with a fainting fit; *mich wandelte die Lust an,* I was seized with a desire. **-lung,** *f.* seizure, fit; impulse; access, touch (*of pity, rage*); slight attack (*of illness*).
anwärmen, *v.a.* heat *or* warm slightly; begin to heat, mull; warm up the engine (*Motor.*).
Anwartschaft, *f.* (prospect of) reversion; expectancy; *in –,* in abeyance; *er hat die – auf seines Vaters Amt,* he has the reversion of his father's office. **-lich,** *adj.* reversionary.
Anwärter, *m.* reversioner, expectant (*Law*), candidate (for a job, *auf eine Stellung*); *see also* Bewerber.
anwedeln, *v.a.* greet *or* welcome (by wagging tail).
anwehen, *v.a.* drift against; blow upon; come over; *Entsetzen wehte ihn an,* horror seized him; (*coll.*) *einem etwas –,* give a p. a gentle hint.
anweichen, *v.a.* soften a little, steep, soak.
anweis-en, *ir.v.a.* direct, instruct; point out, show; assign, allot; designate, appoint; admonish; *sich -en lassen,* take directions *or* advice; *er war auf sich selbst angewiesen,* he was left to his own resources; *ich werde Ihnen Ihr Geld -en,* I shall give you a cheque for your money; *die Beamten sind angewiesen,* the officials have instructions to. **-ung,** *f.* order, instruction, direction, assignment; cheque, bill of exchange; voucher, draft, money-order; advice; method, course; *den Mädchen -ung(en)*

geben, give instructions to the maids; *in einer –ung festgesetzt*, secured by deed of assignment; *methodische –ung*, systematic instruction.
anwend–en, *reg. & ir.v.a.* employ, use, make use of; *–en auf eine S.*, apply to a th.; *viele Mühe bei etwas –en*, take great trouble with *or* bestow great care on a th.; *Vorsicht –en*, take precautions; *–en zu einem Zwecke*, employ for a purpose. **–bar,** *adj.* applicable; practicable; feasible; available. **–barkeit,** *f.* applicability; practicability, feasibility; availability. **–ung,** *f.* use, application; employment; *–ung auf einen bestimmten Fall*, application to a special case; *in der –ung*, in practice; *–ung finden, zur –ung kommen*, be used. **–ungsbereich,** *m.* range of application. **angewandt,** *p.p. & adj.* applied, employed, practical; *angewandte Wissenschaften*, applied sciences; *angewandte und abgezogene Begriffe*, concrete and abstract ideas; *angewandte Chemie*, experimental chemistry; *Schmeichelei ist bei ihm nicht gut angewandt*, flattery is lost upon him.
anwerb–en, 1. *ir.v.a.* recruit, enlist, raise, levy (*troops*); *ein Angeworbener*, a recruit, an enlisted man; *sich –en lassen*, enlist. 2. *v.n.* (*um eine S.*) solicit, apply *or* sue for. **–er,** *m.* recruiting officer. **–ung,** *f.* enlistment, enrolment, engagement, levying, levy.
anwerfen, 1. *ir.v.n.* (*aux.* h.) have the first throw. 2. *v.a.* crank (*an engine*); throw at; throw on; *Kalk –*, roughcast; *den Motor –*, start the engine.
Anwesen, *n.* (-s, -) property; real estate, premises. **–d,** *pr.p. & adj.* present; *jeder –de*, everyone present; *die –den*, those present, the audience; *hochgeehrte –de!* (ladies and) gentlemen! **–heit,** *f.* presence.
anwidern, *v.a.* disgust; *das widert mich an*, it disgusts *or* revolts me; *sich angewidert fühlen*, feel disgusted.
anwinken, *v.a.* beckon to; ease the sheets (*Naut.*).
anwittern, *v.n.* effloresce.
Anwohner, *m.* neighbour.
Anwuchs, *m.* (-es, ¨e) growth; increase; increment; accretion; *junger –*, young copse.
anwünschen, *v.a. einem etwas –*, wish s.th. to happen to a p.; *er wünschte mir viel Gutes an*, he wished me the best of luck.
Anwurf, *m.* (-s, ¨e) rough-cast; deposit (*money*), alluvial deposit; selvage; (*pl.*) reproaches.
anwurzeln, *v.n.* (*aux.* s.) strike *or* take root; be rooted to the ground; *wie angewurzelt*, as if rooted *or* nailed to the spot.
Anzahl, *f.* number, quantity, multitude. **–en,** *v.a.* pay on account; pay a first instalment. **–ung,** *f.* payment on account, instalment, deposit.
anzapfen, *v.a.* broach, tap (*a cask*); tap (*Med.*); (*coll.*) pump (*for news*).
anzaubern, *v.a.* fascinate, bewitch. **angezaubert,** *p.p. & adj.* spellbound.
anzäumen, *v.a.* bridle, put on a bridle.
Anzeich–en, *n.* (-s, -) mark, indication, sign, symptom; token, omen, foreboding, augury. **–enbeweis,** *m.* circumstantial evidence. **–nen,** *v.a.* mark, note; make a note of; signal.
Anzeig–e, *f.* (-n) notice, intimation, report; advertisement, announcement; review (*of a book*); prospectus; *–e bei Gericht*, denunciation; *eine –e machen*, file a declaration; make a report, notify. **–eamt,** *n.* registry office. **–eblatt,** *n.* advertisement sheet *or* journal. **–ebrief,** *m.* letter of advice; circular. **–egerät,** *n.*, **–emittel,** *n.* indicator. **–en,** *v.a.* announce, notify; report, inform; advertise; point out, indicate; advise, intimate; declare, quote (*value, etc.*); (*C.L.*) acknowledge, advise; *einem etwas –en*, inform *or* apprise a p. of a th.; *einen –en*, denounce, inform against; *öffentlich –en*, proclaim. **angezeigt** *p.p. & adj.* indicated, advisable, necessary; *er hielt es für angezeigt*, he considered it advisable. **–enbüro,** *n.* advertising agency. **–epflicht,** *f.* obligation to inform the police. **–er,** *m.* who points out; indicator, pointer; informer; advertiser; exponent (*Math.*). **–erblatt,** *n.* instruction sheet. **–evorrichtung,** *f.* indicating device. **–ung,** *f.* informing; advertising; information (*against*).
Anzett–el, *m.* (-s, -) warp. **–eln,** *v.a.* set up a warp; frame, weave, contrive a plot; plot, scheme; *eine Verschwörung –eln gegen*, plot against. **–ler,** *m.* plotter, intriguer, schemer. **–(e)lung,** *f.* scheming plotting.
anzieh–en, 1. *ir.v.a.* draw, pull (on, in, *etc.*); draw tight, tighten; haul home (*Naut.*); stretch; screw, drive home (*a screw*); put on (*clothes*), dress; suck up, absorb; attract; quote, cite; breed, raise (*cattle, etc.*); cultivate, train (*trees, etc.*); *sich* (*Acc.*) *–en*, dress o.s.; *einen neuen Menschen –en*, turn over a new leaf; *angezogene Stellen*, passages referred to, quotations. 2. *v.n.* (*aux.* h.) draw; make first move (*in chess*); stick, hold fast (*as glue, etc.*); take effect; *Preise ziehen an*, prices rise; (*aux.* s.) draw near, approach; enter upon service *or* upon office; *das Heer kam angezogen*, the army came marching on. **–end,** *pr.p. & adj.* attractive, alluring; astringent; *–ende Kraft*, power of attraction; *–ende Mittel*, astringent medicines. **–er,** *m.* shoehorn; adductor muscle (*Anat.*). **–ung,** *f.* attraction, gravitation; quoting, citing; tightening, **–ungskraft,** *f.*, **–ungsvermögen,** *n.* attraction, power of attraction. **–ungslos,** *adj.* unattractive. **–ungspunkt,** *m.* centre of attraction.
Anzucht, *f.* (¨e) raising, breeding, cultivation, culture. **–schweine,** *n.pl.* breeding-pigs.
Anzug, *m.* (-s, ¨e) 1. suit, dress, clothes, clothing, apparel, attire, garb, costume. 2. approach, entrance (*upon duties*), opening move; *der Feind ist im –e*, the enemy is approaching; *es ist etwas im –*, there is s.th. in the wind *or* brewing; *es ist ein Gewitter im –*, a storm is brewing, coming on *or* imminent. **–smoment,** *n.* initial torque (*Mech.*). **–sstoff,** *m.* suiting. **–stag,** *m.* day of entering upon duty *or* into service.
anzüglich, *adj.* suggestive; personal; offensive; abusive. **–keit,** *f.* suggestive remark; offensiveness; (*pl.*) personalities.
anzünd–en, *v.a.* kindle, light (*a fire, etc.*); set on fire; ignite; inflame. **–er,** *m.* fire-lighter, kindling. **–ung,** *f.* ignition, kindling, lighting.
Aort–a, *f.* (-a, -en) aorta. **–enkammer,** *f.* left ventricle.
apart, 1. *adj.* uncommon, out of the common; singular, odd, remarkable, interesting, (*sl.*) cute. 2. *adv.* separately; *nicht – abgegeben*, not sold separately.
Apath–ie, *f.* apathy. **–isch,** *adj.* apathetic.
Apfel, *m.* (-s, ¨) apple. (*Prov.*) *in den sauern – beißen*, swallow a bitter pill; (*Prov.*) *der – fällt nicht weit vom Stamm*, like father like son. **–äther,** *m.* malic ether. **–auflauf,** *m.* apple souffle. **–baum,** *m.* apple-tree. **–blüte,** *f.* apple blossom. **–branntwein,** *m.* apple brandy, applejack. **–brei,** *m.* apple sauce. **–dorn,** *m.* crab-apple tree. **–garten,** *m.* orchard. **–gehäuse,** *n.* apple core. **–gelee,** *n.* apple jelly. **–grau,** *adj.* dapple-grey. **–häuschen,** *n.* core of an apple. **–kern,** *m.* (apple) pip. **–kuchen,** *m.* apple-tart. **–most,** *m.* new cider. **–mus,** *n.* apple puree. **–presse,** *f.* cider-press. **–saft,** *m.* apple juice (*unfermented*). **–säure,** *f.* malic acid. **–schale,** *f.* apple-paring, apple-peel. **–schimmel,** *m.* dapple-grey horse. **–sine,** *f.* (-n) orange. **–stecher,** *m.* apple corer. **–torte,** *f.* apple-tart. **–wein,** *m.* cider.
Aphongetriebe, *n.* synchromesh transmission (*Veh.*).
Apo–kalypse, *f.* apocalypse; *die –kalyptischen Reiter*, the (four) horsemen of the apocalypse. **–kryph(isch),** *adj.* apocryphal. **–log,** *m.* apologue. **–loget,** *m.* apologist. **–stat,** *m.* apostate. **–stem,** *m.* aposteme, abscess. **–stroph,** *m.* (-s, -e) apostrophe. **–strophe,** *f.* (-en) address, harangue. **–theose,** *f.* apotheosis.
Apost–el, *m.* (-s, -) apostle. **–elamt,** *n.*, **–olat,** *n.* (-s, -e) apostleship. **–elgeschichte,** *f.* Acts of the Apostles. **–olisch,** *adj.* apostolic; *das –olische Glaubensbekenntnis*, the Apostles' Creed; *der –olische Stuhl*, the Apostolic See, the See of Rome; *die –olischen Väter*, the Apostolic Fathers.
Apothek–e, *f.* (-en) chemist's shop, pharmacy, dispensary. **–er,** *m.* (dispensing) chemist, pharmacist; apothecary. **–erbuch,** *n.* pharmacopœia. **–ergarten,** *m.* herb garden. **–ergewicht,** *n.* apothecary's weight. **–erkunst,** *f.* pharmaceutics. **–erwaren,** *f.pl.* drugs. **–erwissenschaft,** *f.* pharmaceutics.

Apparat, *m.* (-(e)s, -e) apparatus; appliance, contrivance; instrument, machine, mechanism, device; set; camera; telephone; *am* –*!* speaking! (*Phone*). **–brett,** *n.* instrument board. **–iv,** *adv.* by means of apparatus. **–ur,** *f.* equipment.

Appell, *m.* (-s, -e) roll-call; parade, inspection; – *haben,* be obedient (*of dogs*); – *abhalten,* call the roll (*Mil.*); *zum – antreten,* fall in for roll-call. **–platz,** *m.* parade ground.

Appell–ant, *m.* (-en, -en) appellant. **–at,** *m.* defendant, respondent. **–ation,** *f.* appeal (*Law*); *er legte –ation ein,* he gave notice of appeal; *seine –ation wurde für unzulässig erklärt,* his appeal was not allowed. **–ationsfreiheit,** *f.* right of appeal. **–ationsklage,** *f.* action upon appeal. **–ationsgericht,** *n.* court of appeal. **–ationsklage,** *f.* action upon appeal. **–ationsrichter,** *m.* appeal judge.

Appetit, *m.* appetite. **–lich,** *adj.* dainty; appetizing. **–los,** *adj.* having no appetite.

applaudieren, *v.a.* & *n.* applaud.

Applikatur, *f.* (-en) fingering (*Mus.*).

applizieren, *v.a.* apply, bestow.

apportieren, *v.a.* retrieve, fetch (*of dogs*).

appret–ieren, *v.a.* dress, finish (*of fabrics*). **–ur,** *f.* dressing; finish.

approbiert, *adj.* certified, approved.

Aprikose, *f.* (-n) apricot.

April, *m.* (-s) April; *einen in den – schicken* or *führen,* make an April fool of a p. **–blume,** *f.* anemone (*Anemone nemorosa*). **–glück,** *n.* fleeting good luck. **–scherz,** *m.* April fooling.

Apside, *f.* (-n) apsis (*Astr.*).

Apsis, *f. pl.* (Apsen), apse.

Aquarell, *n.* (-s, -e) water-colour. **–ieren,** *v.a.* paint in water-colours.

Äquator, *m.* (-s) equator, the line.

Aquavit, *m.* (-) aqua vitae, brandy, spirits.

Äquilibrist, *m.* (-en, -en) tight-rope-walker, trapeze artiste.

Ar, *n. or* (*Bavaria & Austria*) *m.* (-es, -e) 100 square metres.

Ära, *f.* era.

Ärar, *n.* (*Austrian dial.*) (-s) public treasury, exchequer. **–isch,** *adj.* state; public; fiscal.

Arbeit, *f.* (-en) work, labour, toil; task, job, piece of work; performance, workmanship; employment; fermentation; process; energy, effort (*Mech.*); *eingelegte* –, inlaid work; *erhabene* –, embossed *or* raised work, relief; *getriebene* –, chasing; *Hand*–, needle-work; *bei der – sein,* be busy with one's work; *sich an die – machen,* set to *or* about work; *Hand an die – legen* set to work; *schriftliche* –, composition, essay. **–en,** 1. *v.a.* work, make, manufacture, perform, execute, fashion, cultivate (*land*); *sich hindurch –en,* work one's way through; *sich krank –en,* knock o.s. up with work. 2. *v.n.* (*aux.* h.) work, toil, labour; ferment; *–en an,* be busy with *or* employed on; *–en mit,* transact business with; *ich –e daran,* I am at work at it; *das Schiff –et,* the ship labours; *es –et sich schlecht,* work progresses badly. **–er,** *m.* worker, workman, labourer. **–erbewegung,** *f.* working-class movement. **–erfrage,** *f.* labour question. **–erin,** *f.* working woman, factory-girl. **–erpartei,** *f.* Labour Party. **–errat,** *m.* workers' council. **–erschaft,** *f.* working men, working class, proletariat. **–erschutz,** *m.* protection of labour. **–erstand,** *m.* working class, labouring classes. **–ertum,** (*in Nat. Soc. usage had a connotation radically different from 'proletariat'*) an honourable estate or guild of workers who are proud of their position in society. **–erwohnung,** *f.* working-class house. **–geber,** *m.* employer. **–geberschaft,** *f.* employers. **–nehmer,** *m.* employee. **–sabstand,** *m.* working distance. **–sabteilung,** *f.* labour squad, working party. **–sam,** *adj.* hard-working, diligent, industrious. **–samkeit,** *f.* industry, diligence. **–samt,** *n.* Labour Exchange. **–säquivalent,** *m.* mechanical equivalent (*Mech.*). **–saufwand,** *m.* expenditure of work. **–sbeschaffung,** *f.* provision of work for unemployed, works programme. **–sbeschränkung,** *f.* curtailment of work. **–sbeutel,** *m.* workbag. **(s)scheu,** 1. *adj.* work-shy, idle, lazy. 2. *f.* laziness. **–scheue(r),** *m.* shirker. **–sdienst,** *m.* labour service. **–seinheit,** *f.* unit of work, erg (*Mech.*). **–seinsatz,** *m.* mobilization of labour, labour supply, labour pool. **–seinstellung,** *f.* strike. **–sfähig,** *adj.* able-bodied. **–sfeld,** *n.* field of activity, sphere of action. **–sfolge** *f.* working order. **–sfront,** *f.* Nat. Soc. Labour Front (*a public corporation of which membership was compulsory for all employers and workers*). **–sgang,** *m.* operation. **–sgemeinschaft,** *f.* study group. **–sgerüst,** *n.* scaffolding; **–sgesellschaft,** *f.* gang of workmen. **–shaus,** *n.* workhouse; penitentiary. **–shöhe,** *f.* peak performance (*Engin.*). **–shub,** *m.* power stroke (*Engin.*). **–shypothese,** *f.* working hypothesis *or* theory. **–skammer,** *f.* laboratory. **–skästchen,** *n.* (*ladies'*) work-box; tool-box. **–skommando,** *n.* fatigue party (*Mil.*). **–skorb,** *m.* work-basket. **–skräfte,** *f.pl.* hands, labourers, labour. **–slager,** *n.* labour camp. **–sleistung,** *f.* rate of work, achievement, efficiency, performance. **–sloch,** *n.* man-hole (*in boilers, etc.*). **–slohn,** *m.* wages. **–slos,** *adj.* out of work. **–slosenunterstützung,** *f.* unemployment pay, dole. **–smann,** *m.* workman. **–smarkt,** *m.* labour market. **–snachweis,** *m.* **–snachweistelle,** *f.* Labour Exchange. **–sparend,** *adj.* labour-saving. **–spflicht,** *f.* liability for labour service. **–sschule,** *f.* industrial school. **–sspende,** *f.* (*under Nat. Soc.*) a 'voluntary' contribution to combat unemployment. **–stag,** *m.* working-day. **–stakt,** *m. see* **–shub. –steilung,** *f.* division of labour. **–stisch,** *m.* work-table. **–sunfähig,** *adj.* unfit for work, disabled. **–svermögen,** *n.* capacity for work, kinetic energy (*Mech.*). **–swillig,** *adj.* willing to work. **–szeit,** *f.* working hours. **–szeug,** *n.* tools.

archaisch, *adj.* archaic.

archäisch, *adj.* Archaean, Pre-Cambrian, Azoic (*Geol.*).

Archäo–log(e), *m.* (-en, -en) archaeologist. **–logie,** *f.* archaeology. **–logisch,** *adj.* archaeological.

Arche, *f.* (-n) ark; wind-chest (*of an organ*); channel, trough (*Hydr.*); – *Noahs,* Noah's ark.

Archi–, (*in compounds*) **–diakonus,** *m.* (-onen) archdeacon. **–pel,** *m.* (-s, -(e)) archipelago. **–tekt,** *m.* architect. **–tektonisch,** *adj.* architectural. **–tektur,** *f.* (-en) architecture.

Architrav, *m.* (-s, -e) architrave.

Archiv, *n.* (-s, -e) record office; (*also pl.*) archives, records. **–ar,** *m.* (-s, -e) keeper of the archives, registrar. **–stelle,** *f.* record office.

arg, 1. *adj.* (*com.* ärger, *sup.* ärgst) bad, mischievous; wicked, evil, gross; severe; utter, arch, arrant; hard; sad; deceitful; (*coll.*) awful, very; *im ärgsten Falle,* if the worst come to the worst; *einen –en Fehler begehen,* commit a grave error; *ein –er Tabaksraucher,* an inveterate smoker; *das ist zu* –, that is too bad; *es wird immer ärger,* things go from bad to worse; *man hat ihn – mißhandelt,* he has been very badly used *or* cruelly treated; 2. *n.* deceit, malice; *es ist kein – an* or *in ihm,* there is nothing underhand about him, he is not malicious; *ohne* –, without malice; *die Welt liegt im –en,* the world is in a bad way; *ich dachte nichts –es dabei,* I meant no harm by it; *er denkt von jedermann –es,* he thinks ill of everyone. **–heit,** *f.* wickedness, malice. **–list,** *f.* cunning, craftiness, deceitfulness. **–listig,** *adj.* cunning, crafty, deceitful. **–los,** *adj.* unsuspecting, guileless, innocent, harmless. **–losigkeit,** *f.* harmlessness; guilelessness. **–willig,** *adj.* malevolent. **–wohn,** *m.* (*no pl.*) suspicion, mistrust, distrust; *–wohn hegen gegen einen,* suspect a p., be distrustful of a p. **–wohnen,** *usually* **–wöhnen,** *v.a.* suspect, distrust. **–wöhnisch,** *adj.* suspicious, distrustful.

Ärger, *m.* (-s) annoyance, vexation, irritation; anger, chagrin; *einem zum* –, to spite a p. **–lich,** *adj.* annoying, vexatious, provoking, irritating; angry, vexed, put out, irritable, (*coll.*) snappish; crusty (*auf einen,* with a p.; *über etwas* ,about a th.). **–n,** *v.a.* annoy, vex, irritate; put out (of temper); *sich –n über,* lose one's temper; fret; take offence (at *or* over); be annoyed **–nis,** *n.* (-nisses, -nisse) vexation, anger, annoyance; scandal; (*ein*) *–nis*

nehmen an einer S., be scandalized at a th.; *–nis geben*, cause annoyance, shock, hurt.
Arie, *f.* (-n) aria (*Mus.*).
Arier, *m.* Aryan (*abandoned by scientists, but used by Nat. Soc. = non-Jew.*). **–nachweis,** *m.* proof of Aryan descent. **–paragraph,** *m.* Nat. Soc. law (Apr. 1933) excluding 'non-Aryans' from the civil service.
arisch, *adj.* Aryan (*Nat. Soc.* = non-Jewish).
Aristokrat, *m.* (-en, -en) aristocrat. **–ie,** *f.* aristocracy. **–isch,** *adj.* aristocratic.
Arithmet–ik, *f.* arithmetic. **–iker,** *m.* arithmetician. **–isch,** *adj.* arithmetical.
Arkt–is, *f.* the Arctic. **–isch,** *adj.* arctic, northern, North Polar.
arm, *adj.* (*comp.* ärmer, *sup.* ärmst) poor, needy; penniless, impecunious, indigent, (*coll.*) hard-up; meagre, scanty, barren, miserable, lean, low-grade; *die –en*, the poor; *die verschämten –en*, the deserving poor; *–er Sünder*, poor wretch; *ich –er!* unfortunate wretch that I am! *– an einer S.*, destitute of *or* poor in a th.; *– an Schönheit*, wanting in beauty. **–enanstalt,** *f.* alms-house; poor-law institution. **–engesetz,** *n.* poor-law. **–enhaus,** alms-house, workhouse. **–enkasse,** *f.* poor-box; relief fund. **–enpflege,** *f.* poor-relief; charity organization. **–enpfleger,** *m.* relieving officer, almoner. **–enschule,** *f.* charity school, free school. **–envorsteher,** *m.* poor-law guardian. **–enwesen,** *n.* system of providing for the poor, charity organization. **–e(r)sünder,** *m.* (–ensünders, –e(n)-sünder) condemned criminal, condemned man. **–esündergesicht,** *n.* hang-dog look. **–selig,** *adj.* poor, miserable, wretched, needy, paltry; despicable. **–seligkeit,** *f.* wretchedness, misery; paltriness. **–ut,** *f. see* **Armut.**
Arm, *m.* (-es, -e) arm; foreleg (*of a beast*); tributary (*of a river*); beam (*of scales*); branch (*of a candlestick*); shaft (*of a barrow, carriage, etc.*); arm (*of a chair*); shank (*of scissors, etc.*); finger (*of a signpost*); *– der Segelstange*, yard-arm; (*coll.*) *einem unter die –e greifen*, help a p.; *einem in den – fallen*, prevent a p. from doing s.th.; *die –e übereinander schlagen*, fold one's arms; *in die –e schließen*, embrace. **–band,** *n.* bracelet. **–banduhr,** *f.* wrist(let) watch. **–bein,** *n.* armbone, humerus. **–beuge,** *f.*, **–biege,** *f.* bend of the elbow. **–binde,** *f.* armband, brassard, sling. **–blätter,** *n.pl.* dress shields. **–blutader,** *f.* brachial artery. **–bruch,** *m.* fracture of the arm. **–brust,** *f.* (–e *& Austr.* ¨-e) crossbow. **–brustschütze,** *m.* crossbowman, archer. **–gelenk,** *n.* elbow joint. **–geschmeide,** *n.* armlets, bracelets. **–grube,** *f.* **–höhle,** *f.* armpit. **–knochen,** *m. see* **–bein. –korb,** *m.* basket with a handle. **–lehne,** *f.* armrest, arm (*of chair*). **–leuchter,** *m.* chandelier. **–los,** *adj.* without arms. **–nerv,** *m.* brachial nerve. **–schiene,** *f.* arm splint (*Med.*). **–sessel,** *m.*, **–stuhl,** *m.* arm-chair, easy-chair. **–spange,** *f.* bangle. **–spiegel,** *m.* arm badge. **–stütze,** *f.* armrest. **–welle,** *f.* revolution with the arms around the horizontal bar (*Gymn.*).
Armatur, *f.* (–en) armature; fittings, mountings. **–enbrett,** *n.* instrument-board *or* panel.
Armee, *f.* (-n) army. **–befehl,** *m.* army order. **–bericht,** *m.* bulletin, dispatch. **–lieferant,** *m.* army-contractor. **–verordnung,** *f.* military ordinance.
Ärmel, *m.* (-s, -) sleeve; *die – aufkrempeln*, turn *or* roll up one's sleeves; *etwas aus dem – schütteln*, do a th. with the greatest (of) ease. **–aufschlag,** *m.* cuff. **–holz,** *n.* sleeve-board (*for ironing*). **–kanal,** *m.* English Channel.
ärm–er, *see* **arm. –lich,** *adj.* poor, mean, miserable, pitiful, scanty. **–lichkeit,** *f.* poverty, misery, scantiness, meanness, shabbiness.
armier–en, *v.a.* equip (*a vessel*); arm (*a magnet*). **–ung,** *f.* armament, equipment. **–ungskabel,** *n.* armoured cable (*Elec.*).
Armut, *f.* poverty, want, indigence. **–szeugnis,** *n.* evidence of one's incapacity; *sich ein –szeugnis ausstellen*, give oneself away, lay bare one's own weakness.
Arrest, *m.* (-s, -e) arrest, seizure, detention, confinement; *mit – belegen, – legen auf* (*eine S.*), seize, confiscate (a th.); *– geben* (*Dat.*), detain (*after school*); *strenger –*, close confinement. **–ant,** *m.* (-en, -en) prisoner.
arretier–en, *v.a.* arrest, seize. **–hebel,** *m.* catch, check-lever. **–ung,** *f.* apprehension, confiscation; locking device.
Arsch, *m.* (-es, ¨-e) (*Vulg.*) buttocks, hind part; behind, bottom, backside, arse. (*Vulg.*) **–backe,** *f.* buttock. (*Vulg.*) **–lecker,** *m.* lick-spittle, (*Vulg.*) arse-crawler. **–leder,** *n.* breech leather (*patch on seat of trousers*). **–lings,** *also* **ärschlings,** *adv.* backwards, (*Vulg.*), arse first. (*Vulg.*) **–loch,** *n.* arsehole; shit (*said of a p.*).
Arsen, *n.* (-s) arsenic; *gediegenes –*, native arsenic. **–alisch,** *adj.* arsenical. **–butter,** *f.* chloride of arsenic. **–kalk,** *m.* arsenate of lime. **–kies,** *m.* arsenical pyrites. **–saures Salz,** *n.* arsenite.
Art, *f.* (-en) 1. kind, species, variety, type, description, sort; race, clan, stock, breed; 2. nature, manner, method, mode, way; style, fashion; behaviour, propriety, good-breeding; 3. (*In Nat. Soc. usage*) something between *Rasse* and *Volk*, implying spiritual adjustment of the Volk to the race idea. (*This is the idea behind the many almost incomprehensible compounds coined by the Nat. Soc., a few of which are given below.*) *eine – wilder Pflanzen*, a species of wild plants; *einzig in seiner –*, unique; *aus der – schlagen*, degenerate; (*Prov.*) *– läßt nicht von –*, blood is thicker than water, like sire like son; *Fortpflanzung der –*, propagation of the species; *von göttlicher –*, of divine origin; *– des Bodens*, nature of the soil; *das ist bloß eine Redens–*, that is only a figure of speech; *auf diese –*, in this way, at this rate; *auf alle – und Weise*, in every possible way; *der – Leute*, such people; *ein guter Mann in seiner –*, a good fellow in his way. **–bedingt,** *adj.* determined by the type *or* race. **–eigen,** *adj.* fitting, proper, true to type, characteristic. **–en,** *v.n.* (*aux.* h.) acquire, assume a certain quality *or* form; *–en nach*, resemble, take after; *gut geartet*, good-natured. **–fremd,** *adj.* of alien blood, foreign. **–gemäß,** *adj.* true to type. **–gepräge,** *n.* character of the type. **-und-triebgebunden,** *adj.* rooted in the instinct of the type. **–gleichheit,** *f.* identity of species. **–ig,** *adj.* good, well-behaved; polite, courteous, civil, kind, friendly; nice, agreeable, pleasing; pretty; *sei –ig!* be good! *as suffix* = like, resembling (e.g. *balladen–ig*, in ballad style; *gleich–ig*, of the same *or* similar kind; *gut–ig*, good-natured; *bös–ig*, malicious). **–igkeit,** *f.* good behaviour; politeness, courtesy, civility, kindness; prettiness, comeliness; niceness (*of manners*); *er hat ihr allerlei –igkeiten gesagt*, he paid her many compliments. **–merkmal,** *n.* characteristic of the species. **–name,** *m.* specific name. **–ung,** *f.* formation, modification, mode, nature. **–verwandt,** *adj.* of related stock. **–wärme,** *f.* specific heat. **–widrig,** *adj.* contrary to type, repugnant to the type.
Arterie, *f.* (-n) artery. **–nverkalkung,** *f.* arteriosclerosis.
artesisch, *adj.* artesian.
Artikel, *m.* (-s, -) article; goods, commodity; *bestimmter –*, definite article (*Gram.*). **–weise,** *adv.* item by item.
Artikul–ation, *f.* articulation. **–ieren,** *v.a.* articulate (= *move joints*); speak distinctly, articulate.
Artiller–ie, *f.* artillery; gunnery; *leichte –ie*, light artillery; *reitende –ie*, horse artillery. **–iefeuer,** *n.* bombardment, cannonade. **–ieflieger,** *m.* **–flugzeug,** *n.* spotting plane (*Mil.*). **–iekampf,** *m.* artillery duel. **–iepark,** *m.* train of artillery, artillery-park. **–ieschule,** *f.* school of gunnery. **–iewagen,** *m.* tumbrel. **–ist,** *m.* (-en, -en) artilleryman, gunner.
Artischocke, *f.* (-n) artichoke.
Artist, *m.* (-en, -en) artiste. **–isch,** *adj.* artistic.
Arznei, *f.* (*pl.* -en) medicine, drug, physic. **–buch,** *n.* pharmacopœia. **–formel,** *f.* prescription. **–gabe,** *f.* dose. **–glas,** *n.* phial. **–händler,** *m.* druggist, (dispensing) chemist. **–kasten,** *m.* medicine-chest. **–kräftig,** *adj.* medicinal, therapeutic. **–kraut,** *n.* medicinal herb; (*pl.*) simples. **–kunde,** *f.* pharmaceutics. **–mittel,** *n.* remedy; medicine; *Herstellung*

von –mitteln, pharmaceutics, pharmacy. **–mittellehre,** *f.* pharmacology. **–schrank,** *m.* medicine-chest.**–trunk,** *m.* potion, draught. **–vorschrift,** *f.* prescription. **–wein,** *m.* medicated *or* medicinal wine. **–zettel,** *m.* medical prescription.

Arzt, *m.* (-es, ⸚e) doctor, physician, medical man; *ausübender* or *praktizierender* –, medical practitioner. **–gebühr,** *f.* doctor's fee.

ärztlich, *adj.* medical; *–e Hilfe*, medical assistance.

[1]**As,** *n.* A flat (*Mus.*); *As-dur*, A flat major; *As-moll*, A flat minor.

[2]**As,** *n.* (Asses, Asse) ace (*Cards*); grain (*a weight*).

Asant, *m.* (-s); *wohlriechender* –, benzoin; *stinkender* –, asafoetida.

Asbest, *m.* (-(e)s, -e) asbestos; *gemeiner* –, rockwood. **–artig,** *adj.* asbestic. **–pappe,** *f.* asbestos board. **–platte,** *f.* asbestic mat.

Asch–e, *f.* (-e, -en) ash, ashes; *glimmende –e*, embers; *zu –e verbrennen*, burn to ashes, reduce to ashes; *in –e legen*, burn down, destroy by burning; *Friede seiner –e!* may his ashes rest in peace! **–bleich,** *adj.* ashen, pale as ashes. **–enbahn,** *f.* cinder-track. **–enbecher,** *m.* ash-tray. **–enbehälter,** *m.* ash-pan. **–enbrödel,** *n.* Cinderella; slut, scullion. **–engehalt,** *m.* ash content. **–enfarbig,** *adj.* ashen (*in colour*). **–engrube,** *f.* ash-pit. **–enkasten,** *m.* ash-can, dust-bin. **–enkrug,** *m.* funeral urn. **–enpflanze,** *f.* cineraria. **–enraum,** *m. see* **–engrube.** **–ensalz,** *n.* potash. **–ensieb,** *n.* riddle. **–enurne,** *f.* (funeral) urn. **–ermittwoch,** *m.* Ash-Wednesday. **–fahl,** *adj. see* **–bleich.** **–farbe,** *f.* ash-colour. **–farben,** *adj.* ash-coloured. **–grau,** *adj.* ashen (*in colour*); (*sl.*) *bis ins –graue*, till the cows come home. **–ig,** *adj.* ashy.

Aschlauch, *m.* (-(e)s, -e) eschalot, shallot.

äschern, *v.a.* reduce to ashes; strew with ashes.

äs–en, *v.n.* graze (*of deer*), browse. **–ung,** *f.* pasture, grazing, browsing.

aseptisch, *adj.* aseptic.

Aske–se, *f.* asceticism. **–t,** *m.* (-ten,-ten), **–tiker,** *m.* (-ers, -er) ascetic. **–tisch,** *adj.* ascetic.

asozial, *adj.* anti-social.

Aspekt, *m.* (-s, -e) aspect, configuration (*Astr.*).

Asphalt–beton, *m.* asphalt concrete. **–ieren,** *v.a.* asphalt. **–pflaster,** *n.* asphalt pavement.

Aspir–ant, *m.* (-en, -en), aspirant, candidate for a post. **–ate,** *f.*, **–ata,** *f.* aspirate. **–ation,** *f.* aspiration. **–ieren,** *v.a.* aspirate, sound the aspirate; aspire.

Assanierung, *f.* sanitation.

Assekur–ant, *m.* (-en, -en) insurer, underwriter. **–anz,** *f.* (-en) insurance (*fire, etc.*), assurance (*life*); *die –anz validiert auf M.*, the insurance is effected on M. **–anzpolice,** *f.* insurance policy. **–anzprämie,** *f.* insurance premium. **–at,** *m.* (-en, -en) person insured. **–ieren,** *v.a. & n.* insure. **–ierbar,** *adj.* insurable.

Assel, *f.* (-n) wood-louse.

assentier–en, 1. *v.n.* agree, assent. 2. *v.a.* (*Austrian dial.*) declare fit for military service. **–ung,** *f.* agreement, assent; acceptance as A.1 (*Mil.Austr.*).

Assessor, *m.* (-s, -en) professional man (*lawyer, teacher, etc.*) during probationary period, assistant judge, assistant teacher, etc.

Assig–nant, *m.* (-en, -en) (*C.L.*) drawer, giver (*of a draft*). **–nat,** *m.* (-en, -en) drawee. **–nate,** *f.* draft; assignat (= *paper money issued by French revolutionary government*). **–natar,** *m.* assignee. **–nieren,** *v.a.* assign, draw.

Assisen, *f.pl.* assizes. **–gericht,** *n.*, **–gerichtshof,** *m.* court of assizes.

Assistent, *m.* (-en, -en) assistant.

Associé, *m.* (-s, -s) (*C.L.*) (*archaic*) partner.

assort–ieren, *v.a.* sort, assort. (*C.L.*) **–iment,** *n.* assortment.

assoziieren, *v.a.* (*C.L.*) associate; *sich* –, enter into partnership.

Ast, *m.* (-es, ⸚e) bough, branch; knot (*in wood*). **–frei,** *adj.* free from *or* of knots. **–loch,** *n.* knot-hole. **–rein,** *adj.* free of branches. **–verbau,** *m.* abatis (*Mil.*). **–werk,** *n.* branches (*of a tree*).

Äst–chen, *n.* (-s, -) twig, small bough. **–ig,** *adj.* branchy; knotty, gnarled. **–ling,** *m.* fledgeling.

Aster, *f.* (-n) aster.

Ästhet, *m.* (-en, -en) aesthete. **–ik,** *f.* aesthetics. **–iker,** *m.* writer on aesthetics. **–isch,** *adj.* aesthetic.

Astro-log(e), *m.* (-en, -en) astrologer. **–logie,** *f.* astrology. **–logisch,** *adj.* astrological. **–naut,** *m.* (-en, -en) astronaut. **–nom,** *m.* (-en, -en) astronomer. **–nomie,** *f.* astronomy. **–nomisch,** *adj.* astronomical.

Asyl, *n.* (-s, -e) refuge, asylum, sanctuary.

Aszese, *f.* asceticism, *see* **Askese.**

Atelier, *n.* (-s, -s), studio.

Atem, *m.* (-s) breath, breathing; respiration. *kurzer* **–,** shortness of breath; *schwerer* –, asthma; *in – halten*, keep in suspense, keep on the move; *– holen, – schöpfen*, draw breath, breathe; *den – anhalten*, hold one's breath; *außer* –, out of breath, breathless; *in einem* –, in a twinkling; *ein Pferd wieder zu – kommen lassen*, let a horse get its wind; *wieder zu – kommen*, get one's breath back, get a breathing space; *das benimmt* (or *versetzt*) *mir den* –, that takes my breath away. **–bar,** *adj.* breathable. **–gerät,** *n.*, **–schutzapparat,** *m.* respirator. **–holen,** *n.* respiration. **–los,** *adj.* breathless. **–losigkeit,** *f.* breathlessness. **–not,** *f.* asthma; **–pause,** *f.* breathing space, respite. **–raubend,** *adj.* breathtaking (*also fig.*); **–stillstand,** *m.* cessation of respiration. **–zug,** *m.* breath, respiration; *letzter –zug*, the last gasp; *den letzten –zug tun*, breathe one's last.

Athe–ismus, *m.* (-ismus) atheism. **–ist,** *m.* (-en,-en) atheist.

Äther, *m.* (-s) ether. **–isch,** *adj.* ethereal, volatile; *–ische Öle*, essential *or* volatile oils. **–krieg,** *m.* radio war. **–wellen,** *pl.* ether waves (*Rad.*).

Athlet, *m.* (-en, -en) athlete. **–ik,** *f.* athletics. **–isch,** *adj.* athletic.

[1]**Atlas,** *m.* (–asses, –asse & -anten) atlas. **–format,** *n.* atlas folio.

[2]**Atlas,** *m.* (–asses, –asse) satin. **–sen,** *adj.* made of satin. **–band,** *n.* satin ribbon. **–brokat,** *m.* brocaded satin.

atm–en, 1. *v.a. & n.* breathe, inhale; *schwer –en*, breathe heavily, gasp. 2. *n.*, **–ung,** *f.* breathing, respiration. **–ungsapparat,** *m.* respirator. **–ungsgeräusch,** *n.* respiratory murmur. **–ungsorgan,** *n.*, **–ungswerkzeug,** *n.* respiratory organ.

Atmosphär–e, *f.* (-en) atmosphere. **–endruck,** *m.* atmospheric pressure. **–isch,** *adj.* atmospheric.

Atom, *n.* (-s, -e) atom, particle. **–ähnlich, –artig,** *adj.* atomic, atom-like. **–bombe,** *f.* atom bomb. **–gewicht,** *n.* atomic weight. **–kern,** *m.* atomic nucleus. **–lehre,** *f.* atomic theory. **–zerfall,** *m.* **–zertrümmerung,** *f.* nuclear fission.

Ätsch, *int.* (*exclamation of mockery*) serves you right!

Attacke, *f.* (-n) charge, attack (*of cavalry*).

Attent–at, *n.* (-(e)s, -e) assault, attempted murder. **–äter,** *m.* assailant, assassin; (*hum.*) perpetrator.

Attest, *n.* (-es, -e) certificate; attestation. **–ieren,** *v.a.* attest, certify.

Attich, *m.* (-s, -e) dwarf elder (*Sambucus ebulus*).

Attrappe, *f.* dummy, trap.

atypisch, *adj.* non-typical.

ätz–en, *v.a.* corrode; etch; cauterize (*Surg.*); eat into, bite into (*as acid*). **–bar,** *adj.* etchable; corrodible. **–druck,** *m.* etching, engraving. **–end,** *adj.* caustic, corrosive, mordant. **–kalk,** *m.* quicklime. **–kraft,** *f.* causticity, corrosive power. **–kunst,** *f.* art of etching. **–mittel,** *n.* caustic. **–nadel,** *f.* etching-needle. **–natron,** *n.* caustic soda, sodium hydroxide. **–stoff,** *m.* corrosive. **–ung,** *f.* cauterizing, etching. **–wasser,** *n.* nitric acid; aqua fortis. **–wirkung,** *f.* corrosive action.

au, *int.* oh (*exclamation of pain, or simulated pain, as in –weh!* oh!).

Aubo–, abbr. of **Außenbord–,** *e.g.* **–fähre,** *f.* outboard motor ferry.

auch, *conj. & adv.* also, too; even, likewise; (after *wer, was, welcher, wie*, etc. –(so)ever; *wer es – sei*, whoever he (*or* it) may be; *ohne – nur zu fragen*, without so much as asking; – *nicht*, neither, nor . . . neither; *nicht nur . . . sondern* –, not only . . . but also; *sowohl als* –, both . . . and; *und wenn* – (*schon* or *gleich*), even though, even if, although; *wo* –, wheresoever; *und wenn er – bezahlt*, and even if he pay; *es geschehe wann es – wolle*, whenever it may happen; *willst du es – wirklich tun?* will you be sure to do it? *bist du – glücklich?* are you really happy? *das wäre – an der Zeit!* indeed it is high time! *so sehr er – lachte*, however much he laughed.

Audi-enz, *f.* (-en) interview, audience; hearing, reception; *zur -enz kommen*, be admitted to an audience; *-enz beim König*, audience with *or* (*archaic*) of the king. **-enzsaal**, *m.*, **-enzzimmer**, *n.* reception-chamber. **-on**, *n.*, **-onröhre**, *f.* detector valve (*Rad.*). **-onschaltung**, *f.* detector circuit. **-teur**, *m.* (-s, -s) representative of Advocate General's branch at courts martial (*Mil.*). **-tor**, *m.* (-s, -en) 1. judge in ecclesiastical courts; 2. (*Austrian*) *see* **-teur. -torium**, *n.* (-s) lecture-room; audience attending a lecture.

Aue, *f.* (-n) water-meadow; pasture (*Poet.*).

Auer-, (*in compounds*); **-hahn**, *m.* heath cock; wood grouse; capercailzie (*or* capercailye). **-ochs**, *m.* aurochs (*extinct European bison*).

auf, **1.** *prep.* 1. USED WITH DAT. *signifying rest, or limited motion in a place*; on, upon; in; at; – *der Erde liegen*, lie on the ground; – *Erden*, on earth; – *der Stelle*, on the spot, immediately; – *hoher See*, on the high seas; – *der Straße*, in the street; – *seinem Zimmer*, in his room; – *dieser Welt*, in this world; – *dem Markte*, at market; – *der Post*, at the post office; – *der Hochschule*, (up) at the university; – *der Flöte spielen*, play on the flute; – *der Reise*, travelling; – *der Jagd*, hunting; – *der Suche*, seeking, searching for; – *dem Lande wohnen*, live in the country; – *einem Auge blind*, blind in one eye; – *dem nächsten Wege*, by the nearest way. 2. USED WITH ACC. *when signifying motion to a place, or change; or when used not locally, but metaphorically*; on to, into; to, towards; at; for; up, up to; – *die Erde fallen*, fall to the ground; – *sein Zimmer gehen*, go to his room; *-s Land fahren*, travel into the country; – *die Post*, to the post-office; *etwas – die Post geben*, post a th.; – *die Jagd gehen*, go a-hunting; – *einen Berg steigen*, climb a mountain; – *hohen Gewinn ausgehen*, aim high; *den Blick – einen richten*, turn one's eyes to s.o.; – *einen zeigen*, point to a p.; *sich verlassen – einen*, depend on a p.; – *Rechnung*, on account; – *Anfrage*, on application, on inquiry; – *meine Ehre*, upon my honour; – *meine Bitte*, at my request; – *das hin*, on the strength of that; – *deutsch*, in German; *-s neue*, anew; *-s eheste*, as soon as possible; *-s beste*, in the best way possible; – *diese Art*, in this way, at this rate; – *einmal*, suddenly, all at once; – *einen Augenblick*, for a moment; – *jeden Fall*, in any case, at all events; – *keinen Fall*, on no account; *er ist stolz – seine Kinder*, he is proud of his children; *er beging eine Torheit – die andere*, he was guilty of one stupidity after another; – *einen Blick*, at a glance; – *einen Zug*, at one draught; – *ein Haar*, to a T, very accurately; – *eine gewisse Entfernung*, to a certain distance; 5 *Kilogramm – den Quadratzentimeter*, 5 kilo to the square cm.; – *jemandes Gesundheit trinken*, drink to a person's (good) health; *ich bin – morgen eingeladen*, I have an invitation for tomorrow; *es geht – Leben und Tod*, it is a matter of life and death; *es hat nichts – sich*, it doesn't matter much, it's a matter of no consequence; *alle bis – einen*, all but one; *es geht – neun*, it is getting on to nine, it is nearly nine o'clock; – *Befehl des Königs*, by order of the king; *bis – weiteren Befehl*, until further orders; *das geht – meine Kosten*, (*coll.*) that's on me, I pay for that; – *Wache ziehen*, mount guard; *so viel – die Person*, so much per head. **2.** *adv.* up, upwards; open; awake; *Auf!* Get up! – *und ab*, up and down; – *oder ab*, more or less; – *und über*, up to and beyond; *berg–*, up hill; *trepp–*, upstairs; *frisch–!* get moving! (*sl.*) go to it! get cracking! *von Jugend –*, *von klein –*, since childhood; – *und davon gehen*, run away, make off. **3.** *conj.*; – *daß*, in order that; – *daß . . . nicht*, for fear that, (*elevated style*) lest. **4.** *Separable prefix before many verbs*, up, upon; on; open; un-, afresh, anew. *In those cases where a possible compound is not given in the following lists see under the root verb.*

aufarbeiten, **1.** *v.a.* 1. work up, recondition, renovate; elaborate; upholster (*chair, etc.*); 2. work off, finish a task, clear up (*arrears*); use up, finish (*all one's material*), utilize; 3. work open (*a lock, etc.*); **2.** *v.r.* work one's way up.

aufatmen, *v.n.* (*aux.* h.) breathe freely, breathe a sigh of relief; breathe again.

aufbahr-en, *v.a.* lay out (*a corpse*). **-ung**, *f.* lying in state.

Aufbau, *m.* (-(e)s, -ten) building; erection; structure; (*pl.*) superstructure; body, coachwork (*of a vehicle*); disposition, arrangement; construction (*of a drama*); reconstruction; synthesis (*Chem.*); *Bevölkerungs–*, *Rassen–*, *Volks–*, racial groupings within the population; *Alters–*, percentage of age groups within the population. **-en**, *v.a.* erect, build up; base on; rebuild. **-end**, *adj.* synthetic (*Chem.*). **-schule**, *f.* intermediate school.

aufbäumen, 1. *v.a.* wind up (*on a spool, Weav.*). 2. *v.r.* rear up, prance; rebel, struggle (against).

aufbausch-en, *v.a.* puff up. **-ung**, *f.* swelling; exaggeration.

aufbegehren, 1. *v.n.* remonstrate; start up in anger. 2. *n.* strong protest.

aufbehalten, *ir.v.a.* keep on (*one's hat*); keep open (*one's eye*); keep in store.

aufbeißen, *ir.v.a.* bite open.

aufbekommen, *ir.v.a.* get open, manage to open; get *or* receive (*a task to do*); have set (*as an exercise*).

aufbereiten, *v.a.* prepare; process (*food products*), dress (*hides*), refine, separate; wash (*ore*).

aufbesser-n, *v.a.* improve, repair, mend (*clothes*); increase; raise; ameliorate. **-ung**, *f.* amelioration, improvement; increase.

aufbewahr-en, *v.a.* put by, store up; save; preserve, keep. **-ung**, *f.* storage; preservation; **-ungsort**, *m.* depository.

aufbiet-en, *ir.v.a.* cite, summon; proclaim, give notice of; call up, raise (*an army*); exert, strain; *ein Brautpaar -en*, publish banns of marriage; *alles -en*, strain every nerve. **-ung**, *f.* summoning; proclamation (*of banns*); exertion; *unter -ung aller Kräfte*, with the utmost exertion.

aufbinden, *ir.v.a.* untie, loosen; tie on, fasten on; tie up; (*coll.*) *einem etwas –*, impose upon a p., hoax s.o.

aufblähen, 1. *v.a.* puff up; inflate; swell; expand; 2. *v.r.* be puffed up, boast.

aufblasen, *ir.v.a.* blow up, inflate; distend; blow (*a bubble*).

aufblätter-n, *v.a.* open *or* turn over the leaves of a book. **-ung**, *f.* desquamation, exfoliation.

aufbleiben, *ir.v.n.* (*aux.* s.) remain open *or* up; *spät –*, sit up *or* stay up late.

Aufblick, *m.* (-(e)s, -e) upward glance; fulguration, flash, sudden brightening. **-en**, *v.n.* (*aux.* h.) look upwards; flash, glitter, brighten.

aufblitzen, 1. *v.n.* flash; 2. *n.* flash, fulguration.

aufblühen, *v.n.* (*aux.* s.) blossom, unfold; open; flourish; *-de Schönheit*, budding beauty.

aufbrauchen, *v.a.* use up, consume.

aufbrausen, *v.n.* (*aux.* h. & s.) roar; effervesce; ferment; get into a rage; (*coll.*) flare up. **-end** *pr.p.* & *adj.* effervescent, boisterous.

aufbrechen, 1. *ir.v.a.* break open, force open; *Land –*, break *or* plough up land. 2. *v.n.* (*aux.* **s.**) burst open; rise from table; start, depart, set out, move off, break camp. 3. *n.* breaking open; bursting (*of an ulcer*); departure.

aufbrennen, 1. *ir.v.a.* burn up, consume by burning; refine (*metals*). 2. *v.n.* (*aux.* s.) burn up, become brighter (*as a fire*).

aufbring-en, *ir.v.a.* 1. raise (up), lift (up); bring up; rear (*a child*); introduce; levy, muster (*troops, etc.*); summon up (*courage*); bring round, restore to health; raise (*money*); defray (*expenses*); bring forth, utter; produce (*witnesses*); capture, bring in (*a prize, Naut.*); 2. irritate, provoke, enrage; *aufgebracht werden*, get angry, fly into a rage (*über*, at). **-er**, *m.* captor (*Naut.*). **-ung**, *f.* raising, bringing up, rearing; capture (*of a ship*).

Aufbruch, *m.* (-s, ⸚e) break-up; rising from table; departure; breaking up (*Agr.*); revolution, fundamental change, uprising, awakening (*to national or political consciousness*).

aufbürden, *v.a.* burden *or* charge with; impose (on); attribute (to).

aufdämmern, *v.n.* (*aux.* s.) dawn upon.

aufdampfen, *v.n.* (*aux.* s.) evaporate.

aufdecken, 1. *v.a.* uncover; disclose, reveal, expose; discover, detect; spread (*a tablecloth*); turn down (*bed*). 2. *v.n.* lay the cloth *or* table.

aufdonnern, *v.n.* (*coll.*) dress showily *or* vulgarly. **aufgedonnert,** *p.p.* & *adj.* dressed up (to kill).

aufdrängen, 1. *v.a.* push open, force open. 2. *v.r.* obtrude (up)on, force (up)on; *sich einem* –, intrude o.s. upon a p.

aufdrehen, *v.a.* wind (up); unscrew; screw open; turn on, switch on; untwist, unravel.

aufdring-en, *ir.v.a.* press upon, urge upon; obtrude. **-lich,** *adj.* importunate, obtrusive. **-lichkeit,** *f.* importunity, obtrusiveness. **-ling,** *m.* intruder. **-licherweise,** *adv.* obtrusively. **-ung,** *f.* obtrusion, intrusion.

Aufdruck, *m.* (-(e)s, -e) imprint, impress, stamp; upward pressure. **-en,** *v.a.* imprint, impress; affix (*a seal*).

aufdrücken, *v.a.* press open, squeeze open (*as a boil*); impress, affix by pressure; imprint, stamp on; *das Siegel* –, put the seal upon.

aufdunsen, *v.n.* (*aux.* s.) swell up, get bloated. **aufgedunsen,** *p.p.* & *adj.* bloated; turgid (*of style*). **Aufgedunsenheit,** *f.* turgidity.

aufdunsten, *v.n.* evaporate.

aufeinander, *adv.* one after another, successively; one on top of another; one against another. **-folge,** *f.* succession, series. **-folgen,** *v.n.* succeed one another. **-folgend,** *adj.* consecutive, successive. **-legen,** *v.a.* lay one upon another, deposit in layers. **-stoßen,** *v.n.* collide, clash, conflict. **-treiben,** *v.n.* drift together; run foul of another ship (*Naut.*).

Aufenthalt, *m.* (-(e)s, -e) stay, abode, residence, sojourn, whereabouts; stop (*of trains*); halt; delay, hindrance; demurrage (*Naut.*); *ohne* –, without delay. **-sort,** *m.* place of residence, domicile (*Law*), resort. **-sdauer,** *f.* duration of stay, stay (*in a place*).

auferlegen, *v.a.* impose, inflict, enjoin; *einem etwas* –, place s.o. under an obligation; *sich* (*Dat.*) *Zwang* –, force o.s.

aufersteh-en, *ir.v.n.* (*aux.* s.) rise from the dead. **auferstanden,** *p.p.* & *adj.* risen. **-ung,** *f.* resurrection.

auferweck-en, *v.a.* raise from the dead, restore to life; resuscitate. **-ung,** *f.* resuscitation.

aufessen, *v.a.* eat up, consume.

auffädeln, *v.a.* string (*beads*); untwist, unravel.

auffahr-en, 1. *ir.v.n.* (*aux.* s.) mount, rise, ascend, jump up, fly up; start up; drive up; run aground (*Naut.*); fly into a passion, flare up; *in Stellung -en*, drive into position, bring (*guns*) into action. 2. *v.a.* cut up a road (*by driving*); bring up (*guns*); park (*cars*). **-end,** *pr.p.* & *adj.* vehement, irritable irascible. **-t,** *f.* (-ten), approach, drive, driving up; rising ground; ramp, platform; (*Swiss*) Ascension Day.

auffallen, *ir.v.n.* (*aux.* s.) attract attention, be noticeable, strike; fall upon; fall open; *einem* –, strike, astonish a p.; *es fiel uns allen auf*, it struck us all (as strange). **-d,** *pr.p.* & *adj.*, **auffällig,** *adj.* striking, conspicuous, remarkable, noteworthy; extraordinary; shocking; *-d gekleidet*, showily dressed; *-des Licht*, incident light.

auffang-en, *ir.v.a.* catch (*while in motion*); snap up, snatch up; brake (*a dive*) (*Av.*); collect (*rain-water*); gather; intercept (*letters*); deaden (*sound*); break (*a fall*); parry (*a blow*); *wo haben Sie das aufgefangen?* where did you pick that up? **-eglas,** *n.* objective glass (*Opt.*). **-schale,** *f.* collecting dish.

auffärben, *v.a.* re-dye; fresh(en) up, touch up (*colours*).

auffass-en, *v.a.* perceive, conceive, understand, apprehend, comprehend, take in; collect, catch (*rain-water, etc.*); take up, pick up, catch up; interpret. **-ung,** *f.* comprehension, apprehension; interpretation; conception, view. **-ungsgabe,** *f.*, **-ungskraft,** *f.*, **-ungsvermögen,** *n.* power of comprehension, perceptive faculty, intellectual grasp.

auffinden, *ir.v.a.* find out, discover, locate, detect, trace.

aufflackern, *v.n.* (*aux.* s.) flare up.

aufflammen, *v.n.* (*aux.* s.) flame up, blaze up, burst into flames.

auffliegen, *ir.v.a.* (*aux.* s.) fly up, soar, ascend; (*fig.*) end in smoke; fly open (*of doors, etc.*); explode, blow up; *einen Drachen – lassen*, fly a kite.

Aufflug, *m.* (-(e)s, ⸚e) ascent (*Av.*).

aufforder-n, *v.a.* call upon, ask, request, demand, invite, summon; challenge; *eine Dame zum Tanze -n*, ask a lady for a dance; *-nde Blicke*, challenging *or* provocative glances; *man forderte ihn auf, ein Lied zu singen*, he was called on for a song. **-ung,** *f.* request, demand, invitation; challenge; summons, citation; *eine Rechts-ung erlassen*, issue a writ *or* a summons. **-ungsschreiben,** *n.* summons.

aufforsten, *v.a.* afforest. **-ung,** *f.* afforestation.

auffressen, *ir.v.a.* eat up (*of beasts*); devour; corrode.

auffrischen, *v.a.* freshen up, renew; touch up (*Paint.*); revive, (*coll.*) brush up (*memory, etc.*).

aufführ-en, **1.** *v.a.* 1. present, perform, produce, act (*a play, etc.*); play (*a piece, Mus.*); 2. build up, erect; mount (*guns, a guard, etc.*), post (*a sentry*). 3. enter (*in an account*); specify (*in a list, etc.*), quote, state, tabulate, enumerate; *einzeln -en*, specify. **2.** *v.n.* act, behave, conduct o.s. **-bar,** *adj.* that may be erected; that may be acted, actable (*play*). **-ung,** *f.* performance, representation; 2. building; erection; posting (*of a sentry*); mounting (*of guns*); 3. specification, enumeration, adducing (*of reasons*); production (*of witnesses*); 4. conduct, behaviour: *gute -ung*, good manners, good behaviour.

auffüll-en, *v.a.* fill up; refill.

auffüttern, *v.a.* feed up, fatten, rear.

Aufgabe, *f.* (-n) 1. problem, proposition, lesson, exercise; duty. 2. posting (*a letter*); registration (*of luggage, etc.*); 3. surrender (*of a town*); resignation; closing down, abandonment, giving up; 4. (*C.L.*) order, advice; command; *laut* –, as per advice; *wegen – des Geschäfts*, on retiring from business. **-ngebiet,** *n.* field, scope; **-nheft,** *n.* exercise book. **-ort,** *m.* issuing depot; **-vorrichtung,** *f.* feed mechanism.

aufgabeln, *v.a.* (*coll.*) fish *or* ferret out; *wo haben Sie den aufgegabelt?* where did you pick him up?

Aufgang, *m.* (-(e)s, ⸚e) rise, rising, ascension, (*Astr.*) ascent, east; staircase, stairs; upstroke.

aufgären, *v.n.* ferment.

aufgeb-en, *ir.v.a.* 1. give up, deliver, hand in; post (*a letter*); 2. give up, surrender; abandon, relinquish; resign (*an office*); drop (*an acquaintance*); (*coll.*) give up the ghost; 3. propose, propound, ask, put, pose (*a riddle, question, etc*), set (*a task or problem*); 4. (*C.L.*) advise, order, commission, charge, give notice of; *einem etwas -en*, set a p. a task; *das Spiel -en*, throw in the towel, throw up the sponge, throw up one's cards; (*coll.*) *eine S. im letzten Augenblick plötzlich -en*, cry off at the last moment.

aufgeblasen, *p.p.* & *adj. See* **aufblasen**; inflated; puffed up, arrogant. **-heit.** *f.* conceit, arrogance.

Aufgebot, *n.* (-(e)s, -e) public notice; publication (*of banns*), conscription, enrolment (*of troops*); body of men, levy; exertion; *allgemeines* –, levy en masse; *unter – aller Kräfte*, with might and main.

aufgebracht, *see* **aufbringen.**

aufgedonnert, *see* **aufdonnern.**

aufgedunsen, *see* **aufdunsen.**

aufgehen, *ir.v.n.* (*aux.* s.) 1. rise (*of dough, of the sun, etc.*); swell, ferment; dawn (on one); break (*as an abscess*); 2. evaporate; dissolve; be spent *or* consumed; leave no remainder (*Math.*); be merged, disappear; 3. open (*as a door*); come loose *or* untied; untwist, uncurl; break up (*of ice*); 4. come up (*of plants*); open, expand, unfold, sprout; *der Knoten geht auf*, the knot is coming untied; *der Mond ist aufgegangen*, the moon has risen; *jetzt geht mir ein Licht auf*, now it's beginning to dawn on me, I begin to understand; *da geht einem das Herz*

Forms of pp. in **aufge-** *not found here should be sought under inf.*

auf, it does one's heart good; *in Rauch* –, (*fig.*) end in smoke; *in Feuer* –, be consumed by fire; 3 *in* 15 *geht auf*, 3 goes into 15 without remainder; *wechselseitige Schulden – lassen*, set off mutual debts; – *in*, be absorbed in: *ihr Glück geht in dem ihrer Tochter auf*, her happiness is bound up in her daughter's; *Preußen ging in Deutschland auf*, Prussia was merged in Germany.
aufgeklärt, *see* **aufklären;** *-er Despotismus*, enlightened despotism. **-heit,** *f.* enlightenment, open-mindedness.
aufgeknöpft, *p.p. & adj.* (*coll.*) free and easy, chatty, communicative.
Aufgeld, *n.* (-es, -er) (*C.L.*) premium; deposit; advance; earnest money; agio; extra charge.
aufgelegt, *see* **auflegen.**
aufgeräumt, *p.p. & adj.* in high spirits, in good humour, merry; *nicht – sein*, be in low spirits, be depressed, moody, gloomy *or* listless. **-heit,** *f.* cheerfulness, gaiety, good humour *or* spirits.
aufgesessen! 'Mount!' (*Mil.*)
aufgeweckt, *p.p. & adj.* intelligent, bright, clever, quick-witted.
aufgeworfen, *see* **aufwerfen.**
aufgießen, *ir.v.a.* pour upon; infuse; *der Tee ist aufgegossen*, the tea is made.
aufgleit-en, *v.n.* glide up. **-front,** *f.* warm front (*Meteor.*).
aufglühen, *v.n.* flare up.
aufgreifen, *ir.v.a.* snatch up; take up; catch on (*an idea*).
Aufguß, *m.* (-(ss)es, ⁻e) infusion. **-tierchen,** *n.pl.* infusoria.
aufhaben, *ir.v.a.* have on, wear; have open; have to do (*lessons, homework*); *zu viel* –, be overburdened with work; *hast du heute viel auf?* have you got much home work today?
aufhaken, *v.a.* unhook, undo.
aufhalsen, *v.a.* saddle with; *einem etwas* –, thrust a th. upon a p.
aufhalt-en, 1. *ir.v.a.* 1. hold up, stop, delay, arrest, retard, stem, detain; put a stop to; 2. sustain, keep up; hold open; keep open. **2.** *v.r.* stay, stop, dwell on; *sich bei Kleinigkeiten -en*, dwell on trifles; *sich bei einem -en*, stay at a p.'s house; *sich über eine S. -en*, find fault with a th. **-ekraft,** *f.* power of resistance. **-er,** *m.* stopper; retainer; catch (*of a lock*); guyrope (*Naut.*); retardation (*Mus.*). **-erei,** *f.* fault-finding, scoffing. **-ung,** *f.* hindrance, delay, detention; stay; stop, catch, detent.
aufhäng-en, *v.a.* hang up, hang, suspend. **-eboden,** *m.* drying room *or* loft (*for linen*). **-emuskel,** *f.* levator muscle. **-er,** *m.* loop; hanger, rack. **-eschnüre** *f.pl.* drying lines. **-ung,** *f.* suspension.
aufhaschen, *v.a.* snatch up; *Neuigkeiten* –, pick up news.
aufhäuf-en, 1. *v.a.* heap *or* pile *or* store up; amass, accumulate. 2. *v.r.* accumulate, pile up. 3. *n.*, **-ung,** *f.* accumulation.
aufheb-en, 1. *ir.v.a.* 1. lift, raise, hold up; 2. take up, pick up, weigh (*anchor*), seize, capture (*a sentry, etc.*); 3. keep, reserve, put by, preserve, store away, lay up, provide for; 4. abolish, suspend, repeal, annul, cancel (*an order*); invalidate, put an end to, counteract, neutralize; break up; raise (*a siege*); reduce (*fractions*); *einen Verbrecher -en*, apprehend a criminal; *das Kind ist bei ihnen sehr gut aufgehoben*, the child is in good hands with them; *die Tafel wurde aufgehoben*, the guests rose from table; *ein Lager -en*, strike camp; *ein Kloster -en*, suppress a convent; *Handelsgenossenschaft -en*, dissolve partnership; *Stillschweigen -en*, break silence; *der Richter hat den Vertrag aufgehoben*, the judge declared the agreement null and void; *ein Urteil -en*, quash a judgement; *einander -en* or *sich gegenseitig -en*, cancel each other out, neutralize *or* destroy each other; (*Prov.*) *aufgeschoben ist nicht aufgehoben*, put off is not put away, forbearance is not acquittance; (*Prov.*) *besser aufgeschoben als aufgehoben*, better late than never. **2.** *n.* lifting (up), *beim -en der Hände*, on a show of hands; *viel -ens wegen nichts*, much ado about nothing; *machen Sie doch davon kein -ens!* please don't make a fuss about it. **-emuskel,** *m.*, **-er,** *m.* levator muscle (*Anat.*). **-ung,** *f.* lifting *or* taking up; raising, elevation; suspension, suppression, removal (*of restrictions*), abrogation; raising (*of a siege*), breaking up, dissolution, ending, abolition, repeal, annulment, nullification, counter action, neutralization; *bei -ung der Tafel*, when the cloth was removed, at the conclusion of the meal; *-ung eines Befehls*, repeal of an order; *-ung einer Klage*, non-suit; *-ung einer Versammlung*, dissolution of an assembly. **-ungsgericht,** *n.* Court of Cassation.
aufheiter-n, 1. *v.a.* make clear, brighten; cheer, cheer up, gladden. 2. *v.r.* clear, brighten (*sky*); clear up (*weather*); **-ung,** *f.* enlivenment, cheering up; clearing up (*of weather*).
aufhelf-en, *ir.v.a.* aid, succour; *einem -en*, help s.o. up.
aufhell-en, 1. *v.a.* clear, brighten up, light up; heighten (*a tint*); clarify, elucidate, enlighten. 2. *v.r. & imp.* brighten, clear up (*of weather*); settle, clarify (*of liquors*). **-ung,** *f.* clarification; brightening; heightening (*of a tint*); elucidation, explanation, enlightenment, clearing up. **-ungsmittel,** *n.* clearing agent.
aufhetz-en, *v.a.* stir up, incite, instigate, start (*game, etc.*). **-er,** *m.* instigator. **-ung,** *f.* instigation, incitement.
aufhol-en, 1. *v.a.* (*Naut.*) haul up *or* in, hoist; bring (*a ship*) close to the wind. 2. *n.* make up for (*a loss*), draw up to, reduce the distance between (*Racing*). **-er,** *m.* relieving tackle; halyard.
aufhorchen, *v.n.* (*aux.* h.) prick up one ears, listen attentively.
aufhören, 1. *v.n.* (*aux.* h.) cease, stop, end, discontinue, desist from, leave off; *zu zahlen* –, suspend payment; *hör' doch nur auf!* for goodness sake stop! have done! (*coll.*) *da hört doch alles auf!* that beats everything! that's the limit! *in Geldsachen hört die Gemütlichkeit auf*, business is business. 2. *n.* cessation; *ohne* –, incessantly.
aufjagen, *v.a.* start, raise (*game, etc.*); raise (*dust, etc.*); *einen* –, hunt a p. up.
aufjammern, *v.n.* (*aux.* h.) set up a lamentation *or* (*coll.*) wail.
aufjauchzen, aufjubeln, *v.n.* (*aux.* h.) shout for joy.
Aufkauf, *m.* (-s, ⁻e) buying up, purchase in bulk, (*C.L.*) engrossment. **-en,** *v.a.* buy up, purchase in bulk, (*C.L.*) engross; forestall *or* corner (*the market*). **-ung,** *f.* buying up; forestalling.
Aufkäufer, *m.* (*C.L.*) forestaller, engrosser; buying-agent, buying-speculator.
aufkeimen, *v.n.* (*aux.* s.) germinate, bud, sprout. **-end,** *p.p. & adj.* budding, dawning, young, fresh.
aufkett-en, *v.a.* unchain, unfasten the chain.
aufkippen, *v.a. & n.* (*aux.* s.) tilt up.
aufkitten, *v.a.* cement on.
aufklappen, *v.a.* open (*something folded, like a penknife*).
aufklaren, 1. *v.n.* get clear; clear up (*Meteor.*); 2. *v.a.* clear up, make tidy (*the deck, Naut.*).
aufklär-en, 1. *v.a.* clear up; elucidate, explain, enlighten, instruct, inform; scout, reconnoitre (*Mil.*); clarify. 2. *v.r.* clear up (*of weather*), brighten (*of the countenance, etc.*). **-er,** *m.* instructor, enlightener, apostle of culture; scout (*Mil.*). **-ung,** *f.* explanation, clarification, enlightenment; reconnaissance (*Mil.*); *Zeitalter der -ung*, Age of Enlightenment (*18th century*). **-ungsdienst,** *m.* reconnaissance duty (*Mil.*). **-ungsflugzeug,** *n.* reconnaissance plane. **-ungsabteilung,** *f.* reconnaissance patrol.
aufklauben, *v.a.* pick up; glean.
aufklebe-n, 1. *v.a.* stick on, paste on; fasten, affix. 2. *v.n.* (*aux.* h.) adhere, stick. **-etikett(e),** *n.* (*f.*) gummed *or* sticky label.
aufklinken, *v.a.* unlatch (*a door*).
aufknacken, *v.a.* crack (open) (*nuts*).
aufknöpfen, *v.a.* unbutton; button up. *See* **aufgeknöpft.**
aufknüpfen, *v.a.* tie up; string up, (*sl.*) hang (*a criminal*).

Forms of p.p. in **aufge-** *not found here should be sought under inf.*

aufkochen, *v.a.* boil up, warm up, boil again.
aufkommen, 1. *ir.v.n.* (*aux.* s.) rise, get up, come up; recover, convalesce; come into use, come into fashion; grow, thrive, prosper; prevail; approach; *– lassen,* give rise to; *wir dürfen solche Zweifel nicht – lassen,* we must prevent the spread of such doubts; *– für,* accept responsibility for; *nicht – gegen,* be no match for. 2. *n.* getting up, *etc.*; recovery (*from sickness*); introduction (*of a fashion*); rise in the world; yield (*of a tax*).
aufkratz–en, *v.a.* scratch up; raise the nap (*of cloth*); card (*wool*); (*coll.*) *einen –en,* put a p. in good humour. **–er,** *m.* wool-carder.
aufkräusen, *v.n.* form a head (*of beer*).
aufkrempe(l)n, *v.a.* bend back, turn *or* roll up, tuck up (*sleeves, hat brim, etc.*).
aufkriegen, *v.a.* (*coll.*) *see* **aufbekommen.**
aufkünd–igen, *v.a.*; give notice *or* warning (*einem etwas,* to a p. of a th.); recall (*an investment*), call in (*a mortgage*), retract (*a statement*), withdraw (*from an engagement*), renounce (*a p.'s friendship*); *mein Wirt hat mir aufgekündigt,* my landlord has given me notice to move; *ohne aufzukündigen,* without previous notice. **–bar,** *adj.* subject to notice to quit; subject to recall; *–bare Pacht,* tenancy at will. **–igung,** *f.* warning, notice (*of removal, dismissal, withdrawal, etc.*); *–igung einer Hypothek,* calling in of a mortgage. **–igungsbrief,** *m.* written notice (*to quit, etc.*).
auflachen, *v.n.* (*aux.* h.) burst out laughing.
auflad–en, *ir.v.a.* load; charge (*Elec.*); *einem etwas –en,* charge *or* burden s.o. with; *sich* (*Dat.*) *–en,* take upon o.s., saddle o.s. with. **–egeschwindigkeit,** *f.* rate of charging (*Elec.*). **–ekommando,** *n.* loading party. **–elohn,** *m.* packing charges. **–emotor,** *m.* forced induction engine (*Mech.*). **–er,** *m.* packer, loader. **–ung,** *f.* loading, detonating charge.
Auflage, *f.* (-n) 1. edition (*of a book*); circulation (*of newspaper*); 2. tax, duty, impost; contribution, collective fine, levy; 3. judge's order, injunction; 4. superimposed layer; *unveränderte –,* reprint; *verbesserte und vermehrte –,* corrected and enlarged edition; *einem eine – tun,* issue a writ against a person. **–humus,** *m.* superficial layer of humus deposit.
Auflager, *m.* (-s, -) bearing, support (*Engin.*); fixed end support (*of a bridge*). **–n,** *v.a.* 1. lay in stock, store up; 2. mount on bearing. **–ung,** *f.* stratification, deposition. **–ungsschicht,** *f.* stratified *or* deposited layer.
auflassen, *ir.v.a.* leave open; permit a p. to get up *or* out of bed; (*Law*) cede, convey.
auflauer–n, *v.n.* (*aux.* h.) lie in wait (*einem,* for a p.); ambush. **–er,** *m.* spy, eavesdropper, ambusher. **–ung,** *f.* ambush.
Auflauf, *m.* (-es, ⸗e) crowd, mob; riot, uproar; swelling; increase; (*Cook.*) soufflé, light pudding. **–en,** 1. *ir.v.n.* (*aux.* s.) run up; rise, increase, swell, accumulate; run aground; *aufgelaufene Zinsen,* accumulated interest; *eine Rechnung –en lassen,* allow a bill to mount up. 2. *v.r.* get footsore, get blisters *or* get chafed through walking. 3. *n.* germination; rising (*of dough*).
aufleben, *v.n.* (*aux.* s.) revive, be revived, be invigorated; begin afresh.
aufleg–en, *v.a.* put *or* lay on, apply; impose, inflict (*a fine, a tax, etc.*), enjoin (*silence*); publish, issue; show one's hand (*at cards*); lay up (*a ship, stores*); lean (*the elbow*) on; *Bank –en,* hold the bank (*Cards*); *wieder –en,* reprint (*a book*). **aufgelegt,** *p.p.* & *adj.* disposed, inclined *or* in a certain humour; *ich war nicht dazu* (*zum Singen, etc.*) *aufgelegt,* I was not in the mood for it (for singing, *etc.*); *aufgelegte Dampfer,* steamers lying idle. **–ung,** *f.* application (*of a plaster, etc.*); imposition (*of fines, taxes, etc.*); infliction (*of punishment*); laying up (*of a ship*).
auflehn–en, 1. *v.a.* lean (against *or* on). 2. *v.r.* rebel, revolt, mutiny (against); oppose, resist. **–ung,** *f.* revolt, mutiny, rebellion, resistance.
auflesen, *ir.v.a.* glean; gather *or* pick up.
aufleuchten, 1. *v.n.* (*aux.* h.) flash, light up, shine, rise resplendent. 2. *n.* flash, flaring.
aufliegen, 1. *ir.v.n.* (*aux.* s.) lie, lean on, rest upon, weigh on, be on show, be exposed (for sale); be incumbent on. 2. *v.r.* develop bedsores. **aufliegend,** *pr.p.* & *adj.* incumbent.
auflocker–n, 1. *v.a.* loosen (up); shake up (*a feather-bed*); unfix. 2. *v.r.* get loose; relax; disintegrate. **–ung,** *f.* loosening, relaxation.
auflodern, *v.n.* (*aux.* s.) flash, flare up, blaze up, burst into flames.
auflös–en, *v.a.* & *r.* loosen, untie, unravel, solve (*a problem*); reduce (*fractions*); resolve (*a discord*); decompose; analyse (*Gram., Chem.*); break (*a spell*); break up (*an assembly or collection*); dissolve (***partnership, marriage,* & *Chem.***); disband (*troops*); liquefy, decompose, disintegrate. **–bar,** *adj.* soluble. **–barkeit,** *f.* solubility. **–end,** *pr.p.* & *adj.* solvent; *–ende Mittel,* solvents. **–lich,** *adj.* *see* **–bar. –ung,** *f.* loosening; dissolving; dissolution, scattering, disbandment; decomposition; disentanglement, disintegration; solution; analysis; elucidation (*of a mystery*); resolution (*of a discord, of forces*); dénouement; *in –ung begriffen sein,* be in the process of dissolution. **–ungsfähig,** *adj.* soluble, resolvable. **–ungskraft,** *f.* solvent power. **–ungsmittel,** *n.* solvent. **–ungszeichen,** *n.* natural, ♮ (*Mus.*).
aufmach–en, 1. *v.a.* open; undo, untie, unlock; unlace; (*C.L.*) begin (*a new set of books*); fix, get ready; make up, get up, arrange; (*C.L.*) *eine Rechnung –en,* draw up an account; *in Rollen –en,* make up in rolls; *aufgemachtes Leinen,* dressed linen. 2. *v.r.* rise, get up, prepare to start; set out; *sich auf und davon machen,* run away, decamp. **–ung,** *f.* get up (*of a book, etc.*); mise-en-scène, staging; make-up.
Aufmarsch, *m.* (-es, ⸗e) marching up; forming up for deployment, concentration (*of troops*). **–ieren,** *v.n.* (*aux.* s.) deploy; march up; form up (*Mil.*); *–ieren lassen,* draw up, deploy.
aufmerk–en, *v.n.* (*aux.* h.) attend, pay attention to, give heed to. **–sam,** *adj.* attentive, alert, observant; courteous, polite; *einen auf eine S. –sam machen,* call *or* draw a p.'s attention to a th. **–samkeit,** *f.* attention; attentiveness, alertness, watchfulness, vigilance; politeness.
aufmunter–n, *v.a.* cheer up, encourage; arouse, enliven, incite. **–nd,** *pr.p.* & *adj.* rousing, encouraging, animating. **–ung,** *f.* encouragement, incitement; animation.
aufnäh–en, *v.a.* sew on. **–er,** *m.* tuck, false hem.
Aufnahme, *f.* (-n) 1. taking up, reception; assimilation, absorption; 2. admission; enrolment, admittance; 3. exposure (*of a photograph*); snapshot, photograph; survey; 4. loan (*of money*), borrowing; *in – bringen* or *kommen,* bring or come into fashion, favour, *etc.*; *eine – machen,* take a photograph *or* snapshot; *– finden,* meet with a good reception; *Gelände–,* topographical survey, aerial photograph *or* survey. **–fähig,** *adj.* admissible, eligible; capable of absorbing; receptive (*of mind*). **–fähigkeit,** *f.* receptivity. **–prüfung,** *f.* entrance examination. **–schein,** *m.* certificate of admission. **–stellung,** *f.* delaying *or* rallying position (*Mil.*).
aufnehm–en, *ir.v.a.* 1. take up; take in, admit, receive; 2. take photograph (*or* aural record) of; survey, map; shoot (*film*); record (*sound*); 3. hold, contain; absorb; dissolve (*Chem.*); 4. (*C.L.*) draw up (*a statement*); catalogue; raise, borrow (*money*); pick up (*stitches, scent, track*); *in sich –en,* assimilate; appropriate, make one's own; *mit –en in,* embody in; *die Fährte –en,* catch the scent; *es mit einem –en,* be a match for a p.; *gut –en,* take well *or* in good part; *–en für* or *als,* look upon, consider as; *Verbindung –en,* establish contact (*Mil.*). **–er,** *m.* (*C.L.*) receiver, borrower (*of money*).
aufnotieren, *v.a.* note (down), take *or* make a note of.
aufnötig–en, *v.a.*; *einem etwas –en,* force s.th. upon a p. **–ung,** *f.* enforcement, compulsion.
aufopfer–n, 1. *v.a.* sacrifice, offer up. 2. *v.r.* sacrifice o.s., devote o.s., dedicate o.s. (to). **–nd,** *pr.p.* & *adj.* sacrificing; devoted. **–ung,** *f.* sacrificing; (self-)sacrifice; devotion.
aufpass–en, *v.n.* (*aux.* h.) pay attention, attend; watch, be on the alert; fit on (*lid, hat, etc.*); *einem*

-en, waylay a p.; *aufgepaßt!* attention! mind! take care! look out! **-er,** *m.* watcher; overseer; spy.
aufpeitsch-en, *v.a.* lash into a fury; stimulate, (*coll.*) whip up.
aufpflanzen, 1. *v.a.* set up, erect; raise (*a standard*); fix; mount (*guns*); *Seitengewehr pflanzt auf!* fix bayonets! 2. *v.r.*; plant o.s.
aufpfropfen, *v.a.* graft (upon).
aufplustern, *v.r.* ruffle the feathers (*of birds*); give o.s. airs.
aufprägen, *v.a.* imprint, stamp, impress on.
aufprallen, *v.n.* (*aux.* s.) bounce; strike (the ground), rebound.
aufprobieren, *v.a.* try on (*a hat*).
aufprotzen, *v.a.* limber up (*guns*).
aufpumpen, *v.a.* inflate, pump up.
Aufputz, *m.* (-es) finery; ornaments; trimmings; dressing. **-en,** *v.a.* trim up, brush up; make smart; dress up, deck out.
aufquellen, 1. *ir.v.a.* steep, soak. 2. *v.n.* (*aux.* s.) bubble *or* well up; swell, swell up *or* out, expand.
aufraffen, 1. *v.a.* snatch up, collect hastily. 2. *v.r.* pull o.s. together; pick up courage, set to work energetically.
aufragen, *v.n.* (*aux.* h.) jut, tower up, rise on high.
aufräum-en, *v.a.* remove, tidy up, put in order; clear (away *or* up); mop up (*Mil.*); make a clean sweep of; (*C.L.*) *das Lager -en*, clear out the stock. **-ung,** *f.* clearing up, making tidy, mopping up (*Mil.*). **-ungsarbeit,** *f.* salvage work, clearing (*of debris*).
aufrechn-en, *v.a.* reckon up, count up; put to s.o.'s account; specify (*charges*); *gegenseitig -en*, settle accounts. **-ung,** *f.* settling of accounts.
aufrecht, *adj.* erect; straight; upright; honest; *- halten*, hold upright; *- erhalten*, maintain, preserve (*order*); support (*a friend*); uphold (*a doctrine, etc.*); *sich - erhalten*, sit up, hold o.s. up; hold up one's head; (*fig.*) keep up one's courage, maintain one's ground. **-erhaltung,** *f.* maintenance, preservation. **-haltung,** *f.* support. **-sein,** *n.* uprightness. **-stehend,** *adj.* upright, rampant (*Her.*).
aufreden, *v.a.*; *einem etwas -*, talk s.o. into a th.
aufreg-en, 1. *v.a.* stir up; rouse; excite; incite, stimulate, irritate, agitate, enrage; 2. *v.r.* get excited, *etc.* (*coll.*) *Reg dich nicht auf!* (*sl.*) keep your shirt on! **-end,** *pr.p.* & *adj.* exciting; irritant; stimulating. **-ung,** *f.* excitement, agitation. **-ungsmittel,** *n.* irritant, stimulant.
aufreib-en, 1. *ir.v.a.* rub open; rub sore; fret, gall; grind, grate (*sugar, etc.*), wear away (*by friction*); knead thoroughly; destroy, exterminate (*Mil.*). 2. *v.r.* wear o.s. out, worry o.s. to death; *sich gegenseitig -en*, destroy one another. **-er,** *m.* dough-kneader; scraping instrument. **-ung,** *f.* grating; destruction, extirpation.
aufreihen, *v.a.* file (*papers*); string *or* thread (*beads*).
aufreißen, 1. *ir.v.a.* tear *or* rip up *or* open; burst, wrench *or* force open; fling open; slit, cut, crack, split; take up (*a pavement*); break up (*ground*); sketch hastily; *die Augen -*, open one's eyes wide. 2. *v.n.* (*aux.* s.) split open, burst; crack, gape; chap (*of hands with cold*).
aufreiz-en, *v.a.* incite, rouse, stir up, inflame, provoke; (*coll.*) egg on. **-ung,** *f.* provocation; instigation; excitation (*Law*).
aufricht-en, 1. *v.a.* set up, erect; raise, plant (*a standard*); right (*a ship*); (*fig.*) cheer, support, comfort. 2. *v.r.* raise o.s.; *sich im Bett -en*, sit up in bed. **-bar,** *adj.* erectile (*Anat.*). **-ig,** *adj.* sincere, candid, frank, open, honest, upright, straightforward. **-igkeit,** *f.* uprightness, sincerity, *etc.* **-ung,** *f.* erection; establishment.
aufriegeln, *v.a.* unbolt.
Aufriß, *m.* (-(ss)es, -(ss)e) sketch, design, draft, vertical projection, elevation; *perspektivischer -*, perspective view.
aufritzen, *v.a.* slit, rip *or* scratch open; chap (*of hands with cold*).
aufrollen, *v.a.* & *n.* (*aux.* s.) roll up, coil up; unroll; push back; *eine Stellung -*, turn the flank (*Mil. of enemy's position*); *eine Frage -*, open *or* broach a question; *sich aufrollend, pr.p.* & *adj.*, *aufgerollt*, *p.p.* & *adj.*, spiral, convoluted.

aufrücken, *v.n.* (*aux.* s.) advance; close up (*ranks, Mil.*); rise, be promoted.
Aufruf, *m.* (-s, -e) summons; appeal; proclamation. **-en,** *ir.v.a.* call up, summon, call in (*banknotes*); call over (*names*).
Aufruhr, *m.* (-s, -e) tumult, uproar; riot, revolt, mutiny, insurrection. **-akte,** *f.*, **-gesetz,** *n.* riot act. **-stifter,** *m.* agitator. **-zeichen,** *n.* (*Law*) provocative gesture.
aufrühr-en, *v.a.* stir up, incite (*to rebellion*); mention again, bring up, (*coll.*) rake up. **-er,** *m.* agitator, rebel, insurgent, rioter, mutineer. **-erisch,** *adj.* mutinous, rebellious; seditious, inflammatory.
aufrüst-en, *v.n.* & *a.* arm, rearm. **-ung,** *f.* rearmament.
aufrütteln, *v.a.* shake up; arouse.
aufs, = **auf das.**
aufsagen, *v.a.* say, repeat, recite; rescind, recant; renounce, countermand; give notice *or* warning to quit.
aufsässig, *adj.* rebellious, refractory; inimical.
Aufsatz, *m.* (-es, ⸗e) 1. (*anything placed on s.th. else*) top, head-piece; knob; head-dress; year's growth; piece sewed on; attachment, finish, ornament, *etc.*; service, set (*of china, etc.*); centre-piece; tangent-sight (*Artil.*); 2. essay, article (*in a newspaper*); treatise; *vermischte Aufsätze*, miscellaneous essays. **-farbe,** *f.* topping colour; **-höhe,** *f.* elevation (*Artil.*); **-schlüssel,** *m.* box spanner. **-thema,** *n.* subject for an essay. **-winkel,** *m.* angle of sight, tangent elevation (*Artil.*).
aufsaug-en, *v.a.* absorb. **-ung,** *f.* absorption.
aufschauen, *v.n.* (*aux.* h.) look up; glance up.
aufscheuchen, *v.a.* startle, scare (away).
aufschicht-en, *v.a.* pile up, stack (*timber, etc.*); arrange in layers, stratify. **-ung,** *f.* stratification.
aufschieb-en, *ir.v.a.* shove *or* push open; postpone, defer, put off, adjourn, prorogue, delay; (*rare*) procrastinate. **-ung,** *f.* delay; adjournment; respite. **-efenster,** *n.* sash-window.
aufschießen, *ir.v.n.* (*aux.* s.) shoot up (*of plants, animals, etc.*); spring up, leap up.
aufschirren, *v.a.* harness.
Aufschlag, *m.* (-(e)s, ⸗e) striking, percussion, impact; facings (*on a coat*), lapel, revers; cuff; top (*of a boot*); trump card; upward stroke (*in beating time*); service (*Tenn.*); advance, rise, increase (*in price*), highest bid (*at auctions*); additional tax *or* duty; seedlings, saplings; arsis (*Metr.*). **-en, 1.** *ir.v.a.* 1. break *or* beat open; crack (*eggs*); untwist (*a rope*); 2. erect (*scaffolding, etc.*), pitch (*a tent*); 3. open (*a book, the eyes*); look up (*a word, a passage*); 4. turn up (*a card, a table, one's dress, trousers, sleeves, etc.*); advance *or* raise (*the price*); *einem Pferde die Hufeisen -en*, shoe a horse; *ein Gelächter -en*, burst out laughing; *seine Wohnung -en*, establish o.s., make one's home, take up one's abode. **2.** *v.n.* (*aux.* s.) turn up, spring up; fall violently; hit, strike (*of a bullet*); rise in price; *dumpf -en*, thud; **-geschwindigkeit,** *f.* impact velocity (*Artil.*). **-etisch,** *m.* folding table. **-zünder,** *m.* percussion-fuse.
aufschlämmen, 1. *v.a.* make into paste. 2. *v.n.* be suspended (*in liquid, Chem.*).
aufschlemmen *see* **aufschlämmen.**
aufschließ-en, 1. *ir.v.a.* unlock, open (up); disintegrate; (*fig.*) elucidate; disclose. 2. *v.n.* close ranks (*Mil.*). 3. *v.r.* open up, pour out one's heart. **-er,** *m.* opener; turnkey. **-ung,** *f.* opening; disclosure; disintegration, decomposition, hydrolysis.
Aufschluß, *m.* (-(ss)es, ⸗(ss)e) disclosure, information; explanation, elucidation; *- über eine S. geben*, explain a th., give information about *or* give the particulars of a matter. **-reich,** *adj.* informative, instructive.
aufschminken, *v.a.* (*fig.*) paint in false colours.
aufschnappen, 1. *v.a.* snatch *or* snap up (*of dogs*); catch (*a word*). 2. *v.n.* (*aux.* s.) spring, fly open.
aufschneid-en, 1. *ir.v.a.* cut up *or* open; carve; dissect; *ein Buch -en*, cut the leaves of a book. 2. *v.n.* (*aux.* h.) brag, boast, swagger, exaggerate, talk big. **-er,** *m.* boaster, **-erei,** *f.* boasting, exaggeration, bombast.

aufschnellen, 1. *v.a.* jerk *or* fling up. 2. *v.n.* (*aux.* s.) fly up with a jerk.
Aufschnitt, *m.* (-es, -e) cut, slit, slice, incision; *kalter* -, (dish consisting of) cold meat.
aufschnüren, 1. *v.a.* unlace, untie, uncord. 2. *v.r.* come undone (*of parcels*).
aufschrauben, *reg.* & *ir.v.a.* screw on, screw up; screw open, unscrew.
aufschrecken, 1. *v.a.* startle. 2. *ir.v.n.* (*aux.* s.) start up, jump (*with surprise*), be startled.
Aufschrei, *m.* (-s, -e), shriek, scream, yell, shout, outcry. **-en,** *ir.v.n.* (*aux.* h.) cry out, scream, shriek.
aufschreiben, *ir.v.a.* write down, note down, take a note of; enter, book; put *or* charge to a p.'s account; record.
Aufschrift, *f.* (-en) address, direction; inscription; label (*on goods, bottles, etc.*); legend.
Aufschub, *m.* (-(e)s, ⁻e) postponement, deferment, delay; adjournment, reprieve, respite; *Zahlung ohne* –, immediate payment; *die S. leidet keinen* –, the matter is urgent. **-sbefehl,** *m.* reprieve (*Law*). **-sbrief,** *m.* letter of respite.
aufschürzen, *v.a.* tuck up (*a skirt, etc.*); *die Segel* –, furl the sails.
aufschütteln, *v.a.* shake up, disturb by shaking.
aufschütten, *v.a.* heap *or* throw up; pour on; store up; *das Pulver* –, prime a gun.
aufschwatzen, *v.a.* (*coll.*) *einem etwas* –, palm off a th. on to a p., talk a p. into a th.
aufschweißen, *v.a.* weld on, fuse on.
aufschwellen, 1. *v.a.* distend; inflate; puff out. 2. *ir.v.n.* (*aux.* s.) swell; rise; surge up; tumefy (*Med.*); grow turgid.
aufschwemm-en, *v.a.* wash up; deposit (*sand, etc.*); soak, bloat. **-ung,** *f.* suspension, depositing; swelling.
aufschwingen, 1. *ir.v.a.* brandish in the air. 2. *v.r.* soar, rise.
Aufschwung, *m.* (-(e)s) rise; flight (*of fancy, etc.*); progress, prosperity; stimulus, impetus; *einen neuen - nehmen*, receive a fresh impetus, rise again.
aufseh-en, 1. *ir.v.n.* (*aux.* h.) look up *or* upon. 2. *n.* stir, sensation; *er wollte alles -en vermeiden*, he wished to escape notice; *-en erregen*, attract attention; cause a sensation; make a great stir; *-en erregend*, sensational, stirring. **-er,** *m.* overseer, foreman, supervisor, inspector, warden, keeper, attendant, curator.
aufsetz-en, 1. *v.a.* 1. put on (*a hat, a kettle, a patch, etc.*); 2. put down, note; draw up, compose (*letter, etc.*); crown (*a man at draughts*); serve up (*food*); 3. set on *or* up; put *or* pile up; *Dampf -en*, get up steam; *eine Rechnung -en*, draw up a bill, make up an account; *schriftlich* or *etwas Schriftliches -en*, put down in writing, commit to writing; *das setzt allem die Krone auf*, that's the limit, that beats everything; *seinen Kopf -en*, be obstinate about a th.; *einem Hörner -en*, cuckold a p. **2.** *v.r.* sit upright; sit up straight; mount (*on horseback*); establish o.s. (*in business*); oppose, be refractory. **-röhre,** *f.* spout. **-stunde,** *f.* time when the shifts change (*Min.*).
Aufsicht, *f.* inspection, supervision, surveillance, invigilation; care, charge, control, guardianship, custody, keeping; *unter – stehen*, be under supervision; *– führen*, superintend. **-habende(r),** *m.* **-sbeamte(r),** *m.* officer in charge; superintendent; supervisor; inspector. **-sbehörde,** *f.* controlling authority *or* body. **-sbezirk,** *m.* inspectoral district. **-skomitee,** *n.* visiting committee. **-srat,** *m.* board of directors.
aufsitzen, 1. *ir.v.n.* (*aux.* h.) sit *or* rest on; perch, roost (*of birds*); (*Naut.*) run aground; sit up (*at night*); (*aux.* s.) mount horse; *aufgesessen!* to horse! mount! (*Mil.*); *das Ziel – lassen*, aim just below the mark *or* at 6 o'clock of the target; *– lassen*, leave in the lurch. 2. *n.* sitting up; incubation; mounting.
aufspann-en, *v.a.* stretch, bend (*a bow*); open (*a fan, an umbrella, etc.*); pitch (*a tent*); set *or* spread sail (*Naut.*); mount (*an artist's canvas*); string (*a musical instrument*) **-er,** *m.* step-up transformer (*Elec.*).
aufsparen, *v.a.* save, save up, lay by; reserve keep in reserve.
aufspeicher-n, *v.a.* store up; accumulate, lay in stock. **-ung,** *f.* storage, accumulation.
aufsperren, *v.a.* unlock; open wide.
aufspielen, 1. *v.a.* & *n.* (*aux.* h.) strike up (*a tune* or *the music*). 2. *v.r.* give o.s. *or* put on airs, pose (*als*, as).
aufspießen, *v.a.* impale, put on a spit; run through with a sword; gore.
aufsprießen, *ir.v.n.* (*aux.* s.) sprout, spring up, germinate.
aufspringen, *ir.v.n.* (*aux.* s.) leap up, jump up, bound up, spring up; fly *or* burst *or* crack open, split asunder; chap (*of hands with the cold*); rebound. **-d,** *pr.p.* & *adj.* rampant (*Her.*); dehiscent (*Bot.*).
aufspritzen, *v.n.* (*aux.* s.) splash up; squirt up.
aufsprudeln, *v.n.* (*aux.* s.) bubble up, boil up.
Aufsprung, *m.* (-(e)s, ⁻e) bound, leap.
aufspulen, *v.a.* wind on (*a reel, etc.*).
aufspüren, *v.a.* trace out, track; hunt *or* spy out.
aufstacheln, *v.a.* goad, goad on; spur (on); stimulate, incite.
aufstampfen, *v.n.* (*aux.* h.) stamp one's foot.
Aufstand, *m.* (-(e)s, ⁻e) tumult, revolt, rebellion, mutiny, insurrection.
aufständisch, *adj.* rebellious, mutinous, riotous, insurgent, revolutionary.
aufstapeln, *v.a* pile up, heap up, stack, store, accumulate.
aufstechen, *ir.v.a.* prick open, puncture; lance (*Surg.*); retouch (*an engraving*); pay out (*cable*); splice (*ropes*); *das Schiff hat sich aufgestochen*, the ship has broken her back (*Naut.*).
aufsteck-en, *v.a.* fix; affix, pin up; put up (*curtains*); dress (*the hair*); abandon, give up (*coll.*). *In compounds it has the meaning of 'extension piece', something fixed or slipped on*, e.g. **-rohr,** *n.* extension tube; **-blende,** *f.* slip-on lens cover.
aufstehen, *ir.v.n.* (*aux.* s.) stand up; rise, get up; fly up; break cover; right itself (*of a ship*); recover (*from an illness*); (*aux.* h.) stand *or* be open; mutiny (*gegen*, against), rise, revolt; *das Volk steht auf* (*gegen*), the nation rises (*against a tyrant, etc.*).
aufsteig-en, 1. *ir.v.n.* (*aux.* s.) ascend, rise, mount; climb (up), well up (*of water*), take off (*Av.*); *es stieg ein Gedanke in mir auf*, a thought struck me; *der Teig fängt an aufzusteigen*, the dough is rising; 2. *n.* mounting (*a horse, etc.*); ascent; dispersion (*of a fog*). **-end,** *pr.p.* & *adj.* ascending. **-ung,** *f.* ascension (*Astr.*); *gerade -ung*, right ascension; exhalation (*of vapour, etc.*). **-ungsunterschied,** *m.* ascensional difference (*Astr.*).
aufstell-en, 1. *v.a.* set up, erect; install; draw up (*troops*); put *or* make up (*a bed, etc.*); advance (*an opinion*); make (*an assertion*); set (*a trap*); expose (*goods for sale*); post (*sentries*); park (*cars*); bring forward (*instances, etc.*); establish (*a record*); lay down (*a principle*); nominate (*a candidate*); *es läßt sich nichts mit ihm -en*, nothing can be done with him. 2. *v.r.* place o.s. in position, draw up (*in battle-array, etc.*), form up, draw up. **-ung,** *f.* arrangement, disposition, array, formation (*Mil.*); assertion, statement; drawing up, tabulation; list, inventory; nomination (*of a candidate*). **-bahnhof,** *m.* shunting yards (*Railw.*). **-gleis,** *n.* siding (*Railw.*). **-spiegel,** *m.* cheval mirror.
aufstemmen, 1. *v.a.* prop up, support; force open, prize open. 2. *v.r.*; *sich – auf eine S.*, lean upon a th.
Aufstieg, *m.* (-(e)s, -e) ascent (*of mountain or in aeroplane*); step (*of a cycle*); rise; *Preußens* – the rise of Prussia; *im* –, on the up-grade.
aufstimmen, *v.a.* raise the pitch (*Mus.*).
aufstöbern, *v.a.* stir up, start (*game*); hunt up, ferret out; light on, discover (*as result of search*).
aufstören, *v.a.* rouse, disturb.
aufstoßen, 1 *ir.v.a.* knock, kick *or* push open *or* up; knock *or* bump (*gegen*, against); break the skin, graze. 2. *v.n.* (*aux.* s.) belch, repeat; (*Naut.*) run aground; meet with, light upon, chance upon; happen to; ferment; turn acid; *da ist mir etwas Seltsames aufgestoßen*, a strange th. happened to me. 3. *n.* belching, eructation.
aufstößig, *adj.* flat, acid, sour.
aufstreben, *v.n.* (*aux.* s.) rise, aspire (to), soar, struggle upwards. **-d,** *pr.p.* & *adj.* aspiring.

aufstreichen, *ir.v.a.* lay on; spread (*butter on bread, etc.*).
aufstreifen, 1. *v.a.* turn *or* tuck up (*one's cuffs, etc.*); raise, graze (*the skin*). 2. *v.n.* (*aux.* s.) graze, touch the surface.
aufstreuen, *v.a.* strew *or* sprinkle (on).
Aufstrich, *m.* (-(e)s, -e) paste, spread; up-stroke (*of the pen*); up-bow (*Mus.*).
aufstülpen, *v.a.* turn up, cock up (*hat brim, etc.*); put on, clap on (*as a hat*); *aufgestülpte Nase,* turned-up, snub *or* retroussé nose.
aufstützen, 1. *v.a.* prop up, support. 2. *v.r.* lean upon.
aufsuch-en, *v.a.* hunt up, seek out, search for, locate, go in quest of, go to see; look out (*a passage, etc.*); look up (*a p.*.). **-ung,** *f.* search.
auftafeln, *v.a.* dish, serve up (*a meal*).
auftakeln, 1. *v.a.* rig (*a ship*). 2. *v.r.* (*coll.*) tog o.s. up.
Auftakt, *m.* upward beat (*Mus.*); unaccented *or* opening syllable (*or* syllables); anacrusis (*Metr.*); (*fig.*) opening phase, prelude.
auftanken, *v.n.* refuel (*Veh., Av.*).
auftauchen, *v.n.* (*aux.* s.) emerge, appear suddenly, rise to the surface, surface (*of submarines*).
auftauen, *v.n.* (*aux.* s.) thaw; (*fig.*) become talkative *or* sociable, unbend, thaw.
aufteil-en, *v.a.* partition, divide up; distribute, allot. **-ung,** *f.* partition, division, distribution; disintegration.
auftischen, *v.a.* serve up; set on the table; *einem etwas –,* serve *or* regale a p. with a th.
Auftrag, *m.* (-(e)s, ⸗e) commission, order, instruction, charge, mandate; errand, message, task, mission; coat, coating, application (*of colour, paint, etc.*); – *auf* (*Acc.*), order for; *im –e von,* by order of, on behalf of; *einen – ausführen,* execute a commission. **-en,** *ir.v.a.* carry up; serve up (*food*); lay on, apply (*colour*); commission, charge with (*a duty*); wear out (*clothes*); *dick –en,* exaggerate, lay it on thick (*sl.*); *er hat mir Grüße an jeden von Ihnen aufgetragen,* he sent greetings to each of you; *einem eine Arbeit –,* set a p. a task; *das Abendbrot ist aufgetragen,* supper is served *or* on the table. **-geber,** *m.* employer; customer; principal. **-nehmer,** *m.* supplier. **-sbesorger,** *m.* commission agent. **-shandel,** *m.* commission business. **-slenkung,** *f.* allocation of business according to a government plan. **-ssteuerungsstelle,** *f.* compulsory syndicate (*under Nat. Soc.*).
auftreff-en, *v.a.* strike, impinge on. **-geschwindigkeit,** *f.* impact *or* striking velocity. **-punkt,** *m.* point of impact. **-winkel,** *m.* angle of incidence. **-wucht,** *f.* force of impact.
auftreib-en, 1. *ir.v.a.* drive up; raise, start (*game*); hunt up, rummage out, procure (*with difficulty*), get hold of; levy, impress (*troops*); swell up, distend; raise (*prices, money, dust*). 2. *v.n.* (*aux.* s.) run aground. **-eholz,** *n.* roller of a mangle; rolling-pin. **-er,** *m.* beater (*for game*).
auftrennen, 1. *v.a.* undo, rip open. 2. *v.n.* (*aux.* s.) come asunder *or* undone.
auftreten, 1. *ir.v.a.* kick open. 2. *v.n.* (*aux.* s.) tread on; appear, come forward; step forth; occur, be found, crop up (*coll.*); *er trat als Othello auf,* he made his appearance as Othello; *als Schriftsteller –,* come forward as an author; *zum ersten Mal –,* make one's debut; *als Zeuge –,* appear as witness; *sanft* or *leise –,* act *or* proceed cautiously *or* gently. 3. *n.; dies war ihr erstes –,* this was her first public appearance *or* her debut.
Auftrieb, *m.* (-s, -e) buoyancy; lift (*Av.*); (*dial.*) driving cattle to the alpine pasture; impetus, stimulus. **-sbeiwert,** *m.* coefficient of lift (*Av.*).
Auftritt, *m.* (-s, -e) step, doorstep; fire step (*of trench*); appearance; scene (*in a play*); event.
auftrumpfen, *v.a.* trump (*Cards*); exult (*gegen,* over).
auftun, 1. *ir.v.a.* open; disclose. 2. *v.r.* open; blow (*of flowers*); become visible, loom, appear on the horizon; get started *or* established.
auftupfen, *v.a.* mop *or* dab up (*with towel*); press down gently (*goldleaf*).
auftürmen, 1. *v.a.* heap, pile up high. 2. *v.r.* tower up, accumulate.
auftuschen, *v.a.* touch up (*a drawing*).
aufwachen, *v.n.* (*aux.* s.) awake(n), wake up.
aufwachsen, *ir.v.n.* (*aux.* s.) grow up.
aufwägen, *reg. & ir.v.a.* weigh; (*fig.*) outweigh.
aufwall-en, *v.n.* (*aux.* s.) boil up; rage, foam up. **-ung,** *f.* boiling; ebullition; effervescence; emotion; transport; fit.
aufwalzen, *v.a.* wind on rollers; roll out.
aufwälzen, *v.a.* roll up; *einem etwas –,* burden s.o. with a th.
Aufwand, *m.* (-(e)s) expense; expenditure; display; consumption; *viel – machen,* live in grand style. **-gesetz,** *n.* sumptuary law. **-steuer,** *f.* luxury-tax.
aufwärmen, *v.a.* warm up; bring up again, renew (*a dispute, etc.*).
aufwart-en, *v.n.* (*aux.* h.) (*Dat.*) wait on, attend on, serve; call on, pay one's respects to; beg (*of dogs*); *womit kann ich Ihnen –en?* what can I do for you? *kann ich damit –en?* may I offer you some? *ich will gleich damit –en,* you shall have it directly; *einem oft –en,* dance attendance on a p. **-efrau,** *f.* charwoman, help. **-egeld,** *n.*, **-elohn,** *m.* fee for attendance *or* service. **-ung,** *f.* service, attendance; formal visit; (*coll.*) charwoman, help; *einem seine –ung machen,* pay one's respects to a p.
Aufwärter, *m.* attendant, waiter; steward.
aufwärts, *adv.* upward, upwards; *den Fluß –* or *Strom –,* up-stream; *– gerichtet,* erect; *es geht mit ihm –,* he is on the upward grade, he is getting on. **-transformator,** *m.* step-up transformer (*Elec.*). **-zieher,** *m.* adductor (*muscle*).
aufwasch-en, *ir.v.a.* wash up, away *or* off. **-küche,** *f.* scullery. **-wasser,** *n.* dish-water.
aufweck-en, *v.a.* rouse, waken; animate.
aufweichen, *v.a.* soften; soak; mollify; open by fomentation (*Med.*). **-d,** *pr.p. & adj.* emollient.
aufweisen, *ir.v.a.* show, exhibit; point to; produce.
aufwend-en, *reg. & ir.v.a.* spend, expend (upon), devote (to), bestow (upon); *Mühe –en,* take pains (*auf eine S.,* with a th.); *vergebliche Worte –en,* waste one's words *or* breath. **-ung,** *f.* expenditure, employment.
aufwerfen, 1. *ir.v.a.* throw up; cast up (*earth, a rampart, etc.*); throw open (*a door*); raise (*a question*), pose, proclaim; *aufgeworfene Lippen,* pouting lips; *aufgeworfene Nasenlöcher,* distended nostrils. 2. *v.r.*; *sich – zu,* set o.s. up (for); *sich wider* or *gegen einen –,* revolt against a p.
aufwert-en, *v.a.* raise the value of a th., assign a higher value to a th. **-ung,** *f.* revalorization, higher valuation.
aufwickel-n, 1. *v.a.* wind up, roll up; put (*hair*) in curl-papers; unroll, unwind; loosen, let down (*one's hair*); unfurl (*sails*); unwrap (*a parcel*). 2. *v.r.* unravel, unfold. **-spule,** *f.* winding-spool.
aufwieg-eln, *v.a.* stir up, incite to rebellion. **-elei,** *f.*, **-elung,** *f.* incitement, instigation (*to rebellion*). **-ler,** *m.* instigator (*to revolt*), agitator, mutineer. **-lerisch,** *adj.* inflammatory, seditious, mutinous.
aufwiegen, *ir.v.a.* outweigh; counterbalance; compensate for; make up for.
Aufwind, *m.* upcurrent (*Meteor.*).
aufwinden, *ir.v.a.* wind up; hoist (*with a windlass*); haul up, weigh (*anchor*).
aufwirbeln, 1. *v.a.* whirl up; *Staub –,* raise dust, make a stir. 2. *v.n.* (*aux.* s.) rise whirling.
aufwirken, *v.a.* work up; knead (*dough*).
aufwischen, *v.a.* wipe up; wipe away, clear, clean.
aufwollen, *v.n.* (*always used negatively*) wish to open; *das Fenster wollte nicht auf,* the window would not open; *der Deckel will nicht auf,* the lid will not come off.
Aufwuchs, *m.* (-es), growth.
aufwühlen, *v.a.* grub up, root up (*like swine*); (*fig.*) upset, excite.
Aufwurf, *m.* (-s, ⸗e) parapet, mound, ridge.
aufzähl-en, *v.a.* count up; reckon up, enumerate; administer (*blows*). **-ungsreihe,** *f.* frequency distribution (*Statistics*).
aufzäumen, *v.a.* bridle (*a horse*); (*coll.*) *ein Pferd beim Schwanze –,* put the cart before the horse.
aufzehr-en, *v.a.* use up; consume; waste; (*fig.*) eat up, absorb. **-ung,** *f.* consumption, expenditure.
aufzeichn-en, *v.a.* draw, sketch; note down, take

a note of; catalogue, make an inventory of; record. **-ung,** *f.* note, record; sketch, design.
aufzeigen, *v.a.* show, exhibit.
aufzieh-en, 1. *ir.v.a.* 1. draw up, raise, hoist, haul up; draw (*water*); open (*a sluice-gate*); weigh (*anchor*); 2. bring up (*children*); cultivate (*plants*); rear, breed (*cattle, etc.*); assume (*an air*); arrange, plan (*festival*); 3. wind up (*a watch*); put on (*a fiddle-string*); mount (*a print*); undo (*a knot*); set (*a sail*); *gelindere Saiten -en*, come down a peg; draw in one's horns; *andere Saiten -en*, adopt (*or* speak in) a different tone; (*coll.*) *einen -en*, tease *or* make fun of a p. **2.** *v.n.* (*aux.* s.) march, move up, go in procession, draw up *or* near; mount guard; gather, draw on (*of storms*); come to a head (*of ulcers, etc.*). **-brücke,** *f.* drawbridge. **-er,** *m.* levator muscle. **-fenster,** *n.* sash-window. **-karton,** *m.* mounting-board (*for prints*). **-leine,** *f.* release cord, rip cord (*of a parachute*). **-loch,** *n.* winding-hole, keyhole (*of a watch*).
Aufzucht, *f.* breeding, rearing (*of animals*).
aufzucken, *v.n.* (*aux.* h.) start convulsively.
Aufzug, *m.* (-(e)s, ⁻̈e) 1. procession, parade; cavalcade, cortège, suite, train; 2. lift, elevator; hoist, crane, windlass; 3. pageantry, pomp; attire, dress; equipment; (*coll.*) get-up; 4. act (*of a play*); 5. warp (*in weaving*); *erster –, dritter Auftritt*, act one, scene three.
aufzwängen, *v.a.* (*archaic*) *see* **aufzwingen.**
aufzwingen, *ir.v.a.*; *einem eine S. –*, force a th. upon a p.
Aug-e, *n.* (-es, -en); eye; bud, germ; pip, spot (*on cards, dice*); eye (*of a bolt*); lustre (*of precious stones*); face (*of a letter, Typ.*); stitch (*in knitting*); anything resembling an eye (*cavities in bread, whey drops in cheese, grease drops in soup, etc.*); *er hat es ihr an den -en abgesehen*, he anticipated her wishes; *mit scheelen -en ansehen*, look upon with envy; *ich hab' es ihm an den -en angesehen*, I saw it by his face; (*Prov.*) *aus den -en, aus dem Sinn*, out of sight, out of mind; *einem die -en ausstechen*, put a p.'s eyes out; *eine S. im -e behalten*, keep a thing in mind; *mit bloßen -en*, with the naked eye; *einem den Daumen aufs -e setzen*, keep s.o. under one's thumb; *er ist ihm ein Dorn im -e*, he is a thorn in his side *or* flesh; *es fiel mir sogleich ins -e*, it caught my eye at once; *in die -en fallend*, striking, evident; *diese Farbe fällt sehr in die -en*, this is a very glaring colour; *einen ins -e fassen*, have one's eye on a p., keep an eye on a p.; *das paßt wie die Faust aufs -e*, it does not fit at all; *da gehen mir die -en auf*, I begin to see now (*fig.*); *da gehen mir die -en über*, it makes my eyes run (*or* water); *es wird für uns saure -en geben*, we shall meet with black looks; *geh' mir aus den -en!* get out of my sight! (*Prov.*) *keine Krähe hackt der anderen die -en aus*, there is honour among thieves; *in meinen -en*, in my view, in my opinion; *er ist mir aus den -en gekommen*, I have lost sight of him; *komm' mir nicht wieder vor die -en*, never let me see your face again; *er ist mit einem blauen -e davongekommen*, he got off cheaply; *große -en machen*, open one's eyes in surprise; (*sl.*) *einem -en machen*, give a p. the glad eye; *ganz -e und Ohr sein*, be all attention, on the *qui vive*; *er ist ihm wie aus den -en geschnitten*, he is as like him as he can be *or* exactly like him; *es sieht ihm der Schalk aus den -en*, he has a roguish glint in his eye; *aus den -en setzen*, make light of; *in die -en springen*, be obvious *or* manifest; *in die -en stechen*, suit one's fancy, tempt a p.; *einem Sand in die -en streuen*, throw dust into a p.'s eyes, deceive a p.; *-e um -e*, an eye for an eye; *unbewaffnetes -e*, naked eye; *aus den -en verlieren*, lose sight of; *unter vier -en*, tête-à-tête, in confidence; *ein -e zudrücken* wink at, connive at; *kein -e zutun*, not sleep a wink. **-apfel,** *m.* eyeball; apple of one's eye. **-bolzen,** *m.* eyebolt (*Naut.*). (*For other compounds, see* **Augen-.**)
äug-eln, 1. *v.a.* graft, bud (*Hort.*). 2. *v.n.* (*aux.* h.) ogle. 3. *n.* grafting; ogling. **-en,** *v.n.* look round carefully (*of wild animals*). **-ig,** (*in compounds*) = -eyed, *e.g.* **blauäugig,** *adj.* blue-eyed. **-lein,** *n.* little eye; bud (*of a plant*).
augen-ähnlich, *adj.* ocellate, like an eye. **-arzt,** *m.* oculist, ophthalmic surgeon. **-bad,** *n.* eye-douche. **-bader,** *m.* eye-cup. **-betrug,** *m.* optical illusion. **-bild,** *n.* visual image. **-blende,** *f.* blinkers. **-blick,** *m.* moment, instant; *im -blick*, in a moment; *auf einen -blick*, for a moment; *lichte -blicke*, lucid intervals, moments of consciousness; *in diesem -blicke*, at this moment. **-blicklich,** 1. *adj.* instantaneous; immediate; momentary. 2. *adv.* immediately, instantly, forthwith; just now. **-blicks,** *adv. see* **-blicklich. -blicksaufnahme,** *f.* instantaneous photograph, snapshot. **-braue,** *f.* eyebrow. **-drüse,** *f.* lachrymal gland. **-dunkelheit,** *f.* dimness of sight. **-entzündung,** *f.* inflammation of the eye. **-fällig,** *adj.* evident, obvious, conspicuous. **-flimmern,** *n.* twitching of the eye. **-fluß,** *m.* catarrh *or* watering of the eye. **-förmig,** *adj.* eye-shaped; ocellate. **-geschwulst,** *f.* exophthalmia. **-geschwür,** *n.* aegilops. **-gewölk,** *n.* nebula, film on the eye. **-glas,** *n.* eye-glass, monocle. **-heilanstalt,** *f.* ophthalmic hospital. **-heilkunde,** *f.* ophthalmology. **-höhle,** *f.* eye socket, orbital cavity. **-hornhaut,** *f.* cornea. **-kammer,** *f.* chamber of the eye. **-kammerwasser,** *n.* aqueous humour. **-klappe,** *f.* blinkers; patch (*over the eye*). **-leiden,** *n.* eye trouble. **-licht,** *n.* (eye)sight. **-lid,** *n.* (-lider) eyelid. **-liderbrand,** *m.* ulcer on the eyelid, stye. **-liderkrampf,** *m.* twitching of the eyelid. **-loch,** *n.* pupil. **-maß,** *n.* judgement by eye; visual estimate, visual ranging (*Artil.*); *ein gutes -maß haben*, have a sure eye. **-merk,** *n.* object in view, aim; attention; *sein -merk auf eine S. richten*, have a th. in view, direct one's attention to a th. **-nerv,** *m.* optic nerve. **-paar,** *n.* pair of eyes. **-pfropfen,** *n.* bud grafting (*Hort.*). **-pulver,** *n.* anything injurious to the eyes; diamond type; very small *or* illegible handwriting. **-reiz,** *m.* irritation of the eye. **-reizstoff,** *m.* tear gas (*Mil.*) **-ring,** *m.* iris. **-schein,** *m.* appearance; inspection; personal observation; evidence; *in -schein nehmen*, view, inspect; *dem -schein nach*, to all appearance. **-scheinlich,** *adj.* evident, manifest, apparent; *-scheinlicher Beweis*, visible proof. **-scheinseinnahme,** *f.* inquiry *or* investigation on the spot. **-schirm,** *m.* eye-shade. **-schlagader,** *f.* ophthalmic artery. **-schmaus,** *m.* feast for the eyes, delightful sight. **-schützer,** *m.* eye-shade, goggles. **-spiegel,** *m.* ophthalmoscope. **-spritze,** *f.* eye syringe. **-star,** *m.* cataract. **-stechen,** *n.* shooting pains in the eye. **-stern,** *m.* pupil (*of the eye*); favourite, pet, darling. **-täuschung,** *f.* optical illusion. **-träger,** *m.* germinating point (*Hort.*). **-trost,** *m.* eyebright (*Euphrasia officinalis*); (*fig.*) consolation. **-wasser,** *n.* eye-lotion. **-weh,** *n.* pain in the eyes, sore eyes. **-weide,** *f.* welcome sight. **-weite,** range of vision. **-wimper,** *f.* eyelash. **-wurzel,** *f.* wood anemone (*Anemone nemorosa*). **-zahn,** *m.* eye-tooth, canine tooth. **-zauber,** *m.* fascination. **-zeuge,** *m.* eyewitness.
August, *m.* (-s) August (*the month*). **-hafer,** *m.* early oats.
Auktion, *f.* (-en) auction, public sale, (*Scots.*) roup; *in die – geben*, put up for auction. **-ator,** *m.* auctioneer. **-sgebühren,** *f.pl.* auction fees. **-skommissar,** *m.* broker.
Aula, *f.* (-len) great hall.
Aurikel, *f.* (-n) auricula, bear's-ear (*Primula auricula*) (*Bot.*).
aus, 1. *prep.* (*Dat.*) out of; from; of; by; for; on, upon, on account of; in; *– der Mode*, out of fashion; *– Paris kommen*, come from Paris; *er ist – London gebürtig*, he is a native of London; *– Achtung*, out of respect; *– vollem Halse schreien*, scream at the top of one's voice; *was wurde – der Unternehmung?* what was the result of the undertaking? *– unserer Mitte*, from among us; *– jemandes Betragen schließen*, conclude from a p.'s behaviour; *– Erfahrung lernen*, learn by *or* from experience; *bestehen –*, consist of; *– Silber gemacht*, made of silver; *was wird – ihr werden?* what will become of her? *– Ihrem Briefe ersehe ich*, I see by your letter; *– freier Hand*, off-hand, unconstrained; freehand; spontaneously; *– eigener Wahl*, voluntarily, of one's own accord, of one's own free will;

ich sehe – den Zeitungen, I see by *or* from the newspapers; – *dem Englischen übersetzt*, translated from the English; – *Haß*, through hatred; – *vielen Ursachen*, from many causes; – *verschiedenen Gründen*, for many *or* various reasons; – *bloßem Verdacht*, on mere suspicion; – *Mangel an*, for want of; – *Liebe zu*, for love of, out of love for; – *Gehorsam gegen ihn*, in obedience to him; – *Vorsatz*, designedly. 2. *adv.* out, forth; done with, over, ended, past; finished; *jahr– jahrein*, year after year; *höre mich –*, hear me out, let me finish; *er weiß weder – noch ein*, he is at his wit's end; *und damit ist es –*, and there is an end of (*or* to) the matter; *die Kirche ist –*, church is over; *trink es –*, drink it up; (*coll.*) *es ist – mit ihm*, it is all up with him, he is done for; *von Grund –*, thoroughly, radically; *von mir –*, for my part; *von Haus –*, originally. 3. *n.* outside (*football*). 4. *sep. prefix.* out; thoroughly, sufficiently, to the end; stop, cease, finish. (*For compounds not found in the following lists, see the simple verbs and add the appropriate modifying idea.*)

ausarbeit–en, 1. *v.a.* work out, prepare; complete, finish off, perfect, elaborate; compose, draft, write (*a book, etc.*); 2. *v.n.* (*aux.* h.) cease working; cease fermenting. **–er,** *m.* finisher. **–ung,** *f.* perfection, finishing touch; working out, carrying out (*of a plan*); elaboration; composition. *See* **ausgearbeitet.**

ausart–en, *v.n.* (*aux.* s.) degenerate; deteriorate; *die Freiheit artet oft in Anarchie aus*, freedom often degenerates into anarchy. **–ung,** *f.* degeneration; deterioration.

ausästen, *v.a.* prune, trim, clear of branches.

ausatmen, 1. *v.a.* breathe out, exhale. 2. *v.n.* (*aux.* h.) breathe one's last, expire.

ausbaden, *v.a.* (*coll.*) pay; suffer *or* pay the penalty for; *etwas – müssen*, have to suffer for a th.

Ausbau, *m.* (-(e)s) completion (*as of a building*); projecting building; improvement (*of a position, defences, etc., Mil.*); consolidation; extension (*of cultivation, etc.*). **–en,** *v.a.* finish a building; complete, extend, improve; enlarge, cultivate; *ausgebaute Kohlengrube*, exhausted coalpit. **–end,** *pr.p.* & *adj.* expanding; formative.

ausbauch–en, 1. *v.a.* cause to bulge; swell, belly out; hollow out. 2. *v.r.* bulge, project, swell out. **–ung,** *f.* swelling, bulge, protuberance.

ausbeding–en, *ir.v.a.* stipulate; *sich* (*Dat.*) *–en*, reserve for o.s. **–ung,** *f.* reservation; stipulation.

ausbeizen, *v.a.* remove by caustics.

ausbesser–n, *v.a.* mend, repair; improve, restore; darn; refit (*a ship*); *eine Mauer unterhalb –n*, underpin a wall; *es wird ausgebessert*, it is undergoing repair. **–ung,** *f.* repair, mending, restoration. **–ungskosten,** *f.pl.* cost of repairs.

ausbeugen, *v.a.* & *n.*, *see* **ausbiegen.**

Ausbeut–e, *f.* gain; (net) profit, proceeds; produce, production; crop, yield. **–ebogen,** *m.* profit account. **–en,** *v.a.* exploit; draw a profit from, turn to account, make the most of; *ausgebeutet werden*, be taken advantage of. **–er,** *m.* exploiter; **–ertum,** *n.* slave-driving (*i.e. starvation wages and long hours*). **–ung,** *f.* exploitation; working (*of a mine*); cultivation; (*fig.*) spoliation.

ausbiegen, 1. *ir.v.n.* (*aux.* h.) turn aside *or* off; evade, avoid, elude; *einem* or *vor einem –*, make way for a p., get out of the way of a p. 2. *v.a.* bend outwards.

ausbieten, *ir.v.a.* offer for sale; cry (wares.)

ausbild–en, *v.a.* form, develop, cultivate, improve, perfect; train, educate. **–ung,** *f.* improvement, development; formation, cultivation; education; instruction, training; culture; *–ung höherer Lehrer*, training of secondary school teachers; *–ung von Rekruten*, drilling of recruits; *–ung eines Geschwürs*, gathering (*Med.*); *–ung des Körpers*, physical training.

Ausbiß, *m.* (-(ss)es, -(ss)e) outcrop (*Geol.*).

ausbitten, *ir.v.a.* beg for; require, insist on; ask out, invite; *das bitte ich mir aus*, I must insist on this; *darf ich mir das Salz –?* please pass the salt! may I trouble you for the salt? *wir sind heute abend ausgebeten*, we are asked out *or* we have received an invitation for tonight.

ausblas–en, 1. *ir.v.a.* blow out (*a light, etc.*); blow (*an egg*); (*coll.*) *einem das Lebenslicht –en*, kill a p. 2. *v.n.* (*aux.* h.) cease blowing. **–edampf,** *m.* exhaust-steam. **–ehahn,** *m.* blow-off cock, safety-valve (*in steam-engines*).

Ausbläser, *m.* dud (= *shell with weak charge*) (*Artil.*).

ausbleiben, 1. *ir.v.n.* (*aux.* s.) stay away, fail to appear, not come, be absent; be wanting; be left out (*of a word, etc.*); not take place; *eine Gelegenheit blieb nicht lange aus*, an opportunity soon presented itself; *der Puls bleibt ihm aus*, his pulse has stopped; *deine Strafe soll nicht –*, you shall not escape punishment. 2. *n.* non-appearance, absence, non-attendance; non-arrival; – *der Zahlung*, failure to pay.

ausblenden, *v.a.* screen, shield (*Rad.*).

Ausblick, *m.* (-s) outlook, prospect, view; objective lens (*Opt.*).

ausblühen, *v.n.* (*aux.* h.) cease flowering; decay, fade, effloresce; *die Rosen haben ausgeblüht*, the roses are over.

ausblut–en, 1. *v.n.* (*aux.* h.) bleed to death; cease bleeding. 2. *v.a.* *sein Leben –*, bleed to death, die. **–ungskampf,** *m.* battle of attrition.

ausbooten, *v.a.* disembark.

ausbrech–en, 1. *ir.v.a.* break *or* force out; extract; vomit; lop, prune (*trees*); pluck *or* cut off; quarry (*stone*); shell (*peas, etc.*). 2. *v.n.* (*aux.* s.) break out (*as fire, a disease, etc.*); break loose *or* out of prison; break forth, burst out; be cut (*of teeth*); *der Angstschweiß brach ihm aus*, he broke into a cold sweat; *in Tränen –en*, burst into tears, burst out crying.

ausbreit–en, 1. *v.a.* spread, expand, stretch; spread out, extend; broaden out; lay (*tablecloth*); spread abroad, divulge, circulate, propagate; *vor einem –en*, unfold *or* display to a p. 2. *v.r.* go into details; gain ground; spread, extend; branch out, make progress; *sich über eine S. –en*, enlarge on a subject. **–ung,** *f.* spreading, extension; propagation (*of waves, Rad.*); diffusion (*of knowledge, etc.*); promulgation. **–ungsgeschwindigkeit,** *f.* velocity of propagation. **–ungsfähigkeit,** *f.* diffusibility.

ausbrennen, 1. *ir.v.a.* burn out; remove by burning; scorch; cauterize; bake, fire (*bricks, etc.*). 2. *v.n.* (*aux.* h.) cease burning, burn out, go out; (*aux.* s.) be consumed inwardly; *ausgebrannter Vulkan*, extinct volcano. 3. *n.* wear, erosion (*of gun barrel, Artil.*).

ausbringen, *ir.v.a.* bring out; take out (*stains*); hatch; launch; publish, circulate; *eine Gesundheit –*, propose a p'.s health, toast a p.

Ausbruch, *m.* (-(e)s, ¨-e) outbreak, eruption (*of a volcano*); rash (*of measles, etc.*); explosion; elopement; escape (*from prison, etc.*). **–sversuch,** *m.* attempted escape (*from prison*), sally, sortie (*Mil.*); outburst (*of passion, etc.*); *zum – kommen*, break out.

ausbrühen, *v.a.* scald thoroughly (*a vessel*).

ausbrüten, 1. *v.a.* hatch (out), incubate; brood over, plot. 2. *n.* incubation, hatching; plotting.

ausbucht–en, *v.a.* bend out, bow outwards. **–ung,** *f.* indentation; excavation; salient, protrusion.

ausbuddeln, *v.a.* (*coll.*) dig out.

ausbügeln, *v.a.* iron out.

Ausbund, *m.* (-(e)s, ¨-e) selected specimen, pick, embodiment, paragon, quintessence; *sie ist ein – von Schönheit*, she is a paragon of beauty; – *aller Schelme*, arrant knave; – *von Bosheit*, regular demon.

ausbündig, 1. *adj.* excellent, exemplary, downright. 2. *adv.* exceedingly, uncommonly; – *gelehrt*, of profound erudition.

ausbürgern, *v.a.* expatriate, deprive of citizenship.

ausbüßen, *v.a.* expiate fully, make ample amends for.

ausdampf–en, *v.n.* (*aux.* s.) evaporate. (*aux.* h.) cease steaming. **–ung,** *f.* evaporation.

ausdämpfen, *v.a.* (cause to) evaporate, steam, remove *or* clean by steam.

Ausdau–er, *f.* perseverance, persistence, assiduity, endurance. **–ern,** 1. *v.a.* endure; outlast. 2. *v.n.* (*aux.* h.) hold out, last; persevere, be steadfast; be

perennial (*Hort.*). **-ernd,** *pr.p. & adj.* persistent, persevering, steadfast, resolute; perennial (*Hort.*).
ausdehn-en, *v.a. & r.* extend, spread out; enlarge, expand; dilate, distend. **ausgedehnt,** *p.p. & adj.* expanded, extensive; *im ausgedehntesten Sinne,* in the widest sense; *weit ausgedehnt,* widespread. **-bar,** *adj.* expansible, extensible, diffusible; ductile. **-barkeit,** *f.* expansibility; extensibility; ductility. **-ung,** *f.* expansion, extension, elongation; dimension; extent, expanse; comprehension (*of a term*); dilation, distension; *-ung des Herzens,* diastole. **-ungskraft,** *f.*, **-ungsvermögen,** *n.* expansive force, elasticity. **-ungszahl,** *f.* coefficient of expansion.
ausdenk-en, *ir.v.a.* think out, follow out a train of thought; contrive, invent, conceive, devise; *sich* (*Dat.*) *etwas -en,* imagine, think of; *ich kann mir kein passendes Geschenk für ihn -en,* I cannot think of a suitable present for him. **-bar,** *adj.* conceivable, imaginable.
ausdeut-en, *v.a.* interpret, explain; *falsch -en,* misinterpret. **-ung,** *f.* construction, interpretation.
ausdienen, *v.n.* (*aux.* h.) serve (out) one's time; become superannuated; *ausgedienter Soldat,* ex-service man.
ausdörren, *v.a.* dry up, desiccate; season (*timber*).
ausdrechseln, *v.a.* turn (*on a lathe*); mould (*pottery*) (*on the wheel*); elaborate.
ausdrehen, *v.a.* turn out, turn off, switch off, put out (*a lamp, gas*).
Ausdruck, *m.* (-(e)s, ⸗e) expression; phrase, saying, term; *Gesichts-,* facial expression, looks; *Kunst-,* technical term; *veralteter -,* archaism; *überladener -,* pleonasm; *bildlicher -,* figure of speech, figurative expression; *verblümter -,* allegorical expression; *mit -,* with expression (*Mus.*); *zum - kommen,* be manifest(ed), expressed *or* revealed in; *zum - bringen,* express, give expression to. **-sleer, -slos,** *adj.* expressionless, devoid of expression, blank, vacant. **-svoll,** *adj.* full of expression, expressive, significant. **-weise,** *f.* expression, style.
ausdrucken, *v.a.* print in full; finish printing.
ausdrück-en, *v.a.* press *or* squeeze out; express, utter; *nicht mit Worten auszudrücken,* inexpressible. **-lich,** *adj.* express, positive, explicit, intentional; *-licher Befehl,* strict order, special injunction.
Ausdunst, *m.* (-es, ⸗e) evaporation, exhalation; perspiration. **-en,** *v.n.* (*aux.* s.) evaporate, pass off in vapour. **-ung,** *f.* perspiration, evaporation, exhalation.
ausdünst-en, *v.a. & n. see* **ausdunsten. -ung,** *f see* **Ausdunstung.**
auseinander, *adv.* apart; asunder; separately. **-bringen,** *ir.v.a.*, **-tun,** *ir.v.a.* separate suddenly; **-fahren,** *v.n.* scatter (*of crowds*); diverge; *-fahrende Strahlen,* divergent rays. **-fallen,** *v.n.* fall to pieces. **-falten,** *v.a.* unfold. **-gehen,** *v.n.* separate, diverge, differ; disperse, break up; come *or* get loose. **-halten,** *v.a.* distinguish between, keep apart. **-legen,** *v.a.* display; take to pieces; explain. **-nehmen,** *v.a.* dismantle, take apart (*or* to pieces), strip. **-setzen,** *v.a.* discuss, explain, set forth, analyse; *sich mit einem -setzen,* come to terms *or* to an understanding with a p. **-setzung,** *f.* statement, explanation; discussion, argument, altercation. **-sprengen,** *v.a.* disperse. **-ziehen,** *v.a.* pull apart; deploy (*Mil.*).
auserkoren, *adj.* (*Poet.*) chosen, elect, selected.
auserlesen, *p.p. & adj.* picked, selected, select, choice, exquisite.
ausersehen, *ir.v.a.* choose, select, pick out; single out, destine.
auserwähl-en, *v.a.* select, choose; predestine; *die -ten,* the elect; *seine -te,* his intended wife.
ausessen, *ir.v.a.* eat up; pay *or* suffer for (*faults*).
ausfahr-en, 1. *ir.v.a.* take out for a drive; *ausgefahrener Weg,* bad *or* bumpy road. 2. *v.n.* (*aux.* s.) drive out, go for a drive; put to sea; emerge; ascend (*the shaft*) (*Min.*); break out (*as an eruption*); *-ende Lichtstrahlen,* emergent rays; *der Fuß fuhr mir aus,* my foot slipped. **-t,** *f.* drive, gateway; opening (*of a bay*); going out (*in a boat*), sailing; leaving (*a pit, a harbour*); setting out, departure; excursion. **-schacht,** *m.* ascent shaft (*Min.*).
Ausfall, *m.* (-(e)s, ⸗e) 1. falling off; deficiency, deficit, shortage, loss; falling out; shedding; (*Chem.*) precipitation, precipitate; (*Med.*) prolapse, dislocation; (*pl.*) casualties. 2. sally, sortie; pass, lunge; attack; invective. 3. result (*of an enterprise*); issue. **-en,** 1. *ir.v.n.* (*aux.* s.) drop out; be omitted, be deducted; fail to take place; become a casualty (*Mil. etc.*); come out *or* off; sally forth, make a sortie; attack, lunge; (*fig.*) inveigh against; turn out, result; (*Chem.*) precipitate, be deposited; *das Bild ist gut ausgefallen,* the picture has turned out well; *es fiel gegen ihn aus,* it went against him; *er fiel gegen die Zeitung aus,* he attacked the newspaper; *die Schule fällt heute aus,* there is no school today. 2. *n.* (*Chem.*) precipitation. **-end,** *adj.* aggressive, insulting. **-leiter,** *f.* scaling ladder. **-spforte,** *f.*, **-(s)tor,** *n.* postern-gate; sally-port. **-straße,** *f.* arterial road. **-winkel** *m.* angle of reflection (*Opt.*).
ausfäll-en, *v.a.* (*Chem.*) separate, precipitate. **-ig,** *adj.* aggressive, insulting. **-ung,** *f.* (*Chem.*) precipitation.
ausfasern, *v.a.* unravel.
ausfertig-en, *v.a.* draw up (*a deed, report, etc.*); make out (*bills, etc.*); execute (*an order*); carry out (*a plan*); equip, fit out; (*C.L.*) dispatch, expedite; *einen Paß -en,* issue *or* make out a passport; *ein Gesetz -en,* engross law. **-ung,** *f.* drawing up, execution (*of a deed, etc.*); dispatch (*of business*); issuing (*of an order*); engrossment (*of a law*); *in dreifacher -ung,* in triplicate. **-ungstag,** *m.* date (*of issue, of dispatch*).
ausfind-en, (*usually* **-ig machen**) *ir.v.a.* find out, seek out, discover; *ein Mittel -ig machen,* devise an expedient. **-bar,** *adj.* discoverable.
ausflicken, *v.a.* patch up, repair.
ausfliegen, *ir.v.n.* (*aux.* s.) (*coll.*) fly out; escape, run away; leave home; make an excursion; *er ist eben erst ausgeflogen,* he has just now left home.
ausfließen, *ir.v.n.* (*aux.* s.) flow out, run out, discharge; issue, emanate (from).
Ausflucht, *f.* (⸗e) excuse; evasion, shift, subterfuge, loophole; *elende* or *kahle -,* paltry *or* lame excuse; *Ausflüchte machen* (or *suchen*), look for excuses, prevaricate, dodge, shuffle.
Ausflug, *m.* (-(e)s, ⸗e) ramble, trip, excursion, outing; first flight (*of young birds*); entrance (*to a beehive*); *einen - machen,* go for (*or* on) an excursion.
Ausflügler, *m.* (*coll.*) tourist, excursionist, tripper.
Ausfluß, *m.* (-(ss)es, ⸗(ss)e) outflow; discharge; secretion, flux; effluence, emanation; outlet, mouth (*of a river*).
ausfolg-en, *v.a. & n.*; *einem etwas -en* or *-en lassen,* deliver up a th. to s.o., have a th. handed over to a p. **-eschein,** *m.* bill of delivery.
ausfordern, *see* **herausfordern.**
ausforsch-en, *v.a.* search out, inquire after; explore, investigate; hunt out; trace; *einen -en* (*coll.*) pump a p.; *jemandes Meinungen -en,* sound a p. (*as to his views, etc.*). **-ung,** *f.* investigation; inquiry, exploration; sifting; prying out. **-ungsmethode,** *f.* method of investigation.
ausfragen, *v.a.* question, interrogate, examine, sound, pump (*a p.*).
ausfressen, *ir.v.a.* corrode, eat up; (*coll.*) do s.th. forbidden; get into mischief; (*coll.*) *was hat er ausgefressen?* what has he been up to? (*coll.*) *der Junge hat wieder einmal etwas ausgefressen,* the boy has been up to mischief again.
ausfrieren, *ir.v.n.* (*aux.* s.) freeze up thoroughly, congeal; (*aux.* h.) cease to freeze.
Ausfuhr, *f.* export; exportation; *zur - geeignet,* exportable. **-abgabe,** *f.* export duty. **-artikel,** *m.pl.* exports; export goods; **-bewilligung,** *f.* export permit. **-frei,** *adj.* free of export duty. **-handel,** *m.* export trade. (*C.L.*) **-prämie,** *f.* bounty, drawback. **-schein,** *m.* export permit; docket, bill of sufferance. **-waren,** *f.pl.* exports. **-zoll,** *m.* export duty.
ausführ-en, *v.a.* 1. put into effect, execute, carry out, perform; realize; work out; fulfil (*an engagement*); prosecute (*a scheme*); finish (*a picture, a building*); pursue (*a subject*); amplify, enlarge on (*a description*); play (*a part*); 2. export; lead out, take

out; 3. purge, evacuate. **-bar,** *adj.* practicable, feasible; exportable. **-barkeit,** *f.* practicability. **-er,** *m.* exporter; finisher; executor. **-gang,** *m.* excretory duct. **-lich,** 1. *adj.* detailed, circumstantial, full, ample; *-liche Erzählung*, full account. 2. *adv.* in detail, circumstantially, fully, minutely, completely; *-lich schreiben*, write fully. **-lichkeit,** *f.* fullness of detail; completeness, copiousness. **-ung** *f.* 1. execution (*of an order*); accomplishment, realization (*of a plan*); completion (*of a building, etc.*); performance (*of a play, etc.*); fulfilment (*of a contract, etc.*); perpetration (*Law*); prosecution (*of a scheme, etc.*); 2. statement, explanation, exposition (*of a plan* or *scheme*); 3. style, finish, execution, (*C.L.*) quality, description; 4. exportation; 5. excretion, evacuation; *zur -ung bringen*, put into practice, carry into effect. **-ungsmittel,** *n.* purgative.

ausfüll-en, *v.a.* fill out; stuff, pad, make complete; fill up (*time, a form, etc.*); fill (*a place*); supply (*a deficit*). **-masse,** *f.* **-stoff,** *m.* stuff; filling, packing, padding, stuffing. **-ung,** *f.* filling up, completion; filling out, padding.

ausfütter-n, *v.a.* feed up, fatten; line, coat, stuff. **-ung,** *f.* lining; stuffing, padding.

Ausgabe, *f.* 1. expenses, outlay, outgoings, expenditure; issue, publication; delivery (*of letters, etc.*); distribution; *- und Einnahme in Übereinstimmung bringen*, make receipts balance expenses, make both ends meet. **-buch,** *n.* cash-book. **-rechnung** *f.* calculation of expenditure. **-stelle,** *f.* issuing office (*or* depot).

Ausgang, *m.* (-(e)s, ⸚e) departure; exit, outlet, vent, issue, passage out, way out; result, upshot, dénouement, termination, end, ending, close; one's afternoon *or* evening *or* day out, time off (*from duty*); starting-point; *klingender -*, feminine ending (*Metr.*); *stumpfer -*, masculine ending (*Metr.*); *einen - machen*, take a walk; *der Fluß hat drei Ausgänge*, the river branches into three forks; *Unglücksfall mit tödlichem -*, accident with fatal consequences. **-sform,** *f.* initial *or* original form. **-sfront,** *f.* initial position (*Mil.*). **-spunkt,** *m.* point of departure, starting-point. **-szoll,** *m.* export duty.

ausgearbeitet, *adj.* worn out, scrapped (*as tools, etc.*).

ausgeb-en, 1. *ir.v.a.* give out, distribute; deliver (*letters*); deal (*cards*); issue (*bank-notes, proclamations, etc.*); spend (*money*); give (*the word, Mil.*); start, set on foot (*a rumour*). 2. *v.r.; sich für adlig -en*, pass o.s. off for a nobleman; *sich -en*, spend all one has (*energy or money*). 3. *v.n.* (*aux.* h.) produce, yield, bring in; *das Korn gibt nicht aus*, the corn falls short. **-er,** *m.* distributor; drawer (*of a bill, etc.*); utterer (*of a cheque, etc.*); dispenser (*of drugs*).

Ausgebot, *n.* (-(e)s, -e) putting up for sale; first bid (*at an auction*).

Ausgeburt, *f.* (-en) offspring, product; abortion; *- der Hölle*, fiend; diabolical scheme.

Ausgedinge, *n.* reservation, rights reserved.

ausgeglichen, *see* **ausgleichen.**

ausgeh-en, *ir.v.n.* (*aux.* s.) go out; proceed, start, emanate; fail, come to an end, be exhausted, give out (*of wine in a barrel*), run out *or* run short (*of provisions*); come out (*as stains*); fall out (*of hair*); fade (*of colours*); be spent (*of money, etc.*); end in; expire (*of time*); die, wither (*of plants*); aim at; result, terminate; ramify (*Anat.*). *frei -en*, go free; *einen Befehl -en lassen*, issue a decree; *er ist leer ausgegangen*, he has gone away empty-handed; (*B.*) *der heilige Geist geht vom Vater und Sohne aus*, the Holy Ghost proceedeth from the Father and the Son; *ich gehe von dem Grundsatze aus*, I start from the principle that; *-en auf eine S.*, aim at s.th., be bent on s.th.; *auf Bettel -en*, go a-begging; *er ging darauf aus, mich zu ärgern*, his object was to annoy me; *er schwatzte, bis ihm der Atem ausging*, he talked till he was out of breath; *die Geduld geht mir aus*, I lose all patience; *das Wort geht auf ein* s *aus*, the word ends in *s*; *wie wird diese S. -?* how will this matter end? **-anzug,** *m.* lounge-suit; walking-out dress (*Mil.*). **-end,** *pr.p.* & *adj.* outgoing; proceeding; salient (*of an angle*); *-de Waren*, export goods.

ausgenießen, *ir.v.a.* enjoy to the utmost, enjoy thoroughly.

ausgestalt-en, *v.a.* shape, frame, elaborate, develop. **-ung,** *f.* shaping; arrangement of details.

ausgewitzt, *adj.* cunning, wily.

ausgezeichnet, *p.p.* & *adj.* excellent, capital; distinguished.

ausgiebig, 1. *adj.* plentiful, rich, abundant, productive, fertile. 2. *adv.*; *- benutzen*, make full *or* abundant use of.

ausgieß-en, *ir.v.a.* pour out, discharge; diffuse, shed; fill up, load (*a stick with lead*); *die Schale des Zornes über einen -en*, vent one's anger on a p.; *das Kind mit dem Bade -en*, throw away the good with the bad, act without discernment. **-ung,** *f.* effusion; libation; (*B.*) descent *or* coming (*of the Holy Ghost*).

Ausgleich, *m.* settlement, adjustment, arrangement, agreement; compensation, equalization; handicap (*Sport*). **-düse,** *f.* compensating jet (*on a carburettor*). **-en,** *ir.v.a.* make even, equalize; compensate, adjust, make up for (*a loss, etc.*); level; balance; settle (*a dispute, etc.*); harmonize (*differences*); balance (*accounts*); *die Mißverständnisse sind ausgeglichen*, the misunderstandings have been smoothed over; *womit Sie meine Rechnung -en wollen*, balancing thereby my account; *-ende Persönlichkeit*, well-balanced personality; *-endes Wesen*, harmonious nature. **-end,** *pr.p.* & *adj.* compensatory. **-er,** *m.* adjuster; reconciler. **-sgetriebe,** *n.* differential gear (*Engin.*); compensator. **-stelle,** *f.* (*Nat. Soc.*) office for allocation of contracts. **-ung,** *f.* settlement; equalization, adjustment; compensation, balancing, levelling; balance; accommodation, arrangement; *zur -ung dieses Gegenstandes*, in order to close this transaction. **-ungsversuch,** *m.* attempt to bring about a settlement. **-szulage,** *f.* compensation allowance.

ausgleiten, *ir.v.n.* (*aux.* s.) slip, slide.

ausglimmen, *ir.v.n.* (*aux.* h.) go out gradually (*of lights*).

ausglitschen, *v.n.* (*aux.* s.) (*coll.*) = **ausgleiten.**

ausglühen, *v.a.* temper, anneal (*Metall.*).

ausgrab-en, *ir.v.a.* dig up *or* out; disinter, exhume; excavate, unearth; engrave. **-ung,** *f.* excavation.

ausgreifen, 1. *ir.v.a.* pick out (*of a number*); handle, feel. 2. *v.n.* (*aux.* h.) stretch; step out. **-d,** *adj.* extensive; *weit -d*, far-reaching.

Ausguck, *m.* (-s, -e) look-out (*Naut.* & *Mil.*). **-posten,** *m.* observation post.

Ausguß, *m.* (-(ss)es, ⸚(ss)e) effusion, outpouring, sink, gutter, drain; spout (*of a vessel*). **-leitung,** *f.* discharge pipe. **-masse,** *f.* liquid (*or* semi-liquid) compound. **-pfännchen,** *n.* ingot-mould, **-rinnen,** *f.pl.*, **-röhren,** *f.pl.* drain-pipes.

aushacken, *v.a.* hew, hack out; scallop; rough-hew; pick out (*the eyes*).

aushalt-en, 1. *ir.v.a.* hold out, endure, bear, support, suffer; stand (*a test*); sustain (*a siege*); weather, ride out (*a storm*); sustain, prolong (*a note*); withstand (*temptation*); keep (*a mistress*); *es ist nicht zum -en*, it is not to be borne. 2. *v.n.* (*aux.* h.) endure, last, persevere, hold out; *in diesem Hause halten die Dienstboten nicht lange aus*, the servants don't stay long in this house. **-ungszeichen,** pause, hold (*Mus.*).

aushändigen, *v.a.* hand over, deliver up.

Aushang, *m.* (-(e)s, ⸚e) placard, notice; goods hung out for sale *or* show. **-en,** *ir.v.n.* (*aux.* h.) hang out be suspended.

aushäng-en, *v.a.* hang out (*a sign, a flag, etc.*); post up (*a bill*); take off its hinges (*a door*); unship (*a rudder*); make a show of. **-ebogen,** *m.* proof sheet, advance proof (*Typ.*). **-eschild,** *n.* sign-board, sign; pretence, false show; *unter dem -eschild freisinniger Gedanken*, under the pretence of liberal ideas.

ausharr-en, *v.n.* (*aux.* h.) endure to the end; persevere, persist, wait, hold out. **-ung,** *f.* perseverance.

Aushauch, *m.* act of exhaling; exhalation; breath;

Forms of p.p. in **ausge-** *not found here should be sought under inf.*

fume. **-en,** *v.a.* exhale; *seine Seele -en, den Geist -en,* breathe one's last, expire.
aushauen, *ir.v.a.* lop (*trees*); thin (*a forest*); hew out, carve, engrave (*an inscription*); *ausgehauenes Kohlenfeld,* exhausted coalfield.
aushäuten, 1. *v.a.* skin, flay. 2. *v.r.* cast one's skin.
ausheb-en, *ir.v.a.* lift out *or* up; *einen Posten -en,* capture a post (*Mil.*); take *or* dig up (*a plant, etc.*); take off the hinges (*of a door, etc.*); draw out (*with a siphon*); pick out, select; call in, enlist (*recruits*); *sich den Arm -en,* dislocate one's arm; *ein Ausgehobener,* recruit; *die Uhr hebt zum Schlagen aus,* the clock is on the point of striking. **-er,** *m.* ratchet (*Horol.*); trowel; recruiting officer. **-espan,** *m.* composing-stick (*Typ.*). **-ung,** *f.* levy, conscription, draft, recruitment.
aushebern, *v.a.* siphon off.
aushecken, *v.a.* hatch, plot, brew, concoct, devise, contrive; (*Prov.*) *eine Taube heckt keinen Adler aus,* you can't make a silk purse out of a sow's ear.
aushelf-en, *ir.v.n.* (*aux.* h.) help out, aid, assist; accommodate, supply **with**. **-er,** *m.* help, helper; occasional assistant.
ausheilen, *v.a. & n.* heal up; cure completely.
Aushilf-e, *f.* (-en) (temporary *or* improvised) aid *or* assistance; stopgap, makeshift, improvisation. **-slehrer,** *m.* temporary teacher. **-sschauspieler,** *m.* understudy. **-sstellung,** *f.* temporary post. **-sweise,** *adv.* temporarily, as a makeshift.
aushöhl-en, *v.a.* hollow out, excavate; groove, chamfer, flute; undermine; burrow. **ausgehöhlt,** *p.p. & adj.* striate (*Bot.*). **-ung,** *f.* excavation; grooving, fluting, (*of a column, etc.*).
ausholen, 1. *v.a.* obtain information; *einen -,* sound *or* pump a p. 2. *v.n.* (*aux.* h.) lift *or* swing the arm (*for throwing, striking, etc.*); *zu einem Sprunge -,* take a run before jumping, swing, make an enveloping movement (*Mil.*); *weit -,* go far back (*in narrating anything*).
aushorchen, *v.a.* sound, pump.
aushören, *v.a.* hear out, hear to the end.
Aushub, *m.* (-(e)s) levy; choice; excavated material.
aushülsen, *v.a.* shell (*peas, etc.*); husk, peel.
aushungern, *v.a.* starve out; starve.
ausjäten, *v.a.* weed out.
auskämmen, *v.a.* comb out (*manpower, undesirable elements, etc.*), mop up.
Auskauf, *m.* (-(e)s, ⸚e) buying out *or* up; outbidding; ransom. **-en,** *v.a.* buy up, buy out, buy the whole stock; forestall, outbid; *die Zeit -en,* make the most of one's time; *die Gelegenheit -en,* improve the occasion.
auskehl-en, *v.a.* channel, groove, chamfer, flute. **-ung,** *f.* fluting, grooving; chamfer.
auskehr-en, *v.a.* sweep out, sweep clean.
auskeilen, 1. *v.a.* fit *or* provide with wedges; wedge out, squeeze out, pinch out. 2. *v.r. & n.* (*aux.* h.) end in a wedge; peter out, crop out (*Geol.*); *der Gang keilt* (*sich*) *aus,* the lode peters out. (*v.n. only*) kick (*as a horse*).
auskeimen, *v.n.* (*aux.* s.) germinate; cease germinating.
auskeltern, *v.a.* press out (*wine*).
auskennen, *ir.v.a. & r.* know where one is, know one's way about; know about, know what's what; *ich kenne mich nicht mehr aus,* (*coll.*) I am stumped *or* at a loss.
auskerben, *v.a.* notch, indent; mill (*the edge of a coin*). **ausgekerbt,** *p.p. & adj.* engrailed (*Her.*); serrated; crenated (*Bot.*).
auskernen, *v.a.* stone (*fruit*); take out the kernel; shell (*nuts*).
ausklagen, 1. *v.a.* sue for, prosecute. 2. *v.r.* relate all one's grievances.
Ausklang, *m.* (-(e)s, ⸚e) end, termination.
ausklatschen, *v.a.* blab (*or* blurt) out; cease chattering.
ausklauben, *v.a.* pick out *or* over, sort, separate; think out in detail, puzzle out, contrive, devise.
auskleid-en, 1. *v.a.* undress; *-en helfen,* assist in undressing; line, coat, equip; disguise, decorate. 2. *v.r.* take off one's clothes. **-ezimmer,** *n.* dressing-room. **-ung,** *f.* act of undressing; disguise; lining.
ausklingen, *ir.v.n.* (*aux.* h.) cease to sound, die away (*as an echo*); (*fig.*) end in; *die Rede klang in ein Hoch aus,* the speech ended in *or* with cheers.
ausklinken, *v.n.* release (*glider from towing plane*) (*Av.*).
ausklopf-en, *v.a.* beat out (*as dust*); thrash; **-er,** *m.* carpet-beater.
ausklügeln, *v.a.* puzzle out, reason ingeniously, discover after shrewd but hypercritical inquiry.
auskneifen, *v.n.* (*sl.*) do a bunk, hook it, make o.s. scarce.
ausknobeln, *v.a.* settle by dicing; toss for.
auskochen, 1. *v.a.* extract by boiling; decoct; boil thoroughly; scald (*a vessel*). 2. *v.n.* (*aux.* s.) boil over *or* away; (*aux.* h.) cease boiling. **ausgekocht,** *p.p. & adj.,* extracted; (*fig.*) out and out, thorough-paced.
auskommen, 1. *ir.v.n.* (*aux.* s.) 1. come *or* go out; break out (*of fire*); break out of the shell; sprout; become public, be noised abroad; 2. get away, escape; hold good, answer the purpose; 3. agree, live peacefully with, get on with (*a p.*); make do, manage (with), get by (with); *ich kann unmöglich damit -,* I can't possibly manage with so little; *er wird mit dieser Entschuldigung nicht -,* this excuse will not help him. **2.** *n.* act of getting out; peaceable intercourse; livelihood, living; income, subsistence, sufficiency, competence; *ein - treffen,* come to some agreement, find ways and means; *ein gutes - haben,* be well off.
auskömmlich, *adj.* sufficient; *-es Gehalt,* living wage.
auskoppeln, cf. *auskuppeln.*
auskosten, *v.a.* enjoy to the full.
auskramen, *v.a.* display; expose for sale; make a parade of; rummage through, turn out (*a drawer*).
auskratzen, 1. *v.a.* scratch out, erase. 2. *v.n.* (*aux.* s.) (*sl.*) run away, hook it.
auskühlen, *v.a. & n.* (*aux.* s.) cool thoroughly.
Auskult-ant, *m.* (-en, -en) auscultator (*Med.*); young lawyer attending court. **-ation,** *f.* auscultation. **-ator,** *m.* (-s, -en) = **-ant** (*Law*). **-ieren,** *v.a.* auscultate, use the stethoscope; practise auscultation (*Med.*); listen, attend, sit in (*at a court of law*).
auskundschaften, *v.a.* explore; reconnoitre; spy out, ferret out.
Auskunft, *f.* (⸚e), information; intelligence; particulars; *ich fragte ihn um nähere - über,* I asked him for fuller particulars as to. **-ei,** *f.* information bureau, inquiry office. **-sbureau,** *n.* *see* **-ei,** **-smittel,** *n.* expedient, resource. **-stelle,** *f.* information bureau.
auskünsteln, *v.a.* invent, contrive (*with subtlety, with too great art*); elaborate.
auskuppeln, *v.a. & n.* uncouple, disengage, disconnect; declutch, put into neutral gear (*Motor.*).
auslachen, 1. *v.a.* laugh at; deride, laugh to scorn 2. *v.r.* laugh one's fill.
auslad-en, 1. *ir.v.a.* unload; discharge; disembark, land, detrain (*troops*); withdraw *or* cancel an invitation. 2. *v.n.* (*aux.* h.) (*Arch.*) project (*as ornament from a façade*); *-ende Gesten,* expansive *or* sweeping gesture. **-ebrücke,** *f.* jetty, pier. **-ebahnhof,** *m.,* **-erampe,** *f.* railhead. **-ekosten,** *f.pl.* charges for unloading. **-eort,** *m.* port of discharge; landing-place, wharf, quay. **-er,** *m.* lighterman, stevedore; unloader, dock-hand; discharging rod (*Phys.*). **-estation,** *f.* **-estelle,** *f.* place of disembarkation (detraining, debussing, *Mil.*). **-ung,** *f.* unloading; drawing (*of a gun-charge*); projection (*Arch.*).
Auslage, *f.* (-n) outlay, expenses; (*C.L.*) advance; stall, showcase (*for exposure of wares*); exhibit, display (*in shop windows*); guard (*Fenc.*); *die - wieder erstatten,* reimburse; *es lohnt die -n nicht,* it does not pay; *persönliche -n,* out-of-pocket expenses. **-fenster,** *n.* shop-window, show-case.
Ausland, *n.* (-(e)s) foreign country, foreign parts; *im -e,* abroad; *In- und -,* at home and abroad; *Waren vom -e,* foreign goods. **-samt,** *n.* office for giving help and information to aliens. **-sdeutsche(r),** *m.* person of German stock living abroad. **-sdeutschtum,** *n.* those of German stock living abroad. **-spaß,** *m.* passport for abroad. **-swechsel,** *m.* foreign bill.

Ausländ-er, *m.* (-ers, -er) foreigner, alien. **-erei,** *f.* predilection for things foreign; affectation of foreign ways. **-isch,** *adj.* foreign, alien; exotic (*Bot.*).
auslangen, *v.n.* (*aux.* h.) be sufficient, suffice, do; *mit etwas* –, make shift with; *zum Streiche* –, raise the arm to strike; *diese Summe wird schwerlich* –, this sum will scarcely be sufficient; *du wirst mit dieser Entschuldigung nicht* –, this excuse will not help you.
Auslaß, *m.* (-(ss)es, ⸗(ss)e) outlet. **-röhre,** *f.* discharge-pipe.
auslass-en, 1. *ir.v.a.* let out, let go, release; discharge, emit; let off; give vent to; leave out, omit; overlook; melt, render down (*Cook.*); widen, let out, let down (*Dressmaking*); *seine Wut an einem -en*, vent one's anger on a p. **ausgelassen,** *p.p.* & *adj.* wild, unruly, exuberant, unrestrained; gay, frolicsome, wanton. **Ausgelassenheit,** *f.* exuberance, wildness, boisterousness, wantonness, dissoluteness; *ausgelassene Butter*, melted butter. 2. *v.r.* express o.s.; speak one's mind; *er ließ sich nicht weiter aus*, he did not explain himself further. **-ung** *f.* letting out; leaving out, excluding, omission; ellipse, ellipsis (*Rhet.*); elision; expression of opinion, utterance, remark(s). **-ungszeichen,** *n.* apostrophe; mark of elision.
Auslauf, *m.* (-(e)s, ⸗e) running out, leakage; effusion, outflow; projection; continuation, offshoot; mouth (*of a river*); outlet; hen-run; take-off (*or* landing) run (*Av.*); the finish, the tape (*Sport*). **-en,** *ir.v.n.* (*aux.* s.) run *or* flow out, leak; discharge itself into; put to sea, clear a port; spread, run; project (*Arch.*); branch out, diverge; come to an end, run down, cease running (*hour-glass*); *Befehl zum -en*, sailing orders; *die Erbsen laufen aus*, the peas drop (out of the pods); *dünn -en*, taper off; *spitz -en*, end in a point; (*aux.* h.) (*fig.*) end in; *die ganze S. ist auf einen Scherz ausgelaufen*, the whole matter ended in a joke. **-end,** *adj.* outward bound (*Naut.*); **-platz,** *m.* starting-place.
Ausläufer, *m.* errand-boy; printer's devil; sucker, runner, offshoot, stole, stolon (*of plants*); spur (*of a mountain-chain*); branch, ramification.
auslaugen, *v.a.* wash *or* steep in lye; leach, lixiviate, clear of lye.
Auslaut, *m.* (-(e)s) final sound (*at the end of a word or a syllable*); *im* –, when final, at the end (*of a word or a syllable*). **-en,** *v.n.* (*aux.* h.) end in (*a letter or a sound*); *die Wurzelsilbe lautet auf einen Konsonanten aus*, the root-syllable ends in a consonant. **-end,** *pr.p.* & *adj.* final.
ausleben, 1. *v.a.* live to the end of. 2. *v.r.* enjoy life to the full, live a full life. 3. *v.n.* (*aux.* h.) cease to live, die.
ausleer-en, *v.a.* empty; drain, evacuate, clear out (*a room, etc.*); purge (*Med.*); *sich* (*Dat.*) *das Herz -en*, pour out one's heart. **-ung,** *f.* emptying out; clearing, draining; motion *or* action of the bowels, evacuation (*Med.*); excretion. **-ungsmittel,** *n.* purgative, evacuant.
ausleg-en, 1. *v.a.* lay out (*money, etc.*), spend; spread out, display; inlay, veneer, lay (*tiles, etc.*); explain, expound, interpret. 2. *v.r.* stand on guard (*Fenc.*); *eine Stelle falsch -en*, misinterpret a passage; *etwas zum besten -en*, put the best construction on a th.; *es wurde ihm als Stolz ausgelegt*, it was set down to his pride; *Geld auf Zinsen -en*, put money out at interest. **-er,** *m.* expositor, expounder, commentator; jib, beam (*of a crane*); outrigger (*Naut.*). **-ung,** *f.* exposition, construction, interpretation, explanation, exegesis; laying out (*of money*); *buchstäbliche -ung*, literal interpretation.
ausleih-en, *ir.v.a.* lend (out), hire out; *sich* (*Dat.*) *etwas -en*, borrow s.th. **-bibliothek,** *f.* lending library.
auslernen, *v.a.* & *n.* (*aux.* h.) finish one's apprenticeship; finish learning; *man lernt nie aus*, there is always something new to learn, one is never too old to learn. **ausgelernt,** *p.p.* & *adj.* experienced, practised.
Ausles-e, *f.* (-n) selection. assortment, choice; élite, flower, the best, the pick; the choicest wine (= *from selected grapes*). **-en,** *ir.v.a.* select, choose, pick out; sort; read through *or* to the end.
auslichten, *v.a.* clear, thin (*a wood*); prune (*trees*).
ausliefer-n, *v.a.* hand over, deliver *or* give up, relinquish. **-ung,** *f.* surrender, extradition (*of a criminal, etc.*); delivery. **-ungsantrag,** *m.* requisition. **-ungsschein,** *m.* bill of delivery. **-ungsvertrag,** *m.* extradition treaty.
ausliegen, *ir.v.n.* lie out, be displayed for inspection *or* sale; be exhibited; be on show; be generally accessible; (*Fenc.*) be in position.
[1]**auslöschen,** *ir.v.n.* (*aux.* s.). *See* **erlöschen.**
[2]**auslösch-en,** *v.a.* put out, extinguish, quench; efface, obliterate, erase, wipe out, blot out; pay off (*a debt*). **-ung,** *f.* effacement, obliteration, extinction.
auslosen, *v.a.* draw (lots) for; raffle.
auslös-en, *v.a.* 1. loosen, draw out, release; cut out; throw out of gear; 2. redeem (*a pledge*); ransom (*a prisoner*); 3. cause, induce, produce; arouse (*enthusiasm*); awaken, kindle. **-er,** *m.* release, trigger (*Phot.*). **-ung,** *f.* release, redemption; ransom; reimbursement; dislocation; ratchet (*Horol.*); automatic release.
auslüften, *v.a.* air, ventilate.
Auslug, *m.* (-(e)s, -e) look-out (*Naut.*).
ausmachen, *v.a.* 1. shell (*peas, etc.*); open (*oysters*); draw (*poultry*); gut (*fish, etc.*); extinguish, put out (*fire, etc.*); 2. make up, constitute, amount to, come to. 3. decide, arrange, determine; agree upon, settle (*a dispute*); reconnoitre (*Mil.*), find the range (*Artil.*); *es macht nichts aus*, it does not matter; *wir haben es so ausgemacht*, we have settled the matter this way; *was hast du mit ihm auszumachen?* what have you to arrange with him? *einem einen Dienst* –, procure a p. employment; *sie mögen es mit einander* –, let them fight it out between themselves. **ausgemacht,** *p.p.* & *adj.* settled, certain, sure, decided, determined on; *es ist eine ausgemachte Sache*, it is a settled affair; *für ausgemacht annehmen*, take for granted; *was ist ausgemacht worden?* what has been decided on? *ausgemachte Wahrheit*, undeniable truth; *ausgemachter Narr*, downright fool; *ausgemachter Schurke*, confirmed *or* out-and-out rascal. **-d,** *pr.p.* & *adj.* constituent; amounting to.
ausmalen, *v.a.* paint; colour; illuminate; finish (*a picture*); (*fig.*) depict, describe; *sich* (*Dat.*) *etwas* –, imagine s.th. (*in detail*).
Ausmarsch, *m.* (-es, ⸗e) marching out, departure (*of troops*). **-ieren,** *v.n.* (*aux.* s.) march out.
Ausmaß, *n.* (-es, -e) measure; degree, extent; scale, proportion; *in großem -e*, to a great extent.
ausmauern, *v.a.* line with bricks *or* masonry; wall up.
ausmergeln, *v.a.* enervate; exhaust, impoverish (*land*); debilitate, emaciate; *ausgemergelter Wüstling*, worn-out rake.
ausmerz-en, *v.a.* efface, scratch out; reject, suppress, eliminate, expurgate; take away, reject (*Math.*). **-ung,** *f.* abolition, abrogation; elimination, suppression, effacement, proscription.
ausmess-en, *ir.v.a.* measure out; take the dimensions of; survey; gauge. **-er,** *m.* measurer; surveyor. **-ung,** *f.* measuring, measurement; survey; gauging; *die -ung eines Schiffes nehmen*, take a ship's bearings, fix a ship's position.
ausmieten, *v.a.* let out on hire.
ausmisten, *v.a.* cast out the dung, remove the manure, cleanse (*a stable*).
ausmitteln, *v.a.* find out, ascertain; take the average of (*Math.*).
ausmittig, *adj.* eccentric (*Tech.*).
ausmöblieren, *v.a.* fit up, furnish.
ausmünd-en, *v.r.* & *n.* (*aux.* h.) empty, discharge itself, flow, open (into). **-ung,** *f.* mouth (*of a river*), orifice, outlet.
ausmustern, *v.a.* sort out; discharge, reject (*soldiers*); discard, scrap.
Ausnahm-e, *f.* (-en) exception; *ohne -e*, without exception, absolutely. **-eerscheinung,** *f.*, **-efall,** *m.* exceptional case, exception. **-ezustand,** *m.* state of emergency (*Pol.*). **-slos,** *adj.* universal, without exception, invariable, admitting of no exception. **-sweise,** *adv.* by way of exception, exceptionally.

ausnehm-en, 1. *ir.v.a.* take out; draw (*a fowl, a tooth*); except, exclude, exempt; select; *er nimmt alles auf Borg aus,* he takes everything on credit. 2. *v.r.* look, appear; *sich schlecht -en,* look bad, show up ill; *diese Farbe nimmt sich sehr gut aus,* this colour looks very well. **ausgenommen,** *p.p., adj., & prep.* except; excepting, with the exception of, save, barring. **-end,** 1. *pr.p. & adj.* exceptional, extraordinary, uncommon, exceeding. 2. *adv.* exceedingly.

ausnutz-en, *v.a.* wear out; utilize fully, follow up (*a success*), exploit, make the most of, make good use of, take advantage of, turn to account. **-ung,** *f.* utilization, exploitation.

ausnützen = ausnutzen.

auspacken, *v.a.* unpack.

auspeitschen, *v.a.* whip, flog.

auspfänd-en, *v.a.* seize for debt, destrain. **-er,** *m.* distrainer. **-ung,** *f.* distraint.

auspfeifen, *ir.v.a.* hiss (*a play*) off the stage; condemn by hissing.

auspflanzen, *v.a.* plant out, bed out, transplant.

auspichen, *v.a.* coat the inside with pitch. **ausgepicht,** *p.p. & adj.* hardened, seasoned; *ausgepichte Kehle,* well-seasoned throat (*i.e. likes strong drink*); *ausgepichter Magen,* stomach of an ostrich (*i.e. a strong digestion*); (*coll.*) *ausgepichte Gurgel haben,* be a hard drinker.

Auspizien, *n.pl.* auspices.

ausplaudern, 1. *v.a.* divulge, let out (*secrets, etc.*), blab. 2. *v.r.* have a good long chat.

ausplünder-n, *v.a.* pillage, plunder; empty, strip, desolate by plunder. **-er,** *m.* plunderer.

auspolstern, *v.a.* stuff, pad, line; upholster.

ausposaunen, *v.a.* trumpet forth, blazon forth; make universally known; *seinen eignen Ruhm –,* blow one's own trumpet.

ausprägen, 1. *v.a.* stamp, impress; coin. 2. *v.r.* be distinctly marked, strike the eye. **ausgeprägt,** *p.p. & adj.* pronounced, distinct, strongly marked, defined, decided.

auspressen, *v.a.* crush *or* squeeze out; extort, force from.

ausprob-en, -ieren, *v.a.* test, try out, taste.

Auspuff, *m.* exhaust (*Engin.*). **-klappe,** *f.* exhaust valve; **-hub,** *m.*, **-takt,** *m.* exhaust stroke. (*Veh.*). **-rohr,** *n.* **-röhre,** *f.* exhaust-pipe. **-topf,** *m.* silencer.

auspumpen, *v.a.* pump out; exhaust, evacuate.

auspusten, *v.a.* blow out (*candle, etc.*).

Ausputz, *m.* ornamentation, ornaments; trimming. **-en,** 1. *v.a.* adorn, decorate; clean, cleanse, clean out, sweep out; polish up; snuff out (*a candle*); prune (*trees*). 2. *v.r.* deck o.s. out, dress up.

ausquartieren, *v.a.* billet out.

ausradieren, *v.a.* erase, rub out, scratch out.

ausrändeln, ausranden, ausränden, *v.a.* surround with a beading; jag the edges; *ausgerändete Blätter,* crenated leaves (*Bot.*).

ausrangieren, *v.a.* put away as useless, sort out, discard, cast off, reject; shunt to a siding (*Railw.*); *ausrangierte Kleider,* cast-off clothes.

ausräuchern, *v.a.* fumigate; smoke out (*a fox, etc.*).

ausraufen, *v.a.* pull, pluck *or* tear out; *er raufte sich* (*Dat.*) *die Haare aus,* he tore his hair.

ausräum-en, *v.a.* clear out, away *or* off; mop up, remove; clean out, ream, broach (*a hole*). **-ung,** *f.* clearing out, cleansing, removing; reaming.

ausrechn-en, *v.a.* reckon, calculate, compute, make a calculation. **ausgerechnet,** *p.p. & adj.* just, exactly; (*coll. ironic*) that would happen. **-ung,** *f.* computation, calculation.

Ausrede, *f.* (-n) excuse, evasion, subterfuge, pretence; *faule –,* poor excuse; *gerichtliche –,* legal quibble; *nichts als -n,* nothing but evasions; *Sie sind nie um eine – verlegen,* you are never at a loss for an excuse.

ausreden, 1. *v.n.* (*aux.* h.) finish speaking; speak freely; *laß mich –,* let me finish. 2. *v.a. einem etwas –,* dissuade a p. from doing a th., talk a p. out of (*an opinion, etc.*). 3. *v.r.* excuse o.s. from; exculpate o.s.; (*coll.*) wriggle out of; have one's say out.

ausreeden, *v.a.* rig, fit out, equip (*a vessel*).

ausreichen, *v.n.* (*aux.* h.) suffice, do, last, be sufficient. **-d,** *adj.* adequate, sufficient.

ausreifen, *v.a.* ripen, mature. **ausgereift,** *p.p. & adj.* matured, fully ripe.

Ausreise, *f.* journey abroad, departure.

ausreiß-en, 1. *ir.v.a.* pluck *or* tear out; pull up; extract (*a tooth*); *Unkraut -en,* weed; (*fig.*) *er reißt sich kein Bein dabei aus,* he does not kill himself over the job. 2. *v.n.* (*aux.* s.) run away, decamp, abscond; bolt; desert (*Mil.*); tear, split, wear out; *ausgerissene Knopflöcher,* worn-out button-holes; *ausgerissene Deiche,* broken-down dams. **-er,** *m.* deserter; runaway; stray shot, wide (*in shooting*).

ausreit-en, *ir.v.a. & n.* (*aux.* h.) take a ride, go for a ride. **-er,** *m.* outrider.

ausrenk-en, *v.a.* dislocate, sprain. **-ung,** *f.* dislocation, sprain.

ausreuten, *v.a.* root out, clear; eradicate, extirpate.

ausricht-en, *v.a.* make straight *or* level; straighten (out), align; dress (*ranks, Mil.*); co-ordinate, adjust; execute (*an order*); deliver (*a message*); accomplish (*a purpose*); fulfil (*a request, etc.*); go (*an errand*), do (*a job*), see to, execute, accomplish; *Sie können bei ihm viel -en,* you have great influence with him; *nichts -en,* exert o.s. in vain; *damit ist nichts ausgerichtet,* nothing is effected thereby; *richten Sie ihm meinen Gruß aus,* give him my kind regards, present my compliments to him. **-ung,** *f.* performance, execution, delivery; straightening, adjusting, alignment, bringing into line, 'toeing the line'.

ausringen, 1. *ir.v.a.* wring out (*washing, etc.*). 2. *v.n.* (*aux.* h.) finish wrestling; *er hat ausgerungen,* his struggles are over; he is dead.

Ausritt, *m.* (-(e)s, -e) ride, excursion on horseback; departure (*on horseback*).

ausroden, *v.a.* root out, grub up; clear (*a forest*).

ausroll-en, 1. *v.a.* roll out; unroll; 2. *n.* landing run (*Av.*). **-grenze,** *f.* plastic limit (*Tech.*).

ausrott-en, *v.a.* extirpate, exterminate, root out, purge, stamp out, destroy. **-ung,** *f.* destruction, extermination, extirpation. **-ungskrieg,** *m.* war of extermination.

ausrück-en, 1. *v.n.* (*aux.* s.) march out, move out; (*coll.*) escape, decamp. 2. *v.a.* throw out of gear; disengage, uncouple; *eine Zeile -en,* commence a new line (*Typ.*). **ausgerückt,** *p.p. & adj.* out of gear. **-vorrichtung,** *f.* disengaging clutch (*Engin.*).

Ausruf, *m.* (-(e)s, -e) cry; outcry; exclamation; interjection; proclamation; public sale. **-en,** 1. *ir.v.a.* proclaim; publish (*banns*); cry (*for sale*); publish (*by the town-crier*). 2. *v.n.* (*aux.* h.) cry out, call out, ejaculate, exclaim, proclaim, announce. **-er,** *m.* crier, hawker; town-crier, herald. **-ung,** *f.* cry; exclamation, outcry; proclamation, publication (*of banns*). **-ungswort,** *n.* interjection (*Gram.*). **-ungszeichen,** *n.* exclamation mark.

ausruhen, *v.n. & r.* rest, repose.

ausrupfen, *v.a.* pluck out.

ausrüst-en, *v.a.* furnish, equip, fit out; *mit Vernunft ausgerüstet,* endowed with reason. **-ung,** *f.* preparation; outfit, equipment; armament.

ausrutschen, *v.n.* (*aux.* s.) (*coll.*) slip, lose one's footing, skid.

Aussaat, *f.* (-en) sowing; seed; seed-corn; insemination, inoculation.

aussäen, *v.a.* sow (*seed*); disseminate.

Aussage, *f.* (-n) declaration, assertion, statement; deposition, testimony; predicate (*Gram.*); *Zeugen–,* evidence; affidavit; *eine gerichtliche – machen,* give evidence, make a deposition; *– anhören,* receive an audit (*Law*); *eidliche –,* deposition on oath; *seine – beweisen,* prove one's statement; *nach aller –,* by all accounts; *auf seine – hin,* from what he says. **-begriff,** *m.* predicate. **-n,** *v.a.* state, express, declare, assert, affirm, give evidence, testify; *eidlich etwas -n,* make a sworn deposition. **-satz,** *m.* affirmative proposition. **-weise,** *f.* mood (*indicative, subjunctive*).

Aussatz, *m.* leprosy; scab, mange, itch (*in sheep*); tetter (*in horses*); lead (*Bill.*).

aussätzig, *adj.* leprous. **-e(r),** *m.* leper.

aussaug-en, *ir.v.a.* suck out, suck dry; drain, exhaust, impoverish; *ein Kind -en lassen,* allow a

child to suck his (her) fill. **-er,** *m.* sucker; extortioner; parasite; parasitical plant.
ausschaben, *v.a.* scrape out.
ausschacht-en, *v.a.* sink, excavate. **-ung,** *f.* excavation.
ausschälen, *v.a.* shell, peel; blanch (*almonds*).
ausschalt-en, *v.a.* cut out, eliminate, bar, block out, exclude; put out of use *or* circuit; disconnect, switch off (*light*); not take into consideration; *fremde Konkurrenz -en,* keep out foreign competition; *völlig ausgeschaltet,* completely eliminated, quite out of the question. **-er,** *m.* cut-out switch, circuit breaker, commutator, contact breaker. **-ung,** *f.* putting out of circuit, disconnecting; elimination, removal; by-pass.
Ausschank, *m.* (-(e)s, ¨-e) bar, tavern.
ausschärfen, *v.a.* neutralize, deaden.
ausscharren, *v.a.* & *n.* rake *or* scratch up; (*Stud. sl.*) express disapproval by scraping with the feet.
Ausschau, *f.* (*only in the phrase*) *– halten,* watch for, be on the lookout for. **-en,** 1. *v.a.* (*aux.* h.) look out (*nach einem,* for s.o.). 2. *v.n.* look, have an appearance; *traurig -en,* look sad *or* sorrowful.
ausscheid-en, 1. *ir.v.a.* separate; reject; exclude, eliminate; segregate; liberate, crystallize, precipitate (*Tech.*); secrete (*Med.*); *-ende Gefäße,* secretory vessels. 2. *v.n.* (*aux.* s.) drop out, retire, secede, withdraw from (*a body of people, a club, a party, etc.*); *-en aus dem Geschäftsbetrieb,* retire from business. 3. *n.,* **-ung,** *f.* separation; withdrawal, elimination; secession; extraction, precipitation; secretion. **-ungsorgan,** *n.* (-e) excretive organ. **-ungskampf,** *m.,* **-ungsspiel,** *n.* eliminating bout, round, heat (*Sport*).
ausschelten, *ir.v.a.* reprimand, scold, rebuke (*wegen,* for).
ausschenken, *v.a.* pour out; help a p. to (*wine, etc.*); sell, retail (*liquor*).
ausscheuern, *v.a.* scour out, scrub out.
ausschicken, *v.a.* send out; send on an errand; dispatch; *auf Kommando –,* detach (*Mil.*).
ausschieben, *ir.v.a.* shove out; draw out, lengthen (*anything that extends*).
ausschieß-en, 1. *ir.v.a.* shoot out; veer (*of wind*); shoot for (*a prize*); wear (*or* score) (*of a gun*); cast out, reject; discharge (*ballast, etc.*); *ein Revier -en,* shoot all the game in a preserve. 2. *v.n.* (*aux.* s.) sprout, shoot forth. 3. *n.* veering (*of wind*). **-ung,** *f.* act of shooting out, *etc.*; rejection. **-er,** *m.* sorter (*in paper-mills*).
ausschiff-en, 1. *v.a.* put ashore, disembark, land; detrain (*Mil.*). 2. *v.n.* (*aux.* s.) put to sea. **-ung,** *f.* disembarkation; detrainment (*of troops*) (*Mil.*).
ausschirren, *v.a.* unharness.
ausschlachten, *v.a.* cut up for sale (*a carcass*); cannibalize (*a vehicle, etc.*); utilize, exploit; make full use of; capitalize on.
ausschlacken, *v.a.* remove the dross *or* clinker.
ausschlafen, 1. *ir.v.n.* & *r.* (*aux.* h.) sleep one's fill, have one's sleep out, enjoy a good night's rest. 2. *v.a.* sleep off (*effects of drink, etc.*); *seinen Rausch –,* sleep o.s. sober; *guten Morgen! Ausgeschlafen?* good morning! Did you have a good night?
Ausschlag, *m.* (-(e)s, ¨-e) 1. budding, sprouting (*of trees, etc.*); eruption, rash, breaking out (*of skin*); exudation (*on a wall*); efflorescence; border, trimming; 2. turn(ing) of the scale; decisive event, result; 3. throw, deflexion, declination (*of a pointer, compass needle, etc.*); 4. playing off (*a ball, e.g.* drive *in golf,* kick-off *in football;* serve *in tennis*); *eine Feder gibt der Waage den –,* a feather will turn the scale; *der Schlacht den – geben,* decide the issue of a battle; *dies gab den –,* this settled matters; *die Stimme, die den – gibt,* the casting vote. **-en, 1.** *ir.v.a.* 1. strike out, beat, dash *or* knock out; stamp *or* punch out; notch, indent; flatten out; 2. line; hang (*with paper or tapestry*); cover; trim, face (*with fur, etc.*); unfold, lay out, spread; 3. refuse, decline (*an invitation, etc.*); give up (*an inheritance*); ward off, parry (*an attack*). **2.** *v.n.* (*aux.* h.) 1. strike the first blow; play off (*a ball*); lash out (*as horses*); strike the hour; 2. incline to one side, turn, be deflected; (*aux.* s.) 3. burst forth; break out (*in a rash*); show damp, become mouldy; effloresce; sprout, bud; 4. result, turn out; *die Bäume schlagen aus,* the trees are breaking into leaf; *die Wände schlagen aus,* the walls are sweating; *die S. schlägt gut aus,* things will turn out all right; *ein Angebot -en,* reject an offer. **3.** *n.* refusal; renunciation (*of a right*); eruption, rash. **-fieber,** *n.* eruptive fever. **-gebend,** *adj.* decisive, determining (*factor*), telling; casting (*vote*). **-maschine,** *f.* punching-machine. **-swinkel,** *m.* angle of deflection.
Ausschläger, *m.* (-s, -) striker; kicker; server (*of a ball*).
ausschleifen, *ir.v.a.* grind down; whet.
ausschleuder-n, *v.a.* hurl forth. **-maschine,** *f.* centrifuge.
ausschließ-en, *ir.v.a.* shut out, exclude; lock out; excommunicate; debar from; except, exempt; (*Sport*) disqualify, suspend. *ausgeschlossen!* impossible! out of the question! *keiner* or *keinen ausgeschlossen,* no one excepted, without exception. **-lich,** 1. *adj.* exclusive; *-liches Vorrecht,* exclusive privilege. 2. *prep.* exclusive of. **-ung,** *f.* exclusion; expulsion; exemption; excommunication.
ausschlüpfen, *v.n.* (*aux.* s.) slip out, creep out; hatch out.
Ausschluß, *m.* (-(ss)es, ¨-(ss)e) exclusion; exception; exemption; disqualification; *mit – eines Einzigen,* with a single exception; *unter – der Öffentlichkeit,* behind closed doors; in camera.
ausschmelzen, 1. *v.a.* extract by melting; render (*fats*); fuse. 2. *ir.v.n.* (*aux.* s.) melt out.
ausschmücken, *v.a.* adorn, embellish, decorate, (*coll.*) deck out.
ausschnauben, *v.r.* blow one's nose.
ausschneid-en, *ir.v.a.* cut out; excise; cut off; castrate; prune. **ausgeschnitten,** *p.p.* & *adj.* crenate, serrated (*Bot.*); low-necked (*dress*). **-er,** *m.* cutter; retailer. **-ung,** *f.* cutting out, excision.
ausschneuzen, *v.r. see* **ausschnauben.**
Ausschnitt, *m.* (-(e)s, -e) cut, slit, notch, scallop; section, piece cut out; sector (*Geom.*); counterfoil; *Zeitungs–,* newspaper cutting; *– eines Fensters,* embrasure; *Leibchen mit viereckigem –,* bodice with open square neck; *auf den - verkaufen,* sell by retail *or* the yard. **-handel,** *m.* retail business. **-händler,** *m.* haberdasher, retailer.
ausschnitze(l)n, *v.a.* carve out, cut out, whittle out.
ausschöpf-en, *v.a.* scoop, ladle *or* bail (*or less good* bale) out; empty, drain off; exhaust; (*fig.*) deal completely with. **-kelle,** *f.* ladle, scoop, bailer (*or* baler).
ausschoten, *v.a.* shell, pod (*beans, etc.*).
ausschreib-en, 1. *ir.v.a.* write out, write out in full; copy; write to the end, finish (*a letter, etc.*); pirate, plagiarize; publish, announce, proclaim, promulgate; summon; advertise (*a vacant post*); invite (*tenders*); *ausgeschriebene Hand,* fully developed handwriting. 2. *v.r.* exhaust one's power of writing (*of literary men*); *er hat sich ausgeschrieben,* he has written himself out, he has nothing new to say in his books. 3. *n.,* **-ung,** *f.* copy, copying; order, writ. **-er,** *m.* copyist, transcriber; plagiarist. **-erei,** *f.* plagiarism.
ausschreien, *ir.v.a.* & *n.* cry out, exclaim; cry (*wares*); proclaim (*as the town-crier*); cry down.
ausschreit-en, 1. *ir.v.a.* pace *or* step out (*a distance*), traverse. 2. *v.n.* (*aux.* s.) go too far, overstep (*reasonable limits*); *tüchtig -en,* take long strides. **-ung,** *f.* excess, extravagance; transgression; riot.
ausschroten, *v.a.* roll up (*a cask out of the cellar, etc.*); sell by the barrel.
ausschüren, *v.a.* rake out.
Ausschürfwirkung, *f.* abrading action *or* effect (*Tech.*).
Ausschuß, *m.* (-(ss)es, ¨-(ss)e) 1. dross, refuse, waste matter; damaged goods, spoilage, rejects; 2. pick, choice, best part; élite; 3. committee; board; commission; *– des Pöbels,* the lowest rabble; *die größeren und engeren Ausschüsse,* general committees and sub-committees; *geschäftsleitender –,* executive committee, board of management; *allgemeiner –,* general council. **-mitglied,** *n.* member of a board *or* committee. **-papier,** *n.* waste paper. **-stelle,**

f. place where bullet leaves the body. **-waren,** *f.pl.* defective goods, rejects.
ausschütteln, *v.a.* shake out, extract.
ausschütt-en, 1. *v.a.* pour out, empty out; give freely, shed, shower down; *einem sein Herz -en,* unburden one's heart to a p.; *das Kind mit dem Bade -en,* throw the baby out with the bath-water, act without discretion. 2. *v.r.*; *sich vor Lachen -en,* split one's sides with laughter. **-ung,** *f.* pouring out; *-ung von Dividenden,* distribution of dividends.
ausschwären, *ir.v.n.* (*aux.* s.) suppurate.
ausschwärmen, *v.n.* (*aux.* s.) swarm out (*as bees*); proceed in extended line (*Mil.*); (*aux.* h.) settle down, give up one's roving life.
ausschwatzen, *v.a.* blurt *or* blab out.
ausschweben, *v.n.* flatten out (*Av.*).
ausschwefeln, *v.a.* fumigate with sulphur.
ausschweif-en, 1. *v.a.* scallop, indent. 2. *v.n.*(*aux.* h.) splay out; roam about, stray; be prolix, digress; yield to excess; lead a dissolute life. **ausgeschweift,** *p.p.* & *adj.* sinuate, incised, indented (*Bot.*). **-end,** *pr.p.* & *adj.* bulging; extravagant; eccentric; dissolute, licentious. **-ung,** *f.* excess, intemperance, debauch; cut on a slope (*Dressmaking*); aberration (*of mind*); extravagance (*of imagination, etc.*). **-ungskreis,** *m.* line of aberration (*Astr.*).
ausschweißen, *v.a.* hammer, forge *or* weld out; clean metal by firing; (*Hunt.*) bleed.
ausschwemmen, *v.a.* wash away, sluice away, erode by action of water.
ausschwenk-en, *v.a.* rinse, wash out, swill out (*a glass, etc.*); whirl, centrifuge. **-maschine,** *f.* centrifuge, spin-dryer.
ausschwitzen, 1. *v.a.* exude; sweat out. 2. *v.n.* (*aux.* s.) perspire; exude, ooze; (*aux.* h.) stop perspiring.
aussegnen, *v.a.* bless, give benediction *or* absolution to (*at obsequies and churching of women*).
aussehen, 1. *ir.v.n* (*aux.* h.) look (*nach einem,* for *or* out for a p.); look, appear, seem; *er sieht sehr wohl aus,* he looks very well; *er sieht sehr gut aus,* he looks very smart; *wie sieht er aus?* what does he look like? *nach etwas recht Vornehmem -,* have an air of distinction; *es sieht nach etwas aus und kostet wenig,* it makes a great show and costs little; *wie sieht es mit deinem Bruder aus?* how is your brother (doing)? *jetzt sieht es bei ihm wieder besser aus,* things are looking up with him, his affairs are improving; *- wie, - als wenn, - als ob,* look like, seem; *es sieht aus, als ob es regnen wollte* or *es sieht nach Regen aus,* it looks like rain. 2. *n.* appearance, look, air, exterior; *edles -,* noble air; *nach dem - beurteilen,* judge by appearances; *er hat ganz das - danach,* he quite looks it. **-d,** *pr.p.* & *adj.*; *weit -de Pläne,* extensive plans; *weit -de Hoffnungen,* remote hopes; *wohl -d,* healthy looking.
ausseigern, *v.a.* liquate (*Metall.*).
ausseihen, *v.a.* strain, filter.
ausseimen, *v.a.* let run, clarify (*honey*).
außen, *adv.* out, outside, outwardly, without; out of doors; abroad; *nach -, nach - hin,* externally, outwards; *von -, von - her,* from without. **-backenbremse,** *f.* external contraction brake (*Veh.*). **-bord,** *adj.* outboard. **-böschung,** *f.* counterscarp, outside slope. **-dienst,** *m.* outdoor duty, outside duty (*i.e. outside the office or barracks*). **-geltung,** *f.* respect that one commands abroad. **-gewässer,** *n.pl.* extraterritorial waters. **-handel,** *m.* export trade. **-haut,** *f.* skin, fabric (*of an aeroplane, etc.*); hull (*of a ship*). **-linie,** *f.* touchline. **-minister,** *m.* Secretary of State for Foreign Affairs. **-politik,** *f.* foreign policy. **-posten,** *m.* outpost (*Mil.*). **-seite,** *f.* outside, exterior, surface, superficies. **-seiter,** *m.* outsider (*Sport*). **-stände,** *m.pl.* outstanding claims, liabilities. **-stehende(r),** *m.* outsider, non-participant. **-taster,** *m.* outside callipers. **-welt,** *f.* external world, environment. **-winkel,** *m.* external angle.
aussend-en, *ir.v.a.* send out; emit, radiate. **-ling,** *m.* emissary. **-ung,** *f.* act of dispatching; mission; emission, radiation; transmission (*Rad.*).
außer, 1. *prep.* USED WITH DAT. out of, outside, without, beyond; besides, except. *- unserm Bereiche,* outside our scope; *- Betrieb,* out of action, unserviceable; *- Dienst,* retired from active service; *du bist - dir,* you are beside yourself; *alle - einem,* all but one; *- Fassung kommen,* lose all self-control; *- Gebrauch kommen,* become obsolete, go out of fashion; *- (dem) Hause,* out of doors; *- Gefecht setzen,* put out of action (*in a battle*); *- Kraft setzen,* annul, rescind; *- Kurs setzen,* withdraw from circulation; *- Schußweite,* out of range; *- der Zeit,* out of season, untimely; *- Zweifel,* beyond all doubt. USED WITH GEN. (*only in the phrase*); *- Landes,* out of the country, abroad. *N.B. - den Schutz der Gesetze stellen,* place beyond the pale of the law. 2. *conj.* except, unless, save, but; *- daß,* except that, save that; *- wenn,* unless. 3. *prefix*; = external, outer, extra. **-achsig,** *adj.* eccentric (*Tech.*). **-amtlich,** *adj.* non-official, private. **-beruflich,** *adj.* extra-professional. **-dem,** *adv.* besides, moreover, into the bargain; over and above, not to mention. **-dienstlich,** *see* **-amtlich.** **-ehelich,** *adj.* illegitimate. **-gewöhnlich,** *adj.* unusual, extraordinary. **-halb,** 1. *prep.* (*with Gen.*) outside, beyond. 2. *adv.* on the outside, externally. **-etatsmäßig,** *adj.* supernumerary. **-mittig,** *see* **-achsig.** **-ordentlich,** *adj.* extraordinary, unusual, uncommon, exceptional, remarkable, special, singular; *-ordentlicher Professor,* university reader *or* lecturer; *-ordentliche Unkosten,* enormous charges; extra charges. **-planmäßig,** *adj.* extra, not according to schedule. **-sinnlich,** *adj.* supersensual; **-stande,** *adv.*; *er ist -stande,* he is not in a position.
äußer, *adj.* outer, exterior, external, outward; *-e Winkel,* external angles (*Math.*). **-e(s),** *n.* outward appearance; surface; exterior; foreign affairs; *seinem -en nach ist er ein feiner Mann,* to judge from his appearance he is a gentleman; *Minister des -en,* minister of Foreign Affairs. **-lich,** *adj.* external, outward; superficial, extrinsic; *der -liche Wert einer Münze,* the face value of a coin. **-lichkeit,** *f.* formality, superficiality, (*pl.*) externals. **-st,** 1. *adv.* extremely, exceedingly. 2. *adj.* extreme, utmost, uttermost, outermost; *ich werde mein -stes tun,* I will do my utmost; *er wurde aufs -ste gebracht* or *getrieben,* he was driven to extremities; *ich bin aufs -ste gefaßt,* I am prepared for the worst; *zum -sten schreiten,* go the greatest lengths.
äußer-n, 1. *v.a.* utter, express, give voice to; advance (*an opinion, etc.*); manifest; *er -te schon früh einen Hang zur Satire,* he early displayed a turn for satire. 2. *v.r.* express one's opinion; make itself felt; manifest itself; *eine Rückwirkung -te sich bald,* a reaction soon set in. **-ung,** *f.* expression, utterance, remark, saying; manifestation, exhibition.
aussetz-en, 1. *v.a.* 1. set out; display; allow (*a sum of money*); make a settlement on, bequeath; set (*a task*); plant out (*trees, etc.*); 2. put out; eject; post (*sentries*); lower, hoist out (*a boat*); expose (*to cold, etc.*); maroon; disembark (*troops*); *das Ausgesetzte,* allowance; *etwas (an einer S.) -en,* take exception to, find fault with; *daran ist nichts auszusetzen,* there is nothing to find fault with in that; *ein Kind -en,* expose a child; *sich dem Betruge -en,* lay o.s. open to imposition; *die Stimmen -en,* copy the parts from the score (*Mus.*); *die Segel -en,* set the sails; **2.** *v.a.* & *n.* (*aux.* h.) 1. pause, stop, interrupt, suspend, put off, postpone, break down (*Mech.*); 2. have the first move (*at draughts, etc.*); play off (*Bill.*); 3. crop out (*Min.*); *Zahlung -en,* suspend payment; *die Arbeit -en,* interrupt one's work; *der Puls setzt häufig aus,* the pulse is very irregular. **-end,** *pr. p.* intermittent, discontinuous. **-ling,** *m.* foundling. **-ung,** *f.* 1. setting out; settlement (*of a pension, etc.*); landing (*of troops*); exposition (*of goods*); 2. ejection, exposure; exception, censure; 3. intermission, suspension.
Aussicht, *f.* (-en) view, prospect; expectation; *das Haus hat eine - auf den Fluß* or *die Straße,* the house looks over the river *or* faces the street; *einem etwas in - stellen,* hold out a prospect of s.th. to s.o.; *wir haben dies nicht in - genommen,* we do not propose to do this, do not contemplate doing this;

er hat – auf eine gute Stelle, he has a prospect or hopes of a good appointment. **–shäuschen,** *n.* gazebo, belvedere. **–los,** *adj.* hopeless, without prospects. **–losigkeit,** *f.* absence of prospects, hopelessness. **–spunkt,** *m.* observation post, vantage point. **–sreich,** *adj.* promising. **–svoll,** *adj.* promising, full of promise. **–swagen,** *m.* observation-car (*Railw.*).

aussickern, *v.n.* (*aux.* s.) trickle out, ooze out, percolate.

aussieden, *ir.v.a.* extract by boiling.

Aussiedlung, *f.* transfer of population.

aussinnen, *ir.v.a.* contrive, devise, concoct.

aussintern, *v.n. see* **aussickern.**

aussöhn–en, 1. *v.a.* reconcile, expiate. 2. *v.r.*; *sich mit einem –en*, make one's peace *or* make it up with a p. **–bar,** *adj.* reconcilable, expiable. **–ung,** *f.* atonement; reconciliation.

aussonder–n, *v.a.* separate, single out; sort; select; eliminate, reject; secrete, excrete. **–ung,** *f.* separation; selection; secretion, excretion (*Med.*).

aussortieren, *v.a.* sort out, separate; set *or* lay aside.

ausspäh–en, *v.a.* spy out, scout, reconnoitre (*Mil.*).

Ausspann, *m.* (-(e)s, -e) coaching inn, stage. **–en,** 1. *v.a.* spread; stretch; expand; unharness, unyoke. 2. *v.a.* & *n.* relax (*exertions*); slacken (*a spring, etc.*); unfold; *die Post spannt hier aus*, the mail-coach changes horses here. **–ung,** *f.* relaxation; rest.

ausspar–en, *v.a.* spare; leave a space to be filled up (*Paint.*); by-pass (*Mil.*). **–ung,** *f.* hollow, blank, recess.

aussperr–en, *v.a.* shut out, exclude; bar a p.'s entry; lock out (*workmen*). **ausgesperrt,** *p.p.* & *adj.* astride; straddling; locked out (*i.e. refused work by employer*). **–ung,** *f.* lock-out (*from work*).

ausspielen, 1. *v.a.* play out; play to the end; lead (*in cards*); *einen gegen den andern –*, play off one p. against another. 2. *v.r.* exhaust o.s. by playing. 3. *v.n.* (*aux.* h.) lead (*Cards*); play off (*Bill.*); finish playing; *wer spielt aus?* who leads?

ausspinnen, *ir.v.a.* spin out; enlarge upon; devise, plot.

Aussprach–e, *f.* (-en) pronunciation, enunciation, accent, utterance; conversation, discussion, exchange of views; *deutliche –e der Silben*, distinct articulation of the syllables; *richtige –e*, correct pronunciation; *fremdartige –e*, (foreign) accent; *irische –e*, Irish brogue; *öffentliche –e*, public discussion *or* debate. **–ebezeichnung,** *f.* phonetic notation. **–elehre,** *f.* theory of pronunciation **–elehrer,** *m.* teacher of elocution.

aussprech–en, 1. *ir.v.a.* pronounce, articulate; utter, express, declare, state, say; *seine Dankbarkeit –en*, express one's gratitude; *nicht ausgesprochen werden*, be silent *or* mute (*of a letter*); *nicht auszusprechen*, unutterable, unspeakable. 2. *v.r.* speak one's mind; express one's opinion; declare o.s. (*for or against*); manifest; be stamped *or* expressed (*upon one's face*); exhaust (*o.s., or one's subject*) in speaking. **ausgesprochen,** *p.p.* & *adj.* pronounced, avowed, marked, decided, unqualified, outspoken. 3. *v.n.* (*aux.* h.) finish speaking; articulate, enunciate. **–lich,** *adj.* expressible, utterable; pronounceable.

ausspreiten, ausspreizen, *v.a.* extend, stretch apart. **ausgespreizt,** *p.p.* & *adj.* divergent; *mit ausgespreizten Armen*, with arms akimbo; *mit ausgespreizten Beinen*, with straddling *or* widespread legs.

aussprengen, *v.a.* sprinkle; spread (*a report or rumour*); remove by blasting; *ein Pferd –*, put a horse to a gallop.

ausspringen, 1. *ir.v.n.* (*aux.* s.) leap *or* spring out; become dislocated; fly off; escape; (*aux.* h.) stop leaping; *–de Winkel*, salient angles. 2. *v.a.* & *r.*; *sich den Fuß –*, sprain one's ankle; *lassen Sie die Kinder sich –*, let the children romp to their heart's content.

ausspritz–en, 1. *v.a.* squirt *or* put out fire (*with a hose*); syringe; inject (*Med.*). 2. *v.n.* (*aux.* s.) spurt out, squirt out. **–ung,** *f.* ejaculation (*Med., Anat.*).

Ausspruch, *m.* (-(e)s, ¨-e) declaration of opinion, decision, finding, verdict, sentence, award; dictum, maxim, saying, utterance, remark; *– der Geschworenen*, jury's verdict; *– der Schiedsrichter*, award (*of arbitration*); *den – tun* (*über*), pass sentence (on), give a decision (on); express one's opinion (on *or* about).

aussprühen, 1. *v.a.* emit (*sparks*), belch (out *or* forth) (*flames, smoke, etc.*), eject, throw up. 2. *v.n.* (*aux.* s.) be cast up, fly out in sparks.

ausspülen, *v.a.* rinse out, wash out, flush; wash away, erode.

ausspüren, *v.a.* track out, trace.

ausstaffier–en, *v.a.* dress up, deck out, trim, garnish, smarten up; equip, fit out, furnish. **–ung,** *f.* outfit, equipment, trimming, garnishing.

Ausstand, *m.* (-(e)s, ¨-e) strike; arrears, outstanding debt; *Arbeiter–*, strike; *verlorene Ausstände*, bad debts; *in den – treten*, begin a strike, go on strike (*of workmen*).

Ausständ–er, *m.* hive of bees that have outlived the winter. **–ig,** *adj.*, **–isch,** *adj.* on strike; in arrears; *die –ischen*, the strikers.

ausstatt–en, *v.a.* equip, fit out; provide with; portion, settle s.th. on (*a daughter*), give a dowry to; endow; bestow on. **–ung,** *f.* outfit, equipment; fittings; (*coll.*) get-up; scenery (*Theat.*); dowry, portion; *ohne –ung*, portionless, dowerless. **–ungsstück,** *n.* transformation scene (*Theat.*), spectacular play.

ausstäuben, *v.a.* dust, beat out *or* wipe off the dust.

ausstäupen, *v.a.* (*archaic*) flog soundly.

ausstech–en, *ir.v.a.* dig out, cut out (*peat, etc.*), core (*apples*), put out (*the eyes*), open (*oysters*); carve, engrave; (*fig.*) cut out, supplant, outdo, excel, put in the shade, outshine; *hohl –en*, engrave in bas-relief; *ein paar Flaschen Wein mit Freunden –en*, crack a few bottles of wine with one's friends.

ausstecken, *v.a.* put out, display (*a flag, etc.*); mark out (*with pegs*).

aussteh–en, 1. *ir.v.n.* (*aux.* h. & s.) stand out; be outstanding; *mit Waren –en*, keep a stall; *–ende Schulden*, outstanding debts; *ich habe Geld –en*, I have money owing to me; *–endes Gehalt*, arrears of salary; (*aux.* s.) be still expected; *die Sammlung steht noch aus*, the collection is not yet made; *die Antwort steht noch aus*, the answer has not yet come to hand; *die Entscheidung steht noch aus*, no decision has been reached yet. 2. *v.a.* endure, bear; stand, put up with; brook; *ich kann ihn nicht –en*, I can't bear him.

ausssteig–en, *ir.v.n.* (*aux.* s.) get out *or* off, alight (*from a carriage*); disembark (*from a ship*); land; (*sl.*) bail out (*Av.*) **–eplatz,** *m.* arrival platform; landing-stage.

aussteinen, *v.a.* stone (*plums, etc.*).

ausstell–en, *v.a.* exhibit, display, set out; lay out (*a corpse in state*); post (*a sentry*); 2. make out, write out, issue, give (*a bill, cheque, receipt, testimonial, etc.*); 3. take exception to, blame, find fault with; **–er,** *m.* exhibitor; drawer (*of a bill*). **–ung,** *f.* exhibition, show, display; drawing (*of a bill of exchange*); blame, censure; *–ung von Kunstgegenständen*, fine-art exhibition; *–ung von Blumen*, flower-show; *–ung auf dem Paradebette*, lying in state; **–ungstag,** *m.* date of issue (*of a draft*).

aussterbe–n, *ir.v.n.* (*aux.* s.) die out; become extinct (*of a family* or *prehistoric animal*). **ausgestorben,** *p.p.* & *adj.* died out, extinct, gone; (*fig.*) totally deserted; *die Stadt ist wie ausgestorben*, the town is as quiet as the grave. **–stand,** *m.*, **–etat,** *m.*; *auf den –etat kommen* or *gesetzt werden*, *auf dem –etat stehen*, be destined to die out, be moribund, be on the point of extinction.

Aussteuer, *f.* (-n) dowry, marriage portion, trousseau. **–n,** *v.a.* portion, endow; *Ausgesteuerte(r)*, *m.* person no longer eligible (*for dole, etc.*).

Ausstich, *m.* (-(e)s, -e) choice wine. **–ware,** *f.* finest brand, prime quality.

ausstöbern, *v.a.* rummage out (*drawer, etc.*); drive out, beat up (*game*).

ausstopfen, *v.a.* stuff (*birds, chairs*).

Ausstoß, *m.* (-es, ¨-e) expulsion; lunge, thrust, pass (*Fenc.*); tapping (*of a barrel*), first draught (*from a barrel*). **–en, 1.** *ir.v.a.* 1. thrust out, knock out;

expel, eject, eliminate, excrete; tap (*a barrel*), take the first draught (*of beer*); elide, cut off (*a syllable*); remove, relegate; do away with; 2. utter, ejaculate; (*Prov.*) *das heißt dem Fasse den Boden –en*, that finishes *or* settles it; *Gotteslästerungen –en*, utter blasphemies; *einen Seufzer –en*, heave a sigh; *einen Schrei –en*, scream; *einen aus einer Gesellschaft –en*, expel, a p. from a club *or* society. **2.** *v.n.* (*aux.* s.) burst forth; (*aux.* h.) thrust first; make a pass *or* lunge (*Fenc.*). **–produkt,** *n.* waste products. **–rohr,** *n.* torpedo tube (*Nav.*). **–ung,** *f.* expulsion. **–vorrichtung,** *f.* ejector (mechanism).

ausstrahl–en, *v.a.* & *n.* (*aux.* h.) emit rays, radiate, shine forth. **–ung,** *f.* radiation, emanation, emission.

ausstreck–en, 1. *v.a.* reach out, hold out, extend; stretch out, expand, distend. 2. *v.r.* stretch o.s., spread o.s. (out). **–er,** *m.* extensor (*muscle*). **–ung,** *f.* extension, stretching. **–muskel,** *m. see* **–er.**

ausstreichen, 1. *ir.v.a.* obliterate, erase, strike out, cross out (*a word, sentence*); smooth, stroke out; fill up crevices; grease (*a cake-tin, etc.*); *viele Ansätze in einer Rechnung –*, cancel many items in *or* from an account; *einen Namen –*, cross out a name (*on a list*). 2. *v.n.* (*aux.* s.) roam, rove about; *einen Vogel – lassen*, let a bird rise before shooting.

ausstreifen, *v.n.* (*aux.* s.) rove, range, wander about.

ausstreu–en, *v.a.* scatter, spread abroad, disseminate; *den Samen der Zwietracht –en*, sow the seeds of discord. **–ung,** *f.* dissemination; diffusion.

Ausstrich, *m.* (-(e)s, -e) outcrop (*Geol.*); smear (*microscopic preparation*).

ausström–en, 1. *v.a.* pour forth, emit, discharge. 2. *v.n.* (*aux.* s.) stream *or* issue forth; emanate, escape (*of steam, etc.*), radiate (*of rays*), flow out, run out (*of liquids*). 3. *n.*, **–ung,** *f.* outflow, efflux, effluence, effusion, emission, emanation; radiation; escape (*of gas*).

ausstudieren, 1. *v.n.* (*aux.* h.) finish one's studies. 2. *v.a.* study thoroughly. **ausstudiert,** *p.p.* & *adj.* having completed a university course, graduate, qualified.

ausstülp–en, *v.n.* bulge, protrude; evaginate (*Med.*). **–ung,** *f.* protrusion, extroversion.

aussuchen, *v.a.* seek, search out; select, single *or* pick out; *ausgesuchte Ausdrücke*, well-chosen expressions; studied terms; *ausgesuchte Leckerbissen*, choice dainties; *ausgesuchte Höflichkeit*, exquisite politeness.

aussühnen, *v.a.* & *r. see* **aussöhnen.**

aussüßen, *v.a.* sweeten, dulcify, edulcorate (*Chem.*).

austapezieren, *v.a.* paper (*a wall*), line (*a box, etc.*).

Austausch, *m.* (-es -e) exchange; barter; interchange (*of commodities, of ideas*); *im – gegen*, in exchange for. **–bar,** *adj.* interchangeable, exchangeable. **–en,** *v.a.* change, exchange; barter; *Gedanken –en*, exchange ideas. **–stoff,** *m.*, **–ware,** *f.* substitute. **–student,** *m.* exchange student.

austeil–en, *v.a.* distribute (*unter*, among); dispense (*favours, alms, etc.*); divide, allot, apportion (*shares*); issue (*orders*); administer (*the Sacrament*); deal out (*blows*); serve out (*meat, etc.*). **–end,** *pr.p.* & *adj.* distributive. **–er,** *m.* distributor; dispenser. **–ung,** *f.* distribution; apportionment; administration (*of the Sacrament*).

Auster, *f.* (-n) oyster; *–n anstechen* or *aufmachen*, open oysters; *nach –n fischen, –n fangen*, dredge for oysters. **–nbank,** *f.* oyster-bed. **–nfischerei,** *f.* oyster-dredging. **–nlager,** *n. see* **–nbank. –nlaich,** *m.* spat. **–nschale,** *f.* oyster-shell.

austilgen, *v.a.* destroy utterly, exterminate, extirpate, wipe out; eradicate; efface, obliterate.

austoben, 1. *v.n.* cease raging, abate (*of storms*). 2. *v.r.* romp, let off steam, have one's fling; sow one's wild oats.

austönen, *v.n.* (*aux.* h.) die away (*of sound*).

Austrag, *m.* (-(e)s, ⸚e) issue, decision, arbitration, product, end; *eine S. zum – bringen*, determine *or* decide a matter; *eine S. gerichtlich zum – bringen*, go to law; *vor – der S.*, while the case is pending; *gütlicher –*, amicable arrangement. **–en,** 1. *ir.v.a.* deliver, carry (*letters*); distribute; retail (*gossip*); carry child for full time; carry away; wear out (*clothes, etc.*); decide (*a contest, Sport.*), settle (*a quarrel*); *nicht ausgetragenes Kind*, prematurely born child; *eine Streitsache durch Schiedsrichter –en lassen*, leave a disputed matter to arbitration; 2. *v* . (*aux.* h.) cease bearing (*of trees*). **–ung,** *f.* settlement, contest. **–sgericht,** *n.* arbitration court (*between princes of the German Empire*).

Austräger, *m.* light porter; tale-bearer.

austreib–en, *ir.v.a.* drive out, cast out, eject, expel, dislodge (*an enemy*), exorcise; *Schweiß –en*, cause to perspire; *Teufel –en*, cast out devils. **–ung,** *f.* driving out, expulsion, exorcism.

austreten, 1. *ir.v.a.* tread under foot; trample, tread out (*grapes, etc.*); wear out (*shoes, stairs*); widen by treading; *die Kinderschuhe ausgetreten haben*, have put away childish things, have outgrown (*fig.*); *einem die Schuhe –*, supplant a p., cut a p. out. 2. *v.n.* (*aux.* s.) step out; lead off; come forth; withdraw from (*a company*); leave (*the ranks*); secede from (*a church, etc.*); retire from (*an office, etc.*); abscond; desert (*Mil.*); leave the room, be excused (*i.e. go to the lavatory*), ease o.s.; become dislocated; protrude (*as in hernia, etc.*); overflow, break out (*of rivers*); *das ausgetretene Blut*, extravasated blood; *Flüsse sind ausgetreten*, rivers have overflowed their banks; *darf ich bitte –?* may I please leave the room?

austrinken, *ir.v.a.* & *n.* drink up, drain (*a glass, etc.*).

Austritt, *m.* (-(e)s, -e) 1. stepping out; exit; efflux, extravasation; protrusion, prolapsus (*Med.*); emergence (*Astr.*); 2. recession; retiring, retirement (*from an office, etc.*); withdrawal (*from a club*); disappearance, absconding, desertion; 3. outlet, vent, doorstep; porch; antechamber; balcony; 4. discharge, overflow; *– aus diesem Leben*, death. **–sbogen,** *m.* arc of vision. **–serklärung,** *f.* notice of withdrawal. **–skante,** *f.* trailing edge (*of wings. Av.*). **–spunkt,** *m.* point of emergence.

austrockn–en, 1. *v.a.* dry (up), desiccate, parch; season (*timber*); drain (*a marsh*). 2. *v.n.* (*aux.* s.) dry up. **–ung,** *f.* desiccation; drainage (*of land*). **–ungsrinde,** *f.* dried up layer.

auströpfeln, austropfen, *v.a.* drip, ooze out.

austun, *ir.v.a.* put out (*a light*); cancel (*debts*); erase; invest (*money*); send away (*children to school, into service, etc.*), farm out; (*coll.*) pull *or* take off (*clothes*).

ausüb–en, *v.a.* practise (*law, medicine, etc.*); exercise (*authority, privilege*); exert (*influence*); carry on (*a trade*); execute, carry out; commit *or* perpetrate (*crimes*); *Rache an einem –en*, take revenge on a p.; *Druck auf einen –en*, bring pressure to bear on a p. **–end,** *pr.p.* & *adj.* practising; executive; *–ender Arzt*, (general) practitioner. **–ung,** *f.* practice (*opp. to theory*); practice (*of one's profession*); exercise (*of privilege*); execution (*of duty*); perpetration (*of crime*); *in –ung des Dienstes*, in line of duty; *in –ung bringen*, put into practice.

Ausverkauf, *m.* (-(e)s, ⸚e) selling off, clearance sale. **–en,** *v.a.* sell off, sell out; *das Buch war –t*, the book was out of print; *das Theater war –t*, the house was sold out.

auswachsen, 1. *ir.v.n.* (*aux.* s.) shoot, sprout, germinate; grow deformed; attain full growth; heal up *or* over; *er ist hinten ausgewachsen*, he is humpbacked; *ausgewachsenes Fleisch*, proud flesh; *ausgewachsenes Mädchen*, full-grown girl. 2. *v.r.* develop *or* grow (*zu*, into). 3. *v.n.* (*aux.* h.) cease to grow.

Auswahl, *f.* choice, selection; assortment; *eine – treffen*, make a selection; *ohne –*, indiscriminately; *– deutscher Lieder*, selection *or* anthology of German songs.

auswählen, *v.a.* choose, select, single out, fix on. **ausgewählt,** *p.p.*, & *adj.* selected, select, choice; *ausgewählte Soldaten*, picked soldiers; *ausgewählte Gedichte*, selected poems.

auswalzen, *v.a.* roll out.

auswander–n, *v.a.* (*aux.* s.) migrate, emigrate. **–er,** *m.* (-s, -) emigrant. **–ung,** *f.* emigration, migration.

auswärm–en, *v.a.* warm thoroughly; anneal, **–eofen,** *m.* annealing furnace.

auswärt–ig, *adj.* foreign; abroad; outward; *das –ige Amt, Ministerium des –igen,* Foreign Office; *Minister der –igen Angelegenheiten* or *des –igen,* Foreign Secretary; *–iger Berichterstatter,* foreign correspondent (*of a newspaper*); *–iges Mitglied,* corresponding member. **–s,** *adv.* outward, outwards; abroad; out of town, out of doors, away from home; *–s bestimmt,* outward-bound, destined for abroad; *von –s,* from abroad; *–s essen,* go out to eat, eat out; *die Fußspitzen –s setzen,* turn out the toes. **–sdreher,** *m.* supinator muscle (*Anat.*). **–sgekehrt,** *adj.* addorsed (*Her.*).

auswaschen, I. *ir.v.a.* wash, wash up *or* out; rinse, cleanse, edulcorate (*Chem.*); bathe (*Surg.*). 2. *v.n.* & *r.* wash out, run (*of colours*).

auswässer–n, *v.a.* soak, steep. **–ungslinie,** *f.* load water-line.

auswechs–eln, *v.a.* exchange, change (*gegen,* for), interchange, replace; *ausgewechseltes Kind,* changeling; *Gefangene –eln,* exchange prisoners. **–elbar,** *adj.* interchangeable, renewable, replaceable. **–lung,** *f.* change, exchange, interchange, replacement, renewal. **–lungsvertrag,** *m.* treaty for the exchange of prisoners.

Ausweg, *m.* (-(e)s, -e) way out, outlet; opening, vent; means, remedy, expedient, alternative; shift, evasion.

[1]**ausweichen,** *v.a.* soften, soak thoroughly.

[2]**ausweich–en,** **1.** *ir.v.n.* (*aux.* s.) I. turn aside, step aside, shunt (*Locom.*); give place to, make way for, withdraw (*before another*); yield; 2. dodge, elude, evade, avoid, shun; shirk; 3. modulate, change from one key to another (*Mus.*); *einem Stoße –en,* parry a blow. **2.** *n. see* **–ung. –end,** *pr.p.* & *adj.* evasive, elusive. **–(e)platz,** *m.* **–(e)stelle,** *f.* siding (*on a railway*). **–(e)gleis,** *n.*, **–(e)schiene,** *f.* siding rail; switch. **–lager** *n.* storage place in a safe reception area (*against air-raids*). **–stelle,** *f.* lay-by. **–ung,** *f.* yielding; evasion, avoidance, shirking, *etc.*; deviation, deflexion, displacement; soaking; modulation (*Mus.*). **–waren,** *f.pl.* unrationed luxury goods. **–welle,** *f.* secondary frequency (*Rad.*). **–ziel,** *n.* secondary target (*Av.*). **–(e)zungen,** *f.pl.* switches, points (*Railw.*)

ausweiden, *v.a.* eviscerate, draw (*poultry*); *eine Wiese –,* graze (*cattle*) on a meadow.

ausweinen, I. *v.a.* weep; *sich* (*Dat.*) *die Augen –,* cry one's eyes out. 2. *v.r.* cry to one's heart's content, have a good cry. 3. *v.n.* (*aux.* h.) cease weeping.

Ausweis, *m.* (-es, -e) proof, credential, identity card, passport; statement, evidence, certificate, voucher; documentary evidence; tenor, substance, purport, argument; *nach – der Gesetze,* in conformity with the law. **–en,** I. *ir.v.a.* turn out, extradite, expel, banish; show, prove, decide; *die Zeit wird es –en,* time will show. 2. *v.r.*; *sich –en,* identify oneself, prove one's identity; *sich genügend –en,* give a satisfactory account of o.s.; *das wird sich –en,* it will be seen in the end, the end will show, we shall see. **Ausgewiesene(r),** *m.* exile, deportee. **–karte,** *f.* identity card. **–papiere,** *n.pl.* identity card, permit, pass. **–ungsbefehl,** *m.* extradition *or* expulsion order.

ausweit–en, *v.a.* widen, stretch. **–eholz,** *n.* glove-stretcher.

auswendig, *adj.* outside, outward; by heart, by rote, by memory; *– lernen,* commit to memory, learn by heart; *– spielen,* play from memory (*music*); *– wissen,* know by heart; *etwas in- und – kennen,* know a thing thoroughly.

auswerf–en, I. *ir.v.a.* throw out; knock out; discharge, eject; vomit, expectorate; reject; disgorge; cut (*a ditch*); throw up (*a rampart*); throw overboard; hoist out (*a boat*); cast (*anchor*); fix (*a salary*); set apart (*a sum of money*); make an entry, charge (*to an account*); *das Lot –en,* swing the lead, take soundings (*Naut.*). 2. *n.* eruption (*Geol.*). **–er,** *m.* ejector (*of a gun*).

auswert–en, *v.a.* get the full value (from), make full use (of); evaluate, interpret (*aerial photographs, etc.*). **–ung,** *f.* utilization, evaluation, interpretation (*of evidence, photographs, etc.*), computation; *–ung der Lage,* estimate of the situation (*Mil.*).

auswetzen, *v.a.* remove by grinding; (*fig.*) make amends for, make up for, avenge; *eine Scharte –,* wipe out *or* obliterate a dent, blot *or* stain; *einen Schimpf –,* avenge an affront.

auswickeln, I. *v.a.* unwrap; unroll, disentangle. 2. *v.r.* extricate o.s.

auswiegen, *v.a.* weigh out. **ausgewogen,** *p.p.* & *adj.* weighed; calibrated.

auswinden, I. *ir.v.a.* wring out; unscrew. 2. *v.r.* *sich – (aus),* extricate o.s (from).

auswirk–en, I. *v.a.* get, obtain, procure; *sich* (*Dat.*) *etwas –en,* obtain a th. for o.s.; *Gnade einem Verurteilten –en,* secure a pardon for the condemned man. *den Teig –en,* knead dough. 2. *v.r.* operate, take effect; *die Heilung wirkt sich erst nach Monaten aus,* the cure only becomes effective after some months. 3. *v.n.* (*partic. in Perf.*) (*aux.* h.) cease to operate, cease to have any effect. **–ung,** *f.* effect, consequence.

auswischen, *v.a.* wipe out *or* away; efface, rub out; *Staub –,* dust out; (*coll.*) *jemandem einen* (or *eins*) *–,* deal a p. a sudden blow; (*sl.*) dot a p. one.

auswitter–n, I. *v.a.* effloresce, exude; season (*timber, etc.*); scent out (*game*); (*coll.*) smell out, nose out. 2. *v.r.* swarm round the hive (*of bees*); *–n lassen,* season (*timber*). **–ung,** *f.* efflorescence, exudation; weathering, seasoning.

Auswuchs, *m.* (-es, ⸚e) excrescence, protuberance; tumour; (*pl.*) abuses.

auswuchten, *v.a.* balance, compensate.

Auswurf, *m.* (-s, ⸚e) I. throwing out, ejection, discharge; expectoration; excretion; 2. outcast; refuse, dregs, scum, rubbish, trash; excrement; sputum; flotsam, jetsam; *– der Menschheit,* scum of the earth. **–blatt,** *n.*, **–bogen,** *m.* waste sheet (*Print.*). **–stoffe,** *m.pl.* excrement.

auszack–en, *v.a.* notch, indent, scallop, jag; engrail (*Her.*); **ausgezackt,** *p.p.* & *adj.* crenate, denticulate; scalloped (*of postage stamps*). **–ung,** *f.* indentation; denticulation.

auszahl–en, *v.a.* pay out, over *or* away; *bar –en,* pay down in cash. **–ung,** *f.* payment.

auszählen, I. *v.a.* count out. 2. *v.n.* (*aux.* h.) count to the end; finish counting.

auszahnen, *v.n.* (*aux.* h.) have done teething; *das Kind hat ausgezahnt,* the child has cut all its teeth.

auszehr–en, I. *v.a.* consume; waste away; *–ende Krankheit,* wasting disease, consumption; *einen –en,* eat a p. out of house and home. 2. *v.n.* (*aux.* s.) & *r.* waste away; *er zehrt aus,* he is in a decline. **–ung,** *f.* consumption, phthisis.

auszeichn–en, I. *v.a.* mark out, distinguish, treat with distinction; mark, price (*goods*). **ausgezeichnet,** *p.p.* & *adj.* excellent, capital, superb, distinguished. 2. *v.r.* distinguish o.s. (*durch,* by), excel. **–ung,** *f.* distinction; decoration, order; respect, consideration; mark, label. **–ungswert,** *adj.*, **–ungswürdig,** *adj.* worthy of special notice.

auszieh–en, I. *ir.v.a.* pull *or* draw out, extract; draw *or* take off; make an abstract of (*in writing*); make out (*a bill*); take out (*colours*); ink in (*a sketch*); stretch; distil out; concoct; exhaust; leach; *einen –en,* undress a p.; (*coll.*) fleece a p.; *einen Zahn –en,* extract a tooth; *Unkraut –en,* pull up weeds; *den alten Adam* or *Menschen –en,* turn over a new leaf. 2. *v.r.* undress. 3. *v.n.* (*aux.* s.) move, remove (*from a house, a town, etc.*); emigrate; have the move (*Chess, etc.*); march off, set out; take the field (*Mil.*). 4. *n.*, **–ung,** *f.*; extraction (*Chem., Math., Surg., etc.*); abstraction, decoction, infusion; undressing; *im –en begriffen sein,* be on the move. **–er,** extractor (*for ammunition*). **–tisch,** *m.* extension-table. **–tusche,** *f.* drawing ink, Indian ink. **ausgezogen,** *adj.* solid, continuous (*of a line*).

auszier–en, *v.a.* adorn, decorate, ornament; bedeck; *–en eines Schiffes,* dressing of a ship. **–ung,** *f.* decoration.

auszimmer–n, *v.a.* square (*timber*); line (*a shaft*) with timber, revet. **–ung,** *f.* timbering, revetting.

auszinnen, *v.a.* line with tin.

auszirkeln, *v.a.* measure *or* mark out with compasses; *alles –,* do everything by rule.

auszischen, *v.a.* hiss off (*the stage*).

Auszug, *m.* (-(e)s, ⸚e), I. marching *or* going out *or* off; departure, exodus, removal; procession;

emigration; 2. extract; abstract, epitome, summary, abridgement; 3. quintessence, essence, extract, decoction, infusion; 4. drawer, leaf (*of table*), number drawn (*in lottery*); – *der Kinder Israels*, Exodus; *im – darstellen*, epitomize. **-blatt**, *n.*, **-brett**, *n.*, **-platte**, *f.* leaf for an extension table. **-smehl**, *n.* superfine flour. **-sweise**, *adv.* in the form of an abstract *or* extracts.
auszupfen, *v.a.* pluck out; undo (*knots*); unravel, disentangle; *ausgezupfte Leinwand*, lint.
autark, *adj.* economically self-sufficient. **-ie**, *f.* (-n) autarky, self-sufficiency.
authent-isch, *adj.* authentic. **-isieren**, *v.a.* authenticate. **-izität**, *f.* authenticity.
Auto, *n.* (-s, -s) motor-car; – *fahren*, drive a car. **-bahn**, *f.* express motor road. **-brille**, *f.* goggles. **-bus**, *m.* (-sses, -sse) motor-bus. **-droschke**, *f.* taxi(cab). **-fahrer**, *m.* motorist. **-fahrt**, *f.* motor-drive. **-falle**, *f.* speed trap, police trap (against speeding). **-heber**, *m.* car jack. **-hupe**, *f.* motor hooter. **-schuppen**, *m.* garage. **-sport**, *m.* motoring. **-schlosser**, *m.* motor mechanic. **-straße**, *f.* motor road. **-verkehr**, *m.* motor traffic. *As a prefix*: **-biographie**, *f.* autobiography. **-biographisch**, *adj.* autobiographical. **-didakt**, *m.* (-en, en) self-taught person. **-gramm**, *n.* (-s, -e) autograph. **-klav**, *m.* (-s, -en) autoclave, digester (*Med.*). **-krat**, *m.* (-en, -en) autocrat. **-kratie**, *f.* autocracy. **-kratisch**, *adj.* autocratic. **-mat**, *m.* (-en, -en) automaton; penny-in-the-slot machine; self-service restaurant. **-matisch**, *adj.* automatic, self-acting. **-nom**, *adj.* autonomous. **-nomie**, *f.* autonomy. **-typie**, *f.* (-en) half-tone engraving.
Automobil, *n.* (-s, -e) motor-car. **-ist**, *m.* motorist. **-ausstellung**, *f.* motor-show. **-wesen**, *n.* motoring.
Autor, *m.* (-s, -en) author, writer. **-isieren**, *v.a.* authorize, empower. **-itär**, *adj.* authoritarian. **-ität**, *f.* authority; *die besten -itäten*, the persons best qualified to judge. **-schaft**, *f.* authorship.
Aval, *n.* written security, surety, bail. **-isieren**, *v.a.* (*C.L.*) stand security, go bail; endorse *or* guarantee (*a bill of exchange*).
Avanc-e, *f.* (-n) (*C.L. archaic*) advance, money advanced; profit; *mit -e verkaufen*, sell to advantage *or* at a profit; *mit -e bezahlen*, pay in advance. **-ement**, *n.* (-s, -s) preferment, promotion, advance in rank *or* office. **-ieren**, 1. *v.n.* be promoted; *im Dienste -ieren*, rise in the service. 2. *v.a.* put on (*clocks, etc.*).
Ave-Maria, *n.* (-(s), -(s)) Ave Maria, Hail Mary; – *Läuten*, Angelus (*bell*).
Avers, *m.* (-es, -e) obverse, head (*of a coin*).
Aviat-ik, *f.* aviation. **-iker**, *m.* aviator.
Avis, *m. or n.* (-es, -e), **-o**, *n.* (*Austrian*) (-s, -s) (*C.L.*) advice, intelligence. **-brief**, *m.* letter of advice. **-ieren**, *v.a.* (*C.L.*) advise, give notice of. **-o**, *m.* (-s, -s), **-schiff**, *n.* dispatch-boat, advice boat, aviso.
avista, *adv.* (*C.L.*) at sight. **-wechsel**, *m.* draft payable on presentation.
Axt, *f.* (⸚e) axe, hatchet. **-blatt**, *n.* axe-blade. **-stiel**, *m.* handle of an axe.
Az (= abbr. for *Aufschlagzünder*) percussion fuse (*Artil.*).
Azur, *m.* (-s) azure colour, sky blue. **-blau**, *adj.* & *n.* azure, sky blue. **-it**, *m.*, **-stein**, *m.* lapis lazuli. **-n**, *adj.* azure.

B

B, b, *n.* B, b; *b, das B.* 1. B. flat (*the semitone between A and B*) (*Mus.*); 2. flat (*musical symbol showing that the note before which it is placed is to be depressed by a semitone*); *das Quadrat B* or *B-Quadrat*, (♮) natural (*musical symbol cancelling a previous sharp or flat*); *b-moll*, B flat minor; *b-dur*, B flat major.
babbeln, *v.n.* (*coll.*) babble, chatter, prattle.
Babuin, *m.* (-s, -e) baboon.
Baby, *n.* (-s, -s) babe, infant. **-ausstattung**, *f.* layette.
Baccalaureat, *n.* *see* **Bakkalaureat.**
Bacchant, *m.* (-en, -en) worshipper of Bacchus; bacchanal, bacchanal *or* drunken reveller. **-in**, *f.* a priestess of Bacchus; female bacchanal, bacchante. **-isch**, *adj.* bacchantic, bacchic, bacchanalian, drunken, roistering.
Bach, *m.* (-(e)s, ⸚e; *dim.* **Bächlein**, *n.*) brook, stream, rivulet, rill, (*sl.*) the drink (*i.e. the sea*). **-amsel**, *f.* water-ousel, dipper (*Cinclus aquaticus*). **-binse**, *f.* bulrush (*Juncus conglomeratus*). **-fahrt**, *f.* water-course. **-holder**, *m.*, **-holunder**, *m.* guelder rose, water elder (*Viburnum opulus*). **-krebs**, *m.* crayfish, crawfish. **-kresse**, *f.* watercress (*Nasturtium officinale*). **-mücke**, *f.* crane-fly, daddy-long-legs. **-stelze**, *f.* **-stelzchen**, *n.* water-wagtail (*Motacilla*). **-weide**, *f.* crack-willow, osier (*Salix*).
Bach-e, *f.* (-en) wild sow. **-er**, *m.* (-ers, -er) wild boar.
Back, *f.* (-en) & *n.* (-es, -e) forecastle (*Naut.*); mess tin; mess table, mess (*Naut.*). **-bord**, 1. *n.* & *m.* larboard, port; 2. *adv.* aback, abaft (*Naut.*); *-bord das Ruder!* port the helm! **-stag**, *n.* after thwart (*Naut.*).
Back-e, *f.* (-en), **-en**, *m.* (-ens, -en) cheek; bow (*of a ship*); (*pl.*) side-beams; *mit eingefallenen -en*, hollow-cheeked; *dicke -e*, swollen cheek; *die -en vollnehmen*, talk big. **-enbart**, *m.* whiskers. **-enbremse**, *f.* shoe brakes (*Motor.*). **-engrube**, *f.*, **-engrübchen**, *n.* dimple. **-enknochen**, *m.* cheekbone. **-enstreich**, *m.* box on the ear, slap in the face. **-enstreif**, *m.* lappet. **-(en)zahn**, *m.* molar tooth. **-feige**, *f.*, **-pfeife**, *f.* box on the ear. **-ig**, *adj.* (*only in compounds, also* -bäckig, *e.g.* rotbäckig, rotbackig) -cheeked.
back-en, *reg.* & *ir.v.a.* bake (*bread, etc.*), roast, fry; burn, fire (*pottery tiles*); dry (*fruit*); (*coll.*) cake (*as snow on shoes*) (*in this meaning wk. conj.*); (*coll.*) *sein Brot ist ihm gebacken*, there is a rod in pickle for him. **-apfel**, *m.* baking-apple, dried apple. **-fisch**, *m.* girl in her teens, (*sl.*) teen-ager, flapper. **-form**, *f.* cake-tin, patty-pan, pastry-mould. **-mulde**, *f.* kneading-trough. **-obst**, *n.* dried fruit. **-ofen**, *m.* oven. **-pfanne**, *f.* baking-tin; frying-pan. **-pflaume**, *f.* prune. **-pulver**, *n.* baking-powder. **-rädchen**, *n.* pastry cutter. **-schüssel**, *f.* pie-dish, baking-dish. **-stein**, *m.* brick. **-trog**, *m.* kneading-trough. **-werk**, *n.* pastry.
Bäcker, *m.* (-s, -) baker. **-beine**, *n.pl.* knock-knees. **-ei**, *f.* bakery; bakehouse. **-bursche**, *m.*, **-junge**, *m.* baker's boy. **-geselle**, *m.* journeyman baker. **-schabe**, *f.* cockroach.
Bad, *n.* (-es, ⸚er) bath; watering-place; (*pl.*) (mineral) waters; *das Kind mit dem -e ausschütten*, *see* **ausschütten**; *Fuß-*, foot-bath; *Gieß-*, douche; *Schwimm-*, swimming bath; *Schwitz-*, vapour-bath; *Sitz-*, hip-bath; *ins Bad reisen*, go to a watering-place; go to the seaside; *die Bäder brauchen*, take the waters. **-eanstalt**, *f.* baths, bathing-establishment. **-eanzug**, *m.* bathing-costume. **-earzt**, *m.* physician at a watering-place. **-egast**, *m.* visitor at a watering-place. **-ehose**, *f.* bathing-trunks. **-ekappe**, *f.* bathing-cap. **-ekarren**, *m.* bathing-machine. **-ekur**, *f.* treatment at a watering-place; course of mineral waters. **-elaken**, *n.*, *see* **-etuch**. **-emantel**, *m.* bathing-wrap. **-emeister**, *m.* bath attendant. **-en**, *v.a.* & *r.* bathe; *in Blut -en*, wallow in blood; *in Schweiß gebadet*, bathed in perspiration. **-eofen**, *m.* geyser. **-eort**, *m.* watering-place, spa. **-er**, *m.* (*archaic*) barber-surgeon. **-esaison**, *f.* holiday season. **-eschwamm**, *m.* bath sponge. **-estrand**, *m.* bathing beach. **-etuch**, *n.* bath towel. **-ewanne**, *f.* bath-tub. **-ezeit**, *f.* season (*at a watering-place*). **-ezimmer**, *n.* bathroom.
baff, (*coll.*) *ich bin ganz* –, I am dumbfounded *or* speechless.
Bäffchen, *n.* *see* **Beffchen.**
Bagage, *f.* luggage, baggage; (*coll.*) rabble.
Bagatell-e, *f.* (-en) trifle; (*coll.*) small fry. **-sache**, *f.* petty lawsuit. **-schulden**, *f.pl.* trifling debts.
Bagger, *m.* (-s, -) dredger, excavator. **-maschine**, *f.* dredger. **-n**, *v.a.* (*aux.* h.) dredge. **-netz**, *n.* dredging net. **-prahm**, *m.* dredging float *or* raft.

bäh-en, *v.a.* foment; (*Med.*). **-ung,** *f.* fomentation.

Bahn, *f.* (-en) path, (path)way, track, road; course; orbit; trajectory; railway; face (*of a hammer, plane, anvil, etc.*); groove; width (*of fabrics*); *Reit–*, riding-school; *Renn–*, race-course; *Gleit–*, slide; *Kegel–*, skittle alley; *Eis–*, skating rink; *Schlitten–*, sledge run; *sich* (*Dat.*) *– brechen*, force one's way; *die – brechen*, (*fig.*) break the ice, pave the way; *zur – gehen*, go to the station; *auf die – bringen*, take to the station; (*fig.*) put in the right way, start properly; *auf die schiefe – geraten*, be on the downward path; *auf rechter – sein*, be on the right track; *in die richtige – lenken*, *in bestimmte –en lenken*, canalize. (*See also* **Eisenbahn–**). **-anlagen,** *f.pl.* railway installations. **-arbeiter,** *m.* railway worker. **-beamte(r),** *m.* railway official. **-brechend,** *adj.* pioneering, epoch-making; *–brechende Arbeit*, pioneer work. **-brecher,** *m.* pioneer. **-damm,** *m.* railway embankment. **-ebene,** *f.* plane of motion, orbital plane. **-en,** *v.a.* make a way, open a way; smooth, prepare (*the way*), pave the way for; pioneer; *einem den Weg –en zu*, put a p. in the right way for. **-fahrt,** *f.* railway journey. **-frei,** *adj.* (*C.L.*) paid in advance (*of goods transported by rail*). **-geleise, -gleis,** *n.* railway track. **-hof,** *m.* railway station. **-hofsvorsteher,** *m.* station-master. **-körper,** *m.* permanent way. **-lagernd,** *adj.* to be collected (*at railway station*). **-los,** *adj.* pathless, trackless. **-netz,** *n.* railway system. **-renner,** *m.* track racer (*Cycl.*). **-schwelle,** *f.* sleeper. **-sperre,** *f.*, **-steigsperre,** *f.* barrier (*at stations*). **-steig,** *m.* platform (*at railway stations*). **-stollen,** *m.* tunnel. **-strecke,** *f.* section, line. **-wärter,** *m.* signalman.

Bahr-e, *f.* (-en) stretcher, bier, litter; *von der Wiege bis zur –e*, from cradle to grave. **-tuch,** *n.* pall.

Bai, *f.* (-en) bay; *kleine –*, creek, cove.

Baisse, *f.* (-n) (*C.L.*) slump.

Bajonett, *n.* (-s, -e) bayonet; (*das*) *– ab!* unfix bayonets! *das – aufsetzen*, fix bayonets; *mit aufgepflanztem –*, with fixed bayonets; *mit gefälltem –*, at the point of the bayonet. **-ieren,** *v.a.* bayonet.

Bake, *f.* (-n) beacon, landmark.

Bakel, *m.* (-s, -) schoolmaster's cane.

Bakelit, *n.* bakelite.

Bakkalaure-at, *n.* (-(e)s-e) bachelor's degree; B.A., B.Sc. **-us,** *m.* (-us, -us) bachelor (*of arts, etc.*).

Bakteri-en, *f.pl.* bacteria. **-ell,** *adj.* bacterial. **-enforschung,** *f.*, **-enkunde,** *f.* bacteriology. **-ologe,** *m.* bacteriologist. **-ologie,** *f.* bacteriology. **-ologisch,** *adj.* bacteriological.

Balance, *f.* balance, equilibrium.

Balancier, *m.* (-s, -s) beam (*of a balance or engine*); balance-wheel. **-en,** *v.a.* balance. **-maschine,** *f.* beam engine. **-schritt,** *m.* goose-step (*Mil.*). **-stange,** *f.* balancing-pole (*of a tightrope walker*).

balbieren, *v.a.* (*coll.*) *see* **barbieren.**

bald, *adv.* (*comp.* **eher,** *sup.* **am ehesten**) soon, shortly; almost, nearly; easily; *er kam –*, it was not long before he came; *ich wäre – gestorben*, I had nearly died; *so – wie*, as soon as; *es ist – gesagt*, it's easy talking; *– so, – so*, now one way, now another; *– heiter, – traurig*, sometimes merry, sometimes sad; *– das eine, – das andere*, sometimes this, sometimes that. **-ig,** 1. *adj.* early; speedy, quick. 2. *adv.* soon. **-igst, -möglichst,** *adv.* as soon as possible.

Baldachin, *m.* (-s, -e) canopy.

Bälde, *f.*; (*C.L.*) *in –*, soon.

Baldrian, *m.* (-s, -e) valerian. **-säure,** *f.* valeric acid. **-tropfen,** *m.pl.* valerian essence.

Balg, *m.* (-(e)s, ¨-e) 1. husk, pod, follicle, shell, case, skin, slough; 2. cyst; bellows; 3. (*also n.*) imp, brat, urchin; wretch; (*dial.*) illegitimate child; *der dicke –*, paunch; *die Bälge treten*, blow *or* work the bellows (*of an organ*). **-drüse,** *f.* follicular gland. **-en,** *m.* (-ens, -en) bellows (*of a camera*). **-enlinse,** *f.*, **-enniese,** *f.* nozzle of bellows. **-enregister,** *n.* wind-indicator (*in an organ*). **-enschwengel,** *m.* bellows handle. **-entreter, Bälgetreter,** *m.* organ-blower. **-geschwulst,** *f.* encysted tumour. **-kapsel,** *f.* follicle.

Balg-e, *f.* (-n) (*dial.*) wash-tub. **-en,** *v.r.* 1. cast the skin; 2. wrestle, fight; romp, scuffle, (*coll.*) **-erei,** *f.* tussle, scuffle.

balhornisieren, *v.a.* bowdlerize, spoil in the attempt to improve (*after the printer Balhorn*).

Balken, *m.* (-s, -) beam, rafter, joist, girder; baulk; bar, chevron (*Her.*); (*Prov.*) *Wasser hat keine –*, don't trust yourself to the water; *– des Gehirns*, corpus callosum cerebri (*Anat.*). **-anker,** *m.* building clamp, brace. **-band,** *n.* dovetail (*Carp.*). **-decke,** *f.* raftered ceiling. **-gerüst,** *n.* scaffolding. **-lage,** *f.* flooring. **-streif,** *m.* fesse (*Her.*). **-stein,** *m.* corbel. **-waage,** *f.* steelyard, beam balance. **-werk,** *n.* woodwork, timbers, beams (*of a building*), framework.

Balkon, *m.* (-s, -e & -s) balcony.

[1]**Ball,** *m.* (-(e)s, ¨-e) ball; globe, sphere; *den – anspielen*, serve a ball; play off, lead; *den – verschlagen*, serve a fault (*Tenn.*); *den – im Aufsprunge fangen*, catch the ball on the bounce; *einen – machen*, pocket *or* hole a ball (*Bill.*); *ein schön gemachter –*, a good hazard (*Bill.*). **-en,** 1. *v.a.* form into a ball, clench (*fist, etc.*); 2. *v.n.* conglomerate, cluster. **-förmig,** *adj.* spherical, globular. **-ig,** *adj.* slightly convex. **-pritsche,** *f.* battledore. **-schläger,** *m.* racket. **-spiel,** *n.* ball game. **-stock,** *m.* cue; bat. **-ung,** *f.* agglomeration.

[2]**Ball,** *m.* (-(e)s, ¨-e) ball, dance; *auf den – gehen, zu –e gehen*, go to a dance. **-abend,** *m.* ball, soirée. **-dame,** *f.* lady partner at a dance. **-erina, -erine,** *f.* (–nen) ballerina. **-kleid,** *n.* dance dress.

Ballade, *f.* (-n) ballad. **-ndichter,** *m.* ballad-writer. **-ndichtung,** *f.* ballad poetry.

Ballast, *m.* (-es, -e) ballast; *den – einnehmen*, take in ballast; *– abwerfen*, drop ballast; *mit –*, in ballast. **-ladung,** *f.* dead freight.

Ballei, *f.* (-en) bailiwick.

Ballen, *m.* (-s, -) bundle, bale, package; ten reams (*of paper*); a weight, measure (*for flax, silk, etc.*); palm (*of the hand*); ball (*of the foot*); button (*of a foil*); bunion. **-avis,** *m.* (*C.L.*) notification of dispatch of a bale. **-binder,** *m.* packer. **-degen,** *m.* foil. **-eisen,** *n.* ripping-chisel. **-haken,** *m.* packer's hook. **-waren,** *f.pl.* bale-goods. **-weise,** *adv.* in bales.

ballen, *see under* [1]**Ball.**

Ballerina, Ballerine, *see under* [2]**Ball.**

baller-n, *v.a.* (*coll.*) bang, make a noise; fire off, shoot. **-büchse,** *f.* pop-gun.

Ballett, *n.* (-s, -e) ballet. **-euse, -(t)änzerin,** *f.*, ballet-dancer, ballerina.

ballhornisieren, *see* **balhornisieren.**

Ballistik, *f.* ballistics.

Ballon, *m.* (-s, -e & -s) balloon; flask, carboy (*Chem.*). **-gurt,** *m.* balloon cable. **-halle,** *f.* hangar. **-reifen,** *m.* balloon tyre. **-sperre,** *f.* balloon barrage. **-winde,** *f.* winch.

Ballot-age, *f.* balloting; ballot. **-ieren,** *v.n.* (*aux.* h.) vote by ballot.

Balsam, *m.* (-s, -e) balsam, balm, salve, ointment. **-ieren,** *v.a.* embalm, render fragrant. **-ine,** *f.* balsamine (*Impatiens balsamina*). **-isch,** *adj.* balmy; fragrant, soothing. **-kraut,** *n.* balsam herb (*Dianthera repens*), moschatel (*Adoxa moschatellina*).

Balz, *f.* pairing time (*of birds*). **-en,** *v.n.* (*aux.* h.) pair; mate, copulate (*of birds*).

Bambus, *m.* (– & -ses, – & -se) bamboo. **-rohr,** *n.* bamboo cane.

Bammel, *m.* (*coll.*) funk.

bammeln, *v.n.* dangle, hang down.

bamsen, *v.a.* (*coll.*) beat.

banal, *adj.* commonplace, trite, banal. **-ität,** *f.* banality.

Banane, *f.* (-n) banana. **-nfaser,** *f.* plantain-fibre. **-nstecher,** *m.* banana plug (*Rad.*).

Banaus-e, *m.* (-en, -en) narrow-minded fellow; philistine. **-entum,** *n.* narrow-mindedness. **-isch,** *adj.* narrow-minded, limited.

[1]**Band,** *n.* (-(e)s, ¨-er) ribbon, tape, band, strip, strap; bond; hinge; hoop (*of a cask*); swathe (*of a sheaf*); tie-beam (*of a roof, etc.*); ligament (*Anat.*); ligature; bandage; *Schuh–*, shoe-lace; *Zwirn–*, tape; *laufendes –*, conveyor belt, conveyor; *am laufenden –*, *adv.* (*also fig.*) without intermission; *das blaue –*, the Blue Riband. **-age,** *f.* bandage; truss.

-ähnlich, -artig, *adj.* ribbon-like, streaked. **-breite,** *f.* bandwidth (*Rad.*). **-eisen,** *n.* hoop-iron. **-fabrik,** *f.* ribbon factory. **-feder,** *f.* coil-spring. **-haken,** *m.* hasp. **-kupplung,** *f.* rim clutch (*Motor.*). **-krämer,** *m.* haberdasher. **-maß,** *n.* tape measure. **-nudeln,** *f.pl.* ribbon vermicelli. **-reif,** *m.* hoop. **-schleife,** *f.* favour; cockade. **-streif,** *m.* bend (*Her.*); top-knot. **-streifig,** *adj.* banded. **-waren,** *f.pl.* haberdashery. **-wurm,** *m.* tape-worm.

[2]**Band,** *n.* (-(e)s, -e) tie, bond; – *der Freundschaft,* bond of friendship; *eheliches* –, conjugal tie; (*pl.*) fetters, bonds.

[3]**Band,** *m.* (-es, ¨-e) volume, tome; binding (*of a book*).

Bänd-chen, *n.* (-s, -) small ribbon; small volume. **-ereich,** *adj.* in many volumes, voluminous.

Bande, *f.* (-n) band, gang, company; troop, set, pack; border, edge; cushion (*Bill.*); *lustige* –, merry party; *einen Ball dicht an die – spielen,* leave one's ball under the cushion (*Bill.*); *an der – abprallen* (*Bill.*), rebound from the cushion. **-nkrieg,** *m.* guerrilla warfare.

bändig, *adj.* (*in compounds* =) in . . . volumes, *e.g. drei–er Roman,* novel in three volumes.

bändig-en, *v.a.* restrain; subdue, master; break in (*a horse*). **-ung,** *f.* taming, subduing.

Bandit, *m.* (-en, -en) bandit.

bang-e, *adj.* (*comp.* **-er, bänger;** *sup.* **-st, bängst**) afraid, alarmed; timid, anxious. *-e machen,* frighten, terrify; (*coll.*) *-e machen gilt nicht,* I am not to be browbeaten; I won't be bullied; *es ist mir -e um ihn,* I am anxious about him; *es ist mir -e vor ihm,* I am afraid of him; *uns war angst und -e,* we were frightened to death. **-e,** *f.* (*coll.*) fear, worry; (*coll.*) *haben Sie keine -e!* don't worry! **-en,** I. *v.n.* (*aux.* h.) & *imp.* be afraid; *ich -e mich, es -t mir* or *mir -t vor der Zukunft,* I am anxious about the future; *ich -e mich, es -t mir um mein Leben,* I am afraid for my life; *ich -e mich um ihn,* I am anxious about him; *sich -en nach,* long *or* yearn for. **-igkeit,** *f.* anxiety, uneasiness, fear, dread.

bänglich, *adj.* somewhat anxious, rather timid.

[1]**Bank,** *f.* (¨-e) bench, seat, form, pew; sand-bank, reef, shoal; bed, layer, stratum; parapet, banquette, barbette (*Fort.*); *Dreh–,* turning-lathe; *Hobel–,* carpenter's bench; *Fleisch–,* butcher's block; *Fleischer–,* stall, shambles; *auf die lange – schieben,* put aside, defer, keep putting off; *durch die* –, without exception, taking all in all, one and all, in gross; *sich nicht leicht unter die – stecken lassen,* not to be easily put down; *von der – fallen* or *von der – gefallen sein* or *auf der – erzeugt sein,* be a bastard, be an illegitimate child.

[2]**Bank,** *f.* (-en) bank, banking establishment; gambling-bank; *Geld an die – geben* or *bei der – deponieren,* deposit money in the bank; *Geld bei* or *auf der – haben,* have money in the bank; *ein Scheck auf die – von England,* a cheque on the Bank of England; *die – sprengen,* break the bank (*Cards*); *die – halten* or *auflegen,* (*die*) *– machen,* keep *or* hold bank (*Cards*). **-abschluß,** *m.* balance sheet. **-agent,** *m.* exchange broker. **-aktien,** *f.pl.* bank-stock *or* shares. **-aktionär,** *m.* holder of bank-stock. **-anweisung,** *f.* cheque, bank bill. **-beamte(r),** *m.* bank clerk. **-bruch,** *m.* bankruptcy; *-bruch machen,* go bankrupt, fail. **-brüchig,** *adj.* bankrupt, insolvent. **-buch,** *n.* bank book, pass book. **-diskont,** *m.* bank rate. **-(e)rott,** *m., see* **Bank(e)-rott. -fach,** *n.* banking business. **-fähig,** *adj.* negotiable, bankable. **-feiertag,** *m.* bank holiday. **-gewölbe,** *n.* strong-room, bullion-vault, safe-deposit. **-halter,** *m.* casino manager, holder of the bank **-ier,** *m. see* **Bankier. -konto,** *n.* banking account; *ein -konto eröffnen,* open an account at a bank. **-note,** *f.* bank-note; bank-bill (*Amer.*). **-notenausgabe,** *f.* note-issue. **-notenpapier,** *n.* currency paper. **-notenumlauf,** *m.* notes in circulation, paper currency. **-prokura,** *f.* power of attorney to transact banking business. **-schein,** *m. see* **-note. -valuta,** *f.* paper currency **-werte,** *m.pl.* negotiable papers. **-wesen,** *n.* banking. **-zinsfuß,** *m.* bank rate.

Bänkel-gesang, *m.* popular ballad. **-kind,** *n. see* **Bankert. -sänger,** *m.* itinerant singer, singer of popular ballads, rhymester, poetaster. **-sängerei,** *f.* street-minstrelsy, popular balladry.

Bank(e)rott, I. *m.* (-(e)s, -e) bankruptcy, insolvency; – *machen,* go bankrupt, fail; *betrügerischer* –, fraudulent bankruptcy. 2. *adj.* bankrupt. **-befehl,** *m.* fiat in bankruptcy. **-erklärung,** *f.* declaration (*or* act) of bankruptcy.

Bankert, *m.* (-s, -e) bastard, illegitimate child.

Bankett, *n.* (-s, -e) banquet. **-e,** *f.* banquette (*Fort.*); side space (*Railw.*) (= *footpath at side of track*).

Bankier [bɑ̃k'je:], *m.* (-s, -s) banker.

Bann, *m.* I. jurisdiction; (*fig.*) power, constraint; 2. ban, proscription; excommunication; 3. spell, curse, charm; 4. (*pl.* -e) 'regiment' of Hitler Youth (3,000 strong); *kleiner Kirchen–,* interdict; *in den* –, or *in Acht und – tun,* excommunicate; *den – aufheben,* remove an interdict. **-brief,** *m.* interdict. **-bulle,** *f.* **-fluch,** *m.* papal edict *or* bull; anathema. **-en,** *v.a.* I. banish, expel; put under the ban; excommunicate; 2. enchant, charm, captivate; conjure up *or* away; exorcise; 3. fix (*to a certain place* or *within certain limits*), confine; *festgebannt,* rooted to the spot. **-kreis,** *m.* jurisdiction; (*fig.*) (sphere of) influence. **-meile,** *f.* boundary *or* precinct (*of a city*). **-spruch,** *m.* excommunication; exorcism. **-strahl,** *m. see* **-fluch. -wald,** *m.* (*Swiss*), forest preserve (*as protection against avalanches*). **-waren,** *f.pl.* contraband goods, controlled goods (*i.e. distribution subject to war-time controls*). **-wart,** *m.* (*Swiss*) forester, forest-ranger *or* -warden.

Banner, *n.* banner, standard, flag. **-träger,** *m.* standard-bearer.

bannig, *adj.* (*dial.*) extraordinary, very, much.

Bans-e, *f.,* (-en) (*dial.*) barn. **-en,** *v.a.* (*dial.*) pile up sheaves.

[1]**Bar,** *m.* (-e, -e) mastersinger's song.

[2]**Bar,** *f.* (-, -s) drinking and dancing saloon, night club.

bar, *adj.* bare, naked; ready (*of money*); destitute of, devoid of; pure, unmixed; sheer; *-e Zahlung,* cash payment; *-er Ertrag,* net proceeds, proceeds in cash; *– bezahlen,* pay cash; *– liefern,* supply for cash; *gegen* –, for cash; *für -e Münze nehmen,* take at face value; *für -en Ernst nehmen,* believe implicitly; *-es Geld* (or *-geld*), ready money; cash; *-er Unsinn,* sheer nonsense. **-auslage,** *f.* outlay. **-einnahme,** *f.* cash receipts. **-ertrag,** *m.* net proceeds. **-füßer,** *m.* barefooted friar, Franciscan. **-geldlos,** *adj.* paid by cheque, *etc.* (*not in cash*). **-gewinn,** *m.* net proceeds, profit. **-kauf,** *m.* cash purchase. **-laufen,** *n.* prisoner's-base (*a game*). **-preis,** *m.* cash price. **-schaft,** *f.* ready money. **-sendung,** *f.* consignment in specie. **-sortiment,** *n.* wholesale book-store. **-vorrat,** *m.* cash in hand; *-vorrat der Bank,* bullion at the bank; gold reserve. **-vorschuß,** *m.* cash advance. **-zahlend,** *adj.* paying cash; *-zahlende Banken,* specie-banks. **-zahlung,** *f.* cash payment.

Bär, *m.* (-en, -en) bear, (*also fig.* = uncouth fellow); rammer, pile-driver (*Gen.* -s); *junger* –, bear's cub; *der Große* (*Kleine*) –, the Great (Lesser) Bear, Ursa major (minor); (*coll.*) *-en anbinden,* run into debt; (*coll.*) *einen -en abbinden,* pay a debt; *einem einen -en aufbinden,* hoax a p., play a practical joke; *ungeleckter* –, unlicked cub; (*fig.*) rude fellow. **-beißig,** *adj.* quarrelsome, grumpy. **-enartig,** *adj.* ursine. **-enbeißer,** *m.* bulldog. **-enfang,** *m.* bear-hunting; bear-trap. **-enfell,** *n.* bear's skin. **-enführer,** *m.* bear-leader; (*sl.*) cicerone. **-enhatz,** *f.,* **-enhetze,** *f.* bear-baiting. **-enhaut,** *f.* bear-skin; (*coll.*) *auf der -enhaut liegen,* be lazy, lounge about. **-enhäuter,** *m.* idler, sluggard. **-enhüter,** *m.* keeper of bears; Bootes (*Astr.*). (*coll.*) **-hunger,** *m.* ravenous hunger. (*coll.*) **-enkälte,** *f.* extreme cold. **-enklau,** *m.* & *f.* hogweed (*Bot.*); acanthus (*Bot.*). (*coll.*) **-enmäßig,** I. *adj.* very great, enormous. 2. *adj.* very. **-enmütze,** *f.* bearskin cap; busby (*Mil.*). **-enpfeife,** *f.* bourdon pipe (*of an organ*). **-enraupe,** *f.* woolly-bear. **-enzwinger,** *m.* bear garden *or* pit. **-in,** *f.* she-bear. **-lapp,** *m.* club-moss, lycopodium. **-wurz,** *f.* bear's wort, spicknel (*Meum athamanticum*).

Baracke, *f.* (-n) hut, barrack. **-nlager,** *n.* hutment.

Barbar, *m.* (-en, -en) barbarian. **-ei,** *f.* barbarity, cruelty; barbarism. **-isch,** *adj.* barbarous, cruel; barbarian, barbaric; outlandish; (*coll.*) *ich habe -ischen Hunger,* I am fearfully hungry. **-ismus,** *m.* barbarism (*i.e. impurity or vulgarity in speech or writing*).
Barbe, *f.* (-n) barbel (*Icht.*) (*Barbus vulgaris*).
Barbier, *m.* (-s, -e) barber. **-becken,** *n.* shaving-mug. **-en,** *v.a.* shave; (*fig.*) cheat; (*coll.*) *einen über den Löffel -en,* fleece *or* cheat a p. **-messer,** *n.* razor. **-riemen,** *m.* (razor-)strop. **-zeichen,** *n.* barber's pole.
Barchent, *m.* (-s, -e) fustian. **-en,** *adj.* of fustian.
Bard-e, *m.* (-en, -en) bard; minstrel. **-engesänge,** *m.pl.* bardic lays. **-entum,** *n.* bardic writing, patriotic minstrelsy. **-iet,** *n.* (-(e)s, -e) bardic song; patriotic drama by Klopstock. **-isch,** *adj.* bardic.
Barett, *n.* (-s, -e) biretta; cardinal's hat; (*coll.*) mortar-board; skull-cap.
barg, bärge, *see* **bergen.**
Bariton, *m.* (-s, -e) baritone.
Bark, *f.* barque (*Naut.*). **-asse,** *f.* long-boat, launch. **-e,** *f.* Mediterranean fishing craft.
Barlaufen, *n.* prisoner's-base (*a game*).
Bärm-e, *f.* barm, yeast, leaven.
barmherzig, *adj.* compassionate; charitable; *-er Bruder,* monk-hospitaller; *-e Schwester,* sister of mercy; *-er Samariter,* good Samaritan. **-keit,** *f.* compassion, charity, mercy.
Barock, 1. *n.* Baroque (= *17th-cent. art style*), baroque style. 2. *adj.* baroque; quaint, grotesque. **-dichtung,** *f.* baroque poetry (= *German 17th cent.*). **-stil,** *m.* baroque style (*of architecture*).
Baromet-er, *n.* & *m.* (-ers, -er) barometer. **-risch,** *adj.* barometric(al). **-erstand,** *m.* height of the barometer, barometric level.
Baron, *m.* (-s, -e) baron. **-esse,** *f.* titled lady (*i.e. baron's unmarried daughter*). **-in,** *f.* baroness (*i.e. baron's wife*).
Barre, *f.* (-n) 1. bar (*at river's mouth*), barrier, rail; 2. bar, ingot. **-n,** *m.* 1. *see* **Barre** (2); 2. parallel bars (*Gymn.*). **-ngold,** *n.* gold in ingots, gold bullion. **-nhändler,** *m.* bullion-dealer. **-nturnen,** *n.* parallel-bar exercises (*Gymn.*).
Barriere, *f.* (-n) barrier (*Railw.*); toll-bar; frontier post.
Barsch, *m.* (-es, -e) perch (*Icht.*).
barsch, *adj.* rough; rude, tart, brusque, gruff, harsh. **-heit,** *f.* rudeness, roughness, *etc.*
barst, bärste, *see* **bersten.**
Bart, *m.* (-es, ⸚e) beard; wattles (*of a turkey*); whiskers (*of a cat*); barb (*Bot.*); fin, barb (*of fishes*); beard (*of grain*); beard (*of oysters*); wards (*of a key*); *Schnurr-,* moustache; *Backen-,* whiskers; *einen um den - gehen,* cajole s.o.; *in den - brummen,* mutter to o.s.; *er lacht in den -,* he laughs in his sleeve; *sich um des Kaisers - streiten,* quarrel about trifles; fight for a shadow. **-binde,** *f.* moustache-trainer. **-flechte,** *f.* barber's itch; beard-moss (*Bot.*) (*Usnea barbata*). **-geier,** *m.* golden vulture. **-hafer,** *m.* wild oats. **-lappen,** *m.pl.* gills (*Icht.*). **-los,** *adj.* beardless, smooth-faced. **-nelke,** *f.* sweet-william (*Bot.*) (*Dianthus barbatus*). **-salbe,** *f.*, **-wichse,** *f.* cosmetics for the beard. **-weizen,** *m.* bearded wheat.
Barte, *f.* (-n) broad-axe, battle axe; upper jaw of a whale; whalebone.
bärtig, *adj.* bearded, barbellate (*Bot.*).
Baryt, *m.* (-s, -e) barytes, heavy spar. **-artig, -haltig,** *adj.* barytic.
Basalt, *m.* (-(e)s, -e) basalt. **-haltig, -isch,** *adj.* basaltic.
Basar, *m.* (-s, -e) bazaar; sale.
[1]**Base,** *f.* (-n) female cousin; (*Swiss*) aunt. **-nhaft,** *adj.* gossipy. **-nschaft,** *f.* female relatives; (*sl.*) hen party.
[2]**Bas-e,** *f.* (-en) base, pedestal; alkali. **-is,** *f.* (-sen) base, basis. **-isch,** *adj.* basic, basal, alkaline (*Chem.*); radical. **-ieren,** 1. *v.a.* establish, base, ground. 2. *v.n.* be based, grounded *or* founded (*auf,* on).
Basilie, *f.*, **-nkraut,** *n.*, **Basilikum,** *n.* (-s, -s & -ken) basil (*Bot.*).
Basilisk, *m.* (-en, -en) basilisk; cockatrice.
baß, *adv.* (*Poet.*) very, very much, highly, in a high degree, more, rather.
Baß, *m.* (-(ss)es, ⸚(ss)e) bass; bass singer, bass viol, double bass; *begleitender, gebundener -,* thorough-bass. **-(ss)ett,** *n.* (-(e)s, -e) small bass viol. **-(ss)etthorn,** *n.* tenor clarinet. **-(ss)ettstimme,** *f.* baritone voice. **-geige,** *f.* bass-viol; double-bass. **-ist,** *m.* (-en, -en) bass singer. **-pfeife,** *f.* bassoon; drone (*of a bagpipe*). **-posaune,** *f.* trombone. **-saite,** *f.* bass string. **-schlüssel,** *m.* bass clef, bass key. **-stimme,** *f.* bass voice; bass part.
Basset, *m.* (-s, -s) short-legged dog, basset (hound).
Bassin, *n.* (-s, -s) reservoir, dock, basin; tank, cistern, bowl.
Bast, *m.* (-es) inner bark, fibre (*of trees, etc.*), husk (*of flax, etc.*) cuticle of a stag's antler; bast. **-en,** *adj.* made of bast. **-matte,** *f.* bast mat. **-seide,** *f.* raw silk.
basta, *int.* enough; *und damit -!* and there's an end of it!
Bastard, *m.* (-s, -e) bastard; hybrid, mongrel. **-artig,** *adj.* hybrid. **-feile,** *f.* flat file. **-fenster,** *n.* blind window, Flemish window. **-geier,** *m.* white-headed vulture. **-ierung,** *f.* hybridization. **-rasse,** *f.* cross-breed.
Bastei, Bastion, *f.* (-en) bastion, bulwark.
bast-eln, *v.a.* & *n.*, (*rarely v.a.*) occupy o.s. with a constructive hobby, work at as a hobby (*carpentry, radio, but not gardening or needlework*). **-ler,** *m.* amateur *or* home constructor.
Bastonade, (*Austr.*) **Bastonnade,** bastinado; *die - erhalten,* be bastinadoed.
bat, bäte, *see* **bitten.**
Bataillon, *n.* (-s, -e) battalion. **-sbüro,** *n.* battalion orderly room. **-schef,** *m.* battalion commander. **-sstabsquartier,** *n.* battalion headquarters.
Bäting, *see* **Beting.**
Batist, *m.* (-es, -e) cambric. **-en,** *adj.* made of cambric. **-taschentuch,** *n.* cambric handkerchief.
Batterie, *f.* (-n) 1. battery; ordnance; turret of (*naval*) guns; 2. battery (*of electric cells*); *fahrende -,* mounted battery; *reitende -,* troop of horse artillery. **-chef,** *m.*, **-führer,** *m.* battery commander.
Batzen, *m.* 1. small obsolete German coin; 2. lump, clod; (*coll.*) *er hat einen schönen - Geld,* he is well off; *das kostet einen ganzen -,* that cost a pile of money.
Bau, *m.* (-es, *usually* -ten) 1. building, erection, construction; edifice, structure; working (*of a mine*); 2. build, frame, form; 3. (*pl.* -e) burrow (*of rabbit*), earth (*of fox*), form (*of hare*), sett (*of badger*), holt (*of otter*), drey (*of squirrel*), fortress (*of mole*), den; 4. cultivation, culture, agriculture (*especially as suffix*); *Acker-,* agriculture; *Garten-,* horticulture; *Wein-,* wine growing; *Berg-,* mining; *die Kirche ist im - begriffen,* the church is being built *or* is under construction; *öffentliche -ten,* public buildings. **-akademie,** *f.* school of architecture. **-akkord,** *m.* building contract. **-amt,** *n.* Board of Works. **-anschlag,** *m.* builder's estimate. **-art,** *f.* style of architecture; type of construction, design. **-aufseher,** *m.* inspector of buildings; district surveyor. **-bar,** *adj.* capable of cultivation; worth working. **-en,** *see* **bauen.** **-fach,** *n.* architecture, building trade. **-fällig,** *adj.* tumbledown, dilapidated. **-fälligkeit,** *f.* state of decay, dilapidation. **-führer,** *m.* overseer, manager. **-gerüst,** *n.* scaffolding. **-genossenschaft,** *f.*, **-gesellschaft,** *f.* building society. **-gesetz,** *n.* building act; building regulation. **-gewerbe,** *n.* building trade. **-handwerker,** *m.* building artisan. **-herr,** *m.* building contractor, builder. **-holz,** *n.* building timber. **-kasten,** *m.* box of children's bricks. **-kastensystem,** *n.* manufacture of standardized units. **-klotz,** *m.* building-block, brick (*for children*). **-kommission,** *f.* Board of Works. **-kosten,** *f.pl.* building costs, cost of working (*a mine*). **-kunst,** *f.* architecture, structural engineering. **-leute,** *pl.* builders. **-lich,** *adj.* in good repair; structural; *-liche Veränderungen,* structural alterations; *in -lichem Zustande,* habitable. **-lichkeiten,** *f.pl.* buildings. **-meister,** *m.* master-builder **-plan,** *m.* ground plan. **-platz,** *m.*

building-site. **-rat,** *m.* Board of Works; member of this board. **-riß,** *m.* plan, architect's drawing. **-schule,** *f.* school of civil engineering *or* architecture. **-stätte,** *f.*, **-stelle,** *f.* building plot; site. **-stein,** *m.* building stone. **-stil,** *m.* style of architecture. **-stoff,** *m.* building materials. **-unternehmer,** *m.* building contractor. **-verwalter,** *m.* clerk of the works; overseer. **-verwaltung,** *f.* Board of Works. **-werk,** *n.* edifice, building. **-wesen,** *n.* architecture, building, building concerns.

Bauch, *m.* (-es, ⸚e) belly; stomach; abdomen; paunch. *sich* (*Dat.*) *den – halten*, hold *or* split one's sides (*with laughing*); *auf dem –e liegen*, lie flat on one's face; *seinem –e frönen* or *dienen*, *sich den – pflegen*, worship one's belly, lead a life of gluttony; *fauler –*, sluggard; *ein voller –*, *ein leerer Kopf*, a fat belly, a lean brain. **-bedeckung,** *f.*, **-decke,** *f.* abdominal wall. **-binde,** *f.* abdominal bandage. **-bruch,** *m.* abdominal rupture. **-decken-** (*in compounds*) epigastric. **-en, bäuchen,** *v.a.* & *n.* bulge out. **-fell,** *n.* peritoneum. **-fellentzündung,** *f.* peritonitis. **-finne,** *f.*, **-flosse,** *f.* ventral fin. **-fluß,** *m.* diarrhoea; dysentery. **-freiheit,** *f.* ground clearance (*of vehicle*). **-glieder,** *n.pl.* feet (*of birds*), hind feet (*of beasts*). **-grimmen,** *n.* gripes, colic. **-gurt,** *m.* belly-band, girth. **-höhle,** *f.* abdominal cavity. **-ig,** *adj.* bulgy, convex, bellied; ventricose (*Bot.*). **-kneipen,** *n.* gripes. **-landung,** *f.* belly landing (*Av.*). **-redner,** *m.* ventriloquist. **-riemen,** *m.*, *see* **-gurt. -schmerzen,** *m.pl. see* **-weh. -schnitt** *m.* abdominal incision, laparotomy. **-speichel,** *m.* gastric *or* pancreatic juice. **-speicheldrüse,** *f.* pancreas. **-stich,** *m.* tapping the abdomen (*for dropsy*). **-strang,** *m.* umbilical cord. **-ung,** *f.* protuberance, convexity of a column. **-wand,** *f.* abdominal wall. **-weh,** *n.* stomach-ache. **-wirbel,** *m.* lumbar vertebra. **-zirkel,** *m.* callipers.

Bäuche, *see* **Beuche.**

bäuch-ig, *adj. suffix* -bellied. (*coll.*) **-lein,** *n.* (*coll.*) tummy. **-lings** *adv.* lying prone.

bauen, 1. *v.a.* 1. build; construct; erect; 2. till, cultivate (*see* **bebauen**); raise (*flowers, etc.*) (*see* **anbauen**); 3. work (*a mine*); make (*a road*); *wohlgebaut*, well-built, well-made, well-shaped. **2.** *v.r.*; be founded (*auf*, on), rest on. **3.** *v.n.* (*aux.* h.) count rely (*auf*, on); *Leute, auf die man* (*Häuser*) *– kann*, people on whom one can depend. **-er,** *m.* (-s, -) builder, constructor (*especially as second part of compound*), e.g. *Orgelbauer, Schiffsbauer*.

[1]**Bauer,** *m.* (-s & -n, -n) peasant; smallholder, husbandman; knave (*Cards*); pawn (*Chess*). **-nadel,** *m.* old-established peasantry. **-nbrot,** *n.* coarse brown bread. **-nbursche,** *m.* country lad, yokel. **-ndirne,** *f.* country lass, hoyden. **-nfänger,** *m.* sharper (*Cards*), swindler. **-nfängerkniff,** *m.* confidence trick. —**nflegel,** *m.* churl, boor, lout, yokel. **-nfrau,** *f.* farmer's wife. **-nfrone,** *f.* statute labour. **-ngehöft,** *n.* farmstead, farm buildings. **-ngut,** *n.* smallholding. **-nhaus,** *n.* **-nhof,** *m.* farm, farmstead. **-nkittel,** *m.* peasant's smock. **-nknecht,** *m.* farm-hand. **-nkrieg,** *m.* Peasants' War (*especially 1525 in Germany*). **-nschaft,** *f. see* **-nstand. -nschenke,** *f.* village inn, country pub. **-nstand,** *m.* peasant class, peasantry. **-ntisch,** *m.* rustic fare. **-ntracht,** *f.* peasant dress *or* costume. **-ntum,** *n. see* **-nstand. -nvolk,** *n.*, **-sleute,** *pl.* peasants, country-folk. **-nwirtschaft,** *f.* cottage farm, homestead; small-scale farming. **-sfrau,** *f.* peasant woman. **-smann,** *m.* (-sleute) peasant, farmer.

[2]**Bauer,** *n.* & *m.* (-s, -) (bird)cage; aviary.

Bäu(e)r-in, *f.* (-innen) peasant woman, farmer's wife. **-isch,** *adj.* rustic; boorish. **-lich,** *adj.* rural, rustic, country.

Baum, *m.* (-es, ⸚e) tree; pole, beam; boom (*Naut.*); *– der Erkenntnis*, tree of knowledge; *– des Lebens*, *Lebens–*, tree of life; (*Prov.*) *er sieht den Wald vor* (*lauter*) *Bäumen nicht*, he does not see the wood for the trees; *er wird keine Bäume ausreißen*, he won't set the Thames on fire; (*Prov.*) *den – erkennt man an den Früchten*, as the tree is, so is the fruit; (*Prov.*) *auf einen Hieb fällt kein –*, Rome was not built in a day. **-artig,** *adj.* tree-like, dendroid, arborescent. **-axt,** *f.* felling axe. **-brand,** *m.* blight, necrosis. **-elfe,** *f.* dryad, hamadryad. **-ente,** *f.* black-billed whistling duck. **-eule,** *f.* little horned owl. **-fall,** *m.* windfall wood. **-farn,** *m.* tree-fern. **-flechte,** *f.* tree-moss, lichen. **-fraß,** *m.* canker, dry-rot. **-gang,** *m.* avenue (of trees); shady walk. **-garten,** *m.* orchard; tree-nursery. **-geist,** *m.* dryad. **-geländer,** *n.* espalier. **-grassteppe,** *f.* savanna. **-grenze,** *f.* timber line, tree limit. **-gruppe,** *f.* clump of trees. **-hacker,** *m.* woodpecker, nuthatch (*Orn.*). **-harz,** *n.* resin. **-hecke,** *f.* hedgerow. **-heide,** *f.* brier (*Erica arborea*). **-kahn,** *m.* canoe. **-kriecher,** *m.*, **-läufer,** *m.* tree-creeper (*Orn.*). **-krone,** *f.* tree top. **-lang,** *adj.* tall as a lamp-post, strapping, lanky. **-lerche,** *f.* woodlark. **-messer,** 1. *n.* pruning-knife. 2. *m.* dendrometer. **-nachtigall,** *f.* hedge-warbler. **-nymphe,** *f.* wood nymph, hamadryad, dryad. **-öl,** *n.* olive oil sweet oil. **-pflanzung,** *f.* (tree-)nursery, plantation. **-pflege,** *f.* arboriculture. **-rose,** *f.* hollyhock. **-schere,** *f.* garden shears. **-schicht,** *f.* tree zone. **-schlag,** *m.* foliage (*Paint.*). **-schmarotzer,** *m.* tree parasite. **-schröter,** *m.* stag-beetle. **-schule,** *f.* tree-nursery, plantation. **-stamm,** *m.* tree-trunk. **-stark,** *adj.* very strong, robust. **-stein,** *m.* dendrolite, dendrite agate. **-stumpf,** *m.* tree-stump. **-werk,** *n.* foliage (*Paint.*). **-wolle,** *f.* cotton. **-wollen,** *adj.* (made of) cotton. **-woll(en)abfall,** *m.* cotton waste. **-woll(en)fabrik,** *f.* **-woll(en)spinnerei,** *f.* cotton-mill. **-woll(en)faden,** *m.* cotton thread. **-woll(en)garn,** *n.* cotton yarn. **-woll(en)gewebe,** *n.* cotton fabric. **-woll(en)plüsch,** *m.* velours. **-woll(en)samt,** *m.* velveteen. **-woll(en)staude,** *f.* cotton plant. **-woll(en)waren,** *f.pl.*, **-woll(en)zeug,** *n.* cotton-stuff, print, cottons. **-woll(en)watte,** *f.* cotton-wool, cotton wadding. **-zucht,** *f.* arboriculture. **-züchter,** *m.* arborist; nursery-man.

baumeln, *v.n.* (*aux.* h.) dangle, hang, bob, swing; (*sl.*) *am Galgen –*, be hanged.

bäumen, 1. *v.a.* rear, prance. 2. *v.r.* stand on hind legs.

Bausch, *m.* (-es, ⸚e) pad, bolster; bundle; lump; roll; compress (*Surg.*); *in – und Bogen*, in the lump, en gros, wholesale (*also fig.*). **-ärmel,** *m.* puffed sleeve. **-en,** *v.n.* (*aux.* h.) swell out, puff out. **-ig,** *adj.* swelled, puffy, baggy. **-kauf,** *m.* bulk purchase, wholesale purchase. **-summe, -quantum,** (*C.L.*) *see* **Pausch.**

Bauz, Bautz, *int.* smash! bang!

Bazill-us, *m.* (-s, -en) bacillus. **-enlehre,** *f.* bacteriology. **-enträger,** *m.* carrier (*Med.*).

be-, *inseparable unaccented prefix. It is prefixed to verbs, and, among other subtler shifts in meaning, commonly changes an intransitive into a transitive verb* (*e.g.* antworten auf eine Frage, eine Frage beantworten) *or changes the object of the action of a transitive verb; it is also used to form transitive verbs from substantives and adjectives. For possible compounds not found in the following lists see the simple verbs.*

beabsichtig-en, *v.a.* intend, have in view, aim at mean to; *der –te Zweck*, the end in view, the purpose (of).

beacht-en, *v.a.* notice, take notice of, heed, pay attention to; consider, regard, observe, take into consideration; *bitte zu –en*, kindly note. **-enswert,** *adj.* noteworthy, remarkable. **-lich,** *adj.* noteworthy; notable, considerable. **-ung,** *f.* consideration, attention, notice; regard; *zur –ung!* notice! *zur gefälligen –ung*, for your kind attention, kindly notice.

beackern, *v.a.* plough, till, cultivate.

Beamt-e(r), *m.* (-en, -en) official; civil servant. **-enschaft,** *f.* civil service. **-enherrschaft,** *f.* bureaucracy. **-enstand,** *m.* official class. **-entum,** *n.* officialdom. **-enwesen,** *n.*, **-enwirtschaft,** *f.* red tape; officialism.

beängst-igen, *v.a.* alarm, make anxious, fill with anxiety. **-igend,** *pr.p.* & *adj.* terrifying. **-igung,** *f.* anxiety, uneasiness, alarm.

beanlag-en, *v.a.* endow with talents. **-t,** *p.p.* & *adj.* talented, gifted.

beanspruch-en, *v.a.* claim, lay claim to; demand, require; stress, strain. **-ung,** *f.* claim, requirement; stress, strain, sheer.
beanstand-en, *v.a.* object to; contest, appeal against (*an election*). **-ung,** *f.* objection, protest, appeal.
beantragen, *v.a.* move, propose.
beantwort-en, *v.a.* answer, reply to. **-ung,** *f.* answering; answer, reply.
bearbeit-en, *v.a.* till, work, cultivate (*land*); elaborate, manipulate; treat, work at, work up (*a subject*); arrange, adapt, revise, re-edit, compile; machine, finish, fashion, process; *einen -en*, influence a p., belabour a p. **-bar,** *adj.* workable, machinable. **-er,** *m.* compiler, author; elaborator; reviser. **-ung,** *f.* working, machining, processing; treatment; handling (*of a subject*); compilation, editing (*of a book*); revision, adaptation, arrangement; cultivation.
beargwöhnen, *v.a.* suspect, be suspicious of, throw suspicion upon.
beastet, *adj.* branchy.
beaufsichtig-en, *v.a.* inspect, superintend, supervise. **-ung,** *f.* supervision, inspection, invigilation, surveillance, control.
beauftrag-en, *v.a.* commission, empower; order, authorize, charge, instruct; delegate, entrust with. **-te(r),** *m.* deputy, delegate, agent.
beäugeln, *v.a.* eye, quiz, ogle.
beaugenscheinigen, *v.a.* inspect.
bebauen, *v.a.* build on; cultivate, till, work.
beb-en, 1. *v.n.* (*aux.* h.) shake, tremble, shiver, quake; palpitate, oscillate, thrill, quiver; *vor Angst -en*, quake with fear; *vor Frost -en*, shake with cold; *für* or *um jemand -en*, be anxious about a p., *vor jemandem -en*, be frightened of a p. 2. *n.* trembling; tremor, thrill, vibration; tremolo (*Mus.*); *Erd-en, n.* earthquake. **-end,** *pr.p. & adj.* tremulous; shivering. **-enmesser,** *m.* seismograph. **-er,** *m.* tremolo-stop (*in organs*).
beblätter-n, *v.a.* cover with leaves. **-t,** *p.p. & adj.* leafy, foliate.
bebrämen, *v.a.* border, trim (*with fur, etc.*).
bebrillt, *adj.* bespectacled.
bebrüten, *v.a.* incubate, hatch; brood.
Becher, *m.* cup, beaker, goblet, mug: crater (*Astr.*); calix (*Anat.*); cupule, calyx (*Bot.*); *Aschen-*, ash-tray; *Tabaks-*, tobacco-jar; *Würfel-*, dice-box. **-förmig,** *adj.* cup-shaped. **-glas,** *n.* beaker. **-held,** *m.* hard drinker. **-n,** *v.n.* booze, tipple, carouse. **-stürzer,** *m.* toper, hard drinker.
Becken, *n.* basin (*of a port*); pelvis (*Anat.*); cymbal (*Mus.*); vortex (*of a whirlpool*). **-abweichung,** *f.* **-verkrümmung,** *f.* malformation of the pelvis. **-förmig,** *adj.* basin-shaped. **-höhle,** *f.*, **-raum,** pelvic cavity. **-schläger,** *m.* cymbal-player.
bedach-en, *v.a.* roof (*a house*). **-ung,** *f.* roofing.
Bedacht, 1. *m.*, consideration, deliberation, reflection, forethought; *Vor-*, foresight, prudence; *- nehmen auf eine S.*, take s.th. into consideration; *mit -*, advisedly, carefully; *mit gutem -*, after mature reflection. 2. *adj.* intent (on), mindful (of), thoughtful (of); considerate; *auf etwas - sein*, be intent on a th., consider a matter. **-los,** *adj.* inconsiderate. **-sam,** *adj.* considerate. **-samkeit,** *f.* thoughtfulness, consideration, circumspection.
bedächtig, *adj.* circumspect, discreet, prudent, cautious; deliberate, slow. **-keit,** *f.* caution; prudence; circumspection.
bedanken, *v.r.* thank, return thanks for, decline (*with thanks*); *sich bei jemandem -*, thank a p.
Bedarf, *m.* (-(e)s) need, want, requirement, requisites; supply; (*C.L.*) demand; *Kriegs-*, materials of war; *- an einer S.*, need of a th., demand for a th.; *mein -*, all I need; *nach -*, as occasion demands; *bei -*, in case of need. **-sartikel,** *m.*, **-sgegenstand,** *m.* requisites, commodities; utensils. **-sdeckung,** *f.* supply covering all requirements. **-sfall,** *m.* case of need. **-shaltestelle,** *f.* request stop. **-sliste,** *f.* list of things needed. **-snachweis,** *m.* permit to purchase, priority docket. **-swagen,** *m.* tender.
bedauer-lich, *adj.* regrettable, deplorable. **-n,** 1. *v.a.* regret; deplore (*eine S., jemandes Tod*, a th., a p.'s death); pity (*einen wegen*, a p. for); commiserate; sympathize; be sorry for; *bedaure sehr!* I very much regret, I'm sorry I can't. 2. *n.* sorrow, regret; pity, sympathy. **-nswert,** *adj.*, **-nswürdig,** *adj.* regrettable, deplorable, pitiable, unfortunate.
bedeck-en, 1. *v.a.* cover; shelter, protect, screen; escort (*Mil.*); convoy (*Naut.*); cover over *or* up, obscure, hide from view. 2. *v.r.* put on one's hat. **-t,** *p.p. & adj.*; *der Himmel ist -t*, the sky is overcast; *-te Stimme*, husky voice; *-ter Gang*, covered way (*Fort.*); veranda. **-ung,** *f.* covering, cover; protection, escort, convoy, guard; occultation (*Astr.*).
bedenk-en, 1. *ir.v.a.* consider, think (over), ponder (over), reflect (on); bear in mind; provide for (*in one's will, etc.*); *einen mit etwas -en*, bequeath s.th. to a p. 2. *v.r.* deliberate, weigh, consider, hesitate; *sich eines andern -en*, change one's mind; *sich eines Besseren -en*, think better of a thing. 3. *n.* consideration, reflection, deliberation; hesitation, scruple, doubt; *-en tragen*, have misgivings, scruple at, demur at; *ohne -en*, unhesitatingly. **-lich,** *adj.* doubtful, questionable, suspicious; critical, serious, delicate, nice; hazardous, risky. **-lichkeit,** *f.* scruple, doubtfulness; hesitation; seriousness, critical state. **-zeit,** *f.* time for reflection.
bedeppert, *adj.* (*coll.*) flabbergasted, dumbfounded.
bedeut-en, *v.a.* mean, signify, be of importance, imply; direct, enjoin; inform, advise, point out; intimate; give to understand; portend, beckon. **-end,** *pr.p. & adj.* important; significant; considerable; full of meaning; weighty; *nichts -end, nichts zu -en*, of no consequence. **-sam,** *adj.* significant. **-samkeit,** *f.* significance; importance. **-ung,** *f.* meaning; importance; significance; *ein Mann von -ung*, a man of standing *or* of consequence. **-ungsgleich,** *adj.* synonymous. **-ungsleer,** *adj.* devoid of meaning, meaningless, trivial, insignificant. **-ungslos,** *adj.* meaningless, unimportant, insignificant, of no account. **-ungsschwer,** **-ungsvoll,** *adj.* momentous, portentous, of great importance, meaningful, significant.
bedien-en, 1. *v.a.* serve, wait on; attend; fill, do the duty of (*an office*); serve (*guns*); work (*a machine*); *eine Farbe -en*, follow suit (*Cards*); *nicht -en*, revoke (*Cards*). 2. *v.r.* help o.s.; *sich einer S. -en*, make use of a th.; *sich einer Gelegenheit -en*, avail o.s. of an opportunity; *bitte, -en Sie sich*, please help yourself. **-stete(r),** *m.* employee. **-te(r),** *m.* servant. **-tenhaft,** *adj.* servile. **-ung,** *f.* service, attendance attention, servicing; servants; *zu Ihrer -ung*, at your command, for your use. **-tenseele,** *f.* cringing soul, servile character. **-tenzimmer,** *n.* servants' hall. **-ungsknopf,** *m.* control knob (*Rad.*). **-ungsmannschaft** (*eines Geschützes*), *f.* gun crew.
Beding, *m. & n.* (-(e)s, -e) *see* **Bedingung.** **-en,** *reg. & ir.v.a.* stipulate, postulate, limit, restrict; cause, occasion; imply, depend on; bargain, agree on *or* for; settle (*terms, etc.*); *ein Schiff -en*, charter a vessel; *Erfolg -t Fleiß*, success implies hard work; *Fleiß -t Erfolg*, hard work brings success. **-t,** *p.p. & adj.* conditional, qualified, limited; hypothetical; subject to; (*C.L.*) *-t liefern*, supply on sale or return; *von etwas -t sein*, depend on, be affected by a th. **-theit,** *f.* dependence (on); limitation, restrictedness. **-ung,** *f.* stipulation, condition, proviso, terms, restriction; *-ungen einreichen*, make a tender for; *unter der -ung*, on condition, provided; *auf -ungen eingehen*, accept conditions; *unter keiner -ung*, on no account; *unter jeder -ung*, in any case. **-ungslos,** *adj.* unconditional, without conditions. **-ungssatz,** *m.* conditional clause. **-ungsweise,** *adv.* conditionally.
bedräng-en, *v.a.* oppress, afflict, grieve; press hard. **-nis,** *f.* oppression; affliction; distress; trouble, embarrassment. **-t,** *p.p. & adj.* in distress, in difficulties.
bedroh-en, *v.a.* threaten, menace. **-lich,** *adj.* threatening; *-liche Worte*, threats, menaces. **-ung,** *f.* menace, threat; commination (*Law*).
bedrucken, *v.a.* print (on), imprint.
bedrück-en, *v.a.* press; oppress, harass, distress. **-er,** *m.* oppressor. **-t,** *adj.* depressed. **-ung,** *f.* oppression.

bedünken, 1. *v.a. imp.* seem; *mich bedünkt,* methinks, I think, it seems to me. 2. *n.* opinion; *meines –s,* in my opinion, to my way of thinking.
bedürf–en, *ir.v.n.* (*aux.* h.) & *imp.* (*Gen.*) be in want of, need, have need of, require; *es bedarf keines Beweises,* no proof is required; *der Ruhe –en,* need rest. **–nis,** *n.* need, want, lack, necessity, requirement; *Lebens–nisse,* necessaries of life; **–nisanstalt,** *f.* public lavatory. **–nislos,** *adj.* unpretentious, unassuming, frugal. **–nislosigkeit,** *f.* frugality, modesty. **–tig,** *adj.* (*Gen.*) poor, needy, necessitous, in need of, wanting. **–tigkeit,** *f.* indigence, want, need, necessity.
beduseI–n, *v.r.*; (*sl.*) get tipsy. (*sl.*) **–t,** *p.p.* & *adj.* fuddled, tipsy; (*fig.*) confused, muddled.
beehren, *v.a.* honour, confer an honour on; *das Fest mit seiner Gegenwart –,* honour *or* grace the festivity with one's presence; *ich beehre mich Ihnen anzuzeigen,* I have the honour to inform you.
beeidig–en, beeid–en, *v.a.* confirm by oath; put a p. on (his) oath, swear in a p.; *beeidigte Aussage,* sworn disposition, affidavit. **Beeidigung,** *f.* swearing (*a witness*); attestation (*upon oath*).
beeifern, *v.r.* exert o.s. (for), be zealous (about); make (great) efforts (to), endeavour, strive.
beeilen, *v.a.* & *r.* hurry, hasten, make haste.
beeindrucken, *v.a.* impress, make an impression (*upon a p.*).
beeinfluss–en, *v.a.* influence. **–(ß)bar,** *adj.* susceptible, adaptable, modifiable. **–ung,** *f.* influence.
beeinträchtig–en, *v.a.* injure, wrong; prejudice, impair, affect, deteriorate; encroach upon (*another's rights*). **–end,** *pr.p.* & *adj.* prejudicial, detrimental, injurious to, infringing upon. **–ung,** *f.* prejudice; injury; encroachment (on).
beendig–en, beenden, *v.a.* finish, end, terminate, conclude, bring to an end; put a stop to. **–ung,** *f.* finish, end, conclusion, termination, close; issue.
beeng–en, *v.a.* cramp; constrain, hamper, contract; narrow; **–t,** *p.p.* & *adj.*; *ich fühlte mich sehr –t,* I felt ill at ease *or* oppressed; *–te Luft,* close atmosphere.
beerben, *v.a.*; be (*a p.'s*) heir, be heir to, inherit (from).
beerdig–en, *v.a.* bury (*only of human beings*), inter. **–ung,** *f.* burial, interment, funeral. **–ungsfeier,** *f.* funeral service.
Beere, *f.* (-en) berry. **–nähnlich,** *adj.*, **–nartig,** *adj.*, **–nförmig,** *adj.* berry-like; bacciform (*Bot.*). **–nfressend,** *adj.* baccivorous. **–nesche,** *f.* mountain-ash (*Pirus aucuparia*). **–ntragend,** *adj.* bacciferous (*Bot.*).
Beet, *n.* (-(e)s, -e) bed, border.
Beete, *f., see* **Bete.**
befähig–en, *v.a.* enable, qualify. **–t,** *adj.* able (to), capable (of), fit (for), adapted (to); talented, gifted. **–ung,** *f.* qualification; competence, authorization; ability, fitness, capacity; efficiency. **–ungsnachweis,** *m.* certificate of competency.
befahl, *see* **befehlen.**
befahr–bar, *adj.* passable; practicable (*for driving*); navigable, accessible. **–en,** *ir.v.a.* travel over, drive over *or* on; cover with (*gravel, dung, etc.*); navigate (*a river*); *sehr –ener Weg,* much frequented road; *Küsten –en* sail along the coasts; *–ene Leute,* old salts, old tars; *eine Grube –en,* descend into a mine.
Befall, *m.* (-s, ⁻e) attack, infection. **–en,** *ir.v.a.* & *imp.* befall, happen; attack; be seized (by); *von einem Sturme –en werden,* be overtaken by a storm; *von einer Krankheit –en werden,* be taken ill.
befangen, *adj.* embarrassed, disconcerted, (*coll.*) put out; restrained (*in manner*), shy, timid, self-conscious; partial, prejudiced, biased (in favour of), preoccupied (with), engrossed (in); *vom Schlafe –,* overcome with sleep; *in einem Irrtum – sein,* labour under a misapprehension *or* a delusion; *–er Kopf,* narrow-minded person. **–heit,** *f.* constraint, embarrassment; prejudice, bias.
befassen, *v.r.*; *sich mit etwas –,* occupy o.s. with, concern o.s. with, deal with, enter into, engage in; *– Sie sich mit Ihren eigenen Sachen,* mind your own business; *niemand befaßt sich gern mit ihm,* nobody likes to have anything to do with him.
befehd–en, *v.a.* make war upon; attack.
Befehl, *m.* (-(e)s, -e) order, command, mandate; (*C.L.*) commission; *Tages–,* order of the day, general order (*Mil.*); *Ober–,* supreme command (*Mil.*); *auf – des Königs,* by order of the King; *auf wessen –?* by whose orders? *zu –,* yes, sir; very good, sir; ay, ay, sir (*Naut.*); *ich stehe Ihnen zu –,* I am at your service; *stets zu –,* always at your service; *den – übernehmen,* take command (*Mil.*); *einen – überschreiten,* exceed one's orders; *bis auf weiteren –,* till further orders; *gerichtlicher –,* warrant; *mündlicher,* (*schriftlicher*) –, verbal (written) order; *stehender –,* standing orders; *was steht zu Ihrem –?* what is your pleasure? **–en,** 1. *ir.v.a.* (*Dat.*) order, command, dictate, bid; *wie Sie –en,* as you wish; *–en Sie sonst noch etwas?* do you wish for anything else? have you any further orders? 2. *v.r.*; *sich Gott –en,* commend o.s. to God, commit o.s. to God; *Gott befohlen!* good-bye! God be with you! **–end,** *pr.p.* & *adj.* imperative, dictatorial; *–ende Form,* imperative mood; *–ender Ton,* tone of authority **–erisch,** *adj.* haughty, overbearing, imperious. **–igen,** *v.a.* command (*a regiment, an army*); have under one's command; be in command of; *–igt von,* under the command of, led by. **–sausgabe, –serteilung,** *f.* issue of orders. **–sbefugnis,** *f.* authority (*Mil.*). **–sempfang,** *m.* receipt of orders (*Mil.*). **–sempfänger,** *m.* orderly, runner (*Mil.*). **–shaber,** *m.* commanding officer; chief. **–shaberisch,** *adj.* authoritative; imperious, dictatorial. **–sstelle,** *f.* post of command. **–stand,** *m.*, **–stelle,** *f.* command post. **–sübermittlung,** *f.* transmission of orders. **–swidrig,** *adj.* contrary to orders. **–swort,** *n.* word of command.
befeinden, *v.a.* show enmity *or* be antagonistic to, persecute.
befestig–en, *v.a.* fasten, fix, make fast, attach; fortify; establish; strengthen; (*C.L.*) harden, stiffen (*of prices*); *mit Nägeln –en,* nail, nail down; (*B.*) *da wurden die Gemeinden im Glauben –t,* so were the churches established in the faith. **–ung,** *f.* fastening, attachment, fixing; fortification. **–ungsanlagen,** *f.pl.*, **–ungsbauten,** *f.pl.*, **–ungswerke,** *n.pl.*, defences, fortifications. **–ungskunst,** *f.* science of fortification. **–ungsmittel,** *n.* fixing agent (*Chem.*). **–ungspfahl,** *m.* palisade. **–ungsschraube,** *f.* set-screw.
befeucht–en, *v.a.* moisten, damp, dampen, wet; water, irrigate. **–ung,** *f.* moistening; irrigation.
befeuern, *v.a.* fire (*with enthusiasm, etc.*).
Beffchen (Bäffchen), *n.* (*usually pl.*) bands (*of a Protestant clergyman, proctor, etc.*).
befieder–t, *adj.* feathered, fledged. **–ung,** *f.* feathers, feathering.
befiehl, *see* **befehlen.**
befiel, *see* **befallen.**
befind–en, 1. *ir.v.a.* find, deem, consider; think proper. 2. *v.r.* be, fare, feel, find o.s.; *die S. –et sich nicht so,* that is not the real state of affairs *sich in Verlegenheit –en,* be embarrassed; *Sie –en sich in einem seltsamen Irrtume,* you labour under a strange misapprehension; *wie –en Sie sich?* how are you? *wir –en uns hier sehr wohl,* we are very comfortable here; *der Ausgang –et sich unten,* the exit is downstairs. 3. *n.* state of health; condition; state; opinion; *nach –en der S.,* as things turn out; *nach –en,* as you may think fit. **–lich,** *adj.* being, existing; present, situated; *irgendwo –lich sein,* be somewhere or other.
beflaggen, *v.a.* deck with flags.
befleck–en, *v.a.* spot, stain; blot, soil, contaminate; defile, pollute; patch, heel (*shoes, etc.*); *jemandes guten Namen –en,* sully a p.'s reputation. **–ung,** *f.* stain, spot, blot; staining; defilement, contamination, pollution.
befleiß–en, *ir.v.r.* (*rare*), **–igen,** *reg.v.r.* (*Gen.*) apply o.s. to, take great pains with; devote o.s. to; *–ige dich zu gefallen,* take pains to please; *er –igt sich der Kürze,* he studies brevity.
befliß, *see* **befleißen.**
beflissen, *p.p.* (*of* befleißen) & *adj.* (*Gen.*) intent (upon), engaged in, devoted (to); student (of); studious; diligent; *ich habe mich immer beflissen,* I have always sedulously endeavoured; *ein –er der*

Rechte, a student of law. **-heit,** *f.* assiduity. **-tlich,** *adv.* sedulously.
beflügel-n, *v.a.*; accelerate, urge on, lend speed to; *die Angst -t den eilenden Fuß*, fear gives wings to hurrying feet. **-t,** *p.p. & adj.* winged.
beföhle, befohlen, *see* **befehlen.**
befolg-en, *v.a.* obey; comply with, follow, observe; act up to; adhere to (*a custom, a principle*). **-ung,** *f.* following; observance (of), adherence (to).
Beförder-er, *m.* forwarder; forwarding-agent; promoter, instigator, patron. **-lich,** *adj.* favourable, conducive, accessory (to). **-n,** *v.a.* forward, transport, haul; dispatch; further, promote, advance, assist, accelerate; prefer (*to an office*). **-ung,** *f.* forwarding, dispatch, transport, conveyance (*of goods, etc.*); furthering (*of plans*); promotion; advancement; encouragement; *-ung außer der Reihe*, promotion by selection; *-ung nach dem Dienstalter*, promotion by seniority. **-ungsanlage,** *f.* conveyor belt, conveyor. **-ungsmittel,** *n.* means of transport.
befracht-en, *v.a.* freight; charter (*a vessel*); load. **-ung,** *f.* freighting, loading.
befrag-en, 1. *reg. & ir.v.a.* interrogate, question, examine. 2. *v.r.; sich bei einem -en* (*um* or *über eine S.* or *wegen einer S.*) consult with a p. (about a th.) **-ung,** *f.* questioning, interrogation.
befranst, *adj.* fringed.
befrei-en, *v.a.* free, set free, liberate; rescue; release; exempt (*from obligations*), acquit (*of charges, of debts*); disengage, rid, deliver; (*Chem.*) decarbonize (*air*), dehydrogenize, dephosphorize, *etc.* (*with specific reference to the impurity in question*). **-er,** *m.* liberator, deliverer, **-ung,** *f.* liberation; deliverance; release; exemption; immunity; riddance. **-ungsgeld,** *n.* ransom. **-ungskrieg,** *m.* war of independence *or* liberation.
befremd-en, 1. *v.a. & imp.* appear strange, astonish, surprise, create an unfavourable impression. 2. *n.* consternation, surprise, dislike (of), distaste (for). **-end,** *pr.p. & adj.*, **-lich,** *adj.* odd, strange, surprising. **-ung,** *f. see* **-en,** 2.
befreund-en, 1. *v.a.* befriend. 2. *v.r.* become friends; *sich -en mit*, make friends with; reconcile o.s. to. **-et,** 1. *p.p. & adj.* friendly, intimate; allied, akin; *-et sein mit*, be the friend of, be on friendly terms with; *-ete Mächte*, allied powers; *der, die -ete*, friend, intimate, crony. 2. *adv.* on terms of friendship, on friendly *or* intimate terms. **-ung,** *f.* friendly terms; friendship, intimacy; affinity, alliance.
befried-en, *v.a.* pacify. **-ung,** *f.* pacification.
befriedig-en, *v.a.* satisfy; gratify; content, please; appease; *schwer zu -en*, fastidious, hard to please. **-end,** *pr.p. & adj.* satisfactory. **-ung,** *f.* satisfaction; gratification. **-ungspolitik,** *f.* policy of appeasement.
befristen, *v.a.* fix a time, limit; *befristete Einreiseerlaubnis*, entry permit for a stipulated period.
befrucht-en, *v.a.* fertilize; fructify, fecundate, impregnate, stimulate. **-ung,** *f.* fertilization, impregnation, fecundation, fructification; *verborgene* or *unmerkliche -ung*, cryptogamy. **-ungskelch,** *m.* perianth (*Bot.*). **-ungsröhre,** *f.* pistil (*Bot.*). **-ungsschlauch,** *m.* pollen tube (*Bot.*). **-ungsstaub,** *m.* pollen (*Bot.*).
befug-en, *v.a.* empower, authorize. **-nis,** *f.* authorization; authority, right, warrant; powers (*of an envoy, etc.*); faculty; licence; *einem -nis erteilen*, authorize a p.; *seine -nisse überschreiten*, exceed one's powers. **-t,** *p.p. & adj.* authorized; competent; legal, legitimate; *sich für -t halten*, think o.s. entitled (to) *or* justified (in).
befühlen, *v.a.* feel (*the pulse, etc.*); examine by feeling; handle; touch.
befummeln, *v.a.* (*sl.*) handle (clumsily); (*sl.*) investigate; (*sl.*) manage, get done.
Befund, *m.* finding; report, diagnosis; condition, state; *nach ärztlichem -*, according to the medical evidence. **-bericht,** *m.* report; doctor's certificate.
befürcht-en, *v.a.* fear, apprehend; suspect. **-ung,** *f.* (*usually pl.*) fear, apprehension.
befürwort-en, *v.a.* recommend; support, advocate. **-ung,** *f.* recommendation, support.
begab-en, *v.a.* endow (with); bestow upon, give presents to. **-t,** *p.p. & adj.* clever, gifted, talented; endowed. **-ung,** *f.* gift, talent, ability, endowment.
begaffen, *v.a.* stare at, gape at.
begangen, *p.p.* (*of* begeben) *& adj.* used; committed; *-er Weg*, beaten track; *-er Fehler*, mistake that has been made.
Begängnis, *n.* (-nisses, -nisse) funeral; *Leichen-*, obsequies.
begann, begänne, begönne, *see* **beginnen.**
begasen, *v.a.* gas, fumigate.
begatt-en, *v.r.* pair, mate; copulate. **-ung,** *f.* pairing; mating, coition, copulation. **-ungsakt,** *m.* sexual act. **-ungstrieb,** *m.* sexual instinct. **-ungszeit,** *f.* mating time, pairing time; time of fecundation (*Bot.*).
begaunern, *v.a.* swindle, cheat.
begeb-en, 1. *ir.v.a.* (*C.L.*) negotiate, transfer; sell; pass (*a note*); *zu -en*, negotiable. 2. *v.r.* go, proceed (to), set out (for); betake o.s.; set about (*business, etc.*); *sich zur Ruhe -en*, go to bed, retire to rest; *sich auf die Flucht -en*, take to flight; *sich auf den Weg -en*, set out (*on one's journey*); *sich in Gefahr -en*, venture into danger. 3. *impers. v.r.; es begab sich, daß*, it happened *or* chanced that, (*B.*) it came to pass that. 4. *v.r. with Gen.; sich einer S. -en*, give up, renounce *or* forgo a th. **-bar,** *adj.* (*C.L.*) negotiable. **-enheit,** *f.*, **-nis,** *n.* event, occurrence, happening. **-ung,** *f.*, renunciation; (*C.L.*) negotiation.
begegn-en, 1. *v.n.* (*aux.* s.) (*Dat.*) meet, meet with, encounter, light upon; befall, happen, come to pass; obviate, prevent; take steps against; behave towards, treat; *allen Schwierigkeiten zu -en*, obviate all difficulties; *jemandes Wünschen -en*, meet *or* anticipate a p.'s wishes; *einem grob -en*, (*also with aux.* h.) receive *or* treat a p. rudely *or* harshly. 2. *v.r.* meet; concur; *wir -eten einander in dem Wunsche*, we concurred in the desire; *unsere Blicke -eten sich*, our eyes met. **-is,** *n.* occurrence, event. **-ung,** *f.* meeting, encounter; treatment, reception.
begeh-en, *ir.v.a.* traverse; pace off; walk on, frequent (*a road*); celebrate (*a festival*); commit (*an error, etc.*). **-ung,** *f.* traversing, pacing off; celebration, solemnization; commission, perpetration. **-ungssünde,** *f.* sin of commission.
Begehr, *m. & n.* (-s) desire, wish; (*C.L.*) *in -*, in demand; *was ist Ihr -?* what do you want? **-en,** 1. *v.a.* want, desire, demand, long for, hanker after, crave (for), covet: *was -en Sie?* what do you want? (*B.*) *du sollst nicht -en deines Nächsten Weib*, thou shalt not covet thy neighbour's wife; *jemandes Tochter zur Ehe -en*, solicit the hand of a p.'s daughter in marriage; *-t sein*, be in demand, be sought after; (*C.L.*) *Zucker ist wenig -t*, sugar is depressed *or* neglected, little demand for sugar. 2. *n.* desire, demand, request; pretension; *auf Ihr -en*, at your request; by your desire; *was ist Ihr -en?* what can I do for you? **-lich,** *adj.* covetous, desirous. **-lichkeit,** *f.* covetousness; inordinate desire; greediness. **-ung,** *f.* desire; longing (for); hankering (after). **-enswert,** *adj.*, **-enswürdig,** *adj.* desirable.
begeifern, *v.a.* beslaver; (*fig.*) slander, calumniate.
begeister-n, 1. *v.a.* inspire; fill with enthusiasm; animate; enthuse, enliven; enrapture; *von etwas -t sein*, be enthusiastic about, in raptures about *or* over. 2. *v.r.*; *sich für eine S. -n*, be enthusiastic about a th. **-ung,** *f.* enthusiasm, rapture; inspiration.
Begier, *f.*, **-de,** *f.* (-den) eager desire, inordinate longing, avidity; (carnal) appetite, lust, concupiscence; greed. **-ig,** *adj.* eager (*auf* or *nach*, for), desirous (of), covetous (of), greedy (for); lustful; *ich bin -ig zu erfahren, ob, etc.*, I am anxious *or* curious to learn if, *etc.* **-igkeit,** *f.* avidity, eagerness.
begießen, *ir.v.a.* water (*plants, etc.*); sprinkle; wet, moisten; pour over; baste (*meat*); (*coll.*) *sich die Nase -*, drink like a fish; *das muß begossen werden*, we must crack a bottle over that.
Beginn, *m.* beginning, start, commencement, origin, inception. **-en,** 1. *ir.v.a. & n.* begin, start,

commence; set about, undertake; *was wollen Sie –en?* what do you want to do? 2. *n.* undertaking, enterprise, action. **–end,** *pres. p. & adj.* incipient, initiative.

begipsen, *v.a.* plaster over.

beglaubig–en, *v.a.* attest, certify, verify; accredit (*an ambassador*); confirm (*news*); *–te Abschrift,* certified copy. **–ung,** *f.* attestation, verification; *zur –ung dessen,* in testimony thereof. **–ungsbrief,** *m.*, **–ungspapiere,** *n.pl.*, **–ungsschreiben,** *n.* credentials. **–ungseid,** *m.* affidavit. **–ungsschein,** *m.* certificate.

begleich–en, *ir.v.a.* (*C.L.*) balance, pay, settle. **–ung,** *f.* settlement, payment.

begleit–en, *v.a.* accompany, escort; convoy (*Mil.*); *eine Dame nach Hause –en,* see a lady home; *Schwächen –en das Alter,* infirmities attend old age. **–er,** *m.* attendant, escort, guide; companion; accompanist (*Mus.*). **–erscheinung,** *f.* accompanying phenomenon, concomitant symptom. **–schein,** *m.*, **–schreiben,** *n.* letter of advice; covering letter; permit. **–schiff,** *n.* escort vessel. **–stimme,** *f.* second (*Mus.*). **–ung,** *f.* company, escort; attendants, train, retinue; convoy (*Mil.*); accompaniment (*Mus.*). **–wort,** *n.* explanatory remark. **–zettel,** *m.* way-bill.

beglück–en, *v.a.* make happy, bless. **–er,** *m.* benefactor. **–wünschen,** *v.a.* congratulate. **–wünschung** *f.* congratulation. (*zu,* on).

begnad–en, *v.a.* bless (with); favour. **–igen,** *v.a.* pardon. **–igung,** *f.* pardon, reprieve; amnesty. **–igungsgesuch,** *n.* petition for mercy. **–ungsrecht,** *n.* prerogative of mercy, right to pardon.

begnügen, *v.r.* be satisfied (with), acquiesce (in); *sich an einer S. – lassen,* content o.s. with a th.

begönne, begonnen, *see* **beginnen.**

begoß, begösse, *see* **begießen**; *wie ein begossener Pudel,* shamefaced, with one's tail between one's legs.

begraben, *ir.v.a.* bury, inter; entomb; (*fig.*) conceal; (*coll.*) *da liegt der Hund –!* there's the rub!

Begräbnis, *n.* (-nisses, -nisse) burial, funeral; obsequies; burial-place, grave. **–gruft,** *f.* vault, catacomb. **–lied,** *n.* dirge. **–platz,** *m.*, **–stätte,** *f.* cemetery.

begradig–en, *v.a.* straighten (*road or Mil. front*). **–ung,** *f.* straightening.

begrannt, *adj.* bearded, awned, aristate (*Bot.*).

begreif–en, 1. *ir.v.a.* understand, comprehend, conceive, grasp; touch, feel, handle; include, comprise, contain; imply; *etwas schnell –en,* be quick of comprehension; *etwas schwer –en,* be slow; *ich –e nicht, wo er bleibt,* I cannot imagine where he is; *dieses Wort –t mehrere Bedeutungen in sich,* this word has several meanings. *begriffen sein,* be engaged in, be about to do; *das Haus ist im Bau begriffen,* the house is being built *or* is under construction; *im Entstehen begriffen,* nascent; *in fortwährender Aufregung begriffen,* in a state of constant excitement; *mitten in der Arbeit begriffen sein,* be at work; *im Anmarsch begriffen sein,* be approaching, be on the way; *beim* or *im Anziehen begriffen sein,* be just dressing, in the process of dressing. 2. *v.r.*; *das –t sich leicht,* that is easily understood. **–lich,** *adj.* comprehensible, conceivable, intelligible; *einem etwas –lich machen,* make a p. understand *or* see a th. **–licherweise,** *adv.* naturally, of course. **–lichkeit,** *f.* conceivability, intelligibility.

begrenz–en, *v.a.* border, bound (*countries, etc.*); limit, circumscribe; define, confine; *jenes Haus –t unsere Aussicht,* that house obstructs our view. **–bar,** *adj.* limitable; definable. **–t,** *p.p. & adj.* bounded; narrow; limited, circumscribed, local. **–theit,** *f.* narrowness, limitation; finiteness. **–ung,** *f.* limitation; limit, bounds; boundary, delimitation, localization. **–ungslinie,** *f.* line of demarcation.

Begriff, *m.* (-s, -e) idea, notion, concept; comprehension, conception; *einem einen – beibringen,* convey some idea to a p.; *falscher –,* misconception; *schwer* (*schwach*) *von –(en) sein,* be dull (of apprehension), be slow *or* stupid; *sich* (*Dat.*) *einen – machen,* form (for o.s.) an idea; *es ist über seine –e,* it is beyond him, it passes his comprehension; *über alle –e,* exceedingly; *im –(e) sein* or *stehen,* be about to, be on the point of *or* in the act of. **–en,** *see* **begreifen.** **–lich,** *adj.* ideal; abstract; conceptual; *–lich bestimmen,* define. **–sbestimmung,** *f.* definition. **–sbildung,** *f.* abstraction, concept. **–sfach,** *n.* category (*Log.*). **–sgesellung,** *f.* association of ideas. **–sstutzig,** *adj.* dense, dull (witted), stupid, slow. **–svermögen,** *n.* apprehension, intellectual capacity. **–sverwirrung,** *f.* confusion of ideas.

begründ–en, *v.a.* base, found, establish; prove, confirm, substantiate, make good (*an assertion, etc.*), give reasons for; *–ete Zweifel,* well-founded doubts. **–er,** *m.* founder, originator. **–ung,** *f.* founding; foundation, initiation, establishment; proof, reason, motivation.

begrüß–en, *v.a.* greet, welcome, salute, hail. **–ung,** *f.* greeting, welcome, salutation; reception.

begucken, *v.a.* (*coll.*) inspect, look at, peep at.

begünstig–en, *v.a.* favour, patronize; promote; (*Law*) aid and abet. **–ung,** *f.* encouragement, patronage; favouritism; aiding and abetting.

Beguß, *m.* (-(ss)es, ¨(ss)e) icing (*of a cake*); slip (*Pott.*).

begutacht–en, *v.a.* give *or* pass an opinion (on); pass (expert) judgement (on); *–ende Stelle,* body of experts. **–ung,** *f.* expert opinion; judgement, appraisal; examination.

begütert, *adj.* rich, wealthy, well-to-do, well-off; *–er Adel,* landowning nobility.

begütigen, *v.a.* appease, soothe, calm, pacify, propitiate, placate.

behaart, *p.p. & adj.* hairy, hirsute, pilose, crinite (*Bot., Zool.*), villous (*Anat.*).

behäbig, *adj.* corpulent, stout, portly; in easy circumstances, comfortable.

behaft–en, *v.a.* burden, charge, load; infect, affect. **–et,** *p.p. & adj.* subject (to) (*fainting, fits, etc.*); afflicted (with); loaded, burdened, afflicted, infected (by); *mit Schulden –et,* involved in debt; *–ete Güter,* encumbered estates.

behag–en, 1. *v.n.* (*aux.* h.) (*Dat.*) please, suit; *sie ließen es sich –en,* they made themselves comfortable. 2. *n.* comfort, ease; enjoyment, pleasure; *–en an einer S. finden,* take delight in a th. **–lich,** *adj.* comfortable, agreeable, cosy, snug; *er macht es sich –lich,* he makes himself comfortable *or* at home. **–lichkeit,** *f.* comfort, ease; cosiness.

behalmt, *adj.* bladed, stalked (*Bot.*).

behalt–en, 1. *ir.v.a.* keep, retain; maintain; remember; carry (*Arith.*); *im Auge –en,* keep in view *or* in mind, not lose sight of; *seine Fassung –en,* keep cool, keep one's composure *or* temper; *bei sich –en,* keep for o.s.; *für sich –en,* keep to o.s., keep secret; *an sich –en,* retain; *die Oberhand –en,* maintain the upper hand; *recht –en,* be right in the end, carry *or* gain one's point; be victorious; *übrig –en,* have left over; *das Feld –en,* remain master of the field (*Mil.*). 2. *p.p. & adj.*; *wohl–en,* safe and sound; well preserved; *der –ene Kurs,* true course. **–sam,** *adj.* retentive (*of memory*); lasting.

Behält–er, *m.* **–nis,** *n.* (-nisses, nisse) container, case, box; receptacle, reservoir, receiver; bin; shrine (*for relics*); cage (*for wild beasts*); tank, vessel.

behand–eln, *v.a.* handle (*an object, a subject*); treat; deal with; manage, manipulate; work, use (*materials*); dress, attend to (*Med.*); bargain for; *dieser Arzt –elt uns beide,* this physician attends us both; *wie ein kleines Kind –eln,* treat like a baby; *einen redlich –eln,* deal honestly with a p.; *sie versteht es, Kinder zu –eln,* she understands how to manage children; *dies wird im nächsten Kapitel –elt werden,* this will be dealt with in the next chapter; *–elter Betrag,* amount *or* sum agreed upon. **–lung,** *f.* treatment, management, manipulation; dressing (*of wounds*); bargaining; *ärztliche –lung,* medical attention. **–lungsart,** *f.* **–lungsweise,** *f.* (mode *or* method of) treatment, usage, manner of dealing with. **–lungsmittel,** *n.* agents, reagent (*Chem.*).

Behang, *m.* (-(e)s, ¨e) hanging(s); fringe, drapery; appendage. **–en,** *adj.* hung with; having large, hanging ears; *der Hund ist schön –en,* the dog has fine ears.

behängen, 1. *ir. & reg. v.a.* hang (*walls, etc.*); put up (*curtains, hangings, etc.*); cover (with); drape (with). 2. *v.r.*; *sich mit schönem Schmuck* –, adorn o.s. with beautiful jewellery.

beharr-en, 1. *v.n.* (*aux.* h.) continue, persist in, persevere, remain firm *or* steadfast. *auf, bei* or *in etwas –en,* persist in, insist upon, continue to do *or* be steadfast in s.th., stick to a th.; *steif auf seinem Sinne –en,* stick firmly to one's purpose. 2. *n.* perseverance, persistence. **–lich,** *adj.* persistent; constant, unyielding, tenacious, stubborn, firm, persevering; *–licher Fleiß,* assiduity; *–liches Bitten,* importunity; *–licher Eigensinn,* obstinacy, pig-headedness; *ein Mann, der –lich bei seinem Vorsatze bleibt,* a man constant to his purpose. **–lichkeit,** *f.* perseverance, persistence, steadfastness, determination, tenacity, constancy, stability; (*Prov.*) *–lichkeit führt zum Ziel,* perseverance brings success, everything comes to him who can wait. **–ung,** *f.* continuance, perseverance, obstinacy. **–ungsmoment,** *n.* moment of inertia. **–ungsvermögen,** *n.* inertia. **–ungszustand,** *m.* (state of) permanence; persistence; resistance (*of machines*).

behauen, *ir.v.a.* hew; trim, dress, square (*timber, stone*); lop, poll (*trees*); assay (*Min.*); *–er Gang,* exhausted lode.

behaupt-en, 1. *v.a.* maintain, assert, affirm, avouch; keep; make good, prove (*an assertion, etc.*); uphold (*the truth*); *das Feld –en,* remain master of the field; *das will ich –en,* I'll maintain that; *es wird –et,* it is claimed, reported, *or* asserted; *zu viel –en* overstate one's point, go too far; *zu Unrecht –en,* to pretend. 2. *v.r.* hold one's own *or* one's ground, hold out; make good one's position; keep up, be firm (*of prices, etc.*). **–end,** *pr.p.* & *adj.* affirmative. **–ung,** *f.* assertion, statement, proposition, contention; maintenance (*of one's dignity, position, etc.*); *das ist eine bloße –ung,* that is mere conjecture. **–ungssatz,** *m.* affirmative sentence.

Behausung, *f.* lodging; house, dwelling, home, abode.

beheben, *v.a.* remove, eliminate (*difficulties, etc.*).

beheiz-en, *v.a.* heat. **–ung,** *f.* heating.

Behelf, *m.* (-(e)s, -e) help, expedient, makeshift, shift, device; excuse; resource. **–en,** *ir.v.r.* manage (with), contrive; make do (with), content o.s. (*mit,* with); have recourse (to); resort (to); *wir –en uns kümmerlich,* we make shift to live; *er mußte sich mit einer Lüge –en,* he was forced to resort to a lie. **–lich,** *adj.* auxiliary; serviceable; (*rare*) serving as an expedient *or* excuse. **–sbrücke,** *f.* emergency bridge. **–smäßig,** *adj.* temporary, improvised, makeshift, emergency. **–smittel,** *n.* expedient.

behellig-en, *v.a.* importune, bother, molest. **–ung,** *f.* importunity, molestation.

behend, –e, *adj.* agile, nimble, adroit; quick, smart, handy. **–igkeit,** *f.* agility, quickness, adroitness; dexterity; activity.

beherberg-en, 1. *v.a.* lodge, shelter, put up, harbour; quarter (*Mil.*). 2. *n.* **–ung,** *f.* lodging.

beherrsch-en, 1. *v.a.* rule over, govern; control; be master of; have command over, be fully conversant with; *die Festung –t die Stadt,* the fortress commands the city; *er –te die Versammlung,* he dominated the meeting. 2. *v.r.* control o.s., restrain o.s.; control one's feelings, keep one's temper. **–er,** *m.* ruler, master, governor, sovereign, lord. **–t,** *p.p.* & *adj.* dominated, oppressed; overtopped; under control. **–ung,** *f.* rule, command, mastery, control; domination, sway; self-control.

beherz-igen, *v.a.* take to heart; consider well, weigh, ponder. **–igenswert,** *adj.* worthy of consideration, worth heeding. **–igung,** *f.* reflection, consideration. **–t,** *p.p.* & *adj.* brave, spirited, courageous, stout-hearted, plucky; *–t machen,* embolden; *–te Antwort,* spirited *or* bold reply. **–theit,** *f.* courage, daring, pluck, intrepidity.

behex-en, *v.a.* bewitch. **–ung,** *f.* sorcery.

behielt, *see* **behalten.**

behilflich, *adj.* helpful, serviceable, useful; *einem – sein,* help *or* assist a p., lend a p. a helping hand.

behinder-n, *v.a.* hinder, prevent, impede, delay. **–ung,** *f.* impediment, encumbrance, obstacle; prevention; *im –ungsfalle,* in case of being prevented.

behing, *see* **behängen.**

behobeln, *v.a.* plane (*Carp.*).

behorchen, *v.a.* overhear; eavesdrop, listen to.

Behörd-e, *f.* (-n) administrative authority; the authorities; governing body; *höchste –e,* highest authority, government; *Orts–e,* local authority; *zuständige –e,* competent authority. **–lich,** *adj.* official.

Behuf, *m.* (-(e)s, -e) purpose, object, behalf, benefit; use, advantage; *zu diesem –,* for this purpose; *zu meinem –,* on my behalf; *zum –(e) der Armen,* for the benefit of the poor. **–lich,** *adj.* requisite. **–s,** *prep.* (*Gen.*) for the purpose of, in order to, on behalf of.

behülflich, *adj.* (*poet.*) *see* **behilflich.**

behüt-en, *v.a.* guard (*vor,* against), preserve; watch over; defend, protect; keep (from); *der Himmel –e mich vor solchen Gedanken,* heaven preserve me from harbouring such thoughts; (*Gott*) *–e! –e Gott!* certainly not! far from it! God forbid! *Gott –e euch! –' dich Gott!* God save you! may God protect you! **–er,** *m.* guardian; protector. **–ung,** *f.* keeping; protection; preservation.

behutsam, *adj.* careful, cautious, prudent, wary, on one's guard, circumspect; heedful. **–keit,** *f.* care, caution, discretion, circumspection; watchfulness.

bei, 1. *prep.* (*Dat.*) 1. (*proximity in place*) by, near, with, among, at; *Potsdam – Berlin,* Potsdam by *or* near Berlin; *– der Kirche,* near the church; *– einem anklopfen,* knock at a p.'s door; (*fig.*) sound a p.; *–m offenen Fenster,* at the open window; *er wohnt – seinem Vater,* he lives with his father; *– Tische,* at table; *– Hofe,* at court; *– dem Buchhändler,* at the bookseller's; *– der Hand,* at hand, handy; *–m Feuer,* by *or* near the fire; *– einem aushalten,* stand by a p.; *– der Hand nehmen,* take by the hand; *er ergriff sie – den Haaren,* he seized her by the hair; *ich habe kein Geld – mir,* I have no money on *or* about me; *– sich bleiben, – Sinnen bleiben,* control o.s., remain conscious; *die Schlacht – Sedan,* the battle of Sedan; *besiegt – Sedan,* defeated at Sedan; *– einem Glase Wein,* over a glass of wine; *– sich behalten,* keep to o.s.; *er hat stets – dem Prinzen Zutritt,* he has always access to the prince; *sich – der Polizei beschweren,* complain to the police; *– dem Winde segeln,* sail close to the wind; *– uns,* with us, at home, at our house; *er fing –m letzten an,* he began with the last; *bestellen –,* order from *or* through. 2. (*proximity in time*) at, during, while; *–m ersten Anblick,* at the first glance, at first sight; *–m Essen,* at one's meal, at dinner; *–m Spiele,* at play; *– dieser Nachricht,* at this news; *–m Scheiden,* at parting; *– Sonnenaufgang,* at sunrise; *– der Hochzeit,* at the wedding; *– Tage,* by day; *– Licht,* by (candle) light; *– seinen Lebzeiten,* during his lifetime; *– Jahren sein,* be advanced *or* well on in years; *– hellem Tage,* in broad daylight; *– Zeiten,* in good time, early, betimes; *– Gelegenheit,* (up)on occasion, as opportunity offers; *– der Arbeit,* at work, working; *–m Abgang des Zuges,* when the train leaves. 3. (*inner relationship*) in the case of, in connexion with, along with, considering, in the presence of, in spite of; *– all seinem Unglück,* amidst all his misfortunes; *– den Römern,* amongst *or* with the Romans; *er genießt keine große Achtung – uns,* he is not held in very high esteem amongst us; *– Homer,* in Homer; *– guter Gesundheit,* in good health; *– Todesstrafe,* upon pain of death; *das ist – ihm ganz einerlei,* it is all the same to him; *– Gott ist alles möglich,* with God all things are possible; *– diesen Verben steht der Konjunktiv,* these verbs take the subjunctive; *– ihm verliere ich die Geduld,* I lose all patience with him; *– alle dem,* with all that, notwithstanding; *– schlechtem Wetter,* in case of bad weather; *–m besten Willen,* with the best will in the world. 4. (*in many purely idiomatic phrases*) *– seinem Worte nehmen,* take (a p.) at his word; *– seinem Namen nennen,* call (a p.) by his name; *–m Himmel, – Gott schwören,* swear by heaven, by God; *–leibe nicht,* not on your life, by no means, decidedly not; *– weitem besser,* better by far; *– all(e)dem,* for all that, notwithstanding; *– sich überlegen,* consider in one's own mind; *ich war damals – Gelde,* I was well off at that time; *– guter Laune,* in good humour; *nicht – Stimme sein,* be out of voice; – *meiner Seele,* upon my soul; – *näherer Überlegung,* on second thoughts; *Pfeiler – Pfeiler stürzte hin,* pillar upon pillar came crashing down; – *sich denken,* think to o.s.; – *Heller und Pfennig bezahlen,* pay to the last farthing; – *offenen Fenstern schlafen,* sleep with the windows open; *–seite,* aside; *–m Leben erhalten,* keep alive, preserve; *er ist wohl nicht – Troste* or *Verstande,* he is clearly out of his senses. **2.** *adv.* almost, nearly, about, approximately; – *600 Mann,* about 600 men; – *6 Jahr älter,* roughly 6 years older. **3.** *sep. prefix indicating a relationship such as*: near, beside, side by side with; in addition, as accessory *or* help to. *See examples below.*

Beianker, *m.* kedge (*Naut.*).

beibehalt–en, *ir.v.a.* keep, retain, preserve, continue. **–ung,** *f.* retention, continuance.

beibiegen, *ir.v.a.* (*C.L.*) enclose; *beigebogen,* enclosed; (*sl.*) *das werde ich dir schon – !* I'll learn you!

Beiblatt, *n.* (-(e)s, ⁻er) supplement (*to a periodical*).

beibringen, *ir.v.a.* bring forward; produce (*witnesses, etc.*), cite (*authorities*), adduce (*reasons, etc.*), deal, inflict, administer (*blows*), teach, instruct, impart (*knowledge*); *einem Trost –,* comfort a p.; (*coll.*) *dir werde ich's schon noch – !,* I'll teach you!

Beicht–e, *f.* (-en) confession; *seine –e ablegen,* confess, make one's confession. **–en,** *v.a. & n.* confess, go to confession. **–gänger,** *m.,* **–kind,** *n.* penitent. **–iger,** *m.* father confessor. **–stuhl,** *m.* confessional(-box). **–vater,** *m.* father confessor.

beid–e, *adj. & pron.* both, either; *alle –e,* both of them; *keiner von –en,* neither the one nor the other, neither of them; *in –en Fällen,* in either case; *wir –e,* we two, both of us; *–es ist möglich,* both are possible. **–äugig,** *adj.* binocular. **–emal,** *adv.* both times, on both occasions. **–erlei,** *indec. adj.* both kinds, both sorts, either sort, *–erlei Geschlechts,* of either sex; common gender. **–erseitig,** *adj.* on both sides, mutual, reciprocal. **–erseits,** 1. *adv.* reciprocally, mutually. 2. *prep.* (*Gen.*) on both sides. **–händig,** *adj.* ambidextrous. **–lebig,** *adj.* amphibious.

beidrehen, *v.a.* heave to (*Naut.*).

beieinander, *adv.* together.

Beierbe, *m.* (-n, -n) coheir, joint-heir.

Beifahrer, *m.* driver's mate.

Beifall, *m.* (-s) approval, approbation; applause; *einem – zollen* or *spenden,* applaud a p.; – *finden* or *ernten,* meet with approval; *stürmischer –,* loud applause. **–en,** *ir.v.n.* (*aux.* s.) (*Dat.*) come into the mind, occur to one; *jetzt fällt es mir bei,* now it strikes me *or* occurs to me; *einer Meinung –en,* agree with an opinion. **–säußerung,** *f.,* **–sbezeigung,** *f.,* applause; plaudits. **–spender,** *m.* applauder. **–sruf,** *m.* cheer, shout of applause.

beifällig, *adj.* assenting, approving; favourable; incidental; – *aufnehmen,* receive with approval; receive graciously.

Beifilm, *m.* supporting film.

beifolgen, *v.n.* (*aux.* s.) follow; be annexed *or* enclosed. **–d,** *pr.p. & adj.* enclosed, annexed, subjoined, herewith.

beifüg–en, *v.a.* add, enclose, subjoin, append, attach. **–ung,** *f.* addition, appendix; attribute (*Gram.*).

Beifuß, *m.* (-es) mugwort (*Artemisia vulgaris*); truss (*of a sail*).

Beigabe, *f.* supplement, addition, free gift.

beigeben, *ir.v.a.* add, join to, attach to; allot to, appoint (*as an assistant*); (*coll.*) *klein –,* come down a peg, draw in one's horns.

Beigeordnete(r), *m.* assistant, second-in-charge, deputy; town-councillor; *see* **beiordnen.**

Beigerichte, *n.pl.* hors d'œuvre; side-dishes, entremets.

beigeschlossen, *see* **beischließen.**

Beigeschmack, *m.* after-taste, smack, tang, flavour, savour.

beigesellen, *v.a. & r.* associate (with, *Dat.*).

Beiheft, *n.* (-(e)s, -e) supplement.

beiher, *adv.* (*archaic*) beside, besides, moreover.

Beihilfe, *f.* help, aid, assistance, succour; aiding and abetting (*Law*); – *an Geld,* subsidy, allowance; – *an Mannschaft,* auxiliary troops; *staatliche –,* state subsidy.

beiholen, *v.a.* haul aft (*the sheets*) (*Naut.*).

beikommen, *ir.v.n.* (*aux.* s.) get at, get near, come at, come up to, reach; be enclosed *or* annexed; *ihm ist nicht beizukommen,* he is not to be caught (out), there is no getting at him *or* no making an impression on him; *der Festung ist nicht beizukommen,* the fortress is inaccessible; *nicht –,* fall short of; *hierin kommen wir den Engländern nicht bei,* in this respect we are inferior to the English, *sich* (*Dat.*) – *lassen,* dare, presume, imagine, *laß dir nicht –,* don't take it into your head. **–d,** *pr.p. & adj.* (*C.L.*) following; enclosed, annexed; (*C.L.*) *–d erhalten Sie Faktura,* enclosed please find invoice.

Beil, *n.* (-s, -e) hatchet, axe. **–brief,** *m.* ship's register, builder's certificate; grand bill of sale (*Naut.*). **–fertig,** *adj.* finished all but the rigging (*Naut.*). **–stein,** *m.* hatchet-helve. **–träger,** *m.* lictor; halberdier.

Beiladung, *f.* priming charge (*Gun.*).

Beilage, *f.* (-n) addition, enclosure; supplement; appendix; vegetables; *Fleisch mit –,* meat and vegetables.

Beilager, *n.* (*archaic*) nuptials; *das – halten,* celebrate the nuptials, consummate the marriage (*only used of persons of high estate*).

Beiläuf–er, *m.* errand-boy, footboy; supernumerary. **–ig,** 1. *adj.* incidental, casual, parenthetic; approximate; *–ige Bemerkung,* incidental remark; *–ige Berechnung,* rough calculation. 2. *adv.* incidentally, by the way; nearly, roughly.

beileg–en, 1. *v.a.* add, enclose, adjoin; confer (*a title*); attribute, ascribe to, attach (*value, importance to*), settle (*a dispute*); *einem Briefe eine Banknote –en,* enclose a bank-note in a letter, *einem einen Namen –en,* give a name to, *sich einen Namen –en,* assume a name; *einer S. wenig Wert* or *Gewicht –en,* attach little value *or* importance to a matter; *er besitzt alle die Laster, die man ihm –t,* he has all the vices imputed to him; *beigelegte Eigenschaft,* attribute (*Log.*); *sie haben ihren Streit beigelegt,* they have made up their quarrel. 2. *v.n.* heave to, lie to (*Naut.*); come round to (*a p.'s opinion*). **–ung,** *f.* addition; attribution, imputation; conferring (*of a title, etc.*); adjustment, settlement; laying *or* heaving to (*Naut.*).

beileibe, *adv.* (*in the phrase*) – *nicht !* by no means, on no account, (*coll.*) not on your life.

Beileid, *n.* sympathy, condolence; *einem sein – bezeigen,* condole with a p. **–sbezeigung,** *f.* mark of sympathy. **–sbrief,** *m.,* **–sschreiben,** *n.* letter of condolence.

beiliegen, *ir.v.n.* (*aux.* h.) lie with; sleep with, cohabit; accompany, be enclosed; lie to (*Naut.*); *–der Brief,* the enclosed letter.

beimeng–en, *v.a.* add, mix, admix. **–ung,** *f.* impurity, admixture.

beimess–en, *ir.v.a.*; *einem etwas –en,* attribute, ascribe *or* impute s.th. to s.o., charge a p. with s.th.; *einer S. Glauben –en,* believe *or* give credit to s.th. **–ung,** *f.* imputation.

beimisch–en, *v.a.* mix with, admix, add to a mixture. **–ung,** *f.* admixture; impurity; *geringe –ung von,* sprinkling *or* dash of (*Cook*).

beimpfen, *v.a.* inoculate.

Bein, *n.* (-(e)s, -e) leg; bone; *sich* (*Dat.*) *die –e ablaufen* (*nach*), run one's legs off (after), go to a lot of trouble (to get); *er ist mir ein Klotz am –,* he is a millstone round my neck; *er ist gut auf den –en,* he is a good walker; *auf den –en,* on foot, afoot; *sind Sie so früh auf den –en?* are you up so early? *er ist immer auf den –en,* he is always on the move, he never sits down; *auf die –e bringen,* bring up (*children*); raise (*an army*); help a p., set a p. up; *sich auf den –en halten,* keep on one's legs, retain one's balance; *einem auf die –e helfen,* give a man a leg up *or* a helping hand; *wieder auf die –e kommen,* recover one's health, become convalescent; *sich auf die –e machen,* start, set out, be off, (*sl.*) get a move on; *er machte sich schnell auf die –e,* he hastily took to his legs; *ich kann auf keinem –e stehen,* I have not a leg to stand on; *er steht auf sehr schwachen –en,* his affairs are in a shaky condition; *sich kein – ausreißen,* take one's time, not hurry; *mit den –en auf der Erde bleiben,* with one's feet firmly on the ground; *es fuhr* (or *ging*) *mir durch Mark und* –, it went right through me, it sent a shudder through me; *der Schreck ist mir in die –e gefahren*, the fright turned my legs to water; (*sl.*) *kein –!* not a bit, by no means, not at all; *ich will dir –e machen*, I'll make you find your legs; *Stein und – schwören*, swear till one is blue in the face; *er stand mit einem – im Grabe*, he had one leg in the grave; *zu – werden*, ossify; *mit verschränkten –en*, cross-legged. **-ader,** *f.* crural vein. **-ähnlich,** *adj.* osseous; shaped like a leg. **-bruch,** *m.* fracture of the leg. **-brüchig,** *adj.* broken-legged. **-dürr,** *adj.* exceedingly thin, spindly, meagre. **-chen,** *n.* ossicle, small bone. **-ern,** *adj.* of bone. **-fäule,** *f.*, **-fäulnis,** *f.* caries. **-fügung,** *f.* articulation (*of joints*). **-gerippe,** *n.*, **-gerüst,** *n.* skeleton. **-geschwulst,** *f.* osseous tumour. **-gewächs,** *n.* exostosis. **-harnisch,** *m.* greaves, cuisses. **-haus,** *n.* charnel-house. **-haut,** *f.* periosteum. **-hebel,** *m.*, **-heber,** *m.* elevator (*Surg.*). **-höhle,** *f.* bone-socket. **-icht,** *adj.* bony, osseous. **-ig,** *adj.* (*suffix*) = –legged, e.g. *krummbeinig*, bandy-legged. **-ling,** *m.* leg (*of a stocking*). **-kehle,** *f.* hollow of the knee. **-kleid,** *n.* (*usually pl.* -er) trousers, knickers. **-knopf,** *m.* condyle (*Anat.*); bone button. **-lade,** *f.* splint, cradle. **-leder,** *n.* leg (*of a riding-boot*); leather gaiter. **-leim,** *m.* bone-glue. **-mark,** *n.* marrow. **-mehl,** *n.* bone meal. **-röhre,** *f.* tibia (*Anat.*). **-schellen,** *f.pl.* shackles, fetters. **-schiene,** *f.* splint; (*pl.*) greaves. **-schraube,** *f.* the boot (*torture*). **-schwarz,** *adj.* & *n.* bone-black, ivory black.

beinah(e), *adv.* almost, nearly, all but, well-nigh; *as prefix of adj.* = sub-; *– rostfarbig*, subferruginous; *es ist – einerlei* or *– dasselbe*, it is much the same thing; *ich wäre – gestorben*, I was on the point of dying; *– hätte ich es ihr gesagt*, I all but told her.

Beiname, *m.* (-ns, -n) surname; epithet, nickname, sobriquet; *Friedrich II. mit dem –n der Große*, Frederick II known as the Great.

beiordnen, *v.a.* adjoin, coordinate, subordinate; *beigeordnet*, coordinate; coordinative, adjunctive, subordinate.

beipflicht-en, *v.n.* (*aux.* h.); *einem –en*, agree with a p.; *ich pflichte seinen Meinungen bei*, I am of the same opinion, I agree with *or* assent to his views; *einer Maßregel –en*, approve of a measure. **-ung,** *f.* consent; assent; approval.

Beirat, *m.* (-(e)s, ⸗e) adviser, counsellor; council, committee, advisory body.

beirren, *v.a.* mislead, confuse; divert from, lead astray; *er läßt sich nicht* –, he does not let himself be disconcerted, he sticks to his opinion.

beisammen, *adv.* together (= *in the same place*); *seine Gedanken – haben*, have one's wits about one; *nicht – bestehen können*, be incompatible. **-sein,** *n.* union, association, fellowship.

Beisatz, *m.* (-es, ⸗e) addition, admixture, alloy; *er vertraute mir das Geheimnis mit dem –e, daß*, he imparted the secret to me, adding; *ohne* –, unalloyed.

beischießen, *ir.v.a.* contribute, advance (*money*).

Beischiff, *n.* (-(e)s, -e) cock-boat, tender, pinnace, depot ship (*Naut.*).

Beischlaf, *m.* cohabitation, coition; *unehelicher* –, fornication, adultery, concubinage. **-en,** *ir.v.n.* (*aux.* h.) sleep with, cohabit.

Beischläfer, *m.* (-s, -) bedfellow. **-in,** *f.* concubine.

beischlagen, *ir.v.a.* add, subjoin, enclose.

beischließen, *ir.v.a.* enclose; add, annex; *die beigeschlossenen Briefe*, the enclosed letters.

Beischluß, *m.* (-(ss)es, ⸗(ss)e) enclosure.

beischreiben, 1. *ir.v.a.* write by the side of *or* on the margin; add in writing. 2. *n.* appended writ *or* letter.

Beischrift, *f.* annotation, marginal note; postscript; additional writing.

Beischuß, *m.* (-(ss)es, ⸗(ss)e) contribution, additional payment, share.

Beischüssel, *f.* (-n) side-dish, hors d'œuvre, entrée.

Beisein, *n.* presence; *in meinem* –, in my presence; *ohne mein* –, without my being present.

beiseite, *adv.* aside, apart; in an undertone *or* stage-whisper (*Theat.*); *Scherz –!* joking apart! – *bringen*, remove, purloin. **-legen,** *v.a.* lay aside, lay by. **-setzen,** *v.a.* set aside; forget.

beisetz-en, *v.a.* put to, put beside, add, alloy; lay aside; lay to rest, bury, inter; *alle Segel –en*, set the sails, crowd all sails. **-ung,** *f.* burial.

beisitz-en, *ir.v.n.* (*aux.* h.) sit by; sit in (*i.e. attend but take no part in*); have a seat on (*a committee, etc.*). **-er,** *m.* assessor (*i.e. junior lawyer attending courts*); member of a committee *or* syndicate.

Beispiel, *n.* (-s, -e) example, instance, illustration; precedent; *ein – geben*, set an example; *als – anführen*, quote as an illustration, instance; *zum* – (abbr. *z.B.*), for example, for instance, such as, viz., e.g.; *sich* (*Dat.*) *ein – nehmen an einem*, take an example from *or* by a p.; *ein – aufstellen*, set up as an example; *abschreckendes* –, awful warning, deterrent. **-haft,** *adj.* exemplary. **-los,** *adj.* unprecedented, unexampled, unparalleled, unheard of. **-losigkeit,** *f.* extraordinariness, matchlessness, singularity, exceptional condition. **-shalber, -sweise,** *adv.* by way of example, for instance.

beispringen, *ir.v.n.* (*aux.* s.); *einem* –, hasten to a p.'s aid; help, assist, *or* succour a p.

Beisproß, *m.* (-(ss)es, -(ss)e) secondary shoot (*Bot.*).

beiß-en, *ir.v.a.* & *n.* (*aux.* h.) bite; prick, sting; burn, itch; smart; *in eine S. –en*, take a bite out of s.th.; *nicht viel zu –en haben*, be badly off; *in die Angel –en*, take the bait; (*coll.*) *in den sauren Apfel –en*, swallow a bitter pill; (*coll.*) *ins Gras –en*, bite the dust; *auf die Stange –en*, champ the bit; *die Zähne zusammen–en*, gnash one's teeth; *es beißt mich in die Augen*, it makes my eyes smart; *auf der Zunge* –, bite one's tongue. **-end,** *pr.p.* & *adj.* biting, pungent, caustic; mordant, sarcastic; hot, stinging; sharp; acrid; *–ender Witz*, poignant wit; *–ende Schreibart*, sarcastic *or* pungent style. **-beere,** *f.* cayenne pepper, capsicum. **-kohl,** *m.* beet(root). **-korb,** *m.* muzzle. **-zahn,** *m.* incisor. **-zange,** *f.* pincers, nippers.

Beistand, *m.* (-(e)s, ⸗e) 1. help, aid, support, assistance; 2. assistant, helper, supporter, stand-by; second (*in duels*); best man (*at weddings*); counsel; *einem – leisten*, lend a p. a helping hand, give a p. assistance; *rechtlicher* –, *– vor Gericht*, legal adviser, counsel; *ohne* –, unaided. **-sgelder,** *n.pl.* subsidies.

Beiständer, *m.* bystander, assistant; consort vessel.

beistechen, *ir.v.n.* (*aux.* h.) sail close-hauled (*Naut.*).

beisteh-en, *ir.v.n.* (*aux.* h.) (*Dat.*) help, aid, assist, succour; (*coll.*) stand by; *mit Trost –en*, comfort; *Gott stehe mir bei!* God help me! *die –enden*, the bystanders, those present. **-er,** *m.* assistant; backer; second; *see* **Beistand.**

Beisteuer, *f.* (-n) contribution, subsidy, subvention, pecuniary aid. **-n,** *v.a.* contribute (to).

beistimm-en, *v.n.* (*aux.* h.) (*Dat.*) assent to, agree with, concur (with); defer (*to another's judgement*); fall in with; *einem Vorschlage –en*, accede to a proposition. **-ung,** *f.* assent; acquiescence.

Beistrich, *m.* (-s, -e) comma.

Beitel, *m.* (-s, -) chisel.

Beitisch, *m.* (-es, -e) side-table.

Beitrag, *m.* (-s, ⸗e) contribution, subscription; share; premium (*of insurance, etc.*); dues; contingent; *– leisten* or *zahlen*, pay dues; *Beiträge liefern*, contribute (*to a journal*). **-en,** *ir.v.a.* contribute (to *or* towards), bear a share; be conducive to, assist, help (*zu*, towards *or* in); *zur Unterstützung einer Anstalt –en*, contribute towards the support of an institution; *es hat zu meinem Glücke beigetragen*, it has increased my happiness; *das trägt nur bei, ihn zu erbittern*, that will only serve to embitter him.

Beiträger, *m.* (-s, -) contributor.

beitreib-en, *ir.v.a.* collect, recover, requisition, commandeer. **-ung,** *f.* requisition (*Mil.*); foraging.

beitreten, *ir.v.n.* (*aux.* s.) (*Dat.*) agree to, assent to. accede to; enter into (*a treaty, etc.*); join (*a party, a club, etc.*); *einem als Teilhaber im Geschäft* –, enter into partnership with a p.

Beitritt, *m.* accession (to); enrolment, joining (*a society*). **-sgesuch,** *n.* application for membership.

Beiwache, *f.* (-n) *see* **Biwak.**

Beiwagen, *m.* (-s, -) side-car.
Beiweg, *m.* (-s, -e) byway, by-road.
Beiwerk, *n.* (- (e)s, -e) accessories.
Beiwert, *m.* (-(e)s, -e) coefficient, factor.
beiwohn–en, *v.n.* (*aux.* h.) (*Dat.*) be present at, attend (*a meeting, lecture, etc.*); cohabit with, sleep with; *einer S. –en*, be inherent in *or* be peculiar to a th. **–ung,** *f.* presence, attendance; cohabitation.
Beiwort, *n.* (-(e)s, ⸚er) adjective (*Gram.*); epithet (*Rhet.*).
Beiwurzel, *f.* (-n) adventitious root (*Bot.*).
Beizahl, *f.* (-en) numerical coefficient (*Math.*).
beizählen, *v.a.* reckon among, include with, count amongst.
Beiz–e, *f.* (-en) 1. corrosion, maceration; cauterization, pickling; 2. corrosive, caustic, disinfectant, mordant (*Dye.*); pickle; wood-stain; 3. hawking. **–en,** *v.a.* corrode; cauterize (*a wound*); etch (*copper*); steep, macerate; tan, curry (*hides*); mordant (*Dye.*); pickle, blanch, cleanse (*Metall.*); stain (*wood*); fly (*a hawk*); *Fleisch in Essig –en*, steep *or* pickle meat in vinegar; *gebeiztes Fleisch*, pickled meat; *gebeiztes Holz*, stained wood. **–brühe,** *f.* pickling liquor. **–bütte,** *f.*, **–kufe,** *f.* tan-vat, drench pit. **–end,** *pr.p.* & *adj.* corrosive, corroding, caustic, pungent. **–endruck,** *m.* mordant printing. **–farbe,** *f.* mordant colour. **–kraft,** *f.* mordant action. **–mittel,** *n.* corrosive, caustic, mordant, pickler.
Beizeichen, *n.* (-s, -) attribute; symbol; accidental (*sharp or flat*) (*Mus.*); *ein Wappen ohne –*, a plain coat of arms.
beizeiten, *adv.* betimes, early, soon, in (good) time, on time, in good season; *– aufstehen*, be an early riser.
bejah–en, *v.a.* answer in the affirmative, assent to, accept, give consent (to); (*Prov.*) *wer schweigt, bejaht*, silence gives consent *or* means assent; *–ender Satz*, affirmative sentence. **–ung,** *f.* affirmative answer, affirmation, assertion. **–ungssatz,** *m.* see *–ender Satz.*
bejahrt, *adj.* aged, stricken in years.
bejammern, *v.a.* bewail, lament, deplore, bemoan. **–swert,** *adj.*, **–swürdig,** *adj.* lamentable, deplorable.
bejauchzen, bejubeln, *v.a.* cheer loudly, receive with exultation; rejoice *or* exult at, be jubilant over.
bekämpf–en, *v.a.* combat, fight, oppose, resist, stand up against, do battle with; attack (*opinions, etc.*); overcome, subdue, control (*one's passions, etc.*). **–ung,** *f.* combat, fight, opposition, control.
bekannt, *p.p.* (*of* bekennen) & *adj.* known, well-known, renowned, noted; acquainted, familiar; *allgemein –*, commonly known; *er ist wegen seiner Leistungen weit –*, he is famed *or* celebrated for his works; *er ist wegen seiner billigen Preise –*, he is noted for his cheap prices; *ich bin hier selbst nicht –*, I am a stranger here myself; *das ist mir –*, I am aware of that; *sich – machen*, make a name for o.s.; *einen mit jemandem – machen*, introduce s.o. to a p.; *die Sprache ist ihm ebenso – wie seine Muttersprache*, the language is as familiar to him as his mother tongue; *er hat sich mit den besten deutschen Schriftstellern – gemacht*, he has familiarized himself, *or* made himself familiar *or* he is conversant with the best German writers; *als – annehmen* or *voraussetzen*, take for granted. **–e(r),** *m.* acquaintance, friend. **–ermaßen,** *adv.*, **–lich,** *adv.* as is well known, as you know. **–geben, –machen,** *v.a.* make known, notify, advertise, publish; make public; *er hat es in den Zeitungen –gemacht*, he has advertised it in the papers; *es wird hierdurch –gemacht* or *–gegeben*, notice is hereby given. **–machung,** *f.* publication, notification, announcement, intimation; notice, bulletin, advertisement; proclamation. **–schaft,** *f.* circle of acquaintances; connexions; acquaintance, knowledge. **–werden,** 1. *v.n.* become well known, acquire a reputation; get abroad, transpire (*of news*). 2. *n.* publication.
bekehr–en, 1. *v.a.* convert. 2. *v.r.* become converted, mend one's ways, turn over a new leaf. **–bar,** *adj.* convertible. **–er,** *m.* proselytizer, converter; evangelist. **–te(r),** *m.* convert, proselyte. **–ung,** *f.* conversion. **–ungsbote,** *m.* missionary; propagandist. **–ungseifrig,** *adj.*, **–ungslustig,** *adj.* eager to convert, propagandist, proselytizing. **–ungsgeist,** *m.* proselytizing spirit. **–ungssucht,** *f.*, **–ungswut,** *f.* proselytism, propagandism.
bekenn–en, 1. *ir.v.a.* confess, admit, own up (to), acknowledge (*sins, a crime, the truth, the receipt of a letter*); *Farbe –en*, follow suit (*Cards*); (*fig.*) be frank *or* candid, show one's colours. 2. *v.r.*; *sich zu einer Tat –en*, acknowledge having done s.th.; *sich schuldig –en*, plead guilty; *sich zur Schuld –en*, acknowledge a debt; *sich zu einer Religion –en*, profess *or* embrace a religion. **–er,** *m.* one who confesses *or* professes (*a religion*); follower; *Eduard der –er*, Edward the Confessor. **–tnis,** *n.* confession, avowal, acknowledgement; (religious) denomination; *Glaubensbekenntnis*, creed; *schriftliches –tnis*, recognizance; *eidliches –tnis*, affidavit. **–tnisfrei,** *adj.* undenominational. **–tniskirche,** *f.* Confessional Church. **–tnisschriften,** *f.pl.* symbolic books. **–tnisschule,** *f.* denominational school.
beklag–en, 1. *v.a.* lament, bewail, complain, deplore; pity, commiserate; 2. *v.r.* complain (*über eine S.*, of *or* about a th.; *bei einem*, to a p.); make a complaint (about). **–enswert,** *adj.*, **–enswürdig,** *adj.* lamentable, deplorable, regrettable; pitiable. **–te(r),** *m.* defendant, accused.
beklatschen, *v.a.* clap, applaud.
bekleb–en, *v.a.* paste on, stick on, label, placard, cover; line (*with paper*).
bekleckern, *v.a.* & *r.*, **beklecksen,** *v.a.* (*coll.*) blot, spot, blotch, bespatter; daub.
bekleid–en, *v.a.* clothe, dress, attire, array; drape, cover over; hang, paper (*a room*); line, face, revet; invest (*with authority, an office, etc.*); occupy, hold, fill (*an office, post, etc.*). **–ung,** *f.* clothing, clothes, dress; drapery, draping; revetment, casing, sheathing, coating, facing, hangings, tapestry; investiture; tenure, exercise (*of an office*). **–ungsgegenstände,** *m.pl.* wearing apparel.
bekleistern, *v.a.* bedaub, besmear; plaster, paste (over).
beklemm–en, *v.a.* (*p.p. often* beklommen) grip, seize; oppress; *Angst –te mich* or *mir das Herz*, fear gripped me *or* my heart; *–ende Luft*, oppressive atmosphere. **–ung,** *f.* oppression; anxiety; anguish.
beklommen, *p.p.* & *adj.* anxious, uneasy; oppressed; depressed. **–heit,** *f.* uneasiness, anxiety.
beklopfen, *v.a.* beat, tap, knock (on); test by knocking, percuss (*Med.*).
beklügel–n, *v.a.* criticize, (*coll.*) pick holes in.
bekommen, 1. *ir.v.a.* get, receive, have; obtain, catch; *kann ich ein Zimmer –?* can I have a room? *es ist nicht zu –*, it is not to be had; *Lust zu etwas –*, take a fancy to a th.; *ich konnte ihn nicht zu sehen –*, I could not obtain an interview with him; (*coll.*) *einen Korb –*, meet with a refusal *or* rebuff, be rejected *or* snubbed; *Hunger –*, grow hungry; *Furcht –*, grow afraid; *Zähne –*, cut teeth; *das Land zu Gesichte –*, descry land; *eine Krankheit –*, fall ill; *eine ansteckende Krankheit –*, catch a contagious disease; *den Schnupfen –*, catch cold; *etwas wieder –*, recover (*s.th. lost*); *etwas fertig –*, get a th. finished; succeed in doing a th., bring about a th.; *etwas geschenkt –*, have s.th. as a present; *etwas geliehen –*, have s.th. on loan. 2. *v.n.* (*aux.* s.) agree with a p., suit a p.; *wohl bekomm's* (*Ihnen*)! much good may it do you! *diese Speise bekommt mir*, this food agrees with me; *es wird ihm schlecht –*, he will suffer for it, it will not agree with him; *es bekam ihm übel*, it cost him dear; *sie haben einander endlich –*, they have got engaged *or* married at last.
bekömmlich, *adj.* digestible; beneficial, wholesome (*of foods*).
beköstig–en, *v.a.* feed, board. **–ung,** *f.* boarding, catering; board, diet; food, messing (*Mil.*). *Wohnung und –ung*, board and lodging. **–ungsportion,** *f.* daily ration (*Mil.*).
bekräftig–en, *v.a.* strengthen, confirm, corroborate; affirm, assert, aver; ratify (*treaties, etc.*). **–ung,** *f.* corroboration, confirmation; affirmation, sanction. **–ungseid,** *m.* affidavit.
bekränz–en, *v.a.* wreathe, garland, crown with a garland; encircle. **–ung,** *f.* crowning, garlanding.

bekreuz-en, *v.a.* mark with a cross. **-igen,** *v.r.* cross o.s.; make the sign of the cross.
bekriegen, *v.a.*; *einen* –, fight a p., make war upon a p.
bekritt-eln, *v.a.* criticize, censure, carp at; (*coll.*) pick holes in. **-(e)lung,** *f.* carping criticism, fault-finding. **-ler** *m.* fault-finder, carping critic, caviller.
bekritzeln, *v.a.* scribble on *or* over.
bekrust-en, 1. *v.a.* incrust. 2. *v.r.* get *or* be incrusted. **-ung,** *f.* incrustation.
bekümmer-n, 1. *v.a.* afflict, trouble, distress, grieve; seize (*Law*); *um* or *über eine S. -t sein, wegen einer S. -t sein,* be grieved at, troubled at, concerned for, anxious about a th. 2. *v.r.* sorrow, grieve, fret (*über*, over); be anxious (about), trouble (about), concern o.s. (about), care for, mind; *sie ist darüber sehr -t,* she is very upset about *or* over it; *-e dich nicht darüber* never mind that; *das -t mich nicht,* that does not concern me; *ich -te mich nicht um sie,* I took no notice of her; *er -t sich um nichts,* he cares for nothing; *er -t sich gar nicht um mich,* he pays not the slightest attention to me; *-e dich um deine Sachen!* mind your own business! **-nis,** *f.* grief, affliction; solicitude. **-t,** *p.p.* & *adj.* grieved, troubled, afflicted; solicitous, anxious, concerned.
bekund-en, *v.a.* declare, state, depose, testify to, bear witness that; prove, manifest, make manifest, give evidence of, demonstrate. **-ung,** *f.* manifestation, evidence, testimony.
belächeln, *v.a.* smile at.
belachen, *v.a.* laugh at, ridicule. **-swert,** *adj.* laughable, ridiculous.
beladen, *ir.v.a.* load, charge, burden.
Belag, *m.* (-s, ⸚e) 1. slice of meat; spread, filling; *Butterbrot mit* –, sandwich; 2. layer, lining, covering, coating, surface (*of a road*), paving, planking (*of a bridge*); deposit; foil (*of a mirror*); fur (*on the tongue, Med.*); film (*of teeth*).
belager-n, *v.a.* besiege, lay siege to; invest (*a fortress*); beleaguer (*a garrison*). **-er,** *m.* besieger. **-ung,** *f.* siege. **-ungsartillerie,** *f.* siege artillery. **-ungszustand,** *m.* state of siege; martial law; *den -ungszustand verhängen* or *verkünden,* proclaim a state of siege *or* martial law.
Belang, *m.* (-(e)s, -e) importance; interest(s); *nicht von* – or *von keinem* –, of no account, of no consequence, inconsiderable; (*pl.*) affairs, interests. **-bar,** *adj.* actionable (*Law*). **-en,** *v.a.* concern, belong to; *einen gerichtlich -en,* take legal proceedings against, bring an action against, prosecute *or* sue a p.; *was mich -t,* as far as I am concerned, as for me. **-end,** *pr. p.* & *adj.* touching, concerning. **-los,** *adj.* unimportant, insignificant, of no consequence. **-reich,** *adj.* considerable, weighty, momentous, important. **-ung,** *f.* prosecution suit at law.
belassen, *ir.v.a.* leave alone *or* as it was.
belast-en, *v.a.* load, lade, weight, burden, encumber, charge; charge to one's account, debit with; *erblich -et sein,* have an hereditary disposition (towards). **-ung,** *f.* load, burden, stress; charge, debit; *erbliche -ung,* hereditary disposition *or* taint. **-ungsfähigkeit,** *f.* carrying capacity. **-ungsgrenze,** *f.* maximum load. **-ungsspitze,** *f.* peak load. **-ungszeuge,** *m.* witness for the prosecution.
belästig-en, *v.a.* trouble, annoy, bother, molest, pester, harass; *mit Bitten -en,* importune; *um Zahlung -en,* dun. **-end,** *pr.p.* & *adj.* annoying, troublesome, harassing; importunate. **-ung,** *f.* burden, annoyance, nuisance, bother; molestation; importunity.
belaub-en, 1. *v.a.* cover with leaves; foliate (*Arch.*). 2. *v.r.* burst into leaf. **-t,** *p.p.* & *adj.* leafy, covered with foliage. **-ung,** *f.* foliage.
belauern, *v.a.* lie in wait *or* watch for, spy on.
Belauf, *m.* (-(e)s, ⸚e) (*C.L.*) amount, sum; *der ganze* –, sum total; *bis zum -e von,* up to the amount of. **-en,** 1. *ir.v.a.* traverse, cover; inspect. 2. *v.r.*; *sich -en auf,* amount to; (*auf*) *wie hoch beläuft sich das Ganze?* what does it all amount to? what is the sum total?
belausch-en, *v.a.* listen to, overhear, eavesdrop; spy out; *man -t uns,* we are overheard, s.o. is listening. **-er,** *m.* eavesdropper.
beleb-en, *v.a.* enliven, animate, vivify, quicken, revive, resuscitate, invigorate; cheer, elevate; brighten, freshen up (*Colours*). **-end,** *pr.p.* & *adj.* enlivening, invigorating; restorative, cordial; genial; animating. **-t,** *p.p.* & *adj.* lively, animated, bustling, crowded, busy. **-theit,** *f.* animation, liveliness, bustle. **-ung,** *f.* animation, stimulus, revival. **-ungsmittel,** *n.* restorative. **-ungsversuch,** *m.* attempt to restore life.
belecken, *v.a.* lick; (*coll.*) *von der Kultur kaum beleckt,* with hardly a trace of civilized manners.
Beleg, *m.* (-(e)s, -e) 1. proof, evidence, verification; example, illustration, 2. voucher, receipt, document, record, deed; 3. covering, coating, lining, fur; *see* **Belag**; *einen – liefern zu,* furnish evidence of. **-en, 1.** *v.a.* cover, line, face; lay down (*carpets, turf, boards, tiles, etc.*), carpet, board, pave, *etc.*; *mit Dielen* or *Brettern -en,* board; *mit Rasen -en,* turf; *mit Bomben -en,* bomb; *Spiegel -en,* silver a mirror; 2. show proof of, prove, verify; 3. engage, reserve (*a seat*), register o.s. for *or* take a course of lectures; *ein Haus mit Soldaten -en,* quarter soldiers in a house; *eine Stadt mit Truppen -en,* garrison a town; *mit Strafe -en,* inflict a punishment on; *eine Stute -en,* cover a mare; *mit Abgaben -en,* impose taxes on; *mit Beweisen -en,* demonstrate; *können Sie das -en?* can you furnish proof of that? *Geld -en,* invest capital; *-te Zunge,* coated tongue; *-te Stimme,* husky *or* strained voice; *-tes Butterbrot,* sandwich; *ich habe drei Plätze -t,* I have reserved three seats. **-exemplar,** *n.* author's copy. **-schaft,** *f.* staff (*of employees*); personnel, gang, shift (*of workmen*), crew. **-schicht,** *f.* covering layer. **-stelle,** *f.* quotation, citation; evidence, authority. **-stück,** *n.* voucher, record, copy. **-ung,** *f.* billeting (*Mil.*). **-ungen,** *f.pl.* condenser plates (*Elec.*).
belehn-en, *v.a.* invest with (*a fief*), enfeoff. **-te(r),** *m.* vassal. **-ung,** *f.* enfeoffment, investiture.
belehr-en, *v.a.* instruct, enlighten; advise, apprise; *sich -en lassen,* take advice, listen to reason; *man hat mich eines andern -t,* I am otherwise advised; *einen eines Bessern -en,* correct *or* undeceive a p., set s.o. right. **-end,** *pr.p.* & *adj.* instructive; didactic. **-ung,** *f.* instruction; information, advice, correction.
beleibt, *adj.* stout, fat, corpulent. **-heit,** *f.* corpulence, embonpoint.
beleibzüchtigen, *v.a.* (*C.L.*) settle a life annuity on.
beleidig-en, *v.a.* offend, insult, shock; wrong; *gröblich -en,* outrage; *tätlich -en,* assault; *sich -t fühlen, sich für -t halten,* feel hurt *or* insulted. **-end,** *pr.p.* & *adj.* offensive, insulting. **-ung,** *f.* offence; insult, affront. **-ungsklage,** *f.* libel action.
beleih-en, *v.a.* (*C.L.*) lend against security; *ein Gut -en,* lend money on an estate; *Wertpapiere -en,* lend on securities; *sein Grundstück ist hoch beliehen,* his estate is heavily mortgaged. **-bar,** *adj.* accepted as security.
beleimen, *v.a.* glue, cover with glue.
belemmer-n, *v.a.* (*coll.*) confuse; cheat, take in. **-t,** *p.p.* & *adj.* cheated; trashy, rubbishy; *er ist meist der -te,* he is always getting his leg pulled, he lets the wool be pulled over his eyes.
belesen, *adj.* well-read; *ein -er Mann,* a man of wide reading.
beleucht-en, *v.a.* light (up), illuminate, illumine; illustrate, elucidate, clear up, throw light on; arrange the light and shade (*in a picture*); *näher -en,* examine closely. **-ung,** *f.* lighting, illumination; lights (*Paint.*); elucidation, illustration (*of a subject*); examination, inquiry; *Abend-ung,* evening glow, sunset glow; *eingeschränkte -ung,* partial blackout; *freie -ung und Heizung,* no charge for lights and fires. **-ungsanlage,** *f.* lighting system. **-ungseinrichtung,** *f.* lighting installation *or* fixture, light fitting. **-ungskörper,** *m.* light, lamp light fitting, lamp socket. **-ungsschirm,** *m,* reflector. **-ungsspiegel,** *m.* reflecting mirror. **-ungstrupp,** *m.* searchlight squad (*Mil.*).
beleumund-en, *v.a.* give a (*good or bad*) reputation; **-et,** *p.p.* & *adj.* in repute; *übel -et,* in bad repute.

belfern, *v.n.* (*aux.* h.) snarl, yelp; quarrel, scold, nag.

belicht–en, *v.a.* expose to light. **–ung**, *f.* exposure (*Phot.*). **–ungsmesser**, *m.* exposure meter (*Phot.*). **–ungszeit**, *f.* exposure (*time*).

belieb–en, 1. *v.a.* like, choose, wish for; think proper; *–en Sie noch etwas?* would you like anything else? *–en Sie einzutreten*, please walk in. 2. *v.n.* & *imp.* (*aux.* h.) (*Dat.*) please, be pleasing; *was –t Ihnen?* what is your pleasure? what do you wish? *mir –t es nicht*, I don't like it, I don't wish for it; *es –t Ihnen, so zu sagen*, you are pleased to say so; *wie es Ihnen –t*, as you please. 3. *n.* will, pleasure, inclination, discretion; *nach –en*, at will, ad libitum (*Mus.*); *ich stelle es in Ihr –en*, I leave it to your discretion; *nach Ihrem –en, ganz nach –en*, as you please. **–ig**, *adj.* as is agreeable, to your liking, at your pleasure, any (you like), whatever, optional, arbitrary; *in –iger Größe*, of any size you choose; *nehmen Sie einen –igen Maßstab an*, take whatever standard you like; *zu jeder –igen Zeit*, at any time that will suit. **–t**, *p.p.* & *adj.* favourite, popular; *sich bei einem –t machen*, ingratiate o.s. with a p., get into a p.'s good books. **–theit**, *f.* favour, popularity, vogue; preference; *sich großer –theit erfreuen*, enjoy wide popularity.

beliefer–n, *v.a.* furnish, supply. **–ung**, *f.* regular supply.

bellen, *v.n.* (*aux.* h.) bark, bay; *ein –der Husten*, a hacking cough.

Belletrist–ik, *f.* fiction, belles-lettres. **–isch**, *adj.* fictional, belletristic.

belob–en, **–igen**, *v.a.* praise, commend. **–ung**, **–igung**, *f.* praise, commendation.

belohn–en, *v.a.* reward, recompense, remunerate; *mit Undank –en*, repay with ingratitude; *schlecht –t*, ill requited. **–end**, *pr.p.* & *adj.* remunerative. **–ung**, *f.* reward, recompense; commendation.

belüft–en, *v.a.* ventilate, air. **–ung**, *f.* ventilation.

belügen, *ir.v.a.* lie to, tell lies to, deceive by lying.

belustig–en, 1. *v.a.* amuse, entertain, divert. 2. *v.r.* make merry, enjoy o.s.; *sich über etwas –en*, make sport of a th. **–end**, *pr.p.* & *adj.* entertaining, amusing, diverting. **–ung**, *f.* amusement, entertainment, diversion, merry-making.

bemächtig–en, *v.r.* (*Gen.*) take possession of, seize, seize upon, make o.s. master of; *welche Wut –te sich deiner?* what rage possessed you? *sich des Thrones* (*widerrechtlich*) *–en*, usurp the throne. **–ung**, *f.* seizure.

bemäkeln, *v.a.* find fault with.

bemalen, *v.a.* paint (over), colour, stain, bedaub.

bemängel–n, *v.a.* criticize adversely, find fault with. **–ung**, *f.* adverse criticism, fault-finding.

bemann–en, *v.a.* man (*a ship*). **–ung**, *f.* crew (*of a ship*); manning; *volle –ung*, full complement.

bemäntel–n, *v.a.* (*fig.*) cloak, disguise; palliate, smooth over. **–ung**, *f.* cloaking, palliation.

bemeister–n, *v.a.* (& *r. with Gen.*) gain mastery over; master, overcome, surmount (*difficulties, etc.*); make o.s. master of, seize, get possession of. **–ung**, *f.* mastery, seizure.

bemeld–en, *v.a.* (*C.L.*) mention. **–et**, *p.p.* & *adj.* aforesaid.

bemerk–en, *v.a.* notice, observe, perceive; note, mark; remark; *er tat als –te er mich nicht*, he pretended not to see me; *wie unten –t*, as noted below. **–bar**, *adj.* perceptible, noticeable. **–barkeit**, *f.* perceptibility. **–enswert**, *adj.*, **–enswürdig**, *adj.* worthy of note, noteworthy; remarkable. **–lich**, *adj.*; *er möchte sich gern –lich machen*, he is anxious to attract attention; *einem –lich machen*, point out to a p., draw a p.'s attention to. **–ung**, *f.* observation, remark note, comment, annotation; *–ungen am Rande*, marginal notes.

bemessen, *v.a.* ascertain, measure out; mete out, apportion, regulate.

bemitleiden, *v.a.* pity, be sorry for. **–swürdig**, *adj.* pitiable, deplorable.

bemittelt, *adj.* wealthy, in easy circumstances, well off, well-to-do.

Bemme, *f.* (-n) slice of bread and butter, roll (*Saxon dial.*).

bemodert, *adj.* mouldy.

bemogeln, *v.a.*; (*fam.*) *einen –*, take a p. in, cheat a p.

bemoost, *p.p.* & *adj.* mossy; (*sl.*) *bemoostes Haupt*, greybeard; *bemooster Bursch*, student of many terms.

bemüh–en, 1. *v.a.* trouble, give trouble; *darf ich Sie darum –en?* may I trouble you for it? 2. *v.r.* take trouble *or* pains; strive, endeavour; apply (*um*, for); *–en Sie sich doch nicht*, please don't trouble (yourself), don't bother; *sich um einen –en*, interest o.s. on behalf of a p.; *–t sein*, try hard, struggle; *eifrigst –t um*, eagerly bent on. 3. *n.*, **–ung**, *f.* trouble, pains, effort, exertion, endeavour; (*pl.* -ungen), attendance (*of a doctor*), assistance (*of a lawyer*); *seine –ung wurde ihm vergolten*, he was rewarded for his trouble.

bemüßigt, *p.p.*; *sich* (*Acc.*) *bemüßigt sehen* or *fühlen*, feel bound (to) *or* obliged (to).

bemuster–n, *v.a.* sample, match; (*genaue*) **–ung**, (exact *or* dead) match.

bemuttern, *v.a.* mother, nurse, be a mother to.

benachbart, *adj.* (*Dat.*) neighbouring, adjoining, adjacent.

benachrichtig–en, *v.a.* inform, advise, send word, notify, acquaint, apprise. **–ung**, *f.* information, advice, report, notice; communication, notification, intimation, transmission of information. **–ungsschreiben**, *n.* letter of advice.

benachteilig–en, *v.a.* prejudice, injure, hurt, wrong, be of disadvantage to. **–ung**, *f.* injury, hurt, detriment, prejudice.

benadel–t, *adj.* leafy (*of conifers*). **–ung**, *f.* foliage (*of conifers*).

benageln, *v.a.* stud with nails.

benagen, *v.a.* gnaw *or* nibble at.

benamsen, *v.a.* (*coll.*) name, give a name to.

benannt, *p.p.* (*of* benennen) & *adj.* named, called; *–e Zahlen*, concrete numbers (*Arith.*).

benarb–t, *p.p.* & *adj.* scarred, cicatrized. **–ung**, *f.* scar, scarring; return of arable to grass.

benebel–n, *v.a.* befog, fog, fogged; obscure, dim. **–t**, *p.p.* & *adj.* clouded over, fogged; (*sl.*) tipsy, fuddled.

benedei–en, *v.a.* bless; glorify. **–ung**, *f.* benediction; glorification; *die Gebenedeite*, the Blessed Virgin.

Benefiz, *n.* (-es, -e) benefit (performance); (*pl.* -ien) benefice, living, prebend. **–ia(n)t**, *m.* (-ia(n)ten, -ia(n)ten) beneficiary. **–iar**, *m.* (-s, -e) beneficiary (*i.e. holder of a benefice*), prebendary. **–vorstellung**, *f.* benefit performance.

benehmen, 1. *ir.v.a.* take away; *einem den Kopf –*, make a p.'s head swim; *einem die Lust –*, spoil a p.'s pleasure; *einem seinen Irrtum –*, undeceive *or* disabuse a p.; *das benimmt mir den Atem*, that takes my breath away. 2. *v.r.* behave, demean o.s., act; *benimm dich anständig!* behave yourself properly! *sich – mit*, see *sich ins – setzen*. 3. *n.* conduct, behaviour, manners, demeanour; agreement, understanding; *das ist kein –*, that is no way to behave; *feines –*, good manners, gentlemanly behaviour; *sich mit einem wegen einer S. ins – setzen*, get in touch with *or* confer with a p. about a th., come to terms with *or* agree with a p. about a th.; *im – mit Preußen*, in agreement with Prussia.

beneid–en, *v.a.* (*einen um eine S.* or *wegen einer S.*) envy; *ich –e Sie um Ihre Kraft*, I envy (you) your strength; *sie –en ihn*, they are envious of him. **–enswert**, *adj.* enviable.

benenn–en, *ir.v.a.* name, call; designate; *einen Tag –en*, fix a day. **–ung**, *f.* naming, designation, nomenclature, appellation, term, title; denomination; *Brüche unter einerlei –ung bringen*, reduce fractions to a common denominator (*Math.*); *falsche –ung*, misnomer.

benetzen, *v.a.* wet, moisten; sprinkle; humidify; *mit Tau –*, bedew.

Bengel, *m.* (-s, -) 1. club, cudgel; clapper (*of a bell*); 2. (*coll.*) boy, rascal, urchin, unmannerly fellow, boor, hooligan; *süßer kleiner –*, dear little rascal. **–ei**, *f.* rascality; churlishness, rudeness. **–haft**, *adj.* rascally, clownish, boorish, rude.

Benit(zucker), *m.* barley sugar.

benommen, *p.p.* (*of* benehmen) & *adj.* confused,

benumbed, stupified. **-heit,** *f.* numbness; stupefaction; giddiness.
benötigen, *v.a.* require, need, be in want of; *eine S.* –, stand in need of a th.; *das benötigte Geld,* the necessary money.
benutz-en, benütz-en, *v.a.* use, employ, make use of, utilize; profit by, take advantage of; *er -te die Gelegenheit,* he availed himself of the opportunity; *mit Vorteil -en,* profit by *or* from. **-bar,** *adj.* usable; available. **-ung,** *f.* use; utilization; *freie -ung eines Gartens haben,* have the run of a garden.
Benz-in, *n.* (-ins, -ine) petrol, (*Amer.*) gasoline (*Motor.*); benzine. **-inbehälter,** *m.* petrol tank. **-inmotor,** *m.* petrol engine. **-instandmesser,** *m.*, **-inuhr,** *f.* petrol gauge. **-oe,** *f.* benzoin gum. **-oeharz,** *n.* benzoin resin. **-oesäure,** *f.* benzoic acid. **-ol,** *n.* (-ols, -ole) benzole, benzene. **-ollack,** *m.* benzole varnish.
beobacht-en, *v.a.* observe, watch, examine; discharge, perform, do (*one's duty, etc.*); execute, follow, obey (*an order*); *heimlich -en,* shadow, trail. **-er,** *m.* observer. **-ung,** *f.* observation; observance. **-ungsgabe,** *f.* power of observation. **-ungs(kraft)wagen,** *m.* reconnaissance car (*Mil.*). **-ungsstand,** *m.* observation post (*Mil.*). **-ungswarte,** *f.* observation tower (*Mil.*).
beordern, *v.a.* order, command, direct.
bepack-en, *v.a.* pack, load, charge, burden; **-ung,** *f.* load, kit, outfit (*Mil.*).
bepflanzen, *v.a.* plant.
bepflastern, *v.a.* pave; plaster (*Med.*).
bepflügen, *v.a.* plough.
bepudern, *v.a.* powder.
bepunkten, *v.a.* put on points (*i.e.* ration).
bequem, *adj.* (*Dat.*) comfortable, easy, commodious; fitting, suitable, convenient, opportune, proper; easy-going, lazy, indolent; *machen Sie es sich* –, make yourself comfortable *or* at home; *wenn es Ihnen – ist,* if it suits you, at your convenience; *-er Aufgang,* easy ascent; *-e Gelegenheit,* good opportunity; *er ist ein sehr -er Mensch,* he likes to take it easy. **-en,** *v.r.* condescend (to); accommodate o.s. (to), conform (with *or* to), comply (with), submit (to), put up (with); *ich mußte mich dazu -en,* I had to swallow my pride; *sich nach der Zeit -en,* go with the times. **-lichkeit,** *f.* indolence, laziness; ease, comfort; convenience, suitability.
Berapp, *m.* plaster, rough-cast. **-en,** *v.a.* rough-cast, plaster (*a wall*); (*vulg.*) fork out, pay up (for).
beras-en, *v.a.* cover with turf. **-ung,** *f.* sods, turfs.
berat-en, 1. *ir.v.a.* advise, counsel; furnish; *die Welt ist wohl -en,* the world is well ordained; *Sie sind schlecht -en,* you are ill advised; *einen Plan -en,* exchange views about a plan. 2. *v.r.* deliberate, take counsel together; *er beriet sich mit ihm über die* or *wegen der S.,* he conferred with him about the matter. **-end,** *pr.p.* & *adj.* consultative, advisory; *-ender Ausschuß,* advisory committee; *eine -ende Stimme haben,* have a voice (*but not a vote*) in an advisory capacity. **-er,** *m.* adviser, counsellor, consultant. **-schlagen,** *v.n.* & *r.* (*aux.* h.) deliberate; consult, confer with; *es wurde über die S. -schlagt,* the affair is under consideration; *er -schlagte sich mit uns über die Maßregeln,* he discussed the measures with us. **-schlagung,** *f.* consultation, deliberation; conference. **-ung,** *f.* advice; consultation, deliberation. **-ungsstelle,** *f.* advisory board.
berauben, *v.a.* (*einen einer S.*) rob (a p. of a th.); deprive of; divest of.
beräuchern, *v.a.* fumigate, disinfect.
berauschen, 1. *v.a.* intoxicate, enchant. 2. *v.r.* become enraptured (*an,* with).
Berber-is, *f.*, **-itze,** *f.* (–n) barberry.
berech-nen, 1. *v.a.* compute, calculate, estimate (*auf,* at); cast up (*an account*); *deutsche Mark auf englische Pfunde -nen,* calculate the exchange rate of German marks into pounds sterling; *einem etwas -nen,* charge a p. for a th.; *Sie haben mir zu viel -net,* you have charged me too much; *wie -nen Sie das?* how do you arrive at this price? 2. *v.r.*; *sich mit einem -nen,* settle (*accounts*) with, reckon with a p.; *das läßt sich nicht -nen,* that cannot be assessed *or* is incalculable. **-enbar,** *adj.* calculable. **-ner,** *m.* calculator, computer. **-net,** *p.p.* & *adj.* calculated; intended, premeditated; *das war nicht -net,* that was not taken into account; *schlecht -net,* ill-judged. **-nung,** *f.* calculation, computation, account; *außer aller -nung,* incalculable. **-nungsformel,** *f.* formula.
berechtig-en, *v.a.* justify (*a p.*) in, entitle (*a p.*) to; authorize, empower, warrant, qualify (for); *er -t zu den schönsten Hoffnungen,* he bids fair to do well, he shows good promise. **-t,** *p.p.* & *adj.* authorized, entitled (*zu,* to); empowered, qualified; justified, legitimate; *ausschließlich -t,* exclusively privileged. **-ung,** *f.* title, right(s), qualification; justification, authorization, privilege; *bürgerliche -ung,* civil rights; franchise. **-ungsschein,** *m.* authorization, permit.
bered-en, 1. *v.a.* persuade, talk (*a p.*) over; *er wollte sich nicht -en lassen,* he was not to be persuaded; *etwas -en,* talk a matter over. 2. *v.r.* confer (with), talk (*a th.*) over; *sich mit einem -en,* discuss with a p. **-sam,** *adj.* eloquent. **-samkeit,** *f.* eloquence; rhetoric. **-t,** *p.p.* & *adj.* eloquent; talkative; *eine -te Zunge haben,* have a glib tongue, be a fluent speaker; *-tes Schweigen,* eloquent silence. **-ung,** *see* **Besprechung.**
beregt, *adj.* brought up, mentioned, in question; *-e S.*, aforementioned matter, point in question.
Bereich, *m.* & *n.* (-s, -e) scope, range, reach, field, compass; sphere, area, zone, region, domain, province; *außer meinem -e,* beyond my reach, outside my province; *im – der Möglichkeiten,* within the realm of possibility; *im – der Wirklichkeit,* in the sphere of reality.
bereicher-n, 1. *v.a.* enrich, enlarge; *unsere Kenntnisse -n,* enlarge our stock of knowledge. 2. *v.r.* (*coll.*) feather one's nest. **-ung,** *f.* enrichment.
bereif-en, *v.a.* hoop (*casks*); fit with tyres (*motor*). **-t,** *adj.* covered with hoar-frost. **-ung,** *f.* 1. set of tyres; 2. hoar-frost.
bereinig-en, *v.a.* settle, clear up. **-ung,** *f.* settlement.
bereisen, *v.a.* travel through, tour, visit; (*C.L.*) – *lassen,* send a (commercial) traveller.
bereit, *adj.* ready, prepared. **-en,** *v.a.* prepare, make *or* get ready; procure; cause, give; *einem den Untergang -en,* work a p.'s ruin. **-halten,** keep *or* hold in readiness; (*C.L.*) tender (*money*). **-machen,** make ready, prepare. **-s,** *adv.* already, previously. **-schaft,** *f.* readiness, preparation, preparedness; stand-to, alert, stand-by (*Mil.*); squad of mounted police. **-stehend,** *adj.* available, disposable. **-stellen,** *v.a.* provide, have prepared, furnish, make available. **-stellung,** *f.* 1. disposition *or* concentration (of troops) (*Mil.*). 2. preparation; manufacture; dressing. **-willig,** *adj.* & *adv.* ready, willing, eager, prompt; readily, willingly, *etc.*; *-willige Annahme,* due honour *or* acceptance (*of a bill, etc.*). **-willigkeit,** *f.* readiness, willingness, alacrity; *allzu große -willigkeit,* over-readiness, officiousness.
bereit-en, *ir.v.a.* 1. ride over *or* across; 2. train, break in (*a horse*). **-er,** *m.* rough-rider, horse-breaker, trainer; riding-master.
berenn-en, *ir.v.a.* attack, assault, storm, invest, blockade. **-ung,** *f.* assault (*of a fortress*).
bereu-en, *v.a.* repent (*of a th.*), regret; (*archaic*) rue. **-enswert,** *adj.* regrettable. **-ung,** *f.* repentance; regret, remorse.
Berg, *m.* (-es, -e) mountain; hill; *am* or *vor einem -e stehen,* encounter a difficulty, come to a standstill; *da steht der Ochse am -e!* there is the rub! (*mit einer S.*) *hinterm -e halten,* hold back (one's opinions of a th.), keep (a th.) in the dark; (*coll.*) *die Haare standen mir zu -e,* my hair stood on end; *über – und Tal,* across country, over hill and dale; *jetzt ist er sicherlich über alle -e,* he has certainly got clear by now; *wir sind noch nicht über den* –, we are not yet out of the wood *or* round the corner; *unten am -e,* at the foot of the mountain; (*B.*) *-e versetzen,* move mountains; *goldene -e versprechen,* promise great things, make extravagant promises; *zu – fahren,* travel up-stream. **-ab,** *adj.* down-hill (*also fig.*). **-abhang,** *m.* mountain slope, declivity. **-ader,** *f.*

lode, vein. **–ahorn,** *m.* sycamore (*Acer pseudoplatanus*). **–akademie,** *f.* school of mining. **–amt,** *n.* mines office; board of mines. **–an** *or* **–auf** (*latter also fig.*) *adv.* up-hill. **–arbeiter,** *m.* miner. **–bahn,** *f.* mountain *or* alpine railway, **–bau,** *m.* mining. **–beamte(r),** *m.* mining official. **–bewohner,** *m.* highlander. **–bock,** *m.* mountain-goat, wild goat. **–braun,** *n.* umber. **–dachs,** *m.* marmot (*Arctomys*). **–distel,** *f.* spear thistle (*Cirsium lanceolatum*). **–dohle,** *f.* chough (*Pyrrhocorax*). **–drossel,** *f.* redwing (*Turdus iliacus*). **–(e)hoch,** *adj.* as high as mountains, extremely high. **–erz,** *n.* raw ore. **–esalte(r),** *m.* mountain sprite. **–etief,** *adj.* abysmal, extremely deep. **–fach,** *n.* mining profession. **–fahrt,** *f.* excursion into the mountains; voyage up-stream. **–fall,** *m.* landslide. **–farbe,** *f.* ochre. **–fertig,** *adj.* incapacitated (*of miners, usually as result of miners' phthisis*). **–feuer,** *n.* signal fire, beacon. (*coll.*) **–fex,** *m.* enthusiastic alpinist. **–flecken,** *m.* small mountain town; mining village. **–fluß,** *m.* mountain stream; fluorspar. **–freiheit,** *f.* mining rights. **–fried,** *m.* watch-tower, donjon, keep. **–führer,** *m.* alpine guide. **–gang,** *m.* vein, lode. **–gebrauch,** *m.* mining custom. **–geist,** *m.* mountain sprite, goblin, gnome. **–gelb,** *n.* yellow ochre. **–gerichtsordnung,** *f.* miners' code. **–gesetz,** *n.* mining law. **–gipfel,** *m.* summit. **–glas,** *n.* rock-crystal. **–grat,** *m.* mountain ridge, crest. **–grün,** *n.* malachite. **–gut,** *n.* minerals; fossils. **–haar,** *n.* fibrous asbestos. **–hahn,** *m. see* **Auerhahn.** **–halde,** *f.* mountain slope, hillside; slag heap. **–hang,** *m.* mountain slope, hillside. **–harz,** *n.* mineral pitch, asphalt. **–haue,** *f.* miner's pick, pickaxe. **–hauptmann,** *m.* superintendent *or* inspector of mines. **–herr,** *m.* mine-owner. **–holz,** *n.* rockwood, ligniform asbestos. **–huhn,** *n.* red-legged *or* French partridge (*Caccabis rufa*). **–ig,** *adj.* mountainous, hilly. **–kalk,** *m.* carboniferous limestone. **–karren,** *m.* truck (*used in a mine*). **–kamm,** *m.* crest, ridge. **–katze,** *f.* wild-cat; mountain lynx. **–kegel,** *m.* sugar-loaf mountain. **–kessel,** *m.* deep valley, gorge. **–kette,** *f.* mountain chain, range of mountains. **–kiesel,** *m.* rock flint. **–knappe,** *m.* miner, pitman. **–knappschaft,** *f.* miners' guild *or* union. **–krank,** *adj.* 1. *see* **–fertig**; 2. suffering from mountain sickness. **–krankheit,** *f.* mountain sickness. **–kraxler,** *m.* (*coll.*) enthusiastic climber. **–kreide,** *f.* rock lime. **–kristall,** *m.* rock-crystal. **–kunde,** *f.* orology. **–kundige(r),** *m.* orologist; mining expert. **–kupfer,** *n.* native copper. **–land,** *n.* hilly country, upland, highland. **–läufig,** *adj.* in miners' fashion, usual amongst miners. **–lehne,** *f.* mountain slope. **–ler,** *m.* mountain dweller, highlander. **–leute,** *pl.* miners; mountain dwellers. **–mann,** *m.* miner; mountain dweller; *–mann vom Leder,* pitman, underground worker; *–mann von der Feder,* surface worker, clerical worker at a mine. **–männchen,** *n.*, **–männlein,** *n.* gnome. **–männisch,** *adj.* mining; relating to miners. **–meister,** *m.* inspector *or* surveyor of mines. **–nachfahrer,** *m.* controller of mines. **–nymphe,** *f.* oread, mountain sprite. **–öl,** *n.* petroleum, bitumen. **–ordnung,** *f.* mining regulations. **–partie,** *f.* climbing excursion. **–pech,** *n.* mineral pitch, asphalt. **–pecherde,** *f.* bituminous earth. **–predigt,** *f.* (*Christ's*) Sermon on the Mount. **–rat,** *m.* mining board; member of mining board, superintendent. **–recht,** *n.* right to work a mine; mining statutes. **–rot,** *n.* realgar, Indian red, cinnabar. **–rücken,** *m.* ridge, crest. **–rüster,** *f.* wych-elm (*Ulmus montana*). **–rutsch,** *m.* landslide. **–salz,** *n.* rock-salt. **–sattel,** *m.* saddle (= *depression between peaks*). **–schicht,** *f.* layer, stratum. **–schlucht,** *f.* ravine, gorge, glen. **–schotten,** *m.pl.* Scottish Highlanders. **–schüler,** *m.* mining student. **–schwaden,** *pl.* fire damp. **–schwefel,** *m.* native sulphur. **–segen,** *m.* produce *or* revenue from mines. **–steiger,** *m.* climber, mountaineer, alpinist. **–stock,** *m.* massif. **–striche** *m pl.* hachures (*on maps*). **–strom,** *m.* mountain torrent. **–sturz,** *m.* landslide. **–sucht,** *f.* miner's phthisis. **–teer,** *m.* mineral tar, bitumen. **–ulme** *f.* wych-elm (*Ulmus montana*). **–unter,** *adv. see* **–ab.** **–verwalter,** *m.* manager of a mine. **–volk,** *n.* highlanders; miners. **–wand,** *f.* rock face, cliff face, escarpment, bluff. **–wardein,** *m.* mining assayer. **–werk,** *n.* mine; pit; *ein –werk bauen,* sink *or* work a mine. **–werksaktien,** *f.pl.* mining shares. **–wesen,** *n.* mining matters. **–wetter,** *n.* fire-damp. **–wolle,** *f.* mineral wool, asbestos. **–zehnte,** *m.* tithe from the produce of mines. **–zeichen,** *n.* miner's badge (*pick crossed by a hammer*). **–zinn,** *n.* native tin.

Bergamotte, *f.* (-n) bergamot. **–nöl,** *n.* essence of bergamot.

berg–en, 1. *ir.v.a.* save, secure; salve, salvage, rescue, recover; conceal, contain, shelter; *er ist geborgen,* he is safe; *die Segel –en,* strike sails, shorten sail. 2. *v.r.*; *sich –en vor,* save *or* conceal o.s. from, flee from. **–egut,** *n.* flotsam. **–lohn,** *m.* salvage money. **–ung,** *f.* salvage, recovery; sheltering. **–ungsarbeit,** *f.* salvage operations.

Bericht, *m.* (-s, -e) report, account, statement, commentary, (*official*) return; intelligence, information; (*C.L.*) advice. **–en,** *v.a.* report, inform, advise, notify; *einem etwas, einem über eine S. –en,* report upon a matter, inform a p. of, acquaint a p. with a th.; *– erstatten,* present, make *or* hand in a report, report, give an account of; *laut –,* according to my report, as per advice; *bis auf näheren –,* till receipt of details. **–erstatter,** *m.* reporter, newspaper correspondent, commentator (*Rad.*). **–erstattung,** *f.* reporting; report, commentary; information.

berichtig–en, *v.a.* correct, set right, rectify, amend; arrange, adjust, settle (*a bill, etc.*). **–ung,** *f.* correction, emendation, amendment, rectification; adjustment, settlement, payment. **–ungswert,** *m.* correction value.

beriechen, *v.a.* smell, sniff at.

beriesel–n, *v.a.* spray, irrigate. **–ung,** *f.* irrigation.

berindet, *p.p. & adj.* covered with bark, encrusted.

Beritt, *m.* (-es, -e) district (*under the jurisdiction of a mounted officer*); cavalry section (*Mil.*). **–en,** *p.p.* (*of* bereiten) *& adj.* ridden over; mounted, on horseback; *–en machen,* mount (*a force*); *gut –en, schlecht –en,* well *or* badly mounted *or* horsed; *–ene Garde,* horseguards; *–ene Landwehr* or *Miliz,* yeomanry.

Berliner–blau, *n.* Prussian blue. **–säure,** *f.* Prussic acid.

Berlocke, *f.* (-n) pendant, trinket, charm.

Berme, *f.* (-n) berm, fire (*or* firing) step (*Fort.*).

Bernstein, *m.* amber; *schwarzer –,* jet. **–en,** *adj.* made of amber. **–säure,** *f.* succinic acid. **–spitze,** *f.* amber mouthpiece *or* cigarette-holder.

berotzt, *adj.* (*sl.*) drunk.

berst–en, *ir.v.n.* (*aux.* s.) burst, explode, rupture, crack, split. **–druck,** *m.*, **–festigkeit,** *f.* bursting strength.

berüchtigt, *p.p. & adj.* infamous, ill-famed, notorious.

berücken, *v.a.* ensnare, inveigle; impose upon, cheat, (*coll.*) take in; beguile, fascinate, charm, enchant. **–d,** *pr.p. & adj.* fascinating, enchanting; ensnaring.

berücksichtig–en, *v.a.* consider, bear in mind, take into consideration, take into account, allow for, have regard to. **–ung,** *f.* consideration, regard.

Beruf, *m.* (-(e)s, -e) profession, calling, vocation, occupation, pursuit, business, trade, employ, walk of life; function, office; province, faculty; sphere; *der innere –,* the inner voice, divine summons; *seinen – verfehlt haben,* to have missed one's vocation; *es ist mein – nicht,* it is no business of mine. **–en, 1.** *ir.v.a.* 1. call, appoint, nominate; 2. call together, convoke; (*coll.*) tempt providence; 3. blame, censure; *zusammen–en,* convene; *einen zu einem Amte –en,* appoint a p. to an office; *viel –ene Angelegenheit,* much-discussed affair. **2.** *v.r.*; *sich auf einen –en,* appeal to *or* refer to a p.; *sich auf etwas –en,* refer to a th.; *darauf darf man sich nicht –en,* that cannot be taken as a precedent; *sich –en fühlen,* feel called upon (to); *unberufen!* (*coll.*) touch wood! **3.** *p.p. & adj.* competent, qualified; *wohl –en,* of good repute. **–er,** *m.* appellant. **–lich,** *adj.* professional. **–saufklärung,** *see* **–beratung.**

-sbeamtentum, *n.* professional Civil Service. **-sberatung,** *f.* vocational guidance. **-sheer,** *n.* professional army. **-serziehung,** *f.* vocational education. **-sklasse,** *f.* walk of life; *obere -sklassen,* professional classes. **-smäßig,** *adj.* professional. **-sreise,** *f.* official tour. **-sschule,** *f.* trade school, technical college. **-ssoldat,** *m.* professional soldier. **-sstand,** *m.* professional organization; corporate profession, occupational guild. **-sständisch,** *adj.* occupational, corporate. **-stätig,** *adj.* employed, working, in a job. **-sumschulung,** *f.* training for a new profession. **-ung,** *f.* call, summons; vocation; appointment; nomination; convocation; appeal (*Law*); *-ung einlegen,* appeal (*Law*), give notice of appeal; *mit* or *unter -ung auf,* with reference to. **-ungsgericht,** *n.* court of appeal. **-ungsklage,** *f.* action of appeal.

beruh-en *v.n.* (*aux.* h.) rest (on), be based (on), depend (on), be due (to); *dies -t auf einem Irrtum,* this is due to a mistake; *etwas auf sich -en lassen,* let a th. be, leave a th. alone; let the matter drop; *ich will es dabei* or *darauf -en lassen,* I will be satisfied with that, I will let it pass.

beruhig-en, 1. *v.a.* quiet, pacify, soothe, calm, reassure, comfort; mitigate, assuage (*pain, etc.*); compose (*the mind, fears*); lull, bridle, curb (*the passions*). 2. *v.r.* calm down, compose o.s.; make one's mind easy, set one's mind at rest. **-end,** *pr.p.* & *adj.* soothing, *etc.*; sedative. **-ung,** *f.* reassurance, comfort, ease of mind. **-ungsmittel,** *n.* sedative, anodyne.

berühm-t, *p.p.* & *adj.* famous, celebrated, renowned; *sich -t machen,* make a name for o.s., distinguish o.s. **-theit,** *f.* fame, renown, distinction; celebrity, star.

berühr-en, 1. *v.a.* touch, border on, be contiguous; touch (up)on, allude *or* refer (briefly) to. 2. *v.a.* & *n.* concern, affect (*a p.'s interests*); *diese Saite darf nicht -t werden,* no allusion is to be made to this subject; *das -t unangenehm,* that produces an unpleasant effect *or* impression. 3. *v.r.* touch one another, be in contact; *sich -en (mit),* be in accord *or* in harmony (with). **-end,** *pr.p.* & *adj.* contiguous; touching; tangent. **-ung,** *f.* touch, touching, contact; contiguity; collision; reference to (*a subject*); *in -ung kommen,* come in *or* into contact. **-ungsbrücke,** *f.* connecting clamp. **-ungsebene,** *f.* tangential plane. **-ungselektrizität,** *f.* voltaic *or* contact electricity, galvanism. **-ungsempfindung,** *f* perception of contact. **-ungsfläche,** *f.* contact surface. **-ungslinie,** *f.* tangent. **-ungspunkt,** *m.* point of contact (*also fig.*). **-ungsreiz,** *m.* contact stimulus. **-ungsstreifen,** *m.* contact strip (*Elec.*). **-ungsspannung,** *f.* contact potential (*Elec.*). **-ungswinkel,** *m.* angle of contact.

berußen, 1. *v.a.* begrime, blacken with soot. 2. *v.n.* (*aux.* s.) grow sooty.

Beryll, *m.* (-s, -e) beryl; *meergrüner -,* aquamarine.

besabbeln, besabbern, *v.a.* & *r.* (*coll.*) slobber over.

besä-en, *v.a.* sow (*a field, etc.*); inoculate. **-t,** *p.p.* & *adj.* sowed; studded, strewn, covered; *mit Sternen -t,* star-spangled.

besag-en, *v.a.* say, mention, signify, purport, mean; prove; *das hat nichts zu -en, das will gar nichts -en,* that does not mean *or* signify anything, that is not at all important; *das -t die Unterschrift,* that is attested by the signature. **-end,** *pr.p.* & *adj.* to the effect. **-t,** *p.p.* & *adj.* aforesaid. **-termaßen,** *adv.* as before mentioned.

besaiten, *v.a.* string (*an instrument*); *zart besaitetes Gemüt,* sensitive *or* touchy disposition.

besam-en, 1. *v.a.* sow; impregnate. 2. *v.r.* be propagated by seed. **-ung,** *f.* sowing, seeding, insemination, propagation (by seed).

Besan, *m.* (-s, -e) mizzen (*Naut.*); **-baum,** *m.* mizzen-boom.

besänftig-en, 1. *v.a.* appease, soothe, soften, allay, calm, assuage; 2. *v.r.* calm down; *nicht zu -en,* unappeasable, implacable. **-ung,** *f.* appeasement, calming, softening, mitigation. **-ungsmittel,** *n.* palliative; sedative.

besaß, besäße, *see* **besitzen.**

Besatz, *m.* (-es, ⸚e) trimming, border, edge, edging; embroidery, braid, facing, piping. **-spitze,** *f.* braid, braiding. **-streifen,** *m.* cap band (*Mil.*). **-ung,** *f.* garrison (*Mil.*); crew (*Naut.* & *Av.*). **-ungsheer,** *n.* army of occupation.

besaufen, *v.r.* (*vulg.*) get drunk.

beschädig-en, 1. *v.a.* injure, harm, damage, impair; *leicht zu -en,* fragile. 2. *v.r.* hurt o.s., do o.s. an injury. **-ung,** *f.* damage, injury, harm.

beschaff-en, 1. *reg.v.a.* procure, supply, provide. 2. *p.p.* & *adj.* conditioned, constituted; *so ist er -en,* that is his nature; *gut -en,* in good condition, in good circumstances; *so ist die Welt -en,* that is the way of the world; *die S. ist so -en,* the matter stands thus. **-enheit,** *f.* nature, state, condition, quality, constitution, character, disposition; *nach -enheit der Umstände,* according to circumstances. **-enheitswort,** *n.* attribute, adjective. **-ung,** *f.* providing, procuring, procurement; supply; (*C.L.*) *wir bitten um gütige -ung,* please procure for us. **-ungsbedarf,** *m.* demand.

beschäftig-en, 1. *v.a.* occupy, employ, engage, keep busy. 2. *v.r.* occupy o.s., be busy with. **-t,** *p.p.* & *adj.* busy; occupied (with); *bei einem -t sein,* be in the employ of *or* be employed by a p.; *mit etwas -t sein,* be occupied with a th. **-ung,** *f.* occupation, business, pursuit. **-ungslos,** *adj.* unemployed.

beschalen, *v.a.* furnish with a shell *or* cover; lath (*a ceiling*); board (*a floor*).

[1]**beschälen,** *v.a.* peel, husk, pare, bark (*trees*).

[2]**beschäl-en,** *v.a.* cover (*of horses*). **-er,** *m.* stallion, stud-horse.

beschäm-en, *v.a.* shame, make ashamed, confuse, confound, disconcert, abash. **-end,** *pr.p.* & *adj.* disgraceful, shameful. **-t,** *p.p.* & *adj.* ashamed, abashed, confused. **-ung,** *f.* confusion, shame.

beschatten, *v.a.* overshadow; shade.

Beschau, *f.* examination, inspection. **-en,** 1. *v.a.* view, behold; inspect, examine; gaze upon, look at, contemplate; 2. *v.r.* examine o.s., look into one's own heart. **-end,** *pr.p.* & *adj.* contemplative. **-er,** *m.* looker-on, spectator; inspector. **-pflichtig,** *adj.* subject to *or* liable to inspection. **-lich,** *adj.* contemplative, meditative. **-lichkeit,** *f.* contemplation, contemplativeness. **-ung,** *f.* viewing, examination, inspection; contemplation; *bei näherer -ung,* on closer inspection.

Bescheid, *m.* (-(e)s, -e) information, instruction(s), direction(s); knowledge; answer, decision, decree; award; *um eine S.* (*über eine S., von einer S.*) *wissen,* know *or* have knowledge of a th., be acquainted with a th., (*coll.*) know what's what about a th.; *einem - trinken* or *tun,* drink to the health of a p.; *ich weiß hier keinen -,* I am a stranger here; I don't know what to do, I am quite at sea about this; *in einem Hause - wissen,* know one's way about a house; *einem - sagen lassen,* send a p. word, let a p. know; *einem von etwas - geben,* inform a p. of a th.; *gehörig - sagen,* to give a piece of one's mind; *bis auf weiteren -,* till further orders, provisionally. **-en,** 1. *ir.v.a.* allot, assign, apportion; inform, direct, order. *einen über eine S. -en,* inform a p. of a th.; *ich lasse mich -en,* I am open to conviction; *er ist zu seinem Regimente beschieden,* he is ordered to join his regiment; *er beschied mich auf die folgende Woche,* he requested me to call on him the next week; *einen zu sich -en,* send for *or* summon a p.; 2. *v.r.* resign o.s. (to), acquiesce (in), be satisfied (with); *er weiß sich zu -en,* he knows his place; *man muß sich mit wenigem -en,* one must be satisfied with little. 3. *adj.* modest, discreet, unassuming; moderate. **-enheit,** *f.* modesty, diffidence; discretion, moderation.

bescheinen, *ir.v.a.* shine upon, irradiate; illuminate.

bescheinig-en, *v.a.* vouch for, attest, certify; acquit, receipt, acknowledge (receipt of); issue a certificate; *ich will Ihnen den Empfang -en,* I will give you a receipt for it; *ich -e Herrn Z. gern,* I have much pleasure in certifying to Mr. Z. **-ung,** *f.* certificate; voucher; receipt.

beschenk-en, *v.a.* present with; confer upon; *er -te mich mit Schillers Werken,* he made me a present of Schiller's works.

[1]**bescheren,** *ir.v.a.* shear, shave; clip.
[2]**bescher-en,** *reg.v.a.* (*einem etwas*) give (as a share *or* lot *or* present); bestow upon, mete out to, make a present (of); present (with); *zu Weihnachten -en*, give as a Christmas present. **-ung,** *f.* distribution of (Christmas) presents; gift, present; (*coll.*) *eine schöne -ung!* a nice mess, a pretty kettle of fish! a fine business! (*coll.*) *da haben wir die -ung!* now we are in for it! (*coll.*) *die ganze -ung*, the whole lot.
beschick-en, *v.a.* send for *or* to; convey; manage, handle; bring about; put in order, attend to, prepare; tend, charge (*furnace*), take care of; alloy, mix, impregnate; *eine Ausstellung -en*, exhibit, contribute to an exhibition; *den Reichstag -en*, send deputies, return a member to parliament. **-ung,** *f.* sending; conveyance; deputation; alloying, alloy; preparation; *-ung des Landes*, tillage.
beschieden, *see* **bescheiden.**
beschienen, *v.a.* fix with splints; fit with bands of iron; shoe (*a wheel*); lay down rails (*Railw.*).
beschieß-en, 1. *ir.v.a.* fire on; bombard, shell; *der Länge nach -en*, enfilade; rake (with fire) (*Mil.*). 2. *v.n.* (*aux.* s.) become covered with a deposit (*Chem.*). 3. *n.*, **-ung,** *f.* bombardment, shelling, cannonading.
beschiff-en, *v.a.* navigate; ply *or* sail (*a river, etc.*). **-bar,** *adj.* navigable.
beschilft, *adj.* reedy, sedgy.
beschimmeln, *v.n.* grow mouldy.
beschimpf-en, *v.a.* insult, abuse, revile; use abusive language; injure (*a reputation*); call (*a p.*) names. **-end,** *pr.p.* & *adj.* insulting, abusive, derogatory, defamatory; libellous. **-ung,** *f.* insult, abuse, aspersion; affront, outrage; libel.
beschirmen, *v.a.* screen, cover; protect, shelter, defend.
Beschirrung, *f.* harness.
beschlafen, *ir.v.a.* sleep *or* lie with (*a p.*); (*coll.*) *etwas -*, sleep over *or* on s.th.
Beschlag, *m.* (-(e)s, ⸚e) 1. metal fitting, clasp, mounting, cap, sheathing, coating, covering, layer, jacket, lining, rim, knob, plate, stud, *etc.*; shoe (*of a wheel, horse, etc.*); ferrule (*on a stick*); guard (*of a sword*); nails (*of climbing boots*); metal work; 2. mouldiness; moisture, damp, humidity; efflorescence (*Chem.*); 3. seizure, embargo; attachment (*against property of a debtor*); sequestration (*of an income*); distraint (*upon goods*); *in - nehmen, mit - belegen*, confiscate, seize judicially; occupy, take up (*time*); engross (*attention, etc.*); arrest; sequestrate, lay an embargo on, distrain; requisition; *den - aufheben*, remove an embargo, sequestration, *etc.*; release. **-en, 1.** *ir.v.a.* 1. mount; sheath; fit with clasps, studs, nails, tip, horseshoes (*or any metal attachment*); furl (*a sail*); 2. stamp, flatten; square (*timber*); lute (*Chem.*); 3. fix with nails, *etc.* (*sole of a shoe, draping, etc.*); *mit Silber -en*, silver-mounted; *ein mit Leder -ener Koffer*, leather-covered trunk; *scharf -en*, rough-shoe (*a horse*); *mit einem Deckel -en*, fit with a cover. **2.** *v.r.* & *n.* (*aux.* s.) grow mouldy; tarnish, get tarnished; become coated, become covered with moisture, effloresce; *in einer S. gut -en sein*, be well versed in, have a sound knowledge of, be familiar with *or* conversant with a th.; *in allen Künsten gut -en*, well versed in all the arts. **-legung,** *f.*, **-nahme,** *f.* seizure, confiscation, distraint, attachment, sequestration, embargo, commandeering, expropriation. **-nahmen,** *v.a.* seize, confiscate, commandeer, expropriate. **-sbefehl,** *m.* detainer (*Law*). **-(s)verwalter,** *m.*, **-(s)verweser,** *m.* sequestrator.
beschleichen, 1. *ir.v.a.* steal upon, creep up to (stealthily); stalk; surprise; overcome, seize; *ein Gefühl des Ekels beschlich ihn*, a feeling of disgust overcame him. 2. *n.*; *- des Wildes*, deer-stalking.
beschleunig-en, *v.a.* accelerate, hasten, expedite; speed, quicken, force; precipitate; *mein Puls geht -t*, my pulse is fast *or* rapid. **-end,** *pr.p.* & *adj.*; *-ende Kraft*, accelerating force. **-er,** *m.* accelerator (*Motor.*). **-ung,** *f.* acceleration; dispatch, haste, speed. **-ungsmittel,** *n.* accelerator (*Chem.*).
beschließ-en, *ir.v.a.* 1. close, conclude, end, finish, terminate; 2. resolve, determine on, decide; 3. enclose, lock up; *etwas mit einander -en*, agree upon a th. with a p.; *etwas mit Stimmenmehrheit -en*, carry (a motion) with a majority, vote in favour of something. **-er,** *m.*, **-erin,** *f.* butler, housekeeper.
beschlossen, *p.p.* & *adj.* landlocked; sheltered, closed in; resolved; *es wurde beschlossen*, it was agreed *or* resolved. **beschlossenermaßen,** *adv.* as agreed.
Beschluß, *m.* (-(ss)es, ⸚(ss)e) 1. close, end, termination, conclusion; 2. decision, determination; resolve, resolution; decree; custody; *zum -e*, finally, in conclusion, in short; *das Parlament faßte diesen -*, the House passed the following resolution. **-fähig,** *adj.* competent to pass resolutions. *-fähige Anzahl*, quorum; *in -fähiger Anzahl sein*, be *or* constitute a quorum. **-fassung,** *f.*, **-nahme,** *f.* conclusion, decision, determination; decree; passing of a resolution.
beschmieren, *v.a.* (be)smear; spread on, coat; dirty, daub, dedaub; scribble on, scrawl on; grease; *mit Butter -*, butter.
beschmissen, *p.p.* (*of* beschmeißen) & *adj.* fly-blown.
beschmort, *adj.* (*coll.*) drunk, boozed.
beschmutzen, *v.a.* soil, dirty, stain; foul.
beschnarchen, *v.a.* (*coll.*) sleep on *or* over (*before deciding*).
beschneid-en, *ir.v.a.* cut, clip, trim, lop, prune, pare; circumcise; curtail, reduce; *einem das Gehalt -en*, cut down a p.'s salary; (*einem*) *die Gelegenheit -en*, take away an opportunity from a p.; *einem die Flügel -en*, clip a p.'s wings. **-emaschine,** *f.* guillotine; clipper. **-ung,** *f.* cutting, clipping; circumcision; curtailment.
beschnei-en, *v.a.* cover with snow. **-t,** *p.p.* & *adj.* snow-covered, snowy.
beschnitten, *p.p.* & *adj.*; *-e Bäume*, pollards; *-es Papier*, cut paper; *ein -er*, a circumcised p.
beschnüffel-n, beschnupper-n, *v.a.* (*fig.*) sniff at; *er -t alles*, he pokes his nose into everything.
bescholten, *adj.* in disrepute, ill-famed, of ill-repute.
beschön(ig)en, *v.a.* palliate, extenuate; varnish over, gloss over, explain away; *beschönigende Ausdrücke*, extenuating phrases, euphemistic terms.
beschottern, *v.a.* metal, surface, macadamize (*a road*).
beschränk-en, *v.a.* bound, confine, limit, circumscribe, restrict; hem in; *sich auf eine S. -en*, restrict o.s. to a th., be satisfied with a th. **-end,** *pr.p.* & *adj.* restrictive. **-t,** *p.p.* & *adj.* limited, restricted, narrow, circumscribed; narrow-minded; *-te Haftung*, (*C.L.*) limited liability. **-theit,** *f.* narrowness; scantiness; narrow-mindedness; dullness, stupidity. **-ung,** *f.* restraint, restriction; limit, limitation.
beschreib-en, *ir.v.a.* write upon, cover with writing; describe, depict, portray; describe (*a circle, etc.*); *eine Bahn -en*, revolve (*Astron*); *nicht zu -en*, indescribable. **-end,** *pr.p.* & *adj.* descriptive. **-lich,** *adj.* describable. **-ung,** *f.* description, portrayal; (*in compounds often* = -logy *or* -graphy), *-ung des Leibes, der Erde, der Vögel, eines Ortes, der Welt, etc.*, physiology, geography, ornithology, topography, cosmography, *etc.*
beschreien, *ir.v.a.* decry, disparage; render notorious; bewitch, cast a spell on; over-praise; *- Sie es nur nicht!* don't crow over it.
beschreiten, *ir.v.a.* walk on, step over; cross (*a threshold, etc.*); bestride (*a horse*); *den Rechtsweg -*, go to law; *das Ehebett -*, consummate one's marriage.
Beschriftung, *f.* (-en) lettering, labelling; inscription, legend, caption.
beschuhen, *v.a.* provide with shoes, shoe.
beschuldig-en, *v.a.* accuse (*Gen.*, of) charge (with), impute (to). **-er,** *m.* accuser; plaintiff. **-t,** *p.p.* & *adj.*; *der -te*, person accused, defendant. **-ung,** *f.* charge, accusation, impeachment.
beschummeln, *v.a.* (*coll.*) cheat, take in.
beschupp-en, *v.a.* cover with scales, scale. **-t,** *p.p.* & *adj.* covered with scales, scaly.
Beschuß, *m.* fire, bombardment (*Artil.*)
beschütten, *v.a.* throw *or* cast on; pour over; cover with.
beschütz-en, *v.a.* protect, guard, shelter, defend.

-er, *m.* protector, defender, guardian; patron. **-ung,** *f.* protection, defence; patronage.
beschwatzen, *v.a.* persuade, wheedle, talk into.
beschweift, *adj.* tailed.
Beschwer, *n.* (only in the expression *ohne* –), **-de** *f.* (-den) trouble, difficulty; burden, hardship; inconvenience, annoyance; grievance, ground of complaint; complaint, malady, infirmity, pain; molestation; *–de über eine S. führen*, complain of a th.; *Kopf–den*, headache; *körperliche –den*, bodily ailments; *die –den des Alters*, the infirmities of old age. **-debuch,** *n.* book for entering complaints. **-deführer,** *m.* complainant. **-depunkt,** *m.* matter of complaint, grievance. **-deschrift,** *f.* written complaint. **-en,** 1. *v.a.* load, charge, weight, anchor down; burden, encumber, trouble, be troublesome to; clog, lie heavy on (*the stomach*); be a load *or* a weight (*on one's conscience*). 2. *v.r.* complain (*bei einem über einen*, to a p. of *or* about s.o.). **-lich,** *adj.* troublesome; painful; difficult, hard, fatiguing; cumbersome, burdensome, inconvenient; importunate; *einem –lich sein* or *fallen*, inconvenience a p., be a burden *or* trouble to a p.; *das Gehen fällt ihm –lich*, he walks with difficulty. **-lichkeit,** *f.* troublesomeness, burdensomeness; hardship, inconvenience, trouble, toil, difficulty. **-t,** *p.p.* & *adj.* heavy, loaded, encumbered; mortgaged; *–ter Brief*, letter containing money. **-ung,** *f.* burdening, *etc.*; charge, loading, weighting; burden, annoyance, trouble; encumbrance, mortgage.
beschwichtig-en, *v.a.* still, soothe, calm, pacify, appease, allay; hush up; compose (*a quarrel*). **-ung,** *f.* lulling, stilling, appeasing; hushing-up. **-ungsgeld,** *n.* hush-money.
beschwindeln, *v.a.* swindle, cheat.
beschwingt, *adj.* on wings, winged; speedy.
beschwipst, *adj.* (*coll.*) tipsy.
beschwör-en, *ir.v.a.* 1. swear, affirm *or* testify on oath, take one's oath on; 2. conjure; exorcize; entreat, implore, adjure. **-er,** *m.* conjurer, exorcist, magician. **-ung,** *f.* confirmation by oath; exorcism; entreaty, adjuration. **-ungsformel,** *f.* incantation, charm. **-ungskunst,** *f.* exorcism, magic.
beseel-en, *v.a.* animate, inspire, enliven. **-t,** *p.p.* & *adj.* animate; having a soul. **-ung,** *f.* animation.
besegel-n, *v.a.* navigate, sail (*the ocean, etc.*); *die Küste –n*, coast, sail along the coast; *ein Schiff –n*, fit a ship with sails. **-ung,** *f.* fitting with sails; set of sails.
besehen, 1. *ir.v.a.* look at; inspect, examine, (*coll.*) *eine Tracht Prügel* –, get *or* come in for a sound thrashing; *sich* (*Dat.*) *etwas* –, have a look at; visit, view; *zu* –, on view, for inspection. 2. *p.p.; bei Lichte* –, on closer inspection, viewed in the right light.
beseitig-en, *v.a.* put *or* set aside; remove, do away with, eliminate, liquidate; put an end to, settle; explain away, account for. **-t,** *p.p.* & *adj.* removed, eliminated, *etc.*; done away with. **-ung,** *f.* removal; elimination; settlement.
beselig-en, *v.a.* bless; make happy. **-ung,** *f.* blessing; bliss; rapture.
Besen, *m.* (-s, –) broom; (*sl.*) housemaid; slut; (*Prov.*) *neue – kehren gut*, new brooms sweep clean; **-ginster,** *m.* broom (*Cytisus scoparius*) (*Bot.*). **-rein,** *adj.* well-swept. **-reis,** *n.* birch-twig. **-stiel,** *m.* broomstick; *steif wie ein –stiel*, stiff as a ram-rod.
besessen, *p.p.* (*of* besitzen) & *adj.* possessed; frenzied; *der –e*, demoniac, fanatic, madman. **-heit,** *f.* frenzy, madness, demoniacal possession.
besetz-en, *v.a.* 1. put *or* lay on; trim, garnish, border (*with lace, fur, etc.*); set (*with jewels*); lay (*paving stones*); 2. occupy, garrison, man; 3. fill (*an office, vacancy, etc.*); occupy, engage (*a place*); fill the cast (*of a play*). **-t,** *p.p.* & *adj.* engaged (*seat, lavatory*); full up; *es war alles –t*, every seat was engaged *or* taken; *gut –tes Stück*, well-cast play; *jede Stimme war dreimal –t*, each part was sung by three voices; *–tes Gebiet*, occupied territory. **-ung,** *f.* trimming, bordering, edging; (military) occupation; nomination (*to an office*); filling (*of a vacancy*); distribution (*of parts*), cast, casting (*of a play*), **-ungsrecht,** *n.* right of presentation, patronage, advowson.
besicht-igen, *v.a.* inspect; view, review; survey; *einen Leichnam* (*von Amtswegen*) *–igen*, hold an inquest. **-iger,** *m.* inspector, surveyor; visitor. **-igung,** *f.* inspection, review, survey; sightseeing; *–igung einer Leiche*, coroner's inquest. **-igungsbericht,** *m.* inspector's report. **-igungsgebühren,** *f.pl.* surveyor's fees. **-igungsreise,** *f.* tour of inspection.
besied-eln, *v.a.* colonize, settle; *ein Land –eln*, settle in a country; *dicht –elt*, thickly *or* densely populated. **-(e)lung,** *f.* colonization, settlement. **-(e)lungsdichte,** *f.* density of population.
besiegel-n, *v.a.* seal, put one's seal to. **-ung,** *f.* sealing.
besieg-en, *v.a.* defeat, conquer, beat, vanquish, overcome, subdue; surmount (*difficulties*). **-er,** *m.* conqueror, victor. **-ung,** *f.* conquering; conquest.
Besing, *m.*, **Besinge,** *f.*; *schwarze* –, bilberry, myrtle whortleberry; *rote* –, red whortleberry.
besingen, *ir.v.a.* sing, celebrate (in song), praise, laud.
besinn-en, 1. *ir.v.r.*; *sich* (*auf eine S.*) *–en*, recollect, remember, call to mind, think of; *sich eines Besseren –en*, think better of a th.; *sich anders* or *eines andern –en*, change one's mind; *sich –en* (*über eine S.*), consider, deliberate, reflect, ponder; *sich hin und her –en*, rack one's brain; *ohne sich zu –en*, without thinking *or* considering, impulsively; *ohne sich lange zu –en*, without a moment's reflection, without stopping to think. 2. *n.*, *see* **-ung, -lich,** *adj.* thoughtful, reflective, contemplative. **-ung,** *f.* recollection; consciousness; reflection, consideration, deliberation; *wieder zur –ung kommen*, recover consciousness; *sie war nicht bei –ung*, she was unconscious; *einen zur –ung bringen*, bring a p. to his senses. **-ungskraft,** *f.* consciousness; power of recollection. **-ungslos,** *adj.* unconscious, insensible; senseless, inconsiderate, rash. **-ungslosigkeit,** *f.* senselessness; insensibility.
Besitz, *m.* possession; estate, property; *eine S. in – nehmen* or *von einer S. – ergreifen*, take possession of *or* occupy a th.; *in* (*den*) *– setzen*, put in possession of; *im –e einer S. sein*, be in possession of a th.; *sei im –, und du wohnst im Recht*, possession is nine points of the law; *einen aus dem –e bringen* or *treiben*, dispossess, expropriate *or* oust a p. **-anzeigend,** *adj.* possessive (*Gram.*). **-en,** *ir.v.a.* possess, be in possession of, own, be endowed with, hold, occupy; *er –t mein Vertrauen*, he has my confidence. **-end,** *pr.p.* & *adj.*; *die –enden Klassen*, the moneyed *or* propertied classes; the 'haves'. **-entziehung,** *f.* dispossession. **-er,** *m.* owner, possessor; proprietor, principal (*of a business*); master; occupant, occupier; *Grund–er*, land-owner; *den –er wechseln*, change owner *or* hands. **-ergreifung,** *f.* occupancy, seizure. **-los,** *adj.* propertyless; *die –lose Klasse*, the 'have-nots'. **-nahme,** *f.*, **-nehmung,** *f.* taking possession, occupation, seizure, occupancy. **-stand,** *m.* (*C.L.*) active property; *voller –stand bewahrt*, integrity preserved. **-steuer,** *f.* property tax. **-tum,** *n.* (-tums, -tümer) possession, property. **-ung,** *f.* possessions, property; manor, estate; (*pl.*) dominions, dependencies. **-urkunde,** *f.* livery (*Law*).
besoffen, *p.p.* (*of* besaufen) & *adj.* (*vulg.*) drunk.
besohlen, *v.a.* sole (*shoes, etc.*).
besold-en, *v.a.* pay (*wages, salary, etc.*). **-ung,** *f.* payment (*of wages, salary, etc.*); pay, wages, salary, stipend. **-ungsvorschrift,** *f.* pay regulations (*Mil.*)
besonder, *adj.* particular, special, specific; peculiar, separate, distinct; exceptional, odd, strange, singular; *ins–e*, in particular; *jeder Teil ins –e*, each several part; *nichts –es*, nothing particular; nothing unusual; *–e Havarie*, particular *or* simple average (*Naut.*); *–e Wohnung*, separate dwelling; *die –en Eigenschaften einer Pflanze*, the specific qualities of a plant; *die –en Umstände*, the particulars; *meine –e Meinung*, my individual opinion; *das –e*, the concrete (*Log.*); the particular, the extraordinary; *etwas ganz –es*, something quite out of the ordinary.

-heit, *f.* speciality, specialty; particularity, peculiarity, individuality; strangeness, oddness; (*pl.*) details, particulars. **-s,** *adv.* especially, particularly, in particular; apart, separate, severally; peculiarly, exceptionally, extraordinarily; chiefly.

besonnen, *p.p.* (*of* besinnen) & *adj.* prudent, circumspect, discreet, cautious; sensible, rational. **-heit,** *f.* prudence, discretion, circumspection, presence of mind, self-possession.

besorg-en, I. *v.a.* take care of, care for, provide for; procure, fetch; manage, see to, attend to; do, effect, perform, execute, discharge, conduct; *ich werde es -en,* I shall see to it; *seine Schwester -t den Haushalt,* his sister looks after the house; *-en Sie mir drei Plätze,* get three seats for me; *sogar die kleinsten Aufträge -t er schlecht,* he carries out even the smallest job badly. 2. *v.n.* (*aux.* s.) fear, apprehend, be apprehensive of *or* anxious about; *sie ist um ihre Kinder -t.* she is worried about her children; *-tes Aussehen,* careworn look, look of anxiety; *einen -t machen,* alarm a person. **-lich,** *adj.* anxious, solicitous. **-lichkeit,** *f.* fear, anxiety, solicitude; apprehensiveness. **-nis,** *f.* fear, anxiety, alarm, apprehension; *in -nis geraten,* become alarmed. **-niserregend,** *adj.* disquieting, alarming. **-nisvoll,** *adj.* solicitous; apprehensive. **-t,** *adj.* anxious, apprehensive, solicitous; **-theit,** *f.* anxiety, concern, uneasiness, apprehension. **-ung,** *f.* care, management; execution, performance; errand, commission, purchase; *sie hat die -ung meiner häuslichen Angelegenheiten,* she manages my domestic affairs; *-ungen machen,* do the *or* go shopping. **-ungsgebühren,** *f.pl.* commission fees.

bespann-en, *v.a.* span; stretch over, cover with; string (*an instrument*); harness; *mit Ochsen -t,* ox-drawn. **-ung,** *f.* covering fabric; team (*of horses, etc.*).

bespeien, *ir.v.a.* spit on *or* at.

bespiegeln, *v.r.* look at o.s. in a mirror; take an example (*an,* from, by); be mirrored (*in a glass, river, lake*); admire oneself.

besponnen, *p.p.* & *adj.* (*of* bespinnen) covered; *-e Saiten,* covered strings, silver strings (*Mus.*); *-er Knopf,* covered button.

bespotten, bespötteln, *v.a.* jeer at, ridicule.

besprech-en, I. *ir.v.a.* discuss, talk over, arrange, agree upon; criticize, review (*a book*); conjure, speak a charm over. 2. *v.r. sich mit einem -en,* confer with a p.; *sich mit einem über eine S. -en,* discuss a th. with a p. **-ung,** *f.* conversation; discussion, conference, consultation; criticism, review (*of a book*); conjuration; *sich auf eine -ung einlassen,* enter into negotiations.

besprengen, *v.a.* sprinkle, spray.

bespringen, *ir.v.a.* cover (*a mare*).

bespritzen, *v.a.* spray, splash, sprinkle, squirt; bespatter; play on (*with a hose*).

bespülen, *v.a.* wash (against), rinse, ripple over *or* against; *von der See bespült,* sea-washed.

besser, *adj.* (*comp. of* gut) better; *ein -er Herr,* a man in easy circumstances (*middle-class contrasted with working-class*); *er ist nur ein -er Knecht,* he is merely a better sort of labourer (= *not much better than*); *ich habe -es zu tun,* I have something more important to do; *desto -,* so much the better; *- ist -,* it is best to be on the safe side; *sich - in acht nehmen,* be more careful; *- werden,* amend, get better; clear up (*of weather*); *jetzt steht es - mit ihm, geht es ihm -,* his affairs are looking up, he is getting along better; *er hat es -,* he is better off; *eine Wendung zum -n,* a turn for the better; *sich eines -n besinnen,* think better of a th.; *eines -n belehren,* set right; (*sl.*) *- hinauf,* a little higher up, more upwards; *umso -,* so much the better. **-n,** I. *v.a.* make better, better, improve, improve on *or* upon; amend, reform; mend, repair; correct (*passages in a book*); *nicht zu -n,* incorrigible. 2. *v.r.* improve, get better, mend one's ways; *sein Befinden hat sich gebessert,* his health has improved, he is better; *-e dich!* mend your ways! **-ung,** *f.* improvement, amendment, amelioration, betterment; correction, reformation; recovery, convalescence; *gute -ung!* I wish you a speedy recovery! I hope you will soon be better *or* well; *es ist -ung eingetreten,* there is a change for the better. **-ungsanstalt,** *f.* reformatory, remand home. **-ungsfähig,** *adj.* capable of improvement, improvable. **-ungsmittel,** *n.* corrective.

best, *adj.* (*sup. of* gut) best. *mein -er,* my good sir; (*fam.*) my dear fellow; *der erste -e,* the first comer; *ich fand es am -en,* I thought it best; *aufs -e,* in the best possible way, as well as possible; *auf dem -en Weg sein, . . . zu werden,* be well on the way to becoming . . .; *aufs -e benutzen,* make the most of; *ich kann beim -en Willen nicht kommen,* much as I would like to *or* with the best will in the world, I cannot come; *in den -en Jahren,* in the prime of life; *im -en Arbeiten,* in the midst of work; *im -en Spielen,* in the middle of the game; *nach -em* or *meinem -en Wissen,* to the best of my knowledge; *zum -en der Armen,* for the benefit of the poor; *etwas zum -en geben,* give as a treat, treat (*a p.*) to a th., (*coll.*) stand; relate (*a story, etc.*), entertain; *geben Sie uns ein Lied zum -en,* give us a song; *einen zum -en haben,* tease *or* hoax a p., make a fool of a p., (*coll.*) pull a p.'s leg; *etwas zum -en* (or *aufs -e*) *deuten,* put the best construction on a matter; *sprechen Sie zu meinem -en,* speak in my favour, intercede for me. **-enfalls,** *adv.* at best. **-ens,** *adv.* in the best way, as well as possible; *empfehlen Sie mich -ens,* remember me most kindly (to), with my kind regards (to); *-ens empfohlen!* farewell, good-bye! (*on leave taking*), (*fam.*) all the best! *ich danke -ens,* very many thanks, thanks very much, I am greatly obliged. **-leistung,** *f.* record (*athletics, etc.*). **-möglich,** I. *adj.* best possible. 2. *adv.* as well as possible. **-verfahren,** *n.* method of obtaining optimum results. **-wert,** *m.* optimum.

bestall-en, *v.a.* appoint (to), invest (with) (*an office*). **-ung,** *f.* appointment; installation, investiture. **-ungsbrief,** *m.* (letters) patent, diploma, commission.

Bestand, *m.* (-(e)s, ⸗e) existence, duration, continuance; stability, permanency, firmness, certitude-amount, value (*of goods in hand*); stock, supply; strength (*of a unit*) (*Mil.*); (*C.L.*) cash in hand, balance, remainder; (*dial.*) lease of a farm; *Kassen-, barer -,* cash-balance, cash in hand; *von - sein, - haben,* be durable, lasting *or* constant, endure, last; *- eines Waldes,* stand of trees, standing growth of a wood; *der eiserne -,* the necessary constituents; stock contents, basic requirements, the minimum necessary; iron rations (*Mil.*); *in - geben,* let on lease; *der - des Gutes ist,* the estate comprises; *Ausstände und Bestände,* debts and assets (*dial.*) *in - geben,* farm out, let by lease, rent (to). **-(s); aufnahme,** *f.* stock-taking, inventory; timber-survey. **-bildend,** *adj.* gregarious, social. **-buch,** *n.* inventory. **-geld,** *n.* clear account, balance in cash; (*dial.*) rent of a farm. **-los,** *adj.* inconsistent, unstable, shaky; transitory, of no duration. **-losigkeit,** *f.* instability. **-sdichte,** *f.* density of crop. **-sgüte,** *f.* quality of crop. **-teil,** *m.* constituent, ingredient, component; *fremder -teil,* foreign body, foreign matter, impurity.

beständ-ig, I. *adj.* constant, steady, continual, continuous, perpetual, permanent, lasting, stable, settled, unchanging, steadfast; durable, fast (*of dyes*); invariable, faithful, firm; fixed; *wir müssen in der -igen Erwartung leben, daß,* we must live in constant *or* hourly expectation of; *-ige Größen,* constant quantities (*Math.*); *-iges Wetter,* settled weather; *-iger Wind,* steady wind (*Naut.*); *-ige Nachfrage,* steady *or* brisk demand; *-iger Liebhaber,* constant *or* faithful lover. 2. *adv.* continually, perpetually, constantly, faithfully. **-igkeit,** *f.* continuance; permanence, durability, persistency, persistence, stability, steadiness, steadfastness, constancy, faithfulness, perseverance. **-igmachen,** *n.* stabilizing, stabilization.

bestärk-en, *v.a.* confirm, support, corroborate; strengthen, fortify. **-ung,** *f.* corroboration, confirmation; strengthening.

bestätig-en, I. *v.a.* confirm, corroborate, establish, verify, ratify, endorse; sanction, authorize, make valid; acknowledge (*the receipt of a letter*); *gerichtlich -en,* legalize by oath. 2. *v.r.* be confirmed, hold good, prove (to be) true; *die Nachricht -te sich,* the news proved to be true. **-ung,** *f.* confirmation,

corroboration, verification, ratification, acknowledgement, sanction.
bestatt-en, *v.a.* bury, inter. **-ung,** *f.* burial, funeral, interment; *Feuer-ung, f.* cremation.
bestätter-n, *v.a.* convey, forward. **-(er),** *m.* conveyor, forwarder, forwarding agent, carrier. **-ei,** *f.* conveyance, forwarding, carriage (*of goods*).
bestauben, *v.n.* gather dust, get dusty.
bestäub-en, *v.a.* dust (with), powder; pollinate (*Bot.*). **-ung,** *f.* pollination (*Bot.*).
bestaunen, *v.a.* look at with astonishment.
bestech-en, *ir.v.a.* bribe, corrupt; stitch; *das Urteil eines Mannes -en,* prejudice a p. in favour of. **-bar,** *adj.,* **-lich,** *adj.* corrupt, corruptible, bribable, venal. **-barkeit, -lichkeit,** *f.* corruptibility. **-end,** *pr.p. & adj.* attractive, tempting, seductive. **-ung,** *f.* bribery; bribe, corruption, (*sl.*) graft. **-draht,** *m.* tacking thread.
Besteck, *n.* (-(e)s, -e) knife, fork, and spoon; cutlery, (*sl.*) eating irons; set of (*medical*) instruments; instrument case; ship's position *or* reckoning; *das - machen,* fix (a ship's) position, work the reckoning. **-en,** *v.a.* plant with; prick out (*on a chart, etc.*); stick over with; stake (*peas, etc.*).
Besteder, *m.* (-s, -) ship-broker; ship-wright.
besteh-en, 1. *ir.v.a.* undergo, endure; (*coll.*) go through; pass through, overcome; stand (*a test*); pass, get through (*an examination*); *nicht -en,* fail; (*coll.*) get ploughed; *er hat viele Abenteuer bestanden,* he has encountered many adventures; *er hat die Gefahr glücklich bestanden,* he has safely overcome *or* surmounted the danger. 2. *v.n.* (*aux.* s. & h.) stand steadfast, withstand, resist; hold one's own; be, exist; last, continue, persist; subsist; *er hat bestanden* or *er hat die Prüfung bestanden,* he has passed his examination; *diese zwei Sachen können nicht nebeneinander -en,* these two things are inconsistent with one another *or* incompatible; *sein Reich wird nicht -en,* his kingdom will not last; *-en auf* (*einer S.*), insist on, persist in, hold out for; *sie bestanden darauf, ihn zu sehen,* they insisted on seeing him; *auf seinem Kopfe -en,* be obstinate; *-en aus,* consist of, be composed of; *das Werk -t aus sechs Bänden,* the work is complete in six volumes, *-en in* (*Dat.*), consist in; *die Tugend -t im Handeln,* virtue lies in action. 3. *n.* existence, persistence, composition; *bestanden mit,* planted with, covered with (*see* **Bestand**). **-end,** *pr.p. & adj.* existent, subsistent; *die -enden Gesetze,* existing laws; (*C.L.*) *-ende Preise,* ruling prices; *für sich -end,* absolute, independent; *ein zu Recht -ender Vertrag,* a legal contract.
bestehlen, *ir.v.a.* rob, steal from.
besteig-en, *ir.v.a.* climb; mount (*a horse*); scale (*a wall*); board (*a ship*); ascend (*throne*). **-ung,** *f.* ascent, ascension (*to throne*).
bestell-en, *v.a.* 1. order (*goods*), book (*seats*); bespeak; 2. arrange, dispose; set in order, prepare; appoint, constitute; 3. execute (*a commission*), deliver (*a message*); 4. till, cultivate (*land*); *sie -ten einander auf neun Uhr,* they arranged to meet at nine; *man hat ihn zu diesem Amte -t,* he has been appointed to this office; *zu sich -en,* send for; *einen Gruß -en,* send one's compliments *or* kind regards; *haben Sie etwas zu -en?* have you any message, can I take any message from you? *einen Wagen -en,* order a car; *einen Platz -en,* book a seat; *den Acker -en,* till a field; *sein Haus -en,* put one's affairs in order, arrange one's affairs (*before dying*); *mit ihm* or *um ihn ist es schlecht -t,* he is in a bad way. **-arbeit,** *f.* work done to order, contract job. **-buch,** *n.* order-book. **-gebühr,** *f.,* **-geld,** *n.* commission money, carrier's fee. **-ung,** *f.* order, commission; appointment, rendezvous; delivery; message; management, arrangement; cultivation, tillage; *-ung ins Haus,* delivery to the door; *Sonntags gibt es keine -ung,* there is no post on Sundays; *er arbeitet nur auf -ung,* he only takes orders (*i.e. does not supply from stock*), he only works to order. **-ungsbuch,** *n.* order-book. **-wagen,** *m.* delivery van. **-zeit,** *f.* time for tilling; right time for ordering. **-zettel,** *m.* order-form.
besternt, *p.p. & adj.* starry; decorated (*with orders*); marked with an asterisk.
besteuer-n, *v.a.* tax (*people*), impose a duty on (*goods*), assess. **-ung,** *f.* taxation, imposition of taxes, assessment.
bestial-isch, *adj.* bestial, beastly, brutal. **-ität,** *f.* beastliness, bestiality; cruelty.
Bestie, *f.* (-n) beast, brute.
bestielt, *p.p. & adj.* furnished with a handle *or* stalk; pedunculate, petiolate (*Bot.*).
bestimm-en, 1. *v.a.* decide, determine, ascertain; settle, fix, appoint (*a time*); define, allot; *über eine S. -en,* dispose of a th.; *-en zu,* destine, intend for; *wir sind alle dazu -t,* we are all destined to *or* for it; *eine S. für einen Zweck -en,* earmark a th. for a purpose; *ich hatte das Geld für Sie -t,* I had intended the money for you; *einen -en etwas zu tun,* induce a p. to do a th.; *etwas näher -en,* define s.th. more closely, modify *or* qualify a th.; *das Gesetz -t, daß,* the law ordains that. 2. *v.r.*; *sich -en* (*zu einer S.*), determine, resolve on, choose (a th.). **-bar,** *adj.* definable, ascertainable, determinable; appreciable. **-end,** *pr.p. & adj.* determining, deciding; *das -ende dabei war,* what decided the matter was. **-t,** 1. *p.p. & adj.* fixed, appointed, settled, decided, determined; definite, certain, firm, precise, specific, distinct, positive, destined (*by fate*) (*zu,* for); finite, determinate (*Math.*); bound (*nach,* for); *dieses Schiff ist nach Hamburg -t,* this ship is bound for Hamburg; *es war mir vom Schicksal -t,* it was intended for me by fate; *es ist -t in Gottes Rat,* God has decreed *or* willed it; *der -te Artikel,* definite article (*Gram.*); *an dem -ten Tage,* on the appointed day; *-te Antwort,* definite answer; *-tes Gehalt,* fixed stipend *or* salary; *-te Gleichung,* determinate equation; *ganz -t?* are you quite certain? *ganz -t!* most decidedly! 2. *adv.* certainly, assuredly, without doubt. **-theit,** *f.* certainty, exactitude, exactness, precision; definiteness; determination, firmness; *mit -theit,* positively, categorically. **-ung,** *f.* determination; destination; destiny; vocation; designation; statement, definition; regulation, rule; modification, stipulation; diagnosis (*Med.*); analysis (*Chem.*); *gesetzliche -ung,* regulation, ordinance. **-ungstabelle,** *f.* table, key. **-ungsgrund,** *m.* motive. **-ungsmensur,** *f.* students' duel in which combatants represent their 'corps'. **-ungsmethode,** *f.* method of identification *or* determination (*Chem.*). **-ungsort,** *m.* destination. **-ungswort,** *n.* modifying *or* determinating word (*adjective, adverb, etc.*).
bestirnt, *adj.* starry.
bestochen, *see* **bestechen.**
bestohlen, *see* **bestehlen.**
bestoß-en, 1. *ir.v.a.* hit *or* knock against; injure, damage (*by a knock, etc.*); smooth, trim, plane down, rough-file; *Lettern -en,* dress the type. 2. *p.p. & adj.* much worn, rubbed, damaged (*of binding or corners of books*). **-feile,** *f.* rasp. **-hobel,** *m.* jack-plane; dresser (*Typ.*).
bestraf-en, *v.a.* punish. **-ung,** *f.* punishing; punishment; reprimand.
bestrahl-en, *v.a.* shine upon, irradiate; (*Med.*) treat by means of therapy. **-ung,** *f.* irradiation, illumination; ray therapy.
bestreb-en, 1. *v.r.* exert o.s., strive, endeavour. 2. *n.,* **-ung,** *f.* effort, attempt, endeavour, aspiration, striving, exertion.
bestreichen, *ir.v.a.* spread (over), smear, besmear; graze, brush against; sweep, rake (*with shot, etc.*); paint, wash (*with colour*); touch upon; *mit Butter -* butter; *mit Fett -,* grease; *mit Pflaster -,* plaster; *in gerader Linie -,* enfilade; *von der Seite -,* flank; *bestrichener Raum,* danger zone (*Artil.*); *eine Küste -* coast along, sail along the coast.
bestreit-en, 1. *ir.v.a.* dispute, deny; combat, contest, impugn, oppose; 2. be equal to; bear, defray (*expenses*); pay for; *jemandes Bedürfnisse -en.* supply a p.'s wants; *die Kosten der Ausrüstung -en,* cover the costs of the outfit; *ich weiß nicht wie ich diese Ausgaben -en soll,* I do not know how to meet these expenses; *er bestritt die Hälfte des Programms,* he filled half the programme; *er bestritt mir das Recht,* he disputed my right; *das -et niemand,* no one will deny that. **-bar,** *adj.*

disputable controvertible, contestable. **-ung,** *f.* combating; defrayal (*of cost*).
bestreuen, *v.a.* strew, sprinkle over, dust, powder, bestrew.
bestrick-en, *v.a.* ensnare, captivate; charm, fascinate. **-end,** *pr.p. & adj.*; *-endes Lächeln*, captivating smile. **-ung,** *f.* entanglement; captivation.
bestück-en, *v.a.* arm (*a ship*) with guns. **-t,** *p.p. & adj.; -t mit*, mounted with (*guns*). **-ung,** *f.* armament (*of a ship*), guns.
bestürm-en, *v.a.* storm, assault, assail; besiege. **-ung,** *f.* storming; assault.
bestürz-en, *v.a.* perplex, disconcert, confound, dismay. **-t,** *p.p. & adj.* confounded, dismayed, (*coll.*) put out; *-t sein*, stand aghast, be thunderstruck; *-t machen*, startle, surprise; confound, throw into confusion; terrify, dismay; *ein -tes Gesicht machen*, look aghast, be taken aback. **-ung,** *f.* alarm, consternation, dismay, confusion.
Besuch, *m.* (-(e)s, -e) visit, call; company, visitors; attendance; *zu - sein*, be on a visit; *kurzer -*, flying visit; *langer -*, long stay; *einen - abstatten*, pay a visit, make a call; *er hat -*, he has company; *wir haben vielen -*, we have many visitors. **-en,** *v.a.* visit; call on *or* upon; attend; resort to, frequent; *er -t die Kirche regelmäßig*, he attends church regularly; *seine Vorlesungen werden gut* or *sind sehr -t*, his lectures are well attended; *das Theater ist schlecht* or *schwach -t*, the theatre is poorly attended; *ein stark -ter Ort*, a place that is much frequented. **-er,** *m.* visitor. **-skarte,** *f.* (visiting-)card. **-stag, -tag,** *m.* (regular) visiting-day, reception-day, at-home day.
besudel-n, *v.a.* dirty, stain, soil, pollute, contaminate, befoul, sully, defile, besmirch. **-ung,** *f.* defilement, pollution, contamination.
betagt, *p.p. & adj.* aged, stricken in years; due (*of a bill*); *wohl -, hoch -*, well advanced in years.
betakel-n, *v.a.* rig (*a ship*). **-ung,** *f.* rigging (*of a ship*).
betast-en, *v.a.* handle, touch, finger, feel, palpate (*Med.*); *ungeschickt -en*, maul, fumble with. **-ung,** *f.* feeling, fingering touching, *etc.*
betätig-en, 1. *v.a.* set in motion, make to work, set going; prove, give practical proof of, exemplify, show in practice; practise, manifest; *den Hebel -en*, work the handle; *den Knopf -en*, press the button. 2. *v.r.* work, get busy, bestir o.s., take active part in, participate in, be active in; *er -t sich politisch*, he is active politically. **-ung,** *f.* activity, participation (in); manifestation; application.
betäub-en, *v.a.* stun, deafen, stupefy; bewilder, confuse; deaden; anaesthetize (*Med.*). **-end,** *pr.p. & adj.* deafening; narcotic; stupefying. **-t,** *adj.* dizzy, stupefied, torpid. **-ung,** *f.* deafening; bewilderment, stupefaction; numbness, stupor; narcosis; *örtliche -ung*, local anaesthetic. **-ungsmittel,** *n.* narcotic.
betauen, *v.a.* bedew.
[1]**Bete,** 1. *f. & n.* [*pron.* 'be:tə] (-n) stake lost (*at cards*); p. who loses (*at cards*). 2. *adj.*; [*pron.* be:t] (*coll.*) *er ist -*, he has lost the game; he must pay the forfeit.
[1]**Bete,** *f.* (-n) beet, beetroot (*Bot.*); *see* **Beete.**
beteilig-en, 1. *v.a.* give a share *or* an interest to; make a partner of; *bei* or *an einer S. -t sein*, have a share in *or* participate in a th. 2. *v.r.*; take part in, participate in, join in, take an interest in, be interested in, be concerned with; *ich würde mich nicht dabei -t haben, wenn*, I should not have had anything to do with it, if; *die -ten Parteien*, the parties involved. **-te(r),** *m.* accessory (*Law*); *die -ten, pl.* the parties concerned. **-ung,** *f.* share, interest; participation, support; *aus Mangel an -ung*, from lack of support.
bet-en, 1. *v.a.* say in prayer; *sie -ete ihren Rosenkranz (her)*, she told her beads; *er -ete das Vaterunser*, he said the Lord's Prayer. 2. *v.n.* (*aux.* h.) pray, say one's prayers; *vor* (or *nach*) *Tische -en*, say grace; *-en um eine S.*, pray for a th. **-bruder,** *m.* devotee, bigot. **-buch,** *n.* prayer-book. **-er,** *m.* worshipper. **-fahrt,** *f.* pilgrimage. **-glocke,** *f.* angelus (*R.C.*). **-kissen,** *n.* hassock. **-saal,** *m.* chapel, oratory. **-schemel,** *m.* hassock. **-schwester** *f. see* **-bruder.** **-stunde,** *f.* prayer-time; prayer-meeting. **-stundenbuch,** *n.* breviary. **-tag,** *m.* day of prayer *or* thanksgiving, fast-day; Rogation day; *Buß- und -tag*, day of national prayer. **-woche,** *f.* Rogation week.
beteuer-n, *v.a.* assert, aver, protest, asseverate; swear (to); *eidlich -n*, affirm by oath. **-ung,** *f.* protestation, assertion; asseveration.
Beting, *m.* (-s, -e) *or f.* (-e) bitts (*Naut.*); *das Ankertau um die -e schlagen*, bitt the cable.
betiteln, *v.a.* entitle; style, call, name.
Beton, *m.* concrete. **-eisen,** *n.* reinforcing iron, *Eisen-*, *m.* reinforced concrete, armoured concrete. ferro-concrete. **-ieren,** *v.a.* build with concrete. **-maschine,** *f.* concrete mixer.
beton-en, *v.a.* accent, stress, accentuate; emphasize, lay stress on; *-te Silbe*, accented, stressed *or* emphatic syllable. **-ung,** *f.* accentuation; emphasis, stress.
betör-en, *v.a.* infatuate, befool, delude. **-theit,** *f.* besottedness. **-ung,** *f.* infatuation.
Betracht, *m.* respect, regard, consideration, account; (*only used in the following phrases*) *in -*, considering; *in jedem -*, in every respect; *in - kommen*, come into question, be taken into consideration, be of importance; *nicht in - kommen*, be out of the question; *außer - lassen*, leave out of consideration; *in - ziehen*, take into consideration. **-en,** *v.a.* look at, view, consider, contemplate, regard, examine, reflect upon; *alles recht -et*, altogether, taking everything into consideration; *genau -et*, looked at closely. **-er,** *m.* onlooker, spectator. **-ung,** *f.* view, opinion, way of thinking; meditation, contemplation, consideration; reflection, observation; inspection; *in -ung des*, in consideration of, out of regard for; *bei näherer -ung*, looked at more closely; *-ungen machen* or *anstellen über (eine S.)*, meditate *or* reflect on (a th.). **-ungsbücher,** *n.pl.* books of meditation.
beträchtlich, *adj.* considerable, important. **-keit,** *f.* importance.
Betrag, *m.* (-(e)s, ⁻e) amount, sum, total; *eine Rechnung im - von DM.* 10, a bill amounting to 10 marks. **-en,** 1. *ir.v.a.* come to, amount to, (*coll.*) run to; *wieviel beträgt meine Rechnung?* what does my bill come to? how much is my bill? 2. *v.r.* behave, conduct *or* deport o.s.; *sich schlecht -en*, misbehave. 3. *n.* behaviour, conduct, bearing, demeanour.
betrauen, *v.a.*; entrust; *mit einem Amte -*, appoint to an office.
betrauern, *v.a.* mourn for, deplore.
Betreff, *m.* reference, regard; *in - einer S.*, with regard to, as to, touching *or* in respect of a matter; *in dem -*, in that respect, as for that. **-en,** *ir.v.a.* befall, surprise; concern, affect, touch; have to do with; *was mich betrifft*, as for me, so *or* as far as I am concerned. **-end,** *pr.p. & adj.* concerned, in question; with reference to; concerning, regarding, respective; *das -ende Wort*, the word in question; *er las etwas sich -endes*, he read s.th. concerning himself; *ein jeder in seiner -enden Abteilung*, each in his own respective department. **-s,** *adv. & prep.* (*Gen.*) concerning, with regard to, as to, as regards.
betreib-en, 1. *ir.v.a.* urge on, push forward, hasten, follow up; manage, carry on (*a business, etc.*); pursue (*studies, a calling, etc.*). 2. *n.*; *auf -en*, at the instigation (of). **-ung,** *f.* carrying on, management, pushing forward; exercise (*of a profession*); prosecution, pursuit.
betret-en, 1. *ir.v.a.* set foot on *or* in; tread (on); enter upon; follow; enter (*a house*); mount (*a pulpit, etc.*); find, meet with; surprise, catch. 2. *p.p. & adj.* trodden, beaten; startled, surprised, disconcerted. 3. *n.*, **-ung,** *f.* entering, *etc.*; *das -en dieses Weges ist nicht gestattet*, this way is not open to the public, this is a private road; *das -en des Rasens ist verboten*, keep off the grass.
betreu-en, *v.a.* take care of, tend, attend to. **-ung,** *f.* care and control.
Betrieb, *m.* (-(e)s, -e) operation, management (*of a business*); working; trade; industry; workshop, works, factory; undertaking; plant; (*fig.*) activity, bustle; *öffentliche -e*, public utilities. *außer -*,

out of action, not working, closed down; *in – sein*, be working *or* in operation; *in – setzen* or *nehmen*, start, set running, set in motion, set in operation. **–sam,** *adj.* active, industrious. **–samkeit,** *f.* activity, industry. **–sanlage,** *f.* plant (*machinery*). **–sarzt,** *m.* factory doctor. **–sfähig,** *adj.* in working order, in running order. **–sfertig,** *adj.* ready for service. **–sführung,** *f.* works management. **–sgerät,** *n.* rolling-stock (*Railw.*). **–sjahr,** *n.* business-year. **–skapital,** *n.* working capital. **–skosten,** *pl.* operating costs, running costs, working expenses, overheads. **–sleiter,** *m.* manager. **–smaterial,** *n. see* **–sgerät. –smittel,** *n.pl. see* **–skapital. –sordnung,** *f.* regulations, operating instructions. **–spersonal,** *n.* staff. **–srat,** *m.* works council; shop committee. **–sreif,** *adj.* in first-class working order. **–ssicher,** *adj.* safe in operation, reliable, foolproof. **–sstoff,** *m.* fuel, petrol. **–sstoffwechsel,** *m.* basal metabolism (*Physiol.*). **–sstörung,** *f.* breakdown. **–sunfallversicherung,** *f.* workmen's compensation. **–sverhältnisse,** *n.pl.* working conditions. **–swelle,** *f.* driving-shaft. **–szeit,** *f.* working hours, shift. **–szustand,** *m.* operating conditions.

betrinken, *v.r.* get drunk.

betroffen, *p.p.* (*of* betreffen) & *adj.* disconcerted, taken aback, confounded, perplexed, dazed. **–heit,** *f.* perplexity, surprise.

betrogen, *see* **betrügen.**

betrüb–en, *v.a.* grieve, distress, afflict; cast down, depress. **–lich,** *adj.* sad, depressing. **–nis,** *f.* affliction, sorrow, grief, distress, sadness. **–t,** *p.p.* & *adj.* sad, depressed, dejected, distressed, miserable, melancholy, sorrowful; *zu Tode –t*, grieved to death; *–te Gedanken*, gloomy thoughts. **–theit,** *f.*, **–tsein,** *n. see* **Betrübnis.**

Betrug, *m.* (-s; *for pl. see* **Betrügerei**) fraud, deception, swindle, deceit, trickery, imposture; humbug; *frommer –*, white lie.

betrüg–en, *ir.v.a.* cheat, deceive, defraud, dupe; *einen um eine S. –en*, cheat *or* trick a p. out of s.th. **–er,** *m.* deceiver, swindler, cheat, impostor. **–erei,** *f.* cheating, trickery, deceit, fraud, swindle; deceitfulness. **–erisch,** *adj.* deceitful, fraudulent, deceptive; *in –erischer Absicht*, with intent to defraud. *–erischer Bankrott*, fraudulent bankruptcy. **–lich,** *adj.* fraudulent; false, deceptive, illusory, fallacious; *–lich handeln*, cheat, play fast and loose.

betrunken, *p.p.* (*of* betrinken) & *adj.* intoxicated, drunk, inebriated.

Bett, *n.* (-es, -en) bed; channel, bed (*of a river*); layer; lair (*of beasts*); thalamus (*Bot., Anat.*); *Klapp–*, folding bed; *Kranken–*, sick-bed; *Sterbe–*, death-bed; *Wochen–*, child-bed; *ins – gehen, zu – gehen, sich zu – legen*, go to bed; *sich ins – legen*, take to one's bed; *zu – (ins –) bringen*, put to bed; *am –e*, at the bedside; *das – hüten*, be confined to bed; *er muß im – bleiben, er ist ans – gefesselt*, he must stay in bed; *ein – aufschlagen*, put up a bed; *er ist schon im –*, he is already in bed; *das – überziehen*, change the bed. **–behang,** *m.* valance. **–bezug,** *m.* bed-linen. **–decke,** *f.* counterpane, quilt, bedspread, coverlet; blanket; *wollene –decke*, blanket; *gesteppte –decke*, quilt. **–en,** 1. *v.a.* make up a bed; put to bed; embed; *er ist nicht auf Rosen gebettet*, he does not lie on a bed of roses. 2. *v.r.* make one's bed; (*Prov.*) *wie man sich bettet so liegt* or *schläft man*, one must lie in the bed one has made; *er hat sich weich gebettet*, he has married money; *sie –en sich zusammen*, they sleep together. **–flasche,** *f.* hot-water bottle. **–fuß,** *m.* foot of the bed. **–genoß,** *m.* bedfellow. **–gestell,** *n.* bedstead. **–himmel,** *m.* canopy, tester. **–läg(e)rig,** *adj.* bedridden; confined to bed. **–laken,** *n.* sheet. **–pfanne,** *f.* warming-pan. **–pfoste,** *f.*, **–pfosten,** *m.* bedpost. **–säule,** *f.* bedpost. **–sessel,** *m.* sofa-bed. **–stelle,** *f.* bedstead. **–(t)uch,** *n.* sheet. **–ung,** *f.* base, mounting, platform (*Artil.*); ballast, roadbed, bedplate (*Railw.*). **–vorhang,** *m.* bed-curtain. **–vorleger,** *m.* bedside rug. **–wärmer,** *m.* warming-pan; hot-water bottle. **–wäsche,** *f.* bed-linen, bed-clothes. **–zeug,** *n.* bedding; bed-clothes. **–zwillich,** *m.* ticking, striped cotton.

Bett–el, *m.* 1. trash, rubbish, trumpery; 2. begging, mendicancy; *der ganze –el*, the whole (paltry) show; *ist das der ganze –el?* is that all it amounts to? *er ernährt sich vom –el*, he lives by begging. **–elarm,** *adj.* wholly destitute, desperately poor. **–elbrief,** *m.* begging-letter; licence to beg. **–elbruder,** *m.* professional beggar; mendicant (friar). **–elbrüderschaft,** *f.* begging fraternity (*R.C.*). **–elei,** *f.* begging, mendicancy; trash; *sich auf die –elei legen*, have resort to begging. **–elfrau,** *f.*, **–elweib,** *n. see* **Bettlerin. –elgeld,** *n.* alms. **–elkram,** *m.* trumpery, trash. **–elmönch,** *m.* mendicant friar. **–eln,** 1. *v.n.* (*aux.* h.) beg; solicit, importune; *–eln um eine milde Gabe*, beg for alms; *sich aufs –eln legen*, live by begging, go begging; *die Kunst geht –eln*, there's no money to be made with art. 2. *n. see* **Bettelei. –elorden,** *m.* order of mendicant friars. **–elpack,** *n., see* **–elvolk. –elstaat,** *m.* tawdry finery. **–elstab,** *m.* beggar's staff; *an den –elstab bringen*, reduce to beggary; *an den –elstab kommen*, be reduced to beggary, become utterly destitute. **–elstolz,** *m.* baseless *or* unwarranted pride. **–elstudent,** *m* pauper student. **–elsuppe,** *f.* charity soup, watery broth. **–elvogt,** *m.* beadle. **–elvolk,** *n.* beggars; paupers. **–ler,** *m.* (-s, -), **–lerin,** *f.* beggar, pauper. **–lerhandwerk,** *n.* begging, beggar's trade. **–lerstolz,** *m., see* **Bettelstolz.**

betulich, *adj.* attentive, engaging, obliging; busy, active, officious. **–keit,** *f.* officiousness, busy activity.

betun, *ir.v.r.* bestir o.s., be active; behave (= *benehmen*).

betupfen, betüpfeln, *v.a.* dab, dot, spot, touch here and there.

Beuche, *f.* kier-boiling (*Dye.*). **–n,** *v.a.* steep (*in lye*), bowk, buck, kier-boil.

Beug–e, *f.* (-en) bend, bow, curve; bending, flexure; *Knie–e*, knees-bend (*Gymn.*). **–emuskel,** *m.* flexor (muscle). **–en,** 1. *v.a.* bend, bow, flex; deflect, diffract; inflect (*Gram.*); humble. 2. *v.r.* humble o.s., submit; bend low, bow down (before). **–er,** *m.* flexor (muscle *or* tendon) (*Anat.*). **–estellung,** *f.* position of flexion (*Anat.*). **–sam,** *adj.* pliant, flexible. **–samkeit,** *f.* flexibility, pliability, pliancy. **–ung,** *f.* bending, bend, bow, curvature, curve; flexion, flexure (*Anat.*); warping (*of justice, etc.*); divergence; deflection, diffraction (*of light*); inflexion, declension. **–ungsfähig,** *adj.* declinable (*Gram.*). **–ungsfall,** *m.* oblique case (*Gram.*). **–ungsgitter,** *n.* diffraction grating (*Opt.*).

Beul–e, *f.* (-en) bump, lump; tumour, boil, ulcer, swelling; bruise; dent, dint; boss (*Arch.*); *Frost–e*, chilblain; *Leisten–e*, bubo. **–enpest,** *f.* bubonic plague.

beunruhig–en, *v.a.* disturb, upset, disquiet, alarm; harass, trouble, worry; *sich über etwas –en*, be alarmed about s.th. **–ung,** *f.* disturbance, alarm, uneasiness. **–ungsfeuer,** *n.* harassing fire (*Mil.*).

beurkund–en, *v.a.* attest, authenticate (*by documents*), document; prove, verify. **–et,** *p.p.* & *adj.* recorded, registered, documented, documentary. **–ung,** *f.* documentary authentication, verification, documentation.

beurlaub–en, 1. *v.a.* grant *or* give leave of absence; disband (*troops*). 2. *v.r.* excuse o.s., take one's leave; withdraw; *ein Beurlaubter*, man on leave. **–tenstand,** *m.* reserve status (*Mil.*).

beurteil–en, *v.a.* judge, form an opinion of; estimate, value; criticize, review (*a work*); *andere nach sich –en*, judge others by o.s. **–er,** *m.* judge; critic, reviewer. **–ung,** *f.* judgement; valuation, estimation; criticism, review (*of a book*). **–ungskraft,** *f.* (power of) discernment, judgement.

[1]**Beut–e,** *f.* booty, spoil, captured material (*Mil.*); loot, plunder; prey; *–e der Angst*, prey to terror; *eine –e des Todes sein*, be doomed, (*sl.*) be a goner; *auf –e ausgehen*, go marauding *or* plundering. **–egierig,** *adj.*, **–elustig,** *adj.*, **–esüchtig,** *adj.* eager for plunder. **–ezug,** *m.* looting expedition, raid.

[2]**Beut–e,** *f.* (-en) kneading-trough; wooden beehive. **–en,** *v.a.* stock a hive with wild bees. **–enhonig,** *m.* wild honey.

Beutel, *m.* (-s, -) bag, pouch, purse; sac, cyst; pocket (*Bill.*); sieve, sifting machine, bolter *or* boulter (*Mill.*); *Geld–*, purse; *– werfen*, bag, pucker; *seinen – spicken*, line one's pocket; *einem den – fegen* or *schaben*, drain a man's pocket; *tiefer in den – greifen müssen*, have to dip deeper into one's pocket; *das geht an den –*, that touches my (his, *etc.*) pocket; **–bär,** *m.* koala bear. **–faul,** *adj.* stingy. **–gans,** *f.* pelican. **–hase,** *m.* kangaroo. **–ig,** *adj.* baggy, bagged, puckered. **–kasten,** *m.* bolting-hutch (*Mill.*). **–krabbe,** *f.*, **–krebs,** *m.* purse-crab. **–meise,** *f.* penduline titmouse. **–n,** 1. *v.a.* bolt, sift, sieve, shake (*Mill.*); *man hat ihn ordentlich gebeutelt*, he's been properly fleeced. 2. *v.n. & r.* bag, bulge; pucker, crease (*of clothes*). **–perücke,** *f.* bag-wig. **–ratte,** *f.* opossum. **–schneider,** *m.* pickpocket, cutpurse; swindler. **–schneiderei,** *f.* pilfering, swindling. **–star,** *m.* oriole (*Orn.*). **–stolz,** 1. *m.* pride of purse. 2. *adj.* purse-proud. **–tier,** *n.* marsupial. **–werk,** *n.* bolting-mill (*Mill.*).

bevölker–n, *v.a.* people, populate; *dicht* (*spärlich*) *–t*, thickly (sparsely) populated. **–ung,** *f.* population, inhabitants. **–ungsdichte,** *f.* (density of) population.

bevollmächtig–en, *v.a.* empower, authorize; invest with full powers; license, warrant. **–er,** *m.* authorizing body, authority. **–te(r),** *m.* plenipotentiary; attorney (*Law.*); deputy; authorized agent. **–ung,** *f.* authorization; power of attorney; warrant; mandate.

bevor, 1. *conj.* before; *– ich dies tue, muß ich . . .*, before doing this, I must . . . 2. *verb prefix, either adverbial and sep.* (= 1), *or insep.* be– *added to compound verb in* vor–, *the whole prefix becoming insep.*

bevormund–en, *v.a.* (*insep.*) act as a guardian to; hold in tutelage; (*fig.*) patronize; browbeat, domineer over; *der –ete*, ward; *ich lasse mich von niemandem –en*, I won't be browbeaten by anyone. **–ung,** *f.* guardianship, tutelage.

bevorraten, *v.a.* (*insep.*) stock up, pile up reserves (for).

bevorrecht–en, *v.a.* (*insep.*) privilege, give a prior right to; patent. **–ung,** *f.* concession, exclusive privilege, monopoly. **–ungsbrief,** *m.* patent, letters patent.

bevorstehen, 1. *ir.v.n.* (*aux.* h.) (*imp. with Dat.*) (*sep.*) be imminent (*of time*); impend, approach, be at hand, be near; *mir steht Schlimmes bevor*, there's s.th. unpleasant in store for me; *die –de Woche*, the next *or* ensuing week; *das –de Gewitter*, the impending storm. 2. *n.* near approach.

bevorworten, *v.a.* (*insep.*) preface, supply with a foreword.

bevorzug–en, *v.a.* (*insep.*) favour, privilege; prefer. **–t,** *p.p. & adj.* privileged, specially favoured; *–t sein vor einem*, be favoured above another, receive preferential treatment over another. **–ung,** *f.* preference (*given to a p.*), favour (*shown to a p.*), favouritism.

bewach–en, *v.a.* watch over, guard, keep in custody. **–ung,** *f.* watching, guard, custody.

bewachsen, *p.p. & adj.* overgrown; covered with, stocked with.

bewaffn–en, *v.a.* arm, provide with arms, equip; fortify; *bis an die Zähne –et*, armed to the teeth; *mit –eter Hand*, by force of arms; *mit unbewaffneten Augen*, with the unaided eye. **–ung,** *f.* arming; armament, arms, armour, equipment; armature.

bewahr–en, *v.a.* keep, preserve; *–en vor*, guard against, save, protect from; *–e!* by no means! *Gott –e!* God forbid! nothing of the kind! **–anstalt,** *f.* nursery school, kindergarten. **–er,** *m.* keeper, caretaker. **–ung,** *f.* keeping; preservation; conservation. **–ungsmittel,** *n.* preservative; prophylactic. **–heiten,** 1. *v.a.* verify, prove the truth of. 2. *v.r.* turn out *or* prove to be true. **–heitung,** *f.* verification; *zur –heitung dessen*, in faith whereof (*Law*).

bewähr–en, 1. *v.a.* establish as true; prove, confirm, verify, authenticate, certify; approve; 2. *v.r.* prove true; hold good; stand the test; *sich nicht –en*, prove a failure; *das Gerücht –t sich*, the report turns out to be true. **–t,** *adj.* proved, tried, tested, approved, trustworthy; *–ter Freund*, trusty *or* tried friend. **–theit,** *f.* proved excellence, authenticity. **–ung,** *f.* proof; verification, confirmation; trial. **–ungsfrist,** *f.* period of probation.

bewald–et, *p.p. & adj.* woody, wooded. **–ung,** *f.* afforestation.

bewältigen, *v.a.* overcome, overpower; master, accomplish; *ich kann eine solche Portion nicht –*, I can't manage (to eat) such a large portion.

bewandert, *p.p. & adj.* skilled, experienced, versed (*in*, in), proficient (in); well-read; conversant (*in*, with).

bewandt, *p.p. & adj.* such, conditioned; situated, qualified; *bei so –en Umständen*, such being the case, in such circumstances; *so ist die S. –*, that's how it is, so the matter stands. **–nis,** *f.* condition, state of affairs, case; *nach –nis der Umstände*, as circumstances may require; *was es auch damit für eine –nis hat*, be the case as it may; *es hat damit eine ganz andere –nis*, the case is quite different; *es hat damit folgende –nis*, the matter is as follows; *damit hat es eine eigene* or *seine –nis*, the circumstances of the case are peculiar, thereby hangs a tale; *bei solcher –nis*, in such circumstances.

bewarb, *see* **bewerben.**

bewarf, *see* **bewerfen.**

bewässer–n, *v.a.* water, irrigate; wet, soak, moisten. **–ung,** *f.* irrigation; watering. **–ungsanlage,** *f.* irrigation works.

beweg–en, 1. *v.a.* move; stir; put in motion, agitate, shake; excite, affect; *im Kreise –en*, gyrate; *sich zum Mitleid –en lassen*, be moved to pity; *–ende Geschichte*, pathetic *or* touching story; *–ende Kraft*, motive power; *jetzt kann ich die Arme* or *Ellbogen wieder –en*, now my hands are no longer tied. 2. *v.r.*; *sich –en*, move (about), stir, be in motion; take exercise; *sich auf und nieder* or *ab –en*, work up and down (*as a piston*); *sich in gebildeten Kreisen –en*, move in good society; *die Erde –t sich um die Sonne*, the earth revolves around the sun; *der Preis –t sich zwischen DM. 5 und DM. 10*, the price fluctuates between 5 and 10 marks; *sich weiter –en*, move on. 3. *ir.v.a.* induce, persuade, prevail upon; *bewogen werden zu*, be led into *or* induced to; *bewogen von*, actuated by, urged by, moved by; *was bewog ihn dazu?* what made him do it? **–bar,** *adj.* movable (= *able to be moved*); mobile, flexible; easily persuaded. **–barkeit,** *f.*, *see* **–lichkeit.** **–er,** *m.* mover; motor; (*pl.*) motor muscles. **–grund,** *m.* reason (for action), motive, inducement. **–kraft,** *f.* motive power. **–lich,** *adj.* movable, *etc.* (= *able to move*) (*see* **–bar**); versatile, changeable, nimble, active, lively; moving, stirring, touching. **–lichkeit,** *f.* mobility, flexibility, agility, sprightliness, nimbleness, versatility. **–t,** *adj.* agitated, moved, troubled. *es war ein –ter Augenblick*, it was an exciting moment; *–te Zeiten*, stirring times; *–te See*, heavy *or* rough sea. **–theit,** *f.* agitation. **–ung,** *f.* movement, motion; stir, commotion, agitation; motive, stimulus, incitement; emotion; *er tat es aus eigener –ung*, he did it of his own accord *or* free will; *in –ung bringen*, stir up, set *or* put in motion; *in –ung setzen*, set going, actuate; *alle Hebel* or *Himmel und Hölle in –ung setzen*, set every spring in motion, move heaven and earth; *sich* (*Dat.*) *–ung machen* take exercise; *ihre Stimme zitterte vor –ung*, her voice trembled with emotion; *er konnte seine innere –ung nicht verbergen*, he couldn't hide his agitation; *drehende –ung*, rotatory motion; *Hin-und-her-ung*, reciprocating motion; *rückläufige –ung*, retrogression; *–ung der Hände*, gesticulation. **–ungsachse,** *f.* axis of rotation. **–ungsebene,** *f.* plane of motion. **–ungsempfindung,** *f.* kinaesthesia (*Physiol.*). **–ungsfähigkeit,** *f.* power of locomotion. **–ungsfreiheit,** freedom of movement, freedom of manœuvre (*Mil.*). **–ungskraft,** *f.* motive power, impetus, force. **–ungskrieg,** *m.* mobile warfare. **–ungslehre,** *f.* theory of motion, kinetics. **–ungslos,** *adj.*: motionless, immobile. **–ungslosigkeit,** *f.* immobility. **–ungsspiele,** *n.pl.* outdoor games; active games. **–ungstrieb,** *m.* momentum, impetus. **–ungszirkel,** *m.* deferent (*Astr.*).

bewehr–en, *v.a.* arm. **–t,** *p.p. & adj.* armed, **–ung,** *f.* reinforcement (*of concrete*), armour (*on cables*).

beweibt, *adj.* wedded, married.

beweinen, *v.a.* mourn, bewail, lament, bemoan; weep over, deplore. **–swert,** *adj.* deplorable, lamentable.

Beweis, *m.* (-es, -e) proof, evidence; argument, demonstration; – *führen, geben, liefern, beibringen,* or *antreten,* adduce proof, demonstrate, prove; *etwas unter – stellen,* submit s.th. to proof; *zum –e dessen dient,* in support of this is the fact; *schlagender –,* convincing *or* irrefutable proof; *der – hinkte,* it was a lame argument. **–auflage,** *f.* judicial injunction to produce proof; count (*of an indictment*); (point of) argument (*Log.*). **–aufnahme,** *f.* hearing of witnesses. **–bar,** *adj.*, **–lich,** *adj.* demonstrable, provable. **–en,** *ir.v.a.* prove, show, demonstrate, manifest; establish, make good (*a claim, etc.*); *sich dankbar –en,* show one's gratitude, prove oneself grateful. **–führung,** *f.* demonstration, argumentation, reasoning. **–grund,** *m.* argument, reason(s), plea, proof, evidence. **–kraft,** *f.* power of proving *or* of demonstrating; *der Zeuge hat hier keine –kraft,* this witness's evidence is inconclusive. **–kräftig,** *adj.* conclusive, convincing. **–last,** *f.* burden of proof. **–mittel,** *n.* argument, proof, evidence. **–schrift,** *f.* document containing evidence *or* argument. **–stelle,** *f.* quotation in establishment of proof; proof text (*Theol.*). **–stück,** *n.* document, instrument.

bewenden, 1. *ir.v.n.* (*aux.* s.); *es – lassen,* let (*a th.*) be, let take its course; rest satisfied with, acquiesce in (*a matter*). 2. *n.*; *dabei* or *damit hatte es sein –,* there the matter rested.

bewerb–en, *ir.v.r.* apply (*um,* for), seek, compete (for), sue (for), solicit, canvass (*votes*); court *or* woo (*a woman*). **–er,** *m.* applicant (for), candidate (for); competitor, aspirant (to); suitor, wooer. **–ung,** *f.* application, candidature; competition; courtship, wooing. **–ungsschreiben,** *n.* (letter of) application.

bewerfen, *ir.v.a.* throw at, pelt; plaster; bomb; *grob –,* rough-cast; *einen Bahnhof mit Bomben –,* bomb a station.

bewerkstellig–en, *v.a.* achieve, effect, accomplish, bring about, manage, contrive. **–ung,** *f.* effecting; accomplishment, realization, achievement.

bewert–en, *v.a.* value, estimate, assess, rate, evaluate. **–ung,** *f.* valuation, estimation, rating.

Bewetterung, *f.* air conditioning, forced ventilation.

bewickeln, *v.a.* wrap up, envelop; wind round, lap.

bewillig–en, *v.a.* grant, concede, consent to, allow, permit, agree to; *–t werden,* be carried, pass (*of motions*). **–ung,** *f.* grant, permit, licence, concession; permission, consent, sanction.

bewillkommn–en, *v.a.* welcome. **–ung,** *f.* welcoming, welcome; reception.

bewimpert, *adj.* ciliate (*Bot., Physiol.*).

bewinden, *ir.v.a.* wind about; twist round.

bewirk–en, *v.a.* effect, cause, bring about, produce. **–bar,** *adj.* practicable, feasible.

bewirt–en, *v.a.* entertain, show hospitality to, treat. **–ung,** *f.* entertainment, reception, accommodation (*of guests*).

bewirtschaft–en, *v.a.* manage; carry on, cultivate, work (*a farm*). **–ung,** *f.* management; cultivation, farming; control, rationing, regulation of supplies; *Devisenbewirtschaftung,* regulation of foreign exchange.

Bewitterung, *f.* weathering, exposure.

bewitzeln, *v.a.* ridicule, chaff.

bewog, bewöge, bewogen, *see* **bewegen.**

bewohn–en, *v.a.* inhabit, dwell in, live in, reside in, occupy. **–bar,** *adj.* habitable; *nicht –bar,* uninhabitable. **–barkeit,** *f.* habitable condition (*of a house*). **–er,** *m.* inhabitant; occupant, tenant, resident. **–erschaft,** *f.* inhabitants, occupants. **–ung,** *f.* occupation; habitation; residence in.

bewölk–en, 1. *v.a.* cloud, darken. 2. *v.r.* become cloudy *or* overcast, cloud over. **–t,** *p.p.* & *adj.*; *der Himmel war –t,* the sky was overcast. **–ung,** *f.* clouding, cloudiness.

beworben, *see* **bewerben.**

Bewunder–er, *m.* admirer. **–n,** *v.a.* admire; wonder at. **–nswert,** *adj.*, **–nswürdig,** *adj.* admirable; wonderful. **–ung,** *f.* admiration.

Bewurf, *m.* plastering; plaster, rough-cast, stucco.

bewürfe, *see* **bewerfen.**

bewurzel–n, *v.r.* strike *or* take root. **–ung,** *f.* root system; rooting.

bewußt, *adj.* known; conscious of, aware, cognizant of; *–e S.,* matter in question; *sich* (*Dat.*) *einer S. – sein,* be aware *or* conscious of a th. **–los,** *adj.* unconscious, senseless. **–losigkeit,** *f.* unconsciousness, insensibility. **–sein,** *n.* consciousness; knowledge; conviction; *er ist nicht bei –sein,* he is unconscious; *endlich kam er wieder zu(m) –sein,* at last he recovered consciousness *or* (*coll.*) came round; *allmählich kam mir zum –sein daß,* gradually I realized that . . .; *im –sein seiner Pflicht,* convinced of his duty.

bezackt, *adj.* indented.

bezahl–en, *v.a.* pay; discharge, repay (*a debt*); cash (*a bill, etc.*); *man –t für diesen Artikel 5 Mark,* this article costs 5 marks; *etwas teuer –en,* pay dear for a th.; *es macht sich –t,* it pays *or* is lucrative; *im voraus –en,* pay in advance; *bar –en,* pay cash *or* ready money; *auf Heller und Pfennig –en,* pay in full; *du mußt nun die Zeche –en,* now you must foot the bill *or* take the consequences; *–t werden,* be duly honoured (*of bills*). **–bar,** *adj.* payable, to be paid. **–ung,** *f.* payment, settlement; pay; *gegen –ung von,* on payment of.

bezähmen, *v.a.* tame; curb, check, restrain, control, subdue.

bezahnt, *adj.* toothed, indented.

bezauber–n, *v.a.* bewitch, enchant; fascinate. **–ung,** *f.* fascination, charm; enchantment, spell.

bezechen, *v.r.* get drunk.

bezeichn–en, *v.a.* mark, denote, signify; designate, label; term, call, show, characterize; *genau –en,* give exact directions, show clearly. **–end,** *pr.p.* & *adj.* characteristic, significant; *–endes Merkmal,* distinctive mark. **–ung,** *f.* marking, mark; designation, name; sign, specification. **–ungsweise,** *f.* method of notation.

bezeig–en, *v.a.* (*einem etwas*) show, give signs of, manifest; express. **–ung,** *f.* manifestation, display; evidence.

bezetteln, *v.a.* label.

bezeug–en, *v.a.* attest, certify, testify (to); declare; *seine Achtung –en,* pay one's respects. **–ung,** *f.* testimony; attestation.

bezichtigen, *v.a.* accuse of, charge with.

bezieh–en, 1. *ir.v.a.* 1. cover; draw *or* stretch over; *eine Geige mit Saiten –en,* string a violin; *die Betten –en,* change the bed-linen; *ein Sofa mit Stoff –en,* cover a sofa with material; 2. go to (*a place*), take up (*a position*); *ein Haus –en,* move into *or* occupy a house; *sofort zu –en,* vacant possession, ready for immediate occupation; *einen Posten* or *die Wache –en,* take up one's post, mount guard; *eine Stellung –en,* start a job, enter upon one's duties; *die Universität –en,* enter the university; 3. get, gain possession of; receive, obtain, draw (*rations, etc.*); *sein Geld* or *Gehalt –en,* draw one's money *or* salary; *Geld –en,* receive payment, draw a bill; *die Waren aus Birmingham –en,* procure the goods from Birmingham; *er bezog eine Ohrfeige,* he got a box on the ears; 4. bring into relation (with); refer (to); *wir –en uns auf Ihr Schreiben vom 3. d.M.,* we refer to yours of the 3rd inst. (*C.L.*); *der Bezogene,* drawee, acceptor (*of a bill*). **2.** *v.r.* refer, relate, make allusion, appeal (*auf,* to); base (*auf,* on); become cloudy *or* overcast; *das –t sich nicht auf den Gegenstand,* that has no bearing on the subject, that is irrelevant *or* not to the point; *seine Äußerung –t sich nicht auf mich,* his remarks do not refer to me. **–er,** *m.* drawer (*of a bill*); importer (*of goods*); subscriber, customer. **–ung,** *f.* reference (*to a subject*); relation, connexion; respect, bearing; *in dieser –ung,* in this respect; *zu jemandem in –ung treten,* open relations with s.o.; *wir stehen mit ihm in keiner –ung,* we have no relations with him; *in –ung stellen,* bring to bear (*auf,* upon); *unsere –ungen zum Ausland,* our foreign relations; *freundschaftliche –ungen anknüpfen,* enter upon friendly relations (with); *gute* or *einflußreiche –ungen haben,* have good *or* influential connexions; *die –ungen zu einem abbrechen,* break off relations with a p. **–ungsbegriffe,** *m.pl.* correlative ideas. **–ungslos,** *adj.* unconnected, independent. **–ungssatz,** *m.* relative clause. **–ungsweise,** (*abbr.* **bzw.**) *adv.* respectively, or, or else; relatively.

beziffern, 1. *v.a.* number, mark with figures; *der bezifferte Baß*, figured bass (*Mus.*) 2. *v.n.* & *r.* amount to.

Bezirk, *m.* (-(e)s, -e) district, borough; circuit; region, area, precinct; range, compass; (*pl.*) confines, **–samt,** *n.* local government offices, town hall, county hall. **–sbombe,** *f.* (*sl.*) block-buster. **–sgefängnis,** *n.* county jail. **–sgericht,** *n.* county court. **–skommando,** *n.* district command (*Mil.*). **–sregierung,** *f.* local government authority, county council, borough council. **–sumleger,** *m. see* **–sbombe.**

bezog, bezöge, bezogen, *see* **beziehen.** (*C.L.*) **Bezogene(r),** *m.* drawee.

bezollen, *v.a.* levy a toll *or* duty on.

bezuckern, *v.a.* (sprinkle with) sugar (*a cake, etc.*).

Bezug, *m.* (-(e)s, ⸗e) covering; cover, case; set of strings (*Mus.*); relation, reference; supply, purchase, acquisition; (*pl.*) income, emoluments; *in – auf* (*eine S.*), with regard to *or* as to (a th.); *– nehmen auf* (*eine S.*), refer to (a th.) – *haben auf* (*eine S.*), have reference to. **–nahme,** *f.* reference; *mit* (or *unter*) *–nahme auf* (*eine S.*), with reference to *or* respecting (a th.). **–sachse,** *f.* axis of reference. **–sanweis,** *m., see* **–sschein. –sanweisung,** *f.* order (*for goods, etc.*). **–sbedingungen,** *f. pl.* terms of purchase *or* delivery. **–sebene,** *f.* datum level. **–sgröße,** *f.* reference figure. **–sort,** *m., see* **–squelle. –spunkt,** *m.* datum point. **–squelle,** *f.* source of supply. **–sschein,** *m.* permit; licence (*for raw materials*), ration card, coupon, docket, priority voucher (*for controlled goods, petrol, etc.*), indent form (*Mil.*). **–swert,** *m.* relative value.

bezüglich, 1. *adj.* relative, with reference (*auf eine S.*, to a th.); *–e Fürwörter*, relative pronouns. 2. *prep.* (*Gen.*) respecting, referring to, as to.

bezwecken, *v.a.* aim at, have in view, intend, purpose.

bezweifeln, *v.a.* doubt; question, call in question; *nicht zu –*, not to be doubted, indubitable, unquestionable.

bezwing–en, 1. *ir.v.a.* overcome, conquer, vanquish, subdue; master. 2. *v.r.* restrain *or* control o.s. **–bar, –lich,** *adj.* conquerable, vanquishable, reducible. **–er,** *m.* conqueror, subduer. **–ung,** *f.* conquest, reduction.

Bibel, *f.* (-n) Bible; Holy Scriptures. **–auslegung,** *f.* exegesis *or* interpretation of the Bible. **–fest,** *adj.* versed in the Scriptures. (*sl.*) **–husar,** *m.* army chaplain, (*sl.*) sky pilot. **–kunde,** *f.* biblical research. **–lehre,** *f.* Bible teaching, scriptural doctrine. **–sprache,** *f.* scriptural language. **–spruch,** *m.* (biblical) text. **–stelle,** *f.* biblical passage; text; lesson (*read in church*). **–stunde,** *f.* Bible class; Sunday school.

Biber, *m.* (-s, –) beaver, castor. **–bau,** *m.* beaver's hut. **–baum,** *m.* magnolia. **–fell,** *n.* beaver skin. **–geil,** *n.* castor(-eum). **–hut,** *m.* beaver (hat). **–nell(e),** *f.* burnet saxifrage (*Pimpinella*) (*Bot.*). **–pelz,** *m.* beaver fur. **–ratte,** *f.* musk-rat. **–schwanz,** *m.* beaver's tail; flat roofing tile. **–wehr,** *f.* beaver dam. **–zahn,** *m.* projecting tooth.

Biblio–, (*unaccented in compounds*). **–graph,** *m.* (-en, -en) bibliographer. **–graphie,** *f.* bibliography. **–thek,** *f.* (-en) library. **–thekar,** *m.* (-s, -e) librarian.

biblisch, *adj.* biblical, scriptural; *–e Geschichte*, Scriptural (*or* sacred) history.

Bickbeere, *f.* bilberry, whortleberry (*Vaccinium myrtillus*).

bieder, *adj.* upright, honest, honourable; staunch, loyal, trusty; ingenuous; commonplace. **–keit,** *f.* honesty, probity; respectability. **–herz,** *n.* honourable fellow. **–mann,** *m.* man of worth *or* integrity; man of honour; (*pl.*) (*sometimes used ironically*) worthies, philistines. **–meier(stil),** *m.* a homely *or* Early Victorian style. **–meierzeit,** *f.* Early Victorian period (*in Germany 1820–48*).

bieg–en, 1. *ir.v.a.* bend, curve, bow; decline, inflect; diffract, refract (*light*). 2. *v.r.* bend; warp; turn, incline; *sich vor Lachen –en*, double up with laughing; *sich schmiegen und –en*, be yielding, cringe. 3. *v.n.* (*aux.* s.) turn; *er ist um die Ecke gebogen*, he has turned the corner; *auf –en oder Brechen*, by hook or by crook, willy-nilly; *das muß –en oder brechen*, a decision must be reached at all costs. **–bar,** *adj.* pliable, flexible, bendable; declinable. **–barkeit,** *f.* flexibility. **–e,** *f.* (-en) curve, curvature, bend, bow. **–efestigkeit,** *f.* bending strength, transverse strength, flexure. **–emuskel,** *m.* flexor muscle (*Anat.*). **–espannung,** *f.* bending stress. **–sam,** *adj.* flexible, pliant, pliable, supple; lithe; ductile; yielding. **–samkeit,** *f.* pliancy, pliability; suppleness, flexibility; ductility. **–ung,** *f.* curve, curvature; bend, turn, turning, bending, deflection, flexure; declension. **–ungsbeanspruchung,** *f., see* **–espannung. –ungsfähig,** *adj.* declinable (*Gram.*). **–ungsfestigkeit,** *f. see* **–efestigkeit.**

Biene, *f.* (-n) bee; Apis, the Bee (*a southern constellation*); *Arbeits–*, working bee, worker; *faule* or *männliche –*, drone. **–nausbeute,** *f.* output, yield (*from a hive*). **–nbär,** *m.* common bear. **–nbau,** *m., see* **–nzucht. –nbrut,** *f.* larvae of bees. **–nfleiß,** *m.* assiduity; sedulousness. **–nflug,** *m.* stock of bees *or* hives. **–nharz,** *n.,* **–nkitt,** *m.* bee-bread, bee-glue, hive dross, propolis. **–nkönigin,** *f.* queen-bee. **–nkorb,** *m.* beehive. **–nkraut,** *n.* thyme. **–nnährpflanze,** *f.* honey-producing plant. **–nsaug,** *m.* white dead-nettle (*Lamium*) (*Bot.*). **–nschwarm,** *m.* swarm of bees. **–nstand,** *m.* apiary. **–nstock,** *m.* beehive. **–nvater,** *m.* bee-keeper. **–nwabe,** *f.* honeycomb. **–nwachs,** *n.* bees-wax. **–nweide,** *f.* honey-producing plants. **–nweisel,** *m.* queen-bee. **–nzelle,** *f.* cell (*in honeycomb*). **–nzellig,** *adj.* honeycombed. **–nzucht,** *f.* bee-keeping, bee-farming, apiculture. **–nzüchter,** *m.* bee-keeper, apiarist.

Bier, *n.* (-(e)s, -e) beer; ale; *Lager–*, lager (beer); *Flaschen–*, bottled beer; *dünnes –*, small beer; *leichtes –*, bitter, pale ale; *dunkles –*, dark beer; stout; porter; *beim –e sitzen*, sit over one's ale; *etwas wie saures* or *sauer – ausbieten*, get rid of s.th. with difficulty, have s.th. hanging on one's hands; *– vom Faß, – frisch vom Faß*, beer on tap *or* on draught. **–baß,** *m.* coarse bass voice. **–bauch,** *m.* paunch. **–blume,** *f.* froth on beer. **–brauer,** *m.* brewer. **–brauerei,** *f.* brewery. **–bruder,** *m.* heavy drinker, toper. **–eifer,** *m.* great zeal; excessive activity. (*coll.*) **–eifrig,** *adj.* extremely zealous, most studious. **–essig,** *m.* malt vinegar. **–faß,** *n.* beer-barrel. **–filz,** *m.* table mat. **–garten,** *m.* open-air restaurant. **–hahn,** *m.* tap. **–halle,** *f.,* **–haus,** *n.* public house, ale-house, (*vulg.*) pot-house. **–heber,** *m.* beer-machine, beer-pull, pump. **–hefe,** *f.* barm, brewers' yeast. **–idee,** *f.* crazy idea. **–kanne,** *f.* tankard. **–kneipe,** *f.* ale-house, (*coll.*) pub. **–komment,** *m.* students' drinking ritual. **–krug,** *m.* jug, mug, pot. **–reise,** *f.* (*sl.*) pub-crawl. **–schank,** *m.* licence to retail beer; *see also* **–schenke. –schaum,** *m.* froth. **–schenk,** *m.* publican. **–schenke,** *f.* tavern, bar. **–schwengel,** *m. see* **–heber. –seidel,** *n.* beer-glass, beer-mug. **–stube,** *f.* tap-room, bar. **–tonne,** *f.* vat; (*hum.*) big-bellied fellow. **–trichter,** *m.* funnel. **–wirtschaft,** *f.* public house, ale-house. **–zapfer,** *m.* tapster. **–zeitung,** *f.* comic (and crude) programme at students' smoking concert. **–zipfel,** *m.* pendant (on a watch chain).

Biese, *f.* (-n) braid, piping.

Biest, *n.* (-es, -er) beast; (*fig.* & *coll.*) brute (*used particularly of annoying insects, but also, as vulgar abuse, of people*). **–fliege,** *f.* gadfly, botfly, horse-fly. **–milch,** *f.* beestings.

bieten, *ir.v.a.* offer, proffer; bid, wish (*good morning, etc.*); make a bid (*auf eine S.*, for a th.) (*at a sale*); *feil–*, offer for sale; *Trotz –*, bid defiance to, defy; *einem die Spitze –*, resist *or* oppose a p.; *einem die Stirn –*, face s.o. resolutely, put a bold front against s.o.; *wenn sich eine Gelegenheit bietet*, when an opportunity presents itself *or* offers; *Schach –*, check (*chess*); *das dürfte mir niemand –*, I would suffer that from no one; *das lasse ich mir nicht –*, I won't stand (for) that *or* put up with this; *ein Unglück bietet dem andern die Hand*, misfortunes never come singly, it never rains but it pours.

-de(r), *m.*, **Bieter,** *m.* bidder; *der Meist-de*, the highest bidder.
Bigam-ie, *f.* bigamy. **-isch,** *adj.* bigamous.
bigott, *adj.* bigoted. **-erie,** *f.* bigotry.
Bijouterie, *f.* jewellery, trinkets.
Bilanz, *f.* (-en) balance; *die – aufstellen* or *ziehen*, balance the books; *reine –*, net-balance; *rohe –*, rough balance, trial balance. **-bogen,** *m.* balance-sheet. **-ieren,** *v.a.* balance (*an account*). **-prüfer,** *m.* auditor. **-konto,** *n.*, **-rechnung,** *f.* balance account.
Bild, *n.* (-es, -er) picture, image, figure; illustration; portrait; likeness; representation; counterfeit; effigy; idea, simile, metaphor; emblem, symbol; (*pl.*) court-cards; *das gegossene –*, the cast; graven image; *Frauen–*, woman; *Gips–*, plaster cast; *Lebens–*, biography; *Manns–*, man; *Sinn–*, emblem, symbol; *Stein–*, statue; *negatives –*, negative (*Phot.*); *er wurde im –e verbrannt*, he was burnt in effigy; *er spricht in –ern*, he speaks metaphorically; *Gott schuf den Menschen ihm zum –e*, God created man in His own image; (*es bietet sich*) *ein anderes –*, the scene changes; *machen Sie sich einmal ein – davon!* just picture it to yourself! just fancy!; (*coll.*) *ich bin im –e*, I see, I understand, I am clear about it, I'm in the picture. **-aufklärung,** *f.* photographic reconnaissance (*Av.*). **-auswertung,** *f.* interpretation of aerial photographs. **-bericht,** *m.* documentary film. **-en, 1.** *v.a.* 1. form, fashion, shape, mould, model; *eine Figur aus Wachs bilden*, shape a model in wax; *die Kinder bilden einen Kreis*, the children form a circle; 2. be, constitute, compose; 3. educate, train, discipline; cultivate, improve, organize. **2.** *v.r.* 1. form, arise, develop; *Kristalle bilden sich*, crystals form; 2. improve one's mind; *es bildet ein Talent sich in der Stille*, the talented man improves himself in solitude; *gebildeter Mann*, cultivated man. **-end,** *pr.p.* & *adj.* plastic; graphic; composing, component, constituting, constituent; educational, instructive; formative; *-ende Künste*, plastic and graphic arts, fine arts (*including architecture, sculpture, painting*); *-ender Künstler*, sculptor, painter, *or* architect. **-er,** *m.* *see* **-ner. -erachat,** *m.* figured agate. **-eranbetung** *f.* image-worship, idolatry. **-erausstellung,** *f.* exhibition of pictures. **-erbogen,** *m.* picture-sheet. **-erbuch,** *n.* picture-book. **-erdeutung,** f. iconology. **-erdienst,** *m.* idolatry; photo service. **-erfibel,** *f.* illustrated primer. **-erform,** *f.* pattern. **-ergallerie,** *f.* picture gallery. **-erhändler,** *m.* picture-dealer. **-erhandschrift,** *f.* illuminated manuscript. **-erkenner,** *m.* connoisseur of pictures. **-erkundung,** *f.* photographic reconnaissance, photographic survey (*Av.*). **-erleiste,** *f.* picture rail. **-errätsel,** *n.* picture puzzle, rebus. **-erreich,** *adj.* copiously illustrated; figurative abounding in metaphors. **-erschrift,** *f.* hieroglyphics. **-ersprache,** *f.* metaphorical language. **-erstürmend,** *adj.* iconoclastic. **-erstürmer,** *m.* iconoclast. **-erstürmerei,** *f.* iconoclastic riots. **-feld,** *n.* image field (*Phot.*). **-fenster,** *n.* aperture (*Phot.*). **-fläche,** *f.* surface screen, perspective plane; (*coll.*) *auf der -fläche erscheinen*, appear upon the scene; enter the field; come into existence. **-flug,** *m.* photographic reconnaissance flight (*Av.*). **-funk,** *m.* television, radiophoto. **-gestell,** *n.* pedestal. **-gießer,** *m.* bronze-founder. **-größe,** *f.* size of image (*Phot.*). **-hauerkunst,** *f.* sculpture. **-hübsch,** *adj.* extremely pretty. **-lich,** *adj.* pictorial, graphic; figurative, metaphorical. **-los,** *adj.* void of images, amorphous. **-ner,** *m.* modeller, sculptor; (*fig.*) shaper, moulder, organizer. **-nerisch,** *adj.* relating to sculpture; creative. **-nis,** *n.* portrait, likeness; image, effigy; parable. **-plan,** *m.* photographic map. **-sam,** *adj.* plastic, ductile, flexible, easy to shape, adaptive. **-samkeit,** *f.* flexibility, adaptiveness, plasticity. **-sauber,** *adj.* extremely neat, extremely pretty. **-säule,** *f.* statue; *-säule zu Pferde*, equestrian statue. **-schärfe,** *f.* precision, sharpness, focus (*Phot.*). **-schnitzer,** *m.* wood-carver. **-schnitzerei,** *f.* wood-carving. **-schön,** *adj.* most beautiful, very lovely. **-seite,** *f.* face, obverse (*of a coin*), head (*as opposed to 'tail'*). **-stecher,** *m.* engraver **-stein,** *m.* figured stone. (*dial.*) **-stock,** *m.* (**-stöckel,** *n.*) wayside image of the Virgin, wayside shrine. **-streifen,** *m.* reel of film, film strip. **-telegraphie,** *f.* photo-telegraphy. **-teppich,** *m.* figured tapestry. **-übertragung,** *f.*, *see* **-telegraphie. -ung,** *f.* formation, forming; form, fashion, shape; structure, organization, constitution; development, growth, generation; education, training, cultivation, culture, civilization; *Allgemein -ung*, liberal *or* all-round education; *feine -ung*, culture; *höhere -ung*, higher education; *gelehrte -ung*, *f.* classical education; liberal education. **-ungsabweichung,** *f.* deviation from normal development. **-ungsanstalt,** *f.* educational establishment; school. **-ungsfähig,** *adj.* capable of development. **-ungsfehler,** *m.* malformation. **-ungsgang,** *m.* course of instruction. **-ungshemmung,** *f.* arrested development. **-ungsphilister,** *m.* narrow-minded intellectual (*coined by Nietzsche; used by the Nazis as a sneer at the educated classes*). **-ungsroman,** *m.* psychological novel. **-ungsstufe,** *f.* stage of development; degree of culture. **-ungstrieb,** *m.* creative urge, formative power. **-ungswert,** *m.* educational *or* cultural value. **-ungszelle,** *f.* embryonic cell. **-weise,** *adv.* figuratively. **-weite,** *f.* perspective, focal length. **-zeichen,** *n.* symbol.
Billard [*pron.* 'biljart], *n.* (-s, -s) billiards; billiard-table; *-spielen*, play (at) billiards. **-ball,** *m.*, **-kugel,** *f.* billiard-ball. **-beutel,** *m.*, **-loch,** *n.* pocket (*of billiard-table*). **-kellner,** *m.* marker. **-spiel,** *n.* game of billiards. **-stock,** *m.* cue.
Billett [*pron.* bil'jɛt], (-(e)s, -e) ticket (*the normal Austrian and Swiss word for* Fahrkarte). **-ausgabe,** *f.*, **-schalter,** *m.* ticket office, booking office.
billig, *adj.* cheap, moderate, inexpensive, reasonable; right, fair, just; *das ist nicht mehr als –*, that is but fair; *ziemlich –*, rather cheap *or* pretty cheap; *– und schlecht*, cheap and nasty; *ein billiges Verlangen*, a reasonable demand; *eine billige Ausrede*, a paltry *or* cheap excuse; *wir können uns daher – bescheiden*, we may therefore reasonably acquiesce. **-en,** *v.a.* approve of, consent to; sanction, grant. **-ermaßen, -erweise,** *adv.* fairly, in fairness, in justice. **-keit,** *f.* justice, equity, reasonableness; fairness; cheapness; *der -keit gemäß*, in equity. **-keitsgericht,** *n.* court of equity. **-keitsgründe,** *m.pl.* reasons of fairness. **-keitsrecht,** *n.* equity. **-ung,** *f.* approval, consent, sanction, approbation.
Billion, *f.* (-en) billion (*= a million millions*); (*Amer.*) thousand billions (*in U.S.A. billion = a thousand millions*).
Bilse, *f.*, **-nkraut,** *n.* henbane (*Hyoscyamus niger*).
bim-bam, *int.* ding-dong! (*coll.*) *heiliger -bam* dear me! (*expression of great astonishment*). **-mel,** *f.* little tinkling bell. **-meln,** *v.n.* tinkle.
Bims, *m.* polishing. **-e,** *m.pl.* (*coll.*) beating, hiding. **-en,** *v.a.* rub with pumice-stone. **-stein,** *m.* pumice-stone.
bin, *see* **sein.**
binär, *adj.* binary (*Mus., Chem., Math., Astr.*).
Bind-e, *f.* (-en) bandage, sling; band; string, tie, ligature; necktie; protective wrap; sanitary towel; plinth (*Arch.*); fillet (*Bookb.*); *Arm-e*, brassard *Hals-e*, necktie, cravat; *Leib-e*, sash; *Stirn-e*, bandeau; *eine -e vor die Augen tun*, blindfold; (*coll.*) *einen* or *eins hinter die -e gießen*, drink *or* (*sl.*) sink a glass; *die -e fällt mir von den Augen*, the scales fall from my eyes. **-ebalken,** *m.* girder architrave. **-efestigkeit,** *f.* adhesion. **-egewebe,** *n.* connective tissue (*Anat.*). **-eglied,** *n.* connecting link. **-ehaut,** *f.* connective membrane (*Anat.*). **-ehautentzündung,** *f.* conjunctivitis. **-ekalk,** *m.* cement. **-kraft,** *f.* binding power. **-mauer,** *f.* partition wall. **-emittel,** *n.* adhesive cement, binding agent, agglutinant. **-en,** 1. *ir.v.a.* bind, tie, fasten; hoop (*a cask*); thicken (*soup, etc.*); tie up; tie down; restrain; constrain, oblige; 2. *v.n.* unite, combine, consolidate; set, harden; *Garben -en*, make up in sheaves; *Besen -en*, make brooms; (*coll.*) *ich werde ihm nicht alles auf die Nase -en*, I shall not reveal everything to him *or* tell him all my secrets; *einem etwas auf die Seele -en*, solemnly enjoin upon a p. (*to do s.th.*). **gebunden,** *p.p.* & *adj.* bound; latent; *gebundene*

Wärme, latent heat (*Chem.*); *gebundene Rede*, metrical language, metre. 3. *v.r.* bind o.s. (*to a p.*); feel bound *or* compelled (to); make o.s. dependent upon; thicken (*Cook.*). **–end,** *pr.p. & adj.* binding, obligatory (on). **–er,** *m.* binder; ***Faß–er,*** cooper. **–ereifen,** *m.* wheel rim. **–estrich,** *m.* hyphen; tie, legato sign (*Mus.*). **–ewort,** *n.* conjunction; copula. **–ezeichen,** *n. see* **–estrich. –ezeit,** *f.* setting time. **–faden,** *m.* string, twine, pack-thread; *es regnet –faden*, it is raining cats and dogs. **–ig,** *adj.* cohesive, binding. **–igkeit,** *f.* cohesiveness, binding power, consistency. **–ung,** *f.* binding, fastening, linking, adhesion; slur, bind, tie, ligature (*Mus.*); bond, union, combination; agglutination (*Med.*); cement (*Build.*); connexion; obligation; *frei von allen –ungen*, without any obligation. **–ungsmittel,** *n., see* **–emittel. –ungszeichen,** *n. see* **–estrich.**

binnen, 1. *prep.* (*Gen. & Dat.*) within; – *eines Monats*, within a month; – *weniger Stunden*, in a few hours; – *acht Tagen*, in the course of a week; – *kurzem*, ere long, within a short time, shortly. 2. *adv.* within, internal, interior; inner, inland; (*coll.*) *etwas – haben*, have eaten *or* understood s.th. **–deich,** *m.* inner dam *or* dyke. **–druck,** *m.* internal pressure. **–fischerei,** *f.* freshwater fishing. **–gewässer,** *n.* inland water(s). **–hafen,** *m.* inland harbour; basin. **–handel,** *m.* inland trade; domestic trade. **–land,** *n.* inland; interior (*of a country*). **–meer,** *n.* land-locked sea. **–raum,** *m.* inner *or* interior space. **–schiffahrt,** *f.* inland navigation. **–see,** *m.* inland lake. **–stadt,** inland town. **–verkehr,** *m.* overland traffic, inland trade.

Binom, *n.* (-s, -e) binomial. **–isch,** (**–ial** *in compounds*) *adj.* binomial; *–ischer Lehrsatz*, binomial theorem. **–ialkoeffizient,** *m.* binomial coefficient.

Bins–e, *f.* (-en) rush (*Jancus*) (*Bot.*); sedge; bent-grass; *glatte –e*, bulrush. **–enblume,** *f.* flowering rush. **–engras,** *n.* club-rush; sedge. **–enkorb,** *m.* rush basket. **–enwahrheit,** *f.* platitude. **–ig,** *adj.* sedgy, rush-grown.

Bio–, (*in compounds, with chief accent on the foll. word*). **–chemie,** *f.* biochemistry. **–graph,** *m.* (-en, -en) biographer. **–graphie,** *f.* biography. **–graphisch,** *adj.* biographical. **–log(e),** *m.* (-en, –en) biologist. **–logie,** *f.* biology. **–logisch,** *adj.* biological.

Biquadrat, *n.* fourth power (*Math.*).

birg, birgst, birgt, *see* **bergen.**

Birk–e, *f.* (-en) birch-tree (*Betula*). **–en,** *adj.* of birch. **–enbaum,** *m., see* **–e. –enreis,** *n.* birch rod. **–hahn,** *m.* heathcock, black cock. **–henne,** *f.,* **–huhn,** *n.* moor-hen. **–wild,** *n.* black grouse.

Birn–e, *f.* (-en) pear; (electric) bulb; (Bessemer) converter. **–(en)baum,** *m.* pear-tree (*Pyrus communis*). **–enförmig,** *adj.* pear-shaped; pyriform (*Anat.*). **–enmost,** *m.,* **–wein,** *m.* perry.

Birsch, *see* **Pirsch.**

birst, *see* **bersten.**

bis, 1. *prep. or part. added to prep. or adv. and implying extension in time or space*; up to, as far as to; down to; to, till, until; even to; – *dahin*, till then, by that time, so far; to that place; – *hierher*, thus far; *sechs – sieben Kilometer*, six to *or* seven kilometres; – *jetzt*, till now, hitherto, as yet; – *jetzt noch nicht*, not as yet; – *wann bleiben Sie?* how long are you staying; – *an*, up to, even to; – *an den Hals in Schulden stecken*, be over head and ears in debt; *sie wurde rot – an die Ohren*, she blushed up to her ears; – *an* or *in den Tod*, – *zum Tode*, till death; – *ans Ende der Welt*, to the ends of the earth; – *auf*, to, up to, down to, even to; with the exception of, all but; *sie starben alle – auf drei*, they all died except three, all but three died; *sie starben – auf den letzten Mann*, they died to the last man, every single one died; – *auf weiteres*, for the present; *seine Freundlichkeit erstreckte sich – auf die Bedienten*, his kindness extended down to the very servants; *er kam – auf eine Meile von der Stadt*, he came to within a mile of the town; – *auf den heutigen Tag*, till today; – *aufs* or *auf ein Haar*, to a T, exactly; *alles ist bezahlt – auf einige Mark*, all is paid except a few marks; – *gegen* or *nahe an Mitternacht*, till nearly midnight; – *in die Nacht hinein*, right into the night; – *ins Letzte*, to the last detail; – *nach Paris*, as far as Paris; – *über den Kopf ins Wasser gehen*, go beyond one's depth, get out of one's depth; – *über acht Tage warten*, wait till a week has passed, wait for a week; – *um neun Uhr*, till nine o'clock. – *zu dem Betrage von*, to the amount of, amounting to, to the value of; *er wurde – zu Tränen gerührt*, he was moved even to tears; – *zur Verfallzeit*, till due (*C.L.*). 2. *conj.* till; *wartet – ich komme*, wait till I come. **–her,** *adv.* hitherto, up to now, till now. **–herig,** *adj.* until now; hitherto existing, prevailing. **–lang,** *adv.* so far, as yet. **–weilen,** *adv.* sometimes, now and then, occasionally.

Bisam, *m.* musk; *nach – riechend*, musky. **–hirsch,** *m.* musk-deer. **–katze,** *f.* civet-cat. **–körner,** *pl.* musk-seed. **–ratte,** *f.* musk-rat. **–tier,** *n.* musk-deer.

Bischof, *m.* (-s, ⸚e) bishop. **–samt,** *n.* episcopate. **–shof,** *m.* episcopal palace. **–shut,** *m.,* **–smütze,** *f.* mitre. **–sornat,** *m.* bishop's robes. **–ssitz,** *m.* (bishop's) see. **–sstab,** *m.* crosier. **–swürde,** *f.* episcopal dignity; episcopate.

bischöflich, *adj. & adv.* episcopal, episcopalian; pontific, pontifical (*R.C.*); *Seine –e Gnaden*, His Lordship the Bishop.

Bise, *f.* cutting (north-easterly) wind (*esp. in Switzerland*).

bisher, *see* **bis.**

Biskuit, *m.* (-s, -e) rusk, biscuit. **–porzellan,** *n.* biscuit *or* bisque ware.

bislang, *see* **bis.**

Bison, *m.* (-s, -s) bison.

biß, bisse, *see* **beißen.**

Biß, *m.* (-(ss)es, -(ss)e) bite; sting. **–(ss)el,** *n., see* **–chen. –(ss)en,** *m.* morsel, bite, bit; tit-bit; mouthful; *ein fetter* or *ein guter –(ss)en*, a tasty morsel; *keinen –(ss)en*, not a bit; *sich den –(ss)en vom Munde absparen*, stint oneself (*für*, for). **–(ss)enweise,** *adv.* in mouthfuls; in bits, bit by bit. **–(ss)ig,** *adv.* biting; rabid; snappish, sharp, cutting; sarcastic. **–wunde,** *f.* wound caused by a bite *or* snap.

bißchen, (-s, –), (*fam. & dial.*) **bissel,** *n.* (-s, -), *& indec. adj.* a little bit, a morsel; a little; (*used adverbially*) somewhat, rather; *ein – Brot*, a little bread; *kein – Brot*, not a scrap of bread, no bread at all; *sein – Vermögen*, his little fortune; *das ist ein – zuviel verlangt!* that's asking a bit too much, (*sl.*) that's going *or* coming it a bit strong; *ich gehe ein – spazieren*, I'm going for a little *or* short walk; *ein – früh*, rather early; *ein – bange*, somewhat uneasy, rather frightened.

bist, *see* **sein.**

Bister, *m. & n.* (-s, –) bistre.

Bistum, *n.* (-s, ⸚er) bishopric; episcopate; diocese, see.

bisweilen, *see* **bis.**

Bitt–e, *f.* (-en) request, petition, entreaty, prayer, supplication; *demütige –e*, supplication; *dringende –e*, urgent request, solicitation; *die sieben –en des Vaterunsers*, the seven petitions of the Lord's Prayer; *ich hätte noch eine –e an Sie*, I have one more favour to beg of you; *auf seine –e*, at his request; *–e*, please! don't mention it (*in answer to thanks*); *wie, bitte?* I beg your pardon (= what did you say?) *or* surely not (*as a polite contradiction*); *–e, geben Sie mir ein Glas Wasser*, give me a glass of water, please; *darf ich Ihnen helfen? Bitte* (*schön*), May I help you? Please (do); *wünschen Sie noch ein Stück Fleisch? Bitte!* will you have another piece of meat? Yes, please; *ich danke Ihnen für Ihre Freundlichkeit, O, –e, es ist gern geschehen*, many thanks for your kindness. Oh, please don't mention it, you are very welcome. **–en,** *ir.v.a.* ask (for), request; beg, entreat, implore; invite; bid; *für einen –en*, intercede for a p.; *einen um Verzeihung –en*, beg a p.'s pardon; (*einen*) *zu sich* or *zu Gast –en*, invite (a p.) to one's house; *einen um Erlaubnis –en*, ask leave of a p.; *darf ich Sie um Ihren* (*werten*) *Namen –en?* may I ask your name? *er bat um ihre Hand*, he sued for her hand; *ich bitte Sie!* you don't say so! *wenn ich –en darf!* if you please; (*Poet.*) *ein Zeichen bat ich*, I asked for a sign. **–ende(r),** *m. & f.* inviter, petitioner.

-fahrt, *f.* pilgrimage. **-gang,** *m.* procession of pilgrims. **-gebet,** *n.* **-gesang,** *m.* rogation, litany. **-gesuch,** *n.* petition, suit, request. **-schreiben,** *n.*, **-schrift,** *f.* written petition; begging letter; *eine -schrift einreichen (bei)*, petition. **-steller,** *m.*, petitioner, supplicant; suitor (*Law.*). **-weise,** *adv.* as a petition, by way of request. **-wort,** *n.* entreaty.

bitter, *adj.* bitter; sharp, stinging, biting; severe; acrimonious, rancorous; *-e Klage*, bitter complaint; *-e Tränen weinen*, weep bitterly; *-er Ernst*, bitter earnest; *-kalt*, bitterly cold; *Sparsamkeit ist – nötig*, economy is urgently necessary; *er trank einen Bittern*, he drank bitters. **-böse,** *adj.* extremely angry; very wicked. **-erde,** *f.* magnesia. **-feind,** *adj.* very hostile. **-ich,** *m.* yellow succory (*Picris hieracioides*) (*Bot.*). **-kalk,** *m.* magnesium limestone. **-keit,** *f.* bitterness; sarcasm, acrimony, (*pl.*) bitter words. **-lich,** 1. *adj.* bitterish. 2. *adv.* bitterly. **-ling,** *m.* small species of carp; yellow-wort (*Chlora perfoliata*) (*Bot.*). **-klee,** *m.* marsh trefoil, buckbean (*Menyanthes trifoliata*) (*Bot.*). **-kleesalz,** *n.* oxalic acid. **-mandelöl,** *n.* oil of bitter almonds, benzaldehyde. **-mittel,** *n.* bitters. **-salz,** *n.* Epsom salts; sulphate of magnesia. **-säure,** *f.* picric acid. **-spat,** *m.* magnesite. **-stein,** *m.* jade, nephrite. **-stoff,** *m.* bitter principle (*Chem.*). **-süß,** 1. *adj.* bittersweet, 2. *n.* bittersweet, woody nightshade (*Solanum dulcamara*) (*Bot.*). **-tropfen,** *m.pl.* bitters. **-wasser,** *n.* bitter mineral water, sulphatic *or* magnesium sulphate water. **-wurz,** *f.* gentian.

Bitum-en, *n.* bitumen. **-inös,** *adj.* bituminous

Biwak, *n.* (-s, -s) bivouac. **-ieren,** *v.n.* (*aux.* h.) bivouac, camp out.

bizarr, *adj.* bizarre, strange, odd. **-erie,** *f.* (-n) strangeness, oddity.

Blach-feld, *n.* open field, open country. **-mal,** *n.* dross, slag.

Blackfisch, *m.* (-es, -e) cuttle-fish.

blaffen, *v.n.* (*aux.* h.) bark, yelp.

Blage ,*f.* (-n) (*dial.*) noisy child, urchin.

bläh-en, 1. *v.a.* & *r.* inflate, swell out; *er -t sich wie der Frosch in der Fabel*, he puffs himself up like the frog in the fable. 2. *v.n.* (*aux.* h.) cause flatulence; distend, swell; *Erbsen -en*, peas cause flatulence; *sich mit etwas -en*, brag of a th., be puffed up *or* elated about a th. **-end,** *pr.p.* & *adj.* flatulent, windy. **-sucht,** *f.* flatulency. **-ung,** *f.* flatulence, wind.

Blak, *m.* (*dial.*) smoky flame, soot. **-en,** *v.n.* (*aux.* h.) smoke (*of a lamp*). **-ig,** *adj.* smoky (*of a lamp*).

Blam-age, *f.* (-n) shame, disgrace. **-ieren,** 1. *v.a.* expose to ridicule; bring into disrepute, compromise. 2. *v.r.* disgrace o.s.; make o.s. ridiculous, make a fool of o.s.

blanch-ieren, *v.a.* blanch, whiten. **-issure,** *f.* light spot (*in dyeing*).

blank, *adj.* shining; bright, polished; clear, clean; bare, smooth; white (*skin*); *-er Draht*, bare wire, uncovered wire (*Elec.*); *-e Lüge*, flat *or* barefaced lie; *-e Waffe*, cold steel (*Mil.*); *-e Worte*, mere words; *mit einem – stehen*, be at open enmity with a p.; *– beizen*, *v.a.* pickle, dip (*Metall.*). *– putzen*, *– reiben*, scour, polish; *– ziehen*, draw one's sword; *ich bin blank*, (*sl.*) I'm cleaned out. **-ett,** *n.* carte-blanche. **-leder,** *n.* sleek *or* shiny leather. **-o,** *adj.* (*C.L.*) in blank, unprotected; *in -o trassieren*, draw in blank; *Giro in -o*, blank endorsement. **-oakzept,** *n.* acceptance in blank. **-okredit,** *m.* open credit, unlimited credit. **-oscheck,** *m.* blank cheque. **-overkauf,** *m.* sale in blank, open sale, short sale. **-ovollmacht,** *f.* unlimited power (*Law*). **-tran,** *m.* clear cod-liver oil. **-vers,** *m.* blank verse.

Bläschen, *n.* (-s, –) bubble; pustule, pimple, vesicle, small blister; utricle (*Bot.*). **-flechte,** *f.* shingles (*Med.*). **-förmig,** *adj.* vesicular.

Blas-e, *f.* (-en) bubble; blister; pimple, vesicle, pustule, cyst; bladder (*also Anat.*); flaw, bleb (*in metal, glass, etc.*); boiler, copper, still, alembic; *-en ziehen*, blister, raise blisters; *die ganze -e*, (*sl.*) the whole shoot, the whole boiling. **-angriff,** *m.* gas attack (*Mil.*). **-apparat,** *m.* blast apparatus. **-ebalg,** *m.* (pair of) bellows. **-ebalgtreter,** *m.* organ-blower. **-ebaß,** *m.* bassoon. **-efisch,** *m.* bottle-nosed whale. **-eloch,** *n.* spout-hole (*of a whale*); blow-hole (*of a flute*). **-en,** *ir.v.a.* & *n.* (*aux.* h.) blow; sound, play (*trumpets, etc.*); blow (*glass*); *die Flöte -en*, play the flute; *zum Angriffe* or *zum Rückzuge -en*, sound the charge *or* the retreat; *einen Stein -en*, huff (*at draughts*); *einem ins Ohr* or *in die Ohren -en*, whisper in a p.'s ear; (*coll.*) *sie -en in dasselbe* or *ein Horn*, there is a secret understanding between them, they play into one another's hands; (*Prov.*) *was dich nicht brennt, das -e nicht*, let sleeping dogs lie. **-enähnlich,** *adj.*, **-enartig,** *adj.* bladderlike, vesicular. **-enbildung,** *f.* formation of bubbles, blistering. **-enbruch,** *m.* rupture (of the bladder). **-enentzündung,** *f.* cystitis, inflammation of the bladder. **-enfarn,** *m.* bladder fern (*Cystopteris*). **-enfuß,** *m.* thrips (*Ent.*). **-engalle,** *f.* cystic bile. **-engang,** *m.* vesicular *or* cystic duct. **-engärung,** *f.* bubbling fermentation. **-engries,** *m.* gravel (*Med.*). **-engrün,** *n.* sap-green (*artist's colour*). **-enhöhle,** *f.* vesicular cavity. **-enkäfer,** *m.* cantharis (*pl.* cantharides), Spanish fly. **-enkatarrh,** *m.* cystic catarrh, blennorrhoea. **-enkeim,** *m.* blastula. **-enkraut,** *n.* bladderwort. **-enleiden,** *n.* bladder trouble. **-enpflaster,** *n.* blister plaster. **-enrohr,** *n.*, *see* **-(e)rohr.** **-ensäure,** *f.* uric acid. **-enschlagader,** *f.* cystic artery. **-enschnitt,** *m.* lithotomy, cystotomy. **-ensonde,** *f.* catheter. **-enstein,** *m.* calculus (*Med.*). **-ensteinsäure,** *f.* lithic acid. **-ensteinschnitt,** *m.* lithotomy. **-entang,** *m.* seaweed (*Fucus vesiculosus*). **-enziehend,** *adj.* blistering, vesicatory. **-(e)ofen,** *m.* blast furnace. **-ewerk,** *n.* bellows of an organ. **-ig,** *adj.* blistered, vesicular. **-(e)instrument,** *n.* wind-instrument; *Kapelle von -instrumenten*, brass-band. **-(e)kapelle,** *f.* brass-band. **-(e)rohr,** *n.* blow-pipe, pea-shooter.

Bläser, *m.* (-s, –) player on a wind-instrument; trumpeter; blowing machine, blower.

blasiert, *adj.* blasé.

blasonieren, *v.a.* emblazon.

Blasphem-ie, *f.* blasphemy. **-ieren,** *v.a.* & *n.* (*aux.* h.) blaspheme. **-isch,** *adj.* blasphemous.

blaß (*comp.* blasser & blässer; *superl.* blassest & blässest) *adj.* pale, pallid; faint, light (*of colour*); (*coll.*) *keine -e Ahnung*, not the faintest notion, not the foggiest idea; *toten-*, pale as death. **-blau,** *adj.* & *n.* pale blue. **-rot,** *adj.* & *n.* pink.

Bläss-e, *f.* paleness, pallor; blaze (= *white spot on face of horse, cow, etc.*); *von des Gedankens -e angekränkelt*, sicklied o'er with the pale cast of thought. **-(ß)huhn,** *n.* coot (*Fulica atra*) (*Orn.*). **-(ß)lich,** *adj.* rather pale, palish.

Blatt, *n.* (-es, ⸚er) leaf, petal; blade (*of shoulder, grass, oar, saw, sword, axe*); membrane, lamina, flake, plate, layer; newspaper; sheet (*of paper*); *die öffentlichen Blätter*, the (news)papers, the press; *vom -e (weg)spielen*, play music at sight; *Singen vom –*, sight-singing; *ein gutes – haben*, have a good hand (*at cards*); *kein – vor den Mund nehmen*, be plain spoken; *er nimmt kein – vor den Mund*, he does not mince matters; *das steht auf einem andern -e*, that is another matter altogether, that does not concern us here; *das – hat sich gewendet*, the tide has turned; *ein – einschlagen*, turn down a page; *ein unbeschriebenes –*, a clean slate (= *innocent*); an unknown quantity. **-abfall,** *m.* defoliation. **-achsel,** *f.* leaf axil. **-achselständig,** *adj.* axillary (*Bot.*). **-ähnlich,** *adj.* leaf-like; foliaceous. **-ansatz,** *m.* stipule. **-auge,** *n.* leaf-bud. **-bildung,** *f.* scaling (*Metall.*); foliation (*Bot.*). **-brand,** *m.* leaf blight. **-breite,** *f.* breadth (*of cloth*). **-eisen,** *n.* sheet-iron. **-en,** *v.a.* 1. strip *or* clear of leaves. 2. decoy (*deer by imitating call*) (*Hunt.*). **-er,** *see* **Blatter.** **-erde,** *f.* leaf mould. **-feder,** *f.* leaf spring (*Engin.*). **-fleisch,** *n.* pith *or* pulp of plants, parenchyma. **-förmig,** *adj.* leaf-shaped, lamelliform; flaky, laminated. **-gewächs,** *n.* foliage plant. **-gold,** *n.* gold-leaf. **-grün,** *n.* chlorophyll. **-knospe,** *f.* leaf-bud. **-lack,** *m.* shellac. **-laus,** *f.* plant-louse, green-fly, aphid. **-lauskäfer,** *m.* ladybird. **-los,** *adj.* leafless, aphyllous. **-metall,** *n.* sheet metal, metal foil.

-reich, *adj.* leafy, with rich *or* luxuriant foliage, foliose. **-rippe,** *f.* vein of a leaf. **-scheide,** *f.* leaf sheath. **-seite,** *f.* leaf, folio. **-silber,** *n.* silver leaf. **-stellung,** *f.* leaf arrangement (*Bot.*), phyllotaxis. **-stiel,** *m.* leaf-stalk, petiole. **-weise,** *adv.* leaf by leaf. **-werk,** *n.* foliage (*also Paint & Arch.*). **-winkel,** *m.*, *see* **-achsel. -zeichen,** *n.* bookmark. **-zinn,** *n.* tinfoil.

Blätt-chen, *n.* (-chens, -chen) leaflet; blade (*of grass*); small sheet of paper; membrane; fontanel (*Anat.*); (metallic) foil; (*pl.*) lamina. **-er,** *n.pl.*, *see* **Blatt. -erabfall,** *see* **Blattabfall. -ererde,** *see* **Blatterde. -ererz,** *n.* black *or* foliated tellurium. **-erfülle,** *f.* leafiness. **-ergebackene(s),** *n.* puff pastry. **-(e)rig,** *adj.* leafy; foliated; laminated, flaky; *vier-(e)riger Klee*, four-leaved clover. **-erkern,** *m.* laminated core (*Elec.*, *Rad.*). **-erkohle,** *f.* slaty coal. **-erlos,** *see* **blattlos. -ermagen,** *m.* third stomach of ruminants, omasum. **-ern,** 1. *v.n.* (*aux.* h.) turn over the pages. 2. *v.r.* flake off; rise in flakes (*Cook.*). **-erpilz,** *m.*, **-erschwamm,** *m.* mushroom (*Agaricus*). **-erstand,** *m.* foliation. **-erteig,** *m.* puff pastry. **-erwerk,** *n.*, *see* **Blattwerk. -erwuchs,** *m.* foliation.

Blatter, *f.* (-n) pustule, blister, pimple, pock; *die -n*, smallpox; *-n der Schweine*, measles (of pigs); *-n der Schafe*, rot. **-gift,** *n.* vaccine virus, smallpox virus. **-ig,** *adj.* papulous, pustular. **-narbe,** *f.* pockmark. **-narbig,** *adj.* pock-marked. **-nimpfung,** *f.* vaccination.

blau, 1. *adj.* blue; azure (*Her.*); *der -e Montag*, Saint Monday (= *day on which little work is done*); black Monday (*school sl.* = *first day of term*); *-es Auge*, black eye; *mit einem -en Auge davonkommen*, have a narrow escape; come off cheaply; *das -e Band*, the Blue Riband; *die -e Blume*, symbol of Romanticism; *-es Blut*, blue blood, aristocracy; *-e Bohne*, (*Mil. sl.*) bullet; *-er Brief*, official letter of dismissal (*in blue envelope*); *-e Flecke*, bruises; *die -en Jungen(s)*, the boys in blue (*sailors*); *-e Märchen erzählen*, tell incredible *or* tall stories, tell lies; (*coll.*) *sein -es Wunder sehen* or *erleben*, be struck with wonder at seeing a th.; *- machen*, take a holiday; (*coll.*) *- sein*, be drunk *or* (*sl.*) soused *or* sozzled; (*coll.*) *einem (einen) -en Dunst vormachen*, throw dust in a p.'s eyes; *es ward mir - und grün vor den Augen*, I turned giddy; *einen braun und - schlagen*, beat s.o. black and blue. 2. *n.* *das -(e)*, blue (*colour*), blueness, azure; the sky; *ins -e hinein*, haphazard, thoughtlessly, at random; *Fahrt ins -e*, mystery trip; *Berliner -*, Prussian blue; *Königs-* royal blue; (*coll.*) *das -e vom Himmel schwatzen*, talk the hind legs off a donkey; (*fam.*) *er will das -e vom Himmel holen*, he'll go through fire and water. **-äugig,** *adj.* blue-eyed. **-bart,** *m.* Bluebeard, **-beere,** *f.* bilberry, whortleberry (*Vaccinium myrtillus*) (*Bot.*). **-blütig,** *adj.* aristocratic. **-brüchig,** *adj.* blue-brittle (*Metall.*). **-en,** *v.n.* be blue; *der Himmel blaut*, the sky is blue; *soweit die Berge -en*, so far as the blue peaks are seen. **-ente,** *f.* wild duck. **-farbenerz,** *n.* cobalt. **-felche,** *f.*, **-felch(en),** *m.* blue char (*Icht.*). **-fuchs,** *m.* arctic fox. **-grau,** *adj.* livid. **-grün,** *adj.* sea-green. **-holz,** *n.* logwood. **-kohl,** *m.*, **-kraut,** *n.* red cabbage. **-kreuz,** *n.* (*Mil.*) poison gas (diphanyl-arsin). **-meise,** *f.* blue tit(mouse), tomtit (*Parus coeruleus obscurus*) (*Orn.*). **-papier,** *n.* carbon paper, blueprint paper. **-pause,** *f.* blueprint. **-racke,** *f.* roller (*Orn.*). **-salz,** *n.* potassium ferrocyanide. **-säure,** *f.* prussic *or* hydrocyanic acid. **-säureverbindung,** *f.* cyanide. **-schimmel,** *m.* dapple-grey horse. **-spat,** *m.* lazulite. **-specht,** *m.* nuthatch (*Sitta caesia*) (*Orn.*). **-stern,** *m.* bluebell (*Scilla*). **-stich,** *m.* bluish tinge. **-stift,** *m.* blue pencil. **-strumpf,** *m.* bluestocking. **-sucht,** *f.* cyanosis. **-vitriol,** *m.* copper sulphate.

Bläu-e, *f.* blueness; blue; azure (*of sky*). **-en,** 1. *v.a.* dye blue, blue, whiten (*linen, etc.*); beat black and blue. 2. *v.r.* & *n.* (*aux.* h.) grow *or* appear blue. **-lich,** *adj.* bluish. **-ling,** *m.* 'blue' (= butterfly family) (*Lycoenidae*). **-ung,** *f.* bluing, blue-dyeing.

Blech, *n.* (-(e)s, -e) sheet metal; tin-plate; (*sl.*) rubbish, nonsense; *gewalztes -*, rolled metal; *schwarzes (Eisen)-*, sheet-iron; *weißes -*, tin; *Well-*, corrugated iron; (*coll.*) *reines -*, bosh; (*coll.*) *rede doch kein -!* do not talk rubbish! **-en,** *v.a.* & *n.* (*aux.* h.) (*coll.*) pay, shell *or* fork out. **-e(r)n,** *adj.* of sheet-metal *or* tin. **-ner,** *m.* tinker. **-büchse,** *f.*, *see* **-dose**; (*Nav. sl.*) destroyer. **-dose,** *f.* tin can *or* box. **-eisen,** *n.* sheet iron. **-geschirr,** *n.* mess-tin (*Mil.*). **-haube,** *f.*, **-mütze,** *f.* steel helmet, (*coll.*) tin hat. **-instrument,** *n.* brass instrument. **-musik,** *f.* brass band; brass band music. **-schere,** *f.* shears, tin-snips. **-schmied,** *m.* tinsmith, sheet-metal worker. **-zinn,** *n.* tinfoil.

blecken, *v.a.*; *die Zähne -*, show one's teeth (*auf* or *gegen*, at).

Blei, *n.* lead; plummet (*Naut.*); pencil (= *Bleistift*); *gehacktes -*, slugs; *gerolltes -*, sheet-lead; *- in Blöcken*, pig-lead. **-ader,** *f.* lode *or* vein of lead. **-arbeit,** *f.* plumbing; lead smelting. **-arbeiter,** *m.* plumber. **-bergwerk,** *n.* lead-mine. **-blech,** *n.* lead sheet, lead foil. **-blüte,** *f.* arseniate of lead. **-dach,** *n.*, **-dächer,** *pl.* leaden roof; (*pl.*) the leads. **-decker,** *m.* plumber. **-ern,** *adj.* leaden; *er schwimmt wie ein -erner Fisch* (or *eine -erne Ente*), he cannot swim, he swims like a stone. *-erner Schlaf*, leaden wings of sleep. **-essig,** *m.* lead acetate. **-farbig,** *adj.* livid, lead-coloured, leaden. **-feder,** *f.* lead pencil. **-folie,** *f.* lead foil. **-gelb,** *n.* chromate of lead. (*fig.*) **-gewicht,** *n.* dead weight. **-gießer,** *m.* lead smelter. **-glanz,** *m.* galena, lead glance, lead sulphide. **-grau,** *adj.* & *n.* steel grey. **-grube,** *f.* lead-mine. **-gummi,** *m.* pencil eraser, rubber. **-ig,** *adj.* lead-like, leaden. **-kabel,** *n.* lead-covered cable. **-kalk,** *m.*, *see* **-weiß. -kessel,** *m.* vessel lined with lead. **-klumpen,** *m.* pig of lead. **-kolik,** *f.* painter's colic. **-kugel,** *f.* bullet. **-lot,** *n.* plumb-line; lead, plummet; *mit dem -lot untersuchen* (or *ergründen*), take soundings; *mit dem -lot abmessen*, plumb. **-lötung,** *f.* lead soldering. **-mennige,** *f.* red lead, minium. **-mulde,** *f.* pig of lead. **-oxyd,** *n.* lead monoxide. **-recht,** *n.* perpendicular. **-rohr,** *n.*, **-röhre,** *f.* lead-piping. **-rot,** *n.*, *see* **-mennige. -schnur,** *f.* sounding-line. **-schrot,** *n.* lead shot. **-schwer,** *adj.* heavy as lead. **-soldat,** *m.* tin soldier, lead soldier. **-stift,** *m.* lead pencil. **-stiftspitzer,** *m.* pencil sharpener. **-vergiftung,** *f.* lead-poisoning. **-waage,** *f.*, **-wage,** *f.*, plumb-line. **-wasser,** *n.* goulard (water), lead water. **-weiß,** *adj.* & *n.* white lead, lead carbonate. **-wurf,** *m.* plummet; heave of the lead (*Naut.*). **-zucker,** *m.* sugar of lead, lead acetate.

Bleibe, *f.* (-n) (*coll.*) (youth) hostel, shelter; (*sl.*) digs.

bleiben, 1. *ir.v.n.* (*aux.* s.) remain, stay, continue; last, keep; stand, endure; stay away; tarry; be left, remain over. *wird sie lange -?* will she stay long? *wo ist er geblieben?* what has become of him? *sie sind auf dem Schlachtfelde geblieben*, they fell on the battlefield; *auf dem Platze -*, be slain; *es bleibt dabei!* agreed! *es bleibt beim alten*, things go on just as they were, no change will be made; *er bleibt bei seiner Meinung*, he persists in his opinion; *bei der S.* or *Stange -*, keep to the point; *bei der Wahrheit -*, stick to the truth; *der Schuster -t bei seinem Leisten*, the cobbler sticks to his last; (*fig.*) *er blieb dabei*, he insisted; *dabei muß es -*, there the matter must rest; *fern -*, stay away; *sich gleich -*, be always the same; *lassen Sie das -!* leave that alone! *das werde ich wohl -lassen*, I shall take good care not to do this; *gelassen -*, keep one's temper; *ohne Wirkung -*, be without result; *stecken-*, stick fast; *es bleibt uns nichts übrig als*, nothing is left to us but to; *es bleibt unter uns*, this is confidential, we will keep it to ourselves; *bleib mir vom Leibe!* stand off, keep your distance! *davon -*, keep clear of. 2. *n.* stay; *hier ist meines -s nicht*, here is no place for me, I cannot stay here, I must move on. **-d,** *pr.p.* & *adj.* lasting, permanent, abiding, stable; *-de Eindrücke*, lasting impressions; *-de Farbe*, fast colour.

bleich, *adj.* pale, wan, pallid; faint, faded. **-e,** *f.* pallor, paleness; bleaching-ground. **-echt,** *adj.* fast to bleaching. **-en,** 1. *v.a.* bleach; blanch, whiten; *der Ernst, den keine Mühe -et*, that earnestness (of purpose) which is not afraid of any toil; *einen Mohren –en wollen*, attempt the impossible. 2. *v.n.* (*aux.* h. & s.) grow *or* turn pale *or* white; fade; blanch. 3. *n.* bleaching. **–farbig,** *adj.* livid. **–kalk,** *m.* chloride of lime. **–mittel,** *n.* bleaching agent. **–platz,** *m.* bleaching-ground. **–pulver,** *n.* bleaching-powder. **–sucht,** *f.* anaemia; chlorosis, green-sickness. **–süchtig,** *adj.* anaemic. **–wasser,** *n.* chlorine water.

Blend–e, *f.* (-en) blind; blind *or* sham window *or* door; niche (*in a wall*); blende (*Min.*); diaphragm, shutter, stop (*of camera*); (*pl.*) dead-lights (*Naut.*). **–en,** *v.a.* blind (*fig.*), dazzle; deceive, hoodwink; blindfold; shade, screen; hood (*a falcon*). **–end,** *pr.p. & adj.* dazzling, brilliant; delusive; (*coll.*) marvellous. **–enöffnung,** *f.* diaphragm aperture (*Opt.*). **–fenster,** *n.* blind window. **–kappe,** *f.* headlight shield. **–glas,** *n.* darkening glass. **–laterne,** *f.* dark lantern, bull's eye lantern. **–leder,** *n.* blinkers. **–ling,** *m.* (-s, -e) bastard; hybrid; mongrel. **–scheibe,** *f.* diaphragm (*Opt.*). **–ung,** *f.* blinding, dazzling; deception. **–werk,** *n.* delusion, optical illusion; deception; mirage; *das ist lauter –werk*, that's mere deception, it is all eye-wash. **–ziegel,** *m.* facing brick.

Bless–e, *f.* white spot on face of animal; animal with such a spot (*see* **Blässe**). **–(ß)huhn,** *see* **Bläßhuhn.**

bless-ieren, *v.a.* wound. **–ur,** *f.* (-en) wound.

Bleu-el, *m.* (-els, -el) beater; rolling-pin; mallet. **–en,** *v.a.* beat black and blue.

Blick, *m.* (-es, -e) look, glance, gaze; glimpse, view, prospect; appearance; (*pl.*) touches of light (*Paint.*); *einen – tun auf einen*, glance at a p.; *einen – in eine S. tun*, get an insight into a th.; *auf den ersten –*, at first sight; *mit – auf den See*, overlooking the lake; *scharfer –*, penetrating glance, penetration; *verstohlener –*, furtive glance; *der böse –*, the evil eye; *keinen – für etwas haben*, have no eye *or* understanding for a th.; *er wandte keinen – von ihr*, he did not take his eyes off her; *mit dem –e verfolgen*, follow with one's eyes. **–en,** *v.n.* (*aux.* h.) look, glance; shine; *–en lassen*, show; *sich –en lassen*, appear, put in an appearance, let o.s. be seen; *tief –en lassen*, be an eye-opener. **–fang,** *m.* stunt (*advertising*) to catch the eye. **–feld,** *n.* field of vision. **–feuer,** *n.* signal fire; revolving light (*of lighthouse*). **–gold,** *n.* refined gold. **–punkt,** *m.* visual *or* focal point. **–richtung,** *f.* line of sight. **–signal,** *n.* signal fire.

blieb, bliebe, *see* **bleiben.**

blies, bliese, *see* **blasen.**

blind, *adj.* blind; false, sham; hidden; dim, tarnished, dull; blank; without judgement; dazzled; *– auf einem Auge*, blind of *or* in one eye; *–er Bogen*, blank sheet (*Typ.*); (*Prov.*) *–er Eifer schadet nur*, zeal without knowledge is frenzy; *– feuern*, fire with blank; *–es Gefecht*, sham fight; *–er Gehorsam*, blind *or* implicit obedience; *–es Geld*, undecipherable coinage; *–es Glück*, hazard; *–er Kauf*, fictitious purchase; *–e Klippen*, sunken rocks; *–er Lärm*, false alarm; *–er Passagier*, stowaway, deadhead; *–e Patrone*, blank cartridge; *– schießen*, fire in the air; *auf der Maschine – schreiben*, type by touch; *–er Spiegel*, tarnished mirror; *–e Versteigerung*, sham auction; *der –e* (*die –e, etc.*) blind man (woman); *die –e*, spritsail (*Naut.*); *der –e*, dummy (*cards*). **–boden,** *m.* false bottom. **–darm,** *m.* appendix, caecum. **–darmentzündung,** *f.* appendicitis. **–ekuh,** *f.* blind -man's buff. **–enanstalt,** *f.* home for the blind. **–endruck,** *m.*, **–enschrift,** *f.* braille. **–flug,** *m.* blind flight (*Av.*). **–gänger,** *m.* misfire, blind, dud (*Artil.*). **–geborene(r),** *m.* one born blind. **–heit,** *f.* blindness. **–holz,** *n.* wood to be veneered. **–lings,** *adv.* blindly; blindfold. **–leitwert,** *m.* susceptance (*Elec.*). **–schleiche,** *f.* slow-worm, blind-worm; (*fig.*) snake in the grass; **–wert** *m.* (*elektrischer Größen*), wattless *or* imaginary component (of electric values). **–widerstand,** *m.* reactance (*Elec.*).

blink-en, 1. *v.n.* (*aux.* h.) glitter, gleam; twinkle, sparkle. 2. *v.a.* signal (*with lamps*). **–er,** *m.* lamp-signaller. **–feuer,** *n.* flashing light; revolving light; intermittent light; occulting light. **–meldung,** *f.* lamp-signal message. **–verkehr,** *m.* lamp-signal communication. **–zeichen,** *n. see* **–feuer.**

blinz–en, –eln, *v.n.* (*aux.* h.) blink, wink.

Blitz, *m.* (-es, -e) lightning flash; *vom –e berührt*, struck by lightning; *wie vom –e gerührt* or *getroffen*, thunder-struck; *–e zucken*, lightnings flash; *– aus heiterm Himmel*, bolt from the blue; *Potz –! int.* ye gods! *weg wie der –* or *wie ein geölter –*, off like a shot, off like a streak of lightning, off like greased lightning. **–ableiter,** *m.* lightning conductor. **–artig,** *adj.* like lightning, in a flash. **–blank,** *adj.* very bright, shining. **–blau,** *adj.* black and blue. **–(es)eile,** *f.* lightning rapidity. **–en,** *v. imp. & n.* lighten (= *emit lightning*); flash, sparkle; *es blitzt*, it is lightning; you have a gap showing (*girls' sl.*); **–krieg,** *m.* lightning war *or* warfare. **–licht,** *n.* flash-light. **–lichtaufnahme,** *f.* flash-light photograph. **–mädel,** *n.* girl telegraphist with armed forces (*Nat. Soc.*). **–pulver,** *n.* lycopodium. **–sauber,** *adj.* spruce, shining. **–schlag,** *m.* flash of lightning. **–schnell,** *adj.* quick as lightning; like a flash; *die Nachricht verbreitete sich –schnell*, the news spread like wild-fire. **–strahl,** *m.* flash of lightning.

Block, *m.* (-(e)s, ¨-e) block, log; boulder; pad (*of paper*); stocks; block of houses *or* flats; (*Verbrecher*) *in den – legen*, put (criminal) in the stocks. **–en,** *v.a.* stretch (*boots*) over the tree *or* last; block (*hats*). **–form,** *f.* ingot mould. **–haus,** *n.* log hut; blockhouse, pill-box (*Mil.*). **–holz,** *n.* log-timber. **–lehm,** *m.* boulder clay. **–mehrheit,** *f.* coalition majority. **–rad,** *n.* solid wheel. **–säge,** *f.* pit-saw. **–scheide (–rolle),** *f.* pulley. **–schiff,** *n.* raft; hulk. **–schrift,** *f.* block letters. **–stelle,** *f.* signal-box (*Railw.*). **–strecke,** *f.* block (*Railw.*). **–verschluß,** *m.* breech-block mechanism (*Artill.*). **–wagen,** *m.* truck. **–wart,** *m.* block warden (*Nat. Soc.: combining duties of air-raid warden, public relations man and general informer*).

Block–ade, *f.* (-aden) blockade. **–adenbrecher,** *m.* blockade-runner. **–adegeschwader,** *n.* blockading squadron. **–ieren,** *v.a.* block up, obstruct; blockade (*Mil.*); (*sl.*) stymie; *einen Ball –ieren*, send a ball into a corner-pocket, make a coup (*Bill.*). **–ierung,** *f.* blockage, blockade.

blöd, –e, *adj.* stupid, imbecile; bashful, timid, shy; weak (*of eyes*). **–igkeit,** *f.* weak-sightedness; imbecility; bashfulness, coyness, timidity. **–sichtig,** *adj.* weak-sighted. **–sinn,** *m.* imbecility, idiocy; nonsense. **–sinnig,** *adj.* silly; idiotic, imbecile.

blöken, *v.a.* (*aux.* h.) bleat (*sheep*); low (*cattle*).

blond, *adj.* blond (*masc.*), blonde (*fem.*), fair; *der* (*die*) *–e*, fair-complexioned p.; *die –e Bestie*, the blond beast (*Nietzsche's Germanic superman*). **–ine,** *f.* blonde. **–kopf,** *m.* fair-haired person. **–lockig,** *adj.*, **–haarig,** *adj.* fair-haired.

bloß, 1. *adj.* bare, naked, nude, uncovered, unprotected, deprived (of); destitute; pure, mere, sole; *–er Argwohn* or *Verdacht*, mere suspicion; *mit –em Auge*, with the naked eye; *der –e Gedanke*, the mere idea, the very thought; *auf –er Haut*, next to the skin; *im –en Hemd*, wearing nothing but a shirt; *mit –em Kopfe*, bare-headed; *auf einem –en Pferde reiten*, ride barebacked; *mit –em Schwert*, with naked *or* drawn sword; *–e Worte*, empty *or* mere words. 2. *adv.* (*coll.*) merely, only; *– um Ihnen zu gefallen*, simply to please you; *es kostet – eine Mark*, it costs only one mark. **–geben,** *v.r.* expose o.s., betray o.s.; lay o.s. open (to) (*Fenc. & fig.*). **–gestellt,** *adj.* open, unmasked; unprotected. **–legen,** *v.a.* lay bare; (*fig.*) expose, unearth. **–legung,** *f.* denudation, exposure. **–stellen,** *v.a.* expose, unmask; compromise. **–stellung,** *f.* exposure.

Blöße, *f.* (-n) bareness, nakedness; clearing, opening, gap, blank (*in a wood, etc.*); weakness, weak point; *eine – lassen* (or *geben*), leave open *or* unprotected; *sich* (*Dat.*) *eine – geben*, expose o.s., lay o.s. open (*to attack, ridicule, etc.*); *sich* (*Dat.*) *keine – geben*, save one's face.

Bluff, *m.* (-s, -s) bluff, deception, trick. **–en,** *v.a.* bluff.

blüh–en, *v.n.* (*aux.* h.) flower, bloom, blossom; flourish; effloresce; *vier Söhne –ten mir*, I had four sons in the flower of their youth; (*coll.*) *mir –t noch eine Prüfung*, there is still an examination in store for me; *es –t sein Glück*, fortune smiles on him; *das Geschäft –t*, business prospers; *sein Weizen –t*, he is in luck('s way) *or* in clover. **-end,** *pr.p. & adj.* in blossom, blooming; flourishing; florid, flowery; *–endes Alter*, prime of life, flower of one's youth; *–ender Blödsinn*, extravagant nonsense; *–endes Mädchen*, fresh, bright, vigorous *or* unspoiled young girl.

Blüm-chen, -lein, *n.* floweret; scut (*of hare*). (*coll.*) **-chenkaffee,** *m.* very weak coffee.

Blum-e, *f.* (-en) flower, blossom; aroma; bouquet (*of wine*); froth (*on beer*); gloss (*on linen, etc.*); tip of the tail, scut (*Sport*); efflorescence (*Chem.*); figure of speech, metaphor; choice, pick, elite; *durch die –e sprechen*, speak figuratively *or* in metaphors; *die –e von etwas haben*, have the first *or* the pick of a th.; *man streut ihr –en auf den Weg, man bestreut ihr den Weg mit –en*, her path is strewn with roses; *ich bringe dir meine –e*, I drink the first toast to your good health. **-enartig,** *adj.* flowerlike. **-enbau,** *m.* floriculture. **-enbecher,** *m.* calyx. **-enbeet,** *n.* flower-bed. **-enbinde,** *f.* festoon. **-enblatt,** *n.* petal. **-endeckblatt,** *n.* sepal. **-endecke,** *f.* perianth (*Bot.*). **-enduft,** *m.* fragrance, perfume. **-enerde,** *f.* garden-mould. **-enflor,** *m.* show of flowers; flowering time. **-engartner,** *m.* florist. **-engehänge,** *n.*, **-engewinde,** *n.*, **-enschnur,** *f.* festoon, garland. **-engöttin,** *f.* Flora, goddess of flowers. **-engriffel,** *m.* style; pistil (*Bot.*). **-enhändler,** *m.* florist, nursery-gardener. **-enhonig,** *m.* nectar. **-enhülle,** *f.*, *see* **-endecke. -enkelch,** *m.* calyx. **-enkohl,** *m.* cauliflower. **-enkorb,** *m.* flower-basket; corbel (*Arch.*). **-enkorso,** *m.* battle of flowers. **-enkronblatt,** *n.*, *see* **-enblatt. -enkrone,** *f.* corolla. **-enladen,** *m.* flower shop *or* florist. **-enlese,** *f.* anthology, selection. **-enmädchen,** *n.* flower girl. **-enmehl,** *n.* pollen. **-enmuster,** *n.* floral pattern. **-enpfad,** *m.* flower-strewn path. **-enreich.** 1. *adj.* abounding in flowers; florid. 2. *n.* floral kingdom. **-enrohr,** *n.* arrowroot (*Canna Tulema*). **-ensauger,** *m.* humming bird. (*dial*) **-enscherbe,** *f.* flower-pot. **-enseite,** *f.* hairy side (*of leather*). **-enstaub,** *m.* pollen. **-enstengel,** *m.* flower stalk. **-enstiel,** *m.* peduncle. **-enstielständig,** *adj.* pedunculate, peduncular. **-enstock,** *m.* flowering pot-plant. **-enstrauß,** *m.* bunch of flowers, bouquet, nosegay. **-enstück,** *n.* bed of flowers; flower-painting. **-entopf,** *m.* flower-pot. **-enwerk,** *n.* festoons, garlands. **-enzeit,** *f.* flowering season. **-enzucht,** *f.*, *see* **-enbau. -enzüchter,** *m.* florist, nursery-gardener. **-enzwiebel,** *f.* (flower-) bulb. **-ig,** *adj.* flowery.

blüm-eln, *v.n.* (*aux.* h.) be flowery *or* florid (*in style*); fly from flower to flower (*as a bee*). **-erant,** *adj.* pale-blue (*bleu mourant*); (*coll.*) *mir wird ganz –erant*, I feel quite dizzy *or* giddy.

Bluse, *f.* (-n) blouse, smock, tunic; battle-dress (*Mil.*); *gestrickte –*, jumper.

Blut, *n.* blood; race; parentage, birth, lineage; sap, juice (*of plants, etc.*); *bis aufs –*, to the quick; *bis aufs – hassen*; be at daggers drawn; *einen bis aufs – quälen* or *peinigen*, wring a p.'s heart, *– auswerfen*, spit blood; *blaues – in den Adern haben*, have blue blood in one's veins; *– und Boden*, blood and soil (*Nat. Soc. catchword*); *bäses – machen* (or *setzen*), arouse ill feeling; *der Schreck ließ mir das – gerinnen*, fear turned my blood to water; *geronnenes –*, clotted blood, gore; *von gutem –e*, thorough-bred; *junges –*, young thing *or* creature; *mit kaltem –e*, in cold blood; *einem – lassen*, bleed a p.; *es liegt im –e*, it runs in the blood; *Gesicht wie Milch und –*, complexion like lilies and roses; (*nur*) *ruhig –!* calm yourself! steady! *– stillen*, stop the bleeding; *der Schreck ließ mir das – stocken* or *erstarren*, fear made my blood run cold; *Menschen unsers –es*, people of our race. **-abgang,** *m.* loss of blood, haemorrhage. **-ader,** *f.* blood-vessel. **-andrang,** *m.* congestion (*of blood*). **-arm,** *adj.* (*initial stress*) anaemic; (*final stress*) poor as a church-mouse. **-armut,** *f.* anaemia. **-auge,** *n.* bloodshot eye; finger fern (*Comarum palustre*) (*Bot.*). **-ausleerend,** *adj.* depletive. **-auswurf,** *m.* sputum containing blood. **-bad,** *n.* slaughter, massacre, carnage, butchery. **-bann,** *m.* penal judicature. **-befleckt,** *adj.* blood-stained. **-blase,** *f.* blood blister. **-blume,** *f.* bloodflower, arnica (*Haemanthus*) (*Bot.*). **-brechen,** *n.* vomiting of blood. **-buche,** *f.* copper beech (*Fagus*). **-druck,** *m.* blood pressure. **-durst,** *m.* bloodthirstiness. **-dürstig,** *adj.* bloodthirsty. **-egel,** (**-igel**) *m.* leech. **-en,** *v.n.* (*aux.* h.) bleed; shed one's blood, die; suffer; (*coll.*) pay up, pay out; *nur –et das Herz*, my heart bleeds; *fürs Vaterland –en*, die for one's country. **-er,** *m.* bleeder, haemophiliac. **-erguß,** *m.* effusion of blood. **-farbig,** *adj.* crimson. **-farbstoff,** *m.* haemoglobin, blood pigment. **-faserstoff,** *m.* fibrin. **-fluß,** *m.* haemorrhage; menstruation, menses. **-flüssigkeit,** *f.* blood plasma. **-fremd,** *adj.* (*final stress*) utterly strange. **-fülle,** *f.* full-bloodedness; plethora. **-gefäß,** *n.* blood-vessel. **-gericht,** *n.* criminal court. **-gerinnsel,** *n.* blood clot, thrombus (*Med.*). **-gerinnung,** *f.* coagulation, clotting. **-gerüst,** *n.* scaffold for execution. **-geschwulst,** *f.* haemotoma (*Med.*). **-geschwür,** *n.* boil, furuncle, phlegmon. **-getränkt,** *adj.* blood-soaked. **-gier,** *f.* bloodthirstiness. **-gierig,** *adj.* bloodthirsty. **-hochzeit,** *f.* bloodbath, massacre. **-hund,** *m.* bloodhound. **-ig,** *adj.* bloody, sanguinary; cruel; *–ige Tränen weinen*, shed tears of blood; *–ige Schlacht*, bloody battle; *–iger Ernst*, deadly earnestness; *–ig beißen*, draw blood by biting. **-igel,** *see* **-egel, -jung,** *adj.* (*final stress*) very young. **-klumpen,** *m.* clot of blood. **-körperchen,** *n.* blood corpuscle. **-körperchenzählung,** *f.* blood count. **-kreislauf,** *m.* circulation of the blood. **-kuchen,** *m.* blood-residue; placenta (*Med.*). **-lassen,** *n.* bloodletting. **-leer,** *adj.*, **-los,** *adj.* bloodless, anaemic. **-linie,** *f.* blood line (*Heredity*). **-mangel,** *m.* anaemia. **-probe,** *f.* blood test. **-rache,** *f.* vendetta. **-reich,** *adj.* full-blooded plethoric. **-rot,** *n.* haematin, haemoglobin (*Med.*). **-ruhr,** *f.* bloody flux, dysentery. **-rünstig,** *adj.* bloody, bloodthirsty. **-sauger,** *m.* blood-sucker, extortioner; vampire. **-schande,** *f.* incest. **-scheibe,** *f.* corpuscle, blood cell. **-schlag,** *m.* apoplexy. **-schuld,** *f.* capital crime; murder; incest. **-spender,** *m.* blood-donor. **-spucken,** *n.* spitting of blood. **-stein,** *m.* haematite. **-stillend,** *adj.* styptic, blood-sta(u)nching. **-strieme,** *f.* livid weal. **-stuhl,** *m.* block, scaffold. **-sturz,** *m.* violent haemorrhage; bursting of a blood-vessel. **-sucht,** *f.* haemophilia. **-sverwandt,** *adj.* related by blood (*mit*, to). **-sverwandtschaft,** *f.* consanguinity, blood relationship. **-tat,** *f.* bloody deed, murder. **-übertragung,** *f.* blood transfusion. **-umlauf,** *m.* circulation of the blood. **-ung,** *f.* bleeding, haemorrhage. **-unterlaufen,** *adj.* bloodshot. **-unterlaufung,** *f.* effusion of blood. **-urteil,** *n.* sentence of death. **-vergießen,** *n.* bloodshed, slaughter. **-vergiftung,** *f.* blood poisoning, toxaemia. **-(s)verwandte(r),** *m.* blood relation. **-warm,** *adj.* (*initial stress*) at blood-heat. **-wärme,** *f.* blood heat. **-wasser,** *n.* lymph; serum. **-wassergefäß,** *n.* lymphatic vessel. **-wenig,** *adj.* (*final stress*) very little, next to nothing. **-wurst,** *f.* blood pudding. **-zeuge,** *m.* martyr.

Blüt-e, *f.* (–en) blossom, flower; bloom; blossoming time; prime (*of life*). **-enauge,** *n.* flower bud. **-enblatt,** *n.* petal. **-enbüschel,** *m.* fascicle (*Bot.*). **-endecke,** *f.* perianth (*Bot.*). **-endolde,** *f.* umbel (*Bot.*). **-enhülle,** *f.* perianth. **-enhüllenblatt,** *n.* sepal. **-enkätzchen,** *n.* catkin. **-enkelch,** *m.* calyx. **-enknäuel,** *m.* flower cluster. **-knospe,** *f.* bud. **-enkrone,** *f.* corolla. **-enlese,** *f.* anthology. **-enreich,** *adj.* rich in blossoms, full of flowers. **-enstand,** *m.* inflorescence. **-enstaub,** *m.* pollen. **-enstengel,** *m.* flower stalk, peduncle. **-enstiel,** *m.* pedicle. **-enweiß,** *adj.* snow-white. **-eperiode,** *f.*, **-ezeit,** *f.* heyday, blossoming *or* blossom time, golden age. **-ig,** *adj.* (*in compounds* =) 1. flowered, -blossomed; 2. -blooded.

Bö, *f.* (-en) gust, squall. **-ig,** *adj.* gusty, squally.

bob-fahren, *v.n.* bob-sleigh. (**-fahr**)**bahn,** *f.* bob-sleigh run.

[1]**Bock,** *m.* (-(e)s, ⸗e) ram, he-goat, buck; battering-ram; (*Naval sl.*) Diesel engine; lifting jack; coach-box; horse (*for clothes, etc.*), rack; trestle, pile (*of a bridge*; bridge (*Bill.*); vaulting-horse (*Gymn.*); rake, whoremonger, (*sl.*) ram; *einen groben – in der Übersetzung machen*, make a howler in the translation; *den – zum Gärtner machen* or *setzen*, set the fox to keep the geese; *die Schafe von den Böcken scheiden*, separate the sheep from the goats; *einen – schießen*, commit a blunder *or* (*coll.*) bloomer; *– springen*, play at leap-frog; *über den – springen*, jump over the vaulting-horse; *steifer –*, clumsy oaf; *Sünden–*, scapegoat; *weinen, daß einen der – stößt*, sob convulsively. **-bein,** *n.* trestle leg. **-beinig,** *adj.* bowlegged; stubborn, obstinate. **-brücke,** *f.* trestle bridge. **-en,** *v.n.* (*aux.* h.) be on heat; plunge, rear (*as a horse*); be obstinate; sulk. **-ig,** *adj.* obstinate, sulky, refractory; rutting (*of male deer*), on heat; stinking; bumpy (*Av.*). **-käfer,** *m.* capricorn beetle (*Cerambycidae*) (*Ent.*). **-kasten,** *m.* boot (*of a coach*). **-leder,** *n.* buckskin. **-sbart,** *m.* goat's beard (*Tragapogon*) (*Bot.*). **-schemel,** *m.* footboard. **-shorn,** *n.* hartshorn; fenugreek (*Trigonella*) (*Bot.*); *einen ins –shorn jagen*, intimidate a p., bully a p., frighten a p. out of his wits. **-spiel,** *n.* leapfrog. **-sprung,** *m.* caper, gambol; *–sprünge machen*, caper, gambol; frisk. **-wagen,** *m.* box cart.

[2]**Bock,** *m.*, **-bier,** *n.* strong Bavarian beer; bock beer.

Boden, *m.* (-s, – *or* ⸗) ground, soil; floor, base, bottom (*of sea*); basis; attic, loft, garret; *einem – abgewinnen*, gain ground upon a p.; *das schlägt dem Faß den – aus*, that's the limit *or* the last straw; *einen unter den – bringen*, bring a p. to his grave; *Dose mit doppeltem –*, box with a false bottom; *den – ebnen*, prepare *or* clear the ground (*fig.*); *einem den – entziehen*, cut the ground from under a p.'s feet; *– fassen*, obtain a footing; *Fecht–*, fencing room; *Fuß–*, flooring floor; *einen gemeinsamen – finden*, find common ground; *– gewinnen*, gain ground, make headway (*Mil.*); *dem – gleich machen*, level *or* raze to the ground; *zu – schlagen*, knock down; *sich zu – setzen*, settle down deposit. **-bearbeitung,** *f.* cultivation of the soil. **-belag,** *m.* floor covering. **-beschaffenheit,** *f.* condition *or* nature of the soil. **-besitz,** *m.* landed property. **-bestandteile,** *m.pl.* components of the soil. **-bildung,** *f.* soil formation. **-bretter,** *n.pl.* bottom boards; heading (*of casks*); laths (*of bedsteads*). **-erhebung,** *f.* rising ground, undulation. **-fenster,** *n.* attic window. **-fluß,** *m.* soil movement. **-freiheit,** *f.* ground clearance (*of vehicles*). **-fruchtbarkeit,** *f.* soil fertility. **-gekriech,** *n.*, *see* **-fluß. -geschoß,** *n.* attic story *or* floor. **-gestaltung,** *f.* configuration of the ground. **-hefe,** *f.* dregs, grounds. **-hold,** *adj.* favouring *or* adapted to a certain soil (*of plants*). **-kammer,** *f.* garret, attic. **-körper,** *m.pl.* precipitates (*Crystallography*). **-kraft,** *f.* fertility. **-kredit,** *m.* loan on landed property, land credit. **-krume,** *f.* surface soil. **-kultur,** *f.* agriculture. **-kunde,** *f.* science of soils. **-kupfer,** *n.* copper lining, copper bottom. **-los,** 1. *adj.* bottomless; (*fig.*) enormous, excessive, unheard of. 2. *adv.* exceedingly. **-luke,** attic window, sky-light. **-mannschaft,** *f.* ground staff (*Mil.*), ground crew (*Av.*). **-markierung,** *f.* target indicator (*Artil.*). **-meister,** *m.* warehouse manager. **-müdigkeit,** *f.* soil exhaustion. **-personal,** *n.*, *see* **-mannschaft. -probe,** *f.* soil sample. **-punkt,** *m.* bench mark (*Surv.*). **-raum,** *m.* attic. **-reform,** *f.* agrarian reform. **-satz,** *m.* dregs, grounds, sediment, residuum, deposit, precipitate, sludge. **-schätze,** *m.pl.* mineral wealth. **-schicht,** *f.* bottom layer, lowest stratum. **-senkung,** *f.* declivity, subsidence. **-sicht,** *f.* ground visibility. **-ständig,** *adj.* indigenous; (*fig.*) stable, solid, firmly established, permanent; *–ständige Familien*, families of old standing. **-strahlung,** *f.* ground radiation (*Rad.*). **-stein,** *m.* nether millstone. **-stück,** *n.* breech-plate (*of a gun*); heading (*of a cask*). **-treppe,** *f.* attic stairs. **-tür,** *f.* trap-door, door to a loft. **-vag,** *adj.* occurring on *or* adapted to any soil. **-verbesserung,** *f.* soil improvement. **-verfestigung,** *f.* soil stabilization. **-verhagerung,** *f.* soil impoverishment. **-verhältnisse,** *n.pl.* nature of the soil. **-verschluß,** *m.* compactness of the soil. **-welle,** *f.* ground wave (*Rad.*). **-wuchs,** *m.* undergrowth. **-zins,** *m.* ground-rent. **-zünder,** *m.* base percussion fuse (*Gun.*).

bodme-n, *v.a.* insure a ship; raise money on bottomry; floor, plank (*a room*); head (*a cask*). **-rei,** *f.* (*C.L.*) bottomry; *Geld auf –rei austun* (*ausnehmen*), advance (raise) money on bottomry; *–rei auf die Schiffsladung*, respondentia. **-reibrief,** *m.* bottomry bond, respondentia bond. **-reigeber,** (**-reinehmer**) *m.* advancer (raiser) of money on bottomry bonds.

Bofist, *m.* (-s, -e) puff-ball (*Bot.*).

bog, böge, *see* **biegen.**

Bogen, *m.* (-s, – *or* ⸗) 1. bow, bend, curve, curvature; arc; arch, vault; bind, tie (*Mus.*); 2. bow (*violin & archery*); 3. sheet (*of paper*); *äußerer –*, extrados (*Arch.*); *in Bausch und –*, in the lump; *bedruckter –*, printed sheet; *fliegender –*, flying buttress; *der Fluß macht einen –*, the river makes a bend; *gedrückter –*, elliptical arch; *innerer –*, intrados (*Arch.*); *Regen–*, rainbow; *in rohen –*, in quires (*paper*); *schiefer –*, sloping arch; *einen – schlagen*, describe a curve; *einen – spannen*, bend *or* draw a bow; *Spitz–*, ogive (*Arch.*). **-artig,** *adj.* arched, bowed. **-bezeichnung,** *f.* signature, sheet (*Typ.*). **-brücke,** *f.* arched bridge. **-dach,** *n.* vaulted roof. **-fenster,** *n.* bay-window, oriel. **-form,** *f.* folio. **-förmig,** *adj.* curved, arched. **-führung,** *f.* bowing technique, (*Mus.*). **-gang,** *m.* arcade, colonnade. **-größe,** *f.* folio size. **-halle,** *f.* portico. **-instrument,** *n.* bowed instrument (*Mus.*). **-lampe,** *f.* arc-lamp. **-linie,** *f.* curve. **-säge,** *f.* bow-saw. **-schießen,** *n.* archery. **-schluß,** *m.* keystone. **-schuß,** *m.* bowshot; high-angle fire (*Artil.*); *einen –schuß weit*, within bowshot. **-schütze,** *m.* archer. **-sehne,** *f.* bowstring; chord of a segment (*Math.*). **-seite,** *f.* folio-page. **-spitze,** *f.* ogive (*Arch.*). **-strich,** *m.*, *see* **-führung. -tür,** *f.* vaulted door. **-weise,** *adv.* in sheets, by the sheet. **-zahl,** *f.* number of sheets. **-zirkel,** *m.* bow-compasses, callipers.

Bogner, *m.* (-s, –) bow-maker; archer, crossbowman.

Bohle, *f.* (-n) plank, thick board. **-n,** *v.a.* cover with thick planks, board. **-nbahn,** *f.* log road, pile road. **-ndecke,** *f.* raftered ceiling. **-nsäge,** *f.* pit-saw.

Bohne, *f.* (-n) bean; *blaue –n*, bullets; *dicke –n*, broad beans; *Feld–n*, horse-beans; *grüne –n*, French beans, scarlet runners; *keine – wert*, not worth a straw; *weiße –n*, haricot beans. **-nbaum,** *m.* laburnum (*Bot.*). **-nerz,** *n.* pea ore, granular iron ore. **-nhülse,** *f.* bean pod. **-nkäfer,** *m.* weevil. **-nkaffee,** *m.* pure coffee. **-nranke,** *f.* beanstalk. **-nschuß,** *m.* mark on a horse's teeth by which its age can be known. **-nstange,** *f.*, **-stecken,** *m.* bean-pole; *sie ist die reine –nstange*, she is as tall as a lamp-post. **-nstroh,** *n.* bean straw; *grob wie –nstroh*, extremely rude.

bohne(r)-n, *v.a.* wax, polish. **-bürste,** *f.* scrubbing *or* polishing brush. **-lappen,** *m.* polishing cloth. **-wachs,** *n.* floor polish. **-zeug,** *n.* polishing utensils.

bohr-en, 1. *v.a.* bore, drill, pierce, perforate; *ein Schiff in den Grund –en*, sink *or* scuttle a vessel; *das Brett –en, wo es am dünnsten ist*, take the easiest way out, shun trouble; *er –t hartes Holz*, he's got a tough *or* up-hill job, he's up against it; *der Junge –t in der Nase*, the boy picks his nose. 2. *v.n.* (*aux.* h.) pester, worry, harass. **-er,** *m.* drill, borer, augur, gimlet, piercer, perforator, bit; *Dreh–er*, hand-brace; *Meißel–er*, auger; *Nagel–er*, gimlet; *Zwick–er*, gimlet, bradawl. **-käfer,** *m.* death-watch beetle (*Anobiidae*) (*Ent.*). **-knarre,** *f.* ratchet drill. **-ladung,** *f.* blasting charge. **-loch,** *n.* bore hole, gimlet-hole. **-löffel,** *m.* scouring-bit, scoop. **-maschine,** *f.* drilling machine. **-platte,** *f.*, **-scheibe,** *f.* breastplate (*of a drill*). **-schuß,** *m.* blasting shot. **-stange,** *f.* boring-rod, sinker. **-ung,** *f.* bore (*Motor.*); boring; borehole. **-wurm,** *m.* ship's worm, teredo. **-zeug,** *n.* boring tools.

Boje, *f.* (-n) buoy; *die – steht blind*, the buoy is not

visible; *die – wacht*, the buoy is floating. **-nkasten,** *m.* caisson.
Boll-e, *f.* (-en) bulb; onion. **-ig,** *adj.* swollen; bulbous. **-engewächs,** *n.* bulbaceous plant.
Böller, *m.* (-s, –) small cannon.
Bollwerk, *n.* (-(e)s, -e) bulwark, bastion, rampart.
Bolus, *m.* coarse red clay. **-erde,** *f.* bole.
Bolz, *m.* (-es, -e), **-en,** *m.* (-ens, -en) bolt (*Engin.*); crossbow bolt *or* arrow; rivet, pin, peg, billet; bolt (*of a rifle*); firing pin (*of a gun*); heating iron (*for a flat-iron*). **-enbüchse** ,*f.* air-gun. **-(en)gerade,** *adj.* bolt upright. **-enmutter,** *f.* nut (*Engin*). **-enring,** *m.* shackle. **-enscheibe,** *f.* washer (*Engin.*). **-enschloß,** *n.* bar-lock, cylindrical pad-lock.
Bombard-ement, *n.* (-s, -) bombardment, shelling. **-ieren,** *v.a.* bombard, shell, strafe, bomb. **-ierung,** *f.* bombardment, shelling.
Bombast, *m.* bombast; big talk; high-flown language. **-isch,** *adj.* bombastic, pompous (*of language*), inflated, high-flown.
Bombe, *f.* (-n) bomb, shell; bomb-shell (*fig.*); *mit -en belegen*, bomb (*from the air*). **-nabwurf,** *m.* (air) bombing, release of bombs. **-nangriff,** *m.* bombing raid. **-nattentat,** *n.* bomb outrage. **-neinschlag,** *m.* bomb hit. (*fam.*) **-nerfolg,** *m.* huge success. **-nfest,** *adj.* bomb-proof, shell-proof; (*fam.*) *das steht -nfest*, that is absolutely certain. **-nflug,** *m.* bombing raid. **-nflugzeug,** *n.* bomber. **-ngeschwader,** *n.* bombing squadron. **-nklappe,** *f.* bomb door. **-nlast,** *f.* bomb load. **-nmagazin,** *n.* bomb rack. **-npunktwurf,** *m.* pin-point bombing. **-nreihenwurf,** *m.* stick of bombs. **-nschütze,** *m.* bomb aimer, (*Amer.*) bombardier. **-nsicher,** *adj.*, *see* **-nfest.** **-nträger,** *m.*, *see* **-nflugzeug.** **-ntreffer,** *m.* bomb hit. **-ntrichter,** *m.* bomb crater. **-nweiber,** *n.pl.* (*coll.*) evacuees from bombing raids. **-nzielgerät,** *n.* bomb sight. **-r,** *m.*, *see* **-nflugzeug.** **-nzünder,** *m.* fuse, detonator.
Bombierung, *f.* camber.
Bon, [*pron.* bɔ̃:] *m.* (-s, -s) (*C.L.*) check, draft, order, bill.
Bonbon [*pron.* bɔ̃:'bɔ̃:] *m.* or *n.* (-s, -s) sweet, bonbon, (*Amer.*) candy.
Bönhase, *m.* (-n, -n) bungler, botcher; blackleg.
bonifizieren, *v.a.* (*C.L.*) make good, compensate, idemnify.
Bonit-ät, *f.* (*C.L.*) good quality (*of an article*); solvency, credit, reliability (*of a firm*). **-ieren,** *v,a.* appraise (*quality of soil*). **-ierung,** *f.* estimate (*of productivity*).
Bonne, *f.* (-n) nurse; nursery governess.
Bonze, *m.* (-n, -n) (*coll.*) bigwig, party boss. **-ntum,** *n.* political favouritism.
Boot, *n.* (-es, -e) boat; body, hull (*of an aircraft*); *Fähr-*, ferry-boat; *Rettungs-*, lifeboat; *das – aussetzen*, lower the boat. **-sanker,** *m.* kedge, grapnel. **-sdeck,** *n.* boat deck. **-sführer,** *m.*, **-sknecht,** *m.* boatman, sailor. **-shaken,** *m.* boat-hook. **-shaus,** *n.* boathouse. **-sleute,** *pl.* sailors, crew. **-smann,** *m.* boatman, boatswain (*pron.* bos'n). **-sseil,** *n.*, **-stau,** *n.* painter (*Naut.*).
Bor, *n.* boron. **-ax,** *m.* borax. **-salbe,** *f.* boric *or* boracic ointment. **-sauer,** *adj.*; *-saures Salz*, borate. **-säure,** *f.* boric *or* boracic acid.
[1]**Bord,** *m.* (-es, -e) shipboard; edge, border, rim; shore (*of the sea*); *Back-*, larboard; *Steuer-*, starboard; (*N.B. these compounds are n.*); *an –*, aboard, on board; *– an –*, alongside; *über –*, overboard; *frei an –*, (*C.L.*) free on board; *ein Schiff von niedrigem -e*, a vessel deep in the water. **-buch,** *n.* log-book (*Naut., Av.*). **-en,** *v.a.* board (*a ship*), *see* **entern**; edge, border. **-funker,** *m.* wireless operator (*Naut., Av.*). **-ieren,** *v.a.* trim, edge, border. **-ierung,** *f.* border, edging. **-leiste,** *f.* gunwale. **-linie,** *f.* water-line. **-schütze,** *m.* air gunner. **-schwelle,** *f.* kerb stone. **-verständigungsanlage,** *f.* intercommunication equipment (*on aircraft*), (*sl.*) intercom. **-üre,** *f.* border, edging. **-wand,** *f.* ship's side. **-wart,** *m.* flight mechanic. **-zulage,** *f.* hard-lying allowance (*Naut.*).
[2]**Bord, Bort,** *n.* (-es, -e) board, shelf.
Bordell, *n.* (-s, -e) brothel, bawdy-house, disorderly house.
bördeln, *v.a.* border, flange, turn over the rim *or* edge.
Borg, *m.* (-es, -e) borrowing, loan; credit, trust; *auf –*, on credit, (*sl.*) on tick. **-en,** *v.a.* 1. borrow; take on credit; 2. lend; give on trust; *hier wird nicht geborgt*, no credit given, terms cash; (*Prov.*) *-en macht Sorgen*, he who goes borrowing, goes sorrowing. **-er,** *m.* borrower; lender. **-weise,** *adv.* on credit.
Bork-e, *f.* (-en) bark, rind, crust, cortex, scab (*on a wound*). **-ig,** *adj.* barky, scabby. **-enkäfer,** *m.* bark-beetle.
Born, *m.* (-es, -e) (*high style*) spring, well, fountain.
borniert, *adj.* narrow-minded; ignorant. **-heit,** *f.* narrow-mindedness.
Börse, *f.* (-n) 1. purse; 2. (*C.L.*) stock exchange; *die tonangebende –*, the standard market. **-nbericht,** *m.* money-market report. **-nblatt,** *n.* exchange list; commercial newspaper. **-nfähig,** *adj.* negotiable. *-nfähige Papiere*, marketable stocks. **-ngeschäft,** *n.* stock-exchange transaction. **-nkurs,** *m.* rate of exchange. **-nmakler,** *m.* stock-broker. **-nordnung,** *f.* exchange regulations. **-npapiere,** *n.pl.* stocks. **-nschacher,** *m.*, **-spiel,** *n.* speculation. **-nspieler,** *m.* speculator. **-nsprache,** *f.* stock-exchange jargon. **-nzeitung,** *f.* financial *or* commercial paper. **-nzettel,** *m.* stock-list, list of quotations.
borst, *see* **bersten.**
Borst-e, *f.* (-en) bristle; seta (*Bot.*); fissure, crack, **-enartig,** *adj.* bristly; setaceous (*Bot.*). **-enbesen.** *m.* hard *or* stiff broom. **-enfäule,** *f.* swine scurvy. **-enförmig,** *adj.*, *see* **-enartig.** **-ig,** *adj.* bristly; setaceous (*Bot.*), setiform (*Bot.*); (*fig.*) irritable, surly; *-ig werden*, fly into a temper. **-wisch,** *m.* hearth-brush.
börste, bärste, *see* **bersten.**
Bort, *see* [2]**Bord.**
Borte, *f.* (-n) edge, border, edging, trimming, braid, braiding; selvage; *goldene –*, gold lace. **-antrieb,** *m.* rim drive (*Engin.*). **-n,** *v.a.* trim, braid (*a dress, etc.*); *see* **borden.** **-narbeit,** *f.* fringe-making, lace-making.
bös, bös-e, 1. *adj. & adv.* bad, ill; evil, wicked; angry, displeased; sore; cross, ill-tempered; malicious, harmful, noxious, virulent; *er war sehr -e auf mich* (*über eine S.*), he was very angry with me (at *or* about a th.); *-e Augen*, sore eyes; *damit sieht es – aus*, the outlook for it is bad, it is in a bad way; *-er Blick*, evil eye; *viel -es Blut*, much ill-will *or* ill-feeling; *er ist -e dran*, he's in a bad way; *-er Finger*, sore finger; *der -e, der -e Geist* or *Feind*, the evil one, the foul fiend, the Devil; *-e Geister*, evil spirits; *der -e Hund*, the snappish dog; *er meinte es nicht -e*, he meant no harm; *einen -en Ruf haben*, have a bad reputation; *einem -e sein*, be angry *or* annoyed with a p.; *sich -e stellen*, feign anger; *Gutes mit -em vergelten*, return evil for good; *-er Vorsatz*, evil intent, malice; *-e Zunge*, malicious tongue; *-es Weib*, shrew; *-e Zeiten*, hard times. 2. *n.*; *das -e*, evil. **-artig,** *adj.* malicious, ill-natured, malevolent; bad, wicked; virulent. **-artigkeit,** *f.* malignity. **-ewicht,** *m.* (-s, -e *or* -er) villain, rogue, scoundrel, scamp, miscreant. **-lich,** *adj. & adv.*, *see* **-artig**; *-liches Verlassen*, wilful desertion (*Law*). **-willig,** *adj.* malicious, wilful, wicked, malevolent. **-willigkeit,** *f.* malevolence, ill-will, spite.
bösch-en, *v.a.* slope; escarp (*Fort.*). **-ung,** *f.* slope; scarp. **-ungswinkel,** *m.* gradient, angle of slope.
bos-haft, *adj. & adv.* malicious, spiteful, mischievous; malignant, wicked. **-haftigkeit,** *f.* malice, spite. **-heit,** *f.* malice, spite, ill-nature; naughtiness; *aus reiner -heit*, from sheer spite.
Boskett, *n.* (-(e)s, -e) shrubbery, thicket, bosket, bosquet.
Boss-el, *f.* (eln) skittle-ball. **-eln,** 1. *v.n.* (*aux.* h.) play at skittles *or* curling (*on ice*). 2. & **-(el)ieren,** *v.a. & n.* (*aux.* h.) emboss, mould, model. **-elierarbeit,** *f.* embossing, moulding. **-elierwachs,** *n.* modelling-wax. **-(ß)kugel,** *f. see* **-el.**
bot, *see* **bieten.**
Botan-ik, *f.* botany. **-iker,** *m.* (-s, –) botanist.

–isch, *adj.* botanical. **–isieren,** *v.n.* (*aux.* h.) botanize. **–isiertrommel,** *f.* specimen box.
Bot–e, *m.* (-en, -en) messenger; postman, carrier; (*B.*) apostle; herald (*fig.*); *eigener –e*, express messenger; *der hinkende –e kommt nach*, the bad news will follow; *reitender –e*, courier; *die –en des Frühlings*, the heralds of spring; *die Zwölf –en Christi*, Christ's twelve apostles. **–engang,** *m.* errand. **–enjunge,** *m.* errand-boy; carrier. **–enlohn,** *m.* porterage, tip, carrier's fee. **–schaft,** *f.* (-en) message; news, tidings, intelligence; legation, embassy; *frohe –schaft*, joyful tidings; *eine –schaft besorgen*, take a message; *eine –schaft ausrichten*, deliver a message; *Deutsche –schaft*, German Embassy. **–schafter,** *m.* (-s, -) ambassador; *der päpstliche –schafter*, nuncio, (papal) legate.
bote, *see* **bieten.**
botmäßig, *adj.* subject, subordinate, obedient. **–keit,** *f.* dominion, sway, power, jurisdiction.
Böttcher, *m.* (-s, –) cooper. **–ei,** *f.* cooper's trade *or* workshop. **–holz,** *n.* staves. **–lohn,** *m.* cooperage.
Bottich, *m.* (-es, -e) tub, vat, barrel.
Bouillon, *f.* clear soup, broth; beef-tea. **–würfel,** *m.* beef-tea cube (*e.g. Oxo cube*).
Bovist, *m., see* **Bofist.**
Bowle, *f.* prepared cold drink; tureen, bowl (*for such a drink*); *Punsch–*, bowl of punch; *Rotwein–*, claret-cup.
box–en, *v.n. & r.* box. **–er,** *m.* boxer. **–handschuh,** *m.* boxing glove. **–kampf,** *m.* boxing match.
boykottier–en, *v.a.* boycott. **–ung,** *f.* boycotting.
[1]**brach,** *see* **brechen.**
[2]**brach,** *adj.* fallow, unploughed, untilled, uncultivated. **–e,** *f.* fallow ground; fallowness; *er ließ das Feld ein Jahr –liegen*, he let the field lie fallow for one year; *–liegende Gelder*, money that is tied up, resources not being used to good advantage. **–en,** *v.a.* 1. plough *or* break up fallow land; fallow. 2. leave uncropped, let lie fallow. **–et,** *m.* June. **–acker,** *m.*, **–feld,** *n.* fallow land. **–flur,** *f.* tract of fallow land. **–huhn,** *n., see* **–vogel. –legen,** *v.a.* lay fallow; devastate. **–läufer,** *m.*, **–lerche,** *f.* sky-lark (*Alauda arvensis*) (*Bot.*). **–monat,** *m.*, **–mond,** *m.* June. **–schnepfe,** *f., see* **–vogel. –se,** *f.* (-n), **–sen,** *m.* (-s, -) bream (*Icht.*) freshwater bream, carp (*Abramis*); sea-bream, chad (*Pagellus*). **–vogel,** *m.* curlew (*Numenius arquata*) (*Orn.*); *kleiner –vogel*, whimbrel (*Scolopax phaeopus*) (*Orn.*); *großer –vogel*, plover, stone-curlew (*Oedicremus*) (*Orn.*).
bräche, *see* **brechen.**
Brack, *n. & m.* (-es, -e) refuse. **–en,** *v.a.* sort out (*refuse*); beat (*flax*). **–er,** *m.* sorter. **–gut,** *n.* lumber, refuse, trash. **–ig,** *adj.* brackish, briny. **–wasser,** *n.* river mixed with sea-water (*at river's mouth*).
Bracke, *m.* (-n, -n) hound, setter, pointer.
Bram, *m.* (-es, -e) broom (*Cytisus scoparius*) (*Bot.*).
bramarbasieren, *v.n.* swagger, brag.
Bramsegel, *n.* topgallant sail (*Naut.*).
Bräme, *f.* (-n) brim, edge, border; (fur) trimming, undergrowth (*at edge of wood*), hedge.
Branche, *f.* (-n) (*C.L.*) branch, line, department.
Brand, *m.* (-es, ⸚e) burning, combustion, fire, conflagration; firebrand; gangrene, mortification (*Med.*); mildew, blight (*Bot.*); brand; burn; scald; passion, ardour; (*sl.*) intoxication; thirst; *in – geraten* or *kommen*, catch fire; *in – setzen* or *stecken* or *legen*, set on fire, kindle; *in – stehen*, be on fire; *der – greift um sich*, the fire is spreading; *das Haus steht in –*, the house is in flames; *mit – und Mord*, with fire and sword. **–beule,** *f.* carbuncle (*Med.*). **–blase,** *f.* blister. **–bombe,** *f.* incendiary bomb. **–brief,** *m.* threatening letter. **–direktor,** *m.* commander of the fire-brigade. **–er,** *m.* fire-ship; fuse (*Elec.*). **–fackel,** *f.* incendiary torch, firebrand; *–fackel des Krieges*, torch of war. **–fest,** *adj.* fireproof. **–flasche,** *f.* Molotov cocktail (*Mil.*). **–fleck,** *m.* barren patch of land; burn, scald, burn mark; stain (*in porcelain*). **–flecken,** *m.* burn, gangrenous spot. **–fluß,** *m.* lava. **–gasse,** *f.* space between houses. **–ig,** *adj.* burnt; blasted; blighted; gangrenous; *–ig riechen* or *schmecken*, smell *or* taste as if burnt. **–gold,** *n.* refined gold. **–kasse,** *f.* fire-insurance office. **–leger,** *m.* incendiary. **–legung,** *f.* arson. **–mal,** *n.*, **–mark,** *n.* scar from burning; brand; (*fig.*) stigma. **–marken,** *v.a.* brand, stigmatize. **–mauer,** *f.* fire-proof wall. **–mittel,** *n.* remedy for burns. **–opfer,** *n.* burnt offering. **–ordnung,** *f.* fire-regulations. **–pfahl,** *m.* stake. **–probe,** *f.* fire-test, assay. **–rede,** *f.* inflammatory address. **–rohr,** *n.* hose (*of fire-engine*). **–röhre,** *f.* train, fuse. **–rot,** *adj.* fiery red. **–salbe,** *f.* burn ointment. **–satz,** *m.* powder train (*fuse*). **–schaden,** *m.* damage by fire. **–schatzen,** *v.a.* levy contribution from; ravage, plunder. **–schatzung,** *f.* levy; war-contribution. **–schiefer,** *m.* bituminous shale. **–schiff,** *n.* fireship. **–schott,** *m.* fireproof bulkhead. **–silber,** *n.* refined silver. **–sohle,** *f.* welt (*of shoe*). **–stätte,** *f.*, **stelle,** *f.* scene of a fire. **–stein,** *m.* brick. **–stifter,** *m.* incendiary. **–stiftung,** *f.* arson, incendiarism. **–tür,** *f.* fire-proof door. **–versicherung,** *f.* fire-insurance. **–wache,** *f.* fire-guard, fire-watcher (*civil defence*). **–wacht,** *f.* fire-watching. **–wunde,** *f.* burn; scald. **–zeichen,** *n.* brand, mark of burning; beacon fire.
brand–en, *v.n.* break, surge (*of waves*). **–ung,** *f.* breakers; surf; surge.
brannte, *see* **brennen.**
Branntwein, *m.* (-(e)s, -e) spirits, brandy, whisky. **–brenner,** *m.* distiller. **–brennerei,** *f.* distillery. **–geist,** *m.* rectified spirits, alcohol. (*coll.*) **–nase,** *f.* bottle-nose. **–vergiftung,** *f.* alcoholism. (*coll.*) **–zapf,** *m.* drunkard, toper.
Braß, *m.* rubbish, lumber.
[1]**Brasse,** *m.* (-n, -n), **–n,** *m.* (-ns, -n), *see* **Brachse.**
[2]**Brasse,** *f.* (-n) brace (*Naut.*); *die großen –n*, the main braces. **–n,** *v.a.* brace; trim (*the sails*); *dicht beim Winde gebraßt*, close-hauled.
brät, brätst, *see* **braten.**
brat–en, 1. *reg. & ir.v.a. & n.* (*aux.* h.) roast, bake; (*auf dem Roste*) grill, broil; (*in der Pfanne*) fry; (*am Spieße*) roast on a spit; *stark gebraten, durchgebraten*, well done; *wenig* (or *zu wenig*) *gebraten*, underdone; *zu sehr gebraten*, overdone; *sich in der Sonne –en lassen*, get sunburnt, (*coll.*) cook oneself in the sun. 2. *m.* (-ens, -en) roast (meat), joint; *den –en begießen*, baste the meat; *den –en anstecken*, spit the roast; (*coll.*) *den –en riechen*, get wind of a th., smell a rat. **–apfel,** *m.* baked apple. **–enbrühe,** *f.* gravy. **–enfett,** *n.* dripping. (*coll.*) **–enkleid,** *n.*, evening dress. **–enlöffel,** *m.* basting-ladle. **–enrock,** *m.* best coat, dress-coat. **–enspicker,** *m.* skewer. **–enwender,** *m.* turnspit, roasting-jack. **–fisch,** *m.* fried fish. **–hering,** *m.* grilled herring. **–huhn,** *n.* roast chicken. **–kartoffeln,** *f.pl.* fried potatoes, chips. **–ofen,** *m.* roasting oven. **–pfanne,** *f.* frying-pan, baking tin. **–rost,** *m.* gridiron, grill. **–schaufel,** *f.* basting ladle. **–spieß,** *m.* spit. **–wurst,** *f.* frying sausage; fried sausage.
Brätling, *m.* (-s, -e) sprat (*Clupea sprattus*) (*Icht.*); agaric, edible fungus (*Lactarius volemus*) (*Bot.*).
Bratsche, *f.* (-n) viola, tenor violin. **–nschlüssel,** *m.* alto clef (*Mus.*).
Brau, *n. & m.* (**Bräu,** *n. & m.*; *this is the normal form except in the foll. comps.*) (-es, -e) brew; brewery. **–berechtigt,** *adj.* licensed to brew. **–bottich,** *m.* brewing-vat. **–en,** *v.a.* brew. **–er,** *m.* brewer. **–erei,** *f.* (-en) brewery; brewing. **–haus,** *n.* brewery, public house. **–wesen,** *n.* brewing business.
Brauch, *m.* (-es, ⸚e) use; usage, custom. **–bar,** *adj. & adv.* useful; serviceable. **–barkeit,** *f.* utility, usefulness, fitness. **–tum,** *n.* customs, (*Nat. Soc.*) folk-lore. **–en,** 1. *v.a.* need, want, require; (*coll.*) use, make use of, employ; *Sie –en es nur zu sagen*, you only need to mention it; *es –t nur wenig Zeit*, it only takes a short time; *was –en Sie sich zu kümmern?* why need you care? why worry yourself? *das könnt ich grade –en*, that is just my luck; *das kann ich nicht –en*, that is no use to me; *man –t sich nicht zu wundern*, it is not to be wondered at. 2. *imp.* (*Gen.*); *es –t keines Beweises*, no proof is required *or* needed.
bräuchlich, *adj., see* **gebräuchlich.**
Braue, *f.* (-n) brow, eyebrow.

braun, *adj.* brown; tawny; *–es Pferd*, bay horse. **–bär,** *m.* (-en, -en) brown bear (*Ursus arctos*) (*Zool.*). **–bleierz,** *n.* brown phosphate of lead, pyromorphite. **–eisenstein,** *m.*, **–erz,** *n.*, brown iron-ore, limonite, vivianite. **–gelb,** *adj.* yellowish brown, bistre; *–gelbes Pferd*, sorrel horse. **–hemd,** *n.* (*Nat. Soc.*) brownshirt, S.A. man. **–kalk,** *m.* brown spar, dolomite. **–kohl,** *m.* broccoli (*Brassica oleracea*) (*Bot.*). **–kohle,** *f.* brown coal; lignite. **–kohlenhaltig,** *adj.* lignitic. **–rot,** 1. *n.* red ochre, colcothar. 2. *adj.* & *n.* brownish red, russet. **–scheckig,** *adj.* skewbald (*of horse*). **–schwarz,** *adj.* & *n.* dark brown. **–stein,** *m.* manganese dioxide. **–tran,** *m.* blubber, thick cod-liver oil.

Bräun–e, *f.* brown colour, brownness; angina; *entzündliche –e*, quinsy; *häutige –e*, croup. **–en,** 1. *v.a.* tan; brown (*meat, etc.*). 2. *v.r.* (*aux.* h.) grow *or* become brown. **–lich,** *adj.* brownish. **–ung,** *f.* browning, brown dyeing.

Braus, *m.* tumult, bustle, uproar; *in Saus und –leben*, live riotously, lead a gay life. **–e,** *f.* shower bath, douche, spray; rose (*of watering can*); effervescence; aerated water; fermentation (*Chem.*); *in der –e sein*, be fermenting. **–eaufsatz,** *m.* rose (*of a watering can*). **–ebad,** *n.* shower-bath, douche. **–ejahre,** *n.pl.* years of hot-headed youth. **–ekopf,** *m.* hothead. **–elimonade,** *f.* aerated water, (*coll.*) fizzy drink, pop. **–en,** 1. *v.n.* (*aux.* h.) storm, rage, bluster; rush, roar; ferment; effervesce; 2. *v.a.* water, sprinkle; douche, shower; *die Ohren –en mir*, I have a singing in my ears; *vor Zorn –end*, boiling with rage; *–ende Jugend*, impetuous, passionate youth. **–pulver,** *n.* effervescent powder. **–ewasser,** *n.* soda water. **–ewein,** *m.* sparkling wine.

Brausche, *f.* (-n) bruise; bump (*on the head*).

Braut, *f.* (⸚e) fiancée, betrothed, (*coll.*) intended; bride (*only on the wedding-day*); *sie ist –*, she is engaged *or* betrothed; *sie ist meine –*, she is my fiancée; *bitte grüßen Sie Ihr Fräulein –*, please remember me to your fiancée; *– in Haaren*, small fennel-flower. **–ausstattung,** *f.* trousseau. **–bett,** *n.* bridal bed. **–führer,** *m.* best man. **–gemach,** *n.* bridal chamber. **–geschenk,** *n.* wedding present. **–jungfer,** *f.* bridesmaid; species of butterfly. **–kammer,** *f.* bridal chamber. (*Nat. Soc.*) **–kind,** *n.* illegitimate child. **–kleid,** *n.* wedding-dress. **–kranz,** *m.* bridal wreath. **–leute,** *pl.*, *see* **–paar.** **–nacht,** *f.* wedding-night. **–paar,** *n.* engaged couple; bride and bridegroom (*only on the wedding-day*). **–schaft,** *f.* state *or* time of engagement. **–schatz,** *m.* dowry. **–schmuck,** *m.*, **–staat,** *m.* bridal attire. **–vater,** *m.* bride's father; *den –vater machen*, give the bride away. **–zug,** *m.* bridal procession.

Bräut–igam, *m.* (-s, -e) fiancé; bridegroom (*on the wedding-day only*); (*coll.*) intended; *bitte empfehlen Sie mich Ihrem Herrn –igam*, please give my kind regards to your fiancé. **–lich,** *adj.* bridal.

brav, *adj.* excellent; honest, upright; worthy, fine; good, well-behaved; *es ist sehr – von Ihnen, daß Sie*, it is very good of you to *or* that you; *– gemacht!* well done! *–er Kerl*, good fellow, (*coll.*) good sort; *–es Kind*, good *or* well-behaved child. **–heit,** *f.* honesty, uprightness; good behaviour. **–o,** 1. *m.* (-os, -os) bravo. 2. *int.* bravo! cheers! fine! splendid! **–oruf,** *m.* shouts of bravo, cheers.

brech–en, 1. *ir.v.a.* break, break up, break through, break down; pluck, pick, gather (*flowers, etc.*); fracture (*a bone*); quarry (*stones*); blend, mix (*colours, etc.*); fold (*letters*); refract, intercept (*Phys.*); neutralize (*Chem.*); *Bahn –en*, force a passage; (*fig.*) be first in the field, be a pioneer. *nichts zu –en und zu beißen haben*, be starving; *er hat Blut gebrochen*, he has vomited blood; *die Ehe –en*, commit adultery; (*Prov.*) *Not bricht Eisen*, necessity knows no law; *Flachs –en*, beat *or* hackle flax; *sich* (*Dat.*) *das Genick –en*, break one's neck; *einer Flasche den Hals –en*, crack *or* drink a bottle; *etwas übers Knie –en*, do a th. hurriedly, impetuously *or* sketchily; *etwas kurz und klein –en*, break s.th. into tiny fragments; *einen Rekord –en*, break a record (*Sport*); *das Schweigen –en*, break (the) silence; *den Stab über einen –en*, sentence a p. to death; *sein Wort –en*, break one's word *or* promise; *einen Streit vom Zaune –en*, pick a quarrel; *gebrochener Akkord*, arpeggio; *gebrochenes Dach*, curved roof; *gebrochenes Deutsch sprechen*, speak broken German; *gebrochene Farben*, blended colours; *gebrochene Schreibart*, abrupt style; *gebrochene Schrift*, Old English type; *gebrochene Treppe*, staircase with a landing; *gebrochene Tür*, folding door; *gebrochene Zahl*, fraction (*Arith.*). 2. *v.r.* break (*as waves*); be interrupted; be refracted; vomit, be sick; *die Kälte bricht sich*, the cold is abating *or* getting less severe; *das Gute bricht sich Bahn*, the good will always win through. 3. *v.n.* (*aux.* s.) break, be broken, snap off, come apart; rupture; break forth, dawn (*as the day*); *die Augen brachen ihm*, his eyes grew dim, he died; *das Eis brach*, the ice cracked; *das Herz bricht mir*, my heart is breaking; *in den Jahren, wo die Stimme bricht*, at the age when the voice breaks; *er brach mit mir*, he broke off relations with me; *Tränen brachen ihr aus den Augen*, tears gushed from her eyes. 4. *n.* violation; breach; breaking; crushing; vomiting; dressing (*of flax, etc.*); *das ist zum –en*, that's enough to make one sick. **–arznei,** *f.* emetic. **–bar,** *adj.* fragile, brittle. **–barkeit,** *f.* fragility, brittleness; refrangibility (*Phys.*). **–beitel,** *m.* ripping chisel. **–bohnen,** *f.pl.* young kidney beans. **–durchfall,** *m.* diarrhoea with vomiting. **–eisen,** *n.* crowbar. **–er,** *m.* crusher; breaker, heavy sea. **–fieber,** *n.* fever attended with vomiting. **–fliege,** *f.* bluebottle. **–meißel,** *m.* ripping chisel. **–mittel,** *n.* emetic. **–nuß,** *f.* nux vomica. **–punkt,** *m.* point of refraction. **–reiz,** *m.* nausea. **–stange,** *f.*, *see* **–eisen.** **–ruhr,** *f.* cholera. **–stange,** *f.* crowbar, jemmy, handspike. **–ung,** *f.* breaking; refraction; arpeggio (*Mus.*); modification, aberration (*Gram.*). **–ungsebene,** *f.* plane of refraction. **–ungszahl,** *f.* refractive index (*Phys.*). **–weinstein,** *m.* tartar emetic. **–wurz,** *f.*, **–wurzel,** *f.* ipecacuanha. **–zeug,** *n.* wrecking *or* demolition equipment.

Brei, *m.* (-es) pap; pulp, mash; purée; *wie die Katze um den heißen – herumgehen*, beat about the bush; *den – verschütten*, spoil an affair; (*Prov.*) *viele Köche verderben den –*, too many cooks spoil the broth. **–artig, –ig,** *adj.* pappy, pulpy, pasty, viscous. **–umschlag,** *m.* poultice.

breit, *adj.* broad, wide; flat; *einen –en Buckel haben*, (*fig.*) have broad shoulders (*i.e. endure much without complaint*); *sie erzählte mir ein langes und –es darüber, sie erzählte es mir des langen und –en*, she spun me a long yarn about it; *es ist so – wie lang*, it is broad as it is long, it is tantamount to; *die –e Masse Volkes*, the broad masses, the people as a whole; *einen –en Pinsel führen*, have a bold touch (*Paint.*); *–e Segel*, square sails; *weit und –*, far and wide. **–axt,** *f.*, **–beil,** *n.* broad-axe. **–beinig,** *adj.* straddle-legged; straddling. **–blättrig,** *adj.* broad-leafed, latifoliate (*Bot.*). **–brüstig,** *adj.* broad-chested. **–e,** *f.* (-en) breadth, width; gauge (*of a railway line*); latitude; verbosity, prolixity; *in die –e gehen*, grow broader; get stout; *eine in die –e gehende Erzählung*, a story that goes on and on; *um eine Haares–e*, by a hair's breadth. **–eisen,** *n.* sculptor's chisel. **–en,** *v.a.* make broad, widen; spread, extend; flatten out. **–enfeuer,** *n.* sweeping fire (*Mil.*). **–engrad,** *m.* degree of latitude. **–enkreis,** *m.* parallel of latitude. **–füßig,** *adj.* flat-footed. **–köpfig,** *adj.* broad-headed; platycephalous, brachycephalic. **–krempig,** *adj.* broad-brimmed. **–machen,** *v.r.* spread o.s. out, take up a lot of room; (*fig.*) give o.s. airs, swagger, boast. **–nasig,** *adj.* flat-nosed. **–randig,** *adj.* with wide margin (*page*); broad-brimmed (*hat*). **–schlagen,** *v.a. einen zu einer S. –schlagen*, persuade *or* bully a p. to (do) a th.; *ich ließ mich –schlagen*, I gave in, he talked me round. **–schult(e)rig,** *adj.* broad-shouldered. **–seite,** *f.* broadside (*Naut.*). **–spurig,** *adj.* wide gauge (*Railw.*); (*fig.*) swaggering, bombastic, imperious. **–treten,** *v.a.* dilate upon (*a th.*). **–würfig,** *adj.*; *–würfig säen*, sow broadcast.

[1]**Brems–e,** *f.* (-n) brake; *ein Auto mit Vierrad–en*, a car with four-wheel brakes. **–en,** *v.a.* put on *or* apply the brake; retard. **–er,** *m.* brakeman. **–backe,**

f., *see* **-klotz.** **-belag,** *m.* brake lining. **-flüssigkeit,** *f.* brake fluid. **-gitterröhre,** *f.* pentode (*Rad.*). **-hebel,** *m.* brake lever. **-klotz,** *m.* brake-block, brake-shoe, chock, block. **-leistung,** *f.* braking power. **-rad,** *n.* brake-wheel. **-spur,** *f.* skid mark (*on road*). **-stange,** *f.* brake-rod; brake handle (*Cycl.*). **-tritt,** *m.* brake pedal. **-vorrichtung,** *f.*, **-werk,** *n.* braking gear, brake mechanism. **-wagen,** *m.* brake-van (*Railw.*). **-weg,** *m.* stopping distance (*vehicles*). **-wirkung,** *f.* retarding effect.

²**Bremse,** *f.* (-n) horsefly, gadfly (*Tabanidae*).

brenn-en, 1. *ir.v.a.* burn; brand; cauterize; calcine, carbonize; char (*wood*); distil (*spirits*); bake (*bricks*); fire (*pottery*); roast (*coffee*); sting (*as a nettle*); bite (*the tongue, as pepper, etc.*); *sich rein* (or *weiß*) *-en wollen,* try to exculpate o.s. 2. *v.n.* (*aux.* h.) burn, be on fire; sting, smart; *mir -en die Augen,* my eyes smart; *vor Ungeduld -en,* be consumed with impatience; (*coll.*) *wo brennt's denn,* what's the hurry; *es -t mir auf den Nägeln,* I am terribly pressed (with work); *es -t in der Stadt,* there is a fire in the town; *es -t!* fire! **-bar,** *adj.* combustible, inflammable. **-barkeit,** *f.* inflammability, combustibility. **-blase,** *f.* still, alembic. **-end,** *pr.p.* & *adj.* burning; caustic; smarting; pungent; ardent, eager, fiery; *-ende Frage,* burning *or* vital question. **-ebene,** *f.* focal plane. **-docht,** *m.* (lamp-)wick. **-eisen,** *n.* curling-iron; branding iron. **-er,** *m.* distiller; brickmaker; burner. **-erei,** *f.* distillery, kiln. **-geschwindigkeit,** *f.* rate of combustion. **-glas,** *n.* burning-glass, lens. **-haus,** *n.* distillery; bakehouse; foundry. **-holz,** *n.* firewood. **-linse,** *f.*, *see* **-glas.** **-material,** *n.* fuel. **-mittel,** *n.* corrosive, caustic. **-(n)essel,** *f.* stinging nettle (*Urtica*) (*Bot.*). **-ofen,** *m.* kiln **-öl,** *n.* lamp-oil. **-punkt,** *m.* focus; focal point; centre; *im -punkt des Interesses,* in the limelight. **-schere,** *f.* curling-irons. **-spiegel,** *m.* burning-mirror *or* reflector; concave mirror. **-spiritus,** *m.* methylated spirits. **-stahl,** *m.* blister steel. **-stoff,** *m.* fuel, inflammable matter. **-weite,** *f.* focal distance. **-wert,** *m.* calorific value. **-ziegel,** *m.* fire brick.

brenz-eln, *v.n.* (*aux.* h.) smell *or* taste of burning. **-essiggeist,** *m.* acetone (*Chem.*). **-lich,** *adj.*, **-lig,** *adj.* tarry; smelling *or* tasting of burning; risky, risqué, doubtful, (*coll.*) near the knuckle.

Bresche, *f.* (-en) gap, breach; *– schießen in,* make a breach in; *– schlagen,* clear the way, push forward.

Brett, *n.* (-es, -er) board; plank; shelf; tray; (*pl.*) the stage, (*coll.*) the boards; *schwarzes –,* notice-board, blackboard; *mit -ern belegen,* floor (*a room, etc.*); *das – bohren, wo es am dünnsten ist,* take the line of least resistance; *in die -er gehen,* die, come to grief, come to naught; *er ist hoch am -e,* he is at the top of the tree; *an das – kommen,* succeed; *vors – kommen,* be brought to justice; *ein – vor dem Kopfe haben,* be stupid, be a blockhead; *er kann durch ein – sehen,* he can see through a brick wall; *bei jemandem einen Stein im -e haben,* have influence with a p., be in favour with a p., (*coll.*) be well in with a p.; *ein Stück geht über die -er,* a play is put on the stage; *mit -ern täfeln,* panel; (*coll.*) *da ist die Welt mit -ern vernagelt,* there is the end of it, there no headway can be made. **-erbude,** *f.* booth, shed, hut; stall. **-erdach,** *n.* shingle roof. **-ern,** *adj.* made of boards, boarded. **-erverschlag,** *m.*, **-erwand,** *f.* wooden partition. **-erwerk,** *n.* planking. **-erzaun,** *m.* wooden fence, palisade; hoarding. **-mühle,** *f.* saw-mill. **-schuppen,** *m.* wooden shed. **-spiel,** *n.* game played on a board (*chess, draughts, etc.*).

Brettl, *n.*, *see* **Überbrettl.**

Breve, *n.* (-(e)s, -n & -s) (papal) brief.

Brevier, *n.* (-s, -e) breviary.

Brezel, *f.* (*also spelt* **Prezel**) (-n) cracknel, crusty type of roll, pretzel.

brich, brichst, bricht, *see* **brechen.**

Brief, *m.* (-es, -e) letter; epistle, document, charter; paper (*of pins*); (*C.L.*) bill (of exchange), draft, offer; *eingeschriebener –,* registered letter; *frankierter –,* prepaid letter; *– und Geld,* bills and money (*C.L.*); sellers and bidders; *mehr Geld als -e,* buyers over asked and bid; *postlagernder –,* letter to be called for, 'poste restante' letter; *unter – und Siegel,* under hand and seal; *– und Siegel über etwas haben,* have a th. in writing, have a sure pledge; *unbestellbarer –,* dead letter; (*C.L.*) *Wechsel–,* draft; *-e wechseln,* correspond; (*C.L.*) *Ihr werter –,* your favour. **-abgabe,** *f.* delivery of letters. **-ablage,** *f.* letter file. **-adel,** *m.* patent nobility. **-anschrift,** *f.* address. **-aufgabe,** *f.* posting *or* mailing (of) a letter. **-aufgabestempel,** *m.* postmark. **-aufschrift,** *f.* address. **-ausgabe,** *f.* issue of letters (*at the counter*). **-beschwerer,** *m.* paper-weight. **-bestellung,** *f.* delivery of letters. **-bogen,** *m.* sheet of note-paper. **-bote,** *m.* postman. **-einwurf,** *m.* letter-box. **-entwurf,** *m.* first draft of a letter. **-fach,** *n.* 'pigeon-hole', letter-rack. **-form,** *f.* form of a letter; epistolatory style; *in -form brechen,* fold as a letter. **-geheimnis,** *n.* privacy of letters; *das -geheimnis verletzen,* disclose the contents of a private letter. **-gut,** *n.* goods accompanying a bill of lading. **-inhaber,** *m.* holder of a bill of exchange. **-karte,** *f.* letter-card. **-kasten,** *m.* letter-box; pillar-box; mail box (*Amer.*); correspondence column (*in a newspaper*). **-konzept,** *n.* draft of a letter. **-kuvert,** *n.* envelope. **-lich,** *adj.* in writing, by letter; *-licher Verkehr,* correspondence. **-mappe,** *f.* portfolio, writing-case. **-marke,** *f.* postage stamp. **-markenalbum,** *n.* stamp album. **-markenausstellung,** *f.* exhibition of postage-stamps. **-markenkunde,** *f.* philately. **-markensammler,** *m.* philatelist, stamp-collector. **-markensammlung,** *f.* stamp collection. **-ordner,** *m.* letter-file. **-papier,** *n.* notepaper, stationery. **-porto,** *n.* postage. **-post,** *f.* post, mail. **-posttarif,** *m.* postage rates. **-presse,** *f.* copying press, letter press. **-probe,** *f.* sample enclosed in a letter. **-schaften,** *f.pl.* letters, documents. **-schulden,** *f.pl.* arrears of correspondence. **-stecher,** *m.* file. **-steller,** *m.* letter-writer; drawer of a bill; letter writer's guide *or* handbook. **-stempel,** *m.* postmark. **-tasche,** *f.* pocket-book, wallet, portfolio. **-taube,** *f.* carrier-pigeon. **-taubenschlag,** *m.* carrier-pigeon loft. **-träger,** *m.* postman. **-umschlag,** *m.* envelope. **-verkehr,** *m.* postal service. **-waage,** *f.* letter balance *or* scales. **-wechsel,** *m.* correspondence; *sie steht mit ihnen in* or *im -wechsel,* she corresponds *or* is in correspondence with them. **-zensur,** *f.* postal censorship.

Bries, (-es, -e) *n.* thymus (*Anat.*); *see* **Bröschen**; **-eldrüse,** *f.* thymus gland (*Anat.*).

briet, briete, *see* **braten.**

Brigad-e, *f.* (-en) brigade (*German army = two regiments*). **-eführer,** *m.* brigade commander (*in S.S.*). **-ekommandeur,** *m.* brigadier. **-ier,** *m.* *see* **-ekommandeur.**

Brigg, *f.* brig (*Naut.*).

Brikett, *n.* (-(e)s, -e) briquette, pressed coal.

Brikol-e, *f.* rebound (*Bill., Artil.*). **-ieren,** *v.n.* (*aux.* h.) play off the cushion (*Bill.*).

brillant [*pron.* bril'jant], 1. *adj.* brilliant, (*fig.*) excellent, superlative. 2. *m.* (-en, -en) brilliant, diamond. **-ine,** *f.* brilliantine, hair-oil.

Brill-e, *f.* (-en) (pair of) spectacles, eyeglasses, glasses, goggles. *durch die rechte -e sehen,* see things in the right light; *durch eine schwarze -e sehen,* take a gloomy view of everything; *durch eine fremde -e sehen,* see with another p.'s eyes. **-eneinfassung,** *f.* spectacle frame. **-enfutteral,** *n.* spectacle case. **-englas,** *n.* lens. **-enschlange,** *f.* cobra (de capello) (*Naja tripudians*) (*Zool.*).

Brimborium, *n.* (-s, -rien) fuss, pother, (*coll.*) to-do.

bringen, *ir.v.a.* bring, fetch; convey, conduct, take carry; lead, induce, cause; produce, yield; (*Poet.*) bring forth, bear. *einen auf die Bahn –,* see s.o. to the train; *an den Bettelstab –,* reduce to beggary; *an den Mann –,* dispose of (*goods*), find a husband for, marry off; *an sich –,* acquire, take possession of; *an den Tag –,* bring to light; *einen aufs äußerste –,* provoke a p. greatly; *auf die Beine –,* set up, raise (*an army, etc.*); *er bringt es nur auf 50,* he manages to get *or* score 50; *er brachte es nur auf 50 Jahre,* he lived to be only 50 years old; *auf neue Rechnung* –, place to a new account; *einen auf eine S.* –, put a p. in mind of, suggest s.th. to a p.; *auf die Seite* –, put aside, save; *etwas aufs Tapet* –, raise a matter, discuss s.th.; *einen außer sich* –, enrage a p.; *Bescheid* –, bring word; *er brachte es bis zum Major*, he rose to the rank of major; *es dahin* –, bring matters to such a pass; *eine S. fertig* –, accomplish a th., bring a th. about; *jemandem eine Gesundheit* –, drink a p.'s health, toast a p.; *es hoch* –, succeed splendidly; (*sl.*) make the grade; *in Erfahrung* –, ascertain; *in Gang* –, set going; *eine S. ins Gleiche* –, settle a th.; *in Ordnung* –, arrange; *in Rechnung* –, take into account; *ins Reine* –, bring to a conclusion, arrange definitely, settle; *in schlechten Ruf* –, bring into bad repute; *in ein System* –, reduce to a system; *in Verdacht* –, throw suspicion on; *in Verse* –, versify; *es mit sich* –, involve; *das bringt vielen Aufwand mit sich*, this involves great expenditure; *nach Hause* –, see *or* escort home; *ein Opfer* –, make a sacrifice; *übers Herz* –, find in one's heart; *ich kann es nicht über die Lippen* –, I cannot bear to say it; *einen um eine S.* –, deprive a p. of a th.; *ums Leben* –, kill, murder; *sich ums Leben* –, kill o.s., commit suicide; *unter die Erde* –, bring down to the grave; *seine Tochter unter die Haube* –, find a husband for one's daughter, get one's daughter married off; *verschiedene Sachen unter einen Hut* –, bring various things under one heading; *unter die Leute* –, make widely known, circulate; *unter Regeln* –, reduce to rules; *etwas unter sich* or *seine Gewalt* –, get control over s.th.; *etwas vor sich* (*Acc.*) –, lay by, save; *es weit* –, succeed in a high degree; get on in the world; *er bringt es nicht weiter*, he does not get on *or* can get no farther; *einen dazu* –, induce a p. (to); *zu Fall* –, ruin; *zu Papier* –, put (down) on paper; *einen zu sich* –, bring a p. to his senses; *einen wieder zu sich* –, bring a p. back to consciousness; *zum Ausdruck* –, give expression to, express; *zum Schweigen* –, put to silence; *zur Reife* –, bring to fruition; *zur Sprache* –, start *or* broach (*a subject*); *einen zur Vernunft* –, bring a p. to reason; *zur Vollkommenheit* –, bring to perfection; *ein Kind zur Welt* –, give birth to a child, bring a child into the world; *wieder zusammen* –, reunite, rally (*troops*); *eine S. zustande* or *zuwege* –, accomplish a th., bring about s.th.

Brisanz, *f.* explosive power; high explosive. **–granate,** *f.* (-n) high explosive shell.

Brise, *f.* (-n) breeze, light wind.

bröckel–n, *v.a., r.* & *n.* (*aux.* h.) crumble. **–ig,** (*also* **bröcklig**), *adj.* crumbly, crumbling, brittle, friable.

Brocken, *m.* (-s, –) crumb, morsel, fragment; (*pl.*) scraps; (*sl.*) military clothes, uniform. **–sammlung,** *f.* collection of old clothes, scrap. **–weise,** *adv.* in crumbs, piecemeal.

brodeln, *v.n.* (*aux.* h.) bubble, boil up.

Brodem, *m.* steam, vapour, exhalation; foul air (*Min.*).

Brod–erie, *f.* (-n) embroidery. **–ieren,** *v.a.* & *n.* embroider. **–ierung,** *f.*, *see* **–erie.**

Brokat, *m.* (-e)s, -e) brocade.

Brom, *n.* bromine. **–id,** *n.* bromide. **–kalium,** *n.* bromide of potassium. **–silber,** *n.* silver bromide (*Phot.*). **–wasserstoffsäure,** *f.* hydrobromic acid.

Brombeer–e, *f.* (-en) blackberry, bramble (*Rubus*) (*Bot.*). **–strauch,** *m.* bramble, blackberry-bush.

bronch–ial, *adj.* bronchial. **–ialkatarrh,** *m.* bronchial catarrh. **–ien,** *f.pl.* [*pron.* 'brɔnçiən], bronchia. **–itis,** *f.* bronchitis.

Bronn, *m.* (-(e)s, -en), **–en,** *m.* (-ens, -en) (*high style*) spring, well, fountain.

Bronz–e, *f.* (-en) bronze. **–en,** *adj.* bronze. **–ezeit,** *f.* Bronze Age. **–ieren,** *v.a.* bronze, braze.

Brosam, *m.* (-(e)s, -e & -en), **–e,** *f.* (-en) (*usually pl.*) crumb, scrap.

Brosche, *f.* (-n) brooch.

Bröschen, *n.* (-s, –) (*calf's*) sweetbread.

brosch–ieren, *v.a.* stitch together, sew (*as a pamphlet*). **–iert,** *p.p.* & *adj.* in paper cover, in boards, stitched, sewed, unbound. **–üre,** *f.* (-n) pamphlet, booklet.

Brösel, *m.* (-s, -) small morsel, crumb. **–n,** *v.a.* & *n.* crumble.

Brot, *n.* (-es, -e) bread; loaf; (*fig.*) support, livelihood; *alt*(*backen*)*es* –, stale bread; *sein eignes* – *essen*, be one's own master; *er kann mehr als* – *essen*, he is up to a trick or two; *frisch*(*backen*)*es* –, new bread; *die Kunst geht nach* –, art must pay its way; *gesäuertes* –, leavened bread; *sein gutes* – *haben*, be well off; *Kampf ums liebe* –, struggle for a livelihood; *schwarzes* –, black *or* brown bread; *sie spart sich das* – *vom Munde ab*, she is stinting herself; *in* – *bei einem stehen*, be in a p.'s service; *sein* – *verdienen*, earn one's living; *vergessenes* –, anything enjoyed before it has been paid for. **–aufstrich,** *m.* jam, meat-paste (*or anything to spread on bread*); **–beutel,** *m.* haversack. **–erwerb,** *m.* livelihood. **–fruchtbaum,** *m.* bread-fruit tree (*Artocarpus*) (*Bot.*). **–gelehrte(r),** *m.* professional scholar. **–herr,** *m.* master; employer. **–käfer,** *m.* biscuit weevil, bread mite. **–kammer,** *f.* pantry. **–korb,** *m.* bread-basket; *einem den –korb höher hängen*, keep a p. on short rations; underpay *or* take unfair advantage of a p. **–laib,** *m.* loaf. **–los,** *adj.* unemployed; *–lose Künste*, unprofitable *or* unremunerative arts. **–mangel,** *m.* dearth. **–neid,** *m.* professional jealousy. **–rinde,** *f.* crust. **–röster,** *m.* toasting fork. **–schaufel,** *f.* baker's peel. **–scheibe** *f.*, **–schnitte,** *f.* slice of bread. **–schrank,** *m.*, pantry. **–studium,** *n.* study for the purpose of earning a livelihood. **–verwandlung,** *f.* transubstantiation (*Rel.*). **–wurzel,** *f.* yam, cassava (*Dioscorea*) (*Bot.*).

Brötchen, *n.* (-s, –) roll (*of bread*); breakfast-roll; French *or* Vienna roll; *belegtes* –, sandwich; *Schinken–*, ham sandwich.

[1]**Bruch,** *m.* (-(e)s, ⸚e) breach, break; breaking, breakage; fracture; crack, flaw; (*Med.*) rupture, hernia; (*Math.*) fraction; infringement, violation; joint (*of a ruler, etc.*); fold, crease; failure, crash; rubble, debris, scrap; *Ader–*, bursting of a blood-vessel; *Dezimal–*, decimal fraction; *echter* –, proper fraction; *Ehe–*, adultery; *Eingeweide–*, hernia; *gewöhnlicher* –, vulgar fraction; *Knochen–*, fracture; *Neu–*, tillage of fallow land; *Schenkel–*, femoral fracture; *Stein–*, stone quarry. –, *der sich nicht aufheben läßt*, irreducible fraction; *das bedeutet einen – mit deiner ganzen Vergangenheit*, that means a clean break with your past; *einen – einrichten*, set a fracture; (*coll.*) *zu* – or *in die Brüche gehen*, break, fall to pieces, be broken up, get ruined, come to an end; (*coll.*) *in die Brüche kommen*, come to naught, fail; *es kam zwischen uns zum offenen* –, it came to an open quarrel between us; – *machen*, crash (*Av.*). **–band,** *n.* truss. **–beanspruchung,** *f.* breaking stress (*Metall.*). **–belastung,** *f.* breaking load (*Metall.*). **–binde,** *f.* sling. **–blei,** *n.* scrap lead. **–dehnung,** *f.* breaking tension elongation at break (*Metall.*). **–eisen,** *n.* scrap iron. **–fällig,** *adj.* decaying, dilapidated, ruinous. **–fest,** *adj.* unbreakable, crash-proof, elastic. **–festigkeit,** *f.* tensile strength (*Metall.*). **–glas,** *n.* broken glass. **–landung,** *f.* crash-landing (*Av.*). **–last,** *f.* breaking load. **–rechnung,** *f.* fractions (*Arith.*). **–schiene,** *f.* splint. **–sicher,** *adj.* unbreakable. **–strich,** *m.* division sign, fraction stroke (*Math.*); shilling stroke, solidus. **–stück,** *n.* fragment. **–stückweise,** *adv.* fragmentarily, in fragments. **–teil,** *m.* fraction. **–weide,** *f.* crack willow (*Salix fragilis*) (*Bot.*). **–zahl,** *f.* fractional number.

[2]**Bruch,** *m.* (-es, ⸚e) & *n.* (-es, ⸚e *or* ⸚er) bog, fen, marsh, swamp. **–artig,** *adj.* boggy, swampy. **–boden,** *m.* boggy soil. **–dorf,** *n.* village near a swamp. **–ig,** *adj.* boggy, marshy, swampy. **–wasser,** *n.* bog water.

brüchig, *adj.* brittle, fragile; friable; full of cracks, breaks *or* flaws; ruptured.

Brück–e, *f.* (-en) bridge; viaduct; dental arch; *alle –en hinter sich abbrechen*, burn one's boats; (*Prov.*) *dem Feinde muß man goldene –en bauen*, one must leave the way open for reconciliation with the enemy; *eine –e über einen Fluß schlagen*, throw a bridge across a river; *hängende –e*, suspension bridge. **–enbau,** *m.* bridge-building. **–enbogen,**

m. arch of a bridge. **–enboot,** *n.* pontoon. **–engeld,** *n.* bridge-toll. **–enkopf,** *m.* bridgehead. **–enpfeiler,** *m.* pier, pile. **–enstützweite,** *f.* span (*of bridge*). **–enwaage,** *f.* weigh-bridge. **–enzoll,** *m.* bridge-toll.

Bruder, *m.* (-s, ¨) brother; friar; (*Prov.*) *gleiche Brüder, gleiche Kappen,* share and share alike; *nasser –,* heavy drinker; *willst du nicht mein – sein, so schlag ich dir den Schädel ein,* if you're not with me you're against me, (*sl.*) be my buddy or I'll bash your head in; *warmer –,* homosexual; *das ist unter Brüdern DM. 50 wert,* that's cheap at 50 marks. **–liebe,** *f.* brotherly love; *christliche –liebe,* charity. **–mord,** *m.* fratricide. **–rat,** *m.* Consistory of the Confessional Church (*Bekenntniskirche*). **–schaft,** *f. see* **Brüderschaft.** **–volk,** *n.* sister nation. **–zwist,** *m.* fraternal strife.

Brüder, *see* **Bruder:** *barmherzige –,* order of friars devoted to charity; *böhmische –, – vom Gesetz Christi,* Hussites; *graue –,* Cistercians; *– der heiligen Jungfrau,* Carmelites; *Joseph und seine –,* Joseph and his brethren; *meine lieben –,* my dear brethren (*in church*); *mährische –,* Moravian Brethren; *Minder–,* Minorites. **–gemeinde,** *f.* the Moravian Brethren. **–lich,** *adj.* brotherly, fraternal. **–schaft,** *f.* brotherhood, fellowship; *–schaft trinken,* pledge close friendship (change from '*Sie*' form of address to '*Du*').

Brüh–e, *f.* (-n) gravy, sauce, broth; *Fleisch–e,* broth, beef-tea; *viel* or *eine lange –e um etwas machen,* make a long story of a th., spin a th. out; (*coll.*) *in der –e sitzen* or *stecken,* be in a fine mess; *einen in der –e sitzen* or *stecken lassen,* leave a p. in the lurch, (*sl.*) leave a p. to stew in his own juice; *alles in eine –e werfen,* act indiscriminately. **–en,** *v.a.* scald; soak. **–faß,** *n.* scalding-tub. **–heiß,** *adj.* scalding hot. **–näpfchen,** *n.* sauce-boat. **–pfännchen,** *n.* saucepan. **–siedendheiß,** *adj.*; *mir ist –siedendheiß,* I am dreadfully hot. **–warm,** *adj.* scalding hot, boiling hot, piping hot; (*fig.*) red-hot, quite fresh; *eine –warme Neuigkeit,* (*coll.*) hot news; *einem eine S. –warm wiedererzählen,* retail news while it's red-hot.

Brühl, *m.* (-es, -e) swampy meadow, marshy ground.

brüll–en, *v.a.* & *n.* (*aux.* h.) roar, bellow, howl, low, shout, (*coll.*) bawl. **–frosch,** *m.* bullfrog (*Rana catesbyana*) (*Zool.*).

brumm–en, *v.a.* & *n.* (*aux.* h.) growl, grumble; hum, rumble; mutter, mumble; (*coll.*) do time (*in prison*), stay in (*at school*); *in den Bart –en,* mutter to o.s.; grumble to o.s.; *ein Lied vor sich hin –en,* hum a tune to o.s. **–bär,** *m.* **–bart,** *m.* grumbler, (*fig.*) bear (with a sore head). **–baß,** bourdon *m.* (*of an organ*); (*coll.*) deep *or* gruff voice; double bass (*Mus.*). **–eisen,** *n.* Jew's harp. **–er,** *m.* grumbler, growler; bluebottle; (*coll.*) bad singer. **–fliege,** *f.* bluebottle, meat fly (*Musca comitoria*) (*Ent.*). **–ig,** *adj.*, **–isch,** *adj.* grumbling, peevish, grumpy. **–kreisel,** *m.* humming-top, musical top. **–ochse,** *m.* blockhead, dunderhead. **–schädel,** *m.* hangover.

brünett, *adj.* dark-haired, dark-complexioned. **–e,** *f.* brunette.

Brunft, *f.* (¨e) rut, heat (*of animals*), sexual desire. **–en,** *v.n.* (*aux.* h.) rut. **–zeit,** *f.* rutting season.

brünier–en, *v.a.* finish metals with a protective surface, blue (*metals*); brown (*metals*); burnish. **–eisen,** *n.*, **–stahl,** *m.* burnisher, burnishing tool. **–stein,** *m.* burnishing stone, bloodstone.

Brunnen, *m.* (-s, -) spring, well, fountain; mineral spring, spa; *meine Pläne sind in den – gefallen,* my plans have miscarried *or* have come to nothing *or* have ended in smoke; (*Prov.*) *den – zudecken, wenn das Kind hineingefallen ist,* shut the stable-door after the horse has bolted *or* is stolen; *– trinken,* take the waters. **–arzt,** *m.* spa doctor. **–becken,** *n.* basin of a fountain. **–behälter,** *m.* reservoir. **–bohrer,** *m.* sinking auger. **–eimer,** *m.* well-bucket. **–gast,** *m.* visitor at a spa. **–geist,** *m.* spirit (*or* nymph) of a well. **–kresse,** *f.* watercress (*Nasturtium officinale*) (*Bot.*). **–kur,** *f.* treatment at a spa. **–meister,** *m.* master of the pump-room. **–röhre,** *f.* water-pipe. **–schwengel,** *m.* beam, lift (*for the well-bucket*). **–seil,** *n.* well-rope. (*fig.*) **–vergiftung,** *f.* calumniation, defamation; calumny, malicious misrepresentation. **–wasser,** *n.* spring water.

Brunst, *f.* (¨e) ardour, passion; lust; rut. **–zyklus,** *m.* oestrous cycle.

brünstig, *adj.* burning, ardent; lustful, sensual; in heat. **–keit,** *f.* ardour; heat; passion.

brüsk, *adj.* brusque, curt, offhand, blunt.

Brust, *f.* (¨e) breast; chest; bosom; thorax; *komm an meine –,* come to my heart; *er hat es auf der –,* he has difficulty with his breathing; *von der – entwöhnen,* wean; *in seine – greifen,* examine one's conscience; *Kind an der –,* suckling baby; *sich in die – werfen,* give o.s. airs. (*In compounds often* = breast-, of the chest, thoracic, pectoral, mammary; of the lungs.) **–ader,** *f.* thoracic vein *or* gland. **–bein,** *n.* breastbone, sternum. **–beklemmung,** *f.* sense of oppression. **–beschwerde,** *f.* chest complaint. **–bild,** *n.* half-length portrait; bust. **–bräune,** *f.* angina pectoris (*Med.*). **–drüse,** *f.* mammary gland. **–drüsenentzündung** *f.* mastitis (*Med.*). **–entzündung,** *f.* inflammation of the chest. **–feder,** *f.* breast feather (*Orn.*). **–fell,** *n.* pleura. **–fellentzündung,** *f.* pleurisy. **–fellfieber,** *n.* bronchitis. **–fleisch,** *n.* breast, white meat (*of poultry*). **–flosse,** *f.* pectoral fin (*Icht.*); **–flosser,** *pl.* thoracics (*Icht.*). **–gang,** *m.* thoracic duct. **–gefäße,** *n.pl.* mammary glands. **–glas,** *n.* breast-pump; nipple glass. **–harnisch,** *m.* breast-armour, corselet, cuirass. **–haut,** *f.* pleura. **–höhle,** *f.* thoracic cavity. **–kasten,** *m.* chest (cavity). **–knochen,** *m.* breastbone, sternum. **–korb,** *m.*, *see* **–kasten.** **–krank,** *adj.* consumptive. **–krause,** *f.* frill, ruffle. **–latz,** *m.* bib, stomacher, doublet. **–leder,** *n.* leather apron. **–lehne,** *f.*, **–mauer,** *f.* breastwork, parapet railing. **–messer,** *m.* stethometer (*Med.*). **–mittel,** *n.* expectorant. **–reinigend,** *adj.* expectorant. **–schild,** *n.* breastplate; thorax (*Ent.*). **–schwimmen,** *n.* breaststroke. **–stimme,** *f.* chest-voice. **–stück,** *n.* breast, brisket (*of meat*); thorax (*Ent.*). **–ton,** *m.* chest-note; *–ton der Überzeugung,* clear note of conviction. **–tuch,** *n.* neckcloth. **–umfang,** *m.* chest measurement. **–warze,** *f.* nipple. **–warzendeckel,** *m.* nipple-shield. **–wassersucht,** *f.* dropsy of the chest. **–wehr,** *f.* breastwork, rampart, parapet. **–wirbel,** *m.* dorsal vertebra (*Anat.*).

brüst–en, *v.r.* give o.s. airs, boast, brag (*über,* about), plume o.s. (*über,* on); *der Schwan brüstet sich,* the swan stands with outspread wings. **–ig,** *adj.* (*suffix in compounds* =) -breasted, -chested. **–ung,** *f.* breastwork, rampart; (window-)sill.

Brut, *f.* (-en) brood, hatch (*Orn.*), fry (*Icht.* & *Ent.*), spawn (*Icht.*); (*fig.*) rabble, pack, brats; brooding, hatching; *die Henne ist in der –,* the hen is sitting; *– setzen,* spawn, stock with spawn; *die ganze – taugt nichts,* they are a worthless set. **–apparat,** *m.* incubator. **–ei,** *n.* egg for hatching. **–henne,** *f.* brood-hen, sitting hen. **–kasten,** *m.* incubator. **–korn,** *n.* gemma, germ (*Bot.* & *Biol.*). **–ofen,** *m.* incubator. **–pest,** *f.* foul brood (*bees*). **–rahmen,** *m.* brood comb (*bees*). **–sack,** *m.* marsupial pouch (*Zool.*). **–scheibe,** *f.* brood comb (*bees*). **–schrank,** *m.* incubator. **–stätte,** *f.* (*fig.*) breeding-place; hotbed. **–wabe,** *f.* brood comb (*bees*).

brutal, *adj.* & *adv.* brutal. **–ität,** *f.* brutality.

brüt–en, *v.a.* & *n.* (*aux.* h.) sit (*on eggs*); hatch, incubate, brood (*also fig.*); *–ende Sonnenhitze,* brooding heat of the sun; *Rache –en,* be intent on revenge. **–ig,** *adj.* addled.

brutto, *adv.* gross. **–gewicht,** *n.* gross weight. **–registertonnen,** *f.pl.* gross registered tons (*Naut.*).

brutzeln, *v.n.* splutter.

Bub–e, (*South German* **Bub**), *m.* (-en, -en) boy, lad; rogue, scamp; knave (*at cards*). **–enstreich,** *m.*, **–enstück,** *n.* boyish trick; piece of villainy. **–ikopf,** *m.* bobbed hair.

Büb–erei, *f.* (-en) roguery, villainy. **–isch,** *adj.* knavish; villainous.

Buch, *n.* (-es, ¨er) book; quire (*of paper*); full suit (*of cards*); six tricks (*at whist*); *die Bücher abschließen,* close *or* balance the accounts; *zu –e bringen,* book; *ins – eintragen,* book; *einem die Bücher führen,* keep the books for a p.; *rohes –,* book in sheets *or* quires. **-adel,** *m.* patent nobility. **-binder,** *m.* bookbinder. **-bindergold,** *n.* gold leaf. **-deckel,** *m.* binding, cover. **-druck,** *m.* printing; typography. **-drucker,** *m.* printer. **-druckerei,** *f.* printing works, printing-press; printing-office. **-druckerfarbe,** *f.* printers' ink. **-druckerstock,** *m.* vignette, tailpiece (*Typ.*). **-en,** *v.a.* book, enter, put down (to), charge; *das wäre als ein Fortschritt zu -en,* that should be counted *or* reckoned as a step forward. **-führer,** *m.* book-keeper. **-führung,** *f.* book-keeping. **-gelehrsamkeit,** *f.* book-learning. **-halter,** *m.* book-keeper, accountant. **-haltung,** *f.* book-keeping; *einfache -haltung,* single entry; *doppelte -haltung,* double entry. **-handel,** *m.* book trade. **-händler,** *m.* bookseller. **-handlung,** *f.* book-shop. **-macher,** *m.* bookmaker. **-porto,** *n.* bookpost rate. **-stabe,** *see* **Buchstabe. -umschlag,** *m.* jacket. **-ung,** *f.* booking, entry. **-zeichen,** *n.* book-mark.

Buch-e, *f.* (-en) beech tree (*Fagus*). **-en, büchen,** *adj.* beech, beechwood. **-ecker,** *f.*, **-eichel,** *f.*, **-el,** *f.*, **Büchel,** *f.* beech-nut. **-esche,** *f.* hornbeam (*Carpinus betulus*) (*Bot.*). **-fink,** *m.* chaffinch (*Fringilla coelebs*). **-weizen,** *m.* buckwheat (*Fagopyrum*) (*Bot.*).

Bücher, *see* **Buch. -abschluß,** *m.* closing *or* balancing the books. **-bord,** *n.*, **-brett,** *n.* bookshelf. **-ei,** *f.* library. **-folge,** *f.* series of books. **-freund,** *m.* lover of books, bibliophile. **-gestell,** *n.* bookcase, book-shelves. **-halle,** *f.* public library, free library. **-kunde,** *f.* book-lore, bibliography. **-lesezirkel,** *m.* book club. **-mappe,** *f.* brief case. **-mensch,** *m.* bookish *or* unpractical person. **-narr,** *m.* bibliomaniac. **-regal,** *n.* bookshelf; book-stack (*in a library*). **-revisor,** *m.* accountant, auditor. **-sammlung,** *f.* library, collection of books. **-schatz,** *m.* library of rare books. **-schau,** *f.* book reviews. **-schrank,** *m.* bookcase. **-staffel,** *f.* showcase for books. **-ständer,** *m.* book-stand, bookcase. **-stütze,** *f.* book-stand, book-rest. **-sucht,** *f.*, *see* **-wut. -tasche,** *f.* satchel, brief-case. **-verzeichnis,** *n.* list *or* catalogue of books. **-wurm,** *m.* bookworm; (*school sl.*) swot. **-wut,** *f.* bookishness, bibliomania. **-zeichen,** *n.* ex libris, book-plate. **-(bestell)-zettel,** *m.* order-form (for books).

Buchsbaum, *m.* box-tree (*Buxus sempervirens*).

Büchse, *f.* (-n) 1. (cylindrical) box; case, tin, can, tin-can, canister, pyxidium; *mit der - herumgehen,* go round with the collecting box; 2. rifle, carbine; 3. *see* **Buxe, Büx(e). -nfleisch,** *n.* tinned *or* canned meat, (*sl.*) bully beef. **-nkugel,** *f.* rifle-bullet. **-nlauf,** *m.*, **-nrohr,** *n.* rifle-barrel. **-nmacher,** *m.* gunsmith, armourer. **-nmeister,** *m.* master-gunner. **-nmetal,** *n.* gun metal. **-nmilch,** *f.* tinned milk. **-nöffner,** *m.* tin- *or* can-opener. **-nschütze,** *m.* rifleman. **-nstein,** *m.* iron pyrites.

Buchstab-e, *m.* (-ens, -en) letter, character (*Typ.*); type; *großer -e,* capital letter; *-e für -e,* letter by letter, literally; *setz dich auf deine vier -en!* (*vulg.*) find somewhere to put your backside. **-enfolge,** *f.* sequence of letters, alphabet. **-engleichung,** *f.* algebraic equation. **-enmensch,** *m.* pedant. **-enrätsel,** *n.* anagram. **-enrechnen,** *n.* algebra. **-entafel,** *f.* phonetic alphabet (*signalling*). **-enversetzung,** *f.* transposition of letters, metathesis (*Gram.*). **-enwechsel,** *m.* interchange of letters. **-ieren,** *v.a.* spell; *falsch -ieren,* misspell. **-ierung,** *f.* spelling.

buchstäblich, *adj.* literal, verbal, exact; *er nimmt alles -,* he sticks very much to the letter, he is very pedantic.

Bucht, *f.* (-en) bay, creek, inlet, bight; sinus (*Anat., Zool., Bot.*); *die deutsche -,* Bay of Heligoland. **-ig,** *adj.* sinuate (*Bot.*).

Buckel, 1. *m.* (-s, -) hump; humpback; bump (*Phren.*); bulge; (*coll.*) back; *du kannst mir den - runter rutschen,* (*vulg.*) go and chase yourself! *steig mir den - hinauf!* (*vulg.*) you get up my back. 2. *f.* (-n) & *m.* (-s, -) boss, stud, knob; umbo (*of a shield*). **-ig,** *adj.* humpbacked, hunchbacked.

bück-en, *v.r.* stoop, bend, bow, make a bow *or* obeisance; *halte dich nicht so gebückt,* don't stoop so much! *-en und ducken,* bow and scrape. **-ling,** *m.* bow, obeisance. **-lingware,** *f.* (*coll.*) commodity in short supply, 'under the counter' goods.

Bückling, Bücking, *m.* (-s, -e) kipper, bloater, smoked herring.

Buckram, *m.* (-s) buckram.

buddeln, *v.a.* & *n.* (*dial.* & *coll.*) dig.

Bude, *f.* (-n) stall, booth; (*Studs. sl.*) digs, rooms, lodgings, den; (*coll.*) *einem auf die - rücken* or *steigen,* drop in on a p., (*sl.*) blow in; (*coll.*) *Leben in die - bringen,* make things lively, (*coll.*) ginger things up. **-ngeld,** *n.*, **-nzins,** *m.* standing-rent (*for a stall*). (*Studs. sl.*) **-nzauber,** *m.* hectic party in one's room.

Budget, [*pron.* byd'ʒe: *or* 'bʌdʒɛt], *n.* (-s, -s) budget estimate.

Büdner, *m.* (-s, -) (*dial.*) stall-keeper; cottager.

Büfett, *n.* (-s, -e) sideboard, dresser, buffet; refreshment bar; *kaltes -,* cold buffet. **-fräulein,** *n.* waitress, barmaid. **-kellner,** *m.* barman.

Büffel, *m.* (-s, -) buffalo; coarse tufted cloth; lout, clod. **-n,** *v.n.* (*aux.* h.) (*school sl.*) swot, grind, slave. **-ei,** *f.* swotting, grind.

Bug, *m.* 1. (-(e)s, ⸚e) bend, bow; joint, articulation; flexure; 2. (-es, -e) shoulder joint (*of animal*); bow (*of a ship*), nose (*of aircraft*); *Knie-,* bend of the knee; *Vorder-,* shoulder (*of quadrupeds*); *das Pferd ist am - wund,* the horse is collar-galled. **-anker,** *m.* bow-anchor. **-gelenk,** *n.* shoulder joint, shoulder bone. **-lahm,** *adj.* splay-shouldered. **-säge,** *f.* bow saw. **-schütze,** *m.* forward gunner (*Av.*). **-sieren,** *see* **bugsieren. -spriet,** *n.* bowsprit. **-stand,** *m.* forward gun position (*Av.*). **-stange,** *f.* foremast. **-stück,** *n.* brisket (*of beef*); shoulder (*of veal, pork or mutton*).

Bügel, *m.* (-s, -) ring; hoop, bow; guard (*of trigger, sword-hilt, etc.*); stirrup; coat-hanger; gimbals (*Naut.*). **-brett,** *n.* ironing-board. **-eisen,** *n.* flat-iron. **-falte,** *f.* crease (*in trousers*). **-fest,** *adj.* not damaged by ironing. **-n,** *v.a.* iron, press (*with an iron*). **-riemen,** *m.* stirrup-leather.

bugsier-en, *v.a.* tow, take in tow. **-boot,** *n.*, **-dampfboot,** *n.* **-dampfer,** *m.* tug, steam-tug. **-tau,** *n.* tow-rope.

Büh(e)l, *m.* (-s, -) (*Swiss*) hillock.

Buhl-e, *m.* (-en, -en) & *f.* (-en), (*Poet.*) lover, sweetheart; gallant; lady-love, (*now only*) mistress, paramour. **-en,** *v.n.* (*aux.* h.) make love to; woo; have illicit intercourse (*mit,* with); (*fig.*) strive (*um,* for); vie (*mit,* with). **-erei,** *f.* coquetry; love-making; wooing; illicit intercourse. **-erin,** *f.* mistress, courtesan; prostitute, wanton. **-erisch,** *adj.* wanton, lewd; (*Poet.*) amorous. **-schaft,** *f.* (-en) love-affair; amour.

Buhne, *f.* (-n) dam, breakwater; dike, groyne.

Bühne, *f.* (-en) stage; scaffolding, scaffold, platform; theatre; scene of action; arena. **-nanweisung,** *f.* stage-direction. **-nausgabe,** *f.* acting edition. **-nausstattung,** *f.* scenery, décor. **-nbild,** *n.* décor. **-ndichter,** *m.* dramatist, playwright. **-ndeutsch,** *n.* standard German. **-nfieber,** *n.* stage-fright. **-ngerecht,** *adj.* suitable for *or* adapted for the stage. **-nkundig,** *adj.* having theatrical experience. **-nleiter,** *m.* stage manager. **-nmaler,** *m.* scene-painter. **-nmanuskript,** *n.* acting copy. **-nmäßig,** *adj.* scenic, theatrical. **-nschriftsteller,** *m.*, *see* **-ndichter. -nsprache,** *f.*, *see* **-ndeutsch. -nstreich,** *m.* stage-trick. **-nstück,** *n.* stage play. **-nveränderung,** *f.* scene-shifting. **-nwirksam,** *adj.* effective on the stage, good theatre. **-nzubehör,** *n.* properties.

buk, büke, *see* **backen.**

Bukett, *n.* (-(e)s, -e) bunch *or* bouquet (of flowers); bouquet (*of wine*).

[1]**Bull-e,** *m.* (-en, -en) bull, bullock. **-auge,** *n.* porthole (*Naut.*). **-dogge,** *f.*, **-enbeißer,** *m.* bulldog. **-enhetze,** *f.* bull-baiting. **-enhitze,** *f.* (*coll.*) sweltering heat.

[2]**Bulle,** *f.* (-n) seal (*on a deed*); edict, papal bull.

buller-n, *v.n.* boil vigorously; make a noise, (*coll.*) make a fuss **-ig,** *adj.* bubbling, boiling; noisy boisterous.

Bult, *m.*, **Bulten,** *m.* (-en, -en), **Bülte,** *f.* (-n) hillock, grassy hummock.

bum, *int. see* **bums**; *bim, bam,* –, ding-dong (*bell*).
Bumm-el, *m.* (-s, -el) stroll, amble, saunter; *einen -el machen,* go for a stroll. **-elei,** *f.* dawdling, loitering; laziness; negligence, carelessness; (*coll.*) *das ist ja eine tolle -elei,* that is nothing but gross carelessness. **-elig,** *adj.* unpunctual, careless, slow. **-eln,** *v.n.* (*aux.* h.) waste one's time, loaf about, loiter; dawdle, take it easy, slack; saunter, stroll. **-elleben,** *n.* dissipated life; *er führt ein -elleben,* he gads about. **-elzug,** *m.* slow train, local train. **-ler,** *m.* idler, loafer, dawdler, slow-coach.
bums, 1. *int.* bump! crash! bang! 2. *m.* (*sl.*) *auf den – gehen,* go dancing, go to a dance-hall. **-en,** *v.n.* (*aux.* h.) bang against s.th., bump. **-lokal,** *n.* (*sl.*) low dance-hall.
Buna, *n.* synthetic rubber.
Bund, 1. *n.* (-es, -e) bundle; bunch (*of keys, etc.*); truss (*of hay*); knot (*of silk*); hank (*of flax*); bottle (*of straw*); *vier – Radieschen,* four bunches of radishes. 2. *m.* (-es, ⸚e) band, tie; lashing; waist-band (*of a skirt*); league, union, alliance, confederacy, confederation; dispensation, covenant (*B.*); *der deutsche –,* the German Confederation (*1815–66*); *der alte –,* the (*Covenant of the*) Old Testament. *Staaten–,* federation of independent states. **-bruch,** *m.* violation of a treaty. **-brüchig,** *adj.* faithless, covenant-breaking. **-esbahn,** *f.* Federal Railway (*Federal German Republic, Austria and Switzerland*). **-esbruder,** *m.* fellow-member of students' society. **-esein-heit,** *f.* federal unity. **-esgenosse,** *m.* confederate, ally. **-eskanzler,** *m.* Federal Chancellor. (*B.*) **-eslade,** *f.* Ark of the Covenant. **-esrat,** *m.* Federal Council. **-esstaat,** *m.* federal state, centralized Confederacy. **-estag,** *m.* Federal Diet. **-esverwandt,** *adj.* allied by federation. **-holz,** *n.* faggot. **-schuh,** *m.* sandal; clog; symbol of German Peasants' Confederation (*1525*). **-weise,** *adv.* in bundles.
Bünd-el, *n.* (-els, -el) bundle, packet, parcel, bale; (*coll.*) *sein -el schnüren,* pack up one's traps; *sie ist ein -el Nerven,* she is a bundle of nerves. **-eln,** *v.a.* bundle (up), bunch. **-ig,** *adj.* binding, valid, obligatory; convincing, conclusive; concise, laconic, to the point; *kurz und -ig,* short and to the point. **-igkeit,** *f.* conciseness; validity. **-nis,** *n.* alliance, union, league, covenant.
Bunker, *m.* (-s, –) (coal) bunker; dug-out, pill-box (*Mil.*); air-raid shelter. **-n,** *v.a.* coal (*Naut.*).
bunt, *adj. & adv.* coloured, bright, gay; motley, many-coloured, variegated; mottled, spotted; stained (*glass*); (*fig.*) lively, wild, gay, disorderly; *-er Abend,* variety show *or* entertainment; *es ging – zu,* there were fine goings-on; *-e Karte,* court-card; *er macht es (mir) zu –,* he goes too far (for me); *-es Musikprogramm,* musical medley; *-e Reihe machen,* pair off ladies and gentlemen, mix the sexes; *-e Waren,* children's toys; *es wurde immer -er,* the confusion grew worse and worse; *den -en Rock anziehen,* (*archaic*) put on uniform, join the red-coats. **-druck,** *m.* colour printing. **-farbenanstrich,** *m.* protective colouring, camouflage (*Mil.*). **-fleckig,** *adj.* variegated, spotted, speckled. **-gewebe,** *n.* coloured fabric. **-gewür-felt,** *adj.* tartan, chequered. **-heit,** *f.* gayness (*of colours*), motley colouring. **-papier,** *n.* coloured paper. **-scheckig,** *adj.* parti-coloured, chequered, spotted; (*fig.*) mixed, promiscuous. **-schil-lernd,** *adj.* iridescent, opalescent. **-specht,** *m.* spotted woodpecker (*Dryobates*) (*Orn.*). **-stift,** *m.* coloured pencil, crayon.
Bürde, *f.* (-n) burden, load; *von ihrer – entbunden,* delivered; *Würde bringt –,* responsibility brings responsibilities.
Bureau, *n. see* **Büro.**
Burg, *f.* (-en) castle; citadel, stronghold, fortress; (place of) refuge; *eine feste – ist unser Gott* (Luther), God is our refuge (and our strength); *mein Haus: meine –,* (an Englishman's) home is (his) castle. **-bann,** *m.* castle precincts; jurisdiction of a castle. **-dienst,** *m.* feudal service. **-fräulein,** *n.* high-born damsel. **-friede,** *m.* jurisdiction *or* precincts of a (baronial) castle; truce, cessation of party strife. **-gericht,** *n.* baronial court. **-graben,** *m.* castle-moat. **-graf,** *m.* feudal lord, baron. **-lehen,** *n.* baron's fief *or* fee. **-tor,** *n.* castle gate. **-verlies** (*also* **-verließ**) *n.* dungeon. **-vogt,** *m.* steward of a castle, castellan, bailiff. **-vogtei,** *f.* stewardship. **-wache,** *f.* castle guard. **-warte,** *f.* watch-tower.
Bürg-e, *m.* (-en, -en) surety, bail, guarantee; guarantor, warrantor; *-en stellen,* find bail. **-en,** *v.n.* (*aux.* h.) go bail (*für,* for); give bail; vouch (for), guarantee, warrant; *das -t mir für seine Treue,* that assures me of his fidelity; *ich -e für die Güte dieses Artikels,* I guarantee this article to be good. **-schaft,** *f.* security, bail; surety (*rare*); *-schaft leisten,* give security; *-schaft übernehmen,* go bail *or* security; *sichere -schaft,* good security.
Bürger, *m.* (-s, –) citizen, townsman, burgess, burgher; one of the middle class, bourgeois, commoner; *– und Studenten,* town and gown. **-adel,** *m.* patriciate. **-eid,** *m.* citizen's oath. **-frau,** *f.* middle-class woman. **-garde,** *f.* town militia, city volunteers. **-krieg,** *m.* civil war. **-kunde,** *f.* civics, sociology. **-kundlich,** *adj.* concerning civics. **-lich,** *adj.* civic, civil; middle-class, bourgeois; simple, plain, homely; (*Nat. Soc.*) philistine, unheroic, unsoldierly. *sie kann -lich kochen,* she understands plain cooking; *-licher Mittagstisch,* plain lunches; *-liches Drama,* domestic drama, drama of middle-class life; *-liche (Ehren-) rechte,* civil or civic rights; *-liches Gesetzbuch,* code of Civil Law; *-licher Tod,* outlawry, loss of civil rights. **-mädchen,** *n.* middle-class girl. **-meister** *m.* mayor, (*Scot.*) lord provost, (*foreign*) burgomaster. **-pflicht,** *f.* civic duties, duties as a citizen. **-recht,** *n.* civic rights; freedom of a city. **-schaft,** *f.* citizens, townspeople. **-sinn,** *m.* public spirit. **-stand,** *m.* the middle classes, citizens. **-steig,** *m.* pavement, (*Amer.*) sidewalk. **-stolz,** *m.* civic pride. **-tugend,** *f.* public spirit; civic virtues. **-tum,** *n.* middle class. **-versammlung,** *f.* meeting of townspeople. **-vorsteher,** *m,* town councillor, alderman. **-wache,** *f.*, **-wehr,** *f.* city militia; Home Guard.
Büro, *n.* (-s, -s) office, bureau; orderly room (*Mil.*). **-klammer,** *f.* paper-fastener *or* clip. **-krat,** *m.* (-en, -en) bureaucrat. **-kratie,** *f.* bureaucracy. **-fräulein,** *n.* office girl. **-mensch,** *m.* office-drudge. **-vorsteher,** *m.* head *or* chief clerk.
Bursch, *m.* (-en, -en); **-e,** *m.* (-en, -en) youth, boy, lad; fellow, comrade; student (*usually a German student after the first year*); batman, orderly (*Mil.*); *es zogen drei -en wohl über den Rhein,* three students once wandered across the Rhine. **-enbrauch,** *m.* custom among students. **-enbund,** *m.* confederacy of (*German*) students. **-enherrlichkeit,** *f.* the good old student days. **-enkomment,** *m.* ritual of (*German*) student associations. **-enleben,** *n.* student life. **-enlied,** *n.* students' song. **-enschaft,** *f.* (*German*) Students' Association. **-enschaft(l)er,** *m.* member of a Burschenschaft. **-ensprache,** *f.* students' slang. **-ikos,** *adj.* free and easy; wild, boisterous (*as students*); tomboyish, hoydenish (*of girls*).
Bürst-e, *f.* (-en) brush, whisk. **-en,** *v.a.* brush; *sich die Zähne -en,* clean one's teeth. **-enabzug,** *m.* galley-proof (*Typ.*). **-enbinder,** *m.* brush maker. **-enfeuer,** *n.* brush sparking (*Elec.*). **-en-gras,** *n.* beard grass (*Polypogon*) (*Bot.*).
-bürtig, (*in compounds*) born, of birth, native of; e.g. *ritter–,* of noble descent.
Bürzel, *m.* (-s, -) croup, rump; hind part (*of a beast or bird*).
burzeln, *v.n., see* **purzeln.**
Busch, *m.* (-es, ⸚e) bush, shrub; thicket, copse, covert; undergrowth; brushwood; tuft, plume, bunch; shock (of hair); *auf den – klopfen,* fish for information, pump (*a p.*) for information. **-holz,** *n.* undergrowth. **-ig,** *adj.* bushy, shaggy, tufted, dendroid. **-werk,** *n.* shrubbery; brushwood. **-windröschen,** *n.* wood anemone (*Anemone nemorosa*) (*Bot.*).
Büschel, *m.* or *n.* (-s, -) tuft, cluster, bunch, wisp; bundle, sheaf, fascicle (*Bot.*); pencil (*of rays*) (*Opt.*). **-artig,** *adj.* tufted, tasselled, bunchy, clustered; fascicular. **-entladung,** *f.* brush-dis-

charge (*Elec.*). **-förmig,** *adj.*, **-ig,** *adj.*, *see* **-artig.** **-weise,** *adv.* in tufts, in bunches. **-wuchs,** *m.* bushy *or* tufted growth.

Büse, *f.* (-n) small fishing-boat.

Busen, *m.* (-s, -) bosom; breast; heart; gulf, bay; *in seinen* or *sich* (*Dat.*) *in den – greifen*, commune with o.s., examine one's conscience. **-freund,** *m.* bosom friend, intimate friend. **-krause,** *f.* frill, ruffle. **-nadel,** *f.* scarf- *or* tie-pin. **-tuch,** *n.* scarf, neckerchief.

Bussard, *m.* (-(e)s, -e) buzzard (*Butes*) (*Orn.*).

Buß-e, *f.* repentance, penitence; compensation, amends fine, penalty; penance, atonement; *– und Bettag*, day of prayer and repentance. *-e tun*, do penance. **-fällig,** *adj.* liable to punishment, punishable. **-fertig,** *adj.* penitent, repentant, contrite. **-fertigkeit,** *f.* penitence, repentance, contrition. **-hemd,** *n.* hair shirt. **-ordnung,** *f.* penitential regulation. **-prediger,** *m.* preacher of repentance, Lenten preacher. **-predigt,** *f.* penitential sermon. **-tag,** *m.* day of humiliation, day of repentance. **-übung,** *f.* penance. **-zeit,** *f.* time of penance; Lent.

büß-en, *v.a.* & *n.* make amends for, atone for, make good; suffer for, do penance, expiate; repair, mend; *seine Lust -en*, satisfy one's desire; *das sollst du -en*, you will suffer for that. **-er,** *m.* penitent; *Lücken--er*, stopgap. **-ung,** *f.* penance, atonement, expiation.

Busserl, *n.* (-s, –) (*dial.*) kiss. (*dial.*) **-n,** *v.a.* kiss.

Bussole, *f.* (-n) magnetic compass.

Büste, *f.* (-en) bust. **-nhalter,** *m.* brassière.

butt, I. *adj.* (*dial.*) short and thick, stubby, stumpy; blunt; 2. *m.* (-(e)s, -e) flounder (*Pleuronectes flesus*) (*Icht.*). **-e,** *f.* (-n) berry, fruit; (*espec.*) *Hage-e*, rose hip.

Bütt-e, *also* **Butt-e,** *f.* (-en) tub, vat; wooden vessel; basket for carrying on the back; (*coll.*) *Hand von der -e*, hands off! let well alone! **-enpapier,** *n.* hand-made paper. **-enrand,** *m.* deckle-edge (*Paper*). **-ner,** *m.* cooper.

Büttel, *m.* (-s, –) beadle; bailiff; jailer. **-ei,** *f.* jail, jailer's house.

Butter, *f.* butter; (*coll.*) *es ist alles in –*, everything is shipshape *or* fine and dandy; (*coll.*) *ihm ist wohl die – vom Brote gefallen*, he has no more pleasure (in a th.), he has been sadly disillusioned; (*coll.*) *sich* (*Dat.*) *die – vom Brot nehmen lassen*, suffer o.s. to be fleeced; (*coll.*) *sich* (*Dat.*) *nicht die – vom Brot nehmen lassen*, look after one's own interests; *gesalzene –*, salt butter; *– schlagen*, churn butter. **-blume,** *f.* buttercup, ranunculus; marigold. **-brot,** *n.* (slice of) bread and butter; *belegtes -brot*, sandwich; *-brot mit Schinken*, ham-sandwich. **-brotpapier,** *n.* grease-proof paper. **-brühe,** *f.* melted butter, butter sauce. **-büchse,** *f.*, **-dose,** *f.* butter-dish. **-faß,** *n.* churn. **-glocke,** *f.* butter-cooler. **-milch,** *f.* buttermilk. **-n,** *v.a.* butter, spread with butter; churn, turn to butter. **-säure,** *f.* butyric acid (*Chem.*). **-teig,** *m.* short pastry. **-weck,** *m.* buttered roll.

[1]**Butz,** *m.* (-en, -en), **-en,** *m.* (-ens, -en) core (*of fruit*; *of a tumour*); blister (*in glass*). **-enscheibe,** *f.* bull's-eye glass, glass-roundel. **-enscheibenromantik,** *f.* pseudo-Gothic style. **-kopf,** *m.* (*also* **Buttskopf**) (-(e)s, ¨-e) grampus (*Orcinus orca*); (*coll.*) *da steckt der -en*, there's the rub!

[2]**Butz,** *m.* (-es, -e) blow, thud, fall; bogy, bogey, goblin, bogy man. **-e(n)mann,** *m.* (-s, ¨-er) bogy man.

Buxe, Büx(e), *f.* (-(e)n) (*dial.*, *coll.*) trousers. **-n,** *v.a.* pilfer, slip into one's pocket.

C

Except in the ligatures *ch* and *ck* and *sch* this is not a genuine German letter, and occurs only in foreign borrowings. Before the vowels *a*, *o*, and *u* it is now normally replaced by *k*, and before the vowels *ä*, *e*, *i*, and *y* by *z*. Words not found below should be sought under *K*, *Sch*, or *Z*.

C, c, *n.* C, c; key of C (*Mus.*); *C-dur* (*moll*), (the key of) C major (minor); do (*first note of octave*). *C-Schlüssel*, C clef, bass clef.

Café [*pron.* ka'fe] *n.* (-s, -s) café, coffee house, tea-room; *see* **Kaffee.**

Causerie [*pron.* kozə'ri:] *f.* (-n) discussion, chat.

Celesta [*pron.* tʃ] *f.* (-stas & -sten) celeste (*Mus.*).

Cell-o [*pron.* tʃ] *n.* (-os, -os *or* -i) violoncello. **-ist,** *m.* (-en, -en) violoncello player, (violon)cellist.

Cembalo [*pron.* tʃ] *n.* (-s, -s) harpsichord.

Ces [*pron.* ts] *n.* C flat (*Mus.*).

Chagrin [*pron.* ʃa'grɛ̃] I. *m.* (-s, -s) chagrin, mortification. 2. *n.* (-s) shagreen.

Chaiselongue [*pron.* ʃ] *f.* (-s or -n) couch, deck-chair.

Chamäleon [*pron.* k] *n.* (-s, -s) chameleon.

Champagner [*pron.* ʃam'panjər] *m.* (-s) champagne (*wine*), (*coll.*) bubbly; *deutscher –*, sparkling hock or moselle; *herber –*, dry champagne; *stark moussierender –*, sparkling champagne; *– in Eis*, iced champagne. **-bowle,** *f.* champagne-cup.

Champignon [*pron.* ʃ] *m.* (-s, -s) mushroom (*Psalliota*). **-sauce,** *f.* mushroom ketchup.

Chance [*pron.* 'ʃɑ̃:sə] *f.* (-en) (*coll.*) prospect, outlook.

Cha-os [*pron.* k] *n.* chaos. **-otisch,** *adj.* chaotic.

Charakter [*pron.* k] *m.* (-s, -e) character, disposition; nature; title, dignity; type, letter, print (*Typ.*); part (*Theat.*); will-power. **-bild,** *n.* character sketch. **-fest,** *adj.* of strong character; of high moral worth, steadfast, reliable. **-isieren,** *v.a.* characterize; distinguish. **-istik,** *f.* (-en) character sketch, characterization. **-istikum,** *n.*, *see* **-zug. -istisch,** *adj.* characteristic. **-los,** *adj.* of weak character, unprincipled, fickle; nondescript, without character; *-loses Gesicht*, face without character. **-schilderung,** *f.* characterization. **-voll,** *adj.*, *see* **-fest. -zug,** *m.* characteristic, trait.

Charg-e [*pron.* 'ʃarʒə] *f.* (-n) appointment, rank; charge, batch, lot (*Tech.*); *die -n*, non-commissioned officers; the officers of a student association; *die höchsten Hof-n*, the highest court officials. **-ieren,** I. *v.n.* be represented, send representatives (*of student corporations*). 2. *v.a.* charge, stoke (*a furnace*), load (*fire-arms*). **-ierte(r),** *m.* office bearer (*of students' corporation*). **-ierung,** *f.* charge, loading (*of a firearm, etc*).

Charivari [*pron.* ʃ] *m.* or *n.* din, caterwauling.

Chassis [*pron.* ʃa'si:] *n.* (–, –) [*gen.* & *pl. pron.* ʃa'si:s] chassis (*Motor*).

Chauff-eur [*pron.* ʃɔ'fø:r] *m.* (-s, -e) chauffeur, driver (*of a car*). **-ieren,** *v.a.* & *n.* drive (*a motor-car*).

Chauss-ee [*pron.* ʃɔ'se:] *f.* (-n) main road, thoroughfare, highway. **-eebau,** *m.* road-making, road repairs. **-eegraben,** *m.* roadside ditch. **-eewärter,** *m.* road-mender. **-ieren,** *v.a.* macadamize (*road*).

Chef [*pron.* ʃɛf] *m.* (-s, -s) chief, principal, head, manager, (*coll.*) boss; commander (*Mil.*, *Naut.*); *– des Generalstabs*, Chief of General Staff. **-arzt,** *m.* medical superintendent (*in hospital*), senior medical officer (*Mil.*). **-redakteur,** *m.* editor-in-chief.

Chem-ie [*pron.* ç; in South Germany and Austria, k] *f.* chemistry; *angewandte -ie*, applied chemistry. **-ikalien,** *n.pl.* chemicals. **-ikalisch,** *adj.* chemical. **-iker,** *m.* (-s, -), chemist; student *or* teacher of chemistry. **-isch,** *adj.* chemical; *-ische Präparate*, chemicals. *-ische Reinigung* or *Wäsche*, dry-cleaning.

Cherub [*pron.* ç] *m.* (-s, -inen & -im) cherub. **-inisch,** *adj.* cherubic.

Chiff-re [*pron.* 'ʃifər] *f.*, **-er,** *f.* (-n) cipher, code; cryptography. **-reschlüssel, -ernschlüssel,** *m.* cipher-code. **-rieren,** *v.a.* code, (en)cipher.

Chin-a [*pron.* ç] I. *n. See list of Geographical Names.* 2. *f.* Cinchona. **-arinde,** *f.* Peruvian bark, cinchona bark. **-awurzel,** *f.* china-root. **-in,** *n.* quinine; *-in und Ammoniak*, ammoniated quinine.

Chir-omant [*pron.* ç] *m.* (-en, -en) palmist, hand-

reader. **-omantie,** *f.* palmistry, chiromancy **-urg.** *m.* (-en, -en) surgeon. **-urgie,** *f.* surgery. **-urgisch,** *adj.* surgical.
Chlor [*pron.* k] *n.* chlorine. **-ammonium,** *n.* salammoniac, ammonium chloride. **-en,** *v.a.* chlorinate. **-haltig,** *adj.* containing chlorine. **-id,** *n.* (-(e)s, -e) chloride; *-igsaures Salz,* chlorite. **-ieren,** *see* **-en. -kalk,** *m.* chloride of lime, bleaching powder. **-kalzium,** *n.* calcium chloride. **-kohlenoxyd,** *n.* phosgene gas (*Mil.*), carbonyl chloride. **-natrium,** *n.* sodium chloride, common salt. **-oform,** *n.* chloroform. **-oformieren,** *v.a.* chloroform. **-ophyll,** *n.* chlorophyll (*Bot.*). **-räucherung,** *f.* chlorine fumigation.
Choler-a [*pron.* k] *f.* cholera. **-isch,** *adj.* choleric; irascible, hot-tempered.
Chor [*pron.* k] 1. *m.* (-s, ⸚e) choir; chorus. 2. *n.* & *m.* (-s, -e & ⸚e) (*Arch.*) choir, chancel; (*coll.*) pack, throng (*partic. of rowdy children*); *Männer–,* male chorus; *gemischter –,* mixed *or* full chorus; *im – singen,* sing in chorus; (*Poet.*) *das – der Vögel,* the feathered tribe. **-al,** *m.* (-als, -äle) chorale, anthem, hymn. **-bischof,** *m.* suffragan bishop. **-direktor,** *m.* conductor of the chorus; choir-master. **-führer,** *m.* first chorister (*Eccl.*); choragus (*Anc. Theat.*). **-gang,** *m.* aisle. **-gehilfe,** *m.* acolyte. **-gesang,** *m.* chorus; choral singing; anthem; *einstimmiger -gesang,* plain chant, Gregorian chant. **-hemd,** *n.* surplice. **-herr,** *m.* canon, prebendary. **-ist,** *m.* (-en, -en) member of the chorus (*opera, etc.*). **-istin,** *f.* chorus-girl. **-knabe,** *m.* choir-boy, chorister. **-leiter,** *m.* leading *or* first chorister. **-nische,** *f.* apse. **-nonne,** *f.* officiating nun. **-pult,** *n.* lectern. **-rock,** *m.* surplice, cope. **-sänger,** *m.* chorister. **-stuhl,** *m.* choir stall. **-weise,** *adv.* in chorus, tutti.
Chrie [*pron.* ç] *f.* (-n) (school) theme; essay composed according to definite rules (*Rhet.*).
Christ [*pron.* k] *m.* (-en, -en) Christian; *der Heilige –,* Christmas. **-abend,** *m.* Christmas Eve. **-baum,** *m.* Christmas tree. **-dorn,** *m.* holly (*Ilex aquafolium*) (*Bot.*). **-enheit,** *f.* Christendom. **-entum,** *n.* Christianity. **-fest,** *n.* Christmas. **-kind,** *n.* Christ child, baby Jesus. **-lich,** *adj.* Christian; (*sl.*) honest-to-God. **-mette,** *f.* carol service. **-monat, -mond,** *m.* December. **-nacht,** *f.* night before Christmas.
Chrom [*pron.* k] *n.* chromium, chrome, **-atik,** *f.* chromatics, science of colours. **-atisch,** *adj.* chromatic; *-atische Tonleiter,* chromatic scale. **-gelb,** *adj.* & *n.* chrome-yellow, chromate of lead. **-sauer,** *adj.* chromate of; *-saures Salz,* chromate. **-stahl,** *m.* chrome *or* chromium steel (*Metall.*).
Chron-ik [*pron.* k] *f.* (-en) chronicle. **-ika,** *f.* (*B.*) *Bücher der -ika,* Chronicles. **-ikenschreiber,** *m.* chronicler. **-isch,** *adj.* chronic. **-ist,** *m.* (-en, -en) chronicler. **-ologie,** *f.* chronology. **-ologisch,** *adj.* chronological. **-ometer,** *n.* chronometer.
Chrysalide [*pron.* ç] *f.* (-n) chrysalis (*Ent.*).
Cis [*pron.* tsis] *n.* C sharp (*Mus.*).
Clique [*pron.* kli:kə] *f.* (-n) clique, set, coterie.
Couleur [*pron.* kuˈlør] *f.* (-en) (shade of) **colour**; a uniformed students' association; (*coll.*) *das ist dieselbe – in Grün,* that is as near as makes no difference. **-bruder,** *m.* fellow-member of a *Korps* (*q.v.*). **-student,** *m.* student belonging to a uniformed association.
Coupé [*pron.* ku:ˈpe] *n.* (-s, -s) (railway) compartment; carriage.
Cour [*pron.* ku:r] *f.*; *einem Mädchen die – machen* or *schneiden,* court a girl; *eine – halten,* hold a levée. **-fähig,** *adj.* privileged to appear at court. **-macher,** *m.*, **-schneider,** *m.* ladies' man; suitor, admirer.
Courtage [*pron.* kurˈta:ʒə] *f.* (*C.L.*) brokerage.
Cousin [*pron.* ku:ˈzɛ̃] *m.* (-s, -s) (male) cousin. **-e,** *f.* (-en) (female) cousin; *see* **Kusine.**
Creme [*pron.* krɛ:m] *f.* custard; cream (*as in cream chocolates*); cream, paste (*as shoe-cream, hair-cream, tooth-paste, etc.*); *see* **Krem.**
Crin [*pron.* kræ̃] *m.* (-, -s) horsehair.
Curette [*pron.* kyˈrɛt] *f.* curette, scraper (*Surg.*).
Curiosum [*pron.* k] *n.* oddity, curiosity.

D

D, d, *n.* D, d; Re, D (*Mus.*); *D dur,* D major; *D moll,* D minor. **-schieber,** *m.* D-valve (*in steam-engines*). **-Zug,** *m.* through *or* express train.
da, 1. *adv.* 1. there; here; *hier und –,* here and there; now and then; *– ist sein Zimmer,* there is his room; *– bin ich,* here I am; *wer – ?* who goes there? (*Mil.*); *der –,* that *or* this man; *du – !* you there! *– draußen,* out there; *– droben* (or *drunten*), up (*or* down) there; *– herum,* round about here; *von – ging er nach Hause,* from there he went home; *– und dort,* here and there; *wieder –,* here again, back once more; *– sein,* be present, existent, on the spot *or* at hand; *ist schon Post für mich – ?* are there any letters for me yet? (*coll.*) *wenn noch etwas – ist,* if there is anything left *or* over; *für mich ist das gar nicht –,* for me it is non-existent; *-bleiben,* stay; 2. (*Poet.*) where; *ein Ort, – mich niemand kennt,* a place where I am unknown; 3. then, at that time; *– lachte er,* then he laughed; *wenn ich – noch lebe,* if I am still alive then; *ja, – wird man aber fragen,* true, but then people will ask; *– war es zu spät,* by that time it was too late; *von – an* or *ab war er ganz anders,* thenceforth *or* from that time *or* from then onwards he was quite different; 4. (*Poet.*) when; *zu einer Zeit, – alles sich regte,* at a time when all were stirring. **2.** *part.* 1. *generalizing,* -ever, -soever, *or merely emphatic*; *was – kommt,* whatever comes; *es lache, wer – will,* whoever likes may laugh; 2. *after rel. prons.* der, die, das, *to bring out the relative sense*; *alle, die – kamen,* all who came. **3.** (*emphasis on prep.*) *forming a compound with preps., instead of a Dat. or Acc. sing. or pl. pers. or demonst. pron., used with regard to things, but not persons*; *es bleibt -bei,* it remains fixed *or* unchanged, it is settled, there the matter rests; *du erreichst -durch deinen Zweck,* in this way you will achieve your purpose; *ich bin -für,* I'm in favour (of it); *ich habe nichts -gegen,* I haven't anything against it, I have no objection; *-mit wird er nichts ausrichten,* he will achieve nothing by these means; *richte dich -nach,* guide yourself accordingly; *ich wohne gleich -neben,* I live adjoining *or* next door. (*When the preposition begins with a vowel,* r *is interpolated*); *es ist nichts Wahres -ran,* there is no truth in it; *nimm vom Tische alles was -rauf steht,* take everything that is on the table; *er wird nicht klug -raus,* he can't make head or tail of it; *da ist nichts mehr -rin,* there's nothing left in it; *ich kann -rüber nichts sagen,* I have nothing to say about this; *ich würde viel -rum geben wenn . . .,* I would give a great deal if . . .; *-runter kann ich es nicht geben,* I can't give it for less; *dies ist das beste -runter,* this is the best among *or* of them; *er hörte nichts -von,* he heard nothing of it; *er hat mich -vor gewarnt,* he has warned me about, against *or* of it; *ich habe nichts -wider,* I haven't anything against it, I have no objection; *dies kommt noch -zu,* there's this in addition. **4.** *conj.* since, because, inasmuch as; while, whilst; although; *– nun, – doch,* since, since indeed; *– sonst,* whereas; *– hingegen,* while on the other hand *or* on the contrary, whereas; *– sie eine Engländerin ist, muß sie die englische Sprache verstehen,* as she is an Englishwoman she must understand English; *– der Kaiser einsah, daß,* the emperor perceiving that. **-bleiben,** *v.n.* (*sep.*) (*aux.* s.) stay there; be kept in (*at school*). **-sein,** 1. *v.n.* exist, be there; *das ist noch nie -gewesen,* tnat has never existed *or* been done before, is unprecedented; 2. *n.*, *see* **Dasein. -stehen,** *v.n* (*sep.*) be there, stand there; stand forth; *einzig -stehend,* unrivalled, unique.
dabei, *adv.*, *see* **da, 3;** thereby, hereat, therewith, by that, by it, with it, with them; at that place, near, close by; at the same time, in doing so; besides, moreover; in view of it, considering; but, yet, nevertheless, withal; *er ist gescheit und – fleißig,* he is clever and industrious besides; *– sagte er auch,* moreover he said; *– sah er mich an,* with that he looked at me; *ich habe mir nichts Böses – gedacht.* I meant no harm by it; *– bleiben,* persist in, insist

on; – *sein*, be present, take part in; be on the point of; *ich bin* –, I've no objection, I am with you; – *stehen*, stand by *or* near; *die –stehenden*, the bystanders.

Dach, *n.* (-es, ⸚er) roof; shelter, cover; house; dome (*of an engine-boiler*); upper stratum (*Min.*); ceiling (*Av.*); (*coll.*) *eins aufs – bekommen* or *kriegen*, get a dressing down, suffer a hard blow; (*coll.*) *einem aufs –steigen*, blow a p. up, come down upon a p., give s.o. a piece of one's mind; (*Prov.*) *ein Sperling in der Hand ist besser als eine Taube auf dem* –, a bird in the hand is worth two in the bush; *bei ihm ist gleich Feuer im –e*, he is very hot-headed; *ohne* –, houseless; *unter – und Fach*, safely under cover, in safety; (*of a project*) well under way. **-balken,** *m.* rafter, beam; **-blech,** *n.* metal roofing-sheet; girder. **-boden,** *m.* loft, attic. **-decker,** *m.* slater, tiler, thatcher. **-en,** *v.a.* roof. **-fahne,** *f.* weathercock. **-fenster,** *n.* garret window, attic window, dormer window, skylight. **-first,** *m.* (*or dial. f.*) ridge (*of a roof*). **-gesellschaft,** *f.* head firm (*of a combine*), holding company. **-gesperre,** *n.* rafters. **-haut,** *f.* roofing, roof covering. **-kammer,** *f.*, garret, attic. **-luke,** *f.* garret *or* dormer window, scuttle; turret (*Av.*). **-pappe,** *f.* roofing felt. **-reiter,** *m.* ridge, turret (*Arch.*). **-rinne,** *f.* gutter. **-röhre,** *f.* spouting, gutter-pipe, down-pipe. **-schiefer,** *m.*, **-stein,** *m.* roofing slate. **-sparren,** *m.* rafter. **-stroh,** *n.* thatch. **-stube,** *f.*, *see* **-kammer.** **-stuhl,** *m.* woodwork *or* framework of a roof, roof truss, rafters. **-traufe,** *f.* eaves; droppings from the eaves. **-ung,** *f.* roofing. **-wächter,** *m.* roof-spotter. **-werk,** *n.* roofing. **-ziegel,** *m.* tile.

Dachs, *m.* (-es, -e) badger; (*coll.*) *frecher* –, cheeky puppy (*fig.*). **-bau,** *m.* badger's sett *or* earth. **-eisen,** *n.*, **-falle,** *f.* badger-trap. **-hund,** *m.* badger-dog, dachshund.

dachte, dächte, *see* **denken.**

Dachtel, *f.* (*coll.*) box on the ear.

Dackel, *m.* (-s, -) (*coll.*) *see* **Dachshund.**

dadurch, *adv.* thereby, by this means, in that way. *see* **da, 3**; – *daß er es tat*, by doing so.

dafern, *conj.* (*Law, C.L.*) if, in case that, provided.

dafür, *adv.* on behalf of it; in return for *or* instead of it; *see* **da, 3**; *ich kann nichts* –, I can't help it, it's not my fault; *ich stehe Ihnen* – or *ich bin dir gut* –, I will be answerable to you for it, I'll guarantee it; *teurer, – aber auch besser*, dearer, but correspondingly better; – *daß* for the fact that. **-halten,** 1. *v.n.* (*sep.*) hold as an opinion. 2. *n.* opinion, judgement; *nach meinem –halten, meines –haltens*, in my opinion.

dagegen, 1. *adv.* in comparison with; in return *or* exchange for it; on the contrary, on the other hand; *see* **da, 3.** 2. *conj.* on the contrary, on the other hand; but then; *das ist wahr, – läßt sich nicht leugnen*, that is true, on the other hand it cannot be denied. **-halten,** *v.a.* (*sep.*) reproach; reply.

daheim, *adv.* at home; in one's own country.

daher, 1. *adv.* thence, from that place, from there. 2. *conj.* thus, so, hence, for that reason, therefore, accordingly; – *kommt es, daß*, hence it happens that. 3. *sep. prefix with verbs of motion* = along; away. **-schlendern,** *v.n.* (*sep.*) (*aux.* s.) come strolling along.

daherum, *adv.* thereabouts.

dahin, *adv.* thither; to that place, time *or* state; (*used with verbs as sep. prefix* =) away, along; gone, past, lost; *er äußerte sich* –, he spoke to this effect; *bis* –, up to that time, till then; *sein Bestreben geht – daß . . .*, his efforts are bent on . . .; *diese Dinge gehören nicht* –, these things have no bearing on the subject; *meine Meinung geht* –, my opinion is; *mein Glück ist* –, my good fortune is past; *seine Seele ist* –, his soul has departed. **-ab,** *adv.* down there. **-auf,** *adv.* up there. **-aus,** *adv.* out there; *will er –aus?* is that what he is driving at? **-bringen,** *ir.v.a.* carry to a place; bring to a certain point, manage to, contrive to, succeed in (*doing s.th.*); persuade, induce, prevail upon (*persons*); – *habe ich es nie bringen können*, I could never bring it to that. **-ein,** *adv.* in there. **-gegen,** *adv.* on the other hand, on the contrary **-gehen,** pass (*of time*); *er ist –gegangen*, he has died *or* passed on. **-scheiden,** *ir.v.n.* depart this world; *der –geschiedene*, the (dear) departed, the deceased. **-stehen,** *ir.v.n.* be uncertain; *es steht* –, that remains to be seen *or* is still undecided. **-stellen,** *v.a.* *es* or *etwas –gestellt sein lassen*, leave a th. undecided *or* uncertain, offer no opinion on a subject; *es bleibt –gestellt*, it remains undecided, (*coll.*) it has been shelved. **-unter,** *adv.* under there, underneath.

dahin-ten, *adv.* behind, at the back; *ich sehe ihn –ten*, I can see him behind there. **-ter,** *adv.* behind (s.th.), there behind; *es ist –ter gefallen*, it has fallen down behind; *viel Worte und wenig –ter*, much talk and little sense; *er ist –ter her*, he is after it, he takes trouble over it. **-terkommen,** *v.n.* (*aux.* s.) (*sep.*) discover, find out, (*fig.*) get at *or* to the bottom of; **-terstecken,** *v.n.* (*aux.* h.) (*sep.*) be at the bottom of (*fig.*); *es steckt etwas –ter*, there is more there than meets the eye; *es ist* or *steckt nichts –ter*, there is nothing in it.

Dakapo, *n.* (-s, -s) repeat, encore; *–rufen, –verlangen*, call for an encore.

Dalles, *m.* (*coll. Yiddish*) poverty, misfortune; *im – sein, den – haben, an – leiden*, be hard up, be broke.

dalli, *int.* (*dial.*) quick!

Dam-bock, *m.* **-hirsch,** *m.* fallow buck, fallow deer. **-geiß,** *f.*, **-kuh,** *f.* fallow doe. **-kitz,** *m.*, **-kitze,** *f.*, fawn. **-spiel,** *see* **Damenspiel.** **-wild,** *n.* fallow deer.

damal-ig, *adj. & adv.* then, of that time; *die –ige Königin*, the then reigning queen. **-s,** *adv.* then, in those days, at that time.

Damast, *m.* (-es, -e) damask. **-en,** *adj.* damask.

Damasz-ener, 1. *indec. adj.* Damascene. 2. *m.* inhabitant of Damascus. **-enerrose,** *f.* damask rose. **-enerklinge,** *f.* Damascus blade. **-enerpflaume,** *f.* damson. **-ieren,** *v.a.* damask; damascene (*steel, etc.*).

Dame, *f.* (-n) lady; partner (*at a dance*); queen (*at cards & chess*); king (*at draughts*); draughts; (*coll.*) *seine alte* –, his mother; *in die – kommen* or *gehen, eine – machen*, get a king (*at draughts*); *sich eine – machen*, take the queen (*at chess*); *wollen wir eine Partie – spielen* or *ziehen?* shall we have a game at draughts? **-nabteil,** *n. & m.* ladies' compartment, 'for ladies (only)'. **-nbinde,** *f.* sanitary towel. **-nbrett,** *n.* draught-board. **-nfriede,** *m.* treaty of Cambray (*1529*). **-nheld,** *m.* lady-killer; ladies' man. **-npferd,** *n.* lady's horse, palfrey. **-nreitkleid,** *n.* riding-habit. **-nsattel,** *m.* side-saddle. **-nspiel,** *n.* draughts. **-nstein,** *m.* piece (*at draughts*). **-nwahl,** *f.* ladies' choice (*at a dance*). **-nwelt,** *f.* the ladies, the fair sex.

Däm-el, *m.* (-s, –), **-(e)lack,** *m.* (-s, -s) (*coll.*) fathead, fool. **-isch** (*also dial.* **damisch**), **-lich,** *adj.* dull, silly, stupid, foolish. **-lichkeit,** *f.* dullness, silliness, stupidity.

damit, 1. *adv.* therewith, *see* **da, 3,** *es ist aus* –, there's an end of *or* to it; *heraus* –, out with it! (*news*), (*coll.*) fork out! (*money*); *es ist nichts* –, that is no use, (*coll.*) that's no go; *was soll ich* –, what use is that to me? what good is that? 2. *conj.* in order that, that, so that, to; – *nicht*, lest, in order that . . . not, for fear that; – *ich es kurz mache*, in order to be brief; *ich sage es dir nochmals, – du es nicht vergißt.* I repeat it so that you may not forget (it).

Damm, *m.* (-es, ⸚e) dam; dike, dyke; embankment, bank, mole, pier, causeway; perineum (*Anat.*); (*coll.*) *auf den – bringen*, set up, put on one's feet; (*coll.*) *auf dem – sein*, feel up to it *or* things, be in the pink, be O.K. **-bruch,** *m.* breach in a dyke; rupture of the perineum. **-erde,** *f.* mould, humus, surface soil. **-weg,** *m.* causeway.

dämmen, *v.a.* dam (up *or* off); restrain, check, stop, curb.

Dämmer, *m.* dusk, twilight. **-haft,** *adj.*, **-ig,** *adj.* dim, dusky. **-licht,** *n.* twilight. **-n,** *v.n.* (*aux.* h.) dawn, grow light; grow *or* get dark; (*fig.*) dawn on; *vor sich hin –n*, be semi-conscious; *–nde Hoffnung*, gleam of hope. **-schein,** *m.* twilight. **-ung,** *f.* dusk, twilight; dawn. **-ungsfalter,** *m.*, **-ungsschmetterling,** **-ungsvogel,** *m.* hawkmoth. **-zustand,** *m.* semi-consciousness.

Dämon, *m.* (-s, -en) demon. **-isch,** *adj.* demoniac(al); irresistible, overpowering.

Dampf, *m.* (-es, ⸚e) vapour, steam; mist; smoke; (*pl.*) fumes; *das Pferd hat den –*, the horse is broken-winded. **-artig,** *adj.* vaporous. **-bad,** *n.* vapour bath, Turkish bath; fomentation. **-boot,** *n.* steamer, steamboat. **-druck,** *m.* steam pressure. **-er,** *m., see* **-boot.** **-en,** *v.n. & a.* (*aux.* h.) steam, smoke; give off smoke *or* steam *or* fumes; reek; evaporate. **-erzeuger,** *m.* steam-generator. **-esse,** *f.* steam-pipe *or* conduit. **-ig,** *adj.* steamy. **-kessel** *m.* boiler (*Mech.*); steamer (*Cook.*). **-klappe,** *f.* steam-valve. **-kolben,** *m.* piston. **-kolbenstange,** *f.* piston-rod. **-kraft,** *f.* steam power. **-küche,** *f.* steam-kitchen; steam cooking. **-kur,** *f.* course of vapour baths. **-maschine,** *f.* steam-engine. **-messer,** *m.* pressure-gauge, manometer. **-nudeln,** *f.pl.* (s.th. like) vermicelli, noodles. **-pfeife,** *f.* whistle, hooter. **-roß,** *n.* locomotive. **-schiff,** *n.* steamboat, steamer. **-schiffahrt,** *f.* steamboat service. **-schiffahrtsgesellschaft,** *f.* steamship line. **-schiffahrtsverbindung,** *f.* steamer connexion. **-strahl,** *m.* steam jet. **-topf,** *m.* pressure cooker, autoclave. **-ventil,** *n.* steam-valve. **-walze,** *f.* steam-roller. **-wärme,** *f.* heat of vaporization. **-wäscherei,** *f.* steam-laundry.

dämpf-en, *v.a.* damp, smother, suffocate; smooth; attenuate (*Rad., Elec.*); quench, extinguish; deaden (*sound*); soften (*colour*); muffle (*drums*); mute (*a violin*); suppress, quell, depress, subdue; steam (*Cook.*); *mit gedämpfter Stimme*, under o.'s breath, in an undertone. **-er,** *m.* extinguisher, silencer, damper (*in steam-engines*); mute (*on violins*); baffle (*of a loudspeaker*); steam-cooker, pressure cooker; (*fig.*) (*einer S.*) *einen -er aufsetzen*, put a damper (on a th.), tone down, check. **-ig,** *adj.* asthmatic; short-winded. **-pfanne,** *f.* stewing-pan. **-ung,** *f.* quenching, damping, suppression, subduing; smoothing, attenuation (*Rad., Elec.*); steaming. **-ungskreis,** *m.* damping-circuit (*Rad.*).

danach, *adv.* afterwards, thereupon, thereafter; accordingly, according to that; *see* **da, 3;** *es sieht ganz – aus*, it looks very much like it; *er fragt nicht –*, he does not mind *or* care; *seine Kräfte sind nicht –*, his strength is not equal to it; *sehen Sie –!* look to it! *dies ist billig und ist auch –*, the price is low and the quality correspondingly poor; *er wird – handeln*, he will act accordingly.

daneben, 1. *adv.* close by, beside. 2. *conj.* moreover, besides, at the same time, also. *see* **da, 3.** **-gehen,** *v.n.* (*sep.*) go amiss, miss the mark. **-gießen,** *v.a.* spill. **-hauen,** *v.n.* (*sep.*) (*aux.* h.) (*coll.*) bungle, miss fire, be on the wrong scent.

dang, dänge, *see* **dingen.**

danieder, (*also* **darnieder**) *adv.* on the ground; down. **-liegen,** *ir.v.n.* (*sep.*) succumb, perish; be ruined *or* subdued; languish; degenerate; be laid up *or* confined to one's bed.

Dank, 1. *m.* thanks *or* gratitude, reward; recompense; prize; *– abstatten*, see *– sagen*; *mit – annehmen*, accept with gratitude; *einem seinen herzlichsten – aussprechen*, express one's warmest thanks; *Gott sei –!* thank God!; *es (einem) zu -e machen*, give a p. satisfaction; *– vom Haus Österreich*, ingratitude (*i.e. a Hapsburg's gratitude*); *– sagen*, return thanks, thank; *schönen –!* many thanks!; *schlechten – mit etwas verdienen*, be paid with ingratitude for a th.; *Sie würden mich zu – verpflichten, wenn Sie*, you would much oblige me by; *vielen –!* see *schönen –! einem für eine S. – wissen*, be thankful (grateful, obliged) to a p. for a th. 2. *prep.* (*with gen.*) thanks to, owing to; **-adresse,** *f.* vote of thanks. **-bar,** *adj.* grateful, thankful, obliged (*Dat.*, to); profitable, advantageous. **-barkeit,** *f.* gratitude; *zur -barkeit verpflichtet*, bound in gratitude. **-bezeigung,** *f.* proof of gratefulness. **-e!** *int.* thanks! thank you! no thank you! *-e schön!* thank you very much! (*refusal*). **-en,** 1. *v.n.* (*aux.* h.) (*Dat.*) thank, return thanks; *er läßt -en*, he sends his thanks. 2. *v.a.* owe (*s.th. to a p.*), be indebted (*to a p.*) for; decline an offer; *dir danke ich mein Leben*, to you I owe my life; (*C.L.*) *-end erhalten*, received with thanks, paid, settled. **-enswert,** *adj.* deserving of thanks. **-fest,** *n.* thanksgiving festival. **-gottesdienst,** *m.* thanksgiving service; Te Deum (*R.C.*) **-lied,** *n.* hymn of thanksgiving. **-opfer,** *n.* thank-offering. **-predigt,** *f.* thanksgiving sermon. **-rede,** *f.* speech in returning thanks, thanks. **-sagung,** *f.* returning *or* giving thanks, acknowledgement; thanksgiving (*Eccl.*).

dann, *adv.* then, at that time; thereupon; *– und wann*, now and then, occasionally, sometimes; *erst wägen, – wagen*, first ponder then venture, look before you leap; *– erst* or *erst –*, only then, not till then; *selbst –*, even then; *selbst –, wenn er käme*, even in case he should come. **-en,** *adv.*; *von -en*, from that place, thence.

daran, dran, *adv.* thereon, thereat, thereby; *see* **da, 3;** *– ist nicht zu denken*, that cannot be considered; *– glauben*, believe in it; (*coll.*) *– glauben müssen*, have to die; *was liegt –?* what does it matter? *mir ist nichts – gelegen*, it is a matter of indifference to me, it's all one to me; *nahe –*, close by, close to; on the eve of, on the point of; *er war nahe – sein Leben zu verlieren*, he was near losing his life; *ich weiß nicht wie ich – bin*, I don't know what my position *or* task is; *jetzt bin ich –*, now it is my turn; *– sein*, be in for it, be held responsible; *er ist eifrig –*, he is hard at it; *gut (wohl) bei einem – sein*, be in favour with a p., be well off *or* in a good position; *es ist nichts –*, there is nothing in it (*or coll.* to it), it is good for nothing; *übel (schlimm) – sein*, be badly off, be in a bad position; *er tut gut –*, he makes a good job of it, he does it well; *er will nicht gern –*, he does not like the business, he doesn't want to have anything to do with it; *ich zweifle – ob*, I doubt whether. **-gehen,** *v.n.* set to work, set about. **-liegend,** *adj.* adjacent. **-setzen,** *v.a.* risk, stake, venture.

darauf, drauf, *adv.* thereon, thereupon; afterwards, then, next; *see* **da, 3;** *– geht er eben aus*, that is just what he is aiming at, that's just what he is out to do; *– kommt es an*, that's the main point; *besinn dich doch –*, call it to mind, try and recall it; *er besteht –*, he insists on it; *er dringt –*, he insists on it; *er will sich nicht – einlassen*, he won't venture upon it; *ich bin – gefaßt*, I am prepared for it; *etwas – geben*, credit, attach importance to; *gerade – zu*, straight towards; *gleich –*, directly afterwards; *er hält sehr –*, he lays stress upon that; *– will er eben hinaus*, that's just what he's aiming at; *– kommen*, come to speak of, call to mind; *wie kommen Sie –?* what put that idea into your head? how did you hit on that? *ich wollte – schwören*, I would take my oath on it; *es steht der Kopf –*, it is a capital offence; *Sie können sich – verlassen, daß*, you may rest assured that, you may rely *or* depend on; *am Tage –*, on the following day; *den Tag –*, the next day; *eine Woche –*, a week later; *for compounds see* **drauf.** **-folgend,** *adj.* following, ensuing, subsequent. **-hin,** *adv.* thereupon, on the strength of that.

daraus, draus, *adv.* therefrom; thence; hence; *see* **da, 3;** *– folgt*, hence it follows; *ich mache mir nichts –*, I do not care for it much, I'm not particularly keen on it; *was wird am Ende –?* what will come of it in the end? what will be the end of it? *es kann nichts – werden*, nothing can come of it; *– kann ich nicht klug werden*, I cannot make it out, that beats me.

darben, *v.n.* (*aux*, h.) starve, famish; be in want (*an einer S.*, of a th.); *einen – lassen*, starve a p., allow a p. to starve.

darbiet-en, *ir.v.a.* offer, present, hold out, tender. **-ung,** *f.* recital, entertainment, performance.

darbringen, *ir.v.a.* bring, offer, present, make (*a sacrifice, etc.*).

darein, drein, *adv.* therein, thereto, thereinto; *obendrein*, over and above; *sich – ergeben*, submit to; *sich – finden* or *fügen*, accommodate o.s. to a th. **-geben,** *v.a.* (*sep.*) give into the bargain. **-legen,** *v.r.* (*sep.*) meddle, interfere (*in*, with). **-reden,** *v.n.* (*sep.*) interrupt. **-schauen,** *v.n.* (*sep.*) look down upon. **-schicken,** *v.r.* (*sep.*), *see* **-finden.** **-schlagen,** *v.n.* (*sep.*) strike hard *or* at random. **-sehen,** *v.n.* (*sep.*), *see* **-schauen.** **-willigen,** *v.n.* consent (in, to).

darf, darfst, *see* **dürfen.**

Darg, *m.* (-s, -e) peat.
darin, drin, *adv.* therein, in there; in, within; *see* **da, 3**; *mit – begriffen,* included. **–nen** (*usually* **drinnen**), *adv.* there within, inside.
darleg–en, *v.a.* lay down; state, set forth, explain, expound, demonstrate, display, exhibit. **–ung,** *f.* statement, explanation, exposition.
Darleh(e)n, *n.* (-s, –) loan. **–skasse,** *f.* state loan-office.
Darleih–en, *n.* (-s, –) (*Swiss dial.*) loan. **–er,** *m.* lender. **–ung,** *f.* lendings.
Darm, *m.* (-(e)s, ⸚e) gut, intestine, bowel; skin (*of a sausage*); *blinder –, Blind–,* caecum; *dünner –, Dünn–,* small intestine; *der Grimm–, dicker –, Dick–,* colon; *gerader –, Mast–,* rectum. **–bein,** *n.* haunch-bone; ilium (*Anat.*). **–bewegung,** *f.* peristaltic movement *or* motion. **–bruch,** *m.* enterocele; hernia. **–drüse,** *f.* intestinal gland. **–entleerung,** *f.* evacuation of the intestines *or* bowels. **–entzündung,** *f.* enteritis. **–fäule,** *f.* dysentery. **–fell,** *n.* peritoneum. **–fieber,** *n.* gastric fever. **–gang,** *m.* intestinal tract. **–grimmen,** *n.* colic. **–haut,** *f.* intestinal membrane, peritoneum. **–kanal,** *m.* intestinal canal. **–knochen,** *m.*, see **–bein. –kot,** *m.* faeces. **–krankheit,** *f.* enteric. **–lehre,** *f.* enterology. **–saite,** *f.* catgut (*Mus.*). **–schleim,** *m.* mucus. **–schnitt,** *m.* enterotomy. **–spritze,** *f.* clyster-pipe. **–verschließung,** *f.*, **–verschlingung** *f.* stoppage of the bowels. **–würmer,** *m.pl.* ascarides, tapeworms.
darnach, *adv., see* **danach.**
darob, drob, *adv.* on that account.
Darr–e, *f.* (-en) kiln-drying; (*Vet.*) phthisis; roup (*in birds*). **–en,** *v.a.* kiln-dry; smelt (*copper*). **–ofen,** *m.* drying-kiln. **–sucht,** *f.* consumption (*of pets*). **–süchtig,** *adj.* consumptive.
darreich–en, *v.a.* offer, proffer, present, administer (*sacrament*). **–ung,** *f.* offering.
darstell–en, *v.a.* describe; state; represent; display, exhibit; present, produce (*theat.*); educe, prepare (*Chem.*); *sich –en,* present itself (*to the mind, etc.*); *unrichtig –en,* misrepresent. **–bar,** *adj.* presentable, portrayable, representable, educible. **–end,** *adj.* representative, representational. **–er,** *m.* actor. **–erin,** *f.* actress. **–ung,** *f.* exhibition; description; statement; representation; presentation; performance, production (*theat.*); recital; *Christi –ung im Tempel,* presentation of Christ. **–ungsgabe,** *f.* power of representing *or* describing. **–ungsweise,** *f.* manner of representation.
dartun, *ir.v.a.* prove, verify, demonstrate; set forth.
darüber, drüber, *adv.* thereon, on that point; over and above; besides; in the meantime; *see* **da, 3**; *– ist er gestorben,* he died in the meantime *or* while engaged on it; *eher –,* past it rather; *– geht nichts,* nothing surpasses that; *alles geht drunter und drüber,* everything is topsy-turvy; *– hinaus,* beyond that; *sich – (her) machen,* make for a th., fall upon a th.; *– ist er erhaben,* he is above that. **–gelagert,** *adj.* superimposed. **–liegen,** *v.n.* (*sep.*) lie on top of.
darum, drum, *adv.* thereabout; therefore, on that account, for that reason; *see* **da, 3**; *alles drum und dran,* everything connected with it; *es sei –!* let it be so! for all I care! *es ist mir nur – zu tun,* all that I ask *or* my only object is to *or* I am only concerned to; *es ist mir sehr – zu tun,* it is very important that I should. **–bringen,** *v.n.* (*sep.*) deprive (of). **–kommen,** *v.n.* (*sep.*) lose.
darunter, drunter, *adv.* there; less; *see* **da, 3**; *alles ging drunter und drüber,* all was topsy-turvy,
das, 1. *def. art.* the (*nom. & acc. neut. sing.*). 2. *dem. adj. & pron. & rel. pron.* this, that, it; which, that (*nom. & acc. neut. sing.*); *mein Haus und – meines Vaters,* my house and my father's; *– heißt* (abbr. *d.h.*), that is, i.e.; *– heißt doch die S. übertreiben,* but that means exaggerating the affair; *ich bin empört, und – mit Recht,* I am indignant, and indeed with justice. **–jenige, –selb(ig)e,** *see under* **der.**
Dasein, 1. *ir.v.n.* (*aux.* s.), *see* **da.** 2. *n.* presence; existence, life. **–sberechtigung,** *f.* right to exist; *gleichzeitiges –,* coexistence; *Kampf ums –,* struggle for existence.
daselbst, *adv.* there, in that very place.
daß, *conj.* that; *bis –,* till; *– doch,* if only, I wish, would it were that; *– nicht,* lest, for fear that; *– nur nicht,* provided that . . . not; *so –,* so that, so as. *er ist zu stolz als – er es annehmen möchte,* he is too proud to accept it; *für den Fall – ich sterbe,* in case of my death; *nicht – ich wüßte,* not that I know of.
dastehen, *v.n., see* **da.**
datier–en, *v.a.* date; *falsch –en,* misdate; *zurück–en,* antedate; *nach–en,* postdate. **–ung,** *f.* dating (*of a letter*).
Dat–iv, *m.* (-ivs, -ive) dative (*case*). **–o,** *adv.* (*C.L.*) of the date; *bis –o,* up to date, till now; *de –o,* dated, under date (*of*); from today; *a –o,* after *or* from date; of (the) date. **–oscheck,** *m.* dated cheque. **–owechsel,** *m.* day bill. **–um,** *n.* (-s, –ten) date (*of time*); (*pl.*) facts, particulars, data; *welches –um haben wir heute?* what is today's date? *einige wichtige –en,* a few important facts *or* points. **–umgrenze,** *f.* date line (*Geog.*).
Dattel, *f.* (-n) date (*fruit*). **–baum,** *m.*, **–palme,** *f.* date-palm. **–kern,** *m.* date-stone.
Daube, *f.* (-n) stave (*of a cask*); *in –n schlagen,* stave (*a cask*).
Dauer, *f.* length, duration, continuance, permanence, durableness, durability; constancy; longevity; *von kurzer –,* shortlived, ephemeral; *auf die –,* for long, permanent; in the long run; *auf die – gemacht,* made to last; *auf die – von 20 Jahren,* for the term of 20 years. **–apfel,** *m.* winter apple. **–ausscheider,** *m.* chronic carrier (*Med.*). **–befehl,** *m.* standing order (*Mil.*). **–brandofen,** *m.* slow combustion *or* anthracite stove. **–brenner,** *m.* slow combustion burner. **–farbe,** *f.* permanent colour. **–festigkeit,** *f.* endurance, durability, (*Mech.*). **–flug,** *m.* long-distance flight, non-stop flight. **–friede,** *m.* lasting peace. **–haft,** *adj.* durable, permanent, lasting, fast (*of colours*); sound, stout. **–haftigkeit,** *f.* durability; stability, permanence. **–karte,** *f.* season-ticket. **–kraft,** *f.* staying-power. **–lauf,** *m.* long-distance race. **–los,** *adj.* transitory; perishable. **–marsch,** *m.* forced march, endurance test. **–milch,** *f.* sterilized milk. **–n,** *v.n.* (*aux. h.*) last, continue, endure; hold out; keep (*of meat, fruit*); *lange –n,* take a long time; *es –te über eine Stunde ehe,* it was more than an hour before; *das Stück –t mir zu lange,* I find the play too long. **–nd,** *adj.* continuous, constant, enduring, lasting, abiding; persistent, unremitting; perennial (*Bot.*); *kurze Zeit –nd,* shortlived, transient, transitory, passing, fleeting; *lange –nd,* lasting, enduring, protracted, prolonged. **–pflanze,** *f.* perennial plant. **–strom,** *m.* continuous current (*Elec.*). **–träger,** *m., see* **–ausscheider. –versuch,** *m.* endurance test, fatigue test (*Mech.*). **–welle,** *f.* permanent wave (*in hair*). **–wert,** *m.* lasting value. **–wurst,** *f.* hard sausage, smoked sausage.
dauer–n, *v.a. & imp.* make sorry; be sorry for, regret, grieve; *der arme Kerl –t mich,* I am sorry for the poor fellow; *es –t mich, dies getan zu haben,* I regret having done it; *mich –t mein Geld nicht,* I do not mind the expenditure; *sich (Acc.) etwas –n lassen,* grudge *or* begrudge a th.
Daum–en, *m.* (-ens, -en) thumb; cam (*Engin.*); *einem den –en aufdrücken* or *aufs Auge halten* or *setzen,* keep a tight rein on a p., keep a p. under one's thumb; *einem* (or *für einen*) *den –en halten,* keep one's fingers crossed for a p.; *die –en drehen,* twiddle one's thumbs; *über den –en schätzen,* make a rough estimate. **–enbeuger,** *m.* flexor of thumb (*Anat.*). **–endrücker,** *m.* handle, thumb-latch; (*fam.*) protector, patron. **–enklapper,** *f.* castanet. **–enkappe,** *f.* thumb-stall. **–enrad,** *n.* cam-wheel (*Engin.*). **–(en)schraube,** *f.*, **–enstock,** *m.* thumb-screw; *einem –(en)schrauben ansetzen,* (*fig.*) put the screw on a p. **–ensteuerung,** *f.* cam gear (*Engin.*). **–enwelle,** *f.* camshaft (*Engin.*).
Däumling, *m.* (-s, -e) (*also* **Däumerling**) thumb-stall, finger-stall. *See the Index of Names.*
Daun–e, *f.* (-en) down. **–ig,** *adj.* downy. **–endecke,** *f.* eiderdown quilt.
Daus, 1. *n.* (-es, -e & ⸚er) deuce (*dice*); ace (*cards*). 2. *m.* (-es, -e) (*coll.*) *ei der –!* *potz –!* (*sl.*), Great Scott! Wizard! *geputzt wie ein –,* dressed up

to the nines; *ich bin ein – (im Zeichnen)*, I'm a wizard (at sketching).
davon, *adv.* therefrom, thereof, thereby; of, by *or* respecting it, that *or* them; thence; hence, away, off; *bleibt –!* keep off! *was habe ich –?* what do I get by it? *das kommt –*, that's the result; *es ist nicht weit –*, it is not far off. **–bringen**, *v.a.* (*sep.*) save. **–kommen**, *v.n.* (*sep.*) (*aux. s.*) get off, escape; *er kam mit dem bloßen Schrecken –*, he got off with no more than a fright; *mit knapper Not –kommen*, have a narrow escape. **–laufen**, *v.n.* (*sep.*) run away; *es ist zum –laufen*, it is unbearable *or* intolerable; *auf und –laufen*, take to one's heels. **–machen**, *v.r.* (*sep.*) make off, run away, take to one's heels. **–tragen**, *v.a.* (*sep.*) carry off, suffer (damage), win (*prize*), be left with (*injuries*).
davor, *adv.* before it, that *or* them; for, because of *or* from it, that *or* them; against it, that, *or* them; *see* **da, 3**; *– fürchte ich mich nicht*, I am not afraid of it; *hüte dich –*, beware of it; *– behüte uns Gott!* God forbid! *see* **dafür**.
dawider, *adv. see* **da, 3**; to the contrary; *dafür und –*, for and against, the pros and cons. **–reden**, *v.n.* (*sep.*) contradict.
dazu, *adv.* thereto; for that purpose, to that end; moreover, besides, in addition; *see* **da, 3**; *– ist er da*, it is for that purpose that he is there; *noch –*, besides, moreover; *er spricht auch –*, he also has a word to say. **–geben**, *v.a.* (*sep.*) contribute to. **–gehören**, *v.n.* (*sep.*) belong to; *– gehört Zeit*, that requires time; *er gehört mit –*, he is on of the party, he must be counted as well. **–kommen**, *v.n.* (*sep.*) (*aux.* s.) happen, supervene; come by, obtain; *– kommt*, add to this; *nie – kommen*, never find time, never get a chance. **–mal**, *adv.* then, at that time, *von anno –mal*, once upon a time, from time immemorial, (*archaic*) erstwhile, in days of yore. **–tun** *v.a.* (*sep.*) add to; make haste, set about.
dazwischen, *adv.* in between, in the midst of; between times; there between; *see* **da, 3.** **–fahren**, *v.n.* (*aux.* s.) (*sep.*), interpose, interrupt; **–kommen**, *ir.v.n.* (*aux.* s.) (*sep.*) intervene; come between; *wenn nichts –kommt*, if nothing occurs to prevent (it). **–kunft**, *f.* intervention. **–liegend**, *adj.* intermediate. **–reden**, *v.n.* (*sep.*) interrupt (*a conversation*). **–stehen**, *v.a.* (*sep.*) interpose, interpolate. **–treten**, 1. *i.r.v.n.* (*sep.*) step in between, intervene, intercede, interfere, 2. *n.* intervention, intercession.
Debatt–e, *f.* (-en) debate. **–ieren**, *v.a. & n.* debate. **–ierklub**, *m.* debating society.
Debet, *n.* (*C.L.*) debit; *im – stehen*, be on the debit side. **–posten**, *m.* entry on the debit side, item charged *or* debited, charge. **–seite**, *f.* debit side, left-hand side (*of ledger*).
Debit, *m.* sale. **–ant**, *m.* (-en, -en) dealer, agent; retailer. **–ieren**, *v.a.* debit, charge to one's account; *Waren –ieren*, dispose of *or* sell goods. **–ierung**, *f.* charging, debiting; sale, disposal. **–or**, *m.* (-s, -en) debtor. **–kommission**, *f.* commission of bankruptcy. **–masse**, *f.* bankrupt's estate. **–verfahren**, *n.* legal proceedings in bankruptcy.
Debüt, *n.* first appearance. **–ieren**, *v.n.* (*aux.* h.) make one's début.
Dechan–at, *n.* (-s, -e), *see* **Dekanat**. **–t**, *m.* (-en, -en) dean (*Eccl.*).
Decher, *m.* (-s, –) bale *or* number of ten (*esp. of hides*).
dechiffrieren, *v.a.* decode, decipher.
Deck, *n.* (-(e)s, -e) deck (*Naut.*). **–adresse**, *f.* false address, accommodation address. **–bett**, *n.* coverlet, feather-bed (*covering, not mattress*). **–blatt**, *n.* outer leaf (*of cigar*), bract (*Bot.*); amendment (*Mil.*). **–e**, *f.* (-en) cover, coverlet, blanket, quilt, rug, covering; ceiling, roof; skin, envelope, integument, coat (*Anat.*); sounding-board (*Mus.*); cover, pretence, pretext; *geteerte –e*, tarpaulin; *–e eines Buches*, wrapper, jacket; *mit einem unter einer –e stecken*, conspire with a p.; *sich nach der –e strecken*, cut one's coat according to one's cloth, adjust expenditure to income. **–el**, *m.* (-els, -el) lid, cover (*of a box, etc.*); tympan (*Typ.*); operculum (*Bot.*); cornice (*Arch.*); apron (*Artil.*); (*coll.*) hat, straw hat, boater. **–elbecher**, *m.*, **–elkanne**, *f.*, tankard with lid. **–elkorb**, *m.* basket with lid. **–elkrug**, *m.* tankard. **–eln**, *v.a.* cover with a lid. **–en**, 1. *v.a.* cover (*also Mil.*), protect, guard, secure, conceal; reimburse, defray; superpose, coincide with; meet (*a bill*); roof (a building); lay (*the table*); *der Tisch ist gedeckt*, the table is laid; *für sechs Personen –en*, lay covers for six persons; *hinlänglich gedeckt sein*, have sufficient security, be sufficiently covered. 2. *v.r.* be identical, be congruent, coincide (*Math.*). **–enflechter**, *m.* mat-maker. **–engemälde**, *n.*, **–enstück**, *n.* painted ceiling. **–er**, *m.* slater, thatcher; (*in compounds* =) -decker, e.g. *Drei–er*, three-decker (*Naut.*). **–fähig**, *adj.* opaque (*of paint*). **–farbe**, *f.* body colour (*paint*). **–gang**, *m.* covered way. **–haut**, *f.* tegument (*Anat.*) **–hengst**, *m.* stallion. **–ig**, *adj.* imbricate (*Bot., Zool., Icht.*). **–mantel**, *m.* pretence, cloak. **–name**, *m.* pseudonym, code-word, trade name. **–offizier**, *m.* warrant officer (*Naut.*). **–stroh**, *n.* thatch. **–stützen**, *f.pl.* stanchions. **–ung**, *f.* cover, covering; protection, guard (*also fencing & boxing*), defence (*Football*); reimbursement, remittance; funds, resources, security, cover; supply (*of needs*); congruence, coincidence, equality (*Math.*); *in –ung gehen*, take cover. **–ungsgraben**, *m.* slit-trench. **–ungsloch**, *n.* hide-out. **–ungsmaterial**, *n.* roofing material. **–ungstruppen**, *f.pl.* covering party. **–wort**, *n.* code-word. **–zeug**, *n.* table-linen.
dedizieren, *v.a.* dedicate, make a present (of).
deduzieren, *v.a.* deduce, infer.
Defekt, 1. *m.* (-es, -e) defect, deficiency. 2. *adj.* defective, damaged. **–bogen**, *m.* imperfect sheet (*Typ.*). **–iv**, *adj.* defective.
defens–iv, *adj.* defensive; **–ive**, *f.* defence, defensive; *die –ive ergreifen*, take defensive action.
defilier–en, *v.n.* (*aux.* h.) defile, pass in review. *vorbei–en*, march past. **–marsch**, *m.* march past.
defin–ieren, *v.a.* define. **–iert**, *adj.* defined, definite. **–itiv**, *adj.* definite, final, permanent.
Defizit, *n.* (-s, -e) deficit.
Defraud–ant, *m.* (-en, -en) cheat, swindler. **–ieren**, *v.a. & n.* (*aux.* h.) cheat, defraud.
deftig, *adj.* (*coll. & dial.*), capable, strong, sound, proper.
Degen, *m.* (-s, -) 1. sword. 2. (*Poet.*) warrior, fighter, hero, thane; *alter Hau–*, staunch old warrior, experienced fighter. **–fläche**, *f.* flat of the sword. **–gefäß**, *n.* sword-hilt. **–gehänge**, *n.*, **–gehenk**, *n.* sword-belt. **–griff**, *m.* sword-grip. **–klinge**, *f.* sword-blade. **–knopf**, *m.* pommel. **–koppel**, *f.* sword-belt. **–scheide**, *f.* scabbard. **–schneide**, *f.* sword-edge. **–stoß**, *m.* sword-thrust. **–tragvorrichtung**, *f.* sword-frog.
Degener–ation, *f.* degeneration; negative feedback (*Rad.*). **–ieren**, *v.n.* (*aux.* s.) degenerate.
degradieren, *v.a.* degrade, reduce in rank, demote (*Mil.*).
degraissieren, *v.a.* remove fat.
dehn–en, 1. *v.a.* stretch, extend, lengthen, expand, dilate; drawl (*speech*); *gedehnte Silbe*, long syllable. 2. *v.r.* stretch; last long. **–bar**, *adj.* extensible, elastic, ductile, malleable; (*fig.*) vague (*of ideas*). **–barkeit**, *f.* extensibility, flexibility; ductility, malleability. **–fuge**, *f.* expansion joint. **–holz**, *n.* stretcher (*for gloves*). **–maß**, *n.* modulus of elasticity. **–ung**, *f.* extension, lengthening, elongation, expansion, stretching, dilation; stretch, creep (*Metall.*). **–ungszeichen**, *n.* sign indicating long vowel.
Deich, *m.* (-(e)s, -e) dike, dam; embankment. **–anker**, *m.* foundation of a dike. **–en**, *v.a.* dike; dam up. **–graf**, *m.*, **–hauptmann**, *m.* dike-reeve. **–grafschaft**, *f.* dike management, dike administration. **–schoß**, *m.* dike rates. **–strecke**, *f.* section of dike. **–vogt**, *m.* dike-inspector.
Deichsel, *f.* (-n) pole, shaft (*of wagon*), thill. **–gabel**, *f.* shafts (*of a cart, etc.*). **–nagel**, *m.* polepin.
deichseln, *v.a.*; (*coll.*) manage, secure (*sl.*), wangle.
dein, 1. *m. & n. poss. adj. & pron.* (*f. & pl.* -e), your, yours; (*B. & Poet.*) thy, thine. 2. *n.*, *see* **mein**. 3. **–er, –e, –es**, or **der, die, das –e**, or **der, die, das –ige**, *poss. pron.*, yours, thine; your property; your part; *tue das –e* or *–ige*, do your duty; *die –en* or *–igen*, your family *or* people.

-erseits, *adv.* on your side, for your part, as concerns you. **-esgleichen,** *indec. adj. & pron.* the like of you, such as you. **-ethalben,** *adv.*, **-etwegen,** *adv.*, **-etwillen,** *adv.* on your account, for your sake, as far as you are concerned. **-ige,** *see* **-er, -es, -e.**

Deining, *f.* breakers, high seas.

Deis-mus, *m.* deism. **-tisch,** *adj.* deistical.

Deka, *n.* (-s, -) (*Austr. dial.*) *abbr. of* **Dekagramm** (= 10 grammes). **-de,** *f.* (-en) decade. **-disch,** *adj.* decadal, decadic; *-disches Zahlensystem,* decimal system (*Math.*). **-eder,** *n.* (-s, -) decahedron (*Geom.*). **-gramm,** *n.* 10 grammes. **-liter,** *n.* 10 litres.

Dekan, *m.* (-s, -e) dean (*Eccl. & Univ.*). **-at,** *n.* deanery; deanship. **-ei,** *f.* deanery.

dekatieren, *v.a.* hot-press, steam (*cloth*).

Deklam-ation, *f.* declamation. **-ator,** *m.* (-s, en-) declaimer, diseur. **-ieren,** *v.a. & n.* declaim, recite.

deklarier-en, *v.a.* declare; make a declaration; *Waren am Zollamt -en,* declare goods at the customs; *-ter Wert,* registered value (*of a postal packet*).

deklin-abel, *adj.* declinable (*Gram.*). **-ation,** *f.* declension (*Gram.*); declination (*Astr.*). **-ierbar,** *adj.* declinable. **-ieren,** *v.a.* decline, deviate.

Dekokt, *n.* (-es, -e) decoction, infusion.

dekolletier-en, 1. *v.a.* cut a dress low, (leave) bare the neck and shoulders. 2. *v.r.* wear a low-necked dress; go open-necked; *sie -t sich zu sehr,* she wears her dresses too low. **-t,** *p.p. & adj.* low (necked), open-necked.

Dekor-ateur, *m.* (-s, -e), painter and decorator, interior decorator. **-ation,** *f.* (-en), adornment, decoration, order (*Mil., etc.*); scenery (*Theat.*). **-ationsmaler,** *m.* scene painter (*Theat.*). **-ieren,** *v.a.* adorn, decorate; invest with an order.

Dekort, *m.* (-(e)s, -e) (*C.L.*) deduction, discount. **-ieren,** *v.a.* discount, deduct.

Dekret, *n.* (-(e)s, -e) decree, edict, ordinance. **-ale,** *n.* (-alen & -alien) decretal; Papal decree (*R.C.*). **-ieren,** *v.a.* decree, ordain by decree.

deleg-ieren, *v.a.* delegate, depute. **-ierte(r),** *m.* delegate, deputy.

delikat, *adj.* delicate, fine, nice, dainty; delicious. (*coll.*) difficult, ticklish (*problem*). **-esse,** *f.* dainty, delicacy; tact (*sing. only*). **-essenhandlung,** *f.* delicatessen shop.

Delikt, *n.* (-s, -e) crime, offence.

Delinquent, *m.* (-en, -en) delinquent.

delirieren, *v.n.* be delirious, rave.

Delkredere, *n.* (-n) (*C.L.*) guarantee, security.

Delle, *f.* (-n) dent, depression.

Delph-in, *m.* (-(e)s, -e) dolphin. **-isch,** *adj.* Delphian, Delphic; obscure, ambiguous.

Delta, *n.* (-s, -s & -ten) delta. **-förmig,** *adj.* deltoid, triangular.

dem, *Dat. sing. of m. & n. def. art., dem. pron., dem. adj., & rel. pron.*, to the; to it; to whom, to which; *wie - auch sei, - sei wie ihm wolle,* be that as it may; *je nach -,* according as; *zu -,* moreover; *bei alle-,* notwithstanding. **-entsprechend, -gemäß,** *adv.*, accordingly, correspondingly. **-gegenüber,** on the other hand, compared with this, as compared to. **-nach,** *conj.* consequently, accordingly, therefore. **-nächst,** *adv.* thereupon, shortly, soon. **-unerachtet, -ungeachtet,** *conj.* notwithstanding, nevertheless, for all that, in spite of that. **-zufolge,** *conj., see* **demnach.**

Demagog(e), *m.* (-en, -en) demagogue. **-entum,** *n.*, **-ie,** *f.* demagogy. **-isch,** *adj.* demagogic.

Demant, *m.* (*Poet.*), *see* **Diamant.**

demaskieren, *v.a.* unmask.

Dement-i, *n.* (-s, -is) denial (*Politics*). **-ieren,** *v.a.* contradict, deny.

dementsprechend, *see* **dem.**

demgegenüber, *see* **dem.**

demgemäß, *see* **dem.**

Demission, *f.*, **-ieren,** *see* **Dimission, -ieren.**

demnach, *see* **dem.**

demnächst, *see* **dem.**

Demobil-isation, *f.* demobilization. **-isieren,** *v.a. & n.* demobilize. **-machung,** *f.* demobilization.

Demokrat, *m.* (-en, -en) democrat. **-ie,** *f.* (-, -n) democracy. **-isch,** *adj.* democratic

demolieren, *v.a.* demolish.

Demonstr-ant, *m.* (-en, -en) demonstrator. **-ieren,** 1. *v.a.* demonstrate, show. 2. *v.n.* make a demonstration, demonstrate (*Pol.*); feint (*Mil.*). **-ierstock,** *m.* pointer.

demontier-en, *v.a.* dismantle, take apart, strip. **-bar,** *adj.* collapsible.

demoralisieren, *v.a.* demoralize.

demungeachtet, *see* **dem.**

Demut, *f.* humility, meekness, lowliness. **-svoll,** *adj.* humble, meek.

demütig, *adj.* humble, submissive, meek. **-en,** 1. *v.a.* humble; humiliate, abase, bring low; *gedemütigt werden,* be humiliated. 2. *v.r.* submit; stoop, abase o.s., eat humble pie. **-end,** *adj.* humiliating, mortifying. **-ung,** *f.* humiliation, abasement, mortification.

demzufolge, *see* **dem.**

den, 1. *m. acc., def. art., dem. adj., dem. pron. & rel. pron.*, the, this; whom, which. 2. *dat. pl., def. art., & dem. adj.*, to the, to these.

denen, *dat. pl., dem. & rel. pron.*, to them, to whom, to which.

dengeln, *v.a.* whet (*a scythe*).

denk-en, *ir.v.a. & n.* (*aux.* h.) think, reflect; *-e dich in diese Lage!* just imagine yourself in this position. *so lange ich -en kann,* so long as I can remember; *der Mensch -t, Gott lenkt,* man proposes, God disposes; *gedacht, getan* or *getan wie gedacht,* no sooner said than done; *wie Sie -en!* you don't say; *an einen* or *an eine S. -en,* remember (*or* think of) a p. *or* a th., call a p. *or* a th. to mind; *er -t an nichts als,* he only thinks *or* thinks only of, *ich -e gar nicht daran,* I wouldn't think of it; *bitte -e daran, es zu schicken,* please remember to send it; *-' mal an!* you're telling me! (*ironic*)! *sich* (*Dat.*) *-en,* imagine, fancy, conceive, realize; *bei sich -en,* think to o.s.; *wo -en Sie hin?* what are you thinking of? what next; *hin und her -en,* revolve *or* turn over in one's mind; *du kannst dir das nicht -en,* you can't imagine, you have no conception; *es läßt sich -en, daß,* it can be imagined that; *das habe ich mir wohl gedacht,* I thought as much; *man -e sich,* suppose, imagine; *-en Sie sich nur!* only think! just imagine! *- en über etwas,* reflect on a th., ponder a th., hold *or* be of an opinion; (*Poet.*), muse on a th.; *wie -en Sie darüber?* what is your view? (*with* zu *& inf.*) intend, contemplate; *ich -e, morgen abzureisen,* I intend to leave tomorrow; *was -en Sie zu tun?* what do you mean to do? **-art,** *f.* way of thinking; turn of mind; disposition; *er hat eine edle -art,* he is high-minded. **-bar,** *adj.* imaginable, conceivable; *das -bar schönste Verhältnis,* the most beautiful (harmonious) relation conceivable. **-barkeit,** *f.* conceivability. **-faul,** *adj.* mentally sluggish *or* inert. **-freiheit,** *f.* freedom of thought *or* opinion. **-kraft,** *f.* brain power. **-lehre,** *f.* logic. **-lich,** *adj., see* **-bar**; *jede -liche Möglichkeit,* every conceivable possibility. **-mal** (*pl.* **-mäler**], *n.* monument, memorial; benchmark (*Geog.*). **-münze,** *f.* commemorative medal. **-reim,** *m.* mnemonic rhyme. **-schrift,** *f.* record, statement; memorial; memorandum; inscription. **-spruch,** *m.* motto, maxim. **-ungsart,** *f., see* **-art. -vermögen,** *n.* reasoning power. **-weise,** *f., see* **-art. -würdig,** *adj.* memorable, notable. **-würdigkeit,** *f.* memorable occurrence; a th. to be remembered; (*pl.*) memoirs. **-zeichen,** *n.* token, memento, keepsake. **-zettel,** *m.* memorandum, reminder; reprimand; (*coll.*) box on the ear.

denn, 1. *conj.* for, because, then; *er ißt nichts, - er ist krank,* he eats nothing, for he is ill; *mehr - je,* more than ever. 2. *adv.* in that case; *es sei -, daß,* unless, except, provided. 3. (*in comparison, usually to avoid repetition of* als) *er ist größer als Feldherr - als Mensch,* he is greater as a general than as a man; *wer ist reicher - er?* who is richer than he? 4. *part.* (*usually in interr.*); *wo ist er -?* where can he be? I wonder where he is? *wieso -?* how so? *was -?* but what? *was ist - los?* what's the matter?

dennoch, *conj.* yet, still, however, nevertheless, for all that.
Denunz–iant, *m.* (-en, -en), denouncer, informer. **–ieren,** *v.a.* denounce, inform against.
Depesch–e, *f.* (-n) telegram, (*coll.*) wire. **–enreiter,** *m.* dispatch-rider. **–enschlüssel,** *m.* telegraph code. **–ieren,** *v.a.* & *n.* telegraph, wire.
Deplacement, *n.* (-s, -s) displacement (*Naut.*).
Depon–ent, *m.* (-en, -en) depositor, deponent. **–ieren,** *v.a.* deposit (*valuables*); depose (*at a law court*).
Deport–ation, *f.* transportation. **–ieren,** *v.a.* deport, transport.
Deposit–ar, –är, *m.* (-s, -e) trustee. **–eneinlagen,** *f.pl.*, **–engelder,** *n.pl.*, deposits; trust-money. **–enkasse,** bank's branch office; trust funds. **–enschein,** *m.* deposit receipt; paying-in slip. **–um,** *n.* (-ums, -en & -a) deposit; trust (-money).
depossedieren, *v.a.* dispossess.
Depot, *n.* (-s, -s) storehouse, warehouse, repository, depot, (*sl.*) dump; (*C.L.*) deposit. **–schein,** *m.* deposit receipt, pawn-ticket.
Depp, *m.* (-s, -e) (*coll.* & *dial.*) blockhead, nincompoop, ninny.
deprimieren, *v.a.* depress, deject, discourage.
Deput–at, *n.* (-ats, -ate) (extra) allowance, perquisites. **–ation,** *f.* deputation, delegation; committee. **–atlohn,** *m.* payment in kind (*espec. to farm labourers*). **–ierte(r),** *m.* deputy, delegate, member of a deputation *or* delegation.
der, 1. *nom. sing. m., of def. art., dem. adj.* & *pron.* & *rel. pron.*, the; that, this; he, it; who, which, that; – *und* –, such-and-such a one, so and so; – *Narr –!* fool that he is! *unser Vater, – Du bist im Himmel*, our Father who art in Heaven. 2. *Gen.* & *Dat. f. sing., def. art., dem. adj.* & *Dat. sing. f. of dem.* & *rel. pron.*, of the, to the; of *or* to this *or* that; to her, to it; to whom, to which. 3. *Gen. of pl. def. art.* & *dem. adj.*, of the; of these, of those. **–art,** *adv.* in such a way, to such an extent, so much. **–artig,** *adj.* of that kind, such; *nichts –artiges*, nothing of the kind. **–einst,** *adv.* some day, at some future time, in days to come. **–einstig,** *adj.* future. **–en,** (*in compounds* **–ent-**) *see* **deren. –er,** *Gen. pl. of dem. pron.* (= *derjenigen*) of these, of those, of them; *das Geschlecht –er von Bismarck*, the family of the Bismarcks; *die Freunde –er, die* . . ., the friends of those who . . . **–gestalt,** *adv.* in such a manner; to such a degree; *–gestalt, daß*, so that. **–gleichen,** *indec. adj.*, of such kind, such-like; *–gleichen habe ich nie gesehen*, I never saw the like; *–gleichen Tiere gibt es nicht*, there are no such animals; *und –gleichen*, and so forth. **–jenige,** *dem. adj.* & *pron.*, *see* **derjenige. –lei,** *indec. adj.*, *see* **–gestalt. –maleinst,** *adv.* in days to come, hereafter. **–malen,** *adv.* now, at present. **–malig,** *adj.* actual, present. **–maßen,** *adv.* to such an extent, so much. **–o,** *obs. Gen. pl. of* der, die (*used in titles*), *now* deren; your, his; *–o Gnaden*, your Grace; *Seine Majestät haben –o Ministern befohlen*, His Majesty has directed his ministers. **–selbe,** *dem. adj.* & *pron.*, *see* **derselbe. –weil,** *conj.* whilst. **–weile, –weilen,** *adv.* meanwhile. **–zeit,** *adv.* at that time, just now, at the moment. **–zeitig,** *adj.* for the time being, actual, present.
derb, *adj.* firm, solid, strong, powerful, robust, hardy, sturdy, stout; coarse, blunt, rough, rude, uncouth. **–gehalt,** *m.* solid *or* cubic content. **–heit,** *f.* compactness; firmness, sturdiness, solidity; bluntness, rudeness, roughness; (*pl.*) hard words, home truths.
deren, *Gen. sing. f.* & *Gen. pl. m., f.* & *n. of rel. pron.* & *dem. pron.*, of her, of whom, whose, of which, of them; *kaufe keine Blumen, ich habe – genug*, buy no flowers, I have enough of them; *ich sah zwei Mädchen, – Gesichter sehr schön waren*, I saw two girls whose faces were very beautiful. **–thalben,** *adv.*, **–twegen,** *adv.*, **(um) –twillen,** *adv.* for her sake, on her account; on their account; on whose account. (deren *is used for the Gen. sing. f.* & *for the Gen. pl. of all genders of* welcher, *rel. pron.* & *occasionally to avoid ambiguity for the poss. adj.* ihr).
Deriv–at, *n.* (-(e)s, -e), **–ativum,** *n.* (–vums, –va), derivative (*Chem.*). **–ativ,** *n.* (-s, -e) derivative (*Gram.*). **–ieren,** *v.a.* derive.
derjenige, (diejenige, dasjenige, diejenigen) *dem. adj.* & *pron.* that (one); those; such; he, she, it (*before a rel. pron.*).
derlei, *indec. adj.*, *see* **der–.**
dermaßen, *adv.*, *see* **der–.**
dero, *pron.*, *see* **der–.**
derselbe (dieselbe, dasselbe, dieselben), *dem. adj.* & *pron.* (*now usually avoided*), the same, the latter, the selfsame. *der Wein ist gut, ich kann Ihnen denselben empfehlen*, the wine is good, I can recommend it to you; *er sprach von seinen Söhnen und rühmte die Talente derselben*, he spoke of his sons and praised their talents; *ein und* –, one and the same, the very same.
derweil, derweilen, *conj.* & *adv.*, *see* **der–.**
Derwisch, *m.* (-(e)s, -e), dervish.
derzeit, *adv.*, **–ig,** *adj.*, *see* **der–.**
Des, *n.* D flat (*Mus.*); – *dur*, D flat major; – *moll*, D flat minor.
des, *Gen. sing. m.* & *n.* 1. *of def. art.*; 2. (*Poet.*) *of demon. pron.* (*now* dessen); (*Prov.*) *wes Brot ich eß', des Lied ich sing'*, whose bread I eat, his opinion I hold. **–falls,** *adv.* in this *or* that case; in which case; on that account; therefore. **–gleichen,** 1. *indec. adj.* similar, suchlike. 2. *adv.* & *conj.* in like manner, likewise, ditto. **–halb,** *adv.* & *conj.* on this account, for that reason, therefore, hence. **–wegen, –willen,** *adv.* & *conj.*, *see* **–halb;** *eben –wegen*, for that very reason.
designieren, *v.a.* designate.
Desinf–ektion, *f.* disinfection. **–ektionsmittel,** *n.* disinfectant, antiseptic. **–izieren,** *v.a.* disinfect.
despektierlich, *adj.* disrespectful, irreverent.
Despot, *m.* (-en, -en) despot. **–ie,** *f.*, *see* **–ismus. –isch,** *adj.* despotic. **–ismus,** *m.* despotism, despotic power.
dessen, 1. *Gen. sing. m.* & *n. of the dem.* & *rel. pron.*, whose, of whom, of him, of which, of it, of that; whereof. *der Herr, – Haus ich kaufte*, the gentleman whose house I bought; *in – Haus ich wohnte*, in whose house I lived; *die Frau –, der hier gewohnt hat*, the wife of the man who lived here. 2. *Gen. sing. of m.* & *n. sing. poss. adj.* sein, *when this does not refer to subject of sentence*; *er traf seinen Freund und – Sohn*, he met his friend and his (the latter's) son. **–thalben, –twillen,** (*um –thalben* or *–twillen*) *adv.* & *conj.* therefore, on that account, on account of which. **–ungeachtet,** *conj.* nevertheless, for all that, notwithstanding that, in spite of that.
Destill–at, *n.* (-es, -e), distillate. **–ateur,** *m.* (-s, -e) distiller. **–ation,** *f.*, *see* **–ierung. –ierapparat,** *m.*, **–ierblase,** *f.*, **–iergefäß,** *n.* retort, alembic, still. **–ierbetrieb,** *m.* refinery. **–ieren,** *v.a.* distil. **–ierkolben,** *m.* still-head, retort. **–ierofen,** *m.* distilling-furnace. **–ierung,** *f.* distillation.
Destinatar, *m.* (-s, -e) (*C.L.*) consignee.
desto, *adv.* (*used before comparatives*) the, so much; *je mehr, – besser*, the more, the merrier; *je mehr man eine fremde Sprache hört, – besser versteht man sie*, the more one hears a foreign language, the better one understands it; – *besser*, all the better, so much the better; – *eher*, all the sooner; all the more reason; – *mehr*, so much the more; *nichts–weniger*, nevertheless.
desungeachtet, *conj.*, *see* **dessenungeachtet.**
deswegen, deswillen, *adv.* & *conj.*, *see* **des–.**
Deszendenz–prinzip, *n.* evolutionary principle. **–theorie,** *f.* theory of heredity.
Detachiermittel, *n.* spot *or* stain remover, detergent.
Detail, *n.* (-s, -s) detail, particular; (*C.L.*) retail; *ins* – or *auf –s* (*ein*)*gehen*, particularize; *bis ins kleinste* –, (down) to the last detail. **–geschäft,** *n.*, **–handlung,** *f.* retail business. **–handel,** *m.* retail trade. **–lieren,** *v.a.* detail; (*C.L.*) retail. **–list,** *m.* (-en, -en) retailer.
Detektor, *m.* (-s, -en) detector (*Rad.*). **–apparat,** *m.*, **–empfänger,** *m.* crystal set (*Rad.*).
detonieren, *v.a.* detonate.
deucht, deuchte, (*Archaic* & *Poet.*) *see* **dünken.**

Deut, *m.* (-(e)s, -e) farthing, jot, whit, trifle; *keinen – wert,* not worth a fig.
deut–en, 1. *v.a.* explain, expound, interpret. 2. *v.n.* (*aux.* h.) point (*auf,* to *or* at), indicate, signify; bode, augur; *–en auf einen,* point to *or* explain as referring to a p.; *auf gutes Wetter –en,* be a sign of good weather. **–elei,** *f.* (-eien) forced explanation, strained interpretation. **–eln,** *v.a.* subtilize; put a false interpretation on; explain away; twist the meaning. **–bar,** *adj.* explainable, explicable. **–er,** *m.* explainer, interpreter. **–ig,** *adj.* (*suffix* =) significant, capable of such *or* so many interpretations, e.g. *ein–ig,* unequivocal, unmistakable, clear, simple; *viel–ig. adj.* ambiguous, equivocal, indeterminate, obscure. **–lich,** *adj.* distinct, clear, plain, evident; intelligible, articulate. **–lichkeit,** *f.* distinctness, clearness. **–ung,** *f.* interpretation, explanation; meaning, signification; application; *falsche –ung,* misconstruction. **–ungsvoll,** *adj.* problematical; suggestive; ominous.
deutsch, *adj., see the Index of Names.*
Devise, *f.* (-n) device, motto; foreign bill (*of exchange*); *Abteilung für –n,* Foreign Exchange Department. **–ngeschäft,** *n.* business in foreign bills. **–nkurs,** *m.* rate of exchange (*of foreign bills*). **–nschieber,** *m.* currency smuggler, one who evades currency regulations. **–nsperre,** *f.* embargo on foreign exchange.
devot, *adj.* submissive, humble.
Dezember, *m.* (-s, -) December.
Dezennium, *n.* (-s, –nnien) decade.
Dezern–at, *n.* administrative department. **–ent,** *m.* head of an administrative department.
Dezim–al, *adj.* & *n.* decimal; *periodischer –al,* recurring decimal. **–albruch,** *m.* decimal fraction; **–al(bruch)stelle,** *f.* decimal place. **–ieren,** *v.a.* decimate.
diabolisch, *adj.* diabolic(al).
Diagnos–e, *f.* (-n) diagnosis. **–tizieren,** *v.a.* diagnose.
Diagonale, *f.* diagonal.
Diakon, *m.* (-s & -en, -e & -en) deacon. **–at,** *n.* (-(e)s, -e) diaconate. **–issin,** *f.* sister of a Protestant nursing order.
Dialekt, *m.* (-s, -e) dialect. **–frei,** *adj.* free from dialectical peculiarities, pure, standard (*of speech*). **–ik,** *f.* dialectics. **–iker,** *m.* (-s, -) dialectician. **–isch,** *adj.* dialectal, dialectic.
Dialog, *m.* (-s, -e) dialogue.
Diamant, *m.* (-en, -en) diamond. **–en,** *adj.* of diamond, set with diamonds, adamantine; *–ene Hochzeit,* diamond wedding. **–englanz,** *m.* adamantine lustre. **–(en)spitze,** *f.* diamond pencil. **–enschleifer,** *m.* diamond cutter. **–stahl,** *m.* hard steel, tool steel.
diametral, *adj.* diametric(al).
diaphan, *adj.* transparent, diaphanous.
Diapositiv, *n.* lantern slide, transparency.
Diät, 1. *f.* (-en) diet, regimen; (*pl.*) *also* **–engelder,** *n.pl.,* daily payment, daily allowance of money for attendance (*to deputies*). *knappe –,* low diet, short allowance. 2. *adv.*; *– leben,* keep to a diet, be strict in one's diet. **–etik,** *f.* dietetics. **–etisch,** *adj.* dietetic.
diatherm, *adj.* diathermic, diathermal, permeable to heat.
diatonisch, *adj.* diatonic.
dich, *Acc. of* **du.**
dicht, *adj.* close (*in texture, etc.*); thick, dense, compact; tight, close, impervious, impermeable, leakproof (*as vessels*); *– an, – auf, – bei* or *– neben,* close or near by *or* to; *ihm – auf den Fersen,* close to *or* on his heels; *–es Gold,* massive gold; *meine Schuhe sind nicht mehr –,* my shoes let the water in; *–er Wald,* thick wood. *– beim Winde segeln,* hug the wind. **–en,** *v.a.* make close *or* tight; stop up, pack, caulk (*a ship*). **–e,** *f.,* **–heit,** *f.,* **–igkeit,** *f.* closeness, thickness, compactness (*of texture, etc.*), density; tightness; imperviousness. **–emesser,** *m.* **–igkeitsmesser,** *m.* pressure gauge. **–halten,** *v.n.* (*coll.*) keep one's mouth shut, not breathe a word, let go no farther (*of a secret*). **–machen,** (*sl.*) shut up shop, pack up. **–schließend,** *adj.* fitting *or* closing tightly. **–ung,** *f.* caulking, packing (*Mech.*). **–ungsring,** *m.* washer, gasket (*Mech.*).
dicht–en, 1. *v.a.* & *n.* (*aux.* h.) compose (*as an author or a poet*), write poetry; invent, devise. 2. *n.*; meditation, musing; composition of poetry; *das –en und Trachten,* thoughts, aspirations, endeavours, study. **–er,** *m.* poet; writer (of fiction). **–erader,** *f.* poetic vein. **–erfreiheit,** *f.* poetic licence. **–ergott,** *m.* Apollo. **–erisch,** *adj.* poetic(al). **–erling,** *m.* would-be poet, poetaster. **–erroß,** *n.* Pegasus. **–kunst,** *f.* poetry, poetic art, poesy. **–ung,** *f.* poetry; poetical work; poem, fiction. **–ungsart,** *f.* style (*of poetry*). **–ungskraft,** *f.,* **–ungsvermögen,** *n.* poetic power, poetic talent, power of imagination.
dick, *adj.* thick; fat, stout, corpulent; big, bulky, large; swollen, inflated, voluminous; *das –e Ende* (*coll.*), anything unpleasant *or* embarrassing; (*coll.*) *–e Freunde sein,* be close friends; (*coll.*) *etwas – haben,* be fed up with a th.; (*sl.*) *–e Luft,* heavy fire (*Mil.*), dangerous situation, (*sl.*) things are hot; *–e Milch,* curdled *or* sour milk; (*coll.*) *sich mit einer S. – tun,* boast of *or* brag about a th., talk big. **–bäckig,** *adj.* chubby. **–bauch,** *m.* paunch. **–bäuchig,** *adj.* big-bellied, pot-bellied. **–darm,** *m.* colon, great gut, large intestine. **–e,** *f.* thickness; diameter; bigness, bulkiness, size; fatness, corpulence; density, consistency, viscosity; body. **–enmesser,** *m.* callipers. **–fellig,** *adj.* thick-skinned. **–fuß,** *m.* stone curlew (*Pontederia crassipes*) (*Orn.*). **–flüssig,** *adj.* viscid, viscous, thick (*of liquids*), (*coll.*) treacly, syrupy. **–häuter,** *m.* pachyderm, (*coll.*) tank (*Mil.*). **–hülsig,** *adj.* thick-shelled. **–icht,** *n.* (-s, -e) thicket. **–kopf,** *m.* chub (*Icht.*); (*coll.*) blockhead, pig-headed fellow. (*coll.*) **–köpfig,** *adj.* obstinate, stubborn, pig-headed. **–leibig,** *adj.* corpulent; (*fig.*) bulky. **–leibigkeit,** *f.* corpulence; (*fig.*) bulkiness. **–tuer,** *m.* braggart. **–tuerei,** *f.* bragging, boasting (*mit,* of). **–wanst,** *m.* paunch, (*coll.*) belly. **–zirkel,** *m.* callipers.
Didakt–ik, *f.* didactics, the art of teaching. **–iker,** *m.* didactic person teacher of didactics. **–isch,** *adj.* didactic, instructional.
die, 1. *f. sing. Nom. & Acc. of def. art., dem. adj., dem. pron. & rel. pron.,* the; she, her, it; who, whom, that, which. 2. *Nom. & Acc. pl. of def. art., dem. adj., dem. pron. & rel. pron.,* the; they, them; these, those; who, which, that. **–selbe,** *dem. adj. & pron., see* **derselbe. –weil,** *adv. & conj., see* **dieweil.**
Dieb, *m.* (-(e)s, -e) thief, burglar; *haltet den –!* stop thief! **–erei,** *f.* theft, thieving, pilfering, stealing; larceny (*Law*). **–(e)sbande,** *f.* gang of thieves. **–(e)sgeselle,** *m., see* **–shelfer. –(e)sgut,** *n.* stolen goods. **–(e)shehlerei,** *f.* receiving of stolen goods. **–isch,** 1. *adj.* thievish; (*coll.*) capital, excellent, jolly; *–ische Elster,* pilfering magpie. 2. *adv.* (*coll.*) awfully. (*coll.*) *ich habe mich –isch gefreut,* I was awfully bucked, I was jolly glad. **–sgesicht,** *n.* hangdog look. **–shelfer,** *m.* accomplice. **–shöhle,** *f.* den of thieves. **–sschlüssel,** *m.* picklock; skeleton key. **–ssicher,** *adj.* burglar-proof. **–stahl,** *m.* (-(e)s, ⸚e) theft, robbery, burglary; *kleiner –stahl,* petty larceny; *literarischer* or *gelehrter –stahl,* plagiarism.
Diebel, *m.* dowel (pin), peg.
Diele, *f.* (-n) board, plank; floor; hall, vestibule; ceiling; loft. **–n,** *v.a.* floor; board, plank.
Dielektri–kum, *n.* dielectric (*Elec., Rad.*). **–zitätskonstante,** *f.* dielectric constant (*Elec., Rad.*).
dien–en, *v.n.* (*aux. h.*) serve; be of service to; assist; do service (*as a soldier, a servant, etc.*); be good for, serve as, be useful to; *einem –en,* serve a p.; (*Ihnen*) *zu –en,* at your service; *von der Pike auf–en,* rise from the ranks (*Mil.*); *bei einem –en,* be in a p.'s service; *damit ist mir nicht gedient,* that is of no use to me; *mit gleicher Münze –en,* pay (*a p.*) in his own coin: *womit kann ich Ihnen –en?* can I help you? *dieses –e zur Antwort,* this may do *or* serve as an answer; *zu etwas –en,* be fit for s.th.; *das –t zu nichts,* that is of no use; *es soll mir zur Warnung –en,* it will be a warning to me; *wozu –t es?* what is it used for? what is the use of it? **–end,** *pr.p. & adj.* ancillary. **–er,** *m.* (man-)servant, attendant; official; curtsy, bow; *gehorsamer –er!*

your obedient servant; no, thank you! *stummer –er*, dumb-waiter; dinner-wagon, serving table; *–er des Bauches*, belly-worshipper, glutton; *er machte mir einen –er*, he bowed to me; (*Prov.*) *wie der Herr, so der –er*, like master like man. **–erin,** *f.* maidservant, maid. **–ern,** *v.n.* bow and scrape. **–erschaft,** *f.* servants, domestics, attendants. **–ertracht,** *f.* livery. **–lich,** *adj.* serviceable, useful. **–lichkeit,** *f.* serviceableness. **–st,** *m.* (-stes, -ste) service; post, employment, office, situation; good turn; duty; *–st am Kunden*, service to (one's) customers; *den –st aufsagen*, give notice; *außer –st* (*abbr.* a. D.), off duty; unattached; retired (*Mil.*); *Major a. D.*, retired major, ex-major; *außer –st stellen*, place on the retired list, pension off; lay up (*of ships*); *–st bei der Fahne*, active service, service with the colours; *in –st gehen*, go into (domestic) service; *gute –ste*, kind offices; *er hatte –st*, he was on duty; *im –ste*, on duty (*Mil.*); *in aktivem –ste*, on active service, with the colours; *–st leisten*, render a service, help, oblige; *–st nehmen*, enlist; *bei einem im –ste stehen*, be in a p.'s service; *es steht Ihnen zu –sten*, you are welcome to it, it is at your disposal; *was steht Ihnen zu –sten?* what can I do for you? *ein –st ist des andern wert*, one good turn deserves another. **–stalter,** *n.* seniority (in office). **–stanweisung,** *f.* service regulation(s) (*Mil.*). **–stanzug,** *m.*, uniform, livery. **–stbar,** *adj.* serviceable; liable to serve; subservient, subject; *er macht sich alle Welt –stbar*, he makes use of everybody; (*B.*) *–stbare Geister*, ministering spirits, (*hum.*) domestic servants. **–stbarkeit,** *f.* servitude, bondage, subjection. **–stbeflissen,** *adj.* officious, zealous, eager to serve. **–stbezüge,** *m.pl.* official income. **–stbote** *m.* domestic servant. **–steid,** *m.* official oath. **–steifrig,** *adj.* zealous (in service), eager to serve. **–steinkommen,** *n.* pay, salary, stipend. **–stenthebung,** *f.* suspension (from office). **–stentlassung,** *f.* discharge (from office). **–stergeben,** *adj.* devoted. **–stfähig,** *adj.* fit for office *or* service. **–stfertig,** *adj.* ready to serve, obliging. **–stfrei,** *adj.* exempt from service *or* military duty; off duty. **–stgefällig,** *adj.* complaisant. **–stgegenstand,** *m.* military *or* government property. **–stgewalt,** *f.* authority (*by virtue of office*). **–stgrad,** *m.* (military) rank. **–sthabende(r),** *m.* official on duty. **–stherr,** *m.* master, lord; employer. **–stkleidung,** *f.* uniform, livery. **–stleistung,** *f.* service. **–stleute,** *pl.* servants. **–stlich,** *adj.* connected with the service; official; *förderlich und –stlich sein*, be useful, make o.s. useful; *–stliche Stellung*, official position; *–stlich verhindert*, prevented by duty. **–stlohn,** *m.* servant's wages. **–stlos,** *adj.* out of service. **–stmädchen,** *n.*, **–stmagd,** *f.* maidservant, maid, servant girl. **–stmann,** *m.* (*pl.* -männer) out-porter, town porter; (*pl.* -leute) vassal. **–stpersonal,** *n.* servants; officials. **–stpfennig,** *m.* earnest pledge. **–stpflicht,** *f.* liability to service, compulsory military service. **–stpflichtig,** *adj.*, liable for duty *or* service. **–stprämie,** *f.* gratuity (*Mil.*). **–streise,** *f.* duty journey. **–stsache,** *f.* official communication *or* business. **–stschuldig,** *adj.*, *see* **–stpflichtig. –ststelle,** *f.* office, department, headquarters, centre, depot, duty station (*Mil.*). **–ststunden,** *f.pl.* office hours. **–sttauglich,** *adj.* fit for (military) service. **–sttuend,** *adj.* on duty. **–stuntauglich,** *adj.* unfit for (military) service. **–stverwandt,** *adj.*, *see* **–stpflichtig. –stvorschrift,** *f.* instruction, training regulation (*Mil.*). **–stweg,** *m.* official channels. **–stwidrig,** *adj.* contrary to official regulations. **–stwillig,** *adj.* obliging, ready to serve. **–stwohnung,** *f.* official residence. **–stzeit,** *f.* enlistment period. **–stzeugnis,** *n.* written character, testimonial, recommendation. **–stzweig,** *m.* branch of service. **–stzwang,** *m.* compulsion to serve (*Mil.*).

Dienstag, *m.* (-s, -e) Tuesday. **–s,** *adv.* on Tuesdays.

dies, *contraction of* **dieses** (*as n. Nom. or Acc., but not as m. & n. Gen.*). **–er,** *m.* (**–e,** *f.*, **–es,** *n.*, **–e,** *pl.*) *dem. adj. & pron.*, this, that, these, the latter, this one, *etc.*; (*C.L.*) *am* or *den vierten dieses*, on the fourth instant; *vor diesem*, ere now; *einer dieser Tage*, one of these days; *zur Bewahrheitung dieses*, in faith whereof (*Law*). **–bezüglich,** *adj.* referring to this. **–falls,** *adj.* in this case. **–jährig,** *adj.* of this year. **–mal,** *adv.* this time, now. **–malig,** *adj.* this, present. **–seitig,** *adj.* on this side, on our side. **–seits,** *adv. & prep.* (*Gen.*) on this side.

diesig, *adj.* misty, hazy.

Dietrich, *m.* (-s, -e) picklock, skeleton key.

dieweil, *adv. & conj.* (*rare*) meanwhile, as long as, while.

Diffam-ation, *f.* defamation. **–atorisch,** *adj.* defamatory. **–ieren,** *v.a.* defame, calumniate, speak ill of. **–ierung,** *f.* defamation.

Differen-tial, 1. *n.* (-s, -e) differential gear (*Motor.*); differential (*Math.*). 2. *adj.* differential. **–tialgetriebe,** *n.* differential gear. **–tialrechnung,** *f.* differential calculus (*Math.*). **–tiell,** *adj.*, *see* **–tial,** 2. **–z,** *f.* (-en) difference (*also Math.*), misunderstanding. **–zieren,** *v.a.* differentiate, discriminate. (*C.L.*) **–zgeschäft,** *n.*, **–zhandel,** *m.* speculation in futures; *–zgeschäfte machen*, stag.

Dikt-at, *n.* (-s, -e) dictation; *nach –at schreiben*, write from dictation; *Friedens–*, (*usual Nat. Soc. name for*) Versailles Treaty. **–atorisch,** *adj.* dictatorial. **–atur,** *f.* (-en) dictatorship. **–ieren,** *v.a.* dictate. **–atfriede,** *m.* dictated peace (*usually refers to Versailles Treaty*).

Dilator-ium, *n.* writ of respite; postponement. **–isch,** *adj.* dilatory.

Dilemma, *n.* (-s, -s & -ata) dilemma.

Dilett-ant, *m.* (-en, -en) dilettante, amateur. **–antisch,** *adj.* amateurish. **–ieren,** *v.n.* dabble (in), toy (with).

Dill, *m.* (-s, -e), (*dial.*) **–e,** *f.* (-n) anet, dill (*Anethum graveolens*) (*Bot.*).

Dimission, *f.* resignation (*from office*). **–ieren,** *v.n.* resign (*from office*).

dimittieren, *v.a.* discharge (*from office*).

Diner, *n.* (-s, -s) dinner, banquet.

Ding, *n.* 1. (-(e)s, -e) object, thing, matter. 2. (-es, -er) (*contemptuously or jokingly*) creature (*usually refers to a girl*). 3. (-(e)s, -e) old Teutonic tribal assembly (*cf. eisteddfod*); *vor allen –en*, first of all; above all, chiefly, primarily; *das böse –*, whitlow; (*coll.*) *einem ein – drehen*, pull a p.'s leg; *ihr dummen –er*, you silly creatures; (*Prov.*) *aller guten –e sind drei*, all blessings come in threes; *guter –e sein*, be in high spirits; *den –en ihren Lauf lassen*, let things run their course; *das geht mir nicht mit rechten –en zu*, there is s.th. uncanny *or* deceptive; *das – an sich*, the thing in itself (*Phil.*). **–bezug,** *m.* cause and effect. **–brief,** *m.*, **–zettel,** *m.* contract. **–fest,** *adj.* confirmed by law; *einen –fest machen*, apprehend *or* arrest a p. **–en,** 1. *ir.v.a.* bargain for; hire, engage. 2. *v.n.* bargain, haggle. **–glas,** *n.* objective lens (*Opt.*). **–lich,** *adj.* real; concrete, material, objective; judicial (*Law*); *–liche Klage*, real action. **–s,** 1. *n.* (*coll.*) thingamy, thingamybob, what's-its-name. 2. *m.* or *f.* (*coll.*) what's-his (*or* her)-name. **–sda,** 1. *n.* you know where. 2. *m.* or *f.*, *see* **–s,** *m.* or *f.* **–skirchen,** *see* **–sda,** *n.*

Dinkel, *m.* (-s, –) spelt, German wheat.

Diözese, *f.* (-n) diocese.

Diphther-ie, *f.*, **–itis,** *f.*, diphtheria.

Diplom, *n.* (-s, -e) diploma, certificate, patent. **–at,** *m.* (-en, -en) diplomat. **–atiker,** *m.* diplomatist, schemer. **–atie,** *f.* diplomacy. **–atik,** *f.* diplomatics. **–atisch,** *adj.* diplomatic; artful; *–atisch getreue Abschrift*, exact copy. **–ingenieur,** *m.* certified engineer.

dir, *Dat. sing. of* **du,** to you.

direkt, *adv.* direct; at first hand; *–e Fahrkarte* (*nach*), through ticket (for). **–ion,** *f.* direction, management; directory, board of directors. **–ive,** *f.* general instructions, directive. **–or,** *m.* (-s, -en) manager, managing director; principal, head, headmaster. **–orat,** *n.* (-(e)s, -e) governorship, headship, headmastership; governor's residence, headmaster's house. **–orenversammlung,** *f.* headmasters' conference. **–orium,** *n.* directory; board of directors.

Dirig-ent, *m.* (-en, -en) director, leader, manager, conductor (*of an orchestra*). **–entenstock,** *m.*

conductor's baton. **–ieren,** *v.a.* direct, manage; conduct (*Mus.*); *–ierender Arzt,* head physician (*of a hospital*); *–ierender Teilhaber,* managing partner (*of a firm*).
Dirn–dl, *n.* (-s, -n) (*dial.*) young girl. **–dlkleid,** *n.* Austrian or Bavarian costume, peasant dress (*for girls*). **–e,** *f.* (*dial. & poet.*) maid, girl; (*now*) prostitute.
Dis, *n.* D sharp (*Mus.*). *—-dur, n.* D-sharp major. *—-moll, n.* D-sharp minor.
Disharmon–ie, *f.* (-n) discord, disharmony. **–isch,** *adj.* discordant.
Diskant, *m.* (-s, -e) treble, soprano. **–schlüssel,** *m.* treble clef.
Diskont, *m.* (-(e)s, -e), *Austr.* **–o,** *m.* (-os, -os & -i) discount; bank-rate; rebate. **–ieren,** *v.a.* discount; *–ierter Wechsel,* discounted bill.
diskontinu–ierlich, *adj.* discontinuous, intermittent. **–ität,** *f.* discontinuity.
diskret, *adj.* discreet, prudent, tactful, cautious; *in –en Verhältnissen sein,* be in trouble (*of unmarried expectant mothers*). **–ion,** *f.*; *sich auf –ion ergeben,* surrender at discretion. **–ionstage,** *m.pl.* days of grace.
Diskurs, *m.* (-es, -e) discourse.
Diskussion, *f.* discussion; *die Frage steht* or *kommt zur –,* the question is up for discussion.
Diskuswurf, *m.* throwing the discus (*Sport*).
diskutieren, *v.a. & n.* discuss, debate.
Dispens, *m.* (-es, -e) dispensation, exemption. **–ieren,** *v.a.* exempt.
Dispon–enden, *pl.* wares taken 'on sale or return'. **–ent,** *m.* (-en, -en) manager; agent. **–ibel,** *adj.* available, disposable; unattached (*Mil.*). **–ibilitätsgehalt,** *n.* (*archaic*) half-pay (*Mil.*). **–ieren,** *v.a. & n.* (*aux.* h.) dispose, manage, arrange. **–iert,** *p.p. & adj.* disposed (to), with a tendency (towards); *gut –iert,* in a good humour *or* mood.
Disposition, *f.* (-en) disposition, arrangement, management; *zur – stehen,* be at one's disposal; *zur –,* with the reserve (*Mil.*).
Disput–ation, *f.* (-en) debate. **–ieren,** *v.a. & n.* (*aux.* h.) dispute; debate.
Dissertation, *f.* (-en) dissertation, thesis.
Dissident, *m.* (-en, -en) dissenter.
Dissonanz, *f.* (-en) dissonance.
Distanz, *f.* (-en) distance; *– halten,* keep one's distance; remain aloof. **–geschäft,** *n.* business for future delivery, forward contract (*C.L.*).
Distel, *f.* (-n) thistle. **–fink,** *m.* goldfinch (*Carduelis carduelis*) (*Orn.*).
Disziplin, *f.* (-en) discipline; organized branch of knowledge, doctrine, system, theory. **–arisch,** *adj.* disciplinary. **–arstrafordnung,** *f.* disciplinary code. **–arverfahren,** *n.* disciplinary measure. **–ieren,** *v.a.* discipline; train. **–los,** *adj.* undisciplined (*of people*). **–widrig,** *adj.* undisciplined (*of actions*).
Divan, *m., see* **Diwan.**
divers, *adj.* sundry (*C.L.*).
Divid–end, *m.* (-en, -en) dividend, numerator (*Arith.*). **–ende,** *f.* (-n) dividend, share (*C.L.*). **–endenfonds,** *m.* bonus fund. **–ieren,** *v.a.* divide (*durch,* by).
Divis, *n.* (-es, -e) hyphen (*Typ.*). **–ion,** *f.* division (*Math. & Mil.*). **–or,** *m.* (-s, -en) divisor, denominator (*Math.*).
Diwan, *m.* (-s, -s & -e) (Turkish) divan, sofa, couch; council; (*rare*) collection of Oriental poems.
Döbel, *m.* (-s, –) 1. peg, plug, pin, dowel. 2. chub (*Squalius cephalus*) (*Icht.*). **–n,** *v.a.* peg, fasten with dowels; plug (*a wall*).
doch, *adv. & conj.* (*accented if it implies a contradiction or emphatic assertion*) yet, however, nevertheless; for all that, after all, but, at least, though, surely; (*contradicting a negative*) yes; oh! yes. 1. (*unaccented*) *obgleich es verboten ist, geschieht es –,* although it is forbidden, it is done all the same; *du siehst es –?* surely you see it, you can see it, I suppose? *hilf mir –!* do help me! *hättest du das – gleich gesagt!* if you had but said so at once! *seien Sie – ruhig,* do be quiet! *laß es –,* please, let it alone! *er ist – nicht etwa hier?* but surely he isn't here? 2. (*accented*) *du willst nicht kommen? – !* you will not come? Oh, yes, I will! *leugne nicht, du siehst es – !* do not deny it, you cannot help but see it; *sie ist häßlich, aber er liebt sie –,* she is ugly, yet he loves her; *ja –,* yes indeed; yes, yes; but of course; *nein –,* no, no; *nicht –,* certainly not; don't! *also – !* what did I tell you? there you are! that's what I said!
Docht, *m.* (-(e)s, -e,) wick. **–halter,** *m.* wick-holder; burner (*of a lamp*).
Dock, *n.* (-s, -s & -e); dock, dockyard; *Schwimm–,* floating dock; *Trocken–,* dry dock. **–en,** *v.a.* dock (*ships*). **–schiff,** *n.* floating dock.
Dock–e, *f.* (-en) 1. skein, hank, bundle; shock, stook (*of corn*). 2. (*dial.*) doll, smart girl. 3. baluster. 4. spindle (*of a lathe*). **–en,** *v.a.* roll together; wind into skein; shock *or* stook (*sheaves*).
Dodeka–eder, *n.* (-s, –) dodecahedron (*Geom.*). **–disch,** *adj.* dodecahedral.
Dogge, *f.* (-n) a breed of large dog (*incl. mastiff, St. Bernard, Newfoundland, Great Dane*).
Dogma, *n.* (-s, -men) dogma. **–tiker,** *m.* dogmatist. **–tisch,** *adj.* dogmatic. **–tisieren,** *v.n.* dogmatize. **–tismus,** *m.* dogmatism.
Dohle, *f.* (-n) jackdaw (*Corvus monedula*) (*Orn.*).
Dohne, *f.* (-n) bird-snare, gin, springe, noose. **–nstieg,** *m.,* **–nstrich,** *m.* springe-line.
Doktor, *m.* (-s, -en) doctor (*Univ.*). (*coll.*) doctor (*medical practitioner*); physician, surgeon; *einen zum – machen,* confer the doctor's degree on a p.; *den – machen* or (*coll.*) *bauen,* take the degree of doctor; *er hat seinen – in Berlin gemacht,* he took his doctorate at Berlin. **–and,** *m.* (-en, -en) candidate for a doctor's degree. **–arbeit,** *f.* thesis for the doctorate. **–at,** *n.,* **–grad,** *m.,* **–würde,** *f.* doctorate. **–hut,** *m.* academic head-dress, symbol of doctorate; *sich* (*Dat.*) *den –hut holen* or *erwerben,* obtain the doctor's degree.
Dokument, *n.* (-s, -e) document. **–arisch,** *adj.* documentary. **–ieren,** *v.a.* prove (by documents), testify.
Dolch, *m.* (-es, -e) dagger, poniard, dirk. **–stich,** *m.,* **–stoß,** *m.* stab with a dagger; *–stoß von hinten,* stab in the back (*Nat. Soc. view of revolution responsible for defeat in 1918*). **–zahn,** *m.* canine tooth.
Dold–e, *f.* (-en) umbel (*Bot.*). **–ig,** *adj.* umbellate. **–enblütler,** *m.pl.* Umbelliferae (*Bot.*). **–enrebe,** *f.* Virginia creeper (*Ampelopsis quinquefolia*) (*Bot.*). **–entragend,** *adj.* umbelliferous.
doll, *adj.* (*dial. & sl.*) *see* **toll.**
dolmetsch–en, *v.a.* interpret, translate. **–er,** *m.* interpreter.
Dom, *m.* (-(e)s, -e) cathedral; dome, cupola (*Arch.*); (*fig.*) vault, canopy. **–freiheit,** *f.* cathedral close. **–herr,** *m.* prebendary, canon. **–herrnornat,** *m.* canonicals. **–kapitel,** *n.* (cathedral) chapter; dean and chapter. **–kirche,** *f.* cathedral, minster. **–pfaff,** *m.* bullfinch (*Pyrrhula*) (*Orn.*). **–sänger,** *m.* cathedral chorister. **–schule,** *f.* cathedral-school, grammar-school attached to a cathedral. **–stift,** *n.* cathedral chapter; seminary (*Eccl.*).
Domäne, *f.* (-n) domain, demesne; (*fig.*) sphere, ground, field. **–npächter,** *m.* crown-land lessee. **–nwald,** *m.* state forest.
Domin–ante, *f.* (-n) dominant (*Mus.*). **–anz,** *f.* dominance, preponderance. **–ieren,** *v.n.* (*aux.* h.) dominate, be dominant; domineer; (*coll.*) lord it (over).
Domino, 1. *m.* (-s, -s) domino (*cloak*). 2. *n.* (-s, -s) game of dominoes; *– spielen,* play at dominoes. **–steine,** *m.pl.* dominoes.
Domizil, *n.* (-s, -e) domicile, residence; (*C.L.*) address for payment. **–wechsel,** *m.* removal, change of residence; (*C.L.*) addressed bill.
Dommel, *f.* (-n) bittern (*Botaurus stellaris*) (*Orn.*).
Dompteur, *m.* (-s, -e) tamer (*of wild animals*), trainer.
Donner, *m.* (-s, –) thunder; *vom – gerührt,* thunderstruck. **–büchse,** *f.* blunderbuss. **–keil,** *m.* thunderbolt. **–n,** *v.n.* (*aux.* h.) thunder, roar. **–nd,** *adj.* thunderous. **–schlag,** *m.* thunder-clap, thunderbolt (*also fig.*). **–stag,** *m.* Thursday; *grüner –stag, Grün–stag,* Maundy Thursday; *der feiste –stag,* Thursday before Lent. **–stags,** *adv.* on Thursdays. **–strahl,** *m.* flash of lightning. **–wet-**

ter, 1. *n.* thunderstorm. (*fig. coll.*) blowing-up, dressing down. 2. *int.* damn it all! blast!
doof, *adj.* (*coll.*) stupid, simple; tiresome, boring.
Doppel, *n.* (-s, –) duplicate. **-adler,** *m.* two-headed eagle (*Her.*). **-bahn,** *f.* double-track railway. **-bereifung,** *f.* twin tyres. **-bier,** *n.* strong beer. **-bild,** *n.* double image (*Opt.*). **-boden,** *m.* false bottom. **-brechung,** *f.* double refraction (*Opt.*). **-bruch,** *m.* compound fracture (*Surg.*); compound fraction (*Arith.*). **-decker,** *m.* biplane. **-deutig,** *adj.* equivocal, ambiguous. **-ehe,** *f.* bigamy. **-fall,** *m.* alternative. **-farbig,** *adj.* dichromatic. **-fernrohr,** *n.* binoculars. **-flinte,** *f.* double-barrelled gun. **-gänger,** *m.* double (*a p.*). **-gespann,** *n.* four-in-hand. **-gestaltung,** *f.* dimorphism. **-gleisig,** *adj.* double-track (*Railw.*). **-griff,** *m.* double stop (*Mus.*). **-heit,** *f.* doubleness, duality; duplicity. **-herzig,** *adj.* deceitful. **-hub,** *m.* up-and-down stroke (*Engin.*). **-kohlensauer,** *adj.* bicarbonate of. **-kreuz,** *n.* double sharp (*Mus.*). **-lafette,** *f.* twin mounting (*of guns*). **-läufig,** *adj.* double-barrelled. **-laut,** *m.* diphthong. **-lebig,** *adj.* amphibious. **-leiter,** *f.* pair of steps. **-monarchie,** *f.* Dual Monarchy (*Austria-Hungary, 1867–1918*). **-n,** 1. *v.a.* double; sew double; line; sole (*shoes*). 2. *v.n.* (*aux.* h.) double one's stakes; cheat (*at play*). **-pol,** *m.* dipole (*Rad.*). **-punkt,** *m.* colon. **-reihig,** *adj.* double breasted (*of jacket*). **-rumpf,** *m.* twin fuselage (*Av.*). **-rune,** *f.* SS (ᛋᛋ) (*Nat. Soc. symbol*). **-schein,** *m.* conjunction (*Astrol.*). **-schluß,** *m.* dilemma (*Log.*). **-schritt,** *m.* at the double, quick step. **-seitig,** *adj.* bilateral. **-sinn,** *m.* ambiguity. **-sinnig,** *adj.* ambiguous. **-sitzer,** *m.* two-seater (*vehicle*). **-spat,** *m.* Iceland spar. **-spiel,** *n.* duet; double-dealing, trickery. **-steuerung,** *f.* dual control (*Av. & Motor.*). **-stück,** *n.* duplicate. **-t,** *adj.* double, twofold, twin; twice; *in –ter Abschrift*, in duplicate; *–te Buchführung*, double entry (*book-keeping*); *um das –te größer*, double the size, twice as big. **-thochrund,** *adj.* biconvex, convexo-concave. **-tür,** *f.* double door; folding door. **-ung,** *f.* doubling; cheating (*at play*). **-verhältnis,** *n.* duplicate ratio (*Math.*). **-verkehr,** *m.* two-way communication. **-vers,** *m.* distich, couplet. **-währung,** *f.* double standard of currency, bimetallism. **-wesen,** *n.* duality; person with dual nature. **-zentner,** *m.* 100 kilograms. **-zünder,** *m.* combination fuse (*time & percussion*). **-züngig,** *adj.* two-faced, double-dealing, deceitful. **-zylinder,** *m.* twin cylinder (*Motor.*).
Dorf, *n.* (-es, ⸚er) village; *das sind ihm böhmische* or *spanische Dörfer*, that's all Greek to him. **-bengel,** *m.* country bumpkin. **-bewohner,** *m.* villager. **-gemeinde,** *f.* rural parish. **-junker,** *m.* country squire. **-krug,** *m.* village inn. **-pfarrer,** *m.*, **-prediger,** *m.* country parson. **-schaft,** *f.* villagers (*collectively*); village (*community*). **-schenke,** *f.* village inn. **-schulze,** *m.* village magistrate; bailiff, rural justice of the peace.
Dörf-chen, *n.* (-s, -), **-lein,** *n.* (-s, -) little village, hamlet. **-ler,** *m.* villager. **-lich,** *adj.* rustic.
Dorn, *m.* (-es, -en) thorn, prickle, spine; spike, prong; tongue (*of a buckle*); mandrel (*of lathe*); cotter (*Mach.*); punch; *er ist mir ein – im Auge*, he is a thorn in my side *or* flesh; *keine Rose ohne –en*, no rose without a thorn. **-besät,** *adj.* thorny. **-busch,** *m.* brier. **-butte,** *f.* turbot (*Rhombus maximus*) (*Icht*). **-dreher,** *m.* red-backed shrike (*Lanias collurio*) (*Orn.*). **-enhecke,** *f.* thorn hedge. **-enkrone,** *f.* crown of thorns (*Rel.*). **-envoll,** *adj., see* **-ig. -fortsatz,** *m.* spinal process. **-ig,** *adj.* thorny; spiky, spiny, spinous. **-röschen,** *n.* Sleeping Beauty. **-strauch,** *m., see* **-busch.**
dorren, *v.n.* (*aux.* s.) become dry; dry, wither, fade.
dörr-en, *v.a.* dry, desiccate, parch, calcine, bake, kiln-dry. **-obst,** *n.* dried fruit.
Dorsch, *m.* (-es, -e) cod (*Gadus morrhua*) (*Icht.*). **-lebertran,** *m.* cod-liver oil.
dort, (*Poet.* **-en**) *adv.* there, yonder; – *droben*, up there; **-her,** *adv.* from there, thence. **-herum,** thereabout. **-hin,** *adv.* to that place, that way, there, thither; – *hinab*, down there; – *hinauf*, up there; – *hinaus*, out there; *bis – hinaus*, right up to that point; up to the hilt; – *hinein*, in there; – *hinunter*, down there. **-ig,** *adj.* of that place, there. **-selbst,** *adv.* right there.
Dose, *f.* (-n) 1. box, tin, can, tin can. 2. *see* **Dosis. -nbarometer,** *n.* aneroid barometer. **-nentwicklung,** *f.* tank development (*Phot.*). **-nöffner,** *m.* tin-opener, can-opener.
dös-en, *v.n.* (*coll.*) doze, daydream, let one's thoughts wander, be stupid *or* drowsy. **-ig,** *adj.* drowsy, sleepy; absent-minded; stupid, dull. **-igkeit,** *f.* sleepiness, dullness; wool-gathering.
dos-ieren, *v.a.* measure out (*a dose*). **-is,** *f.* (Dosen) dose; *zu starke* or *große –is*, overdose; *zu geringe* or *kleine –is*, underdose.
dossier-en, *v.n.* slope. **-ung,** *f.* slope.
Dost, *m.* (-s, -e) origan (*Origanum*) (*Bot.*); *gemeiner –*, wild marjoram.
dot-al, *adj.* pertaining to a dower *or* dowry. **-algüter,** *n.pl.* glebe lands. **-ation,** *f.* dowry, portion; endowment, bequest. **-ieren,** *v.a.* endow; *neu* or *aufs neue –ieren*, re-endow.
Dotter, *n.* (-s, –) yolk (*of egg*). **-blume,** *f.* marsh-marigold (*Caltha palustris*) (*Bot.*).
Doz-ent, *m.* (-en, -en) university lecturer. **-entur,** *f.* university lectureship. **-ieren,** *v.n. & a.* lecture, teach.
Drache, *m.* (-n, -n) dragon; kite (*latter also*) **-n,** *m.* (-ns, -n)); (*fig.*) termagant, shrew; *einen –n steigen lassen*, fly a kite. **-nkraut,** *n.* dragon's-wort (*Dracontium*) (*Bot.*). **-ntheorie,** *f.* theory of dynamic lift (*Av.*). **-nwurz,** *f., see* **-nkraut.**
Drachme, *f.* (-n) drachm, dram.
Dragee, *f.* (-n) *or n.* (-s, -s) sugar-coated sweetmeat *or* pill.
Dragoner, *m.* (-s, –) dragoon; (*coll.*) virago.
Draht, *m.* (-es, ⸚e) wire, cable; line (*Tele.*); file (*for papers*); thread, grain (*of wood*); (*sl.*) money; (*sl.*) *auf – sein*, be all there, know one's stuff; *blanker –*, bare wire; *besponnener –*, covered wire. **-anschrift,** *f.* telegraphic address. **-antwort,** *f.* telegraphic reply. **-arbeit,** *f.* wire-work; filigree. **-auslöser,** *m.* cable-release (*Phot.*). **-bauer,** *n.* wire cage. **-bericht,** *m.* telegraphic report, telegram, wire. **-en,** 1. *adj.* (made) of wire, wiry. 2. *v.a. & n.* wire, send a telegram. **-fenster,** *n.* wire lattice. **-funk** *m.* radio. **-geflecht,** *n.* wire netting. **-gewebe,** *n.* wire gauze. **-gitter,** *n.* wire grating; trellis. **-haarig,** *adj.* wire-haired (*of dogs*). **-heftung,** *f.* wire sewing *or* stitching (*of books*). **-hindernis,** *n.* wire entanglement. **-leine,** *f.* wire rope. **-lich,** *adj.* transmitted by wire; *–liche Aufträge*, telegraphed orders; *–lich übermitteln*, transmit by wire. **-litze,** *f.* strand (*of wire*). **-los,** *adj.* wireless; *–los verbreiten*, broadcast; *–loser Dienst*, radio news service; *–lose Telegraphie*, wireless telegraphy. **-meldung,** *f.*, **-nachricht,** *f.* telegraphic communication *or* report. **-netz,** *n.* wire gauze *or* netting. **-puppe,** *f.* puppet, marionette. **-saite,** *f.* wire-string (*on violin, etc.*). **-schere,** *f.* wire cutter. **-seilbahn,** *f.* funicular railway. **-sieb,** *n.* wire sieve. **-spinnen,** *n.* wiredrawing. **-stift,** *m.* wire-tack, brad. **-ung,** *f.* wire, telegram. **-verhau,** *m.* wire entanglement; (*soldiers' sl.*) dried vegetables. **-wurm,** *m.* wire-worm. **-zange,** *f.* pliers, nippers. **-zieher,** *m.* wiredrawer; (*fig.*) wire-puller.
dräht-ern, *adj., see* **drahten.** *adj.* **-ig,** *suffix* (e.g. *drei–ig*, of *or* with three strands; *fein–ig*, with fine strands *or* threads).
drainieren, *v.a., see* **Drän–.**
drakonisch, *adj.* rigorous, harsh, Draconic, Draconian.
drall, 1. *adj. & adv.* tight, close-twisted; strapping, buxom, firm, robust; *–e Dirne*, buxom lass. 2. *m.* (-s, -e) rifling (*of a gun*); pitch; twist, torque (*Av.*); angular momentum. **-wirkung,** *f.* twist-effect (*of propeller slip-stream*) (*Av.*).
Drama, *n.* (-s, -en) drama. **-tiker,** *m.* dramatist, playwright. **-tisch,** *adj.* dramatic. **-tisieren,** *v.a.* dramatize. **-turg,** *m.* dramatic producer. **-turgie,** *f.* dramatic theory *or* technique.
dran, *adv., see* **daran.**
Drän, *m.* (-s, -s) draining tube (*Med.*); drainage pipe. **-age,** *f.* drainage. **-ieren,** *v.a. & n.* drain.

drang, dränge, *see* **dringen.**
Drang, *m.* (-(e)s) throng, crowd; pressure; oppression; urgency, stress; hurry; violence; craving, impulse; distress. *ich habe den – zu,* I feel a craving for; *einen heftigen – verspüren,* need the lavatory badly, (*coll. or hum.*) have a sudden call, be taken short; *– nach Osten,* eastward expansion. **–sal,** *n.* (-s, -e) & *f.* (-en), distress, affliction, hardship, oppression. **–salieren,** *v.a.* vex, harass, torment, worry, afflict. **–voll,** *adj.* crowded; oppressed, miserable; *–voll fürchterliche Enge,* close and terrible straits.
drängeln, *v.a.* press, shove.
dräng–en, 1. *v.a.* push, press, urge, hurry; oppress, afflict; *er –t auf Zahlung,* he presses for payment; *es –t mich* or *mich –t's Ihnen meinen Dank auszusprechen,* I cannot refrain from expressing my thanks. *gedrängt, p.p.* & *adj.* crowded, close; urged, compelled (*inner compulsion*); *sich zu etwas gedrängt fühlen,* feel obliged *or* impelled to do s.th.; *gedrängt voll,* crammed full, closely packed. 2. *v.r.* crowd; *sich zu etwas –en,* force o.s. to (do) s.th.; *sich durch–en,* force one's way through. 3. *v.n.* (*aux.* h.) be in a hurry; press (on); *die Zeit –t,* time presses.
dränieren, *see* **Drän.**
drapieren, *v.a.* drape, hang with drapery.
drasch (*also* **drosch**) *see* **dreschen.**
Draß, *n.* dregs, dross.
drastisch, *adj.* drastic.
dräuen, *Poet. for* **drohen.**
drauf, *adj., see* **darauf. –gänger,** *m.* daredevil. **–gängertum,** *n.* pluck, dash. **–gehen,** *v.n.* (*sep.*) be spent, wasted, lost *or* broken, perish, (*coll.*) die. **–geld,** *n.* premium, earnest-money. **–legen,** *v.a.* add to, supplement (*usually money*). **–losgehen,** *v.n.* rush at, go straight for. **–loswirtschaften,** *v.n.* (*sep.*) spend recklessly; **–setzen,** *v.a.* add to, give as an extra; *noch einen –setzen,* take a last drink, (*coll.*) have one for the road.
draus, *adv., see* **daraus.**
draußen, *adv.* outside, out of doors, without; abroad.
drechs–eln, *v.a.* & *n.* (*aux.* h.) turn (*on a lathe*); (*fig.*) elaborate; *Komplimente –eln,* bandy compliments; *gedrechselt, p.p.* & *adj.* elaborate; affected. **–elbank,** *f.* turning-lathe. **–ler,** *m.* (-s, –) turner. **–lerarbeit,** *f.* turnery; turning. **–lerei,** *f.* turner's workshop.
Dreck, *m.* (*fam.* & *dial.*) mud , dirt, mire, filth; dung, excrement, faeces; muck, dregs; *bis über die Ohren im – stecken,* be up to the eyes in mud; (*coll.*) *im – sitzen,* be down and out, be on one's uppers. **–ig,** *adj.* muddy, dirty, filthy; foul, nasty. **–käfer,** *m.* dung-beetle. **–karren.** *m.* muck cart. **–loch,** *n.* pot-hole, slough.
dreesch, *also* **driesch,** 1. *adj.* fallow, uncultivated. 2. *m.* (-es, -e) fallow land. **–ling,** *m.* edible mushroom.
Dregghaken, *m.* grapple (*Naut.*).
Dreh–achse, *f.* axis of rotation. **–bank,** *f.* (turning) lathe. **–bar,** *adj.* revolving, rotary; *–bar eingesetzt,* pivoted. **–bewegung,** *f.* rotary motion, rotation. **–bleistift,** *m.* propelling pencil. **–brücke,** *f.* swing-bridge. **–buch,** *n.* scenario (*Films*). **–bühne,** *f.* revolving stage (*Theat.*). **–ebene,** *f.* plane of rotation. **–eisen,** *n.* chisel, turning tool. **–flügelflugzeug,** *n.* helicopter. **–gelenk,** *n.* pivot. **–gestell,** *n.* pivot mounting. **–kondensator,** *m.* variable condenser (*Rad.*). **–kopf,** *m.* lathe. **–en,** 1. *v.a.* turn, twist, rotate, twirl, wind; distort; *einem eine Nase –en,* hoax a p.; *einen Film –en,* take *or* shoot a film; *einem den Rücken –en,* turn one's back to a p. 2. *v.r.* turn, rotate, revolve; *die Frage –t sich um,* it is a question whether, the question hinges on; *die Sachen können sich –en,* matters may take a (favourable) turn. 3. *v.n.* (*aux.* h.) turn, roll, spin; veer (*of wind*); *an einem Gesetze –en,* twist *or* distort a law. 4. *n.* turning; turn, revolution, rotation; *–en im Kopfe,* giddiness, swimming in the head. **–end,** *pr.p.* & *adj.* turning; rotary, rotatory; giddy. **–er,** *m.* turner, lathe hand; winch; rotator; slow waltz. **–kran,** *m.* derrick. **–krankheit,** *f.* giddiness; staggers (*of sheep*). **–kranz,** *m.* turntable. **–kreuz,** *n.* turnstile. **–moment,** *n.* torque. **–orgel,** *f.* barrel-organ. **–punkt,** *m.* pivot, fulcrum. **–rad,** *n.* fly-wheel. **–scheibe,** *f.* potter's wheel; turnplate, turntable; disk. **–späne,** *pl.* turnings, shavings, swarf. **–spiegel,** *m.* cheval-glass. **–spulinstrument,** *n.* moving-coil instrument (*Elec.*). **–stift,** *m.* mandrel (*of a lathe*). **–strom,** *m.* three-phase current (*Elec.*). **–stahl,** *m.* turning tool. **–stuhl,** *m.* revolving chair; music-stool. **–tisch,** *m.* dumb-waiter, revolving table. **–tür,** *f.* revolving door. **–turm,** *m.* revolving turret. **–ung,** *f.* turn, rotation, revolution; turning, twist, torsion, torque; *halbe –ung der Kurbel,* half-stroke of the crank. **–ungsachse,** *f.* axis of rotation. **–ungsellipsoid,** *n.* spheroid. **–ungsversuch,** *m.* torsion test (*Metall.*). **–ungswinkel,** *m. pl.* co-ordinates (*Math.*), angle of rotation. **–waage,** *f.* torsion balance. **–wuchs,** *m.* spiral grain (*in wood*). **–zahl,** *f.* speed of rotation. **–zahlmesser,** *m.* tachometer, revolution counter. **–zähler,** *m.* turnstile; *see also* **–zahlmesser. –zapfen,** *m.* pivot, gudgeon, journal (*Mach.*).
drei, 1. *num. adj.* three; *ehe man – zählen kann,* in a trice. 2. *f.* three. **–achtel,** *n.pl.* three-eighths. **–armig,** *adj.* three-armed. **–bein,** *n.* tripod. **–blatt,** *n.* trefoil (*Trillium*) (*Bot.*). **–blätterig,** *adj.* three-leaved, trifoliate (*Bot.*). **–bund,** *m.* Triple Alliance. **–dimensional,** *adj.* three-dimensional (*as films, and Nat. Soc. of warfare, i.e. military, economic & psychological*). **–doppelt,** *adj.* triple, treble, threefold. **–drähtig,** *adj.* three-ply, of 3 threads. **–eck,** *n.* triangle. **–eckig,** *adj.* triangular, three-cornered; deltoid (*Bot. Anat.*). **–eckpunkt,** *m.* triangulation point (*Surv.*). **–eckslehre,** *f.* trigonometry. **–einheit,** *f.* triad; trinity. **–einig,** *adj.* three in one, triune. **–einigkeit,** *f.* Trinity. **–einigkeitsbekenner,** *m.* Trinitarian. **–elektrodenröhre,** *f.* triode (*Rad.*). **–er,** 1. *Gen. of* drei; *Tagebuch –er Kinder,* diary kept by 3 children. 2. *m.* an old coin (*now fig.*); *spar deine –er,* save your money; *dafür kriegst du keinen –er,* you won't get a penny for it. **–ergruppe,** *f.* group of three, trio. **–erlei,** *indec. adj.* of 3 kinds, threefold. **–fach,** *adj.* threefold; triple, treble, tri-; *–fache Größe,* trinomial; *–fache Krone,* triple crown, tiara (*of the Pope*). **–faltigkeit,** *f.* Trinity. **–faltigkeitskirche,** *f.* Holy Trinity Church. **–farbendruck,** *m.* three-colour print(ing). **–felderwirtschaft,** *f.* three-field system. **–firner,** *m.* wine 3 years old. **–fuß,** *m.* tripod. **–ganggetriebe,** *n.* three-speed transmission (*Mach.*). **–gesang,** *m.* trio. **–gespann,** *n.* troika. **–gitterröhre,** *f.* pentode (*Rad.*). **–gliedrig,** *adj.* three-membered, in 3 sections; trinomial (*Math.*). **–heit,** *f.* triad; triplicity. **–herrschaft,** *f.* triumvirate. **–hundert,** *num. adj.* three hundred. **–hundertjahrfeier,** *f.* tercentenary celebration. **–hundertste,** *num. adj.* three-hundredth. **–jährig,** *adj.* 3-year-old, triennial. **–jährlich,** 1. *adj.* triennial. 2. *adv.* every 3 years. **–kaiserschlacht,** *f.* the battle of Austerlitz (*1805*). **–kantig,** *adj.* three-cornered, three-edged. **–klang,** *m.* triad (*Mus.*). **–königsabend,** *m.* eve of the Epiphany. **–königsfest,** *n.* Epiphany, Twelfth Night. **–leitersystem,** *n.* three-wire system (*Elec.*). **–mächteabkommen,** *n.* tripartite pact. **–mal,** *adv.* 3 times, threefold, thrice. **–malig,** *adj.* occurring 3 times, repeated 3 times, triple. **–männig,** *adj.* triandrian (*Bot.*). **–master,** *m.* three-master; three-cornered hat. **–monatlich,** *adj.* quarterly. **–namig,** *adj.* trinominal. **–pfündig,** *adj.* weighing 3 pounds. **–polröhre,** *f.* triode (*Rad.*). **–prozentig,** *adj.* at 3 per cent. **–rad,** *n.* tricycle. **–reim,** *m.* triplet. **–satz,** *m.* rule of three. **–schenk(e)lig,** *adj.* three-legged. **–schlag,** *m.* ambling pace (*of a horse*); triple time (*Mus.*). **–schlitz,** *m.* triglyph (*Arch.*). **–schnitt,** *m.* trisection. **–schürig,** *adj.* producing 3 crops a year. **–seemeilenzone,** *f.* three-mile limit. **–seitig,** *adj.* trilateral, three-sided. **–silbig,** *adj.* of 3 syllables, trisyllabic. **–sitzig,** *adj.* provided with 3 seats. **–spännig,** *adj.* yoked with 3 horses. **–sprachig,** *adj.* trilingual. **–sprung,** *m.* hop-skip-and-a-jump. **–ßig,** *num. adj.* thirty; *in den –ßigern,* (*of age*), *in den –ßiger Jahren* (*of dates*), in the thirties. **–ßiger,** *m.* man of 30 years; wine

of 1930. **-ßigjährig,** *adj.* of 30 years; *der -ßigjährige Krieg*, the Thirty Years War (*1618–48*). **-ßigste,** *num. adj.* thirtieth. **-ßigstel,** *n.* thirtieth part. **-ßigstens,** *adv.* in the thirtieth place. **-stellig,** *adj.* with 3 digits *or* places (*Math.*). **-stimmig,** *adj.* in 3 parts (*Mus.*). **-stöckig,** *adj.* three-storied. **-stündig,** *adj.* lasting 3 hours. **-stündlich,** *adv.* every third hour. **-tägig,** *adj.* lasting 3 days; *-tägiges Fieber*, tertian fever. **-teilig,** *adj.* in 3 parts, tripartite. **-verband,** *m.* Triple Entente (*England, France, and Russia*). **-vierteltakt,** *m.* three-four time (*Mus.*). **-wegschalter,** *m.* three-way switch (*Elec.*). **-wertig,** *adj.* trivalent. **-zack,** *m.* trident. **-zackig,** *adj.* three-pronged. **-zehig,** *adj.* tridactylous. **-zehn,** *num. adj.* thirteen. **-zehnte,** *num. adj.* thirteenth. **-zehntel,** *n.* thirteenth part.

drein, *adv.*, *see* **darein.**

dreist, *adj.* bold, daring; audacious, impudent, pert, cheeky. **-igkeit,** *f.* boldness; audacity, assurance; impudence; *Dumm-igkeit, f.* brazen cheek.

Drell, *m.* (-s, -e) *see* **Drillich.**

Dresch-diele, *f.* threshing-floor; **-e** (*coll.*) thrashing. **-en,** *ir. v.a.* thresh; (*coll.*) thrash. **-flegel,** *m.* flail. **-maschine,** *f.* **-mühle,** *f.*, *see* **-werk.** **-tenne,** *f.*, *see* **-diele.** **-werk,** *n.* threshing-machine.

dress-ieren, *v.a.* train; drill; break in; *der Hund ist auf den Mann -iert*, the dog is trained to go for people. **-ur,** *f.* breaking in, training.

driesch, *adj. & m.*, *see* **dreesch.**

Drilch, *m.* (-(e)s, -e), *see* **Drillich.**

[1]**Drill,** *m.* (-es, -e) 1. drill (*Mil.*); 2. *see* **Drillich.** **-bohrer,** *m.* drill, borer. **-egge,** *f.* drill-harrow. **-en,** *v.a.* 1. drill, exercise repeatedly. 2. drill, bore. **-ing,** *see* **Drilling.** **-kraft,** *f.* twisting force, torsion. **-kultur,** *f.* drill-husbandry (*Agr.*). **-maschine,** *f.* ridge-drill (*Agr.*). **-meister,** *m.* drill-sergeant. **-stab,** *m.* torsion bar (*Motor.*). **-ung,** *f.* torsion, twist.

Drillich, Drilch, *m.* (-(e)s, -e) strong ticking, canvas. **-anzug,** *m.* overalls, denims, fatigue dress (*Mil.*).

Drilling, *m.* (-s, -e) triplet (*child*); three-barrelled gun. **-sturm,** *m.* triple turret (*Nav.*).

drin, *adv.*, *see* **darin.**

dring-en, 1. *ir.v.n.* (*aux.* h. & s.) urge, press forward, press, rush; penetrate, pierce; force a way; *durch etwas -en*, force one's way through s.th.; *auf eine S. -en*, insist upon a th.; *in einen -en*, urge strongly upon a p.; *die Zeit -t*, time presses; *gedrungene Gestalt*, stocky *or* thickset build. **-end,** *pr.p. & adj.* pressing, urgent; cogent; *-end ersucht*, earnestly *or* urgently requested. **-lich,** *adj.* urgent, pressing. **-lichkeit,** *f.* urgency. **-lichkeitsantrag,** *m.* urgent motion (*Parl.*). **-lichkeitsliste,** *f.* priority schedule.

drinnen, *aav.* within, indoors.

drisch; drischst; drischt, *see* **dreschen.**

dritt-e, *num. adj.* third; *aus -er Hand*, indirectly; *der -e Stand*, the third estate, the lower classes; *der Wechsel ist schon in -er Hand*, the bill is already endorsed; *zum ersten! zum zweiten! zum -en und letzten!* going, going, gone! *eine Zahl in die -e Potenz erheben*, cube a number (*Math.*); *zu - marschieren*, march in threes; *den -en abschlagen*, play third (*a game*); come in third, take third place (*in a race or competition*); *-es Reich* (*Nat. Soc.*) Third Realm (*the Stefan George & Mueller van den Bruck myth; the first was Charlemagne to Francis II.* (A.D. *800–1806*), *the second was Bismarck's* (*1871–1918*)). **-el,** *n.* third part. **-elsbrot,** *n.* triple mixture bread (*i.e. wheat, barley, & rice*). **-ens,** *num. adv.* thirdly, in the third place. **-(e)halb,** *num. adj.* two and a half. **-letzt,** *adj.* last but two; antepenultimate. **-nächst,** *adj.* next but two.

drob, *adv.*, *see* **darob.**

droben, *adv.* above, up there.

Drog-en, *f.pl.* drugs. **-enhändler,** *m.* druggist. **-enhandlung,** *f.* **-erie,** *f.* drug-store, chemist's shop. **-eriewaren,** *f.pl.* drugs. **-ist,** *m.* (-en, -en) druggist, chemist.

droh-en, *v.a. & n.* (*einem mit einer S.*) threaten, menace. **-brief,** *m.* threatening letter. **-ung,** *f.* threat, menace. **-wort,** *n.* menace, threat.

Drohne, *f.* (-n) drone.

dröhnen, *v.n.* (*aux.* h.) rumble, roar, boom; resound.

drollig, *adj.* droll, amusing, funny, comical, odd.

Dromedar, *n.* (-s, -e) dromedary.

Drommete, *f.*, *see* **Trompete.**

drosch, drösche, *see* **dreschen.**

Droschke, *f.* (-n) cab, hackney-carriage. *Auto-, f.* taxi(-cab). **-ngaul,** *m.* cab-horse. **-nhalteplatz,** *m.* cab-stand. **-nkutscher,** *m.* cabman, cabby.

dröseln, *v.a. & n.* twist.

Drossel, *f.* (-n) 1. thrush, throstle (*Turdus*) (*Orn.*); 2. throttle (*also Motor.*); throat (*Hunt.*). **-ader,** *f.* jugular vein. **-bein,** *n.* collar-bone, clavicle (*Anat.*). **-klappe,** *f.* throttle-valve, butterfly valve, damper. **-kreis,** *m.* rejector circuit (*Rad.*). **-n,** *v.a.* throttle, strangle; choke (*Rad.*); slow down, check, limit. **-spule,** *f.* choke (coil), inductance (*Rad.*).

Drost, *m.* (-es, -e) (*dial.*) high bailiff. **-ei,** *f.* (*dial.*) bailiwick; *Land-ei*, district, province.

drüben, *adv.* over there, on the other side, hereafter (*i.e. after death*), beyond, yonder, opposite; *hüben und* or *wie -*, everywhere, on all sides.

drüber, *adv.*, *see* **darüber.**

Druck, *m.* 1. (-(e)s, ⸚e) compression, pressure, thrust; squeeze; weight, burden; grievance, hardship. 2. (-(e)s, -e) print, printing; impression; type; *- der Schwerkraft*, gravitation; *ein - von drei Atmosphären*, pressure of three atmospheres; *in - geben*, send to be printed, publish; *in - gehen*, go to press. **-beanspruchung,** *f.* compression stress (*Metall.*) **-berichtigungen,** *f.pl.* corrigenda, corrections. **-bogen,** *m.* proof-sheet, proof. **-buchstaben,** *m.pl.* type. **-en,** *v.a.* print; impress, stamp; *er lügt wie gedruckt*, he's a bare-faced liar. **-er,** *m.* printer. **-erei,** *f.* press, printing-press, printing-works. **-erlaubnis,** *f.* imprimatur. **-erschwärze,** *f.* printer's ink. **-feder,** *f.* compression spring. **-fehler,** *m.* misprint, printer's error, typographical error. **-fehlerverzeichnis,** *n.* (list of) errata. **-fertig,** *adj.* ready for (the) press. **-festigkeit,** *f.* compression strength, resistance (*Phys.*). **-freiheit,** *f.* liberty of the press. **-gefälle,** *n.* pressure gradient. **-höhe,** *f.* head of water, height of fall. **-knopf,** *m.* press-button, push-button; bell-push; press-stud, patent fastener. **-kosten,** *f.pl.* expenses of printing. **-kraft,** *f.* pressure (*Phys.*). **-läppchen,** *n.* compress (*Surg.*). **-legung,** *f.* printing. **-lehre,** *f.*, *see* **-messer.** **-luft,** *f.* compressed air. **-messer,** *m.* pressure gauge, manometer. **-model,** *n.* printing-block. **-ölung,** *f.* forced *or* pressure oil feed (*Mach.*). **-ort,** *m.* place of printing *or* publication. **-platte,** *f.* engraving-plate. **-probe,** *f.* proof. **-pumpe,** *f.* forcing-pump, pressure pump. **-punkt,** *m.* pressure point (*Med.*); aerodynamic centre (*Av.*); *-punkt nehmen* (*Mil. sl.*), shirk one's duty. **-sache,** *f.* printed matter, printed papers; (by) book post. **-schraube,** *f.* pusher type propeller (*Av.*). **-schrift,** *f.* type; publication. **-seite,** *f.* printed page. **-stock,** *m.* block (*Typ.*). **-taster,** *m.* signalling key. **-umlaufschmierung,** *f.* pressure lubrication (*Mach.*). **-verband,** *m.* compress. **-versendung,** *f.* book post. **-vorschrift,** *f.* training manual (*Mil.*). **-waage,** *f.* areometer. **-walze,** *f.* printer's roller, cylinder. **-waren,** *f.pl.* (cotton) prints. **-wasserpumpe,** *f.* hydraulic pump. **-welle,** *f.* blast (*of explosive*). **-werk,** *n.* forcing-pump. **-zerstäuber,** *m.* spray gun. **-zugdämpfer,** *m.* quiescent push-pull (*Rad.*).

drück-en, 1. *v.a.* press, push, clasp, squeeze, pinch; oppress, afflict; depress, weigh down; *der Alp -t ihn*, he has a nightmare; *einem Geld in die Hand -en*, slip money into a p.'s hand; *einen im Handel -en*, drive a hard bargain with a p.; *einen ans Herz -en*, clasp a p. to one's heart, embrace a p.; *den Hut ins Gesicht -en*, pull one's hat over one's eyes; *auf den Knopf -en*, press the button; *den Markt -en*, overstock the market; *die Preise -en*, bring down prices; *den Rekord -en*, beat *or* lower the record (*Sport*); (*coll.*) *wo –t dich der Schuh ?* what's the trouble? *der Stiefel –t mich*, the boot pinches me; *die freie Zeit –t ihn*, time hangs heavy on his hands; *gedrückte Stimmung*, depressed mood; (*C.L.*) dullness, flatness (*of the market*); *gedrückte Preise*, low prices. 2. *v.r.* shirk, malinger; sneak away, make o.s. scarce; funk, scrimshank; (*coll.*) *sich vor einer S. –en*, avoid doing a th., get out of a th., shirk a th. (*sl.*) **–eberger,** *m.* shirker, slacker, scrimshanker. (*sl.*) **–ebergerei,** *f.* shirking. **–end,** *pr.p.* & *adj.* heavy, oppressive; *–ende Armut*, extreme poverty; *–ende Hitze*, oppressive *or* sultry heat; *–ende Last*, grievous burden; *–ende Steuer*, heavy taxation; *–ende Verhältnisse*, straitened circumstances; *das –ende benehmen*, make matters easier. **–er,** *m.* latch; trigger, thumb-release.

drucksen, *v.a.* hold back, hesitate, waver.

Drud–e, *f.* (-en) witch. **–enbeutel,** *m.* puff-ball. **–enfuß,** *m.* club moss (*Lycopodium clavatum*) (*Bot.*), drude's foot; pentagram (*symbol* ✡ *against witches and evil spirits*).

drum, *adv.*, *see* **darum**; *mit allem Drum und Dran*, with everything appertaining thereto, (*coll.*) with all the trimmings.

drunt–en, *adv.*, down there, below. **–er,** *adv.*, *see* **darunter. –er und drüber,** *adv.* higgledy-piggledy, upside down.

Drus–e, *f.* (-en) 1. druse, geode; 2. strangles, glanders (*in horses, etc.*); 3. (*dial.*) sediment, dregs, lees. **–ig,** *adj.* suffering from glanders, *etc.* **–enräume,** *m.pl.*, *see* **–e.**

Drüs–e, *f.* (-en) gland; **–enbeule,** *f.* bubo (*Med.*). **–enentzündung,** *f.* adenitis. **–engang,** *m.* glandular duct. **–engeschwulst,** *f.* glandular swelling, struma. **–enkrank,** *adj.* scrofulous. **–enkrankheit,** *f.* glandular disease; scrofula; strangles (*in horses*). **–enkropf,** *m.* goitre. **–ensaft,** *m.* glandular secretion. **–ensekret,** *n.*, *see* **–ensaft. –ig,** *adj.* glandular.

Dschungel, *m.* or *n.* (-s, -) or *f.* (-n) jungle.

du, 1. *pers. pron.* you, (*B.* & *Poet.*) thou; *mit einem auf – und – stehen*, be on intimate terms with a p. 2. *n.*; *dein anderes* or *zweites –*, your other self.

Dua–l, *m.* (-ls, -le), **–lis** (-lis, -le) dual (number). **–lismus,** *m.* dualism. **–listisch,** *adj.* dualistic. **–lität,** *f.* duality.

Dübel, *m.*, *see* **Döbel.**

Dub-lette, *f.* (-n) duplicate, double, doublet. **–lieren,** *v.a.* double concentrate. **–lone,** *f.* (-en) doubloon.

duck–en, 1. *v.a.* & *n.* (*aux.* h.) stoop, duck; humble, humiliate, bring low. 2. *v.r.* duck, stoop, bend down; submit, humble o.s., knuckle under. **–mäuser,** *m.* (-s, –) sneak, coward. **–mäuserig,** *adj.* sneaking, cowardly.

dud–eln, *v.n.* (*aux.* h.) play the bagpipes. **–elei,** *f.* piping. **–elkasten,** *m.* barrel-organ. **–elsack,** *m.* bagpipes. **–elsackpfeifer,** *m.* bagpiper, piper. **–(e)ler,** *m.* (-s, –) bagpiper.

Duell, *n.* (-s, -e) duel; *– auf Degen* or *Pistolen*, duel with swords *or* pistols. **–ant,** *m.* (-en, -en) duellist. **–ieren,** *v.r.* fight a duel.

Duett, *n.* (-s, -e) duet.

Duft, *m.* (-es, ⸚e) scent, odour, smell, aroma; (*Poet.*) fragrance; (*Poet.*) vapour. **–en,** *v.n.* (*aux.* h. & s.) exhale fragrance, be fragrant, smell sweet. **–end,** *pr.p.* & *adj.* fragrant, scented. **–ig,** *adj.* misty, hazy; fragrant, scented, perfumed, odorous, odoriferous. **–los,** *adj.* odourless, inodorous. **–öl,** *n.* aromatic oil. **–stoff,** *m.* aromatic substance, perfume. **–wasser,** *n.* perfume, scent.

Dukaten, *m.* (-s, –) ducat (*an old coin*).

duld–en, 1. *v.a.* suffer, endure, bear patiently; tolerate; (*coll.*) put up with. 2. *n.* sufferance, patient endurance. **–sam,** *adj.* patient, tolerant, long-suffering. **–samkeit,** *f.* toleration, spirit of toleration. **–ung,** *f.* toleration, patience.

Dult, *f.* (-en) (*Austr.* & *Bav. dial.*) fair.

dumm, *adj.* dull, stupid, slow; foolish, silly, ridiculous; (*coll.*) *das ist –*, that is a nuisance *or* awkward; *der –e August*, circus clown; *ein –es Gesicht machen*, be at a loss *or* nonplussed, pretend not to know; *–er Junge* (*if said to an adult*) fool (*the acknowledged word of challenge to a duel*); (*coll.*) *der –e sein, den –en machen*, be the one who pays, (*sl.*) be the sucker; *eine –e S.*, an awkward business; (*coll.*) *–es Zeug !* piffle, stuff and nonsense! **–dreist,** *adj.* impudent, impertinent. **–dreistigkeit,** *f.* impertinence. **–heit,** *f.* stupidity, folly; nonsense; silly action; blunder; (*pl.*) foolish pranks. **–kopf,** *m.*, **–erjan,** *m.*, **–ian,** *m.*, **–rian,** *m.* blockhead, simpleton, noodle.

Dümmling, *m.* (-s, -e) simpleton.

dumpf, *adj.* damp, muggy; stifling, heavy, close (*of air*); dull, hollow, muffled (*of sound*); (*fig.*) dull, apathetic, gloomy; *es macht mir den Kopf ganz –*, it stupefies me *or* makes my head go muzzy, *or* (*sl.*) gets me all flummoxed; *–es Streben*, vague aspirations. **–heit,** *f.* dullness, hollowness, gloominess; stupor, torpor. **–ig,** *adj.* damp, dank, musty, mouldy. **–igkeit,** *f.* dampness, mustiness.

dun, *adj.* (*dial. sl.*) tipsy.

Dun–e, *f.* down (*of birds*). **–ig,** *adj.* downy.

Dün–e, *f.* (-en) dune, sandhill. **–ung,** *f.* surf, swell (*of sea*), ground swell.

Dung, *m.* (-(e)s) dung, manure. **–haufen,** *m.* dung-hill.

düng–en, *v.a.* fertilize, manure. **–ejauche,** *f.* liquid manure. **–emittel,** *n.* fertilizer, artificial manure. **–er,** *m.* manure, dung; *künstlicher –er*, artificial manure. **–erersatz,** *m.* dung salts, saline manure. **–ung,** *f.* manuring.

dunkel, 1. *adj.* dark, obscure, dim, dusky; gloomy; deep, mysterious; *der –ste Tag meines Lebens*, the blackest day of my life; *von dunkler Herkunft*, of doubtful antecedents; *eine dunkle Existenz*, a shady existence; *ein Sprung ins Dunkle*, a leap in the dark. 2. *n.* darkness; obscurity, ambiguity; *im –n*, in the dark (*also fig.*). **–heit,** *f.* darkness; obscurity. **–kammer,** *f.* dark room (*Phot.*). **–mann,** *m.* (-männer) obscurantist. **–n,** 1. *v.n.* (*aux.* h.) grow dark *or* dim. 2. *v.a.* darken, deepen.

Dünkel, *m.* (-s) self-conceit, arrogance; presumption; *– haben*, be self-conceited. **–haft,** *adj.* self-conceited, arrogant.

dünk–en, 1. *ir.v.n.* (*aux.* h.) & *imp.* seem, look, appear; *es –t mich* (or *mir*) or *mich* (or *mir*) *–t*, it seems to me, I fancy; *es dünkte* (*Poet. deuchte*) *ihn* (or *ihm*), it seemed to him, he thought; *tue, was dir gut –t*, do what you think proper. 2. *v.r.* imagine *or* fancy o.s.; *sie dünkt sich schön*, she imagines herself beautiful; *sie –en sich was*, they think a great deal of themselves; *er dünkt sich was Rechtes*, he has a high opinion of himself.

dünn, *adj.* thin, fine; flimsy; slender, slim; weak, diluted (*fluids*); rare (*air*); *–e Ohren haben*, have a quick ear; (*coll.*) *sich – machen*, make o.s. scarce. **–backig,** *adj.* thin-faced, lantern-jawed. **–bewaldet,** *adj.* sparsely wooded. **–bier,** *n.* small beer. **–darm,** *m.* small intestine. **–druckausgabe,** *f.* India paper edition. **–e,** *f.* slenderness, thinness; sparseness; rarity; diluteness. **–en,** *v.a.* thin, dilute. **–flüssig,** *adj.* fluid, watery. **–flüssigkeit,** *f.* low viscosity. **–gesät,** *adj.* sparsely sown, thinly scattered; (*fig.*) scarce. **–häutig,** *adj.* filmy; thin-skinned. **–heit,** *f.* rarity, rareness (*of air*). **–leibig,** *adj.* lank. **–schlagen,** *v.a.* beat out (*metals*). **–schleifen,** *v.a.* grind thin. **–schliff,** *m.* thin section. **–ungen,** *f.pl.* flanks (*Hunt.*).

Dunst, *m.* (-es, ⸚e) vapour, haze; fume, steam; *übler –*, miasma; (*coll.*) *einem einen blauen – vormachen*, humbug a p.; *keinen blassen – davon haben*, not have the haziest notion of. **–artig,** *adj.*, *see* **–förmig. –bild,** *n.*, **–gebilde,** *n.* illusion, phantom. **–bläschen,** *n.* steam globule *or* vesicle. **–en,** *v.n.* (*aux.* h.) rise as vapour, evaporate, steam, smoke, exhale. **–förmig,** *adj.* gaseous, vaporous. **–ig,** *adj.* vaporous, misty, hazy, damp, steamy. **–kreis,** *m.* atmosphere. **–loch,** *n.* airhole, vent, ventilator. **–obst,** *n.* stewed fruit. **–schleier,** *m.* haze.

dünsten, *v.a.* steam, stew.

Dünung, *f.*, *see* **Dün–.**

Duodez, *n.* (-es) duodecimo (*Typ.*). **–fürst,** *m.* petty prince.

Dupli–k, *f.* (-ken) rejoinder (*Law*). **–kat,** *n.* (-(e)s, -e) duplicate. **–zieren,** *v.a.* duplicate, double.

Dur, *n.* major (*Mus.*). **–tonart,** *f.* major key. **–tonleiter,** *f.* major scale.

durch, **1.** *prep.* (*Acc.*) 1. through, across; 2. by, by means of; owing to; 3. (*usually follows its noun*) throughout, during; – *das Fenster sehen,* look through the window; – *den Strom schwimmen,* swim across the river; (*fig.*) – *die Finger sehen,* be indulgent, not be particular; – *die Post,* by post; – *Zufall,* by chance; – *einen Stein gebrochen,* broken by a stone; *das ganze Jahr* –, throughout the year, the whole year, all the year. **2.** *adv.* thoroughly; – *und* –, throughout, through and through, utterly; *fünf Uhr* –, past five o'clock; *ich bin mit der Arbeit* –, I've got through all my work; *er ist mit uns* –, he's finished as far as we're concerned, we've finished with him; (*often implies some verb not expressed*) *der Zug ist schon* –, the train has passed through; *hast du das Buch schon* – ? have you finished the book? *ich muß* –, I must get through (*i.e. past an obstacle*). **3.** *prefix* (*Verbs compounded with* durch *may be either separable or inseparable. In the former case the stress is on the prefix, and the verb is usually intransitive; in the latter the stress is on the root verb, and it is usually transitive*), e.g. *die Feuchtigkeit drang* –, the damp penetrated; *das Gas –drang das ganze Haus,* the gas filled the whole house. **–aus,** *adv.* (*usually not accented on* durch) throughout, thoroughly, quite, completely, absolutely, positively, by all means; *–aus nicht,* by no means, not at all; *weil Sie es –aus wollen,* since you insist upon it; *es ist –aus verschieden,* it is altogether different. **–einander,** 1. *adv.* in confusion, pell-mell, promiscuously. 2. *n.* confusion.
durcharbeiten, 1. *v.a.* (*sep.*) work through, complete, finish, elaborate, perfect; knead (*dough*). 2. *v.n.* (*sep.*) work without a break. 3. *v.r.* (*sep.*) make one's way, get through.
durchätzen, *v.a.* (*sep.*) corrode completely.
durchaus, *see* **durch.**
durchbacken, *v.a.* (*sep.*) bake thoroughly.
durchbeben, *v.a.* (*insep.*) thrill through, shake *or* agitate thoroughly.
durchbeißen, 1. *ir.v.a.* (*sep. & insep.*) bite through; strike home. 2. *v.r.* (*sep.*) fight it out; struggle through.
durchbeizen, *v.a.* (*sep.*) corrode, eat through with a corrosive; macerate, tan.
durchbetteln, 1. *v.r.* (*sep.*) beg one's way, live by begging. 2. *v.a.* (*insep.*) wander through (*a place*) begging.
Durchbiegung, *f.* sag (*Metall.*).
durchbilden, *v.a.* (*sep.*) improve, perfect, develop.
durchblättern, *v.a.* (*sep. & insep.*) turn the pages of, glance at, skim through (*a book*).
Durchblick, *m.* (-(e)s, -e) view, prospect, vista; peep; (*fig.*) penetration. **–en, 1.** *v.n.* (*aux.* h.) (*sep.*) 1. peep *or* peer through; 2. appear through; become visible; *–en lassen,* allow to be noticed, give a hint. **2.** *v.a.* (*insep.*) penetrate *or* pierce with a look, see through.
durchbohren, 1. *v.a.* (*insep.*) bore through, pierce, penetrate, perforate, percolate through. 2. *v.r.* (*sep.*) burrow *or* wriggle through.
durchbraten, *ir.v.a.* (*sep.*) roast thoroughly. *durchgebraten, p.p. & adj.* well done (*of meat*).
durchbrechen, 1. *ir.v.a. & n.* (*aux.* s.) (*sep.*) break through; (*fig.*) appear (*as teeth, buds, etc.*). 2. *v.a.* (*insep.*) break in two (*as a stick*); break *or* come through; breach, pierce, infringe, perforate, punch; *durchbrochene Arbeit,* open work, filigree.
durchbrennen, *ir.v.n.* (*aux.* s.) (*sep.*) burn through, burn a hole, burn out (*electric bulb*), fuse (*Elec.*); (*coll.*) abscond, decamp, elope.
durchbringen, 1. *ir.v.a.* (*sep.*) bring *or* carry through; squander, dissipate; *er hat sein ganzes Vermögen durchgebracht,* he has squandered all his fortune; *die Ärzte hoffen ihn durchzubringen,* the doctors hope to pull him through; *einen Gesetzesvorschlag* –, get a bill passed *or* carried. 2. *v.r.* (*sep.*) maintain o.s., support o.s., get on; *sich ehrlich* –, make shift to gain an honest livelihood; *sich kümmerlich* –, manage barely to make ends meet.
durchbrochen, *adj.* open-work filigree, pierced, perforated; *see* **durchbrechen.**
Durchbruch, *m.* (-(e)s, ⁼e) breach, break-through (*Mil.*); rupture, opening, aperture, eruption, escape, cutting (*of teeth*); (religious) awakening, change for the better; *zum* – *kommen,* burst forth.
durchdacht, *p.p. & adj.* thought out carefully; studied, planned; *see* **durchdenken.**
durchdauern, *v.a.* (*sep. & insep.*) last (over); *den Winter* –, winter (*of plants*); hibernate (*of animals*).
durchdenken, *ir.v.a.* (*sep. & insep.*) think over carefully, reflect on, ponder over.
durchdrängen, *v.a. & r.* (*sep.*) force through.
durchdrehen, *v.a.* (*sep.*) wring, mangle (*washing*), put through the mangle; swing (*propeller*) (*Av.*); (*coll.*) *vollständig durchgedreht sein,* be at one's last gasp, be on one's last legs, be tired to death; be quite crazy.
durchdring–en, 1. *ir.v.n.* (*aux.* s.) (*sep.*) force one's way through; penetrate, pierce; permeate; prevail, get the mastery; accomplish; succeed; *diese Meinung ist durchgedrungen,* this view has prevailed. 2. *v.a.* (*insep.*) penetrate, pierce; permeate, pervade; *er ist von Mut durchdrungen,* he is filled with courage. **–bar,** *adj., see* **–lich. –end,** *pr.p. & adj.* penetrating, piercing, shrill; acute, keen, sharp. **–lich,** *adj.* penetrable, permeable. **–lichkeit,** *f.* penetrability. **–ung,** *f.* penetration, permeation.
durchdrücken, *v.a. & n.* (*sep.*) press or force through; straighten the knees (*in drill*); *ein Gesetz* –, carry a bill with difficulty.
durchduften, *v.a.* (*insep.*) fill with perfume, scent, perfume.
durcheilen, 1. *v.n.* (*aux.* s.) (*sep.*). 2. *v.a.* (*insep.*) hurry through, pass through in haste.
durcheinander, *see* **durch.**
durchfahr–en, 1. *ir.v.n.* (*aux.* s.) (*sep.*) drive *or* pass through (*i.e. without stopping*). 2. *v.a.* (*insep.*) pass through, travel through; (*fig.*) *es durchfuhr mich wie ein Blitz,* it came over me in a flash. **–t,** *f.* passage, transit; gateway; thoroughfare; *–t verboten,* no thoroughfare!
Durchfall, *m.* falling through; diarrhoea (*Med.*); failure, (*sl.*) flop (*at examination or theatre*). **–en,** *ir.v.n.* (*aux.* s.) (*sep.*) fall through; fail, be unsuccessful; be rejected; (*sl.*) be ploughed (*at examination*), be a flop (*Theat.*).
durchfechten, 1. *ir.v.a.* (*sep.*) carry one's point; fight it out. 2. *v.r.* (*sep.*) fight one's way through.
durchfeilen, *v.a.* (*sep.*) file through; give the last polish (*to a work of art, a poem, etc.*).
durchfeuchten, *v.a.* (*insep.*) wet thoroughly, soak, steep.
durchfinden, *ir.v.r.* (*sep.*) find one's way through; master (*a problem*).
durchflammen, *v.a.* (*insep.*) flash through; (*fig.*) animate, fire.
durchfliegen, 1. *ir.v.n.* (*aux.* s.) (*sep.*) fly through, to the end *or* past (*i.e. without stopping*); (*coll.*) plough (*an examination*). 2. *v.a.* (*insep.*) fly through, rush through; skim over, skip (*a book*); *ich habe den Brief nur eben durchflogen,* I have only just glanced through the letter.
durchfluten, *v.a.* (*insep.*) flood, inundate, flow through, stream through, rush through (*water*).
durchforschen, *v.a.* (*insep.*) search through, examine thoroughly, investigate.
durchforst–en, *v.a.* (*sep.*) thin (*a forest*). **–ung,** *f.* thinning (*of a forest*).
durchfressen, 1. *ir.v.a.* (*insep.*) eat through, corrode. 2. *v.r.* (*sep.*) (*coll.*) get out of a difficulty, scrape through.
durchfrieren, 1. *ir.v.a.* (*insep.*) freeze, chill. 2. *v.n.* (*aux.* s.) (*sep.*) be chilled through, feel cold.
Durchfuhr, *f.* (-en) passage through, transit; transport. **–handel,** *m.* transit trade. **–zoll,** *m.* transit duty.
durchführ–en, *v.a.* (*sep.*) convey *or* lead through; accomplish, realize, carry out; modulate (*Mus.*). **–bar,** *adj.* feasible, practicable. **–ung,** *f.* accomplishment; execution, performance, realization.
durchfurcht, *adj.* furrowed, wrinkled.
Durchgang, *m.* (-(e)s, ⁼e) passage through, transit; thoroughfare; passage, alley, opening, duct, gateway; channel (*Naut.*); transit (*Astr., C.L.*); *freier* –, open thoroughfare; – *verboten!* no road! **–sgerechtigkeit,** *f.* right of way; thoroughfare. **–sgut,** *n.*,

–sgüter, *n.pl.* goods in transit. **–shandel,** *m.* trade with transit goods. **–slager,** *n.* transit camp (*Mil.*). **–snote,** *f.* passing-note (*Mus.*). **–sprofil,** *n.* clearance (*Engin.*). **–sschein,** *m.* permit, pass. **–sverkehr,** *m.* transit(-trade), through traffic. **–swagen,** *m.* through carriage. **–swaren,** *f.* transit-goods. **–szoll,** *m.* transit-duty. **–szug,** (*abbr.* **D–Zug**), *m.* through, fast *or* express train, *see* **durchgehen.**

Durchgäng–er, *m.* (-ers, -er) runaway horse; (*fig.*) hothead. **–ig,** *adj.* thorough, radical; general, universal; without exception; prevailing.

durchgeben, *v.a.* (*sep.*) filter, strain; pass (*the word*) down.

durchgebildet, *p.p.* & *adj.* well-trained; *see* **durchbilden.**

durchgehen, 1. *ir.v.n.* (*aux.* s.) (*sep.*) go *or* pass through, be transmitted; pierce; run away, escape, elope; bolt, stampede; pass, be approved; *die Pferde gingen mit uns durch,* the horses bolted; *seine Frau ist ihm durchgegangen,* his wife has run off *or* has left him; *der Antrag ging durch,* the motion was carried; *das geht (mit) durch, das mag so mit –,* that may pass. 2. *v.a.* (*sep.*) (*aux.* h & s.) look over, examine, peruse, check; wear out (*shoes, etc.*); *sich (Dat.) die Füße –,* walk one's feet sore. 3. *v.a.* (*insep.*) (*aux.* h.) go *or* walk through. **–d,** *pr. p.* & *adj.* pervading, piercing; continuous; transmitted; *–der Zug,* through train; *–de Eigenschaft,* general characteristic. **–ds** *adv.* universally, generally; throughout, in every part.

Durchgeseites, *n.* filtrate (*Chem.*); *see* **durchseihen.**

durchgießen, 1. *ir.v.a.* (*sep.*) pour through, filter strain. 2. *v.n.* (*sep.*) percolate.

durchglühen, 1. *v.n.* (*aux.* s.) (*sep.*) burn through; *die Birne ist durchgeglüht,* the bulb is *or* has burnt out. 2. *v.a.* (*insep.*) make red-hot, heat thoroughly, anneal; (*fig.*) inflame, inspire.

durchgraben, *ir.v.a.* (*insep.*) dig through; pierce by digging.

durchgrauen, *v.n.* (*insep.*) fill with horror.

durchgreifen, *ir.v. n.* (*sep.*) (*aux.* h.) proceed without ceremony, take vigorous action, act effectively; *es muß rücksichtslos durchgegriffen werden,* ruthless measures are called for. **–d,** *pr.p.* & *adj.* energetic, thorough, decisive, effectual, sweeping.

Durchguß, *m.* (-(ss)es, ¨-(ss)e) filtration, percolation, strainer, filter, sink; *see* **durchgießen.**

durchhalten, *v.a.* & *n.* (*aux.* h.) (*sep.*) carry on to the end, hold out, endure, stick to a th. through thick and thin, (*sl.*) stick it out.

Durchhang, *m.* sag (*of a wire*) (*Tele.*).

durchhängen, *v.n.* sag, dip.

Durchhau, *m.* opening, clearing, vista (*in a wood*). **–en,** 1. *ir.v.a.* (*sep.* & *insep.*) hew *or* cut through; (*coll.*) *einen –en,* (*sep.*), give a p. a sound thrashing. 2. *v.r.* (*sep.*) hack one's way through.

durchhecheln, *v.a.* (*sep.*) hackle flax thoroughly; (*fig.*) criticize, censure, speak ill of, pull to pieces; *seine Freunde –,* backbite one's friends.

durchheizen, *v.a.* (*sep.*), *see* **durchhitzen.**

durchhelfen, *ir.v.n.* (*sep.*) help (out of a difficulty), give one's support to, assist (*Dat.*); *sich (Dat.) mit etwas –,* succeed by means of, get on by; *sich (Dat.) mühsam –,* work hard to make both ends meet.

durchhitzen, *v.a.* (*sep.* & *insep.*) heat through and through; heat well *or* thoroughly.

durchhöhlen, *v.a.* (*insep.*) hollow out, undermine; excavate.

durchirren, *v.a.* (*insep.*) wander *or* meander through.

durchkämpfen, 1. *v.a.* (*sep.*) fight out *or* to the end; get by fighting; maintain (*a point*). 2. *v.r.* (*sep.*) fight one's way through *or* out; *sich durch Schwierigkeiten –,* valiantly overcome difficulties; *eine Idee muß sich erst –,* an idea must first get itself established *or* accepted.

durchkauen, *v.a.* (*sep.*) chew thoroughly; (*coll.*) repeat over and over again.

durchknabbern, *v.n.* (*sep.*) 'mouse-hole' (*from house to house*) (*Mil.*).

durchkommen, *ir.v.n.* (*aux.* s.) (*sep.*) come *or* get through; succeed, pass (*examinations*); *mit seiner Einnahme –,* make both ends meet. *mit Lügen kommt man nicht durch,* lies won't get you anywhere; *mit diesen Ausflüchten kommst du bei mir nicht durch,* these excuses cut no ice with me; *mit einem –,* succeed with a p.; *er wird in der Prüfung schwerlich –,* he will hardly be able to pass his examination.

durchkönnen, *ir.v.n.* (*aux.* h.) (*sep.*) (*coll.*) be able to get through *or* to pass; *hier kommt man nicht durch,* there's no way through here.

durchkosten, *v.a.* (*sep.*) experience fully, savour.

durchkreuzen, 1. *v.a.* (*insep.*) cross, traverse; (*fig.*) prevent, frustrate, cross, thwart; 2. *v.a.* (*sep.*) cross out, strike out, delete.

Durchlaß, *m.* (-(ss)es, ¨-(ss)e) passage; sieve, filter; opening, outlet; sluice pipe, culvert. **–(ss)en,** 1. *ir.v.a.* (*sep.*) let through, permit to pass; strain; filter; transmit (*light, etc.*). 2. *n.,* see **–(ss)ung.** **–(ss)end,** *pr.p.* & *adj.* pervious; transparent; *nicht –(ss)end,* impermeable. **–kreis,** *m.* acceptor circuit (*Rad.*). **–schein,** *m.* pass, permit.

durchlässig, *adj.* pervious, porous, permeable, penetrable (*für,* to); *–er Kreis,* acceptor circuit (*Rad.*).

Durchlaucht, *f.* (-en) Highness, Serene Highness; *Ew.* (= *Euer*) *–,* (*m.*), *Ihre –,* (*f.*), Your Highness. **–ig,** *adj.* most high, serene, illustrious, august.

Durchlauf, *m.* (-(e)s, ¨-e) passage; sieve, colander; diarrhoea. **–en,** 1. *ir.v.n.* (*aux.* s.) (*sep.*) run *or* pass *or* hurry through, traverse hurriedly; filter. 2. *v.a.* (*sep.*) wear out (*shoes, etc.*); *durchgelaufene Schuhe,* shoes worn into holes. 3. *v.a.* (*insep.*) run all over; peruse hastily, skim over; *es durchläuft mich kalt,* a cold shudder went through me; *ein Gerücht durchläuft die Stadt,* a report is going about the town; *alle Läden –,* hunt through all the shops. **–d,** *adj.* continuous; *–e Strecke,* ship's run (*Naut.*).

durchlesen, *v.a.* (*sep.*) read through *or* over, peruse.

durchleucht–en, 1. *v.n.* (*sep.*) shine through. 2. *v.a.* (*insep.*) fill *or* flood with light, light (up), illuminate, irradiate; X-ray (*Med.*). **–ung,** *f.* illumination; radioscopy.

durchliegen, *ir.v.r.* (*sep.*) get bed-sores.

durchlochen, *v.a.* (*insep.*) punch (*tickets*).

durchlöchern, *v.a.* (*insep.*) perforate, pierce, puncture; (*coll.*) violate, infringe.

durchlüften, *v.n.* (*sep.*) (*aux.* h.) & *v.a.* (*insep.*) ventilate, air.

durchmachen, *v.a.* (*sep.*) finish, accomplish; go through, pass through, experience, suffer; *er hat viel durchgemacht,* he has gone through a good deal, he has had a hard time.

Durchmarsch, *m.* passage of troops; getting all the tricks (*at cards*); (*coll.*) diarrhoea. **–ieren,** *v.n.* (*aux.* s.) (*sep.*) march through. (N.B. *p.p.* **durchmarschiert.**)

durchmess–en, 1. *ir.v.a.* (*insep.*) traverse, pass from end to end; *die Lebensbahn ist bald –en,* life's measure is soon run; 2. (*sep.*) measure in all directions, take the dimensions of. **–er,** *m.* (-s, – diameter; calibre (*Artil.*).

durchmüssen, *v.n.* (*aux.* h.) (*sep.*) (*coll.*) be obliged to pass, be forced to get through *or* finish.

durchmuster–n, *v.a.* (*insep.*) pass in review, inspect, examine, scrutinize, scan. **–ung,** *f.* careful examination, inspection, security.

durchnässen, 1. *ir.v.n.* (*aux.* h.) (*sep.*) let the wet through. 2. *v.a.* (*insep.*) wet thoroughly, drench, soak, steep, saturate; *wir kamen ganz durchnäßt heim,* we got home soaked *or* wet through *or* completely drenched.

durchnehmen, *ir.v.a.* (*sep.*) examine, analyse, go through (*s.th. with a p.*); discuss; *einen gründlich –,* (*coll.*) pull a p. to pieces.

durchpausen, *v.a.* (*sep.*) trace, copy.

durchpeitschen, *v.a.* (*sep.*) whip soundly; (*fig.*) hurry through (*a bill in parliament, a subject in class*).

durchprügeln, *v.a.* (*sep.*) beat *or* thrash (soundly).

durchquer–en, *v.a.* (*insep.*) traverse, cross, (*fig.*) frustrate, thwart. **–ung,** *f.* crossing, traversing.

durchrasen, *v.n.* (*aux.* s.) (*sep.*) & *v.a.* (*insep.*) rush furiously through *or* over, race *or* dash through.

durchrasseln, *v.n.* (*aux.* s.) (*sep.*) (*sl.*) fail in an examination.

durchräuchern, *v.a.* 1, (*sep.*) fumigate; smoke thoroughly (*as sausage*); 2. (*insep.*) fill with smoke (*as a room*).

durchrechnen, *v.a.* (*sep.*) reckon up, count over; revise, check.

durchregnen, 1. *v.n.* (*aux.* h.) (*sep.*) rain through *or* in; *es regnet hier durch,* it rains in here. 2. *v.a.* (*insep.*) drench; *wir waren alle völlig durchgeregnet,* we were all drenched to the skin.

durchreiben, *ir.v.a.* (*sep.*) rub through; rub sore, chafe, gall; *durchgeriebene Kartoffeln,* mashed potatoes.

Durchreise, *f.* journey through, passage, transit; *ich bin nur auf der* –, I am merely passing through. **–n,** 1. *v.n.* (*aux.* s.) (*sep.*) travel through, pass through, traverse. 2. *v.a.* (*insep.*), travel over *or* from end to end. **–nde(r),** *m.* traveller, through passenger (*on train*). **–visum,** *n.* transit visa.

durchreißen, 1. *ir.v.a.* (*insep.*) tear up *or* in two, jerk (*the trigger*). 2. *v.n.* (*aux.* s.) (*sep.*) break, tear, get torn.

durchrieseln, *v.a.* (*imp.*) (*insep.*) flow all over; *es durchrieselt mich,* a thrill goes through me.

durchringen, *v.r.* (*sep.*) (*aux.* h.) struggle through, be acknowledged (*with difficulty*); *er ringt sich zu der Überzeugung durch,* he reaches conviction after a struggle.

Durchriß, *m.* (-(ss)es, -(ss)e) breach, rent.

durchrufen, *v.a.* & *n.* (*aux.* h.) (*insep.*) pass the word down *or* round.

durchrühren, *v.a.* (*sep.*) stir up well agitate; strain.

durchrütteln, *v.a.* (*sep.* & *insep.*) shake thoroughly.

durchs, *adv.* = **durch das.**

durchsacken, *v.a.* (*sep.*) pancake, stall (*Av.*).

durchsagen, *v.a.* (*sep.*) announce, broadcast, transmit (*Rad.*).

durchsättigen, *v.a.* (*insep.*) saturate.

durchsäuern, *v.a.* (*insep.*) leaven thoroughly, acidify.

durchschallen, 1. *v.n.* (*sep.*) (*aux.* h.) resound. 2. *v.a.* (*insep.*) fill with sound.

durchschauen, 1. *v.n.* (*aux.* h.) (*sep.*) see through, look through. 2. *v,a.* (*insep.*) look through *or* over (*items individually*); see through, penetrate, understand, grasp, see into the heart of; *ich durchschaue seine Kniffe,* I see through his game, I am up to his tricks.

durchschauern, *v.a.* (*insep.*) shudder; (*fig.*) fill with horror *or* awe.

durchscheinen, *ir.v.n.* (*aux.* h.) (*sep.*) shine through, be visible through. **–d,** *pr.p.* & *adj.* translucent, diaphanous.

durchscheuern, *v.a.* (*sep.*) scour *or* rub through; wear by rubbing, graze (*knee, etc.*).

durchschieß–en, 1. *ir.v.n.* (*sep.*) (*aux.* h.) shoot *or* fire through (*a window, etc.*); (*aux.* s.) dash, race *or* fly through. 2. *v.a.* (*insep.*) riddle with bullets; interline, space (*between lines*) (*Typ.*); interleave (*a book*); *durchschossen, p.p.* & *adj.* riddled with bullets; interleaved (*book*).

durchschimmern, 1. *v.n.* (*aux.* h.) (*sep.*) glitter, gleam *or* shine through, be dimly visible through.

durchschlafen, 1. *ir.v.a.* (*insep.*) sleep through, pass (in) sleeping. 2. *v.n.* (*sep.*) (*aux.* h.) pass in unbroken sleep, sleep without interruption.

Durchschlag, *m.* (-s, ⸚e) 1. strainer, filter, sieve, colander; 2. carbon copy. **–en,** 1. *ir.v.a.* (*insep.*) beat through; penetrate; (*sep.*) make an opening in; pierce; strain, filter; make carbon copy (*on typewriter*); *man schlägt die Erbsen durch,* one rubs the peas through a strainer. 2. *v.n.* (*sep.*) (*aux.* h.) strike through, penetrate; (*fig.*) be apparent *or* dominant, (*coll.*) tell; be successful *or* effective; take effect (*of medicines*); blot; *schlag durch!* Shake! (*to seal a bargain*); *Papier das nicht durchschlägt,* paper that does not blot *or* that takes ink; *der eine Typus schlägt im Mischling durch,* in the hybrid one type is dominant. 3. *v.r.* (*sep.*) fight one's way through (*an enemy*); struggle through; (*coll.*) rough it; *sich kümmerlich –en,* live from hand to mouth; *–ender Erfolg,* signal *or* outstanding success. **–festigkeit,** *f.* dielectric strength (*Elec.*). **–papier,** *n.* carbon paper. **–skraft,** *f.*, **–swirkung,** *f.* penetrating power *or* force (*of a projectile*). **–spannung,** *f.* breakdown voltage (*Elec.*).

durchschlängeln, *v.a.* (*insep.*) & *r.* (*sep.*) wind through; meander through.

durchschleichen, *ir.v. n.* (*aux.* s.) & *r.* (*sep.*) sneak *or* steal through.

durchschleusen, *v.a.* (*sep.*) pass through the locks (*a ship*); (*sl.*) pour (*tanks, troops, etc.*) through a gap (*Mil.*).

durchschlüpfen, *v.n.* (*aux.* s.) (*sep.*) slip through; escape *or* pass unnoticed.

durchschneid–en, *ir.v.a.* (*sep.*) cut in two, bisect; (*insep.*) cut through *or* across; cross, bisect, intersect; traverse; pierce; *ein Band wird durchgeschnitten,* a ribbon is cut; (*Poet.*) *das Meer wird durchschnitten,* the sea is traversed. **–ung,** *f.* bisection, intersection.

Durchschnitt, *m.* (-(e)s, -e) cut, section; cross-section, profile; cutting (*Railw.*), intersection; average, mean; – *im Kirchenschiffe,* transept; – *eines Gebäudes,* section of a building; *im* –, on the average. **–lich,** *adj.* average, on an average. **–salter,** *n.* average age. **–sansicht,** *f.* section (*Arch.*). **–sbildung,** *f.* average education. **–sertrag,** *m.* average yield. **–sgeschwindigkeit,** *f.* average speed. **–sgröße,** *f.* average size *or* height. **–slinie,** *f.* line of intersection; diameter. **–smensch,** *m.* average person, the man in the street. **–spreis,** *m.* mean cost. **–spunkt,** *m.* point of intersection. **–ssehne,** *f.* secant (*Math.*). **–sverhältnis,** *n.* mean proportion. **–sware,** *f.* article of average *or* mediocre quality. **–szahl,** *f.* mean (*number*). **–szeichnung,** *f.* cross-section, sectional drawing. **–zuwachs,** *m.* mean increment, average accretion.

durchschreiben, *v.n.* (*aux.* h.) (*sep.*) make a copy (*with carbon or tracing paper*).

durchschreien, *ir.v.a.* (*insep.*) fill with cries.

durchschreiten, 1. *ir.v.n.* (*aux.* s.) (*sep.*) stride through from end to end. 2. *v.a.* (*insep.*) cross, traverse, walk across.

Durchschuß *m.* (-(ss)es, ⸚(ss)e) gunshot wound that penetrates right through; woof, weft (*Weav.*); interleaved sheet. **–linien,** *f.pl.* space (*Typ.*), *see* **durchschießen.**

durchschütteln, *v.a.* (*sep.*) shake thoroughly, agitate, mix by shaking.

durchschwängern, *v.a.* (*insep.*) impregnate, saturate.

durchschwärmen, 1. *v.a.* (*insep.*) spend in revelry (*a night, etc.*); roam *or* roister through (*street, etc.*). 2. *v.n.* (*sep.*) (*aux.* s.) rove, ramble about.

durchschweifen, *v.a.* (*insep.*) wander through, roam *or* stroll about aimlessly in.

durchschwelgen, *v.a.* (*insep.*) spend in revelry.

durchschwimmen, 1. *ir.v.n.* (*aux.* s.) (*sep.*) swim through (*a gap, etc.*). 2. *v.a.* (*insep.*) cross (*a river*) by swimming, swim across.

durchschwitz–en, *v.n.* (*aux.* s.) (*sep.*) make wet with sweat, ooze through; *das Hemd ist ganz durchgeschwitzt,* the shirt is soaked with perspiration. **–t,** *adj.* wet with perspiration.

durchsegeln, 1. *v.n.* (*aux.* s.) (*sep.*) sail *or* navigate through; (*coll.*) fail (*an examination*). 2. *v.a.* (*insep.*) sail, sail from end to end.

durchsehen, 1. *ir.v.n.* (*aux.* h.) (*sep.*) see *or* look through; see clearly (*fig.*). 2. *v.a.* (*sep.*) look over, review, revise; scrutinize.

durchseih–en, *v.a.* (*sep.*) strain, filter, percolate. **–er,** *m.* strainer, filter. **–ung,** *f.* filtration.

durchsein, *ir.v.n.* (*sep.*) (*aux.* s.) (*coll.*) have got through a th., be finished with a p. *or* a th.

durchsetzen, 1. *v.a.* (*sep.*) sift, sieve, size (*ore*); accomplish, carry through, put through, succeed with *or* in; *sie hat es bei ihm nicht durchgesetzt,* she has not carried her point with him; *er kann es bei den Behörden nicht* –, he cannot prevail upon the authorities to do it. 2. *v.r.* (*sep.*) make one's way, succeed. 3. *v.a.* (*insep.*) intersperse, mix with, permeate, saturate.

Durchsicht, *f.* perusal, inspection, revision; vista, view. **–ig,** *adj.* clear, transparent, pellucid, diaphanous. **–igkeit,** *f.* transparency; clearness, perspicuity. **–ssucher,** *m.* direct view finder (*Phot.*).

durchsickern, *v.n.* (*aux.* s.) (*sep.*) leak, drip through, ooze through, percolate, trickle through, seep through (*also fig. of news, knowledge, etc.*); *die Nachricht ist durchgesickert,* the news has leaked out.

durchsieben, *v.a.* (*sep.*) sift, sieve, screen; garble, bolt (*flour*); pepper (*with shot, etc.*) (*Mil.*).

durchsieden, *v.a.* (*sep.*) boil thoroughly.

durchsintern, *v.n.* (*sep.*), *see* **durchsickern.**

durchsitzen, 1. *ir.v.a.* (*sep.*) wear out (*trousers, etc.*) by sitting; (*insep.*) spend, pass (*time*), sit through. 2. *v.n.* (*sep.*) be in detention.

durchsollen, *v.n.* (*aux.* h.) (*sep.*) (*coll.*) be under an obligation to pass through.

durchspähen, *v.a.* (*insep.*) examine, explore, peer on all sides.

durchspielen, 1. *v.a.* (*sep.*) play through *or* over (*music, part in a play, etc.*). 2. *v.a.* (*insep.*) spend (*time*) in play *or* playing.

durchsprechen, *v.a.* (*sep.*) talk over *or* out, discuss thoroughly; speak through (*mouth-piece, etc.*).

durchspreng–en, *v.n.* (*aux.* s.) (*sep.*) & *v.a.* (*insep.*) burst through; gallop through. **–t,** *adj.* mixed, interspersed with.

durchspülen, *v.a.* (*sep.*) wash thoroughly, rinse well.

durchspüren, *v.a.* (*sep.*) feel (*a th.*) through (*s.th. else*), be aware of, notice.

durchstaub–en, *v.n.* (*aux.* h.) (*sep.*); *es staubt durch,* the dust is coming in (*at the window, etc.*). **–t,** *p.p.* & *adj.* thoroughly dusty, thick with dust.

durchstech–en, 1. *ir.v.n.* (*aux.* h.) & *a.* (*sep.*) pierce *or* cut through, perforate, prick, stab, gore; cheat (*orig. at cards*). 2. *v.a.* (*insep.*) transfix, thrust through and through; turn over, mix (*with a spade*); dig through (*a bank of earth, etc.*); *durchstochen,* perforated, rouletted (*of postage stamps*); **–erei,** *f.* underhand plotting, intrigue; *–erei treiben,* play into each other's hands. **–ung,** *f.* piercing, perforation; cutting (*of a dike*); *zusammengesetzte –ung,* compound perforation (*of postage stamps*).

durchstehen, *v.n.* (*insep.*) (*aux.* h.) stand one's ground.

Durchstich, *m.* (-s, -e) cut, aperture, slit; intrenchment, canal, ditch; perforation, roulette (*of postage stamps*); *see* **durchstecken.**

durchstöbern, *v.a.* (*insep.*) ransack, rummage through.

durchstoß–en, 1. *ir.v.n.* (*aux.* s.) (*sep.*) break through, pierce, penetrate (*enemy's lines*) (*Mil.*). 2. *v.a.* (*sep.*) push *or* thrust through, break by thrusting *or* stamping *or* hard wear, (*insep.*) transfix, thrust through, stab, gore. **–punkt,** *m.* point of penetration, perforation. **–verfahren,** *n.* blind landing procedure (*Av.*).

durchstrahl–en, 1. *v.n.* (*aux.* h.) (*sep.*) shine through. 2. *v.a.* (*insep.*) irradiate. **–ung,** *f.* irradiation.

durchstreichen, 1. *ir.v.a.* (*sep.* & *insep.*) strike out, cross out, erase, cancel; (*insep.*) roam through. 2. *v.n.* (*aux.* s.) (*sep.*) pass through *or* by rapidly (*as migratory birds*); *–de Linie,* trajectory (*of a comet*).

durchstreifen, *v.a.* (*sep.*) slip past hurriedly, pass fleetingly; (*insep.*) roam through *or* all over.

Durchstrich, *m.* (-s, -e) erasure; passage (*of birds*); *see* **durchstreichen.**

Durchstrom, *m.* multiphase current (*Elec.*).

durchströmen, *v.a.* (*insep.*) & *n.* (*aux.* s.) (*sep.*) stream, flow rapidly *or* run through, perfuse; *mich durchströmte ein freudiges Gefühl,* a feeling of delight thrilled through me.

durchstürmen, 1. *v.n.* (*sep.*) (*aux.* s.) rush through violently. 2. *v.a.* (*insep.*) blow violently through; agitate, convulse (*of feelings*).

durchsuch–en, *v.a.* (*sep.* & *insep.*) search through *or* thoroughly, search everywhere; *gerichtlich –en,* search by order of a court. **–ung,** *f.* search, examination (*baggage, etc.*); (police) raid.

durchtoben, *v.a.* (*insep.*) rage through, ravage.

durchtönen, 1. *v.n.* (*aux.* h.) (*sep.*) sound *or* be audible through (*the wall, etc.*). 2. *v.a.* (*insep.*) resound, ring with.

durchtränk–en, *v.a.* (*insep.*) impregnate, saturate, infiltrate (*mit,* with); *–t mit,* filled with, drenched, saturated *or* impregnated with.

durchträufeln, *v.n.* (*aux.* s.) & *a.* (*sep.*) drop *or* drip through.

durchtreiben, *ir.v.a.* (*sep.*) drive *or* force through; carry through, effect.

durchtreten, *ir.v.a.* (*sep.*) tread through, wear out (*shoes, etc.*); tread thoroughly; *die Weintrauben –,* tread the winepress.

Durchtrieb, *m.* cattle-path; right of way *or* pasture for cattle; *see* **durchtreiben. –en,** *p.p.* & *adj.* sly, artful, cunning, crafty; arrant (*knave*); **–heit,** *f.* cunning, craftiness, slyness.

durchtriefen, durchtröpfeln, *see* **durchtropfen.**

Durchtrift, *f.*, *see* **Durchtrieb.**

Durchtritt, *m.* passage, entrance, *see* **durchtreten. –stelle,** *f.* exit, point of passage.

durchtropfen, *v.n.* (*aux.* s.) (*sep.*) trickle through, drip through (*–tröpfeln suggests smaller drops than –tropfen*).

durchwachen, *v.a.* (*insep.*) watch through, lie awake (*all night*).

durchwachsen, 1. *ir.v.n.* (*aux.* s.) (*sep.*) grow through. 2. *v.a.* (*insep.*) intermingle with, interpenetrate; proliferate. 3. *p.p.* & *adj.* streaked (*Bot.*), marbled, streaky (*of meat*).

durchwandern, 1. *v.n.* (*aux.* s.) (*sep.*) diffuse; 2. *v.a.* (*insep.*) wander through.

durchwärm–en, *v.a.* (*sep.* & *insep.*) warm through *or* thoroughly. **–ig,** *adj.* diathermic.

durchwässern, *v.a.* (*sep.* & *insep.*) irrigate, soak.

durchwaten, *v.n.* (*aux.* s.) (*sep.*) & *a.* (*insep.*) wade through, ford.

durchweben, *v.a.* (*insep.*) interweave; (*fig.*) intersperse; *der Stoff ist mit Blumen durchwebt,* the material has an interweaved *or* interwoven floral pattern; *seine Rede ist mit Flüchen durchwoben,* his speech is interspersed with oaths.

Durchweg, *m.* (-es, -e) thoroughfare, passage. **–(s),** *adv.* throughout, altogether; without exception, always, ordinarily.

durchweichen, *v.a.* (*sep.*) & *n.* (*aux.* s.) (*insep.*) soak through, soften; steep; become soft *or* soaked.

durchwerfen, *ir.v.a.* (*sep.*) cast through; riddle sift, screen, bolt.

durchwinden, 1. *ir.v.a.* (*sep.*) wind through. 2. *v.r.* (*sep.*) wriggle through, manœuvre o.s. through; (*fig.*) overcome (*obstacles*) with difficulty. 3. *v.a.* (*insep.*) entwine.

durchwintern, *v.n.* (*aux.* h.) (*insep.*) pass *or* survive the winter; hibernate.

durchwirken, *v.a.* (*insep.*) interweave, weave in with; knead thoroughly.

durchwischen, *v.n.* (*aux.* s.) (*sep.*) (*Dat.*) slip through, evade, escape.

durchwühlen, 1. *v.a.* (*sep.*) root up; rummage, ransack, turn over. 2. *v.r.* (*sep.*) make *or* force one's way through clumsily. 3. *v.a.* (*insep.*) churn up, tangle up, muddle up, bring into disorder (*as contents of a drawer*).

Durchwurf, *m.* screen, sieve, riddle; *see* **durchwerfen.**

durchwürzen, *v.a.* (*insep.*) spice, season thoroughly; scent; (*fig.*) (*also sep.*) season, make attractive (*of food*).

durchzählen, *v.a.* (*sep.*) count over *or* up.

durchzechen, *v.a.* (*sep.* & *insep.*) carouse through; pass in carousing; *eine durch(ge)zechte Nacht,* a night spent in carousal.

durchzeichnen, *v.a.* (*sep.*) trace; *Papier zum –,* tracing paper.

durchzieh–en, 1. *ir.v.a.* (*sep.*) draw, drag, *or* pull through; pull out of a dive (*Av.*); pass through (*a hole*), thread (*needles*); (*insep.*) traverse, penetrate (*on foot*); interweave, interlace; *mit Gräben –en,* cover with trenches. 2. *v.n.* (*aux.* s. & h.) (*sep.*) go *or* march through. 3. *v.r.* (*sep.*) extend all over *or* through. **–er(hieb),** *m.* hit (*Fenc.*). **–glas,** *n.* slide (*in microscopes.*)

durchzittern, *v.n.* (*insep.*) (*aux.* h.) thrill (through)

Durchzoll, *m.* (-s, ¨-e) transit-duty.

durchzucken, *v.a.* (*insep.*) give a sudden shock to, convulse; flash through.

Durchzug, *m.* (-s, ¨-e) march *or* passage through, circulation, through draught; passage, architrave. (*Arch.*), *see* **durchziehen.**

durchzwängen, *v.a. & r.* (*sep.*) force or squeeze through.

dürf-en, *ir.v.n.* (*aux.* h.) be permitted, have permission *or* authority, be allowed; may, can, dare, venture, be likely; *darf ich fragen?* may I ask? *Sie hätten das nicht tun -en*, you ought not to have done that; *ich habe nicht gedurft*, I didn't dare; *wenn ich bitten darf*, if you please; *darüber -en Sie sich nicht wundern*, you must not be surprised at it; *es darf niemand herein*, no one is admitted; *man darf hoffen*, it is to be hoped; (dürfte, *as polite formula*) *es dürfte sich erübrigen*, it would seem to be superfluous, it is probably not necessary; *jetzt dürfte es zu spät sein*, now it will probably be too late. **-tig,** *adj.* needy, indigent, poor; sorry, paltry, shabby, scanty, insufficient. **-tigkeit,** *f.* poverty, indigence, need, want; insufficiency, scantiness, meagreness.

dürr, *adj*; arid, parched; lean, thin, skinny, meagre; barren, dried, sterile, dead, withered; *-e Worte*, plain *or* blunt language. **-e,** *f.* dryness, drought; leanness; sterility. **-beinig,** *adj.* spindle-shanked. **-futter,** *n.* dry fodder, hay.

Durst, *m.* thirst (*also fig.*); *- haben*, be thirsty; *- stillen*, quench thirst; *das macht -*, that gives one a thirst. **-en,** *v.n.* (*aux.* h.) be thirsty; (*fig.*) thirst; crave, long (*nach*, for); *es -et mich, mich -et*, I am thirsty. **-ig,** *adj.* thirsty, (*fig.*) eager (*nach*, for).

dürsten, *see* **dursten.**

Dusche, *f.* (-n) shower-bath, douche. **-n,** *v.a.* douche, swill.

Düse, *f.* (-n) nozzle; jet; fuel injector (*Av.*).

Dusel, *m.* (*coll.*) stupor; dizziness, sleepiness; (*sl.*) luck; (*coll.*) *im* (*holden*) *- sein*, be day-dreaming; be pleasantly drunk, be half-seas-over; (*sl.*) *- haben*, have undeserved good fortune, (*coll.*) be a lucky dog. **-ig,** *adj.* dizzy, sleepy. **-n,** *v.n.* (*aux.* h.) be half-asleep *or* day-dreaming, doze.

düster, *adj.* dark; gloomy, dusky; sad, mournful, melancholy, dismal. **-heit,** *f.*, **-keit,** *f.* darkness, dusk, gloom, gloominess. **-n,** *v.n.* (*imp.*) (*aux.* h.) get dark, be *or* grow dusky *or* gloomy; lour.

Düt-chen, *n.*, **-e,** *f. see* **Tütchen & Tüte.**

Dutzend, *n.* (-s, -e) dozen. **-mensch,** *m.* commonplace *or* average fellow. **-preis,** *m.* price per dozen; *der -preis ist 20 Mark*, 20 marks a dozen. **-ware,** *f.* cheap *or* mass-produced article. **-weise,** *adv.* by the dozen.

duz-en, *v.a. & r.* be on 'Christian name' terms with (*i.e. using the familiar 'du' rather than the formal 'Sie'*). **-bruder,** *m.* intimate companion, crony. **-fuß,** *m.*; *auf dem -fuß(e) stehen*, be on intimate terms.

dwars, *adv.* athwart, abeam (*Naut.*). **-balken,** *m.* cross-beam. **-linie,** *f.* ships in column *or* in line abreast (*Nav.*). **-schlingen,** *f. pl.* cross-trees.

Dweil, *m.* (-s, -e) mop, swab, scrubber (*Naut.*).

Dynam-ik, *f.* dynamics. **-isch,** *adj.* dynamic(al). **-it,** *n.* or *m.* dynamite. **-omaschine,** *f.* dynamo (*Elec.*).

Dynast, *m.* (-en, -en) feudal lord, ruler, prince. **-ie,** dynasty. **-isch,** *adj.* dynastic(al).

E

E, e, *n.* E, e; E (*Mus.*); *E-dur*, E major; *E-moll*, E minor.

Ebbe, *f.* (-n) ebb, ebb-tide, low tide; decline; *niedrige -*, neap-tide; *die - tritt ein*, the tide is going out; (*fig.*) *- sein*, (*coll.*) be at a low ebb. **-n,** *v.n.* (*aux.* h. & s.) ebb; fall off, decline; *das Meer ebbt*, the tide is going out.

eben, 1. *adj.* even, level, flat, plain, smooth; plane, two--dimensional (*Math.*); open (*country*); *zu ebener Erde*, on the ground floor; *-e Geometrie*, plane geometry; *-er Weg*, level road. 2. *adv. part.* just, even; precisely, exactly, quite certainly; *- wollen, - tun*, be about to (*do a th.*); *das wollte ich - sagen*, that is just what I was going to say, *so-*, even now, just now; *das nun - nicht*, not precisely that, rather the contrary; *an - dem Tage*, on that very day; *es geschieht dir - recht*, it serves you right; *das wäre mir - recht*, that would be just what I should like; *- erst*, only, just, just now. **-baum,** *m.*, *see* **Eben-.** **-bild,** *n.* image, likeness; *das -bild des Schöpfers*, God's image. **-bürtig,** *adj.* of equally high birth, equal. **-bürtigkeit,** *f.* equality (of birth). **-da(selbst),** *adv.*, **-dort,** *adv.* in the same *or* that place, just there; ibidem. **-derselbe,** *pron.* the very same. **-deshalb,** *adv.* for that very reason. **-en,** *see* **ebnen.** **-erdig,** *adj.* flush with the ground *or* floors. **-falls,** *adv.* likewise, also, too. **-kreisig,** *adj.* concentric. **-maß,** *n.* symmetry, proportion, harmony. **-mäßig,** *adj.* symmetrical, proportionate, equal, just. **-so,** *adv.* just so, just as (*when compounded with adv. & indec. adj. written as one word*; *when with epithet as two words*, e.g. *du -sogut wie ich*, you just as well as I; *- so gute Leute wie wir*, just as good people as we are; *-so gut*, just as good, quite as good, equally good; *-sogut*, just as well, quite as well, equally well. **-sogern,** *adv.*; *ich möchte -sogern*, I would just as soon, I would rather. **-solange,** *adv.* just as long. **-solch,** *adj.* similar, like. **-sosehr,** *adv.*, **-soviel,** *adv.* just as much, as many; *das ist -soviel wie . . .*, that is tantamount to. . . . . **-sowenig,** *adv.* just as little, as infrequently.

Eben-baum, *m.* ebony tree. **-holz,** *n.* ebony.

Ebene, *f.* (-n), plain; plane (*Math.*); level, flatness, levelness; *geneigte* (or *schiefe*) -, gradient, inclined plane; (*fig.*) the downward path; *in gleicher - mit*, flush with.

Eber, *m.* (-s, -) wild boar, boar. **-esche,** *f.* rowan, mountain ash (*Sorbus aucuparia*) (*Bot.*). **-fleisch,** *n.* brawn, boar's meat. **-wurz(el),** *f.* carline thistle (*Carlina vulgaris*) (*Bot.*).

ebnen, *v.a.* make even, level; flatten, roll, smooth, plane; *einem die Bahn -*, pave the way for a p.

E-Boot, *n.* motor torpedo boat.

Echo, *n.* (-s, -s) echo; *ein - geben*, echo, resound. **-en,** *v.n.* (*aux.* h.) echo, re-echo, resound. **-lot** *n.* echo-sounding apparatus, sonic depth-finder (*Naut.*).

echt, *adj.* genuine, true, real; pure (*gold*); unadulterated, authentic, legitimate; fast (*of colours*); natural (*hair*); staunch; lawful; *-er Wein*, pure unadulterated wine; *-e und un-e Brüche*, proper and improper fractions (*Math.*); *-e Perlen*, real pearls. **-heit,** *f.* genuineness, authenticity; legitimacy; purity, fastness (*of colours*).

Eck, *n.* (-s, -e) angle; *Drei-*, triangle; *Vier-*, quadrangle; *Acht-*, octagon; *Viel-*, polygon; *über-*, diagonally, *das Deutsche -*, Rhine elbow (*at Coblenz*). **-balken,** *m.* corner-post. **-ball,** *m.* corner-(kick) (*Sport*). **-beschläge,** *m.pl.* (metal) corner pieces. **-brett,** *n.* bracket, corner shelf. **-chen,** *n.* (*coll.*) little way, short distance; *ich will dich ein -chen auf den Weg bringen*, I will go a little way with you. **-e,** *f.* edge; corner, angle; nook; quoin (*Arch.*); *geschliffene -e*, facet; (*coll.*) *eine ganze -e*, a considerable distance; (*coll.*) *um die -e gehen*, die, be no more, (*coll.*) give up the ghost, (*sl.*) kick the bucket; *in die -e stellen*, lay aside, hold over; (*coll.*) *um die -e bringen*, murder, (*sl.*) take for a ride, bump off; *an allen -en und Enden*, everywhere; *von allen -en und Enden* (*her*), from all parts. **-eisen,** *n.* gusset plate. **-ensteher,** *m.* loafer. **-federn,** *f.pl.* pinions. **-holz,** *n.* squared timber. **-ig,** *adj.* angular; cornered; edged; (*fig.*) awkward; squared-tipped (*of airplane wing*). **-loch,** *n.* corner-pocket (*Bill.*). **-säule,** *f.* corner pillar; prism (*Opt., Geom.*). **-säulig,** *adj.* prismatic. **-stein,** *m.* corner-stone; curb-stone; diamonds (*Cards*). **-stütze,** *f.* buttress, stay. **-weise,** *adv.* cornerwise; *-weise schleifen*, cut into facets (*jewellery*). **-zahn,** *m.* eye-tooth, canine-tooth.

Ecker, *f.* (-n) acorn, mast; *Buch-*, beechnut.

edel, *adj.* noble; of noble birth, high-born, well-born; high-minded, lofty, exalted; precious; excellent; electro-positive (*Elec.*); *der* or *die Edle*, person of noble *or* high birth; high-minded man *or* woman; *das Edle*, nobility (*of mind, etc.*), that which is noble; *edler Gang*, rich vein (*of ore*); *edle Teile*, vital parts. **-auge,** *n.*, grafting bud. **-bürger,** *m.* patrician. **-dame,** *f.*, **-frau,** *f.*, titled lady, gentlewoman. **-erz,** *n.*, rich ore. **-falke,** *m.*, (trained) falcon. **-fichte,** *f.* silver pine. **-fräulein,** *n.* titled lady, nobleman's daughter. **-gesinnt,** *adj.* noble-minded. **-hirsch,** *m.* red deer, stag. **-ing,** *m.* (early Germanic), chieftain, aetheling. **-kastanie,** *f.* sweet *or* Spanish chestnut, edible chestnut (*Castanea sativa*) (*Bot.*). **-knabe,** *m.* page. **-knecht,** *m.* squire. **-leute,** *pl.*, *see* **-mann.** **-mann,** *m.* (-leute), nobleman, noble. **-männisch,** *adj.* as an aristocrat. **-marder,** *m.* pine-marten (*Martes*) (*Zool.*). **-metall,** *n.* precious metal. **-mut,** *m.* high-mindedness, generosity, magnanimity. **-mütig,** *adj.* high-minded, noble, magnanimous, generous. **-obst,** *n.* dessert fruit. **-reis,** *n.* scion, graft. **-rost,** *m.* patina (*on old copper*). **-stahl,** *m.* refined steel. **-stein,** *m.* precious stone, gem, jewel. **-steinschleifer,** *m.* diamond-cutter *or* polisher, lapidary. **-tanne,** *f.* silver fir (*Abies picea*) (*Bot.*). **-valuta** *f.* currency with high rate of exchange, hard currency. **-weiß,** *n.* edelweiss, lion's foot (*Gnaphalium leontopodium*) (*Bot.*). **-wild,** *n.* deer; high-class game.

edieren *v.a.* edit, publish.

Edikt, *n.* (-(e)s, -e) edict.

Edle(r), *m.* (-n, -n) nobleman, *see* **edel.**

Efeu, *m.* ivy (*Hedera helix*) (*Bot.*); *mit – bewachsen*, ivy-clad. **-artig,** *adj.* hederaceous.

Effekt, *m.* (-es, -e) effect, power; **-en,** *pl.* effects, (*C.L.*) securities, stocks, bonds. **-enbörse,** *f.* Stock Exchange. **-enhandel,** *m.* stock-exchange business. **-enhändler,** *m.* stockbroker, stock-jobber. **-hascherei,** *f.* straining after effect, sensationalism, showing off, clap-trap. **-iv,** *adj.* effective, real, (*C.L.*) in specie, ready money. **ivbestand,** *m.*, **-ivstärke,** *f.* actual strength, effectives (*Mil.*); effective value (*usually of colours, Dye.*).

effloreszieren, *v.n.* effloresce.

egal, *adj.* alike; even, level; (*coll.*) all one, the same; (*coll.*) *das ist mir ganz –*, I don't care, it's all the same to me. **-isieren,** v.a. equalize, level, flatten (*Dye.*). **-ität,** *f.* equality, evenness, uniformity.

Egel, *m.* (-s, -) leech.

Egg-e, *f.* (-en) harrow; selvage, list, listing. **-en,** *v.a.* harrow.

Ego-ismus, *m.* egoism, selfishness. **-ist,** *m.* (-en, -en) egoist. **-istisch,** *adj.* selfish, egoistical.

egrenieren, *v.a.* gin, clean (*cotton*).

eh, 1. *int.* eh! well! 2. *conj, see* **ehe.**

ehe, *conj.* before, until, (*Poet.*) ere; *– er kommt*, before he comes. **-dem,** *adv.* before this time, formerly, of old, heretofore; (*Law*) ere now. **-malig,** *adj.*, former, past, late, old; *-maliger König*, ex-king. **-mals,** *adv.*, *see* **-dem**; *-mals Professor in*, sometime professor in. **-r,** *adv.* (*comp. of* ehe) sooner, rather; formerly, earlier; *je -r, je lieber*, the sooner the better; *um so -r*, so much the more, all the sooner; *nicht -r bis*, not until, not unless; *ich wollte -r sterben*, I would rather die; *-r alles andere als*, anything but; *das ist -r möglich*, that's more likely; *noch -r*, still more; *-r klein als groß*, small rather than large. **-st,** *adj.* (*sup. of* ehe) earliest, soonest; first; next; *am -sten*, most easily, sooner than anywhere else, first, most nearly; *-ster Tage, mit dem -sten*, very soon, one of these days; *aufs -ste*, as soon as possible, at the earliest opportunity; very soon.

Ehe, *f.* (-n) marriage; matrimony, wedlock; *außer der – geboren*, illegitimate; *aus erster –*, by his *or* her first marriage; *eine – besiegeln*, consummate a marriage; *eine – führen*, live a married life; *eine – schließen*, contract a marriage; (*Prov.*) *-n werden im Himmel geschlossen*, marriages are made in heaven; *eine – vollziehen*, consummate a marriage; *wilde –*, concubinage; *in wilder – leben*, live together. **-band,** *n.* marriage bond, conjugal tie. **-bett,** *n.* nuptial bed. **-brechen,** *ir.v.n.* commit adultery. **-brecher,** *m.* adulterer. **-brecherin,** *f.* adulteress. **-bruch,** *m.* adultery. **-bund,** *m.*, **-bündnis,** *n.* matrimony, marriage tie. **-fähig,** *adj.* marriageable, nubile. **-feind,** *m.* marriage-hater, misogamist, misogynist. **-frau,** *f.* married woman, wife. **-gattin,** *f.* wife, (lawful) spouse. **-gatte,** *m.* husband, (lawful) spouse. **-gemahl,** *m.* husband. **-gemahlin,** *f.* wife. **-gericht,** *n.* divorce court. **-gesetz,** *n.* marriage law. **-glück,** *n.* conjugal bliss. **-hälfte,** *f.* (*coll. & hum.*) better half. **-hindernis,** *n.* obstacle *or* impediment to marriage. **-leben,** *n.* married life. **-leiblich,** *adj.* legitimate, born in wedlock. **-leute,** *pl.* married people; married couple. **-lich,** *adj.* matrimonial, conjugal; *-liche Kinder*, legitimate children, children born in wedlock; *-liches Weib*, wedded wife; *-lich machen*, legitimatize. **-lichen,** *v.a.* marry. **-los,** *adj.* unmarried, single. **-losigkeit,** *f.* celibacy. **-mann,** *m.* (-männer) married man, husband. **-mündig,** *adj.* of marriageable age. **-paar,** *n.* married couple. **-pfand,** *n.* issue, child. **-pflicht,** *f.* conjugal duty. **-recht,** *n.* marriage law. **-schänder,** *m.* adulterer. **-schatz,** *m.* dowry. **-scheidung,** *f.* divorce. **-scheidungsklage,** *f.*, **-scheidungsprozeß,** *m.* divorce suit. **-scheidungsspruch,** *m.* decree absolute (*divorce*). **-scheu,** 1. *f.* aversion to marriage. 2. *adj.* adverse to marriage; misogamic. **-schließung,** *f.* marriage. **-segen,** *m.* nuptial blessing; issue, children. **-stand,** *m.* married state, wedlock. **-standsdarlehen,** *n.* state loan to encourage marriages. **-steuer,** *f.* dowry. **-stifter,** *m.* match-maker. **-tauglich,** *adj.* (*Nat. Soc.*) legally fit to marry. **-trennung,** *f.* judicial separation. **-verbindung,** *f.* matrimonial alliance. **-vergleich,** *m.* marriage contract. **-verlöbnis,** *n.*, **-versprechen,** *n.*, **-verspruch,** *m.* betrothal, engagement. **-vertrag,** *m.* marriage settlement. **-weib,** *n.* wife. **-werber,** *m.* suitor.

ehern, *adj.* brazen, brass, bronze; (*fig.*) *mit -er Stirn*, brazen-faced.

Ehr-e, *f.* (-en) honour; reputation; respect; rank; glory, praise, credit; *einen bei der -e angreifen* or (*coll.*) *packen*, insult, wound a p.'s honour; *au* (*meine*) *-e*, upon my honour; *einem -e bezeigen* or *erweisen*, do *or* show honour to a p.; *bei meiner -e!* I give my word, I swear; *was verschafft mir die -e?* to what do I owe this honour?; *die Prüfung mit -en bestehen*, acquit o.s. creditably in an examination, pass with distinction; *einer die -e rauben* or *eine um die -e bringen*, seduce (a girl); *einen die letzte -e erweisen*, pay one's last respect to a p.; *zur -e gereichen*, redound to a p.'s honour; (*ich*) *hab(e) die -e* (*dial.*) (*rather servile form of greeting*); *mit wem habe ich die -e?* whom have I the honour of speaking to? *in -en halten*, honour; *in allen -en*, in all honour, in good faith; *Ihr Wort in -en*, with due deference to you; *er macht mir keine -e*, he is no credit to me; *sich* (*Dat.*) *eine -e daraus machen*, deem it an honour; *darf ich um die -e bitten?* may I have the honour (*of dancing with you, etc.*)? *-e kann nur mit Blut gewaschen werden*, (national) honour can only be washed in blood; (*C.L.*) *einem Wechsel alle -e widerfahren lassen*, honour *or* meet a bill; *ihm zu -en*, in his honour; *ich rechne es mir zur -e (an), Ihnen zu dienen*, I esteem it an honour to serve you; *ein alter Schriftsteller kommt wieder zu -en*, an old author comes back into favour; *zu -en des Tages*, in honour of the day. **-abschneider,** *m.* slanderer. **-bar,** *adj.* honourable, of good repute; respectable, honest. **-barkeit,** *f.* respectability; propriety; honourableness, good repute; honesty. **-begierig,** *adj.* ambitious. **-beraubung,** *f.* calumniation. **-bewußt,** *adj.* honour-conscious, proud. **-begier(de),** *f.* ambition. **-en,** *v.a.* honour, esteem, revere; (*sehr*) *geehrter Herr*, Sir; dear Sir. **-enamt,** *n.* honorary *or* titular office. **-enamtlich,** *adj.* honorary. **-enbesuch,** *m.* ceremonial *or* formal visit. **-enbezeigung,** *f*, mark of esteem or respect; ovation; (military) salute. **-enbezeugung,** *f.* salute (*Mil.*). **-enbürger,** *m.* freeman (*of a city*). **-endame,** *f.* lady *or* maid of honour. **-endoktor,** *m.* honorary doctor (*of a university*). **-enerklärung,** *f.* (full) apology. **-engabe,** *f.* donation, presentation. **-engast,** *m.* guest of honour. **-engedächtnis,** *n.* pious memory. **-engefolge,** *n.* retinue, escort, suite. **-engehalt,** *n.* (*& dial. m.*) pension. **-engericht,** *n.* court of honour. **-engeschenk,** *n.*, *see* **-engabe,** **-engrab,** *n.* **-engrabmal,** *n.* cenotaph. **-en-**

grad, *m.* honorary degree. **–enhaft,** *adj.* honourable, high-principled. **–enhaftigkeit,** *f.* honourableness. **–enhalber,** *adv.* for honour's sake. **–enhandel,** *m.* affair of honour, duel. **–enklage,** *f.* action for libel. **–enkleid,** *n.* uniform, ceremonial dress. **–enkompanie,** *f.* guard of honour. **–enkränkung,** *f.* affront, insult, slander, libel. **–enlegion,** *f.* Legion of Honour. **–enlüge,** *f.* conventional *or* white lie. **–enmahl,** *n.* dinner *or* banquet in a p.'s honour. **–enmal,** *n.* war memorial, cenotaph. **–enmann,** *m.* man of honour; gentleman. **–enmitglied,** *n.* honorary member. **–enmünze,** *f.* **–enpfennig,** *m.* medal. **–enpforte,** *f.* triumphal arch. **–enplatz,** *m.* place of honour. **–enposten,** *m.* post of honour. **–enpreis,** *m.* 1. price of honour; 2. prize, trophy; 3. speedwell (*Veronica*) (*Bot.*). **–enpunkt,** *m.* point of honour. **–enrat,** *m.* court of honour. **–enrecht,** *n.* code of honour; *bürgerliche –enrechte,* civic *or* civil rights. **–enrettung,** *f.* vindication; apology. **–enrührig,** *adj.* slanderous, libellous, defamatory. **–ensache,** *f.* affair of honour; duel. **–ensäule,** *f.* monument. **–enschänder,** *m.* libeller, slanderer; ravisher. **–enschein,** *m.* promissory note. **(Reichs)–enschild,** *m.* (*Nat. Soc.*) highest civil decoration. **–enschuld,** *f.* debt of honour. (*high style*) **–ensold,** *m.* honorarium. **–enstelle,** *f.* dignity, preferment; post of honour. **–entafel,** *f.* roll of honour. **–entitel,** *m.* honorary title; title of honour. **–envoll,** *adj.* honourable, creditable; *er wurde –envoll erwähnt,* he received honourable mention. **–enwache,** *f.* guard of honour. **–enwächterin,** *f.* chaperon, duenna; *mit ihrer Erzieherin als –enwächterin,* chaperoned by her governess. **–enwert,** *adj.* respectable, honourable. **–enwort,** *n.* word of honour; *auf –enwort,* on parole. **–enwörtlich,** *adj.* on one's word of honour, on parole. **–enzeichen,** *n.* badge of honour; order, medal, decoration; augmentation (*Her.*). **–erbietig,** *adj.* reverential, respectful, deferential. **–erbietung,** *f.* deference, respect, veneration. **–furcht,** *f.* respect, reverence, awe. **–fürchtig,** *adj.* reverential, respectful. **–furchtslos,** *adj.* disrespectful, irreverent. **–furchtsvoll,** *adj.* respectful, reverential. **–gefühl,** *n.* self-respect, sense of honour. **–geiz,** *m.* ambition. **–geizig,** *adj.* ambitious. **–gier,** *f.* inordinate ambition. **–gierig,** *adj.* highly ambitious. **–lich,** *adj.* honest, honourable, reliable; open, true-hearted; *er hat –liche Absichten,* his intentions are honourable (i.e. *he intends to marry the girl*); *ein –liches Begräbnis,* a decent burial; *er meint es –lich* (*mit ihr*), his intentions (towards her) are honourable; *–licher Narr,* harmless ass; (*Prov.*) *–lich währt am längsten,* honesty is the best policy; *mit einem –lich zu Werke gehen,* deal fairly with a p. **–lichkeit,** *f.* honesty. **–los,** *adj.* dishonourable **–losigkeit,** *f.* infamy, dishonesty. **–sam,** *adj.* decent, honourable, respectable. **–sucht,** *f.* ambition. **–süchtig,** *adj.* very ambitious. **–ung,** *f.* mark of honour; token of esteem. **–vergessen,** *adj.* unprincipled, infamous, regardless of honour, despicable, vile. **–vergessenheit,** *f.* infamy, meanness, vileness. **–verlust,** *m.* loss of civil rights. **–widrig,** *adj.* discreditable, despicable, disgraceful. **–würden,** *f.* Reverence; *Ew.* (*Euer*) *–würden,* your Reverence, Reverend Sir. **–würdig,** *adj.* venerable; reverend, sacred. **–würdigkeit,** *f.* venerableness.

ei, *int.* indeed! why! ah! – *was*! nonsense!

Ei, *n.* (-(e)s, -er) egg; (*sl.*) bomb (*Av.*); *hart* (*weich*) *gesottenes –,* hard (soft) boiled egg; *frisches –,* newlaid egg; *faules –,* bad *or* addled egg; *verlorene –er,* poached eggs; *aussehen wie aus dem – geschält* or *gepellt,* be spick and span, look as if one had just stepped out of a bandbox; *sie gleichen sich wie ein – dem andern,* they are as like as two peas *or* pins; (*Prov.*) *das – will klüger sein als die Henne,* don't teach your grandmother to suck eggs; *er ist eben erst aus dem – gekrochen,* he is a greenhorn; he is wet behind the ears; *man muß ihn anfassen* or *behandeln wie ein rohes –,* he is extremely touchy; *ein – zu schälen haben mit,* have a bone to pick with; *kümmre dich nicht um ungelegte –er!* don't anticipate *or* be premature; don't count your chickens before they're hatched. **–dotter,** *m.* & *n.* yolk of egg. **–erauflauf,** *m.* soufflé. **–erbecher,** *m.* egg-cup. **–erbier,** *n.* egg-flip. **–erchen,** *n.* ovule (*Bot.*). **–erkuchen,** *m.*, **–erfladen,** *m.* omelet, pancake. **–erkrebs,** *m.* female crawfish. **–erlegend,** *adj.* oviparous. **–erleger,** *m.pl.* ovipara; *diese Hühner sind gute –erleger,* these hens are good layers. **–erlöffel,** *m.* egg-spoon. **–erpflaume,** *f.* Victoria plum. **–errahm,** *m.* custard. **–ersack,** *m.* ovary (*Anat.*). **–erschale,** *f.* eggshell. **–erschnee,** *m.* whisked *or* beaten white of egg. **–erspeise,** *f.* dish prepared with eggs. **–erstich,** *m.* custard. **–erstock,** *m.* ovary (*Bot.* & *Anat.*). **–förmig,** *adj.* oval, ovoid. **–gelb,** *n.* yolk. **–leiter,** *m.* oviduct, fallopian tube (*Anat.*). **–linie,** *f.* ellipse. **–rund,** *adj.* oval, egg-shaped. **–weiß,** *n.* white of egg, albumen, protein. **–weißhaltig,** *adj.* containing protein. **–weißkörper,** *m.* endosperm (*Bot.*). **–weißstoff,** *m.* protein.

eia, *int.* hey! hey-day! **–popeia,** *int.* & *n.* bye-bye; lullaby, hushaby.

Eibe, *f.* (-n) yew-tree. **–n,** *adj.* yew.

Eibisch, *m.* (-es, -e), marsh-mallow (*Althea officinalis*) (*Bot.*).

[1]**Eich–(e),** *f.* gauge, standard. **–amt,** *n.* office of weights and measures; (*Amer.*) bureau of standards. **–en,** *v.a.* gauge, standardize, graduate, calibrate. **–er,** *m.* gauger, calibrator. **–maß,** *n.* standard, gauge. **–nagel,** *m.* gauge mark. **–fähig,** *adj.* capable of adjustment. **–kurve,** *f.* calibration curve. **–ung,** *f.* gauging, standardization, calibration.

[2]**Eich–e,** *f.* (-en) oak. **–apfel,** *m.* oak apple, oak gall. **–el,** *f.* (-eln) acorn; glans penis (*Anat.*); club (*Cards*). **–elöl,** *n.* nut-oil. **–en,** *adj.* oak, oaken. **–enblatt,** *n.* oak-leaf. **–enfest,** *adj.* firm as an oak. **–elförmig,** *adj.* glandiform. **–elhäher,** *m.* jay (*Garrulus glandarius*) (*Orn.*). **–enlaub,** *n.* oak leaves .**–engalle,** *f.* oak gall, oak apple. **–horn,** *n.*, **–hörnchen,** *n.*, **–kätzchen,** *n.*, **–katze,** *f.* squirrel. **–mast,** *f.* oak mast, acorn mast.

Eid, *m.* (-es, -e) oath; adjuration; execration; *einen – ablegen, leisten* or *schwören,* take an oath, swear, attest; (*einem*) *einen – abnehmen* (*lassen*), put (s.o.) on his oath, swear a p. in; *ich kann einen – darauf ablegen,* I can swear to it. **–brecher,** *m.* perjurer. **–bruch,** *m.* perjury. **–brüchig,** *adj.* perjured, forsworn; *–brüchig werden,* perjure o.s. **–esabnahme,** *f.* administration of an oath. **–esformel,** *f.* form of oath. **–eskräftig,** *adj.* upon oath, sworn, attested. **–esleistung,** *f.* affidavit; taking on oath, act of swearing. **–esstattlich,** *adj.*, *see* **–eskräftig.** **–genossenschaft,** *f.* league, confederacy; Swiss Confederation. **–genössisch,** *adj.* federal; belonging to the Swiss Confederation. **–lich,** *adj.* sworn, by *or* upon oath; *er hat sich –lich verpflichtet,* he is under oath; *–lich erhärten,* depose on oath; *–liche Aussage,* affidavit, sworn deposition. **–schwur,** *m.* oath. **–vergessen,** *adj.* perjured, forsworn. **–verweigernd,** *adj.* non-juring.

Eidam, *m.* (-s, -e), (*archaic*) son-in-law.

Eidechse, *f.* (-n) lizard.

Eider, *m.* (-s, –) **–ente,** *f.* **–vogel,** *m.* eider-duck. **–daunen,** *f.pl.*, **–dunen,** *f.pl.* eiderdown.

Eidotter, *see* **Ei.**

Eifer, *m.* eagerness, zeal; ardour, fervour, passion; (*Prov.*) *blinder – schadet nur,* more haste, less speed. **–er,** *m.* zealot. **–n,** *v.n.* (*aux.* h.) be zealous, act *or* advocate with zeal; endeavour, take great pains (over *or* with); vie (*um,* with), emulate, rival; inveigh, declaim passionately (*gegen,* against), get angry (*über eine S.,* about a th.). **–sucht,** *f.* jealousy. **–süchtelei,** *f.* petty jealousy. **–süchtig,** *adj.* jealous, envious.

eifrig, *adj.* eager, keen, zealous; passionate, ardent; *sich jemandes – annehmen,* interest o.s. warmly for s.o. **–keit,** *f.* zeal; zealousness, officiousness.

eigen, *adj.* (*Dat.*) proper, inherent; own, individual, special; specific, peculiar, characteristic; spontaneous; nice, delicate, particular, exact; odd, strange, curious; ticklish; *–es Gut,* freehold; *–e Leute,* serfs; *aus –em Antriebe,* spontaneously; *–e Aussprache,* peculiar pronunciation; *–e Mund-*

art, idiom; *das ist ihm –*, that is peculiar to him; *– sein* (*Dat.*), belong to, be native to; *ich gab es dir zu –*, I gave it you for yourself; *sich zu – machen*, adopt, utilize, make one's own; *–e Wechsel*, bills of exchange drawn upon o.s.; *auf –e Rechnung*, at one's own risk, on one's own account; *–er Bote*, special messenger. **–art,** *f.* peculiarity, individuality, (*Nat. Soc.*) racial character. **–artig,** *adj.* peculiar, special, individual, original, singular. **–artigerweise,** *adv.* strange to say. **–belastung,** *f.* dead load. **–bericht,** *m.* press report (*from our own correspondent*). **–bewegung,** *f.* spontaneous movement. **–brötelei,** *f.* eccentricity, crankiness. **–brötler,** *m.* crank, eccentric, oddity. **–brötlerisch,** *adj.* eccentric, cranky, odd. **–dünkel,** *m.* self-conceit. **–frequenz,** *f.* fundamental, natural *or* resonant frequency (*Phys.*). **–geräusch,** *n.* needle scratch, surface noise (*gramophone*). **–geschwindigkeit,** *f.* initial velocity (*Phys.*); air speed (*Av.*). **–gesetzlichkeit,** *f.* inner laws, destiny. **–gewicht,** *n.* dead weight, net weight. **–gut,** *n.* freehold. **–händig,** *adj.* with one's own hand; in one's own handwriting; *–händiger Brief*, autograph letter; *einen Brief –händig abgeben*, deliver a letter into the addressee's hands. **–heit,** *f.* peculiarity, oddity, idiosyncrasy; (*in der Sprache*) idiom; trick of speech. **–liebe,** *f.* egotism. **–lob,** *n.* self-praise, (*coll.*) blowing one's own trumpet; (*Prov.*) *–lob stinkt*, self-praise is no recommendation. **–mächtig,** *adj.* arbitrary, autocratic, despotic; unsanctioned, unauthorized; (*coll.*) off one's own bat; *sich* (*Dat.*) *–mächtig Recht verschaffen*, take the law into one's own hands. **–name,** *m.* proper name; proper noun. **–nutz,** *m.* self-interest, selfishness; *Gemeinnutz geht vor –nutz*, (*Nat. Soc. slogan*), the interests of the group come before those of the individual. **–nützig,** *adj.* selfish, self-seeking. **–nützigkeit,** *f.* selfishness. **–s,** *adv.* expressly, on purpose, especially, particularly. **–schaft,** *f.* quality, property, attribute; feature, characteristic peculiarity, character, condition; *Farbe ist eine –schaft des Lichtes*, colour is a property of light; *göttliche –schaft*, divine attribute; *in seiner –schaft als*, in his character of; *gute –schaften*, good points. **–schaftsverkettung,** *f.* correlation. **–schaftswort,** *n.* adjective. **–sinn,** *m.* self-will, obstinacy; caprice, wilfulness. **–sinnig,** *adj.* self-willed, headstrong, stubborn, obstinate; capricious. **–ständig,** *adj.* self-reliant, independent. **–sucht,** *f.* egotism; selfishness. **–süchtig,** *adj.* selfish, egotistical. **–tlich,** 1. *adj.* proper, true, real, essential, intrinsic; *die –tlichen Umstände*, the real circumstances. 2. *adv.* properly *or* strictly speaking, in reality, really, exactly; *was soll das –tlich bedeuten?* what does that really mean? *–tlich habe ich es nicht erwartet*, to tell the truth I did not expect it; *was willst du –tlich?* what exactly do you want? **–ton,** *m.*; *–ton eines Vokals*, characteristic sound of a vowel. **–tum,** *n.* (-tümer), property, belongings; *bewegliches –tum*, movable possessions, goods and chattels; *unbewegliches –tum*, real property. **–tümer,** *m.* owner, proprietor. **–tümlich,** *adj.* (*with initial stress*) belonging exclusively to, proper, characteristic, specific; (*with penultimate stress*) peculiar, original, strange, queer, odd. **–tümlichkeit,** *f.* peculiarity, characteristic. **–tumsrecht,** *n.* right of possession; law of property; copyright; ownership. **–tumssteuer,** *f.* property tax. **–tumstitel,** *m.* title-deed. **–tumsvergehen,** *n.* trespass. **–wärme,** *f.* specific heat. **–wert,** *m.* characteristic number *or* value. **–wille,** *m.* wilfulness. **–willig,** *adj.* self-willed. **–wüchsig,** *adj.* indigenous.

eign–en, 1. *v.r.* be adapted *or* suited *or* qualified (*zu*, for). 2. *v.n.* (*aux.* h.) (*Dat.*) suit, befit, be characteristic of; belong to; (with *für* or *zu*) be qualified *or* suitable for *or* adapted to. **–er,** *m.* owner, proprietor. **–ung,** *f.* aptitude, qualification. **–ungsauslese,** *f.* selection on basis of aptitude test.

Eiland, *n.* (-es, -e), island, isle (*Poet.*).

Eil–e, *f.* haste, speed, dispatch; *große –e*, hurry; *in* (*der*) *–e*, in haste, in a hurry; *es hat keine –e*, there is no hurry, there is plenty of time. **–bote,** *m.* express messenger, courier; *durch –boten*, by special delivery. **–brief,** *m.* express letter. **–en,** *v.n.* (*aux.* s. & h.) & *r.* make haste, hasten, hurry, *Eilt!*, urgent! (*on letters*); *das –t ja nicht*, that is not by any means urgent; *was –en Sie so?* why are you in such a hurry? *sie –en nicht sehr damit*, they take their time over it; (*Prov.*) *–e mit Weile*, slow and steady wins the race. **–fertig,** *adj.* hasty, rash. **–fertigkeit,** *f.* overhaste; hastiness, rashness. **–fracht,** *f.*, **–gut,** *n.* express goods. **–ig,** *adj.* quick, speedy, hurried; *es –ig haben*, be in a hurry; *die S. ist nicht so –ig*, the matter is not so urgent; *–ige Drucksache*, urgent printed matter; *nicht so –ig!* don't be in such a hurry! *sie hatte nichts –igeres zu tun, als die ganze Geschichte zu erzählen*, she could not rest until she had told the whole story. **–igkeit,** *f.*, *see* **Eile. –marsch,** *m.* forced march. **–post,** *f.*, **–sendung,** *f.* express delivery. **–zug,** *m.* express *or* fast train.

Eimer, *m.* (-s, –) pail, bucket. **–kette,** *f.* bucket-chain. **–weise,** *adv.* in bucketsful, by pailfuls.

ein, 1. (eine, ein) *ind. art.* a, an; *was für –*, what sort of. 2. *num. adj.* one, the same; *– für allemal*, once for all; *–er von beiden*, either (of them); *in –em fort, in –em Stücke fort, in –em so hin*, incessantly, continuously, without stopping; *dieses –e Wort sage ich dir noch*, I have just one word more to say to you; *sie sind von –er Größe*, they are the same size; *um –s*, at one o'clock; *es ist halb –s*, it is half-past twelve; *zwanzig und –s sind –undzwanzig*, 20 plus 1 is 21; *zwanzig Knaben und noch –er sind einundzwanzig*, 20 boys and another *or* a further one are 21. 3. *pron.* (-er, -e, -(e)s) one, a person; they, people; a certain portion, some; *– und derselbe*, the very same, one and the same; *es tut –em gut*, it does one good; *so –er*, such a one; *unser –er*, one of us, one such as I; people like ourselves; *manch –er*, many a one; *–er nach dem anderen*, one by one; *–er für alle und alle für –en*, jointly and severally; *noch –s*, another word with you; further, by the way; *noch –s so schön*, as beautiful again; *–s um andere* (*mal*), alternately; *–s ins andere gerechnet*, taking one with the other, all things considered; *–es schickt sich nicht für alle*, the same thing is not suitable for everybody, one man's meat is another's poison. 4. *adv.* & *sep. prefix*, in, into; *Jahr aus, Jahr –*, every year, all the year round; *– und aus gehen*, frequent; *nicht – und aus wissen*, be at one's wit's end. **–er, –ser,** *m.* (-s, -) unit, number below ten, digit; single-sculler, single-seater, etc. **–erlei,** *see* **einerlei, –erseit,** *see* **einerseits. –heit,** *f.*, *see* **Einheit. –ig, –ige, –iges,** *see* **einig. –s,** 1. *adv.* the same, of one mind, at one; *wir sind –s*, we are at one *or* agreed; *wir werden bald –s*, we shall soon agree. 2. *f.* the number one; ace (*dice*). 3. *indec. adj.* one, immaterial, indifferent; *es kommt* or *läuft auf –s hinaus*, it comes to the same thing, it's all one. **–sam,** *see* **einsam. –st,** *see* **einst. –zeln,** *see* **einzeln. –zig,** *see* **einzig.**

einachsig, *adj.* two wheeled, uniaxial.

einackern, *v.a.* plough in.

Einakter, *m.* one act play.

einander, *indecl. pron.* one another, each other; *an–*, in succession; *aus–*, asunder, apart, from each other; *mit einem aus– kommen*, fall out with *or* quarrel with a p.; *bei–*, together; side by side; *durch–*, promiscuously, confusedly, pell-mell; *hinter–*, in succession, one after the other; *mit–*, one with another, on an average; together; *nach–*, successively; *drei Tage nach–*, three days running; *neben–*, side by side; *von–*, apart, asunder.

Einankerumformer, *m.* rotary convertor (*Elec.*).

einarbeiten, 1. *v.a.* train, break in. 2. *v.r. sich in eine S. –*, make o.s. thoroughly acquainted with a th., get used to a th., familiarize o.s. with s.th.; (*coll.*) work *or* break o.s. in.

einarmig, *adj.* one-armed.

einäscher–n, *v.a.* burn *or* reduce to ashes; incinerate; calcine; cremate. **–ung,** *f.* incineration, cremation. **–ungshalle,** *f.* crematorium.

einatm–en, *v.a.* inhale. **–ung,** *f.* inhalation.

einätzen, *v.a.* etch in.

einäugig, *adj.* one-eyed.

Einbahnstraße, *f.* one-way street.

einbalsam-ieren, *v.a.* embalm. **-ierung,** *f.* embalming; embalmment.
Einband, *m.* (-s, ⸚e), binding, cover (of a book); *biegsamer –*, limp cover; *– mit Goldschnitt*, with gilt edges. **-decke,** *f.* cover (*of a book*).
einbändig, *adj.* in one volume.
einbauen, *v.a.* install, fit; *eingebaute Schränke*, built-in cupboards, enclose *or* surround (*with buildings*), build in; dam in.
Einbaum, *m.* (-s, ⸚e), log canoe, primitive boat (*made from a single tree-trunk*).
einbedingen, *ir.v.a.* include in the bargain.
einbegreifen, *ir.v.a.*, comprise, include, contain, imply; *mit einbegriffen*, included, contained, implied.
einbehalten, *ir.v.a. einem etwas –*, keep back s.th. *or* withhold s.th. from s.o.; save; detain.
einbeizen, *v.a.* etch in; pickle (*meat*); soak; vein (*wood or leather*).
einberuf-en, *ir.v.a.* convene, summon; call in (*currency, etc.*); call up (*troops*). **-ung,** *f.* convocation; call to the colours (*Mil.*); *–ung der Reserven*, calling up the army reserve; *–ung einer Konferenz*, summoning of a conference. **-ungsbefehl,** *m.* calling up order *or* papers.
einbett-en, *v.a.* embed, surround with. **-ig,** *adj.*; *–iges Zimmer*, single-bedded room.
einbezieh-en, *v.a.* include, implicate, draw into. **-ung,** *f.* inclusion.
einbieg-en, 1. *ir.v.a.* bend inwards, downwards *or* back, turn down; inflect. **eingebogen,** *p.p. & adj.* inflected; sinuous. 2. *v.n.* (*aux.* s.); *–en in*, turn into *or* to. **-ung,** *f.* bending inwards; inflexion; recess.
einbild-en, *v.a.* (*with Dat. of r. pron.*) fancy, imagine, think, believe; be conceited, flatter o.s., pride o.s. (*auf*, on); presume upon; take into one's head; *eingebildet*, conceited; imaginary. **-ung,** *f.* imagination, conceit, fancy, presumption; *in der –ung vorhanden*, imaginary, fancied; *er leidet an –ungen*, he suffers from delusions *or* hallucinations. **-ungskraft,** *f.* imagination; *seiner –ungskraft freien Lauf lassen*, give a free rein to one's imagination.
einbind-en, *ir.v.a.* bind (*a book*); tie up *or* on; furl (*sails*); take in (*a reef*); *seinem Patenkind etwas –en*, (*archaic*) make a present to one's godchild. **-egeld,** *n.* godparent's christening gift. **-enadel,** *f.* bookbinder's needle, flat awl.
einblas-en, *ir.v.a.* blow *or* breathe into; inject (*steam, etc.*), insufflate; whisper, suggest, prompt, insinuate; blow down (*walls*), blow in (*windows, etc.*). **-ung,** *f.* blowing in; suggestion, insinuation.
Einbläs-er, *m.* (-s, –) prompter, suggester, insinuator. **-erei,** *f.* insinuation.
Einblattdruck, *m.* broadsheet.
einblättrig, *adj.* monophyllous.
einbläuen, einbleuen, *v.a.* dye blue, blue (*washing*) (*usually* einbläuen); knock into a p., drum into (*usually* einbleuen).
Einblendung, *f.* focusing, concentration (*of rays*).
Einblick, *m.* (-es, -e) glance into *or* at; insight; eyepiece (*Opt.*).
einblumig, *adj.* uniflorous.
einbrech-en, 1. *ir.v.a.* break down, pull down; break open, smash in. 2. *v.n.* (*aux.* s.) break in, break into a house, commit burglary; begin, draw on, approach, set in; *die Nacht bricht ein*, night is falling; *bei –ender Nacht*, at nightfall. **-er,** *m.* burglar, housebreaker.
einbrenn-en, *v.a.* brand, cauterize, anneal. **-emaille,** *f.*, **-lack,** *m.* stove enamel.
einbring-en, *ir.v.a.* bring in, house; yield (*profit*), realize *or* fetch (*a price*); capture, seize (*Mil.*); insert, introduce; *etwas wieder –en*, make up for, make good *or* retrieve s.th.; *das Versäumte läßt sich gar nicht mehr –en*, you can't make up for lost time. *was bringt der Posten ein?* what is the post worth? *das Eingebrachte*, dowry. **-lich,** *adj.* profitable.
einbrocken, *v.a.* crumble, break into small pieces; *sich* (*Dat.*) *etwas –*, get into trouble, (*coll.*) put one's foot in it; *er muß nun ausessen, was er sich eingebrockt hat*, he now reaps what he has sown, now he's made his bed he must lie in it.
Einbruch, *m.* (-s, ⸚e) housebreaking, burglary; invasion, inroad; break through, breach (*of enemy's front*), raid, trespass; *– der Nacht*, nightfall; *–sdiebstahl*, burglary. **-sflieger,** *m.* intruder, (*coll.*) tip-and-run raider (*Av*). **-sfront,** cold front (*Meteor.*). **-sicher,** *adj.* burglar-proof. **-sversicherung,** *f.* insurance against burglary.
einbrühen, *v.a.* scald.
einbuchten, *v.a.* groove, indent.
einbürger-n, 1. *v.a.* naturalize; enfranchise; *Wörter –n*, adopt (*foreign*) words (*into a language*); *eingebürgerte Lehnwörter*, naturalized loanwords. 2. *v.r.* become naturalized, acclimatized *or* adopted, come into use, gain vogue; *dies Wort hat sich eingebürgert*, this word has come to stay. **-ung,** *f.* naturalization.
Einbuße, *f.* (-n) loss, damage.
einbüßen, *v.a.* (*an* with *Dat.*) suffer loss (from), lose (on *or* by), forfeit.
eindämmen, *v.a.* dam up; embank; (*fig.*) check; *eingedämmtes Land*, reclaimed land.
eindampfen, *v.n.* (*aux.* s.) boil down *or* away, evaporate, dry by evaporation.
eindämpfen, *v.a.* steam, treat with steam.
eindeck-en, 1. *v.a.* provide with a cover, surface. 2. *v.r.* lay in a store (of); *Italien ist mit Kohlen eingedeckt*, Italy is sufficiently provided with coal. **-er,** *m.* monoplane. **-ung,** *f.* overhead cover, roofing, surfacing. **-ungsangriff,** *m.* saturation raid (*Av.*).
eindeutig, *adj.* clear, plain, unequivocal.
eindeutschen, *v.a.* Germanize, translate into German; *ein Fremdwort –*, give to a foreign word a German appearance (e.g. *Bresche*, *Gruppe*, *Leutnant*, *Möbel*).
eindick-en, *v.a.* thicken, condense, inspissate, coagulate, concentrate. **-ung,** *f.* condensation, thickening, *etc.*
eindorren, *v.a.* dry up, shrink.
eindrängen, 1. *v.a.* squeeze into, force into. 2. *v.r.* crowd in; intrude o.s. into.
eindreh-en, *v.a.* screw in. **-schnecke,** *f.* feed-screw.
eindring-en, *ir.v.n.* (*aux.* s.) enter by force, break in, invade; penetrate, pierce; infiltrate, soak in; (*fig.*) fathom, search into. **-lich,** *adj.* penetrating; affecting, impressive, forcible; intrusive, forward, urgent. **-lichkeit,** *f.* impressiveness; forcefulness, urgency. **-ling,** *m.* intruder, (*coll.*) gatecrasher. **(-ungs)tiefe,** *f.* operational radius (*of raiding aircraft*), depth of penetration (*measured from coast or frontier, not from base*).
Eindruck, *m.* (-(e)s, ⸚e), impression, mark, stamp; *– machen*, produce an impression *or* a sensation. **-en,** *v.a.* imprint, ground in (*cloth*); insert (*printed illustrations in the letterpress*). **-slos,** *adj.* unimpressive. **-svoll,** *adj.* impressive.
eindrück-en, *v.a.* press in, compress, flatten down, squeeze, squash, flatten; shut, close; imprint, impress (*on the memory*). **-lich,** *adj.* impressive, emphatic.
einebn-en, *v.a.* level, even up; flatten, demolish. **-ung,** *f.* levelling.
Einehe, *f.* monogamy.
einen, *v.a.* unite, form into one; *das geeinte Deutschland*, united Germany.
einengen, *v.a.* narrow down, compress, confine, cramp; hem in, limit, define closely.
Einer, *m. see under* **ein-.**
einerlei, 1. *indec. adj.* of one sort, (one and) the same; immaterial, all the same; *– ob*, regardless whether. 2. *n.* monotony, sameness; *ewiges –*, unvarying monotony.
einernten, *v.a.* reap, harvest, gather in; (*fig.*) win, gain, acquire.
einerseits, *adv.* on the one hand *or* side.
einexerzieren, *v.a.* drill thoroughly, train.
einfach, *adj.* simple, single; plain, homely, frugal, modest; *–e Farbe*, primary colour; *–wirkend*, single-actioned. **-heit,** *f.* simplicity, plainness; singleness. **-leitung,** *f.* single-wire circuit (*Elec.*).
einfädeln, 1. *v.a.* thread (*a needle*); devise, manage, contrive; *soll ich Ihnen –?* shall I thread the needle for you? 2. *v.r.* manage to get in, join the line.

einfahr-en, 1. *ir.v.a.* bring or carry in (*on wheels*); run *or* drive into; break in (*horses to harness*), run in (*a new engine*); injure by driving over. 2. *v.n.* (*aux.* s.) drive into, enter, descend (*a mine*). **-t,** *f.* (-ten), entrance, gateway; inlet, harbour mouth, entry; descent (*of a mine*). **-tssignal,** *n.*, **-tszeichen,** *n.* 'up' signal, home signal (*Railw.*).

Einfall, *m.* (-es, ⸗e) falling in, falling down, fall, collapse; downfall, ruin; inroad, invasion, sally (*Mil.*); irruption; incidence (*of light*); sudden idea, brainwave, fancy, notion; *witziger* –, flash of wit; *wunderlicher* –, whim, conceit; *ich geriet auf den* –, it struck me, the idea occurred to me. **-en,** 1. *ir.v. n.* (*aux* s.) fall in; invade, make an inroad, attack, overrun, raid, break in, come in suddenly; chime *or* join in; interrupt; fall down, collapse, fall to ruin; occur (*to one's mind*); alight, roost (*of birds*); fall, be incident (*as light*); *es fiel mir ein*, it occurred to me; *das hätte ich mir nie –en lassen*, I should never have dreamt of such a thing, it would never have entered my head; *wie es ihm gerade einfiel*, as the humour seized him; *es will mir nicht –en*, I cannot remember it; *was fällt dir ein?* what are you thinking of? what do you mean by it? *es fällt mir nicht ein, das zu tun*, I have not the least intention of doing so, (*coll.*) catch me doing that; *eingefallene Augen*, sunken eyes; *Winkel, unter dem ein Lichtstrahl einfällt*, angle of incidence; *das Licht fällt durch das Fenster ein*, the light shines through the window. 2. *v.a. sich* (*Dat.*) *den Schädel –en*, crack one's skull by a fall. **-end,** *pr.p.* & *adj.* incident; *–endes Fenster*, skylight. **-slot,** *n.* perpendicular. **-swinkel,** *m.* angle of incidence.

Einfalt, *f.* simplicity, artlessness, innocence, naïveté. **-spinsel,** *m.* simpleton, silly fool.

einfältig, *adj.* simple, plain; foolish, silly. **-keit,** *f.* simplicity, silliness.

Einfamilienhaus, *n.* villa, self-contained house.

einfangen, 1. *ir.v.a.* seize, catch, capture, apprehend; close, separate by a fence. 2. *v.n.* (*aux.* h.) catch (on).

einfarbig, *adj.* plain, of one colour, self-coloured, monochrome.

einfass-en, *v.a.* border, edge; bind (*carpets*); enclose; frame; mount (*in a frame*); trim (*with lace, etc.*); set (*jewels*); barrel (*beer, etc.*). **-er,** *m.* stonesetter. **-ung,** *f.* enclosing, enclosure; setting; border, trimming, edging, binding; framing, frame, mounting, mount; curb (*of a well*), embankment, fencing, railing. **-ungsband,** *n.*, **(-ß)band,** *n.* binding *or* bordering ribbon.

einfett-en, *v.a.* grease, oil, lubricate. **-ung,** *f.* greasing, oiling, lubrication.

einfeuchten, *v.a.* steep, wet, moisten, damp.

einfinden, *ir.v.r.* appear, make one's appearance; arrive, (*coll.*) turn up.

einflechten, *ir.v.a.* plait, braid; interlace, interweave; adorn with, insert; mention casually, put in (*a word*), interlard (*with oaths, etc.*).

einflicken, *v.a.* patch in, sew on a patch, insert.

einfliegen, 1. *ir.v.a.* test (*a plane*). 2. *v.n.* arrive *or* attack by air. **-er,** *m.* test pilot.

einfließen, *ir.v.n.* (*aux.* s.) flow in *or* into; come in (*of money*); *mit – lassen*, drop in a word, throw in a remark, mention casually.

einflöß-en, *v.a.* cause to flow in; administer, instil, imbue, infuse, inspire with; *einem Mut –en*, inspire a p. with courage; *einem Mitleid –en*, enlist *or* call forth a p.'s sympathy; *einem ein Verlangen –en*, kindle a desire in a p. **-bar,** *adj.* infusible. **-ung,** *f.* infusion.

Einflug, *m.* (-(e)s, ⸗e) test flight; arrival (*at airport*); attack from the air, *see* **einfliegen. -schneise,** *f.* flying lane, air corridor.

Einfluß, *m.* (-(ss)es, ⸗(ss)e), flowing in, influx; influence, effect, bearing, power, sway, credit; *–auf einen ausüben*, exercise influence on a p. **-reich,** *adj.* influential. **-röhre,** *f.* feed-pipe, inlet-pipe.

einflüster-n, *v.a.* whisper to, insinuate. **-ung,** *f.* insinuation, innuendo.

einfordern, *v.a.* call in (*debts*); demand (*payment*); collect (*taxes*).

einförmig, *adj.* uniform, unvaried, monotonous. **-keit,** *f.* uniformity, monotony.

einfressen, 1. *ir.v.a.* eat up, swallow, devour. 2. *v.r.* & *n.* (*aux.* h.) eat into, corrode (*v.r. only*), seize (*of an engine*).

einfried(ig)-en, *v.a.* enclose, fence in, corral. **-ung,** *f.* enclosure; fencing, fence, paling, corral.

einfrieren, *ir.v.n.* (*aux.* s.) freeze in *or* up; be icebound. **eingefroren,** *p.p.* & *adj.* frost-bound; *eingefrorene Kredite*, frozen credits (*C.L.*).

einfüg-en, 1. *v.a.* insert; join together, splice, dovetail, rabbet. 2. *v.r.* become a part *or* member of; fit in, adapt o.s. (to). **-ung,** *f.* fitting in; insertion; dovetailing.

einfühl-en, *v.r.* have a sympathetic understanding (of). **-ung,** *f.* sympathetic understanding; empathy (*Phil.*).

Einfuhr, *f.* (-en) imports; importation; bringing in, housing (*corn, etc.*). **-beschränkung,** *f.* restriction of imports. **-erlaubnis,** *f.* import licence. **-handel,** *m.* import trade. **-liste,** *f.*, **-register,** *n.*, **-tabelle,** *f.* bill of lading: import schedule. **-prämie,** *f.* import bounty. **-schein,** *m.* bill of entry. **-sperre,** f., **-verbot,** *n.* embargo on imports. **-zoll,** *m.* import duty.

einführ-en, *v.a.* introduce, usher in; set up, install, establish; inaugurate, induct (*to a living, etc.*); bring in, import; *in ein Amt –en*, install. **-bar,** *adj.* importable; presentable. **-ung,** *f.* introduction; importation; installation. **-ungsschreiben,** *n.* letter of introduction.

einfüll-en, *v.a.* fill in, fill up; pour in; *in Flaschen –en*, bottle. **-stoff,** *m.* packing, filling, **-trichter,** *m.* funnel.

Eingabe, *f.* (-n) petition, presentation (*of a request, etc.*), application, memorial.

eingabeln, *v.a.* bracket (*with shots*) (*Artil.*); straddle (*with bombs*) (*Av.*).

Eingang, *m.* (-(e)s, ⸗e) entering, entry, arrival, entrance, input (*Rad.*); place of entrance, entrance gate, doorway, hall, passage; orifice (*Anat.*); inlet, mouth (*of a river*); adit (*horizontal entrance of a mine*); introduction; importation; access; beginning, preface, preamble, exordium, prelude, overture, prologue; – *von Geld*, receipt of payment; *nach* –, on receipt *or* payment; *verbotener* –, *kein* –, no admission, no entry; – *der Messe*, introit; *keinen – finden*, not be received, find no acceptance; make no way, have no effect. **-s,** *adv.* on entering; at the beginning *or* outset. **-sbuch,** *n.* book of entries; entrance-book. **-sdeklaration,** *f.* bill of entry. **-srede,** *f.* inaugural speech. **-sspannung,** *f.* input voltage (*Elec.*). **-sstück,** *n.* overture. **-stor,** *n.* entrance-gate. **-svermerk,** *m.* notice of receipt. **-szoll,** *m.* import duty.

eingeb-en, *ir.v.a.* insert; suggest, prompt, inspire (with); hand in, send in, deliver, present, give, administer (*medicine*). **-ung,** *f.* administration; presentation; inspiration, suggestion.

eingebildet, *p.p.* & *adj.* imaginary; conceited, presumptuous, *see* **einbilden.**

eingebogen, *p.p.* & *adj.* inflected, sinuous, crenated.

eingeboren, *p.p.* & *adj.* native, indigenous; inborn, innate; only-begotten (*B.*); *das Recht der –en verleihen*, naturalize. **-e(r),** *m.* native; *er ist kein –er*, he is an alien.

Eingebrachte(s), *n.* capital advanced (*to borrower*); dowry, *see* **einbringen.**

eingedenk, *prep.* mindful of, remembering.

eingefallen, *p.p.* & *adj.* emaciated, sunken, hollow-cheeked, *see* **einfallen.**

eingefleischt, *adj.* incarnate; (*fig.*) inveterate.

eingehen, 1. *ir.v.n.* (*aux.* s.) go in, enter, come in, arrive; decay, perish, wither (*of plants*), die (*of game*), cease, stop, come to an end; enter into (*particulars*); shrink (*of woollen goods*); *auf eine S.*, acquiesce in *or* agree to a th.; *in eine S.* –, investigate *or* look into a th.; *auf den Scherz* –, enter into the spirit of the joke; *er ging eifrig auf* (some times *in*) *die S. ein*, he took up the matter with enthusiasm; *aus- und* –, frequent (*a house*); – *lassen*, give up, leave off, let drop; *er ließ das Geschäft* –, he gave up business; *die Pflanze ist eingegangen*, the plant has withered; *er ist zum ewigen Leben* or *in die ewige Ruhe eingegangen*, he has gone

to his rest, passed away *or* over; *das geht ihm glatt ein*, he likes to hear that; *das will ihm nicht* –, that will not go down with him. 2. *v.a.*; *einen Vergleich* –, come to terms; *eine Wette* –, make a bet. **-d,** *pr. p. & adj.* thorough, searching, exhaustive, exact, in detail. **eingegangen,** *p.p. & adj.* paid, received, in cash; *eingegangene Gelder*, receipts.
eingemacht, *p.p. & adj.* preserved. **-e(s),** *n.* preserve(s); jam; pickles.
eingemeind-en, *v.a.* incorporate. **-ung,** *f.* incorporation.
eingenommen, *p.p. & adj.*, *see* **einnehmen;** *von einem* –, prepossessed in favour of; *er ist sehr von ihr* –, he is infatuated with her; *von sich* –, conceited, full of one's own importance; *gegen einen* –, prejudiced against a p. **-heit,** *f.* predilection, partiality, prepossession; prejudice.
eingeschlechtig, *adj.* unisexual (*Bot.*).
eingeschliffen, *p.p. & adj.* ground in (*of glass-stopper, engine valve, etc.*).
Eingeschlossenheit, *f.* confinement, seclusion; *see* **einschließen.**
eingeschnitten, *p.p. & adj.* incised (*Bot.*); *see* **einschneiden.**
Eingeschränktheit, *f.* limitation, narrowness, narrow-mindedness; frugality.
eingeschrieben, *p.p. & adj.* registered (*as a letter*).
eingesessen, *p.p. & adj.* settled, established, resident.
eingestandenermaßen, *adv.*, *see* **eingestehen.**
Eingeständnis, *n.* (-ses, -se) admission, avowal, confession.
eingestehen, *ir.v.a.* confess, admit, own up; grant, allow; *eingestandenermaßen*, avowedly.
eingestellt, *p.p. & adj.* focused, adjusted (*Opt.*), tuned-in (*Rad.*).
eingestrichen, *p.p. & adj.* once-accented (*Mus.*).
Eingeweide, *n.* (-s, –), intestines; bowels, entrails, viscera. **-geflecht,** *n.* solar plexus (*Anat.*). **-wurm,** *m.* intestinal worm *or* parasite.
Eingeweihte(r), *m.* initiate; (*usually pl.*) the initiated *or* adepts.
eingewickelt, *p.p. & adj.* involute, convolute.
eingewöhnen, 1. *v.a.* accustom to. 2. *v.r.* get used to; settle down.
eingewurzelt, *p.p. & adj.* deep-rooted; inveterate.
eingezogen, *p.p. & adj.* retired, secluded, solitary; retracted; called-up (*Mil.*). *-e Laufräder*, *n.pl.* retracted landing-wheels (*Av.*). **-heit,** *f.* seclusion retirement; solitary life.
eingieß-en, *ir.v.a.* pour in *or* out; infuse (into); cast in; fasten with (*plaster, etc.*); *mit Blei -en*, fill in with lead. **-ung,** *f.* infusion, transfusion.
eingitter-n, *v.a.* fence off, rail in. **-röhre,** *f.* triode (*Rad.*).
Einglas, *n.* monocle.
eingleisig, *adj.* single-track.
eingleder-n, 1. *v.a.* annex, conquer (*territory*), incorporate, 2. *v.r.* fit in, make o.s. part of. **-ung,** *f.* classification, division; insertion.
eingraben, 1. *ir.v.a.* dig in, bury, inter, entrench, furrow; engrave, chase; hide. 2. *v.r.* burrow, entrench o.s.; (*coll.*) dig in; *das Ereignis hat sich tief in mein Gedächtnis eingegraben*, the event is engraved *or* has impressed itself deeply in my memory.
eingravieren, *v.a.* engrave.
eingreif-en, 1. *ir.v.a.* (*aux.* h.) catch, bite (*of an anchor, of a file*), take hold (*of a latch, etc.*); gear together, mesh together, interlock, engage; interfere with, intervene, interrupt; set to work, set about, act; invade, infringe; *ineinander -en*, mesh (*as cog-wheels*), be interdependent; *in jemandes Rechte -en*, encroach on another's privileges; *der Hund greift ein*, the dog picks up the scent; *die Mächte griffen ein*, the powers intervened. 2. *n.* intervention, interference; infringement. **-division,** *f.* reserve division (*Mil.*). **-end,** *adj.* radical, effective; *-ende Maßregeln*, energetic measures.
eingrenzen, *v.a.* localize, limit (*Mech.*).
Eingriff, *m.* (-s, -e), interference, intervention; trespass, infringement, encroachment; invasion; usurpation; catch (*of a lock, etc.*); chemical action; *chirurgischer* –, surgical operation; *einen unerlaubten* – *vornehmen*, perform an illegal operation; (*rare*); *in* or *außer* – *bringen*, throw into *or* out of gear.
Einguß, *m.* (-(ss)es, ¨-(ss)e) pouring in; infusion, potion; drench (*Vet.*); cast, mould; channel, gate, feeder (*Metall.*). **-röhre,** *f.*, **-trichter,** *m.* feed-pipe; furnace-pipe (*Found.*).
einhaken, 1. *v.a.* fasten (*with a hook*); hook in, bite, catch, hold. 2. *v.r.* take a p.'s arm; *sie gingen eingehakt*, they walked arm in arm.
Einhalt, *m.* stop, check, restraint; prohibition; impediment; interruption; – *tun* or *gebieten*, stop, check; order to stop, bring to a standstill. **-en,** 1. *ir.v.a.* follow, observe; adhere to, keep (*a promise*); check, restrain; hold back; gather, pucker (*a seam, etc.*); *die Zeit -en*, be punctual; 2. *v.n.* (*aux.* h.) stop, leave off; pause, desist; *halt ein!* stop! leave off! *mit der Bezahlung -en*, stop payment. **-ung,** *f.* observance (*of feasts, etc.*).
einhallen, *v.a.* berth (*aircraft*).
einhämmern, *v.a.* drum *or* hammer in.
einhändig, *adj.* single-handed. **-en,** *v.a.*; *einem etwas -en*, hand s.th. over to a p.; deliver s.th. to a p. **-ung,** *f.* delivery, consignation. **-ungsschein,** *m.* bill of delivery.
einhängen, 1. *v.a.* hang up, put in; suspend; put on its hinges (*a door*); ship (*a rudder*); skid (*a cart wheel.* 2. *v.r.* engage, click (into position) (*Mach.*); (*coll.*) *sich bei einem* –, take a p.'s arm; *sie gingen eingehängt*, they walked arm in arm.
einhauchen, *v.a.* inhale; inspire (with); breathe into; inculcate, instil.
einhauen, 1. *ir.v.a.* hew *or* cut into *or* open; cut up (*meat*); break open. 2. *v.n.* (*aux.* h.) charge, attack, fall upon (*Mil.*); *in* or *auf den Feind* –, fall upon the enemy; (*coll.*) *tüchtig* –, eat heartily; fall to, (*coll.*) tuck in.
einheb-en, 1. *ir.v.a.* lift into (place), bring to the press (*Typ.*); collect. 2. *n.* imposing (*Typ.*). **-ung,** *f.*, *see* **Einziehung.**
einheften, *v.a.* sew in, stitch in; file (*papers, etc.*); tack together.
einhegen, *v.a.* fence in, enclose.
einheim-isch, *adj.* native, indigenous; endemic; domestic, home-bred, home-made, home; vernacular; *-ische Produkte*, home produce; *-ische Dichtung*, national poetry; *-ische Pflanzen*, indigenous plants; *-isch machen*, naturalize, domesticate, acclimatize; *-isch werden*, settle down, feel at home; *die -ischen*, the natives. **-sen,** *v.a.* get in, bring home, house; (*coll.*) pocket, reap, rake in.
einheiraten, *v.n.* (*sometimes v.r.*); (*sich*) *in ein Geschäft* –, marry into a business.
Einheit, *f.* (-en) unity, oneness, union, uniformity; unit (*Math.*); – *der Handlung*, unity of action; – *von Zeit und Ort*, unities of time and place. **-lich,** *adj.* uniform, homogeneous, centralized, undivided; *-liche Regierung*, centralized government. **-sfront,** *f.* united front, united attitude. **-sgläubige(r),** *m.* unitarian (*Rel.*). **-skurzschrift,** *f.* standard shorthand (*approved by German civil service*). **-slehre,** *f.* monotheism. **-spreis,** *m.* fixed price. **-spreisgeschäft,** *n.*, fixed-price store, (*Amer.*) 5 and 10 cent store. **-sschule,** *f.* standardized primary school.
einheiz-en, *v.a. & n.* (*aux.* h.) light a fire; *wir haben tüchtig eingeheizt*, we have a good fire, we have heated our room well; (*coll.*) *einem -en*, make it warm for a p., speak one's mind to a p.
einhellig. *adj.* unanimous(ly), with one accord.
einhelmig, *adj.* monandrous (*Bot.*).
einher, *adv. & sep. prefix* along, forth (*with words of motion often implying stateliness*). **-gehen,** **-schreiten,** *ir.v.n.* move along, proceed; pace about. **-stolzieren,** *v.n.* strut, stalk along. **-ziehen,** *v.n.* move on.
einhol-en, *v.a.* bring in; haul in *or* home (*a rope*); take in (*sails*); go to meet *or* fetch; obtain (*permission*); seek (*counsel*); collect, gather; overtake, catch up with, make up for (*lost time*); retrieve; *-en gehen*, go shopping. **-er,** *m.* halyard (*Naut.*).
Einhorn, *n.* unicorn.
einhüllen, *v.a.* wrap *or* muffle up *or* in; cover; envelop; embed.
einhutzeln, (*coll.*) *v.a.* shrivel.

einig, *adj.* at one, united, in agreement, unanimous, agreed; *das –e Deutschland,* United Germany; *handels– werden,* come to terms, conclude a bargain; *– sein* or *werden (über eine S.),* agree about *or* upon *(a th.)*; *er ist mit sich selbst nicht darüber –,* he has not made up his (own) mind about it. **–es,** *adj.* (*pl.* **–e**) some, any; (*pl.*) some, sundry, a few; *–e Leute,* some people. **–emal,** *adv.* several times. **–en,** 1. *v.a.* make one, unite, unify. 2. *v.r.* agree, come to terms. **–ermaßen,** *adv.* in some measure, to some extent, somewhat, rather. **–keit,** *f.* unity, union, harmony, concord, agreement, unanimity; (*Prov.*) *–keit macht stark,* union is strength. **–ung,** *f.* unification, union, agreement.

einimpf–en, *v.a.* inoculate, vaccinate; (*fig.*) implant. **–ung,** *f.* inoculation; vaccination.

einigeln, *v.r.* 'hedgehog' (*Mil.*).

einjagen, 1. *v.a.* instil; *einem Schrecken –,* frighten a p., strike terror into s.o.; *einen Hund –,* train a dog for shooting.

einjährig, *adj.* lasting a year; one year old; *–e Pflanze,* annual. **–e(r),** *m.*, **–freiwillige(r),** *m.* (*before 1919*), German one-year volunteer. **–e,** *n.* lower school-leaving certificate (*two years before* Reifezeugnis) (*orig. the educational standard required for one-year volunteers; now required for minor civil service and similar non-academic employment*).

einkalken, *v.a.* lime, lay in *or* dress with lime; join with lime; soak in lime-water.

einkapsel–n, *v.a.* capsule, encyst (*Med.*) **–ung,** *f.* encystment, encapsulation.

einkassieren, *v.a.* cash (*a cheque*), collect, call in (*money, debts*).

Einkauf, *m.* (-(e)s, ⸚e) purchase; buying, marketing. **–en,** *v.a.* buy, purchase, shop for. **–sgeld,** *n.* purchase money. **–spreis,** *m.* cost price; prime cost; **–srechnung,** *f.* account, bill of costs.

Einkäufer, *m.* (-s, –) purchaser, buyer.

einkehl–en, *v.a.* groove; provide with a gutter.

Einkehr, *f.* putting up at an inn; lodging; (*fig.*) (*bei sich selbst*), contemplation. **–en,** *v.n.* (*aux.* s.) enter, stop at, alight; put up at, call at *or* on (*usually an inn*); (*fig.*) *bei* or *in sich –en,* examine o.s., commune with o.s., search one's soul.

einkeilen, *v.a.* wedge in; fasten with wedges, plug; (*fig.*) hem in.

einkellern, *v.a.* lay *or* store *or* deposit in a cellar; lay in *or* up.

einkerben, *v.a.* notch, indent, score; engrail (*Her.*).

einkerker–n, *v.a.* imprison, incarcerate. **–ung,** *f.* incarceration, imprisonment.

einkessel–n, *v.a.* encircle, hem in. **–ung,** *f.* hemming in. **–ungspolitik,** *f.*, *see* **Einkreisungspolitik.**

Einkindschaft, *f.* legal adoption; adjustment of property between children of one father but different mothers.

einklagen, *v.a.* sue for; *eine Schuld –,* sue a p. for debt.

einklammer–n, *v.a.* bracket; insert in brackets, put in parentheses; fasten with cramps, cramp; *das Eingeklammerte,* the words enclosed in brackets. **–ung,** *f.* bracket, parenthesis.

Einklang, *m.* unison, harmony; accord; *in – bringen,* make agree, tune; *im – stehen,* agree.

einklappig, *adj.* univalve, univalvular.

Einklebebuch, *n.* (-(e)s, ⸚er) scrap-book.

einkleid–en, *v.a.* clothe, fit out (*with clothes*), dress; invest with (*a uniform, etc.*), robe; induct into (*an office or order*); lay out (*a corpse*); *eine Lehre in eine Erzählung –en,* embody, wrap up *or* disguise a doctrine in a story; *etwas gut –en,* give a pleasing turn to a th.; *sich –en lassen,* don a uniform, become a soldier; take the veil, enter a monastery. **–ung,** *f.* clothing, investiture; taking of the veil; wording, form (*of words*).

einklemmen, *v.a.* squeeze, jam, pinch; *eingeklemmt,* strangulated (*Med.*).

einklinken, *v.a.* & *n.* (*aux.* s.) latch, engage (*of a catch*); *eingeklinkt,* on the latch.

einknicken, *v.a.* & *n.* (*aux.* s.) break partially, bend in *or* give way (*as the knees*), flex, buckle (*of a wheel*), fold up (*as a carpenter's rule*).

einkochen, *v.a.* thicken by boiling, boil down, condense, evaporate; make jam *or* preserve.

einkommen, 1. *ir.v.n.* (*aux.* s.) come forward (*with a complaint, etc.*), petition, apply to; come in; appear, arrive; *– gegen,* protest against; *mit einer Klage* or *einem Bittschreiben –,* bring an action (*against*); *um eine S. –,* apply for a th.; *er ist um seinen Abschied eingekommen,* he has sent in his resignation; *die eingekommenen Zinsen,* the interest received *or* paid. 2. *n.* income, revenue; emoluments, interest, rent; proceeds; temporalities (*Eccl.*); *jährliches –,* (yearly) income, annuity. **–steuer,** *f.* income-tax. **–steuererklärung,** *f.* income-tax return. **–steuerzuschlag,** *m.* supertax.

einkreis–en, *v.a.* encircle, surround, envelop, invest, isolate; screen (*Rad.*). **–ung,** *f.* encirclement. **–ungspolitik,** *f.* policy of encirclement *or* isolation (*of the enemy*).

einkrimpen, *v.n.* slacken (*of the wind*); *gegen den Wind –,* sail close to the wind (*Naut.*).

Einkristall, *m.* single crystal.

Einkünfte, *f. pl.* income, revenue, rents.

einkuppeln, *v.n.* couple, put in gear.

einkürzen, *v.a.* reduce, shorten, curtail; warp (*a ship*); foreshorten (*Art.*).

einlaben, *v.n.* coagulate.

[1]**einlad–en,** *ir.v.a.* invite; summon, ask in (*auf,* to *or* for). **–end,** *pr.p.* & *adj.* inviting, attractive, tempting. **–ung,** *f.* invitation, summons. **–ungskarte,** *f.* invitation-card. **–ungsschrift,** *f.* invitation, summons.

[2]**einlad–en,** *ir.v.a.* load, ship, lade, freight. **–ung,** *f.* lading. **–ungsplatz,** *m.* wharf.

Einlag–e, *f.* (-en) enclosure (*in a letter, etc.*), insertion; stake (*at play*); deposit, investment (*in a bank*); share, money paid up (*on shares*); filler, stiffening; interlude, addition (*to a programme*); arch-support (*for fallen insteps*). **–eholz,** *n.* wood for inlaying.

einlager–n, *v.a.* store, warehouse, deposit; imbed, stratify, infiltrate. **–ung,** *f.* deposition, deposit; stratification; infiltration.

Einlaß, *m.* (-(ss)es, ⸚(ss)e), admission; inlet; entrance; insertion; wicket-gate. **–(ss)en,** 1. *ir.v.a.* let in, admit; fix in, insert, introduce, countersink (*a screw*); sink; inject (*Med.*); *nicht –(ss)en wollen,* refuse admittance. 2. *v.r.* (*auf* or *in eine S.* or *mit einer S.*) engage in; venture on; meddle with; have dealings with; *ich lasse mich darauf nicht ein,* I will not have anything to do with it; *auf solche Fragen lasse ich mich nicht ein,* I do not discuss such questions; *sich ins Gespräch –(ss)en,* enter into the conversation; *sich auf eine Klage –(ss)en,* answer an accusation. **–geld,** *n.* entrance-money *or* fee. **–karte,** *f.* ticket of admission. **–klappe,** *f.* induction *or* inlet *or* intake valve. **–ofen,** *m.* smelting furnace. **–öffnung,** *f.* intake, inlet (*Motor, Av., etc.*). **–preis,** *m.*, *see* **–geld. –rohr,** *n.*, **–röhre,** *f.* inlet-pipe. **–stück,** *n.* insert. **–tür,** *f.* small gate, wicket, postern. **–ung,** *f.* trimming; injection (*Med.*); answer (*Law*); *see* **Einlaß. –ventil,** *n.*, *see* **–klappe.**

einläßlich, *adj.* (*Swiss dial.*) detailed, minute, special.

Einlauf, *m.* (-(e)s) entering; inlet; arrival; enema (*Med.*). **–en,** 1. *ir.v.n.* (*aux.* s.) come in, arrive; enter (*a harbour*); come to hand (*of dispatches*); pour in (*of orders*); shrink (*of cloth*), be run in (*of engines*). 2. *v.a.*; (*coll.*) *einem das Haus* or *die Tür –en,* be constantly calling at a p.'s house, pester a p. **–echt,** *adj.* unshrinkable. **–hafen,** *m.* port of destination.

einläufig, *adj.* single-barrelled.

einleben, *v.r.* grow *or* get accustomed to, settle down (in), familiarize o.s. with; *sich in eine S. –,* get familiar with *or* enter into the spirit of a th.; *ein tief eingelebter Zustand,* a long-established state of things.

einleg–en, *v.a.* lay, place *or* put in; enclose, fold up, turn inwards; immerse, soak, steep; pickle, preserve; lay in, buy (*for future use*); couch (*spear, lance, etc.*), insert, embed, inlay; *ein (gutes) Wort für einen –en,* intercede for a p., speak on s.o.'s behalf; (*coll.*) put in a good word for a p.; *Berufung –en,* appeal (to), lodge an appeal; *sein Veto -en*, veto; *Verwahrung -en*, enter a protest; *Ehre -en mit*, gain honour by; *eingelegte Arbeit*, inlaid work. **-eholz,** *n.* veneer. **-ekapital,** *n.* deposit; capital. **-er,** *m.* (-ers, -er) inlayer; depositor; pickler; packer, etc. **-erohr,** *n.* liner, sub-calibre barrel (*Artil.*). **-esohle,** *f.* (cork) sock, insole. **-estuhl,** *m.*, *see* **Klappstuhl. -ung,** *f.* laying in; insertion; enclosing; preservation.

einleit-en, *v.a.* begin, start, initiate, open; introduce, preface, prelude; institute (*a lawsuit*); conduct *or* usher in; inject, feed into. **-end,** *pr.p. & adj.* introductory, preliminary. **-ung,** *f.* introduction; preamble; prelude; preface; (*pl.*) preliminary arrangements; preparations. **-ungsrohr,** *n.* delivery *or* feed tube.

einlenken, 1. *v.a.* reduce (*a fracture*), set (*a limb*); lead, guide, *or* turn into (*of conversation, etc.*); turn in *or* back; restore. 2. *v.n.* (*aux.* h.) bend *or* turn in; come round, give in, become more reasonable; return to, resume (*a subject*).

einlernen, *v.a.*; *sich* (*Dat.*) *etwas* –, hammer s.th. into one's head; *einem etwas* –, (*sl.*) hammer s.th. into s.o.'s head, drum s.th. into a p.

einleucht-en, *v.n.* (*aux.* h.) be clear, be intelligible; be evident; *das will mir nicht -en*, I cannot see that; I am not quite clear (*or* satisfied) about it. **-end,** *pr.p. & adj.* evident, obvious, manifest.

einliefern, *v.a.* deliver up, hand over.

einliegen, *ir.v.n.* (*aux.* s.) be enclosed in, be quartered *or* lodge in; *-d finden Sie*, enclosed please find.

einlochen, *v.a.* (*sl.*) put in quod *or* in jug.

einlös-en, *v.a.* ransom, redeem; honour (*a bill*). **-bar,** *adj.* redeemable, realizable. **-ung,** *f.* redemption; ransom; taking up of a bill. **-ungsantrag,** *m.* order to clear (*Books*).

einlöten, *v.a.* solder in.

einlullen, 1. *v.a.* lull to sleep, (*fig.*) lull (into). 2. *v.n.* (*coll.*) drop (*of wind*).

einmach-en, *v.a.* put into; store up, preserve, pickle, bottle; slake (*lime*); knead (*dough*); **eingemacht,** *p.p. & adj.* preserved, pickled; *eingemachtes Obst*, bottled fruit. **Eingemachtes,** *n.* preserves. **-glas,** *n.* preserving bottle *or* jar.

einmal, *adv. & part.* once, one time; formerly; some (*future*) time; one day; *auf* –, all at once, suddenly; – *dies*, – *das*, now this, now that; *es war* –, once upon a time there was . . .; *noch* –, once more, once again; *noch – so gut*, as good again, twice as good; *nicht* –, not even; *heute* –, today for once; *irgend* –, some time or other; *da es nun – so ist*, things being so, as matters stand; *ich bin nun – so*, that is my way *or* my nature; (*after imperatives*) *komm – her*, just come here; *erzähle doch* –, just tell (us); *hören Sie* –, just listen! I say!; (*Prov.*) – *ist keinmal*, once does not mean always, this does not establish a precedent. **-eins,** *n.* multiplication-table. **-ig,** *adj.* happening but once, solitary.

einmännig, *adj.* monandrous (*Bot.*).

Einmarsch, *m.* (-es, ¨-e) marching in, entry. **-ieren,** *v.n.* (*aux.* s.) march in, enter.

einmauern, *v.a.* wall in *or* up; immure, enclose, embed.

einmeng-en, 1. *v.a.* intermix, mix in. 2. *v.r.* interfere, meddle (*in*, with). **-erei,** *f.* meddlesomeness.

einmiet-en, *v.a. & r.* hire, rent; take rooms, engage lodgings; store (*potatoes*). **-er,** *m.* tenant, lodger.

einmischen 1. *v.a.* intermix, mingle, blend; *Nebensachen in einen Prozeß* –, raise collateral issues. 2. *v.r.* meddle with, interfere, involve o.s. (in), step in, intervene; *Nichteinmischungsausschuß*, Non-Intervention Committee (*Spanish Civil War 1936–9*).

einmitten, *v.a.* centre, adjust (*Opt.*).

einmünd-en, *v.n.* (*aux.* h.) discharge into, empty into; run into, flow into; join, enter, fit (in), inosculate with (*Anat.*). **-ung,** *f.* junction, confluence.

einmütig, *adj.* unanimous, of one mind; with one consent, agreed, nem. con. **-keit,** *f.* unanimity.

einnähen, *v.a.* sew in; sew up in.

Einnahme, *f.* (-n) receiving; receipt, income, takings, revenue; capture, conquest, occupation; – *und Ausgabe*, receipts and expenditure. **-quelle,** *f.* source of revenue.

einnehm-en, *ir.v.a.* take in, gather in; take, capture; accept, receive, collect (*money, etc.*); engage, occupy (*room, seat, etc.*); partake (*of a meal*), take (*medicine*); charm, captivate, bewitch, fascinate; *mit -en*, include; *-en für*, interest in, influence in favour of; *-en gegen*, prejudice against; *das Herz -en*, touch the heart; *den Kopf -en*, affect one's head, make giddy *or* faint; *dieser Geruch nimmt mir den Kopf ein*, this smell makes me faint; *wenig -en*, have a small income *or* poor returns; *der Aufsatz nimmt drei Seiten ein*, the essay runs to *or* fills three pages; *seine Liebenswürdigkeit nimmt für ihn ein* or *er nimmt durch seine Liebenswürdigkeit sehr für sich ein*, his charm captivates everybody; *eines anderen Stelle -en*, succeed to another's place *or* replace another; *sich von seiner Leidenschaft -en lassen*, be carried away by one's passion. **eingenommen,** *p.p. & adj.* partial (*für*, to); infatuated (*von*, with); prejudiced (*gegen*, against); bigoted; *er ist für Sie sehr eingenommen*, you stand high in his favour *or* he has a high opinion of you. **-bar,** *adj.* untenable, vulnerable. **-end,** *pr.p. & adj.* taking, captivating, charming, engaging; (*coll.*) fetching. **-er,** *m.* receiver, collector (*of taxes, tolls, etc.*). **-ung,** *f.* taking in; occupation, capture.

einnicken, *v.n.* (*aux.* s.) fall asleep, drop asleep, (*coll.*) nod, drop off.

einnisten, *v.r.* build one's nest; settle a place, settle down; make o.s. at home, (*sl.*) squat. **eingenistet,** *p.p. & adj.* firmly established, inveterate.

Einöde, *f.* solitude, desert, desolate place, wilderness.

einölen, *v.a.* oil, grease, lubricate.

einordnen, *v.a.* arrange, classify, file.

einpack-en, 1. *v.a.* pack, wrap up; put up (*goods*). 2. *v.n.* (*aux.* h.) (*coll.*) pack up, shut up (shop); give up, cry off; (*sl.*) stow it.

einpassen, *v.a. & n.* fit (in); adjust.

einpauk-en, *v.a.* (*coll.*) cram. **-er,** *m.* crammer, coach.

einpeilen, *v.a.* locate (*by direction-finding equipment*), D.F. (*Mil.*).

Einpeitscher, *m.* (-s, –) whip (*Parl.*).

einpfählen, *v.a.* enclose with pales, fence, stockade, picket.

einpfarren, *v.a.* incorporate in a parish.

einpferchen, *v.a.* pen in, coop up, crowd together.

einpflanzen, *v.a.* plant; (*fig.*) implant; inculcate. **eingepflanzt,** *p.p. & adj.* inveterate, innate, implanted.

einpfropfen, *v.a.* cork in *or* up; stuff in, cram in; engraft; implant.

einphasig, *adj.* single-phase (*Elec.*).

einpökeln, *v.a.* salt, pickle; *eingepökeltes Fleisch*, corned meat; *du kannst dich – lassen*, (*vulg.*) go and fry your face!

einpräg-en, *v.a.* imprint, impress; *einem etwas -en*, impress s.th. upon a p.; *sich* (*Dat.*) *etwas -en*, remember *or* note s.th., impress s.th. upon one's memory. **-sam,** *adj.* impressive, easily remembered.

einpuppen, *v.r.* change into a chrysalis (*Ent.*).

einquartier-en, 1. *v.a.* quarter, billet. 2. *v.r.*; *sich bei einem -en*, take up one's quarters in s.o.'s house. **-ung,** *f.* quartering, billeting; soldiers billeted, billetees.

einrahmen, *v.a.* frame; tenter (*cloth*).

einrammen, *v.a.* ram, drive in *or* down.

einrangieren, *see* **einreihen** (*Mil.*).

einräuchern, *v.a.* smoke, fumigate.

einräum-en, *v.a.* give up (*a room, a house*); clear *or* stow away, put away, put in order; furnish (*a room*); (*einem etwas*) *-en*, concede, allow, admit, grant (s.th. to s.o.); (*einem*) *seinen Platz -en*, give up *or* yield one's place to; *einem ein Zimmer -en*, vacate *or* make available a room for s.o. **-ung,** *f.* concession, admission; housing; allowance (*in weighing*).

einrechnen, *v.a.* reckon in *or* add *or* include (in the account); allow for.

Einrede, *f.* (-n) objection, protest, remonstrance, opposition, contradiction; – *tun*, protest against; *keine* –, don't contradict; *ohne* –, without demur. **-n** 1. *v.a.* persuade (*a. p.*) to; talk (*a p.*) over;

convince (*a p.*) of, make (*a p.*) believe; *einem Mut –n,* encourage a p.; *auf einen –n,* keep on talking to s.o., talk at a p., urge s.o.; *lassen sie sich so etwas nicht –n,* do not allow yourself to be persuaded *or* talked into that. 2. *v.n.* (*aux.* h.) interrupt; contradict; object, protest; *rede mir nicht ein!* don't interrupt me! *er läßt sich nicht gern –n,* he does not like to be interfered with *or* to be contradicted.

einreib-en, 1. *ir.v.a.* rub in; smear, embrocate; *sich* (*Dat.*) *den Fuß –en,* rub on *or* into one's foot. 2. *v.r.* rub o.s. (down), rub embrocation in. **–ung,** *f.* liniment, embrocation; rubbing.

einreichen, *v.a.* hand in, deliver, submit (*an account*); present, prefer (*a complaint*); tender (*one's resignation*).

einreih-en, *v.a.* place in a line, row *or* series; align, arrange; enrol, allot to regiments (*Mil.*); lay in little pleats. **–ig,** *adj.* of one row; single-breasted (*Tail.*); unilateral (*Bot.*). **–ung,** *f.* alignment, enrolment.

Einreise, *f.* (-n) journey *or* entry into a country. **–bewilligung,** *f.* **–erlaubnis,** *f.* permission to enter a country; entry *or* entrance permit, visa.

einreißen, 1. *ir.v.a.* tear down; pull down, demolish. 2. *v.n.* (*aux.* s.) rend, tear, burst, get torn; spread, prevail, gain ground; (*coll.*) *es reißt in den Beutel ein,* it is expensive.

einrenk-en, *v.a.* reduce *or* set (*a limb*); (*fig.*) set right. **–er,** *m.* bone-setter.

einrennen, 1. *ir.v.a.* force *or* smash open, run *or* dash against; melt down. 2. *v.n.* (*aux.* s.) run in, down *or* against; *offene Türen –,* beat the air; *sich den Kopf –,* run one's head against a wall.

einricht-en, 1. *v.a.* set right, arrange, prepare, order, adapt, adjust; contrive, dispose, organize, install; furnish (*a house*); set (*a limb*); *gut eingerichtet,* well appointed, comfortable. 2. *v.r.* settle down, establish o.s.; *sich auf eine S. –en,* prepare for s.th.; *er weiß sich einzurichten,* he makes ends meet *or* manages on his income; *sich –en nach,* adapt o.s. to; *sich darnach –en,* take measures accordingly. **–ung,** *f.* arrangement; adjustment; contrivance; institution, establishment, equipment; setting (*Surg.*); accommodation; fittings, furnishings, furniture, household appointments. **–ungskoffer,** *m.* wardrobe-trunk, cabin-trunk.

einriegeln, *v.a.* bolt in, shut up.

Einriß, *m.* crack, rent, fissure, *see* **einreißen.**

einrosten, *v.n.* (*aux,* s.) rust, grow rusty; get rusted up; (*coll.*) get rusty, become dull by inaction, be impaired by inactivity; *eingerostetes Übel,* deeply rooted evil; (*coll.*) *eingerostete Kehlen,* throats too thirsty (to sing *or* speak).

einrück-en, 1. *v.n.* (*aux.* s.) march into, enter; step into (*another's post*), succeed s.o.; report for (military) duty, join up (*Mil.*). 2. *v.a.* insert, put in; advertise; indent (*Print.*), *etwas in die Zeitung –en lassen,* have s.th. inserted in a newspaper. **–ung,** *f.* marching in, entry (*Mil.*); inserting; insertion; advertisement. **–ungsgebühren,** *f.pl.* advertisement fees *or* charges.

einrühren, *v.a.* mix up; stir; beat (*eggs, etc.*); mix in; (*coll.*) *ich habe mir etwas Nettes or eine schöne Suppe eingerührt,* I have got into a nice mess.

einrußen, *v.a.* cover with soot.

einsaitig, *adj.* one-stringed.

einsalz-en, *ir.v.a.* salt down, pickle; *Eingesalzene*(*s*), salt provisions. **–er,** *m.* curer.

einsam, *adj.* lonely, lonesome; solitary, alone. **–keit,** *f.* loneliness, solitude.

einsamm-eln, *v.a.* collect; gather. **–ler,** *m.* gatherer, collector; gleaner. **–lung,** *f.* collection.

einsargen, *v.a.* put in a coffin, (*fig.*) abandon, shelve.

Einsatz, *m.* (-es, ⸚e) insertion, insert; deposit (*on bottle, book,* etc.); supply; share, stake, pledge; pool (*at cards*); charge (*Elec.*); set *or* nest (*of boxes, etc.*); entry, entrance, striking up, effort; sortie (*Av.*); quick response, willingness to obey. *elastischer –,* defence in depth (*Mil.*); *Arbeits–,* labour supply; industrial effort; *mit vollem – arbeiten,* work all out, give of one's best; *Hemd–,* shirt front; *unter – des Lebens,* at risk of one's life. **–becher,** *m.* cup fitting into another. **–bereitschaft,** *f.* initiative, readiness to act *or* (*of aircraft*) to take off. **–besprechung,** *f.* briefing (*Mil.*). **–gewicht,** *n.* gross weight. **–hafen,** *m.* operational base (*Nav. Av.*). **–kessel,** *m. pl.* nest *or* set of kettles. **–truppe,** *f.* air-raid emergency squad. **–verteilung,** *f.* distribution of labour.

einsäuern, *v.a.* leaven; pickle (*in vinegar*), sour, acidify.

einsaug-en, *ir.v.a.* suck in; imbibe, absorb. **–emittel,** *n.* absorbent. **–ung,** *f.* absorption, suction, imbibition.

einschachteln, *ir.v.a.* put in a box; fit one box into another; insert; mix up.

einschalt-en, *v.a.* insert, put in, fit in; interpolate, intercalate; switch on, connect, plug in (*Elec.*), tune in (*Rad.*), put in *or* engage (*gear*) (*Motor.*); *eingeschaltete Stelle,* interpolation; *eingeschalteter Tag,* intercalary day. **–ung,** *f.* insertion; interpolation; intercalation; parenthesis. **–ungszeichen,** *n.* caret.

einschanzen, *v.a. & r.* entrench, fortify.

einschärfen, *v.a.* inculcate, enjoin; (*einem etwas*) impress (s.th.) on (a p.).

einscharren, *v.a.* bury, cover lightly with earth.

einschätzen, *v.a. & r.* assess, estimate, evaluate, value, form an estimate of.

einschenken, *v.a.* pour in; pour out; fill; *schenk ein!* fill your glasses! *einem –,* help a p. to (*wine, etc.*); *einem reinen Wein –,* tell a p. the naked truth.

einschicht-en, *v.a.* stratify, arrange in layers; *eingeschichtet, p.p. & adj.* stratified. **–ig,** *adj.* single-layered.

einschicken, *v.a.* send in, submit, present.

einschieb-en, *ir.v.a.* push in, shove in, put in; insert, introduce, interpolate, intercalate; *eingeschobene Gerichte,* side-dishes, entremets. **–ezeichen,** *n.* parenthesis. **–sel,** *n.* (-sels, -sel) insertion; interpolation, intercalation. **–ung,** *f.* insertion; interpolation.

einschießen, 1. *ir.v.a.* shoot down, batter down (*by artillery fire*); test (*a gun*); deposit, pay in; contribute (*money*). 2. *v.r.* practise shooting. 3. *n.* ranging, adjustment fire (*Artil.*).

einschiff-en, 1. *v.a. & r.* go on board, embark, entrain, embus (*troops*). 2. *v.n.* (*aux.* s.) sail in. **–ung,** *f.* embarkation; entraining.

einschirren, *v.a.* harness.

einschlachten, *v.a.* kill for household use.

einschlafen, *ir.v.n.* (*aux.* s.) go to sleep, fall asleep; die away; get benumbed; *der Fuß ist mir eingeschlafen,* my foot has gone to sleep.

einschläfer-n, *v.a.* lull to sleep; lull into security; narcotize, (*coll.*) put to sleep. **–nd,** *pr.p. & adj.* lulling; somnolent, drowsy; narcotic, soporific, hypnotic; *–nde Mittel,* opiates, sleeping draughts. **–(e)rig,** *adj.* single (*of a bed*).

Einschlag, *m.* (-(e)s, ⸚e) act of driving, beating *or* striking in; thing beaten in; handshake; wrapping up; wrapper, envelope; woof, weft; cooperage; porterage; housing, storing; part turned down *or* in (*as a leaf of a book*), tuck, fold, plait; hasp; impact; bomb-crater; strain, hint, touch, admixture; *Kette und –,* warp and woof; *Rede mit einem leisen – ins Ironische,* speech with a slight touch of irony. **–en,** 1. *ir.v.a.* drive, knock *or* strike in; break, punch *or* burst in; sink in, embed in earth; turn down (*a tuck, a page, etc.*), take in a tuck, shorten (*a dress, etc.*); wrap up, envelop, enclose, bandage; enter upon, adopt, follow (*a course*); take (*a road*); *die Arme –en,* cross one's arms; *Bäume –en,* earth the roots of trees; *Getreide –en,* sack corn; *man hat ihm den Hirnschädel eingeschlagen,* they have knocked out his brains. 2. *v.n.* (*aux.* h.) shake hands (*as token of agreement*), come to an agreement; strike (*of lightning*); succeed, prosper, yield a good crop; (*coll.*) catch on; have reference to, concern; (*aux.* s.) sink in (*of colours*); be checked (*of diseases*); *nicht –en,* fail, miscarry; *schlag ein!* give me your hand on it! **–egarn,** *n.* weft-yarn. **–elupe,** *f.* pocket-lens. **–emesser,** *n.* clasp-knife. **–epapier,** *n.* wrapping paper. **–eseide,** *f.* shot silk. **–sknall,** *m.* report (*of artillery burst*).

einschlägig, *adj.* relative to, relating to, appertaining to, respecting, on the subject, pertinent; competent; appropriate, belonging to; *–e Literatur,* literature on the subject; *jede –e Handlung,* every business *or* firm concerned.
einschlämmen, *v.a. & n.* silt up.
einschleichen, *ir.v.r.* (*aux.* h.) *& n.* (*aux.* s.) creep in, steal in; insinuate o.s. into.
einschleifen, *v.a.* grind in (*a valve*) (*Engin.*).
einschließ–en, 1. *ir.v.a.* comprise, include; lock in *or* up; close up; embed, enclose; (*coll.*) bottle up; encircle, envelop, surround, invest (*Mil.*); confine, form (*an angle*). 2. *v.n.* (*aux.* h.) catch (*of a lock*); fit close. **–lich,** *adj.* included, inclusive. **–ung,** *f.* locking in *or* up; inclusion, comprisal; enclosure; blockade, siege, encirclement, investment, confinement. **–ungszeichen,** *n.* bracket, parenthesis.
einschlucken, *v.a.* swallow, gulp down, absorb.
einschlummern, *v.n.* (*aux.* s.) fall into a slumber, fall asleep; pass quietly away (*i.e. die*).
einschlürfen, *v.a.* sip in.
Einschluß, *m.* (-(ss)es, ⸚(ss)e) enclosure, enclosed letter; parenthesis, inclusion; (*also Geol.*) comprisal; *mit* or *unter – der Kinder,* including *or* inclusive of the children; *Brief mit –,* letter with enclosure; *als –,* under cover. **–klammer,** *f.,* **–zeichen,** *n.* bracket, crotchet.
einschmeichel–n, *v.r.* insinuate o.s., ingratiate o.s. (*bei einem,* with a p.). **–nd,** *pr.p. & adj.* insinuating; catchy (*of music*). **–ung,** *f.* ingratiation, insinuation.
einschmelzen, 1. *reg. & ir.v.a.* melt down. 2. *ir.v.n.* (*aux.* s.) melt (down *or* away), fuse; melt away, diminish by melting.
einschmieren, *v.a.* smear, grease; oil, lubricate.
einschmuggeln, 1. *v.a.* smuggle in; 2. *v.r.* (*coll.*) gate-crash.
einschnapp–en, *v.a. & n.* (*aux.* s.) catch; click *or* snap in, (*fig.*), take offence. **–feder,** *f.* spring-bolt.
einschneid–en, 1. *ir.v.a.* cut into; incise; cut up; notch; make loop-holes. 2. *v.n.* (*aux.* h.) cut (*as a garter*). **–end,** *pr. p. & adj.* incisive, trenchant, decisive, thorough. **–everfahren,** *n.* flash-spotting (*Artil.*). **–ung,** *f.* incision.
einschneien, *v.imp.* snow up; *Züge wurden eingeschneit,* trains were snowed up.
Einschnitt, *m.* (-(e)s, -e) incision; cut; notch, indentation; segment (*Math.*); caesura (*Metr.*); embrasure, emplacement, loop-hole; sector (*of a front*) (*Mil.*); cutting (*Railw.*); harvest; (*fig.*) decisive turning-point.
einschnür–en, 1. *v.a.* cord, lace up, tie up; constrict, strangulate. 2. *v.r.* lace one's stays; *sich eng –en,* lace o.s. tightly. **–ung,** *f.* tight lacing.
einschränk–en, 1. *v.a.* limit, bound, circumscribe; narrow; check, curb; reduce, cut down, curtail, restrict (*rights, etc.*); *in eingeschränktem Sinne,* in a limited sense; strictly speaking; *eingeschränkte Monarchie,* limited monarchy. 2. *v.r.*; *sich auf eine S. –en,* restrict o.s. to a th., retrench. **–end,** *pr.p. & adj.* restrictive. **–ung,** *f.* restriction; retrenchment, curtailment, limitation; *mit –ung,* in a qualified sense, with due allowance, with reservations.
einschreib–en, 1. *ir.v.a.* write in *or* down; inscribe, enter, record, book, note down; register (*a letter*); *in die Matrikel –en,* matriculate; *er schrieb sich ein,* he entered his name; *Gepäck –en lassen,* register luggage. 2. *v.r.* enroll, matriculate (*at a university*); *er ließ sich –en,* he had his name entered; he booked his place. **–ebrief,** *m.* registered letter. **–egeld,** *n.* **–egebühr,** *f.* registration fee. **–esendung,** *f.* registered letter *or* packet. **–ung,** *f,* inscription; enrolment; registration.
einschreit–en, *ir.v.n.* (*aux.* s.) step *or* stride in; interfere, interpose, intervene, take steps; *gerichtlich –en,* take legal steps, proceed (against). **–ung,** *f.* interposition.
einschrumpfen, *v.n.* (*aux.* s.) shrink, shrivel up, contract, dry up, desiccate.
Einschub, *m.* (-(e)s, ⸚e) putting in; thing put in, addition; leaf (*of a dining-table*); insertion; interpolation (*in a text*).
einschüchter–n, *v.a.* abash; intimidate; overawe. **–ung,** *f.* intimidation.
einschulen, *v.a.* school; take, send *or* bring to school; break in (*a horse*); train.
Einschuß, *m.* (-(ss)es, ⸚(ss)e) capital advanced; deposit; share; contribution; payment on account; woof; fall of water (*on a wheel*); point of entrance (*of a bullet*); *– leisten,* lodge a deposit; advance (*a sum of money*).
einschwenken, *v.n.* wheel (round) (*Mil.*).
einsegn–en, *v.a.* consecrate, bless, give benediction (*esp. at confirmation*); confirm; ordain. **–ung,** *f.* consecration; benediction; (Protestant) confirmation; ordination.
einsehen, 1. *ir.v.a.* look *or* see into; look over, examine; perceive, comprehend, understand, realize, conceive; *das sehe ich ein,* I quite see that; *ich sehe gar nicht ein, warum,* I don't at all see why. 2. *v.n.* (*aux.* h.) look into. 3. *n.* insight, inspection; investigation; consideration; judgement; *ein – nehmen,* see, have regard (*auf,* to); *er sollte ein – haben,* he should show some consideration, should be reasonable; (*coll.*) *der Himmel hatte ein –,* the weather favoured us; *sie hat gar kein –,* she is most unreasonable.
einseifen, *v.a.* soap well, lather; (*sl.*) take in, bamboozle, softsoap.
einseitig, *adj.* one-sided, unilateral; partial, biased. **–keit,** *f.* one-sidedness, partiality, narrow-mindedness.
einsend–en, *ir.v.a.* send in; transmit; remit; convey; contribute. *eingesandte Rechnung,* account rendered. **–er,** *m.* remitter; conveyer; contributor; *–er dieses,* our informant *or* correspondent (*Newsp.*). **–ung,** *f.* remittance, contribution.
einsenk–en, *v.a.* sink in; bury, lower into a grave; set (*plants, etc.*), plant. **–er,** *m.* shoot, cutting, slip, layer (*Zool.*). **–ung,** *f.* sinking in; depression; indentation.
Einser, *m., see* **ein–er.**
einsetz–en, 1. *v.a.* put *or* set in; insert; let in (*Dressmaking*); fix, fit, place; set up; step (*masts*); set, plant; institute; nominate, appoint, install; stake, risk, pledge; use, employ, put into action; preserve, bottle (*fruit, etc.*); *seinen ganzen Einfluß –en,* use all one's influence; *einen zum Erben –en,* declare s.o. one's heir; *als Stellvertreter –en,* appoint as a substitute. 2. *v.n.* set in, begin, strike up (*Mus.*). 3. *v.r.* side (with), stand up (for); *sich voll –en,* pull one's weight. **–ling,** *m., see* **Einsenker. –rose,** *f.* rosette (*Arch.*). **–stück,** *n.* joint; junction piece, insert. **–ung,** *f.* institution; investiture, installation; nomination; appointment; staking, pledging. **–ungsworte,** *n.pl.* sacramental words.
Einsicht, *f.* (-en) insight; intelligence, understanding, reason, judgement, discernment; inspection, examination; (*pl.*) views, opinions, judgements; *mit –,* judiciously; *– nehmen in eine S.* or *von einer S.,* examine a th. **–ig,** *adj.* sensible, judicious, prudent. **–nahme,** *f.*; *gegen* or *nach –nahme,* on sight; *zur –nahme,* for inspection, on approval. **–svoll,** *adj.* discerning, judicious.
einsickern, *v.n.* (*aux.* s.) trickle in *or* down; soak into; infiltrate (*also Mil.*).
Einsied–el, *m.* (-els, -el) (*obs.*), *see* **–ler. –elei,** *f.* hermitage. **–ler,** *m.* hermit, recluse, anchorite. **–lerisch,** *adj.* secluded, solitary. **–lerkrebs,** *m.* hermit-crab.
einsilbig, *adj.* monosyllabic; taciturn, laconic; *–es Wort,* monosyllable. **–keit,** *f.* taciturnity.
einsingen, 1. *ir.v.a.* sing to sleep. 2. *v.r.* practise singing, become proficient (*in rendering a piece*) by long *or* repeated singing.
einsinken, *ir.v.n.* (*aux.* s.) sink in; give way (under one's feet).
einsitz–en, 1. *ir.v.n.* (*aux.* h.) stay at home. 2. *v.a.* press down by sitting; *eingesessen, p.p. & adj.* settled, resident, domiciled; *gut eingesessene Lehnstühle,* arm-chairs soft and comfortable through much use. **–er,** *m.* one-seater. **–ig,** *adj.* having but one seat, single-seated.

einsonder-n, *v.n.* secrete internally. **-ungsdrüse,** *f.* endocrine gland (*Anat.*).
einspannen, *v.a.* stretch (*in a frame*); fasten in, fix; harness up, yoke. **Einspänner,** *m.* one-horse vehicle. **einspännig,** *adj.* drawn by one horse.
einsparen, *v.a.* save up (*money*); save (*material*).
einsperren, *v.a.* shut *or* lock up; confine; imprison.
einspielen, *v.r.* practise (*music*); practise (*as a team*), co-ordinate. **eingespielt,** *p.p.* & *adj.* well practised; well co-ordinated; *das Quartett ist gut eingespielt,* the ensemble of the quartet is admirable.
einspinnen, 1. *ir.v.a.* envelop *or* entangle s.th. by spinning; (*sl.*) *einen –,* arrest a p. 2. *v.r.* spin a cocoon (*Zool.*); (*fig.*) seclude o.s. (from), be absorbed (in).
Einsprache, *f.* (-n) objection, protest; mouthpiece (*of a telephone*); – *tun* or *erheben* (*gegen*), protest (against), take exception (to).
einsprechen, 1. *ir.v.a.* (*einem etwas*) inculcate, instil; inspire with; *Mut –,* encourage; *Trost –,* comfort. 2. *v.n.* (*aux.* h.) protest (*gegen,* against); oppose; interrupt (*conversation, etc.*); jam (*Rad.*).
einsprengen, 1. *v.a.* sprinkle; intersperse, intermingle, admix; stratify (*Geol.*); burst open, blast; split, cleave (*by blasting*).
einspringen, *ir.v.n.* (*aux.* s.) leap *or* jump in; catch, snap (*of locks*); bend or turn in; re-enter (*of angles*) (*Math.*); shrink, contract; (*coll., fig.*) help out; step into the breach; – *für einen anderen,* take the place of s.o.; (*Studs. sl.*) *bei einer Verbindung –,* join a students' association.
einspritz-en, *v.a.* inject, squirt in, syringe. **-düse,** *f.* (fuel) injector (*Motor.*). **-er,** *m.* syringe, injector. **-ung,** *f.* injection.
Einspruch, *m.* (-(e)s, ⸗e) protestation, protest, objection; – *tun* or *erheben,* enter *or* raise a protest; protest (against), object (to). **-srecht,** *n.* (right of) veto.
einspurig, *adj.* single-railed, single-track.
einst, *adv.* once, one day; some (*future*) day, some time, in days to come. **-ens,** *adv., see* **einst. -ig,** *adj.* future; former, existing once. **-mals,** *adv.* once, formerly. **-weilen,** *adv.* meanwhile, for the time being, for the present, in the meantime, for a while, just now. **-weilig,** *adj.* provisional, temporary.
einstampfen, *v.a.* pulp, pulverize; ram down.
Einstand, *m.* (-es, ⸗e) entrance (upon an office *or* privilege); membership (*of an association*); deuce (*Tenn.*); – *geben,* pay one's dues *or* footing. **-sberechnung,** *f.* cost-accounting. **-sgeld,** *n.* entrance-fee (*to a club, etc.*); bounty (*Mil.*). **-spreis,** *m.* cost price, prime cost. **-srechnung,** *f.* cost account.
einstanzen, *v.a.* & *n.* emboss, stamp.
einstauben, *v.n.* get dusty.
einstäuben, *v.a.* dust, powder.
einstechen, 1. *ir.v.a.* prick, perforate, puncture; pierce, stick in. 2. *v.n.* (*aux.* s.) stand out to sea.
einsteck-en, *v.a.* stick, put in; pocket, sheathe, hide away; imprison, (*coll.*) run in; (*fig.*) swallow (*an insult*). **-lauf,** *m.* liner, sub-calibre barrel, Morris tube (*Artil.*).
einsteh-en, *ir.v.n.* (*aux.* s.) enter upon; partake of; *in die Miete –en,* take possession of a house; (*aux.* h.) *–en für einen,* be a substitute for s.o.; stand up for s.o.; *–en für* (*einen* or *etwas*), answer for, guarantee, be responsible for. **-er,** *m.* paid substitute (*Mil.*); surety, bail.
einstehlen, *ir.v.r.* introduce o.s. stealthily, steal into, creep into.
einsteig-en, *ir.v.n.* (*aux.* s.) mount, enter, step into, get in, board (*a vehicle*); embark; *–en!* take your seats! **-brücke,** *f.* gangway (*of a ship*), ramp. **-eloch,** *n.,* **-eschacht,** *m.* man-hole. **-estelle,** *f.* starting-place, departure platform.
einstell-en, *v.a.* put in; tune in (*Rad.*), focus (*Opt.*), adjust, set, regulate, standardize; lay up, garage (*a car*); engage, take on (*an employee*), recruit, enlist; stop, cease, discontinue, leave off; do away with; put off, suspend (*payment*); strike (*work*); abolish (*abuses, etc.*); *das Feuer –en,* cease firing (*Mil.*); *die Arbeit –en,* suspend work, (go on) strike; *Fabrikbetrieb –en*: shut *or* close down the factory; *konservativ eingestellt,* with a conservative bias; *die Politik ist wirtschaftlich eingestellt,* the policy is adapted to economic conditions; *auf eine S. –en,* arrange to suit a th., adjust to a th. 2. *v.r.* appear, present o.s.; come, (*coll.*) show up; set in (*of winter, etc.*); *sich wieder –en,* return; *sich auf die Besucher –en*; prepare for the reception of visitors; *sich auf eine Situation –en,* adapt o.s. to a situation. **-bar,** *adj.* adjustable. **-er,** *m.* regulator, thermostat. **-ig,** *adj.* of one digit (*Math.*); *–ige Zahlen,* numerals from 1 to 9. **-(l)upe,** *f.* focusing lens. **-marke,** *f.* reference-mark. **-raum,** *m.* garage. **-scheibe,** *f.* focusing screen. **-schraube,** *f.* set-screw; variable-pitch propeller (*Av.*). **-ung,** *f.* attitude; adjustment, setting; enlistment, engagement; cessation, suspension, stoppage, strike (*from work*), discontinuance; *zeitweilige –ung,* temporary suspension, intermission; *zurückhaltende persönliche –ung,* reserved personal attitude. **-ungsebene,** *f.,* **-ungsfläche,** *f.* focusing screen, plane of reference. **-ungsvermögen,** *n.* provision for adjustment.
Einstich, *m.* (-s, -e) puncture, incision; injection.
einstimm-en, *v.n.* join in (*with the voice*), chime in; agree, harmonize, consent, accord. **-ig,** *adj.* unanimous; (*song*) of one part, for one voice (*Mus.*). **-igkeit,** *f.* unanimity.
einstöckig, *adj.* one-storied (*of a house*).
einstopfen, *v.a.* stuff in; fill (*a pipe*).
einstoßen, *ir.v.a.* push, drive, knock *or* run in; ram (*a charge*); stave (*a cask*); smash, break.
einstreichen, 1. *ir.v.a.* rub into; fill up (*the joints*); draw *or* take in, pocket; *alles –,* clear the board. 2. *v.n.* stroll into; fall into the nets (*of birds*).
einstreuen, 1. *v.a.* strew *or* scatter in, sprinkle, intersperse; interlard; disseminate; *eingestreute Bemerkungen,* occasional remarks. 2. *v.n.*; *dem Vieh –,* bed down cattle.
Einstrich, *m.* (-(e)s, -e); slit, nick; pointing (*of walls*); (*pl.*) traverses (*in a mine*).
einström-en, 1. *v.n.* (*aux.* s.) flow *or* stream in. 2. *n.,* **-ung,** *f.* influx. **-ventil,** *n.* inlet valve.
einstücken, *v.a.* piece in; patch.
einstudieren, *v.a.* practise, study, get up, rehearse (*a play*); *einstudiert werden,* be rehearsed, be in rehearsal.
Einstufung, *f.* classification.
einstülpen, *v.a.* turn in, turn inside out, invaginate.
einstürmen, 1. *v.n.* (*aux.* s.) rush in (*auf einen,* upon s.o.); assail. 2. *v.a.* overthrow, dash in.
Einsturz, *m.* (-es, ⸗e) fall, downfall, crash, collapse, subsidence; – *von Erdmassen,* landslip, land-slide.
einstürzen, 1. *v.n.* (*aux.* s.) fall in, collapse, cave in. – *auf einen* or *etwas,* fall upon s.o. *or* s.th. 2. *v.a.* dash in, demolish (*by falling*).
eintägig, *adj.* lasting one day, ephemeral.
eintanzen, *v.r.* practise dancing, accustom o.s. to one's partner; *sie haben sich gut eingetanzt,* they are dancing well together.
Eintänzer, *m.* gigolo.
eintauchen, 1. *v.a.* dip in, plunge; steep, immerse; imbue. 2. *v.n.* (*aux.* s.) dive, duck, plunge.
Eintausch, *m.* (-es, -e) exchange, barter. **-en,** *v.a.* exchange, receive in exchange. **-ung,** *f.* exchange.
einteil-en, *v.a.* divide; distribute; detail (*Mil.*); classify, arrange; graduate (*a scale*), calibrate. **-ung,** *f.* distribution; division; arrangement, classification. **-ungsgrund,** *m.* principle of a classification.
eintönig, *adj.* monotonous. **-keit,** *f.* monotony.
Eintopfgericht, *n.* hot-pot.
Eintracht, *f.* concord, union; harmony, agreement.
einträchtig, *adj.* harmonious, peaceable, united. **-keit,** *f.* unanimity; harmony.
Eintrag, *m.* (-(e)s, ⸗e) entry, item; woof; (*fig.*) profit, proceeds; (*fig.*) damage, harm, prejudice, detriment, disparagement; (*einem*) – *tun,* prejudice, injure *or* harm (*a p.*); *einem Gesetze – tun,* infringe a law; *es tut ihrer Ehre keinen –,* it is no disparagement to her honour. **-en,** 1. *ir.v.a.* carry in, introduce, gather in; enter, record, post (*in a ledger*), book (*a debt*), register; yield, bring in profit, bring in; produce; work in the woof; *auf Landkarten –en,*

map; *rein –en*, clear, net; *ein Geschäft, welches wenig einträgt*, an unprofitable business; *eingetragene Warenzeichen*, registered trade-marks. **–ung**, *f.* entry, registration.

Einträg–er, *m.* book-keeper, booking-clerk, ledger-clerk. **–lich**, *adj.* lucrative, profitable, productive; *–liche Pfründe*, (*coll.*) fat living.

eintränken, *v.a.* steep, soak, impregnate; (*coll.*) *ich werde es ihm –*, I'll pay him out; I'll make him pay for it.

einträufeln, *v.a.* drip in; add, administer, instil (*drop by drop*).

eintreffen, *ir.v.n.* (*aux.* s.) arrive; happen, be fulfilled, come true.

eintreib–en, *ir.v.a.* drive home (*cattle*), collect (*debts, taxes*), exact (*payment*). **–ung**, *f.* exaction; collection (*of debts, etc.*).

eintreten, 1. *ir.v.n.* (*aux.* s.) enter, go *or* step in; begin, commence; join up (*Mil.*); set in (*of weather, etc.*); happen, take place, occur; set inwards (*of the tide*); make one's appearance; *für einen –*, intercede for *or* in favour of s.o., stand up for s.o.; act as s.o.'s substitute, take the place of s.o.; (*coll.*) stand for s.o.; *eingetretener Hindernisse halber*, on account of unforeseen obstacles; *der Fluß tritt aus den Bergen und in die Ebene ein*, the river issues from the mountains and enters the plain. 2. *v.a.* stamp, tread *or* trample down *or* in; kick open; (*sich*) *einen Dorn in den Fuß –*, run a thorn into one's foot. 3. *n.* beginning; occurrence. **–denfalls**, *adv.* in such an event, if such a state of affairs should come about.

eintrichtern, *v.a.* pour into through a funnel; *einem etwas –*, drum s.th. into a p.'s head.

Eintrieb, *m.* pannage, *see* **eintreiben.**

Eintritt, *m.* (-(e)s, -e) entering on (*an office, etc.*), beginning, accession, commencement, setting in (*of winter, etc.*), appearance, incidence; entry, entrance, admission, ingress; *– ins Heer*, enlisting; *– ins Leben*, outset of life; *–salter*, call-up age (*Mil.*). **–sfähig**, *adj.* admissible. **–sgeld**, *n.* charge for admission, entrance money, admission fee, gate money. **–skarte**, *f.* **–sschein**, *m.* ticket of admission. **–stelle**, *f.* inlet, place of entry.

eintrocknen, *v.n.* (*aux.* s.) dry in, dry up, parch, desiccate; shrink (in drying).

eintröpfeln, *v.a.*, *see* **einträufeln.**

eintun, *ir.v.a.* (*coll.*) put in, up *or* away; put into prison.

eintunken, *v.a.* dip in; sop.

einüben, *v.a.* practise, exercise; train, drill; *sie hat das Stück sorgfältig eingeübt*, she has practised the piece carefully.

einverleib–en, *v.a.* imbibe; incorporate, embody; annex (*land*); *Schleswig wurde –t*, Schleswig was annexed. **–ung**, *f.* incorporation, annexation.

Einvernahme, *f.*, [1]**Einvernehmen**, *n.* hearing (*before the courts*).

[2]**Einvernehmen**, *n.* consent, agreement; understanding; *in gutem – mit*, on good terms with; *sich mit einem ins – setzen*, come to an understanding with a p.

einverstanden, *p.p.* & *adj. see* **einverstehen.**

Einverständnis, *n.* understanding; agreement; consent; *in gutem –se mit einem leben*, be on good terms with s.o.; *heimliches –*, secret understanding, collusion.

einverstehen, *ir.v.r.* (only used as p.p.) *einverstanden*, agreed, understood.

einwäg–en, *v.a.* weigh in *or* out. **–ung**, *f.* amount weighed, sample.

Einwand, *m.* (-(e)s, ⸗e) objection; protest, exception; pretext. **–frei**, *adj.* faultless, unobjectionable, irreproachable, incontestable, perfect, satisfactory; *eine S. –frei feststellen*, establish a th. beyond a doubt *or* beyond question *or* as a fact; *nicht –frei*, doubtful, unsatisfactory, imperfect.

Einwander–er, *m.* immigrant. **–n**, *v.n.* (*aux.* s.) immigrate. **–ung**, *f.* immigration.

einwärts, *adv.* inward(s); *–gehen, die Füße –setzen* or *–stellen*, turn in the toes in walking.

einweben, *reg.* & *ir.v.a.* weave in, interweave; intersperse; *eingewebte* (*eingewobene*) *Erzählung*, episode.

einwechseln, *v.a.* change (*money*); acquire by exchange; *einen Scheck –*, cash a cheque; *sich* (*Dat.*) *Banknoten –*, exchange notes for cash.

einwecken, *v.a.* bottle, preserve.

einweibig, *adj.* monogynous (*Bot.*).

einweichen, *v.a.* soak, steep, macerate.

einweih–en, *v.a.* consecrate, dedicate; inaugurate, initiate, open (*ceremonially*); ordain; *ein Eingeweihter*, initiate, adept; *eingeweiht sein*, be in the secret *or* (*coll.*) in the know. **–ung**, *f.* consecration, dedication, initiation, inauguration, ceremonial opening. **–ungsfeier**, *f.* inaugural ceremony.

Einweisung, *f.* military training. **–sflug**, *m.* paratroops training flight.

einwellig, *adj.* single-phase (*Elec.*).

einwend–en, *reg.* & *ir.v.a.* object, take exception to; oppose; demur; *dagegen läßt sich nichts –en*, there can be no objection to that. **–ung**, *f.* objection; exception; reply; plea; *–ungen vorbringen* (or *machen*) *gegen*, make (*or* raise) objections to *or* against, demur.

einwerfen, *ir.v.a.* throw in *or* down; throw in (*football*); break by throwing, smash; object; interject (*a word*); *einem die Fenster –*, smash a p.'s windows.

einwickeln, *v.a.* wrap up; envelop, enclose; curl (*the hair*); swaddle; *einen – in*, entangle *or* implicate a p. in.

einwiegen, *v.a.* rock to sleep.

einwillig–en, *v.n.* (*aux.* h.) consent *or* agree to, acquiesce in; approve of; subscribe to; permit. **–ung**, *f.* consent in writing, acceptance (*Law*).

einwirk–en, 1. *v.a.* interweave; work in (*patterns*). 2. *v.n.* (*aux.* h.) influence; impress (on), have an effect (on), act (on). **–end**, *pr.p.* & *adj.* influential, effective. **–ung**, *f.* influence, impression, action, effect, reaction (*Chem.*); interweaving.

einwohn–en, 1. *v.n.* be settled, be accustomed (*to one's surroundings*); *wir sind ganz eingewohnt*, we are quite settled. 2. *v.r.* begin to feel at home, settle down. **–end**, *pr.p.* & *adj.* inhabiting; inherent. **–er**, *m.* inhabitant, resident. **–erschaft**, *f.* inhabitants, population. **–erzahl**, *f.* total population. **–erzählung**, *f.* census.

einwollen, *ir.v.n.* (*coll.*) wish to get in; *das will mir nicht ein*, I cannot swallow (*or* understand) that.

Einwurf, *m.* (-(e)s, ⸗e) objection; slit, slot, aperture, opening (*for letters in a pillar-box*); *einen – machen*, make *or* raise an objection, take exception (to); *den – haben*, have the throw in (*football*).

einwurzeln, *v.n.* (*aux.* s.) take root; *tief eingewurzelte Überzeugungen*, deep(ly)-rooted convictions.

Einzahl, *f.* singular (number) (*Gram.*). **–en**, *v.a.* pay in. **–ung**, *f.* payment, deposit, instalment.

einzäun–en, *v.a.* hedge in, fence in. **–ung**, *f.* fence, enclosure; fencing.

einzehr–en, *v.n.* (*aux.* h.) diminish, lose, suffer loss (from evaporation). **–ung**, *f.* loss by evaporation.

einzeichn–en, 1. *v.a.* mark in, note, draw in. 2. *v.r.* enter one's name; subscribe. **–ung**, *f.* added marking, entry; subscription.

Einzel–anführung, *f.* specification. **–arrest** *m.* solitary confinement. **–aufzählung**, *f.* detailed enumeration. **–erscheinung**, *f.* isolated phenomena. **–fall**, *m.* individual *or* particular case. **–gänger**, *m.* individualist, lone-wolf. **–haft**, *f.* solitary confinement. **–handel**, *m.* retail business. **–heit**, *f.* (-heiten), singleness, individuality; detail; (*pl.*) details, particulars. **–kampf**, *m.* single *or* hand-to-hand combat. **–last**, *f.* concentrated load. **–n**, *adj.* single, sole, particular; individual, isolated, detached, separate; *–nes hat mir gefallen*, some things did please me; *die Bände sind –n zu haben*, the volumes are to be had separately; *ins –ne gehen*, enter into particulars; *–n angeben*, specify; *–n betrachten*, individualize; *im allgemeinen und im –nen*, in general and particular; *–n verkaufen*, sell, retail. **–spiel**, *n.* single (*Tenn.*). **–stehend**, *adj.* isolated, scattered. **–verkäufer**, *m*, retailer. **–wesen**, *n.* individual. **–wurf**, *m.* dropping single bombs.

Einzeller, *m.* microbe, bacillus.

einzieh–en, 1. *ir.v.a.* draw in, pull in, get in, take in; retract (*or* raise) (*undercarriage of aircraft*); collect; call up, draft (*Mil.*); absorb, inhale; seize

arrest; suppress, confiscate, remove; withdraw *or* call in (*coins from circulation*); take in, make smaller (*clothes, etc.*), reduce, lessen; fill up, level; *den Faden –en*, thread (*a needle*); *eine Fahne –en*, lower *or* furl a flag; *Erkundigungen –en*, get information; *die Hörner* **–en**, draw in one's horns; (*coll.*) *den Schwanz* **–en**, climb down, give up, call it off. 2. *v.r.* shrink, contract; retire from the world; retrench. 3. *v.n.* (*aux.* s.) enter, march in, move into, take possession (*of a house, lodgings, etc.*); soak in, infiltrate; *eingezogen, p.p. & adj.* retired, solitary. **–bar**, *adj.* retractable; recoverable; liable to confiscation. **–fahrgestell**, *n.*, **–fahrwerk**, *n.* retractable undercarriage (*Av.*). **–ung**, *f.* drawing in, contraction; inhaling, imbibing; collection; confiscation, arresting, suppression; infiltration; tapering (*of a wall*); *–ung der Reserve*, calling up of the army reserve. **–ungsmittel**, *n.* absorbent.

einzig, *adj.* only, single, sole, unique; *– in seiner Art*, unique, peerless; *– und allein*, only, purely and simply. simply and solely; *mein – Geliebter*, my only love, my darling; *er ist doch ganz –*, there is no one like him, he cannot be beaten. **–artig**, *adj.* unique. **–keit**, *f.* **–artigkeit**, *f.* uniqueness.

einzuckern, *v.a.* sugar (over); cover with sugar.

Einzug, *m.* (-(e)s, ⁻e) entry, entrance; moving in (*into a new house, etc.*); *– halten*, enter. **–sgebiet**, *n.* catchment *or* drainage area. **–sschmaus**, *m.* house-warming.

einzwängen, *v.a.* force in, squeeze in, wedge in; pinch; confine; (*fig.*) constrain.

einzwingen, *ir.v.a.* force into.

Eis [*pron.* eːis], *n.* E-sharp (*Mus.*).

Eis *n.* ice; ice-cream; *in – gekühlt*, iced; *zu – werden*, congeal, freeze; *vom –e besetzt*, ice-bound; *gehendes –*, floating ice; *mürbes –*, unsound ice; *der Fluß geht mit –*, large blocks of ice are floating down the river. **–apparat**, *m.* refrigerator. **–artig**, *adj.* icy, ice-like, glacial. **–bahn**, *f.* slide; skating-ice, ice-rink. **–bär**, *m.* polar bear. **–bein**, *n.* pig's trotters, knuckle of pork; (*sl.*) (*pl.*) cold feet. **–beinorden**, *m.* (*sl.*) Order of the cold feet (*Campaign medal for service on the Russian front*). **–berg**, *m.* iceberg. **–bock**, *m.*, **–brecher**, *m.* ice-breaker. **–beutel**, *m.* ice-bag. **–decke**, *f.* sheet of ice, coating of ice. **–dienst**, *m.* iceberg patrol. **–essig**, *m.* glacial acetic acid. **–flöße**, *f.pl.*, **–flacken**, *f.pl.* ice floes. **–frei**, *adj.* free from ice, clear of ice. **–gang**, *m.* drift of ice. **–glas**, *n.* frosted glass. **–glätte**, *f.* icy road conditions. **–grau**, *adj.* hoary. **–heilige(r)**, *m.*; *die drei –heiligen*, May 11th–13th (Mamertus, Pancratius, Servatius; *also called* die drei gestrengen Herrn). **–ig**, *adj.* icy, frigid, glacial. **–kalt**, *adj.* ice-cold, cold as ice. **–kasten**, *m.* refrigerator, ice-box. **–kühler**, *m.* cooler, ice-pail. **–lauf**, *m.* skating. **–läufer**, *m.* skater. **–maschine**, *f.* freezer. **–meer**, *n.* polar sea; *Nördliches* (*Südliches*) *–meer*, Arctic (Antarctic) Ocean. **–mond**, *m.* (*Poet.*) January. **–pickel**, *m.* ice-axe. **–scholle**, *f.* ice floe. **–schrank**, *m.* refrigerator. **–vogel**, *m.* kingfisher. **–zacken**, *m.*, **–zapfen**, *m.* icicle. **–zeit**, *f.* ice-age, glacial period.

Eisbein, *n.* hip-bone (*Anat.*) (*not connected with* Eis).

Eisen, *n.* (-s, –) iron; horseshoe; sword, weapon; iron instrument *or* tool; (*pl.*) irons, fetters; *er schlägt über die –*, he kicks over the traces; *an kaltem – sterben*, die by the sword; *einen in – legen*, put a p. in irons; *Herzen von –*, hearts of steel; *Guß–*, cast iron; *Roh–*, pig-iron; *durch – und Blut*, with blood and iron (*Bismarck*); *Not bricht –*, necessity knows no law; (*Prov.*) *man muß das – schmieden, so lange es heiß ist*, you must strike while the iron is hot; (*coll.*) *etwas zum alten – werfen*, consign s.th. to the rubbish-heap, scrap a th. **–abfall**, *m.* scrap-iron. **–artig**, *adj.* ferruginous. **–bahn**, *f.* railway; railroad (*Amer.*); (*sl.*) *es ist die höchste –bahn*, it is high time, no moment is to be lost. **–bahnabteil**, *n. & m.* compartment. **–bahnaktie**, *f.* railway-share. **–bahndamm**, *m.* embankment. **–bahner**, *m.* railwayman. **–bahnergewerkschaft**, *f.* union of railwaymen. **–bahnfahrt**, *f.* railway-journey. **–bahngesellschaft**, *f.* railway company. **–bahnknotenpunkt**, *m.* junction. **–bahnnetz**, *n.* railway network. **–bahnschwelle**, *f.* sleeper, tie (*Amer.*). **–bahnschienen**, *f.pl.* rails. **–bahnschmöker**, *m.* light reading for the train. **–bahnstollen**, *m.* tunnel. **–bahnstrecke**, *f.* section of railway line. **–bahnübergang**, *m.* level crossing; **–bahnunfall**, *m.* **–bahnunglück**, *n.* railway accident. **–bahnverband**, *m.* National Union of Railwaymen. **–bahnverbindung**, *f.* rail communication. **–bahnwagen**, *m.* railway carriage. **–bahnwesen**, *n.* railways. **–bau**, *m.* iron structure. **–beißer**, *m.* braggart, bully. **–beton**, *m.* reinforced concrete. **–blende**, *f.* pitchblende. **–blau**, *n. & adj.* Prussian blue. **–blech**, *n.* sheet-iron. **–draht**, *m.* iron-wire. **–einlage**, *f.* reinforcement (*ferro-concrete*). **–erde**, *f.* ferruginous earth. **–erz**, *n.* iron-ore. **–feilicht**, *n.* iron-filings. **–fest**, *adj.* hard as iron; inflexible. **–flechtung**, *f.*, *see* **–einlage**. **–fleck**, *m.* iron-stain, iron-mould. **–fresser**, *m.* braggart, bully, fire-eater. **–frischen**, *n.* refining. **–gehalt**, *m.* ferruginous content, amount of iron. **–geld**, *n.* (*Nat. Soc.*) basic minimum quota, priority certificate. **–gießerei**, *f.* iron-foundry. **–glas**, *n.* mica. **–grube**, *f.* iron-mine. **–guß**, *m.* iron casting; cast-iron. **–haltig**, *adj.* containing iron; ferruginous, chalybeate. **–händler**, *m.* ironmonger. **–hart**, *adj.* hard as iron. **–hut**, *m.*, **–hütchen**, *n.* aconite, monkshood (*Aconitum napellus*) (*Bot.*). **–hütte**, *f.* iron-works, forge. **–kies**, *m.* iron pyrites. **–kram**, *m.* old iron. **–meißel**, *m.* cold chisel. **–oxyd**, *n.* ferric oxide. **–oxydul**, *n.* ferrous oxide. **–panzer**, *m.* coat of mail. **–platte**, *f.* armour-plate, iron-plate. **–salz**, *n.* sulphate of iron. **–sau**, *f.* pig of iron. **–säure**, *f.* ferric acid. **–scheck**, *m.* **–schein**, *m.*, *see* **–geld**. **–schimmel**, *m.* iron-grey (*horse*). **–schlacke**, *f.* iron-dross. **–schmied**, *m.* blacksmith. **–walzwerk**, *n.* rolling-mill. **–waren**, *f.pl.* ironmongery, hardware. **–warenhändler**, *m.* ironmonger. **–wasser**, *n.* chalybeate water. **–werk**, *n.* iron-work(s).

eisern, *adj.* iron; hard, strong, inflexible; indefatigable; inalienable (*Law*); *–er Bestand*, reserve stock; iron rations (also *–e Ration*); permanent fund; *mit der –en Stirn*, with head unbowed, undaunted; with brazen effrontery, unblushingly; *der –e Herzog*, the Iron Duke (*Wellington*); *der –e Kanzler*, the Iron Chancellor (*Bismarck*); *–es Kapital*, money sunk on which only the interest is paid; *–es Kreuz*, Iron Cross (*Prussian war medal*); *das –e Tor*, the Iron Gates (*of the Danube*); *–er Fleiß*, untiring energy; *–er Vorhang*, fire-curtain, safety curtain (*in theatres*); iron curtain (*between Eastern and Western Powers*).

eitel, *adj.* vain, conceited; frivolous, empty, idle, futile; (*indecl.*) nothing but, mere, only, *– sein auf eine S.*, be vain *or* conceited about a th.; *eitles Geschwätz*, idle *or* silly talk. **–keit**, *f.* vanity; conceit; *mit –keit, List und Tücke*, with barefaced trickery.

Eiter, *m.* (-s) matter, pus; *dünner –*, gleet; *bösartiger –*, purulent discharge. **–abfluß**, *m.* (purulent) discharge. **–befördernd**, *adj.* suppurative, pyogenic. **–beule**, *f.* abscess, (*fig.*) sink of iniquity. **–bläschen**, *n.* pustule, pimple. **–blase**, *f.* carbuncle. **–brust**, *f.* empyema. **–erzeugend**, *adj.*, *see* **–befördernd**. **–fieber**, *n.* pyaemia. **–fluß**, *m.* running (*from a sore*). **–gang**, *m.* fistula. **–geschwulst**, *f.* abscess. **–ig**, *adj.* purulent. **–n**, *v.n.* (*aux.* h.) suppurate, fester; discharge matter. **–nd**, *pr.p. & adj.* suppurative. **–sack**, *m.* cyst (*of a tumour*). **–ung**, *f.* suppuration, festering. **–vergiftung**, *f.* pyaemia. **–ziehen**, *n.* suppurating.

Ekel, 1. *m.* loathing, disgust, aversion, nausea; *es ist mir zum –*, I am sick of it; I am disgusted with it; (*coll.*) *dieser –* or *dieses –*, that nasty fellow; *wir sind ihnen zum –*, they loathe us. **–haft**, *adj.* loathsome, disgusting, nauseous, offensive; **–haftigkeit**, *f.* loathsomeness. **–ig (eklig)**, *adj.* (*coll.*) disgusting, loathsome unpleasant, nasty, disagreeable. **–n**, 1. *v.n.* (*aux.* h.) arouse disgust, sicken, excite loathing; *mir* or *mich –t davor, es –t mir* or *mich*, I loathe it, it disgusts me. 2. *v.r.*; *sich –n vor einer S.*, loathe a th., be disgusted at a th.

eklatant, *adj.* brilliant, clear, striking.
Eklip–se, *f.* (-sen) eclipse. **–tik,** *f.* ecliptic (*Astr.*). **–tisch,** *adj.* ecliptic.
Eksta–se, *f.* (-n) ecstasy. **–tisch,** *adj.* ecstatic.
Ekzem, *n.* eczema.
Elan, *m.* dash, pluck; (*sl.*) guts.
elast–isch, *adj.* elastic, resilient, springy. **–izität,** *f.* elasticity, resiliency. **–izitätsgrenze,** *f.* elastic limit (*Metall.*).
Elch, *m.* (-(e)s, -e) elk, moose.
Elefant, *m.* (-en, -en) elephant; *wie ein – im Porzellanladen,* like a bull in a china-shop; *aus einer Mücke einen – machen,* make a mountain out of a mole-hill. **–enaussatz,** *m.* elephantiasis (*Med.*). **–enführer,** *m.* mahout. **–enrüssel,** *m.* elephant's trunk. **–enzahn,** *m.* tusk.
elegan–t, *adj.* elegant; smart. **–z,** *f.* elegance, refinement, polish.
Eleg–ie, *f.* (-n) elegy (*poem in elegiac metre* or *melancholy poem in any metre*). **–isch,** *adj.* elegiac, melancholy, mournful; *–ische Verse,* elegiacs; mournful verses, melancholy lines.
elektr–ifizieren, *v.a.* electrify (*railway, etc.*). **–iker,** *m.* electrician. **–izität,** *f.* electricity; *durch –izität töten* or *hinrichten,* electrocute. **–isch,** *adj.* electric; *die –ische,* tramcar; *–isches Feld,* electric field; *–ische Ladung,* electric charge; *–ischer Schlag,* electric shock. **–isieren,** *v.a.* electrify, receive electric treatment. **–isiermaschine,** *f.* electrical machine. **–izitätsgesellschaft,** *f.* electricity-supply company. **–izitätsladung,** *f., see* **–ische Ladung.** **–izitätsleiter,** *m.* conductor. **–izitätsmesser,** *m.* electrometer. **–izitätsstrom,** *m.* electric current. **–izitätswerk,** *n.* power plant. **–izitätszähler,** *m.* electricity meter. **–izitätszeiger,** *m.* electroscope. **–olot,** *n.* electrical depth sounder. **–olyse,** electrolysis; **–omagnetisches Anmessen,** radiolocation. **–onenröhre,** *f.* thermionic valve (*Rad.*), **–onenaussendung,** *f.* emission of electrons. **–otechnik,** *f.* electrical engineering. **–otechniker,** *m.* electrical engineer.
Element, *n.* (-(e)s, -e) element; rudiment, principle; battery, cell (*Elec.*); *in seinem –,* in his element; *chemische –e,* the chemical elements; *–e der Mathematik,* rudiments of mathematics; *die schlechten* or *üblen –e gewannen die Oberhand,* the bad elements gained the upper hand; *das Wüten der –e,* the raging of the elements. **–ar,** *adj.* fundamental, elementary, rudimentary; elemental, violent, irresistible. **–arbuch,** *n.* primer. **–argeist,** *m.* elemental *or* nature-spirit. **–argewalt,** *f.* elemental power. **–arlehrer,** *m.* primary teacher. **–arschule,** *f.* primary school. **–arstein,** *m.* opal. **–arstoff,** *m.* element (*Chem.*). **–prüfer,** *m.* battery tester (*Elec.*).
Elen, *m.* & *n.* (-s, –), **–tier,** *n.* elk.
Elend, 1. *n.* misery, distress, misfortune; want, need, penury; (*coll.*) *sieben Stunden hinterm –,* seven hours from anywhere. 2. *adj.* miserable, wretched, pitiful, ill; *Elender!* wretch! **–ig,** *adj., see* – 2. **–iglich,** *adv.* miserably, wretchedly. **–sviertel,** *n.* slum.
Elf, *m.* (-en, -en), **–e,** *f.* (-en) elf; fairy; goblin. **–enhaft,** *adj.* fairy-like. **–enkind,** *n.* changeling. **–enreigen,** *m.* fairy dance.
elf, *num. adj.* eleven. **–eck,** *n.* hendecagon. **–er,** *m.* the number eleven. **–erlei,** *indec. adj.* of eleven kinds. **–fach,** *adj.* elevenfold. **–mal,** *adv.* eleven times. **–te,** *num. adj.* eleventh. **–tel,** *n.* the eleventh part. **–tens,** *adv.* in the eleventh place.
Elfenbein, *n.* ivory. **–ern,** *adj.* consisting of ivory; made of ivory.
Elger, *m.* harpoon; eel-dart.
elidieren, *v.a.* elide, suppress (*a vowel*).
eliminieren, *v.a.* eliminate.
Elite–kampfgeschwader, *n.* crack bomber squadron. (*Av.*). **–truppen,** *f.pl.* picked troops.
Ell–e, *f.* (-n) ell, yard, yardstick; ulna (*Anat.*); *als hätte er eine –e verschluckt,* straight as a poker *or* ramrod. **–enbreit,** *adj.* an ell broad. **–enhandel,** *m.* draper's trade. **–enlang,** *adj.* an ell long, (*coll.*) extremely long; *er schreibt –enlange Briefe,* he writes interminable letters *or* letters as long as my arm. **–enmaß,** *n.* yardstick. **–enwaren,** *f.pl.* drapery, dry-goods (*Amer.*). **–enweise,** *adv.* by the yard, yard by yard. **–(en)bogen,** *m.* (-s, –) elbow; *mit dem –bogen stoßen,* elbow; *die –bogen frei haben,* have elbow-room. **–bogenbein,** *see* **–bogenknochen.** **–bogenfreiheit,** *f.* elbow-room. **–bogenknochen,** *m.* ulna (*Anat.*). **–bogennerv,** *m.* ulnar nerve.
Eller, *f.* (-n), *see* **Erle.**
Ellip–se, *f.* ellipse; ellipsis. **–senbahn,** *f.* elliptic orbit. **–tisch,** *adj.* elliptical.
Elritze, *f.* minnow (*Phoxinus laevis*) (*Icht*).
Elster, *f.* (-n) magpie (*Pica*) (*Orn.*).
elter–lich, *adj.* parental. **–n,** *pl.* parents; (*coll.*) *nicht von schlechten –n sein,* be first-rate, excellent, fine; (*sl.*) not to be sneezed at. **–nhaus,** *n.* house of one's parents, home. **–nliebe,** *f.* parental love, filial love. **–nlos,** *adj.* orphan, orphaned.
Email [*pron.* eˈmaiːj] *n.* **Emaille,** *f.* enamel. **–lieren** [*pron.* emalˈjiːren] *v.a.* enamel.
emanzipieren, *v.a.* emancipate.
Embolie, *f.* embolism.
Emigr–ant, *m.* (-en, -en), emigrant. **–ieren,** *v.n.* (*aux.* s.) emigrate.
Emi–ssion, *f.* (-en) issuing (*of shares*); emission (*Rad.*). **–ssionsgeschäft,** *n.* issuing firm. **–ttieren,** *v.a.* & *n.* emit.
empfahl, *see* **empfehlen.**
empfand, empfände, *see* **empfinden.**
Empfang, *m.* (-s, ⸚e) reception, receipt (*of a letter, etc.*); *den – bescheinigen,* give a receipt for; *in – nehmen,* receive. **–en,** 1. *ir.v.a.* take, receive; welcome. 2. *v.n.* (*aux.* h.) conceive, become pregnant. **–nahme,** *f.* receipt, reception. **–sanlage,** *f.* (wireless) receiving set. **–sanzeige,** *f.* acknowledgement (*of receipt*). **–sapparat,** *m.* receiver (*Tele.*); receiving set (*Rad.*). **–sdame,** *f.* receptionist. **–sschein,** *m.* receipt. **–(s)stelle,** *f.* receiving station. **–sstörung,** *f.* jamming, interference, atmospherics (*Rad.*). **–stag,** *m.* at-home day.
Empfäng–er, *m.* (-ers, -er) (*C.L.*) receiver, recipient, addressee, consignee; accepter (*of a bill*), payee; receiving set, receiver (*Rad.*). **–lich,** *adj.* susceptible, impressionable, responsive, predisposed. **–lichkeit,** *f.* susceptibility, impressionability, receptiveness. **–nis,** *f.* conception; *unbefleckte –nis,* Immaculate Conception. **–nisverhütend,** *adj.* contraceptive.
empfehl–en, 1. *ir.v.a.* commend, recommend; *–en Sie mich ihm bestens,* give my kind regards to him, remember me to him most kindly; *sich* (*Dat.*) *etwas empfohlen sein lassen,* take good care of a th. 2. *v.r.* take one's leave; bid farewell. (*ich*) *–e mich* (*Ihnen*), (I wish you) good-bye; *sich heimlich –en,* abscond; *sich auf französisch –en,* take French leave; *es empfiehlt sich,* it is advisable. **–bar,** *adj.* recommendable. **–enswert,** *adj.,* **–enswürdig,** *adj.* commendable, advisable, eligible. **–ung,** *f.* recommendation; introduction; compliments; *mit schöner –ung an Sie,* with best compliments to you. **–ungsbrief,** *m.,* **–ungsschreiben,** *n.* letter of introduction; credentials. **–ungskarte,** *f.* business card (*of commercial travellers*); card of introduction.
empfind–eln, *v.a.* (*aux.* h.) be sentimental, (*sl.*) gush over. **–elei,** *f.* sentimentality. **–ler,** *m.* sentimentalist. **–en,** *ir.v.a.* feel, perceive, be sensible of; experience; *übel –en,* take as an offence. **–bar,** *adj.* sensitive; sensible, perceptible. **–barkeit,** *f.* perceptibility, sensitiveness. **–end,** *pr.p.* & *adj.* sensible, sensitive, sentient; perceptive. **–lich,** *adj.* sensitive; tender, delicate, sore, painful; susceptible, irritable, touchy; sharp, severe, grievous; fugitive; sensitized (*Phot.*); *–liche Farbe,* fugitive colour; *das ist seine –liche Stelle,* that is his sore point; *einen –lich verletzen,* wound a p. deeply, hurt s.o.'s feelings grievously. *–lich machen,* *v.a.* sensitize, make sensitive (*Phot.*). **–lichkeit,** *f.* sensibility; sensitiveness; irritability. **–sam,** *adj.* sentimental, sensitive; susceptible; *–same Reise,* sentimental journey. **–samkeit,** *f.* sentimentality, susceptibility; sensitiveness. **–ung,** *f.* sensation, perception; feeling, sentiment. **–ungsfähig,** *adj.* capable of feeling, susceptible. **–ungsfähigkeit,**

f. perceptivity, sensitiveness, perceptive faculty. **-ungskraft,** *f.* power of reception *or* feeling. (*obs.*) **-ungslaut,** *m.* interjection; exclamation. **-ungslos** *adj.* unfeeling; callous; apathetic; insensitive, devoid of feeling, numb. **-ungsvermögen,** *n.* perceptive faculty, **-ungszentrum,** *n.* sense-centre.

empfing, *see* **empfangen.**

empföhle, empfohlen, *see* **empfehlen.**

empfunden, *see* **empfinden.**

Empha-se, *f.* emphasis. **-tisch,** *adj.* emphatic; emphatically.

Empir-ik, *f.* empiricism.

empor, *adv.* & *sep. prefix.* up, upwards, on high, aloft. **-arbeiten,** *v.r.* work one's way up. **-blicken,** *v.n.* look up. **-dringen,** 1. *ir.v.a.* raise, promote. 2. *ir.v.n.* (*aux.* s.) gush forth; rise; *tiefe Seufzer drangen aus ihrer Brust –*, she sighed deeply. **-halten,** *v.a.* hold up. **-heben,** *ir.v.a.* lift up, raise, exalt; elevate (*the Host*). **-helfen,** *ir.v.a.* help up. **-kommen,** *ir.v.n.* (*aux.* s.) rise in the world, get on, prosper, thrive. **-kömmling,** *m.* upstart, parvenue. **-ragen,** *v.n.* stand out, project, tower (*über*, above). **-richten,** *v.r.* rise. **-schnellen,** *v.n.* rise suddenly, jump *or* spring up. **-schwingen,** *ir.v.r.* rise, soar up. **-sehen,** *v.n.* look up. **-steigen,** *v.n.* rise, ascend. **-streben,** *v.n.* (*aux.* h.) aspire, strive upwards. **-strebend,** *pr. p.* & *adj.* aspiring. **-treiben,** *ir.v.a.* force upwards; sublimate (*Chem.*).

Empore, *f.* (-en) choir loft, gallery (*in churches*).

empör-en, 1. *v.a.* rouse to indignation, shock; excite, stir up. 2. *v.r.* be enraged *or* furious; rebel. **-end,** *pr.p.* & *adj.* disgraceful, shocking. **-er,** *m.* insurgent, rebel. **-erisch,** *adj.* mutinous, rebellious. **-ung,** *f.* rebellion, revolt; rising; indignation. **-t,** *p.p.* & *adj.* indignant.

emsig, *adj.* busy, active, industrious; assiduous, eager, diligent. **-keit,** *f.* industry, assiduity; diligence.

emul-gieren, -sieren, -sionieren, *v.a.* & *n.* emulsify.

End-e, *n.* (-es, -en) end; conclusion; close, finish; termination (*of a lease*); result, issue, goal, aim, object, purpose; extremity; tine, point (*of an antler*); wing, flank (*Mil.*); *ein Hirsch von 10 –en* (*Zehn–er*), a stag with 10 antlers *or* points; *Zwölf–er*, royal stag; (*sl.*) old sweat (*soldier with 12 years' service*); *am –e*, in the end, after all, on the whole; finally, at last; perhaps, possibly; *an allen Ecken und –en*, everywhere; *das äußerste –e*, the extremity; *bis ans* or *bis zum –e*, to the last; *bis ans –e der Welt*, to the ends of the earth, the world over; *das dicke –e kommt noch nach*, the disagreeable part has still to come; *alles muß einmal ein –e haben*, there 's an end to everything, everything must come to an end; *letzten –es*, in the long run, when all is said and done, finally, in the final analysis; *das –e vom Liede ist*, the upshot is; *einer S.* (*Dat.*) *ein –e machen*, put an end to a th.; *das nimmt kein –e*, there is no end to it, that goes on for ever; *er faßte es am richtigen* (*verkehrten*) *–e an*, he set about it the right (wrong) way; *von allen –en*, from all quarters (of the globe); *zu –e*, at an end, over; towards the end; *zu –e bringen*, bring to an end, finish; (*Prov.*) *–e gut, alles gut*, all's well that ends well; (*Prov.*) *besser ein –e mit Schrecken als ein Schrecken ohne –e*, better a dreadful ending than endless dread; *zu –e führen*, complete; *zu –e gehen*, come to an end, run short; *zu dem –e*, for the purpose; *zu dem –e, daß*, in order that; *der Tag geht zu –e*, the day is drawing to a close. **-absicht,** *f.* final purpose, ultimate intention. **-bahnhof,** *m.* terminus, railhead. **-bescheid,** *m.* ultimatum; final judgement. **-buchstabe,** *m.* final letter. **-en,** 1. *v.a.* finish, end, put an end to, terminate, conclude; accomplish; *sein Leben –en*, die. 2. *v.r.* come to an end, conclude, close. 3. *v.n.* (*aux.* h.) stop, cease, come to a conclusion, be over, terminate in; die. **-ergebnis,** *n.* ultimate *or* final result, upshot. **-esgenannte(r),** *m.* **-esunterzeichnete(r),** *m.* undersigned. **-geschwindigkeit,** *f.* terminal velocity, striking velocity (*Artil.*). **-gültig,** *adj.* final, definite, conclusive. **-igen,** *v.a.* & *n.*, *see* **-en. -leiste,** *f.* trailing edge (*of wing*) (*Av.*). **-lich.** 1. *adj.* finite, final, conclusive, last, ultimate. 2. *adv,* at last, finally, in short, after all; nimbly. **-lichkeit** *f.* finiteness, limitation. **-los,** *adj.* endless, unending, boundless, infinite. **-losigkeit,** *f.* endlessness, infinity. **-punkt,** *m.* end, terminus, extremity, farthest point, destination. **-silbe,** *f.* final syllable. **-spiel,** *n.* final (*of a tournament*). **-station,** *f.* terminus, railhead (*Railw.*). **-stehend,** *pr.p.* & *adj.* standing at the end; *–stehende Rechnung*, account given below. **-ung,** *f.* ending, termination, end. **-urteil,** *n.* final decree *or* judgement. **-verstärkerröhre,** *f.* output valve (*Rad.*). **-ziel,** *n.* final aim. **-zweck,** *m.* aim, goal, design, purpose.

endemisch, *adj.* endemic.

Endivie, *f.* (–n) endive, chicory.

Energ-ie, *f.* (-ien) energy. **-ieabgabe,** *f.* release of energy. **-ieeinsparung,** *f.* shedding the load (*of electric consumption*). **-ielos,** *adj.* lacking in energy. **-ielosigkeit,** *f.* lack of energy. **-isch,** *adj.* energetic, vigorous.

enfilieren, *v.a.* & *n.* enfilade (*Mil.*).

eng, *adj.* narrow; tight; close; strict; confined; intimate; *–er Atem*, asthma; *–erer Ausschuß*, select committee; *– gebunden*, confined within narrow limits; – or *–er machen*, narrow, tighten; *in –er Verwahrung sein*, be a close prisoner; *im –eren Sinne*, strictly speaking; *–ere Wahl*, select list, short list (*of candidates*); *zur –eren Wahl stehen*, be on the short list. **-begrenzt,** *adj.* limited, small. **-brüstig,** *adj.* narrow-chested; asthmatic, broken-winded. **-e,** *f.* (-en) narrowness, tightness, constriction; narrow place, defile, isthmus, strait; difficulty, dilemma; *einen in die –e treiben*, drive a p. into a corner; corner a p. **-heit,** *f.* narrowness; closeness, tightness; crowded *or* confined state. **-herzig,** *adj.* narrow-minded, strait-laced; illiberal. **-maschig,** *adj.* tightly woven, close-meshed. **-paß,** *m.* narrow pass, defile, bottleneck.

engagieren, 1. *v.a.* engage; take in (*servants, workmen*). 2. *v.r. sich für einen –*, take an interest in a p.; take a p.'s part.

Engel, *m.* (-s, –) angel; (*coll.*) *ein – flog durch das Zimmer*, there was sudden silence in the room *or* in the conversation. **-brot,** *n.* manna. **-gleich,** *adj.* angelic. **-haft,** *adj.* angelic. **-köpfchen,** *n.* cherub's head. **-macher,** *m.*, baby-farmer, baby-killer. **-schar,** *f.* angelic host. **-sgeduld,** *f.* patience of Job. **-sgruß,** *m.* Annunciation; Ave Maria. **-sschatz,** *m.* sweetheart, dear love. **-wurz,** *f.* angelica (*Angelica archangelica*) (*Bot.*).

Engerling, *m.* (-s, -e) larva, grub (*of the cockchafer*).

Engländer, *m.* (*Engin.*) adjustable spanner, monkey-wrench; (*see also List of proper names*).

englisch, *adj.* angelic (*Poet.*); *der –e Gruß*, the Annunciation, Ave Maria; (*see also List of proper names*); *–es Pflaster*, court plaster; *–es Salz*, Epsom salt (magnesium sulphate).

engros, *indec. adj.* wholesale.

Enjambement, *n.* (-s) overflow (*Metr.*).

[1]**Enkel,** *m.* (-s, –) ankle.

[2]**Enkel,** *m.* (-s, –) grandson, grandchild. **-in** *f.* granddaughter. **-kind,** *n.* grandchild.

enorm, *adj.* huge, enormous, tremendous, excessive. **-ität,** *f.* enormity.

ent-, *insep. and unaccented prefix*; *in composition with other words indicates establishment of or entry into a new state or abandonment of an old state. The prefix* emp– *is doublet of* ent– *preceding* f.

entadeln, *v.a.* degrade in rank; dishonour.

entart-en, *v.n.* (*aux.* s.) degenerate, debase, contaminate, deteriorate. **-ung,** *f.* degeneration, deterioration, debasement, contamination.

entäußer-n, *v.r.* (*sich einer S.*) part with, give up, dispose of; deprive o.s. of, divest o.s. of; *er –te sich seiner Vorrechte*, he gave up his privileges. **-ung,** *f.* renunciation; parting with; alienation (*of property*).

entbehr-en, *v.a.* do without, dispense with; be without, lack, miss, want; be deprived of; *ich kann noch etwas –en*, I have still s.th. to spare; *das Gerücht –t jeden Grundes*, the report is without any foundation; *ich kann dich nicht –en*, I cannot do without you, I cannot spare you. **-lich,** *adj.* dispensable, unnecessary, superfluous, spare; *-lich machen,* render superfluous; supersede. **-ung,** *f.* renunciation, self-denial, abstinence; want, privation.

entbieten, *ir.v.a.* bid, send for, command; announce; present, offer; *einem seinen Gruß –,* present one's compliments to a p.; *zu sich –,* send for, summon to one's presence.

entbind-en, *ir.v.a.* (*Gen.* or *von,* from) set free, release, liberate, disengage; absolve, exonerate; evolve (gas); deliver (*Med.*); *entbunden werden,* be confined, give birth (*to a child*), be delivered (of). **-ung,** *f.* releasing, absolving; unbinding, release, disengagement; parturition, delivery, confinement, birth. **-ungsanstalt,** *f.* lying-in hospital, maternity hospital. **-ungskunst,** *f.* obstetrics, midwifery. **-ungsurteil,** *n.* final sentence of acquittal, absolution. **-ungszange,** *f.* obstetric(al) forceps.

entblättern, 1. *v.a.* strip of leaves, defoliate. 2. *v.r.* shed leaves.

entblöden, *v.r.* dare, venture, not be ashamed; *er entblödete sich nicht zu behaupten,* he did not blush to affirm, he had the impudence to maintain.

entblöß-en, *v.a.* denude, bare, strip, divest, expose; uncover (*the head*); unsheath. **-t,** *p.p.* & *adj.* bare, destitute, denuded (*von,* of). **-ung,** *f.* exposing, baring; dismantling; (de)privation.

entbrechen, *ir.v.r.* forbear; abstain from; *sich nicht – können,* not be able to restrain (from).

entbrennen, *ir.v.n.* (*aux.* s.) take fire, be kindled, become inflamed; break out; fly into a passion; *in Liebe –,* fall violently in love.

entbunden, *see* **entbinden.**

entdeck-en, 1. *v.a.* discover, detect, find out; *sein Herz -en,* unbosom o.s. 2. *v.r.* disclose one's presence. **-er,** *m.* discoverer. **-ung,** *f.* discovery; disclosure. **-ungsreise,** *f.* voyage of discovery.

Ente, *f.* (-n) duck; hoax, canard, lying report; (*sl.*) dud (*Gunn.*); *– tauchen,* crash-dive (*of submarine*). **-nbraten,** *m.* roast duck. **-nfang,** *m.* duck decoy. **-njagd,** *f.* duck-shooting. **-npfuhl,** *m.* duck-pond. **-rich,** *m.* (-s, -e) drake.

entehr-en, *v.a.* dishonour, disgrace, degrade; ravish. **-end,** *pr.p.* & *adj.* dishonourable, disgraceful. **-ung,** *f.* dishonouring, defamation; degradation; ravishing, defloration.

enteign-en, *v.a.* expropriate, dispossess. **-ung,** *f.* expropriation; *-ung gegen Entgelt,* expropriation with compensation.

enteilen, *v.n.* (*aux.* s.) hurry away (from).

enteisen, *v.a.* de-ice (*Av.*).

enterb-en, *v.a.* disinherit. **-ung,** *f.* disinheriting.

Enter-er, *m.* boarder (*of a ship*). **-beil,** *n.* boarding axe. **-haken,** *m.* boat-hook, grappling-iron. **-mannschaft,** *f.* boarding party. **-messer,** *n.* cutlass. **-n,** *v.a.* board (*a ship*). **-ung,** *f.* boarding (*a ship*).

entfachen, *v.a.* blow into flame, fan, kindle.

entfahren, *ir.v.n.* (*aux.* s.) escape; slip out from; *tiefe Seufzer entfuhren seiner Brust,* he heaved deep sighs, he sighed deeply.

entfallen, *ir.v.n.* (*aux.* s.) fall out of *or* from, escape *or* slip (*the memory*); *– auf* (*Acc.*), fall to the share of, fall to one (*as a share*); *die S. war mir ganz –,* the affair had quite slipped my memory; *dies entfällt auf mich,* this falls to my share; *auf jeden der Brüder entfiel ein Drittel,* one-third was allotted to each of the brothers.

entfalt-en, 1. *v.a.* unfold, unfurl, display; deploy; develop; evolve. 2. *v.r.* expand. **-ung,** *f.* development, deployment. **-ungszeit,** *f.* opening time (*of a parachute*).

entfärben, 1. *v.a.* deprive of colour; discolour, bleach. 2. *v.r.* change colour, grow pale, fade.

entfasern, *v.a.* string (*beans, etc.*), remove the fibres; unravel.

entfern-en, 1. *v.a.* remove, take away; eliminate, alienate. 2. *v.r.* go away, depart, withdraw, retire; deviate *or* stray from. **-t,** 1. *p.p.* & *adj.* far off, far from; distant, removed, remote; slight, faint; *-te Möglichkeit,* remote *or* off chance; *-tester Anlaß,* slightest occasion. 2. *adv.* at a distance; *weit davon -t, das zu tun,* far from doing so; *nicht im -testen,* not in the least. **-ung,** *f.* distance, range; removal; eccentricity (*Astr.*); *in gewissen -ungen,* at set distances; *kurze* or *nächste -ung,* point-blank range; *Gewehrfeuer auf eine -ung von,* rifle-fire at a range of; *unerlaubte -ung,* absence without leave (*Mil.*). **-ungskraft,** *f.* centrifugal force. **-ungsmesser,** *m.* rangefinder. **-ungspunkt,** *m.* apsis (*Astr.*). **-ungsschalter,** *m.* remote-control switch, safety switch.

entfesseln, *v.a.* unchain; release from, set free, let loose; *entfesselte Elemente,* raging elements; *entfesselte Leidenschaften,* uncontrolled passions.

entfett-en, *v.a.* remove the fat; de-grease; reduce (*of corpulence*). **-ungskur,** *f.* treatment for obesity. **-ungsmittel,** *n.* detergent, scouring agent; remedy for obesity.

entfeucht-en, *v.a.* desiccate. **-er,** *m.* desiccator.

entflamm-en, 1. *v.a.* inflame, kindle. 2. *v.n.* (*aux.* s.) be inflamed, flash, ignite. **-bar,** *adj.* inflammable. **-ungspunkt,** *m.* flash-point.

entfleischt, *p.p.* & *adj.* fleshless; lean; *-e Hände,* lean, scraggy *or* (*sl.*) scrawny hands.

entfliehen, *ir.v.n.* (*aux.* s.) (*Dat.*) run away *or* flee from, escape; pass quickly, fly (*of time*).

entfließen, *ir.v.n.* (*aux.* s.) (*Dat.*) flow from, issue, emanate.

entfremd-en, *v.a.* (*einem etwas*) estrange; alienate (a p. from s.th.). **-ung,** *f.* estrangement, alienation.

entführ-en, *v.a.* carry off; elope with; abduct; kidnap; *sie hat sich von ihm -en lassen,* she has eloped with him; *er -te sie,* he ran away with her. **-ung,** *f.* abduction; elopement; kidnapping.

entgasen, *v.a.* free from gas, extract gas from, degas, decontaminate.

entgegen, 1. *prep.* (*with preceding Dat.*) towards, against, in face of; opposed to, contrary to; *der Wind ist uns –,* the wind is against us, we are going into the teeth of the wind; *auf, ihm –!* up, let us meet him! 2. *adv.* & *sep. prefix, implying opposition or meeting.* **-arbeiten,** *v.a.* & *n.* (*aux.* h.) (*Dat.*) work against, counteract. **-bringen,** *v.a.* offer. **-eilen,** *v.n.* (*aux.* s.) (*Dat.*) hasten to meet. **-gehen,** *ir.v.n.* (*aux.* s.) (*Dat.*) go to meet; face (*a danger, etc.*). **-gesetzt,** *p.p.* & *adj.* contrary, opposite, opposed. **-halten,** *ir.v.a.* hold towards *or* against; oppose, object; contrast, compare (with). **-kommen,** 1. *ir.v.n.* (*aux.* s.) (*Dat.*) advance *or* come to meet; meet half-way. 2. *n.* kindness, willingness to oblige, co-operation. **-kommend,** *adj.* kind, helpful, obliging. **-laufen,** *ir.v.n.* (*aux.* s.) (*Dat.*) run to meet; run counter to. **-nehmen,** *ir.v.a.* accept, receive. **-sehen,** *ir.v.n.* (*aux.* h.) (*Dat.*) look forward to. **-setzen,** *v.a.* (*Dat.* & *Acc.*) set over against; place in opposition to, oppose, contrast, put in competition with. **-setzung,** *f.* comparison; antithesis. **-stehen,** *ir.v.n.* (*aux.* s.) (*Dat.*) stand opposite to; oppose, be opposed to; confront, face (*a foe, etc.*). **-stellen,** 1. *v.a.* set against, place in comparison with, contrast. 2. *v.r.* oppose, face; obstruct, stand in the way of. **-strecken,** *v.a.* stretch out towards. **-treten,** *v.n.* (*aux.* s.) oppose, confront, stand up to, advance towards, come to meet. **-wirken,** *v.n.* (*aux.* h.) (*Dat.*) counteract, check; thwart, repel. **-ziehen,** *ir.v.n.* (*aux.* s.) (*Dat.*) advance towards, go to meet.

entgegn-en, *v.a.* (*einem etwas*) answer, reply; retort. **-ung,** *f.* reply, answer, retort, rejoinder.

entgehen, *ir.v.n.* (*aux.* s.) (*Dat.*) get away from; escape, elude; avoid, evade. *– lassen,* let slip; *es kann Ihnen nicht –,* you cannot fail to observe it.

entgeistern, *v.a.* startle, shock. **entgeistert,** *p.p.* & *adj.* flabbergasted, thunderstruck.

Entgelt, *n.* (& *m.*) recompense; remuneration, reward, compensation; payment. **-en,** *ir.v.a.* pay *or* atone for, suffer for; *einen etwas -en lassen,* make a p. suffer *or* pay for a th.; *er soll mir das -en,* he shall pay for this. **-lich,** *adj.* to be paid; *un-lich,* free of charge. **-ung,** *f.* recompense, atonement, expiation.

entgiften, *v.a.* decontaminate.

entging, *see* **entgehen.**

entgleis-en, *v.n.* (*aux.* s.) run off the rails; (*fig.*) commit a faux pas, (*coll.*) go off the rails; *-en*

lassen, derail (*a train*). **-ung,** *f.* derailment; (*fig.*) slip, blunder, (*Amer.*) boner.
entgleiten, *ir.v.n.* (*aux.* s.) (*Dat.*) slip away, escape (from).
entgöttern, *v.a.* deprive of divine attributes, profane.
entgräten, *v.a.* bone (*a fish*).
enthaar-en, *v.a.* remove hair, depilate. **-t,** *p.p. & adj.* hairless, **-ungsmittel,** *n.* depilatory.
enthalt-en, 1. *ir.v.a.* hold, contain, comprise, include; *wie oft ist 2 in 10 -en?* how many twos are there in ten? how many times does 2 go into 10? 2. *v.r.* refrain *or* abstain (from); *ich konnte mich des Lachens nicht -en*, I could not refrain from *or* help laughing. **-sam,** *adj.* abstemious; abstinent, sober; temperate; continent, chaste. **-samkeit,** *f.* abstemiousness, abstinence; temperance. **-ung,** *f.* abstinence, continence.
enthärten, *v.a.* anneal (*metals*), soften (*water*).
enthaupt-en, *v.a.* behead, decapitate. **-ung,** *f.* beheading, decapitation.
entheb-en, *ir.v.a.* (*einen einer S.*) remove, exonerate, relieve of, free *or* exempt from; *einen seines Amtes -en*, dismiss *or* suspend a p., remove a p. from office. **-ung,** *f.* exemption; dismissal.
entheilig-en, *v.a.* profane, desecrate. **-ung,** *f.* desecration, profanation.
enthüll-en, *v.a.* unveil, expose, uncover; reveal, disclose. **-ung,** *f.* unveiling, exposure; revelation, disclosure.
enthülsen, *v.a.* shell, husk (*peas, etc.*).
Enthusias-mus, *m.* enthusiasm. **-t,** *m.* (-ten, -ten) enthusiast. **-tisch,** *adj.* enthusiastic.
Entjudung, *f.* (*Nat. Soc.*) elimination of Jewish influence, purge of Jews.
entjungfern, *v.a.* ravish, rape, deflower (*a virgin*).
entkeimen, 1. *v.n.* (*aux.* s.) germinate, sprout; spring up. 2. *v.a.* free from germs, sterilize.
entkernen, *v.a.* stone, take out the stone *or* core (*from fruit*).
entkirchlichen, *v.a.* secularize.
entkleiden, *v.a. & r.* undress, strip, unclothe, (*fig.*) divest.
entkohlen, *v.a.* decarbonize.
entkommen, *ir.v.n.* (*aux.* s.) (*Dat.*) get away, escape (from).
entkoppeln, *v.a.* neutralize, decouple (*Rad.*).
entkorken, *v.a.* uncork.
entkräft-en, *v.a.* enfeeble, enervate, weaken, fatigue, exhaust, debilitate, invalidate, refute. **-et,** *p.p. & adj.* weakened, exhausted, effete, invalidated. **-ung,** *f.* weakening, debilitation, enervation, exhaustion; inanition (*Med.*); invalidation.
entkuppeln, *v.a.* uncouple, disconnect, disengage, declutch (*Motor*).
entlad-en, 1. *ir.v.a.* unload, unlade; free from, exonerate; relieve (*of a burden, etc.*); discharge (*electricity, etc.*). 2. *v.r.* explode, burst, go off. **-er,** *m.* discharger (*Phys.*). **-espannung,** *f.* (**-estrom,** *m.*), discharge voltage (current). **-ung,** *f.* unloading; discharge; eruption; explosion.
entlang, 1. *adv. & prep.* (*usually with* an *and following Dat.*; *often with preceding Acc.*) along; *an dem Flusse* – or *den Fluß* –, along the river. 2. *sep. prefix with verbs of motion*, e.g. *-gehen*, go along *or* alongside, *-streifen*, brush, graze.
entlarven, *v.a.* unmask.
entlass-en, *ir.v.a.* set free, dismiss, discharge, release; disband, prorogue, dissolve (*a meeting*); *mit Pension -en*, pension off. **-ung,** *f.* dismissal; discharge; release; *er bat um* or *nahm seine -ung, er ist um seine -ung eingekommen*, he has tendered *or* sent in his resignation. **-ungsantrag,** *m.* resignation, application for discharge. **-ungsschein,** *m.*, **-ungszeugnis,** *n.* certificate of discharge *or* of dismissal; discharge-papers (*Mil.*).
entlast-en, *v.a.* unburden; ease; exonerate; relieve of; discharge (*debt*); (*C.L.*) *einen für etwas -en*, credit a p. with. **-ung,** *f.* discharge (*of a debt*), credit (*to one's account*); relief, exoneration. **-ungsangriff,** *m.* diversionary attack (*Mil.*). **-ungsstraße,** *f.* by-pass (road). **-ungszeuge,** *m.* witness for the defence.
entlauben, *v.a.* strip of foliage, defoliate.
entlaufen, *ir.v.n.* (*aux.* s.) run away, escape (*Dat.*, from); desert.
entlaus-en, *v.a.* delouse. **-ung,** *f.* delousing. **-ungsanstalt,** *f.* delousing centre.
entledig-en, 1. *v.a.* exempt (*Gen.*, from). 2. *v.r.* acquit o.s. of, get rid of, rid o.s. of; *sich seines Versprechens -en*, keep one's word, fulfil one's undertaking; *sich eines Auftrags -en*, execute one's commission. **-ung,** *f.* discharge, performance; acquittance.
entleer-en, *v.a.* empty out, deplete. **-ung,** *f.* evacuation (*of bowels*) (*Med.*).
entlegen, *adj.* remote, distant. **-heit,** *f.* remoteness.
entlehn-en, *v.a.* (*einem etwas, etwas von einem*) borrow; derive (from). **-ung,** *f.* borrowing; loan; *uneingestandene -ung*, plagiarism.
entleiben, 1. *v.a.* kill. 2. *v.r.* commit suicide.
entleihen, *ir.v.a.* (*einem etwas*) borrow (s.th. from a p.).
entloben, *v.r.* (*coll.*) break off an engagement (to marry).
entlocken, *v.a.* (*Dat.*) draw from, elicit from, worm out of.
entlohnen, *v.a.* pay off, pay.
entlüft-en, *v.a.* air, ventilate. **-ung,** *f.* air vent. **-ungsventil,** *n.* air escape, outlet valve.
entmagnetisieren, *v.a.* demagnetize, degauss (*a magnetic mine*) (*Nav.*).
entmann-en, *v.a.* castrate; emasculate; (*fig.*) unnerve, unman. **-ung,** *f.* castration; emasculation.
entmenscht, *adj.* inhuman, barbarous, brutal, brutish.
entmilitarisieren, *v.a.* demilitarize.
entmündig-en, *v.a.* put under tutelage *or* in the care of trustees, interdict. **-ung,** *f.* interdiction.
entmutig-en, *v.a.* discourage, dishearten, daunt; demoralize; *einen durch Blicke -en*, stare a p. out of countenance. **-ung,** *f.* discouragement.
Entnahme, *f.* taking out; drawing (*of money*). **-punkt,** *m.* output terminals (*Rad.*).
entnehm-en, *ir.v.a.* take away *or* from, withdraw; understand from, infer, conclude, learn, gather; (*Geld*) *auf einen -en*, draw upon a p.; *aus einem Buche etwas -en*, quote from a book; *aus jemandes Worten etwas -en*, gather from what a p. has said. (*C.L.*) **-er,** *m.* drawer.
entnerven, *v.a.* enervate, unnerve.
entölen, *v.a.* free from oil, extract the oil.
Entomolog-(e), *m.* (-en, -en) entomologist. **-ie,** *f.* entomology. **-isch,** *adj.* entomological.
entpressen, *v.a.* press *or* squeeze out; *einem etwas* –, extort s.th. from a p.
entpuppen, *v.r.* burst from the cocoon; (*fig.*) reveal o.s. as; turn out to be.
entquellen, *ir.v.n.* (*aux.* s.) (*Dat.* or *aus*) flow forth, issue from.
entrahmen, *v.a.* take off the cream, skim.
entraten, *ir.v.a. & n.* (*aux.* h.) (*Gen.*) (*rare*) dispense with, do without.
enträtseln, *v.a.* solve, make out; decipher, unravel, explain.
entrecht-en, *v.a.* deprive of rights. **-ung,** *f.* deprivation of rights.
entreißen, *ir.v.a.* (*einem etwas*) snatch away, tear away; save *or* rescue from.
entricht-en, *v.a.* pay what is due. *eine Schuld -en*, pay off *or* discharge a debt, settle an account. **-ung,** *f.* payment, due discharge (*of debts, etc.*).
entringen, 1. *ir.v.a.* wrest from, wrench away. 2. *v.r.* break forth (from); *ein Seufzer entrang sich ihrer Brust*, a sigh escaped her, she heaved a sigh.
entrinnen, *ir.v.n.* (*aux.* s.) (*Dat.*) run away, escape from; fly past (*of time*).
entrollen, 1. *v.a.* unfurl, unroll. 2. *v.r.* become unrolled, unroll; (*fig.*) unfold itself.
entrücken, *v.a.* move away, carry off, remove; (*fig.*) enrapture, entrance, carry away; *sich* (*Dat.*) *selbst entrückt sein*, be beside o.s.
entrümpel-n, *v.a.* clear out (for salvage). **-ung,** *f.* 1. removal of lumber from attics; 2. collection of salvage.
entrüst-en, 1. *v.a.* provoke, irritate, make angry,

enrage. 2. *v.r.* become angry *or* indignant; fly into a passion. **–ung,** *f.* indignation, anger, wrath.
entsag–en, *v.r.* & *n.* (*aux.* h.) (*Dat.*) renounce, relinquish; disclaim, waive, abandon; *dem Thron –en,* abdicate. **–ung,** *f.* renunciation, abjuration, resignation; *bei seiner Thron–ung,* on his abdicating the throne.
Entsatz, *m.* relief, succour, rescue; relieving force (*Mil.*).
entschädig–en, *v.a.* indemnify, compensate. **–ung,** *f.* indemnity, compensation, damages, amends. **–ungsforderung,** *f.* claim for damages.
Entschärfungskommando, *n.* bomb-disposal squad.
entschäumen, *v.a.* scum, skim, take off the froth.
Entscheid, *m.* (-(e)s, -e) decision. **–bar,** *adj.* determinable. **–en,** 1. *ir.v.a.* decide, determine, decree, resolve; pass sentence, give judgement; *das entschied,* that clinched matters. 2. *v.r.* make up one's mind, decide; *er entschied sich für mich,* he decided in my favour. **–end,** *pr.p.* & *adj.* decisive; critical, crucial; definite, final. **–ung,** *f.* decision, sentence, judgement; crisis. **–ungsgrund,** *m.* decisive factor. **–ungslos,** *adj.* indecisive. **–ungspunkt,** *m.* crisis, critical point. **–ungsrunde,** *f.* final round (*tournament*). **–ungsschlacht,** *f.* decisive battle. **–ungsspiel,** *n.* deciding game (*Sport*). **–ungsstimme,** *f.* casting vote. **–ungsvoll,** *adj.* decisive; critical; crucial. **–ungszustand,** *m.* critical situation.
entschied, *see* **entscheiden. –en,** 1. *p.p.* & *adj.* decided, determined, resolute, firm, dogmatic, peremptory. 2. *adv.* definitely, decidedly, certainly, **–enheit,** *f.* firmness, energy, determination, decisiveness; *mit –enheit,* decidedly, certainly, categorically.
entschlafen, *ir.v.n.* (*aux.* s.) fall asleep; die, pass away; *der (die) Entschlafene,* the deceased; *er ist sanft –,* he has passed away peacefully.
entschlagen, *ir.v.r.* (*Gen.*) get rid of, give up, part with, divest o.s. of, dismiss from one's mind; decline; *sich der Sorgen –,* banish cares; *sich eines Wunsches –,* renounce a wish.
entschleichen, *ir.v.n.* (*aux.* s.) (*Dat.*) slip off, sneak away; escape.
entschleiern, *v.a.* & *r.* unveil; (*fig.*) reveal.
entschlichten, *v.a.* remove the size, undress (*linen, etc.*).
entschließ–en, *ir.v.r.* make up one's mind, determine (*zu,* upon), decide (*für,* on *or* in favour of) resolve (on). **–ung,** *f.* resolution; fixed purpose.
entschlossen, *p.p.* & *adj.* resolved, resolute; determined, decided, firm. **–heit,** *f.* decision, determination, resolution; fixity of purpose.
entschlummern, *v.n.* (*aux.* s.) fall asleep (*Poet.*), pass away, die.
entschlüpfen, *v.n.* (*aux.* s.) slip away, escape; *eine Gelegenheit – lassen,* let an opportunity slip; *dem Gedächtnis –,* escape one's memory; *das Wort entschlüpfte mir,* the word slipped out.
Entschluß, *m.* (-(ss)es, ¨-(ss)e) resolve, decision, resolution; *einen – fassen,* form a resolution, resolve; *zu einem – kommen,* make up one's mind. **–fassung,** *f.* decision.
entschlüsseln, *v.a.* decode.
entschuld–en, *v.a.* free from encumbrance *or* debts. **–bar,** *adj.* excusable. **–igen,** 1. *v.a.* excuse, exculpate; justify, defend. 2. *v.r.* apologize (*bei,* to; *wegen,* for); *es läßt sich nicht –igen,* it admits of no excuse; *ich bitte mich zu –igen,* please, excuse me; I would rather be excused; *ich muß mich bei ihm –igen, daß ich, etc.,* I must apologize to him for, etc.; *sie läßt sich wegen Unpäßlichkeit –igen,* she begs to be excused on account of indisposition; *–igen Sie,* I beg your pardon; *zu –igen,* excusable. **–igung,** *f.* excuse, apology; *ich bitte (Sie) um –igung,* I beg (your) pardon. **–igungsgrund,** *m.* plea. **–igungsschreiben,** *n.* written apology. **–ung,** *f.* writing off of debt.
entschwinden, *ir.v.n.* (*aux.* s.) (*Dat.*) disappear, vanish.
entseelt, *p.p.* & *adj.* dead, lifeless.
entsenden, *ir.v.a.* send off, dispatch; let fly, hurl.
entsetz–en, 1. *v.a.* displace; (*einen einer Stelle*) dismiss (*a p. from office*); suspend; cashier (*an officer*); depose (*a king, etc.*); relieve (*a garrison, etc.*); frighten, terrify. 2. *v.r.* be horrified, amazed, shocked *or* startled (*vor* or *über,* by). 3. *n.* terror, dread, fright, horror. **–bar,** *adj.* removable (*from office*); relievable (*of a fortress*). **–lich,** *adj.* terrible, dreadful, frightful, horrible, awful, atrocious, shocking. **–lichkeit,** *f.* frightfulness, dreadfulness, heinousness; atrocity. **–ung,** *f.* dismissal; suspension; deposition; relief (*of a garrison*).
entseuchen, *v.a.* disinfect, sterilize.
entsichern, *v.a.* remove *or* release the safety catch of; arm (*a bomb*).
entsinnen, *ir.v.r.* (*sich einer Sache*) recollect, recall, remember (s.th.); *wenn ich mich recht entsinne,* if I remember rightly, if my memory does not fail me *or* serves me right.
entspann–en, 1. *v.a.* relax, relieve (*tension*); uncock (*a pistol*). 2. *v.r.* relax. **–ung,** *f.* relaxation, recreation, rest; easing (*of tension*) (*also fig. of strained relations*).
entspinnen, *ir.v.r.* arise, begin; ensue, develop; *es entspann sich ein Streit (ein Gefecht),* a quarrel arose (a skirmish began).
entsprech–en, *ir.v.n.* (*aux.* s.) (*Dat.*) answer, suit, match; accord with, conform to, comply with, meet (*a demand*); be adequate to; be in accordance with, correspond to (*expectations*); *es entsprach meinen Erwartungen nicht,* it fell short of *or* did not come up to my expectations; *dem Wunsche –en,* comply with the request *or* wish. **–end,** *pr.p.* & *adj.* appropriate, suitable; corresponding, adequate, matching; *dem–end,* accordingly.
entspringen, *ir.v.n.* (*aux.* s.) escape; spring up, rise (*of rivers, etc.*), arise, originate in.
entstammen, *v.n.* (*aux.* s.) (*Dat.*) originate, descend, be descended (from).
entstänkern, *v.a.* deodorize.
entstaub–en, *v.a.* remove dust, dust. **–ung,** *f.* dusting.
entsteh–en, 1. *ir.v.n.* (*aux.* s.) begin, originate (*aus,* in); arise (*aus,* from); be formed, produced *or* generated; grow out of; result (from); break out (*as fire*); *was ist daraus entstanden?* what has come of it? what has been the upshot (of it)? *entstehe was da wolle,* come what may; *eben –end,* incipient, nascent. 2. *n.,* **–ung,** *f.* beginning, rise, origin, genesis; generation, formation. **–ungsart,** *f.,* **–ungsweise,** *f.* nature *or* mode of origin. **–ungsgeschichte,** *f.* history of the origin and rise (of). **–ungszustand,** *m.* nascent, incomplete *or* embryonic state.
entsteigen, *ir.v.n.* (*aux.* s.) (*Dat.*) spring from, arise from *or* out of, emerge, descend from.
entstell–en, *v.a.* deform, disfigure, deface, mutilate, mar; distort (*a meaning, etc.*); garble (*an account*); misrepresent (*facts*). **–t,** *p.p.* & *adj.* disfigured, deformed, distorted. **–ung,** *f.* distortion, misrepresentation; disfigurement.
entstör–en, *v.a.* eliminate interference (*Rad.*). **–kondensator,** *m.* trimming condenser (*Rad.*). **–ung,** *f.* interference elimination (*Rad.*).
entströmen, *v.n.* (*aux.* s.) (*Dat.*) flow, stream *or* gush from, escape (from).
entsühnen, *v.a.* absolve.
enttäusch–en, *v.a.* disappoint, undeceive, disabuse; disillusion. **–t,** *p.p.* & *adj.* disappointed (*von,* in). **–ung,** *f.* disappointment; disillusion.
entthron–en, *v.a.* dethrone.
entvölker–n, *v.a.* depopulate. **–t,** *p.p.* & *adj.* depopulated.
entwachsen, *ir.v.a.* (*aux.* s.) (*Dat.*) outgrow, grow from.
entwaffn–en, *v.a.* disarm. **–ung,** *f.* disarmament.
entwald–en, *v.a.* clear of forests, deforest.
Entwarnung, *f.* 'all-clear' signal (*air-raids*).
entwässer–n, *v.a.* drain; distil, concentrate, rectify; (*Chem.*) dehydrate, desiccate. **–ung,** *f.* draining, drainage; dehydration. **–ungsgraben,** *m.* drain, ditch.
entweder, *conj.* either; *das Entweder — Oder,* alternative.
entwehrt, *adj.* rendered defenceless, disarmed.
entweich–en, *ir.v.n.* (*aux.* s.) leak, escape (*as gas,*

etc.); abscond; evade (*pursuit, etc.*); vanish, disappear. **-ung,** *f.* escape, leakage; elopement; absconding; disappearance. **-ungsventil,** *n.* escape valve.
entweih-en, *v.a.* profane, desecrate, violate. **-ung,** *f.* profanation; defilement; desecration; sacrilege.
Entwelschung, *f.* purification of (German) language from Gallicisms.
entwend-en, *reg. & ir. v.a.* steal, purloin, pilfer; (*sl.*) swipe. **-ung,** *f.* theft, embezzlement.
entwerfen, *ir.v.a.* sketch, trace out; draft; project; draw up (*a document*); frame (*a bill*), outline; plan, design; lay out (*grounds*); *Pläne –*, make plans.
entwert-en, *v.a.* depreciate; debase (*in value*); cancel (*stamps*). **-ung,** *f.* depreciation; cancellation (*of stamps*).
entwick-eln, 1. *v.a.* unroll, unfold, untwist; unwrap; evolve, develop; deploy (*Mil.*); solve; explain; display, give proof of (*ability*); liberate; disengage (*Chem.*). 2. *v.r.* expand; evolve, develop; *es wird sich -eln*, it will be cleared up; *es -elt sich gut*, things (will) turn out well. **-ler,** *m.* developer. **-lung,** *f.* development; evolution; unfolding (*of a plot*); dénouement (*Theat.*); formation (*Phys.*), deployment (*Mil.*). **-lungsablauf,** *m.* course of development. **-lungsapparat,** *m.* developing tank (*Phot.*). **-lungsfähig,** *adj.* capable of development, viable. **-lungshöhe,** *f.* degree of differentiation. **lungsjahre,** *n.pl.* adolescence, puberty. **-lungslehre,** *f.* doctrine of evolution, theory of development, embryology. **-lungsmöglichkeit,** *f.* developmental possibility. **-lungsperiode,** *f.* period of development; (age of) puberty. **-lungsstufe,** *f.* stage of development, phase. **-lungsverlauf,** *m.*, *see* **-lungsablauf.**
entwinden, 1. *ir.v.a.* (*einem etwas*) wrest from; extort. 2. *v.r.* (*Dat.*) extricate o.s. (from); burst away (from).
entwirren, *v.a.* disentangle, unravel; extricate (*from confusion*).
entwischen, *v.n.* (*aux.* s.) (*Dat.*) slip away from, give the slip to, steal away, escape.
entwöhn-en, (*einen einer S., einen von einer S.*) disaccustom, break of (*a habit*); wean (*an infant*). **-ung,** *f.* weaning; disuse.
entwürdig-en, *v.a.* degrade, disgrace, dishonour; profane. **-ung,** *f.* degradation.
Entwurf, *m.* (-(e)s, ⸗e) sketch, outline, draft, rough copy; design, model, project, plan, scheme; *erster –*, first sketch, rough draft; *einen – machen*, make *or* draw up a plan; *einen Gesetz– einbringen* introduce a bill (*in parliament*). **-macher,** *m.* schemer, speculator.
entwurzel-n, *v.a.* root out, uproot, eradicate. **-ung,** *f.* rooting out, uprooting, eradication.
entzerr-en, *v.a.* rectify, equalize. **-er,** *m.* rectifier. **-ung,** *f.* rectification. **-ungsgerät,** *n.* rectifier.
entzieh-en, 1. *ir.v.a.* (*einem etwas*) take away, remove, deprive of, withdraw (from); extract, eliminate. 2. *v.r.* avoid; evade, shun, withdraw from, forsake; *sich der Gerechtigkeit -en*, flee from justice; *sich dem Gehorsam -en*, throw off obedience; *sich seiner Schuldigkeit -en*, evade one's duty. **-ung,** *f.* withdrawal; removal; deprivation; extraction (*Chem.*); *-ung des Gebrauches des Vermögens*, sequestration of property. **-ungskur,** *f.* treatment for drug addicts (*Med.*).
entziffer-n, *v.a.* decipher, decode. **-bar,** *adj.* decipherable, explicable. **-ung,** *f.* deciphering, decoding.
entzück-en, 1. *v.a.* charm, delight, enchant, overjoy. 2. *n.*, **-ung,** *f.* delight, rapture, transport; *zum -en*, ravishing, charming. **-end,** *pr.p. & adj.* delightful, charming. **-t,** *p.p. & adj.* charmed, delighted, enraptured, overjoyed.
entzünd-en, 1. *v.a.* kindle, set fire to, ignite, light; inflame (*Med.*). 2. *v.r.* catch fire, flare up, become inflamed; break out (*as war*). **-bar,** *adj.* inflammable, combustible. **-barkeit,** *f.* inflammability. **-et,** *p.p. & adj.* inflamed. **-lich,** *adj.* inflammatory. **-ung,** *f.* ignition; inflammation. **-ungsherd,** *m.* centre *or* focus of inflammation. **-ungsprobe,** *f.* ignition test. **-ungspunkt,** *m.* flash-point.
entzwei, *adv. & sep. prefix.* in two; asunder apart; torn, broken. **-brechen,** *ir.v.a. & n.* (*aux.* s.) break in two. **-en,** 1. *v.a.* disunite, separate; estrange, alienate, set at variance; *sie sucht die beiden Menschen zu -en*, she is trying to make mischief between the two people. 2. *v.r.* quarrel, fall out. **-gehen,** *ir.v.n.* (*aux.* s.) break. **-schlagen,** *v.a.* smash in two *or* to pieces. **-sein,** *ir.v.n.* be torn *or* broken. **-springen,** *v.a.* crack, split, burst *or* break in two. **-t,** *p.p. & adj.* estranged, divided, at variance, hostile; *sie hatten sich -t*, they had fallen out. **-ung,** *f.* dissension; estrangement, quarrel, hostility.
Enzian, *m.* (-s, -e) gentian (*Bot.*).
Enzykl-ika, *f.* (-iken) encyclic(al). **-opädie,** *f.* encyclopedia. **-opädisch,** *adj.* encyclopedic.
Ephemer-ide, *f.* (-iden) ephemera, mayfly; one-day fever; ephemeris, star calendar, almanack; pamphlet, daily chronicle. **-isch,** *adj.* ephemeral; perishable; short-lived.
Epheu, *see* **Efeu.**
Epidem-ie, *f.* (-ien) epidemic. **-isch,** *adj.* epidemic.
Epigone, *m.* (-n) descendant *or* follower (*of great men*). **-nhaft,** *adj.* decadent. **-ntum,** *n.* decadence in literature *or* art.
Epigramm, *n.* (-s, -e) epigram. **-atisch,** *adj.* epigrammatic, terse, pithy.
Ep-ik, *f.* epic poetry. **-iker,** *m.* epic poet. **-isch,** *adj.* epic. **-os,** *n.* epic poem.
Epi-lepsie, *f.* epilepsy. **-leptiker,** *m.* epileptic. **-leptisch,** *adj.* epileptic. **-log,** *m.* epilogue. **-sode,** *f.* episode. **-sodisch,** *adj.* episodic(al). **-stel,** *f.* (-n), epistle.
Epoch-e, *f.* (-en) epoch; era; *sein Werk machte -e*, his work was epoch-making. **-al,** *adj.* epoch-making.
Eppich, *m.* (-(e)s, -e) celery (*Apium graveolens*) (*Bot.*); (*coll.*) ivy.
Eprouvette, *f.* (*Austrian dial.*) test-tube.
Equip-age, *f.* (-en) carriage, coach, equipage; equipment; suit *or* set of things; crew (*of a ship*). **-ieren,** *v.a.* fit out, equip; man (*a ship*).
[1]**er,** 1. *m. pers. pron.* it, he; *– ist es*, it is he; *– selbst*, he himself. 2. *obs. form of address to inferiors*; *wie heißt –?* what is your name?
[2]**er-** *compounded with verbs is insep. and unaccented; the p.p. loses the* ge-. *It indicates in the main*: (1) *beginning of the action, e.g.* erbleichen, (2) *achievement of the aim set by the action, e.g.* erarbeiten, ermorden.
erachten, 1. *v.a.* think, consider, be of opinion, (*Poet.*) deem, opine. 2. *n.* opinion, judgement; *meinem – nach*; *meines -s* (abbr. *m. E.*) in my opinion.
erarbeiten, *v.a. & r.* gain *or* get by working, earn, achieve by work.
erbarm-en, 1. *v.a.* move to pity; *daß Gott -e!* God help us!; (*archaic*) *imp.* (*with Acc. & Gen.*) *mich -et des Armen*, I pity the poor man. 2. *v.r.* (*with Gen. or* über *with Acc.*), pity, feel pity, have *or* show mercy; *Herr, -e dich unser*, Lord have mercy upon us! 3. *n.* pity, compassion, mercy; *zum -en*, pitiful, wretched; *er sieht zum -en aus*, he looks most wretched. **-end,** *pr.p. & adj.* compassionate. **-er,** *m.* merciful God, God of Mercy. **-ung,** *f.* pity. **-enswert, -enswürdig, -ungswert, -ungswürdig,** *adj.* pitiable. **-ungslos,** *adj.* pitiless, merciless, remorseless. **-ungsvoll** *adj.* full of pity, compassionate.
erbärmlich, *adj.* pitiful, pitiable, miserable, wretched; paltry, contemptible. **-keit,** *f.* misery, wretchedness, pitiableness; lowness, meanness.
erbau-en, 1. *v.a.* build up, raise, erect, construct; edify. 2. *v.r.*; *sich -en an* (*Dat.*), find edification in, be edified by; (*Prov.*) *Rom ist nicht in einem Tage -t worden*, Rome was not built in one day. **-er,** *m.* builder; founder. **-lich,** *adj.* edifying, improving; devotional; *das ist ja recht -lich*, (*ironic*) that's a fine state of affairs. **-ung,** *f.* erection, building, construction; edification. **-ungsschrift,** *f.* devotional book, religious tract. **-ungsstunde,** *f.* hour of devotion.
Erb-e, 1. *m.* (-en, -en) heir; successor; *mutmaßlicher -e*, heir presumptive; *ohne leibliche -en*, without issue. 2. *n.* (-es, -schaften *or* -güter) heritage,

inheritance. (*Nat. Soc. usage combined the biological concept of inheritance with the legal one of heritage. Pride of race and pride in landed property blended and supported each other. In compounds it is nowadays often difficult to isolate and identify the connotation.* **-adel,** *m.* hereditary nobility. **-adlig,** *adj.* noble by birth. **-anlage,** *f.* hereditary factor. **-anspruch,** *m.* claim to an inheritance. **-bar,** *adj* inheritable. **-bedingt,** *adj.* shaped by heritage. **-begräbnis,** *n.* family vault. **-berechtigt,** *adj.* with hereditary title to. **-besitz,** *m.* hereditary possession. **-bild,** *n.* inherited type. **-eid,** *m.* vassal's oath of fealty. **-eigenschaft,** *f.* inherited quality. **-einheit,** *f.* gene (*Biol.*). **-einsetzung,** *f., see* **-ernennung.** **-en,** 1. *v.a.* inherit; *von seinem Vater -en,* succeed to one's father's property. 2. *v.n.* (*aux.* s.); *-en auf,* descend to, devolve on; **-ernennung,** *f.* appointment of an heir. **-erfahrungen,** *f.pl.* genetical data. **-fall,** *m.* heritage, succession; fortune in reversion. **-fällig,** *adj.* hereditary, entailed. **-fälligkeit,** *f.* entail; *die -fälligkeit aufheben,* cut off the entail. **-fehler,** *m.* inherited *or* congenital defect; family failing. **-feind,** *m.* hereditary foe, (*fig.*) sworn enemy, old enemy. **-folge,** *f.* succession (by inheritance); *die -folge bestimmen,* entail. **-folgekrieg,** *m.* war of succession. **-frau,** *f.* lady of the manor. **-genoß,** *m.* joint-heir. **-gerichtsherr,** *m.* lord of the manor. **-gesessen,** *adj.* possessed of real property. **-gesund,** *adj.* of healthy stock. **-grund,** *m.* landed property. **-gut,** *n.* ancestral estate; heirloom. **-herr,** *m.* lord of the manor. **-herrin,** *f., see* **-frau.** **-herrlich,** *adj.* manorial. **-hof,** *m.* entailed estate. **-huldigung,** *f.* (oath of) fealty. **-in,** *f.* heiress. **-krank,** *adj.* congenitally diseased. **-land,** *n.* hereditary land; *die kaiserlichen -lande,* the emperor's patrimonial dominions. **-lasser,** *m.* testator. **-lehen,** *n.* hereditary fief. **-lehre,** *f.* (*Nat. Soc.*) racial biology, theory of race. **-lich,** *adj.* hereditary, inheritable; *-lich besitzen,* possess by inheritance; *-lich belastet,* congenitally tainted *or* afflicted; *-liche Belastung,* congenital taint. **-lichkeit,** *f.* heritability, hereditariness; heredity (*Biol.*). **-los,** *adj.* disinherited, without inheritance; without an heir. **-masse,** *f.* all hereditary factors (*Biol.*); the undivided estate (*Law.*). **-onkel,** *m.* (*hum.*) rich uncle. **-pacht,** *f.* fee-farm, copyhold. **-pächter,** *m.* hereditary tenant, copyholder. **-pflege,** *f.* racial improvement. **-pflicht,** *f.* hereditary duty, homage. **-prinz,** *m.* heir to a reigning prince. **-recht,** *n.* right of succession. **-sasse,** *m.* lord of the manor. **-schaft,** *f.* inheritance, legacy. **-schaftsmasse,** *f.* estate (*Law*). **-schaftsrichter,** *m.* judge of probate court. **-schaftssteuer,** *f.* death duty, legacy duty, probate duty. **-schaftsverfüger,** *m.* testator. **-schaftsverfügerin,** *f.* testatrix. **-schaftsverfügung,** *f.* disposition of property by testament. **-schleicher,** *m.* legacy-hunter. **-schuld,** *f.* charge (*on an estate*), encumbrance. **-setzer,** *m.* testator. **-steuer,** *f.* death duty. **-stück,** *n.* heirloom; germ plasm (*Biol.*). **-sünde,** *f.* original sin. **-teil,** *n.* portion, inheritance. **-tochter,** *f.* (rich) heiress. **-träger,** *m.* bearer of a heritage. **-untertan,** *m.* bondman, serf. **-untertänigkeit,** *f.* serfdom. **-vermögen,** *n.* patrimony. **-zins,** *m.* fee-farm rent, ground-rent; **-zinsmann,** *m.* leaseholder.

erbeben, *v.n.* (*aux.* h. & s.) tremble, shudder (*vor,* at), shake, quiver, quake, vibrate.

erbeten, *v.a.* obtain by prayer; solicit, request.

erbetteln, *v.a.* obtain by begging.

erbeuten, *v.a.* gain *or* take as booty, capture.

erbiet-en, 1. *ir.v.r.* offer; volunteer. 2. *n.* offer. **-ung,** *f.* offer, proffer.

erbitt-en, *ir.v.a.* beg for, request, ask for; prevail upon; *er läßt sich -en,* he is moved by entreaties; *er läßt sich nicht -en,* he is inexorable.

erbitter-n, *v.a.* embitter, provoke, incense, exasperate. **-ung,** *f.* exasperation, animosity. **-t,** *adj.* embittered, bitter, incensed.

erblasen, *v.a.* treat *or* produce in a blast furnace.

erblass-en, *v.n.* (*aux.* s.) grow *or* turn pale, fade; (*Poet.*) die. **-ung,** *f.* pallor.

erbleichen, *ir.v.n., see* **erblassen.**

erblich, *adj.* 1. *see* **Erb-.** 2. *see* **erbleichen.**

erblicken, *v.a.* catch sight of; perceive, see, behold, discover; *das Licht der Welt -,* come into the world; be born.

erblinden, *v.n.* (*aux.* s.) grow blind, lose one's sight.

erbluten, *v.a.* pay for with one's blood.

erbohren, *v.a.* obtain by boring; *Öl -,* strike oil.

erbos-en, 1. *v.a.* make angry, provoke. 2. *v.r.* get angry *or* vexed. **-t,** *p.p.* & *adj.* vexed, angry.

erbötig, *adj.* ready, willing.

erbrechen, 1. *ir.v.a.* break open; break. 2. *v.r.* vomit, be sick. 3. *n.* breaking open, forcing; opening (*a letter, etc.*); vomiting. **-befördernd,** *adj.,* **-erregend,** *adj.* emetic. **-stillend,** *adj.* anti-emetic, antemetic.

erbringen, *ir.v.a.* bring forth, produce, furnish.

Erbse, *f.* (-n) pea; *-n für Bohnen,* tit for tat. **-nbrei,** *m.* pease-pudding. **-ngroß,** *adj.* the size of a pea. **-nprinzessin,** *f.* (*fig.*) delicate, dainty, particular *or* fussy girl (*with reference to the fairy-tale*). **-nschote,** *f.* pea-pod. **-nsuppe,** *f.* pea-soup.

Erchtag, *m.* (*dial.*) Tuesday.

Erd-e, *f.* (*old Gen. & Dat. sing.* -en, *now* -e; -en) earth, ground, soil; the earth, the world; *auf -en,* on earth, alive, in this world; *ihn deckt die kühle -e,* (*coll.*) he's pushing up daisies; *zu ebener -e,* on the ground floor; *über die ganze -e,* all the world over; *gebrannte -e,* terra-cotta; *gelbe -e,* yellow ochre; *der -e gleich machen,* level to the ground; *die -e kauen,* bite the dust; *einen unter die -e bringen,* bring about a p.'s death; *wieder zur -e werden,* return to dust; *auf die -e werfen,* throw upon the ground. **-ableitung,** *f.* earth *or* (*Amer.*) ground connexion (*Rad.*). **-abwehr,** *f.* anti-aircraft defence. **-achse,** *f.* axis of the earth. **-anschluß,** *m.* earth, (*Amer.*) ground (*Rad.*). **-apfel,** *m.* potato. **-arbeiter,** *m.* navvy. **-art,** *f.* kind of earth *or* soil. **-artig,** *adj.* earthy. **-aufklärung,** *f.* ground reconnaissance (*Mil.*) **-bagger,** *m.* bulldozer. **-bahn,** *f.* orbit (*of the earth*). **-ball,** *m.* terrestrial globe, world. **-bau,** *m.* earthwork, embankment; underground work, crypt, cave, vault. **-bearbeitung,** *f.* cultivation of the soil. **-beben,** *n.* earthquake. **-bebenforschung,** *f.,* **-bebenkunde,** *f.* seismology. **-bebenmesser,** *m.* seismometer. **-beere,** *f.* strawberry. **-beschleunigung,** *f.* acceleration due to gravity. **-beschreibung,** *f.* geography. **-boden,** *m.* earth, ground, soil; *dem -boden gleich machen,* raze to the ground. **-bruch,** *m.* subsidence of the ground. **-bürger,** *m.* inhabitant of the earth, mortal. **-durchmesser,** *m.* diameter of the earth. **-eichel,** *f.* peanut, earthnut (*Arachis hypogaea*) (*Bot.*). **-en,** *v.a.* earth, (*Amer.*) ground (*Rad.*). **-enbahn,** *f.* life's course, the ups and down of life. **-(en)bewohner,** *m.,* **-enbürger,** *m.* human being; mortal. **-enfreude,** *f.* earthly joy; worldly pleasure, transitory happiness. **-enge,** *f.* isthmus. **-engeschöpf,** *n.* mortal, human being. **-enkind,** *n.,* **-ensohn,** *m.* mortal. **-enkloß,** *m.* clod of earth; *Got schuf den Menschen aus einem -enkloß,* God formed man of clay. **-enleben,** *n.* mortal life. **-enruhm,** *m.* earthly glory. **-enrund,** *n.* the earth. **-enschoß,** *m.* the interior of the earth. **-enwallen,** *n.* (*Poet.*) earthly pilgrimage. **-enwärts,** *adv.* earthwards. **-enwurm,** *m.* earthworm. **-er,** *m.* earth, (*Amer.*) ground (*Rad.*). **-erschütterung,** *f.* earthquake, earth-tremor. **-fall,** *m.* subsidence, landslide. **-ferne,** *f.* apogee (*Astr.*). **-feuer,** *n.* subterranean fire. **-fläche,** *f.* surface of the earth. **-forscher,** *m.* geologist. **-forschung,** *f.* geology. **-gang,** *m.* vein, lode (*Min.*); tunnel. **-geboren,** *adj.* earth-born, mortal. **-gebunden,** *adj.* grounded (*Av.*). **-gelb,** *n.* yellow ochre. **-geschichte,** *f.* geology. **-geschoß,** *n.* ground floor. **-gürtel,** *m.* zone. **-halbmesser,** *m.* radius of the earth. **-harz,** *n.* bitumen, asphalt; *gelbes -harz,* amber. **-haue,** *f.* pickaxe. **-höhle,** *f.* cavern. **-ig,** *adj.* earthy, terrestrial. **-innere,** *n.* interior of the earth. **-kalk,** *m.* limestone marl. **-kampf,** *m.* land operations (*Mil.*). **-karte,** *f.* map of the world. **-klemme,** *f.* earth *or* (*Amer.*)

ground terminal (*Rad.*). **-kloß,** *m.*, *see* **-enkloß.** **-klumpen,** *m.*, *see* **-kloß.** **-kohle,** *f.* lignite, brown coal, peat. **-körper,** *m.* terrestrial body. **-kreis,** *m.* globe; orb. **-kreislinie,** *f.* horizon. **-krume,** *f.* mould, surface soil. **-kruste,** *f.* earth's crust. **-kugel,** *f.* terrestrial globe. **-kunde,** *f.* geography. **-kundlich,** *adj.* geographical. **-lehre,** *f.* geology. **-leitung,** *f.* earth circuit (*Tele.*); earth wire (*Rad.*), earth connexion, (*Amer.*) ground circuit *or* wire. **-loch,** *n.* dug-out, fox-hole (*Mil.*). **-magnetismus,** *m.* terrestrial magnetism. **-männchen,** *n.* gnome, dwarf. **-maus,** *f.* field-mouse. **-meßkunst,** *f.*, **-messung,** *f.* geodesy. **-mine,** *f.* land mine (*Mil.*). **-mischung,** *f.* soil mixture. **-morchel,** *f.* truffle. **-möve,** *f.* puffin. **-nähe,** *f.* perigee (*Astr.*). **-naturbeschreibung,** *f.* physical geography. **-nuß,** *see* **-eichel.** **-oberfläche,** *f.* surface of the earth. **-öl,** *n.* petroleum, mineral oil, rock oil. **-pech,** *n.* bitumen, asphalt. **-pol,** *m.* pole (*of the earth*). **-reich,** *n.* earth, soil, ground; Earthly Kingdom (*B.*). **-rinde,** *f.* earth's crust. **-riß,** *m.* fissure, cleft in the ground. **-rücken,** *m.* ridge of hills, elevation of land. **-rund,** *n.* (*Poet.*) the earth. **-rutsch,** *m.* landslide. **-sack,** *m.* sandbag (*Mil.*). **-scheibe,** *f.* sphere, the world. **-schicht,** *f.* layer of earth, stratum; *untere -schicht*, subsoil. **-schierling,** *m.* hemlock (*Conium maculatum*) (*Bot.*). **-schluß,** *m.* (accidental) earth (*or Amer.* ground) connexion, short (circuit) to earth *or* ground (*Elec.*). **-schnecke,** *f.* slug. **-scholle,** *f.* clod, glebe. **-schwamm,** *m.* mushroom. **-schwankung,** *f.* earth-tremor. **-spalte,** *f.* crevasse. **-stoß,** *m.* shock (of an earthquake). **-strauch,** *m.* undergrowth. **-strich,** *m.* zone, region; *der heiße, gemäßigte, kalte -strich*, the torrid, temperate, frigid zone. **-stufe,** *f.* terrace; brow of a hill. **-sturz,** *m.* landslide. **-teil,** *m.* continent. **-truppen,** *f.pl.* ground troops, land forces (*Mil.*). **-umschiffung,** *f.*, **-umsegelung,** *f.* circumnavigation of the earth. **-ung,** *f.* earthing (*or Amer.* grounding) terminal (*Rad.*); grounding (*Av.*). **-verbundenheit,** *f.* attachment to *or* contact with soil (*Nat. Soc.*). **-wärts,** *adv.* earthwards. **-weite,** *f.* mean distance of the earth from the sun. **-werk,** *n.* earthwork, rampart. **-zirkel,** *m.* circle on the terrestrial globe. **-zunge,** *f.* isthmus; promontory, cape, headland.

erdacht, *see* **erdenken.**

erdenk-en, *ir.v.a.* think out, devise, invent, excogitate, conceive, imagine. **-bar,** *adj.*, **-lich,** *adj.* imaginable, conceivable; *sich alle -liche Mühe geben*, try one's utmost. **-ung,** *f.* invention, fabrication.

erdicht-en, *v.a.* invent, devise; imagine. **-et,** *p.p.* & *adj.* feigned; fictitious. **-ung,** *f.* fabrication; fiction; feigning. **-ungsgabe,** *f.* inventiveness, imaginativeness.

erdolchen, *v.a.* stab.

erdreisten, *v.r.* dare, venture, presume; *darf ich mich -?* may I be so bold? *sie erdreistete sich, mir zu sagen, etc.*, she had the audacity *or* (*coll.*) cheek to tell me.

erdrossel-n, 1. *v.a.* throttle, strangle. 2. *n.*, **-ung,** *f.* strangulation.

erdrücken, *v.a.* crush *or* squeeze to death; stifle; smother; (*fig.*); crush, overwhelm.

erduld-en, *v.a.* endure, suffer; put up with. **-ung,** *f.* endurance; submission (*to*); toleration (*of*).

ereifern, *v.r.* get excited, be overzealous; lose one's temper.

ereig-nen, *v.r. imp.* occur, happen, come to pass; *es -nete sich, daß wir*, we happened to. **-nis,** *n.* event, occurrence, incident; *auf alle -nisse gefaßt*, prepared for whatever may (*or* might) happen *or* for all eventualities; *sie sieht einem freudigen -nis entgegen*, she is expecting a happy event. **-nislos,** *adj.* uneventful. **-nisreich,** *adj.* eventful.

ereilen, *v.a.* overtake, catch up.

Eremit, *m.* (-en, -en) hermit. **-age,** *f.* hermitage.

ererben, *v.a.* inherit. *ererbte Krankheit*, hereditary disease.

erfahr-en, 1. *ir.v.a.* come to know, learn, hear, be told, discover; experience, suffer, undergo. 2. *p.p.* & *adj.* experienced, seasoned, practised; *-ener Soldat*, seasoned campaigner; *-ener Arbeiter*, skilled workman. **-enheit,** *f.* experience, practice, skill. **-ung,** *f.* (practical) experience, practical knowledge; *auf -ung gegründet, aus -ung entsprungen* or *geschöpft*, experimental, based on empirical data; *in -ung bringen*, learn, ascertain; *aus -ung*, by *or* from experience. **-ungsbeweis,** *m.* practical proof. **-ungsgemäß,** *adv.*, *see* **-ungsmäßig.** **-ungskreis,** *m.* range of experience. **-ungslos,** *adj.* inexperienced. **-ungsmäßig,** *adj.* empirical, from experience. **-ungsreich,** *adj.* experienced. **-ungssatz,** *m.* empirical principle *or* theorem.

erfass-en, *v.a.* lay hold of, seize, grasp; comprehend; *recht -en*, realize, understand correctly; *alle Staatsbürger werden von der Staatskrankenkasse -(ß)t*, all citizens are included in the National Health Insurance scheme. **-(ß)lich,** *adj.* comprehensible.

erfind-en, *ir.v.a.* invent, discover, find out; make up (*a story*); (*Prov.*) *das Pulver hat er nicht erfunden*, he will never set the Thames on fire. **-er,** *m.* inventor, discoverer, designer. **-erisch,** *adj.*, **-sam,** *adj.* ingenious, inventive; (*Prov.*) *Not macht -erisch*, necessity knows no law; (*Prov.*) *Liebe macht -erisch*, love laughs at locksmiths. **-ung,** *f.* invention, discovery, device; fiction. **-ungsgabe,** *f.*, **-ungskraft,** *f.* inventiveness, inventive faculty, ingenuity. **-ungspatent,** *n.* inventor's patent. **-ungsreich,** *adj.*, **-ungsvoll,** *adj.* inventive, ingenious, resourceful.

erflehen, *v.a.* beg for, implore for; *laß dich -!* be moved by my entreaties!

Erfolg, *m.* (-(e)s, -e) success; result, issue, outcome, effect; *alle Bemühungen blieben ohne -*, all efforts proved unavailing; *- haben*, succeed. **-en,** 1. *v.n.* (*aux.* s.) ensue, result, follow (from); *was wird daraus -en?* what will be the result *or* consequence? *die Antwort ist noch nicht erfolgt*, as yet there is no reply; no answer has been received yet. **-los,** *adj.* unsuccessful, ineffectual, unavailing, fruitless, without effect *or* result. 2. *adv.* vainly, in vain. **-reich,** *adj.* successful, fruitful.

erforder-n, *v.a.* require, need; necessitate, render necessary, call for, demand; *handle wie es die S. -t*, act as you think fit *or* according to circumstances. **-lich,** *adj.* requisite, necessary. **-nis,** *n.* requisite, exigency; (*pl.*) necessaries (*of life*); *nach -nis der Umstände*, according to circumstances.

erforsch-en, *v.a.* search into, investigate, explore, fathom. **-er,** *m.* investigator. **-ung,** *f.* investigation, research, exploration.

erfragen, *reg.* & *ir.v.a.* ascertain, inquire into; *er ist nirgends zu -*, no one can tell where he is; *zu - bei . . .*, inquire at. . . .

erfrechen, *v.r.* dare, have the impudence *or* (*coll.*) cheek to, presume (to do).

erfreu-en, 1. *v.a.* gladden, delight, give pleasure (to), cheer, comfort. 2. *v.r.* rejoice, be glad *or* pleased *or* delighted (*über eine S.*, at *or* over a th.); take pleasure, rejoice (*an einer S.*, in a th.), enjoy (*Gen.*). **-lich,** *adj.* delightful; satisfactory, gratifying; *das -lichste für mich ist*, what pleases me most is. **-licherweise,** *adv.* fortunately, happily. **-t,** *adj.* glad, pleased, delighted.

erfrier-en, *ir.v.n.* (*aux.* s.) freeze to death, die from exposure *or* of cold. **erfroren,** *p.p.* & *adj.* frozen to death, (*fig.*) frostbitten; frozen, numb with cold. **-ung,** *f.* frostbite.

erfrisch-en, 1. *v.a.* freshen, refresh. 2. *v.r.* take refreshment. **-end,** *pr.p.* & *adj.* refreshing, cooling. **-ung,** *f.* refreshment; *-ungen (zu sich) nehmen*, take refreshments.

erfüll-en, 1. *v.a.* fill up, impregnate; fulfil, perform, accomplish; comply with (*a request*); realize (*expectations*); *die Bedingungen -en*, satisfy the conditions; *seine Pflicht -en*, do one's duty; *sein Versprechen -en*, keep one's promise; *das Buch -t seinen Zweck*, the book serves its purpose. 2. *v.r.* be fulfilled, come to pass, come true, be realized, take place. **-bar,** *adj.* reasonable, realizable. **-ung,** *f.* fulfilment, accomplishment, performance, realization; *in -ung bringen*, fulfil, accomplish; *in -ung gehen*, come true, be fulfilled, materialize.

(*C.L.*) **–ungsort,** *m.* where a contract is to be fulfilled, destination.

ergänz–en, *v.a.* complete; restore, replenish, supplement, add to; make up (*a deficiency*); **–end,** *pr.p.* & *adj.* supplementary; complementary. **–ung,** *f.* completion; supplement; complement; reserves (*Mil.*); replenishment, restoration. **–ungsamt,** *n.* (*Nat. Soc.*) SS. recruiting office. **–ungsband,** *m.* supplementary volume. **–ungsblatt,** *n.* supplement; supplementary sheet. **–ungsfarben,** *f.pl.* complementary colours. **–ungsheft,** *n.* supplementary number, supplement. **–ungsmannschaft,** *f.* replacements, reserves (*Mil.*). **–ungsnährstoff,** *m.* vitamin. **–ungsstrich,** *m.* dash, ellipsis (*Typ.*). **–ungsstück,** *n.* complement. **–ungsteil,** *m.* integral part. **–ungswahl,** *f.* by-election. **–ungswinkel,** *m.* complement of an angle, supplementary angle (*Math.*).

ergattern, *v.a.* (*coll.*) pick up (*news*); ferret out; hunt up, get hold of (*often by unapproved methods*).

ergeb–en, 1. *v.a.* produce, yield, deliver up, result in, give as a result, show; amount to; *angestellte Untersuchungen haben –en, daß*, tests applied have demonstrated that. 2. *v.r.* surrender (*with* in & *Acc.*), submit, yield, acquiesce (in); (*with Dat.*) devote o.s. to, become addicted to, give way to, take to (*drink, etc.*); (*with* aus) result from; follow; *hieraus ergibt sich*, hence it follows; *sich in den göttlichen Willen –en*, resign o.s. to the will of God; *sich auf Gnade und Ungnade –en*, surrender unconditionally. 3. *p.p.* & *adj.* devoted, loyal, attached; resigned, submissive, humble; *Ihr –ener*, Yours faithfully, Yours truly. **–enheit,** *f.* (*fig.*) resignation, submissiveness; fidelity, loyalty, devotion; *versichern Sie sie meiner –enheit*, present my humble respects to her; *–enheit in Gott*, humility before God, submissive acquiescence in God's will. **–enst,** (*sup.*) *adj.* most devoted, most humble; *Ihr –enster Diener*, your most obedient servant; *ich bitte –enst*, I beg most respectfully; *ich danke –enst*, I am very much obliged. **–nis,** *n.* result, outcome, conclusion, consequence, sequel; yield; product (*Math.*). **–nislos,** *adj.* without result, ineffectual, vain. **–ung,** *f.* submission, resignation, surrender (*Mil.*); *mit –ung*, resignedly, submissively.

ergehen, 1. *ir.v.n.* (*aux.* s.) be issued, published *or* promulgated, (*coll.*) come out; (*über einen*) befall, happen (to a p.); *– lassen*, issue; *ein Urteil – lassen*, pass sentence; *Recht – lassen*, let justice take its course; *etwas über sich – lassen*, bear *or* endure s.th. patiently; (*used imp. with Dat.*) go, fare with; become of; *es erging ihm schlecht*, things went badly with him; *wie würde es dir –?* what would become of you? *möge es ihm wohl –!* may he prosper! *wie ist es Ihnen ergangen?* how did you get on? 2. *v.r.* walk, stroll; *sich im Garten –*, stroll in the garden; *sich – in*, indulge in, dwell upon, launch forth into. 3. *n.* condition, state (*health, prosperity, etc.*).

ergiebig, *adj.* productive, lucrative, fertile, abundant, abounding, rich. **–keit,** *f.* productivity, abundance, richness, fertility.

ergieß–en, *ir.v.r.* overflow, gush forth; empty (into), discharge, flow *or* fall into; break forth; *sich in Tränen –en*, burst into tears. **–ung,** *f.* effusion; efflux; discharge; overflow.

erglühen, *v.n.* (*aux.* s.) glow, kindle.

ergötz–en, 1. *v.a.* delight, please, amuse. 2. *v.r.* enjoy o.s.; *sich an einer S. –en*, take delight in a th., be amused at *or* about s.th. 3. *n.* joy, delight, pleasure, amusement. **–end,** *pr.p.* & *adj.* **–lich,** *adj.* amusing, funny, diverting; delightful. **–ung,** *f.*, *see* **–en,** 3.

ergrauen, *v.n.* (*aux.* s.) grow *or* get grey (*of hair*); dawn (*of the day*).

ergreif–en, *ir.v.a.* lay *or* take hold of, seize, catch grasp; apprehend; effect, touch, move, stir (*feelings*); make use of, avail o.s. of; assume (*the offensive*), enter on, apply o.s. to, take up (*a trade, etc.*); *Besitz von einer S. –en*, take possession of a th.; *die Feder –en*, take up the pen; *die Flucht –en*, take to flight; *die Gelegenheit beim Schopfe –en*, seize *or* take the occasion by the forelock; *das Hasenpanier –en*, take to one's heels; *strenge Maßregeln –en*, have reco
measures; *eine Partei –en*
cause; *auf frischer Tat –e*
Waffen –en, take up arms;
speak. **–end,** *pr.p.* & *adj.*
ing, stirring, impressive
seizure, capture; adoption

ergriffen, *p.p.* & *adj.*
stirred, affected, struck. –

ergrimmen, *v.n.* (*aux.* s
ergrimmt aussehen, look fierce.

ergründ–en, *v.a.* fathom, probe, investigate, look into, explore thoroughly; ascertain, discover, find out, penetrate (*a mystery*), get to the bottom of; *nicht zu –en*, unfathomable, inexplicable. **–lich,** *adj.* fathomable, penetrable. **–ung,** *f.* fathoming, exploration, research.

Erguß, *m.* (-(ss)es, ¨(ss)e) effusion, discharge, outpouring, overflow. **–gestein,** *n.* lava deposit.

erhaben, *adj.* raised, projecting, prominent, elevated, convex; elated; exalted, noble, lofty, illustrious, sublime, stately; *–e Arbeit*, relief, embossed work; *flach –e Arbeit*, bas-relief; *über sein Schicksal –*, superior to one's fate; *ich bin darüber –, so etwas zu tun*, I am above doing such a th. *or* acting in such a way; *das –e*, the sublime. **–heit,** *f.* sublimity, nobility, grandeur, eminence, stateliness; elevation, protuberance, prominence, relief, convexity.

Erhalt, *m.* receipt. **–bar,** *adj.* obtainable; preservable. **–en,** *ir.v.* 1. *a.* get, receive, obtain, save, preserve, keep, maintain, keep up, uphold, support; *einen höheren Preis –en*, fetch a higher price; *wenn sie dieses –en*, when this reaches you; *in Gang –en*, keep going; *Gott –e den König*; God save the King! *sich –en von*, keep alive *or* subsist on; *sich selbst –en*, support o.s.; *sich in Gunst –en bei*, keep in favour with; (*coll.*) keep on the right side of; *sich gut –en*, wear *or* last *or* keep well. 2. *p.p.* & *adj.* preserved; received; (*C.L.*) paid; *–en von dem Zahlmeister*, received from the paymaster; *gut –en*, in good repair *or* condition. **–er,** *m.* preserver, supporter; upholder. **–ung,** *f.* procuring, obtaining, receipt; maintenance, preservation, conservation (*of energy, etc.*). **–ungsmittel,** *n.* means of subsistence. **–ungsumsatz,** *m.* basal metabolism (*Physiol.*). **–ungszustand,** *m.* condition, state of preservation.

erhältlich, *adj.*, *see* **erhaltbar;** *– bei allen Buchhändlern*, to be obtained of all booksellers.

erhängen, *v.a.* & *r.* hang (*a person*).

erhärt–en, *v.a.* harden, set; (*fig.*) confirm, corroborate, prove, verify; *eidlich –en*, affirm upon oath. **–ung,** *f.* corroboration, confirmation, proof; hardening; *eidliche –ung*, affidavit.

erhaschen, *v.a.* snatch (at); seize, catch.

erheb–en, 1. *ir.v.a.* lift *or* raise up, elevate; praise, exalt, extol; set up (*a cry*); promote, advance, raise in rank; levy, gather, collect (*taxes*); bring (*an action against*); raise to a higher power (*Math.*); relieve, set off (*by contrast, Paint.*); *einen in den Adelstand –en*, raise *or* elevate s.o. to the peerage; *Anspruch auf etwas –en*, lay claim to s.th.; *Einspruch –en*, protest, enter a protest; *eine Erbschaft –en*, take possession of an inheritance; *Geld –en*, raise money; *eine Zahl ins Quadrat –en*, square a number; *Zweifel –en*, raise *or* start doubts. 2. *v.r.* raise o.s.; rise, rise up, rebel (*gegen*, against); arise, spring up; assume a superiority (*über einen*, over a p.); *plötzlich erhob sich ein Gemurmel*, a murmur suddenly arose; *ein Gerücht hat sich erhoben*, a rumour is abroad, there is a rumour; *es erhob sich ein heftiger Wind*, a high wind sprang up. **–end,** *pr.p.* & *adj.* elevating, solemn, impressive. **–lich,** *adj.* considerable, weighty, important, cogent. **–lichkeit,** *f.* importance, consequence; weight, cogency. **–ung,** *f.* elevation; raising; collection, levy; promotion; exaltation; involution (*Math.*); rising ground, peak, summit; rising, revolt, rebellion; *nationale –ung*, Nat. Soc. seizure of power 1933; *–ungen anstellen*, make inquiries, set up an official inquiry, survey *or* census. **–ungskosten,** *f.pl.* expenses of collection. **–ungswinkel,** *m.* angle of elevation, slope, gradient.

erheischen, *v.a.* require, demand, claim.

er-n, 1. *v.a.* cheer, brighten, amuse, en-n. 2. *v.r.* clear up; become cheerful, cheer up; ght up (*of facial expression*). **-ung,** *f.* amuse-ment, fun, diversion.
erhell-en, 1. *v.a.* clear up, light up, brighten, illuminate; expose (*to the light, Phot.*). 2. *v.n.* (*aux.* h.) become clear, apparent *or* evident; *daraus -t, daß*, from this it is evident that, hence it appears that. **-ung,** *f.* lighting up; illumination, exposure (*Phot.*).
erheucheln, *v.a.* simulate, feign, (*coll.*) put on.
erhitz-en, 1. *v.a.* heat, warm, make hot; pasteurize (*milk*); excite, inflame. 2. *v.r.* grow hot *or* warm; become heated; get angry, fly into a passion. **-t,** *p.p.* & *adj.* heated; flushed; warm; *ganz -t*, all is in glow, overheated, flushed. **-ung,** *f.* heating; excitement.
erhoffen, *v.a.* hope for, expect, anticipate; *zu -de Freuden*, pleasures in prospect.
erhöh-en, *v.a.* raise, elevate, erect; heighten, increase, enhance (*the value, etc.*); (*coll.*) step up (*production*); extol, exalt. **-t,** *p.p.* & *adj.* increased, heightened, elevated. **-ung,** *f.* elevation; rise, advance, increase, enhancement; swelling, protuberance; rising ground, eminence; exaltation; raising of a note (*Mus.*). **-ungszeichen,** *n.* sharp (*Mus.*).
erhol-en, *v.r.* recover, get better, improve, (*C.L.*) pick up (*of prices*); come to, come round; rest, relax; *sich* (*wegen*) *seines Schadens* or *von seinem Schaden -en an*, retrieve *or* repair a loss by *or* with; *sie -t sich gut*, she is making a good recovery. **-ung,** *f.* recovery, rest, recuperation; recreation, relaxation. **-ungsbedürftig,** *adj.* in need of a change; requiring rest *or* recuperation. **-ungsheim,** *n.* convalescent home. **-ungsort,** *m.* holiday resort. **-ungsreise,** *f.* trip; outing. **-ungsstunde,** *f.* break, playtime (*school*), recreation time, leisure hour. **-ungsurlaub,** *m.* sick leave (*Mil.*).
erhör-en, *v.a.* give a favourable hearing; grant; **-ung,** *f.* favourable hearing, granting (*of a request*).
Erika, *f.* heather (*Erica*) (*Bot.*).
erinner-n, 1. *v.a.* (*einen an eine S.*) remind, call to s.o.'s mind, draw attention to; mention, suggest; admonish; (*dial. N. German*) recall, remember; 2. *v.r.* (*Gen. or* an & *Acc.*) recall, remember, recollect, call to mind; *wenn ich mich recht -e*, if my memory serves me right; *es sei daran -t*, let me remind you of. **-lich,** *adj.* remembered; *es ist mir -lich*, I remember; *so viel mir -lich ist*, so far as I remember; *wie -lich*, a will *or* may be remembered. **-ung,** *f.* remembrance, memory, recollection, reminiscence; reminder, admonition, suggestion, hint; *einem etwas in -ung bringen*, recall s.th. to a p.'s mind; *zur -ung an* (*Acc.*), in remembrance of, in memory of.
erkalt-en, *v.n.* (*aux.* s.) grow cold; cool (down); (*coll.*) cool off (*of feelings, etc.*). **-ung,** *f.* cooling down, loss of heat.
erkält-en, 1. *v.a.* cool, chill; *ich bin stark -et*, I have a bad cold; *er hat sich den Magen -et*, he has a chill on the stomach. 2. *v.r.* catch cold. **-ung,** *f.* cold; chill; cooling, refrigeration.
erkämpfen, *v.a.* gain by fighting.
erkannt, *see* **erkennen.**
erkaufen, *v.a.* buy, purchase; bribe, corrupt; *sich – lassen*, be corruptible, have one's price; *teuer –*, pay dearly for.
erkecken, *v.r.* dare, make bold, be so bold as (to).
erkenn-en, *ir.v.a.* recognize (*an*, by), perceive, know, apprehend, discern, distinguish, understand, take cognizance of; have carnal knowledge of; credit (*C.L.*); judge, decide, pass sentence on (*Law*); diagnose (*Med.*); detect (*Chem.*); *-en lassen*, reveal, exhibit; *zu -en geben*, show, indicate; *sich zu -en geben*, make o.s. known; *der Angeklagte erkannte sich nicht für schuldig*, the prisoner (at the bar) pleaded not guilty; *das Gericht erkannte auf Freisprechung*, the court dismissed the charge; *das Gericht erkannte zu Recht, daß . . .*, the verdict of the court was that . . .; *eine Klage für begründet -en*, find a true bill; *erkannt sein für*, be credited with; *für das Seinige -en*, own to, recognize as one's own; *Sie sind von uns für diesen Betrag erkannt worden*, you have been credited by us for this amount; *-e dich selbst!* know thyself! **-bar,** *adj.* recognizable, perceptible, discernible. **-tlich,** *adj.* grateful; discernible, recognizable. **-tlichkeit,** *f.* gratitude; gratuity. **-tnis,** 1. *f.* knowledge, cognition; perception, understanding, acknowledgement, recognition, realization, recognizance; *zur -tnis kommen*, repent; *der Baum der -tnis*, the tree of knowledge (*B.*). 2. *n.* verdict, finding, sentence, judgement. **-tnisgrund,** *m.* criterion by which something is known. **-tnistheorie,** *f.* theory of cognition. **-tnisvermögen,** *n.* faculty of perception, intellectual power. **-ung,** *f.* recognition; perception, detection; diagnosis (*Med.*); (carnal) knowledge. **-ungskarte,** *f.* identity card. **-ungsmarke,** *f.* identification disk. **-ungswort,** *n.* password, watchword; shibboleth. **-ungszahl,** *f.* index number. **-ungszeichen,** *n.* characteristic symptom, distinctive mark, distinguishing sign, airplane marking, badge (*Mil.*).
Erker, *m.* (-s, –) alcove, balcony. **-fenster,** *n.* oriel, bow (*curved*) *or* bay (*angular*) window.
erkiesen, *ir.v.a.* (*Poet.*) choose, elect.
erklär-en, 1. *v.a.* explain, account for, clear up; declare, announce, pronounce; expound, interpret; define; *ich kann mir das nicht -en*, I cannot account for it; *-en für*, pronounce to be; *in die Acht -en*, outlaw; *den Krieg -en*, declare war. 2. *v.r.* explain o.s.; declare o.s. for (*a party*); make an offer of marriage, propose; *-e dich deutlicher*, explain yourself more clearly; *daraus -t sich sein Benehmen*, that accounts for his conduct; *sich für bankrott -en*, declare o.s. bankrupt; *sich bereit -en*, declare one's willingness. **-bar,** *adj.* explainable, explicable. **-lich,** *adj.* explicable, accountable, understandable, apparent, obvious, evident. **-t,** *p.p.* & *adj.* professed, declared; *deutlich -t*, clearly set forth; *-ter Feind*, open *or* sworn enemy; *-ter Liebling des Publikums*, acknowledged *or* declared favourite with the public. **-ung,** *f.* explanation, interpretation, elucidation; solution (*Math.*); declaration, avowal, (*Law*) deposition; manifesto; *letztwillige -ung*, will. **-ungsschrift,** *f.* commentary. **-ungsversuch,** *m.* attempted explanation.
erklecklich, *adj.* considerable, sufficient.
erklettern, *v.a.* climb up, ascend, scale, reach the summit of.
erklimmen, *ir.v.a. see* **erklettern,** (*also used fig.*).
erklingen, *ir.v.a.* (*aux.* s.) sound, resound, ring out.
erkoren, *p.p.* & *adj.* select, chosen.
erkrank-en, *v.n.* (*aux.* s.) fall sick *or* ill, be taken ill, sicken (*an einer S.*, with s.th.). **-t,** sick, diseased. **-ung,** *f.* illness, sickness.
erkühnen, *v.r.* venture, dare, make bold (to).
erkund-en, *v.a.* ascertain, gain information about; reconnoitre (*Mil.*); explore. **-ung,** *f.* scouting, reconnaissance (*Mil.*), exploration, preliminary survey. **-ungsflugzeug,** *n.* reconnaissance plane.
erkundig-en, *v.r.* inquire, make inquiries (*bei einem*, of *or* from a p.; *wegen einer S.*, about a th.; *nach einem* or *einer S.*, for a p. *or* about a th.); *sich -en lassen*, have inquiries made, send *or* call for information. **-ung,** *f.* inquiry, search; *-ungen einziehen* or *einholen über eine S.*, collect information on *or* about a th.; make inquiries.
erkünstel-n, *v.a.* pretend, feign, affect. **-t,** *p.p.* & *adj.* affected, forced (*of style*); artificial, sham.
Erlag, *m.* (-s, ¨-e) (*Austr. dial.*) payment, deposit. **-schein,** *m.* (*Austr. dial.*) money order, postal order.
erlahmen, *v.n.* (*aux.* s.) become lame; become paralysed; (*fig.*) grow weak, get tired, flag.
erlang-en, *v.a.* reach, attain, acquire, obtain, procure, get; *seinen Zweck -en*, attain one's end, achieve one's purpose; *man konnte es von ihm nicht -en, daß*, he could not be induced to; *mit Mühe -t*, hard-earned; *wieder -en*, recover, retrieve. **-bar,** *adj.* attainable. **-ung,** *f.* attainment, achievement (*of a purpose, etc.*); recovery (*Law*).
Erlaß, *m.* (-(ss)es, -(ss)e) edict, decree, ordinance; deduction, reduction, abatement; allowance; (*C.L.*) remission; pardon, dispensation, exemption,

indulgence (*R.C.*); *allerhöchster* –, imperial *or* royal decree. **–(ss)en,** *ir.v.a.* publish, issue, proclaim; (*einem etwas*) remit, release from; absolve from, exempt from, let off from, pardon; abate (*in price*); *eine Schuld –(ss)en,* forgo *or* remit a debt; (*einem*) *die Strafe –(ss)en,* remit a punishment; *einen Befehl –(ss)en,* give *or* issue an order; *ein Manifest wurde –(ss)en,* a proclamation was issued; *–(ss)en Sie mir Antwort auf die Frage* excuse my (not) answering this question. **–sünde,** *f.* venial sin (*R.C.*). **–(ss)ung,** *f.* remission, release, dispensation.

erläßlich, *adj.* remissible, venial, pardonable; *un–,* indispensable.

erlaub–en, *v.a.* (*einem etwas*) allow, permit; grant *or* give permission to, sanction; *man –e mir,* may I be permitted, I beg leave to; *ich –e mir,* I take the liberty; *sich* (*Dat.*) *–en,* be so free; *er –t sich Frechheiten,* he takes liberties; *das können sie sich –en,* you can afford it; *wenn sie –en,* by your leave; *–en Sie mal!* I beg your pardon (*ironic expression of incredulity*), (*coll.*) how do you arrive at that? where do you get that from? *wem viel –t ist, der soll sich am wenigsten –en,* he to whom much is permitted should be the last to take liberties. **–nis,** *f.* leave, permission, sanction; licence, dispensation; *mit Ihrer –nis,* with your permission; *mit höherer –nis gedruckt,* printed by authority. **–nisbrief,** *m.* licence, letters patent. **–nisschein,** *m.* permit, pass. **–t,** *p.p. & adj.* justifiable, excusable, permitted, sanctioned, allowed; allowable, lawful.

erlaucht, *adj.* illustrious, noble.

erlauschen, *v.a.* overhear; learn by eavesdropping.

erläuter–n, *v.a.* explain, illustrate, commentate, comment on, interpret; *durch Beispiele –n,* illustrate by examples, exemplify. **–er,** *m.* commentator. **–ung,** *f.* explanation, illustration, elucidation; commentary, comment, note; *zur –ung,* in illustration.

Erle, *f.* (-n) alder (*Alnus glutinosa*) (*Bot.*).

erleb–en, *v.a.* experience; witness; live to see; *wir werden nie den Tag –en,* we shall never see the day; *ich habe einen glücklichen Tag –t,* I have had *or* spent a happy day; *hat einer so etwas je –t?* did any one ever see the like? *viele Auflagen –en,* go through many editions; (*coll.*) *du wirst schon was –en,* you will get into trouble, there is trouble in store for you. **–nis,** *n.* experience, adventure; occurrence, event; *widrige –nisse,* adversities.

erledig–en, *v.a.* bring to a close, settle, finish, dispose, carry through, (*coll.*) see through; execute (*a commission*); dispatch (*business*); release, acquit, exempt, discharge, (*Gen.* or *von,* from); vacate (*an office*); remove (*doubts*); (*coll.*) set aside; remove, finish off (*inconvenient persons*); clear off, wind up (*business*); *die S. –t sich hiermit,* the matter is herewith closed. **–t,** *p.p. & adj.* settled; dispatched; in abeyance (*of a fief*); vacant; (*coll.*) finished, done for (*of persons*); *–te Stelle,* vacancy; *–te Pfründe,* vacant living. **–ung,** *f.* execution, completion, settlement, dispatch, discharge, release; vacancy. **–ungsschein,** *m.* receipt, (*archaic*) quittance.

erleg–en, *v.a.* kill, slay, lay low; pay down, deposit. **–ung,** *f.* killing; payment.

erleichter–n, 1. *v.a.* ease, lighten, make easy, facilitate, relieve, alleviate, assuage. 2. *v.r.* relieve o.s.; relieve nature. **–ung,** *f.* facilitation, lightening, easing, relief, mitigation, alleviation.

erleiden, *ir.v.a.* suffer, bear, endure, undergo, sustain. *Schiffbruch –,* be shipwrecked, (*fig.*) come to grief.

erlern–en, *v.a.* learn, acquire. **–ung,** *f.* acquisition (*of knowledge, etc.*).

erlesen, 1. *ir.v.a.* select, choose, elect. 2. *p.p. & adj.* select; selected; choice; *–e Mannschaft,* picked men.

erleucht–en, *v.a.* illuminate, light up; (*fig.*) enlighten; *die –eten,* (*pl.*) the Illuminati. **–ung,** *f.* illumination, enlightenment.

erliegen, *ir.v.n.* (*aux.* h. & s.) (*Dat.* or *unter*) be defeated, succumb to, die of; *zum – kommen,* be worked out *or* exhausted (*of a mine*).

erlischt, *see* **erlöschen.**

erlisten, *v.a.* obtain by cunning, (*sl.*) wangle; (*sich*) *einen Vorteil –,* gain an advantage by trickery.

Erlkönig, *m.* elf-king.

erlogen, *p.p. & adj.* false, untrue, fictitious, fabricated; (*Vulg.*) *das ist erstunken und –,* that's a stinking *or* filthy lie.

Erlös, *m.* (-es, -e) (net) proceeds.

erloschen, *p.p. & adj.* extinguished, expired; extinct, dead; obliterated, effaced, faded, dim, dull, obscure, lifeless; *das Licht ist –,* the light is out; *bei ihm ist alle Scham –,* he is dead to all sense of shame.

erlösch–en, 1. *ir.v.a.* (*aux.* s.) be extinguished, go out; become dull *or* dim; (*fig.*) become extinct; die out, expire, lapse, cease to exist, go out of use, become effaced *or* obliterated. 2. *v.a.* (*aux.* h.) extinguish, put out. **–ung,** *f.* expiration; extinction.

erlös–en, *v.a.* redeem; ransom; (set) free, release; save, deliver, rescue; get (*as proceeds from a sale*). **–er,** *m.* deliverer; redeemer; *der –er,* our Saviour; the Redeemer. **–ung,** *f.* release; redemption; deliverance, salvation.

ermächtig–en, *v.a.* empower, authorize. **–ung,** *f.* authorization, authority, warrant. **–ungsgesetz,** *n.* enabling act.

ermahn–en, *v.a.* admonish, exhort, warn. **–end,** *pr.p. & adj.* hortatory. **–ung,** *f.* admonition, exhortation.

ermang–eln, *v.n.* (*aux.* h.) lack, want, be deficient *or* wanting (*an einer S.,* in a th.); be in want of; fail; *es an nichts –eln lassen,* do one's utmost, spare no pains *or* nothing; (*archaic*) *ich werde nicht –eln zu,* I shall not fail to. **–(e)lung,** *f.* lack, want, deficiency, default, failure; *in –(e)lung eines Besseren,* for the lack *or* want of anything better; *in –(e)lung dessen,* failing which.

ermann–en, *v.r.* pull o.s. together, take courage, take heart. *–e dich!* (*sl.*) pull up your socks.

ermäßig–en, 1. *v.a.* abate, moderate, limit, lessen, lower, reduce (*prices*). 2. *v.r.* be reduced; *die Preise –en sich,* prices are falling. **–ung,** *f.* abatement, moderation, reduction, limitation.

ermatt–en, 1. *v.a.* tire, exhaust, weary, weaken, wear down. 2. *v.n.* (*aux.* s.) faint, grow weary, tired *or* exhausted, fade (*of colours*). **–ung,** *f.* exhaustion, weariness, fatigue, lassitude. **–ungsstrategie,** *f.* strategy of attrition (*Mil.*).

ermess–en, 1. *ir.v.a.* consider, judge, weigh, estimate; 2. *n.* judgement, estimate, estimation, opinion; *meines –ens, nach meinem –en* in my opinion; *nach bestem* or *menschlichem –en,* as far as one can judge. **–(ß)lich,** *adj.* measurable; conceivable.

ermitt–eln, *v.a.* ascertain, find out, determine; *zu –eln,* ascertainable. **–lung,** *f.* determination, inquiry, research. **–lungsverfahren,** *n.* preliminary proceedings (*Law*).

ermöglichen, *v.a.* render *or* make possible *or* feasible, enable, bring about.

ermord–en, 1. *v.a.* murder, assassinate. **–ung,** *f.* murder, assassination.

ermüd–en, *v.a. & v.n.* tire (out), weary, fatigue, exhaust, wear out; *leicht zu –en,* easily tired. 2. *v.n.* (*aux.* s.) get *or* become tired, grow weary. **–end,** *pr.p. & adj.* tiring, wearisome, irksome. **–ung,** *f.* fatigue, weariness. **–ungsfestigkeit,** *f.* fatigue strength (*Metall.*). **–ungsgrenze,** *f.* fatigue limit (*Metall.*), endurance limit.

ermunter–n, *v.a.* awake, rouse, incite, urge on, cheer up, enliven encourage. **–ung,** *f.* encouragement, enlivenment.

ermutig–en, 1. *v.a.* encourage, inspire with courage. 2. *v.r.* take heart *or* courage, summon up courage. **–end,** *adj.* encouraging, reassuring. **–ung,** *f.* encouragement.

ernähr–en, 1. *v.a.* nourish, feed, support, maintain; *sich von einem –en lassen,* depend on s.o. for support. 2. *v.r.* earn one's livelihood; live (by); subsist (*von,* on). **–end,** *pr.p. & adj.* nutritive. **–er,** *m.* bread-winner. **–ung,** *f.* nourishment, food; feeding, nutrition, alimentation; support, maintenance; *schlechte –ung,* malnutrition; *ungenügende –ung,* underfeeding. **–ungsamt,** *n.* Food Office, Ministry of Food. **–ungskanal,** *m.* alimentary canal *or* tract. **–ungskunde,** *f.* dietetics.

–ungsschlacht, *f.* (*Nat. Soc.*) battle for autarky. **–ungsweise,** *f.* feeding habits. **–(ungs)wert,** *m.* nutritive value.

ernannt, *p.p.*, *see* **ernennen;** *der –e*, the nominee.

ernenn–en, *ir.v.a.* nominate, appoint; designate; *einen zum Herzog –en*, create s.o. a duke; *Geschworene –en*, impanel a jury; *er ist zum Professor an der Universität ernannt worden*, he has been appointed professor at the university. **–er,** *m.* nominator. **–ung,** *f.* nomination, appointment; designation. **–ungsbrief,** *m.*, **–ungsurkunde,** *f.* letter of appointment; commission. **–ungsrecht,** *n.* patronage (*of a living*), nomination.

erneu–e(r)n, 1. *v.a.* renew, renovate, repair, replace, restore, refresh, revive; recommence, repeat; *zu –e(r)n*, renewable. 2. *v.r.* become new, recommence; be revived. **–erung,** *f.* renewal, renovation, revival; replacement; repetition. **–t,** *adj.* renewed, *adv.* again, anew.

erniedrig–en, *v.a.* lower, bring low, humble, humiliate, degrade; depress (*a note*) (*Mus.*). **–ung,** *f.* lowering, depression, reduction, humiliation, degradation, abasement. **–ungszeichen,** *n.* mark of depression, flat (♭) (*Mus.*).

Ernst, 1. *m.* earnestness, seriousness, gravity; severity, sternness; *ist es Ihr –? ist es Ihnen – damit?* are you serious *or* in earnest? *im –, in allem* or *vollem –e, allen –es*, in downright earnest, in all seriousness; *das ist nicht Ihr –?* you don't (really) mean that? surely you are joking? *aus einem Spaß – machen*, take a joke in ill part; *mit etwas – machen*, put s.th. into practice; *jetzt wird es (blutiger) –*, now matters are getting serious *or* critical. 2. *adj.* earnest; serious, grave, stern, severe, solemn; *der Preuße sagt 'die Lage ist – aber nicht verzweifelt': der Wiener sagt 'die Lage ist verzweifelt, aber nicht –'*, the Prussian says 'the situation is grave but not hopeless'; the Viennese says 'the situation is desperate but not serious'. **–fall,** *m.* emergency; *im –fall(e)*, when things become serious; in case of emergency. **–haft,** *adj.*, *see* **ernst** 2. *eine Arbeit –haft auffassen*, tackle a job seriously *or* in earnest; *meine –hafte Meinung*, my earnest opinion. **–haftigkeit,** *f.* earnestness, seriousness; gravity; severity, sternness. **–lich,** *adj.* earnest; in earnest, serious; fervent, ardent, eager, intent, forcible; *meine –liche Meinung*, my definite opinion; *einem etwas –lich verbieten*, positively forbid s.o. s.th. **–lichkeit,** *see* **–haftigkeit.**

Ernt–e, *f.* (-n) harvest, crop; (*Prov.*) *ohne Saat keine –e*, as ye have sown so shall ye reap. **–earbeit,** *f.* harvesting. **–edankfest,** *n.* harvest thanksgiving (festival). **–efest,** *n.* harvest-home, harvest-thanksgiving. **–egöttin,** *f.* Ceres. **–ehelfer,** *m.* volunteer harvester. **–emaschine,** *f.* harvester. **–emonat,** *m.*, **–emond,** *m.* August. **–en,** *v.a.* harvest, gather in; reap (*also fig.*). **–er,** *m.* harvester, reaper. **–ereif,** *adj.* fit for harvesting, ripe for the sickle. **–esegen,** *m.* rich harvest. **–eurlaub,** *m.* agricultural leave (*Mil.*). **–ewetter,** *n.* good harvest-weather. **–ezeit,** *f.* harvest-time. **–ing,** *m.* August.

ernüchtern, 1. *v.a.* sober (down); disillusion, disenchant. 2. *v.r.* become sober.

erober–n, *v.a.* conquer; overcome, win, captivate (*hearts, etc.*). **–er,** *m.* conqueror. **–ung,** *f.* conquest, acquisition (*by conquest*). **–ungssucht,** *f.* thirst for conquest.

eröffn–en, 1. *v.a.* open, start, inaugurate; disclose, make known, reveal; inform, notify. 2. *v.r.* open (*one's heart, etc.*); offer, present itself (*as an opportunity*). **–end,** *pr.p.* & *adj.* opening; aperient (*Med.*). **–ung,** *f.* opening, inauguration; beginning, overture; disclosure, communication. **–ungsrede,** *f.* opening address, inaugural speech. **–ungsstück,** *n.* overture (*Mus.*).

erörter–n, *v.a.* discuss, argue (on *or* about), debate; *die S. läßt sich –n*, the subject is open to discussion. **–ung,** *f.* discussion, debate, (*fig.*) ventilation (*of views*); *auf eine –ung eingehen*, enter into a discussion.

erotisch, *adj.* erotic.

erpicht, *adj.* (*auf eine S.*) intent, bent *or* (*coll.*) keen (on); eager (for); passionately attached (to).

erpress–en, *v.a.* extort, blackmail, exact, wring (from); distrain (*Law*). **–er,** *m.* blackmailer, extortioner. **–erisch,** *adj.* extortionate. **–ung,** *f.* blackmail, extortion; exaction.

erprob–en, *v.a.* try, test, prove. **–t,** *p.p.* & *adj.* tried, approved. **–ungsflieger,** *m.* test pilot. (*Av.*).

erquick–en, *v.a.* revive, refresh. **–end,** *pr. p.* & *adj.* refreshing. **–lich,** *adj.* refreshing, comforting, invigorating. **–ung,** *f.* refreshment, comfort. **–ungsmittel,** *n.* restorative.

errat–en, *ir.v.a.* solve (*a riddle*), guess, divine; *ich –e es nicht*, I give it up. **–ung,** *f.* guessing, divining.

erratisch, *adj.* erratic.

errechn–en, *v.a.* reckon out, calculate, compute. **–ung,** *f.* calculation.

erreg–en, *v.a.* excite, stir up, stimulate; agitate, irritate; promote, provoke, cause; inspire (*fear, etc.*). **–bar,** *adj.* excitable, irritable; sensitive. **–barkeit,** *f.* excitability; irritability. **–end,** *pr.p.* & *adj.* exciting, stimulating; *–endes Mittel*, *see* **–ungsmittel;** *–endes Moment*, starting-point o dramatic action. **–er,** *m.* agitator, instigator; exciter (*Elec.*), agent (*Chem.*). **–erstrom,** *m.* induction current *Elec.*). **–erwindung,** *f.* induction winding, choke (*Elec.*, *Rad.*) **–t,** *p.p.* & *adj.* excited; *leicht –t*, irritable, touchy. **–theit,** *f.* agitation; irritability. **–ung,** *f.* agitation; excitement, commotion; excitation, stimulation. **–ungsmittel,** *n.* stimulant.

erreich–en, *v.a.* reach, attain, (*coll.*) get, obtain, gain; arrive at, get up to; fetch (*a price*). **–bar,** *adj.* attainable, accessible, within reach; (*coll.*) get-at-able; *er –t den Zug nicht mehr*, he will not catch the train now; *der Brief –te mich nicht*, I did not get the letter; *bei ihm ist alles zu –en*, you can do anything with him, you can get anything out of him; *wie kann man Sie –en?* how can I get at you? how can you be reached *or* got at? *ich bin telephonisch zu –en* or *–bar*, I am on the phone, you can get me on the phone. **–ung,** *f.* reaching; attainment, achievement.

errett–en, *v.a.* save, rescue, deliver. **–ung,** *f.* rescue, deliverance.

erricht–en, *v.a.* set upright; erect, raise, put up; found, establish, set up; *einen Bund –en*, make an alliance *or* covenant; *ein Testament –en*, draw up a will; *eine Senkrechte –en*, erect a perpendicular (*Math.*); *eine gesellschaftliche Stellung –en*, establish a position in society. **–ung,** *f.* erection, establishment, foundation.

erringen, *ir.v.a.* win, gain, achieve, obtain with difficulty.

erröt–en, 1. *v.n.* (*aux.* s.) blush, redden; *–en machen*, put to the blush. 2. *n.*, **–ung,** *f.* blush, blushing; *–en macht die Häßlichen so schön* (*Lessing*), a blush gives beauty to the plainest.

Errungenschaft, *f.* (-en) acquisition, achievement; gain, advance, progress; *die großartigen –en der Neuzeit*, the splendid achievements of modern times.

ersätt–igen, *v.a.* sate, satiate; satisfy. **–igung,** *f.* sating, satiating; satisfying, satiation, satisfaction. **–lich,** *adj.* satiable, satisfiable.

Ersatz, *m.* substitute; replenishment, reserve (*Sport* & *Mil.*), draft (*Mil.*), replacement, spare (*Motor., etc.*); equivalent; *zum – für*, as compensation for, in exchange for, as a replacement for; *einem – geben*, indemnify a p.; *– leisten*, make amends. **–behörden,** *f.pl.* recruiting authorities. **–blei,** *m.* refill (*for propelling pencil*). **–gewicht,** *n.* equivalent weight. **–heer,** *n.* reserve army. **–leistung,** *f.* indemnification, reimbursement. **–mann,** *m.* substitute, reserve (*Sport.*), deputy. **–mannschaften,** *f.pl.* drafts, replacements (*Mil.*). **–mittel,** *n.* surrogate; substitute, makeshift. **–pflicht,** *f.* liability to repair (*on part of the manufacturer or supplier*), liability for compensation. **–reifen,** *m.* spare tyre (*Motor.*). **–reserve,** *f.* (untrained) army reserve. **–schauspieler,** *m.* double, understudy. **–stück,** *n.*, **–teil,** *m.* spare part, replacement. **–truppen,** *f.pl.* reserve units (*Mil.*).

ersaufen, *ir.v.n.* (*aux.* s.) be drowned; be flooded (*as crops, mine, etc.*).

ersäufen, *v.a.* drown; flood; *die Sorgen im Alkohol –*, drown one's sorrows in drink.

erschaff–en, *ir.v.a.* produce, create; *der –ene,* created being. **–er,** *m.* creator. **–ung,** *f.* creation.
erschallen, *reg. & ir.v.n.* (*aux.* s.) resound, ring; *– lassen,* sound *or* spread abroad; sound, let hear; *es erscholl ein Gerücht,* a report *or* rumour spread.
erschau(d)ern, *v.n.* (*aux.* s.) tremble, shiver, shudder, be seized with horror.
erschauen, *v.a.* (*Poet.*) see, behold.
erschein–en, 1. *ir.v.n.* (*aux.* s.) appear; come out (*as a book*), be published; be evident, seem; *–en lassen,* bring out, publish; *soeben erschienen,* just published; *er ließ es –en,* he made it appear *or* apparent. 2. *n.* appearance, presence. **–ung,** *f.* appearance, figure, apparition, vision (*of spirits*); manifestation; phenomenon; symptom (*Med.*); publication; *äußere –ung,* outward appearance, aspect, look, bearing, presence; *eine glänzende –ung sein,* cut a fine figure; *das Fest der –ung Christi,* Epiphany; *in –ung treten,* appear. **–ungsform,** *f.* outward shape *or* form; phase, manifestation; species. **–ungswelt,** *f.* physical world.
erschieß–en, *ir.v.a.* kill by shooting, shoot dead, shoot; win by shooting; *–en der Entfernung,* ranging fire (*Artil.*). **–ung,** *f.* shooting, execution (*by firing-squad*). **–ungskommando,** *n.* firing-squad.
erschlaff–en, 1. *v.n.* (*aux.* s.) grow slack, slacken; relax, languish, flag. 2. *v.a.* enervate, relax, slacken; *–ende Mittel,* (*pl.*) emollients. **–ung,** *f.* slackening, relaxation; flagging; debility, enervation; effeminacy; (*sl.*) *bis zur –ung,* to the last gasp.
erschlagen, 1. *ir.v.a.* kill, strike dead, slay; *vom Blitz –,* struck by lightning. 2. (*coll.*) *p.p.* dead tired, tired to death, dog tired; thunderstruck, dumbfounded.
erschleichen, *ir.v.a.* obtain surreptitiously; obtain on the 'black market'. **erschlichen,** *p.p. & adj.* surreptitious; *erschlichenerweise,* surreptitiously, by hook or by crook, in an underhand way.
erschließ–en, *ir.v.a.* open, open up, unlock; make accessible, disclose; conclude, infer. **–ung,** *f.* opening up, disclosure; deduction, induction.
erschlug, erschlüge, *see* **erschlagen.**
erschmeicheln, *v.a.* obtain by flattery, wheedle out of (*a p.*).
erscholl, erschölle, erschollen, *see* **erschallen.**
erschöpf–en, *v.a.* drain; exhaust. **–end,** *pr.p. & adj.* exhaustive, full, thorough; exhausting. **–t,** *p.p. & adj.* spent, exhausted, (*coll.*) done up, done in, (*sl.*) fagged; *meine Geduld ist –t,* my patience is exhausted *or* at an end; *–tes Stück Land,* worked-out land. **–theit,** *f.* (state of) exhaustion, collapse. **–ung,** *f.* exhaustion.
erschrak, erschräke, *see* **erschrecken.**
erschreck–en, 1. *ir.v.n.* (*aux.* s.) be frightened, scared, alarmed, terrified *or* startled (*über eine S.* at *or* by a th.). 2. *v.a.* frighten, scare, startle, terrify. 3. *v.r.* give a start, be startled, take fright. **–end,** *pr.p. & adj.* alarming; (*coll.*) *adv.* awfully. **–lich,** *adj.* terrific, terrible, dreadful.
erschrickst, erschrickt, *see* **erschrecken.**
erschrocken, *p.p. & adj.* frightened, scared, terrified, *see* **erschrecken. –heit,** *f.* fright, fear, terror.
erschütter–n, 1. *v.a.* shake violently, convulse, stir, impress, move *or* affect deeply; (*fig.*) shock, unnerve. 2. *v.n.* (*aux.* s.) shake, quake, vibrate. **–ung,** *f.* shaking, shock, vibration, concussion; convulsion, violent emotion. **–ungsreiz,** *m.* contact stimulus. **–ungswelle,** *f.* earth tremor. **–ungszeiger,** *m.* seismograph.
erschweren, *v.a.* make more difficult *or* heavy, aggravate, impede.
erschwing–en, *ir.v.a.* afford, be able to pay, manage. **–lich,** *adj.* within one's means, at a reasonable price, reasonable, attainable.
ersehen, *ir.v.a.* see, perceive, (*rare*) descry; learn, note, observe; distinguish; *sich* (*Dat.*) *etwas –,* choose *or* select s.th. for o.s.; *hieraus ist zu –,* from this it is clear *or* it appears that.
ersehnen, *v.a.* long for, desire greatly.
ersetz–en, *v.a.* replace, take the place of, substitute, displace; repair, restore; compensate, make amends for; make good, make up for; reimburse, repay, indemnify; *sich –en lassen,* be (able to be) replaced; have a substitute provided; *er –t ihn nicht,* he does not take his place, is not equal to him (*his predecessor*); *etwas –t erhalten,* receive compensation. **–bar,** *adj.* replaceable; *nicht –bar,* irreplaceable. **–lich,** *adj.* reparable, retrievable; replaceable. **–ung,** *f.* replacement, substitution, compensation, indemnification, reimbursement; *see* **Ersatz.**
ersichtlich, *adj.* evident, obvious, manifest, visible, perceptible, as may be seen; *hieraus ist –,* from this it appears.
ersinn–en, *ir.v.a.* think out, conceive, devise, invent, excogitate. **ersonnen,** *p.p. & adj.* devised, invented, fabricated. **–lich,** *adj.* imaginable; *auf alle –liche Weise,* in every imaginable, conceivable *or* possible way.
ersitz–en, *ir.v.a.* (*Law*) acquire by (positive) prescription; *er hat sich die Beförderung einfach ersessen,* he obtained promotion solely by virtue of his long service. **–ung,** *f.* possession by prescriptive right, usucaption (*Law*).
erspähen, *v.a.* detect, espy, descry.
erspar–en, *v.a.* save, economize, spare; *du hättest dir die Mühe –en können,* you might have saved *or* spared yourself the trouble. **–nis,** *f.* (-nisse), *n.* (-nisses, -nisse) savings, saving, economy.
ersprieß–lich, 1. *adj.* useful, profitable, beneficial; salutary. 2. *adv.* advantageously. **–lichkeit,** *f.* benefit, advantage, profitableness.
erst, 1. *adj.* first, foremost, prime, leading, best, superior; *der, die* or *das –e beste,* the first that comes; *das –e Buch Moses,* Genesis; *bei –er Gelegenheit,* at the first opportunity; *–er Kommis,* head clerk; *in –er Linie,* in the first place, first of all; *–e Qualität,* prime quality, A 1; *zum –en, fürs –e,* in the first place, for the present, at first, for some time; *zum –en! zweiten! dritten!* going! going! gone! 2. *adv.* at first, first of all, at the beginning; for the first time, not till, only, just; some day *or* time (*in the future*); *– als,* only when; *dann –,* not till then; *eben erst,* just now, only just; *es wurde – heute fertig,* it was only ready today; *er wird es – morgen erfahren,* he will not hear of it till tomorrow; *es muß sich – noch zeigen,* it remains to be seen; *wäre ich nur – da!* if only I were there! *wenn so etwas verboten ist, geschieht es – recht,* if such a thing is forbidden, it is done all the more; *nun – recht,* now more than ever; *– recht nicht,* less than ever, much less still; *das macht es – recht schlimm,* that makes it all the worse; *ich will das – werden,* I want to be that some day; (*Prov.*) *– wägen dann wagen,* look before you leap; (*Prov.*) *– die Arbeit dann das Vergnügen,* business before pleasure. **–aufführung,** *f.* first-night, premiere (*Theat.*). **–druck,** *m.* first edition. **–ens,** *adv.* firstly, in the first place. **–geboren,** *adj.* first-born. **–geburt,** *f.* primogeniture; *Esau verkaufte sein –geburtsrecht,* Esau sold his birthright. **–genannt,** *adj.* first-named, aforesaid, aforementioned, former. **–klassig,** *adj.* first-class, first-rate, A 1. **–lich,** *adv.* firstly, first. **–ling,** *m.* first born, first-production; (*pl.*) first-fruits. **–lingsarbeit,** *f.* first work, beginner's work. **–lingsrede,** *f.* maiden speech. **–lingsroman,** *m.* first novel. **–malig,** *adj.* for the first time. **–milch,** *f.* colostrum. **–rangig,** *adj.*, *see* **–klassig. –strom,** *m.* primary current (*Elec.*).
erstark–en, *v.n.* (*aux.* s.) grow strong *or* stronger, gain strength. **–ung,** *f.* strengthening; *wirtschaftliche –ung,* economic recovery.
erstarr–en, 1. *v.n.* (*aux.* s.) be benumbed, grow stiff, become torpid, congeal, solidify, harden, curdle; be paralysed (*with fear*). 2. *n.* torpidity. **–t,** *p.p. & adj.* benumbed, torpid. **–ung,** *f.* numbness, stiffness, torpidity, freezing, solidification, coagulation.
erstatt–en, *v.a.* refund, restore, make good, return; replace; *Bericht –en,* report, render an account; *wieder –en,* restore, reimburse. **–lich,** *adj.* retrievable, recoverable. **–ung,** *f.* refunding; compensation, restitution; delivery (*of a report*).
erstaun–en, 1. *v.n.* (*aux.* s.) be astonished (*über eine S.,* at a th.). 2. *v.a.* astonish, surprise. 3. *n.* astonishment, amazement, surprise; *höchstes –en,* stupefaction; *in –en setzen,* astonish, amaze;

zum –en, astonishing(ly). **–end,** *pr.p. & adj.* astonishing. **–enswert,** *adj.*, **–enswürdig,** *adj.*, **–lich,** *adj.* surprising, astonishing, amazing, remarkable, marvellous; *das –liche bei der S.*, the surprising thing about it; *er hat –liches geleistet*, his achievement is remarkable.

ersteh–en, 1. *ir.v.n.* (*aux.* s.) (*rare*) arise, rise; *Christ ist erstanden*, Christ is arisen; *es –en mir nichts als Unannehmlichkeiten daraus*, it brings me nothing but unpleasantness. 2. *v.a.* buy, purchase, pick up (*as at an auction*); suffer, endure.

ersteig–en, *v.a.* climb, mount, scale, ascend. **–bar,** *adj.* climbable. **–ung,** *f.* ascent, climbing, scaling.

erstellen, *v.a.* (*rare*), *see* **aufstellen, herstellen.**

ersterben, *ir.v.n.* (*aux.* s.) die; die away, become extinct; fade away; *das Wort erstarb auf seinen Lippen*, the word died on his lips; *erstorbene Glieder*, benumbed limbs.

erstick–en, 1. *v.a.* stifle, suffocate, choke, smother; suppress; *im Keime –t*, nipped in the bud; *ein –tes Lachen*, suppressed laughter. 2. *v.n.* (*aux.* s.) choke, suffocate, be choked *or* suffocated; *in der Arbeit –en*, be snowed under with work. 3. *n.*, **–ung,** *f.* suffocation, asphyxiation, choking, asphyxia; *heiß zum –en*, stiflingly hot; *zum –en voll*, crammed to suffocation. **–ungstod,** *m.* death from suffocation, asphyxiation.

erstrahlen, *v.n.* shine forth, radiate.

erstreb–en, *v.a.* strive for *or* after, aspire to, obtain *or* attain by endeavour. **–ung,** *f.* pursuit (*of an object*), striving, aspiration.

erstreck–en, *v.r.* extend, stretch, run, reach (to) (*auf, bis auf* (*Acc.*) *bis zu, etc.*); *die Summe –t sich auf*, the sum amounts to; *sich gleichweit –en*, coextend. **–ung,** *f.* prolongation (*of a term*); extension.

erstürmen, *v.a.* storm, take by storm *or* assault.

ersuch–en, 1. *v.a.* beg, request, beseech, implore, entreat, supplicate (*um*, for); petition (*formally and politely*). 2. *n.* request, petition, entreaty, solicitation; suit; *auf das –en des Bruders*, at the request of the brother; *auf sein wiederholtes –en*, on his repeated entreaties.

ertappen, *v.a.* catch, detect; surprise; *auf frischer Tat –*, catch red-handed *or* in the act; *bei einer Lüge –*, detect in a lie.

erteil–en, *v.a.* (*einem etwas*) give, impart, confer on, bestow (on), grant, allot, apportion; *Nachricht –en*, send word, inform; *ein Amt –en*, bestow an office; *Rat –en*, give advice; *Unterricht –en*, teach, give instruction. **–ung,** *f.* giving, imparting, bestowing, bestowal, grant; publication (*of an order*). **–ungsakten,** *f.pl.* documentary record.

ertönen, *v.n.* (*aux.* s.) sound, resound; *– lassen*, sound; raise (*the voice*).

ertöten, *v.a.* deaden, smother, stifle; mortify (*the flesh*).

Ertrag, *m.* (-(e)s, ⸚e) produce, yield, output; proceeds, profit, returns, revenue; *reiner –* or *Rein–*, net profit. **–en,** *ir.v.a.* bear, suffer, tolerate, endure, put up with; *dies will ich nicht länger –en*, I will stand *or* bear this no longer. **–los,** *adj.* unproductive. **–reich,** *adj.* productive, fruitful. **–(s)-fähigkeit,** *f.* productivity.

erträg–lich, *adj.* bearable, tolerable, endurable, passable. **–nis,** *n.* (*rare*), *see* **Ertrag.**

ertränk–en, *v.a.* drown; *den Kummer im Wein –en*, drown one's misery in wine. **–ung,** *f.* drowning.

erträumen, *v.a.* dream of, imagine. **erträumt,** *p.p. & adj.* imaginary, chimerical.

ertrinken, *ir.v.n.* (*aux.* s.) drown, be drowned; *der* or *die Ertrunkene*, drowned p.

ertrotzen, *v.a.* (*sich* (*Dat.*) *etwas von einem*) extort from, obtain by insolence, obstinacy, defiance, etc.

ertüchtig–en, *v.a.* make fit *or* vigorous; train, harden, toughen. **–ung,** *f.* training, attainment of physical fitness; *körperliche –ung*, physical training.

erübrig–en, 1. *v.a.* save, lay by; spare, *er hat ein Sümmchen –t*, he has saved *or* put by a small sum; *für dich kann ich eine Stunde –en*, I can spare an hour for you. 2. *v.n.* (*aux.* h.) remain over, be left; *es –t nur noch zu bemerken*, I have only to add. 3. *v.r.* be superfluous *or* unnecessary; *es dürfte sich –en*, it is hardly necessary; *der Gebrauch eines Schlafmittels hat sich –t*, the use of an opiate has become unnecessary. **–t,** *p.p. & adj.* saved; *sein –tes*, his savings. **–ung,** *f.* saving.

erwachen, 1. *v.n.* (*aux.* s.) awake, awaken, wake up. 2. *n.* awakening.

erwachsen, 1. *ir.v.n.* (*aux.* s.) grow up, grow (*aus*, out of, from); spring up, spring from, proceed (*aus*, from); accrue; *der daraus –de Vorteil*, the profit accruing therefrom. 2. *p.p. & adj.* grown up; *der* or *die –e*, adult, grown-up. **–enerziehung,** *f.* adult education.

erwäg–en, *ir.v.a.* consider, weigh, ponder; discuss; *ich will es –en*, I will think it over; *alles wohl erwogen*, on mature consideration. **–ung,** *f.* consideration, reflection, contemplation; deliberation. *in –ung ziehen*, take into consideration; *in –ung dessen*, in consideration of this, with regard to this.

erwählen, *v.a.* choose, elect.

erwähn–en, *v.a.* (*& n.* (*aux.* h.)) (with *Acc. or* (*rare*) *Gen.*) mention, make mention of; call to notice; *es möge hinreichen zu –en*, suffice it to say; *noch ist zu –en*, there remains to be mentioned; *oben –t* above mentioned. **–ung,** *f.* mention; *einer S. –ung tun*, mention a th.; *bei –ung*, at the mention (of); *ehrenvolle –ung*, honourable mention.

erwärm–en, 1. *v.a.* make warm, warm, heat. 2. *v.r. sich –en für eine S.*, take a lively interest in a th., become enthusiastic over *or* about a th. **–ung,** *f.* warming, heating. **–ungskraft,** *f.* heating *or* calorific power.

erwart–en, *v.a.* expect, await, wait for, anticipate; *das läßt sich kaum –en*, that is scarcely to be expected. **–ung,** *f.* expectation, anticipation. **–ungsvoll,** *adj.* expectant, full of hope.

erweck–en, *v.a.* rouse, wake, waken, awaken; arouse, inspire, animate, stir up; *vom Tode –en*, resuscitate, raise (from the dead), restore to life; *er –te bei ihnen den Glauben*, he caused them to believe *or* inspired in them the belief; *Hoffnungen –en*, raise hopes. **–ung,** *f.* awakening; resuscitation; excitation; rousing, revival. **–ungsprediger,** *m.* revivalist.

erwehren, *v.r.* (*Gen.*) guard against, defend o.s. against; resist, refrain from, forbear, (*coll.*) keep off; *ich konnte mich des Lachens nicht –*, I could not help laughing; *sie konnte sich der Tränen kaum –*, she could scarcely restrain her tears.

erweich–en, *v.a.* soften, soak; mellow, mollify; (*fig.*) move, touch; *sich –en lassen*, relent. **–end,** *pr.p. & adj.* softening, emollient. **–ung,** *f.* softening, mollification. **–ungsmittel,** *n.* emollient (*Med.*).

Erweis, *m.* (-es, -e) proof, evidence, demonstration. **–en,** 1. *ir.v.a.* prove; *einem –en*, show, do, pay *or* render (*mercy, honour, favour, etc.*) to a p.; *–en Sie mir diesen Dienst*, do me this service. 2. *v.r.* show *or* prove o.s. (to be), turn out to be; *er erwies sich als einen tüchtigen* (or *als ein tüchtiger*) *Geschäftsmann*, he proved himself to be an excellent man of business; *das Gerücht erwies sich als falsch*, the report turned out to be false. **erwiesen,** *p.p. & adj.* proved, certain; *es ist nichts erwiesen*, nothing is proved; not proven (*Scottish Law*). *erwiesenermaßen*, *adv.* as has been proved. **–bar,** *adj.*, **–lich,** *adj.* demonstrable, provable. **–ung,** *f.* showing, proving, demonstration.

erweiter–n, 1. *v.a.* widen, expand, enlarge, extend; dilate, distend, amplify. 2. *v.r.* grow larger, widen, spread, expand, be extended *or* enlarged; *–ter Selbstschutz* (*Nat. Soc.*), air-raid precautions. **–ung,** *f.* widening, enlargement, extension, amplification; expansion dilatation (*Med.*); *die –ung der Adern*, aneurism (*Med.*).

Erwerb, *m.* acquisition, gain; earnings; profit, returns; industry, business (*by which a livelihood is gained*), livelihood, living; (*as prefix*) commercial (e.g. *–gartenbau, m.* commercial horticulture.). **–en,** *ir.v.a.* gain, obtain, acquire; earn; win. **erworben,** *p.p. & adj.*; *sauer erworben*, hard-earned; *mit Unrecht erworben*, ill-gotten; *das Erworbene*, acquisition, gain; earnings; perquisite (*Law*). **–er,** *m.* acquirer, transferee (*Law*). **–los,** *adj.* (*rare*) unprofitable, (e.g.

-lose Zeiten, times when work is hard to find, hard times.) **-sam,** *adj.* industrious. **-samkeit,** *f.* diligence, industry. **-sfähig,** *adj.* capable of earning a living. **-slos,** *adj.* out of work, unemployed. **-slosenunterstützung,** *f.* unemployment relief, (*coll.*) dole. **-slosigkeit,** *f.* unemployment. **-smittel,** *n.*, **-squelle,** *f.* means of livelihood. **-ssinn,** *m.* acquisitiveness, aptitude for business. **-sstand,** *m.* employed classes. **-stätig,** *adj.* working, in employment. **-sunfähig,** *adj.* incapable of earning a living, unfit for work. **-surkunde,** *f.* title-deed (*Law*). **-szweig,** *m.* branch of industry, line of business.

erwider-n, *v.a.* reply, retort, rejoin, answer (*auf*); return, reciprocate, render in return; requite, repay, retaliate. **-ung,** *f.* reply, answer, retort, rejoinder; return, retaliation, reciprocation, requital. **-ungsschrift,** *f.* rejoinder (*Law*).

erwiesenermaßen, *adv.*, *see* **erweisen.**

erwirken, *v.a.* bring about, effect, achieve, procure, secure.

erwischen, *v.a.* (*coll.*) catch, capture, surprise; *laß dich nicht – !* mind you don't get caught!

erwog, erwöge, erwogen, *see* **erwägen.**

erwünsch-en, *v.a.* wish for, desire. **-t,** *p.p. & adj.* desired; desirable; apropos; *das ist mir sehr –t*, that suits me very well *or* perfectly, I shall be very pleased at that; *persönliche Vorstellung –t*, personal application is desirable *or* requested; *–te Wirkung*, desired effect.

erwürg-en, 1. *v.a.* strangle, choke, throttle; (*Poet.*) slaughter, put to death. 2. *v.n.* (*aux.* s.) choke, be suffocated. **-ung,** *f.* strangling, strangulation; (*Poet.*) slaughter.

[1]**Erz,** *n.* (-es, -e) ore; metal; brass, bronze; *wie aus – gegossen dastehen*, stand like a statue. **-abfälle,** *m.pl.* tailings. **-ader,** *f.* vein of ore, lode. **-ähnlich,** *adj.* metallic. **-anbruch,** *m.* native ore. **-arbeiter,** *m.* metal worker. **-artig,** *adj.* metallic. **-aufbereitung,** *f.* ore dressing. **-beschickung,** *f.*, *see* **-aufbereitung. -beschlagen,** *adj.* brass-bound (*as a desk, etc.*). **-bild,** *n.* bronze statue; brazen image. **-brecher,** *m.* ore *or* rock crusher. **-bruch,** *m.* mine. **-en,** *adj.* brazen, bronze. **-farben,** *adj.* **-farbig,** *adj.* bronze-coloured. **-förderung,** *f.* output of ore, **-führend,** *adj.* ore-bearing. **-gang,** *m.* lode, mineral vein. **-gestein,** *n.* ore-bearing rock. **-gießer,** *m.* brass-founder. **-gießerei,** *f.* brass-foundry; bronze casting. **-grube,** *f.* pit, mine. **-haltig,** *adj.*, **-haltend,** *adj.* containing ore. **-hütte,** *f.* smelting works. **-kunde** *f.* metallurgy; mineralogy. **-lager,** *n.* **-lagerstätte,** *f.* ore *or* mineral deposit. **-mutter,** *f.* matrix. **-ofen,** *m.* smelting furnace. **-pochen,** *n.* crushing of ore. **-probe,** *f.* assay. **-reich,** *adj.* rich in ore. **-scheider,** *m.* ore sorter *or* separator. **-verarbeitung,** *f.*, **-verhüttung,** *f.* ore-smelting.

[2]**Erz-,** *in compounds* = principal; arch-, cardinal, chief, arrant; excellent, very, extremely, high-. **-betrüger,** *m.* arrant cheat. **-bischof,** *m.* archbishop. **-bischöflich,** *adj.* archiepiscopal. **-bistum,** *n.* archbishopric. **-bösewicht,** *m.* arrant rogue. **-dekan,** *m.* archdeacon. **-diakonat,** *n.* archdeaconry. **-dieb,** *m.* inveterate thief. **-dumm** *adj.* extremely stupid. **-engel,** *m.* archangel. **-feind,** *m.* arch-enemy, Satan. **-gauner,** *m.* thorough scoundrel. **-grobian,** *m.* big bully. **-herzog,** *m.* archduke. **-herzogin,** *f.* archduchess. **-herzoglich,** *adj.* archducal. **-herzogtum,** *n.* archduchy. **-kämmerer,** *m.* Lord (High) Chamberlain. **-kanzler,** *m.* Lord (High) Chancellor. **-katholisch,** *adj.* ultra-Catholic. **-ketzer,** *m.* arch-heretic. **-kokette,** *f.* out-and-out flirt, arrant coquette. **-lügner,** *m.* arch-liar. **-lump,** *m.*, *see* **-gauner. -marschall,** *m.* Grand Marshal. **-narr,** *m.* arrant fool. **-schatzmeister,** *m.* Lord (High) Treasurer. **-schelm,** *m.* arrant knave. **-spieler,** *m.* inveterate gambler. **-spitzbube,** *m.* arrant knave. **-stift,** *n.* archbishopric. **-stutzer,** *m.* out-and-out *or* thorough dandy. **-vater,** *m.* patriarch. **-väterlich,** *adj.* patriarchal.

erzähl-en, *v.a.* tell, relate, narrate; *man –t*, people say, it is said. **-bar,** *adj.* fit for recital; (*coll. & hum.*) 'drawing-room' (= *suitable for mixed company*). **-end,** *pr.p. & adj.* narrative; epic (*poem*). **-er,** *m.* narrator; story-teller, writer, novelist. **-ung,** *f.* narration; account, narrative, tale, story, report.

erzeigen, 1. *v.a.* (*einem etwas*) show, manifest, display (*feeling, etc.*); render, do (*kindness*). 2. *v.r.* prove to be.

erzeug-en, *v.a.* procreate, beget (*offpsring*); engender, raise, breed; produce, manufacture; grow; *Dampf –en*, generate steam; *Verdacht –en*, create suspicion; *Verachtung –en*, breed contempt. **-er,** *m.* grower; producer, manufacturer; generator (*Elec.*); begetter, procreator, parent, father, sire. **-erin,** *f.* parent, mother, dam. **-nis,** *n.* product, production, offspring, produce, yield. **-ung,** *f.* begetting; procreation; production; generation (*of steam, electricity, etc.*). **-ungsschlacht,** *f.* (*Nat. Soc.*) struggle for self-sufficiency.

erzieh-en, *ir.v.a.* bring up, train; educate; rear, grow, raise, tend; *wohl erzogen*, well bred, well educated. **-bar,** *adj.* teachable, trainable, educable, rearable. **-er,** *m.* educator; teacher; (private) tutor. **-erin,** *f.* governess, schoolmistress. **-erisch** *adj.* educational. **-lich,** *adj.* educative, pedagogic. **-ung,** *f.* upbringing, education, bringing up, rearing; *schlechte –ung*, bad *or* poor education, ill-breeding. **-ungsanstalt,** *f.* educational establishment. **-ungsart,** *f.* system *or* method of education. **-ungsbeihilfe,** *f.* education allowance. **-ungsfähig,** *adj.* teachable, docile. **-ungskunde,** *f.*, **-ungslehre,** *f.* pedagogy (*as a science*); pedagogics, theory (and practice) of education. **-ungslos,** *adj.* uneducated, without breeding. **-ungsrat,** *m.* educational council, board of governors (*school*). **-ungsroman,** *m.* biographical novel (dealing with the development of character). **-ungswesen,** *n.* educational system.

erzielen, *v.a.* obtain, attain, achieve, produce, realize, strive after.

erzittern, *v.n.* (*aux* s.) tremble violently; shiver, shudder.

erzürnen, 1. *v.a.* irritate, anger, enrage, provoke to anger. 2. *v.r. & n.* (*aux.* s.) get angry, quarrel with, (*coll.*) fall out with.

erzwingen, *ir.v.a.* force, enforce; extort from; gain by force. **erzwungen,** *p.p. & adj.* forced, induced, simulated, affected, artificial; *erzwungenes Lächeln*, forced smile.

[1]**es,** *pers. pron.* 1. (*Nom. & Acc.* of *3rd sing. neuter*); it; *ich bin – müde* or *satt*, I am tired of it; *ich bin – zufrieden*, I am satisfied with it, I have no objection; *er ist – wert*, he is worthy of it, he deserves it; *ich halte – nicht aus*, I can't stand *or* endure it. 2. *Used as a subject of imp. verbs sometimes* = there; *– schneit*, it is snowing, there is snow; *– wird getanzt*, there is dancing; *– gibt Leute*, there are people; *– sagt sich schwer*, it is difficult to say; it is hard to tell; *– friert mich*, I feel cold; *– fröstelt mich*, I am shivering; *– fragt sich, ob*, the question is whether, it is a question if; *– nimmt mich wunder*, I am astonished. 3. *Used demonstratively* = he, she, it, they; *– ist sein erster Versuch*, it *or* this is his first attempt; *– sind Männer von Ansehen*, they are men of position *or* of consequence; *wer ist der Mann? – ist mein Bruder*, who is this man? he is my brother; *wer ist diese Frau? – ist die Mutter*, who is this woman? it is the mother; *– ist eine Freundin von mir*, she is a friend of mine. 4. *Used as dummy subject, the true subject followed the verb, sometimes* = it, there, *etc.*; *sometimes untranslatable*; *– klopft jemand*, somebody is knocking; *– lebe der König;* long live the king! (*Prov.*) *– ist nicht alles Gold was glänzt*, all is not gold that glitters; *– waren ihrer drei*, there were three of them; *– ist nichts so gut*, there is nothing so good; *– ist ein Gott*, there is a God; *– spiele wer da will*, let them play that wish to; *– war einmal ein Mann*, there was once a man; *– sei denn*, unless, provided. 5. *Used to denote a subject that is vague*: *– ruft aus den Tiefen*, a voice is heard from the deep; *– pocht an die Tür*, there is a knock at the door; *– auf der Brust haben*, have something the matter with one's chest *or* breathing; *– riß mich blitzschnell hinunter*, I was carried down as quick as lightning. 6. *Used as completion*

of predicate = so, it; *ich bin* –, it is I; *sie sind* –, it is they; *ich selber bin – nicht mehr*, as for me, I am no longer (*whatever had been referred to earlier*); *wir sind – die es getan haben*, it is we who did it; *keiner will – gewesen sein*, no one would admit to it, no one would acknowledge that it was he; *er ist reich, ich bin – auch*, he is rich and I am too; *er sagt* –, he says so; *ich weiß* –, I know; *ich bat dich, – ihm zu sagen*; *hast du – getan?* I asked you to tell him; did you do so *or* have you done so? *da haben wir's*, now we're getting at it, there's the rub, (*coll.*) that's the snag; – *gut haben*, be well off; – *weit bringen*, make good progress, get on well; *er hat – mit ihr verdorben;* he has annoyed *or* upset her; *er hat – mit mir zu tun*, he has me to deal with, he will have trouble with me; *ich meine – gut mit dir*, I mean well towards *or* by you, I am well disposed towards you; *er treibt – zu bunt*, he goes too far; *er kann – nicht über sich gewinnen*, he can't bring himself to it.

²**es**, *n.* E flat (*Mus.*); *es-dur*, E-flat major; *es-moll*, E-flat minor. *es-es*, *n.* E double flat.

Esche, *f.* (-n), **–nbaum**, *m.* ash, ash-tree (*Fraxinus excelsior*) (*Bot.*). **–n**, *adj.* of ash, ashen.

Esel, *m.* (-s, –) ass, donkey; silly ass, fool, jackass; *hölzerner* –, easel, *wilder* –, onager; *gestreifter* –, zebra; *den* – (*einen*) – *nennen*, call a spade a spade; *dummer –!* silly ass *or* fool! *störrisch wie ein* –, stubborn as a mule; *bepackt* or *beladen wie ein* –, laden like a beast of burden; (*Prov.*) *ein – schilt den anderen Langohr*, the pot calling the kettle black; *den – zu Grabe läuten*, dangle one's feet; *vom Pferde auf den – kommen*, come down in the world; *den Sack schlagen und den – meinen*, say (*or* do) one thing and mean another; *wenn dem – zu wohl wird, geht er aufs Eis*, pride will have a fall. **–ei**, *f.* blunder, folly, stupidity. **–haft**, *adj.* asinine, stupid. **–in**, *f.* she-ass. **–sbrücke**, *f.* (*school sl.*), crib. **–sgeschrei**, *n.* braying of an ass. **–skopf**, *m.* dolt. **–sohr**, *n.* dog's ear, dog-ear (= *turned down corner of page*). **–stritt**, *m.* kick of an ass; cowardly revenge. (*sl.*) **–swiese**, *f.* correspondence column (*in a newspaper*).

Eskadron, *f.* troop (*of cavalry*).

Eskort–e, *f.* (-en) escort, convoy. **–ieren**, *v.a.* escort, convoy.

Espe, *f.* (-n) aspen-tree (*Populus tremula*) (*Bot.*). **–n**, *adj.* aspen. **–nlaub**, *n.* foliage of the aspen; *er zittert wie –nlaub*, he trembles like an aspen leaf.

Esse, *f.* (-n) chimney, chimney-pipe, funnel; forge, smithy. **–naufsatz**, *m.* chimney-pot. **–nfeger**, *m.*, **–nkehrer**, *m.* chimney-sweep.

ess–en, 1. *ir.v.a.* & *n.* (*aux.* h.) eat; take one's meals; mess (*Mil.* & *Naut*); *zu Mittag –en*, lunch, dine (*early*); *zu Abend –en*, dine (*late*), sup; *die Schüssel leer –en*, clean one's plate; *sich satt –en*, eat one's fill; *gern Austern –en*, like oysters; *er ißt täglich dreimal*, he takes three meals a day. 2. *n.* food, meal; eating, feeding. *–en fassen*, draw rations (*Mil.*); *ich kann das fette –en nicht vertragen*, rich food does not agree with me; *das –en abtragen*, clear the table. **–enszeit** *f.* mealtime. **–(ß)bar**, *adj.* eatable, edible. **–(ß)begier**, *f.* craving for food, gluttony. **–(ß)gelage**, *n.* feast, banquet. **–(ß)geschirr**, *n.* mess-tin (*Mil.*). **–(ß)gier**, *f.*, *see* **–(ß)begier**. **–(ß)gierig**, *adj.* ravenous. **–(ß)korb**, *m.* provision-basket, hamper. **–(ß)löffel**, *m.* table-spoon. **–(ß)lust**, *f.* appetite. **–(ß)tisch**, *m.* dining-table. **–(ß)waren**, *f.pl.* eatables, provisions, victuals. **–(ß)zimmer**, *n.* dining-room.

Essenz, *f.* (-en) essence.

Essig, *m.* (-s, -e) vinegar; (*coll.*) *damit ist es –!* the matter has turned out a failure, (*coll.*) it's all up with it! (*sl.*) it's a flop, it's no go. **–artig**, *adj.* vinegar-like; acetic, acetous (*Chem.*). **–äther**, *m.* acetic ether, ethyl acetate. **–bildung**, *f.* acetification. **–geist**, *m.* acetone. **–gurke**, *f.* pickled cucumber *or* gherkin. **–salz**, *n.* acetate. **–sauer**, *adj.* acetic, acetate of (*Chem.*). **–säure**, *f.* acetic acid. **–siederei**, *f.* vinegar works. **Essig- und Ölständer**, *m.* cruet.

Estrich, *m.* (-s, -e) plaster *or* stone floor; pavement, flagstone; top story (*Swiss*).

etablieren, 1. *v.a.* established, set up. 2. *v.r.* set up in business.

Etag–e [*pron.* e:'taʒə], *f.* (-n) floor, story, tier. **–enschlüssel**, *m.* latchkey (*of an apartment*). **–enwohnung**, *f.* flat. **–ere**, *f.* (-n) stand, rack, what-not.

Etappe, *f.* (-n) communications zone (*Mil.*); (*fig.*) stage. **–nanfangsort**, *m.* base (*Mil.*). **–ngebiet**, *n.* lines of communication area (*Mil.*). **–nkommandantur** *f.* L. of C. Commandant's headquarters. **–nlazarett**, *n.* base hospital. **–nort**, *m.* post on L. of C. **–nschwein**, *n.* (*sl.*) base-wallah. **–nstraße**, *f.* military road. **–nverwendungsfähig**, *adj.* suitable for employment on lines of communication; **–nweise**, *adj.* by stages, stage by stage.

Etat [*pron.* e'ta:], *m.* (-s, -s) balance-sheet; budget, estimate; establishment. **–isieren**, *v.a.* estimate (*state expenditure*); (*C.L.*) balance. **–jahr**, *n.* financial year, fiscal year. **–mäßig**, *adj.* on the establishment; permanent (*of an official*). **–sberatung**, *f.* debate on the budget. **–sbuch**, *n.* ledger.

etepetete, *adj.* (*coll.*) finicky, finicking; *darin ist er sehr* –, in that respect he is very particular.

Eth–ik, *f.* ethics. **–iker**, *m.* moral philosopher. **–isch**, *adj.* ethical.

Ethno–, *adj. prefix*; **–graph**, *m.* (-en, -en) ethnographer. **–graphie**, *f.* ethnography. **–graphisch**, *adj.* ethnographic(al). **–log(e)**, *m.* (-en, -en) ethnologist. **–logie**, *f.* ethnology. **–logisch**, *adj.* ethnological, ethnic(al).

Etikett–e, *f.* (-en), etiquette; label, ticket, tag. **–ieren**, *v.a.* label; affix a ticket to, put a ticket on.

etlich–e, *pl. adj.* & *pron.* some, several; a few; *–e Male* (or *–emal*), now and then; (*rare*) *–e und achtzig Jahre*, *achtzig Jahre und –e*, eighty odd; *–e Worte*, a few words. **–es**, *pron. n.* something, sundry things; *ich habe –es hinzuzufügen*, I have a thing or two to add.

Etmal, *n.* (-(e)s, -e) (time *or* work done) round the clock; day's run (*Naut.*).

Etui, [*pron.* e'tvı:] *n.* (-s, -s) case (*for small articles*), box.

etwa, 1. *adv.* nearly, about; perhaps, by chance, perchance; *ist's Ihnen – um 5 Uhr gefällig?* shall we say 5 o'clock? *was – vorkommen mag*, whatever may happen; *wenn sie – hören*, if you should hear by any chance; – *20 Leute*, about 20 people. 2. *part.*; *er wird doch nicht – glauben*, he will not believe, I hope. **–ig**, *adj.* possible, eventual; *–ige Schwierigkeiten*, contingent difficulties, whatever difficulties may arise.

etwas (1 & 2 *often abbrev. to* was), 1. *ind. pron.* (*indec.*) something, some, anything, any; – *Neues*, s.th. new, news; – *Neues?* any news, anything fresh? – *Geld*, some money; – *anderes*, s.th. else; *das ist – anderes*, that is a different matter, that is quite different; *irgend* –, anything, something or other; *in –, um –*, in some measure, in some respects; *wer vieles bringt, wird manchem – bringen* (*Goethe*), he who brings much brings something for most; *das will – sagen*, that is saying a great deal; *er gilt – bei ihm*, he is in high favour with him, he is in his good books; *so* –, such a thing; *so – bedarf Zeit*, such a matter requires time; *nein, so –!* you surprise me, I can't credit it; *nein, so – ist mir doch noch nie vorgekommen!* well, such a thing has never happened to me before. 2. *adv.* somewhat; a little; rather; – *weitschweifig*, rather prolix; *er bildet sich – ein*, he is somewhat *or* rather conceited. 3. *n.* entity; *ein gewisses* –, a certain thing, an indefinable something, something unaccountable.

Etymolog–(e), *m.* (-en, -en) etymologist. **–ie**, *f.* etymology. **–isch**, *adj.* etymological.

euch, *pers. pron.* (*Acc.* & *Dat. pl. of* du) (*in letters* Euch) you, to you.

eu–er (*in letters* & *titles* Euer, *in titles abbr.* Ew.) 1. *pron.* (*Gen. pl. of* du); *–er sind drei*, there are three of you; *ich erinnere mich –er*, I remember you. 2. *poss. adj.* your, your own; *–er Vater*, your father; *–(e)re Mutter*, your mother; *–er Kind*, your child. 3. *poss. pron.* (der, die, das –(e)re *or* –rige) yours, your own. 4. *subst. pl.*; *die –ern, –ren*, or *–rigen*, your relatives, relations *or* people. 5. *n.*; *das –re* or *–rige*, your belongings *or* goods; that which belongs to you *or* to which you are entitled; *ihr müßt das –re* or *–rige tun*, you must do your share *or* play your part. **–(r)erseits,** *adv.* on your side; (you) for your part; as far as you are concerned; you in your turn. **–ersgleichen, –resgleichen,** *indec. adj. or pron.* of your kind, like you. **–erthalben, –rethalben,** *adv.* **–ertwillen, –retwillen,** *adv.* on your account, for your sake.

Eule, *f.* (-n) owl; type of moth; (*coll.*) feather-brush; *–n nach Athen tragen*, carry coals to Newcastle; (*Prov.*) *des einen – ist des anderen Nachtigall*, one man's meat is another man's poison; *eine – unter Krähen*, the butt of everybody. **–nspiegel,** *see the Index of Names.* **–nspiegelei,** *f.* practical joke, tomfoolery.

Euter, *n.* (-s, –) udder.

evakuieren, *v.a.* evacuate, exhaust, empty, create a vacuum.

evangel–isch, *adj.* evangelical; Protestant, Lutheran. **–ium,** *n.* (–iums, -ien) gospel.

Eventu–alität, *f.* eventuality. **–ell,** 1. *adj.* possible. 2. *adv.* possibly, perhaps, if occasion should arise, if necessary.

Evidenz, *f.* certainty, assurance, infallibility, conclusiveness.

Ewer, *m.* (-s, –) fishing smack, coastal craft.

ewig, *adj.* everlasting, eternal; continual, endless; perpetual (*as snow*); *der –e Jude*, the wandering Jew; *das ist – schade*, that is a great pity; *auf –*, for ever, in perpetuity. **–keit,** *f.* eternity; perpetuity; age(s); *von –keit zu –keit, in alle –keit*, world without end, to all eternity. **–lich,** *adv.* for ever, eternally, perpetually, unceasingly.

exakt, *adj.* exact, accurate; *–e Wissenschaften*, mathematical sciences. **–heit,** *f.* exactness, exactitude, precision, punctiliousness.

exaltiert, *adj. & p.p.* over-excited, highly strung.

Exam–en, *n.* (-ens, -ina) examination; *mündliches –en*, oral *or* viva-voce examination, (*coll.*) viva; *ein –en ablegen, ins – gehen* or *steigen*, go in for *or* sit for an examination; *gerade im –en stehen*, he is in the middle of examinations; *das –en machen, das* or *im –en bestehen*, pass an examination; *im –en durchfallen*, (*coll.*) *durch das –en fallen*, fail an examination. **–inand,** *m.* (-en, -en) examinee, candidate. **–inator,** *m.* (-s, -en), examiner. **–inieren,** *v.a.* examine.

Excenter, *see* **Exzenter.**

Exege–se, *f.* exegesis. **–t,** *m.* commentator. **–tik,** *f.* exegetics.

Exemp–el, *n.* (-els, -el) example, model, instance; problem (*Math.*); *zum –el* (abbr. *z. E.*), for instance; *ein –el an einem* or *etwas statuieren*, let a p. *or* s.th. be a warning *or* example; *ein –el statuieren*, be *or* act as a warning, be an example. **–lar,** *n.* (-s, -e), copy (*of a book*); sample, specimen. **–larisch,** *adj.* exemplary; excellent.

Exequien, *n.pl.* obsequies; masses for the dead.

exerzier–en, 1. *v.a. & n.* exercise; drill; 2. *n.* drill. **–meister,** *m.* drill-sergeant, drill-instructor. **–patrone,** *f.* dummy cartridge, blank. **–platz,** *m.* parade ground, drill square, barrack square.

Exerzitium, *n.* (-s, -ien), written homework; devotions.

Exil, *n.* (-(e)s, -e) exile, banishment.

Exist–enz, *f.* (-en) existence; being; *eine sichere –enz*, a secure means of livelihood, an established position; *verfehlte* or *verkrachte –enz*, ne'er-do-well, failure; *dunkle –enz*, shady character. **–enzbedingungen,** *f.pl.* conditions of life. **–enzfähig,** *adj.* capable of existence. **–enzberechtigung,** *f.* right to exist, right to live. **–enzial,** *adj.* existentialist (*Heidegger's philosophy*). **–enzminimum,** *n.* living wage. **–enzmittel,** *n.pl.* means of existence *or* subsistence. **–ieren,** *v.n.* (*aux.* h.) exist, be, live, subsist.

exklusiv, *adj.* exclusive; *–e Gesellschaft*, exclusive society; *–e Trinkgeld*, exclusive of tip, excluding tip.

exkommunizieren, *v.a.* excommunicate.

exmatrikulieren, *v.a.*; *er läßt sich –*, he leaves the university, (*coll.*) he goes down.

exotisch, *adj.* exotic.

Exped–ient, *m.* (-en, -en) forwarder, forwarding agent *or* clerk. **–ieren,** *v.a.* dispatch, forward, send off (*a parcel, etc.*). **–ition,** *f.* dispatch, forwarding, delivery; expedition (*Mil.*); office (*of a journal, etc.*). **–itionsgeschäft,** *n.* hauliers, delivery service.

Experiment, *n.* (-s, -e) experiment; *ein – machen* or *anstellen*, make *or* try an experiment. **–ell,** *adj.* experimental. **–ieren,** *v.n.* (*aux.* h.) experiment.

explizieren, *v.a.* explain.

explo–dieren, *v.n.* explode, detonate. **–sion,** *f.* (-en) explosion, detonation. **–sionsmotor,** *m.* internal combustion engine. **–sivkraft,** *f.* disruptive *or* explosive force. **–sivstoff,** *m.* explosive.

exponier–en, *v.a.* expound, explain; expose; *–te Platte*; exposed plate (*Phot.*); *–te Stelle*, exposed spot *or* situation.

Export, *m.* (-s, -e) export, exportation; (*pl.*) exports, articles of export. **–eur,** *m.* exporter. **–geschäft,** *n.* export house. **–handel,** *m.* export trade. **–ieren,** *v.a.* export.

expreß, 1. *adj.* express, by express. 2. *adv.* on purpose, expressly; by express (*train, etc.*). **–(ss)ionistisch,** *adj.* expressionist (*of art*).

Exspir–ation, *f.* exhalation. **–ationsluft,** *f.* exhaled air. **–ieren,** *v.a. & n.* exhale.

Extase, *f.* (-n) ecstasy.

Extempor–ale, *n.* (-alien), class exercise, test paper; unprepared composition. **–ieren,** *v.a. & n.* extemporize; improvise.

extra, 1. *adj.* extra, additional; special. 2. *adv.* specially, into the bargain. **–ausgabe,** *f.*, **–blatt,** *n.* special edition. **–fein,** *adj.* superfine, of special quality. **–post,** *f.* post-chaise, special mail. **–stunden,** *f.pl.* extra lessons; overtime (*in factories*). **–wurst,** *f.* (*fig. sl.*) something quite special *or* out of the ordinary. **–zug,** *m.* special train.

extrahier–en, *v.a.* extract. **–ung,** *f.* extraction, evolution (*Math.*).

Extrakt, *m.* (-(e)s, -e) extract, essence.

Extrem, 1. *n.* (-s, -e) extreme; *die –e berühren sich*, the extremes meet. 2. *adj.* extreme, exaggerated. **–ität,** *f.* extremity.

Exzellenz, *f.* (-en) excellence; Excellency (*title*); *Ew. –*, Your Excellency.

Exzent–er, *m.* eccentric, cam. **–errad,** *n.* cam gear. **–errolle,** *f.* cam follower. **–risch,** *adj.* eccentric. **–rizität,** *f.* eccentricity.

Exzerp–t, *n.* (-es, -e) excerpt, extract. **–ieren,** *v.a.* make excerpts from, cull passages from. **–tenbuch,** *n.* commonplace book.

Exzeß, *m.* (-es, -e) excess, outrage.

F

F, f, *n.* F, f; F (*Mus.*); *for abbreviations see the Index at the end of the German–English Vocabulary.* (*coll.*) *nach Schema F gehen*, be perfectly in order, (*coll.*) be under control.

Fabel, *f.* (-n) fable, tale, story; plot (*of a drama*). **–dichter,** *m.* writer of fables, fabulist. **–ei,** *f.* fiction, tale. **–gestalt,** *f.* fabulous creature. **–haft,** 1. *adj.* fabulous, mythical; incredible, marvellous, wonderful; (*sl.*) wizard; 2. *adv.* (*sl.*) enormously, fantastically. **–land,** *n.* fairyland. **–lehre,** *f.* mythology. **–n,** *v.a. & n.* (*aux.* h.) tell stories, spin yarns, tell untruths; talk idly (*von*, about). **–schmied,** *m.* romancer, story-teller. **–welt,** *f.*, **–zeit,** *f.* fabulous *or* mythical age. **–wesen,** *n.* fabulous creature.

Fabrik, *f.* (-en) factory, works, mill. **–anlage,** *f.* plant. **–ant,** *m.* (-en, -en) manufacturer. **–arbeit,** *f.* factory work; factory-made articles. **–arbeiter,** *m.* factory hand *or* worker, operative. **–at,** *n.* (-(e)s, -e) manufacture, make; manufactured article, product. **–ation,** *f.* production, manufacture. **–ationsfehler,** *m.* flaw in manufacture. **–besitzer,** *m.* factory owner. **–gold,** *n.* gold-leaf. **–inspektor,** *m.* factory-inspector. **–marke,** *f.*, *see* **–zeichen.** **–mäßig,** *adj.* mass-produced (*of goods*); *–mäßige Herstellung,* bulk processing, mass production. **–stadt,** *f.* manufacturing town. **–waren,** *f.pl.* manufactures. **–wesen,** *n.* factory system. **–zeichen,** *n.* trade-mark.

fabrizieren, *v.a.* manufacture, make.

fabul–ieren, *v.n.* invent stories *or* fables.

Facette, *f.* (-n) facet. **–nschleifer,** *m.* diamond-cutter.

Fach, 1. *n.* (-(e)s, ⁻er) compartment, division; cell (*Bot.*); shelf, partition, pigeon-hole, drawer; panel (*of a door, etc.*); subject, branch, speciality, line, department; *das ist gerade sein –,* that is just his speciality; *von –,* by profession; *das ist nicht mein –* or *schlägt nicht in mein –,* that is not within my province, that is not in my line; *er versteht sein – vollkommen,* he is an expert in his subject; *unter Dach und – bringen,* house, accommodate; put the finishing touches to, get finished; *unter Dach und – kommen,* find shelter *or* accommodation. 2. *suffix in compounds* = -fold (e.g. *hundert–,* hundredfold). **-fache,** *n.* (*suffix with numerals*), e.g. *das Vierfache,* a number four times as large. **–arbeiter,** *m.* skilled worker, specialist. **–artig,** *adj.* cellular. **–arzt,** *m.* specialist. **–ausbildung,** *f.* professional training. **–ausdruck,** *m.* technical term. **–gelehrte(r),** *m.* specialist. **–genosse,** *m,* colleague. **–kenntnis,** *f.* technical *or* specialist knowledge. **–kundig,** *adj.* competent, expert; *–kundige Leitung,* expert guidance, expert opinion. **–lehrer,** *m.* teacher of a special subject, specialist. **–lich,** *adj.* professional; technical; departmental; *–liche Vorbildung,* professional training. **–mann,** *m.* (-leute) expert, specialist; **–männisch,** expert, specialist, professional. **–ordnung,** *f.* classification. **–schaft,** *f.* industrial federation, professional body *or* organization. **–schule,** *f.* trade *or* technical school. (*coll.*) **–simpeln,** *v.n.* talk shop. **–sprache,** *f.* technical language. **–studium,** *n.* special study. **–wand,** *f.* panelled partition. **–weise,** *adv.* by compartments, in compartments; divided into classes. **–werk,** *n.* panelling; framework. **–werkbau,** *m.* half-timbered building. **–wissen,** *n.*, **–wissenschaft,** *f.* special branch of science. **–zeitschrift,** *f.* technical *or* scientific periodical.

fachen, *v.a.* fan; blow violently (*the fire*).

fäch–eln, *v.a.* & *n.* (*aux.* h.) fan. **–er,** *m.* fan. **–erbrenner,** *m.* fantail burner; **–erförmig ausschwärmen,** fan-out, deploy (*Mil.*). **–ergerste,** *f.* bearded barley. **–erpalme,** *f.* fan-palm, palmyra palm.

fächerig, *adj.* divided into compartments, cellular.

Fackel, *f.* (-n) torch, flare, flambeau. **–föhre,** *f.* Scotch pine. **–n,** *v.n.* (*aux.* h.) flare, flicker; (*fig.*) hesitate, dally; *hier wurde nicht lange gefackelt,* not much time was lost, there was not much shilly-shallying.

Façon, *f.* (*now usually* **Fasson**) fashion, style, cut. **–ieren,** *v.a.* fashion, convert. **–ierung,** *f.* conversion.

fad, *adj. see* **fade.**

Fäd–chen, *n.* (-s, –) little thread, filament. **–eln,** 1. *v.a.* thread (*a needle*); string. 2 *v.r.* untwist, become unravelled. 3. *v.n.* (*aux.* h.) be filaceous. **–ig,** *adj.* thread-like, filaceous.

fad–e, *adj.* insipid, flat; vacuous, trite, jejune, dull, stale. **–heit,** *f.* insipidity; staleness; triteness; (*pl.*) inanities, puerilities.

Faden, 1. *m.* (-s, ⁻) thread; string, twine, cord; fibre, filament; hairline (*Opt.*); shred, particle; burr, feather-edge (*of a knife*); thread (*of a discourse, of life, etc.*); cord (128 *cu. ft. of wood*). 2. *m.* (-s, –) fathom (= *6 feet*) (*Naut.*); (*einen*) *am – haben,* have a p. under one's thumb; *die Fäden* (*eines Unternehmens*) *in der Hand halten, alle Fäden in der Hand haben,* hold all the strings (of an enterprise) in one's hand; *an einem – hängen,* hang by a thread; *sie läßt keinen guten – an ihm,* she hasn't a good word to say for him; (*coll.*) *da beißt keine Maus den –* or *die Maus keinen – ab,* that is absolutely definite *or* irrevocable; *ein – Seide,* a bobbin of silk; *kein trockner –,* not a dry stitch; *er hat keinen trocknen – am Leibe,* he is wet through; *in einem – weg,* uninterruptedly. **–ähnlich,** *adj.*, **–artig,** *adj.* thread-like, filiform. **–dorf,** *n.* one-street village. **–förmig,** *adj.*, *see* **–ähnlich.** **–führer,** *m.* thread guide (*Weav.*). **–garn,** *n.* thread. **–gerade,** *adj.*, **–recht,** *adj.* perpendicular; dead straight. **–gold,** *n.* gold-thread. **–holz,** *n.* cord-wood. **–kreuz,** *n.* crosswires, reticule (*Opt.*). **–naß,** *adj.* thoroughly wet. **–nudeln,** *f.pl.* vermicelli. **–scheinig,** *adj.* threadbare, sleazy; (*fig.*) thin, shabby (*of an excuse*). **–weise,** *adv.* by threads, thread by thread. **–ziehend,** *adj.* stringy, ropy, viscous.

fad–en, fäd–en, *v.n.* fade (*Rad.*). **–ing,** *n.* fading (*Rad.*).

Fagott, *n.* (-s, -e) bassoon. **–ist,** *m.* bassoonist.

Fähe, *f.* (-n) female (*of hounds, foxes and wolves*) (*Hunt.*); bitch, vixen, *or* she-wolf.

fähig, *adj.* (*Gen.*) able, capable (of); clever; apt, fit (for); susceptible (of); *– zu einem Amte,* qualified for an office; *sich – machen,* qualify o.s. (*zu,* for); *–er Kopf,* man of parts. **–keit,** *f.* capability, ability; faculty, talent, capacity; (*pl.*) abilities; *das geht über meine –keiten,* that is beyond my power(s), that beats me.

fahl, *adj.* pale, faded, sallow, fawn-coloured, dun; (*rare*) fallow (*as in fallow deer*). **–grau,** *adj.* ashy grey, livid.

fahnd–en, *v.a.* search; *nach einem –en,* search for a p. **–ungsgesuch,** *n.* search warrant.

Fahne, *f.* (-n) flag, standard, banner; colours (*Mil.*); (*archaic*) company, troop, squadron; feather *or* beard (*of a quill*); vane, weather-cock; trail (*of smoke*); *bei der –,* on active service; *Dienst bei der –,* service with the colours, active military service. **–nabzug,** *m.* galley proof (*Typ.*). **–neid,** *m.* oath of allegiance *or* loyalty. **–nflucht,** *f.* desertion. **–nflüchtige(r),** *m.* deserter. **–njunker,** *m.* cadet officer, ensign (*Mil.*). **–nkorrekturen,** *f.pl.* galley proofs (*Typ.*). **–nsatz,** *m.* galley set up for printing; setting up the galley (*Typ.*). **–nstange,** *f.* flagstaff. **–nträger,** *m.* standard-bearer. **–nweihe,** *f.* presentation of colours, consecration of the colours.

Fähn–chen, *n.* (-s, –) pennon, banner (*Bot.*); (*coll.*) *sie trug ein billiges –chen,* she wore a cheap rag of a garment *or* slip of a dress. **–drich,** *m.*, *see* **–rich.** **–lein,** *n.* (*archaic*) troop, squad (*Mil.*), (*Nat. Soc.*) body of 150 'Jungvolk' (wolf-cubs). **–rich,** *m.* officer, cadet, ensign (*Mil.*); midshipman (*Naut.*).

Fähr–de, *f.* (-den), **–lichkeit,** *f.*, (*Poet.*) **–nis,** *f.* danger.

Fähr–e, *f.* (-en) ferry; ferry-boat; *fliegende –e,* flying bridge. **–boot,** *n.* ferry-boat. **–geld,** *n.* fare for ferrying. **–mann,** *m.* ferryman. **–pacht,** *f.* licence to ferry passengers.

fahr–en, 1. *ir.v.n.* (*aux.* s.) go (*in any sort of conveyance*), travel, drive, ride, sail; fare, get on; *Auto –en,* drive a car; *mit dem* or *im Auto –en,* go *or* travel in the *or* by car; *er fährt am besten dabei,* he has the best of the bargain; *er fuhr sehr gut dabei,* he did very well by it, he came off well; *auf* or *mit der Eisenbahn* or *Bahn –en,* go by rail; *über einen Fluß –en,* cross a river; *auf den Grund –en,* run aground; *aus dem Hafen –en,* clear the port; *hinauf–en, herauf–en,* ascend; *hinab–en, herab-en* descend; *mit dem Rad –en, rad–en,* cycle; *zur* or *in die Hölle* or *zum Teufel –en,* go to hell (*or* the devil); *dieses Schiff fährt zweimal wöchentlich,* this ship sails twice a week; *spazieren –en,* go for a drive; *–e wohl!* farewell! (*aux.* s. & h.) move hurriedly *or* violently, flash, shoot; start; (*coll.*) *einem über den Alexanderplatz –en,* slap s.o.'s backside; *aus dem Bette –en* leap out of bed; *einander in die Haare –en,* fly at one another, come to blows; *aus der Hand –en,* slip out of the hand; *mit der Hand –en über,* pass one's hand over; *aus der Haut –en,* lose all patience, lose one's temper, (*sl.*) lose one's wool; *in die Höhe –en,* start up, jump *or* leap up; *in die Kleider –en,* fling one's clothes on; *einem durch den Kopf –en,* (*imp.*) strike one, occur to one; *es fuhr mir ein plötzlicher Schmerz durch den Kopf,* a sudden pain shot through my head; *–en lassen*, let go, abandon, give up; let slip; *die Sorge –en lassen*, banish care; *eine Gelegenheit –en lassen*, let an opportunity slip; *einen (Wind) –en lassen*, drop s.th., let s.th. drop (*periphrastic for*) fart (*vulg.*); (*coll.*) *einem übers Maul –en*, reply rudely, snap *or* take a p. up; *es fuhr mir kalt über den Rücken*, a cold shudder passed through me *or* went down my back *or* spine; *er fuhr in die Tasche*, his hand went to his pocket. 2. *v.a.* drive; convey; take (*by vehicle*); sail, row (*a boat*); ride (*a cycle*); *welchen Betriebstoff fährt er?* what brand of petrol does he use? *Sand –en*, cart sand; *einen über einen Fluß –en*, ferry a p. over a river; *Karussell –en*, ride on the roundabout; *welche Marke fährt er?* what make is his car? *er fährt sehr gut*, he is a good driver; *er fuhr selbst*, he drove himself; *Ski (Schlittschuh) –en*, go ski-ing (skating); *er fuhr die beste Zeit*, he made *or* clocked the best time (*motor racing*). 3. *v.r. es fährt sich gut auf dieser Straße*, this is a good road for driving; *sich müde –en*, tire o.s. by driving; *in diesem Wagen fährt es sich angenehm*, this car rides well. **–end,** *pr.p. & adj.* going, travelling; vagrant; sliding (*Mech.*); *–ender Ritter*, knight errant; *–ende Habe*, movable property, movables; *–ende Artillerie*, mobile artillery; *–ende Post*, stage-coach; *–endes Volk*, tramps, vagrants. **–bahn,** *f.* roadway, track; channel. **–bahndecke,** *f.* road surface. **–bahnteppich,** *m.* wire 'carpet' (*on landing fields*) (*Av.*). **–bar,** *adj.* passable; navigable; practicable; mobile; *–bares Eis*, open ice; *–bare Feldküche*, mobile kitchen (*Mil.*). **–bereich,** *m.* radius of action *or* operation (*vehicles & tanks*) (*Mil.*). **–betrieb,** *m.* traffic. **–brücke,** *f.* flying bridge. **–buch,** *n.* mining journal. **–damm,** *m.* roadway. **–dienst,** *m.* service of trains. **–dienstleiter,** *m.* traffic superintendent (*Railw.*). **–er,** *m.* driver, chauffeur. **–gang,** *m.* carriage-way. **–gast,** *m.* passenger. **–geld,** *n.* fare. **–gelegenheit,** *f.* conveyance. **–geschwindigkeit,** *f.* speed. **–gestell,** *n.* chassis (*Motor.*), under-carriage, landing gear (*Av.*). **–gleis,** *n.* rut. **–heft,** *n.*; *zusammenstellbares –heft*, tourist's circular ticket. **–karte,** *f.* ticket; *eine –karte lösen*, book, take a ticket. **–kartenausgabe** *f.* **–kartenschalter,** *m.* booking-office (*Railw.*). **–kolonne,** *f.* supply train, transport column (*Mil.*). **–ig,** *adj.* fidgety, careless, haphazard, unreliable; *–iges Wesen*, happy-go-lucky ways. **–lässig,** *adj.* negligent; careless. *–lässige Tötung*, accidental homicide. **–lässigkeit,** *f.* negligence, carelessness. **–loch,** *n.* manhole (*in engines*). **–nis,** *f.* movable goods, goods and chattels. **–ordnung,** *f.* rule of the road; cycling regulations. **–plan,** *m.* time-table. **–planmäßig,** *adj.* regular; to schedule; to time. **–post,** *f.* stage-coach. **–prahm,** *m.* tank-landing-craft (*Mil.*). **–preis,** *m.* fare. **–rad,** *n.* (bi)cycle. **–rinne,** *f.* fairway, waterway. **–schacht,** *m.* climbing shaft. **–schalter,** *m.* ticket-office; booking-office (*Railw.*). **–schein,** *m.* ticket. **–straße,** *f.* highway. **–stuhl,** *m.* lift, elevator; hoist; bath-chair, wheel-chair, invalid chair. **–stuhlführer,** *m.* lift attendant *or* lift-boy. **–t,** *f.* (-en) ride, drive, passage, journey, voyage, trip, run; rate of progress; *von der –t abweichen*, alter course; *große –t*, three-quarter speed (*Naut.*); *das Schiff hat harte –t*, she is a fast ship; (*Poet.*) *hohe –t*, prosperous journey; *in –t*, under way (*Naut.*) (*also fig.*); *kleine –t*, dead slow (*Naut.*); *langsame –t*, slow speed (*Naut.*); *die –t nehmen nach*, stand for (*Naut.*); *die –t verfehlen*, lose way (*Naut.*); *wenig –t machen*, make little headway (*Naut.*). **–tausweis,** *m.* ticket. **–tbuch,** *n.* log-book (*Naut.*). **–tflagge,** *f.* blue peter. **–tmaß,** *n.*, **–tmesser,** *m.* log (*Naut.*), air-speed indicator (*Av.*). **–tmesser,** *n.* sheath knife, bowie knife. **–trichtung,** *f.*; *in der –trichtung sitzen*, sit facing the engine. **–tstange,** *f.* driving-bit. **–tunterbrechung,** *f.* break in *or* breaking of the journey. **–tübung,** *f.* cruising manœuvre (*Nav.*). **–tverbot,** *n.* prohibited to traffic. **–tverkauf,** *m.*; *der –tverkauf beginnt um*, the ticket-office opens at, tickets will be sold at. **–wasser,** *n.* navigable water, channel, fairway, lane (through a minefield) (*Mil.*); (*fig.*) element; *der Streit glitt ins politische –wasser ab*, the quarrel wandered off on to politics *or* took a political turn; *in seinem* or *im richtigen –wasser sein*, be in his element. **–weg,** *m.* highroad, carriage road. **–weggerechtigkeit,** *f.* right of way. **–werk,** *n.* landing-gear (*Av.*). **–wind,** *m.* fair wind (*Naut.*). **–zeug,** *n.* vehicle, vessel, craft.

fährig, *adj.* open, passable.

Fährte, *f.* (-n) track, scent, (foot)print, mark, trail; *kalte –*, cold scent; *auf der falschen – sein*, be on the wrong track.

Fäkalien, *n.pl.* faeces, night-soil.

Fakir, *m.* (-s, -e) fakir.

Faksimile, *n.* (-s, -s & -milia) facsimile.

Faktion, *f.* (-en) faction.

Faktis, *n.* rubber substitute.

fakt-isch, *adj.* real, actual, proved by facts; de facto; effective, **–itiv,** *adj.* causative; factitive (*Gram.*). **–or,** *m.* (-s, -en) fact, circumstance; gene (*Biol.*); factor (*C.L. Arith.*); agent, manager, foreman. **–orei,** *f.* factory, agency abroad. **–um,** *n.* (-ums, -en & -a) fact. **–ur(a),** *f.* (-uren) (*C.L.*) invoice; *laut –ura*, as per invoice. **–urenbuch,** *n.* invoice-book. **–urieren,** *v.a.* (*C.L.*) invoice.

Fäkulenz, *f.* sediment, dregs, feculence.

Fakult-ät, *f.* (-en) faculty (*Univ.*). **–ativ,** *adj.* optional.

falb, *adj.* pale yellow, dun, fallow. **–ig,** *adj.* inclining to dun; faded; pale yellow.

Falbel, *f.* (-n) flounce, furbelow.

Falk-e, *m.* (-en, -en) falcon, hawk; *einen –en häubeln (enthäubeln)*, hood (unhood) a hawk; *einen –en steigen lassen*, cast a hawk. **–enaugen,** eyes of a hawk (*fig.*). **–enbeize,** *f.* falconry, hawking. **–enier,** *m.*, **–ner,** *m.* falconer. **–nerei,** *f.* hawking, falconry.

Fall, *m.* (-es, ¨e) fall, tumble, accident; decay, ruin, decline, downfall, failure; waterfall, cataract; case, instance, event; condition, situation; *auf jeden –, auf alle Fälle*, in any case, by all means, at all events; *auf keinen –*, on no account, by no means; *im –e, daß*, in case; *in dem –e*, in that case; *im – der Not*, in case of necessity; (*coll.*) *Knall und –*, like a bolt from the blue; *ich setze den –*, I make the supposition, suppose; *einen – tun*, have a fall; *von – zu –*, as the case may be; (*Prov.*) *Hochmut kommt vor dem –*, pride goes before a fall; *der vorliegende –*, the case in point; *der Wen–*, the accusative case; *der Wer–*, the nominative case; *zu –e bringen*, ruin, seduce; *zu –e kommen*, be ruined. **–en,** 1. *ir.v.n.* (*aux.* s.) fall, tumble; drop, sink, be deposited; decline, abate, subside, decrease, diminish, go down (*of prices*); descend (*Mus.*); die, be killed; die away; be ruined; be seduced; *–en auf* or *an* (*Acc.*) devolve on, descend to; *die Erbschaft fällt an seinen Vetter*, the legacy falls to his cousin; *–en auf* (*Acc.*) hit, light on, occur, turn upon, fall upon; *die Wahl fiel auf ihn*, the choice fell on him, he was chosen; *der Verdacht ist auf ihn gefallen*, suspicion fell upon him; *er fällt mir auf die Nerven*, he gets on my nerves; *das Gespräch fiel auf . . .*, the conversation turned upon . . .; *er ist nicht auf den Kopf gefallen*, he is no fool; *es fällt mir schwer aufs Herz*, it weighs upon my mind; *–en aus*, fall out of, act out of; *das fällt völlig aus dem Rahmen*, that does not fit at all into the picture; *aus den* or *allen Wolken –en*, be thunderstruck; *aus allen Himmeln –en*, become thoroughly disillusioned; *aus der Rolle –en*, act out of part, be inconsistent; *es fiel mir aus der Hand*, it dropped out of my hand; *es fällt mir schwer*, it is difficult for me, I find it hard; *je nachdem es fällt*, according as it turns out; *es fiel die Bemerkung*, the observation was made, it was observed; *es fiel ein Schuß*, a shot was fired; *der Würfel ist gefallen*, the die is cast; *es fielen heftige Reden*, violent language was used; *–en in* (*Acc.*), fall into; meddle with, interrupt; incline to, incur; *es fällt in die Augen*, it catches the eye, it strikes one; *einem in den Arm –en*, seize a p. by the arm, stop a p.; *ins Boot –en!* man the boat! *einem in die Zügel –en*, seize the bridle of another's horse; restrain a p.; *einem in die Rede –en*, interrupt a p.; *einem in die Hände –en*, fall into a p.'s power; *in Ohnmacht –en*, faint, swoon; *mit der Tür ins Haus –en*, blurt out, go at it like a bull at a gate; *das fällt nicht ins Gewicht*, that is of no importance *or* consequence, it is of no great weight; *sein Zeugnis fällt schwer in die Waagschale*, his evidence carries great weight; *in ein Land -en*, invade a country; *in Schlaf -en*, fall asleep; *es fällt ins Pöbelhafte*, it is rather vulgar; *in Schwermut -en*, grow melancholy; *in den Rücken -en*, attack from behind, stab in the back; *er ist beim König in Ungnade gefallen*, he has fallen into disfavour with the king, he has incurred the king's displeasure; *-en lassen*, drop, discard, let fall, put aside; *im Gespräch (ein Wort) -en lassen*, put in a word; *einen Freund -en lassen*, forsake *or* (*coll.*) drop a friend; *etwas vom Preise -en lassen*, take s.th. off the price; *-en über* (*Acc.*), fall *or* stumble over, fall upon; *über den Haufen -en*, fall down; *-en unter*, fall under; fall among; *unter den Tisch -en*, be shelved; (*coll.*) *ich bin fast vom Stengel gefallen*, I was thunderstruck, flabbergasted *or* struck all of a heap; *es fiel mir wie Schuppen von den Augen*, my eyes were suddenly opened, a light *or* the truth suddenly dawned (on me), the scales fell from my eyes; *zu Boden -en*, fall to the ground; come to nothing; *einem zur Last -en*, be a burden *or* troublesome to a p.; *einem zu Füßen -en*, throw o.s. at a p.'s feet; *den Fallenden soll man nicht stoßen*, don't kick a man when he's down; (*Prov.*) *der Apfel fällt nicht weit vom Stamm*, he's a chip of the old block; *die Gefallenen*, the fallen, the victims; *gefallenes Obst*, fallen fruit; windfall; *gefallenes Mädchen*, fallen girl. 2. *v.a. sich wund-en*, fall and hurt o.s.. 3. *n.* subsidence; fall; decay; diminution. **-baum,** *m.* toll-bar, turnpike. **-beil,** *n.* guillotine. **-bö,** *f.* air pocket (*Av.*). **-brücke,** *f.* drawbridge. **-e,** *f.* (-en) trap, snare; pitfall; catch, latch (*of a door*); *eine -e aufstellen gegen Mäuse*, set a trap for mice. **-enleger,** *m.*, **-ensteller,** *m.* trapper. **-fenster,** *n.* sash-window. **-gatter,** *n.* portcullis. **-geschwindigkeit,** *f.* velocity of falling bodies. **-grube,** *f.* trap, pitfall, tank trap (*Mil.*). **-holz,** *n.* fallen wood. **-klappe,** *f.* drop (*on telephone switchboard*). **-obst,** *n.* fallen fruit, windfall. **-reep,** *n.* gangway, companionway (*Naut.*). **-rohr,** *n.* down pipe, waste pipe. **-s,** *adv.* in case, if, supposing that; *allen-s*, see *auf alle Fälle*; *andern-s*, otherwise; *eintretenden-s*, in such an event; *gegebenen-s, gesetzt den -*, in the event that, supposing that; *jeden-s*, see *auf jeden -*; *keines-s*, see *auf keinen -*; *nötigen-s*, see *im -e der Not*; *schlimmsten-(e)s*, if the worst comes to the worst. **-schirm,** *m.* parachute. **-schirmabsprung,** *m.* parachute descent. **-schirmjäger,** *m.pl.* **-schirmtruppen,** *f.pl.* paratroops. **-schirmgriff,** *m.* ripcord (*of parachute*). **-schloß,** *n.* hasp-lock. **-silber,** *n.* precipitated silver, silver precipitate. **-strick,** *m.* snare, noose, gin; (*fig.*) trick, catch, ruse. **-sucht,** *f.* epilepsy. **-süchtig,** *adj.* epileptic. **-tor,** *n.* portcullis. **-tür,** *f.* trap-door. **-werk,** *n.* stamp, press, pile-driver. **-wild,** *n.* carrion. **-winkel,** *m.* gradient, angle of fall, inclination *or* descent.

fäll-en, *v.a.* cause to fall, fell, lay low; shoot, bring down; drop (*a perpendicular*); sink (*a shaft*); pass (*a sentence or judgement*); precipitate (*Chem.*); *mit gefälltem Bajonett angreifen*, charge with fixed bayonets. **-bar,** *adj.* fit for felling; precipitable (*Chem.*). **-er,** *m.*, *see* **-(ungs)mittel.** **-ig,** *adj.* due, payable; (*in compounds* =) ready to fall; (*C.L.*) *-ig werden*, fall due. **-igkeit,** *f.* expiration, maturity (*of bills of exchange*). **-igkeitstag,** *m.* due date. **-ung,** *f.* felling; precipitation (*Chem.*). **-(ungs)mittel,** *n.* precipitant (*Chem.*).

Fall-i(sse)ment, *n.* (-s, -s) (*Austr. & Swiss*) failure, bankrupty. **-ieren,** *v.n.* (*aux.* h.) fail; become bankrupt. **-it,** *m.* (-en, -en) bankrupt. **-itengericht,** *n.* bankruptcy court. **-itenmasse,** *f.* bankrupt's estate *or* assets.

falls, *see* **Fall.**

falsch, 1. *adj.* wrong, false, incorrect, untrue; base, artificial, counterfeit, spurious, pseudo-, adulterated, forged; insincere, deceitful, perfidious, treacherous; blank (*Arch.*); (*coll.*) angry, wroth (*auf einen*, with a p.); - *anführen*, misquote; - *aussprechen*, mispronounce; - *darstellen*, misrepresent; *-er Diskant*, falsetto; *-er Hase*, rissole. *-er König*, usurper, pretender; *-er Mensch*, deceitful person, double-dealer; *-e Münze*, base coin; *-e Rippen*, floating ribs; - *schwören*, perjure; - *singen*, sing out of tune; *-es Spiel*, foul play, trickery; - *spielen*, play out of tune (*Mus.*); cheat (*at cards*); *-er Stein*, spurious stone; *meine Uhr geht -*, my watch is wrong; *Sie sind - unterrichtet*, you have been misinformed; *Sie verstehen mich -*, you misunderstand me; *-e Wechsel*, forged bills of exchange; *-e Zähne*, false teeth, artificial teeth. 2. *m. & n.* dishonesty; *ohne -*, guileless, without guilt; (*B.*) *ohne - wie die Tauben*, harmless as doves; *es ist kein - an ihm*, he is quite open and above board. **-gläubig,** *adj.* heterodox. **-gläubigkeit,** *f.* heterodoxy, heresy. **-heit,** *f.* falsity, falseness; spuriousness; deceit, guile, perfidy; untruth, falsehood, duplicity. **-münzer,** *m.* forger, coiner. **-münzerei,** *f.* counterfeiting, forging, forgery. **-spieler,** *m.* cardsharper, cheat.

fälsch-en, *v.a.* falsify, forge, counterfeit (*coin*); adulterate (*food*). **-er,** *m.* falsifier, forger. **-lich,** *adj.* false, erroneous. **-licherweise,** *adv.* wrongly, falsely, erroneously, by mistake. **-ung,** *f.* falsification, forgery; adulteration.

Falsett, *n.* (-es, -e) falsetto.

fält-eln, *v.a.* lay in small pleats *or* folds; pleat, gather. **-ig,** *suffix* -fold; e.g. *viel-ig*, manifold, various.

Falt-e, *f.* (-en) fold, pleat; bend, flexure; crease, wrinkle; gather (*in dresses, etc.*); hollow (*undulating ground*); *in -en legen*, fold; *-en werfen* or *schlagen*, pucker, get creased; *dieses Kleid wirft keine -en*, this dress does not crease; *die Stirn in -en legen* or *ziehen*, wrinkle *or* knit the brow; *die geheimsten -en des Herzens*, the inmost recesses of the heart. **-boot,** *n.* collapsible boat. **-en,** *v.a.* fold; pleat; double up; clasp together; knit (*the brow*); wrinkle, pucker, ruffle; *mit gefalteten Händen*, with hands clasped (*as in prayer*). **-enfilter,** *n.* filter-paper. **-enfrei,** *adj.*, *see* **-enlos, -enkleid,** *n.* pleated dress. **-enlos,** *adj.* unwrinkled, smooth, without folds *or* creases, plain; open, without hidden blame. **-enmagen,** *m.* third stomach of ruminants. **-ennäher,** *m.* pleater (*on sewing machines*). **-enreich,** *adj.* creased, wrinkled. **-enrock,** *m.* pleated skirt. **-enschlag,** *m.*, **-enwurf,** *m.* (cast of) drapery (*Paint., Sculp.*). **-enweise,** *adv.* in folds *or* pleats. **-er,** *m.* butterfly, moth, lepidopter; third stomach of ruminants. **-ig,** *adj.* folded, pleated, puckered; wrinkled (*forehead*). *In compounds* = in folds; -fold; *see* **-fältig;** *e.g. vier-ig*, with four folds, *mannig-ig*, manifold, various; *Drei-igkeit*, Trinity. **-ung,** *f.* fold, convolution. **-werk,** *n.*, fluting *Arch.*).

Falz, *m.* (-es, -e) fold; furrow, groove, notch; slide-way (*Mach.*); rabbet, lap-joint. **-amboß,** *m.* coppersmith's anvil. **-bein,** *n.* folder, creaser. **-brett,** *n.* folding-board (*Bookb.*). **-en,** *v.a.* fold (*paper*); groove, flute; rabbet, lap (*tin, etc.*); trim (*skins*). **-hobel,** *m.* grooving plane. **-ig,** *adj.* folded; grooved, furrowed. **-schiene,** *f.* slotted rail, tram-rail.

famili-är, *adj.* familiar, intimate; *im -ären Kreise*, in the family circle. **-arisieren,** *v.a.* familiarize. **-arität,** *f.* familiarity.

Familie, *f.* (-n) family; household; lineage; class, genus; *es liegt in der -*. it runs in the family; *- haben*, have children; *von guter - sein*, be of *or* from a good family. **-nähnlichkeit,** *f.* family likeness. **-nangelegenheiten,** *f.pl.* family affairs. **-nanschluß,** *m.*; *er wünscht -nanschluß*, he wishes to be treated like one of the family. **-nanzeigen,** *f.pl.*, **-nnachrichten,** *f.pl.* (announcement of) births, marriages, and deaths (*in newspapers*). **-nbad,** *n.* mixed bathing. **-nbedürftigkeit,** *f.*; *Prüfung der -nbedürftigkeit*, means test. **-nerbstück,** *n.* heirloom. **-nfehler,** *m.* hereditary failing. **-nforschung,** *f.* genealogical investigation. **-nglück,** *n.* domestic happiness. **-nkreis,** *m.* domestic *or* family circle. **-nlos,** *adj.* childless. **-nname,** *m.* surname. **-nrücksichten,** *f.pl.* family considerations. **-nstand,** *m.* family status (*single, married, widowed, etc.*). **-nvater,** *m.* head of a *or* the family, paterfamilias. **-nvermächtnis,** *n.* entail. **-nwappen,** *n.* family coat of arms. **-nzimmer,** *n.* sitting-room. **-nzulage,** *f.* family allowance. **-nzwist,** *m.* family quarrel, domestic discord.

famos, *adj.* (*coll.*) splendid, capital, fine, great; *–er Kerl*, capital fellow.
Famul–us, *m.* (-us, -i) amanuensis.
Fanal, *m.* & *n.* (-(e)s, -e) signal light; beacon (*Mil.*).
Fanat-iker, *m.* (-s, –) fanatic. **–isch,** *adj.* fanatic(al). **–ismus,** *m.* fanaticism.
fand, fände, *see* **finden.**
Fanfar–e, *f.* (-en) fanfare, flourish of trumpets. **–onade,** *f.* vain boasting.
Fang, *m.* (-es, ⸚e) catch, capture; booty, prey; haul, draught; fang, talon, claw, tusk; coup de grâce (*Hunt.*); (*dial.*) snare, trap. **–en,** 1. *ir.v.a.* catch, seize, capture; trap, hook, snare; take prisoner; *leicht Feuer –en*, be inflammable *or* impetuous *or* impressionable *or* excitable; *das Pulver will nicht –en*, the powder will not catch; (*Prov.*) *mit gefangen, mit gehangen*, rogues of a gang on one gibbet must hang. 2. *v.r.* be caught, become entangled; catch, take hold. 3. *v.n.* (*aux.* h.) bite; take hold, clutch (at), seize. **–arm,** *m.* tentacle. **–brief,** *m.* warrant of arrest. **–eisen,** *n.* spring trap. **–faden,** *m.* tentacle. **–garn,** *n.* snaring net. **–gitter,** *n.* suppressor grid (*Rad.*). **–leine,** *f.* leash; harpoon-line; painter (*of a boat*). **–messer,** *n.* hunting knife. **–netz,** *n.*, **–schnur,** *f.* noose, lasso; aiguillette (*on uniforms*). **–spiel,** *n.* cup and ball. **–stoff,** *m.* paper pulp. **–stoß,** *m.* coup de grâce (*Hunt.*); stab; parry. **–vogel,** *m.* decoy-bird. **–zahn,** *m.* fang, tusk.
Fänger, *m.* catcher; captor; weapon for dispatching game; (*pl.*) tusks.
Fant, *m.* (-(e)s, -e) coxcomb, fop.
Fantasie, *f.* (-n) fantasia (*Mus.*).
Farb–e, *f.* (–en) colour, tint, hue; stain, paint, dye; complexion; suit (*Cards*); ink (*Typ.*); (*fig.*) allegiance, party; *–e, auftragen*, apply paint; *die –en zu dick auftragen*, exaggerate; *–e bedienen*, follow suit (*Cards*); *–e, bekennen*, show one's colours; follow suit (*Cards*); *echte –e*, fast colour; *–e halten*, keep its colour, not fade; stick to one's colours. **–band,** *n.* typewriter ribbon. **–deckschicht,** *f.* colour coat (*paint*). **–druck,** *m.* colour print, colour printing. **–echt,** *adj.* of fast colour, unfadeable, fadeless. **–en,** *adj.* (*in compounds with names of substances* =) -coloured; e.g. *gold–en*, golden-coloured. **–enabbeizmittel,** *n.* paint remover. **–enabweichung,** *f.* chromatic aberration. **–enband,** *n.*, **–enbild,** *n.* spectrum. **–enblind,** *adj.* colour-blind. **–enblindheit,** *f.* colour-blindness. **–enbogen,** *m.* iris. **–enbrechung,** *f.* colour refraction; colour blending. **–enbrett,** *n.* palette. **–enbruder,** *m.* member of the same students' club; *see* **Couleur. –endruck,** *see* **–druck. –engrund,** *m.* ground colour. **–enfilm,** *m.*, *see* **–film. –enkasten,** *m.* paint box. **–enkleckser,** *m.* dauber. **–enlehre,** *f.* theory of colours, chromatics. **–enphotographie,** *f.* colour photography. **–enrand,** *m.* iris. **–enreiber,** *m.* colour-grinder. **–enreich,** *adj.* richly coloured. **–enrein,** *adj.* in clear colours. **–enschiller,** *m.* iridescence. **–enschillernd,** *adj.* iridescent. **–ensehen,** *n.* colour vision. **–ensinn,** *m.* (fine) sense of colour. **–enskala,** *f.* colour chart. **–enspiel,** *n.* opalescence. **–(en)stift,** *m.* coloured pencil. **–(en)ton,** *m.* hue, tone, tint; *gedämpfter –enton*, undertone; *mit satten –tönen*, deep-hued. **–entragend,** *adj.* wearing coloured badges; *–entragende Verbindungen*, students' clubs which sport distinctive colours. **–enverdünner,** *m.* paint thinner. **–film,** *m.* colour film. **–flotte,** *f.* dye-bath. **–ig,** *adj.* coloured, colourful; stained; chromatic (*in compounds*) e.g., *ein–ig*, monochrome; *fleisch–ig* flesh-coloured; *die –igen*, the coloured races. **–igkeit,** *f.* colourfulness. **–kasten,** *m.*, *see* **–enkasten. –körper,** *m.* pigment, colouring matter. **–los,** *adj.* colourless, pale; achromatic. **–losigkeit,** *f.* pallor. **–stoff,** *m.* dye-stuff; stain, pigment. **–ton,** *m.* tint, shade. **–tonrichtig,** *adj.* isochromatic (*Phot.*). **–zerstäuber,** *m.* paint spray, spray-gun, atomizer.
Färb–e, *f.* staining, dyeing; dye-house. **–en,** *v.* 1. *v.a.* colour, dye, stain; tinge; *in der Wolle –en*, (*fig.*) engrain; *ein in der Wolle gefärbter Aristokrat*, an out-and-out *or* dyed-in-the-wool aristocrat; *mit Blut gefärbt*, blood-stained; *humoristisch gefärbt*, with a touch of humour; *etwas durch gefärbte Brillen* or *Gläser sehen*, see *or* view a th. through rose-tinted spectacles. 2. *v.r.* blush. **–ehölzer,** *n.pl.* dye-woods. **–emittel,** *n.*, **–estoff,** *m.* colouring matter; pigment; dye-stuff. **–er,** *m.* dyer. **–erei,** *f.* dyer's trade; dye-works; dry-cleaners. **–erwaid,** *m.* dyer's woad. **–ig,** *adj.* (*Austr. dial.*) *see* **farbig. –ung,** *f.* colouring; hue, tinge, shade.
Farc–e, *f.* (-en) farce, farce-meat, stuffing (*Cook.*). **–ieren,** *v.a.* stuff.
Farm, *f.* (-en) settlement (*colonies*). **–er,** *m.* (colonial) settler.
Farn, *m.* (-es, -e) fern. **–kraut,** *n.* fern. **–vorkeim,** *m.* spore of fern.
Farre, *m.* (-n, -n) bullock, young bull, steer.
Färse, *f.* (-n) heifer.
Fasan, *m.* (-s, -e *or* -en) pheasant. **–engarten,** *m.*, **–engehege,** *n.*, **–enhof,** *m.* pheasant-preserve. **–enhund,** *m.* setter. **–enjagd,** *f.* pheasant-shooting. **–erie,** *f.* pheasant-preserve.
Faschier–tes, *n.* (*Austr. dial.*) minced meat. **–maschine,** *f.* mincing machine, mincer.
Faschine, *f.* (-n) fascine (*Fort.*); hurdle, bundle of faggots. **–nbekleidung,** *f.* fascine revetment. **–nmesser,** *n.* matchet, machete.
Fasching, *m.* (-s, -e) (*dial.*) carnival. **–szeit,** *f.* Shrovetide.
Faschi–smus, *m.* fascism. **–st,** *m.* (-en, -en) fascist. **–stisch,** *adj.* fascist.
Fase, *f.* (-n) bevel-edge, chamfer; slender thread. **–nnackt,** *adj.* **–rnackt,** *adj.* stark naked.
[1]**Fasel,** *f.* kidney bean (*Phaseolus vulgaris*) (*Bot.*).
[2]**Fasel,** *m.* (*dial.*) farrow (*of pigs*); brood young of animals. **–n,** *v.n.* (*aux.* h.) bring forth young (*of animals*); yean, farrow. **–hengst,** *m.* stallion. **–ochs,** *m.* bull. **–vieh,** *n.* breeding cattle.
fasel–n, *v.a.* & *n.* (*aux.* h.) talk foolishly, talk twaddle *or* drivel. **–ei,** *f.* drivel, twaddle. **–haft,** *adj.*, **–ig,** *adj.* silly, drivelling. **–hans,** *m.* drivelling fool, babbler, scatterbrain, muddler.
Faser, *f.* (-n) thread, fibre, grain, filament, fluff. **–haut,** *f.* fibrous membrane. **–ig,** *adj.* fibrous, stringy, filaceous. **–knorpel,** *m.* fibrous cartilage. **–n,** 1. *v.a.* unravel, fray. 2. *v.n.* (*aux.* h.) unravel, become frayed. **–nackt,** *see under* **Fase. –stoff,** *m.* fibrin, fibrous material; synthetic textiles. **–ung,** *f.* texture; fibrillation.
Fäserchen, *n.* (-s, –) fibril, filament.
Faß, *n.* (-(ss)es, ⸚(ss)er) cask, barrel, tub, vat, firkin, hogshead, tun, keg; vessel; *drei – Bier*, three casks of ale; *Wein vom –*, wine from the wood; *Bier vom –*, draught-ale; *frisch vom –*, drawn from the wood, on draught; (*coll.*) *das schlägt dem – den Boden aus*, that is the last straw, that is the limit. **–band,** *n.* hoop. **–bier,** *n.* draught-beer *or* ale. **–binder,** *m.* cooper. **–boden,** *m.* head of a cask. **–daube,** *f.* stave. **–faul,** *adj.* tasting of the cask. **–geläger,** *n* bottoms, cask deposit. **–hahn,** *m.* cock, spigot. **–spund,** *m.* bung. **–waren,** *f. pl.* merchandise in casks. **–weise,** *adv.* by *or* in barrels.
Fassad–e, *f.* (-en) façade. **–enkletterer,** *m.* cat-burglar.
fass–en, 1. *v.a.* grasp, seize, hold, lay hold of; contain, include, comprise; (*fig.*) apprehend, comprehend, conceive, (*coll.*) take in; barrel (*beer*); sack (*corn*); hive (*bees*); set, mount, fix; clothe, express (*in a certain form*); form (*a resolve, a liking, etc.*); *– !* (*to a dog*) fetch it! *Abneigung –en*, take a dislike (*gegen*, to); *Anschläge –en*, form plans; *ins Auge –en*, fix one's eyes upon, take a good look at; consider, envisage, keep in mind; (*sl.*) *Essen –en*, come and get it (*soldiers' sl.*); *festen Fuß –en*, settle down, establish o.s.; *das Glas faßt gerade einen halben Liter*, the glass just holds half a litre; *sich* (*Dat.*) *ein Herz –en, Mut –en*, take courage; *in einen Rahmen –en*, frame; *Wurzel –en*, take root. 2. *v.r.* collect o.s., contain *or* compose o.s., pull o.s. together; *sich in Geduld –en*, possess one's soul in patience; *sich kurz –en*, be brief, (*coll.*) cut it short; *es läßt sich nicht in Worte –en*, it is not to be expressed in words; *fasse dich*, compose yourself. **gefaßt,** *p.p.* & *adj.* collected, composed, calm; prepared,

ready; *sich gefaßt machen auf eine S.*, prepare o.s. for a th., resign o.s. to s.th., accept s.th. with composure. **–(ß)bar,** *adj.* comprehensible, tangible. **–(ß)lich,** *adj.* comprehensible, intelligible, conceivable; *leicht –(ß)lich*, easily understood. **–ung** *f.* setting, mounting, frame; socket, lampholder; draft wording, form, style; capacity; composure, self-control; *Ajour- (Kasten-)–ung*, claw- (crown-) setting (*gems*); *in dieser –ung ist es kaum verständlich*, it is scarcely intelligible as it stands; *seine –ung bewahren, nicht aus der –ung kommen*, remain calm, collected *or* composed; *einen aus der –ung bringen*, disconcert, confuse *or* upset a p.; *aus der –ung kommen*, lose one's self-control; *ganz außer –ung sein*, be completely beside o.s. **–ungsgabe,** *f.*, **–ungskraft,** *f.* power of comprehension, mental capacity. **–ungsraum,** *m.*, **–ungsvermögen,** *n.* seating capacity, holding capacity, carrying capacity.

Fasson, *f.* fashion, style, cut. **–eisen,** *n.* steel section.

fast, *adv.* almost, nearly, (well)nigh, close upon; *– nie*, scarcely ever.

fast–en, 1. *v.n.* fast. 2. *n.* fasting; (*pl.*) fast, time of fasting. Lent. **–ensonntag,** *m.* Sunday in Lent. **–enspeise,** *f.* Lenten fare. **–enzeit,** *f.* Lent. **–nacht,** *f.* Shrove-Tuesday; *–nacht halten*, celebrate the end of carnival time. **–nachtsspiel,** *n.* shrovetide farce, carnival play. **–tag,** *m.* fast-day.

Faszikel, *m.* (-s, –) file (*of papers*).

fatal, *adj.* disagreeable, annoying, awkward, unfortunate; *das ist –*, that is a nuisance; *eine –e Geschichte*, an awkward business. **–ismus,** *m.* fatalism. **–ität,** *f.* fatality; ill luck, misfortune.

fatz–en, *v.n.* (*aux.* h.) (*dial.*) play the fool. **–ke,** *m.* (*coll.*) conceited p., fop, coxcomb (*often used in compounds*, e.g. *Patentfatzke*, *m.* dandy).

fauch–en, *v.n.* (*aux.* h.) spit, hiss (*as cats*); puff (*as engine*).

faul, *adj.* decayed, rotten, putrid, stale, bad; lazy, idle, indolent; worthless; brittle; *der –e Fleck*, the sore point; *–es Geschwätz*, idle talk; *–es Fleisch*, proud flesh; *sich auf die –e Haut legen*, eat the bread of idleness; loll in the lap of indolence; *–er Knecht*, ready reckoner; (*C.L.*) *–er Kunde*, bad customer; *–e Küste*, dangerous coast; *–e See*, calm (*Naut.*); *–e Witze*, bad *or* poor jokes; *–er Zauber*, humbug. **–bar,** *adj.* putrescible, corruptible. **–baum,** *m.* breaking buckthorn, berry-bearing alder (*Rhamnus frangula*) (*Bot.*). **–bett,** *n.* (*fig.*) lap of idleness, inactivity. **–brut,** *f.* foul brood (*bees*). **–bütte,** *f.* fermenting trough. **–en,** *v.n.* (*aux.* s.) rot, decompose, putrefy. **–end,** *pr.p.* & *adj.* putrescent, rotting. **–enzen,** *v.n.* (*aux.* h.) idle, lounge; be lazy, laze about. **–enzer,** *m.* sluggard, idler; deck-chair. **–enzerei,** *f.* laziness, sluggishness, idleness, idling. **–fieber,** *n.* putrid fever; (*sl.*) extreme idleness. **–gas,** *n.* sewer gas. **–heit,** *f.* laziness, idleness, sloth. **–ig,** *adj.* putrescent, putrid, rotten, mouldy. **–pelz,** *m.* lazybones, sluggard, idler. **–pfründe,** *f.* sinecure. **–tier,** *n.* sloth (*Bradypus*) (*Zool.*); (*fig.*) sluggard.

Fäul–e, *f.* dry rot, blight. **–en,** *v.a.* cause to putrify. **–nis,** *f.* decay, rottenness, putrefaction, sepsis; (*fig.*) corruption. **–nisbase,** *f.* ptomaine. **–niserregend,** *adj.* septic. **–nisgift,** *n.* septic poison. **–nishemmend, –nishindernd, –nisverhindernd, –niswidrig,** *adj.* antiseptic, aseptic.

Faun, *m.* (-en, -en) faun, satyr. **–a,** *f.* fauna. **–enblick,** *m.* lascivious look. **–enhaft,** *adj.* faun-like; lascivious.

Faust, *f.* (¨e) (clenched) fist; (*coll.*) *das paßt* (*geht*) *wie die – aufs Auge*, that's neither here nor there, that's beside the mark *or* point, it's as like as chalk to cheese; *mit dem Degen in der –*, sword in hand; *auf eigene –*, on one's own responsibility; (*coll.*) off one's own bat; *eiserne* or *gepanzerte –*, mailed fist; *geballte –*, clenched fist; *schwer auf der – liegen*, be hard-mouthed (*of horses*); *einem eine – machen*, shake one's fist at a p. **–ball,** *m.* punch-ball (*game*). **–dick,** *adj.* clumsy, awkward, lumbering, laboured; sly; (*coll.*) *er hat es –dick hinter den Ohren*, he is a sly dog; *das ist –dick gelogen*, that's a thumping lie. **–gelenk,** *n.* wrist. **–handschuh,** *m.* mitten; boxing glove. **–kampf,** *m.* boxing, boxing-match. **–keil,** *m.* flint (weapon *or* tool), stone implement (*Archaeology*). **–pfand,** *n.* dead pledge. **–recht,** *n.* club-law. **–regel,** *f.* rule of thumb. **–schlag,** *m.* punch, blow with the fist; (*pl.*) fisticuffs. **–zeichnung,** *f.* rough sketch.

Fäust–chen, *n.*; *sich* (*Dat.*) *ins –chen lachen*, laugh in one's sleeve. **–el,** *m.* (-els, -el) mallet, miner's hammer. **–ling,** *m.* mitten; early type of pistol. **–lings,** *adv.* with the fist.

Fauteuil, *m.* (-s, -s) arm-chair.

Favor–it, *m.* (-en, -en), **–ite,** *f.*, **–itin,** *f.* favourite.

Faxen, *pl.* (*coll.*) tomfoolery, buffoonery, tricks; (*coll.*) *mach keine – !* don't be a fool! **–macher,** *m.* fool, buffoon.

Fazit, *n.* (-s, -e & -s) result, total, sum, product.

Feb–ruar, *m.* (-s, -e), **–er,** *m.* (*Austr. dial.*) February.

fechs–en, *v.a.* (*dial.*) gather in the vintage. **–er,** *m.* seedling, cutting (*of grape-vines*).

fecht–en, *ir.v.n.* (*aux.* h.) fight; fence; (*coll.*) *–en gehen*, go begging; *mit den Händen –en*, gesticulate. **–boden,** *m.* fencing-room. **–bruder,** *m.* beggar, tramp, mendicant. **–degen,** *m.*, **–eisen,** *n.* foil, rapier. **–er,** *m.* fencer; gladiator. *der sterbende -er*, the dying (Borghese) gladiator. **–erkampf,** *m.* sword-fight; gladiatorial combat. **–ersprung,** *m.* lunge. **–erstellung,** *f.* stance. **–erstreich,** *m.* feint. **–handschuh,** *m.* fencing-glove. **–meister,** *m.* fencing master. **–übung,** *f.* practice with the foils.

Feder, *f.* (-n) feather; plume; quill; pen, (pen) nib; spring; spline (*Mach.*); tongue, slip-feather (*Carp.*); (*pl.*) (*coll.*) bed; *in die – diktieren*, dictate; *das ist aus meiner –*, it is written by me; *die – führen*, act as secretary, do the clerical work; *unter der – haben*, be engaged in writing; *in –n hängen*, be hung on springs; sprung; *er ist soeben aus den –n*, he is just out of bed; (*fig.*) *sich mit fremden –n schmücken*, deck o.s. out in borrowed plumes. **–artig,** *adj.* feathery. **–ball,** *m.* shuttlecock. **–barometer,** *n.* aneroid barometer. **–bett,** *n.* eiderdown. **–blatt,** *n.* spring-plate (*of a lock*). **–brett,** *n.* spring-board (*Gymn.*). **–bund,** *m.* spring shackle (*Mach.*). **–busch,** *m.* tuft *or* plume (of feathers); crest. **–einrichtung,** *f.* spring mechanism. **–förmig,** *adj.* plumiform. **–fuchser,** *m.* quill-driver, scribbler. **–gehäuse,** *n.* spring housing (*Mach.*). **–gewicht,** *n.* feather-weight (*Boxing*). **–halter,** *m.* pen-holder. **–hart,** *adj.* elastic, springy. **–härte,** *f.* elasticity. **–ig,** *adj.* feathered, feathery. **–kasten,** *m.* pencil-case. **–kiel,** *m.* quill. **–kissen,** *n.* feather cushion *or* pillow. **–kleid,** *n.* plumage. **–kraft,** *f.* elasticity. **–lasche,** *f.*, *see* **–band.** **–leicht,** *adj.* light as a feather, very light. **–leinwand,** *f.* swansdown. **–lesen,** *n.* servility, fawning; ceremony; *ohne viel –lesen*, without much ceremony; *nicht viel –lesens machen*, make short work of. **–los,** *adj.* unfledged. **–messer,** *n.* pen-knife. **–n,** 1. *v. n.* be elastic *or* springy; fly *or* spring back; shed feathers, moult. 2. *v.a.* provide with springs. **–nd,** *adj.* resilient, springy; light; moulting. **–nelke,** *f.* feathered pink. **–pose,** *f.* quill. **–ring,** *m.* spring-washer (*Mach.*). **–schloß,** *n.* spring-lock. **–seele,** *f.* pith of a quill. **–spule,** *f.* quill. **–stahl,** *m.* spring steel. **–strich,** *m.*, stroke of the pen. **–stutz,** *m.* tuft of feathers. **–ung,** *f.* spring-suspension, springing; springiness, elasticity. **–vieh,** *n.* poultry. **–waage,** *f.* spring-balance. **–wechsel,** *m.* moulting. **–weg,** *m.* pitch of spring (*Mach.*). **–weiß,** *n.* French chalk, talc. **–werk,** *n.* plumage; spring-mechanism. **–wild,** *n.* wild fowl, winged game. **–wisch,** *m.* feather broom, feather duster. **–wischer,** *m.* pen-wiper. **–wolke,** *f.* cirrus (cloud). **–zeichnung,** *f.* pen-and-ink drawing; plumage markings. **–zug,** *m.*, *see* **–strich.**

Fee, *f.* (-n) fairy. **–nhaft,** *adj.* fairy-like, magical. **–nreigen,** *m.* fairy-ring, fairy dance.

Feg–e, *f.* (-n) riddle, screen, sieve. **–en,** 1. *v.a.* sweep, wipe, clean, cleanse, scour, rub off; purge (*Med.*); winnow; *einem den Beutel –en*, drain a p.'s purse. 2. *v.n.* (*aux.* h. & s.) scamper; sweep over, rush across. **–er,** *m.* sweeper; scourer; (*coll.*) flibbertigibbet; rearguard of convoy (*Nav.*). **–sel,** *n.* sweepings. **–ung,** *f.* cleansing, sweeping, wiping, scouring. **–(e)feuer,** *n.* purgatory. **–elappen,** *m.* mop; dish-clout. **–(e)sand,** *m.* scouring sand.

Feh, *n.* **–e,** *f.* (-en) Siberian squirrel; miniver. **–pelz,** *m.* squirrel coat.

Fehde, *f.* (-n) feud, private warfare; quarrel; – *bieten,* defy. **–brief,** *m.* (written) challenge. **–handschuh,** *m.* gauntlet (*thrown down as a challenge*); *den –handschuh hinwerfen* or *vor die Füße werfen,* throw down the gauntlet, challenge; *den –handschuh aufheben* or *aufnehmen,* accept the challenge.

Fehl, 1. *m.* (-s, -e) (*B.*) fault, blemish, failure. 2. *adv.* & *sep. prefix,* wrong, wrongly, amiss; erroneously; in vain; (*in compounds generally* =) mis-; – *am Platz* or *Ort,* be out of place *or* misplaced; *der Schuß ging –,* the shot went wide of the mark. **–anzeige,** *f.* nil return, negative report. **–bar,** *adj.* fallible. **–barkeit,** *f.* fallibility. **–bestand,** *m.* deficiency, shortage. **–betrag,** *m.* deficit. **–bitte,** *f.* vain request; *eine –bitte tun,* meet with a refusal. **–blatt,** *n.* missing leaf *or* card. **–druck,** *m.* misprint. **–en,** 1. *v.a.* miss. 2. *v.n.* (*aux.* h.) make a mistake, be in the wrong, do wrong, err, blunder; be missing, be absent, be wanting, lack, ail; (*C.L.*) *dieser Artikel –t mir,* I am out of this article; *es –en dem Buch die ersten drei Seiten,* the first three pages of the book are missing; *es –te nur, daß,* all that was wanting was; *es –t ihm noch viel,* he is short of many things; *es –t ihm immer etwas,* he is always ailing; there is always something the matter with him; *ihr –t nichts,* she is quite well; she has all she wants; *es –en im Ganzen 30,* altogether 30 are missing; *es –t uns Geld,* some of our money is missing; *es –t uns an Geld,* we are short of money; *es –t ihm an Mut,* he is wanting in courage; *es –en 10 Minuten bis 12,* it is 10 minutes to 12; *an mir soll es nicht –en,* it will not be my fault; *das –te noch;* that would be too bad, that would be the last straw; *was –t Ihnen?* what is the matter with you? *es –en lassen an* (*Dat.*), be wanting in *or* short in; *er ließ es an nichts –en,* he spared no pains; *weit gefehlt,* far from it, you are making a big mistake. **–end,** *pr.p.* & *adj.* erring, wanting, deficient; *das –ende,* want, deficiency, that which is missing. **–er,** *m.* (-ers, -er) fault, defect, blemish, flaw; mistake, error, blunder; *einen eines –ers beschuldigen,* accuse a p. of a fault; *grober –er,* bad mistake; *dummer –er,* silly mistake. **–erfrei,** *adj.* correct, faultless, flawless, sound. **–ergrenze,** *f.* margin of error, tolerance (*Engin.*). **–erhaft,** *adj.* faulty, defective, imperfect, deficient, incorrect. **–erhaftigkeit,** *f.* faultiness; incorrectness. **–erlos,** *adj.,* *see* **–erfrei. –erquelle,** *f.* source of error. **–fahren,** *ir.v.a.* take the wrong road. **–gang,** *m.* the wrong way; *einen –gang tun,* miss one's way; not succeed. **–gebären,** *v.n.* (*aux.* h.) miscarry. **–geburt,** *f.* miscarriage, abortion. **–gehen,** *ir.v.a.* go astray, go wrong, miss *or* lose one's way; not succeed; make a mistake, fail, err. **–gewicht,** *n.* short weight, underweight. **–greifen,** *ir.v.a.* miss one's hold; make a mistake, err. **–griff,** *m.* blunder, mistake. **–jahr,** *n.* year of a bad harvest; (*coll.*) off year. **–kauf,** *m.* bad bargain. **–landung** *f.* crash landing (*Av.*). **–leiten,** *v.a.* mislead, misguide. **–schießen,** *ir.v.a.* miss one's aim; (*coll.*) *–geschossen!* wrong! mistaken! **–schlag,** *m.* failure; (*coll.*) wash-out; disappointment; wrong stroke. **–schlagen,** *ir.v.n.* (*aux.* h. & s.) miss one's blow; miscarry, fail, come to nothing, be disappointed; *seine Hoffnungen schlugen –,* his hopes were disappointed. **–schließen,** *ir.v.n.* (*aux.* h.) draw a wrong conclusion. **–schluß,** *m.* wrong inference, false conclusion, fallacy. **–schritt,** *m.* false step; error. **–schuß,** *m.* miss; unlucky *or* bad shot. **–spruch,** *m.* miscarriage of justice. **–start,** *m.* false start. **–treffer,** *m.* near miss (*Artil.*). **–treten,** *ir.v.n.* (*aux.* h.) trip, slip, stumble. **–tritt,** *m.* false step; slip, fault; moral lapse; *einen –tritt tun,* miss one's footing, stumble; *das Mädchen hat einen –tritt begangen,* the girl has gone astray *or* (*hum.*) misbehaved, has fallen from grace *or* has lost her virtue. **–urteil,** *n.* misjudgement. **–wurf,** *m.* bad throw, miss. **–ziehen,** *ir.v.n.* (*aux.* h.) draw a blank (*in a lottery*). **–zug,** *m.* wrong move (*Chess, etc.*); blank (*in lotteries*). **–zündung,** *f.* backfire (*Motor.*); misfire (*gun*).

Fehme, *f., see* **Feme.**

Fei, *f.* (-en) *poetic for* **Fee,** fairy. **–en,** *v.a.* charm a p. (*gegen eine S.,* against a th.); make proof against. **gefeit,** *p.p.* & *adj.* charmed; proof (*gegen,* against).

Feier, *f.* (-n) celebration, festival, ceremony; cessation from work, rest; recess, holiday. **–abend,** *m.* time for leaving off work; evening leisure; *–abend machen,* finish work; (*coll.*) knock off (work.). **–gesang,** *m.* solemn hymn. **–jahr,** *n.* sabbatical year. **–kleid,** *n.* festive raiment. **–lich,** *adj.* solemn; festive; *–lich begehen,* solemnize. **–lichkeit,** *f.* solemnity; pomp, ceremony. **–n,** 1. *v.n.* (*aux.* h.) rest, take a holiday; stop work, be idle, strike; like fallow; *da ist nichts zu –n,* there is no time to be lost. 2. *v.a.* celebrate, solemnize; observe; extol, honour. **–stunde,** *f.* festive hour; leisure hour. **–tag,** *m.* holiday; day of rest; festival.

feig–e, *adj.* cowardly, timid, dastardly, faint-hearted; crumbling, rotten (*Min.*); *–e Memme,* poltroon. **–heit,** *f.* cowardice. **–herzig,** *adj.* cowardly, faint-hearted. **–herzigkeit,** *f.* pusillanimity. **–ling,** *m.* coward.

Feig–e, *f.* (-en) fig; *einem die –e weisen,* snap one's fingers at a p.; make an indecent gesture; cock a snoot (*vulg.*). **–blatter,** *f.,* **–warze,** *f.* pimple; boil, tumour. **–bohne,** *f.* lupine, horse-bean. **–enbaum,** *m.* fig-tree. **–enblatt,** *n.* fig-leaf; (*pl.*) subterfuges. **–enkaktus,** *m.* prickly pear.

feil, *adj.* for sale, to be sold; (*fig.*) venal, bribable; mercenary; *dieses Pferd ist mir um keinen Preis –,* I would not sell this horse for any money; *–er Mensch,* hireling; *–e Dirne,* prostitute. **–heit,** *f.* venality; prostitution. **–bieten,** *v.a.* offer for sale. **–haben, –halten,** have for sale, be ready to sell; *Maulaffen –halten,* stand agape with astonishment. **–schen,** *v.a.* & *n.* (*aux.* h.) bargain; (*coll.*) beat down (*the seller to an acceptable price*). **–tragen,** *v.a.* hawk.

Feil–e, *f.* (-en) file; ratchet. **–en,** *v.a.* file, polish. **gefeilt,** *p.p.* & *adj.* filed; (*fig.*) polished, elaborate. **–icht,** *n.,* filings. **–kloben,** *m.,* **–stock,** *m.* hand-vice. **–sel,** *n.* **–späne,** *m.pl.,* **–staub,** *m.* filings.

Feimen, *m.* (-s, –) stack, rick (*of hay, corn*).

fein, *adj.* fine, delicate, thin; polite, cultivated, refined; elegant, distinguished, fashionable; acute, subtle, sly, artful; (*coll.*) beautiful, excellent, capital, fine, grand. *–er Fuchs,* sly dog; *–es Gefühl,* fine feeling; *–er Kopf,* clever person; *–er Mann,* well-bred man; *–er Regen,* drizzling rain; *–e Sitten,* good manners; *–er Ton,* good form; *–er Verstand,* cultivated understanding; *–e Wäsche,* dainty underwear; *–e Welt,* fashionable *or* polite society, people of fashion; *er spricht kein –es Englisch,* he does not speak the Queen's English; (*coll.*) *er ist – heraus,* he is a lucky fellow; *sei mir – klug,* for my sake mind what you're doing; *es ist – warm hier!* it's nice and warm here! **–arbeit,** *f.* precision work. **–bäcker,** *m.* pastry-cook. **–bäckerei,** *f.* confectioner's shop. **–brenner,** *m.* refiner of metals. **–einstellung,** *f.* fine adjustment (*Opt.*); fine tuning (*Rad.*). **–erde,** *f.* garden soil. **–farbe,** *f.* pastel shade. **–fein,** *adj.* superfine. **–feuer,** *n.* refinery. **–fühlend,** *adj.,* **–fühlig,** *adj.* tactful, sensitive; thin-skinned. **–fühligkeit,** *f.,* **–gefühl,** *n.* delicacy, tact. **–gehalt,** *m.* fineness; standard (*gold, etc.*). **–gehaltsstempel,** *m.* hall-mark. **–geschnitten,** *adj.* finely chopped, finely sliced. **–gespitzt,** *adj.* sharp-pointed. **–gezeichnet,** *adj.* finely drawn, with minute detail. **–heit,** *f.* fineness, elegance; politeness, refinement; fine detail; sharpness (*of the senses*); astuteness; delicacy (*of feeling*); finesse, subtlety; purity (*of gold*); closeness of grain (*in wood*); rarity (*of the air*); (*pl.*) niceties (*of language, etc.*). **–hörend,** *adj.,* **hörig,** *adj.* quick of hearing. **–körnig,** *adj.* finely grained. **–kost(handlung),** *f.* delicatessen (shop). **–lunker,** *m.* pinhole (*in castings*). **–macher,** *m.* refiner; finisher. **–malerei,** *f.* miniature painting. **–mechaniker,** *m.* precision tool maker, instrument maker. **–regelung,** *f.,* **–richtung,** *f.* fine adjustment. **–schmecker,** *m.* gourmet, epicure. **–sichtig,** *adj.* sharp-eyed. **–sinnig,** *adj.* sensitive, tasteful, delicate. (*Poet.*) **–sliebchen,** *n.* darling, sweetheart. **–tischler,** *m.* cabinet-maker. **–waage,** *f.* precision balance. **–zeug,** *n.* (paper) pulp. **–zucker,** *m.* refined sugar.

feind, 1. *adj.* hostile. 2. *m.* (-(e)s, -e) enemy, foe; *der* (*alte*) *böse* –, the evil one, the Devil; *abgesagter* –, sworn enemy; *den – stellen,* engage the enemy; *vor dem* –, in the face of the enemy; *zum –e übergehen,* desert to the enemy. **–berührung,** *f.* contact with the enemy. **–beurteilung,** *f.* **–lage,** *f.* estimate of enemy situation. **–flug,** *m.* operational flight (*Av.*). **–lich,** *adj.* (*Dat.*) hostile, inimical, unfriendly; *das –liche Heer,* the enemy; *–liche Ausländer,* enemy aliens. **–lichkeit,** *f.* hostility. **–schaft,** *f.* enmity, hatred, hostility. **–schaftlich,** *adj., see* **–lich. –selig,** *adj.* hostile; malignant. **–seligkeit,** *f.* hostility, animosity, war; *Einstellung der –seligkeiten,* cessation of hostilities, armistice. **–wärts,** *adv.* in the direction of the enemy. **–wirkung,** *f.* air-raid damage.

feist, 1. *adj.* fat, stout, plump; *–er Sonntag,* the last Sunday before Lent. 2. *n.* (-es) fat, suet (*of deer, etc.*). **–e,** *f.* 1. *see* –, 2; 2. *or* **–heit,** *f. or* **–igkeit,** *f.* obesity. **–zeit,** *f.* season for venison (*when deer are fat*).

feixen, *v.n.* (*dial. & coll.*) grin.

Felb–e, *f.* (-en), **–er,** *or* **–inger,** *m.* (-s, –) white willow (*Salix alba*) (*Bot.*).

Felbel, *m.* (-s, –) & *f.* (-n) velveteen.

Felchen, *m.* (-s, –) whitefish (*Coregonus*) (*Icht.*).

Feld, *n.* (-(e)s, -er) field, open country, plain, ground; area, field of action, sphere, scope; battlefield; square (*of a chessboard*); panel; *elektrisches* –, electric field; *ein rotes Kreuz im weißen* –, a red cross on a white ground; *–er* (*pl.*), lands (*of rifling on a barrel*); *abgenutztes* –, scoring of the bore; *das – bebauen,* till the ground; *das – behalten* or *behaupten,* win the day; *freies* –, plain; *über – gehen,* go across country; *– gewinnen,* gain ground; *im freien –e liegen,* bivouac; *noch im weiten –e liegen,* be still very uncertain *or* quite unsettled; *ins – rücken, zu –e ziehen,* go to the front, take the field (*Mil.*); *die S. steht noch im weiten –e,* that is still a long way off *or* very remote; *ein Heer ins – stellen,* take the field with an army. **–ahorn,** *m.* common maple (*Acer campestre*) (*Bot.*). **–arbeit,** *f.* agricultural labour. **–artillerie,** *f.* field artillery. **–arzt,** *m.* medical officer, army surgeon. **–bäckerei,** *f.* field bakery. **–bahn,** *f.* military railway; field *or* narrow-gauge railway. **–bau,** *m.* agriculture, farming, tillage. **–bett,** *n.* camp-bed. **–biene,** *f.* wild bee. **–blume,** *f.* wild flower. **–dichte,** *f.* field strength (*Elec.*). **–dienst,** *m.* service in the field, active service (*Mil.*). **–dienstordnung,** *f.* field-service regulations. **–dienstübung,** *f.* manœuvres, field-day (*Mil.*); *eine –dienstübung abhalten,* hold a field-day. **–ein, –aus,** *adv.* across country, across the fields. **–flasche,** *f.* water-bottle. **–flüchtige(r),** *m.* deserter. **–frucht,** *f.* farm produce; (*pl.*) crops. **–fuß,** *m.* war-footing. **–gehege,** *n.* warren, covert; preserve. **–geistliche(r),** *m.* chaplain to the forces, padre. **–gericht,** *n.* court-martial. **–geschrei,** *n.* war-cry. **–geschütz,** *n.* field gun. **–gottesdienst,** *m.* drumhead service. **–grau,** *adj.* field grey (*uniform of German soldiers*). **–heer,** *n.* field force. **–herr,** *m.* commander-in-chief; general. **–herrnkunst,** *f.* generalship; strategy. **–herrnstab,** *m.* field-marshal's baton. **–huhn,** *n.* partridge. **–jäger,** *m.* chasseur, sharp-shooter; king's messenger (*Mil.*); *berittener –jäger,* mounted courier. **–kessel,** *m.* camp kettle. **–koch,** *m.* army cook. **–koffer,** *m.* valise, hold-all. **–küche,** *f.* field-kitchen. **–lager,** *n.* camp. **–lazarett,** *n.* field hospital, casualty clearing station. **–lerche,** *f.* skylark. **–mark,** *f.* landmark; boundary. **–marschall,** *m.* field-marshal. **–marschmäßig,** *adj.* in full marching order. **–messer,** *m.* land-surveyor. **–musik,** *f.* military music. **–mütze,** *f.* field service cap, forage cap. **–post,** *f.* military post. **–postbrief,** *m.* letter on active service. **–posten,** *m.* outpost, picket. **–postwesen,** *n.* field postal service. **–prediger,** *m.* army chaplain. **–rose,** *f.* wild rose. **–rübe,** *f.* turnip. **–rüster,** *f.* common elm (*Ulmus campestris*) (*Bot.*). **–rute,** *f.* surveyor's pole. **–schaden,** *m.* damage to crops. **–schanze,** *f.* field work. **–scher,** *m.* assistant medical officer (*Mil.*). **–schlacht,** *f.* pitched battle. **–schmiede,** *f.* mobile forge. **–soldat,** *m.* soldier of the line, soldier on active service. **–spat,** *m.* feldspar. **–sperling,** *m.* hedge sparrow. **–stärke,** *f.* field strength (*Elec.*). **–stecher,** *m.* field-glasses, binoculars. **–stein,** *m.* boulder; landmark. **–stiefel,** *m.* field-service boots. **–stück,** *n.* field-piece (*Artil.*). **–stuhl,** *m.* camp-stool. **–ulme,** *f., see* **–rüster. –verpflegung,** *f.* commissariat. **–wache,** *f.* picket, outpost. **–webel,** *m.* sergeant. **–weg,** *m.* lane, field-path. **–weite,** *f.* span, dimension. **–werkstätte,** *f.* 1st echelon workshop. **–wirtschaft,** *f.* agriculture. **–zeichen,** *n.* banner, ensign, standard; signal. **–zeug,** *n.* munition; ordnance, stores. **–zeugmeister,** *m.* master of ordnance, quartermaster. **–zeugmeisterei,** *f.* ordnance depot. **–zug,** *m.* campaign. **–zulage,** *f.* field allowance (*Mil.*).

Felge, *f.* (-n) felloe (*of a wheel*); (wheel-)rim (*Cycl.*). **–n,** *v.a.* provide (*a wheel*) with felloes. **–nbremse,** *f.* calliper brake (*Cycl.*). **–nhauer,** *m.* wheelwright.

Fell, *n.* (-es, -e) skin, hide, pelt, fur, coat (*of animals*); film; *einem das – über die Ohren ziehen,* fleece a p.; (*coll.*) *einem das – gehörig gerben,* tan the hide off a p.; *er hat ein sehr dickes* –, he is very thick-skinned; *– auf dem Auge,* film on the eye; (*Prov.*) *man soll das – nicht verkaufen, ehe man den Bären hat,* don't count your chickens before they're hatched. **–bereiter,** *m.* currier, furrier. **–eisen,** *n.* knapsack. **–händler,** *m.* dealer in hides, furrier. **–werk,** *n.* skins, furs.

Fels, *m.* (-en, -en) rock, crag, cliff. **–abhang,** *m.* rocky slope. **–absturz,** *m.* fall of rocks. **–artig,** *adj.* rocky. **–block,** *m.* boulder. **–boden,** *m.* rocky soil. **–enfest,** *adj.* firm as a rock, unshakeable, adamant; *das steht –enfest,* that is indisputable. **–(en)geröll,** *n.* scree, rubble, debris. **–enhart,** *adj.* hard as rock; stony. **–enhöhle,** *f.* grotto, rock-cave. **–eninsel,** *f.* rocky island. **–enklippe,** *f.* cliff. **–enkluft,** *f.* chasm, cleft in rocks. (*fig.*) **–ennest,** *n.* castle on a rock, rocky refuge. **–(en)öl,** *n.* petroleum. **–enriff,** *n.* ledge of rocks, reef. **–enritze,** *f.* crevice, fissure. **–enschicht,** *f.* layer of rock. **–enschlucht,** *f.* rocky gorge. **–enspitze,** *f.* peak, crag. **–ensteg,** *m.* rocky path, path through rocks. **–enverließ,** *n.* dungeon hewn in a rock. **–enwand,** *f., see* **–wand. –glimmer,** *m.* mica. **–ig,** *adj.* rocky, craggy, rock-like. **–klettern,** *n.* rock climbing. **–klippe,** *f.* rocky ridge, cliff. **–spitze,** *f.* crag. **–sturz,** *m.* fall of rock. **–wand,** *f.* wall of rock, rock face.

Felsen, *m.* (-s, –), *see* **Fels.**

Fem–e, *f.* (*imperial court of justice in Westphalia until 1808*). **–gericht,** *n.* secret court, vehmic court. **–emord,** *m.* political assassination (*20th cent.*). **–recht,** *n.* summary justice.

Fenchel, *m.* (-s) fennel (*Foeniculum vulgare*) (*Bot.*). **–holz,** *n.* sassafras. **–öl,** *n.* oil of fennel, anathol.

Fenn, *n.* (-s, -e) fen, swamp, marsh, bog.

Fenster, *n.* (-s, –) window; *ein blindes* –, mock-window; *bunte* –, stained glass windows; *einem die – einwerfen,* break a p.'s windows; *gemalte* –, see *bunte* –; *gewölbtes* –, bow-window; *er wirft sein Geld zum – hinaus,* he pours his money down the drain. **–angel,** *f.* casement-hinge. **–austritt,** *m.* balcony. **–bank,** *f.* window-ledge *or* sill. **–beschläge,** *m.pl.* iron work of a window. **–bogen,** *m.* arch of a window. **–brett,** *n.,* **–brüstung,** *f.* window-sill. **–flügel,** *m.* casement. **–futter,** *n.* sash *or* frame of a window. **–gardine,** *f.* window-curtain. **–geld,** *n.,* **–steuer,** *f.* window-tax. **–giebel,** *m.* frontal. **–gitter,** *n.* lattice (of a window). **–höhle,** *f.* window-opening. **–jalousie,** *f.* Venetian blind. **–kitt,** *m.* putty. **–kreuz,** *n.* window bars. **–laden,** *m.* (window) shutter. **–mantel,** *m.* heavy window curtain. **–nische,** *f.* embrasure. **–pfeiler,** *m.* pier. **–pfosten,** *m.,* **–säule,** *f.* window-post. **–polster,** *n.* (& *Austr. m.*) window-cushion. **–rahmen,** *m.* window-frame.

-raute, *f.* pane of glass, window-pane. **-riegel,** *m.* sash-bolt, window fastener *or* catch. **-rollen,** *f.pl.* sash-pulleys. **-rose,** *f.* rose-window. **-schiebe,** *f.* window-pane, pane of glass. **-schieber,** *m.* window sash. **-seil,** *n.* window-cord, sash-cord. **-sims,** *m.* window-sill. **-sturz,** *m.* lintel. **-träger,** *m., see* **-sturz.** **-tür,** *f.* glass door, French window. **-überlage,** *f., see* **-sturz.**

Ferge, *m.* (-n, -n) (*Poet.*) ferryman.

Ferialkurs, *m.* (-es, -e) (*Austr. dial.*) holiday course.

Ferien, *pl.* vacation, holidays; *die großen –*, the long vacation, the summer holidays; *in die – gehen,* go away on holiday *or* for the vacation; *er war auf –*, he was on holiday; *– vom Ich,* freedom from every-day cares. **-kolonie,** *f.* holiday camp. **-kurs(us),** *m.* (-kurse) holiday course, vacation course. **-sonderzug,** *m.* holiday special.

Ferkel, *n.* (-s, –) young pig, sucking pig; (*coll.*) pig, swine, dirty person; *eine Tracht –*, a litter of pigs; *– werfen,* farrow. **-maus,** *f.* guinea pig (*Cavia cobaya*) (*Zool.*). **-n,** *v.n.* farrow.

Fermate, *f.* (-n) pause (*ad lib. lengthening of note or rest*); fine (*at conclusion of repeat*) 𝄐 (*Mus.*).

Ferment, *n.* (-(e)s, -e) ferment, enzyme. **-ausscheidung,** *f.* secretion of enzyme. **-ieren,** *v.n.* (*aux.* h.) ferment. **-wirkung,** *f.* fermentation.

fern, *adj.* (*Dat.*) far, distant, far off, remote; *von –*, from afar, at a distance; covertly, secretly; *so–, inso–*, so far as, if, in case; *das sei mir –* or *– von mir,* far be it from me; *inwie–*, how far, in what measure *or* degree; *er steht mir –*, he has no close connexion with me; *dies ist nicht von –e mit jenem zu vergleichen,* this is not in the least to be compared with that. **-amt,** *n.* trunk exchange (*Phone*). **-anruf,** *m.* trunk-call. **-antrieb,** *m.* remote drive. **-ansicht,** *f.* distant view, vista, perspective. **-aufnahme,** *f.* long-range photograph. **-bahn,** *f.* main line. **-bedienung,** *f., see* **-lenkung.** **-bild,** *n.* telephoto. **-drucker,** *m., see* **-schreiber.** **-e,** *f.* (-en) remoteness, distance, distant place *or* time; *aus der –e,* from afar; *in der –e,* in the distance, at a distance, far off; *sich in der –e halten,* keep away *or* out of reach; *in der –e liegend,* remote, uncertain; *das liegt noch in weiter –e,* that is still looming in the distant future. **-empfang,** *m.* long-distance reception (*Rad.*). **-empfänger,** *m.* long-distance receiver. **-er,** *adv.* farther, further, furthermore, moreover, besides; *–er im Amte bleiben,* continue in office; *erstens . . . zweitens . . . –er,* first . . . second . . . and for the rest. **-erhin,** *adv.* for the future, henceforth, henceforward, furthermore. **-fahrer,** *m.* long-distance lorry driver. **-fahrt,** *f.*, **-flug,** *m.* long-distance flight (*of aircraft, etc.*). **-gefühl,** *n.* presentiment, telepathy. **-geschütz,** *n.* long-range gun. **-gespräch,** *n.* trunk-call. **-glas,** *n.* telescope, binoculars, field-glass. **-halten,** 1. *ir.v.a.* keep away *or* off; *einen von sich –halten,* keep a p. at a distance. 2. *v.r.* keep *or* stand aloof (from). **-haltung,** *f.* keeping off, prevention. **-heizung,** *f.* district heating. **-hörer,** *m.* telephone receiver. **-jäger,** *m.* long-range fighter (*Av.*). **-leitung,** *f.* trunk-line. **-lenkung,** *f.* remote control, radio control. **-liegen,** *v.n.* (*aux.* h.) (*Dat.*) be remote from one's desires *or* far from one's thoughts. **-mündlich,** *adj.* by telephone. **-photographie,** *f.* radio photograph *or* photography, telephotography. **-rohr,** *n.* telescope. **-rohraufsatz,** *m.* telescopic sight. **-ruf,** *m.* telephone call. **-ruf 329,** telephone number 329. **-schaltung,** *f., see* **-lenkung.** **-schnellzug,** *m.* de-luxe train. **-schreiber,** *m.* telegraphic recorder, teletype apparatus, teleprinter. **-sehapparat,** *m.* television set. **-sehen,** *n.* television. **-sicht,** *f.* prospect, distant view, vista, perspective. **-sichtig,** *adj.* far *or* long-sighted. **-sprechamt,** *n.* telephone exchange. **-sprechanschluß,** *m.* telephone connexion. **-sprechautomat,** *m.* automatic telephone. **-sprecher,** *m.* telephone. **-sprechwesen,** *n.* telephone service. **-sprechzelle,** *f.* public telephone, telephone box, call box. **-spruch,** *m.* telephone *or* radio message. **-stehende(r),** *m.* outsider. **-steuerung,** *f., see* **-lenkung.** **-trauung,** *f.* marriage by proxy. **-umfang,** *m.* distance range (*of wireless messages*). **-ung,** *f.* distance (*Paint.*). **-unterricht,** *m.* correspondence course. **-verkehr,** *m.* long-distance traffic. **-wirkung,** *f.* long-range effect, telekinesis; *seelische –wirkung,* telepathy. **-zeichnung,** *f.* perspective drawing. **-zug,** *m.* long-distance train, main-line train.

Fernambukholz, *n.* Brazil wood.

Ferner, *m.* (-s, –) (*dial.*) snow mountain, glacier.

Ferse, *f.* (-n) heel; track, footsteps; hind part of a horse's hoof; *die –n zeigen,* take to one's heels, show a clean pair of heels; *einem auf den –n sein* or *auf der – folgen,* be close *or* hard on a p.'s heels; *einem auf die –n treten,* get under a p.'s heels. **-nbein,** *n.* heel-bone. **-nflechse,** *f.* Achilles tendon. **-ngeld,** *n.*; (*coll.*) *–geld geben,* run away, take to one's heels. **-npunkt,** *m.* nadir (*Astr.*). **-nschlag,** *m.* kick (*of a horse*).

fertig, *adj.* ready, prepared; ready to start, complete, finished, done, ruined; ready-made; perfect; skilled, dexterous; accomplished; fluent; *–bringen,* accomplish, achieve, bring about, manage; *sich – halten,* be in readiness, hold o.s. in readiness, be prepared; *sich – machen,* get o.s. ready; *wir sind – miteinander,* it is all over between us; *–!* ready! *ich bin –*, I have done; *er ist –*, he is done for, it is all over with him; *mit etwas – sein,* have done with a th.; have finished s.th.; *–stellen,* get ready, finish, prepare; *– werden,* finish with a th.; *sehen Sie zu, wie Sie – werden,* see what you can do *or* how you can manage; *mit einem – werden,* manage *or* deal with a p.; *man konnte ohne ihn nicht – werden,* there was no getting on *or* doing anything without him, he was indispensable. **-en,** 1. *v.a.* make, manufacture, finish; prepare, make *or* get ready; dispatch. 2. *v.r.* prepare; (*B.*) flee, hasten over. **-er,** *m.* maker; performer; consigner. **-erzeugnis,** *n.* finished product. **-fabrikat,** *n.* manufactured *or* ready-made article. **-häuser,** *n.pl.* prefabricated houses. **-keit,** *f.* skill, dexterity; fluency, knack; completeness; accomplishment; *–keit im Spielen,* execution (*Mus.*). **-machen,** *n.* adjustment (*Typ.*). **-macher,** *m.* finisher; adjuster (*Typ.*); foreman. **-stellung,** *f.* completion. **-ung,** *f.* making, manufacture, fabrication. **-ungskapazität,** *f.* production capacity. **-waren,** *f.pl.* manufactured *or* ready-made goods.

Fes, *n.* F flat (*Mus.*); *m.* fez.

fesch, *adj.* stylish, smart, attractive; (*coll.*) *–er Kerl,* nice fellow (*S. Germany*), smart fellow (*N. Germany*); *–es Mädchen,* lively *or* attractive girl.

Fessel, *f.* (-n) 1. fetter, chain, shackle. 2. fetlock, pastern-joint (*of a horse*); (*pl.*) irons, handcuffs; *einem –n anlegen* or *in –n legen,* put s.o. in irons, handcuff a p. **-ballon,** *m.* captive balloon. **-bein,** *n.* pastern. **-frei,** *adj.*, **-los,** *adj.* unfettered. **-n,** *v.a.* fetter, chain, shackle; fasten, tether, bind; captivate, fascinate, absorb, arrest (*attention*); *ans Bett gefesselt,* confined to bed; *–nde Unterhaltung,* interesting conversation. **-tau,** *n.* mooring rope *or* cable.

fest, 1. *adj., adv. & sep. prefix,* firm, solid, hard, compact; strong, stout, tight, fast, stable; fixed, immovable, rigid, constant, permanent, enduring; (*coll.*) thoroughly; *– angestellt,* appointed to the permanent staff; *–es Auge,* steady eye; (*fig.*) strict eye; *– behaupten,* maintain positively; *Weizen bleibt –*, wheat remains firm *or* steady (*C.L.*); *–er Boden,* firm ground; (*coll.*) *nur – drauf los!* go at it with might and main! *–es Einkommen,* fixed income; *–er Entschluß,* firm resolve; *–e Farben,* fixed colours; *–en Fuß fassen,* gain a (firm) footing; *– gegen,* proof against; *–es Gehalt,* fixed salary; *–e Gesundheit,* robust health; *–er Glaube,* firm belief, unshakeable faith; *–e Grundlage haben,* have a sound basis *or* foundation; *–e Grundsätze,* fixed principles; *–er Handel,* bargain; *einen Handel –machen,* close *or* clinch a bargain; *in –en Händen,* in safe hands; (*C.L.*) not to be sold; *–er Knoten,* tight knot; *–e Körper,* solid bodies; *–er Kunde,* regular customer; *das –e Land,* terra firma, mainland, continent; *–e Masse,* compact mass; *–e Meinung,* firm opinion; *–e Nahrung,* solid food; *–er Ort,* fortress; *–e Preise,* fixed prices; *–er Schlaf,* sound sleep; *so viel steht –*, this (at least) is evident *or* certain;

steif und –, categorically; *–e Stellung*, permanent post (*employment*); secure position (*Mil.*); *– und treu*, steadfast and true; *–es Tuch*, close-woven material; *– davon überzeugt sein*, be firmly convinced; *– umschlossen*, closely surrounded; *–er Wohnsitz*, permanent home, permanent address. 2. *suffix* (*in compounds* =) versed in, e.g. *bibel–*, well-versed in the Scriptures; *sattel–*, firm in the saddle *or* (*coll.*) in one's knowledge. **–backen,** *v.n.* cake together. **–binden,** *ir.v.a.* tie, fasten, bind fast. **–e,** *f.* (-en) firmness, solidity, density; stronghold, prison, fortress; (*B.*) *–e des Himmels*, firmament of heaven. **–fahren,** *v.n.* & *r.* run aground, get bogged down, come to a standstill, stick fast; *sich –fahren*, be in a quandary, (*coll.*) be in a jam. **–frieren,** *v.n.* freeze solid. **–gebannt,** *adj.* spell-bound. **–gehalt,** *m.* solid *or* cubic content. **–haften,** *v.n.* cling right, stick firmly. **–halten,** 1. *ir.v.a.* hold fast; detain, retain, arrest, seize; write down, portray. 2. *v.n.* (*aux.* h.) hold on, cling, adhere to. **–igen,** *v.a.* make fast *or* firm, make solid *or* compact, strengthen, consolidate, secure; settle, establish, confirm. **–igkeit,** *f.* firmness, solidity; soundness, stability; tenacity, durability, steadiness, constancy; strength, resistance consistence, tensile strength. **–land,** *n.* continent, mainland. **–legen,** 1. *v.a.* lay down, fix, determine, define; invest (*money*); 2. *v.r.* tie o.s. down to, commit o.s.; *sich auf eine S. –legen*, undertake to do a th. **–machen,** *v.a.* fasten, fix, tighten, consolidate; make secure, belay (*ropes*); steady, settle. **–meter,** *n.* (*dial.* & *coll. also m.*) cubic metre. **–nageln,** *v.a.* nail up *or* down; *eine Äußerung –nageln*, put a statement on record. **–nahme,** *f.* seizure, arrest. **–nehmen,** *ir.v.a.* seize, arrest, apprehend. **–punkt,** *m.* fixed point, reference point; anchorage. **–setzen,** 1. *v.a.* fix (*a day, etc.*), arrange, establish, stipulate, lay down as a rule; arrest; *der Anfang der Vorstellung ist auf 3 Uhr festgesetzt*, the performance is timed to begin at 3 o'clock. 2. *v.r.* settle; gain a footing (*an*, in). **–setzung,** *f.* establishment; appointment. **–sitzen,** *v.n.* be stuck, sit fast, be attached. **–stehen,** *v.n.* be settled *or* certain, be established as fact. **–stehend,** *adj.* fixed, constant, stationary, stable, well established; old (*custom*). **–stellen,** *v.a.* establish, ascertain, determine; state; confirm (*a fact*); identify (*a p.*). **–stellung,** *f.* statement; stipulation, arrangement, establishment (*evidence, etc.*); identification, confirmation. **–ung,** *f.* fortress; stronghold; citadel. **–ungsanlage,** *f.* fortifications. **–ungshaft,** *f.*, **–ungsstrafe,** *f.* confinement in a fortress (*a more honourable punishment than imprisonment*). **–ungswall,** *m.* rampart. **–werden,** *v.n.* congeal, coagulate.

Fest, *n.* (-es, -e) festival; holiday; feast; fête; banquet; *bewegliches* –, movable feast; (*Prov.*) *man muß die –e feiern wie sie fallen*, Christmas comes but once a year; make hay while the sun shines; strike the iron while it is hot; *ein – geben*, give a banquet *or* treat. **–abend,** *m.* festive evening. **–essen,** *n.* public banquet. **–gabe,** *f.* gift, presentation. **–geber,** *m.* host. **–halle,** *f.* banqueting-hall. **–kleid,** *n.* evening dress, ceremonial dress. **–kommers,** *m.* formal (students') drinking bout, smoker. **–lich,** *adv.* festive, solemn, splendid, magnificent. **–lichkeit,** *f.* festivity, solemnity; *sich –lich kleiden*, dress up (for a party). **–mahl,** *n.*, **–schmaus,** *m.* banquet, feast. **–ordner,** *m.* organizer of a festivity *or* fête, master of ceremonies. **–rede,** *f.* official speech, formal address. **–redner,** *m.* orator of the day, official speaker. **–schmuck,** *m.* decorations; festive attire. **–schrift,** *f.* publication celebrating an event *or* honouring a p. **–spiel,** *n.* festival performance. **–tag,** *m.* holiday, festivity. **–zeit,** *f.* festive season, holidays. **–zug,** *m.* festive procession.

Feston, *n.* (-s, -s) festoon. **–ieren,** *v.a.* festoon.

Festung, *see under* **fest.**

Fetisch, *m.* (-(e)s, -e) fetish. **–anbetung,** *f.*, **–dienst,** *m.*, **–ismus,** *m.* fetishism, idolatry.

Fett, 1. *n.* (-(e)s, -e) fat, grease, lard, dripping; adipose tissue; tallow; *Nieren–*, suet; *Schweine–*, lard; *Braten–*, dripping; (*coll.*) *er hat sein – weg*, he has got his punishment; *– ansetzen*, grow fat; *im eigenen – noch ersticken*, (*coll.*) stew in one's own juice; put on flesh; *– abschöpfen*, skim the cream, keep the best for o.s. 2. *adj.* oily, fatty, greasy; fat, plump, adipose; rich, lucrative, fertile. lush; (*coll.*) *das macht den Kohl nicht* –, that won't make much difference; *–e Pfründe*, fat living; *–er Druck*, bold *or* Clarendon type; *–er Bissen*, (*coll.*) pretty penny, fat pickings, stroke of (good) luck. **–ader,** *f.* varicose vein. **–auge,** *n.* blob of fat (*on soup, etc.*). **–darm,** *m.* rectum. **–druck,** *m.* heavy *or* bold type. **–drüse,** *f.* sebaceous gland. **–e,** *f.*, **–heit,** *f.* fatness, greasiness; richness, **–echt,** *adj.* insoluble in fat. **–en,** *v.a.* grease, oil, lubricate. **–fang,** *m.* grease trap. **–fleck(en),** *m.* grease spot. **–gänge,** *m.pl.* adipose ducts. **–gedruckt,** *adj.* in heavy type. **–gehalt,** *m.* fat-content. **–glanz,** *m.* greasy shine. **–glänzend,** *adj.* greasy, shiny. **–grieben,** *f.pl.* crackling. **–haltig,** *adj.* fatty, containing fat. **–harz,** *n.* oleoresin. **–haut,** *f.* adipose tissue, subcutaneous fatty layer. **–henne,** *f.* stonecrop (*Sedum*) (*Bot.*). **–ig,** *adj.* fatty, greasy; unctuous; adipose. **–igkeit,** *f.* fattiness, greasiness. **–kohle,** *f.* bituminous coal, house coal (*as distinct from steam coal and gas coal*). **–körper,** *m.pl.* fatty bodies. **–kügelchen,** *n.* fat globule. **–leibig,** *adj.* obese, corpulent. **–lösend,** *adj.* fat-dissolving. **–löslich,** *adj.* soluble in fat. **–magen,** *m.* fourth stomach of ruminants. **–näpfchen,** *n.*; (*sl.*) *da habe ich ins –näpfchen getreten*, I dropped a brick, I put my foot into it, I made a mess of it. **–reihe,** *f.* fatty compounds, aliphatic series (*Chem.*). **–sein,** *n.* greasiness, ropiness (*of wine*). **–spritze,** *f.* grease-gun. **–stift,** *m.* wax crayon. **–stoffwechsel,** *m.* metabolism. **–sucht,** *f.* obesity, fatty degeneration. **–ton,** *m.* fuller's earth. **–wanst,** *m.* big paunch. **–wanstig,** *adj.* big-bellied, paunchy. **–zellen,** *f. pl.* adipose cells.

Fetz–en, 1. *m.* (-ens, -en) rag, tatter, scrap, shred, particle. 2. *v.a.* shred. **–er,** *m.* shoddy-machine.

feucht, *adj.* moist, damp, humid, muggy; *–er Brand*, gangrene; (*Poet.*) *–es Weib*, mermaid; (*sl.*) woman of bad reputation; *noch – hinter den Ohren sein*, be wet behind the ears, be green. **–e,** *f.*, **–heit,** *f.* moisture, humidity, dampness, damp. **–igkeit,** *f.* moisture (content), dampness, humidity, humours (*of the body*). **–en,** *v.a.* & *n.* (*aux.* h.) (*usually in compounds with prefix* be- *or* an-) wet, moisten, dampen. (*Studs. sl.*) **–fröhlich,** *adj.* jovial in one's cups, hilarious. **–(e)messer,** *m.*, **–igkeitsmesser,** *m.* hygrometer. **–kalt,** *adj.* clammy. **–kammer,** *f.* wetting-room (*Typ.*). **–ohrig,** *adj.* wet behind the ears.

feudal, *adj.* feudal, aristocratic; (*coll.*) splendid, magnificent, first-rate. **–recht,** *n.* feudal law.

Feuer, *n.* (-s, –) fire, conflagration; furnace, forge, hearth; firing, bombardment; ardour, passion, spirit, vigour, mettle; brilliance, lustre (*jewel*); *– anlegen*, put on fuel; set on fire; *– anmachen, – anzünden*, light a fire; *mit – bestreichen*, rake with fire (*Mil.*); *darf ich Sie um – bitten*, may I ask you for a light? *das – einstellen*, cease firing; *das – eröffnen* or *einschalten*, open fire; *– erhalten*, come *or* be under fire (*Mil.*); *– fangen*, catch fire ;*– geben*, fire (*Mil.*); *einem – geben*, give s.o. a light; *bei gelindem – kochen*, cook on *or* over a slow fire; *in – und Flamme geraten über eine S.*, fire up at a th., get enthusiastic about a th.; (*Prov.*) *Öl ins – gießen*, add fuel to the fire; *lebhaftes* –, rapid firing (*Mil.*); *unter – nehmen*, open fire upon (*Mil.*); *ruhiges* –, deliberate fire (*Artil.*); *im – sein*, be under fire, be fired upon; *bei starkem – kochen*, cook over a hot fire; *– verlegen* or *verkürzen*, decrease the range (*Artil.*); *– vorlegen*, increase the range (*Artil.*); *wirksames* –, effective fire (*Mil.*); *– ohne Zielbeobachtung*, blind fire (*Mil.*). **–anbeter,** *m.* fire-worshipper. **–abriegelung,** *f.* box-barrage. **–arten,** *f.pl.* classification of fire (*Mil.*). **–artig.** *adj.* igneous. **–bake,** *f.* beacon. **–ball,** *m.* fire-ball. **–becken,** *n.* brazier. **–begriffe,** *m. pl., see* **–arten. –bereit,** *adj.* ready to open fire. **–berg,** *m.* volcano. **–bereich,** *m.* danger zone. field of fire (*Mil.*). **–beständig,** *adj.* fire-proof, heat-resistant, incombustible, refractory (*Chem.*).

-bestattung, *f.* cremation. **-bohne,** *f.* scarlet-runner. **-büchse,** *f.* tinder-box; fire-box. **-dienst,** *m.* fire-worship. **-eifer,** *m.* ardent zeal, ardour. **-esse,** *f.* chimney (*of a forge*); furnace, forge. **-fangend,** *adj.* inflammable. **-farbig,** *adj.* flame-coloured. **-fest,** *adj.* fire-proof; *-fester Stahl*, heat-resisting steel; *-fester Ton*, fire-clay; *-fester Ziegel*, firebrick. **-flüssig,** *adj.* molten. **-garbe,** *f.* volley. **-gatter,** *n.* fender; fire guard. **-gefährlich,** *adj.* highly inflammable, combustible. **-hahn,** *m.* hydrant. **-haken,** *m.* pot-hook; poker. **-ig; (feurig)** *adj.* fiery, burning; igneous; ardent, passionate, fervid; *der feurige Busch*, the burning bush; *das feurige Schwert*, the flaming sword; *feurig-flüssig*, *adj.* molten, volcanic. **-kasse,** *f.* fire-insurance office. **-kitt,** *m.* fire-proof cement. **-kraft,** *f.* fire-power (*Mil.*). **-lärm,** *m.* cry of fire, fire-alarm. **-leiter,** *f.* fire-escape. **-leitung,** *f.* fire control (*Artil.*). **-linie,** *f.* firing-line, front-line. **-löschapparat,** *m.*, **-löscher,** *m.*, **-löschgerät,** *n.* fire-extinguisher. **-löschmannschaft,** *f.* fire-fighters, fire brigade. **-löschteich,** *m.* static water tank. **-mal,** *n.* mole, birthmark. **-mann,** *m.* fireman; stoker. **-mauer,** *f.* shaft of a chimney; party-wall, fireproof wall. **-melder,** *m.*, **-meldestelle,** *f.* fire-alarm. **-n,** 1. *v.a.* fire (*a boiler or firearms*); kindle; animate; (*coll.*) fling, throw violently; (*sl.*) fire, sack. 2. *v.n.* burn, spark, glow. **-nelke,** *f.* scarlet lychnis (*Lychnis chalcedonica*) (*Bot.*). **-ordnung,** *f.* fire regulations. **-pfanne,** *f.* chafing-dish; censer. **-probe,** *f.* ordeal by fire; (*fig.*) crucial test. **-rad,** *n.* Catherine-wheel. **-raum,** *m.* combustion chamber, fire-box, furnace. **-rettungsapparat,** *m.* fire-escape. **-rohr,** *n.* firelock. **-rost,** *m.* (fire-)grate. **-rot,** *adj.* red as fire. **-sbrunst,** *f.* fire, conflagration. **-schaden,** *m.* damage caused by fire. **-schein,** *m.* glare of fire, fire-light, gun flash. **-schiff,** *n.* light-ship. **-schirm,** *m.* fire-screen. **-schlund,** *m.* fiery abyss; crater. **-schwaden,** *m.* firedamp (*Min.*). **-schwamm,** *m.* tinder, kindling. **-sgefahr,** *f.* danger of fire. **-sglut,** *f.* blazing heat. **-sicher,** *adj.* fireproof, non-inflammable, incombustible. **-snot,** *f.* distress resulting from fire. **-sperre,** *f.* barrage (*Artil.*). **-spritze,** *f.* fire-engine. **-stätte,** *f.* site of a fire; fire-place. **-stein,** *m.* flint. **-stelle,** *f.* fire-place, hearth. **-stellung,** *f.* firing position; emplacement (*Artil.*). **-strafe,** *f.* death by burning at the stake. **-taufe,** *f.* baptism of fire; *die -taufe erhalten*, be under fire for the first time. **-tod,** *m.* death by (accidental) burning. **-ton,** *m.* fire-clay. **-turm,** *m.* lighthouse. **-ung,** *f.* fuel; firing, heating. **-ungsanlage,** *f.* furnace, fire-place, hearth. **-vergoldung,** *f.* fire gilding. **-versicherung,** *f.* fire-insurance. **-versicherungspolice,** *f.* fire-policy. **-wache,** *f.* fire-station. **-waffe,** *f.* gun; (*pl.*) fire-arms. **-walze,** *f.* creeping barrage (*Artil.*). **-warte,** *f.* lighthouse; beacon. **-wehr,** *f.* fire-brigade. **-wehrmann,** *m.* fireman. **-werk,** *n.* firework; firework display; pyrotechnics. **-werker,** *m.* serjeant-artificer (*guns*) (*Mil.*); gunner (*Nav.*). **-werkerei,** *f.* pyrotechnics. **-zange,** *f.* (fire-)tongs. **-zeichen,** *n.* beacon, signal flash. **-zeug,** *n.* match-box; lighter. **-ziegel,** *m.* firebrick. **-zünder,** *m.* firelighter. **-zusammenfassung,** *f.* concentrated fire (*Mil.*).

Fex, *m.* (-es, -e) crank, faddist; (*usually in compounds*), e.g. *Bergfex*, enthusiastic climber, mountaineering crank.

Fiaker, *m.* (-s, -) (*Austrian*) cab. **-kutscher,** *m.* cabby.

Fiasko, *n.* (-s, -s) failure; fiasco; *- machen*, break down, fail utterly.

Fibel, *f.* (-n) 1. primer, spelling-book. 2. clasp, brooch.

Fib-er, *f.* (-n); fibre; (*also fig.*) *mit jeder - seines Herzens*, with every fibre of his being. **-rin,** *n.* fibrin. **-rös,** *adj.* fibrous.

ficht, fichtst, *see* **fechten.**

Ficht-e, *f.* (-en) spruce, fir (*Picea excelsa*) (*Bot.*). **-en,** *adj.* of spruce-wood, spruce. **-enapfel,** *m.* spruce-cone. **-enbaum,** *m.*, *see* **-e. -enharz,** *n.* common resin. **-enholz,** *n.* spruce-wood. **-enzapfen,** *m.* spruce-cone.

Fick-e, *f.* (-en) (*dial.*) pocket. **-en,** *v.a.* & *n.* make quick movements to and fro; (*vulg.*) copulate, fornicate. **-(e)rig,** *adj.* (*coll.*) restless, shifty. **-fack,** *m.* (-s, -e) (*coll.*) excuse, shift, let-out. **-facker,** *m.* (-s, -) shifty person. **-facke(r)n,** *v.n.* dither, vacillate; do evil, conspire.

Fideikommiß, *n.* (-(ss)es, -(ss)e) entail; *ein - aufheben*, cut off the entail.

fidel [*pron.* fiˈdeːl], *adj.* merry, jolly; *kreuze-*, very merry, very jolly. (*coll.*) **-ität** (*also* **Fidulität**) *f.* jollity.

Fidibus, *m.* (*- or* -sses, *- or* -sse) spill.

Fiduz [*pron.* fiˈduts], *n.* (-es); (*Studs. sl.*) *kein - zu einer S. haben*, have no confidence in a th. **-it,** *int.* (*Studs. sl.*) to your very good health!

Fieber, *n.* (-s, -) fever; *kaltes -*, ague; *aussetzendes -*, intermittent fever; *auszehrendes -*, hectic fever; *- messen*, take the temperature. **-anfall,** *m.* attack of fever. **-artig,** *adj.* febrile. **-frost,** *m.*, shivering fit; chill. **-haft,** *adj.* (*fig.*) feverish. **-haftigkeit,** *f.* feverishness. **-hitze,** *f.* feverishness, fever heat; cauma (*Med.*); *bis zur -hitze*, up to fever point. **-isch,** *adj.* (*fig.*) feverish; febrile. **-kälte,** *f.*, *see* **-frost. -krank,** *adj.* feverish. **-mittel,** *n.* ague powder, febrifuge. **-phantasie,** *f.*, *see* **-wahn. -n,** *v.n.* (*aux.* h.) have a temperature, be feverish; get violently excited. **-rinde,** *f.* cinchona bark, quinine. **-tabelle,** *f.* temperature chart. **-thermometer,** *n.* clinical thermometer. **-traum,** *m.* feverish dream; hallucination. **-wahn,** *m.* delirium.

Fied-el, *f.* (-n) fiddle. **-elbogen,** *m.* bow, fiddle-stick. **-eln,** *v.a.* (*aux.* h.) fiddle, scrape on the fiddle. **-ler,** *m.* fiddler.

Fieder, *f.* (-n) pinnule, leaflet (*Bot.*). **-ig,** *adj.* feathered, plumed; pinnate (*Bot.*). **-n,** *v.a.* feather (*usually p.p.*); *gefiedert*, plumed, feathered; pinnate (*Bot.*).

fiel, fiele, *see* **fallen.**

fieng (*archaic*), *see* **fing.**

fieren, *v.a.* slack, slacken (*Naut.*).

Figur [*pron.* fiˈguːr], *f.* (-en) figure; illustration, diagram; shape, form; image, trope, figure of speech; chessman; court-card; *ein Bild in ganzer -*, a full-length portrait. **-albaß,** *m.* figured bass (*Mus.*). **-almusik,** *f.* florid counterpoint. **-ant,** *m.* (-en, -en) walker-on, super (*Theat.*). **-entanz,** *m.* square dance, figure dance, set dance. **-ieren,** *v.a.* & *n.* (*aux.* h.) figure; cut a figure; *-ierter Stoff*, figured *or* patterned material.

figürlich, *adj.* figurative, metaphorical.

Fikt-ion, *f.* (-en) invention, pretence. **-iv,** *adj.* fictitious, untrue, unreal, imaginary.

Filet [*pron.* fiˈleː], *n.* (-s, -s) netting, net-work; rump-steak, fillet (*beef*), loin (*mutton, veal, pork*); fillet (*of fish*). (*pl.* -en). [*pron.* fiˈleːten] tooling (*Bookb.*).

Filial-e, *f.* (-en) branch (*establishment or office*), affiliated institution. **-geschäft,** *n.*, branch establishment.

Filigran, *n.* (-s, -e) filigree.

Film, *m.* (-s, -e) film (*Phot.* & *cinematograph*); *einen - drehen*, produce a film. **-apparat,** *m.* cinematograph camera. **-atelier,** *n.* film studio. **-en,** *v.a.* & *n.* film, make *or* shoot a film. **-größe,** *f.* film star. **-kasette,** *f.* plate-holder, film-pack (*Phot.*). **-regisseur,** *m.* film producer. **-schauspieler,** *m.* film actor. **-streifen,** *m.* reel of film. **-verleih,** *m.* film distributors. **-vorstellung,** *f.* cinema performance.

Filt-er, *m.* filter. **-erbewegung,** *f.* seepage flow. **-erkuchen,** *m.* residue, sludge. **-ern,** *v.a.* filter, filtrate, strain. **-erpapier,** *n.* filter-paper. **-errest,** *m.*, **-errückstand,** *m.*, *see* **-erkuchen. -erversuch,** *m.* seepage test. **-rat,** *n.*, **-richt,** *n.* filtrate. **-rierapparat,** *m.*, **-riertrichter,** *m.* funnel. **-rieren,** *v.a.* strain, filter. **-rierpapier,** *n.*, *see* **-erpapier. -riertuch,** *n.* straining cloth. **-rierung,** *f.* filtration.

Filz, *m.* (-es, -e) felt; blanket (*Typ.*); tomentum (*Bot.*); (*coll.*) felt hat; (*coll.*) miser, niggard, skin-flint. **-deckel,** *m.* blanket, damper (*Typ.*). **-en,** 1. *adj.* of felt. 2. *v.a.* (line *or* cover with) felt; snub. 3. *v.n.* (*aux.* h.) (*coll.*) be niggardly *or* stingy. **-hut,** *m.* felt hat. **-ig,** *adj.* felt, felt-like, fluffy, downy, nappy; (*coll.*) mean, stingy. **–schuh,** *m.* felt-slipper. **–unterlage,** *f.* blanket (*Typ.*).

Fimmel, *m.* (-s, –) iron wedge; sledge-hammer; (*sl.*) craze.

Finanz [*pron.* fi'nants], *f.* (-en) (*usually pl.*) finance(s), money-matters. **–amt,** *n.* revenue office. **–ausschuß,** *m.* committee of ways and means, finance committee. **–er,** *m.* (*Austr. dial.*) revenue officer, tax-collector. **–iell,** *adj.* financial. **–ieren,** *v.a.* finance, support. **–jahr,** *n.* fiscal year. **–kammer,** *f.* treasury-board. **–klemme,** *f.* financial straits. **–mann,** *m.* financier; financial expert. **–minister,** *m.* Chancellor of the Exchequer, (*Amer.*) Secretary of the Treasury. **–ministerium,** *n.* Treasury. **–rat,** *m.* (Under-)Secretary to the Treasury, Treasury official. **–wesen,** *n.* finance.

Findel–haus, –kind, *see under* **finden.**

find–en, 1. *ir.v.a.* find, discover; meet with, light upon; think, consider, deem; *wie –en Sie diesen Wein?* how do you like this wine? *große Freude an einer S. –en,* take great delight in a th.; *Geschmack an einer S. –en,* relish a th.; *für gut –en,* think proper; *statt–en,* take place. 2. *v.r.* find o.s., be found; be, turn out to be; occur. *sich geschmeichelt –en,* feel flattered; *Sie müssen sich darein –en,* you must comply, you must put up with it; *es fand sich oft,* it often happened, there were often; *es wird sich –en, daß . . .,* it will be seen *or* found that . . .; *es wird sich schon –en,* it will turn out all right, you wait and see; *sich in eine S. –en,* reconcile *or* resign o.s. to a th., put up with a th. **–elhaus,** *n.* foundling-hospital. **–elkind,** *n.* foundling. **–er,** *m.* finder, discoverer. **–erlohn,** *m.* finder's reward. **–ig,** *adj.* clever, resourceful; ingenious. **–igkeit,** *f.* shrewdness, cleverness, resourcefulness, ingenuity. **–ling,** *m.* 1. *see* **–elkind;** 2. erratic block, drift block *or* boulder (*Geol.*). **–ung,** *f.* finding; discovery.

Finesse, *f.* (-n) finesse, stratagem.

fing, finge, *see* **fangen.**

Finger, *m.* (-s, –) finger; digit; *an den (fünf) –n abzählen,* count on the fingers (of one hand); *er faßt es mit spitzen –n an,* he touches it very cautiously; *sich die – wund arbeiten,* work one's fingers to the bone; *bei geraden –n verhungern,* starve on honesty; *er hat überall die – drin* or *dazwischen,* he has a finger in every pie; *an den –n hersagen,* have at one's finger-ends; *einem auf die – klopfen,* rap a p. over the knuckles, rebuke a p.; *er hat* or *macht lange* or *krumme –,* he is light-fingered *or* is given to pilfering; *das Heer der langen –,* light-fingered gentry; *du hast keinen – dabei* or *dafür gerührt,* you didn't raise a finger (to help); *aus den –n saugen,* invent; *einem auf die – sehen,* keep a strict eye upon a p.; watch a p. closely; *durch die – sehen,* not look at too strictly, be tolerant with, wink at; *sich (Dat.) die – verbrennen,* burn one's fingers, get into trouble; *einen um den – wickeln,* twist a p. round one's little finger; *mit –n* or *dem – weisen* or *zeigen auf (einen),* point at *or* to a p., point (a p.) out; *mir zerrinnt das Geld unter den –n,* money runs through my fingers like water. **–abdruck,** *m.* finger-print. **–breit,** *m.* a finger's breadth. **–entzündung,** *f.* whitlow. **–fertigkeit,** *f.* manual skill, dexterity; execution (*Mus.*). **–förmig,** *adj.* digitate, digital. **–futter,** *n.* finger stall. **–gelenk,** *n.* finger-joint. **–hut,** *m.* thimble; foxglove (*Digitalis*) (*Bot.*). **–kraut,** *n.* cinquefoil (*Potentilla*) (*Bot.*). **–nagel,** *m.* fingernail. **–ling,** *m.* fingerstall. **–n,** 1. *v.a. & n. aux.* h.) manipulate; (*coll.*) *ich werde es schon –n,* I'll manage it, (*sl.*) I get it sorted; *er –t nach dem Geld,* his fingers are itching for the money. **–nerven,** *m.pl.* digital nerves. **–platte,** *f.* door-guard, finger-plate. **–probe,** *f.* rule of thumb. **–satz,** *m.* fingering (*Mus.*). **–spitze,** *f.* finger-tip, finger-end; *es juckt ihm in den –spitzen,* (*fig.*) his fingers are itching. **–spitzengefühl,** *n.* instinct, intuition; flair. **–sprache,** *f.* deaf-and-dumb language. **–stock,** *m.* glove-stretcher. **–übung,** *f.* fingering, finger-exercises (*Mus.*). **–zeig,** *m.* sign; indication, hint; cue, tip.

fingier–en, *v.a.* simulate, pretend, feign, invent. **–t,** *p.p. & adj.* assumed, fictitious, imaginary.

Fink, *m.* (-en, -en) finch (*Fringillidae*) (*Orn.*); (*Studs. sl.*) free student (*belonging to no corporation*); (*Swiss dial.*) house-shoe, slipper; (*coll.*) frivolous fellow, rake. **–ler,** *m.* bird-catcher, fowler.

Finn–e, *f.* (-en) fin (*of whales*); claw (*of a hammer*); pimple, pustule, acne; bladder-worm, undeveloped tape-worm (*Med.*). **–ig,** *adj.* pimpled, pustular, measly (*of pigs*). **–wal,** *m.* finback (whale). **–enkrankheit,** *f.* bladder-worm disease.

finster, *adj.* dark, obscure; gloomy, dim; ominous, threatening; morose, sad; *– blicken* or *aussehen,* look black; *– ansehen, mit –n Augen ansehen, ein –es Gesicht machen,* give black looks *or* a black look. **–ling,** *m.* obscurantist, bigot; ignoramus. **–n,** *n.* dark, darkness; *im –n tappen,* grope in the dark (*also fig.*) **–nis,** *f.* darkness; obscurity; gloom; eclipse; *die Macht der –nis,* the power of darkness.

Finte, *f.* (-n) feint (*Fenc.*); trick, wile, artifice

Fips, *m.* (-es, -e) snap of the fingers; fillip; agile little man; nickname for a tailor.

Firlefanz, *m.* (-es, -e) nonsense, foolery, hocus-pocus; frippery. **–er,** *m.* buffoon, trifler. **–erei,** *f.* nonsense, fooling, trifling.

Firm–a, *f.* (-en) firm, business, (commercial) house *or* establishment; (*C.L.*) *unter der –a,* under the style of. **–ainhaber,** *m., see* **–eninhaber. –ieren,** *v.a.* sign (the firm's name). **–enbuch,** *n.* trade directory. **–eninhaber,** *m.* proprietor. **–enschild,** *n.* sign(-board). **–enzeichnung,** *f.* signature.

Firmament, *n.* (-(e)s, -e) firmament, sky, vault of heaven.

firm–eln, *v.a.* confirm (*R.C.*). **–(el)ung,** *f.* confirmation. **–en,** *v.a.* (*Austr. dial.*) *see* **–eln. –ling,** *m.* candidate for confirmation.

Firn, *m.* (-(e)s, -e) old snow, perpetuated snow (*on mountains*), névé; (*pl.* -en *but Austr. dial.* -e); snow-covered mountain; glacier. **–e,** *f.* age, mellowness (*of wine*). **–en,** *v.n.* age (*of wine*). **–er,** *m.* (-s, –) (*Austr. & Bav. dial.*) *see* **Firn** & **Ferner. –blau,** *adj.* icy blue, glacier blue. **–(e)wein,** *m.* old wine, matured wine. **–gürtel,** *m.* region of perpetual snow.

Firnis, *m.* (-sses, -sse) varnish, gloss; (*fig.*) *Bildung als bloßer –,* education that is a mere veneer; *Kultur–,* superficial culture. **–glasur,** *f.* spirit enamel. **–papier,** *n.* glazed paper. **–sen,** *v.a.* (du -sest *or* -(ß)t, gefirnißt) varnish, enamel, lacquer. **–ser,** *m.* varnisher.

First, *m.* (-es, -e), (*dial.*) **–e,** *f.* (-en) ridge (*of a roof or hill*); coping (*of a wall*); roof of a gallery (*Min.*). **–balken,** *m.* ridge-piece. **–enstempel,** *m.pl.* roof props (*Min.*),

Fis, *n.* F sharp. **–is,** *n.* F double sharp (*Mus.*).

Fisch, *m.* (-es, -e) fish; (*pl.*) Pisces (*Astr.*); *gesund wie ein –,* as sound as a bell, right as a trivet; *das sind faule –e,* these are lame *or* paltry excuses, (*coll.*) that won't wash, that cat won't jump; *wie ein – auf trockenem Sand,* like a fish out of water; *stumm wie ein –,* silent as the grave; *nicht –, nicht Fleisch,* neither fish nor flesh. **–adler,** *m.* osprey. **–angel,** *f.* fishing-hook. **–artig,** *adj.* fish-like. **–behälter,** *m.* fish-tub *or* tank, reservoir, aquarium. **–bein,** *n.* whalebone; *weißes –bein,* bone of cuttle-fish. **–beinern,** *adj.* of whalebone. **–beschreibung,** *f.* ichthyology. **–blut,** *n.* sluggishness, apathy; *–blut in den Adern haben,* be phlegmatic. **–blütig,** *adj.* phlegmatic. **–brut,** *f.* fry. **–dampfer,** *m.* steam-trawler. **–en,** *v.a. & n.* (*aux.* h.) fish; *im Trüben –en,* fish in troubled waters; (*coll.*) *dabei ist nichts zu –en,* no *or* nothing good will come of it; *die Brocken aus der Suppe –en,* pick and choose, keep the best for o.s. **–er,** *m.* fisherman, angler. **–erboot,** *n.* fishing-boat, fishing smack. **–erdorf,** *n.* fishing village. **–erei,** *f.* fishing, fishery. **–erhütte,** *f.* fisherman's hut. **–erinnung,** *f.*, **–ergilde,** *f.* fishmongers' company. **–erkorb,** *m.* creel *or* pot (*for catching eels, lobsters, etc.*). **–ernetz,** *n.* fishing-net. **–erring,** *m.* pope's signet ring. **–erzeug,** *n.* fishing-tackle. **–fang,** *m.* fishing; fishery. **–flosse,** *f.* fin. **–geruch,** *m.* fishy smell. **–gräte,** *f.* fish-bone. **–grätenmuster,** *n.* herring-bone pattern. **–grätenstich,** *m.* herring-bone stitch. **–hamen,** *m.* hand-net. **–händler,** *m.* fishmonger. **–ig,** *adj.* fishy. **–kieme,** *f.* gill. **–köder,** *m.* bait. **–konserve,** *f.* pickled *or* canned fish. **-korb,** *m.* creel. **-kunde,** *f.* ichthyology. **-kutter,** *m.* fishing smack. **-laich,** *m.* spawn, hard roe. **-leim,** *m.* fish-glue, isinglass. **-logger,** *m.*, **-lugger,** *m.* fishing smack, drifter. **-milch,** *f.* soft roe, milt. **-netz,** *n.* fishing-net. **-otter,** *m.* & *f.* otter. **-recht,** *n.* fishing right. **-reiher,** *m.* heron. **-reuse,** *f.* trap (*for fish*), bow-net, weir-basket. **-rogen,** *m.* roe. **-satz,** *m.* fry, spawn. **-schuppe,** *f.* fish's scale. **-speck,** *m.* blubber (*from fish*). **-speise,** *f.* fish diet. **-strich,** *m.* spawning; spawn (*of fish*). **-teich,** *m.* fish-pond. **-tran,** *m.* train-oil, fish-oil, whale oil, cod-liver oil. **-wasser,** *n.* fishing-ground; *ärarische -wasser*, State fishing-grounds. **-weib,** *n.* fishwife. **-weiher,** *m.* fish-pond. **-wirtschaft,** *f.* management of fisheries. **-zeug,** *n.* fishing-tackle. **-zucht,** *f.* pisciculture. **-zug,** *m.* catch, haul, draught (*of fish*).

Fisimatenten, *pl.* (*dial.* & *sl.*) excuses, humbug, shuffling.

fisk-alisch, *adj.* fiscal, treasury, state-owned; *-alisches Eigentum*, government property. **-us,** *m.* exchequer, treasury.

Fisole, *f.* (-n) (*Austr. dial.*) runner *or* French bean.

Fist-el, *f.* (-n) fistula (*Surg.*); duct, tube, pipe; falsetto (*voice*). **-eln,** *v.n.* (*aux.* h.) sing falsetto. **-elschnitt,** *m.* syringotomy (*Surg.*). **-elstimme,** *f.* falsetto. **-ulös,** *adj.* fistular, fistulous.

Fittich, *m.* (-(e)s, -e) (*Poet.*) wing, pinion; *einen unter seine -e nehmen*, take a p. under one's wing.

Fitting, *n.* (-s, -s) union, joint (*for pipes, etc.*) (*Plumbing*).

Fitz-e, *f.* (-n) skein; hank; (*dial.*) wrinkle. **-en,** *v.a.* tie up into skeins; fold, lace; (*coll.*) whip, chastise, trounce; (*coll.*) work by fits and starts.

fix, *adj.* 1. fixed, firm, settled; 2. quick, nimble, active, alert, ready, smart; adroit; – *und fertig*, quite ready; *mach -!* be quick! *-er Kerl*, smart fellow; *-e Idee*, fixed idea, monomania; (*Prov.*) *außen -, innen nix*, great show, but no substance. **-age,** *f.* fixing (*Chem. Phot.*). **-ativ,** *n.* fixing agent, fixer, fixative (*Chem.*). **-en,** *v.n.* (*aux.* h.) (*C.L.*) sell on time *or* credit. **-er,** *m.* bear (*Stock Exchange*). **-ieren,** *v.a.* fix, settle, establish; stare at; harden, fix (*Phot.*); *einen -ieren*, stare at a p. **-ierbad,** *n.* fixing solution *or* bath (*Phot.*). **-iermittel,** *n.* fixing agent, fixative. **-stern,** *m.* fixed star. **-um,** *n.* (-ums, -a) fixed sum; fixed stipend *or* salary.

flach, *adj.* flat, plain, level, smooth, even; shallow, superficial; *die -e Hand*, palm, flat of the hand; (*coll.*) *das liegt auf der -en Hand*, that's quite plain *or* evident; *auf dem -en Lande*, in the country, outside the town; (*coll.*) *da kennst du ihn -*, in that respect you do not know him at all; *mit der -en Klinge*, with the flat of the blade; *-e Stelle*, shoal (*Naut.*). **-brenner,** *m.* flat *or* fish-tail burner. **-drehen,** *v.a.* surface (*metal on a lathe*) (*Engin.*). **-en,** *v.a.* flatten, level, smooth. **-feld,** *n.* open field, plain. **-feuer,** *n.* flat-trajectory fire (*Artil.*). **-gänge,** *m.pl.* bottom planks (*of a ship*). **-gedrückt,** *adj.* depressed. **-geschliffen,** *adj.* faceted, tabulated (*of jewels*). **-gründig,** *adj.* shallow. **-heit,** *f.* flatness; shallowness; insipidity. **-kopf,** *m.* blockhead. **-kultur,** *f.* shallow ploughing (*4–6 in. deep*). **-land,** *n.* flat country, lowland, low country, plain. **-relief,** *n.* bas-relief. **-rennen,** *n.* flat race. **-schnitt,** *m.* horizontal section. **-see,** *f.* coastal waters (*under* 100 *fathoms*). **-trudeln,** 1. *v.n.* get into a flat spin (*Av.*). 2. *n.* at spin. **-vertieft,** *adj.* concave. **-wasser,** *n.* shallow water. **-wunde,** *f.* surface wound. **-zange,** *f.* flat-nosed pliers.

Fläch-e, *f.* (-en) flatness, level, expanse, plain; plain surface, area, face, facet; wing (*of aircraft*); superficies; *geneigte -e*, inclined plane. **-enausdehnung,** *f.* square dimension. **-enbelastung,** *f.* wing loading (*Av.*). **-enbrand,** *m.* widespread conflagration. **-enblitz,** *m.* sheet-lightning. **-enbombardierung,** *f.* carpet bombing (*Av.*). **-eneinheit,** *f.* unit of area. **-engröße,** *f.* area. **-eninhalt,** *m.* area, acreage. **-enläufig,** *adj.* fan-shaped. **-enmaß,** *n.* square measure, surface measure. **-enraum,** *m.* area. **-enreich,** *adj.* polyhedral, faceted. **-enschießen,** *n.* echeloned fire, searching fire (*Mil.*). **-enumriß,** *m.* perimeter. **-enwinkel,** *m.* plane angle. **-enzahl,** *f.* square number, number of faces *or* facets. **-enzoll,** *m.* square inch. **-ig,** (*suffix*) -faced, -hedral, (e.g. *acht-ig*, octahedral). **-ner,** *m.* polyhedron.

Flachs, *m.* flax; *wilder -*, dodder. **-ähnlich,** *adj.* flaxen. **-artig,** *adj.* flax-like, flaxen. **-bau,** *m.* flax-growing. **-blond,** *adj.* flaxen-haired. **-brecher,** *m.* flax-scutcher. **-brechmaschine,** *f.* scutching-machine. **-darre,** *f.* flax-drying house. **-farben,** *adj.*, **-farbig,** *adj.* flaxen (coloured). **-haarig,** *adj.* flaxen-haired. **-hechel,** *f.* flax comb. **-kopf,** *m.* flaxen-haired person. **-samen,** *m.* linseed. **-seide,** *f.* dodder. **-stein,** *m.* asbestos. **-werg,** *n.* cotton waste (*for cleansing material in workshops*). **-zurichtung,** *f.* flax-dressing.

flächse(r)n, *adj.* flax, flaxen.

flacker-n, *v.n.* (*aux.* h.) flare, flicker, **-ig,** *adj.* flickering, uncertain.

Fladdermine, *f.*, *see* **Flattermine.**

Fladen, *m.* (-s, –) flat cake; cow dung.

Flader, *f.* (-n) vein (*in metals or wood*), flaw, streak, knot. **-ig,** *adj.* veined, streaked.

Flageolett [*pron.* flaʒoˈlɛt], *n.* (-s, -e) flageolet. **-(t)on,** *m.* flute-like tone.

Flagg-e, *f.* (-en) flag, colours, ensign, standard; defect in spinning; *die -e hissen, heißen* or *setzen*, hoist, break, unfurl *or* run up the flag; *seine -e führen*, show one's colours; *die -e streichen*, strike *or* haul down the colours; (*fig.*) give in; *-e halbstock setzen*, fly the flag at half-mast. **-en,** *v.a.* & *n.* (*aux.* h.) fly a flag, deck with flags, signal with flags; *halbstocks* or *halbmast -en*, hoist the flag at half-mast. **-engala,** *f.*; *-engala setzen*, dress a ship. **-enkopf,** *m.* (mast-head) truck. **-enleine,** *f.* signal-halyard. **-enstange,** *f.*, **-enstock,** *m.* flag-staff, flag-pole. **-entuch,** *n.* bunting. **-enzeichen** *n.* flag signal. **-schiff,** *n.* flag-ship.

Flak, *f.* *see the Index of Abbreviations* (*but has become a word in its own right*) *e.g.* **-posten,** *m.* anti-aircraft spotter. **-stellung,** *f.* anti-aircraft site.

Flakon, *n.* (-s, -s) phial, small bottle, smelling-salts.

Flamberg, *m.* (-(e)s, -e) (*Poet.*) sword, brand.

Flamm-e, *f.* (-en) flame; blaze, light; (*coll.*) sweetheart; *Feuer und -e für eine S. sein*, be wildly enthusiastic about a th.; *-en schlagen*, blaze up. **-en,** 1. *v.n.* (*aux.* h.) flame, blaze, flare, glow. 2. *v.a.* singe; water (*silks, etc.*). **-enbogen,** *m.* electric arc. **-enbombe,** *f.* incendiary bomb, oil bomb. **-enmeer,** *n.* sea of flames. **-ensäule,** *f.* fiery column. **-enstrahl,** *m.* jet of flame. **-entod,** *m.* death by fire. **-enwerfer,** *m.* flame-thrower (*Mil.*). **-enzeichen,** *n.* beacon, signal fire. **-ig,** *adj.* flame-like; watered (*of fabric*), veined, grained (*of wood*). **-kohle,** *f.* steam coal. **-ölbombe,** *f.*, *see* **-enbombe.** **-punkt,** *m.* flash point. **-rohr,** *n.* fire tube, flue.

Flammeri, *m.* (-(s), -s) blancmange.

Flanell, *m.* (-s, -e) flannel. **-en,** *adj.* of flannel.

Flan-eur, *m.* (-s, -e) idler, saunterer. **-ieren,** *v.a.* saunter, meander, dawdle.

Flank-e, *f.* (-en) flank, side; side-vault (*Gymn.*); *-e aufrollen*, turn a flank (*Mil.*); *-en aufdecken*, expose flanks (*Mil.*); *in die -e fallen*, attack (*the enemy*) in the flank. **-enangriff,** *m.* flank attack. **-enbewegung,** *f.* (out)flanking movement. **-enfeuer,** *n.* enfilade fire, flanking fire. **-ieren,** *v. a.* flank, enfilade. **-ierung,** *f.* flanking position, flanking fire.

Flan(t)sch, *m.* (-es, -e), **-e,** *f.* (-en) flange.

Flaps, *m.* (-es, -e) (*coll.*) awkward *or* boorish person. **-ig,** *adj.* boorish, uncouth.

Flasch-e, *f.* (-en) bottle, flask, phial, cylinder; pulley block; *auf -en ziehen*, bottle, put in bottles; *einem Kind die -e geben*, give a child the (feeding) bottle, feed a child from the bottle; bring a child up on the bottle. **-enbier,** *n.* bottled beer. **-enbüchse,** *f.* air-gun. **-engas,** *n.* gas in cylinders. **-enhals,** *m.* neck of bottle, (*coll.*) bottle-neck. **-enheld,** *m.* toper. **-enkappe,** *f.* bottle top *or* cap. **-enkühler,** *m.* ice-pail. **-enkürbis,** *m.* gourd. **-enreif,** *adj.* matured in bottle. **-enschild,** *n.* (bottle-)label.

-enkiste, *f.* crate. **-enspüler,** *m.* bottle-washer. **-enverschluß,** *m.* stopper. **-enzug,** *m.* set of pulleys, block-and-tackle.

Flaschner, *m.* (-s, –) (*dial.*) plumber, tinsmith.

Flaser, *f.* **-ig,** *adj.* (*dial.*) *see* **Flader.**

flatter-n, *v.n.* (*aux.* h. & s.) flutter, hang loose, float in the wind, wave, stream (*of hair*); dangle; ramble; be restless *or* flighty. **-haft,** *adj.* fickle, inconstant, flighty, wavering; volatile. **-haftigkeit,** *f.* inconstancy, fickleness, flightiness, vacillation. **-ig,** *adj.*, *see* **-haft. -geist,** *m.* fickle *or* unstable person. **-mine,** *f.* contact mine, land-mine, booby-trap (*Mil.*). **-ruß,** *m.* lamp black.

flau, *adj.* feeble, weak, faint; insipid, flat, vapid; dull, slack (*of trade*); stagnant; indifferent, half-hearted, lukewarm; *der Wind wird -er*, the wind is dropping; *– machen*, depress (*the exchange*); *die Geschäfte gehen –*, business is dull, trade is slack; *die Platte ist –*, the plate is under-exposed (*Phot.*). **-e,** *f.*, **-heit,** *f.*, **-igkeit,** *f.* flatness; faintness; indifference; dullness, deadness (*of trade*). **(ab)-en,** *v.n.* become weak, dull, slack, indifferent *or* uninteresting. **-macher,** *m.* defeatist, alarmist. **-macherei,** *f.* defeatism. **-te,** *f.*, *see* **Flaute.**

Flaum, *m.* down, fluff; tomentum (*Bot., Anat.*); (*dial.*) fat, lard, suet. **-ig,** *adj.* downy, fluffy, fuzzy; pubescent (*Bot.*). **-feder,** *f.* down feather, plumule. **-haar,** *n.* down, pubescence (*Bot.*).

Flaus, Flausch, *m.* (-es, -e) tuft of wool *or* hair, fleecy woollen material; pilot-cloth, coarse coating. **-rock,** *m.* greatcoat of coarse cloth, duffle-coat.

Flause, *f.* (-n) shift, evasion, trick, humbug, shuffling, false pretence, lie (*usually pl.*). **-nmacher,** *m.* shuffler, humbug.

Flaute, *f.* calm, doldrums, dull weather (*at sea*); depression, slackness (*of trade*).

Fläz, *m.* (-es, -e) (*dial.*) lout, boor, lubber. (*dial.*) **-en,** *v.r.* loll, lounge. **-ig,** *adj.* loutish, uncouth.

Flechs-e, *f.* (-en) tendon, sinew. **-enartig,** *adj.* sinewy. **-enbein,** *n.* tibia (*Anat.*). **-enhaube,** *f.* caul, epicranium (*Anat.*); coif, calotte. **-ig,** *adj.* sinewy.

Flecht-e, *f.* (-en) plait, tress (*of hair*); twist, braid; basket-work, hurdle, hamper; dry scab, tetter, herpes (*Med.*); lichen (*Bot.*). **-en,** 1. *ir.v.a.* plait, braid, twist; wreathe, entwine, interweave, interlace; (*fig.*) interlard; *einen Korb -en*, weave a basket; *geflochtener Zaun*, hurdle, wattle fence; *aus Weidenzweigen geflochten*, wicker; *geflochtener Stuhl*, wicker chair; *aufs Rad -en*, break on the wheel (*torture*). 2. *v.r.* plait; *Binsen -en sich leicht*, rushes plait easily. **-enartig,** *adj.* herpetic (*Med.*); lichenous. **-enausschlag,** *m.* herpetic eruption. **-korb,** *m.* wicker-basket. **-werk,** *n.* wicker-work; wattling; revetment (*Mil.*). **-zaun,** *m.* wattle fence.

Fleck, *m.* (-(e)s, -e) place, spot; plot, piece (*of ground*); blemish, fault, flaw; blot, stain, mark, speck, spot; patch, shred; tripe; *auf dem -e*, on the spot, without delay, at once, post-haste; *blaue -e*, bruises; *– im Auge*, speck in the eye, s.th. in one's eye; *das Herz auf dem rechten – haben*, have one's heart in the right place; *den rechten – treffen*, hit the right nail on the head, strike home; *– schießen*, hit the bull's-eye; *der schwarze –*, bull's-eye; *gehe nicht vom -e*, don't stir! *wir kommen nicht vom –*, we do not get on, we are not making headway; *vom – weg*, see *auf dem -e*. **-en,** *m.* 1. *see* **Fleck**; 2. market-town, country-town. **-en,** 1. *v.a.* spot, stain, mark, soil, speckle; patch. 2. *v.n.* (*aux.* h.) (*usually third person*) blot, spot, stain, soil; *der Stoff -t leicht*, this material marks easily *or* shows marks readily; (*coll.*) make progress; *es will nicht -en*, the work does not get on *or* is unsuccessful; *es -t mir nicht*, I cannot get on with my work; *heute hat es gefleckt*, today I have done a good deal, today I have got on well. **-enfrei,** *adj.*, **-enlos,** *adj.* spotless, stainless, unblemished. **-enkrankheit,** *f.* blight, spot (*Bot.*). **-fieber,** *n.*, *see* **-typhus. -ig,** *adj.* spotted, stained, patchy, mottled. **-schuß,** *m.* point-blank shot. **-schußweite,** *f.* point-blank range. **-seife,** *f.* scouring soap. **-stein,** *m.* scouring stone. **-typhus,** *m.* typhus. **-wasser,** *n.* cleanser, stain remover.

fleddern, *v.a.* (*sl.*) rob (*corpses, etc.*).

Fleder-maus, *f.* bat (*Chiroptera*) (*Zool.*). **-wisch,** *m.* feather-duster; (*coll.*) rapier; flighty female.

Fle(e)t, *n.* (-(e)s, -e) (*dial.*) canal, waterway (*in Hamburg*).

Flegel, *m.* (-s, –) flail; lout, boor, churl. **-ei,** *f.* boorish behaviour, loutishness, rudeness, coarseness, schoolboyish behaviour. **-haft,** *adj.* rude, unmannerly, ungentlemanly, boorish, loutish; tomboyish, hoydenish (*of girls only*). **-jahre,** *n.pl.* teens, adolescence (*applied to boys only aged 13–17 yrs. approx.*); *noch in den -jahren*, still in one's teens, unfledged, unpolished, without manners; *den -jahren entwachsen*, grow up, become less schoolboyish. **-n,** 1. *v.a.* (*dial.*) beat with a flail, thresh. 2. *v.r. sich in einen Stuhl (hin)-n*, loll (inelegantly) in a chair.

flehen, 1. *v.a.* & *n.* (*aux.* h.) implore, entreat, beseech, supplicate; 2. *n.* entreaty, prayers; supplication. **-tlich,** *adj.* suppliant, imploring, beseeching, fervent; *-tlich bitten*, beseech; *-tliche Bitte*, earnest prayer, fervent supplication, entreaty.

Fleisch, *n.* (-es) flesh; meat; flesh *or* pulp (*of fruit*); cellular tissue (*in leaves*); fleshy parts; (*B.*) men, humanity, the flesh (*physical & sensual part of man*); *einem in – und Blut gehen*, become second nature with s.o.; *das ist weder Fisch noch –*, that is neither fish, flesh, fowl, nor good red herring; *gehacktes –*, minced meat; *wildes –*, proud flesh; *ins –*, to the quick; (*B.*) *das – kreuzigen*, mortify the flesh; *das – ist schwach*, the flesh is weak; *den Weg allen -es gehen*, go the way of all flesh; die, perish. **-auswuchs,** *m.* fleshy excrescence; proud flesh. **-bank,** *f.* butcher's stall, shambles. **-beschau,** *f.* meat inspection. **-brühe,** *f.* clear soup; beef-tea, broth; gravy. **-en,** 1. *v.a.* strip of flesh. 2. *v.n.* (*aux.* h.) cut into the flesh, cut deep. **-er,** *m.* butcher. **-ern,** *adj.* fleshy; meaty. **-eslust,** *f.* lust, carnal desire. **-farbe,** *f.* flesh-colour. **-farbig,** *adj.* flesh-coloured. **-faser,** *f.* muscle fibre. **-fliege,** *f.* blow-fly, bluebottle. **-fressend,** *adj.* carnivorous. **-fresser,** *m.* carnivorous animal, carnivore. **-gewächs,** *n.* fleshy tumour *or* excrescence; sarcoma. **-geworden,** *adj.* incarnate. **-hacker,** *m.*, **-hauer,** *m.* butcher. **-halle,** *f.* meat-market. **-ig,** *adj.* like flesh; fleshy, meaty, plump, fat, pulpy. **-igkeit,** *f.* fleshiness. **-kammer,** *f.* larder. **-kloß,** *m.* meat-ball. **-konserve,** *f.* potted *or* tinned *or* canned meat. **-kost,** *f.* meat diet. **-kuchen,** *m.* meat pie. **-lake,** *f.* brine, pickle. **-lappen,** *m.* wattles (*of a cock*). **-lich,** *adj.* carnal, sensual; fleshly. **-lichkeit,** *f.* sensuality, carnal-mindedness. **-los,** *adj.* fleshless, meatless, vegetarian. **-made,** *f.* maggot. **-magen,** *m.* gizzard. **-markt,** *m.* meat-market. **-maschine,** *f.*, *see* **-wolf. -mehl,** *n.* dehydrated meat. **-pastete,** *f.* meat-pie. **-schnitte,** *f.* slice of meat; cutlet, steak. **-speise,** *f.* meat dish. **-suppe,** *f.* broth. **-teile,** *m.pl.* fleshy parts. **-topf,** *m.* flesh-pot (*symbol of good living*) (*usually pl.*). **-vergiftung,** *f.* ptomaine poisoning. **-ware,** *f.* meat. **-werdung,** *f.* incarnation (*Theol.*). **-wolf,** *m.* mincing machine, mincer. **-wunde,** *f.* flesh wound. **-zahn,** *m.* canine tooth.

Fleiß, *m.* diligence, industry, application, assiduity; *mit –*, intentionally; on purpose; *– anwenden*, take pains, exert o.s.; *er hat es mit – getan*, he has done it on purpose; (*Prov.*) *ohne – kein Preis*, hard work brings its reward. **-ig,** *adj.* industrious, hardworking, diligent, assiduous; *-iger Besucher*, frequent *or* regular visitor.

flektieren, *v.a.* inflect (*Gram.*).

flennen, *v.n.* (*aux.* h.) (*dial.*) whine, snivel, blubber.

Flet, *n.*, *see* **Fleet.**

fletsch-en, *v.a.*; *die Zähne -en*, show one's teeth, snarl.

fleuch, fleuchst, fleucht, (*archaic*), *see* **fliehen.**

fleug, fleugst, fleugt, (*archaic*) *see* **fliegen.**

Flexion, *f.* (-en) inflexion (*Gram.*). **-slehre,** *f.* accidence (*Gram.*).

Flibustier, *m.* (-s, –) filibuster, buccaneer, freebooter, pirate.

flicht, flichst, flicht, (*archaic*) *see* **flechten.**

flick-en, 1. *v.a.* patch, mend, repair; bungle;

zusammen–en, patch up; *einem etwas am Zeuge –en*, pick holes in a p.; find fault with a p.; run a p. down. 2. *m.* (-ens, -en) patch.
Flick, *n.* (-s, -e) patch, *see* **Fleck. -arbeit,** *f.*, **-erei,** *f.* patchwork, mending, bungling. **-kasten,** *m.* repair outfit (*Motor.*); sewing-box. **-reim,** *m.* makeshift rhyme. **-schneider,** *m.* jobbing tailor; botcher. **-schuster,** *m.* jobbing cobbler. **-werk,** *n.* patchwork, patched-up job, botched job. **-wort,** *n.* expletive. **-zeug,** *n.* puncture repair outfit; needles, thread, darning wool, etc.
Flieder, *m.* (-s) lilac (*Syringa vulgaris*) (*Bot.*); elder (*Sambucus nigra*) (*Bot.*).
Fliege, *f.* (-n) fly; imperial (*beard*); (*coll.*) flibbertigibbet; *spanische –n*, Spanish fly, cantharides (*Lytta vesicatoria*) (*Ent.*); *von –n beschmissen*, fly-blown; *zwei –n mit einer Klappe* or *einem Schlage treffen*, kill two birds with one stone. **-ndreck,** *m.*, **-nschmiß,** *m.* fly-blow. **-nfalle,** *f.* fly-trap, Venus's fly-trap (*Dionaea muscipula*) (*Bot.*). **-nfänger,** *m.* fly-paper. **-nfürst,** *m.*, **-ngott,** *m.* Beelzebub. **-ngewicht,** *n.* fly-weight (*under 8 st. or 50 kg.*) (*Boxing*). **-nklappe,** *f.*, **-nklatsche,** *f.* fly swatter. **-nkopf,** *m.* turned letter (*Typ.*). **-npilz,** *m.* toadstool (*Amanita muscaria*). **-nschrank,** *m.* meat-safe. **-ntod,** *m.* fly-killer.
flieg–en, 1. *ir.v.n.* (*aux.* s. & h.) fly, rush, dash; (*coll.*) get the sack; (*sl.*) go out on one's neck; *ein Wort –en lassen*, let slip a word; *ein Stein –t durch das Fenster*, a stone flies through the window; *ich –e gerade nach Hause*, I am just rushing home. 2. *v.a.* fly, pilot; *er flog seine eigene Maschine*, he piloted his own machine; *einen Keil –en*, fly in V-formation. 3. *n.* flight; *–en im Verbande*, formation flying. **-end,** *pr.p.* & *adj.* flying, flowing; *–endes Blatt*, flysheet, pamphlet; *–ender Bote*, express courier; *–ende Fahnen*, flying colours; *–ender Fisch*, flying-fish; *–ende Haare*, loose *or* flying hair; *–ender Händler*, itinerant *or* door-to-door salesman, pedlar; *–ende Hitze*, sudden flush; *–ende Kolonne*, flying column; *–endes Personal*, air crew (*Av.*); (*coll.*) *–ende Bombe*, flying-bomb, pilotless aircraft. **-er,** *m.* airman, aviator, pilot; aircraftman 2nd class; aeroplane; short-distance cycle racer, sprinter (*Cycl.*). **-erisch,** *adj.* concerning aviation; *–erischer Nachwuchs*, new generation of airmen. **-erabsturz,** *m.* air accident, aeroplane crash. **-erabwehr,** *f.* anti-aircraft defence. **-erabwehrkanone,** *f.* anti-aircraft gun (*abbr.* **Flak**). **-eralarm,** *m.* air-raid alarm, siren, alert. **-erangriff,** *m.* aerial attack, air raid. **-eraufnahme,** *f.* aerial photograph. **-erausrüstung,** *f.* flying-kit. **-erbeobachtung,** *f.* air reconnaissance. **-erbombe,** *f.* (aerial) bomb. **-erdeckung,** *f.* air umbrella. **-erei,** *f.* aviation. **-erhorst,** *m.* air-base. **-erkampf,** *m.* aerial combat. **-erkanone,** *f.* (*sl.*) air ace. **-erpersonal,** *n.* air-crew. **-erschießen,** *n.* anti-aircraft fire. **-erschule,** *f.* school of aviation. **-erschuppen,** *m.* hangar. **-erschütze,** *m.* air gunner. **-erstation,** *f.* air station. **-erstützpunkt,** *m.* advance airfield, landing ground. **-ertruppe,** *f.* air force, flying corps. **-erwache,** *f.* aircraft spotter (*Mil.*), roof-spotter (*civilian*). **-erwarnungsdienst,** *m.* observer corps. **-erwart,** *m.*, *see* **-erwache. -erwetter,** *n.* (*sl.*) bad flying weather, ceiling zero (*from point of view of ground defenders*).
flieh–en, 1. *ir.v.n.* (*aux.* s.) flee, run away, retreat, escape; *–et ihr Sorgen;* begone, cares! *zu einem –en*, take refuge with a p. 2. *v.a.* shun, avoid, get out of the way of; *–ende Stirn*, receding forehead; *der –ende*, fugitive. **-kraft,** *f.* centrifugal force.
Fliese, *f.* (-n) flagstone; paving stone, tile. **-nwand,** *f.* tiled wall.
Fließ, *n.*, *see* **Vlies.**
fließ–en, *ir.v.n.* (*aux.* h. & s.) flow, run, melt, gutter, trickle down; pass away, elapse (*of time*); be smooth (*of words*); blot; *–en aus*, proceed from, result; *sanft –en*, glide smoothly. **-arbeit,** *f.* work on the assembly line, mass-production (work). **-band,** *n.* conveyor belt. **-end,** *pr.p.* & *adj.* flowing; running; drifting; liquid, fluid; fluent; smooth, easy; *eine Sprache –end sprechen*, speak a language fluently; *–endes Wasser*, running water. **-fähigkeit,** *f.* fusibility. **-laut,** *m.* liquid (*Phonet.*). **-papier,** *n.* blotting-paper. **-sand,** *m.* quicksand.
Flimmer, *m.* glimmer, glitter; tinsel, spangle; (*dial.*) mica. **-n,** *v.n.* (*aux.* h.) glitter, glisten; flicker, sparkle, scintillate; twinkle (*star*); vibrate (*air*); (*soldiers' sl.*) polish; *es –t mir vor den Augen*, my eyes are swimming. **-kiste,** *f.* (*sl.*) flicks.
flink, *adj.* quick, brisk, agile, nimble, alert, lively. **-heit,** *f.* nimbleness, quickness, liveliness.
Flint–e, *f.* (-en) gun, musket, rifle; (*coll.*) *die –e ins Korn werfen*, throw up the sponge. **-enkolben,** *m.* butt-end of a gun. **-enkugel,** *f.* musket-ball. **-enlauf,** *m.* gun-barrel. **-enschaft,** *m.* gun-stock. **-enschrot,** *n.* gun-shot.
flirren, *v.n.* (*aux.* h.) flit about, flicker, whirr, vibrate (*of air*); glitter, sparkle.
Flirt, *m.* (-s, -s) flirtation. **-en,** *v.n.* flirt, make love.
Flitter, *m.* (-s, –) tinsel, spangle. **-gelehrsamkeit,** *f.* sham learning. **-glanz,** *m.* false lustre, empty show, hollow pomp. **-gold,** *n.* tinsel. **-kram,** *m.* cheap finery. **-n,** *v.n.* (*aux.* h.) sparkle, glitter; (*dial.*) flit about. **-schein,** *m.*, *see* **-glanz. -staat,** *m.* tawdry finery. **-werk,** *n.* gewgaw. **-wochen,** *f.pl.* honeymoon.
flitz–en, *v.n.* (*dial.*) move rapidly, flit, dash, scurry. **-bogen,** *m.* toy bow.
flocht, flöchte, *see* **flechten.**
Flock–e, *f.* (-en) flake (*of snow, oats, etc.*); flock (*of wool, hair, etc.*). **-en** 1. *v.n.* & *r.* (*aux.* h.) flake, come down in flakes. 2. *v.a.* beat into flocks, form into flakes. **-enartig, -icht, -ig,** *adj.* flaky, fluffy, filamentous, flocculent. **-enblume,** *f.* knapweed (*Centaurea*) (*Bot.*). **-(en)seide,** *f.* floss silk. **-enstoff,** *m.*, **-entuch,** *n.* coarse cloth. **-feder,** *f.* down. **-wolle,** *f.* waste wool flock.
flog, flöge, *see* **fliegen.**
Floh, *m.* (-s, ⸗e) flea; *jemandem einen – ins Ohr setzen*, send a p. away with a flea in his ear; *lieber einen Sack ⸗e hüten, als . . .*, eat one's hat rather than . . .; (*Prov.*) *er hört die ⸗e husten*, he hears the grass grow. **-farbe,** *f.* puce-colour. **-kraut,** *n.* fleabane (*Pulicaria*) (*Bot.*). **-krebs,** *m.* water flea (*Amphipoda*) (*Ent.*). **-stich,** *m.* fleabite.
flöhen, *v.a.* & *r.* catch fleas; rid of fleas.
Flor, *m.* 1. (-s, -e (*or Austr. dial.* ⸗e)) gauze, crape; nap, pile. 2. riot of bloom; florescence; blossoming time; bevy (*of girls*); flourishing condition, prosperity. **-a,** *f.* Flora (*goddess of flowers*), the vegetable kingdom, flora (*Bot.*). **-artig,** *adj.*, **-ähnlich,** *adj.* gauzy. **-band,** *n.*, **-binde,** *f.* mourning *or* crape band. **-ett,** *m.* (-es, -e (*or Austr. dial.* -s)) coarse silk; silk refuse. **-ettseide,** *f.* sarsanet, *see* **Flockseide. -ieren,** *v.n.* (*aux.* h.) (*C.L.*) flourish, prosper.
Florett, *n.* (-(e)s, -e) foil (*Fenc.*).
Floskel, *f.* (-n) flourish, fine phrase, flowery language. **-n,** *v.n.* (*aux.* h.) use flowery language.
floß, flösse, *see* **fließen.**
Floß, *n.* (*Bav.* & *Austr. m.*) (-es, ⸗e) raft, float; buoy; flowing water; pig iron. **-brücke,** *f.* floating bridge. **-führer,** *m.* raftsman. **-graben,** *m.* canal. **-holz,** *n.* floated *or* rafted timber. **-sack,** *m.* rubber boat (*Mil.*).
Floss–e, *f.* (-en) fin, (*sl.*) hand, foot; float (*on a fishing-net*); pig iron; stabilizer fin; (*Av.*) *Höhen–e*, tailplane (*Av.*). **-(ß)feder,** *f.* fin. **-(ß)füßer,** *m.* pteropod (*mollusc*); pinnipedia (*seals*).
Flöß–e, *f.* (-en) float (*on fishing-net*). **-bar,** *adj.* navigable to rafts. **-en,** *v.a.* float, cause to float; raft (*timber*); (*dial.*) fish with a floating net. **-er,** *m.* raftsman, rafter. **-erei,** *f.* timber transportation (*by river*).
Flöt–e, *f.* (-en) flute; pipe. **-en,** *v.a.* & *n.* (*aux.* h.) play the flute; whistle. **-enartig,** *adj.* flute-like. **-enbläser,** *m.* flute-player, flautist. (*coll.*) **-engehen,** *v.n.* be lost *or* squandered. **-enpfeife,** *f.* open pipe (*in organs*). **-enregister,** *n.*, **-enzug,** *m.* flute-stop (*in organs*). **-ist,** *m.* (-en, -en) flute-player, flautist.
flott, 1. *adj.* floating, buoyant; solvent; lively, brisk, smooth, gay, fast, chic, smart. (*sl.*) snappy; *es ging – her*, there were fine goings-on; *– leben*, lead a fast life; *das Geschäft geht –*, business booms.

2\. *n.* (*dial.*) cream. **–machen,** *v.a.* refloat. **–weg,** *adv.* smartly, promptly; (*coll.*) at one fell swoop.

Flott–e, *f.* (-en) fleet, navy; dye liquor, dye-bath. **–enabkommen,** *n.* naval agreement. **–enbegleiter,** *m.*, **–enbegleitschiff,** *n.* escort vessel, corvette, sloop (*Nav.*). **–enchef,** *m.* commander-in-chief of the navy. **–endienst,** *m.* naval service, service afloat. **–enetat,** *m.* naval estimates (*in parliament*). **–enführer,** *m.* admiral. **–enleitung,** *f.* naval staff. **–enschau,** *f.* naval review. **–enstation,** *f.* home naval base (*e.g. Portsmouth*). **–enstützpunkt,** *m.* naval station (*e.g. Singapore*). **–enverein,** *m.* navy league. **–envorlage,** *f.* navy bill. **–ille,** *f.* flotilla, squadron.

Flöz, *n.* (-es, -e) layer, stratum, deposit; seam, bed; *in –en,* stratified. **–asche,** *f.* clay-marl. **–bau,** *m.* working of a seam. **–gebirge,** *n.* stratified *or* sedimentary rocks (*Geol.*). **–gebirgsarten,** *f.pl.* secondary rocks (*Geol.*). **–lage,** *f.*, **–schicht,** *f.* stratum, bed, layer. **–sandstein,** *m.* new red sandstone.

Fluch, *m.* (-(e)s, ⸚e) curse, oath, imprecation, malediction, execration; – *über dich;* curse you! damn you! **–beladen,** *adj.* under a curse, accursed. **–en,** 1. *v.n.* (*aux.* h.) curse, swear; blaspheme; use bad language; *einem –en,* curse s.o.; *auf einen –en,* call down curses upon a p.; swear at s.o. 2. *v.a.* utter curses, curse, damn, execrate; *einem Böses an den Hals –en,* curse a p., wish s.o. evil. **–enswert,** *adj.*, **–(ens)würdig,** *adj.* accursed, execrable. **–maul,** *n.* blasphemer, foul-mouthed person.

Flucht, *f.* (-en) flight, escape; covey (*of pigeons, etc.*); play, swing (*of a door, hammer, etc.*); row, straight line (*Arch.*); suite (*of rooms*); *Treppen–,* flight of stairs; *sechs Fenster in einer –,* six windows in a row; *die – ergreifen, sich auf die – begeben* or *machen,* run away; take to flight, flee; *in die – schlagen,* put to flight, chase off. **–artig,** *adj.* in full flight. **–bau,** *m.*, **–röhre,** *f.* refuge, retreat (*Sport*). **–holz,** *n.* rule, level. **–ig,** *adj.* perspective. **–linie,** *f.* building line, base-line. **–punkt,** *m.* vanishing point.

flücht–en, 1. *v.a.* (*Poet.*) save by flight, rescue, secure. 2. *v.r.* & *n.* (*aux.* s.) flee, take to flight, escape; *sich –en auf* or *in,* take to (*a tree, etc.*), betake o.s. to, take refuge in; *er –ete* (*sich*) *nach England,* he fled to England. **–er,** *m.* restless *or* changeable person. **–ig,** *adj.* fugitive, runaway; transient, fleeting, non-persistent; volatile (*Chem.*); hasty, hurried, cursory, rough, slight, desultory, superficial; inconsiderate, casual, careless, fickle, changeable, shifting; *–iges Gestein,* brittle *or* friable rock; *–ig werden,* run away, abscond; *–iges Salz,* sal volatile; *–ige Gewänder,* flowing robes; *ich habe das Buch nur –ig durchgeblättert,* I have only just glanced at the book. **–igen,** *v.a.* volatilize. **–igkeit,** *f.* hastiness, transitoriness; carelessness; volatility; inconstancy. **–igkeitsfehler,** *m.* mistake due to inadvertence, slip. **–igmachung,** *f.*, **–igung,** *f.* volatilization (*Chem.*). **–ling,** *m.* fugitive, refugee, deserter. **–lingslager,** *n.* refugee camp.

Fluder, *n.* (-s, –) channel (*of a mill*), mill race.

Flug, *m.* (-(e)s, ⸚e) flying; soaring; flight; flock, swarm, covey; *im –e,* flying, in flight, on the wing; in haste, in passing, briefly; *einen Vogel im –e schießen,* shoot a bird on the wing. **–abwehr,** *f.* anti-aircraft defence. **–asche,** *f.* light ashes. **–bahn,** *f.* line of flight, trajectory. **–bereich,** *m.* operational radius (*Av.*). **–bereit,** *adj.*, *see* **–fertig.** **–bereitschaft,** *f.* war stations (*Av.*). **–besprechung,** *f.* briefing. **–blatt,** *n.* pamphlet, broadsheet; handbill. **–boot,** *n.* seaplane, flying boat. **–feld,** *n.*, *see* **–platz.** **–fertig,** *adj.* ready for flight, ready to take off; very hurried. **–figuren,** *f.pl.* aerobatics. **–fisch,** *m.* flying fish. **–form,** *f.* flying formation. **–früchtler,** *m.* plant with winged seed. **–gast,** *m.* air-passenger. **–hafen,** *m.* aerodrome, airport, airfield, air station. **–hafer,** *m.* wild oats (*Avena fatua*) (*Bot.*). **–halle,** *f.* hangar. **–hörnchen,** *n.* flying squirrel (*Sciuropterus*) (*Zool.*). **–jahr,** *n.* swarm year. **–klar,** *adj.*; *die Maschine ist –klar,* the plane is ready for flight *or* ready to take off. **–kraft,** *f.* power of flight. **–lehre,** *f.* aerodynamics. **–loch,** *n.* entrance to a hive *or* dove-cote. **–meldekommando,** *n.* air-raid precautions headquarters. **–plan,** *m.* air service time-table. **–platz,** *m.* aerodrome, landing ground. **–post,** *f.* air mail. **–s,** *adv.*, *see* **flugs.** **–sand,** *m.* quicksand. **–schein,** *m.* air-ticket. **–schießen,** *n.* shooting at a moving object, shooting on the wing. **–schneise,** *f.* air corridor. **–schnell,** *adj.* very swift. **–schrift,** *f.* pamphlet. **–schule,** *f.* flying school. **–schüler,** *m.* flying trainee. **–strecke,** *f.* distance flown, route (*Av.*). **–streitkräfte,** *f.pl.* air force *or* arm. **–stützpunkt,** *m.* air-base; base ship, parent ship. **–technik,** *f.* aviation. **–technisch,** *adj.* concerning aviation. **–verkehr,** *m.* air traffic; air service; civil aviation. **–wache,** *f.* aircraft spotter. **–wachkorps,** *n.* observer corps. **–waffe,** *f.* air arm. **–wasser,** *n.* spray. **–weite,** *f.* range (*of a projectile*). **–werk,** *n.* flies (*Theat.*). **–wesen,** *n.* aviation, aeronautics. **–wetter,** *n.* flying weather. **–winkel,** *m.* angle of flight (*Ballistics*). **–zeug,** *n.* aeroplane. **–zeugbesatzung,** *f.* air-crew. **–zeugführer,** *m.* pilot. **–zeughalle,** *f.*, *see* **–zeugschuppen.** **–zeugmuster,** *n.* type of aircraft. **–zeugmutterschiff,** *n.* aircraft-carrier, parent ship, depot ship. **–zeugpersonal,** *n.* aircraft maintenance personnel, ground staff. **–zeugrumpf,** *m.* fuselage. **–zeugschlosser,** *m.* aircraft fitter. **–zeugschuppen,** *m.* hangar. **–zeugsteuerung,** *f.* controls (*on an aircraft*). **–zeugträger,** *m.* aircraft-carrier. **–zeugwesen,** *n.* aviation.

Flügel, *m.* (-s, –) wing; vane; arm; flank; sail (*of a windmill*); leaf (*of double door or window*); aisle (*of a church*); casement (*of a window*); fluke (*of an anchor*); blade (*of propeller*); mudguard, wing (*of a car*); lobe (*Anat.*); grand piano; (*coll.*) *die – hängen lassen,* be crestfallen, despond; (*coll.*) with one's tail between one's legs; *sich die – verbrennen,* singe one's wings. **–adjutant,** *m.* aide-de-camp. **–angriff,** *m.* flank attack (*Mil.*). **–bauer,** *m.* maker of grand pianos. **–breite,** *f.* wing-span (*Av.*). **–decke,** *f.* wing-case, elytron (*Zool., Ent.*). **–fenster,** *n.* french window, casement window. **–förmig,** *adj.* wing-shaped. **–haube,** *f.* helmet (*motor*). **–haut,** *f.* wing fabric (*Av.*). **–horn,** *n.* trumpet. **–ig,** *adj.* having wings, winged. **–lahm,** *adj.* broken-winged; winged (*Hunt.*). **–los,** *adj.* wingless. **–mann,** *m.* file-leader, flank-man, end man of a line. **–mutter,** *f.* wing-nut, thumb-nut, butterfly-nut. **–n,** *v.a.* furnish with wings, wing; hit in the wing; *geflügelte Worte,* familiar quotations, household *or* catch phrases. **–offen,** *adj.* wide open. **–pferd,** *n.* winged horse, Pegasus. **–profil,** *n.* airfoil (*Av.*). **–schlag,** *m.* beat of wings. **–schraube,** *f.* propeller; (air)screw. **–stange,** *f.* vane-spindle. **–streckung,** *f.* aspect ratio (*Av.*). **–tuch,** *n.* sails (*of a windmill*). **–tür,** *f.* folding-door. **–zug,** *m.* flank platoon (*Mil.*).

flügge, *adj.* fledged.

flugs, *adv.* quickly, instantly, at once.

Fluh, *f.* (⸚e) (*dial.*) mass of rock; stratum, layer; concrete.

Fluid–um, *n.* (-ums, -a) fluid, liquid; (*fig.*) atmosphere, tone, influence, aura.

Flunder, *m.* (-s, –) & *f.* (-n) flounder (*Limanda flesus*) (*Icht.*).

Flunker–ei, *f.* (*coll.*) lying, sham; bragging. **–n,** *v.n.* (*aux* h.) (*coll.*) tell fibs; brag, boast.

Flunsch, *m.* (*coll.*) pouting expression; *einen – machen,* pout.

Fluor, *n.* fluorine. **–eszenz,** *f.* fluorescence. **–eszieren,** *v.n.* fluoresce.

Flur, 1. *f.* (-en) field, meadow, pasture, plain; common. 2. *m.* (-(e)s, -e) flag, paving-stone; paved floor; vestibule, (entrance-)hall, corridor. **–gang,** *m.* corridor; beating the bounds of a parish. **–grenze,** *f.*, **–scheidung,** *f.* bounds of a parish. **–hüter,** *m.* keeper, ranger. **–schaden,** *m.* damage to crops. **–stein,** *m.* boundary-stone.

Fluß, *m.* (-(ss)es, ⸚(ss)e) river, stream; flow, flux, melting, fusion; molten glass *or* metal; paste (*diamonds*); catarrh, discharge, issue, running; flush (*Cards*); fluency, *weißer –,* whites (*Med.*); **–abwärts,** down-stream. **–arm,** *m.* tributary. **–artig,** *adj.* river-like; catarrhal; rheumatic. **–äther,** *m.* fluoric ether. **–aufwärts,** up-stream. **–bad,** *n.* river bathing *or* bathing-place. **–bett,**

n. channel, river bed. **-eisen,** *n.* ingot iron, soft steel. **-fieber,** *n.* rheumatic fever. **-fisch,** *m.* freshwater fish. **-gebiet,** *n.* river basin. **-knie,** *n.* bend in a river. **-krebs,** *m.* river crayfish. **-lauf,** *m.* course of a river. **-mittel,** *n.* flux (*for soldering, etc.*). **-mündung,** *f.* estuary. **-netz,** *n.* river network. **-nixe,** *f.* water nymph, naiad. **-pferd,** *n.* hippopotamus. **-punkt,** *m.* melting-point. **-reich,** *adj.* abounding in rivers, well watered. **-sauer,** *adj.* fluorated. **-schiffahrt,** *f.* river traffic. **-spat,** *m.* fluor spar, fluorite (*Min.*). **-übergang,** *m.* river crossing, ford, bridge. **-verkehr,** *m.* river traffic.

flüssig, *adj.* fluid, liquid; melted, molten; rheumatic; ready (*of cash*); flowing, fluent; – *machen,* melt, liquefy; convert into ready money; *Geld – machen,* realize money. **-keit,** *f.,* fluid, liquid, liquor; humour (*Vet.*); fluidity. **-keitsbremse,** *f.* hydraulic brake. **-keitsdruck,** *m.* hydraulic pressure. **-keitsmaß,** *n.* liquid measure. **-machung,** *f.* liquefaction, melting, fusing; realization (*of money*). **-werdend,** *adj.* liquescent.

flüster-n, *v.a. & n.* (*aux.* h.) whisper. **-propaganda,** *f.* whispering campaign. **-ton,** *m.* whisper, undertone. **-tüte,** *f.* (*sl.*) megaphone.

Flut, *f.* (-en) flood, deluge, inundation; torrent, stream; high-tide, high-water, flood-tide, incoming *or* rising tide; *Hoch–,* flood-tide, high-water; *Sint–,* the Flood; *Spring–,* spring-tide; *Nipp–,* neap-tide; *– von Worten,* torrent of words. **-bassin,** *n.* tidal basin. **-bett,** *n.* channel; mill-race. **-brecher,** *m.* breakwater. **-en,** *v.n.* (*aux.* h.) flood, stream, flow; be at high water; swell, surge, crowd; *es flutet,* the tide is coming in. **-enuntertrieb,** *m.*, **-enzelle,** *f.* flooding tank (*of submarines*). **-gang,** *m.*, **-gerinne,** *n.* channel, trough (*in mills*), mill-race. **-hafen,** *m.* tidal harbour. **-höhe,** *f.* (high-)water mark. **-karte,** *f.* tide-chart. **-linie,** *f.* high-water mark. **-tabellen,** *f.pl.* tide-tables. **-tor,** *n.* flood-gate. **-wasser,** *n.* tidal water; mill-race. **-wechsel,** *m.*, **-wende,** *f.* turning of the tide. **-welle,** *f.* tidal wave. **-zeichen,** *n.* high-water mark. **-zeit,** *f.* flood-tide, high-water.

focht, föchte, *see* **fechten.**

Fock-mast, *m.* foremast. **-segel,** *n.* foresail. **-stag,** *m.* forestay.

Föder-alismus, *m.* federalism. **-ativ,** *adj.* federative, confederate.

Fohlen, 1. *n.* (-s, –) foal, filly, colt (*foal is newly born, colt & filly till 4–5 years;* Fohlen *till 3 years*). 2. *v.n.* (*aux.* h.) foal.

Föhn, *m.* (-(e)s, -e) warm wind (*in Switzerland*), spring storm. **-ig,** *adj.* sultry, stormy.

Föhre, *f.* (-n) Scots pine (*Pinus sylvestris*) (*Bot.*).

Fokus, *m.* (–, –) focus. **-tiefe,** *f.* focal depth.

Folg-e, *f.* (-en) succession, sequence, series, order; set, suit, suite; sequel, continuation; result, issue, effect, consequence, conclusion, inference; *demzu–e,* see *in–edessen*; *einem Gesuche –e geben,* grant a petition; *in der –e,* subsequently, afterwards, thereafter, in future; *in–edessen,* according to *or* in pursuance of which; *–e von Karten,* sequence, flush; *–e leisten,* obey, comply with, respond to; *die nächste –e dieses Werkes,* the next instalment *or* issue of this work; *die –e sein von,* be due to; *üble –en,* evil results, bad consequences; *zu–e,* in pursuance of, in consequence of; *zur –e haben,* result in, bring about. **-eerscheinung,** *f.* consequence, effect, result. **-eladung,** *f.* explosive set off by sympathetic detonation. **-eleistung,** *f.* obedience. **-en,** *v.n.* 1. (*aux.* s.) *Dat.*) follow (after), ensue (*aus,* from); succeed (*auf* (*Acc.*), to); be derived. 2. (*aux.* h.) obey, attend to, listen to, conform to; *ich bin ihm gefolgt,* I followed him; *ich habe ihm gefolgt,* I was guided by him (*his advice or wishes*), I obeyed him; *was –t daraus?* what will ensue? *seinen Lüsten –en,* follow one's desires; *dem Strom –en,* swim with the stream; *seinem Kopfe –en,* act according to one's lights; persist in one's whim; *–en Sie mir,* take my advice; *er sprach wie –t,* he spoke as follows; *Fortsetzung –t,* to be continued. **-end,** *pr.p. & adj.* subsequent, next; *aufeinander–end,* consecutive; *–ende Woche,* next week; *–endes,* the following (words); *aus* (or *im*) *–enden,* from (*or* in) the following *or* what follows. **-endergestalt** *adv.*, **-endermaßen,** *adv.*, **-enderweise,** *adv.* as follows, in the following manner. **-enlos,** *adj.* without effect, without results. **-enreich,** *adj.* having important consequences, weighty, momentous. **-enschwer,** *adj.* important, grave, momentous, portentous. **-erecht,** *adj.*, **-erichtig,** *adj.* logical, consistent; conclusive. **-erichtigkeit,** *f.* logical consequence, consistency. **-ern,** *v.a.* infer, deduce, conclude, reason out; *falsch –ern,* draw wrong inferences; *hieraus läßt sich –ern,* hence we may infer. **-erung,** *f.* inference, deduction, conclusion, induction, **-esatz,** *m.* conclusion, deduction, corollary. **-eschluß,** *m.* logical result. **-ewidrig,** *adj.* inconsistent, illogical; incoherent. **-ezeit,** *f.* future, time to come, following period; posterity. **-lich,** *adv. & conj.* consequently, hence, therefore, accordingly. **-sam,** *adj.* (*Dat.*) obedient, tractable, docile. **-samkeit,** *f.* obedience, docility.

Foli-ant, *m.* (-en, -en) folio volume. **-e,** *f.* (-en) foil; thin leaf of metal; film, silvering of mirrors; (*fig.*) background, framework, basis of comparison; *mit –e belegte Oberfläche,* silvered surface; *zur –e dienen,* be a foil, set off; *einer S. eine –e geben,* set a th. off. **-ieren,** *v.a.* page (*a book*); silver (*a mirror*). **-o,** *n.* (-os, -ien & -os) folio; page (*of a ledger*); *wir haben ein –o in der Bank,* we have an account with the bank. **-oformat,** *n.* folio size.

Folter, *f.* (-n) torture; *auf die – legen* or *spannen,* put to the rack; (*fig.*) torment. **-bank,** *f.* rack. **-er,** *m.* torturer, tormentor. **-kammer,** *f.* torture-chamber. **-knecht,** *m.* torturer. **-n,** *v.a.* torture, torment. **-ung,** *f.* torture. **-qualen,** *f.pl.* torment, mental anguish.

Fond [*pron.* fõ:], *m.* (-s, -s) ground, bottom; foundation, base, basis, background; back seat (*Motor.*); *– im Handel,* stock-in-trade. *m. sing. & pl.* funds, stock, capital, public funds. **-sbericht,** *m.* stock-exchange news. **-sbesitzer,** *m.* stockholder. **-sbörse,** *f.* stock-exchange. **-smakler,** *m.* stock-broker.

Font-äne, *f.* (-n) fountain. **-anelle,** *f.* fontanel (*Anat.*).

fopp-en, *v.a.* fool, hoax; quiz, chaff, tease, mystify. **-erei,** *f.* teasing, chaffing, quizzing, hoaxing, mystification.

Forc-e, *f.* strong point, strength, forte. **-ieren,** *v.a.* take by assault, force; over-urge, overtax. **-iert,** *adj.* forced, exaggerated, unnatural.

forder-n, *v.a.* demand, ask; claim, require, exact; summon (*Law*); challenge; *wie viel –n Sie dafür?* how much do you want for it? *vor Gericht –n,* summon before a court; *Rechenschaft von einem –n,* call a p. to account; *einen auf Pistolen –n,* challenge s.o. to a duel with pistols; *einen vor die Klinge –n,* challenge s.o. to a duel with swords; *heraus–n,* call out, challenge; *zu viel –n,* overcharge. **-gebühr,** *f.* fee for a summons. **-ung,** *f.* demand; claim, requisition; summons, challenge; *–ungen ausstehen haben,* have outstanding claims *or* claims outstanding; *–ungen an einen stellen,* make claims on a p.; *–ungen geltend machen,* make good one's claims. **-ungssatz,** *m.* postulate.

förder-n, *v.a.* further, promote, advance; benefit, encourage, expedite, hasten, accelerate, dispatch; raise, haul, transport (*Min., etc.*); *zu Tage –n,* bring to light. **-anlage,** *f.* conveying equipment *or* system. **-er,** *m.* (-ers, -er) furtherer, promoter, patron, patroness; conveyor, accelerator. **-gut,** *n.* output, goods delivered. **-kette,** *f.* conveyor. **-klasse,** *f.* class for backward children, special class. **-lich,** *adj.* furthering; promotive (of); conducive (to); beneficial, useful, serviceable, effective; *auf das –lichste,* in the speediest manner possible; in the most helpful way. **-menge,** *f.* output. **-nis,** *n.* furtherance, help. **-quantum,** *n.* output. **-sam,** *adj.*, *see* **-lich. -schacht,** *m.* winding-shaft. **-seil,** *n.* (haulage) rope (*Min.*). **-strecke,** *f.* mine-tramway. **-ung,** *f.* furtherance, help; furthering, advancement, promotion; dispatch; yield, output (*Min.*), hauling (*Min.*). **-ungsmittel,** *n.* aid, auxiliary, adjuvant. **-wagen,** *m.* mine-tram. **-werk,** *n.* hoisting machinery (*Min.*).

Forelle, *f.* (-n) trout. **–nfang,** *m.* trout-fishing.

Forke, *f.* (-n) pitchfork, large fork.

Form, *f.* (-en) form, figure, shape; make, fashion, mode, usage, method of procedure; model, pattern, cut; block, last (*for shoes*); mould; frame, form (*Typ.*); *leidende* (*tätige*) –, *Leide–*, passive (active) voice (*Gram.*); *in gehöriger –*, in due form, in proper shape; *in – Rechtens*, legally; *in aller –*, formally, in due form; *in guter* (*blendender*) –, on *or* in form, in tip-top form (*Sport, etc.*); *in – kommen*, get into form (*Sport*); *in – bleiben*, keep in form (*Sport*); *gegen die –*, contrary to form; *der – wegen*, for form's sake; *über die – schlagen*, block (*hats*); put on the last (*shoes*). **–al,** *adj.* formal; *die –ale Bildung*, formal training (*in contrast to purposive education*). **–alien,** *pl.* formalities. **–alismus,** *m.* formalism. **–alist,** *m.* formalist, pedantic person. **–alität,** *f.* formality; (*pl.*) forms (*of courts, etc.*). **–arbeit,** *f.* casting, mould-making; cast-work. **–artikel,** *m.pl.* moulded goods, plastic goods. **–at,** *n.* (-(e)s, -e) size (*book*), form, shape, format; (*fig.*) importance, weight. **–ation,** *f.* formation; unit (*Mil.*). **–ativ,** *adj.* formative, shaping; morphogenic. **–bar,** *adj.* capable of being shaped, plastic. **–bildung,** *f.* structure. **–brett,** *n.* mould. **–el,** *f.* formula, rule; *Zauber–el*, magic charm, incantation. **–element,** *n.* structural element. **–elhaft,** *adj.* formal, formalized, ceremonious. **–elkram,** *m.* formalities, red-tape. **–ell,** *adj.* formal, stiff. **–en,** *v.a.* form, mould, cast, model, shape, fashion; put on the block (*hats*). **–enausgleich,** *m.* form-association, levelling (*Gram.*). **–enbildung,** *f.* morphology (*Biol., Gram.*). **–engießer,** *m.* moulder in brass. **–enlehre,** *f.* accidence (*Gram.*). **–enmacher,** *m.* pattern-maker; moulder; fashioner. **–enmensch,** *m.* pedant, formalist. **–ensand,** *m.* moulding sand. **–enwesen,** *n.* formality, ceremoniousness; ceremonies. **–erde,** *f.* modelling clay. **–erei,** *f.* moulding operation, moulding shop. **–fehler,** *m.* faux pas, breach of etiquette, social blunder; error in form; informality. **–gebung,** *f.* fashioning; moulding. **–gestaltung,** *f.* shape, form. **–ieren,** 1. *v.a.* form; arrange. 2. *v.r.* fall in (*Mil.*); *Glieder –ieren*, fall in (*Mil.*); *Karree –ieren*, form up in squares (*Mil.*); *in Seiten –ieren*, make up into pages (*Typ.*). **–kopf,** *m.* wig-block. **–kunst,** *f.* plastic art. **–ling,** *m.* briquette. **–los,** *adj.* shapeless, formless; amorphous, amorphic; informal; impolite. **–losigkeit,** *f.* shapelessness, formlessness; amorphousness; unceremoniousness; rudeness. **–rahmen,** *m.* chase (*Typ.*); frame (*Pap.*). **–sache,** *f.* matter of (outward) form, formality. **–stein,** *m.* moulded brick, shaped brick. **–trieb,** *m.* artistic impulse. **–übertragung,** *f.* form-association, levelling (*Gram.*). **–ular,** *n.* (-s, -e) form, blank, schedule; precedent (*Law*). **–ularbuch,** *n.* precedent-book (*Law*). **–ulieren,** *v.a.* formulate. **–ulierung,** *f.* precise wording, formulation, definition. **–ung,** *f.* formation. **–vollendet,** *adj.* perfect in form; highly finished. **–wechsel,** *m.* change of form; (*C.L.*) accommodation-bill. **–widrig,** *adj.* diverging from pattern, contrary to usage, offending against good form, in bad taste, informal. **–zahl,** *f.* form factor.

förm–ig, *suffix* (*in compounds* =) -formed, -shaped. **–lich,** 1. *adj.* formal, ceremonious; downright, express, regular, real. 2. *adv.* really, absolutely, as it were; *–liche Schlacht*, pitched battle; *er hat es –lich darauf abgesehen*, it is clearly his intention. **–lichkeit,** *f.* formality.

forsch, *adj.* (*dial. & coll.*) forthright, outspoken, blatant, crude; strong, vigorous. **–e,** *f.* energy, emphasis.

forsch–en, 1. *v.a. & n.* (*aux.* h.) search (*nach*, after *or* out), seek, inquire; investigate; do research; *einer, der nach Wahrheit –t*, a seeker after truth; *–ender Blick*, searching *or* inquiring glance. 2. *n.* investigation. **–er,** *m.* investigator; research worker; scholar; scientist; scientific investigator. **–erblick,** *m.* searching glance. **–ergeist,** *m.*, **–ersinn,** *m.* inquiring mind. **–kraft,** *f.* penetration. **–ung,** *f.* investigation, inquiry; research. **–ungsamt,** *n.* directorate of scientific research. **–ungsanstalt,** *f.*, *see* **–ungsinstitut.** **–ungsgebiet,** *n.* field of research. **–ungsinstitut,** *n.* research institute *or* station, laboratory. **–ungsreise,** *f.* voyage of discovery *or* exploration. **-ungsreisende(r),** *m.* explorer.

Forst, *m.* (-es, -e) forest, wood. **–akademie,** *f.* school of forestry. **–amt,** *n.* forestry superintendent's office. **–aufseher,** *m.* ranger. **–beamte(r),** *m.* forestry officer. **–bezirk,** *m.* forest range. **–direktion,** *f.* forestry commission. **–fach,** *n.* science of forestry. **–en,** *v.a.*; *einen Wald –en*, afforest a wood. **–frevel,** *m.* infringement of forest laws. **–frevler,** *m.* trespasser in a forest. **–gefälle,** *n.* revenue deriving from forests. **–gesetz,** *n.* forestry law. **–haus,** *n.* ranger's *or* forester's house. **–hut,** *f.* forest supervision. **–hüter,** *m.* forester's assistant, woodman. **–kunde,** *f.* forestry. **–lehrling,** *m.* forestry student. **–lich,** *adj.* relating to forestry. **–mann,** *m.* forester, ranger. **–meister,** *m.* head ranger, chief forester, forestry official. **–meßkunde,** *f.* forest surveying. **–ordnung,** *f.*, **–recht,** *n.* forest laws. **–revier,** *n.* forest range. **–ung,** *f.* afforesting, afforestation; plantation, wood. **–verwalter,** *m.* forestry superintendent. **–verwaltung,** *f.* forest administration. **–wart,** *m.* forest warden. **–wesen,** *n.*, **–wirtschaft,** *f.* forestry. **–wissenschaft,** *f.* science of forestry.

Förster, *m.* (-s, –) forester, game-keeper, forest ranger. **–ei,** *f.* forester's *or* ranger's house.

Fort [*pron.* fo:r], *n.* (-s, -s) fort, fortress, fortification.

fort, 1. *adv.* away, off, gone, forth; forward, onward, on; – *damit!* take it away! *er ist –*, he is off *or* away; *es will mit ihm nicht recht –*, he does not get on; *ich muß –*, I must be off; *mein Mantel ist –*, my coat is gone *or* lost; *all' mein Geld ist –*, all my money is gone *or* spent; – *mit dir!* get out! get off! *und so –*, and so forth, and so on; – *und –*, continually, all the time; *in einem –*, ceaselessly, continuously, uninterruptedly, without stopping; *er schrieb in einem –*, he kept *or* went on writing; 2. *sep. pref.* (*meanings as above*) *see also compounds with* **weg-**. **–an,** *adv.* from this time, henceforth, hereafter.

fortarbeiten, 1. *v.n.* (*aux.* h.) continue *or* go on working. 2. *v.r.* get on (by working).

fortbegeben, *ir.v.r.* withdraw, retire; depart.

Fortbestand, *m.* continuation, continuance, permanence, duration.

fortbestehen, *ir.v.n.* (*aux.* h.) continue, last, endure, persist.

fortbeweg–en, 1. *v.a.* propel, move along *or* on. 2. *v.r.* continue moving, move on, progress. **–ung,** *f.* locomotion (*of animals*), progression.

fortbild–en, *v.r.* continue one's studies. **–ung,** *f.* further education, further development. **–ungsschule,** *f.* continuation school; evening school.

fortbleiben, *ir.v.n.* stay away.

fortbring–en, 1. *ir.v.a.* help on; rear, support, maintain; carry away, remove, transport, convey; *er ist nicht fortzubringen*, you can't get rid of him. 2. *v.r.* make one's way, get on in life. 3. *n.*, **–ung,** *f.* conveyance, removal, transport; rearing; promotion, advance.

Fortdauer, *f.* continuance, permanence, duration; – *nach dem Tode*, existence after death. **–n,** *v.n.* (*aux.* h.) continue, last, endure. **–nd,** *pr.p. & adj.* lasting, permanent, incessant, continuous.

forterben, *v.r.* be inherited *or* transmitted, go down to posterity.

fortfahren, 1. *ir.v.n.* (*aux.* s.) drive off *or* away; depart, set out *or* off; (*aux.* h.) *mit* or *in einer S.* –, continue, proceed, go on with a th. 2. *v.a.* carry away; remove (*in a vehicle*); drive away.

Fortfall, *m.* discontinuing, cessation, abolition. **–en,** *v.n.* (*aux.* s.) be omitted.

fortführ–en, *v.a.* lead forth *or* away; continue, pursue, carry on, keep *or* go on with. **–ung,** *f.* continuation; conveyance; prosecution, pursuit.

Fortgang, *m.* continuation, progress, advance; departure; *die S. wird ihren – nehmen*, the matter will take its course.

fortgehen, *ir.v.n.* (*aux.* s.) go away, depart; go on, continue, proceed, progress.

fortgesetzt, *adj.* continuous, incessant.

forthelfen, *ir.v.a.* help to escape; help on; *sich kümmerlich –*, make shift to live.
forthin, *see* **fortan.**
fortjagen, 1. *v.a.* chase *or* drive off *or* away, dismiss, discharge; drum out (*of the army*); (*coll.*) kick out. 2. *v.n.* (*aux.* h.) continue hunting; (*aux.* s.) gallop *or* ride off.
fortkomm-en, 1. *ir.v.n.* (*aux.* s.) get away, escape; get lost; get on, prosper, make progress, thrive, succeed; *damit kommt man nicht fort,* that will never do; *mach, daß du –st,* (*coll.*) clear out! (*sl.*) beat it! 2. *n.* escape; advancement, progress; prosperity, success.
fortkönnen, *ir.v.n.* (*ellipt.*; *a verb of motion understood*) be able to proceed, go on *or* get away.
fortlassen, *ir.v.a.* (*ellipt.*; *a verb of motion understood*) allow to go; omit, leave out; *nicht –*, not allow to go, stop, detain, keep.
Fortlauf, *m.* progress, advancement; continuation. **–en,** *ir.v.n.* (*aux.* s.) run away, escape; run on; continue. **–end,** *pr.p.* & *adj.* running, continuous, consecutive, successive.
fortleben, 1. *v.n.* live on, survive. 2. *n.* survival, after-life.
fortmögen, *ir.v.n.* (*ellipt.*; *a verb of motion understood*) wish to go *or* leave.
fortmüssen, *ir.v.n.* (*ellipt.*; *a verb of motion understood*) be obliged to go; have to clear out; (*fig.*) die.
fortnehmen, *v.a.* take (away) from, remove from.
fortpflanz-en, *v.a.* propagate, spread, communicate (*disease*), transmit, reproduce. **–ung,** *f.* propagation; reproduction; transmission, communication. **–ungsfähig,** *adj.* generative, reproductive; transmissible, communicable. **–ungsorgane,** *n.pl.* sexual *or* reproductive organs. **–ungstrieb,** *m.* sexual instinct.
Fortreise, *f.* departure. **–n,** *v.n.* (*aux.* s.) depart, set out *or* off (on a journey).
fortreißen, *ir.v.a.* carry away (*by passion, etc.*); sweep away.
fortrücken, *v.a.* & *n.* (*aux.* s.) move away *or* on; advance, progress.
Fortsatz, *m.* continuation; appendix; process (*Anat.* & *Bot.*).
fortschaffen, *v.a.* get rid of, remove, dismiss, discard, discharge.
fortscheren, *v.r.* (*sl.*) beat it, take one's hook.
fortschleichen, *ir.v.a.* & *r.* sneak off, steal away.
fortschreit-en, *ir.v.n.* (*aux.* s.) move *or* step forward, advance, go on, proceed, make progress, improve; *Deutsch für Fortgeschrittene,* German for advanced students; *–en mit,* keep pace with. **–end,** *pr.p.* & *adj.* progressive; *–ende Welle,* travelling wave (*Rad.*). **–ung,** *f.* progression, consecutive chords (*Mus.*).
Fortschritt, *m.* progress, advance, development, improvement; *–e machen,* advance, make progress. **–lich,** *adj.* progressive; (*coll.*) go-ahead.
fortschwemmen, *v.a.* wash away (*of floods*).
fortsehnen, *v.r.* wish o.s. away, wish to be elsewhere.
fortsetz-en, *v.a.* carry on, continue, pursue; *wieder –en,* resume; *nicht –en,* discontinue. **–ung,** *f.* continuation; pursuit, prosecution; *–ung folgt,* to be continued (in our next).
fortstehlen, *v.r.* steal away secretly, abscond, sneak off.
forttreiben, *ir.v.a.* drive away, force out; continue, carry on; *sie treiben es noch immer so fort,* they go on just in the same way.
fortwachsen, *v.n.* continue to grow.
fortwähr-en, *v.n.* (*aux.* h.) last, persist, continue, endure. **–end,** 1. *pr.p.* & *adj.* lasting, continuous, perpetual, incessant, permanent. 2. *adv.* continually, incessantly, without stopping.
fortwollen, *ir.v.n.* (*aux.* h.) (*ellipt.*; *a verb of motion understood*) wish to go away; intend to leave; *es will mit ihm nicht mehr fort,* his affairs are in a bad way.
fortwursteln, *v.n.* (*coll.*) muddle on *or* through.
fortziehen, 1. *ir.v.a.* draw *or* drag along *or* away 2. *v.n.* (*aux.* s.) proceed, move, march on *or* off; depart, leave (*a house*); emigrate, migrate.
Forum, *n.* (-s, -a & -s) tribunal; (*fig.*) judgement seat, bar.
Fossil, *n.* (-s, -ien) fossil. **–ienbildung,** *f.*, **–werden,** *n.* fossilization. **–ienhaltig,** *adj.* fossiliferous.
Foto, *see* **Photo.**
Fötus, *m.* foetus.
Fourage, *f.*, *see* **Furage.**
Fournier, *n.* veneer. **–en,** *v.a.* veneer.
Fracht, *f.* (-en) freight, cargo, load; carriage (*by land*); *in gewöhnlicher –*, at the usual freight; *ausgehende –*, freight outwards; *ein Schiff in – nehmen,* charter a vessel; *in – geben,* freight. **–aufseher,** *m.* supercargo. **–bar,** *adj.* transportable. **–besorger,** *m.* shipping agent. **–brief,** *m.* bill of loading; waybill. **–dampfer,** *m.* cargo boat, freighter. **–empfänger,** *m.* consignee. **–en,** *v.a.* & *n.* (*aux.* h.) load; carry (freight); ship; *wohin habt ihr gefrachtet?* where are you bound for? **–er,** *m.* 1. consigner, shipper; 2. *see* **–dampfer.** **–flug,** *m.* air transport. **–frei,** *adj.* carriage paid. **–gebühr,** *f.*, **–geld,** *n.* freight, carriage, cartage. **–gut,** *n.* lading, cargo, freight, goods, luggage. **–handel,** *m.* carrying-trade. **–liste,** *f.* consignment-sheet, way-bill, freight-note. **–makler,** *m.* shipping *or* forwarding agent. **–raum,** *m.* hold (*of a ship*); freight capacity. **–raumnot,** *f.* lack of shipping space. **–satz,** *m.* freight tariff. **–schiff,** *n.* freighter, cargo-boat. **–stück,** *n.* package. **–verkehr,** *m.* goods-traffic. **–versender,** *m.* consigner. **–wagen,** *m.* wagon *or* van. **–zettel,** *m.*, *see* **–brief.** **–zoll,** *m.* tonnage-dues.
Frächter, *m.*, *see* **Frachter,** 1.
Frack, *m.* (-(e)s, -s & ⸚e) dress-coat; (*coll.*) tail-coat; *– und weiße Binde,* evening dress, (*coll.*) tails. **–anzug,** *m.* dress-suit. **–schoß,** *m.* tail of a dress-coat. **–zwang,** *m.* obligation to wear evening dress.
Frag-e, *f.* (-en) question, query, inquiry; questionable *or* uncertain th., problem; *außer –e sein* or *stehen,* be beyond question, be quite certain; *eine –e bejahen,* answer in the affirmative; *das ist eben die –e,* that is just the point *or* question; *eine –e enthaltend,* interrogatory; *das kommt nicht in –e,* that is out of the question; *die –e nahe legen,* raise the question; *ohne –e,* no doubt, undoubtedly; *peinliche –e,* awkward *or* embarrassing question; *gerichtliche –e,* interrogatory, inquiry; *es ist sehr die –e,* it is very doubtful; *stark in –e sein,* be in great demand; *eine –e stellen* (*an einen*), ask (a p.) a question; *in –e stellen,* call in question, question, doubt; *eine –e tun,* see *eine –e stellen*; *um die –e nicht herumkommen,* not evade the point, (*coll.*) not get past it; *in –e ziehen,* see *in –e stellen.* **–ebogen,** *m.* questionnaire. **–ebuch,** *n.* catechism. **–elehrer,** *m.* catechist. **–eliste,** *f.* list of questions. **–en,** *v.a.* & *n.* (*aux.* h.) ask, inquire (*nach,* for), interrogate, question; consult (*um*); (*C.L.*) *Baumwolle wird* or *ist sehr gefragt,* cotton is in great demand; *er –te mich,* he asked me; *ich –te gar nicht danach,* I did not care a rap about it; (*coll.*) *ich –te den Kuckuck* or *Henker* or *Teufel danach,* I didn't care a damn *or* a tuppenny cuss; *niemand –t nach mir,* nobody cares for me *or* troubles himself about me; *hat jemand nach mir gefragt?* has anyone asked for me? *es –te sich, ob,* the question was whether; *ich –te mich, ob, . . .* I pondered whether . . .; *um Erlaubnis –en,* ask permission; *wegen einer S. –en,* ask concerning a matter; ask about a th.; (*Prov.*) *wer viel –t, erhält viel Antwort,* many questions, many answers. **–end,** *pr.p.* & *adj.* interrogative; interrogatory; *er sah sie –end an,* he looked at her inquiringly. **–epunkt,** *m.* point in question. **–esatz,** *m.* interrogative sentence (*Gram.*). **–(e)selig,** *adj.* fond of asking questions; inquisitive. **–esteller,** *m.* interrogator. **–estellung,** *f.* formulation of a question, questioning. **–eweise,** *adv.* interrogatively, in the form of a question. **–ewort,** *n.* interrogative (*Gram.*). **–ezeichen,** *n.* question mark, interrogation mark. **–lich,** *adj.* questionable, doubtful; *–liche S.,* matter in question; *es ist –lich,* it is open to question. **–los,** *adv.* unquestionably, undoubtedly, beyond all question. **–würdig,** *adj.* questionable, doubtful.
Fragment, *n.* (-(e)s, -e) fragment. **–arisch,** *adj.* fragmentary.
Frakt-ion, *f.* (-en) parliamentary party. **–ionär,**

adj. fractional. **–ionierung,** *f.* fractionation, fractional distillation (*Chem.*). **–ionsbeschluß,** *m.* party resolution, factional motion. **–ionssitzung,** *f.* party meeting. **–ur,** *f.* black letter *or* Gothic type; fracture (*Surg.*); (*fig.*) *–ur sprechen*, talk plain English.

frank, 1. *adj.* free; frank, open; (*usually in the phrase*) *– und frei*, quite frankly, without any restraint. 2. *m.* (*Gen.* -en (*& Austr.* -s)); *pl.* (*coins*) –, (*sum of money*) -en, (*Austr. pl. always* -en) franc. **–atur,** *f.* pre-payment, postage paid. **–en,** *m.* (-ens, -en) (*Swiss*) *see* – 2. **–ieren,** *v.a.* pay the postage *or* carriage; *–ierter Briefumschlag*, stamped envelope. **–ierungszwang,** *m.* obligation to prepay letters. **–o,** *adv.* post-paid, prepaid; carriage-paid; (*C.L.*) *–o* (*bis*) *London*, post-paid *or* carriage-paid to London. **–obrief,** *m.* post-paid *or* prepaid letter. **–ogebühr,** *f.* carriage, postage. **–oprovision,** *f.* no commission charged. **–ospesen,** *pl.* free of cost, no charges. **–overmerk,** *m.* notice of prepayment. **–ozinsen,** *m.pl.* no interest charged. **–tireur,** *m.* franctireur, guerrilla fighter.

Frans–e, *f.* (-en) fringe; valance. **–en,** *v.a.* fringe. **–ig,** *adj.* fringed, frayed.

Franz, *m.* (*sl.*) flier, aviator; air observer; **–band,** *m.* calf-binding; *see the Index of Names.* **–en,** *v.n.* (*sl.*) stooge around (*Av.*).

frapp–ant, *adj.* striking, surprising, staggering. **–ieren,** *v.a.* strike, astound; chill, put on ice (*wine*).

fräs–en, *v.a.* fraise, mill. **–e,** *f.* 1. milling tool *or* machine; 2. Newgate fringe (*beard*). **–er,** *m.* 1, *see* **–e** (1); 2. milling operative.

fraß, fräße, *see* **fressen.**

Fraß, *m.* (-es, -e) feed, fodder (*for beasts*); (*sl.*) grub, prog; (*dial.*) immoderate appetite, voracity, gluttony; caries (*Med.*); corrosion; insect damage. **–mehl,** *n.* frass, larval excrement (*Bot., Ent.*). **–trog,** *m.* feeding-trough.

Fratz, *m.* (-es & (*Austr.*) -en, -en) naughty child, mischievous brat. **–e,** *f.* (-en) grimace; (*coll.*) phiz, mug; (*sl.*) clock, dial (*for face*); prank, antic; caricature; mask (*Arch.*); *–en schneiden*, make *or* pull faces. **–enhaft,** *adj.* grotesque, distorted, contorted, whimsical, burlesque. **–enbild,** *n.* caricature. **–engesicht,** *n.* grotesque *or* distorted face; wry face; mask (*Arch.*).

Frau, *f.* (-en) woman; wife; lady; madam; Mrs.; *meine –*, my wife; *Herr und –*, master and mistress; *die – des Hauses*, lady of the house, mistress; *vornehme –*, gentlewoman, lady; *adlige –*, lady, titled lady; *gnädige –*, madam; *Unsre* (*liebe*) *–*, Our Lady, the Blessed Virgin; *– Scherer* or *– Dr. Scherer*, Mrs. Scherer; *Herr und – Professor Scherer*, Professor and Mrs. Scherer; *wie geht es Ihrer – Gemahlin?* how is your wife? *die – Doktor*, the doctor's wife; *die – Rat*, the councillor's lady; (*often untranslatable, e.g.*) *die – Gräfin*, the countess; her ladyship; *Ihre – Mutter*, your mother; *zur – geben* or *nehmen*, give *or* take in marriage. **–chen,** *n.* (*hum.*) little woman, wifey; (*of dogs*) bitch (*when mother of pups*). **–enabteil,** *n.* (*also m.*) ladies' compartment (*Railw.*). **–enarzt,** *m.* gynaecologist. **–enbewegung,** *f.* feminist movement. **–endienst,** *m.* women's national service (*Nat. Soc.*). **–endistel,** *f.* Scotch thistle. **–eneis,** selenite (*Miner.*). **–enfeind,** *m.* woman-hater. **–enfest,** *n.* Lady Day. **–enfrage,** *f.* question of woman's rights. **–engestalt,** *f.* female character (*in literary works*). **–englas,** *n., see* **–eneis. –engut,** *n.* wife's property. **–enhaar,** *n.* women's hair; maidenhair (*Adiantum capillus-veneris*) (*Bot.*). **–enhaß,** misogyny. **–enheim,** *n.* home *or* refuge for women. **–enheld,** *m.* ladies' man. **–enhemd,** *n.* chemise, vest. **–enherrschaft,** *f.* petticoat government. **–enjäger,** *m.* gay Lothario. **–enkäfer,** *m.* lady-bird. **–enkirche,** *f.* Church of Our Lady. **–enkloster,** *n.* nunnery. **–enliebe,** *f.* woman's love. **–enlyzeum,** *n.* high school for girls. **–enmantel,** *m.* lady's mantle (*Alchemilla vulgaris*) (*Bot.*). **–enmilch,** *f.* mother's milk. **–enraub,** *m.* abduction, (*Poet.*) rape. **–enrechtlerin,** *f.* suffragette. **–enrock,** *m.* skirt. **–ensattel,** *m.* side-saddle. **–enschaft,** *f.* women's organization (*Nat. Soc.*). **–enschuh,** *m.* woman's shoe; lady's slipper (*Cypripedium calceolus*) (*Bot.*). **–enschutz,** *m.* contraceptive pessary. **–ensleute,** *pl.* women, womenfolk. **–enspat,** *m., see* **–eneis. –ensperson,** *f.* female. **–enstand,** *m.* wifehood, married state; womanhood; coverture (*Law*). **–enstift,** *n.* (religious) foundation for women; nunnery. **–enstimme,** *f.* female voice. **–enstimmrecht,** *n.* women's suffrage. **–enstudium,** *n.* admission of women to universities. **–enstühle,** *m.pl.* women's pews (*in church*). **–entag,** *m.* Lady Day. **–entor,** *n.* Gate of Our Lady. **–enverein,** *m.* women's guild. **–enwelt,** *f.* womankind. **–enwerk,** *n.* women's welfare organization. **–enzimmer,** *n.* female, wench; (*archaic*) lady, woman. **–enzwinger,** *m.* harem.

Fräulein, *n.* (*& Swiss f.*) (-s, –) young lady; unmarried lady; Miss (*also to address shop-assistant, officials, etc.*); home governess; *– vom Amt*, operator (*Phone*); *meine –!* young ladies! *gnädiges –*, Miss, madam, Miss (*followed by surname*); *Ihr* or *Ihre – Braut*, your fiancée; *ich habe mit Ihrem* or *Ihrer – Tochter getanzt*, I have danced with your daughter; *Liebes – Lieschen*, dear Miss Lizzie.

frech, *adj.* insolent, impudent, cheeky, shameless, bold, audacious; *mit –er Stirn*, brazen-faced. **–heit,** *f.* insolence, impudence; (*coll.*) cheek; (*sl.*) nerve; insolent behaviour, piece of impudence. (*coll.*) **–dachs,** *m.* cheeky young rascal, impudent fellow.

Fregatte, *f.* (-n) frigate.

frei, 1. *adj.* free, independent (*von*, of); unconfined, uncontrolled, unconstrained; at liberty; frank, outspoken, candid, open; voluntary, spontaneous; vacant, disengaged, exempt, clear; acquitted, exonerated, exempted, prepaid, post-paid, carriage-free, gratis, free of charge, for nothing; bold, loose; *–er Anstand*, easy deportment; *– ausgehen*, get off scot-free; *–e Aussicht*, open view; *die –en Berufe*, the professions; *–e Bühne*, independent theatre; *Freies Deutsches Hochstift*, Frankfort society for the promotion of arts and sciences; *–er Eintritt*, entrance free; *–e Fahrt*, clear road ahead, all clear (*Railw., etc.*); *–es Feld*, open country; (*fig.*) full scope; *auf –en Fuß setzen*, set at liberty; *ins –e gehen*, take the air; *–es Geleit*, safe conduct; *–e Gemeinde*, rationalistic religious community; *Passagiere haben 60 Pfund Gepäck –*, passengers are allowed 60 lb. of luggage free; *–e Hand*, free hand, free rein, full authority; *aus –er Hand*, freehand; off hand; *–er Handwerker*, artisan belonging to no guild; *– ins Haus liefern*, deliver to the door without charge; *unter –em Himmel*, in the open (air); *die –en Künste*, the liberal arts; *–en Lauf lassen* (*einer S., Dat.*), let (a matter) take its own course; *–e Luft*, open air; *sich –machen* (*von*), free o.s. (from); *sich für heute Abend –machen*, arrange to be free for this evening; *sich vom Dienst –machen*, take time off (*from work, etc.*); *morgen ist –*, no school *or* work tomorrow; *ist dieser Platz –?* is this seat taken? *dieser Platz ist –*, this seat is unoccupied; *ich bin so –*, (*coll.*) I don't mind if I do; *darf ich so – sein?* may I take the liberty; *–es Spiel lassen*, *–en Spielraum gewähren*, leave *or* give full scope; *–e Station*, free board and lodging; *–e Stätte*, place of refuge, asylum; *–e Stelle*, vacancy; *Straße –!* make way, please! *aus –en Stücken*, voluntarily, of one's own accord; *–er Tag*, holiday; *–er Teil*, commercial partnership free of all commitments; *–er Tisch*, free board; *zur –en Verfügung sein*, be freely at one's disposal; *–e Zeit*, spare time; *er hat viel –e Zeit*, he has much leisure. 2. *as a verbal prefix it is sep.* **–ballon,** *m.* free balloon. **–bauer,** *m.* independent peasant. **–beuter,** *m.* freebooter, pirate. **–beweglich,** *adj.* mobile, motile. **–billett,** *n.* complimentary ticket, pass. **–bleibend,** *adj.* (*C. L.*) without obligation, without prejudice, subject to alteration; if unsold, if still available. **–bord,** *m.* freeboard (*Naut.*). **–brief,** *m.* permit, licence; patent, charter; carte-blanche. **–denker,** *m.* freethinker. **–denkerei,** *f.* freethinking, latitudinarianism. **–e,** *n.* open air; *im –en*, out of doors. **–eigen,** *adj.* freehold. **–en,** *v.a.* (*obs., survives in*) **Gefreite,** *m.* lance-corporal (*a* *man freed from guard duties*). **–erdings,** *adv.* spontaneously, voluntarily. **–exemplar,** *n.* complimentary *or* presentation *or* specimen copy. **–frau,** *f.* baroness. **–gabe,** *f.* release. **–geben,** *ir.v.a.* set free, release; give a holiday. **–gebig,** *adj.* liberal, generous. **–gebigkeit,** *f.* liberality, generosity. **–gebung,** *f.* emancipation; release. **–geist,** *m.* freethinker; latitudinarian. **–geisterei,** *f.* freethinking. **–gelassen,** *adj.* freed, enfranchised. **–gelassene(r)** *m.* freedman. **–gepäck,** *n.* allowed luggage, luggage conveyed free. **–gesinnt,** *adj.* liberal (*in religion, politics*). **–gläubig,** *adj.* independent in faith. **–graben,** *m.* open drain. **–grenze,** *f.* unrationed allowance. **–gut,** *n.* freehold; goods that are duty-free. **–gutsbesitzer,** *m.* freeholder. **–hafen,** *m.* free port (*outside the bond area*). **–halten,** *ir.v.a.* keep free (*of time or place*); *einen –halten,* stand a p. (*a drink, etc.*), pay a p.'s expenses. **–handel,** *m.* free-trade. **–händig,** *adj.* freehand; unsupported, unassisted, direct (*sale*); voluntary. **–händler,** *m.* free-trader; believer in principles of free-trade. **–handzeichnen,** *n.* freehand drawing. **–heit,** *f.* freedom, liberty; franchise, privilege; immunity; tactical mobility (*Mil.*); licence, charter. (*Under Nat. Soc. it changed its connotation*; *following Nietzsche's* 'Nicht Freiheit wovon, sondern Freiheit wozu' *it no longer meant the constitutional rights of the individual but the freedom and privilege of the state or race*); *in –heit,* at liberty; *ich nehme mir die –heit, Sie darum zu bitten,* I take the liberty of asking you for it; *er erlaubt sich viele –heiten,* he takes a lot upon himself *or* takes liberties. **–heitlich,** *adj.* liberal. **–heitsbrief,** *m.* charter. **–heitsdrang,** *m.* desire for independence. **–heitskampf,** *m.*, **–heitskrieg,** *m.* war of independence. **–heitsstrafe,** *f.* imprisonment. **–heitsurkunde,** *f.* charter. **–heraus,** *adv.* frankly. **–herr,** *m.* baron. **–herrlich,** *adj.* baronial. **–herrin,** *f.*, *see* **–frau. –herrschend,** *adj.* sovereign. **–herzig,** *adj.* open-hearted, frank. **–in,** *f.*, *see* **–frau. –korps,** *n.* volunteer corps. **–lage,** *f.* exposed site, unsheltered position. **–lager,** *n.* bivouac. **–landtomaten,** *f.pl.* outdoor tomatoes. **–länge,** *f.* span, unsupported length. **–lassen,** *ir.v.a.* release, set free, liberate. **–lassung,** *f.* emancipation, release. **–lauf,** *m.* free wheel (*bicycle*). **–legen,** *v.a.* expose, lay open. **–lehen,** *n.* freehold, fee-simple. **–leitung,** *f.* overhead cable (*Elec.*) *or* line (*Tel.*). **–lich,** *adv.* to be sure, of course, certainly, by all means; I confess *or* admit; indeed. **–licht-** *or* **–luftbühne,** *f.* open-air theatre. **–lichtmalerei,** *f.* plein-air painting. **–liegen,** *v.n.* be open *or* exposed; be unencumbered. **–machen,** I. *v.a.* stamp (*letters*), prepay; *Güter –machen,* clear goods; disconnect, disengage, free, liberate, evolve, set free. 2. *n.*, **–machung,** *f.*, freeing, liberation, disengagement, emancipation. **–mann,** *m.* freeman; freeholder. **–marke,** *f.* postage stamp. **–maurer,** *m.* freemason. **–maurerei,** *f.* freemasonry. **–maurerisch,** *adj.* masonic. **–maurerloge,** *f.* masonic lodge. **–meisterschaft,** *f.* freedom of a guild. **–mündig,** *adj.* free-spoken, uninhibited. **–mut,** *m.* frankness, candour, sincerity. **–mütig,** *adj.* candid, frank. **–mütigkeit,** *f.* ingenuousness. **–saß,** *m.* (-(ss)en) yeoman. **–schar,** *f.* irregular troops, guerrilla detachment, volunteer corps. **–schärler,** *m.* (*only applied in praise of Germans, never of the enemy*) volunteer; armed insurgent; guerrilla. **–schein,** *m.* licence. **–schüler,** *m.* public scholar, scholarship holder. **–schweben,** *v.n.* float *or* hover free. **–sinn,** *m.* enlightenment, broadmindedness. **–sinnig,** *adj.* free-thinking, broad-minded, enlightened, liberal (*views*) (*in Germany the implication has usually been 'radical', 'left-wing'*). **–sitz,** *m.* freehold. **–sprechen,** I. *ir.v.a.* acquit, absolve. 2. *n.*, **–sprechung,** *f.* acquittal; absolution; emancipation. **–staat,** *m.* republic; free state; *der irische –staat,* the Irish Free State. **–staatlich,** *adj.* republican. **–stand,** *m.* open position, isolation. **–statt,** *f.*, **–stätte,** *f.* sanctuary, refuge, asylum. **–stehen,** *ir.v.n.* be free; *es steht dir –,* you are at liberty, you may. **–stehend,** *pr.p.* & *adj.* detached, exposed, isolated. **–stelle,** *f.* scholarship, bursary, free place. **–stellen,** *v.a.* give a choice; *einem etwas –stellen,* leave to a p.'s option. **–stellung,** *f.* isolation, exposure. **–student,** *m.* German student who is not a member of an academic corporation. **–stunde,** *f.* leisure hour. **–tisch,** *m.* free board. **–tod,** *m.* suicide. **–tragend,** *adj.* cantilever (*Engin.*). **–treppe,** *f.* outside staircase, front steps. **–truppe,** *f.* volunteer corps. **–übungen,** *f.pl.* physical exercises; callisthenics; (*coll.*) physical jerks, P.T. **–wasser,** *n.* uncontrolled fishing area, water open to public fishing; superfluous water. **–werden,** *v.n.* become free *or* liberated. **–werdend,** *adj.* nascent (*Chem.*). **–willig,** *adj.* voluntary, spontaneous. **–willige(r),** *m.* volunteer. **–willigenschein,** *m.*, **–willigenzeugnis,** *n.* certificate of educational proficiency (*until 1918 qualifying for one year's military service as a volunteer*). **–zeit,** *f.* spare time, leisure. **–zettel,** *m.* warrant; permit; pass. **–zügig,** *adj.* free to move about *or* to live where one likes. **–zügigkeit,** *f.* freedom to live, travel *or* study where one likes.

frei–en, I. *v.a.* woo, court; *nach Geld –en,* set out to marry money *or* to make a wealthy match; (*Prov.*) *jung gefreit hat niemand gereut,* happy the wooing that's not long in doing; (*Prov.*) *schnell gefreit, lange gereut,* marry in haste and repent at leisure. 2. *n.* wooing, courtship. **–er,** *m.* wooer, suitor; *auf –ersfüßen gehen,* be on the lookout for a wife. **–te,** *f.* courtship; *auf der –te sein* or *auf die –te gehen,* be on the lookout for a wife. **–werber** *m.* matrimonial agent; match-maker. **–werbung,** *f.* match-making.

Freitag, *m.* (-s, -e) Friday; *Stiller –,* Good Friday.

fremd, *adj.* strange, foreign; unknown, unfamiliar, unaccustomed; unusual, peculiar, exotic; extraneous, heterogeneous; (*Nat. Soc. usage*) un-German, hostile, inferior; *ich bin hier –,* I am a stranger here; *dies kommt mir sehr – vor,* this seems very strange to me; *es war mir –,* I was not aware of it; *unter –em Namen,* under an assumed name; *–es Gut,* other people's property; *gegen einen – tun,* cut a p. **–artig,** *adj.* strange, odd; unfamiliar; heterogeneous; extraneous (*Chem.*). **–artigkeit,** *f.* heterogeneousness; oddness. **–befruchtung,** *f.* cross-fertilization. **–bestäubung,** *f.* cross-pollination, allogamy. **–blütig,** *adj.* (*Nat. Soc.*) non-German, of inferior stock. **–e,** *f.* foreign country; place away from home; *in der –e,* abroad. **–e(r),** *m.* foreigner, alien; stranger, visitor, guest. **–enbuch,** *n.* visitors' book, hotel register. **–enführer,** *m.* guide; guide book. **–enhaß,** *m.* xenophobia. **–enrecht,** *n.* laws pertaining to aliens. **–enverkehr,** *m.* tourist traffic. **–enzimmer,** *n.* spare room. **–geräusch,** *n.* parasitic noise (*Rad.*). **–gläubig,** *adj.* heterodox. **–heit,** *f.* strangeness, unfamiliarity; peculiarity. **–herrschaft,** *f.* foreign rule. **–körper,** *m.* foreign body. **–ländisch,** *adj.* foreign, extraneous. **–ling,** *m.* stranger, foreigner, alien; (*pl.*) erratic blocks (*Geol.*). **–rassig,** *adj.*, **–stämmig,** *adj.* of different race *or* birth, alien. **–sprache,** *f.* foreign language. **–stoff,** *m.* impurity, foreign matter. **–werden,** *n.* estrangement. **–wort,** *n.* foreign word. **–wörterbuch,** *n.* dictionary of foreign adoptions *or* borrowings.

frenetisch, *adj.* frenzied, frantic, demented, insensate.

frequen–tieren, *v.a.* frequent. **–z,** *f.* attendance; traffic, crowd; frequency, wave-length (*Rad.*). **–z(abhängigkeits)kennlinie,** *f.* frequency characteristics response curve (*Rad.*). **–zwandler,** *m.* frequency changer (*Rad.*).

fress–en, I. *ir.v.a.* & *n.* (*aux.* h.) eat (*of beasts*); feed; devour, consume, destroy; corrode; (*Prov.*) *Vogel friß oder stirb,* it is sink or swim, there is no alternative; *seinen Ärger in sich –en,* swallow one's annoyance; *sie hat einen Narren daran gefressen,* she is infatuated with it *or* dotes upon it; *–ender Gram,* gnawing *or* consuming anxiety; *pflanzen–ende Tiere,* herbivorous animals; *fleisch–ende Tiere,* carnivora. 2. *n.* feed, food, fodder (*for beasts*); *das war ein elendes –en,* (*coll.*) that was a wretched meal; *ein gefundenes –en,* (*coll.*) the very th., a godsend, a gift from the gods; (*coll.*) **–alien,** *pl.* eatables. **–e,** *f.* (*vulg.*) trap, gob (*for mouth*). **–er,** *m.* glutton; voracious eater. **–erei,** *f.* gluttony; feast; (*coll.*) feed, spread. **–(ß)gier,** *f.* voracity, gluttony. **–(ß)beutel,** *m.* feeding bag, nose-bag. **–(ß)lust,** *f.* excessive appetite. **–(ß)sack,** *m.* provender-bag; (*fig.*) glutton. **–(ß)süchtig,** *adj.* voracious. **–(ß)-trog,** *m.* feeding-trough.

Frett, *n.* (-es, -e) (*rare*); **–chen,** *n.* ferret. **–ieren,** *v.n.* ferret, go ferreting.

Freu–de, *f.* (-n) joy, gladness; delight, pleasure, satisfaction; enjoyment, comfort; *plötzlicher Ausbruch der –de*, transport (of joy); *mit –de* or *–den*, gladly, joyfully, with pleasure; *vor –de außer sich sein*, be beside o.s. with joy; *seine –de haben an einer S.*, take delight in a th.; *es macht mir große –de*, it gives me great pleasure; (*Prov.*) *geteilte –de ist doppelte –de*, shared joys are doubled. **–dearm,** *adj.* joyless. **–denbotschaft,** *f.* glad tidings. **–denfeier,** *f.*, **–denfest,** *n.* festival, festivity, feast. **–denfeuer,** *n.* bonfire. **–dengeschrei,** *n.* shouts of joy; cheers. **–denhaus,** *n.* disorderly house, brothel. **–denleer,** *adj.* **–de(n)los,** *adj.*, *see* **–dlos. –denmädchen,** *n.* prostitute. **–denopfer,** *n.* thank-offering. **–denreich,** *adj.* joyous. **–denruf,** *m.* cheer. **–densprung,** *m.* caper. **–denstörer,** *m.* mischief-maker; kill-joy. **–dentag,** *m.* day of rejoicing, red-letter day. **–destrahlend,** *adj.* beaming with joy, radiant. **–detrunken,** *adj.* intoxicated with joy. **–dig,** *adj.* joyful, joyous, glad, cheerful; *einem –digen Ereignis entgegensehen*, be expecting a happy event. **–digkeit,** *f.* joyousness. **–dlos,** *adj.* cheerless, joyless. **–dvoll,** *adj.* glad, delighted. **–en,** 1. *v.a.* & (*usually*) *imp.* make glad, gladden, give pleasure to, delight; *es –t mich,* (*daß*), I am glad (that). 2. *v.r.* rejoice, be glad; *wir –en uns, zu erfahren*, we are pleased to learn; *sich –en über eine S.* or (*Poet.*) *einer S.* (*Gen.*), rejoice at *or* about a th.; *ich –e mich darüber*, I am glad of it; *er –t sich über sein neues Buch*, he is pleased *or* delighted with his new book; *–t euch des Lebens!* let life be joyful! *sich an einer S. –en*, take delight in *or* find pleasure in a th.; *sie –t sich am Glück ihrer Kinder*, she takes delight in the happiness of her children; *sich auf etwas –en*, look forward to s.th.; *wir –en uns auf dein Kommen*, we are looking forward to your visit. 3. *n.*; *das war ein –en*, there were great rejoicings.

Freund, *m.* (-(e)s, -e) friend, acquaintance, companion, comrade; boy friend, gentleman friend (*when used by women*); (*pl.*) Quakers; *– der Wahrheit*, lover of truth; *–e im Glücke*, fair-weather friends; (*Prov.*) *–e erkennt man in der Not*, a friend in need is a friend indeed; *ein – von mir*, a friend of mine; *ich bin kein – von vielen Worten*, I do not like wordiness. **–in,** *f.* girl friend, lady friend (*when used by men*); friend (*when used by women*). **–lich,** *adj.* friendly, kind, affable, amiable, obliging; pleasant, cheerful; *das ist sehr –lich von Ihnen*, that is very kind of you; *–liches Wesen*, obliging, affable *or* kindly manner; *–liches Wetter*, pleasant *or* sunny weather, favourable weather; *–liches Zimmer*, cheerful *or* cosy room; *bitte recht –lich!* smile, please (*photographer's injunction*). **–lichkeit,** *f.* kindness, friendliness, pleasantness, affability. **–los,** *adj.* friendless. **–nachbarlich,** *adj.* neighbourly, companionable. **–schaft,** *f.* friendship; intimacy, acquaintance; friends, acquaintances; amity; *–schaft schließen*, make friends. **–schaftlich,** *adj.* friendly, amicable, cordial. **–schaftlichkeit,** *f.* friendly disposition, camaraderie. **–schaftsbund,** *m.* friendly alliance; bond of friendship. **–schaftsdienst,** *m.* kind service, good offices, friendly turn. **–schaftsversicherung,** *f.* protestation of friendship. (*C.L.*) **–schaftswechsel,** *m.* accommodation-bill.

Frev–el, 1. *m.* (-els, -el) outrage, crime, misdeed; sacrilege, violation; wantonness, wickedness; mischief. **–elhaft,** *adj.*, **–entlich,** *adj.*, **–lerisch,** *adj.* sacrilegious, wicked, criminal, wanton, malicious, outrageous. **–elhaftigkeit,** *f.* wickedness, criminality, wantonness; outrageousness. **–ellust,** *f.* **–elmut,** *m.* **–elsinn,** *m.* malicious *or* mischievous disposition; wantonness. **–eln,** *v.n.* (*aux.* h.) commit a crime, offence *or* outrage (*gegen* or *wider einen*; *an einem*, against a p.); blaspheme; outrage, transgress, trespass. **–eltat,** *f.* outrage. **–elwort,** *n.* wicked word; insult; blasphemy. **–ler,** *m.* criminal; evil-doer, offender, transgressor; outrager; blasphemer.

friderizianisch, *adj.* of Frederick the Great.

Fried–e (Fried–en), *m.* (-ens, -en) peace; tranquillity; harmony. *–en machen* or *schließen*, make peace; *im –en*, in peacetime; *in –en lassen*, let alone, leave in peace; *–en halten*, keep quiet; *in – und Freud*, in peace and amity; (*coll.*) *dem –en ist nicht zu trauen*, I smell a rat; (*Prov.*) *–e ernährt, Un–e verzehrt*, a bad peace is better than a good war; *fauler –e*, hollow truce. **–brüchig,** *adj.* violating the peace. **–emachend,** *adj.* pacifying, pacific. **–ensbruch,** *m.* breach *or* violation of the peace. **–ensbrüchig,** *adj.* guilty of a breach of the peace. **–ensdiktat,** *n.* dictated peace (*referring to Versailles Treaty*). **–ensfest,** *n.* peace celebrations. **–e(ns)fürst,** *m.* Prince of Peace; Christ. **–ensfuß,** *m.* peace-footing (*Mil.*). **–ensgüte,** *f.* pre-war quality. **–ensmäßig,** *adj.* as in peace-time. **–enspfeife,** *f.* pipe of peace. **–ensrichter,** *m.* justice of the peace (*in England*); arbitrator (*when applied to German conditions*). **–ensschluß,** *m.* conclusion of peace. **–ensspruch,** *m.* arbitrational award. **–ensstand,** *m.* peace-time strength, peace establishment (*Mil.*). **–ensstifter,** *m.* mediator, peacemaker. **–ensstörer,** *m.* disturber of the peace; rioter. **–ensstörung,** *f.* disturbance *or* breach of the peace (*Law*). **–ensvermittler,** *m.* mediator. **–ensvertrag,** *m.* peace treaty. **–evoll,** *adj.* peaceful. **–fertig,** *adj.* peaceable, peace-loving; (*B.*) *selig sind die –fertigen*, blessed are the peacemakers. **–fertigkeit,** *f.* peaceableness. **–hof,** *m.* churchyard, cemetery, burial ground. **–lich,** *adj.* peaceable, peaceful, pacific. **–lichkeit,** *f.* peacefulness, peaceableness. **–los,** *adj.* quarrelsome; (*archaic*) outlawed, outcast, proscribed. (*Poet.*) **–sam,** *adj.*, *see* **–lich.**

frier–en, 1. *ir.v.n.* (*aux.* h. & s.) freeze; congeal; *der Fluß ist gefroren*, the river is frozen over. 2. *v.a.* & *imp.* freeze, chill; *hat es gefroren?* did it freeze? *es –t*, there is a frost; *mich –t*, I am cold; *mich –t an den Händen*, my hands are numb with cold; *die Finger sind mir steif gefroren*, my fingers are stiff with cold. 3. *n.* freezing, congelation; shivering, chill, ague. **–punkt,** *m.* freezing-point.

Fries, *m.* (-es, -e) 1. frieze, baize (*coarse woollen cloth*). 2. frieze (*Arch.*).

Friesel, *m.* & *n.* (-s, -n) & *f.* (-n) pustule. **–fieber,** *n.*, **–n,** *pl.* military fever, purples (*Med.*).

Frika–delle, *f.* (-n) meat ball, rissole. **–ndelle,** *f.* (-n) fricandeau (*Cook.*). **–ssee,** *n.* (-s, -s) fricassee. **–ssieren,** *v.a.* mince, make into fricassee.

Friktion, *f.* (-en) friction. **–santrieb,** *m.* friction drive (*Mach.*).

frisch, 1. *adj.* fresh, cool, refreshing; new, unused, recent, raw, green; ruddy (*complexion*); sharp, brisk, vigorous, lively, sprightly, alert; *– gestrichen*, wet paint; *– drauf los!* courage! on them! go to it! *–e Eier*, new-laid eggs; (*Prov.*) *–e Fische, gute Fische*, never put off till tomorrow what you can do today; *– und froh*, happily, joyfully; *es geht ihm – von der Hand*, he is a quick worker; *–e Spur*, hot scent (*Sport*); *auf –er Tat*, in the (very) act; *–e Milch*, new milk; *etwas – wagen*, venture boldly on a th.; (*Prov.*) *– gewagt ist halb gewonnen*, well begun is half done, a good beginning is half the battle; *–e Wäsche anziehen*, change one's linen. **–auf,** *int.* look alive! be quick! (*sl.*) stick it! go it! **–backen,** *adj.*, **–gebacken,** *adj.* newly baked. **–dampf,** *m.* live-steam. **–e,** *f.* freshness; coolness; liveliness, briskness, brightness, vigour; cool spot. **–en,** *v.a.* refine; (*Poet.*) cool, refresh; revive. **–er,** *m.* refiner (*of metals*). **–(en)esse,** *f.* refining furnace refinery. **–feuer,** *n.* refining fire. **–heit,** *f.*, *see* **–e. –herd,** *m.*, **–ofen,** *m.* puddling-furnace. **–ling,** *m.* young boar. **–malerei,** *f.* fresco painting. **–metall,** *n.* virgin metal. **–stahl,** *m.* German steel, natural steel. **–ung,** *f.* metal-refining; renewal, regeneration.

Fris–eur, *m.* (-s, -e), (*Austr. dial.*) **–eurin,** *f.*, **–euse,** *f.*, hairdresser, barber. **–ieren,** *v.a.* dress *or* cut the hair; nap (*cloth*); trim; (*fig.*) cook (*accounts*);

sich –ieren lassen, have one's hair done *or* cut. **–iereisen**, *n.* curling-tongs. **–iermantel**, *m.* dressing-jacket, peignoir. **–iermühle**, *f.* cloth-dressing mill. **–iertisch**, *m.* dressing-table, toilet-table. **–ur**, *f.* (-en) hairdressing; hair-style, coiffure; head-dress; head of hair; trimming.

friß, frißt, *see* **fressen.**

Frist, *f.* (-en) space of time, period, interval; appointed time, term; respite, delay; days of grace; deadline. **–brief**, *m.* letter of respite. **–en**, *v.a.* fix a term for; delay, postpone; (*coll.*) put off; respite; reprieve; *einem das Leben –en*, prolong *or* spare a p.'s life; *so viel haben, um das Leben zu –en* have *or* earn enough to keep body and soul together; *kümmerlich sein Leben –en*, just manage to live. **–(en)weise**, *adv.* at certain times; by intervals; by instalments. **–gesuch**, *n.* motion in arrest of judgement (*Law*). **–los**, *adv.* without respite, immediately, at once; *er ist aus seiner Stellung –los entlassen worden*, he was dismissed without notice; *–lose Entlassung*, summary dismissal. **–mittel**, *n.* palliative. **–tag**, *m.* day of grace *or* respite. **–ung**, *f.* fixing a term; prolongation. **–verlängerung**, *f.* extension of time.

fritt–en, *v.n.* cohere; frit, sinter (*pottery, glass-making, etc.*). **–er**, *m.* coherer (*Rad.*).

frivol, *adj.* frivolous, flippant; indecent, obscene. **–ität**, *f.* frivolity, flippancy; obscenity.

froh, *adj.* glad, joyful, gay, happy; *– sein über* (*eine S.*) rejoice at, be pleased with, be glad about (a th.); *einer S.* (*Gen.*) *– werden*, take pleasure in *or* enjoy a th.; *–en Mutes*, cheerful; *–en Herzens*, glad of heart; *–e Nachricht*, glad news; *–e Botschaft*, good tidings. **–gemut**, *adj.*, *see* **–sinnig. –locken**, *v.n.* (*aux.* h.) rejoice, exult (at), triumph (over), shout for joy; (*B.*) *–locket dem Herrn!* rejoice in the Lord! **–mut**, *m.*, *see* **–sinn. –mütig**, *adj.*, *see* **–sinnig. –sinn**, *m.* cheerfulness, happy disposition. **–sinnig**, *adj.* cheerful, joyful, happy.

fröhlich, *adj.* cheerful, gay, happy, merry, joyous, joyful, gladsome. **–keit**, *f.* cheerfulness, mirth, hilarity, gaiety; gladness, joyfulness.

fromm, *adj.* (*comp.* -er, *sup.* -st, *also* frömmer, frömmst) pious, religious, godly, devout; innocent; harmless; good, gentle; artless; *–es Schaf*, poor simpleton; *–es Pferd*, quiet horse; *–er Wunsch*, pious hope, vain wish; *–er Eifer* or *–e Wut*, religious fanaticism; *–er Knecht*, goodly servant; *–er Held*, valiant hero; (*B.*) *–er und getreuer Diener*, good and faithful servant. **–en**, *v.n.* (*aux.* h.) (*Dat.*) (*archaic*) avail, profit, benefit, be of use; (*survives in*) *was kann es dir –en?* what does it profit you? what good is it to you? *zu Nutz und –en*, for the advantage of.

Frömm–elei, *f.* hypocrisy; bigotry. **–eln**, *v.n.* (*aux.* h.) affect piety. **–elnd**, *pr.p.* & *adj.* canting, hypocritical; *–elnde Sprache*, cant. **–igkeit**, *f.* piety, devoutness, godliness, innocence; meekness. **–ler**, *m.*, **–ling**, *m.* hypocrite; devotee.

Fron, *f.* (-en) compulsory, enforced *or* statute-labour; (*fig.*) drudgery. **–altar**, *m.* high (*or* holy) altar (*R.C.*). **–amt**, *n.* high mass (*R.C.*). **–arbeit**, *f.* socage, statute-labour; drudgery. **–bauer**, *m.* bondman, villein. **–bote**, *m.* beadle. **–dienst**, *m.* compulsory service, statute-labour, villeinage. **–e**, *f.* (-en), *see* **Fron. –en**, *v.n.* (*aux.* h.) slave, drudge. **–fasten**, *pl.* ember-weeks; quarter-fastings (*R.C.*). **–feste**, *f.* public jail. **–frei**, *adj.* exempt from compulsory service. **–geld**, *n.* money paid in lieu of statute-labour. **–herr**, *m.* feudal overlord (entitled to exact socage-service). **–hof**, *m.* socage-farm. **–knecht**, *m.* villein, serf. **–lehen**, *n.* socage-tenure. **–leichnam**, *m.* Corpus Christi. **–pflichtig**, *adj.* obliged to do statute-labour. **–vogt**, *m.* taskmaster. **–weise**, *adv.* in socage.

frön–en, *v.n.* (*aux.* h.) (*Dat.*) be a slave to, pander to (*vice, weakness, etc.*); *jemandes Launen –en* humour a p.'s whims; *der Trunkenheit –en*, be addicted to drink.

Front, *f.* (-en) front, face, frontage, forepart; (*the political use dates from before Nat. Soc., e.g.* Einheitsfront, *united workers' block*, Volksfront, *popular front. Nat. Soc. extended the meaning from 'political organization' or 'body' to include entire political activities of unorganized or quasi-organized sections of the community, e.g.* Arbeitsfront, *labour front* (*i.e. all the workers*), innere Front, *domestic front* (*i.e. propaganda fight against grumblers*)). **–abschnitt**, *m.* sector (*Mil.*). **–al**, *adj.* in *or* to the front, direct. **–alfeuer**, *n.* direct fire. **–angriff**, *m.* frontal attack. **–ausdehnung**, *f.* extent of front held. **–einbuchtung**, *f.* salient (*Mil.*). **–kämpfer**, *m.* front-line fighter, combat veteran. **–länge**, *f.* frontage, front. **–linie**, *f.*; *in –linie*, drawn up abreast (*Nav.*). **–soldat**, *m.*, *see* **–kämpfer. –stärke**, *f.* front-line strength. **–vorsprung**, *m.*, *see* **–einbuchtung. –zulage**, *f.* field allowance (*Mil.*).

fror, fröre, *see* **frieren.**

Frosch, *m.* (-es, ¨-e) frog; cracker (*Firew.*); nut, frog (*of the fiddle-bow*); (*coll.*) *ich habe einen – im Halse*, I have a frog in my throat, I am hoarse; (*coll.*) *sei kein –*, don't (you) be a kill-joy *or* wet-blanket, play the game. **–arten**, *pl.* batrachians, ranidae. **–biß**, *m.* frogbit (*Hydrocharis*) (*Bot.*). **–gequake**, *n.* croaking of frogs. **–keule**, *f.* hind leg of a frog. **–laich**, *m.* frog-spawn; (*sl.*) Scotch broth. **–perspektive**, *f.* 'worm's-eye view'. **–quappe**, *f.*, **–wurm**, *m.* tadpole.

Frost, *m.* (-es, ¨-e) frost; cold, chill, coldness; apathy; feverish shivering; *vom –(e) beschädigt*, frostbitten; *vor – beben*, shiver with cold. **–beule**, *f.* chilblain. **–fieber**, *n.* ague. **–ig**, *adj.* frosty; cold, chilly; cool, stand-offish; frigid (*of behaviour*); *–iger Empfang*, chilly reception. *–ige Antwort*, icy rejoinder. **–igkeit**, *f.* coolness. **–mischung**, *f.* freezing mixture. **–mittel**, *n.* frostbite remedy. **–punkt**, *m.* freezing-point. **–salbe**, *f.* chilblain ointment. **–schaden**, *m.* frost damage. **–schutzmittel**, *n.* anti-freezing agent. **–wetter**, *n.* frosty weather.

fröst–eln, 1. *v.a.* & *imp.* chill, make chilly, cause to shiver; freeze a little; *mich –elt*, I feel chilly, I am shivering, a chill *or* shudder runs down my spine. 2. *v.n.* & *imp.* shiver, feel chilly; *es –elt*, it freezes a little; *ich –ele*, I feel chilly. 3. *n.* shiver, chill; *ein –eln haben*, be shivering, shiver.

frottier–en, *v.a.* & *n.* rub down. **–(hand)tuch**, *n.* bath-towel, Turkish towel.

Frucht, *f.* (¨-e) fruit, crop, harvest; produce; corn, grain; result, effect, product, profit; embryo, foetus (*Med.*); *eingemachte ¨-e*, preserves; *– der Liebe*, love-child. **–abtreibungsmittel**, *n.* abortifacient. **–achse**, *f.* axis of the embryo (*Med.*). **–acker**, *m.* corn-field. **–ansetzen**, *n.* germination. **–auge**, *n.* bud, germ. **–bar**, *adj.* fruitful, fertile, prolific, productive. **–barkeit**, *f.* fruitfulness, fertility, fecundity. **–barmachung**, *f.* fertilization. **–bau**, *m.* cultivation of crops. **–beet**, *n.* hotbed (*of manure*). **–bildung**, *f.* fructification. **–boden**, *m.* placenta, thalamus (*Anat. Bot.*); receptacle (*Bot.*). **–bonbon**, *m.* fruit drop *or* pastille, boiled sweet. **–brand**, *m.* corn-blight; ergot. **–bringend**, *adj.* productive, fertile, fruit-bearing. **–en**, *v.n.* (*aux.* h.) be of use *or* profit, have effect, avail; bear fruit. **–fleisch**, *n.* fruit pulp. **–folge**, *f.*, *see* **–wechsel. –garten**, *m.* orchard. **–gehänge**, *n.*, **–gewinde**, *n.* festoon of fruit (*Arch.*). **–göttin**, *f.* Pomona (*of trees*), Ceres (*of crops*). **–gülte**, *f.* rent to be paid in corn. **–halter**, *m.* matrix, uterus. **–handel**, *m.* fruit-trade; corn-trade. **–haus**, *n.* granary; hothouse. **–häutchen**, *n.* epicarp. **–horn**, *n.* cornucopia. **–hülle**, *f.* husk, pericarp, (*Bot.*); foetal envelope (*Anat.*). **–hülse**, *f.* pod, husk, shell. **–keim**, *m.* germ; embryo. **–kelch**, *m.* calyx (*Bot.*). **–kern**, *m.* kernel. **–knospe**, *f.*, *see* **–auge. –knoten**, *m.* seed-bud, ovary (*Bot.*). **–kopf**, *m.* foetal head (*Anat.*). **–korn**, *n.* seed-corn. **–kuchen**, *m.* foetal placenta (*Anat.*). **–lese**, *f.* harvest, harvesting, gathering (*crops*). **–los**, *adj.* fruitless; sterile; barren; useless, unavailing. **–losigkeit**, *f.* fruitlessness. **–makler**, *m.* cornbroker. **–messer**, 1. *m.* corn-measure. 2. *n.* fruit-knife. **–monat**, *m.* September. **–mus**, *n.* purée. **–presse**, *f.* fruit squeezer *or* press. **–reife**, *f.* fruitage. **–röhre**, *f.* pistil (*Bot.*). **–saft**, *m.* fruit-juice. **–scheuer**, *f.*, **–scheune**, *f.* barn, granary. **–speicher**, *m.* corn-loft, granary. **–tragend,** *adj.* fruit-bearing. **–ung,** *f.* germination, fertilization. **–ungskern,** *m.* fertilized egg. **–ungsvermögen,** *n.* fertility. **–wasser,** *n.* amnion fluid (*Anat.*). **–wechsel,** *m.* rotation of crops. **–zehnte,** *m.* tithe in corn. **–zins,** *m.* rent paid in corn. **–zucker,** *m.* fructose (*Chem.*).

Früchtchen, *n. dim. of* **Frucht**; (*coll.*) scamp, scapegrace.

frug, früge, *see* **fragen.**

früh–(e), *adj.* early; in the morning; soon, speedy; premature; *– morgens, am –en Morgen,* early in the morning; *heute –,* (early) this morning; *morgen –,* tomorrow morning; *übermorgen –,* early the day after tomorrow; *–e Morgenstunden,* small hours (of the morning); *–er Tod,* early *or* untimely death; *– genug ankommen,* arrive in (good) time; *von – bis spät,* from morning till evening, all day long; (*Prov.*) *– ins Bett und – heraus, frommt dem Leib, dem Geist, dem Haus,* early to bed and early to rise makes a man healthy, wealthy, and wise. **–apfel,** *m.* summer apple. **–aufsteher,** *m.* early riser. **–beet,** *n.* hotbed. **–e,** *f.* early hour; (early) morning; *in der –e,* (early) in the morning; *in aller –e,* very early, the first th. in the morning; *bis in die* or *der –,* till the early hours. **–er,** 1. *adj.* (*comp. of* früh) earlier; prior, former; *in –er als 8 Tagen,* in less than 8 days. 2. *adv.* earlier, sooner; formerly, at one time. **–estens,** *adv.* as early as possible; at the earliest; not before, not earlier than. **–gebet,** *n.* morning prayer, matins. **–geburt,** *f.* premature birth. **–gottesdienst,** *m.* morning service. **–jahr,** *n.* spring. **–jahrs–,** *pref.* spring, vernal. **–jahrs(tag-und)nachtgleiche,** *f.* vernal equinox. **–kaffee,** *m.* early morning coffee. **–klug,** *adj.* precocious. **–ling,** *m.* spring; (*fig.*) youth, early prime; animal born in spring; child born too soon. **–lings–,** *pref., see* **–jahrs–.** **–lingshaft,** *adj.*, **–lingsmäßig,** *adj.* spring-like. **–messe,** *f.* early mass, matins. **–mette,** *f.* matins. **–reif,** 1. *adj.* precocious, forward, premature; *–reife Früchte,* forced fruit. 2. *m.* morning frost. **–reife,** *f.* precocity, forwardness, prematurity, earliness (*of ripening*). **–rot,** *n.* dawn, sunrise. **–saat,** *f.* first sowing. **–schoppen,** *m.* morning pint. **–sprenger,** *m.* premature burst (*Artil.*). **–stadium,** *n.* early stage. **–steinzeitlich,** *adj.* paleolithic. **–stück,** *n.* breakfast. **–stücken,** *v.a.* & *n.* breakfast, take breakfast. **–treiberei,** *f.* forcing (*plants*). **–zeit,** *f.* early morning; early epoch; prime. **–zeitig,** *adj.* early, in good time; forward, premature; untimely. **–zeitigkeit,** *f.* precocity; untimeliness. **–zug,** *m.* early *or* morning train. **–zündung,** *f.* premature ignition (*Artil.*); advanced ignition (*Motor.*).

Fuchs, *m.* (-es, ¨e) fox; fox fur; chestnut bay (*horse*), sorrel horse; tortoise-shell butterfly (*Vanessa*) (*Ent.*); red-haired p.; cunning, false *or* sly p.; freshman, (*sl.*) fresher (*Univ.*); fluke (*Bill, etc.*); (*coll.*) *goldener – or Gold–,* gold piece, gold coin; (*coll.*) *alter –,* cunning old devil; (*Studs. sl.*) *krasser –,* raw fresher (*in his first term*); (*Prov.*) *wer den – fangen will, muß früh aufstehen,* the early bird catches the worm. **–affe,** *f.* lemur (*Zool.*). **–balg,** *m.* fox-skin. **–bau,** *m.* foxes' hole, earth, kennel. **–en,** *v.a.* & *r.* (*coll.*) annoy, vex; play a trick on. **–er,** *m.* stock-jobber; fluker. **–grube,** *f.*, **–höhle,** *f.* hole *or* earth of a fox. **–ig,** *adj.* foxy red; (*sl.*) furious. **–jagd,** *f.* foxhunt. **–jäger,** *m.* foxhunter. **–loch,** *n.* funkhole (*Mil.*). **–major,** *m.* older student who looks after the freshers (*in a students' club*). **–pelz,** *m.* fur of a fox; *den –pelz anziehen,* use a dodge. **–rot,** *adj.* foxy red. **–schwanz,** *m.* 1. brush (*tail of a fox*); 2. love-lies bleeding (*Amarantus caudatus*) (*Bot.*); fox-tail grass (*Alopecurus*) (*Bot.*); 3. padsaw. *den –schwanz streichen* or **–schwänzen,** *v.n.*, flatter, fawn, toady, wheedle. **–schwänzer,** *m.* fawner, toady, sycophant. **–stute,** *f.* sorrel mare. (*coll.*) **–(teufels)wild,** *adj.* exceedingly angry, furious.

Füchsin, *f.* vixen.

Fuchsia, Fuchsie, *f.* (-n) fuchsia (*Onagraceae*) (*Bot.*).

Fucht–el, *f.* (-n) sword blade; rod, ferrule; blow; whipping; strict discipline; *einen unter der –el haben* or *in die –el bekommen,* keep a p. under one's thumb. **–eln,** 1. *v.a.* strike with the flat of the sword; beat, whip. 2. *v.n.* (*aux.* h.) brandish a sword *or* switch; gesticulate. **–ig,** *adj.* (*dial.*) angry, furious.

Fuder, *n.* (-s, –) load, cart-load; large measure for wine (*800–1,800 litres according to locality*). **–weise,** *adj.* by cart-loads.

Fug, *m.* (*now used in the phrases*) *mit –,* fittingly, justly; *mit – und Recht,* with full right *or* authority; *mit gutem –,* with good reason. **–e,** *f.* (-en) joint, seam; gap, space (*where bricks, etc., should join*); suture (*Anat., Bot.*); *aus den –en bringen,* put out of joint, unhinge; *die Zeit ist aus den –en,* the times are out of joint; *aus den –en gehen,* fall to pieces. **–en,** *v.a.* & *n.* (*aux.* h.) join, fit together. **–endichtung,** *f.* sealing of joints.

Fug–e, *f.* (-en) fugue (*Mus.*) **–enhaft,** *adj.*, **–iert,** *adj.* fugued, fuguing, fugal (*Mus.*).

füg–en, 1. *v.a.* fit together, join, unite; ordain, will, direct, dispose; add; *wie Gott es –t,* as God ordains. 2. *v.r.* accommodate o.s. to; acquiesce in, submit to; be fitted, suitable *or* proper; come to pass, happen; chance; coincide; *sich in eine S. –en,* accommodate o.s. to *or* submit to a th.; *was sich –t,* what is fitting *or* seemly; *wie es sich –t,* as occasion demands. **–ewort,** *n.* conjunction. **–lich,** *adv.* conveniently, appropriately, properly, rightly, suitably, reasonably, pertinent; *er hätte –lich schweigen können,* he might well have held his tongue; *er konnte es nicht –lich vermeiden,* he could not well avoid it. **–lichkeit,** *f.* suitableness, fitness; pertinence, justice. **–sam,** *adj.* adaptive; pliant, supple, yielding, tractable, docile, obedient, submissive, agreeable. **–samkeit,** *f.* suppleness, submission. **–ung,** *f.* fitting together, joining; joint, articulation; arrangement; dispensation, decree; coincidence, juncture; submission, resignation; *durch eine –ung Gottes,* providentially.

fühl–en, 1. *v.a.* & *n.* (*aux.* h.) feel, perceive, sense, be sensitive to; experience, be aware of; *einem den Puls –en,* feel a p.'s pulse; *einem auf den Zahn –en,* sound a p.'s opinion; *alles, was lebt, –t,* every living creature has perceptions; *Lust –en,* be inclined; *vorher–en,* have a presentiment. 2. *v.r.* feel, have a feeling, consider *or* believe o.s. to be, be conscious of one's worth; *sich müde –en,* feel tired; *sich wohl –en,* feel content, comfortable *or* at ease. 3. *n.* feeling, perception, sensation. **–bar,** *adj.* sensible, tangible, perceptible, susceptible, palpable, tactile, marked, felt. **–barkeit,** *f.* sensibility, susceptibility; perceptibility; tangibility. **–eisen,** *n.* probe (*Surg.*). **–end,** *pr.p.* & *adj.* sensitive; feeling; susceptible. **–er,** *m.* feeler, antenna, tentacle (*Zool.*); (*also fig.*) *die –er ausstrecken,* put out a feeler. **–faden,** *m.*, **–horn,** *n.* feeler (*of insects*). **–kraft,** *f.* faculty of perception, susceptibility. **–los,** *adj.* unreceptive, insensitive (*gegen,* to). **–ung,** *f.* feeling; touch, contact (*Mil.*); feel (*of cloth*); *–ung mit dem Feinde bekommen,* come into touch with the enemy; *in enger –ung mit,* in close touch with; *–ung halten,* keep in touch, maintain contact; *–ung nehmen* (*mit*), get into touch (with). **–ungnahme,** *f.* close touch, contact.

fuhr, führe, *see* **fahren.**

Fuhr–e, *f.* (-en) cart-load, wagon-load; carrying, transport, conveyance; *–e Heu,* load of hay. **–amt,** *n.* transport office. **–geschäft,** *n.* firm of carriers *or* hauliers. **–knecht,** *m.* carter's man, carter. **–lohn,** *m.* carriage, freight, charge for delivery. **–mann,** *m.* carrier, carter, driver, wagoner. **–park,** *m.* transport park (*Mil.*). **–parkkolonne,** *f.* transport and supply column. **–schlitten,** *m.* transport sledge. **–weg,** *m.* highway, roadway. **–wagen,** *m.* freight-wagon. **–werk,** *n.* cart, wagon, vehicle. **–werken,** *v.n.* run a transport business; (*coll.*) fidget, create a disturbance. **–wesen,** *n.* carrying trade; (*coll.*) vehicles; *das –wesen bei einem Heere,* baggage *or* wagon train of an army.

führ–en, 1. *v.a.* conduct, lead, guide, direct, convey, carry, bring; handle, manage, control; drive; deal (*a blow, etc.*); keep (*books*); bear (*a name, title, etc.*); show (*proof*). *den Artikel –en wir nicht,* we do not sell *or* keep that article; *die Aufsicht –en,* superintend; invigilate (*at examinations*); *bei sich –en,* carry about one; *die Bücher –en,* keep the books *or* accounts; *auf das Eis* or *Glatteis –en*, lead into danger; *das Angefangene zu Ende –en*, carry what one has begun through to the end; *die Feder –en*, wield the pen, write; *zu Gemüte –en*, impress on the mind; *zum Munde –en*, raise to one's lips; *ein Gespräch –en*, hold a conversation; *die Haushaltung –en*, run the household; *Klage –en*, complain (*über*, of), bring forward a complaint (*about*); *Krieg –en*, wage war; *aus dem Lande –en*, export; *ins Land –en*, import; *ein Leben –en*, lead a life; *einen hinters Licht –en*, impose on a p.; *mit sich –en* have with one, carry on one's person; *er –te ihn gefangen mit sich*, he led him captive; *die Hand an die Mütze –en*, touch one's cap; *zu nichts –en*, come *or* lead to nothing; *Protokoll –en*, keep the minutes; *sein Rad –en*, wheel one's bicycle; *sonderbare Reden –en*, say strange things, be given to strange utterances; *das Ruder*, *das Regiment*, *die Regierung –en*, sit at the helm, govern, rule; (*also fig.*) have the whip hand (*over*); *ein Schiff –en*, navigate a ship; *im Schilde –en*, have an intention *or* plan; *das Schwert –en*, wear, wield *or* handle the sword; *eine Dame zu Tisch –en*, take a lady in to dinner; *zum Tode –en*, prove fatal; *er –te seine Truppen über die Brücke*, he marched his troops across the bridge; *eine Mauer –en um einen Ort*, enclose a place with a wall; *in Versuchung –en*, lead into temptation; *den Vorsitz –en*, take the chair; *ein Wappen –en*, bear *or* have a coat of arms; *den Beweis –en*, prove, furnish proof; *Waren –en*, have goods in stock, deal in goods; *auf den rechten Weg –en*, put on the right road; *das Wort –en*, be spokesman; *wohin soll das –en?* where is that going to lead us? what are we coming to? *das große Wort –en*, brag, boast; lay down the law; *einen Prozeß –en*, carry on a lawsuit, plead a cause. 2. *v.r.* conduct o.s., behave. **–bar,** *adj.* transportable; manageable. **–er,** *m.* leader; guide; guide-book; conductor; director, manager; chief; driver; pilot (*Av.*); commander (*Nav.*); fugue-theme (*Mus.*). (*Nat. Soc. decree forbade use of the word unless in compounds except for Adolf Hitler. It was the usual way of referring to him, and had the same sort of aura as 'His Majesty'*); **–erprinzip,** *n.* authoritarian principle. **–erschaft,** *f.* guidance, leadership, direction; the leaders. **–erschein,** *m.* driving-licence; pilot's certificate. **–ersitz,** *m.* driving seat, cab; cockpit (*Av.*). **–ung,** *f.* leading, conducting, guiding; conduct, behaviour; leadership; guidance, direction, command, management; keeping (*of books*); *persönliche –ung*, personal record. **–ungszeugnis,** *n.* certificate of good conduct; character, reference.

Füll–e, *f.* abundance; profusion, plenty, fullness, plumpness; intensity, body, depth; *Hülle und –e haben*, have abundance, live at one's ease; *in Hülle und –e*, plentiful, plenty (of). **–en,** *v.a.* fill, fill up, put in, inflate, pour in, charge; *wieder –en*, replenish; *auf Flaschen –en*, bottle. **–apparat,** *m.* filling-apparatus, bottling machine. **–element,** *n.* dry-cell (*Elec.*). **–erde,** *f.* fuller's earth. **–feder,** *f.*, **–federhalter,** *m.* fountain-pen. **–haar,** *n.* hair used for stuffing. **–horn,** *n.* horn of plenty, cornucopia. **–kelle,** *f.* filling-trowel; ladle. **–masse,** *f.* filling material, filling, packing. **–pulver,** *n.* filling charge, TNT (*Artil.*). **–röhre,** *f.* feed-pipe. **–säure,** *f.* accumulator acid, electrolyte. **–sel,** *n.* stopgap, stuffing (*Cook.*). **–strich,** *m.* filling level *or* mark. **–trichter,** *m.* hopper, funnel. **–ung,** *f.* filling, packing; stuffing (*Cook.*), stopping (*Dentist.*); panelling; contents; charge; doubling (*of blossom*) (*Hort.*). **–wort,** *n.* expletive.

Füllen, 1. *n.* (-s, –) foal, filly (*fem.*); colt (*masc.*). 2. *v.n.* (*aux.* h.) foal. **–stute,** *f.* brood-mare. **–zucht,** *f.* foal-breeding.

fummeln, *v.a.* polish; *v.n.* (*coll.*) fumble, grope about.

Fund, *m.* (-(e)s, -e) finding, discovery; thing found, find; *einen – tun*, make a find *or* a discovery. **–büro,** *n.* lost property office. **–geld,** *n.* finder's reward. **–grube,** *f.* mine, shaft (*Min.*); (*fig.*) fund, mine, storehouse, source (*of information, etc.*). **–ort,** *m.* place where a th. is found; locality, habitat (*Bot.*, *Orn.*, *Zool.*). **–recht,** *n.* finder's rights. **–stätte,** *f.* place of discovery.

Fund–ament, *n.* (-s, -e) foundation, basis, base. **–amentalsatz,** *m.* fundamental principle. **–amentalstimme,** *f.* fundamental note (*Mus.*). **–amentieren,** *v.a.* lay the foundation. **–ation,** *f.* foundation, establishment. **–ieren,** *v.a.* found, endow; lay a foundation; establish, consolidate. **–iert,** *p.p.* & *adj.* well-founded, consolidated. **–ierung,** *f.* founding; foundation, establishment, funding.

fündig, *adj.* ore *or* oil bearing, economically worth while (*of a mine, etc.*).

fünf, (*dial.*) **–e** (*when not followed by anything*), *num. adj.* five; *– vom hundert*, five per cent.; *– gerade sein lassen*, wink at a th., be not over-particular; *das –te Rad am Wagen sein*, be superfluous, be in the way *or* not wanted. **–(e),** *f.* (-en), **–er,** *m.* the number five; cinque (*at dice*); fives (*a game*); the lowest mark (*at school*), very poor; a piece *or* note of five (marks, florins, francs, etc.), five pfennig piece, fiver. **–eck,** *n.* pentagon. **–eckig,** *adj.* pentagonal. **–elektrodenröhre,** *f.* pentode (*Rad.*). **–erausschuß,** *m.* committee of five. **–erlei,** *indec. adj.* of five (*sorts, ways, etc.*); *das Wort kann –erlei bedeuten*, the word can have five meanings. **–fach,** *adj.* quintuple, fivefold; *das –fache*, five times the amount. **–füßler,** *m.* pentameter. **–gesang,** *m.* quintet. **–gitterröhre,** *f.* pentagrid (*Rad.*). **–jährig,** *adj.* five-year (-old). **–jährlich,** *adj.* every five years, quinquennial. **–kantig,** *adj.* pentagonal. **–klang,** *m.* fifth (*Mus.*). **–mal,** five times. **–prozentig,** *adj.* of, at *or* yielding five per cent. **–seitig,** *adj.* pentahedral. **–silbig,** *adj.* pentasyllabic. **–stellig,** *adj.* of five digits. **–stimmig,** *adj.* (arranged) for five voices. **–stöckig,** *adj.* five-storied. **–t,** *num. adj.* fifth; *eine –te*, a fifth (*Mus.*). **–tehalb,** *num. adj.* four and a half. **–tel,** *n.* fifth part. **–teln,** *v.a.* divide into fifths. **–tens,** *adv.* fifthly, in the fifth place. **–uhrtee,** *m.* afternoon tea. **–zehn** (*dial.* **funfzehn**) *num. adj.* fifteen. **–zehntel,** *n.* fifteenth (part). **–zig,** (*dial.* **funfzig**) *num. adj.* fifty; *er ist in den –zige(r)n*, he is in the fifties, between fifty and sixty. **–ziger,** *m.* a man of fifty years; wine of the year 1950; *ein vorgerückter –ziger*, a man in the late fifties; *–zigjähriger Mann*, a man of fifty; *–zigjährige Feier*, fiftieth anniversary, golden jubilee. **–zigst,** *num. adj.* fiftieth. **–zigstel,** *n.* fiftieth part. **–zöllig,** *adj.* five inches long.

fungieren, *v.n.* (*aux.* h.) act, function, behave; officiate; discharge (*an office*).

fungös, *adj.* fungous, spongy.

Funk, *m.* (-s) radio, wireless. **–anlage,** *f.* wireless installation. **–apparat,** *m.* wireless set. **–ausstellung,** *f.* wireless exhibition. **–bake,** *f.* radio beacon. **–bastler,** *m.* radio amateur, (*sl.*) ham; home constructor (*of wireless set*). **–betrieb,** *m.* wireless service. **–dienst,** *m.* wireless telegraphic service. **–e,** *m.* (-en, -en), **–en,** *m.* (-ens, -en) spark, sparkle, flash, gleam, scintillation; (*fig.*) bit, particle, jot; (*often dim.* **⁼chen,** *n.*). **–eln,** 1. *v.n.* (*aux.* h.) sparkle, glitter, glisten, twinkle, scintillate, shine, flash. 2. *n.* sparkling; coruscation. **–el(nagel)neu** *adj.*, brand-new. **–empfang,** *m.* wireless reception. **–empfänger,** *m.* wireless receiver. **–en,** *v.a.* broadcast, wireless, transmit. **–enbildung,** *f.* sparking. **–engarbe,** *f.* shower of sparks. **–engeber,** *m.* sparking coil *or* device. **–enentladung,** *f.* spark discharge. **–enfänger,** *m.* spark-catcher (*on locomotives, etc.*). **–enholz,** *n.* touchwood, tinder. **–eninduktor,** *m.* induction coil. **–ensprühend,** *adj.* sparkling, scintillating. **–entelegraphie,** *f.* wireless *or* radio telegraphy. **–er,** *m.* radio-operator, wireless operator, telegraphist. **–feuer,** *n.* radio beacon. **–frequenz,** *f.* radio-frequency. **–gerät,** *n.*, *see* **–apparat.** **–meßstelle,** *f.* radiolocation station. **–messung,** *f.* radiolocation. **–ortung,** *f.* radiolocation. **–peilung,** *f.* radio direction finding. **–röhre,** *f.* wireless valve. **–sender,** *m.* wireless transmitter. **–spruch,** *m.* wireless message, radiogram. **–sprühen,** *n.* scintillation, emission of sparks. **–station,** *f.*, **–stelle,** *f.* wireless station, radio (direction finding) station, broadcasting station. **–strecke,** *f.* spark gap. **–turm,** *m.* wireless mast, radio tower. **–ver-**

bindung, *f.*, **–verkehr,** *m.* wireless *or* radio communication. **–wesen,** *n.* broadcasting. **–zeitung,** *f.* published wireless programme (= *Radio Times*). **–zündung,** *f.* spark ignition.

Funktion, *f.* (-en) function (*also Math.*); *sich in – befinden*, exercise a function; *in – treten*, act, serve, function, officiate. **–är,** *m.* functionary, official. **–ieren,** *v.n.* (*aux.* h.) act, function, operate; (*coll.*) work. **–ierend,** *adj.* in working order. **–sbedingung,** *f.* conditions of activity. **–swert,** *m.* functional value. **–szulage,** *f.* additional emolument, perquisite.

Funsel, *f.* (-) (*coll.*) miserable lamp, guttering candle.

für, 1. *prep.* (*Acc.*) for; instead of, in lieu of; per, in favour of; for the sake of, for the benefit of, on behalf of; in return for, against; *ein – allemal*, once and for all; *an und – sich*, in itself, taken by itself, in the abstract; *–s erste*, in the first place, for the present; *– Ernst halten*, take seriously; *es – gut halten*, consider it (to be) a good thing, deem it advisable; *ich habe es – mein Leben gern*, I like it above all things; *das – und Wider*, the pros and cons; *ich – meine Person*, as for me, I for my part, I for one; *es – einen Schimpf achten*, consider it as an affront; *– sich arbeiten*, work for o.s.; *es hat etwas – sich*, there is s.th. about *or* in it, there is s.th. to be said for it; *– sich leben*, live alone *or* privately; *– sich sprechen*, speak in an undertone; *das ist eine S. – sich*, that is a matter apart; *Stück – Stück*, piece by piece, taken individually; *Tag (Jahr) – Tag (Jahr)* day (year) by *or* after day (year); *was waren das – Fragen?* what kind of questions were those? *was – ein Mann?* what sort of a man? *was – Leute auch da sein mögen*, whatever kind of people may be there; *er hat viele Bücher, aber was – welche!* he has a lot of books, but what trash! *Wort – Wort*, word by word, one word at a time. 2. *adv.* (*Poet. & archaic instead of* vor; *e.g. sich herfür drängen, fürnehm, fürtrefflich*) *– und –*, for ever and ever. (*archaic*) **–baß,** *adv.* further, forward, on. **–bitte,** *f.* intercession; *eine –bitte einlegen*, intercede; *öffentliche –bitte*, public prayers. **–erst,** (*archaic*) *see* **vorerst. –liebnehmen,** *ir.v.n.* (*mit*), be content *or* put up (with); *er nimmt mit allem –lieb*, he puts up with anything; *see* **vorlieb. –sorge,** *f.* precaution; care, solicitude; provision; *liebevolle –sorge*, loving care; *soziale –sorge*, public relief, social welfare, social service. **–sorgeamt,** *n.* public relief *or* welfare office. **–sorgeerziehung,** *f.* child welfare work. **–sorgerin,** *f.* welfare worker, social worker. **–sorgestelle,** *f.*, *see* **–sorgeamt. –sprache,** *f.* intercession; defence (*Law*). **–sprech,** *m.* (*Swiss*) advocate. **–sprechen,** *ir.v.a.* speak in favour of, intercede for. **–sprecher,** *m.* intercessor; advocate. **–wahr,** *adv.* truly, in truth, indeed, verily, forsooth. **–witz,** *m.* pertness, inquisitiveness; *see* **Vorwitz. –wort,** *n.* pronoun.

Furag–e, *f.* forage; fodder. **–eur,** *m.* forager. **–ieren,** *v.n.* (*aux.* h.) go foraging. **–ierungskommando,** *n.* foraging party. **–ierzug,** *m.* foraging expedition.

Furch–e, *f.* (-en) furrow; wrinkle, groove, channel; ridge; **–en,** *v.a.* furrow, plough up; wrinkle, crease, groove, knit (*the brow, etc.*). **–enbildung,** *f.* segmentation, furrowing, cleavage. **–enrain,** *m.* ridge. **–enweise,** *adj.* in furrows. **–ig,** *adj.* furrowed.

Furcht, *f.* (*no pl.*) fear, anxiety, terror, dread, fright, awe; *in – setzen*, terrify, frighten; *– haben*, be afraid; *– vor einem haben*, stand in fear of a p.; *außer sich vor –*, frightened out of one's senses *or* wits; *aus – vor einem Unfalle*, for fear of an accident; *einem – einflößen*, intimidate *or* frighten a p. **–bar,** *adj.* frightful, terrible, awful, dreadful; formidable, fearful; (*coll.*) *er ist –bar klug (freundlich)* he is awfully clever (kind). **–erregend,** *adj.* frightening. **–los,** *adj.* fearless, intrepid. **–losigkeit,** *f.* fearlessness. **–sam,** *adj.* timid, timorous, nervous, fearful, faint-hearted; *–sam machen*, dishearten, intimidate, abash. **–samkeit,** *f.* timidity, faintheartedness; cowardice.

fürcht–en, 1. *v.a. & n.* (*aux.* h.) fear, be afraid of; dread, stand in awe of; *es ist* or *steht zu –en*, it is to be feared. 2. *v.r.* be afraid, stand in fear (*vor*, of). **–erlich,** *adj.* fearful, frightful, horrible, terrible, dreadful, horrid. **–erlichkeit,** *f.* awfulness, frightfulness.

fürder (*archaic*) 1. *adj.* further, onwards. 2. *adv.* henceforward; further.

Furie, *f.* (-n) fury, termagant.

Furier, *m.* (-s, -e) quartermaster-sergeant (*Mil.*).

Furnier, *n.* (-s, -e) veneer. **–en,** *v.a.* inlay, veneer. **–holz,** *n.* wood for inlaying, veneer.

Furore, *n.* sensation; (*sl.*) noise, splash; *der Künstler hat – gemacht*, the artist has created (quite) a sensation.

Fürst, *m.* (-en, -en) prince, sovereign. **–en,** *v.a.* exalt to the rank of prince (*only used in p.p.*). **–entum,** *n.* (-s, ¨er) principality. **–in,** *f.* princess. **–lich,** *adj.* princely; *–liche Durchlaucht*, Serene Highness; (*also fig.*) *–liche Einkünfte*, princely income. **–lichkeit,** *f.* princeliness; magnificence; (*pl.*) princely personages. **–bischof,** *m.* prince-bishop (*with sovereign rights*). **–endiener,** *m.* server of princes; courtier. **–engut,** *n.* crown lands. **–enhaus,** *n.* **–enstamm,** *m.* royal line, dynasty. **–enstand,** *m.* princely rank. **–enwürde,** *f.* sovereign dignity. **–entag,** *m.* diet *or* assembly of princes.

Furt, *f.* (-en) ford.

Furunkel, *m.* (-s, –) furuncle, boil (*Med.*).

Furz, *m.* (-es, ¨e) (*vulg.*) fart. **–en,** *v.n.* fart.

fusch–eln, –en, *v.n.* (*aux.* h.) 1. handle dexterously, make rapid *or* cunning movement (*usually with intent to deceive*); 2. (*dial.*) *see* **pfuschen. –erei,** *f.* sleight-of-hand.

Fusel, *m.* fusel oil; bad *or* unrefined spirits. **–ig,** *adj.* containing fusel oil.

Füsilier, *m.* (-s, -e) (*archaic*) light-infantry soldier, fusilier. **–en,** *v.a.* execute by shooting *or* by firing squad (*Mil.*). **–batallion,** *n.* third battalion in a German infantry regiment.

Fusion, *f.* (-en) fusion, amalgamation, merging.

Fusionspunkt, *m.* fusion *or* melting point.

Fuß, *m.* (-es, ¨e) foot, tarsus (*Anat.*); footing, basis, base; leg (*of chair, etc.*); pedestal; bottom; pedal; stem (*of a glass*); foot (*measure*); *auf den Füßen*, up, not in bed, on one's legs; *auf die Füße bringen*, raise (*troops, etc.*); *sich die Füße abrennen*, run o.s. off one's feet; *sein Haus mit keinem – mehr betreten*, never set foot in his house again; *der Boden brennt mir unter den Füßen*, it's getting too hot for me; *einem den Boden unter den Füßen entziehen*, cut the ground from under a p.'s feet; *den Boden unter den Füßen verlieren*, have the ground cut from under one's feet; *festen –es*, without stirring, unflinchingly; *fest auf den Füßen*, sure-footed; *(festen) – fassen*, gain a (firm) footing, establish o.s.; *einem auf dem –e folgen*, follow hard on a p.'s heels; *auf freiem –e*, at liberty, at large; *auf freien – setzen*, set at liberty; *auf gleichem –e*, on the same footing, on equal terms; *auf großem – leben*, live in grand style; *auf gutem –e stehen*, be on good terms (with); *die S. hat weder Hand noch –*, the th. is without rhyme or reason; *er wehrte sich* or *sträubte sich mit Händen und Füßen*, he defended himself tooth and nail; *einem auf die Füße helfen*, help a p. up, assist a p.; (*coll.*) *er ist (heute) mit dem linken –e zuerst aufgestanden*, (today) he got out of bed on the wrong side, he is irritable or bad-tempered; *sich (Dat.) den – verstauchen*, sprain one's ankle; *auf eigenen Füßen stehen*, be self-supporting *or* independent; *auf schwachen Füßen*, on a weak, unsound *or* shaky foundation; *auf gespanntem –e mit einem*, on bad terms with a p.; *stehenden –es*, immediately; *mehrere – hoch*, several feet high; *mit dem –e stoßen*, kick; *einem auf die Füße treten*, tread on a p.'s toes (*lit. or fig.*) *or* corns (*only fig.*); offend unintentionally; *mit Füßen (unter die Füße) treten*, trample upon; spurn; *trocknen –es*, dry-shod; *sich auf die Füße machen*, take to one's heels; *auf vertrautem –e*, on intimate terms; *vor die Füße werfen*, reject with disdain; *zu –*, on foot; *zu – gehen*, go on foot; walk; *Soldat zu –*, foot-soldier; *schlecht zu –e sein*, be a poor walker, be bad on one's feet; *sich einem zu Füßen werfen*, throw o.s. at a p.'s feet; *sich die Füße wund laufen*, get blisters on one's feet.

-abstreifer, *m.* door-mat, scraper. **-angel,** *f.* man-trap. **-ball,** *m.* football. **-ballen,** *m.* ball of the foot. **-ballmannschaft,** *f.* football team. **-ballspieler,** *m.* football-player, footballer. **-bänder,** *n.pl.* tarsal ligaments; jesses (*Falconry*). **-bank,** *f.* footstool. **-bekleidung,** *f.* footwear. **-beuge,** *f.* **-biege,** *f.* instep. **-blatt,** *n.* flat *or* sole of the foot. **-blech,** *n.* snatch block. **-boden,** *m.* floor; ground; flooring. **-bodenfarbe,** *f.* floor stain. **-bodenwachs,** *n.* floor polish. **-brand,** *m.* trench foot (*Med.*). **-breit,** *m.*; *ein –breit Landes,* a foot of ground; *keinen –breit weichen,* not budge an inch. **-bremse,** *f.* foot-brake (*Motor.*). **-brett,** *n.* pedal. **-decke,** *f.* coverlet (*for the feet*); travelling-rug; bed-side rug. **-eisen,** *n.* trap; fetters, shackles; shoe iron, calkin (*on shoes, etc.*). **-en,** 1. *v.n.* (*aux.* h.) set, have *or* place one's foot on; get a footing, perch, light; depend, rely, rest, stand (*auf,* on). 2. *v.a.* build, base, found (*auf,* on). **-ende,** *n.* foot (*of a bed, etc.*). **-fall,** *m.* prostration; *einen –fall tun vor,* fall prostrate at the feet of. **-fällig,** *adj.* prostrate, on one's knees; *–fällig bitten,* plead humbly. **-fest,** *adj.* sure-footed. **-flasche,** *f.* hot-water bottle, foot-warmer. **-freies Kleid,** skirt that leaves the feet free, ankle-length skirt. **-gänger,** *m.* pedestrian. **-garde,** *f.* footguards (*Mil.*). **-gelenk,** *n.* ankle; fetlock. **-gestell,** *n.* pedestal, base, foot. **-gewölbe,** *n.* arch of the foot; plantar arch (*Arch.*). **-hebel,** *m.* pedal (*Motor.*). **-klaue,** *f.* claw. **-klaviatur,** *f.* pedals (of an organ). **-knöchel,** *m.* ankle bone. **-krank,** *adj.* footsore (*Mil.*). **-kranz,** *m.* base (*of a column*). **-lappen,** *m.* foot wrapping (*to replace socks*); (*sl.*) cabbage (*Mil.*). **-maß,** *n.* size (*of shoes or socks*). **-note,** *f.* footnote, annotation. **-pflege,** *f.* chiropody. **-punkt,** *m.* nadir. **-register,** *n.* pedal-stop (*Organ*). **-reiniger,** *m.* scraper, door-mat. **-reise,** *f.* walking-tour. **-rücken,** *m.* instep. **-sack,** *m.* foot-muff. **-schemel,** *m.* footstool. **-sicher,** *adj.* sure-footed. **-sohle,** *f.* sole of the foot. **-spann,** *m.* instep. **-spitze,** *f.* tiptoe. **-spur,** *f.* footprint, footstep, footmark, track. **-standbild,** *n.* pedestrian statue. **-(s)tapfe,** *f.*, *see* **-spur.** **-steig,** *m.* footway, footpath, (*Amer.*) sidewalk. **-stütze,** *f.* foot-rest. **-taste,** *f.* organ-pedal. **-tour,** *f.* walking-tour. **-tritt,** *m.* kick; step, footboard (*of carriages*). **-volk,** *n.* foot-soldiers, infantry. **-wanderung,** *f.* walking-tour, hike. **-wanne,** *f.* foot bath, slipper bath. **-weg,** *m.* footpath.

Fussel, *f.* (*dial. coll.*) fluff, thread, hair (*on a pen-nib*). **-ig (fußlig)** *adj.* fuzzy, fluffy.

füß-eln, *v.n.* (*aux.* h.) play with the feet (*under the table*); shuffle, trip along; *miteinander –eln,* touch each other's feet (*under the table*). **-er,** *suffix, m.* one having feet. **-ig,** *suffix,* -footed. **-ler,** *suffix, m.* having feet, e.g. *Sechs–ler,* hexameter line (*in verse*); *Vier–ler,* quadruped. **-ling,** *m.* foot of a stocking; sock. **-lings,** *adv.* on, by *or* at the feet; *–lings fallen,* fall (*or* light) on one's feet.

Fustage, *f.* casks, barrels.

futsch, (*coll.*) *int.* gone, lost, ruined, broken.

[1]**Futter,** *n.* (*of animals only except in sl.*) food, fodder, feed; provender, forage; *in gutem – stehen,* be well fed; *– fassen,* go foraging (*Mil.*). **-anbau,** *m.* fodder crop. **-beutel,** *m.* nose-bag, provender bag. **-biene,** *f.* worker bee. **-boden,** *m.* hay-loft. **-bohne,** *f.* horse bean. **-brei,** *m.* mash. **-gerste,** *f.* feed barley. **-hafer,** *m.* feed oats. **-holer,** *m.* forager. **-kammer,** *f.* hay-loft. **-kasten,** *m.* corn-bin. **-korn,** *n.* corn for fodder. **-kraut,** *n.* green fodder. **-krippe,** *f.* crib, manger; (*sl.*) remunerative post. **-n,** *v.n.* (*coll.*) eat heartily *or* ravenously; (*sl.*) tuck in, stuff o.s. **-neid,** *m.* professional jealousy. **-pflanze,** *f.* forage plant, green fodder. **-ration,** *f.* ration, diet. **-rübe,** *f.* turnip (*Brassica rapa*) (*Bot.*). **-sack,** *m.*, *see* **-beutel.** **-saft,** *m.* royal jelly, brood food (*bees*). **-stroh,** *n.* feeding straw. **-schwinge,** *f.* winnowing-fan. **-trog,** *m.* trough, manger. **-wicke,** *f.* common vetch (*Vicia sativa*) (*Bot.*). **-wiese,** *f.* meadow cultivated for fodder. **-wurzel,** *f.* forage root.

[2]**Futter,** *n.* (-s, –) lining, casing, coating, covering; sheath; bushing (*Mach.*). **-al,** *n.* (-(e)s, -e) case; box; sheath. **-holz,** *n.* shim (*Mach.*). **-mauer,** *f.* retaining wall. **-papier,** *n.* lining paper. **-rohr,** *n.* liner (*Artil.*). **-stoff,** *m.*, **-tuch,** *n.*, **-zeug,** *n.* lining material, sateen.

[1]**fütter-n,** *v.a.* feed; give fodder to. **-ung,** *f.* fodder, feed, food, forage, provender.

[2]**fütter-n,** *v.a.* line; cover, pad, coat; stuff. **-ung,** *f.* lining; casing.

Futur, *n.*, *see* **-um.** **-ismus,** *m.* futurism, modernism (*in art*). **-istisch,** *adj.* futuristic, modernistic. **-um,** *n.* (-ums, -a) future tense; ***–um exactum*** future perfect (*Gram.*).

G

G, g, *n.* letter G, G (*Mus.*); *der – -Schlüssel,* the treble clef; *G-dur,* G-major; *G-moll,* G-minor.

gab, gäbe, *see* **geben.**

Gabbro, *m.* gabbro, igneous *or* plutonic rock (*Geol.*). **-chaussierung,** *f.* macadamized surface (*of a road*).

Gabe, *f.* (-n) gift, present, donation; alms, offering; dose (*Med.*); talent, endowment; *Mensch von herrlichen –n,* man of splendid *or* wonderful gifts *or* talents; *milde –,* alms, charity. **-nbringer,** *m.*, **-nspender,** *m.* dispenser of gifts, almsgiver. **-nfresser,** *m.* person who takes bribes; corrupt official.

gäbe, *see* **gang.**

Gabel, *f.* (-n) fork, pitchfork; prong; tendril (*Bot.*); bracket, crutch (*Naut.*); shafts (*of a cart, etc.*), (front *or* rear) fork (*of a bicycle*); bifurcation; *– mit zwei Zinken,* two-pronged fork. **-anker,** *m.* grapnel, small bow-anchor; cramp-iron. **-artig,** *adj.* forked, bifurcated, furcate, dichotomous (*Bot., Zool.*). **-bäume,** *m.pl.*, *see* **-deichsel.** **-bein,** *n.* wish-bone, furcula. **-bildung,** *f.* bracketing (*method of fire*) (*Artil.*). **-deichsel,** *f.* pair of shafts. **-er,** *m.*, *see* **Gabler.** **-förmig,** *adj.*, *see* **-artig.** **-frühstück,** *n.* lunch. **-fuhrwerk,** *n.* wagon with shafts. **-geweih,** *n.* forked antlers. **-hirsch,** *m.*, *see* **Gabler.** **-ig,** *adj.* forked, branched, furcate, bifurcated, fork-like, pronged. **-knochen,** *m.*, *see* **-bein.** **-kopf,** *m.* crown (*Cycl.*). **-maß,** *n.* calliper. **-motor,** *m.* V-engine. **-n,** 1. *v.a.* fork; pitchfork; impale, pierce; gore. 2. *v.r.* fork, branch off, bifurcate, ramify. 3. *v.n.*; (*coll.*) *er –t tüchtig,* he eats heartily. **-nadel,** *f.* hairpin. **-pferd,** *n.* shaft-horse, wheeler. **-röhre,** *f.* branched *or* forked pipe. **-scheiden,** *f.pl.* fork blades (*Cycl.*). **-schwanz,** *m.* puss moth (*Dicranura vinula*) (*Ent.*). **-spaltung,** *f.*, **-teilung,** *f.* bifurcation. **-stich,** *m.* thrust; prod. **-stiel,** *m.* fork-handle. **-ung,** *f.* forking, bifurcation, dichotomy. **-stütze,** *f.* bipod, crutch (*Naut.*), prop. **-zinke,** *f.* prong (*of a fork*).

Gab-ler, *m.* (-lers, -ler) two-year-old stag, brocket. **-lig,** *adj.*, *see* **gabelig.**

gack-eln, -ern, -sen, 1. *v.n.* (*aux.* h.) cackle, cluck; (*sl.*) chatter, prattle. 2. *n.*, **-elei,** *f.* cackling, clucking; chatter.

Gaden, *m.* & *n.* (-s, –) (*dial.*) one-roomed house *or* hut; (*Scots*) single-end.

Gaffel, *f.* (-n), **-baum,** *m.* gaff (*Naut.*).

gaff-en, *v.n.* (*aux.* h.) gape, stare. **-er,** *m.* gaper, idle onlooker *or* bystander.

Gagat, *m.* & *n.* (-s, -e) jet, black amber. **-kohle,** *f.* pitch-coal.

Gage [*pron.* ga:ʒə], *f.* (-n) salary, fee, honorarium (*partic. of actors*).

Gagel, *m.* bog myrtle, sweet gale (*Myrica gale*) (*Bot.*).

gäh, *adj.* (*dial.*), *see* **jäh.**

gähn-en, 1. *v.n.* (*aux.* h.) yawn; gape. 2. *n.* yawning; *–ender Abgrund,* yawning chasm. **-krampf,** *m.* fit of yawning.

Gais, *f.*, *see* **Geiß.**

Gala, *f.* court-, gala- *or* full-dress; (*coll.*) party clothes, evening dress; *sich in – werfen*, dress (*for a party*). **–ball,** *m.* dress ball. **–kleid,** *n.* court-dress, full-dress; (*pl.*) state robes. **–mäßig,** *adj.* festive; formal, pompous. **–uniform,** *f.* full-dress uniform. **–vorstellung,** *f.* gala *or* special performance (*Theat.*). **–wagen,** *m.* state coach. **–zimmer,** *n.* state room.

Galan [*pron.* ga'lan], *m.* (-s, -e) lover, sweetheart; gallant. **–t,** *adj.* courteous, polite (*to ladies*); amorous, gallant; *–tes Abenteuer*, affair of the heart; (*coll.*) *–te Krankheit*, syphilis. **–terie,** *f.* courtesy, gallantry. **–teriearbeit,** *f.* imitation jewellery; (*pl.*) fancy-goods. **–teriedegen,** *m.* dress sword. **–teriewaren,** *f.pl.* fancy-goods, trinkets.

Gal–eere, *f.* (-n) galley. **–eerensklave,** *m.*, **–eerensträfling,** *m.* galley-slave. **–eone,** *f.* (-n) galleon. **–eote,** *f.* (-n) galiot, small coasting-vessel.

Galerie, *f.* gallery (*Theat., Min., Mil.*); balcony (*cheapest theatre seats*); *für die – spielen*, play to the gallery. **–wald,** *m.* fringe of forest.

Galgen, *m.* (-s, –) gallows, gibbet; *geh' an den – !* be hanged to you! *sein Bild ist an den – geschlagen*, he was executed in effigy; *es steht – und Rad darauf*, it is a capital crime. **–bube,** *m.* rascal, rogue, scoundrel, ne'er-do-well; *–förmiges Kreuz*, potence (*Her.*). **–frist,** *f.* short delay, respite. **–gesicht,** *n.* hang-dog look. **–humor,** *m.* grim humour. **–männlein,** *n.* mandrake (*Mandragora*) (*Bot.*). **–schelm,** *m.*, **–schwengel,** *m.*, **–strick,** *m.*, **–vogel,** *m.*, *see* **–bube.**

Galion, *n.* (-s, -e & -s) figurehead (*of a ship*). **–e,** *f.*, *see* **Galeone. –sfigur,** *f.* figurehead.

Galiote, *f.*, **Galjot,** *f.* (-en), *see* **Galeote.**

Gall–e, *f.* (-en) gall, bile; bad temper, asperity, rancour, spite, choler; flaw (*in casting, etc.*), imperfection, defect; marshy *or* stony place (*in fields*); protuberance, swelling (*Bot. & horses*); *seine –e ausschütten*, vent one's spleen; *Gift und –e speien, spucken* or *sein*, give vent to one's rage; *die –e läuft ihm über*, his blood is up; *einem die –e rege* or *heiß machen*, provoke a p.'s anger *or* vindictiveness. **–apfel,** *m.* gall-nut, oak-apple. **–apfelsäure,** *f.* gallic acid. **–artig,** *adj.*, *see* **gallertartig. –eführend,** *adj.* bilious, venomous. **–enader,** *f.* cystic vein (*Med.*). **–enbehälter,** *m.*, *see* **–enblase. –enbitter,** 1. *adj.* bitter as gall. 2. *n.* picromel. **–enblase,** *f.* gall-bladder. **–ebrechen,** *n.* bilious vomiting. **–enfett,** *n.* cholesterin. **–energießung,** *f.* overflow *or* discharge of bile. **–enfieber,** *n.* bilious fever. **–enfluß,** *m.*, *see* **–energießung. –engang,** *m.* bile duct. **–enkrankheit,** *f.* bilious complaint. **–ensäure,** *f.* gallic acid. **–enseife,** *f.* ox-gall soap. **–enstein,** *m.* gall-stone, biliary calculus. **–(en)sucht,** *f.* jaundice. **–(en)süchtig,** *adj.* choleric; melancholic; bilious. **–ig,** *adj.* gall-like; biliary, bilious; bitter; irritable, bad-tempered, spiteful, choleric.

Gallert, *n.* (-(e)s, -e) gelatine; jelly. **–artig,** *adj.* gelatinous, colloidal. **–e,** *f.* (-en) gluten. **–ig,** *adj.*, *see* **–artig. –substanz,** *f.* colloid.

Galimathias, *m.* nonsense, balderdash.

Gallone, *f.* (-n) gallon.

Galmei, *m.* (-(e)s, -e) zinc ore, calamine.

Galon [*pron.* ga'lɔ̃:], *m.* (-s, -s), **–e,** *f.* (-en) (*Austr. dial.*) gold *or* silver lace, braid; galloon. **–ieren,** *v.a.* trim with lace *or* braid; *–ierte Diener*, livery-servants.

Galopp, *m.* (-s, -s & -e) gallop; galop (*dance*); *in – setzen*, put to a gallop; *im –*, at a gallop, galloping; *in gestrecktem –*, at full gallop; *in vollem –*, at full speed; *er erledigte die Arbeit im –*, he raced through the exercise *or* work; *im kurzen – reiten*, canter. **–ade,** *f.* (-n) gallopade (*dance*). **–ieren,** *v.n.* (*aux.* h.) gallop; *–ierende Schwindsucht*, galloping consumption; phthisis florida (*Med.*).

Galosche, *f.* (-n) galosh, overshoe.

[1]**galt, gälte,** *see* **gelten.**

[2]**galt,** *adj.*, *see* **gelt.**

galvan–isch, *adj.* galvanic. **–isieren,** *v.a.* galvanize, electro-plate. **–isierung,** *f.* galvanization, electro-plating. **–ismus,** *m.* galvanism. **–o,** *n.* electrotype, (*coll.*) electro. **–ographie,** *f.* electrotyping. **–oplastik,** *f.* electro-deposition.

Gamasche, *f.* gaiter, legging, spat; *Wickel–*, puttee; (*coll.*) *ich hatte höllische –n*, I was in an awful funk. **–ndienst,** *m.* (*coll.*) square bashing (*Mil.*).

Gambe, *f.* (-n) bass-viol, viola da gamba.

Gams, *f.* (*dial.*), *see* **Gemse.**

Ganerbe, *m.* (-en, -en) (*dial. & archaic*) joint-heir; co-proprietor.

[1]**Gang,** 1. *m.* (-(e)s, ⸚e) motion, movement, action, working, process, procedure; course (*of disease, the planets, a lawsuit, dinner, a river*); progress; action (*of a drama*); flow, cadence (*of verse*); carriage, gait, pace; stroll, walk, march; path, alley, avenue, way, gangway, passage, corridor, gallery, lode, vein, canal, duct (*Anat.*); passage (*of music, of arms*); pass, lunge (*Fenc.*); shift; round (*in boxing*); gear (*Motor.*); stroke (*of an engine*); pitch (*of a screw*). 2. *adj.* (*only in*) *– und gäbe* (*Austr. & Swiss dial. gäng und gäbe*), customary, usual, traditional, the usual thing; *was nicht mehr – und gäbe ist*, what is no longer fashionable *or* customary; *außer – sein*, be out of gear, be idle; *bedeckter –*, sap, mine (*Fort.*); covered way, portico (*Arch.*); *im – bleiben*, keep going *or* moving; *in – bringen*, set going, set in motion, start, introduce, bring into fashion; *– der Dinge*, way of the world; *die S. muß nun ihren – gehen* or *nehmen*, the matter must now take its own course; *– des menschlichen Geistes*, march of human intellect; *erster* (*dritter*) *–*, bottom (top) gear (*Motor.*); *– der Gerechtigkeit*, course of justice; *im –e*, at work, in operation, current; *in vollem –e*, in full swing; *in – kommen*, get going, moving *or* into action; *man lauert auf alle seine Gänge*, all his movements are watched; *offener –*, porch; *das Pferd hat einen guten –*, the horse has good action; *in – setzen*, see *in – bringen*; *toter –*, steering play (*Motor.*); *einen – tun*, go *or* run an errand; *unterirdischer –*, underground passage; *Anzahl der Gänge auf den Zoll*, threads per inch (*of a screw*). **–art,** *f.* gait, walk, action, pace; gange, matrix (*Geol.*). **–bar,** *adj.* practicable, passable; customary, prevalent; (*C.L.*) current; marketable, saleable; pervious; frequented; *–bare Münze*, current coin; *–bare Erklärung*, usual explanation; *–bare Artikel*, staple commodities; *Wasserröhren –bar erhalten*, keep water-pipes in order. **–barmachung,** *f.*; *man beschloß die –barmachung des Weges*, it was decided to make the road practicable. **–bildung,** *f.* lode-formation. **–bord,** *m.* gangway. **–erz,** *n.* vein ore. **–gewicht,** *n.* weight (*driving a clock*). **–haft,** *adj.* in veins *or* streaks. **–häuer,** *m.* lodesman. **–höhe,** *f.* pitch (*of a screw*). **–pfosten,** *m.* baluster. **–rad,** *n.* tread-wheel. **–schaltung,** *f.* gear change (*Motor.*). **–spill,** *n.* capstan; *loses –spill*, crab (*Mach.*). **–unterschied,** *m.* phase difference (*Elec.*). **–wechsel,** *m.* gear lever, gear change (*Motor.*). **–weise,** *adv.* in veins. **–werk,** *n.* driving-gear, machinery, machine; works, movement (*of a clock*). **–woche,** *f.* Rogation week (*R.C.*).

[2]**Gang,** *m.* (-s, -s) gang (*of workmen or criminals*). **–ster,** *m.* (-s, –) gangster.

gäng–eln, 1. *v.n.* (*aux.* h.) toddle. 2. *v.a.* lead by the hand, lead a p. like a child; lead a p. by the nose. **–elband,** *n.* leading-string. **–elwagen,** *m.* go-cart. **–er,** *m.* (-ers, -er) (*rare except in compounds*) goer, walker. **–ig,** *adj.* (*dial.*) saleable, in great demand; quick, fleet; *–iger Hund*, well-trained dog.

Gans, *f.* (⸚e) goose (*in general*), (*properly female only*); *Gänse nudeln*, cram geese; *dumme –*, ninny, silly girl; *goldene –*, foolish young heiress; (*Prov.*) *die Gänse gehen überall barfuß*, human nature is always the same; *er ist so dumm, daß ihn die Gänse beißen*, he can't say boo to a goose; *aussehen wie eine – wenn es blitzt* or *donnert*, look like a dying duck in a thunderstorm. **–er,** *m.* gander.

Gäns–chen, *n.* gosling; silly young girl. **–eadler,** *m.* erne, sea-eagle (*Haliaetus albicilla*) (*Orn.*). **–eblümchen,** *n.*, **–eblume,** *f.* daisy (*Bellis perennis*) (*Bot.*). **–ebraten,** *m.* roast goose. **–efeder,** *f.* goose-feather, quill. **–efett,** *n.* goose oil. **–efüßchen,** *n.pl.* inverted commas, quotation marks. **–egang,** *m.*, *see* **–emarsch. –egekröse,** *n.* goose-giblets. **–egeschnatter,** *n.* cackling of geese. **-ehaft,** *adj.* goose-like; simple, stupid, silly. **-ehaut,** *f.* goose-pimples, goose-flesh, creeps. **-ekiel,** *m.* goose-quill. **-eklein,** *n.* giblets. **-eküchlein,** *n.*, **-eküken,** *n.* gosling. **-eleberpastete,** *f.* pâté de foie gras. **-emarsch,** *m.* single file; follow-my-leader (*game*). **-erich,** *m.* (-s, -e) gander. **-eschmalz,** *n.* goose oil. **-espiel,** *n.* game of fox and geese. **-ewein,** *m.* (*hum.*) water. **-ezucht,** *f.* geese breeding.

Gant, *f.* (-en) (*dial.*) auction of bankrupt's property; *auf die – kommen,* go bankrupt. **-anwalt,** *m.* trustee in bankruptcy. **-buch,** *n.* inventory of a (bankrupt) sale. **-en,** *v.n.* (*aux.* h.) institute a legal execution; *um eine S. -en,* bid for a th. at an auction. **-haus,** *n.* auction-mart. **-mann,** *m.*, **-schuldner,** *m.* bankrupt. **-masse,** *f.* bankrupt's estate. **-mäßig,** *adj.* insolvent. **-recht,** *n.* law of bankruptcy; auction laws.

ganz, 1. *adj.* whole, entire, undivided, complete, intact, full, total; *er blieb -e zwanzig Sekunden unter Wasser,* he stayed under the water for fully twenty seconds *or* (*coll.*) all of twenty seconds; *der -e Betrag,* the full amount, the total; *es ist mein -er Ernst,* I am quite serious; I really mean it; *in -er Figur,* full length; *das -e Haus,* the whole house; *von -em Herzen,* with all my heart; *– machen,* complete, mend; *-er Mann,* true man, downright good fellow; *die -e Nacht hindurch,* all through the night, all night long; *die -e Summe,* see *der -e Betrag*; *die -e Welt,* all the world, the whole world; *-e Zahl,* integer. 2. *adv.* quite, wholly, altogether, entirely, thoroughly, all; perfectly, quite; *– anders,* altogether, entirely *or* quite different; *– besonders,* more especially; *– fremd,* an utter stranger; *sie war – Freude,* she was full of joy; *– und gar,* totally, wholly, absolutely; *– und gar nicht,* not at all, by no means; *– und gar nichts,* nothing at all; *– gewiß,* most certainly; *– gleich,* all the same, quite immaterial *or* identical; *– gut,* quite good, (*coll.*) not at all bad; *– der Ihrige,* yours truly; *– der Mann dazu,* quite the man for it, the right *or* proper man for it; *ich bin – Ohr,* I am all attention; *– wohl,* very well. **-e(s),** *n.* whole, entirety, totality, total; integer (*Arith.*); gross; party, squad (*in mil. commands*); *aufs -e gehen,* go *or* be all out (for); *im -en,* on the whole, taken altogether, in bulk; *im großen und -en,* on the whole, generally speaking, altogether; *im -en genommen,* taking everything into consideration, in general; *im -en verkaufen,* sell wholesale *or* in bulk. **-fabrikat,** *n.* wholly manufactured article. **-heit,** *f.* entirety, totality. **-holz,** *n.* logs, round timber. **-lederband,** *m.* leather *or* calf binding. **-leinenband,** *m.* cloth binding. **-randig,** *adj.* entire (*of leaves*). **-sache,** *f.* entire (*postage stamp*). **-sachen,** *f.pl.* entires (*envelopes, post-cards, wrappers*). **-seide,** *f.* pure silk, all silk. **-wolle,** *f.* pure wool, all wool. **-zeug,** *n.* pulp.

Ganz, Gänz, *f.* (¨-e) pig of iron.

Gänze, *f.* entirety. *See* **Ganzheit.**

gänzlich, *adj.* complete, full, total, entire, whole, thorough (*all form advs. with* -ly).

gar, 1. *adj.* (sufficiently) cooked, tender, well done, well roasted *or* boiled; purified, refined (*of metals*); tanned, dressed (*of skins*); (*dial.*) finished, all gone; *Fleisch, das nicht – ist,* underdone meat; *mehr als –,* overdone. 2. *adv. & part.* entirely, fully, absolutely; very, quite, even, at all; perhaps, I hope; *ist er krank oder – tot?* is he ill or even *or* perhaps dead? *das ist – wohl möglich,* that is indeed quite possible; (*dial.*) *es ist mit ihm – aus,* it is all over with him; *– kein Zweifel,* not the least *or* slightest doubt; *– keiner,* not a single one, none whatever; *– mancher,* many a one to be sure; *– nicht, -nicht,* not at all, by no means; *warum nicht -!* you don't say so! never! *– nichts, -nichts,* nothing at all; *– oft,* very often; *– sehr schlecht,* indeed very bad, very bad indeed; *– selten,* very rarely; *vielleicht gefällt er mir –,* perhaps I may even like him; *– zu,* much too, far too. **-arbeit,** *f.* metal-refining. **-aus,** *m.* (*only used in Nom. & Acc.*) utter ruin; finishing stroke; end; death; *einem den -aus machen,* complete a p.'s ruin, kill s.o., finish a p. off. **-e,** *f.* (*rare*) prepared condition, readiness; mellowness, friability (*of land*). **-eisen,** *n.* refined iron; smelter's iron. **-gekrätz,** *n.*, **-krätze,** *f.* refinery slag. **-koch,** *m.* owner of a cook-shop. **-küche,** *f.* cook-shop, eating-house. **-leder,** *n.* tanned *or* dressed leather. **-machen,** *n.* tanning; refining. **-ofen,** *m.* refining furnace. **-probe,** *f.* assay.

Garag-e, *f.* (-en) (motor-)garage. **-ieren,** *v.a.* (*Austr. & Swiss dial.*) garage.

Garant, *m.* (-en, -en) guarantor. **-ie,** *f.* (-ien) guarantee, security. **-ieren,** *v.a.* (*für eine S.*), guarantee (a th.); warrant.

Garbe, *f.* (-n) sheaf; milfoil, yarrow (*Achillea millefolium*) (*Bot.*); burst (*of fire*) (*Mil.*); beam (*of light*); (*dial.*) neck of beef. **-n,** *v.a.* sheave, bundle. **-nzehnte,** *m.* tithe of sheaves.

gärben, *v.a.* weld (*Metall.*).

Gard-e, *f.* (-en) guards; guards regiment; (*coll.*) *die alte -e,* the old Guard, the 'Die-Hards'; *-e zu Fuß* or *-einfanterie, f.* foot-guards; *-ekavallerie, f.* horse-guards. **-eregiment,** *n.* regiment of the Guards. **-ist,** *m.* (-en, -en) guardsman.

Garderob-e, *f.* (-en) clothes; wardrobe; cloak-room, (*Amer.*) check-room; (*periphrastic for*) closet; *wo ist die -e?* where is the cloak-room? **-enständer,** *m.* hall-stand. **-ier,** *m.* (-s, -s) cloak-room attendant; property-man (*Theat.*). **-iere,** *f.* (-n) cloak-room attendant; wardrobe mistress (*Theat.*).

Gardine, *f.* (-n) curtain; (*coll.*) *hinter schwedischen -n sitzen,* be in jail. **-narm,** *m.*, **-nhaken,** *m.* curtain-hook. **-npredigt,** *f.* curtain-lecture; (*coll.*) telling-off from the wife. **-nstange,** *f.* curtain rail *or* pole.

Gär-e, *f.* fermentation; leaven, yeast; bouquet (*of wine*). **-bottich,** *m.* fermentation vat. **-dauer,** *f.* duration of fermentation. **-fähig,** *adj.* fermentable. **-futter,** *n.* ensilage. **-futterbehälter,** *m.* silo. **-kraft,** *f.* fermentation power. **-lehre,** *f.* zymology. **-mittel,** *n.* leaven, leavening ferment, yeast. **-en,** 1. *ir. & reg. v.n.* (*aux.* h. & s.) ferment; effervesce, work; *es -t in den Köpfen,* (discontent, etc.) is seething in their minds; *es -t im Volk,* the people are restless; *der Wein ist* (or *hat sich*) *zu Essig gegoren,* the wine has turned to vinegar. 2. *n.* fermentation. **-stoff,** *m.*, *see* **-mittel.** **-teig,** *m.* leaven. **-ung,** *f.* fermentation, ferment; *der Teig kommt in -ung,* the dough begins to rise; (*fig.*) *in -ung bringen,* throw into a ferment, cause an upheaval. **-ungsbuttersäure,** *f.* butyric acid. **-ungschemie,** *f.* chemistry of fermentation, zymology. **-ungserregend,** *adj.* zymogenic. **-ungsfähig,** *adj.* fermentable. **-ungsküche,** *f.* dyer's fermenting-vat. **-ungsmittel,** *n.*, **-ungsstoff,** *m.*, *see* **-mittel.** **-ungspilz,** *m.* yeast-germ. **-ungsprozeß,** *m.* process of fermentation. **-ungstechnik,** *f.* zymotechnology. **-ungsverfahren,** *n.* method of fermentation. **-ungsvorgang,** *m.*, *see* **-ungsprozeß.**

Garmond, -schrift, *f.* (*dial.*) long primer.

Garn, *n.* (-s, -e) yarn, thread, twine; net, snare; decoy; *wollenes –,* worsted, wool; *ins – locken,* decoy. **-enden,** *n.pl.* thrums. **-erei,** *f.* yarn-weaving factory *or* department. **-knäuel,** *n.* ball of thread. **-rolle,** *f.* reel of thread. **-spule,** *f.* bobbin, reel. **-strähn,** *m.*, **-strähne,** *f.* hank *or* skein of yarn. **-stricker,** *m.* knitter. **-winde,** *f.* reel, hasp.

Garnele, *f.* (-n) prawn (*large*); shrimp (*small*).

garn-ieren, *v.a.* trim (*a hat, etc.*); garnish (*Cook.*) **-ierung,** *f.* trimming; garnish. **-itur,** *f.* trimming; border; outfit, equipment, set; mounting; fittings, accessories; *zweite -itur,* second uniform.

Garnison, *f.* (-en) garrison; *mit einer – versehen,* garrison (*a town*); *in – liegen,* be quartered (at *or* in). **-dienst,** *m.* garrison duty. **-dienstfähig, -diensttauglich,** *adj.* fit for garrison duty. **-ieren,** *v.n.* be in garrison. **-lazarett,** *n.* military hospital, station hospital. **-verwendungsfähig,** *adj.*, *see* **-dienstfähig.**

Garrott-e, *f.* gar(r)otte. **-ieren,** *v.a.* strangle, throttle, gar(r)otte. **-ierung,** *f.* (Spanish method of) execution by strangulation.

garstig, *adj.* nasty; ugly; horrid; loathsome, detestable; filthy, foul; obscene. **-keit,** *f.* nastiness; vileness; ugliness; filthiness; obscenity.

Garten, *m.* (-s, ⸚) garden. **–arbeit,** *f.* gardening. **–bau,** *m.* horticulture. **–bauausstellung,** *f.* horticultural show. **–beet,** *n.* garden-bed *or* plot. **–bohne,** *f.* kidney bean. **–butterblume,** *f.* ranunculus. **–distel,** *f.* globe artichoke (*Cyanara scolymus*) (*Bot.*). **–erde,** *f.* garden-mould. **–geländer,** *n.* espalier. **–gerät,** *n.* gardening-tools. **–gewächs,** *n.* pot-herb. **–haus,** *n.* summer-house. **–kerbel,** *m.* chervil (*Scandix cerefolium*) (*Bot.*). **–kräuter,** *n.pl.* pot-herbs, vegetables. **–kresse,** *f.* cress (*Lepidium sativum*) (*Bot.*). **–kunst,** *f.* horticulture. **–künstler,** *m.* horticulturist. **–lattich,** *m.* lettuce (*Lactuca sativa*) (*Bot.*). **–laube,** *f.* arbour, summer-house. **–laubenroman:** *m.* trashy sentimental novel (*reference to the* 'Gartenlaube', *a once popular family magazine*). **–lokal,** *n.* tea *or* beer garden. **–messer,** *n.* pruning-knife. **–raute,** *f.* common rue (*Ruta graveolens*) (*Bot.*). **–saal,** *m.* room (*of inn, etc.*) overlooking the garden. **–schädling,** *m.* garden pest. **–spritze,** *f.* garden hose. **–walze,** *f.* garden roller. **–schere,** *f.* garden-shears, pruning-shears. **–wirtschaft,** *f.* 1. horticulture; 2. tea *or* beer garden.

Gärtner, *m.* (-s, –) gardener. **–bursche,** *m.* gardener's man, under-gardener. **–ei,** *f.* gardening; nursery (*Hort.*). **–isch,** *adj.* horticultural. **–kunst,** *f., see* **Gartenkunst.** **–messer,** *n., see* **Gartenmesser.** **–n,** *v.n.* (*aux.* h.) do gardening, work in the garden.

Gas, *n.* (-es, -e) gas; *das – abdrehen,* turn off the gas; (*coll.*) kill (*a p.*), ruin (*a p. economically*) (*with Dat.*); – *ablassen* or *abblasen,* release gas (*Mil.*); – *geben,* (*coll.*) open the throttle, accelerate (*Motor.*). **–abwehr,** *f.* anti-gas defence (*Mil.*). **–anlage,** *f.,* **–anstalt,** *f.* gas works. **–anzeiger,** *m.* gas detector (*Mil.*). **–artig,** *adj.* gaseous. **–austritt,** *m.* escape of gas. **–behälter,** *m.* gasometer, gas-holder. **–beleuchtung,** *f.* gas lighting, gaslight. **–blase,** *f.* blow-hole (*Metall.*). **–brenner,** *m.* gas-burner. **–dicht,** *adj.* gas-tight, hermetically sealed. **–dichte,** *f.* gas density. **–düse,** *f.* gas jet. **–en,** *v.n.* gas, develop gas. **–entbindung,** *f.,* **–entwicklung,** *f.,* **–erzeugung,** *f.* production *or* generation of gas. **–entweichung,** *f.* escape of gas. **–feuerung,** *f.* gas heating. **–flasche,** *f.* gas cylinder. **–förmig,** *adj.* gaseous. **–gemenge,** *n.,* **–gemisch,** *n.* gas mixture (*Motor.*). **–gewinnung,** *f.* gas production. **–glühlicht,** *n.* incandescent light. **–hahn,** *m.* gas tap; (*coll.*) *den –hahn aufdrehen,* put one's head in the gas-oven, commit suicide. **–hebel,** *m.* throttle, accelerator (*Motor.*). **–herd,** *m.,* **–kocher,** *m.* gas cooker, gas stove. **–krank,** *adj.* gassed. **–ig,** *adj.* gaseous. **–krieg,** *m.* gas warfare, chemical warfare. **–leitung,** *f.* gas-pipe. **–maske,** *f.* gas mask. **–messer,** *m.* gas meter. **–ofen,** *m.* gas stove, gas furnace. **–öl,** *n.* Diesel oil. **–olin,** *n.* gasoline, petroleum spirit. **–rest,** *m.* residual gas. **–schleuse,** *f.* gas-proof shelter (*Mil.*). **–schutz,** *m.* anti-gas protection (*Mil.*). **–schwade,** *f.* gas fumes. **–spürer,** *m.* gas sentry (*Mil.*). **–strumpf,** *m.* gas mantle. **–tot,** *adj.* killed by gas, gassed to death. **–tote(r),** *m.* fatal gas casualty. **–uhr,** *f.* gas meter. **–vergiftet,** *adj.* gassed.

gäsch–en, *v.n.* (*aux.* h.) (*archaic*) ferment; froth, foam. **–end,** *pr.p.* & *adj.* effervescing; yeasty. **–t,** *m. see* **Gischt.**

Gasel, *n.* (-s, -e) **Gasele,** *f.* (-n) Persian love poem, ghazel.

Gaskonade, *f.* (-n) bragging, boasting.

Gasse, *f.* (-n) lane, alley; (*Austr. dial.*) street; *auf der –,* in the street; *auf allen –n,* at every street-corner; – *ohne Ausgang,* blind alley; *Hans in allen –n,* busybody; *über die –,* (*Austr. dial.*) outdoor (*sale of liquor for consumption off the premises*). **–nbettler,** *m.* tramp. **–nbube,** *m.* street-arab, urchin, guttersnipe. **–ndieb,** *m.* pickpocket. **–ndirne,** *f.* prostitute. **–nhauer,** *m.* popular song. **–njunge,** *m., see* **–bube.** **–nkehrer,** *m.,* **–nkotführer,** *m.* scavenger, street-sweeper. **–nlaterne,** *f.* street lamp. **–nlaufen,** *n.* running the gauntlet (*Mil.*). **–npöbel,** *m.* street-corner loungers, mob, rag-tag and bobtail. **–nrinne,** *f.,* **–nschleuse,** *f.* gutter. **–ntreter,** *m.* vagabond; street-corner lounger. **–ntroß,** *m.,* **–nvolk,** *n.* scum of the streets, rabble. **–nwirt,** *m.* publican. **–nwitz,** *m.* vulgar joke.

Gast, 1. *m.* (-es, ⸚e) guest, visitor; customer, client; stranger; star (*Theat.*). 2. (-s, -en) sailor, seaman (*usually in compounds, e.g.* Boots–); *einen zu –e bitten,* invite s.o.; *Gäste empfangen,* receive company; *Gäste haben,* have company; *saubrer –,* fine fellow (*ironic*); *schlauer –,* knowing fellow; *seltener –,* queer fish, rara avis; *zu –e sein,* be a guest *or* a visitor. **–bett,** *n.* spare bed. **–erei,** *f.* feast, banquet; (*coll.*) bean-feast, bun-fight. **–frei,** *adj.* hospitable. **–freiheit,** *f.* hospitality. **–freund,** *m.* guest; host. **–freundlich,** *adj.* hospitable. **–freundlichkeit,** *f.* **–freundschaft,** *f.* hospitality; *seine –freundschaft mißbrauchen,* take advantage of his hospitality. **–geber,** *m.* host, landlord. **–geschenk,** *n.* hospitable gift. **–haus,** *n.* restaurant; inn; tavern. **–herr,** *m.* host. **–hof,** *m.* hotel; inn; tavern. **–hofbesitzer,** *m.* hotel proprietor; innkeeper. **–hörer,** *m.* university student not registered for full course. **–ieren,** 1. *v.a.* entertain. 2. *v.n.* (*aux.* h) be a guest star (*Theat.*); take s.o.'s place temporarily. **–kleid,** *n.* dress-suit. **–lich,** *adj.* hospitable. **–lichkeit,** *f.* hospitality. **–mahl,** *n.* (-e (*or Austr. dial.*) ⸚er) banquet, dinner party. **–ordnung,** *f.* regulation for innkeepers. **–pflanze,** *f.* parasite (*Bot.*). **–predigt,** *f.* sermon by a visiting clergyman. **–recht,** *n.* right to hospitality (*of a visitor in a foreign country*); guest's *or* innkeeper's rights, host's privilege; law regulating relations between innkeeper and traveller. **–rolle,** *f.* star part (*played by visiting actor*) (*Theat.*). **–spiel,** *n.* performance by visiting actors (*Theat.*). **–stube,** *f.* visitors' *or* guest room, spare (bed)room; hotel lounge, bar parlour. **–stätte,** *f.* restaurant, café, teashop, public-house. **–tafel,** *f.* **–tisch,** *m.* table-d'hôte. **–wirt,** *m.* landlord, innkeeper, hotel-keeper. **–wirtschaft,** *f., see* **–haus.** **–zimmer,** *n., see* **–stube.**

Gästebuch, *n.* (-(e)s, ⸚er) visitors' book.

gastr–isch, *adj.* gastric. **–onom,** *m.* (-en, -en) gourmet, epicure.

Gat, Gatt, *n.* (-(e)s, -s & -en) hole, narrow opening; stern (*Naut.*).

gäten, *v.a., see* **jäten.**

gätlich, *adj.* (*dial.*) tolerable, middling; convenient; middle-sized.

Gatt–e, *m.* (-en, -en) husband, consort, spouse; mate (*of animals*); (*pl.*) married people. **–en,** *v.a.* & *r.* match, pair, couple, copulate, unite; (*dial.*) sort. **–englück,** *n.* conjugal happiness. **–enrechte,** *n.pl.* marital rights. **–entreue,** *f.* marital fidelity. **–enwahl,** *f.* choice of a mate. **–in,** *f.* (-innen) wife, consort, spouse; mate (*of animals*). **–ung,** *f.* kind, class, type, sort; species; genus, race, breed, family (*of plants*); gender; arm of the service (*Mil.*). **–ungsbastard,** *m.* genus hybrid. **–ungsbegriff,** *m.* generic character. **–ungsmaler,** *m.* genre-painter. **–ungsname,** *m.* generic name, class name; common noun. **–ungsverwandte,** *m.pl.,* allied species, congeners. **–ungswort,** *n. see* **–ungsname.**

Gatter, *n.* (-s, –) railing, fence; grating, lattice, trellis; enclosure; frame (*Paint.*). **–n,** *v.a.* & *n.* (*dial.*) 1. fence; 2. spy out. **–säge,** *f.* machine saw. **–stäbe,** *m.pl.* bars of grating. **–tor,** *n.,* **–tür,** *f.* barred gate, grated door. **–werk,** *n.* lattice-work.

gattieren, *v.a.* classify, sort; mix (*Min., Spinn.*).

Gattung, *f., see* **Gatt–.**

Gau, *m.* (& *n.*) (-(e)s, -e (& *Austr. dial.*) -en) (*dial.* Gäu) district, province, administrative district (*revived by Nat. Soc.*). **–dieb,** *m.* (*dial.*) professional thief, rogue. **–leiter,** *m.* (*Nat. Soc.*) district leader, area commander.

Gauch, *m.* (-(e)s, -e (& *Austr. dial.*) ⸚e) fool, simpleton; oddity, odd fish; (*dial.*) cuckoo. **–bart,** *m.,* **–haar,** *n.* stripling's downy beard. **–heil,** *n.* (& *dial. m.*) scarlet pimpernel (*Anagallis arvensis*) (*Bot.*).

Gaudi, *n.* (*dial.* & *coll.*) fun, spree.

gaufrieren, *v.a.* emboss, goffer (*Pap.*).

gauk–eln, 1. *v.n.* (*aux.* h.) juggle, play tricks; produce illusions; flutter *or* flit about. 2. *v.a.* deceive; get by trickery; *sich in Illusionen -eln*, delude o.s. with foolish hopes. **-elbild,** *n.* illusion, mirage, phantasm. **-elei,** *f.* (-en) conjuring, juggling, legerdemain, trick, illusion; trickery, fraud, imposture. **-elhaft** *adj.* buffoon-like; juggling; delusive, deceptive. **-elmann,** *m.*, **-elmännchen,** *n.* puppet, jack-in-the-box. **-elpossen,** *f.pl.* juggling tricks. **-elspiel,** *n.*, **-elspielerei,** *f.*, **-elwerk,** *n.*, *see* **-elei. -ler,** *m.* (-lers, -ler) juggler, conjurer; buffoon, tumbler; charlatan, impostor. **-lerei,** *f.* jugglery. **-lerisch,** *adj.*, *see* **-elhaft.**

Gaul, *m.* (-e)s, ⁻e) old horse, nag; (*dial.*) carthorse; *elender –*, (miserable) jade; (*Prov.*) *einem geschenkten – sieht man nicht ins Maul*, never look a gift horse in the mouth; beggars must not be choosers; *das bringt einen – um*, that's the last straw, (*sl.*) that's really a bit thick, that's about the limit.

Gaumen, *m.* (-s, –) palate, roof of the mouth; taste; *harter –*, hard palate; *weicher –*, soft palate, velum. **-kitzel,** *m.* tickling of the palate. **-laut,** *m.* palatal (*sound*) (*Phonet.*). **-naht,** *f.* palatine suture (*Anat.*). **-platte,** *f.* plate (*Dentist.*). **-reiz,** *m.*, *see* **-kitzel. -segel,** *n.*, **-vorhang,** *m.* velum, soft palate.

Gauner, *m.* (-s, –) rogue; swindler, cheat, sharper, trickster. **-bande,** *f.* gang of thieves. **-ei,** *f.* swindling, swindle, trickery, imposture. **-herberge,** *f.* thieves' resort, rookery of thieves. **-isch,** *adj.* swindling, cheating; thievish. **-n,** *v.n.* (*aux.* h.) swindle, cheat, trick. **-sprache,** *f.* thieves' Latin. **-streich,** *m.*, **-stück,** *n.* swindle, imposture, rascally trick, sharper's trick. **-welt,** *f.* underworld. **-zinke,** *f.* beggars' *or* thieves' mark (*outside a house*).

Gaup-e, *f.* (-en), **-loch,** *n.* (*dial.*) dormer-window; attic.

Gautsche, *f.* (-n) (*dial.*) swing. **-n,** *v.a.* couch (*Pap.*).

Gaze, *f.* (-n) net, cheesecloth; *feine –*, gossamer. **-papier,** *n.* tissue paper.

ge-, *unaccented prefix forms*: 1. Collective nouns *from substantives, nearly all neuter gender, the root vowel being, if possible, modified*; *e.g.* **Geäder, Geäst, Gebüsch, Gefild(e), Gestein, Gesträuch, Gewässer, Gewölk.** 2. Verbal nouns *denoting repetition or continuation of the action, all neuter gender and without plural*; *e.g.* **Geächze, Gebalge, Geheul, Gerede, Geseufze, Gestöhne, Gewinsel.** 3. Past participles; *e.g.* **geachtet,** *from* achten, **geächtet** *from* ächten, **geboren** *from* gebären, *and nouns from these, e.g.* **Geächtete(r), Erstgeborene(r).** *For any words not given in the following list and particularly in the case of* 3. *above, see the simple words.*

Geächtete(r), *m.* outlaw, proscript.

Geächze, *n.* continual groaning.

Geäder, *n.* blood vessels, veins, arteries, arterial system; marbling. **-t, geadert,** *adj.* veined, grained, marbled.

geaicht, *p.p. & adj.*, *see* **eichen;** *auf eine S. – sein*, understand a th. thoroughly; (*coll.*) *darauf bin ich –*, in this matter I am an expert.

geartet, (*suffix* =) composed, constituted, natured, disposed, formed, conditioned. **-heit,** *f.* nature, disposition, qualities, constitution, attributes, peculiarities.

Geäse, *n.* (-s, –) pasture, fodder *or* feeding ground for deer; deer's mouth.

Geäst, *n.* branches.

Gebäck, *n.* (-(e)s, -e) pastry; confectionery; teabread (*Scots.*); baking, batch.

Gebackene(s), *n.* anything baked; bakery wares, pastry.

Gebalge, *n.* tussle, scuffle.

Gebälk, *n.* beams, framework, joists; timber-work; entablature of a column. **-träger,** *m.* atlas, telamon (*Arch.*).

geballt, *adj.* concentrated; *-e Faust*, clenched fist; *-es Feuer*, concentrated fire (*Artil.*); *-e Ladung*, demolition charge (*Mil.*).

gebar, gebäre, *see* **gebären.**

Gebärd-e, *f.* (-en) air, bearing, appearance, demeanour; gesture, gesticulation. **-en,** *v.r.* behave; conduct *or* deport o.s.; *sich -en als ob*, do as if. **-ig,** *adj.* (*dial.*) of a good bearing *or* countenance, mannerly. **-enkunst,** *f.* mimicry. **-enspiel,** *n.* pantomime, dumb show, miming, gesticulation. **-enspieler,** *m.* mimic. **-ensprache,** *f.* gesture *or* sign language; miming.

gebar-en, 1. *v.r.* (*rare*) behave, conduct o.s. 2. *n.* conduct, behaviour, deportment. **-ung,** *f.* management, running (*of a business*).

gebär-en, 1. *ir.v.a.* bear, bring forth, give birth to; (*ein Kind*) *geboren haben*, be delivered (of a child); *geboren werden*, be born. 2. *n.* parturition; child-bearing; *-ende Frau*, woman in labour; *lebendige Junge -end*, viviparous. **-erin,** *f.* woman in labour, mother. **-anstalt,** *f.* maternity home, lying-in hospital. **-mutter,** *f.* womb, uterus. **-mutterschnitt,** *m.* hysterotomy, Caesarian section.

Gebäude, *n.* (-s, –) building, structure, edifice; *Lehr–*, system. **-steuer,** *f.* property tax, (*Scots.*) burgh rates.

Gebein, *n.* (-(e)s, -e) bones; frame, skeleton; (*pl.*) corpse, body, remains.

Gebelfer, *n.* yelping, barking; brawling, loud abuse.

Gebell, *n.* barking, baying.

geben, 1. *ir.v.a.* give, present, confer, bestow; yield, grant, furnish, produce, emit; render, play, act; show, express, evolve, prove, lead to; *einem den Abschied –*, dismiss *or* discharge a p.; *acht –*, pay attention, give heed; *sich* (*Dat.*) *ein Ansehen –*, give o.s. airs; *sich* (*Dat.*) *das Ansehen –*, assume the appearance of; *auf eine S. etwas –*, set value on *or* attach value to a th., set great store by a th.; *nichts auf eine S. –*, think nothing of a th.; *darauf ist nichts zu –*, that is of no importance whatever; *den Ausschlag –*, be decisive *or* the decisive factor; *Befehl –*, order; *Beifall –*, approve (of), applaud; *ein Beispiel –*, set an example; *Bescheid –*, give information about *or* bring word of s.th.; *zum besten –*, stand (*a drink, etc.*), tell (*a story, joke, etc.*), sing (*a song*), recite (*a poem*), play (*a piece*); *Bewegung –*, impart motion to; *das gibt zu denken*, there's s.th. behind that, that has some significance; *sich* (*Dat.*) *die Ehre –*, do o.s. the honour; *falsch –*, misdeal, deal wrongly (*Cards*); (*coll.*) *Fersengeld –*, run away, decamp; *Feuer –*, fire (*a rifle*); give *or* offer s.o. a light; *frei–*, set at liberty; give a holiday to; *einem einen Freibrief –*, give s.o. carte-blanche; *Frist –*, allow time, grant a respite; *Gewinn –*, yield profit, turn out well; *Gott gebe!* God grant! *einem etwas in die Hand –*, suggest s.th. to s.o.; *Hitze –*, emit *or* throw out heat; *einem das Jawort –*, accept a man's offer of marriage, consent to marry a man; *Karten –*, deal; *wer muß –?* whose deal is it? *der Hund gab Laut*, the dog gave tongue; *sein Leben an etwas –*, stake one's life on s.th.; *in die Lehre –*, apprentice; *ans Licht –*, see *an den Tag –*; *sich* (*Dat.*) *Mühe –*, take pains *or* trouble; *Nachricht –*, send word; *Obacht –*, pay attention (to), take care (of); *in Pension –*, place at a boarding-school; put out to board; *auf die Post –*, post; *Raum –*, make room; *einem recht –*, own that a p. is right; *einem das Recht zu einer S. –*, empower *or* sanction s.o.; *einem gewonnenes Spiel –*, acknowledge one's opponent's victory; throw in one's hand; *dem Pferde die Sporen –*, set spurs to one's horse; *einem Schuld –*, blame s.o., impute blame to *or* accuse s.o.; *an den Tag –*, bring to light, publish; *was wird heute im Theater gegeben?* what play will be performed tonight? what's on at the theatre tonight? *Unterricht –*, teach, instruct; *verloren –*, look upon as lost; renounce (one's claim to); *ein Spiel verloren –*, acknowledge defeat, throw up the sponge; *von sich –*, emit (*a smell, a sound, etc.*), utter; vomit; *einem den Vorzug –*, acknowledge a p.'s superiority *or* priority; show one's preference for a p.; *sein Wort* (*auf eine S.*) *–*, pledge one's word; *gute Worte –*, entreat, persuade; *ein Wort gab das andere*, one word led to another; *die Zeit wird es –*, time will tell *or* show; *Zeugnis –*, bear witness; *auf Zinsen –*, put out at interest; *sich zufrieden –* (*mit*), acquiesce (in); *die Zusage –*, accept (*an invitation, etc.*), promise (*help, etc.*); *gegebenenfalls*, in case (of need), if occasion should arise; *etwas als gegeben voraussetzen*, assume s.th. as fact; *das Gegebene*, known quantity, given number (*Math.*), given fact. 2. *v.r.* acknowledge o.s. to be, behave as if one is; submit; relent; abate; *das gibt sich*, that will pass, that will not last long, that will abate *or* improve; *es gibt sich von selbst*, it is a matter of course; (*coll.*) *so was gibt's*, such things do happen; *sein Eifer wird sich geben*, his zeal will cool; *der Schmerz hat sich gegeben*, the pain has abated; *sich* (*Acc.*) *bloß–*, see *sich preis–*; *sich zu erkennen –*, reveal one's identity; *sich gefangen –*, surrender; *sich kund –*, make o.s. known; *Erstaunen gab sich in aller Mienen kund*, surprise manifested itself *or* was expressed on every face; *sich preis–*, lay o.s. open to, expose o.s. to; *das Tuch gibt sich*, the cloth stretches; *sich verloren –*, admit defeat; *sich zufrieden –*, put up with, submit to, be content with. 3. *v.a. imp. es gibt*, there is, there are; *es gibt Fälle*, there are cases; *es gibt einen guten Grund dafür*, there is a good reason for that; *der größte Prahler, den es gibt*, the greatest braggart living; *es gibt heute Regen*, there will be rain today; *es gab einen Zank*, a quarrel arose; *was gibt's?* what is the matter? (*coll.*) *es wird gleich* (*et*)*was –!* there'll be trouble in a minute! you'll catch it! *gibt es etwas Schöneres?* what is more beautiful? *was gibt's Neues?* what's the news? (*coll.*) *das gibt's nicht!* that is impossible! nonsense! it just isn't done, it's not allowed; *es gibt nichts*, there's nothing here *or* to be had *or* (*sl.*) doing; (*coll.*) *da gibt's nichts*, one cannot deny it, one must admit that; *es gibt nichts derartiges*, there is nothing of the kind *or* like it; *es wird sich schon –*, it will follow in due course; *es gibt viel zu tun*, there's a lot to do *or* to be done. 4. *n.* giving; *das – hat kein Ende bei ihr*, she never leaves off giving; *am – sein*, have the deal (*Cards*); (*B.*) *– ist seliger, denn Nehmen*, it is more blessed to give than to receive. **Gebefall**, *m.* dative case (*Gram.*). **gebefreudig**, *adj.* open-handed, generous, beneficent, bountiful. **Geber**, *m.* giver, donor, dispenser, sender, transmitter (*Tele.*).

Gebet, *n.* (-(e)s, -e) prayer; *das Tisch– sprechen*, say grace; *das – des Herrn*, the Lord's Prayer; *sein – verrichten*, say one's prayers; *ein – sprechen*, offer prayers; (*coll.*) *ins – nehmen*, question closely. **–buch**, *n.* prayer-book, breviary; *des Teufels –buch*, (*hum.*) playing cards. **–formel**, *f.* form of prayer. **–gesang**, *m.* oratorio. **–riemen**, *m.*, **–schnur**, *f.* phylactery (*Jew.*). **–sheilung**, *f.* faith-healing, Christian Science.

gebeten, *see* **bitten.**

Gebettel, *n.* importunity, continual begging.

gebier, gebierst, gebiert, *see* **gebären.**

Gebiet, *n.* (-(e)s, -e) district, area, territory, region, zone, province, sphere, domain, department, branch, field; *– der Gelehrsamkeit*, domain of learning; *auf deutschem –*, on German ground *or* territory.

gebiet–en, 1. *ir.v.a.* (*einem etwas*) command, order, bid. 2. *v.n.* lay down the law; govern, rule; *Ruhe* or *Stillschweigen –en*, impose silence; *die Freundschaft –et*, friendship demands; *Rücksicht scheint geboten*, some consideration seems to be demanded. **–er**, *m.* master, lord, commander, ruler, governor. **–erisch**, *adj.* domineering, dictatorial; imperious, peremptory, commanding, imperative.

Gebild–e, *n.* (-es, -e) creation; creature; product; structure, formation, system, organization, image; pattern (*Weav.*); form, figure. **–brot**, *n.* bread *or* rolls baked in fancy shapes.

gebildet, *p.p.* & *adj.* educated, cultured, well-bred, refined; shaped, fashioned; *die –en*, the cultured *or* educated classes.

Gebimmel, *n.* ringing *or* tinkling of bells.

Gebinde, *n.* (-s, –) bundle; skein; hank, sheaf; cask.

Gebirg–e, *n.* (-es, -e) mountain-chain *or* range, mountains, highlands, rock. **–ig**, *adj.* mountainous. **–ler**, *m.* mountain dweller. **–sart**, *f.* species of rock. **–sbewohner**, *m.* mountain dweller, highlander. **–sjoch**, *n.* saddle (*of a mountain*). **–skamm**, *m.*, **–srücken**, *m.* mountain ridge. **–sstock**, *m.* massif. **–svolk**, *n.* mountain tribe, highlanders. **–svorsprung**, *m.* shoulder of a mountain. **–swand**, *f.* wall of rocks. **–szug**, *m.* mountain-chain, range of mountains.

Gebiß, *n.* (-(ss)es, -(ss)e) set of teeth; denture, set of artificial teeth; bridle-bit; *einem Pferde ein – anlegen*, put a bit on a horse. **–kette**, *f.* curb (*of a bit*).

gebissen, *p.p. of* **beißen.**

Geblase, *n.* trumpeting, blowing.

Gebläse, *n.* (-s, –) blast apparatus, blower, bellows; blowpipe; supercharger (*Motor.*); *das – anlassen*, set the bellows going. **–lampe**, *f.* blow lamp. **–luft**, *f.* blast from the bellows. **–ofen**, *m.* blast-furnace.

geblättert, *adj.* foliate, laminated.

geblichen, *p.p. of* **bleichen.**

geblieben, *p.p. of* **bleiben. –e(n)** *m.pl.* the killed, the (fatal) casualties (*in battle*).

Geblök, *n.* (-(e)s, -e) bleating (*of sheep*); lowing (*of cattle*); bellowing.

geblümt, *adj.* flowered, figured, flowery, mottled, wavy.

Geblüt, *n.* blood, blood system; line, lineage, family, descent, race; *es steckt im –*, it runs in the blood *or* in the family; *Prinz von –*, prince of the blood, prince of the royal line; *zu nahe ins – heiraten*, marry too near of kin.

gebogen, *p.p. of* **biegen** & *adj.* bent, curved, refracted; hooked; arched; vaulted; *–e Nase*, aquiline nose, Roman nose.

geboren, *p.p. of* **gebären** & *adj.* (*abbr.* **geb.**) born; née; by birth, by nature; *unehelich –*, born out of wedlock, illegitimate; *tot–*, stillborn; *–er Deutscher*, German by birth; *–er Londoner*, native of London; *-er Dichter*, born poet; *eine –e N.*, née N.; *was für eine –e ist sie?* what was her maiden name?

geborgen, *p.p. of* **bergen** & *adj.*; *–sein*, be hidden, be in safety *or* out of danger. **–heit**, *f.* (place of) safety *or* security.

geborsten, *p.p. of* **bersten.**

Gebot, *n.* (-(e)s, -e) command, order; precept; (*C.L.*) advance, bid, offer; (*B.*) commandment; *einem zu –e stehen*, be at a p.'s disposal; *die zehn –e*, the ten commandments; *das – der Stunde*, the need of the moment; (*Prov.*) *Not kennt kein –*, necessity knows no law; (*C.L.*) *ein – tun*, make an offer; *das erste – tun*, start a price, give the first bid.

geboten, *p.p. of* **bieten** *and* **gebieten**, & *adj.* necessary, imperative; *es wird – sein*, it seems advisable.

Gebräch, *n.*, *see* **Gebrech.**

gebracht, *p.p. of* **bringen.**

gebrannt, *p.p. of* **brennen** & *adj.*; (*Prov.*) *ein –es Kind scheut das Feuer*, a burnt child dreads the fire; once bit, twice shy; *–er Kalk*, quicklime.

Gebräu, *n.* (-(e)s, -e) brewing, brew, mixture.

Gebrauch, *m.* (-(e)s, ⸗e) employment, use, usage, custom, practice, habit, fashion; *alter –*, ancient (well-established) custom; *außer – kommen*, go out of use, fall into disuse; *wie es der – mit sich bringt*, according to custom; *falscher –*, improper use *or* application, abuse (*of words, etc.*); *in – nehmen*, take into use; *nach – zurückzugeben*, return after use; *Sitten und Gebräuche*, habits and customs; *von einer S. – machen*, make use of a th.; *zum –e*, for use; *zu eigenem –*, for one's personal use. **–en**, *v.a.* use, employ, make use of; *dies ist nicht zu –en*, this is of no use (whatever); *sich –en lassen zu*, lend o.s. to, be instrumental to; *–en Sie mein Wörterbuch noch?* are you still using my dictionary? *ich –e dazu mehrere Tage*, I (shall) want several days for that; *–te Sachen*, second-hand articles, worn garments; *–tes Bad*, spent bath (*Dye*). **–sanweisung**, *f.* directions (for use). **–sdosis**, *f.* usual dose, normal dose. **–sfähig**, *adj.* usable, serviceable. **–sfertig**, *adj.* ready for use. **–sgegenstand**, *m.* commodity. **–sgraphik**, *f.* commercial art. **–smuster**, *n.* patent, registered design. **–smusterschutz**, *m.* registered trade-mark. **–swasser**, *n.* fresh water, tap water. **–swert**, *m.* intrinsic value.

gebräuchlich, *adj.* usual, common, ordinary, in use, customary, current; *–e Orthographie*, current spelling; *nicht mehr –*, no longer used, obsolete; *– sein*, be in use. **–keit**, *f.* usualness, customariness, commonness, frequency.

Gebraus(e), *n.* roaring; singing, ringing.

Gebrech, 1. *n.* (-s, -e) boar's snout; rooting place of wild boars; friable *or* crumbling rock. 2. *adj.* brittle, crumbling, friable (*of rocks*). **-en,** 1. *ir. v.n. imp.* (*pres. & imp. tenses only*) (*Dat.*) (*rare*) lack, be in need of, be wanting; *es soll Ihnen an nichts -en*, you shall want for nothing; *es gebricht ihm an Geld*, he is short *or* in need of money; *wenn es dir an Mut gebricht*, if you are lacking in courage. 2. *n.* infirmity, malady, weakness, defect. **-lich,** *adj.* frail, sickly, weak, feeble, fragile, infirm, decrepit. **-lichkeit,** *f.* frailty, feebleness, weakness, infirmity, decrepitude.

Gebresten, *n.*, *see* **Gebrechen** (2).

gebrochen, *p.p. of* **brechen** & *adj.* broken; bent, deflected; halting, broken (*of speech*); broken in spirit, bowed down; dim, dull, subdued (*of colour, light, etc.*); arpeggiando (*Mus.*).

Gebrüder (*abbr.* **Gebr.**) brothers; *die – Grimm*, the brothers Grimm.

Gebrüll, *n.* roaring, lowing (*of cattle*).

Gebrumm(e), *n.* growling, grumbling, growls; humming, murmuring.

Gebühr, *f.* (-en) fee, tax, rate, charge; duty, due; propriety, seemliness, decency; (*pl.*) dues, money due, taxes; payment, emolument; *nach Standes–*, according to rank; *seine – leisten*, do one's duty; *nach –*, according to merit; *über –*, immoderately, unduly. **-en,** 1. *v.n.* (*aux.* h.) be due, belong of right to; appertain to; *Ehre, dem Ehre -(e)t*, honour to whom honour is due; *Dir -(e)t Majestät und Gewalt*, thine is the majesty and the power. 2. *v.r. & imp.* be fitting *or* proper, becoming; *wie sich's -t*, as it ought to be, in a becoming manner, properly. **-end,** *pr.p. & adj.* due, fit, fitting, proper, appropriate, meet, befitting; *Ihre Tratte soll -enden Schutz finden*, your draft shall be duly honoured. **-endermaßen,** *adv.* properly, duly, in a fitting manner. **-enfrei,** *adj.* tax-free, duty-free, post-free. **-enordnung,** *f.* tariff. **-enpflichtig,** *adj.* liable *or* subject to tax, postage due. **-lich,** *adj.* (*rare*) fitting, suitable, proper; decent, becoming. **-nisse,** *f.pl.* allowances.

Gebund, *n.* (-(e)s, ¨-e) bunch, bundle, skein, truss. **-en,** *p.p. of* **binden** & *adj.* bound, obliged; metrical; combined (with), linked (to); *-ene Wärme*, latent heat; *-ene Noten*, tied notes (*Mus.*); *-ene Rede*, verse, poetry. **-enheit,** *f.* constraint; subjection; affiliation; *-enheit der Auffassung*, narrowness of conception.

Geburt, *f.* (-en) birth, labour, delivery, parturition; (*Poet.*) offspring; origin, family, descent, extraction; *unzeitige –*, abortion; *von –*, by birth; of good birth; *nach Christi –*, A.D.; anno Domini; *vor Christi –*, before Christ, B.C.; *in der – sterben*, die in childbed; *die – abtreiben*, bring about a miscarriage; *von (seiner) – an*, from (his) birth. **-enbeschränkung,** *f.*, **-enregelung,** *f.* birth-control. **-enrückgang,** *m.* fall in the birth-rate. **-enziffer,** *f.* birth-rate. **-sadel,** *m.* nobility of birth, inherited nobility. **-sanzeige,** *f.* announcement of birth. **-sfehler,** *m.* congenital defect. **-shaus,** *n.* birthplace. **-shelfer,** *m.* obstetrician, accoucheur. **-shelferin,** *f.* midwife. **-shilfe,** *f.* midwifery, obstetrics. **-sjahr,** *n.* year of birth. **-skunde,** *f.* obstetrics. **-sland,** *n.* native land. **-slehre,** *f.* obstetrics. **-smal,** *n.* birth-mark. **-snot,** *f.* labour. **-sort,** *m.* birthplace, place of birth. **-srecht,** *n.* birthright. **-sschein,** *m.* birth certificate. **-sschmerzen,** *m.pl.* labour-pains; *in -sschmerzen*, be in labour. **-sstadt,** *f.* native town. **-stag,** *m.* birthday; *einem zum -stag Glück wünschen*, wish a p. many happy returns of the day. **-svorgang,** *m.* parturition. **-swehen,** *f.pl.*, *see* **-sschmerzen.**

gebürtig, *adj.* native (*aus*, of), born in.

Gebüsch, *n.* (-es, -e) bushes, shrubs, shrubbery, thicket, copse, underwood, undergrowth. **-elt,** *adj.* tufted; bushy.

Geck, *m.* (-en, -en) fop, dandy, coxcomb, conceited ass; *einem den -en stechen, den -en mit einem treiben*, sneer, scoff *or* laugh at a p. **-enhaft,** *adj.* foppish, dandified.

gedacht, *p.p. of* **denken** & *adj.*; *der -e Herr*, the aforesaid gentleman; *-e Zahl*, number thought of.

Gedächtnis, *n.* (-(ss)es, -(ss)e) memory, recollection, remembrance; memorial, monument; *starkes, treues –*, retentive memory; *schlechtes, kurzes –*, bad, short memory; *aus dem – hersagen*, recite from memory *or* by heart; *zum – an* (*Acc.*), in remembrance *or* commemoration of; *es ist meinem – entfallen*, it has escaped my memory; *ins – zurückrufen*, call to mind; *wenn mein – mich nicht täuscht*, if my memory serves me right(ly). **-fehler,** *m.* slip of the memory. **-feier,** *f.* commemoration; *kirchliche -feier*, memorial service. **-münze,** *f.* commemorative medal. **-rede,** *f.* speech in commemoration. **-säule,** *f.* monument. **-schwäche,** *f.* loss of memory. **-tafel,** *f.* memorial tablet. **-tag,** *m.* anniversary, commemoration day. **-zeichen,** *n.* keepsake, souvenir, token of remembrance.

gedämpft, *adj.* subdued; *-e Welle*, damped wave (*Rad., etc.*).

Gedank-e, *m.* (-ens, -en) thought, conception, idea, notion; design, purpose, plan; *das bringt mich fast auf den -en*, that makes me almost suppose; *einen auf andere -en bringen*, divert a man's thoughts; make a p. change his mind *or* think of other things; *auf den -en kommen*, hit upon the idea; *sich* (*Dat.*) *etwas aus den -en schlagen*, banish a th. from one's mind; *seine -en nicht beisammen haben*, be absent-minded *or* inattentive; *in -en beiwohnen*, be present in spirit; *in -en sah sie sich*, in fancy she saw herself (a queen, etc.); *in -en vertieft*, engrossed in thought, preoccupied; *seinen -en nachhängen*, muse, day-dream, be lost in thought; *sich* (*Dat.*) *-en über eine S. machen*, worry, be worried *or* uneasy about a th., have misgivings about a th.; *-en sind zollfrei*, opinions are free; *seine -en zusammennehmen*, collect one's thoughts. **-enaustausch,** *m.* exchange of thoughts, interchange of ideas. **-enblitz,** *m.* flash of thought *or* insight, brilliant idea. **-endieb,** *m.* plagiarist. **-enfolge,** *f.* train of thought. **-enfreiheit,** *f.* freedom of thought. **-engang,** *m.*, *see* **-enfolge.** **-enkreis,** *m.* range of ideas. **-enlauf,** *m.*, *see* **-enfolge.** **-enleer,** *adj.* void of ideas. **-enlesen,** *n.* thought-reading. **-enlos,** *adj.* thoughtless. **-enlosigkeit,** *f.* thoughtlessness, frivolity, light-heartedness. **-enlyrik,** *f.* philosophical *or* contemplative poetry. **-enraub,** *m.* plagiarism. **-enreich,** *adj.* full of good ideas, fertile in ideas. **-enreichtum,** *m.* fertility of the mind. **-enspäne,** *m.pl.*, **-ensplitter,** *m.pl.* aphorisms, aperçus. **-enstrich,** *m.* dash, em rule (*Typ.*). **-enübertragung,** *f.* thought-transference, telepathy. **-envoll,** *adj.* thoughtful, pensive; deep in thought. **-envorbehalt,** *m.* mental reservation. **-enwelt,** *f.* world of ideas, ideal world; range of ideas. **-lich,** *adj.* mental, intellectual.

Gedärm, *n.* -(-e)s, -e) (*usually pl.*), **-e,** *n.* (-s, –) intestines, entrails, bowels. **-vorfall,** *m.* prolapsus (*of the intestines*).

Gedeck, *n.* (-(e)s, -e) cover (*at table*); table-linen, cutlery, china, etc. (*for one person*); *– für 20 Personen*, covers for 20 persons, table laid for 20 p.; *trockenes –*, restaurant meal without drinks.

Gedeih, *m.* (*only in*) *auf – und Verderb*, (*or rare*) *auf – und Un–*, for better or for worse. **-en,** 1. *ir.v.n.* (*aux.* s.) increase, develop, grow, thrive, flourish, get on well, prosper, succeed; *das Kind -t prächtig*, the child is developing splendidly; *die Arbeit ist schon weit gediehen*, the work has progressed well; *die S. ist nun dahin gediehen, daß*, the affair has now developed to the point that; *es -t dir nicht zum Heil*, no good will come of it, you won't be any the better for it. 2. *n.* growth, development, vitality, vigour, prosperity, success, increase, advantage; *Gott gebe sein -en dazu!* may God grant his blessing on it! **-lich,** *adj.* thriving, prosperous; salutary, beneficial, profitable, favourable; nutritive, wholesome.

gedenk-en, 1. *ir.v.a.* (*aux.* h.) (*with Gen.*) bear in mind, think of, be mindful of, remember; make mention of; mention (*partic. in one's will*); (*with inf. & zu*) intend, design, propose, plan; *-e mein* or *meiner!* remember me! think of me! *gern -e ich des Tages*, I remember that day with pleasure; *einer S. nicht -en*, pass over a th. in silence; *dessen nicht zu -en, daß*, not to mention that; *ich habe seiner immer nur im Guten gedacht*, I have always thought *or* spoken well of him. 2. *v.a.* (*einem etwas*) remember to the disadvantage of; *ich will es ihm schon –en*, I'll make him pay for it yet, I'll hold that against him. 3. *n.* memory; *einem ein gutes –en bewahren, einen in gutem –en behalten*, have pleasant *or* happy memories of s.o.; *zu Ihrem –en*, in memory of you; *seit Menschen–en*, within living memory, for ages. **–feier,** *f.* commemoration. **–gottesdienst,** *m.* memorial service. **–münze,** *f.* commemorative medal. **–spruch,** *m.* motto, device. **–stein,** *m.* monument, memorial. **–tafel,** *f.* memorial tablet. **–tag,** *m.* commemoration day; anniversary. **–zettel,** *m.* memorandum.

gedeucht, *p.p. of* **dünken.**

Gedicht, *n.* (-(e)s, -e) poem; (*also fig.*) gem, dream (*in extravagant praise of an omelette, a ladies' hat, etc.*). **–form,** *f.*; *in –form*, in verse. **–sammlung,** *f.* anthology. **–et,** *p.p.* written, composed (*as a poem*); packed, sealed, made tight.

gediegen, *adj.* solid, compact, massive; unmixed, pure, native (*Chem.*); true, genuine, thorough; sterling; superior; (*coll.*) splendid, funny; *–e Kenntnisse*, profound erudition; *–e Arbeit*, sound piece of work; *–es Gold*, pure gold; *–er Witz*, capital joke; (*coll.*) *du bist aber –*, you're the limit. **–heit,** *f.* solidity, purity, genuineness; native state (*Chem.*); reliability, thoroughness; sterling quality, intrinsic value.

gedieh, gediehe, gediehen, *see* **gedeihen.**

Gedinge, *n.* (-s, –) bargain, contract; piece-work (*Min.*); (*dial.*) haggling, bargaining; *in – arbeiten*, do piece-work, work by contract. **–arbeit,** *f.* piece-work, contract work. **–geld,** *n.*, **–preis,** *m.* contract price, piece rate.

Gedräng-e, *n.* crowd, press, throng; need, distress, difficulty, dilemma; crowding, pushing, thrusting; *ins –e geraten* or *kommen*, get into a difficulty, tight spot *or* scrape. **–t,** *adj.* crowded, dense, thronged, serried; compact, terse, concise. **–theit,** *f.* terseness.

gedrechselt, *p.p.* & *adj.* pretentious, stilted, highfalutin (*of speech*).

gedreht, *p.p.* & *adj.* contorted, twisted.

gedroschen, *p.p. of* **dreschen.**

gedruckt, *p.p.* & *adj.* printed; *er lügt wie –*, he lies like a gas-meter. **–e(s),** *n.* printed matter, printed papers, print.

gedrückt, *p.p.* & *adj.* oppressed, depressed.

gedrungen, *p.p. of* **dringen** & *adj.* thick-set, stocky, squat, sturdy, compact.

Gedudel, *n.* (-s) tooting, piping, tantara, taratantara.

Geduld, *f.* patience, forbearance, endurance; *jemandes – ermüden*, wear out a p.'s patience; *endlich war meine – erschöpft* or *ging mir die – aus*, at last I lost all patience; *fasse dich in –!* possess your soul in patience! **–en,** *v.r.* have patience, wait patiently; *wollen Sie sich einen Augenblick –en*, kindly wait a few moments. **–ig,** *adj.* patient, forbearing. **–sfaden,** *m.* patience; *der –sfaden reißt*, patience is at an end. **–(s)spiel,** *n.* patience (*Cards*).

gedungen, *p.p. of* **dingen.**

gedunsen, *adj.* bloated, puffy, puffed up; turgid.

gedurft, *p.p.* of **dürfen.**

geehrt, *p.p.* & *adj.*; *–er Herr*, Sir; *Ihr –es vom 16. April*, your favour of April 16.

geeignet, *p.p.* & *adj.* suitable, suited, adapted, appropriate, fit. **–heit,** *f.* **–sein,** *n.* suitability, fitness, appropriateness.

Geest, *f.*, **–land,** *n.* sandy uplands (*partic. North German coastal plain*).

Gefahr, *f.* (-en) danger, peril, hazard, risk; *auf die – hin, ihn zu beleidigen* or, *daß ich ihn beleidige*, at the risk of hurting his feelings; *auf eigene –*, at one's own risk; *auf meine –*, at my own risk; *der – ins Auge sehen*, look danger in the face; *sich einer großen – aussetzen*, expose o.s. to danger, run great risk; *die gelbe –*, the yellow peril; *in – bringen*, endanger; *mit – seines Lebens*, at the risk of his life; *es hat keine –*, there is no danger; *große – laufen*, run great risk; *der – trotzen*, brave the danger; *es ist – im Verzuge*, delay is dangerous; (*C.L.*) *für Rechnung und – von*, for account and risk of. **–bringend,** *adj.* dangerous (*für*, for). **–engeld,** *n.* danger money. **–enzone,** *f.* danger zone, mined area (*Mil.*). **–enzulage,** *f.*, *see* **–engeld. –los,** *adj.* safe, secure, without risk *or* danger. **–voll,** *adj.* perilous, dangerous.

Gefähr-de, *f.* (-den) (*Poet.*) risk, danger. **–den,** *v.a.* endanger, imperil, expose to danger; risk; compromise; *ich bin dabei nicht –det*, I run no risk in the matter. **–dung,** *f.* endangering; danger. **–lich,** *adj.* dangerous, hazardous, perilous, risky; (*fig.*) considerable; enormous; *das –liche Alter*, climacteric, 'change of life'; (*coll.*) *tun Sie doch nicht so –lich!* don't make such a fuss! (*coll.*) *das ist nicht –lich*, that's not very serious, that's nothing much. **–lichkeit,** *f.* danger, risk; insecurity.

Gefahre, *n.* much driving about (*usually implies careless driving*).

Gefährt, *n.* (-(e)s, -e) vehicle, cart; *vierspänniges –*, coach and four, four-in-hand.

Gefährte, *m.* (-en, -en) companion, comrade, associate.

Gefäll, *n.* (-(e)s, -e), **–e,** *n.* (-s, –) fall, drop, descent, incline, slope, gradient, grade; fallen trees, fallen timber; (*pl.*) income, taxes, dues, revenue; *die Mühle hat ein gutes –e*, the mill has a good head of water. **–emesser,** *m.* clinometer. **–holz,** *n.* felled wood; fallen trees. **–wechsel,** *m.* change in gradient (*Railw.*).

Gefallen, *m.* (-s, -) favour, kindness; *tun Sie es mir zu –*, do it to please *or* oblige me, do it for my sake.

[1]**gefall-en,** 1. *ir.v.n.* (*aux.* h.) (*Dat.*) please; *wie es Ihnen gefällt*, as you please; *es gefällt ihm*, he is pleased with it; *das will mir nicht recht –en*, I have misgivings about it; *sich* (*Dat.*) *etwas –en lassen*, put up with a th. *or* submit to a th.; *er läßt sich alles –en*, he puts up with anything; *das lasse ich mir nicht –en*, I will not stand that; (*coll.*) *das lasse ich mir –en*, that is nice, that is splendid; *sich* (*Dat.*) *einen Vorschlag –en lassen*, consent to a proposal; *sich* (*Dat.*) *–en in*, flatter o.s. with; *er gefiel sich in dem Glauben, daß*, he flattered himself in the belief that, he fondly imagined that. 2. *n.* pleasure, liking, preference; *er findet daran kein –en*, it gives him no pleasure. **–sucht,** *f.* coquetry. **–süchtig,** *adj.* coquettish.

[2]**gefallen,** *p.p.* & *adj.* fallen, killed in action; degraded, separated; *das Los ist –*, the die is cast, there is no going back. **–e,** *f.* fallen woman; *die –en*, the fallen, the dead (*Mil.*).

gefällig, *adj.* pleasing, pleasant, agreeable, helpful, obliging, kind, complaisant; (*dial. see* **fällig**) due, payable; *–es Benehmen*, pleasing *or* easy manners; *was ist Ihnen –?* what would you like to have? what can I get you? *Bier –?* would you like some beer? (*said by waiters*); (*C.L.*) *Ihr –es Schreiben*, your favour; (*C.L.*) *Ihrer –en Antwort entgegensehend*, awaiting (the favour of) your reply. **–keit,** *f.* kindness, favour; complaisance; *nur aus –keit für Sie*, only to oblige you *or* as a favour. (*C.L.*) **–keitswechsel,** *m.* accommodation bill. **–st,** *adv.* (*stiff & formal, often threatening*) if you please: *nehmen Sie –st Platz*, sit down, please; pray, be seated; *schicken Sie mir –st*, kindly send me.

gefällst, *see* [1]**gefallen.**

gefällt, *see* [1]**gefallen** (*3rd sing.*) & **fällen** (*p.p.*).

Gefält-el, *n.* gathers, folds, pleats. **–elt,** *p.p.* & *adj.* folded, pleated.

gefangen, *p.p.* & *adj.* captured, caught, captive, imprisoned; *– nehmen*, take prisoner; (*fig.*) captivate; *sich – geben*, surrender, give o.s. up; *– halten*, detain; *– setzen*, imprison; *– sitzen*, be in prison. **–e(r),** *m.* captive, prisoner; *die –e*, female prisoner. **–(en)lager,** *n.* prison camp. **–haltung,** *f.* detention in custody, confinement. **–nahme,** *f.*, **–nehmung,** *f.*, **–setzung,** *f.* arrest, capture, seizure, imprisonment. **–schaft,** *f.* captivity, imprisonment, confinement.

gefäng-lich, *adj.* (*archaic*) imprisoned, captive; *–lich einziehen*, imprison. **–nis,** *n.* prison, gaol, jail; *zu zweijährigem –nis verurteilen*, sentence to two years' imprisonment. **–nisstrafe,** *f.* imprisonment. **–niswärter,** *m.* gaoler, jailer, turnkey. **–niszucht,** *f.* prison discipline.

gefasert, *p.p.* & *adj.* fibrous; *–es Papier*, granite paper.

Gefäß, *n.* (-es, -e) vessel, container, receptacle;

handle, hilt (*of sword*). **–bau,** *m.*, **–bildung,** *f.* vascular structure. **–bündel,** *n.* vascular tissue. **–haut,** *f.* vascular membrane. **–ig,** *adj.* vascular. **–lehre,** *f.* angiology. **–system,** *n.* vascular system.
gefaßt, *p.p.* & *adj.* ready, prepared; composed, calm, collected; written; set (*of stones*); *sich* (*Acc.*) *auf eine S. – machen*, be prepared for a th. **–heit,** *f.* composure, calmness, calm.
Gefecht, *n.* (-(e)s, -e) fight, fighting, battle, combat, action, engagement; *außer – gesetzt werden*, be put out of action, be knocked out; *hinhaltendes –*, containing *or* delaying action; *örtliches –*, local engagement; *das – abbrechen*, cease fire, break off the engagement. **–sabschnitt,** *m.* battle sector. **–sausbildung,** *f.* battle *or* combat training. **–sbefehl,** *m.* operation order. **–sbereitschaft,** *f.* readiness for action, fighting trim. **–sdeck,** *n.* gun deck (*Nav.*). **–sfähig,** *adj.* able to fight, ready to give battle. **–sformation,** *f.* order of battle, battle formation. **–sklar,** *adj.* cleared for action (*Nav.*). **–skopf,** *m.* warhead (*of torpedo*). **–slage,** *f.* tactical conditions. **–slandeplatz,** *m.* advanced air *or* landing field. **–slehre,** *f.* tactics. **–smunition,** *f.* live ammunition. **–sschießen,** *n.* field firing-exercise. **–sstand,** *m.* battle headquarters, operation room, command post. **–sstärke,** *f.* fighting strength. **–sstellung,** *f.* battle station. **–sübung,** *f.* mock battle. **–szweck,** *m.* tactical objective.
gefeit, *adj.* (*gegen*) charmed, proof (against); immune (from).
gefertigt, *adj.* made, manufactured, prepared.
Gefieder, *n.* feathers, plumage. **–t,** *p.p.* & *adj.* feathered; pinnate (*Bot.*).
gefiel, gefiele, *see* **gefallen.**
Gefilde, *n.* (*Poet.*) fields, open country, tract of land; domain; *– der Seligen*, Elysian Fields.
geflammt, *adj.* mottled, wavy.
Geflatter, *n.* fluttering.
Geflecht, *n.* (-(e)s, -e) wickerwork; mesh; texture; plexus (*Anat.*).
gefleckt, *p.p.* & *adj.* spotted, speckled, stained, freckled, maculose.
Geflimmer, *n.* glittering, scintillation; (*sl.*) spit and polish (*Mil.*).
Geflissen-heit, *f.* diligence, assiduity. **–tlich,** 1. *adj.* wilful, intentional, on purpose, premeditated, with malice aforethought (*Law*). 2. *adv.* assiduously, diligently.
geflochten, *p.p.* *of* **flechten.**
geflogen, *p.p.* *of* **fliegen.**
geflohen, *p.p.* *of* **fliehen.**
geflossen, *p.p.* *of* **fließen.**
Geflügel, *n.* poultry, fowl(s). **–händler,** *m.* poulterer. **–pocken,** *f.pl.* chicken-pox (*Med.*). **–t,** *p.p.* & *adj.* winged; *–tes Wort*, familiar quotation, household word. **–zucht,** *f.* poultry-farming.
Geflunker, *n.* (*coll.*) fibbing, lies.
Geflüster, *n.* whispering.
gefochten, *p.p.* *of* **fechten.**
Gefolg–e, *n.* train, attendants, suite, entourage, retinue; consequences; *im –e haben*, be attended with, lead to, result in. **–schaft,** *f.* followers, adherents; *–schaft leisten*, obey, be under the orders of, serve; (*Nat. Soc.*) staff (*of a firm*). **–schaftsgeist,** *m.* (*Nat. Soc.*) team spirit. **–schaftsleute,** *pl.* subordinates, workers. **–schaftsmitglied,** *n.* subordinate, member of staff, worker. **–smann,** *m.* follower; vassal, thane.
gefragt, *p.p.* & *adj.* in demand *or* request; (*C.L.*) asked for, sought after.
gefranst, *adj.* fringed.
Gefräß, *n.* (-es, -e) (*vulg.*) *see* **Fraß. –ig,** *adj.* voracious, greedy. **–igkeit,** *f.* voracity, gluttony, greediness.
Gefreite(r), *m.* lance-corporal (*infantry*) *or* bombardier (*artillery*), able seaman, aircraftman 1st class.
gefrier–en, *ir.v.n.* (*aux.* s.) freeze, congeal. **–apparat,** *m.* ice-machine, freezer. **–fleisch,** *n.* frozen meat. **–punkt,** *m.* freezing-point. **–schutzlösung,** *f.* anti-freeze solution (*Motor.*).
gefroren, *p.p.* *of* **frieren. –e(s),** *n.* ice-(cream).
Gefüg–e, *n.* joining, fitting together; construction, structure, system, frame; articulation, joints; texture; stratification. **–ig,** *adj.* pliant, pliable, flexible; adaptable, tractable, docile; accommodating. **–igkeit,** *f.* pliancy, flexibility, adaptability, tractability.
Gefühl, *n.* (-(e)s, -e) feeling, sentiment, emotion; touch, sense of feeling, consciousness. **–erfüllt,** *adj.*, *see* **–sbetont. –los,** *adj.* unfeeling, hard (-hearted), heartless, apathetic, numb; *–los gegen*, insensible to. **–losigkeit,** *f.* heartlessness; apathy; numbness. **–sart,** *f.* disposition. **–sbetont,** *adj.* sentimental, sensitive. **–smensch,** *m.* emotional character; sentimentalist. **–ssinn,** *m.* sense of touch. **–voll,** *adj.* feeling, tender; affectionate, sensitive; full of expression; sentimental.
geführig, *adj.* good for ski-ing (*of snow*).
gefüllt, *p.p.* & *adj.* filled; double (*Bot.*).
gefunden, *p.p.* *of* **finden.**
Gefunkel, *n.* glittering.
gefurcht, *adj.* furrowed, channelled, grooved, sulcate (*Bot.*).
gegabelt, *adj.* forked, furcate, dichotomous.
Gegacker, *n.* cackle, cackling (*of geese*).
gegangen, *p.p.* *of* **gehen.**
gegeben, *p.p.* & *adj.* given, accepted, acknowledged; traditional, inherited. **–e,** *n.*, **–heit,** *f.* reality, actuality, conditioning factor; (*pl.*) *–heiten*, data. **–enfalls,** *adv.* if occasion arises, in case, if necessary.
gegen, 1. *prep.* (*Acc.*) towards, to, in the direction of; against, opposed to, contrary to, over against, opposite to; compared with; in the presence of; in exchange, in return for, for; about, approximately; *– das Abkommen*, in violation of the agreement; *– bare Bezahlung*, for ready money, for cash; *ich wette 10 – eins*, I lay 10 to one; *– Empfangsbescheinigung*, against a receipt; *er hat etwas davon – mich erwähnt*, he mentioned s.th. about it to me; *die Mode ist so verschieden – früher*, fashion is so different from what it was; *eins – das andere halten*, compare one th. with another; *Heilmittel –*, remedy for; *– dreißig Jahre alt*, about thirty years old, round thirty; *Geld leihen – einen Wechsel*, lend money on a bill; *– hundert Mann*, about a hundred men; *Sie sind jung – mich*, you are young compared with me; *es geht – Morgen*, it is nearly morning; *sich – einen neigen*, bow to a p.; *– Osten*, eastward, towards the east, in the east; *– Quittung*, against a receipt; *– den Strom*, against the current; *– die Vernunft*, in the face of reason; *– diese Zeit*, about this time. 2. *adv.* & *as accented prefix*, contrary, opposing, counter, *etc.* **–absicht,** *f.* opposite intention, cross-purpose. **–angriff,** *m.* counter-attack. **–anklage,** *f.* counter-charge. **–anschlag,** *m.* counterplot. **–arznei,** *f.* antidote. **–bedingung** *f.*; *wir haben zur –bedingung gemacht, daß*, in return, we have stipulated that. **–befehl,** *m.* counter-order; *–befehl geben*, countermand. **–bemerkung,** *f.* reply, criticism. **–beschuldigung,** *f.* recrimination. **–besuch,** *m.* return visit; *einen –besuch machen*, return a visit. **–bewegung,** *f.* reaction, counter-movement. **–beweis,** *m.* counter-evidence. **–beziehung,** *f.*, **–bezug,** *m.* correlation. **–bild,** *n.* contrast; counterpart; antitype. **–böschung,** *f.* counterscarp (*Fort.*). **–dienst,** *m.* service in return. **–druck,** *m.* reaction, resistance; counter-pressure. **–einander,** *adv.* towards *or* against each other, reciprocally; *–einander geneigt*, converging (*Math.*); *–einanderhalten*, *–einanderstellen*, *v.a.* compare, place side by side, bring face to face, confront. **–einanderhaltung,** *f.*, **–einanderstellung,** *f.* comparison; confrontation. **–einanderstoßen,** *n.* shock, collision. **–erklärung,** *f.* counter-declaration; denial, protest. **–farbe,** *f.* complementary colour, contrasting colour. **–forderung,** *f.* counter-claim, set-off. **–frage,** *f.* question in reply to a question. **–füßler,** *m.* dweller in the antipodes, antipode. **–gefühl,** *n.* opposite feeling; aversion. **–gesang,** *m.* antiphony. **–gewicht,** *n.* counterpoise, counterweight; *einem das –gewicht halten*, neutralize a man's influence. **–gift,** *n.* antidote; antitoxin. **–grund,** *m.* objection. **–gruß,** *m.* greeting in return. **–halt,** *m.* counter-pressure; resistance; holdfast, prop. **–halten,** (*sep.*) *v.n.* (*aux.* h.) resist; endure. **–kaiser,** *m.* rival emperor. **–klage,** *f.* recrimination; cross-

action (*Law*). **-kraft,** *f.* reaction, opposing force. **-kurs,** *m.* reciprocal course. **-laufgraben,** *m.* counter-approach (*Mil.*). **-läufig,** *adj.* contra-rotating. **-leistung,** *f.* return, equivalent. **-liebe,** *f.* mutual love; (*coll.*) *er fand mit diesem Vorschlag keine -liebe,* his proposal met with no support *or* was not taken up. **-macht,** *f.* opposing power, adversary. **-maßnahme,** *f.*, **-maßregel,** *f.* counter-measure, preventive measure; (*pl.*) retaliation, reprisals. **-mittel,** *n.* remedy, antidote. **-mutter,** *f.* lock-nut (*Mach.*). **-part,** *m.*; 1. *den -part halten,* maintain the contrary; *see* **-teil.** 2. adversary, antagonist. **-partei,** *f.* (party in) opposition. (*C.L.*) **-posten,** *m.* set-off. **-prall,** *m.* rebound; shock. **-probe,** *f.* check-test, control test. **-rasse,** *f.* (*Nat. Soc.*) misbegotten race (*e.g. Jews, Negroes, even French. 'Rasse' became so pure and holy that it could not be used of the enemy*). **-rechnung,** *f.* check-account, set-off, contra-account; *in -rechnung stehen,* have mutual accounts; *durch -rechnung beglichen* or *saldiert,* counterbalanced by. **-rede,** *f.* contradiction; reply, counter-plea, replication (*Law*). **-reiz,** *m.* counter-irritant. **-revolution,** *f.* counter-revolution. **-richtung,** *f.* reverse direction. **-sang,** *m.* antiphony. **-satz,** *m.* antithesis; contrast; opposition; *im -satze zu,* in opposition to. **-sätzlich,** *adj.* contrary, adverse, opposite. **-schein,** *m.* reflection (*Phys.*); opposition (*Astr.*); counter-deed *or* bond. **-schiene,** *f.* guard-rail. **-schrift,** *f.* refutation; rejoinder. **-see,** *f.* head sea. **-seite,** *f.* opposite *or* reverse side; reverse; opponent, the other party. **-seitig,** *adj.* reciprocal, mutual; *-seitiger Teil,* opposing party; *-seitige Freundschaft,* mutual friendship; *sich -seitig beziehend,* correlative. **-seitigkeit,** *f.* reciprocity; (*C.L.*) *auf -seitigkeit,* mutual; (*coll.*) *das beruht ganz auf -seitigkeit,* I feel just the same. **-sicherheit,** *f.* counter-security, counter-pledge. **-signal,** *n.* answering signal. **-sinn,** *m.* contrary sense; *im -sinne nehmen,* misinterpret. **-sonne,** *f.* parhelion, mock sun. **-spiel,** *n.* counterpart, reverse; opposition; playing against another. **-spieler,** *m.* opponent, antagonist, adversary. **-sprechen,** *n.* two-way communication (*Tele.*). **-stand,** *m.* subject; object; affair; matter, item; *das ist kein -stand,* that is nothing, that is not the difficulty; *er ist der -stand des allgemeinen Gelächters,* he is the general laughing-stock. **-ständig,** *adj.* opposite (*Bot.*). **-ständlich,** *adj.* objective, perspicuous, graphic. **-standsglas,** *n.* object-glass. **-standslos,** *adj.* superfluous, unnecessary, without object, meaningless, unfounded, unsound, devoid of application. **-standswort,** *n.* concrete noun. **-steigerung,** *f.* anticlimax. **-stich,** *m.* counter-thrust. **-stimme,** *f.* counterpart (*Mus.*); dissentient voice. **-stoff,** *m.* antidote, antibody. **-stoß,** *m.* counter-thrust, counter-attack; reaction (*Phys.*). **-strahl,** *m.* reflection, reflected ray (*Phys.*). **-strich,** *m.* stroke against the grain. **-strom,** *m.*, **-strömung,** *f.* eddy, counter-current. **-strophe,** *f.* antistrophe. **-stück,** *n.* counterpart; antithesis; companion picture *or* piece, the other one of a pair. **-subjekt,** *n.* counter-subject (*of a fugue*). **-tausch,** *m.* exchange; interchange. **-teil,** *n.* opposite, contrary, reverse, converse; *er tut gerade das -teil,* he does just the opposite; *das -teil behaupten,* maintain the contrary; *im -teil, -teils,* on the contrary; *ins -teil umschlagen,* turn the tables (*relationship*), turn inside out (*argument, etc.*). **-teilig,** *adj.* contrary, to the contrary, opposite. **-treten,** *v.n.* back-pedal (*Cycl.*). **-über,** 1. *adv.* opposite, face to face, facing, vis-à-vis, abreast; *einander -über,* facing one another; *sich (einer Aufgabe) -über sehen,* be up against (a task). 2. *prep.* (*with preceding Dat.*) opposite (to), over against; opposed to, in the face of; in relation to, as concerns; (*with place names also* -über von, *e.g.* -über von Bremen = Bremen -über). 3. *n.* (-s, -) that which is opposite; vis-à-vis (*p. at table, in railway carriage, etc.*), outlook (*from one's window*), etc. **-überliegend,** *adj.*, **-überstehend,** *adj.* facing, opposite; *-überliegende Winkel,* alternate angles. **-überstellung,** *f.* opposition; comparison; contrast; antithesis; confrontation. **-ufer,** *n.* opposite bank. **-unterschrift,** *f.*, **-unterzeichnung,** *f.* counter-signature. **-verhör,** *n.* cross-examination. **-verkehr,** *m.* traffic from the opposite direction. **-verpflichtung,** *f.* counter-obligation. **-verschreibung,** *f.* collateral deed; counter-bond. **-versicherung,** *f.* counter-security; reinsurance. **-versuch,** *m.* control experiment. **-vorstellung,** *f.* remonstrance. **-vorwurf,** *m.* recrimination. **-wart,** *f.* presence, the present (time); present tense (*Gram.*). **-wärtig,** 1. *adj.* present, actual, current, extant; *die hier -wärtigen,* those present; *-wärtige Preise,* current prices; *einem -wärtig sein,* be present in a p.'s mind; (*C.L.*) *-wärtiges Schreiben,* these presents, the present; (*C.L.*) *mit -wärtigem melde ich Ihnen,* I beg to inform you by the present. 2. *adv.* at present, just now, nowadays. **-wechsel,** *m.* counter-bill of exchange. **-wehr,** *f.* resistance, defence. **-wert,** 1. *m.* equivalent, set-off, counter-value. 2. *adj.* equivalent. **-wind,** *m.* head-wind. **-winkel,** *m.* alternate angle. **-wirkung,** *f.* reaction, counter-action, counter-effect. **-zeichnen,** *v.a.* countersign. **-zeichnung,** *f.* counter-signature. **-zeugnis,** *n.* counter-evidence, contradictory evidence. **-zug,** *m.* counter-move. **-zwangsmittel,** *n.* reprisals.

Gegend, *f.* (-en) region, district; tract of country; neighbourhood; *in unsrer -,* in our parts; *die - um Potsdam,* the environs of Potsdam; *in welcher -?* whereabouts?

gegessen, *p.p. of* **essen.**

Gegirre, *n.* cooing (*of doves*).

geglichen, *p.p. of* **gleichen.**

gegliedert, *p.p. & adj.* jointed; articulate; constructed organically, organized.

geglitten, *p.p. of* **gleiten.**

geglommen, *p.p. of* **glimmen.**

Gegner, *m.* (-s, -) opponent, adversary, enemy, foe. **-isch,** *adj.* hostile, antagonistic, opposing, adverse; *-ische Anstürme,* hostile attacks. **-schaft,** *f.* opponents, antagonists, adversaries; opposition, antagonism.

gegolten, *p.p. of* **gelten.**

gegoren, *p.p. of* **gären.**

gegossen, *p.p. of* **gießen.**

gegriffen, *p.p. of* **greifen.**

Gegrö(h)le, *n.* (*coll.*) cacophony, clamour, caterwauling, hullaballoo, hubbub.

Gehabe, *n.* (*coll.*) fussy, affected *or* pretentious behaviour, mannerisms. **-n,** 1. *ir.v.r.* (*pres. only*) conduct o.s., behave; *gehabt euch wohl!* farewell! 2. *n.* behaviour.

Gehackte(s), *n.* minced meat, mince.

Gehader, *n.* brawling.

Gehalt, 1. *m.* (-s, -e) contents, ingredients; content, capacity; strength, body; proportion, percentage; intrinsic value, merit, import. 2. *n.* (*& Austr. & Bav. m.*) (-(e)s, ⁻er & -e) pay, wages, salary, stipend; allowance; *bei einem im -e stehen,* be in a p.'s pay; *auskömmliches -,* sufficient income, living wage. **-los,** *adj.* worthless, shallow, superficial. **-losigkeit,** *f.* worthlessness, superficiality. **-reich,** *adj.* having body, rich (*in content*), substantial, of value; racy (*of wine*). **-sabzug,** *m.* deduction from salary. **-saufbesserung,** *f.*, **-serhöhung,** *f.*, **-svermehrung,** *f.*, **-szulage,** *f.* increment, increase *or* rise in salary. **-sbestimmung,** *f.* analysis, assay (*Chem., Metall.*). **-sempfänger,** *m.* salaried employee. **-skürzung,** *f.* reduction *or* cut in salary.

gehalten, *p.p. & adj.* bound, obliged; self-controlled, sober, steady; *gut -,* well kept; well treated; *- werden für,* be taken for.

Gehänge, *n.* (-s, -) slope, incline, declivity; hangings, pendants, festoon; hanging ears (*of a dog*). **-schutt,** *m.* scree. **-ton,** *m.* residual clay.

geharnischt, *p.p. & adj.* armoured, violent (*of words*); fiery, testy, barbed, stinging.

gehässig, *adj.* spiteful, malicious, odious; *das -e,* odium. **-keit,** *f.* hatefulness, odiousness; spitefulness, animosity, malice.

Gehau, *n.* (-(e)s, -e) clearing; copse; wood where trees are being felled.

Gehäuse, *n.* (-s, –) box, case, casing, receptacle, shell, housing, capsule, jacket; binnacle; core (*of fruit*); – *einer Reliquie*, shrine.
Geheck(e), *n.* (-(e)s, -e) hatch, brood; covey.
Gehege, *n.* (-s, –) enclosure, enclosed place, precinct; preserve, reservation, plantation; (*fig.*) *einem ins – kommen*, encroach on a p.'s ground *or* rights; (*coll.*) poke one's nose in s.o. else's business.
geheim, *adj.* secret; private, confidential; hidden, concealed, clandestine; underground; (*in titles*) confidential, privy; *im –en, ins–*, secretly; (*B.*) *die –e Offenbarung*, Apocalypse; *–er Rat*, privy council; privy councillor; *see* **–rat**; *–es Siegel*, privy seal; *–e Wissenschaft*, occult science; *–e Tinte*, sympathetic ink; *mit einer S. – tun*, conceal what one is doing; *–er Sinn*, mystical sense. **–bote,** *m.* confidential messenger. **–buch,** *n.* secret journal (*of a commercial house*). **–bund,** *m.* secret society; underground organization; clandestine alliance. **–bündler,** *m.* member of a secret society. **–fach,** *n.* secret drawer, private safe, safe-deposit. **–halten,** *v.a.* keep secret. **–haltung,** *f.* secrecy. **–konto,** *n.* private account. **–lehre,** *f.* esoteric doctrine; *jüdische –lehre*, cab(b)ala. **–mittel,** *n.* secret remedy, patent medicine, nostrum. **–nis,** *n.* secret, mystery; secrecy; arcanum; *öffentliches –nis*, open secret; *ein –nis bewahren*, keep a secret. **–niskrämer,** *m.* mystery-monger. **–niskrämerei,** *f.*, *see* **–tuerei. –nisvoll,** *adj.* mysterious, secretive; (*coll.*) *tu' nicht so –nisvoll*, don't make such a business of it. **–polizei,** *f.* secret police. **–rat,** *m.* privy councillor. **–ratsecken,** *f.pl.* receding hair, frontal baldness. **–ratsviertel,** *n.* fashionable quarter, West End. **–schloß,** *n.* letter-lock. **–schlüssel,** *m.* cipher key *or* code. **–schreibekunst,** *f.* cryptography. **–schreiber,** *m.* private secretary, confidential clerk. **–schrift,** *f.* cipher, code, secret writing. **–sein,** *n.* secrecy. **–sender,** *m.* clandestine *or* pirate radio transmitter; unofficial broadcasting station (*for political propaganda*). **–siegel,** *n.* privy seal. **–sprache,** *f.* secret language, code language. **–tinte,** *f.* invisible *or* sympathetic ink. **–treppe,** *f.* private staircase, backstairs. **–tuer,** *m.*, *see* **–niskrämer. –tuerei,** *f.* secretiveness. **–tuerisch,** *adj.* secretive. **–wirkend,** *adj.* sympathetic; of mystical influence. **–zimmer,** *n.* private cabinet, closet (*of a prince*).
Geheiß, *n.* command, order, bidding, injunction; *auf mein –*, at my bidding.
geh–en, I. *ir.v.n.* (*aux.* s.) go, move, walk, proceed, pass; leave, go away; extend to, reach; run, work *of machinery*); succeed (*imp. with Dat.*); go *or* fare with, be (*in health, etc.*); *das –t nicht an*, that is impossible *or* out of the question; *an die Arbeit –en*, set about *or* begin to work; *– nicht an meine Briefe!* do not touch my letters! *einem an die Hand –en*, assist a p.; give a p. a (helping) hand; *es –t ihm an den Kragen*, it touches him closely, things are getting warm *or* hot for him; *es –t ans Leben*, it is a matter of life and death; *einer S. auf den Grund –en*, get to the bottom of a th.; *auf die Jagd –en*, go (a-)hunting; *aufs Land –en*, go into the country; *auf Leben und Tod –en*, be a matter of life and death; *einem auf den Leim –en*, fall into a p.'s trap, allow o.s. to be hoodwinked; *wie viel Pfennige –en auf eine Mark?* how many pfennigs are there in a mark? *es –t auf Mittag*, it is getting on for midday; *auf die Neige –en*, come to an end, draw to a close; *das –t mir auf die Nerven*, that is getting on my nerves; *auf Reisen* or *auf die Reise –en*, set out on a journey *or* one's travels; *auf bösen Wegen –en*, lead an evil life; *diese Worte gingen auf mich*, these words were aimed *or* directed at me; *– mir aus den Augen*, get out of my sight; *aus den Fugen –en*, get out of joint, come to grief, fall to pieces; *aus dem Wege –en*, step aside, stand out of the way; *das Wasser –t ihm bis an den Hals*, the water came *or* reached up to his neck; *seine Absicht ging dahin*, his intention was; (*coll.*) *er wird d(a)rauf–en*, it will be his death, it will cost him his life; *in diesem Hause –t viel darauf*, the expenses in this house are very great; the upkeep of this house is very high; *sein ganzes Vermögen wird d(a)rauf–en*, it will cost him his whole fortune; *darüber –t nichts*, nothing is better than that: *drunter und drüber –en*, become topsy-turvy, get higgledy-piggledy; *durch den Kopf* or *Sinn –en*, cross one's mind, strike one, occur to one; *das –t mir durch Mark und Bein*, that goes through and through me; *wohin –t es hier?* where does this lead to? *es wird schon –en*, it will be all right, no doubt it will do, that will all come right, it can easily be done; *wie –t's (Ihnen)?* how do you do? how are you? *O, es –t*, Oh, pretty well; *wie wird mir's* or *wird's mir –en?* what will become of me? *es –t gegen Morgen*, it is getting towards morning; *einem gegen den Strich –en*, go against the grain; upset one's plans; *es ist mir gerade so gegangen*, it was just the same with me, the same happened in my case; *das Buch –t gut*, the book sells well; *das Geschäft –t gut*, the business is doing well; *es läßt sich hier gut –en*, the way is easy here; *in die Binsen –en*, come to grief *or* naught; *in die Brüche, in Stücke* or *in Trümmer –en*, go *or* fall to pieces, disintegrate, break down, come to grief, come to naught; *ins einzelne –en*, go into details; *in Erfüllung –en*, come true, be realized, come to pass; *die Preise –en in die Höhe*, prices are rising, soaring *or* rocketing; *einem ins Garn –en*, fall into a p.'s trap, let o.s. be hoodwinked; *mit einem streng ins Gericht –en*, take s.o. to task; *ins vierte Jahr –end*, entering the fourth year; *das –t mit in den Kauf*, that is included *or* is part of the bargain; *in See –en*, put out to sea; *in Seide –en*, wear silk; *in sich –en*, repent, turn over a new leaf; *er ist ins Wasser gegangen*, he has drowned himself; *in die Welt hinaus –en*, launch into the world; *die Zahl –t in die Hunderte*, the number runs into hundreds; *kaputt –en*, get broken; *er kam gegangen*, he came on foot; *etwas –en lassen*, let a th. go, give a th. up; *lassen Sie ihn –en*, leave him alone; *sich –en lassen*, let o.s. go, indulge one's inclinations; speak freely; *wie –t das Lied?* how does the song go *or* run? *der Strom –t mit Eis*, the river is full of drift-ice; *sie –t mit ihm*, she is keeping company with him, he is her young man; *mit der Zeit –en*, march with the times; *nach Brot –en*, go a-begging; seek a livelihood; *das –t nicht nach mir*, I have no say in the matter; *alles –t nach Wunsch*, everything is going as well as we could wish; *die Zimmer –en alle nach der Straße*, all the rooms face *or* overlook the street; *wann –t der Zug nach Hannover?* when does the train for Hanover leave? *das –t mir nahe*, that touches me very closely; *das –t nicht*, that can't be done *or* won't do, that is not possible *or* is impossible; *es –t die Rede*, talk *or* rumour has it, it is said; *schief –en*, go wrong; *schlafen –en*, go to bed; *schwanger –en*, be pregnant, be with child; *mit großen Entwürfen schwanger –en*, be full of great projects; *der Teig –t*, the dough rises; *die Tür –t*, the door opens; *das –t über alles*, that beats everything; *das –t mir über alles*, I like it better than anything; (*coll.*) *das –t über alle Begriffe*, that beats everything, that is beyond belief; *das –t über meine Kraft*, that is beyond my powers; *über Land –en*, go across country; *über Leichen –en*, ride rough-shod over; *die Uhr –t richtig* (or *vor*), the clock is right (*or* fast); *einem um den Bart –en*, wheedle, coax *or* flatter a p.; *wie die Katze um den heißen Brei –en*, be like a cat on hot bricks; *es –t um Geld*, money is at stake, it is a money matter; *es –t um die letzte Entscheidung*, the final decision must be made *or* reached; *es –t um nichts*, there is nothing at stake; *unter die Leute –en*, go into society; *unter die Soldaten –en*, enlist; *verlustig –en* (*with Gen.*), lose (a th.); *es –t ihm von der Hand*, he is a quick and successful worker; *er ist von uns gegangen*, he has departed from us (= died); *vonstatten –en*, go on well, proceed, succeed; *vor Anker –en*, cast anchor; *er ist vor die Hunde gegangen*, he has gone to the dogs; *vor sich –en*, take place, proceed; *– deiner Wege!* get on! be off! *– weiter*, carry *or* go on; (*sl.*) *er wurde gegangen*, he was made to go *or* was dismissed; *es –t ein Sturm*, a strong gale is blowing; *er läßt es sich dort ganz wohl –en*, he enjoys himself very much there; *zu einem –en*, go to see s.o.; *zum Abendmahl –en*, take the holy communion; *zu Fuß –en*, walk, go on foot; *zugrunde –en*, break down, be ruined, be wrecked; *einem zur*

Hand –en, help a p.; *das –t mir zu Herzen*, that touches my heart, I am very sorry about it; *zur Industrie –en*, go into industry; *einem zu Leibe –en*, lay a hand on a p.; *zur Neige –en*, come to an end; *mit sich zu Rate –en*, deliberate, consider; *behutsam zu Werke –en*, set about cautiously. 2. *n.* walking; *das –en wird ihm sauer*, he has difficulty in walking; *des –ens müde sein*, be tired of walking; *das Kommen und –en*, coming and going. **–bar,** *adj.* passable, practicable (*for pedestrians*). **–entfernung,** *f.* walking distance (*usually measured as time*); 3 *Stunden –entfernung*, 3 hours' walk. **–rock,** *m.* frock-coat. **–steig,** *m.* **–weg,** *m.* footpath, pavement, sidewalk.

Gehenk, *n.* (-(e)s, -e) sword-belt; strap (*for hanging s.th. up by*); loop.

geheuer, *adj.* (*only neg. as*) *nicht* –, uncanny, haunted.

Geheul, *n.* howling, lamentation, yelling.

Gehilfe, *m.* (-n, -n) assistant, help, helper; aide-de-camp (*Mil.*).

Gehirn, *n.* (-(e)s, -e) brain; brains, sense; *das kleine* –, cerebellum; *einem das – einschlagen*, knock out a man's brains. **–behälter,** *m.* cranium, skull. **–blatt,** *n.* fontanel. **–entzündung,** *f.* inflammation of the brain, brain-fever. **–erschütterung,** *f.* concussion of the brain. **–erweichung,** *f.* softening of the brain. **–haut,** *f.* cerebral membrane *or* meninges. **–hautentzündung,** *f.* meningitis. **–krankheit,** *f.* brain disorder. **–lehre,** *f.* craniology. **–los,** *adj.* brainless, senseless. **–mark,** *n.* medulla. **–schlag,** *m.* cerebral apoplexy. **–wassersucht,** *f.* hydrocephalus.

gehoben, *p.p. of* **heben** *&* *adj.*; *–e Sprache*, elevated speech, high style; *fünfmal –e Verse*, verses of five beats, pentameters; *–e Stimmung*, high spirits.

Gehöft, *n.* (-(e)s, -e), (*Austr. dial.*) **–e,** *n.* (-s, –) farm, farm buildings, farmstead.

geholfen, *p.p. of* **helfen.**

Gehölz, *n.* (-es, -e) wood, woodland, copse.

gehor–chen, *v.n.* (*aux.* h.) (*Dat.*) obey; *der Vernunft –chen*, listen to reason; *das Schiff –cht dem Ruder*, the ship obeys *or* responds to the tiller. **–sam,** 1. *adj.* obedient, dutiful; submissive; obsequious; *Ihr –samer Diener*, your obedient servant (*at the end of letters to newspapers, etc.*). 2. *m.* obedience, dutifulness; *aus –sam gegen*, in obedience to; *–sam leisten*, obey; *–sam verweigern*, disobey; *der dem Landesfürsten schuldige –sam*, the allegiance due to one's sovereign; *einem den –sam aufkündigen*, renounce allegiance to a p.; *ich verlange –sam*, I will be obeyed; *Verweigerung des –sams*, insubordination. **–samst,** (*sup.*) *adj.* obediently yours (*at the end of a letter, rather servile*); *–samster Diener!* at your service; *melde –samst*, I beg to report (*Mil.*).

Gehör, *n.* hearing; musical ear; *gutes* –, quick ear; *zu – kommen*, be heard; be performed (*of music*); *sich* (*Dat.*) *– verschaffen*, make o.s. heard; *nach dem – singen* (*spielen*), sing (play) by ear; *der Vernunft – geben*, listen to reason; *um – bitten*, crave a hearing; *– schenken*, lend an ear, give a hearing to. **–en,** 1. *v.n.* (*aux.* h.) (*Dat.*) belong to, be owned by, be part of, appertain to; be due to; *das –t nicht hierher*, that is beside the point *or* is irrelevant; *–t das Ihnen?* is it yours? *wo –t dies hin?* where does this go? *er –t mit dazu*, he is one of them; *dazu –t Geld und Zeit*, that requires time and money; *dazu –t Mut*, courage is needed for that; *er –t in die Irrenanstalt*, he ought to be in a madhouse; *es –t zum guten Ton*, it is the polite *or* proper thing to do; *diese –en zu den besten, die ich Ihnen zeigen kann*, these are among the best I can show you; *es –t schon etwas dazu, so etwas zu tun*, (*coll.*) that really takes some doing; *–en unter* (*Acc.*), pertain to, be subject to, fall under; *das –t nicht auf den Tisch*, that does not go on the table. 2. *v.r. & imp.* be suitable *or* proper *or* becoming; *wie sich's –t*, as is right, as is seemly; properly, suitably, duly; *das –t sich nicht*, that isn't the way to behave; *ich verlange nur, was sich –t*, I only ask for what is fair; *so –t es sich*, that is how it should be (done), that is right and proper. **–fehler,** *m.* defect in hearing. **–gang,** *m.* auditory canal. **–ig,** *adj.* belonging to, appertaining to; fitting, suitable; requisite, necessary, proper, fit, due; *nicht zur S. –ig*, irrelevant; *der –ige Respekt*, the proper respect, the respect due (to him, etc.); *–iger Lügner*, thorough liar; *ich hab's ihm –ig gegeben*, I have given him a piece of my mind; *ich habe ihn –ig heimgeschickt*, I have sent him about his business. **–igkeit,** *f.* suitability, fitness, propriety; competence, competency. **–lähmung,** *f.* (partial) deafness. **–lehre,** *f.* acoustics. **–los,** *adj.* deaf. **–mangel,** *m.* defective hearing, deafness. **–nerv,** *m.* auditory nerve. **–sinn,** *m.* (sense of) hearing. **–trichter,** *m.* ear-trumpet.

Gehörn, *n.* (-(e)s, -e) horns, antlers. **–t,** *p.p. & adj.* horned, antlered, horny; *der –te Siegfried*, Siegfried the invulnerable; *der –te Ehemann*, cuckold.

Gehr–e, *f.* (-en), (*dial*) **–en,** *m.* wedge; gusset, gore, triangular field. **–en,** *v.a.* bevel. **–ig,** *adj.* oblique; bevelled. **–hobel,** *m.* bevel-plane. **–holz,** *n.*, **–maß,** *n.* bevel. **–ung,** *f.* mitre, bevel, wedge.

Gehudel, *n.* bungling, botched work.

gehüpft, *p.p.* (*coll.*) *das ist – wie gesprungen*, that's as broad as it's long, it is much of a muchness, six of one and half a dozen of the other.

Geier, *m.* (-s, –) vulture, hawk; *hol' dich der* –, deuce take you! confound you!

Geifer, *m.* drivel, spittle, slaver; venom, wrath; *seinen – auslassen*, vent one's spleen (*an*, upon). **–er,** *m.* vilifier, disparager, scoffer, detractor, carper, caviller, slanderer, traducer. **–läppchen,** *n.*, *see* **–tuch.** **–n,** *v.n.* (*aux.* h.) drivel, slaver, foam at the mouth; (*fig.*) vent one's anger, foam with rage. **–tuch,** *n.* bib.

Geige, *f.* (-n) violin; (*coll.*) fiddle; (*coll.*) *der Himmel hängt ihm voller –n*, he sees the bright side of things, he is full of pleasant anticipations. **–n,** *v.a. & n.* (*aux.* h.) play (on) the violin; (*coll.*) fiddle. **–nbogen,** *m.* (violin-)bow; (*coll.*) fiddle-stick. **–nharz,** *n.* clarified resin, colophony. **–nkasten,** *m.* violin-case. **–nsattel,** *m.*, **–nsteg,** *m.* violin bridge. **–nstimme,** *f.* violin-part. **–nwirbel,** violin-peg. **–r,** *m.* violinist, violin-player, fiddler.

geil, *adj.* luxuriant, rank, voluptuous; lustful, lascivious, in *or* on heat, lewd; *–es Fleisch*, proud flesh; *–er Blick*, wanton glance. **–e,** *f.* (-en), *see* **–heit;** (*dial.*) manure; (*pl.*) testicles (*of animals*). **–en,** *v.n.* (*aux.* h.) lust, be lascivious; ask for presents (in an importunate way). 2. *n.* lasciviousness; (*B.*) importunity. **–heit,** *f.* rankness, luxuriance; lasciviousness, lewdness; rut.

Geisel, *m.* (-s, – & (*Austr.*) -n) *& f.* (-n) hostage *– stellen*, give *or* furnish hostages.

Geiser, *m.* (-s, –) geyser, hot spring.

Geiß, *f.* (-en) (*dial.*) (she *or* nanny) goat, wild goat, doe. **–bart,** *m.* meadowsweet (*Filipendula ulmaria*), goatsbeard (*Spiraea aruncus*) (*Bot.*). **–blatt,** *n.* honeysuckle, woodbine (*Lonicera periclymenum*) (*Bot.*). **–bock,** *m.* he-goat, billy-goat. **–fuß,** *m.* crow-bar, hand-spike; sculptor's veining tool; dentist's implement; goatweed, bishop's weed *or* herb gerard (*Aegopodium podagraria*) (*Bot.*). **–lein,** *n.* kid.

Geißel, *f.* (-n) lash, whip; (*fig.*) scourge; flagellum cilium (*Bot.*, *Zool.*, *Ent.*); cutting reproach *or* sarcasm; *Gottes* –, the scourge of God (Attila) **–brüder,** *m.pl.* flagellants. **–faden,** *m.* flagellum cilium (*Bot.*, *Zool.*, *Ent.*). **–n,** *v.a.* scourge, lash, whip, flagellate; criticize severely, censure, reprimand, condemn. **–ung,** *f.* scourging, lashing, flagellation; (*fig.*) condemnation.

Geist, *m.* (-es, -er (*& Bohemian dial.*) -e) spirit, mind, intellect, intelligence, wit, imagination; genius, soul; morale; essence; ghost, spirit, spectre; *den – aufgeben*, give up the ghost, breathe one's last; *er war von allen guten –ern verlassen*, he had lost all sense of reason; *wir handeln in seinem* –, we are acting according to his intentions; *der heilige* –, the Holy Ghost, the Holy Spirit; *ich weiß, wes –es Kind er ist*, I know what sort of a fellow he is; *voll – und Leben*, witty and vivacious; *der schöne* –, *der Schön–*, bel-esprit, wit; *– einer Sprache*, genius of a language; *es geht ein – in diesem Hause um*, there is a spectre in this house, this house is haunted; *der –, der stets verneint*, the spirit of negation; *dieser Wein hat* –, this wine has body. **-bildend,** *adj.* formative, educative, cultural. **-erähnlich,** *adj.* spectral. **-erbann,** *m.*, **-erbannung,** *f.*, **-erbeschwörung,** *f.* exorcism. **-erbanner,** *m.*, **-erbeschwörer,** *m.* necromancer; exorcist. **-erbild,** *n.* phantom. **-erbleich,** *adj.* pale as a ghost. **-ererscheinung,** *f.* apparition. **-ergeschichte,** *f.* ghost-story. **-erhaft,** *adj.* supernatural; ghostly; ghostlike. **-erglaube,** *m.* belief in ghosts. **-ermüdend,** *adj.* mentally exhausting. **-ern,** *v.n.* haunt. **-erquickend,** *adj.* mentally refreshing. **-erreich,** *n.* spirit-world, the realm of spirits. **-erseher,** *m.* visionary, seer. **-erseherei,** *f.* second sight. **-erstunde,** *f.* witching hour. **-erwelt,** *f.* spirit-world. **-esabwesend,** *adj.* absent-minded. **-esarbeit,** *f.* brain work. **-esarm,** *adj.* poor in spirit, stupid. **-esbildung,** *f.* cultivation of the mind. **-esblitz,** *m.* brain-wave; stroke of genius. **-esfähigkeiten,** *f.pl.* intellectual powers. **-esfreiheit,** *f.* freedom of thought *or* conscience. **-esfrucht,** *f.* literary *or* artistic production. **-esfunke,** *m.* flash of wit. **-esgabe,** *f.* talent, gift. **-esgegenwart,** *f.* presence of mind. **-esgenuß,** *m.* intellectual enjoyment. **-esgeschichte,** *f.* history of ideas. **-esgestört,** *adj.* deranged, unhinged. **-esgröße,** *f.* intellectual greatness; intellectual giant; magnanimity. **-eshaltung,** *f.* mentality, attitude of mind. **-esheld,** *m.* intellectual, literary *or* artistic giant. **-eskraft,** *f.* mental power *or* vigour. **-eskrank,** *adj.* of unsound mind, insane. **-eskrankheit,** *f.* mental disorder, insanity. **-esschwach,** *adj.* feeble-minded. **-esschwäche,** *f.* imbecility. **-esschwung,** *m.* enthusiasm; flight of fancy. **-esstörung,** *f.* mental derangement; mental disorder. **-esträge,** *adj.* intellectually lazy *or* dull. **-esverfassung,** *f.* state of mind, frame of mind. **-esverwandt,** *adj.* congenial. **-esverwirrung,** *f.* mental disturbance *or* unbalance, derangement, delirium. **-eswissenschaften,** *f.pl.* the Arts (*contrasted with 'the Sciences'*). **-eszerrüttung,** *f.* mental disturbance. **-eszustand,** *m.* mental health *or* state. **-ig,** *adj.* spiritual, mental, intellectual; spirituous, volatile, alcoholic; *-ige Arbeit,* brain work; *-ig beschränkt,* stupid; *-iges Eigentum,* intellectual property; *-ige Getränke,* spirits, alcoholic beverages; *er enthält sich aller -igen Getränke,* he is a total abstainer; *-ige Liebe,* platonic love. **-igkeit,** *f.* spirituality; intellectuality; alcoholic content. **-lich,** *adj.* spiritual, religious, sacred; clerical, ecclesiastic; (*B.*) *selig sind, die da -lich arm sind,* blessed are the poor in spirit; *die -liche Behörde,* the ecclesiastical authorities; *-liche Güter,* church lands; *-licher Herr,* clerical gentleman, *-liche Kurfürsten,* spiritual electors; *-liches Lied,* sacred song; *-liche Musik,* sacred music; *-liches Recht,* canon law, *in den -lichen Stand treten,* take (holy) orders, enter the Church. **-liche(r),** *m.* clergyman, minister, priest, pastor, ecclesiastic, divine. **-lichkeit,** *f.* spirituality; priesthood, clergy, the Church. **-los,** *adj.* dull, lifeless, spiritless; senseless, unintellectual. **-losigkeit,** *f.* dullness, mental sluggishness, lifelessness, lack of intellectual interests, spiritlessness. **-reich,** *adj.*, **-voll,** *adj.* ingenious, witty, clever, gifted. **-tötend,** *adj.* soul destroying.

Geitau, *n.* (-e) brail, clew-line (*Naut.*).

Geiz, *m.* avarice; greediness, covetousness, stinginess; inordinate desire; shoot, sucker (*Bot.*). **-en,** *v.n.* (*aux.* h.) covet, be covetous; be stingy; stint, economize; *mit etwas -en,* be economical of a th.; *mit der Gegenwart -en,* make the most of the present; *mit jeder Minute -en,* grudge every minute; *nach einer S. -en,* covet a th., be greedy for a th. **-hals,** *m.*, **-hammel,** *m.*, **-kragen,** *m.* miser, niggard, skinflint. **-ig,** *adj.* avaricious, covetous, stingy, miserly, niggardly; *-ig nach,* covetous of, greedy for.

Gejammer, *n.* wailing, lamentation.

Gejauchze, *n.* rejoicing, jubilation.

Gejohle, *n.* hooting, yelling.

gekachelt, *adj.* tiled.

gekannt, *p.p. of* **kennen.**

Gekeife, *n.* scolding, nagging, squabbling.

gekeimt, *adj.* germinated.

gekerbt, *adj.* crenate.

gekernt, *adj.* having a nucleus.

Gekicher, *n.* tittering.

gekielt, *adj.* carinate, keeled.

Geklapper, *n.* rattling, clatter.

geklappt, *adj.* collapsed, folded.

Geklimper, *n.* jingling, jangling; strumming (*on a piano*).

Geklingel, *n.* tinkling, jangling.

Geklirr(e), *n.* clanking, clanging, clashing.

gekloben, (*archaic*) *p.p. of* **klieben.**

geklommen, *p.p. of* **klimmen.**

Geklöne, *n.* (*coll.*) gossip, chat, tittle-tattle.

Geklopfe, *n.* knocking, banging.

geklungen, *p.p. of* **klingen.**

Geknatter, *n.* rattle, clatter.

geknäult, *adj.* glomerate, coiled.

geknickt, *p.p. & adj.* bent down; geniculate; (*fig.* cast down, subdued, disheartened, morose.

gekniet, *adj.* geniculate, bent, refracted.

gekniffen, *p.p. of* **kneifen.**

Geknirsche, *n.* grinding, gnashing (*of teeth*), crunching.

Geknister, *n.* crackling, rustling, rustle, crepitation.

gekonnt, *p.p. of* **können.**

geköpert, *p.p. & adj.* twilled (*Weav.*); (*coll.*) rich, wealthy.

gekoren, *p.p. of* **kiesen.**

gekörn-elt, *adj.*, **-t,** *adj.* grained, granular, granulated.

Gekose, *n.* (*fam.*) caressing, billing and cooing.

Gekrach(e), *n.* cracking, crash; thunderous noise.

Gekrächze, *n.* croaking.

Gekrätz(e), *n.* waste, refuse, slag, dross, sweeps (*Min.*).

Gekräus-e(l), *n.* curling; curl, ruffle, frill. **-elt,** *adj.* crisped, curled.

Gekreisch(e), *n.* shrieking, shrieks.

Gekritzel, *n.* scrawling, scrawl, scribbling, scribble.

gekrochen, *p.p. of* **kriechen.**

gekröpft, *adj.* off-set (*of tools, etc.*), angulate (*as a cornice*).

Gekröse, *n.* mesentery (*Anat.*); pluck (*of a calf*), entrails, giblets.

gekünstelt, *p.p. & adj.* artificial, affected.

Gelache, *n.* continual laughing.

Gelächter, *n.* laughter; laughing-stock; *in ein schallendes – ausbrechen,* burst out laughing; *wieherndes –,* horse-laugh; *einen zum – machen,* make a p. a laughing-stock, make sport of a p.; *sich dem – aussetzen,* expose o.s. to ridicule, make an exhibition of o.s.

geladen, *p.p. & adj.* charged, loaded; *– !* **load!** (*Mil.*); (*coll.*) *schwer – haben,* be tipsy.

Gelag(e), *n.* drinking-bout, carouse; feast, banquet; revel; *ein – halten,* revel.

Geläger, *n.* dregs, bottoms, deposit.

gelagert, *adj.* beaten down; stratified; mounted on bearings.

Gelände, *n.* arable land; (tract of) country; region; countryside; terrain (*Mil.*); area, territory, ground; *abfallendes* (*aufsteigendes*) –, falling (rising) slope; *bestrichenes –,* beaten zone (*Mil.*); *freies –,* open country; *schwieriges –,* difficult terrain. **-abschnitt,** *m.* sector, area. **-aufnahme,** *f.* aerial photograph, air survey. **-bö,** *f.* ground squall. **-fähig,** *adj.*, **-gängig,** *adj.* suitable for *or* able to traverse rough country, e.g. *-gängiger Wagen,* cross-country vehicle, jeep. **-hindernis,** *n.* natural obstacle. **-kunde,** *f.* topography. **-lauf,** *m.* cross-country run *or* race. **-punkt,** *m.* landmark. **-spiel,** *n.*, **-sport,** *m.* scoutcraft, scouting games. **-verhältnisse,** *n.pl.* nature of the ground.

Geländer, *n.* (-s, –) railing, rails; balustrade, parapet; banister, handrail; trellis, espalier. **-fenster,** *n.* window with balcony. **-säule,** *f.* baluster.

gelang, gelänge, *see* **gelingen.**

gelangen, *v.n.* (*aux.* s.) reach, arrive (at), attain (to); get (to), get admitted to; *in die richtigen Hände –,* get into the right hands; *ans Ziel* or *zu seinem Zwecke –,* attain one's end, accomplish one's purpose; *zur Reife –,* come to maturity; *etwas an einen – lassen,* get a th. delivered, forward, transmit *or* address s.th. to a p.; *auf die Nachwelt* –, be handed down to posterity; *dazu* –, reach the point; *zu Macht und Ansehen* –, reach a position of influence and esteem.

Gelärm(e), *n.* bustle, noise.

Gelaß, *n.* (-(ss)es, -(ss)e) small room, lobby; space.

gelassen, *p.p.* & *adj.* calm, cool, composed, collected; passive, patient; deliberate; – *bleiben*, keep one's temper, remain calm; *scheinbar* –, betraying no emotion. **–heit**, *f.* self-possession, calmness, composure, resignation; even temper, patience; deliberateness.

Gelatin–e, *f.* gelatine. **–efolie**, *f.* sheet *or* leaf gelatine. **–ös**, *adj.* gelatinous.

Gelaufe, *n.* running to and fro, bustle.

geläufig, *adj.* fluent, voluble; ready, easy, familiar, current; *–e Hand*, practised hand; *–e Redensart*, everyday remark, common saying; *–e Zunge*, ready tongue; *er spricht – Deutsch*, he speaks German fluently; *das ist ihm* –, he is familiar *or* conversant with it. **–keit**, *f.* easiness; facility; skill; fluency.

gelaunt, *adj.* disposed; humoured; *wie ist er heute – ?* in what humour is he today? *gut* –, in good humour, sweet-tempered; *schlecht* – or *übel* –, cross, peevish, out of temper, bad-tempered, irritable; *nicht* –, out of spirits *or* temper.

Geläut(e), *n.* ringing *or* peal of bells, chime; baying (*of hounds*).

gelb, 1. *adj.* yellow; *die –e Gefahr*, the yellow peril; *–er Neid*, livid envy; *–e Rübe*, carrot; *–er Verband*, non-affiliated trade union; *er wurde* – (*und grün*) *vor Neid*, he was livid with envy; *es wird ihm grün und – vor den Augen*, he feels dizzy *or* queer. 2. *n. see* **–e**. **–brennsäure**, *f.* pickling acid (*Metall.*). **–e**, 1. *n.* yellow colour; yellow colouring matter; *das –e im Ei*, yolk. **–en**, 1. *v.a.* make yellow. 2. *v.r.* & *n.* (*aux.* h.) turn yellow. **–er**, *m.* (*coll.*) member of a non-affiliated trade union. **–eisenerz**, *n.*, **–erde**, *f.* yellow ochre. **–filter**, *m.* light filter (*Phot.*). **–fuchs**, *m.* sorrel horse. **–gießer**, *m.* brass-founder. **–guß**, *m.* brass-founding. **–kreuzgas**, *n.* mustard gas. **–kupfer**, *n.* yellow metal, brass. **–lich**, *adj.* yellowish. **–lichgrau**, *adj.* drab. **–lichgrauweiß**, *adj.* pepper and salt (*colour*). **–ling**, *n.* chanterella (*Cantharellus cibarius*) (*Bot.*); species of butterfly (*Colias*). **–scheibe**, *f.*, *see* **–filter**. **–schnabel**, *m.* fledgeling; (*fig.*) saucy brat; greenhorn. **–stichig**, *adj.* yellowish, tinged with yellow. **–sucht**, *f.* jaundice. **–weiß**, *adj.* & *n.* cream (*colour*).

Geld, *n.* (-(e)s, -er) coin; money; cash; *anvertrautes* –, money in trust; *ausstehendes* –, money outstanding *or* due; *bares* – (*Bar-*), ready money, cash, money in hand; *bei –e sein*, have plenty of money, be well off; *nicht bei –e sein*, be short of money, be hard up; *falsches* –, counterfeit coin(s); – *zum Fenster hinauswerfen*, throw money down the drain; *viel für sein – bekommen*, get good value for one's money; *für – und gute Worte*, for love or money; *gangbares* –, good *or* current money; *gemünztes* –, coin; – *und Gut*, wealth; *er hat – wie Heu*, he is rolling in wealth; – *auf die hohe Kante legen*, put money on one side *or* aside; *kleines* – (*Klein–*), (small) change; *von seinem – leben*, live on one's income; *nicht mit – zu bezahlen*, invaluable; *öffentliche –er*, public funds; *das kostet ein schönes* –, that will cost a packet; *tägliches* –, daily *or* call money; *totes* –, dead capital; *einen um sein – bringen*, separate a p. from his money; *um sein – kommen*, lose one's money; *mit dem –e um sich werfen*, be free with one's money, fling one's money around. **–abfindung**, *f.* cash settlement; service gratuity (*Mil.*). **–adel**, *m.* monied aristocracy. **–angelegenheit**, *f.* money matter. **–anlage**, *f.* investment. **–anleihe**, *f.* loan. **–anweisung**, *f.* money-order, postal-order. **–beutel**, *m.* purse, money-bag. **–brief**, *m.* letter containing money, registered letter. **–büchse**, *f.* money-box. **–buße**, *f.* fine, penalty. **–einlage**, *f.* money paid in. **–einnehmer**, *m.* cashier, receiver. **–einwurf**, *m.* slot (*for coins*). **–entschädigung**, *f.* indemnity. **–entwertung**, *f.* inflation. **–ersatz**, *m.* reimbursement. **–ertrag**, *m.* revenue. **–erwerb**, *m.* money-making. **–eswert**, *m.* money's worth; (*coll.*) – *und –eswert*, the wherewithal. **–freier**, *m.* fortune-hunter. **–fressend**, *adj.* extravagant. **–gefälle**, *n.pl.* money-dues. **–geizig**, *adj.* avaricious. **–geschäfte**, *n.pl.* money-transactions. **–gier**, *f.* avarice. **–gierig**, *adj.* avaricious. **–handel**, *m.* banking; stock-jobbing. **–herrschaft**, *f.* plutocracy. **–hilfe**, *f.* pecuniary aid; subsidy. **–kasse**, *f.* till. **–kasten**, *m.* strong-box, cash-box. **–katze**, *f.* money-belt, pouch. **–klemme**, *f.* financial straits. **–kurs**, *m.* rate of exchange. **–lade**, *f.* till. **–los**, *adj.* impecunious, poor, badly off. **–macher**, *m.* coiner. **–makler**, *m.* money-broker, bill-broker. **–mangel**, *m.* scarcity of money. **–mittel**, *n.pl.* funds, means, pecuniary resources. **–posten**, *m.* sum of money; item (*in an account-book*). **–prägen**, *n.* coining. **–preis**, *m.* rate of exchange; cash prize. **–protz**, *m.* purse-proud man. **–quelle**, *f.* source of income. **–sache**, *f.* money-matter; (*Prov.*) *in –sachen hört die Gemütlichkeit auf*, business is business. **–schein**, *m.* paper-money, bank-note. **–schneiderei**, *f.* extortion, overcharging, swindling. **–schrank**, *m.* safe. **–sendung**, *f.* remittance. **–stand**, *m.* state of the money-market. **–stolz**, 1. *adj.* purse-proud. 2. *m.* purse-pride. **–strafe**, *f.* fine. **–stück**, *n.* coin. **–sucht**, *f.* avarice. **–süchtig**, *adj.* avaricious. **–umlauf**, *m.* circulation of money. **–umsatz**, *m.* exchange of money. **–verlegenheit**, *f.* financial difficulty, pecuniary embarrassment. **–verlust**, *m.* pecuniary loss. **–vorschuß**, *m.* advance of money. **–verschwendung**, *f.* extravagance, waste of money. **–währung**, *f.* currency. **–wechsel**, *m.* exchange of money. **–wechsler**, *m.* money-changer. **–wert**, *m.* value in money; value of currency. **–wesen**, *n.* monetary matters, finance. **–wucher**, *m.* usury. **–wucherer**, *m.* usurer.

geleckt, *p.p.* & *adj.* very neat; spick and span, spotless, immaculate; (*coll.*) pretty-pretty; *er sah aus wie* –, he was exceedingly well *or* immaculately turned out. **–heit**, *f.* great neatness; exaggerated cleanliness *or* tidiness, spotlessness.

Gelee [*pron.* ʒəˈleː] *n.* (-s, -s) jelly.

Gelege, *n.* nest of eggs, spawn.

gelegen, *p.p. of* **liegen** & *adj.* situated; (*with Dat.*) convenient, opportune, fit, proper; *es ist mir jetzt nicht – hinzugehen*, it does not suit me to go there just now; *zu –er Zeit*, opportunely, in due time; *es kommt mir gerade* –, it just suits me; *es ist mir wenig daran* –, it is a matter of indifference to me; *mir ist daran* –, I am concerned *or* anxious; *es ist nichts daran* –, it is of no importance *or* consequence, it does not matter; *Sie kommen mir sehr* –, you come very opportunely. **–heit**, *f.* occasion, opportunity; favourable moment; (*coll.*) convenience (= W.C.); *die Fahr–heit*, the transport facilities; *gute –heiten*, facilities; *ich werde es ihm bei –heit zurückgeben*, I shall return it to him when I have an opportunity; *bei dieser –heit*, on this occasion; *bei der ersten besten –heit*, at the first opportunity; (*Prov.*) *–heit macht Diebe*, opportunity makes the thief; *es bot sich mir keine günstige –heit*, no suitable *or* favourable opportunity presented itself (to me); *–heit machen*, act as a go-between; *die –heit beim Schopfe packen*, take the occasion by the forelock, not let the opportunity slip. **–heitsarbeiter**, *m.* casual labourer. **–heitsgedicht**, *n.* occasional poem. **–heitskauf**, *m.* bargain. **–heitsmacher**, *m.* go-between; procurer. **–heitsschrift**, *f.* work written for a particular occasion. **–tlich**, 1. *adj.* occasional, incidental; opportune. 2. *adv.* incidentally; at some time or other; at one's convenience; at one's leisure; opportunely, as occasion offers, now and then, by chance; *wenn Sie ihn –tlich sehen*, if you should chance to see him; *ich erfuhr –tlich*, I heard accidentally.

gelehr–ig, *adj.* docile, teachable; intelligent. **–samkeit**, *f.* learning, erudition, scholarship. **–t**, *adj.* learned, scholarly, erudite. **–te(r)**, *m.* learned p., man of learning, scholar, savant. **–tendünkel**, *m.* donnishness. **–tenkreise**, *m.pl.* scholars, the learned world. **–tenrepublik**, *f.* republic of letters. **–tenschule**, *f.* (*archaic*) grammar-school, classical

school. **-tenstand,** *m.* the learned professions. **-tenverein,** *m.* literary society *or* club. **-tenwelt,** *f.* the learned world, scholarly circles, literary and scientific world. **-tenzeitung,** *f.* scholarly journal.
Geleier, *n.* drawling, sing-song delivery, monotonous discourse, speechifying.
geleimt, *adj.* sized (*Pap.*).
Geleise, *n.* (-s, –), *see* **Gleis,** *n.* (-(s)es, -(s)e) rut, track (*of a wheel*), rails, line; (*fig.*) beaten track; *einfaches* (*doppeltes*) –, single (double) track; *auf ein falsches* or *totes – geraten*, get on the wrong track; *das – halten*, follow the track; *im* (*alten*) – *bleiben, sich in ausgefahrenen -en bewegen*, go on in the old way, be in a rut.
Geleit(-e), *n.* (-(e)s, -e) retinue; guard, escort (*Mil.*); convoy (*Nav.*); *einem das – geben*, accompany *or* escort a p. (*Poet.*); *ihm das letzte – geben*, accompany him on his last journey (= bury him) (*Poet.*); *freies* –, safe conduct. **-boot,** *n.* escort vessel. **-en,** *v.a.* accompany, conduct, escort, convoy; *Gott -e dich!* God speed thee; God be with you! **-flotille,** *f.* convoy. **-(s)bediente(r),** *m.* excise-man. **-sbrief,** *m.* advice-note; custom-house receipt; letter of safe-conduct. **-(s)reiter,** *m.* mounted escort. **-schein,** *m.* safe conduct; navicert (*Nav.*). **-schiff,** *n.*, *see* **-boot. -wort,** *n.* preface. **-zug,** *m.* convoy (*Nav.*); *-zug fahren*, sail in convoy. **-zugsicherung,** *f.* convoy escort.
gelenk, 1. *adj. see* **-ig.** 2. *n.* (-(e)s, -e) joint, articulation; wrist; link (*of a chain*); hinge; knot (*Bot.*); *keine -e haben*, be stiff in the joints *or* awkward in movement. **-band,** *n.* ligament of a joint, articular ligament. **-ende,** *n.* head (*of a bone*), articular extremity, condyle. **-entzündung,** *f.* arthritis. **-geschwulst,** *f.* white swelling. **-ig,** *adj.* flexible, pliable, pliant, supple; jointed, articulated, having links; geniculate (*Bot.*); nimble, alert. **-igkeit,** *f.* pliability, flexibility; suppleness; nimbleness. **-kuppelung,** *f.* joint-coupling (*Mach.*). **-puppe,** *f.* jointed doll. **-rheumatismus,** *m.* articular rheumatism, rheumatoid arthritis. **-schmiere,** *f.* joint-oil, synovia. **-stab,** *m.* jointed stick. **-stück,** *n.* joint (*Mach.*). **-verbindung,** *f.* articulation. **-verrenkung,** *f.* dislocation of the joint. **-welle,** *f.* drive shaft (*Mach.*).
gelernt, *adj.* skilled, trained, practised; *-er Arbeiter*, skilled worker.
Geleucht(e), *n.* (*Poet.*) illumination; miner's lamp.
Gelichter, *n.* gang, band, crew, riffraff, rabble.
Geliebt-e(r), *m.* lover, beloved, sweetheart, love, darling; *meine -en!* dearly beloved brethren! (*Eccl.*). **-e,** *f.* sweetheart, darling; mistress.
geliehen, *p.p. of* **leihen.**
gelind(-e), *adj.* soft, gentle, light, light, lenient, mild, tender, smooth; *-e Strafe*, lenient *or* light punishment; *-e gesagt*, putting it mildly; *-e Saiten aufziehen*, relent, be mollified, become lenient. **-igkeit,** *f.*, **-heit,** *f.* mildness, gentleness, leniency, indulgence.
gelingen, 1. *ir.v.n. & imp.* (*aux.* s.) (*Dat.*) succeed (in doing), manage (to do); prosper; *sein Plan ist ihm nicht gelungen*, his plan did not succeed; *es gelang mir nicht, meinen Plan auszuführen*, I was not able to carry out my plan; *es gelingt mir*, I succeed *or* prosper in; (*coll.*) *es ist ihm übel* (*or sl. vorbei-*)*gelungen*, he has had no success, he has failed. 2. *n.* success.
Gelispel, *n.* lisping, whispering.
gelitten, *p.p. of* **leiden.**
gell, 1. (*dial.*) *see* **gelt.** 2. *see* **gellend.**
gell-en, *v.n.* (*aux.* h.) sound shrill, jar, resound; sing (*of ears*); call (*of the quail*); *das Schreien -t mir in den Ohren*, the screaming jars on my ears; *er schrie, daß mir die Ohren -ten*, he screamed so that my ears were singing. **-end,** *pr.p. & adj.* shrill, piercing.
gelob-en, *v.a.* promise solemnly, vow, pledge; *mit Hand und Mund* or *in die Hand -en*, take a solemn oath; *das -te Land*, the Promised Land, the Holy Land; *sich etwas -en*, vow to o.s., pledge o.s., make a solemn resolve.
Gelöbnis, *n.* (-ses, -se) solemn promise, vow.
Gelock(e), *n.* (*coll.*) mass of curls.
gelogen, *p.p. of* **lügen.**
gelöscht, *adj.* quenched; *-er Kalk*, slaked lime.
[1]**gelt,** *adj.* (*dial.*) not giving milk; barren. **-ling,** *m.* one-year-old calf, gelding; eunuch.
[2]**gelt,** (*dial.*) isn't that so? isn't it? don't you think so? eh?
Gelte, *f.* (-n) (*dial.*) pail, bucket, tub (*with one handle*).
gelt-en, *ir.v.n.* (*aux.* h.) mean, matter, carry weight; be worth, be of *or* have value; be valid, hold good; be current, pass for, be considered (as); concern, apply to, be intended for, be aimed at, be the question of; *diese Note gilt einen Takt*, this note is equal to one bar; *diese Briefmarke gilt nicht mehr*, this stamp is no longer valid; (*Prov.*) *der Prophet gilt nichts in seinem Vaterlande*, a prophet is without honour in his own country; *die meisten Stimmen -en*, most votes carry; *was gilt's? was gilt die Wette?* what do you bet? *es gilt!* done! agreed! *das gilt nicht*, that is not allowed *or* does not count *or* is not fair (play); *jetzt gilt's!* now's the time! now for it! *er war tapfer, wo es galt*, he was brave when the moment came; *jetzt gilt's, die Begeisterung zu entflammen*, the main point is now to fire the enthusiasm; *es gilt meine Ehre*, my honour is at stake; *und wenn es mein Leben gilt!* though it cost me my life! *es gilt Sieg oder Tod!* victory or death! *es gilt einen Versuch*, let us take a chance *or* make a trial *or* (*coll.*) have a shot; *es gilt mir gleich*, it is all the same to me; *diese Bemerkung galt mir*, this remark was aimed at *or* intended for me; *eine Kugel kam geflogen, gilt sie mir oder gilt sie dir*, a bullet came flying, is it meant for you or for me? *diese Münze gilt bei uns nicht*, this coin is not current here; *sein Wort gilt viel bei mir*, his word carries great weight with me; (*B.*) *bei Gott gilt kein Ansehen der Person*, God is no respecter of persons; *es gilt für ausgemacht*, it is taken for granted; *er gilt für einen redlichen Mann*, he passes for an honest man, he is supposed to be honest; *der gute Wille gilt für die Tat*, the will is taken for the deed; *das gilt für alle Zeiten*, that always remains true; *-en lassen*, let pass, not dispute, admit; *das will ich -en lassen*, granted! I don't dispute that; *-end machen*, urge, assert, vindicate; *sich -end machen*, maintain one's rights, put o.s. forward, assert o.s., claim recognition, (*coll.*) throw one's weight about, make o.s. felt; hold true; *seine Rechte -end machen* assert one's rights; *was von dir gilt, gilt eben nicht gerade von mir*, what is true of you, is not necessarily true of me. **-ung,** *f.* value, worth, importance; currency, acceptation; respect, recognition; *sich* (*Dat.*) *-ung verschaffen*, make o.s. felt *or* respected, bring one's influence to bear; *ohne -ung*, of no account; *zu -ung gelangen*, become important, come into play. **-ungsbereich,** *m.*, **-ungsgebiet,** *n.* district where (*a law*) is in force, range over which (*a postulate, etc.*) is valid. **-ungstrieb,** *m.* desire to dominate.
Gelübde, *n.* (-s, –) vow. **-opfer,** *n.* votive offering.
gelungen, *p.p. of* **gelingen** *& adj.* well done; (*coll.*) excellent, capital; funny; (*coll.*) *-e Geschichte*, capital story; (*coll.*) *das ist -!* that is splendid! that beats everything! *-er Kerl*, comic fellow.
Gelüst, *n.* (-s, -e) desire, longing, appetite; lust. **-en,** *v. imp. n.* (*aux.* h.) desire, long for, hanker after; *sich* (*Acc.*) *-en lassen*, covet, lust after; (*B.*) *laß dich nicht -en deines Nächsten Weib!* thou shalt not covet thy neighbour's wife (*gen. obs., now it would be* nach deines Nächsten Weib).
Gelz-e, *f.* gelded sow. **-en,** *v.a.* geld, castrate.
gemach, 1. *adj.* comfortable, convenient, easy. 2. *adv.* softly, quietly, gently; gradually, by degrees, slowly; *-!* gently, don't be in (such) a hurry, easy! (*Prov.*) *– geht auch weit*, slow and steady wins the race. 2. *n.* (-(e)s, ⸚er) (*Poet.*) room, apartment, chamber.
gemächlich, *adj.*, *see* **gemach;** *-er Mensch*, easy-going or lackadaisical person; *– leben*, live at ease *or* comfortably. **-keit,** *f.* convenience, comfort, ease.
Gemäch-sel, *n.* (-s, –) clumsy piece of work. **-t(e),** *n.* (-(e)s, -e) 1. creature; 2. (*pl.*) genitals; 3. *see* **-sel.**
gemacht, *p.p. & adj.* affected, simulated. *-e*

Wechselbriefe, bills read for endorsement; *-er Mann*, a p. in an established position *or* whose fortune is assured. **–heit,** *f.* affectation.

Gemahl, *m.* (-(e)s, -e) husband, consort; (*Poet. also* = **–in**). **–in,** *f.* wife, spouse; consort; *wie geht es Ihrer Frau –in, Herr Bolz?* how is Mrs. Bolz? *er erhob sie zu seiner königlichen –in*, he made her his royal consort.

gemahnen, *v.a.* remind (*einen an eine S.*, s.o. of a th.); *used as imp.*: *es gemahnt mich*, it strikes me, it seems to me.

Gemälde, *n.* (-s, –) picture, painting. **–ausstellung,** *f.* exhibition of pictures. **–händler,** *m.* art dealer. **–saal,** *m.* picture gallery.

Gemarkung, *f.* landmark, boundary; district; precincts.

Gemäß, 1. *n.* (-es, -e) measure, moderation; measuring vessel. 2. *adj.* suitable, conformable; *eine mir –e Anschauung*, a view appropriate to me. 3. *prep.* (*with preceding* (*less frequently*) *or following Dat.*) according to, conformably to, in conformity with, in consequence of; *dem Zwecke nicht –*, unsuitable to the purpose; *der Natur –*, according to nature; *dem Befehl –*, in conformity with the order; *– Abschnitt 3*, see para. 3, in consequence of the remarks under para. 3. **–heit,** *f.* (*rare, revived by Nat. Soc.*) conformity, accord, accordance. **–igt,** *adj.* temperate; moderate; *der –igte Gürtel*, the temperate zone.

Gemäuer, *n.* (-s, –) (*Poet.*) masonry; *altes –*, ruins.

gemein, *adj.* common, general, ordinary; low, vulgar, mean, base; belonging in common to; (*dial.*) kind, friendly, condescending. *–es Benehmen*, mean, low *or* base conduct, vulgar behaviour; *–e Brüche*, vulgar fractions; *–e Geschichte*, vulgar *or* indecent story; *auf –e Kosten die Reise machen*, make the journey at joint expense, pool the expenses of the trip; *der –e Mann*, the man in the street; *–e Meinung*, general view, common opinion; *der –e Menschenverstand*, common sense; *das –e Recht*, common law; *mit einem –e S. machen*, make common cause with a p., join a p. in an undertaking; *–er Soldat*, private (soldier); *–e Weide*, common pasture; *– haben mit*, have in common with, share with; *– machen*, make common, popularize, spread, promulgate; *– machen mit*, become friendly with, chum up with, be hail fellow well met; *sich nicht – machen mit*, keep (a p.) at a distance, hold aloof from *or* not to be too familiar with (a p.); *sich – machen*, demean o.s., lower o.s.; *– tun*, behave familiarly, make o.s. familiar; *der Tod ist allen Menschen –*, death is our common fate; *es war ihnen alles –*, they had all things in common. **–acker,** *m.* **–anger,** *m.*, *see* **Gemeindeanger. –de,** *f.*, *see* **Gemeinde. –e,** 1. *f. obs. & Poet. for* **Gemeinde,** *only used now in* **Brüder–e,** Moravian Brethren. 2. *n.* the vulgar, the common-place, that which is mean *or* base. **–e(r),** *m.* (*archaic*) commoner; layman; private (soldier) (*Mil.*); *die –en*, the rank and file (*Mil.*). **–faßlich,** *adj.* intelligible to an ordinary mind, popular, generally comprehensible, easy to understand, elementary. **–gefährlich,** *adj.* dangerous to the public. **–geist,** *m.* public spirit, esprit de corps. **–gültig,** *adj.* generally admitted, current. **–gut,** *n.* common *or* public property. **–heit,** *f.* vulgarity, coarseness, commonness; baseness, mean trick, vileness, meanness. **–herrschaft,** *f.* joint estate; common jurisdiction. **–hin,** *adv.*, **–iglich,** (*archaic*) *adv.* commonly, usually, generally. **–kapitalien,** *n.pl.* joint-stocks. **–kosten,** *pl.* overhead costs. **–nutz,** *m.* common good; (*Nat. Soc.*) *–nutz vor Eigennutz*, service not self (*motto used to justify any arbitrary action against individuals, e.g. elimination of small businesses*). **–nützig,** *adj.* of public benefit, generally useful, beneficial to the community. **–nützigkeit,** *f.* (*partic. Swiss*) voluntary social work, private charity. **–platz,** *m.* commonplace, platitude. **–sam,** *adj.* held in common, common, joint, mutual, combined, together; *–same S. machen*, make common cause. **–samkeit,** *f.* community, common possession; mutuality. **–schaden,** *m.* common nuisance. **–schädlich,** *adj.* generally harmful. **–schaft,** *f.* community; mutual participation, common possession *or* interest; communion; partnership, association; intercourse, (*in Nat. Soc. usage these meanings, denoting relationship between individuals, succumbed before a conception embracing the entirety of a group, race, etc.*, e.g. *Volks–schaft*, the nation as a whole; *Betriebs–schaft*, merger, pool, cartel); *–schaft der Güter* (*Güter–schaft*), community of goods; *–schaft zwischen Seele und Leib*, interaction between soul and body; *–schaft haben mit*, be connected, consort *or* have intercourse with; *etwas in –schaft haben*, hold *or* have s.th. in common; *in –schaft mit*, together with. **–schaftlich,** *adj.* common, mutual; joint, collective, in common; *es geht auf –schaftliche Kosten*, the expenses are borne jointly; *auf –schaftliche Rechnung*, on joint account; *–schaftlich handeln*, act in concert; *sich –schaftlich teilen in eine S.*, be joint partakers of *or* in a th.; *–schaftlich speisen*, dine together; *–schaftlicher Nenner*, common denominator (*Math.*); *die Folgen –schaftlich tragen*, share the consequences. **–schaftlichkeit,** *f.* community of possession; solidarity, joint responsibility. **–schaftsarbeit,** *f.* co-operative work. **–schaftsehe,** *f.* companionate marriage. **–schaftsunfähig,** *adj.* (*Nat. Soc.*) deprived of citizens' rights, asocial. **–schuldner,** *m.* bankrupt. **–sinn,** *m.* public spirit. **–sinnig,** *adj.* public-spirited. **–sprache,** *f.* literary language (*as opposed to dialects*). **–spruch,** *m.* common saying. **–trift,** *f.*, **–weide,** *f.* common. **–verständlich,** *adj.*, *see* **–faßlich. –wesen,** *n.* public affairs; community; commonwealth. **–wirtschaft,** *f.* communal *or* collective farming. **–wohl,** *n.* common weal, public welfare.

Gemeinde, *f.* (-n) community; municipality; corporate body; parish; congregation, parishioners; *christliche –*, Christian communion, the Church; *zur – gehörig*, public, municipal; *von der – ausschließen*, excommunicate. **–abgabe,** *f.* local rates. **–ammann,** *m.* (*Swiss*) mayor. **–anger,** *m.* common, village green. **–arbeiter,** *m.* municipal worker. **–auflagen,** *f.pl.*, see **–abgabe. –ausschuß,** *m.*, **–behörde,** *f.* corporation, local council, parish council. **–bezirk,** *m.* parish, borough, municipality, district. **–haus,** *n.* parish *or* village hall. **–land,** *n.* common. **–rat,** *m.*, *see* **–ausschuß;** alderman, town-councillor; (*Scots*) elder. **–schreiber,** *m.* town-clerk. **–schule,** *f.* council school, elementary school. **–unterstützung,** *f.* parish relief. **–verwaltung,** *f.* local government. **–vorstand,** *m.* local board, town *or* borough council. **–vorsteher,** *m.* mayor. **–weide,** *f.* common. **–werk,** *n.* (*Swiss*) statute labour.

Gemeng–e, *n.* mingling; mixture; aggregation; medley; mêlée, fray (*Mil.*); *Hand–e*, hand-to-hand fight, scuffle; (*sl.*) scrap. **–estoff,** *m.* constituent parts, ingredients. **–sel,** *n.* medley, hotchpotch.

Gemerk, *n.* (-(e)s, -e) mark, token; boundary.

gemessen, *p.p. & adj.* measured; precise, formal, sedate; positive; *–er Befehl*, express *or* strict order. **–heit,** *f.* precision, strictness; measured demeanour.

Gemetzel, *n.* (-s, –) slaughter, carnage, massacre, blood-bath.

gemieden, *p.p. of* **meiden.**

Gemisch, *n.* (-es, -e) mixture, composition, alloy; medley. **–t,** *p.p. & adj.* mixed, diffused, combined. **–twaren,** *f.pl.* (*Austr. dial.*) groceries.

Gemme, *f.* (-n) gem, cameo. **–nabdruck,** *m.*, **–nabguß,** *m.* paste. **–nkundige(r),** *m.*, **–nschneider,** *m.* lapidary.

gemocht, *p.p. of* **mögen.**

Gems–e, *f.* (-en) chamois. **–bock,** *m.* chamois-buck. **–enleder,** *n.* chamois leather. **–tier,** *n.*, **–ziege,** *f.* doe of the chamois.

Gemunkel, *n.* talk, gossip, rumour, tittle-tattle.

Gemurmel, *n.* murmuring, muttering, murmur; *es geht ein –*, it is whispered abroad.

Gemüse, *n.* (-s, –) vegetables, greens. **–bau,** *m.* vegetable gardening. **–garten,** *m.* kitchen *or* vegetable garden. **–gärtner,** *m.* market-gardener. **–händler,** *m.* greengrocer.

gemüßigt, *adj. sich – sehen*, be obliged *or* compelled.

gemußt, *p.p. of* **müssen.**

gemustert, *p.p. & adj.* fancy, patterned, figured; examined.

Gemüt, *n.* (-(e)s, -er) mind, soul, heart, disposition, spirit, feeling, temper; (*fig.*) person, individual, soul. *er ist ganz –*, he is full of feeling; *er hat kein –*, he has no feeling; *sich* (*Dat.*) *etwas zu –e führen*, take a th. to heart; (*hum.*) wrap o.s. around s.th. (*i.e.* eat it); *einem eine S. zu –e führen*, remind a p. of a th., remonstrate with s.o. about a th., bring s.th. home to a p. **–lich**, *adj.* good-natured; genial, jolly, cheerful, hearty; pleasant, agreeable; comfortable, cosy, snug; *nur immer –lich!* take it easy! keep calm! don't get excited! *es ist* (*wir sind* or *befinden uns*) *hier recht –lich*, it is (we feel) very comfortable here. **–lichkeit**, *f.* good-natured, sanguine *or* easy-going disposition, good nature, kindliness, geniality; comfort, cosiness; (*coll.*) *da hört denn doch die –lichkeit auf!* this is too much! that's really too steep, that's more than I can swallow; (*Prov.*) *in Geldsachen hört die –lichkeit auf*, business is business. **–los**, *adj.* devoid of feeling; unfeeling. **–sanlage**, *f.*, **–sart**, *f.*, **–sbeschaffenheit**, *f.* character, disposition, turn of mind, temperament. **–sbewegung**, *f.* emotion, excitement, agitation. **–skrank**, *adj.* melancholic. **–skrankheit**, *f.* melancholia. **–slage**, *f.* frame of mind. **–sleben**, *n.* inner life. **–smensch**, *m.* man of feeling. **–sregung**, *f.* emotion. **–srichtung**, *f.* turn of mind. **–sruhe**, *f.* composure, calmness, peace of mind. **–sstimmung**, *f.*, **–sverfassung**, *f.*, **–szustand**, *m.* frame of mind, humour. **–voll**, *adj.* cheerful, kindly, affectionate; agreeable.

Gen, *n.* (-s, -e) gene, factor (*Biol.*).

gen, *prep.* (*Acc.*), *poet, abbr. from* **gegen**, towards, to; *– Himmel*, heavenwards; *– Westen*, to the west.

genabelt, *adj.* umbilicate (*Bot.*).

genannt, *p.p. of* **nennen**, called, surnamed; referred to, mentioned.

genas, genäse, *see* **genesen.**

genäschig, *adj.* sweet-toothed.

genau, *adj.* tight; close, close-fitting; particular, accurate, minute, exact, precise, scrupulous, strict; sparing, economical; close-fisted, parsimonious. *–er Anschluß*, tight fit; *–es Gewissen*, scrupulous conscience; *sich – an die Vorschriften halten*, follow the instructions closely; *–er Kostenanschlag*, detailed estimate; *es – nehmen*, be punctilious; *es nicht – nehmen*, not to be too particular; *er nimmt es mit der Wahrheit nicht so –*, he takes a rather broad view of the truth; *– genommen*, strictly speaking; *mit –er Not*, with great difficulty; *mit –er Not entkommen*, have a narrow escape; (*coll.*) *der –este Preis*, the lowest price; *nachdem ich es mir – überlegt habe*, after careful consideration; *bei –erer Bekanntschaft*, on closer acquaintance; *–eres*, more precise information; *die Uhr geht –*, the clock keeps accurate time; *– um 3 Uhr*, at 3 precisely; *–e Waage*, accurate scales; *– zur Zeit*, in the very nick of time, on the very dot. **–igkeit**, *f.* accuracy, precision, exactness; economy; closeness, parsimony.

Gendarm, *m.* (-en, -en) gendarme, constable, rural policeman. **–erie**, *f.* constabulary, rural police; police station.

Genealog–ie, *f.* genealogy. **–isch**, *adj.* genealogical.

genehm, *adj.* acceptable, suitable, approved of, agreeable; *wenn es mir – sein wird*, when it will suit me; *– halten*, approve of, agree to, grant. **–igen**, *v.a.* approve of, agree, accede (to), sanction, admit; grant; ratify; (*C.L.*) accept (*a bill*); (*C.L.*) *–igen Sie den Ausdruck meiner vorzüglichen Hochachtung*, please accept the expression of my particular esteem. **–igt**, *p.p. & adj.* approved. **–igung**, *f.* acceptance, approval, assent, approbation, agreement, consent, ratification; authorization; licence, permission, permit. **–igungspflichtig**, *adj.* subject to authorization.

geneigt, *p.p. & adj.* (*with* zu) inclined to, disposed to; having a propensity for; *zur Arbeit nicht –*, disinclined to work; (*with Dat.*) sympathetic towards, favourably inclined towards; *das Glück ist ihm –*, fortune favours him; *–ter Leser*, kind *or* gentle reader; *einem ein –es Gehör geben*, give a p. a favourable hearing. **–heit**, *f.* inclination, propensity, favour; affection; benevolence; slope, incline.

General, *m.* (-s, -e (*less good* ⸚e)) general, (supreme) commander. **–admiral**, *m.* admiral commanding a fleet (*no equivalent British rank*). **–advokat**, *m.*, **–anwalt**, *m.* attorney-general. **–archivar**, *m.* chief archivist (*in England the Deputy Keeper of the Public Record Office*). **–arzt**, *m.* major-general (*of Med. Corps*). **–at**, *n.* (-(e)s, -e) generalship, district under a general. **–auditeur**, *m.* Judge Advocate General. **–baß**, *m.* thorough-bass (*Mus.*). **–beichte**, *f.* universal confession. **–feldmarschall**, *m.* field-marshal, generalissimo. **–feldzeugmeister**, *m.* master-general of the ordnance; commander-in-chief (*Austrian*). **–fiskal**, *m.* attorney- *or* solicitor-general. **–inspektion** *f.* Inspector General's Department. **–intendant**, *m.* theatrical manager. **–isieren**, *v.a.* generalize. **–issimus**, *m.* (–, -mi & -musse) generalissimo. **–ität**, *f.* generality; general officers. **–kasse**, *f.* treasury. **–kommando**, *n.* staff of an army corps, corps headquarters. **–kurs**, *m.* mean course (*Navig.*). **–leutnant**, *m.* lieutenant-general, air marshal, (*Amer.*) major-general. **–major**, *m.* major-general, air vice-marshal, (*Amer.*) brigadier-general. **–nenner**, *m.* common denominator (*Math.*); *Brüche unter den –nenner bringen*, reduce fractions to a common denominator. **–oberst**, *m.* senior general (*no equivalent in British army*). **–pardon**, *m.* general amnesty. **–pause**, *f.* general rest (*Mus.*). **–postdirektor**, *m.* postmaster-general. **–probe**, *f.* dress rehearsal (*Theat.*), full *or* final rehearsal (*Mus.*). **–profoß**, *m.* provost-marshal. **–quittung**, *f.* receipt in full. **–staaten**, *m.pl.* States-General (of Holland). **–stab**, *m.* general staff (*Mil.*). **–stäbler**, *m.* staff officer. **–stabskarte**, *f.* staff map, ordnance map (scale 1:100,000). **–stabsoffizier**, *m.* staff officer. **–streik**, *m.* general strike. **–superintendent**, *m.* (*former designation of a Lutheran bishop*). **–versammlung**, *f.* general meeting, company meeting, meeting of shareholders. **–vollmacht**, *f.* power of attorney (*Law*), full authority.

Gener–ation, *f.* (-en) generation; procreation. **–atorengas**, *n.* producer gas (*Motor*). **–ell**, *adj.* general; universal. **–isch**, *adj.* generic. **–ös**, *adj.* generous, liberal.

Gene–se, *f.* (-sen) genesis, formation. **–tik**, *f.* genetics. **–tisch**, *adj.* genetic.

genes–en, *ir.v.n.* (*aux.* s.) get well *or* better, recover, convalesce; *eines Kindes –en*, be delivered of a child. **–ung**, *f.* recovery; convalescence; *auf dem Wege der –ung* or *der –ung entgegensehend*, in a fair way to recovery, on the road to recovery. **–ungsheim**, *n.* sanatorium. **–ungsurlaub**, *m.* sick leave.

Genever, *m.* Hollands (*gin*).

genial, *adj.* highly gifted, ingenious, gifted with genius. **–ität**, *f.* originality.

Genick, *n.* (-(e)s, -e) nape, back *or* scruff of the neck; *sich* (*Dat.*) *das – brechen*, break one's neck; (*fig.*) bring displeasure upon o.s., ruin one's chances. **–fänger**, *m.* hunting knife. **–krampf**, *m.*, **–starre**, *f.* (cerebrospinal) meningitis (*Anat.*). **–schmerz**, *m.* crick in the neck.

Genie [*pron.* ʒe'ni:], *n.* (-s, -s) genius, capacity; man of genius. **–korps**, *n.* (*archaic*) engineer corps. **–periode**, *f.* period of Storm and Stress (*in German literature 1770–1785*). **–streich**, *m.* stroke of genius; ingenious trick. **–wesen**, *n.* military engineering.

genieren [*pron.* ʒe'ni:rən], 1. *v.a.* embarrass, trouble, bother, be in the way, inconvenience, incommode; *geniert Sie mein Rauchen?* do you mind my smoking? 2. *v.r.* feel awkward *or* embarrassed, be shy; *– Sie sich nicht*, don't disturb yourself; make yourself at home.

genieß–en, *ir.v.a.* (*aux.* h.) eat *or* drink; take (nourishment); enjoy, have the benefit *or* use of; *er –t allgemeine Achtung*, he enjoys everyone's esteem; *dieser Wein ist nicht zu –en*, this wine is not drinkable; *–en Sie doch ein wenig davon*, do taste a little of it; *er hat das Seinige* or *sein Gutes genossen*, he has had his day, he has had his share of the good things of life; *nicht zu –en*, unbearable,

intolerable, destestable. **-bar,** *adj.* eatable, drinkable, palatable, relishable; enjoyable; *er ist heute gar nicht -bar,* he is unbearable today, he is very cross (*or* dull) today. **-er,** *m.* (-ers, -er) epicure, gourmet, gourmand, hedonist, bon viveur.
Genist(e), *n.* 1. nest, hatch, brood; 2. waste, rubbish, sweepings; 3. brushwood, undergrowth; 4. broom, *see* **Ginster.**
Genitiv, *m.* (-s, -e) genitive case. **-isch,** *adj.* genitival.
Genius, *m.* (–, Genien) spirit, guardian angel; – *einer Sprache,* genius of a language; *dem – einer Sprache entsprechend,* idiomatic.
genommen, *p.p. of* **nehmen.**
Genörgel, *n.* grumbling, nagging.
Genoss-e, Genoß, *m.* (-(ss)en, -(ss)en) comrade, companion, colleague, partner, associate; (*coll.*) chum, mate; *-e Pieck,* Comrade Pieck. **-enschaft,** *f.* company, society, guild, fellowship, association; partnership; co-operative society. **-enschaftlich,** *adj.* co-operative. **-(ß)same,** *f.* (*Swiss*) district, parish; village community, model estate.
genoß, genösse, *see* **genießen.**
Genre, *m.* & *n.* (-s, -s) style, kind, genre. **-bild,** *n.* genre-painting. **-maler,** *m.* painter of scenes from everyday life.
genug, *indec. adj.* (*orig. with Gen. & still in some idioms*), enough, sufficient, sufficiently; *es ist über und über –,* there is plenty; *– und über–,* more than enough; *– der Tränen!* no more crying! have done with crying! *– des Streites,* a truce to quarrelling; *– davon!* let us have no more of this! *er ist Manns –,* he is man enough; *ich bin nicht Kenner* or *Künstler –, um zu,* I am not a sufficiently good judge *or* not enough of an artist to; *laß es – sein!* that will do! enough of that! put a stop to it! *es ist an einem –,* one will do. **-sam,** *adj.* (*archaic*) sufficient, plentiful. **-tuend,** *adj.* giving satisfaction, satisfying, satisfactory; atoning. **-tun,** *v.n.* give satisfaction, satisfy. **-tuung,** *f.* satisfaction, compensation; amends, atonement, reparation; *sich* (*Dat.*) *-tuung verschaffen,* take the law into one's own hands; *einem -tuung geben,* give s.o. satisfaction, make amends; fight a duel; apologize.
Genüg-e, *f.* (*only in*) *zur -e,* enough, sufficiently; *um Ihnen -e zu tun* (or *zu leisten*), to satisfy *or* content you, in order to comply with your wishes. **-en,** 1. *v.a.* (*aux.* h.) be enough, suffice, satisfy; (*with Dat.*) *-en lassen* (*an*), be satisfied with; *laß es dir -en,* be content with that; *laß es dir -en, daß,* be content that; *das -t für meine Zwecke,* that will do for my purpose. **-end,** *pr.p.* & *adj.* sufficient, satisfying; satisfactory, fair. **-lich,** *adj.* (*archaic*) *see* **-end. -sam,** *adj.* easily satisfied; contented; unpretentious, unassuming, modest, moderate; frugal. **-samkeit,** *f.* moderation; contentedness.
genung, *adv.* (*poet.,*) *see* **genug.**
Gen-us, *n.* (–, -era) genus; gender.
Genuß, *m.* (-(ss)es, ¨(ss)e) enjoyment, pleasure, delight, gratification, profit, use; taking, partaking (*of food, etc.*); *lebenslänglicher –,* life interest. **-mensch,** *m.* epicure, epicurean, voluptuary. **-mittel,** *n.* (*usually pl.*) luxury. **-recht,** *n.* right of usufruct (*Law*). **-reich,** *adj.* delightful, enjoyable. **-sucht,** *f.* craving for pleasure, pleasure-seeking, epicureanism. **-süchtig,** *adj.* pleasure-seeking, epicurean, sensual.
Genüßling, *m., see* **Genußmensch.**
Geo-, *prefix* (*in compounds*). **-däsie,** *f.* geodesy, surveying. **-dät,** *m.* (-en, -en) geodetic surveyor. **-dätisch,** *adj.* geodetic. **-dynamisch,** *adj.* geodynamic. **-gnostisch,** *adj.* relating to geognosy, geological. **-graph,** *m.* (-en, -en) geographer. **-graphisch,** *adj.* geographical. **-graphisch-Nord,** *n.* true north. **-log(e),** *m.* (-en, -en) geologist. **-logisch,** *adj.* geological. **-meter,** *m.* surveyor. **-metrie,** *f.* geometry. **-metrisch,** *adj.* geometrical.
Georgine, *f.* (-n) bouquet *or* pompom; dahlia (*Hort.*).
Gepäck, *n.* (-(e)s, -e) luggage, (*Amer.*) baggage; kit; *sein – bekleben lassen,* have one's luggage labelled; (*coll.*) *einem ins – fallen,* surprise a p., come upon s.o. unawares; *sein – einschreiben lassen,* have one's luggage registered; *sein – aufgeben,* send one's luggage in advance. **-abfertigung,** *f.* luggage office. **-annahme,** *f.*, **-aufnahme,** *f.*, **-aufbewahrung,** *f.* left-luggage office. **-aufgabe,** *f.* luggage office. **-ausgabe,** *f.* (left-)luggage office (auf-, an- *indicate the receipt or 'in' side,* aus- *the delivery or 'out' side*). **-netz,** *n.* luggage rack. **-schein,** *m.* luggage receipt, cloak-room *or* left-luggage ticket. **-stück,** *n.* parcel, package, bag, case, item (of luggage). **-träger,** *m.* (railway) porter; carrier (*Cycl.*). **-troß,** *m.* second-line transport, baggage train (*Mil.*). **-wagen,** *m.* luggage-van. **-zettel,** *m.* luggage-label.
gepanzert, *adj.* armoured, ironclad; *-er Kraftwagen,* armoured car (*Mil.*).
Gepard, *m.* (-(e)s, -e) hunting leopard (*Acinonyx*) (*Zool.*).
gepfiffen, *p.p. of* **pfeifen.**
gepflegt, *p.p.* & *adj.* cared for, tended, well-groomed. **-heit,** *f.* well-groomed appearance, immaculateness.
Gepflogenheit, *f.* custom, habit, usage.
gepfropt, *p.p.*; *– voll* (*von*), crammed *or* stuffed full of, jammed with, chock-full.
Geplänkel, *n.* skirmishing, skirmish (*Mil.*).
Geplapper, *n.* babbling, chatter.
Geplätscher, *n.* splashing, purling, gurgling.
Geplauder, *n.* small talk; chat, chatter, chatting.
Gepoche, *n.* knocking; beating; bravado; palpitation (*of the heart*).
Gepolter, *n.* rumbling noise, rumble, din.
Gepräge, *n.* stamp, impression, imprint; coinage; feature, character; *einer S.* (*Dat.*) *ihr – aufdrücken,* put a stamp on a th., give a th. its (peculiar) character.
Gepränge, *n.* pageantry, pomp, splendour, ostentatious display.
Geprassel, *n.* crackling; clatter.
gepriesen, *p.p. of* **preisen.**
gepunktet, *adj.* dotted, spotted.
Gequassel, *n.*, **Gequatsch(e),** *n.* empty twaddle, gibberish, balderdash.
gequollen, *p.p. of* **quellen,** & *adj.* soaked, swelled.
Ger, *m.* (-(e)s, -e) spear; javelin.
gerad-e (*in speech the first e is rarely heard*), 1. *adj.* straight, direct; erect, upright; straightforward, honest; even (*numbers*). *fünf -e sein lassen,* not be too particular, stretch a point in favour of; *-er Gang,* erect gait; *das -e Gegenteil,* the very opposite; *-er Kurs,* rhumb line (*Navig.*); *-er Lichtstrahl,* direct ray of light; *-e Linie,* straight line; *-er Mann,* plain man, upright man; *-er Takt,* binary measure (*Mus.*); (*Prov.*) *der -e Weg ist der beste,* honesty is the best policy; *-e Zahl,* even number. 2. *adv.* quite, exactly, just, directly; *er kam -e als ich fortging,* he came just as I was going away; *ich bin -e dabei, den Brief fertig zu schreiben,* I am just about to finish the letter; *-e darum, weil,* just for the very reason; *-e deshalb,* for this very reason; *ich war -e dort,* I happened to be there; *sie stehen einander -e gegenüber,* they are diametrically opposed; *er ist nicht -e mein Freund,* I do not regard him exactly as a friend; *nun -e nicht,* not just now, certainly not now; *nun -e,* now especially, now more than ever; *-e recht,* just right; in the nick of time; *diese Stelle war ihm -e recht,* this situation *or* post was the very th. for him; *-e so,* just so, just like this; *-esogut wie,* just as good as if; *-esoviel wie,* just as much as; *-eso viele wie,* just as many as. 3. *f.* straightness; straight line, the straight (*on race-course*). **-eaus,** *adv.* straight ahead *or* on, right ahead. **-(e)halter,** *m.* orthopaedic apparatus, back-board. **-(e)heraus,** *adv.* bluntly, frankly, **-(e)hin,** *adv.* straight in; rashly, inconsiderately; unceremoniously. **-eweg,** *adv.* plainly, frankly, bluntly. **-ewegs, -enwegs,** (*Austr.*) **-eswegs,** *adv.* straightway, straight away, at once, directly. **-ezu,** *adv.* straight on; immediately, directly; plainly, point-blank, flatly; candidly, frankly; actually; *das ist -ezu Wahnsinn,* that is sheer madness; *-ezu frech,* downright cheeky; *mit einem -ezu sein,* deal plainly with a p. **-flügler,** *m.* Orthoptera (*Ent.*). **-führung,** *f.* slide-bar, slide; guides. **-heit,**

f. straightness; uprightness (*of character*); evenness (*of a number*); rectitude. **–hin,** *see* **–ehin. –läufig,** *adj.* having a straight course, direct; orthopterous (*Ent.*). **–linig,** *adj.* rectilineal, rectilinear. **–sinnig,** *adj.* straightforward, upright, honest. **–zahlig,** *adj.* even-numbered.

gerädert, *adj.* broken on the wheel; (*fig.*) *ich fühle mich wie –*, I'm absolutely done in *or* worn out.

Geräms, *n.* (-es, -e) (*dial.*) framework; porch.

Geranie, *f.*, (-n), **Geranium,** *n.* (-s, -ien) geranium.

gerannt, *p.p. of* **rennen** *&* *adj.* extracted (*Metal.*).

Gerassel, *n.* clatter, rattle, clanking, clash.

Gerät, *n.* (-(e)s, -e) implement, tool, instrument; utensil, vessel; effects, chattels; appliances; furniture; equipment, apparatus. **–schaften,** *f.pl.* implements, utensils. **–(e)turnen,** *n.*, **–übungen,** *f.pl.* gymnastics with apparatus.

gerate–n, 1. *ir.v.n.* (*aux.* s.) get, fall *or* come into, to *or* upon; hit (upon); (*with Dat.*) turn out (well), prosper, succeed, thrive; prove to be; *an eine falsche Adresse –n*, be delivered at the wrong house *or* to the wrong p.; *aneinander –n*, see *sich in die Haare –n*; *außer sich –n*, get worked up, fly into a passion; *an den Bettelstab –n*, be reduced to beggary; *in Brand –n*, catch fire; *alles gerät ihm*, everything succeeds with him, he succeeds in everything; *in Entzücken –n*, go into raptures; *ich bin auf den Gedanken –n*, I hit upon the idea, the thought struck me; *in große Gefahr –n*, run into danger; *in schlechte Gesellschaft –n*, get into bad company; *gut –n*, turn out well, be a success; *sich in die Haare –n*, fall out; come to blows; *wohl –ne Kinder*, well-brought-up *or* well-bred children; *in die Klemme –n*, get into a fix; *unter Räuber –n*, fall among thieves; *an den rechten Mann –n*, fall in with the right p., fall into good hands; *auf den Sand –n*, run aground; *in Schulden –n*, run into debt; *ins Stocken –n*, come to a standstill; *die Torte ist vorzüglich geraten*, the cake has turned out excellently *or* is a great success; *an den Unrechten –n*, catch a Tartar; *in Vergessenheit –n*, become forgotten, sink into oblivion; *in Zorn –n*, fly into a passion. 2. *p.p. of* **raten** *&* **geraten,** *& adj.* successful, prosperous; advisable, advised; guessed; *nicht –n*, unsuccessful; *das –nste wäre*, the best course would be. **–wohl,** *n.*; *aufs –wohl*, at random, haphazard, on the off-chance, in a happy-go-lucky manner.

gerätst, gerät, *see* **geraten.**

gerauht, *adj.* napped (*of fabrics*).

geraum, *adj.* considerable, long; *–e Zeit*, long time; *vor –er Zeit*, some time ago.

geräum–ig, *adj.* roomy, spacious. **–igkeit,** *f.* roominess, spaciousness. **–te,** *n.*, **–de,** *n.* clearing (in a wood).

Geräusch, *n.* (-es, -e) noise; bustle, clamour, stir. **–laut,** *m.* consonant (*not l, m, n, ng, or r*). **–los,** *adj.* noiseless, silent. **–voll,** *adj.* noisy.

Geräusper, *n.* clearing of the throat.

gerb–en, *v.a.* tan, dress (*hides*); refine (*steel*); polish; (*coll.*) thrash; *weiß–en*, taw; refine (*steel*). **–er,** *m.* tanner. **–erei,** *f.* tannery, tan-yard; tanning. **–erlohe,** *f.* tan bark. **–säure,** *f.* tannic acid. **–stahl,** *m.* shear steel; burnisher. **–stoff,** *m.* tannin.

gerecht, *adj.* just, fair, righteous, upright; legitimate, lawful, equitable; fit, right, suitable; skilled; *in allen Sätteln –*, a match for anything; *einem – werden*, do justice to, satisfy *or* compensate a p.; *einer S. – werden*, do justice to a th., take a th. into account, master a th. **–igkeit,** *f.* justice, right; righteousness, fairness, justness; justification; (*einem* or *einer S.*) *–igkeit widerfahren lassen*, do justice to; *der –igkeit ihren Lauf lassen*, let justice run its course. **–same,** *f.* privilege, right, prerogative.

Gerede, *n.* talk; report, rumour; *ins – kommen*, get talked about; *ins – bringen*, cause to be talked about; gossip about; *es geht das –*, the rumour is.

gereichen, *v.n.* (*aux.* h.) bring about, cause, contribute to, redound to; turn out to be, prove to be; *dies gereichte ihm zum Verderben*, this brought about his ruin; *es gereicht ihm zur Ehre*, it does him credit *or* redounds to his honour.

gereizt, *p.p.* *&* *adj.* irritated; vexed. **–heit,** *f.* irritation.

gereuen, *v.a. imp.* cause repentance; *es gereut mich*, I repent (of); I am sorry (for); *es wird (soll) Sie –*, you will (shall) repent it; *sich (Acc.) etwas – lassen*, regret *or* be sorry for s.th.; *er läßt sich keine Mühe –*, he spares no trouble; *sich die Zeit nicht – lassen*, not grudge the time.

Gericht, *n.* (-(e)s, -e) court of justice; judgement, jurisdiction, tribunal; dish, course; *einen beim –e verklagen*, prosecute a p.; *über einen – halten*, sit in *or* pass judgement on (*often fig.*); *mit einem (streng* or *scharf) ins* or *zu – gehen*, haul a p. over the coals, take a p. to task; *das Jüngste –*, the Last Judgement, doomsday; *vor – fordern*, summon; *vor – kommen*, come into court, come before the court(s), come to trial; *vor – stellen*, arraign; *über einen Verbrecher zu – sitzen*, pass judgement on *or* try a criminal, bring a criminal to justice. **–lich,** 1. *adj.* judicial; legal, forensic; *–licher Akkord*, bankrupt's certificate; *–liche Medizin*, forensic medicine; *–liche Schritte*, legal measures; *–liche Tierarzneikunde*, veterinary jurisprudence; *–liches Zeugnis ablegen*, give evidence in a court of law. 2. *adv.* judicially; in legal form; *einen –lich belangen*, sue a p. at law, go to law with s.o.; *–lich gegen einen vorgehen*, start legal proceedings against s.o., take s.o. to court. **–sakten,** *f.pl.* records. **–sbank,** *f.* bench, tribunal. **–sbarkeit,** *f.* jurisdiction. **–sbeamte(r),** *m.* magistrate, justiciary. **–sbefehl,** *m.* writ. **–sbeisitzer,** *m.* judge-lateral, assessor. **–sbezirk,** *m.* circuit, jurisdiction. **–sdiener,** *m.* court usher. **–sferien,** *pl.* vacation. **–sgang,** *m.* legal procedure. **–sgebäude,** *n.* law-court. **–sgebühren,** *f.pl.*, **–sgefälle,** *n.pl.* law charges, costs. **-shandel,** *m.* lawsuit. **–sherr,** *m.* magistrate, judge. **–shof,** *m.* law courts, court of justice, tribunal. **–skanzlei,** *f.* record-office. **–skosten,** *pl.* legal expenses; *einen zu den –skosten verurteilen*, condemn a p. to pay costs. **–sordnung** *f.* legal procedure. **–sperson,** *f.* magistrate, judge, court official *or* officer. **–spflege,** *f.* administration of justice. (*B.*) **–sposaune,** *f.* last trumpet. **–srat,** *m.* justice (*a title*). **–ssaal,** *m.* court room. **–sschreiber,** *m.* clerk of the court. **–ssitzung,** *f.* session. **–ssprache,** *f.* legal jargon. **–ssprengel,** *m.* jurisdiction, circuit. **–sstand,** *m.* competency of a court. **–sstube,** *f.*, *see* **–ssaal. –sverfahren,** *n.* proceedings at law. **–sverfassung** *f.* judicial organization. **–sverhandlungen,** *f.pl.*, legal proceedings. **–sverwalter,** *m.*, **–sverweser,** *m.* administrator of justice, justiciary. **–sverwaltung,** *f.*, **–sverwesung,** *f.* administration of justice. **–svollzieher,** *m.* bailiff, sheriff. **–sweg,** *m.* legal procedure. **–swegen,** *adv.*; *von –swegen*, by warrant. **–szwang,** *m.* legal sanction *or* authority.

gerieben, *p.p. of* **reiben** *&* *adj.* ground, grated; cunning, sly; (*coll.*) *–er Kunde*, wily customer, sly dog.

Geriesel, *n.* (-s) drizzle, rippling.

geriet, geriete, *see* **geraten.**

gering, *adj.* small, little, trifling, slight, scanty, petty, unimportant; mean, low, inferior, humble, modest; *mit –en Ausnahmen*, with but few exceptions; *–e Kenntnisse*, slight *or* meagre knowledge; *–e Kost*, poor fare; *–e Leute*, people in humble circumstances; *–er Preis*, low price; *– schätzen*, estimate at a low value *or* price; *das kostet – geschätzt 3 Mark*, at a low estimate that will cost 3 marks, cf. *–schätzen*; *–er Tiefgang*, shallow draught (*Naut.*); *mein –es Verdienst*, my humble merit; *wir kamen in nicht –e Verlegenheit*, we were not a little embarrassed; *–er Wein*, inferior wine; *ich bin nicht –er als er*, I am as good as he; *–er machen*, lessen, diminish; *nichts –eres als*, nothing short of; *ein –es*, a trifle; *sich (Dat.) nichts –es einbilden*, think a great deal of o.s.; *nicht das –ste*, not the least bit, nothing at all; *nicht im –sten*, not in the least. **–achten,** *see* **–schätzen. –achtung,** *f.*, *see* **–schätzung. –fügig,** *adj.* insignificant, unimportant, trifling, trivial, petty. **–fügigkeit,** *f.* insignificance, paltriness; trifle. **–haltig,** *adj.* of little worth, low-grade, below standard, base, poor, lean. **–heit,** *f.* smallness, meanness, humbleness (*of birth, etc.*); lowness (*of price, etc.*). **–schätzen,** *v.a.* esteem lightly, attach little value to, think little of, scorn, despise. **–schätzig,** *adj.* deprecatory, derogatory, disdainful, scornful, disrespectful, contemptuous. **–schätzung,** *f.* scorn, disdain, contempt.

geringelt, *adj.* ringed, annulate.

Gerinn–e, *n.* (-(e)s, -e) running, flowing; gutter, conduit, mill-race, channel. **–bar,** *adj.* coagulable, congealable. **–en,** *ir.v.n.* (*aux.* s.) curdle, coagulate, congeal, clot. **–sel,** *n.* rivulet; curds; clot, coagulated mass. **–stoff,** *m.* coagulant. **–t,** *adj.* channelled (*Bot.*). **–ung,** *f.* coagulation. **–ungsmittel,** *n., see* **–stoff.**

Geripp–e, *n.* (-es, -e) skeleton; framework; airframe (*Av.*). **–t,** *p.p.* & *adj.* ribbed; groined, fluted, corded; costate; *–tes Papier,* laid paper.

gerissen, *p.p. of* **reißen** & *adj.* (*coll.*) sly, cunning, wily.

geritten, *p.p. of* **reiten.**

Germ, *m.* (*Bav.* & *Austr. dial.*) yeast.

German–e, *m., see the Index of Names.* **–ist,** *m.* (-en, -en) student *or* teacher of German *or* Germanic philology. **–istik,** *f.* German philology.

gern(e), *adv.* (*comp.* lieber; *sup.* am liebsten) with pleasure, willingly, gladly, readily; fain (*archaic*); (*dial.*) often; *ich esse Obst –,* I am fond of fruit; (*es ist*) *– geschehen,* you are very welcome (to it), don't mention it; *das glaube ich –,* that I can readily believe; *gut und –,* easily, very well; *etwas – haben,* like a th.; *ein Mädchen – haben,* be fond of a girl; *so habe ich es –,* that is what I like; (*coll.*) *er kann mich – haben* (*ironic*), I don't care a rap *or* hang about him, he leaves me cold; *herzlich –, von Herzen –,* with all one's heart; *etwas – tun,* like *or* love to do s.th., be fond of doing s.th.; *ich möchte – wissen, ob . . .,* I should like to know if . . .; *nicht –,* reluctantly; unintentionally; *er ist überall – gesehen,* he is welcome everywhere; *ich würde es sehr – sehen, wenn Sie . . .,* I should very much like you to . . ., should be delighted if you . . .; (*dial.*) *er sagte –,* he often said, he used to say; (*dial.*) *der Baum wächst – am Wasser,* this tree tends to grow at the water's edge; (*dial.*) *dieses Holz verfault –,* this wood is apt to rot. **–egroß,** *m.* upstart. **–eklug,** *m.* would-be smart p. **–ewitz,** *m.* would-be wit.

Geröchel, *n.* repeated *or* prolonged rattle.

gerochen, *p.p. of* **riechen.**

Geröll(e), *n.* rubble, gravel, boulders, pebbles, scree, rock-debris, detritus.

geronnen, *p.p. of* (1) **rinnen,** (2) **gerinnen.**

Gerste, *f.* (-n) barley. **–nbrot,** *n.* barley bread, barley loaf. **–nbrühe,** *f.* barley water, barley broth. **–ngraupen,** *f.pl.,* **–ngrütze,** *f.* pearl barley, Scotch barley. **–nkorn,** *n.* barley-corn; sty (*in the eye*). **–nmehl,** *n.* barley flour. **–nsaft,** *m.* (*Poet.* & *hum.*) beer. **–nschleim,** *m.* barley water. **–nzucker,** *m.* barley-sugar.

Gerte, *f.* (-n) sapling, switch, whip, riding cane. **–nhieb,** *m.* stroke of the cane. **–nschlank,** *adj.* slender as a wand.

Geruch, *m.* (-(e)s, ⸚e) smell, odour, aroma, scent, fragrance, savour; (*fig.*) reputation; sense of smell; *im –e der Heiligkeit,* in the odour of sanctity; *er steht in schlechtem* or *üblem –,* he is in bad odour. **–frei,** *adj.,* **–los,** *adj.* odourless; not scented; *–frei machen,* deodorize. **–reich,** *adj.* fragrant. **–sapparat,** *m.* olfactory apparatus *or* organ. **–snerv,** *m.* olfactory nerve. **–ssinn,** *m.* sense of smell. **–swerkzeug,** *n., see* **–sapparat.**

Gerücht, *n.* (-(e)s, -e) rumour, report; *es geht das –,* it is rumoured *or* reported; *das – ist im Umlauf,* the report is abroad; *es ist ein bloßes –,* it is a mere rumour. **–emacher,** *m.* rumour-monger. **–weise,** *adv.* according to report, as rumour has it; *–weise verlautet,* the story goes, it is rumoured.

Gerufe, *n.* repeated shouts, continual calling.

geruh–en, *v.n.* (*aux.* h.) (*rare now except ironically*) condescend, deign, be pleased; *Eure Majestät wollen allergnädigst –en,* may it please Your Majesty; *Seine Majestät haben –t,* His Majesty has signified his pleasure. **–ig,** *adj.* (*Poet.*) perfectly calm. **–sam,** *adj,* leisurely, calm; phlegmatic. **–samkeit,** *f.* leisureliness, imperturbability.

Gerümpel, *n.* lumber, rubbish, trash. **–kammer,** *f.* lumber-room.

Gerund–ium, *n.* (-iums, -ien) gerund. **–iv,** *n.* (-ivs, -ive), **–ivum,** *n.* (-ivums, -iva) gerundive. **–ivisch,** *adj.* gerundial, gerundival.

gerungen, *p.p. of* **ringen.**

gerunzelt, *adj.* wrinkled.

Gerüst, *n.* (-(e)s, -e) scaffold(ing), frame(work); stage, stand, trestle, rack, cradle, crate; stroma (*Biol.*), reticulum; *das – abreißen,* take down the scaffolding. **–brücke,** *f.* trestle-bridge. **–künstler,** *m.* stage carpenter (*Theat.*). **–stange,** *f.* scaffold pole.

Ges, *n.* G-flat.

gesägt, *adj.* serrate, serrated.

gesagt, *p.p.* (*Prov.*) *–, getan,* no sooner said than done. **–e(s),** *n.* what has been said.

gesalzen, *p.p.* & *adj.* salted; (*coll.*) exorbitant (*price*); spicy, smutty, risqué (*joke, etc.*).

gesamt, *adj.* whole, entire, complete; united, joint, common; total, collective; *das –e Volk,* the whole nation, all the people; *alle ins–,* collectively, one and all. **–ansicht,** *f.* general view. **–ausgabe,** *f.* complete edition. **–bedarf,** *m.* total requirement(s). **–betrag,** *m.* sum total. **–bewußtsein,** *n.* collective consciousness. **–blutmenge,** *f.* blood volume. **–e(s),** *n.* the whole, the (sum) total. **–eindruck,** *m.* overall impression. **–einnahme,** *f.* total receipts. **–ertrag,** *m.* entire proceeds, total output. **–forderung,** *f.* total charges *or* claims. **–haft,** *adj.* & *adv.* (*Swiss*) = **gesamt, insgesamt.** **–haltung,** *f.* general attitude. **–heit,** *f.* totality, entirety, generality; the whole; all; *in der –heit genommen,* taken collectively. **–hubraum,** *m.* (cubic) capacity (*of an engine*). **–länge,** *f.* overall-length (*of ship, etc.*). **–macht,** *f.* joint-forces; whole power. (*C.L.*) **–masse,** *f.* total estate. **–staat,** *m.* federal state. **–tonnengehalt,** *m.* total tonnage. **–übersicht,** *f.* general survey, comprehensive view. **–wert,** *m.* aggregate value. **–wille(n),** *m.* collective will. **–wohl,** *n.* public *or* common weal. **–zahl,** *f.* total number, sum total.

gesandt, *p.p. of* **senden.** **–e(r),** *m.* envoy; ambassador, minister; *der päpstliche –e,* the papal nuncio; *er ist ein –er, aber kein geschickter,* he is an ambassador but not a skilful one (*a witticism attributed to Bismarck*). **–schaft,** *f.* embassy, legation. **–schaftlich,** *adj.* ambassadorial, diplomatic; *-schaftlicher Auftrag,* diplomatic mission. **–schaftsgebäude,** *n.* legation. **–schaftspersonal,** *n.* legation staff.

Gesang, *m.* (-es, ⸚e) singing; song; canto; *Lob–,* psalm; *geistliche Gesänge,* sacred songs, psalms, hymns; *des –es Gabe,* the gift of song *or* poesy; *der – der Vögel,* birdsong, singing of the birds; *zweistimmiger –,* (vocal) duet; *mehrstimmiger –,* part-song; *episches Gedicht in 9 Gesängen,* epic poem in 9 cantos. **–buch,** *n.* hymn-book, songbook. **–lehrer,** *m.* singing-teacher. **–lich,** *adj.* vocal, choral. **–skunst,** *f.* vocal *or* choral art. **–stimme,** *f.* vocal part. **–stunde,** *f.,* **–unterricht,** *m.* singing lesson. **–verein,** *m.* choral society, glee club.

Gesäß, *n.* (-es, -e) bottom; seat; breech; buttocks; (*vulg.*) backside. **–wirbel,** *m.* sacral vertebra.

gesättigt, *adj.* saturated (*Chem.*).

Gesaufe, *n.* (*vulg.*) carousing, hard drinking.

Gesäuge, *n.* udder, dugs (*animals with large litter*).

gesäumt, *adj.* bordered, fimbriate; squared (*of timber*).

Gesäusel, *n.* murmuring, rustling.

Geschabsel, *n.* scrapings.

Geschäft, *n.* (-(e)s, -e) business, commerce, trade; transaction, deal, dealings, speculation; commercial firm, business house, office, shop; employment, occupation, calling; *welches – betreiben Sie?* what line of business are you in? *Detail–,* retail business; *Engros–,* wholesale business; (*gut*)*gehendes –,* going concern; *sie geht ins –,* she goes to business; (*fig.*) *ein gewagtes –,* a tricky business; *große –e machen,* do extensive business; *ein gutes – machen,* negotiate a profitable transaction, make a good profit (*with a th.*); *–e halber,* on business; *sich* (*Dat.*) *ein – daraus machen,* do well out of it; *offenes –,* retail business; *das – schließt um 7 Uhr,* the shop *or* office closes at 7 o'clock; *solides –,* sound *or* reliable firm; (*fig.*) *ein unsauberes* –, a dirty business; (*coll.*) *ein natürliches – verrichten*, relieve o.s., do one's business; (*coll.*, *nursery talk*) *ein großes* (*kleines*) –, 'big business' ('little business'). **–ig,** *adj.* busy, active, industrious; officious, fussy. **–igkeit,** *f.* activity, industry, zeal; officiousness. **–lich,** *adj.* business, commercial, mercantile, business-like. **–sabschluß,** *m.* business transaction *or* deal. **–santeil,** *m.* share in a business. **–saufgabe,** *f.* retirement from business, closing down of a firm. **–saufsicht,** *f.* temporary receivership, legal control. **–sauftrag,** *m.* commission. **–sbereich,** *m.* & *n.*; *Minister ohne –sbereich*, minister without portfolio. **–sbericht,** *m.* market *or* company report. **–sbetrieb,** *m.* management. **–sfach,** *n.* line of business. **–sfreund,** *m.* business connexion, correspondent; customer. **–sführer,** *m.* manager, managing director; *–sführender Ausschuß*, executive board. **–sführung,** *f.* executive, management. **–sgang,** *m.* routine. **–sgegend,** *f.* business quarter. **–sgeheimnis,** *n.* trade secret; patent. **–sgehilfe,** *m.* office clerk, assistant. **–sgeist,** *m.* head for business. **–shaus,** *n.* commercial firm. **–sinhaber,** *m.* owner of a firm, principal. **–skapital,** *n.* working capital. **–skenntnis,** *f.* business experience. **–skreis,** *m.* line of business; practice (*of doctors*). **–slage,** *f.* (state of) business, trade *or* the market; commercial status. **–slokal,** *n.* business premises; office; shop; warehouse. **–slos,** *adj.* dull. **–smann,** *m.* (-sleute) business man, tradesman. **–smäßig,** *adj.* business-like. **–sordnung,** *f.* standing orders. **–spersonal,** *n.* staff *or* employees of a firm; clerical staff (*Mil.*). **–sreisende(r),** *m.* commercial traveller. **–sschluß,** *m.* closing-time. **–sschwung,** *m.* briskness of trade. **–ssprache,** *f.* commercial language, mercantile terms. **–sstelle,** *f.* office, bureau. **–sstube,** *f.* office. **–sstunden,** *f.pl.* business hours, office hours. **–steilhaber,** *m.* partner; *stiller –steilhaber*, sleeping partner. **–sträger,** *m.* representative, agent (*of a firm*); chargé d'affaires (*diplomatic*). **–stüchtig,** *adj.* efficient, enterprising; *–stüchtige Dame*, good business woman. **–sübergabe,** *f.* handing over, transfer (*of a business*). **–sübernahme,** *f.* taking over (*of a business*). **–sverbindung,** *f.* business connexion. **–sverkehr,** *m.* commercial intercourse. **–sverlegung,** *f.* removal (*of a business*). **–sverwalter,** *m.* manager. **–sviertel,** *n.* shopping centre *or* district. **–swagen,** *m.* delivery van. **–szeit,** *f.* office-hours. **–szimmer,** *n.* office; orderly room (*Mil.*). **–szweig,** *m.* branch *or* line of business; *besonderer –szweig*, speciality.

geschah, geschähe, *see* **geschehen.**

Geschaukel, *n.* swinging, see-sawing; rolling (*of a ship*); rocking (*of a cradle*).

gescheckt, *adj.* piebald; variegated.

geschehen, 1. *ir.v.n.* (*aux.* s.) take place, happen, come to pass, occur, be done; *es geschehe!* so be it! it will be done! *– ist –*, what is done, is done; *es geschieht mir ein Dienst damit*, it is doing me a good turn; *es kann –, daß*, it may chance that; *das kann nicht ohne große Kosten –*, that cannot be done *or* carried out without great expense; *– lassen*, allow, permit, tolerate, not prevent; *es geschieht ihm recht*, it serves him right; *es ist um ihn –*, he is done for; *es ist ein Unglück –*, a misfortune *or* an accident has happened; *es geschieht ihm unrecht*, he is wronged; *es geschieht viel für die Armen*, a great deal is done for the poor; *es ist so gut wie –*, it is as good as done; *ich weiß nicht, wie mir geschieht*, I don't know what's wrong with me; (*B.*) *Dein Wille geschehe*, Thy will be done; *es geschehe, was da wolle*, whatever may happen. 2. *p.p.* & *adj.*; *–e Dinge sind nicht zu ändern*, what is done, cannot be undone; *nach –er Arbeit*, after one's work is over. **–e(s),** *n.* what is done (and finished with), what has taken place.

Geschehnis, *n.* (-ses, -se) happening, event, occurrence.

Gescheide, *n.* viscera, entrails, guts.

gescheit, *adj.* clever, intelligent, shrewd, sensible; *nicht recht –*, not all there, a little cracked, half-witted; *sei doch –!* do be reasonable! *ich kann nicht – daraus werden*, I cannot make head or tail of it; *daraus kann nichts –es werden*, no good can come of it, it won't lead to anything. **–heit,** *f.* discretion; cleverness; commonsense.

gescheitert, *p.p.* & *adj.* wrecked, frustrated.

Geschenk, *n.* (-(e)s, -e) present, gift, donation; *einem ein – machen mit*, make a p. a present of; *ein – des Himmels*, a heaven-sent blessing, a gift from the gods. **–exemplar,** *n.* presentation copy (*of a book*); *–weise bekommen*, receive as a present.

Geschicht–e, *f.* (-en) history; story; (*coll.*) event; affair, business, concern; *alte –e*, ancient history; *die alte –e!* the old story; (*coll.*) *das sind alte –en*, that is ancient history; *biblische –e*, Scriptural history; *dumme –e*, nuisance; (*coll.*) *eine fatale* or *verflixte –e*, a desperate business, a pretty mess; *die ganze –e*, the whole affair *or* story; (*sl.*) *die ganze –e kostet 5 DM*, the whole caboodle costs 5 marks; *Heiligen–e* legends of saints; (*coll.*) *mache doch keine –en!* don't make a fuss! don't be so silly! *neuere –e*, modern history; *eine schöne –e!* (*ironic*) a nice th. indeed! a pretty business! (*coll.*) *schwierige –e*, difficult task. **–enbuch,** *n.* story-book. **–lich,** *adj.* historical, historically true; *er hat –lich denken gelernt*, he has learned to see things in historical perspective. **–lichkeit,** *f.* authenticity; historical relevance. **–sbuch,** *n.* history book; historical work. **–sforscher,** *m.* historian. **–sforschung,** *f.* historical research. **–sklitterung,** *f.* biased historical account. **–skunde,** *f.* historical science. **–skundig,** *adj.* versed in history. **–(s)schreiber,** *m.*, historiographer, annalist. **–surkunde,** *f.* record. **–swissenschaft,** *f.* science of history.

geschichtet, *adj.* stratified, laminated.

Geschick, *n.* (-es, -e) fate, destiny; fitness, knack, aptness, skill, ability, aptitude; *– zu* or *für etwas haben*, have a knack *or* aptitude for, be skilful *or* clever at s.th.; *dieser Rock hat kein –*, this coat is badly cut *or* is a bad fit; *etwas ins – bringen*, set a th. right, put a th. in order. **–lichkeit,** *f.* skill, dexterity, adroitness, aptitude, fitness. **–t,** *p.p.* & *adj.* fit, adapted, apt, capable, adept, able, dexterous. **–theit,** *f.*, *see* **–lichkeit.**

Geschiebe, *n.* (-s, –) 1. boulder detritus. 2. pushing, shoving. **–mergel,** *m.* boulder clay. **–formation,** *f.* detrital *or* unstratified deposit. **–lehm,** *m.* glacial loam.

geschiefert, *adj.* exfoliated.

geschieht, *see* **geschehen.**

geschienen, *p.p. of* **scheinen.**

Geschimpfe, *n.* nagging, continual abuse.

Geschirr, *n.* (-(e)s, -e) crockery, dishes, china, earthenware, table ware; implements, utensils, apparatus; harness (*of horses*); horse and cart, equipage; parachute harness; *das – abräumen* (*abwaschen*), (*abtrocknen*), clear away (wash), (dry) the dishes *or* crocks; *sich ins – legen, ins – gehen*, pull hard (*of horses*); *also fig.* exert o.s., put one's back into it. **–brett,** *n.* (cupboard *or* pantry) shelf. **–kammer,** *f.* harness-room; pantry. **–(r)einigen,** *n.* washing-up (the crocks).

geschissen, *p.p. of* **scheißen.**

geschlängelt, *adj.* tortuous.

Geschlecht, *n.* (-(e)s, -er) sex; genus, kind, species, race, family, stock, generation; gender (*Gram.*), *aus altem -e*, from an old line *or* family; *kommende –er*, future generations; *männliches –*, male sex; masculine gender (*Gram.*); *das menschliche –*, the human race; *das sächliche –*, the neuter gender (*Gram.*); *das schöne* (*schwache*), (*zarte*) –, the fair (weaker), (*no English equivalent*; *implies 'soft-hearted'*, *'melting'*) sex. **–erkunde,** *f.* genealogy. **–erwesen,** *n.* aristocracy, patricians. **–lich,** *adj.* sexual; generic. **–los,** *adj.* asexual; neuter (*Gram.*). **–sadel,** *m.* hereditary nobility, nobility of blood. **–sakt,** *m.* sexual intercourse, coition. **–salter,** *n.* generation. **–sart,** *f.* genus, kind, species, race; generic character. **–sbaum,** *m.* pedigree. **–sfolge,** *f.* lineage. **–sglied,** *n.* one of a family *or* generation; sexual organ; (*pl.*) genitals (*Anat.*). **–skrank,** *adj.* suffering from venereal disease. **–skrankheit,** *f.* venereal disease. **–slinie,** *f.* lineage, pedigree. **–slos,** *adj.*, *see* **–los.** **–slust,** *f.* carnal desire. **–smerkmal,** *n.* sex characteristic. **–sname,** *m.* family name, surname; genus. **–sorgan,** *n.* sex organ, genitals. **-sregister,** *n.* genealogical table, pedigree. **-sreif,** *adj.* pubescent, fully developed. **-sreife,** *f.* puberty. **-sreizend,** *adj.* aphrodisiac. **-ssystem,** *n.* Linnaean system (*Bot.*). **-stafel,** *f.* genealogical table. **-steile,** *m.pl.* sex organs, genitals, private parts. **-strieb,** *m.* sex instinct *or* desire. **-sverhältnis,** *n.* sex ratio. **-sverkehr,** *m.* sexual intercourse. **-swahl,** *f.* sexual selection. **-swappen,** *n.* family arms. **-swort,** *n.* article (*Gram.*).

geschlichen, *p.p. of* **schleichen** *& adj.* (*coll.*) *das kommt mir gerade –*, that's the very thing I want.

geschliffen, *p.p. of* **schleifen** *& adj.* polished, polite; (*sl.*) well-trained (*Mil.*). **-heit,** *f.* polish, refinement; elegance (*of style*).

Geschlinge, *n.* pluck, giblets, offal; festoon, garland, scroll; (*coll.*) twirls, twiddly-bits.

geschlossen, *p.p. of* **schließen**; whole, complete, unbroken, closed, continuous; united, unanimous, consistent; *–e Kette*, endless chain; *–e Gesellschaft*, private circle; club. **-heit,** *f.* compactness, inclusiveness, uniformity; resolution, determination, doggedness, tenacity (of purpose).

Geschluchze, *n.* inordinate *or* prolonged sobbing.

geschlungen, *p.p. of* **schlingen.**

Geschmack, *m.* (-(e)s, ⸚e) taste, flavour; savour, relish; fancy, liking; good taste; *dies hat einen guten –*, this tastes good; *– an einer S. finden*, relish, like, *or* take a fancy to a th.; *einer S. keinen – abgewinnen können*, not be able to acquire a taste for a th. *or* to develop a liking for a th.; *der – des 18. Jahrhunderts*, 18th-century taste; *über den – läßt sich nicht streiten*, there is no accounting for tastes; *die Geschmäcke* (also fam. *Geschmäcker*) *sind verschieden*, tastes differ. **-lich,** *adj.* as regards taste. **-los,** *adj.* tasteless, insipid, flat, stale; in bad taste. **-losigkeit,** *f.* lack of good taste, bad taste; *das ist eine –losigkeit*, that is in bad taste; *–losigkeiten*, platitudes, inanities; tactlessness, bad form. **-sbecher,** *m.*, **-sknopse,** *f.* taste bud. **-snerv,** *m.* gustatory nerve. **-(s)sache,** *f.*; *das ist –(s)sache*, that is a matter *or* question of taste. **-ssinn** *m.* sense of taste; refinement, good taste. **-sverirrung,** *f.* error in taste, misguided taste; outrage, travesty. **-voll,** *adj.* tasteful, refined, stylish, elegant. **-widrig,** *adj.* in bad taste, inelegant, vulgar.

Geschmatze, *n.* champing, smacking of lips, noisy eating.

Geschmause, *n.* banqueting, feasting, revelling.

Geschmeid-e, *n.* jewellery, jewels, trinkets. **-ig,** *adj.* soft, supple, pliant, ductile, pliable, flexible, malleable; smooth, yielding, tractable, versatile. **-igkeit,** *f.* suppleness, flexibility; softness, malleability; tractability. **-ehändler,** *m.* jeweller. **-ekästchen,** *n.* jewel-case *or* casket.

Geschmeiß, *n.* dung, dirt, droppings; fly-blow, eggs (*of insects*); vermin; (*fig.*) scum, rabble, dregs of society.

Geschmetter, *n.* flourish (*of trumpets*); warbling (*of a canary*).

Geschmier(e), *n.* scrawl, smear(ing), greasing; daub. **-t,** *p.p. & adj.* well-oiled, smooth; (*coll.*) *das geht wie –t*, that comes off very well.

geschmissen, *p.p. of* **schmeißen.**

geschmolzen, *p.p. of* **schmelzen.**

Geschmorte(s), *n.* stew.

Geschmus(e), *n.* fawning, wheedling, honeyed words, (*coll.*) soft soap.

geschnäbelt, *adj.* beaked; rostrate.

Geschnarche, *n.* snoring.

Geschnatter, *n.* cackling, chatter.

geschniegelt, *p.p. & adj.* spruce, trim, smart, dressed-up; *– und gebügelt*, spick-and-span.

geschnitten, *p.p. of* **schneiden.**

geschnoben, (*rare*) *p.p. of* **schnauben.**

Geschnörkel, *n.* embellishment, trappings, arabesques; bombast, preciosity, flamboyance, mannerisms.

geschoben, *p.p. of* **schieben.**

gescholten, *p.p. of* **schelten.**

Geschöpf, *n.* (-es, -e) creature; production, creation.

geschoren, *p.p. of* **scheren.**

Geschoß, *n.* (-(ss)es, -(ss)e) projectile, missile, bullet. shell; shoot, sprout (*Bot.*); story, floor; *– ansetzen*, ram. **-aufschlag,** *m.* impact (*of shell*). **-aufzug,** *m.* shell-hoist (*Mil.*). **-bahn,** *f.* trajectory. **-bö,** *f.* shell blast. **-kammer,** *f.* magazine (*Nav.*). **-garbe,** *f.* cone of fire, dispersion. **-raum,** *m.* chamber (*of a gun*). **-sicher,** *adj.* shell-proof. **-treibend,** *adj.* ballistic. **-trichter,** *m.* shell-crater, shell-hole. **-vorrat,** *m.* ammunition supply. **-wirkung,** *f.* burst effect (*of projectile*).

geschossen, *p.p. of* **schießen.**

Geschräge, *n.* paling; hurdle.

geschraubt, *p.p. & adj.* screwed, twisted; stilted, affected. **-heit,** *f.* affectation.

Geschrei, *n.* (-s, -e) screams, shrieks, cries, shouting, screaming; outcry, clamour, fuss, ado, stir; discredit, disrepute; noises of animals (*as braying, crowing, etc.*); *ins – bringen*, bring into disrepute; *es geht ein –*, there is a rumour, it is rumoured; *– hinter einem her*, halloo, hue and cry; *ins – kommen*, get talked about, get a bad name; *viel – um, über, von* or *wegen etwas machen*, make a great fuss *or* stir over s.th.; *viel – um nichts*, (*Prov.*) *viel – und wenig Wolle*, much ado about nothing.

Geschreib-e, *n.* pen-pushing, quill-driving, scribbling. **-sel,** *n.* scribble, scrawl; pot-boiler; writing deficient in form and contents.

geschrieben, *p.p. of* **schreiben.**

geschrieen, *p.p. of* **schreien.**

geschritten, *p.p. of* **schreiten.**

geschult, *adj.* trained.

geschunden, *p.p. of* **schinden.**

Geschür, *n.* dross, scoria.

Geschütz, *n.* (-es, -e) gun, cannon; piece (of ordnance); (*fig.*) *grobes* or *schweres – auffahren*, bring all one's guns into play; throw one's weight about; *das – auffahren lassen*, bring the gun into action; *das – aufpflanzen*, mount the guns; *das – richten*, lay the gun. **-aufstellung,** *f.* disposition of guns (*Nav.*), gun emplacement (*Artil.*). **-bedienung,** *f.* gunners, gun-crew. **-bettung,** *f.* gun platform, mounting. **-donner,** *m.* thunder of the guns. **-einschnitt,** *m.* gun pit. **-feuer,** *n.* barrage, cannonade. **-führer,** *m.* gun layer, gun captain (*Nav.*). **-gießerei,** *f.* gun-foundry. **-guß,** *m.* gun-metal. **-instandsetzung,** *f.* maintenance and repair of guns. **-kampf,** *m.* artillery duel. **-ladung,** *f.* propellent (charge). **-pforte,** *f.* port-hole (*Nav.*). **-probe,** *f.* firing test. **-protze,** *f.* carriage of a gun, limber. **-rohr,** *n.* barrel of a gun. **-salve,** *f.* salvo, broadside (*Nav.*), volley of artillery. **-stand,** *m.* gun emplacement, firing position. **-turm,** *m.* gun turret. **-weite,** *f.* range. **-wesen,** *n.* artillery, ordnance.

geschützt, *p.p. & adj.* protected, patented.

Geschwader, *n.* (-s, –) squadron (*Nav.*), group (*Av.*). **-flug,** *m.* mass formation flight.

Geschwafel, *n.* (*coll.*) twaddle, silly talk.

Geschwätz(e), *n.* idle *or* empty talk, babble; tittle-tattle, gossiping; rigmarole; *was soll dies –?* what is the meaning of this babble? **-ig,** *adj.* talkative, garrulous, loquacious, babbling (*brook*). **-igkeit,** *f.* talkativeness, loquaciousness, loquacity.

geschweift, *p.p. & adj.* cranked, arched, curved, tailed.

geschweig-e, *adv.* not to mention, let alone; much less; far from; to say nothing of; *ich habe ihn nicht gesehen, –e denn gesprochen*, I have not seen him, much less spoken to him; *sie mag mich nicht zum Freunde, –e zum Geliebten*, she doesn't want my friendship, much less my love. **-en,** *ir.v.n.* (*aux.* h.) (*Gen.*) (*archaic*) pass by in silence, say nothing of, not mention, omit; *anderer Vorzüge zu –en*, not to speak of other advantages.

geschwiegen, *p.p. of* **schweigen.**

geschwind, *adj.* quick, swift, fast, speedy, rapid; prompt, immediate; *sie wußte nicht, was sie – sagen sollte*, she did not know at the moment what to say; *mach' –!* be quick! **-igkeit,** *f.* rapidity, haste, quickness; speed, rate, velocity; headway (*Naut.*); *in der –igkeit*, hurriedly, on the spur of the moment; *Anfangs–igkeit*, initial velocity; *volle –igkeit*, full speed; (*Prov.*) *–igkeit ist keine Hexerei*, sleight of hand is no magic. **-igkeitsgrenze,** *f.* speed limit. **-igkeitsmesser,** *m.* speedometer (*Motor.*), air-speed indicator (*Av.*). **-igkeitssteigerung,** *f.*

acceleration. **-igkeitsverminderung,** *f.* retardation. **-schritt,** *m.* double-quick step, at the double.

Geschwirr(e), *n.* whirring, whizzing; buzz.

Geschwister, *pl.* brother(s) and sister(s); *sie sind –*, they are brother and sister; *meine –*, my brother(s) and sister(s). **-kind,** *n.* nephew *or* niece; first cousin. **-lich,** *adj.* brotherly, sisterly. **-liebe,** *f.* love for brother(s) and sister(s). **-mord,** *m.* fratricide.

geschwollen, *p.p. of* **schwellen.**

geschwommen, *p.p. of* **schwimmen.**

geschwor-en, *p.p. of* **schwören. -(e)ne(r),** *m.* juryman. **-(e)nen,** *pl.* jury; *einen vor die –(e)nen stellen*, send a p.'s case to the assizes. **-(e)nenbank,** *f.* jury-box. **-(e)nengericht,** *n.* jury. **-(e)nenliste,** *f.* jury-list; panel; *auf die –(e)nenliste setzen*, empanel. **-(e)nenobmann,** *m.* foreman of the jury.

[2]**geschworen,** *p.p. of* **schwären,** festered, ulcerated.

Geschwulst, *f.* (¨-e) swelling, tumour.

geschwunden, *p.p. of* **schwinden.**

geschwungen, *p.p. of* **schwingen.**

Geschwür, *n.* (-(e)es, -e) ulcer, abscess, boil, running sore; *in ein – verwandeln*, ulcerate, form into an abscess; *bösartiges –*, malignant ulcer. **-bildung,** *f.* ulceration. **-ig,** *adj.* ulcerous. **-öffnung,** *f.*, **-schnitt,** *m.* opening *or* lancing of an abscess.

gesegn-en, *v.a.* (*Poet. & dial.*) (*einem etwas*) bless; *Gott –e es!* God's blessing on his gifts (*grace after meal*); *–ete Mahlzeit!* (*a greeting at mealtimes*; *no English equivalent nearer than 'good appetite'!*); *–eten Leibes*, with child.

Geselchte(s), *n.* (*Bav. & Austr. dial.*) smoked meat.

Gesell-(e), *m.* (-en, -en) companion, comrade, partner, mate, fellow, brother member (*of a society*); journeyman. **-en,** *v.a. & r.* join, associate, ally, associate (o.s.) with; keep company with; (*Prov.*) *gleich und gleich –t sich gern*, birds of a feather flock together. **-enherberge,** *f.* workingmen's lodging-house. **-enjahre,** *n.pl.*, *see* **-enzeit. -enverein,** *m.* journeymen's union. **-enzeit,** *f.* time of service as journeyman. **-ig,** *adj.* social, sociable; companionable; (*coll.*) chummy; gregarious (*Bot.*); *–iger Verein*, club, society; *–ige Zusammenkunft*, *–iges Beisammensein*, *–iger Abend*, social gathering *or* evening; *man lebte –ig*, there was much social life. **-igkeit,** *f.* sociability, good fellowship, social life. **-igkeitstrieb,** *m.* social *or* gregarious instinct. **-schaft,** *f.* society, association; fellowship, club; (*C.L.*) company, partnership; party, social gathering; high society; (*coll.*) *die ganze –schaft*, the whole lot, the whole crowd; *geschlossene –schaft*, club; *– schaft mit beschränkter Haftung* (*abbr. G.m.b.H.*) limited liability company; *die –schaft Jesu*, the Jesuit Order; *einem –schaft leisten*, keep a p. company; *schlechte –schaft verdirbt gute Sitten*, evil communications corrupt good manners; *mit einem in –schaft treten*, enter in(to) partnership with a p.; *sich in –schaft zeigen*, appear in society. **-schafter,** *m.* companion; associate, partner; member of a society *or* company; *er ist ein guter –schafter*, he is good company; *stiller –schafter*, sleeping partner. **-schafterin,** *f.* lady companion. **-schaftlich,** *adj.* social, sociable, companionable, gregarious, co-operative; *–schaftliche Produktion*, co-operative *or* joint production; *–schaftlicher Schliff*, social graces, good manners, cultured *or* refined behaviour. **-schaftlichkeit,** *f.* sociable disposition, sociability; social life. **-schaftsanzug,** *m.* evening-dress, party frock. **-schaftsbank,** *f.* joint-stock bank. **-schaftsdame,** *f.* lady companion; chaperone. **-schaftsfond,** *m.* joint-stock. **-schaftsgeist,** *m.* social spirit. **-schaftsglied,** *n.* member of a society. **-schaftshaus,** *n.* club-house, casino. **-schaftslehre,** *f.* sociology. **-schaftsreise,** *f.* conducted tour. **-schaftsschicht,** *f.* social stratum, group, class. **-schaftsspiel,** *n.* party game, round game. **-schaftsverderber,** *m.* kill-joy. **-schaftsvertrag,** *m.* deed of partnership. **-schaftswidrig,** *adj.* anti-social. **-schaftswissenschaft,** *f.* sociology. **-schaftszimmer,** *n.* reception-room, drawing-room; club-room.

Gesenk, *n.* (-(e)s, -e) stamp, die, swage. **-e,** *n.* (-es, -e) slope, declivity; hollow, cavity, pit, sump; bottom (*of a pit*) (*Min.*). **-schmiede,** *f.* drop forge. **-tiefe,** *f.* depth of a subterranean shaft (*Min.*).

gesessen, *p.p. of* **sitzen.**

Gesetz, *n.* (-es, -e) law, statute, commandment, decree; precept; strophe; *das natürliche, göttliche, bürgerliche –*, the natural, divine, civil law; *ein – geben, bekannt machen, umgehen, aufheben, halten, brechen, übertreten*, make, promulgate, evade, repeal, keep, break, infringe a law; *zum –e werden*, become law, pass into law; *ein – tritt in Kraft*, a law comes into force *or* becomes effective; *ein – in Kraft setzen* or *in Kraft treten lassen*, put a law into effect; *das – anrufen*, appeal to the law. **-antrag,** *m.* motion, bill. **-buch,** *n.* statute-book; code; *bürgerliches –buch*, civil code. **-entwurf,** *m.* draft of a bill (*Parl.*). **-eskraft,** *f.* force of law, legal power *or* sanction; *–eskraft erhalten* (*erlangen*), be enacted, be put on the statute-book. **-eskundig,** *see* **-kundig. -esschärfe,** *f.* rigour of the law. **-esvorlage,** *f.*, *see* **-entwurf. -gebend,** *adj.* legislative; *–gebender Körper*, legislative assembly *or* body, legislature. **-geber,** *m.* legislator, lawgiver. **-gebung,** *f.* legislation. **-gültig,** *adj.*, **-kräftig,** *adj.* legally sanctioned, having the force of the law. **-kundig,** *adj.* versed in law; *–kundiger Lord*, law-lord. **-lich,** *adj.* legal, statutory, lawful, legitimate; *–lich geschützt*, protected by law; copyright, patented. **-lichkeit,** *f.* legality, lawfulness. **-los,** *adj.* lawless, illegal; anarchical. **-losigkeit,** *f.* lawlessness, illegality; anarchy. **-mäßig,** *adj.*, lawful, legitimate, legal; according to laws, regular, in accordance with theoretical principles. **-mäßigkeit,** *f.* legality; conformity, regularity. **-sammlung,** *f.* code *or* body of laws. **-t,** *see* **gesetzt, -tafel,** *f.* table of laws; *die* (*mosaischen*) *–tafeln*, decalogue. **-übertretung,** *f.* infringement of the law. **-vollstrecker,** *m.*, **-vollzieher,** *m.* executor of the law, sheriff. **-vorschlag,** *m.* bill, motion (*Parl.*). **-widrig,** *adj.* unlawful, illegal.

gesetzt, 1. *p.p. & adj.* fixed, set, placed, established; in type, set up (*Typ.*); mature, steady, calm, serious, sedate; *von –eren Jahren*, arrived at years of discretion, of a certain maturity; *–en Benehmens*, of sedate behaviour. 2. granted, supposing, in case; *–enfalls* or *– den Fall*, take the case, let us suppose; *– es sei wahr*, supposing it to be true; *–, daß du recht hättest*, supposing *or* granted that you were right. **-heit,** *f.* steadiness, sedateness.

Gesicht, *n.* 1. (*no pl.*) sight; eyesight; eye; 2. (-(e)s, -er) face, countenance, visage, physiognomy, look; (*fig.*) appearance, aspect; grimace; 3. (-(e)s, -e) sight; vision, apparition; *die S. kriegt ein anderes –*, the matter takes on a different complexion; *wie aus dem –e geschnitten*, (looking) very much like; *aus dem – verlieren*, lose sight of; *einem ins –*, to a p.'s face; *ins – fassen*, face; *allen guten Sitten ins – schlagen*, act contrary to good manners, behave abominably; *seine Behauptung schlägt den Tatsachen ins –*, his statement flatly contradicts the facts, the facts give the lie to his statement; *kurzes – haben*, be short-sighted; *ein böses – machen*, look angry *or* ill-tempered; *ein freundliches – machen*, have a sympathetic appearance; *ein langes – machen*, pull a long face; *ein saures – machen*, look surly; *–er schneiden*, make faces, pull faces; *–e sehen*, see visions; *das – verlieren*, lose one's sight; *das – wahren*, save one's face; *zu – bekommen*, catch sight of; *das steht gut zu –e*, that is becoming *or* looks well; *zweites –*, second sight. **-sausdruck,** *m.* facial expression. **-sbildung,** *f.* physiognomy. **-seindruck,** *m.* visual impression. **-sfarbe,** *f.* complexion. **-sfehler,** *m.* visual defect. **-sfeld,** *n.* field of view. **-skreis,** *m.* (mental) range, horizon; *seinen –skreis erweitern*, enlarge the range of one's ideas; *er ist seit Jahren aus meinem –skreis verschwunden*, I have lost sight of him for years; *das liegt außer seinem –skreis*, that is beyond him *or* his mental horizon. **-skrem,** *m.* face cream. **-slinie,** *f.* facial line, lineament; visual line, level; outer line of a work (*Fort.*). **-snerv,** *m.* optic nerve; facial nerve. **-spunkt,** *m.* point of view, viewpoint, aspect. **-srose,** *f.* erysipelas. **-sschmerz,**

m. face-ache. **-sschwäche,** *f.* weakness of sight. **-ssinn,** *m.* sense of sight. **-stäuschung,** *f.* optical illusion. **-swahrnehmung,** *f.* sight, visual perception. **-sweite,** *f.* visible range. **-swinkel,** *m.* facial angle, optic angle; angle of vision. **-szug,** *m.* feature, lineament.

Gesims, *n.* (-es, -e) cornice, moulding; shelf, ledge; – *an einer Tür,* lintel; – *an Fenstern,* window-sill; – *an einer Mauer,* entablature, pediment.

Gesind-e, *n.* (*archaic*) domestic servants; (*dial.*) farm-hands. **-el,** *n.* rabble, mob, (*coll.*) rag-tag and bobtail. **-eamt,** *n.* registry office for servants. **-elohn,** *m.* servants' wages. **-eordnung,** *f.* regulations governing rights and duties of servants. **-estube,** *f.* servants' hall.

gesinn-t, *adj.* minded, disposed, affected; *der Regierung* or *gegen die Regierung gut oder übel –t* (or *gut–t, übel–t*) well- or ill-disposed towards the government; *sie sind alle gleich –t,* they are all of the same mind; *anders –t,* of different opinion; *österreichisch –t,* having Austrian sympathies; *den Engländern freundlich –t,* Anglophil; *Gustav Adolf war protestantisch –t,* Gustavus Adolphus had Protestant sympathies; *ein königlich –ter,* a royalist; *feindlich –t,* ill-disposed, antipathetic, hostile, inimical; *wie ist er –t?* what are his views? to what party does he belong? **-ung,** *f.* disposition; sentiment; conviction; mind, way of thinking; intention; *politische, religiöse –ung,* political, religious views *or* opinions; *treue –ung,* loyalty; *knechtische –ung,* servility; *er zeigt nie seine wahre –ung,* he never shows his true face. **-ungsbildung,** *f.* (*Nat. Soc.*) political training, inculcation of approved ideas. **-ungsgenosse,** *m.* partisan; follower; political friend. **-ungslos,** *adj.* unprincipled, characterless. **-ungslosigkeit,** *f.* lack of character. **-ungslump,** *m.* turncoat, time-server; (*sl.*) rat. **-ungstreu,** *adj.* loyal, true-hearted, constant, staunch. **-ungstüchtig,** *adj.* sycophantic, fawning, cringing. **-ungstüchtigkeit,** *f.* sycophancy, obsequiousness. **-ungswechsel,** *m.* change of opinion, face *or* front, change in one's opinions.

gesitt-et, *adj.* mannered; well-bred, polished, polite; cultured; moral. **-ung,** *f.* good manners, good breeding, culture; morality.

Gesöff, *n.* (*sl.*) hooch.

gesoffen, *p.p. of* **saufen,** (*vulg.*) drunk.

gesogen, *p.p. of* **saugen.**

gesonnen, *p.p. of* **sinnen**; – *sein,* intend, be inclined, resolved *or* disposed (to do); *was sind Sie – zu tun?* what have you in mind (to do)? *ich bin – abzureisen,* it is my intention to leave.

gesotten, *p.p. of* **sieden.**

gespalten, *adj.* cleft.

Gespan, 1. *m.* (-(e)s & -en, -e(n)) (*archaic & dial.*) colleague, assistant, comrade; 2. (-(e)s, -e) Hungarian local official.

Gespann, *n.* (-(e)s, -e) team, yoke (*of horses, etc.*); horse-drawn vehicle, carriage *or* coach and horses; *ungleiches –,* (*fig.*) bad match, incongruence, incongruity, disparity. **-t,** *p.p. & adj.* stretched, tight, taut, strained, under tension, cocked (*firearm*); intent, eager, anxious; *mit –ter Aufmerksamkeit,* with close attention; *in der –testen Erwartung,* in the most tense expectation; *ich bin sehr auf den Ausgang –t,* I am anxiously awaiting the result; *–te Verhältnisse,* strained relations; *mit –ten Blicken,* with eager looks; *auf –tem Fuße mit einem stehen,* be on bad terms with s.o.; (*coll.*) *ich bin –t, ob er es tut,* I wonder whether he will do it. **-heit,** *f.* tension, estrangement, bad terms.

Gesparr(e), Gespärre, *n.* framework; rafters.

Gespenst, *n.* (-es, -er) ghost, spectre, phantom, apparition; *es geht ein – in diesem Hause um,* this house is haunted; *das – der Arbeitslosigkeit,* the spectre of unemployment. **-erartig,** *adj.* spectral. **-ererscheinung,** *f.* ghostly apparition, hallucination. **-ergeschichte,** *f.* ghost-story. **-erglaube,** *m.* belief in ghosts. **-erhaft,** *adj., see* **-ig, -isch. -erreich,** *n.* spirit-world. **-erschiff,** *n.* phantom ship. **-erspuk,** *m.* witchery. **-erstunde,** *f.* witching-hour, midnight hour. **-ig,** *adj.,* **-isch,** *adj.* ghostly, ghostlike.

Gesperr(e), *n.* (-(e)s, -e) brood of pheasants, etc. (*Hunt.*). **-e,** *n.* (-s, –) safety catch, ratchet(-wheel) (*of a watch*), catch, clasp; encumbrance, resistance.

gespickt, *p.p. & adj.* larded (*Cook.*); (*fig.*) *ein wohl–er Geldbeutel,* a well-lined purse.

Gespiel-e, 1. *m.* (-en, -en) playmate. 2. *n.* continual playing; (*archaic*) playmate. **-in,** *f.* (-innen) playmate.

gespie(e)n, *p.p. of* **speien.**

Gespinst, *n.* (-es, -e) spun yarn; web, cocoon; tissue (*of lies, etc.*); *von feinem –e,* fine-spun; (*Prov.*) *wie das –, so der Gewinnst,* no pains, no gains.

gesponnen, *p.p. of* **spinnen.**

Gespons, 1. *m.* (-es, -e) (*Poet. & hum.*) bridegroom, husband; 2. *n.* (-es, -e) (*Poet. & hum.*) bride, wife; (*genders sometimes used indifferently*); (*coll.*) better-half.

Gespött, *n.* mockery, derision; laughing-stock; *aller Leute – sein, allen Leuten zum – dienen,* be the laughing-stock of everyone; *einen zum – machen, sein – mit einem treiben,* make a laughing-stock of s.o. **-el,** *n.* mockery, quizzing.

Gespotte, *n.* continual jeering, derision.

Gespräch, *n.* (-(e)s, -e) conversation, talk, discussion, discourse; dialogue; call (*Phone*); *sich* (*Acc.*) *mit einem in ein – einlassen, ein – mit einem anknüpfen,* enter into conversation with a p.; *es ist das – der ganzen Stadt,* it is the talk of the town, it is all over the town; *das – auf* (*einen Gegenstand*) *bringen,* lead the conversation round to (a subject), bring (a subject) into the conversation. **-ig,** *adj.* talkative, communicative; garrulous; (*coll.*) chatty. **-igkeit,** *f.* talkativeness; garrulousness, garrulity. **-sgegenstand,** *m.,* **-sstoff,** *m.* topic (*of conversation*), subject. **-sweise,** *adv.* in the course of conversation.

gespreizt, *p.p. & adj.* spread out, wide apart; (*fig.*) stilted, affected, pompous; *mit –en Beinen,* with legs astraddle. **-heit,** *f.* affectation, pomposity.

Gesprenge, *n.* blasting; precipitous slope (*Min.*); buttressed wall.

gesprengt, *p.p. & adj.* split.

gesprenkelt, *adj.* speckled, mottled.

Gespritze, *n.* spouting, spurting, squirting, playing (*of fire-engines, etc.*).

gesprochen, *p.p. of* **sprechen.**

gesprossen, *p.p. of* **sprießen.**

Gesprudel, *n.* spluttering, bubbling; bubbling noise; bubbling spring.

gesprungen, *p.p. of* **springen.**

Gest, *f.* (*dial.*) yeast, balm.

gestachelt, *adj.* prickly, thorny.

Gestade, *n.* (-s, –) (*Poet.*) bank, shore, beach.

gestaffelt, *adj.* staggered, distributed; echeloned (*Mil.*).

Gestalt, 1. *f.* (-en) form, shape; figure, build, frame, stature; air, manner, aspect; fashion, kind, character; (*in psychological contexts* 'Gestalt' *should not be translated. Nat. Soc. further perverted its meaning to 'ideal type', 'usage', 'concept'*); *Arznei in – von Pulver,* medicine in powder form; *folgender–,* in the following manner; *solcher–, daß,* in such a way as to; *das Abendmahl unter beiden –en* or *in beiderlei –,* communion in both kinds; *sich in seiner wahren – zeigen,* show one's true character *or* colours; *nach – der Sachen,* according to circumstances. 2. *adj.* (*rare*) shaped; *bei so –en Sachen,* such being the case. **-änderung,** *f.* metamorphosis. **-en,** 1. *v.a.* form, fashion, mould, shape. 2. *v.r.* take shape, appear; turn out; *es –ete sich zu seinem Besten,* it turned out to his advantage. **-end,** *pr.p. & adj.* formative. **-et,** *p.p. & adj.*; *wohl–eter Mensch,* well-proportioned man. **-lehre,** *f.* morphology. **-los,** *adj.* shapeless, formless, amorphous; immaterial; misshapen. **-prägend,** *adj.* (*Nat. Soc.*) capable of shaping destiny. **-ung,** *f.* formation, forming, construction, shaping, fashioning, modelling; form, figure, shape, configuration; condition, state, organization. **-ungsfähig,** *adj.* modifiable, variable, plastic. **-ungskraft,** *f.* creative power, power of *or* gift for organization. **-ungstrieb,** *m.* creative impulse. **-ungsvermögen,** *n.* variability. **-verwandlung,** *f.* trans-

figuration. **-werdung,** *f.* (*Nat. Soc.*) emergence, realization, incarnation.
Gestammel, *n.* stammering, stuttering.
gestand, gestände, *see* **gestehen.**
gestanden, *p.p. of* (1) **stehen,** (2) **gestehen.**
Gestände, *n.* (-s, –) aerie, eyrie, nest (*of hawks, herons, etc.*).
geständ-ig, *adj.* confessing; *–ig sein*, confess, plead guilty; *–iger Verbrecher*, approver (*Law*). **-nis,** *n.* admission, acknowledgement, confession, avowal.
Gestänge, *n.* poles, rods, bars, rails, stakes, transmission shafts, antlers; articulated rod (*Mach.*).
Gestank, *m.* (-(e)s, ¨-e) bad smell, stench, stink; *die Luft mit – erfüllen*, poison the air.
gestatt-en, *v.a.* permit, allow, grant, consent to; *–en Sie!* excuse me! may I pass? **-ung,** *f.* permission, consent.
gestaucht, *adj.* compressed; dammed up.
Gest-e, *f.* (-en) gesture. **-ikulieren,** *v.n.* (*aux.* h.) gesticulate.
gesteh-en, 1. *ir.v.a.* own, confess, acknowledge, admit, grant. *offen gestanden*, to speak frankly, to tell the (plain) truth. 2. *v.n.* coagulate, curdle, congeal, clot. **-ungskosten,** *pl.* cost of production, prime cost, working costs. **-ungspreis,** *m.* cost price.
Gestein, *n.* (-(e)s, -e) rocks, mineral; (*Poet.*) rock, stone; *taubes –*, deads (*Min.*). **-gang,** *m.* vein, streak, lode. **-skunde,** *f.*, **-slehre,** *f.* mineralogy petrology; geology. **-sunterlage,** *f.* rocky subsoil.
Gestell, *n.* (-(e)s, -e) stand, rack, frame (*of umbrella, spectacles, etc.*), framework, support, holder, chassis, bedstead; hearth, crucible. **-macher,** *m.* wheelwright. **-ung,** *f.* reporting (for duty) (*Mil.*). **-ungsaufschub,** *m.* deferment (of call-up). **-ungsbefehl,** *m.* enlistment *or* mobilization order.
gest-ern, 1. *adv.* yesterday; *–ern vor vierzehn Tagen*, yesterday fortnight; *–ern abend*, last night, yesterday evening; *–ern früh*, yesterday morning; early yesterday; (*coll.*) *ich bin nicht von –ern*, I wasn't born yesterday, I know what I'm about. 2. *n.* yesterday; the past; *das leidige –ern*, tiresome routine; *das ewige –ern* or *ewig –rige*, established custom, everyday routine. **-rig,** *adj.* of yesterday; *der –rige Tag*, yesterday; (*C.L.*) *wir beziehen uns auf unser Gestriges*, we refer to our letter of yesterday.
gesternt, *adj.* decorated *or* patterned with stars, starred.
gestiefelt, *p.p.* & *adj.* booted; *–er Kater*, Puss in Boots; *– und gespornt*, booted and spurred; quite ready.
gestiegen, *p.p. of* **steigen.**
gestielt, *adj.* helved; stalked, stemmed, petiolate, pedunculate (*Bot., Zool.*).
gestikulieren, *see* **Geste.**
Gestirn, *n.* (-(e)s, -e) star; stars, heavenly body, constellation. **-forscher,** *m.* astronomer. **-kultus,** *m.* astrology. **-lehre,** *f.*, astronomy. **-stand,** *m.* constellation. **-t,** *adj.* starry, starred; *suffix* –fronted, –browed.
gestoben, *p.p. of* **stieben.**
Gestöber, *n.* (-s) drift (*of dust or snow*); storm.
gestochen, *p.p. of* **stechen.**
gestohlen, *p.p. of* **stehlen;** (*coll.*) *der* or *das kann mir – bleiben*, he *or* that does not interest me in the slightest, (*coll.*) I don't care two hoots for him *or* that.
Gestöhn(e), *n.* moaning, groaning.
Gestolper, *n.* tottering, stumbling.
gestorben, *p.p. of* **sterben.**
Gestotter, *n.* stammering, stuttering.
gestrahlt, *p.p.* & *adj.* stellate, radiate.
Gestrampel, *n.* wriggling, fidgeting with one's legs.
gestrandet, *adj.* ashore, aground (*Naut.*).
Gestrauchelte(r), *m.* petty offender, s.o. who has slipped *or* fallen.
Gesträuch, *n.* (-(e)s, -e) shrubs, bushes, shrubbery, thicket.
gestreckt, *adj.* procumbent, trailing, stretched, attenuate.
gestreift, *adj.* streaky, striped.
gestreng(e), *adj.* (*archaic*) severe, strict, austere, puissant (*usually in titles*); (*coll.*) *die 3 –en Herren*, the 3 severe days in May (*North Germany*: *May 11, 12, 13, Mamertus, Pancratius, Servatius*; *South Germany*: *Bonifatius, May 14, instead of Mamertus*).
gestrichen, *p.p. of* **streichen** & *adj.* painted; *–es Maß*, level measure; strike-measure, strickle measure (*Mill.*).
gestrig, *adj.*, *see* **gestern.**
Gestrudel, *n.* boiling (*of a whirlpool*); bubbling up.
Gestrüpp, *n.* (-(e)s, -e) bushes, underwood, undergrowth, brushwood, thicket, scrub.
Gestübe, Gestübbe, *n.* combustible dust; mixture of charcoal *or* coal-dust with earth, etc. (*Smelting*).
Gestühl, *n.* pew(s).
Gestümper, *n.* bungling; bungled work.
gestund-en, *v.a.* (*C.L.*) (*einem etwas*) grant delay *or* respite (*in payment*). **-ung,** *f.* respite, delay (*in payment*).
Gestürm, *n.* (*Swiss dial.*) commotion, hurly-burly; gabble.
Gestüt, *n.* (-(e)s, -e) stud, stud-farm. **-hengst,** *m.* stallion; stud-horse. **-stute,** *f.* brood-mare. **-zeichen,** *n.* brand of a stud.
Gesuch, *n.* (-(e)s, -e) application, petition, (formal) request; suit. **-steller,** *m.* applicant, petitioner. **-t,** *adj.* choice; far-fetched, affected (*style*); (*C.L.*) sought after, in demand.
Gesudel, *n.* dirty work; daub, scrawl.
Gesumm(e), *n.* humming, buzzing.
gesund, *adj.* healthy, sound, well; financially sound, solvent; wholesome, beneficial, salutary, salubrious; *–er Menschenverstand*, common sense; *wieder – werden*, get well again, be restored to health; (*coll.*) *das ist ihm –!* that serves him right! **-beterei,** *f.*, **-beten,** *n.* faith-healing. **-brunnen,** *m.* mineral spring *or* well. **-en,** *v.n.* (*aux.* s.) regain *or* recover one's health. **-heit,** *f.* health; wholesomeness, soundness; *bei guter –heit sein*, be in good health; *in bester –heit*, in the best of health; *wie steht es um Ihre –heit* or *mit der –heit?* how is your health? *eine –heit ausbringen*, propose *or* give a toast; *auf Ihre –heit!* your (very good) health! (*zur*) *–heit!* God bless you! (*to a p. sneezing*). **-heitlich,** *adj.* concerning health; hygienic, sanitary. **-heitsamt,** *n.* Public Health Department, Ministry of Health. **-heitsdienst,** *m.* medical service. **-heitshalber,** *adv.* for the sake of health. **-heitskunde,** *f.*, **-heitslehre,** *f.* hygiene. **-heitspaß,** *m.*, *see* **-heitsschein. -heitspflege,** *f.* care of health, sanitation, hygiene; *öffentliche –heitspflege*, public health service. **-heitsschädlich,** *adj.* injurious to health, noxious. **-heitsschein,** *m.* certificate of (good) health, clean bill of health. **-heitswidrig,** *adj.*, *see* **-heitsschädlich. -heitszustand,** *m.* state of health (*of a p.*); sanitary condition (*of a place*). **-ung,** *f.* recovery, convalescence.
gesungen, *p.p. of* **singen.**
gesunken, *p.p. of* **sinken.**
Getäf-el, *n.* wainscot, wainscoting; inlaying, panelling; honeycomb (*bees*); *–el eines Fußbodens*, parquet flooring, inlaid wooden floor. **-er,** *n.* (*Swiss dial.*), *see* **-el.**
getan, *p.p. of* **tun;** *gesagt, –*, no sooner said than done.
Getändel, *n.* trifling, dallying, toying.
Geteiltheit, *f.* state of separation *or* division.
Getier, *n.* animals, beasts; (*coll.*) animal.
getigert, *adj.* striped, marked; watered (*fabrics*).
Getön, *n.* noise, din, clamour, clang. **-t,** *p.p.* & *adj.* tinted.
Getös(e), *n.*, **Getose,** *n.* (deafening) noise, din, uproar, turmoil.
getragen, *p.p.* & *adj.* solemn, grave, ceremonious.
Getrampel, *n.* stamping, trampling.
Getränk, *n.* (-(e)s, -e) drink, beverage; potion; *geistiges –*, (spirituous) liquor; (*pl.*) spirits. **-t,** *adj.* impregnated, saturated.
Getratsch(e), Geträtsch(e), *n.* (*coll.*) meaningless talk, twaddle, gossip, tittle-tattle.
getrau-en, *v.r.* dare, venture; trust, feel confident; *ich –e mich* (not *mir*) *nicht dahin*, I dare not go there, I don't trust myself there; *ich –e mir* (not *mich*) *den Schritt nicht*, I don't trust myself to take this step; *ich –e mich* (or *mir*) *nicht*,

dieses zu tun, I dare not do that, I hesitate to do that.

Getreide, *n.* corn, grain, cereals. **–art,** *f.* cereal. **–bau,** *m.* corn-growing. **–boden,** *m.* cornland; granary. **–börse,** *f.* corn-exchange. **–brand,** *m.* smut *or* blight on corn. **–brennerei,** *f.* grain distilling *or* distillery. **–fege,** *f.* winnowing machine. **–fuhre,** *f.* wagon-load of corn. **–händler,** *m.* corn-merchant. **–kammer,** *f.* granary. **–kümmel,** *m.* cumin-brandy (*made of rye*). **–land,** *n.* corn-growing country; cornland. **–mähmaschine,** *f.* reaper. **–speicher,** *m.* *see* **–kammer.**

Getrennt-heit, *f.* **–sein,** *n.* separation. **–schreibung,** *f.* uncial, printed writing, printing (*opp.* cursive writing).

getreu, *adj.* faithful, true, trusty, loyal; (*archaic*) accurate; *–es Gedächtnis*, retentive memory; *unsern lieben –en*, to our trusty and well-beloved (subjects, vassals, etc.). **–lich,** *adj.* faithfully, truly, loyally.

Getriebe, *n.* driving, drift; motion, agitation, bustle, busy life; motive power, drive, machinery, mechanism, spring, works; gear, pinion, gearing, gear-box, linkage, transmission; – *des Lebens*, bustle of life; – *der Menschen*, busy life of men; – *einer Uhr*, movement of a watch; – *zum Abstoßen*, disconnecting gear. **–bremse,** *f.* flywheel-brake. **–gehäuse,** *n.*, **–kasten,** *m.* gear-box, gear-casing, transmission housing. **–lehre,** *f.* kinetics. **–welle,** *f.* transmission shaft.

getrieben, *p.p. of* **treiben** *&* *adj.*; *–e Arbeit*, chased work.

getroffen, *p.p. of* **treffen** *&* **triefen.**

getrogen, *p.p. of* **trügen.**

getrost, *adj.* confident, hopeful; comforted, of good cheer; *–en Mutes*, of good courage.

getrösten, *v.r.* (*with Gen.*) (*archaic*) hope for, be confident, wait patiently; be solaced (*mit*, by).

getrübt, *adj.* dull, cloudy, turbid, opaque.

getrunken, *p.p. of* **trinken.**

Getue, *n.* (*coll.*) doings, goings-on; pretence; affectation; fuss, bother; (*coll.*) *was soll nur das –?* what's the good of all that fuss?

Getümmel, *n.* tumult; bustle, turmoil.

getüpfelt, *adj.* dotted, spotted, pitted (*Bot.*).

Geübtheit, *f.* skill, dexterity, practice.

Gevatter, *m.* (-s, -n) godfather, sponsor; (*dial.*) intimate friend, neighbour, relative (*now implies a snobbish sneer*); – *Schneider und Handschuhmacher*, shop-keepers and such-like people; – *stehen*, stand godfather *or* sponsor; *einen zu* or *zum – bitten*, ask a p. to stand sponsor (to); *er steht bei einem meiner Kinder –*, he is godfather to one of my children; *sie ist meine –in*, she is my godmother. **–schaft,** *f.* sponsorship; sponsor. **–geschenk,** *n.* christening present. **–schmaus,** *m.* christening feast. **–sleute,** *pl.* sponsors. **–smann,** *m.* godfather.

gevier-t, 1. *adj.* quartered; squared; quaternary. 2. *n.* (-(e)s, -e), **–te,** *n.* (-tes, –) square; quadrature; *ins –te bringen*, square; *es mißt 3 Zentimeter im –t*, it is 3 centimetres square. **–teilt,** *adj.* quartered. **–tmaß,** *n.* square measure. **–tmeter,** *n.* (*coll.* *&* *Austr.*, *Swiss* *&* *Bav. dial. m.*) square metre. **–tschein,** *m.* quartile aspect (*Astr.*). **–twurzel,** *f.* square root.

Gewächs, *n.* (-es, -e) plant, vegetable, herb; vintage, growth; tumour (*Med.*); *ausländisches –*, exotic plant; *eigenes –*, home produce; *heuriges –*, this year's vintage. **–haus,** *n.* greenhouse, hothouse, conservatory. **–kunde,** *f.*, **–lehre,** *f.* botany.

gewachsen, *p.p.* *&* *adj.*; *einem* or *einer S. – sein*, be a match for a p. *or* equal to a th.

gewagt, *adj.* risky, daring.

gewählt, *adj.* selected, choice.

gewahr, *adj.*; *etwas* or (rare) *einer S. – werden*, perceive, become aware of; see; *ich wurde meines Irrtums* or *meinen Irrtum bald –*, I soon became aware of my mistake. **–en,** *v.a.* (*&* *n. with Gen.*) (*Poet.*) *see* – **werden.** **–sam,** 1. *m.* (-es, -e) charge, custody. 2. *n.* (-(e)s, -e) prison.

Gewähr, *f.* security, surety; warrant, guarantee, bail; *ohne –*, no responsibility taken; – *leisten* (*für eine S.*), go bail (for a th.), guarantee (a th.). **–en,** *v.a.* (*einem etwas*) grant, accord, concede, vouchsafe; give, furnish, impart; *Vergnügen –en*, afford pleasure; *–en lassen*, let alone, let (*a p.*) have his own way, leave to go on as it will, indulge (*a p.*); *laß ihn –en!* let him do as he likes! *laß mich –en!* let me alone! don't interfere! leave it to me! **–leisten,** *v.a.* guarantee, vouch for, warrant. **–leistung,** *f.* acceptance of responsibility, granting security, offering surety, undertaking to guarantee, giving bail. **–schaft,** *f.* warranty, guaranty. **–schein,** *m.* warrant, bond. **–smangel,** *m.* default of bail. **–smann,** *m.* authority, informant; *zuständiger –smann*, competent authority. **–ung,** *f.* granting, concession; grant (*Law*); *er hat die –ung seiner Bitte erlangt*, his request has been granted.

gewahrt, *p.p.* protected, preserved.

Gewalt, *f.* (-en) power, authority, dominion, might; force, violence; *einem – antun*, do a p. violence; *einem Mädchen – antun*, violate *or* ravish a girl; *sich* (*Dat.*) *– antun*, restrain *or* constrain o.s.; lay violent hands upon o.s., commit suicide; *einer Stelle – antun*, distort the sense of a passage (*in a book, etc.*); *ausübende –*, executive power; *höhere –*, act of God *or* Providence, force majeure; *in der – haben*, master, be master of, have command of, have in one's power; *sich in der – haben*, have control of o.s., have self-control; *mit –*, by force, forcibly, perforce; *mit* (*aus*) *aller –*, with all one's might; *sie wollen mit aller – neue Länder entdecken*, they are determined to discover new countries. **–anmaßung,** *f.* usurpation of power. **–brief,** *m.* power of attorney; warrant. **–friede,** *m.* enforced *or* dictated peace. **–geber,** *m.* client, constituent, p. authorizing. **–haber,** *m.* holder of power, p. in authority, autocrat, dictator. **–herrschaft,** *f.* despotism. **–herrscher,** *m.* despot. **–ig,** *adj.* powerful, potent, mighty, strong, forcible, intense, violent; big, vast, prodigious, huge, immense, enormous; *–iges Verbrechen*, atrocious crime; *sich –ig irren*, be widely mistaken; *–ig reich*, enormously rich; *–ig lieb haben*, be excessively fond of; *die –igen der Erde*, the rulers of the earth. **–marsch,** *m.* forced march. **–maßregel,** *f.* violent *or* illegal measure. **–mensch,** *m.* man of authority; man who abuses authority; violent *or* brutal man. **–sam,** *adj.* vigorous, forcible, violent, powerful; *–sam verfahren*, use violence; *–same Schritte*, strong measures; *eines –samen Todes sterben*, die a violent death. **–samkeit,** *f.* violence. **–streich,** *m.* violent *or* illegal measure, arbitrary act, bold stroke, coup de main. **–sturm,** *m.* mass attack (*Mil.*). **–tat,** *f.* deed of violence, outrage, atrocity. **–tätig,** *adj.* violent, brutal, outrageous; *–tätiger Angriff*, assault; *–tätiger Mensch*, brutal man. **–tätigkeit,** *f.* violence, act of violence. **–träger,** *m.* attorney; plenipotentiary.

gewalzt, *p.p.* rolled, milled.

Gewand, *n.* (-(e)s, ⸚er *&* (*Poet.*) -e) garment, dress, raiment, robe, vestment. **–händler,** *m.* woollen-draper. **–haus,** *n.* drapers' hall; clothiers' *or* woollen merchants' exchange (market). **–ung,** *f.* (-en) drapery.

gewandt, *p.p. of* **wenden** *&* *adj.* active, agile, nimble; clever, adroit, skilled, skilful, versatile; – *in* (*einer S.*), good at *or* at home in (a th.). **–heit,** *f.* adroitness, dexterity, agility; versatility, fluency, knack, cleverness, skill.

gewann, gewänne, *see* **gewinnen.**

gewärtig, *adj.* (*with Gen.*) awaiting, expecting, expectant; *einer S. – sein*, expect *or* hope for a th.; *ich bin von ihm jeder Unfreundlichkeit –*, I expect every unpleasantness at his hands; (*archaic*) *ich bleibe Ihrer Befehle –*, I shall attend to your orders. **–en,** *v.a.* be prepared for, be resigned to, expect, look forward to; *es ist zu –en*, it is to be expected.

Gewäsch(e), *n.* (*coll.*) idle talk, twaddle.

Gewässer, *n.* (-s, –) waters, flood; *die – fallen*, the floods subside. **–kunde,** *f.* hydrology

Gewebe, *n.* weaving; web, (textile) fabric; texture; tissue; (*dial.*) cells (*of bees*); *das – der Adern*, plexus; *ein – von Lügen*, a tissue *or* pack of lies. **–lehre,** *f.* histology. **–verletzung,** *f.* lesion (*Med.*). **–waren,** *f.pl.* textiles, textile goods.

geweckt, *p.p.* & *adj.* lively, alert, bright, sprightly; clever, wide-awake. **–heit,** *f.* sprightliness, liveliness, vivacity.

Gewehr, *n.* (-(e)s, -e) rifle, musket; tusk (*of a boar*); (*Poet.*) weapon, arms; *Seiten–*, sword, side-arms; *– ab!* order arms! *an die –e!* stand to (your arms)! *– über!* shoulder arms! *ins – rufen*, call to arms; *präsentiert das –!* present arms! *Seiten– pflanzt auf;* fix bayonets! *das – strecken*, lay down one's arms; *die Mannschaft trat unters –*, the men stood to their arms; *zum – greifen*, take up *or* fly to arms. **–appell,** *m.* rifle inspection. **–feuer,** *n.* firing, rifle-fire. **–geschoß,** *n.* rifle bullet. **–kammer,** *f.* armoury. **–kolben,** *m.* butt. **–kreuz,** *n.* gun-rack. **–lauf,** *m.* gun-barrel. **–riemen,** *m.* rifle-sling. **–schein,** *m.* gun licence. **–stärke,** *f.* combatant *or* rifle strength.

Geweih, *n.* (-(e)s, -e) horns, antlers; *ein – aufsetzen*, cuckold, deceive one's husband. **–kronleuchter,** *m.* chandelier. **–zacken,** *m.* prong *or* process of antlers.

geweiht, *p.p.* (*of* **weihen**) & *adj.* sacred; 2. antlered, horned.

gewellt, *p.p. of* **wellen**; corrugated (*iron*); wavy, undulating.

Gewende, *n.* (-s) turn of the plough; length of the furrow; *ein – machen*, turn the plough.

Gewerb–e, *n.* (-(e)s, -e) trade, business, calling, profession, industry, vocation, occupation; *er war seines –es ein Tischler*, he was a joiner by trade. **–eaufsicht,** *f.* factory inspection. **–eaufsichtsbeamter,** *m.* factory inspector. **–eausstellung,** *f.* industrial exhibition, industries fair. **–efreiheit,** *f.* liberty to exercise a trade. **–efleiß,** *m.* industry; industrial activity. **–egericht,** *n.* industrial council. **–ekammer,** *f.* Chamber of Commerce. **–ekrankheit,** *f.* occupational disease. **–ekunde,** *f.* technology. **–ekundige(r),** *m.* technologist. **–ekundlich,** *adj.* technological. **–eordnung,** *f.* trade regulations. **–esalz,** *n.* common salt. **–eschein,** *m.* trade licence. **–eschule,** *f.* trade school. **–eschüler,** *m.* pupil of a trade school. **–esteuer,** *f.* tax paid for carrying on a trade; profit-tax. **–esteuerpflichtig,** *adj.* subject to licence, liable to tax on an occupational basis. **–etreibend,** *adj.* manufacturing, industrial. **–etreibende(r),** *m.* manufacturer, artisan, tradesman. **–everein,** *m.* tradesmen's union. **–lich,** *adj.* industrial; professional. **–sleute,** *pl.* tradespeople, tradesmen. **–smäßig,** *adj.* professional; *–smäßige Bettelei*, professional begging; *–smäßige Prostitution*, prostitution. **–stätig,** *adj., see* **–lich.** **–szweig,** *m.* branch of industry, line of business.

Gewerk, *n.* (-(e)s, -e) (*archaic*) works, machinery; guild, corporation, craft. **–e,** *m.* (-en, -en) member of miners' union; (*Austr. dial.*) manufacturer. **–schaft,** *f.* trade(s)-union. **–schaftler,** *m.* trade(s)-unionist. **–schaftlich,** *adj.* & *adv.*; *–schaftlich organisierte Arbeiter*, workers united in a trade(s)-union. **–schaftsbund,** *m.* Trade(s)-Union Congress (*Brit.*); Federation of Labor (*Amer.*). **–schaftskongress,** *m.* Trade(s)-Union Congress (T.U.C.). **–schaftswesen,** *n.* trade(s)-unionism. **–verein,** *m.* trade(s)-union.

gewesen, *p.p. of* **sein**, *mein –er Freund*, my friend that was, my former friend; *–e Schönheit*, one-time beauty, faded beauty.

gewichen, *p.p. of* **weichen.**

Gewicht, *n.* (-(e)s, -e) weight, heaviness; gravity, importance, moment; stress, load; *das – nicht haben*, be short in weight; *an – haben*, weigh; *schwer ins – fallen*, (*fig.*) be of *or* carry great weight, be of great importance, weigh heavily with; *das – halten*, be full weight; *– auf etwas legen*, consider a th. to be important, set (great) store by a th.; *spezifisches –*, specific gravity (*Phys.*): *totes –*, tare; *an – verlieren*, lose (in) weight; *volles – geben*, give full weight. **–eicher,** *m.* assizer of weights. **–heber,** *m.* weight-lifter, strong man. **–ig,** *adj.* heavy; weighty, important, momentous; forcible, impressive. **–igkeit,** *f.* weightiness, weight, full weight; importance. **–kunst,** *f.*, **–lehre,** *f.* statics. **–sabgang,** *m.* loss in weight. **–sabnahme,** *f.* decrease in weight. **–sanalyse,** *f.* gravimetric(al) analysis (*Chem.*). **–sklasse,** *f.* weight (*Sport*). **–ssatz,** *m.* set of weights. **–sverlust,** *m., see* **–sabnahme.** **–szunahme,** *f.* increase in weight. **–voll,** *adj.* weighty, ponderous; full of importance.

gewickelt, *p.p.* (*coll.*) *schief – sein*, be completely mistaken, be altogether on the wrong track.

gewiegt, *adj.* experienced, skilled; clever, shrewd.

Gewieher, *n.* neighing; (*fig.*) horse-laugh.

gewiesen, *p.p. of* **weisen.**

gewillt, *adj.* willing, disposed, inclined; *– sein*, be determined, intend.

Gewimmel, *n.* swarming, crawling; crowd, swarm, multitude, throng.

Gewimmer, *n.* whining, wailing, moaning, whimpering.

Gewinde, *n.* (-s, –) winding, coil, skein (*of thread*), festoon, garland, wreath; worm, (screw) thread; labyrinth (*of the ear*); whorl (*of shells*). **–bohrer,** *m.* screw tap. **–steigung,** *f.* screw pitch.

Gewinn, *m.* (-(e)s, -e) gaining, winning; earnings, gain, profit, prize, winnings; yield, proceeds, produce; *der reine –* (*Rein–*), net profits; *Gewinn- und Verlustkonto*, profit and loss account; *mit – verkaufen*, sell to advantage; *– abwerfen*, yield a profit; *das ist schon (ein) –*, that is s.th. gained. **–anteil,** *m.* share in the profits, dividend. **–bar,** *adj.* obtainable, gainable. **–beteiligung,** *f.* profit-sharing. **–bringend,** *adj.* profitable, lucrative. **–en,** 1. *ir.v.a.* win, gain, obtain, acquire, earn; prevail over, conquer; produce, extract, reclaim, prepare (*Chem.*); *es –t das Ansehen, als wenn*, it seems as if; *Boden –en*, gain ground; *einen für (eine S.) –en*, interest a p. in, win a p. over to; *das Freie –en*, gain the open (field); *Interesse –en für eine S.*, interest o.s. *or* become interested in s.th.; *einen lieb –en*, become fond of a p.; *das große Los –en*, win *or* draw the first prize; *die Oberhand –en*, get the mastery of, get the upper hand of; *ich habe Ehrfurcht vor ihm gewonnen*, he has inspired me with respect; *den Vorsprung –en*, gain an advantage (over), gain a lead (on); (*Prov.*) *wie gewonnen, so zerronnen*, easy come, easy go; *–endes Lächeln*, winning *or* ingratiating smile; *einen zum Freunde –en*, gain a p. as a friend. 2. *v.n.* (*aux.* h.) *er –t bei näherer Bekanntschaft*, he improves on closer acquaintance; *an Klarheit –en*, gain in clarity; *ich konnte es nicht über mich –en*, I could not bring myself to (do it). **–er,** *m.* winner, gainer. **–ler,** *m.* profiteer. **–liste,** *f.* prize list. **–los,** *adj.* profitless, unprofitable. **–nummer,** *f.* winning number. **–rechnung,** *f.* profit account. **–reich,** *adj.* profitable, lucrative. **–sucht,** *f.* greed, greediness, avarice. **–süchtig,** *adj.* greedy, avaricious. **–ung,** *f.* gaining; gain, produce, production; extraction (*Chem.*).

Gewinsel, *n.* whining, moaning, whimpering.

Gewinst, *m.*, (-es, -e) winnings, takings, gain, profit.

Gewirbel, *n.* whirling; roll (*of drums*); roulade (*Mus.*); warbling.

Gewirk–e, *n.* weaving; web, texture. **–t,** *adj.* woven.

Gewirr(e), *n.* confusion, entanglement; maze, jumble, tangle; whirl (*of ideas*).

gewiß, 1. *adj.* (*with Gen.*) sure, certain, assured, positive, true, undoubted; stable, steady, fixed; *ein –(ss)er*, a certain p., s.o.; *das –(ss)e*, certainty; *sein –(ss)es haben*, have a fixed income; *er behauptete es als –*, he asserted it as a fact; *ich bin dessen –*, I am sure of it; *seine Stimme ist mir –*, I am sure of his vote; *seiner S. – sein*, be sure of what one says; be sure of one's facts *or* one's ground, know a th. thoroughly. 2. *adv.* certainly, surely, indeed, to be sure, no doubt, of a surety; *das ist – ein Streich von ihm*, that is a trick of his, I'll be bound; *du hast – kein Geld?* I'll warrant you have no money; *Sie wollten uns – überraschen?* you hoped to surprise us, didn't you? *wußten Sie, daß er fort war? – !* did you know he had gone? Of course I did! Certainly! To be sure! **–(ss)ermaßen,** *adv.* to a certain degree, to some extent, so to speak, as it were. **–heit,** *f.* certainty, assurance, proof, certitude; *ich werde mir –heit darüber verschaffen*, I shall make certain on that point, I shall put an end to all doubt about that. **–lich,** *adv.* certainly, surely, assuredly.

Gewissen, *n.* conscience; *einem* (*schwer*) *aufs – fallen*, bring it home to s.o.'s conscience; *Sie haben es auf dem –*, you are morally responsible for it *or* have it on your conscience; *er macht sich kein – daraus zu betrügen*, he does not scruple to cheat; *enges –*, touchy conscience; *einem ins – reden*, appeal to a p.'s conscience; *er hat es getan, um sich mit seinem – abzufinden*, he did do it to soothe his conscience; (*Prov.*) *ein gutes – ist ein sanftes Ruhekissen*, a good conscience sleeps through thunder; *sich* (*Dat.*) *ein – über eine S. machen*, make a th. a matter of conscience, have scruples about a th.; *ein weites – haben*, be not over-scrupulous, have an obliging conscience. **–haft,** *adj.* conscientious; scrupulous. **–haftigkeit,** *f.* conscientiousness. **–los,** *adj.* unprincipled, unscrupulous. **–losigkeit,** *f.* lack of principle, unscrupulousness. **–sangst,** *f.* qualms of conscience. **–sbiß,** *m.* twinge of conscience; *usually pl.* **–sbisse,** pangs of conscience; remorse. **–sehe,** *f.* morganatic marriage, cohabitation. **–sfrage,** *f.* moral issue, difficult case, question of conscience. **–sfreiheit,** *f.* freedom of conscience. **–sfreund,** *m.* spiritual father, father confessor. **–slehre,** *f.* casuistry. **–spflicht,** *f.* bounden duty. **–sprüfung,** *f.* self-examination. **–srüge,** *f.* remorse. **–srührung,** *f.* compunction. **–sskrupel,** *m.* moral scruple. **–svorwurf,** *m.* self-reproach. **–szwang,** *m.* moral constraint. **–szweifel,** *m.* doubt, scruple, qualm.

Gewitter, *n.* (-s, –) thunderstorm, tempest, storm; *es steigt ein – auf, ein – ist im Anzuge*, a thunderstorm is gathering. **–haft,** *adj.* stormy, sultry, oppressive. **–luft,** *f.* sultriness before a thunderstorm, thunder in the air. **–n,** *v.n. imp.*; *es –t*, it thunders, there is a thunderstorm. **–regen,** *m.* downpour, thunder-shower. **–schlag,** *m.* thunderclap. **–schwanger,** *adj.*, **–schwer,** *adj.*, **schwül,** *adj.* sultry. **–schwüle,** *f.* sultriness. **–wolke,** *f.* thundercloud.

gewitz–igt, –t, *adj.* taught by experience; shrewd.

gewoben, *p.p. of* **weben.**

Gewoge, *n.* waving; fluctuation; rocking; (*Poet.*) waves.

gewogen, *p.p. of* 1. **wiegen**; 2. **wägen** & *adj.*; (*einem*) well-disposed (towards), friendly, affectionate; *sich* (*Dat.*) *einen – machen*, secure *or* gain a p.'s affection *or* favour; (*coll.*) *bleib mir –!* think of me from time to time! I'll be glad to hear from you (*farewell*). **–heit,** *f.* goodwill; affection, attachment.

gewöhn–en, *v.a.* & *r.* accustom, habituate; inure, familiarize, train, break in; domesticate; *sich –en*, get into the habit of; *sich an eine S. –en*, get accustomed to a th. **–lich,** *adj.* usual, customary, ordinary, average, general, commonplace; common, vulgar; *das –liche*, the usual th.; *–liche Frau*, everyday woman; vulgar woman; *–liche Leute*, ordinary people; *etwas über das –liche hinaus*, s.th. out of the common *or* the ordinary. **–t,** *p.p.* & *adj.* accustomed, habituated, trained; *ich habe mich –t, früh aufzustehen*, I have trained myself *or* have made it my habit to get up early. **–ung,** *f.* custom, habit; accustoming, habituation; *–ung an das Klima*, acclimatization; *–ung der Haustiere*, domestication of animals.

Gewohn-heit, *f.* habit, custom, usage, fashion, wont; *zur –heit werden*, grow into a habit; *aus –heit*, from habit; *aus der –heit kommen*, fall into disuse; get out of practice; *nach seiner –heit*, according to his custom. **–heitsmäßig,** 1. *adj.* customary, habitual, routine; *–heitsmäßiger Bummler*, inveterate loafer. 2. *adv.* as is the *or* his *or* their custom. **–heitsmensch,** *m.* creature *or* slave of habit. **–heitsrecht,** *n.* prescriptive law *or* right. **–heitssäufer,** *m.*, **–heitstrinker,** *m.* habitual *or* confirmed drunkard. **–heitssünde,** *f.* habitual *or* besetting sin. **–heitstier,** *n.*; (*Prov.*) *der Mensch ist ein –heitstier*, man is a creature of habit. **–t,** *p.p.* & *adj.* in the habit of, accustomed to, used to, inured to; usual; (*Prov.*) *jung –t, alt getan*, what is bred in the bone comes out in the flesh; *–t sein*, be used to; *ich bin es nicht –t*, I am not used to it; *–t werden*, get used to; *–te Bedingungen*, usual conditions; *in –ter* or *auf –te Weise*, in the usual way, as usual.

Gewölbe, *n.* (-s, –) vault, arch; cellar; *bombensicheres –*, bomb-proof cellar; *Kreuz–*, groined vault (*Arch.*). **–ähnlich,** *adj.*, **–artig,** *adj.* arch-like, vault-like. **–bock,** *m.* centring of a vault. **–bogen,** *m.* arch of a vault. **–fenster,** *n.* skylight; bow-window. **–pfeiler,** *m.* buttress; shaft of an arch. **–schlußstein,** *m.* keystone. **–stein,** *m.* vaulting-stone. **–stütze,** *f.* flying buttress. **–winkel,** *m.* haunch of an arch.

Gewölk(e), *n.* clouds.

gewönne, gewonnen, *see* **gewinnen**; (*Prov.*) *wie gewonnen, so zerronnen*, easy come, easy go.

geworben, *p.p. of* **werben** & *adj.* raised, levied *–e Truppen*, hired soldiers, levies.

geworden, *p.p. of* **werden.**

geworfen, *p.p. of* **werfen** & *adj.*; *–es Gut*, jetsam (*Naut.*).

Gewühl, *n.* rooting up; tumult, bustle, throng, crowd.

gewunden, *p.p. of* **winden** & *adj.* winding, wound, spiral, twisted; sinuous, contorted, tortuous. **–heit,** *f.* sinuosity.

gewürfelt, *adj.* chequered, tessellate, tessellated, tessellar.

Gewürge, *n.* bloody battle, slaughter; laborious task.

Gewürm, *n.* worms; reptiles; vermin.

Gewürz, *n.* (-es, -e) spice, condiment, seasoning. **–artig,** *adj.* spicy, aromatic. **–essig,** *m.* aromatic vinegar. **–fleisch,** *n.* curry, ragout. **–haft,** *adj.* **–ig,** *adj.* spiced, seasoned, spicy, aromatic. **–händler,** *m.*, **–krämer,** *m.* grocer. **–kram,** *m.* groceries. **–kuchen,** *m.* (spiced) gingerbread *or* cake. **–nelke,** *f.* clove. **–reich,** *adj.* spicy, aromatic. **–waren,** *f.pl.* groceries.

gewußt, *p.p. of* **wissen.**

gezackt, *adj.* notched, serrated.

Gezäh–(e), *n.* (-(e)s, -e) set of tools (*of miners*). **–kasten,** *m.* tool-box (*of miners*).

gezähnelt, gezähnt, gezahnt, *adj.* notched, cogged, toothed, serrated; indented, dentate (*Bot.*); perforated (*of postage stamps*).

Gezanke, Gezänk, *n.* quarrel, squabble; quarrelling, wrangling.

Gezappel, *n.* struggling, kicking; floundering.

gezeichnet, *p.p.* & *adj.* signed; drawn, sketched.

Gezeiten, *f.pl.* tide(s). **–hub,** *m.* difference between high and low water. **–tafel,** *f.* tide-tables (*Naut.*).

gezeitet, *p.p.* & *adj.* timed.

Gezelt, *n.* (-(e)s, -e) (*Poet.*) tent, canopy.

Gezeter, *n.* screaming, strident outcry.

Gezeug, *n.* set of tools.

Geziefer, *n.* vermin, insects.

geziehen, *p.p. of* **zeihen.**

geziem–en, *v.r.* & *n.* (*aux.* h.) *imp.* be suitable, befit, become; *es –t sich nicht für ihn*, it is not the proper th. for him to do; *wie es sich –t*, as is fit *or* becoming. **–end,** *pr.p.* & *adj.*, **–lich,** *adj.* proper, becoming, suitable, seemly; *mit –ender Ehrfurcht*, with due reverence; *sich –end aufführen*, behave properly.

Gezier–e, *n.* affectation; prudery. **–t,** *adj.* affected; prim; studied. **–theit,** *f.* affectation; studied mannerism, airs.

Gezirp(e), *n.* chirping.

Gezisch–(e), *n.* hissing; whizzing. **–el,** *n.* whispering; backbiting, scandalmongering.

gezogen, *p.p. of* **ziehen** & *adj.* rifled, twisted; *–e Geschütze*, rifled cannon; *–er Lauf, –es Rohr*, rifled barrel; *–e Wechsel*, drawn bills, drafts; *in die Länge –*, drawn out, spun out.

Gezücht, *n.* (-(e)s, -e) brood, breed; race, set, lot, crew.

Gezweig, *n.* branches (*of a tree*).

gezweit, *adj.* binary, bipartite.

Gezwitscher, *n.* chirping, twittering.

gezwungen, *p.p. of* **zwingen** & *adj.* forced, compulsory, overstrained, unnatural, constrained, affected; *–es Wesen*, affected manners; *– lachen*, force *or* affect a laugh. **–heit,** *f.* constraint; affectation; stiffness.

gib, gibst, gibt, *see* **geben.**

gibberig, *adj.* (*dial.*); *nach einer S. – sein,* hanker after a th.
Gicht, *f.* (*no pl.*) gout, arthritis; (*pl.* -en) furnace-mouth. **-artig,** *adj.* gouty (*swelling*). **-brüchig,** *adj.* (*archaic*) paralytic, palsied; (*B.*) *der -brüchige,* the man of the palsy. **-brüchigkeit,** *f.* palsy. **-er,** *pl.* (*dial.*) convulsive fits, convulsions. **-erisch,** *adj.* convulsive. **-gas,** *n.* blast-furnace gas. **-ig,** *adj.*, **-isch,** *adj.* gouty; arthritic (*person*). **-rose,** *f.* rhododendron, peony (*Paeonia*) (*Bot.*). **-ung,** *f.* charging a furnace.
Giebel, *m.* (-s, –) gable, gable-end; pediment; (*Poet.*) summit. **-balken,** *m.* roof-tree. **-dach,** *n.* gabled roof. **-feld,** *n.* pediment, tympanum (*Arch.*). **-fenster,** *n.* attic- *or* dormer-window; gable-window. **-ig,** *adj.* gabled. **-schwalbe,** *f.* house-martin (*Delichon urbica*) (*Orn.*).
Gier, *f.* eagerness, avidity, inordinate desire, greed. **-en,** *v.n.* (*aux.* h.) long (*nach einer S.*, for a th.); be greedy for; deviate from course, sheer, yaw (*Naut.*). **-brücke,** *f.* trail- *or* flying-bridge. **-fähre,** *f.* trail-ferry. **-ig,** *adj.* eager, greedy, covetous (*nach,* for *or* of). **-igkeit,** *f.* eagerness, greediness. (*coll.*) **-ling,** *m.*, **-laps,** *m.* greedy person, glutton. **-sch,** *m.* goatsfoot, goutweed (*Aegopodium podagraria*) (*Bot.*). **-tau,** *n.* towing cable.
gieß-en, 1. *ir.v.a.* pour, water, shed, spill, sprinkle; cast, mould, found; *Öl auf die Wogen -en,* pour oil on troubled waters; *Öl ins Feuer -en,* add fuel to the flames, make things worse; *es -t sich schlecht aus diesem Topf,* this pot pours badly; (*sl.*) *eins hinter die Binde -en,* put one (*a drink*) down the hatch, wrap o.s. round (*a pint, a whisky, etc.*); *er stand da wie aus Erz gegossen,* he stood there rooted to the spot. 2. *v.n. imp.*; *es -t,* it is pouring with rain; (*coll.*) *es -t wie mit Scheffeln* or *mit Mollen,* it is raining cats and dogs. **-bach,** *m.* mountain torrent. **-bett,** *n.* casting bed. **-er,** *m.* founder, caster, moulder; pouring vessel, ewer. **-erei,** *f.* foundry; casting. **-erz,** *n.* bronze. **-form,** *f.* mould. **-haus,** *n.*, **-hütte,** *f.* foundry. **-kanne,** *f.* watering-can. **-kannenaufsatz,** *m.*, **-kopf,** *m.* rose of a watering-can. **-kasten,** *m.* casting-mould. **-loch,** *n.* spout. **-mutter,** *f.* mould, matrix. **-ofen,** *m.* casting *or* foundry furnace. **-pfanne,** *f.* ladle. **-rinne,** *f.* gutter, kitchen-sink. **-tiegel,** *m.* melting-pot, crucible. **-waren,** *f.pl.* cast-metal goods.
Gift, *n.* (-(e)s, -e) poison, toxin, virus, venom; (*coll. & dial. also m.*) virulence, malice, fury; (*coll.*) *darauf kannst du – nehmen,* that's as sure as fate, that's a dead certainty; *voll – und Galle,* full of vicious malice; *– und Galle speien,* wreak fire and fury on, foam with rage; *schleichendes –,* slow poison; (*coll.*) *einen – auf jemanden haben,* be angry *or* furious with s.o. **-abtreibend,** *adj.* antitoxic, antidotal. **-arznei,** *f.* antidote. **-blase,** *f.* venom sac (*Zool.*). **-erz,** *n.* arsenic ore. **-frei,** *adj.* non-poisonous. **-gas,** *n.* poison gas. **-hahnenfuß,** *m.* marsh crowfoot (*Ranunculus sceleratus*) (*Bot.*). **-haltig,** *adj.* poisonous, venomous, toxic. **-hauch,** *m.* blight. **-ig,** *adj.* poisonous, venomous, virulent, toxic; pernicious; malignant, spiteful; (*coll.*) angry, furious. **-igkeit,** *f.* virulence, poisonousness; (*coll.*) anger, wrath. **-kies,** *m.* arsenic pyrites. **-kunde,** *f.*, **-lehre,** *f.* toxicology. **-los,** *adj.* harmless, non-poisonous. **-mehl,** *n.* flowers of arsenic; arsenic trioxide. **-mischer,** *m.* poisoner. **-mittel,** *n.* antidote. **-mord,** *m.* poisoning. **-nebel,** *m.* toxic smoke (*Mil.*). **-pilz,** *m.* poisonous toadstool. **-pflanze,** *f.* poisonous plant. **-schlange,** *f.* poisonous snake. **-schwamm,** *m.*, *see* **-pilz.** **-stachel,** *m.* poisonous sting. **-stein,** *m.* white arsenic. **-stoff,** *m.* virus. **-trank,** *m.* poisoned drink. **-zahn,** *m.* poison-fang. (*fig.*) **-zunge,** *f.* venomous tongue.
Gigant, *m.* (-en, -en) giant (*Myth.*). **-isch,** *adj.* gigantic, colossal.
Gigerl, *m. or n.* (-s, –) (*Austr. dial.*) fop, dandy, masher.
Gilb-e, *f.* yellowish colour; yellow ochre; dyer's weed (*Reseda luteola*) (*Bot.*). **-en,** *v.n.* turn yellow. **-hard,** *m.* October.
Gilde, *f.* (-n) guild, corporation. **-brief,** *m.* charter of a corporation. **-nhalle,** *f.* guild hall.
Gilling, *f.* (-e & -s) **Gillung,** *f.* (-en & -s) counter (*Naut.*).
giltig, *adj.*, *see* **gültig.**
giltst, gilt, *see* **gelten.**
Gimpel, *m.* (-s, –) bullfinch (*Pyrrhula*) (*Orn.*); dunce, ninny, noodle, simpleton.
ging, ginge, *see* **gehen.**
Ginster, *m.* (-s, –) the genus *Genista* (*British varieties are* petty whin *and* needle furze) *N.B. not broom or gorse* (*Bot.*).
Gipfel, *m.* (-s, –) summit, top (*of a mountain*), peak; pinnacle, climax, height, zenith, apex; (*Swiss dial. also*) tree-top. **-blüte,** *f.* terminal flower. **-höhe,** *f.* ceiling (*Av.*). **-leistung,** *f.* record. **-n,** *v.r. & n.* (*aux.* h.) culminate, reach the zenith *or* climax, rise to a peak; *seine Behauptungen -ten darin,* his assertions culminated in this. **-punkt,** *m.* limit. **-ständig,** *adj.* terminal, apical (*Bot.*).
Gips, *m.* (-es, -e) gypsum; plaster of Paris, stucco, calcium sulphate. **-abdruck,** *m.*, **-abguß,** *m.* plaster cast *or* impression. **-anwurf,** *m.* plastering. **-bild,** *n.* plaster figure. **-brennen,** *n.* calcination of plaster. **-decke,** *f.* plaster ceiling. **-en,** *v.a.* plaster. **-er,** *m.* plasterer, stucco-worker. **-guß,** *m.* plaster casting. **-malerei,** *f.* painting in fresco. **-mörtel,** *m.* plaster, stucco. **-verband,** *m.* plaster of Paris dressing (*Surg.*).
Giraffe, *f.* (-n) giraffe.
Gir-ant [*pron.* ʒiˈrant], *m.* (-en, -en) (*C.L.*) endorser. **-at,** *m.* (-en, -en) endorsee. **-ieren,** *v.a.* put into circulation; *einen Wechsel -ieren,* endorse a bill (*auf* or *an,* in favour of). **-ierbar,** *adj.* endorsable. **-o** [*pron.* ˈʒiːroː], *n.* (-os, -os *or* (*Austr.*) Giri) endorsement; *sein -o geben,* endorse; *unausgefülltes -o,* blank endorsement; *sein -o verweigern,* refuse to back a bill; *ohne -o,* unendorsed. **-oabteilung,** *f.* cheque department. **-obank,** *f.* transfer *or* clearing bank. **-ogeschäft,** *n.* clearing-house business. **-okonto,** *n.* current account. **-overkehr,** *m.*, *see* **-ogeschäft.** **-ozettel,** *m.* bank statement.
Girlande, *f.* (-n) garland.
girren, *v.n.* (*aux.* h.) coo.
Gis, *n.* G-sharp (*Mus.*).
gisch-en, *v.n.* (*rare*) foam, froth, boil, bubble, ferment, effervesce. **-t,** *m.* foam, froth, spray; fermentation.
Giß, *f.* (-en) & *m.* (-es, -e) estimated position (*Navig.*). **-(ss)en,** *v.n.* estimate one's position; *gegißter Kurs,* dead reckoning course. **-(ss)ung,** *f.* dead reckoning.
Gitarre, *f.* (-n) guitar.
Gitter, *n.* (-s, –) grating, lattice, railing, bars, fence, trellis; grid, control electrode (*Rad.*). **-bett,** *n.* cot. **-brücke,** *f.* girder bridge. **-drossel,** *f.* grid resistor (*Rad.*). **-fenster,** *n.* lattice window, barred window. **-n,** *v.a.* lattice; grate; rail in; *das gegitterte B,* A-sharp (*Mus.*). **-kreis,** *m.* grid *or* input circuit (*Rad.*). **-kreisimpedenz,** *f.* input impedance (*Rad.*). **-tor,** *n.* iron gate. **-tür,** *f.* grated door. **-werk,** *n.* trellis-work; grating. **-zaun,** *m.* iron fence, railings.
Glac-é [*pron.* glaˈseː], *m.* kid (*leather*). **-éhandschuhe,** *m.pl.* kid gloves. **-épapier,** *n.* glazed paper. **-ieren,** *v.a.* glaze, gloss; freeze. **-is** [*pron.* -ˈsiː], *n.* glacis (*Mil.*). **-isabhang,** *m.*, **-isböschung,** *f.* slope of the glacis (*Fort.*).
Glanz, *m.* brightness, lustre, gleam, gloss, glossiness, polish, glitter, shine; splendour, glamour, distinction, magnificence; *– der Gesundheit,* radiant health; *– eines Stoffes,* gloss of a fabric; *mit – bestehen,* pass (*examination*) with distinction. **-bürste,** *f.* polishing brush, buffing wheel. **-farbe,** *f.* brilliant colour. **-firnis,** *m.* glazing varnish. **-gold,** *n.* gold-foil. **-kattun,** *m.* glazed calico. **-kohle,** *f.* anthracite. **-leder,** *n.* patent leather. **-leinwand,** *f.* glazed linen, **-leistung,** *f.* brilliant performance, outstanding achievement, record. **-los,** *adj.* lustreless, dull, mat, dim, dead. **-papier,** *n.* glazed paper. **-periode,** *f.* palmy days; most brilliant period. **-punkt,** *m.* brightest point, climax; *der -punkt des Tages,* the culminating point *or* the great attraction of the day. **-schleifen,** *v.a.* burnish, polish. **-seite,** *f.* bright side. **-um-**

leuchtet, *adj.* radiant. **–voll,** *adj.* splendid, glorious, brilliant. **–zeit,** *f.*, *see* **–periode. –zwirn,** *m.* glacé thread.

Glänz–e, *f.* gloss, glaze; glossing-machine, polishing material, polisher. **–en,** 1. *v.n.* (*aux.* h.) shine, glitter, glisten, gleam, sparkle; be distinguished *or* outstanding; (*Prov.*) *es ist nicht alles Gold, was –t,* all is not gold that glitters; *er will gern –en,* he likes to shine *or* to show off, he loves display; *durch Abwesenheit –en,* be conspicuous by absence. 2. *v.a.* gloss, glaze; polish, burnish. **–end,** *pr.p.* & *adj.* shiny, shining, glossy, glittering, lustrous, brilliant, splendid; *–ende Tat,* glorious deed.

[1]**Glas,** *n.* (-es, ⸚er) glass; drinking-glass, tumbler; mirror, (*pl.*) eyeglasses; *ein – Wein,* a glass of wine; *ein Wein–,* a wine-glass; *er trank 3 – Bier,* he drank 3 glasses of beer; *er kaufte 3 Gläser,* he bought 3 tumblers; *die Gläser des Hirsches,* the eyes of the stag; *unter – und Rahmen bringen,* frame; (*Prov.*) *Glück und –, wie leicht bricht das,* happiness is fragile as glass; *zu tief ins – gucken* or *schauen,* drink too much. **–ähnlich,** *adj.*, **–artig,** *adj.* glassy, vitreous. **–auge,** *n.* glass eye. **–birne,** *f.* glass bulb, globe (*for electric lights*). **–blaseröhre,** *f.* blowpipe. **–brennen,** *n.* annealing. **–einsetzen,** *n.* glazing. **–en,** *see* [2]**Glas. –er,** *m.* glazier. **–erkitt,** *m.* putty. **–fabrik,** *f.* glass-works. **–faser,** *f.* spun glass. **–flasche,** *f.* glass bottle; decanter. **–gebläse,** *n.* glass-blower's blowpipe. **–geschirr,** *n.* glass, glassware. **–gespinst,** *n.* glass-wool *or* fibre. **–glanz,** *m.* vitreous lustre. **–glocke,** *f.* bell-jar, glass cover. **–grün,** *adj.* bottle-green. **–harmonika,** *f.* musical glasses. **–haus,** *n.* hothouse, greenhouse, conservatory. **–haut,** *f.* cellophane. **–hell,** *adj.* diaphanous. **–hütte,** *f.* glass-works. **–ieren,** *v.a.* glaze, glass; enamel, varnish; ice (*Cook.*). **–ig,** *adj.* glassy, vitreous; *ein –iger Blick,* a glassy stare. **–kasten,** *m.* glass case; show-case. **–kitt,** *m.*, *see* **–erkitt. –kolben,** *m.* flask (*Chem.*). **–koralle,** *f.* glass bead. **–körper,** *m.* vitreous humour (*of the eye*). **–malerei,** *f.* glass-painting, painting on glass. **–ofen,** *m.* glass-furnace. **–papier,** *n.* glass-paper, sand-paper (*Carp.*). **–perle,** *f.* glass bead. **–röhre,** *f.* glass tube. **–scheibe,** *f.* pane of glass. **–scherbe,** *f.* piece of broken glass; (*pl.*) cullet. **–schirm,** *m.* glass-shade *or* screen. **–schleifen,** *n.* glass cutting *or* grinding. **–schrank,** *m.* cupboard with glass doors *or* for glassware. **–splitter,** *m.* splinter of glass. **–stock,** *m.* glass beehive. **–sturz,** *m.*, *see* **–glocke. –tafel,** *f.* plate *or* square *or* pane of glass. **–tiegel,** *m.*, **–topf,** *m.* crucible, glass-melting pot. **–ur,** *f.* glaze, gloss, varnish, enamel; icing (*Cook.*). **–wolle,** *f.*, *see* **–gespinst. –zylinder,** *m.* lamp-chimney.

[2]**Glas,** *n.* (-es, -en) half-hour bell (*Naut.*); *es schlägt 8 –en,* it is 8 bells (*Naut.*). **–en,** *v.a.* strike the (ship's) bell.

Gläs–chen, *n.* (-s, –) little glass; *ein –chen zuviel* or *über den Durst,* a drop too much. **–ern,** *adj.* of glass; vitreous, glassy, crystalline; *ein –erner Blick,* a glassy stare.

Glast, *m.* (-es, -e) (*dial.* & *Poet.*) radiance.

glatt, (*comp.* -er, *sup.* -est, *better than* glätter, glättest, *which also occur*). 1. *adj.* smooth, even, flat, flush; polished, slippery, glossy; plain, bare; sleek; (*fig.*) bland, oily, flattering, sweet; (*Swiss dial.*) splendid, capital; *es ist zu – zum Gehen,* it is too slippery for walking; *–es Geschäft,* (*C.L.*) even (*without profit or loss*) business; *–es Gesicht,* smooth *or* sleek face; *–es Kinn,* smooth *or* clean-shaven chin; *–e Lüge,* bare faced lie; *– machen,* smooth, polish; *–e Stirn,* unfurrowed forehead; *–er Unsinn,* sheer nonsense; *–e Worte,* smooth *or* oily words; *–e Zunge,* smooth tongue. 2. *adv.* smoothly; quite, entirely; plainly; unhesitatingly. *er hat alles – abgemacht,* he has settled the whole business; *– abschlagen,* give a flat refusal; *ein Geschäft – abwickeln,* settle a business easily; *die S. ging ganz –,* the affair went (off) very smoothly *or* without the slightest hitch; *– heraussagen,* tell bluntly, plainly *or* frankly; *ihm – ins Gesicht,* to his face; *– landen,* land smoothly. **–eis,** *n.* (sheet) ice, frost, slippery surface; *aufs –eis führen,* mislead, lead up the garden path. **–heit,** *f.*, *see* **Glätte. –köpfig,** *adj.* bald (-headed). **–legen, –machen,** *v.a.* (*coll.*) clear (*a debt*). **–rasiert,** *adj.* clean-shaven. **–stellen,** *v.a.* (*C.L.*) clear (*a debt*) **–sitzen,** fit close. **–weg,** *adv.* plainly, flatly, openly. **–züngig,** *adj.* smooth-tongued.

Glätt–e, *f.* smoothness; polish, gloss; slipperiness; plainness; politeness, sleekness; litharge. **–en,** 1. *v.a.* smooth; plane, flatten; mangle, calender, (*Swiss dial.*) iron (*clothes*); glaze; polish, burnish. 2. *v.r.*, become smooth *or* calm (*as waves*). **–er,** *m.* burnisher; polisher; polishing-tool. **–eisen,** *n.* smoothing-iron. **–werkzeug,** *n.* smoothing-, polishing-, *or* burnishing-tool.

Glatz–e, *f.* (-en) bald spot *or* patch, bald head, tonsure. **–ig,** *adj.* bald-pated, bald. **–kopf,** *m.* bald-pate, bald-headed person.

glau, *adj.* (*dial.*) bright, lively, quick. (*Poet.*) **–äugig,** *adj.* bright-eyed; keen-sighted.

Glaub–e, –en, *m.* (*Gen.* -ens) faith, confidence, trust, belief, credence; religious faith, creed; *von seinem –en abgehen,* see *–en verleugnen*; *einen –en bekennen,* profess a religion; *in gutem –en,* in good faith; *etwas im guten –en tun,* do s.th. with no ulterior motives *or* without mental reservations; (*einem* or *einer Behauptung*) *–en schenken,* give credence to (s.o. *or* an assertion); (*Prov.*) *der –e macht selig,* faith alone makes happy; *etwas auf Treu und –en annehmen,* believe a th. implicitly, accept s.th. on trust *or* in good faith; *seinen –en verleugnen,* abjure one's faith, become an apostate. **–en,** *v.a.* & *n.* *aux.* h.) believe, trust, have faith in, give credence to; think, suppose, imagine; *ich –e es nicht,* I don't believe it; *ich –te ihn gerettet,* I thought he was saved; *wenn man es ihm –en soll,* if he is to be believed; *an eine S. –en,* believe in a th.; *an einen –en,* have faith in a p.; *einem –en,* believe a p.; *er wollte –en machen, daß . . .,* he would have it believed that . . .; *ich –e Ihnen aufs Wort,* I take your word for it; (*obs.* & *Poet.*) *einen Gott –en,* believe in a God; *an Gott –en,* believe *or* trust in God; *das ist nicht zu –en,* that is incredible; *ich –e wohl,* I dare say, I should think so, indeed; (*coll.*) *er mußte daran –en,* he lost his life. **–ensabfall,** *m.* apostasy. **–ensartikel,** *m.* article of faith, dogma. **–ensbekenntnis,** *n.* confession of faith, creed; *apostolisches –ensbekenntnis,* the Apostles' creed. **–ensbruder,** *m.*, *see* **–ensgenoss(e). –enseifer,** *m.* religious zeal. **–ensfreiheit,** *f.* religious liberty. **–ensgenoss(e),** *m.* co-religionist; fellow-believer. **–ensgericht,** *n.* inquisition. **–enslehre,** *f.* religious dogma *or* doctrine, dogmatic *or* doctrinal theology. **–ensmeinung,** *f.* religious opinion. **–enspartei,** *f.* denomination, sect. **–ensrichter,** *m.* inquisitor. **–enssatz,** *m.* dogma. **–ensschwärmer,** *m.* fanatic. **–ensschwärmerei,** *f.* fanaticism. **–ensspaltung,** *f.* schism. **–ensstark,** *adj.* truthful; deeply religious. **–ensstreit,** *m.*, **–ensstreitigkeit,** *f.* religious controversy. **–ensverleugner,** *m.* renegade. **–ensvoll,** *adj.*, *see* **–ensstark. –answert,** *adj.*, *see* **–würdig. –enswut,** *f.* fanaticism. **–enszeuge,** *m.* martyr. **–enszwang,** *m.* religious intolerance, persecution. **–haft,** *adj.* **–haftig,** *adj.* **–lich,** *adj.* credible, probable, likely; authentic; true. **–haftigkeit,** *f.*, **–lichkeit,** *f.* credibility; authenticity; probability. **–ig,** *adj.* (*dial. for* **gläubig**) believing, religious, credulous. **–würdig,** *adj.* worthy of belief, credible, authentic. **–würdigkeit,** *f.* credibility; authenticity.

Glaubersalz, *n.* (-es) Glauber's salt(s), sodium sulphate.

gläubig, *adj.* believing, full of faith, devout; credulous. **–e(r),** *m.*, **–e,** *f.* believer; *die –en,* the (true) believers, the faithful. (*C.L.*) **–er,** *m.* creditor. **–keit,** *f.* faith, confidence.

gleich, 1. *adj.* same, like, equal, equivalent; alike, similar, resembling; proportionate, adequate; even, level, straight; *ich achte mich ihm –,* I consider myself to be his equal; *von –em Alter,* of the same age; *sich* (*Dat.*) *– bleiben,* be always o.s. *or* the same; *–er Boden,* level ground; *ins –e bringen,* arrange, put right *or* in order; (*Prov.*) *–e Brüder, –e Kappen,* like pot, like cover; (*Prov.*) *– und – gesellt sich gern,* birds of a feather flock together;

das gilt mir –, see *das ist mir –*; *– gut*, equally good; *es kommt aufs –e hinaus*, it comes to the same thing in the end, it is all one; *einem –kommen*, reach a p.'s level; *–machen*, level; *dem Boden –machen*, make flush with the ground, raze; *in –em Maße*, to the same degree *or* extent; *einem mit –er Münze zahlen*, see *es mit –em vergelten*; *das ist mir –*, that is all the same *or* all one to me; *das sieht ihm –*, that is just like him; *die Tochter sieht ihrer Mutter –*, the daughter resembles her mother; *sich einem – stellen*, put o.s. on a par with another; *am –en Strange ziehen*, have the same end in view; *ich werde ein –es für dich tun*, I will do as much for you; *es einem –tun*, do the same as, imitate *or* rival a p.; *es einem –tun wollen*, vie with a p.; *einem –es mit –em vergelten*, pay a p. off in the same coin, (*coll.*) give tit for tat; *in –er Weise*, likewise, in the same way; *von –em Werte*, equivalent; *in –em Werte stehen*, be at par; *zu –er Zeit*, at the same time. 2. *adv.* alike, equally, exactly, just; immediately, at once, instantly, directly, presently; *– als ich ihn sah*, as soon as I saw him; *– als ob*, just as if; *– alt*, of the same age; *– anfangs*, at the very beginning; *– bei der Hand*, prompt, ready, at hand; *– darauf*, see *– nachher*; *das ist – geschehen*, that is easily *or* soon done; *– jetzt*, at once, just now; *– nachher*, immediately afterwards; *– viel*, just as much; *ich bin – wieder zurück*, I shall return immediately; *willst du – still sein!* be quiet this minute! *Frequently used idiomatically as a more or less meaningless particle, e.g. ich dachte es –*, I thought as much; *wie ist doch – der Name?* what is the name now? what did you say your name was *or* is? 3. *conj.* although; *ist er – nicht reich, so tut er doch . . .*, although he is not rich, yet he acts . . .; *wären Sie – mein Vater*, even though you were my father. **–altrig,** *adj.* of the same age. **–artig,** *adj.* of the same kind, homogeneous; similar, analogous. **–bedeutend,** *adj.* synonymous; equivalent, convertible, homologous; *–bedeutende Wörter*, synonyms. **–berechtigt,** *adj.* having equal right, equally entitled. **–berechtigung,** *f.* equality of right(s). **–bleibend,** *adj.* constant, invariable. **–bürtigkeit,** *f.* equality of birth. **–e,** *f.* (*rare*) evenness, equality; *etwas in die –e* (*usually* ins -e) *bringen*, settle a th.; *Tag-und-Nacht–e*, equinox. **–en,** 1. *ir.v.n.* (*aux.* h.) (*Dat.*) equal; match, be equal to; resemble, be like; *die Zwillinge –en einander völlig*, the twins are absolutely alike; *etwas* (*Dat.*) *–en wie ein Ei dem andern*, be as like as two peas. 2. *v.a.* cause to be equal, equalize; adjust; make alike; smooth, level; (*B.*) *ihr sollt euch ihnen nicht –en*, ye shall not do as they. **–entfernt,** *adj.* equidistant. **–er,** *m.* (*archaic*) equator; equalizer, leveller. **–ergestalt,** *adv.*, **–ermaßen,** *adv.* **–erweise,** *adv.* in like manner, likewise. **–falls,** *adv.* & *conj.* likewise, also, in the same way, even, in like case. **–farbig,** of the same colour, isochromatic. **–flächig,** *adj.* isohedral (*Math.*). **–förmig,** *adj.* uniform, homogeneous, isomorphous, monotonous. **–förmigkeit,** *f.* uniformity. **–geltend,** *adj.* (*Dat.*) equivalent (to), tantamount (to). **–geschlechtlich,** *adj.* homosexual. **–gesinnt,** *adj.* like-minded, congenial, compatible. **–gestaltet,** *adj.*, **–gestaltig,** *adj.* of the same shape, isomorphic. **–gestimmt,** *adj.* tuned to the same pitch, congenial. **–gewicht,** *n.* balance, equilibrium, equipoise; *das europäische –gewicht*, the balance of power in Europe; *labiles –gewicht*, unstable equilibrium; *einem das –gewicht halten*, counterbalance a p.'s influence, cope with a p.; *im –gewicht erhalten*, balance (equally), keep in equal balance; *das –gewicht verlieren*, lose one's balance; *das –gewicht wiederherstellen*, redress the balance; *das –gewicht aufheben*, turn the scales, upset the balance; *im –gewicht ruhend*, well-poised. **–gewichtslehre,** *f.* statics. **–gewichtspunkt,** *m.* centre of gravity. **–gewichtsstange,** *f.* balancing pole. **–giltig,** *adj.* (*Austr. dial.*), **–gültig,** *adj.* indifferent (*gegen*, to), unconcerned (about), apathetic (towards); *mir ist es –gültig*, it is all the same *or* a matter of indifference to me. **–gültigkeit,** *f.* indifference; unconcern. **–heit,** *f.* equality, parity, identity, similarity; *Freiheit, –heit, Brüderlichkeit*, liberty, equality, fraternity; *–heit vor dem Gesetz*, parity in the eyes of the law; *die –heit der Winkel in einem Dreieck*, the identity of the angles in a triangle. **–heitszeichen,** *n.* sign of equality, (*coll.*) equals sign (=). **–klang,** *m.* unison; consonance, identity of sound. **–kommend,** *adj.* equivalent (to). **–läufig,** *adj.*, **–laufend,** *adj.* parallel. **–lautend,** 1. *adj.* identical, corresponding, consonant; (*C.L.*) *–lautende Abschrift*, duplicate. 2. *adv.* in conformity; consonantly. **–machen,** *v.a.* make equal, equalize; *dem Erdboden –machen*, raze to the ground. **–machung,** *f.* razing, levelling; equalization. **–maß,** *n.* symmetry; proportion; commensurateness, uniformity. **–mäßig,** *adj.* proportionate, symmetrical; equal, uniform, constant, level, regular, even, homogeneous; *–mäßige Verteilung*, uniform distribution; *von –mäßigem Körperbau*, with a well-proportioned figure; *–mäßig marschieren*, march at a steady pace. **–mut,** *m.* (*rarely f.*) equanimity. **–mütig,** *adj.* even-tempered, calm. **–mütigkeit,** *f.*, *see* **–mut.** **–namig,** *adj.* of the same name, having the same denominator (*Math.*), correspondent (*Math.*); homonymous. **–nis,** *n.* image, simile, similitude; comparison; allegory; parable; *Christi –nisse*, the parables of Christ; *in –nissen reden*, speak in riddles. **–nisrede,** *f.* parable, allegory. **–nisweise,** *adv.* allegorically, symbolically. **–niswort,** *n.* figurative *or* symbolic expression *or* saying. **–richter,** *m.* rectifier (*Rad.*). **–sam,** *adv.* as if, as it were, as though; almost. **–schaltung,** *f.* political coordination, bringing into line, elimination of opponents. **–schenk(e)lig,** *adj.* isosceles (*Math.*). **–schritt,** *m.* same step; spondee (*Metr.*); *–schritt halten*, keep step (*Mil.*). **–seitig,** *adj.* equilateral; reciprocal. **–stand,** *m.* deuce (*Tenn.*). **–stellung,** *f.* equalization; comparison. **–stimmig,** *adj.* in unison; unanimous; congenial. **–strom,** *m.* direct current (*Elec.*). **–teilig,** *adj.* equally divided; divisible into equal parts; isometric (*Chem.*). **–ung,** *f.* equation (*Math., Astr.*); equalization; adjusting, sizing; levelling; *–ung des ersten (zweiten) (dritten) Grades*, simple (quadratic) (cubic) equation (*Math.*). **–viel,** *adv.* no matter, all the same; all one. **–weit,** *adj.* equidistant; parallel; *er ist –weit davon entfernt, Unrecht zu tun, als*, he is as far from doing wrong as. **–wertig,** *adj.* equivalent. **–wie,** *conj.* & *adv.* just as, even as. **–wink(e)lig,** *adj.* equiangular. **–wohl,** *conj.* & *adv.* nevertheless, notwithstanding, yet, for all that, however. **–zeitig,** 1. *adj.* contemporary; simultaneous, synchronous. 2. *adv.* together, at the same time; *–zeitig geschehend*, coincident. **–zeitigkeit,** *f.* coexistence, simultaneousness; synchronism. **–zu,** *adv.* straightway; without ceremony.

Gleis, Gleise, *n.*, *see* **Geleise.**

Gleisner, *m.* (-s, –) hypocrite, dissembler, double-dealer, pharisee. **–ei,** *f.* hypocrisy; shamming; simulation. **–isch,** *adj.* hypocritical.

Gleiße, *f.* fools'-parsley (*Aethusa cynapium*) (*Bot.*).

gleißen, (*reg.* &) *ir.v.n.* (*aux.* h.) glisten.

gleit–en, (*reg.* &) *ir.v.n.* (*aux.* s. & h.) glide, slide; slip, skid; creep (*Metal*); *–ende Reime*, gliding rhymes, i.e. rhymes in which the rhyming vowels stand in the last syllable but two (*e.g.* unmerited, inherited; *reisende, preisende*); *–ende Preise* (*Löhne*), sliding scale of prices (wages). **–bahn,** *f.* slide, chute; slip(s); slipway (*Shipbuilding*). **–boot,** *n.* hydroplane. **–ertruppen,** *f.pl.* airborne *or* glider-borne troops (*Mil.*). **–flug,** *m.* gliding flight; *im –flug niedergehen*, plane down. **–flugzeug,** *n.* glider (*Av.*). **–frei,** *adj.*, *see* **–sicher.** **–kufe,** *f.* landing skid (*Av.*). **–lager,** *n.* friction *or* sliding bearing (*Mach.*). **–schiene,** *f.*, **–stange,** *f.* skid, guide, slide-bar. **–schutzreifen,** *m.* nonskid tyre (*Motor.*). **–sicher,** *adj.* non-skidding, non-slipping. **–ungszahl,** *f.* shear modulus (*Engin.*).

Gletscher, *m.* (-s, –) glacier. **–bildung,** *f.* glacial formation. **–brand,** *m.* sunburn (*from reflected rays*). **–brille,** *f.* snow-goggles. **–eis,** *n.* glacial ice. **–salz,** *n.* Epsom salts. **–schliff,** *m.* glacial erosion, rock polished by glaciers. **–schutt,** *m.* moraine. **–spalte,** *f.* crevasse. **–zeit,** *f.* glacial period.

glich, gliche, *see* **gleichen.**

Glied, *n.* (-(e)s, -er) limb, member; rank, file (*Mil.*); term (*Math. & Log.*); link (*of chains*); joint (*Anat.*); *äußere –er einer Verhältnisgleichung*, extremes (of a ratio); *–er formieren*, fall in (*Mil.*); *ich habe meine geraden –er gerettet*, I escaped without any bones broken *in –ern links*, left wheel (*Mil.*); *männliches –*, penis; *die –er recken*, stretch o.s.; *in Reih und –*, formed up (*on parade, for battle*), in formation; *kein – rühren können*, not be able to move hand or foot; *mit steifen –ern erwachen*, wake up stiff in every joint; *aus dem –e treten*, step out of the ranks (*Mil.*); *Vettern im dritten –e*, third cousins. **-abnahme,** *f.* amputation of a limb. **–buße,** *f.* indemnification for bodily injury (*Law*). **–erabstand,** *m.* space between the ranks (*Mil.*). **–erband,** *n.* articular ligament. **–erbau,** *m.* formation, structure, organization; articulation; frame. **–erfuge,** *f.* articulation. **–erfüß(l)er,** *m.pl.*, *see* **–ertiere. –ergicht,** *f.* arthritis. **–erhülse,** *f.* loment (*Bot.*). **–erlahm,** *adj.* paralytic, palsied. **–erlähmung,** *f.* paralysis. **–ern,** 1. *v.a.* segment; joint, articulate; construct, form, arrange, classify, organize; form into ranks *or* files, form up. 2. *v.r.* be composed of, be divided into, form. **–erpuppe,** *f.* puppet, marionette, jointed doll. **–erreißen,** *n.*, **–erschmerz,** *m.* shooting pains, growing pains, rheumatism. **–erschwund,** *m.* atrophy of the limbs. **–ersucht,** *f.* (*dial.*) rheumatism. **–ertiere,** *n.pl.* arthropods, articulated animals (*Zool.*). **–erung,** *f.* organization, arrangement, formation, classification, articulation; scansion; forming into files; structure, **–erweise,** *adv.* by joints, by links; in files. **–erzucken,** *n.*, **–erzuckung,** *f.* convulsion. **–maßen,** *f.pl.* limbs; *gesunde –maßen haben*, be sound of limb; *Mann von starken –maßen*, powerfully built man. **–(e)rig,** *adj.* limbed, jointed; *groß–erig*, large-limbed. **–staat,** *m.* constituent state (*in a federation*). **–wasser,** *n.* synovial fluid (*Anat.*). **–weise,** *adv.* limb by limb; in files.

glimm–en, (*reg. &*) *ir.v.n.* (*aux.* h.) glimmer, glow, smoulder; *–ende Asche*, embers. **–er,** *m.* faint glow, glimmer; mica. **–erig,** *adj.* glimmering; micaceous. **–ern,** *v.n.* glimmer, shine dimly. **–erschiefer,** *m.* mica-slate, micaceous schist. **–lampe,** *f.*, **–licht,** *n.* fluorescent lamp *or* light. (*coll.*) **–stengel,** *m.* cigar, cigarette.

Glimpf, *m.* 1. (*archaic*) indulgence, mildness, forbearance, gentleness; *mit –*, without harm *or* evil consequences; *mit Fug und –*, with right and justice; *sich mit – aus der S. ziehen*, extricate o.s. from a matter unscathed. 2. (*pl.* –e) (*Swiss dial.*) bodkin. **–ig,** *adj.* (*Swiss dial.*) pliant, pliable, elastic. **–lich,** 1. *adj.* forbearing, indulgent, moderate, easy, light, gentle, fair. 2. *adv.* without difficulty *or* unpleasantness; *er ist –lich davongekommen*, he got off scot-free.

Glitsch–e, *f.* (-en) (*coll.*) slide. **–en,** *v.n.* (*aux.* h. & s.) (*coll.*) slide; glide; slip. **–erig,** *adj.* **–ig,** *adj.* slippery.

glitt, glitte, *see* **gleiten.**

glitzern, *v.n.* (*aux.* h.) glitter, glisten, sparkle; twinkle (*of stars*).

Glob–us, *m.* (-us & -usses, -en & -usse) globe.

Glock–e, *f.* (-en) bell, gong; glass shade; bell jar (*Chem.*); any bell-shaped article; (*dial.*) clock; *etwas an die große –e hängen*, blaze a th. abroad, make a great fuss about a th.; *die –en läuten*, ring the bells; (*Prov.*) *er hat die –en läuten hören, weiß aber nicht, wo sie hängen*, he's been told, but doesn't take it in *or* doesn't see the point *or* doesn't grasp the idea; (*coll.*) *einem sagen, was die –e geschlagen hat*, give a p. a sound dressing-down *or* scolding; *sie weiß, was die –e geschlagen hat*, she knows how the matter stands; *–e zehn werde ich da sein*, I shall be there on the stroke of ten. **–enblume,** *f.* Canterbury-bell, harebell, (*Scots*) bluebell (*Campanula rotundifolia*) (*Bot.*). **–enboje,** *f.* bell buoy (*Naut.*). **–enförmig,** *adj.* bell-shaped. **–engeläute,** *n.* peal of bells; *er hielt unter –engeläute seinen Einzug*, all the bells were ringing as he made his entry. **–engießer,** *m.* bell-founder. **–enhammer,** *m.*, *see* **–enklöppel. –enklar,** *adj.* clear as a bell. **–enklöppel,** *m.* clapper of a bell. **–enläuter,** *m.* bell-ringer. **–enschlag,** *m.* chime, stroke of the hour; *mit dem –enschlag*, punctually, (*coll.*) on the dot. **–enschwengel,** *m.*, *see* **–enklöppel. –enspeise,** *f.* bell-metal. **–enspiel,** *n.* chime(s), carillon. **–enstube,** *f.*, **–enstuhl,** *m.* bell-loft, belfry. **–entonne,** *f.*, *see* **–enboje. –enturm,** *m.* steeple, belfry, campanile. **–enzieher,** *m.* bell-ringer; bell-pull. **–enzug,** *m.* bell-rope; bell-stop (*in organs*). **–ig,** *adj.* bell-shaped, campanulate.

Glöckner, *m.* (-s, –) sexton, bell-ringer.

glomm, glömme, *see* **glimmen.**

Glor–ie, *f.* (-ien) glory; halo; (*coll.*) *einen seiner –ie entkleiden*, debunk. **–ienschein,** *m.* halo. **–ifizieren,** *v.a.* glorify. **–iole,** *f.* halo. **–ios,** *adj.* glorious; (*coll.*) excellent, capital. **–reich,** *adj.* glorious, illustrious.

Gloss–ar, *n.* (-ars, -are *or* -arien) glossary. **–ator,** *m.* commentator; annotator. **–e,** *f.* gloss, annotation; sarcastic comment; *über alles –en machen*, carp *or* sneer at everything. **–ieren,** *v.a.* gloss, comment on, supply with marginal notes.

Glottis, *f.* (-es) glottis. **–schlag,** *m.* glottal stop (*Phonet.*).

glotz–en, *v.n.* (*aux.* h.) gape; stare, goggle. **–äugig,** *adj.* goggle-eyed.

Glück, *n.* (-(e)s, *as pl.* **–sfälle, –sumstände** *are often used*) luck, fortune, good luck; success, prosperity; happiness; fate, chance; *– ab!* (*aviator's greeting*) good luck! happy landing! *– auf!* good luck! *auf – oder Unglück*, for better or for worse; *alles auf das – ankommen lassen*, leave everything to chance; *Gott gebe – dazu*, may God grant his blessing on it; (*Prov.*) *– und Glas, wie leicht bricht das*, fortune is brittle as glass; *auf gut – tun*, do at random *or* at a venture, take a chance, chance it; *– haben*, be lucky, succeed; *sein – machen*, succeed, make one's fortune; *Jagd nach dem –*, fortune-hunting; *da können Sie von – sagen*, you may call *or* count yourself lucky; (*Prov.*) *jeder ist seines –es Schmied*, every one is the architect of his own fortune; *es war ein –*, it was lucky; *dem –e im Schoß sitzen*, be a favourite of Fortune; *sein – verscherzen*, forfeit one's chance of happiness; (*Prov.*) *mancher hat mehr – als Verstand*, Fortune favours fools; *viel – !* see *– auf! – im Winkel*, modest happiness, quiet serenity; (*einem*) *– wünschen*, congratulate (a p.); *ich wünsche Ihnen viel – zum Geburtstage*, I wish you many happy returns of the day; *ich wünsche Ihnen – zum neuen Jahre*, I wish you a happy New Year; *– zu!* see *– auf! zum –e*, fortunately, by good fortune; *zu meinem –e*, luckily for me. **–bringend,** *adj.* fortunate, auspicious, propitious. **–en,** *v.n.* (*aux.* h. & s.) *imp.* (*einem*) prosper, succeed, turn out well; *es –t ihm alles*, everything succeeds with him; *es –te nicht*, it failed *or* miscarried; *es wollte mir nirgends –en*, I failed everywhere; *es ist ihm geglückt*, he has been successful. **–haft,** *adj.* *see* **–bringend. –lich,** *adj.* fortunate, lucky, prosperous, successful; auspicious; happy; *–liche Reise!* bon voyage! *sich –lich schätzen*, count *or* consider o.s. lucky, congratulate o.s.; *ich war so –lich, ihn zu sehen*, I was fortunate enough to see him; *wenn ich –lich zurückkomme*, if I return safely; *–lich vonstatten gehen*, go *or* come off well; (*Prov.*) *dem –lichen schlägt keine Stunde*, to the happy, time is swift. **–licherweise,** by good fortune, fortunately, happily, luckily. **–sbahn,** *f.* high road to fortune. **–sbote,** *m.*, **–sbotschaft,** *f.* glad tidings. **–selig,** *adj.* blissful, radiant, very happy, highly blessed. **–seligkeit,** *f.* bliss, happiness, rapture. **–sfall,** *m.* (-sfälle; *often used as pl. of* Glück, *q.v.*) lucky chance, stroke of luck. **–sgöttin,** *f.* Fortune, Fortuna. **–sgüter,** *n.pl.* earthly goods, good things of this world, wealth. **–shafen,** *m.* safe port. **–sjägerei,** *f.* fortune-hunting. **–skind,** *n.* Fortune's favourite, lucky person. **–sklee,** *m.* 4-leafed clover. (*coll.*) **–spilz,** *m.* lucky fellow, lucky chap, lucky dog. **–srad,** *n.* Fortune's wheel; roulette wheel. **–sritter,** *m.* adventurer, fortune-hunter. **–sschweinchen,** *n.* lucky mascot. **–sspiel,** *n.* game of chance *or* hazard. **–sspinne,** *f.* money spider. **–sstand,** *m.* prosperity, bliss. **–strahlend,** *adj.* radiantly happy. **–sstern,** *m.* lucky star. **–umstände,** *m.pl.* (*often used as pl. of* Glück, *q.v*). fortunate circumstances. **–swechsel,** *m.* vicissitude.

-swurf *m.* lucky shot *or* dip. **-verheißend,** *adj.*, **-weissagend,** *adj.* propitious, auspicious, of good augury. **-wünschend,** *pr.p. & adj.* congratulating, congratulatory. **-wünschung,** *f.*, **-wunsch,** *m.* congratulation, good wishes, felicitation; compliments (of the season); *einem seinen -wunsch abstatten, einem seine (besten) -wünsche aussprechen,* congratulate a p.; *herzlichste* or *beste -wünsche (zu),* heartiest congratulations (on). **-wunschschreiben,** *n.* congratulatory letter.

Gluck-e, *f.* (-en) sitting hen. **-en,** *v.n.* cluck (*as hens*). **-henne,** *f.* hen with chicks.

glucksen, *v.n.* (*aux.* h.) gurgle (*like water*), sob.

glüh-(e), *adj.* (*Poet.*) glowing, shining, **-behandlung,** *f.* annealing. **-birne,** *f.* electric bulb. **-e,** *f.* (*archaic*) glow, gleam. **-en,** 1. *v.a.* make red-hot; anneal; mull (*wine*). 2. *v.n.* (*aux.* h.) glow; burn; *vor Wonne -en,* beam with *or* be in a rapture of joy. **-end,** *pr.p. & adj.* glowing, ardent, fervent; *-ende Kohle,* live coal; (*coll.*) *wie auf -enden Kohlen sitzen,* be on thorns. **-draht,** *m.*, **-faden** *m.* filament (*of electric lamp, etc.*). **-frischen,** *n.* tempering (*Metall.*). **-heiß,** *adj.* red- *or* white-hot. **-hitze,** *f.* red-heat, white-heat. **-kathodenröhre,** *f.* thermionic valve. **-kolben,** *m.* retort (*Chem.*). **-kopf,** *m.*, *see* **-zünder.** **-licht,** *n.* incandescent light. **-ring,** *m.* retort stand, tripod. **-strumpf,** *m.* incandescent mantle. **-wein,** *m.* mulled wine; negus. **-wind,** *m.* sirocco. **-wurm,** *m.* glow-worm. **-zünder,** *m.* (sparking) plug (*Motor.*).

glup-en, *v.n.* (*aux.* h.) (*dial. & coll.*) look sullen, scowl, lour, glower. **-sch,** *adj.* sullen, louring, glowering, surly.

Glut, *f.* (-en) heat, embers; glow, ardour, passion; fire; incandescence. **-asche,** *f.* embers. **-auge,** *n.* fiery eye. **-esse,** *f.* forge. **-hauch,** *m.* scorching breath. **-hitze,** *f.* red *or* white heat. **-meer,** *n.* ocean of fire. **-pfanne,** *f.* chafing-dish; coal-pan. **-zange,** *f.* fire-tongs.

Glykose, *f.* glucose.

Glyptik, *f.* gem-engraving, glyptography.

Glyzine, *f.* wistaria (*Wistaria cinensis*) (*Bot.*).

Gnad-e, *f.* (-en) favour; grace; clemency, mercy; pardon; quarter (*Mil.*); goodwill, kindness; *(einem) -e angedeihen lassen,* see *einem eine -e widerfahren lassen*; *zu -en annehmen,* take into favour; *sich auf -e und Un-e ergeben,* surrender unconditionally; *-e für Recht ergehen lassen,* show mercy; *-e erlangen bei einem,* see *-e finden vor einem*; *eine -e erweisen,* show *or* grant a favour; *Ew.* (*Euer*) or *Eure -en,* your Honour, your Grace; *-e finden vor einem,* find favour in a p.'s eyes; *einem eine -e gewähren,* see *eine -e erweisen*; *durch Gottes -e,* by the grace of God; *Wir, von Gottes -en, König von,* We, by the grace of God, king of; *Königtum von Gottes -en,* divine right of kings; *zu -en halten,* excuse, pardon (graciously); (*archaic*) *halten zu -en!* if it pleases your Lordship! *um -e rufen,* cry out for mercy; *in -e stehen,* be in favour; *einem eine -e widerfahren lassen,* pardon a p. **-en,** *v.n.* be gracious, show grace *or* mercy; (*only in*) *-e uns Gott!* God have mercy upon us! *dann -e dir Gott!* (*threat*) then God have mercy on you (*if you do what you propose*). **-enbezeichnung,** *f.* favour. **-enbild,** *n.* wonder-working *or* miraculous image, shrine. **-enbrief,** *m.* letter of pardon; warrant, diploma. **-enbrot,** *n.* bread of charity, pittance; *-enbrot essen,* live on sufferance. **-enfrist,** *f.* respite. **-engehalt,** *n.*, **-engeld,** *n.* allowance, pension. **-engeschenk,** *n.* donation. **-engesuch,** *n.* appeal for mercy, petition for leniency *or* reprieve. **-enkette,** *f.* chain of honour, decoration. **-enlohn,** *m.* gratuity, pension. **-enmittel,** *n.* means of grace (*offered by the Church*). **-enordnung,** *f.* divine ordinance. **-enort,** *m.*, **-enplatz,** *m.* place of pilgrimage. **-enreich,** *adj.* merciful, gracious. **-ensold,** *m.* pension, gratuity. **-enstoß,** *m.* finishing stroke, death-blow, coup de grâce. **-entisch,** *m.* (*Poet.*) altar. **-enwahl,** *f.* predestination. **-enweg,** *m.* way of mercy, act of grace; *auf dem -enwege erlassen,* remit as an act of grace. **-enzeichen,** *n.* token of favour.

gnädig, *adj.* merciful, kind; favourable, gracious, condescending; *Gott sei uns -!* God have mercy upon us! *er ist noch - davongekommen,* he has, after all, got off easily *or* cheaply; he has had a narrow escape; *machen Sie es - mit ihm!* do not be too hard on him! *du bist aber -!* (*ironical*) you are a nice one! *-er Herr,* Sir; *-e Frau,* Madam; *aller-st,* (*slightly old-fashioned*) most gracious.

gnarren, *v.n.* (*aux.* h.) (*dial.*) snarl; grizzle, whine.

gnatz-ig, *adj.* (*coll.*) irritable, grumpy. **-kopf,** *m.* cross-patch.

gneisig, *adj.* containing gneiss.

Gnom, *m.* (-en, -en) gnome. **-e,** *f.* (-en) maxim, apophthegm. **-enhaft,** *adj.* dwarfish, deformed, misshapen. **-iker,** *m.* writer of sententious poetry. **-isch,** *adj.* sententious.

Gockel, *m.* (-s, -), **-hahn,** *m.* (-s, ¨-e) (*dial.*) rooster, cock.

gokeln, *v.n.* (*dial.*) play with fire.

Gold, *n.* gold; *nicht mit - zu bezahlen,* above price; (*Prov.*) *es ist nicht alles -, was glänzt,* all is not gold that glitters; (*Prov.*) *eigener Herd ist -es wert,* there's no place like home; (*Prov.*) *Morgenstunde hat - im Munde,* the early bird catches the worm. **-ader,** *f.* vein of gold; hemorrhoidal vein. **-ammer,** *f.* yellow-hammer (*Emberiza citrinella*) (*Orn.*). **-anstrich,** *m.* gilding. **-apfel,** *m.* golden pippin. **-arbeiter,** *m.* goldsmith. **-artig,** *adj.* golden, gilt. **-barren,** *m.* gold ingot. **-blatt,** *n.*, **-blättchen,** *n.* gold leaf. **-borte,** *f.* gold lace. **-braun,** *adj. & n.* chestnut, auburn. **-butt,** *m.* plaice. **-chen,** *n.* (*coll.*) darling, love, sweetheart. **-druck,** *m.* gold lettering. **-en,** *adj.* gold, golden, gilt; *er ist noch -en gegen seinen Bruder,* he is an angel compared with his brother; (*coll.*) *-ene Berge versprechen,* make extravagant (and rash) promises; (*coll.*) *sich (Dat.) -ene Berge versprechen,* cherish exaggerated hopes, expect to find Tom Tiddler's ground; (*Prov.*) *dem Feinde -ene Brücken bauen,* leave a way open for reconciliation, give an enemy a chance to escape, leave a loophole open; (*sl.*) *-ene Füchse,* gold pieces, yellow-boys; *-enes Herz,* heart of gold; *-ene Hochzeit,* golden wedding; *-ene Medaille,* gold medal; *der -ene Mittelweg,* the golden mean; *-ene Regel,* golden rule (*Matt.* 7. 12: *whatsoever ye would that men should do to you, do ye even so to them*); *der -ene Schnitt,* sectio aurea (*Math.* $AB{:}AC = AC{:}BC$); *Buch mit -enem Schnitte,* gilt-edged book; *-ene Zeit,* golden age, idyllic age. **-erde,** *f.* auriferous earth. **-erz,** *n.* gold ore. **-finger,** *m.* ring-finger. **-firnis,** *m.* gold varnish, gold size. **-fisch,** *m.* goldfish; (*coll.*) rich heiress. **-flimmer,** *m.* gold dust *or* grains (*as found in alluvial deposits*). **-flitter,** *m. & f.* tinsel. **-fuchs,** *m.* yellow-dun horse; (*sl.*) gold coin. **-führend,** *adj.* gold-bearing, auriferous. **-gefäße,** *n.pl.*, **-geschirr,** *n.* gold plate. **-gehalt,** *m.* gold content, proportion of gold. **-gespinst,** *n.* spun gold. **-gewicht,** *n.* troy weight. **-gewinn,** *m.* gold-output. **-glanz,** *m.* golden lustre *or* sheen. **-gries,** *m.* gold-dust. **-grube,** *f.* gold-mine; (*also fig.* = *highly profitable undertaking*). **-grund,** *m.* gold size. **-haar,** *n.* golden hair; goldilocks (*Bot.*). **-hähnchen,** *n.* golden-crested wren (*Orn.*); yellow anemone (*Bot.*). **-haltig,** *adj.* containing gold, gold-bearing, auriferous. **-ig,** *adj.* golden (*colour*); (*dial.*) sweet, precious, darling. **-käfer,** *m.* rose-beetle. **-kies,** *m.* auriferous pyrites. **-kind,** *n.* sweet child, cherub. **-klumpen,** *m.* nugget, gold ingot. **-lack,** *m.* gold varnish; wallflower (*Cheiranthus cheiri*) (*Bot.*). **-lauter,** *adj.* pure as gold. **-legierung,** *f.* gold alloy. **-leim,** *m.* gold size. **-leiste,** *f.* gilt cornice. **-macher,** *m.* alchemist. **-macherkunst,** *f.* alchemy. **-mark,** *f.* German coinage. **-milz,** *f.* golden saxifrage (*Chrysosplenium alternifolium*) (*Bot.*). **-münze,** *f.* gold coin; gold medal. **-niederschlag,** *m.* precipitate of gold. **-plattierung,** *f.* gold-plating. **-pressung,** *f.* gilt tooling (*Bookb.*). **-probe,** *f.* gold assay. **-regen,** *m.* laburnum (*Cytisus laburnum*) (*Bot.*). **-reich,** *adj.* rich in gold. **-rute,** *f.* golden rod (*Solidago virga-aurea*) (*Bot.*). **-sachen,** *f.pl.* jewellery. **-schale,** *f.* cupel (*Chem.*). **-schaum,** *m.* gold leaf; tinsel. **-scheider,** *m.* gold-refiner. **-scheidewasser,** *n.* aqua regia. **-schlag,** *m.* gold leaf, gold foil.

–schläger, *m.* gold-beater. **–schlägerhaut,** *f.* gold-beater's skin. **–schmied,** *m.* goldsmith. **–schnitt,** *m.* gilt edge (*of a book*). **–stange,** *f.* gold ingot. **–stein,** *m.* chrysolite, olivine. **–stoff,** *m.* gold brocade; tinsel. **–stück,** *n.* gold coin. **–stufe,** *f.* piece of gold ore. **–tresse,** *f.* gold lace. **–überzug,** *m.* gold wasn; coating of gold. **–waage,** *f.* scales for weighing gold, gold-balance; (*coll.*) *er legt alles* or *jedes Wort auf die –waage*, he weighs every word, is overparticular *or* is touchy. **–währung,** *f.* gold standard. **–waren,** *f.pl.* jewellery. **–wasser,** *n.* choice Danzig brandy, gold cordial. **–wirker,** *m.* gold weaver. **–wolf,** *m.* jackal.

1**Golf,** *m.* (-(e)s, -e) gulf. **–strom,** *m.* the Gulf Stream.

2**Golf,** *n.* golf (*game*). **–platz,** *m.* golf links. **–spieler,** *m.* golfer.

Goller, *m.*, *see* **Koller.**

Göller, *m.* (-s, –) (*Swiss dial.*) collar.

gölte, *see* **gelten.**

Gondel, *f.* (-n) gondola; nacelle (*of an aircraft*). **–n,** *v.a.* go in a gondola; (*coll.*) travel, go boating. **–führer** (& *Austr. dial* **–ier**), *m.* gondolier.

Gong, *m.* & *n.* (-s, -s) gong.

gönn-en, *v.a.* not to envy, not to grudge, allow, grant, permit; favour; wish; *ich –e es ihm*, I do not begrudge it him; *ich –e es ihm nicht*, I grudge it him; *einem alles Gute –en*, wish a p. all happiness; *sie –t sich das liebe Brot nicht*, she grudges herself the very bread she eats; *er –t sich nie einen Augenblick Ruhe*, he never allows himself a moment's rest; *ich will mir einige Tage Erholung –en*, I shall take a few days off; *–en Sie mir die Ehre Ihres Besuches*, favour me with a visit; *–en Sie mir das Wort*, permit me to speak. **–er,** *m.* patron, protector; well-wisher. **–erhaft,** *adj.* patronizing. **–erschaft,** *f.* patrons; patronage.

Göpel, *m.* (-s, –) winch; capstan; horse-gin; whim. **–hund,** *m.* whim-beam. **–knecht,** *m.* whim-stopper. **–rad,** *n.* pulley.

gor, göre, *see* **gären.**

Gör, *n.* (-(e)s, -en), **–e,** *f.* (*dial.*) small child, brat; little girl; (*coll.*) *ein niedliches –*, a pretty little thing.

Gösch, *m.* (-es, -e) & (*Austr.*) *f.* (-en) jack (*small flag*) (*Naut.*); inset (*in a flag*). **–stock,** *m.* jack-staff.

Gose, *f.* Goslar-beer, pale and light ale.

goß, gösse, *see* **gießen.**

Gosse, *f.* (-n) gutter, drain; *einen aus der – auflesen*, rescue a p. from the gutter. **–nstein,** *m.* gutter-stone; sink (*in a kitchen*).

Gotik, *f.*, *see the Index of Names.*

Gott, *m.* (-es, ¨er) God; god. *bei –!* by God! I swear; *– befohlen!* good-bye! adieu! *– bewahre* or *behüte!* heaven forbid! not if I can help it; *– sei Dank!* thank God! thank goodness; *daß sich – erbarme!* the Lord have mercy upon us! (*coll.*) *leben wie – in Frankreich*, live a life of carefree abandon; *– gebe!* God grant! *von –es Gnaden*, by the grace of God; *großer –!* great Scot! great heavens! (*dial.*) *grüß' (dich) –!* good day! *so wahr mir – helfe!* so help me God; (*Prov.*) *– hilft denen, die sich selbst helfen*, God helps those who help themselves; *Herr –!* Good gracious! *leider –es!* alas! sad to say; *lieber –!* O Lord! (*in prayers*); (*coll.*) *den lieben – einen guten Mann sein lassen*, not to worry about anything, trust in providence, let matters slide; *mein –!* good Heavens! *O mein –!* O God! *– steh' uns bei!* God help us! (*Prov.*) *–es Wege sind wunderbar*, the ways of providence are strange; *weiß –!* God knows! *wann er kommt, das weiß –*, when he will come God only knows; *will's –!* so God will! please God! *um –es Willen*, heaven forbid! for heaven's sake! *wollte –!* would to God! **–ähnlich,** *adj.* godlike, divine. **–begnadet,** *p.p.* & *adj.* divinely favoured; *ein –begnadeter Dichter*, a divinely inspired poet. **–ergeben,** *adj.* resigned to God's will, devout. **–esacker,** *m.* graveyard, churchyard. **–esdienst,** *m.* divine service, public worship; *dem –esdienste beiwohnen*, attend divine service; *den –esdienst verrichten*, officiate (at divine service). **–eserde,** *f.* the earth; consecrated ground. **–esfahrt,** *f.* pilgrimage. **–esfurcht,** *f.* fear of God, piety. **–esfürchtig,** *adj.* pious; God-fearing. **–esgelehrte(r),** *m.* divine, theologian. **–esgelehrsamkeit,** *f.* divinity, theology. **–esgericht,** *n.*, **–esurteil,** *n.* divine judgement; ordeal. **–esgnadentum,** *n.* theory of the divine right of kings. **–eshaus,** *n.* place of worship, church, chapel. **–eslade,** *f.* poor-box. **–eslästerer,** *m.* blasphemer. **–eslästerlich,** *adj.* blasphemous. **–eslästerung,** *f.* blasphemy. **–eslehre,** *f.* theology, divinity. **–esleugner,** *m.* atheist. **–esleugnung,** *f.* atheism. **–eslohn,** *m.* God's reward; *um einen –eslohn*, for the love of God, for charity, for no reward. **–espfennig,** *m.*, **–esgeld,** *n.* earnest-money. **–esreich,** *n.* Kingdom of God; theocracy. **–estisch,** *m.* the Lord's table, communion-table. **–esverächter,** *m.* impious person. **–esweisheit,** *f.* theosophy. **–eswelt,** *f.* God's wide world. **–eswort,** *n.* the Bible, God's word. **–gefällig,** *adj.* pleasing to God. **–gefälligkeit,** *f.* piety. **–gesandte(r),** *m.* the Messiah. **–gläubige,** *pl.* followers of modern German cult of non-Christian theism. **–heit,** *f.* deity; divinity; godhead. **–lob,** *int.* thank God! thank goodness! **–los,** *adj.* irreligious, ungodly, godless; wicked, impious. **–losigkeit,** *f.* ungodliness. **–mensch,** *m.* God incarnate, Christ. **–seibeiuns,** *m.* (*euphemism for*) the devil. **–selig,** *adj.* godly, pious; blessed. **–seligkeit,** *f.* godliness, piety, devotion. (*coll.*) **–sjämmerlich,** *adj.* very wretched; most pitiable. (*coll.*) **–sträflich,** *adv.* awfully. **–vergessen,** *adj.* ungodly, impious; godforsaken, miserable, wretched. **–verhaßt,** *adj.* abominable, odious. **–verlassen,** *adj.* godforsaken. **–voll,** *adj.* (*coll.*) splendid, capital, funny.

gött–erhaft, *adj.* god-like. **–erbild,** *n.* image of a god, god-like figure. **–erbote,** *m.* messenger of the gods, Mercury, Hermes. **–erbrücke,** *f.* rainbow, bow of Iris. **–erburg,** *f.* valhalla. **–erdämmerung,** *f.* twilight of the gods. **–erdienst,** *m.* polytheism. **–erfunken,** *m.* divine spark. **–ergestalt,** *f.* divine form. **–ergleich,** *adj.* divine, godlike, godly. **–erglück,** *n.* unsurpassed happiness. **–erhaus,** *n.* temple. **–erleben,** *n.* life like the gods. **–erlehre,** *f.* mythology. **–erlust,** *f.* exquisite pleasure. **–ersage,** *f.* myth. **–ersitz,** *m.* abode of the gods, Olympus. **–erspeise,** *f.* ambrosia (*Myth.*); trifle with whipped cream, any exquisite dish (*usually sweet*). **–erspruch,** *m.* oracle. **–ertrank,** *m.* nectar (*Myth.*). **–erwelt,** *f.* the gods; Olympus; paganism. **–erwesen,** *n.* mythology; divine being. **–erwonne,** *f.* divine bliss; exquisite delight. **–erwort,** *n.* oracle. **–erzeichen,** *n.* omen, augury. **–erzeit,** *f.* mythological age, golden age. **–in,** *f.* goddess. **–lich,** *adj.* godlike, divine, godly; (*coll.*) most excellent, capital; *das –liche*, the divine essence, godliness; *das –liche im Menschen*, the divine spark in man. **–lichkeit,** *f.* divinity; godliness.

Götze, *m.* (-n, -n) idol, false deity. **–nbild,** *n.* graven image, idol. **–ndiener,** *m.* idolator. **–ndienst,** *m.* idolatry. **–nopfer,** *n.* an idolatrous sacrifice. **–ntempel,** *m.* temple of an idol, heathenish temple. **–nzertrümmerer,** *m.* iconoclast.

Goudron, *m.* asphalt.

Gouvern–ante, *f.* (-en) governess; (*dial.*) manageress. **–ement,** *n.* (-s, -s) government, province. **–eur,** *m.* (-s, -e) governor, commandant.

Grab, *n.* (-(e)s, ¨er) grave, tomb, sepulchre; (*fig.*) death, destruction, ruin; *einen ins – bringen*, cause a p.'s death; *ein feuchtes –*, a watery grave; *einen zu –e geleiten*, attend a p.'s funeral; *die Kirche des heiligen –es*, Church of the Holy Sepulchre; *er nimmt sein Geheimnis mit ins –*, he carries his secret with him to the grave; *am Rande des –es stehen*, have one foot in the grave, be at death's door; *er schaufelt sich selbst sein –*, he is digging his own grave; *einen* (or *eine Hoffnung*) *zu –e tragen*, bury s.o. (*or* one's hopes); *treu bis über das – hinaus*, faithful unto death. **–ähnlich,** *adj.*, **–artig,** *adj.* sepulchral. **–denkmal,** *n.* tomb. **–esrand,** *m.* brink of the grave. **–esstille,** *f.* deathly silence. **–esschlummer,** *m.* sleep of death. **–esstimme,** *f.* sepulchral voice. **–geläute,** *n.* knell, tolling of bells. **–geleite,** *n.* funeral procession. **–gerüst,** *n.* catafalque. **–gesang,** *m.* dirge. **–gewölbe,** *n.*

vault, tomb. **-hügel,** *m.* mound, tumulus. **-legung,** *f.* (*archaic*) interment, funeral, burial. **-lied,** *n.* dirge. **-mal,** *n.* tomb, monument. **-platte,** *f.*, *see* **-stein.** **-rede,** *f.* burial sermon, funeral oration. **-schändung,** *f.* desecration of graves. **-schrift,** *f.* epitaph. **-stätte,** *f.* burial-place, sepulchre, tomb, family vault, graveyard, cemetery; (*pl.*) catacombs. **-stein,** *m.* tombstone, gravestone, **-tuch,** *n.* winding-sheet, shroud, pall.

grabbeln, *v.n.* (*aux.* h.) (*dial.*) grope, fumble.

grab-en, *ir.v.a.* dig, ditch, trench; (*archaic*) engrave; *einem eine Grube -en*, lay a snare for a p.; (*Prov.*) *wer andern eine Grube gräbt, fällt selbst hinein,* the biter bit; *es ist mir ins Gedächtnis gegraben,* it is deeply imprinted *or* impressed on my mind *or* memory. **-meißel,** *m.* graving tool, chisel. **-scheit,** *n.* (*dial.*) spade, shovel. **-stichel,** *m.*, *see* **-meißel.**

Graben, *m.* (-s, ⸚) ditch; trench; moat; dike, drain, canal; (*coll.*) *über den – sein,* be out of danger; *erster –,* front trench (*Mil.*); *zweiter –,* support trench (*Mil.*); *dritter –,* reserve trench (*Mil.*). **-bagger,** *m.* excavator, mechanical digger. **-bekleidung,** *f.* revetment (*Fort.*). **-böschung,** *f.* counter-scarp. **-brücke,** *f.* culvert. **-kampf,** *m.* trench-fighting. **-krieg,** *m.* trench fighting *or* warfare. **-rost,** *n.* duck-board. **-schere,** *f.* tenaille (*Fort.*). **-sohle,** *f.* trench bottom. **-stufe,** *f.* firestep, berm (*Mil.*). **-wehr,** *f.* parapet (*Fort.*). **-zieher,** *m.* ditcher. **-zug,** *m.* lines of ditches *or* trenches.

Gräber, *m.* (-s, –) digger; graving tool, spade. **-fund,** *m.* relics (of *or* in a tomb).

gräbst, gräbt, *see* **graben.**

Gracht, *f.* (-en) (*dial.*) ditch, drain, canal.

Grad, *m.* (-(e)s, -e) degree, rank; grade, rate; stage, step; power (*Math.*); *ein Vetter zweiten -es,* second cousin; *ein Winkel von 30 –,* an angle of 30°; *Wärme von 30 – Celsius,* temperature of 30° centigrade; *unter 30 – nördlicher Breite,* latitude 30° N.; *in hohem -e,* highly, extraordinarily; *im höchsten –,* exceedingly; *im höchsten – zerstreut,* absent-minded to a degree; *bis zu einem gewissen -e,* to a certain extent *or* degree, up to a certain point; *hoher – der Kultur,* high level of civilization. **-abteilung,** *f.* map square. **-abzeichen,** *m.* badge of rank (*Mil.*). **-ation,** *f.* gradation; comparison (*Gram.*). **-bogen,** *m.* protractor, sextant. **-buch,** *n.* nautical almanac. **-einteilung,** *f.* graduation. **-feld,** *n.* map square. **-ieren,** *v.a.* refine (*gold*); graduate (*salt*). **-ierhaus,** *n.*, **-ierwerk,** *n.* graduation works (*salt*). **-leiter,** *f.* scale. **-linig,** *adj.*, *see* **gerade.** **-messer,** *m.* graduator. **-messung,** *f.* measurement of degrees. **-netz,** *n.* grid (*maps*). **-ual,** *n.* (-s, -e) gradual, grail (*R.C.*). **-uell,** *adj.* gradual. **-uieren,** *v.a.* & *n.* (*aux.* h.) graduate, take a *or* one's degree. **-uierte(r),** *m.* graduate (*of a university*). **-weise,** *adv.* gradually, by degrees. **-zahl,** *f.* compass-bearing, direction.

Grädigkeit, *f.* concentration, density (*Chem.*), number of degrees.

Graf, *m.* (-en, -en) earl (*in England*), count (*foreign*); *– und Gräfin W.,* the Earl and Countess of W. **-enwürde,** *f.* earldom. **-schaft,** *f.* earldom; shire, county. **-schaftsgericht,** *n.* county court.

Gräf-in, *f.* (-innen) countess. **-lich,** *adj.* belonging to an earl *or* count.

Gral, *m.* grail.

Gram, 1. *m.* grief, sorrow, affliction. 2. *adj.* (*only used with* sein *or* werden) *einem – sein,* be angry *or* cross with a p., dislike a p., bear s.o. a grudge. **-gefurcht,** *adj.* care-worn (*face*). **-voll,** *adj.* sorrowful, melancholy, gloomy, sad.

gräm-en, 1. *v.a.* grieve; (*usually*) 2. *v.r.* grieve (for), worry *or* fret (*über eine S.,* about *or* at a th.); *sich zu Tode -en,* die of grief *or* of a broken heart. **-lich,** *adj.* peevish, morose, sullen.

Gramm, *n.* (-s, -e) (*abbr. g.*) gram, gramme.

Grammat-ik, *f.* (-iken) grammar; *vergleichende -ik,* comparative grammar; *elementare -ik des Deutschen,* German primer. **-iker,** *m.* grammarian. **-isch,** *adj.*, **-ikalisch,** *adj.* grammatical; *-ischer Fehler,* grammatical mistake.

Grammophon, *n.* (-s, -e) gramophone. **-platte,** *f.* record.

Gran, *n.* & (*Austr.*) *m.*, **Grän,** *n.* (-(e)s, -e) grain (*Pharm.*). **-alien,** *f.pl.* granulated metal (*Metall.*). **-ieren, -ulieren,** *see* **granieren** & **granulieren.**

Granat, *m.* (-(e)s, -e & -en) garnet (*jewel*); (-(e)s, -e) (*dial.*) shrimp. **-apfel,** *m.* pomegranate. **-baum,** *m.* pomegranate tree. **-stein,** *m.* garnet.

Granat-e, *f.* (-en) grenade, shell (*Mil.*); *mit -en beschießen,* shell, bombard (*Mil.*). **-einschlag,** *m.* shell-burst. **-splitter,** *m.* shell splinter. **-loch,** *n.*, **-trichter,** *m.* shell crater *or* hole. **-werfer,** *m.* (trench) mortar (*Mil.*).

Grand, *m.* fine gravel, coarse sand. **-ig,** *adj.* gravelly. **-mehl,** *n.* whole meal.

Grand-e, *m.* (-en, -en) grandee. **-ezza,** *f.* sententiousness, solemn gravity. **-ios,** *adj.* splendid, magnificent.

granieren, *v.a.* pulverize, granulate.

Granit, *m.* (-(e)s, -e) granite; *da beißt er auf –,* he is running his head against a brick wall. **-en,** *adj.* granitic. **-artig,** *adj.*, **-förmig,** *adj.* granitic.

Grann-e, *f.* (-en) awn, beard, arista (*of corn*); whiskers (*of a cat*); needle (*Bot.*); bristle. **-ig,** *adj.* bearded.

Grans, *m.* (-es, ⸚e), **Gransen,** *m.* (-s, –) (*dial.*) bow (*of a ship*).

grantig, *adj.* (*dial.*) angry, bad-tempered.

granul-ieren, *v.a.* granulate. **-ös,** *adj.* granular.

Graph-ik, *f.* (-en) graphic arts. **-iker,** *m.* commercial artist, illustrator. **-isch,** *adj.* graphic; *-ische Farben,* printing inks. **-it,** *m.* (-s, -e) graphite, black lead, plumbago. **-itschmiere,** *f.* graphite lubricant. **-itspitze,** *f.* carbon (*of arc lamp*). **-ologe,** *m.* (-n, -n) graphologist, hand-writing expert.

grapsch-en, graps-en, *v.a.* (*coll.*) snatch, grab, clutch; take away secretly.

Gras, *n.* (-es, ⸚er) grass; (*coll.*) *ins – beißen,* bite the dust, be killed; (*coll.*) *er hört das – wachsen,* he fancies he knows everything, he thinks he is very clever, he fancies himself, he is a know-all; *darüber ist – gewachsen,* that is all forgotten; *ins – tun,* put out to grass. **-affe,** *m.* young fool, stupid young boy *or* (*usually*) girl. **-anger,** *m.* grass-plot, green. **-artig,** *adj.* gramineous, herbaceous. **-ebene,** *f.* grassy plain, prairie, steppe, savanna. **-en,** 1. *v.n.* (*aux.* h) graze (*of animals*). 2. *v.a.* cut *or* mow grass; *nach einer S. -en,* aspire to a th.; *in einer S. -en,* satisfy o.s. with a th. **-er,** *m.* haymaker. **-fleck,** *m.* grass plot; grass-stain. **-fressend,** *adj.* herbivorous, graminivorous. **-fütterung,** *f.* feeding on grass. **-halm,** *m.* blade of grass. **-hüpfer,** *m.* (*dial.*) grasshopper. **-ig,** *adj.* grassy, grass-grown. **-land,** *n.* meadow-land. **-mäher,** *m.*, **-mähmaschine,** *f.* grass-cutter. **-milbe,** *f.* harvest-tick *or* bug. **-mücke,** *f.* bird of the warbler family (*Silviidae*) (*Orn.*) (*British examples are Greater* (& *Lesser*) *Whitethroat* (*Silvia communis* (& *curraca*)), *Blackcap* (*Silvia atricapilla*), *and Hedge-sparrow* (*Accentor modularis*)). **-platz,** *m.* grass-plot, lawn, green. **-rost,** *m.* mildew. **-schnecke,** *f.* slug. **-scholle,** *f.* turf, sod. **-stück,** *n.* grass-plot, lawn, green. **-ung,** *f.* grazing. **-weide,** *f.* pasture. **-wirtschaft,** *f.* dairy farming.

Gräs-chen, *n.* (-chens, -erchen) blade of young grass, (*pl.*) young grass, tender grass shoots. **-er,** *m.* grass cutter.

graß, *adj.* (*archaic*), *see* **gräßlich.**

grassieren, *v.n.* (*aux.* h.) prevail, spread, rage (*of diseases*).

gräßlich, *adj.* terrible, shocking, horrible, monstrous, ghastly.

Grat, *m.* (-es, -e) edge; ridge (*of a mountain*); roof-tree; spine, burr (*on metal*), tongue (*Carp.*), groin (*Arch.*). (*dial.* & *Poet.*) **-tier,** *n.* chamois.

Grät-e, *f.* (-en) fish-bone. **-en,** *v.n.* (*aux.* h.) remove fish-bones. **-enschritt,** *m.* herring-bone step (*in ski-ing*). **-ig,** *adj.* full of fish-bones, bony.

Grat-ial(e), *n.* (-s, -e & -en) thank offering, thanks-giving, donation; gratuity. **-ias,** *n.* grace, thanks-giving; *das -ias sprechen,* return thanks. **-ifikation,**

f. gratification; supplement, gratuity. **-is,** *adv.* free of charge. **-isbeilage,** *f.* free supplement. **-isexemplar,** *n.* presentation copy, specimen copy.

Grätsche, *f.* (-n) straddle, splits. **-n,** *v.a.* straddle, do the splits.

Gratul-ant, *m.* (-en, -en) well-wisher, congratulator. **-ation,** *f.* congratulation. **-ationsschreiben,** *n.* congratulatory letter. **-ieren,** *v.a.* (*einem zu etwas*) congratulate (a p. on a th.).

grau, I. *adj.* grey, grizzled, hoary; colourless, vague, sombre; venerable, ancient; *der -e Alltag,* drab everyday routine; *-es Altertum,* remote antiquity; *-er Bär,* grizzly bear; (*coll.*) *das -e Elend,* hangover; (*coll.*) *darüber lasse ich mir keine -en Haare wachsen,* I do not trouble my head about that; I do not let that worry me; *- in - malen,* paint a black picture; *das -e Männchen,* man in a grey coat (*the devil*); *-e Vorzeit,* prehistoric time, the dim, distant past; *seit -er Vorzeit,* from time immemorial; *-e Zeiten,* olden time(s), times of yore; *-e Zukunft,* dim future. 2. *n.* grey colour; dawn. **-bart,** *m.* greybeard. **-blau,** *adj.* & *n.* greyish-blue, slate-blue. **-braun,** *adj.* dun. **-braunstein,** *m.* manganite. **-brot,** *n.* brown bread. **-chen,** *n.* Neddy (*pet name for a donkey*). **-guß,** *m.* cast iron. **-en,** *v.n.* (*aux.* h.) grow grey; dawn. **-haarig,** *adj.* grizzled, grey-haired. **-lich,** *adj.* grizzly, greyish. **-pappel,** *f.* white poplar. **-rock,** *m.*; *Bruder -rock,* Grey Friar. **-rötlich,** *adj.* sorrel, roan (*horse*). **-schimmel,** *m.* grey horse. **-tier,** *n.* ass, donkey. **-werk,** *n.* (*archaic*) calabar, grey (Siberian) squirrel skin.

grau-en, I. *v.n.* & *imp.* (*einem*) have a horror of; have an aversion to; dread; be afraid of; shudder at; *es -t mir vor . . .,* I shudder at; *mir -'s vor dir,* I shudder to look at you; *mir -t vor Gespenstern,* I am terrified of ghosts; *es -t mir, wenn ich daran denke,* I shudder to think of it. 2. *n.* horror, dread, fear, terror; *es wandelte ihn ein -en an,* he was seized with fear. **-enhaft,** *adj.*, **-envoll,** *adj.* horrible, awful, dreadful, ghastly. **-lich,** *adj.* horrible, horrifying; timorous, nervous. **-s,** *m.*, *see* **Graus.**

graul-en, I. *v.r.* (*coll.*) be afraid, fear, shudder (*esp. of ghosts, the dark, etc.*); (*coll.*) *einen weg-en,* frighten a p. away. 2. *imp.*; *es -t mir davor,* I am afraid of it, I shudder at the thought of it.

gräulich, *adj.* greyish.

Graupe, *f.* (-n) hulled grain, pearl barley, groats. **-ngrütze,** *f.* barley-groats. **-nschleim,** *m.* barley water. **-nsuppe,** *f.* barley-broth.

Graup-el, *f.* (-eln) sleet, hail. **-eln,** *v.n.* & *imp.* sleet, hail. **-elerz,** *n.* granular ore. **-elwetter,** *n.* sleety weather. **-ig,** *adj.* granular.

[1]**Graus,** *m.* coarse sand, gravel, rubble; (*dial.* **Grus, Gruß**) bad *or* dirty coal; *in - zerfallen,* fall into decay.

[2]**Graus,** *m.* horror. **-am,** *adj.* cruel, inhuman, fierce; horrible, terrible, gruesome. **-amkeit,** *f.* cruelty, ferocity. **-en,** I. *v.n.* & *imp.* feel horror, shudder; *mir* or *mich -t,* I shudder; (*Swiss dial.*) I loathe it, it disgusts me. 2. *n.* horror, terror, awe, dismay. **-enerregend,** *adj.*, horrifying, horrid, awful. **-enhaft,** *adj.*, **-ig,** *adj.* horrible, horrid, gruesome, dreadful, hideous.

Grav-eur, *m.* (-s, -e) engraver. **-ieren,** *v.a.* engrave; aggravate. **-ierend,** *pr.p.* & *adj.* suspicious. **-ierer,** *m.* engraver. **-ierkunst,** *f.* art of engraving. **-iermeißel,** *m.* graver. **-ierzeug,** *n.* engraving tools. **-üre,** *f.* engraving.

Grav-is, *m.* grave accent. **-ität,** *f.* gravity, solemnity. **-itätisch,** *adj.* grave, ceremonious. **-itieren,** *v.n.* (*aux.* h.) gravitate. **-itation(skraft),** *f.* force of gravity.

Grazi-e, *f.* (-en) grace, gracefulness, charm; (*pl.*) the Graces. **-ös,** *adj.* graceful, charming.

Greif, *m.* (-(e)s, -e) griffin, condor.

greif-en, I. *ir.v.a.* & *n.* (*aux.* h.) seize, grasp, catch, catch hold of, snatch, grab; comprehend; touch; strike (*Mus.*); *man kann es mit Händen -en,* it is as clear as day; *es ist völlig aus der Luft gegriffen,* that is pure invention; *Platz -en,* get a foothold, establish itself, take root; *die Zahl ist zu hoch gegriffen,* the figure has been fixed too high, the estimate is excessive; *in ein Wespennest -en,* bring a hornets' nest about one's ears. 2. *n.* (*aux.* h.) have effect; prevail; feel; handle; bite (*of an anchor*); *an den Hut -en,* raise one's hat, touch one's cap; *einem ans Leben -en,* make an attempt on a p.'s life; *auf dem Klavier falsch -en,* strike a false note on the piano; *ineinander-en,* interlock, mesh, interlace; *ins Leere -en,* clutch at a straw; *nach dem rettenden Strohhalm -en,* clutch at a straw; (*einem*) *in die Seele -en,* touch a p. to the quick; *in die Tasche -en,* put one's hand into one's pocket, foot the bill, pay for; *-en nach,* snatch at; *um sich -en,* gain ground, spread; (*fig.*) *einem unter die Arme -en,* help a p., give a p. one's support; *einem unter das Kinn -en,* chuck a p. under the chin; *-en zu,* have recourse to; *zur Flasche -en,* reach for the bottle, take to drink; *zu den Waffen -en,* take up arms. **-bar,** *adj.* seizable, tangible, palpable; (*C.L.*) to hand. **-er,** *m.* catcher; grab. **-fuß,** *m.* prehensile foot, gnathopod. **-haken,** *m.* grapple. **-holz,** *n.* wooden handle. **-klaue,** *f.* hind claw, talon. **-schwanz,** *m.* prehensile tail. **-waffe,** *f.* prehensile weapon. **-zange,** *f.* grip-strap (*bridging. Mil.*). **-zirkel,** *m.* callipers.

grein-en, *v.n.* (*aux.* h.) (*coll.*) cry, weep, whine, whimper, grizzle.

greis, I. *adj.* (*poet.*) hoary, venerable, aged, senile. 2. *m.* (-es, -e) old man. **-enalter,** *n.* old age, senility. **-enhaft,** *adj.* senile. **-enhaftigkeit,** *f.* senility.

grell, *adj.* dazzling; glaring, crude (*of colours*); harsh, piercing, loud, strident, shrill (*sounds*); *- gegen eine S. abstechen,* contrast strongly with a th. **-e,** *f.* **-heit,** *f.* harshness; vividness; glaringness.

Gremi-um, *n.* (-ums, -en) panel, board.

Grenz-e, *f.* (-en) frontier; boundary, limit, border, edge; end, term, extreme point, limitation, threshold; *alles hat seine -en,* there is a limit to everything; *meine Geduld ist nicht ohne -en,* there are limits to my patience; *die -en des Möglichen überschreiten,* exceed the bounds of possibility; *einer S. feste -en ziehen* or *setzen,* set a limit to s.th. **-acker,** *m.* boundary-field. **-belastung,** *f.* critical load. **-bestimmung,** *f.* boundary settlement. **-bewohner,** *m.* borderer. **-bezeichnung,** *f.* demarcation. **-en,** I. *v.n.* (*aux.* h.) border (*an* (*with Acc.*), on); adjoin; be bounded by. 2. *v.a.* border; limit. **-dichte,** *f.* density limit. **-enlos,** *adj.* boundless, unlimited infinite, immeasurable. **-enlosigkeit,** *f.* boundlessness; infinitude. **-fall,** *m.* limiting case, extreme case; border-line case. **-festung,** *f.* frontier fortress. **-frequenz,** *f.* cut-off frequency (*Rad.*). **-gegend,** *f.* frontier region, borderland. **-gemeinschaft,** *f.* contiguity. **-land,** *n.* **-mark,** *f.* borderland, frontier-country. **-linie,** *f.* boundary-line, border-line, line of demarcation. **-mal,** *n.* landmark. **-mauer,** *f.* party-wall. **-scheide,** *f.* boundary. **-schicht,** *f.* boundary layer (*Meteor.*). **-schraube,** *f.* locking screw, stop (*Mach.*). **-stadt,** *f.* frontier town. **-stein,** *m.* landmark; boundary-stone. **-verkehr,** *m.* frontier traffic. **-wache,** *f.* frontier-guard (*troops*). **-wächter,** *m.* frontier-guard (*soldier*). **-wert,** *m.* limit, limiting value, threshold value (*Math.*). **-winkel,** *m.* critical angle. **-zoll,** *m.* transit duty, customs. **-zwischenfall,** *m.* frontier incident.

Greu-el, *m.* (-els, -el) horror, abomination, outrage; *es ist mir ein -el,* I abominate it, I loathe it. **-eltat,** *f.* atrocity, horror, horrible deed. **-lich,** *adj.* horrible, abominable, detestable, frightful, atrocious, heinous, dreadful. **-elmärchen,** *n.* atrocity story (*propaganda*). **-elnachricht,** *f.* false *or* exaggerated report of atrocities.

Grieben, *f.pl.* (*also dial.* **Griefe** *f.*) cracklings, greaves, tallow refuse.

Griebs, *m.* (-es, -e) (*dial.*) core (*of fruit*); (*dial.*) Adam's apple.

Grien, *n.* (-s) (*Swiss dial.*) gravel.

grienen, *v.n.* (*dial.*), *see* **grinsen.**

gries, *adj.* (*dial.*) grey. **-eln,** *v.n. imp.* (*dial.*) shudder, shiver. **-gram,** *m.* grouser, grumbler, morose *or* surly fellow; ill-humour. **-grämig,** *adj.*, **-grämisch,** *adj.*, **-grämlich,** *adj.* peevish, morose, sullen, surly, grousing, grumbling.

Grieß, *m.* (-es, -e) semolina; gravel, grit, coarse sand; groats, grits. **-brei,** *m.*, thick (semolina) gruel. **-eln,** *v.a.* & *n.* (*aux.* h.) break into small pieces, grind; grumble. **-ig,** *adj.* gritty, gravelly. **-kohle,** *f.* singles, smalls, slack (*coal*). **-mehl,** *n.* groats. **-pudding,** *m.* semolina-pudding. **-stein,** *m.* urinary calculus, gravel (*Med.*). **-wärtel,** *m.* (*archaic*) marshal (*tournament*).

[1]**griff, griffe,** *see* **greifen.**

[2]**Griff,** *m.* (-(e)s, -e) grip, grasp; hold, catch; hand-hold *or* foot-hold (*mountaineering*); handful; handle, knob, hilt (*of a sword*), haft; fret (*of guitars*); touch (*Mus.*); rounce (*Typ.*); talons, claws, clutch (*Orn.*), art, trick, artifice; (*pl.*) *-e*, manual of arms (*Mil.*); *etwas zum – bereitlegen*, lay a th. ready to hand; *etwas im -e haben*, have a *or* the right feel for a th., know a th. by the touch; be good at a th.; *-e klopfen*, (*sl.*) do rifle drill (*Mil.*); *das war ein kühner –*, that was a bold stroke; *einen falschen – tun*, play a wrong note; make a mistake; *einen – nach der* or *in die Tasche tun*, go to one's pocket. **-brett,** *n.* fret-board, finger-board (*of a violin, guitar, etc.*); key-board (*of a piano*). **-el,** *m.* stylus, graver; slate-pencil; style, pistil (*Bot.*); *mit ehernem -el eingetragen* (*fig.*), recorded ineffaceably *or* indelibly. **-elartig,** *adj.*, **-elförmig,** *adj.* styloid; *-elförmiger Fortsatz*, styloid process (*Anat.*). **-ellos,** *adj.* without styles *or* pistils, acephalous. **-ig,** *adj.* (*dial.*) graspable, handy. **-igkeit,** *f.* gripping capacity, grip; *-igkeit der Reifen*, tyre grip (*Motor.*). **-loch,** *n.* keyhole of wind-instruments. **-stück,** *n.* stock (*of pistol, etc.*).

Grill-e, *f.* (-en) cricket (*Ent.*); whim, fad, caprice, vagary, crotchet; melancholy thought; *die -e zirpt*, the cricket chirps; *sich* (*Acc.*) *mit -en plagen*, *-en fangen*, be low-spirited *or* in low spirits, have a bee in one's bonnet, worry unnecessarily. **-enfänger,** *m.* capricious person, crank; pessimist. **-enhaft,** *adj.*, **-ig,** *adj.* whimsical, capricious. **-enhaftigkeit,** *f.* fancifulness, capriciousness.

Grimasse, *f.* (-n) grimace.

Grimm, 1. *m.* anger, fury, rage. 2. *adj.* (*poet*), *see* **-ig.** **-darm,** *m.* colon (*Anat.*). **-darmanhang,** *m.* appendix (*Anat.*). **-darmentzündung,** *f.* colitis (*Med.*). **-en,** 1. *v.n.* (*imp.*) (*aux.* h.) (*rare*) enrage, infuriate; *es -t mich im Bauche*, I have the *or* a stomach-ache. 2. *n.* stomach-ache, gripes; colic. **-ig,** *adj.* enraged, furious, wrathful, violent, fierce, grim; *es ist -ig kalt*, it is bitterly cold; *-ige Schmerzen*, excruciating pain. *-iger Hunger*, fierce *or* gnawing hunger. **-igkeit,** *f.* fury, ferocity, grimness. **-schnaubend,** *adj.* breathing fire and fury, raging.

Grind, *m.* (-(e)s, -e) scab, scurf, mange; head (*of stag, etc.*) (*Hunt.*). **-ig,** *adj.* scabbed, scabby, scurfy.

Grinsel, *n.* (-s, -(n)) (*Austr. dial.*) back-sight (*of rifle*).

grinsen, 1. *v.n.* (*aux.* h.) grin, simper, smirk, sneer, (*coll.*) cry, whimper, grizzle; *cf.* **greinen.** 2. *n.* grin, smirk, sneer.

Grippe, *f.* (-n) influenza, (*coll.*) flu.

Grips, *m.* (*coll.*) brains, sense; (*dial.*) neck; *einen beim – packen*, seize s.o. by the scruff of the neck; (*coll.*) *er hat keinen – im Kopf*, he is an empty-headed fellow.

Grit, *m.* (-s, -e) sandstone.

grob, *adj.* (*comp.* gröber, *sup.* gröbst) coarse, rude, uncivil, clumsy, uncouth, rough, gross; big, thick; *einen – anfahren*, address a p. rudely; handle a p. roughly; *aus dem -en arbeiten*, roughhew; *-er Fehler*, bad mistake; *-es Geschütz*, big or heavy guns; *-er Scherz*, broad joke; *-e Schrift*, bold hand *or* type; *aus dem Gröbsten heraus sein*, have got over the worst; *-e Stimme*, deep *or* gruff voice; *etwas in -en Umrissen schildern*, give a rough picture of a th., depict a th. in broad outline. **-arbeiter,** *m.* heavy *or* unskilled worker. **-faserig,** *adj.* coarse grained *or* fibred. **-gewicht,** *n.* gross weight. **-heit,** *f.* coarseness, roughness, grossness, rudeness, insolence; *-heiten sagen*, say rude things. **-ian,** *m.* (-(e)s, -e) rude fellow, boor, brute. **-jährig,** *adj.* broad-ringed (*of timber*). **-keramik,** *f.* earthenware. **-körnig,** *adj.* coarse-grained. **-lunker,** *m.* cavity (*Metall.*). **-schlächtig,** *adj.* uncouth, coarse. **-sieb,** *n.* wide meshed *or* coarse sieve. **-schmied,** *m.* blacksmith. **-sicherung,** *f.* main fuse (*Elec.*). **-sinnig,** *adj.* crude, coarse-grained, lacking refinement. **-sinnlich,** *adj.* gross, grossly sensual, voluptuous.

gröblich, *adv.* rather coarsely, grossly, rudely; *– beleidigen*, insult grossly; (*sich*) *– irren*, make a bad *or* big mistake; *sich – vergehen*, commit a *faux pas*, (*coll.*) put one's foot in it.

Gröbs, *m. see* **Griebs.**

Groden, *m.* (-s) (*dial.*) reclaimed land, alluvial land.

Grog, *m.* (-s, -s) grog.

gröhlen, grölen, *v.a.* (*aux.* h.) bawl, squall.

Groll, *m.* anger, resentment, animosity, rancour; *einen – auf einen haben*, harbour resentment against s.o.; *einen alten – hegen*, nurse an old grievance, bear a grudge. **-en,** *v.n.* (*aux.* h.) (*usually Dat. but also with* auf (*Acc.*), gegen *or* mit) bear ill-will, be resentful, be angry with; rumble, roll, peal (*of thunder*).

[1]**Gros,** *n.* [*pron.* gro:] gross; *en –*, wholesale; *– der Armee*, main body. **-gewicht,** *n.* brutto weight.

[2]**Gros,** *n.* [*pron.* grɔs] (-ses, -se) gross, twelve dozen.

Groschen, *m.* (-s, –) smallest Austrian coin (*100 = Schilling*); (*coll.*) penny, ten-pfennig piece; *keinen – wert*, not worth a jot; *einen schönen* or *hübschen – verdienen*, earn a pretty penny. **-schreiber,** *m.* penny-a-liner, quill-driver.

groß, (*comp.* größer, *sup.* größt) 1. *adj.* tall, high; large, big, vast, huge, great; important, capital, eminent, grand; *einen – ansehen, anschauen, anblicken* or *angucken*, stare at a p. in surprise; *– auftreten*, lord it, assume airs; *-e Augen machen*, stare (in surprise); *-e Bohnen*, broad beans; *-er Buchstabe*, capital letter; *– denken*, think nobly; *die -deutschen*, pan-Germans, advocates of a Greater Germany (*including Austria*); *-e Fahrt machen* (*Naut.*), sail full speed ahead; *-e Ferien*, long vacation; *auf -em Fuße leben*, live extravagantly *or* in a grand style; *im -en und ganzen*, on the whole, generally (speaking); *-es Geld*, money in large denominations; *die -e Welt*, the fashionable world; *im -en handeln*, carry on wholesale trade; *-es Hauptquartier*, General Headquarters (*Mil.*); *-e Havarie*, general average; *-e Kinder*, grown-up children; *-e Kleinigkeit*, mere trifle; *der Große Kurfürst*, Friedrich Wilhelm, Elector of Brandenburg (1640–88); (*etwas*) *-es leisten*, achieve great things; *das -e Los*, first (lottery) prize, winning draw; *-es machen*, (*nursery talk*) do one's big business (*= evacuate the bowels*); *nicht – nötig haben*, have no great need of; *-er Ozean*, Pacific; *-e Quarte*, major fourth (*Mus.*); *-er Rat*, full council; *-e Rosinen im Kopf haben*, have one's head full of great ideas *or* fantastic plans; *– sprechen*, boast, talk big, brag, draw the long bow; *-e Stücke auf einen halten*, have a high opinion of s.o.; *in -er Uniform*, in full dress; *– werden*, grow big *or* tall. 2. *n.* gross, *see* [2]**Gros.** **-e(r),** *m.* grandee. **-admiral,** *m.* Admiral of the Fleet. **-angelegt,** *adj.* large-scale. **-angriff,** *m.* large-scale attack. **-artig,** *adj.* grand, splendid, imposing, grandiose, noble, magnificent; sublime, egregious. **-artigkeit,** *f.* grandeur. **-aufnahme,** *f.* close-up (*Phot.*). **-betrieb,** *m.* large-scale operation (*Mil.*); large-scale concern (*industry*); bustling throng; wholesale business. **-einsatz,** *m.* large-scale operation (*Mil.*). **-elterlich,** *adj.* concerning, belonging to *or* coming from grandparents. **-eltern,** *pl.* grandparents. **-enkel,** *m.* great-grandson. **-enkelin,** *f.* great-granddaughter. **-enteils,** *adv.* mainly, mostly, to a great extent, in large part. **-fabrikation,** *f.* large-scale manufacture. **-funkstelle,** *f.* high-power radio station. **-fürst,** *m.* grand-duke (*Russian*). **-gesinnt,** *adj.* high-minded. **-gewehr,** *n.* big *or* heavy gun. **-gewerbe,** *n.*, *see* **-fabrikation.** **-gliederig,** *adj.* large-limbed. **-grundbesitz,** *m.* estates, landed property. **-grundbesitzer,** *m.* landed proprietor. **-handel,** *m.* wholesale trade. **-händler,** *m.* wholesale dealer *or* merchant. **-handlung,** *f.* wholesale warehouse *or* firm. **-herrlich,** *adj.* seignorial; most excellent.

–herzig, *adj.* magnanimous. **–herzigkeit,** *f.* magnanimity. **–herzog,** *m.* grand duke (*German*). **–herzoglich,** *adj.* grand-ducal. **–herzogtum,** *n.* grand-duchy. **–hirn,** *n.* cerebrum. **–industrie,** *f.* wholesale manufacture, large-scale industrial enterprise. **–industrielle(r),** *m.* wholesale manufacturer; industrial magnate. **–ist,** *m.* wholesale dealer. **–jährig,** *adj.* of age; *–jährig werden,* come of age. **–jährigkeit,** *f.* majority, coming of age, full age. **–kammerherr,** *m.*, **–kämmerer,** *m.* lord chamberlain. **–kampfschiff,** *n.* capital ship. **–kanzler,** *m.* Lord High Chancellor. **–kaufmann,** *m.* wholesale merchant. **–knecht,** *m.* foreman on a farm. **–leibig,** *adj.* big-bellied. **–lippig,** *adj.* thick-lipped. **–luke,** *f.* main hatch (*Naut.*). **–macht,** *f.* great power. **–mächtig,** 1. *adj.* high and mighty. 2. *adv.* enormously. **–mannssucht,** *f.* megalomania. **–maschig,** *adj.* wide-meshed. **–maul,** *n.* braggart. **–mäulig,** *adj.* bragging, swaggering. **–meister,** *m.* grand master (*of an order*). **–mut,** *f.* magnanimity; generosity; *–mut üben,* show generosity. **–mütig,** *adj.* magnanimous; generous. **–mutter,** *f.* grandmother. **–mütterlich,** *adj.* of, by *or* pertaining to a grandmother. (*coll.*) **–nasig,** *adj.* bottle-nosed; arrogant. **–oheim,** *m.*, **–onkel,** *m.* great-uncle. **–oktav,** *n.* large octavo; full organ. **–prahler,** *m.* boaster, braggart. **–prahlerei,** *f.* bragging, boasting; boast. **–protzig,** *adj.* purse-proud. **–quart,** *n.* large quarto. **–raum,** *m.* (*Nat. Soc.*) extra-territorial sphere of influence. **–raumkarte,** *f.* small-scale map. **–raumpolitik,** *f.* (*Nat. Soc.*) foreign policy affecting areas adjacent to a power, expansionist policy within sphere of influence. **–reihenanfertigung,** *f.* mass production. **–reinemachen,** *n.* (spring) cleaning. **–schatzmeister,** *m.* grand-treasurer; Lord High Treasurer. **–schiffahrtsweg,** *m.* canal for sea-going vessels. **–schnauzig,** *adj.*, **–schnäuzig,** *adj.* (*sl.*) boasting, swaggering, cock-a-hoop. **–seite,** *f.* hypotenuse. **–siegelbewahrer,** *m.* Keeper of the Great Seal (*in England the Lord Chancellor*). **–sprecher** *m.* boaster, swaggerer. **–sprecherei,** *f.* magniloquence, boasting, bragging. **–sprecherisch,** *adj.* boastful, bragging, swaggering; grandiloquent. **–spurig,** *adj.* arrogant, conceited. **–staat,** *m.* great power. **–stadt,** *f.* large town (*over 100,000 inhabitants*). **–städter,** *m.* inhabitant of a large town. **–städtisch,** *adj.* of a large town; fashionable. **–stadtroman,** *m.* novel of metropolitan society. **–steingrab,** *n.* megalithic burial place. **–tante,** *f.* great-aunt. **–tat,** *f.* great deed, exploit, achievement, feat. **–tuer,** *m.* braggart. **–tuerei,** *f.* swaggering. **–tun,** *v.n.* brag, boast, swagger, give o.s. airs; *sich* (*Acc.*) *mit einer S. –tun,* brag *or* boast of a th. **–vater,** *m.* grandfather. **–väterlich,** *adj.* of, by *or* pertaining to a grandfather. **–vaterstuhl,** *m.* high-backed arm-chair, easy-chair. **–wild,** *n.* big game, deer. **–würdenträger,** *m.* high dignitary. **–zahlforschung,** *f.* statistics. **–ziehen,** *v.a.* bring up, rear (*children, etc.*). **–zügig,** *adj.* on a generous *or* large scale; in bold outlines; grandiose; noble, grand.

Größ–e, *f.* (–en) size, dimension, bulk, largeness, greatness, bigness; height, tallness; quantity, value, power; magnitude (*Astr.*); celebrity, star; *von mittlerer –e,* of medium size; *in natürlicher –e,* life-size; *bekannte* or *gegebene –e,* known quantity. **–enlehre,** *f.* mathematics. **–enordnung,** *f.* order of magnitude. **–enverteilungskurve,** *f.* (frequency) distribution curve (*statistics*). **–enwahn,** *m.* megalomania; (*coll.*) swelled head. **–er,** *adj.* (*comp. of* groß) bigger, larger, higher, taller, greater. **–tenteils,** *adv.* for the most part, mostly, chiefly. **–tmöglich,** *adj.* as large as possible, greatest possible. **–twert,** *m.* maximum value.

Grossist, *see* **groß.**

grotesk, *adj.* grotesque. **–e,** *f.* (-en) grotesque(ness).

Grotte, *f.* (-n) grotto.

grub, grübe, *see* **graben.**

Grübchen, *n.* (-s, –) dimple; lacuna. **–bildung,** *f.* pitting (*Metall.*).

Grub–e, *f.* mine, pit, hole, cavity; ditch, depression, excavation, quarry; (*einem*) *eine –e graben,* lay a snare for; (*Prov.*) *wer andern eine –e gräbt, fällt selbst hinein,* the biter will be bitten; *in die –e fahren,* (*B.*) go down to the grave. **–enarbeiter,** *m.* miner. **–enaxt,** *f.* miner's pick. **–enbau,** *m.* underground working. **–enbesitzer,** *m.* mine-owner. **–enblende,** *f.*, **–enlicht,** *n.*, *see* **–enlampe.** **–engas,** *n.* firedamp, marsh gas, methane. **–engezähe,** *n.* miner's tools. **–engut,** *n.* minerals. **–enklein,** *n.* smalls, slack (*coal*). **–enlampe,** *f.* miner's (safety) lamp. **–enschlacke,** *f.* slag. **–ensteiger,** *m.* overseer of a mine. **–enwasser,** *n.* seepage. **–enwetter,** *n.* damp, fire-damp.

Grüb–elei, *f.* (-en) musing, meditation, brooding. **–eln,** *v.n.* (*aux.* h.) (*über*) brood, meditate, muse (on *or* over), rack one's brains (about *or* over); *–elnde Vernunft,* carping criticism. **–ler,** *m.* over-subtle reasoner, melancholy brooder, one lost in futile speculation. **–lerisch,** *adj.* brooding, melancholy, hypercritical.

Grude, *f.* (-n) lignite coke.

Gruft, *f.* (¨-e) vault, tomb, (*poet.*) grave. **–gewölbe,** *n.* vault. **–kirche,** *f.* crypt.

Grum(me)t, *n.* aftermath, second crop (*of hay*).

grün, 1. *adj.* green, verdant; fresh, young, vigorous; raw, unripe, immature, inexperienced; *–e Bekanntschaft,* short acquaintance; *– bleiben,* remain alive (*remembrance*); *es wird mir – und gelb vor den Augen,* I have an attack of giddiness; *– und gelb vor Neid,* green with envy; *– und gelb vor Wut,* see red; *– und gelb vor Ärger* (*Zorn*), be beside o.s. with annoyance (anger); *einen – und gelb schlagen,* beat a p. black and blue; *–e Häute,* undressed skins; *der –e Heinrich,* (*Austr. dial.*) police van; (*coll.*) *dasselbe in –,* practically the same, as near as no matter, (*sl.*) as near as dammit; *–er Junge,* greenhorn; *bei Mutter Grün schlafen,* camp out, sleep in the open; (*coll.*) *einem nicht – sein,* not be well-disposed *or* be ill-disposed towards a p.; *er setzt sich an meine –e Seite,* he makes his appeal to my feelings *or* my better nature *or* knows which is my soft spot; *vom –en Tisch aus,* only in theory. 2. *n.* green colour, verdure; *im –en,* in the country, in rural surroundings. **–ästung,** *f.* pruning. **–donnerstag,** *m.* Maundy Thursday. **–e,** *n.* greenness, verdure; green (*golf, etc.*); nature; verdigris; spade (*cards*). **–en,** *v.n.* sprout, become green. **–heit,** *f.* inexperience. **–kern,** *m.* green rye *or* spelt. **–kohl,** *m.* (green) kale. **–kram,** *m.*, **–kraut,** *n.* greens. **–kramladen,** *m.* greengrocer's. **–kreuz,** *n.* asphyxiating gas (*Mil.*). **–lich,** *adj.* greenish; *ins –liche fallend,* of a greenish hue. **–ling,** *m.* green agaric (*Tricholoma equestre*) (*Bot.*); greenhorn. **–rock,** *m.* hunter, huntsman; gamekeeper; chasseur. **–schnabel,** *m.* greenhorn. **–span,** *m.* verdigris, copper acetate. **–specht,** *m.* green woodpecker (*Picus viridis*) (*Orn.*). **–zeug,** *n.* herbs.

Grund, *m.* (-es, ¨-e) ground, earth, soil; land, estate, terrain; sediment, bottoms, dregs, lees; bottom, base, foundation, basis, fundus, groundwork, rudiments, elements, first principles; reason, cause, motive, argument; background, ground, priming (*Paint.*); *an – laufen,* see *auf den – fahren*; *auf – meiner Vollmacht,* in virtue of my authority; *wir sitzen am* or *auf dem –e,* we are aground; *auf den – fahren,* run aground; *einer S. auf den – gehen,* get to the root of a matter, investigate a matter thoroughly, solve, find out; *auf – von,* according to, on account of, on the strength of, on the basis of; *aus dem –e,* fundamentally, thoroughly, utterly; *aus welchem –e?* for what reason? why? *die Nachricht entbehrt jedes –es,* the news is without any foundation; *die ersten Gründe einer Wissenschaft,* the rudiments of a science; *im –e,* at bottom, after all, really, fundamentally; *im –e genommen,* actually; *in – und Boden,* thoroughly, radically; *liegende Gründe,* landed property; *des Meeres tiefe Gründe,* the depths of the ocean, the deep; *ich habe hier keinen – mehr,* I am quite out of my depth here; *von – aus,* in its essentials, completely; see *aus dem –e; zu –e,* see *zugrunde*; *– zur Klage,* cause for complaint. **–akkord,** *m.* fundamental chord (*Mus.*). **–angeln,** *n.* bottom-fishing. **–anstrich,** *m.* first coat, undercoat, ground coat (*Paint.*).

–ausbildung, *f.* basic training (*Mil.*). **–balken,** *m.*, **–baum,** *m.* foundation-beam; keel (*of a ship*). **–baß,** *m.* thorough-bass (*Mus.*). **–bau,** *m.* foundation; substructure; underpinning. **–bedeutung,** *f.* original meaning. **–bedingung,** *f.* fundamental *or* primary condition. **–begriff,** *m.* fundamental principle, basic idea *or* concept. **–beschaffenheit,** *f.* fundamental quality. **–besitz,** *m.* real estate, landed property. **–besitzer,** *m.* landed proprietor. **–besitztum,** *n.* (*höheres or freies*) free tenure. **–bestandteil,** *m.* primary *or* essential component *or* constituent. **–blei,** *n.* sounding-lead, plummet. **–böse,** *adj.* thoroughly bad. **–bruch,** *m.* (soil) subsidence. **–buch,** *n.* land register. **–ebene,** *f.* ground-plane. **–ehrlich,** *adj.* thoroughly honest. **–eigenschaft,** *f.* fundamental property *or* character. **–eigentum,** *n.* landed property. **–einheit,** *f.* absolute *or* fundamental unit. **–einkommen,** *n.* land-revenue. **–eis,** *n.* ground-ice; (*vulg.*) *ihm geht der Arsch mit –eis,* he's frightened out of his wits. **–entwurf,** *m.* first draft, rough sketch. **–falsch,** *adj.* radically wrong, absolutely false. **–farbe,** *f.* ground colour, priming; primary colour. **–fest,** *adj.* solid; real, landed. **–feste,** *f.* (*fig.*) basis, foundation. **–firnis,** *m.* priming-varnish. **–fläche,** *f.* base, basis; area (*Geom.*). **–form,** *f.* original *or* primary form. **–gedanke,** *m.* fundamental idea. **–gehalt,** *n.* basic pay *or* salary. **–gerechtigkeit,** *f.* territorial jurisdiction, land-owner's rights, easement. **–geschwindigkeit,** *f.* ground speed (*Av.*). **–gesetz,** *n.* statute. **–hefe,** *f.* sediment. **–herr,** *m.* lord of the manor. **–ieren,** 1. *v.a.* size, prime, apply ground coat (*Paint.*), impregnate. 2. *n.* grounding; priming (*Paint.*). **–ierfarbe,** *f.* priming colour. **–irrtum,** *m.* fundamental mistake *or* error. **–kapital** *n.* (original) stock. **–kette,** *f.* ground-warp (*Weav.*). **–kraft,** *f.* main strength. **–kreis,** *m.* circumference of the base (*Geom.*). **–lage,** *f.* foundation, base, basis; rudiments, groundwork, fundamentals. **–legend,** *adj.* fundamental; *die –legende wissenschaftliche Ausgabe,* standard (critical) edition. **–legung,** *f.* laying the foundation. **–lehre,** *f.* fundamental doctrine; first principles. **–linie,** *f.* outline; groundline, base-line; datum line, point of reference. **–los,** *adj.* bottomless, unfathomable, boundless; unfounded, groundless, causeless. **–mauer,** *f.* foundation-wall. **–mörtel,** *m.* concrete. **–pfeiler,** *m.* main support; foundation-pillar, principal axis. **–pflicht,** *f.* fundamental duty. **–preis,** *m.* basic price. **–recht,** *n.* landlord's privilege *or* right; fundamental law. **–rechte,** *n.pl.* rights of man. **–regel,** *f.* fundamental rule; axiom; first principle (*of a science*). **–register,** *n.*, *see* **–buch.** **–rente,** *f.* ground-rent. **–riß,** *m.* outline, sketch, design, plan, cross-section, ground-plan (*of a building*); epitome, compendium. **–satz,** *m.* principle; rule of conduct; axiom. **–sätzlich,** *adj.* fundamental, (based) on principle; *ich tue das –sätzlich niemals,* I have made a point never to do this. **–satzlos,** *adj.* unprincipled. **–säule,** *f.* pedestal, foot, basis, support. **–schelm,** *m.* arrant rogue. **–schlamm,** *m.* bottom mud. **–schlecht,** *adj.* radically bad, thoroughly bad *or* wicked. **–schoß,** *m.* land-tax. **–schuld,** *f.* mortgage on land. **–schule,** *f.* elementary school. **–schwelle,** *f.* ground-sill (*Arch.*); railway-sleeper. **–see,** *f.* ground-swell. **–stein,** *m.* foundation- *or* corner-stone. **–steinlegung,** *f.* laying of the foundation-stone. **–stellung,** *f.* original *or* first position; as you were! (*Mil. command*). **–steuer,** *f.* land-tax, ground rent. **–stimme,** *f.* bass voice. **–stock,** *m.* matrix. **–stoff,** *m.* element, base, radical (*Chem.*); raw material, pulp (*paper-making*). **–stoffwechsel,** *m.* basal metabolism. **–strich,** *m.* down-stroke (*opp. to hair-stroke*). **–stück,** *n.* real estate; piece of land, site; *Haus mit –stücken,* messuage. **–stürzend,** *adj.* destructive, revolutionary; *–stürzende Änderungen,* fundamental *or* radical changes. **–stütze,** *f.* main support, basis. **teilchen,** *n.* fundamental particle, atom. **–ton,** *m.* key-note. **–trieb,** *m.* natural impulse. **–übel,** *n.* fundamental evil, the root of all evil. **–unterschied,** *m.* basic difference. **–ursache,** *f.* primary cause. **–vermögen,** *n.* primitive force; landed property; real estate; capital fund. **–verschieden,** *adj.* entirely *or* fundamentally different. **–verschiedenheit,** *f.* radical difference. **–wahrheit,** *f.* fundamental truth. **–wasser,** *n.* subsoil *or* underground water. **–werksteuer,** *f.* ground-rent. **–wesen,** *n.* primary essence (*of a th.*). **–zahl,** *f.* cardinal number; unit. **–zehnte,** *m.* land-tithe. **–zins,** *m.* ground-rent. **–zug,** *m.* main feature, characteristic.

gründ–en, 1. *v.a.* establish, found, (*C.L.*) promote, float; sound, fathom; *see also* **grundieren**; ground (*a pupil*); base (*an argument*); *gegründete Ansprüche,* established claims. 2. *v.r.* rest, be based, rely (*auf* (*Acc.*), on). 3. *v.n.* (*aux.* h) sound, feel the bottom; *stille Wasser –en tief,* still waters run deep. **–er,** *m.* founder; (*C.L.*) promoter, jobber. **–erjahre,** *n.pl.* years of reckless financial speculation (*following Franco-German War, 1871–74*). **–ertum,** *n.* speculative mania. **–lich,** *adj.* thorough, solid, well-founded, profound, radical, fundamental; *–liche Kenntnisse in einem Fache haben,* be thoroughly grounded *or* versed in a subject. **–lichkeit,** *f.* thoroughness, solidity, profundity. **–ling,** *m.* gudgeon (*Gobis fluviatilis*) (*Icht.*). **–ung,** *f.* foundation, establishment; commercial *or* financial enterprise; priming, first coat (*paint*); founding.

grüneln, *v.n. imp.* (*dial.*); *es grünelt,* there is a smell of young leaves.

grünen, *v.n.*, *see* **grün.**

grunz–en, 1. *v.n.* (*aux.* h.) grunt. 2. *n.* grunt. **–er,** *m.* grunter.

Grupp–e, *f.* (-en) group, section, class, cluster; squad, army group (*Mil.*). wing (*Av., British*), squadron (*Av. Amer.*). **–enfeuer,** *n.* volley firing (*Mil.*). **–enschaltung,** *f.* series-parallel connexion (*Elec.*). **–enweise,** *adv.* in groups *or* clusters; in sections *or* squads (*Mil.*). **–ieren,** *v.a.* group, classify. **–ierung,** *f.* grouping, arrangement, classification, organization.

Grus, *m.* grit, fine gravel; debris; smalls, (coal) slack. **–sand,** *m.* coarse sand, gravel. **–tee,** *m.* tea-dust.

grusel–ig, *adj.* uncanny, creepy, gruesome. **–n,** 1. *v.imp.*; *mich –t's, es –t mir,* my flesh creeps. 2. *n.* horrors, creeps.

Gruß, *m.* (-es, ⸚e) greeting, salutation, salute; *mit bestem Gruß Ihr,* yours very truly; *einen – ausrichten,* convey a p.'s kind regards. **–formel,** *f.* form of salutation.

grüß–en, *v.a.* greet; salute; present compliments to; *–en lassen,* send one's respects, compliments *or* kind regards (to); *bitte –en Sie ihn von mir,* please remember me to him, give him my kind regards; *meine Mutter läßt deine Schwester herzlich –en,* my mother sends her love to your sister; *er läßt euch alle –en,* he desires to be remembered to you all; *– Gott!* (*dial.*) greetings! farewell! **–fuß,** *m.*; *mit einem auf dem –fuß stehen,* have a nodding acquaintance with s.o.; know s.o. just to speak to.

Grütz–e, *f.* (-en) groats; (*coll.*) *–e im Kopfe haben,* be clever, be all there; *rote –e,* fruit-flavoured blancmange. **–brei,** *m.* gruel. **–kopf,** *m.* blockhead. **–schleim,** *m.*, *see* **–brei.**

Gschaftelhuber, *m.* (*dial.*) busybody.

Guardian, *m.* (-s, -e) (convent) prior; *Vater–,* father superior.

Guck, *m.* (-(e)s, -e) (*dial.*) look, peep. **–en,** *v.n.* (*aux.* h.) look, peep, peer; *der Schelm –t ihm aus den Augen,* his looks bespeak the rogue he is. **–er,** *m.* peeper; eyeglass, spy-glass; *Opern–er,* opera glass. **–kasten,** *m.* (*archaic*) peep-show. **–loch,** *n.* peep-hole, spy-hole.

Gugelhupf, *m.* (-(e)s & -en, -e(n)) (*Austr. dial.*) sort of cake.

guillotinieren, *v.a.* guillotine.

Gulasch, *n.* stewed steak (flavoured with paprika). **–kanone,** *f.* (*Mil. sl.*) field-kitchen.

Gulden, *m.* (-s, –) florin, guilder.

gülden, *adj.* (*Poet.*) golden.

Gülle, *f.* liquid manure.

Gully, *m.* (-s, -s), street drain.

Gült–e, *f.* (*dial.*) ground-rent; revenues of an estate; payment in kind. **–buch,** *n.*, **–register,** *n.* rent-roll. **-herr,** *m.* lord of the manor. **-ig,** *adj.* valid, binding, good, legal; authentic, current; admissable, applicable, available; *-ig für* or *nach*, available for; *eine Anklage für -ig erklären*, bring in a true bill (*Law*); *-ig machen*, render valid, ratify. **-igkeit,** *f.* validity, legality; availability; *Fahrkarten mit dreißigtägiger -igkeit*, tickets available for thirty days; *Behauptung von allgemeiner -igkeit*, statement of universal validity. **-igkeitsdauer,** *f.* period of validity.

Gummi, 1. *n.* rubber, india-rubber, gum. 2. *m.* (-s, -s) india-rubber (eraser), (*coll.*) rubber. **-absatz,** *m.* rubber heel. **-arabikum,** *n.* gum (Arabic). **-artig,** *adj.* rubber-like, gummy. **-band,** *n.* elastic (band), rubber band. **-baum,** *m.* gum tree. **-druck,** *m.* offset (printing). **-eren,** *v.a.* gum, rubberize; *-erte Briefumschläge*, adhesive envelopes; *-erte Etikette*, gummed label; *-erter Stoff*, proofed fabric. **-ersatz,** *m.* synthetic rubber, rubber substitute, factice. **-federung,** *f.* rubber absorber (*Motor.*). **-gutt,** *n.* gamboge. **-harz,** *n.* gum-resin. **-kabel,** *n.* insulated cable. **-knüppel,** *m.* rubber truncheon. **-lösung,** *f.* rubber solution *or* cement. **-mantel,** *m.* mackintosh, waterproof. **-reifen,** *m.* rubber tyre. **-schlauch,** *m.* rubber tube *or* tubing, hose. **-schlauchboot,** *n.* rubber dinghy. **-schleim,** *m.* mucilage, gum. **-schuhe,** *m.pl.* galoshes, overshoes. **-seilstart,** *m.* catapult take-off (*gliders*). **-stempel,** *m.* rubber stamp. **-stiefel,** *m.pl.* gum boots. **-überzug,** *m.* film of rubber. **-zelle,** *f.* padded cell. **-zug,** *m.* elastic.

Gumpe, *f.* sump, grease-trap; (*dial.*) pool, deep (*in a watercourse*).

Gundel-kraut, *n.* wild thyme (*Thymus serpyllum*) (*Bot.*). **-beere,** *f.*, **-rebe,** *f.*, **Gundermann,** *m.* ground ivy (*Nepeta hederacea* or *glechoma*) (*Bot.*).

gunksen, *v.a.* (*dial.*) nudge, push.

Günsel, *m.* common bugle (*Ajuga reptans*) (*Bot.*).

Gunst, *f.* favour, goodwill, kindness, affection, partiality; credit, advantage; (*archaic*) leave, permission; *sich um jemandes – bewerben*, court a p.'s favour; *einem eine – erweisen*, do a p. a favour; *bei einem in – stehen*, be in favour with s.o.; (*archaic*) *mit –*, with (your) permission, by (your) leave; *es geht hier alles nach –*, everything goes by favour here; *zu -en von*, in favour of, on behalf of, (*C.L.*) to the credit of; *see also* **zugunsten. -bezeigung,** *f.* act of favour *or* kindness.

günst-ig, *adj.* favourable, propitious; kind, friendly, gracious; convenient, advantageous; *bei einer S. -ig abschneiden*, show up to advantage in a matter; *einen -ig für jemand stimmen*, win a p.'s good opinion *or* favour for another. **-ling,** *m.* favourite, minion. **-lingswesen,** *n.*, **-lingswirtschaft,** *f.* favouritism.

Gurgel, *f.* (-n) throat, gullet, pharynx; *einem die – abschneiden*, cut s.o.'s throat; (*vulg.*) *durch die – jagen*, squander in drink; *einem die – zuschnüren*, (*fig.*) strangle a p., ruin a p. economically. **-ader,** *f.* jugular vein. **-bein,** *n.* collar bone, clavicle. **-klappe,** *f.* uvula. **-n,** *v.n.* (*aux.* h.) gargle; gurgle. **-mittel,** *n.*, **-wasser,** *n.* gargle.

Gurke, *f.* (-n) cucumber, gherkin; (*vulg.*) snitch, boko. **-nhobel,** *m.* cucumber slicer. **-nsalat,** *m.* cucumber salad; (*Prov.*) *was versteht der Bauer von -salat?* this is quite above his head. (*coll.*) **-nzeit,** *f.* (*Saure-nzeit* or *Zeit der sauren -n*) silly season.

Gurre, *f.* (-n) (*dial.*) nag, jade.

gurren, *v.n.* (*aux.* h.) coo.

Gurt, *m.* (-(e)s, -e) girth, girdle, belt; strap, webbing, harness (*parachute, etc.*), machine-gun belt. **-anzug,** *m.* Norfolk suit. **-en,** *v.n.* fill ammunition *or* cartridge belt. **-enzuführung,** *f.* belt-feed (*machine guns*). **-förderer,** *m.* belt conveyor. **-gehenk,** *n.* s.th. hanging from a belt; trinkets, chatelaine; sword-belt. **-sims,** *m.* plinth (*of a pillar*). **-strippe,** *f.* cinch strap (*harness*). **-werk,** *n.* parachute harness. **-zufuhr,** *f.*, *see* **-enzuführung.**

Gürt-el, *m.* (-els, -el) belt, girdle, sash; waistband; cordon; zone (*Geog.*); fascia (*Arch.*). **-elbahn,** *f.* ring railway (*in large towns*). **-elkette,** *f.* chatelaine. **-elrose,** *f.* shingles (*Med.*). **-elschnalle,** *f.* belt buckle. **-eltier,** *n.* armadillo (*Dasypodidae*) (*Zool.*). **-en,** 1. *v.a.* gird, girdle. 2. *v.r.* put on one's belt; make (o.s.) ready, prepare (o.s.) for; prepare to leave. **-ler,** *m.* brassfounder, brass-worker.

Guß, *m.* (-(ss)es, ⸚(ss)e) gush, downpour, torrent; spout, gutter; pouring out; casting, founding; cast, fount (*Typ.*); icing (*Cook.*); *schmiedbarer –*, malleable cast iron; *aus einem –*, homogeneous, a perfect whole, harmonious. **-abdruck,** *m.* plate, stereotype plate (*Typ.*); cast. **-block,** *m.* ingot. **-eisen,** *n.* cast iron, pig iron. **-eisern,** *adj.* (made of) cast iron. **-form,** *f.* (casting-)mould. **-mutter,** *f.* matrix (*Typ.*). **-regen,** *m.* (*also* Regen–) heavy shower, downpour (of rain). **-stahl,** *m.* cast steel. **-stein,** *m.* (*dial.*) sink, gutter. **-stück,** *n.* casting. **-waren,** *f.pl.* castings.

gut, (*comp.* besser, *sup.* best) 1. *adj.* good, excellent, desirable, beneficial; pleasant, kind, friendly, good-natured; respectable, virtuous; *-er Absatz*, ready sale; *sein -es Auskommen haben*, make *or* earn a good deal of money; *fröhlich und -er Dinge sein*, be cheerful and in good spirits; (*Prov.*) *Ende –, alles –*, all's well that ends well; *für – finden*, think proper; *– und gern*, quite willingly, easily; *in -em Glauben*, in good faith, bona fide; *etwas auf — Glück tun*, do s.th. and hope for the best, do s.th. at a venture; *kein -es Haar an einem lassen*, run a p. down, pull a p. to pieces; not have a good word to say for a p.; *es – haben*, be well off; *für – halten*, approve of; *in -er Hand bei einem sein*, be in good hands with s.o.; *-er Hoffnung sein*, live in hope(s); be with child, be in the family way; *kurz und –*, in short; *zu -er Letzt*, finally, in the last resort; *ein -es Mädchen*, a good-natured girl; *-en Mutes*, be of good cheer *or* in good spirits; *der -e Ort*, (Jewish) cemetery; *-er Rechner*, a p. quick at figures; (*es ist*) *schon –*, all right! that will do, enough, you need not say any more; *es mag für diesmal – sein*, I will overlook it this time, I will for this once take no notice of it; *lassen Sie es – sein*, never mind, let it pass, do not mention it; no more of it; *einem – sein*, be favourably disposed towards *or* care for a p. *or* love a p.; *sie ist ihm –*, she loves him; *sie sind wieder –*, they have made it up *or* are friendly again; *– sein zu*, be good for; *wozu ist das –?* what is the use of that? *stehst du* (*dich*) *– mit ihm?* are you on friendly terms with him? *die -e Stube*, the best room, parlour, drawing-room; *eine -e Stunde*, fully *or* quite an hour, an hour at least; *-e Tage haben*, have an easy life; *die -en Taktteile*, the strong accents (*Mus.*); *ein -es Teil der Schuld liegt an mir*, I am largely responsible; *das hat -e Wege*, we need not trouble about that yet, there is plenty of time for that, that is (still) a long way off; *das hat -e Weile*, see *-e Wege*; *es wird schon noch alles – werden*, it will, no doubt, all turn out well; *er wird bald wieder –*, his anger passes quickly; *-es Wetter*, fine weather; *es ist sein -er Wille*, it is his wish *or* his own free will; *-e Worte*, fair words, be conciliatory; (*Prov.*) *ein -es Wort findet eine -e Statt*, a good word goes a long way; *zu –*, see *zugute*. 2. *adv.* well, good; *so – wie*, as well as; *so – wie kein Haar*, practically no hair; *sie ist so – schuld daran wie ich*, she is as much to blame as I am; *es ist so – als hätte er sie geheiratet*, he has as good as married her; *– 25 DM*, quite 25 marks; *– eine Viertelstunde*, fully a quarter of an hour; *Sie haben – reden*, it is easy for you to talk; *den Klugen ist – predigen*, a word is enough to the wise. 3. *n.* (-es, ⸚er) good thing, blessing; property, possession; (*C.L.*) goods, commodity, (*Amer.*) freight; country-seat, estate, farm; rigging (*Naut.*); *– und Blut*, life and property; *jenseits von – und Böse* (*Nietzsche*), beyond good and evil; *ein erworbenes –*, an acquisition; *– und Geld, Geld und –*, wealth, possessions; *Hab und –*, all one's property, goods and chattels; *ein heimgefallenes –*, escheat (*Law*); *das hochwürdige –*, the consecrated bread, the Host; *Gesundheit ist das höchste – auf Erden*, the finest thing on earth *or* life's most precious gift is good health; *laufendes* (*stehendes*) *–*, running (standing) rigging (*Naut.*); (*Prov.*) *unrecht – gedeiht nicht*, ill-gotten gain never prospers. **-achten,** *n.* (expert) opinion, judgement, verdict; (legal) advice; estimate; *nach Ihrem*

-*achten*, according to your advice; as you think proper, in (your) estimation. **-achter,** *m.* surveyor, valuer, assessor. **-achtlich,** *adv.* authoritative. **-artig,** *adj.* good-natured, benign, mild (*of fevers*). **-aufgelegt,** *adj.* well disposed, in good humour. **-befinden,** *n.* pleasure, discretion; approval; *nach Ihrem -befinden*, upon your own terms, as you think fit. **-denkend,** *adj.* well-meaning. **-dünken,** *n.* opinion, estimation, discretion; *nach -dünken*, at discretion. **-e,** *n.* good quality, goodness; *das -e an der S.*, the good thing about it; *das -e an der Geschichte*, the best of the joke; *eine S. zum -en* ***lenken***, give a matter a favourable turn, prevent a misunderstanding *or* catastrophe; *an das -e* ***glauben***, have faith in (man's, God's) goodness; *zum* ***-en reden***, conciliate, speak fair; *im -en handeln*, act willingly *or* in a friendly manner, be amicable; ***-es***, good, good things, everything good; *-es mit* ***Bösem*** *vergelten*, repay good with evil; *nur -es sagen*, only say nice things; *was bringst du -es?* what pleasant surprises have you brought? *er hat auch sein -es*, he has his good points too. **- eingerichtet,** *adj.* well-furnished, well-equipped. **-gelaunt,** *adj.* in a good temper, good-humoured, in good spirits. **-gemeint,** *adj.* well-meant, well intentioned. **-gesinnt,** *adj.* friendly, right-minded, loyal. **-gewicht,** *n.* allowance, tret. **-gläubig,** *adj.* credulous. **-haben,** 1. *v.n.* be in *or* have credit with; *ich habe eine Menge Geld bei ihm -*, he owes me a lot of money. 2. *n.* credit, balance, outstanding debt; *ich habe noch ein kleines -haben bei Ihnen*, a small sum still stands to my credit with you; *nicht abgehobenes -haben*, unclaimed balance. **-heißen,** *v.a.* approve, sanction. **-heißung,** *f.* approbation, approval, consent, sanction. **-herzig,** *adj.* good-hearted; kind-hearted. **-machen,** *v.a.* make amends for, make up for. **-mütigkeit,** *f.* good nature. **-sagen,** 1. *v.n.* be *or* go security (for), be responsible (for) *or* answerable (for). 2. *see* **-sagung.** **-sager,** *m.* surety, bondsman. **-sagung,** *f.* security. **-sbesitzer,** *m.* landowner, squire, gentleman farmer, landed proprietor. **-schein,** *m.* voucher. **-schließend,** *adj.* tight fitting (*of lids*). **-schreiben,** *v.a.* credit; *einem etwas -schreiben*, put s.th. to a p.'s account, place s.th. to a p.'s credit. **-schrift,** *f.* credit(ing); *zur -schrift*, to the credit of my (our) account. **-sein,** *see* **-sagen.** **-sherr,** *m.* squire, lord of the manor. **-sherrlich,** *adj.*; *-sherrliche Privilegien*, manorial rights. **-shof,** *m.* estate, farm. **-situiert,** *adj.* well-placed, in easy *or* comfortable circumstances. **-spflichtig,** *adj.* liable to socage-service. **-stehen,** (*für*), *see* **-sagen.** **-steuer,** *f.* property-tax. **-sverwalter,** *m.* manager of an estate, steward. **-szwang,** *m.* manorial authority. **-tat,** *f.* charitable act, benediction. **-tun,** *v.n.* do *or* behave well, do right *or* good. **-willig,** *adj.* voluntary; obliging, willing; *etwas -willig tun*, do a th. of one's own free will. **-willigkeit,** *f.* willingness.

Güt-e, *f.* kindness, goodness; excellence, purity, quality; *auf dem Wege der -e*, see *in -e*; *durch* (*die*) *-e des Herrn Dr. W.*, through the kindness of Dr. W., by the kind offices of Dr. W.; (*coll.*) *erster -e*, of the first rank, first-rate; *eine Dummheit erster -e*, a first-class piece of stupidity; *haben Sie die -e*, be so kind as (to); *in* (*der*) *-e*, voluntarily, amicably; *wollen Sie es in -e tun?* will you do it without compulsion? will you do it amicably? *meine -e!* (*periphrastic for* mein Gott!) good gracious! good lord! **-erabfertigung,** *f.* goods office. **-erabtretung,** *f.* surrender of a bankrupt's estate. **-eranschlag,** *m.* valuation of goods. **-erbahnhof,** *m.* goods station, goods yard, (*Amer.*) freight yard. **-erbestätter,** *m.* carrier, carter, conveyor of goods; forwarder, dispatcher. **-erbrief,** *m.* bill of lading. **-erflugzeug,** *n.* freight carrying aircraft. **-ergemeinschaft,** *f.* joint property (*of husband and wife*). **-erhandel,** *m.* estate-agency; real-estate business. **-ermasse,** *f.* bankrupt's assets. **-erpacker,** *m.* stevedore. **-erschuppen,** *m.* goods depot. **-erspedition,** *f.* goods department, forwarding agency, carriers, carters. **-erverkehr,** *m.* goods traffic. **-ervertreter,** *m.* trustee. **-erwagen,** *m.* goods van, luggage van, truck, (*Amer.*) freight car. **-erzug,** *m.* goods train, (*Amer.*) freight train. **-estufe,** *f.* grade, quality. **-everhältnis,** *n.* efficiency. **-ig,** *adj.* good, kind, gracious; benevolent, charitable; indulgent; *-ig gegen einen*, good to a p.; *seien Sie so -ig und geben es ihm*, kindly give it to him; *mit Ihrer -igen Erlaubnis*, with your kind permission; *der Brief, den Sie mir -igst geschrieben haben*, the letter which you were kind enough to write me; *-iger Himmel!* Good Heavens! Gracious Heaven! **-igkeit,** *f.* goodness, kindness, graciousness; benevolence. **-ler,** *m.* (*dial.*) smallholder. **-lich,** *adj.* amicable, friendly; *-licher Vergleich*, amicable settlement; *sich* (*Dat.*) *-lich tun an einer S.*, enjoy s.th., revel in a th.; *-lich beilegen*, settle amicably.

Guttapercha, *f.* (*Austr. n.*) gutta-percha.

Gymnas-ialbildung, *f.* classical education. **-ialdirektor,** *m.* grammar-school headmaster. **-iallehrer,** *m.* grammar-school master. **-iast,** *m.* (-en, -en) grammar-school boy, secondary school boy (*on the classical side*). **-ium,** *n.* (-iums, -ien) grammar-school, secondary school (*with classical bias*); *Mädchen-ium*, high school for girls. **-tik,** *f.* gymnastics. **-tisch,** *adj.* gymnastic.

Gynäkolog-e, *m.* (-en, -en) gynaecologist.

H

H, h, *n.* H, h; B, si (*Mus.*).

Haar, *n.* (-(e)s, -e) hair; filament; nap, pile; wool; hairy *or* woolly side of skins; trifle; *an den -en herbeiziehen*, drag in willy-nilly; *das ist an den -en herbeigezogen*, that is far-fetched; *sein Leben hing an einem -*, his life hung by a thread; *auf ein -*, *aufs -*, to a T, exactly; *das - aufwickeln*, curl one's hair; *ein - in einer S. finden*, be turned against a th.; find fault with a th.; *deshalb lasse ich mir keine grauen -e wachsen*, I do not take that much to heart; *es ist kein gutes - an ihm*, there is no redeeming feature about him; there is not a good word to be said for him; *sie läßt kein gutes - an ihm*, she won't admit that he has a single good quality, she runs him down unmercifully; *mit Haut und -(en)*, completely, entirely, altogether; lock, stock and barrel; *sie liegen sich fortwährend in den -en*, they are always at loggerheads; (*coll.*) they get in each other's hair; *einem gern in die -e wollen*, wish to pick a quarrel with a p.; *man hat ihm kein - gekrümmt*, they have not touched a hair of his head; *-e lassen müssen*, come to harm, suffer loss, be fleeced, be cheated; *die -e standen* or *stiegen mir zu Berge*, my hair stood on end; ***um ein -***, within an ace; *um ein - wäre er umgekommen*, he escaped death by a hair's breadth; *nicht* (*um*) *ein -*, (*um*) *kein -*, not a jot, not in the least; *-e auf den Zähnen haben*, be bare-faced *or* brazen. **-ader,** *f.* capillary vein. **-aufsatz,** *m.* false hair, toupee. **-(auf)wickler,** *m.* curling-pin; curl-paper; curling-tongs. **-balg,** *m.* hair follicle. **-beize,** *f.* depilatory. **-beutel,** *m.* hair bag; (*coll.*) *einen -beutel haben*, be tipsy. **-besatz,** *m.* hairy covering. **-bleiche,** *f.* hair bleach(ing). **-bürste,** *f.* hair-brush. **-büschel,** *m.* tuft of hair. **-drüse,** *f.* sebaceous gland. **-en,** *v.r.* & *n.* (*aux.* h.) lose hair; shed hair. **-esbreite,** *f.* hair's breadth. **-farbe,** *f.* colour of the hair; hair-dye. **-färbestoff,** *m.* hair-dye. **-farn,** *m.* maiden-hair fern (*Adiantum capillus veneris*) (*Bot.*). **-faser,** *f.* filament. **-faserig,** *adj.* capillary. **-feder,** *f.* down (*on birds*); hair-spring. **-fein,** *adj.* fine as a hair; delicate; capillary. **-flechte,** *f.* braid of hair. **-förmig,** *adj.* capillary. **-gefäß,** *n.* capillary vessel. **-ig,** *adj.* hairy, haired; of hair; hirsute; pilose (*Bot.*); hazy, obscured (*Naut.*); (*coll.*) strange, unprecedented, scandalous, shocking. **-klauberei,** *f.* hair-splitting. **-klein,** *adj.* to a hair, to a nicety, minute;

–*klein alles erzählen*, tell without missing any of the details. **–kopf,** *m.* head of hair. **–kranz,** *m.* tonsure. **–krause,** *f.* toupet; tonsure. **–locke,** *f.* curl; lock of hair. **–lockerungsmittel,** *n.* depilatory agent. **–los,** *adj.* hairless, bald; napless (*of cloth*). **–nadel,** *f.* hairpin. **–pflege,** *f.* hair-dressing. **–pinsel,** *m.* camel-hair brush. **–putz,** *m.* head-dress; coiffure; hair-ornament. **–röhrchen,** *n.* capillary tube. **–röhrchenanziehung,** *f.* capillary attraction. **–salbe,** *f.* brilliantine. **–scharf,** *adj.* very *or* dead sharp; very fine; extremely precise *or* accurate. **–scheitel,** *m.* crown of the head; parting of the hair. **–schneiden,** *n.* haircut. **–schopf,** *m.* tuft of hair. **–schuppen,** *f.pl.* scurf. **–schweif,** *m.* tail of a comet, coma. **–schwund,** *m.* loss of hair. **–sieb,** *n.* hair sieve (*Cook.*). **–spalterei,** *f.* hair-splitting. **–stern,** *m.* comet. **–sträubend,** *adj.* (*fig.*) hair-raising; atrocious, shocking. **–strich,** *m.* up-stroke (*in writing*). **–tour,** *f.*, **–tracht,** *f.* coiffure. **–tragend,** *adj.* capillary (*Bot.*). **–wachs,** *n.*, *see* **–salbe.** **–wasser,** *n.* hair-lotion. **–wechsel,** *m.* moulting. **–wickel,** *m.* curl-paper. **–wild,** *n.* fur (*opp. of* fin *and* feather); ground game; *–wild und Federwild*, fur and feather. **–wuchs,** *m.* growth of hair; coat (*of animals*). **–zange,** *f.* tweezers. **–zopf,** *m.* pigtail; plait.

Hab–e, *f.* property, goods, possessions, effects, fortune; *– und Gut*, goods and chattels, all one's property; *fahrende –e*, movables; *liegende –e*, immovable property, immovables. **–enichts,** *m.* (– & -es, -e) 'have-not'; person, class *or* nation without resources (*translation of Lloyd George's coinage*). **–erecht,** *m.* (*dial.*) arguer, dogmatist, dogmatical p.

hab–en, 1. *ir.v.a.* have; possess; hold; bear; *Acht –en auf*, pay attention to; *er hat das so an sich*, that is just his manner; *Anwendung –en auf*, apply to; *auf sich –en*, be of significance *or* consequence, signify; *im Auge –en*, have in view; *Aussicht –en auf*, command a view of; have expectations of; *bei sich –en*, have about *or* with one; *zum besten –en*, make a fool of, mock; *was will er dafür –en?* what price does he ask for it? *dafür ist er nicht zu –en*, he will have nothing to do with it; *ich habe nichts dagegen*, I have no objection to it; *ein Datum –en*, bear a date; *nichts davon –en*, get nothing from, gain *or* derive no benefit from; *was habe ich davon?* what do I get out of it? *Durst –en*, be thirsty; *Eile –en*, be in a hurry; admit of no delay; *fertig –en*, have finished, be done with; *das hat etwas für sich*, that has its points, there's s.th. to be said for it; *im Gang –en*, have in full swing; *gern –en*, like, be fond of; *etwas im Griff –en*, know a thing by the touch, have the feel of a th.; *er hat es gut*, he has a fine time *or* a pleasant life of it; *wo –en Sie es her?* where have you picked that up? where did you get that from? *hinter sich –en*, have done with, be past *or* through; be backed up by, have at one's disposal; *das hat es in sich*, there's a catch *or* difficulty in it; *lieb–en*, love; *lieber –en*, prefer; *am liebsten –en*, prefer above all; *sie –en es miteinander*, there is an affair between them, they are in love with each other; *–e Mut!* take courage! pluck up courage! *Nachsicht –en*, be indulgent, make allowance for; *nötig –en*, need; *Recht* (*Unrecht*) *–en*, be right (wrong); *es hat seine Richtigkeit*, there is s.th. in it, it is not entirely false; *nichts zu sagen –en*, not mean *or* signify much; *es satt –en*, be sick of a th., (*coll.*) be fed to the teeth with a th., (*vulg.*) have had a belly-full; *den Schaden –en*, bear the cost, meet *or* foot the bill; *am Schnürchen –en*, have at one's fingers' ends; *wer hat* (*die*) *Schuld?* who is to blame? *Gott habe ihn selig*, God rest his soul! *statt –en*, take place; *etwas zu tun –en mit*, have to deal with, be concerned with; *es nicht für ungut –en*, not take amiss; *er hat viel von seinem Vater*, he takes a great deal after his father; *wen meinst du vor dir zu –en?* whom do you think you are speaking to? *vor sich –en*, have still to do, have in sight; *Sie –en die Wahl*, take your choice; you may choose; (*coll.*) *hat sich was!* there's no question of it, not a hope! 2. *v.r.* behave; (*coll.*) *sich darum –en*, grieve for a th.; (*coll.*) *–e dich doch nicht so!* do not make such a fuss! do not be so foolish; (*dial.*) there is, it is; *es hat sich nichts zu danken*, there's nothing to thank me for, you're welcome to it. 3. *n.* (*C.L.*) credit; creditors; *Soll und –en*, debit and credit. **–gier,** *f.*, **–sucht,** *f.* covetousness, avarice, greediness, greed, avidity. **–gierig,** *adj.*, **–süchtig,** *adj.* avaricious, covetous, greedy. **–haft,** *adj.* (*only in*) *einer S.* (*Gen.*) *–haft werden*, get hold of, obtain, take possession of, seize *or* take a th. **–schaft,** *f.*, **–seligkeit,** *f.* (*usually pl.*) all that a p. has, belongings, property, fortune, effects; kit (*Mil.*).

Haber, *m.* (*dial.*) = **Hafer.** **–feldtreiben,** *n.* popular lynch justice (*among Bavarian peasants*). **–geiß,** *f.* (*dial.*) bogy, spectre.

Habicht, *m.* (-(e)s, -e) hawk. **–sauge,** *n.* hawk-eye, keen eyesight. **–sfang,** *m.* hawk-catching; claw *or* pounce of a hawk. **–sinseln,** *f.pl.* the Azores. **–snase,** *f.* hooked nose.

Habilit–ation, *f.* inauguration (*into academic career*) (*Univ.*). **–ationsschrift,** *f.* inaugural dissertation. **–ieren,** *v.r.* qualify for inauguration as *or* become recognized as academic lecturer (*Univ.*).

habituell, *adj.* habitual.

Hachse (*also* **Haxe**) *f.* (-n) back of the knee, lower leg; hock, leg (*of veal or pork*).

Hack, *m.* (*dial.*) hack, stroke (*with an axe, etc.*); *– und Pack*, rag, tag and bobtail. **–bau,** *m.* hoeing. **–e,** *f.* (-en) pickaxe, pick, mattock, hoe; hoeing time *or* season. **–(e)bank,** *f.* chopping-block. **–(e)beil,** *n.* chopper. **–(e)brett,** *n.* chopping-board; dulcimer (*Mus.*); (*sl.*) piano. **–emack,** *m.*, **–epack,** *m.*, *see* **–mack.** **–en,** *v.a.* chop, hash, mince, hack; hoe; cleave (*wood*), pick, peck up; *Gehacktes*, *n.* minced meat, mince. **–epeter,** *m.* (*dial.*) minced pork. **–er,** *m.* (also **Häcker,** *m.*) (*dial.*) vine-grower. **–fleisch,** *n.* minced meat. **–frucht,** *f.* root crops. **–fruchtbau,** *m.* cultivation of root crops. **–klotz,** *m.*, *see* **–bank.** **–mack,** *m.* hotch-potch, medley; rabble; rag, tag, and bobtail. **–messer,** *n.* chopping-knife, cleaver, chopper.

Hacke, *f.* (-n), **–n,** *m.* (-ns, -n) afterpiece, shoulder, heel (*of stocking, boot, etc.*); *die –n zusammenschlagen*, click one's heels; (*coll.*) *sich* (*Dat.*) *die –n nach einer S. ablaufen*, run one's feet off for a th.; *er tritt mir unter die –n*, he gets under my feet *or* heels; *er ist mir dicht auf den –n*, he is hard on my heels.

Häck–erling, *m.* **–sel,** *m.* (*& Austr. n.*) chopped straw, chaff; anything chopped fine. **–erlingsschneider,** *m.*, **–selmaschine,** *f.* chaff-cutter.

[1]**Hader,** *m.* (-s, -n) (*dial.*) rag, tatter, (*pl.*) rags (*Pap.*). **–lump,** *m.* disgraceful fellow, ragamuffin. **–nbrei,** *m.* rag pulp (*Pap.*).

[2]**Hader,** *m.* quarrel, brawl, dispute, strife. **–er,** *m.* grumbler, wrangler, brawler; fang, tusk. **–geist,** *m.* spirit of contention. **–n,** *v.n.* (*aux.* h.) wrangle, strive, quarrel, squabble, dispute. **–süchtig,** *adj.* quarrelsome.

Hafen, *m.* (-s, ⸚) port, harbour; haven; refuge; (*dial.*) earthen vesseel, pot; *einen – anlaufen*, make for port (*Naut.*); (*Prov.*) *jeder – findet seinen Deckel*, every pot has its lid. **–abgabe,** *f.* harbour-dues. **–amt,** *n.* port authority. **–anker,** *m.* moorings. **–arbeiter,** *m.* docker, longshoreman. **–baum,** *m.* harbour-boom. **–becken,** *n.* wet dock. **–brücke,** *f.* pier, mole. **–damm,** *m.* pier, jetty, breakwater, mole. **–dock,** *n.* basin, wet dock. **–gäste,** *m.pl.* foreign vessels in a port. **–gatt,** *n.* harbour-mouth. **–gebühr,** *f.*, **–geld,** *n.* harbour-dues, anchorage (dues). **–lotse,** *m.* harbour-pilot. **–räumer,** *m.* dredger. **–sperre,** *f.* blockade, embargo; boom. **–spesen,** *pl.*, **–zoll,** *m.* port-dues. **–stadt,** *f.* seaport (town).

Hafer, *m.* oats; (*coll.*) *der – sticht ihn*, he is uppish, insolent *or* (*coll.*) cocky. **–artig,** *adj.* avenaceous. **–bau,** *m.* growing of oats. **–brei,** *m.* oatmeal porridge. **–flocken,** *f.pl.* rolled oats. **–grütze** *f.* groats. **–mehl,** *n.* oatmeal. **–schleim,** *m.* oatmeal gruel. **–spreu,** *f.* oat-chaff. **–stroh,** *n.* oat-straw; *grob wie –stroh*, very rude. **–zins,** *m.* avenage, rent paid in oats.

Haff, *n.* (-(e)s, -e) lagoon (*Baltic*).

Hafner, *m.* (-s, –) (*dial.*) potter.

[1]**Haft,** *m.* (-(e)s, -e) fastening, clasp, clamp, tie; crotchet.

[2]**Haft,** *f.* custody, arrest; imprisonment, confinement; *zur – bringen,* put under arrest; *aus der – entlassen,* discharge from custody; *in enger –,* in close custody. **–bar,** *adj.* responsible, liable, answerable. **–barkeit,** *f.* liability, responsibility. **–befehl,** *m.,* **–brief,** *m.* warrant for arrest. **–dauer,** *f.* term of imprisonment. **–en,** *v.n.* (*aux.* h.) cling to, adhere to, stick; remain; be fixed; *–en für,* go bail for, bear the blame *or* loss; be responsible for; answer for, be liable for; *Schulden –en auf dem Gute,* the estate is encumbered *or* mortgaged; *es –et ein Verdacht auf ihm,* suspicion rests on him; *es –et nichts an ihm* or *bei ihm,* it goes in at one ear and out at the other, it goes over him like water off a duck's back. **–fähigkeit,** *f.* adhesion. **–festigkeit,** *f.* adhesive strength, adhesiveness, tenacity. **–geld,** *n.* (*dial.*) earnest money; retaining fee. **–hohlladung,** *f.* limpet bomb, sticky bomb. **–mittel,** *n.* adhesive. **–pflicht,** *f.* liability, responsibility; *solidare –pflicht,* solidarity; *mit beschränkter –pflicht,* limited (liability). **–pflichtgesetz,** *n.* employers' liability act. **–pflichtig,** *adj.* bound, liable, responsible. **–vermögen,** *n., see* **–fähigkeit.** (*C.L.*) **–ung,** *f.* liability, security, bail; *mit beschränkter –ung,* limited (liability).

Häftling, *m.* (-s, -e) prisoner.

Hag, *m.* (-(e)s, -e) hedge, fence; enclosure; (*Poet.*) bush, grove, coppice; grass-plot, meadow. **–ebuche,** *f.* hornbeam (*Carpinus betulus*) (*Bot.*). **–ebüchen,** *adj.,* **–ebuchen,** *adj.* coarse; clumsy; unheard-of, preposterous. **–ebutte,** *f.* hip, haw. **–edorn,** *m.* (*dial.*) hawthorn (*Crataegus monogyna*) (*Bot.*). **–estolz,** *m.* (-es *and* -en, -en) (old) bachelor.

Hagel, *m.* hail; (*archaic*) grape- *or* case-shot; *ein – von Schimpfworten,* a storm of abuse. **–korn,** *n.* hailstone; stye (*in the eye*). **–kugel,** *f.* grape-shot. **–n,** *v.n. imp.* hail; *es –te Schläge,* blows rained down. **–schaden,** *m.* damage done by hail. **–schlag,** *m.* hailstorm. **–schloßen,** *f.pl.* hailstones. **–wetter,** *n.* hail-storm.

hager, *adj.* haggard; thin, lean, lank; meagre, unproductive. **–keit,** *f.* leanness, meagreness.

Häher, *m.* (-s, –) jay (*Garrulus glandarius*) (*Orn.*).

Hahn, *m.* (-(e)s, ⸚e, *or rare except in mechanical sense* -en) cock; stopcock, tap, spigot, (*Amer.*) faucet; (*archaic*) cock (*on a gun, etc.*); *danach kräht kein –,* nobody cares two hoots about it; *– im Korbe sein,* be cock of the roost *or* walk; *der rote –,* fire, incendiarism; *einem den roten – aufs Dach setzen,* set fire to a man's house; *den – am Gewehr spannen,* cock a gun. **–enbalken,** *m.* roost; collar-beam; upper cross-beam of gable. **–enbart,** *m.* wattles. **–enei,** *n.* cock's egg, chimera, mare's nest; (*coll.*) very small egg. **–enfuß,** *m.* ranunculus (*Bot.*). **–engeschrei,** *n.* cock-crowing; cock-crow. **–engewicht,** *n.* bantam weight (*Sport*). **–enkamm,** *m.* cockscomb; carob tree (*Erythrima abessinica*) (*Bot.*); common cockscomb (*Celosa eristata*) (*Bot.*); yellow rattle (*Rhinanthus cristagalli*) (*Bot.*). **–enkampf,** *m.* cock-fight. **–enplan,** *m.* cockpit. **–enruf,** *m.,* **–enschrei,** *m.* cock-crowing, cock-crow. **–enschlagen,** *n.* cock-shy. **–enschlüssel,** *m.* key of a stop-cock. **–entritt,** *m.* copulation (*of fowl*); tread *or* cicatricule (*of eggs*); spring-halt (*Vet.*). **–rei,** *m.* (-s, -e) cuckold. **–reischaft,** *f.* cuckoldom.

Hai, (-(e)s, -e), **–fisch** *m.* shark; (*also fig.* = *unscrupulous money-maker*).

Hain, *m.* (-(e)s, -e) (*Poet.*) grove, sylvan glade, bosket, boscage. **–ampfer,** *m.* blood-wort (*Rumex sanguineus*) (*Bot.*). **–buche,** *f.* hornbeam (*Carpinus betulus*) (*Bot.*). **–bund,** *m.* poetic coterie of Göttingen undergraduates 1770–4.

Häk–chen, *n.* (-s, –) little hook, crochet; apostrophe; **–(e)lig,** *adj.* hooked; barbed; prickly; (*dial.*) captious, critical, tricky. **–elarbeit,** *f.* crochet-work. **–elei,** *f.* crochet-work; chaffing, teasing, taunting, fault-finding, quarrelling. **–elgarn,** *n.* crochet-thread. **–elhaken,** *m.,* **–elnadel,** *f.* crochet-needle. **–eln,** 1. *v.a.* crochet. 2. *v.r.* attach o.s. to, cling, stick to, get caught up (*on a hook*); tease, chaff, taunt; censure.

Hak–en, 1. *m.* (-ens, -en) hook; grappling-iron; catch, difficulty; *die S. hat einen* or *ihren –en,* there is a catch *or* snag in it; *ein rechter –en,* a right hook (*Boxing*); (*Prov.*) *was ein –en* or *Häkchen werden will, krümmt sich beizeiten,* as the twig is bent the tree will grow; *–en schlagen,* double (*as hares*); take evasive action (*Av.*). 2. *v.a.* hook; grapple. 3. *v.r.* get caught *or* hooked up (*an,* on). 4. *v.n. & imp. da –t es,* there's the rub *or* the snag. **–enbüchse,** *f.* arquebus. **–enförmig,** *adj.* hooked. **–enkreuz,** *n.* swastika, fylfot. **–enkreuzler,** *m.* (*Austr.*) Nazi, Hitlerite. **–ennase,** *f.* aquiline *or* hooked nose. **–enschlüssel,** *m.* picklock. **–enspieß,** *m.* harpoon. **–enzahn,** *m.* canine *or* eye tooth. **–ig,** *adj.* hooked.

Halali, *int. & n.* (-s, -(s)) mort, kill, death (*hunting*). **–blasen,** *v.n.* sound a mort.

halb, 1. *adj.* half; (*as prefix*) semi-, demi-; *–e Fahrt,* half-speed (*Naut.*); *mit –em Ohre zuhören,* listen with half one's attention, listen inattentively; *zum –en Preise,* at half the price, (at) half-price; *es schlägt –,* the half-hour strikes; *diese Uhr schlägt voll und –,* this clock strikes the (full) hours and half-hours; *mit –er Stimme,* in an undertone; mezza voce (*Mus.*); *–e Stunde,* half an hour; *alle –en Stunden,* every half-hour; *der –e Ton,* semitone; *– so viel,* half as much; *– zehn,* half-past nine. 2. *adv.* by halves, half; *– und –,* so-so, middling; almost, tolerably; *– und – dazu entschlossen,* half decided on; *– so viel,* half as much; *noch –mal so viel,* half as much again; *noch (ein) –mal so groß (lang),* half as big (long) again; *weder – noch ganz,* neither one thing nor another. **–amtlich,** *adj.* semi-official. **–arier,** *m.* (*Nat. Soc.*) half-Jew (*distinguished from 'Halbjuden' by fact that Jewish parent was Christian at time of marriage*). **–art,** *f.* sub-species. **–batzig,** *adj.* (*Swiss dial.*) mediocre. **–bau,** *m., see* **–pacht.** **–befahren,** *adj.*; *–befahrenes Volk,* common (*i.e. not* able) seamen. **–bild,** *n.* half-length portrait, bust. **–bildung,** *f.* superficial culture; smattering of education. **–bleiche,** *f.* cream-colour, half-white, off-white. **–bruder,** *m.* half-brother. **–bürtig,** *adj.* half-caste; *–bürtige Geschwister,* (illegitimate) stepbrother *or* sister. **–dach,** *n.* lean-to roof. **–deck,** *n.* quarter-deck. **–deckend,** *adj.* semi-opaque. **–dunkel,** *n.* dusk, semi-darkness, twilight. **–durchlässig,** *adj.* semi-permeable. **–durchmesser,** *m.* radius. **–durchsichtig,** *adj.* semi-transparent. **–edelstein,** *m.* semi-precious stone. **–e (-r)** *or* **(-s)** *f., m. or n.* (-en) half, moiety; *ein –es bestellen,* order a small beer; *einen –en bestellen,* order half a litre of wine. **–er,** *prep.* (*with preceding Gen.*) for, on account of, on behalf of, because of, for the sake of; *sicherheits–er,* in order to be safe, for the sake of safety. **–erhaben,** *adj.* in basso relievo. **–flügler,** *m.pl.* hemiptera (*Ent.*). **–franzband,** *m.* half-calf binding. **–gar,** *adj.* underdone. **–geschoß,** *n.* entresol, mezzanine. **–gesicht,** *n.* profile. **–gott,** *m.* demigod. **–gut,** *n.* alloy of equal parts of tin and lead. **–heit,** *f.* incompleteness; imperfection; lukewarmness; indecision; supineness; superficiality. **–hemd,** *n.* front, dicky. **–hose,** *f.* knickerbockers; bloomers (*of women*) **–ieren,** *v.a.* cut in halves, halve, bisect. **–insel,** *f.* peninsula. **–jahr,** *n.* half-year, six months. **–jährig,** *adj.* lasting six months; six months old. **–jährlich,** *adj.* occurring every six months, half-yearly. **–kenner,** *m.* dabbler. **–kettenfahrzeug,** *n.* half-tracked vehicle. **–kreis,** *m.* semicircle. **–kreisförmig,** *adj.* semicircular. **–kugel,** *f.* hemisphere. **–lasierend,** *adj.* semi-transparent. **–laut,** *adj.* in an undertone. **–leder,** *n.* half-calf. **–ling,** *m.* half-breed, hybrid, mongrel. **–mensch,** *m.* demi-man; centaur; brute. **–messer,** *m.* radius. **–monatsschrift,** *f.* fortnightly (review *or* magazine). **–mond,** *m.* half-moon. **–pacht,** *f.* half-share farming. **–part,** *m.* halves; *auf –part eintreten,* go halves. **–pergamentband,** *m.* half-vellum. **–pferd,** *n.* centaur; meadow-sorrel. **–rund,** *adj.* semicircular. **–schatten,** *m.* half-shade, half-shadow, penumbra. **–scheid,** *f.,* (*dial.*) **–schied,** *f.* moiety, half. **–schlächtig,** *adj.* hybrid; undecisive. **–schlag,** *m.* mongrel, mixed breed. **-schreitig,** *adj.* chromatic (*Mus.*). **-schuh,** *m.* shoe. **-schürig,** *adj.* of second shearing; premature, imperfect; inferior; *-schüriges Lob*, half-hearted praise. **-schürigkeit,** *f.* inferiority; half-heartedness. **-seide,** *f.* silk mixed with cotton. **-seite,** *f.* half-page (*Typ.*). **-silber,** *n.* platina. **-sopran,** *m.* mezzo-soprano. **-stiefel,** *m.* ankle-boot. **-stocks,** *adv.* half-mast. **-strumpf,** *m.* sock. **-täglich,** *adj.* occurring twice a day; lasting twelve hours. **-trauer,** *f.* half-mourning. **-uniform,** *f.* undress uniform. **-verdeck,** *n.* quarter-deck. **-vers,** *m.* half-line, hemistich. **-vokal,** *m.* semi-vowel. **-wagen,** *m.* chaise. **-wegs,** *adv.* half-way; (*coll.*) tolerably, to a certain extent. **-welt,** *f.* demi-monde. **-wisserei,** *f.* superficial *or* imperfect knowledge. **-zeit,** *f.* half-time (*Sport*). **-zug,** *m.* half-platoon (*Mil.*).

Halde, *f.* (-n) (*Poet.*) slope, declivity, hill-side; slag-heap, dump.

half, *see* **helfen.**

Halfa, *f.* esparto grass, alpha grass.

Hälfte, *f.* (-n) half, moiety; middle; *bessere –*, better half, wife; *um die – teurer*, half as dear again.

Halfter, *f.* (-n) *Austr. sometimes m. or n.* (-s, –) halter. **-geld,** *n.* groom's gratuity at the purchase of a horse. **-n,** *v.a.* put the halter on. **-tasche,** *f.* holster.

Hall, *m.* (-(e)s, -e) sound, resonance, peal, clang, acoustics. **-en,** *v.n.* (*aux.* h.) sound, resound, echo, clang.

Hall-e, *f.* (-en) hall, great room; public room; market, bazaar, large shop; covered court (*Tenn.*); hangar (*Av.*); *Trink-e*, pump-room (*at a watering-place*). **-enbad,** *n.* indoor baths.

Hallig, *f.*, **Halling,** *f.* (-en) *dial.* small island (*Schleswig-Holstein*).

hallo, 1. *int.* hullo! 2. *n.* (*coll.*) hullabaloo, din.

Halm, *m.* (-(e)s, -e) blade; stalk, stem, straw; *Getreide auf dem –*, green corn; standing corn. **-früchte,** *f.pl.* cereals. **-ig,** *adj.* stalky. **-knoten,** *m.* joint *or* node of a stalk. **-lese,** *f.* **gleaning.** **-ziehen,** *n.* drawing lots.

Halogen, *n.* (-s, -e) halogen, halide of, haloid (*Chem.*). **-ieren,** *v.a.* halinate, halogenate. **-silber,** *n.* haloid silver. **-id,** *n.* (-s, -e), **-verbindung,** *f.* halogen compound.

Hals, *m.* (-es, ⸚e) neck; throat; tongue (*voice of a hound*); *einem den – abdrehen* or *abschneiden*, bring a p. to ruin; *sich* (*Dat.*) *die Schwindsucht an den – ärgern*, worry o.s. into a decline; *am – aufhängen*, hang by the neck; *das geht ihm an den –*, that may cost him his head; *sich* (*Dat.*) *etwas an den – reden*, bring s.th. upon o.s. by inconsiderate talk; *sich einem an den – werfen*, thrust *or* force o.s. on a p.; *etwas auf dem -e haben*, be troubled, encumbered *or* plagued with a th.; *sich* (*Dat.*) *etwas auf den – laden* or *ziehen*, bring a th. upon o.s., bring s.th. down on one's head; *auf dem -e sitzen*, importune, be a burden to; *aus vollem -e*, heartily, with all one's might; *aus vollem -e schreien*, scream at the top of one's voice; *bis an den –*, up to the eyes; *böser –*, sore throat; *den – brechen*, break one's neck; *einem den – brechen*, ruin a p.; *einer Flasche den – brechen*, crack a bottle; *– geben*, give tongue; *es wird ja nicht den – kosten*, it is not a matter of life and death *or* a vital *or* serious *or* hanging matter; *einen langen – machen*, crane one's neck; *die Lüge blieb ihm im -e stecken*, the lie stuck in his throat; *einem über den – kommen*, surprise a p.; *über – und Kopf*, headlong; *– über Kopf*, head over heels, precipitately; *einem um den – fallen*, fall on a p.'s neck, embrace a p.; *es geht um den –*, it is a matter of life and death, it is a vital issue; *einem den – umdrehen*, wring a p.'s neck; *er kann den – nicht voll genug kriegen*, he is insatiable; *bleiben Sie mir damit vom -e*, don't pester me with that; *sich* (*Dat.*) *vom -e schaffen*, rid o.s. of; *das wächst mir zum -e heraus*, I am sick and tired of that. **-abschneider,** *m.* cut-throat; usurer. **-abschneiderisch,** *adj.* cut-throat (*competition*). **-ader,** *f.* jugular vein. **-arterie,** *f.* carotid artery. **-band,** *n.* collar; necklace. **-bein,** *n.* collar-bone, clavicle. **– und Beinbruch!** (*hum.*) good luck! all the best! **-binde,** *f.* neck-tie, cravat, scarf. **-bräune,** *f.* quinsy. **-brechen,** *n.* breakneck exploit. **-brechend,** *adj.*, **-brecherisch,** *adj.* breakneck, dangerous, perilous. **-brüchig,** *adj.* capital (*crime*). **-dreher,** *m.* wryneck (*Jynx tortilla*) (*Orn.*). **-drüse,** *f.* tonsil. **-e,** *f.*, *see* **-ung.** **-eisen,** *n.* iron collar, pillory. **-en,** *v.a.* (*archaic*) embrace; gybe (*Naut.*). **-entzündung,** *f.* tonsillitis, angina, sore throat. **-gehänge,** *n.* necklace, pendant. **-gericht,** *n.* capital court. **-geschmeide,** *n.* necklace. **-kappe,** *f.* cowl. **-koppel,** *f.* yoke. **-krause,** *f.* frill, ruff (*for the neck*). **-recht,** *n.* power over life and death. **-röhre,** *f.* wind-pipe, trachea. **-sache,** *f.* matter of life and death. **-schlagader,** *f.*, *see* **-arterie.** **-schleife,** *f.* (neck-)tie, cravat. **-schlinge,** *f.* noose. **-schmuck,** *m.* necklace. **-starre,** *f.* stiffness of the neck. **-starrig,** *adj.* stiff-necked, stubborn, obstinate, headstrong. **-starrigkeit,** *f.* obstinacy, stubbornness. **-stimme,** *f.* falsetto. **-strafe,** *f.* capital punishment. **-stück,** *n.* neck (*of meat*). **-sucht,** *f.* bronchitis. **-tuch,** *n.* scarf, neckerchief, muffler. **-ung,** *f.* (*dial.*) dog collar, leash (*Hunt.*). **-verbrechen,** *n.* capital crime. **-weh,** *n.* sore throat. **-wirbel,** *m.* cervical vertebra. **-zäpfchen,** *n.* uvula.

Halt, 1. *m.* (-(e)s, -e) hold, holding; footing, support; stability, firmness; purchase; stop, halt; *Mensch ohne inneren –*, unbalanced, vacillating *or* unstable p.; *– geben*, support; *– machen*, stop, halt. 2. *adv.* & *part.* (*dial.*) in my opinion, I think; *er wird – nicht kommen*, I don't think he will come; *er ist – ein Bummler*, he is a loafer when all is said and done. **-bar,** *adj.* tenable, defensible; strong, firm, stable; durable, lasting, permanent, fast; valid. **-barkeit,** *f.* defensibility; durability, stability, firmness; strength, endurance, wear; validity. **-egurt,** *m.* parachute harness. **-ekabel,** *n.* mooring rope. **-en,** 1. *ir.v.a.* hold, keep, retain; detain, keep back, constrain; contain, include; observe, perform, celebrate; endure, hold out against; think, deem, consider; *das Abendmahl -en*, celebrate *or* administer Holy Communion; *auf eine S. -en*, insist upon a th., lay stress upon a th.; *große Stücke auf einen -en*, think highly *or* make much of a p.; *er hält auf frische Luft*, he is particular about fresh air, (*coll.*) he is a fresh-air fiend; *ein Auto -en*, keep *or* run a car; *Freundschaft -en*, live on friendly terms; *Frieden -en*, keep peace; *-en für*, look upon *or* as, consider, think, take to be; *-en gegen*, hold against, contrast with; *er hält sein Auto gut*, he keeps his car in good order, he maintains his car well; *Hochzeit -en*, celebrate one's marriage; *in Ehren -en*, hold in honour; *in Ordnung -en*, keep in order; *Inventur -en*, take stock; *Mahlzeit -en*, dine, sup, be at table; *es mit einem -en*, side with a p.; *Mund -en*, not divulge, keep one's mouth shut; *eine Note -en*, sustain a note (*Mus.*); *rechts* (*links*) *-en!* keep to the right (left)! *eine Rede -en*, make *or* deliver a speech, speak (*in public*); *einen schadlos -en*, indemnify a p.; *sich schadlos -en*, recover one's losses; *Schritt -en*, keep pace, walk in step; *Stich -en*, stand the test; *ein Kind über die Taufe -en*, stand sponsor to a child; *Vorlesungen -en*, deliver *or* give lectures; *Wasser -en*, be watertight; *-en Sie das wie Sie wollen*, please yourself (about that); *einen bei seinem Worte -en*, hold *or* keep a p. to his word; *im Zaume -en*, keep a tight hand on; *eine Zeitschrift -en*, subscribe to a periodical; *eine Zeitung -en*, take in a newspaper; *einen zum besten -en*, tease, make a fool of *or* deceive s.o.; *-en zu Gnaden*, (*archaic*) at your pleasure; *ich -e ihm das zugute*, I excuse that in him. 2. *v.n.* (*aux.* h.) stop, halt; hold out, stand firm; insist on; *-en an*, stick *or* adhere to; *an sich -en*, restrain o.s.; *auf seine Ehre -en*, be jealous of one's honour; *auf Träume -en*, believe in dreams; (*coll.*) *dicht -en*, keep quiet about, keep one's mouth shut; *das Eis hält noch nicht*, the ice does not bear yet; *das kann nicht lange -en*, that cannot last long; *es hält schwer*, it is difficult; *der Stoff hält nicht*, the material does not wear well; *ich -e nicht viel von ihm*, I do not think much of him. 3. *v.r.* hold out, last, keep good; behave; take (good *or* bad) care of o.s.; *ich hielt mich an ihn*, I depended upon him *or* relied on him; *sich bereit -en*, hold o.s. in readiness; *die Festung hält sich*, the fortress holds out; *sich links -en*, keep to the left; *die Preise -en sich*, prices remain steady; *das Wetter hält sich*, the weather continues fair (*or* bad); *sich zu Hause -en*, stay at home *or* indoors; (*sich*) *zu einer Partei -en*, hold with *or* support a party; *gehalten*, bound, obliged, reserved, sustained, supported, sober, staid, calm. **-eplatz,** *m. see* **-estelle. -epunkt,** *m.* aiming point, point of aim; halt (= *small station*) (*Railw.*). **-er,** *m.* holder, keeper, owner; hold, support, clamp; reservoir, receptacle; (*coll.*) penholder. **-estelle,** *f.* stopping place, stop, halting place, resting place; *-estelle für Taxis*, taxi-stand. **-etau,** *n.* guy-rope. **-ezahn,** *m.* catch, pin. **-ig,** *adj.*, yielding, rich (*of ore*); *as a suffix* (*in compounds* =) holding, containing, *e.g.* **eisen-ig,** *adj.* **erz-ig,** *adj.* containing iron *or* ore. **-los,** *adj.* without support, unstable, unsteady, loose, straggling; rootless; vain; unprincipled. **-losigkeit,** *f.* instability, unsteadiness; emptiness; want of principle(s). **-machen,** *v.n.*, *see* **Halt machen. -nagel,** *m.* linch-pin. **-signal,** *n.* block-signal. **-ung,** *f.* holding, keeping, maintenance, support, prop; bearing, attitude, conduct, behaviour, morale; deportment, carriage, posture; mien; fulfilling, delivery (*of speeches, etc.*); harmony (*of colour, etc.*); *Charakter ohne sittliche -ung*, unstable character; *mit -ung*, with restraint, composedly; *-ung bewahren*, maintain one's self-control; *-ung der Börse*, state of 'Change, feeling on 'Change; *-ung einer Zeitung*, (political) attitude *or* standpoint of a paper. **-ungslos,** *adj.* unsteady, unprincipled.

hältst, hält, *see* **halten.**

Halunke, *m.* (-n, -n) rascal, scamp.

Hämatit, *m.* (-s, -e) blood-stone.

Hamen, 1. *m.* (-s, –) fishing-hook; fishing *or* prawning net. 2. *v.a.* net.

Hamfel, Hampfel, *f.* (*dial.*) handful.

hämisch, *adj.* malicious, mischievous, spiteful; *-es Wesen*, malice, spitefulness; *-es Lachen*, mischievous *or* sardonic laugh; *-e Freude*, malignant joy.

Hämling, *m.* (-s, -e) eunuch.

Hammel, *m.* (-s, – & ¨) wether; mutton; *süßer –*, duck, pet (*of a child*); (*coll.*) *um auf besagten – zurückzukommen*, to return to our subject. **-braten,** *m.* roast mutton. **-fleisch,** *n.* mutton, lamb. **-keule,** *f.* leg of mutton. **-rippchen,** *n.pl.* mutton chops. **-schlegel,** *m.* leg of mutton. **-sprung,** *m.* division (*Parl.*). **-talg,** *m.* mutton dripping, mutton suet.

Hammer, *m.* (-s, ¨) hammer; forge; knocker; malleus (*of ear*) (*Anat.*); *zwischen – und Amboß*, twixt the devil and the deep blue sea; *unter den – kommen*, come under the hammer, come up for auction. **-bahn,** *f.* face of a hammer. **-eisen,** *n.* hammered iron, wrought iron. **-fisch,** *m.*, **-hai,** *m.* hammer-headed shark. **-herr,** *m.* owner of a foundry. **-hütte,** *f.* forge; ironworks. **-schlag,** *m.* stroke with a hammer; hammer-scale, iron oxide. **-schloß,** *n.* percussion-lock. **-schmied,** *m.* blacksmith. **-stiel,** *m.* handle of a hammer. **-werfen,** *n.* throwing the hammer (*Sport*). **-werk,** *n.* foundry, ironworks.

hämmer-bar, *adj.* malleable. **-er,** *m.* hammerer. **-lein,** *n.*, **-ling,** *m.* gnome; demon; merry Andrew; *Meister -lein, Meister -ling*, Jack Ketch, hangman. **-n,** *v.a.* & *n.* (*aux.* h.) hammer, forge.

Hämorrhoid-en, *f.pl.* **-alknoten,** *m. pl.* haemorrhoids, piles.

Hampel-mann, *m.* (-(e)s, ¨er) jumping Jack, puppet. **-n,** *v.n.* (*aux.* h.) dither, prance about, flounder.

Hamster, *m.* (-s, –) hamster, German marmot (*Zool.*); hoarder (*of food, etc.*). **-er,** *m.* hoarder. **-n,** *v.a.* hoard.

Hand, *f.* (¨e) hand; handwriting; side, direction; source, origin; (*pl.*) workmen; *die letzte – an eine S. anlegen*, give *or* put the finishing touch *or* touches to a th.; *– anlegen* (*an etwas*), set to work (upon s.th.); *an Händen und Füßen gebunden*, bound hand and foot; *ein Kind an der – führen*, lead a child by the hand; *einem etwas an – geben* (*C.L.*), place s.th. at a p.'s disposal; *einem an die – gehen*, see *zur – gehen*; *einen an der – haben*, have s.o. to hand (*ready to give assistance*); *– an sich legen*, commit suicide; *an – von*, with the aid of, on the basis of, by means of; *auf eigene –*, on one's own responsibility; at one's expense; *auf die – geben*, pay into a p.'s hand, give earnest; *auf Händen und Füßen laufen*, go on all fours; *es liegt* (*klar*) *auf der –*, it is very plain *or* obvious; *einem auf die – sehen*, watch a p. closely; *auf* (*den*) *Händen tragen*, treat with great tenderness, do all one can for a p.; *aus der –*, quickly, adroitly; *Nachricht aus erster –*, first-hand information; *aus freier –*, spontaneously, voluntarily; *etwas aus der – geben*, waive one's rights to a th., leave a th. to others; *ich habe es aus guter –*, I have it on good authority; *aus* (or *von*) *der – in den Mund leben*, live from hand to mouth; *aus öffentlicher –*, from public funds; *einem etwas aus den Händen spielen*, make a p. lose a th.; *aus zweiter – kaufen*, buy second-hand; *die – ballen*, clench one's fist; *bei der –*, at hand, in readiness; *er ist stets mit der Antwort bei der –*, he is always ready with an answer, he always has an answer pat; *flache –*, palm of the hand; *freie –*, liberty of action; *– und Fuß haben*, be to the purpose, be well set up, be well said *or* done, be to the point; *das hat weder – noch Fuß*, I can make neither head nor tail of it; *darauf gebe ich* (*dir*) *die –*, I promise it, here's my hand on it; *sich* or *einander die Hände geben*, shake hands; *hinter der –*, saved, laid by; past, subsequently; *Hände hoch!* hands up! *hohle –*, palm of the hand; *fest in der –*, in *or* under one's control, (*coll.*) under one's thumb; *in die Hände klatschen*, clap one's hands; *schwer in der – liegen*, pull hard at the bit; *in die – nehmen*, undertake (the direction *or* execution of); *einem etwas in die Hände spielen*, help a p. to gain a th. (*without one's assistance being apparent*); *seine Hände im Spiel haben*, have a hand *or* finger in the affair; *in andere Hände übergehen*, fall into other hands; *küß die Hand* (*Austrian form of greeting ladies*); *an die linke – antrauen lassen*, contract a morganatic marriage; *Ehe zu linken –*, left-handed *or* morganatic marriage; *milde –*, generosity; *Geld mit vollen Händen ausgeben*, spend money extravagantly *or* recklessly; *das ist mit Händen zu greifen*, that is quite obvious, (*coll.*) that sticks out a mile *or* is as clear as daylight; *mit leeren Händen*, empty-handed; *mit stürmender –*, by storm, by assault; *nach der – kaufen*, buy in the lump; *die Hände in den Schoß legen*, do nothing, remain idle; *tote –*, mortmain (*Law*); *über die – mit*, not on good terms with; *unter der –*, privately, underhand; *unter den Händen haben*, have in hand; *einem unter die Hände kommen*, fall into a p.'s power; *alle Hände voll zu tun haben*, have one's hands full; *die – abziehen von*, abandon, withdraw support from; *von der – gehen*, be easy, quick *or* off-hand; *die Arbeit geht von der –*, the work progresses rapidly; *von guter –*, on good authority; *von der – schlagen* or *weisen*, reject *or* refuse out of hand; *vor der –*, for the present, just now; meanwhile; *vor die – nehmen*, take in hand, set to work; (*Prov.*) *eine – wäscht die andere*, one good turn deserves another; *einem zur – gehen*, give a p. a helping hand; *zur linken – antrauen*, see *an die linke –*; *zur – sein*, be at hand *or* ready. **-anlasser,** *m.* hand *or* self-starter (*Motor.*). **-anlegung,** *f.* seizure (*Law*). **-arbeit,** *f.* manual work *or* labour; needlework. **-arbeiter,** *m.* mechanic; workman, manual labourer. **-auf,** *n.* knock-on (*Rugby football*). **-aufheben,** *n.* show of hands. **-ausgabe,** *f.* pocket-edition. **-ballen,** *m.* ball of the thumb. **-baum,** *m.* lever. **-becken,** *n.* wash-handbasin. **-beil,** *n.* hatchet. **-bewegung,** *f.* gesture, gesticulation. **-bibliothek,** *f.* reference library. **-bohrer,** *m.* gimlet. **-breit,** *adj.* of a hand's breadth. **-bremse,** *f.* hand-brake (*Motor.*). **-buch,** *n.* handbook, manual, cyclopaedia; compendium, vademecum; *-buch für Reisende*, travellers' guide; *-buch des feinen Tons*, guide to etiquette. **-decke,** *f.* small cover; saddle-cloth. **-dienst,** *m.* service by manual labour. **-druck,** *m.* manual pressure. **-eisen,** *n.* handcuff; *einem -eisen anlegen* manacle *or* handcuff a p. **-el,** *m.*, *see* **Handel** *and* *compounds.* **-exemplar,** *n.* author's copy; copy in regular use. **-fackel,** *f.* torch. **-fäustel,** *m.* miner's hammer. **-fertig,** *adj.* skilful with one's hands. **-fertigkeit,** *f.* manual skill *or* dexterity. **-fesseln,** *f.pl.* handcuffs. **-fest,** *adj.* strong, sturdy, stalwart; binding; *einen -fest machen,* take a p. into custody; *-festes Pferd,* manageable horse; a horse well broken in; *-feste Lüge,* convincing lie. **-feste,** *f.* bond, affidavit (*Law*), (*archaic*) signed and sealed document. **-feuerwaffe,** *f.* rifle, pistol, etc.; *-feuerwaffen,* small-arms. **-fläche,** *f.* palm *or* flat of the hand. **-förmig,** *adj.* hand-shaped. **-galopp,** *m.* canter. **-gebrauch,** *m.* daily use. **-geld,** *n.* earnest; bounty (*Mil.*); pocket-money; deposit, advance (*C.L.*). **-gelenk,** *n.* wrist; *etwas aus dem -gelenk schütteln,* do s.th. with remarkable ease *or* without preparation. **-gemein,** *adv.* hand to hand; in close combat; grappling; *-gemein werden,* come to blows *or* close quarters, grapple. **-gemenge,** *n.* hand-to-hand fight, scrimmage, scuffle, affray. **-gepäck,** *n.* hand- *or* portable luggage. **-gerecht,** *adj., see* **-lich.** **-geschöpft,** *adj.* hand-made (*paper*). **-gewehr,** *n., see* **-waffe.** **-granate,** *f.* hand-grenade. **-greiflich,** *adj.* palpable, obvious, evident; downright. **-griff,** *m.* handle; grip, hold, grasp; manipulation; sleight of hand; knack. **-habe,** *f.* handle; hold; (*fig.*) ways and means, pretext, chance. **-haben,** *ir. v.a.* (*insep.*) handle, manipulate; manage, operate; deal with, administer; maintain; *gut zu -haben,* handy, easily handled *or* managed. **-habung,** *f.* handling; use, operation, management; administration. **-karren,** *m.* hand-barrow, hand-cart, truck. **-kauf,** *m.* purchase in the lump; retail *or* cash transaction. **-klapper,** *f.* castanet. **-koffer,** *m.* portmanteau, suit-case. **-korb,** *m.* work-basket; hand-basket. **-krause,** *f.* wrist-ruffle. **-kurbel,** *f.* crank handle. **-kuß,** *m.* kissing of the hand. **-langer,** *m.* handyman, helper; jobber, under-worker, workman's mate; drudge, hack. **-langerdienst,** *m.* work of an underling, fetching and carrying; work of a literary hack; drudgery. **-lehen,** *n.* free *or* hereditary fief. **-leiter,** *f.* small ladder, stepladder, steps. **-leuchter,** *m.* portable candlestick. **-lexikon,** *n.* pocket dictionary. **-lich,** *adj.* easily managed, tractable; handy, manageable, wieldy; moderate. **-lohn,** *m.* wages of manual labour. **-maschinengewehr,** *n.* sub-machine gun, tommy gun. **-mehr,** *n.* majority (*by show of hands*); *durch offnes -mehr gewählt,* elected by show of hands. **-nähmaschine,** *f.* hand sewing-machine. **-pferd,** *n.* right-hand (*or* near-side) horse of a team; led horse. **-pflege,** *f.* manicure. **-reichung,** *f.* charity; help, aid. **-rücken,** *m.* back of the hand. **-schellen,** *f.pl.* handcuffs, manacles. **-schlag,** *m.* shaking hands (*as a pledge*). **-schreiben,** *n.* autograph-letter; autograph. **-schrift,** *f.* handwriting; signature; manuscript; bond. **-schriftendeutung,** *f.* graphology. **-schriftenkunde,** *f.* palaeography. **-schriftlich,** *adj.* in manuscript; in writing; in long hand. **-schuh,** *m.* glove; *den -schuh aufnehmen,* accept the challenge. **-schuhmacher,** *m.* glover. **-schuldschein,** *m.* promissory note. **-schwärmer,** *m.* squib (*Firew.*). **-seite,** *f.* near side (*in driving, etc.*). **-siegel,** *n.* signet. **-spake,** *f.* capstan bar (*Naut.*). **-spiel,** *n.* keys in an organ. **-steuerung,** *f.* hand-change (*of gears*) (*Motor.*). **-streich,** *m.* coup de main, sudden attack, surprise onslaught. **-stück,** *n.* specimen of a handy size. **-tasche,** *f.* (lady's) handbag; attaché case. **-tasten,** *f.pl.* finger-board (*Mus.*). **-teller,** *m.* palm of the hand. **-trommel,** *f.* tambourine. **-tuch,** *n.* towel. **-tuchdrell,** *m.* towelling. **-umdrehen,** *n.* instant, moment; *im -umdrehen,* in a flash, in the twinkling of an eye, (*coll.*) in a jiffy. **-verkäufer,** *m.* retailer. **-versuch,** *m.* small scale test. **-voll,** *f.* handful. **-vollweise,** *adv.* by *or* in handfuls. **-waffen,** *f.pl.* small-arms. **-wagen,** *m.* hand-cart, barrow. **-wahrsager,** *m.* chiromancer. **-wahrsagerei,** *f.* palmistry, chiromancy. **-warm,** *adj.* luke-warm, tepid. **-weberei,** *f.* hand-loom weaving. **-werk,** *n.* handicraft; trade; calling; guild; *er ist seines -werks ein Schneider,* he is a tailor by trade; *ein -werk betreiben,* follow a trade; *einem das -werk legen,* forbid a p. to exercise his trade; put a stop to a p.'s activities; *einem ins -werk pfuschen,* encroach upon a p.'s business, compete with a p.; *sein -werk verstehen,* understand one's business, be up to one's work; (*Prov.*) *-werk hat goldenen Boden,* trade lays the foundation for all prosperity. **-werker,** *m.* mechanic, artisan; workman. **-werkerstand,** *m.* labouring class, artisans. **-werkerverein,** *m.* working men's club. **-werksälteste(r),** *m.* president of a corporation, master of a guild. **-werksbursche,** *m.* travelling artisan, journeyman. **-werksgenoß,** *m.* fellow-tradesman. **-werksinnung,** *f.* guild. **-werksjunge,** *m.* apprentice. **-werksleute,** *pl.* artisans, craftsmen, mechanics. **-werksmäßig,** *adj.* mechanical, by rote, by rule of thumb, without thinking; professionally, workmanlike. **-werksmeister,** *m.* master-mechanic. **-werkszeug,** *n.* tools, instruments. **-werkszunft,** *f.* guild. **-wörterbuch,** *n.* pocket dictionary. **-wurzel,** *f.* wrist. **-zeichen,** *n.* monogram; initials, mark (*in lieu of signature*). **-zeichnung,** *f.* drawing, sketch, preliminary study (*for a painting, etc.*).

Händ-edruck, *m.* clasp of the hand, handshake. **-eklatschen,** *n.* clapping of hands, applause. **-eringen,** *n.* wringing of the hands (*despair or embarrassment*). **-espiel,** *n.* gesticulation. **-ewaschen,** *n.* washing the hands. **-ig,** *suffix* (*in compounds* =) -handed.

Handel, *m.* (-s, ¨) trade, traffic, commerce; transaction, business; affair; lawsuit, action; bargain; (*pl.*) difference, quarrel, dispute, fray; *abgekarteter* –, got-up *or* staged *or* preconcerted affair; *den – aufkündigen* or *aufsagen,* go back on *or* break a bargain; *– mit dem Auslande,* foreign trade; *in den – bringen,* put on the market; *ein böser* –, a bad business; *einen – mit einem eingehen,* make a bargain with s.o.; *sich in einen – einlassen,* see *einen – schließen*; *– im Großen,* wholesale trade; *nicht im* –, not for sale; privately printed and published; *– im Kleinen,* retail trade; *in den – kommen,* be put on the market; *einen – machen,* see *einen – schließen*; *den – an sich reißen,* capture the market; *einen – schließen,* make *or* conclude a bargain; *Händel mit einem suchen,* pick a quarrel with a p.; *– treiben,* trade; *– und Wandel,* trade in general; general behaviour. **-n,** 1. *v.n.* (*aux.* h.) behave, act; treat (*von,* of); bargain, negotiate, haggle (*um,* about *or* for); deal, trade, traffic (*mit,* in); *mit sich -n lassen,* be easy to deal with; be ready to bargain; *er hat wie ein Vater an mir gehandelt,* he has been *or* acted like a father to me; *ich werde gegen Sie so -n, wie Sie gegen mich -n,* I will treat you as you treat me; *als es zu -n galt,* when it came to the point, when the moment came to act; *hier wird nicht gehandelt,* prices are fixed, no reduction; *erst -n und dann reden,* act first and talk afterwards; *die -nden Personen des Dramas,* the characters appearing in the play. 2. *v.r. & imp. es -t sich um,* the question is, it is a question of; *um was -t es sich?* what is the point in question, what is it all about? *wovon -n die Aufsätze?* what is the subject of the essays? **-sabgabe,** *f.* duty. **-sadreßbuch,** *n.* commercial *or* trade directory. **-samt,** *n.* Board of Trade. **-sangelegenheit,** *f.* trade matter. **-sartikel,** *m.* commodity, merchandise; (*pl.*) goods. **-sausdruck,** *m.* commercial term. **-sbeflissene(r),** *m.* (merchant's *or* commercial) clerk, apprentice in a business house. **-sbericht,** *m.* commercial report, trade returns. **-sbilanz,** *f.* balance of trade. (*C.L.*) **-sbillett,** *n.* note. **-sblatt,** *n.* trade journal. **-sbrief,** *m.* commercial letter. **-sbuch,** *n.* ledger; account-book. **-sbündnis,** *n.* trading agreement. **-seinig,** *adj.*, **-seins,** *adj.* in agreement; *-seinig werden,* come to terms. **-sfach,** *n.* line of business, branch of trade. **-sfaktorei,** *f.* trading post. **-sfirma,** *f.* commercial firm. **-sflagge,** *f.* merchant flag. **-sflotte,** *f.* merchant shipping, mercantile marine. **-sflugwesen,** *n.* civil aviation. **-sfreiheit,** *f.* free trade; freedom of trade. **-sfreund,** *m.* business colleague, correspondent. **-sgärtner,** *m.* market-gardner, florist. **-sgeist,** *m.* commercial spirit, business mind. **-sgenoß,** *m.* partner. **-sgenossenschaft,** *f.* partnership; trading company. **-sgericht,** *n.* (commercial) arbitration tribunal, commercial court. **-sgeschäft,** *m.* commercial *or* business transaction; commercial firm *or* undertaking. **-sgesellschaft,** *f.* trading company; partnership in trade. **-sgesetz,** *n.* commercial law. **-sgesetzbuch,** *n.* commercial code. **-sgesetzgebung,** *f.* commercial legislation. **-sgewicht,** *n.* avoirdupois weight. **-shaus,** *n.* business house, trading firm. **-sherr,** *m.* business magnate, head of a commercial house. **-shochschule,** *f.* commercial college. **-skammer,** *f.* Chamber of Commerce. **-skapital,** *n.* stock in trade; trading capital. **-skollegium,** *n.* Board of Trade. **-skorrespondent,** *m.* city correspondent (*newspaper*). **-skorrespondenz,** *f.* commercial correspondence. **-skreise,** *m.pl.* the merchants, business circles, the commercial world. **-skrieg,** *m.* economic warfare. **-skrise,** *f.* trade crisis. **-slage,** *f.* state of trade. **-sleute,** *pl.* tradespeople; merchants. **-smann,** *m.* merchant; business man; trader, dealer. **-smarine,** *f.* merchant navy. **-sministerium,** *n.*, (**-sminister,** *m.*) Ministry (Minister) of Commerce (*Germany*); (President of the) Board of Trade (*England*); Department of (Secretary of) Commerce (*America*). **-splatz,** *m.* trading centre, centre of commerce. **-spolitik,** *f.* trade *or* commercial policy. **-srat,** *m.* (member of) Board of Trade. **-srecht,** *n.* commercial law; trading licence. **-sregister,** *n.* commercial register-general; *Eintragung in das -register,* (certificate of) incorporation (of joint-stock companies). **-sreise,** *f.* business journey *or* trip. **-sreisende(r),** *m.* commercial traveller; *Gasthof für -sreisende,* commercial hotel. **-ssache,** *f.* commercial affair; lawsuit relating to commerce. **-schiedsgericht,** *n.* commercial court of arbitration. **-sschiff,** *n.* merchantman, trading-vessel, trader, tramp (steamer). **-sschiffahrt,** *f.* merchant marine *or* shipping. **-sschule,** *f.* commercial school. **-ssperre,** *f.* embargo on trade. **-sstand,** *m.* the business classes; the merchants, the commercial world. **-sstatistik,** *f.* Board of Trade returns. **-sstörer,** *m.* surface raider. **-süblich,** *adj.* in normal commercial usage. **-sumsatz,** *m.* trade turnover. **-sverbindung,** *f.*, **-sverein,** *m.* commercial union. **-sverbindungen,** *f.pl.* business connexions. **-sverbot,** *n., see* **-ssperre.** **-sverkehr,** *m.* business dealings. **-sverordnung,** *f.* trading regulation. **-svertrag,** *m.* commercial treaty, trade agreement. **-svertreter,** *m.* commercial representative, consul. **-svorrat,** *m.* stock in trade. **-swaren,** *f. pl.* merchandise, commodities. **-swechsel,** *m.* trade-bill. **-sweg,** *m.* trade-route; (*pl.*) trade channels. **-swesen,** *n.* commerce, trade, business. **-szeichen,** *n.* trade-mark, brand. **-szweig,** *m.* branch of trade, line of business. **-treibend,** *adj.* trading, commercial.

Händ-el, *pl. of* Handel; **-ler,** *m.* (-s, -) dealer, merchant, trader, retailer; *fliegender -ler,* hawker; (*often in compounds,* e.g. *Kohlen-ler, m.* coal-dealer; *Tee-ler, m.* tea-merchant; *Fisch-ler, m.* fishmonger). **-elsucht,** *f.* quarrelsomeness, pugnacity. **-elsüchtig,** *adj.* quarrelsome, pugnacious.

Handlung, *f.* (-en) action, deed, performance, act, transaction; business, trade, commerce; shop; firm; *dramatische -,* plot (*of a play*); *heilige -,* religious observance (*mass, christening, etc.*); *strafbare -,* punishable offence; *Blumen-,* flower shop; *Drogen-,* chemist's shop. **-sgehilfe,** *m.* clerk (*in a shop*). **-sgesetz,** *n., see* **Handelsgesetz.** **-sinhaber** *m.* proprietor of a shop, merchant. **-sreisende(r),** *m.* commercial traveller. **-sspesen,** *pl.*, **-sunkosten,** *pl.* business expenses. **-sweise,** *f.* mode of procedure, action *or* operation; way of acting, attitude, conduct, behaviour. **-szeichen,** *n.* trade-mark.

hanebüchen, *adj., see* **hagebüchen.**

Hanf, *m.* hemp (*Cannabis sativa*) (*Bot.*); *im - sitzen,* be in clover, sit pretty. **-bau,** *m.* hemp-culture. **-en,** *adj,* hempen. **-öl,** *n.* hemp-seed oil. **-samen,** *m.* hemp-seed.

hänf-en, *adj.* hempen. **-ling,** *m.* linnet (*Linota cannabina*) (*Orn.*).

Hang, *m.* (-(e)s, ⸚e) slope, incline, declivity; inclination, bias, propensity; bent, disposition; *einen - zu etwas haben,* be prone *or* inclined to a th. *or* to do a th. **-en,** *ir.v.n.* (*aux.* h. & s.) (*in the pres. tense the correct forms of this verb have practically disappeared from colloquial speech, and are replaced by forms of* hängen) hang, be suspended, dangle (*an with Dat.,* from); slope; cling, adhere; catch, clog, stick, be caught; be pending, remain undecided; be attached, given *or* devoted (*an with Dat.,* to); turn upon, depend on; *bis zu* or *auf etwas -en,* hang down to; *an einem Haar -en,* hang by a thread; *alles was drum und dran hing,* everything connected with it; (*coll.*) *er hängt bei mir,* he owes me money.

Hangel-, (*in compounds*). **-leiter,** *f.* horizontal ladder (*Gymn.*). **-n,** *v.n.* travel along a horizontal bar hanging by the hands (*Gymn.*). **-tau,** *n.* rope horizontally suspended (*Gymn.*).

häng-en, 1. *v.a.* cause to hang, hang (up), suspend, attach, fasten; (*coll.*) *den Mantel nach dem Winde -en,* sail with the wind, be a time-server; *einem den Brotkorb höher -en,* keep s.o. on short commons; *sein Herz an eine S. -en,* set one's heart on a th. 2. *v.n.* (*aux.* h.) (*in pres. tense see note under* **hangen**) *aneinander-en,* hang *or* stick together, be firmly attached to one another; *sehr am Gelde -en,* be very fond of money; (*coll.*) *an der Strippe -en,* have a long telephone call, hang on to the line; *-en bleiben,* catch, be caught on, get *or* be stuck; not to advance, remain pending; *die S. bleibt -en,* there's a hitch in the matter, the affair does not quite come off; *-en lassen,* give up, discontinue, let drop; (*sl.*) *mit einem -en,* have a quarrel with s.o. 3. *v.r.* hang o.s.; *sich an einen -en,* hang round s.o.'s neck, pursue *or* pester a p.; *sich an etwas -en,* depend *or* rely on a th. **-e,** *f.* drying room, loft, tenter (*Weav.*). **-ebauch,** *m.* paunch, pot-belly. **-eboden,** *m.* drying-loft, hanging-loft. **-ebrücke** *f.* suspension-bridge. **-egerüst,** *n.* hanging scaffold. **-ekette,** *f.* drag-chain. **-elampe,** *f.* hanging lamp. **-eleuchter,** *m.* lustre, chandelier. **-ematte,** *f.* hammock. **-emuskel,** *m.* suspensory muscle. **-end,** *pr.p.* & *adj.* hanging, pendulous, suspended. **-enswert,** *adj.* deserving to be hanged. **-eohren,** *n.pl.* drooping *or* flapping ears. **-er,** *m.* pendant, hanger. **-eriemen,** *m.* brace. **-eriß,** *m.* fingerhold (*mountaineering*). **-eschloß,** *n.* padlock. **-eseil,** *n.* leash. **-ewaage,** *f.* suspension-scale. **-eweide,** *f.* weeping willow (*Salix babylonica*) (*Bot.*). **-ewerk,** *n.* suspended work, trussing. **-ig,** *adj.* (*Swiss dial.*) = **anhängig.** **-sel,** *n.* anything by which a th. can be hung up; clothes-loop.

Hanke, *f.* (-n) (*archaic*) haunch (*of a horse*) **-ntief,** *adj.* low in the hind-quarters.

hänseln, *v.a.* make a fool of, chaff, tease.

Hantel, *f.* (-n) & (*dial.*) *m.* (-s, -) dumb-bell. **-n,** *v.n.* (*aux.* h.) exercise with dumb-bells.

hantier-en, 1. *v.a.* handle, wield, manipulate, operate; manage. 2. *v.n.* (*aux.* h.) busy o.s., occupy o.s., bustle about. **-ung,** *f.* business, management, handling, manipulation.

hantig, *adj.* (*Austr. dial.*) bitter, sharp, harsh; quarrelsome.

haper-ig, *adj.* embarrassing, frustrating. **-n,** *v.n.* & *imp.* come to a standstill, stick fast, go *or* be amiss *or* wrong; *es -t am Gelde,* lack of money is the stumbling block; *da -t es,* there's the rub *or* snag; *es -t mit der S.,* there's a hitch in the matter; the affair is at a standstill.

Happ-en, 1. *m.* (-ens, -en), **Häppchen,** *n.* mouthful, morsel, titbit; (*coll.*) *mit einem einen -en essen,* eat s.th. with a p. 2. *v.n.* (*aux.* h.) snap, bite. **-ig,** *adj.* greedy; (*coll.*) great, large, excessive, crude.

Här-chen, *n.* (-s, -) little hair; cilium; *man hat ihm kein -chen gekrümmt,* not a hair of his head has been touched. **-en,** *adj.* (*archaic*) made of hair; *-enes Gewand,* hairshirt.

Häre-sie, *f.* (-n) heresy. **-tiker,** *m.* (-s, -) heretic. **-tisch,** *adj.* heretical.

Harf-e, *f.* (-n) harp; corn-screen. **-en,** 1. *n.* (*aux.* h.) play the harp. 2. *v.a.* screen (*corn*). **-enist,** *m.* (-en -en), **-enspiel,** *n.* harp-playing. **-enspieler,** *m.* harpist. **-ner,** *m.* harper, harpist.

Haring, *m.* (*dial.*), *see* **Hering.**

Harke, *f.* (-n) rake; (*coll.*) *einem zeigen, was eine - ist,* give a p. a good dressing down, give a p. a piece of one's mind, bring s.o. to his senses. **-n,** *v.a.* & *n.* rake.

Harlekin, *m.* (-s, -e) Harlequin, clown. **-ade,** *f.* harlequinade, buffoonery.
Harm, *m.* grief, sorrow, affliction. **-los,** *adj.* harmless; inoffensive.
härmen, 1. *v.a.* afflict, grieve. 2. *v.r.* feel wretched, grieve, pine, fret, worry.
Harmon-ie, *f.* (-n) harmony; agreement, concord, union. **-iegesetz,** *n.* tonal law; (*pl.*) laws of harmony. **-ielehre,** *f.*, **-ik,** *f.* harmony. **-ieren,** *v.n.* (*aux.* h.) harmonize (*sounds*); (*fig.*) get on well together, sympathize *or* be in keeping with. **-ika,** *f.* (-kas & -ken) *orig.* musical glasses, *now* concertina; harmonica. **-ikazug,** *m.* corridor-train. **-isch,** *adj.* harmonious; harmonic; *-ische Komponenten* or *Teilschwingungen*, harmonics (*Rad.*); *-isch stimmen*, attune. **-isieren,** *v.a.* & *n.* attune, harmonize, bring into harmony *or* accord, **-ium,** *n.* (-iums, -ien) harmonium, parlour-organ.
Harn, *m.* urine; *den – lassen* or **-en,** *v.n.* (*aux.* h.) urinate, make water; (*incorrect though frequently used*) micturate. **-abfluß,** *m.* incontinence, urgency, enuresis, micturition. **-beschwerden,** *f.pl.* urinary disorder. **-blase,** *f.* (urinary) bladder. **-blasengang,** *m.* urethra. **-blasengries,** *m.* gravel. **-brennen,** *n.*, **-drang,** *m.* scalding in the bladder, micturition. **-fluß,** *m.* discharge of urine; *unwillkürlicher -fluß, see* **-abfluß. -gang,** *m.* ureter. **-kunde,** *f.* urinology, urology. **-leiter,** *m.* ureter; catheter. **-plätze,** *m.pl.* urinals. **-probe,** *f.* urine sample, uric test. **-röhre,** *f.* urinary passage, urethra. **-ruhr,** *f.* polyuria (*diabetes insipidus*). **-säure,** *f.* uric acid. **-stein,** *m.* stone in the bladder, urinary calculus. **-stoff,** *m.* urea (*Chem.*) **-treibend,** *adj.*; *-treibendes Mittel*, diuretic. **-vergiftung,** *f.* uraemia. **-verhaltung,** *f.* retention of urine. **-zapfer,** *m.* catheter. **-zwang,** *m.* strangury, dysuria.
Harnisch, *m.* (-(e)s, -e) (suit of) armour; *in – jagen* or *bringen*, enrage, provoke; *in – geraten*, fly into a passion.
Harpun-e, *f.* (-n) harpoon; *abschießbare -e*, gun-harpoon. **-engeschütz,** *n.* harpoon-gun, whaling-gun. **-ier,** *m.* (-s, -e) harpooner. **-ieren,** *v.a.* harpoon.
Harpyie, *f.* (-n) harpy, witch. **-nartig,** *adj.* witch-like.
harren, *v.n.* (*aux.* h.) (*with Gen. or usually* auf *and Acc*). look forward to impatiently; wait for, await; stay, tarry: (*obs.*) *ich harre des Herrn*, I trust confidently in the Lord; *diese Aufgabe harrt auf* or *nach Erledigung*, it's high time this job was finished.
harsch, 1. *adj.* harsh, rough, hard; frozen, crusted (*of snow*). 2. *m.* frozen snow. **-en,** *v.n.* (*aux.* h. & s.) harden; become frozen *or* crusted.
hart, *adj.* (*comp.* härter, *sup.* härtest) hard, difficult; harsh, rough, severe, stern, austere; obstinate; stiff, firm, solid, tough, hardy; crude (*Paint.*); calcareous (*as water*) (*Chem.*). *– an*, close by, near to; *– am Feind*, in the face of the enemy; *– anfassen*, deal with severely, treat roughly; *es kommt mir – an*, see *es fällt mir –*; *– Backbord!* hard a-port! (*Naut.*); *– bedrängt*, hard-pressed, hard beset; *-er Dreiklang*, major third; *es fällt mir –*, it is hard for me; *-es Futter*, corn, oats, *etc.* as fodder; *-es Geld*, specie, coin; *– gewöhnt sein*, be accustomed to rough it; *es wird – halten*, it will be no easy matter *or* be attended with difficulties; *es wird – hergehen*, there will be a stiff fight; *-e Kälte*, severe frost; *-e Laute*, harsh *or* discordant sounds; *-en Leib haben*, be constipated; *einem – im Magen liegen*, be heavy on one's stomach; *das Fieber hat ihn – mitgenommen*, the fever has left severe after-effects, (*coll.*) has pulled him down badly; *-es Mittel*, severe measure, drastic remedy; *-e Not*, dire necessity; *eine -e Nuß zu knacken*, a tough nut to crack; *– Ruder!* full helm! (*Naut.*); *-en Schädel haben*, be thick-headed; *-e Stirn*, brazen face; *-e Strafe*, harsh punishment; *wetter–*, weather-resisting; *-es Wort*, unkind word. **-borste,** *f.* crack, fissure (formed in hardening). **-fleischig,** *adj.* brawny, muscular. **-geld,** *n.* coins; specie. **-gesinnt,** *adj.* hard-hearted. **-gesotten,** *adj.*; hard-boiled (*egg*); *-gesottener Sünder*, hardened sinner, confirmed sinner. **-gläubig,** *adj.* sceptical. **-gummi,** *m.* vulcanized india-rubber, vulcanite, ebonite. **-guß,** *m.* chilled work, case-hardened castings. **-häutig,** *adj.* thick-skinned; (*fig.*) callous, unfeeling. **-herzig,** *adj.* hard-hearted. **-herzigkeit,** *f.* hard-heartedness. **-holz,** *n.* close-grained *or* hard wood. **hörig,** *adj.* (*dial.*) hard of hearing. **-köpfig,** *adj.* obstinate, adamant. **-lage,** *f.*; *in -lage legen*, put the helm over (*Naut.*). **-leibig,** *adj.* constipated, costive. **-lot,** *n.* hard solder. **-löten,** *v.a.* braze. **-mäulig,** *adj.* hard-mouthed; unruly. **-meißel,** *m.* cold chisel. **-näckig,** *adj.* stiff-necked, stubborn, obstinate, tenacious. **-näckigkeit,** *f.* obstinacy. **-pappe,** *f.* fibre board. **-schalig,** *adj.* hard-shelled, testaceous. **-schnaufen,** *n.* roaring (*Vet.*). **-sehnig,** *adj.* sinewy. **-ung,** *m.* January. **-waren,** *pl.* hardware. **-zinn,** *n.* pewter.
Härt-e, *f.* (-en) harshness; severity, rigour; hardness, temper (*Metall.*) hardiness; roughness, crudeness; hardship. **-en,** *v.a.* harden, solidify, congeal; case-harden; temper. **-egrad,** *m.* (degree of) temper. **-eparagraph,** *m.* hardship clause. **-eprobe,** *f.*, **-eprüfung,** *f.*, **-eversuch,** *m.* hardness test (*Metall.*). **-ung,** *f.* hardening tempering.
Hartschier, *m.* (*Austr. dial.*), *see* **Hatschier.**
Harz, *n.* (-es, -e) resin, rosin, gum. **-elektrizität,** *f.* negative electricity. **-en,** 1. *v.a.* (*aux.* h.) collect *or* tap resin (*from pines*). 2. *v.n.* exude resin; (*Swiss dial.*) stick; be difficult. **-förmig,** *adj.* resiniform. **-galle,** *f.* resinous exudation (*of wood*). **-gebend,** *adj.* resiniferous. **-gummi,** *n.* (& *m.*) resinous gum. **-haltig,** *adj.* resinoid. **-ig,** *adj.* resinous; like resin. **-kohle,** *f.* resinous coal. **-reißen,** *n.*, **-scharren,** *n.* extraction of resin (*from trees*). **-stoffe,** *m.pl.* resinoids. **-talgseife,** *f.* household, yellow *or* washing soap. **-tragend,** *adj.* resiniferous.
Hasard, *n.*, **-spiel,** *n.* game of chance, betting game, gambling. **-ieren,** *v.a.* risk, chance, hazard.
Hasch-ee, *n.* (-ees, -ees) hash, minced meat. **-ieren,** *v.a.* hash, mince (*Cook.*).
haschen, 1. *v.a.* snatch, seize. 2. *v.n.* (*aux.* h.); *– nach*, snatch at; strain after, aim at. 3. *n.* catching; tig (*game*).
Häschen, *n.* (-s, –) young hare, leveret, (*sl.*) novice pilot (*Av.*).
Häscher, *m.* (-s, –) (*archaic*) sheriff's officer, (bum) bailiff, catch-pole; (*Poet.*) persecutor. **-ei,** *f.* police-practices; (*sl.*) the cops.
Hascherl, *n.* (-s, –) (*Austr. dial.*) beggar, poor wretch, creature *or* devil.
Hase, *m.* (-n, -n) hare; (*fig.*) coward, (*sl.*) funk; *einem -n das Fell abziehen*, skin a hare; *einen -n aufjagen*, start a hare; *falscher –*, meat loaf, meat roll, mock duck; (*coll.*) *heuriger –*, greenhorn; *sehen, wie der – läuft*, see how the cat jumps *or* how the wind blows; (*coll.*) *da liegt der – im Pfeffer*, there's the snag, that's the difficulty; (*coll.*) *mein Name ist –*, I do not know, I have not the faintest notion; (*Prov.*) *viele Hunde sind des -n Tod*, it is no use *or* good fighting against such odds. **-nartig,** *adj.* leporine. **-nbalg,** *m.*, **-nfell,** *n.* hareskin. **-nbraten,** *m.* roast hare. **-nfuß,** *m.* (*fig.*) poltroon, coward. **-nfüßig,** *adj.* cowardly. **-nhaft,** *adj.* faint-hearted, timid, cowardly; leporine. **-nhatz,** *f.*, **-nhetze** *f.* hare-hunting. **-nherz,** *n.* coward. **-nhund,** *m.* harrier. **-njagd,** *f.*, *see* **-nhatz**; *dies ist ja keine -njagd*, there is no hurry about that, that can take its time. **-nklein,** *n.* jugged hare (*Cook.*). **-nkurven,** *f.pl.* evasive action (*Av.*). **-nlager,** *n.* hare's form *or* lair. **-nöhrchen,** *n.pl.* inverted commas. **-npanier,** *n.*; *das -npanier ergreifen*, take to one's heels. **-npfeffer,** *m.* jugged hare (*Cook.*). **-nscharte,** *f.* harelip. **-nweibchen,** *n.* female *or* doe hare.
Hasel, *f.* (-n), *see* **-strauch. -huhn,** *n.* black-cock, hazel-hen (*Tetrastes bonasia*) (*Orn.*). **-maus,** *f.* dormouse (*Muscardinus avellanarius*) (*Zool.*). **-n,** *adj.* hazel-wood. **-nuß,** *f.* hazel-nut. **-nußfarbig,** *adj.* nut-brown. **-strauch,** *m.* hazel, hazel-bush (*Corylus avellana*) (*Bot.*).
Haspe, *f.* (-n) hasp, hinge; staple. **-l,** *m.* (-s, –) & *f.* (-n) reel, winder; whim, windlass, winch; hinge-pin; turnstile. **-ln,** 1. *v.a.* (*aux.* h.) wind

(*on a reel, etc.*). 2. *v.n.* (*coll.*) hurry, hustle, fidget about; chatter.

Haß, *m.* hate, hatred, enmity. **–(ss)en,** *v.a.* hate. **–(ss)enswert,** *adj.*, **–(ss)enswürdig,** *adj.* hateful, odious. **–erfüllt,** *adj.* seething with hatred.

hässig, *adj.* (*Swiss dial.*) irritable, disagreeable.

häßlich, *adj.* ugly, hideous, repulsive, ill-favoured; nasty, odious, loathsome, offensive; *–es Gesicht,* ugly face; *–e Antwort,* nasty answer; *–es Benehmen,* bad behaviour; *–e Geschichte,* unpleasant affair; *–e Gesinnung,* nasty mind; *–er Geruch,* offensive smell; *–e Sitte,* objectionable custom; *–es Wetter,* bad *or* dirty weather; *– von Gestalt,* ill-formed; *– gegen einen,* unpleasant *or* disagreeable to a p. **–keit,** *f.* ugliness, unsightliness, loathsomeness; nastiness, offensiveness.

Hast, *f.* haste, hurry; precipitation. **–en,** 1. *v.n.* hurry, hasten, rush along, be in a hurry. 2. *v.r.* make haste. **–ig,** *adj.* hasty, hurried; rash, precipitate; irritable, passionate; *sie fiel ihm –ig in die Rede,* she interrupted him abruptly. **–igkeit,** *f.* hastiness; hurry; rashness, impetuosity; passionateness; irritability.

hätschel–n, *v.a.* coddle, pamper; coax, caress, fondle.

Hatschier, *m.* (-s, -e) (*archaic*) halbardier; body-guard.

hatte, hätte, *see* **haben.**

Hatz, *f.* (-en) hunt, coursing; pack of hounds; rout, tumultuous revelry.

Hau, *m.* (-(e)s, -e) (*archaic*) cutting, felling; stroke, blow; place where wood is felled; (*pl.*) (*coll.*) beating, thrashing. **–bar,** *adj.* fit for felling. **–degen,** *m.* broadsword; experienced fighter, bruiser, bully, fire-eater. **–e,** *f.* (-en) hoe, mattock, pickaxe. **–en,** 1. *ir.v.a.* hew, cut, chop, fell; carve, chisel; whip, lash; break (*stones*); strike, beat; *Fleisch –en,* cut up meat (for sale); *einen hinter die Ohren –en,* box a p.'s ears; *einen übers Ohr –en,* cheat *or* outwit a p. 2. *v.r.* fight. 3. *v.n.* (*aux.* h.) cut; strike; *um sich –en,* lay about one; *über die Schnur* or *den Strang –en,* kick over the traces; *nach einer S. –en,* strike at a th.; *–en und stechen,* cut and thrust; (*Prov.*) *das ist weder gehauen noch gestochen,* that is neither one thing nor the other, neither fish nor flesh; (*coll.*) *in die Pfanne –en,* put to the sword, cut to pieces; *in die Eisen –en,* overreach (*of a horse*). **–er,** *m.* wild boar; cutting instrument; tusk; (*Austr. dial.*) vine-grower; *Stein–er,* stone-cutter; *Bild–er,* sculptor, **–hammer,** *m.* miner's pick. **–land,** *n.* clearing, newly cultivated land. **–meißel** *m.* cutting chisel. **–zahn,** *m.* boar's tusk.

Haub–e, *f.* (-en) cap, coif, hood, bonnet, cowl, head-dress; tuft, crest, top (*birds*); cupola, dome; cowling, windshield (*aircraft*); cabin roof; bonnet (*Motor.*); crown, coping (*of a wall*); motoring *or* flying helmet; *unter die –e bringen,* provide a husband for, marry off; *unter die –e kommen,* find a husband, get married; *die –e aufklappen,* raise the bonnet (*Motor.*). **–engeschoß,** *n.* projectile with a false cap. **–enkram,** *m.* millinery. **–enlerche,** *f.* crested lark (*Galerida cristata*) (*Orn.*). **–enschachtel,** *f.* hat-box, bandbox. **–enstock,** *m.*, **–enkopf,** *m.* milliner's block.

Haubitze, *f.* (-en) howitzer.

Hauch, *m.* (-(e)s, -e) breath, exhalation, breathing; breeze; puff; whiff; aspiration (*Gram.*); tinge, touch; haze; bloom. **–bildung,** *f.* bloom. **–dünn,** *adj.* extremely thin (*coating*). **–en,** 1. *v.n.* (*aux.* h.) breathe, exhale, respire. 2. *v.a.* breathe out, exhale; blow; aspirate. **–laut,** *m.* spirant, aspirate. **–zart,** *adj.* extremely delicate. **–zeichen,** *n.* mark of aspiration.

Hauder–er, *m.* (-ers, -er) (*dial.*) hackney-coachman, hired driver, cabby; (*fig.*) slow-coach. **–n,** *v.n.* (*aux.* h.) (*dial.*) ply for hire; go in a jog-trot style.

Häuer, *m.* (-s, –) pickman; miner.

Hauf–e, *m.* (-ens, -en), **–en,** *m.* (-ens, -en) heap, pile, hoard; large sum, great number, batch, agglomeration; crowd, body, swarm; mass, multitude; *ein –en Arbeit,* a mass of work; *Steine auf –en legen,* pile stones; *Heu auf –en setzen,* stack hay; *ein –en Geld,* a pile of money; *gemeiner –e,* rabble; *der große –e,* the masses of the people, the masses, the rank and file; *in –en,* in heaps, by heaps; *dort kommen sie in hellen –en,* there they are advancing in large bodies; *in –en legen* or *setzen,* see *auf –en*; *ein –en Schulden,* a pile of debts; *einen –en setzen,* (*vulg.*) evacuate the bowels; *über den –en schießen,* shoot out of hand; *über den –en fallen,* tumble down, perish; *über den –en stoßen,* overthrow; *alle Bedenken über den –en werfen,* throw all scruples aside *or* overboard. **–endorf,** *n.* clustered village. **–enweise,** *adv.* in heaps; in crowds. **–enwolke,** *f.* cumulus.

Häuf–chen, *n.* little heap, *etc.*; *wie ein –chen Unglück,* like a bundle of misery. **–eln,** *v.a.* earth (*potatoes*); form into little heaps; divide into piles. **–en,** 1. *v.a.* accumulate, amass, heap up; pile, earth up. 2. *v.r. imp.* accumulate, increase. **–ig,** 1. *adj.* copious, abundant, numerous; frequent, repeated; *nicht –ig,* infrequent. 2. *adv.* frequently, often, repeatedly; abundantly. **–igkeit,** *f.* frequency; quickness (*of the pulse*). **–igkeitskurve,** *f.* frequency (distribution) curve. **–lein,** *n.* (-s, –) small group; little band; small body *or* troop of men.

Haupt, *n.* (-(e)s, ¨-er) (*pl. with numbers often* –; e.g. *drei – Rinder,* three head of cattle) head; leader, chief, principal; *einem das – abschlagen,* behead a p.; (*sl.*) *bemoostes –,* old student; *entblößten –es,* with head bared; *an – und Gliedern,* root and branch; *aufs – schlagen,* defeat totally; *mit gesenktem –,* with bowed head; *zu Häupten,* at the head of. **–ader,** *f.* cephalic vein. **–agentur,** *f.* head *or* general agency. **–altar,** *m.* high altar. **–anschluß,** *m.* (main) switchboard (*Phone.*) **–arm,** *m.* main gallery (*Min.*). **–artikel,** *m.* principal article; leader (*in a newspaper*). **–aufgebot,** *n.* general levy. **–augenmerk,** *n.*; *sein –augenmerk auf* (*eine S.*) *richten,* direct one's special attention to (a th.). **–bahn,** *f.* main line (*Railw.*). **–bahnhof,** *m.* central station. **–balken,** *m.* main girder, architrave; (*pl.*) principals. **–begriff,** *m.* fundamental idea. **–belastungszeit,** *f.* peak load. **–bestand,** *m.* principal crop **–bestandteil,** *m.* chief constituent. **–betrag,** *m.* sum total. **–beweis,** *m.* main proof. **–buch,** *n.* ledger; *das –buch abschließen,* balance the ledger. **–buchstabe,** *m.* capital letter. **–draht,** *m.* primary wire. **–einfahrt,** *f.*, **–eingang,** *m.* main entrance. **–erbe,** *m.* major beneficiary (*of a will*). **–fach,** *n.* principal subject, main subject. **–farbe,** *f.* primary colour; dominant colour. **–feder,** *f.* mainspring. **–fehler,** *m.* main defect; capital fault. **–flügel,** *m.* main wing (*Arch.*). **–frage,** *f.* main issue *or* question. **–geschoß,** *n.* first floor, principal story. **–gesims,** *n.* entablature (*Arch.*). **–gewinn,** *m.* first prize. **–gläubiger,** *m.* chief creditor. **–grind,** *m.* scald (*Med.*). **–grund,** *m.* main motive, chief reason; foundation, basis. **–grundsatz,** *m.* fundamental *or* leading principle. **–haar,** *n.* hair of the head. **–hahn,** *m.* cock of the roost; main cock (*of pipes*); (*Studs. sl.*) jolly fellow, the life of the party. **–handlung,** *f.* principal action, main plot (*drama*); main *or* head shop. **–inhalt,** *m.* general *or* principal contents, synopsis. **–jagd,** *f.* grand chase, battue. (*coll.*) **–kerl,** *m.*; *er ist ein –kerl,* he is a splendid fellow. **–kessel,** *m.* main boiler. **–kissen,** *n.* pillow. **–knoten,** *m.* main plot. **–ladung,** *f.* detonating charge. **–lager,** *n.* principal camp; headquarters. **–land,** *n.* mainland; mother country. **–laster,** *n.* ruling vice. **–lehre,** *f.* main doctrine, cardinal doctrine. **–lehrer,** *m.* senior master. **–leidenschaft,** *f.* ruling passion. **–leidtragende(r),** *m.* chief mourner. **–leiter,** *m.*, **–leitung,** *f.* principal conductor; main (*gas, water, etc.*). **–linie,** *f.* axis (*Mil.*). **–los,** *adj.* headless; without a leader. **–mahlzeit,** *f.* chief meal. **–mann,** *m.* 1. (*pl.* -leute) captain; (Roman) centurion; 2. (*pl.* -männer) responsible local government official. **–mannschaft,** *f.* captaincy; first eleven, first fifteen, etc. (*Sport*). **–masse,** *f.* bulk. **–mast,** *m.* main mast. **–menge,** *f.* bulk. **–merkmal,** *n.* main feature, principal characteristic. **–moment,** *n.* main point. **–nahrung,** *f.* staple food. **–nenner,**

m. common denominator. **–niederlage,** *f.* general defeat; central warehouse. **–nutzung,** *f.* final yield (*Forestry*). **–pastor,** *m.* chief clergyman, pastor primarius. **–person,** *f.* principal person; leading character (*Theat.*). **–post,** *f.*, **–postamt,** *n.* general post-office. **–prämie,** *f.* first prize. **–probe,** *f.* dress rehearsal (*Theat.*), general rehearsal (*Mus.*). **–punkt,** *m.* main point; cardinal point; chief feature. **–quartier,** *n.* headquarters; *großes –quartier*, general headquarters (G.H.Q.). **–quelle,** *f.* main source; fountain-head. **–querbalken,** *m.* architrave. **–quittung,** *f.* general receipt. **–raum,** *m.* after-hold (*Naut.*). **–register,** *n.* index; main stop (*Org.*). **–richtung,** *f.* main direction. **–rippe,** *f.* midrib (*of leaf*). **–rohr,** *n.* main (supply-pipe). **–rolle,** *f.* leading character *or* part (*Theat.*). **–ruder,** *n.* stroke-oar. **–ruderer,** *m.* stroke. **–sache,** *f.* chief item, main point; (*pl.*) essentials; *in der –sache*, in the main, chiefly; *der –sache nach*, in substance. **–sächlich,** 1. *adj.*; essential, principal, main. 2. *adv.* essentially, chiefly, mainly, especially, particularly, above all; *es kommt –sächlich darauf an*, the main point is. **–sängerin,** *f.* prima donna. **–satz,** *m.* main point; leading theme (*Mus.*); axiom; principal clause, principal sentence (*Gram.*). **–schelm,** *m.* arrant rogue. **–schiff,** *n.* flagship. **–schlacht,** *f.* decisive battle. **–schlagader,** *f.* aorta (*Anat.*). **–schlußschaltung,** *f.* series winding (*Elec.*). **–schlüssel,** *m.* master-key. **–schmuck,** *m.* head adornment *or* ornament; principal ornament. **–schuld,** *f.* principal fault; *die –schuld trifft ihn*, it is mainly his fault. **–schuldiger,** *m.* chief offender. **–schuldner,** *m.* principal debtor. **–schule,** *f.* intermediate school. **–schwingung,** *f.* fundamental oscillation. **–segel,** *n.* mainsail. **–seite,** *f.* principal side, front, façade (*of a building*); face (*of a coin*). **–spaß,** *m.* capital joke. **–spule,** *f.* primary winding (*Elec.*). **–stadt,** *f.* metropolis, capital. **–städtisch,** *adj.* metropolitan. **–stamm,** *m.* main stem, bole; leading *or* elder branch (*of a race*); chief tribe. (*fig.*) **–stärke,** *f.* strongest point. **–steuer,** *f.* poll-tax; principal tax. **–stimme,** *f.* falsetto, head-voice; leading voice, solo. **–stollen,** *m.*, *see* **–arm.** **–straße,** *f.* principal street, high street; highway, main road. **–streich,** *m.* master-stroke. **–strom,** *m.* main stream; primary current (*Elec.*). **–stromkreis,** *m.* primary circuit (*Elec.*). **–stück,** *n.* principal piece; head-piece; head; chapter, section; chief article; important point. **–stütze,** *f.* main support, mainstay. **–summe,** *f.* principal sum; sum total. **–sünde,** *f* cardinal sin; besetting sin. **–ton,** *m.* key-note; principal accent, chief stress. **–treffen,** *n.*, *see* **–schlacht.** **–treffer,** *m.* first (lottery-)prize. **–trumpf,** *m.* best trump. **–tugend,** *f.* cardinal virtue. **Haupt- und Staatsaktion,** *f.* type of baroque drama; (*fig.*) great to-do *or* pother. **–unterschied,** *m.* main *or* characteristic difference. **–untersuchung,** *f.* trial (*Law*). **–ursache,** *f.* principal cause. **–verbrechen,** *n.* capital crime; major offence. **–verdienst,** *m.* chief merit. **–verkehrszeit,** *f.* peak hour, rush hour. **–verlesen,** *n.* (*Swiss dial.*) roll-call (*Mil.*). **–verwendungsgebiet,** *n.* chief use *or* field of application. **–verzeichnis,** *n.* general catalogue. **–wache,** *f.* main-guard; main guard-house. **–welle,** *f.* transmission shaft (*Engin.*). **–werk,** *n.* principal work, masterpiece. **–wirkung,** *f.* main effect. **–wissenschaft,** *f.* fundamental science. (*coll.*) **–witz,** *m.* capital joke. **–wort,** *n.* noun, substantive; chief word. **–wunde,** *f.* wound in the head; dangerous wound. **–wurzel,** *f.* tap-root. **–zahl,** *f.*, **–zahlwort,** *n.* cardinal number. **–zeuge,** *m.* principal witness. **–zug,** *m.* leading *or* principal feature; main direction (*of a lode*) (*Min.*). **–zweck,** *m.* chief object. **–zweig,** *m.* main branch.

Häupt–el, *n.* (-s, -(n)) (*dial.*) head of lettuce (*or similar plant*). **–elsalat,** *m.* lettuce, green salad. **–ling,** *m.* (-s, -e) chief, leader. **–lings,** *adv.* head-foremost, head over heels, headlong.

Haus, *n.* (-es, ⸚er) house, residence, dwelling; home; housing, casing, frame, shell; household, family, race; firm; *sie wohnen – an –*, they live next door to each other; *aus gutem –e*, of a good family; *außer – essen*, feed away from home; *auf ihn kannst du Häuser bauen*, you may pin your faith on him, you may trust him implicitly; *sein – bestellen*, prepare for death, put one's affairs in order; *ein neues – beziehen*, move to a new house; *mit der Tür ins – fallen*, do a th. awkwardly, go like a bull at a gate; *ein großes – machen*, live in great style, keep open house; *der Herr vom –e*, the master of the house; *– und Hof*, one's all, house and home; *sie trieben ihn von – und Hof*, they drove him from hearth and home; *das – hüten*, stay at home, stay indoors; *nach –e*, homeward, home; *öffentliches –*, house of ill-repute, disorderly house; *von –e*, from home; *von –e aus*, from the very beginning, fundamentally, originally; *von –e aus Vermögen haben*, have property of one's own; *von –e aus begabt sein*, be innately gifted, be born clever; *mit herzlichen Grüßen von – zu –*, with our kind regards to all of you; *zu –e*, at home; *wo sind Sie zu –e?* what nationality are you? where do you come from? *nirgends zu –e sein*, have no fixed abode; know no subject thoroughly; *er is überall zu –e*, he is well up in everything; he is very widely read; *er fühlt sich wie zu–e*, he feels quite at home; *tut als ob ihr zu–e wäret*, make yourself at home; *bleibt mir damit zu–e!* don't bother me about that, keep that to yourself! **–altar,** *m.* domestic altar; (*fig.*) **–altäre,** *pl.* hearth and home, native land. **–andacht,** *f.* family prayers. **–angelegenheiten,** *f.pl.* family affairs. **–angestellte,** *f.* & *m.* housemaid, domestic (servant); *pl.* domestics, servants. **–apotheke,** *f.* family medicine-chest. **–arbeit,** *f.* indoor work; domestic work; home work (*of schoolchildren*). **–arrest,** *m.* confinement to one's own house. **–arznei,** *f.* household remedy. **–arzt,** *m.* family doctor. **–backen,** *adj.* home-baked; homely, plain; prosaic, pedestrian; *–backenes Brot*, home-made bread; *–backener Verstand*, plain common sense, humdrum intelligence. **–bedarf,** *m.* household necessaries; *für den –bedarf*, for the house, for family use; *nicht über den –bedarf*, not above the ordinary requirements of the family; for everyday use. **–bediente(r),** *m.* indoor servant. **–besitzer,** *m.* owner, landlord. **–bettelei,** *f.* begging from door to door. **–bewohner,** *m.* tenant. **–biene,** *f.* domestic bee. **–bier,** *n.* home-brewed ale. **–brauch,** *m.* family custom; domestic use. **–brief,** *m.* conveyance, deeds of house purchase. **–brot,** *n.* household bread. **–buch,** *n.* housekeeping-book. **–dame,** *f.* housekeeper, lady's companion. **–diener,** *m.* house servant (*in an inn*), manservant. **–drache,** *m.* shrew, scold, vixen. **–durchbruch,** *m.* mouse-holing (*Mil.*). **–durchsuchung,** *f.* domiciliary visit (*by the police*). **–eigentümer,** *m.*, *see* **–besitzer.** **–einbrecher,** *m.* house-breaker, burglar. **–einrichtung,** *f.* domestic furnishings. **–en,** *v.n.* (aux. h.) house, lodge, reside, dwell; manage badly, ransack, wreak havoc, cause a turmoil; (*Swiss dial.*) save, economize. **–er,** *m.* (*Austr. dial.*), *see* **–halter.** **–fideikomiß,** *n.* family trust. **–flur,** *m.* (*or Austr. f.*) hall, vestibule. **–frau,** *f.* mistress of the house; housewife; landlady. **–freund,** *m.* family friend. **–friede,** *m.* domestic peace, family concord. **–friedensbruch,** *m.* intrusion, trespass (*Law*). **–gebrauch,** *m.* domestic use, family custom. **–geld,** *n.* rent. **–genosse,** *m.* fellow-lodger, member of the same family. **–genossen,** *pl.*, **–genossenschaft,** *f.* family, household. **–gerät,** *n.* household utensils. **–gesinde,** *n.* (*archaic*) domestic servants. **–glück,** *n.* domestic bliss *or* happiness. **–gott,** *m.* household deity (*Roman* = penates). **–gottesdienst,** *m.* (family) prayers, family worship. **–grille,** *f.* cricket (*Gryllus domesticus*) (*Ent.*). **–halt,** *m.* household; housekeeping; household budget. **–halten,** 1. *ir.v.n.* keep house; husband, economize; *sie hält ihm –*, she keeps house for him; *gut –halten*, be a good housekeeper. 2. *n.* housekeeping; management. **–hälter,** *m.*, **–halter,** *m.* householder, housekeeper. **–hälterin,** *f.* housekeeper. **–hälterisch,** *adj.* economical, thrifty. **–haltsfarbe,** *f.* dye for home use, dolly dye. **–haltsgeld,** *n.* housekeeping money *or* allowance. **–haltsplan,** *m.* budget.

–haltstarif, *m.* household tariff (*electricity*). **–haltung,** *f.*, *see* **–halt** & **–halten.** 2, economy. **–haltungsschule,** *f.* school of domestic science. **–herr,** *m.* master of the house, head of the family; landlord. **–hoch,** *adj.* as high as a house, very high. **–ieren,** *v.n.* (*aux.* h.) hawk, peddle. **–ierer,** *m.* pedlar. **–ierhandel,** *m.* hawking, peddling, colportage (*of books, pamphlets*). **–industrie,** *f.* cottage industry. **–jungfer,** *f.* (*archaic*) housemaid. **–kapelle,** *f.* private chapel; private orchestra. **–kleid,** *n.* house-dress. **–knecht,** *m.* porter; boots (*at an inn*). (*sl.*) **–knochen,** *m.* house-key, latch-key. **–kost,** *f.* household fare. **–kreuz,** *n.* family burden, skeleton in the cupboard; (*sl.*) wife. **–lehrer,** *m.* private tutor. **–lehrerin,** *f.* governess. **–leute,** *pl.* caretaker and his family, people employed in the house; *see* **–mann.** **–lich,** *adj.* *Swiss dial.*) economical. **–mädchen,** *n.* housemaid; maid. **–magd,** *f.* housemaid, maid of all work. **–mann,** *m.* (-männer) house-porter, caretaker; *see* **–leute.** **–mannskost,** *f.* plain *or* homely fare. **–marke,** *f.* trade mark. **–meier,** *m.* majordomo. **–meister,** *m.* house-steward; caretaker. **–miete,** *f.* (house-)rent. **–mittel,** *n.* home-made (herbal) remedy. **–müll,** *n.* domestic *or* household refuse. **–mutter,** *f.* mother of a family; matron. **–mütterlich,** *adj.* matronly. **–mütze,** *f.* smoking cap. **–nummer,** *f.* street number. **–orden,** *m.* Royal Order. **–ordnung,** *f.* rule of the house, daily routine. **–pflanze,** *f.* indoor plant. **–postille,** *f.* book of family devotions. **–prediger,** *m.* family chaplain. **–rat,** *m.* household furniture, utensils, etc. **–recht,** *n.* domestic right; domestic authority; *sein –recht brauchen*, turn an intruder out of doors. **–regel,** *f.* custom of the house. **–regiment,** *n.* discipline of a household, home discipline. **–riegel,** *m.* bolt of the street-door. **–rock,** *m.* house coat, indoor gown. **–schabe,** *f.* cockroach. **–schatz,** *m.* privy purse (*of a prince*); family scrap-book. **–schlüssel,** *m.* front-door key. **–schuh,** *m.* slipper. **–schwalbe,** *f.* house-martin. **–schwamm,** *m.* dry-rot. **–segen,** *m.* (*coll.*) children. **–sorge,** *f.* domestic care. **–stand,** *m.* household. **–suchung,** *f.* domiciliary visit (*by the police*), police raid. **–suchungsbefehl,** *m.* search-warrant. **–taufe,** *f.* private baptism. **–teufel,** *m.* termagant, shrew. **–tier,** *n.* domestic(ated) animal. **–trauung,** *f.* private wedding. **–truppen,** *f.pl.* household troops, life guards. **–tuch,** *n.* home-spun. **–tür,** *f.* street-door, front-door. **–tyrann,** *m.* domestic tyrant. **–übel,** *n.* family affliction. **–unke,** *f.* rush-toad; (*fig.*) home-bird. **–unkosten,** *pl.* household expenses. **–unterstützung,** *f.* out-door relief. **–vater,** *m.* father of a family. **–verstand,** *m.*; (*coll.*) horse-sense. **–vertrag,** *m.*, *see* **–brief.** **–verwalter,** *m.* steward. **–vogt,** *m.* steward; keeper of a city-prison, gaoler. **–vogtei,** *f.* city-prison. **–wanze,** *f.* bed-bug. **–wappen,** *n.* family arms. **–wart,** *m.* (house-)porter, caretaker. **–wäsche,** *f.* household washing. **–wesen,** *n.* domestic concerns; household. **–wirt,** *m.* master of a house; landlord, host. **–wirtin,** *f.* mistress of a house; landlady, hostess. **–wirtschaft,** *f.* housekeeping; domestic economy. **–zins,** *m.* house-rent. **–zucht,** *f.* home discipline.

Häus–chen, *n.* (-s, -) small house, cottage; *aus dem –chen*, beside o.s., confused, overcome; *sie ist vor Freude ganz aus dem –chen*, she is beside herself with delight; *aufs –chen gehen*, (*coll.*) go out to the lavatory. **–erin,** *f.* (*Austr.* (*dial.*), *see* **Haushälterin.** **–erkampf,** *m.* house-to-house fighting. **–ermakler,** *m.* house agent, real estate broker. **–ler,** *m.* cottager; landless labourer. **–lich,** *adj.* domestic, domesticated, home-loving, homely; economical, thrifty; *–liche Aufgaben*, home work, home lessons (*of school-children*); *–licher Kreis*, domestic circle; *im –lichen Kreise*, by the fireside; *–licher Unterricht*, private tuition; *sich –lich niederlassen an einem Orte*, make one's home in a place. **–lichkeit,** *f.* domesticity, family life; simplicity, frugality.

Hausen, *m.* (-s, –) sturgeon (*Acipenser huso*) (*Icht.*). **–blase,** *f.* isinglass, fish-glue. **–rogen,** *m.* spawn of sturgeon, caviare.

Hauss–e, *f.* [*pron.* 'ho:sə] (*C.L.*) rise, advance, boom. **–en,** *v.n.* (*aux.* h.) speculate on a rise, bull.

haußen, *adv.* (*dial.*) outside, out of doors; (*fig.*) distasteful, detestable, irksome.

Haut, *f.* (¨e) hide; skin; cuticle, dermis, integument, membrane; film, flurry, bloom; outer planking (*of a ship*); *treue alte –*, good old soul; *er kann aus seiner – nicht heraus*, he cannot change his nature; *es ist um aus der – zu fahren, es ist zum Ausderhautfahren*, it's enough to drive one mad (*with impatience*); *naß bis auf die –*, wet to the skin, sopping wet; *auf der bloßen – tragen*, wear next to the skin; *ehrliche –*, honest fellow; *mit ganzer –*, safe, unharmed; *mit – und Haar*, altogether, utterly, thoroughly, out and out; *er kam mit heiler – davon*, he escaped uninjured, he got off scot-free; (*Prov.*) *die – ist allweg näher als das Hemd*, charity begins at home; *er ist bloß noch – und Knochen*, he is a mere bag of bones *or* nothing but skin and bones; *auf der faulen – liegen*, be idle, take it easy; *lustige –*, (*sl.*) cheerful cuss; *einem die – über die Ohren ziehen*, flay a p., fleece *or* cheat a p.; *ich möchte nicht in seiner – stecken*, I should not like to be in his place *or* skin; *seine – (selbst) zu Markte tragen*, do at one's own risk, risk one's life; *seine – teuer verkaufen*, sell one's life dearly; *sich seiner – wehren*, defend one's own life, look after o.s. **–abschürfung,** *f.* excoriation. **–artig,** *adj.* skin-like. **–ausschlag,** *m.* eruption, rash. **–bläschen,** *n.* papula, eczema. **–drüse,** *f.* miliary gland. **–drüsenkrankheit,** *f.* scrofula. **–entzündung,** *f.* dermatitis. **–falten,** *f.pl.* wrinkles. **–farbe,** *f.* complexion. **–fleck,** *m.* spot, blotch. **–flügler,** *pl.* hymenoptera (*order of insects*). **–gewebe,** *n.* outer tissue, cuticle (*of plants*). **–krankheit,** *f.* skin disease. **–lehre,** *f.* dermatology. **–leim,** *m.* hide glue. **–pflege,** *f.* care of the skin, cosmetics. **–reinigend,** *adj.*; *–reinigende Mittel*, skin lotion, complexion milk, cosmetics.

Häut–chen, *n.* (-s, –) membrane; film. **–en,** 1. *v.a.* skin. 2. *v.r.* cast *or* shed the skin; moult; *die Schlange –ete sich*, the snake was sloughing its skin. **–ig,** *adj.* membranous, cutaneous, cuticular; *in compounds* = skinned. **–ung,** *f.* skinning, moulting, casting *or* shedding of the skin, sloughing, desquamation.

Havarie, (-n) **Haverei,** *f.* damage by sea; average; *große –*, gross average; *kleine –*, particular average; *– erleiden*, suffer (sea-)damage. **–ren,** 1. *v.a.* injure; *–rter Dampfer*, damaged steamer. 2. *v.n.* make average.

Havelock, *m.* (-s, -s); ulster (*coat*).

Heb–e, *f.* (-en) lever, pulley, jack. **–amme,** *f.* midwife. **–ärztlich,** *adj.* obstetric. **–arzneikunst,** *f.* obstetrics. **–arzt,** *m.* accoucheur. **–earm,** *m.* lever, piston. **–eband,** *n.* truss. **–ebaum,** *m.* lever, jack, hand-spike, crowbar. **–ebock,** *m.* lifting gear, crane. **–edaumen,** *m.* cam. **–eeisen,** *n.* crowbar; elevatory (*Surg.*). **–efahrzeug,** *n.* salvage vessel (*Naut.*). **–ekran,** *m.* hoisting winch. **–ekunde,** *f.* obstetrics. **–el,** *m.* (-els, -el) lever; *den –el ansetzen*, set about, tackle; *alle –el in Bewegung setzen*, take all steps (to), use all means at one's disposal. **–elade,** *f.* crane. **–elarm,** *m.* arm of a lever. **–elführung,** *f.* lever-guide. **–elkraft,** *f.* leverage, purchase. **–eln,** *v.a.* & *n.* (*aux.* h.) lever, move with a lever. **–elpunkt,** *m.* bearing. **–elverhältnis,** *n.* leverage. **–emuskel,** *m.* elevator (*Anat.*). **–en,** 1. *ir.v.a.* lift, raise, elevate, heave; draw up, siphon (*liquids*); exalt; levy; make prominent; remove, put an end to, cancel, settle (*disputes*). 2. *v.r.* rise; *die Tür aus den Angeln –en*, take the door off its hinges; *die Welt aus den Angeln –en*, put the world out of joint; *den Ertrag –en*, increase output *or* yield; *die Farbenwirkung –en*, enhance the colouring; *Wein aus dem Faß –en*, siphon *or* draw wine from the cask; *in den Himmel –en*, laud to the skies; *den Mut –en*, inspire with courage, give courage *or* heart to; *aus dem Sattel –en*, unhorse; *einen Schatz –en*, unearth a treasure; *ein Schiff –en*, refloat a ship; *aus der Taufe –en*, stand sponsor to; *eine Dame aus dem Wagen –en*, help a lady out of a carriage; *das –t sich*, that cancels out, that makes us quits; *es –t mich beim bloßen Zusehen*, the mere sight of it makes my gorge rise; *–' dich weg von mir Satan!* get thee behind me Satan! (*B.*); *ihr Busen hob sich*, her bosom was heaving; *unsere Forderungen –en sich*, our demands balance each other; *der Handel –t sich wieder*, trade *or* business is improving *or* reviving; *die Preise –en sich*, prices are looking up; *der Teig –t sich*, the dough is rising; *in gehobener Stellung*, in an elevated position; *gehobener Stil*, exalted style; *in gehobener Stimmung*, in an excited *or* enthusiastic frame of mind, in high spirits; *ein fünfmal gehobener Vers*, a verse of five beats *or* stresses. **–er,** *m.* lifter, raiser, heaver; elevator (*Anat.*); siphon. **–ern,** *v.a.* siphon, pipette. **–epunkt,** *m.* fulcrum, point of leverage. **–erolle,** *f.* register of dues and taxes (*Law*). **–eschraube,** *f.* lifting screw. **–estelle,** *f.* inland revenue office. **–ewerk,** *n.* **–ezeug,** *n.* jack, lifting gear. **–ewinde,** *f.* windlass. **–ig,** *adj.*; *ein fünf–iger Vers*, a verse of five stresses. **–ung,** *f.* raising, lifting; improvement, encouragement; cancelling, solution; revenue, tax; elevation, rising ground; arsis (*Mus.*), accented syllable, accent, beat (*Metr.*). **–ungsfähig,** *adj.* capable of bearing an accent (*of syllables*). **–ungskammer,** *f.* inland-revenue department.

Hech–el, *f.* (-eln) hackle, flax-comb; censurer; *durch die –el ziehen*, censure severely. **–elbank,** *f.* hackling-bench. **–elei,** *f.* hackling; heckling, carping. **–eln,** *v.a.* hackle, dress (*flax*); censure severely, catechize, slate, criticize, heckle. **–elung,** *f.* hackling; censure, catechism; slashing criticism. **–ler,** *m.* hackler; heckler, censurer; satirist.

Hechse, *f.* (-n), *see* **Hachse.**

Hecht, *m.* (-(e)s, -e) pike (*Esocidae*) (*Icht.*); (*coll.*) *feiner –*, fop, dandy.

Heck, *n.* (-(e)s, -e) after-deck, stern; (*dial.*) lattice-work fence; gate in such fence. **–enschütze,** *m.* rear gunner (*Av.*).

Heck–e, *f.* (-en) 1. hedge, hedgerow, copse, inclosure; brush-wood; *lebendige –e*, quickset hedge; *dichte –e*, thick-set (hedge); *tote –e*, paling, fence. 2. hatch, brood, breed; breeding-time; breeding-cage. **–en,** *v.a. & n.* (*aux.* h.) hatch, breed; produce. **–enbeschneider,** *m.*, **–enbinder,** *m.* hedger. **–engang,** *m.* lane between hedges. **–enreiter,** *m.* highwayman. **–enrose,** *f.* dog-rose (*Rosa canina*) (*Bot.*). **–enschere,** *f.* hedge-clipper. **–enschlehe,** *f.* sloe. **–enschütze,** *m.* sniper (*Mil.*). **–ensichel,** *f.* bill-hook. **–enspringer,** *m.* hedge-hopper, low-flying aircraft (*Av.*). **–enzaun,** *m.* quickset hedge. **–ig,** *adj.* covered with hedges *or* copses. **–jäger,** *m.* poacher. **–männchen,** *n.* money-spinner; mandrake. **–münze,** *f.* **–pfennig,** *m.* lucky penny, nest-egg. **–zeit,** *f.* pairing time.

Hede, *f.* (-n) tow, oakum. **–n,** *adj.* of tow *or* oakum.

Hederich, *m.* (-(e)s, -e) hedge-mustard (*Raphanus raphanistrum*) (*Bot.*).

Heer, *n.* (-(e)s, -e) army, troops; host, multitude. *das wilde, wütende –*, Wodan's (*or* Arthur's) chase; *stehendes –*, standing army; *Dienst im aktiven –e*, service with the colours. **–bann,** *m.* (*archaic*) summons to arms; general levy; levies. **–esabteilung,** *f.* army division. **–esbericht,** *m.* army communiqué. **–esbetreuung,** *f.* army welfare. **–esdienst,** *m.* military service. **–eseinrichtung,** *f.* army organization. **–esflucht,** *f.* desertion. **–esflüchtig,** *adj.*; *–esflüchtig werden*, desert. **–esfolge,** *f.* (compulsory) military service; *–esfolge leisten*, join the army. **–esgefolge,** *n.* camp followers. **–eshaufen,** *m.* host, army. **–esleitung,** *f.* army command; *oberste –esleitung*, Supreme Command. **–esmacht,** *f.* military forces; troops. **–esschar,** *f. see* **–schar.** **–estruppen,** *f.pl.* G.H.Q. troops. **–eszeitung,** *f.* army gazette. **–eszug,** *m.*, *see* **–zug.** **–flucht,** *f.* desertion. **–flügel,** *m.* flank. **–führer,** *m.* commander-in-chief. **–lager,** *n.* camp, encampment; (*fig.*) party, faction, group. **–schar,** *f.* host, legion; *die himmlischen –scharen*, the heavenly host; *der Herr der –scharen*, the Lord of Hosts. **–schau,** *f.* military review, parade. **–spitze,** *f.* vanguard. **–straße,** *f.* military road; highway. **–verpflegungsamt,** *n.* commissariat. **–wagen,** *m.* baggage-wagon; Charles's Wain (*Astr.*). **–wesen,** *n.* military affairs. **–wurm,** *m.* army-worm, grass-worm, snake-worm (*migrating host of larvae of Sciara militaris*). **–zug,** *m.* campaign.

Hef–e, *f.* (-en) yeast, barm; leaven; dregs, sediment; *bis auf die –e, bis zur –e*, to the very dregs; *die –e des Volks*, the scum of the people. **–e(n)brot,** *n.*, **–e(n)gebäck,** *n.* leavened bread, *or* pastry. **–e(n)teig,** *m.* leavened dough. **–ig,** *adj.* barmy, yeasty; yeast-like; full of lees.

Heft, *n.* (-(e)s, -e) haft, handle, hilt; stitched *or* paper-covered book, exercise book, copy-book; *einem das – in die Hand geben*, allow a p. to have all his own way; *einem das – entwinden* or *aus der Hand nehmen*, wrest the power from s.o.; *das – in der Hand haben*, be at the helm of affairs; *die Zeitschrift erscheint in zwanglosen –en*, the periodical appears in irregular instalments. **–e,** *f.* tying up (*vine-tendrils*). **–el,** *m. & n.* (*Austr. f.*) hook and eye. **–eln,** *v.a.* fasten (*with hooks and eyes*), hook up. **–en,** *v.a.* fasten; stitch, tack (*sewing*); pin; hook; *den Blick auf etwas –en*, fix *or* glue one's eyes on s.th.; *er –et sich an meine Fersen*, he sticks to my heels. **–faden,** *m.* basting *or* stitching thread. **–klammer,** *f.* paper-fastener. **–lade,** *f.* bookbinder's sewing frame *or* press. **–nadel,** *f.* stitching-needle. **–nagel,** *m.* wire tack. **–pflaster,** *n.* sticking *or* adhesive plaster, court-plaster. **–schnur,** *f.* pack-thread. **–stich,** *m.* tacking stitch (*sewing*). **–ung,** *f.* fastening, attaching, stitching. **–zwecke,** *f.* drawing-pin. **–zwinge,** *f.* clip.

heftig, *adj.* forcible, violent, severe, vigorous, intense, vehement, fierce, furious, impetuous; passionate, fervent. **–keit,** *f.* vehemence, violence, fierceness, intensity, impetuosity, ardour.

Hege, *f.* preservation, protection, care; preserve, reserve; close-season. **–n,** *v.a.* hedge *or* fence about, enclose, protect, preserve, shelter, cherish, take care of; (*Poet.*) comprise, contain; *–n und pflegen*, cherish and protect, foster with great care; *Verdacht –n*, harbour suspicion; *Zweifel –n*, entertain doubts. **–r,** *m.* keeper; forester; (*dial.*) hoarder; (*dial.*) small-holder, cottager. **–holz,** *n.*, *see* **–wald.** **–meister,** *m.* head gamekeeper. **–reiter,** *m.* gamekeeper. **–säule,** *f.* landmark. **–schlag,** *m.*, *see* **–wald.** **–stätte,** *f.* preserve. **–tiere,** *n.pl.* preserved game. **–wald,** *m.* plantation, reservation. **–wasser,** *n.* fish-preserve. **–weide,** *f.*, **–wiese,** *f.* enclosed meadow. **–zeit,** *f.* close-season (*for game*).

Hehl, *n.* concealment, secrecy; *er macht kein – daraus*, he makes no secret of it; *ohne –*, openly, frankly, without subterfuge. **–en,** *v.a.* conceal, make a secret of. **–er,** *m.* concealer; receiver (of stolen goods); (*sl.*) fence; (*Prov.*) *der –er ist so schlimm wie der Stehler*, the receiver is as bad as the thief. **–erei,** *f.* receiving stolen property.

hehr, *adj.* (*poet.*) exalted, lofty, majestic, sublime; august, sacred; *hoch und –*, high and commanding, lofty and dignified, imposing.

heida, heisa, *int.* cheers!

[1]**Heid–e,** *f.* (-en) heath, moorland, moor; Scotch heather *or* ling (*Calluna vulgaris*) (*Bot.*), bell heather (*Erica cinerea*) (*Bot.*), cross-leaved heather (*Erica tetralix*) (*Bot.*). **–eginster,** *m.* gorse, furze (*Ulex europæus*) (*Bot.*). **–ehahn,** *m.* blackcock (*Lyrurus tetrix*) (*Orn.*). **–ekorn,** *n.*, buckwheat. **–ekraut,** *n.* Scotch heather, *see* [1]**–e.** **–eland,** *n.* heath, moorland. **–elbeere,** *f.* bilberry; whortleberry (*Vaccinium myrtillis*) (*Bot.*). **–elerche,** *f.* woodlark (*Lullula arborea*) (*Orn.*). **–elhahn,** *m.*, *see* **–ehahn.** **–emehl,** *n.* buckwheat flour. **–e(n)röschen,** *n.* rock rose (*Helianthemum nummularium*) (*Bot.*). **–schnucke,** *f.* North German moorland sheep.

[2]**Heid–e,** *m.* (-en, -en), **–in,** *f.* heathen, pagan; *Juden und –en*, Jews and Gentiles; *zu –en machen*, heathenize. (*coll.*) **–enangst,** *f.* mortal fright, (*coll.*) blue funk. **–enapostel,** *m.* apostle to the Gentiles. **–enbekehrer,** *m.* missionary. **–enbekehrung,** *f.* conversion of heathens, foreign

missions, missionary work. **-enbild,** *n.* idol. **-enchrist,** *m.* heathen proselyte (*of early Christianity*). (*coll.*) **-engeld,** *n.* enormous sum of money, (*sl.*) a devil of a lot of money. **-enhaar,** *n.* first hair (*of newborn infant*). (*coll.*) **-enlärm,** *m.* fearful *or* (*sl.*) hell of a noise, hullabaloo. (*coll.*) **-enmäßig,** *adj.* very large, very great, very much; *-enmäßig viel Geld*, an enormous sum of money, a mint of money. **-entum,** *n.* heathendom; paganism; pagans. **-nisch,** *adj.* heathenish, pagan.

heidi, *int.* look sharp! keep your chin up! (*sl.*) – *gehen*, get lost.

heikel, heiklig, *adj.* ticklish, difficult, critical; delicate; dainty, fastidious, particular, (*coll.*) choosy.

heil, 1. *adj.* unhurt, safe and sound, whole, intact, unscathed; healed, well, cured, restored; *seine Wunde ist* –, his wound is healed up. 2. *n.* prosperity, happiness, welfare; salvation, redemption; *das ewige* –, eternal salvation; *im Jahre des -s*, in the year of grace, in the year of our Lord; *sein – versuchen*, try one's luck, take one's chance; *es war mir zum* –, it was lucky for me, fortunately. 3. *int.* hail! good luck! – *dem König!* long live the king! God save the king! – *dir!* hail! – *dem Volke, welches, usw.*, happy the people that, *etc.*; – *dem Manne, der* . . ., blessed be the man who . . .; *Sieg* –*!* (*Nat. Soc. acclamation*) To Victory! *Ski* –*!* Good ski-ing! **-and,** *see* **Heiland. -anstalt,** *f.* sanatorium, hospital, asylum, convalescent home, nursing home (*usually* mental home, lunatic asylum). **-bad,** *n.* mineral bath. **-bar,** *adj.* curable; remediable. **-behandlung,** *f.* treatment, cure. **-bringend,** *adj.* salutary blessing. **-bringer,** *m.* bringer of blessings; Saviour. **-brunnen,** *m.* mineral springs, spa. **-butt,** *m.* halibut (*Hippoglossus vulgaris*) (*Icht.*). **-en,** 1. *v.a.* heal, cure, make well; *die Zeit -t alle Wunden*, time cures everything. 2. *v.n.* (*aux.* s.) grow well, heal, be cured; *das -t von selbst*, that will get well by itself *or* without treatment. **-end,** *pr.p. & adj.* healing, curative, remedial. **-froh,** *adj.* overjoyed, delighted. **-gymnastik,** *f.* remedial *or* orthopaedic gymnastics. **-kraft,** *f.* healing power. **-kräftig,** *adj.* curative; medicinal, therapeutic; *-kräftige Eigenschaft*, medicinal property. **-kraut,** *n.* medicinal herb. **-kundig,** *adj.* skilled in medicine. **-kunst,** *f.*, **-kunde,** *f.* medical science, medicine, therapeutics. **-künstler,** *m.* quack doctor. **-los,** *adj.* wicked, abandoned, godless; heinous, terrible, disastrous, dreadful; wretched; hopeless; (*coll.*) very large, enormous; *-lose Angst*, terrible fright; *-los viel Geld*, no end of money. **-losigkeit,** *f.* wickedness; wretchedness. **-mittel,** *n.* remedy; medicament. **-mittellehre,** *f.* pharmacology, materia medica. **-pflanze,** *f.*, *see* **-kraut. -pflaster,** sticking-plaster. **-plan,** *m.* mode of treatment. **-praktikant,** *m.* (-en, -en) quack doctor. **-prozeß,** *m.* healing process, cure; recovery. **-quelle,** *f.* mineral springs, medicinal waters. **-sam,** *adj.* healing; wholesome, salutary, beneficial; *die Lektion wird ihm sehr -sam sein*, the lesson will do him a great deal of good. **-samkeit,** *f.* wholesomeness, salutariness, salutary effect; recovery. **-sarmee,** *f.* Salvation Army. **-sbotschaft,** *f.* Christ's message to the world. **-serum,** *n.* antitoxic serum, antitoxin. **-sfroh,** *see* **-froh. -sgeschichte,** *f.* Passion and Salvation of Christ. **-stätte,** *f.*, *see* **-anstalt** (*usually for tubercular cases*). **-stoff,** *m.*, *see* **-mittel. -ung,** *f.* healing, curing, cure, recovery. **-verfahren,** *n.* medical treatment. **-wasser,** *n.* medicinal *or* mineral water. **-wissenschaft,** *f.* (the science of) medicine.

Heiland, *m.* (-(e)s, -e) Saviour.

heilig, *adj.* holy, godly, sacred, hallowed; solemn, venerable, august; *der -e Abend*, Christmas Eve; *das -e Abendmahl*, the Lord's Supper, holy communion; *-es Bein*, os sacrum; *der -e Geist*, the Holy Ghost; *den Sonntag – halten*, keep the Sabbath day (holy); *-e Jungfrau*, the Blessed Virgin (Mary); *-er Ort*, holy *or* sacred place; *-e Pflicht*, sacred duty; *die -e Schrift*, the Scriptures; *-er Vater*, the Holy Father, the Pope; *hoch und – versprechen*, promise solemnly; *-e Woche*, Passion Week; *-iger Zorn*, righteous anger. **-abend,** *m.* Christmas Eve. **-e(r),** *m.*, **-e,** *f.* saint; (*coll.*) *wunderlicher -er*, queer fellow, odd fish. **-e(s),** *n.* holy *or* sacred thing. **-en,** *v.a.* hallow, sanctify, consecrate; keep holy sanction, justify; (*Prov.*) *der Zweck -t die Mittel*, the end justifies the means; *geheiligt werde Dein Name*, hallowed be Thy name; *durch die Zeit geheiligt*, time-honoured. **-enbild,** *n.* image *or* picture of a saint. **-enblende,** *f.* niche for image of a saint. **-enbuch,** *n.* book of legends of saints, martyrology. **-endienst,** *m.* worship of saints; hagiolatry. **-engeschichte,** *f.* hagiology. **-englanz,** *m.* halo. **-enhaus,** *n.*, **-enkapelle,** *f.* chapel of a saint; shrine. **-enkalender,** *m.* calendar of saints. **-enschein,** *m.* halo (*of glory*), glory, gloriole; (*Paint.*) aureola; nimbus. **-halten,** 1. *v.a.* keep holy. 2. *n.*, **-haltung,** *f.* religious observance. **-keit,** *f.* holiness, godliness, sanctity, sacredness; *im Geruch der -keit*, in the odour of sanctity; *Seine -keit*, His Holiness. **-machend,** *adj.* sanctifying. **-sprechung,** *f.* canonization. **-tuerei,** *f.* sanctimoniousness. **-tum,** *n.* (-s, ⸚er) holy place, shrine, sanctuary; relic. **-tumsraub,** *m.* sacrilege. **-ung,** *f.* consecration, sanctification.

heim, 1. *adv.* home, homeward. 2. *n.* (-(e)s, -e) home; dwelling, abode; domicile; hostel; *eignes – haben*, own one's own house; *ein – gründen*, set up house; – *und Herd*, hearth and home. **-abend,** *m.* club night, weekly meeting. **-at,** *f.* (-en) home, native place *or* country, homeland. **-atkunde,** *f.* local history and topography. **-atkunst,** *f.* regional *or* local art. **-atland,** *n.* mother-country. **-atlich,** *adj.* native, belonging to one's home. **-atlos,** *adj.* homeless. **-atrecht,** *n.* rights of a native *or* naturalized p. **-atschein,** *m.* certificate of domicile. **-atschlag,** *m.* homing loft (*pigeons*). **-atschuß,** *m.* (*Mil. sl.*) a Blighty one (*1914–18 war*; a wound that ensured repatriation). **-atschutz,** *m.* preservation of beauty-spots (*cf. National Trust*). **-atsgesetz,** *n.* law of settlement. **-at(s)hafen,** *m.* port of registry (*Naut.*). **-begeben,** *v.r.* go *or* betake o.s. home. **-chen,** *n.* cricket. **-elig,** *adj.* comfy, intimate, cosy, snug. **-fahrt,** *f.* return *or* journey home. **-fall,** *m.* devolution, reversion, escheat (*Law.*). **-fallen,** *v.n.* revert (to). **-fällig,** *adj.* revertible, devolving. **-führen,** *v.a.* lead home; *die Braut -führen*, bring home one's bride, carry off the bride. **-führerin,** *f.*, *see* **-leiterin. -führung,** *f.* (*einer Braut*) bringing home a bride. **-gang,** *m.* going home; (*usually*) death. **-gegangene(r),** *m.*, *f.* the deceased. **-gehen,** *v.n.* (*aux.* s.) go home; die. **-isch,** *adj.* home-bred, domestic; homelike; native, national, indigenous; *-ische Industrie*, home industry; *sich -isch machen*, make o.s. at home, settle down; *sich -isch fühlen*, feel at home. **-kehr,** *f.*, *see* **-kunft. -kehrer,** *m.* returned soldier. **-kommen,** *ir.v.n.* (*aux.* s.) return home. **-krieger,** *m.* arm-chair warrior, carpet knight. **-kunft,** *f.* return home. **-leiterin,** *f.* matron (*of a hostel*). **-leuchten,** *v.a.* light home; (*fig. & poet.*) *einem -leuchten*, send a p. about his business, give a p. a piece of one's mind. **-lich,** *adj.* secret, concealed; stealthy, underhand, furtive, secretive, close; private, secluded; comfortable, snug; *-lich lachen*, laugh secretly, laugh in one's sleeve; *-lich tun*, effect a mysterious and knowing air. **-lichhaltung,** *f.* keeping secret; concealment. **-lichkeit,** *f.* secrecy; secret; privacy. **-lichtuerei,** *f.* **-lichtun,** *n.* affectation of secrecy, mystification. **-reise** *f.* homeward voyage; return. **-ritt,** *m.* ride home. **-ruf,** *m.*, **-rufung,** *f.* call *or* summons home, recall. **-schaffung,** *f.* repatriation. **-schule,** *f.* boarding school. **-sehnen,** *v.r.* be homesick. **-stätte,** *f.* home(stead); toft (*Law*); *-stätte für arme Greise*, home for the aged poor; *-stätte für Irrsinnige*, lunatic asylum. **-suchen,** *v.a.* visit, frequent; haunt, infest, overrun; afflict; punish. **-suchung,** *f.* visitation; affliction. **-tücke,** *f.* malice; underhand trick. **-tückegesetz,** *n.* (*Nat. Soc.*) law against malicious gossip. **-tükkisch,** *adj.* malicious, mischievous, crafty, treacherous, insidious. **-wärts,** *adv.* homeward, home. **-weg,** *m.* way home, return home; *auf dem -wege*, coming home, on the way home. **-weh,** *n.*

homesickness. **–wehr,** *f.* Home Defence Force; Austrian fascist party. **–wesen,** *n.* home, household. **–zahlen,** *v.a.* (*einem etwas*) pay a p. out (for s.th.) *or* back in his own coin, be revenged on (a p. for s.th.).

Hein, *m.*; (*coll.*) *Freund –*, Death.

heint, *adv.* (*dial.*) tonight, last night; today.

Heinz, *m.* (-en, -en), **–e,** *f.* (-n) rack *or* trestle for drying hay.

Heinzelmännchen, *n.* goblin, brownie, imp.

Heirat, *f.* (-en) marriage; nuptials, wedding, match; *– aus Liebe*, love-match; *die – ist rückgängig gemacht*, the match is broken off, the wedding *or* marriage will not take place; *auf – ausgehen*, look out for a wife. **–en,** *v.a.* & *n.* (*aux.* h.) marry, get married, wed (*high style*); take in marriage; *zum zweiten Male –en*, marry again *or* a second time; (*nach*) *Geld –en*, marry (for) money; *in die Stadt –en*, marry a townsman; *aufs Land –en*, marry a farmer; *nach London –en*, marry a Londoner. **–santrag,** *m.* offer of marriage, proposal; *einer Dame einen –santrag machen*, propose to a lady. **–sanzeige,** *f.* announcement of marriage. **–sfähig,** *adj.* marriageable. **–sgesuch,** *n.* offer of marriage. **–sgut,** *n.* marriage portion, dowry. **–skandidat,** *m.* suitor, wooer. **–skonsenz,** *m.* (marriage) licence. **–skontrakt,** *m.* marriage-settlement. **–slustig,** *adj.* eager to marry. **–smacher,** *m.*, **–sstifter,** *m.* matchmaker. **–sschein,** *m.* marriage certificate *or* lines. **–svermittler,** *m.* go-between, matchmaker, matrimonial agent. **–s(vermittlungs)bureau,** *n.* matrimonial agency.

heisch–en, *v.a.* (*poet.*) ask, demand, request, require. **–esatz,** *m.* postulate; optative clause (*Gram.*).

heiser, *adj.* hoarse, husky. **–keit,** *f.* hoarseness.

heiß, *adj.* hot, burning, boiling, torrid; ardent, passionate, fervid, vehement; *der Boden wird mir zu –*, things are getting too hot for me; *wie die Katze um den –en Brei*, like a cat on hot bricks; *–er Dank*, warm(est) thanks; *das Eisen schmieden solange es – ist*, strike the iron while it's hot; *–e Gebete*, fervent prayers; (*coll.*) *einem die Hölle – machen*, terrify a p., aggravate a p.'s alarm; *–er Kampf*, fierce combat; *–e Kastanien*, roasted chestnuts; *einem den Kopf – machen*, alarm *or* perturb a p.; *–e Liebe*, ardent love; *es lief mir – und kalt über den Rücken*, I went all hot and cold; *mir ist –*, I feel hot; *was ich nicht weiß, macht mich nicht –*, ignorance is bliss; *–e Zone*, torrid zone. **–blütig,** *adj.* hot-blooded (*Zool.*); hot-blooded, hot-tempered, choleric. **–brühen,** *v.a.* scald. **–dampf,** *m.* superheated steam. **–geliebt,** *adj.* dearly beloved. **–hunger,** *m.* ravenous hunger, voracious appetite. **–hungrig,** *adj.* ravenously hungry, voracious. **–kühlung,** *f.* cooling by evaporation. **–laufen,** *v.n.* (*aux.* s.) & *r.* overheat (*of engines*). **–luftbeize,** *f.* hot air treatment. **–sporn,** *m.* hotspur, firebrand. **–wasserheizung,** *f.* water heater, hot-water system. **–wasserspeicher,** *m.* hot-water tank (*usually with electric immersion heater fitted*).

[1]**heiß–en,** 1. *ir.v.a.* command, enjoin, bid, order, direct; name, call, denominate; *einen gehen –en*, bid s.o. go; *er hieß ihn hereinkommen*, he bade him come in; *tue, wie dir geheißen*, do as you are bid; *gut–en*, approve of; *einen willkommen –en*, welcome a p.; *wer hat Sie das geheißen?* who bade you do that, who told you to do that? *jemanden einen Lügner –en*, call a p. a liar. 2. *v.n.* (*aux.* h.) be called *or* named; mean, signify; *das –t*, that is (to say), that is equal to; *er heißt*, his name is; *wie –en Sie?* what is your name? *ich will ein Schuft –en, wenn . . .*, I'm a Dutchman if . . ., I'll eat my hat if . . .; *wie –t das auf Deutsch?* what is that in German? what is the German for this? *er lachte laut auf, was soviel –en sollte als*, he laughed outright, as much as to say; *das –e ich lügen*, that's what I call a lie; *das –t gelaufen*, I call that good running; *was soll das –en?* what is the meaning of this? what do you mean? *das will wenig –en*, that is of little consequence; *das will schon etwas –en*, that is saying a good deal. 3. *v.n.imp.*; *es –t*, it is said *or* reported, they say; *damit es nicht –e*, that it may not be said; *wie es im Liede –t*, as the song says; *hier –t es mit Recht*, one may well say here; *jetzt –t es Mut!* courage is called for here.

[2]**heißen,** *v.a.*, *see* **hissen.**

Heister, *m.* (-s, –), *also f.* (-n) sapling, young tree, (*dial.*) young beech-tree.

heiter, *adj.* clear, bright; serene, calm, unruffled; happy, gay, merry, cheerful, glad; *– werden*, grow bright, clear up; (*coll.*) become interesting; *–es Gemüt*, cheerful *or* happy disposition; *–e Stimmung*, merry *or* jovial mood; *–es Wetter*, fine, sunny weather; *wie ein Blitz aus –em Himmel*, like a bolt from the blue. **–keit,** *f.* brightness; cheerfulness; clearness, serenity.

heiz–en, 1. *v.a.* & *n.* heat; make a fire; *mit Holz* or *Steinkohlen –en*, burn wood *or* coal; *dieses Zimmer läßt sich gut –en*, this room is easily heated; *diese Kohlen –en gut*, this coal gives a good heat. **–anlage,** *f.* heating-installation. **–anzug,** *m.* electrically heated flying suit (*Av.*). **–apparat,** *m.* heating-apparatus, heater. **–bar,** *adj.* heatable, easily heated; *–bare Zimmer*, rooms with heating. **–batterie,** *f.* low-tension battery (*Rad.*). **–draht,** *m.*, **–faden,** *m.* filament (*Rad.*). **–er,** *m.* stoker, fireman; heating-apparatus. **–gas,** *n.* fuel gas. **–kammer,** *f.* stokehold. **–kissen,** *n.* electric pillow, pad *or* blanket. **–kraft,** *f.* heating power. **–loch,** *n.*, *see* **–kammer.** **–mantel,** *m.* steam jacket. **–material,** *n.* fuel. **–platte,** *f.* hot-plate. **–raum,** *m.* stokehole. **–röhre,** *f.* fire-tube. **–sonne,** *f.* electric fire. **–strom,** *m.* filament current (*Rad.*). **–ung,** *f.* heating; fuel, firing; steam; *die –ung abdrehen* (or *aufdrehen*), turn off (*or* on) the steam. **–vorrichtung,** *f.* heating appliance. **–wert,** *m.* calorific value.

Hekatombe, *f.* (-n) hecatomb.

Hektar, *n.* (*Austr. also m.*) (-s, -e), **–e,** *f.* (-n) (*Swiss dial.*) hectare.

hektisch, *adj.* hectic.

Hekto-, (*in compounds*). **–gramm,** *n.* hectogramme. **–graph,** *m.* hectograph; duplicator. **–liter,** *n.* & (*Austr.*) *m.* hectolitre.

Held, *m.* (-en, -en) hero; champion; famous person; principal person; *– eines Romans*, hero *or* chief character of a novel. **–enalter,** *n.* heroic age. **–enbahn,** *f.* heroic career. **–enbuch,** *n.* collection of medieval heroic poems. **–endichter,** *m.* epic poet. **–endichtung,** *f.* heroic *or* epic poetry. **–engedicht,** *n.* heroic epic. **–engeist,** *m.* heroic spirit. **–enhaft,** *adj.* heroic. **–enkeller,** *m.* (*sl.*) air-raid shelter, funk-hole. **–enkühn,** *adj.* brave as a hero of old. **–enlied,** *n.* heroic song, *see* **–engedicht.** **–enmäßig,** *adj.*, **–enmütig,** *adj.* heroic, valiant. **–enmut,** *m.* heroism, valour, heroic spirit. **–enrolle,** *f.* part of the hero (*Theat.*). **–ensage,** *f.* heroic saga *or* legend. **–ensinn,** *m.* heroism, heroic spirit. **–enstück,** *n.* heroic feat. **–entat,** *f.* heroic deed, bold exploit. **–entod,** *m.* death in battle. **–entum,** *n.* heroism; heroic age. **–enverehrung,** *f.* hero-worship. **–enweib,** *n.* heroic woman, heroine. **–enzug,** *m.* heroic trait; expedition. **–in,** *f.* heroine. **–isch,** *adj.* heroic; *–ische Dichtung*, (medieval) heroic *or* epic poetry.

helf–en, *ir.v.n.* (*aux.* h.) (*Dat.*) help, aid, assist, succour, promote, support; be of use, avail, profit, do good to; remedy; deliver; *hilf Gott!* Heaven preserve me! *so wahr mir Gott –e!* so help me God! (*B.*) *was hülfe es dem Menschen, wenn*, what is a man profited if; *da ist nicht zu –en*, nothing can be done about it; *dem ist nicht* (*mehr*) *zu –en*, he is past help; that is irremediable; *ich kann mir nicht –en*, I cannot help it, I have no alternative; *es hilft nichts*, it is of no use, it is *or* does no good; *es hilft Ihnen nichts zu . . .*, it is of no use for you to . . .; *einem zu seinem Rechte –en*, see that a p. gets his rights; *einem auf die Spur –en*, put a p. on the track; *er weiß sich zu –en*, he can take care of himself, he is never beaten *or* nonplussed. **–er,** *m.* helper, assistant. **–erin,** *f.* nurse. **–ershelfer,** *m.* accomplice, abettor.

Helge, *f.* (-n), **–n,** *m.* (-s, –) (*dial.*) *see* **Helling.**

Helio-, (*in compounds*) **–graph,** *m.* heliograph. **–gravüre,** *f.* photogravure. **–trop,** *m.* (-s, -e) heliotrope. **–zentrisch,** *adj.* heliocentric.

hell, *adj.* clear, bright, shining, brilliant, luminous, pellucid; distinct; ringing, high (*of pitch*); light, fair (*hair*); pale (*ale*); *–e Augenblicke*, lucid intervals; *–e Farben*, light colours; *seine –e Freude an einer S. haben*, take a real pleasure in a th.; *–es Gelächter*, loud laugh, ringing laughter, hearty laugh; *in –en Haufen*, in large numbers, in full force; *–er Kopf*, clear-headed person; *–er Mittag*, broad noon(day); *–er Neid*, pure jealousy; *–er Tag*, fine day; *am –en, lichten Tage*, in broad daylight; *–e Tränen*, big tears; *–e Verwunderung, –e Verzweiflung, –er Wahnsinn*, sheer astonishment, despair, madness; *–e Wahrheit*, plain truth; *es wird schon –*, it is getting light, dawn is breaking. **–auf,** *adv.* loudly, noisily (*used only with* lachen). **–äugig,** *adj.* bright-eyed; clear-sighted. **–blond,** *adj.* very fair; ash-blond. **–braun,** *adj.* light brown. **–denkend,** *adj.* clear-headed. **–dunkel,** 1. *adj.* dim, half-lit, dusky. 2. *n.* (*dial.*) twilight, dusk; chiaroscuro. **–e,** 1. *f.*, *see* **–igkeit.** 2. *n.* light ale; *ein –es*, a glass of pale ale. **–en,** 1. *v.a.* (*Poet.*) make clear *or* bright; clarify, elucidate. 2. *v.r.* (*Poet.*) become bright, clear up. **–igkeit,** *f.* clearness, brightness, intensity of light; splendour; loudness. **–färben,** *v.a.* tint. **–farbig,** *adj.* light-coloured. **–hörig,** *adj.* keen of hearing. **–(l)euchtend,** *adj.* luminous. **–(l)icht,** *adj.*; *am –(l)ichten Tage*, in broad daylight. **–rot,** *adj.* light *or* bright red. **–schreiber,** *m.* teleprinter. **–sehen,** *n.* clairvoyance. **–sehend,** *adj.* clear-sighted, keen-sighted, wide-awake. **–seher,** *m.*, **–seherin,** *f.* clairvoyant(e). **–seherisch,** *adj.* **–sichtig,** *adj.* clairvoyant. **–violett,** *adj.* mauve.

Hellebard–e, *f.* (-en) halberd, halbert. **–ier,** *m.* (-s, -e) halberdier.

Heller, *m.* (-s, –) small coin; (*B.*) mite; *kein roter –*, not a farthing; *auf* or *bei – und Pfennig*, to the last farthing; *der letzte –*, the last farthing; *ich schere mich keinen roten – darum*, I don't care a brass farthing about it.

Helling, *f.* (*pl.* -en & Helligen) & *m.* (-s, -e) slip, slip-way (*Shipbuilding*).

[1]**Helm,** *m.* (-(e)s, -e) helmet, (*archaic*) helm, casque; dome, cupola; **–artig,** *adj.* helmet-like; galeate(d) (*Bot.*). **–beschlag,** *m.* helmet furnishings. **–busch** *m.* crest *or* plume of a helmet. **–dach,** *n.* vaulted roof, cupola. **–fenster,** *n.*, **–gitter,** *n.* eye-piece, eye-slit (of helmet). **–gewölbe,** *n.* vaulted roof. **–kamm,** *m.* crest. **–kolben,** *m.* distilling flask. **–schieber,** *m.* beaver, visor. **–strauß,** *m.*, **–stutz,** *m.* crest, plume. **–sturz,** *m.* visor. **–visier,** *n.* visor.

[2]**Helm,** *m.* & *n.* (-(e)s, -e) handle, helve.

Helot(e), *m.* (-en, -en) helot. **–entum,** *n.* helotry, helotism. **–isch,** *adj.* slave-like, slavish.

Hemd, *n.* (-(e)s, -en) shirt; undervest (*man*), chemise, vest (*woman*); *bis aufs – ausziehen*, rob of everything, plunder completely; *im bloßen –e*, in one's shirt; *kein* (*ganzes*) *– am* or *auf dem Leib* (*mehr*) *haben*, not have a shirt to one's back; (*Prov.*) *das – ist mir näher als der Rock*, blood is thicker than water; charity begins at home; *alles bis aufs – verlieren*, lose everything, not have a thing left; *das – wechseln*, put on a clean shirt. **–ärmel,** *m.*, *see* **–särmel. –ärmelig,** *adj.*, *see* **–särmelig. –brust,** *f.*, **–einsatz,** *m.* shirt-front, dicky. **–(en)knopf,** *m.* shirt button; stud. (*coll.*) **–enmatz,** *m.* (*hum.*) little child with nothing on but a shirt. **–hose,** *f.* combinations, cami-knickers. **–knopf,** *m.* stud. **–kragen,** *m.* shirt-collar. **–krause,** *f.* frill. **–leinwand,** *f.* shirting. **–särmel,** *m.* shirt sleeve. **–särmelig,** *adj.* in shirt-sleeves. **–schlitz,** *m.* shirt-opening.

Hemisphär–e, *f.* (-en) hemisphere. **–isch,** *adj.* hemispherical.

hemm–en, *v.a.* hem in; check, stop, arrest, dog, obstruct, inhibit, hinder, retard; slow up *or* down, delay; prohibit; put on the drag *or* brake; stop, deaden (*Naut.*); curb, restrain (*passions, etc.*). **–e,** *f. see* **–schuh, –kette. –feder,** *f.* stopper (*Horol.*). **–kette,** *f.* drag-chain. **–nis,** *n.* check, obstruction, obstacle, hindrance, impediment. **–schuh,** *m.* drag, block, wedge. **–ung,** *f.* restraint, check; inhibition, suppression; checking, stopping, retardation; escapement (*of a watch*); jam, stoppage (*of a gun*). **–ungsbildung,** *f.* arrested development, malformation, structural defect. **–ungslos,** *adj.* unchecked, unrestrained. **–ungsspruch,** *m.*, **–ungsurteil,** *n.* arrest of judgement.

Hendel, *n.* (-s, -(n)) (*Austr. dial.*) chicken.

Hengst, *m.* (-es, -e) stallion; jackass (*male of the horse, zebra, camel, or ass*). **–füllen,** *n.* male colt. **–geld,** *n.* covering-fee.

Henkel, *m.* (-s, –) handle (*of a basket, pot, etc.*); ring, ear, lug; hook; shank (*of a button*). **–ig,** *adj.* with a handle, handled. **–korb,** *m.* basket with handles. **–krug,** *m.* jug, mug. **–napf,** *m.* **–schale,** *f.*, **–topf,** *m.* casserole.

henk–en, *v.a.* (*archaic*) hang (*a p. on the gallows*) **–er,** *m.* hangman, executioner; *was zum –er!* what the deuce! (*vulg.*) *geh zum –er! scher' dich zum –er!* go to the devil! (*vulg.*) *hol' euch der –er!* devil take you! (*vulg.*) *ich frage den –er danach, ich schere mich den –er drum*, I don't care a damn about it; (*coll.*) *daraus werde der –er klug*, I cannot make head or tail of it. **–ersbeil,** *n.* executioner's axe. **–ersfrist,** *f.*, *see* **Galgenfrist. –shand,** *f.*; *von –shand sterben*, die at the hands of the executioner. **–ersknecht,** *m.* tormentor, torturer. **–ersmahl,** *n.*, **–ersmahlzeit,** *f.* last meal (before execution); (*coll.*) farewell dinner. **–erstrick,** *m.* halter, rope for hanging.

Henne, *f.* hen; *junge –*, pullet.

her, *adv.* 1. hither, here, this way; *– damit!* out with it! hand it over! *wo hat er das –?* where did he get that (from)? *die Hand –*, give me your hand! *hin und –*, to and fro, hither and thither, up and down, there and back; *ich dachte lange hin und –*, I turned the matter over in my mind for a long time; *hin und – sprechen*, debate, argue; *hinter einem – sein*, follow close upon s.o.'s heels, pursue a p., pester a p., be after a p.; (*fig.*) press *or* urge a p.; *hinter einer S. – sein*, be hot in pursuit of s.th.; *rings um uns –*, round about us; *von oben* (*unten*) *–*, from above (below); *weit –*, from afar; *nicht weit – sein*, be inferior, indifferent, mediocre, middling, insignificant, unimportant *or* of little value; (*coll.*) be no great shakes, not be up to much; (*coll.*) *wo sind Sie –?* where do you come from? *– zu mir!* come over here! 2. since, ago (*of time*); *von alters –*, from time immemorial, of old; *vom Anfange –*, from the very beginning; *von früher –*, from some time earlier, from earlier times; *von je –*, always; *von meiner Jugend –*, dating from my youth; *wie lange ist es –?* how long ago is it? *noch keine Viertelstunde –*, not a quarter of an hour ago. 3. *prefix* (a) *to prepositions* (*used adverbially*), *is unaccented*; *see* **herab, heran, herauf, heraus, herbei,** *etc.*: *it refers the indicated motion in the direction of the speaker, cf. its opposite* **hin**; (b) *to verbs, it takes the accent and is separable*; *both as a simple prefix and as a component of the compound prefixes of* (*a*) *it usually implies the notion of 'hither'. Many compounds are of course quite idiomatic.*

herab, *adv.* & *sep. prefix* (*indicates movement downwards as seen by the person below*), down, down here; down from; downward; (*with preceding Acc.*) *den Berg –*, down (from) the mountain; *die Treppe –*, down (the) stairs; *von oben –*, from above; in a superior way *or* tone. **–bemühen,** 1. *v.a.* (*einen*) give (a p.) the trouble of coming down. 2. *v.r.* take the trouble of coming down. **–drücken,** *v.a.* press down, depress. **–drücker,** *m.* depressor muscle (*Anat.*). **–fließen,** *v.n.* flow *or* run down. **–gehen,** *v.n.* extend downward. **–hängend,** *adj.* pendent, pendulous; flowing. **–kommen,** *ir.v.n.* (*aux.* s.) come down; be reduced in circumstances, be brought low. **–lassen,** 1. *ir.v.a.* lower, let down. 2. *v.r.* condescend, deign, stoop. **–lassend,** condescending, affable. **–lassung,** *f.* condescension; courtesy; affability. **–laufen,** *v.n.* run down (*as clocks*). **–mindern,** *v.a.* decrease, reduce, diminish. **–rieseln,** *v.n.* trickle down. **–schießen,** 1. *v.a.* shoot down (*birds, aircraft, etc.*). 2. *v.n.* come shooting *or* running down. **–sehen,** *ir.v.n.* (*aux.* h.) look down (*auf einen* or *etwas*, upon a p. *or* a th.), despise. **–senken,** *v.a.* lower. **–setzen,** *v.a.* lower, degrade; undervalue, minimize, disparage; abate, decrease, reduce (*in price*); *zu –gesetzten Preisen*, at reduced prices. **–setzung,** *f.* degradation, reduction, abatement, decrease; disparagement, undervaluation, depreciation. **-sinken,** *ir.v.n.* (*aux.* s.) sink down; drop, fall; debase *or* degrade o.s. **-steigen,** *ir.v.n.* (*aux.* s.) descend, step down; dismount. **-stimmen,** *v.a.* lower; tune lower; deject, depress; moderate (*one's pretensions, etc.*); *er muß die Saiten etwas -stimmen,* he must come down a peg or two. **-stimmung,** *f.* lowering, lowering of the pitch (*Mus.*); dejection, depression. **-transformieren,** *v.a.* step down (*Elec.*). **-wollen,** *ir.v.n.* wish to come down. **-wünschen,** *v.a.* call down (*blessings, curses*) upon. **-würdigen,** 1. *v.a.* degrade, abase; depreciate. 2. *v.r.* lower o.s., demean o.s., stoop. **-würdigung,** *f.* degradation, abasement; disparagement.

Herald-ik, *f.* heraldry. **-isch,** *adj.* heraldic.

heran, *adv.* & *sep. prefix* (*indicates movement approaching the speaker*), on, near, along(side), up to, upwards; *er ging an sie -,* he went up to them; *nur -!* come on! advance! **-bilden,** *v.a.* bring up, train, educate. **-führen,** *v.a.* bring up, concentrate (*forces*) (*Mil.*). **-gehen,** *v.n.* approach; *an den Gegner scharf -gehen,* press one's opponent closely, (*sl.*) pile into one's opponent. **-kommen,** *ir.v.n.* (*aux.* s.) come on *or* near, approach, get near to, near, come alongside (*Naut.*); set in; *Dinge an sich -kommen lassen,* bide one's time. **-kunft,** *f.* approach. **-machen,** *v.r.* (*an*) undertake, set about (*a task*), approach (*a p. in order to obtain s.th.*). **-nahen,** *v.n.* (*aux.* s.) draw near, approach. **-pirschen,** *v.r.* stalk up (to) (*Hunt.*). **-reichen,** *v.n.* (*aux.* s.) reach up to. **-reifen,** *v.n.* (*aux.* s.) grow to maturity, grow up. **-rücken,** *v.n.* (*aux.* s.) push onward, advance, draw near. **-schaffen,** *see* **-führen.** (*sl.*) **-schlängeln,** *v.r.* come quietly *or* sneaking up. **-schleichen,** *v.n.* sneak up, creep forward. **-treten,** *ir.v.n.*; *an einen -treten,* approach a p. **-wachsen,** *ir.v.n.* (*aux.* s.) grow up; *das -wachsende Geschlecht,* the rising generation. **-ziehen,** 1. *ir.v.a.* & *n.* (*aux.* s.) draw near. 2. *v.a.* draw on *or* along, tow; draw into, bring into play, bring up; requisition, detail (*Mil.*); interest in; quote; call upon, refer to. **-zieher,** *m.* adductor muscle (*Anat.*).

Herauch, (*Austr. also*) **Heerauch, Höhenrauch,** *m.* haze.

herauf, *adv.* & *sep. prefix* (*indicates movement upwards as seen by the person above*), up, up to(wards), upwards, from below. **-beschwören,** *v.a.* conjure up; bring on, cause, occasion. **-blicken,** *v.n.* (*aux.* h.) glance up *or* upwards. **-kommen,** *ir.v.n.* (*aux.* s.) come up; *-kommen in der Welt,* get on *or* rise in the world; *-kommen lassen,* order up. **-müssen,** *v.n.* be obliged to come up. **-setzen,** *v.a.* put up (*prices*); *der Schüler wurde -gesetzt,* the pupil was put up (*in class*). **-steigen,** 1. *ir.v.a.* mount (*stairs, etc.*). 2. *ir.v.n.* come up (*as a storm*), break, dawn (*of day*). **-ziehen,** 1. *v.a.* draw up. 2. *v.n.* (*aux.* s.) draw near, approach.

heraus, *adv.* & *sep. prefix* (*indicates movement from inside a place as seen by the person outside*), out, from within, forth, from among; *-!* turn out! (*Mil.*); *- damit!* out with it! speak out! *- aus den Federn!* get up! get out of bed! (*coll.*) *er ist fein* (or *schön*) *heraus,* he is a lucky fellow, he is well out of it; *von innen -,* from within; (*coll.*) *er hat es -,* he has found it out; he understands it, (*coll.*) he's tumbled to it; *rund* or *frei -,* flatly, bluntly, fearlessly; *da -,* this way out. **-arbeiten,** 1. *v.a.* work out. 2. *v.r.* extricate o.s. **-beißen,** 1. *v.r.* extricate o.s. 2. *v.a.* lay stress on; *er beißt immer den Offizier heraus,* he won't let anyone forget that he is an officer. **-bekommen,** *ir.v.a.* find out, get out, make out, elicit, arrive at, solve; get back in exchange; *einen Nagel aus dem Holz -bekommen,* get *or* pull a nail out of the wood; *ein Geheimnis aus einem -bekommen,* worm a secret out of s.o.; *ich bekomme eine Mark -,* I get a mark change; *er kann die Aufgabe nicht -bekommen,* he is unable to solve the problem. **-bilden,** *v.a.* develop. **-bildung,** *f.* formation, evolution. **-bringen,** *ir.v.a.* find out, solve; bring out, get out; publish, issue; *seine Kosten -bringen,* cover one's expenses; *ein Buch -bringen,* bring out *or* publish a book. **-drängen,** *v.a.* drive out. **-fahren,** *ir.v.n.* (*aux.* s.) drive *or* sail out; rush, fly *or* burst out; slip out (*as an unpremeditated remark*). **-finden,** 1. *ir.v.a.* find out, discover. 2. *v.r.* find one's way out; see one's way clearly. **-fordern,** *v.a.* challenge; provoke; defy; demand categorically; *einen zum Zweikampf -fordern,* challenge s.o. to a duel; *-forderndes Benehmen,* defiant conduct. **-forderung,** *f.* challenge; provocation. **-fühlen,** *v.a.* discover *or* select by touch *or* feeling. **-gabe,** *f.* giving back *or* up, delivering up; setting free; editing (*of a book*), issue, publication. **-geben,** *ir.v.a.* give up, deliver up, hand out; edit, publish; give change; *können Sie mir -geben?* can you give me change? **-geber,** *m.* editor, publisher. **-gehen,** *v.n.* go out, come out, leave; lead *or* open out (*auf,* on to); *aus sich nicht -gehen,* be reserved *or* taciturn. **-greifen,** *v.a.* choose, single out. **-hängen,** 1. *v.a.* hang out (*washing, flags, etc.*). 2. *v.n.* hang out (*as tongue with thirst*); (*vulg.*) *das hängt mir zum Halse heraus,* I am fed up with it, I have had my fill of it; (*vulg.*) I've had a belly-full. **-heben,** *ir.v.a.* lift *or* take out; haul out, raise; render prominent, make conspicuous, lay stress on; throw into relief, set off; *eine Dame aus dem Wagen -heben,* help a lady *or* give a lady a hand out of the car. **-holen,** *v.a.* get, drag *or* force from *or* out of; *aus einem Menschen* (or *Motor*) *das Äußerste -holen,* force a person (*or* a motor) to the limit. **-kehren,** *v.a., see* **-beißen**; *er kehrt den Offizier nicht heraus,* he does not flaunt his rank. **-kommen,** *ir.v.n.* (*aux.* s.) come out *or* forth; issue; appear; be issued; become known, be published; prove correct, amount to, be of use, yield profit; *was wird dabei -kommen?* what will be the use of it? what will be the upshot? *es muß ganz natürlich -kommen,* it must appear quite natural; *so -kommen als ob,* seem as if; *aus sich -kommen,* loosen up, thaw out; *aus etwas -kommen,* recover from, get over; *das kommt dabei - wenn man lügt,* that is the result of telling lies; *es kommt auf eins -,* it is all the same in the end, it is all one. **-lesen,** *ir.v.a.* deduce from what one reads, read between the lines. **-locken,** *v.a.* entice out, elicit, lure out. **-machen,** 1. *v.a.* get *or* take out (*stains, etc.*). 2. *v.r.* get on, prosper; *sie hat sich sehr -gemacht,* she has developed wonderfully. **-müssen,** *ir.v.n.* be obliged to come *or* go out. **-nehmen,** *ir.v.a.* take out, draw forth; extract, remove; *sich* (*Dat.*) *etwas -nehmen,* presume, make (so) bold, venture; *sich* (*Dat.*) *-nehmen,* choose, take for o.s., usurp. **-platzen,** *v.n.* (*aux.* s.) blurt out. **-pressen,** *v.a.* squeeze, wring *or* force out; express, extrude. **-putzen,** *v.a.* dress up, decorate, set off, (*coll.*) doll up. **-ragen,** *v.n.* jut out, protrude, project. **-reden,** 1. *v.n.* (*aux.* h.) speak freely. 2. *v.r.* make excuses. **-reißen,** *ir.v.a.* pull out, tear out, weed out, extract; free, deliver, extricate; *einen aus seinem Schlendrian -reißen,* shake a p. out of his idleness. **-rücken,** 1. *v.a.* move out, (*coll.*) fork out (*money*). 2. *v.n.* (*aux.* s.) march out, come forth; *mit der Sprache -rücken,* speak out freely, come out with. **-rufen,** *v.a.* call before the curtain (*Theat.*); turn out (*the guard*) (*Mil.*). **-sagen,** *v.a.* speak one's mind; *rund -gesagt,* to put it bluntly, in plain words. **-schälen,** *v.a.* obtain by peeling, shell, sift, pick out; *aus verworrenen Überlieferungen den geschichtlichen Kern -schälen,* sift *or* pick out what is historically true from a mass of confused evidence. **-scheren,** *v.n.* peel off (*from a formation in flight*) (*Av.*). **-schlagen,** 1. *v.a.* strike out, beat out; *Funken aus dem Stein -schlagen,* strike sparks from the stone; *Geld -schlagen,* make money, make a profit; *die Kosten -schlagen,* recover expenses; *möglichst viel -schlagen aus einer S.,* make the most of a th., derive the greatest possible benefit from a th. 2. *v.n.* burst forth; *die Flammen schlugen zum Dach heraus,* the flames shot up *or* broke through the roof. **-setzen,** *v.a.* set out, expose; object. **-stecken,** *v.a.* put *or* hang out (*flags, etc.*); put *or* stick (*tongue*) out at, (*fig.*) say, utter, or do (*s.th.*) tactlessly or heedlessly; (*sl.*) shoot off one's mouth, put one's foot in it. **-stehen,** *ir.v.n.* (*aux.* h.) stand out, project. **-stellen,** 1. *v.a.* put out, expose, lay out; lay down, expound. 2. *v.r.* turn out, appear, prove (*als wahr oder falsch*, true *or* false); *im Laufe der Untersuchung stellte sich –, daß . . .*, in the course of the inquiry it appeared that . . . . **–streichen,** *ir.v.a.* expunge, efface; extol, praise. **–treten,** 1. *ir.v.a.* step out, retire, emerge; protrude. 2. *n.* protuberance. **–tun,** *ir.v.a.* put out, take out. **–wachsen,** *ir.v.n.* (*aux.* s.) grow out, develop, sprout; (*coll.*) *das wächst mir zum Halse –, see* **–hängen. –wickeln,** 1. *v.a.* unwrap. 2. *v.r.* extricate o.s. **–ziehen,** 1. *ir.v.a.* extract, remove. 2. *v.n.* (*aux.* s.) march out. 3. *v.r.* extricate o.s. (*from a scrape*).

herb, *adj.* acid, sharp, tart, acrid; astringent; (*fig.*) harsh, dry (*of wine*); austere; unpleasant; bitter; *–e Not*, dire necessity; *–er Tod*, grim death. **–e,** *f.* acidity; harshness, austerity, severity. **–heit,** *f.*, **–igkeit,** *f.* bitterness, acerbity, harshness. **–lich,** *adj.* somewhat bitter, rather harsh.

herbei, *adv. & sep. prefix* (*indicates movement from a remoter to a nearer place with reference to the speaker or the point contemplated by him*), hither, here, near, on, this way, into the vicinity of; *–, ihr Leute!* gather round, folks! **–bringen,** *ir.v.a.* bring on *or* up; produce. **–führen,** *v.a.* bring about, up *or* near; induce, cause, give occasion for, give rise to. **–lassen,** *ir.v.r.* condescend to do a th.; *mein Bruder will sich nicht dazu –lassen*, my brother scorns to do it. **–rufen,** *v.a.* call in. **–schaffen,** *v.a.* bring near, collect; raise (*money*); procure, produce; furnish, provide. **–strömen,** *v.n.* gather *or* flock round. **–ziehen,** 1. *ir.v.a.* draw *or* pull near, towards. 2. *v.n.* (*aux.* s.) draw *or* march near, approach; *er zieht seine Beispiele an den Haaren –*, his examples are far-fetched *or* fantastic.

herbemühen, 1. *v.a.* induce (a p.) to come. 2. *v.r.* take the trouble to come.

Herberg–e, *f.* (-en) shelter, lodging, quarters; inn, hostel; *einem –e geben*, lodge a p. **–en,** *v.a. & n.* (*aux.* h.) shelter, harbour, lodge; entertain (*wishes, views, etc.*). **–smutter,** *f.*, **–svater,** *m.* hostel warden.

herbestellen, *v.a.* order to come; send for (*a p.*).

herbringen, *ir.v.a.* bring hither, in *or* up; establish; transmit (*from ancestors*); *hergebracht*, handed down (*to our own times*), traditional, customary, established (*by traditional usage*); *hergebrachter Ton, hergebrachtes Wesen*, conventionalism; *hergebrachte Gewohnheit*, ancient *or* established custom.

Herbst, *m.* (-es, -e) autumn; fall (*Amer.*); harvest season; (*dial.*) vine harvest; *der – ist eingebracht*, the vine harvest is gathered. **–eln,** *v.n. imp., see* **–en** (2). **–en,** 1. *v.a.* (*dial.*) gather the vine harvest. 2. *v.n. imp.*; *es –et*, there are signs of autumn; *so oft es –et*, always when autumn comes. **–lich,** *adj.* autumnal. **–lichkeit,** *f.* autumnal season; autumnal look. **–ling,** *m.* autumn fruit; animal born in autumn. **–färbung,** *f.* autumnal tints. **–furche,** *f.* autumn ploughing. **–leute,** *pl.* (*dial.*) harvesters; vintagers. **–mäßig,** *adj.* autumnal. **–monat,** *m.*, **–mond,** *m.* September. **–rose,** *f.* hollyhock (*Althaea rosea*) (*Bot.*). **––Tagundnachtgleiche,** *f.* autumnal equinox. **–zeitlose,** *f.* meadow saffron, autumn crocus (*Colchicum autumnale*) (*Bot.*).

Herd, *m.* (-(e)s, -e) hearth, fireplace, fireside; kitchen-range, cooking stove; seat, focus (*of rebellion, disease, etc.*); centre; source; saddle (*of a block*) (*Naut.*); (*Prov.*) *eigner – ist Goldes wert*, there's no place like home; *Heim und –*, hearth and home. **–eisen,** *n.* poker. **–geld,** *n.* house tax. **–guß,** *m.* open sand casting. **–löffel,** *m.* assaying ladle. **–platte,** *f.* hot-plate. **–steuer,** *f.*, **–zins,** *m., see* **geld.**

Herde, *f.* (-n) drove, flock, herd; crowd, multitude; *der – folgen*, follow the crowd, be guided by herd instinct. **–ntier,** *n.* gregarious animal. **–nweise,** *adv.* in flocks *or* herds.

herein, *adv. & sep. prefix* (*indicates movement into a place as seen by the person inside*) in, in here; inward; *–!* come in! *hier –*, this way, in here; *von (dr)außen –*, from without. **–brechen,** *v.n.* (*aux.* s.) set in, befall, overtake, fall. **–bestellen,** *v.a.* order to come *or* be brought in. **–bitten,** *v.a.* invite (*a p.*) to come in. **–bringen,** *v.a.* gather in (*crops*), harvest. **–dürfen,** *ir.v.n.* be allowed to come in. **–fallen,** *ir.v.n.* (*aux.* s.) fall into; come to grief; (*coll.*) be taken in, be disappointed. **–lassen,** *ir.v.a.* admit; *laß ihn –!* let him come in! bid him come in! **–legen,** *v.a.* lay in; (*coll.*) deceive, take in, do. **–müssen,** *ir.v.n.* (*aux.* h.) be obliged to come in; *die Stühle müssen –*, the chairs must be brought in. (*fig.*) **–schneien,** *v.n.* arrive unexpectedly, (*coll.*) drop in. **–treten,** *v.n.* step in, enter. **–wollen,** *ir.v.n.* wish to come in.

hererzählen, *v.a.* go over, rehearse, relate, recite, narrate.

herfahren, 1. *ir.v.n.* (*aux.* s.) come, travel, approach, arrive; move hastily along; *über einen –*, pounce upon, attack *or* inveigh against a p. 2. *v.a.* bring, drive.

herfallen, *ir.v.n.* (*aux.* s.) fall towards; *über einen –*, assail a p., fall upon a p. (*with blows, angry words*).

herfinden, *ir.v.r.* find one's way to a place.

herfließen, *ir.v.n.* (*aux.* s.) flow on, up *or* towards, issue *or* proceed (from), originate (in).

herfür, *adv.* (*Poet.*), *see* **hervor.**

Hergang, *m.* way here; course of events, circumstances, proceedings; occurrence; *der ganze – der S.*, the details of the story, the whole story.

hergeben, *ir.v.a.* give up, deliver; give away, hand over; *geben Sie mir gefälligst das Brot her*, I'll thank you to pass me the bread; *ich will mich nicht dazu –*, I will not lend myself *or* be a party to that, I will have nothing to do with it; *Waren – für*, sell goods at.

hergebracht, *adj., see* **herbringen.**

hergehen, *ir.v.n.* (*aux.* s.); (*generally used as v. imp.*) come to pass, happen; go on, be going on, be carried on; *vor etwas –*, go before *or* at the head; *über etwas –*, set to *or* set about s.th.; *es geht über ihn her*, he is attacked *or* fallen upon; *da geht es heiß her*, there is hot work going on there; *es geht lustig her*, things are going on merrily; *es geht armselig bei ihm her*, he lives in a poor way *or* is badly off; *so geht es (in der Welt) her*, that's the way of the world, such is life; (*dial.*) *geh' her*, come along.

hergehör–en, *v.n.* (*aux.* h.) belong to (*this place, the matter in question*); be to the purpose; *diese Bemerkungen gehören nicht (hier)her*, these remarks are out of place (here). **–ig,** *adj.* apposite, pertinent.

herhalten, 1. *ir.v.a.* hold out, tender. 2. *v.n.* (*aux.* h.) pay, suffer (for), bear the brunt (of); *sein Beutel muß –*, he has to pay, (*coll.*) his pocket will have to stand it.

herholen, *v.a.* fetch; *weit hergeholt*, far-fetched.

Hering, *m.* (-s, -e) herring; tent-peg; weedy fellow, little shrimp; *geräucherter –*, smoked herring, bloater; *gesalzener –*, pickled herring; *gedörrter –*, kipper(ed) (herring); *geschichtet wie die –e*, packed like sardines. **–fang,** *m.* herring-fishery. **–sjäger,** *m.* herring-smack. **–smilch,** *f.* soft roe.

herkommen, 1. *ir.v.n.* (*aux.* s.) come hither *or* near, approach, advance; be caused by, be the consequence (of), originate (in), arise (from), be derived *or* descended (from), be transmitted, be established as a custom; *wo kommt dies Wort her?* what is the origin *or* derivation of this word? *wo soll die Zeit –?* how shall we find the time? 2. *n.* origin, extraction, descent; tradition, custom, usage.

herkömmlich, *adj.* traditional, customary, usual.

herkönnen, *ir.v.n.* (*aux.* h.) be able to come *or* go.

Herkunft, *f.* coming, arrival; origin, descent, extraction; *von unsicherer – sein*, have doubtful antecedents; (*C.L.*) *– Deutschland*, made in Germany.

herladen, *ir.v.a.* summon, invite.

herlallen, *v.n.* (*aux.* h.) say in a faltering *or* halting manner.

herlassen, *ir.v.a.* permit to *or* allow to *or* let come.

herlaufen, *ir.v.n.* (*aux.* s.) run (*hither or near*); *hinter einem –*, run about after s.o. *hergelaufener Kerl*, worthless vagabond, vagrant.

herlegen, *v.a.* (*C.L.*) lay down *or* put down (*here*).

herleiern, *v.a.* recite *or* deliver in a monotonous sing-song manner.

herleit-en, 1. *v.a.* lead, conduct hither; derive (*von*, from); draw from, deduce; refer to (*cause or origin*). 2. *v.r.* be derived from, originate in, date from. **-ung,** *f.* derivation; deduction.
herlesen, *ir.v.a.* read off, recite.
Herling, *m.* (-s, -e) unripe grape; wild grape; (*B.*) sour grape.
herlocken, *v.a.* entice, lure, decoy.
hermachen, *v.r.* (*über etwas*) set about; work at, (*coll.*) tackle; (*über einen*) fall upon, set about (a p.).
Hermaphrodit, *m.* (-en, -en) hermaphrodite.
Hermarsch, *m.* march hither; approach.
Herme, *f.* (-n) bust.
Hermelin, 1. *n.* (-s, -e) stoat, ermine (*Putorius ermineus*) (*Zool.*); cream-coloured horse. 2. *m.* (-s, -e) ermine (*fur*).
hermetisch, *adj.* air-tight, hermetic; – *verschlossen*, hermetically sealed.
hermüssen, *v.n.* (*aux.* h.) have to *or* be obliged to come *or* appear.
hernach, *adv.* afterwards, hereafter, after this *or* that; –*?* what next? then? *den Tag* –, the day after.
hernehm-en, *ir.v.a.* take, get, draw from (*somewhere*); deduce, derive; (*coll.*) *einen -en*, take a p. to task. **-ung,** *f.* deduction.
hernennen, *ir.v.a.* name in succession, call over, recite.
hernieder, *adv. & sep. prefix*, down.
Hero-enalter, *n.* heroic age. **-enkultus,** *m.* hero-worship. **-in,** *n.* (-s) heroin (*drug*). **-in(e),** *f.* (-inen) heroine. **-isch,** *adj.* heroic. **-ismus,** *m.* heroism. **-s,** *m.* (-s, -en) hero, demigod.
Herold, *m.* (-(e)s, -e) herald; harbinger. **-sfiguren,** *f.pl.* heraldic figures. **-skunst,** *f.* **-swissenschaft,** *f.* heraldry, heraldic art. **-smantel,** *m.*, **-srock,** *m.* tabard.
Herr, *m.* (-n, -en) master; lord; gentleman; sir (*in address*); Mr. (*before proper names*); (*fam.*) *sein alter* –, his father *or* governor; *die alten -en* (*einer Verbindung*), 'old boys', former students; *ich habe* (*es*) *-n Doktor B. versprochen*, I have promised (that to) Doctor B.; *sein eigner – sein*, stand on one's own feet; (*Prov.*) *gestrenge -en regieren nicht lange*, tyranny is shortlived; *die drei gestrengen -en, see* **gestreng**; *der – Gott*, God, our Lord, Lord God; *den großen -n spielen*, lord it; *das Haus des -n*, the House of God; *Hochgeehrter* –, Sir, Dear Sir; *der junge* –, the young master, son of the house; (*Prov.*) *wie der –, so der Knecht*, like master, like man; – *der Lage sein*, be master of the situation; *meine -en*, Gentlemen; *der – der Schöpfung*, the lord of creation; – *zur See sein*, rule the waves; *einer S., von einer S.* or *über eine S. – sein*, be master of a th., have at one's disposal *or* in one's power; *selig im -n sterben*, die blessed in the eyes of God; *der Tag des -n*, the Lord's day; *Ihr – Vater*, your father; *einer S. – werden*, overcome *or* master s.th. **-enabend,** *m.* stag party, smoking concert. **-enarbeit,** *f.* compulsory service; *dieser Schneider macht nur -enarbeit*, this tailor makes men's wear only. **-enartikel,** *m.pl.* gentlemen's outfitting. **-enbank,** *f.* peers' bench. **-enbier,** *n.* strong beer. **-enbrot,** *n.*; *-enbrot essen*, be in service, be dependent. **-endiener,** *m.* gentleman's servant. **-endienst,** *m.* lord's service; forced service; service (*in a family*). **-endoppelspiel,** *n.* men's doubles (*Tenn.*). **-enfahrer,** *m.* owner-driver (*of a motor-car*), amateur driver (*car-racing*). **-engülte,** *f.* tax paid to the lord of the manor. **-enhaus,** *n.*, **-enhof,** *m.* manor(-house); mansion; country house; castle. **-enleben,** *n.* aristocratic life; *ein -enleben führen*, live like a lord, live in grand style. **-enlos,** *adj.* out of service *or* employment (*of servants*), without a master, ownerless; *-enlose Güter*, lost property, unclaimed goods. **-enmoral,** *f.* code of morality for men (but not women) *or* for masters (but not servants). **-enpfarre,** *f.* benefice in private patronage. **-enrecht,** *n.* seigneurial right. **-enreiten,** *n.* owners up, gentlemen's race (*Sport*). **-enreiter,** *m.* gentleman rider, *see* **-enfahrer. -enschneider,** *m.* men's tailor. **-enschnitt,** *m.* Eton crop. **-ensitz,** *m.*, *see* **-enhaus**; *im -ensitz reiten*, ride astride (*opp.* side-saddle). **-enstand,** *m.* rank of a lord; gentry. **-gott,** *m.* Lord God; (*ach*) *-gott!* Lord! Good God! good heavens! good gracious! *den -gott einen guten Mann sein lassen*, let matters take their course; (*Prov.*) *er lebt wie der -gott in Frankreich*, he lives like a fighting cock. **-gottsfrühe,** *f.* crack of dawn. **-gottskäferchen,** *n.* lady-bird. **-gott(s)schnitzer,** *m.* carver of crucifixes. **-in,** *f.* lady, mistress. **-isch,** *adj.* domineering; imperious; dictatorial; masterful. **-je!** *int.* goodness gracious! **-lich,** *adj.* magnificent, splendid, glorious, capital, excellent, delicious, grand. **-lichkeit,** *f.* splendour, magnificence, grandeur, glory, excellence; *-lichkeit Gottes*, majesty of God. **-nhuter,** *m.* Moravian; (*pl.*) the Moravian brethren. **-nhutertum,** *n.* Moravianism. **-schaft,** *f.* dominion, mastery, control, power, government, sovereign authority, command; manor, estate, domain; master and mistress, employers (*of servants*); p. *or* persons of rank; *sich der -schaft bemächtigen*, secure mastery *or* control; (*etwas*) *unter seine -schaft bringen*, bring (a th.) under one's rule *or* dominion, subdue a th.; *ist die -schaft zu Hause?* are your master and mistress (is your master *or* mistress) at home? *hohe -schaften*, people of high rank, illustrious persons; *die junge -schaft*, the children of the master *or* lord; *meine -schaften!* ladies and gentlemen! *die -schaft über sich verlieren*, lose one's self-control. **-schaftlich,** *adj.* belonging to *or* referring to a lord *or* master, seigneurial, manorial; fit for a lord, lordly, high-class; *-schaftliche Gefälle*, seigneurial revenues; *-schaftlicher Befehl*, lord's command; *-schaftliche Wohnung*, 'desirable' residence, mansion. **-schaftshaus,** *n.*, *see* **-enhaus. -schaftsrecht,** *n.* sovereign authority; jurisdiction.
herrechn-en, *v.a.* reckon up, enumerate. **-ung,** *f.* enumeration, specification.
herreichen, *v.a.* reach, hand (to).
Herreise, *f.* journey hither, homeward journey, return journey.
herrichten, *v.a.* prepare, get ready, fit up, put in order.
herrücken, *v.n.* (*aux.* s.) approach *or* draw near push on.
herrühren, *v.n.* (*aux.* h.) (*von*) originate (in), proceed, flow (from).
hersagen, *v.a.* recite, repeat, rehearse; tell (*one's beads*); *das Tischgebet* –, say grace.
herschaffen, *reg. v.a.* bring hither; move near; produce, procure.
herrsch-en, *v.n.* (*aux.* h.) rule, reign, govern, be lord *or* master of; prevail, be prevalent, be in vogue; exist; *es -t Schweigen*, silence reigns; '*komm her!' -te er*,' approach!' he ordered haughtily. **-end,** *pr.p. & adj.* ruling; predominant, dominant, prevailing. **-begier,** *f.*, **-begierde,** *f.*, *see* **-sucht. -begierig,** *adj.*, *see* **-süchtig. -er,** *m.* ruler, sovereign, lord, despot, monarch, prince, governor; *willkürlicher -er*, despot; *unumschränkter -er*, autocrat; *Selbst-er*, autocrat. **-erbinde,** *f.* diadem. **-erblick,** *m.* commanding look, authoritative bearing. **-erfamilie,** *f.* reigning family, dynasty. **-ergeist,** *m.* authoritative attitude. **-ergeschlecht,** *n.*, *see* **-erfamilie. -erstab,** *m.* sceptre. **-erstuhl,** *m.* throne. **-erwille,** *m.* sovereign will. **-erwillkür,** *f.* despotism. **-erwort,** *n.* word of command. **-gier,** *f.*, **-lust,** *f.* **-sucht,** *f.* love of power, lust for power. **-süchtig,** *adj.* fond of power, tyrannical.
herschießen, 1. *ir.v.n.* (*aux.* s.) rush along, run, *or* fly to. 2. *v.a.* advance (*money*).
herstammen, *v.n.* (*aux.* s.) descend, come, be derived (*von*, from).
herstell-en, *v.a.* place here; set up, establish, raise; produce; *das läßt sich leicht -en*, that can be easily effected *or* produced; (*wieder*)*-en*, re-establish, repair, restore; *er ist wieder ganz hergestellt*, he is quite restored to health again. **-er,** *m.* producer, manufacturer. **-ung,** *f.* production, manufacture, preparation, restoration. **-ungskosten,** *f.pl.* cost of manufacture *or* of production. **-ungsmittel,** *n.* restorative.
Herstrich, *m.* down-bow (*Mus.*); return of migratory birds.
herstürzen, *v.n.* (*aux.* s.) rush, plunge in (*über with Acc.*, upon).

herüber, *adv. & sep. prefix (indicating movement across s.th. as seen by the p. approached)* over, to this side, across.

herum, *adv. & sep. prefix (indicates* (a) *movement around as seen from the centre,* (b) *vague movement round about with no reference to a centre,* (c) *approximate time or amount)* round, round about, around, about; (*coll.*) finished, over; *er wohnt gleich um die Ecke –,* he lives just round the corner; *um das Haus –,* round about the house; *hier –,* hereabouts; *in der ganzen Stadt –,* all over the town; *um zehn DM –,* round (about) *or* about *or* roughly ten marks; *rings* or *rund –,* all round; *überall –,* everywhere; *um die Zeit –,* about that time. **–betteln,** *v.n.* (*aux.* h.) go about begging. **–bringen,** *ir.v.a.* bring *or* get round; induce, persuade; *see* **–kriegen. –drehen,** 1. *v.a.* turn round; misconstrue. 2. *v.r.*; *sich –drehen,* turn over (*in bed*); hinge, turn *or* depend (*um,* on). **–drücken,** *v.r.* hang around, loiter; (*um*) evade, dodge, run away from. **–fahren,** *ir.v.n.* (*aux.* s.) drive *or* sail around; dart, fly *or* rush about; (*mit den Händen*) gesticulate, wave one's arms about. **–fragen,** *v.n.* (*aux.* h.) make inquiries, ask everyone. **–führen,** *v.a.* lead *or* show around, show over; *an der Nase –führen,* lead by the nose. **–geben,** *ir.v.a.* hand *or* pass round. **–gehen,** *ir.v.n.* (*aux.* s.) go round; make the round (*Mil.*); surround; wander *or* walk about; be current (*of reports*); be prevalent; *die Mauer ging einst um die ganze Stadt –,* the wall once enclosed the whole town; *es geht mir im Kopf –,* it is on my mind; *–gehen lassen,* send *or* pass round; *ich lasse mir die S. im Kopfe –gehen,* I am carefully considering the matter. **–holen,** *v.a.* bring over *or* round. **–irren,** *v.n.* (*aux.* s.) wander about. **–kommen,** *ir.v.n.* (*aux.* s.) come round (*a corner, etc.*); go *or* travel about; become known; *Leute, die viel in der Welt –gekommen sind,* people who have seen much of the world; *um etwas nicht –kommen,* not be able to avoid; *wir kommen um die Tatsache nicht – daß . . .,* we cannot escape *or* ignore the fact that . . .; *mit etwas –kommen,* finish a th., get a th. done. **–kriegen,** *v.a.* (*coll.*) win round, talk over. **–langen,** *v.a., see* **–gehen. –laufen,** *ir.v.n.* (*aux.* s.) run about, rove, tramp. **–liegen,** *v.a.* lie round, surround (*as a wall*), lie around (*untidily*). **–lungern,** *v.n.* lounge about. **–reichen,** *v.a. & n.* hand *or* pass round. **–reißen,** *v.a., see* **–werfen;** *das Steuer –reißen,* change course suddenly, change one's policy *or* (*coll.*) tune. (*auf einer S.*) **–reiten,** *v.n.* (*aux.* s.) harp upon (a th.), ride a hobby-horse. **–schiffen,** *v.n.* (*aux.* s.) sail about; *um (ein Kap) –schiffen,* sail round, double (a cape). **–schweifend,** *pr.p. & adj.* wandering; vagrant, **–schwenken,** *v.n.* (*aux.* s.) wheel (*Mil.*). **–streichen,** *ir.v.n.* (*aux.* s.) rove about. **–tanzen,** *v.n.* dance attendance (*um,* on). **–tasten,** *v.n.* grope about. **–tragen,** *ir.v.a.* carry around; *seinen Kummer mit sich –tragen,* nurse one's grief. **–treiben,** *ir.v.r.* dawdle, loiter about, prowl around, rove *or* gad about; cruise around, (*sl.*) stooge around (*Av.*). **–werfen,** 1. *ir.v.a.* cast around, turn sharply; *see* **–reißen.** 2. *v.r.*; *sich (im Bette) –werfen,* toss about(in bed). **–ziehen,** 1. *ir.v.a.* draw *or* pull round. 2. *v.r.* surround; run along; *sich mit etwas –ziehen,* have s.th. on one's mind. 3. *v.n.* (*aux.* s.) wander about; have no fixed abode. **–ziehend,** *pr.p. & adj.* itinerant, strolling; nomadic.

herunter, *adv. & sep. prefix (meaning similar to* **herab** *and* **hernieder,** *with fig. uses implying deterioration)* down, downward; off; *– mit ihm!* down with him! *den Hut –!* off with your hat! hats off! **–bringen,** *ir.v.a.* get down; lower, reduce. **–drücken,** *v.a.* lower, depress; put down (*aircraft*). **–handeln,** *v.a.* beat down (*in price*). **–hauen,** *v.a.* (*coll.*) box (*ears*). **–holen,** *v.a.* fetch down; shoot down (*Av.*). **–klappen,** *v.a.* turn *or* fold down. **–kommen,** *ir.v.n.* (*aux.* s.) come down; alight; be reduced (*in circumstances*); be run down (*in health*); decline, decay, fall off, become depraved, come down in the world. (*coll.*) **–kriegen,** *v.a.* get down; lower, reduce. **–langen,** *v.a., see* **–hauen. –lassen,** *v.a.* lower, let down. **–leiern,** *v.a.* recite in a sing-song manner. **–machen,** *v.a.,* **–putzen,** *v.a.* (*coll.*) abuse, upbraid, give a thorough scolding. **–reißen,** *v.a.* pull *or* tear down; pull to pieces, disparage; throw off (*one's clothes*). **–rutschen,** *v.a.* slide *or* slip down; *du kannst mir den Buckel –rutschen,* (*coll.*) I snap my finger at you; (*vulg.*) go and fry your face. **–schlucken,** *v.a.* swallow, gulp; stomach (*insults, etc.*); smother, suppress (*what one would like to say*). **–sein,** *v.n.* be run down (*in health*), be low (*in spirits*), be low-spirited, depressed *or* despondent; be in a bad way. **–setzen,** *v.a.* reduce, lower (*prices*); depreciate, disparage; degrade. **–werfen,** *ir.v.a.* throw down *or* off; throw (*a rider*). **–wirtschaften,** *v.a.* ruin by bad management, bring to ruin. **–ziehen,** 1. *ir.v.a.* pull down. 2. *v.n.* (*aux.* s.) march down, descend.

hervor, (*archaic* **herfür**) *adv. & sep. prefix (expressing movement forward as seen from out in front)* forth; out; *– mit euch! kommt –!* come out, you! advance! **–brechen,** *v.n.* (*aux.* s.) rush out, break through; sally forth, debouch (*Mil.*). **–bringen,** *ir.v.a.* bring forth, produce, yield; generate, beget; utter; elicit. **–bringung,** *f.* production; procreation; utterance. **–gehen,** *ir.v.n.* (*aux.* s.) go *or* come forth, issue, proceed, result, arise; come off (*victorious, etc.*); *es geht daraus –,* hence it follows. **–heben,** *ir.v.a.* bring into prominence; set off, display, call special attention to, emphasize, stress. **–leuchten,** *v.n.* (*aux.* h.) shine forth; become clear *or* evident, be conspicuous *or* distinguished. **–locken,** *v.a.* draw, lure *or* entice out. **–machen,** *v.r.* appear, make one's appearance. **–ragen,** *v.n.* (*aux.* h.) project, stand out, be prominent, jut forth; rise above, overtop, tower up; exceed, surpass. **–ragend,** *pr.p. & adj.* prominent, protruding, outstanding, salient; distinguished; (*coll.*) excellent, splendid, superlative. **–ragung,** *f.* projection, protuberance, promontory, prominence, eminence. **–ruf,** *m.* encore, recall (*Theat.*). **–rufen,** *ir.v.a.* evoke, call forth; cause, bring about, occasion; encore (*actors and singers*). **–schießen,** *v.n.* shoot up, appear suddenly. **–springen,** *v.n.* project. **–stechen,** *ir.v.n.* (*aux.* h.) stand out, jut out; be conspicuous; **–stechend,** outstanding, characteristic, glaring, conspicuous, striking. **–stehen,** *ir.v.n.* (*aux.* s.) project, be prominent *or* outstanding. *–stehende Backenknochen,* high cheek-bones. **–treten,** *ir.v.n.* (*aux.* s.) step forth *or* forward; come forward; stand out, be prominent; *–treten lassen,* throw into bold relief. **–tun,** *ir.v.r.* distinguish o.s., excel; come into prominence.

herwagen, *v.r.* venture near, venture to come to a place.

Herweg, *m.* way here, way back (*as seen from the starting place*).

Herz, *n.* (-ens, -en) heart; breast, bosom; feeling, sympathy; mind, spirit; courage; centre; vital part; marrow, pith (*Bot.*); core, kernel; hearts (*Cards*); darling; *es will ihm das Herz abdrücken,* it will break his heart; *aus dem –en,* sincerely, earnestly; *sein – ausschütten,* open one's heart, unbosom o.s.; *es brennt mir auf dem –en,* it wrings my heart; *etwas übers – bringen,* bring o.s. to do s.th., reconcile o.s. to a th., find it in one's heart to do; *ans – drücken,* press to one's bosom; *sich das – erleichtern,* unburden o.s.; *aufs – fallen,* weigh on a p.; *schwer aufs – fallen,* oppress *or* worry a p.; *sich (Dat.) ein – fassen,* take courage; take heart; *ein – zu einem fassen,* repose confidence in a p.; *flammendes –,* bleeding heart (*Bot.*); *das – am* or *auf dem rechten Fleck haben,* have one's heart in the right place; *frisch vom –en weg reden,* speak one's mind freely; *von ganzem –en,* with all my heart; *einem einen Stich ins – geben,* grieve a p. deeply; *von –en gehen,* be genuine; *von –en gern,* with the greatest of pleasure; *im Grund seines –ens,* at the bottom of his heart; *einem von –en gut sein,* love a p. dearly; *auf dem –en haben,* have on one's mind; *das – zu einer S. haben,* find it in one's heart *or* bring o.s. to do a th.; *mit halbem –en bei einer S. sein,* be half-hearted about a th.; *Hand aufs – !* cross your heart! *sein – an eine S. hängen,* set one's heart on a th.; *von –en kommen,* come from the heart, be heart-felt *or* sincere; *einem etwas ans – legen,* urge *or* enjoin a th. on a p.; *kein – im Leibe haben*, be without a heart *or* without feelings, be heartless; *leichten –ens*, light-heartedly, without misgivings; *es liegt mir am –en*, I have it at heart; *seinem –en Luft machen*, give vent to one's feelings *or* opinions; *mit dem –en bei einer S. sein*, have one's heart in a thing; *mit – und Hand*, sincerely, earnestly; *ein Mann (recht) nach meinem –en*, a man according to my own heart; *sich (Dat.) zu –en nehmen*, take to heart; *sein – in die Hände nehmen*, take heart *or* courage; *sich (Dat.) das – aus dem Leibe reden*, talk to one's heart's content; *einem ans – rühren*, touch a p. to the quick; *ins – schließen*, become fond of; *einen ins – schließen*, take s.o. to one's heart; *es schneidet mir ins –*, it cuts me to the quick *or* wrings my heart; *ein – und eine Seele*, bosom friends; *ich weiß, wie es ihm ums – ist*, I know how he feels; *es fällt mir ein Stein vom –en*, that's a load off my mind; *ein Kind unter dem –en tragen*, be with child; *von –en*, heartily, cordially; (*B.*) *wes das – voll ist, des gehet der Mund über*, out of the abundance of the heart the mouth speaketh; *einem ans – gewachsen sein*, be very dear to a p.; *es zerreißt mir das –*, it wrings my heart; *das – auf der Zunge haben*, wear one's heart on one's sleeve. **–ader**, *f.* aorta (*Anat.*). **–allerliebst**, *adj.* dearest, beloved. **–as**, *n.* ace of hearts (*Cards*). **–beben**, *n.* palpitation of the heart. **–bein**, *n.* breast bone, sternum. **–beklommen**, *adj.* anxious. **–beutel**, *m.* pericardium. **–beutelentzündung**, *f.* pericarditis. **–bewegend**, *adj.* pathetic; moving, touching, stirring. **–blatt**, *n.* unopened leaf bud, young leaf (*Bot.*); darling; hearts (*Cards*). **–blut**, *n.* life's blood, (*fig.*) heart blood, heart's blood. **–bräune**, *f.* angina pectoris (*Med.*). **–bube**, *m.* knave of hearts (*Cards*). **–dame**, *f.* queen of hearts (*Cards*). **–drücken**, *n.*; *er stirbt nicht an –drücken*, he cannot hold his tongue *or* peace. **–eleid**, *n.* grief, sorrow, affliction. **–en**, *v.a.* press to one's heart, caress, embrace. **–ensangelegenheit**, *f.* love-affair, affair of the heart. **–ensangst**, *f.* anguish of mind, deep anxiety. **–enseinfalt**, *f.* simple-mindedness. **–ensergießung**, *f.*, **–enserguß**, *m.* outpouring of the heart, unbosoming, confidences. **–ensfreude**, *f.* great joy; heart's delight. **–ensfreund**, *m.* bosom friend, (*archaic*) dear heart. **–ensfroh**, *adj.* heartily glad. **–ensfülle**, *f.* depth of feeling. **–ensgut**, *adj.* kind-hearted. **–ensgüte**, *f.* kind-heartedness. **–enskind**, *n.* darling. **–enskönigin**, *f.* girl of one's choice, lady-love. **–enslust**, *f.* great joy; *nach –enslust*, to one's heart's content. **–ensnot**, *f.*, **–enspein**, *f.*, **–ensqual**, *f.* great distress. **–enswunsch**, *m.* heartfelt desire. **–erfreuend**, *adj.* cheering, comforting, gladdening. **–ergreifend**, *adj.* affecting, moving. **–erhebend**, *adj.* heart-stirring. **–erquickend**, *adj.*, *see* **–erfreuend**. **–erschütternd**, *adj.* appalling. **–erweiterung**, *f.* dilatation of the heart, hypertrophy. **–fehler**, *m.* organic disease of the heart. **–fell**, *n.* pericardium. **–fibern**, *f.pl.* heart-strings. **–förmig**, *adj.* heart-shaped. **–gegend**, *f.* cardiac region. **–grube**, *f.* pit of the stomach, epigastrium (*Anat.*). **–haft**, *adj.* courageous, valiant, bold, stout-hearted, brave; hearty, goodly. **–haftigkeit**, *f.* courage, bravery, manliness. **–ig**, *adj.* charming, sweet, lovely, dear, beloved. **–igkeit**, *f.* loveliness, sweetness, charm. **–innig**, *adj.*, **–inniglich**, *adj.* hearty, heartfelt, cordial. **–kammer**, *f.* ventricle of the heart. **–klappe**, *f.* valve of the heart. **–klopfen**, *n.* palpitation of the heart; *mit –klopfen*, with beating heart. **–könig**, *m.* king of hearts (*Cards*). **–krampf**, *m.* spasm of the heart. **–krank**, *adj.*, **–leidend**, *adj.* suffering from heart trouble, with a weak heart. **–lich**, *adj.* hearty, cordial, affectionate, heartfelt, sincere; *–lich gern*, most willingly, with all one's heart. *–lich wenig*, (*coll.*) mighty little; *–lich langweilig*, (*coll.*) awfully dull; *–lich dumm*, (*coll.*) extraordinarily stupid; *wir haben es –lich satt*, we are heartily sick of it; *die –lichsten Grüße*, hearty greetings; *das –lichste Beileid*, heartfelt *or* deepest sympathy. **–lichkeit**, *f.* cordiality, affection, sincerity. **–lieb**, *adj.* very dear, dearly beloved. **–liebchen**, *n.* sweetheart. **–los**, *adj.* heartless, unfeeling, unsympathetic. **–muschel**, *f.* cockle (*Cardium edule*) (*Mollusc*). **–ohr**, *n.* auricle. **–pochen**, *n.* severe palpitations. **–reiz**, *m.* cardiac stimulant. **–schlächtig**, *adj.* broken-winded. **–schlag**, *m.* heart beat; heart attack *or* failure. **–stoß**, *m.* finishing blow. **–stück**, *n.* crossing frog (*Railw.*). **–tätigkeit**, *f.* heart-action, heart beat. **–verfettung**, *f.* fatty (degeneration of the) heart. **–verknöcherung**, *f.* ossification of the heart. **–vorhof**, *m.*, **–vorkammer**, *f.* auricle. **–weh**, *n.* heart-ache; grief. **–wurzel**, *f.* taproot (*Bot.*). **–zerreißend**, *adj.* heart-rending.

herzahlen, *v.a.* pay down.

herzählen, *v.a.* reckon up, enumerate.

herzaubern, *v.a.* conjure up.

herziehen, 1. *ir.v.a.* draw, pull *or* entice near *or* hither. 2. *v.n.* (*aux.* h.) draw near, move in this direction; come to live with *or* near (the speaker); *– über einen*, criticize a p. sharply, attack a p. (*in speech or writing*), speak *or* write badly of a p.

Herzog, *m.* (-(e)s, -e *or* ⸚e) duke. **–in**, *f.* duchess. **–lich**, *adj.* ducal. **–tum**, *n.* duchy, dukedom.

herzu, *adv.* & *sep. prefix* (*meaning much the same as* **heran, herbei**) up, up to, near, here, towards, hither. **–laufen**, *v.a.* run up, come up running.

Herzug, *m.* up-train.

Hetäre, *f.* (-n) (Greek) courtesan.

hetero–dox, *adj.* heterodox. **–doxie**, *f.* heterodoxy, heresy. **–gen**, *adj.* heterogeneous; *–gene Befruchtung*, cross-fertilization; *–gene Bestäubung*, cross-pollination; *–gene Zeugung*, heterogenesis.

Hetz–e, *f.* (-n) chase, pursuit, hunt; baiting; instigation, agitation; wild *or* mad rush. (*coll.*) *eine ganze –e*, a great multitude, rabble, mob. **–bahn**, *f.*, *see* **–garten**. **–blatt**, *n.* (*sl.*) 'rag' (*newspaper*), gutter press, yellow press; *see* **–schrift**. **–en**, 1. *v.a.* hunt, course, run after, pursue; agitate, provoke, incite, bait, set on, (*coll.*) egg on; *fast zu Tode gehetzt*, almost worried to death; (*coll.*) *mit allen Hunden gehetzt sein*, be full of craft, be up to every trick. 2. *v.n.* (*aux.* h.) rush, hurry. **–er**, *m.* instigator, inciter, baiter. **–erei**, *f.* baiting, harassing; stirring up strife; setting on, inciting; *–erei der Prüfungen*, rush and worry of examinations. **–erisch**, *adj.* inflammatory, stirring up. **–garten**, *m.* bullring, bear garden, baiting-place. **–hund**, *m.* staghound, sporting dog. **–jagd**, *f.* hunt, chase, coursing; rush, great hurry; (*coll.*) *wir leben in der reinen –jagd*, we are driven off our feet. **–redner**, *m.* agitator. **–schrift**, *f.* inflammatory writing *or* pamphlet. **–zeit**, *f.* hunting season.

Heu, *n.* hay; *Geld wie –*, money in abundance; money like dirt. **–bar**, *adj.* yielding hay (*as a meadow*). **–baum**, *m.* hay-pole. **–boden**, *m.* hay-loft. **–bühne**, *f.* (*Swiss dial.*), *see* **–boden**. **–bund**, *n.*, **–bündel**, *n.* bottle *or* truss of hay. **–diele**, *f.* (*Swiss dial.*), *see* **–boden**. **–en**, 1. *v.a.* make hay. 2. *n.* haymaking. **–er**, *m.* haymaker. **–ernte**, *f.* hay-harvest; hay-making season. **–ert**, *m.*, **–et**, *m.* (*dial.*). July. **–feim**, *m.*, **–feime**, *f.*, **–feimen**, *m.* haystack, hayrick. **–fieber**, *n.* hay fever. **–gabel**, *f.* pitchfork. **–gewinn**, *m.* hay-crop. **–miete**, *f.* hayrick, haystack. **–monat**, *m.*, **–mond**, *m.* July. (*sl.*) **–ochse**, *m.* blockhead. **–pferd**, *n.* *see* **–schrecke**. **–reiter**, *m.* (*dial.*) rack for drying hay. **–scheide**, *f.* haycock. **–schober**, *m.* hayrick, haystack, barn. **–schnupfen**, *m.*, *see* **–fieber**. **–schrecke**, *f.* grasshopper; (*B.*) locust. **–sense**, *f.* scythe. **–stadel**, *m.*, **–stock**, *m.* (*Swiss dial.*), *see* **–schober**. **–zehnte**, *m.* tithe paid in hay.

Heuch–elei, *f.* (-en) hypocrisy, dissimulation; cant. **–eln**, 1. *v.a.* feign, affect, simulate. 2. *v.n.* (*aux.* h.) dissemble, sham, play the hypocrite; pose (*as a saint*). **–elrede**, *f.* hypocritical *or* dissembling speech. **–elschein**, *m.*, **–elwerk**, *n.* hypocrisy, sham, false pretence; (*Poet.*) *mit falschem –elschein*, with a dissembling voice *or* mien. **–eltränen**, *f.pl.* crocodile tears. **–ler**, *m.* hypocrite, dissembler. **–lerisch**, *adj.* hypocritical; false, deceitful; dissembling.

Heuer, *f.* (-n) (*Naut.*) hire; wages (*of seamen*). **–baas**, *m.* seaman's agent. **–ling**, *m.* (*dial.*) hired man, hireling; day-labourer. **–n**, *v.a.* charter, engage, hire (*sailors*).

heu–er, *adv.* (*Austr. dial.*) (in) this year. **–rig**, *adj.*

(*Austr. dial.*) of this year; this year's, current; *–riger (Wein)*, new wine; *–rige Kartoffeln*, new potatoes. **–rige(r)**, *m.* 1. new wine; 2. tavern (*kept by the grower, the usual tavern in Vienna's suburbs*); *zum –rigen gehen*, go out for a drink. **–rigenschenke**, *f.*, *see* **–rige(r)** (2).

heul–en, *v.n.* (*aux.* h.) howl, yell, scream, roar, cry; hoot (*of sirens*) (*B.*) *–en und Zähneklappen*, weeping and gnashing of teeth; *mit den Wölfen –en*, do at Rome as the Romans do. **–boje**, *f.* whistling buoy (*Naut.*). **–(e)meier**, *m.*, **–(e)michel**, *m.*, **–suse**, *f.*, **–trine**, *f.* cry-baby. **–kreisel**, *m.* humming-top. **–sirene**, *f.* (factory-)hooter. **–tonne**, *f.*, *see* **–boje.**

heut–e, *adv.* today, this day; *–e abend*, tonight; *–e früh*, this morning; *das ist nicht von gestern und –e*, there is nothing new in that; (*Prov.*) *–e mir, morgen dir*, every one in his turn; *–e morgen*, this morning; *nicht von –e auf morgen zu erwarten*, not to be expected overnight; *–e nacht*, this night, tonight; (*Prov.*) *–e rot, morgen tot*, here today, gone tomorrow; *–e über ein Jahr*, a year hence; *–e über vierzehn Tage* or *in vierzehn Tagen*, today fortnight; *–e über vier Wochen*, a month (from) today; *von –e an*, from today; *–e vor acht Tagen*, a week ago today. **–ig**, *adj.* of today, of the present time; present, actual, modern; *mit der –igen Post*, by today's mail; *–igentags*, nowadays, at the present time; *am –igen Tag*, today, on this day; (*C.L.*) *Ihr –iges*, your favour of today; *unterm –igen*, under this day's date.

Hexa–eder, *n.* (-s, –), hexahedron, cube. **–meter**, *m.* (dactylic) hexameter (verse). **–metrisch**, *adj.* hexametrical.

Hex–e, *f.* (-en) witch, sorceress, enchantress; hag. **–en**, *v.n.* (*aux.* h.) conjure, practise sorcery; *ich kann nicht –en*, I cannot work miracles. **–enbann**, *m.* witch's curse *or* spell. **–enbesen**, *m.* witch's broom. **–enbrut**, *f.* covey of witches. **–enbuch**, *n.* conjuring-book. **–englaube**, *m.* belief in witchcraft. **–enkessel**, *m.* witch's cauldron; (*fig.*) hurly-burly, hubbub. **–enkraut**, *n.* enchanter's nightshade (*Circaea lutetiana*) (*Bot.*). **–enkreis**, *m.* magic circle; fairy-ring. **–enküche**, *f.* witch's kitchen. **–enkunst**, *f.* witchcraft, magic art. **–enmehl**, *n.* lycopodium. **–enmeister**, *m.* wizard, sorcerer, magician. **–enprobe**, *f.* witches' ordeal. **–enprozeß**, *m.* witchcraft trial. **–enpulver**, *n.*, *see* **–enmehl.** **–enritt**, *m.* witches' ride. **–ensabbat**, *m.* witches' Sabbath. **–enschuß**, *m.* lumbago. **–enwesen**, *n.* witchcraft, witchery. **–enzunft**, *f.*, *see* **–enbrut.** **–erei**, *f.* witchcraft, sorcery, magic; (*Prov.*) *Geschwindigkeit ist keine –erei*, sleight-of-hand requires no magic; *das ist keine –erei*, there is nothing wonderful in that; *–erei treiben*, practise witchcraft.

hie, *adv.* (*archaic*), *see* **hier**; *– und da*, here and there, now and then; *– Welf, – Weibling!* a Guelph, a Ghibelline! **–nieden**, *adv.* (*Poet.*) here below, in this world, on earth. **–sig**, *adj.*, *see* **hiesig.**

hieb, hiebe, *see* **hauen.**

Hieb, *m.* (-(e)s, -e) blow, stroke, hit, slash, cut, gash; cutting remark; *der – sitzt*, the blow goes home; (*Prov.*) *auf den ersten – fällt kein Baum*, Rome was not built in a day; *auf – und Stich gehen*, cut and thrust (*Fenc.*); *freien – haben*, have the right of felling timber. **–er**, *m.*, *see* **–waffe.** **–fechten**, *n.* fighting with swords *or* sabres; *Hieb- und Stoßfechten*, cut and thrust. **–reif**, *adj.* fellable, ready for felling (*trees*). **–satz**, *m.* yield (*from felling*); amount felled. **–waffe**, *f.* weapon, broadsword. **–wunde**, *f.* gash, slash, sword wound.

hielt, hielte, *see* **halten.**

hieng, *archaic for* **hing.**

hier, *adv.* here; present; in this place; at this point; *– und da*, now and then, from time to time; *– und dort*, here and there; *für – bestimmt*, bound for this place; *– herum*, hereabouts; *von – ab*, starting here, from this point *or* place; (*coll.*) *er ist nicht von –*, he isn't all there; *– Karl*, Charles calling *or* speaking (*Phone*). (*In the following compounds* hier- *is nowadays normal in North Germany,* hie- *is archaic. In South Germany & Austria* hie- *is still common, being in fact preferred where the second component commences with a consonant, e.g.* hiegegen.) **–amts**, *adv.* (*Austr. dial.*) at *or* from this office (*official style*). **–an**, *adv.* hereupon, on, at *or* by this. **–auf**, *adv.* hereupon, upon this, at this; up here; after that, afterwards, then. **–aus**, *adv.* out of this, from here, from this, hence, hereby, by this. **–bei**, *adv.* hereby, in doing so, herewith; by, at, in, during *or* with this; enclosed. **–durch**. *adv.* through this place, through here; by this means; this way; by this, due to this, hereby, thereby. **–ein**, *adv.* in(to) this place, in(to) this. **–für**, *adv.* for this, for it, instead of this. **–gegen**, *adv.* against this *or* it; in return for this. **–her**, *adv.* to this place, this way, hither, here, to me; *bis –her*, hitherto, till now, up to now; so far, thus far; *nicht –her gehörend*, not to the purpose, off the mark. **–herum**, *adv.* hereabouts, in this neighbourhood. **–hin**, *adv.* in this direction, this way; hither; *bald –hin bald dorthin*, hither and thither, now here now there. **–in**, *adv.* herein; in this, inside. **–lands**, *adv.* in this country. **–mit**, *adv.* herewith, (along) with this; saying *or* doing this. **–nach**, *adv.* after this; hereupon; hereafter; according to this. **–nächst**, *adv.* next to this, after this; close by. **–neben**, close by; besides. **–orts**, *adv.* here, in *or* of this place. **–sein**, *n.* being here, sojourn here; presence. **–selbst**, *adv.* here, in this very place; local (*in addresses*). **–über**, *adv.* over here; concerning *or* regarding this; about this, hereat; on this account. **–um**, *adv.* about *or* round this place, hereabout; about *or* concerning this. **–unter**, *adv.* hereunder; under *or* beneath this *or* it; in *or* by this; among these. **–von**, *adv.* hereof, of *or* from this. **–wider**, *adv.* against this. **–zu**, *adv.* to this; hereto; add to this, in addition to this, moreover, to it, for it. **–zulande**, *adv.* in this country. **–zwischen**, *adv.* between; between these things.

Hier–archie, *f.* (-ien) hierarchy. **–archisch**, *adj.* hierarchical. **–atisch**, *adj.* hieratic, sacerdotal. **–oglyphe**, *f.* hieroglyph(ic). **–oglyphenschrift**, *f.* hieroglyphic *or* hieratic writing.

hiesig, *adj.* of this place *or* country, local, native, indigenous.

hieß, hieße, *see* **heißen.**

hieven, *v.a.* (*Naut.*) heave, haul.

Hift, *m.* (-(e)s, -e) (*rare*) sound given by the hunting-horn, bugle-call. **–horn**, *n.* hunting-horn.

hilf, hilfst, hilft, *see* **helfen.**

Hilf–e, *f.* (-en) help, aid, assistance, succour, support; relief, auxiliary, accessory; redress, remedy; *–e leisten*, render assistance *or* aid; *einen um –e bitten*, ask a p. for help, call in a p.'s assistance; *zur –e dienend*, auxiliary; *erste –e*, first aid; *–e finden in einer S.*, be helped by a th.; *–en geben*, give a hand (*Gymn.*); *einem zu –e kommen*, come to a p.'s aid; *–e leisten* (*with Dat.*) help, aid, assist, succour; *wo keine –e mehr ist*, past remedy; *mit –e der Nacht*, under cover of night *or* darkness; *etwas zu –e nehmen*, make use of a th. **–(e)leistung**, *f.* assistance, help; rescue work, salvage (*Naut.*). **–eruf**, *m.* cry *or* appeal for help. **–lich**, *adj.* (*dial.*) beneficial, salutary. **–los**, *adj.* helpless, defenceless, destitute. **–losigkeit**, *f.* helplessness. **–reich**, *adj.* helpful, benevolent, charitable. **–sameise**, *f.* worker ant. **–sarbeiter**, *m.* temporary worker, assistant. **–sbedürftig**, *adj.* requiring help; needy, indigent. **–sbedürftigkeit**, *f.* destitution. **–sbegriff**, *m.* supplementary *or* postulated concept. **–sbeischiff**, *n.* supply ship, tender. **–sbereit**, *adj.* helpful, co-operative, obliging; beneficent, philanthropic. **–sbereitschaft**, *f.* helpfulness, goodwill; solidarity, collaboration. **–sbetrieb**, *m.* sideline, auxiliary undertaking. **–sbischof**, *m.* suffragan bishop. **–sbuch**, *n.* elementary text-book, manual; book of reference. **–sdienst**, *m.* auxiliary air-raid precaution service. **–sfallschirm**, *m.* pilot parachute. **–sfrist**, *f.* days of grace. **–sgeld**, *n.* subsidy. **–sgerätewagen**, *m.* breakdown lorry. **–sgrund**, *m.* subsidiary reason. **–skasse**, *f.* relief fund. **–skraft**, *f.* additional helper *or* worker, assistant. **–slehrer**, *m.* assistant teacher *or* master (on probation); replacement teacher, teacher on supply, part-time teacher **–slinie**, *f.* auxiliary line (*Math.*); ledger-line (*Mus.*). **–smaßnahmen**, *f.pl.* emergency measures, first-aid. **-smittel,** *n.* remedy; expedient, resource, auxiliary means; *letztes -smittel,* last resort. **-spolizei,** *f.* special constabulary, auxiliary police. **-sprediger,** *m.* deputy clergyman, locum (tenens). **-squelle,** *f.* resources; expedient. **-ssatz,** *m.* lemma (*Math.*). **-sschiff,** *n.* auxiliary vessel, armed trawler. **-sschule,** *f.* special school (for backward children). **-ssprache,** *f.* auxiliary language (*Esperanto, Ido*). **-struppen,** *pl.* auxiliaries. **-swache,** *f.* first-aid station. **-sweise,** *adv.*, in an auxiliary, subsidiary, *or* ancillary capacity. **-swissenschaft,** *f.* auxiliary science. **-swörterbuch,** *n.* special vocabulary *or* glossary. **-szeitwort,** *m.* auxiliary verb. **-szug,** *m.* special *or* extra train.

Himbeer-e, *f.* raspberry. **-gelee,** *n.* raspberry jam. **-saft,** *m.* raspberry juice. **-strauch,** *m.* raspberry-bush *or* cane.

Himmel, *m.* (-s, –) heaven; heavens, sky, firmament; canopy, tester; *–!* good heavens! *am –,* in the sky; *bedeckter –,* overcast sky; *– und Hölle in Bewegung setzen,* move heaven and earth; *das Blaue vom – herunterlügen,* lie impudently, swear black is white; *dem – sei Dank, daß wir . . .!* thank heaven, we . . .! *aus allen –n fallen,* be bitterly disappointed *or* utterly disillusioned; *vom – fallen,* come *or* appear out of the blue; *wie vom – gefallen sein,* be astounded; *unter freiem –,* in the open air; *gerechter –!* good heavens! (*bis*) *in den – heben,* praise to the skies; *heiterer –,* clear sky; *ein Blitz aus heiterem –,* a bolt from the blue; *du lieber –!* heavens above! (*excl. of dismay*); *im siebenten – schweben,* be in the seventh heaven, be beside o.s. for joy; *es stinkt zum –,* it stinks to high heaven; *die Bäume wachsen nicht in den –,* there is a limit to everything; *so weit der – blaut* or *reicht,* everywhere under the sun; *weiß der –,* heaven only knows; *um –s Willen!* for heaven's sake! **-ab,** *adv.* from heaven, from on high. **-an,** *adv.* heavenwards, to the skies. **-angst,** *adv.* (*coll.*) terribly frightened. **-bett,** *n.* four-poster bed. **-blau,** *adj.* & *n.* sky-blue, azure, cerulean. **-brot,** *n.* manna. **-ei,** *f.* affected piety, canting manner. **-fahrt,** *f.* ascension; *-fahrt Christi,* Ascension Day; *Mariä -fahrt,* Assumption (of the Blessed Virgin). **-fahrtskommando,** *n.* (*sl.*) suicide squad, death-or-glory squad. **-hoch,** *adj.* sky-high, very high; *-hoch jauchzend,* shouting to the skies with delight. **-n,** *v.n.* (*aux.* h.) turn up the eyes, affect piety. **-reich,** *n.* kingdom of heaven; bliss. **-sachse,** *f.* celestial axis. **-sangel,** *f.*, *see* **-spol.** **-sbahn,** *f.* orbit. **-sbeschreiber,** *m.* astronomer. **-sbild,** *n.* heavenly image; constellation. **-sbogen,** *m.* (*Poet.*) vault of heaven; rainbow. **-sbraut,** *f.* (*Poet.*) nun. **-sbreite,** *f.* latitude. **-sbrot,** *n.*, *see* **-brot.** **-schlüssel,** *m. see* **-sschlüssel.** **-schreiend,** *adj.* crying to heaven, most atrocious *or* revolting. **-serscheinung,** *f.* portent in the skies. **-sfeste,** *f.* (*Poet.*) firmament. **-sfeuer,** *n.*, **-sglut,** *f.* divine inspiration; lightning. **-sgabe,** *f.* heavenly gift, blessing. **-sgegend,** *f.*, *see* **-srichtung.** **-sgewalt,** *f.* heavenly power; supernatural *or* irresistible power. **-sgewölbe,** *n.* firmament. **-sglobus,** *m.* celestial globe. **-shaus,** *n.* firmament; house (*Astrol.*). **-sheer,** *n.* heavenly host. **-shöhe,** *f.* solar altitude (*vertical angle a star makes with the horizon*). **-skarte,** *f.* star chart. **-skönigin,** *f.* (*Poet.*) Virgin Mary, mother of God. **-skörper,** *m.* celestial body. **-skost,** *f.* ambrosia; the Sacrament. **-skugel,** *f.* celestial globe, firmament. **-skunde,** *f.* astronomy. **-slänge,** *f.* astronomical longitude. **-slauf,** *m.* motion of the heavenly bodies. **-sleiter,** *f.* Jacob's ladder. **-slicht,** *n.* celestial orb; (*pl.*) luminaries; *das große -slicht,* the sun. **-sluft,** *f.* ether. **-spförtner,** *m.* St. Peter. **-spol,** *m.* celestial pole. **-spunkt,** *m.* zenith. **-srand,** *m.* horizon. **-sraum,** *m.* the heavens, space. **-srichtung,** *f.* cardinal point, point of the compass; direction. **-sschlüssel,** *m.*, **-sschlüsselchen,** *n.* keys of heaven, cowslip (*Primula veris*). **-sschrift,** *f.* sky writing (*Av.*). **-sspeise,** *f.*, *see* **-skost.** **-sstrich,** *m.* climate; latitude, zone, region. **-strank,** *m.* nectar. **-(s)stürmend,** *adj.* titanic. **-(s)stürmer,** *m.* Titan. **-swächter,** *m.*, *see* **-spförtner.** **-swagen,** *m.* the Great Bear, Charles's Wain. **-szeichen,** *n.* sign of the zodiac. **-szelt,** *n.* (*Poet.*) canopy *or* vault of heaven. **-szirkel,** *m.* celestial sphere. **-träger,** *m.* canopy bearer; Atlas. **-wärts,** *adj.* heavenwards. **-weit,** *adv.* miles apart; *unsere Ansichten sind -weit von einander* or *verschieden,* our views differ widely *or* are diametrically opposed.

himmlisch, *adj.* heavenly, celestial, divine; ethereal, beatific; (*coll.*) splendid, beautiful, lovely, capital; *-e Fügung,* divine ordinance, decree of Providence; *die -en Mächte,* the powers above; *die -en,* the Celestials, the gods; *-e Sehnsucht,* longing for heaven, spiritual yearning; (*coll.*) *ein -er Abend,* a lovely evening.

hin, 1. *adv.* (a) *expressing motion away from the speaker or point contemplated; usually with reference to a definite goal;* hence, thither, that way, over there; (b) *expressing duration of time into the future;* on, along; (c) *sometimes implying motion with no reference to direction;* along; (d) (*coll.*) gone, lost; spent; exhausted, broken; undone; *auf die Gefahr –,* at the risk of; *auf Ihr Wort –,* (relying) on your word; *auf ein Ziel –,* directed towards a goal; *bis zum Baum –,* up as far as the tree; *ich wage es darauf –,* then *or* on the strength of that I shall risk it; *– und her,* to and fro, there and back, backwards and forwards; *– und her laufen,* run to and fro, run all over the place; *hin- und herlaufen,* run there and back; *– und her überlegen* or *denken,* rack one's brains about, turn over in one's mind; *nach vielem Hin- und Herschreiben,* after much correspondence; *Mode –, Mode her, ich werde . . .,* however the fashion may change (*or* in spite of fashion), I shall . . .; *er weiß weder – noch her,* he is at his wit's end, he does not know where to turn; *– und her ist gleich weit,* it's as broad as it's long; *– ist –,* what is gone (lost, passed) is gone, it is no good crying over spilt milk; *nach . . . –,* to *or* towards . . .; *oben –,* along the upper part, on the surface; (*coll.*) *er ist –,* he is lost, undone, ruined *or* dead; *über das ganze Feld –,* all over the field; *still vor sich –,* quietly to oneself without interruption; *es ist noch weit –,* it is still a long way off; *– und wieder,* now and then, from time to time; *– und zurück,* there and back, outward and return. 2. *prefix to verbs and to preps.* (*used adverbially*), *it has opposite meaning to* her (*q.v.*), *referring the motion away from the speaker; in compounds with verbs* hin *is sep. and has the accent; with preps. or advs. it is insep. and the accent is on the prep. or adv.*

hinab, *adv.* & *sep. prefix* (*movement downwards as seen from the starting place above*), down (there), downward(s); *– mit dir!* down! (*to dogs*); *etwas weiter –,* a little lower (down); *den Strom –,* down the river, down-stream. **-lassen,** *ir.v.a.* let down, lower. **-schlängeln,** *v.r.* wind down (*the hill*). **-steigen,** *ir.v.n.* (*aux.* s.) descend. **-stürzen,** 1. *v.n.* (*aux.* s.) fall down (*from a precipice*). 2. *v.a.* throw down, precipitate.

hinan, *adv.* & *sep. prefix* (*rising movement to a summit or elevated position*) up (to), upward. **-klettern,** *v.n.*, **-steigen,** *ir.v.n.* (*aux.* s.) mount, ascend, climb up.

hinarbeiten, 1. *v.n.* (*aux.* h.) (*auf eine S.*) aim at (a th.), struggle towards (a th.). 2. *v.r.* work one's way towards, attain with difficulty.

hinauf, *adv.* & *sep. prefix* (*movement upwards as seen from the starting point below*), upward(s), up (to); *bis –,* up to; *da –, dort –,* up there; *den Fluß –,* up the river, up-stream; *sich – arbeiten,* work one's way up. **-setzen,** *v.a.* put up (*prices, pupil in class*). **-steigen,** *ir.v.n.* (*aux.* s.) mount, ascend. **-stimmen,** *v.a.* raise the pitch of (*Mus.*); raise, increase (*one's pretensions, etc.*). **-transformieren,** *v.a.* step-up (*voltage*) (*Elec.*).

hinaus, *adv.* & *sep. prefix* (*movement outwards as seen from inside*), out, outside, forth; *vorn –,* out in front; *hinten –,* out at the back; *– mit ihm!* turn him out! *dort –,* out there; (*dar*)*über –,* beyond; *ich weiß nicht, wo –,* I don't know the way out; I don't know what to do *or* which way to turn; *zum Fenster –,* out of the window; *über den Termin –,* beyond the time limit. **-beißen,** *v.a.* (*coll.*) drive out, eject. **-gehen,** *ir.v.n.* (*aux.* s.) go *or* walk out; *über eine S. -gehen,* surpass, exceed, go beyond *or* transcend a th.; *auf etwas* (*Acc.*) *-gehen,* aim at a th.; end in a th.; look out on a th.; *das Zimmer geht auf den Garten -,* the room looks out over *or* out on to the garden; *die Rede ging darauf -,* the conversation turned on; the drift *or* purport of the speech was. **-kommen,** *ir.v.n.*, **-laufen,** *ir.v.n.* (*aux.* s.) come out, run out; terminate in a certain way; *auf eins* (or *dasselbe*) *-kommen* or *-laufen,* come *or* amount to the same th.; *darauf kommt* or *läuft es -,* that is what it is coming to; *die Rede kam* or *lief darauf -,* *see* **-gehen. -ragen,** *v.n.* jut out, project. **-reichen,** *v.n.* (*aux.* h.) stretch out (*über,* beyond). **-rücken,** *v.a.*, **-schieben,** *ir.v.a.* defer, postpone, (*coll.*) put off. **-schießen,** *v.n.* go beyond, exceed; (*weit*) *über das Ziel -schießen,* be too much of a good thing, go too far. **-setzen,** 1. *v.a.* put off, postpone, defer; put out (*of doors*). 2. *v.r.* sit down outside, take one's seat outside. **-sollen,** *v.n.* have to go out; have a certain aim; *wo soll das -?* where is this to end? **-werfen,** *ir.v.a.* throw out, expel, eject. **-wollen,** *ir.v.n.* wish to go out; aim at; end in; *wo wollte er -?* what was he driving at? *wo will das -?* what will be the end *or* upshot of it? *hoch -wollen,* aim high *or* at great things, have extravagant ambitions. **-ziehen,** 1. *ir.v.a.* stretch out, draw *or* drag out, prolong, protract. 2. *v.n.* (*aux.* s.) march out, go out.

hinbegeben, *ir.v.r.* move, betake o.s., repair (*zu,* to).

hinbestellen, *v.a.* order *or* appoint to a place.

Hinblick, *m.* (*only in*) *im* or *in - auf,* with *or* in regard to, with a view to. **-en,** *v.n.* (*aux.* h.) (*auf* (*with Acc.*) or *nach*) look towards, glance at, view.

hinbringen, 1. *ir.v.a.* bring *or* carry away; spend, squander; *die Zeit -,* pass *or* spend the time. 2. *v.r. sich kümmerlich -,* make shift to live, eke out a miserable existence.

hinbrüten, *v.n.* (*aux.* h.) be lost in day-dreams.

Hind-e, *f.* (-en), (*Poet.*) **-in,** *f.* hind, doe.

hindenken, *ir.v.n.* (*aux.* h.) let one's thoughts run away with one; *wo denken Sie hin?* what are you thinking of? that is out of the question.

hinder-n, *v.a.* hinder, impede, hamper, prevent, stop, obstruct; embarrass, cross, thwart; *was -t mich* (*daran*), *daß ich es tue* or *mich, es zu tun,* what prevents me from doing it? *sie -t mich am* or *beim Schreiben,* she prevents me from writing. **-lich,** *adj.* (*Dat.*) hindering, obstructive, embarrassing, troublesome, in the way. **-nis,** *n.* hindrance, impediment, obstacle, bar, check, barrier; fence (*racing*). **-nislauf,** *m.* obstacle-race. **-nisrennen,** *n.* steeplechase, hurdle-race. **-ung,** *f.* prevention, hindering.

hindeut-en, *v.n.* (*aux.* h.) point, show the way; *auf eine S. -en,* intimate a th., point to *or* hint at a th. **-ung,** *f.* (*auf eine S.*) hint, hinting (at a th.), intimation (of a th.).

hindrängen, *v.a.* crowd *or* push towards.

hindurch, *adv. & sep. prefix,* through; throughout; across; *den ganzen Tag -,* all day long; *lange Zeit -,* for a long time. **-dringen,** *v.n.* penetrate, permeate. **-lassen,** *ir.v.a.* let through, let pass; transmit.

hinein, *adv. & sep. prefix* (*penetration into s.th., sometimes as seen from the outside, but often figurative*), into, inside, from out here. *-! nur -!* step in! go in! *ins Blaue -,* see *in den Tag -*; (*bis*) *in sein Herz -,* to the bottom of his heart; *ins Leere -,* see *in den Tag -*; *in die Luft -,* see *in den Tag -*; *mitten -,* (right) in the middle; *bis tief in die Nacht -,* far into the night; *bis in die Stadt -,* right into the town; *in den Tag -,* thoughtlessly, at random. **-arbeiten,** *v.r.* work one's way into; *sich in eine S. -arbeiten,* make o.s. perfectly acquainted, familiarize o.s. with a matter. **-beziehen,** *v.a.* include, draw in, incorporate. **-dringen,** *v.n.* penetrate, force one's way in. **-erstrecken,** *v.r.* extend into. **-finden,** *ir.v.r.* see one's way, understand, become familiar with. **-gehen,** *ir.v.n.* (*aux.* s.) go into, be contained. **-gelangen, -geraten,** *v.n.* get in, enter, penetrate. **-knien,** *v.r.* (*coll.*) get down to. **-lassen,** *v.a.* allow to come in *or* enter. **-leben,** *v.r.*; *sich in eine S. -leben,* gradually accustom o.s. to a th. (*coll.*) **-legen,** *v.a.* (*einem etwas*) or (*einen*) get *or* land (a p.) into a mess, bamboozle (a p.). **-ragen,** *v.n.* project into, extend into, be embedded in. **-reden,** 1. *v.n.* (*aux.* h.) (*in einen*) lecture (a p.); *ins Blaue -reden,* talk without thinking, talk nonsense; *in alles mit -reden wollen,* wish to have a say, a voice *or* a finger in everything. 2. *v.r.*; *sich in Zorn -reden,* talk o.s. into a passion. **-reiten,** *ir.v.a. see* **-legen,** (*einen*). **-stecken,** *v.a.* invest, support with (*one's money*); *die Nase überall -stecken,* poke one's nose in everywhere. **-verlegen,** *v.a.* place *or* transfer into, project. **-tun,** *ir.v.a.* put into; add to; mix with; *einen Blick -tun,* glance into. **-wollen,** *ir.v.n.* (*aux.* h.) wish *or* be willing to go in; *das will mir nicht in den Kopf -,* I cannot get that into my head, that is beyond me. **-ziehen,** *v.a.* pull, draw *or* drag in, involve, implicate.

hinfahr-en, 1. *ir.v.n.* (*aux.* s.) go away, depart; cease; die; drive, sail *or* cycle by, near, along; pass; *fahre hin, Mitleid!* farewell, pity! *mit der Hand über eine S. -en,* pass one's hand over a th. 2. *v.a.* convey to. **-t,** *f.* journey there, passage out, outward journey; decease.

Hinfall, *m.* falling down; fall; decay. **-en,** *ir.v.n.* (*aux.* s.) fall down; decay.

hinfällig, *adj.* falling down, declining; deciduous (*Bot.*); ready to fall, decaying; frail, feeble, weak, perishable; untenable (*of opinions*); *- werden,* come to nothing, fail. **-keit,** *f.* decrepitude, frailty, feebleness; weakness (*of arguments*).

hinfinden, *ir.v.r.* find one's way to a place.

hinfort, *adv.* henceforth, in future.

hing, hinge, *see* (1) **hangen;** (2) **hängen.**

Hingabe, *f.* giving away; surrender, submission; abandonment, resignation; devotion.

Hingang, *m.* (*archaic*) departure; decease.

hingeb-en, 1. *ir.v.a.* give up, surrender, resign; sacrifice; *sein Leben für einen -en,* sacrifice one's life for a p. 2. *v.r.* resign o.s. to, give o.s. up to; indulge in; submit, yield (*of a girl to a man's demands*), *sie hat sich ihm hingegeben,* she gave herself to him. **-end,** *adj.* devoted, self-sacrificing. **-ung,** *f.* surrender; resignation; devotion. **-ungsvoll,** *adj.*, *see* **-end.**

hingegen, *adv. & conj.* on the contrary, on the other hand; whereas.

hingehen, *ir.v.n.* (*aux.* s.) go to that place; go there, proceed; pass, elapse; *es geht hin,* it is passable; *es mag -,* it may pass; *etwas - lassen,* let a th. pass, wink at a th.

hingehören, *v.n.* belong to.

hingeraten, *ir.v.n.* (*aux.* s.) fall *or* light on *or* come *or* get to a place by chance *or* accident; *wo ist er -?* what has become of him?

hingerissen, *see* **hinreißen.**

hingestreckt, *see* **hinstrecken.**

hinhalt-en, *ir.v.a.* proffer, tender; hold out *or* off; put off, delay, retard; contain (*the enemy*); *einen -en,* keep a p. in suspense, put a p. off; *-ender Widerstand,* delaying action *or* tactics. **-ung,** *f.* holding forth; putting off; delay.

hink-en, *v.n.* (*aux.* h. & s.) limp, go lame, hobble; be imperfect; *auf* or *mit dem linken Fuß -en,* limp with the left leg; *auf beiden Seiten -en,* waver between two alternatives; *es -t mit ihm,* things are going ill with him; *die S. -t,* there is a hitch in the matter; *der -ende Bote,* bad news; *-ende Verse,* halting verse.

hinkommen, *ir.v.n.* (*aux.* s.) come *or* get there, arrive at; *nirgends -,* not go anywhere, never go out; *wo ist er hingekommen?* what has become of him?

Hinkunft, *f.* (*rare*) arrival there; *in -,* in future.

hinlangen, 1. *v.a.* (*einem etwas*) hand over, give, pass (s.th. to s.o.). 2. *v.n.* (*aux.* h.) reach, arrive at, be adequate, suffice.

hinlänglich, *adj.* sufficient, adequate; *-es Auskommen,* sufficient means, a competence, living wage.

hinlaufen, *ir.v.n.* (*aux.* s.) run there *or* away; *er mag -,* let him have his way.

hinlegen, 1. *v.a.* lay down; put away. 2. *v.r.* lie down.

hinmachen, (*coll.*) *v.n.*; *da hat der Hund hinge-*

macht, the dog has made a *or* done its mess (*used only of animals and small children*); (*aux.* s.) go *or* get there; (*aux.* h.) hurry.
Hinmarsch, *m.* march there, outward march.
Hinnahme, *f.* acceptance, receiving, reception.
hinnehmen, *ir.v.a.* take, accept; take upon o.s., submit to; bear, suffer, put up with. **hingenommen,** *adj.* preoccupied, carried away by.
hinneigen, *v.r.* & *n.* (*aux.* h.) incline to; bend *or* lean towards.
hinnen, *adv.* (*only in*) *von* –, away from here, from hence; *von – scheiden,* depart from hence, depart this life.
hinpassen, *v.n.* (*aux.* h.) (*in*) fit, suit, be fit for.
hinreichen, 1. *v.a.*, *see* **–langen.** 2. *v.n.* (*aux* h.) reach the desired point; suffice, be sufficient, do. **–d,** *pr.p.* & *adj.* sufficient, adequate, enough.
Hinreise, *f.* outward journey; *Hin- und Rückreise,* the double journey, outward and return journey.
hinreißen, *ir.v.a.* carry along; overpower, overcome; delight, charm, transport; *sich – lassen,* allow o.s. to be carried away, give way to. **–d,** *adj.* ravishing, enchanting, charming, thrilling, exciting.
hinricht–en, *v.a.* execute, put to death; spoil, ruin. **–ung,** *f.* execution.
hinrotzen, *v.n.* (*sl.*) crash, crack up (*vehicles, aircraft*).
hinschaffen, *v.a.* transport, convey, move.
hinscheiden, *ir.v.n.* (*aux.* s.) depart, pass away, die; *der Hingeschiedene,* the deceased; *das – Seiner Majestät,* the passing of His Majesty.
Hinschied, *m.* (*Swiss dial.*) departure, death.
hinschießen, *ir.v.n.* (*aux.* h.) shoot towards; (*aux.* s.) rush, haste along, fly away.
hinschlachten, *v.a.* murder (*on a large scale*); butcher.
hinschlagen, *ir.v.n.* (*aux.* s.) fall down heavily; (*coll.*) *lang* –, fall full length; (*coll.*) *da schlag einer lang hin;* (you could) knock me down with a feather!
hinschlängeln, *v.r.* wind, meander along.
hinschleichen, *v.n.* creep along.
hinschleppen, *v.a.* drag on *or* along.
hinschmachten, *v.n.* (*aux.* s.) languish on *or* away; linger on.
hinschmeißen, (*coll.*) *ir.v.a.* throw *or* fling down.
hinschwinden, *ir.v.n.* (*aux.* s.) pass away, vanish, dwindle; *–d,* evanescent.
hinsehen, *ir.v.n.* (*aux.* h.) look towards *or* at, watch.
hinsetzen, 1. *v.a.* set *or* put down, put away. 2. *v.r.* sit down.
Hinsicht, *f.* view, consideration, reference, respect, regard; *in – auf,* with regard to, concerning; *in mancher* or *vieler* – or *in vielen –en,* in many respects; *Sie haben in dieser – recht,* you are right in this respect *or* on this point. **–lich,** *prep.*, **–s,** *prep.* (*Gen.*) with regard to, as to, touching.
hinsiechen, *v.n.* go into a decline.
hinsinken, *ir.v.n.* (*aux.* s.) sink *or* fall down, collapse, swoon, faint.
hinstellen, *v.a.* put *or* place (down); set down *or* forth, bring forward, represent; *das wollen wir doch nicht so schroff* –, let us not be too positive about this.
hinstreben, *v.n.* (*aux.* h.) tend (*nach,* towards), strive (after).
hinstrecken, 1. *v.a.* knock down, lay low *or* out, kill. 2. *v.r.* lie down *or* stretch out at full length.
Hinsturz, *m.* falling headlong; precipitation.
hinstürzen, *v.n.* (*aux.* s.) fall headlong, tumble down; rush forward, hasten to.
hintan–setzen, *v.a.*, **–stellen,** *v.a.* treat slightingly, neglect. **–setzung,** *f.* neglecting; disregard; slighting.
hinten, *adv.* behind; in the rear, at the back, at the end; aft (*Naut.*); *von* –, from behind; *von – angreifen,* attack in the rear; *– anfügen,* add, append, annex; (*nach*) *– hinaus wohnen,* live at the back of a house; *es hieß Herr B. – und vorn,* it was always Mr. B. here, Mr. B. there, Mr. B. everywhere; *ich habe doch – keine Augen,* I haven't eyes in the back of my head. **–drein,** *adv.*, **–nach,** *adv.* after, afterwards, after the event; behind, in the rear; as an afterthought; last. **–über,** *adv.* (leaning) backwards.
hinter, 1. *adj.* & *insep. prefix,* hind, hinder back; posterior; *der –e,* (*vulg.*) the posterior, hind quarters, bottom, bum, backside, arse. 2. *prep.* & *sep. prefix,* (*with more or less literal meanings*) *and insep. prefix* (*with figurative meanings*): (*the former are mostly omitted here*) after; *– dem Berge halten,* keep one's thoughts secret, dissemble; *er brachte die Strecke in kurzer Zeit – sich,* he covered the distance in a short time; *immer – einem her sein* or *hergehen,* be always at a p.'s heels, be constantly urging *or* worrying a p.; *– eine S. kommen,* find a th. out, discover a th.; *– das* or *–s Licht führen,* dupe, deceive, take in; *sich – die Arbeit machen,* set to work with a will; *ich werde es mir – die Ohren schreiben,* I shall take good care to remember it, I shall certainly not forget it; *er hat es faustdick – den Ohren,* he is a very cunning *or* shrewd fellow; *ihm – die Schliche kommen,* be up to his tricks *or* wiles; *– sich sehen,* look back; *er steckt – der S.*, he is behind the matter; *es steckt etwas – der S.*, there is more in the matter than meets the eye; *er steckt sich – mich,* he shelters behind me *or* uses me as his mouthpiece; *er steht – mir zurück,* he is inferior to me *or* does not come up to my level; *das hätte ich nicht – ihm gesucht,* I should not have thought him capable of that (*or coll.*) thought it of him. **–achse,** *f.* rear axle (*Motor.*). **–ansicht,** *f.* back-view, rear elevation (*Arch.*). **–aus,** *adv.* astern (*Naut.*). **–backe,** *f.* buttock; (*pl.*) (*vulg.*) backside, bottom, bum, arse. **–backenzahn,** *m.* molar, grinder. **–bein,** *n.* hind leg; *sich auf die –beine setzen* or *stellen,* stand on one's hind legs; show fight, dig one's feet in. **–bleiben,** *ir.v.n.* (*aux.* s.) (*insep.*) remain behind, survive. **–bliebene(r),** *m.* bereaved, dependant, survivor. **–bliebenenversorgung,** *f.* dependants' allowance. **–bringen,** *ir.v.a.* 1. (*insep.*) (*einem etwas*) inform (a p. of a th.) secretly, give information of; bring a charge against; *er hat es mir –bracht,* he has informed me about it. 2. (*sep.*) (*coll.*) bring to the rear. **–bringer,** *m.* informer, spy, tell-tale. **–bringung,** *f.* (secret) information. **–darm,** *m.* rectum. **–deck,** *n.* poop (*Naut.*). **–drein,** *adv.* after; afterwards; too late; behind, at the end, bringing up the tail. **–e,** *m.*, *see* – 1. **–einander,** *adv.* one after another, in succession; *–einander weg,* without stopping to draw breath, uninterruptedly; *fünfmal –einander,* five times running. **–einanderschaltung,** *f.* connexion in series (*Elec.*). **–essen,** *v.a.* (*sep.*) (*coll.*) eat down, eat reluctantly *or* with difficulty. **–fuß,** *m.* hind foot. **–gaumen,** *m.* soft palate. **–gaumenlaut,** *m.* guttural *or* velar sound (*Phonet.*). **–gedanke,** *m.* mental reservation, ulterior motive. **–gehen,** *ir.v.a.* 1. (*sep.*) (*coll.*) go *or* walk to the rear. 2. (*insep.*) deceive, cheat, impose on. **–glied,** *n.* rear rank (*Mil.*); minor proposition (*Log.*); consequent (*Math.*). **–grund,** *m.* background, distance (*landscape, pictures*); (*pl.*) hidden difficulties, moot *or* tricky points, (*sl.*) snags (*of problems*). **–gründig,** *adj.* recondite, profound, enigmatical, cryptic, impenetrable. **–halt,** *m.* ambush, trap (*Mil.*). **–halten,** *ir.v.a.* (*insep.*) hold back, be reserved, conceal, deceive. **–haltig,** *adj.* **–hältig,** *adj.* reserved, close; malicious, insidious. **–hand,** *f.* hind quarter (*of a horse*). **–haupt,** *n.*, *see* **–kopf.** **–haus,** *n.* rear building, back premises. **–her,** *adv.* behind; in the rear; after(wards). **–hof,** *m.* back yard. **–kante,** *f.* trailing edge (*Av.*). **–kopf,** *m.* back of the head; occiput (*Anat.*). **–lader,** *m.* breech-loader. **–lage,** *f.* (*Swiss dial.*) deposit, pledge. **–land,** *n.* hinterland. **–lassen, 1.** *ir.v.a.* 1. (*sep.*) (*coll.*) permit to go *or* pass to the rear. 2. (*insep.*) leave behind; leave word *or* instructions *or* a message; bequeath; *die –lassenen,* the survivors *or* heirs. **2.** *p.p.* & *adj.* posthumous. **–lassenschaft,** *f.* testator's estate. **–lastig,** *adj.* tail-heavy (*Av.*). **–legen,** *v.a.* 1. (*sep.*) (*coll.*) relegate to the rear. 2. (*insep.*) deposit; consign (*as a pledge*). **–leger,** *m.* depositor. **–legte(s),** *n.* deposit. **–legung,** *f.* deposition. **–leib,** *m.* hind quarters, back; abdomen. **–leiste,** *f.*, *see* **–kante.** **–list,** *f.* fraud; cunning, artifice, wile. **–listig,** *adj.* cunning, deceitful, insidious, artful, wily. **–mann,** *m.* rear-rank man; backer, supporter, (*coll.*) cover; endorsers (*of cheques*); *wer ist mein –mann?* who plays

after me? (*Cards*). **–mast,** *m.* mizzen-mast. **–n,** *m.* (*coll.*), *see* **–e. –rad,** *n.* back wheel(*Motor.*). **–rücks,** *adv.* backwards; from behind; secretly, insidiously, stealthily. **–saß, –sasse,** *m.* (-(ss)en, -(ss)en), **–säß,** *m.* (*Swiss dial.*) copyholder; smallholder, small farmer. **–satz,** *m.* apodosis (*Gram.*). **–schiff,** *n.* stern (*of a ship*). **–schlingen,** *ir.v.a.* (*coll.*), *see* **–essen. –schlucken,** *v.a.* (*coll.*), *see* **hinunterschlucken. –sinnen,** (*Swiss dial.*) *ir.v.r.* be moody *or* melancholy. **–sinnig,** (*Swiss dial.*) *adj.* crazy; gloomy, melancholy. **–sitz,** *m.* back seat, pillion. **–st,** *superl. adj.* hindmost, last. **–ste,** *m.* (*coll.*), *see* **–e. –steven,** *m.* stern post. **–stück,** *n.* hind *or* back piece. **–tau,** *n.* stern-fast (*mooring cable*) (*Naut.*). **–teil,** *n.* hind part, back part; buttock, crupper (*of horse*), stern (*of a ship*). **–treffen,** *n.* reserve; rearguard; *ins –treffen kommen,* be pushed into the background, fall behind, take a back seat. **–treiben,** *ir.v.a.* 1. (*sep.*) (*coll.*) drive to the rear; 2. (*insep.*) hinder, baffle, thwart. **–treibung,** *f.* frustration, thwarting. **–treppe,** *f.* backstairs. **–treppenpolitik,** *f.* backstairs politics. **–treppenroman,** *m.* cheap thriller *or* shocker. **–trinken,** *v.a.* (*coll.*), *see* **–schlucken. –tür,** *f.* back-door; escape hatch; (*fig.*) loophole, escape, outlet. **–verdeck,** *n.* quarterdeck. **–wäldler,** *m.* backwoodsman, squatter. **–wand,** *f.* back wall; back cloth (*Theat.*). **–wärts,** *adv.* backwards; behind. **–ziehen,** *ir.v.a.* (*insep.*) defraud (of), embezzle.

hintaumeln, *v.n.* totter *or* reel along.

hintrauern, *v.a.* pass in sorrow *or* mourning.

hinträumen, *v.a. & n.* dream away, day-dream.

hintreten, *ir.v.n.* (*aux.* s.) step along, tread; step up (*vor, zu,* to).

Hintritt, *m.* departure, death (*high style*).

hintun, *ir.v.a.* (*coll.*) put *or* place; *wo soll ich es –?* where shall I put it? what shall I do with it?

hinüber, *adv. & sep. prefix,* over there, across, beyond, to the other side; (*coll.*) dead; broken, worn-out, useless; *da –,* over there, that way; *er ist –,* he is dead; *die Vase ist –,* the vase is broken; *das Kleid ist –,* the dress is worn out, (*sl.*) this dress has had it. **–bringen, –schaffen,** *ir.v.a.* (*sep.*) bring across; transpose (*Math.*). **–reißen,** *ir.v.a.* carry over. **–wechseln,** *v.n.* move over (*to another place*), go *or* change over; *zu einer andern Partei –wechseln,* go over to another party, change one's allegiance; *ins Lager der Feinde –wechseln,* desert *or* go over to the enemy.

Hinundher-Bewegung, *f.* oscillating motion. **–biegeversuch,** *m.* reverse bending test (*Metall.*).

hinunter, *adv. & sep. prefix,* down, downwards; downstairs, below, from up here. **–gehen,** *ir.v.n.* go down. **–schauen,** *v.n.* look down. **–schlucken,** *v.a.* swallow, gulp down. **–spülen,** *v.a.* wash down. **–stürzen,** *v.a.* fall, rush *or* fly down (*stairs, etc.*); gulp hurriedly, throw down one's throat.

hinwagen, *v.r.* venture to go (*to a place*).

hinweg, 1. *adv. & sep. prefix,* away, forth off. 2. *n.* way there *or* to a place, outward trip; *– mit euch!* be off! begone! **–gehen,** *ir. v.n.* (*aux.* s.) go away; (*über eine S.*) pass over, disregard, ignore, treat lightly *or* with indifference, regard as unimportant. **–kommen,** *ir.v.n.* (*aux.* s.)(*über eine S.*) get over. **–raffen,** *v.a.* snatch away. **–sehen,** *ir.v.n.* (*aux.* h.) look away; (*über eine S.*) manage to see over (*an obstacle*); take no notice of, overlook. **–setzen,** *v.r.* (*über eine S.*), *see* **–gehen** (*über eine S.*).

Hinweis, *m.* indication; hint, allusion; *unter – auf* (*Acc.*), with reference to. **–en,** *ir.v.a.* show (*the way*) to; *auf eine S. –en,* point to, towards *or* at, refer *or* allude to; *–end,* pointing to, alluding to; *–endes Fürwort,* demonstrative pronoun (*Gram.*). **–ung,** *f.* direction, instruction.

hinwelken, *v.n.* wither away, droop.

hinwerfen, *ir.v.a.* throw, fling to *or* down; write *or* jot down *or* sketch hastily; drop (*a word*); make (*a remark*); *hingeworfene Worte,* casual words, occasional utterances.

hinwieder, *adv.,* **hinwiederum,** *adv.* again, once more; on the other hand, in return.

hinwollen, *ir.v.n.* (*aux.* h.) want to go to; aim at, tend to; *ich merke, wo er hin will,* I see what he is driving at.

hinzahlen, *v.a.* pay down (*cash*).

hinzeichnen, *v.a.* sketch (roughly).

hinziehen, 1. *ir.v.a.* draw along, extend, protract; draw to(wards), attract. 2. *v.n.* (*aux.* s.) move off *or* along; move to; pass away, depart; draw out, drag on *or* out, last a long time, go on indefinitely.

hinzielen, *v.n.* (*aux.* h.); *auf eine S. –,* aim at a th., be intended for a th.

hinzu, *adv. & sep. prefix* (*movement into the neighbourhood of or as an addition to s.th.*), to, towards, near; in addition, besides, moreover. **–fügen,** *v.a.* add to, append. **–fügung,** *f.* addition; apposition (*Gram.*). **–gehören,** *v.n.* (*aux.* h.) be one of; belong to. **–gießen,** *ir.v.a.*pour into (in addition), add. **–kommen,** *ir.v.n.* (*aux.* s.) be added, come up to; *es kommt noch –, daß, usw.,* add to this, that, *etc.* **–kommend,** *adj.* additional, accessory, adventitious. **–nahme,** *f.* addition, inclusion, combination. **–setzen,** 1. *v.a.* add (*a remark, etc.*). 2. *v.r.* join (*others*) at their table. **–träufeln,** *v.a.* add drop by drop. **–treten,** *ir.v.n.* (*aux.* s.) join (*others already there*); supervene. **–tritt,** *m.* approach, accession. **–tun,** 1. *ir.v.a.* add. 2. *n.* addition. **–ziehen,** *ir.v.a.* take in addition; take into consultation. **–ziehung,** *f.*; *unter –ziehung der Spesen,* including all expenses, all charges included.

Hiobs-botschaft, *f.* (-en), **–post,** *f.* (-en) bad news, ill tidings.

Hippe, *f.* (-n) sickle, hedging *or* pruning knife, billhook, scythe; (*dial.*) bread roll, croissant; (*dial.*) goat.

Hippursäure, *f.* hippuric acid.

Hirn, *n.* (-(e)s, -e) brain; brains, intellect; brains (*Cook.*), *see* **Gehirn**; *Klein–,* cerebellum. **–anhang,** *m.* pituitary gland. **–deckel,** *m.* cranium. **–erschütterung,** *f.* concussion of the brain. **–falte,** *f.* cephalic *or* cerebral lobe. **–geburt,** *f.,* **–gespinst,** *n.* fancy, whim, chimera, phantom; bogey *or* bogy. **–haut,** *f.* meninges; *die obere* (*untere*) *–haut,* the dura (pia) mater. **–hautentzündung,** *f.* meningitis. **–holz,** *n.* cross-cut timber. **–kammer,** *f.* brain-cell, cerebral ventricle. (*coll.*) **–kasten,** *m.* brain-box, pate. **–lappen,** *m., see* **–falte. –los,** *adj.* brainless, silly. **–losigkeit,** *f.* empty-headedness. **–schädel,** *m.* skull, cranium. **–schädelfuge,** *f.,* **–schädelnaht,** *f.* suture. **–schädelhaut,** *f.* pericranium. **–schale,** *f.* skull, cranium. **–schnitt,** *m.* cross-section (*timber*). **–teil,** *n.* brain substance. **–verbrannt,** *adj.* (*coll.*) mad, crazy, crack-brained, (*coll.*) crack-pot. **–verletzung,** *f.* contusion of the brain. **–windung,** *f.* cerebral convolution.

Hirsch, *m.* (-es, -e) stag, hart; (red) deer; *der – schreit* or *röhrt,* the stag bellows. **–bock,** *m.* stag, buck. **–braten,** *m.* venison. **–brunft,** *f.,* **–brunst,** *f.* rutting (of deer). **–fänger,** *m.* hunting-knife, bowie knife. **–fleisch,** *n.* venison. **–geweih,** *n.* antlers. **–horn,** *n.* hartshorn. **–hornsalz,** *n.* carbonate of ammonia. **–käfer,** *m.* stag-beetle (*Lucanidae*) (*Ent.*). **–kalb,** *n.* fawn. **–keule,** *f.* haunch of venison. **–kuh,** *f.* hind, doe. **–leder,** *n.* buckskin, doeskin, deerskin. **–ledern,** *adj.* deerskin, buckskin, doeskin. **–sprung,** *m.* capriole (*haute école*). **–wurz,** *f.* mountain parsley (*Peucedanum cervaria*) (*Bot.*). **–ziege,** *f.,* **–antilope,** *f.* sasin, black buck, Indian gazelle (*Antilope cervicapra*) (*Zool.*). **–ziemer,** *m.* saddle of venison.

Hirse, *f.* millet. **–brei,** *m.* millet gruel. **–korn,** *n.* millet seed; stye (*on the eye*). **–(n)fieber,** *n.* miliary fever.

Hirt, *m.* (-en, -en), (*Poet.*) **–e,** *m.* (-en, -en) herdsman, shepherd; pastor; *der Herr ist mein –e,* the Lord is my shepherd; *ich bin der gute –e,* I am the Good Shepherd; *wie der – so die Herde,* like master like man. **–en,** *v.n.* (*Swiss dial.*) tend flocks. **–enamt,** *n.* pastorate. **–enbrief,** *m.* pastoral letter. **–endichtung,** *f.* pastoral poetry, bucolic poetry. **–enflöte,** *f.* Pan's pipe. **–engedicht,** *n.* pastoral poem, bucolic eclogue. **–engott,** *m.* Pan. **–enhund,** *m.* sheep-dog. **–enknabe,** *m.* shepherd boy. **–enleben,** *n.* pastoral life, idyllic existence. **–enlied,** *n.* pastoral song. **–enpfeife,** *f.,* **–enrohr,** *n. see* **–enflöte. –enspiel,** *n.,* **–enstück,** *n.* pastoral (play). **–enstab,** *m.* shepherd's staff *or* crook; bishop's crozier. **–entasche,** *f.,* **–entäschel,** *n.*

shepherd's purse (*Capsella bursa-pastoris*) (*Bot.*). **–envolk,** *n.* pastoral tribes. **–in,** *f.* shepherdess.
Hiss–e, *f.* (-en) pulley, tackle. **–en,** *v.a.* hoist, set (*sail*). **–etau, (Hißtau),** *n.* halyard.
hist, *int.* left! (*call to horse*); *der eine will –, der andere hott,* one pulls one way, the other another.
Histörchen, *n.* (-s, –) funny story, anecdote.
Histor–ie, *f.* (-ien) history; (*archaic*) story, narrative. **–ienmalerei,** *f.* historical painting. **–iker,** *m.* historian. **–isch,** *adj.* historic(al).
Hitsche, *f.* (-n) (*dial.*) footstool; small sledge.
Hitz–e, *f.* heat; ardour, fervour, passion; *in die –e bringen,* put into a temper; *in der ersten –e,* in the first flush (of enthusiasm); *in der –e des Gefechts,* in the heat of the moment; *in –e geraten,* fly into a passion; *in der –e trinken,* drink when one is hot. **–blase,** *f.*, **–blatter,** *f.* heat rash. **–blütig,** *adj.* choleric. **–ebeständig,** *adj.* unaffected by heat, heat-resisting. **–eempfindlich,** *adj.* sensitive to heat. **–eferien,** *f. pl.* half-holiday from school during heat wave. **–efrei,** *adj.* no school on account of heat. **–egrad,** *m.* temperature. **–emesser,** *m.* pyrometer. **–ewelle,** *f.* heat-wave, hot spell. **–ig,** *adj.* hot; (*fig.*) fiery, ardent, fervent, passionate; hot-headed, hasty, choleric; *–iges Fieber,* high fever; *–iger Kopf,* excitable fellow; *–ige Krankheit,* acute malady *or* disease; *–ige Worte,* heated words. **–igkeit,** *f.* heat, rut; ardour, passion, temper, vehemence. **–kopf,** *m.* hot-headed person. **–köpfig,** *adj.* hot-headed. **–pocken,** *f. pl.* *see* **–blase.** **–schlag,** *m.* heat-stroke.
hob, höbe, *see* **heben.**
Hobel, *m.* (-s, –) plane. **–n,** *v.a.* plane, smooth; take the rough off. **–bank,** *f.* joiner's bench. **–späne,** *m.pl.* shavings.
Hobo–e, *f.* (-en) (*archaic*) hautboy. **–ist,** *m.* (-en, -en) oboe-player.
hoch, 1. *adj.* (*when followed by* e *of the inflected cases* ch *becomes* h, *as*: hoher, hohe, hohes, *or* der, die, das Hohe; *comp.* höher; *sup.* höchst) high; tall, lofty; noble, sublime; proud; expensive, dear; deep; great; (raised) to the power of (*Math.*); *2 hoch 3 gleicht 8,* 2 to the power of 3 *or* 2 cubed equals 8; *das Hohe,* the sublime; *der hohe Adel,* the peerage, the nobility; *–es Alter,* advanced *or* old age; *in hohem Ansehen stehen, ein hohes Ansehen genießen,* enjoy great respect *or* high esteem; *– aufhorchen,* prick up one's ears; *hoher Baß,* bass-baritone; *hohe Blüte,* full bloom; *in hoher Blüte stehen,* be very prosperous, be at the height of (its) prosperity; *die Dichtung stand in hoher Blüte,* it was a golden age of poetry; *hoher Eid,* solemn oath; *hohe Farbe,* bright colour; *hohe Flut, –flut,* high-tide *or* -water; *ein hoher Fünfziger,* a man well on in the fifties; *der Rhein geht –,* the Rhine runs high; *hoher Genuß,* great enjoyment; *hoher Gewinn,* big prize (*in a lottery*); *zu – gegriffen sein,* be set *or* fixed too high, be estimated at too high a figure; *Hände –!* hands up! *es geht – her,* things are pretty lively, there is great excitement; *hohe Herrschaften,* people of high rank; *– hinaus-* or *hinaufwollen,* be ambitious; *hohe Jagd,* deer stalking, hunting large game; *– an Jahren,* advanced in years; (*coll.*) *auf die hohe Kante legen,* put aside, put on one side, save; *wenn es – kommt,* at (the) most; *einen –leben lassen,* toast, drink a p.'s (very good) health, give three cheers for a p.; *– lebe der König!* long live the king! *drei Mann –,* three men deep; *die Hohe Messe,* high mass; *hohes Neujahr,* feast of Epiphany; *– und niedrig,* rich and poor; *– oben im Norden, im hohen Norden,* in the far north; *die hohe Obrigkeit,* the powers that be, the authorities; *die Hohe Pforte,* the Sublime Porte; *die hohe Schule, haute école,* equestrian gymnastics, advanced horsemanship; *hohe See,* open sea, the high seas; *hoher Sinn,* nobility of mind; *der Geldkurs steht –,* cash is at a high premium; *– zu stehen kommen,* cost dear; *bei hoher Strafe,* under a heavy penalty; *hohe Summe,* large sum (of money); *– anrechnen,* value greatly; *– am Tage* or *hoher Tag,* broad daylight; *– und heilig* or *teuer versprechen,* swear by all that is holy; *die hohe Woche,* Holy Week; *hohe Worte machen,* make fine phrases; *das ist ihm zu –,* that is too deep *or* profound for him, that is beyond him. 2. *n.* cheer; toast; anticyclone, high (pressure) (*Meteor.*). **–achten,** *v.a.* respect, esteem. **–achtung,** *f.* esteem, respect, regard; *in* or *mit vorzüglicher –achtung, –achtungsvoll,* yours respectfully, yours faithfully (*at the end of a letter*). **–adelig,** *adj.* aristocratic. **–altar,** *m.* high altar. **–amt,** *n.* high mass. **–angriff,** *m.* high-level attack (*Av.*). **–ansehnlich,** *adj.* of the highest reputation, most honourable. **–antenne,** *f.* outside aerial (*Rad.*). **–bahn,** *f.* overhead railway, high-level railway. **–bau,** *m.* superstructure, building above ground (*as opp. to excavation*); *Hoch- und Tiefbau,* underground and surface engineering. **–bejahrt,** *adj.*, **–betagt,** *adj.* aged, advanced in years. **–betrieb,** *m.* intense activity; (*fam.*) hustle, bustle. **–bewegt,** *adj.* deeply agitated; stormy, rough. **–burg,** *f.* stronghold. **–decker,** *m.* high-wing monoplane (*Av.*). **–deutsch,** *adj.* High German, standard German. **–druck,** *m.* high pressure; relief-printing; *mit –druck an einer S. arbeiten,* work energetically at a th. **–ebene,** *f.* tableland, plateau. **–edelgeboren,** *adj.* high-born; honourable (*archaic title*). **–ehrwürden,** *m.* (*abbr.* **Ew.**) Your Reverence. **–ehrwürdig,** *adj.* right reverend. **–email,** *n.* embossed enamel. **–empfindlich,** *adj.* highly sensitive (*Phot.*). **–entzückt,** *adj.* ecstatic, in ecstasy. **–erfreut,** *adj.* highly delighted. **–erhaben,** *adj.* sublime; in high relief. **–fahren,** *v.n.* rise *or* start up (suddenly). **–fahrend,** *adj.* haughty. **–farbig,** *adj.* highly coloured. **–fein,** *adj.* superfine, exquisite, choice. **–fliegend,** *adj.* soaring, lofty, ambitious. **–frequenz,** *f.* high-frequency. **–gebenedeit,** *adj.* most blessed (*Virgin*). **–gebietend,** *adj.* (*archaic*) in high authority; high and mighty; dread. **–gebirge,** *n.* high mountain-chain. **–gebirgspflanze,** *f.* alpine plant. **–geboren,** *adj.* high-born; Right Honourable. **–geehrt,** *adj.* highly honoured, highly respected; *–geehrter Herr,* (Dear) Sir (*in letter*). **–gefühl,** *n.* exultation, delight, enthusiasm; *im –gefühl des Sieges,* exulting in one's victory. **–gehen,** *v.n.* rise, soar, mount, (*coll.*) fly into a temper. **–gehend,** *adj.* high (*of waves*). **–gelag(e),** *n.* banquet. **–gelehrt,** *adj.* very learned. **–gelobt,** *adj.* highly praised; magnified, blessed. **–geneigt,** *adj.* most gracious. **–genuß,** *m.* rapture, ecstasy, delight; luxury, treat. **–gericht,** *n.* supreme penal court; place of execution, gallows. **–gesang,** *m.* hymn, anthem. **–geschätzt,** *adj.* highly esteemed. **–geschürzt,** *adj.* with skirts tucked up, (*fig.*) free-and-easy, sportive. **–gesinnt,** *adj.* high-minded, noble. **–gespannt,** *adj.* exaggerated; at high tension. **–gewässer,** *n.*, *see* **–wasser.** **–glanz,** *m.* high-gloss, brilliance, polish. **–gradig,** *adj.* to a high degree, extreme, intense; high-grade, high quality. **–halten** *v.a.* (*sep.*) think highly of, cherish; *jemandes Andenken –halten,* cherish the memory of a p. **–haus,** *n.* skyscraper (*Arch.*). **–herzig,** *adj.* high-minded, noble, magnanimous. **–kantig,** *adj.* on edge, edgewise. **–konjunktur,** *f.* business prosperity, boom. **–konzentriert,** *adj.* highly concentrated. **–lage,** *f.* high altitude. **–land,** *n.* highland, upland. **–länder,** *m.* highlander. **–leistung,** *f.* heavy duty, high capacity. **–leitung,** *f.* overhead line *or* wire (*Tele.*). **–meister,** *m.* Grand Master. **–molekular,** *adj.* of high molecular weight (*Chem.*). **–mut,** *m.* pride, arrogance, haughtiness; (*Prov.*) *–mut kommt vor dem Fall* pride will have a fall. **–mutig,** *adj.* courageous, intrepid. **–mütig,** *adj.* proud, arrogant, haughty. **–mutsteufel,** *m.* demon of pride. **–näsig,** *adj.* haughty, arrogant, supercilious, (*coll.*) stuck-up. **–nehmen,** *v.a.* (*coll.*) 1. take (a p.) in, trick. 2. scold.. **–notpeinlich,** *adj.* penal, capital; *–notpeinliches Gericht,* criminal court (*for capital offences*); *–notpeinliche Halsgerichtsordnung,* penal code (*involving death penalty*). **–ofen,** *m.* blast furnace. **–prozentig,** *adj.* of a high percentage, in a large degree. **–ragend,** *adj.* towering. **–rot,** *adj.* bright *or* deep red, crimson. **–ruf,** *m.* cheer; *sie wurden mit lauten –rufen begrüßt,* they were loudly cheered. **–rund,** *adj.* convex. **–schätzen,** *v.a.* (*sep.*) esteem highly (N.B. *– schätzen,* set a high value on, make a high estimate of). **–schätzung,** *f.* high esteem. **–schule,** *f.* college, university;

technische –schule, school of technology, polytechnic; *–schule für Landwirtschaft*, agricultural college; *–schule für Musik*, academy of music. **–schüler,** *m.* university student. **–schulwesen,** *n.* university affairs. **–schwanger,** *adj.* advanced in pregnancy; (*coll.*) far gone. **–seeflotte,** *f.* ocean-going fleet, battle fleet. **–seeschlepper,** *m.* sea-going tug. **–selig,** *adj.* late, deceased, of blessed memory. **–silo,** *m.* silo. **–sinn,** *m.* high-mindedness. **–sinnig,** *adj.* high-minded. **–sommer,** *m.* midsummer. **–spannung,** *f.* high tension *or* voltage (*Elec.*). **–spannungsleitung,** *f.* high-tension cables. **–sprache,** *f.* standard educated speech; literary language. **¨–st,** *see* **höchst. –sprung,** *m.* high jump (*Sport*). **–stämmig,** *adj.* tall, lofty (*of trees*); standard (*of roses*). **–stand,** *m.* high-water mark; high standing; fine condition; prosperity; high prices. **–stapelei,** *f.* fraud, swindling, embezzlement. **–stapler,** *m.* swindler. **–stehend,** *adj.* eminent, notable. **–stift,** *n.* cathedral chapter, bishopric; academy. **–straße,** *f.* main route *or* artery (*for traffic*); *–straßen des Luftverkehrs*, main airways. **–strebend,** *adj.* aspiring, aiming at great things, ambitious. **–ton,** *m.* high pitch; principal accent (*Metr.*). **–tönend,** *adj.* high-sounding, high-flown, grandiloquent. **–tonig,** *adj.* having the principal accent. **–tönig,** *adj.*, *see* **–näsig** & **–tönend. –tourist,** *m.* mountaineer, alpinist. **–trabend,** *adj.* bombastic, pompous, high-sounding. **–traber,** *m.* high-stepping horse. **–trächtig,** *adj.*, **–tragend,** *adj.* great with young (*of animals*). **–verdient,** *adj.* highly meritorious, most worthy. **–verrat,** *m.* high treason. **–verräter,** *m.* traitor, rebel, treasonable felon. **–verräterisch,** *adj.* treasonable. **–verzinslich,** *adj.* bearing high rates of interest. **–wald,** *m.* mountain *or* high-altitude *or* alpine forest; tree-covered mountain slope. **–wasser,** *n.* high-water, flooding. **–wasserstand,** *m.* high-water mark, flood level. **–weide,** *f.* alpine pasture, alp. **–wertig,** *adj.* of high value, first-rate, high-grade, highly qualified, excellent; of high valence (*Chem.*). **–wild,** *n.* deer, game. **–wirksam,** *adj.* highly active, highly effective. **–wohlgeboren,** *adj.* (*archaic*), *Ew. –wohlgeboren*, Right Honourable Sir, Your Honour, Your Reverence, Reverend Sir. **–wohllöblich,** *adj.*, **–würden** (*in titles*); *Ew. –würden*, Your Reverence, Reverend Sir. **–würdig,** *adj.* right reverend; *das –würdigste Gut*, the Host (*R.C.*). **–zahl,** *f.* exponent (*Math.*). **–zeit,** *f.*, *see* **Hochzeit. –ziehen,** 1. *ir.v.n.*(*sl.*)pull the nose up, zoom (*Av.*). 2. *v.a.* (*die Maschine*) *–ziehen*, climb (*Av.*).

höch–lich, *adv.* highly, exceedingly, greatly, mightily; grievously. **–st,** 1. *adj.* (*see* **hoch**) highest, uppermost, utmost, maximum, extreme; *–ste Not*, direst need, last extremity; *das ist das –ste, was ich geben kann*, that is the utmost I can give; *es in einer S. aufs –ste bringen*, bring a th. to the height of perfection; *wenn es aufs –ste kommt*, if the worst comes to the worst; *es ist mit ihnen aufs –ste gekommen*, they are reduced to the last extremity; *das Leben ist der Güter –stes nicht*, life is not man's most precious possession (*Schiller*); *es ist –ste Zeit*, it is high time. 2. *adv.* most, at the most, very, extremely, in the highest degree; *–st schädlich*, highly injurious; *–st gemein*, grossly vulgar; *diese Vögel fliegen am –sten*, these birds fly highest. 3. *n.* record, maximum. **–stbelastung,** *f.* maximum load (*Mech.*). **–steigen,** *adj.*; *in –steigener Person*, in person. **–stens,** *adv.* at most, at the utmost *or* outside; at best. **–stfahrt,** *f.* full speed, top speed (*Naut.*). **–stgeschwindigkeit,** *f.* top speed (*Motor.*); *zulässige –stgeschwindigkeit*, speed limit. **–stgrenze,** *f.* limit. **–stleistung,** *f.* best performance, maximum output, record; *die bisherige –stleistung noch übertreffen*, beat the record. **–stmaß,** *n.* maximum. **–stpreis,** *m.* maximum price. **–stsatz,** *m.* maximum rate. **–stschußweite,** *f.* maximum range. **–stwahrscheinlich,** *adv.* most probably *or* likely, in all probability.

Hochzeit, *f.* (-en) wedding, marriage; pairing (*of birds*); *– machen* or *halten*, get married, celebrate one's wedding. (*dial.*) **–er,** *m.* bridegroom. (*dial.*) **–erin,** *f.* bride. **–lich,** *adj.* nuptial, bridal. **–sbett,** *n.* bridal bed. **–sfeier,** *f.*, **–sfest,** *n.* wedding celebration. **–sflug,** *m.* nuptial flight (*insects*). **–sgedicht,** *n.* epithalamium. **–sgeschenk,** *n.* wedding present. **–sgewand,** *n.* bridal dress, wedding-garment. **–sgott,** *m.* Hymen. **–smahl,** *n.* wedding breakfast. **–sreise,** *f.* honeymoon. **–sschmaus,** *m.*, *see* **–smahl.**

Hock–e, *f.* (-n) heap of sheaves, stook; squatting posture. **–en,** 1. *v.n.* (*aux.* h.) crouch; squat; *immer hinter dem Ofen* or *zu Hause –en*, hug the fire, be a stay-at-home. 2. *v.a.* set up (*sheaves*) in heaps *or* stooks. **–er,** *m.* stool. **–ergrab,** *n.* prehistoric grave.

Höcker, *m.* (-s, –) protuberance, eminence, hump, knob, tubercle (*Bot.*); *einen – haben*, be hunchbacked; (*B.*) *ich will die – eben machen*, I will make the crooked places straight. **–hindernis,** *n.* dragons' teeth, tank obstacle (*Mil.*). **–ig,** *adj.* humpy, knobby, knotty, nodulated, gibbous; uneven; hunchbacked. **–tier,** *n.* animal with a hump.

Hode, *f.* (-n) *or m.* (-n -n), **–n,** *m.* (-ns, -n) testicle. **–nsack,** *m.* scrotum.

Hof, *m.* (-es, ¨-e) yard, court-yard; farm; country house, manor; palace, court; ring *or* circle (*round the eyes*), halo, corona, aureole (*Opt.*); *einem den – machen*, pay court to a p. **–arzt,** *m.* court physician. **–bauer,** *m.* peasant proprietor. **–beamte(r),** *m.* court official. **–besitzer,** *m.* owner of an estate, freeholder. **–brauch,** *m. see* **–gebrauch. –dame,** *f.* maid of honour, lady in waiting. **–dichter,** *m.* court poet; poet laureate. **–dienst,** *m.* office at court; socage. **–fähig,** *adj.* (*coll.*) presentable. **–fart,** *f.*, *see* **Hoffart. –fräulein,** *n.* maid of honour. **–gänger,** *m.* (*archaic*) day-labourer. **–gebrauch,** *m.* court etiquette. **–gefolge,** *n.* retinue. **–gerät,** *n.* farming implements. **–gericht,** *n.* high court of justice. **–gesinde,** *n.* servants of a royal household; servants on a farm *or* estate. **–gut,** *n.* domain, demesne. **–haltung,** *f.* royal household. **–herr,** *m.* lord of the manor. **–hörig,** *adj.* manorial. **–hund,** *m.* watch-dog. **–jäger,** *m.* royal gamekeeper. **–junker,** *m.* page; equerry. **–kammer,** *f.* exchequer. **–kanzlei,** *f.* court chancery. **–kapelle,** *f.* court musicians. **–kaplan,** *m.* court chaplain. **–kasse,** *f.* prince's privy purse, civil list. **–kavalier,** *m.* gentleman in waiting; courtier. **–künste,** *f.pl.*, *see* **–ränke. –leute,** *pl.* courtiers; bondsmen, socagers. **–lieferant,** *m.* purveyor (by special appointment) to His Majesty. **–macher,** *m.* wooer. **–manier,** *f.* court manner, court atmosphere. **–mann,** *m.* courtier. **–männisch,** *adj.* obsequious, fawning, sycophantic. **–marschall,** *m.* court marshal; Lord Chamberlain (*in England*). **–mäßig,** *adj.* courtly. **–meier,** *m.* farm-steward; tenant farmer. **–meister,** *m.* (*archaic*) private tutor; steward. **–meisterei,** *f.* steward's house; tutorship; (*coll.*) pedantry. **–meistern,** 1. *v.n.* act as private tutor; play the pedant. 2. *v.a.* censure, find fault with, criticize. **–narr,** *m.* court fool *or* jester. **–prediger,** *m.* court chaplain; *ordentlicher –prediger*, chaplain in ordinary. **–ränke,** *m.pl.* court intrigues. **–rat,** *m.* Privy Councillor. **–raum,** *m.* courtyard; yard. **–schatzmeister,** *m.* royal treasurer. **–schranz(e),** *m.*, **–schranze,** *f.* courtier, flunkey, lickspittle. **–schulze,** *m.* wealthy (Westphalian) farmer. **–sitte,** *f.* court etiquette. **–staat,** *m.* household of a prince; court-dress. **–tor,** *n.* yard-gate. **–tracht,** *f.* court-dress. **–trauer,** *f.* court mourning. **–tür,** *f.* yard-door. **–wesen,** *n.* court ways; court affairs. **–wohnung,** *f.* flat (in a large block) overlooking the court-yard.

höfeln, *v.n.* (*Dat.*) (*Swiss dial.*), *see* **hofieren.**

Hof–fart, *f.* arrogance, pride, haughtiness. **–färtig,** *adj.* haughty, arrogant.

hoff–en, 1. *v.a.* & *n.* (*aux.* h.) hope; expect, look for; *ich –e es*, I hope so; *ich –e es von ihm*, I expect it of him; *auf eine S. –en*, hope for a th.; *was man –t glaubt man gern*, the wish is father to the thought; *der Mensch –t solang er lebt*, while there's life there's hope; *es ist* (or *steht*) *zu –en*, it is to be hoped. 2. *n.* hoping, expecting; (*Prov.*) *–en und Harren macht manchen zum Narren*, he who lives on hope dies of hunger. **–entlich,** *adv.* it is to be hoped. **–nung,** *f.* hope, expectation; *zu den schönsten –nungen berechtigen*, justify the fondest hopes; *–nung geben auf eine S.*, hold out hopes for a th.; *guter –nung sein*, be of good cheer; be confident; be with child, be pregnant; *einem –nung auf eine S. machen*, give a p. a reason to hope *or* expect; *noch am Grabe pflanzt der Mensch die –nung auf* (*Schiller*), hope springs eternal in the human breast. **–nungslos,** *adj.* hopeless; past all hope. **–nungslosigkeit,** *f.* hopelessness, despair. **–nungsreich,** *adj.*, **–nungsvoll,** *adj.* promising, hopeful. **–nungsschimmer,** *m.*, **–nungsstrahl,** *m.* ray of hope.

-höffig, *suffix*, rich in, *e.g.* **erdölhöffig,** *adj.* oil bearing (*Min.*). **–lich,** *adj.* rich, yielding (*Min.*).

hofieren, *v.n.* (*aux.* h.) (*Dat.*) pay court to, flatter.

höf–isch, *adj.* courtly; *die –ische Lyrik*, courtly lyric; *das –ische Epos*, court epic. **–lich,** *adj.* polite, civil, courteous. **–lichkeit,** *f.* politeness, courtesy, civility. **–lichkeitsbezeigung,** *f.* mark of respect. **–ling,** *m.* courtier.

Höft, *n.* (-es) (*dial.*) foreland, headland; stage.

Höhe, *f.* (-n) height, altitude, elevation, loftiness; summit, top, high place, hill, mountain; amount (*of money*); dearness (*of price*); (level of) volume (*Rad.*); pitch (*Mus.*); upper register (*Mus.*); intensity, brilliancy; *auf der – sein*, be at the height of one's powers, be in tip-top form; be up to date, be well informed; *auf der – von*, in the latitude of; *auf der – von Dover*, off Dover; *aus der –*, from on high, from up aloft; *in die – fahren*, start up, jump up *or* to one's feet; get excited; *die – gewinnen*, reach the summit; *auf gleicher –*, on a level; *in der –*, aloft, above, on high (*B.*); *in die –*, aloft, upward, up; *in die – gehen*, rise, soar; (*coll.*) blow up (*of a p.*); *alle Artikel gehen in die –*, everything is going up (*in price*); *lichte –*, head room; *die – von einem Kap nehmen*, weather a cape; *die – der Sonne nehmen*, take an observation (of the sun's altitude); *die – des Meeres*, offing; *in die – richten*, raise; *das ist* (*doch wirklich*) *die –*, that is the (absolute) limit, that beats everything; *von der –*, from above. **–nanzug,** *m.* high-altitude flying suit (*Av.*). **–natmer,** *m.* high-altitude oxygen apparatus (*Av.*). **–ndarstellung,** *f.* relief (*on maps*). **–nfestigkeit,** *f.* altitude fitness (*of airmen*). **–nflosse,** *f.* tail-plane, stabilizer (*Av.*). **–nklima,** *n.* alpine climate. **–nkrankheit,** *f.* mountain sickness, air sickness. **–nkreis,** *m.* parallel of latitude. **–nlader,** *m.* supercharger, (*sl.*) blower (*Av.*). **–nlage,** *f.* altitude. **–nlinie,** *f.* contour (line). **–n(luft)kurort,** *m.* mountain resort. **–nmesser,** *m.* height finder, altimeter. **–nmeßkunst,** *f.*, **–nmessung,** *f.* art of measuring heights, altimetry, hypsometry. **–nmotor,** *m.* supercharged engine (*Av.*). **–nrauch,** *m.* haze; *see* **Herauch.** **–nrichtfeld,** *n.*, **–nrichtung,** *f.* (angle of) elevation (*Artil.*); *dem Geschütz die –nrichtung geben*, elevate the gun. **–nrücken,** *m.* ridge, crest. **–nruder,** *n.* elevator (*Av.*). **–nschichtlinie,** *f.* contour (line). **–nsonne,** *f.* ultra-violet lamp. **–nsteuer,** *n.*, *see* **–nruder.** **–nstrahlung,** *f.* cosmic radiation. **–nverhältnis,** *n.* interval (*Mus.*). **–nzug,** *m.* ridge of hills, mountain chain. **–punkt,** *m.* culminating point, acme, zenith, climax. **–r,** *comp. adj.*, *see* **hoch**; *–re Berufe*, learned professions; *–re Bildung*, liberal education; *–rer Blödsinn*, utter nonsense; *–re Gewalt*, act of God; *–re Mädchenschule*, high school for girls, secondary school for girls; *–rer Offizier*, superior officer; *–re Schule*, secondary school, grammar school, high school (*Amer.*); *von –rer Warte*, from an exalted, pre-eminent, sovereign position *or* point of view. **–rwertig,** *adj.* polyvalent (*Chem.*).

Hoheit, *f.* (-en) sublimity, nobility, grandeur, majesty; supreme power, sovereignty; high rank; Highness (*title*). **–sgewässer,** *n.pl.* territorial waters. **–srechte,** *n.pl.* sovereign rights. **–svoll,** *adj.* majestic. **–szeichen,** *n.* national colours *or* markings, insignia.

Hohe–lied, *n.* (*B.*) Song of Solomon, Song of Songs. **–priester,** *m.* (*ein –rpriester, des –npriesters, die –npriester, zwei –priester*) high priest. **–priesterlich,** *adj.* pontifical; *–priesterliche Gewänder*, pontifical robes.

höher, *comp. adj. see* **Höhe.**

hohl, *adj.* hollow, concave; dull, vain, shallow, empty; fistulous (*Med.*); *die –e Hand*, the hollow of the hand, palm; *–e Seite*, weak side. **–äugig,** *adj.* hollow-eyed. **–ausgeschliffen,** *adj.* hollow-ground (*knives, lenses*). **–backig,** *adj.* hollow-cheeked. **–drüsen,** *f.* follicle (*Med.*). **–erhaben,** *adj.* concavo-convex. **–fläche,** *f.* concave surface, concavity. **–gang,** *m.* fistula, canal (*Anat.*). **–geschliffen,** *adj.* hollow-ground, concave. **–geschoß,** *n.* shell, hollow projectile. **–geschwür,** *n.* fistula. **–guß,** *m.* hollow casting. **–hand,** *f.* hollow of the hand, palm. **–kehle,** *f.* hollow, furrow, groove, channel. **–köpfig,** *adj.* empty-headed. **–kugel,** *f.* shell (*Artil.*); hollow ball. **–linse,** *f.* concave lens. **–maß,** *n.* dry measure; liquid measure; cubic measure. **–naht,** *f.*, *see* **–saum.** **–raum,** *m.* hollow space, cavity, well; lacuna. **–rund,** *adj.* concave. **–rundung,** *f.*, **–ründe,** *f.* concavity. **–saum,** *m.* hemstitch, drawn-thread work. **–schiene,** *f.* U-shaped rail. **–schliff,** *m.* hollow grinding (*knives, lenses*). **–spiegel,** *m.* concave mirror. **–stab,** *m.* catheter. **–stempel,** *m.* matrix. **–treppe,** *f.* spiral staircase. **–weg,** *m.* gorge, defile, sunken road, narrow pass. **–walze,** *f.* hollow cylinder. **–zahn,** *m.* hemp-nettle (*Galeopsis tetrahit*) (*Bot.*); milk-tooth. **–ziegel,** *m.* gutter-tile. **–zirkel,** *m.* inside callipers.

Höhl–e, *f.* (-en) cave, cavern, grotto, den, burrow, cavity, hollow, hole, ventricle (*Anat.*). **–en,** *v.a.* hollow out, excavate. **–enbewohner,** *m.* cave-dweller, cave-man, troglodyte. **–entiere,** *n.pl.* troglodytic animals, fossil animals found in caves. **–ig,** *adj.* hollow, cavernous, honeycombed, porous. **–ung,** *f.* excavation, cavity; chamber, hollow, concavity, socket.

Hohn, *m.* scorn, disdain, derision, mockery; sneer, insult; *einem zum –e*, in defiance of a p.; *das spricht der Wahrheit –*, that flies in the face of truth; *zum Spott und – werden*, become an object of derision. **–gelächter,** *n.* derision, mockery. **–lächeln,** *v.n.* (*aux.* h.) (*sep.*), **–lachen,** *v.n.* (*aux.* h.) (*insep.*) scoff, mock, jeer, deride, sneer. **–rede,** *f.* scornful language, insulting speech. **–sprechen,** *v.n.* (*sep.*) (*aux.* h.) (*with Dat.*) defy, flout, fly in the face of.

höhn–en, *v.a.* scoff, sneer *or* laugh at; treat with scorn. **–isch,** *adj.* scornful, sneering, insulting, sarcastic.

Hök–er, *m.* (-ers, -er) huckster, costermonger, hawker. **–erei,** *f.* hawking, huckstering; huckster's shop. **–ern,** *v.n.* (*aux.* h.) retail (*small provisions*); hawk, huckster; *schimpfen wie ein –erweib*, swear like a trooper, scold like a fishwife.

Hokuspokus, *m.* hocus-pocus.

hold, *adj.* gracious, friendly; pleasing, charming, lovely; favourable, propitious; *–er Friede*, gentle peace; *mein –es Mädchen*, my sweet girl; *einem – sein*, favour a p., be kind to a p. **–e,** *f.*, **–in,** *f.* darling, sweetheart. **–(an)lächelnd,** *adj.* sweetly smiling. **–selig,** *adj.* most gracious, most lovely, most charming, sweet. **–seligkeit,** *f.* sweetness, charm, loveliness; graciousness.

Holder, *m.* (*dial.*), *see* **Holunder.** **–n,** *adj.* of elder-wood. (*dial.*) **–blüte,** *f.*, **–blust,** *m.*, *n. or f.* elder-blossom.

holen, *v.a.* fetch, go *or* come for; get, catch, haul (*Naut.*); *Atem –*, draw breath; *– lassen*, send for; *sich* (*Dat.*) *bei einem Rat –*, consult a p., ask a p. for advice; *sich* (*Dat.*) *bei einem Trost –*, seek comfort from a p.; *sich* (*Dat.*) *einen Korb –*, get turned down (flat) (*by a girl*); (*coll.*) *sich* (*Dat.*) *eine Nase –*, come in for a rebuke; get snubbed; *sich* (*Dat.*) *eine Erkältung –*, catch a cold; *hol's* (*hol'dich*) *der Teufel!* the devil take it (you)! confound it (you)!

Holk, Hulk, *m.* (*dial.*) (-es, -e) hulk, boat, barge.

holla, *int.* halloo! holla! (*coll.*) *und damit –!* and there's an end of it!

Holländer, *m.* (-s, –) (*dial.*) dairy-farmer; cylindrical paper-mill. **–ei,** *f.* dairy-farm. **–n,** 1. *v.a.* grind (rags) into pulp by means of a 'Holländer'. 2. *v.n.* skate in the Dutch way.

Holle, *f.* (-n) (*dial.*) comb, wattle, crest.

Höll–e, *f.* (-en) hell, the infernal regions; (*dial.*)

space behind the stove, hot place in a furnace; *Himmel und –e aufbieten*, move heaven and earth; *einem die –e heiß machen*, terrify a p.; *in die –e kommen, zur –e fahren*, go to hell. **–enangst,** *f.* mortal fright *or* anxiety. **–enbrand,** *m.* hell-hound, regular devil, utter scoundrel; insatiable thirst. **–enbrut,** *f.* scum, wretches, outcasts. **–enfahrt,** *f.* (Christ's) descent into hell. **–enfürst,** *m.* prince of hell, Satan. **–enhund,** *m.* hell-hound, Cerberus. **–enlärm,** *m.* infernal noise. **–enmächte,** *f.pl.* powers of darkness. **–enmaschine,** *f.* infernal machine. **–enpein,** *f.*, **–enqual,** *f.* torments of hell; excruciating pain, agony. **–enrachen,** *m.*, **–enschlund,** *m.* jaws of hell, bottomless pit. **–enstein,** *m.* lunar caustic, silver nitrate. **–enwut,** *f.* fury, satanic rage. **–enzwang,** *m.* hell-charm, cabalistic incantation, book of black magic. **–isch,** 1. *adj.* hellish, infernal; terrific, abominable. 2. *adv.* (*coll.*) very, dreadfully, awfully; *das –ische Feuer*, the fires of hell; *–ische Qualen*, torments of hell; (*coll.*) *–isch gescheit*, devilish(ly) clever; (*coll.*) *–ische Angst*, mortal fear.

Holler, *m. see* **Holder.**

[1]Holm, *m.* (-(e)s, -e) (*dial.*) islet, holm, eyot *or* ait; hill, hillock.

[2]Holm, *m.* (-(e)s, -e) cross-beam, transom, spar, stout rail; helm, haft, handle; upright (*of a ladder*); (parallel) bar (*Gymn.*).

holper–ig, *adj.* (*also* **holprig**) rough, uneven, bumpy; clumsy, stammering, stumbling. **–n,** *v.n.* (*aux.* h.) jolt, stumble.

holterpolter, holterdiepolter, *adv.* helter-skelter; pell-mell; *das ging –*, it was done with a great rumpus.

Holunder, Hollunder, *m.* (-s, –) elder (*Sambucus canadensis*) (*Bot.*); *spanischer –*, lilac. **–beere,** *f.* elder-berry. **–blüte,** *f.* elder-blossom. **–strauch,** *m.* elder-bush.

Holz, *n.* (-es, ⸚er) wood; timber; piece of wood; firewood; thicket, grove, copse; lumber (*Amer.*); (*Prov.*) *wo man – haut, da fallen Späne*, from chipping come chips. **–abfall,** *m.* waste wood. **–alkohol,** *m.* methyl alcohol, wood spirit. **–anbau,** *m.* afforestation. **–apfel,** *m.* crab-apple. **–arbeiter,** *m.* woodworker. **–arm,** *adj.* destitute of wood. **–art,** *f.* species of wood. **–artig,** *adj.* ligneous; woody. **–bar,** *adj.* that may be felled. **–bau,** *m.* cultivation of timber; timber-work; wooden building. **–beize,** *f.* wood-stain. **–beizen,** *n.* wood-staining. **–bildhauer,** *m.*, **–bildner,** *m.* wood-carver *or* engraver. **–birne,** *f.* wild pear. **–blasinstrument,** *n.* wood-wind instrument (*Mus.*). **–bock,** *m.* sawing trestle; capricorn-beetle, tick. **–boden,** *m.* wooden floor; wood-loft; soil for timber growing. **–bohrer,** *m.* auger, drill, bit; wood-beetle. **–brandmalerei,** *f.* poker-work. **–brei,** *m.* wood-pulp. **–bündel,** *n.* faggot. **–druck,** *m.* block-print (*Typ.*). **–en,** *v.n.* (*aux.* h.) fell, cut *or* gather wood; castigate, (*coll.*) pile into; play rough, foul (*Sport*), charge (*in football*). **–erei,** *f.* (*coll.*) thrashing, beating; rough *or* foul play (*Sport*). **–fäller,** *m.* woodcutter. **–faser,** *f.* wood fibre, grain. **–faserstoff,** *m.* cellulose. **–fäule,** *f.*, **–fäulnis,** *f.* dry-rot. **–feu(e)rung,** *f.* firewood. **–frei,** *adj.*; *–freies Papier*, rag paper, paper free from wood-pulp. **–frevel,** *m.* vandalism (*in cutting timber*); infringement of forest laws. **–fuhre,** *f.* carrying *or* conveying wood; cart-load of wood. **–gas,** *n.* producer gas. **–gefälle,** *n.pl.* yield from felling. **–geist,** *m.*, *see* **–alkohol. –gerechtigkeit,** *f.* rights over a wood; free supply of wood (*from forest, etc.*). **–gleite,** *f.* timber-shoot. **–hacker,** *m.* woodcutter. **–häher,** *m.* jay (*Garrulus glandarius*) (*Orn.*). **–handel,** *m.* timber-trade. **–händler,** *m.* timber-merchant; lumber-merchant (*Amer.*). **–hau,** *m.* site of felling. **–hauer,** *m.* woodcutter; lumberjack (*Amer.*). **–hof,** *m.* wood-yard, timber-yard; lumber-yard (*Amer.*). **–icht, –ig,** *adj.* woody, ligneous, tough as wood. **–imprägnierung,** *f.* preservation of wood. **–instrument,** *n.* wood-wind instrument (*Mus.*). **–klotz,** *m.* wood(en) block. **–kopf,** *m.* wooden-headed person. **–kohle,** *f.* charcoal. **–lager,** *n.* wood-yard, timber-yard. **–meißel,** *m.* wood chisel. **–mosaik,** *f.* wood-inlaying. **–nagel,** *m.*, *see* **–pflock. –nager,** *m.* wood-worm. **–obst,** *n.* wild fruits. (*dial.*) **–pantine,** *f.*, **–pantoffel,** *m.* clog. **–papier,** *n.* wood-pulp paper. **–pflaster,** *n.* wood block *or* parquet flooring. **–pflock,** *m.* peg, dowel. **–platz,** *m.*, *see* **–lager. –recht,** *n.* right to gather wood (*Law*). **–reich,** *adj.* well-wooded. **–säure,** *f.* ligneous acid. **–scheit,** *n.* billet *or* log of (fire)wood. **–schlag,** *m.* felling area, trees marked for felling. **–schlägel,** *m.* mallet. **–schläger,** *m.* woodcutter; woodman; lumberman (*Amer.*). **–schliff,** *m.*, *see* **–brei. –schneider,** *m.* wood-carver *or* wood-block engraver. **–schnepfe,** *f.* woodcock (*Scolopax rusticola*) (*Orn.*). **–schnitt,** *m.* woodcut, wood engraving. **–schnitzer,** *m.* wood-carver. **–schober,** *m.* wood-stack. **–schuh,** *m.* wooden shoe, clog, patten. **–schwelerei,** *f.* charcoal burning. **–späne,** *m.pl.* shavings. **–splitter,** *m.* splinter. **–stamm,** *m.* tree-trunk. **–stich,** *m.*, *see* **–schnitt. –stock,** *m.* wood-block (*Engr.*). **–stoff,** *m.* cellulose, wood pulp. **–stoß,** *m.* wood-pile. **–täf(e)lung,** *f.* wood panelling. **–taube,** *f.* wood-pigeon, ring dove (*Columba palumbus*) (*Orn.*). **–taxe,** *f.* royalty on timber. **–trift,** *f.* forest pasture; raft. **–ung,** *f.* cutting *or* gathering of wood; wood, forest, thicket, copse; felling area. **–verbindung,** *f.* joint. **–verkohlung,** *f.* charcoal burning. **–wand,** *f.* wooden partition *or* wall. **–ware,** *f.* wooden article. **–weg,** *m.* timber track (*for bringing down felled timber*), woodcutter's track; (*fig.*) wrong track *or* tack; (*sehr* or *stark*) *auf dem –wege sein*, be quite on the wrong tack, be utterly at fault. **–werk,** *n.* woodwork, timbers, framework; wainscoting. **–wolle,** *f.* wood wool, fine shavings. **–wurm,** *m.* death-watch beetle. **–zapfen,** *m.* plug, bung. **–zeit,** *f.* felling season. **–zucht,** *f.* forest-culture. **–zunder,** *m.* touchwood, tinder, punk.

hölzern, *adj.* wooden; (*fig.*) stiff, awkward.

homo–gen, *adj.* homogeneous, uniform. **–genität,** *f.* homogeneity. **–log,** *adj.* homologous. **–nym,** 1. *adj.* homonymous. 2. *n.* (-s, -e) homonym.

Homöopath, *m.* (-en, -en) homoeopath. **–isch,** *adj.* homoeopathic.

honett, *adj.* (*archaic*) respectable, honourable.

Honig, *m.* honey; *Scheiben–*, honey in combs; *ausgelassener –, geseimter –*, liquid *or* strained honey; *einem – ums Maul schmieren*, wheedle (into doing s.th. *or* out of a p.), cajole, inveigle; (*Prov.*) *– im Munde, Galle im Herzen, außen – innen Galle*, honeyed words, hard heart. **–bau,** *m.* bee-keeping, apiculture. **–behälter,** *m.*, **–behältnis,** *n.* nectary (*of flowers*); honey pot. **–biene,** *f.* honey bee, worker bee. **–erzeugend,** *adj.* honey-producing. **–gefäß,** *n.* honey-pot; nectary. **–kelch,** *m.* nectary. **–kuchen,** *m.* gingerbread. **–magen,** *m.* honey-sac, pollen basket (*of bees*). **–monat,** *m.*, **–mond,** *m.* honeymoon. **–saft,** *m.* nectar. **–säure,** *f.* oxymel. **–scheibe,** *f.* honeycomb. **–schleuder,** *f.* honey extractor. **–seim,** *m.* virgin honey. **–stein,** *m.* mellite. **–steinsäure,** *f.* mellitic acid. **–süß,** *adj.* sweet as honey, mellifluous. **–tau,** *m.* honeydew. **–trank,** *m.* mead. **–wabe,** *f.* honeycomb. **–wasser,** *n.* hydromel. **–wochen,** *f.pl.*, *see* **–monat. –worte,** *n.pl.* honeyed words. **–zelle,** *f.* honey-cell; alveolus.

Honneurs, *n.pl.*; *die – machen*, salute (*Mil.*); do the honours.

Honor–ar, *n.* (-s, -e) fee, honorarium; *–ar für Vorlesungen*, lecture fee; *–ar für ärztlichen Rat*, fee for professional medical attendance. **–arprofessor,** *m.* honorary professor, professor honoris causa. **–atioren,** *pl.* people of rank, notables, dignitaries. **–ieren,** *v.a.* honour (*a bill*); pay a fee. **–ig,** *adj.* (*Studs. sl.*) generous, honourable.

Hopfen, 1. *m.* (-s, –) hop (*Bot.*); hops; (*Prov.*) *an ihm ist – und Malz verloren*, nothing can be done with him, all trouble is thrown away on him. 2. *v.a.* mix with *or* impregnate with hops. **–bau,** *m.* hop culture. **–bauer,** *m.* hop-grower. **–ernte,** *f.* hop-picking. **–stange,** *f.* hop-pole; (*fig.*) lanky p.

hopp, *int.* up! jump! jump to it! quick! away! hop it! beat it! **-la!** mind! steady! clumsy! (*on stumbling*).

Hoppelpoppel, *n.* (-s, –) egg-flip, scrambled egg dish.

Hop-s, 1. *m.* (-ses, -se) hop, skip, jump. 2. *int.*, *see* **hopp.** 3. *adv.* gone, away. **-sen,** *v.n.* (*aux.* h.) hop, jump, limp. **-ser,** *m.* hop, jump; hop, skip, and jump; quick waltz, schottische, galop, polka.

horch-en, *v.n.* (*aux.* h.) (*Dat. or auf & Acc.*) listen, give ear to, hearken; be an eavesdropper, spy. **-er,** *m.* listener; eavesdropper; (*Prov.*) *-er an der Wand hört seine eigne Schand'*, eavesdroppers hear no good of themselves. **-gerät,** *n.* sound locator (*Mil.*), hydrophone (*Nav.*). **-posten,** *m.* listening post (*Mil.*). **-sam,** *adj.* attentive, heedful.

Hord-e, *f.* (-en) horde, troop, tribe, gang; trestle, hurdle, lattice. **-enweise,** *adv.* in hordes.

hör-en, *v.a. & n.* (*aux.* h.) hear; listen; listen to; listen-in to (*radio*), attend (*lectures*), obey; *-en auf einen* or *eine S.*, heed *or* obey a p. *or* th.; *alles -t auf mein Kommando!* (*Mil.*) wait for the word of command! *der Hund -t auf den Namen . . .*, the dog answers to the name of . . .; (*Prov.*) *wer nicht -en will, muß fühlen*, pay attention or take the consequences; *er -t sich gern*, he likes to hear himself talk, he likes to hear the sound of his own voice; *ein Kolleg -en*, attend a course of lectures; *einen kommen -en*, hear a p. coming; *das läßt sich -en*, that sounds all right, there is s.th. in that, that is worth considering; *sich -en lassen*, let o.s. be heard speak, sing, *etc.*, before company; *von sich -en lassen*, give news of o.s., write; *laß dann und wann von dir -en*, let us hear from you now and then; (*coll.*) *-en Sie mal*, I say! *auf diesem Ohre -e ich nicht*, I am deaf in this ear; *ich habe sagen -en*, I have heard it said, I have been told; *schwer -en*, be hard of hearing; *soviel* (*wie*) *ich -e*, from all I hear; *er will nicht -en*, he will not listen; *man kann sein eignes Wort nicht -en*, one cannot hear o.s. speak. **-bar,** *adj.* audible; *nicht -bar*, inaudible. **-barkeit,** *f.* audibility. **-bericht,** *m.* running commentary (*Rad.*). **-bild,** *n.* sound picture (*Rad.*). **-ensagen,** *n.* hearsay, rumour. **-er,** *m.* hearer; university student; receiver, headphones (*Phone, Rad.*); (*pl.*) radio audience, listeners. **-erschaft,** *f.* hearers, students, audience. **-fehler,** *m.* mistake in hearing, misapprehension. **-folge,** *f.* feature programme (*Rad.*). **-frequenz,** *f.* audiofrequency (*Rad.*). **-ig,** *adj.* belonging to, a slave to. **-ige(n),** *pl.* bondsmen. **-igkeit,** *f.* bondage, serfdom. **-muschel,** *f.* earpiece (*Phone*). **-nerv,** *m.* auditory nerve. **-rohr,** *n.*, **-trichter,** *m.* ear-trumpet; stethoscope. **-saal,** *m.* auditorium, lecture-room. **-samkeit,** *f.* acoustics. **-spiel,** *n.* radio drama. **-weite,** *f.* ear-shot, within hearing.

Horizont, *m.* (-(e)s, -e) horizon; *das geht über meinen -*, that is beyond me. **-al,** *adj.* horizontal. **-albomben,** *v.n.* make a low-level bombing attack (*Av.*). **-ale,** *f.* horizontal line, level. **-ierung,** *f.* levelling mechanism (*Artil.*).

Hormon, *n.* (-s, -e) hormone.

Horn, *n.* (-(e)s, ⸚er) horn; bugle; feeler (*of insects*); hard *or* horny skin; (*dial.*) hoof (*of horses*); (*dial.*) cape, headland; *sich* (*Dat.*) *die Hörner ablaufen* or *abstoßen*, learn by experience; *einem die Hörner bieten* or *zeigen*, oppose *or* offer resistance to a p., show one's claws; *mit einem in ein* or *dasselbe* or *das gleiche - blasen*, agree with a p., conspire with a p.; *den Stier an* or *bei den Hörnern packen* or *fassen*, take the bull by the horns; *Hörner tragen*, be a cuckold; *einem* (*die*) *Hörner aufsetzen*, cuckold s.o., make a cuckold of s.o.; *- des Überflusses*, cornucopia. **-artig,** *adj.* horny, like horn. **-auswuchs,** *m.* horny excrescence. **-baß,** *m.* horn-stop (*in organs*). **-baum,** *m.* hornbeam (*Carpinus betulus*) (*Bot.*). **-bläser,** *m.* horn-blower, bugler, trumpeter. **-blende,** *f.* hornblende, amphibole. **-brille,** *f.* horn-rimmed spectacles. **-flügel,** *m.* elytra (*of insects*). **-förmig,** *adj.* horn-shaped, corniform. **-füßig,** *adj.* hoofed. **-hart,** *adj.* as hard as horn. **-haut,** *f.* horny skin; cornea (*Anat.*). **-häutig,** *adj.* callous. **-häutigkeit,** *f.* callosity. **-ig,** *adj.* horny; horn-like; callous. **-ist,** *m.* horn player. **-klee,** *m.* bird's-foot trefoil (*Lotus corniculatus*) (*Bot.*). **-kraut,** *n.* mouse-ear, chickweed (*Cerastium vulgatum*) (*Bot.*). **-leiste,** *f.* ventral ridge (*of a feather*). (*coll.*) **-ochs,** *m.* blockhead. **-signal,** *n.* bugle-call. **-spaltig,** *adj.* cloven-hoofed. **-ung,** *m.* (-s, -e) February. **-vieh,** *n.* horned cattle; (*vulg.*) silly ass, blockhead.

Hörn-chen, *n.* (-s, -) cornicle, little horn; crescent; croissant. **-en,** 1. *v.a.* furnish with horns; *gehörntes Wild*, horned *or* antlered game; *der gehörnte Siegfried*, horny Siegfried (*with horny skin*). 2. *v.r.* cast *or* shed the antlers. **-ern,** *adj.* horny, of horn. **-erschall,** *m.* bugle sound, sound of horns. **-ertragend,** *adj.* horned. **-erträger,** *m.* cuckold.

Hornis, *m. & f.* (-sse), **-se,** *f.* (-ssen) hornet.

Horoskop, *n.* (-s, -e) horoscope; *einem das - stellen*, cast s.o.'s horoscope.

Horst, *m.* (-es, -e) eyrie *or* aerie; air-station, (air) base (*Av.*); tuft; shrubbery, thicket. **-en,** *v.n.* (*aux.* h.) build an eyrie, nest (*of birds of prey*).

Hort, *m.* (-(e)s, -e) day-nursery, play centre; (*Poet.*) safe retreat, refuge; shield, protection; protector; (*Poet.*) hoard, treasure. **-en,** *v.a.* hoard (*money*). **-nerin,** *f.* nursery school teacher. **-ung,** *f.* hoarding (*of money*), reluctance to spend.

Hortensie, *f.* (-n) hydrangea (*Hortensis*) (*Bot.*).

Hos-e, *f.* (-en) (*usually in pl.*) trousers, shorts, knickers; thigh (*of horses and poultry*); water spout; (*dial.*) tub, pail; firkin; *Knie-en*, breeches, knickerbockers; drawers (*for ladies*); plus-fours; *lederne -en*, leather breeches; (*coll.*) *sie hat die -en an*, she wears the breeches *or* is master of the house; *die -n durchsitzen*, sit through the seat of one's trousers; (*coll.*) *das Herz fiel ihm in die -en*, his heart fell into his boots; (*sl.*) *sich auf die -en setzen*, work hard at one's studies; (*vulg.*) *die -en voll haben*, be frightened out of one's wits, be in a blue funk; (*coll.*) *einem die -en stramm* or *straff ziehen*, give a boy a sound beating. **-enbandorden,** *m.* Order of the Garter. **-enboden,** *m.* seat of trousers. **-enboje,** *f.* breeches buoy (*Naut.*). **-engurt,** *m.*, **-engürtel,** *m.* waistband. **-enklappe,** *f.*, **-enlatz,** *m.* fly. **-enlos,** *adj.* unbreeched. **-enlose(r),** *m.* sansculotte. (*coll.*) **-enmatz,** *m.* little boy in first trousers. **-ennaht,** *f.* seam of the trouser-leg. **-enrock,** *m.* divided skirt. **-enrolle,** *f.* man's part (*for actress*) (*Theat.*). **-enschlitz,** *m.* fly. **-enstrecker,** *m.* trouser-press. **-entasche,** *f.* trouser pocket. **-enträger,** *m.pl.* braces; suspenders (*Amer.*). **-enzeug,** *n.* trousering (material).

Hosp-ital, *n.* (-itals, -itäler *or Austr. dial.* -itale) hospital, home for aged *or* infirm. **-italit,** *m.* inmate (*of a hospital or home*). **-italität,** *f.* hospitality. **-itant,** *m.* (-en, -en) guest listener (*at lectures, etc.*). **-itieren,** *v.n.* (*aux.* h.) sit in at (*lectures, lessons, etc.*); supervise (*a p.'s work*). **-iz,** *n.* (-es, -e) hostel; *christliches -iz*, temperance hostel *or* hotel.

Hostie, *f.* (-n) consecrated wafer, the Host. **-ngefäß,** *n.* pyx. **-nhäuslein,** *n.* tabernacle. **-nteller,** *m.* paten.

Hotel, *n.* (-s, -s) hotel. **-ier,** *m.* (-s, -s) hotelkeeper.

hott, 1. *int.* gee up! to the right! (*to horses*). 2. **-ehü,** *n.* (-s, -s) horsie, gee-gee (*children's word for horse*). **-o,** *n.* (-s, -s), *see* **-ehü.**

Hotte, *f.* (-n) (*dial.*) vintager's butt; fruit-measure.

Hotzel, *f.*, **-n,** *v.n.*, *see* **Hutzel.**

hu, *int.* (*expressing horror*) ugh! hugh!

hü, *int.* whoa! (*to horses*).

Hub, *m.* (-(e)s, ⸚e) lifting, raising, heaving; lift; impetus; stroke (*of a piston, etc.*); *aufgehender -*, upstroke (*Engin.*). **-brücke,** *f.* drawbridge. **-höhe,** *f.* difference between high and low tides. **-länge,** *f.* (length of) stroke. **-raum,** *m.* cylinder capacity, piston displacement (*Engin.*). **-schrauber,** *m.* helicopter (*Av.*). **-werk,** *n.* hoisting gear. **-zähler,** *m.* indicator (*of an engine*).

Hube, *f.* (-n) (*dial.*) hide (*of land*). *See* **Hufe.**

Hübel, *m.* (-s, -) (*dial.*) hillock.

hüben, *adv.* (*dial.*) on this side; *- und drüben*, far and near, on all sides.

hübsch, *adj.* pretty, charming, fine, handsome, nice; (*coll.*) good, proper; fair, considerable; *-e runde Summe*, good round sum; *-es Vermögen*, considerable fortune; *sei - artig!* there's a good boy (or girl)! *das will ich - bleiben lassen*, I will leave it nicely as it is, I'll take good care not to interfere; *es ist nicht -*, it is not fair, not nice.

Hucke, *f.* (-n) load (*carried on back*); *einem die – vollügen*, tell a p. a pack of lies (*or* rain blows on a p.). **-n,** *v.n.a.* hump, carry on one's back; (*dial.*) *see* **hocken. -pack,** *adv.* pick-a-back.

Hudel, *m.* (-s, -(n)) rag, tatter; trash; (*dial.*) ragamuffin, scoundrel. **-ei,** *f.* botched work; bungling. **-ig,** *adj.* ragged; paltry; botched, bungled. **-n,** 1. *v.a.* do negligently, botch, bungle, scamp; vex, tease, torment. 2. *v.n.* (*aux.* h.) be untidy *or* slap-dash. **Hud(e)ler,** *m.* bungler.

Huf, *m.* (-es, -e) hoof. **-beschlag,** *m.* horse-shoeing; horseshoes. **-eisen,** *n.* horseshoe. **-eisenförmig,** *adj.* horseshoe (-shaped). **-haar,** *n.* fetlock. **-hammer,** *m.* shoeing hammer. **-kratze,** *f.* hoof-pick. **-lattich,** *m.* coltsfoot (*Tussilago farfara*) (*Bot.*). **-nagel,** *m.* shoeing-nail, hobnail. **-schlag,** *m.* horse's kick; beating of hoofs. **-schmied,** *m.* farrier. **-tier,** *n.* hoofed animal (*Ungulata*).

Hufe, *f.* (-n) hide (*of land*). **-ngeld,** *n.* land-tax. **-nmeister,** *m.* collector of land-rents.

Hufner, *m.*, **Hüfner,** *m.* (-s, –) smallholder.

Hüft-e, *f.* (-en) hip, haunch. **-ader,** *f.* sciatic vein. **-bein,** *n.*, **-blatt,** *n.* hip bone. **-bruch,** *m.* fracture of the hip. **-gelenk,** *n.* hip joint. **-pfanne,** *f.* socket of the hip-joint. **-schmal,** *adj.* narrow-hipped. **-schmerz,** *m. see* **-weh. -stück,** *n.* haunch (*of meat*). **-verrenkung,** *f.* dislocation of the hip. **-weh,** *n.* sciatic pains, sciatica.

Hügel, *m.* (-s, –) hill, hillock, knoll. **-ab,** *adv.* downhill. **-an,** *adv.*, **-auf,** *adv.* uphill. **-ig** (**hüglig**) *adj.* hilly. **-kette,** *f.* chain of hills. **-land,** *n.* hilly *or* rolling country (*200–500 metres*).

Huhn, *n.* (-(e)s, ¨er) fowl, hen; (game) bird; (*coll.*) chap, fellow; (*pl.*) poultry; *junges –*, chicken, pullet; (*coll.*) *ich habe ein Hühnchen mit dir zu pflücken* or *zu rupfen*, I have a bone to pick with you; (*sl.*) *er ist ein blindes –*, he is as blind as a bat; *er ist ein verrücktes –*, he is a crazy loon; (*sl.*) *unsolides –*, loose fish; a man too fond of drink; *zwei Völker Hühner*, two covies of partridges.

Hühner, *see* **Huhn** (*in compounds generally*) chicken, hen; (*sl.*) *vor die – gehen*, go to the dogs. **-artig,** *adj.* gallinaceous. **-auge,** *n.* corn (*on the foot*); *einem auf die -augen treten*, tread on a p.'s corns, offend *or* upset a p. **-blindheit,** *f.* night-blindness. **-braten,** *m.* roast chicken. **-brühe,** *f.* chicken broth. **-brust,** *f.* pigeon chest. **-ei,** *n.* hen's egg. **-farm,** *f.* poultry farm. **-händler,** *m.* poulterer. **-haus,** *n.* hen-house, fowl-house. **-hof,** *m.* poultry-yard. **-hund,** *m.* pointer; setter. **-jagd,** *f.* partridge shooting. **-korb,** *m.* hencoop. **-leiter,** *f.*, **-stiege,** *f.* hen-roost; (*coll.*) very steep and narrow staircase, breakneck stairs. **-markt,** *m.* poultry-market. **-seuche,** *f.* pip. **-stall,** *m.* hen-house, chicken-run. **-stange,** *f.* hen-roost, perch. **-vieh,** *n.* poultry. **-zucht,** *f.* poultry rearing, chicken farming.

hui, 1. *int.* (*expressing pleasure, surprise, disgust*) ho!, ha!, oh!, pooh! 2. *m. in einem* or *im –*, in a twinkling, in a trice, in a flash.

Huld, *f.* (-en) (*archaic*) grace, favour, charm, kindness; graciousness. **-göttin,** *f.*, **-in,** *f.*; *die drei -göttinen*, the three Graces. **-igen,** *v.n.* (*aux.* h.) (*Dat.*) do homage, swear allegiance; pay homage *or* one's respects to; hold, embrace, subscribe to (*an opinion, etc.*), indulge in (*alcohol, etc.*); *dem Fortschritte -igen*, believe in progress; *einer Dame -igen*, pay one's attentions to *or* court a lady. **-igung,** *f.* homage, oath of allegiance; admiration, respect, marked attention; favour; *-igung leisten*, do homage. **-igungseid,** *m.* oath of allegiance *or* fealty. **-igungspflichtig,** *adj.* bound in homage. **-reich,** *adj.*, **-voll,** *adj.* gracious, benevolent; favourable.

hülfe, 1. *see* **helfen.** 2. *f. see* **Hilfe.**

Hülle, *f.* (-n) cover, covering, envelope, wrapper, wrapping, integument; pod, husk, sheath (*Bot.*); raiment, jacket, tunic; cortex; veil, cloak, mask; *irdische –*, mortal frame, body; *sterbliche –*, mortal remains; *– der Nacht*, cover of night; *die – und die Fülle*, food and shelter, all that is needed; *in – und Fülle*, in plenty, in abundance; *die – fiel mir von den Augen*, the scales fell from my eyes. **-n,** 1. *v.a.* wrap (up), cover, envelop; hide; *in Dunkel -n*, veil in obscurity; *in Flammen gehüllt*, enveloped in flames; *die Sonne war in dichte Nebel gehüllt*, the sun was veiled *or* hidden in mist. 2. *v.r.* wrap o.s. up, muffle o.s.; *sich in Schweigen -n*, be wrapped in silence.

Hüls-e, *f.* (-en) pod, shell, husk; case, casing, housing, capsule, socket; shell *or* cartridge case. **-en,** *v.a.* hull, shell, husk. **-enartig,** *adj.* leguminous. **-enfrucht,** *f.* legume, legumen. **-ig,** *adj.*, *see* **-enartig.**

human, *adj.* humane; affable. **-ismus,** *m.* humanism. **-istisch,** *adj.*; *-istische Bildung*, classical education. **-itär,** *adj.* humanitarian. **-itarier,** *m.* humanitarian. **-ität,** *f.* humanitarianism, liberal culture, high-mindedness. **-itätsduselei,** *f.* sentimental humanitarianism.

Humbug, *m.* humbug, balderdash, swindle.

Humm-el, *f.* (-n) bumble-bee; (*fig.*) tomboy, romp, hoyden; *-eln im Hintern haben*, (*coll.*) have ants in one's pants, be restless *or* fidgety.

Hummer, *m.* (-s, – *or Austr. dial.* -n) lobster. **-salat,** *m.* lobster salad. **-schere,** *f.* claw of a lobster.

Humor, *m.* sense of humour; humorous vein, comicality; *feiner –*, *versteckter –*, sly humour; *derber –*, broad humour; *heiterer –*, gay humour; *ausgelassener –*, boisterous humour. **-eske,** *f.* humorous sketch, witty story. **-ist,** *m.* (-en, -en) humorist, comedian; funny *or* facetious p. **-istisch,** *adj.* humorous, facetious.

hump-eln, *v.n.* (*aux.* h. & s.) hobble, limp. **-elei,** *f.* hobbling along, limping. **-elrock,** *m.* hobble-skirt.

Humpen, *m.* (-s, –) bumper, tankard, bowl.

Humus, *m.* vegetable mould, humus. **-boden,** *m.* humus soil, arable land. **-decke,** *f.* leaf-mould.

Hund, *m.* (-(e)s, -e) dog, hound, (*fig.*) cur, beast, scoundrel; miner's truck; (*coll.*) *auf dem -e sein*, be wretched *or* miserable; be down and out; (*coll.*) *auf den – kommen*, go to the dogs; *wie ein begossener –*, (or *Pudel*), with his tail between his legs, crestfallen; (*Prov.*) *-e die viel bellen, beißen nicht*, his bark is worse than his bite; (*Prov.*) *blöder – wird selten fett*, faint heart ne'er won fair lady; *wie – und Katze leben*, live a cat-and-dog life; *kein – nimmt ein Stück Brot von ihm*, no one will have anything to do with him, he is beneath contempt; (*coll.*) *da liegt der Knüppel beim -e*, that goes without saying; (*coll.*) *da liegt der – begraben*, there's the rub! that's the snag *or* the root of the matter; (*coll.*) *damit lockt man keinen – hinter dem Ofen vor*, that has no appeal; *mit allen -en gehetzt sein*, be wily, be up to all the tricks *or* dodges; *wer mit -en zu Bette geht, steht mit Flöhen auf*, as you make your bed, so you must lie in it; (*Prov.*) *kommt man über den –, so kommt man auch über den Schwanz*, with most of it done the rest will be easy; *unter allem – sein*, be as bad as it can be, be worse than awful. **-earbeit,** *f.* drudgery, slaving. **-eartig,** *adj.* canine. **-ebellen,** *n.* barking of dogs. **-eelend,** *adj.* very miserable *or* wretched; *-eelend aussehen* (*sich fühlen*), look (feel) like nothing on earth. **-efutter,** *n.* dog's food, dog biscuits; (*fig.*) miserable fare. **-egattung,** *f.* breed of dog. **-ehütte,** *f.* dog-kennel. **-ekälte,** *f.* bitter cold. (*coll.*) **-ekerl,** *m.* scamp, scoundrel. **-ekoppel,** *f.* leash, lead, leash *or* pack (of hounds). **-ekot,** *m.* dog manure. **-ekuchen,** *m.* dog biscuit. **-eleben,** *n.* dog's life, wretched existence. **-eliebhaber,** *m.* dog-fancier. **-emüde,** *adj.* dead *or* dog tired. **-erennen,** *n.* greyhound race. **-escheu,** *adj.* afraid of dogs. **-estaupe,** *f.* (canine) distemper. **-esteuer,** *f.* dog licence. **-etrab,** *m.* jog-trot. **-ewache,** *f.* dog watch (*Naut.*). **-ewärter,** *m.* kennel-man. (*coll.*) **-ewetter,** *n.* wretched *or* beastly weather, weather not fit to turn a dog out. **-ezucht,** *f.* breeding, training of dogs. **-saffe,** *f.* baboon. **-sblume,** *f.* dandelion. **-sdolde,** *f.* fool's parsley (*Aethusa cynapium*) (*Bot.*). (*vulg.*) **-sfott,** *m.* low scoundrel, mean cur. **-sföttisch,** *adj.*, **-sgemein,** *adj.* very mean, low *or* vulgar; (*sl.*) lousy. **-sgleiße,** *f. see* **-sdolde. -shai,** *m.* dogfish. **-smiserabel,** *adj.* most wretched. **-smüde,** *adj. see* **-emüde. -srose,** *f.* dog rose, wild brier (*Rosa canina*) (*Bot.*). **-sstern,** *m.* Sirius. **-stage,** *pl.* dog-days. **-swut,** *f.* rabies, hydrophobia.

hundert, 1. *num. adj.* hundred. 2. *n.* (-s, -e) hundred; *zu –en,* in *or* by hundreds; *–e von Pferden,* hundreds of horses; *zehn vom –,* ten per cent.; *es geht in die –e,* it runs into hundreds; *– und aber –,* hundreds and hundreds; *zwei (einige) – Zigaretten,* two (several) hundred cigarettes; *– gegen eins wetten,* bet *or* lay a hundred to one. **–er,** *m.* hundred, three-figure number; hundred (mark, franc, dollar, *etc.*) note. **–erlei,** *indec. adj.* of a hundred kinds; (*coll.*) of all kinds. **–fach,** *adj.,* **–fältig,** *adj.* hundred-fold. **–fuß,** *m.,* **–füßler,** *m.* centipede. **–jahrfeier,** *f.* centenary. **–jährig,** *adj.* centenary, centenarian; *der –jährige Krieg,* the hundred years' war; *die –jährige Feier von Schillers Geburt,* the centenary celebration of Schiller's birth, the hundredth anniversary of Schiller's birthday. **–jährlich,** *adj.* centennial. **–mal,** *adv.* a hundred times, (*fig.*) very often. **–malig,** *adj.* done a hundred (*or fig.*) very many times. **–pfünder,** *m.* hundred-pounder (*Artil.*). **–prozentig,** *adj.* & *adv.* hundred per cent.; complete(ly), entire(ly), utterly. **–schaft,** *f.* an organized body of a hundred men. **–st,** *adj.* hundredth; *vom –sten ins Tausendste kommen,* muddle up things, give a garbled account, not keep to the point; *das weiß der –ste nicht,* not one in a hundred knows that. **–stel,** *n.* hundredth part. **–stens,** *adv.* in the hundredth place. **–tausend,** *num. adj.* a *or* one hundred thousand; *–tausende von Exemplaren,* hundreds of thousands of copies.

Hünd–in, *f.* bitch. **–isch,** *adj.* fawning, cringing.

Hüne, *m.* (-n, -n) giant. **–nbett,** *n.,* **–ngrab,** *n.* prehistoric grave, barrow, cairn, mound. **–ngestalt,** *f.* colossal figure. **–nhaft,** *adj.* gigantic.

Hung–er, *m.* hunger; appetite; starvation, famine; *vor –er,* or *–ers sterben,* die of hunger, starve to death; *–er haben,* be hungry; (*Prov.*) *–er ist der beste Koch,* hunger is the best sauce. **–erblockade,** *f.* hunger-blockade. **–erjahr,** *n.* year of famine. **–erkandidat,** *m.* unemployed graduate (*teacher, etc.*). **–erkur,** *f.* fasting cure, lowering diet. **–erleider,** *m.* starveling; needy wretch; poor devil. **–erlohn,** *m.* starvation wages. **–ern,** 1. *v.n.* (*aux.* h.) hunger, be hungry; fast, starve; *ich –ere,* I am starving myself; I go hungry; *–ern nach einer S.,* long for a th. 2. *v.a. imp.*; *mich –ert, es –ert mich,* I am hungry. **–erpfote,** *f.*; (*coll.*) *an den –erpfoten saugen,* be extremely hard up, have nothing to eat. **–ersnot,** *f.* famine. **–erstreik,** *m.* hunger strike. **–ertod,** *m.* death from starvation. **–ertuch,** *n.* black cloth covering the altar in Lent; (*coll.*) *am –ertuche nagen,* live in extreme poverty *or* misery. **–erturm,** *m.* (*archaic*) dungeon. **–rig,** *adj.* hungry, starving; poor (*of soil*); *nach* or *auf etwas –rig sein,* have a craving for s.th. **–rigkeit,** *f.* hunger, appetite; starvation.

hunten, *adv.* (*dial.*) below, down here.

Hupe, *f.* (-n) motor-horn, siren, hooter. **–n,** *v.n.* hoot, toot, sound the horn. **–nsignal,** *n.* signal with the horn, hooting.

Hupf, *m.* (-es, -e) hop, jump. **–en,** (*archaic* & *dial.*) *see* **hüpfen.** **–er,** *see* **Hüpfer;** (*coll.*) *das ist gehupft wie gesprungen,* there is not the least *or* slightest difference, that is all the same.

hüpf–en, *v.n.* (*aux.* h. & s.) hop; frisk about; jump, leap, skip; *das Herz –te ihr vor Freude,* her heart leapt with joy. **–er,** *m.* (*dial.*) grasshopper. **–spiel,** *n.* hopscotch. **–steinspiel,** *n.* ducks and drakes.

Hürde, *f.* (-n) hurdle; fence (*Racing*); fold, pen. **–ngeflecht,** *n.* trellis-work. **–nlager,** *n.* sheep-fold, pen. **–nrennen,** *n.* hurdle-race.

Hure, *f.* (-n) prostitute, whore, harlot. **–n,** *v.n.* (*aux.* h.) whore, fornicate. **–nbalg,** *m.* & *n.,* **–nkind,** *n.* bastard. **–nhaus,** *n.* brothel. **–nwirt,** *m.* brothel keeper. **–r,** *m.* whoremonger, fornicator. **–rei,** *f.* (*archaic*) prostitution, fornication, harlotry.

hürnen, *adj.* (*obs.*) horny, impenetrable, invulnerable.

hurr, 1. *int.* swish! 2. *m.* whirr, scurry. **–en,** *v.n.* (*dial.*) hurry, scurry.

hurra, *int.* hurra(h)! **–schreien,** *v.n.* cheer. **–geschrei,** *n., see* **–ruf.** **–patriotismus,** *m.* jingoism, chauvinism. **–ruf,** *m.* cheer.

hurtig, *adj.* quick, swift, speedy, agile, nimble; presto (*Mus.*); (*coll.*) *mach' –!* be quick! **–keit,** *f.* swiftness, agility, promptness; dash.

Husar, *m.* (-en, -en) hussar. **–enjacke,** *f.* dolman. **–en(pelz)mütze,** *f.* busby.

husch, 1. *int.* quick! *etwas – – machen,* do s.th. hurriedly, carelessly, sketchily; skimp a th.; *– war er weg,* he was gone in a flash. 2. *m.* (-es, -e) brief moment, short spell, hurry; *see also* **–e;** *im –,* all of a sudden; *im – zu einem kommen,* pay a fleeting visit to s.o., drop in on s.o. for a moment. **–e,** *f.* (*dial.*) sudden shower. **–(el)ig,** *adj.* hasty, fleeting, superficial. **–en,** *v.n.* (*aux.* s.), **–eln,** *v.n.* (*aux.* s.) slip hurriedly (past, in, out, *etc.*), flit; *sich in einen Mantel –eln,* huddle *or* swathe o.s. in a coat.

Hüsing, *n.* (-(e)s, -e) *or f.* (-e) housing (*Naut.*).

hussa(h), *int.* huzza! *– rufen,* urge on.

hüst, *int.* (*dial.*) left! (*drover's call to horses*).

hüsteln, *v.n.* (*aux.* h.) cough slightly, clear one's throat.

husten, 1. *v.n.* (*aux.* h.) cough, have a cough. 2. *v.a.* cough (up); (*coll.*) *ich werde dir etwas –,* you can whistle for it; (*coll.*) *auf etwas –,* turn up one's nose at a th. 3. *m.* cough. **–anfall,** *m.* fit of coughing. **–bonbon,** *m.* (*or Austr. n.*) cough sweet, lozenge. **–fieber,** *n.* catarrhal fever. **–krampf,** *m.* convulsive cough. **–mittel,** *n.* cough cure **–stillend,** *adj.* pectoral.

[1]**Hut,** *m.* (-(e)s, ⸚e) hat; cap, cover, lid; top of a mushroom; coping; *den – vor einem abnehmen,* take off one's hat to a p., (*also fig.* = to respect a p.); *verschiedene S. unter einen – bringen,* reconcile conflicting opinions, bring different things under one heading, reduce different things to a common formula; *den – im Genick haben,* have *or* wear one's hat on the back of one's head; *etwas* or *einen unterm –e haben,* have s.th. *or* a p. in one's power; *– mit hohem Kopfe,* high-crowned hat; (*coll.*) *du kriegst was auf den –,* you'll get your knuckles rapped; *schlaffer –,* slouch hat; *den – (vor Freude) schwingen,* toss one's cap in the air (for joy); *den – aufs Ohr setzen,* cock one's hat on one side *or* over one ear; *unter einem –e stecken,* be in the same boat; *den – in die Augen* or *ins Gesicht ziehen,* pull one's hat (down) over one's eyes. **–boden,** *m.* crown of a hat. **–form,** *f.* hat-block. **–futteral,** *n.* hat box. **–krempe,** *f.* brim. **–los,** *adj.* without a hat, bare-headed. **–macher,** *m.* hatter. **–schachtel,** *f.* hat-box. **–schleife,** *f.* cockade. **–schnur,** *f.* hat-band *or* -string; (*coll.*) *das geht doch über die –schnur,* that is past a joke, that's going too far. **–zucker,** *m.* loaf sugar.

[2]**Hut,** *f.* (-en) keeping, guard, protection, shelter; charge, care; tending (*of cattle*); (*dial.*) pasture, pasturage; right of pasture; flock, herd; *unter meiner –,* in my care; *in Gottes – sein,* be in God's keeping *or* under God's protection; *auf der –* or *auf seiner – sein,* be careful *or* on one's guard. **–ung,** *f.* pasture; pasturage. **–ungsrecht,** *n.* right of common.

Hütchen, *n.* (-s, –) capsule; extinguisher; *Zünd–,* percussion-cap.

hüt–en, 1. *v.a.* watch, guard, take care of, tend, keep; *das Vieh –en,* tend the cattle; *einen vor einer S. –en,* defend *or* preserve a p. from s.th.; *das Bett (Zimmer, Haus) –en,* be confined to one's bed (one's room, the house); *er –ete ihn wie seinen Augapfel,* he cherished him as the apple of his eye; *–e deine Zunge!* guard your tongue! 2. *v.r.* be on one's guard, take care, beware (of), shun; *–en Sie sich vor ihm!* (or *vor Taschendieben!*) be on your guard against him! (*or* against pickpockets!); *ich –e mich vor seiner Gesellschaft,* I shun his society, I keep away from him; *ich werde mich –en, das zu tun,* I shall take good care not to do that! **–er,** *m.* keeper, guardian, custodian, warden; herdsman. **–ung,** *f.* guarding (*vor,* against), preserving, protecting.

Hutsche, *dial. f.* (-n), *see* **Hitsche;** *also Austr. dial.* swing. **–n,** *v.n.* (*aux.* h.) slip, slide; swing.

Hutte, *f.* (-n) (*Swiss dial.*) basket.

Hütte, *f.* (-n) cottage, hut, chalet, cabin, shelter, shed; (*B.*) tent, tabernacle; forge, foundry, works, mill, kiln, furnace; poop (*Naut.*). **–nafter,** *m.* slag, waste matter. **–namt,** *n.* superintendent's office (*at a foundry*). **-narbeiter,** *m.* foundry-worker. **-nbau,** *m.* smelting works, foundry. **-nkoks,** *m.* metallurgical coke. **-nbewohner,** *m.* cottager. **-nkunde,** *f.* metallurgy. **-nleute,** *pl.* smelters, foundrymen. **-nmehl,** *n.* white arsenic. **-nrauch,** *m.* furnace smoke, (arsenical) fumes, white arsenic. **-nrevier,** *n.* mining district. **-nspeise,** *f.* ore for smelting. **-nwerk,** *n.* foundry, smelting works. **-nwesen,** *n.* metallurgy, smelting. **-nwirt,** *m.* hut-warden (*on mountains*).

Hutzel, *f.* (-n) (*dial.*) dried fruit (*esp.* pears); wild pear; shrivelled old hag. **-ig,** *adj.* shrivelled, wrinkled. **-männchen,** *n.* goblin. **-n,** 1. *v.a.* dry (*fruit*). 2. *v.n.* (*aux.* s.) shrivel, shrink, become wrinkled.

Hyäne, *f.* (-n) hyena; – *des Schlachtfeldes*, plunderer, despoiler (*of corpses and wounded*).

Hyazinth, *m.* (-(e)s, -e) hyacinth, jacinth (*precious stone*). **-e,** *f.* (-n) hyacinth (*flower*).

Hybrid-e, *f.* (-n) & *m.* (-n, -n) hybrid, mongrel, cross. **-(isch),** *adj.* hybrid, mongrel.

Hydrant, *m.* (-en, -en) hydrant, fire-point, stand-pipe.

Hydrat, *n.* (-(e)s, -e) hydrate, hydroxide. **-ation,** *f.* hydration. **-isieren,** *v.a.* hydrate, form hydrates from. **-wasser,** *n.* water of hydration.

Hydraul-ik, *f.* hydraulics. **-isch,** *adj.* hydraulic.

Hydrier-anlage, *f.* hydrogenation plant. **-en,** *v.a.* hydrogenate, hydrogenize. **-ung,** *f.* hydrogenation. **-werk,** *n. see* **-anlage.**

Hydro-chinon, *n.* hydroquinone (*Phot.*). **-chlorsäure,** *f.* hydrochloric acid. **-genisieren,** *v.a. see* **hydrieren.** **-genschwefel,** *m.* hydrogen sulphide. **-lyse,** *f.* hydrolysis. **-lytisch,** *adj.* hydrolytic. **-meter,** *n.* hydrometer. **-metrisch,** *adj.*; *-metrische Waage*, aerometer. **-pisch,** *adj.* dropsical (*Med.*). **-statik,** *f.* hydrostatics.

Hyetometer, *n.* rain-gauge.

Hygien-e, *f.* hygiene, sanitation. **-isch,** *adj.* hygienic, sanitary.

Hymn-e, *f.* (-en), **-us,** *m.* (-en) hymn, anthem. **-isch,** *adj.*, **-enhaft,** *adj.* hymnic, hymnal. **-enbuch,** *n.* hymn-book, hymnary, hymnal. **-endichtung,** *f.* hymnology, hymnody.

Hyper-bel, *f.* (-n) hyperbola (*Math.*); hyperbole. **-belfunktion,** *f.* hyperbolic function (*Maths.*). **-boreer,** *m.*, **-boreisch,** *adj.* Hyperborean. **-kritisch,** *adj.* overcritical, exceptionally critical. **-nervös,** *adj.* highly strung, oversensitive.

Hypno-se, *f.* hypnosis; *für -se empfänglich*, hypnotizable; *durch -se*, hypnotically. **-tisch,** *adj.* hypnotic; *-tische Mittel*, hypnotics; *-tischer Zustand*, hypnotic state; trance. **-tiseur,** *m.* hypnotist. **-tisieren,** *v.a.* hypnotize. **-tisierung,** *f.* hypnotization. **-tismus,** *m.* hypnotism; *Anhänger des -tismus*, hypnotist.

Hypochond-er, *m.* (-ers, -er) hypochondriac. **-rie,** *f.* hypochondria. **-risch,** *adj.* hypochondriac(al).

Hypokrit, *m.* (-en, -en) hypocrite. **-isch,** *adj.* hypocritical.

Hypotenuse, *f.* (-n) hypotenuse.

Hypothek, *f.* (-en) mortgage; *eine – aufnehmen*, raise money on mortgage; *mit -en belastet*, encumbered with mortgages. **-arisch,** *adj.*, mortgage; *-arischer Gläubiger*, mortgagee. **-engläubiger,** *m.* mortgagee. **-enschuldner,** *m.* mortgager.

Hypo-these, *f.* (-n) hypothesis. **-thetisch,** *adj.* hypothetical.

Hyster-ie, *f.* hysteria. **-isch,** *adj.* hysterical; *einen -ischen Anfall bekommen*, go (off) into hysterics.

I

I, i, 1. *n.* I, i. 2. *int.*; – *bewahre!* by no means! nothing of the kind! – *wo!* certainly not! nonsense!

Iah, *n.* bray of an ass. **-en,** *v.n.* bray, hee-haw (*like an ass*).

Iamb-us, *m.* **-isch,** *adj.*, *see* **Jamb-us, -isch.**

I-Barren, *m.* wire bar (*Metall.*).

ich, 1. *pers. pron.* I; – *selbst*, I myself; – *bin es*, it is I; – *Elender!* miserable wretch that I am! 2. *n.* self; ego; *mein zweites* or *anderes* –, my other self; my double. **-heit,** *f.* the individual(ity) (*as philosophical entity*), self; selfishness, egotism. **Ich-Roman,** *m.* novel in the first person. **-sucht,** *f.* selfishness.

Ickerchen, *n. pl.* toothy-pegs, megs (*children's word for teeth*).

Ideal, 1. *n.* (-s, -e) ideal; model, pattern; *er ist das – eines Redners*, he is a model orator. 2. *adj.* ideal, conceptual, abstract; imaginary, Utopian; perfect; *-er Mensch*, – *angelegter Mensch*, man of ideals, idealist; *-er Ratschlag*, council of perfection; *-er Schauspieler*, perfect actor. **-isieren,** *v.a.* idealize. **-ismus,** *m.* idealism. **-ist,** *m.* idealist. **-istisch,** *adj.* idealistic. **-ität,** *f.* ideality, conceptual realm.

Idee, *f.* (-n) idea; notion, conception; thought, fancy; intention, purpose; (*coll.*) *keine -!* by no means, certainly not! *keine* (*blasse*) – *von einer S. haben*, not have the faintest notion of *or* be altogether in the dark about a th. **-ll,** *adj.* existing in idea, hypothetical, imaginary. **-narm,** *adj.* devoid of ideas. **-ngehalt,** *m.* thought content, value of the ideas (contained). **-ngeschichte,** *f.* history of ideas *or* thought. **-nhaft,** *adj.* in idea. **-nkreis,** *m.* circle of ideas. **-nreich,** 1. *n.* realm of ideas. 2. *adj.* rich in ideas. **-ntausch,** *m.* exchange of ideas. **-nverbindung,** *f.* association of ideas, **-nwelt,** *f.* ideal world, world of ideas.

Iden, *pl.* Ides (*in ancient Rome, the 15th day of March, May, July, October, and the 13th of the other months*).

ident-ifizieren, *v.a.* identify. **-isch,** *adj.* identical. **-ität,** *f.* identity. **-itätsnachweis,** *m.* identification papers.

Ideolog-ie, *f.* ideology. **-isch,** *adj.* ideological.

Idioblast, *m.* (-en, -en) germ plasm.

Idiom, *n.* (-s, -e) dialect, speech habits, manner of speech. **-atisch,** *adj.* dialectal, showing *or* referring to speech peculiarities (*of a class or group*); idiomatic.

Idiosynkrasie, *f.* fixed aversion, allergy, antipathy.

Idiot, *m.* (-en, -en) idiot. **-ie,** *f.* idiocy. **-isch,** *adj.* idiotic. **-ismus,** *m.* idiom; (*rare*) stupid behaviour.

Idiotikon, *n.* (-kons, -ken *or* -ka) dialect dictionary.

Idyll, *n.* (-s, -e), **-e,** *f.* (-en) idyll. **-enhaft,** *adj.*, **-isch,** *adj.* idyllic, pastoral.

Igel, *m.* (-s, –) hedgehog; harrow; spiky brush; surly *or* irritable p. **-artig,** *adj.*, **-ig,** *adj.* prickly. **-stellung,** *f.* hedgehog position (*Mil.*).

igitte, (*dial.*) *int.* (*of abhorrence*) how nasty! how disgusting!

Ignor-ant, *m.* (-en, -en) ignoramus. **-anz,** *f.* ignorance. **-ieren,** *v.a.* ignore, (*coll.*) cut.

ihm, *pers. pron.* (*Dat. sing. of* er, es) (to) him, (to) it.

ihn, *pers. pron.* (*Acc. sing. of* er) him; it. **-en,** (*Dat. of* sie, *pl.*) (to) them; (*with cap.*, *Dat. of* Sie) (to) you.

ihr, 1. *pers. pron.* 1. (*Nom. pl. of* du) ye, you. 2. (*Dat. of* sie, *f. sing.*) (to) her, (to) it. **2.** *poss. adj.* (*and pron.*) (ihr, ihre, ihr) her(s); its; their(s); (*with cap.*) your(s). **-e,** (der, die, das -e), *see* **-ige.** **-er, 1.** *pers. pron.* 1. (*Gen. of* sie, *f. sing.*) of her, of it. 2. (*Gen. of* sie, *pl.*) of them; (*with cap.*) of you; *es waren -er viele*, there were many of them; *Gott wird sich -er erbarmen*, God will have compassion on them. **2.** *poss. adj.* (*Gen. & Dat. sing. & Gen. pl. of* ihr) of her, to her; of their; (*with cap.*) of your. **-erseits,** *adv.* in her (its, their) turn; for her (its, their) part; as far as she (it, they) are concerned; (*with cap.*) for your part, in your turn. **-esgleichen,** *indec. adj.* of her (its, their) kind; like her (it, them); (*with cap.*) of your kind; like you. **-ethalben,** *adv.*, **-etwegen,** *adv.*, **-etwillen,** *adv.* on her (its, their) account *or* behalf; for her (its, their) sake; so far as she (it, they) are concerned; (*with cap.*) on your account, *etc.* **-ige,** (der, die, das -ige; die -igen) *poss. pron.* hers, its, theirs; (*with cap.*) yours; *das -ige*, your property; your duty, *etc.*;

die –igen, your family; *ich verbleibe stets der* (*die*) *–ige*, I remain yours (very) truly *or* sincerely, *etc.* (*at the end of a letter*).
Ikterus, *m.* jaundice (*Med.*), chlorosis (*Bot.*).
Ilk, *m.* (-s, -e) (*dial.*), *see* **Iltis.**
illegitim, *adj.* unlawful, illegal; spurious, illegitimate. **–ität,** *f.* illegitimacy.
illoyal, *adj.* disloyal. **–ität,** *f.* disloyalty.
Illumin–ation, *f.* (-en) illumination. **–ieren,** *v.a.* illuminate (*a town, books*).
Illus–ion, *f.* (-en) illusion, self-deception. **–ionist,** *m.* (-en, -en) fantast, visionary, dreamer. **–orisch,** *adj.* illusory, illusive.
illustrieren, *v.a.* illustrate.
Iltis, *m.* (-ses, -se) polecat, fitchet.
im, *contraction of* **in dem.**
imaginär, *adj.* imaginary; floating (*capital*); *–e Größe*, imaginary quantity (*Math.*).
Imber, *m.* ginger.
Imbiß, *m.* (-(ss)es, -(ss)e) light meal, snack; light refreshments, (*Swiss dial.*) lunch. **–halle,** *f.* refreshment-bar.
imitieren, *v.a.* imitate, match.
Im–ker, *m.* (-s, –) bee-keeper, apiarist. **–kerei,** *f.* bee-keeping. **–kern,** *v.a.* keep *or* rear bees. **–me,** *f.* (-n) (*dial. & poet.*) bee.
immateriell, *adj.* immaterial.
Immatrikul–ation, *f.* matriculation, enrolment. **–ieren,** *v.a.* matriculate; enrol; *er ist an der Universität B. –iert*, he is a matriculated student at the University of B.; *sich –ieren lassen*, matriculate.
immediat, *adj.* immediate. **–isieren,** *v.a.* make free from intermediate control, make directly responsible to the ultimate authority. **–bericht,** *m.*, **–eingabe,** *f.* direct report *or* petition (*to the highest authority without mediation*).
immens, *adj.* immense, enormous.
immer, 1. *adv.* always, ever, every time; perpetually, continually; more and more (*with compar.*); nevertheless, yet, still; *auf –*, for ever; *– besser*, better and better; *– und ewig*, for ever and ever, eternally; *– fort!* further! forward! go on! *– gerade aus*, keep straight ahead; *– mehr*, more and more; *noch –*, still; *– schlimmer*, worse and worse; *– weiter!* on and on! *– weniger*, less and less; *wenn* (*auch*) *–*, although; *wer* (*auch*) *–*, who(so)ever; *wie –*, as usual; *wie auch –*, howsoever; *– wieder*, again and again; *wo* (*auch* or *nur*) *–*, where(so)ever; *– zu!* keep on! 2. *part.*; *er mag es – tun*, he is welcome to do it; *laß ihn nur – kommen*, he can come for all I care, as far as I am concerned he can come; *er ist doch – dein Vater*, after all he is your father; *er kommt doch wohl noch nicht, wir wollen uns – setzen*, he won't be here yet, let us take our seats; *was er nur – haben mag!* what can be the matter with him! *mag – sein Name vergessen werden, doch . . .*, although his name may be forgotten, yet. . . . **–dar,** *adv.* always, ever (more), for ever (and ever). **–fort,** *adv.* continually, constantly, perpetually, evermore. **–grün,** 1. *n.* large (lesser) periwinkle (*Vinca major* (*minor*)) (*Bot.*). 2. *adj.* evergreen. **–hin,** *adv. & part.* for all that, still, nevertheless; in spite of everything; no matter; after all; *mag es –hin so sein*, be that as it may; *tue es –hin*, well, you may do it, I do not object; *–hin mag die Welt wissen*, the world is welcome to know. **–während,** *adj.* endless, eternal, everlasting, perpetual. **–zu,** *adv. & int.* always, all the time; continually; *es regnet –zu*, it rains without stopping.
Immis, *m.* (*dial.*), *see* **Imbiß.**
immobil, *adj.* immovable; not ready for war. **–iarvermögen,** *n.* landed property. **–ien,** *pl.* real estate, immovables, dead stock.
Immortelle, *f.* (-n) everlasting flower, immortelle (*Helychrysum*) (*Bot.*).
immun, *adj.* immune (*from disease*), exempt (*from taxes*). **–isieren,** *v.a.* immunize, render immune. **–ität,** *f.* immunity, exemption. **–reaktion,** *f.* immune reaction (*Med.*).
Imperat–iv, *m.* (-s, -e) imperative mood. **–orisch,** *adj.* imperious.
Imperial–ismus, *m.* imperialism. **–fraktur,** *f.* great primer (*Typ.*).
impertinen–t, *adj.* impertinent, insolent. **–z,** *f.* insolence, impertinence.
impf–en, *v.a.* inoculate, vaccinate; graft (*Hort.*); (*fig.*) *einem den Haß ins Herz –en*, inspire s.o. with hate. **–arzt,** *m.* vaccinating physician, inoculator. **–gesetz,** *n.* vaccination act. **–ling,** *m.* child that has been *or* is about to be vaccinated. **–reis,** *n.* graft-twig (*Hort.*). **–schein,** *m.* certificate of vaccination. **–stoff,** *m.* vaccine, serum, lymph. **–ung,** *f.* inoculation, vaccination. **–zwang,** *m.* compulsory vaccination.
implizieren, *v.n.* implicate (*a p.*), imply (*s.th.*).
imponderab–el, *adj.* imponderable. **–ilien,** *n.pl.* imponderable substances, (*fig.*) imponderables.
imponieren, *v.n.* (*aux.* h.) (*einem*) impress (a p.). **–d,** *pr.p. & adj.* imposing, impressive.
Import, *m.* (-(e)s, -e) importation, imports. **–e,** *f.* imported Havana cigar; **–en,** *pl.* imported goods, imports. **–ieren,** *v.a.* import. **–ware,** *f.* imported article.
imposant, *adj.* impressive, imposing, majestic.
Impost, *m.* (-es, -en) impost; (*pl.*) taxes, duties, customs.
Impotenz, *f.* impotency.
imprägnier–en, *v.a.* saturate, proof, impregnate. **–bad,** *n.* impregnating bath. **–ung,** *f.* impregnation, proofing.
Imprimatur, *n.* Press! *einem Druckbogen das – erteilen*, mark a sheet for press; authority to print (*R.C.*).
Improvis–ator, *m.* (-s, -en) improviser. **–ieren,** *v.a.* improvise.
Impuls, *m.* (-es, -e) impulse. **–iv,** *adj.* impulsive.
imputieren, *v.a.* impute, charge with.
Ims, *m. see* **Imbiß.**
imstande, *adv.* capable (of); able, in a position (to).
in, *prep. expressing rest or motion in a place* (*Dat.*); in, at; *implying motion to or towards* (*Acc.*); into, to, within; *– der besten Absicht*, with the best intentions; (*coll.*) *– die Binsen gehen*, come to grief; *– die Breite gehen*, spread, swell; get more and more; *– Erscheinung treten*, come to pass; *– etwas*, a little, somewhat; *– Fahrt*, under way (*Naut.*); *– aller Frühe*, very early, at daybreak; *– Geschäften ausgehen*, to go out on business; *– die Kirche gehen*, go to church; *– kurzem*, shortly, soon, in a short time; *– die Länge gehen*, run to length, go on and on; *zehn Fuß – die Länge*, ten feet long; *– Musik setzen*, set to music; *– die Nacht hinein*, late into the night; *– den Schlaf singen*, sing to sleep; *– der Schule*, at school; *– Schutz nehmen*, take under protection; *– (die) See stechen*, put to sea; (*coll.*) *das hat es – sich*, there is a lot to it, it is difficult; *– Vergessenheit geraten*, become forgotten. **–begriff,** *m.* **–dem,** *adv., etc.*, *see* **Inbegriff, indem,** *etc.*
inadäquat, *adj.* inadequate.
inaktiv, *adj.* inactive, inert, neutral, passive. **–ieren,** *v.a.* put out of action, render inactive, incapacitate.
Inangriffnahme, *f.* start, beginning made (with a th.), setting about (a th.).
Inanspruchnahme, *f.* laying claim to; requisition (*Mil.*); being very busy; *zur – des Kredits*, for using credit; *überaus starke geschäftliche –*, heavy business claims on one's time.
inartikuliert, *adj.* unarticulated; inarticulate.
Inaugenscheinnahme, *f.* inspection, scrutiny.
inaugurieren, *v.a.* inaugurate.
Inbegriff, *m.* (-s, -e) contents; embodiment, essence; tenor, purport; summary, abstract, epitome; sum, total, aggregate; *mit –*, including; *mit – der Spesen*, inclusive of charges. **–en,** *adv.* including, included, inclusive of, implied.
Inbetrieb–nahme, *f.*, **–setzung,** *f.* starting, opening, setting to work.
Inbrunst, *f.* ardour, fervour.
inbrünstig, *adj.* ardent, fervent.
Inc. . . . *For words beginning with* **Inc** *see under* **Ink . . .** or **Inz. . . .**
indeklinabel, *adj.* indeclinable.
Indelikatesse, *f.* indelicacy.
indem, 1. *adv.* just then, meanwhile. 2. *conj.* during the time that, whilst, while, in *or* on (doing), as, in that, by (doing); since, because; *ich gewähre es, – ich hoffe*, I grant it in the hope that.

indemni–sieren, *v.a.* indemnify, recompense. **–tät,** *f.* indemnity, exemption.
indes, indessen, 1. *adv.* meantime, meanwhile; *lesen sie –*, read in the meantime. 2. *conj.* however, nevertheless, none the less; (*archaic*), whilst, while.
Indeterminismus, *m.* free will (*Phil.*).
Index, *m.* (-(es), -e *or* Indices), index; *auf den – setzen*, proscribe (*a book*). **–ziffer,** *f.* index (number) (*Statistics*).
Indienststellung, *f.* mobilization; *– eines Schiffes*, commissioning of a (war-)ship.
indifferen–t, *adj.* passive, neutral, indifferent; *–es Gas*, inert gas. **–tismus,** *m.* neutrality, indifference. **–z,** *f.* passivity, ineffectiveness.
indigen, *adj.* indigenous, native. **–at,** *n.* (-(e)s, -e) right of a native; denizenship.
indignieren, *v.a.* offend, make indignant, arouse indignation.
Indigo, *m.* indigo. **–blau,** *adj.* & *n.*, **–tin,** *n.* indigo blue.
Indikativ, *m.* (-s, -e) indicative (mood).
indiskret, *adj.* inquisitive, prying, tactless, (*coll.*) nosy. **–ion,** *f.* inquisitiveness.
indisponibel, *adj.* not to be disposed of, not available.
indisponiert, *adj.* indisposed, out of sorts; disinclined (from).
Indisziplin, *f.* lack of discipline. **–iert,** *adj.* undisciplined.
Individu–alität, *f.* (-en) individuality, personality. **–ell,** *adj.* individual, personal, single, special. **–um,** *n.* (-ums, -en) individual, (*coll.*) doubtful *or* shady character *or* customer.
Indizienbeweis, *m.* (-es, -e) circumstantial proof *or* evidence.
Indoss–ement, (*Austr. dial.* **–ament**), *n.* (-es, -e) (*C.L.*) indorsement. **–ant,** *m.*, **–ent,** *m.* indorser. **–ieren,** *v.a.* indorse.
Indukti–on, *f.* (-en) induction (*Log.* & *Elec.*) **–onsapparat,** *m.* inductor; magneto, induction coil. **–onselektrizität,** *f.* induced electricity. **–onsfunken,** *m.* induction spark. **–onsspule,** *f.* inductance (coil) (*Rad.*). **–onsstrom,** *m.* induction current, induced current. **–vität,** *f.* inductance (*Elec. unit*).
Induktor, *m.*, *see* **Induktionsapparat.**
industri–alisieren, *v.a.* industrialize. **–alisierung,** *f.* industrialization. **–e,** *f.* (-en) industry. **–ell,** *adj.* industrial, manufacturing. **–eausstellung,** *f.* industrial exhibition, industries fair. **–ebezirk,** *m.* industrial *or* manufacturing district. **–elle(r),** *m.* manufacturer, producer, factory owner. **–epapiere,** *n.pl.* shares in industrial undertakings. **–eritter,** *m.* (*archaic*) swindler, fraudulent speculator. **–estaat,** *m.* industrial *or* manufacturing country.
induzier–en, *v.a.* induce (*Log.* & *Elec.*). **–t,** *p.p.* & *adj.* induced, secondary.
inegal, *adj.* unequal; uneven.
ineinander, *adv.* & *sep. prefix.* into one another, into each other. **–flechten,** *ir.v.a.* interlace. **–fügen,** *v.a.* join. **–greifen,** *ir.v.a.* (*aux.* h.) mesh, work together; co-operate.
Inempfangnahme, *f.* reception, receiving.
Inexistenz, *f.* subsistence, inherence, immanence.
infam, *adj.* infamous. **–ie,** *f.* infamy.
Infant, *m.* (-en, -en) infante. **–il,** *adj.* infantile, childish, retarded. **–in,** *f.* infanta.
Infanter–ie, *f.* infantry. **–ieflieger,** *m.* army co-operation plane. **–ist,** *m.* (-en, -en) infantryman.
Infektions–krankheit, *f.* infectious disease. **–träger,** *m.* carrier.
Infel, *f.* mitre, *see* **Inful.**
infer–ieren, *v.a.* deduce, infer. **–ioritätskomplex,** *m.* inferiority complex.
infiltrieren, *v.n.* infiltrate.
Infinit–esimalrechnung, *f.* infinitesimal calculus. **–iv,** *m.* (-ivs, -ive), **–ivus,** *m.* (–, -ive) infinitive (mood).
infizieren, *v.a.* infect.
inflat–ionistisch, *adj.* inflationary. **–ionszeit,** *f.* inflation period. **–orisch,** *adj.* inflationary.
Influenz, *f.* induction (*Elec.*). **–a,** *f.* influenza, (*coll.*) flu.
infolge, *prep.* as a result of, in consequence of, owing to. **–dessen,** *adv.* hence, consequently, because of that.
inform–ieren, *v.a.* inform, give information, brief (*Law, Mil.*). **–atorisch,** *adj.* informative, instructive.
Inful, *f.* (-n) (bishop's) mitre. **–ieren,** *v.a.* invest (with episcopal robes).
Infus, *n.* (-es, -e & -a), **–ion,** *f.* (-en) infusion, decoction. **–ionstierchen,** *n.pl.*, **–orien,** *pl.* infusoria.
Ingangsetzung, *f.* starting (*of a machine*).
Ingenieur [*pron.* inʒenɪ'øːr], *m.* (-s, -e) engineer. **–schule,** *f.* school of engineering. **–wesen,** *n.* engineering.
ingleichen, *adv.* & *conj.* (*archaic*) likewise, also.
Ingreß, *m.* (-(ss)es, -(ss)e), entry, admission (*into religious order, etc.*).
Ingrimm, *m.* rage, anger, wrath. **–ig,** *adj.* furious, very angry; fierce.
Ingwer, *m.* ginger. **–bier,** *n.* ginger-ale.
Inhaber, *m.* possessor, holder, proprietor; occupant, bearer (*of a bill*); *– einer Pfründe*, incumbent. **–aktie,** *f.* bearer share.
inhaft–ieren, *v.a.* take into custody, arrest. **–nahme,** *f.* arrest.
inhalieren, *v.a.* inhale.
Inhalt, *m.* contents; content, capacity, extent, area, volume; tenor, subject, purport, substance, sense, meaning. **–lich,** *adj.* with regard to the contents. **–reich,** *adj.*, **–schwer,** *adj.* weighty, full of meaning, significant. **–sangabe,** *f.*, **–sanzeige,** *f.*, **–sverzeichnis,** *n.* (table of) contents, summary; index. **–sanzeiger,** *m.* fuel gauge. **–sermittlung,** *f.* determination of volume. **–(s)leer,** *adj.*, **–(s)los,** *adj.* empty, trivial, meaningless, of little consequence. **–smaß,** *n.* measure of capacity, cubic measure. **–svoll,** *adj.*, *see* **–schwer.**
inhärent, *adj.* inherent.
inhib–ieren, *v.a.* check, stop, hinder, inhibit; *einen Prozeß –ieren*, stay proceedings. **–itorium,** *n.* inhibition (*Law*).
Initial, *n.* (-s, -e), *usually* **–e,** *f.* (-en) capital letter; (*latter only*) initial *or* apical cell (*Bot.*). **–zünder,** *m.* primer (*Artil.*).
Initiativ–e, *f.* (-en) initiative, first step, (*Swiss*) right of initiative, obligatory referendum (*Pol.*). *aus eigener –e*, on one's own initiative; *–e ergreifen*, take the initiative; *private –e*, private enterprise. **–antrag,** *m.* private bill (*Parl.*).
injizieren, *v.a.* inject.
Injurie, *f.* (-n) insult, slander, libel. **–nklage,** *f.* action for libel *or* slander.
inkarn–at, 1. *adj.* flesh-coloured, incarnative. 2. *n.* flesh-colour, pink. **–iert,** *adj.* incarnate, embodied.
Inkass–ant, *m.* (-en, -en) (*Austr. dial.*) cashier. **–o,** *n.* (-s, -s & -) (C.L.) encashment, cashing; *das –o besorgen*, collect, cash, get cashed, procure payment. (*C.L.*) **–obüro,** *n.* encashment office. (*C.L.*) **–ogeschäft,** *n.* collection business, collection of bills. (*C.L.*) **–ospesen,** *pl.* expenses of collection. **–owechsel,** *m.* bill to be cashed.
Inklination, *f.* dip (*of magnetic needle*); inclination, predilection.
inkohärent, *adj.* incoherent.
inkomplett, *adj.* incomplete.
inkonsequen–t, *adj.* inconsistent, contradictory. **–z,** *f.* (-en) inconsistency, contradiction.
Inkrafttreten, *n.* coming into force.
Inkretion, *f.* internal secretion, endocrine secretion (*Med.*).
inkulan–t, *adj.* (*C.L.*) unaccommodating. **–z,** *f.* incivility, brusqueness.
Inkulp–ant, *m.* (-en, -en) (*archaic*) prosecutor. **–at,** *m.* (-en, -en) (*archaic*) accused, defendant.
Inkunabel, *f.* (-n) early printed book, (*pl.*) incunabula.
Inland, *n.* inland, interior; native country, home; *im In- und Auslande*, at home and abroad; *fürs – bestimmt*, for home consumption.
Inländ–er, *m.* (-s, –) native. **–isch,** *adj.* inland; indigenous, native, home-bred, home-made; home; *–isches Fabrikat*, home produce (*not foreign*).
Inlaut, *m.* (-(e)s, -e) medial sound; *im –*, medially.

Inlett, *n.* (-(e)s, -e; & *Austr. dial.* -s, -en) bed-tick *or* ticking.
inliegend, *pr.p.* & *adj.* enclosed, herewith.
inmitten, *adv.* & *prep.* (*Gen.*) in the midst of.
inne, *adv.* & *sep. prefix.* within; *mitten* –, right in the middle *or* midst. **–behalten,** *ir.v.a.* keep back *or* for o.s. **–haben,** *ir.v.a.* occupy, possess, hold, be master of; know, understand, be thoroughly acquainted with, have at one's fingers' ends. **–halten,** 1. *ir.v.a.* hold, maintain, keep to. 2. *v.n.* stop, pause, leave off. **–werden,** 1. *ir.v.n.* (*with Gen.*) perceive, become conscious *or* aware of, learn. 2. *n.* perception. **–wohnen,** *v.n.* dwell *or* be inherent in.
innen, *adv.* within, inside; – *und außen,* through and through. **–architektur,** *f.* inside decoration. **–backenbremse,** *f.* internal expanding brake (*Motor.*). **–dienst,** *m.* garrison duty (*Mil.*). **–druck,** *m.* internal pressure. **–durchmesser,** *m.* inside diameter. **–einrichtung,** *f.* inside decoration, furnishing. **–fläche,** *f.*, *see* **–seite. –lunker,** *m.* blow-hole (*Metall.*). **–leben,** *n.* inner life. **–leitung,** *f.* inside wiring, piping, etc. **–minister,** *m.* Secretary of the Interior (*Amer.*), Home Secretary (*Eng.*). **–ministerium,** *n.* Department of the Interior (*Amer.*), Home Office (*Eng.*). **–politik,** *f.* domestic *or* home policy. **–politisch,** *adj.* relating to home affairs. **–raum,** *m.* interior (space). **–seite,** *f.* inner surface, inside; palm (of hand). **–welt,** *f.* the world within us, inner life. **–winkel,** *m.* internal angle.
inner, *adj.* interior, internal, inner, inward, intestine, domestic; intrinsic, spiritual; *–e Angelegenheiten eines Staates,* internal affairs of a state; *–e Schiffsladung,* inboard cargo; *das –e Auge,* the mind's eye; *–es Leiden,* internal complaint; *–e Mission,* home mission; *die –e Stimme,* inner voice, conscience; *–er Verbrauch,* home consumption; *–er Wert,* intrinsic value. **–e(s),** *n.* interior, inside; inner self, heart, soul, core; *das –e der Erde,* the bowels of the earth; *Ministerium des –en, see* **Innenministerium**; *das –e der Stadt,* the centre of the town; *im tiefsten –en,* in the inmost recesses of the heart. **–halb,** *adv.* & *prep.* (*Gen.*) within, inside; *–halb eines Jahres,* within a year (*but with Dat. when Gen. form is not recognizable, e.g.* –halb vier Jahren). **–lich,** *adj.* interior, inner, inward, internal; profound, heartfelt, sincere, cordial, intrinsic; mental; *–lich anzuwenden,* to be taken internally. **–lichkeit,** *f.* inwardness, subjectivity, subjectiveness; cordiality, warmth. **–politisch,** *adj.* of internal policy, of home affairs, domestic. **–st,** *adj.* (*sup. of* inner) inmost, innermost; *meine –ste Überzeugung,* my firm *or* deepest conviction; *das –ste,* inner man *or* self; bottom of the heart *or* soul, core, intrinsic nature, innermost part; *im –sten,* in one's heart, at heart. **–t,** (*Swiss dial.*), *see* **–halb.**
innig, *adj.* intimate, heartfelt, sincere, earnest, cordial, fervent, ardent; *–e Freundschaft,* close friendship; – *lieben,* love deeply *or* sincerely; *–e Mischung,* intimate mixture. **–keit,** *f.* cordiality, sincerity, fervour, ardour, intimacy. **–lich,** *adv., see* **innig.**
Innung, *f.* guild, corporation. **–sbrief,** *m.* charter of a guild. **–smitglied,** *n.* member of a corporation. **–swesen,** *n.* guild system.
inoffiziell, *adj.* unofficial.
ins, *contr. for* **in das. –besondere,** *adv.* especially, particularly, in particular. **–geheim,** *adv.* secretly, privily. **–gemein,** *adv.* in common; usually, generally. **–gesamt,** *adv.* all together, in a body, collectively. **–künftige,** *adv.* in the time to come, henceforth, in *or* for the future.
Insasse, *m.* (-n, -n) inmate; inhabitant; passenger.
Inschrift, *f.* (-en) inscription; legend, caption. **–enkunde,** *f.* art of deciphering inscriptions, epigraphy. **–lich,** 1. *adj.* epigraphic. 2. *adv.* according to *or* by the inscription *or* records.
Insekt, *n.* (-(e)s, -en) insect. **–enartig,** *adj.* of the insect kind. **–enfraß,** *m.* damage *or* ravage by insects. **–enfressend,** *adj.* insectivorous. **–enkenner,** *m.* entomologist. **–enkunde,** *f.*, **–enlehre,** *f.*, **–ologie,** *f.* entomology. **–enmittel,** *n.*, **–enpulver,** *n.* insect powder, insecticide.
Insel, *f.* (-n) island. **–bewohner,** *m.* islander. **–chen,** *n.* isle, islet. **–gruppe,** *f.* archipelago. **–meer,** *n.* archipelago. **–reich,** 1. *n.* island realm (*usually refers to Denmark*). 2. *adj.* dotted with islands. **–volk,** *n.* islanders, insular race.
Inser–at, *n.* (-(e)s, -e) advertisement. **–atenteil,** *m.* & *n.* advertisement columns (*of newspaper*). **–ent,** *m.* (-en, -en) advertiser. **–ieren,** *v.a.* insert an advertisement, advertise. **–tion,** *f.* advertisement.
insgeheim, *see* **ins–.**
insgemein, *see* **ins–.**
insgesamt, *see* **ins–.**
Insignien, *pl.* insignia, regalia, badge of office *or* mark of dignity.
inskünftige, *adv., see* **ins–.**
insofern, 1. *adv.* to that extent, so far. 2. *conj.* in so far as, inasmuch as, according as.
Insolvenz, *f.* insolvency. **–erklärung,** *f.* declaration of insolvency.
insonderheit (*archaic*) *adv.* separately, apart; especially, particularly.
insoweit, *adv., see* **insofern.**
Inspekt–ion, *f.* inspection, supervision. **–eur,** *m.* (-s, -e), **–or,** *m.* (-s, -en) inspector, supervisor.
inspirieren, *v.a.* inspire.
Inspiz–ient, *m.* (-en, -en) stage-manager (*Theat.*); inspector. **–ieren,** *v.a.* inspect, superintend.
Install–ateur, *m.* (-s, -e), plumber, electrician, fitter. **–ieren,** *v.a.* install, fit, put in.
instandhalt–en, *v.a.* keep in repair, maintain, keep up. **–ung,** *f.* repair, maintenance, upkeep.
inständig, *adj.* urgent, pressing, earnest (*only used of requests, etc.*); – *bitten,* beseech, implore.
instand–setzen, *v.a.* repair, do up, make ready, prepare; enable. **–setzung,** *f.* getting ready; repair. **–stellung,** *f.* (*Swiss dial.*), *see* **–setzung.**
Instanz, *f.* (-en) court (of justice); stage (*of proceedings*); *höhere* –, superior court; *letzte* –, last resort; *von der* – *abgewiesen,* out of court; *von der* – *entbunden,* discharged (*not acquitted*). **–enweg,** *m.* official channels; stage of appeal. **–enzug,** *m.* successive appeal.
Inste, *m.* (-n, -n) (*dial.*), *see* **Instmann.**
instehend, *adj.* herein contained.
Inster, *m.* & *n.* (-s) (*dial.*) pluck, tripe, entrails, offal.
Instinkt, *m.* (-(e)s, -e) instinct. **–artig,** *adj.*, **–iv,** *adj.*, **–mäßig,** *adv.* instinctive.
insti–tuieren, *v.a.* institute. **–tut,** *n.* (-s, -e) institute (*of science or learning*), academy.
Inst–mann, *m.* (-es, -leute) (*dial.*) cottager.
instruieren, *v.a.* instruct, brief; *einen Prozeß* –, draw up *or* prepare a case (*Law*).
Instrument, *n.* (-(e)s, -e) instrument. **–al,** *adj.* instrumental. **–enbrett,** *n.* dashboard (*Motor.*). **–ieren,** *v.a.* instrument, score (*Mus.*).
Insul–aner, *m.* (-s, –), islander, island dweller. **–ar,** *adj.* insular.
inszenier–en, *v.a.* stage, produce (*Theat.*). **–ung,** *f.* mise en scène, staging, production (*Theat.*).
Integral–rechnung, *f.* integral calculus. **–zahl,** *f.* integer.
Intell–ekt, *m.* (-s, -e) intellect. **–ektuell,** *adj.* intellectual; *die –ektuellen, pl.* the intelligentsia. **–igent,** *adj.* intelligent. **–igenz,** *f.* intellect, brains, intelligence, understanding, cleverness; intelligentsia, intellectuals. **–igenzblatt,** *n.* (*archaic*) advertiser (*newspaper*).
Intend–ant, *m.* (-en, -en) director, superintendent; administrative officer (*Mil.*). **–antur,** *f.* superintendent's office *or* department; (*archaic*) Quartermaster-General's Department, commissariat (*Mil.*). **–anz,** *f.* board of management.
Intensi–tät, *f.* (-en) intensity. **–v,** *adj.* thorough, intensive.
interess–ant, *adj.* interesting. **–e,** *n.* (-es, -en) interest; advantages; (*pl.*) (*archaic*) interest (*on money*); *–e an einer S. nehmen,* take an interest in a th., be interested in a th.; *er hat –e für,* he is interested in. **–engemeinschaft,** *f.* community of interests; pooling agreement. **–enpolitik,** *f.* policy based on (commercial) interests. **–ensphäre,** *f.* sphere of

influence. **–ent,** *m.* (-en, -en) interested party, vested interests. **–ieren,** 1. *v.a.* interest. 2. *v.r.* be interested *or* take an interest (in). **–iert,** *p.p.* & *adj.* interested; selfish, self-interested; *an einer S. –iert sein,* have an interest in a th.

Interim, *n.* interim *or* provisional measure; interim, intervening period. **–istisch,** *adj.* provisional. (*C.L.*) **–sanleiheschein,** *m.* scrip. **–skonto** *n.* suspense account. **–sregierung,** *f.* provisional government, interregnum. **–sschein,** *m.* sight-entry. **–swechsel,** *m.* bill ad interim, provisional bill of exchange.

interkonfessionell, *adj.* interdenominational, undenominational.

interkurrent, *adj.* intermittent, spasmodic.

intermediär, *adj.* intermediate, intermediary.

intern, *adj.* internal. **–at,** *n.* (-s, -e) boarding school. **–e,** *m. or f.* boarder (*in boarding school, etc.*). **–ieren,** *v.a.* intern, confine, detain; isolate (*cases of infectious disease*). **–ierung,** *f.* internment; isolation. **–ist,** *m.* specialist for internal diseases.

interpolieren, *v.a.* interpolate.

Interpret, *m.* (-en, -en) interpreter. **–ieren,** *v.a.* interpret, explain, expound.

interpun–gieren, –ktieren, *v.a.* punctuate. **–ktion,** *f.* punctuation. **–ktionszeichen,** *n.* punctuation mark.

Intervall, *n.* (-s, -e) interval (*Mus.*).

intervenieren, *v.n.* intervene.

Interview, *n.* interview. **–en,** *v.a.* interview.

intim, *adj.* intimate, familiar; *–e Bekanntschaft,* close connexion; *–e Freunde,* fast *or* close friends. **–ität,** *f.* intimacy, familiarity. **–us,** *m.* (-us, -i) intimate friend, chum.

Intoleranz, *f.* intolerance.

intonieren, *v.a.* intone, intonate.

Intrade, *f.* (-n) prelude (*Mus.*); (trumpet-) flourish.

intransitiv, 1. *adj.* intransitive. 2. *n.* (-s, -e), **–um,** *n.* (-ums, -a) intransitive verb.

intrig–ant. 1. *adj.* plotting, scheming, designing. 2. *m.* intriguer, plotter. **–e,** *f.* intrigue. **–ieren,** *v.a.* intrigue, plot, scheme.

intus, *adj.* inner, inward; (*coll.*) *– haben,* have understood, know full well.

invalid, –e, *adj.* disabled. **–e,** *m.* disabled soldier, unemployable (*through old age or disability*). **–enliste,** *f.* retired *or* superannuated list. **–enrente,** *f.* old age *or* disability pension. **–enversicherung,** *f.* old-age insurance. **–ieren,** *v.a.* invalidate. **–ierung,** *f.* invalidation, disallowance. **–ität,** *f.* disability (*of a workman, soldier*).

Invariante, *f.* (-n) invariable (*Math.*).

Invent–ar, *n.* (-ars, -are (& *Austr.* -arien)) inventory, stock-list; *ein –ar von einer S. aufnehmen,* take, make *or* draw up an inventory of a th.; *lebendes –ar,* livestock; *totes –ar,* fixtures. **–ieren,** *v.a.* list, inventory, schedule. **–ur,** *f.* stock-taking; (*C.L.*) *–ur machen,* take stock. **–uraufnahme,** *f., see* **–ur.** **–urausverkauf,** *m.* stock-taking sale.

investier–en, *v.a.* invest (with). **–ung,** *f.* investment.

investigieren, *v.a.* investigate.

Investition, *f.* (capital) investment.

inwärt–ig, *adj.* internal, inward. **–s,** *adv.* inwards, internally.

inwendig, *adj.* interior, inside, inward; *in- und auswendig kennen,* know thoroughly, know completely by heart.

inwiefern, *adv.* **inwieweit,** *adv.* to what extent, in what way *or* respect, how far.

inwohn–en, *v.n.* (*aux.* h.), **–end,** *pr.p.* & *adj.* (*archaic* & *dial.*) *see* **innewohnen.** **–er,** *m.* (*archaic* & *dial.*) dweller, inhabitant.

Inzest, *m.* (-es, -e) incest, endogamy, inbreeding. **–uös,** *adj.* incestuous.

Inzicht, *f.* (-en) (*archaic*) accusation; grounds for suspicion.

inzid–ent, *adj.* casual, incidental, incident (to). **–entien,** *pl.* incidentals. **–enz,** *f.* incidence. **–enzwinkel,** *m.* angle of incidence. **–ieren,** *v.n.* (*mit*) incident (on a line) (*Math.*); *eine Linie –iert mit einer anderen,* one line is incident on another (*Math.*)

Inzucht, *f.* inbreeding; endogamy.

inzwischen, *adv.* & *conj.* in the meantime, meanwhile.

Ion, *n.* (-s, -en) ion. **–enbildung,** *f.* formation of ions. **–engeschwindigkeit,** *f.* ionic velocity. **–enspaltung,** *f.* ionization. **–isieren,** *v.a.* ionize.

Iper, *f.* (-n) common elm (*Ulmus campestris*) (*Bot.*).

ird–en, *adj.* earthen, made of earth *or* clay; *–enes Geschirr,* earthenware, crockery; *–ene Pfeife,* clay-pipe. **–isch,** *adj.* earthly, worldly, terrestrial, mortal, perishable; *–isches Dasein,* temporal existence; *–ische Dinge,* earthly things, temporal affairs; *–isch gesinnt,* worldly-minded; *–ische Hülle, –ische Überreste,* mortal remains.

irgend, *adv.* any, some; perhaps; about, nearly; (*before a pron., adj. or pronominal adv. often* =) soever, at all, ever, *etc.*; *wer – anständig ist,* a person with any pretensions to respectability; *wenn ich – kann,* if I possibly can; *wenn – möglich,* if at all possible. **– einer** (*Austr. dial.* –einer) *pron.* anybody, someone; *auf – eine* (*Austr. dial.* –eine) *Art,* in some way or other, somehow; *– ein anderer,* someone else; *um – einer Ursache willen,* for some reason or other; *ist – eine Hoffnung vorhanden?* is there any hope (at all)? **– einmal,** *adv.* at any time, ever. **– etwas,** anything at all. **– jemand,** *see* **– einer.** **–wann,** *adv.* some time or other. **–wer,** *pron., see* **– einer.** **–wie,** *adv.* somehow, anyhow, in any way. **–wo,** *adv.* anywhere, somewhere. **–woher,** *adv.* from some place or other, from anywhere. **–wohin,** *adv.* to some place or other.

irisierend, *adj.* iridescent.

Iron–ie, *f.* (-ien) irony. **–isch,** *adj.* ironical. **–isieren,** *v.a.* treat with irony.

irr–(e), *adj.* in error, wrong; astray, wandering, lost; in perplexity, confused, puzzled, disconcerted; wavering, doubtful; delirious, insane; *er redet –e,* he is raving; *an einem ganz –e werden,* not know what to make of a p., have one's doubts about a p., lose confidence in a p. **–e** *f.* mistaken course, error, (*only in*) *in die –e führen,* lead astray; *in die –e gehen,* go astray. **–block,** *m.* erratic block (*Geol.*). **–e(r),** *m.* madman, lunatic. **–eführen,** *v.a.* lead astray, mislead, deceive. **–egehen,** *v.n.* (*aux.* s.) go astray, lose one's way. **–elaufen,** *n.* miscarriage (*of letters, etc.*). **–eleiten,** *v.a., see* **–eführen.** **–emachen,** *v.a.* bewilder, confuse, puzzle. **–en,** 1. *v.n.* (*aux.* h. & s.) go astray, lose one's way; err, be mistaken *or* deceived. 2. *v.a.* mislead, lead astray, deceive; disturb, puzzle; vex. 3. *v.r.* be mistaken, be wrong; commit an error; *sich in einem –en,* be mistaken about a p., be disappointed in a p. **–enanstalt,** *f.,* **–enhaus,** *n.* lunatic asylum. **–enarzt,** *m.* psychiatrist, alienist. **–fahrt,** *f.* going astray; wandering about, vagary. **–gang,** *m.* aberration, bootless errand; maze, labyrinth. **–gängig,** *adj.* labyrinthine, intricate. **–garten,** *m.* maze. **–glaube,** *m.* heresy. **–gläubig,** *adj.* heterodox, heretical. **–ig,** *adj.* erroneous, false, incorrect, wrong. **–igerweise,** *adv.* by mistake, erroneously. **–igkeit,** *f.* erroneousness. **–köpfig,** *adj.* crack-brained, crazed. **–läufer,** *m.* lost letter, letter delivered to wrong address. **–lehre,** *f.* false doctrine, heresy. **–licht,** *n.* (-er), will-o'-the-wisp, jack-o'-lantern. **–lichtelieren,** *v.n.* (*aux.* h.) dart about like a will-o'-the wisp. **–pfad,** *m.* wrong path. **–sal,** *n.* erring, sin, error; labyrinth, maze. **–sinn,** *m.* insanity, madness, delirium. **–sinnig,** *adj.* insane, mad. **–stern,** *m.* comet. **–tum,** *m.* (-s, ¨er) error, mistake, false step, fault, erroneous idea; *einem seinen –tum benehmen,* undeceive a p., disabuse a p.'s mind; (*C.L.*) *–tum vorbehalten,* errors excepted. **–tümlich,** 1. *adj.* erroneous, mistaken, false. 2. *adv.* mistakenly, erroneously, by mistake. **–ung,** *f.* error, mistake; misunderstanding, difference. **–wahn,** *m.* delusion, erroneous opinion; insanity. **–weg,** *m.* wrong way. **–wisch,** *m. see* **–licht**; (*also coll.*) flibbertigibbet, flighty p.

irreal, *adj.* unreal, imaginary.

irritieren, *v.a.* irritate, annoy; upset, disturb, make insecure.

Isabellfarbe, *f.* buff, dun, cream-colour.

Ischias, *f.* sciatica.
Isogon, *n.* (-s, -e) equiangular and equilateral polygon.
Isol–ation, *f.* insulation, isolation. **–ator,** *m.* (-s, -en) insulator, insulating material (*Elec.*). **–ieren,** *v.a.* isolate; screen (*Rad.*). **–ierung,** *f.* insulation, isolation, lagging. **–ierband,** *n.* insulating tape. **–ierbaracke,** *f.* isolation hospital. **–ierflasche,** *f.* vacuum *or* thermos flask. **–ierhaft,** *f.* solitary confinement. **–ierschicht,** *f.* insulating layer. **–ierzelle,** *f.* padded cell, solitary confinement *or* punishment cell.
isomorph, *adj.* isomorphic, isomorphous.
ißt, issest, ißt, *see* **essen.**
ist, *see* **sein. –ausgabe,** *f.* actual issue. **–bestand,** *m.* stock in hand. **–eingänge,** *m.pl.*, **–einnahmen,** *f.pl.* clear income, net receipts. **–stand,** *m.*, **–stärke,** *f.* effective strength, actual strength (*Mil.*).
itz–e, –o, –t, *adv.* (*archaic & dial.*) now, at present. **–ig,** *adj.* (*dial.*) the same; *–ig und allein,* solely, by itself.
Itzig, *m.* (*pej.*) Jew.

J

J, j, *n.* J, j.
ja, 1. *adv. & part.* yes; truly, really; indeed, certainly, by all means, of course, (*archaic*) forsooth; even; well; you know; (*with emphasis*) *nimm dich – in acht,* be sure to take care; *geh – nicht dahin,* do not go there on any account; *das mußt du – tun,* you must do that without fail *or* in any case *or* at all events *or* come what may; *sei doch – so gut!* please be so good *or* kind; *daß du es – nicht wieder tust,* see to it *or* make sure *or* mind that you don't do that again; *– doch!* to be sure, really; *– freilich, see* **–wohl;** *wenn –,* if so, if this is the case. (*without emphasis*) *er ist – mein Freund, aber . . .,* he is indeed my friend although . . .; *ich gebe mir – Mühe,* I do take pains; *da ist er –!* well, there he is; *Sie sehen – ganz blaß aus,* you certainly look quite pale; *– wenn es sein muß,* if it must needs be; *wenn er – kommt,* if indeed he come at all, even if he should come; *ich sage es –,* I am telling you; *ich wünsche, daß du es tust, – ich bitte darum,* I wish, I even beg you to do it, (*archaic*) I wish, nay I beg, that you would do it; *warum schreibst du nicht? Ich schreibe –,* Why are you not writing? But I am! *er ist hier – zu Hause,* this is his home, you know; *ich habe es dir – schon gesagt,* well, I have told you before; *– was ich sagen wollte,* by the way I was going to tell you; *– was wollen sie denn eigentlich?* well, what do you want anyway? 2. *n.* (-s, -s) assent, consent, approval; affirmation; *– sagen,* give one's consent; *mit einem – beantworten,* answer in the affirmative. **–wohl,** *int.* yes indeed! surely! to be sure, certainly, of course. **–wort,** *n.* affirmation; consent; *einem sein* or *das –wort geben,* accept an offer of marriage.
jach, (*Poet. & archaic*) *see* **jäh.**
jachern, jachtern, *v.n.* (*aux.* h.) (*dial.*) romp, roister.
Jacht, *f.* (-en) yacht.
Jäckchen, *n.* (-s, –) vest, jacket *or* short coat for children.
Jacke, *f.* (-n) jacket; coat; jerkin; (*coll.*) *einem die – voll klopfen,* thrash a p. soundly; (*coll.*) *einem die – voll lügen,* stuff a p. with lies; *das ist – wie Hose,* that is all one *or* all the same, there is no difference.
Jagd, *f.* (-en), chase, hunt, pursuit; hunting, shooting, hunting-party, hunting expedition; the huntsmen, hounds, the hunt; *auf die – gehen,* go hunting *or* shooting; *– machen auf* (*Acc.*), give chase to, hunt, chase *or* run after; *hohe –,* deer-stalking. **–aufseher,** *m.* gamekeeper. **–bar,** *adj.* fit for the chase, fair game. **–berechtigt,** *adj.* licensed to shoot. **–berechtigung,** *f.* shooting-licence. **–beute,** *f.* bag, booty, quarry. **–bezirk,** *m.* hunting-ground, preserve. **–flieger,** *m.* fighter pilot (*Av.*). **–flinte,** *f.* sporting gun, (*archaic*) fowling piece. **–flugzeug,** *n.* fighter (plane) (*Av.*), pursuit plane (*Amer.*). **–freund,** *m.* sportsman. **–frevel,** *m.* poaching. **–geleit,** *n.* fighter escort. **–gerät,** *n.*, **–zeug,** *n.* hunting outfit. **–gerecht,** *adj.* skilled in the chase; broken in (*of dogs*). **–gerechtigkeit,** *f.* shooting rights. **–geschichte,** *f.* (hunter's) tall story. **–geschwader,** *n.* fighter (*or Amer.* pursuit) group (*Av.*). **–gesellschaft,** *f.* shooting-party. **–gesetz,** *n.* game law. **–gewehr,** *n.* sporting-gun. **–grenze,** *f.* boundary of a hunting district. **–gründe,** *m.pl.*; *in die ewigen –gründe,* into eternity, in *or* to the Elysian fields. **–haus,** *n.* shooting-box. **–horn,** *n.* hunting-horn. **–hund,** *m.* hound, setter. **–karte,** *f.* shooting-licence. **–kundig,** *adj.* skilled in hunting. **–kunst,** *f.* huntsmanship. **–leute,** *pl.* huntsmen, hunters. **–partie,** *f.* hunting-party, hunting expedition. **–pferd,** *n.* hunter. **–recht,** *n.* game-laws. **–revier,** *n., see* **–bezirk. –schein,** *m.* shooting licence. **–schloß,** *n.*, **–sitz,** *m.* hunting lodge. **–schutz,** *m.*, **–sicherung,** *f.* fighter escort (*Av.*). **–staffel,** *f.* fighter (*or Amer.* pursuit) squadron *or* unit (*Av.*). **–stück,** *n.* picture of a hunt, *etc.*; hunting-piece (*Mus.*). **–tasche,** *f.* game-bag. **–verband,** *m.* fighter (*or Amer.* pursuit) formation (*Av.*). **–zeit,** *f.* shooting season. **–zusammenkunft,** *f.* meet (*Hunt.*).
jagen, 1. *v.a.* chase, pursue, drive; *ein Witz jagte den anderen,* one witty remark followed the other; *einen auf die Straße –,* drive a p. into the street; *aus dem Hause –,* turn out of doors; *einem eine Kugel durch den Kopf –,* blow a p.'s brains out; *in die Flucht –,* put to flight. 2. *v.n.* (*aux.* s. & h.) hunt, chase; go *or* drive at full speed, rush, race, gallop; *nach einer S. –,* pursue with all one's might, (*coll.*) go all out to get; *davon –,* scamper away; *vorbei –,* gallop past, sweep by; (*auf*) *Hasen –,* go coursing hares, go hare-shooting; (*auf*) *Füchse –,* go fox-hunting; (*auf*) *Rotwild –,* go deer-stalking; *gut gejagt haben,* have had good sport. 3. *n.* hurry, rush, hot pursuit, galloping; hunting, chasing, shooting; shooting preserve, game reserve.
Jager, *m.* (-s), flying jib (*Naut.*), herring-smack.
Jäger, *m.* (-s,–), hunter, huntsman, sportsman; gamekeeper; rifleman, fusilier, yager (*Mil.*); fighter (pilot *or* plane) (*Av.*). **–ei,** *f.* huntsmanship, (*archaic*) venery, woodcraft. **–gehege,** *n.* hunting-ground. **–haus,** *n.* gamekeeper's house. **–joppe,** *f.* shooting-jacket. **–latein,** *n.* huntsmen's slang; tall stories. **–mäßig,** *adj.* huntsmanlike. **–meister,** *m.* chief ranger; master of hounds. **–smann,** *m.* hunter, huntsman. **–sprache,** *f.* hunting jargon.
jäh, *adj.* rapid, sudden, quick, hasty, rash, precipitate; steep, precipitous; *–es Ende,* sudden *or* violent end; *–e Flucht,* headlong flight; *–er Schrecken,* panic; *–er Tod,* sudden death; *–e Höhe,* precipitous peak. **–e,** *f.*, **–heit,** *f.* haste, precipitation; abruptness, suddenness; steepness, declivity; precipice. **–lings,** *adv.* abruptly; suddenly, precipitously, in violent haste. **–stotzig,** *adj.* (*dial.*) precipitous. **–zorn,** *m.* violent temper, sudden anger. **–zornig,** *adj.* irascible, hot-tempered.
Jahn, *m.* (*dial.*) strip of land, swath.
Jahr, *n.* (-(e)s, -e) year; *alle –e,* see *– für –*; *er ist schon bei –en,* he is already advanced in years; (*B.*) *fette –e,* prosperous years; *– für –,* year by year, every year; *in die –e kommen,* begin to grow old, be getting on in years; *in den besten –en,* in the prime of life; *es geht ins vierte – daß,* it is more than three years since; *zwei –e lang,* for two (whole) years; *nach –en,* after many years; *seit –en,* for years; *seit einigen –en,* of late years, for some years; *seit undenklichen –en,* since time immemorial, time out of mind; *übers –,* a year hence, next year; *über – und Tag,* a year and a day, (sometime) in the future; *ein – ums* or *übers andere,* every year, year after *or* by year; *vor einem –e,* a year ago; *vor –en,* years ago; *vor – und Tag,* quite a year ago; a long time ago; *zu –en kommen,* begin to grow old. **–anleihe,** *f.* annuity. **–aus,** *adv.*; *–aus, –ein,* year after year. **–buch,** *n.* year-book, annual, almanac. **–ein,** *adv., see* **–aus. –elang,** *adv.* (lasting) for years

–esabonnement, *n.* annual subscription (*to a journal*). **–esabschluß,** *m.* annual balance-sheet. **–esbeitrag,** *m.* annual subscription (*to a society*). **–esbericht,** *m.* annual report. **–(es)feier,** *f.*, **–(es)fest,** *n.* annual celebration, anniversary. **–esfolge,** *f.* (*nach*, in) chronological order. **–esfrist,** *f.* space of a year; *innerhalb –esfrist*, within a year. **–(es)gehalt,** *n.*, *see* **–(es)lohn. –eshälfte,** *f.* half-year. **–esklasse,** *f.* mobilization (*or coll.*) call-up group (*Mil.*). **–(es)lohn,** *m.* annual wages. **–esring,** *m.* annual circle (*in a tree*). **–estag,** *m.* anniversary. **–esviertel,** *n.* quarter of a year. **–esvierteltag,** *m.* quarter-day. **–eswechsel,** *m.*, **–eswende,** *f.* new year; *Wünsche zum –eswechsel*, New Year's greetings. **–eszahl,** *f.* date, year. **–eszeit,** *f.* season. **–fünft,** *n.* lustrum, quinquennium, quinquenniad, quinquennial period. **–gang,** *m.* age group, year's class, year of publication; year's vintage. **–gänger,** *m.* (*Swiss dial.*) p. born in same year, coeval. **–gebung,** *f.* judicial declaration of a p.'s majority (*Law*). **–geld,** *n.* yearly allowance; annuity, yearly dues. **–hundert,** *n.* (-s, -e) century. **–hundertfeier,** *f.* centenary. **–hundertwende,** *f.* turn of the century. **–markt,** *m.* annual fair. **–schuß,** *m.*, *see* **–wuchs. –tausend,** *n.* (-s, -e) millennium. **–weise,** *adv* annually. **–wuchs,** *m.* year's growth. **–zehnt,** *n.* (-s, -e) decennium, decade.

jähr–en, *v.r.*; *es* or *der Tag –t sich heute, daß . . .*, it is a year today since, **–ig,** *adj.* a year old; lasting a year; a year ago; (*usually in compounds, e.g.*) *zwei–ig*, two years old; *ein Zwei–iger*, a two-year old (boy). **–lich,** 1. *adj.* yearly, annual. 2. *adv.* every year, per annum. **–ling,** *m.* yearling (*animal*), annual (*plant*).

Jalousie, *f.* (-n), venetian blind.

Jamb–e, *m.* (-en, -en), **–us,** *m.* (-us, -en) iambus. **–isch,** *adj.* iambic.

Jammer, *m.* lamentation; misery, distress, wretchedness; *es ist ein –*, it is a pity. **–n,** 1. *v.n.* (*aux.* h.) (*über*) lament, mourn, grieve; moan, cry, wail. 2. *v.a.* (*pers. & impers.*) pity, feel sorry for; move to pity; (*B.*) *meine Seele –te der Armen*, my soul was grieved for the poor; *mich –t seine Not*, I pity his misery; *meine Freunde –n mich*, I pity my friends; *es –t mich*, I am moved to pity. **–bild,** *n.* picture of misery. **–blick,** *m.* piteous look. **–geheul,** *n.*, **–geschrei,** *n.* wail of lamentation. **–gesicht,** *n.* piteous look, rueful countenance. **–gestalt,** *f.* pitiable figure *or* object. **–lappen,** *m.* (*coll.*) sissy. **–leben,** *n.* miserable *or* wretched life. **–lied,** *n.* song of lamentation; dirge. **–nswert,** *adj.*, **–nswürdig,** *adj.* lamentable. **–ruf,** *m.* piteous wail. **–schade,** *adv.* a thousand pities, a very great pity. **–tal,** *n.* (*Poet.*) vale of tears *or* woe. **–voll,** *adj.* lamentable, woeful, pitiable, wretched, deplorable, miserable. **–zustand,** *m.* piteous condition.

jämmer–lich, *adj.* pitiable, miserable, wretched, deplorable. **–lichkeit,** *f.* wretchedness; pitiable condition. **–ling,** *m.* miserable wretch.

Janhagel, *m.* rabble, mob.

Janitschar, *m.* (-en, -en) janizary, janissary.

janken, *v.n.* (*dial.*) whine (*nach einer S.*, for a th.), hanker (after a th.).

Jänner, *m.* (*Austr. dial.*) *see* **Januar.**

Januar, *m.* (-s, -e) January.

jappen, japfen, *v.n.* (*aux.* h.) (*dial.*) gape; pant; yawn.

Jargon [*pron.* ʒarˈgɔ̃:] *m.* (-s, -s) jargon, parlance; gibberish.

Jasmin, *m.* (-s, -e) jasmine, jessamine; *gemeiner –*, white syringa.

Jaspis, *m.* (-ses, -se) jasper.

Jaß, *m.* a Swiss card game. **–(ss)en,** *v.n.* play this game.

jät–en, *v.a.* weed. **–hacke,** *f.*, **–haue,** *f.* hoe.

Jauche, *f.* (-n) dung water, liquid manure; ichor (*Med.*).

jauchze–n, *v.n.* (*aux.* h.) rejoice, shout with joy; exult, triumph. **–r,** *m.* shout (of joy).

jaulen, *v.a.* (*coll.*) whine, howl (*of dogs*).

Jause, *f.* (-n) (*Austr. dial.*) afternoon tea. **–n,** *v.n.* have *or* take tea.

Jazz, *m.* jazz. **–kapelle,** *f.* dance band.

[1]**je,** 1. *adv.* ever, always, at all times, at any time, at every time; in any case; at a time, each, apiece; (*before comparatives* =) the; *– zwei*, two at a time, in pairs; *er gab ihnen – zwei Äpfel*, he gave them two apples each; *– einer um den andern*, always one after another, alternately; *– nach*, according to, depending on; *– nachdem*, according as; according to circumstances, that depends; *– eher, – lieber* or *desto lieber* or *um so lieber*, the sooner the better; *ich habe sie – länger – lieber*, the longer I know her the more I love her. 2. *int.* well! ah! why! *– nun!* well now! well then! well really! **–doch,** *adv.* however, notwithstanding, nevertheless, yet. **–her,** *adv.* (*only in*) *von –her*, from time immemorial, ever since, all along. **–längerjelieber,** *m.* (*& Austr. n.*) honeysuckle, woodbine (*Lonicera caprifolium*) (*Bot.*). **–mals,** *adv.* ever, at any time. **–mand,** *indef. pron.* (*Acc.* -mand *&* -manden; *Gen.* -mandes; *Dat.* -mand *&* -mandem), somebody, someone; *sonst –mand*, somebody *or* anybody else; *irgend –mand*, anyone, anybody; *–mand Fremdes*, some stranger. **–weilen,** *adv.* (*archaic*), *see* **–weils. –weilig,** *adv.* actual, at the moment, for the time being, momentary; respective; *der –weilige Direktor*, the headmaster at the time being considered, (whoever may be) the headmaster at the moment. **–weils,** *adv.* at any given time, at times, from time to time.

[2]**je,** (*abbr. of* **Jesus**), *int.* heavens! gracious! *–mine! Herr –mine!* good gracious!

jed–enfalls, *adv.* at all events, in any case, by all means, however. **–er, –e, –es,** 1. *adj.* each, every, either, any; *auf –en* or *in –em Fall*, *see* **–enfalls,** *zu –er Zeit*, at all times; *an –em Orte*, in every place, everywhere; *–e leiseste Berührung*, the least *or* slightest touch; *–e beliebige Sorte*, any kind that you may choose. 2. *pron.* (ein -er, eine -e, ein -es) each, each one, every, either; everyone, everybody; *alles und –es, alle und –e*, one and all; *–e zehn Minuten*, every ten minutes; *–em das Seine*, to every man his due; (*Prov.*) *–er ist seines Glückes Schmied*, every man is the architect of his own fortune; (*Prov.*) *–er ist sich selbst der Nächste*, charity begins at home. **–erlei,** *indec. adj.* of every *or* any kind. **–ermann,** *pron.* everyone, everybody. **–erzeit,** *adv.* at any time, always. **–esmal,** *adv.* each time, every time, always; *–esmal wenn*, whenever, as often as. **–esmalig,** *adj.* existing, actual, in each case, then being; *wie es die –esmaligen Zustände erheischen*, according to the prevailing circumstances, as circumstances demand. **–weder, –wede, –wedes,** *pron.* (*Poet.*), *see* **jeglich–.**

jedoch, *see* [1]**je–.**

jeglich–er, –e, –es, *adj. & pron.* (*elevated style*), every, each; everyone; *–en Geschlechts*, of both sexes, of either sex.

jeher, *see* [1]**je–.**

Jelängerjelieber, *see* [1]**je–.**

jemals, *see* [1]**je–.**

jemand, *see* [1]**je–.**

jemine, *see* [2]**je.**

jen–er, –e, –es, 1. *dem. adj.* that; *auf –er Seite des Flusses*, on the other side of the river; *in –em Leben, in –er Welt*, in the life to come, in the other world. 2. *dem. pron.* that one, the former; *–e, welche*, those who; *bald dieses, bald –es*, now onc thing, now another. **–seit,** *prep.* (*Gen.*), *see* **–seits. –seitig,** *adj.* opposite; ulterior. **–seits,** 1. *prep. & adv.* on the other side (of), beyond, across; yonder. 2. *n.* the next world, the life to come, the hereafter.

jerum, *int.* (*for* **Jesus**); *o – !* dear me!

jetz–ig, *adj.* present, now existing, actual, modern; *–iger Zeit*, nowadays; *der –ige König*, the reigning *or* present king; *zum –igen Kurs*, at the current rate of exchange. **–t,** 1. *adv.* now, at present, at the present time; *gleich –t, gerade –t*, instantly, this very moment; *für –t*, for the present; *von –t an*, from this time, henceforth; *bis –t*, till now, up to now, as yet, hitherto; *nur –t erst, eben –t*, only just, just now. 2. *n.* the present, the present time. **–tzeit,** *f.* present, the present day.

jeweil–en, –ig, –s, *see* [1]**je–.**

Joch, *n.* (-(e)s, -e) yoke; cross-beams, transom,

pile (*bridges*); (*fig.*) burden, load; saddle (*mountains*), mountain ridge; land measure; *ins – spannen*, yoke; *sich ins – spannen*, work hard, slave; *zwei – Ochsen*, two pair *or* two yoke of oxen. **–bein,** *n.* cheek bone. **–brücke,** *f.* pile-bridge. **–en,** *v.a.* yoke. **–hölzer,** *n.pl.* crossbars. **–spannung,** *f.* span (*of bridge*). **–straße,** *f.* mountain pass. **–träger,** *m.* cross-beams.

Jockei, *m.* (-s, -s) jockey.

Jod, *n.* iodine; *mit – behandeln*, **–ieren,** *v.a.* iodate (*Chem.*), iodize (*Med.*, *Phot.*). **–id,** *n.* iodide. **–kalium,** *n.* potassium iodide. **–oform,** *n.* iodoform. **–tinktur,** *f.* tincture of iodine.

jod–eln, *v.n.* (*aux.* h.) yodel. **–ler,** *m.* (-ers, -er), yodeler.

Johannis–beere, *f* red-currant. **–brot,** *n.* carob-bean. **–käfer,** *m.*, **–wurm,** *m.*, **–würmchen,** *n.* glow-worm. **–kraut,** *n* St. John's wort (*Hypericum perforatum*) (*Bot.*). **–nacht,** *f.* midsummer night. **–tag,** *m.* midsummer day. **–trieb,** *m.* second bloom; late love.

johlen, *v.n.* (*aux.* h.) howl, yell, bawl, hoot.

Jolle, *f.* (-n) dinghy, jolly-boat. **–nführer,** *m.* boatman, waterman.

Jongl–eur, *m.*(-s, -e) juggler. **–ieren,** *v.a. & n.* juggle.

Joppe, *f.* (-n) jerkin, jacket.

Jot, *n.* (-s, -s) letter J. **–a,** *n.* (-as) iota; jot, whit.

Journal, *n.* (-s, -e) newspaper; (*C.L.*) daybook. **–ist,** *m.* (-en, -en) journalist. **–ismus,** *m.*, **–istik,** *f.* journalism.

jovial, *adj.* jovial. **–ität,** *f.* joviality.

Jubel, *m.* rejoicing, exultation, jubilation. **–feier,** *f.*, **–fest,** *n.* jubilee. **–gesang,** *m.* song of rejoicing. **–greis,** *m.* lively old man, (*coll.*) gay old spark. **–jahr,** *n.* jubilee; (*coll.*) *alle –jahre einmal*, once in a blue moon. **–n,** *v.n.* (*aux.* h.) rejoice, shout with joy, exult. **–paar,** *n.* couple celebrating their silver *or* golden wedding. **–ruf,** *m.* acclamation, shout of joy. **–schmaus,** *m.* celebration banquet. **–tag,** *m.* day of rejoicing, jubilee.

Jubil–ar, *m.* (-s, -e), p. celebrating his jubilee. **–äum,** *n.* (-äums, -äen), jubilee, anniversary. **–ieren,** *v.n.* (*aux.* h.) exult, (*coll.*) crow over; shout with joy.

juch, –he, –hei(sa), –heirassa(ssa), *int.* hurrah! **–heien, –zen,** *v.n.* shout for joy. **–zer,** *m.* shout of joy.

Juchten, 1. *n.* (*& Austr. dial. m.*) Russia leather. 2. *adj.* in *or* made of Russia leather. **–band,** *m.*, **–einband,** *m.* Russia(n)-leather binding.

juck–en, 1. *v.n.* (*aux.* h.), *v.a. & imp.* itch, irritate; scratch, rub; *es –t mich* or *mir am Arm*, my arm itches; *die Ohren –en ihm*, he is inquisitive; *es –t mir in den Fingern*, my fingers itch to be at (him, it, *etc.*); *das Fell –t ihn* or *ihm*, he is itching for a fight; *die Hand –t ihm*, he expects a tip *or* present; (*Prov.*) *wen's* or *wem's –t, der kratze sich*, let those whom the cap fits wear it. 2. *v.r.* (*dial.*) scratch o.s. 3. *subst. n.* itching, itch.

Jucker, *m.* (-s, –) carriage horse. **–zug,** *m.* four-in-hand.

Jude, *m.*, *see the Index of Names.*

Jugend, *f.* youth, adolescence; early period; young people; (*Prov.*) *– hat keine Tugend*, you cannot put an old head on young shoulders; boys will be boys. *von – auf*, from the earliest years. **–alter,** *n.* (days of) youth. **–bewegung,** *f.* youth movement. **–blüte,** *f.* bloom of youth. **–ertüchtigung,** *f.* physical training of youth. **–erziehung,** *f.* education of youth, early education. **–feuer,** *n.* ardour of youth. **–freund,** *m.* friend of one's youth, school-friend, chum. **–fülle,** *f.* exuberance of youth. **–fürsorge,** *f.* young people's welfare. **–gefährte,** *m.*, **–genosse,** *m.* companion of one's youth. **–gericht,** *n.* juvenile court. **–herberge,** *f.* youth hostel. **–jahre,** *n.pl.* early years. **–kraft,** *f.* youthful strength. **–kräftig,** *adj.* fresh, vigorous. **–lich,** *adj.* youthful, juvenile; *–licher Verbrecher*, juvenile delinquent, young criminal. **–liche(r),** *m. & f.* boy *or* girl; (*pl.*) young people, juveniles. **–lichkeit,** *f.* youthfulness. **–liebe,** *f.* early love, first love, calf-love; old sweetheart, old flame. **–pflege,** *f.*, *see* **–fürsorge. –schöne,** *f.*, **–schönheit,** *f.* bloom of youth. **–schriften,** *f.pl.* books for the young. **–streich,** *m.* youthful prank, *–streiche machen*, sow one's wild oats. **–wachstum,** *n.* early growth. **–werk,** *n.* early work (*of a writer*), (*pl.*) juvenilia. **–wert,** *adj.* fit for juveniles (*Film*). **–zeit,** *f.* youth, early days.

juhe! (*int.*) (*Swiss dial.*) *see* **juchhe.**

Jul– (*in compounds*) Yule. **–block,** *m.* Yule log. **–fest,** *n.* Christmas festivities. **–feuer,** *n.* ceremonial fire for the winter solstice. (*dial.*) **–klapp,** *n.* Christmas present traditionally thrown in at window. **–monat,** *m.*, **–mond,** *m.* December.

Juli, *m.* (-s) July.

jung, *adj.* (*comp.* jünger, *sup.* jüngst) young, youthful; new, fresh; recent; early; *–e Erbsen*, green peas; *–es Blut*, young person, youngster; *–er Boden*, reclaimed land; *–er Morgen*, early morning; *–er Wein*, new wine; *die –e Frau*, newly married woman, young wife, bride; (*Prov.*) *– gewohnt, alt getan*, what is bred in the bone will come out in the flesh. **–brunnen,** *m.* fountain of youth. **–e,** *m.* (-en, -en *or* (*dial. & coll. pl.* –ens *or* -s)) boy (*der –e*, the boy; *ein –e*, a boy), lad, youth; apprentice; errand *or* message boy; *alter –e!* old fellow! old boy! *mein lieber –e!* my dear fellow *or* chap! *die blauen –s*, the boys in blue. **–e(s)** *n.* (-en, -e(n)) young, offspring (*of animals*), cub, puppy, calf, whelp, *etc.*; *ein –es* a young one; *–e werfen*, *see* **jungen. –en,** *v.a.* bring forth young (*of animals*). **–enmäßig,** *adj.* boyish. **–enhaft,** *adj.* boyish. **–fer,** *f.* (-n) virgin, maid, young girl; (*archaic*) miss; lady's maid; *alte –fer*, old maid. **–fernerde,** *f.* virgin soil. **–fernfahrt,** *f.* maiden voyage (*of a ship*). **–ferngeburt,** *f.* parthenogenesis. **–fernglas,** *n.* selenit. **–fernhaft,** *adj.*, *see* **jüngferlich. –fernhäutchen,** *n.* hymen (*Anat.*). **–fernkäfer,** *m.* ladybird. **–fernkind,** *n.* illegitimate *or* natural child; first-born. **–fernkranz,** *m.* bridal wreath. **–fernmetall,** *n.* native metal. **–fernraub,** *m.* rape. **–fernräuber,** *m.* ravisher. **–fernrede,** *f.* maiden speech. **–fernschaft,** *f.* maidenhood, virginity. **–fernschänder,** *m.* ravisher. **–fernschwarm,** *m.* swarm of young bees. **–fernstand,** *m.* virginity; spinsterhood. **–fernzeugung,** *f.*, *see* **–ferngeburt. –frau,** *f.* virgin; maid, maiden; Virgo (*Astr.*); *heilige –frau*, Blessed Virgin; *–frau von Orleans*, Maid of Orleans; *von der –frau Maria geboren*, born of the Virgin Mary. **–fräulich,** *adj.* maidenly, modest, coy, chaste, pure, virginal. **–fräulichkeit,** *f.* maidenliness, virginal purity, coyness. **–frauschaft,** *f.* (*rare*) maidenhood; virginity. **–gesell(e),** *m.* bachelor; junior journeyman. **–gesellenstand,** *m.* bachelorhood. **–herr,** *m.* (*archaic*) young nobleman. **–mädchen,** *n.* (*Swiss dial.*) girl. **–mädel,** *n.* (*Nat. Soc.*) young member of girls' organization, Nazi 'Girl Guide'. **–mann,** *m.* (-männer & –mannen) (*Nat. Soc.*) pupils of political training establishment, party probationers *or* cadets. **–mannschaften,** *f.pl.* companies of youth. **–steinzeit,** *f.* neolithic age. **–tertiär,** *n.* miocene period. **–vieh,** *n.* young cattle. **–wuchs,** *m.* young growth. **–wuchsgrenze,** *f.* timber line. **–zeitlich,** *adj.* recent.

jüng–er, 1. *adj.* (*comp. of* jung) younger; later; junior; puisne. 2. *m.* disciple; follower, adherent; (*B.*) *die zwölf –er*, the apostles. **–erschaft,** *f.* disciples. **–ferlich,** *adj.* maidenly, coy, timid, prudish. **–ling,** *m.* young man, youth; adolescent, stripling. **–st,** 1. *adj.* (*sup. of* jung) youngest; latest, last; recent; *zu –st*, finally, in the end; *das –ste Gericht, der –ste Tag*, Judgement Day, doomsday; *Ihr –stes Schreiben*, your last letter; *sie ist nicht mehr die –ste*, she is no longer as young as she was *or* not as young as she used to be. 2. *adv.* lately, recently, the other day; *aus dem –st Gesagten*, from what has just been said. **–stenrecht,** *n.* right of juniority (*opp. to primogeniture*). **–stens, –sthin,** *see* **–st** (2).

Juni, *m.* June.

Junker, *m.* (-s, –) country squire; titled landowner; (*pl.*) Junkers, aristocratic landowners (*in Prussian territories*). **–haft,** *adj.*, **–lich,** *adj.* cavalier; like a young nobleman. **–herrschaft,** *f.* squirearchy, junkerdom. **-schaft,** *f.* body of young noblemen *or* squires; squirearchy, junkerdom. **-tum,** *n.* system of squirearchy, aristocratic ownership of landed estates in Prussian eastern provinces, manners and way of life characteristic of petty nobility.

Jur-a, 1. (*in compounds*) **-akalk,** *m.* Jurassic *or* oolitic limestone. 2. *pl.* (*of* **Lat.** jus) law; *-a studieren,* study law. **-at,** *m.* deponent (*on oath*). **-ato,** *adv.* upon oath. **-idisch,** *adj.* juridical. **-ist,** *m.* (-en, -en) lawyer; law student. **-istisch,** *adj.* legal, in law, juridical; *-istische Fakultät,* faculty of law, board of legal studies.

just, 1. *adv.* just, exactly; just now, only just, even now. 2. *adj.* proper, right; *nicht –,* uncanny; *das ist – nicht nötig,* that is not altogether necessary. **-ieren,** *v.a.* adjust; justify (*Typ.*). **-iergewicht,** *n.* standard. **-ierschraube,** *f.* adjusting *or* set screw. **-ierwaage,** *f.* adjusting balance. **-ifizieren,** *v.a.* justify. **-itiar** (*Austr.* **-itiär**), *m.* (-s, -e) justiciary.

Justiz, *f.* administration of the law. **-amt,** *n.* court of law. **-beamte,** *m.* officer of justice. **-kollegium,** *n.*, **-hof,** *m.*, **-kammer,** *f.* court *or* chamber of justice. **-kommissär,** *m.* (*archaic*) attorney-at-law. **-minister,** *m.* Minister of Justice (*combines the functions of British Lord Chancellor, Attorney-General and Solicitor-General*). **-mord,** *m.* judicial murder, execution of an innocent person. **-palast,** *m.* Law Courts. **-pflege,** *f.* administration of justice. **-rat,** *m.* King's *or* Queen's Counsel. **-versehen,** *n.* miscarriage of justice. **-wachtmeister,** *m.* court officer *or* attendant. **-wesen,** *n.* judicial *or* legal affairs, judicature; the law.

Juwel, *n.* & *m.* (-s, -e & -en) jewel, gem, precious stone; (*pl.*) jewellery; (*also fig.*) treasure, priceless gift (*of a friend, servant, etc.*). **-ier,** *m.* (-s, -e) jeweller.

Jux, *m.* (-es, -e) (*coll.*) lark, spree, practical joke; (*dial.*) filth, muck. **-en,** *v.a.* (*coll.*) lark, frolic, play practical jokes; (*coll.*) *einen -en,* pull a p.'s leg.

K

See also under **C.**

K, k, *n.* K, k.

Kabal-e, *f.* (-en) intrigue, conspiracy, cabal; *-en schmieden,* hatch a plot, intrigue.

Kabarett, *n.* (-s, -e) cabaret; entré dish. **-ist,** *m.* cabaret artiste.

Kabbal-a, *f.* cab(b)ala, Jewish oral tradition; occult lore. **-istisch,** *adj.* cab(b)alistic, occult, esoteric.

Kabbel-ei, *f.* (-eien) (*dial.*) squabble, quarrel. **-n,** *v.n.* (*aux.* h.) & *r.* (*dial.*) bandy words, squabble, quarrel; *die See -t* or *geht -n,* the sea is choppy. **-ig,** *adj.* choppy (*of sea*). **-ung,** *f.* choppiness (*of sea*).

[1]**Kabel,** *n.* (-s, –) cable; *oberirdisches –,* overland cable; *unterirdisches –,* underground cable; *unterseeisches –,* submarine cable. **-ar,** *f.* messenger (*Naut.*). **-aufführung,** *f.* point where cable emerges. **-brunnen,** *m.* cable manhole. **-dampfer,** *m.* cable layer, cable-laying vessel. **-depesche,** *f.* cable(gram); *eine -depesche senden,* cable. **-gatt,** *n.* (-s, -e) cable locker (*Naut.*). **-klüse,** *f.* hawse-pipe (*Naut.*). **-länge,** *f.* cable's length (*120 fathoms*). **-legung,** *f.* laying of a (telegraphic) cable. **-n,** *v.a.* & *n.* (*aux.* h.) cable, send a cablegram. **-muffe,** *f.* cable coupling. **-nachricht,** *f.* news *or* information sent by cable. **-seil,** *n.*, *see* **-tau.** **-tanz,** *m.* sailor's hornpipe. **-tau,** *n.* cable. **-verbindung,** *f.* cable splice (*Naut.*).

[2]**Kabel,** *f.* (-n) (*dial.*) lot, share.

Kabeljau, *m.* (-s, -s & -e) cod. **-(leber)tran,** *m.* cod-liver oil.

Kabine, *f.* (-n) cabin (*Naut.*), cockpit (*Av.*); bathing hut, cubicle.

Kabinett, *n.* (-s, -e) cabinet; body of ministers; collections (*of coins, gems, etc.*); section *or* department (of a museum); private room; water-closet; (*archaic*) *aufs – gehen,* go to the lavatory. **-auslese,** *f.* choice wine. **-photographie,** *f.* cabinet photograph. **-sbefehl,** *m.* order in council. **-sfrage,** *f.* vital question; question involving the cabinet; *die —sfrage stellen,* appeal to the confidence of the House (*Parl.*); *aus einer S. eine -sfrage machen,* make a vital issue of a matter. **-sjustiz,** *f.* high-handed *or* warped justice. **-sminister,** *m.* cabinet minister. **-sorder,** *f.*, *see* **-sbefehl.** **-srat,** *m.* cabinet council. **-ssiegel,** *n.* privy seal. **-ssitzung,** *f.* cabinet meeting. **-stück,** *n.* museum piece *or* specimen.

Kabriolett, *n.* (-(e)s, -e) cab, cabriolet.

Kabuse, *f.* (-n) (*coll.* & *dial.*) shack, shanty, small hut; galley, caboose (*Naut.*), *see* **Kombüse.**

Kachel, *f.* (-n) (glazed) tile. **-ofen,** *m.* tiled stove.

Kacke, *f.* (*vulg.*) excrement, stool. **-en,** *v.n.* (*aux.* h.) go to stool.

Kadaver, *m.* (-s, –) carcass, corpse. **-fliege,** *f.* carrion-fly; **-gehorsam** *m.* utter subordination, slavish obedience, abject submissiveness.

Kadenz, *f.* (-en) cadence (*Mus.*).

Kader, *m.* & *n.* cadre.

Kadett, *m.* (-en, -en) cadet; midshipman. **-enanstalt,** *f.* officer's training-school, cadet college. **-enkorps,** *n.* cadet corps. **-enschule,** *f.* military academy. **-enschulschiff,** *n.* training-ship.

kadu-k, *adj.* frail, broken (down). **-zieren,** *v.n.* condemn (as failed *or* worthless); destroy, break down.

Käfer, *m.* (-s, –) beetle; (*sl.*) young girl, wench; (*sl.*) *sie ist ein netter –,* she is a nice bit of stuff *or* skirt. **-artig,** *adj.* coleopterous. **-larve,** *f.* grub. **-schnecke,** *f.* Chitonidae (*Mollusc.*).

Kaff, *n.* & *m.* (-(e)s, -e) (*dial.*) chaff; rubbish, nonsense, bosh; (*n. only*) (*coll.*) hamlet, god-forsaken village.

Kaffee, 1. *m.* coffee; (mid-morning) coffee, afternoon tea. 2. *n.* coffee-house, café; *eine Tasse – trinken,* take a cup of coffee; *wollen Sie morgen nachmittag zum – zu uns kommen?* will you come to tea tomorrow? *– verkehrt,* more milk than coffee. **-base,** *f.*, *see* **-schwester.** **-bohne,** *f.* coffee-bean. **-brenner,** *m.* coffee-roaster. **-brötchen,** *n.* breakfast roll. **-dick,** *n.* (*dial.*) coffee grounds. **-geschirr,** *n.* coffee-service. **-grund,** *m.* coffee-grounds. **-haus,** *n.* café. **-kanne,** *f.* coffee-pot. (*coll.*) **-klatsch,** *m.* gossip over a cup of coffee, afternoon-tea party. **-kränzchen,** *n.* coffee party. **-löffel,** *m.* coffee-spoon. **-maschine,** *f.* coffee-percolator. **-mühle,** *f.* coffee-mill *or* grinder; (*sl.*) dog fight (*Av.*). **-muhme,** *f.*, *see* **-schwester.** **-röster,** *m.*, **-schütter,** *m.*, **-trommel,** *f.* coffee-roaster. **-satz,** *m.* coffee-grounds. (*coll.*) **-schwester,** *f.* coffee lover; gossip. **-seiher,** *m.* coffee-strainer. **-trichter,** *m.* coffee-filter. **-sorten** *f.pl.* brands of coffee. **-topf,** *m.* coffee-pot.

Käfig, *m.* (-s, -e) cage; bird-cage; (*sl.*) prison; *im goldenen –,* in a gilded cage.

Kaftan, *m.* (-s, -e (& *Austr. dial.*) -s) caftan.

kahl, *adj.* bare, naked; unfledged (*of birds*); callow; dismantled (*of ships*), denuded; sterile, barren, leafless; paltry, poor, sorry, threadbare; empty, (*sl.*) skint; *-e Ausflucht,* poor excuse; *– bestehen,* come off poorly; *-es Geschwätz,* empty *or* idle talk. **-bäuche,** *m.pl.* apodes (*Icht.*). **-fleckig,** *adj.* having threadbare spots. **-geschoren,** close cropped. **-heit,** *f.* baldness, alopecia; bleakness; barrenness. **-köpfig,** *adj.* bald-headed. **-schlag,** *m.*, **-trieb,** *m.* complete deforestation, clearing.

Kahm, (*dial.*) **Kahn,** *m.* mould (*on liquids*). **-en,** *v.n.* (*aux.* h. & s.) grow mouldy. **-ig,** *adj.* mouldy, stale, ropy (*of wine*).

Kahn, *m.* (-(e)s, ⸚e) boat, barge, canoe, skiff; scapha (*Surg.*); *see* **Kahm.** **-bein,** *n.* scaphoid bone, navicular bone. **-fahren,** *v.n.* (*aux.* h.) go boating. **-fahrt,** *f.* boat trip.

Kai, *m.* (-s, -e (& *Austr. dial.* -s)) quay, wharf; embankment. **-arbeiter,** *m.* docker, longshoreman. **-gebühr,** *f.*, **-geld,** *n.* wharfage, pier-money.

Kaiman, *m.* (-s, -e (& *Austr. dial*) -s) alligator, cayman.

Kaiser, *m.* (-s, –) emperor; *der frühere* –, the ex-Kaiser; *den – einen guten Mann sein lassen*, let matters take their course; *sich um des –s Bart streiten*, quarrel about nothing; *auf den alten – borgen*, borrow with no intention of repaying, abuse one's credit; (*B.*) *gebt dem – was des –s ist*, render unto Caesar the things which are Caesar's; (*Prov.*) *wo nichts ist, hat (selbst) der – sein Recht verloren*, where nought's to be got, kings lose their scot; you cannot get blood out of a stone. **–adler,** *m.* imperial eagle (*Aquila heliaca*) (*Orn.*). **–bart,** *m.* dundreary, mutton-chop whiskers. **–blau,** *n.* smalt. **–format,** *n.* imperial (paper) (22″ × 32″). **–haus,** *n.* imperial family *or* house. **–in,** *f.* empress; *die –inmutter* or *–inwitwe*, the Dowager Empress. **–krone,** *f.* imperial crown; crown imperial (*Fritillaria imperialis*) (*Bot.*). **–lich,** *adj.* imperial; *die –lichen*, the imperial troops; *–lich-königlich, adj.* royal and imperial (*title of the Hapsburgs*); (*gut*) *–lich gesinnt*, siding with the emperor; supporting the imperial party. **–ling,** *m.* would-be emperor; golden agaric (*Amanita caesarea*) (*Bot.*). **–los,** *adj.*; *die –lose Zeit*, Interregnum (1150–73). **–mantel,** *m.* cloak, ulster; mother-of-pearl butterfly (*Argynnis paphia*) (*Ent.*). **–pracht,** *f.* imperial state *or* splendour. **–reich,** *n.* empire. **–schlange,** *f.* boa-constrictor. **–schnitt,** *m.* Caesarean section *or* operation. **–schrift,** *f.* great primer (*Typ.*). **–schwamm,** *m.*, *see* **–ling.** **–stadt,** *f.* imperial town. **–treu,** *adj.* loyal to the emperor. **–tum,** *n.* (-s, -er) empire; imperial dignity; reign. **–wetter,** *n.* glorious weather. **–würde,** *f.* imperial dignity.

Kajak, *m.* & *n.* (-s, -e & -s) folding *or* collapsible canoe, light canoe (*of Esquimaux*).

Kaje, *f.* (-n) (*dial.*) dyke, embankment.

Kajüte, *f.* (-n) cabin, berth; *erste* –, saloon.

Kakadu, *m.* (-s, -s (& *rare*) -e) cockatoo.

Kakao, *m.* cocoa (*the product*); cacao (*the tree & seed*); (*coll.*) *einen durch den – ziehen*, make s.o. look ridiculous.

Kakerlak, *m.* (-s & -en, -en) cockroach; (*dial.*) albino.

Kako–, (*in compounds*) bad. **–kratie,** *f.* bad government. **–phonie,** *f.* cacophony.

Kak–tee, *f.*, **–tus,** *m.* (–, -teen, (& *Austr. dial.*) -tusses, -tusse) cactus.

Kalander, *m.* calendering machine, glazing rollers (*Pap.*). **–n,** *v.a.* calender.

Kalauer, *m.* (-s, –) (*coll.*) pun, stale joke, chestnut. **–n,** *v.a.* make puns.

Kalb, *n.* (-(e)s, ⸚er) calf; fawn; (*fig.*) ninny; *ein – abbinden*, wean a calf; (*fig.*) *das – ins Auge schlagen*, tread on someone's toes; *das goldene – anbeten*, worship the golden calf; (*B.*) *mit fremdem –e pflügen*, plough with another p.'s heifer, profit by another's work, plagiarize. **–e,** *f.* (-en) heifer. **–en,** *v.n.* (*aux.* h.) calve. **–erig,** *adj.* giggling. **–ern,** *v.n.* behave foolishly; snigger, titter, giggle. **–fell,** *n.* calfskin; drum; *dem –fell folgen*, follow the call of the army, follow the colours. **–fleisch,** *n.* veal. **–leder,** *n.* calf (leather); *in –leder gebunden*, bound in calf. **–sbraten,** *m.* roast veal. **–sbröschen,** *n.*, **–sdrüse,** *f.*, *see* **–smilch.** **–skeule,** *f.*, **–sschlegel,** *m.* leg of veal. **–skotelett,** *n.* veal cutlet. **–smilch,** *f.* sweetbread. **–snierenbraten,** *m.* loin of veal. **–spergament,** *n.* vellum. **–sschnitte,** *f.*, **–sschnitzel,** *n.* veal cutlet.

Kälber–drüse, *f.* calf's sweetbread. **–lab,** *n.*, **–magen,** *m.* rennet. **–n,** *v.n.* (*aux.* h.) be frolicsome, romp. **–ne(s),** *n.* veal. (*dial.*) **–stoß,** *m.* leg of veal.

Kaldaunen, *f.pl.* (*dial.*) intestines, tripe.

Kalebasse, *f.* (-n), calabash.

Kalender, *m.* (-s, –) calendar, almanac; *das steht nicht in meinem* –, that is nothing to me, I know nothing of that; *rot im – angestrichener Tag*, red-letter day. **–block,** *m.* tear-off calendar. **–rechnung,** *f.*; *Russische –rechnung*, old style.

Kalesche, *f.* (-n) light carriage.

Kalfak–ter, *m.* (-s, –), **–tor,** *m.* (-s, -en) boilerman, caretaker; toady, spy.

kalfatern, *v.n.* (*aux.* h.) caulk (*Naut.*).

Kali, *n.* (*abbr. of* **–um**) potash; *ätzendes* – caustic potash, potassium hydrate; *blausaures* –, cyanide of potassium; *chlorsaures* –, chlorate of potassium. **–alaun,** *n.* alum. **–bikarbonat,** *n.* bicarbonate of potash. **–blau,** *n.* Prussian blue. **–dünger,** *m.* potash manure, fertilizer. **–hydrat,** *n.* potassium hydrate. **–lauge,** *f.* potash lye, caustic lye. **–nitrat,** *n.* saltpetre, nitre, potassium nitrate. **–pflanze,** *f.* glasswort, alkaline plant. **–saltpeter,** *n.*, *see* **–nitrat.** **–um,** *n.* potassium.

Kaliber, *n.* (-s, –) calibre, bore, gauge; (*coll.*) sort, kind, quality. **–mäßig,** *adj.* true to gauge. **–zirkel,** *m.* callipers.

kalibrieren, *v.a.* take the size, gauge; calibrate.

Kalif, *m.* (-en, -en) caliph. **–at,** *n.* (-(e)s, -e) caliphate.

Kaliko, *m.* (-s, -s) calico.

Kalk, *m.* (-(e)s, -e) lime, limestone, chalk, calcium; *ätzender* or *gebrannter* –, quicklime, unslaked *or* anhydrous lime; *gelöschter* –, slaked lime; *kohlensaurer* –, carbonate of lime; *verwitterter* –, see *gelöschter* –; *– brennen*, calcine lime; *mit – bewerfen*, roughcast. **–ablagerung,** *f.* calcareous deposit, lime deposit. **–anlagerung,** *f.* calcification. **–anwurf,** *m.* plaster, parget of lime. **–artig,** *adj.* calcareous, chalky, limy. **–boden,** *m.* calcareous soil. **–brennen,** *n.* lime-burning. **–brennerei,** *f.* lime-kiln. **–bruch,** *m.* limestone quarry. **–düngung,** *f.* liming (*the soil*). **–en,** *v.a.* dress *or* cover with lime, whitewash. **–erde,** *f.* calcareous earth, calcium oxide. **–farbe,** *f.* distemper. **–fels,** *m.* limestone. **–grube** *f.* lime-pit. **–haltig,** *adj.* calcareous, hard (*of water*). **–hütte,** *f.* lime-kiln. **–hydrat,** *n.* slaked lime. **–ig,** *adj.* chalky, calcareous, hard (*of water*). **–kelle,** *f.* trowel. **–kies,** *m.* limestone gravel. **–malerei,** *f.* fresco-painting. **–milch,** *f.* slaked lime, whitewash. **–mulde,** *f.* mortar-trough. **–ofen,** *m.* lime-kiln. **–pfeife,** *f.* clay-pipe. **–schicht,** *f.* chalk layer. **–stein,** *m.* limestone. **–tünche,** *f.* whitewash. **–wand,** *f.* plaster-wall.

kälken, *v.n.*, *see* **kalken.**

Kalkül, *m.* (-s, –e) calculation, assessment, estimate.

kalkulieren, *v.a.* calculate, reckon, estimate.

Kall, *m.* (*dial.*) chatter, prattle. **–en,** (*dial.*) chatter, prattle.

Kalle, *f.* (*vulg.*) lover, mistress.

Kalligraph, *m.* (-en, -en) calligraphist. **–ie,** *f.* calligraphy.

kall–ös, *adj.* callous, hard, hardened (*Med., Bot.*). **–us,** *m.* (–, -sse) callosity, hardening (*of skin*) (*Med., Bot.*).

Kalmäuser, *m.* (-s, –) grumbler, grouser, misanthrope. **–ei,** *f.* moping, misanthropy. **–n,** *v.n.* (*aux.* h.) mope.

Kalme, *f.* calm, windless period (*Naut.*). **–ngürtel,** *m.* doldrums (*Naut.*).

Kalmus, *m.* (-se) calamus (*Acorus calamus*) (*Bot.*).

Kalomel, *n.* mercurious chloride, calomel.

Kalori–e, *f.* (-en) thermal unit, calorie. **–fer,** *n.* (-s, -s) heating element, radiator. **–metrie,** *f.* measurement of heat.

Kalotte, *f.* (-n) (priest's) skull-cap.

kalt, *adj.* (*comp.* kälter, *sup.* kältest) cold, cool, chill, chilly; frigid, indifferent, callous, passionless, restrained, calm; *–e Angst*, chill of terror; *– bleiben*, keep cool, keep one's temper; *–en Blutes*, in cold blood; *–er Brand*, gangrene, mortification; *–e Ente*, cold punch; *–e Fährte*, cold scent (*Hunt.*); *–es Fieber*, ague; *– keilen*, quarry without blasting; *–e Küche*, cold dishes, cold foods; *–e Schale*, *see* **–schale;** *–er Schlag*, lightning that strikes without igniting; *mir ist* –, I am cold; *– stellen*, put into cold storage; shelve (*a th.*), *see* **–stellen;** *es überläuft mich –, es läuft mir – über den Rücken*, a cold shudder runs down my back; *–e Zone*, frigid zone. **–blütig,** *adj.* cold-blooded; calm, composed, deliberate. **–blütigkeit,** *f.* cold-bloodedness; composure. **–blütler,** *m.* cold-blooded animal. **–brüchig,** *adj.* brittle from cold; cold-short (*Metall.*). **–gezogen,** *adj.* cold-drawn (*Metall.*). **–grundig,** *adj.*, **–gründig,** *adj.* cold (*of land*).

-herzig, *adj.* hard-hearted. **-luftfront**, *f.* cold front (*Meteor.*). (*coll.*) **-machen**, *v.a.* kill (*a p.*). **-nadelarbeit**, *f.* dry-point etching. **-schale**, *f.* cold fruit soup. **-schmied**, *m.* coppersmith, wrought-iron worker. **-sinn**, *m.* coldness, indifference, insensibility. **-sinnig**, *adj.* cold, indifferent. **-stellen**, *v.a.* remove (*a p.*) from office, debar (*a p.*) from having influence, make (*a p.*) innocuous *or* incapable of interfering. **-verarbeitung**, *f.* cold working (*Metall.*). **-walzen**, *n.* cold rolling (*Metall.*). **-wasserheilanstalt**, *f.* hydropathic (establishment). **-wasserkur**, *f.* hydropathic treatment.

Kälte, *f.* cold, coldness, chill, chilliness; coolness, frigidity, indifference; *vor – zittern*, shiver with cold. **-beständig**, *adj.* resistant to cold, non-freezing. **-beständigkeit**, *f.* non-freezing quality. **-empfindlich**, *adj.* sensitive to cold. **-erzeugend**, *adj.* frigorific. **-erzeugung**, *f.* refrigeration. **-festigkeit**, *f.*, *see* **-beständigkeit**. **-n**, *v.a.* make cold; *mit Eis –n*, ice. **-grad**, *m.* degree of frost. **-industrie**, *f.* cold-storage industry. **-maschine**, *f.* refrigerator. **-mischung**, *f.* freezing-mixture. **-welle**, *f.* cold spell. **-wüste**, *f.* tundra.

kalzi-nieren, *v.a.* calcine. **-um**, *n.* calcium.

kam, kam(e)st, käme, *see* **kommen**.

Kamarill-a, *f.* (-en) camarilla, court-party.

kamb-ieren, *v.n.* deal in bills, do exchange business. **-ist**, *m.* money-changer, financier.

kambrisch, *adj.* Cambrian (*Geol.*).

Kambüse, *f. see* **Kombüse**.

Kamee, *f.* (-n), **Kameo**, *m.* (-s, -n) cameo.

Kamel, *n.* (-s, -e) camel; (*coll.*) blockhead, numskull, dolt; *Mücken zu -en machen*, make mountains out of molehills. **-abteilung**, *f.* camel corps. **-garn**, *n.* mohair. **-hengst**, *m.* male camel. **-kuh**, *f.*, **-stute**, *f.* female camel. **-ziege**, *f.* Angora goat.

Kamelie, *f.* (-n) camellia.

Kamelopard, *m.* (-en *or* -(e)s, -e(n)) giraffe, (*archaic*) camelopard.

Kamelott, *m.* (-(e)s, -e) Angora cloth, camlet,

Kamera, *f.* (*pl.* -s) camera (*Phot.*).

Kamerad, *m.* (-en, -en) comrade, mate, companion, colleague, fellow (worker, *etc.*); (*fam.*) chum. **-schaft**, *f.* comradeship, fellowship, companionship, camaraderie; (*Nat. Soc.*) squad of Hitler Youth. **-schaftlich**, 1. *adj.* companionable, friendly. 2. *adv.* as comrades. **-schaftlichkeit**, *f.*, *see* **-schaftsgefühl**. **-schaftsehe**, *f.* companionate marriage. **-schaftsgefühl**, *n.*, **-schaftsgeist**, *m.* camaraderie, fellow-feeling. **-schaftshaus**, *n.* students' union.

Kameral-ien, *pl.*, *see* **-istik**. **-ist**, *m.* (-en, -en) student of public affairs. **-istik**, *f.* public finance and administration. **-wesen**, *n.* financial side of government. **-wissenschaft**, *f.*, *see* **-istik**.

kamig, *adj.*, *see* **kahmig**.

Kamille, *f.* (-n) camomile (*Matricaria chamomilla*)

Kamin, *m.* (-s, -e) chimney (*also mount.*); fireplace, fireside. **-aufsatz**, *m.* mantelpiece, overmantel. **-besen**, *m.* hearth-brush. **-ecke**, *f.* chimney-corner. **-feger**, *m.* chimneysweep. **-feuer**, *n.* open fire. **-gerät**, *n.* fire-irons. **-gesims**, *n.* mantelpiece. **-gestell**, *n.* fire-dogs. **-gitter**, *n.* fender; fire-guard. **-kehrer**, *m.*, *see* **-feger**. **-platte**, *f.* back of a chimney. **-rost**, *m.* grate. **-schirm**, *m.* fire-screen. **-sims**, *n.*, *see* **-gesims**. **-teppich**, *m.* hearth-rug. **-vorsatz**, *m.*, **-vorsetzer**, *m.* fender, fireguard, fire screen.

Kamm, *m.* (-es, ⸚e) comb; ridge (*of hills*); crest (*of waves*); cog, cam, tappet; mane (*of a horse*); back of neck (*of oxen*); tuft, crest (*of birds, etc.*); comb (*of a cock*); pecten (*Zool.*); weaver's reed, carding machine (*for wool*); (*dial.*) stalk (*of grapes*); *enger –*, fine comb; *der – schwillt ihm*, he bristles up *or* is carried away by his anger; he gives himself airs *or* grows arrogant; (*sl.*) he gets cocky; *alle* (*alles*) *über einen – scheren*, treat *or* judge all (everything) alike. **-artig**, *adj.* pectinate. **-flossen**, *f.pl.* pectinals. **-flosser**, *m.* pectinal (*Ichth.*). **-förmig**, *adj.* comb-like, crested, pectinate. **-garnstoff**, *m.* worsted cloth. **-haar**, *n.* mane. **-(m)acher**, *m.* comb-maker. **-(m)uschel**, *f.* scallop (*Pectinidae*) (*Mollusc.*). **-rad**, *n.* cog-wheel. **-wellen**, *f.pl.* white horses (*on waves*). **-wolle**, *f.* combed wool for weaving into worsted. **-zahn**, *m.* tooth of a comb; tooth *or* cog of a wheel.

kämmel-n, *v.a.* comb finely, card (*wool*). **-ung**, *f.* wool-carding.

kämm-en, 1. *v.a.* comb; card (*wool*), mesh (*of gears*), dovetail, splice. 2. *v.r.* comb one's hair. **-erei**, *f.* wool-combing (*see also* **Kämmerei**). **-ling**, *m.* combings (*of wool*). **-(m)aschine**, *f.* wool-combing machine.

Kammer, *f.* (-n) small unheated room; chamber (*of a gun, etc.*); cavity, hollow, ventricle (*of the heart*); chamber (*of deputies, etc.*), board; clothing depot (*Mil.*); *Stube und –*, sitting-room and bedroom; *dunkle –*, camera obscura; *Dunkel–*, dark-room (*Phot.*); *erste –*, Upper House, House of Lords; *zweite –*, Lower House, House of Commons *or* Deputies; *Speise–*, larder, pantry. **-archiv**, *n.* the rolls. **-beamte(r)**, *m.* finance clerk. **-bediente(r)**, *m.* valet de chambre. **-dame**, *f.* lady of the bedchamber. **-degen**, *m.* dress-sword. **-diener**, *m.* valet, groom, personal servant. **-er**, *m.* president of the exchequer (*see also* **Kämmerer**). **-frau**, *f.*, **-fräulein**, *n.* lady's maid, chambermaid. **-gefälle**, *n.pl.* revenues of a prince's domains. **-gericht**, *n.* supreme court (*in Prussia*). **-gut**, *n.* crown land. **-herr**, *m.* chamberlain; gentleman of the bedchamber. **-jäger**, *m.* vermin-destroyer; rat-catcher. **-jungfer**, *f.*, *see* **-frau**. **-kapelle**, *f.* private chapel; prince's private musicians. **-kätzchen**, *n.* (*hum.*) chambermaid. **-klappe**, *f.* ventricular valve (*of heart*). **-knabe**, *m.* page. **-kollegium**, *n.* board of finance. **-lehen**, *n.* fief of the crown. **-musik**, *f.* chamber music. **-pächter**, *m.* crown-land tenant. **-rat**, *m.* counsellor of the exchequer. **-sänger**, *m.*, **-sängerin**, *f.* court singer (*also as title given to singers*). **-schreiber**, *m.* clerk to the exchequer. **-spiele**, *n.pl.* intimate theatre. **-ton**, *m.* concert-pitch (*Mus.*). **-tuch**, *n.* cambric. **-verhandlungen**, *f.pl.* debates in the chamber. **-wasser**, *n.* aqueous humour (*of eye*). **-zahlmeister**, *m.* keeper of the privy purse. **-zofe**, *f.*, *see* **-frau**.

Kämmer-chen, *n.* (-s, –) cosy little room, closet. **-ei**, *f.* chamberlain's office; (city) treasury, finance department; wool-combing. **-er**, *m.* (*archaic*) chamberlain; (city) treasurer. **-lein**, *n.* (-s, –) *see* **-chen**.

Kamp, *m.* (-(e)s, ⸚e) (*dial.*) enclosure, preserve. **-ieren**, *see* **kampieren**.

Kampanje, *f.* (-n) (*archaic*) poop (*Naut.*). **-treppe**, *f.* companion(way) (*Naut.*).

Kämpe, *m.* (-n, -n) (*Poet.*) champion, warrior, knight; (*dial.*) hog.

kampeln, *v.n.* (*dial.*) quarrel, squabble, tussle.

Kampescheholz, *n.* campeachy-wood, logwood.

Kampf, *m.* (-(e)s, ⸚e) combat, fight, contest, engagement, battle, conflict, action; struggle, strife; *– ums Dasein*, struggle for existence; *– bis aufs Messer*, war to the knife; *wo der – am heißesten tobt*, the thick of the battle *or* fight; *– der Anschauungen*, conflict of opinions; *– auf Leben und Tod*, fight to the death; *– um die Macht*, struggle for power. **-bahn**, *f.* stadium, arena. **-begier(de)**, *f.* pugnacity. **-begierig**, *adj.* pugnacious, bellicose. **-bereit**, *adj.* ready for action. **-erprobt**, *adj.* veteran, tried in battle. **-fähig**, *adj.* effective (*Mil.*), in fighting trim; *ein Schiff -fähig machen*, clear a ship for action. **-fertig**, *adj.* ready for action *or* for combat. **-flieger**, *m.* member of aircrew. **-flugzeug**, *n.* military, operational, *or* (*Amer.*) combat aircraft. **-front**, *f.* front line (*Mil.*). **-gas**, *n.* poison gas (*Mil.*). **-gefährte**, *m.*, **-genoß**, *m.* comrade in arms. **-geschrei**, *n.* war-cry, battle-cry. **-geschwader**, *n.* fighter squadron. **-gier**, *f.*, *see* **-begier(de)**. **-hahn**, *m.* fighting cock; (*fig.*) pugnacious fellow. **-lage**, *f.* tactical situation. **-lust**, *f.* pugnacity. **-lustig**, *adj.* pugnacious, bellicose. **-mittel**, *n.pl.* weapons, war materials. **-ordnung**, *f.* order of battle. **-platz**, *m.* battle field; scene of action, arena, cockpit; *den -platz betreten*, enter the lists. **-preis**, *m.* prize (*contested for*); (*C.L.*) cut price. **-raum**, *m.* battle area. **-richter**, *m.* umpire. **-spiel**, *n.* jousting, tilting, tournament; prize-fighting, prize-fight; (*pl.*) athletic contest, sports meeting. **-stoff**, *m.* poison gas (*Mil.*). **-übung**, *f.* manœuvres (*Mil.*). **-unfähig**, *adj.* disabled; *-unfähig machen*, knock out, put out of action. **-wagen**, *m.* armoured car, tank. **-wagenfalle**, *f.*, **-wagengraben**, *m.* tank trap, anti-tank ditch. **-zweck**, *m.* tactical objective.

kämpf-en, 1. *v.n.* (*aux.* h.) fight, combat; strive, struggle, contend with, do battle; *um eine S. -en*, fight for (*or* in order to obtain *or* keep) a th.; *für eine S. -en*, fight for (*or* in the interests of *or* on the side of) a th. 2. *v.a.* fight (*a battle*). **-er**, *m.* combatant, fighter, warrior; champion; prize-fighter, pugilist; spring-stone, abutment (*Arch.*); *alte -er*, (*Nat. Soc.*) old *or* original party member. **-erisch**, *adj.* warlike, bellicose, pugnacious.

Kamp-fer, *m.* camphor. **-fern**, *v.a.* camphorate. **-fersauer**, *adj.* camphorated. **-hen**, *n.* camphene.

kampieren, *v.a.* camp (out), be encamped; (*coll.*) *auf dem Sofa -*, shake down on the sofa.

Kanal, *m.* (-s, ⸚e) canal; ditch, conduit, drain, sewer; cutting; channel; *Ärmel-*, English Channel. **-arbeiter**, *m.* navvy. **-dampfer**, *m.* cross-channel steamer. **-gas**, *n.* sewer gas. **-inseln**, *f.pl.* Channel Islands. **-isation**, *f.* canalization, drainage, sewerage. **-isieren**, *v.a.* drain, canalize. **-netz**, *n.* canal system. **-schiffahrt**, *f.* canal-navigation. **-schleuse**, *f.* canal-lock. **-wasser**, *n.* sewage.

Kanapee, *n.* (-s, -s) sofa, settee.

Kanarien-hahn, *m.* cock canary. **-hecke**, *f.* aviary. **-männchen**, *n. see* **-hahn**. **-vogel**, *m.* canary. **-weibchen**, *n.* hen canary.

Kanaster, *m.* (*archaic*), *see* **Knaster**.

Kandare, *f.* (-n) curb, bridle (*of a bridge*); (*fig.*) *an die - nehmen*, take in hand, take a strong line with; (*ein Pferd*) *an die - legen* or **-n**, *v.a.* put on the curb *or* bridlebit, curb (*a horse*). **-nstange**, *f.* curb bit.

Kandelaber, *m.* (-s, -) candelabrum, chandelier.

kandeln, *v.a.* groove, channel, flute.

Kandelzucker, *see* **Kandiszucker**.

Kandid-at, *m.* (-en, -en) candidate, applicant; probationer; *cand. phil.* = *Kandidat der Philosophie*, final year arts student; *aufgestellter -at*, nominee; *als -aten aufstellen*, nominate; *als -at* (*für eine Stelle*) *auftreten*, stand *or* apply (for a post), come forward as a candidate. **-atur**, *f.* (-en) candidature, application. **-ieren**, *v.n.* be a candidate (for), stand *or* apply (*for a post*).

kand-ieren, *v.a.* candy. **-iert**, *p.p.* & *adj.* candied. **-is(zucker)**, *m.* sugar candy.

Kaneel, *m.* cinnamon.

Kanevas, *m.* (-ses, -se) canvas.

Känguruh, *n.* (-s, -s) kangaroo.

Kaninchen, *n.* (-s, -) rabbit. **-bau**, *m.* rabbit-burrow. **-gehege**, *n.* rabbit-warren. **-höhle**, *f.*, *see* **-bau**. **-kasten**, *m.*, **-stall**, *m.* rabbit-hutch.

Kanister, *m.* (-s, -) petrol can *or* tin.

Kanker, *m.* (-s, -) canker (*on trees*).

kann, kannst, *see* **können**.

Kanne, *f.* (-n) can, tankard, mug, jug, pot, canister; quart, litre (*liquid measure*); (*studs. sl.*) *in die - steigen*, be called upon to drink (*students' drinking ritual*); *es gießt mit -n*, it is raining cats and dogs. **-gießer**, *m.* (*coll.*) pot-house politician, tub-thumper. **-gießerei**, *f.* political hot air. **-nbürste**, *f.* bottle-brush. **-nweise**, *adv.* by quarts *or* pots. **-nzinn**, *m.* pewter.

Kännel, *m.* (-s, -) (*Swiss dial.*) roof gutter.

kannel-ieren, *v.a.* channel, flute, groove. **-iert**, *p.p.* & *adj.* fluted. **-üre**, *f.* (-n) flute, groove (*of a pillar*); (*pl.*) fluting.

Kannibal-e, *m.* (-en, -en) cannibal. **-isch**, *adj.* cannibal, ferocious; (*sl.*) enormous, extraordinary; (*sl.*) *ich habe -en Hunger*, I am ravenously hungry; (*sl.*) *-e Hitze*, terrific heat.

kannte, kanntest, *see* **kennen**.

Kanon, *m.* (-s, -s) canon (*of Holy Scriptures*); canon, round (*Mus.*). **-ikat**, *n.* (-(e)s, -e) prebend, canonry. **-iker**, *m.*, (*Austr. dial.* **-ikus**, *m.* (*pl.* -iki)) prebendary, canon. **-isch**, *adj.* canonical. **-isieren**, *v.a.* canonize. **-issin**, *f.* canoness.

Kanon-ade, *f.* (-n) cannonade, bombardment. **-e**, *f.* (-en) cannon, gun; (*sl.*) *ein Paar -en*, a pair of riding-boots; *gezogene -e*, rifled gun; *die -en fest machen*, house the guns; *eine -e auffahren*, mount a gun; *eine -e abnehmen*, dismount a gun; *eine -e richten*, lay a gun; *eine -e vernageln*, spike a gun; *die -en einholen*, haul the guns home; (*fig.*) *große -e*, (*sl.*) big gun, big bug, big noise; (*sl.*) *unter aller -e*, beneath contempt, quite worthless. **-enboot**, *n.* gunboat, naval sloop *or* pinnace. **-endonner**, *m.* boom, peal *or* roar of cannon; cannonade. **-enfeuer**, *n.* artillery fire, cannonade. **-enfieber**, *n.* nervousness under fire; (*coll.*) *-enfieber haben*, get cold feet. **-enfutter**, *n.* cannon fodder. **-engießerei**, *f.* gun-foundry. **-engut**, *n.* gun-metal. **-enkeller**, *m.* casemate. **-enkugel**, *f.* cannon-ball. **-enlauf**, *m.* barrel of a cannon. **-enofen**, *m.* high-pressure furnace. **-enschlag**, *m.* bursting-charge; maroon (*fireworks*). **-enschuß**, *m.* cannon-shot; *mit -enschüssen begrüßen*, honour with a salute. **-enstiefel**, *m. pl.* jackboots. **-ier**, *m.* (-s, -e) gunner. **-ieren**, *v.a.* & *n.* cannonade, bombard.

Kantate, *f.* (-n) cantata.

Kant-e, *f.* (-en) edge, corner; edging, lace, brim, border, margin, selvage (*of cloth*); crust (*of bread*); *spitze -e*, corner; *flache -e*, face, side; *Geld auf die hohe -e legen*, put money by, save money; *an allen Ecken und -en*, on all sides, everywhere; *mit -en besetzen*, trim with lace. **-el**, *m.* & *n.* square ruler. **-en**, *m.* (*dial.*) crust (*of a loaf*). **-en**, *v.a.* furnish with edges, edge, border; turn on edge, tilt, cant; square (*a stone*); *nicht -en*, this side up (*on boxes*). **-enbesatz**, *m.* trimming, edging. **-enkleid**, *n.* dress trimmed with lace. **-enlänge**, *f.* length of side. **-enschienen**, *f.pl.* edge-rails (*Railw.*). **-enweise**, *adv.* on edge, edgewise. **-enwinkel**, *m.* angle formed by two planes. **-haken**, *m.* (-s, -) cant-hook; (*sl.*) *einen beim -haken fassen*, seize a p. by the scruff of the neck. **-holz**, *n.* squared timber. **-ig**, *adj.* edged, cornered, angular, squared.

Kanter, *m.* canter. **-n**, *v.n.* & *a.* canter.

Kantharide, *f.* Spanish fly.

Kantine, *f.* (-n) canteen, mess.

Kanton, *m.* (-s, -e) (Swiss) canton; district, province. **-ieren**, *v.n.* (*archaic*) be quartered *or* billeted, be in cantonment (*Mil.*). **-ierung**, *f.* cantonment, billet. **-ist**, *m.* (-en, -en); (*sl.*) *unsicherer -ist*, shifty fellow, unreliable customer.

Kantönligeist, *m.* (*Swiss dial.*) narrow particularism.

Kantor, *m.* (-s, -en) precentor; choir-master; organist; cantor (*Jew.*). **-at**, *n.* (-(e)s, -e) precentorship; organist's house. **-ei**, *f. see* **-at**; class of choristers.

Kantschu, *m.* (-s, -s) short whip, knout.

Kanu, *n.* (-s, -s) canoe.

Kanüle, *f.* (-n) hypodermic syringe; tube (used in tracheotomy) (*Med.*).

Kanzel, *f.* (-n) pulpit; turret, cockpit (*Av.*); chair (*Univ.*); *sich von der - ablesen lassen*, have the banns published. **-ieren**, *v.a.* cross out, delete, cancel. **-mäßig**, *adj.* suited to the pulpit. **-rede**, *f.* sermon. **-redner**, *m.* preacher.

Kanz-lei, *f.* (-en) chancellery, lawyer's office, government office. **-leiarchiv**, *n.* rolls, archives, government records. **-leibeamte(r)**, *m.* chancery clerk, government official. **-leidekret**, *n.* departmental order. **-leidiener**, *m.* government servant, tipstaff. **-leiformat**, *n.* foolscap. **-leigerichtshof**, *m.* court of chancery. **-leimäßig**, *adj.* in legal style. **-leipapier**, *n.* foolscap paper. **-leipersonal**, *n.* staff (*of a public office*). **-leischreiben**, *n.* writ of chancery. **-leisprache**, *f.*, **-leistil**, *m.* chancery language, legal language, officialese. **-ler**, *m.* chancellor. **-list**, *m. see* **-leibeamte(r)**.

Kaolin, *m. or n.* china clay, porcelain clay.

Kap, *n.* (-s, -e & -s) cape (*Geog.*).

Kapaun, *m.* (-s, -e) (*coll.*) capon; quarrelsome youngster. **-en**, *v.a.* castrate.

Kapazität, *f.* (-en) capacity (*also Elec.*), capacitance (*Elec.*); authority; *Professor Z. war eine - ersten Ranges auf dem Gebiete der englischen Sprach-*

wissenschaft, Professor Z. was a leading authority in the field of English philology.
Kap-ee, *n.* (*coll.*) *schwer von -ee sein*, be dull of comprehension, be slow on the uptake. **-ieren**, *v.a.* (*sl.*) take in, understand, grasp, tumble to.
Kapellan, *m.* (*Austr. dial.*), *see* **Kaplan.**
Kapell-e, *f.* (-en) chapel; band, orchestra; church choir; cupel (*gold refining*). **-enabfall**, *m.* loss in cupellation. **-engold**, *n.* fine gold. **-ieren**, *v.a.* refine, cupel (*gold, etc.*). **-meister**, *m.* bandmaster, conductor. **-enofen**, *m.* assay furnace. **-enraub**, *m.*, **-enzug**, *m.*, *see* **-enabfall.**
[1]**Kaper**, *m.* (-s, –) pirate, freebooter, corsair, privateer, sea raider. **-ei**, *f.* privateering. **-n**, *v.a.* capture (*a ship*); (*fig.*) win *or* gain by trickery; *sie hat endlich einen Mann gekapert*, she has secured a husband at last. **-brief**, *m.* letter of marque (and reprisal). **-schiff**, *n.*, *see* [1]**Kaper.**
[2]**Kaper**, *f.* (-n) caper. **-nsoße**, *f.*, **-ntunke**, *f.*, caper sauce. **-nstrauch**, *m.* *Capparis spinosa* (*Bot.*).
kapillar, *adj.* capillary. **-aktiv**, *adj.* tending to reduce surface tension. **-inaktiv**, *adj.* tending to increase surface tension. **-ität**, *f.* capillary attraction. **-gefäß**, *n.* capillary (vessel).
Kapital, 1. *n.* (-s, -e & -ien) capital, principal, stock, funds; *eingeschossenes* –, deposit; *eisernes* –, capital invested *or* sunk; *imaginäres* –, floating capital; – *aus einer S. schlagen*, profit by a th.; *totes* –, unemployed capital; – *und Zinsen*, principal and interest; *Umsatz von -ien*, stock operations. 2. *pref.* (= large, extraordinary); *-hirsch*, royal stag; *-verbrechen*, capital crime. 3. *adj.* (*as pref.*). **-abfindung**, *f.* lump sum settlement. **-abwanderung**, *f.*, *see* **-flucht.** **-anlage**, *f.* investment. **-bildung**, *f.* formation of (new) capital. **-flucht**, *f.* flight of capital (to foreign markets). **-isieren**, *v.a.* capitalize. **-ismus**, *m.* capitalism. **-ist**, *m.* (-en, -en) capitalist; stockholder. **-istisch**, *adj.* capitalist(ic). **-kräftig**, *adj.* well provided with capital, wealthy, sound (*of a business*). **-markt**, *m.* stock market. **-rente**, *f.* unearned income, revenue, annuity. **-sabgabe**, *f.* capital levy. **-seinschuß**, *m.* capital deposited *or* paid in. **-steuer**, *f.* property tax. **-zins**, *m.* interest on capital.
Kapitäl, *n.* (-s, -e *or* -er) (*Austr. dial.*), *see* **Kapitell.** **-chen**, *n.* small capitals (*Typ.*).
Kapitän, *m.* (-s, -e) captain (*Navy*), skipper (*also sport*). **-leutnant**, *m.* lieutenant (*Navy*).
Kapitel, *n.* (-s, –) chapter (*book*); chapter (*Eccl.*); topic; *das ist ein – für sich*, that is another story; *ein – halten*, hold a chapter, convene the canons. **-fest**, *adj.* well-versed. **-haus**, *n.* chapter-house. **-n**, *v.a.* (*coll.*) lecture, reprimand. **-weise**, *adv.* by chapters, chapter by chapter.
Kapitell, *n.* (-s, -e) capital (*Arch.*).
Kapitul-ant, *m.* (-en, -en) (*archaic*) re-enlisted soldier. **-ation**, *f.* (-en) capitulation; (*archaic*) (re-)enlistment. **-ieren**, *v.n.* (*aux.* h.) capitulate, surrender; (*archaic*) (re)engage, (re)enlist.
Kaplan, *m.* (-s, ⸚e) chaplain, assistant priest (*R.C.*).
kapores, *adj.* (*sl.*) spoilt, broken; – *gehen*, get broken, *etc.*
Kapotte, *f.* (-n) hood.
Kapp-e, *f.* (-en) cap, hood, cowl; dome (*Arch.*); (*archaic*) hooded mantle, cape; crown (*of a tooth*); horn (*of a sea-mine*); coping; bonnet (*Fort.*); toe-piece (*of shoe*); heel-plate; sheath, calyptra (*Bot.*); *Tarn-e*, invisible cloak; (*coll.*) *etwas auf seine -e nehmen*, answer for a th., make o.s. responsible *or* shoulder the responsibility for a th.; (*Prov.*) *gleiche Brüder gleiche -en*, birds of a feather flock together. **-en**, *v.a.* chop, sever, cut away (*partic. Naut.*); lop, top, trim (*a hedge*); castrate, caponize. **-enförmig**, *adj.* hood-shaped, cowled, cucullate (*Bot., Zool.*). **-enmantel**, *m.* hooded cloak, cape. **-enmine**, *f.* horned mine (*Nav.*). **-enrobbe**, *f.* hooded seal. **-enstiefel**, *m.pl.* top-boots. **-fenster**, *n.* dormer window. **-hahn**, *m.* capon. **-kragen**, *m.* cowl, hood. **-naht**, *f.* hem; flat seam. **-zaum**, *m.* cavesson (*harness*).
Käppi, *n.* (-s, -s) military cap, kepi, shako.
Kapriole, *f.* (-n) caper, capriole (*haute école*).
kapriz-ieren, *v.r.* be obstinate (*auf*, about). **-iös**, *adj.* capricious.
Kapsel, *f.* (-n) cover, case, box, capsule; detonator; (*hum. sl.*) bed. **-artig**, *adj.*, **-förmig**, *adj.* capsular. **-tragend**, *adj.* capsulated, capsuliferous.
Kaput, *m.* (-s, -e) (*Austr. & Swiss dial.*) soldier's greatcoat *or* cape.
kaputt, *adj.* (*coll.*) done up, exhausted, played out, dead; lost, spoilt, ruined, broken in pieces; – *sein*, be broken, *etc.*; – *gehen*, get broken, come to pieces, *etc.*
Kapuz-e, *f.* (-en) cowl; cape, hood. **-inade**, *f.* popular sermon, tirade, severe lecture. **-iner**, *m.* capuchin monk, (*Austr. coll.*) coffee with little milk. **-inerkresse**, *f.* nasturtium (*Tropaeolum majus*) (*Bot.*). **-inerpredigt**, *f.*, *see* **-inade.**
Karabin-er, *m.* (-ers, -er) carbine, rifle. **-erhaken**, *m.* swivel. **-ier**, *m.* (-s, -s) carbineer, carabineer, dragoon. **-iere**, *m.* (-(s), -ieri) Italian gendarme.
Karaffe, Karaffine, *f.* (-n) (cut-glass) carafe, decanter.
Karambol-age, *f.* (-n) cannon (*Bill.*). **-ieren**, *v.n.* cannon, collide.
Kar-at, *n.* ((-e)s, -e) carat. **-atieren**, *v.a.* alloy (*gold*). **-atgewicht**, *n.* troy weight. **-ätig**, *suffix*, e.g. *zehn-ätig*, ten carat.
Karausche, *f.* (-n) crucian, carp (*Carassius vulgaris*) (*Icht.*).
Karawan-e, *f.* (-en) caravan. **-serei**, *f.*, (*Austr. dial.* **-serai**, *f.*) caravanserai.
Karbatsche, *f.* (-n) whip, scourge. **-n**, *v.a.* whip, flog.
Karbid, *n.* (-(e)s, -e) carbide. **-lampe**, *f.* carbide lamp (*Cycl. etc.*).
Karbol, *n.* (*coll.*) *see* **-säure.** **-ineum**, *n.* creosote. **-säure**, *f.* phenol, carbolic acid. **-seife**, *f.* carbolic soap.
Karbonade, *f.* (-n) chop, cutlet.
Karbonsäure, *f.* carbonic acid.
Karborund, *m.* (-s, -e) carborundum.
Karbunkel, *m.* (-s, –) carbuncle, furuncle. **-krankheit**, *f.* anthrax.
Kärcher, *m.* (-s, –) (*dial.*) *see* **Kärrner.**
Kardan-gelenk, *n.* universal joint. **-ische Aufhängung**, *f.* gimbals. **-welle**, *f.* jointed shaft.
Kardätsche, *f.* (-n) carding-comb; curry-comb, curry-brush, horse-brush. **-n**, *v.a.* card (*wool*); curry (*a horse*).
Kard-e, *f.* (-n) teasel (*Dipsacus sativus*) (*Bot.*); teasel brush; carding instrument. **-en**, **-ieren**, *v.a.* card *or* comb wool.
Kardeel, *f.* (-e) strand of a hawser (*Naut.*).
Kardinal, 1. *m.* (-s, ⸚e) cardinal (*R.C.*); type of American finch (*Cardinalis*) (*Orn.*). 2. *adj.* cardinal, chief, principal. **-zahlen**, *f.pl.* cardinal numbers.
Karenz, *f.* (-en) (*C.L.*) interval before benefits become available.
karessieren, *v.a.* caress, fondle, hug.
Karfiol, *m.* (-s, -e) (*Austr. dial.*) cauliflower.
Kar-freitag, *m.* Good Friday. **-woche**, *f.* Holy Week, Passion Week.
Karfunkel, *m.* (-s, –) carbuncle, almandite (*gem*); (*coll. also for* Karbunkel).
karg, *adj.* (*comp.* kärger *or* karger; *sup.* kärgst *or* kargst (*Austr. dial. only the latter*)) scanty, poor, meagre; sterile (*soil*); miserly, niggardly, parsimonious, stingy; *-e Antwort*, short answer. **-en**, *v.n.* (*aux.* h.) be stingy, be very economical; *mit etwas -en*, be sparing of a th. **-heit**, *f.* parsimony, stinginess; poverty (*of soil*); meagreness, scantiness.
kärglich, *adj.* scanty, poor, paltry, wretched; *-e Kost*, scanty rations, short commons.
kariert, *p.p. & adj.* chequered, checked; *-e Artikel*, checks; tartans (*Scottish*).
Karik-atur, *f.* (-en) caricature. **-ieren**, *v.a.* caricature.
Karkasse, *f.* (-n) carcass; form (*for hats*); tread (*of tyres*).
karm-esin, 1. *adj.* crimson. 2. *n.* crimson. **-in**, *n.* (*& Austr. dial. m.*) carmine. **-oisin**, *adj.*, *see* **-esin.**
Karneol, *m.* (-s, -e) carnelian (*gem.*).
Karneval, *m.* (-s, -e (*& Austr. dial.*) -s) carnival, Shrovetide festivities.

Karnickel, *n.* (-s, –) (*coll. & Austr. dial.*) rabbit, bunny; scapegoat; (*coll.*) *wer war das –?* who began it (*the trouble*)? who is to blame? (*coll.*) *das – hat angefangen,* the cat did it.
Karnies, *n.* (-es, -e) cornice, moulding (*Arch.*); pelmet, valance, curtain runner.
Karo, *n.* (-s, -s) diamond (*shape*), diamonds (*cards*).
Kaross–e, *f.* (-n) state-coach. **–erie,** *f.* body, bodywork (*motor-car*). **–ier,** *m.* (-s, -s) coach-horse.
Karotte, *f.* (-n) carrot.
Karpfen, *m.* (-s, –) carp.
Karr–e, *f.* (-en), **–en,** 1. *m.* (-s, –) cart, wheelbarrow, barrow; car, truck; carriage (*Typ.*); (*fig.*) *den –en fest fahren,* come to a deadlock in s.th., get stuck; *an demselben –en ziehen,* be in the same boat; *den –en einfach laufen lassen,* let matters take their course. 2. *v.a.* cart. **–enbaum,** *m.* shaft of a cart. **–enführer,** *m.* drayman, carter. **–engabel,** *f.* cart-shafts. **–engaul,** *m.* cart-horse. **–enschieber,** *m.* worker with a wheelbarrow, barrowman.
Karree, *n.* (-s, -s) square (*Mil.*); set (*Danc.*); *offenes –,* hollow square.
Karrer, *m.* (*Swiss dial.*), *see* **Kärrner.**
Karrete, *f.* (-n) (*Austr. dial.*) old rickety and bumpy cart *or* carriage.
Karrette, *f.* (-n) (*Swiss dial.*) wheelbarrow.
Karriere [*pron.* kari'ɛːrə], *f.* (-n) career; course; full gallop; – *machen,* get on well in the world, be quickly promoted.
karriert, *adj.* (*Austr. dial.*), *see* **kariert.**
Karriol, *n.* (-s, -s), **–e,** *f.* (-n) two-wheel(ed) chaise, gig; dog-cart; curricle. **–en,** *v.n.* move about, tear about quickly, drive madly *or* recklessly.
Kärrner, *m.* (-s, –) (*archaic*) carter, carrier, drayman.
Karst, *m.* (-es, -e) mattock, two-pronged fork. **–en,** *v.a.* hoe, work with a mattock. **–hans,** *m.* (*archaic*) peasant.
[2]**Karst,** *m.* chalky formation (*Geol.*).
Kartätsche, *f.* (-n) canister-shot, case-shot, grape-shot, shrapnel.
Karte, *f.* (-n) card, postcard, visiting *or* playing-card; map, chart (*Naut.*); ticket (of admission); menu, bill of fare; *ein Spiel –n,* a pack of cards; *seine –n aufdecken,* show one's hand; *eine – ausspielen,* play one's card; *–n geben,* deal the cards; *–n hinlegen,* disclose one's cards; *–n legen,* tell one's fortune; *–n mischen,* shuffle the cards; *alles auf eine – setzen,* stake everything on one throw, put all one's eggs in one basket; *–(n) spielen,* play cards; *–n schlagen,* tell fortunes by cards; (*coll.*) *einem in die –n sehen,* spy out *or* discover a p.'s designs; *die –n durchschauen,* be in the secret *or* in the plot; *aus einer – spielen,* play the same game; *angelegte –,* concerted plan; *–n abheben,* cut cards; *seine – abgeben,* leave one's (visiting) card; *nach der – speisen,* dine à la carte. **–n,** 1. *v.n.* (*aux.* h.) play at cards. 2. *v.a.* concert, plot, contrive, bring about. **–nblatt,** *n.* (single) card. **–nbrief,** *m.* letter-card. **–nfolge,** *f.* sequence; *–nfolge von 5 –n,* quint. **–nhaus,** *n.* house of cards; chimerical project; chart room (*Naut.*). **–nkunde,** *f.* map-reading. **–nkunststück,** *n.* card-trick. **–nlegerin,** *f.* fortune-teller (with cards). **–nnetz,** *n.* map grid. **–nschläger,** *m.,* **–nschlägerin,** *f.* fortune-teller (with cards). **–nspiel,** *n.* card-playing; card game; pack of cards. **–nwerk,** *n.* atlas. **–nzeichen,** *n.* conventional sign. **–nzeichner,** *m.* cartographer.
Kartei, *f.* (-en) card-index, filing-cabinet.
Kartell, *n.* (-s, -e) (*C.L.*) cartel, trust, combine, syndicate, ring; agreement between enemies; challenge (*to single combat*). **–schiff,** *n.* ship with a flag of truce. **–träger,** *m.* second, bearer of a challenge (*for a duel*).
Kartoffel, *f.* (-n) potato; *junge –,* new potato; *gebratene –,* fried potato; *gestampfte* or *gequetschte –,* mashed potato; *gekochte –,* boiled potato; *–n schälen,* peel potatoes; *–n stecken,* plant potatoes. **–ausschuß,** *m.* small potatoes. **–bau,** *m.* potato growing. **–brei,** *m.* mashed potatoes. **–fäule,** *f., see* **–pest.** **–flocken,** *f.pl.* potato crisps. **–käfer,** *m.* Colorado beetle. **–kloß,** *f.* potato-dumpling. **–mehl,** *n.* potato flour, farina. **–pest,** *f.* potato-rot. **–kraut,** *n.* potato-tops *or* stalks. **–mus,** *n.* mashed potatoes. **–puffer,** *m.* potato pancake. **–schale,** *f.* potato peel(ing).
karto–graphisch, *adj.* cartographic(al), map-making; *–graphische Verlagsanstalt,* publishing house for maps. **–mantie,** *f.* art of fortune-telling by cards. **–thek,** *f.* card-index.
Karton, *m.* (-s, -s) cardboard, pasteboard, (*coll.*) cardboard box; boards (*Bookb.*); cartoon. **–age,** *f.* boarding, packing, wrapping, cardboard box. **–ieren,** *v.a.* bind in boards. **–iert,** *p.p. & adj.* with stiff paper covers *or* cloth-backed boards.
Kartusch–e, *f.* (-en) cartridge, charge. **–munition,** *f.* semi-fixed ammunition (*Artil.*). **–raum,** *m.* powder chamber.
Karussell, *n.* (-s, -e) roundabout, merry-go-round.
Karzer, *n.* (*& Austr. dial. m.*) (-s, –) lock-up, prison (*School & Univ.*).
Kaschemme, *f.* (-n) tavern, pot-house, (*sl.*) low dive.
Käscher, *m.* (-s, –) *see* **Kescher.**
Kaschmir, *m.* (-s, -e) cashmere.
Käs–e, *m.* (-es, –) cheese; curds; flower (*of cauliflower*); seed (*of poplars or mallows*); crown (*of artichokes*); (*coll.*) nonsense, rubbish, balderdash; *Schweizer–e,* Gruyère. **–eblatt,** *n.* local newspaper, (*coll.*) local rag. **–ebutter,** *f.* curds; cream-cheese. **–eform,** *f.* cheese-mould. **–eglocke,** *f.* cheese-dish, cheese-cover. **–elab,** *n.* rennet. **–elaib,** *m.* whole cheese. **–emade,** *f.,* **–emilbe,** *f.* maggot, cheese-mite. (*sl.*) **–emesser,** *n.* large knife, sword, (*hum.*) cheese cutter, cut-throat. **–en,** 1. *v.a.* turn into cheese, make curds. 2. *v.r. & n.* (*aux.* h. & s.) curdle, curd, coagulate. **–epappel,** *f.* mallow. **–erei,** *f.* dairy; trade of cheese-making. **–esäure,** *f.* lactic acid, caseic acid. **–estange,** *f.* cheese-straw. **–estoff,** *m.* casein. (*dial.*) **–ewasser,** *n.* whey. **–ig,** *adj.* caseous, cheesy; curdled; sallow (*of the complexion*).
Kasel, *f.* (-n) chasuble.
Kasematte, *f.* (-n) casemate, barbettes; gun turret (*Nav.*).
Kaserne, *f.* (-n) barracks. **–narrest,** *m.* confinement to barracks. **–nhof,** *m.* barrack-square. **–nhofblüten,** *f.pl.* barrack-room expressions; N.C.O.'s howlers.
Kasimir, *m.* (*rare*), *see* **Kaschmir.**
Kasino, *n.* (-s, -s) casino, clubroom, officers' mess (*Mil.*).
Kasko, *m.* (-s, -s) (*C.L.*) hull (*of ship*). **–versicherung,** *f.* insurance on hull (*i.e. not on cargo*).
Kasperletheater, *n.* Punch and Judy show.
Kass–a, *f.* (-en) (*archaic & Austr. dial. for* **Kasse**).
Kassation, *f.* cashiering, military degradation. **–surteil,** *n.* reversal of judgement, quashing, annulment.
Kass–e, *f.* (-en) cash-box, till, safe; cash-desk, counting-house, pay-office; ticket-office, booking-office, box-office; ready money, cash (in hand); *schlecht bei –e sein,* be hard up; *gut bei –e sein,* be in funds, (*sl.*) be flush; *–e machen,* make up the cash account; *die –e führen,* keep the cash, act as treasurer; *gegen –e verkaufen,* sell for cash. **–enabschluß,** *m.* closing cash account, cash balance. **–enanweisung,** *f.* treasury bill. **–enarzt,** *m.* panel doctor. **–enbeamte(r),** *m.* cashier. **–enbeleg,** *m.* cash voucher. **–enbestand,** *m.* balance in hand. **–enbetrug,** *m.* embezzlement (*of public money*). **–enbilanz,** *f.* balance in cash. **–enbote,** *m.* bank-messenger. **–enbuch,** *n.* cash-book. **–enführer,** *m.* cashier. **–engehilfe,** *m.* teller. **–enordnung,** *f.* finance regulations. **–enprüfer,** *m.* auditor. **–enprüfung,** *f.* auditing. **–enschein,** *m.* treasury bill, bank-note; receipt. **–enschrank,** *m.* fire-proof safe. **–enstück,** *n.* box office draw, (*coll.*) hit (*Theat.*). **–ensturz,** *m.* audit; adding up the cash; *–ensturz machen,* make up the cash. **–entisch,** *m.* counter. **–enübersicht,** *f.* balance-sheet. **–enverwalter,** *m.,* **–enwart,** *m.* treasurer. **–enzettel,** *m., see* **–enschein.**
Kasserolle, *f.* (-n) stew-pot, casserole.
Kassette, *f.* (-n) cash-box, deed-box; casket, coffer; (film-pack) adapter, plate-holder (*Phot.*).
Kassi–a, –e, *f.* (-en) cassia. **–enblüte,** *f.* cassia bud. **–enöl,** *n.* oil of cassia.

Kassiber, *m.* (-s, –) clandestine communication between prisoners; letter smuggled into a prisoner's cell.
Kassier, *m.* (-s, –e) (*S. German*) *see* **–er. –en,** *v.a.* receive money, cash (*a bill*); annul, quash (*a will, a judgement*); cashier, dismiss (*Mil.*); *see* **Kassation. –er,** *m.* cashier, treasurer, (*Naut.*) purser. **–ung,** *f.* cashiering, annulment, quashing, cassation.
Kastagnette [*pron.* -tan'jɛtə] *f.* (-n) castanet.
Kastanie, *f.* (-n) chestnut; *eßbare –, Edel–,* sweet chestnut; *Roß–,* horse-chestnut; (*Prov.*) *anderen die –n aus dem Feuer holen,* be made a cat's-paw of, do s.o. else's dirty work. **–nbaum,** *m.* chestnut-tree; *bitterer* (*wilder*) *–nbaum, see* **Roß–. –nbraun,** *adj.* chestnut (brown), auburn, maroon.
Kästchen, *n.* (-s, –), *see* **Kasten;** little box, casket; alveolus.
Kaste, *f.* (-n) caste; corporation. **–ntum,** *n.* caste system. **–ngeist,** *m.* caste feeling *or* prejudice. **–nwesen,** *n.* caste system.
Käste, *f.* (-n) (*dial.*), *see* **Kastanie.**
kastei–en, *v.a.* & *r.* castigate *or* mortify (o.s.). **–ung,** *f.* castigation, mortification (*of the flesh*); penance.
Kastell, *n.* (-(e)s, -e) fort, citadel, castle. **–an,** *m.* (-s, -e) castellan, steward.
Kasten, *m.* (-s, – (& *Austr. dial.* ¨)) box, chest, case, housing, crate, coffer; locker, press, cupboard; hutch; boot (*of a coach*); setting (*of jewels, etc.*); pillar-box; body, frame (*of coaches, etc.*), wind-chest, sounding-board (*Organ*); (*dial.* & *coll.*) fund; (*sl.*) guard-room, detention barracks, clink, jug (*Mil.*); (*coll.*) tumbledown house; unseaworthy ship, hulk; old crock, boneshaker (*vehicle*); crate (*Av.*); blowzy female; *– der Zähne,* socket of teeth; *Bau–,* box of bricks.
Kästenbaum, *m.* (*dial.*), *see* **Kastanienbaum.**
Kastr–at, *m.* (-en, -en) eunuch. **–ieren,** *v.a.* castrate; *–ierte Bücher,* expurgated texts *or* editions of books.
Kasualien, *pl.* occasional emoluments, incidental fees.
Kasuar, *m.* (-s, -e) cassowary (*Orn.*).
Kasuistik, *f.* casuistry.
Kasus, *m.* (–, –) case (*Gram.*); incident.
Kata–falk, *m.* (-s, -e) tomb of state; catafalque. **–kombe,** *f.* (-n) catacomb. **–log,** *m.* (-s, -e) catalogue, list. **–logisieren,** *v.a.* catalogue. **–lysator,** *m.* (-s, -en) catalyst, catalytic agent. **–lyse,** *f.* catalysis. **–pultieren,** *v.a.* launch (*aircraft*) by catapult (*Av.*). **–rakt,** *m.* (-(e)s, -e) waterfall, cataract, rapids; (*also* **–rakta,** *f.* **–rakte,** *f.* (–)) cataract (of the eye). **–strophe,** *f.* catastrophe. **–strophal,** *adj.* catastrophic.
Katarrh, *m.* (-s, -e) catarrh, cold in the head; *–alfieber,* feverish cold; catarrh of cattle.
Kataster, *n.* (& *Austr. dial. m.*) (-s, –) land-register. **–amt,** *n.* land-registry office.
Kate, *f.* (-n) (tied) cottage.
Katech–ese, *f.* catechizing. **–et,** *m.* (-en, -en) catechist, religious instructor (*R.C.*). **–etisch,** *adj.* catechetic(al), socratic. **–isieren,** *v.a.* catechize. **–ismus,** *m.* (-mus, -men) catechism.
Kategor–ie, *f.* (-ien) category. **–isch,** *adj.* categorical, positive, unconditional.
Kater, *m.* (-s, –) tom-cat; (*sl.*) hang-over; *der gestiefelte –,* Puss in boots; *moralischer –,* qualms of conscience, self-reproach. (*sl.*) **–idee,** *f.* crazy idea.
kathartisch, *adj.* cathartic, purgative, cleansing, purifying.
Kathed–er, *m.* & *n.* (-s, –) rostrum, desk (*for lectures*); (*fig.*) chair (*Univ.*); *vom –er,* ex cathedra. **–erblüte,** *f.* lecturer's howler. **–erheld,** *m.* theorizer. **–ersozialismus,** *m.* academic socialism. **–erweisheit,** *f.* theoretical knowledge, unpractical views. **–rale,** *f.* (-n) cathedral.
Kathete, *f.* (-n) small side of a rectangular triangle (*Geom.*).
Katheter, *m.* (-s, –) catheter, bougie (*Surg.*).
Kathode, *f.* (-n) cathode. **–nröhre,** *f.* thermionic valve. **–nstrahl,** *m.* cathode ray.
Kathol–ik, *m.* (-en, -en) (Roman) Catholic. **–isch,** *adj.* catholic; all-embracing; *–isch werden,* turn (Roman) Catholic. **–izismus,** *m.* Roman Catholicism.
Kätner, *m.* (-s, –) cottager, farm labourer.
katschen, *v.n.* (*Austr. dial.*) smack one's lips, eat noisily.
Katt–anker, *m.* kedge (*Naut.*). **–block,** *m.* cathead (*Naut.*). **–en,** *v.a.* cat (*the anchor*) (*Naut.*).
Kattun, *m.* (-s, -e) cotton, calico; *ostindischer –,* chintz. **–en,** *adj.* (made of) calico *or* cotton. **–papier,** *n.* chintz paper. **–wolle,** *f.* cotton (wool).
Kätzchen, *n.* (-s, –) kitten; catkin (*Bot.*).
Katz–e, *f.* (-en) cat; (*coll.*) puss; (*dial.*) battering-ram; pouch *or* money-bag; *wie die –e um den heißen Brei gehen,* beat about the bush; *falsch wie eine –e,* false as a serpent, sly as a fox; (*coll.*) *das ist für die –e,* that is to no purpose, is fruitless *or* in vain, that is as good as useless; *sie vertragen sich wie –e und Hund,* they lead a cat and dog life; *sieht doch die –(e) den Kaiser an,* a cat may look at a king; (*Prov.*) *die -e läßt das Mausen nicht,* what is bred in the bone will out in the flesh; *wenn die –e fort ist, tanzen die Mäuse,* when the cat's away the mice will play; (*Prov.*) *bei Nacht sind alle –en grau,* all cats are grey in the dark; *neunschwänzige –e,* cat-o'-nine-tails; (*coll.*) *die –e läuft ihm den Rücken hinauf,* it gives him the creeps, it makes his flesh creep; (*Prov.*) *die –e im Sack kaufen,* to buy a pig in a poke. **–balgen,** *v.r.* brawl. **–balgerei,** *f.* scuffle, scrap, brawl. **–buckeln,** *v.n.* (*aux.* h.) cringe, toady (*vor,* to). **–enartig,** *adj.* cat-like, feline. **–enauge,** *n.* cat's-eye (*semi-precious stone* & *traffic indicator*), red light, rear reflector (*cycle*). **–enbalken,** *m.* ridge pole, roof-tree. **–enbuckel,** *m.* crouching position, arched back; broken back (*of a ship*); *einen –enbuckel machen,* arch one's back, make a profound reverence. **–enfreundlich,** *adj.* friendly to one's face only. **–enfreundschaft,** *f.* cupboard love. **–engedächtnis,** *n.* bad memory. **–engeschlecht,** *n.* cat tribe, feline family. **–englimmer,** *m.,* **–engold,** *n.* yellow mica. **–enjammer,** *m.* hang-over; (*coll.*) *einen moralischen –enjammer haben,* have qualms of conscience *or* a touch of compunction; resolve to mend one's ways. (*coll.*) **–enkopf,** *m.* box on the ear; *see also* **Kattblock. –enleben,** *n.* the nine lives of a cat. **–enmusik,** *f.* caterwauling, catcalls. **–enpfötchen,** *n.* mountain everlasting *or* catsfoot (*Antennaria dioica*) (*Bot.*). **–ensilber,** *n.* Argentine mica. **–ensprung,** *m.* a stone's throw. **–ensteg,** *m.,* **–ensteig,** *m.* barrow path; cat walk. (*coll.*) **–entisch,** *m.* children's table; *am –entische essen,* eat at the little folk's table, eat alone in a corner (*punishment for children*). **–entritt,** *m.* cat-like tread, stealthy footsteps. **–enwäsche,** *f.* cat-lick; superficial wash.
kauder–n, *v.n.* (*aux.* h.) gobble (*as a turkey*); talk gibberish; act as middleman *or* go-between, profiteer. **–welsch,** *n.* gibberish, nonsense, jargon. **–welschen,** *v.n.* talk gibberish, jabber.
Kaue, *f.* (-n) pithead; *Wasch–,* pithead baths.
kau–en, 1. *v.a.* chew, masticate; mouth (*one's words*); *die Nägel* or *an den Nägeln –en,* bite one's nails. 2. *n.* mastication, chewing; *das –en auf dem Gebiß,* champing the bit. **–gummi,** *n.* chewing gum. **–magen,** *m.* gizzard. **–pfeffer,** *m.* betel nut. **–tabak,** *m.* chewing tobacco, quid. **–werkzeug,** *n.pl.* masticators. **–zahn,** *m.* grinder, molar tooth.
kauern, *v.n.* (*aux.* s.) & *r.* squat, crouch, cower. **–d,** *adj.* couchant (*Her.*).
Kauf, *m.* (-(e)s, ¨e) buying, purchase; bargain *einen – abschließen,* complete a purchase; *durch – an sich* (*Acc.*) *bringen,* acquire by purchase; *leichten –es davonkommen,* get off lightly; *durch –,* by purchase; *in den – geben,* throw into the bargain, (*coll.*) throw in; *in den –,* over and above, into the bargain; *einen wohlfeilen* or *guten – machen,* get a bargain; *in* (*den*) *– nehmen,* make allowance for; (*mit*) **in** *– nehmen,* put up with; *– auf, nach* or *zur Probe,* sale on appro.; *– ist –,* a bargain is a bargain; *einem in den – treten,* outbid s.o.; *– mit Vorbehalt,* qualified purchase; *zum –,* for sale. **–bar,** *adj.* for sale, purchasable, that may be bought *or* sold. **–brief,** *m.* bill of sale. (*C.L.*) **–buch,** *n.* accounts book. **–en,** *v.a.* & *n.* (*aux.* h.) buy, purchase; (*sl.*

sich (*Dat.*) *einen Affen –en*, get tipsy; *das –en geistlicher Ämter*, simony; *auf Borg* or *Kredit –en*, buy on credit; *einen Beamten –en*, bribe *or* buy over an official; *bei wem –en Sie gewöhnlich?* with whom do you deal as a rule? (*coll.*) *was ich mir dafür –e!* that cuts no ice with me; *für teures Geld –en*, pay a lot for; (*coll.*) *sich* (*Dat.*) *einen –en*, call a p. to account, explain one's attitude in no uncertain terms; (*coll.*) *auf Stottern –en*, buy on the never never. **–enswert,** *adj.* worth buying. **–fahrer,** *m.* merchantman. **–fahrtei,** *f.* (*archaic*) sea trade. **–fahrteiflotte,** *f.* merchant fleet. **–fahrteischiff,** *n.* merchantman, merchant ship. **–geld,** *n.* purchase-money. **–gut,** *n.* merchandise. **–handel,** *m.* commerce, trade, traffic. **–haus,** *n.* warehouse, stores. **–herr,** *m.* merchant. **–kontrakt,** *m.*, bill of sale. **–kraft,** *f.* purchasing power. **–kräftig,** *adj.* able to buy, wealthy, moneyed. **–kraftüberhang,** *m.* surplus purchasing power. **–laden,** *m.* shop, store. **–leute,** *see* **–mann.** **–lustig,** *adj.* keen to buy; *die –lustigen, pl.* the buyers. **–mann,** *m.* (-s, -leute) merchant; tradesman, shopkeeper. **–männisch,** *adj.* mercantile, commercial; *–männischer Angestellte(r)*, clerk (*in business concern*); *–männische Regel*, rule of business; *in –männischer Hinsicht*, commercially, from a business point of view. **–mannschaft,** *f.* body of merchants *or* tradesmen; Chamber of Commerce. **–mannsdeutsch,** *n.* commercial German. **–mannsgeist,** *m.* commercial spirit. **–mannsgut,** *n.* merchandise. **–mannsinnung,** *f.* trading company, guild. **–mannsjunge,** *m.* merchant's *or* shopkeeper's apprentice. **–mannsstand,** *m.* merchant class. **–muster,** *n.* salesman's sample. **–platz,** *m.* market-place, market. **–preis,** *m.* purchase-money, cost price, first cost. **–recht,** *n.* right of purchase. **–schilling,** *m.* earnest-money. **–steuer,** *f.* stamp duty on conveyance (*Law*). **–vertrag,** *m. see* **–kontrakt.** **–weise,** *adv.* by purchase. **–zwang,** *m.* obligation to purchase; *ohne –zwang*, on approval, without obligation to purchase; inspection invited.

Käuf–er, *m.* (-ers, -er) purchaser, buyer. **–lich,** 1. *adj.* marketable; saleable, to be bought, for sale; venal, corruptible 2. *adv.* by purchase; *–lich erwerben* or *an sich* (*Acc.*) *bringen*, buy, acquire by purchase; *–lich überlassen*, sell.

Kaul–e, *f.* (*dial.*), *see* **Kuhle.** **–barsch,** *m.* species of perch (*Acerina cernua*) (*Icht.*). **–quappe,** *f.* tadpole.

kaum, *adv.* hardly, scarcely, barely, with difficulty; no sooner . . . than; only just, just now; – *noch*, just a moment ago; – (*der Gefahr*) *entgehen* or *entwischen*, have a very narrow escape; – *war er fort, da* or *so* . . ., he was no sooner gone than. . . .

kaupeln, *v.n.* (*aux.* h.) (*Austr. dial.*) barter, swap.

kausal, *adj.* causal, causative. **–konjunktion,** *f.* causal conjunction (*Gram.*). **–nexus,** *m.* connexion between cause and effect, causality. **–satz,** *m.* causal clause (*Gram.*). **–verbum,** *n.* causative verb, factitive verb (*Gram.*).

Kausch(e), *f.* (-en) eyelet, thimble (*on rope*) (*Naut.*).

kaust–ifizieren, *v.a.* cauterize, corrode. **–ik,** *f.* (art of) etching. **–ika,** *pl.* corrosive substances, caustics. **–isch,** *adj.* caustic, corrosive; biting, satirical, mocking.

Kautel, *f.* (-en) caution; precaution; reservation.

kauter–isieren, *v.a.* cauterize, sear. **–ium,** *n.* (-iums, -ien) cautery; caustic.

Kaution, *f.* (-en) security, guarantee, bail; caution money; *unter* –, under bond; *gegen gute* –, on good security; – *legen* or *stellen*, go bail, stand security. **–sfähig,** *adj.* able to give bail *or* provide security. **–sversicherung,** *f.* guaranty-insurance.

Kautschuk, *m.* & *n.* (-s, -e) caoutchouc, (india)-rubber. **–milch,** *f.* rubber latex.

Kauz, *m.* (-es, ⸚e) screech-owl; queer fellow, eccentric.

Kavalier, *m.* (-s, -e) cavalier, gallant, knight; gentleman, ladies' man. **–mäßig,** *adj.* gentlemanly. **–tuch,** *n.* breast-pocket handkerchief; (*coll.*) handkerchief to show, not to blow.

Kavaller–ie, *f.* (-ien) cavalry, horsemen, horse (*collect.*). **–ist,** *m.* (-en, -en) cavalryman, trooper.

Kavent, *m.* (-en, -en) guarantor. **–ieren,** *v.n.* (*aux.* h.) give security for, guarantee.

Kaviar, *m.* caviare; (*Prov.*) – *fürs Volk*, caviare to the general.

Kebs–e, *f.* (-en) concubine, mistress. **–ehe,** *f.* concubinage. **–kind,** *n.* illegitimate child, bastard. **–weib,** *n.*, *see* **–e.**

keck, *adj.* bold, daring, audacious; pert, forward, impudent, cheeky; (*dial.*) firm, sound (*of fruit*); *mit –er Stirn*, with brazen assurance. **–heit,** *f.* boldness, audacity; pertness; impudence. **–lich,** *adv.* boldly; pertly.

Kegel, *m.* (-s, –) cone; skittle, ninepin; shoulder-bone (*of a horse*); (*archaic*) illegitimate child; depth (*of type*) (*Typ.*); *mit Kind und* –, with bag and baggage. **–bahn,** *f.* skittle- *or* bowling-alley. **–förmig,** *adj.*, *see* **–ig.** **–getriebe,** *n.* bevel pinions (*Mach.*). **–ig,** *adj.* conical, cone-shaped, tapering. **–junge,** *m.* marker (*at ninepins*). **–kugel,** *f.* skittle-ball. **–kupplung,** *f.* cone clutch (*Motor.*). **–n,** 1. *v.n.* (*aux.* h.) play at ninepins *or* skittles; roll head over heels, turn a somersault. **–rad,** *n.* bevel wheel (*Mach.*). **–scheiben,** *v.n.* (*dial.*), **–schieben,** *v.n.* play at skittles *or* ninepins. **–schnitt,** *m.* conic section; *Lehre von den –schnitten*, conics. **–schub,** *m. see* **–bahn.** **–spiel,** *n.*, **–sport,** *m.* (game of) skittles, skittle-playing. **–stumpf,** *m.* truncated cone. **–ventil,** *n.* conical valve.

Kegler, *m.* (-s, –) skittle-player.

Kehl–e, *f.* (-en) throat, gullet, throttle; fluting, channel, gutter; gorge (*Fort.*), breast of a bastion; *aus voller –e*, heartily, loudly, at the top of one's voice; *ihm geht's an die –e*, he is up against it; *in die unrechte –e kommen*, go down the wrong way; *einem die –e zuschnüren* or *abschneiden*, strangle or bleed s.o. (*through usury*); *einem das Messer an die –e setzen*, hold a knife at a p.'s throat; *ein Vermögen durch die –e jagen*, squander a fortune in drink, pour one's fortune down the drain. **–ader,** *f.* jugular vein. **–bräune,** *f.* quinsy. **–deckel,** *m.* epiglottis (*Anat.*). **–entzündung,** *f.* laryngitis. **–drüse,** *f.* thyroid gland. **–en,** *v.a.* flute, hollow, groove, channel. **–hauch,** *m.* aspirate 'h', spirant. **–hobel,** *m.* grooving plane. **–ig,** *adj.* grooved, fluted; *tausend–ig*, of a thousand voices. **–knochen,** *m.*, **–knorpel,** *m.*, **–kopf,** *m.* larynx. **–kopfbänder,** *n.pl.* vocal chords. **–kopfeingang,** *m.* glottis. **–kopfspiegel,** *m.* laryngoscope. **–kopfverschlußlaut,** *m.* glottal stop (*Phonet.*). **–lappen,** *pl.* wattles. **–laut,** *m.* guttural sound (*Phonet.*). **–leiste,** *f.* moulding (*Arch.*). **–riemen,** *m.* throat latch (*Harness*). **–rinne,** *f.* gutter. **–schweißnaht,** *f.* fillet weld (*Metall.*). **–stimme,** *f.* guttural voice. **–ung,** *f.* channel, groove, fluting, moulding. **–ziegel,** *m.* gutter-tile.

Kehr–e, *f.* (-en) turning, winding, turn, bend, corner; side *or* flank vault (*Gymn.*); (*dial.*) *ganz aus der –e*, quite wrong, in the contrary direction. [1]**–en,** 1. *v.a.* turn; *das Schwert in die Scheide –en*, put the sword into the scabbard; *einem den Rücken –en*, turn one's back on s.o.; *eine S. zum besten –en*, make the best of a th.; *die rauhe Seite nach außen –en*, show one's worst side, behave brusquely, be abrupt *or* blunt; *das Oberste zu unterst –en*, turn everything upside down; *die Maschinen –en*, reverse the engines. 2. *v.r.* turn; *sich –en an* (*Acc.*), regard, heed, mind, pay attention to, follow; *an ihn –e ich mich nicht*, I pay no attention to him; *sich zur Buße –en*, become penitent; *in sich* (*Acc.*) *–en*, retire into o.s., brood, meditate, commune with o.s. **–aus,** *m.*, *see* [2]**kehren.** **–bild,** *n.* negative (*Phot.*). **–punkt,** *m.* apsis (*Astr.*). **–reim,** *m.* refrain. **–seite,** *f.* reverse (side), back (*of the sheet*); drawback, disadvantage. **–t,** about turn!; (*Amer.*) about face! (*Mil.*); *–t machen*, wheel *or* face about (*Mil.*); turn back. **–tunnel,** *m.* loop-tunnel. **–twendung,** *f.* about turn (*Mil.*), turn (*Av.*). **–um,** *see* **–reim** & **–wieder;** *im –um*, in a twinkling of the eye. **–wert,** *m.* reciprocal value. **–wieder,** *n.* & *m.* blind alley.

[2]**kehr–en,** *v.a.* sweep, brush; turn out (*a room*); (*Prov.*) *neue Besen –en gut*, new brooms sweep clean; *–e vor deiner eignen Tür!* mind your own business! **–aus,** *m.* last dance. **–besen,** *m.* broom,

besom. **–bürste,** *f.* brush. **–icht,** *m.* (& *n.*) dust, rubbish, refuse, sweepings. **–ichteimer,** *m.*, *see* **–ichtkasten.** **–ichthaufen,** *m.* rubbish heap, dump. **–ichtkasten,** *m.* dust-bin, rubbish bin, refuse bin.

keif–en, *v.n.* (*aux.* h.) scold, upbraid, chide, nag. **–isch,** *adj.* scolding, quarrelsome.

Keil, *m.* (-(e)s, -e) wedge; gusset, gore (*dressmaking*); keystone (*of an arch*); clock (*of a stocking*); bolt, thunderbolt; key, dowel, cotter, pin; (*Mech.*); V-formation (*Av.*); quoin (*Typ.*); *pl.* (*dial.*) thrashing. *das spitze Ende eines –es*, the thin end of the wedge; (*dial.*) *es gibt –e!* they are coming to blows! (*dial.*) *–e kriegen*, get thrashed; (*Prov.*) *auf einen groben Klotz gehört ein grober –*, give tit for tat; (*Prov.*) *ein – treibt den andern*, it is just one thing after another. **–ähnlich,** *adj.*, **–artig,** *adj.*, see **–förmig.** **–en,** 1. *v.a.* wedge, fasten with a wedge, key (*Mach.*); cleave, split with a wedge; (*dial.*) thrash; induce (a p. to do a th.); win (a p.) over; *ein um sich –ender Gaul*, a kicking horse. 2. *v.r.* come to blows. **–erei,** *f.* fight, fisticuffs, rough-and-tumble, (*sl.*) scrap. **–flosse,** *f.* triangular tail fin (*Av.*). **–förmig,** *adj.* wedge-shaped, cuneiform, sphenoidal, cuneate. **–hacke,** *f.* pickaxe, mattock. **–inschrift,** *f.* cuneiform inscription. **–kissen,** *n.*, *see* **–polster.** **–nute,** *f.* keyway (*Mach.*). **–polster,** *n.* (& *Austr. m.*) wedge-shaped bolster. **–schrift,** *f.* cuneiform characters. **–welle,** *f.* keyed shaft (*Mach.*).

Keiler, *m.* (-s, –) wild boar (*of more than a year*).

Keim, *m.* (-(e)s, -e) germ; bud, spore, sprout, shoot, nucleus; embryo; origin; *im –e ersticken*, nip in the bud. **–anlage,** *f.* blastoderm. **–drüse,** *f.* gonad. **–en,** *v.n.* (*aux.* h. & s.) germinate, sprout, bed; arise, spring up, develop, begin to show itself, stir; *im –en*, in embryo. **–frei,** *adj.* sterile, free from germs, sterilized, disinfected, aseptic; *–frei machen*, sterilize (*Med.*). **–hülle,** *f.* perisperm. **–kapsel,** *f.*, **–korn,** *n.* spore. **–knospe,** *f.* germinal bud, ovule. **–kraft,** *f.* vitality, viability. **–lager,** *n.* stroma. **–ling,** *m.* germ, seedling, embryo. **–sack,** *m.* amnion. **–stock,** *m.* ovary. **–tötend,** *adj.* disinfectant, antiseptic, germicidal; *–tötendes Mittel*, germicide, disinfectant, antiseptic. **–träger,** *m.* carrier (*Med.*). **–ung,** *f.* germination. **–wurzel,** *f.* radicle. **–zelle,** *f.* germ cell, spore.

kein, *adj* no, not a, not one, not any; (*coll.*) – *Gedanke!* no such thing! that is not to be thought of! nonsense! *– einziger*, not a single one; *– Mensch*, no one; *auf –en Fall*, *see* **–esfalls;** *es ist –e so wichtige S.*, it is not so important a matter; *er ist – Student mehr*, he is no longer a student; *–e halbe Stunde vor dem Anfang der Prüfung*, within half an hour of the beginning of the examination; *es sind noch –e acht Tage*, it is not a week yet; *– Geschäftstag*, dies non. **–er, –e, –es,** *pron.* no one, not anyone, none; *er ist –er der Stärksten*, he is not of the strongest; *–er von beiden*, neither of them; *er gibt –em etwas nach*, he is inferior to none; *–es dieser Bücher gefällt ihm*, he does not like any of these books. **–erlei,** *indec. adj.* of no sort, not any; *auf –erlei Weise*, by no means whatever, in no way at all. **–erseits,** *adv.* on neither side. **–esfalls,** (*less good* **–enfalls**), *adv.* in no case, on no account. **–eswegs,** *adv.* by no means, not at all. **–mal,** *adv.* not once, never; (*Prov.*) *einmal ist –mal*, once does not count, the exception proves the rule.

Keks, *m.* & *n.* (– & -es, – & -e) biscuit.

Kelch, *m.* (-es, -e) cup, goblet, chalice; calyx (*Bot.*); (*Prov.*) *zwischen Lipp' und –es Rand schwebt der finstern Mächte Hand*, there's many a slip 'twixt cup and lip. **–artig,** *adj.* cup-like, cup-shaped. **–blatt,** *n.* sepal. **–glas,** *n.* crystal goblet. **–narbe,** *f.* umbril, eye (*Bot.*). **–weihe,** *f.* consecration of the communion-cup.

Kelle, *f.* (-n) trowel; scoop, ladle; fish-slice. **–n,** *v.a.* scoop, ladle.

Kell–er, *m.* (-ers, -er) cellar; tavern, wine-cellar; *Küche und –er*, food and drink. **–erei,** *f.* cellarage, wine-cellar. **–erer,** *m.* keeper of a wine cellar. **–ergeschoß,** *n.* basement. **–ergewölbe,** *n.* vault. **–erhals,** *m.* covered entrance to a cellar. **–erknecht,** *m.* cellar-man. **–erlager,** *n.* stand for casks. **–ermeister,** *m.*, *see* **–erer.** **–ermiete,** *f.* cellarage. **–erschnecke,** *f.* slug. (*C.L.*) **–erwechsel,** *m.* kite, accommodation bill. **–erwohnung,** *f.* basement dwelling. **–erzins,** *m.* cellarage. **–ner,** *m.* waiter. **–nerin,** *f.* barmaid. (*coll.*) **–nern,** *v.n.* act as a waiter *or* waitress, serve up food *or* drink.

Kelter, *f.* (-n) wine-press; *die – treten*, work the wine-press, tread the grapes. **–n,** *v.a.* tread *or* press (*grapes*). **–faß,** *n.*, **–zuber,** *m.* tub which receives the pressed juice, wine-dosser. **–haus,** *n.* press-house.

Kem(e)nate, *f.* (-n) (*archaic*) ladies' bower.

kenn–en, *ir.v.a.* know, be acquainted with; have cognizance of; *wir –en uns*, we know one another *or* each other; *von Ansehen –en*, know by sight. **–bar,** *adj.* knowable, distinguishable, recognizable, discernible; distinct, conspicuous. **–enlernen,** *v.a.* get to know, become acquainted (with), make the acquaintance (of). **–enswert,** *adj.* worth knowing. **–er,** *m.* (-ers, -er) connoisseur, judge, expert, specialist. **–erauge,** *n.*, **–erblick,** *m.* eye *or* glance of a connoisseur *or* expert. **–erschaft,** *f.* connoisseurs; connoisseurship. **–karte,** *f.* identity card. **–licht,** *n.* navigation light (*Av.*, *Naut.*). **–linie,** *f.* graph, characteristic, curve. **–musik,** *f.* signature tune. **–tlich,** *adj.* (easily) recognizable, discernible, distinguishable; conspicuous, marked, distinct (*an einer S.*, by a th.); *–tlich machen*, make known. **–tlichmachung,** *f.* characterization, labelling. **–tnis,** *f.* (-se) knowledge, information; notice, cognizance. *zur –tnis nehmen* or *–tnis nehmen von*, take cognizance *or* notice *or* note of; *einen in –tnis setzen von*, apprize a p. of; *einem etwas zur –tnis bringen* or *geben*, bring s.th. to s.o.'s notice, inform a p. about s.th.; *sich von etwas in –tnis setzen*, inform o.s. about s.th.; *Mann von vielen –tnissen*, man of wide *or* much knowledge; *er hat gute philologische –tnisse*, he knows a great deal about philology, he has a thorough knowledge of philology. **–tnisnahme,** *f.* getting information, taking cognizance of; information; (*C.L.*) *zu Ihrer –tnisnahme*, for your information *or* guidance. **–tnisreich,** *adj.* well-informed, learned. **–ung,** *f.* recognition signal (*Av.*, *etc.*), landmark, beacon (*Naut.*), characteristic. **–wert,** *m.* characteristic value. **–wort,** *n.* password, code word, motto. **–zahl,** *f.* reference number, constant, characteristic, code number. **–zeichen,** *n.* distinguishing mark, characteristic; sign, token, symptom; criterion. **–zeichnen,** *v.a.* mark, characterize. **–ziffer,** *f.* *see* **–zahl;** index of a logarithm, coefficient.

kenter–n, *v.a.* capsize, overturn; list, heel over (*Naut.*). **–haken,** *m.* grappling-iron.

Keramik, *f.* (-en) ceramics, pottery.

Kerb–e, *f.* (-en) notch, nick, indent, indentation, groove; *er haut in dieselbe –e wie ich*, he is working along *or* on the same lines as I am; *in die –e pfropfen*, graft in the cheek (*Hort.*). **–eisen,** *n.* wire-gauge. **–en,** *v.a.* notch, indent, dent, mill (*the edge of coins*). **gekerbt,** *p.p.* & *adj.*, crenate(d) (*Bot.*). **–holz,** *n.* notched stick; tally; *viel auf dem –holz haben*, have a lot to answer for; *etwas bei einem auf dem –holz haben*, be on a p.'s books, be in debt to a p. for s.th., have s.th. put on the slate by a p.; *das kommt nicht aufs –holz*, there will be no charge for this. **–ig,** *adj.* notched, jagged, indented, grooved. **–ling,** *m.*, *see* **–tier.** **–maschine,** *f.* crimping-iron. **–schlag(versuch),** *m.* notched bar impact test (*Metall.*). **–schnitzerei,** *f.* chip-carving. **–tier,** *n.* insect. **–tierkunde,** *f.*, **–tierlehre,** *f.* entomology. **–zähigkeit,** *f.* notch(ed bar) impact strength (*Metall.*). **–zähnig,** *adj.* notched, crenate, indented.

Kerbel, *m.* (-s, –) chervil (*Anthriscus & Chaerophyllum*) (*Bot.*).

Kerf, *m.* (-s, -e), **–e,** *f.* (-n), *see* **Kerbtier.**

Kerker, *m.* (-s, –) (*archaic & poet.*) prison, dungeon; (*Austr. dial.*) imprisonment with hard labour. **–artig,** *adj.*, **–haft,** *adj.*, **–mäßig,** *adj.* prison-like. **–fieber,** *n.* jail-fever. **–haft,** *f.* imprisonment. **–meister,** *m.* gaoler, jailer. **–turm,** *m.* donjon, keep.

Kerl, *m.* (-(e)s, -e & (*coll. & dial.* -s)) fellow; (*coll.*) chap; *ein ganzer –*, a man indeed, a fine fellow; (*sl.*) *sie ist ein lieber –*, she is a dear.

Kern, *m.* (-(e)s, -e) kernel, core, pip, stone (*of fruit*); pith (*of wood*), heartwood; heart, essence, root (*of a matter*); best part; élite, flower, picked men (*of an army*); (*dial.*) grain (*of corn*); nucleus (*Physics*). **-artig,** *adj.* kernel-like, nuclear. **-beißer,** *m.* hawfinch. **-bewegung,** *f.* nuclear motion (*Physics*). **-deutsch,** *adj.* thoroughly German, German to the core. **-echt,** *adj.* true to type. **-en,** 1. *v.a.* take the core *or* kernel out, stone (*fruit*); churn. 2. *v.r.* curdle, turn to butter. **-faul,** *adj.* rotten at the core; utterly lazy, bone idle. **-fest,** *adj.* very firm *or* solid. **-fleisch,** *n.* choice meat; pulp, pith. **-gehäuse,** *n.* core. **-geschoß,** *n.* armour-piercing bullet. **-gestalt,** *f.* fundamental form. **-gesund,** *adj.* thoroughly sound *or* healthy. (*coll.*) fit as a fiddle. **-haft,** *adj.* substantial, sound, healthy, robust, solid; pithy, vigorous, energetic, forcible. **-haus,** *n.* core. **-holz,** *n.* heartwood. **-ig,** *adj.* full of kernels *or* pips; *see* **-haft. -ladung,** *f.* main charge (*Artil.*), nuclear charge (*Phys.*). **-ladungszahl,** *f.* atomic number. **-leder,** *n.* best *or* bend leather. **-ling,** *m.* seedling. **-mehl,** *n.* best grade flour, firsts. **-obst,** *n.* stone fruit, fruit with a core. **-physik,** *f.* nuclear physics. **-punkt,** *m.* essential *or* decisive point; strong point (*Mil.*). **-rohr,** *n.* liner (*Artil.*). **-schatten,** *m.* umbra (*Astr.*). **-schuß,** *m.* point-blank shot. **-schußweite,** *f.* point-blank range. **-schwarz,** *adj.* pitch-black. **-seife,** *f.* best quality soap, curd soap. **-spruch,** *m.* pithy saying. **-stäbchen,** *n.* chromosome. **-stück,** *n.* principal item. **-teilung,** *f.* nuclear fission. **-truppen,** *f.pl.* picked troops. **-wuchs,** *m.* seedling. **-wüchsig,** *adj.* sprung from seed.

Kerze, *f.* (-n) candle, taper; sparking plug (*Motor.*). **-ngerade,** *adj.* straight as a ramrod, bolt upright. **-ngießer,** *m.*, **-nzieher,** *m.* chandler. **-nhalter,** *m.* candlestick. **-nlicht,** *n.* candle-light. **-nstärke,** *f.* candle-power.

Kescher, *m.* (-s, –) fishing net.

keß, *adj.* (*coll.*) bold, saucy, forward.

Kessel, *m.* (-s, –) kettle; cauldron, copper, boiler; retort (*Chem.*); valley, depression, hollow (*Geol.*); cover, burrow, den, kennel (*of wild animals*); excavation; crater; basin (*of a fountain, etc.*); pocket (*of troops*) (*Mil.*). **-asche,** *f.* potash. **-dampf,** *m.* live steam. **-flicker,** *m.* tinker. **-gestell,** *n.* kettle-stand. **-gewölbe,** *n.* cupola. **-haken,** *m.* pothook. **-haus,** *n.* boiler-house. **-jagen,** *n.* battue-shooting. **-kohle,** *f.* steam coal. **-macher,** *m.* coppersmith; boiler-maker. **-n,** *v.n.* (*aux.* h.) hollow out; root up the ground (*of boars*). **-pauke,** *f.* kettle-drum. **-schlacht,** *f.* encircling battle (*Mil.*). **-schmied,** *m.*, *see* **-macher. -stein,** *m.* deposit, scale (*on boilers*), fur (*on kettles*). **-tal,** *n.* valley enclosed by mountains. **-treiben,** *n.* battue-beating (*hunted game*), encirclement and extermination (*Mil.*); hunting down (*of a criminal*). **-wagen,** *m.* tanker, fuel truck.

Keßler, *m.* (-s, –) (*dial.*) brazier, coppersmith, boilermaker, tinker.

Ketsch, *f.* (-en) ketch (*Naut.*).

Kette, *f.* (-n) chain; necklace; track (*of tracked vehicles*) (*Mil.*); series, train, concatenation; covey (*of birds*); flight (*of 3 aircraft*); chain, range (*of mountains*), cordon (*Mil.*); (*archaic*) chain (*measure = 10 metres*); (*pl.*) fetters, bondage, slavery; *an die – legen,* chain up; *in –n legen* or *schlagen,* fetter; *in der – stehen,* stand in a queue; *– und Schuß,* warp and woof. **-ln,** *v.a.* fasten with a chain; embroider with chain-stitch; link together *or* pick up (stitches). **-lhaken,** *m.*, **-lnadel,** *f.* embroidery needle. **-n,** *v.a.* chain, fetter; connect with; link *or* tie to. **-nantrieb,** *m.* chain drive (*Motor.*). **-nbrüche,** *m. pl.* compound fraction (*Arith.*). **-nbrücke,** *f.* suspension-bridge. **-nfaden,** *m.* warp (*Weav.*). **-nfeier,** *f.*; *Petri –nfeier,* St. Peter's chains, Lammas (*R.C.*). **-ngebirge,** *n.* mountain-chain. **-ngelenk,** *n.* link (*of a chain*). **-nglied,** *n.* link (*of a chain*), member. **-nhandel,** *m.* transaction passing through hands of numerous middlemen. **-nhemd,** *n.*, *see* **-npanzer. -nhund,** *m.* yard dog; watch-dog. **-nkasten,** *m.* chain cover (*Cycl.*). **-nkugel,** *f.* chain-shot. **-npanzer,** *m.* coat of mail. **-nrad,** *n.* sprocket wheel. **-nraucher,** *m.* chain smoker. **-nregel,** *f.* chain-rule, double rule of three. **-nschluß,** *m.* sorites, chain-syllogism (*Log.*). **-nstich,** *m.* chain-stitch. **-ntriller,** *m.* sustained shake (*Mus.*). **-nwirkung,** *f.* chain reaction (*atomic fission*).

Kett-faden, *m.*, **-garn,** *n.* warp.

Ketzer, *m.* (-s, –) heretic. **-ei,** *f.* heresy. **-gericht,** *n.* (court of) inquisition. **-haft,** *adj.*, **-isch,** *adj.* heretical, heterodox. **-macherei,** *f.* intolerance of dissentients. **-meister,** *m.* grand inquisitor. **-richter,** *m.* inquisitor. **-riecher,** *m.* heresy-hunter. **-verbrennung,** *f.* burning of heretics, auto-da-fé.

keuch-en, *v.n.* (*aux.* h.) pant, gasp, puff, wheeze. **-husten,** *m.* whooping-cough.

Keule, *f.* (-n) club; pestle; hind leg, thigh (*of a beast*); leg (*of meat*). **-n,** *v.a.* (*Swiss dial.*) slaughter (*beasts*). **-nförmig,** *adj.* club-shaped. **-nschlag,** *m.* blow of a club. **-nschwingen,** *n.* club swinging (*Gymn.*). **-nstück,** *n.* cut off the leg (*of meat*).

Keuper, *m.* red marl, keuper (*Geol.*).

keusch, *adj.* chaste, pure, virgin, maidenly. **-heit,** *f.* chastity, purity, virginity, continence; *Priesterin der –heit,* vestal virgin. **-heitsgelübde,** *n.* vow of chastity.

Kichererbse, *f.* (-n) chick-pea (*Cicer arietinum*) (*Bot.*).

kichern, *v.n.* (*aux.* h.) giggle, titter.

Kicks, *m.* (-es, -e), **-er,** *m.* miss (*Bill.*). **-en,** *v.n.* miss the ball (*Bill.*).

Kiebitz, *m.* (-es, -e) lapwing, peewit, green plover (*Vanellus cristatus*) (*Orn.*). **-en,** *v.n.* (*aux.* h.) look over players's shoulders as a spectator (*cards*).

[1]**Kiefer,** 1. *m.* (-s, –) jaw; jawbone; mandible. 2. (*in compounds* =) maxillary. **-ig,** (*suffix*) e.g. *gross–ig,* large-jawed. **-muskel,** *m.* maxillary muscle. **-sperre,** *f.* lockjaw. **-winkel,** *m.* angle of the jaw.

[2]**Kiefer,** *f.* (-n) Scots pine (*Pinus silvestris*) (*Bot.*), stone pine (*Pinus pinea*) (*Bot.*). **-n,** *adj.* (made of) pine. **-nholz,** *n.* pine-wood, yellow pine, pitch-pine. **-nspanner,** *m.* pine beauty (*butterfly*). **-zapfen,** *m.* pine-cone.

Kieke, *f.* (-n) (*dial.*) foot-warmer.

kiek-en, *v.a.* (*dial. & coll.*) peep. (*sl.*) **-er,** *m.* telescope, spy-glass; *einen auf dem –er haben,* keep one's eye on s.o.; *etwas auf dem –er haben,* have one's eye on s.th. (*coll.*) **-indiewelt,** *m.* (-s, -s) jackanapes, greenhorn.

Kiel, *m.* (-s, -e) 1. quill (pen). 2. keel; carina, keel (*Bot.*); *den – legen,* lay down the keel; *mit breitem –,* broad-bottomed; *auf ebenem –,* on an even keel. **-bett,** *n.* coarse feather-bed. **-brüchig,** *adj.* broken-backed (*of a ship*). **-feder,** *f.* quill feather. **-en,** 1. *v.a.* feather (*an arrow*). 2. *v.n.* (*aux.* h.) become fledged. **-flosse,** *f.* tail fin. **-förmig,** *adj.* keel-shaped; carinate (*Bot.*). **-geld,** *n.* keelage. **-holen,** *v.a.* careen (*a vessel*); (*archaic*) keelhaul (*a sailor*). **-kropf,** *m.* (*dial.*) changeling; abortion, monster. **-linie,** *f.*; *in –linie fahren,* sail line-ahead. **-oben,** *adv.* bottom up. **-raum,** *m.* ship's hold. **-recht,** *n.* keelage. **-richtung,** *f.* head. **-schwein,** *n.* keelson. **-wasser,** *n.* wake (*of a ship*). **-wasserströmung,** *f.* back wash.

Kieme, *f.* (-n) gill (*of fish*); branchia. **-natmend,** *adj.* gill-breathing.

Kien, *m.* (-(e)s, -e) resinous pine-wood; pine-resin; (*coll.*) nonsense, rubbish. **-apfel,** *m.* pine cone. **-baum,** *n.* Scots pine. **-en,** *adj.* (made of) pine. **-harz,** *n.* pine resin. **-holz,** *n.* resinous wood. **-ig,** *adj.* resinous. **-öl,** *n.* oil of turpentine. **-ruß,** *m.* lamp-black. **-span,** *m.* pine torch.

Kiepe, *f.* (-n) (*dial.*) wicker basket (*carried like rucksack*), dosser.

Kies, *m.* (-es, -e) gravel; shingle, scree; pyrites; quartz; (*sl.*) money. **-artig,** *adj.*, gravelly; pyritous. **-boden,** *m.* gravelly soil. **-brenner,** *m.* pyrites burner. **-eln,** *v.a.* cover *or* lay with gravel. **-grube,** *f.* gravel-pit. **-ig,** *adj.* gravelly; gritty. **-sand,** *m.* coarse sand. **-weg,** *m.* gravel path.

Kiesel, *m.* (-s, –) pebble, flint; silex, silica; (*dial. & coll.*) top (*plaything*). **-artig,** *adj.* siliceous. **-erde,** *f.* siliceous earth, silica. **-glas,** *n.* flint-glass.

-grund, *m.* pebbly ground *or* bottom. **-gur,** *f.* infusorial earth (*Geol.*). **-hart,** *adj.* hard as flint. **-herz,** *n.* flinty *or* hard heart. **-n,** *v.n. see under* **Kies**; (*dial. & coll.*) play (whip and) top. **-ig,** *adj.* flinty, pebbly, siliceous. **-sand,** *m.* coarse gravel. **-sandstein,** *m.* siliceous sandstone. **-sauer,** *adj.* silicic, silicate of. **-säure,** *f.* silicic acid. **-stein,** *m.* pebble, flint. **-stoff,** *m.* silicon.

[1]**kiesen,** *ir.v.a.* (*archaic & poet.*) select, choose, elect.

[2]**kiesen,** *see* **kieseln.**

kikeriki, 1. *int.* cock-a-doodle-doo! 2. *m.* (-s, -s) cock.

Kilo-gramm, *n.* (-s, -e) kilogram. **-meter,** *n.* kilometre. (*coll.*) **-meterfresser,** *m.* road hog. **-meterzähler,** *m.* cyclometer, mileage meter. **-wattstunde,** *f.* kilowatt hour.

Kilt, *m.* (*dial.*) nocturnal visit. **-en,** *v.a.* pay a nocturnal visit to one's sweetheart. **-gang,** *m.*, *see* **Kilt.**

Kimm, *f.* (*m. is common though incorrect*) horizon (*Naut.*); bilge (*of a ship*). **-e,** *f.* (-en) border, brim, chime *or* chimb; saw-cut, kerf, notch, nick; back-sight (*of rifle*); *über -e und Korn feuern,* fire over open sights (*Mil.*). **-en,** *v.a.* provide with a brim *or* chime; nick, notch. **-ung,** *f.* mirage. **-wasser,** *n.* bilge-water.

Kind, *n.* (-(e)s, -er) child; offspring; *ein – abtreiben,* procure abortion; *an -esstatt annehmen,* adopt; (*Prov.*) *das – mit dem Bade ausschütten,* reject the good together with the bad; *ein – bekommen,* have a child; *Berliner –,* native of Berlin; (*Prov.*) *wenn das – ertrunken ist, wird der Brunnen zugedeckt,* lock the stable door when the horse is gone; *wes Geistes – ist er?* what sort of a person is he? *eines -es genesen,* be delivered of a child; *– des Glückes,* lucky person; *-er Gottes,* the pious, all mankind; *ein – unter dem Herzen haben,* be carrying *or* pregnant; *ich komme mit – und Kegel,* I am coming, bag and baggage; *er hat weder – noch Kegel,* he has neither kith nor kin; *sie wird kein – mehr haben,* she is past child-bearing; *– und Kindes–,* children and grandchildren, progeny, descendants; *kleines –,* infant, baby; *– der Liebe,* natural *or* illegitimate child; *mein –!* my dear, my dear child! *– im Mutterleibe,* embryo, foetus, unborn child; *nachgeborenes –,* posthumous child; *das – beim rechten* or *bei seinem Namen nennen,* call a spade a spade; *ein – stillen,* give suck to a child; *ein – aus der Taufe heben,* stand sponsor to a child; *– des Todes,* one doomed to death; *totgeborenes –,* still-born child; *unmündiges –,* minor; *von – auf,* from childhood, from infancy; (*wieder*) *zum – werden,* grow childish. **-bett,** *n.* childbed; *ins -bett kommen,* be brought to bed. **-betterin,** *f.* lying-in woman, woman that has just been delivered. **-bettfieber,** *n.* puerperal fever. **-elbier,** *n.* (*dial.*) christening-feast. **-elmutter,** *f.* (*dial.*) midwife. **-eln,** *v.n.* (*aux.* s.) (*dial.*) fondle, stroke; trifle, act childishly. **-eramme,** *f.* wet-nurse. **-erbett,** *n.* crib, cot. **-erbewahranstalt,** *f.* day-nursery. **-erbrei,** *m.* pap. **-erdieb,** *m.* kidnapper (of children). **-erei,** *f.* nonsense, stupidity, childishness, childish behaviour; (*fig.*) trifle. **-erernährung,** *f.* baby *or* infant feeding. **-erfeind,** *m.* child-hater. **-erfrau,** *f.*, **-erfräulein,** *n.* nurse, nursery governess, nanny. **-erfürsorge,** *f.* child welfare. **-ergarten,** *m.* kindergarten. **-ergärtnerin,** *f.* kindergarten teacher. **-erhort,** *m.* day-nursery, crèche, nursery school. **-erhusten,** *m.* whooping cough. **-erjahre,** *n.pl.* (years of) childhood. **-erkrankheiten,** *f.pl.* children's ailments, (*fig.*) teething troubles. **-erlähmung,** *f.* infantile paralysis. **-erlätzchen,** *n.* bib. **-erlehre,** *f.* instruction in the catechism; Sunday-school (teaching). **-erleicht,** *adj.* very easy, child's play. **-erlieb,** *adj.* fond of children. **-erliebe,** *f.* love of children; filial love. **-erlieder,** *n.pl.* nursery rhymes. **-erlos,** *adj.* childless. **-ermädchen,** *n.*, *see* **-erfrau. -ermord,** *m.* infanticide; *der Bethlehemitische -ermord,* the Massacre of the Innocents. **-erpferd,** *n.* hobby-horse. **-erposse,** *f.* childish trick, foolery. **-erraub,** *m.* kidnapping. **-erreich,** *adj.* prolific, having many children. **-erreime,** *m.pl.* nursery rhymes. **-erschreck,** *m.* bogy (man). **-erschuhe,** *m.pl.* children's shoes; *die -erschuhe ausgetreten, ausgezogen* or *abgelegt haben* or *den -erschuhen entwachsen sein,* be no longer a child, have put away childish things; *noch in den -erschuhen stecken,* be still a child, be tied to one's mother's apron-strings; not have progressed *or* advanced *or* not be developed beyond the early stages, be still in its beginnings *or* infancy. **-erseife,** *f.* nursery soap, baby-soap. **-erspiel,** *n.* children's game; child's play, easy matter; trifle; *es ist kein -erspiel,* it is not easy, that is no joke. **-erspott,** *m.* laughing-stock. **-ersterblichkeit,** *f.* infant mortality. **-erstube,** *f.* nursery; early education; *gute -erstube,* good breeding, upbringing *or* manners. **-ertag,** *m.* Innocents' Day. **-ertaufe,** *f.*, *see* **-taufe. -erverse,** *m.pl.* nursery rhymes. **-erwagen,** *m.* perambulator, (*coll.*) pram. **-erwärterin,** *f.*, *see* **-erfrau. -erwäsche,** *f.* baby-linen. **-erwiege,** *f.* cradle. **-erzahl,** *f.*; *Beschränkung der -erzahl,* birth-control. **-erzahn,** *m.* milk-tooth. **-erzeug,** *n.* playthings, trifles; baby-linen. **-erzucht,** *f.* bringing up children. **-erzulage,** *f.* children's allowance. **-esalter,** *n.* infancy, childhood. **-esannahme,** *f.* adoption. **-esbeine,** *n.pl.*; (*only in*) *von -esbeinen an,* from infancy *or* earliest childhood. **-eskind,** *n.* grandchild; (*pl.*) grandchildren; posterity. **-esliebe,** *f.* filial love. **-esmord,** *m.* murder of new-born child by mother. **-esmörderin,** *f.* woman guilty of infanticide; infanticide. **-esnot,** *f.* labour, travail; *in -esnöten sterben,* die in childbed. **-espflicht,** *f.* filial duty. **-esräuber,** *m.* baby-snatcher. **-esrecht,** *n.*, **-esteil,** *n.* portion of inheritance due to a child. **-esstatt,** *f.*; *Annahme an -esstatt,* adoption. **-estötung,** *f.* infanticide (*among primitive peoples*). **-eswasser,** *n.* amniotic fluid. **-haft,** *adj.* childlike, childish. **-heit,** *f.* childhood, infancy; *von -heit an,* from infancy *or* childhood. **-isch,** *adj.* childish. **-lich,** *adj.* childlike; filial. **-schaft,** *f.* relation of a child to its parents; filiation; (*B.*) adoption. **-skopf,** *m.* childish person, fool; numskull; *sei kein -skopf!* don't be (so) childish! **-slage,** *f.* foetal position. **-spech,** *n.* meconium. **-taufe,** *f.* christening, baptism.

Kin-ematograph, *m.* (-en, -en) cinematograph. (*coll.*) **-o,** *n.* (-os, -os) cinema, the pictures, (*Amer.*) motion pictures, movies, kino. **-obesucher,** *m.* cinema-goer, film fan.

Kineti-k, *f.* kinetics. **-sch,** *adj.* kinetic.

Kinkerlitzchen, *n.pl.* (*coll.*) trifles, trivialities; *– machen,* make a silly fuss.

Kinn, *n.* (-(e)s, -e) chin; lower jaw; spout (of a gutter). **-backe,** *f.*, **-backen,** *m.* jaw, mandible. **-backendrüse,** *f.* submaxillary gland. **-backenkrampf,** *m.* lockjaw, trismus. **-backenzahn,** *m.* molar tooth. **-bart,** *m.* beard on the chin; imperial, goatee. **-grube,** *f.* dimple; mental fossa. **-haken,** *m.* upper-cut (*Boxing*). **-kette,** *f.*, **-reif,** *m.* curb. **-kettenstange,** *f.* curb-bit. **-lade,** *f.* jaw-bone, maxilla. **-riemen,** *m.* chin-strap.

Kino, *see* **Kin-.**

Kipf, *m.* (-es, -e), **-el,** *n.* (-s, –) (*dial.*) (horn-shaped) roll, croissant.

Kipp-e, *f.* (-en) edge, brink, verge; dangerous situation; (*dial.*) see-saw; (*sl.*) fag-end; *auf der -e stehen,* be in a critical position, hang in the balance, be on the verge (*of falling, of disaster*). **-elig,** *adj.*, *see* **-lig. -eln,** 1. *v.r.* (*dial.*) wrangle. 2. *v.n.* (*aux.* h. & s.) (*coll.*) topple, wobble, see-saw. **-en,** 1. *v.a.* tilt, tip over, upset, tip up; (*dial.*) cut the edges off, clip, lop. 2. *v.n.* (*aux.* h. & s.) tip *or* topple over, lose one's balance; upset, overturn. **-er,** *m.* (-s, –) tip-cart, tip-truck; (*archaic*) money-clipper. **-erei,** *f.* (*dial.*) usury. **-ern,** *v.n.* (*aux.* h.) (*dial.*) carry on usury. **-hebel,** *m.* rocker arm (*Motor, etc.*). **-kessel,** *m.* swivel pan. **-lager,** *n.* rocker bearing. (*coll.*) **-lig,** *adj.* doubtful, undecided; dangerous; *-liges Gleichgewicht,* labile equilibrium. **-schalter,** *m.* tumbler switch. **-schwimmer,** *m.* carburettor float (*Motor.*). **-spannung,** *f.* saw-tooth *or* time-base voltage (*Rad.*). **-vorrichtung,** *f.* tipping, rocker *or* swivelling device *or* mechanism; hinge-fitting. **-wagen,** *m.* tip-cart *or* wagon.

Kirch–e, *f.* (-en) church; *streitende –e*, church militant; *herrschende –e*, established church. **–enablaß**, *m.* indulgence (*R.C.*). **–enälteste(r)**, *m.* churchwarden, elder, vestryman. **–enamt**, *n.* church office, ecclesiastical function; eldership. **–enbann**, *m.* excommunication; interdict; *in den –enbann tun*, excommunicate, interdict. **–enbekleidung**, *f.* pulpit-hangings. **–enbesuch**, *m.* attendance at church. **–enbesucher**, *m.* churchgoer. **–enbuch**, *n.* parish register. **–enbuße**, *f.* penance imposed by the church. **–enchor**, *m.* choir. **–endiener**, *m.* church officer; sexton; sacristan, verger. **–endienstlich**, *adj.* pertaining to the church service; *–endienstliche Handlungen*, religious observances *or* ceremonies. **–enfahne**, *f.* banner used in church ceremonies. **–enfluch**, *m.* anathema. **–enfreiheit**, *f.* ecclesiastical immunity. **–enfrevel**, *m.* sacrilege. **–enfriede**, *m.* union of the members of the church; security of church property. **–enfürst**, *m.* ecclesiastical prince, high dignitary of the church; prelate. **–engebet**, *n.* common prayer. **–engebetbuch**, *n.* book of common prayer, prayer-book. **–engebiet**, *n.* diocese. **–engebrauch**, *m.* church rite *or* observance. **–engefäß**, *n.* church vessel; (*pl.*) church plate. **–engeld**, *n.* church fund; (*pl.*) church property. **–engemeinde**, *f.* parish; congregation. **–engemeinschaft**, *f.* church-membership. **–engerät**, *n.* sacred vessels *or* garments. **–engericht**, *n.* ecclesiastical court, consistory. **–engesang**, *m.* hymn; chorale; *liturgischer –engesang*, psalmody; *Gregorianischer –engesang*, Gregorian chant. **–engeschichte**, *f.* ecclesiastical history. **–engesetz**, *n.* canon; (*pl.*) decretals. **–engesetzlich**, *adj.*, **–engesetzmäßig**, *adj.* canonical. **–englaube**, *m.* creed, dogma. **–engrund**, *m.* glebe. **–enjahr**, *n.* ecclesiastical year. **–enkonvent**, *m.* convocation. **–enkonzert**, *n.* recital of sacred music. **–enlehen**, *n.* ecclesiastical fief. **–enlehre**, *f.* church doctrine. **–enlehrer**, *m.* father of the church; one of the early fathers. **–enlicht**, *n.*; *kein –enlicht sein*, be dull *or* stupid, be not a very bright spark. **–enlied**, *n.* hymn. **–enmaus**, *f.*; *arm wie eine –enmaus* or *die reine –enmaus sein*, be as poor as a church mouse, be extremely poor. **–enmusik**, *f.* sacred music. **–enordnung**, *f.* liturgy, ritual. **–enornat**, *n.* canonicals. **–enrat**, *m.* consistory, church committee, ecclesiastical court; member of a consistory *or* church committee. **–enraub**, *m.* sacrilege. **–enrecht**, *n.* canon law. **–enrechtlich**, *adj.* canonical. **–enregiment**, *n.*, **–regierung**, *f.* church government; hierarchy. **–ensache**, *f.* ecclesiastical affair. **–ensänger**, *m.* chorister. **–ensatz**, *m.* ecclesiastical tenet. **–ensatzung**, *f.* rule of the church. **–enschänder**, *m.* sacrilegious person. **–enschiff**, *n.* nave. **–ensitz**, *m.* pew. **–enspaltung**, *f.* schism. **–enstaat**, *m.* Papal territory, Pontifical State. **–ensteuer**, *f.* church-rate. **–enstreit**, *m.*, **–enstreitigkeit**, *f.* religious controversy; dissension in the church. **–enstuhl**, *m.* pew. **–entrennung**, *f.* schism. **–entür**, *f.* church door. **–envater**, *m.* father of the church; *die –enväter*, the early fathers. **–enversammlung**, *f.* synod; convocation; vestry. **–envorschrift**, *f.* church law; ordinance of the church; liturgy. **–envorstand**, *m.* vestry board. **–envorsteher**, *m.* churchwarden; *Versammlung der –envorsteher*, vestry-meeting. **–enwesen**, *n.* church matters. **–gang**, *m.* procession to church, church-going; *–gang halten*, be churched. **–gänger**, *m.* churchgoer. **–halle**, *f.* church porch. **–hof**, *m.* churchyard; cemetery, graveyard. **–lich**, *adj.* ecclesiastical; *–liches Begräbnis*, Christian burial. **–ner**, *m.* sexton, verger, sacristan. **–spiel**, *n.* parish; *nicht zu einem –spiele gehörig*, extra-parochial. **–sprengel**, *m.* diocese. **–turm**, *m.* church tower *or* steeple. **–turmspitze**, *f.* steeple, spire. **–turmspolitik**, *f.* parochialism, parish-pump politics. **–weih(e)**, *f.* consecration *or* dedication of a church; church-festival.

Kirmes, (-sen), (*dial.*) **Kirmse, Kermse**, (-n), (*Austr.*) **Kirmeß**, (-(ss)en) *f.* church festival; *see* **Kirchweihe.**

kirnen, *v.a.* churn (*butter*).

kirr–e, *adj.* tame; familiar; tractable, submissive. **–en**, 1. *v.a.* tame, make tractable; bring to heel; bait, decoy; allure. 2. *v.n.* (*dial.* (*aux.* h.) coo. **–ung**, *f.* taming; baiting, luring; bait, allurement.

Kirsch, *m.* *see* **–branntwein.** **–e**, *f.* (-en) cherry; (*Prov.*) *mit ihm ist nicht gut –en essen*, he is not an easy man to deal with *or* to get on with; *sich wie reife –en verkaufen*, sell like hot cakes. **–baum**, *m.* cherry-tree. **–branntwein**, *m.*, **–geist**, *m.* cherry-brandy. **–kern**, *m.* cherry-stone. **–kuchen**, *m.* cherry-tart. **–saft**, *m.* cherry-juice. **–wasser**, *n.* cherry-brandy.

Kissen, *n.* (-s, –) cushion, pillow, bolster, pad, padding. **–bezug**, *m.*, **–überzug**, *m.*, **–ziehe**, *f.* pillow-slip *or* case, cushion cover.

Kist–e, *f.* (-en) box, chest, coffer, trunk, crate, packing-case; (*sl.*) job, matter, affair; (*sl.*) crate (*for aircraft*); *eine –e Zigarren*, a box of cigars; (*sl.*) *die –e wird gemacht*, the job is on. **–enbrett**, *n.*, thin board. **–enpfand**, *n.* daughter's portion (*Law*). **–enweise**, *adv.* by the case, in single cases.

Kitsch, *m.* rubbish, trash; daub (*of pictures*). **–ig**, *adj.* rubbishy, trashy, inartistic, showy.

Kitt, *m.* (-(e)s, -e) cement; putty; lute, luting; (*sl.*) *der ganze –*, the whole shoot, the whole boiling. **–en**, *v.a.* glue, cement, lute, (fasten with) putty.

Kittel, *m.* (-s, –) smock, overall; frock, blouse; (*dial.*) jacket (*of a suit*); *hinter jedem – herlaufen*, trail after every skirt.

Kitz, *n.* (-es, -e), (*Austr.*) **–e**, *f.* (-en) kid, fawn.

Kitz–el, *m.* tickle, itching, itch, tickling, titillation; (inordinate) desire, appetite; *der –el sticht ihn danach*, he has a longing for it. **–elig**, *adj.*, *see* **–lig.** **–eln**, *v.a.* tickle, titillate; gratify, flatter (*vanity, etc.*). **–ler**, *m.* (-s, –), clitoris (*Anat.*). **–lig**, *adj.* ticklish, delicate, difficult, tricky, critical.

klabastern, *v.a.* (*dial.*) blunder along.

Klabautermann, *m.* bogy man, evil man (*Naut.*).

Klack, *m.* (-(e)s, ⸚e) (*dial.*) crack, chap (*in skin*).

klack(s), *int.* slap-bang!

Kladde, *f.* (-n) rough draft, rough copy; rough notebook, scribbling jotter; (*C.L.*) daybook, log.

Kladderadatsch, *m.* (*coll.*) mess, muddle, mix-up; desolation, havoc, damage, mischief.

klaff–en, *v.n.* (*aux.* h. & s.) gape, yawn; split open; chap (*of skin*); be ajar; *hier –t ein Widerspruch*, there is an irreconcilable contradiction here. **–end**, *pr. p.* & *adj.* gaping, yawning, (wide) apart, ajar; dehiscent (*Bot.*).

kläff–en, *v.n.* (*aux.* h.) bark, yelp; clamour, be quarrelsome, brawl. **–er**, *m.* yelping dog; brawler; grumbler, fault-finder.

Klafter, *f.* (-n) fathom (*archaic*), cord (*of wood*), span (*with outstretched arms*). **–holz**, *n.* cord-wood. **–n**, *v.n.* & *a.* span (with outspread arms *or* wings); cord up (*wood*). **–tief**, *adj.* many fathoms deep. **–weise**, *adv.* by the cord *or* fathom.

klag–bar, *adj.* actionable (*Law*); *–bar machen*, sue; *–bar werden*, go to law. **–e**, *f.* (-en) complaint; lament, lamentation; grievance, ground of complaint; suit, action, accusation, impeachment, indictment; *eine –e eingeben, anhängig machen* or *anstellen*, bring an action (*wider* or *gegen*, against); *–e auf Schadenersatz*, action for damages; *mit einer –e abgewiesen werden*, be nonsuited; *–e über, gegen* or *wider einen führen*, complain of a p.; bring an action against a p. **–(e)gesang**, *m.* threnody; *see* **–elied.** **–(e)geschrei**, *n.* wailing, lamentation. **–elied**, *n.* dirge, lamentation, elegy. **–elustig**, *adj.* litigious; querulous. **–emauer**, *f.* wailing wall (*at Jerusalem*). **–en**, 1. *v.a.* bewail, complain about, bemoan; *einem eine* S. or *sein Leid –en*, complain to a p. of a th.; (*um*) *einen Toten –en*, mourn for s.o. 2. *v.n.* (*aux.* h.) complain, lament (*über, um*, for); sue, go to law; *auf Schadenersatz –en*, sue for damages. **–end**, *pr.p.* & *adj.* complaining; plaintive; *der –ende*, the plaintiff. **–enswert**, *adj.* lamentable, deplorable. **–epunkte**, *m.pl.* counts of an indictment; grievances. **–esache**, *f.* subject of complaint; action at law. **–eschrift**, *f.* writ, written complaint. **–estimme**, *f.* plaintive voice. **–esucht**, *f.* litigiousness, disposition to complain, querulousness. **–esüchtig**, *adj.* litigious; querulous. **–eton**, *m.* plaintive *or* doleful accent. **–eweib**, *n.* (hired) mourner. **-los,** *adj.* uncomplaining; irreproachable, indemnified; *-los stellen,* give satisfaction, indemnify. **-weise,** *adv.* by way of complaint. **-würdig,** *adj.* lamentable, pitiful, woeful.

Kläg-er, *m.* (-ers, -er) plaintiff, complainant, accuser. **-erei,** *f.* litigiousness; constant complaining. **-erisch,** *adj.* relating to the plaintiff; litigious; *der -erische Advokat,* plaintiff's counsel. **-lich,** *adj.* lamentable, deplorable, pitiable; doleful, plaintive; miserable, wretched, pitiful.

Klamauk, *m.* (*coll.*) din, upheaval, rumpus, hullabaloo.

klamm, 1. *adj.* tight, close, compact, narrow; stiff (*with cold*), numb; (*dial.*) clammy; scarce; short (*esp. of money*). 2. *f.* (-en) ravine, gorge, cañon, canyon. **-er,** *f.* (-ern) clamp, clasp, cramp, (paper) clip, (clothes) peg; *eckige -er,* bracket (*Typ.*); *runde -er,* round bracket; parenthesis (*Typ.*); *löse zuerst die -er auf;* get rid of the brackets first (*Math.*). **-eraffe,** *m.* spider-monkey (*Ateles*) (*Zool.*); (*sl.*) pillion-rider (*Motor.*). **-erausdruck,** *m.* parenthetical expression. **-erfuß,** *m.* prehensile claw. **-erhaken,** *m.* grasping *or* clasping hook. **-ern,** 1. *v.a.* fasten, clip, clasp, clinch, clamp. 2. *v.r.* cling (*an,* to). **-erwurzel,** *f.* clinging root.

Klamotten, *f.pl.* (*coll.*) belongings, goods and chattels.

Klampe, *f.* (-n) clamp, cramp, clasp, holdfast; (*pl.*) cleats (*Naut.*).

Klampfe, *f.* (-n) guitar, lute.

klang, klang(e)st, klänge, *see* **klingen.**

Klang, *m.* (-(e)s, ¨-e) sound, tone, ringing, clang; ring; timbre (*Mus. & Phonet.*); *von gutem -e,* of good repute; *keinen guten - haben,* sound badly; be held in ill repute; *mit Sang und -,* with great pomp, with much ado; *ohne Sang und -,* clandestinely. **-boden,** *m.* sounding-board. **-farbe,** *f.* timbre. **-fülle,** *f.* sonority. **-lehre,** *f.* acoustics. **-lich,** *adv.* in respect of (its) sound. **-los,** *adj.* soundless, mute, unaccented; secret; without (a word of) praise. **-malerei,** *f.* onomatopoeia. **-reich,** *adj.* sonorous, full-sounding, rolling. **-stufe,** *f.* interval (*Mus.*). **-voll,** *adj., see* **-reich.** **-wort,** *n.* onomatopoeic word.

klapp, *int.* bang! clack! **-arm,** *m.* hinged arm. **-bar,** *adj.* folding, hinged, collapsible. **-bett,** *n.* camp-bed, folding-bed. **-blende,** *f.* drop shutter. **-brücke,** *f.* drawbridge. **-e,** *f.* (-en) flap, lid, valve, trap, hatch; ramp (*on landing craft*) (*Naut.*); damper; key, stop (*Mus.*); cuff, turn-up; (*sl.*) bed; (*sl.*) mouth; *eine Flöte mit elf -en,* an eleven-keyed flute; (*Prov.*) *zwei Fliegen mit einer -e treffen,* kill two birds with one stone; (*sl.*) *in die -e gehen* or *steigen,* go to bed; (*sl.*) *halt deine -e,* shut your trap! shut up! **-en,** 1. *v.a.* flap, strike together. 2. *v.n.* (*aux.* h.) clap, flap; clatter, rattle; (*coll.*) tally, fit, suit, work well, work out, be all right, (*sl.*) come off, click; (*coll.*) *alles -te famos,* everything went off splendidly; (*coll.*) *wenn es zum -en kommt,* if things come to a head. **-enhorn,** *n.* cornet-à-piston. (*sl.*) **-enschrank,** *m.* (telephone) switchboard. **-(en)-stiefel,** *m.* top-boot. **-enventil,** *n.* flap valve. **-er,** *f.* (-n) rattle; clapper; flier (*Weav.*). **-erbein,** *n.* skeleton, Death. **-erdürr,** *adj.* thin as a rake. **-(e)rig,** *adj.* clattering, rattling; weak, shaky, rickety. (*coll.*) **-erkasten,** *m.* old *or* out-of-tune piano; bone-shaker (*car*). **-ern,** *v.n.* (*aux.* h.) clatter, rattle; click; chatter (*teeth*); *ihm -ern die Zähne,* his teeth are chattering; *-ern gehört zum Handwerk,* you must blow your own trumpet; (*B.*) *Heulen und Zähne-ern,* weeping and gnashing of teeth. **-erschlange,** *f.* rattlesnake. **-erstorch,** *m.* stork (*partic. the one that brings babies*). **-fenster,** *n.* trap *or* skylight window. **-hornvers,** *m.* limerick. **-hut,** *m.* opera-hat. **-kamera,** *f.* folding-camera. **-kragen,** *m.* turn-down collar. **-messer,** *n.* jack-knife. **-(p)ult,** *n.* folding-desk. **-sitz,** *m.* tip-up seat. **-stuhl,** *m.* camp-stool, folding-chair. **-tisch,** *m.* folding-table. **-tür,** *f.* trap-door.

Klaps, *m.* (-es, ¨-e (& *Austr.* -e)) smack, clap, slap; (*coll.*) *du hast wohl einen -?* you're cracked *or* crackers, I should think. **-en,** *v.a.* slap, smack.

klar, 1. *adj.* clear, limpid, transparent; bright, light-coloured; pure, serene; distinct, plain, lucid, evident; fine (ground) (*of sugar, sand, etc.*); ready (*Naut.*); (*N.B. with verbs: used as an adverb with literal meanings, as a sep. pref. when figurative*); *- zum Gefecht,* ready *or* clear for action; *an sich -,* self-evident; *noch nicht im -en sein,* not yet see one's way about a th.; *ins -e kommen mit einem,* come to a clear understanding with s.o.; *einen ins -e setzen,* set a p. right; *etwas ins -e setzen,* clear up a point; *er muß sich darüber - werden,* he must make up his mind about it; *einem -en Wein einschenken,* tell s.o. the plain truth. 2. *n.* (*dial.*) white of an egg. **-äugig,** *adj.* clear-eyed. **-blickend,** *adj.* clear-sighted. **-heit,** *f.* clearness, lucidity, clarity; brightness, transparency, purity; fineness. **-ieren,** *v.a.* clear a ship (at the custom-house). **-kochen,** *v.a.* boil till clear. **-legen, -machen, -stellen,** *v.a.* explain, clear up, elucidate; *die Rettungsboote - machen,* get the lifeboats away; *die Riemen - machen,* ship the oars; *Holz - machen,* cut wood up (small). **-text,** *m.* text in clear (*not in code*).

Klär-e, *f.* (*Poet.*) clearness, purity, brightness; clarifier; clear liquid. **-en,** 1. *v.a.* clear, clarify, purify, defecate, decant. 2. *v.r.* settle, become clear. **-anlage,** *f.* purification *or* filter plant. **-becken,** *n.* filter bed. **-flasche,** *f.*, **-gefäß,** *n.*, **-kessel,** *m.* clarifier, decanting flask, settling tank. **-lich,** *adv.* (*archaic*) clearly. **-mittel,** *n.* clarifying agent. **-sel,** *n.* clarified sugar, filtered syrup. **-ung,** *f.* clarification, elucidation.

Klarinett-e, *f.* (-en) clarinet. **-ist,** *m.* (-en, -en) clarinet-player.

Klass-e, *f.* (-en) class, form (*school*); rank, order, division, grade, quality, type; (*C.L.*) *Wechsel erster -e,* A1 bill. **-enälteste(r),** *m.* top-boy (of the form). **-enbewußt,** *adj.* class-conscious. **-eneinteilung,** *f.* classification. **-enkampf,** *m.* class war(fare), class-conflict. **-enlehrer,** *m.* form-master. **-enordnung,** *f.* classification. **-enzimmer,** *n.* schoolroom, classroom. **-ieren,** *v.a.* size (*ore*). **-ifizieren,** *v.a.* classify.

Klass-ik, *f.* classical period (*of art, literature, etc.*). **-iker,** *m.* classical author, classical scholar, classic (*work of literature*). **-isch,** *adj.* classical, (*coll.*) classic; *ein -isches Beispiel,* a classic example.

Klatsch, 1. *m.* (-es, -e) slap, smack; crack (*of a whip*); (*coll.*) tittle-tattle, gossip. 2. *int.* crack! smack! **-base,** *f.* gossip, tale-bearer. **-e,** *f.* (-en) fly-swatter; gossip. **-en,** 1. *v.a. & n.* (*aux.* h.) clap, applaud; gossip, chat, spread stories, tell tales, blab; clatter, slap; swat (*flies*); *Beifall -en,* applaud; *in die Hände -en,* clap one's hands. **-erei,** *f.* gossip, tittle-tattle. **-haft,** *adj.* gossiping, gossipy. (*vulg.*) **-maul,** *n., see* **-base.** **-mohn,** *m.* corn-poppy (*Papaver rhoeas*) (*Bot.*). **-naß,** *adj.* sopping *or* soaking wet. **-nest,** *n.* gossip-shop. **-rose,** *f., see* **-mohn.** **-sucht,** *f.* love of gossipping. **-weib,** *n., see* **-base.**

klaube-n, *v.a.* pick, pick out, sort, cull; *Worte -n,* split hairs. **-rei,** *f.* picking, culling; (*pl.*) minutiae; *Wort-rei,* hair-splitting, cavilling.

Klau-e, *f.* (-en) claw, talon, fang; fluke (*of an anchor*); hoof, paw, clutch; jaws (*of death*), (*sl.*) hand, paw, mitt; (*sl.*) handwriting, fist. **-en,** *v.a.* claw, clutch; (*sl.*) pilfer, pinch. **-enfett,** *n.* neat's-foot oil. **-enförmig,** *adj.* ungulate. **-enhieb,** *m.* stroke, blow (*of a paw or talon*). **-enkupplung,** *f.* dog clutch. **-enöl,** *n., see* **-enfett.** **-enseuche,** *f.* foot-and-mouth disease (*Vet.*). **-ensteuer,** *f.* tax on cattle. **-ig,** *adj.* having claws, fangs *or* clutches.

Klaus-e, *f.* (-en) closet; cell, hermitage, (*coll.*) den; mountain-pass, defile. **-el,** *f.* (-eln) clause; stipulation, proviso, condition; musical period. **-(e)ner,** *m.* hermit, recluse. **-ur,** *f.* confinement, seclusion, cloister; *unter -ur,* under supervision (*as examinations*). **-urarbeit,** *f.* class exercise (*under examination conditions*); examination-paper, test-paper.

Klaviatur, *f.* (-en) key-board, keys (*of a piano*).

Klavier, *n.* (-s, -e) piano. **-auszug,** *m.* pianoforte arrangement, (*dial.*) **-en,** strum (*on the piano*). **-lehrer,** *m.* pianoforte teacher. **-schule,** *f.* manual of exercises for the piano. **-spieler,** *m.* pianist. **-stimmer,** *m.* piano tuner. **-stuhl,** *m.*

music-stool. **-stunde,** *f.* piano-lesson. **-vortrag** *m.* pianoforte recital.

kleb-en, 1. *v.a.* paste, glue, gum, stick. 2. *v.n.* (*aux.* h.) stick, adhere (*an*, to); *es bleibt nichts bei ihm -en*, nothing will stick with him, he has a memory like a sieve; *am Irdischen -en*, be worldly-minded; *an der Scholle -en*, be bound to the soil; (*coll.*) *einem eine -en*, give a p. a clout; (*coll.*) *schon seit 3 Jahren -en*, have been insured *or* covered (*i.e.* sticking on insurance stamps) for 3 years; *-en bleiben*, stick, stay stuck; stay down (*at school*). **-äther,** *m.* collodion. **-eband,** *n.*, *see* **-estreifen. -eblatt,** *n.* poster. **-eflugzeug,** *n.* intruder aircraft. **-efrei,** *adj.* non-tacky. **-(e)garn,** *n.* springe. **-elack,** *m.* fabric dope (*Av.*). **-(e)mittel,** *n.* *see* **-stoff. -(e)pflaster,** *n.* adhesive *or* sticking-plaster; court-plaster. **-er,** *m.* bill-poster; adhesive; (*fig.*) sticker (= *persistent p.*); gum; gluten. **-(e)rig,** *adj.* adhesive; sticky, viscid, viscous, glutinous; clammy, tacky. **-(e)rigkeit,** *f.* stickiness, viscidity, viscosity, tackiness. **-erute,** *f.* lime-twig (*for catching birds*). **-estreifen,** *m.* adhesive tape. **-ezettel,** *m.* poster; gummed label. **-fähig,** *adj.* adhesive. **-kraft,** *f.* adhesive strength *or* property. **-sand,** *m.* luting sand. **-scheibe,** *f.* adhesive disk. **-stoff,** *m.* adhesive, gum, glue, agglutinant.

kleckern, *v.n.* (*dial.*) trickle, dribble, drop (*one's food*), spill (*one's drink*), slobber; (*sl.*) lay mines (*Nav.*).

Kleck-s, *m.* (-es, -e) blot, (ink) stain, spot, blotch, blur; *voller -se*, full of blots. **-sen,** 1. *v.n.* (*aux.* h.) blot, stain, blur. 2. *v.n.* splutter, make blots (*of pens*); daub, scrawl. **-ser,** *m.* scrawler, scribbler, dauber. **-serei,** *f.* scrawl, untidy writing; daubing, daub (*bad painting*). **-sig,** *adj.* blotty, blotchy, blurred.

Klee, *m.* clover, trefoil, shamrock; (*rare*) clubs (*Cards*); *eine S. über den grünen – loben*, boost a th., laud s.th. to the skies. **-blatt,** *n.* clover-leaf; trio, triplet. **-blattbogen,** *m.* trefoil arch (*Arch.*). **-salz,** *n.* sorrel-salt, potassium acid oxalite, salts of lemon. **-salzkraut,** *n.* wood-sorrel (*Oxalis acetosella*) (*Bot.*). **-säure,** *f.* oxalic acid.

Klei, *m.* clay, loam, marl. **-acker,** *m.* clay-land. **-ig,** *adj.* clayey, loamy; *see also* **Kleie.**

kleib-en, 1. *ir.v.a.* daub (*wattles*), smear; (*dial.*) stick, glue, paste. 2. *v.n.* (*aux.* h.) (*dial.*) stick, adhere. **-er,** *m.* daub; daub and wattle worker; nuthatch (*Sitta europaea*) (*Orn.*). **-erlehm,** *m.* daub (*for wattles*). **-(er)werk,** *n.* daub and wattle (*fence, wall, etc.*).

Kleid, *n.* (-(e)s, -er) frock, dress, gown; garb, (*pl.*) clothes, garments; (*Prov.*) *-er machen Leute*, fine feathers make fine birds; *abgetragene -er*, cast-off clothing; *Reit-*, (riding) habit. **-en,** 1. *v.a.* clothe, dress; deck, adorn, cover; fit, suit, become; give expression to, express (in words), couch. 2. *v.r.* get dressed, dress o.s.; *sich gut -en*, dress well. **-erablage,** *f.* cloak-room. **-erbehälter,** *m.* wardrobe. **-erbezugschein,** *m.* clothing coupon. **-erbügel,** *m.* clothes- *or* coat-hanger. **-erbürste,** *f.* clothes-brush. **-ergeld,** *n.* clothing allowance. **-erhandel,** *m.* old-clothes trade. **-ernarr,** *m.* fop, dandy. **-erordnung,** *f.* sumptuary law affecting (clerical) dress. **-erpflock,** *m.* clothes-peg. **-erpuppe,** *f.* lay-figure (*as used by artists*), tailor's dummy. **-erschrank,** *m.* wardrobe. **-erschützer,** *m.* dress-guard (*Cycl.*). **-erständer,** *m.* hall-stand, hat and coat stand. **-erstoff,** *m.* clothing material, dress material, cloth. **-ertrödel,** *m.* old-clothes business. **-ertrödler,** *m.* old-clothes man. **-erverleiher,** *m.* theatrical costumer. **-erverwahrer,** *m.* keeper of the wardrobe. **-erzimmer,** *n.* dressing-room; wardrobe. **-sam,** *adj.* fitting well, becoming; *nicht -sam*, unbecoming. **-ung,** *f.* clothing, clothes, dress; costume, garb; drapery. **-ungsstück,** *n.* article of clothing *or* dress, garment; (*pl.*) clothes, wearing apparel.

Klei-e, *f.* bran. **-enmehl,** *n.* pollard. **-ig,** *adj.* branny; *see also* **Klei.**

klein, 1. *adj.* little, small, tiny, minute, diminutive; insignificant, petty; mean, narrow-minded; exact; scanty; neat, nice; minor (*Mus.*). *die -e*, the little girl; sweetheart; (*rare*) *see* **-heit**; *der -e*, the little boy; *das -e*, the (little) child, the little one; *die -en.* the children, the young folk; *– anfangen*, begin in a small way, make a modest start; *-e Anzeigen*, small advertisements (*in newspaper*); *-e Augen machen*, look tired; *-e Auslagen*, petty expenses; *bei -em*, by degrees; *– beigeben*, give way; *ein* or *etwas -es bekommen*, have a baby; *ein – bißchen*, a very little, a tiny bit; to a slight extent *or* degree; *von einem – denken*, think little of a p., have a poor opinion of s.o.; (*Prov.*) *wer das -e nicht ehrt, ist des Großen nicht wert*, look after the pence and the pounds will look after themselves; *-e Fahrt*, dead slow (*Naut.*); *ins -e gehen*, enter into details; *-es Geld*, small change; *groß und –*, children and adults; (*fig.*) high and low; *Leute, bei denen es – hergeht*, people who are badly off; *im -en*, on a small scale, in miniature; in detail; retail; *bis ins -ste*, down to the very last detail; (*coll.*) *er läßt sich nicht – kriegen*, he will not let himself be beaten, he does not give in; *-e Leiden*, petty annoyances; *die -en Leute*, see *der -e Mann*; *sich – machen*, humble o.s.; *der -e Mann*, the lower middle-class, the poorer classes, the common man; *-e Propheten*, minor prophets; *das ist ihm ein -es*, that is a trifle to him; *eine -e Stunde*, barely an hour; *-e Terz*, minor third; *über ein -es*, in a short time, after a while; *um ein -es zu kurz*, a shade too short; *um ein -es*, by a hair's breadth, very nearly; *-es Verbrechen*, petty crime, minor offence; *von – ab*, *an* or *auf*, from infancy *or* childhood, from an early age; *ein – wenig*, see *ein – bißchen*; *– werden*, grow small, diminish, decrease, subside; become docile *or* tractable. 2. *n.* giblets (*Cook.*); broken fragments. **-arbeit,** *f.* detail. **-auto,** *n.* light car. **-bahn,** *f.* light *or* narrow-gauge railway. **-bauer,** *m.* smallholder. **-betrieb,** *m.* small business; work on a small scale. **-bild,** *n.* miniature. **-bogenform,** *f.* small folio. **-bürger,** *m.* petty bourgeois, little man; philistine. **-bürgerlich,** *adj.*; *-bürgerliche Ansichten*, narrow-minded views. **-denkend,** *adj.* narrow-minded, petty. **-deutsch,** *adj.*; *die -deutschen*, politicians (before 1866) who wished for a united Germany excluding Austria. **-empfänger,** *m.* midget receiver (*Rad.*). **-en,** *v.a.* crush, pulverize. **-ern,** *v.a.* reduce (*fractions*) (*Math.*). **-flugzeug,** *n.* light aeroplane. **-garten,** *m.* allotment. **-gefüge,** *n.* fine structure. **-geistig,** *adj.* small *or* narrow minded. **-geld,** *n.* small change, change. **-gewerbe,** *n.* small-scale industry, **-gläubig,** *adj.* of little faith, faint-hearted. **-grundbesitz,** *m.* small estate. **-gut,** *n.* petty wares. **-handel,** *m.* retail trade. **-händler,** *m.* retailer. **-heit,** *f.* littleness, smallness; pettiness, meanness, insignificance; trifle. **-herzig,** *adj.* faint-hearted; narrow-minded. **-hirn,** *n.* cerebellum. **-holz,** *n.* firewood, sticks, kindling, matchwood. **-igkeit,** *f.* trifle, detail, bagatelle, small matter; *sich mit -igkeiten abgeben*, fritter one's time away; busy o.s. with trifles; *es kommt mir auf eine -igkeit nicht an*, I shall not mind paying a little. **-igkeitskrämer,** *m.* pedant, pundit, pettifogger. **-igkeitskrämerei,** *f.* pedantry, hair-splitting. **-kaliberschießen,** *n.* miniature *or* sub-calibre rifle shooting. **-kind,** *n.* toddler, pre-school child (*under six years*). **-kinderbewahranstalt,** *f.* day-nursery, crèche. **-kinderschule,** *f.* infant school. **-kinderwäsche,** *f.* baby-linen. **-kohle,** *f.* slack, small coal. **-kraftrad,** *n.* auto-cycle. **-kraftwagen,** *m. see* **-auto. -körnig,** *adj.* fine-grained. **-kram,** *m.* trifle, bagatelle, small matter. **-krämerei,** *f.* pedantry. **-krieg,** *m.* guerrilla warfare. **-kunstbühne,** *f.* intimate theatre, cabaret. **-laut,** *adj.* meek, subdued, quiet; low-spirited, dejected. **-lebewesen,** *n.* micro-organism. **-lich,** *adj.* paltry, mean, petty, trivial. **-lichkeit,** *f.* meanness, pettiness, paltriness. **-maler,** *m.* miniature-painter. **-maschig,** *adj.* fine meshed. **-messer,** *m.* micrometer. **-mühle,** *f.* crushing *or* pulverizing mill. **-mut,** *m.* (*rare f.*) despondency, pusillanimity. **-mütig,** *adj.* faint-hearted; dejected, despondent. **-od,** *see* **Kleinod. -pferd,** *n.* pony. **-rentner,** *m.* small investor. **-schmied,** *m.* (*dial.*) tool-maker, mechanic. **-siedler,** *m.* smallholder. **-siedlung,** *f.* smallholding. **-staat,** *m.* minor state, petty state. **-staaterei,** *f.* particularism. **-stadt,** *f.* small provincial town (*under 20,000 inhabitants*).

-städtisch, *adj.* provincial. **-steller,** *m.* by-pass (*of gas burner*). **-stmaß,** *n.* minimum. **-stoßen,** *v.a.* pound (*in a mortar*). **-verkauf,** *m.* retail trade. **-vieh,** *n.* small livestock (*viz.* sheep, goats, pigs). **-ware,** *f.* hardware. **-wechsel,** *m.* bill under one's hand, promissory note. **-wild,** *n.* small game.

Kleinod, *n.* (-s, -e *or* -ien) jewel, gem; treasure.

Kleister, *m.* paste, size, gum, adhesive. **-ig,** (**kleistrig**), *adj.* pasty, sticky. **-n,** *v.a.* paste. **-tiegel,** *m.*, **-topf,** *m.* paste-pot.

Klemm-e, *f.* (-en) clip, clamp, vice, hold-fast; terminal (*Elec.*); defile, narrow pass; difficulty, dilemma, straits, fix, tight corner; *in der -e sein, sitzen* or *stecken,* be in a fix, a jam *or* a corner; *in die -e geraten* or *kommen,* get into *or* land o.s. in a fix, etc. **-en,** 1. *reg.* & *ir.v.a.* squeeze, pinch, cramp; press; (*sl.*) pilfer, pinch, swipe. 2. *v.r.* get jammed *or* locked, jam, bind; get pinched, pinch. **-enspannung,** *f.* terminal voltage. **-er,** *m.* pince-nez, eye-glasses; clip (*Cycl.*). **-haken,** *m.* cramp-iron, hold-fast. **-schraube,** *f.* set-screw, binding-screw. **-ung,** *f.* stoppage (*of a gun*).

Klempner, *m.* plumber, sheet-metal worker. **-ei,** *f.* plumber's trade *or* workshop. **-(ei)arbeit,** *f.* plumbing. **-n,** *v.n.* (*aux.* h.) do sheet-metal work, work in sheet-metal, do plumbing.

Klepper, *m.* (-s, -) nag, hack.

Kler-iker, *m.* (-s, -) cleric, priest, clergyman (*R.C.*). **-isei,** *f.* clerical set, clergy, (*coll.*) hangers-on. **-us,** *m.* clergy (*R.C.*).

Klett-e, *f.* (-n) bur, burdock (*Arctium lappa*) (*Bot.*); *sich wie eine -e an einen hängen* or *wie eine -e an einem hängen,* stick to a p. like a leech. **-en,** *v.r.* stick to, adhere, hang on to. **-enbombe,** *f.* sticky *or* limpet bomb.

kletter-n, *v.n.* (*aux.* h. & s.) climb, clamber; scramble up. **-er,** *m.* climber, mountaineer. **-pflanze,** *f.* climber, creeper. **-rose,** *f.* rambler. **-stange,** *f.* climbing pole; greasy pole. **-vögel,** *m.pl.* climbers, scansores.

klieb-en, *reg.* & *ir.v.a.* (*dial.*) cleave, split. **-eisen,** *n.* cleaver. **-holz,** *n.* sawed timber. **-ig,** *adj.* fit for splitting.

klieren, *v.n.* (*coll.*) scrawl, scribble.

Klima, *n.* (-s, -s *or* (*Austr. dial.*) -te) climate. **-anlage,** *f.* air-conditioning plant. **-kterium,** *n.* climacteric, change of life. **-tisch,** *adj.* climatic.

Klimbim, *m.* & *n.* (*coll.*) pother, fuss and bother; festivity, party, goings-on.

Klimme, *f.* (-n) wild grape.

klimm-en, *reg. or* (*usually*) *ir.v.n.* (*aux.* h. & s.) climb (*auf eine S.*); aspire to (*nach einer S.*); *er ist bis zum Gipfel des Ruhms geklommen,* he has reached *or* raised himself to the pinnacle of fame. **-ziehen,** *n.*, **-zug,** *m.* climbing hand over hand (*Gymn.*); pulling up (*on the horizontal bar*) (*Gymn.*).

klimper-n, *v.n.* (*aux.* h.) jingle, jangle, clink, tinkle; strum. **-kasten,** *m.* (*coll.*) poor piano. **-klein,** *adj.* (*dial.*) tiny, very small.

Klinge, *f.* (-n) blade; sword; *vor die - fordern,* challenge; *mit der - entscheiden,* decide by the sword; *über die - springen,* be put to the sword; *einen über die - springen lassen,* put s.o. to the sword; *eine gute - führen* (or *schlagen*), be a good swordsman, (*fig.*) be able to defend o.s. *or* to hold one's own.

Kling-el, *f.* (-eln) small bell, handbell. **-elbeutel,** *m.* collection-bag, offertory bag. **-elknopf,** *m.* bell-push. **-eln,** *v.n.* (*aux.* h.) tinkle, ring; *es -elt,* there is a ring at the door; *es wurde nach dem Diener geklingelt,* the bell was rung for the servant. **-elschnur,** *f.* bell-rope. **-eltransformator,** *m.* bell transformer (*Elec.*). **-elzug,** *m.* bell-pull. **-en,** *ir.v.n.* (*aux.* h.) (*usually 3rd pers. only*) ring, chime, sound, tinkle, clink; *diese Frage -t sonderbar,* this is a strange question; *die Gläser -en lassen,* touch glasses (*in drinking*); *die Ohren -en mir,* there is a ringing in my ears, my ears are burning; *-t es nicht, so klappert's doch,* it's s.th. at any rate, even though it isn't very good; it is better than nothing. **-end,** *pr.p.* & *adj.* resonant, ringing; (*B.*) *tönendes Erz oder -ende Schelle,* sounding brass or a tinkling cymbal; *-ende Worte,* high-sounding words; *-ende Münze,* (hard) cash, ready money; *mit -endem Spiele,* drums beating, with full band, triumphantly; *-ender Reim,* feminine rhyme (*Metr.*). **-klang,** *m.*, **-ling,** *n.* ding-dong, jangle.

Klin-ik, *f.* (-en) clinical hospital, nursing-home. **-iker,** *m.* clinical physician. **-ikum,** *n.* (-ums, -ken) clinical hospital; clinical lecture *or* demonstration. **-isch,** *adj.* clinical.

Klink-e, *f.* (-en) latch, door handle, bolt, pawl; jack (*Elec.*). **-en,** *v.a.* & *n.* (*aux.* h. & s.) press the latch.

Klinker, *m.* (-s, -) (Dutch) clinker, hard brick. **-bau,** *m.* brick building; clinker construction (*of boats*). **-boot,** *n.* clinker-built boat.

Klinse, (*Austr. dial.* **Klinze**), *f.* (-n) cleft, crack, chink, gap, fissure.

Klipp, 1. *m.* (-(e)s, -e) clip, clasp. 2. *int.* snip, snap; *-klapp!* click-clack! (*coll.*) *- und klar,* quite clear, obvious. **-kram,** *m.* paltry trinkets, toys, small wares. **-schenke,** *f.* tavern, pot-house. **-schuld,** *f.* paltry debt. **-schule,** *f.* infant-school.

Klipp-e, *f.* (-en) crag, rock, reef; obstacle, snag; *blinde -e,* sunken rock. **-enbock,** *m.* wild goat. **-(en)fisch,** *m.* dried cod. **-enreihe,** *f.* ledge of rocks, reef. **-enwand,** *f.* rocky wall, escarpment. **-er,** *m.* sculptor's mallet; fast-sailing merchantman; flying-boat. **-ig,** *adj.* rocky, craggy.

klirren, *v.n.* (*aux.* h. & s.) clink, clank, clash, jingle, clatter; *mit -den Sporen,* with clanking spurs.

Klisch-ee, *n.* (-s, -s) stereotype-plate, block; electro, cliché (*Typ.*); cliché, hackneyed phrase. **-ieren,** *v.a.* stereotype, cut *or* make a block (*Typ.*).

Klistier, *n.* (-s, -e) enema, (*rare*) clyster. **-en,** *v.a.* give an enema (to). **-spritze,** *f.* enema.

klitsch, 1. *int.* slap! slop! splash! 2. *m.* (-es, -e) soggy mass, (*coll.*) doughy bread, sad cake. (*dial., coll.*) **-e,** *f.* poor farm; hovel. **-en,** 1. *v.n.* (*aux.* h.) splash, make a splashing *or* slapping sound. 2. *v.a.* slap, smack. **-(e)naß,** *adj.* sopping wet. **-ig,** *adj.* (*coll.*) doughy, soggy, sad (*Cook.*); sodden, clayey.

Klitter, *m.* blur, smudge, mess. **-n,** *v.a.* & *n.* (*aux.* h.) enter into details; smear, daub, smudge. **-schuld,** *f.* (*dial.*) accumulated debt.

Kloake, *f.* (-n) sewer, sink, drain, cesspool; cloaca (*Zool., Orn.*). **-ntiere,** *n.pl.* monotremes (*Zool.*).

klob, klobest, klöbe, *see* **klieben.**

Klob-en, *m.* (-ens, -en) log, billet (*of wood*); block, pulley; hand-vice, clamp; staple; cheek (*of a balance*); pivot (*of hinge*). **-en,** *v.a.*, **klöben,** *v.a.* (*rare*), *see* **kleiben. -enholz,** *n.* wood billets, logs. **-ig,** *adj.* clumsy, crude, loutish, boorish.

klomm, klomm(e)st, klömme, *see* **klimmen.**

klönen, *v.n.* (*coll.*) talk and talk, talk at great length; complain, (*coll.*) moan.

Klopfe, *f.*, *see* **Kloppe.**

Klöpfel, *m.* (-s, -), *see* **Klöppel** (2).

klopf-en, 1. *v.a.* & *n.* (*aux.* h.) beat, pound, break (*stones*), beetle; knock, tap, rap; pulsate, palpitate, throb; *es -t,* there is a knock at the door; *einem auf die Finger -en,* rap s.o. over the knuckles; *sanft -en,* tap, pat; *die Form -en,* plane down (*Typ.*); *auf den Busch -en,* beat (*for game*); *bei einem auf den Busch -en,* pump *or* sound a p. 2. *n.* knocking, beating, throbbing, palpitation. **-er,** *m.* (carpet) beater; (door) knocker. **-fechter,** *m.* rowdy, pugilist; controversialist. **-fechterei,** *f.* pugilism; polemics. **-fest,** *adj.* anti-pinking, anti-knock (*Motor.*). **-holz,** *n.* mallet, beetle; planer (*Typ.*). **-käfer,** *m.* death-watch beetle (*Anobidae*). **-see,** *f.* heavy, chopping sea. **-wert,** *m.* octane number (*of petrol*).

Kloppe, *f.* (*dial.*) beating, blows.

Klöppel, *m.* (-s, -) 1. bobbin; 2. tongue *or* clapper (*of a bell*); (door) knocker; mallet, cudgel, drumstick. **-arbeit,** *f.* pillow lace. **-ei,** *f.* lace-making. **-garn,** *n.* thread used in lace-making. **-holz,** *n.* bobbin. **-kissen,** *n.* lace pillow. **-maschine,** *f.* bobbin, loom. **-n,** *v.a.* & *n.* make pillow lace; *geklöppelte Spitzen,* pillow lace. **-spitze,** *f.* pillow lace.

Klöpplerin, *f.* (-nen) lace-maker.

Klops, *m.* (-es, -e) (*dial.*) meat ball.

Klosett, *n.* (-s, -e) lavatory, toilet, (water-)closet (W.C.). **-muschel,** *f.* lavatory pan. **-papier,** *n.* toilet-paper.

Kloß, *m.* (-es, ⁻e) clod, lump; meat ball; dumpling. **-ig,** *adj.* clodlike; doughy.
Kloster, *n.* (-s, ⁻) monastery, nunnery, convent, cloister; *ins – gehen*, take the veil (*of women*), turn monk. **-bogen,** *m.* Gothic arch. **-bruder,** *m.* friar. **-frau,** *f.*, **-fräulein,** *n.* nun. **-gang,** *m.* cloister(s). **-gelübde,** *n.* monastic vow. **-gemeinde,** *f.* fraternity, sisterhood. **-gut,** *n.* estate belonging to a convent. **-leben,** *n.* monastic life. **-leute,** *pl.* conventuals, monks, nuns. **-ordnung,** *f.* monastic discipline. **-schule,** *f.* monastery school. **-schwester,** *f.* lay sister; nun. **-vorsteher,** *m.* superior of a monastery. **-wesen,** *n.* monasticism, monastic affairs.
klösterlich, *adj.* monastic, conventual.
Klotz, *m.* (-es, ⁻e) block; log, lump (*of wood*); butt, stump; lout, clod; *ein – am Bein*, a millstone round one's neck; (*Prov.*) *auf einen groben – gehört ein grober Keil*, rudeness must be met by rudeness; the biter must be bit. **-bremse,** *f.* block brake. **-holz,** *n.* knotty wood. **-ig,** *adj.* in chunks, lumpish; knotty, coarse-grained; rude, boorish; (*sl.*) big, heavy, unwieldy, enormous; (*sl.*) *-ig viel* or *-es Geld kosten*, cost no end of money. **-kopf,** *m.* (*dial.*) blockhead.
Klub, *m.* (-s, -s) club; clubroom. **-sessel,** *m.* easy-chair.
Klucke, *f.* (*dial.*) sitting *or* broody hen.
kluckern, *v.n.* gurgle, babble (*as water*).
Kluft, 1. *f.* (⁻e) cleft, fissure, gap, cleavage; chasm, gulf, ravine, abyss, gorge; log of wood; pincers, tongs. 2. *f.* (-en) (*sl.*) duds, togs, rig-out (*Mil.*). **-ig,** *adj.*, *see* **klüftig.**
klüft-en, *v.a.* (*dial.*) cleave, split. **-ig,** *adj.* (*also* **kluftig**) cleft, split; cracked. **-ung,** *f.* cleaving, segmentation.
klug, *adj.* (*comp.* klüger, *sup.* klügst) intelligent, clever, smart, cunning, shrewd, clear-sighted, wise, sagacious, sensible, prudent. (*coll.*) *er ist nicht recht –*, he is half-crazy; he is half-witted; *aus etwas – werden*, see through *or* understand a thing; *daraus kann ich nicht – werden*, I can make neither head nor tail of it; *nun bin ich genau so – wie vorher*, I am just as wise as I was; *ich bin dadurch um nichts klüger*, I am not a whit the wiser for it; (*Prov.*) *durch Schaden wird man –*, a burnt child dreads the fire; *das Klügste wäre nun wohl*, it would probably be best. **-heit,** *f.* prudence, discretion, good sense; intelligence, cleverness, sagacity, shrewdness. **-heitslehren,** *f.pl.*, **-heitsregeln,** *f.pl.* rules of prudence; worldly wisdom. **-heitsrücksicht,** *f.* consideration of prudence. **-schnack,** *m.* know-all, wiseacre.
Klüg-elei, *f.* sophistry, casuistry, quibbling, chicanerie, special pleading, cavilling, hypercriticism. **-eln,** *v.n.* (*aux.* h.) brood, ponder; split hairs, quibble. **-ler,** *m.* (-s, –) sophist, caviller, carper, quibbler, wiseacre. **-lich,** *adv.* prudently, sensibly, wisely, shrewdly.
Klump, *m.* (-(e)s, –e) (*rare*), *usually* **-en,** *m.* (-ens, -en) mass, clod, clot, lump; ingot, nugget (*of gold*); cluster, heap, ball; *pl.* clogs, pattens; *-en Blut*, clot of blood; *alles in -en hauen*, smash everything to pieces; *auf einem -en*, all of a heap. **-en,** *v.r.* cake *or* clot together, get lumpy. **-(e)rig,** *adj.*, *see* **-ig. -enweise,** *adv.* in lumps *or* clusters. **-fuß,** *m.* club-foot. **-ig,** *adj.* clotted, in lumps, lumpy, caked (*flour*).
Klümp-chen, *n.* (-s, – & -erchen) little lump *or* clot; small particle, globule, nodule; *-chen bilden*, clot; (*coll.*) (*wie*) *ein -chen Unglück*, (like) a picture of misery. **-(e)rig,** *adj.* lumpy, clotted; *-(e)rig werden*, clot.
Klüngel, *m.* (-s, –) clique, coterie, faction; *der ganze –*, the whole bunch, clique *or* gang.
Klunker, *f.* (-n) & *m.* (-s, –) tassel; cake *or* clod (*of dirt*). **-ig,** *adj.* caked with mud, spattered with dirt, bedraggled. (*dial.*) **-milch,** *f.* clotted milk, sour milk. **-n,** *v.n.* (*aux.* h.) (*also* **klunken**) (*dial.*) dangle, draggle.
Klupp-e, *f.* (-en) pincers, nippers, tongs; callipers; (*Austr. dial.*) clothes-peg; die-stock. **-en,** *v.a.* squeeze into a slit *or* fissure, pinch. **-ieren,** *v.a.* & *n.* measure the girth (of). **-zange,** *f.* forceps.
Klus, *f.* (-en) (*Swiss dial.*) gorge, ravine, chasm.
Klüse, *f.* (-n) hawse, hawse-pipe (*Naut.*).
Klutter, *f.* (-n) decoy-whistle, bird-call.
Klüver, *m.* (-s, –) jib (*Naut.*); fan-tail (*of windmill*). **-baum,** *m.* jib-boom. **-fall,** *m.* jib-halyards. **-schote,** *f.* jib-sheet, head-sheet. *-schoten los!* ease off the jib!
Klystier, *n.*, *see* **Klistier.**
knabbern, *v.a.* & *n.* (*aux.* h.) nibble, gnaw, munch.
Knabe, *m.* (-n, -n) boy, lad; *alter –*, old boy, old fellow; old fogy; *braver –*, fine lad. **-nalter,** *n.* boyhood. **-nhaft,** *adj.* boyish. **-nhaftigkeit,** *f.* boyishness. **-nkraut,** *n.* orchis (*Bot.*). **-nschule,** *f.* boys' school. **-nstreich,** *m.* boyish trick. **-nzeit,** *f.* youth, boyhood.
Knack, 1. *m.* (-(e)s, -e) cracking noise; crack, split, break; underwood, undergrowth. 2. *int.* crack! snap! **-beere,** *f.* wild strawberry (*Fragaria viridis*) (*Bot.*). **-en,** *v.a.* & *n.* (*aux.* h) crack, break; solve (*riddles*); click, crackle, crepitate. **-er,** *m.* (*coll.*) *alter -er*, old fogy, old codger, greybeard. **-ern,** *v.n.* (*aux.* h.) crackle. **-mandel,** *f.* almond in the shell. **-s,** *int.* & *m.*, *see* **Knack;** (*coll.*) *er hat seinen -s weg* or *seine Gesundheit hat einen -s bekommen*, his health has suffered permanent injury; *ein alter -s*, an old dodderer. **-sen,** *v.n.* (*aux.* h.) crack, break. **-wurst,** *f.* saveloy.
Knagge, *f.* stay, bracket; cam, tappet (*Mach.*).
Knall, *m.* (-(e)s, -e) report, bang, pop, clap; detonation, explosion; (*coll.*) *– und Fall*, all at once, immediately, without warning. **-bonbon,** *m.* & *n.* (Christmas) cracker. **-büchse,** *f.* popgun. **-effekt,** *m.* coup de théâtre, unexpected turn in events. **-en,** *v.n.* (*aux.* h.) burst, explode, detonate, fulminate, pop; *mit der Peitsche -en*, crack the whip; (*aux.* s.) *der Pulverturm -te in die Luft*, the powder-magazine blew up with a loud report. **-erbse,** *f.* cracker (*firew.*). **-gas,** *n.* oxyhydrogen gas. **-gasgebläse,** *n.* oxyhydrogen blowpipe. **-gold,** *n.* fulminating gold. **-ig,** *adj.* glaring, striking; (*sl.*) crazy, crackers. **-kapsel,** *f.* fog-signal (*Railw.*). **-körper,** *m.* detonator. **-pulver,** *n.* fulminating powder. **-quecksilber,** *n.* fulminate of mercury. **-rot,** *adj.* & *n.* glaring red. **-salpeter,** *m.* ammonium nitrate. **-satz,** *m.* explosive mixture. **-scheu,** *adj.* gun-shy. **-signal,** *n.*, *see* **-kapsel. -silber,** *n.* fulminating silver. **-zündmittel,** *n.* primer, detonator.
knapp, *adj.* close-fitting; narrow, tight, close; scanty, scarce; poor, shabby, meagre, paltry, barely sufficient; accurate, exact, concise, terse; *sein -es Auskommen* or *– sein Auskommen haben*, have barely enough to live on; *das Geld ist – bei ihm*, money is scarce with him; *– halten*, keep on short allowance, keep a tight rein (*on a p.*); *-e Kost*, barely sufficient food; short rations; *eine -e Mehrheit*, a bare majority; *mit -er* (*Mühe und*) *Not*, barely, only just, with great difficulty; *– sitzen*, be close-fitting, fit tight, be a tight fit; *-er Stil*, concise style; *-er Wind*, scant wind; *-e Zeiten*, hard times; (*sl.*) *aber nicht zu –!* and how! *es geht – zu* or *her* (*in diesem Hause*), they live very poorly, they are economizing as much as possible. **-en,** *v.n.* (*aux.* h.) pinch, be stingy. **-heit,** *f.* scantiness, shortage, scarcity; tightness, narrowness; conciseness, terseness.
Knapp-e, *m.* (-en, -en) page, esquire; miller's boy *or* apprentice; miner. **-schaft,** *f.* body of miners. **-schaftskasse,** *f.* miners' fund. **-schaftsrente,** *f.* miners' pension.
knapsen, *v.n.* (*aux.* h.), *see* **knappen.**
Knarr-e, *f.* (-en) creaking noise; rattle; ratchet; (*sl.*) rifle (*Mil.*). **-en,** *v.a.* & *n.* (*aux.* h.) creak, squeak; groan; rattle; crackle.
Knast, *m.* (-(e)s, -e) (*dial.*) knot (*in wood*); stub, stump, crust (*of bread*); *also* = **-er** (2); (*sl.*) *einen – sägen*, snore. **-er,** *m.* 1. tobacco. 2. *alter -er*, old curmudgeon. **-ern,** *v.n.* (*aux.* h.) crackle, crunch; grumble, grouse. **-erbart,** *m.*, *see* **-er** (2).
knattern, *v.n.* (*aux.* h.) rattle, clatter, crack; *das – des Gewehrfeuers*, rattle of musketry; *das – der Motorräder*, clatter of the motor-bikes.
Knäuel, *n.* & *m.* (-s, –), (*dial.*) **Knaul,** *m.* & *n.* (-s, -e & ⁻e) ball, hank, clew, skein, tangle; coil, convolu-

tion; fascible, spireme, knob, knot, guard; crowd, throng; Scleranthus (*Bot.*). **–binse,** *f.* common rush (*Juncus conglomeratus*) (*Bot.*). **–förmig,** *adj.* ball-shaped, globular, glomerate, in a coil, coiled, convoluted. **–n,** *v.a. & r.* form into a ball, ball up, gnarl, coil up.

Knauf, *m.* (-(e)s, ⸗e) capital (*Arch.*); knob; pommel (*of a sword's hilt*).

knaupeln, *v.a. & n.* (*aux.* h.) nibble; crunch; scrabble.

Knauser, *m.* (-s, –) miser, skinflint, niggard. **–ei,** *f.* stinginess, cheese-paring, niggardliness. **–ig,** *adj.* niggardly, mean, stingy, close-fisted, cheese-paring, churlish. **–n,** *v.n.* (*aux.* h.) be stingy *or* niggardly, stint, grudge.

knautschen, *v.a.* crumple, crease; eat noisily.

Knebel, *m.* (-s, –) branch, shoot, slip; club, cudgel, stick; toggle, cross-bar, frog; gag (*for the mouth*); clapper (*of a bell*); twisted moustache; (*dial.*) knuckles of clenched fist. **–bart,** *m.* (twisted) moustache. **–gebiß,** *n.* snaffle-bit. **–n,** *v.a.* fasten with a toggle; gag, (*fig.*) suppress; *die Presse –n,* muzzle the press.

Knecht, *m.* (-(e)s, –e) servant, farm-hand, menial; trestle, jack (*Mech.*); *fauler –,* ready reckoner; *– Ruprecht,* Santa Claus, St. Nicholas; *lieber ein kleiner Herr als ein großer –,* better a big fish in a little pond than a little fish in a big pond; *wie der Herr so der –,* like master like man. **–en,** *v.a.* reduce to servitude, subjugate, enslave. **–isch,** *adj.* menial; slavish; servile, crawling. **–sarbeit,** *f.*, **–sdienst,** *m.* menial work, drudgery. **–schaft,** *f.* servitude, slavery. **–ssinn,** *m.* servile spirit. **–ung,** *f.* enthralment, subjugation; servitude.

Kneif, (*Austr. dial.* **Kneip**), *m.* (-s, -e) cobbler's knife.

kneif–en, 1. *v.a.* pinch, squeeze, nip, gripe; cog (*dice*); *den Schwanz zwischen die Beine gekniffen,* with its tail between its legs; *Preise –en,* force down prices; *den Wind –en,* hug the wind. 2. *v.n.* (*aux.* h. & s.) flinch, withdraw; shirk, dodge (*work, etc.*). **–er,** *m.* pince-nez, eyeglasses; dodger, shirker. **–zange,** *f.* cutting pliers, nippers, pincers; tweezers.

Kneip–e, *f.* (-n) tavern, public-house, (*coll.*) pub; saloon, bar; beer party; *auf der –e,* in the bar. **–en,** 1. *v.a.* (*dial.*) pinch, nip; *es –t ihm im Bauche,* he has a pain in his stomach; *mit glühenden Zangen –en,* torture with red-hot tongs. 2. *v.n.* (*aux.* h.) go drinking, (*sl.*) go on the beer; booze, tipple. 3. *n.* colic, gripes. **–abend,** *m.* (students') drinking party. **–bruder,** *m.* toper, tippler. **–erei,** *f.* hard drinking; (*sl.*) boozing. **–lied,** *n.* drinking-song. **–wart,** *m.* (student) in charge of the drinks. **–wirt,** *m.* publican.

Kneller, *m.* (*dial.*) cheap tobacco, (*coll.*) weed.

knet–bar, *adj.* capable of being kneaded, plastic. **–e,** *f.* plasticine. **–en,** 1. *v.a.* knead, mill, pug. 2. *n.* kneading, moulding. **–er,** *m.* churn, dough mixer.

knick, 1. *int.* crack! 2. *m.* (-(e)s, -e) crack, break, flaw; bend (*of a road*); (*dial. with pl. also* –s) quickset hedge. **–beinig,** *adj.* knock-kneed. **–en,** 1. *v.a.* bend, fold (*paper*); crack, break; *einen –en,* break a p., break a p.'s spirit *or* resistance; *Eier –en,* crack eggs; *einen Hasen –en,* break the neck of a hare. 2. *v.n.* (*aux.* h. & s.) crack, break; buckle, sag; (*fig.*) be broken *or* cast down (*of courage, hope, etc.*); be niggardly; *geknicktes Dasein,* blighted life; *geknickter Mann,* broken man. **–er,** *m.* miser, niggard; grumbler, grouser; clasp-knife; (*dial.*) marble, taw. **–erei,** *f.* niggardliness. **–(e)rig,** *adj.* mean, stingy, niggardly. **–ern,** *v.n.* (*aux.* h.) be mean *or* stingy; chaffer, higgle; crackle; (*dial.*) play marbles. **–festigkeit,** *f.* buckling strength (*Metall.*). **–flügel,** *m.* gull-wing (*Av.*). **–last,** *f.* buckling load. **–punkt,** *m.* break (*in a curve*). **–s,** *m.* (-ses, -se) crack. **–sen,** 1. *v.a. see* **–en.** 2. *v.n.* (*aux.* h.) curtsy, make a curtsy. **–stütz,** *m.* bent-arm rest (*Gymn.*). **–ung,** *f.* bending, buckling, flexion. **–versuch,** *m.* buckling test (*Metall.*).

Knie, *n.* (-s, – *or dial.* -e) knee; bend, salient, elbow; bent, angle, joint; (*Poet.*) *euch lege ich's auf die –,* I leave my fate in your hands, I leave the decision with you; *etwas übers – brechen,* hurry a matter unduly, rush one's fences, make short work of a th.; *auf* or *in die – fallen* or *sinken,* go down on one's knees; *einen auf* or *in die – zwingen,* force a p. to his knees; *ein Kind übers – legen,* put a child across one's knee; *mir schlottern die –,* my knees are knocking. **–band,** *n.* garter; ligament of the knee. **–beuge,** *f.* bend of the knee, popliteal space; knees-bend (*Gymn.*). **–beugung,** *f.* genuflexion. **–binde,** *f.* knee bandage, knee-cap (*Surg.*). **–bügel,** *m.* leather cover for the knee (*Min.*). **–decke,** *f.* coachman's apron. **–fall,** *m.* genuflexion; *einen –fall tun,* make, do *or* pay obeisance. **–fällig,** *adv.* upon one's knees. **–flechse,** *f.* hamstring. **–frei,** *adj.* leaving the knees free; *–freier Rock,* knee-length skirt. **–galgen,** *m.* gibbet. **–geige,** *f.* viola da gamba. **–gelenk,** *n.* knee-joint. **–hoch,** *adj.* up to the knees; knee-high. **–holz,** *n.* scrub. **–hose,** *f.* shorts, breeches, knickerbockers, plus-fours. **–kehle,** *f., see* **–beuge.** **–kissen,** *n.* hassock. **–n, –en,** *v.n.* (*aux.* h.) be on one's knees, be kneeling, kneel; (*aux.* s.) go down on one's knees. **–end,** *pr.p. & adj.* kneeling, on one's knees; with bended knees. **–riem(en),** *m.* shoemaker's stirrup; (*hum.*) *Meister –riem,* cobbler. **–rohr,** *n.* elbow bend (*of a pipe*). **–scheibe,** *f.* knee-cap, patella. **–schützer,** *m.* knee-pad. **–stück,** *n.* knee-piece, angle-joint (*of a pipe*), *see* **–rohr**; three-quarter length portrait.

kniff, kniff(e)st, kniffe, *see* **kneifen.**

Kniff, *m.* (-(e)s, -e) crease, fold, dent; trick, dodge, device, artifice, stratagem; *geheime –e,* underhand dealings. **–en,** *v.a.* (*dial.*) fold, crease. **–ig,** *adj.* tricking, intriguing. (*coll.*) **–lich,** *adj.*, **–(e)lig,** *adj.* difficult, intricate, tricky.

knipsen, 1. *v.a.* (*aux.* h.) punch (*a ticket*); (*coll.*) *einen –,* take a snapshot of a p. 2. *v.n.* click, snap one's fingers.

Knirps, *m.* (-es, -e) dwarf, pigmy, manikin; *kleiner –,* little chap. **–ig,** *adj.* stunted, dwarfish, tiny.

knirschen, *v.a. & n.* (*aux.* h.) crunch, gnash; grind, grate, creak; crackle, rustle; *mit den Zähnen –,* gnash *or* grind one's teeth.

knist–ern, *v.n.* (*aux.* h.) crackle, rustle; crepitate (*Chem.*). **–ergold,** *n.* tinsel. **–(e)rig,** *adj.* crackling, crisp.

Knittel, *m., see* **Knüttel.**

Knitter, *m.* (-s, –) crease, rumple. **–frei,** *adj.* non-creasing, crease-resisting. **–gold,** *n.* tinsel. **–ig,** *adj.* creased, wrinkled, crumpled, (*fig.*) irritable. **–n,** 1. *v.n.* (*aux.* h.) crackle, rustle. 2. *v.a.* crumple, crease, ruck. 3. *v.r.* become crumpled, creased *or* rucked.

Knobel, *m.pl.* dice, (*dial.*) knuckles. **–n,** *v.n.* throw dice (*um eine S.,* for a th.).

Knoblauch, *m.* garlic.

Knöchel, *m.* (-s, –) knuckle; ankle (bone); (*dial.*) *pl.* dice, bones. **–chen,** *n.* ossicle; small joint. **–gelenk,** *n.* ankle-joint. **–n,** *v.n.* (*aux.* h.) play with dice. **–spiel,** *n.* game with dice.

Knoch–en, *m.* (-ens, -en) bone; *in –en verwandeln, zu –en werden,* ossify; *stark von –en,* bony, strong-limbed; *seine –en schonen,* take good care of o.s.; *naß bis auf die –en,* wet to the skin; *bis in die –en,* to the core, through and through; *er ist nichts als Haut und –en,* he is a mere bag of bones, he is all skin and bones. **–enartig,** *adj.* bony, osseous. **–enband,** *n.* ligament. **–enbau,** *m.* skeleton, frame. **–enbeschreibung,** *f.* osteology, osteography. **–enbrand,** *m.* necrosis. **–enbruch,** *m.* fracture (*of a bone*). **–endünger,** *m.*, **–endungmehl,** *n.* bone manure. **–endürr,** *adj.* dry as a bone. **–enfäule,** *f.*, **–enfäulnis,** *f.* caries. **–enfortsatz,** *m.* bony process, apophysis. **–enfraß,** *m.* caries. **–enfuge,** *f.* symphysis. **–enfügung,** *f.* articulation of the bones. **–engebäude,** *n.*, **–engerippe,** *n.* **–engerüst,** *n.* skeleton. **–engelenk,** *n.* joint, articulation. **–engewebe,** *n.* bony tissue. **–enhart,** *adj.* hard as brick. **–enhaus,** *n.* charnel-house. **–enhaut,** *f.* periosteum. **–enhautentzündung,** *f.* periostitis. **–enkohle,** *f.* animal charcoal, bone black. **–enkunde,** *f., see* **–enlehre.** **–enlager,** *n.* bone bed. **–enlehre,** *f.* osteology. **–enleim,** *m.* bone glue. **–enmann,** *m.* (*Poet.*) Death (*as a skeleton*). **–enmark,** *n.* marrow. **–enmarksentzündung,** *f.*

osteomyelitis. **–enmehl,** *n.* bone-meal. **–ennaht,** *f.* suture (*Anat.*). **–enöl,** *n.* neat's-foot oil. **–enpfanne,** *f.* glenoid cavity. **–ensäure,** *f.* phosphoric acid. **–enschwarz,** *n.* bone black. **–enschwund,** *m.* atrophy of the bones. **–enverbindung,** *f.*, *see* **–enfügung.** **–enwuchs,** *m.* ossification. **–ig,** *adj.* & *suffix.* bony, osseous; big-boned.

knöch–(e)rig, *adj.* thin and bony, scraggy, fleshless. **–ern,** *adj.* bony, of bone, osseous.

Knödel, *m.* (-s, –) (*dial.*) dumpling.

Knoll–e, *f.* (-en), **–en,** *m.* (-ens, -en) clod, lump; dumpling (*Cook.*); protuberance, knot, knob, nodule; bulb, tuber (*Bot.*). **–enartig,** *adj.* bulbous, globular. **–enfäule,** *f.* potato rot, tuber rot. **–engewächs,** *n.* bulbous plant. **–enzwiebel,** *f.* corm. **–fuß,** *m.* club-foot. **–ig,** *adj.* knotty, knobby; tuberous; bulbous, lumpy.

Knopf, *m.* (-es, ⸚e) button, knob, stud, boss, head (*of a pin*); pommel; (*Austr. dial.*) knot; (*dial.*) bud; (*Swiss dial.*) dumpling; (*coll.*) fellow; *mit zwei Reihen Knöpfe,* double-breasted; (*vulg.*) *Knöpfe haben,* have money *or* dough; *übersponnene Knöpfe,* covered buttons; (*coll.*) *den – auf dem Beutel halten,* be mean *or* stingy; *die Knöpfe bekommen,* be made a lance-corporal, get one's stripe; (*coll.*) *mit den Knöpfen herausrücken,* pay up; (*coll.*) *der – geht ihm auf,* at last he understands, the penny has dropped. **–loch,** *n.* buttonhole. (*dial.*) **–nadel,** *f.* pin. **–naht,** *f.* suture (*Surg.*).

knöpf–en, *v.a.* button, (*dial.*) tie in a knot. **–er,** *m.* button-hook. **–ig,** *adj.* provided with buttons, buttoned. **–stiefel,** *m.* buttoned boot.

knorke, *adv.* (*dial., sl.*) splendid, top-hole, first-rate, priceless, pucka, wizard.

Knorpel, *m.* (-s, –) cartilage, gristle. **–artig,** *adj.*, **–ig,** *adj.* gristly, cartilaginous. **–band,** *n.* fibrocartilage, synchondrosis (*Anat.*). **–gelenk,** *n.* cartilaginous joint, symphysis (*Anat.*). **–werk,** *n.* scroll, volute (*Arch.*).

Knorr–en, *m.* (-ens, -en) knotty excrescence *or* protuberance; knot, gnarled branch, tree stump. **–bremse,** *f.* pneumatic brake. **–ig,** *adj.* knotty, knobbed, gnarled.

Knorz, *m.* (-es -e) knot (*in wood*). **–ig,** *adj.* knotty.

Knosp–e, *f.* (-en) bud; burgeon, gemma, gemmule; *pl.* leafage (*of a capital*) (*Arch.*). **–en,** *v.n.* (*aux.* h.) bud, sprout, gemmate. **–enartig,** *adj.* bud-like. **–enbehälter,** *m.* conceptacle (*Bot.*). **–enbildung,** *f.* gemmation. **–entragend,** *adj.* gemmiferous. **–entreiben,** *n.* budding (forth), gemmation. **–ig,** *adj.* bud-like; covered with buds, budding, gemmate.

Knöt–chen, *n.* (-s, –) nodule, little lump, pimple; tubercle. **–chenausschlag,** *m.* heat rash. **–erich,** *m.* knotgrass, knotweed (*Polygonum aviculare*) (*Bot.*).

Knot–e, *m.* (-en, -en) boor, clod-hopper, lout, cad. **–en,** I. *m.* (-ens, -en) knot; knot (*Naut.*); bun (*of hair*); node, nodule, joint; knob, condyle (*Anat.*); ganglion; growth, tubercle (*Med.*); tangle, plot, difficulty; *zehn –en laufen,* make ten knots; *einen –en knüpfen, schlingen* or *schürzen,* tie a knot; *einen –en lösen,* undo a knot; solve a difficulty; *den –en durchhauen,* cut the knot (*fig.*); *das Ding hat einen –en,* there is a hitch in the affair; (*coll.*) *da steckt der –en,* there is the snag. 2. *v.a.* & *n.* (*aux.* h.) knot, tie in a knot. **–enader,** *f.* sciatic vein. (*vulg.*) **–enleben,** *n.* dissolute life. **–enlösung,** *f.* winding up of the plot, development, dénouement, catastrophe (*Theat.*). **–enpunkt,** *m.* nodal point; junction (*Railw.*). **–enschürzung,** *f.* working up of the dramatic plot, complication, epitasis (*Theat.*). **–enstock,** *m.* knobbed stick, knotty stick. **–enstrick,** *m.* Franciscan's girdle. **–enstück,** *n.* knot (*in wood*). **–ig,** *adj.* knotty; articulate, joined (*Bot.*); gnarled, nodular; tubercular (*Med.*); boorish, caddish, uncouth, rude, vulgar, coarse.

Knöterich, *see* **Knöt–.**

Knubb–e, *f.* (-en), (*Austr. dial.*) **–en,** *m.* (-ens, -en) knot (*in wood*). **–ig,** *adj.* huge.

Knuff, *m.* (-(e)s, ⸚e) buffet, cuff, thump, push, shove. **–en,** *v.a.* cuff, buffet, pommel; push. (*coll.*) **–ig,** *adj* rude, churlish, crusty, cross.

knüll(e), *adj.* (*sl.*) drunk, soused. **–en,** *v.a.* crumple, crease, ruck.

knüpf–en, I. *v.a.* fasten together, attach, join, knit together, knot, unite; (*coll.*) string up (*on gallows*); *sich –en an* (*Acc.*), be connected with, be associated with (*in one's mind*); *ein Bündnis –en,* form an alliance.

Knüppel, *m.* (-s, –) club, cudgel, truncheon, sculptor's *or* carpenter's mallet; billet (*of wood*), round timber, log; wire bar (*Metall.*); French roll (*Bak.*); joystick (*Av.*); boor; *der – liegt beim Hunde,* there is no choice, that goes without saying; *einem einen – zwischen die Beine werfen,* put difficulties in a p.'s way. **–brücke,** *f.* rustic bridge. **–damm,** *m.* corduroy road. **–dick,** *adv.* again and again, time and again, time without number; thick as hail, in quick succession; (*coll.*) *er hat es –dick hinter den Ohren,* he is a thorough scoundrel; *–dick voll,* crammed full; *ich hab's –dick,* I'm sick of it. **–holz,** *n.* logs, faggots. **–steig,** *m.*, **–weg,** *m.*, *see* **–damm.** **–stock,** *m.* knotted stick.

knuppern, *v.a.* & *n.*, *see* **knabbern** & **knuspern.**

knurr–en, *v.n.* (*aux.* h.) growl, snarl; grumble, rumble; *mein Magen –t, mir –t der Magen,* my tummy is rumbling. **–ig,** *adj.* growling, grumbling, disagreeable, snarling, irritable.

knusp–(e)rig, *adj.* crisp, crunchy, crackling; *ein –riges Mädchen,* (*sl.*) a snappy piece, a nice bit of stuff. **–ern,** *v.a.* nibble, crunch.

Knute, *f.* (-n) knout; (*fig.*) terrorism; *die – bekommen,* be knouted. **–n,** *v.a.* lash with the knout.

knutschen, I. *v.a.* crumple; 2. *v.r.* (*coll.*) cuddle, squeeze.

Knüttel, Knittel, *m.* (-s, –) cudgel, club; mallet. **–vers,** *m.* doggerel.

knütten, *v.a.* & *n.* (*aux.* h.) (*dial.*) knit.

Kobalt, *m.* cobalt. **–blau,** *adj.* & *n.* cobalt blue, smalt. **–spiegel,** *m.* transparent cobalt ore. **–stahl,** *m.* high-speed steel (*Metall.*). **–stufe,** *f.* piece of cobalt ore.

Kob–el, *m.* (-s, –) (*dial.*) shed, hut, dove-cote. **–en,** *m.* (-ens, -en) shed, hut; pigsty. **–er,** *m.* (*dial.*) two-handled basket, hamper.

Kobold, *m.* (-(e)s, –e) goblin, hobgoblin, elf, sprite. **–streich,** *m.* impish *or* mischievous trick.

Kobolz, *m.* (*only in*) (*einen*) *– schießen,* go head over heels, turn a somersault.

Koch, *m.* (-es, ⸚e) cook; (*Prov.*) *viele Köche verderben den Brei,* too many cooks spoil the broth; (*Prov.*) *Hunger ist der beste –,* hunger is the best sauce. **–apfel,** *m.* cooking apple. **–birne,** *f.* stewing pear. **–buch,** *n.* cookery book. **–echt,** *adj.* fast to boiling (*of dyes*). **–en,** I. *v.a.* & *n.* (*aux.* h.) cook; boil; stew; seethe; ripen (*of grapes*); *er –t vor Wut,* he is seething with rage; *die –ende Brandung,* the raging *or* boiling surf; *sie –t schlecht,* she is a bad cook; *gekochtes Obst,* stewed fruit; (*Prov.*) *es wird überall mit Wasser gekocht,* people are the same everywhere; *hier wird auch nur mit Wasser gekocht,* you cannot expect the impossible; *dies Fleisch –t sich gut* this meat boils well. 2. *n.* cooking, boiling; *zum –en bringen,* bring to the boil (*Cook.*) *or* to boiling-point (*Chem.*); (*fig.*) bring to a head, rouse, inflame (*tempers, spirits, etc.*). **–er,** *m.* cooker, boiler, digester. **–gefäß,** *n.*, **–gerät,** *n.*, **–geschirr,** *n.* cooking vessels *or* utensils, pots and pans, mess tin (*Mil.*). **–herd,** *m.* kitchen-range, cooking-stove. **–kelle,** *f.*, **–löffel,** *m.* ladle. **–kessel,** *m.* cauldron, copper, digester. **–kiste,** *f.* haybox. **–kunst,** *f.* culinary art. **–obst,** *n.* fruit for stewing. **–punkt,** *m.* boiling-point. **–salz,** *n.* table salt. **–topf,** *m.* cooking-pot, saucepan. **–vergütung,** *f.* ageing at 100° C. (*Metall.*). **–wein,** *m.* cooking-wine. **–zeug,** *n.* kitchen utensils. **–zucker,** *m.* brown sugar.

Köcher, *m.* (-s, –) quiver, golf bag.

Köchin, *f.* (-nen) (female) cook.

koddrig, *adj.* (*dial.*) shabby, dishevelled, unkempt; impudent, cheeky; ill, amiss; (*vulg.*) *–e Schnauze,* insolence, big mouth.

Köder, *m.* (-s, –) bait, lure, decoy; *auf den – anbeißen,* take the bait, bite. **–n,** *v.a.* bait, lure, decoy, entice.

Kod–ex, *m.* (-es, -e & -ices) codex, old manuscript; code (*of laws*). **–ifizieren,** *v.a.* codify, systematize (*laws, etc.*). **–izill,** *n.* (-s, -e) codicil.

Kofel, *m.* (-s, –) (*dial.*) summit, knoll.
Kofen, *m.* (*dial.*), *see* **Koben.**
Kofent, *m.* (-s, -e) small beer.
Koffein, *n.* caffeine.
Koffer, *m.* (-s, –) trunk, coffer, portmanteau, suitcase, bag. **–grammophon,** *n.* portable gramophone. **–träger,** *m.* porter. **–zettel,** *m.* luggage label.
Kog, *see* **Koog.**
Kohä–renz, *f.* coherence. **–rieren,** *v.n.* cohere. **–rierend,** *adj.* cohesive. **–sion,** *f.* cohesion, cohesiveness. **–sionskraft,** *f.* cohesive power.
Kohl, *m.* (-(e)s, -e) cabbage, kale, (*archaic*) cole; (*coll.*) rigmarole, stuff and nonsense, twaddle, bosh; *Blumen–*, cauliflower; *Braun–*, *Grün–*, (curly) kale; *Rot–*, red cabbage; *Weiß–*, common cabbage, drumhead; *Sprossen–*, *Rosen–*, (Brussels) sprouts; *Wirsing–*, savoy cabbage; *Feder–*, curly kale; *aufgewärmter –*, same old story; (*coll*) *– machen*, blunder; (*coll.*) *das macht den – nicht fett*, that does not help us much; (*coll.*) *schöne Worte machen den – nicht fett*, fair words butter no parsnips. **–dampf,** *m.* (*sl.*) hunger; *–dampf schieben*, be hungry. (*coll.*) **–en,** *v.n.* (*aux.* h.) talk nonsense (*see also under* **Kohle**). **–kopf,** *m.* head of cabbage; blockhead. **–rabi,** *m.* (-(s), -s (& *Austr. dial.* –)) kohlrabi. **–rübe,** *f.* swede, turnip, rape. **–same,** *m.* cole-seed. **–stengel,** *m.*, **–strunk,** *m.* cabbage-stalk. **–weißling,** *m.* cabbage butterfly.
Kohl–e, *f.* (-en) charcoal; coal; carbon; *abgeschwefelte –e*, coke; *ausgebrannte –en*, cinders; *glimmende –en*, embers; *glühende –e*, live coal; *–en einnehmen*, coal (*of ships*); *zu –e werden*, become charred *or* carbonized; *in –e verwandeln*, char, carbonize; *zu –e verbrennen*, be reduced to cinders; *auf* (*glühenden*) *–en sein* or *sitzen*, be on thorns *or* tenterhooks; *mit der Hand in die –en schlagen*, burn one's fingers (by a foolish undertaking); (*B.*) *feurige –en auf jemandes Haupt sammeln*, heap coals of fire on a p.'s head. **–en,** *v.a.* & *n.* (*aux.* h.) (*see also under* **Kohl**) char, make charcoal; carbonize; blacken, turn black, burn badly (*of a cigar or wick*); coal (*a ship*) (*Naut.*). **–enabbau,** *m.* coal-mining, working of coal. **–enarbeiter,** *m.* coal-miner, pitman, collier. **–enbank,** *f.* coal-bed. **–enbecken,** *n.* coalfield; brazier. **–enblende,** *f.* anthracite. **–enbergbau,** *m.* coal-mining. **–enbergwerk,** *n.* coal-mine, colliery. **–enbogenlampe,** *f.* arc lamp. **–enbrenner,** *m.* charcoal-burner. **–enbrennerei,** *f.* charcoal-burning; charcoal-kiln. **–endampf,** *m.*, **–endunst,** *m.* charcoal fumes. **–eneimer,** *m.* coal-scuttle, bucket *or* box. **–e(n)fadenbirne,** *f.* carbon filament lamp. **–enflöz,** *n.* coal-seam. **–engas,** *n.* coal gas; producer gas (*Motor.*). **–engestübe,** *n.* coal-dust, slack. **–engrube,** *f.* coal-mine. **–engrus,** *m.* slack, small coal. **–enhaltig,** *adj.* carboniferous, containing coal. **–enhütte,** *f.* charcoal-kiln. **–enhydrat,** *n.* carbohydrate. **–enhydratabbau,** *m.* carbohydrate metabolism. **–enkalk,** *m.* carboniferous limestone. **–enkasten,** *m.* coal-box, coal-scuttle. **–enklein,** *n.* small coal, slack. **–enlager,** *n.* colliery. **–enlösche,** *f.* coal-dust. **–enluke,** *f.* coaling hatch (*Naut.*). **–enmeiler,** *m.* charcoal pile. **–enmulm,** *m.* coal-dust, slack. **–enofen,** *m.* charcoal-kiln; coal-stove. **–enoxyd,** *n.* carbon monoxide. **–enpapier,** *n.*, *see* **–epapier.** **–enrevier,** *n.* coal-mining district. **–ensauer,** *adj.*; *–ensaures Soda*, carbonate of soda; *–ensaurer Kalk*, calcium carbonate; *–ensaures Wasser*, aerated water. **–ensäure,** *f.* carbonic acid. **–ensäuregas,** *n.* carbon dioxide. **–enschiefer,** *m.* bituminous shale. **–enschiff,** *n.* collier, coal barge. **–enschuppen,** *m.* coal-shed. **–enstation,** *f.* coaling-station. **–enstift,** *m.* carbon (*for arc-lamp*). **–enstoff,** *m.* carbon. **–enstoffstahl,** *m* carbon steel (*Metall.*). **–enwasserstoff,** *m.* (*Chem.*) hydrocarbon. **–enwerk,** *n.* colliery. **–enwerkstoff,** *m.* coal by-product *or* derivate. **–enzeche,** *f.* coal-pit, colliery. **–epapier,** *n.* carbon paper. **–estift,** *m.* charcoal pencil. **–ezeichnung,** *f.* charcoal drawing. **–ezinksammler,** *m.* dry cell (*Elec.*). **–ig,** *adj.* carbonite, carbonous. **–meise,** *f.* great tit (*Parus major*) (*Orn.*). **–(pech)rabenschwarz,** *adj.* jet black. (*coll.*) **–rabe,** *m.*, *see* **Kolkrabe.** **–schwarz,** *adj.* coal-black.
Köhler, *m.* (-s, –) charcoal-burner. **–ei,** *f.* charcoal-burning; charcoal kiln. **–glaube,** *m.* blind faith. **–irrtum,** *m.* belief founded on ignorance.
Kohorte, *f.* (-n) cohort.
Koitus, *m.* coition, copulation.
Koje, *f.* (-n) berth, bunk; stand, stall (*in a market, etc.*).
Kokain, *n.* cocaine.
Kokarde, *f.* (-n) cockade.
Kokerei, *f.* carbonization *or* coking plant.
kokett, *adj.* coquettish, flirtatious. **–e,** *f.* (-en) flirt, coquette, demi-monde. **–erie,** *f.* coquetry, flirting. **–ieren,** *v.a.* (*aux.* h.) flirt, coquet.
Kokille, *f.* mould, die. **–nguß,** *m.* chill casting.
Kokon, *n.* (-s, -s) cocoon.
Kokos–baum, *m.*, **–palme,** *f.* coconut palm. **–faser,** *f.* coir, coconut fibre. **–fett,** *n.* coconut oil. **–nuß,** *f.* coconut.
Koks, *m.* (-es, -e) (*Austr. dial. also f.*) coke; (*sl.*) = *Kokain*, snow; (*sl.*) = *Geld*, dough.
Kolb–en, I. *m.* (-ens, -en) club, mace, mallet; butt-end, butt (*of rifle*); burnisher; soldering-iron; piston (*Engin.*); flask, still, demijohn, retort, alembic; spadix (*Bot.*); feeler (*Ent.*); immature stag's horn. 2. *v.n.* (*aux.* h.) grow horns (*as young stag*), develop a head (*as maize or rushes*). **–enaufgang,** *m.* up-stroke of a piston. **–enbolzen,** *m.* gudgeon pin (*Motor.*). **–enförmig,** *adj.* club-shaped. **–enhirsch,** *m.* stag with knags for horns. **–enhub,** *m.*, **–enlauf,** *m.* piston-stroke. **–enkappe,** *f.* butt-plate (*of rifle*). **–enniedergang,** *m.* down-stroke of the piston. **–enschieber,** *m.*, *see* **–enventil.** **–enspiel,** *n.* motion of the piston. **–enstange,** *f.* piston-rod. **–enstreich,** *m.* blow with a club *or* butt-end. **–entragend,** *adj.* spadiceous (*Bot.*). **–enträger,** *m.* mace-bearer; retort stand (*Chem.*). **–enventil,** *n.* piston-valve. **–ig,** *adj.* club-like; knotty, knobby, nodular.
Kolibri, *m.* (-s, -s) humming-bird.
kolier–en, *v.a.* filter, strain. **–tuch,** *n.* filter, strainer.
Kolk, *m.* (-(e)s, -e) (*dial.*) deep hole, depression, pool. **–rabe,** *m.* common raven (*Corvus corax*) (*Orn.*).
kollationieren, *v.a.* collate, check (against).
Kolleg, *n.* (-s, -ien) (course of) lectures; *also* = **–ium**; *– halten* or *lesen*, give (*or* deliver) a course of lectures, lecture (*über* *S.*, on a th.); *– hören*, hear (*or* attend) a course of lectures *or* a lecture; *– belegen*, register for a course of lectures; *– schinden*, attend lectures without paying fees; *– schwänzen*, cut lectures; *– testieren*, testify to attendance at lectures; *– nachschreiben*, take (down) lecture notes. **–e,** *m.* (-en, -en), colleague; *Herr –e* or *Lieber –e*, *form of address in academic circles*. **–geld,** *n.* lecture-fee. **–heft,** *n.* lecture notebook. **–ial,** *adj.*, (*archaic*) **–ialisch,** *adj.* friendly, as a good colleague; *–ialisch verkehren*, be on good terms with one's colleagues. **–ialität,** *f.* esprit de corps among colleagues. **–ium,** *n.* (-iums, -ien) corporation, council, board, staff, teaching body; *also* = **Kolleg.**
Kollekt–aneen, *pl.* literary gleanings, miscellany, collectanea. **–aneenbuch,** *n.* commonplace-book. **–e,** *f.* collection; flag day; collect, short prayer (*Eccl.*). **–iv,** *adj.* collective. **–ivismus,** *m.* collectivism. **–ivvertrag,** *m.* collective agreement. **–or,** *m.* commutator (*Elec.*). **–ur,** *f.* (-en) (*Austr. dial.*) assembly *or* collecting point, depot, dump.
[1]**Koller,** *n.* (-s, –) jerkin, doublet; waistcoat; bodice.
[2]**Koller,** *m.* (-s) frenzy, rage, choler; staggers (*Vet.*). **–gang,** *m.* crushing rollers (*Mill.*). **–ig,** *adj.* afflicted with the staggers; crazy, raving. **–n,** I. *v.n.* (*aux.* h.) have the staggers; be furious, rage, rave; rumble (*as abdominally*); coo (*of pigeons*); gobble (*turkeys*); (*aux.* s.) roll (about). 2. *v.a.* grind. **–stein,** *m.* millstone, roller.
Kollett, *n.* (-(e)s, -e *or* (*dial.*) -s), *see* [1]**Koller.**
kollidieren, *v.n.* (*aux.* s.) come into collision (with), collide, clash, conflict (*as lectures, etc. held at the same time, or opposing views*), be incompatible.
Kollier [*pron.* kɔli′eː], *n.* (-s, -s) necklace.

kollieren, *v.a.* lay (*a ball*) under the cushion (*Bill.*).
Kollo, *n.* (-s, -s & Kolli) (*archaic*) bale, bundle, parcel, package.
Kollodium, *n.* (-s) collodion.
kolludieren, *v.n.* (*aux.* h.) act in collusion with.
Kolon, *n.* (-s, -s & –) colon (*Typ. & Anat.*).
kolon–ial, *adj.* colonial. **–ialminister,** *m.* Secretary of State for the Colonies, Colonial Secretary (*Eng.*). **–ialministerium,** *n.* Colonial Office. **–ialwaren,** *f.pl.* groceries. **–ialwarenhändler,** *m.* provision merchant, grocer. **–ialzucker,** *m.* cane sugar. **–ie,** *f.* (-n) colony. **–isieren,** *v.a.* colonize. **–ist,** *m.* (-en, -en) colonial settler.
Kolonne, *f.* (-n) column (*Mil.*). **–ngebiet,** *n.* rear area (*Mil.*). **–nstaffel,** *f.* rear echelon (*Mil.*).
Kolophonium, *n.* colophony, rosin.
Kolor–atur, *f.* (-en) coloratura (*Mus.*); (*pl.*) grace-notes (*Mus.*). **–atursängerin,** *f.* coloratura soprano, prima-donna. **–ieren,** *v.a.* colour; illuminate. **–it,** *n.* colouring, hue, shade, colour effect.
Koloß, *m.* (-(ss)es, -(ss)e) colossus. **–(ss)al,** *adj.* colossal, gigantic, huge, enormous; (*coll.*) extremely, immensely; (*coll.*) *er hat –(ss)ales Schwein,* he has fantastic luck; *freut mich –(ss)al,* I'm devilish pleased.
Kolport–age, *f.* door-to-door sale of books; colportage (*especially of religious tracts*); sensational rubbish, pandering to the public (*of literature*). **–ageroman,** *m.* penny-dreadful, shocker. **–eur,** *m.* (-s, -e) itinerant bookseller, hawker; (*fig.*) newsmonger. **–ieren,** *v.a.* hawk, sell in the streets; spread, disseminate (*news*).
[1]**Kolter,** *m.* (-s, –) quilt, coverlet.
[2]**Kolter,** *n.* (-s, –) ploughshare.
Kolumne, *f.* (-n) column (*Typ. & Arch.*). **–nmaß,** *n.* scale, ruler (*Typ.*). **–ntitel,** *m.* running title, heading. **–nweise,** *adv.* in columns. **–nziffer,** *f.* folio.
kombin–ieren, *v.a.* combine, join forces (with); scheme, devise, think out. **–ation,** *f.* (-en) surmise, conjecture; combination, team work; scheme, project, gambit; combinations (*underclothing*), flying-suit (*Av.*). **–ationslehre,** *f.* (permutations and) combinations (*Math.*).
Kombüse, *f.* (-n) galley, caboose.
Komet, *m.* (-en, -en) comet. **–enbahn,** *f.* orbit of a comet. **–enschweif,** *m.* tail of a comet. **–ensystem,** *n.* cometary system.
Komfort [*pron.* kɔm'fo:r *or* kɔm'fɔrt], *m.* ease, luxury. **–abel,** *adj.* luxurious, comfortable; *–able Wohnung,* luxurious apartment (*usual in advertisements*). **–wohnung,** *f.* luxury flat.
Komi–k, *f.* comicality; fun, funny ways, humour. **–ker,** *m.* comedian, comic writer. **–sch,** *adj.* comical, funny, droll, humorous; peculiar, queer, strange; *ein –scher Kauz,* a queer fish; *–sches Epos* mock-heroic *or* burlesque epic.
Komit–at, *m. & n.* (-(e)s, -e) suite, attendance; county (*in Hungary*). **–ee,** *n.* (-ees, -ees) committee, board.
Komma, *n.* (-s, -s & -ta) comma, decimal point.
Kommand–ant, *m.* (-en, -en) commander (*of a ship*), commandant (*of a garrison*). **–antur,** *f.* commandant's office, garrison headquarters. **–eur,** *m.* (-s, -e) commanding officer (*of military unit*). **–ieren,** *v.a. & n.* (*aux.* h.) give orders, be in command. (*C.L.*) **–itär,** *m.* (-s, -e) branch manager; (*Swiss dial.*) = **–itist. –ite,** *f.* (-n) branch establishment. **–itgesellschaft,** *f.* limited partnership; company in which liability of one partner is limited (*in commendam*). **–itist,** *m.* partner with limited liability. **–itsumme,** *f.* amount for which limited partner is liable. **–o,** *n.* (-s, -s) (word of) command, order; command, authority; squad, detachment. **–obrücke,** *f.* bridge (*Naut.*). **–opfeife,** *f.* boatswain's whistle. **–oturm,** *m.* control tower, conning tower, fighting top.
kommen, 1. *ir.v.n.* (*aux.* s.) come, arrive; approach, get to, draw near, reach; arise, proceed from; come about, result, fall out, happen, take place, occur; *sie sind mir abhanden gekommen,* I have lost *or* mislaid them; *es kann nicht anders –, als daß er,* he cannot but; (*Studs. sl.*) *einem etwas –,* drink to a p.'s health; *frei –,* get off free; *so wie es gerade kommt,* just as it turns out; *gegangen* or *geritten –,* come on foot *or* on horseback; *wie gerufen –,* come opportunely; *– Sie hierher,* come this way, come over here; *wenn es hoch kommt,* at the most; *es kann – daß,* it is possible that; *zu kurz –,* come off a loser, not get enough; *einen – lassen,* send for a p.; *etwas – lassen,* order a th.; *mir kam der Gedanke,* the thought occurred to me *or* crossed my mind; *er kommt und kommt nicht,* he still does not come; (*etwas*) *– sehen,* foresee, see it coming; *kommt mir nicht so,* do not speak to me *or* treat me in that way; . . . *daß es soweit – konnte,* . . . that things could get so bad; *weit –,* make great progress; *es ist weit mit ihm gekommen,* he has fallen very low; *wie* or *woher kommt es, daß . . . ?* how do you explain that . . .? *der soll mir wieder –!* just let him show his face here again! *wieviel* or *wie hoch kommt das Stück? Das Stück kommt 3 Mark,* how much is each piece? Each piece costs 3 marks; *es mag – was will, es komme wie es will,* whatever may happen; *die –de Fracht,* freight home *or* inwards; *–de Geschlechter,* future generations; *–de Woche,* next week; *an den Bettelstab –,* be reduced to poverty *or* beggary; *an die S. –,* reach the heart of the affair; *an das Licht* or *den Tag –,* be brought to light, become known, be found out; *nun kommt es* (or *die Reihe*) *an mich,* now it is my turn; *etwas an sich* (*heran*) *– lassen,* await s.th. quietly; *an jemandes Stelle –,* succeed to a p.'s post; *ans Land* or *Ufer –,* land, reach the shore; *wie kamen Sie darauf?* how did you (come to) think of that? *auf eine S. –,* think of, hit upon *or* come to mention a th.; *auf die Welt –,* be born; *wieder auf die Füße –,* fall on one's feet; *au seine Kosten –,* recover one's expenses, reimburse o.s.; *ich kam in die Schule,* I was sent to school; *einem* or *einer S. auf die Spur –,* be on a p.'s tracks *or* on the track of s.th.; *auf den Gedanken –,* have the idea, occur to one (to); *einer S. auf den Grund –,* get to the bottom of a matter; *nicht auf einen Namen – können,* be unable to remember a name; *er ist mir aus den Augen gekommen,* I have lost sight of him, I have not seen *or* met him again; *es kam mir aus dem Sinn* or *den Gedanken,* I forgot, it slipped my mind *or* memory; *außer Fassung* or *aus der Fassung –,* lose one's self-control; *aus der Mode –,* go out of fashion; *durch eine Prüfung –,* pass *or* get through an examination; *hinter das Geheimnis –,* penetrate the secret; *hinter seine Schliche –,* see through his tricks; *hinter die Wahrheit –,* discover *or* get at the truth; *ins Gerede* or *in der Leute Mund –,* be talked of, get a bad name; *in Verlegenheit –,* be embarrassed, get into trouble; *in Verfall –,* decay; *es kam mir in den Sinn,* it occurred to me, I remembered; *in Gang, Bewegung, Fahrt* or *Schwung –,* be set going, get under way; *in den Himmel –,* go to Heaven; *einem in den Weg* or *die Quere –,* cross *or* thwart a p.; *in die unrechte Kehle –,* go down the wrong way; *über etwas ins reine* or *klare –,* come to an agreement, arrive at a clear understanding about a th.; *nicht in Frage –,* be no question of; *in die Lage –,* be put in a position (to); *in die Schule –,* start school; *sie kommt in die Wochen,* she is near her time; *– Sie mir nicht damit,* (*coll.*) don't you come that one on me; *– Sie gut nach Hause!* get home safely! *über eine S. –,* come upon a th.; get over a th.; *Furcht kam über mich,* I was seized with fear; *um eine S. –,* lose a th.; *ums Leben –,* lose one's life; *unter die Leute –,* be spread abroad *or* made known (*of news*); mix with people, meet people; *von Kräften –,* lose one's strength; *von Sinnen –,* lose consciousness; go mad; *nicht vom Fleck* or *von der Stelle –,* not get any farther, not move from the spot; be at a standstill; *sie – mir nicht von der Seite,* they never leave me; *das kommt davon,* that comes of it, that is the result; *vor einen –,* come into a p.'s presence; *zur Ausbildung –,* develop; *es zum Äußersten – lassen,* let matters come to the worst; *einem zu Gesicht –,* be seen by s.o., come to a p.'s notice; *zu etwas –,* attain to, come to, get, obtain; find time for; *er wird schon zu etwas –,* he will no doubt make his way in the world; *wie kamen Sie dazu?* how did you

come to (do) that? how did you come by that? how did you get this? *ich komme nicht dazu*, I have no time (to); *dazu kommt noch*, besides, add to that; *zu Falle* or *Schaden* –, be ruined; *zum Militär* –, join the army; *zu nichts* –, not achieve anything, do no good; *einen zur Rede* or *zu Worte – lassen*, allow a p. to speak; *zu Kräften* –, recover strength; *zu Atem* –, get one's breath (back); *zur Besinnung* or *zu sich* –, come to one's senses; *zu Vermögen* or *Geld* –, come into a fortune; *es ist mir zu Ohren gekommen*, I have been told; *zu Tage* –, come to light, be discovered, become known; *wenn es zum Treffen kommt*, when it comes to the point, when matters come to a head, when it becomes urgent *or* crucial; *nie zur Ruhe* –, never get a rest, never get any peace; *komm zur S.*, come to the point! *zur Sprache* –, be discussed; *einem hoch zu stehen* –, cost a p. dear; *zur Überzeugung* –, reach the conviction; *zu einer Vereinbarung* –, come to a settlement; *zur Verwendung* –, be used, be put into use; *zum Vorschein* –, appear; *zustatten* or *zugute* –, be of use, be serviceable; *sich* (*Dat.*) *etwas zuschulden – lassen*, be guilty of *or* incur the blame for a th.; *er kam mit dem Finger zwischen die Türe*, his finger was squeezed *or* pinched in the door. 2. *n.* coming, arrival.

Kommende [*pron.* –ˈmɛndə], *f.* (-en) prebend.

Komment [*pron.* –ˈmɑ̃:], *m.* (-s, -s) (*archaic*) students' customs; code of corporate behaviour, Bacchanalian ritual (*among German students*); (*sl.*) *– reiten*, be a stickler for formality. **–mäßig**, *adj.* in conformity with students' code. **–widrig**, *adj.* contrary to students' code.

Komment–ar, *m.* (-s, -e) commentary. **–ieren**, *v.a.* comment on *or* upon; furnish with notes, annotate.

Kommers [*pron.* –ˈmɛrs], *m.* (-es, -e) festive evening (*among students*), students' social gathering. **–ieren**, *v.n.* hold a beer party. **–buch**, *n.* students' song book. **–lied**, *n.* students' song.

Kommilitone, *m.* (-n, -n) fellow-student.

Kommis [*pron.* –ˈmi:], *m.* (*C.L.*) clerk.

Kommiß, *m.* (-(ss)es, –) (*coll.*) army, soldiering, barracks, uniform; (*coll.*) *er ist beim* –, he is a soldier; *zum – kommen*, join up, be drafted *or* conscripted. **–brot**, *n.* army bread. (*sl.*) **–hengst**, *m.* martinet. **–mütze**, *f.* service cap. **–stiefel**, *m.pl.* army boots, (*sl.*) ammo boots.

Kommiss–ar (*Austr. dial.* **–är**), *m.* (-s, -e) deputy, delegate, commissary, commissioner, police inspector. **–ariat**, *n.* (-s, -e) territory *or* office of commissioner, (*dial.*) police station. **–arisch**, *adj.* provisional. **–ion**, *f.* commission, committee; percentage; *eine –ion erteilen*, give an order; *eine –ion einsetzen* or *ernennen*, appoint a commission *or* committee. **–ionär**, *m.* (-s, -e) (commission) agent. **–ionsbericht**, *m.* report of a commission *or* committee. **–ionsbuch**, *n.* order-book. **–ionsgebühr**, *f.* commission (charges). **–ionsgeschäft**, *n.* commission business, business on commission.

Kommittent, *m.* (-en, -en) (*C.L.*) person *or* party giving an order; employer of an agent (*commission business*), consignor.

kömmlich, *adj.* (*dial.*) convenient, comfortable.

kommod, *adj.* (*coll.*) comfortable, cosy, snug. **–e**, *f.* (-n) chest of drawers.

kömmst, kömmt, (*dial.*), *see* **kommen.**

kommun–al, *adj.* communal, municipal. **–albeamte(r)**, *m.* local official. **–alsteuer**, *f.* (local) rate. **–e**, *f.* (*sl.*) the Communist Party, Reds, Bolshies. **–ikant**, *m.* communicant (*Theol.*). **–ion**, *f.* (holy) communion. **–ismus**, *m.* communism. **–ist**, *m.* (-en, -en) communist. **–istisch**, *adj.* communist. **–izieren**, *v.n.* communicate (*Phys. & Theol.*).

Komöd–iant, *m.* (-en, -en) comedian; actor; (*fig.*) buffoon, clown, humbug, mountebank. **–ie**, *f.* (-n) comedy; play, (*fig.*) farce.

Kompa(g)nie, *f.* (-n) company, squadron (*Mil.*); (*C.L.*) company. **–chef**, *m.*, **–führer**, *m.* company commander. **–geschäft**, *n.* joint-business, partnership; *ein –geschäft gründen* (*auflösen*), go into (dissolve) partnership. (*sl.*) **–mutter**, *f.* sergeant.

Kompagnon, *m.* (-s, -s) partner, associate; *stiller* –, sleeping-partner.

kompakt, *adj.* compact, solid.

Kompar–ation, *f.* comparison (*Gram.*). **–se**, *m.* (-sen, -sen) super (*Theat.*). **–serie**, *f.* mute actors, supers.

Kompaß, *m.* (-(ss)es, -(ss)e) compass. **–häuschen**, *n.* binnacle. **–peilung**, *f.* compass bearing. **–strich**, *m.* point of the compass.

kompet–ent, 1. *adj.* competent; authoritative. 2. *m*, (-en, -en) competitor, rival. **–enz**, *f.* competence; competition; *–enz eines Falliten*, bankrupt's allowance. **–enzstreit**, *m.* question of jurisdiction.

Kompil–ator, *m.* (-s, -en) compiler. **–ieren**, *v.a.* compile.

Komplement–är *m.* (*C.L.*) unlimited partner of company '*in commendam*'. **–ärfarbe**, *f.* (-n) complementary colour. **–winkel**, *m.* complement of an angle.

Komplet, *n.* (-s, -s) ensemble (*Dressm.*).

komplett, *adj.* complete, all included; *–es Frühstück*, full breakfast.

Komplex, *m.* (-es, -e) complex; *Minderwertigkeits–* inferiority complex; *der ganze Häuser–*, the whole block (of houses.)

Kompliment, *n.* (-s, -e) compliment; greeting; bow, obeisance; *keine –e!* no ceremony! *ohne viel –e!* please do not stand on ceremony! **–ieren**, *v.a.* pay one's compliments *or* respects.

Kompliz–e, *m.* (-en, -en) accomplice. **–ieren**, *v.a.* complicate. **–iert**, *adj.* complicated, intricate.

Komplott, *n.* (-(e)s, -e) plot; *ein – schmieden*, hatch a plot.

Kompo–nente, *f.* (-n) component, ingredient, constituent. **–nieren**, *v.a. & n.* compose, set to music (*Mus.*). **–nist**, *m.* (-en, -en) composer. **–siteur**, (-s, -e) *m.* (*Austr. dial.*) = **–nist. –sition**, *f.* composition, composing. **–situm**, *n.* (-tums, -ta) compound (*Gram.*).

Kompott, *n.* (-s, -e) stewed *or* preserved fruit.

Kompresse, *f.* (-n) compress, poultice (*Med.*).

Komprette, *f.* (-n) pill, tablet.

komprimier–en, *v.a.* compress. **–bar**, *adj.* compressible.

Komprom–iß, *m. or n.* (-(ss)es, -(ss)e) compromise. **–ittieren**, 1. *v.a.* compromise. 2. *v.r.* commit *or* compromise o.s.

Komteß, –(ss)e, *f.* (-ssen) daughter of a count.

Komtur, *m.* (-s, -e) (Grand) Commander of an order. **–ei**, *f.* estate (under jurisdiction) of a knightly order.

Kondens–ation, *f.* condensation. **–ator**, *m.* (-s, -en) condenser. **–atorkette**, *f.* high-pass filter (*Rad.*). **–ieren**, *v.a.* condense. **–milch**, *f.* condensed *or* tinned milk. **–streifen**, *m.* vapour trail (*Av.*). **–wasser**, *n.* condensed water, water of condensation.

Kondition, *f.* (-en) condition, stipulation; (*coll.*) situation; (*archaic*) *in – gehen*, enter service. **–ieren**, *v.n.* (*aux.* h.); (*archaic*) *bei einem –ieren*, be in a p.'s employment.

Konditor, *m.* (-s, -en) pastry-cook, confectioner. **–ei**, *f.* confectioner's shop, café. **–eiwaren**, *pl.* confectionery.

Kondol–enz, *f.* (-en) condolence. **–enzbesuch**, *m.* visit of condolence. **–enzbrief**, *m.* letter of condolence. **–ieren**, *v.n.* condole (with), express one's sympathy (with)

Kondom [*pron.* –ˈdɔm], *m.* (-s, -s) condom, rubber sheath, contraceptive.

Kondukt [*pron.* –ˈdukt], *m.* (-(e)s, -e) funeral train, cortège. **–eur**, *m.* (-s, -e) (*Swiss & Austr. dial.*), (tram *or* bus) conductor. **–or**, *m.* (-s, -en) (electrical) conductor.

Konfekt [*pron.* –ˈfɛkt], *n.* (-(e)s, -e) confectionery, chocolates, sweets, sweetmeats, (*Amer.*) candy.

Konfektion, *f.* (-en) ready-made clothes. **–är**, *m.* (-s, -e) outfitter, clothier. **–sartikel**, *m.pl.*, *see* **Konfektion. –sgeschäft**, *n.* ready-made clothier's. **–swaren**, *f.pl.*, *see* **Konfektion.**

Konfer–enz, *f.* (-en) conference. **–ieren**, *v.n.* (*aux.* h.) confer together, meet for *or* go into conference, discuss.

Konfession, *f.* (-en) confession (of faith), creed; denomination. **–ell,** *adj.* confessional. **–slos,** *adj.* atheistic, free-thinking.
Konfirm–and, *m.* (-en, -en), **–andin,** *f.* (-innen), candidate for confirmation. **–andenunterricht,** *m.* confirmation classes. **–ieren,** *v.a.* confirm.
konfiszieren, *v.a.* confiscate.
Konfitüren, *pl.* jam, marmalade, preserves; sweetmeats, confectionery.
konform, *adj.* corresponding, coinciding, uniform, in agreement.
konfus, *adj.* puzzled, confused, muddled.
kongenial, *adj.* congenial, like-minded.
Konglomerat, *n.* (-(e)s, -e) conglomerate (*Geol.*); conglomeration, aggregation, accumulation, lump, mass.
Kongreß, *m.* (-(ss)es, -(ss)e) congress. **–mitglied,** *n.* member of congress. **–polen,** *n.* Russian Poland (1815–1918).
Kongru–enz, *f.* (-en) congruity, perfect equality. **–ieren,** *v.n.* (*aux.* h.) agree; coincide, be congruent (*Math.*).
König, *m.* (-s, -e) king; regulus (*Chem.*); *der Drei –stag,* Twelfth Day; *die heilige drei –e,* the three Magi; (*B.*) *das erste Buch der –e,* the first book of Kings; *zum – machen* or *einsetzen,* make *or* create king; *er wurde zum – gewählt,* he was elected king; *Herz–,* king of hearts (*Cards*); *des –s Rock* (*tragen*), the king's uniform (wear the king's coat (*archaic*)). **–in,** *f.* queen; *–inmutter,* queen mother; *–inwitwe,* queen dowager. **–lich,** *adj.* royal, kingly *or* queenly, regal, sovereign; *–lich Gesinnte(r),* royalist; (*coll.*) *sich –lich freuen,* be as happy as a king; (*coll.*) *sich –lich unterhalten,* enjoy o.s. immensely; *Ew. –liche Hoheit,* Your Royal Highness. **–reich,** *n.* kingdom, realm. **–sadler,** *m.* golden eagle. **–sblau,** *adj.* royal blue. **–shof,** *m.* royal palace *or* court. **–skerze,** *f.* mullein (*Verbascum thrapsus*) (*Bot.*). **–skrankheit,** *f.* king's evil, scrofula. **–skrone,** *f.* royal crown; crown-flower. **–smann,** *m.* royalist. **–smord,** *m.*, **–smörder,** *m.* regicide. **–ssäure,** *f. see* **–swasser.** **–sschießen,** *n.* (rifle) shooting competition. **–sschuß,** *m.* best shot. **–ssitz,** *m.* throne; royal residence. **–ssohn,** *m.* prince of royal blood. **–sstab,** *m.* sceptre. **–streu,** *adj.* loyal to the throne. **–swasser,** *n.* aqua regia (*Chem.*). **–swürde,** *f.* royal dignity; kingship. **–tum,** *n.* kingship, royalty; monarchial principle; *–tum von Gottes Gnaden,* kingship by divine right *or* by divine grace.
kon–isch, *adj.* conical. **–izität,** *f.* taper.
Konjug–ation, *f.* (-en) conjugation. **–ieren,** *v.a.* conjugate (*Gram*).
Konjunkt–iv, *m.* (-s, -e) subjunctive (*Gram.*). **–ur,** *f.* conjuncture, trend, trade cycle, industrial fluctuation, state of business; (*coll.*) favourable turn of the market, boom; *die günstige –ur ausnützen,* make the most of a favourable opportunity; *eine gute –ur versäumen,* miss a good chance. **–urbericht,** *m.* report on business conditions. **–urforschung,** *f.* study of trade cycles *or* industrial *or* business fluctuations. **–urgewinn,** *m.* market profit. **–urritter,** *m.* profiteer. **–urschwankung,** *f.* market vacillation. **–urverkauf,** *m.* seasonal sale.
konkav, *adj.* concave. **–ität,** *f.* concavity.
Konkord–anz, *f.* (-en) concordance; agreement. **–at,** *n.* (-(e)s, -e) concordat, treaty between (R.C.) Church and State.
konkret, *adj.* concrete, real, tangible.
Konkubinat, *m.* or *n.* (-(e)s, -e) concubinage.
Konkurr–ent, *m.* (-en, -en) competitor; rival. **–enz,** *f.* (-en) competition; rivalry, opposition. **–enzfähig,** *adj.* able to compete, competitive. **–enzieren,** *v.n.* (*aux.* h.) (*Swiss & Austr. dial.*) compete (with). **–enzkampf,** *m.* competition, struggle for survival. **–enzlos,** *adj.* exclusive. **–enzprüfung,** *f.* competitive examination. **–ieren,** *v.n.* (*aux.* h.) compete (with); be concurrent (with). **–ierend,** *pr.p. & adj.* competitive, concurrent.
Konkurs, *m.* (-es, -e) bankruptcy, insolvency, failure; *es ist ein – eröffnet worden,* a fiat of bankruptcy has been issued; *Erkennung des –es,* judicial assignment of an involvent's property; *in – gehen* or *geraten,* go bankrupt, fail; *– anmelden,* declare o.s. bankrupt; *– erklären,* file a petition. **–behörde,** *f.* commission of bankruptcy. **–erklärung,** *f.* declaration of insolvency. **–eröffnung,** *f.* opening of bankruptcy proceedings. **–gericht,** *n.* court of bankruptcy. **–masse,** *f.* estate of a bankrupt. **–ordnung,** *f.* regulations concerning insolvency, bankruptcy law. **–verfahren,** *n.* proceedings in bankruptcy. **–verwalter,** *m.* accountant in bankruptcy, receiver of a bankrupt's estate, liquidator, (*Amer.*) judicial factor.
können, 1. *ir.v.a.* know, understand (*how to do a th.*); have skill in; have power, be able to; *er kann nichts,* he knows nothing; he can do nothing; *laufe was du kannst,* run as fast as you can; *Englisch –,* know English. 2. *v.n.* (*aux.* h.) be able, be capable of, be permitted (to), be in a position (to); *es kann sein,* it may be; *ich kann mich irren,* I may be mistaken; *ich konnte nichts als,* I could do nothing but; *ich konnte nicht anders als,* I could not but, I could not help; *was kann ich dafür?* how can I help it? *er kann nichts dafür,* it is not his fault; *ich kann nicht umhin zu bemerken,* I cannot help *or* avoid remarking; *ich kann nicht mehr,* I can do no more; I am quite knocked up *or* I am all in; *sie kann gut deklamieren,* she recites well *or* is a good reciter; *er kann gut reiten,* he knows how to ride, he rides well; *ich kann nicht anders,* I cannot act otherwise; *nicht weiter –,* be at a standstill; *man kann hoffen,* it is to be hoped; *solche Leute – bei Hofe viel,* such people have great influence at court; *das Gekonnte wieder vergessen,* forget what one has once known. 3. *n.* ability, faculty, knowledge, power.
Könner, *m.* (-s, –) adept, efficient fellow.
Konnex, *m.* (-es, -e) connexion; contact. **–ion,** *f.* (*usually in pl.* –ionen) connexion; *–ionen haben,* have influential contacts, connexions *or* friends.
Konnossement, *n.* (-(e)s, -e) (*C.L.*) bill of lading.
konnte, konntest, *see* **können.**
Konrektor, *m.* (-s, -en) deputy *or* assistant headmaster.
Konsens, *m.* (-es, -e) consent, assent, approval.
konsequen–t, 1. *adj.* consistent, consequent (*Log.*); persistent; *–ter Naturalismus,* thoroughgoing naturalism. 2. *adv.* by natural sequence; consequently. **–z,** *f.* consistency; result, consequence; *–zen tragen,* accept responsibility, acknowledge the consequences; *–zen ziehen,* draw conclusions.
Konserv–ator, *m.* (-s, -en) keeper, curator (*of museum*). **–atorist,** *m.* music student. **–atorium,** *n.* school of music. **–en,** *f.pl.* tinned food. **–enbüchse,** *f.*, **–endose,** *f.* can, tin. **–enfabrik,** *f.* cannery. **–enverpflegung,** *f.* tinned rations (*Mil.*).
Konsign–ation, *f.* consignment, delivery (*from wholesaler to retailer*). **–ieren,** *v.a.* consign, deliver, forward.
Konsilium, *n.* (-iums, -ien) consultation (of experts); expert opinion.
konsisten–t, *adj.* firm, solid, durable, viscious; *-tes Fett,* grease, solid lubricant. **–z,** *f.* consistency, consistence, body, viscosity.
Konsistorium, *n.* (-iums, -ien) consistory; (Lutheran) Church Council.
konskri–bieren, *v.a.* levy (troops). **–bierte(r),** *m.* conscript. **–ption,** *f.* conscription.
Konsole, *f.* (-n) console; corbel (*Arch.*); bracket.
konsolidieren, *v.a.* consolidate; *konsolidierte Staatspapiere,* consolidated funds, consols.
konson–ant, 1. *adj.* consonant; agreeing. 2. *m.* (-en, -en) consonant (*Phonet.*). **–anz,** *f.* agreement, concord (*Mus.*).
Konsort–en, *m.pl.* associates, accomplices, parties (*Law*); *Z. und –en,* Z. and those he consorts with, Z. and his like. **–ium,** *n.* syndicate, association.
Konstabler, *m.* (-s, –) (*dial.*) constable; (*archaic*) armourer. **–kammer,** *f.* gun-room.
konstan–t, *adj.* constant, permanent, stable, invariable, persistent, stationary. **–z,** *f.* constancy, permanence, stability.
konstatieren, *v.a.* state, confirm, establish, verify, substantiate.
konsterniert, *adj.* disconcerted, amazed, stupified, taken aback.

konstitu-ieren, *v.a.* constitute, establish. **-tionell,** *adj.* constitutional (*Pol.*). **-tionswasser,** *n.* water of crystallization (*Chem.*). **-tiv,** *adj.* structural, fundamental, intrinsic; (*Law*) conclusive, probative, evidential.

konstru-ieren, *v.a.* construct, design, invent. **-kteur,** *m.* designer, constructor. **-ktiv,** *adj.* constructional, structural. **-ktivismus,** *m.* modernism, cubism (*Arch.*).

Konsul, *m.* (-s, -n) consul; *General-*, consul-general. **-arisch,** *adj.* consular. **-at,** *n.* (-(e)s, -e) consulate. **-ent,** *m.* (-en, -en) counsel, advocate, consultant. **-tativ,** *adj.* advisory. **-tieren,** *v.a.* consult.

Konsum, *m.* consumption. **-ent,** *m.* (-en, -en) user, consumer. **-genossenschaft,** *f.* **-verein,** *m.* co-operative society. **-ieren,** *v.a.* consume, use.

Kontakt, *m.* (-s, -e) contact, terminal (*Elec.*). **-mittel,** *n.* catalyst (*Chem.*). **-schlüssel,** *m.* ignition key (*Motor.*). **-schnur,** *f.* flex.

kontant, *adj.* ready, ready money, in cash. **-en,** *pl.* cash; ready money.

Konter-admiral, *m.* rear-admiral. **-band,** *adj.* contraband. **-bande,** *f.* contraband, smuggled goods. **-eskarpe,** *f.* counterscarp (*Fort.*). **-fei,** *n.* (-(e)s, -e) (*archaic*) portrait, likeness. **-revolution,** *f.* counter-revolution, forces of reaction. **-tanz,** *m.* square-dance, quadrille.

Konting-ent, 1. *n.* (-(e)s, -e) contingent, quota. 2. *adj.* contingent, incidental, accidental, chance. (*C.L.*) **-entieren,** *v.a.* fix the quotas, allocate, ration. **-enz,** *f.* contingency, uncertainty.

kontinu-ierlich, *adj.* continuous. **-ität,** *f.* continuity.

Konto, *n.* (-s, -s *or* Konten) account, credit; *– geben* or *nehmen*, give *or* take credit; *ein – saldieren*, balance an account; *Akontozahlung*, payment on account. **-auszug,** *m.* statement of account. **-inhaber,** *m.* person with a banking account. **-korrent,** *n.* (-(e)s, -e) current account. **-saldo,** *n.* balance account.

Kontor [*pron.* -ˈtɔr], *n.* (-s, -e) (*archaic*) counting-house, trading post (*in foreign country*), office. **-ist,** *m.* clerk.

kontra, 1. *adv.* & *pref.* counter, contra. 2. *n.* (-s, -s) argument *or* reason (put forward) against (s.th.), credit side of an account; (*C.L.*) *per –*, against which. **-baß,** *m.* double-bass, bass-viol. **-buch,** *n.* pass-book, customer's book. **-fagott,** *n.* double bassoon (*organ stop*). **-hage,** *f.* (-n) (*archaic*) challenge to a duel. **-hent,** *m.* (-en, -en) contracting party, party to a contract; (*archaic*) opponent (in a duel). **-hieren,** *v.a.* & *n.* (*aux.* h.) contract, bargain (*mit*, for), stipulate; (*archaic*) challenge to a duel. **-punkt,** *m.* counterpoint. **-punktisch,** *adj.* contrapuntal (*Mus.*).

kontrakt, 1. *adj.* contracted, stiffened (*Med.*). 2. *m.* (-(e)s, -e) contract, bargain. **-brüchig,** *adj.* breaking a contract. **-lich,** *adj.* by contract; *-lich verpflichtet*, bound by contract. **-ur,** *f.* (-en) muscular contraction, shortening (*Med.*).

konträr, *adj.* adverse, antithetical. **-farbe,** *f.* contrasting colour.

Kontrast, *m.* (-es, -e) contrast, opposition. **-ieren,** *v.a.* & *n.* contrast.

Kontroll-e, *f.* (-en) control, supervision, revision, examination; muster, army-list. **-abschnitt,** *m.* counterfoil. **-amt,** *n.* board of control. **-eur,** *m.* (-s, -e) controller, comptroller. **-gesellschaft,** *f.* (*C.L.*) holding company. **-ierblatt,** *n.* counterfoil (*of exchequer bills*). **-ieren,** *v.a.* check, supervise, control. **-schein,** *m.*, *see* **-abschnitt.** **-uhr,** *f.* control clock.

Kontumaz, *f.* (*Law*) contempt of court, contumacy. **-ieren,** *v.a.* condemn *or* convict in absentia.

Kontur, *f.* (-en) contour, outline.

Konven-ienz, *f.* (-en) suitability, propriety; custom, convenience. **-ieren,** *v.n.* be proper *or* convenient *or* suitable; (*mit einem*), agree upon, come to an arrangement (with a p.).

Konvent, *m.* (-(e)s, -e) convention, assembly. **-ion,** *f.* convention, usage; arrangement, agreement. **-ionalstrafe,** *f.* demurrage, penalty for breach of contract. **-ionell,** *adj.* conventional, traditional; formal, ceremonious.

Konversations-lexikon, *n.* encyclopaedia. **-stück,** *n.* society comedy (*Theat.*).

Konvert-ierung, *f.* (-en) conversion (*C.L.* & *Rel. etc.*). **-it,** *m.* (-en, -en) convert.

konvex, *adj.* convex. **-ität,** *f.* convexity.

Konvikt, *n.* (-(e)s, -e) hostel (*R.C.*).

Konvoi, *m.* (-s, -s) convoy (*Nav.*).

Konvolut, *n.* (-(e)s, -e) bundle *or* sheaf of papers.

konzedieren, *v.a.* concede, allow, acknowledge, make a concession.

Konzentr-at, *n.* concentration, concentrate (*Chem.*). **-ationslager,** *n.* concentration camp. **-ieren,** 1. *v.a.* concentrate, condense. 2. *v.r.*; *sich rückwärts -ieren*, fall back (*Mil.*); (*hum.*) flee, run away. **-isch,** *adj.* concentric.

Konzept, *n.* (-(e)s, -e) rough copy, first draft, notes (*of a speech, etc.*); *einen aus dem -e bringen*, confuse *or* disconcert a p., put a p. out; *aus dem -e ablesen*, read (*a speech*) from one's notes; *aus dem -e kommen*, become confused, lose the drift; *ins* or *in sein – passen*, fit *or* suit his plans. **-buch,** *n.* notebook, scribbling-book. **-papier,** *n.* scribbling-paper.

Konzern, *m.* (-s, -e) (*C.L.*) combine.

Konzert, *n.* (-(e)s, -e) concert; concerto. **-besucher,** *m.* concert-goer. **-flügel,** *m.* grand piano. **-haus,** *n.* concert hall. **-ieren,** *v.n.* give *or* play in a concert. **-meister,** *m.* impresario.

Konzession, *f.* (-en) concession, allowance; grant, patent, licence; *einander -en machen*, make mutual allowances; *eine – haben*, be licensed. **-iert,** *adj.* licensed, authorized. **-sausgabe,** *f.*, **-ssteuer,** *f.* licence-fee, licence.

Konzil, *n.* (-s, -e *or* -ien), (*Austr. dial.*) **-ium,** *n.* (-iums, -ien) (church-)council.

konzip-ieren, 1. *v.a.* draw up, plan, draft. 2. *v.n.* conceive, become pregnant (*archaic*). **-ient,** *m.* drawer-up (*of a document*), draughtsman.

Koog, *m.* (-(e)s, Köge) reclaimed land, polder.

Köper, *m.* twill, tweel.

Kopf, *m.* (-es, ¨-e) head; top, crown; title, heading; pommel; talented person, thinker; brains, abilities; *– an –*, shoulder to shoulder, packed tight; *auf den –*, a head, each; *er ist nicht auf den – gefallen*, he is no fool, he is all there *or* wide awake; (*coll.*) *einem auf den – kommen* or *steigen*, take a p. to task; *seinen* or *sich einen – aufsetzen*, be obstinate (about); *ich lasse mir nicht auf den – spucken*, I won't stand for it; *auf dem – stehen*, be topsy-turvy, in confusion *or* in a muddle; *der – steht darauf*, it is a capital offence; *auf den – stellen*, turn upside down, bring into confusion; *und wenn du dich auf den – stellst*, wriggle how you may, whatever you do; *aus dem -e*, by heart, from memory; *sich* (*Dat.*) *etwas aus dem -e schlagen*, banish *or* dismiss s.th. from one's thoughts *or* mind; *den – aus der Schlinge ziehen*, get out of the scrape, slip one's head out of the noose; *sich blutige Köpfe holen*, suffer a severe rebuff; *mir brennt der –*, my head is singing; *es geht ihm zu viel durch den –*, he has too much to think of; (*coll.*) *mit dem -e durch die Wand wollen*, batter one's head against a brick wall; *einen eigensinnigen – haben*, be obstinate; *die Köpfe erhitzten sich*, tempers ran high; *fähiger –*, clever fellow; *fauler –*, shiftless fellow; *seinen – für sich haben*, be obstinate; *es gilt seinen –*, see *es geht um seinen –*; *– haben*, have sense; *den – hängen lassen*, be despondent *or* disgruntled; *– hoch!* chin up! *im -e behalten*, remember; *etwas im -e haben*, be preoccupied with a th.; *etwas noch frisch im -e haben*, have s.th. still fresh in one's mind; *immer Grillen* or *große Rosinen im -e haben*, be full of crazy ideas; *er hat Grütze im -e*, he has his wits about him; *er hat weiter nichts im -e als . . .*, his mind runs perpetually on . . .; *Stroh im -e haben*, be scatter-brained *or* a scatter-brain; *sich* (*Dat.*) *in den – setzen*, take into one's head; *in den – steigen*, go to a p.'s head; *das will mir nicht in den –*, I cannot understand that; I cannot credit that; *mit dem – bezahlen*, pay for with one's life; *nach dem eignen -e leben*, follow one's own inclinations; *mir steht der – nicht danach*, I have no inclination for it; *nach Köpfen stimmen*, count heads; *den – oben behalten*, keep one's courage, spirits *or* (*sl.*) pecker up; *pro –*, see *auf den –*; *– oder Schrift?* heads or tails?; *nicht wissen wo einem der – steht*, not know whether one is on one's head or one's feet; *über Hals und –, Hals über –*, head over heels, precipitately, headlong; *einem über den – wachsen*, be too much for s.o.; *einem über dem – zusammenstürzen*, fall about one's ears; *es geht um seinen –*, his life is at stake; *um einen – größer*, a head taller; *ein Brett vor dem –e haben*, be very stupid; *einem den – vor die Füße legen*, behead a p.; *wie vor den – geschlagen sein*, be dazed; *einen vor den – stoßen*, offend *or* hurt a p., give offence to a p.; *einem den – waschen*, reprimand a p. sharply, give a p. a piece of one's mind *or* a dressing-down; *sich* (*Dat.*) *den – zerbrechen* (*über*), rack one's brains (about); *einem zu –e steigen*, go *or* fly to a p.'s head (*of wine*); *einem den – zurechtsetzen*, bring a p. to his senses; *von – bis Fuß* or *bis zu den Füßen*, from top to toe *or* head to foot; (*Prov.*) *was man nicht im –e hat, muß man in den Beinen* or *Füßen haben*, use your head to save your heels; who falls short in the head must be long in the heels. **–arbeit,** *f.* brain-work. **–baum,** *m.* lopped tree, pollard. **–bedeckung,** *f.* headgear. **–besteuerung,** *f.* capitation tax. **–blüte,** *f.* aggregate blossom, capitulum (*Bot.*). **–drüse,** *f.* cephalic gland. **–düngung,** *f.* top dressing. **–ende,** *n.* head (*of a bed, etc.*). **–fest,** *adj.* constant, steady, persevering. **–fieber,** *n.* brain-fever. **–füßer,** *m.* cuttle fish (*Cephalopoda*). **–geld,** *n.* poll-tax, capitation fee. **–gewand,** *n.* amice (*Eccl.*). **–grind,** *m.* scald-head, porrigo (*Med.*). **–haar,** *n.* hair of the head. **–hänger,** *m.* low-spirited person. **–haube,** *f.* tuft, crest, hood. **–haut,** *f.* scalp. **–hörer,** *m.* earphones (*wireless*), headset (*Tele.*). **–kissen,** *n.* pillow. **–kissenbezug,** *m.* pillow-case. **–kohl,** *m.* common *and* red cabbage. **–länge,** *f.* head (*horse-race*). **–lastig,** *adj.* nose-heavy (*Av.*), down by the bow (*Naut.*). **–los,** *adj.* headless; acephalous; impetuous; confused. **–nicken,** *n.* nod. (*vulg.*) **–nuß,** *f.* cuff, box on the ear. **–pfühl,** *m.* bolster; pillow. **–putz,** *m.* coiffure; head adornment. **–rechnen,** *n.* mental arithmetic. **–rose,** *f.* erysipelas (*Med.*). **–salat,** *m.* cabbage- *or* garden-lettuce. **–scheu,** *adj.* alarmed, startled, timid, restless, uneasy (*as horses*). **–schmerz,** *m.*, **–schmerzen,** *m.pl.* headache. **–schütteln,** *n.* misgiving, disapproval. **–schützer,** *m.* Balaclava helmet. **–sprung,** *m.* header. **–stand,** *m.* standing on one's head (*Gymn.*). **–station,** *f.* terminus, railhead. **–stehen,** *v.n.* (*sep.*) (*aux.* h.) stand on one's head; be upside down *or* inverted; be amazed *or* staggered. **–steinpflaster,** *n.* cobbled pavement. **–steuer,** *f.* poll-tax. **–stimme,** *f.* falsetto. **–sturz,** *m.* nose-dive (*Av.*). **–tuch,** *n.* kerchief, shawl, scarf. **–über,** *adv.* head foremost, headlong, precipitously. **–unter,** *adv.* head down. **–waschen,** *n.* shampooing. **–wasser,** *n.* hair wash *or* lotion, shampoo. **–weh,** *n.* headache. **–weide,** *f.* pollard willow. **–zahl,** *f.* number of persons. **–zerbrechen,** *n.* pondering, cogitation, rumination. **–zeug,** *n.* headgear, head-dress.

köpf–en, 1. *v.a.* behead; poll, lop, top, truncate, pollard. 2. *v.n.* (*aux.* h.) form a head (*of plants*). **–ig,** *adj.* headstrong; (*in compounds* =) -headed, capitate, -cephalous. **–lings,** *adv.* headlong, head first.

Kop–ie, *f.* (-ien) copy, reproduction, transcript, carbon copy, contact print. **–ieren,** *v.a.* copy. **–iermaschine,** *f.* copying-press. **–iertinte,** *f.* copying ink. **–ist,** *m.* (-en, -en) copyist.

Koppe, *f.* (*dial.*), *see* **Kuppe.**

Koppel, 1. *f.* (-n) pack, string, leash (*of dogs*), paddock, enclosure; (*Austr. dial.*) sword-belt. 2. *n.* sword-belt. **–n,** *v.a.* couple, join, leash, tie *or* harness together, link, unite; fence, enclose; hobble. **–balken,** *m.* tie-beam. **–band,** *n.* leash. **–kette,** *f.* drag-chain. **–kurs,** *m.* dead-reckoning (*Navig.*). **–recht,** *n.* right enjoyed in common with others. **–schloß,** *n.* buckle. **–ung,** *f.* coupling, linkage; double-main (*organ stop*). **–weide,** *f.* enclosed pasture. **–wirtschaft,** *f.* rotation of crops.

Kopplung, *see* **Koppelung.**

Kopul–ation, *f.* (-en) union, mating, marriage, pairing, grafting. **–ativ,** *adj.* copulative; *–ative Bindewörter*, copulative conjunctions (*Gram.*). **–ieren,** 1. *v.a.* unite, pair, mate, graft, marry. 2. *v.n.* pair, mate.

kor, korest, köre, *see* **kiesen.**

Korall–e, *f.* (-en) coral. **–en,** *adj.* coralline. **–enbank,** *f.*, *see* **–enriff.** **–enfischer,** *m.* coral-diver *or* -fisher. **–enriff,** *n.* coral reef. **–enschnur,** *f.* string of coral beads, coral necklace.

koramieren, (ad) Koram nehmen, *v.a.* (*archaic*) take to task.

koranzen, *see* **kuranzen.**

Korb, *m.* (-(e)s, ⸚e) basket, hamper, crate, pannier; (*fig.*) refusal, dismissal; rejection; *einen – bekommen*, receive a refusal, be turned down; *einem einen – geben*, reject s.o.'s offer of marriage, turn s.o. down; *Hahn im –e sein*, be cock of the walk. **–blütler,** *m.pl.* compositae (*Bot.*). **–er,** *m.* (*Swiss dial.*) basket maker. **–flasche,** *f.* carboy, demijohn. **–flechter,** *m.* basket maker. **–flechterei,** *f.* basket-work. **–gitter,** *n.* hurdle. **–möbel,** *n.pl.* wicker furniture. **–sessel,** *m.*, **–stuhl,** *m.* wicker chair. **–wagen,** *m.* basket-carriage. **–weide,** *f.* osier (*Salix viminalis*) (*Bot.*).

Kord, *m.* (-(e)s, -e) corduroy. **–hose,** *f.* corduroy trousers, cords.

Korde, *f.* (-n) (ornamental) cord, piping. **–l,** *f.* (-n) (*dial.*) cord, twine, string.

Kordon, *m.* (-s, -s (*& Austr. dial.* -e)) cord, line; cordon, barrier, barricade.

Korduan, *m.* (-s, -e) (*archaic*) cordwain, cordova leather.

kör–en, *v.a.* assay, inspect, select (*animals for breeding*). **–hengst,** *m.* selected stallion.

Korinthe, *f.* (-n) (dried) currant.

Kork, *m.* (-(e)s, -e) cork, stopper. **–en,** 1. *adj.* of cork, corky, suberous. 2. *v.a.* cork (up). **–enzieher,** *see* **–zieher.** **–form,** *f.* model in cork. **–geld,** *n.* corkage. **–gürtel,** *m.* lifebelt. **–stöpsel,** *m.* cork(-stopper). **–teppich,** *m.* linoleum. **–weste,** *f.* life jacket. **–zieher,** *m.* corkscrew; spin, spiral dive (*Av.*).

Korn, *n.* (-(e)s, ⸚er (= grains) & -e (= cereals)) grain, corn, cereal; seed, kernel; rye; standard (*of metal*); foresight (*of a rifle*) (*pl. also -e*); *aufs – nehmen*, (take) aim at, sight; fix one's eye on, fix with one's eye, (*fig.*) make the target of one's remarks; *von gutem Schrot und –*, of full measure and good quality; *Mann von altem* or *echtem Schrot und –*, man of the good old stamp *or* of the right sort; *die Flinte ins – werfen*, throw in one's hand, throw in the towel. **–ähre,** *f.* ear of corn; spica (*Astr.*). **–artig,** *adj.* frumentaceous. **–bau,** *m.* cultivation of cereals. **–bildung,** *f.* crystallization, granulation. **–blume,** *f.* corn-flower (*Centaurea cyanus*) (*Bot.*). **–boden,** *m.* granary. **–börse,** *f.* corn-exchange. **–brand,** *m.* blight, smut. **–branntwein,** *m.* whisky. **–fege,** *f.* winnowing machine. **–förmig,** *adj.* granulated, granular. **–fraß,** *m.*, *see* **–brand.** **–garbe,** *f.* sheaf of corn. **–kammer,** *f.* granary. **–kasten,** *m.*, **–lade,** *f.* corn-bin. **–mutter,** *f.* ergot. **–rade,** *f.* corn-cockle, corn campion (*Agrostemma* or *Lychnis githago*) (*Bot.*). **–reich,** *adj.* abounding in corn. **–schnaps,** *m.* rye whisky. **–speicher,** *m.* granary. **–spitze,** *f.* dead-centre (*Mach.*).

Körn–chen, *n.* (-s, –) granule, spore; (*fig.*) *kein –chen*, not the least, not a grain (*of truth, etc.*). **–eln,** *v.a.* granulate. **–elung,** *f.*, *see* **–ung.** **–en,** 1. *v.a.* granulate; grain (*leather*), tool (*metal*). 2. *v.r.* form into grains, granulate; run to seed. **–erfressend,** *adj.* granivorous. **–ig,** *adj.* granular, crystalline, granulated, grained; gritty, pebbly. **–ung,** *f.* granulation; graining, tooling.

Kornett, 1. *m.* (-(e)s, -e (*& Austr. dial.* -s)) standard bearer, (*archaic*) cornet (*Mil.*). 2. *n.* (-s, -e) cornet (*Mus.*).

Korona, *f.* (-nen) (*Univ. sl.*) circle of listeners, audience; (*Astr.*) corona.

Körper, *m.* (-s, –) body; bulk, matter, compound, substance; carcass, corpse; *der gesetzgebende –*, legislative body; *flüssiger –*, liquid substance; *fester –*, solid matter, solid body. **–anlage,** *f.* constitution; temperament. **–bau,** *m.* bodily structure, frame, build; *von kräftigen –bau*, of sturdy physique, of robust build. **–beschaffen-**

heit, *f.* physique. **–bildung,** *f.* physique; formation of the body, physical structure. **–chen,** *n.* particle, corpuscule, corpuscle. **–farbe,** *f.* pigment. **–fülle,** *f.* corpulence, plumpness. **–gehalt,** *n.* & *m.* solid content, body. **–größe,** *f.* stature. **–haft,** *adj.* corporeal. **–haltung,** *f.* bearing, carriage, deportment. **–inhalt,** *m.* solid content (*Math.*). **–kraft,** *f.* physical strength. **–kultur,** *f.* physical culture. **–lehre,** *f.* somatology; solid geometry, stereometry (*Math.*). **–lich,** *adj.* bodily, physical; corporeal, solid, substantial, material; corpuscular; *–liche Anlage,* constitution, temperament; *–licher Winkel,* solid angle; *–licher Eid,* verbal oath, oath taken in person; *–liche Strafe,* corporal punishment; *–lich leidend,* physically ailing; *das –liche,* materiality. **–lichkeit,** *f.* corporeality, concreteness. **–los,** *adj.* incorporeal. **–losigkeit,** *f.* immateriality. **–maß,** *n.* cubic measure. **–messung,** *f.* stereometry. **–pflege,** *f.* beauty culture, personal hygiene. **–reich,** *n.* material world. **–schaft,** *f.* corporate body, corporation. **–schulung,** *f.* physical training, culture *or* exercise. **–schwäche,** *f.* debility, frailness. **–stärke,** *f.* physical strength. **–stellung,** *f.* posture. **–stimmung,** *f.* temperament, disposition, constitution. **–stoff,** *m.* organic matter. **–strafe,** *f.* corporal punishment. **–teilchen,** *n.* particle, molecule. **–übung,** *f.* physical exercise, gymnastics. **–verletzung,** *f.* bodily injury. **–wärme,** *f.* body heat. **–welt,** *f.,* *see* **–reich.** **–winkel,** *m.* solid angle. **–zahl,** *f.* cubic number.

Korporal, *m.* (-s, -e) corporal. **–schaft,** *f.* section, squad (*Mil.*).

Korps [*pron.* ko:r], *n.* (–, – [*Gen.* & *pl. pron.* ko:rs]) army corps, students' club *or* association (*aristocratically exclusive and given to duelling*); *fliegendes –,* flying column. **–bruder,** *m.,* **–bursch,** *m., see* **–student.** **–geist,** *m.* esprit de corps; party spirit (*Pol.*). (*coll.*) **–student,** *m.* member of a Korps.

Korpus, 1. *m. or n.* (-us, -ora) body, totality, entirety, mass. 2. *f.* long primer (*Typ.*).

korrekt, *adj.* correct, proper, irreproachable. **–heit,** *f.* correctness. **–ionshaus,** *n.* remand home. **–iv,** *adj.* correctional, corrective. **–ivmittel,** *n.* corrigent, corrective. **–or,** *m.* (-s, -en) press-corrector, proof reader. **–ur,** *f.* (-en) correction, revision, proof (sheet) (*Typ.*). **–urabzug,** *m.,* **–urbogen,** *m.* printer's proof, proof-sheet. **–urzeichen,** *n.* (mark of) correction.

Korrespond–ent, *m.* (-en, -en) correspondent. **–enz,** *f.* correspondence, agreement. **–enzbüro,** *n.* press-agency. **–ieren,** *v.n.* correspond, exchange letters; agree with.

korrigieren, *v.a.* correct, rectify; read (*proofs*).

korrumpieren, *v.a.* corrupt.

Korsar, *m.* (-en, -en) pirate, corsair.

Korsett, *n.* (-(e)s, -e) corset, stays. **–stange,** *f.* corset-busk *or* bone.

Koryphäe, *m.* (-n, -n) star, celebrity, authority; leader of a choir *or* dramatic company.

Koschenille, *f.* cochineal.

kos–en, 1. *v.a.* caress, fondle. 2. *v.n.* (*aux.* h.) talk amorously *or* intimately; make love. **–ig,** *adj.* intimate, cosy. **–ename,** *m.* pet name.

Kosinus, *m.* (–, –) cosine (*Math.*).

Kosmet–ik, *f.* cosmetics. **–isch,** *adj.* cosmetic.

kosm–isch, *adj.* cosmic. **–os,** *m.* (-os) universe. **–opolit,** *m.* (-en, -en) cosmopolitan. **–opolitisch,** *adj.* cosmopolitan.

Kossat, Kossäte, *m.* (-en, -en) cottager, cotter, cottar.

Kost, *f.* food, diet, fare, victuals, board; *in* (*der*) *– sein* (*bei*), board (with); *in* (*die*) *– geben* or *tun,* put out to board; *einen in* (*die*) *– nehmen, einem die – geben,* board a p.; *kräftige –,* substantial *or* rich food; *schmale –,* slender *or* scanty fare, poor living, poor diet; *– und Wohnung* (or *Logis*), board and lodging *or* residence; *Wertpapiere in – nehmen,* accept securities for a short-term loan. **–en,** 1. *v.a.* taste; try, experience, make trial of. 2. *n.* tasting. **–frei,** *adj.* with free board. **–gänger,** *m.* boarder. **–geber,** *m.* boarding-house keeper. **–geld,** *n.* board allowance; alimony (*Law*); *–geld bekommen,* be on board-wages (*of servants*). **–happen,** *m.,* **–probe,** *f.* taste, trial, sample, morsel. **–regel,** *f.* diet, regimen. **–schule,** *f.* boarding school. **–verächter,** *m.*; *kein –verächter sein,* eat anything and everything, enjoy one's food.

kost–bar, *adj.* precious; valuable, costly, expensive; *-barer Witz,* capital joke. **–barkeit,** *f.* costliness; object of value, valuable. **–en,** 1. *pl.* cost(s), expense(s), expenditure, charge(s); *es geht auf meine –en,* it is at my expense, charge it to me, put it down to my account; *die –en bestreiten* or *tragen, für die –en aufkommen,* defray *or* meet the expenses; *einem –en machen,* put a p. to expense; *in die* or *zu den –en verurteilen,* condemn a p. to pay all costs (*Law*); *die –en herausschlagen,* recover expenses; *auf die –en kommen,* recover expenses; be satisfied (with), receive satisfaction (over) (*a transaction*); *sich in –en stürzen,* incur (great) expense; *ich habe es auf meine –en erfahren,* I have learned it to my cost; *auf –en seiner Ehre,* at the expense of his honour. 2. *v.a.* cost; require; *es –et mich 10 Pfennig,* it cost me 10 pfennigs; *es –et mich* or *mir einen schweren Kampf,* it costs me a hard struggle; *es –et Zeit,* it takes time; *es –e was es wolle,* at any cost *or* price. **–enanschlag,** *m.* estimate (of cost). **–enaufwand,** *m.* expenditure. **–enausgleichung,** *f.* balance of expenses. **–enberechnung,** *f.* calculation of cost, costing. **–enersatz,** *m.* compensation for outlay. **–enfrei,** *adj.,* **–enlos,** *adj.* free, without charge, for nothing. **–enordnung,** *f.* tariff. **–enpflichtig,** *adj.* liable for costs (*Law*). **–enpreis,** *m.* cost price, prime cost; *unter –enpreis verkaufen,* sell at a loss. **–enpunkt,** *m.* (matter of) expense(s); *was den –enpunkt anbetrifft,* as to expenses. **–spielig,** *adj.* expensive, costly, dear. **–spieligkeit,** *f.* costliness, expensiveness.

köstlich, *adj.* costly, precious, valuable; exquisite, excellent, delicious, tasty, dainty; *das ist – !* that's capital! that's a good joke!

Kostüm, *n.* (-s, -e) costume, fancy-dress; tailor-made dress, coat and skirt, two-piece. **–ball,** *m.,* **–fest,** *n.* fancy-dress ball; *historisches –fest,* historical pageant. **–ieren,** *v.a.* dress; dress up, disguise, drape. **–kunde,** *f.* study of historical costumes. **–probe,** *f.* dress-rehearsal.

[1]**Kot,** *n.* (-(e)s, -e), *also* **–e,** *f.* (-en) (*dial.*) hut, cot, hovel, shed. **–saß,** *m.,* **–sasse,** *m. see* **Kätner.**

[2]**Kot,** *m.* dirt, filth; mire, mud; muck, manure, droppings, dung; excrement, faeces. **–abgang,** *m.* defaecation. **–ausführend,** *adj.* laxative, aperient, purgative, cathartic. **–blech,** *n.,* **–flügel,** *m.* mudguard, wing, fender (*Motor.*). **–grube,** *f.* sewer; cesspool. **–ig,** *adj.* dirty, muddy, mucky; filthy, faecal.

Kote, *f.* (-n) contour (*of a map*).

Köte, *f.* (-n) (*dial.*), **–ngelenk,** *n.* (-(e)s, -e) fetlock.

Kotelett, *n.* (-(e)s -e) cutlet, chop; *Kalbs–,* veal cutlet; *Hammel–,* mutton chop. **–e,** *f.* (-n), *see* **–**; *also* mutton-chop whiskers.

Kotenschopf, *m.* (-es, ⸗e) *see* **Köte.**

Köter, *m.* (-s, –) cur; mongrel.

Kothurn, *m.* (-s, -e) cothurnus, buskin.

kotieren, 1. *v.a.* (*C.L.*) quote (*prices, etc.*). 2. *v.n.* measure altitude (*Geogr.*).

Kötner, *m., see* **Kätner.**

Kotze, *f.* (-n) *also* **Kotzen,** *m.* (-s, –) (*dial.*) coarse blanket, woollen cape.

Kötze, *f.* (-n) (*dial.*) basket (for the back).

kotzen, *v.r.* & *n.* (*aux.* h.) (*vulg.*) vomit, spew.

Krabbe, *f.* (-n) crab; shrimp; (*coll.*) little child, lively girl. **–lig,** *adj.* lively; itchy. **–ln,** 1. *v.n.* (*aux.* h. & s.) clamber, grope, crawl, creep. 2. *v.a.* & *n.* (*aux.* h.) & *imp.* itch, tickle; scratch; *es –t mir am Halse,* my neck itches.

Krach, *m.* (-(e)s, -e & *coll.* ⸗e) crash; noise, din; quarrel, sharp difference of opinion; bankruptcy, failure, commercial crisis; *mit einem einen – bekommen,* fall out with a p.; *mit Ach und –,* with great difficulty. **–en,** 1. *v.n.* (*aux.* h. & s.) crack, burst, crash, roar; fail, be ruined. 2. *v.a.* crack (*nuts, etc.*). 3. *n.* crack, crash, roar. 4. *m.* (*Swiss dial.*) gorge, ravine. **–er,** *m.* (*coll.*) old dodderer. **–erl,** *n.* (*Austr. dial.*) aerated water, (*coll.*) pop. (*dial.*) **–mandel,** *f.* soft-shelled almond.

krächz-en, *v.n.* (*aux.* h.) croak, caw; *die Krähe* –*t*, the crow caws; *der Rabe* –*t*, the raven croaks.
Kracke, *f.* (-n) (*dial.*) jade, nag; screw.
Kraft, 1. *f.* (⸚e) strength; power, force, vigour, energy; efficacy, validity; (*C.L.*) worker, employee; *aus allen Kräften*, with all one's might; *außer* – *setzen*, annul, abrogate; *bewegende* –, moving force, motive power; *was in meinen Kräften liegt*, as far as I can; *in* – *setzen*, enforce (*a law, etc.*), execute (*judgement, etc.*); *in* – *treten*, come into force; *in voller* –, in full force; *mit der* – *der Verzweiflung*, with strength born of despair; *nach besten Kräften*, to the best of one's ability; *das geht über meine Kräfte*, that is outside my power *or* too much for me; *zu Kräften kommen*, regain one's strength. 2. *prep.* (*Gen.*) in *or* by virtue of, on the strength of, by authority of. **–anlage,** *f.* power-plant, power-station. **–anstrengung,** *f.* effort. **–antrieb,** *m.* power drive. **–aufbietung,** *f.*, **–aufwand,** *m.* exertion, expenditure of energy. **–ausdruck,** *m.* strong language. **–äußerung,** *f.* manifestation of strength *or* energy. **–bedarf,** *m.* (*of a machine*) power requirement. **–brühe,** *f.* beef-tea. **–droschke,** *f.* taxi-cab. **–einheit,** *f.* unit of force *or* work. **–fahrer,** *m.* motorist. **–fahrschule,** *f.* school of motoring. **–fahrzeug,** *n.* motor vehicle. **–feld,** *n.* field of force (*Physics.*). **–fülle,** *f.* exuberance. **–lastwagen,** *m.* motor lorry. **–lehre,** *f.* dynamics. **–los,** *adj.* weak, feeble, powerless; ineffectual, impotent; null, invalid. **–mensch,** *m.* he-man. **–messer,** *m.* dynamometer. **–mittel,** *n.* forceful means; powerful remedy. **–probe,** *f.* trial of strength. **–quelle,** *f.* source of power *or* energy; generator unit. **–rad,** *n.* motor-cycle. **–sammler,** *m.* accumulator. **–schlepper,** *m.* tractor. **–sprache,** *f.* powerful, forceful *or* pithy language. **–stoff,** *m.* fuel, petrol, (*Amer.*) gas. **–stoffförderung,** *f.* fuel feed (*Motor.*). **–stoffverbrauchsatz,** *m.* rate of fuel consumption. **–übertragung,** *f.* power transmission. **–verlust,** *m.* loss of power. **–voll,** *adj.* vigorous, powerful; pithy. **–wagen,** *m.* motor-car, motor vehicle, (*Amer.*) automobile. **–werk,** *n.* power-station. **–winde,** *f.* power-winch.
Kräfte–einsatz, *m.* commitment of forces (*Mil.*). **–verteilung,** *f.* distribution of forces (*Mech.*). **–vieleck,** *n.* polygon of forces (*Mech.*). **–zersplitterung,** *f.* division of forces (*Mil.*).
kräftig, *adj.* strong, powerful, energetic, vigorous, robust; pithy, forcible, forceful; efficacious, effective; valid; strengthening, nourishing. **–en,** *v.a.* strengthen, invigorate; enforce; harden, steel. **–keit,** *f.* robustness; energy; efficaciousness; validity, full force. **–ung,** *f.* strengthening.
Kragen, *m.* (-s, – (& *dial.* ⸚)) collar; cape; neck; *Geiz*–, miser; *Klapp*–, turn-down collar; *Steh*–, stand-up collar; *weicher* –, soft collar; *am* – *packen*, collar, seize by the scruff of the neck; *beim* – *nehmen* or *fassen*, call to account; *es geht ihm an den* –, it will cost him his life, he will be called to account; *und sollte es mir auch den* – *kosten*, though I should have to die for it. **–knopf,** *m.* collar-stud. **–patten,** *f.pl.*, **–spiegel,** *m.* patch, facing, collar insignia (*Mil.*).
Krag–stein, *m.* (-(e)s,-e) corbel, console, bracket (*Arch.*). **–träger,** *m.* cantilever beam (*Engin.*).
Kräh–e, *f.* (-en) crow; rook; *die* –*e krächzt*, the crow caws; (*Prov.*) *eine* –*e hackt der andern die Augen nicht aus*, there's honour among thieves. **–en,** *v.n.* (*aux.* h.) screech, squawk; *danach* –*t kein Hahn*, nobody troubles about it. **–enauge,** *n.* nux vomica, (*dial.*) corn (*on the foot*). **–enfüße,** *m.pl.* bad writing, scrawl; crow's feet, wrinkles. **–ennest,** *n.* crow's nest (*Naut.*).
Krakeel, *m.* (-s, -e) (*coll.*) squabble, quarrel, brawl, (*coll.*) row. **–en,** *v.n.* (*aux.* h.) brawl, (*coll.*) kick up a row. **–er,** *m.* rowdy, brawler.
Krakelfüße, *m.pl.* (*coll.*) illegible handwriting, scrawl.
Krall–e, *f.* (-en) claw, talon, clutch; *die* –*en zeigen*, (*fig.*) show one's claws *or* teeth; *in die* –*en bekommen*, (*fig.*) get one's claws on. **–en,** *v.n.* (*aux.* h.) claw; clutch, scratch; (*coll.*) steal; (*dial.*) clamber. **–enförmig,** *adj.* claw-shaped. **–ig,** *adj.* claw-like, clawed.
Kram, *m.* (-(e)s, ⸚e) small wares; stuff, rubbish, trumpery, trash, odds and ends, lumber; (*coll.*) affair, business; retail trade; shop; (*dial.*) childbed; (*coll.*) *das taugt nicht in meinen* –, that will not do for me; *es paßte nicht in seinen* –, it did not suit his purpose; *das verdirbt mir den ganzen* –, that spoils all my plans; *den* – *zumachen*, shut up shop. **–bude,** *f.*, *see* **–laden.** **–en,** *v.n.* (*aux.* h.) rummage, fumble; (*dial.*) hawk, sell; (*dial.*) be brought to childbed; *man hat immer etwas zu* –*en*, there is always something to be done *or* to be put in order. **–er,** *m.* (*dial.*), *see* **Krämer.** **–handel,** *m.* retail trade. **–laden,** *m.* small shop, retail shop, stall. **–waren,** *f.pl.* haberdashery.
Krämer, *m.* (*dial.* **Kramer**), (-s, –) shopkeeper, retailer, tradesman, grocer; haberdasher. **–ei,** *f.* shopkeeping, retailing; trading. **–geist,** *m.* petty *or* mercenary spirit. **–bude,** *f.* **–laden,** *m.* haberdashery stall. **–latein,** *n.* dog-Latin. **–seele,** *f.* petty individual, mercenary creature. **–volk,** *n.* nation of shopkeepers.
Kram(me)tsvogel, *m.* fieldfare (*Turdus pilaris*) (*Orn.*).
Krampe, *f.* (-n) staple, U-bolt.
Krampf, *m.* (-(e)s, ⸚e) cramp, spasm, convulsion, fit; (*coll.*) thieving, pilfering; *in Krämpfen*, in (spasmodic) fits. **–ader,** *f.* varicose vein. **–artig,** *adj.*, *see* **–haft.** **–en,** *v.a.* & *r.* clench, clasp convulsively, contract; (*coll.*) thieve, pilfer. **–haft,** *adj.* convulsive, spasmodic; (*fig.*) frantic, desperate, frenzied; –*haft schluchzen*, sob convulsively, be seized with a fit of sobbing; –*haftes Lachen*, convulsions of laughter; –*hafte Zuckung*, convulsion. **–haftigkeit,** *f.* convulsiveness, frenzy. **–husten,** *m.* convulsive cough. **–lindernd,** *adj.*, **–stillend,** *adj.* sedative, soothing.
Kran, *m.* (-(e)s, -e (& *Austr.* ⸚e)) crane, hoist; (*dial.*) cock, faucet (*Mach.*). **–ausleger,** *m.* crane-jib. **–bahn,** *f.* gantry. **–geld,** *n.* cranage.
krängen, *v.n.* heel over (*Naut.*).
Kranich, *m.* (-s, -e) crane (*Grus grus*) (*Orn.*).
krank, *adj.* (*comp.* kränker *sup.* kränk(e)st) ill, sick, ailing, diseased; – *zu Bett liegen*, be ill in bed; *sich* – *melden*, report sick (*Mil.*); – *an einer S.*, ill with; – *werden*, fall *or* be taken ill; *sich* – *stellen*, feign illness; *sich* – *lachen* (*über eine* S.), split one's sides with laughing; *es war zum* –*lachen*, it was absurdly funny, it made us shriek with laughter. **–en,** *v.n.* (*aux.* h.); *an einer S.* –*en*, suffer from, be ill with. **–enanstalt,** *f.* hospital. **–enauto,** *n.* motor ambulance. **–enbericht,** *m.* bulletin; hospital report. **–enbesuch,** *m.* sick visiting; doctor's visit. **–enbett,** *n.* sick-bed. **–engeld,** *n.* medical *or* sick benefit, sick pay (*Mil.*). **–enhaus,** *n.* infirmary, hospital. **–enkasse,** *f.* health insurance. **–enkost,** *f.* invalid diet. **–enlager,** *n.*, *see* **–nbett.** **–enpflege,** *f.* sick-nursing. **–enpflegerin,** *f.*, *see* **–enschwester.** **–enrevier,** *n.* sick-bay, medical centre (*Mil.*). **–enschein,** *m.* sick report (*Mil.*), doctor's certificate *or* (*coll.*) note. **–enschwester,** *f.* nurse. **–enstube,** *f.* sick-room; sick-bay (*Mil.*). **–entrage,** *f.* stretcher, litter. **–enträger,** *m.* stretcher bearer. **–enurlaub,** *m.* sick-leave (*Mil.*). **–enwagen,** *m.* ambulance. **–enwärter,** *m.* male nurse, hospital orderly. **–enzimmer,** *n.* sick-room. **–enzug,** *m.* hospital train. **–e (r),** *m.*, **–e,** *f.* invalid, patient, casualty. **–haft,** *adj.* pathological, unhealthy, diseased, abnormal, morbid. **–haftigkeit,** *f.* diseased state, morbidity. **–heit,** *f.* (-en) illness, sickness, disease, malady, complaint; *sich* (*Dat.*) *eine* –*heit zuziehen*, contract a disease; *eine* –*heit bekommen, in eine* –*heit* (*ver*)*fallen*, fall ill; *an einer* –*heit sterben*, die of an illness. **–heitsentscheidung,** *f.* crisis. **–heitserreger,** *m.* pathogenic agent. **–heitserscheinung,** *f.* pathological symptom. **–heitsfall,** *m.* case of sickness. **–heitshalber,** *adv.* on account of sickness, owing to illness. **–heitsherd,** *m.* seat of disease. **–heitslehre,** *f.* pathology. **–heitsstoff,** *m.* morbid *or* contagious matter. **–heitsträger,** *m.* carrier (*Med.*). **–heitsübertragung,** *f.* infection. **–heitsverlauf,** *m.*, **–heitsvorgang,** *m.* course of disease. **–heitsvortäuschung,** *f.* malingering. **–heitszeichen,** *n.* symptom. **–heitszustand,** *m.* state of disease, morbid state, case.

kränk-bar, *adj.* easily aggrieved, susceptible, touchy. **-e,** *f.* (*dial.*) epilepsy, falling sickness. **-elei,** *f.* sickliness. **-eln,** *v.n.* (*aux.* h.) be sickly, ailing, in bad *or* poor health *or* poor in health. **-en,** 1. *v.a.* vex, grieve, insult, offend, provoke, injure, wrong; impair, detract from. 2. *v.r.* worry, fret; *das -t,* that hurts; *jemandes Rechte -en* or *einen an seinen Rechten -en,* encroach upon a p.'s rights; *es -te mich tief,* it cut me to the quick; *gekränkte Unschuld,* injured innocence; *auf eine -ende Art,* insultingly. **-lich,** *adj.* sickly, ailing, poorly, infirm. **-ung,** *f.* insult, offence, wrong, outrage, mortification, vexation.

Kranz, *m.* (-es, ¨-e) garland, wreath, triumphal wreath *or* crown, corona; (*fig.*) virginity, innocence; cornice; festoon, cincture (*Arch.*); brim (*of a glass, etc.*), rim (*of wheel*), (mounting) ring, border, areola; edge, crest, ridge; valance; group, circle (*of onlookers, etc.*); *- von schönen Frauen,* circle of beautiful women, galaxy of beauty; *einen - spenden,* send a wreath (*funeral*). **-brenner,** *m.* (gas-)ring. **-förmig,** *adj.* wreath-like; coronoid. **-gesims,** *n.* cornice. **-jungfer,** *f.* bridesmaid. **-los,** *adj.* uncrowned; deflowered. **-spende,** *f.* funeral wreath.

Kränz-chen, *n.* (-s, -) little garland; small gathering, bee, coffee-party; girls' *or* ladies' club. **-en,** *v.a.* (*poet.*) crown, wreathe, garland, bedeck.

Krapfen, *m.* (-s, -) fritter; doughnut.

Krapp, *m.* madder (*dye*).

kraß, *adj.* crass, flagrant, blatant, gross; *-(ss)e Unwissenheit,* gross ignorance; *-(ss)er Fuchs,* freshman, fresher; *-(ss)er Widerspruch,* flagrant contradiction; *-(ss)e Lüge,* blatant untruth; *-(ss)er Philister,* crass materialist. **-heit,** *f.* blatancy, crudeness, flagrancy.

Kratz, *m.* (-es, -e (& *coll.* ¨-e)) scratch, score, striation. **-beere,** *f.* (*dial.*) bramble, blackberry. **-bürste,** *f.* scrubbing-brush; scratch-brush, wire-brush; (*fig.*) irritable p., cross-patch. **-bürstig,** *adj.* irritable, quick-tempered, cross; (*sl.*) snooty. **-e,** *f.* (-en) scraper; carding-comb. **-eisen,** *n.* scraping-iron; (mud) scraper. **-en,** *v.a.* & *n.* (*aux.* h.) scratch, scrape, striate; card, tease; grate, be harsh *or* tart to the taste; scrawl, scribble; itch, tickle; *sich hinter dem Ohr -en,* scratch one's head; *der Rauch -t mir im Halse,* the smoke affects my throat; *auf einen Haufen -en,* scrape together into a heap. **-er,** *m.* scraper, scratcher (*p. or th.*); intestinal worm; *see* **-wunde.** **-fuß,** *m.* bow, obeisance. **-füßler,** *m.* sycophant, toady, cringer, obsequious person. **-ig,** *adj.* scratchy; easily offended, irritable, gruff. **-maschine,** *f.* carding-machine. **-wunde,** *f.* surface wound, scratch.

Krätz-e, *f.* (-en) itch, scabies, scab, mange; scrapings, clippings, skimmings, dross (*Metal*); (*dial.*) **-en,** *pl.* basket. **-er,** *m.* bad *or* sour wine. **-ig,** *adj.* scabious, psoric (*Med.*); scabby; rough, fibrous. **-salbe,** *f.* ointment against the itch.

krauchen, *v.n.* (*coll. for*) **kriechen.**

krauen, *v.a.*, **kraueln,** *v.a.* rub *or* scratch gently.

kraulen, *v.n.* (*aux.* h.) swim the crawl.

kraus, *adj.* curly, crinkled, crisp, crisped, curled, corrugated; irregular, ruffled; intricate; *ein -es Durcheinander,* an inextricable tangle; *ein -es Gesicht machen, die Stirne - ziehen,* knit one's brows; *er macht (treibt) es zu -,* he carries things too far. **-e,** *f.* (-en) frill, ruff, ruffle. **-en,** 1. *v.a.*, *n.* & *r.* (*aux.* h.), *see* **kräuseln.** **-eminze,** *f.* peppermint. **-gummi,** *m.* crêpe rubber. **-kopf,** *m.* curly-head; curly-headed person. **-putz,** *m.* rough-cast. **-salat,** *m.* endive. **-tabak,** *m.* shag.

kräus-eln, 1. *v.a.* curl, crisp, crinkle, crimp, goffer, pucker; mill (*coin*); fold, plait. 2. *v.r.* & *n.* (*aux.* h.) curl, be ruffled; *sich das Haar -eln lassen,* have one's hair curled. *gekräuselt, p.p.* & *adj.* curly, crimped. **-eleisen,** *n.* crimping-iron, curling-tongs. **-en,** *pl.* head (*Brew.*).

Kraut, *n.* (-(e)s ¨-er) herb, plant, vegetable, weed, leaves *or* tops of a plant; sumac; (*dial.*) cabbage; (*dial.*) purée; (*Prov.*) *gegen den Tod ist kein - gewachsen,* there is no cure for death; (*Prov.*) *Muß ist ein bitter -,* necessity is painful, compulsion is unpleasant; *durcheinander wie - und Rüben,* higgledy-piggledy; *ins - schießen,* run to leaf; *das macht das - nicht fett,* that does not help, that makes things no better. **-artig,** *adj.* herbaceous. **-en,** 1. *v.a.* & *n.* (*aux.* h.) hoe, weed. 2. *n.* weeding. **-er,** *m.* eccentric, crank, oddity. **-förmig,** *adj.* herb-like; dendroid (*Min.*). **-fressend,** *adj.* herbivorous. **-garten,** *m.* kitchen-garden. **-hacke,** *f.* hoe. **-junker,** *m.* country bumpkin, clod-hopping squire.

Kräut-erbuch, *n.* herbal. **-erkäse,** *m.* green cheese. **-erkenner,** *m.* herbalist, botanist. **-erkenntnis,** *f.* botanical knowledge. **-erkunde,** *f.*, **-erlehre,** *f.* botany. **-ersammler,** *m.* herbalist. **-ersuppe,** *f.* vegetable soup. **-ertee,** *m.* herb tea. **-erwein,** *m.* medicated wine. **-erwerk,** culinary herbs. **-icht,** *n.* (-(e)s, -e) leaves *or* tops of vegetables. **-ler,** *m.* (*Austr. dial.*) greengrocer.

Krawall, *m.* (-s, -e) (*coll.*) row, uproar, riot. **-en,** *v.n.* (*aux.* h.) kick up a row; riot. **-macher,** *m.* rowdy, hooligan.

Krawatte, *f.* (-n) (neck)tie, cravat. **-nmacher,** *m.* (*coll.*) moneylender, usurer.

kraweelgebaut, *adj.* carvel-built (*of boats*).

kraxeln, *v.n.* (*aux.* s.) (*coll.*) climb, clamber.

Kräze, *f.* (*Swiss dial.*) basket; *see* **Krätze.**

Kreatur, *f.* (-en) creature, created man, (*Poet.*) all living creatures; vassal, dependant; *feile -,* hireling.

Krebs, *m.* (-es, -e) crab, crayfish; Cancer (*Astr*); cancer (*Med.*); canker (*Bot.*); unsold copy remainder; (*B.*) breastplate (of faith); (*pl.*) crustaceans; *Wendekreis des -es,* Tropic of Cancer. **-artig,** *adj.* crustaceous; cancerous, cankerous. **-bildung,** *f.* cancerous growth. **-eln,** *v.n.* crawl, clamber. **-en,** *v.n.* (*aux.* h.) catch crayfish; go to a lot of trouble in vain; (*sl.*) turn to one's own advantage. **-gang,** *m.* crab's walk; movement backwards, retrogression, decline. **-gängig,** *adj.* retrograde. **-geschwür,** *n.* cancerous growth *or* swelling. **-rot,** *adj.* red as a lobster *or* turkey-cock. **-schaden,** *m.* (*archaic*) cancerous sore; (*fig.*) inveterate evil. **-schere,** *f.* crayfish's *or* crab's claw.

Kredenz, *f.* (-en) sideboard. **-en,** *v.a.* (*archaic*) taste (*wine before serving*); (*Poet.*) offer, serve, present. **-er,** *m.* foretaster; cupbearer. **-teller,** *m.* salver. **-tisch,** *m.* sideboard, serving table.

Kredit, *m.* (-(e)s, -e) credit; reputation, trust; *laufender -,* open credit; *den - übertreiben,* overdraw one's account, exceed one's credit. **-anstalt,** *f.* bank. **-ausweitung,** *f.* (*euphemistic for*) inflation. **-brief,** *m.* letter of credit. **-fähig,** *adj.* solvent, sound. **-fähigkeit,** *f.* solvency. **-ieren,** 1. *v.a.* credit, give on trust. 2. *v.n.* (*aux.* h.) give credit. **-ierung,** *f.* crediting, placing to a p.'s credit. **-iv,** *n.* (-s, -e) credentials, warrant, authority. **-posten,** *m.* credit entry. **-saldo,** *m.* credit balance.

kregel, *adj.* (*dial.*) sound, hale; lively, brisk.

Kreid-e, *f.* (-en) chalk; crayon; calcium carbonate, whiting; (*coll.*) *bei einem in die -e geraten,* get into a p.'s debt; (*coll.*) *mit 12 Mark bei einem in der -e stehen,* owe a p. 12 marks; (*coll.*) *tief in der -e stehen* or *sitzen,* be crippled with debts; *mit doppelter -e anschreiben,* overcharge. **-efels, m** chalk cliff. **-eformation,** *f.*, **-egebilde,** *n.* chalk-formation; cretaceous group. **-en,** *v.a.* chalk; cover with chalk. **-e(n)artig,** *adj.* chalky. **-estift,** *m.* chalk, crayon. **-eweiß,** *adj.* deathly pale, white as a sheet. **-ezeichnung,** *f.* chalk, crayon *or* pastel drawing. **-ig,** *adj.* chalky, cretaceous.

kreieren, *v.a.* create, make.

Kreis, *m.* (-es, -e) circle, ring, orbit; circuit, district; sphere, range, zone (*of action, etc.*); *städtischer (ländlicher) -,* urban (rural) district; *einen - ziehen,* describe a circle (*Geom.*); *das liegt außer meinem -e,* that is not within my province *or* ken; *im -e seiner Familie,* in the bosom of his family; *alles geht mit mir im -e herum,* my head is swimming; *in allen -en des Lebens,* in every walk of life; *die höchsten -e,* the upper ten (thousand), the aristocracy; *sich in einen - stellen* or *treten,* form a circle; *seine -e weiter ziehen,* enlarge one's horizon; *sich im -e bewegen,* revolve, turn round and round;

not get on, not get nearer one's goal; *sich im –e drehen*, revolve, rotate; *im –e um etwas herumgehen*, turn *or* revolve round s.th. **–abschnitt,** *m.* segment (of a circle). **–amtmann,** *m.* chairman of a district council. **–arzt,** *m.* local doctor. **–ausschnitt,** *m.* sector (of a circle) (*Math.*). **–bahn,** *f.* orbit. **–beamte(r),** *m.* district civil officer. **–behörde,** *f.* local *or* district council. **–bewegung,** *f.* circular *or* rotary motion. **–bogen,** *m.* circular arch; arc (of a circle). **–brief,** *m.* circular letter; proclamation. **–einteilung,** *f.* division into districts. **–en,** *v.n.* (*aux.* h.) move in circles *or* a circle, circle, revolve, whirl round; circulate; *die Flasche –en lassen*, pass the bottle round. **–förmig,** *adj.* circular, round, annular. **–fuge,** *f.* round canon (*Mus.*). **–gang,** *m.* circular movement. **–gericht,** *n.* district-court; county court, petty sessions (*Eng.*). **–hauptmann,** *m.* (*dial.*) prefect of a district. **–lauf,** *m.* rotation, revolution; circulation; course, cycle, circuit, orbit; series, succession (*of the seasons, etc.*). **–leitung,** *f.* closed circuit (*Elec., Rad.*). **–linie,** *f.* circumference. **–messung,** *f.* cyclometry. **–ordnung,** *f.* district regulations. **–richter,** *m.* district judge. **–ring,** *m.* annular space, ring. **–rund,** *adj.* circular. **–säge,** *f.* circular saw. **–schluß,** *m.* circular argument, vicious circle. **–schule,** *f.* district *or* county school. **–stadt,** *f.* chief town of a district, market town. **–ständig,** *adj.* cyclic. **–strom,** *m.* circuit current (*Elec.*). **–tag,** *m.* local council meeting. **–umfang,** *m.* circumference, periphery. **–verkehr,** *m.* traffic circle. **–viertel,** *n.* quadrant.

kreischen, *ir.v.n.* (*aux.* h.) shriek, screech, scream; hiss, sizzle; grate, be glaring; *–de Stimme*, shrill voice.

Kreisel, *m.* (-s, –) (spinning) top, gyroscope; *den – treiben*, spin a top. **–förmig,** *adj.* top-shaped, turbinate. **–frequenz,** *f.* angular velocity. **–horizont,** *m.* artificial horizon (*Naut.*). **–kompaß,** *m.* gyro-compass. **–n,** *v.r. & n.* (*aux.* h.) revolve, spin, whirl round; spin a top. **–pumpe,** *f.* centrifugal pump. **–rad,** *n.* turbine, rotor. **–verdichter,** *m.* turbo-compressor.

kreiß–en, 1. *v.n.* (*aux.* h.) be in labour. 2. *n.* labour (pains). **–ende,** *f.* woman in labour. **–saal,** *m.* labour ward.

Krem, *m.* (-s, -e) *& f.* (-e) cream (filling), custard. **–e,** *f.* ointment, (face) cream, (tooth) paste, (shoe) polish; (*dial.*) cream (*of milk*).

kremieren, *v.a.* cremate.

Kremp–e, *f.* (-en) brim, edge, border, flange. **–el,** 1. *m.* (*coll.*) lumber, trash, rubbish; stuff. 2. *f.* card, carding-comb. **–(e)ler,** *m.* wool-carder, (*dial.*) rag-and-bone man. **–eln,** *v.a.* card; *see* **–en.** **–en,** *v.a.* turn up, put a brim to (*a hat*).

Kremser, *m.* (-s, –) (*dial.*) charabanc.

Kren, *m.* (*Austr. dial.*) horse-radish.

krepieren, 1. *v.n.* (*aux.* s.) die (*of animals, & vulg.*); explode; burst (*of shells*). 2. *v.a.* (*dial.*) annoy, irritate.

Krepp, *m.* (-s, -e) crêpe, crape. **–en,** *v.a.* crêpe, crisp, crinkle; nap (*cloth*); curl, wave. **–(p)apier,** *n.* crêpe paper.

kreß, *adj.* orange (coloured).

Kresse, *f.* (-n) cress (*Lepidium sativum*) (*Bot.*).

Krethi; *– und Plethi*, all the world and his wife; rag tag, and bobtail; Tom, Dick and Harry.

Kretscham, *m.* (-s, -e) (*dial.*) village tavern.

kreuch, kreuchst, kreucht, *see* **kriechen.**

Kreuz, *n.* (-es, -e) cross, crucifix, crosier; cross-bar; small of the back, loins, rump; croup, crupper; club (*Cards*); sharp (*Mus.*); dagger, obelus (*Typ.*); (*fig.*) burden, affliction; *ans – schlagen*, fix *or* nail to the cross; (*sich*) *das – brechen*, break one's back; *drei –e hinter einem machen*, be glad to see the back of s.o.; *ins – legen*, lay cross-wise; *ins – segeln*, tack; *das – machen*, cross o.s., make the sign of the cross; *das – nehmen*, take up one's cross; go on a crusade; (*in*) *die – und Quere, – und quer*, in all directions; *ein – schlagen*, see *das – machen*; *über –*, across, crosswise; *zu –e kriechen*, humble o.s., repent. **–abnahme,** *f.* descent *or* deposition from the cross. **–arm,** *m.* cross-bar. **–band,** *n.* notched joint (*Carp.*); postal *or* newspaper wrapper; *unter –band*, as printed matter, by book-post. **–bein,** *n.* sacrum. **–beinig,** *adj.* cross-legged. **–berg,** *m.* Calvary **–bild,** *n.* effigy of the Cross. **–blütler,** *m.pl.* cruciferous plants. **–brav,** *adj.* thoroughly honest *or* good. **–bube,** *m.* knave of clubs. **–dame,** *f.* queen of clubs. **–en,** 1. *v.a.* mark with a cross; thwart, cross; hybridize, interbreed. 2. *v.r.* make the sign of the cross; intersect; cross one another; meet; clash. 3. *v.n.* (*aux.* h.) cross; cruise; tack about. **–er,** *m.* groat, farthing; cruiser (*Nav.*). **–dorn,** *m.* buckthorn (*Rhamnus cathartica*) (*Bot.*). **–erhöhung,** *f.* elevation of the cross. **–esstamm,** *m.* Holy Rood. **–fahrer,** *m.* crusader. **–feuer,** *n.* cross-fire (*Mil.*). **–fidel,** *adj.* merry as a cricket, pleased as Punch. **–förmig,** *adj.* cruciform, cross-shaped. **–gang,** *m.* cloisters; cross-lode (*Min.*). **–gelenk,** *n.* universal joint (*Mach.*). **–gegend,** *f.* lumbar region. **–gewölbe,** *n.* cruciform vault. **–gitter,** *n.* grating, lattice. **–heer,** *n.* army of the cross *or* of crusaders. **–holz,** *n.* cross piece (*Carp.*). **–igen,** *v.a.* crucify. **–igung,** *f.* crucifixion. **–kirche,** *f.* church on cruciform plan; church of the Holy Cross. **–kopf,** *m.* big-end (*Motor.*). **–lahm,** *adj.* suffering from azoturia (*Vet.*); (*fig.*) *–lahm sein*, have the back-ache. **–mast,** *m.* mizzen (*when square-rigged*) (*Naut.*). **–maß,** *n.* T-square; gauge (*Typ.*). **–naht,** *f.* cross-stitched seam. **–otter,** *f.* viper, adder. **–peilung,** *f.* cross-bearing. **–predigt,** *f.* crusading sermon. **–punkt,** *m.* point of intersection. **–ritter,** *m.* crusader. **–schmerz,** *m.* lumbago. **–schnabel,** *m.* crossbill (*Loxia curvirostra*) (*Orn.*). **–schraffierung,** *f.*, **–schraffur,** *f.* cross-hatching. **–spinne,** *f.* garden spider. **–stab,** *m.* crosier. **–stelle,** *f.* crossing, intersection. **–stellung,** *f.* pas croisé (*Danc.*). **–stenge,** *f.* mizzen topmast (*Naut.*). **–stich,** *m.* cross-stitch. **–ung,** *f.* crossing; cross-breeding, inter-breeding, hybridization; road crossing, cross-roads, intersection. **–unglücklich,** *adj.* thoroughly wretched, miserable, despondent *or* downcast. **–ungspunkt,** *m.* (point of) intersection. **–verhör,** *n.* cross-examination; *ein –verhör mit einem anstellen* or *einen ins –verhör nehmen*, cross-examine a p. **–verweisung,** *f.* cross-reference. **–weg,** *m.* crossing, cross-roads; way *or* stations of the Cross (*Theol.*). **–weise,** *adv.* crosswise, transverse, across. **–woche,** *f.* Rogation-week. **–worträtsel,** *n.* crossword puzzle. **–zeichen,** *n.* sign of the cross. **–zug,** *m.* crusade.

Kribbel, *m.* itching, irritation, impatience. **–n,** *v.a. & n.* (*aux.* h.) (*coll.*) crawl, swarm; itch, tickle, prickle, tingle, irritate. **–ig,** *adj.* irritable, touchy, impatient. **–kopf,** *m.* irritable person, hothead. **–krankheit,** *f.* ergot poisoning.

Kribskrabs, *m.* (*& n.*) hotch-potch, medley, gibberish.

Krick–elei, *f.* (*dial.*) scrawl, scribble; provocations, annoyances; fretfulness, peevishness, cavilling. **–eln,** *v.n.* (*aux.* h.) be fretful, querulous, peevish, *or* captious; scrawl, scribble.

Krida, *f.* (*Austr. dial.*) bankruptcy. **–r,** *m.* (-rs, -re) bankrupt.

Kriech, *m.* creep (*Metall.*). **–en,** *ir.v.n.* (*aux.* h. & s.) creep, crawl; cringe, sneak, fawn; *aus dem Ei –en*, be hatched. **–er,** *m.* sneak, cringing person. **–erei,** *f.* servility, fawning, cringing. **–erisch,** *adj.* fawning, cringing. **–funken,** *m.* flash-over, surface discharge (*Elec.*). **–geschwindigkeit,** *f.* creep rate (*Metall.*). **–pflanzen,** *f.pl.* creepers. **–tiere,** *n.pl.* reptiles.

Krieg, *m.* (-(e)s, -e) war, warfare; strife; *den – wieder anfangen*, resume hostilities; *– beginnen*, go to war; *einem Lande den – erklären*, declare war against a country; *– im Frieden*, large-scale manœuvres; (*mit einem* or *gegen einen*) *– führen*, wage *or* make war (upon *or* against a p.); *geistiger –*, psychological warfare; *im –e*, in time of war, in war-time; *im –e sein*, be at war; *– in der Luft*, aerial warfare; *in den – ziehen*, go to war; *– bis aufs Messer* or *– auf Tod und Leben*, war to the knife; *ein Land mit – überziehen*, invade, carry war into a country; *– zu Lande*, land warfare; *– zur See*, maritime *or* naval warfare. **–en,** *v.n.* (*aux.* h.) (*rare*) wage war, **–er,** *m.* warrior, soldier. **–erdenkmal,** *n.* war-memorial. **–ergrab,** *n.* war-grave. **–erisch,**

adj. warlike, martial. **–erverein,** *m.* ex-serviceman's *or* old comrades' association. **–erwaise,** *f.* war orphan. **–führend,** *adj.* belligerent. **–führung,** *f.* conduct of war, strategy; warfare. **–sakademie,** *f.* military academy; staff college. **–sanleihe,** *f.* war loan. **–sartikel,** *m.pl.* articles of war. **–saufgebot,** *n.* draft. **–saufruf,** *m.* call to arms. **–sausrüstung,** *f.* war equipment. **–sauszeichnung,** *f.* war decoration. **–sbaukunst,** *f.* (*archaic*) fortification, military engineering. **–sbedarf,** *m.* military stores. **–sbehörde,** *f.* military authorities. **–sbeil,** *n.* battle-axe; *das –sbeil begraben,* bury the hatchet. **–sbereit,** *adj.* prepared for war. **–sbereitschaft,** *f.* readiness for war. **–sbericht,** *m.* war communiqué. **–sberichterstatter,** *m.* war correspondent. **–sbeschädigt,** *adj.* wounded, disabled. **–sbeseitigung,** *f.* elimination of war. **–sbesoldung,** *f.* war-pay. **–sblinde(r),** *m.* blind ex-serviceman. **–sdenkmünze,** *f.* war-medal. **–sdienst,** *m.* military service. **–sdienstpflichtige(r),** *m.* one liable for conscription. **–sdienstverweigerer,** *m.* conscientious objector. **–sentschädigung,** *f.* war indemnity. **–serklärung,** *f.* declaration of war. **–seröffnung,** *f.* commencement of hostilities. **–setat,** *m.* military estimates. **–sfähig,** *adj.* fit for active service. **–sfahne,** *f.* regimental colours. **–sfall,** *m.* case of war. **–sflotte,** *f.* navy. **–sfreiwillige(r),** *m.* war-time volunteer. **–sführung,** *f.* conduct of war. **–sfuß,** *m.* war footing; *auf* (*dem*) *–sfuß,* on a war footing, (*fig.*) in open hostility; *auf –sfuß setzen,* mobilize; put (*a ship*) in commission. **–sgebiet,** *n.* war area. **–sgefährte,** *m.*, **–sgenosse,** *m.* comrade in arms. **–sgefangene(r),** *m.* prisoner of war. **–sgefangenschaft,** *f.* captivity. **–sgeist,** *m.* martial spirit. **–sgeleit,** *n.* military escort. **–sgerät,** *n.*, **–sgerätschaften,** *f.pl.* warlike stores, war material. **–sgericht,** *n.* court-martial. **–sgerichtlich,** *adv.* by court-martial. **–sgerichtsrat,** *m.* judge advocate. **–sgerücht,** *n.* rumour of war. **–sgeschichte,** *f.* military history; war story. **–sgeschrei,** *n.* rumour of war; battle-cry. **–sgesetz,** *n.* martial law. **–sgetös,** *n.*, **–sgetümmel,** *n.* (*Poet.*) din of war. **–sgewinnler,** *m.* war profiteer. **–sglück,** *n.* fortune of war; military success. **–sgott,** *m.* god of war, Mars. **–sgräberfürsorge,** *f.* war graves commission. **–sgreuel,** *m.pl.* atrocities of war. **–shafen,** *m.* naval base *or* station. **–shandwerk,** *n.* profession of arms, military profession. **–sheer,** *n.* field-army, (*B.*) host. **–sheld,** *m.* great warrior. **–sherr,** *m.* commander-in-chief, generalissimo, war lord. **–shetzer,** *m.* warmonger. **–shinterbliebene(n),** *m.pl.* next-of-kin of war casualties. **–sindustrie,** *f.* war industry. **–skamerad,** *m.*, *see* **–sgefährte.** **–skind,** *n.* war-baby. **–sknecht,** *m.* mercenary. **–skonterbande,** *f.* contraband of war. **–skost,** *f.* war-time rations. **–skunde,** *f.*, **–skunst,** *f.* military science; art of war, tactics, strategy. **–slage,** *f.* strategic situation. **–slärm,** *m.* rumours of war. **–slazarett,** *n.* military hospital. **–slist,** *f.* stratagem. **–slüge,** *f.* lying war propaganda. **–slustig,** *adj.* bellicose. **–smacht,** *f.* fighting strength, war potential; forces, troops. **–smarine,** *f.* navy. **–smarschmäßig,** *adj.* in full marching order. **–sminister,** *m.* Secretary of State for War (*Eng.*); Secretary of War (*Amer.*). **–sministerium,** *n.* War Office, War Department. **–smüdigkeit,** *f.* war-weariness. **–smusik,** *f.* martial music. **–snotwendigkeit,** *f.* military necessity. **–sopfer,** *n.* war casualty. **–sorden,** *m.* war-time decoration. **–spflicht,** *f.*, *see* **–sdienst.** **–spflichtig,** *adj.* liable for military service. **–sration,** *f.* war-time rations. **–srat,** *m.* council of war. **–recht,** *n.* martial law; *–srecht über einen halten* or *ergehen lassen,* try a p. by court-martial. **–srente,** *f.* war pension. **–sruf,** *m.* war-cry; summons to arms. **–sschaden,** *m.* war damage. **–sschauplatz,** *m.* seat of war, theatre of operations. **–sschiff,** *n.* man-of-war, warship. **–sschuld,** *f.* war guilt. **–sschuldverschreibung,** *f.* war-bond. **–sschule,** *f.* military academy. **–sschüler,** *m.* officer cadet. **–sspiel,** *n.* manœuvre; prisoner's base (*game*). **–sstärke,** *f.* war-time establishment. **–steilnehmer,** *m.* combatant; *ehemaliger –steilnehmer,* ex-serviceman. **–strauen,** *v.a.* *sich –strauen lassen,* make a war-time marriage. **–strauung,** *f.* war-time wedding. **–stüchtigkeit,** *f.* military efficiency. **–sübung,** *f.* manœuvres. **–sunbrauchbar,** *adj.* unfit for service (*equipment*). **–suntauglich,** *adj.* unfit for active service (*personnel*). **–sverbrecher,** *m.* war-criminal. **–sverluste,** *m.pl.* casualties. **–sverpflegungsamt,** *n.* commissariat department. **–sversehrte(r),** *m.* & *f.*, *see* **–sbeschädigte(r).** **–sverwendungsfähig,** *adj.* fit for active service. **–svolk,** *n.* troops, forces. **–svorrat,** *m.* warlike stores. (*archaic*) **–swagen,** *m.* war chariot. **–swesen,** *n.* military affairs. **–swille,** *m.* will for war. **swirtschaft,** *f.* war economy. **–swucher,** *m.* war profiteering. **–szeit,** *f.* war-time. **–sziel,** *n.* war aim. **–szone,** *f.* battle area. **–szucht,** *f.* military discipline. **–szufälle,** *m.pl.* contingencies of war. **–zug,** *n.* military expedition. **–szulage,** *f.* field-allowance. **–szustand,** *m.* state of war; military preparedness. **–szweck,** *m.* war aim; *für –szwecke,* for purposes of war, for military purposes.

kriegen, 1. *v.n.* *see* **Krieg.** 2. *v.a.* (*coll.*) obtain, gain, get; *ich will dich schon –,* I shall get hold of you and make you do it; I'll pay you off yet; (*coll.*) *das werden wir schon –,* we shall manage that all right; we shall get it before long.

krimin–al, 1. *adj.* criminal, penal. 2. *n.* (-s, -e) (*Austr. dial.*) prison. **–alabteilung,** *f.*, **–algericht,** *n.* criminal court. **–algerichtsbarkeit,** *f.* criminal jurisdiction. **–algesetzbuch,** *n.* penal code. **–algesetzgebung,** *f.* penal legislation. **–alist,** *m.* (-en, -en) authority on criminal law. **–alpolizei,** *f.* criminal investigation department, plain clothes police. **–alpolizist,** *m.* detective. **–alrecht,** *n.* criminal law. **–alroman,** *m.* detective novel. **–alverfahren,** *n.* criminal prosecution. **–alvergehen,** *n.* indictable offence. **–ell,** *adj.* criminal, culpable.

krimmel–n, *v.n.* (*aux.* h.); (*dial.*) (*only in*) *es –t und wimmelt,* crawling swarms (of).

Krimmer, *m.* (-s, –) astrakhan, Persian lamb (skin).

Krimp–e, *f.* shrinking; *in die –e gehen,* shrink. **–en,** 1. *v.a.* shrink (*cloth*). 2. *v.r.* & *h.* (*aux.* s.) shrink; back (*of wind*); shrivel. **–frei,** *adj.* non-shrinking.

Krimskrams, *m.* (*coll.*), *see* **Kribskrabs.**

Krimstecher, *m.* (-s, –) (*archaic*) field-glass.

Kringel, *m.* (-s, –) ring-shaped roll, cracknel (*Bak.*); ring, circle, kink, loop (*in rope*).

Kripp–e, *f.* (-en) crib, manger, feeding trough; (*dial.*) hurdle-work, fence; crèche, day-nursery. **–en,** *v.a.* fence with hurdles; strengthen (*a dike*) with hurdle-work. **–enbeißer,** *m.* crib-biter, wind-sucker, unsound horse. **–enreiter,** *m.* parasite. **–ensetzer,** *m.*, *see* **–enbeißer.** **–enspiel,** *n.* nativity play.

Kris–e, –is, *f.* (*pl.* Krisen) crisis, turning point; (*C.L.*) depression; (*coll.*) dole. **–eln,** *v.n. imp.* take a critical turn, approach a crisis. **–enfürsorge,** *f.* unemployment relief. **–enhaft,** *adj.* critical.

krispeln, *v.a.* crinkle, grain (*leather, etc.*).

Kristall, 1. *m.* (-s, -e) crystal. 2. *n.* *see* **–glas.** **–ähnlich,** *adj.*, **–artig,** *adj.* crystal-like, crystalline. **–bau,** *m.* crystal structure. **–bildung,** *f.* crystallization. **–empfänger,** *m.* crystal set (*Rad.*). **–en,** *adj.* crystal clear; crystalline, crystal-like. **–fläche,** *f.* crystal face. **–flasche,** *f.* cut-glass decanter. **–gitter,** *n.* crystal lattice. **–glas,** *n.* cut-glass, crystal. **–hell,** *adj.*, **–klar,** *adj.* clear as crystal; transparent. **–in,** *adj.*, **–inisch,** *adj.* crystalline (*Geol.*). **–isch,** *adj.*, *see* **–en.** **–isierbar,** *adj.* crystallizable. **–isieren,** *v.a.* crystallize. **–isierung,** *f.*, **–isation,** *f.* crystallization. **–kunde,** *f.*, **–(l)ehre,** *f.* crystallography. **–wasser,** *n.* water of crystallization.

Krit–erium, *n.* (-iums, -ien) criterion. **–ik,** *f.* (-en) criticism; review; critique; *einer –ik unterziehen,* criticize; review (*a book*); *aufbauende –ik,* constructive criticism; *wohlwollende –ik,* favourable criticism; *ungünstige –ik,* adverse criticism, stricture; *unter aller –ik,* beneath contempt. **–ikaster,** *m.* carping critic, fault-finder. **–iker,** *m.* critic, reviewer. **–iklos,** *adj.* uncritical, undiscriminating. **–isch,** *adj.* critical; grave, serious; *–ische*

Temperatur, critical temperature; *das –ische Alter*, change of life, menopause, climacteric. **–isieren,** *v.a.* criticize; review; censure; *abfällig –isieren*, disparage, impugn, decry, vilify, speak ill of.

Kritt–elei, *f.* carping criticism. **–(e)ler,** *m.* fault-finder, grouser, niggling critic. **–(e)lig,** *adj.* fault-finding, captious. **–eln,** *v.n.* (*aux.* h.) criticize, carp (at), find fault (with).

Kritz, *m.* (-es, -e) scratch, scrawl. **–elei,** *f.* scrawl, scribble. **–eln,** 1. *v.a.* scribble, scrawl, scratch. 2. *v.n.* (*aux.* h.) scratch, splutter (*as pens*). **–(e)lig,** *adj.* scrawly, spidery.

kroch, kroch(e)st, kröche, *see* **kriechen.**

Krok–i, *n.* (-is, -is) sketch map (*Mil.*). **–ieren,** *v.a.* & *n.* sketch, make a sketch map (*Mil.*).

krollen, *v.a.* & *r.* (*dial.*) crisp, curl (up).

Kron–e, *f.* (-en) crown; coronet; (*fig.*) diadem, king, kingdom; tonsure, (*fig.*) head; chandelier; florin; corona (*Anat., Arch., Bot.*); perianth (*Bot.*); crest (*of waves* & *Fort.*); top, tree-top, highest point, crowning work, paragon; glory, halo; *das setzt der S. die –e auf*, that puts the lid on it; *das setzt seiner Treulosigkeit die –e auf*, that puts the finishing touch to his perfidy; *das setzt seinen Verdiensten die –e auf*, that is his crowning merit; *dem Verdienste seine –e*, honour to whom honour is due; (*coll.*) *was ist ihm in die –e gefahren?* what has upset *or* offended him? **–anwalt,** *m.* counsel for the crown, public prosecutor; attorney-general. **–beamte(r),** *m.* officer of the crown. **–bewerber,** *m.* aspirant to the crown. **–enartig,** *adj.* coronal; coronary. **–enbein,** *n.* frontal bone. **–engold,** *n.* 18-carat gold. **–enlos,** *adj.* uncrowned; apetalous (*Bot.*). **–enträger,** *m.* crowned head, sovereign. **–erbe,** *m.* heir to the crown. **–glas,** *n.* crown-glass (*Opt.*). **–gut,** *n.* crown-lands, royal domain. **–lehen,** *n.* fief of the crown. **–leuchter,** *m.* lustre, chandelier. **–prinz,** *m.* crown-prince; *der englische –prinz*, the Prince of Wales; *die englische –prinzessin*, Princess Royal. **–rat,** *m.* Privy Council. **–räuber,** *m.* usurper. **–rede,** *f.* speech from the throne. **–sbeere,** *f.* (-n) (*dial.*) cranberry. **–schatz,** *m.* crown jewels. **–werk,** *n.* outworks (*Fort.*). **–zeuge,** *m.* king's evidence; chief witness.

krön–en, *v.a.* crown; honour, exalt, put the finishing touch (to); cap, overtop, surmount; *gekrönter Dichter*, poet laureate. **–ung,** *f.* coronation, crowning. **–ungsfeier(lichkeit),** *f.* coronation ceremony. **–ungsinsignien,** *pl.* regalia. **–ungsmünze,** *f.* coronation medal. **–ungszug,** *m.* coronation procession.

Kropf, *m.* (-(e)s, ⸚e) crop, craw, maw (*of birds*); wen, goitre (*Med.*); excrescence (*Bot.*); bunches, glanders (*Vet.*); bow (*of ships*); projecting part, top (*of a wall*). **–ader,** *f.* varicose vein. **–artig,** *adj.* goitrous. **–drüse,** *f.* thyroid gland. **–ig,** *adj.* strumous, goitrous. **–mittel,** *n.* antistrumatic. **–rohr,** *n.* bent tube. **–stein,** *m.* corner-stone. **–sucht,** *f.* cretinism. **–taube,** *f.* pouter pigeon.

kröpf–en, 1. *v.a.* bend at right angles, form a knee (*Tech.*); cram (*poultry*). 2. *v.n.* (*aux.* h.) gorge, feed (*of birds of prey*). **–er,** *m.* male pouter pigeon. **–ung,** *f.* corner-moulding; cramming; crank (*Mach.*).

Kroppzeug, *n.* rag, tag and bobtail; (*dial.* & *coll.*) small children; *das kleine –*, pack of young brats.

Kroquis, *n.* (–, –) (*Austr. dial.*), *see* **Kroki.**

Krösel–eisen, *n.* glazier's iron; croze (-iron). **–n,** *v.a.* trim (*glass*).

Kröt–e, *f.* (-en) toad; malicious person; bitch; jade, wench; (*sl.*) coin; (*sl.*) *ich habe nur noch ein paar –en in der Tasche*, I have only a few coppers in my pocket; (*vulg.*) *niedliche kleine –e*, pretty wench. **–ig,** *adj.* malicious; obstinate, self-willed.

Krück–e, *f.* (-en) crutch; (*fig.*) prop; scraper, rake; bridge (*Bill.*); *an –en gehen*, walk with crutches; *einem die –e reichen*, do everything to help a p. **–(en)stock,** *m.* crutch; crooked-stick.

Krug, *m.* (-(e)s, ⸚e) pitcher, jug; mug, pot, jar, urn; public-house, tavern; (*Prov.*) *der – geht so lange zum Wasser bis er bricht*, the pitcher goes so often to the well that it comes home broken at last.

Krüger, *m.* (-s, –) publican, innkeeper.

Kruke, *f.* (-n) stone jar *or* (hot-water) bottle; oddity, queer card *or* fish.

Krulle, *f.* (-n) (*archaic*) ruffle, ruff.

krüll–en, *v.a.* (*dial.*) shell (*peas*). **–tabak,** *m.* curly cut.

Krume, *f.* (-n) crumb (*of bread*); young shoot; vegetable mould.

Krüm–el, *n.* & *m.* (-s, –), *see* **Krume.** **–(e)lig,** *adj.* crumbling, friable, crumbly, crumby. **–eln,** *v.r.* & *n.* (*aux.* h.) crumble; *sich –eln*, crumble away. **–elschokolade,** *f.* broken chocolate. **–elzucker,** *m.* granulated sugar.

krumm, *adj.* (*comp.* -er *or* ⸚er, *sup.* -st *or* ⸚st) crooked, bent, curved, wry, bow, bandy, twisted, bowed, arched; indirect, circuitous; artful, dishonest; *einen – ansehen*, look askance at a p.; *–er Buckel*, flunkyism, fawning, sycophancy; *–e Finger machen*, be light-fingered; *eine –e Haltung haben*, stoop; *–e Knie*, knock-knees; (*coll.*) *sich – legen* (also *– liegen*), cut down one's expenses, draw in one's horns, cut one's coat according to one's cloth; (*coll.*) *– liegen*, suffer want; *–e Linie*, curve; *–es Maul*, wry mouth; *–er Rücken*, see *–er Buckel*; (*einen*) *– und lahm schlagen*, beat (a p.) unmercifully; *– sitzen*, cower, loll; *–e Wege*, crooked *or* underhand ways; *– werden*, grow crooked, warp. **–ästig,** *adj.* gnarled. **–beinig,** *adj.* bow *or* bandy-legged. **–buckel,** *m.* hunchback. **–e,** 1. *m.* (*dial.*) hare (*Hunt.*). 2. *f.* (-n) (*dial.*) sickle, billhook. **–e(r),** *m.* & *f.* hunchback. **–faserig,** *adj.* cross-grained. **–halsig,** *adj.* wry-necked. **–holz,** *n.* dwarf mountain pine; knee-timber, scrub. **–horn,** *n.* animal with crumpled horns; cornet (*Mus.*). **–linig,** *adj.* curvilinear, non-linear. **–nasig,** *adj.* hook-nosed. **–nehmen,** *v.n.* take amiss. **–säbel,** *m.* scimitar. **–stab,** *m.* crook; crosier; (*fig.*) episcopal authority. **–zirkel,** *m.* bow-compasses, callipers.

Krümm–e, *f.* (-en) crookedness; winding, intricacy; curvature; circuitous way. **–en,** 1. *v.a.* bend, curve, crumple; *niemand soll dir ein Haar –en*, no one shall hurt a hair of your head. 2. *v.r.* grow crooked, warp, stoop, bend down; wriggle, writhe, wind, meander; cringe, grovel, fawn; *sich vor Schmerzen –en*, writhe with pain; *sich vor Lachen –en*, double up with laughter; (*Prov.*) *auch ein Wurm –t sich*, even a worm will turn. **–er,** *m.* pipe-joint, bend, elbow; harrow (*Agr.*). **–ung,** *f.* bend, curve, curvature, flexure; turn, winding; crookedness, sinuosity; contortion. **–ungshalbmesser,** *m.* radius of curvature.

krumpeln, krümpeln, *v.a.* crumple, crinkle, ruffle, pucker.

Krümper–pferd, *n.* reserve horse (*Mil.*). **–system,** *n.* short-service training of conscripts.

Krupp, *m.* (*coll.*) croup (*Med.*).

Kruppe, *f.* (-n) crupper, croup (*of a horse*).

Krüppel, *m.* (-s, –) cripple; *zum – machen*, cripple, maim. **–haft,** *adj.*, **–ig,** *adj.* crippled, maimed, deformed, stunted. **–wuchs,** *m.* scrub, dwarf timber.

Krust–e, *f.* (-en) crust, scab, scale, incrustation, scurf; fur (*on a boiler, etc.*); *sich mit –e überziehen*, become (in)crusted; *Anstoß–e*, kissing crust. **–enartig,** *adj.* crust-like, crusty, crustaceous. **–enbildung,** *f.* incrustation. **–entiere,** *n.pl.* crustaceans. **–ig,** *adj.* crusty, crusted.

Krypt–a, –e, *f.* (-en) crypt. **–ogame,** *f.* cryptogam. **–ogamisch,** *adj.* cryptogamous (*Bot.*).

Kübel, *m.* (-s, –) bucket, pail, tub, vat. **–wagen,** *m.* jeep (*Mil.*). **–system,** *n.* bucket-system (*in mines*). **–träger,** *m.* hodman.

kub–ieren, *v.a.* take the cubic measure of; cube. **–ikberechnung,** *f.* cubature. **–ikgehalt,** *m.* volume. **–ikmaß,** *n.* cubic measure. **–ikwurzel,** *f.* cube-root. **–ikzahl,** *f.* cube; *auf die –ikzahl erheben*, cube, raise to the third power. **–isch,** *adj.* cubic, cubical. **–ismus,** *m.* cubism. **–us,** *m.* (–, Kuben) cube.

Küche, *f.* (-n) kitchen; cooking, cookery, culinary art; *eine gute – führen*, keep a good table; *die schwarze –*, alchemist's laboratory; *bürgerliche –*, plain fare, plain cooking; *kalte –*, cold meat; (*coll.*) *in des Teufels – kommen*, get into a hell of a mess. **–n,** *v.n.* (*Swiss dial.*) bake cakes. **–nabfall,** *m.* kitchen refuse. **–nbulle,** *m.* (*sl.*) mess sergeant (*Mil.*). (*coll.*) **–ndragoner,** *m.* (*hum.*) strong kitchen-wench. **-neinrichtung,** *f.* kitchen-furniture. **-nfee,** *f.* (*hum.*) good fairy in the kitchen (= cook). **-ngarten,** *m.* vegetable *or* kitchen-garden. **-ngerät,** *n.*, **-ngeschirr,** *n.* kitchen utensils. **-ngewächs,** *n.* garden produce. **-nherd,** *m.* (kitchen-)range. **-nkräuter,** *pl.* culinary herbs. **-nlatein,** *n.* dog-latin. **-nmädchen,** *n.* kitchen maid, scullion. **-nmeister,** *m.* head-cook, chef. **-npersonal,** *n.* kitchen staff. **-nrost,** *m.* kitchen-grate; gridiron. **-nschabe,** *f.* cockroach. **-nschrank,** *m.* kitchen-cupboard *or* dresser. **-nzettel,** *m.* bill of fare, menu.

Kuchen, *m.* (-s, –) cake; tart; pastry; clot (*of blood*); placenta; (*coll.*) *ja –!* what a hope! **-bäcker,** *m.* pastry-cook. **-blech,** *n.* baking tin. **-bürste,** *f.* pastry brush. **-form,** *f.* cake-tin. **-teig,** *m.* cake-mixture.

Küchlein, *n.* (-s, –) chicken, chick.

Küchler, *m.* (-s, –) pastry-cook.

Kücken, *n.* (-s, –), *see* **Küchlein**; *also* young girl.

Kuckuck, *m.* (-(e)s, -e) cuckoo; (*coll.*) *der – und sein Küster,* Old Nick; *hol' ihn der –!* devil take him! *zum –!* confound it! hang it! *wie, zum –, soll ich das anfangen?* how in the world am I to set about it? *das mag der – wissen,* how the deuce should I know? heaven only knows! **-sblume,** *f.* ragged robin (*Lychnis flos-cuculi*) (*Bot.*). **-sei,** *n.*; (*fig.*) *einem ein -sei ins Nest legen,* render s.o. a doubtful service, sow the seeds of future trouble for a p. **-suhr,** *f.* cuckoo clock.

Kuddelmuddel, *m.* (*coll.*) motley crowd, medley.

Kufe, *f.* (-n) vat, tub, barrel; runner *or* skid (*of a sledge*).

Küfer, *m.* (-s, –) cellarman; (*dial.*) cooper.

Kugel, *f.* (-n) ball, globe, sphere, globule; bullet; *mit goldenen -n schießen,* let one's money talk; *-n und Granaten,* shot and shell; *matte –,* spent bullet; *sich* (*Dat.*) *eine – durch den Kopf jagen,* blow one's brains out; *man hat ihm eine schwarze – geworfen,* he was black-balled; *die schwarze – ziehen,* have bad luck; (*Prov.*) *eine jede – trifft ja nicht,* not every bullet hits home; *-n wechseln,* exchange shots; (*Prov.*) *eine jede – hat ihren Zweck,* every bullet has its billet. **-abschritt,** *m.* spherical segment. **-ähnlich,** *adj.* spherical; spheroidal. **-artig,** *adj.* globular. **-ausschnitt,** *m.* cone with spherical base. **-bahn,** *f.* trajectory; bowling-green. **-blitz,** *m.* ball lightning. **-büchse,** *f.* shot-gun. **-dicke,** *f.* ball-calibre. **-dreieck,** *n.* spherical triangle. **-dreieckslehre,** *f.* spherical trigonometry. **-fang,** *m.* butts. **-fest,** *adj.* bullet-proof. **-fläche,** *f.* surface of a sphere. **-form,** *f.* spherical form; bullet-mould. **-förmig,** *adj.* globular, spherical. **-gelenk,** *n.* ball and socket (joint), ball joint. **-gewölbe,** *n.* cupola. **-haube,** *f.* spherical calotte. **-helm,** *m.* tholus, cupola (*Arch.*). **-ig,** *adj.* spherical, globular, globose. **-kalotte,** *f.*, **-kappe,** *f.*, *see* **-haube.** **-lage,** *f.* position of bullet (*in wound*). **-lager,** *n.* ball-bearing. **-loch,** *n.* pocket (*Bill.*). **-los,** *n.* decision by ballot. **-n,** 1. *v.n.* (*aux.* s.) roll; (*aux.* h.) bowl; ballot. 2. *v.a.* roll; make globular, form into a ball. 3. *v.r.* roll, assume a globular form; (*coll.*) *sich -n vor Lachen,* double up with laughter; (*coll.*) *das ist zum -n,* that is extremely funny. **-patrone,** *f.* ball-cartridge. **-regen,** *m.* shower of bullets. **-rund,** *adj.* quite round, round as a ball. **-schaltung,** *f.* ball-jointed gear **-schnitt,** *m.* spherical section. **-schreiber,** *m.* ball-point pen. **-spiel,** *n.* bowling, bowls. **-stoßen,** *v.n.* (*& n.*) put(ting) the shot *or* weight. **-ventil,** *n.* ball-valve. **-wahl,** *f.* election by ballot. **-wand,** *f.* target. **-wechsel,** *m.* exchange of shots. **-zange,** *f.* ball-extractor, bullet-forceps. **-zapfen,** *m.* ball-pivot.

Kügelchen, *n.* (-s, –) globule, globulet.

Kuh, *f.* (⸚e) cow; female of deer, elephant, *etc.*; *blinde –,* blindman's-buff; *er sieht es an wie die – das neue Tor,* he stares at it like a stuck dummy; (*B.*) *fette* or *magere Kühe,* fat *or* lean kine; (*coll.*) *dumme –,* silly goose! *junge –,* heifer; *Milch–,* milch-cow; anything lucrative. **-blume,** *f.* marsh-marigold (*Caltha palustris*) (*Bot.*). **-fladen,** *m.* cow-dung. **-fuß,** *m.* crowbar; (*archaic*) old gun, rifle. **-glocke,** *f.*, *see* **-schelle.** **-handel,** *m.* shady business, wire-pulling, log-rolling. **-haut,** *f.* cowhide; (*coll.*) *das geht auf keine -haut,* that beggars description. **-hessig,** *adj.* knock-kneed (*Vet.*). **-hürde,** *f.* cow-stall. **-magd,** *f.* dairy-maid. **-molken,** *f.pl.* whey. **-pocken,** *f.pl.* cow-pox. **-pockenimpfung,** *f.* vaccination. **-pockenstoff,** *m.* vaccine lymph. **-reigen,** *m.*, **-reihen,** *m.* dance (music) of Alpine cowherds. **-schelle,** *f.* cow-bell. **-schluck,** *m.* (*vulg.*) large draught (*of beer, etc.*). **-stall,** *m.* cow-shed, byre. **-weide,** *f.* cattle pasture.

Küher, *m.* (*Swiss. dial.*) cowherd.

kühl, *adj.* cool; fresh; (*fig.*) lukewarm, unconcerned, indifferent, half-hearted, unmoved; (*Berlin sl.*) *eine -e Blonde,* a glass of pale ale. **-anlage,** *f.* cold-storage plant. **-apparat,** *m.* refrigerator. **-bottich,** *m.* cooling vat. **-e,** 1. *n.*; *des Morgens -e,* morning freshness; *im -en sitzen,* sit in the shade. 2. *f.* coolness; coldness; freshness, cool; half-heartedness, indifference. **-eimer,** *m.*, **-faß,** *n.* cooler. **-en,** 1. *v.a.* cool, chill, refresh; refrigerate; *sein Mütchen an einem -en,* vent one's rage on a p. 2. *v.r. & n.* (*aux.* h.) grow cool. **-er,** *m.* radiator (*Motor.*), cooler, refrigerator, condenser. **-erhaube,** *f.* bonnet (*Motor.*). **-halle,** *f.*, **-haus,** *n.* cold store, cold-storage depot. **-mantel,** *m.* water-jacket (*Motor.*). **-mittel,** *n.* cooling draught; refrigerant. **-ofen,** *m.* cooling furnace, annealing oven. **-raum.** *m.* refrigerating *or* cold-storage chamber. **-schlange,** *f.* condensing coil. **-schrank,** *m.* refrigerator. **-te,** *f.* fresh breeze (*Naut.*). **-trank,** *m.* cooling drink. **-wasser,** *n.* cooling water. **-ung,** *f.* cooling, freshness, breeze; refrigeration.

Kuhle, *f.* (-n) deep hole, pit.

kühn, *adj.* bold, brave, daring, audacious; *– machen,* embolden. **-heit,** *f.* boldness, daring, dash, intrepidity; audacity. **-lich,** *adv.* boldly.

Kujon, *m.* (-s, -e) scoundrel, rogue. **-ieren,** *v.a.* treat shabbily, exploit.

Küken, (*dial.*), *see* **Kücken.**

Kukuruz, *m.* (*Austr. dial.*) maize.

kulan-t [*pron.* kuːˈlɑnt], *adj.* (*C.L.*) accommodating, obliging, fair. **-z,** *f.* fair dealing, readiness to oblige.

Kule, *f.*, *see* **Kuhle.**

Kuli, *m.* (-s, -s) coolie.

Kulisse, *f.* (-n) wing; scene (*Theat.*); space in a stock-exchange set apart for unofficial business; connecting-link (*of a railway engine*); *in die – sprechen,* make an aside; *hinter den -n,* behind the scenes, in secret; *hinter die -n schauen,* know the ins and outs of, have a glimpse behind the scenes; *das ist nur –,* that is only outward show. **-nfieber,** *n.* stage-fright. **-ngeschwätz,** *n.* green-room talk. **-nmaler,** *m.* scene-painter. **-nreißer,** *m.* sensational actor, ranter. **-nreißerei,** *f.* playing to the gallery. **-nschieber,** *m.* scene-shifter. **-ntür,** *f.* stage-door. **-ntisch,** *m.* extending table.

Kulm, *m.* (-s, -e) (*dial.*) summit, knoll. **-inieren,** *v.n.* (*aux.* h.) culminate; reach the climax. **-inationspunkt,** *m.* culminating point, culmination, zenith, pinnacle, acme.

Kult, (-(e)s, -e) worship; cult.

kult-ivieren, *v.a.* cultivate, till. **-iviert,** *adj.* cultured. **-ur,** *f.* cultivation, afforestation, forest plantation; culture; civilization (N.B. *Orig. with connotations of 'learning' & 'literary', Nat. Soc. perverted it in two directions*: (1) 'folklore', 'race culture'; (2) 'decadent intellectualism', 'western democratic materialism'); *in -ur nehmen,* bring under cultivation. **-urarbeit,** *f.* cultural work. **-urbolschewismus,** *m.* (*Nat. Soc.*) intellectual (and artistic) nihilism. modernism (in art), decadence. **-urell,** *adj.* cultural. **-urfähig,** *adj.* cultivable, arable. **-urfeindlich,** *adj.* hostile to culture, barbarous. **-urfilm,** *m.* documentary. **-urgebiet,** *n.* civilized region. **-urgeschichte,** *f.* history of civilization. **-urgeschichtlich,** *adj.* relating to the history of civilization. **-urgut,** *n.* cultural value. **-urkammer,** *f.* (*Nat. Soc.*) 'Chamber of Culture' (*acting as censor over all cultural life*). **-urkampf,** *m.* Bismarck's struggle with Catholicism. **-urkreis,** *m.* cultural field. **-urkunde,** *f.* study of cultural development. **-urmensch,** *m.* civilized man.

-urpflanze, *f.* cultivated plant. **-urstaat**, *m.* civilized state. **-urstufe**, *f.* stage of civilization. **-urträger**, *m.* upholder of culture. **-urvolk**, *n.* civilized nation. **-us**, *m.*, *see* **Kult**. **-usminister**, *m.* Minister of Public Worship and Education.

Kumme, *f.* (-n) (*dial.*) basin, bowl.

Kümmel, *m.* (-s, -) caraway *or* cumin(-seed). **-n**, 1. *v.a.* flavour with caraway. 2. *v.n.* (*aux.* h.) (*sl.*) tipple, soak (spirits). **-brot**, *n.* bread flavoured with caraway-seeds. **-käse**, *m.* cheese flavoured with caraway-seeds. **-kuchen**, *m.* seed-cake. (*coll.*) **-(schnaps)**, *m.* kümmel (*liqueur*). **-türke**, *m.* philistine, 'petit bourgeois'; braggart.

Kummer, *m.* grief, sorrow, sadness, trouble, worry, care; (*dial.*) rubble, rubbish, heap; *mit – behaftet*, careworn; *– und Sorge*, trouble and worry; *– und Not*, grief and misery; *Hunger und – leiden*, be in dire distress; *sich* (*Dat.*) *– machen über eine S.*, grieve about a th.; *das ist mein geringster –*, that is the least of my troubles; *einem viel – bereiten* or *verursachen*, cause a p. much grief; *das macht mir wenig –*, I do not worry (my head) about that; (*dial.*) *sie hatte –, es könnte ihm etwas passieren*, she feared s.th. might happen to him. **-frei**, *adj.*, **-los**, *adj.* untroubled, without a care in the world. **-voll**, *adj.* sorrowful, doleful; grievous, painful.

kümmer-lich, 1. *adj.* miserable, wretched, pitiful; poor, stunted, scanty, needy; *-lich leben*, live a wretched *or* miserable existence; *-liches Einkommen*, meagre income. 2. *adv.* scarcely, barely, with great trouble. **-n**, 1. *v.a.* grieve, afflict, trouble; concern; *was -t mich das?* what is that to me? what do I care? 2. *v.r.* (*um*) mind, pay heed (to), care (for), worry, be worried (about); (*über*) grieve (for); *ich -e mich nicht darum*, I do not trouble my head about it; *-n Sie sich nicht um ihn*, do not take any notice of him; *-n Sie sich nicht um Dinge, die Sie nichts angehen!* do not poke your nose into other people's business! mind your own business! *-e dich nicht um ungelegte Eier!* do not count your chickens before they are hatched! 3. *v.n.* wilt, starve, be stunted. **-ling**, *m.* stunted *or* undersized creature, plant, etc. **-nis**, *f.* grief, anxiety, care; annoyance, affliction.

Kump, *n.* (-s, -e), **-en**, *m.* (-s, –) (*dial.*), *see* **Kumpf**.

Kumpan, *m.* (-s, -e) (*Poet.*) companion, fellow, crony.

Kumpel, *m.* (*dial.*) coal-miner.

Kumpf, *m.* (-(e)s, -e & ⸚e) (*dial.*) deep basin, bowl; feeding trough.

Kum(me)t, *n.* (-(e)s, -e) horse-collar. **-pferd**, *n.* draught-horse.

kund, *indec. pred. adj.* known, public; *die S. ist –*, it is generally known; *– und zu wissen sei hiemit*, know all men by these presents. **-bar**, *adj.* (*dial.*) notorious, (well-)known; manifest. **-barkeit**, *f.* notoriety, publicity. **-e**, 1. *f.* (-en) information, notice; news, tidings, intelligence; (*in compounds*) knowledge, science; *-e von etwas nehmen*, take cognizance of a th. 2. *m.* (-en, -en) customer, client; (*sl.*) tramp, fellow; *schlauer* or *geriebener -e*, sharp *or* sly one *or* customer; *fester -e*, regular customer; *zufälliger -e*, chance buyer; *du bist mir ja ein netter -e*, well, you're a nice fellow. **-enfang**, *m.* touting. **-enfänger**, *m.* tout. **-ensprache**, *f.* thieves' slang. **-enzahl**, *f.* number of customers, connexions, custom. **-geben**, 1. *v.a.* notify, inform; announce, proclaim, publish, set forth. 2. *v.r.* prove o.s. *or* itself (to be), become manifest. **-gebung**, *f.* demonstration, rally; proclamation, announcement, manifestation. **-ig**, *adj.* (*Gen.*) skilful, versed, experienced, expert, learned; (*in*) (well-)informed (about); familiar (with); *einer S. -ig*, thoroughly acquainted with a th.; *ein des Weges -iger*, one who knows the way; *die -igen*, people who know, the initiated. **-machen**, *v.a.* (*Austr. & Swiss dial.*) *see* **-geben**. **-machung**, *f.* proclamation, publication, declaration, announcement, notification. **-schaft**, *f.* custom, patronage; customers, clientele; (*C.L.*) goodwill; knowledge, notice, information; reconnaissance, reconnoitring; *auf -schaft ausgehen*, go out to reconnoitre, go scouting; *-schaft einziehen*, collect information; *einem seine -schaft zuwenden*, patronize *or* give one's custom to a p. **-schaften**, *v.n.* (*aux.* h.) scout, spy, reconnoitre. **-schafter**, *m.* spy, scout, explorer. **-werden**, *v.n.* become known *or* public, come to light, transpire. **-tun**, 1. *v.a.*, *see* **-geben**. 2. *v.r.* declare o.s. (to be).

künd-bar, *adj.* (*C.L.*) recallable, terminable. **-en**, *v.a.* (*poet.*) publish, announce; (*also dial.* = **-igen**). **-ig**, *adj.*, *see* **kund**. **-igen**, 1. *v.n.* give notice *or* warning. 2. *v.a.* recall, call in (*money*); *ich habe meinem Diener gekündigt*, I have given my servant notice (to leave); *der Diener -igte zum Monatsersten*, the servant gave his notice for the first of the month; *den Waffenstillstand -igen*, call off *or* denounce the armistice. **-igung**, *f.* (previous) notice, warning; *often used for* **-igungsfrist**, *f.* time for giving notice, period of notice; *halbjährige -igung*, six-months' notice.

künftig, 1. *adj.* future; coming, to come, next; *-e Zeiten*, time(s) to come; *-e Woche*, next week; *das -e Leben*, the future life; *das -e*, the future; *seine -e Frau*, his wife to be; his intended. 2. *adv.*; *ins -e*, for the future, in future, henceforth, hereafter. **-hin**, *adv.*, *see* – 2.

Kunkel, *f.* (-n) distaff; (*archaic*) womankind. **-lehen**, *n.* petticoat tenure (*Law*). **-magen**, *m.pl.* maternal relations (*Law*).

Kunst, *f.* (⸚e) art, skill, dexterity, ingenuity, trick, knack, artifice, sleight-of-hand; (*archaic*) machine, engine, waterwork; *angewandte –*, applied art; *bildende Künste*, pictorial *or* graphic arts; (*Prov.*) *– geht nach Brot*, art follows the public; *brotlose –*, profitless business, thankless task; *darstellende –*, representational art; *die freien Künste*, the liberal arts; *handwerksmäßige Künste*, mechanical arts; *das ist keine –*, that is easy enough; *er ist mit seinen Künsten zu Ende*, he is at his wits' end; *nach –, nicht nach Gunst gehen*, depend on merit rather than influence; *redende Künste*, rhetorical arts; *schöne Künste*, fine arts; *schwarze –*, black art, magic, necromancy; mezzotint (*Engr.*); *seine – an einer S. versuchen*, try one's skill *or* one's hand at a th. **-akademie**, *f.* art school. **-anlage**, *f.* artistic bent. **-anstalt**, *f.* art printing-works. **-arbeit**, *f.* work of art; artificial work. **-arm**, *m.* artificial arm. **-ausdruck**, *m.* technical term. **-ausstellung**, *f.* art exhibition. **-bäcker**, *m.* fancy baker, confectioner. **-ballade**, *f.* literary ballad. **-beflissene(r)**, *m.* student of art. **-beilage**, *f.* pictorial *or* art supplement. **-bein**, *n.* artificial leg. **-brut**, *f.* artificial incubation. **-butter**, *f.* synthetic butter, margarine. **-dichtung**, *f.* literary poetry (*opp. folk-poetry*). **-druckerei**, *f.* fine art printers. **-dünger**, *m.* artificial manure, fertilizer. **-epos**, *n.* literary epic. **-erziehung**, *f.* aesthetic education. **-fasern**, *f.pl.* synthetic textiles. **-fehler**, *m.* technical error. **-fertig**, *adj.* skilful. **-fertigkeit**, *f.* artistic *or* technical skill. **-fliegen**, *v.n.* stunt-flying, aerobatics (*Av.*). **-flug**, *m.* stunt-flight. **-freund**, *m.* lover *or* patron of the fine arts. **-gärtner**, *m.* florist, horticulturist, nursery-gardener. **-gärtnerei**, *f.* horticulture. **-gefühl**, *n.* artistic feeling, taste for art. **-gegenstand**, *m.* objet d'art. **-gemäß**, *adj.* artistic, aesthetically satisfying **-genoß**, *m.*, **-genosse**, *m.* fellow-artist. **-genuß**, *m.* (artistic) treat; *es war ein musikalischer -genuß*, it was a musical treat. **-gerecht**, *adj.* correct, skilful. **-geschichte**, *f.* history of art. **-geschmack**, *m.* artistic taste. **-geübt**, *adj.* skilled, skilful. **-gewerbe**, *n.* arts and craft, applied art, useful art. **-gewerbeschule**, *f.* school of arts and crafts. **-gewerbler**, *m.* worker in arts and crafts. **-glanz**, *m.* artificial lustre. **-graben**, *m.* canal, conduit, aqueduct. **-griff**, *m.* knack, trick, artifice, craft, device. **-gummi**, *n.* synthetic rubber. **-halle**, *f.* art gallery. **-handel**, *m.* fine art trade. **-händler**, *m.* art dealer. **-handlung**, *f.* print-shop, picture shop, fine-art dealers. **-handwerk**, *n.* skilled craft. **-handwerker**, *m.* skilled craftsman. **-harz**, *n.* synthetic resin, plastic. **-höhle**, *f.* man-made grotto. **-horn**, *n.* celluloid. **-kenner**, *m.* connoisseur. **-kniff**, *m.* artifice, trick, dodge. **-kritik**, *f.* art-criticism. **-lauf**, *m.*, **-laufen**, *n.* figure-skating. **-leder**, *n.* imitation leather. **-liebhaber**, *m.* art lover, amateur artist; dilettante. **-liebhaberei**, *f.* artistic hobby. **-los**, *adj.* tasteless, inartistic, crude; artless, naive, natural; unsophisticated. **-losigkeit,** *f.* lack of artistry, tastelessness, poor taste; artlessness. **-mäßig,** *adj.* artistically sound *or* correct. (*archaic*) **-meister,** *m.* hydraulic engineer. **-mittel,** *n.* artificial means. **-museum,** *n.* art-gallery. **-pause** *f.* pause for effect; (*iron.*) awkward pause. **-periode,** *f.* golden age of art, period in the history of art. **-pflege,** *f.* promotion of art. **-poesie,** *f.*, *see* **-dichtung.** **-produkt,** *n.* artificial product. **-prosa,** *f.* rhythmic prose. **-reich,** *adj.* artistic; ingenious. **-reiter,** *m.* circus-rider. **-richter,** *m.* critic. **-sammlung,** *f.* art collection. **-schloß,** *n.* combination-lock. **-schlosser,** *m.* art-metal worker. **-schreiner,** *m.* cabinet-maker. **-schule,** *f.* school of art; artists' coterie. **-seide,** *f.* artificial silk, rayon. **-sinn,** *m.* artistic sense, taste for art. **-sinnig,** *adj.* appreciative of art. **-sprache,** *f.* artificial language; literary language; technical language. **-springen,** *n.* acrobatics; fancy diving. **-stecher,** *m.* engraver. (*archaic*) **-steiger,** *m.* surveyor of waterworks (*Min.*). **-stein,** *m.* artificial stone. **-stickerei,** *f.* art needlework, embroidery. **-stoff,** *m.* plastics, synthetic products. **-stopferei,** *f.* invisible mending. **-stück,** *n.* clever trick, feat, cunning device; *das ist kein -stück!* there is nothing clever in that! **-tischler,** *m.* cabinet-maker. **-trieb,** *m.* mechanical instinct (*of animals*); artistic instinct. **-verein,** *m.* art-club. **-verfahren,** *n.* artistic process. **-verlag,** *m.* fine-art publishers. **-verleger,** *m.* fine-art publisher. **-verständige(r),** *m.* expert on art; connoisseur. **-voll,** *adj.* *see* **-reich.** **-wabe,** *f.* comb foundation (*Beekeeping*). **-wart,** *m.* curator of an art-gallery. **-werk,** *n.* work of art, artistic production; (*archaic*) machine, engine; waterwork. **-widrig,** *adj.* inartistic, inelegant, barbarous, uncouth. **-wissenschaft,** *f.* aesthetics. **-wolle,** *f.* artificial wool, shoddy. **-wort,** *n.* technical term. **-zweig,** *m.* branch of art.

Künst-elei, *f.* (-en) affectation, mannerism, artificiality, affected ways; artificial method *or* work; elaboration. **-eln,** 1. *v.a.* elaborate; overrefine, subtilize. *gekünstelt* *p.p.* & *adj.* artificial, elaborate, affected. 2. *v.n.* (*aux.* h.); *-eln an einer S.*, bestow great pains on a th. **-ler,** *m.* artist; virtuoso; artiste, performer (*Theat.*). **-lerisch,** *adj.* artistic. **-lerlaufbahn,** *f.* artistic career, career of an artist. **-lerlos,** *n.* artist's unhappy lot. **-lertum,** *n.* artistic gift, power, greatness *or* genius. **-lerverein,** *m.* society of artists, artists' club. **-lerwerkstatt,** *f.* studio. **-lich,** *adj.* artificial; imitated, false, synthetic; *-liche Atmung*, artificial respiration; *-liches Auge*, artificial eye; *-liche Befruchtung*, artificial insemination; *-liche Beleuchtung*, artificial lighting; *-liche Blumen*, artificial flowers; *-licher Diamant*, paste (diamond); *-liche Glieder*, artificial limbs; *-liche Haare*, false hair; *-liche Zähne*, artificial teeth, dentures; *-lich* (*in die Höhe*) *treiben*, force (*vegetables, flowers*).

kunterbunt, *adj.* topsy-turvy, higgledy-piggledy; gaudy, parti-coloured; (*coll.*) *er redet -es Zeug*, he talks incoherent rubbish; (*coll.*) *bei X. geht es – her* or *zu*, at X.'s things are pretty hectic.

Küp-e, *f.* (-en) large tub, vat, copper, boiler; dyeing liquor. **-er,** *m.* (*dial.*), *see* **Küfer.**

Kupee, *n.* (-s, -s) compartment (*Railw.*). **-koffer,** *m.* (-s, –) dressing-case.

Kupfer, *n.* (-s, –) copper; copper vessels; copper coin; (*archaic*) copperplate print; *in – stechen*, engrave on copper; *mit – beschlagen*, copper-bottomed. **-ader,** *f.* vein of copper (*Min.*). **-bergwerk,** *n.* copper-mine. **-beschlag,** *m.* copper sheathing. **-blatt,** *n.* copper-foil. **-blech,** *n.* sheet-copper. **-draht,** *m.* copper-wire. **-druck,** *m.* copperplate (printing *or* print). **-erz,** *n.* copper-ore. **-farben,** *adj.*, **-farbig,** *adj.* copper-coloured. **-feilicht,** *n.* copper-filings. **-frischen,** *n.* copper-refining. **-gang,** *m.* copper-lode. **-gehalt,** *m.* copper content. **-(geld),** *n.* copper money; *nur etwas -geld*, only a few coppers. **-gewinnung,** *f.* extraction of copper. **-grün,** *n.* verdigris. **-haltig,** *adj.* cupreous, cupriferous. **-hütte,** *f.* copper-works. **-ig,** *adj.* cupreous, coppery, copper-like. **-kalk,** *m.* oxide of copper. **-kies,** *m.* copper pyrites. **-legierung,** *f.* copper alloy. **-münze,** *f.* copper coin; (*coll.*) *ein paar -münzen*, a few coppers. **-n,** 1. *adj.* copper; *-ner Kessel*, copper kettle. 2. *v.a.* line *or* mount with copper. **-oxyd,** *n.* black oxide of copper, cupric oxide. **-oxydul,** *n.* red oxide of copper, cuprous oxide; *salzsaures -oxydul*, cuprous chloride. **-platte,** *f.* copperplate. **-probe,** *f.* assay of copper ore, test for copper. **-rost,** *m.* verdigris. **-rot,** 1. *adj.* copper-coloured. 2. *n.* red oxide of copper. **-röte,** *f.* virgin copper; copper-colour. **-sammlung,** *f.* collection of engravings. **-schmied,** *m.* brazier, coppersmith. **-sinter,** *m.* copper scale. **-stechen,** *n.* engraving on copper. **-stecher,** *m.* (copperplate) engraver. **-stich,** *m.* (copperplate) engraving. **-tiegel,** *m.* copper crucible. **-verhüttung,** *f.* copper-smelting. **-verkleidung,** *f.* copper-sheathing. **-vitriol,** *n.* copper sulphate, blue vitriol.

kupier-en, *v.a.* (*Austr. dial.*) cut off; dock (*tail*), (*archaic*) punch (*tickets*), clip; adulterate (*wine*); *-tes Gelände*, broken ground.

Kupp-e, *f.* (-en) top, summit, knoll; round head (*of a nail*); finger-end. **-el,** *f.* (-eln) cupola, dome. **-ig,** *adj.* with a round *or* rounded end.

Kupp-elei, *f.* match-making; pandering. **-elgelenk,** *n.* coupling-link. **-eln,** *v.n.* pander, procure; *v.a.* couple, join, tie together, unite. **-elpelz,** *m.*; *sich einen -elpelz verdienen*, bring about a match, succeed in bringing (*lovers*) together. **-elstange,** *f.* connecting-rod, tie-rod. **-elwort,** *n.* hyphenated word. **-ler,** *m.* match-maker; procurer, pander, go-between. **-lerin,** *f.* (*as* **-ler,** *but* procuress). **-lung,** *f.* coupling, joint, clutch (*Motor.*). **-lungs(fuß)hebel,** *m.* clutch-pedal (*Motor.*).

[1]**Kur,** *f.* (-en) (course of) treatment, cure; course of baths, taking the waters; *die – schlägt an*, the cure is taking effect; *sich in die – begeben*, undergo medical treatment; *in der – haben*, treat; *er war in Karlsbad zur* (or Swiss *in der*) –, he was drinking the waters *or* undergoing treatment at Karlsbad; *eine – machen*, undergo treatment; (*fig.*) *in die – nehmen*, work on, (*sl.*) give (*a p.*) the works; *mein Freund ging zur – nach Reichenhall*, my friend went to Reichenhall for his health *or* to be treated. **-anstalt,** *f.* sanatorium. **-bad,** *n.* curative baths, spa. **-gast,** *m.* patient, visitor (*at a spa*). **-haus,** *n.* pump-room, spa hotel, casino. **-ieren,** *v.a.* cure; *er ist -iert*, he is cured, his health is restored; *sich -ieren lassen*, receive medical attention *or* treatment, get cured. **-liste,** *f.* list of visitors (*at a spa*). **-ort,** *m.* health resort, watering-place, spa. **-pfuscher,** *m.* quack. **-pfuscherei,** *f.* quack practices. **-saal,** *m.* pump-room, casino. **-taxe,** *f.* tax on visitors.

[2]**Kur,** *f.* courting; (*einer Dame*) *die – machen* or *schneiden*, make love to, court *or* woo (a lady).

[3]**Kur,** *f.* *only in compounds*; **-brandenburg,** *n.* electorate of Brandenburg. **-erbe,** *m.*, *see* **-prinz.** **-fürst,** *m.* elector (*in the German Empire*). **-fürstenbank,** *f.* electoral bench. **-fürstentag,** *m.* diet. **-fürstentum,** *n.* electorate. **-fürstlich,** *adj.* electoral. **-hessisch,** *adj.* of the electorate of Hesse. **-hut,** *m.* electoral crown. **-länder,** *n.pl.* electoral domains. **-pfalz,** *f.* the Palatinate; *der -fürst von der Pfalz* or *von -pfalz*, the Elector Palatine. **-prinz,** *m.* elector's heir. **-recht,** *n.* right of electing (*the emperor*). **-würde,** *f.* electoral dignity, electorship.

kurant [*pron.* kuː'rant] 1. *adj.* current, in demand. 2. *n.* currency; current coin, coin of the realm. 3. *m.* (-en, -en) (*Swiss dial.*), *see* **Kurgast.**

kuranzen, koranzen, *v.a.* (*coll.*) scold, punish.

Küraß, *m.* (-(ss)es, -(ss)e) cuirass. **-(ss)ier,** *m.* cuirassier, dragoon.

Kurat-el, *f.* (-en) guardianship, tutelage, protection; *einen unter -el stellen*, put a p. in charge of a guardian. **-or,** *m.* (-s, -en) curator, guardian, commissioner, (*Austr. dial.*) executor, trustee. **-orium,** *n.* board of trustees, governing body; (semi-official) board.

Kurbel, *f.* (-n) handle, crank; starting-handle (*Motor.*); winch. **-bewegung,** *f.*, **-ei,** *f.* twisting and turning, (*sl.*) dog-fight (*Av.*). **-gehäuse,** *n.*

crank-case. **-getriebe,** *n.* crank-action *or* mechanism. (*sl.*) **-kasten,** *m.* film-camera. **-lager,** *n.* crank-bracket. **-mast,** *m.* extending *or* telescopic mast. **-n,** *v.n.* (*aux.* h.) crank, turn (*the winch*); reel off, wind; *einen Film -n,* run off *or* take a film. **-pumpe,** *f.* reciprocating pump. **-rad,** *n.* hand-wheel. **-stange,** *f.* connecting-rod (*in locomotives*). **-welle,** *f.* crankshaft. **-zapfen,** *m.* crank-pin.

Kurbett-e, *f.* curvet (*of a horse*). **-ieren,** *v.n.* curvet.

Kürbis, *m.* (-ses, -se) pumpkin, gourd. **-baum,** *m.* calabash-tree. **-flasche,** *f.* gourd. **-gewächse,** *n.pl.* cucurbitaceous plants.

kür-en, *v.a.* (*archaic & poet.*) choose, elect. **-turnen,** *n.* exercises at discretion, free gymnastics.

Kurfürst, *see* [3]**Kur.**

Kuri-alstil, *m.* (*archaic*) legal *or* official style. **-e,** *f.* (-en) curia; papal court; legislative assembly; *Herren-e,* assembly of nobles.

Kurier, *m.* (-s, -e) courier; express messenger; (*als*) - *reiten,* ride express. **-stiefel,** *m.* jack-boot.

kurieren, *see* [1]**Kur.**

kurios, *adj.* (*archaic*) singular, odd, curious, strange; *mir ist ganz - zu Mute,* I feel queer. **-ität,** *f.* curiosity; rarity.

Kurr-e, *f.* (-en) trawl, dredge, trammel (*fishing*); (*dial.*) turkey-hen. **-en,** *v.a. & n.* (*aux.* h.) (*dial.*) coo; gobble. (*dial.*) **-ig,** *adj.* fiery, untamed, excitable; moody, surly. **-hahn,** *m.* (*dial.*) turkey-cock.

Kurrend-aner, *m.* (*archaic*) itinerant choir-boy. **-e,** *f.* (-n) 1. (*archaic*) itinerant boys' choir; 2. round robin, circular letter.

kurrent, *adj.* cursive. **-schrift,** *f.* script, running hand; italics. **-schuld,** *f.* running score.

Kurs, *m.* (-es, -e) 1. (*C.L.*) (rate of) exchange, quotation; circulation. 2. course (*of a ship*); *welchen - geben Sie für diesen Wechsel?* what rate do you give for this bill? *die -e sind gefallen,* the exchange has fallen; *der - ist pari,* exchange is at par; *in - setzen,* circulate; *außer - setzen,* call in; *rechtweisender -,* true course; *mißweisender -,* magnetic course; *den - besetzen* or *bestimmen,* plot a course; *den - absetzen* or *nehmen,* shape a course; *vom - abkommen* or *abweichen,* deviate from course. **-änderung,** *f.* change of course. **-bericht,** *m.* market quotations. **-buch,** *n.* time-table, railway guide. **-festsetzung,** *f.* rate-fixing. **-ieren,** *v.n.* (*aux.* h.) circulate, be current. **-makler,** *m.* stockbroker. **-notierung,** *f.* quotation of exchanges. **-schwankungen,** *f.pl.* fluctuations in the exchange. **-stand,** *m.* rate of exchange. **-steuerung,** *f.* auto-pilot (*Av.*). **-sturz,** *m.* fall in prices. **-us,** *m.* (-, Kurse) course (*of lectures, etc.*), course of instruction. **-weiser,** *m.* radio beacon (*Naut.*). **-wert,** *m.* exchange value. **-zettel,** *m.* stock-exchange list.

Kürsch, *m.* or *n.* fur (*Her.*). **-ner,** *m.* (-s, -) furrier. **-nerei,** *f.* furrier's trade; furriery. **-nerware,** *f.* furs and skins.

kursiv, *adj.* in italics; *- gedruckt,* italicized. **-druck,** *m.*, **-schrift,** *f.* italics.

Kursus, *see* **Kurs-us.**

Kurtine, *f.* (-n) curtain (*Fort.*).

Kurtisan, *m.* (-s, -e) (*archaic*) courtier; parasite. **-e,** *f.* courtesan.

Kurve, *f.* (-n) curve, bend, turn; *in die - gehen,* bank (*Av.*); *gezogene -,* climbing turn (*Av.*); *ballistische -,* trajectory. **-n,** *v.n.* turn, bank, go into a turn. **-nbild,** *n.*, **-ndarstellung,** *f.* graph. **-ngleitflug,** *m.* spiral glide (*Av.*). **-nkampf,** *m.* dog-fight (*Av.*). **-nkampftüchtig,** *adj.* manœuvrable (*of aircraft*). **-nschar,** *f.* set *or* system of curves *or* graphs.

kurz, (*comp.* kürzer, *sup.* kürzest) 1. *adj.* short, brief; abrupt; summary, concise, compendious, concentrated; *- abbrechen,* break off *or* end abruptly; *- abfertigen,* be short with, dismiss abruptly; *- abweisen,* cut (*a p.*) short; *- angebunden sein,* be curt *or* brusque; *-en Atem haben,* be asthmatic *or* short of breath; *binnen -em,* within a short time; *- und bündig,* concise, succinct; *- danach* or *darauf,* a little while *or* not long afterwards; *- eingekocht,* boiled down *or* away, concentrated; *sich - fassen,* be brief, express o.s. briefly; *-es Futter,* corn, oats, *etc.* (*opp. to langes Futter,* hay, straw, *etc.*); *-er Galopp,* canter; *- und gut,* in a word, in short, to come to the point; *einen - halten,* keep a p. short (*of money, etc.*); *in -em,* soon, shortly, ere long; *- und klein hauen* or *schlagen,* cut to pieces, smash to bits, beat to a jelly; (*coll.*) *etwas - kriegen,* get the knack of a thing; *über - oder lang,* sooner or later; *um es - zu machen,* to sum up, to be short, to cut a long story short; *-es Papier,* short(-dated) bills; *-en Prozeß mit einem* (*einer S.*) *machen,* make short work of a p. (a matter); *ihr wird die Schürze zu -,* she is in the family way; *seit -em,* lately; *-e Sicht,* short sight; (*C.L.*) short-date; *der langen Rede -er Sinn,* the pith of the matter; *- treten,* mark time; *vor -em,* recently, the other day, only just, not long ago; *bis vor -em,* until quite recently; *- vorher,* a little while before, a short time previously; *-e Wechsel,* (*pl.*), see *-es Papier*; *den Kürzeren ziehen,* get the worst of it, be the loser; *zu - kommen,* come off badly. 2. *adv.* in short, in a word, briefly. **-ab,** *adv.* briefly, in a few words, abruptly. **-angriff,** *m.* tip-and-run raid (*Av.*). **-arbeit,** *f.* short-time (work). **-ärmelig,** *adj.* short-sleeved. **-armig,** *adj.* short-armed; short-beamed. **-atmig,** *adj.* short-winded, asthmatic; broken-winded. **-brüchig,** *adj.* brittle, short (*of pastry*). **-dauernd,** *adj.* transient, short-lived, brief. **-e,** *f.* (-n, -n) (*dial.*) shorts. **-erhand,** *adv.* briefly, abruptly; *-erhand abtun,* make short work of. **-flügelig,** *adj.* brachypterous. **-form,** *f.* abbreviation. (*C.L.*) **-fristig,** *adj.* at short sight, short-dated; of short duration, for a limited time. **-gefaßt,** *adj.* brief, concise; compact, succinct. **-geschichte,** *f.* short story. **-geschoren,** *adj.* close-cropped. **-haarig,** *adj.* short-haired. **-lebig,** *adj.* shortlived. **-schäd(e)ig,** *adj.* brachycephalic. **-schäftig,** *adj.* short-bodied. **-schließer,** *m.* earth switch *or* cut-out (*Elec.*). **-schluß,** *m.* short circuit (*Elec.*). **-schlußklemme,** *f.* shunt (*Elec.*). **-schreiber,** *m.* short-hand-writer. **-schrift,** *f.* shorthand, stenography. **-schuß,** *m.* short (*Artil.*). **-sichtig,** *adj.* near-sighted, short-sighted; of short date (*as bills*). **-sichtigkeit,** short *or* near sightedness, myopia. **-silbig,** *adj.* short-spoken, reserved, taciturn; *-silbiger Mann,* man of few words. **-sinnig,** *adj.* narrow-minded, **-streckenläufer,** *m.* sprinter. **-um,** *adv.* in short, to sum up. **-waren,** *f.pl.* haberdashery. **-weg,** *adv.* simply, plainly, offhand, curtly; only; *einen -weg Fritz nennen,* call a p. simply Freddy. **-weil,** *f.* pastime, amusement; *seine -weil mit einem haben,* make sport of a p., (*coll.*) rag a p. **-weilig,** *adj.* entertaining, amusing, pleasant. **-wellen,** *f.pl.* short waves (*Rad.*). **-wellensender,** *m.* short-wave transmitter (*Rad.*).

Kürz-e, *f.* shortness, brevity, conciseness; short space of time; short syllable; *in -e,* shortly, soon; *in aller -e,* with all possible dispatch; *sich der -e befleißigen,* be brief; (*Prov.*) *in der -e liegt die Würze,* brevity is the soul of wit. **-el,** *n.* (-s, -) logogram, grammalogue (*Shorthand*). **-en,** *v.a.* shorten; abbreviate, abridge; curtail, cut, diminish; simplify (*Maths.*); (*dial.*) *einen um etwas -en,* withhold s.th. from a p., refuse to grant s.th. to a p. **-lich,** *adv.* lately, not long ago, recently. **-ung,** *f.* shortening; abbreviation; retrenchment, reduction, cut. **-ungsfett,** *n.* shortening (*Cook.*).

kusch-eln, *v.r.* cuddle *or* snuggle up (to *or* against). **-en,** *v.r. & n.* (*aux.* h.) crouch, lie down; (*fig.*) do as one is told, submit; *kusch* (*dich*)*!* (lie) down! (*to dogs*).

Kusine, *f.* (female) cousin.

Kuß, *m.* (-(ss)es, ¨-(ss)e) kiss; (*Prov.*) *einen - in Ehren kann niemand verwehren,* an innocent kiss comes never amiss. **-echt, -fest,** *adj.* kiss-proof (*of lipstick*). **-hand,** *f.* blown kiss; *jemandem eine -hand zuwerfen,* kiss one's hand to a p., throw s.o. a kiss; (*coll.*) *mit -hand tun,* do with alacrity.

küssen, *v.a. & n.* (*aux.* h.) & *v.r.* kiss; *er küßte sie* (*ihre Hand* or *ihr die Hand*), he kissed her (her hand); *er küßte sie auf die Stirn,* he kissed her (on the) forehead; *sie küßten sich heiß,* they kissed

passionately. **–erig,** *adj.* **küßlich,** *adj.*, **küßrig,** *adj.* kissable, made for kissing.
Küste, *f.* (-n) coast, shore; *das Land längs der –*, the littoral; *an der – hinfahren*, coast, sail along a coast; *die – entlang*, coastwise; *angesichts der Waliser –*, off the Welsh coast. **–naufnahme,** *f.* coastal survey. **–nbefeu(e)rung,** *f.* shore lights. **–nfahrer,** *m.* coaster, coasting vessel. **–nfahrt,** *f.* coasting. **–nhandel,** *m.* coastal trade. **–nland,** *n.* littoral. **–nlotse,** *m.* inshore pilot. **–nprovinz,** *f.* maritime province. **–nschiffahrt,** *f.* coastal shipping. **–nschutzflottille,** *f.* light coastal forces (*Nav.*). **–nstrich,** *m.* coastline, strip of coast. **–ntelegraph,** *m.* semaphore. **–nversetzung,** *f.* change in the coastline. **–nwache,** *f.* coastguard; coastguard station.
Küster, *m.* (-s, –) verger, sexton, sacristan.
Kustos, *m.* (–, Kustoden) keeper, custodian, curator; catchword (*Typ.*); direction (*Mus.*).
Kute, *f.* (-n) (*dial.*) pit, hole.
Kutsch–bock, *m.* coachman's seat, box. **–e,** *f.* (-en) carriage, coach. **–en,** *see* **–ieren.** **–er,** *m.* coachman, driver, (*sl.*) pilot (*Av.*). (*coll.*) **–er(spiel),** *n.* game with a very good hand (*Cards*). **–ieren,** *v.n.* (*aux.* h. & s.) go driving, drive (in) a carriage *or* coach. **–kasten,** *m.* boot, box (*under the seat of a coach*).
Kutte, *f.* (-n) cowl; *die – anlegen*, don the cowl, turn monk; (*Prov.*) *die – macht nicht den Mönch*, all is not gold that glitters.
Kuttel, *f.* (-n) (*dial.*) entrails. **–fleck,** *m.* (-(e)s, -e) tripe, offal. **–kraut,** *n.* (*Austr. dial.*) thyme.
Kutter, *m.* (-s, –) cutter (*Naut.*).
Kuvert, *n.* (-(e)s, (*with French pronun.*) -s, (*otherwise*) -e) (*archaic*) envelope, wrapper; cover (*plate, knife, fork, etc.*); *trockne –*, dinner exclusive of wine. **–ieren,** *v.a.* put in an envelope, pack for posting.
Küvette, *f.* tray, trough, vessel, wash-bowl; draining trench (*Fort.*); (inner) dust cover (of watch-case).
Kux, *m.* (-es, -e) mining share.

L

L, l, *n.* L, l.
Lab, *n.* rennet. **–drüse,** *f.* peptic gland. **–en,** *v.a.* coagulate *or* curdle with rennet. **–kraut,** *n.* galium. **–magen,** *m.* fourth stomach of ruminants, rennet-bag.
Labb–e, *f.* (-en) hanging lip; (*vulg.*) mouth, gob; long-tailed gull (*Orn.*). **–(e)rig,** *adj.* insipid, pappy. **–ern,** *v.a.* & *n.* (*aux.* h.) lap, lick up, slobber; talk twaddle, blab.
Lab–e, *f.* (-en) (*Poet.*) refreshment; tonic; comfort. **–en,** 1. *v.a.* refresh, revive, restore; comfort, delight. 2. *v.r.*; *sich mit Speisen –en*, take some refreshment; *sich an einer Speise –en*, enjoy a dish thoroughly; *seine Augen –ten sich an dem Anblick*, he feasted his eyes on the sight. 3. *v.n.* (*dial.*), *see* **labbern.** **–ebecher,** *m.*, **–ekelch,** *m.*, **–etrunk,** *m.* refreshing draught, cordial. **–mittel,** *n.* refreshment, restorative. **–sal,** *n.* (-s, -e), **–ung,** *f.*, *see* **–e.**
Laberdan, *m.* (-s, -e) salted cod.
labil, *adj.* variable, unstable, changeable, unsteady, vacillating, unsettled. **–ität,** *f.* instability.
Labor–ant, *m.* (-en, -en) laboratory assistant. **–atorium,** *n.* (-iums, -ien) laboratory. **–ieren,** *v.n.* (*aux.* h.) (*an* or *unter with Dat.*) be afflicted with, suffer from, labour under; do laboratory work.
[1]**Lach–e,** *f.* (-en) notch; blaze, face (*on a tree*). **–en,** *v.a.* cut *or* blaze trees. **–baum,** *m.* marked *or* blazed tree; boundary-tree.
[2]**Lache,** *f.* (-n) pool, puddle.
[3]**Lach–e,** *f.* laugh, laughter; *eine –e aufschlagen*, burst out laughing. **–en,** 1. *v.n.* (*aux.* h.) laugh; *über einen* or *eine S. –en*, laugh at a p. *or* a th.; *aus vollem Halse –en*, laugh heartily *or* uproariously; *–en daß einem die Augen übergehen*, laugh until the tears come; *in die Faust –en* or *sich* (*Dat.*) *ins Fäustchen –en*, laugh in one's sleeve; *du kannst wohl –en*, you may consider yourself lucky; *hier ist nichts zu –en*, there is nothing to laugh at; *das ist nicht zum –en*, that is no laughing matter *or* no joke; *ihm –t das Herz im Leibe*, his heart leaps for joy, his heart rejoices; *das Glück –t ihm*, Fortune smiles upon him; (*Prov.*) *wer zuletzt –t, –t am besten*, those laugh best who laugh last. 2. *a.*; *sich tot, schief, krumm, krank* or *bucklig, sich* (*Dat.*) *einem Buckel* or *den Buckel voll –en*, die *or* split one's sides with laughing, laugh o.s. silly. 3. *n.* laughter, laugh; *das ist zum –en*, that is ridiculous; *einen zum –en bringen*, make s.o. laugh; *sich des –ens nicht erwehren können*, not be able to restrain one's laughter *or* to contain o.s. for laughter; *nicht aus dem –en kommen*, not be able to stop laughing; *sich* (*Dat.*) *das –en verbeißen*, choke one's laughter; *unter –en*, laughingly. **–anfall,** *m.* laughing fit. **–end,** *pr.p.* & *adj.* laughing, smiling; pleasant, glad. **–gas,** *n.* laughing-gas. **–haft,** *adj.* laughable, ridiculous. **–krampf,** *m.* fit *or* paroxysm of laughter. **–lustig,** *adj.* cheery, light-hearted, merry, hilarious. **–taube,** *f.* collared turtle dove (*Turtur risorius*) (*Orn.*); (*sl.*) merry girl.
läch–eln, 1. *v.n.* (*aux.* h.) smile (*über einen* or *eine S.*, at a p. *or* a th.); *einem –eln*, smile upon *or* at a p.; *albern –eln*, simper, snigger; *geziert –eln*, smirk; *höhnisch* or *spöttisch –eln*, sneer. 2. *v.a.* smile (*approval, etc.*). 3. *n.* smile; simper; sneer. (*sl.*) **–erbar,** *adj.*, *see* **–erlich.** **–erig,** *adj.* (*dial.* & *coll.*) giggly. **–erlich,** *adj.* laughable; ridiculous; droll, comical; *sich –erlich machen*, make a fool of o.s.; *etwas ins –erliche ziehen*, make s.th. appear ridiculous; *einen –erlich machen*, make fun of *or* ridicule s.o., turn a p. into ridicule; *mir ist gar nicht –erlich zu Mute*, I am in no laughing mood; *–erlich billig*, ridiculously cheap. **–erlichkeit,** *f.* absurdity, ridicule; *er kümmert sich nicht um solche –erlichkeiten*, he does not bother about such trivialities. **–ern,** *v.a.*, (*coll.*) *es –ert mich*, it makes me laugh.
Lachs, *m.* (-es, -e) salmon; a Danzig brandy. **–brut,** *f.* salmon fry. **–farben, –farbig,** *adj.* salmon-pink. **–forelle,** *f.* salmon-trout. **–reuse,** *f.* salmon-weir. **–schinken,** *m.* lightly salted and smoked cut of lean pork.
Lachter, *n.* (-s, –) & *f.* (-n) (*archaic*) fathom.
Lack, *m.* (-(e)s, -e) varnish, lacquer, lac; *der – der Zivilisation*, the veneer of civilization. **–arbeit,** *f.* japanned *or* lacquered work. **–en,** *see* **–ieren.** **–farbe,** *f.* enamel paint. **–firnis,** *m.* lacquer, varnish. **–ieren,** *v.a.* lacquer, varnish, enamel, japan; (*coll.*) cheat, impose upon, hoodwink, dupe, hoax, take in; (*coll.*) *da war ich der –ierte*, I was the dupe *or* (*coll.*) the mug. **–leder,** *n.* patent leather.
Lackmus, *n.* litmus.
Lade, *f.* (-n) box, chest, case; drawer; sounding board (*of organs*).
Lad–ebaum, *m.* derrick, jib. **–ebereit,** *adj.* ready to take in cargo. (*C.L.*) **–ebrief,** *m.* bill of lading; *see also under* **laden.** **–ebühne,** *f.* loading platform. **–edamm,** *m.* jetty, landing stage. **–efähig,** *adj.* serviceable (*of ammunition*). **–egeld,** *n.* charge for lading. **–egewicht,** *n.* deadweight tonnage (*Naut.*). **–ehemmung,** *f.* jam, stoppage (*machine-gun*). **–elinie,** *f.* load-line, Plimsoll('s) mark. **–eloch,** *n.* chamber (*Artil.*). **–emaschine,** *f.* battery charger (*Elec.*). **–en,** 1. *ir.v.a.* load, lade, freight; load (*a gun*); charge (*Elec.*); *blind –en*, load with blank cartridge; *scharf –en*, load with ball; *ins Schiff –en*, ship; (*sl.*) *er hat schwer* or *schief geladen*, he is half-seas-over; *auf sich* (*Acc.*) *–en*, bring down upon o.s., incur; *ein Verbrechen auf sich –en*, commit a crime. 2. *m. see* **Laden.** **–eplatz,** *m.* wharf, landing stage, loading point. **–er,** *m.* loader; longshoreman. **–erampe,** *f.* loading-platform. **–eraum,** *m.* (ship's) hold; chamber (*Artil.*). **–eschein,** *m.*, *see* **–ebrief.** **–espannung,** *f.* charging voltage (*Elec.*). **–estation,** *f.* battery-charging station. **–estock,** *m.* rammer, ramrod. **–estörung,** *f.*, *see* **–ehemmung.** **–estreifen,** *m.* cartridge belt (*machine-gun*), cartridge-clip (*rifle*). **–estrom,** *m.* charging current (*Elec.*). **–etisch,** *m.* loading tray

(*Artil.*). **-ung,** *f.* loading, lading; freight, cargo; load, burden; charge (*ammunition & Elec.*); *in -ung liegendes Schiff*, vessel taking in cargo; *in -ung liegen nach*, be loading for; *die -ung anbrechen*, break bulk; *-ung einnehmen*, take on cargo *or* freight; *ohne -ung*, empty, in ballast; *volle -ung*, full freight; *geballte -ung*, concentrated charge; Bangalore torpedo (*Mil.*); *gestreckte -ung*, distributed charge. **-ungsfähigkeit,** *f.* tonnage (*of a ship*). **-ungsflasche,** *f.* Leyden jar. **-ungsinteressent,** *m.* part-owner of a cargo. **-ungsraum,** *m.*, *see* **-eraum. -ungsverzeichnis,** *n.* ship's manifest, freight-list.

lad-en, *ir.v.a.* invite; cite, summon. **-ebrief,** *m.* summons (*Law*); *see also under* **Lad-. -egeld,** *n.* fee paid for a summons (*Law*). **-ung,** *f.* invitation; summons, citation.

Laden, *m.* (-s, - & ¨-) 1. shutter, window-shutter. 2. shop, stall, store; *einen - anlegen*, set up a shop; *einen - halten*, keep a shop; *dieser Artikel verkauft sich gut im -*, this article sells well over the counter. **-bank,** *f.* counter. **-besitzer,** *m.* shopkeeper. **-dieb,** *m.* shoplifter. **-diebstahl,** *m.* shoplifting. **-diener,** *m.* (*archaic*), *see* **-gehilfe. -einbruch,** *m.* smash-and-grab raid. **-fenster,** *n.* shop-window, show-case. **-gaumer,** *m.* (*Swiss dial.*), *see* **-hüter. -gehilfe,** *m.* shop-assistant. **-hüter,** *m.* (*sl.*) white elephant, drug in the market. **-inhaber,** *m.*, *see* **-besitzer. -kasse,** *f.* cash-desk, till. **-mädchen,** *n.* (*Austr. dial.* **Ladnerin,** *f.*) shop-girl. **-preis,** *m.* selling price, retail price; published price (*of books*). **-schluß,** *m.* shop-closing, closing-time. (*sl.*) **-schwengel,** *m.* counter-jumper. **-tisch,** *m.* counter. **-tochter,** *f.* (*Swiss dial.*), *see* **-mädchen.**

lädieren, *v.a.* hurt, injure.

Ladnerin, *see* **Ladenmädchen.**

lädst, *see* **laden.**

Ladung, *see* **Lade** and [2]**laden.**

Lafette, *f.* (-n) gun-carriage; *auf die - bringen* or *heben*, mount a gun; *von der - abheben*, dismount a gun. **-nkreuz,** *n.* outriggers, gun-legs. **-nrücklauf,** *m.* recoil. **-nschwanz,** *m.* trail. **-nsporn,** *m.* trail spade. **-nwand,** *f.* bracket *or* cheek.

Laffe, 1. *f.* (*dial.*) bowl (*of a spoon*). 2. *m.* (-n, -n), fop, dandy, (*fig.*) puppy. (*fig.*) **-nmäßig,** *adj.* puppyish.

lag, läge, *see* **liegen.**

Lage, *f.* (-n) situation, position, site, locality, location, attitude, posture; guard (*Fenc.*); state, condition, circumstances; layer, stratum, course (*Arch.*); covering, film, coat (*of paint*); harmonic arrangement (*of a chord*) (*Mus.*); register, compass (*Mus.*); position (*of fingering with stringed instruments*); quire (*of paper*); round (*of drinks*); *Oktav-*, common chord, *Terz-* (*Quint-*), 1st (2nd) inversion; *in der - sein*, be in a position (to); *bei dieser - der Dinge* or *dieser Sach-*, in these circumstances; *eine schlimme* or *böse -*, a difficult situation; *das ändert die (ganze) -*, that puts (quite) a new face on things; *nach - der Dinge*, as things stand; *einen in eine schiefe* or *mißliche - bringen*, misrepresent a p.'s position, put a p. in an awkward position; *außer -*, off one's guard (*Fenc.*); *ein Schiff mit drei -n*, a three-decker; *volle -*, broadside (*Naut.*). **-beziehung,** *f.* relative position. **-fest,** *adj.* stable. **-festigkeit,** *f.* stability. **-nfeuer,** *n.* salvo, continuous fire. **-nstaffel,** *f.* mixed-style relay race (*Swimming*). **-nweise,** *adv.* in layers; in tiers; in strata. **-plan,** *m.* plan of a site.

Lägel, *n.* (-s, -) (*dial.*) barrel, keg, cask; hank (*of cord*); cringle (*Naut.*).

Lager, *n.* (-s, - & *C.L.* ¨-) 1. storehouse, warehouse, depot, dump, store, stock, supply. 2. camp, encampment; (*fig.*) party, side. 3. stratum, stroma, layer. 4. couch, bed; lair, den, hole, cover, *etc.* (*of beasts*). 5. dregs, sediments. 6. bearing (*Engin.*); *auf(s) - bringen*, warehouse, put into store; *das - aufnehmen*, take an inventory of stock in hand; *auf - haben*, stock, have on hand, keep in stock; *dies fehlt auf -*, this is out of stock; *ein - aufschlagen* (*abstecken*), pitch (mark out) a camp, pitch one's tent *or* tents; *- abbrechen*, strike camp; *ein - beziehen*, move into camp; *ins feindliche - übergehen*, go over to the enemy; *ein unruhiges - haben*, be a restless sleeper, have a restless night; *vom - aufstehen*, rise from a bed of sickness. **-arrest,** *m.* confinement to camp *or* barracks, (*sl.*) jankers (*Mil.*). **-aufnahme,** *f.* stock-taking, inventory. **-aufseher,** *m.* store-keeper. **-bestand,** *m.* inventory, stock. **-beständig,** *adj.* unaffected by storage. **-bier,** *n.* beer brewed for keeping, lager (beer). **-buch,** *n.* stock-book. **-büchse,** *f.* bushing (*Engin.*). **-diener,** *m.* warehouse-clerk. **-fest,** *adj.*, *see* **-beständig. -feuer,** *n.* camp-fire. **-förmig,** *adj.* in layers *or* strata. **-gebühren,** *f.pl.*, **-geld,** *n.* charge for storage, warehouse charges. **-getreide,** *n.* grain laid *or* flattened by wind *or* rain. **-haus,** *n.* warehouse. **-holz,** *n.* fallen timber, tree uprooted by storm. **-hütte,** *f.* camp-hut; barrack. **-ist,** *m.* warehouse-clerk, store-keeper. **-kosten,** *f.pl.* warehouse charges. **-leben,** *n.* camp-life. **-miete,** *f.*, *see* **-geld. -n,** 1. *v.n.* (*aux.* h. & s.) & *v.r.* lie down, rest; camp, be encamped; be stored *or* deposited, be in store; lie spread out. 2. *v.a.* lay down; deposit, pile, place, post; encamp (*troops*), pitch (*tents*); store, lay up. 3. *n.*, *see* **-ung. -obst,** *n.* fruit for keeping. **-platz,** *m.* storage place, depot, dump; bed (*Geol.*); camping place, camp site; resting-place. **-raum,** *m.* store-room, warehouse. **-reibung,** *f.* bearing friction (*Engin.*). **-schale,** *f.* bearing-housing, axle-box. **-statt,** *f.*, **-stätte,** *f.* resting-place; couch, bed; lodging; encampment. **-ung,** *f.* arrangement; orientation; recumbent position; encampment; storing, storage, deposition, warehousing; stratification. **-wache,** *f.* camp-guard. **-wand,** *f.* solid rock wall. **-wein,** *m.* wine for keeping; wine that keeps. **-zapfen,** *m.* trunnion, journal (*Engin.*).

lägerig, *suffix* (*in compounds* =) -lying, *e.g.* **bettlägerig,** *adj.* lying in bed, confined to one's bed.

Lagune, *f.* (-n) lagoon.

lahm, *adj.* lame, crippled; paralysed, (*archaic*) halt; weak, impotent, paltry; *ein -er, eine -e*, a lame person, a cripple; *eine -e Entschuldigung*, a poor excuse. **-en,** *v.n.* (*aux.* h. & s.); *- gehen*, walk with a limp, be lame, limp. **-heit,** *f.* lameness. **-legen,** *v.a.* paralyse, bring to a standstill, make useless. **-schießen,** *v.a.* damage *or* cripple (*a vehicle, etc.*) by gunfire (*Mil.*).

Lähm-e, *f.* spring-halt (*Vet.*). **-en,** *v.a.* cripple, lame, disable, paralyse; stop, hinder. **-ung,** *f.* lameness, paralysis, palsy.

Lahn, *m.* (-(e)s, -e) metal foil, tinsel. **-tresse,** *f.* gold *or* silver lace.

Lai, *n.* (-s, -s) (*usually pl.*) lay, song (*of Celtic and Old French minstrels*).

Laib, *m.* (-(e)s, -e) loaf (*of bread*); *ein - Käse*, a whole cheese.

Laich, *m.* (-(e)s, -e) spawn. **-e,** *f.* spawning-time. **-en,** *v.n.* (*aux.* h.) spawn. **-kraut,** *n.* pond-weed (*Pontamogeton*). **-teich,** *m.* breeding-pond. **-zeit,** *f.*, *see* **-e.**

Laie, *m.* (-n, -n) layman; novice, uninitiated p., amateur; (*pl.*) the laity. **-nbruder,** *m.* lay-brother. **-ngüter,** *n.pl.* temporalities. **-nhaft,** *adj.* lay, belonging to the laity; uninitiated, non-professional, amateur. **-npriester,** *m.* lay-reader. **-nrichter,** *m.* lay-judge, magistrate, (*Engl.*) justice of the peace. **-nspiel,** *n.* amateur theatricals. **-nstand,** *m.*, **-nwelt,** *f.* laity, laymen.

Lakai, *m.* (-en, -en) lackey, flunkey. **-enhaft,** *adj.* flunkey-like, cringing. **-ensitz,** *m.* dicky, rumble.

Lake, *f.* (-n) brine, pickle.

Laken, *m.* & *n.* (-s, -) (*dial.*) dust-cloth, sheet; tablecloth; shroud.

lakonisch, *adj.* laconic.

Lakritz-en, *m.* (-en, -en), (*Austr. dial.* **-e,** f. (-n)) (Spanish) liquorice.

lala, (*coll.*); *so -*, so-so, middling, pretty well, not so bad, nothing to boast of, (*sl.*) not so dusty.

lallen, *v.a.* & *n.* (*aux.* h.) stammer; babble, speak indistinctly.

Lama, 1. *m.* (-(s), -s) lama (*Buddhist priest*). 2. *n.* (-(s), -s) llama.

Lambertsnuß, *f.* filbert, hazel-nut.

Lamell-e, *f.* (en) lamella, lamina, lamination (*Elec.*);

layer, segment. **-enkupplung,** *f.* plate-clutch (*Motor.*). **-ieren,** *v.a.* laminate; *-ierter Kern,* laminated core.

lament-ieren, *v.n.* complain, whine, murmur, (*coll.*) moan, (*sl.*) belly-ache. **-o,** *n.* (-(s), -s) lamentation, wail.

Lametta, *f.* lametta, angels' hair (*decoration on Christmas-trees*).

laminieren, *v.a.* flatten (*metal*), laminate.

Lamm, *n.* (-(e)s, ¨er) lamb. **-braten,** *m.* roast lamb. **-(e)sgeduld,** *f.* patience of Job. **-fell,** *n.* lamb's skin. **-fleisch,** *n.* lamb. **-en,** *v.a.* (*aux.* h.) lamb. **-fromm,** *adj.*, **-herzig,** *adj.* gentle as a lamb. **-zeit,** *f.* lambing-time.

Lämmer-chen, *n.* lambkin; (*pl.*) lambs' tails, fleecy clouds; catkins. **-geier,** *m.* lammergeyer, great bearded vulture (*Gypaetus barbatus*) (*Orn.*). (*coll.*) **-hüpfen,** *n.* dancing, frisking, frolicking (*young girls without male partners*). **schwänzchen,** *n.* lamb's tail, yarrow (*Bot.*); (*coll.*) *lustig wie ein -schwänzchen,* as merry as a cricket. **-wolke,** *f.* cirrus. **-wolle,** *f.* lamb's-wool.

Lampe, *f.* (-n) lamp; (*pl.*) footlights (*Theat.*) **-nbrenner,** *m.* burner. **-ndocht,** *m.* (lamp-) wick. **-nfaden,** *m.* lighting filament. **-nfassung,** *f.* light- *or* lamp-fitting. **-nfieber,** *n.* stage-fright. **-ngestell,** *n.* lamp-post. **-nglocke,** *f.* lampshade, globe. **-nhell,** *adj.* lit up *or* lighted by lamps. **-nlicht,** *n.* lamplight, artificial light. **-nruß,** *m.* lamp-black. **-nschein,** *m.*, **-nschimmer,** *m.* light of a lamp. **-nschirm,** *m.* lampshade. **-nzylinder,** *m.* (lamp-)chimney.

Lampion, *m.* & *n.* (-s, -s) Chinese lantern.

Lamprete, *f.* (-n) lamprey; (*coll.*) tit-bit, luxury.

lancier-en, *v.a.* fling, thrust, push, launch. **-rohr,** *n.* torpedo-tube.

Land, 1. *n.* land (*as opp. to water*); country (*as opp. to town*); soil, earth, ground, arable land. 2. *n.* (-(e)s, ¨er & (*poet.*) -e) country, region, realm, territory, province, state; *an – gehen* or *ans – steigen,* land, go ashore; *auf das – gehen,* go into the country; *auf dem* (*Austr. dial. am*) *-e,* in the country; *aus aller Herren Ländern,* from all countries, from all over the world; *außer -es,* abroad; *– der Elfen,* fairyland; *festes –,* terra firma, mainland; *seitdem sind viele Tage ins – gegangen,* since then much water has flowed under the bridges; *plattes* or *flaches –,* low country, plain; *– und Leute regieren,* govern a country; *– sehen,* be near one's goal; *– der Träume* dreamland; *über –,* by land, overland; *des -es verwiesen,* exiled; *vom -e stoßen,* put to sea, push off from the bank; *Einfalt* (or *Unschuld* or *Gänschen*) *vom -e,* simple country maid, country cousin; *zu -e,* by land. **-adel,** *m.* landed gentry. **-ammann,** *m.* (*pl.* -männer) (*Swiss dial.*) cantonal president. **-anker,** *m.* shore-anchor. **-anwachs,** *m.* alluvium. **-arbeit,** *f.* agricultural labour. **-arbeiter,** *m.* farm labourer, farm-hand. **-arzt,** *m.* country doctor. **-aus,** *adv.*; *-aus, -ein,* far afield. **-bank,** *f.* farmer's bank. **-bar,** *adj.* fit for landing; accessible. **-bau,** *m.* agriculture. **-besitz,** *m.* landed property. **-besitzer,** *m.* landed proprietor. **-bewohner,** *m.* country dweller. **-bezirk,** *m.* country district. **-buch,** *n.* land register. **-bund,** *m.* Farmers' Union. **-ebahn,** *f.* runway (*Av.*). **-edeck,** *n.* flying deck (*Naut.*). **-edelmann,** *m.* country squire. **-eerlaubnis,** *f.* landing permit. **-egeschwindigkeit,** *f.* landing speed (*Av.*). **-eigentum,** *n.* landed property. **-eigentümer,** *m.*, **-eig(e)ner,** *m.* landed proprietor. **-einwärts,** *adv.* up country, inland. **-eklappe,** *f.* landing flap (*Av.*). **-en,** 1. *v.n.* (*aux.* h. & s.) land, disembark, get ashore, alight; touch down (*Av.*). 2. *v.a.* land (*troops, a blow*). **-enge,** *f.* isthmus. **-erad,** *n.* landing wheel (*Av.*). **-erbe,** *m.* heir to landed property. **-erziehungsheim,** *n.* country boarding-school. **-esangehörigkeit,** *f.* nationality. **-esanleihe,** *f.* domestic loan. **-esarchiv,** *n.* national archives. **-esart,** *f.* soil and climate of a country; national character and customs. **-esaufnahme,** *f.* ordnance survey; topography. **-esaufnahmestelle,** *f.* survey office. **-esbank,** *f.* national bank. **-esbeschaffenheit,** *f.*, *see* **-esart.** **-esbeschreibung,** *f.* topography. **-esbrauch,** *m.* national custom. **-eserzeugnis,** *n.* home produce. **-esfarben,** *f.pl.* national colours. **-esflagge,** *f.* national flag. **-esfürst,** *m.* reigning prince, sovereign. **-esgebiet,** *n.* national territory. **-esgebrauch,** *m.*, *see* **-esbrauch.** **-esgericht,** *n.* assize court. **-esgesetz,** *n.* law of the land. **-esgewächs,** *n.* home-grown produce, indigenous flora. **-esgrenze,** *f.* national boundary *or* frontier. **-esherr,** *m.* ruler, sovereign. **-esherrlich,** *adj.* sovereign. **-esherrschaft,** *f.* sovereignty, the crown. **-eshuldigung,** *f.* oath of fealty. **-esindustrie,** *f.* home industry. **-eskammer,** *f.* finance board. **-eskasse,** *f.* public treasury. **-eskind,** *n.* native; *preußisches -eskind,* native of Prussia, born in Prussia. **-eskirche,** *f.* established church. **-eskollegium,** *n.* provincial council. **-kunde,** *f.* study of national customs. **-esmünze,** *f.* legal coin *or* tender. **-esmutter,** *f.* sovereign princess. **-esobrigkeit,** *f.* supreme authority, government. **-esordnung,** *f.* government regulation. **-espolizei,** *f.* national police. **-esregierung,** *f.* central government. **-esschützen,** *m.pl.* local defence units. **-essitte,** *f.* national custom. **-essprache,** *f.* vernacular. **-estracht,** *f.* national costume *or* dress. **-estrauer,** *f.* public *or* national mourning. **-esüblich,** *adj.* customary, usual. **-esvaluta,** *f.* lawful currency. **-esvater,** *m.* sovereign; students' ritual. **-esvermessung,** *f.* topographical survey. **-esverrat,** *m.* high treason. **-esverräter,** *m.* traitor. **-esverteidigung,** *f.* home defence. **-esverwalter,** *m.*, *see* **-esverweser.** **-esverwaltung,** *f.* provincial administration. **-esverweisung,** *f.* banishment, exile. **-esverweser,** *m.* governor, viceroy. **-esverwiesen,** *adj.* banished, exiled. **-eswährung,** *f.* standard currency. **-eswohl,** *n.* national welfare. **-flucht,** *f.* migration from the country (*to the towns*). **-flüchtig,** *adj.* fugitive; *-flüchtig werden,* flee one's country. **-flüchtigkeit,** *f.* voluntary exile. **-flugzeug,** *n.* land-plane. **-frachtwesen,** *n.* (over)land carrying trade. **-fremd,** *adj.* foreign *or* strange to *or* a stranger in a country; quite strange *or* new. **-friede(n),** *m.* public peace (*proclaimed by the Emperor in medieval times*); (*coll.*) *dem -frieden nicht trauen,* be upon one's guard. **-gängig,** *adj.* current; epidemic. **-geistliche(r),** *m.* country clergyman. **-gemeinde,** *f.* village community; country parish. **-gemeindeordnung,** *f.* local government regulations. **-gericht,** *n.* county court, petty sessions. **-graf,** *m.* (-en, -en) count. **-grenze,** *f.* landmark; boundary. **-gültig,** *adj.* valid, legal; *-gültiges Gesetz,* common law, law of the land. **-gut,** *n.* estate, manor, country-seat. **-haus,** *n.* villa, country house, week-end house. **-heer,** *n.* land-forces. **-helfer,** *m.* (*Nat. Soc.*) youngster during year's land service. **-hilfe,** *f.* (*Nat. Soc.*) land service for girls; land-girl. **-hunger,** *m.* expansionist urge (*Pol.*). **-jäger,** *m.* gendarme; rural policeman. **-jahr,** *n.* (*Nat. Soc.*) year of compulsory service on the land. **-junker,** *m.* country squire. **-karte,** *f.* map. **-kartenkunde,** *f.* map-reading. **-kennung,** *f.* navigational aids (*in coastal waters*). **-krämer,** *m.* country shopkeeper; pedlar. **-krankheit,** *f.* endemic disease. **-kreis,** *m.* rural district. **-krieg,** *m.* land warfare. **-kundig,** *adj.* knowing the country well; well-known, notorious. **-kutsche,** *f.* stage-coach. **-läufig,** *adj.* customary, ordinary, current. **-leben,** *n.* rural *or* country life. **-leute,** *pl.* country people, peasant farmers. **-macht,** *f.* land-forces. **-mann,** *m.* (*pl.* -leute) farmer, peasant. **-messer,** *m.* surveyor. **-miliz,** *f.* yeomanry, provincial militia. **-mine,** *f.* landmine (*Mil.*). **-nähe,** *f.* landfall (*Naut.*). **-nahme,** *f.* annexation of territory. **-partie,** *f.* picnic, excursion. **-pastor,** *m.*, **-pfarrer,** *m.* country parson. **-pfarre,** *f.* country living *or* parsonage. (*B.*) **-pfleger,** *m.* governor, prefect. **-plage,** *f.* scourge, calamity. **-polizei,** *f.* rural police, gendarmerie. (*coll.*) **-pomeranze,** *f.* buxom country wench. **-ralle,** *f.* corncrake, land-rail (*Crex crex*) (*Orn.*). **-rasse,** *f.* indigenous breed. **-rat,** *m.* district magistrate, chairman of rural district council; cantonal government (*in Switzerland*). **-ratte,** *f.* (*coll.*) landlubber. **-recht,** *n.* provincial law *or* jurisdiction. **-rechtlich,** *adj.* according to provincial law. **-regen,** *m.* widespread and persistent rain. **-reiter,** *m.* mounted gendarme. **-rente,** *f.* ground-rent. **-rentmeister,** *m.* land-steward. **-richter,** *m.* county-court judge. **-rücken,** *m.* ridge of hills. **-rutsch,** *m.* landslide. **-sasse,** *m.* freeholder; feudal lord. **-sässig,** *adj.* having freehold *or* feudal rights. **-schaft,** *f.* (-en) landscape, scenery; district, region; estates (*Hist.*). **-schaftlich,** *adj.* provincial; scenic, of the landscape. **-schaftsaufnahme,** *f.* landscape-photograph. **-schaftsbank,** *f.* agricultural bank. **-schaftsbild,** *n.* scene, landscape. **-schaftselement,** *n.* feature of the landscape. **-schaftsgärtnerei,** *f.* landscape-gardening. **-schaftsmaler,** *m.* landscape-painter. **-schaftsmalerei,** *f.* landscape-painting. **-schnecke,** *f.* common snail. **-schreiber,** *m.* (*Swiss dial.*) magistrate's clerk. **-schule,** *f.* village-school. **-schulheim,** *n.* country boarding school. **-see,** *m.* inland lake. **-ser,** *m.* (*coll.*) infantryman, foot-slogger; private, common soldier. **-seuche,** *f.* epidemic. **-sgemeinde,** *f.* (*Swiss dial.*) annual assembly of all voters in a canton. **-sitz,** *m.* country-seat. **-sknecht,** *m.* trooper, mercenary, (16th century) lansquenet; *fluchen wie ein -sknecht,* swear like a trooper. **-smann,** *m.* (*pl.* -sleute) compatriot, fellow countryman; *was für ein -smann sind Sie?* what is your native country? *er ist Ihr -smann,* he is a countryman of yours. **-smannschaft,** *f.* student organization with local affiliations. **-spitze,** *f.* cape, headland, promontory. **-stände,** *m.pl.* representative body, provincial diet. **-ständisch,** representative (of the people), elected; *-ständische Verfassung,* representative government, constitution. **-steuer,** *f.* land-tax. **-straße,** *f.* high-road, main road, highway. **-strecke,** *f.* tract of land, region. **-streicher,** *m.* tramp, vagrant. **-streicherei,** *f.* vagrancy. **-strich,** *m. see* **-strecke.** **-sturm,** *m.* Home Guard (*men over 45*), local militia. **-tag,** *m.* provincial diet (*Pol.*). **-tier,** *n.* land animal. **-transport,** *m.* overland transport. **-truppen,** *f.pl.* land-forces. **-ung,** *f.* landing, disembarkation. **-ungsboot,** *n.* landing barge *or* craft, assault boat (*Mil.*). **-ungsbrücke,** *f.* landing-stage, pier, jetty. **-ungsplatz,** *m.* landing place. **-ungstruppen,** *f.pl.* landing force, beach assault troops. **-verschickung,** *f.* evacuation to the country. **-vogt,** *m.* provincial governor. **-volk,** *n.* country people; peasantry. **-wärts,** *adv.* landward; *tief -wärts,* far inland. **-weg,** *m.* land route. **-wehr,** *f.* militia, yeomanry; Territorial Reserve (*men between 35 and 45*). **-wind,** *m.* off-shore wind. **-wirt,** *m.* farmer. **-wirtschaft,** *f.* farming, agriculture, husbandry. **-wirtschaftlich,** *adj.* agricultural. **-wirtschaftsrat,** *m.* agricultural council. **-zeichen,** *n.* landmark. **-zunge,** *f.* spit (of land). **-zwang,** *m.* (*Law*) breach of the peace, public nuisance.

Landauer, *m.* (-s, -) landau.

Länd-e, *f.* landing place. **-en,** *v.a.* bring (*a corpse*) ashore, find (*a corpse*) washed ashore; (*Swiss dial.*) *see* **landen.** **-erbeschreibung,** *f., see* **-erkunde.** **-erei,** *f.* landed property, estates. **-ergier,** *see* **-ersucht.** **-erkunde,** *f.* geography. **-erkundlich,** *adj.* geographical. **-erkampf,** *m.* international contest (*Sport.*). **-erraub,** *m.* appropriation *or* annexation of territory. **-ersucht,** *f.* urge towards territorial aggrandizement, love of conquest, land-grabbing. **-ler,** *m.* slow country waltz. **-lich,** *adj.* rural, rustic; (*Prov.*) *-lich, sittlich,* other countries, other customs; do in Rome as the Romans do; *-lich, schändlich,* rural and bad. **-lichkeit,** *f.* rusticity.

lang, 1. *adj.* (*comp.* länger, *sup.* längst) long; tall; high, lofty; prolonged, protracted, lengthy; ropy (*of wine*); *am längsten* or *aufs längste,* at farthest, at the latest, *see also* **läng-st;** *auf die -e Bank schieben,* put off, postpone, protract, delay; *das -e und Kurze der S.,* the long and the short of the matter; *ein -es und breites* (*Austr. with caps.*) *reden* or *schwatzen,* talk at great length; *sich des -en und breiten über etwas aussprechen,* discuss a th. from all angles; *-e Finger machen,* steal, pilfer; *er machte ein -es Gesicht,* he pulled a long face *or* was disgruntled; *einen -en Hals machen,* crane one's neck; (*coll.*) *eine -e Leitung haben,* be slow on the uptake; *-e Ohren machen,* be inquisitive; *-e Nase machen,* mock, jeer; *der -en Rede kurzer Sinn,* to cut a long story short; *seit -em,* for a long time; *auf -e Sicht,* long-dated (*bills*); far-sighted; *den lieben -en Tag,* the live long day; *vor -en Jahren* or *vor -er Zeit,* long ago; *-e Wellen,* long waves, low frequencies (*Rad.*); *ihm wird die Zeit -,* time hangs heavy on his hands; *er kommt auf längere Zeit,* he is going to stay some time; *die längste Zeit,* not very much longer, not any longer. 2. *adv.* & *prep.* (*preceded by Acc.*); long; for, during; *eine Zeit -,* for a time; *drei Jahre -,* for three years; *sein Leben -,* all his life, till the end of his days; *jahre-,* for years; *tage-,* for days together; *meilen-,* for miles; *den Fluß - gehen* (*coll. for* entlang), walk along the river. 3. **-(e),** *adv.* (*comp.* länger, *sup.* am längsten, längst) *see also* **längst-;** a long while, long; by far; *auf -e,* for a long time; *nicht -(e) darauf,* shortly after; *den muß man nicht erst -(e) fragen,* he does not wait to be asked; *wer wird erst -(e) fragen?* who would hesitate?; (*coll.*) *es ist für mich -e gut,* it is quite good enough for me; *-e machen,* be long about *or* in doing; (*coll.*) *er wird es nicht mehr -e machen,* he has not long to live; *-e nicht so gut,* not nearly so good; *er kommt noch -e nicht,* he will not be here for a long time yet; *es ist noch -e nicht fertig,* it is not nearly ready; *er ist noch -e kein Goethe,* he is far from being a Goethe; *ohne sich -e zu besinnen,* without any hesitation; *schon -e bereit,* ready long ago; *schon -e her,* a long time ago; *schon -e vorbei,* all over *or* past, long since; *so -e als,* as long as; *so -e bis,* until; *über kurz oder -,* sooner or later; *von -e her,* of long standing, of old; *je länger je lieber,* the longer the better; *länger machen,* lengthen; prolong, extend; *wenn er es noch länger so macht,* if he goes on in this way; *schon länger,* for some time. **-anhaltend,** *adj.* continuous, enduring. **-atmig,** *adj.* long-winded. **-blätterig,** *adj.* long-leaved, macrophyllous. **-brennweite,** *f.* long focus. **-dauernd,** *adj.* lasting, continuous. **-en,** 1. *v.n.* (*aux.* h.) be sufficient, suffice; reach; *nach einer S. -en,* reach for *or* stretch out the hand for a th.; *das Geld wird nicht -en,* the money will not suffice; *das Kleid -t kaum bis an die Knie,* the dress scarcely reaches the knees; *-e zu!* help yourself! *es -t so weit es kann,* it will go as far as it can; *-en und bangen in schwebender Pein,* longing and fearing in pain and suspense; *in die Tasche -en,* put one's hand in one's pocket. 2. *v.a.*; *einem eine* (*Ohrfeige*) *-en,* box a p.'s ears, give s.o. a clout; *-e mir den Hut!* reach *or* pass me my hat. **-erwünscht,** *adj.* long-wished-for. **-eweile,** *f.* (*see also* **-weile**), tediousness, tedium, boredom, ennui; *aus -e(r)weile, aus lauter -erweile,* from (sheer) boredom, to pass the time; *-eweile empfinden,* feel bored. **-ezeit,** *f.* (*Swiss dial.*) home-sickness. (*coll.*) **-finger,** *m.* thief, pickpocket. (*coll.*) **-fingerig,** *adj.* long-fingered; light-fingered. **-fertig,** *adj.* long-dated (*bills*), long-term (*weather forecast, etc.*). **-gespitzt,** *adj.* running to a point. **-gestielt,** *adj.* long-stalked, long-handled. **-gestreckt,** *adj.,* **-gezogen,** *adj.* elongated, extended, long-drawn-out. **-haarig,** *adj.* long-haired; shaggy. **-haus,** *n.* main aisle (*of a church*). **-hin,** *adv.* long, far. **-holz,** *n.* timbers, beams and planks (*Naut.*). **-jährig,** *adj.* of long standing; *-jähriger Freund,* old friend; *-jährige Erfahrung,* long experience. **-köpfig,** *adj.* dolichocephalic. **-kreis,** *m.* oval, ellipse. (*C.L.*) **-laufend,** *adj.* long-sighted. **-lebig,** *adj.* long-lived. **-lebigkeit,** *f.* longevity. **-loch,** *n.* slot. **-mut,** *f.,* **-mütigkeit,** *f.* forbearance, patience, long-suffering. **-mütig,** *adj.* long-suffering, forbearing, patient. **-ohr,** *m.* (-(e)s, -e) & *n.* (-(e)s, -en) long-eared p. *or* beast; ass; (*Prov.*) *ein Esel nennt den anderen -ohr,* the pot calls the kettle black. **-rund,** *adj.* oval. **-sam,** *adj.* slow; tardy; *-sam backen,* bake in a slow oven; *-sam kochen,* simmer; *-sam begreifend,* dull of comprehension; *-sam laufen,* tick over (*of an engine*). **-sambinder,** *m.* slow-setting cement. **-samkeit,** *f.* slowness, tardiness; dullness. **-schaftig,** *adj.* long-boled (*trees*). **-schiff,** *n.* nave (*Arch.*). **-schläfer,** *m.* late-riser; (*coll.*) slug-abed. **-schliff,** *m.* fibrous (wood) pulp. **-schwanz,** *m.* long-tailed animal; long-tailed tit (*Aegithalus caudatus rosens*) (*Orn.*). **-schwelle,** *f.* ground-plate (*Railw.*). **-sein,** *n.* ropiness (*of wine*). **-sichtig,** *adj.* long-sighted; (*C.L.*) of long date. **-stielig,** *adj.* long-stemmed, long-stalked; long-handled; (*coll.*) tiresome, tedious, circumstantial. **-streckenflug,** *m.* long-distance flight. **-streckenjäger,** *m.* long-range fighter (*Av.*). **-streckenläufer,** *m.*, **-streckler,** *m.* long-distance runner. **-tau,** *n.* drag-rope. **-weile,** *f.*, *see* **-eweile. -weilen,** 1. *v.a.* tire, bore, weary. 2. *v.r.* be bored. **-weilig,** *adj.* boring, tedious, irksome; *-weilige Person,* bore. **-weite,** *f.* range. **-wellen,** *f.pl.* long waves (*Rad.*). **-wierig,** *adj.* lengthy, protracted, tedious, wearisome; lingering, chronic. **-zeile,** *f.*; *stabreimende -zeile,* alliterative (long) line (*Metr.*). **-zeitzünder,** *m.* delayed-action fuse (*Artil.*). **-ziehen,** *n.* lengthening; drawing out (*Mus.*).

Läng-e, *f.* (-en) length; size; longitude; duration, quantity (*Metr.*); (*fig.*) tedious passage (*in a book, etc.*); *der -e nach,* lengthwise; longitudinally; *-e über alles,* overall length; *um eine -e,* (*win*) by a length; *Berlin liegt unter 13° östliche -e,* Berlin is long. 13° E.; *auf die -e,* in the end, in the long run; *in die -e ziehen,* 1. *v.a.* elongate, draw out; protract, spin out. 2. *v.n.* drag on; *der -e lang* or *nach hinfallen,* fall at full length; *20 Fuß in der -e,* 20 feet long. **-elang,** *adv.*, see *der -e lang.* **-enabweichung,** *f.* error in range (*Artil.*), variation in longitude. **-enausdehnung,** *f.* elongation, extension, linear expansion. **-enbruch,** *m.* longitudinal fracture (*Surg.*). **-endurchschnitt,** *m.* longitudinal section. **-eneinheit,** *f.* unit of length. **-enfaser,** *f.* grain (*in wood*). **-engrad,** *m.*, **-enkreis,** *m.* degree (circle) of longitude. **-enmaß,** *n.* linear measure. **-enmessung,** *f.* linear measurement. **-enschnitt,** *m. see* **-schnitt. -enunterschied,** *m.* difference of length *or* longitude. **-ezeichen,** *n.* macron (*Metr.*). **-lich,** *adj.* longish; oblong. **-lichrund.** oval, elliptical, ovate. **-s,** *adv.* & *prep.* (*Gen. or Dat.*) along, alongside; *-s des Flusses* or *dem Flusse,* along the river's bank; *-s der Küste,* along the shore. **-sachse,** *f.* longitudinal *or* longer axis. **-sfeuer,** *n.* enfilade fire (*Artil.*). **-slager,** *n.* axial *or* thrust bearing (*Engin.*). **-sschiffs,** *adv.* fore and aft (*Naut.*). **-sschnitt,** *m.* longitudinal section. **-sseit(s),** *adv.* & *prep.* (*with Gen.*) alongside (*Naut.*). **-st,** *adv.* long ago, long since; *ich hätte es -st sagen sollen,* I ought to have mentioned it long ago; *see also* **lang(e)** (3); *ich weiß es schon -st,* I have known it for a long time. **-stens,** *adv.* at the furthest *or* at the most; at the latest; *er kommt -stens in einer Woche zurück,* he will return in a week at the latest; *es hat am* or *zum -sten gedauert,* it must not go on any longer.

längen, *v.a.* & *r.* lengthen, extend, stretch; roll out (*dough*); thin (*soup*).

Langette, *f.* (-n) scalloping, scallop.

Languste, *f.* (-n) lobster.

Lanthan, *n.* lanthanum.

Lanze, *f.* (-n) lance, spear, harpoon; *die - einlegen,* couch the spear; *eine - für einen brechen* or *einlegen,* stand up for a p., champion a p.'s cause; *Schwadron von 100 -n,* squadron of 100 lancers. **-nblatt,** *n.* head *or* blade of a lance. **-nbrechen,** *n.*, *see* **-nstechen. -nförmig,** *adj.* lanceolate (*Bot.*). **-nreiter,** *m.* lancer; uhlan. **-nschuh,** *m.* bucket of a lance. **-nstechen,** *n.* joust, tournament, tilting. **-ttbogen,** *m.* Gothic arch (*Arch.*). **-tte,** *f.* (-n) lancet. **-ttförmig,** *adj.* lanceolate (*Bot.*).

lapidar, *adj.* lapidary; concise, pithy.

Lappalie, *f.* (-n) trifle, bagatelle; bauble.

Lapp-en, 1. *m.* (-ens, -en) rag, cloth, duster; patch; lobe (*Anat., Bot.*), flange, (*Mech.*) (*pl.*) ears (*of hounds*); (*pl.*) wattles; (*sl.*) *durch die -en gehen,* abscond; (*sl.*) clear out, beat it, do a bunk. 2. *v.a.* (*coll.*) patch, mend. 3. *v.n.* flap, hang, dangle. **gelappt,** *p.p.* & *adj.* lobed, lobulate. **-enhaut,** *f.* web (*between toes*). **-enlos,** *adj.* acotyledonous (*Bot.*). **-erei,** *f.*, *see* **Läpperei. -ern,** *v.a.* & *n.*, *see* **läppern. -ig,** *adj.* flabby, flaccid; ragged, tattered; lobed, lobate, lobular. **-ohrig,** *adv.* lop-eared.

Läpp-chen, *n.* (-s, -), small flap *or* lobe. **-erei,** *f.* trifle, frippery. **-ern,** *v.a.* & *n.* (*aux.* h.) (*coll.*) lap, sip; (*coll.*) *sich zusammenläppern,* mount up, accumulate. **-erschulden,** *f.pl.* petty debts. **-erweise,** *adv.* little by little, in driblets. **-isch,** *adj.* silly, childish, foolish, trifling.

Lärche, *f.* (-n) larch (*Larix europœa*) (*Bot.*).

Laren, *m.pl.* household gods, Lares.

Larifari, *n.* & *int.* prattle, nonsensical talk; stuff and nonsense! fiddle-sticks!

Lärm, *m.* noise, din, uproar, row; bustle; alarm; fuss; *blinder -,* false alarm; *- blasen* or *schlagen,* sound *or* raise the alarm; *viel - um nichts,* much ado about nothing. **-apparat,** *m.* alarm. **-en,** *v.a.* (*aux.* h.) make a noise *or* an uproar; be noisy; bluster. **-end,** *adj.* noisy, loud, unruly. **-er,** *m.* noisy person; blusterer, roisterer, rowdy. **-zeichen,** *n.* alarm (signal).

Larve, *f.* (-n) mask, (*archaic*) face; larva, grub; (*Poet.*) spectre, ghoul; *einem die - abziehen* or *abnehmen,* unmask a p.; (*archaic*) *jedes hübsche Lärvchen,* every pretty face. **-nmantel,** *m.* domino. **-nzustand,** *m.* chrysalis state.

las, läse, *see* **lesen.**

lasch, *adj.* lax, limp; *see* **laß**; loose, flabby, languid.

Lasche, *f.* (-n) flap, lappet; tongue (*of a shoe*); groove; joint, fishplate (*Railw.*). **-n,** *v.a.* sew in a lappet; join wood in a groove. **-nkette,** *f.* sprocket chain.

Lase, *f.* (-n) (*dial.*) pitcher, jug, can (*with spout*).

las-ieren, *v.a.* glaze (*paint, pott., etc.*). **-ur,** 1. *f.* glazing, transparent coating. 2. *m.* lapis-lazuli. **-urblau,** *adj.* azure, sky-blue. **-urfarbe,** *f.* transparent colour; glaze. **-urit,** *n.*, **-urstein,** *m.* lapis-lazuli.

laß, *adj.* lax, slack; weary; spiritless; (*B.*) slothful. **-heit,** *f.* laziness; weariness. **-gut,** *n.* (*dial.*) leasehold (*dial.*) **-pflichtig,** *adj.* subject to ground-rent. **-sünde,** *f.* venial sin. (*dial.*) **-zins,** *m.* ground-rent.

lassen, 1. *ir.v.a.* let; leave alone, desist *or* refrain from; leave, relinquish, part with, let go; abandon; *keinen guten Faden* or *kein gutes Haar an einem -,* have not a good word to say for a p.; *einen nicht aus den Augen -,* not let a p. out of one's sight; *aus der Hand -,* drop; *aus den Händen -,* let go *or* slip; *einen aus dem Hause -,* let a p. out, see a p. to the door; *außer acht -,* disregard, take no notice of; *alles beim Alten -,* leave matters as they were; *einen bei seiner Meinung -,* let a p. keep his opinion; *wenn Sie es mir nicht billiger -, so laß ich's,* if you cannot let me have it any cheaper, I will leave it; *Blut -,* bleed, let blood; *wir wollen es dabei -,* we will leave it at that; *laß das,* leave that alone; *Haar* or *Haare -,* pay dearly, lose heavily (*gambling*), be fleeced; *einem freie Hand -,* give a p. a free hand; *das läßt alles weit hinter sich,* that knocks everything into a cocked hat; *ich ließ ihn in die Stube,* I let him enter the room; *ich ließ ihn in der Stube,* I left him in the room; *sein Leben - für,* lay down *or* lose one's life for; *das muß man ihm -,* we must grant him that, one must give him credit for that; *laß nur!* never mind! *mit sich reden -,* listen to reason, be reasonable; *laß (es) gut sein,* never mind; *laß das Spaßen!* no more nonsense! *aus dem Spiele -,* leave out of the question; *sie ließ ihren Tränen freien Lauf,* she abandoned herself to tears, she gave vent to her tears; *unerwähnt -,* pass over in silence *or* without mention; *von etwas -,* renounce, abandon *or* relinquish a th.; *ich kann von ihm nicht -,* I cannot give him up *or* part from him; *laß die Hände davon!* hands off! don't meddle with that! *von seiner Meinung -,* change one's opinion; *vom Stapel -,* launch; *tun, was man nicht - kann,* do what one cannot help doing; *Wasser -,* make *or* pass water; *Wein vom Fasse -,* draw wine from a cask; *laß das Weinen!* stop crying! *man muß ihm nicht allen Willen -,* one must not let him have all his own way; *einem Zeit -,* give a p. time; *sich Zeit -,* take time; *einen zur Ader -,* see *Blut -*; *zu sich -,* admit to one's presence; *laß mich zufrieden!* let me alone! don't bother me! *When governing the inf.* (*to which it frequently gives a passive sense*) = cause, make, effect; get *or* have done; order, command; let, permit, allow, (*archaic*) suffer; *sich abschrecken* –, be intimidated; *einem eine S. ahnen* –, give a p. an inkling of a th.; *er hat sich einen Zahn ausziehen* –, he has had a tooth extracted; *das läßt sich nicht biegen*, that cannot *or* must not be bent; *sich bitten* –, wait to be asked *or* pressed; (*etwas*) *bleiben* –, leave a th. alone; *das läßt sich denken*, I should think so, that is very natural; *laß dich nicht erwischen*, don't get caught; *fahren* –, let slip, let go; *fallen* –, drop; *fragen* –, have inquiries made; *das laß ich mir gefallen*, that will suit me; *das laß ich mir nicht gefallen*, I will not put up with that; *gehen* –, let go; *gelten* –, allow, admit as valid; *geschehen* –, allow to happen; *grüßen* –, send greetings *or* kind regards to; *gut sein* –, let pass, approve; *sich hören* –, speak, sing, play, *etc.*, in company; – *Sie von sich hören*, let us hear from you; *das läßt sich hören*, that sounds good, that's the thing! *kommen* –, send for; *liegen* –, leave behind; *es läßt sich nicht leugnen*, there is no denying; *das läßt sich machen*, that can be done all right; *ich werde mir nichts merken* –, I shall seem to know nothing, I shall not show it; *darüber läßt sich weiter reden*, that admits of further discussion; *ich lasse mich nicht leicht rühren*, I am not easily moved; *einem sagen* –, send a p. word; *ich habe mir sagen* –, I have been told; *sich* (*Dat.*) *nichts sagen* –, be deaf to entreaty, take no advice; *laß dir das gesagt sein*, let me tell you once and for all; *ich werde mir das gesagt sein* –, I shall take due notice of it; *sich sehen* –, show o.s., put in an appearance; *etwas sein* –, refrain from doing s.th., not do s.th.; *fünf gerade sein* –, not be too particular; *die Zügel schießen* –, let the reins loose; *laß dir's gut schmecken*, I hope you enjoy it (= *the food*), good appetite! *einen Brief schreiben* –, have a letter written; *ins Reine schreiben* –, have a fair copy made; *alle Minen springen* –, do one's utmost; *das hätte ich mir nicht träumen* –, I would not have dreamt such a thing were possible; *der Wein läßt sich trinken*, the wine is drinkable *or* is not bad; – *Sie sich trösten*, be comforted; *das läßt sich leicht tun*, that may easily be done, we can easily have that done; *es läßt sich nicht übersetzen*, it cannot be translated, it defies translation; *das läßt sich nicht umgehen*, that cannot be avoided; *laß dir's* or *dich's nicht verdrießen*, do not let yourself be dissuaded *or* put off; *sich keine Mühe verdrießen* –, make every effort, take great pains; *der Richter ließ die Zeugen verhören*, the judge caused the witnesses to be examined; *laß dich nicht verführen*, do not be led astray; *seine Worte – mich vermuten*, his words give *or* lead me to suppose; *diese Blumen – sich nicht verpflanzen*, these flowers will not bear transplanting; *er ließ das Heer vorrücken*, he ordered the army to advance; *Milde walten* –, show clemency, be indulgent; *warten* –, keep waiting; *einen wissen* –, inform a p., let a p. know. 2. *v.n.* (*aux.* h.) (*archaic & dial.*) look, appear, become, suit; *es läßt ihr nicht übel*, it is rather becoming to her; *du läßt jünger denn je*, you look younger than ever. 3. *n. unser Tun und* –, our commissions and omissions, our behaviour *or* conduct.

lässest, läßt, *see* **lassen.**

läss–ig, *adj.* inactive, indolent, sluggish, lazy, idle; careless, negligent. **–igkeit,** *f.* laziness, indolence; negligence. **–(ß)lich,** *adj.* pardonable, venial; *–(ß)liche Sünden*, venial sins, peccadilloes.

Last, *f.* (-en) load, burden, weight; cargo, freight, tonnage; charge, encumbrance, tax, impost; onus, trouble; (approx.) 2 tons (*measure of shipping tonnage*); hold (*Naut.*); *das Schiff ist bei seiner* –, the ship is freighted; *die – brechen*, break bulk; *zur – fallen*, be a burden to *or* a charge on; *der Gemeinde zur – fallen*, come upon the parish; *einem etwas zur – legen*, lay s.th. to a p.'s charge, charge *or* tax a p. with a th.; *einem zur – schreiben*, charge to a p.'s account; (*C.L.*) *zu –en von*, to the debit of; *nach Abzug der –en*, deducting all charges; *ein Schiff von 200* –, a ship of 400 tons burden. **–adie,** *f.* (-n) wharf, quay. **–auto,** *n.* motor-lorry. **–bar,** *adj.* (*poet.*) capable of bearing a burden; *–bare Tiere*, beasts of burden. **–en,** *v.n.* (*aux.* h.) weight on, press heavily upon; oppress; encumber, burden. **–enaufzug,** *m.* goods lift *or* elevator. **–enfrei,** *adj.* unburdened; free of taxes *or* charges. **–engebühr,** *f.* tonnage. **–er,** *m.* army lorry. **–flugzeug,** *n.* freight carrier (*Av.*). **–ig,** *adj.* freighted; weighted; of 2 tons burden (*Naut.*); *ein gleich–iges Schiff*, a ship upon an even keel; *ein zwei–iges Schiff*, a vessel of 4 tons burden; *schwanz–ig*, tail-heavy (*Av.*). **–igkeit,** *f.* burden, tonnage (*Naut.*); trim (*of a ship in the water*), trimming (*Av.*). **–kahn,** *m.* lighter, barge. **–(kraft)wagen,** *m.*(motor-)lorry. **–pferd,** *n.* pack-horse. **–sand,** *m.* ballast-sand. **–schiff,** *n.* cargo-boat. (*C.L.*) **–schrift,** *f.* debit-item. **–tier,** *n.* beast of burden; *wie ein –tier arbeiten*, work like a nigger *or* slave, slave, drudge. **–träger,** *m.* porter. **–wagen,** *m.* truck, van, lorry. **–zug,** *m.* goods *or* freight train; motor-lorry and trailers.

Laster, *n.* (-s, –) vice; depravity; (*coll.*) slut, slattern, trollop. **–haft,** *adj.* vicious, wicked. **–haftigkeit,** *f.* viciousness, wickedness. **–höhle,** *f.* den of iniquity. **–knecht,** *m.* slave to vice. **–leben,** *n.* life of wickedness.

Läster–er, *m.* (-s, –) slanderer, calumniator; blasphemer. **–lich,** *adj.* blasphemous, slanderous, abusive; scandalous, shameful, disgraceful, abominable. **–maul,** *n.* slanderer, scandalmonger; *einem das –maul stopfen*, stop a man's abusive mouth. **–n,** *v.a. & n.* slander, defame (*auf* or *über*); revile (*wider* or *gegen*); blaspheme. **–süchtig,** *adj.* slanderous, blasphemous. **–ung,** *f.* slander, calumny, blasphemy. **–zunge,** *f.* slanderous tongue.

lästig, *adj.* burdensome, troublesome, irksome, annoying, tedious; *einem – fallen*, hinder *or* inconvenience a p.; (*sl.*) be a pain in the neck; *–er Ausländer*, undesirable alien. **–keit,** *f.* irksomeness, inconvenience, annoyance.

Lasur, *see* **lasieren.**

Laterne, *f.* (-n) lantern, lamp; street lamp. **–nanzünder,** *m.* lamplighter; (*sl.*) pathfinder, target-marking aircraft (*Av.*). **–nhalter,** *m.* lamp-bracket (*Cycl.*). **–npfahl,** *m.* lamp-post; (*coll.*) *mit dem –npfahl winken*, give a broad hint.

Latsch, *m.* (-s, -e) slovenly fellow, slut; (*dial.*) weak coffee; [1]**–e,** *f.* (-n), (*usually pl.*) slipper; down-at-heel shoe; feathered foot (*of fowl*). **–en,** *v.n.* (*aux.* h.) shuffle along, drag one's feet, slouch. **–gang,** *m.* shuffling, slouching. **–ig,** *adj.* shuffling; negligent, slovenly.

[2]**Latsche,** *f.* (-n) dwarf-pine.

Latte, *f.* (-n) lath, batten; sapling; (*coll.*) *lange* –, lanky p. **–ngestell,** *n.* crate. **–npunkt,** *m.* bench mark (*Surv.*). **–nsteg,** *m.* duck-boards; trestle bridge. **–nverschlag,** *m.* boarded *or* wooden partition. **–nwerk,** *n.* trellis. **–nzaun,** *m.* paling; railing.

Lattich, *m.* (-(e)s, -e) genus *Lactuca*; lettuce (*Lactuca sativa*).

Latwerge, *f.* (-n) electuary.

Latz, *m.* (-es, ¨-e (*& Austr. dial* -e)) bib; flap. **–schürze,** *f.* apron, pinafore.

lau, *adj.* lukewarm, tepid; mild (*of weather*); indifferent, half-hearted. **–heit,** *f.*, **–igkeit,** *f.* lukewarmness, tepidity; indifference. **–warm,** *adj.*, *see* **lau.**

Laub, *n.* (-(e)s, -e) foliage, leaves. **–baum,** *m.* deciduous tree. **–dach,** *n.* leafy canopy. **–decke,** *f.* carpet of leaves. **–e,** *f.* (-en) summer-house, pergola, bower, arbour, loggia, covered way, arcade box (*in theatre*). **–endach,** *n.* roof of an arbour. **–engang,** *m.* arcade, pergola, covered way. **–engarten,** *m.* allotment. **–enkolonie,** *f.* allotments. **–entfaltung,** *f.* foliation. **–erde,** *f.* vegetable *or* leaf mould. **–fall,** *m.* fall of the leaf, defoliation. **–förmig,** *adj.* leaf-shaped, foliate. **–frosch,** *m.* tree-frog. **–gehänge,** *n.*, **–gewinde,** *n.* festoon, garland. **–gitter,** *n.* lattice-work, trellis. **–grün,** *adj.* leaf-green. **–holz,** *n.* deciduous trees. **–hütte,** *f.* bower, (*B.*) tabernacle. **–hüttenfest,** *n.* Feast of Tabernacles (*Jew.*). **–ig,** *adj.* leafy, foliate, foliaceous. **–käfer,** *m.* (*Swiss dial.*) cockchafer. **–los,** *adj.* leafless. **–reich,** *adj.* leafy. **–säge,** *f.* fretsaw. **-sägearbeit,** *f.* fretwork.

-verzierung, *f.* foliage (*Art.*). **-wald,** *m.* deciduous forest. **-werk,** *n.* foliage, leaves, trees (*Paint., etc.*); crocket (*Arch.*).

Lauch, *m.* (-(e)s, -e) leek (*Allium porrum*) (*Bot.*).

Laue, *f.* (-nen) (*Swiss dial.*) avalanche, landslide.

[1]**Lauer,** *f.* ambush, look-out, lurking-place; *auf der – sein* or *liegen* lie in wait, be on the watch *or* look-out, lurk. **-er** (*also* **Laurer**), *m.* spy, lurker. **-n,** *v.n.* (*aux.* h.) watch, observe keenly, be on the look-out; lie in ambush, lurk, lie in wait for; (*coll.*) await with impatience (*auf einen* or *etwas*, a p. *or* a th.).

[2]**Lauer,** *m.* wine of the second press; sour wine.

Lauf, *m.* (-(e)s, ⸗e) course, career, way; current, circulation, flow; track, path, orbit; progress, movement, running, action, pace; barrel (*of a rifle*); bed (*of a river*); run, arpeggio (*Mus.*); (*dial.*) rutting season; leg, foot (*of furred game*); *freien – lassen,* give full scope to, give vent *or* free play to, indulge; *der Gerechtigkeit ihren* (or *freien*) *– lassen,* let justice take its course; *– der Begebenheiten,* course of events; *das ist der – der Welt,* that is the way of the world, such is life; *einen einzelnen – machen,* run a heat; *am Ende seines –es,* at the close of his career; *in vollem –e,* at top speed, at full gallop; *ein Gewehr mit zwei Läufen,* a double-barrelled gun. **-achse,** *f.* free (running) axle, carrying axle (*Railw.*). **-bahn,** *f.* career; racecourse; course, tract, runway; track, wake (*of torpedo*). **-band,** *n.* tread (*of a tyre*). **-bohne,** *f.* scarlet runner. **-brett,** *n.* running-board; carriage (*of a press*) (*Typ.*) **-bretter,** *n. pl.* duck-boards. **-brief,** *m.* circular. **-brücke,** *f.* footbridge, plank bridge; gangway. **-bursche,** *m.* errand-boy, messenger-boy; printer's devil. **-en,** 1. *ir.v. n.* (*aux.* h. & s.) run; go; (*dial.*) walk, move; flow, ooze, leak, run out, run down, gutter; extend, stretch; be in circulation; rut; rise (*of dough*); pass, elapse, go by *or* on (*of time*); *einem in die Arme –en,* rush *or* fall into a p.'s arms; come across a p. unexpectedly, run into *or* across s.o.; *zu Ende –en,* run out, come to an end, expire; *das läuft ins Geld,* that runs into money; *es läuft ein Gerücht, daß,* it is rumoured that; *auf den Grund –en,* run aground; *Hals über Kopf –en,* run head over heels; *sehen wie der Hase läuft,* see how the cat jumps; *gelaufen kommen,* come running; *–en lassen,* let go, set free; let (*s.th.*) slide; *ein Pferd –en lassen,* give a horse its head; *es läuft mir eiskalt über den Rücken,* it makes my flesh creep; *hinter die Schule –en,* play truant; *vom* or *von Stapel –en,* be launched; *der Teig läuft,* the dough is rising; *das läuft wider die gesunde Vernunft,* that flies in the face of reason; *die Augen –en ihm voll Wasser,* his eyes fill with tears; *der Wechsel läuft noch,* the bill has still some time to run; *um die Wette –en,* run for a wager; race. 2. *v.a.* contract by running; run; *die Sonne läuft ihre Bahn,* the sun moves in its orbit; *Gänge* or *Wege –en,* run errands; *Gefahr –en,* run a risk; *sich müde –en,* tire o.s. out; *es läuft sich hier schlecht,* this is not a good place for running; *Schlittschuh –en,* skate; *Spießruten –en,* run the gauntlet; *Sturm –en,* charge into the attack, assault, storm; *sich die Füße wund –en,* get sore-footed, get a blister. **-end,** *adj.* current, running, continuous, consecutive; *auf dem –enden bleiben* or *sein,* be well acquainted with, keep abreast (of affairs), be up to date; *–ende Ausgaben,* running expenses; *das –ende Band,* conveyor belt, assembly line; *die –enden Geschäfte,* the course of affairs, the daily business; *das –ende Gut,* running tackle, halyards and sheets (*Naut.*); *das –ende Jahr,* current year; *vom 3. –enden Monats,* of the 3rd inst.; *–ende Nummer,* serial number; *zum –enden Preise,* at the current rate of exchange, at the market price; *–ende Rechnung,* current account; *der –ende Termin,* the present quarter; *–ende Wechsel,* bills in circulation. **-erei,** *f.* running about *or* to and fro. **-feld,** *n.* runway (*Av.*). **-feuer,** *n.* heath *or* grass fire; running fire (*Mil.*); train of gunpowder; *sich wie ein –feuer verbreiten,* spread like wildfire. **-fläche,** *f.* bearing surface, journal (*Mech.*). **-gang,** *m.* gangway, catwalk, gallery; corridor (*Railw.*). **-getriebe,** *n.* moving parts, mechanism. **-gewicht,** *n.* sliding weight, counterpoise. **-graben,** *m.* communication trench (*Mil.*). **-grabenspiegel,** *m.* trench-periscope. **-junge,** *m., see* **-bursche.** **-käfer,** *m.* ground-beetle (*Carabidae*). **-karren,** *m.* (*dial.*) wheelbarrow. **-katze,** *f.* cranecrab, overhead tackle. **-kran,** *m.* travelling crane. **-kundschaft,** *f.* casual customers. **-masche,** *f.* ladder (*in stockings*), dropped stitch. **-paß,** *m.* dismissal; *einem den –paß· geben,* dismiss a p., give s.o. (his, *etc.*) marching orders. **-planke,** *f.* gangway. **-rad,** *n.* carrying wheel (*Railw.*); rotor (*of turbine*), caster; bogie (*Engin.*), landing wheel (*Av.*). **-schiene,** *f.* guide-rail. **-schritt,** *m.* double time; *im –schritt,* at the double. **-seele,** *f.* bore (*of gun*). **-steg,** *m.* footbridge, footpath, gangway. **-walzen,** *f.pl.* cylinders, runners. **-werk,** *n.* drive (assembly), movement (*of a clock*). **-zaum,** *m.* leading-string. **-zeit,** *f.* rutting season; time (*Sport*); currency (*C.L.*). **-zettel,** *m.* circular letter of inquiry; post-office circular (*to recover mis-delivered letters*).

Läuf-er, *m.* (-s, –) runner, courser, racer; footman; messenger; half-back (*football*), three-quarter (back) (*Rugby*); bishop (*Chess*); tendril, shoot, sucker; stair-carpet, table-runner, drugget; slider (*of mathematical instruments*); overhead tackle (*of crane*); rotor (*of turbines & electric motors, etc.*); run, glissando (*Mus.*); (*pl.*) genus *Cursores* (*Orn.*). **-erstange,** *f.* stair-rod. **-erzug,** *m.* move with the bishop. **-ig,** *adj.,* **-isch,** *adj.* ruttish; in, on *or* at heat (*of dogs*). **-te,** *obs. pl. of* **Lauf,** *only in compounds,* e.g. *Zeit–te,* times.

läufst, läuft, *see* **laufen.**

Laug-e, *f.* (-en) lye, buck, leach; (*coll.*) *einem den Kopf mit scharfer –e waschen,* give a p. a good dressing down *or* scolding; *die –e seines Spottes,* his biting sarcasm, his caustic wit. **-en,** 1. *v.a.* soak *or* steep in lye, leach, lixiviate, buck. 2. *v.n.* (*aux.* h.); *das Faß –t,* the cask leaves a taste. **-(en)artig,** *adj.* lixivial, alkaline. **-enasche,** *f.* alkaline ashes, potash. **-enhaft,** *adj., see* **-enartig.** **-ensalz,** *n.* alkaline salt, alkali, soda. **-enwasser,** *n.* lye, suds, liquor, alkaline solution.

Laun-e, *f.* (-en) mood, humour, temper, frame of mind; whim, caprice; *gleiche –e,* even temper; *bei* (*guter*) *–e,* in a good humour *or* mood, in good spirits; *nicht bei –e,* out of temper, in a bad mood, not in the mood (for); *er hat heute seine –e,* he is in one of his moods today; *–e des Glückes,* freak of fortune. **gelaunt,** *adj.* disposed; *gut gelaunt,* in good humour. **-enhaft,** *adj.* moody, capricious, changeable. **-enhaftigkeit,** *f.* moodiness, capriciousness; waywardness. **-ig,** *adj.* humorous, comical, funny, droll; (*in compounds* =) -humoured, -tempered. **-isch,** *adj.* ill-humoured, bad-tempered, peevish, grumpy, moody.

Laurer, *m., see* **Lauerer.**

Laus, *f.* (⸗e) louse; (*vulg.*) *einem eine – in den Pelz setzen,* give a p. trouble, cause annoyance to s.o.; *eine – läuft ihm über die Leber,* he is very annoyed *or* angry. (*fam.*) **-bub(e),** *m.* little rogue *or* rascal, (*coll.*) young devil. **-büberei,** *f.* mischievousness. **-ejunge,** *m.* (*dial.*) lout, hobbledehoy. **-en,** *v.a.* delouse; (*vulg.*) fleece. **-erei,** *f.* (*coll.*) trumpery thing; unpleasantness. **-ig,** *adj.* (*vulg.*) lousy, miserable; perishing, awful.

Lausch-e, *f.* (*archaic*) lurking, eavesdropping, lying in wait; hiding-place; cosy nook. **-en,** *v.n.* (*aux.* h.) listen to, eavesdrop, spy, take careful note of; (*dial.*) lie in wait for; (*dial.*) doze, slumber. **-er,** *m.pl.* ears (*of the wolf, fox, deer, etc.*). **-ig,** *adj.* snug, cosy. **-platz,** *m.* lurking-place. **-posten,** *m.* listening post (*Mil.*).

Läuschen, *n.* (*dial.*) doggerel *or* verse anecdote.

läuse-frei, *adj.* free of vermin, deloused. **-kraut,** *n.* louse-wort, larkspur (*Bot.*). **-pulver,** *n.* insect-powder, insecticide. **-sucht,** *f.* Herodian *or* pedicular disease; lice disease (*of plants*).

laut, 1. *adj.* loud, noisy, audible, sonorous; open, public. 2. *adv.* forte (*Mus.*), aloud; *– werden,* become known, get about *or* abroad; become noisy; give tongue (*of hounds*); *– werden lassen,* divulge, betray, breathe a word (of *or* about); *seine Gefühle – werden* *lassen*, show or express one's feelings; *ich sage es* – ,I say it openly. 3. *m.* (-(e)s, –e) sound, tone; speech; *keinen – von sich geben*, not utter a sound; *– geben*, give tongue (*hounds*). 4. *prep.* (*with Gen. except in formal phrases*) according to, in accordance with, by the terms of; in consequence of, in virtue of; *– Angabe*, according to statement, as advised; *– Befehl*, *– des Befehls*, as ordered, by order; (*C.L.*) *– Bericht*, as per advice, as advised; *– Faktura* or *Rechnung*, as per invoice; *– Verfügung*, as directed. **–angleichung,** *f.* assimilation of sounds. **–bar,** *adj.* audible; known, notorious, public. **–bezeichnung,** *f.* sound-notation. **–bildung,** *f.* articulation. **–en,** *v.n.* (*aux.* h.) sound, run, read; *die Worte –en so*, the words run thus *or* as follows; *das –et seltsam*, that sounds strange; *wie –et sein Name?* what is his name? *wie –et das dritte Gebot?* what does the third commandment say? *die Antwort –ete günstig*, the answer was favourable; *das Urteil –et auf ein Jahr Gefängnis*, the verdict was for one year's imprisonment; *sein Urteil –et dahin, daß . . .*, his opinion is that . . .; *auf den Inhaber –ende Aktien*, shares made out to bearer. **–er,** *m.* (*archaic*) sound (*Phonet.*). **–gesetz,** *n.* phonetic law. **–getreu,** *adj.* phonetically correct. **–heit,** *f.* loudness, sonorousness. **–ieren,** *v.n.*, read phonetically. **–lehre,** *f.* phonology; phonetics. **–lich,** *adj.* phonetic. **–los,** *adj.* silent, mute; hushed, inaudible; speechless; *es herrschte –lose Stille*, all was hushed. **–losigkeit,** *f.* silence. **–malerei,** *f.*, **–nachahmung,** *f.*, **–nachbildung,** *f.* onomatopœia. **–physiologie,** *f.* physiology of speech. **–schrift,** *f.* phonetic spelling *or* script. **–schwund,** *m.* disappearance of a sound. **–spaltung,** *f.* differentiation of sounds. **–sprecher,** *m.* loud-speaker. **–stand,** *m.* phonetic structure (*of a language*). **–stärke,** *f.* intensity *or* volume of sound, signal-strength, volume (*Rad.*). **–stärkeregler,** *m.* volume-control (*Rad.*). **–tafel,** *f.* sound-chart. **–umschrift,** *f.* phonetic transcription. **–verhältnis,** *n.* interrelation of sounds. **–verschiebung,** *f.* sound-shifting, Grimm's law; *erste –verschiebung*, Germanic sound-shift; *zweite –verschiebung*, High-German sound-shift. **–verstärker,** *m.* audio-amplifier (stage) (*Rad.*). **–wandel,** *m.* **–wechsel,** *m.* sound change, mutation. **–zeichen,** *n.* phonetic symbol.

Laute, *f.* (-n) lute. **–nist,** *m.* (-en, -en), **–nschläger,** *m.*, **–nspieler,** *m.* lute-player, lutenist.

läut–en, 1. *v.a.* & *n.* (*aux.* h.) ring, peal, toll, sound; *zur Kirche –en*, ring the bells for church; *der Fernsprecher –et*, that is the telephone bell; *etwas –en hören*, hear a rumour of. 2. *n.* ringing, tolling. **–(e)werk,** *n.* electric bell, alarm bell.

lauter, 1. *adj.* clear; pure, unmixed, unalloyed, undefiled; genuine, true, candid, unvarnished, reliable, honest; *–e Absichten*, disinterested motives. 2. *adv.* (*used as indec. adj.*) only, nothing but, pure and simple, downright, mere, sheer, rank; *er trinkt – Wein*, he drinks nothing but wine; *es sind – Lügen*, it is all lies; *aus – Neid*, out of sheer envy; *er sieht den Wald vor – Bäumen nicht*, he cannot see the wood for the trees. **–keit,** *f.* purity, clearness; uprightness, integrity, sincerity.

läuter–n, *v.a.* purify, refine, clear, clarify, strain, rectify (*spirits*); purge; thin (*a wood*); (*fig.*) ennoble. **–bottich,** *m.* refining vat. **–feuer,** *n.* purifying fire; purgatory fire. **–tuch,** *n.* filter. **–ung,** *f.* purification; refining, clarification. **–ungsprozeß,** *m.* refining-process. **–vorrichtung,** *f.* clarifying apparatus.

Lavendel, *m.* lavender. **–geist,** *m.* essence of lavender. **–öl,** *n.* spike-oil.

lavieren, *v.n.* (*aux.* h.) tack (*Naut.*); (*fig.*) wriggle (through), wangle.

Lawine, *f.* (-n) avalanche.

lax, *adj.* lax, loose; *–e Moral*, easy morals; *–e Sitten*, loose living. **–heit,** *f.* laxity, looseness. **–ieren,** 1. *v.n.* take an aperient *or* laxative. 2. *v.a.* purge. **–iermittel,** *n.* aperient, laxative, purge.

Lazarett, *n.* (-s, -e) military hospital, sick bay. **–fieber,** *n.* hospital fever. **–gehilfe,** *m.* hospital orderly. **–schiff,** *n.* hospital-ship. **–wagen,** *m.* ambulance. **–zug,** *m.* hospital-train.

Laz(z)arone, *m.* (-(n) & -s, -n) beggar, pauper.

leb–en, 1. *v.n.* (*aux.* h.) live, be alive, exist, pass one's life; dwell, live; *es –t alles an ihm*, he is full of life; *er –t auf großem Fuße*, he lives in (a) grand style; *für sich –en*, live alone; (*B.*) *der Gerechte wird seines Glaubens –en*, the just shall live by faith; *so wahr Gott –t*, as sure as there is a God; *er ist sein Vater, wie er leibt und –t*, he is the living image of his father; *er hat zu –en*, he is provided for *or* he has enough to live on; *–en lassen*, drink (to) the health of; *er –t in dem Glauben*, he firmly believes, he is convinced; *sein Andenken –t im Herzen des Volkes*, his memory lives on in the people's hearts; (*in*) *der Hoffnung –en*, live in hope of; *in den Tag hinein –en*, live for the moment *or* in a happy-go-lucky way; *es –e der König! der König soll –en! der König –e hoch!* long live the king! *so etwas –t nicht!* things like that don't happen, (*sl.*) you're telling me! *–en von*, feed on, subsist on; support o.s. *or* live by; *von der Hand in den Mund –en*, live from hand to mouth; *so wahr ich –e*, as sure as I am alive; *er weiß zu –en*, he is a man of the world, (*coll.*) he knows his way around; *wie Hund und Katze –en*, lead a cat-and-dog life; *–(e) wohl! –en Sie wohl!* farewell! 2. *v.r.*; *sich satt –en* or *sich satt gelebt haben*, be weary of life; *hier –t sich's gut*, it is pleasant living here. 3. *n.* (-ens, -en) life, existence; activity, vivacity, liveliness, stir; living flesh, the quick; biography; *am –en bleiben*, survive; *am –en sein*, be alive; *das geht ihm ans –en*, that will cost his life, his life is in danger; *auf –en und Tod*, a matter of life and death; *Kampf auf –en und Tod*, mortal combat; *aus dem –en gegriffen*, taken from real life; (*coll.*) *ein neues –en beginnen*, turn over a new leaf; *bei meinem –en*, as I live; *bei Leib und –en*, upon pain of death; *bis aufs –en*, to the quick; (*coll.*) *–en in die Bude bringen*, make things lively *or* interesting, stir things up a bit; *für sein –en gern tun*, be very willing to do; *ich darf es für mein –en nicht tun*, I dare not do it for the life of me; *es gilt sein –en*, his life is at stake; *im öffentlichen –en stehen*, be a public figure; *in diesem und in jenem –en*, in this life and the life to come *or* hereafter; *ins –en rufen*, call into existence, originate, start, establish; *ins –en setzen*, give birth to; *ins –en treten*, be born; be started *or* established, set up; *sein –en lassen*, lay down one's life, die; *nach dem –en*, from life; *einem nach dem –en trachten*, be after a p.'s blood; *sich* (*Dat.*) *das –en nehmen*, commit suicide, kill o.s.; *einem Kind das –en schenken*, give birth to a child; *ums –en bringen*, kill, make away with; *ums –en kommen*, lose one's life, die, perish; *Zeit meines –ens*, all my life long. **–ehoch,** *n.* cheering, cheer; toast; *ein dreimaliges –ehoch ausbringen*, drink to *or* propose a p.'s health. **–emann,** *m.* man of the world, worldling; epicurean. **–end,** *pr.p.* & *adj.* living, alive; lively; (*B.*) *die –enden und die Toten*, the quick and the dead; *der –ende Bestand*, inventory of livestock (*Agr.*); *–ende Bilder*, tableaux vivants; *–ende Blumen*, natural flowers; *–ende Hecken*, quickset hedges; *–ende Sprachen*, living *or* modern languages; *unter den noch –enden*, among the survivors. **–endgebärend,** *adj.* viviparous. **–endgewicht,** *n.* live weight (*of cattle*). **–endig,** *adj.* living, live, alive; active, lively, vivacious; *–endige Anteilnahme*, warm interest; *fünf –endige Kinder*, five children living; *–endige Kraft*, kinetic energy; *bei –endigem Leibe*, while still alive; (*B.*) *der –endige Odem*, the breath of life; *es wird schon –endig auf der Straße*, the street is already astir; *–endige Unterhaltung*, animated conversation; *das –endige Werk*, below the waterline (*Naut.*). **–endiggebärend,** *adj.* viviparous. **–endigkeit,** *f.* animation, liveliness, vivacity. **–endigmachend,** *adj.* vivifying, enlivening; *–endigmachende Gnade*, quickening grace (*Theol.*). **–ensabend,** *m.* decline of life, old age. **–ensabriß,** *m.* biographical sketch. **–ensalter,** *n.* age. **–ensart,** *f.* manners, good breeding; *ohne –ensart*, ill-bred. **–ensaufgabe,** *f.* life-work. **–ensbahn,** *f.* course, career. **–ensbaum,** *m.* tree of life. **–ensbedingung,** *f.* condition essential for life; condition of vital importance. **–ensbedürfnisse,** *n.pl.* necessaries of life. **–ensbejahend,** *adj.* optimistic, virile. **-ensbeschreibung,** *f.* biography. **-ensbild,** *n.* sketch of a p.'s life, short biography. **-ensblüte,** *f.* prime of life. **-ensdauer,** *f.* duration of life, durability, lifetime, life-span; *auf -ensdauer,* for life; (*C.L.*) *zu erwartende -ensdauer,* expectation of life. **-ensende,** *n.* end of life; *bis an mein -ensende,* to the end of my days. **-enserhaltungstrieb,** *m.* instinct of self-preservation. **-ensfähig,** *adj.* capable of living; viable, full of vitality. **-ensfähigkeit,** *f.* viability, vitality. **-ensfrage,** *f.* vital question. **-ensfremd,** *adj.* ill-equipped for life; unsociable, retiring, solitary. **-ensfreudig,** *adj.,* **-ensfroh,** *adj.* light-hearted, vivacious. **-ensführung,** *f.* manner of living, conduct. **-ensgefahr,** *f.* danger to life; *mit -ensgefahr,* at the risk *or* peril of one's life. **-ensgefährlich,** *adj.* perilous, highly dangerous. **-ensgefährte,** *m.,* **-ensgefährtin,** *f.* life's companion, partner for life; husband, wife. **-ensgeist,** *m.* spirit of life; (*pl.*) animal spirits; *die -ensgeister wecken,* put life into. **-ensgeschichte,** *f.* biography. **-ensgewohnheiten,** *f.pl.* lifelong habits. **-ensglut,** *f.* vital energy. **-ensgroß,** *adj.* life-sized. **-ensgröße,** *f.* life-size. **-ensgüter,** *n.pl.* earthly possessions. **-enshaltung,** *f.* standard of living *or* life. **-enshauch,** *m.* breath of life; life. **-ensholz,** *n.* lignum vitae. **-ensinteresse,** *n.* vital interest (*usually pl.*). **-ensjahr,** *n.* year (of one's life). **-ensklugheit,** *f.* worldly wisdom. **-enskraft,** *f.* vigour, vital energy; vitality; *voll -enskraft und -enslust,* full of animal spirits. **-enskreis,** *m.* surroundings. **-enskunde,** *f.* biology. **-enslage,** *f.* position of life; *in jeder -enslage,* in every emergency, in all situations. **-enslang,** *adj.* lifelong; for life. **-enslänge,** *f., see* **-ensdauer.** **-enslänglich,** *adj.* lifelong, for life, perpetual; *-enslängliches Gnadengehalt,* life pension *or* pension for life; *-enslängliches Mitglied,* life-member; *-enslängliche Rente,* life annuity; *-enslängliche Zwangsarbeit,* penal servitude for life. **-enslauf,** *m.* curriculum vitae, personal record. **-enslehre,** *f.* biology; precept, rule of life. **-enslinie,** *f.* line of life (*Palmistry*). **-ensluft,** *f.* vital air; oxygen. **-enslust,** *f.* vivacity, exhilaration, high spirits, zest. **-enslustig,** *adj.* cheerful, gay; high-spirited. **-ensmark,** *n.* (*fig.*) vitals. **-ensmittel,** *n. pl.* food; provisions, foodstuffs, victuals, nourishment. **-ensmittelkarte,** *f.* ration-card. **-ensmittelknappheit,** *f.* food-shortage. **-ensmittelversorgung,** *f.* food-supply. **-ensmüde,** *adj* dispirited, dejected, disconsolate, despondent, depressed. **-ensmut,** *m.* high-spirits, exhilaration, energy. **-ensnerv,** *m.* (*fig.*) mainspring. **-ensnotdurft,** *f.* (bare) necessaries of life. **-ensnotwendigkeit,** *f.* vital necessity. **-ensordnung,** *f.* diet, regimen. **-ensprozeß,** *m.* animal economy, vital functions. **-ensraum,** *m.* environment, milieu, living space. **-ensregel,** *f.* rule of conduct, maxim, precept. **-ensrente,** *f.* life-annuity. **-ensretter,** *m.* life-saver, oxygen apparatus. **-ensstellung,** *f.* life appointment. **-ensstil,** *m.* mode of life. **-ensstrafe,** *f.* capital punishment. **-ensstufe,** *f.* stage of life. **-enstrieb,** *m.* vitality, vital instinct *or* impulse. **-enstrunken,** *adj.* exuberant, boisterous, full of vitality. **-ensüberdrüssig,** *adj.* sick of life. **-ensunterhalt,** *m.* livelihood, living, subsistence. **-ensverrichtungen,** *f.pl.* vital functions. **-ensversicherung,** *f.* life-insurance. **-ensversicherungsgesellschaft,** *f.* life-insurance office, life-insurance company. **-ensvoll,** *adj.* vigorous, active, vivacious, spirited, lively. **-ensvorgang,** *m.* vital process. **-enswahr,** *adj.* true to life, life-like. **-enswahrscheinlichkeit,** *f.* expectation of life. **-ensweg,** *m.* path through life; vital tract (*Anat.*). **-ensweise,** *f.* mode of life, way of living, habits. **-ensweisheit,** *f.* practical wisdom. **-enswerk,** *n.* life-work. **-enswichtig,** *adj.* vital, essential. **-enszeichen,** *n.* sign of life. **-enszeit,** *f.* age; lifetime; *auf -enszeit,* for life; *bei -enszeit,* during life, in life. **-ensziel,** *n.,* **-enszweck,** *m.* aim in life. **-ewesen,** *n.* living being *or* creature, organism. **-ewohl,** *n.* farewell. **-haft,** *adj.* lively, vivacious, spirited, active, sprightly, gay, brisk; bright, vivid, brilliant; *eine -hafte Straße,* a busy street; *-haft vor Augen haben,* have a clear picture of; *-haft bedauern,* regret very much. **-haftigkeit,** *f.* liveliness, vivacity, sprightliness, gaiety, *etc.* **-ig,** *suffix* (*in compounds*) = lived. **-kuchen,** *m.* gingerbread. **-los,** *adj.* lifeless, inanimate, dull, heavy, spiritless. **-tag,** *m,*; (*all*) *mein -tag,* in all my life; *meine -tage,* all the days of my life. **-zeiten,** *f.pl.* life, lifetime.

Leber, *f.* (-n) liver; *frei von der - weg sprechen,* speak one's mind frankly *or* plainly. **-anschwellung,** *f.* enlargement of the liver. **-beschwerde.** *f.* liver-complaint. **-blume,** *f.* a form of crowfoot, (*Anemone hepatica*) (*Bot.*). **-braun,** *adj. & n.* liver-coloured. **-entzündung,** *f.* hepatitis (*Med.*). **-fleck(en),** *m.* mole, birth mark. **-gang,** *m.* hepatic duct. **-krank,** *adj..* suffering from a liver-complaint. **-moose,** *n.pl.* liverworts (*Bot.*). **-tran,** *m.* cod-liver oil. **-wurst,** *f.* liver-sausage.

Lebkuchen, *see* **Leb-kuchen.**

lechzen, *v.n.* (*aux. h.*) be parched with thirst; *nach einer S. -,* languish, long *or* yearn for a th.; *nach Blut -,* thirst for blood.

leck, 1. *adj.* leaky, leaking; *- werden,* spring a leak. 2. *n.* (*& m.*) (-(e)s, -e) leak; leakage; *ein(en) - bekommen,* spring a leak. [1]**-en,** *v.n.* (*aux.* h.) let in water, leak; (*aux.* s.) leak, run, drip *or* trickle out; gutter (*as a candle*).

[2]**lecken,** *v.n.* (*archaic*) (*B.*) *wider den Stachel -,* kick against the pricks.

[3]**leck-en,** *v.a.* lick; *an den Fingern -en, sich* (*Dat.*) *die Finger -en,* lick one's fingers; *sich* (*Dat.*) *die Finger nach etwas -en,* desire something greedily; *das ist wie geleckt,* that is very neat *or* spruce. **-arsch,** *m.* (*vulg.*) lickspittle, toady, (*vulg.*) arse-crawler. **-er,** 1. *m.* gourmet, sweet-tooth; fawner, toady; tongue (*of furred game*) (*Hunt.*). 2. *adj.* nice, tasty, delicious; dainty, fastidious. **-erbissen,** *m.* dainty morsel, titbit. **-erei,** *f.* daintiness, fastidiousness; delicacy, dainty, titbit. **-erhaft,** *adj.* lickerish, fastidious. **-erli,** *n.pl.* (*Swiss dial.*) gingerbread. **-ermaul,** *n.* sweet-tooth, epicure. **-ern,** *v.n.* (*aux.* h.) be fastidious, be fond of dainty food; *nach einer S. -ern,* long *or* crave for a th., hanker after a th.

Leder, *n.* (-s, -) leather; skin; leather apron, leather seat of trousers; football; *ungegerbtes -,* undressed leather; *lohgares -,* tanned leather; *weiches -,* kid; *zugerichtetes -,* dressed *or* curried leather; (*coll.*) *einem das - gerben,* give a p. a good tanning. **-abfälle,** *m.pl.* leather cuttings. **-arbeiter,** *m.* leather worker. **-artig,** *adj.* leathery, tough. **-band** 1. *m.* leather binding. 2. *n.* leather strap *or* thong. **-bereitung,** *f.* leather-dressing. **-ei,** *f.* leather-work. **-er,** *m.* (*dial.*) tanner. **-gamaschen,** *f.pl.* leggings. **-gelb,** *adj. & n.* buff (-coloured). **-handel,** *m.* leather trade. **-haut,** *f.* cutis vera, corium, derma (*Anat.*). **-hosen,** *f.pl.* leather shorts. **-koffer,** *m.* leather trunk. **-n,** 1. *adj.* leather, leathery; coriaceous; (*coll.*) dull, tedious. 2. *v.a.* tan, curry, dress (*leather*); garnish *or* trim with leather; (*coll. & dial.*) thrash, tan. **-riemen,** *m.* leather strap *or* belt; strop (*for shaving*). **-ring,** *m.* leather washer. **-rücken,** *m.* leather back. **-scheibe,** *f., see* **-ring.** **-schmiere,** *f.* dubbing. **-streifen,** *m.* leather thong. **-überzug,** *m.* leather case. **-waren,** *f.pl.* leather goods. **-zeug,** *n.* leather equipment (*Mil.*). **-zucker,** *m.* (*weißer*) marshmallow; *schwarzer* (*brauner*) *-zucker, m.* liquorice.

ledig, *adj.* unmarried, single, (*Poet.*) empty, devoid (of), free, unencumbered, untrammelled; exempt (from), (*dial.*) unoccupied, vacant; *-es Frauenzimmer,* spinster; *-er Mann,* bachelor; (*dial.*) *-es Kind,* illegitimate child; *-e Mutter,* unmarried mother; *-er Stand,* celibacy; (*coll.*) single blessedness; *aller Pflichten los und -,* exempt from all duties; *los und - sprechen,* absolve, acquit; *- bleiben,* remain single, (*coll.*) be left on the shelf (*of girls*); *ich bleibe -,* I shall not marry. **-enheim,** *n.* home for bachelors. **-ensteuer** *f.* bachelor's tax. **-lich,** *adv.* only, solely, merely, purely, simply. **-sprechung,** *f.* acquittal; granting the freedom of a company.

Lee, *f.* lee, lee-side (*Naut.*); *das Ruder in - !* ease the

helm! *in – fallen*, drive to leeward. **–gierig,** *adj.* carrying lee helm (*Naut.*). **–segel,** *n.* studding-sail.
leer, *adj.* empty, vacant, void, unoccupied, blank; inane; idle, unfounded; hollow, vain; *–es Blatt*, clean sheet of paper; *mit –en Händen*, empty-handed; *– ausgehen*, leave empty-handed; *–er Raum*, empty space, blank space; vacuum; *–es Stroh*, threshed straw; *–es Stroh dreschen*, beat the air, pour water into a sieve; *–es Gerücht*, unfounded report. *– laufen*, run idle, tick over (*Mach.*); *see* **–laufen. –darm,** *m.* jejunum. **–e,** *f.* void, emptiness, vacancy, blank; vacuum; nothingness. **–en,** *v.a.* empty, evacuate, clear, clear out, pour out; *der Saal leerte sich in fünf Minuten*, the room was cleared in five minutes. **–faß,** *n.* emptying vat. **–gang,** *m., see* **–lauf. –gebrannt,** *p.p. & adj.* burnt out. **–gewicht,** *n.* dead weight, weight empty, tare. **–heit,** *f.* emptiness, futility; inanition (*Med.*). **–gut,** *n.* empties. **–lauf,** *m.* running idle, idling, ticking-over (*Mach.*). **–laufen,** *v.n.* empty (*tank, etc.*). **–schraube,** *f.* drain plug. **–stehend,** *adj.* unoccupied. **–ung,** *f.* emptying, clearing, clearance, evacuation. (*C.L.*) **–verkauf,** *m.* short sale.
Lefze, *f.* (-n) lip (*of animals*).
legal, *adj.* legal, lawful. **–isieren,** *v.a.* legalize, validate. **–isierung,** *f.* legalization. **–ität,** *f.* legality.
Legat, 1. *m.* (-en, -en) legate. 2. *n.* (-(e)s, -e) legacy; *bedingtes –*, contingent bequest. **–ar,** *m.* legatee. **–ion,** *f.* legation, embassy.
Legel, *m.* (*Austr. dial.*), *see* **Lägel.**
leg–en, 1. *v.a.* lay, put, place; deposit; set, sow, plant (*potatoes, etc.*); *Hand an eine S. –en*, turn one's hand to a th., take s.th. in hand; *Hand an einen –en*, lay hands on a p.; *Hand an sich –en*, commit suicide; *einem (etwas) ans Herz –en*, bring (s.th.) home to a p., impress (s.th.) upon a p.; *an die Kette –en*; chain up; *an den Tag –en*, make known, show; *Geld auf die hohe Kante –en*, put money aside; *großen Wert auf seine S. –en*, attach great importance to a th.; *Geld auf Zinsen –en*, invest capital; *etwas aus der Hand –en*, put a th. down, lay a th. aside; *Eier –en*, lay eggs; *einen Fußboden –en*, lay a floor; *einem das Handwerk –en*, put a stop to a p.'s activities, put a spoke into a p.'s wheel, put a spanner in the works; *in Asche –en*, reduce to ashes; *Bresche in etwas* (*Acc.*) *–en*, force a breach, batter in (*Mil.*); *einem Einquartierung ins Haus –en*, quarter soldiers on a p.; *einem Worte in den Mund –en*, ascribe words to a p. falsely; *die Hände in den Schoß –en*, sit with one's hands in one's lap, fold one's hands, be idle; *einem die Karte(n) –en*, tell a p.'s fortunes from cards; *einem etwas nahe –en*, bring s.th. home to a p., give a broad hint, make a pointed suggestion; *einen Teppich –en*, lay a carpet; *unter Siegel -en*, deliver under seal; *von sich –en*, lay aside; *einem den Kopf vor die Füße –en*, strike off a p.'s head; *ein Schloß vor die Tür –en*, put the bolt on the door; *zur Last –en*, charge with; *zur Schau –en*, expose to view. 2. *v.r.* lie down; cease, die down; subside, abate, settle, slacken, be quiet; *sich auf eine S. –en*, apply o.s. to, give o.s. up to *or* devote o.s. to a th.; *sich aufs Bitten –en*, implore *or* entreat earnestly; *sich auf die faule Haut –en*, take it easy, be lazy; *sich auf die Seite* or *aufs Ohr –en*, lay o.s. to rest; *sich ins Mittel –en*, interpose, intercede; *sich mächtig ins Zeug –en*, (*coll.*) go all out for; *sich vor Anker –en*, cast anchor; *sich schlafen –en*, go to bed. (*dial.*) **–egeld,** *n.* entrance-fee. **–(e)henne,** *f.* laying-hen. **–er,** *m.* good layer, laying hen. **–eröhre,** *f.* ovipositor. **–ezeit,** *f.* laying-season.
Legende, *f.* (-n) legend, myth; inscription, caption, legend. **–nhaft,** *adj.* legendary, mythical.
legier–en, *v.a.* alloy; thicken (*soup*). **–ung,** *f.* alloy(ing).
Legion, *f.* (-en) legion. **–är,** *m.* (-s, -e) legionary.
Legislat–ive, *f.* legislature. **–orisch,** *adj.* legislative. **–ur,** *f., see* **–ive.**
legitim, *adj.* legitimate, lawful. **–ation,** *f.* authority (to act); acknowledgement of legitimacy, proof of identity. **–ieren,** 1. *v.a* prove the identity of; authorize; legitimize; make lawful. 2. *v.r.* prove one's identity. **–ität,** *f.* legitimacy, legality. **–ationskarte,** *f.*, **–ationspapiere,** *n.pl.* identity card, identification papers.
Lehde, *f.* (-n) (*dial.*) waste *or* fallow land.
Leh(e)n, *n.* (-s, –) fief, feudal tenure; *als – besitzen* or *zu – tragen*, hold in fee; *zu – geben*, invest with; *unbedingtes* or *freies –*, fee simple. **–bauer,** *m.* peasant holding land on feudal tenure. **–besitz,** *m.* copyhold. **–dienst,** *m.* feudal service, vassalage, socage. **–erbe,** 1. *m.* successor to a fief. 2. *n.* hereditary fief. **–hof,** *m.* court-leet. **–(s)adel,** *m.* feudal nobility. **–(s)brief,** *m.* bill of enfeoffment; title-deed. **–seid,** *m.* oath of allegiance. **(s)entsetzung,** *f.*, **–seinziehung,** *f.* seizure of distraint upon a fief, dispossession. **–sfall,** *m.* escheat of a fief. **–sfolge,** *f.* succession to a fief; feudal obligation to serve in war; *–sfolge leisten*, follow one's liege lord to war. **–sfrei,** *adj.* allodial; *ein Gut –frei machen*, alienate an estate in mortmain. **–(s)gut,** *n.* property held in fee. **–sherr,** *m.* feudal lord, liege lord. **–sleute,** *pl.* vassals, feudal tenants. **–smann,** *m.* vassal. **–spflicht,** *f.* homage, fealty. **–(s)recht,** *n.* feudal law. **–ssystem,** *n.*, **–sverschaffung,** *f.* feudal system. **–sträger,** *m.* feudal tenant. **–streue,** *f.* allegiance. **–sverhältnis,** *n.* vassalage, socage. **–swesen,** *n.* feudalism.
Lehm, *m.* (-(e)s, -e) loam, clay; mud. **–artig,** *adj.* loamy. **–arbeit,** *f.*, **–bau,** *m.* mud-walling, wattle daubing. **–boden,** *m.* loamy *or* clay soil; clay floor. **–grube,** *f.* clay *or* loam-pit. **–hütte,** *f.* mud-hut. **–ig,** *adj.* loamy, clayey, argillaceous. **–schicht** *f.* loam-coat(ing). **–stein,** *m.* (unbaked) clay brick. **–wand,** *f.* mud wall. **–ziegel,** *m.* sun-dried brick.
Lehn–e, *f.* (-n) arm *or* back (*of a chair*), support, rest, prop; hand-rail, balustrade, railing; gallows (*Typ.*); (*dial.*) slope, inclined plane, declivity. **–en,** *v.a. & n.* (*aux.* h. & s.) lean (against), recline, rest (upon); *der eine Gang –t sich mit dem andern*, one lode runs into another (*Min.*). **–fenster,** *n.* window with embrasure *or* breastwork. **–satz,** *m.* lemma (*Math.*). **–sessel,** *m.*, **–stuhl,** *m.* easy chair, arm-chair. **–wort,** *n.* loan-word.
Lehr, *n.* (-(e)s, -e) pattern, model, gauge, *see* **–e. –amt,** *n.* teacher's post, professorship; teaching profession. **–anstalt,** *f.* educational establishment. **–aufgabe,** *f.* programme of work; *–aufgabe der Obersekunda*, work to be done in the Upper Fifth. **–auftrag,** *m.* professorship; *einen –auftrag erhalten*, be appointed professor. **–befähigung,** *f.* qualification to teach (*a subject*). **–begriff,** *m.* system; outline, manual of science. **–behelf,** *m., see* **–mittel. –beruf,** *m.* teaching *or* scholastic profession. **–bogen,** *m.* centre, centering (*Arch.*). **–brief,** *m.* indentures. **–brett,** *n.* templet, template; mould, pattern. **–buch,** *n.* text-book. **–bursche,** *m.* apprentice. **–e,** *f.* (-en) instruction, lesson, precept, teaching, warning; moral, doctrine, dogma, tenet, theory, science; apprenticeship; gauge (*Engin.*); *in die –e geben* or *tun*, apprentice to; *er ist bei Herrn N. in der –e*, he is serving his time with Mr. N.; *in die –e gehen*, work as an apprentice; *laßt euch dies zur –e dienen!* let this be a warning to you! *die –e Christi*, Christ's teaching; *die –e vom Schall*, the theory of sound. **–en,** *v.a.* (*einen etwas*) teach, instruct; inform; show, prove; take the calibre of; *einen lesen –en*, teach a p. to read; *so wurde es mir gelehrt*, that was the way I was taught; *die Zeit wird es –en*, time will show. **–er,** *m.* teacher, schoolmaster, instructor, tutor. **–erbildungsanstalt,** *f., see* **–erseminar. –erhaft,** *adj.* pedantic, didactic, doctrinaire. **–erin,** *f.* woman teacher. **–erkollegium,** *n.* staff (*of a school*). **–erprüfung,** *f.* examination for teachers. **–erschaft,** *f.* body of teachers; staff. **–erseminar,** *n.* (teachers) training college. **–erstand,** *m.* scholastic profession; members of the teaching profession. **–erstelle,** *f.* post of teacher. **–erstellung,** *f.* status of teachers. **–ertag,** *m.* teachers' conference. **–erwelt,** *f.* scholastic world. **–erzeugnis,** *n.* teacher's diploma. **–fach,** *n.* subject, branch of study. **–fähig,** *adj.* capable of teaching. **–film,** *m.* instructional *or* educational film. **–freiheit,** *f.* freedom of teaching. **–gang,** *m.* course (*of*

instruction). **–gebäude,** *n.* system (*of a science, etc.*). **–gedicht,** *n.* didactic poem. **–gegenstand,** *m.* subject taught, branch of study. **–geld,** *n.* fees, apprentice's premium; *–geld bezahlen,* (*fig.*) pay for one's experience. **–gerüst,** *n.* matrix, frame, scantling (*Arch.*). **–grund,** *m.* principle, basis (*of a science, etc.*). **–haft,** *adj.* didactic; schoolmasterly; instructive. **–herr,** *m.* master (*of an apprentice*). **–jahre,** *n.pl.* years of apprenticeship; *seine –jahre durchmachen,* serve out one's time. **–junge,** *m.* apprentice. **–kanzel,** *f.* (*Austr. dial.*) *see* **–stuhl. –körper,** *m.* teaching staff, professoriate. **–kraft,** *f.* teacher. **–kunst,** *f.* pedagogics, art of teaching. **–kurs, –kursus,** *m.* course of instruction. **–ling,** *m.* apprentice, pupil, novice, tyro. **–lingsstand,** *m.* apprenticeship, novitiate. **–mädchen,** *n.* girl-apprentice. **–mäßig,** *adj.* didactic, dogmatic. **–meinung,** *f.* dogma; hypothesis. **–meister,** *m.* teacher, instructor; master of a trade. **–meisterlich,** *adj.* preceptorial; pedantic, doctrinaire. **–mittel,** *n.* educational aids, apparatus (*for instruction*). **–plan,** *m.* course of instruction; school curriculum. **–probe,** *f.* (time of) probation, novitiate, trial lesson. **–reich,** *adj.* instructive. **–saal,** *m.* lecture-room; class-room, school-room. **–satz,** *m.* thesis, dogma, doctrine, proposition, theorem, precept. **–spruch,** *m.* maxim, adage. **–stand,** *m.* scholastic profession. **–stelle,** *f.* apprenticeship. **–stoff,** *m.* subject matter (of instruction). **–stuhl,** *m.* professorial chair. **–stunde,** *f.* period of instruction, lesson, lecture. **–tätigkeit,** *f.* educational work, teaching. **–tochter,** *f.* (*Swiss dial.*), *see* **–mädchen. –vertrag,** *m.* indentures. **–weise,** *f.* method of teaching. **–widrig,** *adj.* heterodox. **–zeit,** *f.* apprenticeship. **–ziel,** *n.* standard of achievement (*in a subject*). **–zwang,** *m.* compulsory indoctrination, compulsory education.

Lei, *f.* (-en) (*dial.*) slate (*e.g. Erpeler Lei, Lorelei*).

Leib, *m.* (-(e)s, -er) body; abdomen belly; womb; waist, trunk; *toter –,* corpse (*of a man*); carcass (*of an animal*); *es ging ihm an – und Leben,* his life was at stake; *am ganzen –e zittern,* tremble all over; *kein Hemd auf dem –e haben,* not have a shirt to one's back; *bei –e nicht!* (*Austr. dial.*), (*usually*) *beileibe nicht!* not on your life; not on any account! *bei lebendigem –e,* while (still) alive; *gut bei –e sein,* be plump *or* fat; *Gefahr für – und Leben,* danger to life and limb; *gesegneten –es,* pregnant, with child, in the family way; *harten –es sein,* be constipated; *der – des Herrn,* the Host, the consecrated wafer *or* bread; *mit – und Seele,* with heart and soul. (*vulg.*) *sich* (*Dat.*) *den – vollschlagen,* eat one's fill, stuff o.s.; *bleib mir vom –e! drei Schritt vom –e!* keep off! *bleib mir damit vom –e!* don't bother me about that; (*scharf*) *zu – gehen* or *rücken,* attack a p. sharply, become aggressive; close in on s.o. **–arzt,** *m.* physician in ordinary (*to the king, etc.*). **–binde,** *f.* waistband, sash; abdominal belt *or* bandage, body-belt. **–buch,** *n.* favourite book. **–bürge,** *m.* hostage. **–bursch,** *m.* elder student who has a younger one to fag for him. **–chen,** *n.* bodice, vest, corset. **–diener,** *m.* officer's servant, batman (*Mil.*); page, valet de chambre. **–eigen,** *adj.* in bondage, thrall *or* villeinage. **–eigene(r),** *m.* serf, bondman. **–eigenschaft,** *f.* bondage, serfdom. **–en,** (*only in*) *wie er leibt und lebt,* the very image of (him), his very self. **–erl,** *n.* (*dial.*) rissole. **–esbeschaffenheit,** *f.* (physical) constitution. **–eserbe,** *m.* legitimate heir; offspring; (*pl.*) issue. **–esfrucht,** *f.* foetus, embryo, (*Poet.*) offspring; *Abtreibung* or *Tötung der –esfrucht,* procuring abortion. **–esgebrechen,** *n.*, **–esfehler,** *m.* bodily infirmity *or* deformity. **–esgröße,** *f.* stature. **–eskraft,** *f.*; *aus –eskräften,* with might and main, with all one's might; *er schrie aus –eskräften,* he shouted at the top of his voice. **–esnahrung,** *f.* food; *–esnahrung und –esnotdurft,* bodily needs, necessities of life. **–esöffnung,** *f.* opening of the bowels, motion. **–espflege,** *f.* care of the body. **–(es)schüssel,** *f.* bed-pan. (*coll.*) **–essen,** *n.* favourite dish. **–esstellung,** *f.* posture, attitude. **–esstrafe,** *f.* corporal punishment. **–esübung,** *f.* (*usually pl.* –en) physical exercise, gymnastics. **–fuchs,** *m.* freshman who acts as fag to an older student. **–garde,** *f.* bodyguard, life-guards. **–gedinge,** *n.* jointure, dower, appanage, settlement, (*dial.*) pension, life-annuity. **–geleit,** *n.* safe-conduct. (*coll.*) **–gericht,** *n.* favourite dish. **–gurt,** *m.*, **–gürtel,** *m.* body *or* abdominal belt. **–haftig,** *adj.* embodied, real, true, incarnate; *–haftig erscheinen,* appear in person. **–ig,** *adj.* (*dial.*) fat, corpulent; (*otherwise only as suffix*) having such-and-such a body, *e.g. dickleibig,* corpulent. **–jäger,** *m.* prince's own huntsman *or* game-keeper; chasseur (*Mil.*). **–knecht,** *m.* groom of the royal stables. **–kompa(g)nie,** *f.* colonel's own company, first company of a regiment. **–lich,** *adj.* bodily, material, corporeal, somatic; consanguineous; temporal; *sein –licher Sohn,* his own son; *mit –lichen Augen sehen,* see with one's own eyes; *–licher Bruder,* own brother; *–licher Vetter,* cousin german; *ihr –licher Sohn,* her own son; (*B.*) *–liche Güter,* carnal things; earthly goods; *–licher Tod,* natural death. **–lichkeit,** *f.* corporeality. **–los,** *adj.* incorporeal. **–pacht,** *f.* lease for life. **–regiment,** *n.* prince's own regiment. **–rente,** *f.* (life) annuity; *bedingte –rente,* contingent annuity. **–rock,** *m.* (*archaic*) frock-coat, dress-coat. **–schmerz,** *m.* (*usually pl.* -en), **–schneiden,** *n.* stomach-ache, gripes, colic. **–speise,** *f.*, *see* **–gericht.** (*coll.*) **–spruch,** *m.* favourite saying *or* maxim. **–standarte,** *f.* (*Nat. Soc.*) Hitler's body-guard. (*coll.*) **–stück,** *n.* favourite piece, favourite tune *or* air (*Mus.*). **–ung,** *f.* inner face of arches and wall openings (*windows, doors, etc.*) (*Arch.*). **–wache,** *f.* bodyguard. **–wächter,** *m.* soldier of the bodyguard; satellite. **–wäsche,** *f.* linen, underwear. **–weh,** *n.*, *see* **–schmerz. –zucht,** *f.* (*archaic*), *see* **–gedinge. –züchter,** *m.*, **–züchterin,** *f.* life-annuitant.

Leich, *m.* (-(e)s, -e) (*archaic*) lay; *die Lieder und Leiche der Minnesinger,* the songs and lays of the minnesingers.

Leichdorn, (-s, ⸗er (*& Austr. dial.* -e)) (*dial.*) corn (*on the foot*).

Leich–e, *f.* (-en) dead body, corpse, cadaver, (*dial.*) funeral; omitted word(s) (*Typ.*); (*dial.*) *zur –e gehen,* attend a funeral. **–enacker,** *m.* (*dial.*) churchyard, burying-ground, cemetery, necropolis. **–enbegängnis,** *n.* funeral. **–enbegleiter,** *m.* mourner. **–enbegleitung,** *f.* funeral procession. **–enbeschauer,** *m.* coroner. **–enbesorger,** *m.*, **–enbestatter,** *m.* undertaker. **–enbestattung,** *f.*, *see* **–enbegängnis. –enbitter,** *m.* one who invites to a funeral. **–enbittergesicht,** *n.*, **–enbittermiene,** *f.* woebegone look. **–enblaß,** *adj.* pale as death. **–enchor,** *m.* funeral dirge, requiem. **–endieb,** *m.* body-snatcher. **–endienst,** *m.* burial-service, obsequies, exequies. **–enfarbe,** *f.* pallor of death. **–enfeier,** *f.* obsequies, exequies, funeral service. **–enfeld,** *n.* field strewed with corpses, battlefield. **–enfledderer,** *m.* looter of corpses. **–enfrau,** *f.* layer-out. **–engebräuche,** *m.pl.* funeral rites. **–engeleit,** *n.*, *see* **–enbegleitung. –engepränge,** *n.* funeral pomp. **–engeruch,** *m.* cadaverous smell. **–engerüst,** *n.* catafalque. **–engesang,** *m.* dirge. **–engewand,** *n.*, *see* **–enhemd. –engewölbe,** *n.*, **–engruft,** *f.* burial-vault, catacomb. **–engift,** *n.* ptomaine. **–enhaft,** *adj.* corpse-like, cadaverous. **–enhalle,** *f.* mortuary, morgue. **–enhemd,** *n.* shroud, winding sheet. **–enmahl,** *n.* funeral banquet **–enmusik,** *f.* dead march, funeral music. **–enöffnung,** *f.* post-mortem examination. **–enpredigt,** *f.* funeral sermon. **–enräuber,** *m.* one who loots corpses. **–enrede,** *f.* funeral oration. **–enschädigung,** *f.* desecration of corpses. **–enschau,** *f.* coroner's inquest, post-mortem examination. **–enschauer,** *m.* coroner. **–enschleier,** *m.* shroud. **–enschmaus,** *m.*, *see* **–enmahl. –enstarre,** *f.* rigor mortis. **–enstein,** *m* tombstone. **–enträger,** *m.* bearer. **–entuch,** *n.* winding-sheet, shroud, pall. **–enuntersuchung,** *f.* post-mortem examination, coroner's inquest. **–enverbrennung,** *f.* cremation. **–enwagen,** *m.* hearse. **–enwurm,** *m.* maggot. **–enzug,** *m.* funeral procession. **–nam,** (-s, -e) *m.* dead body, corpse, cadaver, remains; (*hum.*) *seines –nams pflegen*, do o.s. well.

leicht, *adj.* light, easy, free, facile, nimble; mild, small (*of beer*); slight, moderate, gentle, trifling, insignificant, superficial; fickle, frivolous, careless, flighty; weak, feeble, faint; *–en Absatz finden*, be disposed of easily, sell readily; *etwas auf die –e Achsel nehmen*, take *or* treat a th. lightly; *es kann – anders kommen*, it may easily turn out otherwise; *–e Bewegung*, easy *or* graceful movement; *mit –er Bewegung des Kopfes*, with a slight movement of the head; *–er Bruder*, loose character; *–en Fußes*, light-footed, trippingly; *–en Kaufs davon kommen*, get *or* come off lightly; *es sich* (*Dat.*) *– machen*, take the easy way out; *– möglich*, very probably; *etwas – nehmen*, make light of a th.; *ich kann es nicht – tun*, I cannot well do it; *außer ihm wird es nicht – jemand tun*, there is no one except himself who is likely to do it; *das kommt nicht – zweimal vor*, that is unlikely to happen again; *das kann – sein*, that is very possible; *–er Sinn*, cheerful temperament; *– über eine S. hinweggehen*, treat a th. superficially, pass over a th. lightly; *es wird* or *ist mir –er ums Herz*, I feel easier in my mind, I am *or* feel relieved; *die Arbeit geht ihr – von der Hand*, the work comes easily to her; *– zu Mute*, cheerful, in good *or* high spirits. **–athletik,** *f.* athletics. **–beweglich,** *adj.* easily movable, changeable, very mobile. **–blütig,** *adj.* sanguine. **–en,** *v.a.* weigh (*the anchor*), *see* **[2]lichten. –er,** *m.* lighter, barge (*Naut.*). **–ergeld,** *n.* lighterage. **–ern,** *v.a.* unload (*a ship*). **–faßlich,** *adj.* easily understood, popular. **–fertig,** *adj.* frivolous, thoughtless, inconsiderate, unscrupulous, wanton, loose. **–fertigkeit,** *f.* frivolity, thoughtlessness, wantonness; **–flugzeug,** *n.* light aeroplane. **–flüssig,** *adj.* easily fusible, easily dissolved; thinly liquid. **–fuß,** *m.* gay spark, happy-go-lucky fellow. **–füßig,** *adj.* nimble, light-footed. **–geschürzt,** *adj.* lightly draped (*i.e. the Muse*). **–gewicht,** *n.* light-weight (*Sport*). **–gläubig,** *adj.* credulous. **–gläubigkeit,** *f.* credulity. **–heit,** *f.* lightness. **–herzig,** *adj.* cheerful. **–hin,** *adv.* lightly, casually, carelessly, superficially. **–igkeit,** *f.* agility, facility; ease, readiness. **–lebig,** *adj.* light-hearted, happy-go-lucky, easy-going. **–lich,** *adv.* easily, lightly. **–löslich,** *adj.* easily soluble. **–matrose,** *m.* ordinary seaman. **–metall,** *n.* light metal. **–sinn,** *m., see* **–sinnigkeit. –sinnig,** *adj.* thoughtless, careless, rash, frivolous. **–sinnigkeit,** *f.* thoughtlessness, rashness, indiscretion. **–verderblich,** *adj.* perishable (*of goods*). **–verständlich,** *adj.* easy to understand. **–verwundete(n),** *pl.* walking wounded.

leid, 1. *adj.* painful, disagreeable (*only predicatively with* sein, tun, werden, *and Dat.*); (*Swiss dial.*) *used attributively*, unpleasant, bad; *es ist* or *tut mir –*, I am sorry, I regret; *einem etwas – machen*, make a p. repent of a th., spoil a th. for s.o., spoil a p.'s pleasure in a th.; *es wird dir einmal – werden*, you will one day be sorry for it; *laß dir das nicht – sein*, do not regret having done it. 2. *n.* (*archaic* **–s,** *n.*; *Austr. dial.* **–es,** *n.*) harm, hurt, injury, wrong; pain, sorrow, grief, mourning; *in Lieb und –*, through thick and thin; *einem ein – tun* or *zufügen*, harm *or* injure s.o.; *sich* (*Dat.*) *ein –(s) antun*, commit suicide; *einem sein – klagen*, pour out one's trouble to a p.; *vor – vergehen*, die of a broken heart; *um einen – tragen*, mourn *or* be in mourning for a p.; *keinem zu –e und keinem zu Liebe*, without fear or favour. **–eform,** *f.* passive voice (*Gram.*). **–en,** 1. *ir.v.a.* suffer, bear, endure, undergo, put up with, tolerate; allow, permit, admit; *–en mögen* or *können*, like; *ich kann ihn nicht –en*, I cannot stand him; *ich mag ihn wohl –en*, I rather like him; *Hunger –en*, suffer from hunger; *Schaden –en*, sustain loss *or* injury; *er ist bei uns wohl gelitten*, he is very popular with us; *es litt mich nicht*, I could not remain quiet; *es litt mich dort nicht länger*, I could not bear to stay there any longer. 2. *v.n.* (*aux.* h.) suffer, be in pain; *an etwas –en*, suffer from, be subject *or* liable to; *seine Gesundheit wird darunter –en*, his health will suffer from it; *sie ist sehr –end*, she is ailing *or* very poorly; *er ist herz– (augen–) –end*, he suffers from a weak heart (weak eyes). 3. *n.* suffering, pain, torment; affliction, malady, ailment, chronic complaint, disease; *das –en Christi*, the Passion of our Lord; *der Mensch ist zum –en geboren*, man is born to trouble. **–end,** *pr.p.* & *adj.* ailing, suffering; passive; *das –ende Zeitwort*, passive verb; *–ender Gehorsam*, passive obedience; *der* (or *die*) *–ende*, the patient, the sufferer. **–ensbecher,** *m.* cup of sorrow. **–ensbruder,** *m., see* **–ensgefährte. –enschaft,** *f.* (-en) passion. **–enschaftlich,** *adj.* passionate, vehement; enthusiastic. **–enschaftsfrei,** *adj.*, **–enschaftslos,** *adj.* apathetic, dispassionate; calm. **–enschaftslosigkeit,** *f.* apathy. **–ensgefährte,** *m.*, **–ensgenosse,** *m.* fellow-sufferer, companion in misfortune. **–ensgeschichte,** *f.* tale of woe; Christ's Passion. **–enskelch,** *m., see* **–ensbecher. –ensprobe,** *f.* ordeal, trial. **–ensstationen,** *f.pl.* the stations of the cross. **–ensweg,** *m.* way of the cross; life of suffering. **–enswoche,** *f.* Passion Week. **–er,** *adv.* & *int.* unfortunately, I am sorry to say; alas! *–er Gottes!* most unfortunately! *–er sehen wir, daß . . .*, we are sorry to see that . . ., we see that unfortunately . . .; *–er müssen wir zugeben*, we must reluctantly admit; *–er muß ich gehen*, I am afraid I have to go. **–ig,** *adj.* tiresome, unpleasant, nasty, disagreeable; grievous, distressing; abominable, loathsome, shocking, accursed; *–iger Trost*, cold comfort, poor consolation; *der –ige Teufel*, Satan himself. **–karte,** *f.* (*Swiss dial.*) mourning card. **–lich,** *adj.* tolerable, passable, middling, mediocre; *ich bin noch so –lich weggekommen*, I have got off rather easily. **–sam,** *adj.* (*dial.*) tolerant, patient; tolerable. **–tragend,** *adj.* mourning; *der –tragende*, mourner. **–voll,** *adj.* full of grief, sorrowful. **–werken,** *v.n.* (*with Dat.*) (*Swiss dial.*) make difficulties (for), annoy. **–wesen,** *n.*; *zu unserm –wesen*, to our sorrow.

Leier, *f.* (-n) lyre (*see also* **–kasten**); Lyra (*Astr.*); *immer die alte –*, the same old story; *immer bei der alten – bleiben*, be always harping on the same thing. **–förmig,** *adj.* lyre-shaped; lyrate (*Bot.*). (*coll.*) **–kasten,** *m.* barrel-organ, hurdy-gurdy. **–kastenmann,** *m.* organ-grinder. **–n,** *v.a.* & *n.* (*aux.* h.) grind a barrel-organ; turn (with) a winch; drawl on; *einem die Ohren voll –n*, din perpetually into a p.'s ears; *besser geleiert als gefeiert*, anything is better than nothing.

Leih–e, *f.* loan; (*coll.*) pawnshop. **–en,** *ir.v.a.* lend; loan; borrow, hire; *er –t es mir*, he lends it to me; *ich –e es mir von ihm*, I borrow it from him. **–bibliothek,** *f.*, **–bücherei,** *f.*, lending *or* circulating library. **–haus,** *n.* loan-office, pawnshop. **–schein,** *m.* pawn-ticket; library ticket. **– und Pacht,** lease-lend. **–weise,** *adv.* as a loan.

Leikauf, *m.* (-(e)s, -̈e) (*dial.*) drink to seal a bargain.

Leim, *m.* (-(e)s, -e) glue; size; bird-lime; gelatine; *– sieden*, boil glue; do unprofitable work; (*coll.*) *auf den – gehen*, fall into the trap; (*coll.*) *auf den – krieche* (or *gehe*) *ich nicht*, I shall not let myself in for that, you will not catch me there; (*coll.*) *aus dem –e gehen*, fall to pieces, come to grief. **–artig,** *adj.* glutinous, gelatinous. **–en,** *v.a.* glue; size; (*coll.*) trick, deceive. **–farbe,** *f.* water-paint, distemper. **–fuge,** *f.* glued joint. **–ig,** *adj.* gluey, viscous, glutinous. **–kitt,** *m.* plastic wood. **–ring,** *m.* grease band (*on fruit trees*). **–rute,** *f.* lime-twig. **–sieder,** *m.* glue-maker; (*hum.*) bore. **–stoff,** *m.* gluten. **–tiegel,** *m.*, **–topf,** *m.* glue-pot. **–zucker,** *m.* glycocoll, glycocin.

Lein, *m.* (-(e)s, -e) flax; linseed. **–bau,** *m.* cultivation of flax. **–e,** *f.* (-en) cord, line, rope; (dog's) lead, leash; *an der –e haben*, hold by a string; (*fig.*) have in one's power; *von einem an der –e gehalten werden*, be in a p.'s leading-strings; *Hunde sind an der –e zu führen*, dogs must be kept on a lead; *–e ziehen*, hang out a clothes line; (*coll.*) *–eziehen*, clear off *or* out, (*vulg.*) do a bunk. **–en,** 1. *adj.* linen. 2. *n.* (-ens, -en) linen; linen goods. **–enband,** *m.* cloth binding; *biegsamer –enband*, limp-cloth binding. **–engarn,** *n.* linen yarn. **–enpapier,** *n.* linen-paper. **–(en)weber,** *m.* linen-weaver. **–(en)weberei,** *f.* manufacture of linen; linen-factory.

-(en)zeug, *n.* linen. **-fink,** *m.* (*dial.*) linnet. **-firnis,** *m.* printer's varnish. **-kraut,** *n.* wild flax (*Linaria vulgaris*) (*Bot.*). **-kuchen,** *m.* oil-cake. **-öl,** *n.* linseed-oil. **-pfad,** *m.* towing-path. **-same(n),** *m.* flax-seed, linseed. **-tuch,** *n.* linen cloth; sheet. **-wand,** *f.* linen, linen cloth; canvas (*Paint.*); screen (*Films*); *grobe -wand,* sackcloth, bale-cloth; *gesteifte -wand,* buckram; *auf -wand ziehen,* mount on canvas.

leis(e), *adj.* low, soft, gentle; slight, faint, imperceptible; fine, delicate; *- schlafen,* sleep lightly, be a light sleeper; *- auftreten,* tread noiselessly; proceed cautiously; *- berühren,* touch lightly upon; treat superficially; *mit -r Stimme,* in a low voice, in an undertone; *nicht der -ste Laut,* not the least sound; *nicht die -ste Ahnung,* not the faintest idea, *or* suspicion; *nicht im -sten zweifeln,* not have a shadow of doubt. **-treter,** *m.* sneak, grovel, fawn. **-treterei,** *f.* sneaking, obsequiousness, fawning.

Leist, *m.* (-es, -e) (*Swiss dial.*) club, association.

Leiste, *f.* (-n) ridge, beading, moulding, fillet; ledge; carina (*Bot. & Zool.*); (*dial.*) slope, incline; groin (*Anat.*). **-nbruch,** *m.* rupture (in the groin), inguinal hernia; **-ngegend,** *f.* inguinal region. **-nwerk,** *n.* coping; beading, moulding.

leist-en, *v.a.* do, fulfil, carry out, perform, accomplish; effect, realize; afford, give; produce; *Beistand -en,* render assistance; *Bürgschaft -en,* give bail; *Buße -en,* do penance; *Dienste -en,* render service; *den Eid der Treue -en,* take the oath of allegiance; *Ersatz -en,* supply a substitute, act as substitute; *er wird nie etwas -en,* he will never do any good; *Folge -en,* obey; *einer gerichtlichen Aufforderung Folge -en,* answer a summons; *Gesellschaft -en,* keep (s.o.) company; *Gewähr -en,* vouch for, guarantee; *Hilfe -en,* help, assist (*coll.*) give a hand; *mehr -en als zu erwarten war,* do more than was expected; *tüchtiges -en,* do extremely well; *Verzicht auf eine S. -en,* renounce, give up *or* do without a th.; *Widerstand -en,* offer resistance; *Zahlung -en,* make payment, pay a debt; (*coll.*) *ich kann mir das -en,* I can afford (to do) it; (*coll.*) *er hat sich einen neuen Hut geleistet,* he has treated himself to a new hat. **-ung,** *f.* performance, execution; achievement, accomplishment, work; payment; production, output, result, effect; *tüchtige -ung,* creditable performance, excellent piece of work; *gegen -ung einer Bürgschaft,* on bail. **-ungsarbeit,** *f.* piece work. **-ungsfähig,** *adj.* fit, able; efficient, productive. **-ungsfähigkeit,** *f.* capacity for work; efficiency; (*C.L.*) solvency; power (*Mech.*) **-ungsfaktor,** *m.* power factor (*Elec.*). **-ungsgrundsatz,** *m.* Bedaux principle. **-ungsmesser,** *m.* output meter (*Elec.*). **-ungsprüfung,** *f.* efficiency test.

Leisten, *m.* (-s, -) shoemaker's last, boot-tree; *auf* or *über den - schlagen,* put on the last; *alles über einen - schlagen,* treat all alike; *sie sind alle über einen - geschlagen,* they are all of the same stamp. **-arbeit,** *f.* routine work, mass-production job.

Leit-artikel, *m.* leading article, leader. **-bar,** *adj.* manageable, conductible, ductile, flexible, versatile. **-blech,** *n.* deflecting plate, baffle. **-e,** *f.* (-n) (*dial.*) declivity, slope (*of a hill*). **-en,** *v.a.* lead, guide, conduct; train, direct; manage, oversee, preside over, govern; *sich -en lassen,* allow o.s. to be led, be tractable *or* docile; be actuated (*von,* by); *nicht -end,* non-conducting; *die -enden Kreise,* influential persons, the governing classes, those in authority. **-er,** 1. *m.* leader, guide, conductor; director, manager, governor, principal, head. 2. *f.* (-n) ladder; scale, gamut (*Mus.*). **-erartig,** *adj.*, **-erförmig,** *adj.* scalariform (*Bot., Zool.*). **-erbaum,** *m.*, *see* **-erstange. -ernetz,** *n.* conducting network (*Elec.*). **-erschleife,** *f.* armature (*Elec.*). **-ersprosse,** *f.* rung of a ladder. **-erstange,** *f.* ladder upright. **-erwagen,** *m.* rack-wagon. **-faden,** *m.* guide, manual; text-book, primer. **-fähig,** *adj.* conductive (*Elec.*). **-fähigkeit,** *f.* conductivity, conductance. **-feuer,** *n.* leading light (*Naut.*); slow-match, safety-fuse. **-flosse,** *f.* tail fin (*Av.*). **-fossil,** *n.* characteristic fossil. **-gedanke,** *m.* main idea, keynote. **-gerade,** *f.* director, generator (*Math.*). **-hammel,** *m.* bell-wether. **-kante,** *f.* leading edge (*Av.*). **-kauf,** *m.* *see* **Leikauf. -linie,** *f.* directrix (*Geom.*). **-motiv,** *n.* leitmotiv. (*Mus.*). **-riemen,** *m.* driving-rein; leading strings. **-satz,** *m.* guiding principle. **-schiene,** *f.* live rail (*Railw.*). **-seil,** *n.* guide-rope. **-stab,** *m.*, **-stange,** *f.* guide-rod. **-stelle,** *f.* army post-office. **-stern,** *m.* guiding-star; pole-star. **-strahl,** *m.* radius vector (*Geom.*). **-tier,** *n.* leader (*Hunt.*). **-ung,** *f.* leading, guidance, direction; administration, directorate; command, control, management, charge, care; conduit, pipe, piping, tubing, duct; (*dial.*) tap, stand-pipe; line, wire, lead, cable, circuit (*Elec.*); supply, conduction, transmission (*Phys.*); *-ung der öffentlichen Angelegenheiten,* conduct of public affairs; *die -ung haben,* lead, be in *or* have charge of; *die -ung in die Hand nehmen,* take the lead, take charge, take the reins; (*coll.*) *eine lange -ung haben,* be slow *or* dull of comprehension. **-ungsaufseher,** *m.* lineman (*Phone.*). **-ungsbehörde,** *f.* committee of management, directorate. **-ungsdraht,** *m.* conducting-wire. **-ungsfähigkeit,** *f.* conductivity, conductance (*Elec.*). **-ungsfehler,** *m.*, *see* **-ungsstörung. -ungsnetz,** *n.* supply network (*Elec.*). **-ungsrohr,** *n.* supply-pipe; conduit, main. **-ungsschnur,** *f.* flex, lead (*Elec.*). **-ungsspannung,** *f.* line voltage. **-ungsstörung,** *f.* line-fault (*Phone.*), circuit fault (*Phone.*). **-ungsvermögen,** *n.*, *see* **-ungsfähigkeit. -ungswasser,** *n.* tap-water. **-vermerk,** *m.* indication of route. **-werk,** *n.* tail unit, empennage (*Av.*). **-zaum,** *m.* bridle, rein.

Lekt-ion, *f.* (-en) lesson; rebuke; *einem eine -ion lesen,* give a p. a lecture *or* a good scolding. **-or,** *m.* (-s, -en) lecturer, lector, teacher (of mother tongue abroad); publisher's reader. **-üre,** *f.* (-n) reading; reading matter, books, literature. **-ürestunde,** *f.* lesson to discuss home reading.

Lemma, *n.* (-s, -s) assumption, proposition, lemma (*pl.* lemmata) (*Log.*); caption, legend, heading.

Lemur(e), *m.* (-s, -(e)n) maki, lemur (*Zool.*); evil spirit, ghost, spook.

Lende, *f.* (-n) loin, loins; haunch, hip, (*coll.*) thigh. **-nbraten,** *m.* roast sirloin; rump of beef. **-ngegend,** *f.* lumbar region. **-nknochen,** *m.* hip-bone. **-nlahm,** *adj.* hobbling, crippled, worn out (*from walking*); (*fig.*) halting, lame (*as an excuse*). **-nschurz,** *m.* loin cloth. **-nstück,** *n.* loin, fillet. **-nwirbel,** *m.* lumbar vertebra.

lenk-en, *v.a.* turn, guide, direct; navigate, pilot; lead, control, manage; steer, drive; *-en (in),* turn (into); *einen Wagen -en,* drive a car; *die Schritte -en,* wend one's way; turn, go; *das Gespräch auf einen Gegenstand -en,* turn the conversation upon a subject; *die Aufmerksamkeit auf sich -en,* attract attention, call attention to o.s.; (*Prov.*) *der Mensch denkt, Gott -t,* man proposes, God disposes. **-ballon,** *m.* dirigible (balloon). **-bar,** *adj.* dirigible, (*fig.*) tractable, manageable, docile. **-er,** *m.* ruler, disposer; guide. **-gehäuse,** *n.* steering gear housing. **-knüppel,** *m.* joy-stick (*Av.*). **-luftschiff,** *n.* dirigible (airship). **-rad,** *n.* steering-wheel (*Motor*); front wheel (*Cycl.*). **-sam,** *adj.* tractable, manageable, docile; flexible. **-samkeit,** *f.* manageableness, docility. **-säule,** *f.* steering column. **-seil,** *n.* guide-rope. **-stange,** *f.* tie-rod; (*pl.*) steering suspension (*Motor.*), handlebars (*Cycl.*). **-stelle,** *f.* planning office. **-ung,** *f.* controlling, control, direction, governing, ruling; management; steering. **-stock,** *m.* steering arm. **-zaum,** *m.* bridle, rein.

Lenz, *m.* (-es, -e) (*Poet.*) spring; prime, bloom (*of life*); (*pl.*) years (*of age*). **-en,** *v. imp.* spring comes, become spring. **-haft,** *adj.*, **-lich,** *adj.* vernal, spring-like. **-ing,** *m.* **-mond,** *m.* March.

lenz, 1. *adj.* (*dial.*) dry, empty. 2. *f.* (*Austr. dial.*) indolence; leisure. **-en,** *v.a.* pump (*bilges*), blow (*tanks of submarine*); run before the wind, scud (*Naut.*); (*Austr. dial.*) laze, be idle; lounge, loaf. **-pumpe,** *f.* bilge-pump.

Leopard, *m.* (-en, -en) leopard, panther.

Lepra, *f.* leprosy. **-kranke(r),** *m.* & *f.* leper.

Lerche, *f.* (-n) lark; *eine - schießen,* take a toss, fall head over heels; *-n streichen,* catch larks with a net.

-ngarn, *n.* net for catching larks. **-nherd,** *m.* decoy for larks. **-nstreichen,** *n.* netting of larks. **-nstrich,** *m.* migration of larks. **-nwirbel,** *m.* warbling of larks.

lern-en, 1. *v.a.* learn; study; (*dial.*) teach; *ich habe ihn kennengelernt,* I have got to know him, I have made his acquaintance *or* become acquainted with him; *ich habe vieles entbehren -en* or *gelernt,* I have learnt to do without many things. 2. *v.r.*; *die Verse -en sich leicht,* the verses are easy to learn; *gelernt,* trained, expert, skilled. 3. *n.* learning, study; *das -en wird ihm schwer,* he learns with difficulty. **-begierig,** *adj.* studious, eager to learn. **-eifer,** *m.* zeal for learning. **-fähig,** *adj.* capable of learning, teachable; intelligent. **-fleiß,** *m.* application, diligence in studying. **-freiheit** *f.* uncontrolled study (*as in German universities*). **-zeit,** *f.* time for study; apprenticeship.

Les-art, *f.* version, reading; *kritischer Text mit allen abweichenden -arten,* critical text with all variants. **-bar,** *adj.* legible; readable, worth reading. **-barkeit,** *f.* legibility. **-eabstand,** *m.* reading distance. **-ebuch,** *n.* reading-book, reader. **-efibel,** *f.* primer. **-efreund,** *m.* great reader. **-egesellschaft,** *f.* reading circle, literary society; book-club. **-ehalle,** *f.* reading-room. **-ekränzchen,** *n.*, **-ekreis,** *m.* reading circle. **-elampe,** *f.* reading-lamp. **-elupe,** *f.* reading-glass. **-elust,** *f.* love of reading. **-en,** 1. *ir.v.a.* (*also v.n. aux.* h.) read; lecture (*über einen Gegenstand,* on a subject); *einem den Text, die Epistel, ein Kapitel* or *die Leviten -en,* reprimand a p. severely, give s.o. a dressing down, read the riot act; *die Messe -en,* say mass; *für sich -en,* read to o.s.; *sich leicht -en lassen,* be easily read, be very readable; *das Buch liest sich gut,* the book is easy to read *or* is well printed; the book is interesting reading *or* is very readable; *seine Schrift ist nicht zu -en,* his handwriting is unreadable *or* illegible; *es liest sich wie, . . .* it reads like . . .; *was liest du aus diesem Briefe?* what do you understand from this letter? *er hat viel gelesen,* he has read much, he is well read; *heute wird nicht gelesen,* there are no lectures today (*Univ.*). 2. *n.* reading. **-enswert,** *adj.*, **-enswürdig,** *adj.*, worth reading. **-eprobe,** *f.* rehearsal (*Theat.*); sample text, extract (*in a bookseller's catalogue*). **-epult,** *n.* reading-desk, lectern. (*coll.*) **-eratte,** *f.* bookworm. **-erkreis,** *m.* readers (*collect.*), public (*for newspapers & periodicals*). **-erlich,** *adj.* legible. **-erlichkeit,** *f.* legibility. **-erschaft,** *f.* readers (*collect.*). **-esaal,** *m.* reading-room. **-estoff,** *m.* reading-matter. **-estücke,** *n.pl.* selections for reading. **-estunde,** *f.* reading-lesson; hour for reading. **-ewelt,** *f.* reading public. **-ewut,** *f.* mania for reading. **-ezeichen,** *n.* book-mark(er). **-ezeit,** *f.* time taken to read. **-ezimmer,** *n.* reading-room. **-ezirkel,** *m.* reading circle; book-club. **-ung,** *f.* reading; *der Gesetzentwurf kam zur* (*ersten, zweiten*) *-ung,* the bill was read (for the first, second time).

Lese, *f.* (-n) gleaning; gleanings; gathering, collecting; harvest; vintage. **-holz,** *n.* fallen wood. **-n,** 1. *ir.v.a.* gather, collect, glean; pick, cull, select; *Ähren -n,* glean; *Wein -n,* gather grapes; *den Acker -n,* clear the ground of stones. 2. *n.* gathering, gleaning. **-zeit,** *f.* vintage-time.

Lett-en, 1. *m.* (-s, -) potter's clay, loam. 2. *adj.* of clay. **-ig,** *adj.* clayey, loamy.

Letter, *f.* (-n) letter, character; type; *lateinische* or *deutsche -n,* Roman *or* Gothic type. **-ndruck,** *m.* printing, letterpress. **-ngut,** *n.*, **-nmetall,** *n.* type-metal.

Lettner, *m.* (-s, -) rood-loft, wood screen (*between nave and choir in church*).

letzen, *v.a.* (*Poet.*) gratify, refresh, comfort; *sich -* (*an einer S.*), enjoy *or* relish (a th.).

letzt, 1. *adj.*, last, latest, ultimate, final; extreme; *-en Endes,* in the last analysis, when all's said and done; *-e Erklärung,* ultimatum; *zu guter -,* in the end, finally, to sum up, to cap it all; *die -e Hand an etwas legen,* put the finishing touches to a th.; *bis auf den -en Mann,* to a man, to the last man; *-en Mittwoch,* last Wednesday; *-e Nachrichten,* stop-press news; *-e Ölung,* extreme unction (*R.C.*); (*coll.*) *der -e Schrei sein,* be all the rage; *das -e Wort behalten,* have the last word; *in -er* or *der -en Zeit,* of late, recently, lately; *in den -en Zügen liegen,* be breathing one's last; *er wäre der -e, dem ich vertraute,* he is the last man I would trust; *der -e* (*in*) *der Klasse,* bottom in *or* of the class; *den -en beißen die Hunde,* devil take the hindmost; *das -e,* the last thing, the end, the last extremity; *mein -es,* my deathblow, my end, the death of me; *sein -es hergeben,* do one's utmost, give of one's best; *er gäbe das -e hin,* he would sacrifice everything *or* his all. 2. *adv.* lately, of late, in the last place. **-ens,** *adv.* finally, lastly, in the last place; lately, of late, recently. **-ere(r),** *m.*, **-ere,** *f.*, **-ere(s),** *n.* (*der, die, das -ere*) the latter. **-erwähnt,** *adj.*, **-genannt,** *adj.* last-named *or* mentioned, latter. **-hin,** *adv.* lately, of late, latterly, recently; lastly, in the last analysis. **-lich,** *adv.* lastly, at last, finally, to conclude; lately, the other day. **-verstorben,** *adj.* late; *der -verstorbene,* the late, the deceased. **-willig,** 1. *adj.* testamentary; *-willige Verfügung,* last will and testament; *ohne -willige Verfügung gestorben,* died intestate. 2. *adv.* by will.

Leu, *m.* (-en, -en) (*Poet.*) lion.

Leucht-e, *f.* (-n) luminary, light, lamp; (*fig.*) outstanding figure, shining light, star. **-en,** 1. *v.n.* (*aux.* h.) shine, light, illuminate, radiate, emit *or* give light; beam, gleam, glow, burn, glare, glimmer; phosphoresce (*of the sea*); lighten; *einem die Treppe hinunter -en,* light a p. downstairs; *in alle Winkel -en,* shine a light into all the corners; *-en wie die Sonne,* shine forth as the sun; *sein Auge -ete vor Zorn,* his eye flashed with anger. 2. *n.* shining, burning; glare, glow, illumination, coruscation; phosphorescence. **-end,** *pr.p. & adj.* shining, brilliant, bright, luminous, lustrous; lucid; *ein leuchtendes Beispiel,* an illuminating example. **-er,** *m.* candlestick. **-erarm,** *m.* branch of a chandelier. **-erkrone,** *f.* chandelier. **-erscheinung,** *f.* luminosity, phosphorescence. **-fähig,** *adj.* luminous. **-fallschirm,** *m.* parachute-flare. **-farbe,** *f.* luminous paint. **-feuer,** *n.* beacon, flare (*Av.*), light (*Naut.*). **-gas,** *n.* coal gas (for lighting). **-geschoß,** *n.*, **-granate,** *f.* star shell (*Artil.*). **-käfer,** *m.* glow-worm, fire-fly. **-kraft,** *f.* luminosity, illuminating power. **-kugel,** *f.* fire-ball; star-shell, Very light. **-öl,** *n.* lamp oil, naphtha, kerosene. **-pfad,** *m.* flare path (*Av.*). **-pistole,** *f.* Very pistol. **-röhre,** *f.* neon tube, fluorescent tube. **-schiff,** *n.* lightship. **-schild,** *n.* illuminated sign. **-schirm,** *m.* fluorescent screen. **-spur,** *f.* tracer (fire). **-spurgeschoß,** *n.*, **-spurgranate,** *f.* tracer shell. **-stab,** *m.* flash-lamp, torch. **-stein,** *m.* Bologna-stone; lithophosphor. **-stoff,** *m.* luminous matter. **-tonne,** *f.* light buoy. **-turm,** *m.* lighthouse. **-uhr,** *f.* luminous clock *or* watch. **-wurm,** *m.* glow-worm. **-zifferblatt,** *n.* luminous dial.

leugn-en, 1. *v.a.* deny; disavow, gainsay, recant, retract; *nicht zu -en,* undeniable; *das Gesagte -en,* eat one's words. 2. *n.*, **-ung,** *f.* disavowal.

Leumund, *m.* reputation; character; *guter -,* good name. **-szeugnis,** *n.* testimonial, certificate of good conduct.

Leut-e, *pl.* people, persons, folk, crowd, public, the world; servants, hands, rank and file, men; *ausgediente -e* ex-service men; (*leib*)*eigene -e,* serfs; *-e von Stand,* gentlefolk, persons of standing *or* quality; *vor allen -en,* openly, before all the world; *unter die -e kommen,* go into society, get about; become widely known; *es fehlt ihm an -en,* he is short-handed; *er kennt seine -e,* he knows whom he has to deal with, he is a good judge of character; *wir sind geschiedene -e,* it is all over between us; *Kleider machen -e,* clothes make the man. **-enot,** *f.* shortage of hands. **-eschinder,** *m.* extortioner, bloodsucker, slave-driver. **-estube,** *f.* servants' quarters. **-priester,** *m.* (*Swiss*) lay priest (*R.C.*). **-selig,** *adj.* affable, familiar; kind, genial; popular. **-seligkeit,** *f.* kindness; affability, geniality, good nature; popularity.

Leutnant, *m.* (-s, -s (& *Austr. dial.*) -e) second lieutenant (*Mil.*), pilot officer (*Av.*); – *zur See*, sub-lieutenant (*Nav.*); *Ober–*, first lieutenant; *General–*, lieutenant-general. **–sstelle,** *f.* lieutenant's commission, lieutenancy.

Levit, *m.* (-en, -en) Levite; *einem die* (*Austr. dial.* den) *–en lesen*, lecture a p.

Levkoje, *f.* (-n) stock, gillyflower (*Matthiola incana*) (*Bot.*).

Lexik–alien, *pl.* things connected with a dictionary. **–alisch,** *adj.* from a lexicographic standpoint. **–ograph,** *m.* (-en, -en) compiler of a dictionary, lexicographer. **–on,** *n.* (-ons, -a & -en) dictionary, encyclopaedia; *ein wandelndes –on*, a walking encyclopaedia.

Libell, *n.* (-s, -e) libel. **–ist,** *m.* (-en, -en) libeller, lampooner.

Libelle, *f.* (-n) dragon-fly (*Ent.*); spirit-level.

licht, 1. *adj.* light, luminous, shining, bright; lucid, clear; pale; thin, sparse, open; *–e Augenblicke*, lucid intervals; *–e Fassung von Juwelen*, open setting of jewels; *–e Höhe*, clearance (*of bridges, etc.*); *–e Maschen*, wide meshes; *am –en Tage*, in broad daylight; *–e Weite*, width in the clear; – *werden*, grow clear; get light, dawn; *–e Zukunft*, bright future. 2. *n.* (-(e)s, -er) light, illumination; lighting, highlight (*Paint.*); luminary; (*dial.*) opening, window; eye (*of game*); *ans – bringen*, bring to light; divulge; *ans – kommen*, come to light; *ans – treten*, become known, be published; *jetzt geht mir ein – auf*, now I begin to see, now it dawns on me; *einem ein – aufstecken über eine S.*, open a p.'s eyes to a fact; *einem aus dem –e gehen*, stand out of s.o.'s light; *bei –e*, by day, in daylight; *bei –e besehen* or *betrachtet*, looked at closely, on careful consideration, taking everything into account; – *geben*, give light; enlighten; *er ist ein großes –*, he is an outstanding figure; *er ist kein großes –*, he is pretty stupid; *einen hinters – führen*, take a p. in, humbug *or* dupe a p., impose on a p.; *in milderndem – sehen*, see through rose-tinted spectacles; *in ein falsches – setzen, stellen* or *rücken*, misrepresent; *einem* (*sich* (*Dat.*) *selbst*) *im –e stehen*, stand in a p.'s (one's own) light; – *machen*, strike a light, light; switch on (*electric light*); (*Prov.*) *wo viel – ist, ist starker Schatten*, the brighter the light, the deeper the shadow; *sein – unter den Scheffel stellen*, hide one's light under a bushel; *das – der Welt erblicken*, see the light of day; (*B.*) *es werde –!* let there be light! 3. *n.* (-(e)s, -e (& *Austr. dial.*) -er) candle, taper, dip. **–anlage,** *f.* lighting-plant. **–bad,** *n.* solar bath, insolation (*Med.*). **–beständig,** *adj.* fast to light, non-fading. **–beugung,** *f.* refraction. **–bild,** *n.* photograph. **–bilderkundung,** *f.* photographic reconnaissance (*Mil.*). **–bildervortrag,** *m.* lantern lecture. **–bildkunst,** *f.* photography. **–bildlich,** *adj.* photographic. **–bildner,** *m.* photographer. **–bildung,** *f.* production of light, photogenesis. **–blau** (*etc.*), *adj.* & *n.* light blue (*etc.*). **–blick,** *m.* ray of hope. **–blond,** *adj.* ash-blond. **–bogen,** *m.* arc (*Elec.*). **–bogenbildung,** *f.* arcing. **–brechend** *adj.* refracting, refractive, dioptric. **–brechung,** *f.* refraction of light. **–bündel,** *n.*, **–büschel,** *m.* pencil of light. **–dämpfer,** *m.* extinguisher. **–dicht,** *adj.* light-proof, light-tight. **–druck,** *m.* collotype. **–durchlässig,** *adj.* transparent, translucent. **–echt,** *adj.* fadeless, non-fading, fast to light. **–empfindlich,** *adj.* sensitive to light, sensitized (*Phot.*); *–empfindlich machen*, sensitize. **–en,** 1. *v.a.* thin out, clear (*a wood*); thin (*the ranks*); 2. *v.r.* grow *or* become thinner, get brighter *or* clearer, clear up (*see also* **lichten**). **–erbaum,** *m.* Christmas-tree. **–erglanz,** *m.* brightness, brilliancy (of light). **–erloh,** 1. *adj.* blazing. 2. *adv.* ablaze; *–erloh brennen*, be ablaze. **–farben,** *adj.* **–farbig,** *adj.* light-coloured. **–form,** *f.* mould for candles. **–geschwindigkeit,** *f.* velocity of light. **–gestalt,** *f.* phase (*of moon, etc.*); bright *or* beautiful figure. **–gießer,** *m.* chandler. **–glanz,** *m.* lustre, brightness. **–heilverfahren,** *n.* sun-ray treatment. **–hell,** *adj.* lighted up; very bright. **–hieb,** *m.* thinning (*a wood*). **–hof,** *m.* well of a court; halation (*Phot.*). **–hoffrei,** *adj.* non-halation (*Phot.*). **–hütchen,** *n.* extinguisher. **–jahr,** *n.* light-year (*Astr.*). **–kegel,** *m.* cone of light, search-light beam. **–körper,** *m.* luminary. **–kranz,** *m.* corona (*of sun*). **–kreis,** *m.* luminous circle, halo. **–leer,** *adj.*, **–los,** *adj.* dark, obscure, sombre, unlit, dusky, murky, dingy. **–lehre,** *f.* optics. **–leitung,** *f.* lighting circuit. **–maschine,** *f.* dynamo (*Motor.*), lighting generator. **–messe,** *f.*, **–meß,** *f.* Candlemas. **–messer,** *m.* photometer. **–messen,** *n.* flash-spotting (*Artil.*). **–nelke,** *f.* lychnis. **–pausapparat,** *m.* photographic copying apparatus. **–pause,** *f.* blue-print, photostatic reproduction. **–punkt,** *m.* luminous point, focus; (*fig.*) ray (*of hope*). **–putze,** *f.* snuffers. **–quelle,** *f.* source of light. **–reklame,** *f.* illuminated advertisement *or* advertising. **–schacht,** *m.* light-shaft. **–schein,** *m.* lustre, glow. **–schere,** *f. see* **–putze.** **–scheu,** *adj.* shunning the light, aphotic; (*fig.*) furtive, skulking. **–schirm,** *m*, lamp-shade, eye-protector, screen. **–schlag,** *m.*, *see* **–hieb,** **–schwingung,** *f.* light-wave. **–seite,** *f.* (*fig.*) bright side. **–spiel,** *n.* (cinematograph) film. **–spieltheater,** *n.* cinema, picture house. **–spur,** *f*, luminous trail. **–spurgeschoß,** *n.* tracer bullet. **–stärke,** *f.* intensity of light. **–strahl,** *m.* ray, beam (*of light*), streamer (*of the aurora borealis*). **–strahlenbrechung,** *f.* refraction of light. **–strahlenmesser,** *m.* actinometer. **–strahlung,** *f.* radiation. **–stumpf,** *m.* candle-end. **–telegraphie,** *f.* heliograph signalling. **–träger,** *m.* candle-holder, candlestick. **–trunken,** *adj.*, **–umflossen,** *adj.* bathed in light, radiant. **–undurchlässig,** *adj.* opaque. **–ung,** *f.* clearing, glade. **–voll,** *adj.* resplendent, luminous; clear, illuminating, lucid. **–weite,** *f.* clearance, width in the clear. **–welle,** *f.* wave of light. **–zeichen,** *n.* illuminated sign. **–zerstreuung,** *f.* dispersion of light. **–zieher,** *m.* chandler. **–zug,** *m.* candle-mould.

lichte–n, *v.a.* lighten, unload; weigh (anchor). **–r,** *m.* lighter, barge. **–rgeld,** *n.* lighterage.

Lid, *n.* (-(e)s, -er) lid, eyelid; *die –er schließen*, close one's eyes.

lider–n, *v.a.* (*archaic*) garnish, line *or* pack with leather. **–ung,** *f.* packing, washer, gasket; gas check, obdurator (*Artil.*).

lieb, *adj.* dear, beloved; valued, esteemed; attractive, charming, agreeable, delightful; (*also used pleonastically in familiar phrases*) *um das –e Brot arbeiten*, work for one's bare subsistence; *so ein –es Ding*, such a dear *or* darling; *unsere –e Frau*, Our Lady, the Virgin Mary; *der –e Gott*, God (Almighty); *das weiß der –e Himmel*, heaven only knows; *das Kind ist gar zu –*, the child really is too sweet for anything; *er will sich – Kind bei mir machen*, he is trying to ingratiate himself with me *or* to curry favour with me; *wenn Ihnen Ihr Leben – ist*, as you value your life; *ich habe meine –e Not mit ihm*, I have no end of trouble with him; *das ist aber – von Ihnen*, that is indeed most kind of you; *es ist mir –, daß*, I am glad that; *es ist mir nicht –*, I am sorry, I regret; *es wäre mir –*, I should like, I should be glad; *das wäre Ihnen gewiß nicht –*, you would not like that, I'm sure; *es mag ihm – oder leid sein*, whether he like it or not; *den –en langen Tag*, the livelong day; *ach, du –e Zeit!* good gracious! dear me! **–e(r),** *m.*, **–e,** *f.*, **–e(s),** *n.*; (*coll.*) *mein –er*, my dear fellow; *meine –e*, my dear woman *or* girl; *meine –en*, my beloved ones; dear friends! *etwas –es*, anything *or* something pleasing; *einem –es und Gutes tun* or *erweisen*, be very kind to a p.; *ich weiß nur –es und Gutes von ihm*, I can only speak well of him; *nicht wissen, was man einem* (*alles*) *–es antun soll*, overwhelm a p. with kindness. **–äugeln,** *v.n.* (*insep.*) (*mit einem*) ogle, (*sl.*) give (a p.) the glad eye; toy (*with an idea*). **–chen,** *n.* sweetheart, pet, darling, love. **–den,** *f.* (*archaic form of address among sovereigns*); *Euer –den*, my dear prince. **–e,** *f.* love, affection, fondness; kindness, favour, charity; beloved, love; *Lieb und Leid*, *in –e und Leid*, in joy and grief, for better or for worse; *Lieb und Lust*, pleasure and delight, heart's delight; *abgöttische –e*, idolatry; *aus –e*, for love; *kindliche –e*, filial love *or* piety; *christliche –e*,

Nächsten–e, love for others; (*sl.*) *meine brüderliche –e*, my brother; *–e zur S.*, love of the cause; *–e zum Vaterlande*, love of one's country; *ein Kind der –e*, a love-child, illegitimate child; *mit –e tun*, do gladly; *mit Lust und –e tun*, do with all one's heart; *tun Sie mir die –e*, have the kindness to, oblige me by; *mir zu –e*, for my sake; (*Prov.*) *eine –e ist der andern wert*, one good turn deserves another; (*Prov.*) *alte –e rostet nicht*, old love is never forgotten; (*Prov.*) *–e macht erfinderisch*, love will find out a way, love laughs at locksmiths. **–edienerei,** *f.* cringing servility, adulation. **–edienern,** *v.n.* (*aux.* h.) cringe, fawn, grovel. **–eleer,** *adj.* loveless, lacking in love. **–elei,** *f.* (-en) flirtation. **–eln,** *v.n.* (*aux.* h.) flirt, dally, trifle with. **–en,** 1. *v.a.* love, be fond of; like; fancy, cherish (*an idea, etc.*); *meine geliebte Frau*, my dearly beloved wife. 2. *v.n.* (*aux.* h.) be in love. **–end,** *pr.p.* & *adj.* loving, fond, affectionate; *Deine Dich –ende Schwester*, your loving *or* affectionate sister; *Dein Dich –ender Wilhelm*, yours affectionately, William. **–enswert,** *adj.* worthy of love. **–enswürdig,** *adj.* kind, amiable, charming. **–enswürdigkeit,** *f.* amiability, kindness, charm. **–er,** 1. *compar. adj.*, *see* **lieb.** 2. *adv.* (*compar. of* gern) rather, sooner; *je länger je –er*, the longer the better; *ich täte es –er selbst*, I would rather do it myself; *es ist mir –er*, I prefer; *–er sterben als leiden*, better die than suffer; *um so –er, weil*, so much the more so since; *es ist mir nur um so –er*, I only like it all the better; *warum nicht –er gar vierzig?* why not rather forty (and have done with it)? **–esabenteuer,** *n.* love-affair, liaison, intrigue. **–esangelegenheiten,** *f.pl.* love-affairs. **–esantrag,** *m.* proposal. **–esapfel,** *m.* tomato. **–esband,** *n.* bond of love. **–esbedürfnis,** *n.* desire for love. **–esbeteu(e)rung,** *f.* protestation of love. **–esblick,** *m.* loving glance. **–esbote,** *m.* harbinger of love. **–esbrief,** *m.* love-letter. **–esdienst,** *m.* good turn, kind act, act of kindness; *einem einen –esdienst erweisen*, do a p. a kindness. **–eserklärung,** *f.* declaration of love. **–esfrühling,** *m.* dawn of love. **–esgabe,** *f.* gift parcel; (*pl.*) comforts (*for troops*). **–esgedicht,** *n.* love-poem. **–esgeschichte,** *f.* love-story; love-affair, romance. **–esgeständnis,** *n.* protestation of love. **–esglück,** *n.* success in love, lover's bliss. **–esglut,** *f.* amorous rapture. **–esgott,** *m.* Cupid, Amor, Eros; (*pl.*) amoretti, cupids, putti (*Arch.*). **–esgöttin,** *f.* Venus, Aphrodite. **–esgras,** *n.* quaking grass. **–eshandel,** *m.* love affair, intrigue. **–esheirat,** *f.* love-match. **–esknoten,** *m.* lovers' knot. **–eskrank,** *adj.* love-sick, lovelorn. **–eskummer,** *m.* lover's grief. **–eskünste,** *f.pl.* artifices of love. **–eslied,** *n.* love-song. **–eslust,** *f.* pleasure of love. **–esmahl,** *n.* love-feast, agape; banquet; regimental dinner. **–esmühe,** *f.*; *Verlorene –esmüh*, Love's Labour 's Lost. **–esnot,** *f.*, **–espein,** *f.* torment *or* pains of love. **–espaar,** *n.* lovers, couple. **–espfand,** *n.* love-token; pledge of love; (*Poet.*) child. **–espfeil,** *m.* love-dart, Cupid's dart. **–espflicht,** *f.* Christian duty. **–esqual,** *f.* pangs of love. **–esrausch,** *m.* transport of love. **–esritter,** *m.* knight-errant; gay Lothario, Don Juan. **–esroman,** *m.* love-story; erotic novel. **–esschwur,** *m.* pledge of love. **–essehnsucht,** *f.* love-sickness. **–esspiel,** *n.* amorous play, dalliance, flirtation. **–(es)stöckel,** *m.* lovage (*Levisticum officinale*) (*Bot.*). **–estat,** *f.* labour of love. **–estrank,** *m.* love-potion, philtre. **–estreue,** *f.* constancy. **–estrunken,** *adj.* crazed with love. **–esverhältnis,** *n.* love-affair. **–eswerben,** *n.*, **–eswerbung,** *f.* wooing, courtship. **–eswerk,** *n.* work of charity, Christian act. **–esworte,** *n.pl.* loving words. **–eszauber,** *m.* love-spell. **–eszeichen,** *n.* love-token. **–evoll,** *adj.* loving, kind, affectionate. **–frauenkirche,** *f.* church of Our Lady. **–frauenmilch,** *f.* a choice Rhenish wine. **–gewinnen,** *v.a.* (*sep.*) take a fancy to, grow fond of. **–haben,** *v.a.* (*sep.*) be fond of, like, love. **–haber,** *m.* lover, admirer, gallant; dilettante, amateur; fancier; *–haber finden*, find buyers. **–haberausgabe,** *f.* edition de luxe. **–haberei,** *f.* inclination, fondness, fancy, liking, partiality; hobby, favourite amusement; dilettantism. **–haberpreis,** *m.* fancy price. **–haberkonzert,** *n.* amateur concert. **–haberrolle,** *f.* lover's part (*Theat.*). **–habertheater,** *n.* private theatre; amateur theatricals, dramatic club. **–haberwert,** *m.* collector's value, sentimental value. **–kosen,** (*insep.*) *v.a.* pet, caress, fondle, hug. **–kosung,** *f.* caress; caressing, petting. **–lich,** *adj.* lovely; charming, delightful, pleasing, sweet. **–lichkeit,** *f.* charm, sweetness, pleasantness. **–ling,** *m.* darling, dear, favourite, pet. **–lingsidee,** *f.* pet idea. **–lingsnahrung,** *f.* favourite food. **–lingssohn,** *m.* favourite son. **–los,** *adj.* loveless; unloving, unkind, hard-hearted. **–losigkeit,** *f.* uncharitableness, unkindness. **–reich,** *adj.* loving, kind. **–reiz,** *m.* charm, attractiveness. **–reizend,** *adj.* charming, winning. **–sam,** *adj.* pleasant. **–schaft,** *f.* love-affair, amour; sweetheart, (*coll.*) flame; *flüchtige –schaft*, flirtation. **–st,** 1. *sup. adj.*, *see* **lieb**; *meine –ste Beschäftigung*, my favourite occupation; *der* or *die –ste* dearest, beloved, lover, love, sweetheart; *das –ste*, the most precious th. 2. *adv. sup.* of gern; *das esse ich am –sten*, this is my favourite dish; *am –sten haben*, love *or* like best. **–tätig,** *adj.* charitable, beneficent. **–wert,** *adj.* (*archaic*) highly esteemed, beloved.

Lied, *n.* (-(e)s, -er) song; lay, ballad; air, tune, ditty; *geistliches –*, hymn, psalm; *das Hohe – (Salomonis)*, Song of Solomon, Song of Songs; *immer das alte –*, always the same old story; *davon kann ich auch ein – singen*, there's s.th. I can say about that; (*Prov.*) *wes Brot einer ißt, des – er singt*, never quarrel with your bread and butter; *ein anderes – anstimmen*, change one's tune; *das – ist aus*, it is all over; *das Ende vom –e*, the end of the matter, the upshot. **–erabend,** *m.* ballad concert, song recital. **–erbuch,** *n.* song-book; hymn-book. **–erdichter,** *m.* lyric poet; song writer. **–erkranz,** *m.* choral society; collection of song. **–erreich,** *adj.* tuneful. **–ersammlung,** *f.*, *see* **–erbuch.** **–ersänger,** *m.* ballad singer. **–ertafel,** *f.* glee club, choral society. **–haft,** *adj.* lyrical, tuneful.

Liederjan, *m. see* **liederlicher Mensch.**

liederlich, *adj.* slovenly, disorderly; lewd, dissolute, immoral, loose; (*dial.*) wretched, miserable; *–er Mensch, Kerl, Patron* or *Bruder*, rake, loose-liver, debauchee; *–e Person*, sloven, slut; loose woman. **–keit,** *f.* slovenliness, disorderliness; debauchery, dissoluteness, loose living, immoral conduct.

Liedrian, *m. see* **liederlicher Mensch.**

lief, liefe, *see* **laufen.**

Liefer–ant, *m.* (-en, -en), contractor, purveyor; supplier, furnisher, caterer. **–bar,** *adj.* available for delivery. **–er,** *m.*, *see* **–ant.** **–frist,** *f.*, *see* **–ungsfrist.** **–schein,** *m.*, *see* **–ungsschein.** **–n,** *v.a.* deliver, hand over, furnish, supply, afford; produce, yield; *eine Schlacht –n*, give battle; *ein Werk in Heften –n*, publish a work in numbers; *einen Beweis –n*, furnish proof; *zu –n in 8 Tagen an Herrn . . .*, to be delivered in 8 days to Mr. . . .; (*coll.*) *er ist geliefert*, he is lost, ruined *or* done for. **–ung,** *f.* delivery, supply; issue, part, number (*of a work*); lot, parcel, car-load, cargo; *auf –ung*, on delivery; *zahlbar bei –ung*, payable on delivery; *sofortige –ung*, for immediate delivery; *eine –ung ausschreiben*, invite tenders for a contract; *–ung in Naturalien*, payment in kind. **–(ungs)bedingungen,** *f.pl.* specifications, terms of contract *or* delivery. **–(ungs)frist,** *f.* term for delivery. **–ungsgeschäft,** *n.* contract business, time bargain. **–(ungs)preis,** *m.* agreed price, contract price. **–(ungs)schein,** *m.* delivery note, receipt. **–(ungs)vertrag,** *m.* contract. **–(ungs)wagen,** *m.* delivery van. **–ungsweise,** *adv.* in numbers *or* parts. **–ungswerk,** *n.* serial. **–(ungs)zeit,** *f. see* **–(ungs)frist.** **–wagen,** *m. see* **–(ungs)wagen.**

lieg–en, *ir. v.n.* (*aux.* h. & *dial.* s.) lie, rest, repose, be recumbent; be situated, be; lodge, be quartered *or* billeted; *es –t an Ihnen*, it depends on you; it is your fault; *so viel an mir –t*, as far as I am concerned, as far as lies in my power; *an wem –t die Schuld?* whose fault is it? *woran – es, daß . . .?*

how does it come that . . .? *es –t nun einmal daran, daß* . . ., that is due to the fact that . . .; *es –t nichts daran*, it does not matter, it is of no consequence; *daran –t mir nichts*, that does not interest me, I don't care; *es –t (mir) viel (wenig) daran*, it matters a great deal (little) (to me); *das –t mir am Herzen*, it is of interest to me, I am deeply interested in that; *der Hund –t an der Kette*, the dog is on the chain; *es –t am Tage*, it is obvious *or* as clear as day; *auf Flaschen –en*, be in bottles; *auf der Hand –en*, be plain *or* obvious; *der Ton –t auf der letzten Silbe*, the accent is on the last syllable; *einem auf der Tasche –en*, be a heavy expense *or* burden to a p.; *einem auf der Zunge –en*, be on the tip of a p.'s tongue; *da –t der Hund begraben*, (*coll.*) that's the snag; *–en bleiben*, stay in bed; remain, lie over, stand over, be left on one's hands, not sell; be left *or* forgotten; break down (*as a car*); *unter der Last –en bleiben*, sink under the burden; *es –t mir fern*, far be it from me; *gefangen –en*, be *or* lie in prison; *–en haben*, have in stock; possess, have ready; *da –t der Hase im Pfeffer*, there's the rub, that's the fly in the ointment; *es –t schon hinter uns*, it is over *or* done with, that's past history; *es –t schon darin*, it is implied; *es –t in meiner Absicht*, it is my intention; *es –t im Blute*, it runs in the blood; *das Pferd –t schwer in der Faust*, the horse is hard-mouthed; *einander in den Haaren –en*, be at loggerheads; *einem in den Ohren –en*, din into s.o.'s ears; *das –t mir noch immer im Sinne*, I cannot get that out of my head *or* mind; *krank –en*, lie ill in bed; *–en lassen*, let lie, leave lying about, leave behind; leave off, discontinue; *laß das –en!* leave that alone! *einen links –en lassen*, neglect, disregard *or* cold-shoulder a p.; *das –t mir nicht*, that is not in my line, that does not suit me; *nach Osten –en*, face east; *nahe –en*, be *or* lie near *or* close, be proximate; *see also* **naheliegen**; *wie –t die S.?* what is the position? how does the matter stand? *immer über den Büchern –en*, be always poring over one's books; *das Schiff –t vor Anker*, the ship lies *or* rides at anchor; *klar vor Augen –en*, be apparent; *vor einer Festung –en*, besiege a fortress; *zu Bett –en*, keep one's bed; *einer S. zugrunde –en*, underlie *or* be the basis of a th.; *einem zur Last –en*, be a burden *or* nuisance to a p., importune a p.; *klar zutage* or *zu Tage –en*, be obvious. **–egeld**, *n.* demurrage. **–ekur**, *f.* rest-cure. **–enbleiben**, *see* **–en bleiben** *above*. **–end**, *pr.p. & adj.* recumbent, prostrate, horizontal; situated; *–endes Geld*, idle money; *–ende Güter*, *pl.* real estate, landed property; *–ende Schrift*, italics; *see also* **gelegen. –enlassen**, 1. *see* **–en lassen** *above*. 2. *n.* discontinuance. **–eplatz**, *m.* berth, staple (*of a ship*). **–er**, *m.* ship lying up; ship's caretaker; large water butt. **–estuhl**, *m.* deck-chair. **–etag**, *m.* lay-days (*Naut.*) **–ezeit**, *f.* time of lying (*of wine*); quarantine; *see also* **–etag**; *extra –ezeit*, days of demurrage.

lieh, liehe, *see* **leihen.**

lies, liesest, liest, *see* **lesen.**

ließ, ließe, *see* **lassen.**

Liga, *f.* (-gen) league. **–spiel**, *n.* league-match (*Sport*).

Liguster, *m.* (-s) privet (*Bot.*).

liier–en, *v.a.* ally, unite, combine. **–te(r)**, *m. & f.* confidant, ally. **–ung**, *f.* alliance, union.

Likör, *m.* (-s, -e) liqueur, (*coll.*) highball. **–bonbon**, *n.* brandy-ball.

lila, 1. *adj. & n.* lilac(-coloured), pale violet; (*coll.*) *es geht mir –*, I'm pretty well, not bad *or* so so. 2. **–(k)** *m.* (-(k)s) lilac (*Bot.*).

Lilie, *f.* (-n) lily; fleur-de-lis (*Her.*). **–nartig**, *adj.* liliaceous. **–nbaum**, *m.* magnolia. **–nblaß**, *adj.* lily-white. **–nhand**, *f.* lily-white hand. **–nhaut**, *f.* lily-white skin.

Lim–etta, *f.* (-etten) lime (*Bot.*). **–onade**, *f.* lemonade, lemon squash. **–one**, *f.* (-onen) citron; *süße –one*, lime; *saure* or *eigentliche –one*, lemon. **–onensaft**, *m.* lemon-juice, lime juice.

Limit, *n.* (-(e)s, -e), **–e**, *f.* (-en), *see* **–um. –ieren** (*C.L.*) *v.a.* limit, restrict, control (*prices*). **–um**, *n.* (-ums, -a) (*C.L.*) fixed price, reserve price, price limit *or* ceiling.

lind (*Austr. dial.* **–e**), *adj.* soft, gentle, mild; smooth, scoured. **–ern**, *v.a.* mitigate, alleviate, soften, ease; soothe, allay, palliate, relieve, temper, moderate. **–ernd**, *pr.p. & adj.* soothing, palliative; *–erndes Mittel*, anodyne. **–erung**, *f.* alleviation, mitigation, palliation; relief, comfort. **–erungsmittel**, *n.* palliative, anodyne.

Linde, *f.* (-n) lime-tree, (*Poet.*) linden (tree). **–n**, *adj.* made of linden-wood. **–nallee**, *f.*, **–ngang**, *m.* avenue of lime-trees. **–nblütentee**, *m.* lime-blossom tea.

Lindwurm, *m.* (-s, ⸚er) (*Poet.*) dragon.

Linea–l, 1. *n.* (-s, -e) ruler, rule, straight edge. **–r**, *adj.* linear. **–rmaßstab**, *m.* linear scale. **–rzeichnung**, *f.* line-drawing, outline.

Linie, *f.* (-n) line; rank (*Mil.*); equator (*Naut.*); lineage, descent, ancestry; row; *krumme –*, curve; *dicke* or *breite –n*, full strokes; *punktierte –*, dotted line; *gestrichelte –*, line of dashes; *–n ziehen*, rule (*paper, etc.*); *in gerader –*, in a straight line; as the crow flies, in the direct line; *auf der ganzen –*, all along the line; *in der ersten –*, in the first rank; *in erster –*, first of all, above all, primarily; *in letzter –*, finally, in the last analysis; *in vorderster –*, in the front rank, in the firing line; *auf gleicher – mit*, on the same footing as; *– halten*, keep in line; write straight; *eine mittlere – einhalten*, follow a middle course. **–nblatt**, *n.* lined sheet (*guide lines in writing*). **–nförmig**, *adj.* linear. **–npapier**, *n.* ruled paper. **–nrichter**, *m.* linesman (*Footb.*). **–nschiff**, *n.* ship of the line, battleship. **–nspannung**, *f.* line voltage (*Elec.*). **–ntaufe**, *f.* christening of sailors on crossing the line. **–numschalter**, *m.* commutator, switch (*Elec.*). **–nzug**, *m.* plotted line, curve, graph.

–linig, *suffix*, lined, e.g. *gerad–*, in a straight line.

lin(i)ier–en, *v.a.* rule (lines). **–feder**, *f.* ruling- *or* drawing-pen.

link, *adj.* left; left-hand; sinister (*Her.*); clumsy, awkward; (*dial.*) left-handed; *–e Seite*, wrong side (*of cloth, etc.*), reverse (*of coins*); *–er Hand*, *see* **–erhand**; *sich zur –en Hand trauen lassen*, contract a morganatic marriage. **–e**, *f.* left hand, left; left wing, the Left (*Pol.*); *zur –en*, on *or* to the left; *mit dem –en Bein aufstehen*, get out of bed on the wrong side. **–e(r)**, *m.* left-handed blow *or* punch, left; *gerader –er*, straight left (*Boxing*). **–erhand**, *adv.* on the left. **–isch**, *adj.* awkward, clumsy. **–s**, *adv. & prep.* (*with Gen.*) to the left, on the left; wrong side out; inside out; *nach –s*, to the left; *–s schwenkt!* left wheel! *–s um!* left turn! *–s um kehrt!* left about turn! *alles –s anfangen*, do everything the wrong way; *–s liegen lassen*, cold-shoulder; *–s eingestellt*, with left-wing sympathies; (*coll.*) *da sind Sie weit –s*, there you are wide of the mark *or* very much mistaken. **–saußen(stürmer)**, *m.* outside left (*Footb.*). **–sdrall**, *m.* counter-clockwise rifling (*of gun*). **–sdrehend**, *adj.* levorotatory. **–sdrehung**, *f.* levorotation, left-handed polarization. **–sgängig**, *adj.*, *see* **–släufig. –sgewinde**, *n.* left-handed screw. **–shänder**, *m.*, (*coll.*) **–ser**, *m.* left-handed person. **–shändig**, *adj.* left-handed. **–sher**, *adv.* from the left. **–sherum**, *adv.* round to the left. **–shin**, *adv.* to the left. **–släufig**, *adj.* counter-clockwise, anti-clockwise. **–srheinisch**, *adj.* on the left bank of the Rhine. **–sum**, *see* **–s um** *above*.

linnen, *adj. & n.* linen; *see* **Leinen.**

Linol–eum, *n.* linoleum. **–schnitt**, *m.* lino-cut (*Typ.*).

Linon, *m.* (-s, -s) (French) lawn.

Linse, *f.* (-n) lentil; lens (*Opt.*); pendulum-bob; (*coll.*) money, (*sl.*) dough, tin. **–nförmig**, *adj.* lenticular, lens-shaped. **–ngericht**, *n.* pea soup, mess of pottage (*cf.* Gen. xxv. 29 ff.). **–nglas**, *n.* lens. **–npaar**, *n.* paired lenses.

Lipp–e, *f.* (-en) lip; labium; edge, border; *sich* (*Dat.*) *die –en ablecken*, smack one's lips, (*coll.*) lick one's chops; *es soll nicht über meine –en kommen*, it shall not pass my lips, I shall not speak of it; *sich* (*auf*) *die –en beißen*, bite one's lips (*in anger*); *die –en hängen lassen*, mope, sulk; *die –en aufwerfen* or *schürzen*, curl one's lip (*in scorn*); sneer; (*sl.*) *eine –e* *riskieren*, be pert, saucy *or* cheeky; *die –en spitzen*, purse one's lips; *das Herz auf den –en haben*, wear one's heart on one's sleeve; *einem auf den –en schweben*, be on the tip of one's tongue; *zwischen –' und Kelches Rand schwebt der finstern Mächte Hand*, many a slip 'twixt cup and lip; *Ablesen von den –en*, lip-reading (*by the deaf and dumb*). **–enbekenntnis,** *n.* lip-service. **–enblütler,** *m.* labiate flower (*Bot.*). **–enlaut,** *m.* labial (*Phonet.*). **–endienst,** *m.* lip-service. **–enförmig,** *adj.* labiate. **–enpomade,** *f.* lip-salve. **–enstift,** *m.* lipstick. **–ig,** *adj.* (*in compounds*), -lipped, *e.g.* *dünn–ig*, thin-lipped.

liquid, *adj.* (*C.L.*) liquid, payable, due; *–e Forderungen*, debts due. **–a,** *f.* liquid (sound) (*Phonet.*). **–ation,** *f.* charge, fee, costing; liquidation, winding up (*of a business*). **–ator,** *m.* (-s, -en) liquidator, administrator (*of an estate*); receiver (*in bankruptcy cases*). **–ieren,** *v.a.* liquidate, wind up, settle; charge (*a fee*). **–ierung,** *f.*, *see* **–ation.**

lismen, *v.a.* & *n.* (*Swiss dial.*) knit.

lispel–n, *v.a.* & *n.* (*aux.* h.) lisp; whisper, murmur softly. **–laut,** *m.*, **–ton,** *m.* lisped *or* whispered sound.

List, *f.* (-en) cunning, craftiness, artfulness; artifice, device, stratagem, trick, ruse; *arge –*, arrant cunning; (*Prov.*) *– gegen –, – über –*, diamond cut diamond. **–ig,** *adj.* crafty, cunning, deceitful, sly; (*coll.*) astute. **–igkeit,** *f.* craftiness.

Liste, *f.* (-n) list, register, schedule, roll, catalogue; panel (*of jurors*); *schwarze –*, black list; *eine – führen*, keep a register; *in eine – eintragen*, enrol, register. **–nführung,** *f.* keeping a register, registry. **–npreis,** *m.* catalogue price. **–nwahl,** *f.* 'ticket' election.

Litanei, *f.* (-en) litany; *– (von Klagen)* jeremiad.

Liter, *n.* (*Austr. dial. m.*) (-s, –) litre.

Litera, *f.* (-as & -ä) (*archaic*) letter. **–risch,** *adj.* literary. **–t,** *m.* (-en, -en) man of letters, literary man, writer; (*pl.*) literati. **–tentum,** *n.* world of letters. **–tur,** *f.* literature; letters. **–turangaben,** *f.pl.* bibliographical data. **–turblatt,** *n.*, **–turzeitung,** *f.* literary journal, (literary and critical) review. **–turgeschichte,** *f.* history of literature. **–turhistoriker,** *m.* historian of literature. **–turnachweis,** *m.* reading list, books consulted.

Litewka, *f.* (-ken) battledress blouse *or* tunic.

Litfaßsäule, *f.* (-n) advertisement pillar, erection for posting bills.

Lithograph–ie, *f.* (-ien) lithograph; lithography. **–ieren,** *v.a.* lithograph. **–isch,** *adj.* lithographic.

litt, litte, *see* **leiden.**

Liturg–ie, *f.* (-ien) liturgy; responses (*Eccl.*). **–isch,** *adj.* liturgical.

Litz–e, *f.* (-en) braid, cord, lace, piping; heddle (*Weav.*); strand (*of wire*), flex. **–en,** *v.a.* (*Swiss dial.*) fold *or* turn up. **–enbesatz,** *m.* braiding; lace-trimming. **–endraht,** *m.* stranded wire.

Livree, *f.* (-n) livery.

Lizen–tiat, *m.* (-en, -en) licentiate. **–z,** *f.* licence; poetic licence. **–zieren,** *v.a.* license.

Lob, *n.* praise, commendation, eulogy, applause; fame, reputation; *einem – erteilen, spenden* or *zollen*, give praise to s.o., praise a p.; *des –es voll*, full of praise; *über alles – erhaben*, above *or* beyond praise; *zum –e (Gen.)*, in praise of; *zu seinem –e sagen*, tell *or* say to his credit *or* in his praise; *Gott sei –!* Heaven be praised! **–en,** *v.a.* praise, commend, laud; (*B*) glorify, extol; (*dial.*) value, estimate; *das ist an ihm zu –en*, that is praiseworthy in him; *über den grünen Klee –en*, laud to the skies; *sich –end über einen aussprechen*, speak highly of a p.; *ich –e mir den Frieden!* thank goodness for peace! *da –e ich mir ein warmes Bett!* there is nothing like a warm bed! *das Werk –t den Meister*, the work reflects honour upon its maker; *gelobt sei Gott!* God be praised! **–enswert,** *adj.*, **–enswürdig,** *adj.* praiseworthy, laudable, commendable. **–esam,** *adj.* (*Poet.*) honourable, worthy; laudable; (*Poet.*) *Kaiser Rotbart –esam*, the noble emperor Frederic Barbarossa. **–eserhebung,** *f.* high praise, encomium. **–gesang,** *m.* song of praise, hymn of praise, panegyric. **–hudelei,** *f.* fulsome praise, base flattery. **–hudeln,** *v.a.* (*insep.*) flatter; praise fulsomely *or* extravagantly. **–hudler,** *m.* toady, flatterer, sycophant. **–lied,** *n.*, *see* **–gesang.** **–preisen,** *v.a.* (*insep.*) praise, extol. **–preisung,** *f.* praise, glorification. **–rede,** *f.* panegyric, eulogy. **–singen,** *ir.v.n.* (*aux.* h.) (*sep.*) (*B.*) (*einem*) sing praises to. **–spruch,** *m.* eulogy.

löblich, *adj.* praiseworthy, laudable, commendable; (*archaic, as form of address*) estimable, honourable, worthy.

Loch, *n.* (-es, ¨-er) hole, opening, cavity, orifice, aperture; gap, breach; slot; pore, eye; pocket (*Bill.*); perforation, puncture, leak; (*sl.*) prison, clink, jug; den, hovel; (*vulg.*) arse; foramen (*Anat.*); (*coll.*) *einem ein – in den Bauch reden* or *fragen*, pester a p. with chatting *or* with questions; *sich ein – in den Bauch reden*, talk one's head off, talk to no avail; (*coll.*) *einen ins – stecken* or *setzen*, put s.o. in clink *or* jug; *aus dem – jagen*, draw, unearth (*foxes, etc.*); *ins – spielen*, pocket (*Bill.*); (*hum.*) *einem zeigen wo der Zimmermann das – gelassen hat*, show a p. the door; *ein – zumachen*, stop a hole; (*coll.*) pay a debt; *ein – mit dem andern zustopfen, ein – aufmachen um das andere zu schließen, ein – zu- und ein anderes aufmachen*, rob Peter to pay Paul, borrow money to pay a debt; *aus einem anderen – pfeifen*, change one's tune; (*coll.*) *er pfeift auf dem letzten –*, he is on his last legs. **–bohrer,** *m.* borer; auger, piercer. **–eisen,** *n.* punch (*metal-worker's tool*). **–en,** *v.a.* perforate, pierce, punch. **–er,** *m.* punch, perforator (*for office use*). **–fraß,** *m.* pitting (*Metall.*). **–lehre,** *f.*, *see* **–winkel.** **–säge,** *f.* pad-saw, keyhole *or* compass-saw. **–ung,** *f.* punching, perforation (*of tickets, etc.*). **–weite,** *f.* width of opening, inside diameter. **–winkel,** *m.* hole-gauge. **–zange,** *f.* punch (*conductor's, etc.*).

Löch–elchen, *n.* (-s, –) small hole; eyelet; foramen (*Anat.*); dimple. **–(e)rig,** *adj.* full of holes; porous; perforated; (*fig.*) untenable, shaky (*of arguments*).

Lock–e, *f.* (-en) lock (*of hair, etc.*), curl, ringlet; flock (*of wool, etc.*); *sich (Dat.) –en brennen lassen*, have one's hair curled (*with irons*); *in –en legen*, curl. **–en,** *v.a.* & *r.* curl. **–enhaar,** *n.* curly hair. **–enkopf,** *m.* curly head (*also person*). **–enköpfig,** *adj.* curly-headed. **–enwickel,** *m.* **–enwickler,** *m.* curl-paper. **–enwulst,** *m.* mass of thick curly hair. **–ig,** *adj.* curly.

lock–en, *v.a.* & *n.* (*aux.* h.) attract, entice, coax, decoy, allure, tempt, bait; *einem Tränen aus den Augen –en*, bring tears to a p.'s eyes; *aus einem –en*, draw, entice *or* wrest from a p.; *einen Hund –en*, call *or* whistle to a dog; (*coll.*) *damit kann man keinen Hund vom Ofen –en*, that's no use whatever, that won't catch on. **–mittel,** *n.* bait, lure, inducement. **–pfeife,** *f.* bird-call. **–ruf,** *m.* call-note (*of a bird*). **–speise,** *f.* bait, lure. **–spitzel,** *m.* agent provocateur; (*Amer.*) stool-pigeon. **–ung,** *f.* attraction, enticement, allurement. **–vogel,** *m.* decoy-bird; (*fig.*) tempter, allurer.

locker, *adj.* loose, slack; light, spongy, porous; lax, frivolous, disorderly, dissolute; *–er Boden*, light soil; *– werden*, get, work *or* grow loose; (*coll.*) *er läßt nicht –*, he will not give in *or* give way, he holds fast *or* remains firm, he insists; *– machen*, loosen, relax; *– leben*, lead a dissolute life; *–er Gesell* or *Zeisig*, dissolute fellow, scamp, good-for-nothing, rake, rip. **–heit,** *f.* looseness; lightness, sponginess, porosity; dissipation, licentiousness, crapulence, libertinism, laxity. **–n,** 1. *v.a.* loosen, slacken; break up (*soil*). 2. *v.r.* (be)come *or* work loose; give way; relax.

Lode, *f.* (-n) young shoot, sprout, sprig, sapling, young tree.

Loden, *m.* (-s, –) coarse woollen cloth. **–joppe,** *f.* woollen jacket. **–mantel,** *m.* waterproof woollen overcoat.

lodern, *v.n.* (*aux.* h.) blaze, flame *or* flare up; (*fig.*) glow, burn.

Löffel, *m.* (-s, –) spoon; ladle, scoop, dipper, bucket (*of excavator*); ear (*of hare or rabbit*); *kommen Sie zu einem – Suppe zu uns*, come and take pot-luck with us; (*coll.*) *einen über den – barbieren*, cheat a p., do a p. down; *tun als hätte man die Weisheit mit –n gegessen*, play the wiseacre, make a great show of wisdom *or* learning. **–bohrer**, *m.* spoon bit. **–ente**, *f.* shoveler (*Spatula clypeata*) (*Orn.*). **–förmig**, *adj.* spoon-shaped, cochlear(iform). **–gans**, *f.*, **–reiher**, *m.* spoon-bill, pelican (*Platalea leucorodia*) (*Orn.*). **–kraut**, *n.* scurvy grass (*Cochlearia*) (*Bot.*). **–n**, *v.a.* & *n.* (*aux.* h) spoon up; ladle out; (*Studs. sl.*) *sich –n*, drink in response to a toast; return a favour. **–stiel**, *m.* spoon-handle. **–weise**, *adv.* in spoonfuls, spoonful by spoonful.

log, löge, *see* **lügen.**

Log, *n.* (-s, -e), **–e**, *f.* (-n) log (*Naut.*). **–buch**, *n.* log(-book), ship's log (*Naut.*). **–gast**, *m.* log-heaver. **–gen**, *v.n.* (*aux.* h.) heave the log. **–ger**, *m.* lugger (*Naut.*). **–leine**, *f.* log-line.

Logarithm–us, *m.* (-men) logarithm. **–isch**, *adj.* logarithmic. **–entafel**, *f.* table of logarithms.

Log–e, [*pron.* 'lo:ʒə] *f.* (-en) (private) box (*in theatre*); Freemason's lodge. **–enbruder**, *m.* (brother) mason. **–enmeister**, *m.* master of a lodge (*Freem.*). **–enschließer**, *m.* **–enwärter**, *m.* attendant (*in the theatre*). **–ieren**, 1. *v.n.* (*aux.* h.) lodge, dwell, stay, put up. 2. *v.a.* lodge, accommodate, put up. **–ierzimmer**, *n.* spare room, guest-room. **–is**, *n.* lodging(s), (*sl.*) digs; mess-deck, crew space (*Naut.*).

Logi–k, *f.* (-ken) logic. **–ker**, *m.* logician. **–sch**, *adj.* logical.

loh, *adj.* (*archaic*) blazing, flaming, flaring, burning. **–e**, *f.* (-en) blaze, flame, flare; (*fig.*) ardour. **–en**, *v.n.* blaze *or* flare up, flame.

Loh–e, *f.* (-en) tanning-bark, tan (liquor), ooze. **–beize**, *f.* tanning, tan liquor. **–brühe**, *f.* ooze, tannin. **–en**, *v.a.* steep in, treat *or* prepare with; tan. **–farbe**, *f.* tan (*colour*). **–farben**, **–farbig**, *adj.* tan(-coloured). **–faß**, *n.* tan-vat. **–gar**, *adj.* tanned. **–gerber**, *m.* tanner. **–gerberei**, *f.* tannery; tanning. **–grube**, *f.* tan-pit. **–rinde**, *f.* tanning-bark.

Lohn, *m.* (& *n.*) (-(e)s, ⸚e) reward, recompense, compensation, requital; payment, salary, wages; – *drücken*, undercut wages; (*Prov.*) *Undank ist der Welt(en) –*, one meets with nothing but ingratitude in this world; *bei einem in – und Brot stehen*, to be in a p.'s pay *or* service; *der Arbeiter ist seines –es wert*, the labourer is worthy of his hire. **–amt** *n.* trade board. **–arbeit**, *f.* hired labour. **–arbeiter**, *m.* labourer, workman. **–diener**, *m.* hired servant, extra help. **–drückerei**, *f.* sweating. **–empfänger**, *m.* wage-earner. **–en**, *v.a.* & *n.* (*aux.* h.) remunerate, reward, recompense, compensate, requite; pay, repay, be worth; *einen –en*, (*archaic*) pay a p. (*for work*); *einem etwas –en*, reward *or* requite a p. for s.th.; *einem mit Undank –en*, repay a p. with ingratitude; *Gott –' es dir!* may God reward you for it! *es –t die Mühe* or *sich der Mühe*, it is worth the trouble; *das –t sich nicht*, that does not pay, that is not worth while; *es –t (sich) nicht darüber zu reden*, it is not worth talking about. **–end**, *pr.p.* & *adj.* remunerative, lucrative, profitable; advantageous, worthwhile. **–erhöhung**, *f.* rise in wages. **–handwerk**, *n.* piece-work. **–herabsetzung**, *f.* reduction in wages. **–kampf**, *m.* wages disagreement. **–kutsche**, *f.* hackney-cab. **–kutscher**, *m.* cabman. **–liste**, *f.* wages-sheet, pay-roll. **–satz**, *m.* rate of pay. **–schreiber**, *m.* literary hack. **–steuer**, *f.* tax on wages, income tax. **–stopp**, *m.* wage ceiling, figure at which wages are pegged. **–tag**, *m.* pay-day. **–tüte**, *f.* pay packet *or* envelope. **–vereinbarung**, *f.* wage agreement. **–zuschlag**, *m.* additional *or* extra payment; wage increment.

löhn–en, *v.a.* pay (*wages, etc.*). **–ung**, *f.* pay, payment, wages. **–ungsappell**, *m.* pay parade (*Mil.*). **–ungstag**, *m.* pay-day.

lokal, 1. *adj.* local; suburban; *–es*, local concerns, local news. 2. *n.* (-(e)s, -e) (*Austr. dial.* **–e** *n.* (-s, –)) public house, (*coll.*) pub; locality, place; premises. **–bahn**, *f.* local *or* suburban railway. **–behörden**, *f.pl.* local authorities. **–blatt**, *n.* local (news-) paper. **–farbe**, *f.* natural colour; (*fig.*) local colour. **–isieren**, *v.a.* localize, locate, determine the position. **–ität**, *f.* locality; *–itäten eines Hauses*, ins and outs of a house. **–kenntnis**, *f.* knowledge of a place, familiarity with a district. **–patriotismus**, *m.* local patriotism; parochialism. **–sage**, *f.* local tradition, local legend. **–verhältnisse**, *n.pl.* local conditions. **–wirkung**, *f.* local action. **–zug**, *m.* local *or* suburban train.

loko–, *adv.* on the spot, local (*C.L.*) **–geschäft**, *n.* spot-business. **–verkehr**, *m.* local trade. **–waren**, *f.pl.* (*C.L.*) spots, spot goods.

Lokomo–bile, *f.* (-n) traction engine. **–tive**, *f.* (-n) locomotive, train engine. **–tivführer**, *m.* engine-driver. **–tivschuppen**, *m.* engine-shed.

Lokus, *m.* (–, – & -se) (*sl.*) rear, bog, W.C.

Lolch, *m.* (-(e)s, -e) darnel, ray-grass (*Lolium*) (*Bot.*).

Lombard, *m.* & *n.* (-s, -e) (*C.L.*) loan against security; (*dial.*) pawn shop; loan office; deposit-bank. **–bestände**, *m.pl.* advances of money on security. **–geschäft**, *n.* loan business on securities. **–ieren**, *v.a.* (*C.L.*) lombard; pawn; deposit security against a loan; lend *or* advance against security. **–zettel**, *m.* pawn ticket. **–zinsfuß**, *m.* pawnbroker's rate of interest.

Lomber, *n.* ombre (*Cards*).

Lompenzucker, *m.* *see* **Lumpenzucker.**

Lorbeer, *m.* (-s, -en) laurel, bay (*Bot.*); (*fig.*) fame, repute; *auf seinen –en ausruhen*, rest on one's laurels. **–baum**, *m.* laurel, bay-tree. **–kranz**, *m.* laurel-wreath. **–rose**, *f.* oleander (*Kalmia augustifolia*) (*Bot.*). **–spiritus**, *m.* bay rum.

Lorch, *m.* (-(e)s, -e) (*dial.*), *see* **Lurch.**

Lore, *f.* (-n) truck, trolley, lorry.

Los, *n.* (-es, -e) lot, share, allotment, portion; fate, destiny; chance, fortune, hazard; lottery ticket *or* prize; *das große – gewinnen*, win the first prize; *das – ist geworfen*, the die is cast; *das – ziehen*, draw lots; *durchs – entscheiden*, decide by lot; *ihm wurde ein glückliches – zuteil*, his lot was a happy one; *nach dem –e*, by lot. **–en**, *v.n.* (*aux.* h.) draw lots (*um*, for). **–topf**, *m.* urn for lots *or* tickets; urn of fate; *aus dem –topf*, fortuitously, (*coll.*) out of the hat. **–ung**, *f.* casting lots. *See also* **losen** *below.*

los, *predic. adj.* & *adv.* loose, slack; flowing, dishevelled; free, disengaged, released; *etwas* (or *einen*) *– sein*, be rid of a th. (*or* a p.); *– werden* (*Acc.* or *von*) get loose *or* free from, get rid of; *der Gefangene ist –*, the prisoner is free *or* at large *or* has escaped; *der Anker ist –*, the anchor drags; *aller Bande –*, free of all restraint; *– und ledig*, rid of once and for all; (*coll.*) *nur – !* fire away! go on! (*coll.*) *was ist – ?* what is the matter? what is wrong? what's up? *der Teufel ist –*, hell is let loose; *es muß etwas – sein*, something must be afoot, there is s.th. in the wind; (*coll.*) *hier ist viel –*, there is plenty going on *or* doing here; (*coll.*) *mit seinem Wissen ist nicht viel –*, his knowledge is nothing to boast of *or* is not up to much; (*coll.*) *etwas – haben*, know what one's talking about, be a clever fellow; *die '– von Rom-Bewegung'*, the 'Away from Rome' movement. *As a sep. pref.* los *has the meaning of (a) separation; (b) commencement; (c) violence, lack of restraint; with last meaning it can be added adverbially to most verbs of action, not listed here*, e.g. *drauf – leben*, live from hand to mouth, live carelessly; *wacker drauf – lügen*, lie shamelessly; *sie lärmten drauf –*, they made an awful row; *– trinken !* drink up! drink to your heart's content! drink your fill! *frisch drauf – !* courage! at him! go on! (let us) go at it with a will! **–arbeiten**, 1. *v.a.* loosen, work loose, disengage. 2. *v.r.* extricate o.s., get free. 3. *v.n.* (*aux.* h.) work on *or* away. **–bekommen**, *ir.v.a.* loosen; get *or* set free; (*coll.*) get to understand. **–binden**, *ir.v.a.* untie, detach, undo, loosen, unfurl. **–brechen**, 1. *ir.v.a.* break off *or* loose. 2. *v.n.* (*aux.* s.) break loose *or* away, break *or* burst forth *or* out; rush off. **–brennen**, 1. *ir.v.a.* discharge, fire (off) (*a gun*); let off (*fireworks*). 2. *v.n.* (*aux.* s.) go off (*as a gun*). **–bringen**, *ir.v.a.* get loose *or* off; disengage; loosen. **–bröckeln**, *v.a.*, *r.* & *n.* (*aux.* s.) crumble off. **–donnern**, *v.n.* (*aux.* h.) thunder out *or* away. **–drehen**, *v.a.*

untwist, twist off. **–drücken,** 1. *v.a.* loosen, detach. 2. *v.a.* & *n.* (*aux.* h.) fire (off) (*a gun*), shoot (*an arrow*); *er legte an und drückte* –, he took aim and fired. **–e,** *see* **lose** *below*. **–en,** *see* **Los** *above* & **losen** *below*. **–eisen,** *v.a.* (*coll.*) clear, free, extricate; (*einen*) *–eisen*, get (s.o.) out of a jam. **–fahren,** *ir.v.n.* (*aux.* s.) depart, set off; come off, come loose; *auf einen –fahren*, fly (out) at a p.; *gerade auf das Land –fahren*, make straight for land. **–feuern,** *v.a.* discharge, shoot. **–geben,** *ir.v.a.* set free, liberate. **–gehen,** 1. *ir.v.n.* (*aux.* s.) set out, begin; come off, become loose; (*auf einen*) fly at, attack (a p.); charge (*the enemy*); explode, go off. 2. *n.* explosion, deflagration; *verspätetes –gehen*, hang-fire; *vorzeitiges –gehen*, premature; *da ging das Zanken* –, then they begin to quarrel; *frisch auf etwas –gehen*, set about a th. with a will; *es geht bald* –, things will soon start, it will not be long now; *dieses Gewehr geht schwer* –, this gun is stiff on the trigger; *es geht auf den Winter* –, winter is drawing near. **–gelöst,** *p.p.* & *adj.* detached, *see* **–lösen.** **–haben,** *v.a.*; (*coll.*) *viel – haben*, be pretty bright. **–haken,** *v.a.* unclasp, unhook. **–hauen,** *v.a.* cut loose *or* away. **–helfen,** *ir.v.n.* (*einem*) help (a p.) to get free. **–kauf,** *m.* buying off, ransom. **–kaufen,** *v.a.* redeem, ransom; *sich –kaufen*, buy o.s. off (*Mil.*). **–ketten,** *v.a.* unchain. **–kitten,** *v.a.* unseal, detach. **–knallen,** *v.a.* & *n.* (*aux.* s.) explode, let off. **–knüpfen,** *v.a.* untie, unknot. **–kommen,** *ir.v.n.* (*aux.* s.) get loose; get rid of; get free, be set free, escape; get away, take off (*Av.*). **–lassen,** *ir.v.a.* let loose, let go, release, set free; let off (*a gun*); utter, break out into; (*coll.*) *einen Brief –lassen*, write a letter; (*coll.*) *eine Rede –lassen*, deliver a speech; (*coll.*) *einen Witz –lassen*, make a joke; *laß mich – !* let go! let me go! *Hunde –lassen*, set dogs on, unchain *or* unleash dogs. **–lassung,** *f.* release. **–legen,** 1. *v. a.* loosen. 2. *v.n.* (*aux.* h.) (*coll.*) begin, set about; inveigh (against). **–lösen,** 1. *v.a.* loosen, detach, untie, separate; set free, liberate. 2. *v.r.* disengage o.s., become detached; peel off. **–lösung,** *f.* separation, dissociation. **–löten,** *v.a.* unsolder. **–machen,** 1. *v.a.* loosen, make loose; undo, unfasten, cast off, unmoor, disengage; detach, separate; set at liberty, free. 2. *v.r.* get away; disengage *or* extricate o.s. (from); get rid (of); get free (from); *ich kann mich nicht von ihm –machen*, I cannot get away from him. **–mäulig,** *adj.* abusive, slanderous, scurrilous, foul-mouthed. **–platzen,** *v.n.* (*aux.* s.) burst *or* blurt out; explode. **–reißen,** 1. *ir.v.a.* pull *or* tear off *or* away; separate. 2. *v.r.* break loose, break away; part anchor, go adrift (*Naut.*); tear o.s. away (*von*, from). 3. *v.n.* (*aux.* s.) snap; break off *or* loose. **–ringen,** *v.r.* free o.s., break free, struggle free. **–sagen,** *v.r.* (*von*), renounce, give up, withdraw (from), *ich sage mich von der S.* –, I will have nothing more to do with the matter. **–sagung,** *f.* renunciation, withdrawal. **–scheibe,** *f.* idler pulley. **–schießen,** 1. *ir.v.a.* fire off, discharge; (*coll.*) fire away. 2. *v.n.* (*aux.* s.) *auf einen –schießen*, fly at, *or* rush upon a p. **–schlagen,** 1. *ir.v.a.* knock off; sell (cheap), sell off. 2. *v.n.* (*aux.* h.) (*auf einen*) attack, belabour (a p.). **–schnallen,** *v.a.* unbuckle. **–schneiden,** *ir.v.a.* cut off *or* loose. **–schrauben,** *v.a.* unscrew, screw off. **–schütteln,** *v.a.* shake off, shake loose. **–spannen,** *v.a.* unbend, relax; unyoke, unharness. **–sprechen,** 1. *ir.v.a.* acquit, absolve; release, free (*from an obligation, etc.*); *die Kirche hat das Recht –zusprechen*, the church has power to absolve from sin. 2. *n.* absolution; acquittal, discharge. **–sprechung,** *f.* acquittal; absolution; release. **–sprengen,** 1. *v.a.* blast off *or* loose. 2. *v.n.* (*aux.* s.) gallop (*auf einen*, towards, up to *or* at a p.). **–springen,** *ir.v.n.* (*aux.* s.) fly off, burst loose, crack; *–springen auf* (*Acc.*), fly at, rush upon. **–steuern,** *v.n.* set course for, direct (*remarks*) at. **–stürmen,** *v.n.* (*aux.* s.) rush (*auf eine S.*, upon *or* at a th.); rush forth; *auf seine Gesundheit –stürmen*, play ducks and drakes with one's health. **–stürzen,** *v.n.* (*auf*) dash (at), pounce (upon). **–trennen,** *v.a.* undo, unsew, unstitch; rip off, tear apart, sever, separate. **–ung,** *f.* fumets, droppings (*Hunt.*). **–werden,** *see* **– werden** *above*. **–werfen,** *v.a.* cast off, unmoor. **–wickeln,** 1. *v.a.* unwind, untwist, uncurl, unravel. 2. *v.r.* extricate o.s. (from). **–winden,** 1. *ir.v.a.* untwist; wrench loose. 2. *v.r.* wriggle free. **–ziehen,** 1. *ir.v.a.* draw off, pull loose. 2. *v.n.* (*aux.* s.) set out, march away; (*aux.* h.) *auf, über* or *gegen einen –ziehen*, rail at *or* inveigh against a p.

lösbar, *see* **lösen.**

Lösch–e, *f.* coal *or* charcoal dust, slack, dross; cinder, clinker. **–en,** 1. *ir.v.n.* (*aux.* s.) go out, be extinguished. 2. *v.a.* extinguish, quench, put out; blot out, liquidate, discharge, cancel (*a debt*); efface, obliterate; slake (*lime, one's thirst*); *ein nicht zu –ender Durst*, an unquenchable thirst; *dies Papier –t die Tinte*, this paper absorbs the ink. **–blatt,** *n.* sheet of blotting-paper. **–boot,** *n.* fire-boat. **–dienst,** *m.* fire-fighting service. **–eimer,** *m.* fire-bucket. **–er,** *m.* extinguisher; blotter. **–gerät,** *n.* fire-fighting apparatus, fire extinguisher. **–gruppe,** *f.* **–mannschaft,** *f.* fire brigade, fire-fighting squad. **–mittel,** *n.* chemical extinguisher. **–papier,** *n.* blotting-paper, blotter. **–schaum,** *m.* foam-extinguisher. **–ung,** *f.* cancellation. **–wesen,** *n.* fire department. **–zug,** *m.* fire-brigade.

lösch–en, *v.a.* unload, discharge, lighten (*a ship*); *Waren –en*, discharge (*cargo*). **–arbeit,** *f.* unloading, discharging. **–er,** *m.* docker, longshoreman. **–gebühren,** *f.pl.* **–geld,** *n.* landing charges, wharfage. **–platz,** *m.* wharf; port of delivery. **–ung,** *f.* unloading, discharge, disembarkation (*Naut.*). (*C.L.*) **–ungsspesen,** *pl.* landing charges.

lose, 1. *adj.* loose, slack, movable, not firm *or* fixed, unsteady; vagrant; wanton, dissolute, frivolous, irresponsible, mischievous, roguish, naughty; *–s Band*, loose string, slight connexion; *– Blätter*, loose *or* unbound sheets; *–s Gesindel*, vagabonds, blackguards; *–s Geschwätz*, irresponsible chatter; *–s Haar*, flowing *or* dishevelled hair; *–r Kalk*, untempered mortar; *–s Mädchen*, frivolous *or* roguish, immodest *or* loose girl; (*coll.*) *ein –s Maul haben*, have a loose *or* abusive tongue. *– Reden*, loose talk; *–r Streich*, reckless prank; *–r Vogel*, indecent, disolute *or* bawdy fellow, rake, libertine. 2. *n.* free end (*of rope*) (*Naut.*).

los–en, *v.n.* (*dial.*) listen, overhear, eavesdrop. **–ung,** *f.* watchword, sign, countersign, parole, signal; takings (*of a business*). *See also* **Los.** **–ungsbuch,** *n.* cash book (*for daily sales*). **–ungswort,** *n.* watchword.

lös–en, *v.a.* loosen, slacken, untie, unbind, relax; detach, disconnect, dissociate, break off, give up, absolve from; annul, cancel, dissolve (*also Chem.*); solve, answer (*a riddle, etc.*), resolve (*Math.*); redeem, ransom; discharge, fire (*a shot*), take, buy (*a ticket*); *diese Arznei –t den Schleim von der Brust*, this medicine loosens the phlegm; *eine Ehe –en*, dissolve *or* annul a marriage; *eine Frage –en*, settle a question; *Gefangene –en*, set prisoners free; *Geld aus etwas –en*, realize money on a th.; *den Knoten eines Schauspieles –en*, unravel the plot of a play; *ein Pfand –en*, redeem a pledge; *Rätsel –en*, solve *or* guess riddles; *eine Schwierigkeit –en*, settle *or* overcome a difficulty; *ein Siegel –en*, break a seal; *sein Verhältnis zu einem –en*, break off all connexion with a p.; *eine Verlobung –en*, break off an engagement; *sein Versprechen –en*, fulfil one's promise; *die Verwirrung –en*, dispel the confusion; *einen Widerspruch –en*, resolve a contradiction; *den Zauber –en*, break the spell; *die Zunge –en*, make a p. speak; *Zweifel –en*, clear away doubts. 2. *v.r.* free o.s., get loose; dissolve; *sich von etwas –en*, withdraw *or* dissociate o.s. from s.th.; *die Freundschaft –t sich*, the friendship goes to pieces; *der Verband –t sich*, the bandage gets loose; *Zucker –t sich in Wasser*, sugar dissolves in water; *sie –te sich in Tränen*, she dissolved into tears; *das Rätsel –t sich sehr einfach*, the riddle is easy to solve. **–bar,** *adj.* soluble (*Chem.*); solvable, resolvable (*Math.*); detachable. **–egeld,** *n.* ransom. **–emittel,** *n.* expectorant; solvent; means of redemption. **–end,** *pr. part.* & *adj.* solvent, expectorant, purgative.

–eschlüssel, *m.* power of forgiving sins, St. Peter's key. **–lich,** *adj.* soluble, easily dissolved. **–lichkeit,** *f.* solubility (*Chem.*). **–ung,** *f.* loosening; firing (*of guns*); solution, explanation, dénouement, solving, unravelling (*of a plot*); (*Poet.*) ransom, redemption (*of a pledge*); absolution; solution (*Math.*, *Chem.*); resolution (*Math.*); (*dial.*) receipts, yield; *das wäre die beste –ung,* that would be the best solution (*of the difficulty*); *die –ung des Rätsels,* the answer to the riddle. **–ungsdichte,** *f.* concentration. **–ungsmittel,** *n.* solvent.

Löß, *m.* loess (*Geol.*).

Losung, *f. see under* **Los, los,** & **losen.**

Lot, *n.* (-(e)s, -e) perpendicular (line); plumb-line, plummet, sounding-lead; solder; (*archaic*) small weight (= 10 grams); (*coll.*) *er ist nicht ganz im –,* he is not all there; *es gehen 100 auf ein –,* they are as light as a feather. **–en,** *v.a.* & *n.* (*aux.* h.) sound, take soundings, plumb; test for perpendicular (*Carp.*). **–leine,** *f.* plumb-line. **–recht,** *adj.* perpendicular, vertical. **–ung,** *f.* sounding.

Löt–e, *f.* soldering; solder. **–bar,** *adj.* solderable. **–en,** 1. *v.a.* solder, braze. 2. *n.* soldering, brazing. **–blei,** *n.* soft solder. **–fett,** *n.*, **–flüssigkeit,** *f.* flux. **–kolben,** *m.* soldering-iron *or* bit, copper bolt. **–ig,** *adj.* weighing half an ounce, of due alloy, of full weight; *das feinste Silber ist 16–ig,* the finest silver is of 12 dwt. **–igkeit,** *f.* fineness (*of silver*). **–lampe,** *f.* blow-lamp. **–mittel,** *n.* solder. **–naht,** *f.*, **–stelle,** *f.* soldered joint. **–rohr,** *n.* blowpipe. **–ung,** *f.* soldering, brazing. **–wasser,** *n.* chlorate of zinc.

Lotse, *m.* (-n, -n) pilot. **–n,** *v.a.* pilot; (*coll.*) get (*a p.*) to a place. **–ngebühr,** *f.*, **–ngeld,** *n.* pilotage.

Lotter, *m.*, *see* **–bube. –bett,** *n.* (*archaic*) couch; (*fig.*) *auf dem –bett liegen,* be sunk in indolence. **–bube,** *m.* rascal, good-for-nothing rapscallion; (*dial.*) vagabond. **–ei,** *f.* (-en) laziness, slovenliness; vagabondage; disorderly life. **–ig,** *adj.* slovenly, sluttish, slatternly, dissolute. **–leben,** *n.* dissolute life. **–n,** *v.n.* loaf about, sow one's wild oats. **–wirtschaft,** *f.* hugger-mugger, maladministration, mismanagement, disreputable goings-on.

Lotterie, *f.* (-n) lottery; *in der – spielen,* take a lottery-ticket; (*coll.*) have a flutter. **–gewinn,** *m.* winning number; prize in a lottery. **–los,** *n.* lottery-ticket. **–rad,** *n.*, **–trommel,** *f.* lottery-wheel.

Löw–e, *m.* (-en, -en) lion; Leo (*Astr.*). **–enanteil,** *m.* lion's share. **–enartig,** *adj.*, *see* **–enhaft. –enbändiger,** *m.* lion-tamer. **–engrube,** *f.* lions' den. **–enhaft,** *adj.* leonine. **–enherz,** *n.* (*fig.*) valour, fortitude; man of mettle, Cœur de Lion. **–enhöhle,** *f.*, *see* **–engrube. –enmaul,** *n.* snapdragon (*Antirrhinum*) (*Bot.*). **–enmut,** *m.* lion-hearted *or* stout-hearted courage. **–enstärke,** *f.* stubborn, invincible, unsurpassed *or* sovereign strength. **–enzahn,** *m.* dandelion (*Taraxacum officinale*) (*Bot.*). **–in,** *f.* lioness.

loyal, *adj.* loyal. **–ität,** *f.* loyalty.

Luch, *n.* (-(e)s, -e) & *f.* (¨-e) (*dial.*) marsh, bog; *– und Bruch,* moorland.

Luchs, *m.* (-es, -e) lynx. **–en,** *v.a.* & *n.* (*aux.* h.) (*coll.*) watch intently, scrutinize; pry, be all eyes. (*coll.*) *etwas –en,* steal *or* pilfer a th. **–auge,** *n.* lynx-eye (*also fig.*). **–äugig,** *adj.* lynx-eyed, sharp-eyed.

Lücke, *f.* (-n) gap, break, breach, opening, space, cavity, hole, interstice, lacuna; blank, omission, deficiency, deficit; hiatus; *eine – schließen,* (*fig.*) step into the breach. **–nbüßer,** *m.* stopgap, stand-by, makeshift (*things*); stand-in (*person*). **–nhaft,** *adj.* defective, incomplete; full of gaps, broken, interrupted; fragmentary, meagre. **–nlos,** *adj.* uninterrupted, unbroken, complete, consistent.

lud, lüde, *see* **laden.**

Luder, *n.* (-s, –) (*archaic* & *dial.*) carrion; bait, lure, decoy; (*vulg.*) low scoundrel, wretch; slattern, slut, hussy, low jade; (*coll.*) rascal, scamp; (*vulg.*) *das ist unter allem –,* that is unspeakably abominable. **–haft, –ig,** *adj.* disgusting. **–leben,** *n.* dissolute life. **–mäßig,** *adj.* execrable; lewd. **–n,** 1. *v.a.* lure, bait. 2. *n.* (*aux.* h.) feed on carrion; lead a dissolute life.

lüderlich, (*coll.*) *see* **liederlich.**

Lue–s, *f.* syphilis. **–tisch,** *adj.* syphilitic.

Luft, *f.* (¨-e) air, atmosphere; breeze, zephyr, breath; relief; *keine – bekommen,* not be able to breathe; *an die – bringen,* air; (*coll.*) *dicke –,* great danger, threatening atmosphere; *die – erneuern,* ventilate, air (*a room, etc.*); *in die – fliegen,* be blown up; *in freier –,* in the open air; *– geben,* blow (*tanks*) (*Naut.*); *an die – gehen,* go into the open air; *in die – gehen,* go up in the air, blow up (*with anger*); *aus der – greifen,* fabricate, invent; *gute – haben,* draw well (*of a chimney, etc.*); *das hängt* or *schwebt in der –,* that has no foundation; that is still undecided; *– lenzen,* pump out air (*from tanks*) (*Naut.*); *es liegt in der –,* it is in the air; *– machen* (*with Dat.*) air, give air (to); loosen, undo, unbutton; tidy up, bring order to; lop, prune; set free, relieve, disengage; *sich – machen,* give vent to (*anger, etc.*); *die – ist rein,* the coast is clear; *einem – schaffen,* give a p. breathing space; give (*or* gain) time for a p.; (*frische*) *– schöpfen* or (*coll.*) *schnappen,* get a breath of (fresh) air; *er ist mir* or *für mich –,* he just does not exist for me, as far as I am concerned he might not be there; *einen an die – setzen,* throw *or* turn a p. out; *in die – sprechen,* (*coll.*) talk to no purpose; *in die – sprengen,* blow up. **–abschluß,** *m.* hermetic seal. **–abwehr,** *f.* anti-aircraft, air defence. **–angriff,** *m.* air-raid, aerial attack. **–antenne,** *f.* overhead aerial. **–artig,** *adj.* aeriform; gaseous. **–aufklärung,** *f.* air-reconnaissance. **–aufnahme,** *f.*, *see* **–bild. –auftrieb,** *m.* air buoyancy, air-pressure. **–ballon,** *m.* balloon. **–behälter,** *m.* compressed-air tank; airsack (*Orn.*). **–bereifung,** *f.* pneumatic tyres. **–beschaffenheit,** *f.* climatic conditions. **–bewegung,** *f.* flow of air. **–bild,** *n.* vision, fancy; aerial *or* air photograph. **–blase,** *f.* bubble; vesicle (*Bot.*), air-bladder (*Icht.*). **–bremse,** *f.* air *or* pneumatic brake. **–dicht,** *adj.* air-tight, hermetically sealed. **–dichte,** *f.* density of the air, atmospheric pressure. **–dichtigkeitsmesser,** *m.* manometer. **–dienstuntauglich,** *adj.* grounded (*Av.*). **–drahtzuleitung,** *f.* aerial feeder (*Rad.*). **–druck,** *m.* atmospheric pressure; blast (*of explosion*). **–druckbremse,** *f.* compressed air *or* pneumatic brake. **–druckgefälle,** *n.* pressure gradient. **–druckpumpe,** *f.* air-compressor, pneumatic pump. **–düse,** *f.* air-vent. **–erkundung,** *f.* aerial reconnaissance. **–fahrer,** *m.* airman. **–fahrt,** *f.* aviation; aeronautics, air-navigation. **–fahrtminister,** *m.* air-minister. **–fahrwesen,** *n.* aviation. **–fahrzeug,** *n.* aircraft. **–feuchtigkeit,** *f.* humidity of the atmosphere. **–feuchtigkeitsmesser,** *m.* hygrometer. **–flotte,** *f.* air-fleet. **–förmig,** *adj.* gaseous, aeriform. **–gang,** *m.* air-duct (*Bot.* & *Zool.*). **–gebilde,** *n.*, **–gestalt,** *f.* vision, phantom. **–gefahr,** *f.* air-raid danger. **–gefäß,** *n.* air-vessel (*Bot.*, *Orn.*, *Ent.*); (*pl.*) the lungs. **–gefecht,** *n.* air *or* aerial combat. **–geist,** *m.* spirit of the air, sylph; astral body (*Theosophy*). **–gekühlt,** *adj.* air-cooled. **–geräusche,** *n.pl.* atmospherics, static (*Rad.*). **–gespinst,** *n.* airy nothing, chimera. **–gewehr,** *n.* air-gun, air-rifle. **–gleichgewichtslehre,** *f.* aerostatics. **–gitter,** *n.* balloon barrage. **–hafen,** *m.* airport. **–hahn,** *m.* air-cock, air-valve. **–heizung,** *f.* hot-air heating, controlled ventilation. **–herrschaft,** *f.* air-supremacy. **–hülle,** *f.* atmosphere. **–ig,** *adj.* airy, breezy, windy; vaporous, gaseous; light, thin, flimsy; flighty, unsteady. **–ikus,** *m.* (–, -se) (*coll.*) harum-scarum; wind-bag. **–kabel,** *n.* overhead cable. **–kampf,** *m.* aerial combat. **–kissen,** *n.* air *or* pneumatic cushion. **–klappe,** *f.* ventilation-flap; air-valve. **–krankheit,** *f.* air-sickness. **–kreis,** *m.* atmosphere. **–krieg,** *m.* aerial war(fare). **–kurort,** *m.* health resort. **–landetruppen,** *f.pl.* airborne troops. **–leer,** *adj.* exhausted, void of air; *–leerer Raum,* vacuum. **–leiter,** *m.* overhead aerial, (*Amer.*) antenna. **–leitung,** *f.* overhead wire(s), **–linie,** *f.* bee-line; *in der –linie,* as the crow flies. **–loch,** *n.* air-hole, vent, breathing-hole; air-pocket (*Av.*); register (*of a chimney*); stigma (*Ent.*). **–meer,** *n.* atmosphere. **–messer,** *m.* aerometer. **–meßkunst,** *f.* aerometry. **–photobrief,** *m.* airgraph. **-post,** *f.* airmail. **-pumpe,** *f.* pneumatic pump. **-raum,** *m.* air space; atmosphere. **-reifen,** *m.* pneumatic tyre. **-reiniger,** *m.* air-filter. **-reise,** *f.* flight. **-reisende(r),** *m.* air-passenger. **-reklame,** *f.* sky-writing. **-rohr,** *n.* vent-pipe. **-röhre,** *f.* air-tube; trachea, windpipe (*Anat.*); air-vessel (*Bot.*). **-röhrenäste,** *m.pl.* bronchiae, bronchial tubes. **-röhrendeckel,** *m.* epiglottis. **-röhrenentzündung,** *f.* bronchitis. **-röhrenkatarrh,** *m.* tracheal catarrh. **-röhrenkopf,** *m.* larynx. **-röhrenschnitt,** *m.* tracheotomy. **-rüstung,** *f.* air armament. **-sack,** *m.* (wind) sleeve, wind direction indicator. **-sauger,** *m.* aspirator. **-saugpumpe,** *f.* suction pump. **-säure,** *f.* carbonic acid. **-schacht,** *m.* air-shaft (*in tunnels*). **-schaukel,** *f.* swing-boat. **-scheu,** *adj.* afraid of fresh air. **-schicht,** *f.* layer of air. **-schiff,** *n.* airship. **-schif(f)fahrt,** *f.* aerial navigation, aeronautics. **-schlange,** *f.* paper streamer. **-schlauch** *m.* (inner) tube (*of tyre*). **-schloß,** *n.* castle in the air. **-schöpfen,** *n.* respiration, drawing breath. **-schraube,** *f.* propeller, air-screw. **-schutz,** *m.* (passive) air defence, air-raid precautions. **-schutzbottich,** *m.* static water tank. **-schutzbunker,** *m.*, **-schutzkeller,** *m.*, **-schutzraum,** *m.* air-raid shelter. **-schutzwart,** *m.* air-raid warden. **-schwere,** *f.* specific gravity of the air. **-schwingung,** *f.* vibration of the air. **-sicherung,** *f.* air umbrella (*Av.*). **-späher,** *m.* spotter, air-sentry. **-sperre,** *f.* balloon barrage. **-spiegelung,** *f.* mirage. **-sport,** *m.* amateur flying. **-sprung,** *m.* leap, caper, spring. **-stauung,** *f.*, **-stockung,** *f.* airlock. **-stöpsel,** *m.* valve. **-störung,** *f.* atmospherics, static (*Rad.*). **-stoß,** *m.* gust of air. **-strahl,** *m.* air-stream, slipstream (*Av.*). **-streitkräfte,** *f.pl.* air forces. **-strom,** *m.*, **-strömung,** *f.* slipstream, air current. **-strudel,** *m.* air-eddy (*Meteor.*). **-stützpunkt,** *m.* air-base (*Av.*). **-tanken,** *v.n.* refuel in the air. **-teilchen,** *n.* particle of air. **-trocken,** *adj.* air-dried, seasoned. **-tüchtig,** *adj.* airworthy (*Av.*). **-veränderung,** *f.* change of air. **-verbindung,** *f.*, **-verkehrslinie,** *f.* air-way, air-route. **-verdichter,** *m.* air-compressor. **-verdrängung,** *f.* displacement of air. **-verdünnung,** *f.* rarefaction of the air. **-verflüssigung,** *f.* production of liquid air. **-verkehr,** *m.* air-traffic. **-vermessung,** *f.* aerial survey. **-verteidigung,** *f.* air-defence. **-waage,** *f.* aerometer. **-waffe,** *f.* (German) air force. **-wechsel,** *m.* ventilation. **-weg,** *m.* respiratory tract; air route *or* passage; *auf dem -weg,* by air. **-widerstand,** *m.* air resistance. **-wirbel,** *m.* vortex. **-wurzel,** *f.* aerial *or* exposed root (*Bot.*). **-ziegel,** *m.* air-dried brick. **-zufuhr,** *f.* air-supply. **-zug,** *m.* draught, current of air. **-zurichtung,** *f.* air-conditioning. **-zutritt,** *m.* access of air. **-zwischenraum,** *m.* air-gap.

Lüft-chen, *n.* (-s, -) breath of wind, gentle breeze, zephyr. **-en,** 1. *v.a.* air (*a room*), ventilate, expose to the air; raise, reveal, lay bare, disclose; loosen; *den Schleier eines Geheimnisses -en,* unveil a secret; *den Hut -en,* raise one's hat. 2. *v.r.* take the air. **-er,** *m.* ventilator, air-hole. **-ung,** *f.* airing, ventilation; raising (*as a veil*), disclosure. **-ungsanlage,** *f.* ventilating-fan (*Min.*); air-circulating plant.

[1]**Lug,** *m.* (*obs. only in*) *- und Trug,* falsehood and deceit.

[2]**Lug,** *m.* (-(e)s, -e) opening; peep-hole, spy-hole. **-en,** *v.n.* (*aux.* h.) show, be visible; peep out, (*dial.*) look, peep, spy. **-aus,** *m.* (*dial.*), **-insland,** *m.* (*dial.*) watch-tower, lookout.

Lüg-e, *f.* (-en) lie, falsehood, untruth; *einen -n strafen,* give the lie to a p.; *fromme -e,* white lie; *-en haben kurze Beine,* you will not get anywhere with lying. **-en,** 1. *ir.v.a. & n.* (*aux.* h.) lie, (*coll.*) fib, tell a lie *or* fib, deceive, be false; sham; *in seinen Beutel -en,* lie to one's own advantage; *ich will gern gelogen haben,* I wish I could deny it, it is unfortunately all too true; *daß ich nicht -e,* to tell the truth, really; (*coll.*) *einem die Haut, die Jacke* or *die Ohren voll -en,* cram a p. with lies; *er -t das Blaue vom Himmel herunter, er lügt daß sich die Balken biegen, er -t wie gedruckt,* he lies like a gas-meter. 2. *n.* lying, deceitfulness. **-enbold,** *m.* habitual liar. **-enfürst,** *m.*, **-engeist,** *m.* Satan. **-engewebe,** *n.* tissue of lies. **-enhaft(ig),** *adj.* lying, false, untrue; deceitful, mendacious **-enhaftigkeit,** *f.* mendacity; falseness. **-enmaul,** *n.* brazen *or* barefaced liar. **-enprophet,** *m.* false prophet. **-envater,** *m.*, *see* **-enfürst. -ner,** *m.* liar; *er wurde zum -ner an mir,* he did not keep his word to me, he deceived me; *einen zum -ner machen,* call s.o. a liar, make a p. out to be a liar. **-nerisch,** *adj.*, *see* **-enhaft.**

Lugger, *m.* lugger (*Naut.*), *see* **Logger.**

luisch, *adj.*, *see* **luetisch.**

Luke, *f.* (-n) dormer-window; (*dial.*) trap-door; hatch (*Naut.*). **-ndeckel,** *m.* hatch-cover (*Naut.*). **-nöffnung,** *f.* hatchway (*Naut.*).

lullen, *v.a. & n.* (*aux.* h.) sing, lull (*to sleep*).

Lümmel, *m.* (-s, -) lout, ruffian, boor, hooligan. **-ei,** *f.* boorishness, loutish behaviour. **-haft,** *adj.* loutish, ruffianly, boorish. **-n,** *v.r.* (*& n.*) behave badly; loll about indecorously *or* in an unseemly manner.

Lump, *m.* (-(e)s & -en, -e(n)) scamp, rascal, scoundrel. **-en,** 1. *m.* (-ens, -en) rag, tatter, clout; (*pl.*) ragged clothes, rags and tatters; lumber, trash; thingamy, thingumajig, thingumbob, thingummy; (*dial.*) handkerchief. 2. *v.n.* (*sl.*) go on the binge. 3. *v.a.* (*coll.*) *ich will mich nicht -en lassen,* I do not intend to act shabbily, I will do the thing decently *or* come down handsomely. **-azius,** *m.* (-, -ziusse) **-azivagabundus,** *m.* (*sing. only*) (*hum.*) vagabond, tramp, scoundrel. **-enbaron,** *m.* shabby-genteel person. **-enbrei,** *m.* paper pulp, first stuff (*Pap.*). **-engeld,** *n.* paltry sum; *um ein -engeld,* dirt-cheap. **-engesindel,** *n.* riff-raff, rabble, rag-tag and bobtail. **-enhändler,** *m.* rag-and-bone man. **-enhund,** *m.*, **-enkerl,** *m.* hobbledehoy, ragamuffin, scoundrel, (*sl.*) rotter, cad. **-enkram,** *m.*, *see* **-enzeug. -enpack,** *n.*, *see* **-engesindel. -ensammler,** *m.* ragpicker; rag-and-bone man; (*coll.*) last tram *or* last bus (*at night*). **-envolk,** *n.*, *see* **-engesindel. -enwolf,** *m.* rag-tearing machine, devil (*Pap.*). **-enwolle,** *f.* shoddy. **-enzeug,** *n.* trash, stuff. **-enzucker,** *m.* lump *or* loaf sugar. **-erei,** *f.* rascality; shabby trick, meanness; triviality, trifle, bagatelle. **-ig,** *adj.* ragged, tattered, shabby; mean, stingy; paltry, trifling, miserable; base; (*coll.*) *die -igen paar Mark,* those few miserable marks.

lunarisch, *adj.* lunar.

Lünette, *f.* (-n) skylight, fanlight (*above doors and windows*); lunette (*Fort.*).

Lunge, *f.* (-n) lung(s); lights; *aus voller - schreien,* shout at the top of one's voice; *auf - rauchen,* inhale (smoke). **-nbläschen,** *n.* vesicle of the lungs. **-nbraten,** *m.* (*dial.*) loin (of beef). **-nentzündung,** *f.* pneumonia, **-nfell,** *n.* pleura. **-nfellentzündung,** *f.* pleurisy. **-nfieber,** *n.* pulmonary fever. **-nflügel,** *m.* lobe of the lungs. **-nheilstätte,** *f.* sanatorium for consumptives. **-nkammer,** *f.* right ventricle (*of heart*). **-nkrank,** *adj.* consumptive. **-nkrankheit,** *f.*, *see* **-nleiden. -nlappen,** *m.*, *see* **-nflügel. -nleiden,** *n.* pulmonary disease. **-npfeifer,** *m.* whistler, roarer (*horse*). **-nschützer,** *m.* respirator. **-n(schwind)sucht,** *f.* tuberculosis, phthisis. **-nsüchtig,** *adj.* consumptive.

Lunger-er, *m.* (-ers, -er) loafer, loiterer, idler. **-n,** *v.n.* (*aux.* h. & s.) idle, loll, lounge *or* loiter about; (*dial.*) crave (*nach,* for).

Lunker, *m.* cavity, pipe (*Metall.*). **-n,** *v.n.* develop cavities. **-ung,** *f.* porosity.

Lünse, *f.* (-n) linch-pin, axle-pin.

Lunte, *f.* (-n) slow-match, fuse; fox's brush; (*coll.*) *- riechen,* smell a rat.

Lupe, *f.* (-n) magnifying glass; *unter die - nehmen,* examine closely.

lupfen (*dial.*), **lüpfen** (*Austr. dial.*) *v.a.* lift, raise.

Luppe, *f.* (-n) loop, ball, lump (*ore*), bloom (*Found.*). **-nfeuer,** *n.* smelting-furnace.

Lurch, *m.* (-(e)s, -e) batrachian; amphibious animal.

Lust, *f.* (⸚e) pleasure, joy, delight; fancy, inclination, desire, wish, longing; lust, carnal pleasure;

mirth, fun; *die – kommt* or *wandelt mich an*, I have taken a fancy (to), I am in the mood (for), I feel inclined (to); *seine – büßen*, gratify one's desire; *– an einer S. finden* or *seine – an einer S. haben*, take pleasure in a th.; (*keine*) *– haben* (*zu*), (not) be inclined, like *or* want (to do); be in a (no) mood, have a (no) mind (*for a th.* or *to do a th.*); *nach Herzens–*, to one's heart's content; *in – und Leid*, in joy and sorrow; *mit – und Liebe bei einer S. sein*, have one's heart in a matter; *einem – zu etwas machen*, excite a p.'s desire for a th., give s.o. a taste for a th.; *einem die – nehmen* (*an* or *zu*), spoil a p.'s pleasure (in a th.); *er arbeitet, daß es eine – ist*, it is a treat *or* pleasure to see how he works; *ich hatte nicht übel –*, I had a good mind to . . .; *die – dazu ist ihm vergangen*, his wish for it is gone; *er zeigte wenig –*, he showed little liking. **–barkeit,** *f.* amusement, entertainment, diversion, pleasure; sport. **–barkeitssteuer,** *f.* entertainment tax. **–dirne,** *f.* prostitute. **–fahrt,** *f.* excursion, trip, outing. **–feuer,** *n.* bonfire. **–garten,** *m.* pleasure-grounds *or* garden. **–gefühl,** *n.* pleasurable sensation. **–häuschen,** *n.* summer-house. **–ig,** *adj.* merry, gay, joyous, jolly, jovial; amusing, funny, droll, comical; *–iger Bruder*, jolly fellow, joker, merry-andrew; *–ige Geschichte*, funny story, lark; *sich über einen –ig machen*, make fun of a p.; *da geht es –ig her!* merry goings-on there! *–ige Person*, clown, fool (*Theat.*); *das kann ja –ig werden*, (*ironic*) this is a nice state of affairs. **–igkeit,** *f.* gaiety, mirth, merriment, fun, jollity. **–igmacher,** *m.* buffoon, wag, clown, jester, merry-andrew. **–los,** *adj.* (*C.L.*) dull, inactive (*of market*). **–losigkeit,** *f.* dullness, flatness (*of the market*). **–mord,** *m.* murder and rape, sex murder. **–ort,** *m.* place of amusement; pleasure-grounds. **–partie,** *f.* pleasure trip. **–schiff,** *n.* yacht, pleasure-boat. **–schloß,** *n.*, **–sitz,** *m.* country seat. **–seuche,** *f.* (*archaic*) venereal disease. **–spiel,** *n.* comedy. **–verderber,** *m.* kill-joy, spoil-sport. **–wandeln,** *v.n.* (*aux.* h. & s.) *insep.* stroll, go for a stroll *or* walk.

lüst–en, *v.a. imp.*; (*archaic*) *es –et mich sehr danach* I covet it, I would fain have *or* do it. **–ern,** 1. *adj.* greedy (for); desirous, covetous (of); lustful, lascivious, lewd; *–erne Erzählungen*, indecent, ribald, bawdy, smutty *or* Rabelaisian stories; *mit –ernen Augen*, with shameless, suggestive, prurient, lascivious, lustful, lecherous *or* salacious glances. 2. *v.a. imp.*, *see* **–en. –ernheit,** *f.* concupiscence, lasciviousness, prurience, lubricity; lust, greed. **–ling,** *m.* voluptuary, sensualist; debauchee.

Lüst–er, *m.* (-ers, -er) lustre, gloss; chandelier. **–erglanz,** *m.* lustre, sheen, glaze, gloss. **–rin,** *m.* (-s, -e) lustrine.

lutsch–en, *v.n.* (*aux.* h.) (*coll.*) suck. (*coll.*) **–er,** *m.*, **–beutel,** *m.*, **–pfropfen,** *m.* teat, dummy, comforter.

lütt, lüttje, *adj.* (*dial.*) small, little, wee; *lüttje Lage*, (*dial.*) beer with brandy.

Lutter, *m.* singlings (*brandy*).

Luv, *f.* luff, weather side (*Naut.*); *die – gewinnen*, gain the weather side. **–en,** *v.n.* (*aux.* h.) luff, ply to windward. **–küste,** *f.* weather-shore. **–seite,** *f.* weather side (*Naut.*); windward slope (*of a hill*). **–wall,** *m.* weather-shore. **–wärts,** *adv.* windward, weather. **–winkel,** *m.* drift angle, allowance for wind.

luxur–ieren, *v.n.* luxuriate, revel, wallow. **–iös,** *adj.* luxurious.

Luxus, *m.* (–) luxury, sumptuousness, extravagance. **–artikel,** *m.* luxury article; (*pl.*) luxuries, fancy goods. **–ausgabe,** *f.* edition de luxe. **–auto,** *n.* saloon-car. **–(ein)band** *m.* superior *or* fancy binding. **–steuer,** *f.* duty on luxuries. **–verbot,** *n.* sumptuary law. **–waren,** *f.pl.* fancy goods. **–zug** (*abbr.* **L-Zug**) *m.* saloon-train.

Lymph–e, *f.* (-en) lymph, vaccine. **–bahn,** *f.* lymph tract *or* duct. **–drüse,** *f.* lymphatic gland. **–gefäß,** *n.* lymphatic vessel, lymph duct. **–körperchen,** *n.* lymph-corpuscle, leucocyte.

lynch–en, *v.a.* lynch. **–justiz,** *f.* mob-law.

Lyr–a, *f.* (-en) lyre, harp; Lyra (*Astr.*). **–ik,** *f.* lyric poetry. **–iker,** *m.* lyric poet. **–isch,** *adj.* lyric(al).

Lyssa, *f.* rabies.

Lyzeum, *n.* (-s, -zeen) girls' secondary school *or* high school.

M

M, m, *n.* M, m; *see Index of Abbreviations at end.*

Maar, *n.* (-es, -e) crater, (*Scots*) corrie.

Maat, *m.* (-s, -s & -en) mate, petty-officer (*Naut.*); (*coll.*) comrade, pal. **–schaft,** *f.* (*dial.*) mates, crew, clique.

Machandelbaum, *m.* (*dial.*) juniper.

Mach–art, *f.* (-en) pattern, type, sort, kind, style. **–e,** *f.* making, production, manufacture; workmanship; (*fig.*) show, pretence, sham; *in die –e nehmen*, take in hand, set about; *in der –e sein*, be in hand; *einen in der –e haben*, tell tales about a p.; (*coll.*) *er versteht sich auf die –e*, he knows how to beat the big drum *or* blow his own trumpet.

mach–en, 1. *v.a.* make, do; manufacture, fabricate, create; cause, effect, produce; constitute, amount *or* come to; *drei mal drei –t neun*, three times three are nine; *was –t die Rechnung?* how much does the bill come to? *so –t es jeder*, everyone does the same; *–e es mir nicht noch einmal so*, do not let me catch you doing it a second time; *was –en Sie?* how are you? what are you up to *or* doing? *was –t das?* what does that matter? *das –t nichts*, that is of no consequence, never mind; *das –t mir nichts*, that is nothing to me; *–(e), daß du fort kommst*, get out of here; *lassen Sie mich nur –en*, just let me have my own way; *Anspruch auf eine S. –en*, lay claim to s.th.; *er –t es zu arg*, he goes too far; *große Augen –en*, stare; *sich* (*Dat.*) *einen Begriff davon –en*, form an idea about a th., have any conception of s.th.; *einem Beine –en*, chase s.o. off, put one's toe behind a p.; *sich bei einem beliebt –en*, ingratiate o.s. with a p.; *ein Ende –en*, put an end to; *Epoche –en*, make a sensation; be epoch-making; *Ernst –en* (*mit einer S.*), set about (a th.) seriously; *fertig –en*, finish; *Feuer –en*, light a fire; *einem Freude –en*, give a p. pleasure; *einen Gang –en*, take a walk, go an errand; *sich* (*Dat.*) *allerlei Gedanken –en*, be full of queer notions; *sein Glück –en*, make his fortune; *sich* (*Dat.*) *die Haare –en lassen*, have one's hair done; *den großen Herrn –en*, play the fine gentleman; *Holz –en*, chop wood; *einem den Kopf warm –en*, cause a p. anxiety, give s.o. trouble; *da ist nichts zu –en*, nothing can be done in the matter; *bitte Platz –en!* please make room! *gemeinsame S. –en*, make common cause, act in concert; *einem Schmerz –en*, cause a p. pain, grieve a p.; *– schnell!* make haste! (*coll.*) get a move on! *Spaß –en*, joke, jest; *ein Vermögen –en*, make a fortune; *sich* (*Dat.*) *viel zu schaffen –en*, give o.s. a lot of trouble; *einen weiten Weg –en*, come a long way; *ohne viel Wesens zu –en*, without great ceremony; *– zu!* see *– schnell! sich an eine S. –en*, set about *or* apply o.s. to s.th., take s.th. in hand; *wir wollen uns auf die Beine –en*, we are about to set off *or* go *or* start; *sich auf den Weg –en*, set out, depart; *ich –e mir nichts daraus*, I do not care (about it), it does not worry me; *sich* (*Dat.*) *viel* (*wenig*) *aus etwas –en*, care much (little) about a th., make much (little) of a th. attach great (little) importance to a matter; *sich aus dem Staube –en*, take to one's heels; *ich –e mir ein Vergnügen daraus*, it is a pleasure to me; *er –t in Zucker* (*Wolle*), he deals in sugar (wool); *ins Bett* (*in die Hosen*) *–en*, soil the bed, (one's trousers); *einen zum Feind –en*, make an enemy of a p.; *etwas zu Gelde –en*, turn s.th. into money, sell a th.; *sich* (*Dat.*) *etwas zum Gesetze –en*, make it a rule *or* law for o.s.; *einen zum König –en*, make a p. a king. 2. *v.r.* do well, get on; come right, happen; *es –t sich nicht, es läßt sich nicht –en*, it cannot be done, it is not practicable *or* feasible; *es wird sich schon –en*, it will come right in time; *der Junge –t sich jetzt*, the boy is doing nicely *or* getting on well; *das –t sich*, business is looking up; (*coll.*) *es –t sich ja*, not too badly, not bad, pretty well; (*coll.*) *wird ge–t*, it shall be done, I (*or* we) shall do it; *das ist ihm wie ge–t*, that suits him perfectly, that fits him like a glove; *ge–te Begeisterung*, simulated enthusiasm; *ge–te Blumen*, artificial flowers; *ein ge–ter Mann*, a made man. **–enschaften,** *f.pl.* machinations, intrigues. **–erei,** *f.* making, make; bungling; *Gleich–erei*, levelling (system). **–erlohn,** *m.* cost of *or* charge for making. **–werk,** *n.* poor *or* inferior work, clumsy *or* botched piece of work.

Macht, *f.* (¨e) might, strength, authority, influence, power, potency; forces; *aus eigner –*, on one's own responsibility, by one's own authority; *einem – zu etwas geben*, authorize *or* empower a p. to do a th.; *es steht nicht in meiner –*, it is not in my power; *mit aller –*, with all one's might, with might and main; (*Prov.*) *– geht vor Recht*, might is right; *See–*, sea power; *die Westmächte*, the Western Powers; *die europäischen Großmächte*, the great European Powers. **–befugnis,** *f.* competency. **–bereich,** *m.* sphere of influence. **–frage,** *f.* trial of strength. **–gebot,** *n.* authoritative *or* despotic order. **–haber,** *m.* lord, ruler, authority. **–haberisch,** *adj.* dictatorial, despotic. **–herrscher,** *m.* despot. **–kreis,** *m.*, *see* **–bereich. –los,** *adj.* powerless, weak, impotent. **–losigkeit,** *f.* impotence, powerlessness, weakness. **–politik,** *f.* power politics. **–probe,** *f.*, *see* **–frage. –spruch,** *m.*, *see* **–wort. –stellung,** *f.* strong position, political power, predominance. **–trieb,** *m.* lust for power. **–übernahme,** *f.* seizure of power. **–verhältnis,** *n.* balance of power. **–voll,** *adj.* effective. **–vollkommenheit,** *f.* plenitude of power, authority, absolute power; *aus eigner –vollkommenheit*, on one's own authority. **–wort,** *n.* emphatic words, peremptory order, word of command, authoritative decision, decree.

mächtig, 1. *adj.* mighty, strong, powerful; vast, huge, immense, thick, (*coll.*) intense. 2. *adv.* (*coll.*) extremely. *einer S. – sein*, be master of *or* have the mastery of a th.; *sie ist des Deutschen vollkommen –*, she is thoroughly conversant with German, she has a thorough command of German. **–keit,** *f.* mightiness, size, extent, thickness; richness, power, depth.

Mädchen, *n.* (-s, –) girl; (*dial.*) servant (girl); maiden, maid; sweetheart; *gefallenes –*, fallen girl; *spätes –*, old maid; *– für alles*, maid-of-all-work, general servant. **–haft,** *adj.* girlish; maidenly. **–handel,** *m.* white-slave traffic. **–heim,** *n.*, **–herberge,** *f.* hostel for young girls. **–held,** *m.*, **–jäger,** *m.* rake, rip, libertine, gay Lothario. **–kammer,** *f.* servant's bedroom. **–lyzeum,** *n.* secondary school for girls. **–name,** *m.* maiden name. **–raub,** *m.* rape. **–räuber,** *m.* ravisher. **–schändung,** *f.* violation, seduction (*of a girl under the age of 16 years. Law*). **–zimmer,** *n.* servant's room.

Mad–e, *f.* (-en) maggot, mite; worm. **–ig,** *adj.* worm-eaten; maggoty; (*sl.*) *einen –ig machen*, give a p. a good scolding, make mincemeat of a p.

Mädel, *n.* (-s, –) girl, (*Scots*) lass.

madonnen–haft, *adj.* Madonna-like. **–bild,** *n.* image of the Virgin Mary. **–kultus,** *m.*, **–verehrung,** *f.* worship of the Virgin.

mag, magst, *see* **mögen.**

Magazin, *n.* (-s, -e) warehouse; storehouse, depot, dump, repository; magazine (*of gun*); magazine, periodical. **–aufseher,** *m.*, **–verwalter,** *m.* depot *or* warehouse superintendent. **–ieren,** *v.a.* warehouse, store.

Magd, *f.* (¨e) maid, maidservant, general servant; (*B.*) handmaid; (*poet.*) maiden, virgin. **–lich,** *adj.* (*poet.*) virginal. **–tum,** *n.* (*poet.*) virginity.

Mägd–lein, *n.* (*poet.*) little girl. **–eherberge,** *f.* servants' hostel. **–estube,** *f.* servant's room.

Magen, *m.* (-s, – & *dial.* ¨) stomach; maw, gizzard; *sich* (*Dat.*) *den – verderben*, get indigestion, upset one's stomach; (*coll.*) *etwas* or *einen im – haben*, hate the mention of *or* be fed to the teeth with a th. *or* a p. **–arznei,** *f.* stomachic. **–ausgang,** *m.* pylorus. **–beschwerden,** *f.pl.* indigestion, stomach trouble. **–bewegung,** *f.* gastric movement. **–bitter,** *m.* bitters. **–brei,** *m.* chyme. **–brennen,** *n.* heart-burn, pyrosis. **–eingang,** *m.* cardia. **–entzündung,** *f.* gastritis. **–erkältung,** *f.* chill on the stomach. **–fieber,** *n.* gastric fever. **–flüssigkeit,** *f.* gastric fluid. **–gegend,** *f.* epigastrium. **–grube,** *f.* pit of the stomach. **–knurren,** *n.* rumbling in the bowels, (*coll.*) tummy rumbles. **–krankheit,** *f.* disorder of the stomach. **–krebs,** *m.* cancer of the stomach. **–lab,** *n.* rennet. **–leiden,** *n.* gastric complaint. **–mittel,** *n.*, *see* **–arznei. –mund,** *m.*, *see* **–eingang. –pförtner,** *m.*, *see* **–ausgang. –rohr,** *n.* esophagus. **–saft,** *m.* gastric juice. **–säure,** *f.* acidity. **–schlund,** *m.*, *see* **–rohr. –schmerzen,** *m.pl.* stomach-ache. **–schnitt,** *m.* gastrotomy. **–schwäche,** *f.* dyspepsia. **–stärkung,** *f.* stomachic, tonic. **–tropfen,** *m.pl.* cordial, drops. **–verstimmung,** *f.* stomach upset.

mager, *adj.* thin, lean, spare; poor, meagre, scanty; sterile; *–er Kalk*, poor lime; *–e Lauge*, weak lye (*Dye.*); *–er Stoff*, short pulp (*Pap.*); *das –e*, the lean (*of meat*). **–keit,** *f.* leanness; poorness. **–kohle,** *f.* semi-bituminous *or* non-coking coal. **–milch,** *f.* skim milk.

Mag–ie, *f.* magic. **–ier,** *m.* (-s, –) magician; (*pl.*) Magi. **–iker,** *m.* magician. **–isch,** *adj.* magic(al).

Magist–er, *m.* (-ers, -er) schoolmaster; tutor, (*Scots*) dominie; *–er der freien Künste*, Master of Arts (*M.A.*). **–erhaft,** *adj.* pedantic, didactic, pragmatical. **–rat,** *m.* borough *or* municipal council, local authority. **–ratur,** *f.* magistracy. **–ratsmitglied,** *n.*, **–ratsperson,** *f.* town-councillor.

Magnat, *m.* (-en, -en) magnate, grandee.

Magnes–ia, *f.* magnesia, magnesium oxide; *doppeltkohlensaure –ia*, bicarbonate of magnesia. **–ium,** *n.* magnesium. **–iumlicht,** *n.* flash-light. **–iumsulphat,** *m.* Epsom salt.

Magnet, *m.* (-s & -en, -e & -en) magnet, loadstone; magneto (*Motor.*). **–apparat,** *m.* magneto. **–eisenerz,** *n.* magnetite. **–feld,** *n.* magnetic field. **–isch,** *adj.* magnetic; *–ische Abweichung*, declination; *–ischer Schlaf*, mesmeric trance. **–iseur,** *m.* (-s, -e) mesmerist. **–isieren,** *v.a.* magnetize. **–isierungsstärke,** *f.* intensity of magnetization. **–ismus,** *m.* magnetism; mesmerism. **–ismusmenge,** *f.* intensity of magnetization. **–kies,** *m.* magnetic pyrites. **–nadel,** *f.* magnetic needle, compass needle. **–schalter,** *m.* ignition switch (*Motor.*). **–spule,** *f.* electromagnet, solenoid. **–stab,** *m.* bar magnet. **–stein,** *m.* lodestone. **–zündung,** *f.* magneto-ignition.

Mahagoni, *n.* mahogany.

Mahd, 1. *f.* (-en) mowing; swath; hay crop; haymaking time. 2. *n.* (-es, ¨er) (*Swiss*) alpine pasture.

[1]**mäh–en,** *v.a.* & *n.* (*aux.* h.) mow, cut, reap. **–der,** *m.* (*dial.*) mower, reaper. **–drescher,** *m.* combine. **–erlohn,** *m.* mower's *or* reaper's wages. **–(e)zeit,** *f.* mowing time. **–feuer,** *n.* shifting fire (*Mil.*). **–maschine,** *f.* reaping-machine, lawn-mower.

[2]**mähen,** *v.n.* (*aux.* h.) bleat.

Mahl, *n.* (-(e)s, -e & ¨er) meal, repast, banquet. **–zeit,** *f.* meal-time, meal; *gesegnete –zeit!* I hope you will enjoy your meal; (*coll.*) *Prost –zeit!* that's a pretty kettle of fish!

mahl–en, *reg.* & *ir.v.a.* & *n.* (*aux.* h.) grind, mill, pound, crush, bray, beat (*Pap.*), powder, pulverize; disintegrate; (*Prov.*) *wer zuerst kommt, –t zuerst*, first come, first served. **–feinheit,** *f.* fineness of grinding. **–gang,** *m.* grinding mill. **–geld,** *n.* miller's fee. **–knecht,** *m.* miller's man. **–korn,** *n.* grist. **–mühle,** *f.*, **–werk,** *n.* grinding-mill. **–stein,** *m.* millstone. **–zahn,** *m.* molar.

mählich, *archaic*, *see* **allmählich.**

Mahlschatz, *m.* (*archaic*) dowry.

Mahlstrom, *m.* maelstrom, vortex, whirlpool.

Mähn–e, *f.* (-en) mane. **–enbusch,** *m.* helmet-plume.

mahn–en, *v.a.* remind; warn, admonish; exhort;

dun; *einen an seine Pflicht –en*, remind s.o. of his duty; *einen wegen einer Schuld –en*, press a p. for payment, demand payment from a p. **–er,** *m.* admonisher; dun. **–brief,** *m.*, **–schreiben,** *n.* demand-note, request to pay, dunning letter, reminder. **–gebühr,** *f.* library fine. **–mal,** *n.* memorial (stone, *etc.*). **–ruf,** *m.* warning cry. **–ung,** *f.* reminder; warning, admonition; dunning. **–zettel,** *m.* reminder, demand-note.

Mahr, *m.* (-(e)s, -e) (*dial.*) nightmare.

Mähre, *f.* (-n) jade, hack.

Mai, *m.* (-s, -e) (*poet.* -en, -en) May; *des Lebens –*, springtime of life. **–baum,** *m.* maypole. **–blume,** *f.* lily of the valley (*Convallaria majalis*) (*Bot.*). **–bowle,** *f.* punch seasoned with woodruff. **–e,** *f.* (-en) & *Austr. dial. m.* (-en, -en) maypole; may-day festivities; greenery, leaves (*for decoration*); (*dial.*) birch twigs, birch sapling. **–en,** *m.* (-ens, -en) (*Swiss*) posy, bouquet. **–enblüte,** *f.* (*fig.*) blossom-time, spring-time. **–enkönigin,** *f.* Queen of the May. **–ensäß,** *n.* (-es, -e) (*Swiss*) spring pasture. **–feier,** *f.* Mayday celebration. **–glöckchen,** *n.*, *see* **–blume.** **–käfer,** *m.* cockchafer (*Melolontha vulgaris*) (*Ent.*). (*sl.*) **–käfern,** *v.n.* (*aux.* h.) ponder, ruminate, puzzle over, rack one's brains. **–kätzchen,** *n.* catkin (*of birches, etc.*). **–kraut,** *n.* woodruff. **–trank,** *m.*, *see* **–bowle.**

Maid, *f. poet. for* **Magd, Mädchen.**

Mais, *m.* Indian corn, maize. **–kolben,** *m.* corn-cob.

Maisch–e, *f.* (-en) mash; mashing. **–bottich,** *m.*, mash(ing)-tub *or* -vat. **–en,** *v.a.* mash.

Majestät, *f.* (-en) majesty. **–isch,** *adj.* majestic. **–sbeleidigung,** *f.* lèse-majesté. **–sbrief,** *m.* letter patent, charter. **–srecht,** *n.* sovereign prerogative. **–srechte,** *n. pl.* regalia.

Major, *m.* (-s, -e) major (*Mil.*), squadron-leader (*Av.*). **–at,** *n.* (-s, -e) primogeniture; entail. **–atserbe,** 1. *m.* heir through primogeniture. 2. *n.* inheritance attached to primogeniture. **–atsgut,** *n.* property entailed on the eldest child. **–atsherr,** *m.* owner of an entailed estate. **–enn,** *adj.* of age. **–in,** *f.* major's wife. **–isieren,** *v.n.* outvote, carry the vote, carry by a majority. **–isierung,** *f.* outvoting. **–ität,** *f.* majority (*of votes, etc.*). **–itätsbeschluß,** *m.* resolution carried by a majority. **–srang,** *m.* majority, field rank (*Mil.*).

Majuskel, *f.* (-n) capital (letter), upper case, majuscule; small cap (*Typ.*).

makadamisieren, *v.a.* macadamize, metal (*roads*).

Makel, *m.* (-s, –) stain, spot, blemish, flaw, defect, fault. **–ig,** *adj.* spotted, stained. **–los,** *adj.* spotless, immaculate, faultless, pure.

Mäk–elei, *f.* (-en) fault-finding, censoriousness; *–elei im Essen*, fastidiousness, daintiness. **–elig,** *adj.* censorious, critical; fastidious, dainty. **–eln,** *v.n.* find fault with, criticize (in a carping spirit); *–le nicht an ihm!* don't run him down so! **–ler,** *m.* fault-finder, caviller (*see also* **Makler**).

mak–eln, *v.n.* (*aux.* h.) act as a broker *or* go-between, negotiate; *mit seinem Gewissen –eln*, compound with one's conscience. **–ler,** (*Swiss* **Mäkler**), *m.* (-s, –) broker, middleman, jobber, agent, negotiator. **–lergebühr,** *f.* brokerage. **–lerschaft,** *f.* broker's business.

Makkaron–i, *pl.* macaroni. **–isch,** *adj.* macaronic, burlesque (*of verse, etc.*).

Makrele, *f.* (-n) mackerel.

Makrone, *f.* (-n) macaroon.

Makul–atur, *f.* (-en) waste paper, scrap. **–aturbogen,** *m.* waste sheet (*Typ.*). **–ieren,** *v.a.* pulp (*paper*).

[1]**Mal,** *n.* (-(e)s, -e & ¨-er) sign, mark; landmark, monument; token; stigma, stain, spot, mole; goal; starting-point (*Sport*). **–baum,** *m.* boundary-tree. **–graben,** *m.* **–grube,** *f.* boundary-ditch. **–mann,** *m.* scratch (*Sport*). **–pfahl,** *m.*, **–säule,** *f.* boundary post *or* mark. **–stein,** *m.* boundary-stone; monumental stone. **–zeichen,** *n.* mark, sign; memorial.

[2]**Mal,** 1. *n.* (-(e)s, -e) point of time, time, bout, turn; *das erste –*, the first time; *zum dritten –e*, for the third time; *dieses eine –*, this once; *mit einem –e*, all at once, suddenly; *zu verschiedenen –en*, at different times; *ein ums andre –*, by turns, alternately; *ein – über das andre*, again and again, time and again, time out of number, time after time; *zwei – fünf ist zehn*, twice five are ten; *often compounded, see* allemal, diesmal, einmal, zweimal, *etc.*, erstemal, etlichemal, letztenmal, *etc.*, manchmal, wievielmal, x-mal, *etc.* 2. *adv.* & *part.* (*dial.* & *coll. for* einmal) once; just; *es ist nun – nicht anders in der Welt*, that is the way of the world, you see; *sie ist nicht – hübsch*, she is not even pretty; *hör' – !* just listen! *sag' –*, just tell me; *kommen Sie – her!* just come here! **–nehmen,** *v.a.* multiply. **–zeichen,** *n.* multiplication sign.

mal–en, 1. *v.a.* paint; portray, represent, delineate; *sich –en lassen*, sit for one's portrait, have one's portrait painted; (*Prov.*) *wenn man den Teufel an die Wand –t, dann kommt er*, talk of the devil and he'll appear; *sie ist zum –en*, she is a picture; *es ist wie gemalt*, it is like a picture *or* as pretty as a picture. 2. *v.r.* be reflected. **–er,** *m.* (-s, –) painter, artist. **–erei,** *f.* painting; picture. **–erfarbe,** *f.* artists' colour, paint. **–ergold,** *n.* painter's gold; ormolu. **–erisch,** *adj.* picturesque, artistic; pictorial, graphic. **–erkunst,** *f.* art of painting. **–erleinwand,** *f.* artist's canvas. **–ermeister,** *m.* master (house-)painter. **–erpinsel,** *m.* paint-brush. **–erscheibe,** *f.* palette. **–erschule,** *f.* school of painting *or* painters; school for painters, school of art. **–erstaffelei,** *f.* easel. **–kasten,** *m.* paint-box.

Mall, *n.* (-es, -e) model, mould (*Naut.*). **–brief,** *m.* building contract (*Naut.*).

Malter, *m.* & *n.* (-s, –) (*archaic*) corn-measure (*about* 150 *litres*); cord (*of wood*). **–n,** *v.a.* cord (*wood*).

Malvasier, *m.* malmsey (*grape or wine*).

Malve, *f.* (-n) mallow (*Bot.*). **–nartig,** *adj.* malvaceous (*Bot.*). **–nfarbig,** *adj.* mauve, heliotrope.

Malz, *n.* (-es, -e) malt; (*Prov.*) *an ihm ist Hopfen und – verloren*, he is (quite) hopeless. **–auszug,** *m.* malt extract. **–bier,** *n.* malt-beer, ale. **–bonbon,** *m.* & *n.* cough-lozenge. **–bottich,** *m.* malt-vat. **–darre,** *f.* malt-kiln. **–en,** *v.a.* & *n.* (*aux.* h.) malt. **–kaffee,** *m.* malt-coffee. **–milch,** *f.* malted milk. **–schrot,** *m.* & *n.* crushed malt, grist. **–tenne,** *f.* malt-floor. **–zucker,** *m.* maltose (*Chem.*).

mälz–en, *v.a.* & *n.*, *see* **malzen.** **–er,** *m.* maltster. **–erei,** *f.* malting; malt-house.

Mama, *f.* (-s) mamma.

Mammon, *m.* mammon, lucre, money bags, worldly riches. **–sdiener,**, *m.* **–sknecht,** *m.* mammon-worshipper, worldling.

Mammut, *n.* (-(e)s, -s & -e) mammoth.

mampfen, *v.n.* (*aux.* h.) (*coll.*) eat with one's mouth full.

Mamsell, *f.* (-en) (*coll.*) miss, damsel; shopgirl; housekeeper, stewardess (*on a farm*).

[1]**man,** *indef. pron.* (*used only in the Nom. sing.*; *in other cases of singular an oblique case of* einer *is used*) one, they, people, we, you, a person, someone, somebody; *– sagt*, it is said, they say; *– lasse mich in Frieden*, let me alone; *– hat mir gesagt*, I was *or* have been told; *– erlaube mir*, I beg leave (to); *– muß es tun*, it must be done; *das kann – nicht wissen*, there is no knowing; *– schneide AD im Punkte B*, bisect *AD* at the point *B*.

[2]**man,** *adv.* (*dial.*) only, but; (*coll.*) *das ist – wenig*, that is but little; *geh – ja nicht hin!* mind you do not go!

manch, (-er, -e, -es) *ind. adj.* & *pron.* many a, many a one; *– einer*, many a man, many a one; *das habe ich – liebes mal gehört*, I have heard that many a time; *das wird –em leid sein*, that will grieve many a one. **–e,** *pl.* many; some, several. **–erlei,** *indec. adj.* various, sundry, divers; *auf –erlei Art*, in various ways; *er sagte mir –erlei*, he told me many things. **–es,** *pron. subst. n.* many a thing, many things; *ich habe Ihnen gar –es zu erzählen*, I have a good deal to tell you; *–es ist dabei zu bedenken*, many things must be considered in this matter. **–mal,** *adv.* sometimes, now and again, from time to time.

Mand–ant, *m.* (-en, -en) principal, client. **–at,** *n.*

(-(e)s, -e) mandate; authorization, brief, (*Austr. dial.*) order to pay. **–atar,** *m.* (-s, -e) attorney, proxy, mandatory. **–atarmacht,** *f.* mandatory authority *or* power. **–atsgebiet,** *n.* mandated territory.

[1]**Mandel,** *f.* (-n) almond (*Bot.*); tonsil (*Anat.*). **–bräune,** *f.* quinsy. **–entzündung,** *f.* tonsillitis. **–kern,** *m.* almond. **–kleie,** *f.* ground almonds. **–öl,** *n.* oil of almonds.

[2]**Mandel,** *f.* (-(n) & *Austr. dial. m.* (-s, -n)) set of 15; 15 sheaves. **–n,** *v.a.* put up in heaps *or* shocks of 15 sheaves; count by fifteens. **–weise,** *adv.* by fifteens.

Mandoline, *f.* (-n) mandolin.

Mandragora, *f.* (-ren) mandrake (*Bot.*).

Manege, *f.* (-n) riding-school, circus ring.

Manen, *pl.* manes, shades.

Mangan, *n.* manganese. **–sauer,** *adj.* manganate of. **–säure,** *f.* manganic acid.

Mang–e, *f.* (-en) (*dial.*),[1] **Mang–el,** *f.* (-eln) mangle, wringer; rolling-pin; calender, rolling-press. **–en** (*dial.*), **–eln,** *v.a.* wring, mangle, calender.

[2]**Mangel,** *m.* (-s, ⸚) want, need, lack, dearth, scarcity, deficiency; absence, defect, blemish, flaw, fault, shortcoming; *an einer S. – haben* or *leiden*, be in want of a th.; *aus – an*, for want of, in default of; *in – geraten*, be reduced to want. **–erkrankung,** *f.* malnutrition, vitamin deficiency. **–haft,** *adj.* defective (*also Gram.*); imperfect, faulty; deficient, incomplete. **–haftigkeit,** *f.* defectiveness; imperfection, faultiness. **–n,** 1. *v.n.* (*aux.* h.) & *imp.* want, be wanting *or* deficient, lack; *an mir soll es nicht –n*, I shall do my part, I shall not fail; *er läßt es sich* (*Dat.*) *an nichts –n*, he denies himself *or* goes short of nothing; *es –t mir an barem Gelde*, I am in need of ready money; *wegen –nder Nachfrage*, in absence of demand. **–s,** *prep.* (*with Gen.*) for want of, in default of; *–s Annahme*, for non-acceptance. **–ware,** *f.* commodity in short supply.

Mangold, *m.* (-s, -e) silver *or* stock beet, mangelwurzel.

Manie, *f.* (-n) mania; madness; *es ist ihm zur – geworden*, it is a mania with him.

Manier, *f.* (-en) manner, way; deportment; fashion, habit; mode, style; mannerism; grace notes (*Mus.*); (*usually pl.*) manners, good behaviour; *mit guter –*, with a good grace; *das ist keine –*, that is not the way to behave. **–iert,** *adj.* affected, stilted, pretentious, meretricious, extravagant, ornate, florid, flamboyant, pompous, bombastic, bizarre, grandiloquent, highfalutin. **–iertheit,** *f.* affectation, mannerism. **–lich,** *adj.* civil, polite, mannerly, genteel, well-bred.

Manifest, *n.* (-es, -e) manifesto; ship's manifest (*Naut.*). **–ant,** *m.* (-en, -en) demonstrator. **–ationseid,** *m.* (*archaic*) sworn declaration of insolvency. **–ieren,** *v.a.* manifest; declare; (*archaic*) swear an affidavit to one's insolvency (*Law*); make a demonstration, demonstrate (*für*, in favour of; *gegen*, against).

Mani–küre, *f.* manicure; manicurist. **–küren,** *v.a.* manicure.

Manip–el, *f.* (-n) maniple (*Eccl.*). **–ulation,** *f.* manipulation, treatment. **–ulieren,** *v.a.* manipulate, treat, work.

Manko, *n.* deficit, deficiency, short measure *or* weight, shortage.

Mann, *m.* 1. (-(e)s, ⸚er) man; husband. 2. (-es, -en) (*poet.*) retainer, vassal; *die Soldaten standen drei – hoch*, the soldiers were drawn up three deep; *mit dreitausend –*, with three thousand troops; *tausend – zu Fuß*, a thousand foot(soldiers) *or* infantrymen; *alle – an Deck!* all hands on deck! (*Naut.*); *so viel auf den –*, so much per *or* a head; *an den – bringen*, find a purchaser for, dispose of; *seine Tochter an den – bringen*, dispose of one's daughter in marriage; *seinen – finden*, find one's match; *so viel für den –*, so much a *or* per head; *– für –*, one and all; *– gegen –*, hand to hand (*fight*); *der gemeine –*, the common people, the man in the street; *er ist –s genug*, he is man enough; *den lieben Gott einen guten – sein lassen*, let things take their course; *der kleine –*, see *der gemeine –*; *wenn Not an den – kommt* or *am – ist*, in case of necessity, if the worst comes to the worst; *wollen Sie den vierten – machen?* will you make the fourth? (*cards*); *mit – und Maus untergehen*, go down with all hands; *einen – nehmen*, marry; *du wärst nie mein –*, you would never do for me, you are not the man for me; *seinen – stehen* or *stellen*, hold one's own, stand one's ground; *du bist ein – des Todes, wenn . . .*, you are a dead man if . . .; *das Volk erhob sich wie ein –*, the nation rose as one man; *der wilde –*, the wild man of the woods; (*Prov.*) *ein – ein Wort*, an honest man is as good as his word. **–bar,** *adj.* marriageable; able to bear fruit. **–barkeit,** *f.* sexual maturity, puberty, marriageable age, (wo)manhood, (wo)man's estate. **–esalter,** *n.* (years of) manhood. **–eskraft,** *f.* manly vigour, virility. **–esreife,** *f.* puberty, maturity. **–esstamm,** *m.* male line. **–esstolz,** *m.* manly pride. **–eswort,** *n.* honest man's word. **–eswürde,** *f.* manly dignity. **(e)szucht,** *f.* (military) discipline. **–haft,** *adj.* manly, brave, valiant; resolute. **–haftigkeit,** *f.* manliness; bravery. **–heit,** *f.* manhood, virility; manliness, courage, valour. **–loch,** *n.* man-hole. (*coll.*) **–sbild,** *n.* man, male. **–schaft,** *f.* (body of) men, personnel, troops, crew; team (*sport*). **–schaftskost,** *f.* troops' rations. **–schaftsrennen,** *n.* team-race. **–schaftsschlitten,** *m.* bob-sleigh. **–sen,** *n.* (-s, –) (*coll.*) man, body; (*pl.*) menfolk. **–shoch,** *adj.* tall as a man. **–sleute,** *pl.* menfolk, men. **–sperson,** *f.* man, male. **–stoll,** *adj.* mad about *or* on men. **–streu,** *f.* eryngo, sea-holly (*Eryngium maritimum*) (*Bot.*). **–svolk,** *n.*, *see* **–sleute.** **–weib,** *n.* virago; mannish woman. **–weibisch,** *adj.* gynandrous, hermaphrodyte.

Männ–chen, *n.* (-s, – & -erchen) little man, manikin; male (*of beasts, birds, etc.*); *mein –chen*, my dear hubby; *–chen machen*, sit up, beg (*as a dog*); *–erchen sehen*, see pink elephants. **–erchor,** *m.* male chorus. **–erkleidung,** *f.* man's dress. **–erriege,** *f.* men's section (*Gymn.*). **–erstimme,** *f.* man's voice, male part. **–ertreu,** *f.* an alpine orchid (*Nigritella nigra*) (*Bot.*). **–ervolk,** *n.* men. **–erwürde,** *f.* dignity of the male. **–in,** *f.* virago; (*B.*) woman; *Lands–in*, (fellow-) countrywoman. **–isch,** *adj.* masculine, mannish, unwomanly. **–lein,** *n.* little fellow; *–lein und Weiblein*, man, woman, and child. **–lich,** *adj.* male, manly; (*Gram.*) masculine; bold, valiant; *–liche Kleidung*, man's clothes. **–lichkeit,** *f.* manhood, virility; masculinity, maleness; manliness, bravery.

mannig–fach, *adj.*, **–faltig,** *adj.* various, manifold, diverse, multifarious. **–faltigkeit,** *f.* multiplicity, variety, diversity.

männiglich, *indec. adj.* (*Law*) every man, everybody; one and all; individually and collectively.

Manometer, *n.* (-s, –) manometer; steam-gauge, pressure-gauge.

Manöv–er, *n.* (-ers, -er) manœuvre; military exercise; (*fig.*) trick, feint. **–rieren,** 1. *v.n.* (*aux.* h.) manœuvre. 2. *n.* manœuvring, manœuvres. **–erkrieg,** *m.* mock war. **–erkartusche,** *f.* blank (cartridge). **–rierfähig,** *adj.* manœuvrable. **–rierfreiheit,** *f.* freedom of manœuvre.

Mansarde, *f.* (-n) attic. **–ndach,** *n.* mansard-roof. **–nfenster,** *n.* attic-window, dormer-window. **–nstübchen,** *n.*, **–nzimmer,** *n.* attic. **–nwohnung,** *f.* garret.

Mansch, *m.* (-(e)s, -e) mixture; squash, slop, slush. **–en,** *v.a.* & *n.* (*aux.* h.) paddle about, splash, slop about; mix up, knead. **–erei,** *f.* dabbling, splashing, mixing, kneading.

Manschette, *f.* (-n) cuff; sleeve (*Mach.*); (*coll.*) *–n haben* (*vor*), be afraid, in awe *or* in fear (of). **–nfieber,** *n.* funk. **–nknopf,** *m.* cuff-link.

Mantel, *m.* (-s, ⸚) overcoat, top coat; cloak, gown, robe, pallium (*also Zool.*); mantle, pall; envelope, sheathing, case, shell, jacket, casing; outer cover (*of a tyre*); (*fig.*) mantle, cloak, pretence; *den – nach dem Winde hängen*, temporize, trim one's sails according to the wind; *einer S. ein Mäntelchen umhängen*, cloak *or* palliate a th. **–geschoß,** *n.* shell (*Artil.*). **–gesetz,** *n.* skeleton law. **–sack,** *m.* portmanteau, valise. **–schicht,** *f.* protective layer.

-stoff, *m.*, **-tuch,** *n.* mantling, coat-material. **-tarif,** *m.* skeleton agreement. **-zeug,** *n.*, *see* **-stoff.**

Mantille, *f.* (-n) mantilla.

Mantsch, *m.*, **-en,** *see* **Mansch.**

Manu-al, *n.* (-s, -e) handbook; (*C.L.*) journal, day-book; keyboard (*Mus.*); organ-manual. **-ell,** *adj.* manual (*skill*).

Manufaktur, *f.* (-en) manufacture, manufacturing, making; hand-made article; (*archaic*) factory. **-ist,** *m.* (-en, -en) manufacturer; maker; dealer in textiles. **-waren,** *f.pl.* textiles, drapery, (*Amer.*) dry-goods. **-warenhändler,** *m.* dealer in textiles *or* (*Amer.*) dry-goods, (linen-)draper, mercer.

Manuskript, *n.* (-(e)s, -e) manuscript; copy (*Typ.*); *Bühnen–*, acting copy; *als – gedruckt*, printed for private circulation only; *den Bühnen gegenüber als – gedruckt*, acting rights reserved.

Mappe, *f.* (-n) portfolio, letter- *or* writing-case; music-case; file.

Mär, *f.* (-en) news, tidings, rumour, report, story. **-chen,** *n.* (-s, –) fairy-tale; fable, legend; tale, story; fib. **-chenhaft,** *adj.* fabulous, legendary; (*fig.*) fictitious. **-chenwelt,** *f.* fabulous world, world of romance, Wonderland. **-e,** *f.*, *see* **Mär.**

Maras-mus, *m.* (–, -men) marasmus, wasting, bodily decay. **-tisch,** *adj.* marasmic, wasted, decrepit.

Marbel, Märbel, *m.* (-s, –), *see* **Marmel.**

Marder, *m.* (-s, –) pine marten (*Zool.*); marten-fur.

Margarin-e, *f.* margarine. **-sauer,** *adj.* margaric, margarate of.

Marien- (*for compounds see* **Maria** *in Index of Proper Names*).

Marille, *f.* (-n) (*Austr. dial.*) apricot.

Marine, *f.* (-n) navy (*in Germany, combined navy & merchant fleet*); *bei der – dienen*, serve in the navy; *in –kreisen*, among naval experts. **-akademie,** *f.* Royal Naval College. **-artillerie,** *f.* naval artillery (*in Germany, coastal artillery*). **-blau,** *adj.* navy blue. **-etat,** *m.* naval estimates. **-flugwesen,** *n.* Fleet Air Arm. **-flugzeug,** *n.* seaborne aircraft, plane of the Fleet Air Arm. **-infanterie,** *f.* marines. **-maler,** *m.* marine *or* sea-painter. **-minister,** *m.* First Lord of the Admiralty (*Eng.*); Secretary of the Navy (*U.S.A.*). **-ministerium,** *n.* Admiralty (*Eng.*), Navy Department (*U.S.A.*). **-offizier,** *m.* naval officer. **-soldat,** *m.* marine. **-station,** *f.* naval base. **-truppen,** *f.pl.* marines. **-werft,** *f.* navy-yard, government dockyard. **-wesen,** *f.* naval affairs.

marinieren, *v.a.* pickle.

Marionette, *f.* (-n) puppet. **-nspiel** *n.* puppet-show. **-ntheater,** *n.* marionette- *or* puppet-theatre.

[1]**Mark,** *f.* (-en) boundary, frontier, limit; border, border-country, marches; wood *or* pasture held in common; touch(line) (*Rugby football*); *die – = die – Brandenburg*, Brandenburg Marches. **-baum,** *m.* boundary-tree. **-en,** *v.a.* settle a boundary. **-graf,** *m.* margrave. **-gräfin,** *f.* margravine. **-scheide,** *f.* boundary, surface limits of a mine. **-scheider,** *m.* mining surveyor. **-stein,** *m.* boundary-stone, landmark, (*fig.*) limit; deciding factor, turning point. **-ung,** *f.* boundary, demarcation; common land.

[2]**Mark,** *f.*, (-stücke & (*as measure of value*) – (*e.g.* 5 –, 5 marks)) mark (*coin*). **-rechnung,** *f.* calculation in marks. **-schein,** *m.*; *100–schein*, 100-mark note. **-stück,** *n.* mark piece. **-währung,** *f.* currency of Germany.

[3]**Mark,** *n.* marrow; pith; pulp; core, heart, medulla, essence; mettle, strength, vigour; – *in den Knochen haben*, be of great strength; *durch – und Bein dringen*, penetrate to the very marrow, cut to the quick; *ins – treffen*, cut to the quick. **-erschütternd,** *adj.* blood-curdling. **-holz,** *n.* pithy wood. **-ig,** *adj.* pithy; vigorous, emphatic. **-los,** *adj.* marrowless; pithless; (*fig.*) spineless, spiritless. **-strahlen,** *pl.* medullary rays. **-zelle** *f.* medullary cell.

markant, *adj.* striking, prominent, (well-)marked, characteristic.

Marke, *f.* (-n) mark, token, sign; countermark, label, chit, counter, ticket; brand, trade-mark; quality, sort, growth, make; (postage) stamp. **-nalbum,** *n.* stamp album. **-nartikel,** *m.*, **-nware,** *f.* proprietary article. **-nring,** *m.* graduated ring. **-nsammler,** *m.* stamp collector, philatelist. **-nschutz,** *m.* trade-mark, registration.

Märker, *m.* (-s, –) frontier dweller, Brandenburger.

Marketender, *m.* (-s, –) canteen proprietor, (*archaic*) sutler. **-in,** *f.* camp-follower. **-n,** *v.n* (*aux.* h) keep a canteen, sell to the troops.

markier-en, *v.a.* mark, label, stamp, brand, indicate, (*coll.*) simulate. **-t,** *p.p.* & *adj.* marked, distinguished, prominent; clearly defined. **-ung,** *f.* marking (*of footpaths, etc.*), route indicator. **-ungsboje,** *f.* sea-marker.

Markise, *f.* (-n) blind, awning.

Markör, *m.* (-s, -s) billiard-marker, billiard-hall attendant, (*Austr. dial.*) waiter.

Markt, *m.* (-(e)s, ⸚e) market, market-place; market-town; mart, emporium; bargain, business, trade; *Jahr–*, (yearly) fair; *seine Haut zu –e tragen*, risk one's life; *zu –e* or *auf den – bringen*, put on the market, offer for sale; *eine Anleihe auf den – bringen*, issue a loan; *auf den – kommen*, come to market. **-bericht,** *m.* market report. **-bude,** *f.* stall, stand, booth. **-en,** *v.n.* (*aux.* h.) (*dial.*) haggle, bargain (*um eine S.*, for a th.); market, sell in the market. **-fähig,** *adj.* marketable, saleable. **-flecken,** *m.* small market-town. **-freiheit,** *f.* right of holding a market. **-gängig,** *adj.* current; *–gängiger Preis*, market-price. **-gebühren,** *pl.* market dues. **-geld,** *n.* stall rent. **-gut,** *n.* market wares. **-halle,** *f.* covered market; market-hall. **-helfer,** *m.* porter, packer. **-korb,** *m.* shopping basket. **-lage,** *f.* state of the market. **-leute,** *pl.* stall holders. **-ordnung,** *f.* market-regulation(s). **-platz,** *m.* market-place. **-preis,** *m.* current *or* market-price. **-recht,** *n.* market-regulations; *see* **-freiheit.** **-schreier,** *m.* quack, charlatan. **-schreierisch,** *adj.* charlatan, showy. **-schwankung,** *f.* fluctuation of the market. **-wert,** *m.* market-value, value on the open market. **-zettel** *m.* market-report, price-list.

Marmelade, *f.* (-n) jam.

Marmel(-stein), *m.* (*Poet.* & *archaic*) marble; marble (*boys' toy*). **-n,** *v.a.* marble, vein (*Paint.*); play marbles.

Marmor, *m.* (-s, -e) marble. **-band,** *m.* marbled binding. **-bild,** *n.* marble statue *or* bust. **-bruch,** *m.*, **-grube,** *f.* marble quarry. **-glatt,** *adj.* as smooth as marble. **-ieren,** *v.a.* marble, grain, vein, mottle. **-iert,** *p.p.* & *adj.* marbled, mottled; *–iertes Papier*, marble paper; *mit –iertem Schnitt*, marbled-edged (*Bookb.*). **-n,** *adj.* marble, marble-like, made of marble. **-platte,** *f.* marble slab. **-säule,** *f.* marble column. **-schleifer,** *m.* marble-polisher. **-schnitt,** *m.* marbled edges (*of book*).

marod-e, *adj.* weary, exhausted, tired out, knocked-up; unfit to march. **-eur,** *m.* (-s, -e) marauder, pillager. **-ieren,** *v.n.* (*aux.* h.) loot, pillage.

Marone, *f.* (-n) sweet chestnut.

Marotte, *f.* (-n) whim, fancy, fad, caprice, hobby-horse.

Mars, *m.* & *f.* (–, -e(n)) crow's nest, top (*Naut.*); *der große –*, main-top. **-schoten,** *f.pl.* topsail-sheets. **-segel,** *n.* topsail.

[1]**Marsch,** *f.* (-en) alluvial land, fen, marsh. **-boden,** *m.* alluvial soil, marshland. **-(en)bewohner,** *m.*, *see* **-länder.** **-fieber,** *n.* malaria. **-hof,** *m.* fen-farm. **-ig,** *ad*. marshy. **-länder,** *m.* fen-dweller.

[2]**Marsch,** 1. *m.* (-es, ⸚e) march; marching; march (*Mus.*); *verdeckte Märsche*, stolen marches; *den – schließen*, bring up the rear; *auf dem –*, on the march, (*fig.*) under way, in progress; *sich auf den – begeben* or *in – setzen*, march away *or* off, set out; *den – blasen*, strike up a march; (*coll.*) *einem den – blasen*, send a p. about his business; *in Gewaltmärschen*, in forced marches. 2. *int.* – *!* march! forward! be off! *– ! – !* double! **-anzug,** *m.* marching kit. **-befehl,** *m.* marching orders. **-bereit,** *adj.* ready to move. **-bereitschaft,** *f.* readiness to march. **-fähig,** *adj.* fit for marching. **-fahrt,** *f.*

cruising speed (*Naut.*). **-folge,** *f.* order of march. **-gepäck,** *n.* full pack, full marching order. **-geschwindigkeit,** *f.* rate of marching, (marching) pace, cruising speed. **-ieren,** *v.n.* (*aux.* h. *&* s.) march. **-kolonne,** *f.* column on the march, column of route. **-lager,** *n.* bivouac. **-leistung,** *f.* distance marched. **-linie,** *f.* line of march. **-mäßig,** *adj.* in marching order. **-ordnung,** *f.* order of march. **-pause,** *f.* halt on the march. **-route,** *f.* (*usually fig.*) orders, instructions. **-spitze,** *f.* head of the column. **-tag,** *m.* day of departure. **-tempo,** *n.* march time (*Mus.*).

Marschall, *m.* (-s, ¨-e) marshal. **-sstab,** *m.* marshal's baton.

Marstall, *m.* (-s, ¨-e) stables.

Marter, *f.* (-n) torture; torment, agony, pang. **-er,** *m.* torturer, tormenter, (*dial.*) martyr. **-l,** *n.* (*dial.*) memorial tablet. **-bank,** *f.* rack. **-gerät,** *n.* instruments of torture. **-geschichte,** *f.* martyrology. **-holz,** *n.* the Cross. **-kammer,** *f.* torture-chamber. **-n,** *v.a.* torment; torture, inflict torture on; inflict martyrdom on; *sich* (*Dat.*) *den Kopf* (*zer*)*–n*, rack one's brain. **-pfahl,** *m.* the stake. **-tod,** *m.* death by torture, painful death. **-voll,** *adj.* excruciating. **-werkzeuge,** *n.pl.*, *see* **-gerät. -woche,** *f.* Passion week.

Märty-rer, *m.* (-s, –), **-rerin,** *f.* martyr. **-rertum,** *n.*, **-rium,** *n.* (-iums, -ien) martyrdom. **-rergeschichte,** *f.* martyrology. **-rertod,** *m.* martyrdom; *den –rertod sterben*, suffer martyrdom.

Marunke, *f.* (-n) (*Austr. dial.*) egg-plum.

März, *m.* March. **-lich,** *adj.* Marchlike, of March; *vor–lich*, pre-1848. **-(en)bier,** *n.* strong beer. **-feld,** *n.* national assembly of the Franks. **-tage,** *m.pl.* revolution of 1848. **-veilchen,** *n.* sweet violet.

Masch-e, *f.* (-en) mesh, stitch; interstice; (*dial.*) bow, bow-tie; link (*of mail*); *eine –e fallen lassen* (*aufnehmen*), drop (pick up) a stitch (*in knitting*). **-en,** *v.a.* net. **-endraht,** *m.* wire-netting. **-enfest,** *adj.* ladder-proof (*hosiery*). **-enpanzer,** *m.* chain-mail. **-enweite,** *f.* width of mesh. **-enwerk,** *n.* network. **-ig,** *adj.* meshy, meshed, netted, reticulated.

Maschin-e, *f.* (-en) machine, engine, machinery; apparatus; typewriter; *eine –e anlassen*, start an engine; *eine –e abstellen*, stop an engine; *mit der – geschrieben*, typewritten. **-ell,** *adj.* mechanical. **-enanlage,** *f.* power-plant. **-enantrieb,** *m.* mechanical drive; *mit –enantrieb*, power-driven. **-enbauer,** *m.* mechanical engineer. **-enbauschule,** *f.* engineering school. **-enfabrik,** *f.* engineering-works. **-enfett,** *n.* lubricating grease. **-enführer,** *m.* engine-driver. **-engarn,** *n.* machine-spun yarn, (mule-)twist. **-engebäude,** *n.*, **-enhaus,** *n.* engine-room, engine-shed. **-engewehr,** machine-gun. **-engewehrschütze,** *m.* machine-gunner. **-engondel,** *f.* power-gondola (*Av.*). **-enkunde,** *f.* **-enlehre,** *f.* (science of) mechanical engineering. **-enmäßig,** *adj.* mechanical, automatic. **-enmeister,** *m.* mechanical engineer; machinist; engine driver (*Railw.*); stage-mechanic; machine minder (*Typ.*). **-enpapier,** *n.* machine-made paper. **-enpersonal,** *n.* engine-room staff. **-enpistole,** *f.* sub-machine gun, tommy gun. **-enraum,** *m.*, **-ensaal,** *m.* engine-room. **-ensatz,** *m.* generating plant, generator, power unit; machine-set type (*Typ.*). **-enschaden,** *m.* engine trouble. **-enschlosser,** *m.* fitter, mechanic. **-enschmiere,** *f.* lubricating grease. **-enschreiber,** *m.* typist. **-enschrift,** *f.* typescript. **-enschriftlich,** *adj.* typewritten. **-enstand,** *m.* engine-driver's cab. **-enwebstuhl,** *m.* power-loom. **-enwerk,** *n.* machinery. **-enwesen,** *n.* engineering. **-enzeichnen,** *n.* engineering drawing. **-enzentrale,** *f.* central power-plant. **-erie,** *f.* machinery, works, drive, wheels. **-ist,** (-en, -en) *m.* machinist; engineer; mechanic, fitter, artificer.

Maser, *f.* (-n) *&* *m.* (-s, –) vein, streak; speck, speckle, spot; gnarl, burr, knot (*of wood*). **-fleck,** *m.* speckle, vein. **-holz,** *n.* veined wood, bird's-eye wood. **-ig,** *adj.* mottled, grained, streaky, speckled. **-kegel,** *m.*, **-knollen,** *m.*, **-knoten,** *m.*. knob, burr (*in wood*). **-n,** 1. (*pl.*) measles. 2. *v.a.* grain, vein. 3. *v.r.* become streaky, mottled *or* knotty. **-ung,** *f.* veining, graining.

Mask-e, *f.* (-en) mask; disguise; pretence, pretext; camouflage, screen; fancy dress *or* costume; *einem die –e abnehmen* or *vom Gesicht reißen*, unmask a p.; *die –e fallen lassen* or *von sich werfen*, drop pretence, show one's true face, come into the open. **-enanzug,** *m.*, **-enkleid,** *n.* fancy dress; disguise, costume. **-enball,** *m.*, **-enfest,** *n.* fancy-dress ball. **-entänzer,** *m.* masked dancer. **-enverleih,** *m.* hire of fancy costumes *or* theatrical properties. **-enzug,** *m.* fancy-dress parade. **-erade,** *f.* disguise, fancy dress, masquerade. **-ieren,** *v.a.* mask, camouflage; put on a mask, disguise. **-ierung,** *f.* camouflage, screening.

maß, mäße, *see* **messen.**

Maß, 1. *n.* (-es, -e) measure, measurement, size, dimension, gauge; index, extent, degree, criterion, standard, rate; metre, time (*Mus.*); proportion, moderation; (*pl.*) limit, bounds, height; *auf –e*, to size; *– für –*, tit for tat; *das kleinste gemeinsame –*, least common measure (*Math.*); *in dem –e als*, in the same manner as, to the same extent as; *in dem – daß*, to such an extent that; *in gleichem –e*, to the same extent; *in großem –e*, to a large extent, on a large scale; *in hohem –e*, in a high degree, highly; *in höherem –e*, to a greater extent; *in rechtem –*, in due proportion; *in reichem –e*, in full measure; *in solchem –e*, to such an extent, to such a degree; *in verjüngtem –e*, on a reduced scale, in miniature; *in vollem –e*, amply, completely; *alles mit –(en)*, everything in moderation; *Anzug nach –*, suit made to measure; *nach dem –e*, in proportion to, according to; *einem (das) – zu einem Rock nehmen*, measure a p. *or* take a p.'s measurement for a coat; *das rechte – haben*, be the right size; *das geht über alles –*, that exceeds all bounds; *das – überschreiten*, go too far; *das – ist voll*, my patience is exhausted; *das – vollmachen*, fill the cup to the brim; *weder – noch Ziel halten* or *kennen*, know no bounds. 2. *m.* *&* *f.* (*dial.* *&* *archaic*) measure, pot, tankard; *zwei – Bier*, two tankards of beer. **-e,** *f.* (-en) (*archaic, still used in stock phrases*), *see* **Maß**; *in solcher –e*, see *in solchem –e*; *mit –en*, with propriety, in moderation, moderately; *ohne –en*, excessively; *über die –en, über alle –en*, beyond measure, out of all bounds, exceedingly; (*and in compounds*) *bekannter–en*, as is well known; *beliebiger–en*, as one pleases; *der–en*, in such a manner; *einiger–en*, to some *or* a certain extent; *folgender–en*, in the following way, as follows; *gehöriger–en*, duly; *gewisser–en*, in some degree, to a certain extent; *hergebrachter–en*, according to custom; *solcher–en*, in such a manner; *verabredeter–en*, according to agreement; *versproch(e)ner–en*, according to promise. **-analyse,** *f.* volumetric analysis (*Chem.*). **-arbeit,** *f.* made to measure. **-einheit,** *f.* unit of measure. **-flüssigkeit,** *f.* standard solution (*Chem.*). **-gabe,** *f.* measure, proportion; *nach –gabe seiner Kräfte*, according to his powers. **-gebend,** *adj.*, **-geblich,** *adj.* authoritative, decisive, controlling, conclusive, determining; standard; *–gebenden Orts*, in an authoritative quarter; *die –gebenden Kreise*, influential circles, those in authority. **-gefäß,** *n.* measuring vessel, standard measure. **-halten,** *v.n.* observe moderation, keep within bounds *or* limits. **-haltend,** *adj.* moderate, temperate. **-haltung,** *f.* moderation, restraint, sobriety. **-kanne,** *f.*, **-krug,** *m.* tankard, quart-pot, litre-mug. **-liebchen,** *n.* ox-eye daisy (*Chrysanthemum leucanthemum*) (*Bot.*). **-los,** *adj.* boundless, immoderate, extravagant, exorbitant. **-losigkeit,** *f.* want of moderation, extravagance, vehemence. **-nahme,** *f.* measure; precaution, preventive measure; mode of acting. **-regel,** *f.* measure, step, expedient; *die nötigen (Vorsichts)–regeln ergreifen* or *treffen*, take steps accordingly, take the necessary precautions; *gesetzliche –regeln ergreifen*, take legal steps. **-regeln,** *v.a.* reprimand, take to task; inflict disciplinary punishment on. **-regelung,** *f.* reprimand, disciplinary punishment. **-röhre,** *f.* burette

(*Chem.*). **-schneiderei,** *f.* bespoke tailoring. **-stab,** *m.* ruler, rule, measure; standard; scale; criterion; representative fraction (*on maps*); *in großem -stabe,* on a large scale; *verjüngter -stab,* reduced scale; *in vergrößertem -stabe,* on an enlarged scale. **-verhältnis,** *n.* proportion; (*pl.*) dimensions. **-voll,** *adj.* moderate, sober, temperate, tempered. **-werk,** *n.* tracery (*Arch.*).

Mass-age, *f.* (-n) massage. **-ieren,** *v.a.* massage.

Massak-er, *n.* (-s, –) massacre. **-rieren,** *v.a.* massacre.

Mass-e, *f.* (-en) mass, heap, quantity, number; multitude, the masses, the people; lump, block, bulk; substance, paste, dough; pulp, stuff (*Pap.*); property, estate, assets; *in -en aufstellen,* mass (*Mil.*); *-e der Nation,* bulk of the nation; *sich zur -e melden,* lodge a claim (*on a bankrupt's estate*); *Kreditoren der -e,* creditors of the estate; *bei der -e einkommen,* claim on the estate; (*Prov., C.L.*) *die -e muß es bringen,* small profits and large returns. **-egläubiger,** *pl.* bankrupt's creditors. **-enabsatz,** *m.* wholesale. **-enartikel,** *m.* wholesale article. **-enaufgebot,** *n.* levy en masse, general levy (*Mil.*). **-enaussperrung,** *f.* general lock-out. **-enbeeinflussung,** *f.* propaganda. **-enbildung,** *f.* massing, concentration (*Mil.*). **-enfabrikation,** *f.* mass-production. **-enfeuer,** *n.* concentrated fire (*Artil.*). **-engrab,** *n.* common grave. **-engüter,** *n.pl.* bulk articles. **-enhaft,** *adj.* in a mass, in large quantities, wholesale; bulky, enormous. **-enmord,** *m.* general massacre, wholesale murder. **-enquartier,** *n.* billets for a large number. **-enteilchen,** *n.* particle, corpuscle, molecule. **-enverbrauch,** *m.* bulk consumption. **-enverkauf,** *m.* bulk sale. **-enversammlung,** *f.* mass-meeting. **-enverwalter,** *m.* (official) receiver. **-enweise,** *adv.* en masse, in large numbers, in heaps; in a lump, wholesale. **-eschulden,** *pl.* bankrupt's debts. **-ieren,** *v.a.* mass, concentrate (*troops, etc.*). **-ig,** *adj.* bulky, clumsy, heavy, solid. **-iv,** 1. *adj.* massive, solid. 2. *n.*(-(e)s, -e) massif (*mountain*).

Massel, *f.* (-n) pig, slab (*of iron*).

Maßholder, *m.* (-s, –) (*dial.*) common maple (*Acer campestre*) (*Bot.*).

mäßig, 1. *adj.* moderate; frugal, modest, reasonable, temperate, middling; andante (*Mus.*). 2. *adv.* fairly, moderately; *zu -em Preise,* at a reasonable figure. 3. *as suffix* = -like (*e.g.* **helden-,** like a hero). **-en,** 1. *v.a.* moderate, temper; ease, mitigate, allay, assuage; restrain, check; *den Schritt -en,* slacken one's pace; *gemäßigte Zone,* temperate zone. 2. *v.r.* restrain o.s., keep one's temper, be moderate; *-e dich!* calm yourself! do not lose your temper! **-keit,** *f.* moderation, temperance, frugality; mediocrity; *strenger -keitsverein,* total-abstinence society. **-ung,** *f.* moderation, restraint.

Maßlieb, *n.* (-(e)s, -e), *see* **Maßliebchen** *under* **Maß.**

[1]**Mast,** *m.* (-es, -e(n)) mast, pole, pylon, tower; *einen – absegeln,* carry away a mast; *einen – einsetzen,* set up a mast; *der große –,* mainmast; *der vordere –,* foremast; *der hintere –,* mizzen-mast. **-baum,** *m.* mast. **-er,** *suffix, e.g.* **Drei-er,** *m.* three-master. **-korb,** *m.* (round-)top, crow's-nest. **-topp,** *m.* masthead. **-verankerung,** *f.* mooring (*of airships*). **-wächter,** *m.* masthead look-out (man) (*Naut.*). **-wurf,** *m.* clove hitch (*knot*).

[2]**Mast,** *f.* mast, acorns, beech-nuts, *etc.*; feeding-stuff, fattening (*pigs, etc.*); *zur – halten, auf der – haben,* fatten. **-darm,** *m.* rectum. **-feder,** *f.* tail feather. **-futter,** *n.* fattening (food). **-geld,** *n.* pannage. **-ig,** *adj.* sleek, fat, well-fed; thick (*of corn, etc.*), lush (*of pasture*). **-kalb,** *n.* fatted calf. **-kur,** *f.* fattening diet. **-nutzung,** *f.* pannage. **-recht,** *n.* right of pannage. **-ung,** *f.* fattening; fattening food. **-vieh,** *n.* fattened cattle. **-zeit,** *f.* time for fattening cattle.

mäst-en, 1. *v.a.* feed, fatten, cram; (*B.*) *das gemästete Kalb schlachten,* kill the fatted calf. 2. *v.r.* overfeed, live on the fat of the land. **-ung,** *f.* fattening.

Mastix, *m.* (-(es), -e) (gum) mastic.

Matador, *m.* (-s, & -en, -e(n)) matador; (*coll.*) eminent person; crack player, champion; (*sl.*) big shot.

Material, 1. *n.* (-s, -ien) material, matter, substance, stuff; stock, plant; equipment, material (*Mil.*); (*pl.*) (raw) materials, ingredients, products; experimental data; *rollendes –,* rolling stock (*Railw.*); *liegendes –,* railway-plant. 2. *adj.* material. **-anforderung,** *f.* indent *or* requisition for stores (*Mil.*). **-iendepot,** *n.* supply depot, ordnance stores (*Mil.*). **-isieren,** *v.a.* & *r.* materialize. **-ismus,** *m.* materialism. **-ist,** *m.* (-en, -en) materialist, sensualist, worldling; (*dial.*) druggist, grocer. **-istisch,** *adj.* materialistic. **-prüfungsamt,** *n.* testing laboratory. **-schaden,** *m.* material damage. **-schlacht,** *f.* battle in which superior equipment is decisive. **-waren,** *f.pl.* household goods; (*dial.*) groceries, colonial produce; drugs.

Materi-e, *f.* (-en) matter, stuff, substance; subject, cause; pus (*Med.*). **-ell,** *adj.* material, real; materialistic; *-eller Mensch,* matter-of-fact person; materialist.

Mathemat-ik, *f.* mathematics. **-iker,** *m.* (-s, –) mathematician. **-isch,** *adj.* mathematical.

Matjeshering, *m.* (-s, -e) white herring.

Matratze, *f.* (-n) mattress.

Mätresse, *f.* (-n) (kept) mistress, concubine. **-nwirtschaft,** *f.* petticoat government.

Matrikel, *f.* (-n) roll, register; matriculation; *in die – eintragen,* matriculate. **-schein,** *m.* certificate of matriculation.

Matrize, *f.* (-n) matrix, mould; die, stencil.

Matrone, *f.* (-n) matron, elderly lady.

Matrose, *m.* (-n, -n) sailor, seaman, naval rating. **-nheuer,** *f.* sailor's wages. **-nkragen,** *m.* sailor-collar. **-ntanz,** *m.* sailor's hornpipe.

Matsch, *m.* (-es, -e) (*coll.*) mash, squash, pulp; mud, mire, slush; 100 (*Cards*); *– machen,* make all the tricks; *– werden,* lose all the tricks (*at cards*). **-en,** *v.a.* squash, mash, bruise; splash; capot (*Cards*). **-ig,** *adj.* sloppy, mashed, muddy, slushy.

matt, 1. *adj.* faint, weak, dim, feeble, languid; flat, stale, exhausted, insipid, jejune, tasteless; dull, mat, tarnished, dead, subdued, lifeless; spent (*of balls, bullets, etc.*); checkmate (*at chess*); *die Eisenbahnaktien waren ziemlich –,* railway shares were rather dull; (*C.L.*) *-e Haltung,* faint demand. 2. *n.* mate (*Chess*); *einen – machen* or *setzen,* checkmate a p.; *Schach* (*und*) *–,* check-mate. **-äugig,** *adj.* dim-eyed. **-beize,** *f.* tarnishing pickle. **-blau,** *adj.* & *n.* pale blue. **-geschliffen,** *adj.* frosted, ground. **-glanz,** *m.* dull finish. **-glas,** *n.* frosted glass. **-gold,** *n.* old gold. **-heit,** *f.* dullness, faintness. **-herzig,** *adj.* faint-hearted, spiritless. **-ieren,** *v.a.* frost, deaden, dull, delustre, tarnish. **-igkeit,** *f.* feebleness, weakness, languor, lassitude, debility. **-rot,** *adj.* & *n.* dull red. **-scheibe,** *f.* focusing screen, ground glass screen (*Phot.*), fluorescent screen. **-setzen,** *v.a.* checkmate; (*fig.*) thwart, frustrate, deprive of influence. **-weiß,** *adj.* & *n.* dull white.

[1]**Matte,** *f.* (-n) mat; matting. **-nflechter,** *m.* mat-maker, strawplaiter. **-nzeug,** *n.* matting.

[2]**Matte,** *f.* (-n) (*dial. Poet.*) alpine meadow, mead. **-nklee,** *m.* red clover.

Matur-a, *f.* (*Austr. dial.*), *see* **-itätsexamen.** **-ität,** *f.* maturity, ripeness. **-itätsexamen,** *n.* school-leaving examination. **-itätszeugnis,** *n.* (school-)leaving certificate.

Matz, *m.* (-es, ¨-e) brat, kid, nipper; *oder ich will – heißen,* or I'm a Dutchman, or my name is not (*one's own name*).

Mätzchen, *n.* (-s, –) (*coll.*) nonsense, silly excuses; *mache keine –!* don't play the fool!

Matze, *f.* (-n), **-n,** *m.* (-ns, -n) unleavened bread.

mau, *adj.* (*sl.*) middling, rather bad, indifferent, wretched.

mauen, *v.n.* (*aux.* h.) mew.

Mauer, *f.* (-n) wall; battlement. **-absatz,** *m.* offset. **-anker,** *m.* cramp-iron. **-anschlag,** *m.* placard, poster. **-arbeit,** *f.* masonry. **-blende,** *f.* niche. **-blümchen,** *n.* (*coll.*) 'wallflower'.

-brecher, *m.* battering-ram. **-dach,** coping. **-hut,** *m.* **-kappe,** *f.* coping(-stone). **-kalk,** *m.*, **-kitt,** *m.* mortar. **-kelle,** *f.* trowel. **-klammer,** *f.* cramp-iron. **-krone,** *f.* mural crown. **-mantel,** *m.* lining of a wall. **-n,** 1. *v.n.* build (*with stone* or *brick*), make a wall, (*fig.*) play a waiting game, stone-wall. 2. *v.a.* wall up *or* in, immure. **-pfeffer,** *m.* stonecrop (*Sedum*) (*Bot.*). **-polier,** *m.* foreman bricklayer, head-mason. **-putz,** *m.* plastering, rough-cast. **-schwalbe,** *f.*, **-segler,** *m.* swift (*Micropus apus*) (*Orn.*). **-speise,** *f.* mortar. **-stein,** *m.* building stone; brick. **-werk,** *n.* masonry, stonework; brickwork; (*collect.*) walls. **-ziegel,** *m.* brick. **-zinne,** *f.* battlement.

Mauke, *f.* (-n) scurf, malanders (*Vet.*).

Maul, *n.* (-s, ⸚er) mouth, jaws, muzzle (*of animals*); (*vulg. also of persons*); (*fig.*) tongue; peristoma (*Bot.*); *das – aufreißen,* talk big, blow one's own trumpet; *kein Blatt vors – nehmen,* speak one's mind, not mince one's words; *alle bösen Mäuler des Dorfes,* all the scandalmongers *or* gossips of the village; *sein – zu brauchen wissen,* have a flippant tongue; *er ist nicht aufs – gefallen,* he has a nimble tongue, he is always ready with an answer, he can talk himself out of anything; *einem geschenkten Gaul sieht man nicht ins –,* don't look a gift horse in the mouth; *ein grobes (loses) –,* a coarse (loose) tongue; *ein großes – haben,* be a windbag *or* tub-thumper, brag, make empty promises; *halt's – !* hold your tongue! shut up! *das – hängen* (or *hängen lassen*), see *ein schiefes – ziehen*; *Maul- und Klauenseuche, f.* foot and mouth disease; *er redet wie es ihm ins – kommt,* he says whatever comes into his head; *in der Leute Mäuler kommen,* become the talk of the town; *einem nach dem –e reden,* echo a p.'s views; *ein (schiefes) – ziehen* or *machen,* look disappointed *or* sulky, pull a wry face, have a hang-dog look; *sich selbst aufs – schlagen,* contradict o.s.; *das – nach etwas spitzen,* have one's tongue hanging out for s.th.; *einem übers – fahren,* shout a p. down; *sich (Dat.) das – verbrennen,* be too ready with one's tongue; *das – vollnehmen,* see *das – aufreißen.* **-affe,** *m.* inquisitive person, nosy parker; *–affen feilhalten,* stand gaping with one's mouth open; stand lounging about *or* with one's hands in one's pockets. **-beerbaum,** *m.* mulberry tree. **-en,** *v.n.* (*coll.*) sulk, pout, mope. **-esel,** *m.* hinny. **-faul,** *adj.* slow of speech, laconic, taciturn. **-fertigkeit,** *f.* loquacity. **-held,** *m.* braggart, boaster. **-knebel,** *m.* gag. **-korb,** *m.* muzzle. **-schelle,** *f.* slap on the face, box on the ear. **-sperre,** *f.* lock-jaw, tetanus. **-tasche,** *f.*, *see* **-schelle.** **-tier,** *n.* mule. **-trommel,** *f.* Jew's harp. (*coll.*) **-werk,** *n.*; (*vulg.*) *ein gutes –werk haben,* have the gift of the gab. **-wurf,** *m.* (-s, ⸚e) mole; (*coll.*) *wie ein –wurf schlafen,* sleep like a top. **-wurfshaufen** *or* **-wurfshügel,** *m.* molehill.

Mäulchen, *n.* (-s, –) pursed lips, (*fam.*) kiss; *– machen,* purse one's lips.

Maur-er, *m.* (-s, –) mason, bricklayer, builder; (*Frei*)*–er,* (free)mason. **-erarbeit,** *f.* masonry. **-ergesell(e),** *m.* journeyman mason. **-erhandwerk,** *n.* building-trade. **-erei,** *f.* masonry; freemasonry. **-erisch,** *adj.* masonic. **-erkelle,** *f.* mason's trowel. **-ermeister,** *m.* building contractor. **-erpolier,** *m.* foreman bricklayer. **-erzunft,** *f.* bricklayers' union.

Maus, *f.* (⸚e) mouse; ball of the thumb; hairy mole; (*coll.*) *liebe kleine –,* my little darling; (*Prov.*) *wenn die Katze nicht zu Hause ist, tanzen die Mäuse,* when the cat's away the mice will play; (*Prov.*) *mit Speck fängt man Mäuse,* good bait catches fine fish; *Mäuse im Kopfe,* a bee in one's bonnet; (*coll.*) *da beißt keine – den Faden* or *die – keinen Faden ab,* nothing can be changed, that's settled and done with. **-efalle,** *f.* mouse-trap. **-ekatze,** *f.* mouser. **-eloch,** *n.* mouse-hole. **-en,** 1. *v.n.* (*aux.* h.) catch mice. 2. *v.a.* pilfer, pinch. **-etot,** *adj.* stone-dead, dead as a doornail. **-fahl, -farben, -farbig, -grau,** *adj.* drab, dun. **-ig,** *adj.* mousy, smelling of mice.

mauscheln, *v.n.* (*aux.* h.) talk with a Jewish accent.

Mäus-chen, (-s, –) little mouse, mousie; funny-bone; (*coll.*) *mein –chen,* little duckie, my darling. **-chenstill,** *adj.* quiet as a mouse, stock-still, so that one could hear a pin drop. **-e,** (*in compounds interchangeable with* Maus, Mause-) **-eartig,** *adj.* mouselike; murine. **-edreck,** *m.* mouse-dung. **-efalk(e),** *m.* buzzard. **-efalle,** *f.* mouse-trap. **-efänger,** *m.* mouse-catcher, mouser. **-efraß,** *m.* damage done by mice; (*coll.*) bald patch. **-egift,** *n.* ratsbane. **-erich,** *m.* male mouse.

Maus-e, -er(ung), *f.* moulting; moulting-season; *in der –er sein,* be moulting. **-en,** *v.r.*, **-ern,** *v.r.* moult, (*fig.*) be a turncoat, change sides. **-erfeder,** *f.* shed feather. **-erig,** *adj.* (*Swiss dial.*) peevish, bad-tempered. **-erzeit,** *f.* moulting-season. **-ig,** *adj.* cheeky, cocky; *sich –ig machen,* poke one's nose in everywhere, be uppish *or* cocky, put on airs.

Maut, *f.* (-en) (*dial.*) duty, excise, toll; custom-house. **-amt,** *n.* custom-house. **-frei,** *adj.* duty-free. **-ner,** *m.* customs-officer.

Maxim-al-, (*in compounds*) maximum. **-albelastung,** *f.* maximum load. **-albetrag,** *m.* highest amount; (*C.L.*) limit. **-algewicht,** *n.* maximum weight. **-alleistung** *f.* maximum output. **-e,** *f.* (-en) maxim, principle. **-um,** *n.* (-ums, -a) maximum (amount).

Mäzen, *m.* (-s, -e) Mæcenas, patron. **-at,** *n.*, **-atentum,** *n.* patronage. **-isch,** *adj.* generous, patronizing.

Mechan-ik, *f.* (-en) mechanics; (*coll.*) mechanism. **-iker,** *m.* (-s, –) mechanic, fitter, artificer. **-isch,** *adj.* mechanical; *–ische Beanspruchung,* mechanical strain *or* wear; *–ischer Webstuhl,* power-loom. **-isierung,** *f.* mechanization. **-ismus,** *m.* mechanism, works.

meckern, *v.n.* (*aux.* h.) bleat; (*fig.*) grumble, grouse, carp.

Medaill-e, *f.* (-en) medal; seal; *die Kehrseite der –e,* the dark side of the picture; *Inhaber der goldenen –e,* gold medallist. **-on,** *n.* (-s, -s) locket, medallion.

media, *adv.* (*C.L.*) middle, middle of the month. **-wechsel,** *m.* bill due on the 15th of the month.

Median-, (*in compounds*). **-ader,** *f.* median vein (*Anat.*). **-folio,** *n.* demi-folio. **-größe,** *f.* median size. **-oktav,** *n.* demi-octavo.

Mediante, *f.* (-n) mediant (*Mus.*).

Medik-ament, *n.* (-(e)s, -e) medicine, drug, physic, medicant. **-us,** *m.* (–, Medizi) medical man, doctor.

meditieren, *v.n.* meditate.

Medium, *n.* (-iums, -ien) (psychic) medium; agent (*Phys.*).

Medizin, *f.* (-en) (science of) medicine; (*coll.*) physic, medicine, medicament; *gerichtliche –,* forensic medicine, medical jurisprudence. **-al,** *adj.* medicinal. **-albehörde,** *f.* Board of Health. **-algewicht,** *n.* troy weight. **-alrat,** *m.* medical officer (*of Board of Health*). **-alwaren,** *f.pl.* medicinal drugs. **-alwein,** *m.* medicated wine. **-ball,** *m.* medicine ball. **-er,** *m.* medical man; medical student. **-isch,** *adj.* medical; medicinal; *–ische Fakultät,* faculty of medicine; *–ische Seife,* medicated soap. **-mann,** *m.* medicine-man, magician.

Meer, *n.* (-es, -e) sea; ocean; *am –e liegend,* maritime; *am –e,* on the seashore; at *or* by the seaside; *auf dem –e,* (out) at sea, on the sea, on the main; *das – betreffend,* marine; *das hohe –,* the main, the high sea(s); *ein Tropfen im –e,* a drop in the ocean; *ein – von Tränen,* a flood of tears; *auf offenem –e,* on the high seas; *übers – gehen,* go overseas; *unter dem –e,* submarine; *vom –e bespült,* washed by the sea, sea-girt; *das weite –,* the open sea. **-bake,** *f.* buoy, beacon. **-bewohnend,** *adj.* marine. **-busen,** *m.* gulf, bay. **-deich,** *m.* sea-wall. **-enge,** *f.* straits, channel, narrows. **-esalge,** *f.* seaweed, alga. **-esarm,** *m.* arm of the sea, inlet. **-esboden,** *m.* bottom of the sea, sea bottom, (*coll.*) Davy Jones's locker. **-esbrandung,** *f.* surf, breakers. **-esfläche,** *f.* surface of the sea. **-esflut,** *f.* waves of the sea. **-esgebiet,** *n.* maritime basin. **-esgrund,** *m.*, *see* **-esboden.** **-eshöhe,** *f. see* **-esspiegel.** **-eskunde,** *f.* oceanography, hydrography. **-esküste,** *f.* sea-coast, sea shore. **–(es)leuchten,** *n.* marine phosphorescence. **–esschlund,** *m.* the deep. **–esspiegel,** *m.* sea-level, surface of the sea; *über dem –esspiegel*, above sea-level. **–esstille,** *f.* calm at sea; dead calm. **–esstrand,** *m.* beach. **–esstrom,** *m.*, **–esströmung,** *f.* ocean-current. **–eswoge,** *f.* billow. **–fahrt,** *f.* sea-trip, cruise, sea-voyage. **–fräulein,** *n.*, **–frau,** *f.* mermaid, siren. **–gestade,** *n.* sea-coast. **–gewächs,** *n.* marine plant. **–gott,** *m.* sea-god, Neptune. **–gras,** *n.* sedge (*Zostera*) (*Bot.*); seaweed. **–greis,** *m.*; *alter –greis*, Old Man of the Sea; old fogy. **–grün,** *adj.* & *n.* sea-green, glaucous. **–hafen,** *m.* seaport. **–handel,** *m.* maritime trade. **–herrschaft,** *f.* maritime supremacy. **–jungfer,** *f.* mermaid, siren. **–katze,** *f.* long-tailed monkey (*Cercopithecus*) (*Zool.*). **–kohl,** *m.* sea-kale (*Crambe*) (*Bot.*). **–muschel,** *f.* sea-shell. **–rettich,** *m.* horse-radish (*Armoracia lapathifolia*) (*Bot.*). **–schaum,** *m.* meerschaum. **–schwalbe,** *f.* tern. **–schwein,** *n.* porpoise. **–schweinchen,** *n.* guinea-pig (*Cavia porcellus*) (*Zool.*). **–stern,** *m.* starfish. **–strandbewohnend,** *adj.* maritime. **–straße,** *f.* strait. **–tang,** *m.* seaweed. **–umflossen,** *adj.*, **–umschlungen,** *adj.* sea-girt. **–ungeheuer,** *n.* sea-monster. **–wärts,** *adv.* seawards. **–weib,** *n.*, **–weibchen,** *n.* mermaid, siren. **–wunder,** *n.* sea-monster, (*fig.*) miracle.

Megäre, *f.* (-n) vixen, shrew, termagant.

Mehl, *n.* (-s, -e) flour, meal, farina (*Bot.*); dust, powder. **–artig,** *adj.* flour-like; floury, mealy; farcinaceous. **–beutel,** *m.* bolter, sifter. **–brei,** *m.* meal-pap. **–faß,** *n.* meal-tub; flour-barrel. **–früchte,** *pl.* cereals. **–gebend,** *adj.*, **–haltig,** *adj.* farinaceous. **–kleister,** *m.* flour paste. **–kloß,** *m.* plain dumpling. **–körper,** *m.* endosperm. **–kreide,** *f.* infusorial earth. **–sack,** *m.* flour-bag. **–speise,** *f.* (*Austr. dial.*) pudding. **–suppe.** *f.* gruel. **–tau,** *m.*, *see* **Meltau.** **–teig,** *m.* dough. **–wurm,** *m.* meal-worm. **–zucker,** *m.* caster *or* castor sugar.

mehr, 1. *ind. num. adj.* & *adv.* more; *– als einer*, more than one; *– als zehn Uhr*, past ten; *– groß als klein*, tall rather than short; *und andere –*, and a few others; *– bereit*, readier; *und dergleichen –*, and the like, et cetera; *immer –*, more and more; *je – er hat, je – er will*, the more he has, the more he wants; *je – ich ihm gebe, desto – verlangt er*, the more I give him, the more he asks; *kein Kind –*, no longer a child; *kein Wort –!* not another word! *nicht lange –*, *nicht – lange*, not much longer; *nicht –*, no more, no longer; *es ist nicht mehr als billig*, it is only fair; *nichts –*, nothing more, nothing further; *noch –*, even more, still more; *– noch*, what is more; (*dial.*) *nur –*, nothing but, only; *– rechts*, farther to the right; *um so –*, so much the more; *um so – als*, all the more as. 2. *n.* (-e) majority; increase; surplus, excess. **–achsenantrieb,** *m.* multiple-axle drive. **–arbeit,** *f.* overtime. (*Marx*: surplus work, work producing profit for the employer; *see* **–wert**). **–aufwand,** *m.*, **–ausgabe,** *f.* additional expenditure. **–bändig,** *adj.* in several volumes. **–bedarf,** *m.* surplus demand. **–betrag,** *m.* surplus, excess, increased yield. **–bieter,** *m.* outbidder, higher bidder. **–deutig,** *adj.* ambiguous. **–deutigkeit,** *f.* ambiguity. **–drehung,** *f.* multirotation. **–einnahme,** *f.* surplus of receipts. **–en,** *v.a.*, *see* **mehren.** **–enteils,** *adv.* for the most part, mostly. **–ere,** *adj.*, *see* **mehrere.** **–erlei,** *indec. adj.* of more than one kind, various, diverse, sundry, divers. **–fach,** *adj.* manifold, multiple; several, numerous, repeated(ly), more than once. **–fachzünder,** *m.* combination fuse. **–farbendruck,** *m.* colour-printing. **–farbig,** *adj.* polychromatic. **–forderung,** *f.* increased demand, higher claim. **–frontenkrieg,** *m.* war on several fronts. **–gebot,** *n.* overbid; higher bid. **–genannt,** *adj.* mentioned *or* named several times, aforesaid. **–gewicht,** *n.* overweight, excess weight. **–gitterröhre,** *f.* multiple grid valve (*Rad.*). **–gliederig,** *adj.* complex (*Math.*). **–heit,** *f.* majority, plurality. **–heitsbeschluß,** *m.* majority decision. **–jährig,** *adj.* several years old. **–kosten,** *pl.* additional expenses. **–lader,** *m.* magazine rifle, repeater. **–leistung,** *f.* increased efficiency *or* output. **–malig,** *adj.* repeated, reiterated. **–mals,** *adv.* again and again, repeatedly, more than once, several times. **–motorig,** *adj.* multi-engined. **–phasenstrom,** *m.* polyphase current (*Elec.*). **–samig,** *adj.* polyspermous. **–scheibenkupplung,** *f.* multiple-drive clutch. **–seitig,** *adj.* polygonal, many-sided. **–silbig,** *adj.* polysyllabic. **–stellig,** *adj.* with more than one digit. **–stimmig,** *adj.* arranged for several voices; part (*song*). **–stufe,** *f.* comparative degree (*Gram.*). **–stündig,** *adj.* of several hours' duration. **–tägig,** *adj.* of several days. **–umsatz,** *m.* increase of the turnover. **–verbrauch,** *m.* increased consumption. **–wert,** *m.* (*Marx*) ratio between work necessary for workers' needs and work producing profit for employer (*see* **–arbeit**); surplus value. **–wertig,** *adj.* polyvalent (*Chem.*). **–zahl,** *f.* majority; plural (*Gram.*). **–zehig,** *adj.* polydactyl. **–zweckflugzeug,** *n.* multi-purpose aircraft.

mehr–en, *v.a.* & *r.* increase, augment; multiply, propagate, grow. **–er,** *m.* augmenter, enlarger, increaser; factor (*Arith.*). **–ung,** *f.* multiplication; augmentation, increase.

mehrere, *pl. adj.* several; *– schöne Blumen*, several fine flowers; *–s*, various *or* sundry things.

meiden, *ir.v.a.* avoid, shun, flee from.

Meier, *m.* (-s, –) steward (*of an estate*); tenant of a (dairy-)farm, (dairy-)farmer. **–ei,** *f.* (dairy-)farm; farmhouse. **–eierzeugnisse,** *n.pl.* dairy-produce. **–gut,** *n.*, **–hof,** *m.*, *see* **–ei.** **–haus,** *n.* farmhouse.

meiern, *v.a.* (*coll.*) cheat; (*coll.*) *einen –*, take a person in, pull the wool over s.o.'s eyes.

Meile, *f.* (-n) league; (*7,500 metres, 4.6 English miles*); *englische –*, English mile (*1,524 metres*); *geographische –*, geographical mile (*7,420 metres*); *nautische – (See–)*, nautical mile (*1,852 metres*). **–nbreit,** *adj.* a mile broad; extending for miles. **–ngeld,** *n.* mileage. **–nstein,** *m.* milestone. **–nstiefel,** *m.pl.* seven-league boots. **–nweit,** *adv.* for miles, miles away.

Meiler, *m.* (-s, –) charcoal-kiln *or* pile. **–kohle,** *f.* charcoal. **–köhler,** *m.* charcoal-burner.

mein, (–, -e, –) 1. *poss. adj.* my, mine; *–es Wissens*, so far as I know; *dieser – Sohn*, my son here; *die –en*, my family, my people; *das –e*, my share, my property *or* belongings; *–e vielen Freunde*, my numerous friends. 2. *poss. pron.* mine; *dieses Haus ist –*, this house is mine; *– ist die Schande*, mine is the shame. 3. *old Gen. sing. of* ich; *see* **–er**; *gedenke –*, think of me; *vergiß – nicht!* do not forget me! 4. *n.* my own, my property; *das – und Dein*, what is mine and what is thine. **–e,** (der, die, das -e), **–er, –e, –es; –ige** (der, die, das -ige), *poss. pron.* mine; *nicht dein Bruder, sondern –er* or *der –ige*, not your brother but mine; *das –ige*, my own, my share, my property; *die –(ig)en*, my family; *ich habe das –ige getan*, I have done my part. **–er,** *Gen. of* ich, *see* – 3; *erbarme dich –er*, have pity upon me; *ich war –er nicht mehr mächtig*, I had lost control over myself. **–erseits,** *adv.* for my part, so far as I am concerned. **–esgleichen,** *indec. adj. or pron.* my equals, such as I, people like me. **–esteils,** for my part, as for me. **–ethalben,** *adv.*, **–etwegen,** *adv.*, **–etwillen,** *adv.* for my sake; so far as I am concerned, for all I care; by all means.

Meineid, *m.* perjury; *einen – leisten* or *schwören*, perjure o.s., commit perjury. **–ig,** *adj.* perjured; *–ig werden*, commit perjury, perjure o.s.; *der –ige*, perjurer.

mein–en, *v.a.* & *n.* (*aux.* h.) 1. be of the opinion, believe, think, suppose; mean, intend, purpose; deem fitting; *es böse mit einem –en*, mean no good to a p.; *den Sack schlagen und den Esel –en*, put the blame on an innocent p.; *er –t es gut*, he means well; *damit sind Sie gemeint*, that is meant for you; *wenn Sie es so –en*, if you look at it in that way; *wenn Sie es wirklich so –en*, if that is really what you mean; *so war es nicht gemeint*, it was not meant in that way; *was –en Sie dazu?* what do you think of it? *was –en Sie damit?* what do you mean by that? *wie –en Sie?* what did you say? I beg your pardon? *das will ich –en*, I should think so indeed;

er –te wunder, was er täte, he thought he was doing great things; *sie –t wunder, wer sie ist*, she thinks she is the last word. 2. (*Poet.*) love; *Freiheit, die ich –e*, Freedom that I love. **–ung,** *f.* opinion, view, belief; idea, notion, thought; meaning, significance; intention; *nach meiner –ung, meiner –ung nach*, in my opinion; *einem anderen eine bessere –ung von jemandem beibringen*, make a p. think better of s.o. else; *wir sind einer –ung*, we are of one opinion, we share the same opinion; *keine –ung für eine Ware haben*, have no inclination to purchase an article; *in guter –ung geschehen*, take place with the best intentions; *die öffentliche –ung*, public opinion; *einem seine –ung sagen*, give a p. a piece of one's mind; *der –ung sein, daß . .*, be of the opinion that . . .; *vorgefaßte –ung*, preconceived notion, prejudice. **–ungsäußerung,** *f.* expression of opinion. **–ungsaustausch,** *m.* interchange of ideas; comparing notes. **–ungsstreit,** *m.* conflict of opinion. **–ungsverschiedenheit,** *f.* difference of opinion, divergence of views; dissension, disagreement. **–ungswechsel,** *m.* change of opinion *or* mind.

Meise, *f.* (-n) titmouse (*Paridae*) (*Orn.*).

Meißel, 1. *m.* (-s, –) chisel. 2. *f.* (-n) (*dial.*) plug *or* wad of lint, pledget (*Surg.*). **–n,** *v.a.* chisel, carve.

meist, 1. *adj.* (*sup. of* mehr) most; *die –en*, most people; *die –en Schüler lesen gut*, most of the pupils read well; *seine –e Zeit*, most of his time; *das –e*, the most (part). 2. *adv.* generally, usually, most, mostly, *see* **–ens**; *am –en*, most of all, for the most part. **–begünstigung,** *f.* preference, preferential treatment. **–begünstigungsklausel,** *f.* most-favoured-nation clause. **–betrag,** *m.* maximum amount. **–bietend,** *adj.* bidding highest; *–bietend verkaufen*, sell to the highest bidder, sell by auction. **–bietende(r),** *m.* highest bidder. **–enorts,** *adv.* nearly *or* almost everywhere. **–ens,** *adv.*, **–enteils,** *adv.* generally, usually, mostly, for the most part, as a rule; *ich bin –ens um sechs Uhr zu Hause*, I am generally in at six o'clock; *es waren –ens junge Leute*, they were for the most part young people. **–gebot,** *n.* highest bid, best offer.

Meister, *m.* (-s, –) master, chief, leader, (*sl.*) boss; champion (*Sport*); shipwright (*Naut.*); *am Werke erkennt man den –*, the master's hand is seen in the finished work; (*Prov.*) *Übung macht den –*, practice makes perfect; *er hat in ihm seinen – gefunden*, he has met his match in him; *– in einer S. sein*, excel in a th.; (*Prov.*) *es ist noch kein – vom Himmel gefallen*, no man is born a master of his craft; *– vom Stuhl*, master of the lodge: *seiner Gefühle – werden*, get one's feelings under control; *einen zum – machen*, grant s.o. the freedom of a company. **–arbeit,** *f.* masterly performance. **–dieb,** *m.* expert thief. **–gesang,** *m.* poetry of the mastersingers. **–gesell,** *m.* master-journeyman. **–grad,** *m.* degree of M.A.; grade of master (*Freem.*); freedom (*of a guild*). **–haft,** 1. *adj.* masterly, excellent, perfect, skilful. 2. *adv.* in a masterly manner. **–haftigkeit,** *f.* mastery; masterliness. **–hand,** *f.* master's hand. **–in,** *f.* mistress, master's wife; woman champion (*Sport*). **–lich,** *adj. & adv.*, *see* **–haft.** **–los,** *adj.* (*Swiss dial.*) headstrong. **–n,** *v.a.* master; rule, control; censure, find fault with; correct, put right; *er kann seine Zunge nicht –n*, he cannot keep a rein on his tongue. **–recht,** *n.* freedom of a company. **–sänger,** *m.* mastersinger. **–schaft,** *f.* mastery, eminent skill; freedom (*of a guild, etc.*); masters of a lodge *or* trade-guild; championship. **–schaftskampf,** *m.* championship bout. **–schütze,** *m.* marksman, crack-shot. **–singer,** *m.*, *see* **–sänger.** **–spieler,** *m.* virtuoso; champion. **–streich,** *m.* masterly stroke. **–stück,** *n.* masterpiece. **–ton,** *m.* melody of a song by a mastersinger. **–werk,** *n.*, *see* **–stück.** **–zug,** *m.* master-stroke (*Chess, Pol.*).

Melancho–lie, *f.* melancholy, melancholia. **–liker,** *m.* p. of melancholy disposition. **–lisch,** *adj.* melancholy.

Melange, *f.* mixture, blend; (*Austr. dial.*) coffee with milk.

Melasse, *f.* (-n) molasses, treacle.

meld–en, 1. *v.a.* inform, advise, apprise of, notify; report, announce; send word; recount, tell; mention; *einen –en*, announce a p.; report a p. (*to the police, etc.*); *Sie haben zu– en*, it is your call (*cards*). 2. *v.r.* announce o.s.; com forward, make a claim (*of creditors*); report (*Mil.*); *sich –en lassen*, send in one's name *or* card, have o.s. announced; *sich zu einer S.* or *für eine S. –en*, apply for a th.; *sich zu einer Prüfung –en*, enter for an examination; *man muß sich zeitig –en*, early application is necessary; *der Winter –et sich dieses Jahr zeitig*, winter is setting in early this year; *der Hunger –et sich*, hunger makes itself felt; *sich zum Wort –en*, announce one's wish to speak, catch the chairman's eye. **–eamt,** *n.* registration office. **–eboot,** *n.* dispatch boat. **–edienst,** *m.* intelligence service. **–efrist,** *f.* final date for applications. **–egänger,** *m.* messenger, runner. **–ehund,** *m.* messenger dog. **–ekette,** *f.* relay of runners. **–eläufer,** *m.*, *see* **–egänger.** **–enswert,** *adj.* worth reporting. **–epflicht,** *f.* obligation to report. **–equadrat,** *n.* reference square (*map*). **–er,** *m.* dispatch-rider, runner, messenger; alarm (equipment). **–ereiter,** *m.* mounted orderly; dispatch-rider **–eschluß,** *m.* closing date for entries (*Sport*). **–estelle,** *f.* reporting office. **–evorschriften,** *f.pl.* regulations for applicants. **–ezettel,** *m.* registration form, message form. **–ung,** *f.* message, advice, notice, notification; announcement, news, report.

melier–en, *v.a.* mix, mingle, blend, mottle; shuffle; *grau meliert*, mixed with gray, (*coll.*) pepper and salt. **–papier,** *n.* mottled *or* marbled paper.

Melinit, *n.* picric acid, melinite (*Chem.*).

Melior–ation, *f.* soil enrichment. **–ieren,** *v.r.* ameliorate.

Melisse, *f.* (-n) balm, balm-mint.

Meliszucker, *m.* (coarse) loaf-sugar.

melk, *adj.* milch. **–eimer,** *m.*, *see* **–kübel.** **–en,** 1. *reg. & ir.v.a.* milk; (*coll.*) drain, impoverish; *frisch gemolkene Milch*, new milk. 2. *v.n.* (*aux.* h.) (*dial.*) give milk. **–erei,** *f.* (*dial.*) milking; dairy (-farm). **–kübel,** *m.* milking-pail. **–kuh,** *f.* milch-cow (*also fig.*). **–maschine,** *f.* milking-machine. **–schemel,** *m.* milking-stool. **–vieh,** *n.* milch-cattle. **–zeit,** *f.* milking time.

Melod–ie, *f.* (-n) melody, tune, air. **–ik,** *f.* melodics. **–isch,** *adj.* melodious.

Melone, *f.* (-n) melon; (*coll.*) bowler hat. **–nkürbis,** *m.* squash; pumpkin.

Meltau, *m.* mildew, blight.

Membran(e), *f.* (-en) membrane; diaphragm (*Phone.*).

Memme, *f.* (-n) coward, poltroon. **–nhaft,** *adj.* cowardly.

Memoire, *n.* (-s, -s) memorial address *or* publication. **–n,** *pl.* memoirs, reminiscences.

Memor–abilien, *pl.*, *see* **Denkwürdigkeiten.** (*C.L.*) **–andum,** *n.* (-s, -da & -den) note, memorandum; notebook. (*C.L.*) **–ial,** *n.* (-(e)s, -e & -en) daybook; memorandum book; (*einem*) *ein –ial einreichen*, present a memorial to s.o., petition a p. **–ieren,** *v.a. & n.* memorize, commit to memory, learn by heart. **–ierstoff,** *m.* matter to be committed to memory.

Menag–e [*pron.* mən'ɑʒə], *f.* (-n) set of dishes; cruet; (*dial.*) household, mess (*Mil.*). **–ieren,** 1. *v.a.* manage, treat with consideration; economize, save. 2. *v.r.* restrain o.s.

Meng–e, *f.* (-n) quantity, number, amount, a great many *or* deal, mass; multitude, crowd; *eine ganze –e*, quite a lot; *in großer –e*, in abundance, abundantly; *eine –e Geld, Geld in –en* or *in –e*, plenty of money, money in abundance, (*coll.*) lots of money; *eine –e Bücher*, a great many books; *Freunde die –e*, hosts of friends; *eine große –e Wasser*, a large body of water; *die –e muß es bringen*, small profits, quick returns. **–en,** 1. *v.a.* mix, mingle, blend, admix (*unter eine S., mit einer S.*, with a th.); shuffle (*cards*); *eins ins andere –en*, give a garbled account. 2. *v.r.* mix, mingle; meddle with, interfere in; *sich unter die Zuschauer –en*, mix with the crowd of spectators; *er –t sich in alles*, he meddles in everything, he pokes his nose in everywhere, he is a busybody. **–enbestimmung,** *f.* quantitative determination *or* analysis. **–enmäßig,**

adj. quantitative. **–enverhältnis,** *n.* ratio, proportion. **–futter,** *n.*, **–korn,** *n.* mash; mixed grain *or* fodder. **–sel,** *m.* medley; mess, hodge-podge. **–teil,** *m.* ingredient. **–ung,** *f.* mixture, blend; hybridization.

Mennig, *m.*, **–e,** *f.* minium, red lead.

Mensch, 1. *m.* (-en, -en) human being, man, person; (*pl.*) people, mankind; *kein* –, nobody, not a soul; *eine Menge –en*, a crowd of people; *es wohnen 10,000 –en in dieser Stadt*, this town has 10,000 inhabitants; *einzelner* –, individual; *der –gewordene Gott*, God incarnate; *unter die –en kommen*, see something of the world, mix in society; *einen neuen –en anziehen*, turn over a new leaf; *der innere* –, the inner man; (*Prov.*) *der – denkt, Gott lenkt*, man proposes, God disposes. 2. *n.* (-es, -er) (*vulg.*) wench, hussy, slut. **–eln,** *v.imp.* (*coll.*) show human imperfections. **–enaffe,** *m.* anthropoid ape. **–enähnlich,** *adj.* anthropoid, anthropomorphous. **–enalter,** *n.* generation, age. **–enart,** *f.* race of men, kind *or* species of man; *das ist –enart*, such are men, such is human nature. **–enbedürfnis,** *n.* human need; men needed. **–enbestand,** *m.* manpower, personnel. **–enblut** *n.* human blood. **–endieb,** *m.* kidnapper. **–enfamilie,** *f.* human race. **–enfeind,** *m.* misanthropist. **–enfeindlich,** *adj.* misanthropic. **–enfressend,** *adj.* anthropophagous. **–enfresser,** *m.* man-eater, cannibal. **–enfreund,** *m.* philanthropist. **–enfreundlich,** *adj.* affable, sociable, philanthropic. **–engattung,** *f.* human species. **–engedenken** *n.*; *seit –engedenken*, from time immemorial; since human records began. **–engeschlecht,** *n.* human race, mankind. **–engestalt,** *f.* human shape *or* form. **–engewühl,** *n.* throng of men, large crowd. **–enhändler,** *m.* slave-dealer. **–enhaß,** *m.* misanthropy. **–enheil,** *n.* man's welfare; salvation of mankind. **–enkenner,** *m.* one who understands his fellow-men, keen observer of human nature. **–enkenntnis,** *f.* knowledge of human nature. **–en(s)kind,** *n.* human being; (*coll.*) fellow. **–enkunde,** *f.*, *see* **–enlehre.** **–enleben,** *n.* lifetime, human life; life of man. **–enlehre,** *f.* anthropology. **–enleer,** *adj.* deserted. **–enliebe,** *f.* philanthropy, charity; love of one's fellow man. **–enmaterial,** *n.* man-power (*Mil.*). **–enmenge,** *f.* crowd, mob. **–enmöglich,** *adj.* humanly possible; *er hat das –enmöglichste getan*, he had done the utmost possible, he has done all that is humanly possible; **–enopfer,** *n.* human sacrifice. **–enpack,** *n.* rabble. **–enraub,** *m.* kidnapping, (*Poet.*) rape. **–enrecht,** *n.* rights of man, human rights; natural law, human law. **–enreich,** *adj.* populous. **–enscheu,** *adj.* unsociable, shy. **–enschinder,** *m.* extortioner. **–enschlag,** *m.* race of men, type *or* breed of men. **–enseele,** *f. es war keine –enseele zu erblicken*, not a living soul was to be seen. **–ensohn,** *m.* Son of Man. **–entroß,** *m.* crowd. **–entum,** *n.* mankind, humanity. **–enverächter,** *m.* cynic. **–enverstand,** *m.* human understanding; *gesunder –enverstand*, common sense. **–enwerk,** *n.* (fugitive *or* transitory) works of man. **–enwohl,** *n.* human weal. **–enwürde,** *f.* human dignity. **–enwürdig,** *adj.* worthy of a human being. **–heit,** *f.* human race, humanity, mankind; *der Abschaum* or *Auswurf der –heit*, the scum of the earth. **–lein,** *n.* mannikin, homunculus. **–lich,** *adj.* human; humane; *ein –liches Rühren*, bodily needs, a human urge; *nach –lichem Ermessen*, as far as can be foreseen; (*Prov.*) *irren ist –lich*, to err is human; *–lich gesprochen*, humanly speaking; *etwas –liches begehen*, be guilty of a human weakness; *es ist ihm etwas –liches begegnet*, he has gone the way of all flesh; (*hum.*) he has had an accident in his trousers. **–lichkeit,** *f.* human nature; humanity, humaneness; (*also pl.*) human weakness, human frailties. **–werdung,** *f.* incarnation, anthropogenesis.

menstruieren, *v.n.* (*aux.* h. & s.) menstruate.

Mensur, *f.* (-en) measure; measuring vessel; mensuration; students' duel; proper distance between two duellists (*Fenc.*); measure (*Danc.*); duration of a note (*Mus.*); standard size and thickness (*of organ-pipes, wind instruments*). **–glas,** *n.* measuring glass.

Mentalität, *f.* (-en) mentality, way of thinking.

Menü, (*Austr. & Swiss dial.*) **Menu,** *n.* (-s, -s) bill of fare; table d'hôte.

Menuett, *n.* (-s, -e) minuet.

Mergel, *m.* marl. **–boden,** *m.* marly soil. **–grube,** *f.* marl-pit. **–ig,** *adj.* marly. **–n,** *v.a.* manure with marl.

merkantil, *adj.* mercantile. **–isch,** *adj.* commercial. **–ismus,** *m.* controlled economy, system of state control of all economic life.

merk–en, 1. *v.a. & n.* (*aux.* h. *with* auf) mark, note, observe, notice, perceive; *–e wohl! wohlgemerkt!* take notice! mark my words!; *auf eine S.* or *einen –en*, pay attention to a th. *or* a p.; *ich –te, wo er hinaus wollte*, I could see what he was driving at. 2. *v.a.* (*with Dat. & Acc.*) bear in mind, make a note of; *sich* (*Dat.*) *–en*, remember, bear in mind; *sich* (*Dat.*) *nichts –en lassen*, act as if one knew nothing, act as if nothing had happened, take no notice of a th. **–bar,** *adj.* noticeable, perceptible, evident. **–blatt,** *n.* leaflet, instruction sheet, pamphlet. **–buch,** *n.*, **–büchlein,** *n.* notebook, memorandum-book. **–enswert,** *adj.* remarkable. **–er,** *m.* judge, censurer (*of the old mastersingers*); keen nose, faculty of observation. **–lich,** *adj.* marked, noticeable, appreciable, visible, perceptible. **–mal,** *n.* sign, mark, indication, symptom, feature, characteristic, criterion. **–malsträger,** *m.* gene. **–punkt,** *m.* reference point, landmark. **–satz,** *m.* maxim. **–tinte,** *f.* marking ink. **–wort,** *n.* catchword; cue (*Theat.*). **–würdig,** *adj.* remarkable, noteworthy, striking, strange, curious, peculiar. **–würdigerweise,** *adv.* strange to say. **–würdigkeit,** *f.* strangeness, peculiarity, curiosity; salient point. **–zeichen,** *n.* mark, sign, stamp, characteristic.

Merle, *f.* (-n) (*dial.*) blackbird.

Merzschaf, *n.* cast-off sheep.

meschugge, *inv. adj.* (*sl.*) crazy, cracked.

Mesmer, *m.* (-s, –) (*Swiss dial.*), *see* **Mesner.**

Mesner, *m.* (-s, –) sacristan, sexton (*R.C.*).

Meß–amt, *n.* celebration of mass. **–buch,** *n.* missal. **–bude,** *f.* stall at a fair. **–diener,** *m.* acolyte. **Mess–e,** *f.* (-n) mass (*R.C.*); mass (*Mus.*); fair, market; wardroom (*Naut.*); *hohe –(ss)e*, high *or* grand mass; *stille –(ss)e*, low mass; *in die –(ss)e gehen, die –(ss)e hören*, go to mass; *die –(ss)e lesen*, say mass; *die –(ss)e besuchen* or *beziehen*, attend the fair; *die –(ss)e beschicken*, send goods to the fair. **–(ss)ebesucher,** *m.* visitor to a fair. **–(ss)ezeit,** *f.* fair-season. **–freiheit,** *f.* right to hold a fair. **–fremde(r),** *m.* visitor at a fair. **–gerät,** *n.* ornaments and utensils used in celebrating mass. **–gewand,** *n.* vestment, chasuble. **–gut,** *n.* goods exhibited at a fair. **–hemd,** *n.* alb, alba. **–kelch,** *m.* chalice. **–opfer,** *n.* (sacrifice of the) mass; host. **–stand,** *m.* booth at a fair. **–tuch,** *n.* corporal, communion cloth. **–wein,** *m.* consecrated wine. **–woche,** *f.* fair-week. **–zeit,** *f.* fair-time.

mess–en, *ir.v.a. & n.* (*aux.* h.) measure, gauge, survey; be a certain size; *mit der Elle –en*, measure by the yard; *er maß mich vom Scheitel bis zur Sohle*, he eyed me from top to toe, he took stock of me; *an ihm gemessen bist du klein*, measured against him *or* compared with him you are small. 3. *v.r.*; *sich –en mit*, compete with, try one's strength with, try conclusions with; *sich mit einem nicht –en können*, be no match for a p. **–(ß)bar,** *adj.* measurable, commensurable. **–(ß)analyse,** *f.* volumetric analysis. (**–(ß)band,** *n.* measuring tape, tape measure. **–(ß)bild,** *n.* scale drawing. **–(ß)brücke,** *f.* Wheatstone bridge (*Elec.*). **–(ß)einteilung,** *f.* graduation. **–er,** measurer, surveyor; gauge, meter. **–(ß)flug,** *m.* test flight (*Av.*). **–(ß)gerät,** *n.* measuring instrument, range-finder, gauge. **–(ß)holz,** *n.* measuring rod, fathom. **–(ß)kanne,** *f.* liquid measure. **–(ß)keil,** *m.* pipe gauge **–(ß)kette,** *f.* surveyor's chain. **–(ß)kreis,** *m.* graduated circle, map protractor. **–(ß)kunst,** *f.* surveying. **–(ß)latte,** *f.* surveyor's rod *or* pole **–(ß)leine,** *f.* measuring line. **–(ß)rohr,** *n.*, **–(ß)röhre,** *f.* burette (*Chem.*). **–(ß)scheibe,** *f.* sextant, quadrant. **–(ß)stelle,** *f.* **computing centre**

(*Surv.*). **–(ß)tisch,** *m.* plane table. **–(ß)tischblatt,** *n.* ordnance-survey map (1:25,000); **–(ß)trupp,** *m.* survey section (*Mil.*). **–(ß)verfahren,** *n.* range finding, ranging. **–ung,** *f.* measurement; measuring, mensuration, survey.

Messer, *n.* (-s, –) knife; *das große – führen,* draw the long bow; *das – sitzt ihm an der Kehle,* he is face to face with ruin; *Krieg bis aufs –,* war to the knife. **–bank,** *f.*, **–bänkchen,** *n.* knife-rest. **–griff,** *m.*, **–heft,** *n.* knife-handle. **–held,** *m.* cut-throat. **–klinge,** *f.* blade. **–rücken,** *m.* back of a knife. **–scheide,** *f.* knife-case, knife-sheath. **–schmied,** *m.* cutler. **–(schmiede)waren,** *f.pl.* cutlery. **–spitze,** *f.* point of a knife. **–stecher,** *m.* cut-throat. **–stich,** *m.* stab. **–stiel,** *m.* knife-handle.

Messing, *n.* (-s, -e) brass; *mit – löten,* braze. **–beschlag,** *m.* brass mounting. **–blech,** *n.* sheet brass. **–draht,** *m.* brass wire. **–en,** *adj.* brazen, of brass. **–geschirr,** *n.* brass utensils. **–gießer,** *m.* brass founder. **–hütte,** *f.* brass-foundry. **–isch,** *adj.*, brass. **–schmied,** *m.* brazier. **–waren,** *f.pl.* brass goods. **–werk,** *n.*, *see* **–hütte.**

Met, *m.* (-(e)s, -e) mead.

Metall, *n.* (-(e)s, -e) metal; timbre (*of the voice*); *edle –e,* precious metals; *unedle –e,* base metals. **–abfall,** *m.* scrap-metal. **–arbeiter,** *m.* metal-worker. **–auftrag,** *m.* metallic coating. **–beschlag,** *m.* metal sheathing *or* plating, **–bestand,** *m.* bullion. **–bürste,** *f.* wire-brush. **–en,** *adj.* metal, brass; *ein –ener Klang,* a metallic sound; *das hat einen –enen Beigeschmack,* that smacks of bribery. **–fadenlampe,** *f.* metal-filament lamp. **–farbe,** *f.* metallic pigment. **–folie,** *f.* metal foil. **–führend,** *adj.*, *see* **–haltig. –gehalt,** *m.* metal content. **–gemisch,** *n.* alloy. **–geld,** *n.* specie. **–glanz,** *m.* metallic lustre. **–gold,** *n.* Dutch metal. **–haltig,** *adj.* metalliferous. **–isch,** *adj.* metallic; *eine –ische Stimme,* a harsh, jarring *or* strident voice. **–kunde,** *f.* metallurgy. **–oxyd,** *n.* metallic oxide. **–probe,** *f.* assay. **–spritzverfahren,** *n.* metallization. **–urg,** *m.* (-en, -en) metallurgist. **–urgie,** *f.* metallurgy. **–versetzung,** *f.* alloy; alloying. **–waren,** *f.pl.* hardware.

Meta–morphose, *f.* (-n) metamorphosis. **–pher,** *f.* (-n) metaphor. **–phrastisch,** *adj.* periphrastic, circumlocutory. **–physik,** *f.* metaphysics. **–physisch,** *adj.* metaphysical.

Meteor, *n.* (-s, -e) meteor. **–olog(e),** *m.* (-en, -en) meteorologist. **–ologie,** *f.* meteorology. **–stein,** *m.* aerolite, meteorite.

Meter, *n.* (*Swiss & Austr. dial., elsewhere coll. m.*) (-s, –) metre; *nach –n messen,* measure by metres. **–kilogramm,** *n.* kilogram-meter. **–maß,** *n.* metric measure; tape measure. **–sekunde,** *f.* meters per second. **–system,** *n.* metric system. **–weise,** *adv.* by the metre. **–zentner,** *m.* 100 kilos (*approx.* $\frac{1}{10}$ ton).

Method–e, *f.* (-en) method; way, manner; process. **–enlehre,** *f.*, **–ik,** *f.* theory of method, methodology. **–isch,** *adj.* methodical. **–ismus,** *m.* Methodism. **–istisch,** *adj.* Methodist.

Metr–ik, *f.* versification; prosody. **–isch,** *adj.* metrical; metric (*cf.* **Meter**). **–um,** *n.* (-ums, -en & –a) metre.

Metropol–e, *f.* (-en) metropolis. **–it,** *m.* (-en, -en) archbishop. **–itankirche,** *f.* Cathedral.

Mette, *f.* (-n) matins; early morning service. **–nglöcklein,** *n.* matins bell.

Mettwurst, *f.* (⸚e) German sausage.

[1]**Metze,** *f.* (-n) (*archaic*) prostitute.

[2]**Metz–e,** *f.* (-en), **–en,** *m.* (-s, –) peck (= 3.44 *litre*).

Metz–elei, *f.* (-en) massacre; butchery. **–eln,** *v.a.* butcher; massacre, cut to pieces. **–elsuppe,** *f.* (*dial.*) broth. **–ge,** *f.* slaughter-house, shambles. **–gen,** *v.a.* (*dial.*) slaughter. **–ger,** *m.* (*dial.*) butcher. **–gerei,** *f.* (*dial.*) butcher's shop. **–ger(s)-gang,** *m.* (*dial.*) fool's errand.

Meuch–elmord, *m.* assassination. **–elmörder,** *m.* assassin. **–elmörderisch,** *adj.* assassin-like; dastardly. **–eln,** *v.a.* assassinate. **–elrotte,** *f.* band of assassins. **–ler,** *m.* assassin. **–lerisch,** *adj.*, **–lings,** *adv.* treacherous(ly), dastardly.

Meute, *f.* (-n) pack of hounds, (*fig.*) gang, pack, rabble. **–rei,** *f.* (-en) mutiny. **–rer,** *m.* mutineer. **–risch,** *adj.* mutinous. **–rn,** *v.n.* mutiny.

miauen, *v.n.* (*aux.* h.) mew; caterwaul.

mich, *Acc. of* **ich,** me.

mied, miede, *see* **meiden.**

Mieder, *n.* (-s, –) bodice, corset.

Miene, *f.* (-n) countenance; air, look, expression; bearing, mien; *fromme –,* pious looks; *sich* (*Dat.*) *die – geben als ob,* affect to; *gute – zum bösen Spiele machen,* make the best of a bad job, make a virtue of necessity; *kecke –,* bold front; *– machen,* look as if, seem; threaten; *der Feind machte – uns anzugreifen,* the enemy showed signs of attacking us; *er machte – fortzugehen,* he was just making a move to leave; *saure –,* scowl; *er verzog keine –,* he remained unmoved. **–ndeuter,** *m.*, **–nforscher,** *m.* physiognomist. **–nspiel,** *n.* play of the features, changing expression; pantomime, dumb show; *Mienen- und Gebärdenspiel,* by-play (*of an actor*).

Miere, *f.* chickweed.

mies, *adj.* (*coll.*) out of sorts, poorly; poor, bad, wretched; *das Wetter ist –,* the weather is miserable *or* wretched. **–ekatze,** *see* **Mieze.** (*coll.*) **–epeter,** *m.* (*coll.*) cross-patch, sour-puss. **–epetrig,** *adj.* morose, churlish, sullen, moody, grumpy, irritable, disgruntled. **–macher,** *m.* (*coll.*) grouser, defeatist, alarmist.

Miesmuschel, *f.* (-n) mussel.

[1]**Miete,** *f.* (-n) (*dial.*) mite.

[2]**Miete,** *f.* (-n) stack, shock, rick (*of corn, etc.*), clamp (*of potatoes*).

[3]**Miet–e,** *f.* (-en) hire; rent; lease; *die –e aufsagen,* give notice; *fällige –e,* rent due; *in der –e haben,* have on hire, hold on lease; *in –e nehmen,* hire, rent; *rückständige –e,* arrears of rent; *zur –e geben,* let out; *zur –e wohnen,* be a tenant, live in lodgings. **–ausfall,** *m.* loss of rent. **–bar,** *adj.* rentable, for hire. **–besitz,** *m.* tenancy. **–en,** *v.a.* hire, rent, lease; engage (*a taxi, etc.*); charter (*a ship*). **–er,** *m.* tenant, lodger, lessee. **–erschaft,** *f.* tenantry. **–erschutz,** *m.* rent control *or* restriction. **–frei,** *adj.* rent-free. **–herr,** *m.* landlord. **–kutsche,** *f.* hackney carriage. **–ling,** *m.* hireling, mercenary. **–preis,** *m.* charge for hire, rent. **–(s)auto,** *n.* taxi (cab). **–(s)bedingung,** *f.* terms of hire *or* lease. –(s)haus, *n.* tenement (house). **–skaserne,** *f.* (*coll.*) large block of flats. **–(s)kontrakt,** *m.* lease; charter. **–(s)leute,** *pl.* lodgers. **–(s)lohn,** *m.* servants' wages. **–(s)mann,** *m.* lodger, tenant. **–(s)truppen,** *f.pl.* mercenaries. **–(s)vertrag,** *m.*, *see* –(s)**kontrakt. –(s)wohnung,** *f.* rented house; flat, lodgings. **–weise,** *adv.* on hire. **–wert,** *m.* rental value. **–wucher,** *m.* extortionate rent. **–zins,** *m.* rent.

Mieze, *f.* (-n) pussy, puss.

Migräne, *f.* (-n) sick headache.

Mikro–be, *f.* (-n), **–bie,** *f.* (-bien) microbe. **–biologie,** *f.* bacteriology. **–brief,** *m.* airgraph (letter). **–kopie,** *f.* microfilm. **–kosmus,** *m.*, **–kosmos,** microcosm. **–meter,** *m.* micrometer. **–organismus,** *m.* micro-organism. **–phon,** *n.* microphone. **–skop,** *n.* microscope. **–skopisch,** *adj.* microscopic; *–skopisch untersuchen,* examine under the microscope.

Milbe, *f.* (-n) mite (*Acarus*) (*Ent.*).

Milch, *f.* milk; emulsion; milt, soft roe; juice (*Bot.*); *saure –, geronnene –, dicke –,* curdled milk, sour milk; *abgerahmte –,* skimmed milk; *wie – und Blut,* like cream and roses; *in die – geben,* put out to nurse. **–ader,** *f.* lacteal vein. **–ähnlich,** *adj.*, **–artig,** *adj.* milk-like, milky, lacteal. **–bart,** *m.* greenhorn, milksop. **–brei,** *m.* milk-pap. **–brot,** *n.*, **–brötchen,** *n.* French roll. **–bruder,** *m.* boy raised by the same nurse. **–drüse,** *f.* lacteal *or* mammary gland. **–eimer,** *m.* milk-pail. **–en,** *v.n.* give milk; emulsify. **–er,** *m.* milter, male fish; (*dial.*) milker, dairy-hand. **–ferkel,** *n.* sucking pig. **–fieber,** *n.* lacteal fever. **–frau,** *f.* dairy-woman. **–gebend,** *adj.* lacteal. **–gefäß,** *n.* milk pan; lacteal vessel (*Anat.*). **–geschäft,** *n.*, **–laden,** *m.* dairy. **–gesicht,** *n.* baby face. **–gewinnung,** *f.* milk production. **–glas,** *n.* opalescent *or* frosted glass; glass for milk. **–haltig,** *adj.* lactiferous. **–händler,** *m.* milkman.

-ig, *adj.* milky. **-kaffee,** *m.* coffee with milk. **-kuh,** *f.* milk cow. **-kur,** *f.* milk diet. **-lab,** *n.* rennet. **-leistung,** *f.* milk yield. **-magd,** *f.*, **-mädchen,** *n.* dairy-maid, milkmaid. **-mann,** *m.* milkman, dairyman. **-messer,** *m.* lactometer. **-napf,** *m.* milk saucepan. **-ner,** *m.*, *see* **-er.** **-pan(t)scher,** *m.* adulterator of milk. **-pulver,** *n.* dried milk. **-rahm,** *m.* cream. **-ruhr,** *f.* infantile diarrhoea. **-saft,** *m.* milky juice, chyle; latex. **-sauer,** *adj.* lactate of. **-säure,** *f.* lactic acid. **-schwester,** *f.* foster-sister. **-straße,** *f.* Milky Way. **-suppe,** *f.* (*sl.*) pea-soup fog. **-topf,** *m.* milk-jug. **-vieh,** *n.* dairy cattle. **-warze,** *f.* nipple. **-wasser,** *n.* whey. **-weiß,** *adj.* milk-white. **-wirtschaft,** *f.* dairy-farm(ing). **-zahn,** *m.* milk-tooth. **-zucker,** *m.* sugar of milk, lactose.

mild-(e), *adj.* mild, soft, mellow, tender; gentle, kind; liberal, generous, charitable; *-e Beiträge,* donations, benefactions; *-e Früchte,* mellow fruit; *-e Gabe,* charitable gift, alms; *seine -e Hand auftun,* show one's generosity *or* clemency; *-e Stiftung,* charitable institution; benefaction; *-e Strafe,* light punishment. **-e,** *f.* mildness, gentleness, *etc.*; kindness, clemency; (*archaic*) generosity. **-ern,** *v.a.* soften, moderate, ease, mitigate, alleviate, assuage, temper; extenuate, mollify, qualify, tone down; *-ernde Umstände,* extenuating circumstances. **-erung,** *f.* mitigation, alleviation; mollification; moderation; qualification (*of a statement*). **-erungsausdruck,** *m.* euphemism. **-erungsgründe,** *m.pl.* extenuating circumstances. **-erungsmittel,** *n.* lenitive, mitigant, palliative, demulcant. **-herzig,** *adj.* tender *or* kind-hearted, charitable. **-herzigkeit,** *f.* kind-heartedness. **-tätig,** *adj.* generous, benevolent, beneficent. **-tätigkeit,** *f.* beneficence, liberality, generosity.

Milieu, *n.* (-s, -s) surroundings, background, environment, local colour. **-einfluß,** *m.* influence of environment. **-schilderung,** *f.* description of the background.

Militär, 1. *m.* (-s, -s) (*coll.*) military man, soldier. 2. *n.* the military, soldiery, army, soldiers. **-anwärter,** *m.* long-service N.C.O. entitled on discharge to low-grade civil-service employment. **-arzt,** *m.* army doctor, medical officer. **-beamte(r),** *m.* military official. **-behörden,** *pl.* military authorities. **-bevollmächtigte(r),** *m.* military plenipotentiary. **-dienst,** *m.* active service. **-dienstpflicht,** *f.* liability to serve in the army. **-etat,** *m.* army estimates. **-frei,** *adj.* exempt from military service. **-fromm,** *adj.* battle-trained (*of horses*). **-geistliche(r),** *m.* army chaplain. **-gericht,** *n.* military court, court-martial. **-gerichtsbarkeit,** *f.* military jurisdiction. **-größe,** *f.* minimum height for military service. **-herrschaft,** *f.*, **-hoheit,** *f.* military control. **-isch,** *adj.* military, soldierly, martial; *-isches Aussehen,* soldierly *or* martial bearing; *-isch besetzt,* occupied by troops. **-kapelle,** *f.* military band. **-macht,** *f.* military power. **-maß,** *n.* minimum height for military service. **-musik,** *f.* martial music; military band. **-musiker,** *m.* bandsman. **-pflicht,** *f.* compulsory military service, conscription. **-pflichtig,** *adj.* liable for military duty. **-recht,** *n.* military law. **-staat,** *m.* militarized state. **-stand,** *m.* profession of arms. **-stiefel,** *m.pl.* field service boots, (*coll.*) ammo boots. **-tauglich,** *adj.* fit for military service. **-verwaltung,** *f.* army administration. **-vorlage,** *f.* army bill.

Militarismus, *m.* militarism.

Miliz, *f.* (-en) militia; yeomanry. **-soldat,** *m.* militiaman.

Mill-iarde, *f.* milliard, (*U.S.A.*) billion. **-iardär,** *m.* multi-millionaire. **-ion,** *f.* million. **-ionär,** *m.* (-s, -e) millionaire. **-ionenfach,** *adj.* millionfold.

Milz, *f.* (-en) spleen; *mich sticht die –,* I have the stitch, I have a stitch in my side. **-brand,** *m.* anthrax. **-krank,** *adj.* splenetic. **-krankheit,** *f.*, *see* **-sucht.** **-stechen,** *n.* stitch (in the side). **-sucht,** *f.* (*archaic*) spleen, melancholia. **-süchtig,** *adj.* (*archaic*) splenetic, melancholic.

Mim-e, *m.* (-en, -en) mimic actor. **-en,** *v.a.* & *n.* act (*in plays*), feign, pretend. **-ik,** *f.* mimicry, miming. **-iker,** *m.* mimic. **-isch,** *adj.* mimic.

Mimose, *f.* (-n) mimosa. **-nhaft,** *adj.* highly sensitive, (*coll.*) touchy.

minder, *adj.* less; smaller, lesser, inferior, minor; *nicht mehr, nicht –,* neither more nor less; *– gut,* inferior, of lower quality. **-bedarf,** *m.* smaller demand. **-begabt,** *adj.* handicapped. **-bemittelt,** *adj.* of moderate means. **-betrag,** *m.* deficiency, deficit. **-einnahme,** *f.* drop in earnings *or* receipts. **-gewicht,** *n.* short weight. **-heit,** *f.* minority. **-jährig,** *adj.* under age; *er ist -jährig,* he is a minor. **-jährige(r),** *m.* minor. **-jährigkeit,** *f.* minority. **-n,** 1. *v.a.* diminish, abate, lessen. 2. *v.r.* grow less. **-ung,** *f.* decrease, diminution. **-wertig,** *adj.* inferior, less valuable, of poor quality. **-wertigkeitsgefühl,** *n.* inferiority complex. **-zahl,** *f.* minority.

mindest, *adj.* least, smallest, lowest, minimum; *nicht das -e,* not at all, nothing at all; *zum -en,* at least, at the very least; *nicht im -en,* not in the least, not at all, by no means. **-betrag,** *m.* minimum (amount), lowest sum. **-bietende(r),** *m.* lowest bidder. **-ens,** *adv.* at least. **-lohn,** *m.* minimum wage. **-maß,** *n.* indispensable minimum. **-preis,** *m.* minimum price.

Mine, *f.* (-n) mine; refill, lead (*for propelling pencil*); *auf eine – stoßen* or *laufen,* hit a mine; *-n ausbauen,* clear a minefield (*Mil.*); *-n räumen,* sweep for mines (*Naut.*); *alle -n springen lassen,* leave no stone unturned. **-nabweiser,** *m.* paravane (*Naut.*). **-naktie,** *f.* mining share. **-nauge,** *n.* shaft of a mine. **-nfalle,** *f.* booby trap (*Mil.*). **-nfeld,** *n.* mine-field. **-ngang,** *m.* tunnel, gallery. **-ngasse,** *f.* lane in a minefield. **-nhalle,** *f.* mine-chamber. **-nhals,** *m.* entrance to a gallery. **-nhund,** *m.* truck. **-nleger,** *m.* minelayer. **-enräumer,** *m.* minesweeper. **-nsperre,** *f.* minefield. **-nstolle,** *f.* gallery (*in a mine*). **-nsuchboot,** *n.*, **-nsucher,** *m.* mine-sweeper. **-nwerfer,** *m.* trench mortar (*Mil.*).

Mineral, *n.* (-s, -e & -ien) mineral. **-isch,** *adj.* mineral. **-kunde,** *f.*, **-lehre,** *f.* mineralogy. **-og(e),** *m.* (-en, -en) mineralogist. **-ogie,** *f.* mineralogy. **-ogisch,** *adj.* mineralogical. **-öl,** *n.* mineral oil, petroleum. **-quelle,** *f.* mineral spring. **-reich,** 1. *n.* mineral kingdom. 2. *adj.* rich in minerals. **-stoffwechsel,** *m.* inorganic metabolism. **-wasser,** *n.* (-wässer) mineral water.

Min-eur, *m.* (-s, -e) sapper, miner. **-eurpflug,** *m.* deep plough. **-ieren,** *v.a.* mine; undermine, sap.

Miniatur, *f.* (-en) miniature. **-ausgabe,** *f.* pocket-edition. **-bild,** *n.* miniature.

minim-al, *adj.* minimum; minute, tiny. **-albetrag,** *m.* minimum amount, lowest rate. **-alsatz,** *m.* lowest rate. **-um,** *n.* (-ums, -ma) minimum; depression (*Meteor.*).

Minister, *m.* (-s, –) minister; *– des Äußeren* or *Auswärtigen,* Minister of Foreign Affairs; *bevollmächtiger –,* plenipotentiary; *erster –,* Prime Minister, premier; *– ohne Geschäftsbereich,* minister without portfolio; *– des Inneren,* Minister for Home Affairs; Home Secretary. **-ial,** *adj.*, *see* **-iell.** **-ialdirektor,** *m.* head of a government department. **-ialerlaß,** *m.* ministerial order; order in Council. **-ialgebäude,** *n.* Government offices. **-ialrat,** *m.* senior civil servant. **-ium,** *n.* (-iums, -ien) ministry; government department; *-ium des Inneren,* Home Office; *im -ium sein,* be in the cabinet, be in office, hold office. **-iell,** *adj.* ministerial. **-präsident,** *m.* president of cabinet council; Prime Minister. **-rat,** *m.* cabinet council.

Ministr-ant, *m.* (-en, -en) acolyte. **-ieren,** *v.n.* minister, officiate.

Minn-e, *f.* (*archaic* & *Poet.*) love. **-en,** *v.a.* & *n.* (*aux.* h.) love, woo. **-elied,** *n.*, **-esang,** *m.* medieval German love poetry; *-esangs Frühling,* early medieval lyrics. **-esänger,** *m.*, **-esinger,** *m.* minnesinger (*German lyric poet of the 12th to 14th centuries*). **-ig(lich),** *adj.* lovely, charming; lovable.

minor-enn, *adj.* under age, minor. **-ennität,** *f.* minority (*of a person*). **-ität,** *f.* minority. **-itätsgutachten,** *n.* minority report. **-itätenproblem,** *n.* problem of minorities.

minus, 1. *adv.* minus. 2. *n.* deficit, deficiency; shortage. **–betrag,** *m.* minus quantity, discount. **–elektrizität,** *f.* negative electricity. **–kel,** *f.* (-n) small letter; minuscule. **–seite,** *f.* debit side (*also fig.*). **–zeichen,** *n.* minus sign (—).

Minut–e, *f.* (-en) minute; *auf die –e genau*, exactly to the minute; *ein Grad dreißig –en*, 1° 30′ (*angle*). **–enlang,** *adj.* for (several) minutes. **–enweise,** *adv.* every minute. **–enzeiger,** *m.* minute-hand. **–ig,** *adj. suffix*, e.g. *fünf–ig*, for *or* lasting (for) 5 minutes. **–iös,** *see* **minuziös.** **–lich,** *adj. suffix*, e.g. *fünf–lich*, every five minutes.

minuziös, *adj.* minute, tiny; painstaking, petty.

Minze, *f.* mint (*Mentha*) (*Bot.*).

mir, *Dat. of* **ich,** me, to me; *ein Buch von –*, a book belonging to me *or* written by me; a book of mine; *jetzt ist es an –*, now it is my turn; *von – aus*, as far as I am concerned, for all I care; *– nichts, dir nichts*, without more ado; unceremoniously; *laß – das bleiben*, do not do that, just leave that alone; *wie du –, so ich dir*, what's sauce for the goose is sauce for the gander; tit for tat; (*Prov.*) *heute –, morgen dir*, everyone in his turn.

Mirabelle, *f.* (-n) yellow plum.

Mirakel, *n.* (-s, –) miracle. **–spiel,** *n.* (medieval) miracle play.

Misanthrop, *m.* (-en, -en) misanthropist. **–isch,** *adj.* misanthropic.

misch–en, 1. *v.a.* mix, mingle; blend, combine, compound; adulterate, alloy; shuffle (*Cards*). 2. *v.r.* mix (with people), join in; blend, combine, be miscible; interfere *or* meddle with; *sich in fremde Angelegenheiten –en*, meddle in other people's affairs; *sich ins Gespräch –en*, join in the conversation; *die Karten betrügerisch –en*, stack the cards; *gemischte Spirituosen*, compounded spirits; *mit gemischten Gefühlen*, with mixed feelings; *gemischte Gesellschaft*, very mixed company; *gemischte Schule*, mixed school. **–art,** *f.* mongrel, cross-breed. **–bar,** *adj.* miscible, mixable, combinable. **–barkeit,** *f.* miscibility. **–bestand,** *m.* mixed crop. **–ehe,** *f.* mixed marriage. **–farbe** *f.* mixed *or* combination colour. **–futter,** *n.* mixed fodder. **–gericht,** *n.* ragout. **–ling,** *m.* mongrel, cross (breed), hybrid, half-caste. **–masch,** *m.* & *adv.* medley, hotchpotch. **–maschine,** *f.* mixer. **–rasse,** *f.* mongrel race, cross-breed. **–ung,** *f.* mixture; compound; composition; combination; blend, alloy. **–ungsverhältnis,** *n.* ratio of components. **–ungsverwandtschaft,** *f.* chemical affinity. **–volk,** *n.* mixed race *or* breed. **–wald,** *m.* mixed woodland.

miserabel, *adj.* wretched, miserable; vile, base rascally.

Misogyn, *m.* (-en, -en, & *Austr. dial.* -(e)s, -e) misogynist.

Mispel, *f.* (-n) medlar (*Mespilus germanica*) (*Bot.*).

miß–, *prefix* = mis-, dis-, bad, ill, amiss, false, wrong; *cannot be described as either sep. or insep.*; *p.p. is best without* ge–, *e.g.* mißachtet, *though both other forms occur, e.g.* gemißhandelt, mißgetönt; *inf. is sometimes as sep., sometimes as insep., e.g.* mißzustimmen, zu mißbilden, *depending on the stress*; *sep. when the contrast with its opposite is emphasized.* **–achten,** *v.a.* (*p.p.* –achtet, *also* ge––achtet) disregard, undervalue, esteem lightly; neglect, slight, despise, disdain. **–achtung,** *f.* disregard, disrespect, disdain, neglect. **–arten,** *v.n.* (*p.p.* –(ge)artet) (*aux.* s.) degenerate. **–artung,** *f.* degeneracy. **–begriff,** *m.* misconception, wrong idea. **–behagen,** 1. *v. imp.* (*p.p.* –behagt) (*aux.* h.) (*Dat.*) displease. 2. *n.* discomfort, displeasure, discontent. **–behaglich,** *adj.* disagreeable, uncomfortable, unpleasant. **–bilden,** *v.a.* (*p.p.* –gebildet) deform, malform. **–bildung,** *f.* deformity malformation, disfigurement. **–billigen,** *v.a.* (*p.p.* –billigt, *also* ge–billigt) disapprove (of), object to; disallow, condemn. **–billigung,** *f.* disapprobation, disapproval. **–brauch,** *m.* misuse; abuse, malpractice, unauthorized use. **–brauchen,** *v.a.* (*p.p.* –braucht, *also* ge–braucht) misuse, abuse; (*p.p.* –braucht) take advantage of, outrage; *den Namen des Herrn –brauchen*, take the Lord's name in vain. **–bräuchlich,** *adj.*, **–bräuchlicherweise,** *adv.* wrong, perverted, improper. **–deuten,** *v.a.* (*p.p.* –deutet, *also* ge–deutet) misinterpret, misconstrue. **–deutung,** *f.* misinterpretation. **–(ss)en,** *see* **missen.** **–erfolg,** *m.* failure. **–ernte,** *f.* bad harvest. **–(ss)etat,** *f.* (*B.*) sin, misdeed, crime. **–(ss)etäter,** *m.* criminal, offender, evil-doer, sinner. **–fallen,** 1. *ir.v.n.* (*p.p.* –fallen) (*aux.* h.) (*Dat.*) displease, be displeasing, offend; *es –fällt mir*, I dislike it. 2. *n.* displeasure, dissatisfaction. **–fällig,** *adj.* unfavourable, disparaging; unpleasant, displeasing, disagreeable, offensive; *sich –fällig äußern über* (*Acc.*), find fault with. **–farbig,** *adj.* discoloured. **–färbung,** *f.* discoloration. **–gebären,** *ir.v.a.* miscarry; *–geboren*, abortive. **–gebilde,** *n.* monster. **–geburt,** *f.* abortion; monster. **–gelaunt,** *adj.* bad-tempered, ill-humoured. **–geschick,** *n.* misfortune, bad luck, mishap. **–gestalt,** 1. *f.* monster. 2. *adj.* deformed; misshapen. **–gestalten,** *v.a.* (*p.p.* –gestaltet) disfigure, mutilate, deform. **–gestimmt,** *p.p.* & *adj.* bad-tempered. **–glücken,** *v.n.* (*p.p.* –glückt) (*aux.* s.) (*Dat.*) not succeed, fail, miscarry. **–gönnen,** *v.a.* (*p.p.* –gönnt) (*einem etwas*) begrudge, grudge, envy. **–greifen,** *ir.v.n.* (*p.p.* –gegriffen) (*aux.* h.) miss; mistake, blunder. **–griff,** *m.* blunder, mistake; failure. **–gunst,** *f.* envy, jealousy, grudge; (*rare*) ill-will, disfavour. **–günstig,** *adj.* envious, jealous. **–handeln,** 1. *v.n.* (*aux.* h.) (*p.p.* –gehandelt) do wrong. 2. *v.a.* (*p.p.* –handelt) abuse, ill-treat. **–handlung,** *f.* abuse, ill-treatment, maltreatment, ill-usage; misdeed. **–heirat,** *f.* misalliance. **–hellig,** *adj.* dissentient, disagreeing, dissonant, discordant. **–helligkeit,** *f.* (*usually pl.*) disagreement, dissension, difference. **–jahr,** *n.* bad year *or* season. **–kennen,** *ir.v.a.* (*p.p.* -(ge)kannt) (*archaic*) misjudge, mistake. **–klang,** *m.* dissonance, discord. **–kredit,** *m.* discredit, bad reputation; *in –kredit bringen*, discredit, bring into ill repute. **–laut,** *m.* discord, cacophony. **–leiten,** *v.a.* (*p.p.* –leitet, *also* –geleitet) mislead. **–lich,** *adj.* doubtful, precarious, uncertain; unpleasant, awkward, difficult, delicate; critical, unfortunate, dangerous; disagreeable; *es sieht mit ihm –lich aus*, he seems in a bad way. **–lichkeit,** *f.* difficulty; uncertainty; peril, risk; perplexity; critical condition, fatality. **–liebig** *adj.* unpopular, not in favour; *etwas –liebig aufnehmen*, take s.th. amiss *or* ill; *sich –liebig machen bei einem*, incur the displeasure of a p., get into a p.'s bad books. **–liebigkeit,** *f.* ill-favour; disgrace. **–lingen,** 1. *ir.v.n.* (*aux.* s.) & *imp.* (*p.p.* –lungen) (*Dat.*) fail, miscarry, prove unsuccessful. 2. *n.* failure, miscarriage. **–mut,** *m.* ill-humour, discontent; despondence. **–mutig,** *adj.* discontented; bad-tempered, sullen, peevish, cross. **–raten,** (*p.p.* –raten) 1. *ir.v.n.* (*aux.* s.) (*Dat.*) turn out badly, miscarry, fail; cross. 2. *v.a.* (*einem etwas*) dissuade (a p.) from (a th.). 3. *adj.* naughty, ill-bred, badly brought up. **–stand,** *m.* nuisance, inconvenience; grievance; *–stände beseitigen*, remedy abuses. **–stimmen,** 1. *v.a.* (*p.p.* –gestimmt) put out of temper, upset, depress. 2. *v.n.* (*aux.* h.) be discordant *or* inharmonious. **–stimmung,** *f.* ill-humour, depression; dissension, friction, strife. **–ton,** *m.* discord, dissonance. **–tönen,** *v.n.* (*p.p.* –getönt) be dissonant *or* out of tune. **–tönend,** *pr.p.* & *adj.*, **–tönig,** *adj.* out of tune, discordant. **–trauen,** 1. *v.n.* (*p.p.* –traut, *also* ge–traut) (*aux.* h.) (*Dat.*) mistrust, distrust, suspect. 2. *n.* suspicion, mistrust, distrust; *–trauen in einen setzen*, suspect a p.; *–trauen gegen sich selbst*, diffidence, misgivings, lack of self-confidence. **–trauensvotum,** *n.* vote of no confidence. **–trauisch,** *adj.* distrustful; suspicious. **–vergnügen,** *n.* displeasure, discontent, dissatisfaction. **–vergnügt,** *adj.* discontented, displeased. **–verhältnis,** *n.* disproportion, disparity, incongruity, inadequacy; unfriendly relations tension. **–verständlich,** *adj.* misleading, ambiguous. **–verständnis,** *n.* misunderstanding, misconception, mistake, error; unfriendly relations. **–verstehen,** *ir.v.a.* (*p.p.* –verstanden) misunderstand, mistake; *in nicht –zuverstehender Weise*, in an unmistakable manner. **-wachs,** *m. see* **-ernte. -wachsen,** *adj.* misshapen, ill-formed. **-wuchs,** *m.* malformation (of growth). **-weisung,** *f.* magnetic declination; *-weisender Kurs,* magnetic *or* compass course. **-wirtschaft,** *f.* maladministration, mismanagement.

Missal, *n.* (-s, -e), **-e,** *n.* (-es, -en) missal.

missen, *v.a.* be *or* do without, dispense with; miss, feel the lack of.

missest, mißt, miß, *see* **messen.**

Misse-tat, -täter, *see under* **miß-.**

Mission, *f.* (-en) mission; *Innere -,* home mission. **-ar** (*Austr. dial.* **-är**) (-s, -e) missionary. **-sanstalt,** *f.* mission-house. **-sgesellschaft,** *f.*, **-sverein,** *m.* missionary society.

Mist, *m.* (-es, -e) dung, manure, muck; haze (*Naut.*); (*sl.*) trash, bosh, twaddle. **-en,** *v. imp. es -et,* there is a haze (*Naut.*). **-beet,** *n.* hotbed. **-beetkasten,** *m.* forcing frame. (*vulg.*) **-fink,** *m.* dirty child; filthy person. **-fuhre,** *f.* load of manure. **-gabel,** *f.* pitch-fork, dung-fork. **-haufen,** *m.* dunghill, dung-heap. **-ig,** *adj.* (*coll.*) caddish, low-down, shabby, scurvy, vile; (*Naut.*) hazy, misty; (*dial.*) filthy. **-jauche,** *f.* liquid manure. **-käfer,** *m.* dung-beetle. **-stock,** *m.* (*Swiss dial.*) dunghill. **-vieh,** *n.* (*vulg.*) filthy beast. **-wagen,** *m.* muck-cart.

Mistel, *f.* (-n) mistletoe.

Miszellaneen, Miszellen, *f.pl.* miscellanies.

mit, 1. *prep.* (*Dat.*) with; along with, in company with, at the same time with; by; at; to; *- Absicht tun,* do intentionally; *- voller Dampfkraft,* at full steam *or* speed; *- Gewalt,* by force; *- dem Glockenschlage,* on the dot; *- 15 Jahren,* at the age of 15; *- einem Male* or *- einemmal,* suddenly, all at once; *- Namen,* by name; *- der Post,* by post; *- Protest,* under protest; *- jemand reden,* speak to a person; *- einem Schlage,* at a blow; *- Tinte schreiben,* write in ink; *was ist - ihm?* what has happened to him? what is the matter with him? *- Verlust,* at a loss; *was hat er - ihr vor?* what plans has he regarding her? *- Vorsicht,* with caution, cautiously; *- einem Worte,* in a word. 2. *adv.* along with, together *or* in company with; jointly, likewise; also; simultaneously; *die Kosten sind - berechnet,* the charge is included; *das ist - die beste Lösung,* that is one of the best solutions; *- dabei sein,* be (one) of the party, be there too, be concerned in a matter; *das gehört - dazu,* that belongs to it also; that is part of it; *da kann ich nicht -,* that is beyond me, that is too much for me (*i.e.* my understanding); I cannot manage that (*i.e.* exceeds my powers *or* pocket); *ich will -,* I want to go (*or* come) too; *willst du nicht - fahren?* would you not like to ride with us (*or* them) (*i.e.* do you prefer to walk?). 3. *prefix with nouns and some adjs.* = fellow-, joint-, co-; *sep. prefix with practically any verb* = in company with, in common with, simultaneously. **-angeklagte(r),** *m.* codefendant (*Law*). **-arbeiten,** *v.n.* (*aux.* h.) (*an with Dat.*) assist, collaborate, work together, cooperate; contribute to. **-arbeiter,** *m.* assistant, colleague, collaborator, co-worker, contributor (*to a journal*). **-bedacht,** *adj.* also remembered (in the will); *der -bedachte,* co-legatee. **-begreifen,** *ir.v.a.* comprise, include, comprehend. **-besitz,** *m.* joint property. **-besitzen,** *ir.v.a.* possess in common, share in the ownership of. **-besitzer,** *m.* joint-owner *or* proprietor. **-bestimmen,** *v.n.* (*aux.* h.) have a voice in (*a decision*). **-beteiligt,** *adj.* taking part in, having a share *or* an interest in (*with others*). **-beteiligte(r),** *m.* interested party, partner. **-beten,** *v.n.* (*aux.* h.) join in prayer. **-bewegung,** *f.* collateral *or* associated movement. **-bewerben,** *ir.v.a.* compete (with), enter into competition (for). **-bewerber,** *m.* competitor; rival. **-bewohner,** *m.* fellow-lodger. **-bringen,** *ir.v.a.* bring along with (one); *für diese Stellung bringt er gar nichts mit,* he has not any qualifications for this post; *das -gebrachte,* bride's dowry. **-bringsel,** *n.* (*coll.*) present, souvenir, memento. **-bürge,** *m.* co-surety, joint security. **-bürger,** *m.* fellow-citizen. **-dasein,** *n.* coexistence. **-dürfen,** *ir.v.n.* (*aux.* h.) (*ellipt.*) be allowed to accompany, have permission to join. **-eigentum,** *n.* joint-property. **-eigentümer,** *m.* joint-proprietor. **-einander,** *adv.* with one another, together, jointly. **-einbegriffen,** *adj.* included, inclusive. **-empfinden,** 1. *ir.v.a.* have compassion, feel for, sympathize with. 2. *n.* sympathy, fellow-feeling, compassion. **-erbe,** *m.* co-heir. **-erben,** *v.n.* (*aux.* s.) inherit conjointly. **-erleben,** *v.a.* witness, experience at first hand. **-essen,** *ir.v.n. & a.* (*aux.* h.) eat *or* dine with, share a meal with. **-esser,** *m.* blackhead (*Med.*). **-folgen,** *v.n.* (*aux.* s.) follow without delay. **-fühlen,** *v.n.* sympathize (with), feel for; *ein -fühlendes Herz,* a feeling heart. **-führen,** *v.a.* bring *or* carry along with. **-geben,** *ir.v.a.* give to a departing guest; impart; give as dowry; *einem einen Führer -geben,* send a guide with a p. **-gefangene(r),** *m.* fellow-prisoner. **-gefühl,** *n.* sympathy, pity, compassion. **-gehen,** *ir.v.n.* (*aux.* s.) go with, accompany; be with; agree with; *mit dem Redner -gehen,* be carried away by the speaker, be in complete agreement with the speaker; *das geht noch -,* this is to be added as well; (*coll.*) *eine S. -gehen heißen,* steal a th.; *-gegangen, -gefangen, -gehangen,* together through thick and thin. **-genosse,** *m.* co-partner; consort; companion. **-gift,** *f.* dowry. **-giftjäger,** *m.* fortune-hunter. **-glied,** *n.* (-s, -er) member. **-gliederversammlung,** *f.* meeting of all members, general meeting. **-gliedschaft,** *f.* membership; fellowship. **-gliedskarte,** *f.* membership card. **-hafte,** *m.* (-n, -n) (*Swiss dial.*) underwriter. **-halten,** 1. *ir.v.a.* share, hold conjointly with. 2. *v.n.* be one of a party, be there; side with; *ich halte mit,* I will join you; *ich kann nicht -halten,* I cannot keep up (the pace). **-helfen,** *ir.v.a. & n.* (*aux.* h.) cooperate with; help, assist. **-helfer,** *m.* assistant; accomplice (*Law*). **-herausgeber,** *m.* co-editor. **-herrschaft,** *f.* joint-dominion. **-herrschend,** *adj.* co-dominant. **-herrscher,** *m.* co-regent. **-hilfe,** *f.* co-operation, assistance, aid. **-hin,** *adv. & conj.* consequently, therefore, hence. **-hören,** *v.n.* (*aux.* h.) overhear; intercept (*Tele.*). **-kämpfer,** *m.* fellow-soldier, comrade in arms. **-kommen,** *ir.v.n.* (*aux.* s.) accompany, come along with; be able to follow (*the lesson, etc.*); keep up with. **-können,** *ir.v.n.* (*aux.* h.) (*ellipt.*) be able to go with *or* keep up with. **-läufer,** *m.* time-server, 'fellow-traveller' (*Pol.*). **-laut(er),** *m.* consonant (*Gram.*). **-leid,** *n.* pity, compassion; sympathy; *-leid mit einem haben,* have pity on a p., be indulgent towards s.o.; *er rief mein -leid an,* he appealed to my sympathy. **-leiden,** *ir.v.n.* (*aux.* h.), suffer at the same time; feel for, pity, suffer with; sympathize. **-leidenschaft,** *f.* sympathy (*Med.*); *in -leidenschaft ziehen,* affect, involve, implicate. **-leidenswert,** *adj.*, **-leidenswürdig,** *adj.* pitiable, piteous. **-leidig,** *adj.* sympathetic, compassionate. **-leidsbezeigung,** *f.* condolence. **-leidslos,** *adj.* pitiless, ruthless, unfeeling. **-leidsvoll,** *adj.* sympathetic, feeling. **-machen,** 1. *v.a.* take part in, conform to, join. 2. *v.n.* (*aux.* h.) participate; do as others do; *er macht alles -,* he joins in everything; *ich mache nicht -,* I shall keep out of it; *alle Moden -machen,* follow every fashion; *er hat viel -gemacht,* he has seen a good deal of life, he has gone *or* been through a lot; *du kannst nichts Besseres tun als -machen,* it will be best for you to do the same. **-mensch,** *m.* (-en, -en) fellow-creature; one's neighbour (*B.*). **-müssen,** *ir.v.n.* (*aux.* h.) (*ellipt.*) be obliged to go with, be forced to join. **-nahme,** *f.* carrying, taking. **-nehmen,** *ir.v.a.* take with one; treat harshly, criticize severely; weaken, exhaust, tire out; desolate (*a country*); profit by; *jemanden im Wagen -nehmen,* give a p. a ride *or* a lift; *auf der Reise einen Ort -nehmen,* call at a place on one's way; *einen Verdienst -nehmen,* take the opportunity of doing a stroke of business *or* of turning an honest penny; *das ist immer -zunehmen,* that is not by any means to be neglected *or* refused; *die Kritiker haben ihn sehr -genommen,* the critics have been very hard on him; *die Krankheit hat ihn sehr -genommen,* the illness has pulled him down very much. **-nehmer,** *m.* follower (*Mach.*), catch (*Mach.*), axle stay

(*Veh.*). **-nichten,** *adv.* by no means. **-rechnen,** 1. *v.a.* include in the reckoning. 2. *v.n.* (*aux.* h.) *das rechnet nicht –*, that does not count. **-reden,** 1. *v.n.* (*aux.* h.) join in the conversation; put in a word. 2. *v.a.*; *hier habe ich auch ein Wort –zureden*, I have also a word to say in this matter; *Sie haben hier nichts –zureden*, you have no say in this matter. **-reisen,** *v.n.* (*aux.* h.) travel in company with. **-reisende(r),** *m.* fellow-traveller, travelling companion. **-reißen,** *ir.v.a.* tear *or* drag along with; (*fig.*) carry with *or* sweep along (*as enthusiasm, etc.*). **-samt,** *prep.* (*Dat.*) together with. **-schuld,** *f.* complicity, share of guilt. **-schuldig,** *adj.* implicated in *or* accessory to a crime. **-schuldige(r),** *m.* accessory, accomplice. **-schuldner,** *m.* joint-debtor. **-schüler,** *m.* schoolfellow, classmate, fellow-pupil; *sie war meine –schülerin*, she and I were at school together. **-schwingen,** *v.n.* vibrate in resonance, be resonant. **-sollen,** *ir.v.n.* (*aux.* h.) (*ellipt.*) be obliged to accompany; *er soll mit*, he is to go *or* is supposed to be going with (us, him, them). **-spielen,** *v.a. & n.* (*aux.* h.) join in a game; take a hand (*at cards*); accompany (*Mus.*); play a part, take part; *ihm wurde übel –gespielt*, a dirty *or* shabby trick was played on him. **-spieler,** *m.* partner; accompanist (*Mus.*). **-sprechen,** participate, join in (the conversation), have s.th. to say; come into consideration, be involved, be a factor; *das wird freilich auch dabei –sprechen*, that is of some consequence, too. **-stimmen,** *v.n.* (*aux.* h.) vote as others do, add one's vote. **-tag,** *see* **Mittag.** **-täter,** *m.* accomplice. **-täterschaft,** *f.* complicity. **-te,** *see* **Mitte.** **-teilbar,** *adj.* communicable; contagious (*Med.*). **-teilbarkeit,** *f.* communicability. **-teilen,** 1. *v.a.* (*einem etwas*) communicate, impart, pass on (s.th. to s.o.); inform, apprise, notify (s.o. of a th.); tell (s.o. s.th.). 2. *v.r.* communicate one's thoughts, unbosom o.s.; spread, communicate itself, be contagious. **-teilsam,** *adj.* communicative. **-teilung,** *f.* announcement, pronouncement, communication, information, news, intimation, notification, notice, note, intelligence. **-tel,** *see* **Mittel.** **-ten,** *see* **mitten.** **-tragen,** *v.a.* carry with others; share (*a burden or loss*). **-tun,** *ir.v.n.* (*aux.* h.) (*ellipt.*) take part in, join *or* help in doing. **-unter,** *see* **mitunter.** **-unterschreiben, -unterzeichnen,** *v.a. & n.* (*aux.* h.) add one's signature, countersign. **-unterschrift,** *f.* joint-signature. **-verantwortlich,** *adj.* sharing responsibility, guilty with others. **-verschworene(r),** *m.* fellow-conspirator, accomplice. **-welt,** *f.* the age we live in, our age, our own times, the present generation, our contemporaries. **-wirken,** *v.n.* (*aux.* h.) co-operate, concur, assist, contribute towards, collaborate, take part, take a part in (*a concert, etc.*). **-wirkende(n),** *pl.* members (of the cast), actors, players. **-wirkung,** *f.* co-operation, assistance, participation. **-wissen,** 1. *ir.v.n.* (*aux.* h.); *um eine S. –wissen*, have cognizance of, be privy to, know of a th. 2. *n.* cognizance; *ohne mein –wissen*, without my knowledge, unknown to me. **-wisser,** *m.* one in the secret; confidant, accessory. **-wisserschaft,** *f.* collusion, complicity. **-zählen,** *see* **-rechnen.** **-zweck,** *m.* (-(e)s, -e) secondary aim.

Mittag, 1. *m.* (-s, -e) midday, noon; meridian; (*archaic*) south; *gegen –*, towards noon; (*poet.*) southerly; *heller –*, broad noon; *zu – essen*, take one's midday meal, have lunch *or* dinner; lunch, dine. 2. *n.* (*coll.*) dinner, lunch; *– machen*, break for lunch. **-essen,** *n.* midday meal, lunch, (early) dinner. **-mahlen,** *v.n.* (*Austr. dial.*) *see zu – essen.* **-s,** *adv.* at noon; at dinner *or* lunch-time. **-sausgabe,** *f.* noon edition. **-sgesellschaft,** *f.* luncheon party. **-sglut,** *f.*, **-shitze,** *f.* midday heat. **-shell,** *adj.* bright as noonday. **-shöhe,** *f.* meridian altitude; *–shöhe der Sonne*, the sun's altitude. **-skreis,** *m.* meridian. **-slänge,** *f.* meridional longitude. **-slinie,** *f.* line of the meridian. **-smahl,** *n.* midday meal. **-spause,** *f.* lunch-hour. **-sruhe,** *f.*, **-sschlaf,** *m.*, **-sschläfchen,** *n.* siesta, after-dinner nap. **-ssonne,** *f.* midday sun. **-sstunde,** *f.* noon; dinner-hour. **-stisch,** *m.* midday meal; luncheon club, private restaurant supplying midday meals; *der –stisch kostet hier 5 Mark*, the charge for dinner here is 5 marks. **-szeit,** *f.* noontide. **-wärts,** *adv.* (*Poet.*) southerly.

mittäg-ig, *adj.* midday, noontide. **-lich,** *adj.* occurring (regularly) at noon; meridional; southerly.

Mitt-e, *f.* (-en) middle, centre; midst; mean, medium; *–e Fünfzig, –e der Fünfziger*, in the middle fifties, between 50 and 60 years of age; *goldene –e*, golden mean; *die (rechte) –e halten*, observe the happy mean; *–e Januar*, in the middle of January; *in die –e nehmen*, attack on *or* from both sides (*Mil.*); *das Reich der –e*, the Middle Kingdom, China; *richtige –e*, happy medium; *einer aus unserer –e*, one of our circle. **-efünfziger,** *m.* man in his middle fifties. **-el, -en, -er-, -ler,** *see* **Mittel, mitten, Mitter-, Mittler.** **-fasten,** *pl.* mid-Lent. **-schiffs,** *adv.* amidships. **-sommer,** *m.* (*dial.*) midsummer. **-woch,** (-s, -e) Wednesday. **-wochs,** *adv.* every Wednesday, on a Wednesday.

Mittel, 1. *n.* (-s, –) remedy, medicine; expedient, way, measure, means; average, mean, median (*Maths.*); medium, agent (*Phys.*); (*pl.*) means, wealth, property, resources, money; *das arithmetische –*, the arithmetical mean; *bescheidene –*, moderate means; *meine – erlauben es nicht*, I cannot afford it; *alle ersinnlichen – anwenden*, employ every possible means; *hier gibt es kein –*, there is no help for it, nothing can be done; *sich ins – legen*, interpose, mediate, intercede; *das – nehmen*, take the average; *neue – anwenden*, change one's tactics; *er hat reichliche –*, he is very well off; *ein unfehlbares –*, a specific; *kein – unversucht lassen, alle – und Wege versuchen*, explore every avenue, leave no stone unturned; *er war nicht heikel in der Wahl seiner –*, he was not choosy about the means he employed; (*Prov.*) *der Zweck heiligt die –*, the end justifies the means. 2. *adj.* (mittler, mittelst; *rarely used in the positive, see* **mittler**) middle, mid, central; mean, average, intermediate. **-alter,** *n.* Middle Ages. **-alt(e)rig,** *adj.* middle-aged. **-alterlich,** *adj.* medieval. **-arrest,** *m.* light field-punishment (*Mil.*). **-bar,** *adj.* mediate; indirect; collateral. **-barkeit,** *f.* indirectness. **-darm,** *m.* intestine. **-decker,** *m.* mid-wing monoplane (*Av.*). **-ding,** *n.* something between, intermediate thing. **-ernte,** *f.* average crop. **-farbe,** *f.* secondary colour. **-fehler,** *m.* mean error. **-finger,** *m.* middle finger. **-flüssig,** *adj.* semi-fluid, viscous. **-fuß,** *m.* metatarsus (*Anat.*). **-gebirge,** *n.* medium altitude *or* sub-alpine mountains. **-geschwindigkeit,** *f.* mean velocity. **-gewicht,** *n.* middle-weight (*Boxing*). **-glied,** *n.* middle phalanx (*Anat.*); middle term (*Log.*); intermediate member. **-groß,** *adj.* medium sized. **-größe,** *f.* medium size. **-gut,** *adj.* middling, of medium quality; second-rate. **-hand,** *f.* metacarpus (*Anat.*). **-hart,** *adj.* medium *or* fairly hard. **-hochdeutsch,** *n.* Middle High German. **-höhe,** *f.* mean height. **-klassen,** *f.pl.* the middle school (*about 14-year olds*). **-kraft,** *f.* resultant (force) (*Dyn.*). **-lage,** *f.* middle position. **-ländisch,** *adj.* Mediterranean. **-latein,** *n.* Medieval Latin. **-läufer,** *m.* centre half (*Footb.*). **-leib,** *m.* thorax. **-linie,** *f.* centre line, axis, equator. **-los,** *adj.* without means, destitute. **-mächte,** *f.pl.* Central (European) Powers. **-maß,** *n.* average, mean; middling size. **-mäßig,** *adj.* average, middling, moderate, indifferent, mediocre, tolerable, fair. **-mäßigkeit,** *f.* mediocrity. **-meer,** *n.* Mediterranean Sea. **-partei,** *f.* centre party (*Pol.*). **-preis,** *m.* average price. **-punkt,** *m.* centre; central point, focus; *nach dem –punkte der Schwere streben*, gravitate. **-s, -st,** *prep.* by means of, through, with the help of. **-salz,** *n.* neutral salt (*Chem.*). **-satz,** *m.* middle term (*Log.*); middle movement (*Mus.*). **-schicht,** *f.* intermediate layer. **-schiff,** *n.* middle aisle (*Arch.*). **-schule,** *f.* intermediate school; (*Austr. dial.*) secondary school. **-schwein,** *n.* main keelson (*Naut.*). **-schwer,** *adj.* medium weight. **-schwert,** *n.* centre-board (*Naut.*). **-smann,** *m.* (-smänner),

-sperson, *f.* mediator, go-between; middleman; umpire (*Sport*). **-sorte,** *f.* medium quality **-staaten,** *m. pl.* secondary states. **-stand,** *m.* middle classes. **-ständig,** *adj.* intermediate, perigynous (*Bot.*). **-stark,** *adj.* moderately strong. **-steinzeit,** *f.* mesolithic age. **-stellung,** *f.* mid position, balance. **-stimme,** *f.* baritone; mezzo-soprano. **-straße,** *f.* middle course, mean, compromise; *die goldne -straße*, the golden mean; *ich halte mich auf der -straße*, I steer the middle course. **-streckenlauf,** *m.* medium-distance race. **-streckler,** *m.* medium-distance runner. **-stück,** *n.* middle piece; central portion; interlude (*Mus.*). **-stufe,** *f.* intermediate step *or* stage, middle grade. **-stürmer,** *m.* centre forward (*Footb.*). **-ton,** *m.* mediant (*Mus.*). **-wand,** *f.* partition wall. **-weg,** *m.*, *see* **-straße;** *einen -weg einschlagen*, adopt a middle course, make a compromise. **-wert,** *m.* average *or* mean (value), median. **-wort,** *n.* (*archaic*) participle (*Gram.*). **-zeit,** *f.* mean time. **-zustand,** *m.* intermediate state *or* condition.

mitten, *adv.* (*used with a prep. following*) midway; *– am Tage*, in broad daylight; *– auf*, in the midst *or* middle of; *– aus*, from amidst *or* among; *–drein*, into the centre; *–drin*, in the centre; *–drunter*, in their midst; *–durch*, through the middle, right through; *– entzwei* or *hindurch*, in two, broken in the middle; *– in*, see *– auf*; *– in der Luft*, in mid-air; *– in der Nacht*, in the middle of the night; *–inne* (*Austr. dial. – inne*), right in the middle, amidst; *– unter*, amongst, amidst, in the midst of.

Mitter-nacht, *f.* midnight; (*archaic & poet.*) North. **-nächtig,** *adj.* nocturnal; midnight; gloomy. **-nächtlich,** *adj.* (happening every) midnight; (*archaic*) northern. **-nachts,** *adv.* at midnight. **-nachtssonne,** *f.* midnight sun.

mittler, (*comp. of* mittel *which it has supplanted*) middle, central, medium, average, mean; middling, mediocre; *–e Abweichung*, *f.* standard deviation (*Statistics*); *–e Ortszeit*, local time; *Person von –en Jahren*, middle-aged person; *–e Schnelligkeit*, average speed; *–e Streuung*, *f.* mean scatter (*Statistics*). **-weile,** *adv.* meanwhile, in the meantime.

Mittler, *m.* (-s, –) mediator, intercessor; third party; *unser –*, Christ. **-in,** *f.* mediatrix. **-tod** *m.* expiatory death.

mitunter, *adv.* sometimes, at times, occasionally, now and then.

Mixtur, *f.* (-en) mixture (*Pharm.*).

Möb-el, *n.* (-els, -el) piece of furniture; (*pl.*) furniture; (*coll.*) *altes –el*, old fogy, fixture, stick-in-the-mud (*said of an old family servant*). **-elhändler,** *m.* furniture dealer. **-ellack,** *m.* cabinet varnish. **-elpolitur,** *f.* furniture polish. **-elspediteur,** *m.* furniture-remover, warehouseman. **-elspeicher,** *m.* repository, pantechnicon. **-eltischler,** *m.* cabinet-maker, joiner. **-elwagen,** *m.* furniture van, removal van, pantechnicon van. **-lieren,** *v.a.* furnish; *–lierte Zimmer zu vermieten*, furnished apartments to let; (*coll.*) *ein –lierter Herr*, a man living in furnished rooms.

mobil, *adj.* movable, mobile; active, nimble; *– machen*, put in motion; mobilize (*troops*); *es wurde – gemacht*, the reserves were called out; *für eine S. – machen*, make an appeal for a th., rouse support *or* sympathy for a th. **-e,** *n.*; *Perpetuum –e*, perpetual motion. **-iar,** *n.* furniture. **-iarerbe,** *m.* heir to personal property. **-iarmasse,** *f.* movable property of a bankrupt. **-ien,** *pl.* movables, goods and chattels. **-isieren,** *v.a.* mobilize. **-isierung,** *f.*, **-machung,** *f.* mobilization.

mochte, möchte, *see* **mögen.**

Modd-er, *m.* (*dial.*) bog, marsh, mire. **-rig,** *adj.* (*dial.*) boggy, marshy, swampy.

Mod-e, *f.* (-en) fashion, mode, vogue; custom; *–e werden* (or *sein*), come into (*or* be in) fashion; *die –e angeben*, set the fashion; *die –e mitmachen*, follow the fashion; *nach der –e*, in the latest style *or* fashion; *aus der –e kommen*, go out of fashion. **-eartikel,** *m.pl.* novelties, fancy goods. **-eausdruck,** *m.*, *see* **-ewort.** **-edame,** *f.* lady of fashion. **-ehans,** *m.*, **-enarr,** *m.* fop, dandy. **-ekram,** *m.*, *see* **-eartikel.** **-epuppe,** *f.* woman dressed in the extreme fashion. **-ern,** *see* **modern.** **-eschau,** *f.* dress *or* fashion show, mannequin parade. **-eschöpfung,** *f.* latest creation. **-eschriftsteller,** *m.* popular writer. **-esucht,** *f.* craze for the latest fashion. **-etorheit,** *f.* fashionable craze. **-ewaren,** *f.pl.*, *see* **-eartikel.** **-ewelt,** *f.* fashionable world. **-ewort,** *n.* vogue-word. **-e(n)-zeitung,** *f.* fashion magazine. **-isch,** *adj.* fashionable, stylish. **-istin,** *f.* milliner.

Model, *m.* (-s, –) pattern, block, mould, matrix. **-n,** 1. *v.a.* figure, work patterns (on stuffs); shape, form, mould. 2. *v.r.*; *sich –n nach einem*, model o.s. on a p., take a p. for one's model. **-tuch,** *n.* stencilled pattern (*for embroidery*). **-ung,** *f.* forming, shaping, moulding.

Modell, *n.* (-s, -e) model; mould, form; pattern, sample; artist's (living) model; *ein – abnehmen*, take a cast; *als – dienen*, serve as a model *or* prototype; *– stehen*, pose for an artist. **-ierbogen,** *m.* cutting-out pattern. **-ieren,** *v.a.* model, mould, form, fashion. **-ierer** (*also* **Modelleur**) *m.* modeller; pattern-maker. **-iermasse,** *f.* modelling clay, plasticine. **-puppe,** *f.* lay-figure. **-tischler,** *m.* pattern-maker. **-zeichnung,** *f.* drawing from life *or* casts; drawing of models (*Engin.*).

Moder, *m.* dry rot, mould, mouldering, decay, rottenness; mother (*on wine, etc.*); damp, close air; (*dial.*) bog, mire. **-erde,** *f.* mould, compost, rotten earth. **-fleckig,** *adj.* mildewed. **-geruch,** *m.* musty smell. **-luft,** *f.* musty air. **-wasser,** *n.* stagnant water. **-ig** (*Austr. dial.* **modrig**), mouldy, musty, putrid, rotten, decaying; (*dial.*) boggy. **-n,** *v.n.* (*aux.* s. & n.) putrefy, rot, decay, moulder.

modern, *adj.* modern; fashionable, up-to-date; *die –e*, the modern trend. **-isieren,** *v.a.* modernize, bring up-to-date. **-ität,** *f.* modernity.

Modifi-kation, *f.* (-en) modification. **-zieren,** *v.a.* modify, qualify. **-zierung,** *f.* modification.

Modul, *m.* module (*Arch.*), modulus (*Math.*); *see also* **Model.**

Modu-lation, *f.* (-en) modulation, intonation. **-lationsfähigkeit,** *f.* adaptability (*of voice*). **-lieren,** *v.a.* modulate; *–lierte Trägerwelle*, modulated carrier (*Rad.*).

Mod-us, *m.* (-us, -i) mood (*Gram.*), mode, manner, way of doing.

mogel-n, *v.a.* (*coll.*) cheat (*at cards*). (*coll.*) **-ei,** *f.* cheating, trickery.

mög-en, *ir.v.a. & n.* (*aux.* h.) want, wish, like, desire, have a mind to, be inclined; be allowed, be able, be permitted *or* at liberty; (*as modal auxiliary* =) may, might; *ich mag nicht*, I would rather not; *ich mag das nicht*, I do not like that; *ich mag nicht nach Hause*, I do not want to go home; *es mag geschehen*, very well, I do not care; *wie dem auch sein mag*, be that as it may; *was ich auch (immer) tun mag*, no matter what I do; *wer mag das sein?* who might that be? *–e kommen was da will*, come what may; *möge es ihm wohl bekommen!* much good may it do him! *–e er sich wohl in Acht nehmen!* let him beware *or* look out! *leiden –en*, like well enough; *sich –en*, be fond of each other; (mögen *used for p.p.* gemocht, *when immediately preceded by an inf.*); *ich hätte es ihm nicht sagen –en*, I should not have liked to tell him; *ich habe es nicht tun –en*, I did not like *or* care to do it; *es mochte wohl schon 4 Uhr sein*, it was perhaps as late as 4 o'clock; *das Haus mochte noch etwa 100 Meter weiter entfernt sein*, the house may have been *or* was perhaps another 100 yards farther off; *X, Y, Z, und wie sie alle heißen mochten*, X, Y, Z, or whatever their names might have been; *ich mochte es ihm nicht sagen*, I did not like to tell him; *ich möchte gern*, I should like; *ich möchte lieber*, I would *or* had rather; *ich möchte am liebsten*, (most of all) I would prefer; *ich ließ ihm sagen, er möchte zu mir kommen*, I sent him word to call on me; *das möchte schwer zu beweisen sein*, (I fear) it will be difficult to prove that; *man möchte aus der Haut fahren*, it is enough to make one lose one's temper; *das Herz möchte mir zerspringen*, my heart is ready to break; *möchte es doch geschehen!* how I wish it would happen! **-lich,** *adj.* possible; practicable, feasible; *er gab alle*

–lichen Versprechungen, he made all kinds of promises; *alles –liche*, everything possible, all sorts *or* kinds of things, every conceivable thing; *das –liche tun*, do everything in one's power; *das ist eher –lich*, that is more likely to be feasible; *das einzige mir –liche Mittel*, the only means in my power; *das ist leicht –lich*, that may well be so; *etwas –lich machen*, render s.th. feasible; *nicht –lich!* not really, surely not, it can't be; *so schnell wie* or *als –lich*, as quickly as possible; *womöglich*, if it is *or* should be possible. **–lichenfalls,** *adv.*, **–licherweise,** *adv.* as far as *or* if possible; possibly, perhaps. **–lichkeit,** *f.* possibility, feasibility, practicability; contingency; potentiality; *außerhalb des Bereichs der –lichkeit*, outside the bounds of possibility; *einem die –lichkeiten bieten zu*, give a p. a chance to; *es ist keine –lichkeit (vorhanden)*, there is no chance; *nach –lichkeit*, as far as possible, as far as lies in one's power; *einem die –lichkeit verschaffen*, make it possible for a p., put s.o. in the way of. **–lichkeitsfall,** *m.* possibility, contingency. **–lichkeitsform,** *f.* subjunctive *or* conditional mood (*Gram.*). **–lichst,** *adv.* as much as (is) possible; *–lichst bald*, as soon as possible; *mit –lichster Geschwindigkeit*, with the greatest possible speed *or* the greatest speed possible; *sein –lichstes tun*, do one's utmost.

Mohn, *m.* (-s, -e) poppy (*Papaver*) (*Bot.*). **–blume,** *f.* poppy. **–kapsel,** *f.*, **–kopf,** *m.* poppy-head. **–saft,** *m.* poppy-juice, opium. **–same(n),** *m.* poppy-seed. **–säure,** *f.* meconic acid. **–stoff,** *m.* narcotic.

Mohr, *m.* (-en, -en) Moor; Negro. **–isch,** *adj.* Moorish.

Möhre, *f.* (-n), **Mohrrübe,** *f.* (-n) carrot.

Moir–é, *m.* & *n.* (-s, -s) moiré, watered *or* shot silk; moreen. **–ieren,** *v.a.* water, cloud (*silk*).

mok–ant, *adj.* sarcastic, sneering, mocking. **–ieren,** *v.r.* mock, sneer (*über einen*, at a p.).

Mokka, *m.* (-s, -s), **–kaffee,** *m.* Mocha (coffee). **–tasse,** *f.* small coffee-cup.

Molch, *m.* (-es, -e) salamander; (*fig.*, *coll.*) monster.

Mole, (*dial.* **Molo,** *m.*) *f.* (-n) mole, breakwater; jetty, pier.

Molek–el, *f.* (-n), **Molek–ül,** *n.* (-s, -e), molecule. **–ularbewegung,** *f.* molecular motion. **–ulargewicht,** *n.* molecular weight. **–ularkraft,** *f.* molecular energy. **–ularphysik,** *f.* molecular physics. **–ulartheorie,** *f.* molecular theory. **–ularwärme,** *f.* molecular heat. **–ülbau,** *m.* molecular structure.

molk, mölke, *see* **melken.**

Molk–e, *f.* (-en), **–en,** *m.*(-s, –) whey. **–enartig,** *adj.* wheyish. **–enkur,** *f.* diet of whey and whey products. **–ensäure** *f.* lactic acid. **–entrank,** *m.* posset. **–erei,** *f.* dairy. **–ereierzeugnisse,** *n.pl.* dairy-produce. **–ereigenossenschaft,** *f.* dairy-farmers' association. **–ig,** *adj.* containing *or* like whey.

moll, *adj.* & *n.* minor (*Mus.*). *a-moll*, A minor. **–akkord,** *m.* minor chord. **–tonart,** *f.* minor key. **–tonleiter,** *f.* minor scale.

Moll, *m.* (-(e)s, -e & -s) mull (*muslin*).

Molle, *f.* (*dial.*), *see* **Mulde;** beer-glass, glass cf beer; (*dial.*) bed (*cf.* **mollig**); (*coll.*) *mit –n gießen*, rain cats and dogs.

mollig, *adj.* soft, cosy, (*coll.*) comfortable, rounded; pleasant, snug; (*dial.*) chubby, buxom.

Molluske, *f.* (-n) mollusc.

Moment, 1. *m.* (-s, -e) moment, instant; *– mal!* (*coll.*) just a moment, (*sl.*) half a tick *or* mo. 2. *n.* moment (*Phys.*); force, impetus, impulse; motive, factor, instance, point of view; *das ausschlaggebende –*, the decisive factor; *das erregende –*, the initial impulse (bringing about the development of the dramatic action), the starting-point of the plot; *das psychologische –*, the psychological motive (*determining action of any kind*); *Trägheits–*, moment of inertia (*Phys.*); *Dreh–*, torque. **–an,** *adj.* momentary; for the present, just now. **–aufnahme,** *f.* snapshot. **–verschluß,** *m.* instantaneous shutter (*Phot.*).

Monad–e, *f.* (-en) monad, atom, radical element, ultimate unit. **–enlehre,** *f.* theory of monads, monadium (*Phil.*, *esp. Leibniz*).

Monarch, *m.* (-en, -en) monarch. **–engeschlecht,** *n.* princely line. **–ie,** *f.* monarchy. **–isch,** *adj.* monarchical. **–ist,** *m.* (-en, -en) monarchist, royalist. **–istisch,** *adj.* pro-monarchic, royalist.

Monat, *m.* (-s, -e) month; *vor anderthalb –en*, a month and a half ago, six weeks ago; (*C.L.*) *laufenden –s*, of the current month (*abbr.* inst.); *alle zwei –e*, every second month, alternate months; *– für –*, month after month. **–elang,** *adj.* for months. **–ig,** *suffix* (*in compounds* =) of so many months; *nach einer sechs–igen Reise*, after a six-months' tour; *ein drei–iges Kind*, a child of three months. **–lich,** *adj.* monthly; menstrual, every month; *eine drei–liche Zeitschrift*, a quarterly magazine; *–liche Lieferung*, monthly instalment (*of a publication*); *–liche Zahlung*, monthly instalment (*of payments*); *er bekommt sein –liches (Gehalt) am 15.*, his salary is paid monthly on the 15th; *das –liche*, menstrual period. **–sabschluß,** *m.* monthly balance. **–saufstellung,** *f.* monthly statement. **–sbericht,** *m.* monthly report. **–sfluß,** *m.* menses; *Aufhören des –sflusses*, menopause. **–sfrist,** *f.* space *or* respite of a month; *binnen –sfrist*, within a month. **–sgarderobe,** *f.* fashionable lady's gowns (*sold second-hand in almost new condition*). **–sgehalt,** **–geld,** *n.*, monthly salary *or* wages. **–sheft,** *n.* monthly number (*of a periodical*). **–skarte,** *f.*, monthly season-ticket. **–srate,** *f.* monthly quota *or* instalment. **–sschrift,** *f.* monthly magazine; *Halb–sschrift*, fortnightly review *or* magazine; *Drei–sschrift*, quarterly. **–stag,** *m.* day of the month, date. **–swechsel,** *m.* (student's) monthly allowance. **–szeiger,** *m.* calendar-hand (*on a clock*). **–szeit,** *f.* monthly period (*Med.*). **–weise,** *adv.* month by month, monthly; *die Zahlung erfolgt –weise*, the payment will be made by monthly instalments.

Mönch, *m.* (-es, -e) monk, friar; spindle (*of spiral staircase*). **–isch,** *adj.* monastic, monkish. **–skutte,** *f.* cowl, capuche; *ohne –skutte*, unfrocked, uncowled; *die –skutte anlegen*, turn monk. **–skloster,** *n.* monastery. **–slatein,** *n.* dog-Latin. **–sorden,** *m.* monastic order. **–splatte,** *f.* (monastic) tonsure. **–stum,** *n. see* **–tum.** **–swesen,** *n.* monachism, monasticism, monastic life. **–szucht,** *f.* monastic discipline. **–tum,** *n.* monasticism.

Mond, *m.* (-es, -e) moon; satellite; lune (*Geom.*); (*Poet.*) month; (*coll.*) bald patch *or* spot; *der – nimmt ab*, the moon is waning *or* on the wane; *den – anbellen*, give way to impotent rage; *auf dem – sein*, be up in the clouds; (*coll.*) *hinter dem –e sein*, be behind the times; *ein Loch in den – bohren*, swindle one's creditors; *nach dem – verlangen*, cry for the moon; *unter dem –e*, sub-lunary; *zunehmender –*, waxing moon. **–bahn,** *f.*, moon's orbit. **–beglänzt,** *adj.* moonlit. **–beschreibung,** *f.* selenography. **–(es)glanz,** *m.* light of the moon. **–enschein,** *m.* (*Poet.*) *see* **–schein.** **–finsternis,** *f.* eclipse of the moon. **–fläche,** *f.*, *see* **scheibe.** **–flecken,** *m.pl.* lunar markings. **–förmig,** *adj.* moon-shaped; lunate (*Bot.*). **–gebirge,** *n.* mountains of the moon. **–hell,** *adj.* moonlit. **–hof,** *m.* halo round the moon. **–jahr,** *n.* lunar year. **–kalb,** *n.* premature issue; (*fig.*) moon-calf, born fool. **–nacht,** *f.* moonlight night. **–phasen,** *f.pl.* phases of the moon. **–scheibe,** *f.* face of the moon. **–schein,** *m.* moonlight; (*coll.*) bald spot. **–sichel,** *f.* crescent moon. **–stein,** *m.* moonstone, selenite. **–strahl,** *m.* moonbeam. **–sucht,** *f.* sleep-walking, somnambulism. **–süchtig,** *adj.* given to sleep-walking, somnambulistic; (*fig.*) moon-struck. **–tafeln,** *f.pl.* lunar tables. **–umlauf,** *m.* lunar revolution. **–viertel,** *n.* quarter of the moon; quadrature (*Astr.*). **–wechsel,** *m.* change of the moon. **–zirkel,** *m.* lunar cycle.

mondän, *adj.* modish, in the vogue. **-e,** *f.* mondaine, woman moving in the fashionable world, worldly woman.
Moneten, *pl.* (*sl.*) money.
monieren, *v.a.* warn, remind; censure, criticize; object to, deplore.
Mono-gamie, *f.* monogamy. **-gam(isch),** *adj.* monogamous. **-gonie,** *f.* asexual reproduction. **-gramm,** *n.* monogram. **-graphie,** *f.* monograph, treatise, study. **-kel,** *n.* monocle. **-log,** *m.,* (-s, -e) monologue, soliloquy. **-phasisch,** *adj.* single-phase. **-pol,** *n.* (-s, -e) monopoly; *-pol treiben,* monopolize. **-polisieren,** *v.a.* monopolize. **-theismus,** *m.* monotheism. **-ton,** *adj.* monotonous, humdrum; (*coll.*) constant. **-tonie,** *f.* monotony.
Monstranz, *f.* (-en) monstrance, pyx (*Eccl.*).
monstr-ös, *adj.* monstrous, hideous, odious, frightful, misshapen. **-osität,** *f.* deformity, uncouthness, monstrosity, unsightliness, repulsiveness. **-um,** *n.* (-s, -en & *Austr. dial.* -a) monster, horror.
Monsun, *m.* (-s, -e) monsoon.
Mon-tag, *m.* Monday; *der blaue -tag,* holiday Monday; (*Prov.*) *-tag wird nicht wochenalt,* Monday does not outlast the week. **-tägig,** *adj.* (happening) on a Monday. **-täglich,** *adj.* every Monday, on Mondays. **-tags,** *adv.* on Monday; every Monday. **-tagsblatt,** *n.,* **-tagszeitung,** *f.* Monday paper. **-tagspost,** *f.* Monday's post *or* mail.
Mont-age [*pron.* mɔ̃ˈtɑʒə] *f.* (-n) setting *or* fitting up, erection, assembly, assembling, assembly-line. **-agegestell,** *n.* jig. **-agehalle,** *f.* assembly-shop. **-agerampe,** *f.* assembly-line. **-eur,** *m.* (-s, -e), (engine) fitter, mechanic, rigger. **-ieren,** *v.a.* erect, set *or* fit up, assemble, install, mount; clothe, equip (*soldiers*). **-ierhebel,** *m.* tyre-lever. **-ierung,** *f.* mounting, adjusting, erection, assembling, setting up; mount, setting (*of jewels, etc.*); clothing, equipment (*Mil.*). **-ierungskosten,** *pl.* assembly costs, charge for installation. **-ur,** *f.* (-en) uniform, livery, regimentals.
Montan-aktien, *f.pl.* mining-shares. **-industrie,** *f.* mining-industry. **-werte,** *m.pl., see* **-aktien.**
Monument, *n.* (-(e)s, -e) monument. **-alausgabe,** *f.* imposing, elaborate *or* de luxe edition. **-albau,** *m.* imposing structure. **-alwirkung,** *f.* imposing effect, impression of size, grandeur, etc.
Moor, *n.* (-s, -e) bog, fen, swamp, peat-bog. **-bad,** *n.* mud-bath. **-boden,** *m.* marshy soil. **-eiche,** *f.* bog-oak. **-ente,** *f.* fen-duck (*Aythya nyroca*) (*Orn.*). **-erde,** *f.* peaty soil. **-gegend,** *f.* fen-country, marshy land. **-gras,** *n.* sedge. **-huhn,** *n.* moor-cock; red grouse (*Lapogus*) (*Orn.*). **-ig,** *adj.* marshy, boggy, swampy. **-kultur,** *f.* marshland cultivation. **-torf,** *m.* turf, peat. **-wasser,** *n.* brackish water.
Moos, *n.* (-es, -e) moss, lichen; (*dial.*) peat-bog; (*Stud. sl.*) money, cash, dough; *irländisches -* Carragheen moss. **-bedeckt,** *adj.,* **-bewachsen.** *adj.* moss-grown. **-beere,** *f.* cranberry (*Vaccinium oxycoccus*) (*Bot.*). **-grün,** *adj.* moss-green. **-ig,** *adj.* mossy, moss-grown.
Mop, *m.* (-(e)s, -s) mop. **-pen,** *v.a. & n.* mop.
Mops, *m.* (-es, ⸚e) pug. **-en,** I. *v.a.* (*sl.*) pilfer, pinch, swipe. 2. *v.r.* (*sl.*) be bored; *sich schauderhaft -en,* be bored stiff. **-ig,** *adj.* pug-nosed; (*sl.*) boring; cocky; (*sl.*) *sich -ig machen,* assert o.s.
Moral, *f.* morals, morality, ethics, moral philosophy; moral, lesson; morale; *die - lesen,* point the moral. **-isch,** *adj.* moral; *-ische Betrachtungen anstellen,* moralize; *einen -ischen Druck auf einen ausüben,* bring moral pressure to bear on s.o.; (*coll.*) *einen -ischen* (*Kater*) *haben,* have qualms of conscience; *eine -ische Ohrfeige,* a dressing-down; *-isch unmöglich,* morally impossible. **-isieren,** *v.n.* (*aux.* h.) moralize. **-ist,** *m.* moral philosopher, moralist. **-ität,** *f.* morality; morality play. **-pauke,** *f.* reprimand, lecture; *jemandem eine -pauke halten,* read the riot act to s.o. **-philosophie,** *f.* moral philosophy, ethics.
Moräne, *f.* (-n) moraine.
Morast, *m.* (-es, ⸚e & -e) morass, quagmire, bog, mire. **-ig,** *adj.* muddy, boggy.
Morchel, *f.* (-n) morel (*edible fungus*).
Mord, *m.* (-es, -e) murder, assassination, homicide; (*sl.*) *das ist ja -,* it is a terrible business; *das ist der rein(st)e -,* that is a hopeless, impossible *or* perilous task; *Zeter und - schreien,* scream for help; *der - des Ehemannes an der Frau,* the murder of his wife by the husband; *- an dem Ehemann,* her murder of her husband; *einen - begehen,* commit a murder; *es gibt - und Totschlag,* it will end in bloodshed, there will be serious trouble. **-anschlag,** *m.* murderous attack, attempt on a p.'s life. **-axt,** *f.,* **-beil,** *n.* murderous weapon, battle-axe. **-begierig,** *adj., see* **-gierig. -brenner,** *m.* incendiary who endangers life. **-brennerei,** *f.* incendiarism, arson, (*Scots*) wilful fire-raising. **-bube,** *m.* assassin, cut-throat. **-en,** *v.a.* murder; slay, kill. **-falle,** *f.* lethal trap. **-geschichte,** *f.* tale of woe, (*coll.*) cock-and-bull story. **-geselle,** *m.* accessory to a murder; assassin. **-gier,** *f. see* **-lust. -gierig,** *adj.* bloodthirsty. **-io,** *int.* murder! help! **-kommission,** *f.* homicide squad. **-lust,** *f.* pathological urge to murder, bloodthirstiness. **-nacht,** *f.* night of a murder. **-rächer,** *m.* avenger of blood. **-raupe,** *f.* carnivorous caterpillar. **-schlacht,** *f.* bloody battle. (*coll.*) **-sgeschrei,** *n.* fearful outcry. (*coll.*) **-skalt,** *adj.* (*coll.*) terribly cold. (*coll.*) **-skerl,** *m.* devil of a fellow. **-slärm,** *m., see* **-sspektakel.** (*coll.*) **-smäßig,** *adj.* awful, enormous, terrific. (*coll.*) **-sspektakel,** *m.* hullabaloo, awful din. **-sucht,** *f. see* **-lust. -süchtig,** *see* **-gierig.** (*coll.*) **-swenig,** *adv.* precious little. **-tat,** *f.* murder, murderous act. **-versuch,** *m.* attempt at murder. **-waffe,** *f.* murderous weapon.
Mörder, *m.* (-s, -) murderer, (*fig.*) destroyer. **-grube,** *f.* den of thieves *or* cut-throats; (*coll.*) *aus seinem Herzen keine -grube machen,* wear one's heart upon one's sleeve, be very outspoken. **-isch,** *adj.* murderous, bloody. (*coll.*) **-lich,** *adj.* fearful, terrible; cruel; (*sl.*) enormous; *sie haben ihn -lich verhauen,* they beat him within an inch of his life.
Morelle, *f.* (-n) morello (*cherry*).
Mores, *pl.* morals; good manners; (*coll.*) *einen - lehren,* teach a p. manners.
morganatisch, *adj.* morganatic, left-handed (*marriage*).
Morgen, I. *m.* (-s, -) morning, daybreak, dawn, (*archaic & poet.*) east; *alle -,* every morning; *anbrechender -,* dawn; *des -s,* in the morning, of a morning; *am frühen -,* early in the morning; *gegen -,* towards daybreak, (*Poet.*) turned eastwards; *gestern -,* yesterday morning; *guten -,* good morning; *heute -,* this morning; *eines schönen -s,* one fine morning; *vorgestern -,* the morning before yesterday; *es wird -,* day *or* dawn is breaking. 2. *n.* (-s, -) the next day, the morrow. 3. measure of land (*local variations from 0·6 to 0·9 acres.* 4. *adv.* tomorrow; *- früh,* tomorrow morning; *- über acht Tage* or *- in acht Tagen,* tomorrow week; *- ist auch ein Tag,* there is always tomorrow; that is enough for today. **-andacht,** *f.* morning prayers, matins. **-ausgabe,** *f.,* **-blatt,** *n.* morning paper. **-brot,** *n.* (*dial.*) breakfast. **-d,** *adj.* (*archaic*) *see* **morgig. -dämmerung,** *f.* daybreak, dawn; *in der -dämmerung,* in the early twilight. **-dlich,** *adj.* in *or* of the morning, matutinal, fresh as the morn. **-essen,** *n.* (*Swiss dial.*) breakfast. **-gabe,** *f.* bridegroom's gift to bride on the day after marriage; dowry. **-grauen,** *n.* dawn *or* break of day, crack of dawn. **-kleid,** *n.* house-gown. **-land,** *n.* East; Orient, Levant. **-ländisch,** *adj.* eastern, oriental. **-luft,** *f.* morning breeze *or* air; *-luft wittern,* have wind of an advantage. **-post,** *f.* first *or* morning post. **-rock,** *m.* dressing-gown, housecoat, kimono. **-rot,** *n.,* **-röte,** *f.* dawn, sunrise, aurora; (*fig.*) youthful bloom, prime. **-s,** *adv.* in the morning, every morning. **-segen,** *m.* morning prayer, matins. **-seite,** *f.* eastern aspect. **-sonne,** *f.* morning sun; rising sun. **-stern,** *m.* morning star; medieval cudgel. **-stille,** *f.* calmness of the dawn. **-stunde,** *f.*; (*Prov.*) *-stunde hat Gold im Munde,* the early bird catches the worm. **-tau,** *m.* morning dew. **-trunk,** *m.* early morning drink. **-wache,** *f.* morning watch (*Naut.*). **-wind,** *m.* morning breeze; east wind. **-zeitung,** *f., see* **-blatt.**

morgig, *adj.* next day, of tomorrow.
moros, *adj.* morose, glum, ill-tempered.
Morphin, *n.* (*Austr. dial.*), *see* **Morphium.**
Morphium, *n.* morphine, morphia. **–einspritzung,** *f.* morphia injection. **–spritze,** *f.* syringe for injecting morphia; morphia injection. **–sucht,** *f.* morphinism. **–süchtige(r),** *m.* & *f.* morphia addict.
morsch, *adj.* decaying, decayed, decomposed, rotten; frail, fragile, tender. **–en,** *v.n.* decay, rot, crumble. **–heit,** *f.* rottenness, decay.
morse–n, *v.a.* & *n.* transmit in the morse code. **–schrift,** *f.* Morse code. **–zeichen,** *n.* morse signal.
Mörser, *m.* (-s, –) mortar; howitzer (*Artil.*). **–keule,** *f.* pestle. **–n,** *v.a.* grind with mortar and pestle. **–stößel,** *m.* pestle.
Mörtel, *m.* (-s, –) mortar; plaster, cement; *mit – bewerfen,* plaster. **–arbeit,** *f.* stucco-plastering. **–kelle,** *f.* trowel. **–träger,** *m.* hodman. **–trog,** *m.* hod.
Mosaik, *f.* & *Austr. dial. n.* (-s, -e), **–arbeit,** *f.* mosaic(-work), inlaid work. **–fußboden,** *m.* tesselated pavement.
Mosch, *m.* (*dial.*) waste, rubbish, scraps.
Moschee, *f.* (-n) mosque.
Moschus, *m.* musk. **–geruch,** *m.* musky odour. **–ochse,** *m.* musk-ox. **–tier,** *n.* musk-deer.
Moskito, *m.* (-s, -s) mosquito.
Most, *m.* (-es, -e) (*dial.*) fruit juice, new wine, must; cider; *wissen, wo Barthel den – holt,* be in the know, be behind the scenes. **–en,** *v.a.* make cider *or* must. **–kelter,** *f.,* **–presse,** *f.* wine-press; cider-press.
Mostrich, *m.* (*dial.*) French mustard.
Mot–ette, *f.* (-n) motet (*Mus.*). **–ion,** *f.* (-en) movement, exercise; motion (*in parliament, etc.*); *sich* (*Dat.*) (*eine kleine*) *–ion machen,* take some exercise. **–iv,** *n.* (-s, -e) motive; subject, theme, motif (*Mus.*). **–ivieren,** *v.a.* motivate. **–ivierung,** *f.* motivation.
Motor, *m.* (-s, -en) motor, engine; *elektromagnetischer –,* dynamo; *hochverdichteter –,* high-compression engine; *sternförmiger –,* radial engine; *untersetzter –,* geared motor; *der – setzt aus* or (*sl.*) *muckt* or *stottert,* the engine cuts out; *der – springt an,* the engine picks up; *den – voll beanspruchen,* run the engine full out. **–aufhängung,** *f.* engine suspension. **–ausfall,** *m.* engine failure. **–boot,** *n.* motor-boat, motor-launch, speed-boat. **–defekt,** *m.* engine failure. **–drehmoment,** *n.* engine torque. **–enanlage,** *f.* power-plant. **–enbetriebsstoff,** *m.* motor fuel. **–(en)gondel,** *f.* engine nacelle (*Av.*). **–enhalle,** *f.,* **–enhaus,** *n.* engine-house, power-house. **–haube,** *f.* bonnet, hood (*Motor.*), engine cowling (*Av.*). **–ig,** *adj. suffix,* -engined, *e.g. zwei–ig,* twin-engined. **–isch,** *adj.* motor, motive, kinetic. **–isieren,** *v.a.* motorize. **–kraftwagen,** *m.,* **–lastwagen,** *m.* motor-lorry. **–pflug,** *m.* motor-plough. **–rad,** *n.* motor-cycle. **–schaden,** *m.* engine trouble *or* failure. **–segler,** *m.* power glider (*Av.*). **–störung,** *f., see* **–schaden.** **–unfall,** *m.* motor accident.
Mott–e, *f.* (-en) moth; *du hast die –en,* you've a bee in your bonnet. **–enfraß,** *m.* damage done by moths. **–enpulver,** *n.* insect-powder, insecticide.
moussieren, *v.n.* effervesce, sparkle, froth, fizz; *–der Champagner,* sparkling champagne, (*sl.*) bubbly.
Möwe, *f.* (sea-)gull, mew.
Muck, *m.* (-(e)s, -e) faint *or* suppressed sound; *keinen – tun,* not utter a sound; *nicht – sagen,* (*coll.*) not say boo to a goose. **–e,** *f.* whim, crotchet, caprice, mood; sulks; *ein Pferd das –en hat,* a vicious horse; *er hat seine –en,* he has his peculiarities; *das Ding hat seine –en,* the matter has its snags; *einem die –en vertreiben,* cure a p. of his whims. **–en,** *v.n.* (*aux.* h.) utter a low sound; grumble, mutter, be up in arms; budge, move, stir, flinch; sulk; *–e nicht!* not a word *or* sound! hush! don't stir! **–er,** *m.* (-s, –) bigot, hypocrite. **–erei,** *f.* cant, hypocrisy. **–erhaft,** *adj.,* **–erisch,** *adj.* canting, hypocritical, self-righteous, pharisaical, bigoted. **–ern,** *v.n.* (*aux.* h.) (*coll.*) be a bigot *or* hypocrite; whine hypocritically. **–ertum,** *n.* cant, bigotry, hypocrisy. **–isch,** *adj.* cross, peevish. **–s,** *m.* (-es, -e), *see* **–.** **–sen,** *v.n.* (*aux.* h.) & *v.r. see* **–en.** **–ser,** *m.* grumbler, grouser. **–smäuschenstill,** *adj.* quiet as a mouse.
Mücke, (*dial.*) **Mucke,** *f.* (-n) gnat, midge; fly; (*archaic*) foresight (*of a gun*); (*Prov.*) *aus einer – einen Elefanten machen,* make a mountain of a molehill; *–n seihen und Kamele verschlucken,* strain at a gnat and swallow a camel; (*Prov.*) *mit Geduld und Spucke fängt man eine Mucke,* softly, softly, catchee monkey. **–nfett,** *n.* mare's nest, pigeon's milk; *einen nach –nfett schicken,* send a p. on a fool's errand. **–nflor,** *m.,* **–nnetz,** *n.* mosquito-net. **–nseiger,** *m.,* **–nsieber,** *m.* fidgety *or* fussy person. **–nstich,** *m.* midge *or* gnat-bite.
müd–e, *adj.* weary, tired, exhausted, fatigued, (*coll.*) worn out; *ich bin des Wartens –e,* I am tired of waiting; *ich bin –e auf ihn zu warten* I am tired of waiting for him; *ich bin es –e,* I am tired of it; *zum Umfallen –e,* tired to death; *sich –e arbeiten,* work till one is tired; *lebens–e,* weary *or* sick of life. **–igkeit,** *f.* weariness, fatigue, exhaustion, lassitude; *von der –igkeit übermannt werden,* be overcome with exhaustion.
[1]**Muff,** *m.* (-es, -e) muff (*for the hands*). **–e,** *f.* (-en) socket, coupling, sleeve (*Tech.*).
[2]**Muff,** *m.* (*dial.*) mouldy *or* musty smell; mould, mildew; grumbler, grouser. **–el,** *m.* mouth, snout, muzzle; grumbler, grouser; gabbler, mumbler, mutterer. **–eln,** *v.a.* & *n.* (*aux.* h.) mumble, mutter, gabble; champ (*one's food*); mope, sulk; grumble, grouse; smell musty *or* fusty (*also* müffeln). **–en** *v.n.* (*aux.* h.) *see* **–eln.** **–ig,** *adj.* (*also* müffig) mouldy, musty, fusty; cross, sulky, disgruntled, glum. **–lig,** *adj.* (*dial.*) cross, sulky, disgruntled, glum.
Müffchen, *n.* (-s, –) mitten, muff.
Muffel, *f.* (-n) muffle, crucible (*Chem.*). **–ofen,** *m.* muffle-furnace.
müffeln, *v.n. see* **muff–eln.**
Müh–e, *f.* (-en) trouble, pains, toil, labour, effort; *sich* (*Dat.*) *–e geben,* take pains (*mit* or *um,* with *or* over); *es lohnt die –e,* it is quite worth while; *einem –e machen,* give a p. trouble, make trouble for a p.; *sich –e machen,* see *sich –e geben*; *machen Sie sich keine –e!* do not go to any trouble; *sich die –e nehmen,* take the trouble (to); *mit –(e) und Not,* barely, only just, with difficulty; *keine –e* or *–en scheuen,* spare no pains; *sich jeder –e unterziehen,* go to no end of trouble; *sich* (*Acc.*) *keine –e verdrießen lassen,* spare no pains; *die* or *seine –e umsonst haben,* have all the trouble in vain *or* to no purpose; *nicht der –e wert,* not worth while. **–en,** *v.r.* (*mit einer S.*) take pains *or* trouble (about a th.). **–elos,** *adj.* easy, effortless. **–elosigkeit,** *f.* ease, easiness, facility. **–evoll,** *adj.* laborious, difficult, troublesome, irksome. **–ewaltung,** *f.* care, trouble *or* pains (taken), assiduity; *für seine –ewaltung,* for the trouble he has taken. **–sal,** *n.* & *f.* toil, difficulty, trouble, hardship, affliction, distress. **–sam,** *adj.* troublesome, laborious, difficult, hard, painful, irksome, intricate; assiduous, painstaking; *sich –sam ernähren,* struggle hard to get a living. **–samkeit,** *f.* difficulty, trouble, irksomeness. **–selig,** *adj.* difficult, hard, laborious, toilsome. **–seligkeit,** *f.* irksomeness, hardship, misery.
muhen, *v.n.* (*aux.* h.) low (*of cows*).
Mühl–e, *f.* (-en) mill; crusher, grinder; game played with draughtsmen; *das ist Wasser auf seine –e,* that is grist to his mill. **–bach,** *m.* mill-stream. **–bursche,** *m.* miller's man. **–enarbeiter,** *m.* mill-hand. **–enbauer,** *m.* millwright. **–enrad,** *n., see* **–rad.** **–enflügel,** *m.* sail of a windmill. **–enstein,** *m., see* **–stein.** **–enteich,** *m., see* **–teich.** **–enwehr,** *n., see* **–wehr.** **–espiel,** *n.* game played on a board with counters. **–graben,** *m.* mill-race. **–rad,** *n.* mill-wheel. **–steiger,** *m.* headman *or* inspector of mills. **–stein,** *m.* millstone. **–steinkragen,** *m.* ruffle. **–teich,** *m.* mill-pond. **–wasser,** *n.* mill-race. **–wehr,** *n.* mill-dam. **–werk,** *n.* grinding mechanism. **–zwang,** *m.* obligation to have one's corn ground at a certain mill.

Muhme, *f.* (-n) (*archaic*) aunt; elderly female relation.
Mulatte, *m.* (-n, -n) mulatto.
Muld-e, *f.* (-en) tray, trough, mould, tub, bowl, hollow, basin (*also Geol.*); depression, re-entrant (*Geol.*); *eine -e Blei*, a pig of lead; (*coll.*) *es gießt wie mit -en* it is raining cats and dogs. **-enblei,** *n.* pig-lead. **-enförmig, -ig,** *adj.* trough *or* basin-shaped.
Müll, Mull, *m.* dust, sweepings, rubbish, refuse; humus, mould. **-abfuhr,** *f.* removal of refuse, emptying dust-bins. **-eimer,** *m.* dust-bin. **-erde,** *f.* humus soil, leaf mould. **-haufen,** *m.* rubbish *or* refuse heap. **-kasten,** *m.* dust-bin. **-kutscher,** *m.* dustman. **-verbrennungsofen,** *m.* incinerator. **-wagen,** *m.* dust-cart.
Mull, *m.* & *n.* (-(e)s, -e) mull (*muslin*).
Müller, *m.* (-s) miller; meal-worm (*Ent.*). **-ei,** *f.* miller's trade. **-esel,** *m.* drudge; dunce. **-gesell,** *m.*, **-knappe,** *m.* miller's man *or* apprentice. **-in,** *f.* miller's wife.
Mulm, *m.* (-(e)s, -e) decay, rot; rotten wood; mould, humus; ore-dust. **-en,** 1. *v.a.* pulverize. 2. *v.n.* (*aux.* s.) turn to dust, crumble. **-ig,** *adj.* worm-eaten, decayed; friable, earthy, dusty; (*fig.*) precarious.
Multipli-kation, *f.* multiplication. **-kationszeichen,** *n.* multiplication sign. **-kator,** *m.* (-s, -en) multiplier. **-zieren,** *v.a.* multiply (*mit*, by).
Multipl-um, *n.* (-ums, -a) multiple.
Mul-us, *m.* (-i) (*Studs. sl.*) fresher, university entrant.
Mumi-e, *f.* (-en) mummy. **-enhaft,** *adj.* mummy-like. **-fizieren,** *v.a.* mummify, embalm.
Mumm, *m.*; (*sl.*) *keinen – (in den Knochen) haben*, have no guts or spunk.
[1]**Mumme,** *f.* a kind of strong (*Brunswick*) beer.
[2]**Mumme,** *f.* (-n) disguise, mask; masquerader. **-ln,** *v.n.* (*aux.* h.) mumble; champ, munch. **-lgreis,** *m.* old fogy. **-n,** *v.a.* muffle up; mask, disguise. **-nkleid,** *n.* fancy-dress, costume. **-nschanz,** *m.*, **-nspiel,** *n.* masquerade. **-r,** *m.* masquerader, mummer. **-rei,** *f.* mummery; fancy-dress ball.
Mummel, *f.* (-n) (*dial.*) water-lily.
Mumpitz, *m.* (*sl.*) bosh, balderdash, stuff, nonsense.
Mund, *m.* (-es, -e & ⸗er) mouth; muzzle, os, orifice, opening, aperture, vent; *sich (Dat.) eine S. am -e absparen*, stint o.s. of food for a th.; *den – aufsperren*, stand gaping; *einem über den – fahren*, cut a p. short; *nicht auf den – gefallen sein*, have a ready tongue; *im -e führen*, always be talking about; *den – halten*, hold one's tongue; *reinen – halten*, keep a secret; *an seinem – hängen*, hang on his words; *von* or *aus der Hand in den – leben*, live from hand to mouth; *einem etwas in den – legen*, suggest to a p. what to say; attribute a statement to s.o., have *or* make (*a character*) say s.th.; *in aller (Leute) – sein*, be much talked of, be on everybody's lips; *Sie nehmen mir das Wort aus dem -e*, that is just what I was going to say, you took the words out of my mouth; *ich mag das Wort nicht in den – nehmen*, I cannot bring myself to use that word; *kein Blatt vor den – nehmen*, call a spade a spade, not choose one's words; *einem nach dem -e reden*, flatter a p., say what s.o. expects of one; *auf den – schlagen*, contradict flatly; *er ist wie auf den – geschlagen*, he is quite dumbstruck; *einem etwas in den – schmieren*, leave a p. no choice but to believe s.th.; *den – spitzen*, screw up one's mouth; *einem das Wort im -e umdrehen*, twist a p.'s words *or* meaning; *sich den – verbrennen*, put one's foot in it; *den – voll nehmen*, brag, boast, talk big; *einem den – wässerig machen*, make s.o.'s mouth water. **-art,** *f.* idiom, dialect. **-artlich,** *adj.* dialectal, provincial. **-bäcker,** *m.* royal baker. **-bedarf,** *m.* provisions, victuals. **-en,** *v.n.* (*aux.* h.) taste good, be appetizing; *ich lasse es mir -en*, I fall to heartily; *es -et mir*, I relish that, I like it. **-faul,** *adj.* tongue-tied; taciturn. **-fäule,** *f.* thrush (*Med.*). **-fertig,** *adj.* ready with one's tongue. **-gerecht,** *adj.* easy (to pronounce); palatable, fit *or* suitable for eating; (*fig.*) suitable, attractive. **-harmonika,** *f.* mouth-organ. **-höhle,** *f.* oral cavity. **-klappe,** *f.* epiglottis. **-klemme,** *f.* lockjaw. **-knebel,** *m.* gag. **-koch,** *m.* royal cook. **-loch,** *n.* blow-hole (*of a flute*). **-pflege,** *f.* dental care. **-raub,** *m.* pilfering food, picking. **-schenk,** *m.* cupbearer. **-sperre,** *f.* lockjaw. **-stellung,** *f.* position of the mouth (*Phonet.*). **-stück,** *n.* mouth-piece; tip (*of cigarettes*): bridle-bit; (*vulg.*) mouth, tongue. **-teil,** *m.* allowance, ration. **-tot,** *adj.* dead in law; prevented from speaking; *einen -tot machen*, silence a p.; reduce a p. to silence. **-tuch,** *n.* (table)-napkin, serviette. **-voll,** *m.* mouthful. **-vorrat,** *m.* victuals, provisions. **-wasser,** *n.* mouth-wash, gargle. **-werk,** *n.* (*coll.*) glib tongue; (*coll.*) *er hat ein gutes -werk*, he has the gift of the gab. **-winkel,** *m.* corner of the mouth.
Münd-el, *m.* (*Austr. dial. n.*), (*when applying to a girl also f.*) (-eln) ward, minor. **-elgeld,** *n.*, **-elgut,** *n.* property of a ward *or* minor. **-elsicher,** *adj.* absolutely safe (*of investments, etc.*), gilt-edged (*of securities*). **-elstand,** *m.* pupilage. **-ig,** *adj.* of age; *-ig werden*, come of age; *einen für -ig erklären, einen -ig sprechen*, declare a p. of age; *der -ige*, person who has attained his majority, p. no longer a minor. **-igkeit,** *f.* majority. **-igmachung,** *f.*, **-igsprechung,** *f.* declaring (*a person*) of age; (*fig.*) emancipation.
münd-en, *v.n.* (*aux.* h.) flow, run, fall, empty *or* discharge (into). **-lich,** *adj.* oral, verbal, by word of mouth; viva-voce; *-liche Auskunft*, information by word of mouth; *-licher Verkehr*, personal intercourse; *-liche Prüfung*, oral *or* viva-voce examination. **-lichkeit,** *f.* oral proceedings (*Law*); oral character (*of anything*). **-ung,** *f.* mouth (*of a river*), estuary; opening, aperture, outlet, orifice; muzzle (*of gun*). **-ungsfeuer,** *n.* gun-flash. **-ungsfeuerfrei,** *adj.* flashless. **-ungsgebiet,** *n.* delta. **-ungsgeschwindigkeit,** *f.* muzzle velocity. **-ungsknall,** *m.* muzzle blast. **-ungsrohr,** *n.* torpedo tube. **-ungswaag(e)rechte,** *f.* chord of trajectory (*Artil.*).
mund-ieren, *v.a.* make a fair copy of; engross (*Law*). **-ierung,** *f.* engrossing. **-um,** *n.* (-ums, -a) fair copy.
Munition, *f.* (-en) ammunition, military *or* naval stores; *– vorbringen*, bring up ammunition. **-sarbeiter,** *m.* munition-worker. **-saufzug,** *m.* ammunition hoist. **-seinsatz,** *m.* expenditure of ammunition. **-sergänzung,** *f.*, **-sersatz,** *m.* replenishment of ammunition. **-skammer,** *f.* magazine. **-skolonne,** *f.* ammunition-column *or* train. **-slager,** *n.* ammunition depot *or* dump. **-snachschub,** *m.*, **-sversorgung,** *f.* ammunition-supply.
munkel-n, *v.a.* & *n.* (*aux.* h.) whisper, mutter; do s.th. in the dark; *man -t*, it is rumoured; *ich habe davon -n hören*, I have heard it rumoured; (*Prov.*) *im Dunkeln ist gut -n*, night is the friend of lovers; *das Wetter -t*, the weather is threatening.
Münster, *n.* (& *rare m.*) (-s, –) cathedral, minster.
munter, 1. *adj*, wide-awake; lively, alive, brisk, vigorous; gay, cheerful, blithe, merry; bright, gay (*of colours*); allegro (*Mus.*); *du bist wohl nicht ganz –*, are you mad? *gesund und –*, hale and hearty; *er war schon –*, he was already up and doing; *er war früh –*, he was astir early. **-keit,** *f.* liveliness, sprightliness; cheerfulness, gaiety.
Münz-e, *f.* (-n) coin, coinage; small change; medal; mint; *-en schlagen*, coin, strike coins; *bare -e*, ready cash; *falsche -e*, base coin; *landesübliche -e*, local currency; *klingende -e*, hard cash; *einem mit gleicher -e zahlen*, pay a p. in his own coin; *für bare -e nehmen*, take for gospel truth, believe implicitly, take at its face value. **-amt,** *n.* directory of the mint. **-anstalt,** *f.* mint. **-beschickung,** *f.* alloyage. **-einheit,** *f.* monetary unit, standard of currency. **-en,** *v.a.* &*n.* (*aux.* h.) coin, mint money; forge; *gemünztes Geld*, specie; *es war auf ihn gemünzt*, that was meant for *or* aimed at him. **-(en)sammlung,** *f.* collection of coins. **-er,** *m.* coiner, minter, forger. **-fälscher,** *m.* coiner, forger. **-fälschung,** *f.* uttering false coin. **-fernspre-**

cher, *m.* coin-box telephone; telephone-kiosk. **-freiheit,** *f.* right to strike coinage. **-fuß,** *m.* standard (*of coinage*). **-gehalt,** *m.* standard of alloy, fineness (*of coins*). **-gewicht,** *n.* standard weight. **-herr,** *m.* mint-master. **-justierer,** *m.* mint-assayer. **-kabinett,** *n.* collection of coins. **-kenner,** *m.* numismatist. **-kunde,** *f.* numismatics. **-kunst,** *f.* art of coining. **-meister,** *m., see* **-herr.** **-prägung,** *f.* coinage. **-presse,** *f.* coining-press. **-probe,** *f.* assay (*of coin*). **-rand,** *m.* edge *or* rim of a coin. **-recht,** *n.*, **-regal,** *n., see* **-freiheit.** **-schlag,** *m.* coinage. **-schrift,** *f.* inscription on a coin. **-stecher,** *m.* die-sinker. **-stempel,** *m.* die. **-stück,** *n.* coin; planchet. **-verbrechen,** *n.*, **-verfälschung,** *f.* uttering base coin. **-vertrag,** *m.* monetary convention. **-wardein,** *m.* assay-master. **-wert,** *m.* nominal value. **-wesen,** *n.* monetary system. **-zeichen,** *n.* mint mark.

mürb-e, 1. *adj.* mellow; tender, ripe, soft; well-cooked; crisp, brittle, friable, short (*of pastry*); unsound (*of ice*); suffering from dry-rot; unnerved; pliable; *-e machen*, make pliable, cause to yield; unnerve; (*coll.*) soften up (*Mil.*), break (*a p.'s spirit*); (*vom Schicksal*) *-e gemacht*, broken, battered; *-e werden*, give in. 2. *f.*, **-heit,** *f.*, **-igkeit,** *f.* mellowness; tenderness; dry-rot; friability; suppleness. **-(e)braten,** *m.* roast sirloin. **-ekuchen,** *m.* shortbread, shortcake. **-(e)teig,** *m.* short pastry.

Mur-bruch, *m.* (*dial.*) landslip. **-(e),** *f.* scree. **-gang,** *m., see* **-bruch.**

murksen, 1. *v.n.* (*coll.*) botch *or* bungle one's work. 2. *v.a.* (*hum.*) rub out, do for, do in (*murder*).

Murmel, *f.* (-s, –) (*dial.*) marble (*boys' toy*). **-spiel,** *n.* game at marbles.

murmel-n, *v.a. & n.* (*aux.* h.) murmur, mutter. **-tier,** *n.* marmot; *schlafen wie ein -tier*, sleep like a top.

murr-en, *v.n.* (*aux.* h.) murmur, grouse, grumble (*über*, at). **-kater,** *m.*, **-kopf,** *m.* grouser, grumbler. **-köpfig,** *adj., see* **mürrisch.**

mürrisch, *adj.* surly, morose, sullen, disgruntled, bad-tempered.

Mus, *n.* (-es, -e) purée, pulp, jam; stewed fruit; *zu – schlagen*, beat to a jelly. **-artig,** *adj.* pulpy, pasty, thick.

Muschel, *f.* (-n) mussel; shell; ear-piece (*Phone*); conch (*Anat.*); thumb (*of a latch*); lavatory pan *or* pedestal, wash-hand basin. **-ig,** *adj.* conchoidal. **-artig, -förmig,** *adj.* shell-like, conchoidal. **-gehäuse,** *n.* shell (*of mussels, etc.*). **-ig,** *adj., see* **-artig.** **-kalk,** *m.* shell lime(stone) (*Geol.*). **-kenner,** *m.* conchologist. **-kunde,** *f.* conchology. **-linie,** *f.* conchoid (*Math.*). **-rauschen,** *n.* humming of a shell. **-schale,** *f., see* **-gehäuse.** **-schieber,** *m.* side-valve (*Motor.*). **-tier,** *n.* mollusc, shell-fish.

Mus-e, *f.* (-en) muse. **-enalmanach,** *m.* poetical annual. **-enberg,** *m.* Parnassus, Helicon. **-enborn,** *m., see* **-enquell.** **-enfreund,** *m.* poetry lover, patron of poetry. **-engott,** *m.* Apollo. **-enquell,** *m.* Hippocrene. **-enroß,** *n.* Pegasus. **-ensitz,** *m.* seat of the Muses; academy, university. **-ensohn,** *m.* poet; university student. **-enstadt,** *f.* university town. **-eum,** *n.* (-eums, -een) museum. **-isch,** *adj.* sacred *or* devoted to the Muses, favoured by the Muses; poetic, musical, artistic.

Musik, *f.* music; band; *in – setzen*, set to music; (*coll.*) *ohne – abziehen*, steal *or* sneak away; *da kommt die –*, there comes the band. **-alien,** *pl.* music (books), printed music. **-alienhandlung,** *f.* music-shop. **-alisch,** *adj.* musical, musically gifted; *-alisches Gehör*, good ear for music. **-alität,** *f.* musicality. **-ant,** *m.* (*poet.*) musician; performer; *herumziehende -anten*, itinerant musicians; (*coll.*) *hier liegt ein -ant begraben!* I tripped over s.th.; *da sitzen die -anten!* there's the rub! **-antenknochen,** *m.* funny-bone. **-aufführung,** *f.* musical performance. **-begleitung,** *f.* musical accompaniment. **-direktor,** *m.*, **-dirigent,** *m.*, **-meister,** *m.* conductor; bandmaster (*Mil.*). **-drama,** *n.* opera. **-er,** *m.* composer, musician, bandsman. **-fest,** *n.* music(al) festival. **-freund,** *m.* music lover. **-instrument,** *n.* musical instrument. **-kenner,** *m.* connoisseur of music. **-korps,** *n.* band (of musicians). **-lehrer,** *m.* music teacher. **-liebhaber,** *m.* music lover, amateur musician. **-mappe,** *f.* music-case. **-meister,** *m.* director of music, bandmaster. **-saal,** *m.* concert hall. **-schule,** *f.* school *or* academy of music; music primer. **-stimme,** *f.* part (*in music*). **-stunde,** *f.* music lesson. **-unterricht,** *m.* music lesson. **-us,** *m.* (-us, -er *or* Musizi) (*archaic*), *see* **-er.** **-verein,** *m.* musical society. **-werk,** *n.* musical work, composition; musical box. **-wissenschaft,** *f.* musicology.

mus-isch, *see under* **Mus-e.** **-ivisch,** *adj.* inlaid, mosaic.

musizier-en, *v.n.* (*aux.* h.) play *or* have music; *des Abends wurde stets -t*, we always had music in the evenings.

Muskat, *m.* (-s, -e), **-e,** *f.* (-en) mace, nutmeg. **-eller(wein),** *m.* muscatel, muscadel. **-enblüte,** *f.* mace. **-nuß,** *f.* nutmeg.

Muskel, *m.* (-s, -n), *or f.* (-n) muscle. **-ansatz,** *m.* strenuous work. **-anstrengung,** *f.* muscular exertion. **-band,** *n.* ligament. **-bau,** *m.* muscular structure. **-binde,** *f.* ligament, fascia. **-eiweiß,** *n.* myosia. **-faser,** *f.* muscular *or* muscle fibre. **-gewebe,** *n.* muscular tissue. **-haut,** *f.* muscular membrane. **-ig,** *adj.* muscular, with muscles, sinewy. **-kater,** *m.* stiffness (after exertion). **-kraft,** *f.* muscular strength. **-lehre,** *f.* myology. **-magen,** *m.* gizzard. **-mann,** *m.* skinned figure (*for study of muscles*). **-schwund,** *m.* atrophy of the muscles. **-sehne,** *f.* tendon. **-stark,** *adj.* muscular. **-stärke,** *f.* muscular strength. **-stoff,** *m.* sarcosine. **-zergliederung,** *f.*, **-zerlegung,** *f.* myotomy. **-zerrung,** *f.* sprained muscle. **-zucker,** *m.* inositol.

Musket-e, *f.* (-en) musket. **-ier,** *m.* (-s, -e) musketeer.

Muskul-atur, *f.* (-en) muscular system. **-ös,** *adj.* muscular, brawny, sinewy.

muß, mußt, *see* **müssen.** **Muß,** *n.* (*Austr. dial. m.*) (*indec.*) necessity, compulsion; *es ist kein – dabei*, there is no real need for it; (*Prov.*) *– ist eine harte Nuß*, necessity is a hard master; *das harte –*, inalienable necessity; *– ist ein bitter Kraut*, compulsion is always unpleasant *or* is hard to swallow. **-baier,** *m.* native of Franconia. **-pole,** *m.* (*Nat. Soc.*) Pole against his own wishes, subject of a district annexed by Poland. **-preuße,** *m.* native of Hanover, Schleswig-Holstein, or other district annexed by Prussia.

Muße, *f.* leisure, spare time; *in* (*aller*) *–*, *mit –*, at (one's) leisure, in a leisurely manner; *– haben*, have leisure, be at leisure. **-stunde,** *f.* leisure hour. **-zeit,** *f.* spare time.

Musselin, *m.* (-s, -e) muslin. **-en,** *adj.* muslin.

müssen, *ir.v.n. aux. of mood*, be obliged to, have to, must; (*preceded by inf.* müssen *is used for p.p.* gemußt); *ich muß fort* (*ellipt.*), I must go *or* leave; *der Brief muß zur Post* (*ellipt.*), the letter must go to the post *or* must be posted; *ich muß lachen*, I cannot help laughing; *es muß gewiß schon spät sein*, it must be late already; *er muß bald kommen*, he will certainly be here soon; *wenn es geschehen muß*, if it is inevitable; *das muß wahr sein*, that is (inevitably *or* undeniably) true; that is doubtless true; *das muß man sagen*, one has to acknowledge it, it must be admitted, to be sure; *ich muß, ich mag wollen oder nicht*, I must, whether I want to or not; *was sein muß, muß sein*, what has to be, cannot be averted; *eine Frau wie sie sein muß*, a woman such as one would wish, a model wife; a paragon of a woman; *kein Mensch muß –*, no one has to submit to compulsion; *es mußte sich gerade so fügen, daß . . .*, chance would have it that . . .; *er mußte sündigen*, he could not help sinning; *nach meiner Berechnung müßte er bald hier sein*, I reckon he must be *or* cannot help but be here before long; *du müßtest vor Scham in den Erdboden sinken*, you must have hidden *or* surely had to hide your face in shame; *ich müßte mich sehr irren, wenn . . .*, I should be very much mistaken if . . .; *er kommt noch, er müßte denn krank sein*, he is sure to come, unless he is ill; *er hätte fleißiger sein* –, he ought to have been more diligent; *ich habe es tun* –, I had to do it; *Sie* – *wissen*, you ought to know.

müßig, *adj.* idle, lazy; unemployed, at leisure; *eine* –*e Frage*, a question not worth asking, an idle question; *sich* –*e Gedanken machen*, speculate idly; – *gehen*, idle, be idle; – *hinbringen*, idle away; –*es Kapital*, unproductive capital; *sein Geld* – *lassen*, let one's capital lie idle; *es wäre* –, it would not be worth while; it would be superfluous. **–en,** only in *sich gemüßigt sehen*, find o.s. compelled, be left with no alternative but. **–gang,** *m.* idleness, sloth, indolence; (*Prov.*) –*gang ist aller Laster Anfang*, idleness is the root of all evil; –*gang ist des Teufels Ruhebank*, the devil finds work for idle hands. **–gänger,** *m.* idler, loafer.

mußte, müßte, *see* **müssen.**

Mußteil, *m.*, (*Austr. dial.*) **Musteil,** *m.* (-s, -e) widow's portion.

Muster, *n.* (-s, –) model, ideal, paragon, pattern, design, sample, specimen, type, standard, example; – *ohne Wert*, sample with no commercial value; *sich* (*Dat.*) *zum* – *nehmen*, take as a model; *nach* – *machen*, make to (a) pattern; *nach* –, according to pattern, as per sample. **–anlage,** *f.*, **–betrieb,** *m.* model plant. **–aussetzen,** *n.* designing. **–bild,** *n.* paragon, model, ideal. **–buch,** *n.* book of patterns. **–gültig,** *adj.*, **–haft,** *adj.* model, exemplary, perfect; classical, standard. **–karte,** *f.* pattern-card, sample card. **–klammer,** *f.* paper-fastener. **–knabe,** *m.* model boy, prig. **–lager,** *n.* showroom(s); store of samples. **–leistung,** *f.* splendid achievement, record. **–mäßig,** *adj.* standard, typical. **–n,** *v.a.* survey, examine, criticize, muster; (*archaic*) pass in review, inspect (*Mil.*); figure, pattern; *gemusterter Stoff*, patterned *or* figured stuff. **–probe,** *f.* pattern. **–sammlung,** *f.* anthology; specimen collection. **–schule,** *f.* model school. **–schüler,** *m.* model pupil. **–schutz,** *m.* registered design, trademark, patent, copyright. **–sendung,** *f.* parcel of samples. **–stück,** *n.* model, pattern; specimen, perfect example. **–ung,** *f.* examination; inspection, review (*Mil.*). **–wort,** *n.* paradigm (*Gram.*). **–zeichner,** *m.* pattern-maker, designer. **–zeichnung,** *f.* design.

Mut, *m.* courage, pluck, fortitude, boldness, mettle, spirit; state of mind, mood, humour; *einem* – *einflößen*, see *einem* – *zusprechen*; *mir fiel* or *sank der* –, my heart failed me; – *fassen*, summon *or* pluck up courage, take heart; *frischer* – *zur Tat*, a high spirit of endeavour; *gutes* or *guten* –(*e*)*s sein*, be of good courage *or* cheer, be full of hope; *einem* – *machen*, see *einem* – *zusprechen*; *den* – *sinken lassen*, be discouraged; *nur nicht den* – *verlieren!* do not lose courage, never say die! *wie ist dir zu* –*e?* (*see also* **zumute**) how do you feel? *einem* – *zusprechen*, inspire a p. with courage. **–beseelt,** *adj.*, *see* **–voll. –en,** 1. *v.n.* (*aux.* s.) *only p.p.* gemutet *or* gemut; minded, disposed; *wohl gemut sein* (*see also* **wohlgemut**), be of good cheer. 2. *v.a.* demand, sue for, claim. (*um*) *eine Grube* –*en*, stake a claim (*Min.*); (*archaic*) *das Meisterstück* –*en*, submit a masterpiece to one's guild. **–er,** *m.* petitioner, claimant. **–erfüllt,** *adj.*, *see* **–voll. –ig,** *adj.* courageous, brave, valiant, stout-hearted; spirited, mettlesome; –*ig!* courage! (*Prov.*) *dem* –*igen gehört die Welt*, Fortune favours the brave. **–jahr,** *n.* (*archaic*) year in which journeyman submits his masterpiece; journeyman's travel year. **–los,** *adj.* despondent, spiritless, discouraged, dejected. **–losigkeit,** *f.* despondency, dejection. **–maßen,** *v.a.* (*insep.*) have an idea of, guess, suppose, presume, surmise, conjecture. **–maßlich,** *adj.* probable, conjectural, presumable, supposed, apparent. **–maßlichkeit,** *f.* probability. **–maßung,** *f.* guess, surmise, conjecture, supposition, suspicion. **–maßungsweise,** *adv.* at *or* as a guess. **–ung,** *f.* application, appeal; demand for a concession, claim (*Min.*). **–voll,** *adj.* full of courage, filled with courage, very courageous, high-spirited. **–wille,** *m.* wantonness, mischievousness; petulance. **–willig,** *adj.* wanton, mischievous, petulant; *sich* –*willig in Gefahr begeben*, rush headlong into danger; –*willige Beschädigung*, wanton damage. **–willigerweise,** *adv.* wantonly, out of mischief.

Mütchen, *n.* (*coll.*) *sein* – *kühlen*, vent one's anger (on).

mutieren, *v.a.* (*aux.* h.) change, break (*as the voice*).

[1]**Mutter,** *f.* (¨) mother; matrix (*Found.*); *sie fühlt sich* –, she is pregnant, she is with child; *eine ledige* –, an unmarried mother; *ein Mädchen zur* – *machen*, put a girl in the family way; *bei* – *Grün übernachten*, sleep *or* pass the night in the open; *sie wird* –, she is going to become a mother, she is having a child; –*s Geburstag*, mother's birthday; (*coll.*) *er hat's dort wie bei* –*n*, he is treated as one of the family. **–band,** *n.* ligament of the womb. **–baum,** *m.* parent tree. **–biene,** *f.* queen-bee. **–boden,** *m.*, *see* **–erde. –bruder,** *m.* maternal uncle. **–erde,** *f.* mother earth; native soil; garden mould, top-soil. **–fieber,** *n.* puerperal fever, milk fever. **–freuden,** *f.pl.* maternal joy; –*freuden entgegensehen*, be expecting, be in a certain condition. **–füllen,** *n.* filly. **–fürsorge,** *f.* maternity welfare. **–gesellschaft,** *f.* parent company (*C.L.*). **–gottes,** *f.* Blessed Virgin. **–hals,** *m.* neck of the uterus (*Anat.*). **–haus,** *n.* chief *or* head office. **–kind,** *n.* mother's pet *or* darling. **–kompaß,** *m.* master compass. **–korn,** *n.* (-e) ergot. **–kuchen,** *m.* placenta. **–lamm,** *n.* ewe lamb. **–land,** *n.* mother country. **–lauge,** *f.* mother-lye, mother-liquor. **–leib,** *m.* womb, uterus; *vom* –*leibe an*, from birth. **–liebe,** *f.* mother-love. **–los,** *adj.* motherless. **–mal,** *n.* (-e) birth-mark, mole. **–milch,** *f.* mother's milk; *mit der* –*milch einsaugen*, have bred in the bone. **–mord,** *m.* matricide. **–mund,** *m.* orifice of the uterus. **–pferd,** *n.* mare. **–pflicht,** *f.* maternal duty. **–rohr,** *n.* Fallopian tube. **–schaf,** *n.* ewe. **–schaft,** *f.* motherhood, maternity. **–scheide,** *f.* vagina. **–schiff,** *n.* parent ship, depot ship. **–schoß,** *m.* mother's lap, (*fig.*) womb. **–schutz,** *m.* antenatal care. **–schwein,** *n.* sow. **–schwester,** *f.* maternal aunt. **–seelenallein,** quite *or* all alone. **–söhnchen,** *n.* mother's darling (boy); spoilt child. **–sprache,** *f.* mother tongue, native tongue. **–stand,** *m.* maternity. **–stelle,** *f.*; –*stelle vertreten an* or *bei einem*, be a mother to a p. **–stock,** *m.* parent stem (*Hort.*). **–substanz,** *f.* matrix, stroma. **–tag,** *m.* Mothering Sunday. **–teil,** *m.* maternal inheritance. **–trompeten,** *f.pl.* Fallopian tubes. **–wehen,** *f.pl.* birth-pangs. **–witz,** *m.* mother-wit, common-sense.

[2]**Mutter,** *f.* (-n) female screw, (screw-)nut. **–gewinde,** *n.* female thread (*screw*). **–nschlüssel,** *m.* wrench. **–schraube,** *see* [2]**Mutter.**

Mütter-beratungsstelle, *f.* antenatal centre. **–chen,** *n.* (-s, –) mummy; little old woman. **–lich,** *adj.* motherly, maternal. **–licherseits,** *adv.* on the mother's side. **–lichkeit,** *f.* motherliness. **–verschickung,** *f.* evacuation of expectant mothers (*from air-raids*).

Mütze, *f.* (-n) cap; calyptra (*Bot.*); (*dial.*) second stomach of ruminants; *die* – *vor einem abziehen*, acknowledge a p.'s superiority; (*coll.*) *das war ihm nicht nach der* –, that did not suit him, he did not like that; *eine* – *Wind*, a capful of wind (*Naut.*). **–nband,** *n.* cap strap, chin strap. **–nschild,** *n.*, **–nschirm,** *m.* peak of a cap.

Myriade, *f.* (-n) myriad.

Myrrhe, *f.* (-n) myrrh.

Myrte, *f.* (-n) myrtle; *eine jungfräuliche* –, a bridal wreath.

Myst-erium, *n.* (-ums, -erien) mystery. **–eriös,** *adj.* mysterious. **–ifizieren,** *v.n.* mystify. **–ik,** *f.* mystics, mysticism. **–iker,** *m.* mystic. **–isch,** *adj.* mystic(al).

Myth-e, *f.* (-en) myth, fable. **–enbildung,** *f.* formation of myths. **–enforschung,** *f.*, **–enkunde,** *f.* mythology. **–enhaft,** *adj.*, **–isch,** *adj.* mythical. **–ologie,** *f.* mythology. **–ologisch,** *adj.* mythological. **–os, –us,** *m.* (-os *or* -us, -en) myth.

N

N, n, N, n; *for abbreviations see Index of Abbreviations at end.*

na, *int.* well! come now! – *also*! what did I tell you! – *gut!* all right! if that is what you think; – *!* – *!* come, come! well, well! surely not! – (*und*) *ob!* I should think so! rather! most certainly! (*sl.*) and how! –, *so was!* well, that is a nice thing! come now! oh, nonsense! –*nu!* there now! well, I never! what next!

Nabe, *f.* (-n) nave, hub (*of a wheel*); boss (*Av.*).

Nabel, *m.* (-s, ¨ & –) navel; hilum (*Bot.*); umbo, boss (*of shield*); nombril (*Her.*). **–binde,** *f.* navel-bandage. **–bruch,** *m.* omphalocele. **–förmig,** *adj.* umbilicate. **–schnur,** *f.*, **–strang,** *m.* umbilical cord, funiculus.

nach, 1. *prep.* (*with Dat.*) (*precedes the word it governs*) after, behind, following; towards, to; (*sometimes follows the word it governs*) in conformity with, according to, as regards, after the manner of; on the authority of; by; at; in; for, considering; *im Jahre . . . – Christi Geburt,* in the year . . . of our Lord; – *Empfang des Gegenwärtigen,* on receipt of this; – *Tisch,* after the meal; *ein Viertel – fünf,* a quarter past five; – *einer Woche,* after a week; – *langer Zeit,* after a long interval, a long time afterwards; *die Flucht – Ägypten,* the flight into Egypt; – *außen,* outward, externally; – *Deutschland bestimmte Postsendungen,* the mails for Germany; *eine Frage –,* a question as to; *die Jagd – dem Glück,* the pursuit of happiness; – *Hause,* home; – *oben,* upwards, on high; – *rechts* (*zu*), toward the right; – *der Stadt,* to *or* into town; – *Süden,* towards the south, southwards; – *allem was ich höre,* according to all that I hear, as far as my information goes; *seinem Aussehen –,* to judge by his appearance; – *Belieben,* at one's discretion; – *dem Gedächtnis,* from memory; – *französischem Geschmacke,* in the French fashion *or* style; *sich – dem Gesetz richten,* conform to the law; *meiner Meinung –,* in my opinion; *nur dem Namen – kennen,* know by name only; – *der Natur zeichnen,* draw from nature; – *Noten spielen,* play from music *or* from sight; – *alphabetischer Ordnung,* in alphabetical order; – *der Regel,* according to the rule(s); generally, as a rule; – *der Reihe, der Reihe –,* in turn, by turns; – *dem Schein urteilen,* judge by appearances; – *meiner Uhr,* by my watch; *der Wirklichkeit –,* in reality; – *Wunsch,* as one desires; – *einem ausschauen,* to look (out) for a p.; – *einer S. fragen,* inquire for *or* about a th.; – *Tabak riechen,* smell of tobacco; *schicken –,* send for; – *mehr schmecken,* tempt one to eat more, (*coll.*) be morish; – *Diktat schreiben,* write from dictation; – *Brot schreien,* cry for bread; *sich – einer S. umsehen,* look round for a th.; *werfen –,* throw at; – *sich ziehen,* bring on, be followed by, cause. 2. *adv.* & *sep. prefix,* after, behind; afterwards; – *und –,* little by little, by degrees, by and by, gradually; – *wie vor,* now *or* as much *or* the same as ever *or* before, as usual; *mir – !* follow me! (*As a prefix, may be used with most verbs and many abstract nouns formed from verbs. Compounds not found below should be derived by adding 'after'* (*in space or time*) *to the root verb.*) **–achten,** *v.n.* (*aux.* h.) (*Dat.*) act in conformity with, observe, live up to. **–achtung,** *f.* observance; rule; *dies diene Ihnen zur –achtung,* let this serve for your guidance. **–äffen,** *v.a.* & *n.* (*aux.* h.) (*Dat.* & *Acc.*) ape, mimic. **–äfferei,** *f.*, **–äffung,** *f.* aping, mimicry. **–ahmen,** *v.a.* & *n.* (*aux.* h.) (*Dat.*) imitate, copy; *einen –ahmen,* imitate *or* mimic s.o.; *einem –ahmen in . . .,* imitate a p. in . . ., follow a p.'s example in . . .; *nachgeahmt,* imitated, copied, counterfeit, artificial. **–ahmend,** *pr.p.* & *adj.* imitative; mimic. **–ahmenswert,** *adj.* worthy of imitation. **–ahmer,** *m.* imitator, counterfeiter. **–ahmerei,** *f.* mimicry; slavish imitation; plagiarism. **–ahmung,** *f.* imitation; counterfeiting, forgery. **–ahmungstrieb,** *m.* imitative instinct. **–arbeit,** *f.* (-en) subsequent *or* additional work, extra work; copy, replica; last finish, retouching, repair. **–arbeiten,** *v.a.* & *n.* (*aux.* h.) (*Dat.*) work from *or* according to, copy; touch up, retouch; make good; *einem Muster –arbeiten,* work from a pattern; *ein Muster –arbeiten,* reproduce *or* make a replica of a model; *das Versäumte –arbeiten,* make good *or* catch up the work missed *or* omitted. **–arten,** *v.n.* (*aux.* s.) (*Dat.*) resemble, take after. **–bar,** *m.* (-s & –n, -n), neighbour; *nächster –bar,* next-door neighbour. **–bardivision,** *f.* division on the flank (*Mil.*). **–bardorf,** *n.* neighbouring village. **–barhaus,** *n.* adjoining house, house next door. **–barlich,** *adj.* neighbouring; adjoining, adjacent; neighbourly, friendly; *mit einem –barlich verkehren,* live on neighbourly terms with a p. **–barschaft,** *f.* neighbourhood, vicinity; neighbours; *in der nächsten –barschaft,* in the immediate neighbourhood; *die ganze –barschaft,* all the neighbours. **–barskind,** *n.* child next door. **–barsleute,** *pl.* neighbours. **–barstaat,** *m.* neighbouring state. **–bartruppen,** *pl.* adjacent troops. **–behandlung,** *f.* after-treatment. **–besserer,** *m.* (-s, –) corrector, improver. **–bessern,** *v.a.* mend, improve, repair; replenish; touch up. **–bess(e)rung,** *f.* touching-up; repair; later improvement. **–bestellen,** *v.a.* order subsequently, repeat an order; order a fresh supply. **–bestellung,** *f.* additional *or* repeat order. **–beten,** *v.a.* & *n.* (*aux.* h.) (*Dat.*) (*fig.*) repeat mechanically, echo. **–beter,** *m.* blind adherent. **–bezahlen,** *v.a.* pay later; pay the rest. **–bezahlung,** *f.* additional *or* subsequent payment. **–bild,** *n.* copy, imitation, counterfeit; after-image. **–bilden,** *v.a.* copy, imitate, reproduce; counterfeit. **–bildung,** *f.* copy, imitation, facsimile, replica, reproduction; counterfeit. **–blättern,** *v.a.* turn over the leaves (*of a book*), look through (*a book*). **–bleiben,** *ir.v.n.* (*aux.* s.) remain behind; be left over; survive; lag behind; be kept in (*at school*); *–bleiben lassen,* detain, keep in (*a schoolboy*); *–bleiben müssen,* have to stay in, be kept in (*at school*). **–bleibend,** *pr.p.* & *adj.* residual, residuary; redundant, superfluous. **–bleiber,** *m.* child kept in (*after school*). **–bleibsel,** *n.* remainder, surplus, remains, residuum. **–blicken,** *v.n.*; *einem –blicken,* look *or* gaze after a p., follow a p. with one's eyes. **–blüte,** *f.* (-n) second blossom(ing); aftergrowth (*Agr.*); (*fig.*) aftermath. **–brenner,** *m.* hangfire (*Artil.*). **–bürge,** *f.* (-en), **–bürgschaft** *f.* (-en) collateral security. **–datieren,** *v.a.* post-date (*a letter*). **–dem,** 1. *adv.* afterwards, hereafter; *je –dem,* according to circumstances; that depends. 2. *conj.* after, according as, according to the way that; *je –dem es kommt,* just as it comes; *je –dem er sich benimmt,* that depends on how he behaves himself, according to his behaviour. **–denken,** 1. *ir.v.n.* (*aux.* h.); *über* (*eine S.*) *–denken,* think, reflect, consider, ponder *or* muse (on), meditate (on), cogitate (over). 2. *n.* reflection, meditation, consideration. **–denklich,** *adj.* reflective, thoughtful, pensive, meditative. **–dichtung,** *f.* imitation, paraphrase, free rendering. **–drängen,** 1. *v.a.* & *n.* (*aux.* h.) press, crowd, push. 2. *v.r.* press after, push after, follow eagerly. 3. *n.* pursuit, pressure (*on the enemy*). **–dringen,** *ir.v.n.* (*aux.* s.) press after, pursue hotly. **–druck,** *m.* stress, emphasis; energy, vigour, force; reprint, reprinting, reproduction (*of a book*); pirated edition; *–druck verboten,* copyright reserved; *mit –druck handeln,* act with energy; *mit –druck sagen,* say emphatically; *–druck auf eine S. legen,* lay stress upon a th. **–drucken,** *v.a.* reprint; republish; pirate (*a book*). **–drucker,** *m.* piratical printer *or* publisher; literary pirate. **–drücken,** *v.a.* urge forward, push. **–drücklich,** *adj.* energetic, vigorous, forcible, emphatic; *–drücklich sagen,* say emphatically; *–drücklich handeln,* act energetically. **–drücklichkeit,** *f.* forcibleness; emphasis; energy. **–drucksvoll,** *adj.* emphatic, forcible, impressive. **–dunkeln,** *v.n.* grow darker, darken; deepen (*Paint.*); sadden (*Dye.*). **–eifer,** *m. see* **–eiferung.** **–eiferer,** *m.* rival; emulator. **–eifern,** *v.n.* (*aux.* h.) (*Dat.*) emulate. **–eiferung,** *f.* emulation. **–eilen,** *v.n.* (*aux.* s.) hasten after, pursue. **–einander,** *adv.* one after another, successively, by turns, in turn; *fünf Tage –einander*, for five days running *or* on end. **–einanderfolgend,** *adj.* successive. **–empfinden,** *ir.v.a.* enter into *or* appreciate, feel for, sympathize with. **–empfindend,** *pr.p. & adj.* sympathetic, receptive. **–empfindung,** *f.* appreciation, sensitivity, receptivity, sympathy. **–en,** *see* **Nachen.** **–erbe,** *m.* next heir. **–ernte,** *f.* second crop; gleaning. **–erzählen,** *v.a.* (*einem etwas*) repeat what one has heard; *dem Englischen –erzählt*, imitated *or* adapted from the English; *schlimme Geschichten werden ihm –erzählt*, terrible reports are being circulated about him. **–exerzieren,** *v.n.* (*aux.* h.) do extra drill; (*coll.*) do a th. after all others have finished. **–fahr,** *m.* (-s & -en, -en) (*Poet.*) descendant; successor. **–färben,** *v.a.* re-dye. **–feiern,** *v.n. & a.* celebrate after the event. **–folge,** *f.* succession (*in office, etc.*); reversion; sequence, following; *–folge Christi*, imitation of Christ. **–folgen,** *v.n.* (*aux.* s.) (*Dat.*) follow, pursue; succeed; imitate. **–folgend,** *pr.p. & adj.* following, consecutive, subsequent; *das –folgende*, that which follows. **–folger,** *m.* successor, follower, imitator. **–folgerschaft,** *f.* successors. **–folgestaaten,** *m.pl.* succession states. **–forderung,** *f.* (-en) subsequent claim; extra charge. **–forschen,** *v.n.* (*aux.* h.) inquire *or* search after; trace; investigate. **–forscher,** *m.* inquirer, investigator. **–forschung,** *f.* quest, search, investigation; research. **–frage,** *f.* (-n) inquiry; demand, request; *Dank für gütige –frage*, thanks for the kind inquiries; *–frage anstellen*, make inquiries; *–frage halten*, inquire after; *Angebot und –frage*, supply and demand; *starke –frage nach Kaffee*, great demand for coffee. **–fragen,** *reg. & ir.v.* (*aux.* h.) (*Dat.*) inquire about *or* after; *er fragt nicht danach*, he cares nothing about it. **–fühlen,** *v.a.* feel for *or* with, sympathize with (*a p.*); *ich kann es ihm so recht –fühlen*, I know well what he must have felt, I can fully enter into his feelings. **–gärung,** *f.* secondary fermentation. **–geben,** *ir. v.n.* (*aux.* h.) give way, yield, submit, give in (*to a p.*); stretch; *einem nichts –geben*, be in no way inferior to a p.; *die Kurse haben weiter –gegeben*, exchange rates have declined further. **–gebend,** *pr.p. & adj.* compliant, yielding, indulgent. **–geboren,** *p.p. & adj.* posthumous; born later. **–gebot,** *n.* subsequent *or* higher bid. **–gebühr,** *f.* (-en) surcharge, excess postage. **–geburt,** *f.* afterbirth, placenta (*Med.*). **–gehen,** *ir.v.n.* (*aux.* s.) (*Dat.*) be behind, follow; lose, be slow (*of clock*); trace, inquire into, investigate; pursue (*a line of enquiry*); mind, attend to; apply o.s. to; be addicted to. **–gehends,** *adv.* afterwards, hereafter, subsequently. **–gelassen,** *adj.* posthumous (*work, etc.*). **–gemacht,** *adj. & p.p.* imitated, false, counterfeited, sham. **–geordnet,** *p.p. & adj.* subordinate. **–gerade,** *adv.* by degrees, gradually, at length; by this time, by now, after all. **–gesang,** *m.* epode. **–geschmack,** *m.* after-taste. **–gewiesenermaßen,** *adv.* as has been proved. **–giebig,** *adj.* flexible, pliable, tractable, yielding, supple, soft; obliging, compliant, indulgent, easy-going. **–giebigkeit,** *f.* yielding *or* weak disposition; softness, tractability, complaisance, indulgence; subservience. **–gießen,** *ir.v.a.* pour afterwards; add (by pouring); refill, replenish. **–grübeln,** *v.n.* (*aux.* h.) (*Dat.*) ponder over, muse (on), investigate laboriously. **–guß,** *m.* refilling, replenishing. **–hall,** *m.* echo, resonance, reverberation, (*fig.*) efficacy; response. **–hallen,** *v.n.* (*aux.* h.) echo, resound. **–halten,** *ir.v.n.* (*aux.* h.) last, hold out. **–haltig,** *adj.* lasting; persistent, protracted, sustained; effective. **–haltigkeit,** *f.* permanence, durability. **–hangen,** *ir.v.n.* (*aux.* h.), **–hängen,** *v.n.* (*aux.* h.) (*einer S.*) give way to, give o.s. up to (a th.); indulge in *or* be addicted to (a th.); *seinen Gedanken –hängen*, be immersed in one's thoughts, muse. **–hause,** *adv.* home(ward). **–hausegehen,** *v.n. & subst. n.* walk home. **–heizen,** *v.n.* stoke the fire, make *or* make up the fire, put on coal. **–helfen,** *ir.v.n.* (*aux.* h.) (*Dat.*) lend a helping hand, help, assist; prompt. **–her,** *adv.* afterwards, later (on), hereafter, subsequently. **–herig,** *adj.* subsequent, later, future, posterior. **–hilfe,** *f.* aid, help, assistance; coaching; repair, patching up. **–hilfekurs(us),** *m.* supplementary course. **–hilfestunden,** *f.pl.* private tuition, (private) coaching. **–hinken** 1. *v.n.* (*aux.* s.) (*Dat.*) lag behind; *nachgehinkt kommen*, be too late; imitate clumsily. 2. *n.* time-lag. **–holen,** *v.a.* make up for; retrieve, recover; overtake; finish (*a job*). **–hut,** *f.* rearguard (*Mil.*). **–hutgefecht,** *n.* rearguard action. **–impfung,** *f.* reinoculation. **–jagen,** 1. *v.n.* (*aux.* s.) (*Dat.*) pursue, hunt *or* chase (after). 2. *v.a.* send after; *einem ein Telegramm –jagen*, send a telegram after a p., (*coll.*) chase a p. with a telegram. **–kauen,** *v.a.* (*coll.*) *einem etwas –kauen*, repeat s.th. mechanically, echo the views of another p. **–kinder,** *n.pl.* children of a subsequent marriage (*Law*). **–klang,** *m.* echo, resonance; reverberation; after-effect; reminiscence. **–klingen,** *ir.v.n.* (*aux.* h.) resound, echo; die away (*sound*). **–komme,** *m.* (-n, -n) descendant, offspring, successor; *ohne –kommen*, without issue. **–kommen,** *ir.v.n.* (*aux.* s.) (*Dat.*) come after, follow on, come later, (re-)join, overtake; act up to, fulfil, perform, observe, comply with, accede to; *seinen Verbindlichkeiten –kommen*, fulfil one's engagements; *seinem Versprechen –kommen*, keep one's promise; *Ihrem Wunsche –kommend*, in compliance with your wish(es); *gehen Sie nur voran, in fünf Minuten werde ich –kommen*, go on ahead and I will join you in five minutes. **–kommenschaft,** *f.* posterity, descendants, successors, offspring, progeny; *ohne –kommenschaft*, without issue, childless. **–kömmling,** *m.* (-s, -e) descendant; later child. **–kriegs-,** *prefix*, post-war. **–kur,** *f.* rest after treatment, convalescence. **–laß,** *m.* (-(ss)es, -(ss)e & ¨-(ss)e) heritage, legacy, deceased's estate; literary remains; relaxation, intermission; remission, reduction, rebate, discount, deduction; annealing. **–laßgericht,** *n.* probate-court. **–laßsteuer,** *f.* death duty. **–laßversteigerung,** *f.* disposal of an estate by auction. **–laßverwalter,** *m.* executor. **–lassen,** 1. *ir.v.a.* leave (behind), bequeath; relax, mitigate, discontinue, remit, reduce (*price*); grant, yield, give up; temper, anneal (*Metal.*); *etwas vom* (or *am*) *Preise –lassen*, allow a discount, make a reduction in the price. 2. *v.n.* (*aux.* h.) slacken, give way *or* over, grow less, slow up, fall off, subside, abate; flag, weaken, decline, fail, diminish; cease; *die Kälte läßt nach*, the cold is abating; *lassen Sie doch nach!* do stop! (*C.L.*) *die Nachfrage läßt nach*, the demand is growing less brisk *or* quietening off; *im Fleiße –lassen*, become less diligent; *nachgelassene Werke*, posthumous works, literary remains. 3. *n.* remission; relaxation, abatement, weakening, flagging. **–lassenschaft,** *f.* estate, inheritance. **–lässig,** *adj.* negligent, slovenly, careless, remiss, neglectful; indolent, supine. **–lässigerweise,** *adv.* carelessly, through carelessness. **–lässigkeit,** *f.* negligence, carelessness; inaccuracy, remissness. **–lauf,** *m.* last drips, tails (*Distillery*). **–leben,** 1. *v.n.* (*aux.* h.) (*Dat.*) conform to, live up to. 2. *n.* after life. **–legen,** *v.a.* add to, lay on more, make up the fire. **–lese,** *f.* gleanings, gleaning; remains; supplement, addenda; *–lese halten*, glean. **–lesen,** *ir.v.a. & n.* (*aux.* h.) glean; read after, re-read; look up (*in a book*); *beim –lesen*, on reading again. **–leuchten,** *v.n.* phosphoresce, be luminous. **–liefern,** *v.a.* deliver *or* furnish subsequently, (add as a) supplement. **–lieferung,** *f.* subsequent delivery, supplement. **–lösen,** *v.a.* take a supplementary ticket. **–machen,** *v.a.* copy, imitate; mimic, counterfeit; *das soll mir einer –machen;* I defy anyone to do the same! *mach es mir –*, do as I do; *–gemachte Blumen*, imitation flowers. **–mahd,** *f.* (*dial.*) aftermath. **–malig,** *adj.* subsequent. **–mals,** *adv.* afterwards, subsequently. **–messen,** *ir.v.a.* measure again; check measurements, verify. **–mittag,** *m.* (-(e)s, -e) afternoon; *eines –mittags*, one afternoon, of an afternoon; *heute –mittag*, this afternoon. **–mittägig, –mittäglich,** *adj.* (taking place in the) afternoon, post-prandial. **–mittags,** *adv.* in the afternoon; p.m. **–mittagsschläfchen,** *n.* afternoon nap, siesta. **–mittagssitzung,** *f.* afternoon session. **–mittagsvorstellung,** *f.* afternoon performance, matinée (*Theat.*). **–nahme,** *f.* cash on delivery; *unter –nahme Ihrer Spesen,* carrying your charges forward. **–nahmebetrag,** *m.* amount to be collected on delivery, C.O.D. **–nahmegebühr,** *f.* collection-fee. **–nahmesendung,** *f.* parcel to be paid for on delivery, C.O.D. parcel. **–name,** *m.* (-ns, -n) surname. **–nehmen,** *ir.v.a.* charge forward, collect charges on delivery. **–ordnen,** *v.a.* subordinate, place subordinate to; rearrange; *die –geordneten Stellen,* the subordinate offices *or* grades. **–plappern,** *v.a.* repeat mechanically. **–porto,** *n.* (-s, -s *or -porti*) postage due, excess postage, surcharge. **–prüfen,** *v.a.* check, verify, make sure; control, examine, test. **–prüfung,** *f.* verification, testing, checking. **–rechnen,** *v.a. & n.* (*aux.* h.) check, verify (*a calculation*), audit. **–rechner,** *m.* auditor. **–rede,** *f.* epilogue; rumour, gossip; calumny; *in üble –rede bringen,* slander s.o., injure a p.'s reputation. **–reden,** *v.a. & n.* (*aux.* h.) repeat (*what another has said*); *einem etwas* or *Übles –reden,* speak ill of a p., slander a p. **–reder,** *m.* slanderer. **–redner,** *m.* later speaker. **–regeln,** *v.a.* adjust. **–richt,** *f.* (-en) news, communication, account, information, report, advice, notice; *amtliche –richt,* official report; *ausführliche –richt,* detailed account; *öffentliche –richt,* (public) advertisement; *einem –richt geben,* let s.o. know, advise a p., send a p. word; *über eine S. –richt einziehen,* obtain information regarding s.th.; *nach allen –richten,* by all accounts. **–richtenabteilung,** *f.* intelligence department (*Mil.*). **–richtenamt,** *n.* information-bureau. **–richtenbüro,** *n.* press-agency. **–richtendienst,** *m.* radio news service; signals (*Mil.*), intelligence service (*Mil.*). **–richtenhelferinnen,** *f.pl.* women auxiliaries for signals duties (*German Air Force*). **–richtenjäger,** *m.* reconnaissance fighter (*Av.*). **–richtensperre,** *f.* ban on news, news black-out. **–richtentruppen,** *f.pl.* corps of signals (*Mil.*). **–richtenwesen,** *n.* news *or* (*Mil.*) intelligence service, communications (system). **–rücken,** *v.n.* (*aux.* s.) move forward *or* up, follow. **–ruf,** *m.* (-(e)s, -e) posthumous fame, memory; memorial address, obituary notice, in memoriam. **–rufen,** *ir.v.a. & n.* (*aux.* h.); *einem –rufen,* call after a p. **–ruhm,** *m.* fame after death. **–rühmen,** *v.a.*; *einem etwas –rühmen,* praise a p. for s.th., say s.th. to s.o.'s credit. **–sagen,** *v.a.* repeat mechanically, repeat after (a p.); speak *or* say of; *das muß ich ihm zum Ruhme –sagen,* I must say that in his praise *or* to his credit. **–satz,** *m.* minor term *or* proposition (*Log.*); final clause (*Gram.*); postscript. **–schauen,** *v.a.*; *einem –schauen,* gaze after a p.; (*coll.*) *schau mal nach, ob er kommt,* just look and see if he is coming. **–schicken,** *v.a.* send on, forward; *Bitte –schicken,* please forward, to be forwarded. **–schieben,** *ir.v.a.* shove from behind, push along; send in (*reserves*) (*Mil.*). **–schieber,** *m.* caudal disk (*Ent.*). **–schießen,** 1, *ir.v.a.*; *einem –schießen,* shoot at s.o. going away; *Gelder –schießen,* make a subsequent payment. 2. *v.n.* (*aux.* s.) dart after; spring up later, bud a second time. **–schlag,** *m.* following blow; grace-note (*Mus.*). **–schlagen,** 1. *ir.v.a. & n.* (*aux.* h.) consult (*a book*), look up (*a word*), refer to; counterfeit (*coins*). 2. *v.n.* (*aux.* s.) take after, resemble. **–schlagewerk,** *n.* work of reference, reference book. **–schleifen,** 1. *ir.v.a.* resharpen, regrind. 2. *v.a. reg.* drag *or* trail along *or* behind. **–schleppen,** *v.a.* drag *or* trail after; tow (*Naut.*). **–schlüssel,** *m.* master-key, skeleton key, picklock. **–schmecken,** *v.n.* (*aux.* h.) leave a taste *or* an aftertaste; taste of. **–schreiben,** *ir.v.a. & n.* (*aux.* h.) write from dictation; take notes (*of a lecture*); write *or* take down, copy, transcribe, write out. **–schrift,** *f.* postscript; transcript, copy. **–schub,** *m.* (-(e)s, ¨e) supplement; new batch; replacement, fresh supply, relief, reserves, reinforcement. **–schubfahrtruppe,** *f.* Army Service Corps. **–schubgut,** *n.* supplies (*Mil.*). **–schublinie,** *f.* line of communications (*Mil.*). **–schuß,** *m.* additional *or* further payment; new shoot. **–schwatzen,** *v.a.* (*aux.* h.) repeat (*gossip*). **–sehen,** 1. *ir.v.n.* (*aux.* h.) look after, follow with one's eyes (*einem,* a p.); look for *or* up; *sieh nach, daß es geschieht,* see that it is done; *sieh nach, ob etwas darin ist,* look *or* see if there is anything in it. 2. *v.a.* look into, examine, investigate, attend to; inspect, check, revise, overhaul; (*einem etwas*) *–sehen,* overlook, take no notice of, condone, excuse *or* pardon (a th. in a p.). 3. *n.*; *das* (*leere*) *–sehen haben,* have one's trouble for nothing, be too late; *nun bleibt uns* (*Dat.*) *das –sehen,* now we may whistle for it. **–senden,** *v.a.* send after, forward, re-direct (*letters*); *Bitte –senden,* please forward. **–setzen,** 1. *v.a.* set, put *or* place after *or* behind; think less of. 2. *v.n.* (*aux.* s.) (*Dat.*) follow, pursue, hunt after; *mir wird nachgesetzt,* I am being pursued. **–setzung,** *f.* hot pursuit; disregard. **–sicht,** *f.* indulgence, forbearance, leniency, clemency, pity; respite; *–sicht haben mit* or *üben gegen,* be indulgent toward, make allowance for; *gegenseitige –sicht üben,* bear and forbear. **–sichtig,** *adj.* considerate, forbearing, indulgent, lenient. **–sichtigkeit,** *f.* good nature, indulgence. **–sichtsvoll,** *adj.,* *see* **–sichtig.** **–silbe,** *f.* suffix. **–sitzen,** *v.n.* stay in (*after school*), be kept in; *einen –sitzen lassen,* keep in (*after school*); *er mußte –sitzen,* he was kept in. **–sommer,** *m.* Indian summer. **–speise,** *f.* dessert, sweet. **–spiel,** *n.* (-s, -e) epilogue; voluntary (*Mus.*); (*fig.*) sequel. **–sprechen,** *ir. v.a. & n.* (*aux.* h.) (*einem*) repeat another's words; mimic a p. **–spüren,** *v.n.* (*aux.* h.) (*Dat.*) track, trace, spy on, investigate. **¨st,** *see* **nächst.** **–stehen,** *ir.v.n.* (*aux.* h.) follow; *einem –stehen,* fall short of, be inferior to, make way for; *–stehende Worte,* the following words; *wie –stehend bemerkt,* as mentioned below. **–stellen,** 1. *v.n.* (*aux.* h.) (*Dat.*) lie in wait for; waylay. 2. *v.a.* place after; put back (*clocks*), adjust. **–stellschraube,** *f.* adjusting screw. **–stellung,** *f.* (*usually pl.*) snare; ambush; pursuit, persecution. **–stoßen,** *ir.v.a. & n.* (*aux.* h.) push forward; thrust after, pursue. **–streben,** *v.n.* (*aux.* h.) (*Dat.*) strive after, aspire to, emulate. **–suchen,** 1. *v.a. & n.* (*aux.* h.) look *or* search for, seek; *um eine S. –suchen,* apply, sue *or* petition for s.th., solicit s.th. 2. *n.,* **–suchung,** *f.* search, inquiry; application. **–t,** *see* **Nacht.** **–teil,** *m.* (-s, -e) disadvantage, drawback, prejudice, inconvenience, detriment, damage, injury, loss; *sich im –teil befinden,* be at a disadvantage, have the worst of it; *er ist dabei sehr im –teil,* it is greatly to his disadvantage. **–teilig,** *adj.* disadvantageous, prejudicial, detrimental, injurious, hurtful, disparaging, derogatory; *–teilig sprechen von,* speak unfavourably *or* disparagingly of. **–tigall,** *see* **Nachtigall.** **–tisch,** *m.* (-es, -e) dessert. **–tönen,** *v.n.* (*aux.* h.) resound, (re-)echo, reverberate. **–trab,** *m.* rear, rearguard (*Mil.*). **–traben,** *v.n.* (*aux.* s.) (*einem*) follow at a trot, trot at someone's heels. **–trag,** *m.* (-(e)s, ¨e) supplement, addendum, postscript; codicil. **–tragen,** *ir.v.a.* (*einem etwas*) carry after; add, append; (*fig.*) bear a grudge (against), be resentful (of); pay up (*arrears*); *einen Posten in eine Rechnung –tragen,* enter an additional item into an account. **–trägerisch,** resentful, vindictive. **–träglich,** 1. *adj.* supplementary, additional, further, later, extra, subsequent, *–träglicher Einfall,* afterthought. 2. *adv.* subsequently, later. **–tragsetat,** *m.* supplementary estimate. **–tragszahlung,** *f.* additional payment. **–treten,** *ir.v.n.* (*aux.* s.) (*Dat.*) follow after; follow closely, follow (in the footsteps of). **–treter,** *m.* follower, adherent. **–trupp,** *m.* rearguard. **–tun,** *ir.v.a.* (*einem etwas*) imitate, do in imitation, do the same *or* the like, copy, emulate. **–untersuchung,** *f.* check-up, follow-up. **–urlaub,** *m.* (-(e)s) extension of leave. **–vermächtnis,** *n.* codicil (*to a will*). **–wägen,** *v.a.* weigh again, check the weight. **–wahl,** *f.* (-en) by-election. **–wehen,** *f.pl.* after-pains; (*fig.*) after-effects, evil *or* painful consequences. **–weinen,** *v.a. & n.* (*aux.* h.) (*Dat.*) bewail, mourn, lament (*loss or death*). **–weis,** *m.* (-es, -e) proof, demonstration, evidence; agency. **–weisbar,** *adj.* authenticated, demonstrable, manifest, evident, traceable, detectable, assignable. **–weis(e)amt,** *n.* inquiry office, information office. **–weisen,** *ir.v.a.* (*einem etwas*) point out, show, detect, trace, identify, indicate, demonstrate, refer to; prove, authenticate, ascertain, establish. **–weiser,** *m.* director; index, pointer. **–weis(e)zahl,** *f.* folio-number. **–weis(e)zeichen,** *n.* reference mark, asterisk, direction (*Mus.*). **–weislich,** *adj.* evident, demonstrable; authentic. **–weisung,** *f.* demonstration, detection, proof; information, reference. **–welt,** *f.* posterity, future generations; *die späteste –welt*, the remotest ages. **–wiegen,** *v.a.* *see* **–wägen.** **–wirken,** *v.a.* & *n.* (*aux.* h.) take effect afterwards, produce an after-effect. **–wirkung,** *f.* after-effect, secondary effect. **–wort,** *n.* epilogue, concluding remarks. **–wuchs,** *m.* second growth; young wood; (*fig.*) new blood, rising generation, recruits; *der junge –wuchs*, the rising generation. **–zahlen,** *v.a.* pay afterwards *or* in addition. **–zählen,** *v.a.* count over again, count (*one's change*); check. **–zahlung,** *f.* additional payment. **–ziehen,** I. *ir.v.a.* drag along; trace again (*lines*); pencil (*eyebrows*); tighten (*screws*). 2. *v.n.* (*aux.* s.) (*nach einem*) march after, follow. **–zotteln,** *v.n.* (*aux.* s.) (*Dat.*) (*coll.*) lag behind. **–zug,** *m.* (*archaic*) rearguard (*Mil.*). **–zügler,** *m.* (-s, –) straggler, laggard; camp follower. **–zündung,** *f.* retarded ignition (*Motor.*).

Nachen, *m.* (-s, –) skiff, small boat.

nächst, I. *adj.* (*sup. of* nah, *q.v.*) next, nearest, closest, shortest; *im –en Augenblick*, the next moment; *der –e beste*, the first that comes; *die –en Beziehungen*, the most intimate relations; *die –en Freunde*, the closest *or* most intimate friends; *bei –er Gelegenheit*, at the first opportunity; *mit –em*, as soon as possible, very soon; *das –e Mal*, the next time; (*C.L.*) *–en Monat*, proximo; *–er Nachbar*, next-door neighbour; *–e Stadt*, nearest town; *der –e Weg*, the nearest way, the shortest cut; *–ster Zeit*, very soon; *der –e Zweck*, the immediate object *or* purpose; (*Prov.*) *jeder ist sich selbst der –e*, charity begins at home; *das –e*, what is nearest, that which touches one closest. 2. *adv.* next; soon: *am –en*, nearest; *fürs –e*, for the present. 3. *prep.* (*Dat.*) next to, next after. **–best(e),** *m.* second-best. **–dem,** *adv.* after that, besides. **–e(r),** *m.* (*B.*) fellow man *or* creature, neighbour. **–enliebe,** *f.* (Christian) charity, love for one's fellow-men. **–ens,** *adv.* shortly, very soon. **–folgend,** *adj.* succeeding, immediately following; *–folgender Tag*, next day. **–liegend,** *adj.* nearest at hand. **–treffer,** *m.* near-hit, near-miss. **–vorhergehend,** *adj.* immediately preceding.

Nacht, *f.* (¨e) night; darkness; *bei –*, in the night, during the night, at night; *bei – und Nebel davon gehen*, escape under cover of darkness *or* the night; (*Prov.*) *bei – sind alle Katzen grau*, all cats are grey in the dark; *des –s*, see *bei –*; *gute – sagen*, bid good-night; *in der –*, see *bei –*; *in tiefer –*, at dead of night; *mit einbrechender –*, at nightfall; *Märchen von 'Tausendundeiner –'*, the Arabian Nights; *über –*, during the night; *über – bleiben*, stay the night; *über – kommen*, come unexpectedly; *es wird –*, it grows dark; *einem – vor den Augen werden*, go black before one's eyes, become unconscious; *zu – essen*, have supper, sup. **–angriff,** *m.* night-attack. **–anzug,** *m.* night-clothes, pyjamas. **–arbeit,** *f.* night-work. **–blindheit,** *f.* night-blindness. **–blütler,** *m.* night-flowering plant. **–dienst,** *m.* night-service; night duty. **–en,** *v.n.* (*aux.* h.) & *imp.*; *es –et*, night is coming on *or* is drawing in, it is getting dark. **–essen,** *n.* supper. **–eule,** *f.* screech-owl. **–falter,** *m.* moth. **–feier,** *f.* vigil. **–flug,** *m.* night flight. **–gebet,** *n.* evening-prayer. **–geschirr,** *n.* chamber(-pot). **–gleiche,** *f.* equinox. **–haus,** *n.* binnacle (*Naut.*). **–hemd,** *n.* nightshirt (*men*); night-dress, night-gown (*women*). **–jacke,** *f.* bed-jacket. **–jäger,** *m.* night-fighter (*Av.*). **–kerze,** *f.* night-light. **–kleid,** *n.* night-dress *or* -gown, (*coll.*) nightie. **–lager,** *n.* night's lodging, quarters, bed; *ein –lager aufschlagen*, bivouac (*Mil.*). **–leben,** *n.* night-life. **–licht,** *n.* night-light. **–lokal,** *n.* night-club. **–mahl,** *n.* (*Austr. dial.*) supper. **–mahlen,** *v.n.* (*Austr. dial.*) have supper. **–mahr,** *m.* nightmare. **–mette,** *f.* nocturn (*Eccl.*). **–musik** *f.* serenade. **–mütze,** *f.* night-cap; (*coll.*) dolt **–pfauenauge,** *n.* emperor-moth. **–quartier,** *n.* quarters for the night; *einem –quartier geben*, put a p. up for the night. **–ruhe,** *f.* sleep, night's rest. **–runde,** *f.* night-patrol. **–s,** *adv.* by night, at night, in the night. **–schatten,** *m.* nightshade (*Solanum*) (*Bot.*). **–schicht,** *f.* night-shift. **–schlafend,** *adj.*; (*coll.*) *bei dieser –schlafenden Zeit*, at this time of night, when everyone is asleep. **–schwärmer,** *m.* moth; night reveller. **–seite,** *f.* dark *or* seamy side. **–stuhl,** *m.* night-stool, commode. **–tisch,** *m.* bed-side table. **–topf,** *m., see* **–geschirr.** **–übung,** *f.* night-manœuvres (*Mil.*). **–uhr,** *f.* clock with illuminated dial. **–viole,** *f.* dame's violet (*Bot.*). **–wache,** *f.* night-watch; vigil; beat (*of policemen*). **–wächter,** *m.* night-watchman; stupid person; (*sl.*) *unter dem –wächter*, beneath criticism. **–wandeln,** I. *v.n.* (*aux.* h.) (*insep.*) walk in one's sleep. 2. *n.* sleep-walking, somnambulism. **–wandler,** *m.* sleep-walker, somnambulist. **–wandlerisch,** *adj.*; *mit –wandlerischer Sicherheit*, with absolute certainty. **–zeug,** *n.* night-clothes, night-things.

nächt–elang, *adv.* for whole nights, for nights together. **–en,** (*archaic*) *see* **–igen.** **–ens,** *adv.* (*Poet.*), *see* **nachts.** **–ig,** *adj.* dark, gloomy, like night. **–igen,** *v.n.* pass *or* spend the night. **–igung,** *f.* putting up for the night, providing night-shelter. **–lich,** I. *adj.* nightly, nocturnal; gloomy, dismal; *bei –licher Weile*, at night-time. 2. *adv.* at night.

Nachtigall, *f.* (-en) nightingale; *die Nachtigall singen lehren wollen*, (*coll.*) teach one's grandmother to suck eggs. **–enschlag,** *m.* song of the nightingale.

Nack–edei, *m.* & *n.* (-(e)s, -e & -s) (*coll.*) naked child. **–end,** *adj.*, **–ig,** *adj.* (*archaic*), **–icht,** *adj.* (*dial.* & *coll.*) naked.

Nacken, *m.* (-s, –) nape of the neck, neck; scrag (*of mutton, etc.*); *einem auf dem* or *im – sitzen* or *liegen*, be at a p.'s heels, press *or* harass a p. (*Mil.*); be a burden to a p., pester a p.; *den – unter das Joch beugen*, submit to the yoke; *einen harten – haben*, be unyielding, indomitable, recalcitrant *or* refractory; *den Feind im – haben*, have the enemy hard on one's heels; *den Schelm im – haben*, be full of mischief. **–haar,** *n.* back hair. **–schlag,** *m.* blow from behind; (*fig.*) disaster; abuse (*of one absent*); *–schläge bekommen*, be in great trouble. **–stachel,** *m.* dorsal spine (*Icht.*). **–starre,** *f.* stiff neck. **–wirbel,** *m.* cervical vertebra (*Anat.*).

nackt, *adj.* naked, bare, nude; callow (*of birds*); *mit –em Auge*, with the naked *or* unaided eye; *– und bloß*, stripped, fleeced, bereft, penniless, destitute; *das –e Leben retten*, barely escape with one's life; *–e Lüge*, bare-faced lie; *die –e Wahrheit*, the plain, blunt *or* unadorned truth; *die –en Wände*, the bare walls; *mit –en Worten*, in plain words, bluntly, openly. **–heit,** *f.* nakedness, nudity; (*pl.*) nudes (*Art*). **–kultur,** *f.* nudism. **–stengelig,** *adj.* non-leafy (*Bot.*).

Nadel, *f.* (-n) needle, pin; point; pinnacle; striker (*of a gun*); *mit –n befestigen*, pin; *Brust–*, brooch; *Haar–*, hairpin; *Häkel–*, crochet hook; *das ist mit der heißen – genäht*, that was done in a hurry, that was a rush job ; *Näh–*, (sewing-)needle; *Sicherheits–*, safety-pin; *wie auf –n sitzen*, be on thorns; *Spick–*, larding-needle; *Steck–*, pin; *Stopf–*, darning-needle; *Strick–*, knitting-needle. **–abweichung,** *f.* magnetic declination. **–arbeit,** *f.* needle-work. **–ausschlag,** *m.* deflexion of needle (*Magnet.*). **–baum,** *m.* conifer. **–brief,** *m.* paper of pins. **–buch,** *n.* needle-case. **–förmig,** *adj.* needle-shaped, acicular. **–futteral,** *n.* needle-case. **–geld,** *n.* pin-money, dress-allowance. **–holz,** *n.* conifers, conifer forest. **–holzteer,** *m.* pine tar. **–kissen,** *n.* pin-cushion. **–knopf,** *m.*, **–kopf,** *m.* pin's head. **–n** I. *v.n.* (*aux.* h.) shed foliage (*of conifers*). 2. *v.a.* sew up, stitch (*wounds*). **–öhr,** *n.* (-(e)s, -e) eye of a needle. **–spitze,** *f.* point of a needle. **–stein,** *m.* load-stone. **–stich,** *m.* prick; stitch; acupuncture (*Med.*); (*fig.*) pin-prick, petty annoyance. **–stockung,** *f.*

repeating groove (*on a gramophone record*). **-wald,** *m.* coniferous forest. **-ware,** *f.* pins and needles. **-zahl,** *f.* azimuth reading.

Nadler, *m.* pin- *or* needle-maker.

Nagel, *m.* (-s, ⸚) nail, stud, (carpet) tack; spike, peg; *keinen – breit*, not an inch; *es brennt mir auf den Nägeln*, the matter is urgent, I am hard pressed; *einen – haben*, have a high opinion of o.s.; (*coll.*) *an den – hängen*, shelve, give up, abandon; *an den Nägeln kauen*, chew one's nails (*with rage* or *impatience*); *den – auf den Kopf treffen*, hit the nail on the head; *ein – zu meinem Sarge*, a cause of deep concern *or* sorrow, the death of me; *sich* (*Dat.*) *die Nägel schneiden*, cut one's nails; *der – zieht an*, the nail holds *or* goes home. **-bohrer,** *m.* gimlet. **-bürste,** *f.* nail-brush. **-feile,** *f.* nail-file. **-fest,** *adj.* nailed, immovable, tight; *niet- und -feste Gegenstände*, fixtures. **-förmig,** *adj.* unguiform. **-geschwür,** *n.* whitlow. **-gras,** *n.* chickweed. **-kuppe,** *f.* nail-head, head of a nail. **-n,** *v.a.* nail; *ich -e ihn fest*, (*coll.*) I'll pin him down. **-neu,** *adj.* brand-new. **-pflege,** *f.* manicure. **-politur,** *f.* nail-varnish. **-probe,** *f.*; *die -probe machen*, show that one's glass is empty by ringing it with the finger-nail; (*fig.*) crucial test; *nicht die -probe ist im Glase geblieben*, not a heel-tap is left in the glass. **-schere,** *f.* nail-scissors. **-schmied,** *m.* nail-maker. **-schmiede,** *f.* nail-forge. **-weiß,** *n.* lunula, moon (*of the nail*). **-wurzel,** *f.* root of a nail. **-zange,** *f.* nippers. **-zieher,** *m.* nail-extractor. **-zwang,** *m.* (*coll.*) ingrowing nails.

Näg-elchen, *n.* (-s, –), **-lein,** *n.* (-s, –) tack, brad; (*dial.*) clove.

nage-n, *v.a.* & *n.* (*aux.* h.) gnaw, nibble; corrode, erode, eat into; rankle; *-nde Sorgen*, carking cares; *Kummer nagt an ihm*, he is eaten up with worry; *am Hungertuche -n*, be starving *or* destitute. **-r,** *m.*, **-tier,** *n.* rodent. **-zahn,** *m.* incisor tooth.

Näglein, *n.* (-s, –), *see* **Nägelchen.**

Nagler, *m.* nailer, nail-maker.

nah-(e), *adj.* (*with Dat.*) & *adv.* (*comp.* näher, *sup.* nächst) near, close, neighbouring, adjoining, adjacent; approaching, impending, imminent; *-e an*, nearly, almost, about; *see also* -e bei; *-e aneinander*, close to one another, contiguous; *-e bei*, close to; *-e dabei*, nearby; *-(e) daran sein*, be on the point of, almost happen that; *– und fern*, far and wide; *-er Freund*, close friend; *-e Gefahr*, impending danger; *das Weinen war ihr sehr -e*, she was very nearly crying; (*when, with verbs,* -(e) *has literal meaning of proximity, or when it is preceded by* zu, sehr, *etc., it is written separately: when it has a figurative meaning, it is used as a separable prefix.*) *-e Stadt*, neighbouring town; *wie – sind Sie verwandt?* how closely are you related?; *von -em ansehen*, look at closely, peer at. **-aufnahme,** *f.* close-up. **-ebei,** *adv.* near, close by, nearby. **-egehen,** *v.n.* (*aux* s.) grieve, affect; *sich -egehen lassen*, take to heart. **-ekommen,** *v.n.* (*aux.* s.) (*with Dat.*) approach, come near to *or* into close contact with, get at; resemble. **-elegen,** *v.a.* suggest, urge upon, make plain, bring home. **-eliegen,** *v.n.* suggest itself, be obvious *or* natural. **-eliegend,** *pres. part.* & *adj.* nearby, adjacent, neighbouring; obvious, manifest. **-en,** *v.r.* & *n.* (*aux.* s.) (*Dat.*) (*Poet.*) approach, come up, draw near. **-estehen,** *v.n.* be closely connected *or* friendly (with). **-etreten,** *v.n.* (*aux.* s.), *see* **-ekommen**; *einem -etreten*, hurt a p.'s feelings; *der Wahrheit zu -e treten*, violate the truth. **-ezu,** *adv.* nearly, almost, well-nigh. **-kampf,** *m.* hand-to-hand fighting, close combat; clinch (*Box.*). **-kampfjäger,** *m.* short-range fighter (*Av.*). **-kampfwaffe,** *f.* short-range weapon (*Mil.*). **-verkehr,** *m.* local traffic.

Näh-e, *f.* nearness, proximity; neighbourhood, surroundings, vicinity; propinquity; *in der -e*, near (to), close by *or* at hand; *in nächster -e*, at one's elbow; within call; *in erreichbarer -e*, within reasonable distance, within striking distance; *in der -e betrachten*, look at closely. **-er,** (*comp. of* nah(e)) *adj.* & *adv.* nearer, closer; more precise, more detailed, more intimate, more direct, shorter; (*also used as a separate prefix with meanings similar to compound verbs with* nahe–) *e.g. -erbringen*, explain, elucidate; *-ertreten*, become intimate with, get familiar with; *-ere Auskunft*, further information, more particulars; *-ere Bekanntschaft*, close acquaintance; greater familiarity, intimacy; *mit einem -er bekannt werden*, become closely acquainted with a p.; *bei -erer Betrachtung*, on further consideration; *darauf kann ich nicht -er eingehen*, I cannot go into further details; *um der Sache -er zu kommen*, to come to the point, to get to the root of a matter; *-eres Objekt*, direct object (*Gram.*); *-ere Rechte*, prior rights *or* claims; *treten Sie -er*, step this way! *die -ere Umgebung*, the immediate vicinity; *-ere Umstände*, particulars, details. **-ere(s),** *n.* details; particulars; *das -ere wollen Sie ersehen aus . . .*, for particulars please refer to . . .; *des -eren*, with regard to details *or* further particulars. **-ern,** 1. *v.a.* bring *or* place near. 2. *v.r.* approach, draw near. **-erung,** *f.* approximation (*Math.*). **-erungswert,** *m.* approximate value.

näh-en, 1. *v.a.* & *n.* (*aux.* h.) sew, stitch; do needlework; *einen Saum -en*, hem; *überwendlich -en*, overcast, whip-stitch. **-arbeit,** *f.* needlework. **-erei,** *f.* sewing; needlework. **-erin,** *f.* needlewoman, seamstress. **-garn,** *n.* sewing-cotton. **-kasten,** *m.*, **-kästchen,** *n.* workbox, sewing-box. **-korb,** *m.* work-basket. **-kränzchen,** *n.* sewing-bee. **-maschine,** *f.* sewing-machine. **-nadel,** *f.* (sewing-)needle. **-schule,** *f.* school of needlework. **-seide,** *f.* sewing-silk. **-unterricht,** *m.* sewing-class. **-wachs,** *n.* cobbler's wax. **-zeug,** *n.* sewing things, workbox. **-zwirn,** *m.* sewing-thread.

näher, *comp. adj., see* **näh-er. -n,** *see* **näh-ern. -ung,** *see* **Näh-erung.**

nahm, nahmest, nähme, *see* **nehmen.**

nähr-en, 1. *v.a.* feed, provide *or* supply with nourishment; nurse, suckle; keep, support; nourish; (*fig.*) cherish; entertain (*hope, etc.*); *ein Handwerk, das seinen Mann -t*, a trade by which a man may support himself. 2. *v.r.* gain a livelihood; maintain *or* keep o.s., support o.s. (by), live (on), feed on; *sich kümmerlich -en*, earn a scanty living, have great difficulty in making both ends meet. 3. *v.n.* (*aux.* h.) be nourishing. **-boden,** *m.* fertile soil; culture-medium. **-end,** *pr.p.* & *adj.* nutritious, nutritive, nourishing, nutrient. **-gang,** *m.* alimentary canal. **-geschäft,** *n.* nutrition. **-kräftig,** *adj.* nutritious. **-mittel,** *n.* nutriment, nutrient; (*usually pl.*) articles of food; prepared foodstuffs. **-mutter,** *f.* foster-mother. **-präparat,** *n.* patent food. **-saft,** *m.* nutrient juice, chyme, sap. **-salz,** *n.* nutrient salt. **-stand,** *m.* the producers, the peasants. **-stoff,** *m.* nutrient. **-ung,** *f.* feeding; nourishment, sustenance, nutrition; livelihood. **-wert,** *m.* nutritive value.

nahr-haft, *adj.* nourishing, nutritious, nutritive; alimentary; productive (*district, etc.*); (*fig.*) lucrative. **-ung,** *f.* nourishment, nutriment, food; support, sustenance, livelihood; *in -ung setzen*, give employment to, find work for; *seiner -ung nachgehen*, strive to gain a livelihood. **-ungsaufnahme,** *f.* absorption of food. **-ungsbedarf,** *m.* food requirement. **-ungsbedürfnis,** *n.* need of nourishment. **-ungsbrei,** *m.* chyme. **-ungsflüssigkeit,** *f.* chyle. **-ungsfreiheit,** *f.* agrarian self-sufficiency, independence of foodstuffs from abroad. **-ungskanal,** *m.* alimentary canal. **-ungsmangel,** *m.* scarcity of food. **-ungsmittel,** *n.* article of food; (*pl.*) means of subsistence, food supplies; food, victuals, foodstuffs. **-ungsmittelchemie,** *f.* chemistry of food. **-ungsmittelfälschung,** *f.* adulteration of food. **-ungsmittelkarte,** *f.* ration card. **-ungsmittelkunde,** *f.* science of nutrition. **-ungsmitteluntersuchung,** *f.* food research. **-ungsmittelzufuhr,** *f.* food-supply. **-ungssorgen,** *f.pl.* struggle for livelihood, difficulty in making both ends meet; *-ungssorgen haben*, make a precarious living, struggle for a living. **-ungsstoff,** *m.* foodstuff, nutritive substance. **-ungsverweigerung,** *f.* hunger-strike; sitiophobia (*Med.*). **-ungsvorschrift,** *f.* diet, regimen. **-ungswert,** *m.* nutritive *or* food value.

Naht, *f.* (⸗e) seam; suture (*Anat.*, *Bot.*, *Surg.*); join, joint, juncture, fissure; edge; sector boundary (*Mil.*); *aufgetrennte –*, split down the seam; *die – ist aufgegangen*, the seam has come undone; (*coll.*) *einem auf die – fühlen* or *gehen*, sound a p.; *einem auf die Nähte rücken*, press home one's attack on a p. **–kompagnie,** *f.* contact company (*Mil.*). **–los,** *adj.* seamless. **–stelle,** *f.* boundary between sectors (*Mil.*).

Nähterin, *f.* (*dial.*) *see* **Näherin.**

naiv, *adj.* naive, naïve, ingenuous, artless, simple. **–e,** *f.* ingénue (*Theat.*). **–ität,** *f.* naivety, naïvety, naïveté, simplicity, ingenuousness.

Najade, *f.* (-n) naiad, water-nymph.

Nam–e (*Austr. dial. also* **–en**) *m.* (-ens, -en) name, title, denomination; noun, appellation; character, reputation, good name; *Eigen–e*, proper noun; *Gattungs–e*, collective noun; *auf –en meiner Frau*, under my wife's name; (*C.L.*) *auf den –en lautend*, not negotiable, payable to order; *dem –en nach*, by name; *Dinge* or *das Kind beim rechten* or *richtigen –en nennen*, call a spade a spade, not mince matters; *seinen –en daruntersetzen*, set one's name to s.th.; *den –en zu etwas hergeben*, allow one's name to be associated with s.th.; *in Gottes –en*, in the name of God, for God's sake; *im –en des Königs*, in the king's name, by order of the king; *irrtümlicher –e*, misnomer; *sich einen großen –en machen*, gain a name for o.s.; *er geht unter dem –en*, he is known by the name of; *unter unsern vereinten –en*, under our joint signature; *wie ist Ihr* (*werter*) *–e?* what is your name? **–enchrist,** *m.* nominal Christian. **–enforschung,** *f.* study of (place *or* personal) names. **–engebung,** *f.* naming, nomenclature; christening. **–enkunde,** *f.*, *see* **–enforschung. –enlos,** *adj.* anonymous, nameless; ineffable, unspeakable, inexpressible, indescribable, dreadful. **–ennennung,** *f.* specifying by name, giving (of) the name. **–enregister,** *n.* index of names, list of names, roll. **–ens,** *adv.* called, named, by name of, in the name of. **–ensaufruf,** *m.* roll-call. **–enschild,** *n.* name-plate, scutcheon. **–ensfest,** *n. see* **–enstag. –enskarte,** *f.* visiting-card. **–enstag,** *m*, Saint's day, name-day (*R.C.*), (*coll.*) birthday (*R.C.*). **–ensvetter,** *m.* namesake. **–enszug,** *m.* signature, monogram. **–entausch,** *m.* change of name; metonymy. **–entlich,** *adj.* (*rare*) & *adv.* by name, particularly, especially. **–enverzeichnis,** *n.*, *see* **–enregister. –enwechsel,** *m.*, *see* **–entausch. –haft,** *adj.* well-known, noted, renowned, worth mentioning, noteworthy, considerable; *–haft machen*, name, specify. **–haftmachung,** *f.* designation, specification.

nämlich, 1. *adj.*; *der, die, das –e*, the (self-)same; *dieser –e Mensch*, the very man. 2. *adv.* namely, that is (to say), of course, (*archaic*) to wit. **–keit,** *f.* sameness, identity.

Nänie, *f.* (-n) elegy, dirge.

Nanking, *m.* (-s, -e & -s) nankeen.

nannte, nanntest, *see* **nennen.**

nanu, *int.*, *see* **na.**

Napf, *m.* (-es, ⸗e) basin, bowl. **–kuchen,** *m.* large cake.

Näpfchen, *n.* (-s, –) little bowl *or* basin; cup, cupule (*Bot.*, *Zool.*); cuvette (*Med.*).

Narb–e, *f.* (-n) scar; cicatrice (*Med.*); seam; grain (*in leather*); stigma, hilum (*Bot.*). **–en,** 1. *m.* (-s, –) grain (*of leather*). 2. *v.a.* scar, mark, grain (*leather*). 3. *v.r.*; *sich –en*, cicatrice, form a scar. **–enbildung,** *f.* cicatrization; pitting (*of metals*). **–enlos,** *adj.* unmarked; unscarred. **–enseite,** *f.* grain-side (*of leather*). **–envoll,** *adj.*, **–ig,** *adj.* scarred; marked, pitted; embossed, grained.

Narde, *f.* (-n) nard, spikenard. **–nöl,** *n.* nard-oil.

Narko–se, *f.* (-sen) narcosis, anaesthesia. **–tikum,** *n.* (-kums, -ka) narcotic. **–tisch,** *adj.* narcotic, anaesthetic; *–tische Mittel*, narcotics. **–tisieren,** *v.a.* narcotize, anaesthetize.

Narr, *m.* (-en, -en) fool, clown, jester, buffoon; *ein – von Hause aus*, a born fool; *den – abgeben*, play the fool; (*coll.*) *einen –en an einem fressen*, dote on a p., take a great fancy to a p.; *einen zum –en haben* or *halten*, make a fool of a p.; *sich zum –en hergeben* or *machen*, make a fool of oneself, make oneself a laughing-stock; (*Prov.*) *jedem –en gefällt seine Kappe*, everyone like his own hobby best; (*Prov.*) *ein – kann mehr fragen, als sieben Weise beantworten können*, a fool may ask more questions in one hour than a wise man can answer in seven years. **–en,** 1. *v.n.* (*aux.* h.) play the fool, fool. 2. *v.a.* make a fool of, dupe (*a p.*). **–enfest,** *n.* All Fools' Day. **–engeschwätz,** *n.* stuff and nonsense. **–enhaus,** *n.* madhouse. **–enkappe,** *f.* fool's cap, cap and bells. **–enseil,** *n.*; *einen am –enseil führen*, make a fool of a p., lead a p. by the nose. **–ensicher,** *adj.* foolproof. **–en(s)posse,** *f.* (*usually pl.*) foolery, tomfoolery, silly trick; *–enspossen treiben*, fool about, play the fool, play mad pranks. **–enstreich,** *m.* foolish trick, stupid act. **–etei,** *f.* madness, folly, fooling, tomfoolery. **–heit,** *f.* foolishness, folly, craziness, madness.

Närr–in, *f.* mad *or* foolish woman. **–isch,** *adj.* foolish, crazy, silly, mad; strange, peculiar, eccentric, ridiculous; *man möchte –isch werden*, it is enough to drive one mad; *ganz –isch auf eine S. sein*, be a complete fool about *or* dote on a th.

Narziß, *m.* (-(ss)es, -(ss)e) one lost in self-admiration. **–mus,** *m.* narcissism, self-worship.

Narzisse, *f.* (-n) narcissus; *gelbe –*, daffodil.

nas–al, *adj.* nasal (*Phonet.*). **–alieren,** *v.a.* nasalize, speak through the nose. **–allaut,** *m.* nasal (sound) (*Phonet.*). **–führen,** *v.a.* fool, bamboozle, dupe. **–horn,** *n.* (-s, -e & ⸗er) rhinoceros. **–ig,** *suffix* (*also* **-näsig**), e.g. *hoch–ig*, *hochnäsig*, proud, haughty, (*coll.*) stuck-up; *groß–ig*, *großnäsig*, with a big nose. **–lang,** *adj.*, *see* **nasenlang.** (*dial.*) **–tuch,** *n.* handkerchief.

nasch–en, *v.a.* & *n.* (*aux.* h.) eat sweets *or* dainties (*on the sly*); nibble, pick, pilfer (*food*); *gern –en*, have a sweet tooth. **–haft,** *adj.* sweet-toothed, fond of sweet things. **–katze,** *f. see* **Näscher. –lust,** *f.* fondness for dainties. **–maul,** *n.*, *see* **Näscher. –werk,** *n.* sweets, (*Amer.*) candy.

Näsch–er, *m.* (-ers, -er) sweet tooth. **–erei,** *f.* eating sweets on the sly; sweets.

Nase, *f.* nose, snout, proboscis; scent (*dog, etc.*); nozzle, spout; (*archaic*) beak (*of a ship*); tappet, cam (*Mach.*); (*fig.*) rebuke; *einem* (*etwas*) *an der – ansehen*, see by a p.'s face; *an der – herumführen*, lead by the nose; *einem etwas auf die – binden*, (*coll.*) put one over on a p., (*sl.*) pull a fast one; *einem auf der – herumtanzen*, do as one likes with a p., ride rough-shod over a p.; *auf der – liegen*, be laid up, be ill; *Mund und – aufsperren*, gape, stand aghast; (*vulg.*) *einem die Würmer aus der – ziehen*, worm a secret out of a p.; (*sl.*) *sich* (*Dat.*) *die – begießen*, booze, guzzle; *eine – bekommen*, be rebuked *or* snubbed; *in die – bekommen*, get on the scent (*of dogs*); *einem eine – drehen*, cock a snook at a p.; *eine feine – haben*, have a good nose for *or* a keen sense of smell; (*also fig.*) not miss much; *in die – steigen*, become noticeable (*of smells*); *das sticht mir in die –*, I hanker *or* crave after that; *einem eine lange – machen*, cock a snook *or* put one's fingers to one's nose at a p.; *mit langer – abziehen*, come away disappointed; *einen mit der – auf etwas stoßen*, bring a th. forcibly to a p.'s notice, rub a p.'s nose in s.th.; *der – nachgehen*, follow one's nose; *die – (über etwas) rümpfen*, turn up one's nose (at s.th.); *er steckt die – gern in Bücher*, he keeps his nose buried in his books; *seine – in jeden Quark* or *Dreck stecken*, poke one's nose into everything; *er trägt die – hoch*, he carries his nose in the air; *er hat sich viel Wind um die – wehen lassen*, he has knocked around a good deal; *einem etwas unter die – reiben*, cast s.th. in a p.'s teeth, fling a th. in a p.'s face, bring a th. home to a p., rub s.th. in; (*sl.*) *die – voll haben*, be fed up (with) *or* sick to death (of); *mir vor der –*, under my very nose; *einem die Tür vor der – zumachen*, slam the door in a p.'s face; *zieh* or *zupf dich an deiner* (*eignen*) *–!* mind your own business! *sich die – zuhalten*, hold one's nose. **–lang** *see* **–nlang. –nbein,** *n.* nasal bone. **–nbluten,** *n.* nose-bleeding. **–nflügel,** *m.* side *or* wing of the nose. **–ngewächs,** *n.* nasal polypus. **–nhöhle,** *f.* nasal cavity. **–nklemmer,** *m.*, **–nkneifer,** *m.*

pince-nez. **-nknorpel,** *m.* cartilage of the nose. (*coll.*) **-nlang,** *adj.*; *alle -nlang,* very frequently, every minute. **-nlänge,** *f.*; (*mit einer*) or (*um*) *eine -nlänge voraus sein,* win by a short head. **-nlaut,** *m.* nasal (sound) (*Phonet.*). **-nleiste,** *f.* leading edge (*of wing*) (*Av.*). **-nloch,** *n.* nostril. **-nrücken,** *m.* bridge of the nose. **-(n)rümpfen,** *n.* turning up the nose; sneering. **-nsattel,** *m.* bridge of the nose. **-nscheidewand,** *f.* nasal septum. **-nschleim,** *m.* mucous (discharge from the nose). **-nspitze,** *f.* tip of the nose. **-nstüber,** *m.* snub, snubbing, rap on the knuckles. **-nton,** *m.* nasal sound; twang. **-nwärmer,** *m.* comforter, muffler; (*coll.*) short pipe. **-weis,** *adj.* pert, saucy, impertinent, (*coll.*) cheeky. **-weisheit,** *f.* pertness, forwardness, sauciness; impudence, (*coll.*) cheek.

näs-eln, *v.n.* (*aux.* h.) snuffle, sniff; scent (*of dogs*); speak through the nose, nasalize. **-ig,** *suffix, see* **nas-ig.**

nasführen, Nashorn, nasig, *see* **nas-.**

naß, 1. *adj.* (*comp.* nässer, *also Austr. dial.* nasser, *sup.* nässest, *also Austr. dial.* nassest) wet, damp, humid, moist, rainy, liquid; *es wird -(ss)e Augen setzen* or *geben,* many a tear will be shed about it; *er hat das Bett - gemacht,* he has wet the bed; *-(ss)er Boden,* marshy *or* low-lying ground; *ein -(ss)er Bruder,* a tippler, toper, drunkard, sot *or* (*sl.*) boozer; (*dial. & coll.*) *für -,* (*sl.*) buckshee; *ein -(ss)es Grab,* a watery grave; *Vergoldung auf -(ss)em Wege,* water-gilding; *- werden,* get soaked *or* drenched. 2. *n.* (*Poet.*) humidity, wetness; liquid, water. **-dampf,** *m.* saturated *or* wet steam. **-fest,** *adj.* proof against damp, damp-proof. **-kalt,** *adj.* raw, damp and cold. **-verfahren,** *n.* wet process.

nassauern, *v.a.*; (*coll.*) *bei einem -,* sponge on a p.

Nässe, *f.* wet, wetness, dampness, moisture, humidity. **-n,** 1. *v.a.* wet, moisten, soak. 2. *v.n. & imp.* (*aux.* h.) ooze, discharge (*of wounds*); make *or* pass water; drizzle.

naszierend, *adj.* nascent (*Chem.*).

Nation, *f.* (-en) nation. **-al,** *adj.* national. **-albewußtsein,** *n.* national consciousness. **-alcharakter,** *m.* national character. **-ale,** *n.* (*archaic*) form giving personal particulars. **-alfarben,** *f. pl.*, **-alflagge,** *f.* national colours *or* flag. **-alfeiertag,** *m.* national holiday. **-algefühl,** *n.* patriotic feelings. **-alhymne,** *f.* national anthem. **-alitätenstaat,** *m.* federation. **-almannschaft,** *f.* national team. **-alökonom,** *m.* (political) economist. **-alökonomie,** *f.* political economy. **-alrat,** *m.* (Swiss) representative assembly. **-alsachen,** *f.pl.* domestic *or* home affairs. **-alsozialismus,** *m.* National Socialism. **-alsozialist,** *m.* National Socialist, (*coll.*) Hitlerite, Nazi. **-alsozialistisch,** *adj.* National Socialist. **-alstolz,** *m.* national pride. **-altracht,** *f.* national costume. **-alversammlung,** *f.* National Assembly.

Nativität, *f.* (-en) nativity; horoscope; *einem die - stellen,* cast a p.'s horoscope. **-ensteller,** *m.* astrologer.

Natrium, *n.* (-s) sodium. **-hydrat,** *n.* caustic soda. **-nitrat,** *n.* Chili saltpetre. **-sulfat,** *n.* Glauber's salts.

Natron, *n.* (-s) soda, sodium hydroxide *or* hydrate; *kohlensaures -,* sodium carbonate; *doppelkohlensaures -,* sodium bicarbonate; *salpetersaures -,* Chili saltpetre, sodium nitrate; *salzsaures -,* sodium chloride. **-lauge,** *f.* caustic soda solution, soda-lye.

Natter, *f.* (-n) adder, viper; *eine - am Busen nähren,* cherish a snake in one's bosom.

Natur, *f.* (-en) nature, disposition, constitution, essence; temperament, temper, frame of mind; (natural) scenery; *sie ist etwas bequemer -,* she is of a rather easy-going disposition; *hitzige -,* fiery temperament; *in -,* see *in -a*; *es liegt in der - der S.,* it is in the nature of things; *nach der - zeichnen,* draw from life *or* from nature; *es ist seiner - nach kalt,* it is naturally *or* by nature cold; *von - (aus),* by nature; *ein von - fester Ort,* a natural stronghold; *das ist mir von - zuwider,* I have a natural aversion to that; *es geht mir wider die -,* it goes against the grain; *der - seinen Tribut zahlen,* pay one's debt to nature; *einem zur zweiten - werden,* become second nature with a p. **-a,** *f.*; *in -a bezahlen,* pay in kind. **-alien,** *pl.* natural produce, fruits of the soil; natural history specimens. **-aliensammlung,** *f.* natural history collection, museum of natural curiosities. **-alisieren,** *v.a.* naturalize; *sich -alisieren lassen,* become naturalized. **-alisierung,** *f.* naturalization. **-alismus,** *m.* naturalism; natural religion. **-alistisch,** *adj.* naturalistic. **-allasten,** *pl.* charges to be paid in kind. **-alleistung,** *f.* payment *or* delivery in kind. **-allohn,** *m.* remuneration in kind. **-alverpflegung,** supply of provisions (*Mil.*). **-alzins,** *m.* tithe. **-anlage,** *f.* disposition, temperament; talent, gifts. **-arzt,** *m.* nature-healer, quack. **-begebenheit,** *f.* natural phenomenon. **-beobachtung,** *f.* study of nature. **-beschreibung,** *f.* natural description. **-bleiche,** *f.* grass bleach, sun bleach. **-bursche,** *m.* child of nature. **-butter,** *f.* real butter. **-dichtung,** *f.* nature-poetry. **-dienst,** *m.* natural religion, worship of nature. **-ell,** 1. *n.* (-s, -e) nature, disposition, temper. 2. *adj., see* **natürlich.** **-ereignis,** *n.*, **-erscheinung,** *f.* natural phenomenon. **-erzeugnis,** *n.* natural product. **-farbe,** *f.*, **-farbig,** *adj.* natural colour; self-colour; *-farbene Wolle,* natural wool. **-fehler,** *m.* natural defect. **-forscher,** *m.* naturalist, scientist; natural philosopher. **-gefühl,** *n.* feeling for nature. **-gemäß,** *adj.* conformable to nature, natural. **-geschichte,** *f., see* **-kunde.** **-gesetz,** *n.* law of nature, natural law. **-getreu,** *adj.* true to nature, true to life, life-like, natural. **-glaube,** *m.* natural religion. **-heilkunde,** *f.* nature cure. **-heilkundige(r),** *m.* nature healer. **-historiker,** *m.* writer of natural history. **-kind,** *n.* child of nature. **-kraft,** *f.* natural force; natural strength. **-kunde,** *f.* natural history. **-lehre,** *f.* natural philosophy, physics. **-mensch,** *m.* primitive man, uncivilized man; nature worshipper. **-notwendig,** *adj.* physically necessary. **-notwendigkeit,** *f.* physical necessity. **-produkte,** *n.pl.* natural products. **-recht,** *n.* natural right, natural law, law of nature. **-reich,** *n.* kingdom of nature; nature. **-religion,** *f.* natural religion. **-schutz,** *m.* preservation *or* conservation of natural beauty and wild life. **-schutzgebiet,** *n.* preserve, sanctuary, national trust property. **-schutzpark,** *m.* national (preserved) park. **-seltenheit,** *f.* natural curiosity. **-spiel,** *n.* freak of nature, sport (*Biol.*). **-stoff,** *m.* native *or* natural substance. **-trieb,** *m.* instinct. **-verehrung,** *f.* worship of nature. **-volk,** *n.* primitive race. **-wahr,** *adj.* true to nature, true to life. **-widrig,** *adj.* unnatural; abnormal. **-wissenschaft,** *f.* (natural *or* physical) science. **-wissenschaft(l)er,** *m.* scientist. **-wissenschaftlich,** *adj.* scientific. **-wolle,** *f.* native, natural *or* unprocessed wool. **-wüchsig,** *adj.* indigenous, original, natural, unforced. **-wunder,** *n.* prodigy. **-zustand,** *m.* natural *or* primitive state.

natürlich, 1. *adj.* natural, native, innate; normal, genuine, unaffected, uninhibited, artless; *ein -es Bedürfnis befriedigen,* satisfy nature's call, ease nature; *-e Tochter,* natural *or* illegitimate daughter; *eines -en Todes sterben,* die a natural death; *-e Tonleiter,* natural key (*without sharp or flat*); *-e Zuchtwahl,* natural selection (*Biol.*); *das geht ganz - zu,* that is quite natural *or* normal; *das geht nicht - zu,* there is something strange *or* uncanny in this; *in -em Zustand,* in a state of nature, naked. 2. *adv.*, **-erweise,** *adv.* of course, certainly, naturally. **-keit,** *f.* naturalness, genuineness, artlessness, simplicity.

Naut-ik, *f.* art of navigation; nautical affairs. **-iker,** *m.* navigator. **-isch,** *adj.* nautical.

Navig-ation, *f.* navigation. **-ationsoffizier,** *m.* navigator, pilot. **-ationsraum,** *m.* chart-room. **-ationschule,** *f.* naval college. **-ieren,** *v.a.* navigate.

ne, *see* **nee.**

Nebel, *m.* (-s, -) mist, fog, haze; *der - fällt,* the mist comes down; *künstlicher -,* smoke-screen; *- legen* or *abblasen,* lay a smoke-screen; *bei Nacht und -,* stealthily, like a thief in the night. **-artig,** *adj.* misty; (*fig.*) ill-defined. **-bank,** *f.* fog-bank.

-boje, *f.* smoke-buoy. **-bombe,** *f.* smoke-bomb. **-fleck,** *m.* nebula (*Astr.*); nebulous spot on the eye (*Med.*). **-geschoß,** *n.* smoke-shell (*Mil.*). **-grau,** *adj.* misty grey. **-haft,** *adj.* hazy, nebulous, dim. **-horn,** *n.* fog-horn. **-ig,** *adj.* (*also* **neblig**) foggy, misty, hazy. **-kappe,** *f.* magic cloak of invisibility; shroud of mist. **-krähe,** *f.* hooded crow. **-monat,** *m.*, **-mond,** *m.* (*poet.*) month of fogs, November. **-n,** *v.n.* (*aux.* h.) be *or* grow foggy; lay a smoke-screen; *es nebelt,* it is foggy. **-regen,** *m.* drizzle. **-schleier,** *m.* veil of mist; smoke-screen. **-schwaden,** *m.* damp fog. **-stern,** *m.* nebula. **-ung,** *m.* (*poet.*) November. **-wand,** *f.* smoke-screen (*Mil.*). **-wetter,** *n.* foggy weather.

neben, *adv. & prep.* (*with Acc. when expressing motion absolutely; with Dat. when expressing rest or limited motion*) beside, near, next to, by the side of, close to; with, in addition to, besides; *– mir,* at my side, beside me; in addition to me; in competition with me, compared with me; *stellen Sie es – mich,* put it beside me; *er stand* (*ging*) *– mir,* he stood (walked) by my side; *er trat – mich,* he came up to me; *– andern Dingen,* amongst other things. **-abschnitt,** *m.* adjoining sector (*Mil.*). **-absicht,** *f.* secondary objective *or* aim. **-achse,** *f.* secondary *or* lateral axis. **-amt,** *n.* sub-office; subsidiary appointment. **-an,** *adv.* close by, alongside, next-door. **-angriff,** *m.* diversionary attack (*Mil.*). **-anschluß,** *m.* extension (*Phone*), shunt (*Elec.*). **-arbeit,** *f.* work of secondary importance; extra work. **-ausgang,** *m.* side-exit. **-bedeutung,** *f.* secondary meaning. **-bedingung,** *f.* secondary factor, accessory factor. **-begriff,** *m.* subordinate *or* collateral idea. **-bei,** *adv.* close by, adjoining; by the way, incidentally, besides, moreover, by the by. **-beruf,** *m.*, **-beschäftigung,** *f.* incidental occupation, sideline, avocation. **-bestandteil,** *m.* secondary *or* accessory ingredient *or* constituent. **-beweis,** *m.* additional, collateral *or* corroborative proof. **-blatt,** *n.* stipule, bract (*Bot.*). **-buhler,** *m.* rival, competitor. **-buhlerschaft,** *f.* rivalry. **-durchmesser,** *m.* conjugate diameter. **-einander,** 1. *adv.* side by side, abreast, close together, in proximity *or* juxtaposition. 2. *n.* coexistence; *–einander bestehen,* coexist; *–einander stellen,* place side by side; *–einander gestellt,* in juxtaposition. **-einanderliegen,** *n.* contiguity. **-einanderschaltung,** *f.* parallel connexion (*Elec.*). **-einanderstehen,** *n.* juxtaposition. **-einanderstellen,** *v.a.* compare. **-einanderstellung,** *f.* juxtaposition, comparison. **-eingang,** *m.* side-entrance. **-einkünfte,** *f.pl.*, **-einnahme,** *f.*, **-erwerb,** *m.* perquisites, casual emoluments *or* earnings, additional income. **-einteilung,** *f.* subdivision. **-erbe,** *m.* co-heir. **-ergebnis,** *n.* subsidiary result. **-erzeugnis,** *n.* by-product, residual product. **-fach,** *n.* subsidiary subject. **-farbe,** *f.* secondary *or* complementary colour. **-figur,** *f.* subordinate figure (*Paint.*); accessory. **-fluß,** *m.* tributory, affluent. **-folge,** *f.* indirect result, secondary effect. **-forderung,** *f.* accessory claim. **-frage,** *f.* secondary question, question of less importance. **-frau,** *f.*, *see* **-weib.** **-gang,** *m.* byway, passage; side lode, lateral vein (*Min.*). **-gasse,** *f.* side-street, lane. **-gebäude,** *n.* outbuilding, annex; adjacent building. **-gebühren,** *f.pl.* extras, supplementary fees. **-gedanke,** subordinate idea; mental reservation. **-gelaß,** *n.*, **-gemach,** *n.* closet, box-room, small room; adjoining room. **-geleise,** *n.* siding (*Railw.*); (*fig.*) side-track. **-geräusch,** *n.* interference, atmospherics, jamming (*Rad.*). **-geschmack,** *m.* accompanying taste, incidental flavour, after-taste. **-gewinn,** *m.* extra *or* incidental profit. **-gleis,** *n.* siding (*Railw.*). **-handlung,** *f.* subordinate *or* subsidiary action (*Drama*); (*fig.*) episode, side-show. **-haus,** *n.* adjoining house, house next-door. **-her,** *adv.*, **-hin,** *adv.* by the side of, alongside; by the way, incidentally; along with, side by side with. **-hergehend,** *adj.* additional, secondary, accessory, subordinate, minor. **-interesse,** *n.* subordinate interest. **-kammer,** *f.*, *see* **-gemach;** auricle (*of heart*). **-kläger,** *m.* co-plaintiff. **-kosten,** *pl.* extras, incidental expenses. **-linie,** *f.* collateral line (*Genealogy*); branch line (*Railw.*). **-mann,** *m.* next man (*in line*); man right *or* left of one (*Mil.*). **-mensch,** *m.* fellow-creature. **-niere,** *f.* adrenal gland (*Anat.*). **-person,** *f.* subordinate character (*Theat.*); person of no consequence. **-postamt,** *n.* branch post-office. **-posten,** *m.* incidental item of expense. **-produkt,** *n.* by-product, residual product. **-reaktion,** *f.* secondary *or* side reaction. **-regierung,** *f.* collateral government. **-rolle,** *f.* subordinate part *or* role (*Theat. & fig.*). **-sache,** *f.* matter of secondary importance; non-essential, accessory. **-sächlich,** *adj.* unimportant, immaterial; accidental, incidental, accessory, subsidiary; *eine –sächliche Rolle spielen,* be of secondary importance. **-sächlichkeit,** *f.* unimportance, insignificance; subordination. **-satz,** *m.* subordinate *or* dependent clause (*Gram.*). **-schluß,** *m.* shunt (*Elec.*). **-schößling,** *m.* sucker, off-shoot. **-sonne,** *f.* mock-sun, parhelion. **-sprechen,** *n.* cross-talk (*Rad.*). **-sproß,** *m.*, *see* **-schößling.** **-ständig,** *adj.* accessory, collateral. **-stehend,** *adj.* proximate, following, annexed, in the margin; *der –stehende,* bystander; *wie –stehend,* as per margin. **-strafe,** *f.* additional punishment. **-straße,** *f.* side-street, by-road. **-strom,** *m.* tributary, feeder; shunt-current (*Elec.*). **-titel,** *m.* subtitle. **-ton,** *m.* secondary stress. **-treppe,** *f.* service- *or* backstairs. **-tür,** *f.* side-door. **-umstand,** *m.* accidental circumstance, minor *or* accessory detail, incident. **-ursache,** *f.* incidental cause; secondary reason. **-verdienst,** 1. *m.* incidental gain, extra profit, perquisites. 2. *n.* additional merit. **-versicherung,** *f.* collateral assurance, underwriting. **-weg,** *m.* by-way, side- *or* branch-road; (*pl.*) (*fig.*) indirect means. **-weib,** *n.* concubine. **-weibig,** *adj.* perigynous (*Bot.*). **-widerstand,** *m.* shunt, shunt resistance (*Elec.*). **-winkel,** *m.* adjacent angle. **-wirkung,** *f.* secondary effect *or* action. **-wort,** *n.* adverb (*Gram.*). **-wurzel,** *f.* adventitious root. **-zimmer,** *n.* next *or* adjoining room. **-zweck,** *m.* secondary aim. **-zweig,** *m.* side-branch; lateral branch.

nebst, *prep.* (*Dat.*) with, together *or* along with, in addition to, besides, including.

neck-en, *v.a.* tease, chaff; irritate, provoke; *was sich liebt, das –t sich,* lovers are fond of teasing. **-erei,** *f.* banter, raillery, chaffing, teasing. **-isch,** *adj.* fond of teasing, roguish; droll, queer, odd, funny.

nee, *int.* (*dial. & coll.*) no.

Neffe, *m.* (-n, -n) nephew.

Neg-ation, *f.* (-en) negation (*Math.*). **-ativ,** 1. *adj.* negative (*Math., Elec., Phot.*); (*coll.*) fruitless, unsuccessful. 2. *n.* (-s, -e), **-ativbild,** *n.* negative (*Phot.*). **-ativlack,** *m.* photographic varnish. **-ieren,** *v.a.* deny, answer in the negative, negative (*a proposal*). **-ierung,** *f.* denial, negation.

Neger, *m.* (-s, –) Negro. **-in,** *f.* Negro (woman, girl, etc.). **-artig,** *adj.*Negroid. **-braun,** *adj.* dark-brown. **-chor,** *m.* Negro-minstrels. **-handel,** *m.* slave-trade.

Negligé, [*pron.* negli'ʒe:], *n.* (-s, -s) négligé, dishabille; (*archaic*) informal dress, undress.

Negozi-ant, *m.* (-en, -en) negotiator, agent, trader, merchant. **-ieren,** 1. *v.a.* arrange, bring about, negotiate (*bills*). 2. *v.n.* negotiate, traffic.

nehm-en, *ir.v.a.* take; seize, appropriate, capture, lay hold of; receive, accept; *etwas an sich –en,* take s.th. into one's safe keeping; *einen Anfang –en,* begin; *Anstand –en,* hesitate (to), demur (at); *etwas auf sich* (*Acc.*) *–en,* take upon o.s., undertake a th., assume (*a charge or burden*); *eine Verantwortung auf sich –en,* shoulder a responsibility; *die Folgen auf sich –en,* answer for the consequences; (*coll.*) *etwas auf seine Kappe –en,* accept responsibility for s.th.; *Augenschein* (*von etwas*) *–en,* (*etwas*) *in Augenschein –en,* view *or* inspect (a th.); *einen beim Worte –en,* take a p. at his word; *–t euch ein Beispiel daran,* let this be an example to you; *ein Ende –en,* come *or* be brought to an end, cease, terminate; *ein ehrenvolles Ende –en,* die an honourable death; *es ernst mit einer S. –en,* be serious about a th.; *–en wir den Fall,* let us assume *or* suppose; *nicht für ungut –en*, not take amiss; *es genau –en*, be very particular *or* pedantic; *ein Boxer ist hart im –en*, a boxer takes punishment well; *ein Hindernis –en*, take *or* clear an obstacle; *nimm dich in Acht!* take care! *etwas in Angriff –en*, make a beginning with s.th., take a th. in hand; *in Anspruch –en*, make demands on, engross, absorb (*attention*); take up (*time*); *in Empfang –en*, accept, receive; *einen ins Gebet –en*, speak seriously to a p., take s.o. to task; (*mit*) *in* (*den*) *Kauf –en*, take into the bargain; *in Kost –en*, board (*a p.*); *etwas in seine Obhut –en*, take s.th. under one's charge *or* care; *ein Haus in Pacht –en*, take a lease on a house; *Interesse –en*, take an interest; *ich lasse es mir nicht –en*, I (must) insist upon it, I will not be talked out of it, I will not renounce that *or* (*coll.*) give it up; *er weiß seine Leute zu –en*, he understands how to handle people; *sich* (*Dat.*) *die Mühe –en*, take the trouble; *den Mund voll –en*, talk big, brag; *sie –en sich beide nichts*, there is nothing to choose between them, the one is as good as the other; *Partei –en* (*für einen*), side (with a p.), take a p.'s part; *Platz –en*, take a seat; *Reißaus –en*, decamp; *Rücksicht –en*, show consideration; *Schaden –en*, suffer damage; *einem die Sicht –en*, block *or* obscure s.o.'s view; (*coll.*) *er ist vom Stamme Nimm*, he has a grasping nature; *Stellung zu einer S. –en*, express *or* make clear one's attitude towards s.th.; *etwas über sich –en*, accept responsibility for carrying out s.th., take a th. upon o.s.; *Urlaub –en*, be granted leave; *das Wort –en*, begin to speak; *es* or *das nimmt mich Wunder*, it astonishes me, I am surprised at it; *zu sich –en*, take into one's house; take (food), eat (s.th.); *eine zur Frau –en*, make s.o. one's wife; *etwas zur Hand –en*, see *in Angriff –en*; *sich* (*Dat.*) *etwas zu Herzen –en*, take a th. to heart; *im Grunde genommen*, after all, at bottom; *streng* or *genau genommen*, strictly speaking.

Nehrung, *f.* (-en) narrow tongue of land.

Neid, *m.* (-es) envy; grudge; jealousy; *das muß ihm der Neid lassen*, (even) his worst enemy must admit that; *vor – vergehen*, die with envy; *– gegen einen hegen*, be envious of a p.; *blaß*, *gelb* or *grau vor – werden*, become green with envy. **–en**, *v.a.* & *n.* (*aux.* h.) envy; *einem etwas –en*, envy *or* begrudge a p. s.th. **–enswert**, *adj.* enviable. **–er**, *m.*, **–hammel**, *m.*, **–hart**, *m.* envious p. **–isch**, *adj.* envious, jealous (*auf einen*, of a p.). **–los**, *adj.* not envious, ungrudging.

Neidnagel, *m.* (*dial.*) see **Niednagel.**

Neig–e, *f.* (-n) slope, decline, declivity; sediment, dregs; depression, wane; *auf der –e sein*, *zur* or *auf die –e gehen*, come *or* draw *or* be coming to an end, run short, be on the decline; *den Becher bis zur –e leeren*, drain the cup to the dregs; *ein Faß auf die –e setzen*, tilt a barrel. **–en**, 1. *v.a.* tilt, bend (over); incline, bow, lower. 2. *v.r.* & *n.* (aux. h.) bend over, bow, dip, lean; slope, incline; decline, wane, draw to a close; be inclined to, tend; *der Tag –t sich dem Ende zu*, the day is drawing to a close; *er –t zu Erkältungen*, he is very apt to catch cold, he is subject *or* prone to chills; *der geneigte Leser*, the sympathetic *or* kind reader; *ein geneigtes Ohr*, a ready *or* sympathetic ear. **–ung**, *f.* inclination, preference, disposition, propensity, tendency, bias; taste (*for art, etc.*), liking; incline, declivity; bow(ing), bend(ing); slope, gradient, tilt, slant; dip, pitch, list (*of ship*); inclination (*Math.*, *Astr.*); *–ung haben* or *fassen zu*, take a fancy to. **–ungsebene**, *f.*, **–ungsfläche**, *f.* inclined plane. **–ungsehe**, *f.*, **–ungsheirat**, *f.* love-match. **–ungslinie**, *f.* gradient. **–ungslot**, *n.* axis of incidence. **–ungsmesser**, *m.* clinometer. **–ungsnadel**, *f.* dipping needle. **–ungswinkel**, *m.* angle of inclination.

nein, *adv.* no; *mit – beantworten*, answer in the negative; *– und abermals –!* no! a thousand times no! *– doch!* no, indeed! no, certainly not!

Nekro–log, *m.* (-s, -e) obituary (notice), necrology. **–mant**, *m.* (-en, -en) necromancer. **–mantie**, *f.* necromancy. **–se**, *f.* necrosis, gangrene, mortification (*Med.*).

Nelke, *f.* (-n) pink, carnation (*Dianthus caryophyllus*) (*Bot.*), clove; *gefüllte –*, double carnation; *Gewürz–*, clove (*Eugenia caryophyllata*) (*Bot.*). **–nöl**, *n.* oil of cloves. **–npfeffer**, *n.* allspice, pimento.

nenn–en, *ir.v.a.* name, call, term, style, denominate; mention by name, quote, speak of; enter (*Sport*); *das –e ich . . .*, that is what I call . . .; *ich hörte ihn –en*, I heard his name mentioned; *einer, der nicht genannt sein will*, one who does not wish his name to be known, who wishes to remain anonymous; *Karl, genannt der Kühne*, Charles surnamed the Bold; *diese sogenannten Doktoren*, these so-called doctors; *obengenannt*, above-mentioned; *das Kind beim Namen –en, ein Ding beim rechten Namen –en*, call a spade a spade. **–bar**, *adj.* nameable, speakable, mentionable. **–belastung**, *f.* nominal load. **–enswert**, *adj.* worth mentioning, noteworthy, important, considerable. **–er**, *m.* denominator. **–fall**, *m.* nominative case (*Gram.*). **–form**, *f.* infinitive (*Gram.*). **–geld**, *n.* entry-fee (*Sport*). **–leistung**, *f.* rated output *or* power. **–ung**, *f.* naming, nomination, mention, registration, entry (*Sport*). **–ungsliste**, *f.* list of competitors. **–ungsschluß**, *m.* close of entries (*Sport*). **–wert**, *m.* nominal value, face value; denomination (*of a coin*); (*C.L.*) *zum –wert*, at par. **–wort**, *n.* noun, substantive.

Neolog–ie, *f.*, **–ismus**, *m.* (-mus, -men) neology, neologism, verbal innovation, newly coined word.

neppen, *v.a.* & *n.* (*sl.*) diddle, swindle, take in, try it on, do brown.

Nereide, *f.* (-n) nereid, sea-nymph.

nergeln, *see* **nörgeln.**

Nerv, *m.* (-(e)s & -en, -en) nerve; (*archaic*) sinew; string (*of a bow*); vein (*of leaf*); fibre, filament; *einem auf die –en fallen* or *gehen*, get on a p.'s nerves. **–atur**, *f.* venation (*of leaf*). **–enanfall**, *m.* attack of nerves, fit. **–enanregung**, *f.* nerve impulse. **–enaufregung**, *f.* nervous excitement. **–endurchschneidung**, *f.*, *see* **–enschnitt. –enentzündung** *f.* neuritis. **–enfaser**, *f.* nerve fibre. **–enfieber**, *n* (*archaic*) typhus; (unspecified) nervous disease. **–engewebe**, *n.* nerve tissue. **–enheilanstalt**, *f.* clinic for nervous diseases. **–enknoten**, *m.* ganglion. **–enkrank**, *adj.* neurotic, neurasthenic. **–enkrankheit**, *f.* neurosis, neurasthenia. **–enkunde**, *f.*, **–enlehre**, *f.* neurology. **–enlähmung**, *f.* nervous paralysis. **–enleiden**, *n.* nervous complaint. **–ennaht**, *f.* nerve seam *or* suture. **–enreiz**, *m.* nervous irritation. **–enschmerz**, *m.* (*usually pl.*) neuralgia. **–enschnitt**, *m.* neurotomy. **–enschock**, *m.* shock. **–enschwach**, *adj.* nervous, neurasthenic. **–enschwäche**, *f.* nervous debility, neurasthenia. **–enstrang**, *m.* nerve-centre. **–ensystem**, *n.* nervous system. **–enzelle**, *f.* nerve cell. **–enzentrum**, *n.* nerve-centre. **–enzerrüttung**, *f.* shattered nerves. **–enzucken**, *n.* nervous twitching. **–enzusammenbruch**, *m.* nervous breakdown. **–ig**, *adj.* veined, ribbed; sinewy, pithy. **–ös**, *adj.* nervous, excitable, (*coll.*) nervy. **–osität**, *f.* nervousness.

Nerz, Nörz, *m.* (-es, -e) mink (*Zool.*).

Nessel, *f.* (-n) nettle; *Bren(n)–*, stinging nettle; *Taub–*, dead-nettle; (*coll.*) *er hat sich in die –n gesetzt*, he has put his foot in it. **–ausschlag**, *m.* nettle-rash, urticaria (*Med.*). **–brand**, *m.* nettle-sting. **–fieber**, *n.*, **–sucht**, *f.*, *see* **–ausschlag. –tuch**, *n.* unbleached calico.

Nest, *n.* (-es, -er) nest; eyrie, eyry, aerie *or* aery; nidus; (*fig.*) home, haunt, den; (*fig.*) small country town, village; hole, emplacement (*Mil.*); cluster, rosette (*Min.*); (*coll.*) bed; *die Polizei fand das – leer*, the police found the bird(s) flown; *Krähwinkel ist ein rechtes* or *elendes –*, K. is a godforsaken hole; *–er ausnehmen*, go bird-nesting; *sein eignes – beschmutzen*, foul one's own nest; (*Prov.*) *eigen – ist stets das Best'*, there's no place like home. **–feder**, *f.* down. **–flüchter**, *m.* autophagous bird; (*pl.*) autophagi. **–förmig**, *adj.* nidiform. **–häkchen**, *n.* nestling; spoilt child, baby pet of the family. **–hocker**, *m.* insessorial *or* heterophagous bird; (*pl.*) insessores. **–küchlein**, *n.* nestling; (*fig.*) pet. **–ling**, *m.* nestling.

Nestel, *f.* (-n) string, thread, thong, (tagged) lace, strap. **-beschlag,** *m.* tag (*of a lace*). **-loch,** *n.* eyelet-hole. **-n,** *v.a.* lace up, fasten with a lace. **-nadel,** *f.* bodkin.

nett, *adj.* pleasant, amiable, kind; nice, pretty, neat, spruce, trim, tidy, (*coll.*) clear, unambiguous; *-e Zustände,* (*iron.*) a fine state of affairs. **-igkeit,** *f.* neatness, spruceness; prettiness; kindness.

netto, *adv.* (*C.L.*) net, clear (of all charges); *– Kassa im voraus,* net cash in advance. **-betrag,** *m.* net amount. **-einnahme,** *f.*, **-gewinn,** *m.* net profits. **-ertrag,** *m.* net proceeds, net yield. **-gewicht,** *n.* net weight. **-preis,** *m.* net price; *–preis drei Schillinge,* three shillings net. **-registertonnen,** *pl.* net register tonnage (*Naut.*).

Netz, *n.* (-es, -e) net, netting, mesh, gauze; lattice, network; (*pl.*) toils; caul, reticulum, plexus; reticule (*Opt.*); electric mains; *ein – von Lügen,* a tissue *or* tangle of lies; *ins – locken,* win over. **-anschluß,** *m.* connexion to mains (*Elec.*). **-artig,** *adj.* reticular. **-auge,** *n.* compound eye (*Ent.*). **-ball,** *m.* lawn-tennis. **-brumm,** *m.* mains hum (*Rad.*). **-empfänger,** *m.* mains receiver (*Rad.*). **-flügler,** *m.pl.* neuroptera (*Ent.*). **-förmig,** *adj.* reticular. **-funk,** *m.* relay service (*Rad.*). **-gerät,** *n.* mains-set (*Rad.*). **-gleichrichter,** *m.* A C. eliminator (*Rad.*). **-haut,** *f.* retina; omentum (*Anat.*). **-hautspiegel,** *m.* ophthalmoscope. **-hemd,** *n.* cellular shirt. **-magen,** *m.* reticulum, second stomach of ruminants. **-spannung,** *f.* mains *or* line voltage. **-stecher,** *m.* mains plug (*Elec.*). **-steller,** *m.* snarer. **-stoff,** *m.* cellular cloth. **-stricker,** *m.* net maker. **-werk,** *n.* network; reticulation (*Arch.*).

netz-en, *v.a.* wet, moisten, sprinkle, soak, steep, humidify. **-kasten,** *m.*, **-kessel,** *m.*, **-ständer,** *m.* steeping-tub, immersion vat *or* tank.

neu, *adj.* new, fresh; recent, modern, novel, latest; *die –(er)e Geschichte,* modern history; *–e Mode,* latest fashion; *–en Mut schöpfen,* gain fresh courage; *was gibt's –es?* what is the news? *aufs –e,* anew, afresh, again, once more; *von –em,* see *aufs –e*; (*with finite verbs usually written separately; with participles used attributively usually as a prefix.*) *– aufgelegt,* reprinted; *etwas – machen,* renovate; *ein Schauspiel – besetzen,* re-cast a play; *–hinzugekommene Mitglieder,* newly enrolled members; *ein –eröffnetes Geschäft,* a recently established business; *die –eren,* the moderns; *die –eren Sprachen,* modern languages; *in –erer Zeit, in –ester Zeit,* in recent times, of late years. **-angekommen,** *adj.* newly arrived. **-angekommene(r),** *m.* new arrival. **-anschaffung,** *f.* new purchase, acquisition. **-ansiedlung,** *f.* resettlement. **-artig,** *adj.* new-style, new-fashioned, novel. **-auflage,** *f.* new edition, reprint. **-backen,** *see* **-gebacken.** **-bau,** *m.* building in course of erection; reconstruction. **-bauten,** *m.pl.* new buildings. **-bearbeitung,** *f.* revised edition, revision. **-bekehrte(r),** *m.* neophyte. **-bildung,** *f.* new growth, new formation; neologism. **-bruch,** *m.* ground newly broken and cleared. **-druck,** *m.* reprint. **-einstellung,** *f.* adjustment; appointment. **-erdings,** *adv.* latterly, recently. **-(e)rer,** *m.* innovator. **-erlich,** *adj.* recent, late; repeated, renewed. **-ern,** *v.n.* (*aux.* h.) innovate; modernize. **-erung,** *f.* innovation. **-erungssüchtig,** *adj.* fond of innovations. **-estens,** *adv.* very recently. **-gebacken,** *adj.* newly baked, freshly made, fresh; (*fig.*) newly-fledged, new-fangled; *der –gebackene,* upstart. **-geboren,** *adj.* new-born. **-gestaltung,** *f.* reorganization, modification. **-gier(de),** *f.* curiosity, inquisitiveness. **-gierig,** *adj.* curious, inquisitive. **-griechisch,** *adj.* modern Greek. **-heit,** *f.* novelty, newness. **-hochdeutsch,** *n.* Modern High German. **-igkeit,** *f.* news, piece of news; new production; novelty; *–igkeiten des Tages,* current events. **-jahr,** *n.* New Year; *Prosit –jahr!* A happy New Year! **-jahrstag,** *m.* New-Year's day. **-jahrswunsch,** *m.* New-Year's greeting (card). **-land,** *n.*, *see* **-bruch**; (*fig.*) new territory; new departure. **-lateinisch,** *adj.* Neo-latin. **-lich,** *adv.* recently, the other day, a day or two ago (*in E. Germany*); the other week, a week or so ago (*in W. Germany*). **-ling,** *m.* novice, beginner, tyro, neophyte; stranger. **-metall,** *n.* virgin metal. **-modisch,** *adj.* fashionable, novel; new-fangled. **-mond,** *m.* new moon. **-orientierung,** *f.* new course (*esp. in politics*); new approach, new policy. **-philolog(e),** *m.* modern language specialist. **-platoniker,** *m.* Neoplatonist. **-regelung,** *f.* rearrangement. **-reich,** *adj.*, **-reiche(r),** *m.* parvenu, (wealthy) upstart, nouveau riche. **-silber,** *n.* German silver, nickel silver, argentine. **-sprachler,** *m.*, *see* **-philologe.** **-steinzeitlich,** *adj.* neolithic. **-vermählt,** *adj.* newly married. **-wahl,** *f.* new *or* second election. **-zeit,** *f.* modern times. **-zeitlich,** *adj.* modern.

neun, 1. *num. adj.* nine; *alle –(e) schieben,* throw down the whole nine (*at skittles*). 2. *f.* (-en) number nine. **-auge,** *n.* lamprey. **-eck,** *n.* nonagon. **-eckig,** *adj.* nonagonal. **-er,** *m.* the figure nine; one of nine. **-erlei,** *indec. adj.* of 9 different sorts. **-fach,** *adj.*, **-fältig,** *adj.* ninefold. **-jährig,** *adj.* 9 years old. **-jährlich,** *adj.* recurring every ninth year, novennial. **-mal,** *adv.* 9 times. (*iron.*) **-malklug,** *adj.* would-be clever, sapient. **-malkluge(r),** *m.* know-all. **-monatlich,** *adj.* every 9 months. **-stimmig,** *adj.* for 9 voices (*Mus.*). **-t,** *adj.* ninth. **-tehalb,** *indec. adj.* eight and a half. **-teilig,** *adj.* of nine parts. **-tel,** *n.* (*Swiss dial. m.*) ninth part. **-tens,** *adv.* in the ninth place, ninthly. **-zahl,** *f.* ennead. **-zehn,** *num. adj.* nineteen. **-zig,** *num. adj.* ninety; *ein mittlerer –ziger,* a man in the middle nineties; *in den –ziger Jahren,* in the nineties, in the last decade of the century, between (18)90 and (19)00. **-zigjährig,** *adj.* 90 years old. **-zigjähriger,** *m.* nonagenarian. **-zigst,** *num. adj.* ninetieth. **-zigstel,** *n.* ninetieth part.

Neur-algie, *f.* neuralgia. **-algisch,** *adj.* neuralgic. **-asthenie,** *f.* neurasthenia. **-astheniker,** *m.* neurasthenic. **-in,** *n.* neurine. **-om,** *n.* neuroma. **-ose,** *f.* neurosis.

neutr-al, *adj.* neutral, impartial. **-alisieren,** *v.a.* neutralize, saturate. **-alität,** *f.* neutrality. **-alitätserklärung,** *f.* declaration of neutrality. **-alitätsverletzung,** *f.* violation of neutrality. **-um,** *n.* (-ums, -a & -en) neuter (*Gram.*).

nicht, 1. *adv.* not; *was man dort – alles hört!* what surprising things one hears there! *und ich auch –,* not even I, nor I; *bitte –!* please don't! *– doch!* no, but no, don't! certainly not! *durchaus –,* not at all, by no means, on no condition; in no way, not in the least; *– einmal,* not even, not so much as; (*ganz und*) *gar –,* see *durchaus –*; *– mehr,* not any longer, no longer; *noch –,* not (as) yet; (*sl.*) *das ist – ohne,* that's not bad, that's not so dusty, that's not to be sneezed at; *– wahr?* is it not so? isn't it? aren't you? *– weniger als,* no *or* not less than; *wo – . . .,* unless, if not . . .? 2. *part.*; *– ?* is it not? 3. (*archaic & poet.*) to be sure, (*or often redundant*) *wie schön ist – die Eintracht!* how beautiful is concord! (is it not?); *wie liebte ich ihn –!* how I did love him! (didn't I?); *verhüt' es Gott, daß ich nicht Hilfe brauche!* God forbid that I should need help! 4. (*archaic.*) *n.* naught, nothing; *mit –en* (*see also* **mitnichten**), by no means, not at all; (*see also* **zunichte**). **-achtung,** *f.* disregard, disrespect. **-amtlich,** *adj.* unofficial. **-anderskönnen,** *n.* inability to do otherwise. **-anerkennung,** *f.* disavowal; repudiation (*of debts*). **-angreifend,** *adj.* non-corroding, inert. **-angriffspakt,** *m.* non-aggression pact. **-annahme,** *f.* non-acceptance. **-arisch,** *adj.* (*Nat. Soc.*) non-Aryan, Jewish. **-beachtung,** *f.* non-observance. **-beamtet,** *adj.* unestablished, not on the permanent staff. **-bezahlung,** *f.*, *see* **-zahlung.** **-brennbar,** *adj.* uninflammable, non-inflammable. **-duldung,** *f.* intolerance. **-eignung,** *f.* unfitness, unsuitableness. **-eingeweihte(r),** *m.* uninitiated *or* uninformed p. **-einhaltung,** *f.* non-compliance. **-einmischung,** *f.* non-interference. **-eisen,** *adj.* nonferrous. **-erscheinen,** *n.* non-appearance; default (*Law*). **-flüchtig,** *adj.* non-volatile. **-gebrauch,** *m.* disuse, lack of use. **-haltbar,** *adj.* unstable. **-haltung,** *f.* non-observance; adjournment (*of a meeting, etc.*). **Nicht-Ich,** *n.* non-ego, world of objective reality (*Phil.*). **-ig,** *adj.* null, void; invalid; vain, futile, idle, empty; transitory; perishable; *-ig machen*, annul, abolish; *für (null und) -ig erklären*, quash, annul, declare (null and) void. **-igkeit,** *f.* nullity, invalidity, invalidation, nothingness; futility, vanity. **-igkeitsbeschwerde,** *f.*, **-igkeitsklage,** *f.* plea of nullity. **-igkeitserklärung,** *f.* annulment. **-leiter,** *m.* non-conductor (*Phys.*). **-löslich,** *adj.* insoluble. **-metall,** *n.* metalloid. **-mitglied,** *n.* non-member. **-periodisch,** *adj.* aperiodic. **-raucher,** *m.* non-smoker. **-reduzierbar,** *adj.* irreducible. **-rostend,** *adj.* rust-proof, stainless. **-s,** *see* **nichts. -sein,** *n.* non-existence, nullity. **-vollziehung,** *f.* non-execution, non-fulfilment. **-vorhandensein,** *n.* absence, lack; non-existence (*Phil.*). **-wesentlich,** *adj.* non-essential. **-wissen,** *n.* ignorance. **-wollen,** *n.* unwillingness. **-zahlung,** *f.* non-payment; *-zahlung eines Wechsels*, dishonouring of a bill. **-zielend,** *adj.* intransitive (*Gram.*). **-zutreffende(s),** *n.* that which does not apply *or* is inapplicable.

Nichte, *f.* (-n) niece.

nichts, 1. *ind. & indec. pron.* nothing, (*archaic*) naught; *- als*, nothing but, nothing short of; *es ist - daran* or *- an der S.*, there is no truth in it, it is of no consequence; *- anderes*, nothing else; *- der Art*, nothing of the kind; no such things; *- daraus machen*, not take too seriously; *- dergleichen*, no such thing; *für - achten*, think little *or* nothing of; (*ganz und*) *gar -*, nothing at all, nothing whatever; *es ist - Gutes an ihm*, there is no good in him; *sich in - unterscheiden*, show no difference whatever, be completely identical, be the same in all respects; *- mehr*, nothing more, no more; *mir -, dir -*, quite coolly, without more ado, bold as brass; (*coll.*) *es ist - damit*, it is no go; *wissen Sie - Neues?* have you no news? *- nützen*, be of no use; *mit der S. ist es -, es kann aus der S. - werden*, nothing can come of it; *das hat - zu sagen, das schadet -*, that does not matter at all, that is of no consequence; *sonst -?* nothing more? nothing else? is that all? *es bleibt mir weiter - übrig*, I have no alternative, I have no choice in the matter; *um -*, for nothing; *um - und wieder -*, without any cause whatever, for no reason in the world; *um - gebessert*, in no wise improved, in no way better; *- für ungut!* don't take it amiss; *so viel wie -*, next to nothing; *- von dem!* no such thing; *- (mehr) davon!* not a word of that! *ich habe - davon*, it does not benefit me at all, I get nothing out of it; *- weniger als*, anything but; *- wert*, of no value, valueless; *wenn es weiter - ist*, if that is all, if it is nothing more than that; *es zu - bringen*, fail to achieve anything. 2. *n.* nothingness, emptiness, void, nothing, chaos; insignificance, trifle, bagatelle, cipher; *vor dem - stehen*, be past hope, be face to face with ruin, not have a leg to stand on. **-bedeutend,** *adj.* insignificant. **-destominder, -destoweniger,** *adv.* nevertheless, notwithstanding. **-er,** *m.*, **-nutz,** *m.* (-es, -e) good-for-nothing, ne'er-do-well, scamp. **-nutz(ig),** *adj.* useless, worthless, good-for-nothing. **-nutzigkeit,** *f.* uselessness, futility; worthlessness. **-sagend,** *adj.* meaningless, insignificant, indeterminate, vague, colourless. **-tuer,** *m.* idler, loafer, slacker. **-tun,** *n.* idling, idleness, indolence, listlessness, inaction. **-würdig,** *adj.* worthless, base, vile. **-würdigkeit,** *f.* worthlessness; baseness; (*pl.*) base actions.

Nichts, *n.* flowers of zinc, zinc oxide.

Nick, *m.* (-es, -e) nod. **-en,** *v.n.* (*aux.* h.) nod; (*coll.*) doze, snooze. **-er,** *m.*, *see* -; hunting-knife. **-erchen,** *n.* nap, snooze.

[1]**Nickel,** *m.* (-s, -) (*dial.*) dwarf; pigheaded fellow; scamp. **-mann,** *m.* water-sprite.

[2]**Nickel,** 1. *n.* (*Austr. dial. m.*) nickel. 2. *m.* small coin, copper; (*coll.*) *ein paar -*, a few coppers. **-ocker,** *m.* nickel-ochre. **-oxydul,** *n.* nickelous oxide. **-stahl,** *m.* nickel-steel. **-überzug,** *m.* nickel-plating.

nid, (*dial.*), *see* **nied.**

nie, *adv.*, **-mals,** *adv.* never, at no time; *- und nimmer*, never at any time; *noch -*, never before *or* yet; *fast -*, hardly ever. **-mand,** *indec. pron.*, *see* **niemand.**

nied, *prep. & adv.* (*dial.*) below, beneath. **-en,** *adv.* (*Poet.*) here below, here on earth. **-er, -rig,** *see* **nieder, niedrig.**

nieder, 1. *adj.* low, inferior, mean, base, vulgar; *hoch und -*, high and low, great and small, rich and poor; *der -e Adel*, the gentry; *ein -er*, one of low birth; *die -en*, inferiors. 2. *adv. & sep. prefix*, down; low; *auf und -*, up and down; *- mit den Verrätern!* down with the traitors! **-beugen,** *v.a.* bend down, depress; humiliate. **-brechen,** *ir.v.a. & n.* (*aux.* s.) break down, reduce to submission. **-brennen,** *ir.v.a. & n.* (*aux.* s.) burn down (*to the ground*). **-brüllen,** *v.a.* howl down. **-bücken,** *v.a. & r.* bow down, stoop, grovel. **-deutsch,** *adj.* Low German, North German. **-druck,** *m.* low pressure. **-drücken,** *v.a.* press *or* weigh down, keep down, depress; overwhelm, oppress (*see* **-gedrückt**). **-fahren,** 1. *ir.v.n.* (*aux.* s.) descend. 2. *v.a.* knock over, run down. **-fahrt,** *f.* descent. **-fall,** *m.*, **-fallen,** *n.* downfall; prostration. **-fallen,** *ir.v.n.* (*aux.* s.) fall down; settle, alight (*of birds*); precipitate (*Chem.*); *vor einem -fallen*, fall at a p.'s feet. **-frequenz,** *f.* low frequency (*Elec.*), audio- *or* speech-frequency (*Rad.*). **-gang,** *m.* downfall, decline; setting (*of the sun*); down-stroke (*Mech.*); companion-way (*Naut.*). **-gedrückt,** *adj.* depressed. **-gedrücktkugelig,** *adj.* spheroidal. **-gehen,** *ir.v.n.* (*aux.* s.) go down, descend, sink; set (*of the sun*); land, alight (*Av.*); burst, break out (*of a storm*). **-gelassene(r),** *m.* (*Swiss dial.*) permanent resident. **-geschlagen,** *p.p. & adj.* dejected, depressed, low-spirited, cast-down. **-geschlagenheit,** *f.* depression, dejection, low spirits. **-halten,** *ir.v.a.* hold *or* keep down, suppress; fasten *or* peg down; neutralize *or* pin down (*troops*). **-holen,** *v.a.* haul down *or* lower (*a flag*). **-holz,** *n.* undergrowth, brushwood, scrub. **-jagd,** *f.* coursing. **-kämpfen,** *v.a.* overcome, overpower, subdue, silence (*enemy's fire*), destroy (*troops*), reduce (*a fort*); *die Gebrechen des Alters -kämpfen*, get the better of the infirmities of old age. **-kommen,** *ir.v.n.* (*aux.* s.) be confined, lie in (*of women*). **-kunft,** *f.* (-en & ¨-e) delivery, confinement. **-lage,** *f.* warehouse, depot; (*C.L.*) agency, branch establishment; defeat, overthrow. **-lande,** the Netherlands *or* Low Countries. **-länder,** *m.* Netherlander, Dutchman. **-lassen,** 1. *ir.v.a.* let down, lower. 2. *v.r.* sit down; settle, establish oneself; alight. **-lassung,** *f.* lowering; settling, establishment; settlement, colony. **-legen,** 1. *v.a.* lay *or* put down, deposit, store, warehouse; resign, abdicate, (*coll.*) knock off (*work*); *ein Kind -legen*, put a child to bed. 2. *v.r.* lie down, go to bed. **-legung,** *f.* deposition; abdication; resignation. **-machen,** *v.a.*, **-metzeln,** *v.a.* cut down, slay, massacre, wipe out. **-reißen,** *ir.v.a.* pull down, demolish; precipitate (*Chem.*). **-ringen,** *v.a.* overpower, overcome. **-rollen,** *v.n.* (*aux.* s.) roll down; *der Vorhang rollt -*, the curtain falls. **-schießen,** 1. *ir.v.a.* shoot down. 2. *v.n.* (*aux.* s.) shoot *or* rush down. **-schlag,** *m.* precipitation; down-stroke; knock-out (*Sport*); beat, fall (*Mus.*); sediment, deposit, precipitate (*Chem.*); rainfall (*Meteor.*); (*fig.*) result, outcome, upshot. **-schlagen,** *ir.v.a.* strike *or* knock down, cast down (*eyes*); knock out (*in boxing*); prostrate; deposit, precipitate (*Chem.*); fell; quiet, pacify; condense (*of steam*); put down, quell; quash, cancel, refute; dishearten, depress (*see* **-geschlagen**). **-schlagend,** *pr.p. & adj.* disheartening, depressing. **-schlagmittel,** *n.* precipitant, precipitating agent. **-schlag(s)messer,** *m.* rain-gauge. **-schlagung,** *f.* cancellation (*of debts or taxes*); suppression (*of rebellion*). **-schlagwasser,** *n.* condensed water, condensate, water of condensation. **-schmettern,** *v.a.* strike down, dash to the ground; (*fig.*) crush, overwhelm; depress; *-schmetternde Worte*, shattering words. **-schreiben,** *v.a.* write down. **-schreien,** *v.a.* shout down. **-schrift,** *f.* written copy, notes. **-senken,** 1. *v.a.* let down. 2. *v.r.* sink, fall (*night*). **-setzen,** 1. *v.a.* set *or* put down; deposit; ground (*arms, Mil.*). 2. *v.r.*

sit down. **-sinken,** *v.a.* sink down, drop. **-spannung,** *f.* low voltage, low tension. **-steigen,** *ir.v.n.* (*aux.* s.) descend, step down. **-stoßen,** 1. *v.a.* knock down. 2. *v.n.* (*aux.* s.) swoop down. **-strecken** 1. *v.a.* stretch to the ground, prostrate; cut down, knock down. 2. *v.r.* lie down. **-strich,** *m.* downstroke; down-bow (*Mus.*). **-stürzen,** 1. *v.a.* precipitate, throw *or* hurl down. 2. *v.n.* (*aux.* s.) fall violently. **-tracht,** *f.* meanness, baseness. **-trächtig,** *adj.* low, base, mean, abject, vile. **-trächtigkeit,** *f.* base act, vile action. **-treten,** *ir.v.a.* tread *or* trample down; wear down (*heels of shoes*). **-ung,** *f.* lowland, plain, low ground, marsh. **-wald,** *m.* undergrowth, brushwood, coppice, copse. **-wärts,** *adv.* downwards; *-wärts gekehrt,* reversed (*Her.*). **-werfen,** 1. *v.a.* throw down; put down, suppress, overcome, crush (*a rising*). 2. *v.r.* prostrate o.s. **-werfung,** *f.* suppression.

niedlich, *adj.* pretty, nice, dainty, neat, elegant; (*coll.*) *das ist ja recht –*, that's a fine state of affairs, a nice mess indeed! **-keit,** *f.* prettiness, niceness, neatness.

Niednagel, *m.* (-s, ¨-) agnail, hangnail, torn quick (*of nail*).

niedrig, *adj.* low; lowly, inferior, humble, obscure; base, abject, vile, vulgar; mean; *hoch und –*, great and small; one and all; (*C.L.*) *-e Prämie*, short premium; *– halten*, keep down (*prices*); *von -em Stande*, of low birth; of poor standing; *von einem – denken*, have a poor *or* low opinion of a p. **-er,** *adj. comp.* lower; inferior; *eine S. -er hängen*, show a th. in its true light, (*sl.*) debunk a th.; *ausländische Fond. gingen -er*, foreign stocks fell. **-keit,** *f.* lowness; lowliness; baseness. **-wasser,** *n.* low tide.

niemals, *adv.*, *see under* **nie.**

niemand, *ind. pron.* (-(e)s, (*Dat.* -em *or* (*archaic*) -en), *Acc.* – *&* -en) nobody, no one; *– anders*, no one else; *– Fremdes*, no stranger. **-sland,** *n.* no-man's-land (*Mil.*).

Niere, *f.* (-n) kidney; nodule, concretion (*Min.*); (*pl.*) loins; *wandernde –*, floating kidney; *einen auf Herz und -n prüfen*, subject a p. to a thorough examination, (*sl.*) pump a p. **-nbraten,** *m.* roast loin. **-nentzündung,** *f.* nephritis. **-nfett,** *n.* suet. **-nförmig,** *adj.* reniform, kidney-shaped. **-ngrieß,** *m.* renal gravel. **-stein,** *m.* renal stone. **-nstück,** *n.* loin of veal. **-ntalg,** *m.* suet.

nies-eln, *v.n.* (*imp.*) drizzle; (*dial.*) dawdle. **-en,** 1. *v.n.* (*aux.* h.) sneeze; *auf etwas -en*, sniff at a th., turn one's nose up at s.th. 2. *n.* sneeze; sneezing. **-fieber,** *n.* hay fever. **-kraut,** *n.* sneezewort (*Achillea ptarmica*) (*Bot.*). **-pulver,** *n.* sneezing-powder; sternutative, snuff. **-wurz,** *f.* hellebore (root).

Nieß-brauch, *m.* usufruct, benefit. **-brauchen,** *v.a.* enjoy the usufruct. **-braucher,** *m.* usufructuary. **-nutz,** *m.*, **-nutzer,** *m.*, *see* **-brauch, -braucher.**

Niet, *n. &* *m.* (-(e)s, -e), **-e,** *f.* (-en) rivet; *– und nagelfest*, nailed fast, firmly fixed. **-en,** *v.a.* rivet. **-nagel,** *m.* rivet. **-stelle,** *f.* riveted joint, riveting.

Niete, *f.* (-n) blank (*in a lottery*), failure, (*sl.*) wash-out, flop; *see also* **Niet.**

Nilpferd, *n.* hippopotamus.

Nimbus, *m.* nimbus cloud (*Meteor.*); nimbus, halo, aura, aureole; prestige, respect, solemnity.

nimm, nimmst, nimmt, *see* **nehmen;** (*coll.*) *er ist vom Stamme Nimm*, he is very greedy, grasping *or* rapacious.

nimmer, *adv.* never, nevermore, at no time; (*dial.*) no more, no longer; *nun und –*, never, at no time, not now nor ever afterwards; *nie und –*, never at any time, at no time. **-leinstag,** *see* **-mehrstag. -mehr,** *adv.* nevermore; never, not at all. **-mehrstag,** *m.* (*coll.*) when the cows come home, doomsday, the Greek Calends. **-müde,** *adj.* indefatigable. **-satt,** 1. *adj.* insatiable. 2. *m.* glutton. **-wiedersehen,** *n.*; *auf -wiedersehen*, farewell for ever; *er verschwand auf -wiedersehen*, he disappeared and was not seen any more.

Nipp, *m.* (-(e)s, -e) nip, sip. **-en,** *v.a. &* *n.* (*aux.* h.) sip, taste; (*dial.*) tipple; (*dial.*) nod, snooze; *er -t zu gern*, he is too fond of tippling. **-flut,** *f.* neap-tide.

Nippel, *m.* (-s, –) nipple (*of a valve*), jet.

Nipp-es, *f.pl.*, **-sachen,** *f.pl.* knick-knacks, trinkets. **-tisch,** *m.* what-not.

nirgend(s), -(s)wo, *adv.* nowhere, nowhere at all; *ich komme – mehr hin*, I do not go anywhere any more.

Nische, *f.* (-n) niche, recess.

Niß, *f.* (-(ss)e), **Nisse,** *f.* (-n) nit. **-(ss)ig,** *adj* lousy, nitty; (*fig.*) mean.

nist-en, *v.n.* (*aux.* h.) nest, build a nest. **-kasten,** *m.* nesting-box.

Nitr-at, *n.* (-(e)s, -e) nitrate. **-ieren,** *v.a.* nitrate. **-oglyzerin,** *n.* nitroglycerine. **-olsäure,** *f.* nitrolic acid. **-ozellulose,** *f.* nitrocellulose, guncotton.

Niveau [*pron.* niˈvoː] *n.* (-s, -s) level; standard; *– haben*, be above the average.

nivellier-en, *v.a.* level, grade. **-ung,** *f.* levelling. **-apparat,** *m.*, **-instrument,** *n.* levelling-instrument, level (*Surv.*). **-libelle,** *f.*, **-waage,** *f.* spirit-level.

Nix, *m.* (-es, -e) water-sprite. **-e,** *f.* (-en) water-nymph.

nix, (*dial. & coll.*) *see* **nichts.**

nobel, 1. *adj.* (*comp.* nobler) noble, high-born; distinguished, grand, stylish, extravagant, expensive; (*coll.*) generous, open-handed; (*coll.*) *sich – zeigen, geben* or *machen*, be very free with one's money.

Nobis-haus, *n.*, **-krug,** *m.* (*sl.*) purgatory.

noch, *adv. &* *part.* still, yet; in addition, besides, further; *wenn er auch – so lange bleibt*, if he stays ever so long; *– dazu*, moreover, in addition, into the bargain; *– einer*, another, one more; *– einmal*, once more, over again; *– einmal so viel*, as much again; *– eins*, just one more point, just one final remark; *– etwas*, s.th. else, some(thing) more; *– etwas?* anything else? *– immer*, still; *– nicht*, not yet; *– nie*, never (before); *nur –*, only; *das fehlte nur –*, that was all that was wanting, that is the last straw; *– vor kurzem*, until recently; *weder . . . – . . .*, neither . . . nor . . .; *– lieber wollte ich*, I should even prefer; *weil er . . ., ist er – nicht . . .*, because he . . ., it does not follow that he. . . . **-geschäft,** *n.* put, call (*Stock Exchange*). **-malig,** *adj.* second, repeated. **-mal(s)** *adv.* once more, (once) again.

Nock, *n.* (-(e)s, -e) *or f.* (-en) arm (*of a yard. Naut.*), end (*of mast or spar*). **-takel,** *n.* yard-tackle.

Nöck, *m.* (-(e)s, -e), *see* **Nix.**

Nocke, *f.* (-n), (*Austr. dial.*) **-rl,** *n.* (-s, -(n)) dumpling.

Nocken, *m.* (-s, –) cam, lifter. **-welle,** *f.* camshaft.

nöl-en, *v.a.* (*dial.*) dawdle, drawl. (*coll.*) **-peter,** *m.*, **-suse,** *f.* slowcoach.

Nomad-e, *m.* (-en, -en) nomad. **-enhaft, -isch,** *adj.* nomadic.

Nomen, *n.* (-s, Nomina) noun, substantive. **-klatur,** *f.* nomenclature, technical terms.

Nomin-albetrag, *m.* nominal sum *or* figure. **-alsatz,** *m.* nominal price. **-alwert,** *m.* nominal *or* face value. **-ativ,** *m.* (-s, -e) nominative. (*C.L.*) **-ell,** *adj.* nominal, on paper.

None, *f.* (-n) ninth (*Mus.*); nones (*R.C.*).

Nonius, *m.* vernier. **-einteilung,** *f.* vernier scale.

Nonne, *f.* (-n) nun; night-moth; white nun (*Orn.*); pot-mould (*Found.*). **-nkloster,** *n.* nunnery, convent. **-nweihe,** *f.* taking the veil.

Nopp-e, *f.* (-en) burl (*in cloth*). **-en,** *v.a.* burl, pick (out the knots). **-zange,** *f.* burling iron.

Nord, *m.* north; (*Poet.*) (-(e)s, -e) north wind; *– zum Westen*, north by west (*Naut.*). **-en,** *m.* the North. **-ersonne,** *f.* midnight sun. **-isch,** *adj.* northern; Norse, Nordic. **-kap,** *n.* North Cape. **-länder,** *m.* Northerner; Scandinavian; (*pl.*) northern nations. **-ländisch,** *adj.* northern, arctic. **-landreise,** *f.* arctic expedition, Scandinavian journey. **-licht,** *n.* aurora borealis, northern lights. **-mark,** *f.* (*Nat. Soc.*) Schleswig-Holstein. **-östlich,** *adj.* north-east(ern). **-ostseekanal,** *m.* Kiel Canal. **-pol,** *m.* North Pole. **-polarkreis,** *m.* arctic circle. **-polfahrer,** *m.*, **-polforscher,** *m.* arctic explorer. **-polfahrt,** *f.*

arctic expedition. **-schein,** *m.* zodiacal light. **-see,** *f.* North Sea. **-stern,** *m.* polar star. **-wärts,** *adv.* northward.

nördlich, 1. *adj.* northern, northerly; arctic, septentrional; *-e Breite,* north latitude; *-e Halbkugel,* northern hemisphere; *-e Lage,* northern aspect; *das -e Eismeer,* Arctic Ocean; *- liegen von,* lie (to the) north of. 2. *prep.* (*with Gen.*) *- des Meeres,* to the north of the sea; *-st, am meisten -,* northernmost.

Nörg-elei, *f.* nagging; grumbling, (*coll.*) grousing. **-eln,** *v.n.* (*aux.* h.) grumble; nag, grouse. **-ler,** *m.* grumbler, fault-finder, carper, malcontent. **-lig,** *adj.* grumbling, grousing, carping, fault-finding.

Norm, *f.* (-en) rule, standard, model, norm, criterion; signature (*Typ.*). **-al,** *adj.* normal, standard, regular; perpendicular, at right angles; (*coll.*) *er ist nicht -al,* he is not right in the head. **-albelastung,** *f.* normal load. **-ale,** *f.* perpendicular (line). **-alelement,** *n.* standard cell (*Elec.*). **-alerweise,** *adv.* normally. **-alfluglage,** *f.* level flight (*Av.*). **-algeschwindigkeit,** *f.* normal speed, permitted speed. **-algewicht,** *n.* standard weight. **-alkerze,** *f.* standard candle. **-alklasse,** *f.* scratch (*Sport*). **-almaß,** *n.* standard measure. **-alnull,** *n.* (mean) sea-level (*Surv.*). **-alspur,** *f.* standard gauge. **-alstärke,** *f.* proof strength (*of spirits*). **-aluhr,** *f.* standard clock. **-alzeile,** *f.* direction line (*Typ.*). **-alzeit,** *f.* mean, standard *or* correct time. **-ativ,** *adj.* authoritative, standard. **-en,** *v.a.,* (*archaic*) **-ieren,** *v.a.* standardize, regulate. **-ung,** *f.* standardization.

Nörz, *m.* (*Austr. dial.*), *see* **Nerz.**

Nößel, *m.* & *n.* (-s, -) (*archaic*) pint.

Not, 1. *f.* (⸚e) need, want, distress, misery; necessity, exigency, emergency, trouble, urgency, difficulty, peril, danger; *aus -,* from necessity; *aus der - eine Tugend machen,* make a virtue of necessity; (*Prov.*) *- bricht Eisen,* necessity is the mother of invention; *wenn es die - erfordert,* if need be; (*Prov.*) *wenn die - am größten, ist Gottes Hilfe am nächsten,* man's extremity is God's opportunity; *- haben,* find it difficult; *die S. hat -,* the matter is urgent; *wir hatten unsere liebe -, um . . .,* we had no end of trouble with . . .; *es hat keine - damit,* it is not urgent; do not worry; *in - sein,* be in distress *or* danger; (*coll.*) be dishonoured (*of a cheque*); *in Nöten sein,* be in trouble, be hard pressed; (*Prov.*) *- kennt kein Gebot,* necessity knows no law; (*Prov.*) *in der - frißt der Teufel Fliegen,* beggars can't be choosers; *- leiden,* suffer want; *einen Wechsel - leiden lassen,* dishonour a bill; *er macht uns viele -,* he causes us much anxiety; *wenn - an (den) Mann geht* or *am Mann ist,* if need be, in case of need, when necessity *or* the need arises, when help is needed, when it gets urgent *or* pressing, when the worst comes to the worst; *mit (knapper) -,* with difficulty, only just, scarcely, barely, narrowly; *ohne -,* unnecessarily, needlessly, without cause; *über -,* more than necessary; *von Nöten* (see *vonnöten*) *sein,* be necessary *or* needful; *zur -,* at a pinch, at the worst, if need be, in an emergency. 2. *pred. adj.* needful, necessary; *es ist* or *tut -,* it is necessary; *es täte -,* if it were necessary; *wenn es - tut,* in case of necessity; *mir tut es - daß . . .,* I have need of . . ., I need to . . .; *Friede tut uns -,* we need peace. **-adresse,** *f.* emergency address. **-anker,** *m.* sheet-anchor. **-ausgang,** *m.* emergency exit. **-bau,** *m.* temporary structure. **-behelf,** *m.* makeshift; expedient, last resort *or* resource. **-bremse,** *f.* emergency brake; communication cord (*Railw.*) **-brücke,** *f.* temporary bridge. **-durft,** *f.* necessaries, necessity, pressing need; *seine -durft verrichten,* ease o.s., relieve nature. **-dürftig,** *adj.* scanty; needy, necessitous, indigent, hard up; makeshift; *-dürftig reparieren,* make rough-and-ready repairs. **-dürftigkeit,** *f.* indigence, want. **-erbe,** *m.* legal heir. **-fall,** *m.* case of emergency; *-falls,* or *im -fall,* in case of need, if necessary. **-flagge,** *f.* flag of distress. **-gedrungen,** *adj.* compulsory, forced; necessarily, perforce. **-geld,** *n.* emergency (issue of) money. **-gemeinschaft,** *f.* emergency association. **-gesetz,** *n.* provisional *or* emergency decree. **-hafen,** *m.* harbour of refuge. **-helfer,** *m.* helper in need, one of 14 catholic saints. **-hemd,** *n.* magic shirt. **-hilfe,** *f.* help in need, emergency service. **-jahr,** *n.* year of scarcity. (*C.L.*) **-klausel,** *f.* distress-clause. **-lage,** *f.* distress, calamity. **-landen,** *v.n. insep.* make a forced landing (*Av.*). **-landeplatz,** *m.* emergency landing ground. **-landung,** *f.* forced landing. **-leidend,** *adj.* needy, suffering, poor, distressed; dishonoured (*of bills*); *-leidende(r), m.* sufferer. **-leine,** *f.* communication cord (*Railw.*). **-lüge,** *f.* unavoidable lie, white lie. **-luke,** *f.* escape hatch. **-mast,** *m.* jury-mast. **-mittel,** *n.* shift, expedient. **-nagel,** *m.* makeshift, stopgap. **-pfennig,** *m.* savings; nest-egg; *einen -pfennig zurücklegen,* lay by (money) for a rainy day. **-recht,** *n.* right of necessity. **-reif,** *adj.* immature, unripe, prematurely ripened, forced. **-ruf,** *m.* cry of distress, emergency call (*Phone*). **-sache,** *f.* case of necessity, urgent case. **-schlachtung,** *f.* forced slaughter (*of diseased or starving animals*). **-schrei,** *m.* cry of distress, shout for help. **-sender,** *m.* transmitter of SOS messages. **-signal,** *n.* distress signal, SOS. **-sitz,** *m.* emergency seat, dickey-seat (*Motor.*). **-stand,** *m.* state of distress, critical state, emergency. **-standsarbeiten,** *f.pl.* relief works. **-standsgesetz,** *n.* Emergency Powers Act, emergency bill. **-taufe,** *f.* private baptism (*in emergency*). **-tür,** *f.* emergency exit. **-verband,** *m.* temporary dressing, first field dressing (*Mil.*). **-verordnung,** *f.* emergency decree. **-wassern,** *v.n.* make a forced landing on the sea, (*sl.*) ditch a plane. **-wehr,** *f.* self-defence; *Totschlag aus -wehr,* justifiable homicide (*Law*). **-wendig,** *adj.* necessary, urgent, essential, indispensable, inevitable; *das -wendige,* necessaries. **-wendigenfalls,** *adv.* in case of necessity. **-wendigerweise,** *adv.* necessarily, of necessity. **-wendigkeit,** *f.* urgency, necessity. **-wurf,** *m.* jettisoning (*of bombs*) (*Av.*). **-zeichen,** *n.* distress signal. **-zucht,** *f.* indecent assault, rape, violation, ravishment. **-züchtigen,** *v.a.,* **-züchten,** *v.a.* (*insep.*) rape, ravish, violate; assault (*Law*). **-zwang,** *m.* force of circumstances.

Nota, *f.* (-s) note, memorandum, bill; (*C.L.*) *in - nehmen,* book; *sich* (*Dat.*) *etwas ad -m nehmen,* take note of a th.

Notab-eln, -ilitäten, *f.pl.* notables; (*coll.*) big shots.

Notar, *m.* (-s, -e) notary; *öffentlicher -,* notary public, commissioner for oaths. **-iat,** *n.* (-(e)s, -e) notary's office. **-iell,** *adj.,* **-isch,** *adj.* notarial; attested by a notary; *-iell beglaubigt,* officially signed and attested; *-ielle Vollmacht,* power of attorney.

Note, *f.* (-n) note, memorandum; diplomatic note; bank-note; musical note; mark *or* report (*at school*); (*pl.*) music; *ganze -,* semibreve; *geschwänzte -,* quaver; *gute -,* high *or* good marks, a good report (*school*); *halbe -,* minim; *in -n setzen,* set to music; *nach -n spielen,* play at sight; (*coll.*) *nach -n,* thoroughly, with a vengeance; *persönliche -,* personal trait *or* stamp; *schwarze -,* crotchet. **-nausgabe,** *f.* issue of (bank-)notes. **-naustausch,** *m.* exchange of notes (*Pol.*). **-nbank,** *f.* bank of issue, issuing bank. **-nbeilage,** *f.* musical supplement. **-nbezeichnung,** *f.* musical notation. **-nblatt,** *n.* sheet of music. **-ndruck,** *m.* music-printing; printed music. **-nhalter,** *m.* music-stand. **-nhandlung,** *f.* music-shop. **-nlesen,** *n.* reading of music. **-nlinie,** *f.* line (*Mus.*). **-npapier,** *n.* music-paper. **-nständer,** *m., see* **-nhalter. -nschlüssel,** *m.* clef (*Mus.*). **-nsystem,** *n.* staff (*Mus.*). **-numlauf,** *m.* circulation of (bank-)notes.

notier-en, 1. *v.a.* note, make *or* take a note of; (*C.L.*) quote, state (*prices*). 2. *v.n.* (*C.L.*) be quoted at; *die Anleihe -t 83,* the loan is quoted at 83. **-ung,** *f.* quotation (*of prices*).

notifizieren, *v.a.* notify.

nötig, *adj.* needful, necessary, required; *etwas - haben,* need a th., be *or* stand in need of a th.; require a th.; (*coll.*) *er hat es sehr -,* he needs the lavatory badly; *- machen,* necessitate; *das -e besorgen,* do all that is necessary; *das zum Leben -e,* the necessities of life. **-en,** *v.a.* necessitate; oblige, force, coerce, compel, urge, entreat, press; *sich -en lassen,* stand upon ceremony, need pressing; *lassen*

Sie sich nicht lange –en, do not wait to be asked, help yourself. **–enfalls,** *adj.* if need be. **–ung,** *f.* compulsion, coercion, constraint; entreaty.
Notiz, *f.* (-en) notice, cognizance; note, memorandum. **–block,** *m.* scribbling pad, jotter. **–buch,** *n.* notebook.
notorisch, *adj.* notorious, acknowledged.
Novell–e, *f.* (-en) short story, short novel; supplementary law *or* clause, amendment (*Law*); *die –en des Justinian*, the constitutions *or* laws of Justinian. **–enartig,** *adj.*, **–enhaft,** *adj.* in the manner of a short story. **–ette,** *f.* anecdote, sketch. **–ieren,** *v.a.* (*Austr. dial.*) amend, modify, reorganize. **–ist,** *m.* writer of short stories *or* sketches. **–istisch,** *adj.*, *see* **–enartig**; fictional; diverting; mawkish.
November, *m.* November.
Nov–ität, *f.* (-en) novelty; new publication. **–ize,** *m.* (-n, -n) *or f.* (-n) novice, probationer, acolyte. **–iziat,** *n.* (-es, -e) novitiate. **–um,** *n.* (-a) unheard-of fact; *see* **–ität**; (*Law*) fresh evidence.
nu, 1. *int.* (*dial. & coll.*) well! well now! 2. *m. & n.* moment, instant; *im* or *in einem –*, in an instant, in a trice, in no time.
Nuance, *f.* shade, tint, hue, tinge, cast (*Dye.*). **–nabstufung,** *f.*, **–nskala,** *f.* range of shades.
nüchtern, *adj.* (on an) empty (stomach); sober, temperate, moderate, calm, reasonable, sensible, clear-headed; (*dial.*) flat, insipid, dry, dull, jejune, prosaic, Philistine; *wieder – werden*, sober up; *–es Urteil*, sober *or* dispassionate judgement. **–heit,** *f.* sobriety, calmness; prosiness; emptiness, dullness, dryness.
Nucke, *f.*, **Nücke,** *f.* (-n) (*dial.*) whim, fad, crotchet, fancy; wilfulness, obstinacy.
Nuckel, *m.* (*coll.*) comforter, dummy (*for babies*). **–n,** *v.n.* (*aux.* h.) (*coll.*) suck.
Nudel, *f.* (-n) vermicelli, macaroni, (*Amer.*) noodles; stuffing (*for poultry*). **–brett,** *n.* pastry-board. **–holz,** *n. see* **–walze. –n,** *v.a.* cram, feed up; stuff (*poultry*); (*vulg.*) *ich bin genudelt*, I am full. **–suppe,** *f.* vermicelli soup. **–walze,** *f.* rolling pin.
null, 1. *indec. adj.* nil, null; *– und nichtig*, null and void; *– und nichtig machen*, annul. 2. *f.* (-en) naught, zero, cipher; blank; *er ist eine wahre –*, he is a nobody *or* a mere cipher. **–ifizieren,** *v.a.* nullify, invalidate. **–ität,** *f.* nullity, invalidity; insignificance. **–partie,** *f.* love-set (*Tenn.*). **–punkt,** *m.* zero, nadir. **–spiel,** *n.* love-game (*Tenn.*). **–stellung,** *f.* zero-position. **–strich,** *m.* zero-mark. **–zeit,** *f.* zero-hour (*Mil.*).
Numer–ale, *n.* (-s, -alien (*Austr. dial.* –, -alia)) numeral adjective. **–ieren,** *v.a.* number; *–ierter Sitz*, reserved seat. **–ierung,** *f.* numbering, numeration; notation. **–isch,** *adj.* numerical. **–us,** *m.* (–, -i) number (*Gram.*).
Nummer, *f.* (-n) number; part, issue, copy (*of a journal*); lottery-ticket; size (*in clothing*); event (*Sport.*); *eine große – sein*, be influential, have influence; *eine gute – haben*, be well thought of; *keine – haben*, have no say, be without influence; (*coll.*) *nette* or *feine –*, a nice sort *or* specimen (*ironically*); (*coll.*) *er ist auf – Sicher*, he is in jug *or* the clink. **–n,** *v.a., see* **numerieren. –nfolge,** *f.* numerical order. **–nscheibe,** *f.* dial (*Phone*). **–nschild,** *n.* number-plate (*Motor.*).
nun, 1. *adv.* now, at present; then, henceforth; *von – an*, henceforth; *– erst gestand er*, it was only then that he confessed; *– und nimmer*, never, nevermore. 2. *part.* now, well; *er mag – kommen oder nicht*, whether or not he comes; *–, und?* and then what? *– also?* well then! *– ja!* that's true enough, granted; *wenn –*, supposing, now if. 3. (*coll. & dial.*) *conj.* (= *da*) *– es einmal so ist*, since it is so; *– du mich kennst*, now that you know me. **–mehr,** (*archaic*) **–mehro,** *adv. & conj.* now, at present, by this time; henceforth, then, since then. **–mehrig,** *adj.* present, actual.
Nuntius, Nunzius, *m.* (–, -ien & (*Austr. dial.*) -ii) (papal) nuncio.
nur, *adv. & part.* only, but, merely, solely, alone, except, scarcely; *geh – !* do go! *er mag – gehen!* let him go by all means, he is quite at liberty to go! *so viel ich – kann*, as much as ever I can; *laßt mich – machen!* (just) let me do it! let me alone! *sehen Sie –, was Sie gemacht haben*, just look at what you have done; *– mehr*, (*coll. & Austr. dial.*) still, only; *– nicht ängstlich!* do not fear! *alle, – er nicht*, all except him; *alles, – nicht das*, anything but *or* rather than that; *nicht – . . ., sondern auch . . .*, not only . . ., but also; *– noch eine Zeile*, only one line more; *– so*, easily, rapidly, perfectly; *die Federn flogen – so*, the feathers were flying fast; *es klappte – so*, everything fitted in admirably; *es ging – so*, it went off first-rate *or* without a hitch; *– so tun*, pretend to do, do a th. without taking any trouble about it; *was –*, whatever (*as Acc. separated by subject*); *– weiter!* carry on! that is all right so far! *wenn –*, if only, provided that, would that; *wer – (immer)*, whoever (*as Acc. separated by subject*); *wie –*, however (*as Acc. separated by subject*); *wie kommt er – hierher?* however did he get here? *wo –* wherever (*as Acc. separated by subject*); *wo du – hinkommst*, wherever you may go; *– zu!* go on! make a start! (*coll.*) get *or* jump to it! **–flügelflugzeug,** *n.* flying wing (*Av.*).
Nuß, *f.* (¨(ss)e) nut (*also Mech.*); walnut; *taube –*, empty nut; *keine taube – wert*, not worth a straw *or* fig; *harte –*, (*fig.*) hard nut, difficult task; *Nüsse auskernen*, shell nuts; (*coll.*) *ich will ihm eine harte – zu knacken geben*, I will give him a hard nut to crack; (*coll.*) *wir haben noch eine – miteinander zu knacken*, I have still a crow to pluck with you. **–baum,** *m.* walnut-tree. **–braun,** *adj. & n.* nut-brown, hazel. **–kern,** *m.* kernel (*of a nut*). **–knacker,** *m.* nutcracker(s); (*coll.*) *alter –knacker*, old fogy. **–kohle,** *f.* small coal, (kitchen) nuts. **–schale,** *f.* nutshell; small boat. **–staude,** *f.* hazel-tree.
Nüstern, *f.pl.* nostrils (*of horses*).
Nut, *f.* (-en), (*coll.*) **–e,** *f.* (-n) groove, furrow, rabbet, slot, flute; *– und Zapfen*, mortise and tenon. **–en,** *v.a.* groove. **–hobel,** *m.* rabbet- *or* grooving-plane.
Nutsch–e, *f.* suction filter (*Chem.*). **–beutel,** *m.* feeding-bottle. **–en,** *v.n.* (*rare*) filter by suction, (*dial.*) suck. **–er,** *m.* (-s, -) (*coll.*) suckling.
nutz–(e), (nütze), 1. *adj.* useful, of use, profitable; *das ist zu nichts –*, that is good for nothing *or* quite useless. 2. *m.* (*archaic*) *see* **–en,** 3; *sich (Dat.) etwas zu –e machen*, turn s.th. to advantage, profit by a th.; (*Poet.*) *zu – und Frommen*, for the benefit *or* good of, to the advantage of. **–anwendung,** *f.* utilization; practical application. **–arbeit,** *f.* effective work (*Mech.*). **–bar,** *adj.* usable, fit for use, useful, profitable, productive, effective. **–barmachung,** *f.* utilization. **–bringend,** *adj.* profitable, advantageous. **–effekt,** *m.* efficiency (*Mech.*). **–en,** 1. *v.a.* make use of, use, exploit. 2. *v.n.* (*aux.* h.) (*Dat.*) be of use, be profitable; *was –t es, daß . . .?* what avails it, that . . .? *zu etwas –en*, be good for s.th. 3. *m.* profit, gain, use, advantage; *–en bringen* or *tragen*, yield a profit; *mit 30% –en verkaufen*, dispose of with a profit of 30 per cent., make 30 per cent. on a sale; *von –en*, of use, profitable; *großer Umsatz, kleiner –en*, a large turnover with small profit; *–en aus einer S. ziehen*, turn a th. to advantage. **–garten,** *m.* kitchen-garden. **–holz,** *n.* commercial timber. **–kraft,** *f.* effective power. **–last,** *f.* loading capacity, working *or* pay load. **–leistung,** *f.* effective work, useful power (*Mech.*). **–los,** *adj.* useless, unprofitable. **–losigkeit,** *f.* futility, uselessness. **–nießen,** *v.a.* (*insep.*) derive profit from; have the usufruct of. **–nießer,** *m.* beneficiary, usufructuary. **–nießung,** *f.* usufruct. **–pflanze,** *f.* useful plant, plant useful as fodder. **–ung,** *f.* produce, yield, revenue, usufruct. **–ungsdauer,** *f.* useful life. **–ungsrecht,** *n.* right of use. **–vieh,** *n.* domestic cattle. **–wert,** *m.* economic value.
nütz–e, *adj., see* **nutz. –en** (*see also* **nutzen**) 1. *v.n.* be of use; be profitable, serve for; *wozu –t das?* what good is that? what is the good of that? 2. *v.a.* use, make use of, utilize. **–lich,** *adj.* useful, of use, serviceable, profitable, advantageous, conducive; *das Angenehme mit dem –lichen verbinden*, combine pleasure with profit. **–lichkeit,** *f.* utility,

usefulness, advantage, profitableness. **–lichkeitsprinzip,** *n.*, **–lichkeitssystem,** *n.* utilitarianism. **–lichkeitsrücksichten,** *f.pl.* considerations of utility, practical considerations.
Nymph–e, *f.* (-n) nymph, fairy, elf; chrysalis, pupa (*Zool.*). **–omanie,** *f.* nymphomania.

O

O, o, 1. *n.* O, o. 2. *int.* oh! O! *das A und O,* the beginning and end, the whole *or* entire. *For abbreviations see Index of Abbreviations at end.*
Oase, *f.* (-n) oasis.
[1]ob, *conj.* if, whether; *es fragt sich –,* I wonder whether, it is a question whether; *wer weiß, – er nicht krank ist,* who knows but he may be ill; *– er wohl wieder kommt?* will he come back, do you think? *(na) und–!* rather! I should say so! (*sl.*) and how! *als –,* as if; *nicht als –,* not that; *tun als –,* pretend, make believe; *– . . ., – nicht,* whether . . . or not. **–gleich, –schon, –wohl, –zwar,** *conj.* (*in older German often separated by subject, e.g. ob er gleich müde war,* although he was tired) although, though, albeit, notwithstanding.
[2]ob, *prep.* (*with Dat.*) (*dial.*) over, above, on, upon; (*with Gen. or Dat.*) (*archaic*) on account of; (*dial.*) *Rothenburg – der Tauber,* Rothenburg on Tauber; *er zürnte mir – meines Freimuts,* he was angry with me on account of my frankness; *er zürnte – solchem Frevel,* he was angry at such sacrilege. **–acht,** *f.* superintendence, attention, care, heed; *etwas in –acht nehmen,* take heed of s.th.; *–acht auf einen geben,* keep a watchful eye on s.o., take care of s.o.; *–acht!* take care! look out! **–bemeldet, –berührt, –besagt, –genannt,** *adj.* abovementioned, aforesaid. **–dach,** *n.* shelter; lodging; *unter –dach bringen,* place under shelter. **–dachlos,** *adj.* homeless. **–dachlose(r),** *m.* casual (pauper), homeless p.; *Asyl für –dachlose,* house of refuge; casual ward. **–duktion,** *see* **Obduktion. –en, –er, –erst,** *see* **oben, ober, oberst. –gleich,** *see* **[1]ob–. –hut,** *f.* keeping, guardianship, care, protection; *in –hut nehmen,* take care of. **–ig,** *see* **obig. –liegen,** *ir.v.n.* (*sep.*) 1. (*aux.* h.) (*Dat.*) (*rare*) be incumbent on, be one's duty (to), have the task of; apply o.s. to, be devoted to; *es liegt mir –,* it is incumbent on me *or* is my duty; *er liegt seinen Studien –,* he applies himself to his studies. 2. (*aux.* s.) (*Dat.*) (*B.*) prevail over. **–liegenheit,** *f.* duty, obligation. **–ligat,** *see* **obligat. –macht,** *f.* (*archaic*) supreme power *or* authority. **–mann,** *m.* overseer, head man, foreman (*of a jury*); chairman; (*dial.*) umpire. **–rig,** *see* **obrig. –schon,** *see* **[1]ob–. –siegen,** *v.n.* (*sep.*) (*aux.* h.) (*Dat.*) triumph *or* be victorious over, get the better of, conquer. **–walten,** *v.n.* (*sep.*) (*aux.* h.) prevail, predominate, rule, control; exist. **–wohl, –zwar,** *see* **[1]ob–.**
Obdach, *see* **[2]ob–.**
Obduktion, *f.* post-mortem examination.
obduzieren, *v.n.* hold a post-mortem examination.
Obedienz, *f.* obedience (*R.C.*).
O-Beine, *n.pl.* bandy legs.
oben, *adv.* above, aloft, overhead, on high; upstairs; at the top; on the surface; *– abschöpfen,* skim (off); (*fig.*) treat superficially; *den Kopf – behalten,* remain calm and collected; *von – bis unten,* from top to bottom; (*coll.*) *mir steht die ganze Wirtschaft bis hier –,* I am heartily sick of the whole concern; *dort –,* up there; *– erwähnt,* mentioned above, aforesaid; *von – herab behandeln,* treat with condescension; *nach –,* upward, up, upstairs, on high; *von – nach unten,* downward, from above; *von –,* from the top. **–an,** *adv.* at the top, at the head; in the first place. **–auf,** *adv.* at the top *or* head, above; on the surface; uppermost; *–auf sein,* be in great form. **–drein,** *adv.* over and above, in addition, into the bargain, what is more. **–erwähnt,** *adj.*, **–gesagt,** *adj.* aforesaid, above-mentioned. **–hin,** *adv.* on the surface; superficially, cursorily, perfunctorily; *etwas –hin abtun,* half-do, do perfunctorily. **–hinaus,** *adv.*; *–hinaus wollen,* have extravagant *or* ambitious notions.
ober, 1. *prep.* (*Dat.*) (*Austr. dial.*) over, above, beyond. 2. *adj.* situated above, upper, higher, superior; supreme, chief, principal, senior, leading; *der –e,* the head, chief *or* superior; *die –(e)n,* one's betters; those in authority; *das –e,* the top; *das –e zu unterst kehren,* turn everything upside-down *or* topsy-turvy. 3. *m.* (-s, –) trump knave, highest knave; (head) waiter; (*Herr*) *–!* waiter! **–appellationsgericht,** *n.* High Court of Appeal. **–arm,** *m.* upper arm. **–armbein,** *n.* humerus (*Anat.*). **–armgelenk,** *n.* shoulder joint. **–armknochen,** *m.*, *see* **–armbein. –arzt,** *m.* head-physician. **–aufseher,** *m.* inspector-general. **–aufsicht,** *f.* superintendence. **–bau,** *m.* superstructure; roadbed (*Railw.*). **–bauch,** *m.* epigastrum (*Anat.*). **–baumeister,** *m.* building contractor, master of works. **–befehl,** *m.* supreme command. **–befehlshaber,** *m.* commander-in-chief. **–bett,** *n.* coverlet, down-quilt, duvet. **–boden,** *m.* topsoil; garret. **–bootsmaat,** *m.* boatswain's mate (*Naut.*). **–bootsmann,** *m.* chief boatswain's mate (*Naut.*). **–bramsegel,** *n.* main-royal (*Naut.*). **–bürgermeister,** *m.* lord mayor (*England*); lord provost (*Scotland*). **–deck,** *n.* upper deck. **–deutsch,** *adj.* Upper German, South German. **–feldwebel,** *m.* regimental sergeant-major, warrant officer class 1 (*Mil.*); chief petty officer (*Nav.*); flight-sergeant (*Av.*). **–feuerwerker,** *m.* chief gunner's mate (*Artil.*). **–fläche,** *f.* surface area. **–flächenhärtung,** *f.* case-hardening. **–flächenreibung,** *f.* skin-friction. **–flächenspannung,** *f.* surface-tension. **–flächlich,** *adj.* superficial; *nach –flächlicher Schätzung,* at a rough estimate. **–führer,** *m.* (*Nat. Soc.*), major-general (of S.S.). **–gärtner,** *m.* head-gardener. **–gefreiter,** *m.* corporal (*Mil.*); leading seaman (*Nav.*); leading aircraftman (*Av.*). **–gericht,** *n.* (*Swiss dial.*) supreme *or* high court. **–geschoß,** *n.* upper story. **–gewalt,** *f.* supreme power *or* authority; supremacy, sovereignty. **–glied,** *n.* major term (*Log.*). **–gurt,** *m.* top boom (*Naut.*). **–halb,** *adv. & prep.* (*Gen.*) above, at the upper part of. **–hand,** *f.* back of the hand; metacarpus, wrist; (*fig.*) upper hand, ascendancy; *die –hand haben,* have the upper hand, predominate, prevail; (*coll.*) be top dog; *die –hand gewinnen,* get the better (*über einen,* of a p.). **–hals,** *m.* cervical region. **–haupt,** *n.* head, chief, master, sovereign; vertex. **–haus,** *n.* House of Lords, upper house *or* chamber; upper stories. **–haut,** *f.*, **–häutchen,** *n.* cuticle, epidermis. **–heizer,** *m.* leading stoker. **–hemd,** *n.* (dress) shirt. **–herr,** *m.* supreme lord, sovereign. **–herrlich,** *adj.* sovereign. **–herrschaft,** *f.* sovereignty, supremacy. **–hofgericht,** *n.* supreme court of judicature. **–hofmarschall,** *m.* lord marshal. **–hofmeister,** *m.* Lord High Steward; tutor to a prince. **–in,** *f.* (-nen) Mother Superior (*R.C.*); hospital matron. **–irdisch,** *adj.* above ground, surface; aerial; overhead (*cable*). **–jägermeister,** *m.* master of the hunt *or* of hounds. **–kämmerer,** *m.*, **–kammerherr,** *m.* lord high chamberlain. **–kanzleidirektor,** *m.* head of a chancellery. **–kellner,** *m.* head-waiter. **–kiefer,** *m.*, **–kinnlade,** *f.* upper jaw. **–kirchenrat,** *m.* High Consistory (*Protestant*); member of a High Consistory. **–klasse,** *f.* upper class (*of society*): (*pl.*) upper *or* fifth and sixth forms (*school*). **–kleid,** *n.* outer garment. **–kommando,** *n.* supreme *or* high command. **–körper,** *m.* upper part of the body, trunk. **–land,** *n.* upland, highland. **–länder,** *m.* highlander; South German. **–landesgericht,** *n.* Provincial Court, Court of Appeal. **–lastig,** *adj.* top-heavy. **–lauf,** *m.* upper course (*of a river*). **–leder,** *n.* uppers (*of boots*). **–lehrer,** *m.* senior

assistant master, secondary school teacher; headmaster (*in Austria*). **–leib,** *m.* upper part of the body, trunk; bodice (*of a dress*). **–leitung,** *f.* direction, management; overhead system (*Elec.*). **–leutnant,** *m.* (1st) lieutenant (*Mil.*); flying-officer (*Av.*); *–leutnant zur See*, lieutenant (*Nav.*). **–licht,** *n.* skylight, fanlight. **–lippe,** *f.* upper lip. **–macht,** *f.* superiority, ascendancy; supreme authority. **–pfarrer,** *m.* rector. **–postmeister,** *m.* postmaster-general. **–präsident,** *m.* lord lieutenant, highest civil official of a province. **–priester,** *m.* high priest. **–priesterlich,** *adj.* pontifical. **–priestertum,** *n.* pontificate. **–prima,** *f.* Upper VI. **–primaner,** *m.* upper-sixth-form boy. **–realschule,** *f.* modern *or* non-classical secondary school. **–rinde,** *f.* outer bark; upper crust. **–s,** *n.* (*Austr. dial.*) whipped cream. **–satz,** *m.* major term (*of a syllogism*). **–schenkel,** *m.* thigh. **–schenkelbein,** *n.*, **–schenkelknochen,** *m.* femur (*Anat.*). **–schicht,** *f.* upper stratum (*Geol.*); (*fig.*) upper classes. **–schiedsrichter,** *m.* referee (*Tenn.*). **–schlächtig,** *adj.* overshot (*of a mill*). **–schule,** *f.* modern *or* non-classical secondary school. **–schwingung,** *f.* harmonic, overtone. **–seite,** *f.* top side, right side. **–sekundaner,** *m.* upper-fifth-form boy. **–st,** *see* **oberst. –staatsanwalt,** *m.* attorney-general. **–stallmeister,** *m.* master of the horse. **–steuermann,** *m.* first mate. **–stimme,** *f.* treble, soprano. (*coll.*) **–stübchen,** *n.* head; *bei ihm stimmt was nicht im –stübchen*, he is not quite right in the top story. **–studiendirektor,** *m.* head-master of a secondary school. **–studienrat,** *m.* senior assistant master. **–stufe,** *f.* higher *or* highest grade; upper school. **–tertianer,** *m.* upper-fourth-form boy. **–ton,** *m.* harmonic, overtone. **–trumpf,** *m.* matador (*Cards*). **–vormundschaftsgericht,** *n.* Court of Chancery (*Eng.*). **–wärts,** *adv.* upwards. **–wasser,** *n.* upper water (*weir*); (*fig.*) *–wasser haben* or *bekommen*, have *or* get the upper hand. **–wasserverdrängung,** *f.* surface displacement. **–zähne,** *m.pl.* upper teeth. **–zeug,** *n.* outer garments. **–zimmermeister,** *m.* chief shipwright (*Nav.*).

Obers, *see* **ober.**

oberst, 1. *adj.* (*sup. of* ober) top, topmost, uppermost, highest; chief, head, first, principal, supreme; *–e Heeresleitung*, supreme command; *er ist der –e* or *er sitzt zu – in seiner Klasse*, he is top *or* head of his form. 2. *m.* (-en *&* -s, -en) colonel (*Mil.*); group-captain (*Av.*). **–leutnant,** *m.* lieutenant-colonel (*Mil.*); wing-commander (*Av.*).

obgleich, *conj.*, *see under* [1]**ob.**

Obhut, *f.*, *see under* [2]**ob.**

obig, *adj.* above, foregoing, above-mentioned.

Objekt, *n.* (-s, -e) object. **–abstand,** *m.* working distance. **–glas,** *n.* (microscopic) slide *or* mount. **–iv,** 1. *adj.* objective, impartial, dispassionate. 2. *n.* (-s, -e) objective case (*Gram.*); object lens, objective (*Opt.*). **–ivität,** *f.* objectivity, impartiality. **–träger,** *m.* slide, mount, stand.

Oblate, *f.* (-n) wafer (*Conf.*); consecrated wafer, Host (*Rel.*). **–nschachtel,** *f.* pyx (*Rel.*). **–nteller,** *m.* patent (*Rel.*).

obliegen, *see* [2]**ob–.**

oblig–at, *adj.* obligatory, indispensable, necessary; *mit –ater Flöte*, with flute obligato. **–ation,** *f.* obligation; bond, debenture, promissory note. **–atorisch,** *adj.* obligatory, compulsory. **–ationsinhaber,** *m.* bond-holder. **–ationskonto,** *n.* debenture book. **–ationsschein,** *m.* bond. **–ationsschuldner,** *m.* obligor (*Law*). **–o,** *n.* (-s, -s) obligation to pay; liability; engagement (*C.L.*).

Obmacht, *see* [2]**ob–.**

Obmann, *see* [2]**ob–.**

Obo–e, *f.* (-n) oboe. **–ist,** *m.* oboe player.

Obrigkeit, *f.* (-en) ruling body, government, authorities; magistrate; *von –s wegen*, by order of the authorities. **–lich,** *adj.* magisterial, authoritative, official, governmental; *–licher Befehl*, government order; *–liche Genehmigung*, official permission; *–lich gestempelt*, with the official stamp.

Obrist, *m.*, *archaic for* **Oberst** (*Mil.*).

obschon, *see* [1]**ob–.**

Observ–anz, *f.* (-en) observance, conformance; usage, convention, custom. **–atorium,** *n.* (-ien) observatory.

obsiegen, *see* [2]**ob.**

obskur, *adj.* obscure; *eine –e Größe*, (*coll.*) a dark horse. **–ant,** *m.* (-en, -en) obscurantist.

Obst, *n.* (-es, -arten) fruit. **–bau,** *m.* fruit-growing. **–baum,** *m.* fruit-tree. **–en,** *v.n.* (*aux.* h.) pick, pluck *or* gather fruit. **–ernte,** *f.* fruit crop. **–garten,** *m.* orchard. **–händler,** *m.* fruiterer. **–kern,** *m.* kernel, stone, pip. **–kuchen,** *m.* fruit-tart, flan. **–ler,** *m.* (-s, –) (*Austr. dial.*) fruiterer. **–lese,** *f.* fruit gathering. **–most,** *m.* fruit drink, unfermented fruit juice. **–mus,** *n.* fruit puree. **–reich,** *adj.* abounding in fruit. **–schale,** *f.* skin, peel, paring. **–wein,** *m.* fruit drink, fermented fruit juice. **–züchter,** *m.* fruit-grower. **–zucker,** *m.* l(a)evulose, l(a)evo-rotatory glucose.

Öbstler, *m. see* **Obst–ler.**

Obstruktion, *f.* blockage, stoppage, obstruction; constipation. **–sstelle,** *f.* (*coll.*) bottle-neck.

obszön, *adj.* obscene. **–ität,** *f.* obscenity; smutty joke.

obwalten, *see* [2]**ob.**

obwohl, *see* [1]**ob.**

obzwar, *see* [1]**ob.**

Ochs–(e), *m.* (-en, -en) ox, bull, bullock; (*fig.*) duffer, blockhead; *die –en hinter den Pflug spannen*, put the cart before the horse; *er steht da wie der –e am Berge* or *vorm neuen Tor*, (*coll.*) he stands there like a duck in a thunderstorm. **–en,** *v.n.* (*aux.* h.) (*sl.*) cram, swot. **–enauge,** *n.* bull's eye (*Naut.*); ox-eye (*Bot.*); oval *or* round window (*Arch.*); fried egg. **–enbraten,** *m.* roast beef. **–enfiesel,** *m. see* **–enziemer. –enfleisch,** *n.* beef. **–enfrosch,** *m.* bull-frog. **–engespann,** *n.* ox-team. **–enhaft,** *adj.* cxlike, bovine; stupid. **–enklauenöl,** *n.* neat's foot oil. **–enkopf,** *m.* (*fig.*) blockhead. **–enpost,** *f.* (*coll.*) slow journey. **–enschwanz,** *m.* ox-tail. **–entreiber,** *m.* drover. **–enwagen,** *m.* ox-wagon. **–enziemer,** *m.* (*archaic*) bull's pizzle; horsewhip. **–enzunge,** *f.* ox-tongue.

Ocker, *m.* ochre (*Min.*). **–gelb,** *n.* yellow earth.

Ode, *f.* (-n) ode. **–ndichter,** *m.* writer of odes.

öd–(e), *adj.* waste, empty, bare, bleak, desolate, deserted; (*coll.*) tedious, dull, dreary. **–e,** *f.* (-en) desert, solitude, waste. **–en,** *v.r.* be bored. **–land,** *n.* wasteland, barren land, fallow land.

Odem, *m.* (*poet. for*) **Atem.**

Ödem, *n.* (-s, -e) oedema (*Path.*). **–atös,** *adj.* oedematic, oedematose, oedematous.

oder, *conj.* or; or else, otherwise; *– aber*, or instead, or on the other hand.

Odermennig, *m.* agrimony (*Bot.*).

Ofen, *m.* (-s, ⁼) stove, oven, furnace, kiln; mine-chamber (*Min.*); *hinter dem – hocken*, be a stay-at-home; *damit lockt man keinen Hund hinterm – vor*, that has no attraction at all, that leaves (me, him, *etc.*) quite cold; (*B.*) *der feurige –*, the fiery furnace. **–bank,** *f.* fireside seat, chimney-corner. **–emaille,** *f.* stove enamel. **–farbe,** *f.* black-lead. **–geld,** *n.* charge for using baker's oven. **–hocker,** *m.* stay-at-home, mollycoddle. **–kachel,** *f.* Dutch tile. **–klappe,** *f.* damper. **–loch,** *n.* stove-vent. **–rohr,** *n.* stove-pipe; recess for keeping things warm. **–röhre,** *f.* cooking oven. **–rost,** *m.* grate. **–schaufel,** *f.*, **–schippe,** *f.* fire-shovel. **–schirm,** *m.* fire-screen. **–schwärze,** *f.* black-lead, stove-polish. **–setzer,** *m.* stove-fitter. **–trocknung,** *f.* stoving, kiln-drying. **–tür,** *f.* oven door. **–vorsetzer,** *m.* fender. **–ziegel,** *m.* fire-brick.

offen, *adj.* open; frank, outspoken, candid, clear, overt, sincere; public, vacant, free, spaced, denuded, bare; *–er Brief*, unsealed letter, open letter; *–er Dampf*, live steam; *–es Eis*, loose ice; *bei –en Fenstern schlafen*, sleep with the windows open; *–es Feuer*, open fire; *–e Flamme*, open *or* naked flame; *–e Fragen*, unsolved problems; *– gesagt*, *– gestanden*, frankly speaking; *– halten*, hold *or* keep open (*see* **–halten**); *–e Handelsgesellschaft*, private firm; *– lassen*, leave open (*see* **–lassen**); *eine Stelle – lassen*, leave a blank; *–er Leib*, open bowels; *–e Police*, floating policy; *–e Rechnung*, current account; *auf –er See*, on the open sea; *–en Sinn für eine S. haben*, be receptive to a th.; *–e*

Stadt, unfortified town; – *stehen*, stand, remain *or* be open (*see* **–stehen**); *–e Stelle*, vacancy, gap; *eine –e Stelle besetzen*, fill a vacancy; *auf –er Straße*, in the open street, in public; *auf –er Strecke*, on the open road; between stations (*Railw.*); *bei –er Szene*, in the middle of the performance (*Theat.*); *–e Tafel halten*, keep open house; – *zu Tage liegen*, be evident; *–e Türen einrennen*, fight shadows; *mit –em Visier*, openly, without ulterior motive; *–er Wechsel*, blank cheque; *–er Wein*, wine from the barrel; *–e Zeit*, open season (*Hunt.*). **–bar,** *adj.* manifest, evident, plain, obvious, palpable; declared (*enemy*). **–baren,** *v.a.* disclose, reveal, manifest, discover; proclaim, publish; *sein Herz –baren*, open one's heart, unbosom o.s.; *geoffenbarte Religion*, revealed religion. **–barung,** *f.* manifestation; disclosure; revelation. **–barungseid,** *m.* oath of manifestation, pauper's oath. **–barungsglaube,** *m.* belief in revealed religion. **–halten,** *v.n.* (*Dat.*) (*fig.*) keep *or* leave open *or* undecided; reserve the right (to). **–heit,** *f.* frankness, candour. **–herzig,** *adj.* candid, frank, sincere. **–herzigkeit,** *f.* frankness, candour, sincerity; (*hum.*) *sein Rock hat einige –herzigkeiten*, his coat is more holy than righteous. **–kundig,** *adj.* public, well-known, evident, notorious; *etwas –kundig werden lassen*, allow a thing to become public *or* to get abroad. **–lassen,** *v.a.* leave unfinished, unsettled *or* undecided. **–sichtlich,** *adj.* obvious, apparent. **–stehen,** *v.n.* (*Dat.*) be at liberty (to), be allowed; remain unpaid; remain unsettled *or* undecided. **–stehend,** *adj.* open, undecided.

offensiv, *adj.* offensive, aggressive. **–e,** *f.* offensive, attack (*Mil.*); *die –e ergreifen*, assume the offensive.

öffentlich, *adj.* public, open; – *bekannt machen*, proclaim; *–es Geheimnis*, open secret; *–e Hand*, public enterprise; *–es Haus*, brothel, disorderly house; *–e Person*, public figure; *–es Recht*, law applying to public bodies; *–e Schule*, free *or* state school; *–e Vorlesung*, open *or* public lecture. **–keit,** *f.* publicity; public; *sich in die –keit flüchten*, rush into print; *an* or *vor die –keit treten*, appear publicly *or* in public; publish, be published, come before the public.

offer–ieren, *v.a.* bid, tender, (make an) offer. **–t,** *n.* (-(e)s, -e) (*Austr. dial.*), **–te,** *f.* (-en) offer, tender, bid, proposal; *billige –te*, low offer.

Offiz–ial, *m.* (-s, -e) ecclesiastical official. **–ialverteidiger,** *m.* poor defendant's counsel. **–iant,** *m.* (-en, -en) minor official. **–iell,** *adj.* official; on the authority of the state, authoritative. **–ier,** *m.* (-s, -e) (military) officer; all the chessmen except the king and pawns; *er ist –ier geworden*, he has obtained his commission; *–ier vom Dienst*, orderly officer (*Mil.*). *zur Disposition gestellter –ier*, officer on the retired list; *vom Gemeinen zum –ier emporsteigen*, rise from the ranks. **–ierkorps,** *n.* body of officers, the officers. **–ier(s)anwärter,** *m.*, officer cadet. **–ier(s)bursche,** *m.* orderly, batman. **–ier(s)deck,** *n.* quarter-deck (*Naut.*). **–ier(s)kasino,** *n.* officers' club. **–ier(s)messe,** *f.* officers' mess (*Mil.*), ward-room (*Naut.*). **–ier(s)patent,** *n.* commission. **–in,** *f.* workshop; laboratory; dispensary, chemist's shop; printing-office *or* shop. **–inell,** *adj.* medicinal, officinal. **–iös,** *adj.* semi-official.

öff–nen, *v.a.* & *r.* open; unlock, unseal; reveal, disclose; dissect (*a body*); *einem die Wege –nen*, pave the way for a p.; *dem Laster Tür und Tor –nen*, give full licence to vice. **–nend,** *pr.p.* & *adj.* opening; aperient, laxative. **–nung,** *f.* opening, hole, aperture, gap; mouth, orifice; outlet; dehiscence (*Bot.*); evacuation (*Med.*); dissection (*Med.*). **–nungsmittel,** *n.* aperient.

oft, *adv.* (sup. öfter, *comp.* öftest) often, frequently; *so – du kommst*, every time you come; *wie – ist 3 in 6 enthalten?* how many times does 3 go into 6? **–malig,** *adj.* frequent, repeated. **–mals,** *adv.* often, frequently, repeatedly.

öfter, 1. *adj.* (*comp. of* oft, *q.v.*); repeated; *sein –es Kommen*, his repeated *or* frequent visits. 2. *adv.* more frequently; oftener; *je – ich ihn sehe, desto mehr ...* the more I see of him, the more . . . *etc.*; –s, *des –en*, often, frequently, oftentimes, sometimes, several times, not infrequently.

Oheim, [1]**Ohm,** (*Poet.* & *dial.* **Öhm**) *m.* (-s, -e) uncle.

[2]**Ohm,** *m.* & *n.* (-es, -e) & *f.* (-e) (*archaic*) liquid measure (= *about 35 gallons*).

[3]**Ohm,** *n.* (-(s), –) ohm (*Elec.*).

Öhm–d, *n.* (*dial.*) second mowing (*of grass*). **–en,** *v.a.* & *n.* mow for the second time.

ohn, *archaic for* **ohne**; **–erachtet, –gefähr,** *etc.* (*archaic*), *see* **ungeachtet, ungefähr,** *etc.*

ohne, *prep.* (*Acc.*) without, apart from; but for, not to speak of; but that, except, save; besides; – *Arbeit*, out of work; (*C.L.*) – *Bericht*, for want of advice; – *daß*, without, but that, save; besides; – *daß ich es wußte*, without my knowledge, unknown to me; *sie treffen sich selten – daß sie sich zanken*, they seldom meet without quarrelling; – *Frage*, doubtless; – *Jahr*, no date (*of publication*); (*coll.*) *die S. ist nicht –*, there is a good deal to be said for that, it is not at all bad; – *weiteres*, without more ado, forthwith, at once. **–dem,** *adv.* (*archaic*), **–dies,** *adv.*, **–hin,** *adv.* besides; all the same, anyhow, moreover. **–(e)maßen,** *adv.* (*archaic*) beyond measure. **–gleichen,** *adj.* unequalled. **–haltflug,** *m.* non-stop flight (*Av.*).

Ohn–macht, *f.* (-en) faint, fainting fit, swoon, syncope, unconsciousness; impotency, impotence, powerlessness, weakness; *in –macht fallen*, swoon; *es wandelte ihn eine –macht an*, he was seized with a fainting fit, he fell down in a swoon. **–mächtig,** *adj.* swooning, unconscious; faint, weak, helpless, powerless, feeble; *–mächtig werden*, faint, swoon. **–machtsanfall,** *m.* fainting fit.

Ohr, *n.* (-(e)s, -en) ear; auricle; hearing; handle; (*coll.*) *sich aufs – legen*, lie down, go to sleep *or* to bed; *die –en aufmachen, aufsperren* or *auftun*, see *die –en spitzen*; *einen bei den –en nehmen*, (*coll.*) pin a p.'s ears down; *ganz – sein*, be all ears; *ein geneigtes – finden*, obtain a sympathetic hearing; *die –en hängen lassen*, be discouraged, look crestfallen; *er hat es (faustdick) hinter den –en*, he is very wily, he is a sly *or* cunning dog; *sich hinter den –en kratzen*, scratch one's head (*embarrassed or puzzled*); *sich (Dat.) etwas hinter die –en schreiben*, note a th., take a th. to heart; *noch nicht trocken hinter den –en*, still wet behind the ears; *ein – in ein Buch einschlagen*, turn down the corner of a page; *es klingt mir in den –en*, my ears are tingling *or* burning, someone is walking over my grave; *einem in den –en liegen*, importune a p., keep dinning (*s.th.*) into a p.'s ears; *einem einen Floh ins – setzen*, unsettle a p.'s mind; *lange –en machen*, listen inquisitively; *einem sein – leihen*, give *or* lend a p. one's ear, listen to a p.; be (secretly) influenced by a p.; *die –en spitzen*, prick up one's ears; *die –en steif halten*, keep up one's courage, keep one's spirits up; *bis über die –en*, up to the eyes; *sie wurde bis über die –en rot*, she blushed up to the roots of her hair; *bis über die –en verliebt*, head over heels in love; *einen übers – hauen*, cheat a p., (*sl.*) do a p. in the eye; *einem das Fell über die –en ziehen*, fleece a p.; *sich die Nacht um die –en schlagen*, not get a wink of sleep, toss and turn all night; *einem sein – verschließen*, refuse to listen to a p.; *einem die –en vollschreien*, din in a p.'s ears; *vor meinen –en*, in my hearing; *einem zu –en kommen*, come to a p.'s knowledge *or* hearing; *zu einem – hinein, zum andern hinaus*, in at one ear and out at the other. **–band,** *n.* ligament of the ear. **–blatt,** *n.* lobe of the ear. **–enarzt,** *m.* ear specialist. **–enbeichte,** *f.* auricular confession. **–enbläser,** *m.* tale-bearer, scandal-monger, slanderer. **–(en)brausen,** *n.* buzzing in the ears. **–endiener,** *m.* flatterer, toady. **–(en)drüse,** *f.* parotid gland. **–enfällig,** *adj.* sounding impressive. **–enhöhle,** *f.* cavity of the ear. **–enklingen,** *n.* ringing in the ears. **–enleiden,** *n.* disease of the ear. **–(en)nerv,** *m.* auditory nerve. **–enqualle,** *f.* auricula (*Mollusc.*). **–enreißen,** *n.* earache. **–ensausen,** *n.* buzzing in the ears, tinnitus (*Med.*). **–enschmalz,** *n.* ear-wax, cerumen. **–enschmaus,** *m.* musical treat. **–enschmerz,** *m.* earache. **–entasse,** *f.* two-handled mug. **–enschützer,** *m.pl.* ear-muffs. **–enspiegel,** *m.* otoscope (*Med.*).

–entrommel, *f.* eardrum. –entrompete, *f.*, *see* –trompete. (en)zerreißend, *adj.* ear-splitting. –enzeuge, *m.* auricular witness. –eule, *f.* horned owl. –feige, *f.* slap in the face, box on the ear. –feigen, *v.a.* (*insep.*) box (a p.'s) ears. –finger, *m.* (*dial.*). little finger. –förmig, *adj.* auriculate (*Bot.*); auriform. –gang, *m.* auditory canal. –gehänge, *n.* ear-ring. –hammer, *m.* mallet. –ig, *adj.* with (long) ears, (long-)eared. –kanal, *m.*, *see* –gang. –kreis, *m.* helix. –läppchen, *n.* lobe of the ear. –leiste, *f.* helix. –muschel, *f.* external ear, pinna, ear conch, auricle. –ring, *m.* ear-ring. –schnecke, *f.* cochlea. –speicheldrüse, *f.* parotid gland. –speicheldrüsenentzündung, *f.* mumps. –trommel, *f.* eardrum. –trompete, *f.* Eustachian tube (*Anat.*). –wurm, *m.* earwig (*Ent.*).

Öhr, *n.* (-(e)s, -e) eye (*needle*), eyelet; handle, lug, catch. –en, *v.a.* perforate (*needles*).

Okkasion, *f.* opportunity, occasion; (*C.L.*) (good) bargain.

Okkupation, *f.* (-en) occupation, seizure.

Ökonom, *m.* (-en, -en) farmer, agriculturist; manager, steward, housekeeper. –ie, *f.* economics; economy; domestic economy, housekeeping; farming. –iegebäude, *n.* farm-building(s). –isch, *adj.* economic, economical.

Okt–aeder, *n.* (-s, –) octahedron. –aedrisch, *adj.* octahedral. –ant, *m.* octant. –av, *n.* (-s, -e) octavo; *breites –av*, crown octavo. –avband, *m.* octavo volume. –ave, *f.* (-en) octave (*Mus.*). –ett, *n.* octet. –avieren, *v.n.* be overblown (*of a note on a wind instrument*). –ober, *m.* October. –ogon, *n.* (-s, -e) octagon. –ogonal, *adj.* octagonal.

oktroyieren, *v.a.* dictate, impose (on) from above, force (upon).

okul–ar, 1. *adj.* ocular. 2. *n.* (-s, -e) eyepiece (*Opt.*), binoculars. –arschätzung, *f.* visual estimate. –ieren, *v.a.* graft, inoculate (*Bot.*). –iermesser, *n.* grafting-knife.

ökumenisch, *adj.* oecumenical.

Okzident, *m.* occident.

Öl, *n.* (-s, -e) oil; petroleum; olive-oil; *ätherische –e*, essential oils; *fette –e*, fatty oils; *heiliges –*, chrism; *flüchtige –e*, see *ätherische –e*; *– ins Feuer gießen*, pour oil on the flames; *– auf die Wellen gießen*, pour oil on the waters; *in – malen*, paint in oil(s). –ablaß, *m.* oil drain *or* outlet. –abscheider, *m.* oil trap. –anstrich, *m.* coat of oil-paint. –badblech, *n.* oil bath (*Motor.*). –bauer, *m.* owner of an olive-grove. –baum, *m.* olive-tree; *wilder or falscher –baum*, oleaster. –beere, *f.* olive. –behälter, *m.* oil-receptacle (*in a lamp*), oil-tank. –berg, *m.* Mount of Olives. –blatt, *n.* olive-leaf. –bohrung, *f.* oil-well. –druck, *m.* oil pressure; oleography. –druckbild, *n.* oleograph, chromolithograph. –druckstoßdämpfer, *m.* oil *or* oleo shock-absorber. –en, *v.a.* oil, lubricate; anoint (*Eccl.*). –er, *m.* lubricating point, nipple; oil-can. –fangblech, *n. see* –badblech. –farbe, *f.* oil-colour. –farbendruck, *m.* oleography; oleograph. –feuerung, *f.* oil-fuel. –firnis, *m.* oil-varnish, boiled oil. –fläschchen, *n.* oil-cruet. –garten, *m.* olive-garden *or* grove. –geläge, *n.*, *see* –schlamm. –gemälde, *n.* oil-painting. –gewinnung, *f.* oil production. –götze, *m.* phlegmatic *or* impassive person, bore; blockhead; *steh doch nicht da wie ein –götze!* don't stand there like a stuffed dummy. –haltig, *adj.* oily. –händler, *m.* oilman, oil-merchant. –handlung, *f.* oil-shop. –ig, *adj.* oily; (*fig.*) unctuous. –kelter, *f.* oil-press. –kohle, *f.* carbon (*inside cylinders*) (*Motor.*). –kuchen, *m.* oilcake. –leitung, *f.* oil pipe-line. –lese, *f.* olive-harvest. –malerei, *f.*, painting in oil. –meßstab, *m.* dipstick. –motor, *m.* oil-engine, diesel engine. –papier, *n.* transparent (oiled) paper, grease-proof paper. –quelle, *f.*, *see* –bohrung. –ruß, *m.* lamp-black. –saat, *f.* rape-seed. –same(n), *m.* linseed, rape-seed. –sauer, *adj.*; *–saures Salz*, oleate. –säure, *f.* oleic acid. –schiefer, *m.* shale (*Min.*). –schläger, *m.* oil-miller; oil-presser. –schlamm, *m.* sludge, oil-foots *or* dregs. –stand, *m.* oil-level. –stein, *m.* oilstone. –süß, *n.* glycerin(e), glycerol. –tuch, *n.* oilcloth. –ung, *f.* oiling, lubrication; anointment (*Eccl.*); *letzte –ung*, extreme unction. –ventil, *n.* lubricating valve. –zeug, *n.* oilskin (clothing), oilskins (*Naut.*). –zucker, *m.*, *see* –süß. –zweig, *m.* olive branch (*symbol of peace and goodwill*).

olim, 1. *adv.*, *see* **ehemals**. 2. *n.*; (*coll.*) *seit –s Zeit*, from time immemorial, from the year dot; *zu –s Zeiten*, in days of yore.

Oliv–e, *f.* (-n) olive. –enöl, *n.* olive-oil. –grün, *adj.* olive green.

Oma, *f.* (–, -s) (*nursery talk*) grandma, granny.

ominös, *adj.* ominous.

Onanie, *f.* onanism, masturbation, self-abuse. –ren, *v.n.* masturbate.

ondulieren, *v.a.* wave (*hair*).

Onkel, *m.* (-s, –) uncle; (*sl.*) old chap; (*sl.*) *er ist ein gemütlicher –*, he is a jolly old boy.

Onomatopöie, *f.* onomatopoeia.

Oolith, *m.* (-(e)s & -en, -e(n)) oolite.

Opa, *m.* (-s, -s) (*nursery talk*) gran(d-)dad, grandpa.

opak, *adj.* opaque.

opal–eszierend, *adj.* opalescent. –glanz, *m.* opalescence. –isierend, *adj.*, –schillernd, *adj.* opalescent.

Oper, *f.* (-n) opera; opera-house. –ette, *f.* (-n) operetta, musical comedy. –nbuch, *n.* libretto. –ndichter, *m.* libretto-writer. –nglas, *n.*, –ngucker, *m.* opera-glass. –nhaft, *adj.* in the style of an opera, stagy. –nmusik, *f.* operatic music. –nsänger, *m.*, –nsängerin, *f.* operatic singer. –ntext, *m.*, *see* –nbuch.

Oper–ateur, *m.* (-s, -e) operator (*cinematograph, etc.*); operating surgeon. –ation, *f.* (military) operation, (surgical) operation. –ationssaal, *m.* operating theatre. –ationsgebiet, *n.* theatre of operations (*Mil.*). –ationsplan, *m.* plan of campaign. –ationsziel, *n.* tactical objective. –ativ, *adj.* operative. –ieren, 1. *v.a.* & *n.* operate; perform an operation (*Surg.*). 2. *v.n.* operate, manœuvre (*Mil.*); effect; *sich –ieren lassen*, undergo an operation.

Opfer, *n.* (-s, –) offering, sacrifice; victim, martyr; *ein – werden* or (*einem*) *zum – fallen*, fall a victim (to a p.); *ich habe ihm viele – gebracht*, I have made many sacrifices for him; *sein Leben dem Lande zum – bringen*, make the supreme sacrifice. –altar, *m.* sacrificial altar. –bereit, *adj.* unselfish, self-forgetful. –binde, *f.* fillet. –brot, *n.* consecrated bread *or* wafer; showbread (*of Mosaic ritual*). –dienst, *m.* worship by sacrifices. –freudig, *adj.* self-sacrificing. –gabe, *f.* offering. –gebet, *n.* offertory. –gebrauch, *m.* sacrificial rite. –geist, *m.* readiness to make sacrifices. –geld, *n.* money-offering. –lamm, *n.* sacrificial lamb; the Lamb (Jesus); (*fig.*) innocent victim. –n, *v.a.* & *n.* (*aux.* h.) sacrifice, offer as a sacrifice, offer up, immolate; *einem* (or *einer S.*) *etwas –n*, sacrifice *or* give up s.th. for a p. (*or* for a cause); *sich für etwas –n*, sacrifice o.s. for a th. –priester, *m.* sacrificer. –schale, *f.* dish for receiving the blood of the victim. –stätte, *f.* place of sacrifices. –stock, *m.* poor-box, collection box. –teller, *m.* collection plate, offertory. –tier, *n.* victim. –tod, *m.* sacrifice of one's life; expiatory death (*of Christ*). –trank, *m.*, *see* –wein. –ung, *f.* offering sacrifice. –wein, *m.* oblation-drink; libation. –willig, *adj.*, *see* –freudig. –willigkeit, *f.* readiness to make sacrifices, self-sacrificing devotion.

Opi–at, *n.* (-(e)s, -e) opiate. –um, *n.* opium. –umtinktur, *f.* laudanum.

Oppo–nent, *m.* (-en, -en) objector (*in disputations*). –nieren, *v.a.* object, resist, oppose. –sition, *f.* opposition (*Pol.* & *Astr.*). –sitionell, *adj.* opposed, opposing.

opportun, *adj.* opportune. –ität, *f.* expediency. –itätspolitik, *f.* political time-serving.

optieren, *v.a.* choose, decide, opt (*für*, in favour of).

Opt–ik, *f.* optics; periscope, gun-sight. –iker, *m.*, (*archaic*) –ikus, *m.* optician. –isch, *adj.* optic(al); *–ische Brechung*, refraction; *–ische Täuschung*, optical illusion.

optim–al, *adj.* optimum, maximum, highest, best, most favourable. –at, *m.* (-en, -en) dignitary. –ismus, *m.* optimism. –istisch, *adj.* optimistic. –um, *n.* (-ums, -tima) optimum, best.

Orakel, *n.* (-s, –) oracle. –haft, *adj.* oracular,

cryptic. **-n,** *v.a.* speak in riddles. **-spruch,** *m.* oracle, oracular decree.
Orange, 1. *f.* (-n) orange. 2. *adj.* & *n.* orange-yellow; orange. **-at,** *n.* candied-peel. **-nblüte,** *f.* orange-blossom. **-nschale,** *f.* orange-peel.
Orang-Utan, *m.* (-s, -e & -s) orang-outang.
Oratorium, *n.* (-s, -ien) oratorio (*Mus.*); oratory (*R.C.*).
Orches-ter, *n.* (-s, –) orchestra; band; place for orchestra in theatre. **-trieren,** *v.a.* orchestrate, score.
Orchidee, *f.* (-n) orchid.
Ordal, *n.* (-s, -ien) (*usually pl.*) (judgement by) ordeal.
Orden, *m.* (-s, –) order; decoration, distinction, medal. **-sband,** *n.* ribbon of an order. **-sbruder,** *m.* member of an order; friar, monk. **-sburg,** *f.* castle of (*Teutonic, etc.*) order; (*Nat. Soc.*) training school for political leaders. **-sgelübde,** *n.* vow, profession; *das -sgelübde ablegen*, take the (monastic) vows. **-shaus,** *n.* religious house. **-skleid,** *n.* monastic garb *or* habit. **-sregel,** *f.* statute(s) of an order. **-sritter,** *m.* knight of an order. **-sschwester,** *f.* sister, nun. **-szeichen,** *n.* badge, order. **-tlich,** *adj.* orderly, neat, tidy; regular, steady; ordinary, proper, usual; respectable, decent; downright, out-and-out, really, seriously; *sie haben ihn -tlich durchgeprügelt*, they thrashed him soundly; *ich bin -tlich froh*, I am really *or* downright glad; *ein -tlicher Kerl*, a decent fellow; *-tliches Mädchen*, respectable girl; *-tliche Mahlzeit*, proper *or* (*coll.*) decent meal; *-tlicher junger Mann*, steady young fellow; *-tliches Mitglied*, ordinary *or* full member; *-tlicher Professor*, university professor; *-tliche Schlacht*, pitched battle; *-tlich schlagen*, beat regularly (*of the pulse, etc.*); *waschen Sie ihm -tlich den Kopf*, give him a good blowing up *or* dressing down. **-tlichkeit,** *f.* orderliness; respectability.
Order, *f.* (-n), (*archaic or dial.*) **Ordre** (-s) order, command (*Mil., C.L.*); *bis auf weitere –*, until further orders; (*coll.*) *– parieren*, obey, carry out orders; (*C.L.*) *eine – erteilen*, place an order; (*C.L.*) *an – stellen*, endorse; *für mich an die – des* or *von . . .*, pay to the order of. . . .
Ordin-ale, *n.* (-s, -alia), **-alzahl,** *f.* ordinal (number). **-är,** *adj.* common, ordinary, base, inferior, low, vulgar; *-äre Gattungen*, inferior qualities; (*C.L.*) *-äre Havarie*, petty average; *-ärer Mensch*, vulgar fellow; *-ärer Preis*, published price (*of books*). **-ariat,** *n.* form-mastership, professorship. **-arium,** *n.* budget, standing charge. **-arius,** *m.* (–, -arien) professor, form-master; ordinary (*Eccl.*). **-ärpreis,** *m.* sale *or* net price. **-ate,** *f.* (-en) ordinate, offset, *y*-axis (*Geom.*). **-ation,** *f.* ordination, investment; surgery hours. **-ationszimmer,** *n.* doctor's surgery. **-ieren,** *v.a.* ordain; *sich -ieren lassen*, take (holy) orders. **-iert,** *p.p.* & *adj.* in (holy) orders.
ordn-en, *v.a.* arrange, (set *or* put in) order, classify, sift, sort; regulate, settle, organize. **-er,** *m.* organizer, regulator, arranger, director; prefect, monitor (*schools*); (letter) file. **-ung,** *f.* arrangement, regulation; classification, order, array; tidiness, orderliness; class, rank, succession, series; *auf -ung halten*, enforce good order; *aus der -ung*, disarranged, out of order; *geöffnete -ung*, extended order (*Mil.*); *geschlossene -ung*, close order (*Mil.*); *in -ung*, in order, correct, right, settled, arranged; *nicht in* (*der*) *-ung*, not in order, out of order, faulty, wrong; *etwas in -ung bringen*, arrange *or* settle a th., put a th. straight *or* in order; *nach der -ung*, in order, in succession; *zur -ung!* Order, Order! Chair! **-ungsdienst,** *m.* security police. **-ungsgemäß,** *adj.* orderly, regular, according to order. **-ungsliebe,** *f.* orderliness, tidiness (*of a p.*). **-ungslos,** *adj.* disorderly. **-ungsmäßig,** *adj.* orderly, methodical; duly, lawful, in order. **-ungsruf,** *m.* call to order (*Parl.*). **-ungssinn,** *m.* orderliness, sense of order. **-ungsstrafe,** *f.* fine, penalty for breach of the peace. **-ungswidrig,** *adj.* disorderly; contrary to orders, illegal, irregular. **-ungszahl,** *f.* ordinal (number), atomic number, electron number (*Phys.*), number in a series.

Ordonnanz, *f.* (-en) orderly, runner; (*archaic*) order, instruction; announcement; *auf – sein*, be on orderly duty. **-dienst,** *m.* orderly duty. **-offizier,** *m.* orderly officer, staff officer, administrative officer.
Ordre, *see* **Order.**
Organ, *n.* (-s, -e) organ; organon; agent, agency; mouthpiece of opinion, publication, periodical, journal (*expressing specific views*); voice. **-iker,** *m.* organic chemist. **-isation,** *f.* organization. **-isator,** *m.* organizer. **-isatorisch,** *adj.* organizing. **-isch,** *adj.* organic. **-isieren,** *v.a.* organize; (*sl.*) organize, get hold of, pinch, swipe. **-isiert,** *p.p.* & *adj.* organized, affiliated to an organization. **-ismus,** *m.* (-men) organism. **-ist,** *m.* (-en, -en) organist.
Orgel, *f.* (-n) organ (*Mus.*). **-bauer,** *m.* organ-builder. **-chor,** *n.* organ-loft. **-geschütz,** *n.* multiple-barrel gun. **-konzert,** *n.* organ-recital. **-n,** *v.a.* (*aux.* h.) play the organ; grind a barrel-organ; (*contemptuously*) play *or* sing badly. **-pfeife,** *f.* organ-pipe. **-pult,** *n.* organ-desk. **-punkt,** *m.* pedal-note. **-register,** *n.* organ-stop. **-spiel,** *n.* organ-playing. **-spieler,** *m.* organist. **-stimme,** *f.* organ-stop. **-treter,** *m.* bellows-blower. **-zug,** *m.* organ-stop.
orgi-astisch, *adj.* wild, dissolute, crapulous, sybaritical. **-e,** *f.* (-en) orgy, dissipation, debauch(ery).
Orient, *m.* (-s) orient. **-ale,** *m.* oriental. **-alisch** *adj.* oriental, eastern. **-ieren,** 1. *v.a.* locate, fix, orient; (put) right, orientate, inform, give direction to, determine the trend of. 2. *v.r.* get *or* find one's bearings, find one's way about, learn how the land lies; *darüber muß ich mich noch -ieren*, I must make myself acquainted with the matter; *eine Politik nach gewissen Grundsätzen -ieren*, guide policy along certain channels, give a policy a certain bias; *religiös -iert*, with a religious bias; *falsch -iert*, incorrectly informed. **-ierung,** *f.* orientation, direction; information. **-ierungsvermögen,** *n.* sense of direction.
origin-al, 1. *adj.* original, initial; genuine, innate, inherent. 2. *n.* (-s, -e) original, oddity, eccentric. **-alität,** *f.* originality, inventiveness; peculiarity. **-alausgabe,** *f.* first edition. **-al(hand)-schrift,** *f.* autograph, author's own hand. **-ell,** *adj.* creative, inventive, original; odd, queer, peculiar, eccentric.
Orkan, *m.* (-s, -e) hurricane, gale, typhoon.
Ornat, *m.* (-(e)s, -e) official robes, gown, vestments, canonicals; (*coll.*) *in vollem –*, in fully array.
[1]**Ort,** *m.* 1. (-(e)s, -e) place, spot, point, site. 2. (-(e)s, ⁻er) region, locality; (*usually n.*) coal-face, head of a working (*Min.*); locus (*Geom.*); *an allen -en*, everywhere; *am angegebenen –*, as mentioned above, loc. cit.; *geeigneten -es empfehlen*, recommend in the proper quarter; *– der Handlung*, scene of action (*Theat.*); *der Plan ist höheren -es genehmigt*, the authorities have approved of the project; *recht am -e*, in the right place; *das ist hier sehr am -e*, that is very appropriate *or* quite suitable here; *an – und Stelle*, on the spot; *am unrechten -e*, in the wrong place, out of place, misplaced; *vor – arbeiten*, work at the face, work at the head of a gallery, prolong the gallery (*Min.*). **-en,** *v.n.* locate, fix the position, pin-point (*by direction-finding equipment, radar, etc.*). **-sangabe,** *f.* indication of place, address. **-sangelegenheit,** *f.* local concern. **-sanruf,** *m.* local call (*Phone*). **-sansässig,** *adj.* resident in the locality. **-sbehörde,** *f.* local authorities. **-sbeschaffenheit,** *f.* nature of a place. **-(s)beschreibung,** *f.* topography. **-sbestimmung,** *f.* position-finding, orientation, bearing. **-schaft,** *f.* (inhabited) place; village; market-town. **-scheit,** *n.* splinter-bar, swingle-tree. **-sfest,** *adj.* fixed, stationary, permanent. **-sfremd,** *adj.* strange to a place, unknown in a place. **-sgedächtnis,** *n.* sense of direction. **-sgespräch,** *n.* local call (*Phone*). **-sgruppe,** *f.* local branch. **-skenntnis,** *f.* local knowledge, knowledge of a place. **-skundig,** *adj.* acquainted with a locality. **-sname,** *m.* place-name. **-squartier,** *n.* billet (*Mil.*). **-ssässig,** *adj.* local. **-ssender,** *m.* local transmitter. **-ssinn,** *m.* sense of direction. **-ssteuer,** *f.* local rate. **-stein,**

m. boundary stone, corner-stone. **–süblich,** *adj.* the local custom, customary in a place. **–sunterkunft,** *f.* billets (*Mil.*). **–sveränderung,** *f.* change of place *or* habitat, migration, locomotion. **–sverkehr,** *m.* local traffic. **–sverweisung,** *f.* expulsion *or* banishment from a place. **–svorstand,** *m.* local authorities, mayor. **–svorsteher,** *m.* village magistrate, mayor. **–swechsel,** *m.* migration, change of habitat. **–szeit,** *f.* local time. **–szulage,** *f.*, **–szuschlag,** *m.* local bonus. **–ung,** *f.* orientation, location, position-finding. **–ungsgerät,** *n.* radar equipment.

²**Ort,** *m.* (& *n.*) (-(e)s, -e) (*dial.*) shoemaker's awl.

Örtchen, *n.* (*coll.*) lavatory.

Ortho–graphie, *f.* orthography, spelling. **–graphisch,** *adj.* orthographical; *–graphische Reform,* spelling reform.

örtlich, *adj.* local, endemic; *einen Streit – begrenzen,* localize a conflict; *–e Betäubung,* local anaesthetic; *–e Korrosion,* pitting. **–keit,** *f.* place, locality.

Öse, *f.* (-n) ring, loop, eye, eyelet; lug, ear, hook, catch; *Haken und –n,* hooks and eyes. **–nschraube,** *f.* eyebolt.

Osmo–se, *f.* osmosis. **–tisch,** *adj.* osmotic.

Ost, *m.* east; (-es, -e) (*Poet.*) East wind; – *zu Nord,* east by north. **–en,** 1. *m.* east, the East, Orient. **–elbier,** *m.* Junker, Prussian land-owner. **–elbisch,** *adj.* located east of the Elbe. **–frage,** *f.* problem of German minorities beyond the Eastern frontier. **–hilfe,** *f.* subsidies to maintain the large estates of the Eastern provinces. **–indienfahrer,** *m.* East-Indiaman (*Naut.*). **–isch,** *adj.* Alpine (*Ethn.*). **–jude,** *m.* Polish *or* Galician Jew. **–mark,** *f.* (*Nat. Soc.*) Austria. **–raum,** *m.* (*Nat. Soc.*) Eastern Europe (*claimed as German sphere of influence*). **–see,** *f.* Baltic (Sea). **–wärts,** *adv.* eastward.

Oster–n, *f.pl.* (*but used as sing.*) Easter; Passover; *–n fällt dies Jahr früh,* Easter is early this year; *nächstes –n,* next Easter. **–abend,** *m.* Easter Eve. **–ei,** *n.* Easter egg. **–ferien,** *pl.* Easter vacation. **–fest,** *n.* Easter; *–fest der Juden,* Passover. **–fladen,** *m.* Passover bread. **–hase,** *m.* (fabulous) hare that lays the Easter eggs. **–lamm,** *n.* paschal lamb (*Jew.*). **–monat,** *m.*, **–mond,** *m.* April. **–montag,** *m.* Easter Monday. **–(sonn)tag,** *m.* Easter Sunday. **–woche,** *f.* Holy Week.

österlich, *adj.* of Easter, paschal.

östlich, *adj.* eastern, easterly, oriental.

Oszill–ation, *f.* oscillation, vibration. **–ieren,** *v.n.* (*aux.* h.) oscillate, vibrate.

Otter, 1. *m.* (-s, –) (& *rare*, *f.* (-n)) otter. 2. *f.* (-n) viper, adder.

Ouvertüre, *f.* (-n) (*Austr. dial.* **Ouverture**) overture (*Mus.* & *fig.*).

Oxhoft, *n.* (-(e)s, -e) hogshead.

Oxyd, *n.* (-(e)s, -e) oxide. **–ation,** *f.* oxidation. **–ationsmittel,** *n.* oxidizing agent. **–beschlag,** *m.* coating of oxide. **–haut,** *f.* oxide film. **–ieren,** *v.a.* & *n.* (*aux.* h. & s.) oxidize. **–ierung,** *f.* oxidation. **–ul,** *n.* (-s, -e) protoxide; *Eisen–ul,* ferrous oxide.

Ozean, *m.* (-s, -e) ocean; (*hum.*) *dem – Tribut zahlen,* be seasick. **–dampfer,** *m.* liner. **–fahrt,** *f.* ocean cruise. **–flug,** *m.* trans-oceanic flight. **–isch,** *adj.* oceanic. **–ographie,** *f.* oceanography.

Ozon, *n.* ozone; *in – verwandeln,* ozonify. **–isieren,** *v.a.* ozonize.

P

P, p, *n.* P, p; *for abbreviations see at the end of the German–English Vocabulary.*

Paar, 1. *n.* (-s, -e) pair, couple, brace; *20 – Rebhühnchen,* 20 brace of partridges; *ein – Pistolen,* a brace of pistols; *ein – Strümpfe,* a pair of stockings; *sie sind ein schönes –,* they are a handsome couple; *sie werden wohl ein – werden,* it looks like a match; *zu –en treiben,* scatter, rout, put to flight. 2. *adj.* (*rare or dial.*) like, matching; *– oder unpaar,* odd or even; (*dial.*) *–e Zahlen,* even numbers. 3. *num. adj.* (*indec.*) some, a few; *die – Mark,* those few shillings; *mit ein – Worten,* in a few words; *in ein – Tagen,* in a few days; **–en,** 1. *v.a.* sort, match; pair, couple, join, mate, unite. 2. *v.r.* pair, couple, copulate, mate. *gepaart, p.p.* & *adj.* conjugate (*Bot.*); paired. **–ig,** *adj.* in pairs, paired, even. **–ling,** *m.* each of a pair, allelomorph. **–mal,** *adv.* several times. **–ung,** *f.* pairing, matching; coupling, mating; conjugation. **–ungsausfall,** *m.* product of mating, offspring. **–weise,** *adv.* by *or* in pairs, in couples, two by two. **–zeher,** *m.* artiodactyl. **–zeit,** *f.* mating season.

Pacht, *f.* (-en) & *m.* (-(e)s, -e) tenure, lease; rent; *in – geben,* let on lease; *in – nehmen,* take a lease of, take on lease; *in – haben,* have on lease. **–bar,** *adj.* farmable, tenantable. **–bauer,** *m.* tenant-farmer. **–besitz,** *m.* tenure on lease. **–brief,** *m.*, *see* **–vertrag. –en,** *v.a.* lease, rent; farm; (*fig.*) monopolize; *sich* (*Dat.*) *etwas –en,* (*sl.*) commandeer. **–er,** *m.*, *see* **Pächter. –frei,** *adj.* rent-free. **–geld,** *n.* (farm) rent. **–gut,** *n.*, **–hof,** *m.* farm, leasehold estate. **–herr,** *m.* landlord. **–leute,** *pl.* tenants, tenantry. **–ung,** *f.* leasing *or* renting, farming; leasehold estate. **–vertrag,** *m.* lease, deed of conveyance. **–weise,** *adv.* on lease. **–wert,** *m.* rental value. **–zins,** *m.* rent.

Pächter, *m.* (-s, –) farmer; tenant, leaseholder, lessee. **–schaft,** *f.* tenancy; tenantry.

Pack, 1. *m.* & *n.* (-(e)s, -e & ¨-e) packet, parcel, package, pack, bundle, bale; baggage (*Mil.*); *mit Sack und –,* with bag and baggage. 2. *n.* mob, rabble, pack; (*Prov.*) *– schlägt sich, – verträgt sich,* the mob is fickle. **–darm,** *m.* rectum. **–eis,** *n.* pack-ice. **–en,** *m.* (-s, –) bale. **–en,** 1. *v.a.* pack (up); stow away; lay hold of, seize, come to grips with, pounce on, grasp, (*fig.*) thrill; affect. 2. *v.r.* pack off, clear out, be gone; *–' dich!* be gone! get away! clear out! **–end,** *pr.p.* & *adj.* thrilling, stirring, gripping, absorbing, affecting. **–er,** *m.* packer. **–esel,** *m.* pack-ass, sumpter *or* baggage mule; (*fig.*) drudge. **–garn,** *n.* packthread. **–haus,** *n.* warehouse; packing-room. **–hof,** *m.* custom-house; bonded warehouse; office, goods-office. **–kasten,** *m.* packing-case. **–korb,** *m.* crate, hamper. **–kosten,** *pl.* charges for packing. **–lack,** *m.* & *n.* sealing wax. **–leinen,** *n.*, **–leinwand,** *f.* packing-cloth, sacking. **–nadel,** *f.* packing-needle. **–papier,** *n.* packing *or* wrapping paper; brown paper. **–pferd,** *n.* pack-horse, baggage-horse. **–stoff,** *m.* packing (material). **–tasche,** *f.* saddle-bag. **–träger,** *m.* (*dial.*) porter. **–ung,** *f.* packing, wrapper; poultice; lagging (*of pipes*). **–wagen,** *m.* baggage waggon, luggage-van, goods-van. **–zeug,** *n.*, *see* **–stoff.**

Pädagog–(e), *m.* (-en, -en) pedagogue. **–ik,** *f.* pedagogy, educational theory. **–isch,** *adj.* educational.

Padde, *f.* (-n) (*dial.*) frog; toad.

paddel–n, *v.n.* (*aux.* h.) paddle. **–boot,** *n.* canoe.

Paff, 1. *m.* (-s, -e) bang, pop. 2. *int.* pop! bang! plop! **–en,** *v.n.* (*aux.* h.) puff, smoke; (*vulg.*) *daß es* (*nur so*) *–t,* with a vengeance.

Page, *m.* (-n, -n) page. **–nkopf,** *m.* bobbed hair.

pagin–ieren, *v.a.* number the pages. **–ierung,** *f.* pagination.

Pagode, *f.* (-n) pagoda.

Pair, *m.* (-s, -s) peer. **–ie,** *f.*, **–schaft,** *f.* peerage. **–sschub,** *m.* nomination of new peers (*for political purposes*), (wholesale) creation of peers.

Paket, *n.* (-s, -e) packet, package, parcel, bundle. **–annahme,** *f.* parcels receiving-office. **–ausgabe,** *f.* parcels issuing office. **–beförderung,** *f.* parcels-delivery. **–boot,** *n.* mail-boat, steam-packet. **–ieren,** *v.a.* & *n.* parcel up, wrap up, make into a parcel. **–karte,** *f.* parcel form. **–post,** *f.* parcel-post.

Pakt, *m.* (-s, -e & -en), (*archaic*) **–um,** *n.* (-ums, -en) pact, agreement, compact. **–ieren,** *v.n.* (*aux.* h.) agree (on), come to terms (about).

Palast, *m.* (-es, ⸚e) palace. **-artig,** *adj.* palatial. **-dame,** *f.* lady in waiting. **-revolution,** *f.* court-revolution.
Palatschinke, *f.* (-en) (*usually pl.*) (*Austr. dial.*) pancakes.
Paletot, *m.* (-s, -s) overcoat; greatcoat.
Palette, *f.* (-n) palette.
Palisad-e, *f.* (-en) palisade, stockade. **-ieren,** *v.a.* fence in, palisade.
Palisanderholz, *n.* rosewood.
[1]**Palm-e,** *f.* (-en) palm(-tree). **-(en)gewächse,** *n.pl.* palms. **-enstärke,** *f.* sago. **-in,** *n.* coconut butter. **-insäure,** *f.* palmic acid. **-kätzchen,** *n.* (*dial.*) willow catkin (*Bot.*). **-nußöl,** *n.* coconut oil. **-sonntag,** *m.* Palm Sunday. **-wedel,** *m.* palm branch (*symbol of victory*). **-weide,** *f.* sallow (*Salix capraea*) (*Bot.*). **-woche,** *f.* Holy Week.
[2]**Palme,** *f.* (-n) palm (*measure*); (*archaic*) hand-breadth.
Pampelmuse, *f.*, *see* **Pompelmuse.**
Pamphlet, *n.* (-(e)s, -e) lampoon. **-ist,** *m.* pamphleteer; lampoonist.
Panaschier-system, *n.* alternative voting, proportional representation (*Pol.*). **-t,** *adj.* mottled. **-ung,** *f.* mottling, variegation (*in plants*).
Pandekten, *pl.* pandects. (*coll.*) **-reiter,** *m.*, **-wurm,** *m.* student of law.
Paneel, *n.* (-s, -e) panel; wainscot. **-ieren,** *v.a.* wainscot, panel.
Panier, *n.* (-s, -e) banner, standard.
panieren, *v.a.* dress (*meat, fish*), sprinkle with egg, bread-crumbs, *etc.*
Pan-ik, *f.* panic. **-isch,** *adj.*; *-ischer Schrecken,* panic. **-ikartig,** *adj.* panicky. **-ikzustand,** *m.* state of panic.
Panne, *f.* (-n) puncture, break-down (*Motor*).
Panoptikum, *n.* (-s, -ken) waxworks.
panschen, (*Austr. dial.*) *see* **pantschen.**
Pansen, *m.* (-s, –) paunch, belly; first stomach of ruminants.
Pantine, *f.* (-n) (*dial.*) clog, patten.
Pantoffel, *m.* (-s, – & -n) slipper; *dem Papste den – küssen,* kiss the pope's toe; (*coll.*) *unter dem – stehen,* be henpecked. **-blume,** *f.* slipper-wort (*Calceolaria*) (*Bot.*). **-held,** *m.* henpecked husband. **-regiment,** *n.* petticoat government. **-tierchen,** *n.* slipper animalcule (*Paramaecium*) (*Zool.*).
Pantomime, *f.* (-n) mime, pantomime; dumb show.
pantschen, 1. *v.a.* adulterate, mix. 2. *v.n.* (*dial.*) dabble, splash.
Panzen, (*dial.*) *see* **Pansen.**
Panzer, *m.* (-s, –) armour, cuirass, coat of mail; armour plating *or* plate; tank (*Mil.*). **-abwehr,** *f.* anti-tank defence. **-abwehrkanone,** *f.* anti-tank gun. **-batterie,** *f.* armoured battery. **-blech,** *n.* armour-plate. **-brechend,** *adj.* armour-piercing. **-büchse,** *f.* anti-tank rifle. **-drehturm,** *m.* revolving gun turret (*of tank*). **-faust,** *f.* anti-tank weapon, bazooka. **-gewölbe,** *n.* strong-room, vault (*of a bank*). **-glas,** *n.* bullet-proof glass. **-granate,** *f.* armour-piercing shell. **-hemd,** *n.* coat of mail. **-kabel,** *n.* armoured cable (*Elec.*). **-kampfwagen,** *m.* tank. **-kraftwagen,** *m.* armoured car, tank. **-kreuzer,** *m.* pocket battleship. **-kuppel,** *f.*, *see* **-turm. -macher,** *m.* armourer. **-mine,** *f* anti-tank mine. **-pflug,** *m.* bulldozer. **-n,** 1. *v.a.* arm, armour, plate (*a ship*). 2. *v.r.* put on armour; arm o.s. (*against*); *gepanzert, p.p.* & *adj.* armoured; *gepanzerte Faust,* mailed fist. **-platte,** *f.* armour-plate. **-prahm,** *m.*, *see* **-träger. -schiff,** *n.* armoured vessel, dreadnought. **-träger,** *m.* tank-landing ship. **-truppe,** *f.* tank corps. **-turm,** *m.* gun turret (*of a tank*). **-ung,** *f.* armour-plating. **-waffe,** *f.* tank force (*Mil.*). **-wagen,** *m.* tank, armoured car. **-wanne,** *f.* hull (*of tank*). **-weste,** *f.* bullet-proof vest. **-zug,** *m.* armoured train.
Päonie, *f.* (-n) peony.
Papagei, *m.* -(s & -en, -en) parrot. **-enhaft,** *adj.* parrot-like. **-enkrankheit,** *f.* psittacosis.
Papier, *n.* (-s, -e) paper; document; (*pl.*) identity papers; (*C.L.*) stocks, securities; *das steht nur auf dem –,* that is only on paper; *gemachtes –,* bills ready for endorsement; *Staats-e,* government bonds, stocks; *zu – bringen,* write down; put on paper *or* record; *fettdichtes –,* grease-proof paper; *geglättetes –,* calendered paper, glazed paper; *geleimtes –,* sized paper; *gemasertes –,* grained paper; *geprägtes –,* embossed paper; *geripptes –,* laid paper; *gewelltes –,* corrugated paper; *lichtempfindliches –,* sensitized paper. **-abfälle,** *m.pl.* waste paper. **-abgänge,** *m.pl.* paper waste. **-adel,** *m.* patent nobility. **-blatt,** *n.*, **-bogen,** *m.* sheet of paper. **-en,** *adj.* (made of) paper; papery, paper-like; *-ener Stil,* unnatural, artificial *or* wooden style. **-fabrik,** *f.* paper-mill. **-geld,** *n.* paper money, bank-note(s). **-händler,** *m.* stationer. **-handlung,** *f.* stationer's shop. **-korb,** *m.* waste-paper basket. **-masse,** *f.* paper pulp, stuff. **-schlange,** *f.* paper streamer. **-schnitzel,** *n.pl.* paper shavings. **-tüte,** *f.* paper bag. **-umlauf,** *m.* paper circulation. **-waren,** *f.pl.* stationery. **-wert,** *m.* nominal *or* paper value. **-zeichen,** *n.* watermark. **-zeug,** *n.*, *see* **-masse.**
Papillote, *f.* (-n) curl-paper.
Papis-mus, *m.* popery. **-tisch,** *adj.* popish.
Papp, *m.* (-es, -e) (*dial.* & *coll.*) pap; paste. **-band,** *m.* (binding in) boards. **-bogen,** *m.* sheet of card-board *or* pasteboard. **-einband,** *m.* binding in boards. **-e,** *f.* (-n) pasteboard, cardboard, millboard; *also dial., see* **Papp.** *in -e gebunden,* bound in boards; (*coll.*) *nicht von -e,* considerably, thorough, sound. **-en,** 1. *v.a.* (*coll.*) stick, paste; *see also* **päppeln** & **pappeln.** 2. *adj.* pasteboard. **-(en)deckel,** *m.* pasteboard, millboard (cover). **-enstiel,** *m.* trifle; (*coll.*) *um einen -enstiel,* for a mere song, dirt-cheap. (*fam.*) **-erlapapp!** *int.* bosh! rubbish! nonsense! fiddlesticks! **-ig,** *adj.* sticky, pasty, pappy. **-masse,** *f.* papier-mâché. **-schachtel,** *f.* card-board box. (*coll.*) **-schädel,** *m.* blockhead, dunce. **-schnee,** *m.* soggy *or* caking snow (*that sticks to bottom of skis*).
Pappel, *f.* (-n) poplar. **-n,** *adj.* of poplar wood. **-allee,** *f.*, **-gang,** *m.* avenue of poplars.
pappeln, *v.a.* (*coll.*) babble, blether.
päppeln, *v.a.* feed a child (with pap), put (child) on the bottle; (*fig.*) coddle.
Paprika, *m.* red pepper.
Papst, *m.* (-es, ⸚e) pope, pontiff; Holy Father. **-tum,** *n.*, papacy. **-krone,** *f.* tiara, triple crown. **-würde,** *f.* papal dignity, papacy, pontificate.
päpst-isch, *adj.* popish. **-ler,** *m.* papist. **-lich,** *adj.* papal, pontifical; *-licher Stuhl,* Holy See.
Para-bel, *f.* (-n) parable, simile; parabola (*Geom.*). **-bolisch,** *adj.* parabolic; figurative, allegorical. **-bolspiegel,** *m.* parabolic reflector. **-digma,** *n.* (-s, -men) paradigm (*Gram.*).
Parad-e, *f.* (-en) parade; display; (military) review; parry, ward (*Fenc.*); *eine -e abnehmen,* take the salute, hold a review; *einem in die -e fahren,* upset a p.'s calculations, put a spoke in s.o.'s wheel. **-eanzug,** *m.* full-dress uniform, gala uniform. **-eaufstellung,** *f.* review order. **-ebett,** *n.* catafalque; *auf dem -e bett liegen,* lie in state. **-emarsch,** *m.* march past. **-eplatz,** *m.* parade ground. **-eschritt,** *m.* goose-step, slow march. **-estückchen,** *n.*; *das ist sein -estückchen,* that is his show-piece. **-ieren,** 1. *v.n.* (*aux.* h.) parade, make a show; *see also* **parieren.** 2. *v.a.* parade, show off, make a show of.
Paradeis, 1. *n.* (*archaic*) *see* **Paradies.** 2. *m.* (–, -er), **-er,** *m.* (-s, –), **-apfel,** *m.* (*dial.*) tomato.
Paradies, *n.* (-es, -e), paradise; (*sl.*) upper gallery, the gods (*Theat.*). **-isch,** *adj.* heavenly, delightful. **-apfel,** *m.* (*Austr. dial.*) tomato. **-vogel,** *m.* bird of Paradise.
paradox, *adj.* paradoxical. **-on,** *n.* (-ons, -a) paradox.
Paragraph, *m.* (-en, -en) paragraph. **-enreiter,** *m.* stickler for the letter of the law.
parallel, *adj.* parallel. **-e,** *f.* parallel (*Math.*); (*fig.*) parallel, comparison. **-erscheinung,** *f.* analogous form. **-fall,** *m.* parallel case. **-ismus,** *m.* co-existence, coincidence; analogy, analogue; pleonasm, tautology. **-ität,** *f.* parallelism, coextension.

-kreis, *m.* parallel (*of latitude*). **-linie,** *f.* parallel (line). **-schaltung,** *f.* parallel connexion (*Elec.*). **-stelle,** *f.* parallel passage, literary parallel. **-trapez,** *n.* trapezium.

Paraly-se, *f.* paralysis. **-sieren,** *v.a.* paralyse. **-tiker,** *m.* paralytic. **-tisch,** *adj.* paralytic, paralysed.

Paranuß, *f.* (¨(ss)e) Brazil-nut.

Paraph-e, *f.* (-n) flourish, paraph. **-ieren,** *v.a.* sign (*with a flourish*); sign provisionally.

Parasit, *m.* (-en, -en) parasite. **-är,** *adj.*, **-isch,** *adj.* parasitic.

parat, *adj.* (*coll.*) prepared, ready.

Paratyphus, *m.* paratyphoid fever.

Pärchen, *n.* (-s, –) (loving) couple, lovers.

pardautz, *int.* bang! crash!

Pard-el, *m.* **-er,** *m.* (-s, -) leopard, panther.

Pardon, 1. *m.* (-s, -s) pardon, grace, clemency, mercy; *keinen – geben*, give no quarter. 2. *int.* (*dial.*) excuse me!

Parenthese, *f.* (-n) parenthesis, brackets.

Parforce-jagd, *f.* hunting with hounds, coursing. **-kur,** *f.* drastic cure. **-ritt,** *m.* steeplechase.

Parfum [*pron.* par'fø] *n.* (-s, -s), *usually* **Parfüm,** *n.* (-(e)s, -e) perfume, scent. **-fläschchen,** *n.* scent-bottle. **-ieren,** *v.a.* scent, perfume.

pari, *adv.* at par; *unter –*, below par. **-tät,** *f.* (*C.L.*) parity; (religious) equality. **-tätisch,** *adj.* on a footing of equality; *–tätische Schule*, undenominational school; *Baden ist ein –tätischer Staat*, in Baden there is religious equality. **-wert,** *m.* par value, nominal value.

parieren, 1. *v.a.* & *n.* (*aux.* h.) parry, ward off (*Fenc.*); rein in (*a horse*), draw rein. 2. *v.n.* (*aux.* h.) (*Dat.*) obey, follow; *Order –*, obey orders, be obedient.

Park, *m.* (-(e)s, -e) park; depot, dump, distributing point (*Mil.*). **-anlagen,** *f.pl.* public gardens, pleasure-grounds. **-aufseher,** *m.* park-keeper. **-en,** *v.a.* & *n.* park (*motor-cars*). **-ieren,** *v.a.* & *n.* (*Swiss dial.*), *see* **-en.** **-platz,** *m.* parking place, car-park. **-verbot,** *n.* no parking!

Parkett, *n.* (-(e)s, -e) parquet (floor); (orchestra) stalls (*Theat.*). **-ieren,** *v.a.* inlay, lay with parquet. **-wachs,** *n.* floor polish.

Parlament, *n.* (-(e)s, -e) parliament. **-är,** *m.* (-s, -e) bearer of a flag of truce, intermediary. **-ärflagge,** *f.* flag of truce, white flag. **-arier,** *m.* member of parliament. **-arisch,** *adj.* parliamentary. **-arismus,** *m.* parliamentism. **-ieren,** *v.n.* (*aux.* h.) parley (*Mil.*); (*coll.*) talk round the subject. **-sbeschluß,** *m.* vote of parliament, parliamentary decision *or* enactment. **-sferien,** *pl.* recess. **-smitglied,** *n.* member of parliament (M.P.). **-ssitzung,** *f.* parliamentary session.

Parod-ie, *f.* (-n) parody, travesty. **-ieren,** *v.a.* parody, travesty.

Parole, *f.* (-n) parole; password; watchword.

Paroli, *n.* (-s, -s) double stakes; *einem ein – bieten*, defy s.o.; get one's own back on a p.

Part, *n.* & (*Austr. dial.*) *m.* (-(e)s, -e) part; share; *halb– machen*, go halves, share equally. **-iell,** *adj.* partial, in part; special; one-sided. **-ieren,** *v.a.* part, divide, distribute.

Parte, *f.* (-n) (*Austr. dial.*) obituary notice.

Partei, *f.* (-en) faction, party following; part, side; plaintiff *or* defendant (*Law*); tenant; *– ergreifen* or *nehmen für*, side with; *es mit keiner – halten, sich zu keiner – schlagen*, stand aside from the conflict, not take sides, remain neutral; *sich zwischen den -en halten*, sit on the fence; *in einer S. – sein*, be an interested party. **-abzeichen,** *n.* party insignia *or* badge. **-anhänglichkeit,** *f.* partisanship. **-buch,** *n.* membership-book. **-buchbeamte(r),** *m.* official appointed on party grounds. **-führer,** *m.* party leader. **-gänger,** *m.* partisan, follower. **-geist,** *m.* party spirit. **-genosse,** *m.* fellow member (of a party) (*associated now irredeemably with Nat. Soc. Party*). **-getriebe,** *n.* party manœuvres. **-herrschaft,** *f.* party rule. **-isch,** *adj.*, *see* **-lich.** **-leitung,** *f.* party headquarters. **-lich,** partial, biased, prejudiced, one-sided; factious. **-lichkeit,** *f.* partiality, bias. **-los,** *adj.* impartial, neutral. **-losigkeit,** *f.* impartiality, neutrality. **-nahme,** *f.* partisanship. **-sucht,** *f.* factiousness. **-tag,** *m.* party conference. **-ung,** *f.* division *or* split into parties, disunity, disagreement. **-wesen,** *n.* party system.

Parterre, 1. *n.* (-s, -s) ground-floor; pit (*Theat.*); 2. *adv.* on the ground floor; *erstes –*, stalls (*Theat.*). **-loge,** *f.* lower box (*Theat.*). **-wohnung,** *f.* ground-floor flat.

partial, *adj.* (*Austr. dial.*), *see* **part-iell.**

Partie, *f.* (-n) parcel, batch, lot; passage (*in a book or piece of music*); part (*Theat.* & *Mus.*); party, picnic, excursion; game (*of whist, etc.*); set (*Tenn.*); match (*Sport*); *in –n von 6 bis 12 Stück*, in lots of from 6 to 12 pieces; *in –n billiger*, cheaper in bulk; *eine – machen*, go on an excursion, have an outing; play a game; *eine gute – machen*, marry well, make a good match; *sie hat mehrere –n ausgeschlagen*, she has refused several offers of marriage; *bei, mit* or *von der – sein*, (*coll.*) be in on a th.; *– mit Spiel vor*, advantage set (*Tenn.*). **-geld,** *n.* expenses (*for the table, cards, etc.*) at play; *wir spielen nur ums –geld*, we are only playing for the table (*Bill.*) (*i.e. there are no stakes*). **-ll,** *adj.*, *see* **part-iell.** **-preis,** *m.* special price for the lot *or* set. **-waren,** *f.pl.* substandard goods; remainders (*books*).

partiell, *see* **Part.**

Partikel, *f.* (-n) particle (*Gram.*).

Partikular, *m.* (-s, -e) (*Swiss dial.*), *see* **Partikülier.** **-isieren,** *v.a.* particularize. **-ismus,** *m.* particularism, separatist movement (*Pol.*). **-ist,** *m.* separatist. **-recht,** *n.* special law.

Partikülier (*Austr. dial.* **Partikulier**), *m.* (-s, -s) private individual, man of private means.

Partisan, *m.* (-s, -e) partisan, follower.

Partisane, *f.* (-n) halberd.

Partitur, *f.* (-en) full score (*Mus.*).

Partizip, *n.* (-s, -e & -ien), **-ium,** *n.* (-iums, -ien) participle (*Gram.*). **-ial,** *adj.* participial (*Gram.*).

partizipieren, *v.n.* (*aux.* h.) participate, share (*an einer S.*, in a th.).

Partner, *m.* (-s, –), **-in,** *f.* (-innen) partner. **-schaft,** *f.* partnership.

partout, *adv.* (*coll.*) by all means, at any cost.

Parze, *f.* (-n) destiny, fate; *die –n*, the Fates, the weird sisters.

Parzell-e, *f.* (-en) parcel, lot (*of ground*), allotment. **-ieren,** *v.a.* parcel out, divide into lots.

Pasch, *m.* (-es, -e & ¨-e) dice; doublets (*at dice*); *einen – setzen*, make the numbers at each end the same (*dominoes*); *– werfen* or *würfeln*, throw doublets (*at dice*). **-en,** 1. *v.n.* (*aux.* h.) throw doublets (*at dice*); (*Austr. dial.*) clap one's hands, slap. 2. *v.a.* smuggle. **-er,** *m.* smuggler. **-erei,** *f.* smuggling.

Pascha, *m.* (-s, -s) pasha, pacha.

pascholl, *int.* (*coll.*) vamose! vamoos(e)! hop it!

Paspel, *m.* (-s, –) & *f.* (-n) piping, edging (*on a dress, etc.*). **-ieren,** *v.a.* pipe (*a dress*).

Pasquill, *n.* (-s, -e) lampoon. **-ant,** *m.* lampooner, satirist. **-ieren,** *v.a.* & *n.* (*aux.* h.) lampoon.

Paß, *m.* (-(ss)es, ¨(ss)e) pace, amble; pass, defile, passage; narrows (*Naut.*); passport, papers, pass, permit; measuring glass; *den – gehen*, amble, pace; *einem den Lauf– geben*, send a p. about his business; 2. *adv.* fitly, suitably, well; (*coll.*) *das kommt mir zu –* (usually *zu–*), that suits me perfectly. **-(ss)abel,** *adj.* passable, tolerable, admissible, practicable. **-(ss)age,** **-(ss)agier,** *see* **Passage. Passagier.** **-amt,** *n.* passport-office. **-(ss)en,** **-(ss)ieren,** *see* **passen, passieren.** **-gang,** *m.* amble. **-gänger,** *m.* ambler, ambling nag. **-höhe,** *f.* height of a pass. **-kontrolle,** *f.*, **-revision,** *f.* examination of passports. **-lich,** *adj.* fit, suitable, seemly, proper. **-stelle,** *f.* passport-office. **-zwang,** *m.* necessity for a passport.

Passag-e, [*pron.* pa'saʒə] *f.* (-n) passage, thoroughfare; covered way, arcade; passage (*Mus., etc.*). **-ier,** *m.* (-s, -e) passenger, traveller; *blinder –ier*, stowaway. **-ierdampfer,** *m.* passenger-steamer. **-ierfahrt,** *f.* tour, trip, cruise. **-ierflugzeug,** *n.* air-liner. **-iergut,** *n.* passenger's luggage. **-ierverkehr,** *m.* passenger-traffic.

Passah, *n.* (-s) Passover.

Passant, *m.* (-en, -en) passer-by.

Passat, *m.* (-(e)s, -e), **-wind,** *m.* (-s, -e) trade-wind.
Passe, *f.* (-n) yoke (*of dress*).
passen, 1. *v.n.* (*aux.* h.) & *r.* fit, be fit, be convenient; suit, be suited, be suitable, be proper, seemly *or* becoming; correspond with, harmonize with; pass (*at cards*); *das paßt*, that will do; *das paßt wie die Faust aufs Auge*, that's not at all suitable *or* is entirely out of keeping; *das paßt mir ausgezeichnet*, that suits me admirably; – *auf* (*Acc.*), notice, be attentive to, watch, wait for; fit on *or* into; *paß auf!* take care! look out! *er paßt in jede Gesellschaft*, he is fit for any society; *das paßt in seinen Kram*, that suits his purpose exactly; *der Schlüssel paßt zum Schloß*, the key fits the lock; *er paßt gar nicht zum Kaufmann*, he will never make a business-man; *dies paßt nicht zur S.*, this is beside the question; *zueinander* –, be well matched, suit each other, go well together, harmonize. 2. *v.a.* adapt, adjust; fit on. **-d,** *pr.p.* & *adj.* appropriate, fit, fitting, suitable; becoming, apt, proper, seemly; convenient, opportune, to the purpose; *das -de Wort*, the right word; *für -d halten*, think proper; *dazu -d*, matching, fitting.
Passepartout, *m.* & *n.* (-(s), -s) master-key, free ticket; mount (*for photos, etc.*).
passier-en, 1. *v.a.* pass, travel over, through *or* across; cross; (*durch ein Sieb*) *-en*, sieve, filter, strain, pass through a sieve. 2. *v.n.* (*aux.* s.) pass muster, be tolerable, get past *or* through, pass; be current; (*coll.*) come to pass, take place, happen, occur; *nicht zu -en*, impassable; *-en für*, pass as; *es mag -en*, it will (just) *or* may do; (*coll.*) *was ist ihm -t?* what has happened to him? (*coll.*) *ist nichts Neues -t?* is there no news? **-bar,** *adj.* passable, traversable. **-gefecht,** *n.* running fight. **-gewicht,** *n.* mint-allowance, tolerated deficiency. **-schein,** *m.* pass, permit.
Passion, *f.* (-en) passion (*also Rel.*), passionate devotion. **-iert,** *p.p.* & *adj.* impassioned. **-sbetrachtung,** *f.* Lenten meditation. **-sblume,** *f.* passion-flower. **-spredigt,** *f.* Good Friday sermon. **-sspiel,** *n.* Passion play. **-swoche,** *f.* Holy Week.
passiv, 1. *adj.* passive, inert, inactive; *-er Widerstand*, passive resistance; ca'canny; *-e Bilanz*, debit balance; *-es Wahlrecht*, eligibility for election. 2. *n.* (-s, -e & *Austr. dial.* -a) *see* **-um. -isch,** *adv.* passively. **-ität,** *f.* passivity, inertness, inactivity. (*C.L.*) **-seite,** *f.* left side (*of ledger*). **-um,** *n.* (-ums, -a) passive voice; passive verb; (*pl.*) (*also* -en) liabilities; debts; (*C.L.*) *Aktiva und -a*, assets and liabilities.
paßlich, *adj.*, *see* **Paß.**
Passus, *m.* (–, –) passage (*in a book*), paragraph; case, instance.
Past-a, -e, *f.* (-en) paste; impress, replica, facsimile. **-ete,** *f.* (-n) pie, pastry; (*coll.*) *da haben wir die -ete!* here's a pretty kettle of fish! **-etenbäcker,** *m.* pastry-cook.
Pastell, 1. *m.* (-s, -e) pastel, crayon. 2. *n.* (-s, -e) pastel *or* crayon drawing. **-farben,** *f.pl.* pastel colour, coloured crayons. **-farbig,** *adj.* pastel-coloured, of delicate shade.
pasteurisieren, *v.a.* pasteurize.
Pastille, *f.* (-n) pastille, lozenge.
Pastinak, *m.* (-(e)s, -e), **-e,** *f.* (-n) parsnip.
Pastor, *m.* (-s, -en) pastor, clergyman, minister. **-al,** *adj.* pastoral. **-ale,** *n.* idyll, eclogue, pastoral. **-alschreiben,** *n.* pastoral (letter). **-at,** *n.* (-s, -e) parsonage, vicarage, (*Scots*) manse; incumbency. **-in,** *f.* minister's wife.
Pat-chen, *n.* (-s, –) godchild. **-e,** 1. *m.* (-en, -en) godfather, sponsor; godchild. 2. *f.* (-n) *see* **-in. -engeld,** *n.*, **-engeschenk,** *n.*, **-engroschen,** *m.* christening-gift. **-enkind,** *n.* godchild. **-enpfennig,** *m.*, *see* **-engeld. -enschaft,** *f.* sponsorship. **-enstelle,** *f.* sponsorship; *bei einem Kinde -enstelle vertreten*, stand sponsor to a child, act as godparent to a child. **-in,** *f.* godmother.
Patent, 1. *n.* (-s, -e) (letters) patent; charter; commission (*Mil.*); *ein – anmelden*, apply for a patent; *ein – nehmen*, take out a patent. 2. *adj.* (*coll.*) fine, splendid, (*sl.*) top-hole, tip-top. **-amt,** *n.* patent-office. **-anmeldung,** *f.* application for a patent. **-anwalt,** *m.* patent-attorney *or* agent. **-beschreibung,** *f.* patent-specification. **-brief,** *m.* letters patent; licence. **-dauer,** *f.* life of a patent. (*sl.*) **-fatzke,** *m.* dandy, fop. **-gebühr,** *f.* patent-fee. **-ieren,** *v.a.* patent; grant a patent to; *etwas -ieren lassen*, take out a patent (for). **-inhaber,** *m.* patentee. **-listen,** *f.pl.* register of patents. **-schutz,** *m.* patent-laws. **-träger,** *m.* patentee. **-verletzung,** *f.* infringement of a patent. **-verschluß,** *m.* patent stopper, patent cork.
Paternoster, *n.* (-s & *Austr. dial.* –, –) paternoster. **-aufzug,** *m.* hoist, lift. **-werk,** *n.* bucket chain.
path-etisch, *adj.* lofty, elevated, solemn, expressive. **-ogen,** *adj.* pathogenic. **-ogenese,** *f.* pathogenesis. **-olog(e),** *m.* pathologist. **-ologie,** *f.* pathology. **-ologisch,** *adj.* pathological. **-os,** *n.* solemnity, fervour, ardour, vehemence, emotion, transport, animation, exuberance.
Patient *m.*, (-en, -en), **-in,** *f.* (-innen) patient; – *sein*, be under (medical) treatment.
Patin-a, *f.* patina, verd-antique; *-iert* or *mit -a überzogen*, patinated, patinous.
Patri-arch, *m.* (-en, -en) patriarch. **-archalisch,** *adj.* patriarchal. **-monium,** *n.* (–, -nien) patrimony. **-ot,** *m.* (-en, -en) patriot. **-otisch,** *adj.* patriotic. **-otismus,** *m.* patriotism; *Hurrahpatriotismus*, jingoism.
Patrize, *f.* (-n) punch, counter-die.
Patriz-ier, *m.* (-s, –) patrician. **-isch,** *adj.* patrician. **-iertum,** *n.* patricians, the upper class. **-ierherrschaft,** *f.* aristocratic government, rule of the upper-class clique.
Patron, *m.* (-s, -e) patron; patron saint; (*coll.*) fellow; *Schiffs–*, master *or* owner of a ship; *unzuverlässiger* –, shifty fellow; *lustiger* –, jolly dog. **-at,** *n.* (-en, -en) advowson. **-atsberechtigt,** *adj.* having the gift of a living *or* the right of presentation. **-atsherr,** *m.* patron of a living (*Eccl.*). **-atsrecht,** *n.* patronage.
Patrone, *f.* (-n) cartridge, round (of ammunition) (*Mil.*); pattern, stencil, mandrel; *scharfe* –, ball-cartridge; *Platz–*, blank cartridge; *Exerzier–*, dummy-cartridge. **-nauswerfer,** *m.* ejector. **-nauszieher,** *m.* extractor. **-nform,** *f.*; *in -nform*, in tubes. **-ngurt,** *m.* cartridge-belt, bandolier. **-nhülse,** *f.* cartridge-case. **-ntasche,** *f.* cartridge pouch. **-ntrommel,** *f.* cartridge drum.
Patrouill-e, *f.* (-en) patrol (*Mil.*). **-ieren,** *v.n.* (*aux.* h. & s.) patrol. **-engang,** *m.* patrol-line, beat.
patsch, 1. *int.* slap! smack! 2. *m.* (-es, -e) (*coll.*) smack, clap; (*dial.*) hand. **-e,** *f.* (-en) (*coll.*) hand; beater; slap on the face, box on the ears; mire, mud, slush; dilemma, difficulty, fix, mess; (*coll.*) *einen in die -e bringen*, get a p. into a scrape; (*coll.*) *in die -e geraten*, get into hot water; (*coll.*) *in der -e sitzen*, be in a fix; (*coll.*) *einen in der -e sitzen lassen*, leave a p. in the lurch. **-en,** 1. *v.n.* (*aux.* h. & s.) make a slapping noise, clap; splash *or* paddle about; patter down (*of rain*). 2. *v.a.* smack, slap, pat, tap; splash. **-(e)naß,** *adj.* soaked to the skin. **-hand,** *f.*, **-händchen,** *n.* tiny hand (*of a baby*).
Patschuli, *n.* patchouli.
patt, *indec. adj.*; & *n.* (-s, -s) stalemate (*chess*); – *machen* or *setzen*, stalemate; – *sein*, be stalemated.
Patte, *f.* (-n) lapel, revers (*of coat*), flap (*of pocket*); (*dial.*) paw.
patz-en, *v.n.* (*coll.*) make blots, botch, (*sl.*) codge. **-ig,** *adj.* rude, impudent, insolent; *sich -ig tun* behave insolently.
Pauk-e, *f.* (-n) kettle-drum (*Mus.*); tympanum (*Anat.*); (*sl.*) lecture, harangue, dressing-down, rebuke; *mit -en und Trompeten*, with drums beating and trumpets sounding, with full honours; (*iron.*) ignominiously. **-en,** 1. *v.n.* (*aux.* h.) beat the kettledrum; (*sl. also v.a.*) cram, swot; fight a duel; thump, drum (*auf*, on). **-ant,** *m.* (-en, -en) duellist. **-arzt,** *m.* doctor at a students' duel. **-boden,** *m.* fencing-floor. **-enfell,** *n.* tympanic membrane; drum-skin, drumhead. **-enhöhle,** *f.* tympanic cavity. **-enklöppel,** *m.*, **-enschläger,** *m.*, **-enschlegel,** *m.* drumstick. **-enwirbel,** *m.* roll of the kettle-drum. **-er,** *m.* kettle-drummer; duellist;

(*sl.*) school-teacher; coach, crammer. **–erei,** *f.* duel; (*sl.*) cramming, swotting. **–handschuh,** *m.* fencing-glove. **–komment,** *m.* duelling rules.

Paus–back, *m.* (-(e)s, -e) chubby-faced person. **–backe,** *f.* chubby face. **–backig** (*Austr. dial.* **–bäckig**), *adj.* chubby-faced.

Pausch–ale, *n.* (-ales, -alien) lump sum. **–algebühr,** *f.* flat rate. **–alieren,** *v.n.* estimate in the lump. **–(al)kauf,** *m.* wholesale purchase. **–(al)-summe,** *f.*, *see* **–ale.** **–quantum,** *n.* bulk.

Pausche, *f.* (-n) pommel (*of saddle, etc.*).

[1]**Paus–e,** *f.* (-en) pause, stop, interruption, rest (*also Mus.*); interval (*Theat. & Mus.*); break, play-time, recess (*schools*); *ganze –e*, semibreve rest; *halbe –e*, minim rest; *viertel –e*, crotchet rest. **–enlos,** *adj.* without pause, uninterrupted. **–enzeichen,** *n.* interval signal (*Rad.*). **–ieren,** *v.n.* (*aux.* h.) pause.

[2]**Paus–e,** *f.* tracing; traced design; blue print. **–en,** *v.a.* trace, calk. **–leinwand,** *f.* tracing-cloth. **–papier,** *n.* tracing-paper, carbon paper.

Pavian, *m.* (-s, -e) baboon.

Pavillon, *m.* (-s, -s) pavilion, arbour.

Pazif–ismus, *m.* pacificism. **–ist,** *m.* (-en, -en) pacifist. **–izieren,** *v.n.* (*mit einem*) come to an agreement.

Pazisz–ent, *m.*; *die –enten*, the contracting parties. **–ieren,** *v.n.* make a contract.

Pech, *n.* pitch; cobbler's wax; (*coll.*) hard *or* bad luck; *– haben*, be unlucky; (*Prov.*) *wer – angreift, besudelt sich*, who touches pitch will be defiled. **–artig,** *adj.* bituminous. **–blende,** *f.* pitchblende. **–draht,** *m.* cobbler's thread. **–dunkel,** *adj.* pitch-dark. **–erde,** *f.* bituminous earth. **–fackel,** *f.* torch. **–ig,** *adj.* bituminous; pitchy. **–kohle,** *f.* bituminous coal; jet. **–nelke,** *f.* catch-fly (*Bot.*). **–(raben)schwarz,** *adj. & n.* pitch-black. (*coll.*) **–strähne,** *f.* run of bad luck. **–tanne,** *f.* common spruce; American pitch-pine. **–uran,** *n.* pitch-blende. (*coll.*) **–vogel,** *m.* unlucky person.

Pedal, *n.* (-s, -e) pedal. **–harfe,** *f.* double-actioned harp.

Pedant, 1. *m.* (-en, -en) pedant. 2. *adj.* (*Austr. dial.*), *see* **–isch.** **–isch,** *adj.* pedantic; precise, crotchety.

Pedell, *m.* (-s & -en, -e(n); *Austr. dial.* -(e)s, -e) beadle, porter, janitor, proctor's man, (*Univ. sl.*) bulldog.

Pegel, *m.* (-s, –) water-gauge, tide-gauge, water-mark. **–stand,** *m.* water-mark *or* level.

peil–en, *v.a.* take bearings, get a fix; take soundings, sound; *das Land –en*, take the bearings of the coast; *die Sonne –en*, take the sun's altitude. **–er,** *m.* bearing-compass, direction finder. **–funk,** *m.* radio-beam; radar, direction finding (*Rad.*). **–gerät,** *n.* direction finding *or* radar equipment. **–lot,** *n.* plummet. **–stange,** *f.* sounding-rod. **–station,** *f.*, **–stelle,** *f.* radar station. **–ung,** *f.* (radio) bearing; direction-finding (*Rad.*); sounding; *optische –ung*, visual bearing.

Pein, *f.* pain, agony, torture, torment. **–igen,** *v.a.* torture; torment, harass. **–iger,** *m.* torturer, tormentor; (*coll.*) plague. **–igung,** *f.* torture; torment. **–lich,** *adj.* painful, distressing, embarrassing; precise, painstaking, exact, meticulous, minute; capital, penal, on pain of death (*Law*); (*obs.*) by torture; *–liche Frage*, awkward question; *–liche Gerichtsbarkeit*, criminal jurisdiction; *einen in –liche Untersuchung nehmen*, try a p. for his life; *–lich anklagen*, accuse on a capital charge; *–lich befragen*, put to torture; *–lich genau*, scrupulously exact. **–lichkeit,** *f.* painfulness; exactness, precision, carefulness. **–voll,** *adj.* painful, excruciating.

Peitsche, *f.* (–n) whip, lash, scourge; cat-o'-nine-tails; *mit der – klatschen* or *knallen*, crack a whip. **–n,** 1. *v.a.* (horse-) whip, flog, scourge, lash; sweep *or* drive along. 2. *v.n.* flap (*of sails*); pelt (*of rain*). **–ngriff,** *m.* whip-handle *or* stock. **–nhieb,** *m.* lash *or* cut with a whip. **–nknall,** *m.* crack of a whip. **–nriemen,** *m.*, **–nschnur,** *f.* thong of a whip. **–nstiel,** *m.*, *see* **–ngriff.**

pekuniär, *adj.* pecuniary.

Pelerine, *f.* cape.

Pelikan, *m.* (-s, -e) pelican.

Pell–e, *f.* (-en) (*dial.*) peel, skin, husk. (*dial.*) **–en,** *v.a. & n.* peel, skin; *wie aus dem Ei gepellt*, spick and span. **–kartoffeln,** *f.pl.* potatoes in their jackets.

Peloton, *n.* (-s, -s) (*archaic*) file, platoon, firing party (*Mil.*).

Pelz, *m.* (-es, -e) fur, pelt, hide, skin; fur coat; (*coll.*) skin; *Faul–*, lazy-bones; *einem den – ausklopfen*, give a p. a good thrashing; (*vulg.*) *einem Läuse in den – setzen*, give s.o. cause for anxiety; (*coll.*) *einem (dicht) auf den – rücken*, importune a p.; (*coll.*) *einem den – waschen*, blow a p. up, give a p. a dressing down; *einem (eins) auf den – brennen*, fire a shot at a p. **–besetzt,** *adj.* trimmed with fur. **–en,** *v.a.* skin; graft, inoculate; (*coll.*) thrash. **–futter,** *n.* fur lining. **–händler,** *m.* furrier. **–ig,** *adj.* furry. **–mantel,** *m.* fur coat. (*dial.*) **–märtel,** *m.*, **–nickel,** *m.* Santa Claus. **–tiere,** *n.pl.* (*collect.*) fur-bearing animals. **–ware,** *f.*, **–werk,** *n.* furriery, furs.

Pendel, *n. & m.* pendulum. **–ausschlag,** *m.* amplitude (*Phys.*). **–länge,** *f.* length of pendulum. **–linse,** *f.* pendulum-bob. **–n,** *v.a.* oscillate, swing, vibrate, undulate. **–schlagwerk,** *n.* pendulum-tup. **–schwingung,** *f.* oscillation. **–uhr,** *f.* pendulum-clock. **–ung,** *f.* oscillation, swinging. **–verkehr,** *m.* shuttle-service.

Pennal, 1. *n.* (-s, -e) pencil case; (grammar-) school. 2. *m.* (*Studs. sl.*) (*also* **Pennäler**) grammar-school boy. **–ismus,** *m.* fagging (system).

Penn–e, *f.* (-en) tramps' lodging-house; (*coll.*) school. (*coll.*) **–bruder,** *m.* tramp. (*sl.*) **–en,** *v.n.* sleep.

Pension, *f.* (-en) (retiring) pension; boarding-house; board and lodging; *mit – verabschiedet*, pensioned off. **–är,** *m.* (-s, -e) pensioner; boarder (*at school or boarding house*). **–at,** *n.* (-s, -e) boarding-school. **–ieren,** *v.a.* pension (off). **–ierte(r),** *m.* pensioner. **–ierung,** *f.* pensioning, superannuation. **–ist,** *m.* (-en, -en) (*Austr. dial.*) pensioner. **–sbeitrag,** *m.*, superannuation *or* pension fund contribution. **–sberechtigung,** *f.* right to a pension. **–sfonds,** *m.*, **–skasse,** *f.* superannuation-fund. **–sliste,** *f.* retired list. **–spreis,** *m.* terms for residents. **–sstand,** *m.*; *in den –sstand treten*, be pensioned off, retire on a pension.

Pens–um, *n.* (-ums, -a & -en) task, lesson; curriculum.

Penta–eder, *n.* (-s, –) pentahedron. **–gramm,** *n.* pentacle.

per, *prep.*; *– Achse*, by road (transport); *– Adresse*, care of; *– Dampf*, by rail *or* steamer; (*coll.*) *– Fuß*, on foot; *zweimal – Jahr*, twice a year; (*C.L.*) *– Kasse*, on payment in cash; *– Post*, by post.

pereat, 1. *int.* (*Studs. sl.*) down with . . .! 2. *n.* (-s, -s); *einem ein – bringen*, throw mud at *or* hiss a p.; *ein – dem . . .!* three groans for . . .!

peremptorisch, *adj.* peremptory.

perennierend, *adj.* perennial.

perfekt, 1. *adj.* perfect, complete, settled. 2. *n.* (-s, -e), **–um,** *n.* (-s, -s) perfect tense (*Gram.*).

perfid–(e), *adj.* perfidious, insidious. **–ie,** *f.*, **–ität,** *f.* perfidy, perfidiousness; insidiousness.

perforieren, *v.a.* perforate.

Pergament, *n.* (-(e)s, -e) parchment, vellum. **–en,** *adj.* (of) parchment. **–papier,** *n.* thick vellum; grease-proof paper. **–rolle,** *f.* parchment scroll.

Pergamin, *n.* imitation parchment.

Period–e, *f.* (-en) period; sentence, phrase; repetend (*Mus.*); cycle (*Elec.*); menstrual period, menses (*Med.*). **–isch,** *adj.* periodic(al); *–ischer Dezimalbruch*, recurring decimal; *–isches System*, periodic law (*Chem.*); *–isch erscheinende Zeitschrift*, periodical (magazine). **–izität,** *f.* periodicity.

Peri–petie, *f.* climax, turning-point (*of dramatic action*) (*Theat.*). **–pherie,** *f.* periphery, circumference; *–pherie einer Stadt*, outer suburbs *or* outskirts of a town. **–skop,** *n.* (-s, -e) periscope.

Perl, *f.* nonpareil, pearl (*Typ.*). **–e,** *f.* (-en) pearl; bead; sparkling bubble; (*fig.*) gem, jewel; *–en vor die Säue werfen*, cast pearls before swine. **–en,** 1. *v.n.* (*aux.* h.) sparkle, glisten; ripple (*laughter*); form bubbles, effervesce. 2. *v.n.* (*aux.* s.) appear in drops *or* beads; *die Träne –t aus ihrem Auge*, the tear-drop rolled from her eye. **–enband,** *n.*, *see* **–enkette.** **–enbank,** *f.* bank of pearl-oysters.

-enfischer, *m.* pearl-fisher *or* diver. **-englanz,** *m.* pearly *or* nacrous lustre. **-enkette,** *f.*, **-enschnur,** *f.* string of pearls, pearl necklace *or* necklet. **-enstickerei,** *f.* beading. **-graupe,** *f.* pearl-barley. **-huhn,** *n.* guinea-fowl. **-ig,** *adj.* (of) pearl, nacrous. **-muschel,** *f.* pearl-oyster. **-mutter,** *f.* mother of pearl. **-samen,** *m.* seed pearl. **-ustrieren,** *v.a.* examine closely, investigate.

permanen-t, *adj.* permanent, lasting, enduring, durable. **-z,** *f.* permanency, permanence, persistence, durability, stability; *sich in -z erklären,* prolong one's (power, authority, *etc.*) *or* sit *sine die* (*Pol.*). **-zkarte,** *f.* (*Austr. dial.*) season-ticket.

permut-ieren, *v.r.* permute, exchange, interchange. **-ation,** *f.*, **-ierung,** *f.* permutation.

Perpendik-el, *m.* & *n.* (-s, –) perpendicular (line); pendulum; plummet-line. **-ular, -ulär,** *adj.* perpendicular.

perplex, *adj.* (*coll.*) confused.

Perron, *m.* (-s, -s) (*archaic & dial.*) railway platform.

Persenning, *f.* (-en) tarpaulin.

Person, *f.* (-en) person, personage; role, character, part (*Theat.*); *stumme –,* silent part; *lustige –,* clown, fool (*Theat.*); *juristische –,* corporation, body politic; *klein von –,* of short stature; *die handelnden -en,* dramatis personae; *in –,* personally, personified; *von – kennen,* know by sight; *ich für meine –,* I for my part; *die beteiligten -en,* the parties (*Law*); *ohne Ansehen der –,* without respect of persons. **-al,** 1. *n.* staff, assistants, officials, personnel, crew, servants, attendants. 2. *adj.*, *see* **-ell.** **-alarrest,** *m.* attachment of a person. **-albeschreibung,** *f.* personal description. **-alien,** *n.pl.* personalties; particulars of a person. **-aliter,** *adv.* in person, personally. **-ell,** *adj.* personal. **-enaufzug,** *m.* passenger lift. **-enbahnhof,** *m.* passenger station. **-enbeförderung,** *f.* conveyance of passengers. **-enkraftwagen,** *m.* private motor-car, passenger vehicle. **-enname,** *m.* proper name *or* noun. **-enstand,** *m.* number in family; legal status. **-enverkehr,** *m.* passenger-traffic. **-enverwechs(e)lung,** *f.* mistaken identity. **-enverzeichnis,** *n.* register of persons; dramatis personae. **-enwaage,** *f.* weighing-machine. **-enzug,** *m.* passenger-train, local train. **-ifizieren,** *v.a.* personify, impersonate.

persönlich, 1. *adj.* personal; *-e Meinung,* private opinion; *– werden,* make personal remarks, become personal (*in a quarrel*). 2. *adv.* in person, personally; *– haften,* be individually answerable. **-keit,** *f.* personality, individuality; personage. **-keitsbewußt,** *adj.* self-assured.

Perspektiv, *n.* (-s, -e) telescope, field-glass. **-e,** *f.* (-en) perspective; prospect (*of the future*). **-isch,** *adj.* perspective.

Pertinenz-ien, (*pl. of* Pertinens, *n.*) belongings, appurtenances.

Perücke, *f.* (-n) wig; *einem in die – fahren,* show a p. up as he really is, strip s.o. of all his pretensions. **-nstock,** *m.* wig-block.

pervers, *adj.* perverse, unnatural. **-ion,** *f.* perversion. **-ität,** *f.* perversity, aberration.

Perz-eption, *f.* perception. **-eptorisch,** *adj.* perceptual, perceptive. **-ipieren,** *v.a.* perceive, apprehend, conceive of; collect (*money, rent, etc.*) (*Law*).

Pesel, *m.* (-s, –) (*dial.*) (unheated) parlour.

pesen, *v.n.* (*dial.*) hurry, rush.

Pessar, *n.* (-s, -e) pessary.

Pessimis-mus, *m.* pessimism. **-t,** *m.* (-en, -en) pessimist. **-tisch,** *adj.* pessimistic.

Pest, *f.* (-en) plague, pestilence; contagion, epidemic; pest, nuisance; *daß dich die –!* a plague on you! *einen wie die – fliehen,* avoid s.o. like the plague. **-artig,** *adj.* pestilential. **-beule,** *f.* bubo (*Med.*); (*fig.*) plague-spot. **-geruch,** *m.*, **-hauch,** *m.* pestilential smell *or* stench. **-haus,** *n.* plague hospital. **-ilenz,** *f.* pestilence. **-ilenzialisch,** *adj.* pestilential. **-krank,** *adj.* plague infected, plague-stricken.

Petersilie, *f.* parsley; (*coll.*) *ihm ist die – verhagelt,* he has come unstuck *or* come a cropper; *sie pflückt –,* she is on the shelf, she is a wallflower.

Petrefakt, *n.* (-(e)s, -e(n)) fossil. **-enkunde,** *f.* palaeontology.

Petroleum, *n.* petroleum, crude oil, mineral oil, rock oil; paraffin(-oil), lamp oil, (*Amer.*) kerosene. **-quelle,** *f.* petroleum-spring, oil-well.

Petschaft, *n.* (-s, -e) seal, signet. **-ring,** *m.* signet-ring. **-stecher,** *m.* seal-engraver.

Petsche, *f.* drying rack *or* frame.

Petto, *m.*; *in – haben,* have in mind, intend.

Petz, *m.* Bruin. **-e,** *f.* (-n) she-bear; (*dial.*) bitch; (*coll.*) sneak, tell-tale. **-en,** *v.a.* (*aux.* h.) (*sl.*) tell tales, inform (against); (*sl.*) sneak, shop.

Pfad, *m.* (-es, -e) path, lane. **-er,** *m.* (*Swiss dial.*), *see* **-finder.** **-finder,** *m.* Boy Scout. **-finderin,** *f.* Girl Guide. **-finderbund,** *m.* Boy Scouts Association. **-findertum,** *n.* Scouting.

Pfaff-(e), *m.* (-en, -en) priest; cleric, parson. **-engeschmeiß,** *n.*, **-engezücht,** *n.* priests, clerics (*contemptuously*). **-enherrschaft,** *f.* clerical rule. **-enknecht,** *m.* slavish adherent of the clergy. **-enplatte,** *f.* priest's tonsure. **-entum,** *n.* clericalism; (*collect.*) priests. **-enwirtschaft,** *f.* clerical control.

pfäff-isch, *adj.* priest-like; clerical; priest-ridden.

Pfahl, *m.* (-s, ⸚e) stake, stick, post, pole, pile, prop, picket; pillory; *in meinen vier Pfählen,* within my own four walls, in my own house; *ein – im Fleische,* a thorn in the flesh. **-bau,** *m.* lake-dwelling, building on piles. **-bauer,** *m.* pile-builder; lake-dweller. **-bauten,** *m.pl.* lake-dwellings. **-bürger,** *m.* citizen; Philistine; stick-in-the-mud. **-dorf,** *n.*, lake-village. **-graben,** *m.* palisaded ditch. **-gründung,** *f.* pile foundation. **-hecke,** *f.* palisade, paling. **-jochbrücke,** *f.* trestle-bridge, pile bridge. **-ramme,** *f.*, **-rammler,** *m.* pile-driver. **-rost,** *m.* pile support *or* framework. **-werk,** *n.* paling, stockade, palisade; timber-work. **-wurzel,** *f.* tap-root (*Bot.*). **-zaun,** *m.* paling, railing, rail *or* picket fence.

pfähl-en, *v.a.* enclose (with a paling), fence in; prop, support, tie up, train (*on stakes*); impale. **-ung,** *f.* impalement.

Pfalz, *f.* imperial palace; surrounding territory. **-graf,** *m.* Count Palatine. *See Index of Names.*

Pfand, *n.* (-es, ⸚er) pledge, security, forfeit, pawn; mortgage; deposit, guarantee; *Pfänder spielen,* play at forfeits; *auf – geben,* supply against security; *zum -e setzen,* pawn, mortgage; pledge (*one's honour, word*). **-brief,** *m.* (deed of) mortgage, mortgage bond. **-geber,** *m.* pawner, mortgager. **-gebühr,** *f.* interest on mortgage; pledge-money. **-gläubiger,** *m.* mortgagee. **-haus,** *n.* pawnshop, pawn-office. **-hinterlegung,** *f.* deposit. **-kontrakt,** *m.* mortgage deed *or* bond. **-leiher,** *m.* pawnbroker. **-leihgeschäft,** *n.* pawnbroker's business; pawnshop. **-lösung,** *f.* redemption *or* recovery of a pledge. **-recht,** *n.* lien; hypothecary law. **-rechtlich,** *adj.* hypothecary. **-schein,** *m.* pawn-ticket. **-schuld,** *f.* debt on a mortgage. **-schuldner,** *m.* mortgagor. **-sicherheit,** *f.* collateral security. **-stück,** *n.* pledge. **-vertrag,** *m.*, **-verschreibung,** *f.* mortgage deed. **-weise,** *adv.* by pawn *or* mortgage.

pfänd-bar, *adj.* distrainable. **-en,** *v.a.* seize, distrain, take in pledge. **-er,** *m.* (*dial.*) executor, bailiff. **-erspiel,** *n.* game of forfeits. **-ung,** *f.* seizure, distraint, attachment, distress. **-ungsbefehl,** *m.* distress warrant.

Pfann-e, *f.* (-en) pan, bowl, caldron, copper, boiler; socket (*Anat.*); (*coll.*) *den Feind in die -e hauen,* cut the enemy to pieces; *etwas auf der -e haben,* have s.th. pat. **-enflicker,** *m.* tinker. **-enhaus,** *n.* salt-works. **-enschmied,** *m.* tinsmith. **-enstein,** *m.* boiler scale. **-enwerk,** *n.* salt-works. **-enziegel,** *m.* pantile. **-kuchen,** *m.* pancake; fritter; (*dial.*) doughnut.

Pfänner, *m.* (-s, –) salt-manufacturer.

Pfarr-acker, *m.* glebe land. **-amt,** *n.* incumbency. **-besetzungsrecht,** *n.* patronage. **-bezirk,** *m.* parish. **-buch,** *n.* parish register. **-e,** *f.* (-en), **-ei,** *f.* (church) living; parsonage, vicarage; parish. **-er,** *m.* clergyman, parson; rector, vicar; minister; priest. **-erin,** *f.* parson's wife. **-gefälle,** *n.pl.* revenues of a living. **-gut,** *n.* glebe land. **-haus,** *n.* parsonage; rectory, vicarage; (*Scots*) manse. **-kind,** *n.* parishioner. **-kirche,** *f.* parish church. **-land,** *n.* glebe land. **-schule,** *f.* church school, village school. **-zehnte,** *m.* parochial tithe.

Pfau, *m.* (-(e)s & -en, -e & -en) peacock; *der – schlägt* (*ein*) *Rad*, the peacock spreads its tail. **-enauge,** *n.* peacock-butterfly (*Ent.*); spot in a peacock's tail. **-enrad,** *n.*, **-enschweif,** *m.* peacock's tail *or* fan.

Pfeffer, *m.* (-s, –) pepper; (*Prov.*) *da liegt der Hase im –*, there's the rub *or* snag; (*coll.*) *im – sein*, be in a pickle *or* a jam; (*coll.*) *wo der – wächst*, far away, Jericho. **-artig,** *adj.* peppery. **-büchse,** *f.* pepper-caster *or* box. **-fresser,** *m.* toucan (*Orn.*). **-gurke,** *f.* (pickled) gherkin. **-korn,** *n.* pepper-corn. **-kuchen,** *m.* gingerbread. (*coll.*) **-land,** *n.* Jericho. **-ling,** *m.* (-s, -e), *see* **Pfifferling. -minze,** *f.* (pepper)mint (*plant*). **-minz,** 1. *m.* (-es, -e) essence of peppermint. 2. *n.* (-es, -e) peppermint (*sweet*). **-n,** *v.a.* pepper; season with pepper; (*coll.*) throw, fling, let fly; *die Preise sind gepfeffert*, the prices are exorbitant; *gepfefferte Witze*, spicy jokes; *gepfefferte Worte*, bitter *or* biting words. **-nuß,** *f.* ginger biscuit. **-staude,** *f.*, **-strauch,** *m.* pepper-plant. **-streuer,** *m.*, *see* **-büchse.**

Pfeif-e, *f.* (-en) pipe; blowpipe; organ-pipe; whistle; *eine -e stopfen*, fill a pipe; *nach jemandes -e tanzen*, dance to a p.'s tune: (*Prov.*) *man muß sich -en schneiden, während man im Rohr sitzt*, make hay while the sun shines. **-en,** *ir.v.a.* & *n.* (*aux.* h.) whistle, squeal, hiss, wheeze; sing, howl, squeak; *tanzen müssen wie jemand -t*, have to dance to another's tune; *also daher -t der Wind?* so that's the way the wind is blowing! (*coll.*) *ich will dir eins* or *was -en!* you may whistle for it! I'll put your nose out of joint! *-en auf etwas*, not care a straw for a th.; (*coll.*) *darauf -e ich*, I do not care (two hoots); *auf dem letzten Loch -en*, be at the end of one's tether. **-enbohrer,** *m.* pipe-borer. **-enerde,** *f.* pipe-clay. **-enform,** *f.* pipe-mould. **-enförmig,** *adj.* tubular. **-enhalter,** *m.* pipe-rack. **-enkopf,** *m.* pipe-bowl. **-enspitze,** *f.* mouth-piece (*of a pipe*). **-enstiel,** *m.* pipe stem. **-enstrauch,** *m.* (white) syringa. **-enstummel,** *m.* short pipe. **-enton,** *m.* pipe-clay, Fuller's earth. **-enwerk,** *n.* organ-pipes. **-er,** *m.* piper; whistler.

Pfeil, *m.* (-s, -e) arrow, dart; bolt, shaft; camber (*of an arch*). **-förmig,** *adj.* arrow-shaped; swept back (*of aircraft wings*). **-gerade,** *adj.* straight as an arrow. **-geschwind,** *adj.*, *see* **-schnell. -regen,** *m.* shower of arrows. **-richtung,** *f.* (*in the*) direction of the arrow. **-schnell,** *adj.* swift as an arrow. **-schuß,** *m.* bowshot. **-spitze,** *f.* arrow-head; (*fig.*) spearhead. **-verhältnis,** *n.* ratio of rise to span (*of an arch*).

Pfeiler, *m.* (-s, –) pillar; prop; upright; door-post, jamb; pier. **-brücke,** *f.* pier bridge. **-weite,** *f.* space between two pillars.

Pfennig, *m.* (-s -e) one-hundredth part of a mark; farthing; (*Prov.*) *wer den – nicht ehrt, ist des Talers nicht wert*, take care of the pennies and the pounds will take care of themselves. **-fuchser,** *m.* skin-flint, money-grubber. **-fuchserei,** *f.* stinginess. **-weise,** *adv.* in pennyworths.

Pferch, *m.* (-es, -e) fold, pen. **-en,** *v.a.* pen, fold, coop up; pack closely, cram.

Pferd, *n.* (-es, -e) horse; vaulting-horse; knight (*Chess*); *zu -e*, mounted, on horseback; *zu -e!* to horse! *vom -e auf den Esel kommen*, come down in the world; *nicht* or *keine vier, sechs* or *zehn -e bringen mich dahin*, wild horses could not drag me there; *das – beim Schwanze aufzäumen, das – hinter den Wagen spannen*, put the cart before the horse; *auf hohem – sitzen*, be on one's high horse; *sich aufs hohe – setzen*, get on one's high horse. **-earbeit,** *f.* drudgery. **-eausstellung,** *f.* horse show. **-ebändiger,** *m.* horse-breaker. **-ebehang,** *m.* harness, trappings. **-ebeschlag,** *m.* horse-shoeing; horseshoes. **-ebespannt,** *adj.* horse-drawn. **-ebestand,** *m.* effective force of horses *or* cavalry. **-ebremse,** *f.* horse-fly, cleg. **-edecke,** *f.* horse-blanket. **-edünger,** *m.* horse manure. **-efleisch,** *n.* horseflesh. **-efuß,** *m.* club-foot; (*fig.*) cloven foot. **-efutter,** *n.* fodder, provender. **-egeschirr,** *n.* harness. **-ehändler,** *m.* horse-dealer. **-ehuf,** *m.* horse's hoof. **-ejunge,** *m.* stable-boy. **-eknecht,** *m.* ostler, groom. **-ekoppel,** *f.* paddock. **-ekraft,** *f.* horse-power; *Maschine von 20 -ekräften*, 20 horse-power machine. **-ekrippe,** *f.* manger. **-ekum(me)t,** *n.* horse-collar. **-elänge,** *f.*; *um 2 -elängen*, by 2 lengths. **-emäßig,** *adj.* (*sl.*) excessive. **-emilch,** *f.* mare's milk. **-emist,** *m.* horse manure, horse droppings. **-erennen,** *n.* horse-race; horse-racing. **-eschau,** *f.* horse show. **-eschweif,** *m.* horse's tail. **-eschwemme,** *f.* horse-pond. **-eseuche,** *f.* murrain. **-estall,** *m.* stable. **-estärke,** *f.* horse-power. **-estriegel,** *m.* curry-comb. **-eträнke,** *f.* horse-pond, watering-place. **-e(transport)wagen,** *m.* horse-box. **-everleiher,** *m.* keeper of livery stables. (*coll.*) **-everstand,** *m.* horse sense. **-ewechsel,** *m.* relay of horses. **-ezucht,** *f.* horse breeding. **-ig,** *adj.* *suffix* horse-power; *ein 50 -iger Motor*, a 50 horse-power engine.

Pfette, *f.* (-n) purlin, templet (*Arch.*).

pfiff, pfiffest, pfiffe, *see* **pfeifen.**

Pfiff, *m.* (-es, -e) whistle, whistling; nip (*of wine, spirits, etc.*); trick; *einen – tun*, give a whistle; *einem auf den – gehorchen*, come at a p.'s call; *den – verstehen*, know *or* be up to all the tricks (of the trade); *keine -e!* no nonsense! **-ig,** *adj.* sly, artful, cunning, crafty. **-igkeit,** *f.* cunning, artfulness, craftiness. (*coll.*) **-ikus,** *m.* (–, -se) sly dog, artful dodger.

Pfifferling, *m.* (-s, -e) kind of mushroom; chanterelle; *keinen – wert*, not worth a rap *or* a straw.

Pfingst-en, *n.* (-ens, -en) & *pl. indec.* (*Austr. dial. f.*) Whitsuntide, Pentecost. **-abend,** *m.* Whit Saturday. **-ferien,** *pl.* Whitsun holidays, Whitsuntide recess (*Parl.*). **-fest,** *n.*, *see* **-en. -lich,** *adj.* Pentecostal; Whitsun-. **-montag,** *m.* Whit-Monday. **-ochs,** *m.*; *geputzt wie ein -ochs*, dressed up to the nines. **-rose,** *f.* peony. **-sonntag,** *m.* Whit-Sunday. **-tage,** *m.pl.* Whitsun holidays. **-woche,** *f.* Whitsun week.

Pfirsich, *m.* (-s, -e) & (*dial.*) *f.* (-e), **-e, Pfirsche,** *f.* (-en) peach. **-kern,** *m.* peach-stone.

Pflänz-chen, *n.* (-s, –) (*fig.*) tender plant; (*coll.*) *ein nettes -chen*, a pretty young th. **-ling,** *m.* young plant, seedling, sapling.

Pflanz-e, *f.* (-en) plant; (*coll.*) person, fellow; *du bist eine saubere -e!* you're a nice so-and-so! **-dolch,** *m.*, **-eisen,** *n.* dibble. **-en,** *v.a.* plant; (*fig.*) implant. **-enanatomie,** *f.* phytotomy. **-enart,** *f.* species of plants. **-enbeet,** *n.* bed (*of plants*). **-enbildung,** *f.* organization of plants. **-enbuch,** *n.* herbal, flora. **-enbutter,** *f.* vegetable butter. **-enchemie,** *f.* chemistry of plants. **-endaunen,** *f.pl.* kapok. **-eneiweiß,** *n.* vegetable protein. **-enerde,** *f.* vegetable mould, humus. **-enesser,** *m.* vegetarian. **-enfarbe,** *f.* vegetable dye. **-enfaser,** *f.* vegetable fibre. **-enfressend,** *adj.* graminivorous, herbivorous. **-engarten,** *m.* botanical garden. **-engattung,** *f.* genus of plants. **-engift,** *n.* vegetable poison. **-engrün,** *n.* chlorophyll. **-enhändler,** *m.* nurseryman, florist. **-enhaus,** *n.* greenhouse, conservatory. **-enkenner,** *m.* botanist. **-enkost,** *f.* vegetarian diet. **-enkunde,** *f.* botany. **-enleben,** *n.* vegetable life, vegetation; *ein -enleben führen*, vegetate. **-enlehre,** *f.* botany; book on botany. **-enöl,** *n.* vegetable oil. **-enreich,** 1. *n.* vegetable kingdom. 2. *adj.* rich in flora. **-enreste,** *m.pl.* fossil plants. **-ensaft,** *m.* sap. **-ensammlung,** *f.* herbarium. **-ensäure,** *f.* vegetable acid. **-enschädling,** *m.* plant pest. **-enschleim,** *m.* mucilage. **-enstecher,** *m.* dibble. **-enstoff,** *m.* vegetable matter; (*pl.*) vegetable remains. **-enstoffwechsel,** *m.* plant metabolism. **-ensystem,** *n.* classification of plants. **-entier,** *n.* zoophyte. **-enverbreitung,** *f.* distribution of plants. **-enwachstum,** *n.* vegetation, plant growth. **-enwelt,** *f.* flora. **-enwuchs,** *m.* vegetation. **-enzelle,** *f.* plant cell. **-enzucht,** *f.* plant cultivation. **-enzüchter,** *m.* nurseryman. **-er,** *m.* planter; settler, colonist. **-erde,** *f.* compost. **-holz,** *n.* dibble. **-kartoffel,** *f.* seed potato. **-lich,** *adj.* vegetable. **-reis,** *n.* scion. **-schule,** *f.* nursery; plantation. **-stadt,** *f.* daughter-town, development area. **-stätte,** *f.* (*fig.*) hotbed, source, nucleus. **–stock,** *m.* dibble. **–ung,** *f.* planting; plantation; settlement, colony.

Pflaster, *n.* (-s, –) plaster; patch; pavement, paving; (*fig.*) amends, sop; *eingelegtes –*, tessellated pavement; *englisches –*, court-plaster; *das – treten*, loaf about; (*coll.*) *London ist ein teures –*, London is an expensive place. **–er,** *m.* paviour, paver. **–geld,** *n.* road charges. **–kasten,** *m.* (*hum.*) sawbones, medical orderly (*Mil.*). **–n,** *v.a.* put a plaster on; pave; (*Prov.*) *der Weg zur Hölle ist mit guten Vorsätzen ge–t*, the way to hell is paved with good intentions. **–ramme,** *f.* paving-beetle. **–stein,** *m.* paving-stone, cobble stone. **–treter,** *m.* loiterer, loafer, street-corner lounger. **–ung,** *f.* paving.

Pflästerchen, *n.* (-s, –) patch; *Schönheits–*, beauty-patch.

Pflaume, *f.* (-n) plum; *gedörrte –*, prune; *geschmorte –n*, stewed prunes. **–nkern,** *m.* plum-stone. **–nmus,** *n.* plum jam. **–nweich,** *adj.* soft as butter, (*fig.*) spineless.

Pfleg–e, *f.* (-n) care, attention; rearing, tending, nursing; bringing up, fostering, cultivation, culture, encouragement (*of arts, etc.*); guardianship; *Kranken–e*, sick-nursing; *in die –e geben*, put out to nurse (*of babies*); put out to board (*bei*, with); *in* (*seine*) *–e nehmen*, take charge of; *–e des Haares*, care of the hair. **–eamt,** *n.* guardianship; public assistance office. **–eanstalt,** *f.* convalescent home, nursing home. **–ebedürftig,** *adj.* needing care. **–ebefohlen,** *adj.* committed to the care of; *der* or *die –ebefohlene*, charge, ward. **–eeltern,** *pl.* foster-parents. **–ekind,** *n.* foster-child. **–emutter,** *f.* foster-mother; nurse. **–en,** 1. *v.a.* (*reg.*) (*with Gen. archaic except in stock phrases*) tend, nurse, cherish, care for, attend to, take care of; cultivate, foster, go in for (*also poet. & archaic irreg.*); *er –te seines Amtes*, he performed the duties of his office; *einen hegen und –en*, cherish and love a p.; *Freundschaft mit jemandem –en*, cultivate a p.'s friendship; *er –te seinen Bauch*, he lived well, he pampered himself; *wir pflogen Rat*(*s*) *miteinander*, we consulted (with) each other; *sie –ten der Ruhe*, they rested, they took a rest, they took their ease, they took it easy; *Umgang mit einem –en*, see a good deal of a p.; be on terms of intimacy with s.o.; associate with a p.; *gepflogene Unterhandlungen*, negotiations conducted; *gepflegtes Äußere*, well-groomed appearance; *gepflegter Garten*, well cared for *or* well tended garden. 2. *v.n.* (*with inf.*) (*reg. only*) used to, be accustomed to, be in the habit of, be given to; *er –te zu sagen*, he used to say, he would say; *er –te der erste zu sein*, he was usually *or* used to be the first. **–er,** *m.*, **–erin,** *f.* nurse; guardian, curator. **–esohn,** *m.* foster-son. **–etier,** *n.* (animal) foster-parent. **–etochter,** *f.* foster-daughter. **–evater,** *m.* foster-father. **–ling,** *m.* foster-child; ward, charge. **–lich,** *adj.*, *see* **–sam**; (*dial.*) usual, customary. **–sam,** *adj.* careful, attentive. **–schaft,** *f.* guardianship; trust (*Law*).

Pflicht, *f.* (-en) duty, obligation; *einen in – nehmen*, bind a p. by oath; *in – stehen*, be bound by oath, be subject to; *es für seine – halten*, think it *or* hold it to be one's duty (to); *einem etwas zur – machen*, make it a p.'s duty to do a th., make a p. responsible for (doing) s.th.; *einen zu seiner – anhalten*, compel a p. to do his duty, hold a p. to his duty; *– und Schuldigkeit*, bounden duty. **–anker,** *m.* sheet- *or* main anchor. **–arbeit,** *f.* compulsory work. **–eifer,** *m.* zeal. **–enlehre,** *f.* ethics, moral philosophy. **–erfüllung,** *f.* performance of a duty. **–gefühl,** *n.* sense of duty. **–gemäß,** *adj.* conformable to duty; dutiful, loyal, conscientious; as in duty bound. **–gesetz,** *n.* moral law. **–ig,** *adj.* obligatory, binding, beholden. **–jahr,** *n.* (*Nat. Soc.*) compulsory domestic service. **–leistung,** *f.* performance of duty; oath of allegiance. **–mäßig,** *adj.* dutiful. **–schuldig,** *adj.* in duty bound. **–teil,** *m.* lawful share; inalienable (portion of) inheritance, entail (*Law*). **–treu,** *adj.* conscientious, dutiful. **–treue,** *f.* fealty; faithfulness to duty. **–vergessen,** *adj.* disloyal, undutiful, unfaithful. **–vergessenheit,** *f.* dereliction of duty; disloyalty, falsity. **–verletzung,** *f.* violation of duty. **–vorlesung,** *f.* lecture prescribed as compulsory. **–widrig,** *adj.* contrary to duty; undutiful, disloyal.

Pflock, *m.* (-(e)s, ¨e) (tent-)peg; (wooden) pin, stake, picket; plug; (*coll.*) *einige ¨e zurückstecken*, come down a peg, climb down.

pflöcken, *v.a.* fasten with pegs, peg.

pflog, pflöge, (*archaic*) *see* **pflegen.**

pflücken, *v.a.* pluck, pick, gather, cull; (*archaic*) pluck (*fowls, etc.*); (*coll.*) *ich habe ein Sträußchen* (*Hühnchen*) *mit ihm zu –*, I have a crow to pluck with him.

Pflug, *m.* (-(e)s, ¨e) plough; *Land unter dem –e*, arable land, land under the plough. **–dienst,** *m.* socage. **–eisen,** *n.* coulter. **–land,** *n.* arable land. **–messer,** *n.*, *see* **–eisen. –schar,** *f.* ploughshare. **–sterz,** *m.*, (*Austr. dial.* **–sterze,** *f.*) plough-handle. **–tiefe,** *f.* depth of furrow. **–treiber,** *m.* ploughboy.

pflüg–bar, *adj.* arable, ploughable. **–en,** *v.a.* & *n.* (*aux.* h.) plough; till; *mit fremdem Kalb*(*e*) *–en*, plough with another man's heifer; *den Sand* or *das Wasser –en*, beat the air; *sich –en durch*, plough through (*as a ship through the waves*). **–er,** *m.* ploughman.

Pfört–chen, *n.* (-s, –) little door; wicket-gate. **–ner,** *m.* porter, doorkeeper, gateman; turnkey; pylorus (*Anat.*).

Pfort–e, *f.* (-en) gate, door, opening, orifice, entrance; porthole (*Naut.*); *die Hohe –e*, the Sublime Porte. **–ader,** *f.* portal vein.

Pfoste, *f.* (-n), **–n,** *m.* (-ns, -n) post, pale, stake; jamb (*of doors*); main-piece (*of rudders*).

Pfote, *f.* (-n) paw; (*coll.*) scrawl; fist, mitt, paw; *sich die –n verbrennen*, burn one's fingers; *einem etwas auf die –n geben, einen auf die –n klopfen*, rap o.s. over the knuckles.

Pfriem, *m.* (-(e)s, -e), (*Austr. dial.* **–e,** *f.* (-en)), **–en,** *m.* (-ens, -en) awl, bradawl; German broom (*Bot.*). **–en,** *v.a.* bore. **–engras,** *n.* esparto grass.

Pfropf, *m.* (-(e)s, -e & ¨e), **–en,** *m.* (-ens, -en) stopper, cork, bung, plug; clot, thrombus, embolus (*Med.*); wad, wadding, tampon; tampion (*Artil.*); (*coll.*) tubby p. **–bastard,** *m.* graft hybrid (*Bot.*). **–en,** *v.a.* cram into, stuff full of; cork, plug; graft. **–engeld,** *n.* corkage. (*coll.*) **–envoll,** *adj.* full to overflowing, stuffed *or* crammed tight, packed (*with people*). **–enzieher,** *m.* corkscrew. **–messer,** *n.* grafting knife. **–reis,** *n.* graft, scion, shoot, slip. **–spalt,** *m.* graft-slit.

Pfröpfling, *m.* (-s, -e) shoot (for grafting), scion.

Pfründ–e, *f.* (-en) benefice, living; prebend; maintenance, keep (*in an institution*); (*fig.*) sinecure. **–enbesetzungsrecht,** *n.* advowson. **–enbuch,** *n.* register of livings. **–enertrag,** *m.* income of a living. **–enhandel,** *m.* simony. **–er,** *m.* (*Swiss dial.*) *see* **–ner. –haus,** *n.* institution, old people's home. **–ner,** *m.* beneficiary; prebendary; incumbent, beneficed clergyman.

Pfuhl, *m.* (-(e)s, -e) pool; puddle, slough; *Sünden–*, sink of corruption; *Höllen–*, bottomless pit.

Pfühl, *m.* (& *n.*) (-(e)s, -e) (*poet.*) bolster, pillow, cushion; couch; torus, column-moulding.

pfui, *int.* fie! shame! *– schäme dich!* fie upon you! *– über ihn!* shame on him! *– rufen*, cry shame.

Pfulmen, *m.* (-s, –) (*Swiss dial.*) pillow.

Pfund, *n.* (-(e)s, -e) pound (*weight*); half a kilogram (*unofficial except in Austr.*); pound (*sterling*); (*B.*) talent; *drei – Fleisch*, three pounds of meat; (*fig*). *sein – vergraben*, hide one's talent. **–geld,** *n.* poundage. **–gewicht,** *n.* pound-weight. **–ig,** *adj.* (*coll.*) splendid, fine, first-rate. (*sl.*) **–s-** (*prefix indicating approval*). (*sl.*) **–sessen,** *n.* excellent food. **–skerl,** *m.* fine fellow. **–weise,** *adv.* by the pound.

-pfünd–er, *m. subst. suffix* (-ers, -er) -pounder, *i.e.* **Sechs–er,** *m.* six-pounder (*Artil.*). **–ig,** *adj. suffix*; -pounder; *ein sechs–iges Geschütz*, a six-pounder cannon.

pfusch–en, *v.a.* & *n.* (*aux.* h.) blunder, bungle, botch; *in etwas* (*Acc.*) *–en*, meddle with *or* dabble in a th.; *einem ins Handwerk –en*, meddle without authority with s.o.'s work. **–er,** *m.* bungler, dabbler; inferior tradesman. **–erei,** *f.* bungling, scamped work. **–erhaft,** *adj.* clumsy, bungling, unworkmanlike.

Pfütz–e, *f.* (-en) puddle, slough, pool, pot-hole, mud-hole. **–eimer,** *m.* bailer, baling *or* bailing bucket (*Min.*). **–en,** *v.a.* pump out water (*Min.*). **–ig,** *adj*, muddy, miry, full of puddles.

Phänomen, *n.* (-s, -e) phenomenon, (*coll.*) miracle. **–al,** *adj.* phenomenal; remarkable, prodigious. **–ologisch,** *adj.* phenomen(al)istic (*Phil.*).

Phantas–ie, *f.* (-ien) imagination, fancy, inventiveness; fantastic vision, chimera, whim; reverie, impromptu, improvisation (*Mus.*). **–iepapier,** *n.* fancy coloured paper, decorative paper. **–iereich,** *adj.* imaginative, fanciful. **–ieren,** *v.a.* & *n.* (*aux.* h.) indulge in reveries *or* fancies; imagine, dream; rave, ramble, be delirious; improvise (*Mus.*). **–ievoll,** *adj.*, *see* **–iereich.** **–t,** *m.* (-en, -en) visionary; dreamer; oddity. **–tisch,** *adj.* fanciful; fantastic.

Phantom, *n.* (-s, -e) phantom, chimera; manikin, anatomical model (*Med.*).

Pharisäer, *m.* (-s, –) Pharisee, hyocrite. **–tum,** *n.* pharisaism.

Pharma–kologie, *f.* pharmacology. **–kopöe,** *f.* pharmacopoeia. **–zeut,** *m.* (-en, -en) apothecary, druggist, pharmacist. **–zeutisch,** *adj.* pharmaceutical. **–zie,** *f.* pharmacy.

Pharo(spiel), *n.* faro.

Phase, *f.* (-n) phase (*Elec.*, *of moon, etc.*). **–nänderung,** *f.* phase-change. **–ngleich,** *adj.* of the same *or* of like phase. **–nmesser,** *m.* phasemeter. **–nunterschied,** *m.* phase difference. **–nverzögerung,** *f.* phase lag.

Philanthrop, *m.* (-en, -en) philanthropist. **–isch,** *adj.* philanthropic.

Philist–er, *m.* (-ers, -er) Philistine; unimaginative p.; vulgarian; (*Studs. sl.*) townsman; *–er und Studenten*, town and gown. **–erei,** *f.* Philistinism; narrow-mindedness, lack of imagination, pedantry. **–erhaft,** *adj.*, **–rös,** *adj.* philistine, pedantic, unimaginative, uncultured, narrow-minded. **–erium,** *n.* (*Studs. sl.*) life after leaving the university; (*collect.*) old students, graduates; *ins –erium treten*, go down. **–ertum,** *n.* humdrum existence, everyday routine.

Philolog–(e), *m.* (-en, -en) philologist, linguist. **–ie,** *f.* philology, language studies. **–isch,** *adj.* philological, linguistic. **–enverband,** *m.* classical (*or* modern language) association.

Philosoph, *m.* (-en, -en) philosopher; – *von Sanssouci*, King Frederick II (the Great) of Prussia. **–ie,** *f.* philosophy. **–ieren,** *v.n.* (*aux.* h.) philosophize. **–isch,** *adj.* philosophical.

Phiole, *f.* (-n) phial, vial.

Phlegma, *n.* phlegm; apathy, sluggishness, dullness. **–tiker,** *m.* (-s, –) phlegmatic person. **–tisch,** *adj.* phlegmatic.

Phon–etik, *f.* phonetics. **–etiker,** *m.* phonetician. **–etisch,** *adj.* phonetic.

Phos–gen, *n.* phosgene gas. **–phat,** *n.* phosphate. **–phor,** *m.* phosphorus. **–phorblei,** *n.* lead phosphide. **–phoreszenz,** *f.* phosphorescence. **–phoreszieren,** *v.n.* phosphoresce. **–phorhaltig,** *adj.* phosphated. **–phorig,** *adj.* phosphorous. **–phorisch,** *adj.* phosphoric. **–phorit,** *m.* phosphate of lime. **–phorsauer,** *adj.* phosphate of. **–phorsäure,** *f.* phosphoric acid. **–phorwasserstoff,** *m.* phosphoretted hydrogen.

Photo, *n.* (-s, -s) photo. **–apparat,** *m.* camera. **–brief,** *m.* airgraph (letter). **–chemie,** *f.* photochemistry. **–geschäft,** *n.* photographic-materials shop. **–graph,** *m.* (-en, -en) photographer. **–graphie,** *f.* photograph; photography. **–graphieren,** *v.a.* photograph. **–graphisch,** 1. *adj.* photographic. 2. *adv.* by photography. **–gravüre,** *f.* heliogravure. **–händler,** *m.* dealer in photographic materials. **–kopie,** *f.* photographic copy, photoprint, photostat. **–montage,** *f.* photographic layout. **–sphäre,** *f.* photosphere (*Astr.*). **–therapie,** *f.* sun-ray treatment. **–typie,** *f.* printing with phototypes. **–zelle,** *f.* selenium cell.

Phras–e, *f.* (-en) phrase (*also Mus.*); catch-word; *leere –en*, empty talk, clap-trap. **–endrescher,** *m.* phrase-monger. **–enhaft,** *adj.* ambling, long-winded, prosy, prolix, verbose. **–ierung,** *f.* phrasing (*Mus.*).

phrenetisch, *adj.* frenzied, frantic, demented, insensate.

Physik, *f.* physics, physical science, natural philosophy. **–alisch,** *adj.* physical. **–er,** *m.* (-ers, -er) physicist, physical scientist. **–um,** *n.* pre-medical (examination).

physisch, *adj.* physical, natural, material, bodily.

Physio–gnomie, *f.* physiognomy. **–log(e),** *m.* (-en, -en) physiologist. **–logie,** *f.* physiology. **–logisch,** *adj.* physiological.

Pian–ino, *n.* (-s, -s) upright piano. **–ist,** *m.*, **–istin,** *f.* pianist. **–o,** 1. *adv.* piano, gently. 2. *n.* (-os, -os), **–oforte,** *n.* (-s, -s) piano(forte). **–ola,** *n.* (-s, -s) pianola, player piano.

Pich–elei, *f.* tippling; carouse. **–eln,** *v.n.* (*aux.* h.) (*coll.*) tipple, tope. **–en,** *v.a.* pitch, smear with pitch. **–wachs,** *n.* heel-ball.

Pick, *m.* (-s, -e) picking; peck; (*dial.*) secret grudge (*see* **Pik, Pike**). **–e,** *f.* (-en) pickaxe, pick. **–el,** *m.* (-s, –) 1. pimple. 2. pickaxe, ice-axe. **–elflöte,** *f.* piccolo. **–elhaube,** *f.* (-n) spiked helmet. **–elhering,** *m.* (-s, -e) pickled herring; clown, buffoon. **–(e)lig,** *adj.* pimply, blotched. **–en,** *v.a.* & *n.* (*aux.* h.) peck, pick; (*coll.*) stick, bind, be sticky *or* tacky. **–nick,** *n.* (-s, -e & (*Austr. dial.*) –s) picnic.

Piek, *f.* (-en) peak (*of sail; also narrow fore-part of hold*) (*Naut.*). **–en,** *v.n.* (*dial.*) prick. **–fein,** *adj.* (*sl.*) especially good, tip-top.

piep–(s), 1. *int.* tweet! peep! 2. *m.* (-s, -se) chirp, chirrup; (*coll.*) *nicht – sagen*, not utter a sound, be mum. (*sl.*) **–e,** *adj.*; *das ist mir ganz –e*, that's all the same to me, I do not care a damn. **–en,** *v.n.* (*aux.* h.) chirp, cheep, squeak; (*coll.*) *es ist zum –en*, it's a scream, it is quite ludicrous; (*coll.*) *bei dir –t es wohl*, you are off your head. **–matz,** *m.*, *see* **–vogel.** **–sen,** *v.n.*, *see* **–en**; be poorly, be off colour. **–sig,** *adj.* chirping, squeaking, piping; (*coll.*) weakly, ailing, poorly. (*coll.*) **–vogel,** *m.* dicky-bird.

piesacken, *v.a.* (*sl.*) worry, harass, torment.

Piet–ät, *f.* reverence, devotion, attachment; piety. **–ätlos,** *adj.* irreverent, disrespectful. **–ätvoll,** *adj.* reverent, devout. **–ismus,** *m.* form of evangelical devotional piety. **–istisch,** *adj.* pietistic.

Pik, 1. *m.* (-s, -s) pique; rancour, grudge (*see* **Pick, Pike**); peak (*of mountain*); (*coll.*) *einen – auf jemanden haben*, bear s.o. a grudge. 2. *n.* (-s, -s) spade (*cards*). **–ant,** *adj.* piquant, pungent, biting, highly seasoned *or* spiced; (*coll.*) racy, spicy. **–anterie,** *f.* spicy *or* racy joke *or* story. **–as,** *n.* ace of spades. **–e,** *f.* (-en) pike, lance; (*fig.*) *see* **Pik, Pick**; *von der –e auf dienen*, rise from the ranks. (*coll.*) **–en,** *v.a.*, **–sen,** *v.a.* prick. **–enier,** *m.* (-s, -e) pikeman. **–ee,** *m.* quilting; cotton fabric, pique. **–ett,** *n.* (-(e)s, -e) piquet (*Cards*); (*Swiss dial.*) squad, picket (*Mil.*). **–ieren,** 1. *v.a.* pique, nettle, annoy; transplant, plant out. 2. *v.r.* pique o.s. (*auf eine S.*, upon a th.); make it a point (of honour) to do a th., set one's mind on doing a th. **–iert,** *p.p.* & *adj.* offended, hurt, piqued; touchy.

Pikkolo, *m.* (-s, -s) boy waiter. **–flöte,** *f.* piccolo.

Pikrinsäure, *f.* picric acid.

Pilger, *m.* (-s, –) pilgrim. **–n,** *v.n.* (*aux.* h. & s.) go on a pilgrimage. **–fahrt,** *f.*, **–schaft,** *f.* pilgrimage.

Pille, *f.* (-n) pill; *eine bittere – versüßen*, sugar a pill. **–ndreher,** *m.* scarabaeus (*Ent.*); (*hum.*) apothecary.

Pilot, *m.* (-en, -en) pilot (*Naut.* & *Av.*). **–schirm,** *m.* pilot parachute.

Pilz, *m.* (-es, -e) mushroom, fungus; upstart; *in die –e gehen*, go mushroom gathering; (*coll.*) run away, disappear. **–artig,** *adj.*, **–haft,** *adj.*, **–ig,** *adj.* fungoid, mushroom-like. **–keim,** *m.* fungus spore. **–kunde,** *f.* mycology.

Piment, *m.* & *n.* (-(e)s, -e) allspice, pimento, Jamaica pepper. **–rum,** *m.* bay rum.

Pimpel–ei, *f.* (*coll.*) effeminacy. **–ig,** *adj.* soft, flabby, effeminate; weakly; sickly; whining, complaining. **–n,** *v.n.* (*aux.* h.) whine, complain; (*sl.*) be a cissy; be sickly. (*coll.*) **–fritz,** *m.*, **–liese,** *f.* delicate *or* sickly person; (*sl.*) cissy, sissy.

Pimpernuß, *f.* (-nüsse) pistachio *or* bladder-nut (*Staphylæa*).

Pimpf, *m.* (-(e)s & -en, -e) (*Nat. Soc.*) (*analogous to*) wolf-cub.

Pinasse, *f.* (-n) pinnace.

Pinguin, *m.* (-s, -e) penguin (*Aptenodytes*) (*Orn.*).

Pinie, *f.* (-n) stone-pine (*Pinus pinea*) (*Bot.*). **–nkern,** *m.*, **–nnuß,** *f.* pine-kernel. **–nzapfen,** *m.* pine-cone.

Pinke, *f.* (-n) (*sl.*) money; (*dial.*) blacksmith. **–ln,** *v.n.* (*coll.*) piddle. **–pank,** *int.* cling! clang!

Pinne, *f.* (-n) drawing-pin, brad, tack; pivot (*of compass needle*); tiller (*Naut.*); quill feather. **–n,** *v.a.* fasten with tacks.

Pinscher, *m.* (-s, –) fox-terrier, rough-haired terrier.

Pinsel, *m.* (-s, –) (paint-)brush; simpleton, noodle. **–ei,** *f.* daubing; stupidity. **–führung,** *f.* brush-work, touch. **–n,** *v.a.* & *n.* (*aux.* h.) brush; paint; daub; play the fool. **–stiel,** *m.* brush handle. **–strich,** *m.* stroke of the brush, brushwork.

Pinzette, *f.* forceps, tweezers, pincers, nippers.

Pionier, *m.* (-s, -e) engineer, sapper (*Mil.*); (*fig.*) pioneer. **–park,** *m.* engineer stores (*Mil.*).

Pipe, *f.* (-n) butt, wine cask.

Pips, *m.* pip (*in fowls*).

Pirat, *m.* (-en, -en) pirate. **–erie,** *f.* piracy.

Pirol, *m.* (-s, -e) golden oriole (*Orn.*).

Pirsch, *f.* hunting, deer-stalking. **–en,** *v.a.* stalk, hunt. **–er,** *m.* deer-stalker, hunter.

Pisang, *m.* (-s, -e) banana, plantain(-tree).

pispern, *v.n.* (*aux.* h.) (*dial.*) whisper.

Piss–e, *f.* (*vulg.*) piss; *die kalte –e*, strangury (*Med.*). **–en,** *v.n.* (*aux.* h.) (*vulg.*) piss. **–oir, Pißort,** *m.* urinal.

Pistazie, *f.* (-n) pistachio-nut *or* tree.

Piste, *f.* (-n) path, beaten track, cinder track (*for cycle racing*).

Pistill, *n.* (-s, -e) pistill (*Bot.*); pestle.

Pistol, *n.* (-s, -e), **–e,** *f.* (-en) pistol; *wie aus der –e geschossen*, like a shot from a gun; *einem die –e auf die Brust setzen*, hold a pistol to a p.'s head. **–engriff,** *m.* pistol grip. **–enschußweite,** *f.* (in, within) pistol-shot. **–entasche,** *f.* holster.

Piston, *n.* (-s, -s) piston (*Mach.*); cornet-à-piston (*Mus.*).

pitsch(e)naß, *adj.* (*coll.*) wet through, sopping wet, wet to the skin.

pittoresk, *adj.* picturesque.

Pivot–lafette, *f.* pivot mounting, rotating mount. **–lager,** *n.* trunnion bearing. **–zapfen,** *m.* trunnion.

Plack, *m.* (-es, -e), **–e,** *f.* (-en), **–en,** *m.* (-ens, -en) (*dial.*) patch, piece; blot, stain; *see also* **Plage.** **–en,** 1. *v.a.* (*dial.*) patch, stick; post up, placard; flatten, ram down. 2. *v.a.* & *r. see* **plagen.** **–erei,** *f.* vexation; toil, drudgery; extortion, oppression.

pladdern, *v.n.* (*dial.*) rain in torrents.

Pläd–eur, *m.* (-s, -e) defendant. **–ieren,** *v.n.* plead (*a cause*). **–oyer,** *n.* (-s, -s) speech for the defence.

Plag–e, *f.* (-en) vexation; misery; drudgery; trouble, nuisance, annoyance, bother; plague, pest, calamity, torment; (*Prov.*) *jeder Tag hat seine –e*, sufficient for the day is the evil thereof; *durch –en bewegen zu*, worry into (*doing, etc.*); *durch –en einen um etwas bringen*, worry s.o. out of a th. **–en,** 1. *v.a.* plague torment; vex, annoy; worry, trouble, bother, harass. 2. *v.r.* toil and moil, drudge; be troubled; *sich –en mit*, take trouble about; *geplagt werden von*, be afflicted with (*a disease*). **–(e)geist,** *m.* tormentor; tiresome p., pest, nuisance, plague.

Plagge, *f.* (-n) (*dial.*) sod, turf.

Plagia–r, *m.* (-rs, -re) *see* **–tor.** **–t,** *n.* (-tes, -te) plagiarism; *ein –t begehen*, plagiarize. **–tor,** *m.* (-s, -en) plagiarist.

Plaid, *m.* & *n.* (-s, -s) plaid, travelling-rug.

plaidieren, *v.n.* (*Austr. dial.*) *see* **plädieren.**

Plakat, *n.* (-(e)s, -e) bill, placard, poster. **–ankleber,** *m.* bill-sticker. **–anschlag,** *m.* bill-posting. **–farbe,** *f.* poster colour. **–ieren,** *v.a.* post *or* stick bills. **–ierung,** *f.* bill-posting. **–kunst,** *f.* poster design. **–malerei,** *f.* poster-painting. **–säule,** *f.* advertisement pillar. **–schrift,** *f.* poster-lettering. **–träger,** *m.* sandwich-man.

plan, 1. *adj.* plain, clear, open; level, flat, plane, horizontal. 2. *m.* (-(e)s, ⸚e) plane, plain; arena, battle-field; glade, clearing (*in a wood*); ground-plan (*Arch.*); map, chart, plan, design, diagram; project, intention, scheme, plot; *auf den – treten*, appear, turn up, put in an appearance; *der grüne –*, the greensward, meadow; *tief durchdachter –*, carefully thought-out scheme; *gedruckter –*, prospectus; *entgegengesetzte Pläne*, cross-purposes; *Pläne schmieden*, make plans. **–en,** *v.a.* plan, project; plot, scheme, design, work out. **–feuer,** *n.* curtain of fire (*Artil.*). **–film,** *m.* flat film, film-pack (*Phot.*). **–hammer,** *m.* planishing-hammer. **–ieren,** *v.a.* level, plane, grade, smooth; size (*paper*). **–ieramboß,** *m.* planishing-anvil. **–iermasse,** *f.* size (*Pap.*). **–ierpresse,** *f.* size-press. **–ierung,** *f.* levelling, grading. **–ierwasser,** *n.* size; glue-water. **–konvex,** *adj.* planoconvex. **–liegend,** *adj.* non-curling (*Phot.*). **–los,** *adj.* without a fixed plan, planless, purposeless, desultory. **–losigkeit,** *f.* lack of design *or* purpose, desultoriness. **–mäßig,** *adj.* according to plan, methodical, systematic; to scale. **–pause,** *f.* blue-print. **–quadrat,** *n.* map square *or* grid. **–schießen,** *n.* map fire (*Artil.*). **–sektor,** *m.* map protractor. **–spiegel,** *m.* plane mirror. **–stelle,** *f.* map position. **–um,** *n.* road-bed. **–ung,** *f.* planning. **–unterlage,** *f.* map table. **–voll,** *adj.* planned, systematic, concerted. **–wirtschaft,** *f.* planned economy, economic planning. **–zeichnen,** *n.* map-drawing; plotting; field-sketching. **–zeiger,** *m.* map-reading scale.

Plan–e, *f.* awning, tarpaulin; tilt (*of a cart*). **–wagen,** *m.* covered wagon, tilt-cart.

Planet, *m.* (-en, -en) planet; asteroid. **–arisch,** *adj.* planetary. **–arium,** *n.* orrery. **–enbahn,** *f.* orbit of a planet. **–enjahr,** *n.* planetary year. **–enstand,** *m.* position of planets; aspect (*Astrol.*).

planieren, *see* **plan.**

Plank–e, *f.* (-en) plank, board; fence of boards. **–enwerk,** *n.* planking, sheathing.

Plänk–elei, *f.* (-en) skirmishing. **–eln,** *v.n.* (*aux.* h.) skirmish. **–ler,** *m.* skirmisher.

plan(t)sch–en, *v.a.* & *n.* (*aux.* h.) (*coll.*) splash, paddle. **–becken,** *n.* paddling pool. **–erei,** *f.* splashing.

Plantage, *f.* plantation.

Plapper–ei, *f.* (-eien) babbling, prattle, chatter, blether. **–haft,** *adj.* talkative, chatty, gossipy. **–haftigkeit,** *f.* garrulity. **–liese,** *f.*, **–maul,** *n. see* **–tasche.** **–n,** *v.a.* & *n.* (*aux.* h.) babble, chatter, prattle, jabber; rattle off. **–tasche,** *f.* chatterbox, prattler, gossip.

plärren, *v.n.* (*aux.* h.) blubber, bawl, cry.

Plast–ik, *f.* plastic art, sculpture. **–iker,** *m.* sculptor. **–ilin,** *n.*, **–ilina,** *f.* plasticine. **–isch,** *adj.* plastic, formative; *–ische Landkarte*, relief map.

Platane, *f.* (-n) plane-tree.

Platin, *n.* platinum. **–ieren,** *v.a.* cover, combine *or* coat with platinum. **–chlorid,** *n.* platinum chloride. **–draht,** *m.* platinum wire. **–haltig,** *adj.* platiniferous. **–ichlorid,** *n.* platinic chloride. **–ochlorid,** *n.* platinous chloride.

Platon–iker, *m.* (-s, –) Platonist. **–isch,** *adj.* Platonic, unworldly, spiritual.

platsch, *int.* splash! **–en,** *v.n.* (*aux.* h.) splash; (*aux.* s.) fall plump. **–naß,** *adj.* sopping wet, drenched.

platt, 1. *adj.* flat, flattened, plain, level, even; dull, stale, insipid, silly; vulgar; downright; low (*of a dialect*); *– abschlagen*, give a flat refusal; *–es Benehmen*, boorish manners; *– auf der Erde liegen*, lie flat on the ground; *das –e Gegenteil*, quite the contrary; *–es Gespräch*, dull discourse; *ich sagte es ihm – heraus*, I told it him straight out; *–es Land*, flat *or* open country; *–e Scherze*, low *or* vulgar jokes; *– schlagen*, flatten; (*sl.*) *ich war ganz –*, I was quite dumbfounded *or* taken aback; *–e Wahrheit*, plain *or* naked truth; *–er Widerspruch*, downright *or* flat contradiction. 2. *n.* Low German, North-German dialect(s). **–deutsch,** *adj.* & *n.* Low-German, the North-German dialects. **–e,** *f.* (-en) plate; dish; tray, salver; bald head, tonsure; clearing in a wood; blaze, mark; sheet (*of metal*); lamina, lamella; slab, tile, flagstone; plinth (*Arch.*); planchet, disk; gramophone record; photographic plate; platform; plateau, tableland; smooth slope of rock, sandbank; leaf (*of a table*); *kalte –e*, (plate of) cold meat;

in -en brechen, flake off. **-en,** *v.a.* flatten, level; laminate (*wire*). **-enabdruck,** *m.*, **-enabzug,** *m.* stereotyped proof. **-enbelag,** *m.* layer *or* covering of slabs *or* tiles. **-endruck,** *m.* stereotype (*printing*). **-enförmig,** *adj.* plate-like; lamelliform. **-engeräusch,** *n.* surface scratch (*gramophone*). **-engummi,** *n.* sheet-rubber. **-enhalter,** *m.* plate-holder (*Phot.*). **-enkamera,** *f.* plate camera. **-enkassette,** *f.* plate-holder (*Phot.*). **-enpulver,** *n.* flake powder. **-enrille,** *f.* groove (*of gramophone record*). **-enrüstung,** *f.* plate-armour. **-enschrift,** *f.* stereotype. **-enspieler,** *m.* record player. **-enteller,** *m.* turntable (*gramophone*). **-enwechsel,** *m.* record changing (*gramophone*). **-erdings,** *adv.* absolutely, decidedly, positively, by all means; *-erdings nicht*, not by any means, in no case. **-fisch,** *m.* flat-fish; plaice, flounder. **-form,** *f.* platform. **-fuß,** *m.* flat foot. **-fußeinlage,** *f.* arch-support. **-füßig,** *adj.* flat-footed. **-gedrückt,** *adj.* flattened. **-heit,** *f.* flatness, levelness; triviality, dullness, staleness, insipidity; trite expression, platitude. **-ieren,** *v.a.* plate. **-kopf,** *m.* empty head, shallow pate. **-ler,** *see* **Schuhplattler.** **-mönch,** *m.* (-es, -e) black-cap (*Sylvia atricapilla*) (*Orn.*). **-stich,** *m.* satin-stitch. **-weg,** *adv.*, *see* **-zu.** **-ziegel,** *m.* flat tile. **-zu,** *adv.* flatly, roundly, peremptorily.

Plätt-e, *f.* (-en) (*dial.*) flat-iron. **-bolzen,** *m.* heater for a smoothing-iron. **-brett,** *n.* ironing-board. **-eisen,** *n.* (smoothing *or* flat)iron. **-en,** *v.a.* iron (*clothes*). **-erin,** *f.*, **-frau,** *f.* ironer. **-stahl,** *m.*, *see* **-bolzen.** **-wäsche,** *f.*, **-zeug,** *n.* ironing, linen (to be) ironed.

Platz, *m.* (-es, ⸗e) place, spot, site, location; room, space; stand (*for carriages*); (market) square; seat (*Theat.*, *etc.*); post; *am -e*, in this place, here; suitable, pertinent, opportune; *nicht am -e*, unwanted, uncalled for, irrelevant; *500 blieben auf dem -e*, 500 were slain; *immer auf dem -e sein*, be always on the alert; be ready for anything; *den – behaupten*, hold one's ground, gain the upper hand, carry all before one; *– da!* make way there! *fester –*, fortress, fortified place; *freier –*, open space, esplanade; *– greifen*, gain ground, spread, take effect; *einen guten – haben*, have a good seat (*Theat.*); *hier ist kein – mehr*, there is no more room here; *– machen*, make way, clear the way (for), make room; *– nehmen*, sit down; be seated, take a seat. **-angst,** *f.* agoraphobia (*Path.*). **-anweiserin,** *f.* theatre attendant, usherette. **-bedarf,** *m.* local wants. **-feuer,** *n.* airfield lights. **-geschäft,** *n.* local business. **-karte,** *f.* seat ticket. **-kommandant,** *m.*, **-major,** *m.* local commandant, town-major. **-mangel,** *m.* shortage *or* lack of space. **-notierung,** *f.* spot quotation (*C.L.*). **-nummer,** *f.* atomic number (*Chem.*). **-raubend,** *adj.* taking up too much space. **-runde,** *f.* circling flight (*before landing* (*Av.*)). **-verkauf,** *m.* sale on the spot. **-wart,** *m.* groundsman. **-wechsel,** *m.* change of place, migration; local bill (*C.L.*).

Plätz-chen, *n.* (-s, –) pastille, drop, lozenge, tablet, tabloid; fancy cake, chocolate, *etc.* **-en,** *v.a.* & *n.* (*aux.* h.) (*dial.*) smack, slap; blaze (*trees*).

platz-en, *v.n.* (*aux.* s.) burst, explode, detonate; *einem ins Zimmer* (*herein*)*-en*, burst into a p.'s room; (*mit etwas*) *heraus-en*, burst out (with s.th.), blurt out (s.th.). **-patrone,** *f.* blank cartridge. **-regen,** *m.* cloudburst, downpour.

Plauder-ei, *f.* chat, small talk, tittle-tattle, gossip; talk, commentary (*Rad.*). **-er,** *m.* conversationalist, talker; chatterer, chatterbox. **-haft,** *adj.* chatty, talkative, loquacious. **-haftigkeit,** *f.* loquacity. **-hans,** *m.*, **-liese,** *f.*, **-maul,** *n.*, *see* **-tasche.** **-n,** *v.n.* (*aux.* h.) converse, chat, talk, chatter, gossip, have a chat; *aus der Schule -n*, tell tales (out of school). **-tasche,** *f.* chatterbox, gossip. **-stündchen,** *n.* cosy chat. **-ton,** *m.* conversational tone.

Plaue, *f.* (-n) (*Austr. dial.*) *see* **Plane.**

Plausch, *m.* (-es, -e) (*dial.*) chat. (*dial.*) **-en,** *v.n.* chat.

plausibel, *adj.* plausible, feasible, specious; *– machen*, make plausible, give colour to.

plauz, 1. *int.* bang! smash! 2. *m.* (-es, -e) crash, bang; (*coll.*) beating, spanking. (*coll.*) **-en,** *v.n.* fall down with a bang.

Pleb-ejer, *m.* (-s, –) plebeian. **-ejisch,** *adj.* plebeian, low, vulgar. **-iszit,** *n.* (-s, -e) plebiscite. **-s,** *m.* (& *Austr. dial. f.*) plebs; mob, rabble.

Pleite, 1. *f.* (-n) (*sl.*) bankruptcy; failure; *– machen*, go bankrupt. 2. *adj.* bankrupt; (*coll.*) *– gehen*, go smash, fail (*in business*). (*coll.*) **-geier,** *m.* misfortune, mischance.

Plejade, *f.* pleiad.

Plempe, *f.* (-n) (*Mil. sl.*) short sword; (*coll.*) thin coffee, wishy-washy drink. **-rn,** 1. *v.n.* (*dial.*) lounge about. 2. *v.a.* (*coll.*) splash, spray, water.

Plenum, *n.* full assembly, plenary session.

Pleuelstange, *f.* connecting rod, piston rod (*Mach.*).

Plicht, *f.* (-en) cockpit (*Naut.*).

plinkern, *v.n.* (*coll.*) blink, wink.

Plins-e, Plinz-e, *f.* (*Austr. dial.*) (-en) fritter, pancake, omelette. **-en,** *v.n.* (*dial.*) weep, cry.

Pliozän, *n.* & *adj.* pliocene (*Geol.*).

Pliss-ee, *n.* (-s, -s) pleating. **-ieren,** *v.a.* pleat.

Plomb-e, *f.* (-en) lead, seal, plug, stopping *or* filling (*for a tooth*). **-ieren,** *v.a.* affix lead seal to; plug; fill, stop (*a tooth*).

Plötze, *f.* (-n) roach (*Leuciscus rutilus*) (*Icht.*).

plötzlich, 1. *adj.* sudden, abrupt. 2. *adv.* all at once. **-keit,** *f.* suddenness, abruptness.

Pluder-hosen, *f.pl.* baggy trousers, wide breeches, plus-fours. **-n,** *v.n.* be baggy, bag (*of clothes*).

Plumeau, *n.* (-s, -s) feather bed.

plump, 1. *adj.* heavy, bulky, shapeless, unwieldy, (*coll.*) podgy; clumsy, awkward, gross; rude, blunt, coarse, ill-bred; ponderous (*style*); *-e Schmeichelei*, gross flattery; *ein -es Wesen haben*, have blunt manners; *– heraussagen*, blurt out. 2. *m.*, *see* **-s,** 1. **-en,** *see* **-sen.** **-heit,** *f.* shapelessness, heaviness, unwieldiness, clumsiness; bluntness. **-s,** 1. *m.* (-ses, -se) thump, thud, heavy fall. 2. *int.* plump! bump! thump! thud! **-sack,** *m.* knotted handkerchief (*in a game*), the knot; (*fig.*) clumsy lout. **-sen,** *v.n.* (*aux.* h. & s.) fall plump *or* with a thud, plump down; blurt out; bounce (into).

Plunder, *m.* lumber, old clothes, trash, rubbish, junk. **-kammer,** *f.* lumber-room. **-kram,** *m.* litter, lumber. **-mann,** *m.* rag-and-bone man.

Plünder-er, *m.* (-ers, -er) plunderer. **-n,** *v.a.* plunder, pillage, sack; despoil, rob. **-ung,** *f.* plundering, looting, pillage, sack; *der -ung preisgeben*, give up to pillage, allow to be sacked.

Plural, *m.* (-s, -e) plural. **-isch,** *adj.* in the plural. **-wahlrecht,** *n.* plural vote.

Plus, 1. *n.* plus, surplus. 2. *adv.* plus, more, in addition. **-betrag,** *m.* surplus. **-macher,** *m.* financial schemer, profiteer. **-quamperfekt(um),** *n.* pluperfect (*Gram.*). **-zeichen,** *n.* plus *or* addition sign (+).

Plüsch, *m.* (-es, -e) plush. **-teppich,** *m.* Wilton carpet.

pluster-n, *v.n.* & *r.* ruffle one's feathers, bristle. **-ig,** *adj.* tousled.

Pneu, *m.* (-s, -s), **-matik,** *m.* (-s, s) & *Austr. dial. f.* (-en) (pneumatic) tyre. **-matisch,** *adj.* pneumatic.

Pöbel, *m.* mob, populace, rabble. **-haft,** *adj.* vulgar, low, plebeian. **-haftigkeit,** *f.* vulgarity, coarseness. **-haufe,** *m.* rabble. **-herrschaft,** *f.* mob-rule. **-justiz,** *f.* lynch-law. **-n,** *v.n.* behave in a vulgar manner, indulge in a slanging match.

Poch, *n.* & *m.*, *see* **-spiel.** **-e,** *pl.* (*dial.*) thrashing. **-en,** 1. *v.a.* crush, pound, batter. 2. *v.a.* & *n.* (*aux.* h.) knock, rap; beat, throb (*of the heart*); play poker; *man -t*, there is a knock at the door; *mir -t das Herz*, my heart beats *or* throbs; *auf eine S. -en*, brag about, boast of *or* presume upon a th.; rely on a th. **-erz,** *n.* crude ore. **-hammer,** *m.* crusher. **-mehl,** *n.* pulverized ore. **-mühle,** *f.* stamping-mill. **-satz,** *m.*, **-schlamm,** *m.*, **-schlick,** *m.* ore sludge. **-schlägel,** *m.*, *see* **-hammer.** **-spiel,** *n.* poker (*cards*). **-werk,** *n.* stamping-mill.

Pock-e, *f.* (-en) pock; pockmark; *die -en*, (*pl.*) smallpox. **-engift,** *n.* smallpox virus. **-enholz,** *n.* lignum vitae. **-enimpfung,** *f.* vaccination. **-enkrank,** *adj.* suffering from smallpox. **-enlymphe,** *f.* vaccine. **-ennarbe,** *f.* pockmark. **-ennarbig,**

adj. pockmarked. **–holz,** *see* **–enholz. –ig,** *adj., see* **–ennarbig.**
Podagra, *n.* gout, podagra.
Podest, *m.* & *n.* (-es, -e) landing (*of staircase*); stage, platform.
Podex, *m.* (-(es), -e) posterior, buttocks, backside.
Podium, *n.* (-ums, -ien) rostrum, platform.
Poe–sie, *f.* (-n) poetry; piece of poetry, poem. **–sielos,** *adj.* without poetry, unpoetical; prosaic, dull, commonplace. **–t,** *m.* (-ten, -ten) (*high style*) poet. **–tik,** *f.* theory of poetry, poetics. **–tisch,** *adj.* poetic.
Pogge, *f.* (-n) (*dial.*) frog. **–nstuhl,** *m.* toadstool.
Point–e [*pron.* poˈɛ̃:tə], *f.* (-en) point (*of a joke*). **–ieren,** *v.a.* give point to, express in a pointed manner, emphasize.
Pokal, *m.* (-s, -e) goblet, cup; trophy. **–spiel,** *n.* cup-tie (*Sport*).
Pökel, *m.* brine, pickle. **–faß,** *n.* salting-tub *or* vat. **–fleisch,** *n.* salt(ed) *or* pickled meat. **–hering,** *m.* pickled herring. **–n,** *v.a.* salt, cure, pickle.
pokulieren, *v.n.* (*aux.* h.) drink, booze, carouse.
Pol, *m.* (-s, -e) pole (*Astron.* & *Magnet.*); terminal (*Elec.*). **–ar,** *adj.* polar. **–arbär,** *m.* polar bear. **–arforscher,** *m.* polar explorer. **–arforschung,** *f.* polar exploration. **–arfuchs,** *m.* arctic fox. **–argegend,** *f.* polar regions. **–argürtel,** *m.* frigid zone. **–arisationsebene,** *f.* plane of polarization. **–arisationsfarbe,** *f.* colour of polarized light. **–arisator,** *m.* polarizer. **–arisieren,** *v.a.* polarize. **–arität,** *f.* polarity. **–arkreis,** *m.* polar circle. **–arländer,** *n.pl.* arctic regions. **–arlicht,** *n.* northern lights, aurora borealis. **–armeer,** *n.* Arctic ocean; *südliches –armeer*, Antarctic ocean. **–arstern,** *m.* Pole star, (*Poet.*) loadstar, lodestar. **–arstrom,** *m.* arctic current. **–höhe,** *f.* latitude. **–klemme,** *f.* terminal, binding-screw (*Elec.*). **–schuh,** *m.* pole piece (*Elec.*). **–stein,** *m.* loadstone, lodestone. **–wechsler,** *m.* transformer (*Elec.*).
Polder, *m.* (-s, –) reclaimed land.
Polem–ik, *f.* (-en) polemics, controversy. **–iker,** *m.* controversialist. **–isch,** *adj.* polemic. **–isieren,** *v.n.* carry on a controversy; (*gegen eine S.*) controvert (s.th.).
Police, *f.* (-n) (insurance) policy.
Polier, *m.* (-s, -e) building trade foreman.
polier–en, *v.a.* polish, burnish; furbish. **–er,** *m.* burnisher, French-polisher. **–mittel,** *n.* polish. **–rot,** *n.* (jeweller's) rouge, colcothar. **–scheibe,** *f.* polishing wheel, buff-wheel **–stahl,** *m.* burnisher. **–stock,** *m.* polishing stick, buff-stick. **–wachs** *n.* polishing wax.
Poliklinik, *f.* outpatients' department (*of hospital*).
Polit–ik, *f.* politics; policy. **–ikaster,** *m.* armchair politician. **–iker,** *m.* (-s, –) politician. **–ikus,** *m.* (*fig.*) diplomatist, sly old fox. **–isch,** *adj.* political; politic. **–isieren,** 1. *v.n.* dabble in *or* talk politics. 2. *v.a.* give political character to, make politically-minded.
Politur, *f.* (-en) polish, gloss, lustre, varnish; *er hat viel –*, he is a very polished man.
Polizei, *f.* police; police-station; *berittene –*, mounted police. **–amt,** *n.* police-station. **–aufsicht,** *f., see under* **–lich. –beamte(r),** *m.* police-officer. **–behörde,** *f.* police (authorities). **–diener,** *m.* policeman. **–gefängnis,** *n.* cells, lock-up. **–gericht,** *n.* police-court, magistrate's court. **–kommissar, –kommissär,** *m.*, **–leutnant,** *m.* inspector of police. **–lich,** *adj.* police; *–lich verboten*, forbidden, prohibited; *unter –licher Bedeckung* or *–lichem Schutz*, with *or* under police protection; *unter –licher Aufsicht stehen*, be under police supervision, (*coll.*) on ticket of leave; *–liche Anmeldung* (*Abmeldung*), report of (change of) address to the police. **–präsidium,** *n.* police headquarters. **–richter,** *m.* magistrate. **–spitzel,** *m.* police spy. **–strafe,** *f.* fine. **–streife,** *f.* police raid. **–stunde,** *f.* closing time, curfew. **–truppe,** *f.* constabulary, police-force. **–(ver)ordnung,** *f.* police regulation(s). **–wache,** *f.* police-station. **–wachtmeister,** *m.* police sergeant. **–widrig,** *adj.* contrary to police regulations, unlicensed, unauthorized; (*hum.*) *er ist –widrig dumm*, he is intolerably stupid.
Polizist, *m.* (-en, -en) policeman, constable. **–in,** *f.* policewoman.
Polizze, *f.* (-n) (*Austr. dial.*) see **Police.**
Poller, *m.* bollard, mooring post (*Naut.*).
Polster, *n.* & (*Austr. dial.*) *m.* (-s, –) cushion, pillow. bolster; stuffing, pad, padding. **–bank,** *f.* cushioned bench. **–förmig,** *adj.* pulvinate (*Arch., Bot.*). **–kammer,** *f.* padded cell. **–klasse,** *f.* upholstered class (*in German trains the first and second*). **–möbel,** *n.pl.* upholstered furniture. **–n,** *v.a.* stuff, pad, cushion, upholster. **–sessel,** *m., see* **–stuhl. –sitz,** *m.* cushioned seat. **–stuhl,** *m.* easy chair. **–ung,** *f.* upholstery, stuffing, padding.
Polter–abend, *m.* eve-of-the-wedding party. **–geist,** *m.* noisy and mischievous spirit, hobgoblin. **–kammer,** *f.* lumber-room. **–n,** *v.n.* (*aux.* h. & s.) make a noise, knock, rattle; rumble, thunder; bluster, scold.
poly–andrisch, *adj.* polyandrous (*Bot.*). **–chrom(atisch),** *adj.* polychromatic, polychrome. **–gamie,** *f.* polygamy. **–gam(isch),** *adj.* polygamous. **–glotte,** *f.* polyglot (*Bible, dictionary, etc.*). **–glott(isch),** *adj.* polyglot. **–gonal,** *adj.* polygonal, multangular. **–morph,** *adj.* polymorphous. **–morphie,** *f.* polymorphism. **–p,** *m.* (-pen, -pen) polyp (*Zooph.*); polypus (*Med.*); (*Studs. sl.*) policeman. **–phon(isch),** *adj.* polyphonic. **–technik,** *f.* polytechnics. **–techniker,** *m.* engineering student. **–technikum,** *n.* technical *or* engineering college.
Pomad–e, *f.* (-en) hair-oil, brilliantine, pomade; (*sl.*) coolness, ease. **–enhengst,** *m.* dandy, fop. **–ig,** *adj.* (*coll.*) phlegmatic, indifferent, leisurely, easy-going, lazy.
Pomeranze, *f.* (-n) (Seville) orange. **–nlikör,** *m.* curaçao.
Pomp, *m.* pomp. **–haft,** *adj.* pompous, stately. **–ös,** *adj.* splendid, magnificent.
Pompelmuse, *f.* (-n) grape-fruit.
ponieren, *v.a.* postulate, assume; (*Studs. sl.*) pay for.
Ponton, *m.* (-s, -s) pontoon. **–brücke,** *f.* pontoon bridge.
Pony, *m.* & *n.* (-s, -s & (*Austr. dial.*) Ponies) pony; fringe (*hair style*).
Popanz, *m.* (-es, -e) bugbear, bogy, scarecrow.
Pope, *m.* (-n, -n) priest of the Greek church.
Popel, *m.* (-s, –) (*dial.* & *coll.*) nasal mucus; guttersnipe. **–n,** *v.n.* (*coll.*) pick one's nose.
Popo, *m.* (-s, -s) (*coll.*) backside, bottom, behind.
popul–är, *adj.* popular; *sich –är machen*, make o.s. a general favourite, ingratiate o.s. with everyone; *–ärwissenschaftliche Vorlesung*, scientific lecture for the general public. **–arisieren,** *v.a.* popularize, bring (down) to the level of the masses. **–arität,** *f.* popularity.
Por–e, *f.* (-en) pore, foramen. **–enzelle,** *f.* guard cell. **–ös,** *adj.* porous, permeable. **–osität,** *f.* porosity.
Porphyr, *m.* (-s, -e) porphyry.
Porree, *m.* (-s, -s) leek.
Port, *m.* (-(e)s, -e) harbour, port.
Port–al, *n.* (-s, -e) portal, main entrance. **–echaise,** *f.* sedan chair. **–efeuille,** *n.* portfolio. **–emonnaie,** *n.* purse. **–epée,** *n.* sword-knot. **–epéefähnrich,** *m.* ensign. **–ier** *m.* (-s, -s & *Austr. dial.* -e) porter, doorkeeper. **–ière,** *f.* door curtain. **–en,** 1. *v.a.* (*Swiss dial.*) nominate (for election). 2. *v.r.* interest o.s., show an interest (*für*, in).
Portion, *f.* (-en) portion, helping, ration; *eine – Tee und zwei Tassen*, a pot of tea and two cups; *zwei –en Kaffee*, coffee for two; *eine – Frechheit*, a good dose of cheek. **–enweise,** *adv.* in rations *or* portions; gradually, bit by bit; by the plateful.
Porto, *n.* (-s, -s & Porti) postage; mail charges. **–frei,** *adj.* prepaid, post-free. **–kasse,** *f.* petty cash. **–pflichtig,** *adj.* subject to postage. **–satz,** *m.* rate of postage. **–vergütung,** *f.* refunding of postage. **–zuschlag,** *m.* excess postage.
Porträt, *n.* (-(e)s, -e) portrait, likeness. **–ieren,** *v.a.* portray, paint a portrait of. **–maler,** *m.* portrait-painter. **–malerei,** *f.* portrait-painting.
Portulak, *m.* (-s, -e & -s) purslane (*Bot.*).
Porzellan, *n.* (-s, -e) china, china-ware, porcelain. **–aufsatz** *m.* china service. **–blau** *adj.* & *n.* china-

blue. **-brennerei,** *f.* porcelain works. **-en,** *adj.* (of) porcelain, china. **-erde,** *f.* china-clay, kaolin. **-geschirr,** *n.* china-ware. **-handlung,** *f.*, **-laden,** *m.* china-shop; (*coll.*) *wie der Elefant im -laden*, like a bull in a china-shop. **-malerei,** *f.* painting on china. **-ofen,** *m.* porcelain-kiln. **-schnecke,** *f.* cowrie (*Zool.*).

Posament, *n.* (-(e)s, -en) gold *or* silver lace, braid, gimp, galloon. **-ier,** *m.*, (*Austr. dial.*) **-ierer,** *m.* maker *or* seller of gold lace, *etc.*, haberdasher. **-ierwaren,** *f.pl.* haberdashery.

Posaun-e, *f.* (-en) trombone; (*fig.*) trumpet; *letzte -e*, last trump(et), trump of doom. **-en,** *v.a.* & *n.* (*aux.* h.) play the trombone; trumpet, sound, proclaim aloud; (*coll.*) *er -t seinen eigenen Ruhm aus*, he blows his own trumpet. **-enbläser,** *m.* trombone player. (*coll.*) **-enengel,** *m.* angel with puffed-out cheeks; chubby baby. **-ist,** *m.* trombonist.

Pos-e, *f.* (-en) pose, attitude; quill; (*coll.*) feather; (*coll.*) *'raus aus den -en!* get out of (your) bed! **-ieren,** *v.n.* (*with Dat.*) pose, sit (for); strike an attitude *or* pose.

Position, *f.* (-en) position, station; entry, item (*Accounting*). **-slicht,** *n.* navigation light, recognition light.

positiv, 1. *adj.* positive; *-e Größe*, positive *or* affirmative quantity; *-es Recht*, statute law; *-es Wissen*, exact science; *nichts -es*, nothing definite. 2. *m.* (-s, -e) positive (*degree*) (*Gram.*). 3. *n.* (-s, -e) portable organ, harmonium; positive (picture); print (*Phot.*).

Positur, *f.* (-en) posture; defensive attitude; *sich in - setzen* or *stellen*, strike an attitude; put o.s. on one's guard.

Poss-e, *f.* (-en) farce; jest, joke, foolery. **-en,** *m.* (-s, -) trick, hoax, practical joke; *-en reißen*, play the fool, play tricks; *-en treiben mit*, play tricks on; *einem etwas zum -en tun*, do a th. to vex a p. **-enhaft,** *adj.* comical, farcical. **-enreißer,** *m.* buffoon, jester, tomfool. **-enspiel,** *n.*, **-enstück,** *n.* farcical comedy (*Theat.*); tomfoolery. **-ierlich,** *adj.* droll, quaint, comic, funny, waggish.

Post, *f.* (-en) post-office; postal service; post, mail; (*Poet.*) news; *Haupt-*, General Post-Office; *Hiobs-*, bad news; *mit der - fahren*, travel by post-chaise; *mit der heutigen -*, by today's post; *mit umgehender* or *wendender -*, by return of post; *auf die - geben* or *tragen*, (take *or* send to the) post; *mit der - schicken*, send by post, mail. **-adreßbuch,** *n.* post-office directory. **-alisch,** *adj.* postal. **-amt,** *n.* post office. **-annahme(stelle),** *f.* receiving-office (*for parcels, etc.*). **-annahmestempel,** *m.* stamp of collecting office. **-anweisung,** *f.* postal order, money-order. **-auftrag,** *m.* cash on delivery order. **-ausgabestempel,** *m.* stamp of delivery-office. **-auto,** *n.* motor-bus (*carrying mail as well*). **-beamte(r),** *m.* post-office official *or* clerk. **-beförderung,** *f.* postal delivery. **-beförderungsdienst,** *m.* postal service. **-behörde,** *f.* post-office authorities. **-(bestell)bezirk,** *m.* postal district. **-bote,** *m.* postman. **-dampfer,** *m.* mail-boat, packet (steamer). **-debit,** *n.* postal delivery of newspapers. **-diebstahl,** *m.* mail robbery. **-dienst,** *m.* postal service, mail-service. **-dienststunden,** *f.pl.* post-office hours of business. **-direktion** *f.* General Post-Office. **-einlieferungsschein,** *m.* post-office receipt, certificate of posting. **-fach,** *n.* post-office box. **-festkonto,** *n.* post-office deposit account. **-flugzeug,** *n.* mail-plane. **-frei,** *adj.* postage paid; post-free. **-gebühr,** *f.* postal charge. **-gebühren,** *f.pl.* postal rates. **-gefälle,** *f.pl.* post-office revenues. **-gehilfe,** *m.* post-office assistant. **-geld,** *n.* postage. **-gut,** *n.*, *see* **-sachen.** **-halter,** *m.* (*archaic*) keeper of post-horses *or* posting house. **-haltestelle,** *f.* stage. **-handbuch,** *n.* post-office guide. **-haus,** *n.* (*archaic*) posting house *or* post stage. **-hilfsstelle,** *f.* sub-office (*in a shop, etc.*). **-horn,** *n.* posthorn, postilion's horn. **-karte,** *f.* postcard; *-karte mit (Rück)Antwort*, reply postcard; *Ansichts-karte*, picture postcard. **-kasten,** *m.* letter-box, post-box. **-konto,** *n.* post-office account. **-kutsche,** *f.* mail *or* stage coach; post-chaise. **-lagernd,** *adv.* to be called for; poste restante. **-marke,** *f.* postage-stamp. **-meister,** *m.* postmaster. **-nachnahme,** *f.*; *gegen -nachnahme*, cash on delivery. **-ordnung,** *f.* post-office regulation(s). **-paket,** *n.* postal package. **-quittung,** *f.* certificate of posting. **-regal,** *n.* post-office monopoly. **-reisende(r),** *m.* passenger by mail-coach. **-reiter,** *m.* courier. **-sachen,** *f.pl.* post, mailed goods. **-sack,** *m.* mail-bag. **-schalter,** *m.* post-office counter. **-scheck,** *m.* postal cheque. **-scheckkonto,** *n.* post-office transfer *or* cash account. **-schein,** *m.* post-office receipt; certificate of posting. **-schiff,** *n.* mail-steamer, packet-boat. **-schließfach,** *n.* post-office box. **-schluß,** *m.* last collection, post-office closing time. **-sendung,** *f.* letter *or* parcel sent by post. **-sparkasse,** *f.* post-office savings-bank. **-sparschein,** *m.* savings-certificate. **-sperre,** *f.* interruption of postal services. **-stempel,** *m.* post-mark. **-stunden,** *f.pl.* hours of business at a post-office. **-tag,** *m.* mail-day. **-verbindung,** *f.* postal communication. **-verkehr,** *m.* postal traffic. **-vermerk,** *m.* official note by the post-office. **-vertrag,** *m.* postal convention. **-verwalter,** *m.* chief clerk (*of a small post-office*). **-verwaltung,** *f.* postal administration. **-wagen,** *m.* mail-coach, stage-coach; post-office van. **-wechsel,** *m.* (*archaic*) change of post horses. **-wendend,** *adv.* by return of post. **-wertzeichen,** *n.* postage-stamp. **-wesen,** *n.* postal affairs *or* system; postal service. **-zahlschein,** *m.* postal order. **-zeichen,** postmark. **-zug,** *m.* mail-train. **-zustellung,** *f.* postal delivery. **-zwang,** *m.* postal privilege.

post-datieren, *v.a.* post-date. **-glazial,** *adj.* post-glacial. **-numerando,** *adv.* payable on receipt. **-skript,** *n.* (-(e)s, -e), **-skriptum,** *n.* (-tums, -te & -ta) postscript, P.S. **-um,** *adj.* posthumous.

Postament, *n.* (-s, -e) pedestal, base.

Posten, 1. *m.* (-s, -) entry, item; parcel, lot; post, position, situation, station, place; sentry, guard, sentinel, picket, outpost; (*C.L.*) *kleiner -*, small item; *starker -*, strong picket (*Mil.*); *- zu Pferde*, vedette; *auf -*, on guard-duty; *auf dem - sein*, be at one's post; (*fig.*) be fighting fit, feel well; *nicht auf dem - sein*, (*coll.*) feel seedy *or* groggy, not be up to the mark; *- stehen*, be on guard *or* sentry duty; *- aufstellen*, post a sentry; *- ablösen*, change guard, relieve sentries. **-dienst,** *m.* sentry-duty. **-jäger,** *m.* place-hunter. **-kette,** *f.*, **-linie,** *f.* outposts, cordon. **-stand,** *m.* sentry post. 2. *v.n.* (*Swiss dial.*) go *or* run errands.

postieren, 1. *v.a.* post, place. 2. *v.r.* take up one's stand.

Postille, *f.* (-n) book of prayers *or* sermons.

Postill(i)on, *m.* (-s, -e) postilion.

Postul-at, *n.* (-at(e)s, -ate) postulate. **-ieren,** *v.a.* postulate.

Poten-tat, *m.* (-en, -en) potentate. **-tial,** 1. *adj.*, *see* **-tiell.** 2. *n.* (-s, -e) potential, voltage (*Elec.*). **-tialexponent,** *m.* index (*Math.*). **-tialsprung,** *m.* potential difference (*Elec.*). **-tiell,** *adj.* potential, latent. **-z,** *f.* (-en) power (*Math.*); potency; *zweite -z*, square; *dritte -z*, cube. **-zexponent,** *m.* index. **-zieren,** *v.a.* raise to a higher power (*Math.*). **-zierung,** *f.* involution. **-zreihe,** *f.* exponential series (*Math.*).

Pott, *m.* (-(e)s, ⸚e) (*dial.*) pot. **-asche,** *f.* potash, potassium carbonate. **-aschefluß,** *m.* crude potash. **-fisch,** *m.*, **-wal,** *m.* sperm-whale. **-fischtran,** *m.* sperm oil. **-lot,** *n.* graphite, black-lead.

potz (*in exclam.*) **-tausend! - Wetter!** *int.* good God! good gracious!

Poule, *f.* pool (*game*).

poussieren, 1. *v.a.* promote, push. 2. *v.n.* court, flirt. 3. *v.r.* push one's way in the world.

Prä, *n.* preference; (*coll.*) *ein - vor einem haben*, come *or* rank first, have an advantage over s.o. **-ambel,** *f.* preamble. **-bende,** *f.*, *see* **Pfründe.** **-dikant,** *m.* preacher. **-dikat,** *n.* (-(e)s, -e) predicate (*Gram.*); report (*school*), marks. **-disponieren,** *v.a.* predispose. **-fekt,** *m.* (-(e)s & *Austr. dial.* -en, -en) prefect, governor. **-fix,** *n.* (-es, -e) prefix. **-judiz,** *n.* (-es, -e) prejudice. **-judizieren,**

v.a. prejudice, prejudge. **-lat,** *m.* (-en, -en) prelate. **-liminar,** *adj.* preliminary. **-liminarien,** *pl.* preliminaries. **-ludieren,** *v.a.* & *n.* prelude. **-ludium,** *n.* (-s, -dien) prelude (*Mus.*). **-mie,** *f.* (-n) premium, prize; bonus, subsidy. **-miengeschäft,** *n.* option-business. **-mien(lohn)system,** *n.* bonus system of payment. **-mienschein,** *m.* premium bond. **-miieren,** *v.a.* award a prize (to). **-misse,** *f.* (-n) premise. **-numerando,** *adv.* payable in advance. **-numerant,** *m.* subscriber. **-numerieren,** *v.a.* subscribe. **-parand,** *m.* (-en, -en) trainee. **-parat,** *n.* (-es, -e) preparation (*Anat., Chem., Pharm.*); patent medicine. **-parieren,** *v.a.* & *r.* prepare, dissect. **-pariertisch,** *m.* dissecting table. **-position,** *f.* preposition (*Gram.*). **-rie,** *f.* (-n) prairie. **-rogativ,** *n.* (-s, -e), **-rogative,** *f.* (-n) prerogative. **-sens,** *n.* (-sentia) present tense. (*Gram.*). **-sentant,** *m.* presenter, holder (*of a bill*). **-sentieren,** *v.a.* present, offer. **-sentierteller,** *m.* tray, salver. **-senz,** *f.* presence. **-senzbibliothek,** *f.* reference library. **-senzliste,** *f.* list of participants, muster-roll (*Mil.*). **-senzstärke,** *f.* effective strength, effectives (*Mil.*). **-ses,** *m.* (-ses, -siden & -sides), **-sident,** *m.* (-en, -en) president; chairman; moderator. **-sidialerlaß,** *m.* presidential decree. **-sidieren,** *v.n.* (*aux.* h.) (*with Dat.*) preside (over); (*Swiss dial. v.a.*). **-sidium,** *n.* (-s, -dien) presidency; chair. **-tendent,** *m.* claimant, pretender. **-teritum,** *n.* (-s,-ta)preterite, past tense (*Gram.*). **-torianer,** *m.pl.* praetorian guards. **-tur,** *f.* praetorship. **-ventivimpfung,** *f.* immunization. **-ventivkrieg,** *m.* preventive war. **-zedens,** *f.* (-denzien) precedence, precedent. **-zedenzfall,** *m.* precedent. **-zipitieren,** *v.a.* precipitate. **-zis,** *adj.* precise, exact, punctual. **-zisieren,** *v.a.* make precise, define, limit. **-zision,** *f.* precision; punctuality. (*C.L.*) **-ziswechsel,** *m.* bill drawn and payable on the same day.

Pracht, *f.* pomp, display, state; splendour, magnificence; luxury; *das ist eine –!* that is splendid! *das ist eine – von einem Becher,* that is a magnificent goblet. **-ausgabe,** *f.* édition de luxe. **-bau,** *m.*, **-gebäude,** *n.* splendid building. **-bett,** *n.* state bed. **-exemplar,** *n.* fine specimen. **-kerl,** *m.* splendid fellow, (*coll.*) sport, brick. **-liebe,** *f.* love of splendour. **-liebend,** *adj.* fond of show, ostentatious. **-stück,** *n.* choice piece, fine specimen, (*coll.*) beauty. **-voll,** *adj.* splendid, glorious, magnificent, gorgeous, beautiful, fine.

prächtig, *adj.* magnificent, splendid; gorgeous, sumptuous, brilliant, superb, glorious, lovely, excellent, fine, capital.

Prädik-ant, -at, *see* **Prä-dikant,** *etc.*

prädisponieren, *see* **prä-disponieren.**

Präfekt, *see* **Prä-fekt.**

Präfix, *see* **Prä-fix.**

präg-en, *v.a.* coin; stamp, emboss; (*fig.*) imprint, impress (on); *sich* (*Dat.*) *etwas ins Gedächtnis* (*ein*)*-en,* impress s.th. on one's memory. **-eanstalt,** *f.* mint. **-edruck,** *m.* embossed printing. **-eform,** *f.* matrix. **-(e)recht,** *n.* right of coinage. **-stock** (*Austr. dial.* **-estock**), *m.* die, matrix. **-ung,** *f.* stamping, stamp, character; coining, coinage.

pragmatisch, *adj.* pragmatic.

prägnan-t, *adj.* pregnant (*with meaning*); suggestive, significant, pithy, terse; precise, exact. **-z,** *f.* terseness, precision.

prahl-en, *v.n.* (*aux.* h.) boast, brag, swagger, show off, be loud (*of colours*); *mit einer S. -en,* parade *or* make a parade of *or* boast of a th. **-er,** *m.* boaster, braggart, swaggerer. **-erei,** *f.* boast(ing), bragging; ostentation. **-erisch,** *adj.* boastful, bragging, ostentatious, swaggering. **-hans,** *m.* braggart, swaggerer, boaster. **-sucht,** *f.* love of boasting, ostentation.

Prahm, *m.* (-(e)s, -e), **-e,** *f.* (-en) barge, lighter, punt. **-geld,** *n.* lighterage.

praien, *see* **preien.**

Präjudiz, -ieren, *see* **Prä-judiz,** *etc.*

Prakt-ik, *f.* (-iken) practice; (manner of) execution, exercise; (*pl.*) machinations, tricks. **-ikant,** *m.* probationer, laboratory assistant. **-iker,** *m.* practitioner; practical man, experienced person, expert. (*coll.*) **-ikus,** *m.* old hand *or* stager. **-ikum,** *n.*(-s,-ka & -ken) laboratory course, course of practical work; practical handbook, laboratory manual. **-isch,** *adj.* practical, experimental; useful, serviceable; *-ischer Arzt,* general practitioner. **-izieren,** *v.a.* & *n.* (*aux.* h.) practise (*one's profession*); *einem etwas aus der Tasche -izieren,* extract s.th. from a p.'s pocket.

Prälat, *see* **Prä-lat.**

präliminar, -ien, *see* **prä-liminar,** *etc.*

Praline, *f.* (-n), **Praliné,** *n.* (-s, -s) chocolate (cream).

prall, 1. *adj.* tight; taut, tense, stretched; stuffed out; chubby, plump, well-rounded; *-e Sonne,* full glare of the sun. 2. *m.* (-s, -e) shock, collision; rebound, bounce, recoil, reflection; backstroke. **-en,** *v.n.* (*aux.* h. & s.) rebound, recoil, bounce, dash against, be reflected; ricochet (*Artil.*). **-blech,** *n.* baffle. **-heit,** *f.* tightness, tension. **-kraft,** *f.* elasticity, resilience. **-schuß,** *m.* ricochet. **-triller,** *m.* mordent (*Mus.*). **-winkel,** *m.* angle of reflection.

prälud-ieren, -ium, *see* **prä-ludieren,** *etc.*

Prämie, *see* **Prä-mie.**

Prämisse, *see* **Prä-misse.**

prang-en, *v.n.* (*aux.* h.) make a show, look fine, be resplendent; glitter, shine, sparkle; be displayed, be exhibited; boast; crowd all sails; *die Bäume -en in vollem Blätterschmucke,* the trees are decked in rich foliage. **-er,** *m.* (-s, –) pillory, whipping-post; *an den -er stellen,* (put in the) pillory; (*fig.*) expose publicly.

Pranke, *f.* (-n) clutch, claw, fore-paw.

pränumer-ando, -ant, -ieren, *see* **prä-numerando,** *etc.*

Präpar-at, -ieren, *see* **Prä-parat,** *etc.*

Präposition, *see* **Prä-position.**

Prärie, *see* **Prä-rie.**

Prärogativ, *see* **Prä-rogativ.**

Präsen-s, -tieren, -z, *see* **Prä-sens,** *etc.*

Präsid-ent, -ieren, *see* **Prä-sident,** *etc.*

prassel-n, *v.n.* (*aux.* h. & s.) (*3rd pers. only*) patter; crackle; rustle; rattle; *Hagel -t an das Fenster,* hail rattles against the window; *Feuer -t im Kamin,* fire crackles in the grate.

prass-en, *v.n.* (*aux.* h.) feast, revel, carouse; live in debauchery. **-er,** *m.* glutton, reveller; spendthrift; rake. **-erei,** *f.* feasting, revelry; debauchery, dissipation.

Prätendent, *see* **Prä-tendent.**

Präteritum, *see* **Prä-teritum.**

Prätur, *see* **Prä-tur.**

präventiv, *see* **prä-ventiv.**

Praxis, *f.* practice, usage, custom; exercise, execution, application; patients, clients. **-versuch,** *m.* trial in practice, experiment on a practical scale.

Präzedenz, *see* **Prä-zedenz.**

Präzipität, *see* **Prä-zipität.**

Präzision, *see* **Prä-zision.**

predig-en, *v.a.* & *n.* (*aux.* h.) preach; (*coll.*) rant, discourse, sermonize; (*Prov.*) *Gelehrten ist gut -en,* a word to the wise is enough. **-er,** *m.* preacher, clergyman, minister; *der -er in der Wüste,* a voice crying in the wilderness. **-erorden,** *m.* Dominican Order. **-erseminar,** *n.* theological college. **-t,** *f.* (-ten) sermon; (*coll.*) lecture; *in die* or *zur -t gehen,* go to church; *eine -t halten,* preach a sermon; *einem eine tüchtige* (*Moral*)*-t halten,* give a p. a good lecture. **-tamt,** *n.* holy orders.

preien, *v.a.* hail (*a ship*).

[1]**Preis,** *m.* (-es, -e) price, cost, charge; fee, fare, rate, terms; reward, prize; praise, glory; *– und Ehre sei Gott!* praise and glory be to God! *die -e halten sich,* prices are well maintained; *hoch im –,* dear; *im -e von,* at the price of; *leidlicher –,* fairly good price; *Schleuder–,* ruinous price, dirt-cheap; *stehender –,* fixed price; *um diesen –,* at this price *or* rate; *um jeden –,* at any price, at all costs; *um keinen –,* not for all the world, not at any price; *unter dem -e,* below cost (price); *zivile -e,* reasonable prices, moderate charges; *zu jedem -e losschlagen,* sell at any price. **-abbau,** *m.*, **-abschlag,** *m.* reduction of price(s). **-angabe,** *f.*, **-ansatz,** *m.* quotation of prices; *ohne -angabe,* not priced, not marked. **-aufgabe,** *f.*, *see* **-ausschreiben.** **-aufschlag,** *m.* rise of price(s).

-ausschreiben, *n.* open competition. **-bewerber,** *m.* competitor. **-bewerbung,** *f.* competition. **-bildung,** *f.* price control. **-drückerei,** *f.* close bargaining. **-en,** *ir.* (*& obs. reg.*) *v.r.* praise, commend, extol, exalt, laud, glorify; *Gott sei gepriesen!* glory be to God!; *sich glücklich -en,* call *or* consider o.s. lucky. **-erhöhung,** *f.* increase *or* rise in prices. **-ermäßigung,** *f.* reduction of price; reduced price. **-frage,** *f.* subject *or* question set for competition; matter of price. **-gabe,** *f. see* **-gebung. -geben,** *ir.v.a.* give up, surrender, hand over; reveal, expose; abandon, sacrifice; *alles -geben,* let everything go to rack and ruin *or* slide; *sich -geben,* deliver o.s. up; prostitute o.s.; (*dem*) *Wind und* (*den*) *Wellen -gegeben,* at the mercy of the wind and waves. **-gebung,** *f.* surrender, abandonment; exposure; prostitution. **-gekrönt,** *adj.* awarded the prize, prize-winning. **-gericht,** *n.* tribunal, committee of adjudicators, the judges. **-krönen,** *v.a.* award a prize to. **-kurant,** *m., see* **-liste. -lage,** *f.* price range; *in jeder -lage,* at all prices. **-lich,** *adj.* (*poet.*) praiseworthy, estimable. **-liste,** *f.* price-list, list of prices. **-nachlaß,** *m.* rebate, discount. **-notierung,** *f.* quotation. **-richter,** *m.* judge, arbiter, umpire. **-satz,** *m.* valuation, estimate. (*C.L.*) **-schere,** *f.* relation between prime costs and selling price of product. **-schießen,** *n.* shooting-match. **-schrift,** *f.* prize essay. **-schwankung,** *f.* fluctuation of prices. **-stopp,** *m.* price pegging, ceiling price. **-sturz,** *m.* sudden fall in price(s), slump. **-tafel,** *f.* price ticket *or* label; price list. **-träger,** *m.* prize-winner. **-treiberei,** *f.* forcing up of prices, profiteering. **-verteilung,** *f.* distribution of prizes. **-verzeichnis,** *n., see* **-liste. -wert,** *adj.,* **-würdig,** *adj.* praiseworthy; worth the money *or* price, good value. **-zuschlag,** *m.* supplement.

[2]**Preis,** *m.* (-es, -e), **-e,** *f.* (-en) border(ing), edging.

Preiselbeere, *f.,* (*Austr. dial.* **Preißelbeere**) (-n) red bilberry; red whortleberry, cranberry.

prell-en, 1. *v.a.* make rebound; toss (in a blanket); bang, bruise; *sich* (*Dat.*) *die Hand -en,* bruise one's hand; (*fig.*) humbug, dupe, cheat, swindle. 2. *v.n.* (*aux.* h. *&* s.) *see* **prallen. -er,** *m.* cheat, swindler; back-stroke, rebound. **-erei,** *f.* cheating, trickery; imposition, overcharging, swindle, cheat, fraud. **-bock,** *m.* buffer (*Railw.*), stop. **-schuß,** *m.* ricochet (*Artil.*). **-stein,** *m.* kerb(stone), guard-stone.

Premier, *m.* (-s, -s) prime minister. **-e,** *f.* first night, first performance (*Theat.*). **-minister,** *m. see* **-.**

presbyter-ianisch, *adj.* presbyterian. **-ium,** *n.* (-iums, -ien) presbytery.

preschen, *v.n.* (*coll.*) hurry, scurry.

Presenning, *f. see* **Persenning.**

preß-bar, *adj.* compressible. **-baum,** *m.* lever (*of a press*). **-brett,** *n.* pressing-board. **-(ss)e,** *f.* (-en) press; gloss, lustre; journalism, the press; (*coll.*) coach, crammer, tutorial college; *in* or *unter der -(ss)e,* in the press, being printed; *die -(ss)e knebeln,* restrict (*or* do away with) the liberty of the press. **-(ss)efreiheit,** *f.* freedom of the press. **-(ss)eknebelung,** *f.* muzzling of the press. **-(ss)en,** *v.a.* press, squeeze, strain, extrude; stamp; compress; cram; urge, dun; oppress, depress; *das -t ihm Tränen aus den Augen,* that draws tears from him; *Matrosen -(ss)en,* (im)press sailors; *gepreßt voll,* overcrowded, crammed full; *mit gepreßter Stimme,* in a choked voice. **-(ss)erecht,** *n.* press law. **-(ss)estelle,** *f.* publicity *or* propaganda department. **-(ss)estimme,** *f.* press comment, review. **-form,** *f.* mould. **-glanz,** *m.* gloss. **-glas,** *n.* moulded glass. **-(ss)ieren,** *v.n.* (*aux.* h.) be urgent; *es -(ss)iert sehr,* there is no time to be lost; *es -(ss)iert nicht,* there is no hurry. **-(ss)ion,** *f.* pressure. **-kohle,** *f..* briquette. **-kopf,** *m.* brawn, chawl. **-lauge,** *f.* expressed liquor. **-luft,** *f.* compressed air. **-luftanlage,** *f.* air compressor. **-lufthammer,** *m.* pneumatic hammer. **-ölschmierung,** *f.* compression lubrication. **-stempel** *m.* press die, dolly. **-stoff,** *m.* moulded plastic compound. **-teil** *m.* pressed section. **-torf,** *m.* pressed peat. **-tuch,** *n.* filter-cloth. **-walze,** *f.* pressure roller. **-(ss)ung,** *f.* pressing, pressure, compression.

Prick-e, *f.* (-en) lamprey (*Icht.*). **-(e)lig,** *adj.* prickly; pungent. **-eln,** *v.a. & n.* (*aux.* h.) prick, prickle, sting, itch; be pungent. **-elnd,** *pr.p. & adj.* tickling, prickling; sharp, pungent; piquant, spicy.

Priel, *m.* (-(e)s, -e), **-e,** *f.* (-en) rill; channel.

Priem, *m.* (-(e)s, -e), **-e,** *f.* (-en) quid, chew, (*vulg.*) chaw. **-en,** *v.n.* chew (tobacco). **-tabak,** *m.* chewing tobacco.

pries, priesest, priese, *see* **preisen.**

Priester, *m.* (-s, –) priest. **-amt,** *n.* priesthood, priest's office. **-beffchen,** *n.* clergyman's bands. **-binde,** *f.* fillet. **-gewand,** *n.* vestment. **-hemd,** *n.* alb, surplice. **-herrschaft,** *f.* hierarchy. **-in,** *f.* priestess. **-lich,** *adj.* priestly, sacerdotal. **-rock,** *m.* cassock, vestment. **-schaft,** *f.,* **-tum,** *n.* priesthood, clergy. **-weihe,** *f.* ordination, consecration of a priest.

Prim-a, 1. *f.* (-en) sixth form; (*Austr. dial.*) lowest form (*of secondary school*). 2. *adj.* (*C.L. & coll.*) prime, first grade, first rate. **-aner,** *m.* (-s, –) sixth-form boy. **-aqualität,** *f.,* **-asorte,** *f.* first *or* prime quality. **-är,** *adj.* primary, idiopathic (*Med.*). **-ärelement,** *n.* primary cell (*Elec.*). **-ärkreis,** *m.* primary circuit (*Elec.*). **-arius,** *m.* (–, -arien) (*Austr. dial.*) chief surgeon. **-arschule,** *f.* (*Swiss dial.*) public elementary school. **-ärwicklung,** *f.* primary winding (*Elec.*). **-as,** *m.* (-as, -aten) primate. **-at,** *m. & n.* primacy. **-avista,** *adv.* at sight (*Mus.*). **-aware,** *f.* superior *or* high-grade goods. **-awechsel,** *m.* first (*bill*) of exchange. **-e,** *f.* prime (*Eccl., Typ., Fenc.*); prima (*Mus.*). **-el,** *f.* (-eln) primrose, primula. **-itiv,** *adj.* primitive, original; simple. **-itiven,** *pl.* primitive peoples *or* races. **-itivität,** *f.* primitiveness. **-us,** *m.* head (boy) *or* top (boy) of the form. **-geld,** *n.* primage (*Naut.*). **-zahl,** *f.* prime number.

Prinz, *m.* (-en, -en) prince; – *von Geblüt,* prince of the blood. **-enerzieher,** *m.,* **-enhofmeister,** *m.* tutor to a prince. **-essin,** *f.* (*coll.* **-eß** *f.*) princess. **-eßunterrock,** *m.* princess slip. **-gemahl,** *m.* prince consort. **-lich,** *adj.* princely. **-regent,** *m.* prince regent.

Prinzip, *n.* (-s, -e *&* -ien) principle; *-ien,* rudiments; *im –,* on principle, essentially. **-al,** *m.* (-s, -e) principal, chief; employer, head (*of a firm*), manager. **-iell,** *adj.* on *or* in principle, fundamental. **-ienfrage,** *f.* question of principle. (*coll.*) **-ienreiter,** *m.* stickler for principles, pedant, dogmatist.

Prior, *m.* (-s, -en) prior. **-in,** *f.* prioress. **-ität,** *f.* priority. **-itätsaktie,** *f.* preference share. **-itätsanleihe,** *f.* loan on a mortgage. **-itätsanspruch,** *m.* priority claim. **-itätsbeleg,** *m.* certified copy of documents. **-itätsobligation,** *f.* preference bond, debenture. **-itätspapiere,** *n.pl.* preferential stock.

Prise, *f.* (-n) prize (*Naut.*); pinch (*of snuff*). **-ngelder,** *n.pl.* prize-money. **-ngericht,** *n.,* **-nhof,** *m.* prize-court. **-nkommando,** *n.* prize crew (*Naut.*). **-nmannschaft,** *f.* boarding party (*Naut.*). **-nrecht,** *n.* right of capture.

Prism-a, *n.* (-as, -en) prism. **-aförmig,** *adj.* prismoidal. **-atisch,** *adj.* prismatic. **-englas,** *n.* prismatic binocular. **-enspektrum,** *n.* prismatic spectrum.

Pritsch-e, *f.* (-en) (harlequin's) wooden sword; bat; back-seat (*of a sledge*); plank-bed; guard-bed (*Mil.*). **-en,** *v.a. & n.* (*aux.* h.) slap, beat, drub; *ich bin gepritscht,* my hopes are dashed, I have been let down. **-enwagen,** *m.* light carriage. **-meister,** *m.* harlequin.

privat, *adj.* private; personal, confidential. **-abkommen,** *n.,* **-abmachung,** *f.* private agreement *or* understanding. **-angestellte(r),** *m.* employee of a private firm. **-dozent,** *m.* (unsalaried) university lecturer. **-eigentum,** *n.* personal property. **-gelehrte(r),** *m.* independent scholar. **-im,** *adv.* privately; separately, tête-à-tête; private and confidential. **-isieren,** *v.n.* (*aux.* h.) live on one's independent means. **-issimum,** *n.* (-ums, -ma) private class for selected students (*Univ.*). **-kasse,** *f.*

privy purse. **–klage,** *f.* civil action. **–klinik,** *f.* nursing home. **–kolleg,** *n.* lectures for which a fee is charged (*Univ.*). **–leben,** *n.* private life, personal life. **–lehrer,** *m.* private tutor. **–mann,** *m.* private person. **–meinung,** *f.* personal opinion. **–person,** *f.* private individual *or* person. **–recht,** *n.* civil law. **–rücksichten,** *f. pl.* personal grounds (*aus*, on). **–schatulle,** *f.* privy purse. **–stunde,** *f.* private lesson. **–unterricht,** *m.* private coaching. **–wirtschaft,** *f.* private enterprise.

Privileg–(ium), *n.* (-(ium)s, -ien) privilege, patent. **–ieren,** *v.a.* privilege.

pro, *prep.* for, per; – *Stück*, a piece; – *Mille*, per thousand.

prob–at, *adj.* proved, approved, tried; good, excellent. **–e,** *f.* (-en) trial, test, experiment; probation, proof, ordeal; exhibition, demonstration (*of skill*); pattern, sample, specimen, test-piece, assay; rehearsal (*Theat.*); (trade) mark, stamp; *eine –e ablegen*, give proof of; *auf –e*, on probation, on trial; *die –e bestehen*, stand the test; *es gilt die –e!* let us try it! *–e halten*, see *die –e bestehen*; *die –e machen auf eine S.* or *auf die Richtigkeit einer S.*, prove a th. (*Arith.*); *auf die – stellen*, (put to the) test; *zur –e*, as a sample; on approval. **–eabdruck,** *m.*,**–eabzug,** *m.* proof (sheet). **–earbeit,** *f.* sample of work; test, exercise (*in schools*). **–ebelastung,** *f.* test load. **–ebogen,** *m.* pattern-sheet. **–edruck,** *m.* proof(-sheet); **–eexemplar,** *n.* specimen copy. **–efahrt,** *f.* trial trip *or* run. **–efest,** *adj.*, **–ehaltig,** *adj.* proof, standard. **–eflug,** *m.* trial flight. **–ejahr,** *n.* year of probation. **–ekandidat,** *m.* probationer, assistant master (*during year of probation*). **–en,** *v.a. & n.* rehearse. **–enummer,** *f.* specimen number *or* copy. **–esendung,** *f.* sample sent on approval. **–estab,** *m.* test-piece, sample (*Metal.*). **–estück,** *n.* sample, pattern, specimen. **–eweise,** *adv.* on approval, on trial, as a specimen. **–ezeit,** *f.* time of probation; noviciate. **–ierbar,** *adj.* testable. **–ieren,** *v.a.* test, prove, put to the test *or* proof, assay, taste; (*coll.*) attempt, try; *Rollen –ieren*, rehearse; (*Prov.*) *–ieren geht über Studieren*, practice is better than theory. **–ierer,** *m.* assayer, analyst. **–ierdame,** *f.*, **–ierfräulein,** *n.*, **–iermamsell,** *f.* mannequin. **–ierglas,** *n.* test-tube. **–iernadel,** *f.* touch-needle. **–ierofen,** *m.* assay-furnace. **–ierröhre,** *f.* test-tube. **–ierstein,** *m.* touchstone. **–iertiegel,** *m.* crucible. **–ierwaage,** *f.* assay-balance.

Problem, *n.* (-s, -e) problem. **–atik,** *f.* uncertainty, ambiguity, difficulty (in arriving at a solution). **–atisch,** *adj.* problematic.

Probst, *m. see* **Propst.**

Produkt, *n.* (-(e)s, -e) produce; product, result. **–enbörse,** *f.* produce-exchange. **–enhandel,** *m.* trade in home produce. **–ionsausfall,** *m.* fall in production. **–ionsfähigkeit,** *f.* productivity, productive capacity. **–ionsgenossenschaft,** *f.* co-operative association (of producers). **–ionsmenge,** *f.* output. **–ionsmittel,** *n.pl.* means of production. **–iv,** *adj.* productive. **–ivität,** *f.* productiveness, productivity.

Produz–ent, *m.* (-ten, -ten) grower, producer; manufacturer. **–ieren,** 1. *v.a.* produce, grow; yield, bring forward, furnish (*proofs*). 2. *v.r.*, perform, exhibit *or* appear in public; show off.

profan, *adj.* profane, secular. **–bau,** *m.* secular building. **–ieren,** *v.a.* profane. **–ierung,** *f.* profanation.

Profeß, *f. &* (*Austr. dial.*) *m.* (-(ss)es, -(ss)e) profession, vow (*Rel.*); – *tun*, take vows, take the veil.

Profess–ion, *f.* (-en) trade; profession; *Spieler von –ion*, a professional gambler. **–ional,** *m.* (-s, -e) professional (sportsman). **–ionell,** *adj.*, **–ioniert,** *adj.* by trade; in business as. **–ionist,** *m.* (*Austr. dial.*) tradesman, artisan. **–or,** *m.* (-s, -en) university professor; *ordentlicher –or*, professor in ordinary; *außerordentlicher –or*, assistant professor. **–orisch,** *adj.* professorial. **–ur,** *f.* professorship, academic chair.

Profi, *m.* (-s, -s) (*see* **Professional**) (*coll.*) pro.

Profil, *n.* (-s, -e) profile, side-view, section. **–dicke,** *f.* airfoil section (*Av.*). **–eisen,** *n.*, **–stahl,** *m.* sectional *or* structural iron (*or* steel), iron girders. **–ieren,** *v.a.* outline, sketch in profile. **–iereisen,** *n.*, *see* **–eisen.** **–iert,** *adj.* streamlined. **–ierung,** *f.* fairing (*Av.*).

Profit, *m.* (-(e)s, -e) profit, (net) proceeds. **–abel,** *adj.* profitable. **–ieren,** *v.a. & n.* (*aux.* h.) make *or* clear a profit, profit, gain. **–lich,** *adj.* (*coll.*) profit-seeking; (*dial.*) mean, stingy. **–macher,** *m.* profiteer. **–macherei,** *f.* profiteering.

Profos, Profoß, *m.* (-en, -en, (*or Austr. dial.* -es -e)) (*archaic*) provost (*Mil.*).

Prognos–e, *f.* (-en) prognosis (*Med.*); forecast (*Meteor.*). **–tikon,** *n.* (-kons, -ka & -ken) prognostic. **–tizieren,** *v.a. & n.* (*aux.* h.) prognosticate, predict, foretell.

Programm, *n.* (-s, -e) programme, prospectus; lecture, paper (*read annually in German schools*). **–atisch,** *adj.*, **–gemäß,** *adj.*, **–mäßig,** *adj.* according to plan *or* programme. **–musik,** *f.* incidental music.

Progymnasium, *n.* (-s, -ien) secondary school with curtailed (classical) curriculum.

prohib–ieren, *v.a.* check, forbid, prohibit. **–ition,** *f.* (-en) prohibition. **–itivzoll,** *m.* prohibition duty. **–itorium,** *n.* writ of prohibition.

Projekt, *n.* (-(e)s, -e) project, plan, proposal. **–ieren,** *v.a.* project, plan, propose, design. **–il,** *n.* (-s, -e) projectile. **–ionsapparat,** *m.* magic lantern, projector. **–ionsmattscheibe,** *f.* ground-glass screen. **–ionsschirm,** *m.* screen.

projizieren, *v.a.* project (*a picture*), throw on the screen.

proklamieren, *v.a.* proclaim.

Prokur–a, *f.* (*C.L.*) proxy, procuration, power of attorney. **–ator,** *m.* (-s, -en) proxy, attorney, procurator. **–ist,** *m.* (-en, -en) confidential *or* head clerk, deputy.

Prolet, *m.* (-en, -en) commoner, one of the masses; (*coll.*) clod, lout, cad. **–ariat,** *n.* (-(e)s, -e) proletariat, the lower classes, the workers. **–arier,** *m.* (-s, –) worker, member of the working classes, proletarian. **–arisch,** *adj.* proletarian, lower-class. **–arisieren,** *v.a.* proletarianize.

Prolog, *m.* (-s, -e) prologue.

prolong–ieren, *v.a.* prolong; renew (*a bill*). (*C.L.*) **–ationsgebühr,** *f.* renewal fee.

Promemoria, *n.* (-s, -s & -rien) memorandum; memorial.

Promen–ade, *f.* (-en) promenade; walk, (*coll.*) stroll. **–ieren,** *v.n.* go *or* take a walk *or* a stroll.

Promesse, *f.* (-n) (*C.L.*) promissory note.

prominent, *adj.* prominent, outstanding; *die –en*, the leading figures *or* personages.

Promo–tion, *f.* (-en) graduation (*Univ.*). **–ionsschrift,** *f.* doctoral dissertation. **–vieren,** 1. *v.a.* confer a degree. 2. *v.n.* (*aux.* h.) graduate, take a degree.

prompt, *adj.* prompt, punctual, ready, quick; – *bezahlen*, pay without delay, pay cash. **–heit,** *f.* promptitude.

Pronomen, *n.* (-ens, -ina) pronoun (*Gram.*).

Propag–anda, *f.* propaganda, publicity. **–ieren,** *v.a.* propagate, publicize.

Propeller, *m.* (-s, –) propeller. **–antrieb,** *m.*; *mit –antrieb*, propeller-driven. **–bö,** *f.* slipstream (*Av.*). **–flügel,** *m.* propeller blade. **–nabe,** *f.* propeller hub. **–steigung,** *f.* propeller pitch.

Proph–et, *m.* (-en, -en) prophet; (*sl.*) *Moses und die –eten*, ready cash; *die kleinen –eten*, the minor prophets; (*Prov.*) *ein –et gilt nichts in seinem Vaterlande*, a prophet has no honour in his own country. **–etie,** *f.*, *see* **–ezeiung.** **–etin,** *f.* prophetess. **–etisch,** *adj.* prophetic. **–ezeien,** *v.a.* prophesy. **–ezeiung,** *f.* prophecy.

proportion–al, *adj.* proportionate, proportional. **–ale,** *f.* (-en); *mittlere –ale*, mean proportional, middle term. **–alwahlrecht,** *n.* (*Austr. & Swiss dial.* **Proporzwahlrecht**), proportional representation. **–iert,** *adj.* proportional; well-proportioned.

Propst, *m.* (-es, ⸗e) prior; provost. **–ei,** *f.* diocese, jurisdiction *or* dwelling of a provost.

Prosa, *f.* prose. **–dichtung,** *f.* prose fiction, novel-writing. **–iker,** *m.* (-s, –), **–ist,** *m.* (-en, -en) prose-writer. **–isch,** *adj.* in prose; prosaic.

Proselyt, *m.* (-en, -en) proselyte. **-enmacherei,** *f.* proselytism.
prosit, prost, *int.* cheers! your health! (*coll.*) – *Mahlzeit*, good appetite! (*coll.*) you may whistle for it! you won't get it! – *Neujahr!* a Happy New Year.
Prospekt, *m.* (-(e)s, -e) prospectus; prospect, (distant) view; back-cloth (*Theat.*); organ screen. **-us,** *m.* prospectus.
prostitu-ieren, *v.r.* prostitute. **-ierte,** *f.* prostitute. **-tion,** *f.* prostitution.
Proszeniumsloge, *f.* stage-box (*Theat.*).
protegieren, *v.a.* patronize.
Protekt-ionswirtschaft, *f.* protectionism. **-orat,** *n.* protectorate.
Protest, *m.* (-es, -e) protest; (*C.L.*) *zu – gehen lassen*, dishonour (*a cheque*); (*C.L*) *mit – zurückkommen*, be dishonoured; (*C.L.*) *– mangels Annahme*, protest for non-acceptance; *– erheben*, protest, raise a protest; *– einlegen*, lodge a protest. **-ant,** *m.* Protestant. **-antisch,** *adj.* Protestant. **-antismus,** *m.* Protestantism. **-erhebung,** *f.* resolution in protest. **-ieren,** 1. *v.n.* (*aux.* h.) protest (*gegen etwas*, against s.th.). 2 *v.a.* protest (*a bill, etc.*) *einen Wechsel -ieren lassen*, have a bill protested. **-versammlung,** *f.* indignation meeting.
Prothese, *f.* artificial limb.
Protokoll, *n.* (-s, -e) record, report, protocol, minutes; *im –*, upon record; *in das – eintragen*, see **-ieren**; (*das*) *– führen*, take down the minutes; *zu – geben*, depose, state in evidence; *zu – nehmen*, draw up an official report of, take down (*a deposition, etc.*). **-ant,** *m.*, *see* **-führer. -arisch,** *adj.* in the minutes, on record. **-aufnahme,** *f.* record, report (*of a meeting*). **-buch,** *n.* minute-book. **-eintragung,** *f.* minute; entry in the minute-book. **-führer,** *m.* clerk of the minutes, recorder, registrar. **-ieren,** *v.a.* keep the minutes, register, record.
Protz, *m.* (-en, -en) ostentatious person, snob, (*coll.*) swell. **-en,** *v.n.* be a snob, be purse-proud, put on airs, flaunt one's wealth. **-enhaft,** *adj.* snobbish, ostentatious, purse-proud. **-entum,** *n.* snobbism, snobbishness. **-ig,** *adj.*, *see* **-enhaft.**
Protz-e, *f.* (-en) limber (*Artil.*). **-gestell,** *n.* limber-frame. **-kasten,** *m.* limber-box.
Provenienz, *f.* origin, source, derivation.
Proviant, *m.* provisions, victuals, provender, forage, supplies, stores. **-amt,** *n.* supply depot (*Mil.*). **-ieren,** *v.a.* provision, victual, supply (*troops*). **-kolonne,** *f.* supply column (*Mil.*). **-lager,** *n.* ration store (*Mil.*). **-sack,** *m.* haversack. **-schiff,** *n.* store-ship. **-wagen,** *m.* ration truck. **-wesen,** *n.* commissariat.
Provinz, *f.* (-en) province, provinces; *in der – leben*, live in the country. **-ial,** 1. *adj.* provincial, regional. 2. *m.* provincial, father superior (*Rel.*). **-ialismus,** *m.* (-men) provincialism, dialect word. **-iallandtag,** *m.* provincial diet. **-iell,** *adj.* provincial, narrow-minded, unenlightened. **-ler,** *m.* provincial, country cousin, country bumpkin.
Provis-ion, *f.* (-en) commission, brokerage. **-ionsfrei,** *adj.* free of commission. **-or,** *m.* (-s, -en) dispenser; chemist's *or* pharmacist's assistant. **-orisch,** *adj.* provisional, temporary. **-orium,** *n.* (-s, -ien) provisional *or* temporary arrangement.
Provo-kation, *f.* (-en) provocation. **-zieren,** *v.a.* provoke; challenge.
Prozedur, *f.* procedure; proceeding (*at law*).
Prozent, *n.* (*Swiss m.*) (-s, -e) per cent., percentage; *zu sechs –*, at six per cent.; *wie viel –?* what percentage? *zu hohen -en*, at a high rate of interest. **-ig,** *adj. suffix* percent(age); *drei -ige Rente*, three per cent. stock. **-isch,** *adj.* (expressed as) percentage. **-satz,** *m.* percentage, rate of interest. **-ual,** *adj.*, *see* **-isch.**
Prozeß, *m.* (-(ss)es, -(ss)e) action, lawsuit, proceedings; operation, procedure, process; *einen – anfangen mit jemandem, einem einen – anhängen, einen – gegen jemanden anhängig machen*, institute (legal) proceedings against a p.; *im – liegen*, be at law, be involved in a lawsuit; *einem den – machen wegen*, put a p. on his trial for; *einen – führen*, conduct a case; *kurzen – machen mit*, make short work of; *der – schwebt noch*, the case is still pending *or* sub judice; *einen – gewinnen*, gain one's case. **-bevollmächtige(r),** *m.* mandatary. **-fähig,** *adj.* actionable. **-führer,** *m.* plaintiff; plaintiff's counsel. **-(ss)ieren,** *v.n.* (*aux.* h.) carry on a lawsuit, be at *or* go to law (with), litigate. **-(ss)ion,** *f.* procession. **-kosten,** *pl.* law-costs. (*coll.*) **-krämer,** *m.* litigious person. **-süchtig,** *adj.* litigious, fond of litigation.
prüde, *adj.* prudish. **-rie,** *f.* prudishness, prudery.
prüf-en, *v.a.* try, test, examine, assay; inspect, investigate; audit, check (*an account*); *geprüfte Lehrerin*, certificated teacher; *schwergeprüft*, sorely tried; (*einen auf*) *Herz und Nieren -en*, (*B.*) try the heart and the reins; (*coll.*) put a person to a severe test; *die Richtigkeit von etwas -en*, verify a th. **-er,** *m.* examiner, inspector, tester, assayer; test-cock (*Mach.*). **-glas,** *n.* test-tube. **-ling,** *m.* examinee, candidate. **-meister,** *m.* technical supervisor (*Mil.*). **-stand,** *m.* test-bench. **-stein,** *m.* touchstone, criterion, test. **-ung,** *f.* examination investigation; check, test, trial; affliction; temptation; (*Studs. sl.*) *in die -ung steigen*, sit *or* take one's examinations; *die -ung bestehen*, pass an examination; *in der -ung durchfallen*, fail an examination; (*in*) *einer -ung unterliegen*, fail to get through a test, succumb to temptation. **-ungsarbeit,** *f.* examination paper. **-ungsausschuß** *m.*, **-ungsbehörde,** *f.* board of examiners, examination board. **-ungsbestimmungen,** *f.pl.* **-ungsordnung,** *f.* regulations for the conduct of an examination. **-ungsfach,** *n.* examination subject. **-ungskommission,** *f.*, *see* **-ungsausschuß -ungszeugnis,** *n.* certificate, diploma.
Prügel, *m.* (-s, –) cudgel, stick; (*pl.*) thrashing, caning; *eine Tracht –*, a sound thrashing; *mit einem – drein schlagen*, resort to violent measures. **-ei,** *f.* beating; fight, (*coll.*) row, scrap. **-n,** 1. *v.a.* cane, thrash. 2. *v.r.* fight (*of boys*), (*coll.*) scrap. **-junge,** *m.*, **-knabe,** *m.* scapegoat; *den -knaben für jemanden abgeben*, be the scapegoat for s.o. **-strafe,** *f.* corporal punishment; whipping, caning, birching. **-weg,** *m.* corduroy road (*Mil.*).
Prunk, *m.* pomp, splendour, state, show; ostentation. **-bett,** *n.* bed of state. **-en,** *v.n.* (*aux.* h.) show off; (*mit*) make a show of, parade. **-gemach,** *n.*, *see* **-saal. -gewand,** *n.* state attire. **-haft,** *adj.* ostentatious, showy. **-liebend,** *adj.* given over to display. **-los,** *adj.* unostentatious, unpretentious. **-saal,** *m.* state hall. **-stück,** *n.* show-piece. **-sucht,** *f.* ostentation. **-süchtig,** *adj.* ostentatious. **-voll,** *adj.* splendid, gorgeous.
prusten, *v.n.* (*aux.* h.) snort; sneeze violently; burst out laughing.
Pseudonym, 1. *n.* (-s, -e) pseudonym, nom-de-plume, assumed name. 2. *adj.* pseudonymous, fictitious.
Psych-iater, *m.* psychiatrist. **-isch,** *adj.* psychic(al). **-oanalyse,** *f.* psycho-analysis. **-olog(e),** *m.* (-en, -en) psychologist. **-ologisch,** *adj.* psychological. **-ose,** *f.* psychosis. **-otechnik,** *f.* industrial psychology.
Pubertät, *f.* puberty.
publi-ce, *adv.* publicly. **-k,** *adj.* public. **-kation,** *f.* publication, publishing; published paper *or* book. **-kum,** *n.* public; audience, bystanders; readers; *das große* or *breite -kum*, the general public; (*pl. also* Publika) open *or* public lecture. **-zieren,** *v.a.* publish; make public, promulgate; prove (*a will*). **-zist,** *m.* political writer, newspaper-writer, journalist. **-zistik,** *f.* (political) journalism.
puddel-n, *v.a.* puddle (*metal*); (*dial.*) paddle, splash; potter about. **-eisen,** *n.* puddled iron. **-ofen,** *m.* puddling furnace.
Pudding, *m.* (-s, -e & -s) pudding.
Pudel, *m.* (-s, –) poodle; drudge, (*sl.*) skivvy; blunder; miss (*at skittles*); (*Studs. sl.*) university beadle, bulldog; *wie ein begossener – abziehen*, withdraw abashed, slink off with one's tail between one's legs. **-mütze,** *f.* fluffy cap. **-n,** *v.n.* (*aux.* h.) miss (*at skittles*). **-nackt,** *adj.* stark naked. **-närrisch,** *adj.* droll, funny; silly. **-naß,** *adj.* drenched, sopping wet.

Puder, *m.* (-s, –) toilet powder. **–ig,** *adj.* powdered, powdery. **–mantel,** *m.* (*archaic*) peignoir. **–n,** *v.a.* powder. **–quaste,** *f.* powder-puff.

puff, 1. *int.* puff! bang! 2. *m.* (-(e)s, –e & *Austr. dial.* ⸗e) bump, crash, bang; cuff, thump, blow; push, nudge; (*pl.* –e) pouffe; (*sl.*) brothel; *er kann einen* (*guten*) – *vertragen*, he can stand a good deal, he is thick-skinned. 3. *n.* backgammon. **–ärmel,** *m.* puffed sleeve. **–bohne,** *f.* horsebean. **–brett,** *n.* backgammon-board. **–en,** *v.a.* & *n.* (*aux.* h.) pop, puff; shoot, push, nudge; thump, whack, cuff; puff out, pad; play backgammon; (*coll.*) *daß es –t*, with a vengeance. **–spiel,** *n.* backgammon.

Puffer, *m.* buffer, cushion; (*dial.*) potato-fritter; popgun. **–batterie,** *f.* balancing battery (*Elec.*). **–staat,** *m.* buffer state.

Pulle, *f.* (-n) (*dial.*) bottle.

pullen, *v.n.* (*dial.*) row; pull *or* rein in (*a horse*); (*coll.*) piddle.

Puls, *m.* (-es, -e) pulse; *erhöhter* –, high pulse; *einem den – fühlen*, feel a person's pulse, (*fig.*) sound a p. **–ader,** *f.* artery; *die große –ader*, aorta. **–en,** *v.n.*, (*Austr. dial.* **–ieren**), (*aux.* h.) pulsate. **–schlag,** *m.* pulsation, pulse (beat). **–stillstand,** *m.*, **–stockung,** *f.* cessation of the pulse. **–wärmer,** *m.* mitten, wristlet.

Pult, *n.* (-(e)s, -e) desk, lectern, reading-desk. **–dach,** *n.* lean-to roof.

Pulver, *n.* (-s, –) powder; gunpowder; *zu – und Blei verurteilt*, condemned to be shot; (*coll.*) *er hat das – nicht erfunden*, he will never set the Thames on fire; *ein Schuß* –, a whiff of powder; *sein – unnütz verschießen*, labour in vain; *sein* – (*vorzeitig*) *verschießen*, shoot one's bolt; *er ist keinen Schuß – wert*, he is not worth powder and shot, he is a worthless fellow; *er hat – gerochen*, he has been in the front line. **–artig,** *adj.* powdery. **–dampf,** *m.* powder-smoke. **–faß,** *n.* powder-barrel *or* keg; *auf dem –faß sitzen*, sit on top of a volcano. **–form,** *f.*; *in –form*, pulverized. **–ig,** (*also* **pulvrig**), *adj.* powdery. **–isieren,** *v.a.* pulverize. **–kammer,** *f.* powder-magazine. **–korn,** *n.* percussion primer; grain of powder. **–ladung,** *f.* powder charge. **–n,** 1. *v.a.* pulverize, reduce to powder. 2. *v.n.* fire, shoot (*with a gun*). **–satz,** *m.* powder train. **–scheu,** *adj.* timorous. **–schnee,** *m.* dry powdery snow. **–turm,** *m.* powder-magazine.

Pummel, *m.* (*coll.*) plump little person. (*coll.*) **–ig,** *adj.* plump, chubby.

Pump, *m.* (-(e)s, -e) hollow sound; (*sl.*) credit, trust, tick; (*sl.*) *auf* –, on tick. **–e,** *f.* (-en) pump; *Saug- und Druck–e*, suction and forcing-pump. **–en,** *v.a.* & *n.* (*aux.* h.) pump; (*sl.*) borrow, lend, give *or* take on tick. **–enschwengel,** *m.* pump-handle. **–hosen,** *f.pl.* baggy trousers, plus-fours. **–hub,** *m.* pump-lift. **–kasten,** *m.* pump-cistern (*Min.*). **–kolben,** *m.* piston, sucker of a pump. **–stiefel,** *m.* barrel *or* chamber of a pump; top-boot. **–werk,** *n.* pumping apparatus.

Pumpernickel, *m.* (-s, –) black Westphalian rye-bread.

Punkt, *m.* (-(e)s, -e) point, dot, spot, place; period, full stop; article, head, topic, item, matter, subject; *auf dem –e, wo die Sachen stehen*, as matters stand; *das trifft auf den – zu*, that is right to a T, that hits the nail on the head; – *für* –, point by point, item by item; *in vielen –en*, in many respects; *sich in einem – schneiden*, intersect at a point (*Geom.*); *den – aufs i setzen*, dot one's *i*'s, be meticulous; *nach –en siegen*, win on points (*Boxing*); *der springende* –, the salient point; *auf dem toten* –, at a deadlock, at dead centre (*Mech.*); – *zehn Uhr*, on the stroke of ten; *der wunde* –, the weak *or* sore point. **–ation,** *f.* draft agreement. **–ball,** *m.* punch-ball. **–feuer,** *n.* converging *or* concentrated fire (*Artil.*). **–frei,** *adj.* unrationed. **–ieren,** *v.a.* point, dot; puncture; punctuate; tap (*Med.*); spot, speckle, stipple; *den Frieden –ieren*, stipulate the conditions *or* draw up preliminaries of peace; *–ierte Linie*, dotted rule. **–ierung,** *f.* punctuation; tapping (*Med.*). **–ierkunst,** *f.* geomancy; stippling. **–iernadel,** *f.* stipple. **–ierrädchen,** *n.* dotting-wheel. **–ion,** *f.*, *see* **–ur** (*Surg.*). **–linie,** *f.* dotted line. **-pflichtig.** *adj.* available on points (*rationing*). **–roller,** *m.* massage roller. **–schrift,** *f.* braille. **–schweißung,** *f.* spot-welding. **–sieg,** *m.* victory on points (*Boxing*). **–system,** *n.* points (rationing) scheme. **–um,** *n.* full stop; end, ending; *und damit –um!* enough! let us have no more of it! there's an end of it! **–ur,** *f.* puncture (*Surg.*); (*pl.*) points (*Typ.*). **–weise,** *adv.* point by point.

pünktlich, *adj.* punctual, prompt, on time; precise, painstaking, accurate; *–er Gehorsam*, strict obedience. **–keit,** *f.* punctuality; *mit militärischer –lichkeit*, with military precision.

Punsch, *m.* (-es, -e & ⸗e) punch (*drink*). **–bowle,** *f.*, **–schüssel,** *f.* punch-bowl.

Punz–e, *f.* (-en), (*Austr. dial.*) **–en,** *m.* (-ens, -en) punch (*tool*). **–arbeit,** *f.* tooling. **–en,** *v.a.* punch (*leather*); chase, chisel, stamp, emboss. **–ieren,** *v.a.* hallmark.

Pup, *m.* (-(e)s, -e), **–s,** *m.* (-ses, -se) (*vulg.*) fart. **–(s)en,** *v.n.* break wind, (*vulg.*) fart.

Pupill–(e), 1. *m.* (-en, -en). 2. **–e,** *f.* (-en) (*archaic*) orphan, ward. 3. **–e,** *f.* (-en) pupil (*of the eye*). **–arisch,** *adj.* pupil(l)ar(y). **–enerweiterung,** *f.* dilation of the pupil. **–engelder,** *n.pl.* property of a ward *or* of a minor. **–engericht,** *n.* court of chancery.

Pupp–e, *f.* (-en) doll, puppet (*also fig.*); lay figure, dummy; chrysalis, pupa (*Ent.*); stack, stook (*hay, corn*); (*sl.*) *bis in die –en*, till the cows come home. **–engesicht,** *n.* pretty face, face like a doll. **–enhaus,** *n.*, **–enstube,** *f.* doll's house. **–enhülle,** *f.* cocoon. **–enspiel,** *n.*, **–entheater,** *n.* puppet-show; puppet-play. **–enstand,** *m.* chrysalis condition. **–enwagen,** *m.* doll's pram. **–enzustand,** *m.*, *see* **–enstand.**

puppern, *v.n.* (*aux.* h.) (*dial.*) throb; tremble, palpitate.

pur, *adj.* pure, genuine, sheer.

Püree, *n.* (-s, -s) & *f.* (–, -s) purée, mash.

Purg–anz, *f.* (-en) (*Austr. dial.*), **–ativ,** *n.* (-s, -e) purgative, laxative, aperient. **–ieren,** *v.a.* & *n.* (*aux.* h.) purge; boil off.

Puritan–er, *m.* Puritan. **–isch,** *adj.* puritan(ical).

Purpur, *m.* purple; crimson, deep red; purple *or* scarlet robe. **–n,** *adj.* purple, crimson, scarlet, deep red. **–farben,** *adj.*, **–farbig,** *adj.* purple, crimson. **–hut,** *m.* cardinal's hat. **–rot,** *adj.* & *n.* crimson, scarlet.

purren, 1. *v.n.* (*aux.* h.) purr, hum, buzz. 2. *v.a.* call out the watch (*Naut.*); poke, stir up (*fire*), (*fig.*) tease, incite.

Pürsch, *f.*, *see* **Pirsch.**

purzel–n, *v.n.* (*aux.* s.) tumble (*head over heels*). **–baum,** *m.* somersault; *einen –baum schlagen*, turn a somersault. **–taube,** *f.* tumbler (pigeon).

pussel–ig, (*also* **pußlig**), *adj.* (*dial.*) sweet, darling, pretty; fiddling, footling. **–n,** *v.n.* (*coll.*) potter about, fiddle (about *or* with), footle.

Puste, *f.* (*coll.*) breath; (*coll.*) *er hat keine – mehr, die – geht ihm aus*, he is out of breath. **–n,** *v.a.* & *n.* (*aux.* h.) puff, blow, pant; huff (*Draughts*); (*coll.*) *darauf puste ich*, I snap my fingers at it. **–rohr,** *n.* blowpipe; pea-shooter.

Pustel, *f.* (-n) pustule, pimple.

put, *int.* chuck! chuck! **–chen,** *n.*, **–hahn,** *m.*, **–huhn,** *n.*, **–put,** *n.* (-s, –) (*nursery talk*) chuckie chuck-chuck.

Pute, *f.* (-n) (*dial.*) turkey-hen; (*iron.*) conceited woman. **–r,** *m.* turkey-cock. **–rbraten,** *m.* roast turkey. **–rrot,** *adj.* (as) red as a turkey-cock.

Putsch, *m.* (-es, -e) armed (up)rising, riot; (*Swiss dial.*) push, shove. **–en,** (*aux.* h.) riot. **–ist,** *m.* rioter.

putt, *see* **put.**

Putte, *f.* (-n) putto (*usually pl.* putti) (*Art*).

Putz, *m.* attire, ornaments, finery, trimming; dress, adornment; plaster, rough-cast; *im* –, in full dress; *dem – ergeben*, fond of dress, dressy. **–en,** 1. *v.a.* clean, cleanse, scour, polish, brighten, burnish; dress, adorn; snuff (*a candle*), trim (*a lamp*), blow *or* wipe (*one's nose*), brush (*one's teeth*); groom (*a horse*); prune, lop; pluck (*fowls*); plaster, rough-cast (*a wall*). 2. *v.r.* dress up. 3. *v.n.* be ornamental *or* dressy. **–arbeit,** *f.* plasterwork. **–artikel** *m. l.* millinery. **–er,** *m.* scourer, cleaner;

polisher. **-frau,** *f.* charwoman. **-händlerin,** *f.* milliner. (*coll.*) **-ig,** *adj.* funny, queer, quaint, droll, curious; (*dial.*) small, tiny. **-kram,** *m.* millinery, finery; toilet wares. **-laden,** *m.* milliner's shop. **-lappen,** *m.* duster, polishing cloth. **-leiste,** *f.* (decorative) window-frame. **-macherin,** *f.* milliner. **-mittel,** *n.* cleaner, detergent. **-pulver,** *n.* scouring powder. **-schachtel,** *f.* bandbox. **-schere,** *f.* (candle) snuffers. **-stein,** *m.* bath brick. **-stock,** *m.* cleaning-rod (*of a gun*). **-sucht,** *f.* love of dress *or* finery. **-süchtig,** *adj.* very fond of dress. **-tuch,** *n.* polishing cloth. **-waren,** *f.pl.* millinery. **-werg,** *n.*, **-wolle,** *f.* cotton waste. **-zeug,** *n.* cleaning utensils *or* materials.

Pygmä-e, *m.* (-en, -en) pigmy. **-enhaft,** *adj.*, **-isch,** *adj.* pigmy.

Pyjama, *n.* (& *m.*) (-s, -s) pyjamas.

Pyramid-e, *f.* (-en) pyramid; stack (*of rifles*); *-e ansetzen, die Gewehre in -en (zusammen)setzen,* pile arms (*Mil.*). **-al,** *adj.* pyramidal; (*coll.*) towering, overwhelming. **-enwürfel,** *m.* octahedron.

Pyrit, *m.* (-es, -e) pyrites.

pyro-gen, *adj.* pyrogenic. **-metrie,** *f.* pyrometry. **-phor,** *adj.* pyrophoric, pyrophorus. **-silin,** *n.* gun-cotton, nitro-cellulose, pyroxylin. **-technik,** *f.* pyrotechnics, fireworks.

Q

Q, q, *n.* Q, q; (*see Index of Abbreviations*).

Quabb-e, *f.* (-n) fatty growth, wen; tadpole; quagmire (*see* **Quebbe**). **-el,** *m.* (-els, -el) flabby mass. **-elig, -ig, -lig,** *adj.* flabby, jelly-like. **-eln,** *v.n.* (*aux.* h.) wobble, quiver, quake, shake (*like jelly*); be flabby (*of flesh*); (*dial.*) *ich -ele,* I feel queasy.

Quack-elei, *f.* (-en) silly talk; nonsense. **-eln,** *v.n.* (*aux.* h.) chatter, babble (*see* **quakeln**); be irresolute, shilly-shally; waver. (*coll.*) **-elfritz,** *m.*, **-elliese,** *f.* (*dial.*) irresolute and fussy person; niggler. **-salber,** *m.* quack, charlatan. **-salberei,** *f.* quackery. **-salbern,** *v.n.* (*aux.* h.) practise quackery; dabble (*mit,* in); (*an einem*) doctor a p.

Quaddel, *f.* (-n) itchy swelling *or* lump. **-sucht,** *f.* nettle-rash.

Quad-er, *m.* (-ers, -er) & *f.* (-ern) squared stone; freestone, ashlar. **-erstein,** *m.* ashlar. **-erwerk,** *n.* bound masonry. **-rant,** *m.* (-en, -en) quadrant. **-rat,** 1. *n.* (-s, -e) square; natural (*Mus.*); quadrat (*Typ.*); block (*of houses*); *zum* or *auf das* or *ins -rat erheben,* square (*a number*); *im -rat der Entfernung,* as the square of the distance. 2. *adj.*, *see* **-ratisch.** **-rätchen,** *n.* M-quadrat (*Typ.*); *halbes -rätchen,* N-quadrat. **-ratförmig,** *adj.* square. **-ratisch,** *adj.* square, quadratic; tetragonal. **-ratmeter,** *n.* square metre. **-ratpyramide,** *f.* pentahedron. **-ratschein,** *m.* quartile (*Astr.*). **-ratur,** *f.* quadrature, squaring (*of the circle*). **-ratwurzel,** *f.* square root. **-rieren,** *v.a.* square (*Math.*). **-riga,** *f.* (-en) quadriga, four-in-hand. **-rille,** *f.* quadrille. **-rillion,** *f.* a million million million million, 10 to the power of 24. **-rupel,** *adj.* quadruple.

quak-eln, *v.n.* (*dial.*) chatter, babble, blether. **-en,** *v.n.* (*aux.* h.) quack (*ducks*); croak (*frogs*); *see also* **-eln.**

quäken, *v.n.* squeak; *-de Stimme,* squeaky voice.

Quäker, *m.* (-s, -) Quaker. **-bund,** *m.* Society of Friends. **-speisung,** *f.* Friends Relief Organization.

Qual, *f.* (-en) torment, torture, agony, pangs, pain; affliction. **-voll,** *adj.* very painful, agonizing, excruciating; full of anguish.

quäl-en, 1. *v.a.* torture, torment; agonize, afflict, distress, cause pain; pester, molest, harass, annoy, worry; *zu Tode -en,* kill by (slow) torture; (*fig.*). worry the life out of. 2. *v.r.* toil, slave, drudge. **-er,** *m.* tormentor, torturer; bore. **-erei,** *f.* tormenting; torments, torture; vexation, annoyance, pestering, persecution; drudgery. **-erisch,** *adj.* tormenting; vexatious. **-geist,** *m.* tormentor, bore, nuisance, plague, pest.

qualifizieren, 1. *v.a.* qualify, fit; mark, denote. 2. *v.r.*; *sich für eine* or *zu einer S.* – (show *or* prove o.s. to) be fit *or* suitable for a th.

Qualit-ät, *f.* (-en) quality; grade, brand, sort; capture of castle by bishop or knight (*chess*); *kleine -ät,* capture of bishop by knight (*Chess*). **-ativ,** *adj.* qualitative. **-ätsarbeit,** *f.* high quality work(man)-ship). **-ätsstahl,** *m.* high-grade steel. **-ätsware,** *f.* high-class article.

Qualle, *f.* (-n) jelly-fish, medusa; (*vulg.*) phlegm, gob.

Qualm, *m.* thick *or* dense smoke; fumes. **-en,** 1. *v.n.* (*aux.* h.) steam; smoke; be in a towering rage. 2. *v.a.* smoke (*cigars, etc.*) heavily. **-er,** *m.* inveterate smoker. **-ig,** *adj.* steaming; smoky.

Qualster, *m.* (-s, –), (*vulg.*) *see* **Qualle** (*vulg.*).

Quandel, *m.* (-s, –) chimney vent (*in a kiln*).

quängeln, *v.n.*, *see* **quengeln.**

Quant-entheorie, *f.* quantum theory. **-ität,** *f.* (-en) quantity (*also Metrics*), amount. **-itativ,** *adv.* numerical, quantitative. **-itätsbestimmung,** *f.* quantitative determination. **-itieren,** *v.n.* measure syllables (*Metrics*). **-um,** *n.* (-ums, -en & *Austr. dial.* -a) quantity; share, portion, amount, quota; quantum (*Phys.*).

Quappe, *f.* (-n) eel-pout; tadpole.

Quarantäne, *f.* quarantine; – *halten,* undergo *or* be subjected to quarantine; *in – liegen,* be in quarantine; *die – auferlegen, in – versetzen, unter – stellen, der – unterwerfen,* put *or* place in quarantine. **-maßregeln,** *f.pl.* quarantine regulations.

Quark, *m.* curd, curds; slime, slush, filth; (*fig.*) trifle, rubbish, trash; (*sl.*) *du verstehst einen – davon,* you understand damn-all about it; *den alten – aufrühren,* (*fig.*) stir up mud. **-ig,** *adj.* containing curds; dirty. **-käse,** *m.* soft *or* cream cheese.

Quarr-e, *f.* (-en) (*dial.*) squalling child, nagging wife, shrew; (*Prov.*) *erst die Pfarre, dann die -e,* first a living, then a wife. **-en,** *v.n.* (*aux.* h.) whine, squall, squawk; croak (*frogs*); nag. **-ig,** *adj.* squalling, whining, squeaking, nagging.

Quart, 1. *n.* (-(e)s, -e) (*archaic*) quart (= *approx.* 1 *litre*); quarto (*Typ.*). 2. *f.* (-en), *see* **-e.** **-a,** *f.* (-en) third form (*in secondary schools*). **-al,** *n.* (-als, -ale) quarter (*of a year*); **-alabschluß,** *m.* quarter's balance, quarterly stock-taking. **-algeld,** *n.* quarterly allowance. **-algericht,** *n.* quarter-sessions. **-aliter,** *adv.* quarterly, every quarter; in quarterly instalments. **-alkündigung,** *f.* three months' notice. **-al(s)tag,** *m.* quarter-day. **-alweise,** *adj.* quarterly. **-an,** *adj.* every fourth day. **-aner,** *m.* third-form boy. **-är,** *adj.* quaternary (*Geol.*). **-ant,** *m.*, **-band,** *n.* quarto volume. **-blatt,** *n.*, **-bogen,** *m.* quarto sheet. **-e,** *f.* (-en) carte, quart (*Cards, Fenc.*); fourth (*Mus.*). **-ett,** *n.* (-(e)s, -e), quartet(te) (*Mus.*), four (*Cards*). **-format,** *n.* quarto. **-stoß,** *m.* thrust in carte (*Fenc.*).

Quartier, *n.* (-s, -e) lodging, quarters, billet; (*dial.*) district, ward; watch below decks (*Naut.*); (*archaic*) quarter, mercy, clemency (*Mil.*); *in – liegen bei . . .,* be quartered upon . . .; *– nehmen,* take lodgings. **-arrest,** *m.* confinement to quarters (*Mil.*). **-en,** *v.a.* quarter, billet, lodge. **-geber,** *m.* host. **-macher,** *m.* billeting officer (*Mil.*). **-meister,** *m.* quartermaster. **-sfrau** *f.* landlady. **-zettel,** *m.* requisition for billets.

Quarz, *m.* (-es, -e) quartz. **-drüse,** *f.* crystallized quartz. **-haltig,** *adj.* quartziferous. **-ig,** *adj.* quartzy, of quartz. **-kristall,** *n.* rock-crystal.

quasi, *adv.* as it were, so to speak, in a way. **-gelehrte(r),** *m.* would-be scholar. **-modogeniti,** *m.* Low Sunday.

quassel-n, *v.a.* & *n.* (*aux.* h.) (*sl.*) prattle, chatter, blether. (*sl.*) **-strippe,** *f.* prattler, bletherer; telephone.

Quast, *m.* (-es, -e), **-e,** *f.* (-en) tuft, tassel; soft brush, puff. **-enbehang,** *m.* tasselled hangings. **-ig,** *adj.* tasselled.

Quäst-or, *m.* (-s, -en) quaestor, university finance officer. **-ur,** *f.* (-en) university finance office.

Quatember, *m.* (-s, –) quarter-day, ember-day; (*in compounds* =) quarterly.

quatern-är, *adj. see* **quartär. –e,** *f.* (-n) quaternity, run *or* set of four.
quatsch, 1. *int.* splash! squash! 2. *m.* (*dial.*) squashy mess, mash; (*coll.*) twaddle, nonsense, rubbish, bosh. 3. *adj.* silly, stupid, nonsensical. **–en,** 1. *v.n.* (*aux.* h. & s.) (*dial.*) splash, flounder; (*coll.*) (*aux.* h.) talk nonsense *or* bosh, twaddle. 2. *v.a.* (*dial.*) crush, squash. (*coll.*) **–kopf,** *m.* twaddler.
Quecke, *f.* (-n) couch-grass (*Agropyrum repens*) (*Bot.*).
Quecksilber, *n.* quicksilver, mercury. **–chlorür,** mercurous chloride, calomel. **–dampf,** *m.* mercury vapour. **–ig,** *adj.* lively, restless, mercurial. **–legierung,** *f.* amalgam. **–n,** *adj.* of quicksilver. **–oxyd,** *n.* mercuric oxide. **–oxydul,** *n.* mercurous oxide. **–salbe,** *f.* mercurial ointment, blue ointment. **–säule,** *f.* column of mercury.
Quell, *m.* (-(e)s, -e) (*Poet.*), **–e,** *f.* (-en) spring, source, fountain, well; fountain-head, origin; authority; (*sl.*) fix (*Navig.*); *aus guter –e haben* or *wissen,* have on good authority. **–bottich,** *m.* steeping-vat. **–en,** 1. *v.ir.n.* (*aux.* s. & h.) gush, well (up); issue, flow *or* arise from, originate *or* spring from; swell, expand; *die Augen –en ihm fast aus dem Kopfe,* his eyes are popping out of his head; *Tränen –en ihr aus den Augen,* tears well from her eyes. 2. *v.reg. & ir.a.* cause to swell; soak, steep. **–enangabe,** *f.* (list of) references (to one's authorities). **–enfinder,** *m.* water-diviner. **–enforschung,** *f.* study of sources, original research. **–enmäßig,** *adj.* on good authority, according to the most reliable sources, authentic. **–ennachweis,** *m., see* **–enangabe. –enreich,** *adj.* well-watered. **–gebiet,** *n.* headwaters. **–reif,** *adj.* steeped *or* soaked sufficiently. **–sand,** *m.* quicksand, drift-sand. **–ung,** *f.* swelling, soaking, tumefaction. **–wasser,** *n.* spring water.
Quendel, *m.* wild thyme.
Quengel-ei, *f.* wrangling, whining, nagging. **–ig,** *adj.* (*also* **quenglig**), querulous. **–n,** *v.n.* (*aux.* h.) wrangle; grumble, nag; whine; (*sl.*) belly-ache, moan.
Quent, *n.* (-(e)s, -e) (*archaic*) drachm, dram.
quer, 1. *adj.* cross, transverse, lateral, oblique, slanting, diagonal. 2. *adv.* athwart, across; crosswise, obliquely; *kreuz und –,* hither and thither, to and fro, in all directions; *es kommt mir –,* I am put out by this, it thwarts my plans *or* puts a spoke in my wheel. **–ab,** *adv.* on the beam (*Naut.*). **–achse,** *f.* transverse axis. **–axt,** *f.* twibill, mattock. **–balken,** *m.* cross-beam, transom: architrave; bar (*Her.*). **–baum,** *m.* cross-bar. (*sl.*) **–beet,** *adv.* across country (*of tanks, etc.*). **–durch,** *adv.* across; *er ist –durchgelaufen,* he ran across; *er ist – durch die Felder gelaufen,* he ran across the fields. **–durchschnitt,** *m.* transverse section *or* diameter (*of a conic section*). **–e,** *f.* diagonal; oblique *or* transverse direction (*rarely used except in stock phrases*); *die –e, in die –e, der –e nach,* athwart, across, crosswise; *die Länge und die –e,* the length and breadth; *einem in die –e kommen,* cross a p.'s path, thwart s.o.'s designs, queer a p.'s pitch; *alles ist der –e gegangen,* everything has gone wrong. **–ein,** *adv., see* **–ab. –en,** *v.n. & a.* cross (over), cut across; traverse (*Mountaineering*). **–faser,** *f.* transverse fibre. **–feldein,** *adv.* cross-country. **–feldeinlauf,** *m.* cross-country running *or* run. **–feldeinritt,** *m.* point-to-point racing *or* meeting. **–fell,** *n.* diaphragm. **–feuer,** *n.* enfilading fire (*Mil.*). **–flöte,** *f.* flute. **–format,** *n.* broadside (*Typ.*). **–frage,** *f.* interposed *or* interjected question. **–gang,** *m.* traverse, alley way, (*sl.*) cut. **–giebel,** *m.* side gable. **–holz,** *n.* transom; bail (*Crick.*). **–kopf,** *m.* contrary fellow; crank. **–köpfig,** *adj.* contrary, cranky. **–kraft,** *f.* shearing force. **–leiste,** *f.* cross-piece, strut, transverse ridge. **–linie,** *f.* diagonal. **–pfeife,** *f.* fife. **–ruder,** *n.* aileron (*Av.*). **–säge,** *f.* cross-cut saw. **–sattel,** *m.* side-saddle. **–schiff,** *n.* transept. **–schiffs,** *adv.* athwartships (*Naut.*). **–schläger,** *m.* ricochet (*Artil.*). **–schnitt,** *m.* cross-section, transverse section, profile, cross-cut. **–schott,** *n.* (transverse) bulkhead. **–schub,** *m.* lateral thrust. **–stange,** *f.* cross-bar. **–steuer,** *n.* aileron control (*Av.*). **–stollen,** *m.* transverse gallery (*Min.*). **–straße,** *f.* crossroad, side-street. **–strich,** *m.* dash, stroke, break (*Typ.*); (cross-)line (*in fractions*); disappointment, frustration; *einen –strich machen durch,* frustrate, thwart, nip in the bud. **–summe,** *f.* total of the digits of a number. **–treiberei,** *f.* intrigue. **–über,** *adv.* diagonally *or* nearly opposite, right across. **–wall,** *m.* traverse (*Fort.*). **–wand,** *f.* partition, transverse wall. **–welle,** *f.* transverse shaft.
Querul-ant, *m.* (-en, -en) querulous person, grumbler. **–ieren,** *v.n.* (*aux.* h.) be querulous *or* contentious, grumble.
Quese, *f.* (-n) (*dial.*) blister, blood-blister.
Quetsch-e, *f.* (-en) crusher, presser, wringer; (*dial.*) plum (*see* **Zwetschge**); (*coll.*) cramped space, poky hole. **–en,** *v.a.* crush, bruise, contuse; press, squeeze, squash, pinch, nip; knead; *einen Ball an die Bande –en,* strike a ball against the cushion (*Bill.*). **–hahn,** *m.* pinch-cock, spring clip. **–kartoffeln,** *f.pl.* mashed potatoes. **–kommode,** *f.* (*sl.*) squeeze-box. **–laut,** *m.* affricate (*Phonet.*). **–ung,** *f.* crushing; bruise; cushion (*Bill.*). **–werk,** *n.* crushing-mill. **–wunde,** *f.* contused wound.
Queue [*pron.* kø:], 1. *n.* (-s, -s) cue (*Bill.*). 2. *f.* (-s) queue.
quick, 1. *adj.* (*dial.*) lively, brisk. 2. *m.* (*dial.*) quicksilver. **–arbeit,** *f.* amalgamation. **–born,** *m.* fountain of youth (*Poet.*). **–brei,** *m.* amalgam. **–en,** *v.a.* amalgamate. **–erz,** *n.* mercury ore. **–wasser,** *n.* mercurial solution.
Quidam, *m.* (-s, –) a certain person, somebody, so-and-so.
Quiek, *int. & m.* (-es, -e) squeak, squeal. **–en,** (*coll.*) **–sen,** *v.n.* (*aux.* h.) squeak, squeal.
quietschen, *v.n.* (*coll.*) scream, squeak, creak.
quill, quillst, quillt, *see* **quellen.**
Quint-a, *f.* (-en) second form, (*Austr. dial.*) fifth form. **–aner,** *m.* second-form boy. **–e,** *f.* (-en) fifth (*Mus.*); first string, E string (*of violins*); quinte (*Fenc.*); quint (*Cards*); trick, feint. **–essenz,** *f.* quintessence, pith. **–ett,** *n.* (-s, -e) quintette (*Mus.*).
Quirl, *m.* (-(e)s, -e) whisk, agitator, beater; whirl, whorl (*Bot.*); one year's growth of firs; restless person; (*fig.*) whirlwind. **–en,** 1. *v.n.* (*aux.* h. & s.) whirl. 2. *v.a.* whisk, beat, stir, agitate, twirl.
quitt, *adj.* (*only pred.*) quits, even; rid, free; *mit einem – sein,* be square with a p. **–ieren,** *v.a.* receipt (*a bill*), give a receipt; quit, leave, abandon; *–ierte Rechnung,* receipted bill. **–ung,** *f.* receipt.
Quitte, *f.* (-n) quince. **–ngelb,** *adj. & n.* brilliant *or* bright yellow. **–ngelee,** *n.* quince marmalade.
quoll, quollest, quölle, *see* **quellen.**
Quot-e, *f.* (-en) quota, share; contingent. **–ient,** *m.* (-en, -en) quotient. **–ieren,** *v.a.* quote (*prices*).

R

R, r, *n.* R, r; *see Index of Abbreviations.*
Raa, *f., see* **Rahe.**
raba-ntern, –ngen, –schen, –stern, *v.n.* (*coll.*) move about noisily, be busy, be restless.
Rabatt, *m.* (-(e)s, -e) discount, deduction, rebate allowance; *davon geht noch – ab,* discount to be deducted; *einem – unterworfen,* subject to a discount. **–e,** *f.* facing (*of a coat*); cuff; ridge, border, bed (*Hort.*). **–ieren,** *v.a.* reduce in price, make a deduction, allow discount on. **–marke,** *f.* discount-ticket.
rabatzen, *v.n.* (*coll.*), *see* **rabantern,** *etc.*
Rabbi, *m.* (-s, -nen & -s), **–ner,** *m.* (-s, –) rabbi. **–nisch,** *adj.* rabbinical.
Rabe, *m.* (-n, -n) raven, crow; Corvus (*Astr.*); *weißer –,* rare bird, black swan, blue moon; *alt wie*

ein –, as old as the hills; *er stiehlt wie ein –*, he steals like a magpie. **–naas,** *n.* carrion; (*fig.*) gallows-bird. **–neltern,** *pl.* unnatural parents. **–nhaar,** *n.* raven (black) hair. **–nkrähe,** *f.* carrion crow. **–nmutter,** *f.* cruel mother. **–nschwarz,** *adj.* & *n.* jet-black, pitch-black *or* dark; *–nschwarze Locken*, raven locks. **–nstein,** *m.* place of execution, gallows. **–nvater,** *m.* harsh father.

rabiat, *adj.* furious, raving, rabid, mad with rage.

Rabulist, *m.* (-en, -en) pettifogger, hair-splitter. **–erei,** *f.* pettifogging, chicanerie, hair-splitting.

Rach–e, *f.* vengeance, revenge; *–e an einem nehmen*, revenge o.s. on a p. **–edurst,** *m.* vengefulness, vindictiveness. **–eengel,** *m.* avenging angel. **–egöttin,** *f.* Fury. **–eschnaubend,** *adj.* breathing fire. **–gier,** *f.*, *see* **–edurst.** **–gierig,** *adj.*, *see* **–süchtig.** **–sucht,** *f.*, *see* **–edurst.** **–süchtig,** *adj.* vindictive; (re)vengeful, resentful.

Rachen, *m.* (-s, –) jaws (*of beasts*); throat, mouth; yawning abyss. **–bein,** *n.* jaw-bone, inferior maxilla. **–bräune,** *f.* quinsy. **–förmig,** *adj.* ringent, labiate (*Bot.*). **–höhle,** *f.* pharynx, pharingeal cavity. **–katarrh,** *m.* sore throat, pharyngitis. (*coll.*) **–putzer,** *m.* (*coll.*) acid wine, strong spirits.

räch–en, I. (*archaic ir.*) *v.a.* avenge, revenge. 2. *v.r.* take revenge (*an*, on); *es wird sich an ihm –en*, it will come *or* be brought home to him, it will take its toll, he will pay *or* suffer for it. **–er,** *m.* avenger.

Rachiti–s, *f.* rickets. **–sch,** *adj.* rickety.

Racker, *m.* (-s, –) rogue, rascal, scamp. **–zeug,** *n.* pack of rogues. **–n,** *v.n.* & *r.* (*coll.*) drudge, toil, slave, wear o.s. out.

Racket, *n. see* **Rakett.**

Rad, *n.* (-s, ⸚er) wheel; bicycle, (*coll.*) cycle, bike; *das – an der Welle*, wheel and axle; *ein – schlagen*, turn a cartwheel; spread the tail (*of peacocks*); (*fig.*) *unter die ⸚er kommen*, go to the dogs; *das – der Geschichte*, the wheels of history; (*coll.*) *bei ihm fehlt ein –*, he's got a screw loose; *zum –e verurteilen*, condemn to be broken on the wheel; *aufs – flechten*, break on the wheel; *das – laufen lassen*, coast (*Cycl.*); *das fünfte – am Wagen sein*, be redundant, be out of place, not be wanted. **–achse,** *f.* axle-tree. **–antrieb,** *m.* gear drive. **–arm,** *m.* spoke. **–ber,** *f.* (-en) (*Austr. dial.*) wheel-barrow. **–bewegung,** *f.* rotation, rotary motion. **–bremse,** *f.* hub brake. **–dampfer,** *m.* paddle-steamer. **–drehung,** *f.* rotation, torsion. **–eber,** *f.*, **–eberge** *f. see* **–ber.** **–ebrechen,** *v.a.* (*insep.*) mangle *or* murder (*a language*). **–eln,** *v.n.* (*aux.* s.) (*coll.*) cycle, ride a bicycle. **–emacher,** *m. see* **–macher.** **–fahren,** *v.n.* (*aux.* h. & s.) cycle, ride a bicycle. **–fahrer,** *m.* cyclist. **–fahrerzug,** *m.*, *see* **–fahrzug.** **–fahrweg,** *m.* cycle track. **–(fahr)zug,** *m.* cycle platoon (*Mil.*). **–felge,** *f.* rim, felly, felloe. **–fenster,** *n.* rose-window. **–förmig,** *adj.* rotate (*Bot.*); wheel-shaped. **–gelenk,** *n.* pivot joint. **–ial,** *adj.* radial. **–kappe,** *f.* hub-cap. **–körper,** *m.* hub. **–kranz,** *m.* rim. **–lafette,** *f.* wheeled gun carriage. **–lenker,** *m.* guide rail (*Railw.*). **–ler,** *m.* (*coll.*) cyclist. **–linie,** *f.* cycloid (*Geom.*). **–macher,** *m.* wheelwright. **–mantel,** *m.* outer cover (*Cycl.*); cycling cape. **–nabe,** *f.* hub (*of a wheel*). **–reifen,** *m.* tyre. **–rennbahn,** *f.* cycling track. **–rennen,** *n.* cycle-race. **–schaufel,** *f.* sweep (*of a water-mill*); paddle-board; *bewegliche –schaufel*, feathering paddle. **–scheibe,** *f.* pulley. **–schlagen,** *v.n.* spread the tail (*of peacocks*); turn a cartwheel; (*coll.*) *das ist zum –schlagen*, that is enough to drive one silly; that is screamingly funny **–schuh,** *m.* wheel-drag. **–speiche,** *f.* spoke. **–sperre,** *f.* drag-chain. **–sporn,** *m.* tail-wheel (*Av.*). **–sport,** *m.* cycling. **–spur,** *f.* track of a wheel, rut, wheel mark. **–stand,** *m.* wheel-base. **–sturz,** *m.* camber. **–welle,** *f.* (paddle *or* pulley)-shaft. **–zahn,** *m.* cog. **–zug,** *m.*, *see* **–fahrzug.**

Radau [*pron.* ˈdau], *m.* (*coll.*) noise, row, hullabaloo. **–bruder,** *m.* rowdy.

Räd–chen, *n.* (-s, –) small wheel; caster; (*coll.*) *bei dir ist ein –chen locker*, you've got a screw loose. **–eln,** *v.a.* mill; trace with a perforating wheel. **–elsführer,** *m.* ringleader. **–erfahrzeug,** *n.* wheeled vehicle. **–erkasten,** *m.* gear-box. **–erkettenfahrzeug,** *n.* half-track vehicle. **–(e)rig,** *adj. suff.* -wheeled; *e.g. vier–(e)rig*, four-wheeled. **–ern,** *v.a.* (*rare*) furnish with wheels; (*archaic*) break on the wheel; sift, screen; *wie gerädert sein*, be fagged out, knocked up. **–ertierchen,** *n.* rotifer, wheel-animalcule. **–erwerk,** *n.* gearing, gears, wheels, clockwork.

Rade, *f.* (-n) cockle (*Agrostemma githago*) (*Bot.*).

radier–en, *v.a.* etch; erase, rub out. **–gummi,** *n.* india-rubber. **–kunst,** *f.* (art of) etching. **–messer,** *n.* eraser, penknife. **–nadel,** *f.* etching-needle, dry needle. **–ung,** *f.* etching.

Radieschen, *n.* radish.

radik–al, I. *adj.* radical, root, basic, fundamental, inherent; utterly, ruthlessly. 2. *n.* radical, root. **–ale(r),** *m.* radical (*in politics*). **–alessig,** *m.* glacial acetic acid. **–alismus,** *m.* radicalism. **–and,** *m.* (-en, -en) number of which root is to be found (*Math.*).

Radio, *n.* (& *Swiss dial. m.*) (-s, -s) radio, wireless. **–aktiv,** *adj.* radio-active. **–anlage,** *f.* wireless installation. **–apparat,** *m.*, **–gerät,** *n.* wireless set, radio. **–gramm,** *n.* radio telegram. **–peilung,** *f.* radiolocation, radar. **–publikum,** *n.* listeners, radio audience. **–sendung,** *f.* transmission. **–technik,** *f.* radio technology. **–telegraphie,** *f.* wireless telegraphy. **–wesen,** *n.* broadcasting.

Radium, *n.* radium.

Rad–ius, *m.* (-ien) radius (*Math.*, *Anat.*). **–izieren,** *v.a.* extract the root of.

Räf, *n.* (-s, -e) (*Swiss dial.*), *see* **Reff.**

Raff, *m.* (-(e)s, -e) (*coll.*) grab, handful.

Raffel, *f.* (-n) raffle-net (*for turbot*); rattle; chatter-box; grater, scraper; flax-comb. **–n,** I. *v.a.* rake, ripple (*flax*); grate, scrape. 2. *v.n.* chatter, gossip.

raff–en, I. *v.a.* snatch up, carry off, gather up. 2. *v.n.* (*aux.* h.) snatch (*nach*, at). **–gier,** *f.* greed, rapacity. **–gut,** *n.* stolen goods. **–holz,** *n.* wind-fallen wood. **–ig,** *adj.* grasping, greedy, covetous. (*sl.*) **–ke,** *m.* profiteer. **–zahn,** *m.* laniary *or* canine tooth (*of carnivores*); projecting front tooth.

Raffin–ade, *f.* refined sugar. **–ation,** *f.* refining. **–erie,** *f.* refinery. **–ieren,** *v.a.* (*aux.* h.) refine, purify. **–ierofen,** *m.* refining furnace. **–iert,** *adj.* refined; artful, cunning, crafty; *–ierte Bosheit*, studied malice.

ragen, *v.n.* tower (up), project.

Ragout, *n.* (-s, -s) stew, hotch-potch.

Rah–(e), *f.* (-en) yard, spar (*Naut.*); spreader; *große –*, main yard. **–schiff,** *n.* square-rigged vessel. **–segel,** *n.* square sail.

Rahm, *m.* cream; soot; *– ansetzen*, form cream; *– abnehmen*, skim the cream. **–en,** I. *v.n.* (*aux.* h.) form cream. 2. *v.a.* skim. **–farbig,** *adj.* cream-coloured. **–ig,** *adj.* creamy; sooty. **–käse,** *m.* cream cheese.

Rahmen, I. *m.* (-s, –) frame, housing, casement (*of windows*); surroundings, milieu; compass, scope. 2. *v.a.* frame (*see also* **Rahm**). **–antenne,** *f.* frame-aerial, loop aerial (*Rad.*). **–arbeit,** *f.* welted footwear. **–erzählung,** *f.* stories within a story. **–gesetz,** *n.* skeleton law. **–heer,** *n.* cadre. **–rohr,** *n.*; *oberes –rohr*, cross-bar (*Cycl.*). **–schuh,** *m.* welted shoe. **–spiegel,** *m.* framed mirror. **–stickerei,** *f.* frame-embroidery. **–sucher,** *m.* view finder (*Phot.*). **–vertrag,** *m.* skeleton agreement. **–werk,** *n.* framework.

Rain, *m.* (-(e)s, -e) balk, ridge, bank (*between fields*); (*Poet.*) limit, border, edge. **–en,** *v.a.* fix boundaries (*of fields*), demarcate. **–farn,** *m.* tansy (*Tanacetum vulgare*) (*Bot.*). **–stein,** *m.* boundary-stone. **–weide,** *f.* privet (*Ligustrum vulgare*) (*Bot.*).

rajolen, *v.a.*, *see* **rigolen.**

räkeln, *v.r.*, *see* **rekeln.**

Rakete, *f.* (-n) rocket; *Fallschirm–*, parachute flare. **–nantrieb,** *m.* rocket propulsion. **–nflugzeug,** *n.* rocket-plane. **–nwerfer,** *m.* rocket-apparatus (*on lifeboats, etc.*).

Rakett, *n.* (-(e)s, -e & *Austr. dial.* -s) racket.

Ralle, *f.* (-n) (water-)rail (*Rallus aquaticus*) (*Orn.*).

Ramm, *m.* (-(e)s, -e) (*dial.*) ram. **–bär,** *m.*, **–bock,** *m.*, *see* **–e.** **–dösig,** *adj.* excitable, hysterical. **–e,** *f.* pile-driver, drop hammer, rammer. **–el,** *m.*, *see* **–e;** (*dial.*) *see* **–;** (*dial.*) lout. **–elei,** *f.* (*vulg.*)

randiness; fornication. **-elig,** *adj.* (*dial.*) in heat, (*vulg.*) randy. **-elkammer,** *f.* nuptial chamber. **-eln,** 1. *v.a.* ram in, thrust, jam together. 2. *v.n.* (*aux.* h.) rut, be in heat. **-en,** *v.a.* drive in, ram in; ram (*a ship*); beat *or* stamp down (*the soil*). **-ler,** *m.* buck hare *or* rabbit. **-sporn,** *m.* ram (*Naut.*).

Rampe, *f.* (-n) platform, slope, ramp, ascent; drive, approach; apron (*of stage*). **-nlichter,** *n.pl.* footlights (*Theat.*).

ramponieren, *v.a.* (*coll.*) spoil, damage, smash, bash.

Ramsch, *m.* (-es, ¨-e) odds and ends; job lot, rubbish; students' quarrel; *im* –, in the lump, in bulk. **-en,** *v.a.* buy in the bulk, buy cheap; (*Studs. sl.*) challenge. **-geschäft,** *n.* junk-shop. **-verkauf,** *m.* jumble sale. **-waren,** *f.pl.* sale-price goods, odds and ends.

ran, *see* **heran.**

Rand, *m.* (-es, ¨-er) edge, brink, verge, border, brim, rim, flange, lip; margin, ledge; (*coll.*) *das versteht sich am -e* that is a matter of course; *außer – und Band sein,* out of hand, unmanageable; *bis zum -e voll,* full to the brim, brimful; *dunkle ¨-er um die Augen,* dark rings under one's eyes; *am -e des Grabes,* on the brink of the grave; (*sl.*) *den – halten,* hold one's tongue; *zwischen Lipp' und Kelches – schwebt der dunklen Mächte Hand,* there's many a slip 'twixt cup and lip; *am -e des Todes,* at death's door; *am -e des Verderbens,* on the verge of ruin; (*coll.*) *zu -e kommen mit,* accomplish a th.; *nicht zu -e kommen,* make vain efforts. **-bemerkung,** *f.* marginal note, gloss, (*fig.*) aside. **-gebirge,** *n.* mountains bordering a plateau. **-ig,** *adj. suff.* with a . . . border, edge, *or* margin. **-leiste,** *f.* ledge. **-schrift,** *f.* marginal inscription, edge-legend (*on coins*). **-siedlung,** *f.* new estate on the outskirts of a town. **-ständig,** *adj.* marginal, peripheral. **-stein,** *m.* kerb-stone. **-steller,** *m.* margin stop (*Typewriter*). **-verzierung,** *f.* ornamental border. **-widerstand,** *m.* induced drag (*Av.*). **-zacken,** *m.* edging, fringe. **-zeichnung,** *f.* marginal sketch.

Randal [*pron.* -ˈdaːl], *m.* (-s, -e) (*Studs. sl.*) row, brawl. (*sl.*) **-ieren,** *v.n.* kick up a row.

Rande, *f.* (*Swiss dial.*) beetroot.

ränd-eln, -ern, *v.a.* border, edge; mill (*coins*). **-(e)rig,** *adj. suff.* with a . . . margin. **-elrad,** *n.* milling tool.

Ranft, *m.* (-(e)s, ¨-e) crust (*of bread*); (*Poet.*) edge, border.

rang, rangest, ränge, *see* **ringen.**

Rang, *m.* (-(e)s, ¨-e) rank, station, position, order, class, degree, grade; tier, row, circle (*Theat.*); *einem den – ablaufen,* outrun, outstrip, outdo *or* get the better of a p.; *ersten -es,* first-class, first-rate; *erster –,* dress-circle (*Theat.*); *zweiter –,* upper circle (*Theat.*); *einem den – streitig machen,* dispute s.o.'s position. **-abzeichen,** *n.* badge of rank (*Mil.*). **-älteste(r),** *m.* senior officer (*Mil.*). **-erhöhung,** *f.* promotion. **-klasse,** *f.* class position (*in order of merit*). **-liste,** *f.* Army List; table (*Sport*). **-mäßig,** *adj.* according to rank. **-ordnung,** *f.* order of precedence, hierarchy, order of merit. **-streit,** *m.* dispute for precedence. **-stufe,** *f.* degree, order, grade. **-sucht,** *f.* social ambition. **-unterschied,** *m.* distinction of rank. **-verlust,** *m.* degradation, loss of rank (*Mil.*).

Range, *m.* (-n, -n), *f.* (-n) young scamp (*boys*); tomboy, romp, hoyden (*girls*). **-nhaft,** *adj.* wild, boisterous, obstreperous, headstrong, ungovernable.

rangier-en [*pron.* rã'ʒiːren] 1. *v.a.* arrange, rank, classify; shunt (*trains*); *nach der Größe -t,* arranged *or* classified according to size. 2. *v.n.* (*aux.* h.) (have a certain) rank; *-en mit,* be classed with, rank with. **-bahnhof,** *m.* shunting yard, marshalling yard (*Railw.*). **-geleise,** *n.*, **-gleis,** *n.* siding (*Railw.*). **-lokomotive,** *f.*, **-maschine,** *f.* shunting engine (*Railw.*). **-meister,** *m.* yard-master.

rank, 1. *adj.* (*dial.*) slim, slender; crank (*ship*). 2. *m.* (-es, ¨-e) (*dial.*) turning, bend (*in road*); (*usually in the pl.*) crookedness, intrigue, trick; wile, artifice, machination; *Ränke schmieden* or *spinnen,* hatch plots, intrigue; (*Swiss dial.*) *den – ausfinden,* find a way out. **-e,** *f.* (-en) tendril, runner, climber, shoot. **-en,** *v.r.* & *n.* (*aux.* h. & s.) creep, climb; send forth tendrils. **-engewächs,** *n.* creeper, climber. **-enverzierung,** *f.*, **-enwerk,** *n.* scroll, interlaced ornament. **-ig,** *adj.* having tendrils.

Ränke, *m.pl.*, *see* **Rank** 2. **-schmied,** *m.* intriguer, plotter, schemer. **-sucht,** *f.* deceitfulness, insincerity, shiftiness, duplicity, guile. **-süchtig,** *adj.* deceitful, shifty, artful, sly, designing, scheming.

rann, rannest, ränne *or* **rönne,** *see* **rinnen.**

rannte, ranntest, *see* **rennen.**

Ranunkel, *f.* (-n) ranunculus, buttercup, crowfoot.

Ranzen, *m.* (-s, –), **Ränzel,** *n.* (-s, –) knapsack, satchel, schoolbag; (*vulg.*) belly, paunch; *seinen Ranzen schnüren,* pack one's traps.

ranz-en, *v.n.* rut, be in rut (*Hunt.*). **-er,** *m.* (*coll.*) dressing down, wigging. **-zeit,** *f.* rut, rutting season.

ranzig, *adj.* rancid, rank. **-keit,** *f.* rancidity.

Ranzion, *f.* (-en) ransom. **-ieren,** *v.a.* redeem, ransom, buy off.

Rappe, *m.* (-n, -n) black horse; (*coll.*) *auf Schusters -n reiten,* go on Shanks's pony.

Rappel, *m.* (*coll.*) fit of madness, rage; whim, craze; (*coll.*) *er hat einen –,* he is cracked *or* loopy. **-ig,** *adj.* crazy, excitable, headstrong. **-kopf,** *m.* crazy person, hothead. **-köpfig,** *adj.* crack-brained, mad. **-n,** 1. *v.n.* (*aux.* h.) rattle, make a noise; (*coll.*) *es -t bei ihm,* he is cracked *or* dotty. 2. *v.r.* (*coll.*) make progress *or* headway, be on the mend; pull o.s. together.

Rappen, *m.* (-s, –) (*Swiss dial.*) centime.

Rapport, *m.* (-s, -e) report, notice, announcement; *sich zum – melden,* come in to report, make one's report. **-ieren,** *v.a.* report, announce, make an announcement *or* a report.

Raps, *m.* (-es, -e) rape, colza (*Brassica napus*) (*Bot.*). **-acker,** *m.* field of rape. **-öl,** *n.* rape-oil.

Raptus, *m.* (–, -se), *see* **Rappel.**

Rapunze, *f.* (-n), **-l,** *m.* & *f.* (-n) lamb's lettuce, rampion (*Varianella olitoria*) (*Bot.*).

rar, *adj.* rare, scarce; exquisite; (*coll.*) *Sie machen sich –,* you are quite a stranger. **-ität,** *f.* rarity, curiosity, curio.

rasan-t, *adj.* flat, grazing (*Artil.*). **-z,** *f.* flat trajectory, flatness of trajectory.

rasaunen, *v.n.* (*dial.*) make a noise, raise a hullabaloo.

Rasch, *m.* (-es, -e) serge.

rasch, *adj.* quick, swift, speedy, rapid, hasty, impetuous, rash; lively, brisk, nimble. **-heit,** *f.* quickness, liveliness; rashness.

rascheln, *v.n.* (*aux.* h.) rustle, crackle.

ras-en, *v.n.* (*aux.* h.) rave, rage; be mad *or* delirious; (*coll.*) speed, scorch. **-end,** *pr.p.* & *adj.* raving; furious; mad, frantic; (*coll.*) very, exceedingly; *-end hungrig,* furiously hungry; *einen -end machen,* enrage a p., drive a p. mad; *es ist zum -endwerden,* it is enough to drive one mad. **-er,** *m.* (*coll.*) reckless driver, (*vulg.*) tear-arse. **-erei,** *f.* fury, rage, frenzy; raving, madness; mad act; (*coll.*) reckless driving, speeding, scorching.

Ras-en, *m.* (-ens, -en) lawn, turf, sward; sod; grass (plot); *auf dem -en,* on the lawn; *unter dem –,* under the sod, in the grave. **-enbekleidung,** *f.* turf-lining, sod-revetment (*Fort.*). **-enbleiche,** *f.* bleaching-ground; sun bleaching. **-eneisenerz,** *n.*, **-eneisenstein,** *m.* limonite, bog iron ore. **-enhacke,** *f.* sod-cutter. **-enhügel,** *m.* grassy knoll. **-enmähmaschine,** *f.* lawn-mower. **-enplagge,** *f.* sod, turf. **-enplatz,** *m.* lawn, grass plot, green. **-ensport,** *m.* outdoor sport *or* game. **-ensprenger,** *m.* lawn-sprinkler. **-enstück,** *n.* sod; grass plot. **-enwalze,** *f.* lawn-roller. **-ig,** *adj.* grassy, turf-covered.

rasier-en, *v.a.* shave; raze (*Mil.*); *sich -en lassen,* get shaved. **-apparat,** *m.* safety-razor. **-flechte,** *f.* ringworm, barber's rash. **-klinge,** *f.* razor-blade. **-messer,** *n.* razor; *-messer geschliffen und abgezogen,* razors ground and set. **-pinsel,** *m.* shaving-brush. **-seife,** *f.* shaving-soap *or* -stick. **-zeug,** *n.* shaving-things.

Räson, *f.* reason, common sense; *er will keine – annehmen,* he will not listen to reason. **-eur,** *m.*

(-s, -e) grumbler; argumentative person. **-ieren,** *v.n.* (*aux.* h.) (*archaic*) reason, argue; complain, grumble.
Raspel, *f.* (-n) rasp, grater. **-n,** *v.a.* rasp, scrape, grate; (*coll.*) *Süßholz -n,* say sweet nothings, flirt, spoon. **-späne,** *m.pl.* filings, scrapings.
Rass-e, *f.* (-en) race, breed; *von reiner -e,* thoroughbred; *das Mädchen hat -e,* the girl has quality. **-ehund,** *m.* pedigree dog. **-enhaß,** *m.* race-hatred. **-enhygiene,** *f.* eugenics. **-enkampf,** *m.* racial conflict. **-enkreuzung,** *f.* cross-breeding. **-enkunde,** *f.* ethnology. **-enmischung,** *f.* miscegenation. **-erein,** *adj.* pure-bred, thoroughbred. **-ereinheit,** *f.* racial purity. **-ig,** *adj.* thoroughbred, (*coll.*) fine, superior. **-isch,** *adj.* racial.
Rassel, *f.* (-n) rattle. **-n,** *v.n.* (*aux.* h. & s.) rattle, clatter; clank, clash; (*sl.*) be ploughed (*in an examination*); *mit den Ketten -n,* clank one's chains.
Rast, *f.* (-en) rest, repose; halt (*on march*); resting place; (*dial.*) stage (*of a journey*); stay; bosh (*of blast-furnace*); *ohne - und Ruh,* restlessly, never at rest. **-en,** *v.a.* & *n.* (*aux.* h.) rest, halt. **-gärung,** *f.* incomplete fermentation. **-los,** *adj.* restless, indefatigable. **-losigkeit,** *f.* restlessness. **-ort,** *m.* resting place, halting place. **-tag,** *m.* day of rest.
Rastelbinder, *m.* (-s, -) (*dial.*) itinerant tinker.
Raster, *m.* (-s, -) screen (*for photo-engraving*). **-n,** *v.a.* print by screen-process. **-tiefdruck,** *m.* autotypy; screen-process.
Rastral, *n.* (-s, -e) pen for ruling music.
Rasur, *f.* (-en) erasure.
Rat, *m.* (-(e)s) 1. (*pl.* -schläge) counsel, advice, suggestion. 2. (*pl.* Beratungen) deliberation, consultation; remedy, means, expedient, ways and means. 3. (*pl.* -sversammlungen) senate, assembly, board, council. 4. (*pl.* ⁻e) councillor. 5. (*pl.* -sherrn) alderman, senator; *um- fragen,* ask advice; *Frau -,* councillor's wife; *mit einem zu -e gehen,* go into consultation with a p.; *da ist guter - teuer,* that is a very difficult case, it is a critical situation; *etwas zu -e halten,* be sparing with a th., not waste a th.; *sich* (*Dat.*) *- holen* or (*archaic*) *-s erholen bei,* consult (*a p.*); turn to (s.o.) for advice; (*Prov.*) *kommt Zeit kommt -,* all in good time; *-s pflegen,* see *zu -e gehen*; *- schaffen,* devise means; *vortragender -,* privy councillor, counsellor; *mit - und Tat,* by word and deed; *- wissen,* know what to do; *da wußt' ich keinen - mehr,* then I was at my wit's end; *zu -e ziehen,* consult, (*coll.*) call in (*a doctor, etc.*). **-en,** *ir.v.a.* & *n.* (*aux.* h) (*with Dat.*) advise, counsel, commend, give advice; guess, conjecture, solve (*a riddle*); (*obs.*) help; *einem etwas* or *zu einer S. -en,* advise s.o. on a th.; *damit ist mir nicht geraten,* that does not help me much; *laß dir -en,* be advised; *er läßt sich von niemand -en,* he will not listen to anyone; *geschehenen Dingen ist nicht zu -en,* what's done can't be undone, it's no use crying over spilt milk; *ich wußte mir nicht zu -en,* I was at my wit's end; *einem etwas zu -en geben,* give a p. s.th. to think about, give a p. a nut to crack; *hin und her -en,* make random guesses; (*coll.*) *-e mal!* have a guess! *geraten,* *adj.* advisable, advantageous; *geraten!* you have guessed it! right! **-erei,** *f.* guess-work. **-geber,** *m.* adviser, counsellor; counsel (*Law*). **-haus,** *n.* town-hall, guild-hall. **-los,** *adj.* perplexed, helpless, embarrassed, at a loss, at sea. **-sam,** *adj.* advisable, commendable, expedient, fit, useful, (*dial.*) prudent. **-samkeit,** *f.* advisability, expediency; suitability. **-sbeschluß,** *m., see* **-serlaß.** **-schlag,** *m.* advice, counsel, suggestion. **-schlagen,** *v.n.* (*aux.* h.) (*insep.*) deliberate, consult (together). **-schluß,** *m.* resolution, decision; decree; *die -schlüsse der Vorsehung,* the decrees of Providence; *die -schlüsse Gottes,* the ways of the Lord. **-sdiener,** *m.* summoner. **-serlaß,** *m.* decree of the council. **-sherr,** *m.* (-(e)n) senator; alderman, town-councillor. **-skeller** *m.* town-hall cellar (restaurant). **-ssaal,** *m.* council chamber. **-sschreiber,** *m.* town-clerk. **-ssitzung,** *f.* council meeting. **-sstube,** *f.* council-chamber. **-sversammlung,** *f.* council meeting. **-swahl,** *f.* local government election.
rät, *see* **raten.**
Rate, *f.* (-n) instalment; rate, quota; *in -n,* by instalments. **-ngeschäft,** *n.* hire-purchase business. **-nkauf,** *m.* hire-purchase. **-nweise,** *adv.* by instalments.
Räte-regierung, *f.* (-en) Soviet government. **-republik,** *f.* Soviet republic.
ratifizieren, *v.a.* ratify.
Rät-in, *f.* councillor's *or* senator's wife. **-lich,** *adj.* advisable, expedient; useful; wholesome.
Ration, *f.* (-en) ration, rations, portion. **-al,** *adj.* rational, sensible. **-alisierung,** *f.* rationalization, simplification. **-alismus,** *m.* rationalism. **-alistisch,** *adj.* rationalistic. **-ell,** *adj.* expedient, economical, rational, reasonable, scientific. **-ieren,** *v.a.* ration.
Rätsel, *n.* (-s, -) riddle, puzzle, conundrum, problem, mystery, enigma; *das ist mir ein -,* that puzzles me, that beats me. **-frage,** *f.* riddle, conundrum. **-haft,** *adj.* puzzling, enigmatical, mysterious, incomprehensible, obscure. **-spruch,** *m.,* **-wort,** *n.* enigma, cryptic remark.
rätst, *see* **raten.**
Ratte, *f.* (-n) rat; miss, mis-throw (*skittles*). **-nfänger,** *m.* rat-catcher; *-nfänger von Hameln,* the Pied Piper of Hamelin. **-ngift,** *n.* ratsbane, rat poison. **-nkahl,** *adj.* bald as a coot, quite bare. **-nkönig,** *m.* (*fig.*) a perfect maze, tangle, farrago, jumble, concatenation. **-nschwanz,** *m.* rat-tail (file).
rätten, *v.a.* riddle, screen, sift, sieve.
rattern, *v.a.* clatter, rattle.
Ratz, *m.* (-es, -e) (*dial.*) rat; marmot; polecat; *schlafen wie ein -,* sleep like a top *or* log.
Ratze, *f.* (-n) (*coll.*), *see* **Ratte.** **-kahl,** *adj., see* **rattenkahl.**
Raub, *m.* (-(e)s, (*rare*) -e) robbery; plundering, pillaging, rapine; rape; piracy; prey, spoil, loot, booty; *Kinder-,* kidnapping; *auf - ausgehen,* go on the prowl; *gewaltsamer -,* robbery with violence; *zum -e werden,* fall victim *or* a prey (to); *ein - der Flammen werden,* be consumed by fire. **-anfall,** *m.* highway robbery. **-bau,** *m.* exhaustion of the soil; uncontrolled cutting (*of woods*); despoiling a mine. **-en,** 1. *v.a.* steal, plunder, abduct, ravish; take away, deprive of. 2. *v.n.* (*aux.* h.) rob; pillage. **-fisch,** *m.* predatory fish. **-gesindel,** *n.* pack of thieves. **-gier,** *f.* rapacity. **-gierig,** *adj.* rapacious. **-gut,** *n.* booty; stolen goods. **-krieg,** *m.* predatory war. **-mord,** *m.* murder and robbery. **-ritter,** *m.* robber knight. **-schiff,** *n.* pirate-ship, corsair. **-sucht,** *f.* rapacity. **-süchtig,** *adj.* rapacious. **-tier,** *n.* beast of prey. **-vogel,** *m.* bird of prey. **-wirtschaft,** *f.* ruinous exploitation. **-zug,** *m.* predatory incursion, raid.
Räuber, *m.* (-s, -) robber, thief; pirate; brigand; sucker (*Hort.*). **-bande,** *f.* gang of thieves, band of robbers. **-ei,** *f.* robbery; depredation; brigandage. **-geschichte,** *f.* penny-dreadful; cock-and-bull story. **-hauptmann,** *m.* robber chief. **-höhle,** *f.* den of thieves. **-isch,** *adj.* thievish, rapacious, predatory. **-pack,** *n.* gang of robbers.
rauch, *adj.* (*used mainly in compounds*) shaggy. **-füßig,** *adj.* hairy-footed; plumiped (*Orn.*). **-waren,** *f.pl.,* **-werk,** *n.* furs, peltry. **-warenhändler,** *m.* furrier.
Rauch, *m.* smoke; fume, vapour, steam; (*dial.*) soot; (*Poet.*) haze; *in den - hängen,* smoke (-dry); (*fig.*) disregard; *in - aufgehen,* go up in smoke, (*fig.*) end in smoke, come to nothing. **-artig,** *adj.* smoky. **-belästigung,** *f.* smoke nuisance *or* pollution. **-bombe,** *f.* smoke-shell. **-dicht,** *adj.* smoke-tight. **-en,** 1. *v.n.* (*aux.* h.) smoke, fume, reek. 2. *v.a.* smoke. **-end,** *adj.* smoking, fuming. **-er,** *m.* smoker; (*coll.*) smoking-compartment. **-erabteil,** *n.* (& *m.*) smoking-compartment. **-fahne,** *f.* trail of smoke. **-fang,** *m.* chimney flue. **-farben,** *adj.* smoke-coloured, dingy. **-faß,** *n.* censer. **-fleisch,** *n.* smoked meat. **-frei,** *adj.* smokeless. **-gas,** *n.* flue-gas, gas of combustion. **-geschwärzt,** *adj.* smoke-stained. **-helm,** *m.* smoke helmet. **-ig,** *adj.* smoky. **-kammer,** *f.* smoking-room, smoke chamber, smoke-box (*in engines*). **-kanal,** *m.* smoke-flue, funnel. **-los,** *adj., see* **-frei.** **-nächte,** *f.pl.* nights

when spirits walk. **-opfer**, *n.* incense offering. **-pfanne**, *f.* incense burner. **-pulver**, *n.* fumigating powder. **-säule**, *f.* pillar *or* column of smoke. **-schieber**, *m.* damper, register (*of furnace*). **-schrift**, *f.* sky-writing (*Av.*). **-schwach**, *adj.* smokeless. **-schwaden**, *m.pl.* wisps of smoke. **-schwarz**, *adj.* black as soot. **-stube**, *f.* smoke-room. **-tabak**, *m.* tobacco. **-verbot**, *n.* ban on smoking. **-verbrennung**, *f.* consumption *or* elimination of smoke. **-verzehrer**, *m.* smoke-consumer, eliminator *or* remover. **-vorhang**, *m.*, **-wand**, *f.* smoke-screen (*Mil.*). **-werk** (*usually* **Räucherwerk**), *n.* incense. **-wirbel**, *m.pl.* swirl of smoke. **-zimmer**, *n.* smoke-room. **-zug**, *m.* flue.

räucher-n, 1. *v.a.* fumigate, smoke; smoke-dry, cure; *geräucherte Heringe*, smoked herrings, bloaters. 2. *v.n.* (*aux.* h.) burn incense. **-apparat**, *m.* fumigator. **-essig**, *m.* aromatic vinegar. **-faß**, *n.* censer. **-ig**, *adj.* smoky; tasting of smoke. **-kammer**, *f.* smoking *or* curing-room. **-kerze**, *f.* fumigating candle. **-pulver**, *n.* fumigating powder. **-ung**, *f.* fumigation; smoking, curing (*of food*). **-waren**, *f.pl.* smoked goods *or* food. **-werk**, *n.* perfumes, scents, perfumery; frankincense (*B.*).

Räud-e, *f.* (-en) scab, mange (*of dogs*), rubbers (*of sheep*). **-ig**, *adj.* scabby; mangy; (*fig.*) rotten, lousy, foul.

rauf, *adv.* & *sep. prefix*, (*coll.*) *see* **darauf, herauf.**

Raufe, *f.* (-n) hay-rack; hackle.

rauf-en, 1. *v.a.* pluck, pull out; *sich die Haare -en*, tear one's hair. 2. *v.r.* fight, scuffle, tussle. **-bold**, *m.*, **-degen**, *m.* bully, brawler, rowdy. **-erei**, *f.*, **-handel**, *m.* scuffle, fight, brawl. **-lust**, *f.*, **-sucht**, *f.* pugnacity. **-lustig**, *adj.* pugnacious.

rauh, *adj.* rough, uneven, rugged; inclement, cold, raw; coarse, unfinished; rude; hoarse, harsh; (*dial.*) raw, uncooked; *aus dem -en arbeiten*, rough-hew; *-e Behandlung*, harsh treatment; *-es Benehmen*, rude behaviour; *-e Gegenden*, wild, mountainous countryside; *-es Klima*, bleak climate; (*coll.*) *in -en Mengen*, in a large quantity; *-er Pfad*, rugged *or* bumpy path; *-e Sitten*, coarse manners; *-e Stimme*, harsh voice; *-e Tugend*, austere virtue; *-er Wind*, biting wind; *die -e Wirklichkeit*, harsh reality, the hard facts. **-bank**, *f.* jack-plane (*Carp.*). **-bein**, *n.* (*fig.*) rough diamond, tough egg. **-beinig**, *adj.* caddish, loutish. **-e**, *f.*, *see* **-zeit.** **-(h)eit**, *f.* rudeness, coarseness; hoarseness, harshness; inclemency, acerbity. **-en**, 1. *v.a.* roughen; card, tease, nap, dress (*cloth*). 2. *v.n.* (*aux.* h.) & *r.* (*dial.*) moult. **-frost**, *m.* (*dial.*), *see* **-reif.** **-haarig**, *adj.* hirsute; wire-haired (*dog*). **-igkeit**, *f.* roughness, unevenness, ruggedness. **-nächte**, *see* **Rauchnächte.** **-reif**, *m.* rime, hoar-frost. **-zeit**, *f.* moulting season.

Rauke, *f.* hedge mustard (*Eruca sativa*) (*Bot.*).

Raum, 1. *m.* (-(e)s, ⸚e) room, space; place; area; expanse; capacity, volume; hold (*of a ship*); accommodation; (*fig.*) scope, opportunity, sphere; *bestrichener* –, danger zone (*Mil.*); *feuerleerer* or *gedeckter* –, dead space (*Mil.*); *luftleerer* –, vacuum; – *geben*, give way (to), indulge (in), grant, yield (to); *seinen Neigungen – geben*, follow one's bent *or* one's inclinations; *einer Hoffnung – geben*, indulge in a hope. 2. *adj.*; (*Naut.*) *-e See*, open sea; *-er Wind*, following *or* favourable wind; *-es Feld*, open *or* clear field. **-analyse**, *f.* volumetric analysis. **-beständig**, *adj.* of constant volume, incompressible. **-bewetterung**, *f.* air conditioning. **-bild**, *n.* stereoscopic *or* panoramic picture, three-dimensional diagram. **-einheit**, *f.* unit of volume. **-en**, *v.n.* (*aux.* h.) veer *or* draw aft (*of wind*). **-ersparnis**, *f.* economy of space. **-flugzeug**, *n.* stratosphere aircraft. **-gehalt**, *m.* volumetric content. **-geometrie**, *f.* solid geometry. **-gewinn**, *m.* progress, advance, ground gained (*Mil.*). **-inhalt**, *m.* capacity, volume. **-kunst**, *f.* interior decoration. **-lehre**, *f.* geometry. **-mangel**, *m.* lack of space *or* room. **-maß**, *n.* measure of capacity. **-meter**, *n.* cubic metre. **-politik**, *f.* (*Nat. Soc.*) geopolitics. **-raffer**, *m.* telephoto lens. **-temperatur**, *f.* room temperature. **-verschwendung**, *f.* waste of space. **-welle**, *f.* propagating *or* non-directional wave (*Rad.*).

räum-en, *v.a.* clear away, remove; sell off (cheap), clear, clean up; make room, quit, leave, evacuate; *aus dem Wege -en*, remove (*obstacles*), make away with, liquidate (*a p.*); *das Feld -en*, quit the field; *beiseite -en*, put aside. **-boot**, *n.* mine-sweeper. (*Nav.*). **-ig**, *adj.* (*dial.* & *Poet.*) roomy, spacious. **-lich**, *adj.* spatial; volumetric, three-dimensional, in space; *-liches Sehen*, stereoscopic vision; *-liche Wirkung*, stereoscopic effect (*Opt.*). **-lichkeit**, *f.* extent, space; spaciousness; locality; (*pl.*) rooms, premises. **-pflug**, *m.* bulldozer. **-te**, *f.* offing, open sea; ship's hold, loading space; *die -te suchen*, stand out to sea. **-ung**, *f.* removing, clearing, leaving, quitting, removal; evacuation (*of population*). **-ungsausverkauf**, *m.* clearance sale.

raunen, *v.a.* & *n.* (*aux.* h.) whisper; *man raunt sich* (*Dat.*) *ins Ohr*, it is whispered, there is a rumour.

raunzen, *v.n.* (*coll.*) grumble, find fault, niggle, nag.

Raupe, *f.* (-en) caterpillar; grub, maggot; caterpillar track (*vehicle*); helmet crest; (*coll.*) whim, fancy, crazy notion. **-n**, *v.a.* clear of caterpillars. **-nantrieb**, *m.* caterpillar-drive. **-nfahrzeug**, *n.* full-tracked vehicle. **-nfraß**, *m.* damage done by caterpillars. **-ngängig**, *adj.* tracked (*of vehicles*). **-nhelm**, *m.* dragoon's crested helmet. **-nkette**, *f.* caterpillar-track. **-nschlepper**, *m.* caterpillar-tractor.

raus, *adv.* & *sep. prefix*, *coll. for* **heraus.** **-reißer**, *m.* good selling line. **-schmeißer**, *m.* (*sl.*) chucker-out.

Rausch, *m.* (-es, ⸚e) drunken fit, drunkenness, intoxication; delirium, frenzy, transport, ecstasy; *einen – haben*, be drunk; *im -e*, in one's cups; *sich* (*Dat.*) *einen – trinken*, get tipsy; *seinen – ausschlafen*, sleep it off; *im ersten* –, in the first rapture, transport *or* flush (of enthusiasm). **-beere**, *f.* crowberry (*Empetrum nigrum*) (*Bot.*). **-en**, *v.n.* (*aux.* h.) rush; rustle, murmur, roar, thunder; (*Poet.*) sough; (*aux.* s.) move with a rustle, swish. **-end**, *pr.p.* & *adj.* rustling; thundering, noisy; *-ender Beifall*, thunderous applause; *-ende Vergnügungen*, boisterous pleasures. **-gelb**, *n.* orpiment. **-gift**, *n.* narcotic. **-gold**, *n.* tinsel. **-mittel**, *n.* intoxicant. **-pfeife**, *f.*, **-werk**, *n.* loud alto (*in organs*). **-silber**, *n.* silver-leaf.

räuspern, *v.r.* (*aux. h.*) clear one's throat.

[1]**Raute**, *f.* rue (*Ruta*) (*Bot.*).

[2]**Raut-e**, *f.* lozenge(-shaped figure), diamond (*Cards*), rhombus, rhomb(oid); facet. **-en**, *v.a.* cut into facets. **-enbauer**, *m.* knave of diamonds (*Cards*). **-enfläche**, *f.* rhomb; facet. **-enförmig**, *adj.* rhomboid, rhombic, lozenge-shaped; *-enförmig schneiden*, cut in facets. **-ig**, *adj.* rhomboid, diamond-shaped; faceted.

Rayon, *m.* (-s, -s) radius, range (*Artil.*); district, area. **-ieren**, *v.a.* allocate, distribute. **-chef**, *m.* departmental head *or* manager.

Razz-ia, *f.* (-ien & *Austr. dial.* -ias) police-raid.

Reag-enz, *n.* (enzien) reagent. **-enzglas**, *n.* test-tube. **-enzpapier**, *n.* test-paper, litmus paper. **-ieren**, *v.a.* react, show a reaction; counteract; (*fig.*) *nicht -ieren auf*, not respond to.

Reaktion, *f.* (-en) reaction. **-är**, *adj.* & *m.* (-ärs, -äre) reactionary. **-smoment**, *n.* (engine) torque. **-sträge**, *adj.* slow to react, unresponsive.

real, *adj.* real, actual, substantial; material. **-e**, *n.* (-en) reality, something real. **-gymnasium**, *n.* secondary school with scientific bias. **-ien**, *pl.* realities, real facts, exact sciences; institutions and customs. **-injurie**, *f.* assault and battery. **-isieren**, *v.a.* realize, sell, convert into money; *einen Verkauf -isieren*, effect a sale. **-ismus**, *m.* realism. **-istisch**, *adj.* realistic. **-ität**, *f.* reality; (*pl.*) (*dial.*) real estate, landed property. **-iter**, *adv.* in reality. **-katalog**, *m.* subject catalogue. **-kenntnisse**, *f.pl.* factual knowledge. **-kredit**, *m.* mortgage. **-lexikon**, *n.* encyclopaedia. **-obligation**, *f.* mortgage (bond). **-politik**, *f.* realist politics. **-schule**, *f.* science *or* modern secondary school. **-steuer**, *f.* tax on real estate and commercial transactions. **-wert**, *m.* actual value.

Reb-e, *f.* (-en) vine, grape tendril. **-bau**, *m.* vine growing. **-eln**, *v.n.* (*dial.*) gather grapes. **-enbekränzt**, *adj.* vine-clad. **-engeländer**, *n.* vine-trellis. **-engott,** *m.* Bacchus. **-enhügel,** *m.* vine-clad hill, vine-yard. **-ensaft,** *m.* grape-juice; (*Poet.*) wine. **-enumsponnen,** *adj., see* **-enbekränzt.** **-huhn,** *n.* partridge. **-hühnervolk,** *n.* cóvey of partridges. **-laus,** *f.* phylloxera vastatrix. **-pfahl,** *m.* vine-prop. **-stock,** *m.* vine.

Rebell, *m.* (-en, -en) rebel; mutineer. **-ieren,** *v.n.* (*aux.* h.) rebel, revolt, mutiny. **-ion,** *f.* rebellion. **-isch,** *adj.* rebellious.

Rechen, 1. *m.* (-s, –) rake; rack (*for clothes*); grating (*of a weir*). 2. *v.a.* rake. **-stiel,** *m.* rake handle.

Rechen-aufgabe, *f.* sum, problem. **-brett,** *n.* abacus. **-buch,** *n.* arithmetic book. **-exempel,** *n., see* **-aufgabe.** **-fehler,** *m.* miscalculation, arithmetical error. **-heft,** *n.* sum book, arithmetic book. **-kammer,** *f.* audit-office. **-knecht,** *m.* ready reckoner. **-kunst,** *f.* arithmetic. **-künstler,** *m.* person good at figures. **-lehrer,** *m.* arithmetic teacher. **-maschine,** *f.* adding *or* calculating-machine. **-pfennig,** *m.* counter (*at cards*). **-schaft,** *f.* account; *einem -schaft schuldig sein,* be accountable to a p.; *einen zur -schaft ziehen* or *fordern,* call a p. to account; *-schaft ablegen* or *geben,* answer *or* account for, give an account of; *sich der -schaft entziehen,* dodge *or* evade the consequences. **-schaftsbericht,** *m.* statement of accounts. **-schieber,** *m.,* **-stab,** *m.* slide-rule. **-stelle,** *f.* computing centre. **-stunde,** *f.* arithmetic lesson. **-tabelle,** *f.* ready reckoner. **-zettel,** *m.* computing table.

rechn-en, 1. *v.a.* & *n.* (*aux.* h.) count, calculate, reckon, compute, figure, estimate, do sums; esteem, consider, hold (to be); rank, class (*zu* or *unter* with *or* among); (*auf eine S.* or *einen*) *-en,* count, depend *or* rely upon (a th. *or* a p.); *an einer Aufgabe -en,* work out a sum; *falsch -en,* miscalculate; *gegen einander -en,* balance, compare; *eins fürs* or *ins andre gerechnet,* taking *or* counting each (item) separately, omitting nothing; with one th. and another, considering everything; *alles in allem gerechnet,* considering everything, all in all; *-en lernen,* learn arithmetic; *mit etwas -en,* count upon *or* rely upon a th., reckon with a th.; *mit ihm ist nicht zu -en,* he cannot be relied on, there is no relying on him, you do not know where you are with him; *wir müssen damit -en, daß . . .,* we must take into account that . . ., we must be prepared for . . .; *mit dazu gerechnet,* inclusive of, thrown in; *eins zum andern -en,* add to, include, group *or* classify one thing with another; *wir -en es uns zur Ehre, daß,* we deem it an honour that. 2. *n.* arithmetic. **-er,** *m.* p. good at figures, reckoner, arithmetician. **-erisch,** *adj.* mathematical, analytical. **-ung,** *f.* calculation, computation; sum; account, bill, invoice, (*coll.*) reckoning; calculus; opinion; *-ung ablegen,* render an account; *eine -ung ausgleichen* or *aufgehen lassen,* strike a balance; *auf eigne -ung,* at one's own risk; *auf -ung und Gefahr,* for account and risk; *auf seine -ung kommen,* benefit (from *or* by), profit (from); *auf jemandes -ung setzen* or *stellen,* charge, place *or* put to a p.'s account; *eine -ung begleichen,* see *eine -ung saldieren*; *jemandem einen Strich durch die -ung machen,* frustrate a p.'s plans, put an end to a p.'s game; *seine -ung bei einer S. finden,* profit *or* benefit by a th., reap advantage from a th.; *-ung führen,* keep an account; *die -ung geht nicht auf,* the sum will not come out; *halbe -ung,* joint account, half-share; *in -ung bringen* or *stellen,* see *auf -ung setzen*; *auf* or *in feste -ung liefern,* supply and charge to account; *in -ung stehen mit,* have a running *or* ledger account with; *in -ung ziehen,* take into account; *laufende -ung,* current account; *laut -ung,* as per account; *die -ung ohne den Wirt machen,* reckon without one's host; *eine -ung saldieren,* settle, clear *or* square an account; *-ung tragen* (*with Dat.*), allow for, take into account, make allowances for. **-ungsabnahme,** *f.* audit(ing of accounts). **-ungsabschluß,** *m.* balancing *or* closing of accounts, balance-sheet. **-ungsart,** *f.* method of calculation; *die vier -ungsarten,* the four rules (*Arith.*). **-ungsauszug,** *m.* abstract *or* statement of accounts. **-ungsbeleg,** *m.* voucher. **-ungsbetrag,** *m.* sum total of an account, invoice amount. **-ungsbuch,** *n.* account-book. **-ungsfehler,** *m.* error in calculation. **-ungsführer,** *m.* accountant, book-keeper. **-ungsjahr,** *n.* financial *or* fiscal year. **-ungskammer,** *f.* government audit-office. **-ungsmäßig,** *adj.* in conformity with the books, according to calculation. **-ungsprüfer,** *m.* auditor, comptroller. **-ungsprüfung,** *f.* auditing. **-ungsrat,** *m.* senior government auditor *or* actuary. **-ungsrevisor,** *m.* auditor, actuary; *vereidigter -ungsrevisor,* chartered accountant. **-ungsstelle,** *f.* accounting-office. **-ungsvorlage,** *f.* submission of account. **-ungswesen,** *n.* book-keeping, accountancy, auditing, actuarial matters.

recht, 1. *adj.* right, right-hand; proper, correct, fitting, befitting, agreeable, suitable; true, real, thorough, genuine; just, lawful, legitimate; *mein -er Bruder,* my own brother (*opp. to half-brother*); *das geht nicht mit -en Dingen zu,* there is something not quite right there; *-e Ehefrau,* lawful wife; *der -e Glaube,* the true faith; *mir ist es –,* I agree to *or* with it, I am agreeable, that suits me fine; *wenn es Ihnen – ist,* if it is agreeable to you; *ist es so –?* will that do? *-er Winkel,* right angle; *zu -er Zeit,* in time, punctually; *zur -en Zeit,* in good time, just in time, in the nick of time. 2. *adv.* well, right; greatly, remarkably, very; quite, exactly, really, downright; *wenn ich es – bedenke,* when I come to think about it *or* to consider it properly; *– behalten,* be right in the end; *– und billig,* just and reasonable, fair; *nicht mehr als – und billig,* only fair; *erst –,* all the more, more than ever, especially; *– gern,* most willingly, with pleasure; *das geschieht dir –,* that serves you right; *– gut,* very good, quite well; *– haben,* be (in the) right; (*iron.*) *da kommst du mir – !* just what I expected; *es tut mir – leid,* I am truly sorry; (*so*) *– als ob,* just as if; *schlecht und –,* fairly good, not bad; *ich weiß nicht – wie . . .,* I do not quite know how . . .; *sie kommen – zeitig,* you (have) come very early (*see* **-zeitig**). 3. *n.* (-es, -e) right, privilege; claim, title; law; justice; administration of justice; *bürgerliches –,* civil code; *das gemeine –,* common law; *das geschriebene –,* statute law; *Gewohnheits–,* prescriptive law; *im -e sein,* be in the right; *mit –,* justly, rightly, with reason; *mit – sagen,* be correct in saying; *mit vollem* or *gutem –,* for good reasons; *Natur–,* natural law; *ohne –,* unjustly; *– sprechen,* dispense justice; (*Prov.*) *tue – und scheue niemand,* do (what is) right and shame the devil; *– über Leben und Tod,* power over life and death; *sich* (*Dat.*) *selbst – verschaffen,* take the law into one's own hands; *von -s wegen,* by right, in justice, by virtue of law; *einem – widerfahren lassen,* do a p. justice; *zu – bestehen,* be legitimate *or* valid; *zu seinem – kommen,* come into one's own. **-e,** *f.* right hand; right side; the Conservatives, the Right (*in politics*); *mit erhobener -en,* with the right hand uplifted; *zur -en,* on *or* to the right. **-e(r),** *m.* the right p., the very man; *Sie sind der -e,* you are the very man; (*iron.*) *du bist mir der -e!* you're a fine fellow, indeed! I wouldn't have thought it of you; *an den -en kommen,* light on the right man; meet with one's match; *mit einem blitzschnellen -en* (i.e. *Schlag*), with a lightning right (*Boxing*). **-e(s),** *n.* the proper, appropriate *or* real th.; *er dünkt sich etwas -es,* he thinks himself somebody; (*iron.*) *das half ihm auch 'was -es!* that was a great help, I'm sure! *etwas -es können,* understand one's job; *nichts -es wissen,* not know anything properly, (*coll.*) have no idea; *das -e meinen,* have the right idea; *das -e treffen,* hit the mark; *zum* or *nach dem -en sehen,* see that everything is all right *or* in order. **-eck,** *n.* rectangle. **-eckig,** *adj.* rectangular. **-en,** *v.n.* (*aux.* h.) go to law, litigate; contest, dispute, remonstrate, demand one's right. (*obs.*) **-ens** (*Gen. of* Recht); *es ist -ens,* it is right and proper; *ein Schein -ens,* a semblance of justice; *das ist bei uns -ens,* such is the law with us, that is the law of the land; *im Wege -ens,* by legal proceedings, by law. **-erhand,** *adv.* on the right-hand side. **-fertigen,** *v.a.* & *r.* (*insep.*) justify, vindicate, exculpate (o.s.). **-fertigung,** *f.* justification, vindication. **-geben,** *v.n.* admit, support, prove right. **-gläubig,** *adj.* orthodox. **-gläubigkeit,** *f.* orthodoxy. **-haben,** *v.n.* be right. **-haber,** *m.*

dogmatic person; disputer. **-haberei,** *f.* disputatiousness, obstinacy. **-haberisch,** *adj.* obstinate, positive, dogmatic(al). **-läufig,** *adv.* clockwise, running the normal course. **-lich,** *adj.* just, fair; honest, upright; lawful, legal, judicial; legitimate; proper. **-lichkeit,** *f.* integrity, honesty; fair play. **-linig,** *adj.* rectilinear. **-los,** *adj.* unjust, illegal; outside the pale of the law, outlawed; illegitimate. **-losigkeit,** *f.* illegality; outlawry. **-mäßig,** *adj.* legal, lawful, legitimate; just. **-mäßigkeit,** *f.* legality; legitimacy. **-s,** *adv.* on the right hand; to the right; *nach -s,* to the right; *-s halten!* keep to the right! *gleich -s um die Ecke,* (take) the first turning to the right; *die erste Straße -s,* the first street on the right; *-sher, von -s her,* from the right side; *-shin, nach -s hin,* towards *or* on the right; *-s schwenkt!* right wheel! (*Mil.*); *-s um (kehrt)!* right (about) turn! **-saltertümer,** *n.pl.* legal antiquities. **-sanhängig,** *adj.* pending judicial decision. **-sanspruch,** *m.* legal claim. **-sanwalt,** *m.* counsel, solicitor, attorney, lawyer. **-sausdruck,** *m.* legal term. **-saußen(stürmer),** *m.* outside right (*Footb.*). **-sbeflissene(r),** *m.* law-student. **-sbefugnis,** *f.* competency of a court. **-sbeistand,** *m.* counsel; legal adviser. **-sbelehrung,** *f.* summing up. **-sbeständig,** *adj.* valid, legal. **-sbetreuung,** *f.* legal aid, poor man's lawyer. **-sbeugung,** *f.* defeating the ends of the law. **-sboden,** *m.* legal basis. **-schaffen,** *adj.* righteous, upright, just, honest; solid, thorough, (*coll.*) mighty, mightily. **-schaffenheit,** *f.* integrity, honesty, uprightness; thoroughness. **-schreiben,** *v.n.* (*sep.*) spell correctly; (*but cf. er kann nicht - schreiben,* he cannot write properly, his writing is bad). **-schreibung,** *f.* spelling, orthography. **-sdrall,** *m.* clockwise rifling. **-sdrehend,** *adj.* clockwise, dextrorotatory. **-sdrehung,** *f.* clockwise rotation. **-seingriff,** *m.* encroachment upon a p.'s rights. **-seinwand,** *m.* demurrer, traverse, plea. **-ser,** *m.* (*coll.*) right-handed p. **-serfahren,** *adj.* versed in the law *or* in jurisprudence. **-sfähig,** *adj.* competent. **-sfähigkeit,** *f.* competence, legal rights. **-sfall,** *m.* suit, case. **-sfrage,** *f.* legal question, point of law. **-sgang,** *m.* legal procedure; proceedings. **-sgängig,** *adj.,* see **-sdrehend.** **-sgefühl,** *n.* sense of justice. **-sgelehrsamkeit,** *f.* jurisprudence. **-sgelehrt,** *adj.* versed in jurisprudence. **-sgelehrte(r),** *m.* lawyer, jurist. **-sgemäß,** *adv.* according to law. **-sgewinde,** *n.* right-hand thread. **-sgleichheit,** *f.* equality in the eyes of the law. **-sgrund,** *m.* legal argument. **-sgrundsatz,** *m.* legal maxim. **-sgültig,** *adj.* legal, valid, good in law. **-sgültigkeit,** *f.* validity (*Law*). **-sgutachten,** *n.* counsel's opinion. **-shandel,** *m.* (legal) action, lawsuit. **-shänder,** *m.* right-handed p. **-shändig,** *adj.* right-handed. **-sher,** *adv.,* see *von -s her.* **-shin,** *adv.,* see *nach - s hin.* **-sinnen (stürmer),** *m.* inside right (*Footb.*). **-skniff,** *m.* quibble, lawyer's dodge. **-skraft,** *f.* force of law; *-skraft erteilen,* confirm, validate. **-skräftig,** *adj.* legal, valid. **-slauf,** *m., see* **-sdrehung.** **-släufig,** *adj.* right-hand, to the right, clockwise. **-smittel,** *n.* legal remedy. **-snachfolger,** *m.* assign. **-sperson,** *f.* body corporate. **-spflege,** *f.* administration of justice. -(s)**sprechung,** *f.* administration of justice; jurisdiction. **-ssatz,** *m.* legal maxim. **-ssäure,** *f.* dextro-acid (*Chem.*). **-sschwenkung,** *f.* movement to the right (*Mil.*). **-ssprache,** *f.* legal terminology. **-sspruch,** *m.* sentence, judgement, verdict. **-sstaat,** *m.* constitutional state. **-ssteuerung,** *f.* right-hand drive (*Motor.*). **-sstreit,** *m.* action, lawsuit. **-stitel,** *m.* legal title **-sungültig,** *adj.* illegal, invalid. **-surkunde,** *f.* legal document; patent. **-sverdreher,** *m.* pettifogging lawyer, caviller. **-sverfassung,** *f.* judicial system, code of laws, judicature. **-svertreter,** *m.* proxy. **-sverwalter,** *m.* administrator of justice. **-svorbehalt,** *m.* legal reservation. **-swahrer,** *m.* (*Nat. Soc.*) lawyer. **-sweg,** *m.* course of law, legal procedure; *den -sweg beschreiten,* go to law, take legal proceedings *or* steps; *unter Ausschluß des -sweges,* admitting of no appeal. **-sweisend,** *adj.* true (*of a course*) (*Navig.*). **-swidrig,** *adj.* illegal. **-swissenschaft,** *f.* jurisprudence. **-szuständigkeit,** *f.* competence. **-szwang,** *m.* legal compulsion. **-wink(e)lig,** *adj.* rectangular. **-zeitig,** *adj.* prompt, timely, opportune, seasonable, in (good) time, punctually, in due course.

Reck, *n.* (-(e)s, -e) horizontal bar (*Gymn.*), rack, stretcher. **-e,** *m.* (-n, -n) valiant warrior, hero. **-en,** 1. *v.a.* stretch, extend; rack; *die Glieder -en,* stretch one's limbs; *den Kopf in die Höhe -en,* crane one's neck. 2. *v.r.* stretch o.s. **-enhaft,** *adj.* valiant, doughty. **-probe,** *f.* elongation test.

Redakt-eur, *m.* (-s, -e & -s) editor. **-ion,** *f.* editing; editor's office; editorial staff; drawing up (*of deeds, etc.*); *nach Schluß der -ion eingelaufene Nachrichten,* stop-press news. **-ionell,** *adj.* editorial. **-ionsschluß,** *m.* time of going to press; *-ionsschluß machen,* (*coll.*) put a paper to bed.

Red-e, *f.* (-n) words, talk, discourse, conversation; speech, address, oration; utterance, report, rumour; *alltägliche -e(weise),* common parlance; *die -e fiel* or *kam auf diesen Gegenstand,* the conversation turned upon this subject; *gebundene -e,* verse, poetry; *-e und Gegen-e,* assertion and contradiction, pros and cons; *die -e geht,* it is said, rumour has it; *gehobene -e,* elevated style; *eine -e halten,* make a speech; *in die -e fallen,* interrupt a p.; *in -e stehen,* be under discussion, be in question; *wovon ist die -e?* what are you talking about? what is the point at issue? *davon kann keine -e sein,* that is out of the question; *darüber -e (und Antwort) stehen,* be answerable for it, give an account of it; *der in -e stehende Gegenstand,* the subject under discussion *or* in question; *ungebundene -e,* prose; *nicht der -e wert,* not worth mentioning; *es wird die -e davon sein,* we shall speak of it, we shall turn to this point; *einen zur -e kommen lassen,* let a p. speak; *zur -e stellen,* call to account, take (a p.) to task. **-ebegabt,** *adj.* eloquent. **-efertig,** *adj.* fluent, eloquent, glib. **-efigur,** *f.* figure of speech, metaphorical expression. **-efluß,** *m.* flow of words, fluency, volubility. **-efreiheit,** *f.* liberty of speech. **-egabe,** *f.* fluency, (*coll.*) gift of the gab. **-egewandt,** *adj.,* see **-efertig.** **-egewandtheit,** *f.* fluency. **-ekunst,** *f.* rhetoric. **-elustig,** *adj.* fond of talking, talkative. **-en,** 1. *v.a.* & *n.* (*aux.* h.) speak; talk; converse; discourse; *sich (Dat.) einen Prozeß an den Hals -en,* let one's tongue get one into trouble; *Sie haben gut -en,* it is all very well for you to talk; *einem ins Gewissen -en,* admonish a p. seriously, appeal to a p.'s conscience; *in den Tag hinein -en,* talk at random; *etwas in den Wind -en,* beat the air; *in die Wolle hinein -en,* talk into the blue; *ein langes und breites über eine S. -en,* discuss s.th. at great length; *darüber läßt sich -en,* we can talk about that (later), that must be discussed; *mit sich -en lassen,* listen to reason; *viel von sich -en machen,* cause a great stir; *einem nach dem Munde -en,* echo a p.'s opinion, talk in a way that suits *or* pleases s.o.; *-en wie einem der Schnabel gewachsen ist,* talk without inhibitions, (*sl.*) shoot off one's mouth; *sich um den Hals -en,* talk a noose round one's neck; *aus ihm -et die Verzweiflung,* his is the language of despair; (*einer Person* or *Sache*) *das Wort -en,* put in a (good) word for, advocate, recommend. 2. *subst. n.* talking, speaking; speech; *viel -ens von etwas machen,* make a great pother *or* fuss about a th.; *all' Ihr -en ist umsonst,* you are wasting your words; *das -en wird ihm schwer,* he speaks with difficulty. **-end,** *pr.p.* & *adj.* speaking; expressive; *die -ende Person,* the interlocutor *or* speaker; *-ende Künste,* poetry and music, the communicative arts. **-ensart,** *f.* expression, phrase; idiom, figure of speech; phraseology; *bloße -ensarten,* empty talk *or* phrases. **-erei,** *f.* rubbish, nonsense, empty talk. **-escheu,** *adj.* reticent, taciturn. **-eschmuck,** *m.* rhetorical embellishment. **-eschrift,** *f.* parliamentary shorthand. **-eschwulst,** *m.* bombast. **-eschwung,** *m.* rhetorical flight. **-eteil,** *m.* part of speech (*Gram.*). **-eübung,** *f.* exercise in speaking, declamation. **-eweise,** *f.* manner of speaking, mode of expression, style. **-ewendung,** *f.* turn of speech, phrase, idiom. **-lich,** *adj., see* **redlich.** **-ner,** *m.* (-s, -) orator, speaker. **-nerbühne,** *f.* platform, rostrum. **-nergabe,** *f.* oratorical gift, (*hum.*) gift of the gab.

-nerisch, *adj.* oratorical, rhetorical. **-nerkunst,** *f.* rhetoric. **-nertalent,** *n., see* **-nergabe. -selig,** *adj.* talkative, loquacious, chatty. **-seligkeit,** *f.* talkativeness, loquacity.
redigieren, *v.a.* edit, prepare for the press, revise.
redlich, *adj.* honest; sincere, upright, candid, just. **-keit,** *f.* honesty; sincerity.
Redoute, *f.* (-n) redoubt (*Fort.*); fancy-dress ball.
Reduktion, *f.* (-en) reduction, diminution. **-sventil,** *n.* reduction valve.
reduzier-bar, *adj.* reducible. **-en,** 1. *v.a.* reduce (*auf* (*Acc.*), to). **-t,** *p.p.* & *adj.* reduced, vestigial; *er sieht sehr -t aus,* he looks very down-at-heel. 2. *v.r.* be(come) reduced, atrophy.
ree, *int.* about ship! (*Naut.*).
Reede, *f.* (-n) roadstead, roads (*Naut.*); *auf der - liegen,* ride at anchor (*in the roads*). **-n,** *v.a.* fit out ship. **-r,** *m.* shipowner. **-rei,** *f.* shipping-office; shipping company *or* line; fitting out of a merchantman; *-rei betreiben,* be in the shipping trade. **-reiflagge,** *f.* house flag.
Reef, *n., see* **Reff,** 2.
Reeling, *f., see* **Reling.**
reell [*pron.* re'ɛl] *adj.* real, essential; safe, sound, solid, respectable; honourable, fair, honest, just; *-e Bedienung,* fair dealing; *-es Geschäft,* respectable *or* reliable firm; *-e Waren,* sound wares. (*C.L.*) **-ität,** *f.* solidity, reliability.
Reep, *n.* (-(e)s, -e) (*dial.*) rope. **-schläger,** *m.* rope-maker.
Refektorium, *n.* (-s, -ien) refectory.
Refer-at, *n.* (-(e)s, -e) lecture, talk, report (*usually verbal*); abstract, review (*of a book*). **-endar,** *m.* (-s, -e) junior barrister; teacher on probation. **-endum,** *n.* (*Swiss dial.*) plebiscite. **-ent,** *m.* expert adviser, reporter; reviewer; lecturer, reader of a (scholarly) paper (at a meeting). **-enz,** *f.* (-en) reference, testimonial; referee (*person supplying a reference*). **-ieren,** *v.a.* & *n.* (*aux.* h.) report, read a paper, give a lecture; sum up.
Reff, *n.* (-s, -e) 1. frame for carrying loads on the back. 2. reef (*Naut.*). 3. (*coll.*) crone, baggage. **-en,** *v.a.* reef (*Naut.*).
Reflekt-ant, *m.* (-en, -en) prospective purchaser *or* customer. **-ieren,** *v.a.* & *n.* (*aux.* h.) consider, ponder, reflect (*über,* upon); think of buying; *auf* (*eine S.*) *-ieren,* have (a th.) in view, have one's eye on (a th.).
Reflex, *m.* (-es, -e) reflex, reflection. **-bewegung,** *f.* reflex action *or* movement. **-ion,** *f.* reflection, contemplation; reflex. **-ionswinkel,** *m.* angle of reflection. **-kette,** *f.* chain of reflexes. **-licht,** *n.* reflected light. **-iv,** *adj.*, **-iv(um),** *n.* reflexive (*pronoun*) (*Gram.*); reflex (*response*).
Reform, *f.* (-en) reform. **-ation,** *f.* reformation. **-ator,** *m.* (-s, -en) (religious) reformer. **-atorisch,** *adj.* reformatory. **-er,** *m.* (social) reformer. **-ieren,** *v.a.* reform. **-ierte(r),** *m.* Calvinist, member of the Reformed Church. **-kleidung,** *f.* rational dress.
refrakt-är, *adj.* refractory. **-ion,** *f.* refraction. **-or,** *m.* (-s, -en) refracting *or* astronomical telescope.
refrigieren, *v.a.* & *n.* freeze, refrigerate.
¹Regal, *n.* (-(e)s, -ien) royal prerogative. **-ieren,** *v.a.* & *r.* regale (o.s.) (*mit,* with); treat (*mit,* to).
²Regal, *n.* (-s, -e) book-shelf; portable organ.
reg-e, *adj.* astir, in motion, moving, movable; lively, alert, quick, nimble, brisk, active; industrious, enthusiastic, zealous; *-e machen,* stir up, excite; *-e sein,* be up and doing; *der Wunsch wurde in ihm -e,* he was seized with a desire to; *-e Kauflust,* brisk demand; *-er Verstand,* alert *or* active mind. **-en,** 1. *v.a.* move, stir; animate, rouse. 2. *v.r.* stir, move, be in motion, be active; make itself felt; *er darf sich nicht -en,* he must not move; *es -t sich kein Lüftchen,* not a breath of air is stirring. **-sam,** *adj.* active, nimble, agile, quick, mobile. **-samkeit,** *f.* agility, activity, alertness. **-ung,** *f.* motion, movement; stirring, impulse; agitation, emotion. **-(ungs)los,** *adj.* still, motionless.
Regel, *f.* (-n) rule, standard; regulation, precept, principle, law; menses, menstruation (*Med.*); *in der -,* as a rule, usually, ordinarily; *-n des Fußballspieles,* rules of football. **-bar,** *adj.* adjustable, variable. **-buch,** *n.* book of rules. **-detri,** *f.* rule of three (*Arith.*). **-last,** *f.* permissible load, normal load. **-los,** *adj.* irregular, anomalous. **-losigkeit,** *f.* irregularity. **-mäßig,** 1. *adj.* regular, well proportioned; ordinary, normal. 2. *adv.* regularly, always. **-mäßigkeit,** *f.* regularity, uniformity, conformity to law. **-n,** 1. *v.a.* regulate, adjust, settle, arrange, fix, order, determine, govern. 2. *v.r.* *sich -n nach,* be ruled *or* guided by. **-recht,** *adj.* according to rule; normal, regular, orderly; proper, correct; thoroughgoing; *-rechte Schlacht,* pitched battle. **-spur,** *f.* standard gauge (*Railw.*). **-tank,** *m.* trimming *or* compensating tank (*Naut.*). **-ung,** *f.* adjustment, regulation, settlement. **-widerstand,** *m.* variable resistor, rheostat (*Rad.*). **-widrig,** *adj.* contrary to rule, irregular, abnormal; foul (*Sport*). **-zelle,** *f. see* **-tank.**
Regen, *m.* rain; shower; downpour; precipitation (*Meteor.*); *vom - in die Traufe,* out of the frying-pan into the fire. **-anlage,** *f.* automatic fire-extinguishing plant. **-bogen,** *m.* rainbow. **-bogenfarben,** *f.pl.* prismatic colours; *in den -bogenfarben,* iridescent. **-bogenhaut,** *f.* iris (*Anat.*). **-decke,** *f.* rainproof cover, tarpaulin. **-dicht,** *adj.* waterproof, rainproof. **-fall,** *m.* rainfall, precipitation. **-fang,** *m.* rainwater cistern. **-faß,** *n.* water-butt. **-flut,** *f.* torrent of rain. **-guß,** *m.* downpour. **-haut,** *f.* oilskin. **-mantel,** *m.* waterproof, mackintosh. **-messer,** *m.* rain-gauge. **-pfeifer,** *m.* golden plover (*Orn.*). **-schauer,** *m.* shower (of rain). **-schirm,** *m.* umbrella. **-schirmgestell,** *n.* umbrella frame. **-schirmständer,** *m.* umbrella-stand. **-schwanger,** *adj.*, **-schwer,** *adj.* rain-bearing (*cloud*). **-tag,** *m.* rainy day. **-tonne,** *f* water-butt. **-tropfen,** *m.* rain-drop. **-verdeck,** *n.* carriage-hood. **-wasser,** *n.* rain-water. **-wetter,** *n.* rainy weather. **-wurm,** *m.* earthworm. **-zeit,** *f.* rainy season.
Regener-at, *n.* reclaimed substance. **-ieren,** *v.a.* reclaim, recover, salve, regenerate.
Regent, *m.* (-en, -en) regent; sovereign, reigning prince. **-schaft,** *f.* regency, regentship.
Reg-ie [*pron.* re'ʒi:], *f.* (-ien & *Austr. dial.* -ieen) state monopoly; management, administration; production (*Theat.*). **-iebetrieb,** *m.* state *or* public undertaking. **-iekosten,** *f.pl.* government expenses. **-iespesen,** *pl.* administrative *or* operating costs. **-ieverschluß,** *m.* bond. **-isseur,** *m.* (-s, -e) stage-manager, producer.
regier-en, 1. *v.a.* regulate, conduct, manage, steer; rule, govern. 2. *v.n.* (*aux.* h.) reign, rule. **-erei,** *f.* misgovernment, red-tape. **-ung,** *f.* government, reign, rule, administration, management, direction. **-ungsantritt,** *m.* accession (*to the throne*). **-ungsbeamte(r),** *m.* government official, civil servant; (*Swiss dial.*) cantonal government. **-ungsbezirk,** *m.* administrative area. **-ungsbildung,** *f.* formation of a cabinet. **-ungsblatt,** *n.* official journal. **-ungsform,** *f.* form of government. **-ungsgebäude,** *n.* government offices. **-ungsgegner,** *m.* member of the opposition. **-ungskreise,** *m.pl.* government circles. **-ungspartei,** *f.* party in power. **-ungspaß,** *m.* diplomatic passport. **-ungsrat,** *m.* administrative adviser, privy councillor. **-ungsseite,** *f.*; *von -ungsseite,* issuing from the government. **-ungssitz,** *m.* seat of government. **-ungswechsel,** *m.* change of government. **-ungszeit,** *f.* reign.
Regiment, *n.* 1. (-s, -e) power, authority; *das - haben* or *führen,* rule, command, have control; *sie führt das -,* she wears the breeches. 2. (-s, -er) regiment (*of soldiers*). **-sarzt,** *m.* regimental medical officer. **-sbefehl,** *m.* regimental order. **-schef,** *m.* colonel-in-chief, honorary colonel. **-skapelle,** *f.*, **-smusik,** *f.* military *or* regimental band. **-skommandeur,** *m.* regimental commander, colonel. **-sschreiber,** *m.* orderly-room sergeant. **-stisch,** *m.* officers' mess. **-suniform,** *f.* regimentals. **-s(un)kosten,** *pl.* government expense; (*iron.*) other people's expense (*auf,* at).
Regisseur, *see* **Regie.**
Regist-er, *n.* (-ers, -er) table of contents, index;

register, record; list, catalogue; damper; stop (*Org.*); *alle –er spielen lassen* or *ziehen*, make every effort; do one's utmost, leave no stone unturned; *ins alte –er gehören*, be obsolete, old-fashioned *or* out of date; *ich stehe bei ihr im schwarzen –er*, I am in her bad books. **–erstimme,** *f.*, **–erzug,** *m.* register (*Org.*). **–ertonnen,** *f.pl.* tons burden, register tons (*Naut.*). **–rande,** *f.* (-n) order-book. **–rator,** *m.* registrar, recorder. **–ratur,** *f.* registry *or* record-office; filing cabinet. **–rieren,** *v.a.* register, record, index, file, place on record. **–rierapparat,** *m.* recording-apparatus. **–rierballon,** *m.* pilot-balloon (*Meteor.*). **–rierkasse,** *f.* cash register. **–rierthermometer,** *n.* self-registering thermometer.

Reglement [*pron.* reglə'mɑ̃] *n.* (-s, -s) regulation(s); by-law. **–arisch,** *adj.*, *see* **–mäßig.** **–ieren,** *v.a.* bring under official control *or* supervision. **–mäßig,** *adj.* according to regulations. **–widrig,** *adj.* contrary to regulations.

Regler, *m.* (-s, –) regulator, trimmer, compensator; governor (*Mach.*); corrector (*Artil.*). **–tank,** *m.* trimming tank (*Naut.*). **–teilung,** *f.* correction scale (*Artil.*).

regn–en, *v.a.* & *n.* (*aux.* h.) & *imp.* rain. **–erdüse,** *f.* spray nozzle. **–erisch,** *adj.* rainy, showery.

Regre–ß, *m.* (-sses, -sse) recourse, remedy; (*C.L.*) *–ß nehmen an* (*Dat.*), make claim on *or* come upon (*the endorser*). **–ßanspruch,** *m.*, **–ßrecht,** *n.* right of recovery, right to compensation. **–ssiv,** *adj.* regressive, degenerate. **–ßnehmer,** *m.* claimant. **–ßpflichtig,** *adj.* liable for compensation.

regul–är, *adj.* regular. **–ativ,** *n.* (-s, -e) regulation, rule. **–ator,** *m.* governor, regulator, compensator, trimmer. **–ierbar,** *adj.* adjustable. **–ieren,** *v.a.* regulate, adjust, control. **–ierhebel,** *m.* choke (control) (*Motor.*), adjusting handle, lever *or* knob. **–ierschraube,** *f.* adjusting screw, set-screw. **–iervorrichtung,** *f.* regulating device.

Reh, *n.* (-(e)s, -e) roe (deer); *ein Rudel –e*, a herd of deer. **–blatt,** *n.* shoulder of venison. **–bock,** *m.* roebuck. **–braten,** *m.* roast venison. **–braun,** *adj.*, **–farben,** *adj.*, **–farbig,** *adj.* fawn(-coloured). **–fell,** *n.* doeskin. **–fleisch,** *n.* venison. **–geiß,** *f.* doe. **–kalb,** *n.*, **–kitz,** *n.*, **–kitze,** *f.* fawn. **–keule,** *f.* haunch of venison. **–leder,** *n.* doeskin, buckskin. **–ling,** *m.* chanterelle. **–posten,** *pl.* buckshot. **–rücken,** *m.* saddle of venison. **–schlegel,** *m.*, *see* **–keule.** **–wild,** *n.* deer. **–ziege,** *f.* doe. **–ziemer,** *m.* loin of venison.

Rehe, *f.* founder (*Vet.*); (*dial.*) (-n) plough-tail; (*dial.*) doe.

Reib–e, *f.* (-n), **–eisen,** *n.* grater, scraper, rasp. **–en,** 1. *ir.v.a.* rub, grate, scour, grind; bray, pulverize; gall, chafe; *sich* (*Dat.*) *die Hände wund –en*, rub the skin off one's hands, chafe one's hands; *einem etwas unter die Nase –en*, tell s.o. a th. to his face, bring a th. home to a p.; *ein ganz geriebener Kerl*, a smooth customer. 2. *v.r.* *sich an einem –en*, provoke, annoy, irritate, vex a p. **–ahle,** *f.* reamer, broach. **–elaut,** *m.* fricative (consonant), spirant. **–epulver,** *n.* abrasive powder. **–er,** *m.* rubber, grater, grinder, pestle. **–erei,** *f.* provocation, (constant) friction. **–festigkeit,** *f.* resistance to abrasion. **–fläche,** *f.* rubbing *or* striking surface; cartridge base. **–keule,** *f.* pestle. **–maschine,** *f.*, **–mühle,** *f.* grating machine, grinding mill. **–schale,** *f.* mortar. **–sel,** *n.* scourings, scrapings. **–stein,** *m.*, *see* **–keule.** **–stellen,** *pl.* abrasion marks. **–ung,** *f.* rubbing, friction; abrasion, attrition; trituration; (*fig.*) clash, difficulty, tension. **–ungsbeiwert,** *m.* coefficient of friction. **–ungsbremse,** *f.* friction-brake. **–ungselektrizität,** *f.* frictional electricity. **–ungsfläche,** *f.* cause of annoyance, source of irritation. **–ungskoeffizient,** *m.* coefficient of friction. **–ungskupplung,** *f.* friction-clutch. **–ungslos,** *adj.* free from friction, smooth, smooth-running. **–ungsverlust,** *m.* loss by friction. **–ungswiderstand,** *m.* frictional resistance. **–zünder,** *m.* friction primer.

reich, *adj.* rich, wealthy; abundant, copious; opulent, full, ample, exuberant, plentiful, fertile, abounding in, concentrated; *– an* (*Dat.*) *Erfahrung*, rich in experience; *–e Anzahl*, large number; *ein –er*, a rich man; *die –en*, the well-to-do people, the wealthy. **–begütert,** *adj.* owning large estates. **–beschenkt,** *adj.* richly endowed. **–besetzt,** *adj.* well-spread (*table*). **–golden,** *adj.* old-gold. **–haltig,** *adj.* copious, abundant, plentiful, profuse; comprehensive. **–haltigkeit,** *f.* copiousness, abundance, plentifulness. **–lich,** *adj.* ample, profuse, copious, plentiful, abundant; *–lich Zeit haben*, have plenty of time; *sein –liches Auskommen haben*, be well off. **–lichkeit,** *f.* plentifulness, abundance. **–tum,** *m.* (-s, ¨er) riches, wealth; opulence, abundance; richness. **–verziert,** *adj.* profusely decorated; florid.

Reich, *n.* (-(e)s, -e) state, realm, empire, kingdom; reign; *Deutsches –*, Germany; *das Dritte –*, the Third Reich; *– der Geister*, realm of spirits, spirit world; *das – Gottes*, the Kingdom of God; *das Heilige Römische – (Deutscher Nation)*, the Holy Roman Empire (843–1806); *das deutsche Kaiser–*, the German Empire (1871–1918); *das – der Mitte*, China; *das – der Schatten*, the shades, Hades, the underworld; *Pflanzen–*, vegetable kingdom; *Tier–*, animal kingdom. **–s–,** (*as a prefix* =) (*until* 1918) imperial; (*subsequently*) National, Federal; State (*in contrast to the separate States*). **–sacht,** *f.* imperial ban; *in die –sacht tun*, outlaw. **–sadler,** *m.* German eagle, imperial eagle. **–sangehörige(r),** *m.* German natural *or* subject. **–sangehörigkeit,** *f.* German nationality. **–angelegenheiten,** *f.pl.* national affairs, Federal business. **–sanleihe,** *f.* German government loan. **–sanwalt,** *m.* public prosecutor. **–sanzeiger,** *m.* official gazette. **–sapfel,** *m.* imperial orb. **–sarbeitsminister,** *m.* German Minister of Labour. **–sarchiv,** *n.* National Records Office. **–sarmee,** *f.* imperial army. **–sautobahn,** *f.* arterial motor-road. **–sbahn,** *f.* German railways. **–sbank,** *f.* German National Bank. **–sbanner,** *n.* ex-service mens' association (1924–33). **–sbehörden,** *f.pl.* federal authorities. **–sbund,** *m.* national league. **–sbürger,** *m.* German subject *or* national. **–sdeutsche(r),** *m.* German (*not Austrian*). **–sehrenmal,** *n.* national cenotaph. **–serbhofgesetz,** *n.* (*Nat. Soc.*) law of entail. **–sfarben,** *f.pl.*, **–sflagge,** *f.* national colours *or* flag. **–sfrei,** *adj.* subject to the emperor only. **–sfreiherr,** *m.*, **–sfürst,** *m.* baron, prince of the Holy Roman Empire. **–sgebiet,** *n.* territory of the Reich. **–sgericht,** *n.* Supreme Court of Justice. **–sgesetz,** *n.* federal law. **–sgesundheitsamt,** *n.* Department of Public Health. **–shaushalt,** *m.* Federal budget. **–sheer,** *n.* German army. **–shilfe,** *f.* government subsidies. **–skammergericht,** *n.* Supreme Court (*of Holy Roman Empire*). **–skanzlei,** *f.* State Chancery. **–skanzler,** *m.* Chancellor. **–skleinodien,** *n.pl.* imperial insignia, crown jewels. **–skulturkammer,** *f.* (*Nat. Soc.*) Chamber for Arts and Culture. **–skursbuch,** *n.* German railway guide. **–skurzschrift,** *f.* official shorthand system. **–sland,** *n.*; *die –lande*, the imperial provinces (*Alsace and Lorraine*, 1871–1918). **–slehen,** *n.* fief of the empire. **–smarine,** *f.* German navy. **–smark,** *f.* German Mark, stabilized currency (*after* 1924). **–sminister,** *m.* Federal Minister; *–minister des Auswärtigen*, Reich Minister of Foreign Affairs; *–sminister des Innern*, Reich Minister of the Interior. **–sministerium,** *n.* Ministry of the Reich. **–soffen,** *adj.* open to all Germans (*as athletic contest*). **–spartei,** *f.* National(ist) Party (1871–1933). **–spost,** *f.* German postal service. **–spostdirektion,** *f.* Postmaster General's Department. **–spräsident,** *m.* President of the Republic. **–srat,** *m.* Federal Council (1918–33). **–srecht,** *n.* federal law. **–sritter,** *m.* knight of the (Holy Roman) Empire. **–srundfunkgesellschaft,** *f.* German Broadcasting Company. **–ssender,** *m.* German radio station. **–sstadt,** *f.* imperial city. **–sstände,** *m.pl.* princes and dignitaries of the Imperial Diet. **–sstatthalter,** *m.* federal representative in the states. **–stag,** *m.* Imperial Diet (*of Holy Roman Empire*); German Parliament. **–stagsabgeordnete(r),** *m.* member of Parliament. **–stagsabschied,** *m.* recess of an Imperial Diet. **–struppen,** *f.pl.* imperial troops. **–sun-**

mittelbar, *adj.*, *see* **–sfrei. –sverband,** *m.* National Federation. **–sverfassung,** *f.* constitution of the Reich. **–sverkehrswoche,** *f.* Safety First Week. **–sverweser,** *m.* Imperial Administrator (*1848–49*). **–swährung,** *f.* standard currency. **–swappen,** *n.* imperial arms. **–swehr,** *f.* German army and navy (*1919–35*).

reich–en, 1. *v.a.* reach; (*einem etwas*) *–en,* give, present, pass, hand; *das Abendmahl –en,* administer the sacrament; *Almosen –en,* bestow alms; *einem die Hand –en,* hold out one's hand to a p.; *er kann ihm das Wasser nicht –en,* he is not fit to hold a candle to him, he is no match for him. 2. *v.n.* (*aux.* h.) reach, extend to; suffice, be enough, last, hold out; *–en nach,* stretch out one's hand for *or* towards; *das –t,* that will do; *–t das nicht?* is that not enough? *er –t mir bis an die Schulter,* he comes to my shoulder. **–weite,** *f.* reach, range, coverage.

reif, *adj.* ripe, mature, mellow; fully developed, ready; *– werden,* ripen, become ripe, mature; season, mellow; *ein Mann in –eren Jahren,* a middle-aged man. **–e,** *f.* maturity, puberty; ripeness, mellowness; *zur –e bringen,* ripen. **–ei,** *n.* mature ovum. **–en,** 1. *v.a.* ripen. 2. *v.n.* (*aux.* s.) mature, ripen, mellow. **–eprüfung,** *f.* leaving examination, school certificate examination. **–ezeugnis,** *n.* (school) leaving certificate. **–ezustand,** *m.* maturation, ripeness. **–lich,** *adj.* careful, mature, thorough.

[1]**Reif,** *m.* (-(e)s, -e) hoar-frost; bloom (*on fruit*). **–en,** *v.n. & imp.* be covered *or* become white with hoar-frost.

[2]**Reif,** *m.* (-(e)s, -e) (*poet.*), *see* **–en,** *m.* **–eln,** *v.a.* flute, channel (*Arch.*). **–(e)lung,** *f.* flute, fluting, groove (*Arch.*). **–en,** 1. *m.* (-ens, -en) ring, circle, collar, hoop, tyre; *– legen um,* hoop (*a cask, etc.*); *den – schlagen* or (*mit dem*) *– spielen,* trundle *or* drive a hoop. 2. *v.a.* (*dial.*) hoop; put a rim on. 3. *v.n.* play with a hoop. **–enpanne,** *f.*, **–enschaden,** *m.* puncture (*of tyre*). **–enspiel,** *n.* trundling the hoop. **–enspringen,** *n.* jumping through hoops. **–rock,** *m.* crinoline.

Reigen, *m.* (-s, –) round dance; roundelay; *den – eröffnen,* lead the dance, (*fig.*) take the lead.

Reih–e, *f.* (-en) row, rank, line, file; order, tier, range, suite, progression, set, series, succession, sequence, train (*of thought, etc.*); string (*of beads*); innings (*Crick.*); *die –e ist an mir, ich bin an der –e,* it is my turn; *Sie werden an die –e kommen, die –e kommt an dich,* your turn will come; *aus* or *außer der –e,* out of turn, out of order; *bunte –e,* paired off, ladies and gentlemen alternately; *– und Glied,* rank and file; *in –en,* in file (*Mil.*), in series (*Elec.*); *in einer –e,* in a row *or* line; *nach der –e, der –e nach,* in succession, successively, in rotation, in turn, by turns. **–en,** 1. (*dial.*) *m.* (-ens, -en), see **Reigen;** *der nächtliche –en,* the nocturnal dance. 2. *m.* arch of the foot. 3. *v.a.* arrange in a row *or* series; range; string (*pearls, etc.*); tack, baste. 4. *v.r.* rank, form a row. **–enband,** *m.* volume in a series. **–endorf,** *n.* Franconian form of settlement. **–enfabrikation,** *f.*, **–enfertigung,** *f.* serial production. **–enfolge,** *f.* (order of) succession, order, sequence, series. **–enhäuserbau,** *m.* ribbon building *or* development. **–enherstellung,** *f.*, *see* **–enfertigung. –enmotor,** *m.* in-line engine. **–enschaltung,** *f.* series-connexion (*Elec.*). **–enschlußmotor,** *m.* series motor (*Elec.*). **–enstandmotor,** *m.*, *see* **–enmotor. –entanz,** *m.* round dance. **–enweise,** *adv.* in rows; by turns. **–enwurf,** *m.* stick of bombs (*Av.*). **–faden,** *m.* tacking thread. **–ig,** *adj. suff.* -breasted (*of a coat*). **–um,** *adv.* in succession, in *or* by turns.

Reiher, *m.* (-s, –) heron. **–beize,** *f.* heron-hawking. **–busch,** *m.* tuft of heron's feathers. **–feder,** *f.* aigrette. **–horst,** *m.*, **–stand,** *m.* heronry. **–schnabel,** *m.* cranesbill (*Bot.*).

Reim, *m.* (-s, -e) rhyme; *männlicher* or *stumpfer –,* masculine rhyme; *weiblicher* or *klingender –,* feminine rhyme; *rührender –,* identical rhyme. **–en,** *v.a., r., & n.* (*aux.* h.) rhyme; (*fig.*) make sense, agree (with), tally (with). **–er,** *m.* rhymer, versifier. **–erei,** *f.* doggerel. **–geklingel,** *n.* jingle. **–kunst,** *f.* rhyming. **–los,** *adj.* unrhymed. **–schmied,** *m.* rhymester, poetaster. **–silbe,** *f.* rhyming syllable. **–spruch,** *m.* proverb in rhyme. **–weise,** *adv.* in rhymes; in couplets. **–wort,** *n.* rhyming word.

[1]**rein,** 1. *adj.* clean, clear, neat, tidy; genuine, pure, chaste; undiluted, unalloyed; (*C.L.*) net; kosher (*Jew.*); (*coll.*) quite, absolutely, sheer, mere; *–e Bahn machen,* clear the way, clear away impediments, make a clean sweep; *–e Bilanz,* clear balance; *–e Gesichtsfarbe,* clear complexion; *–er Gewinn,* net profit; *– heraus,* clearly and to the point; *etwas ins –e bringen,* clear a th. up, put a th. in order; (*coll.*) get to the bottom of a th.; *eine Rechnung ins –e bringen,* clear *or* settle an account; *ins –e kommen,* come to an understanding; *etwas ins –e schreiben,* make a fair copy of a th.; *ich bin mit mir im –en,* I have made up my mind; *–e Lüge,* downright lie; *aus –em Mitleid,* out of sheer compassion; *–en Mund halten,* hold one's tongue, keep a secret; *– nichts,* nothing whatever; *–en Tisch machen,* make a clean sweep (of); *– unmöglich,* quite impossible; *einem –en Wein einschenken,* tell a p. the plain *or* unvarnished truth. **–druck,** *m.* clean proof. **–e,** *f.* (*Poet.*), *see* **–heit. –erbig,** *adj.* homozygotic. **–ertrag,** *m.* net proceeds, yield *or* profit. (*coll.*) **–(e)weg,** *adv.* completely, altogether. (*C.L.*) **–gewicht,** *n.* net weight. **–gewinn,** *m.* net profit, net yield. **–gewinnung,** *f.* purification. **–heit,** *f.* purity, pureness, chastity; cleanness, cleanliness, clearness. **–igen,** *v.a.* clean, cleanse; purify; purge; disinfect; refine, clear, clarify, rectify; *er –igte sich von jedem Verdacht,* he cleared himself of all suspicion. **–igend,** *adj.* detergent. **–iger,** *m.* cleanser; refiner; purifier. **–igung,** *f.* purification; cleaning, cleansing; refinement, rectification; purging; disinfection; *chemische –igung,* dry cleaning; *Mariä –igung,* Purification of the Virgin (*R.C.*); *monatliche –igung,* menses, menstruation. **–igungseid,** *m.* oath of purgation. **–igungsmittel,** *n.* cleanser, detergent; purgative. **–igungsopfer,** *n.* lustration. **–kultur,** *f.* bacilli-culture, (*fig.*) the purest form. **–lich,** *adj.* clean, neat, tidy, clean-cut, distinct. **–lichkeit,** *f.* cleanliness, neatness, tidiness. **–(e)machefrau,** *f.* charwoman. **–(e)machen,** *n.* clean (*the house*), tidy up, scrub (*floors*); (*fig.*) clean up. **–rassig,** *adj.* pure-bred. **–schrift,** *f.* fair copy. **–waschen,** *v.a.* clear, vindicate.

[2]**rein,** *adv. & sep. prefix, coll. for* **herein.** (*sl.*) **–fall,** *m.* disappointment, let down, sell. (*sl.*) **–fallen,** *v.n.* be unsuccessful.

Reineclaude, *f.* (*Austr. dial.*), *see* **Reneklode.**

[1]**Reis,** *n.* (-es, -er) twig, sprig; shoot, scion. **–besen,** *m.* besom, birch-broom. **–holz,** *n.* brushwood. **–ig,** *n.* twigs; brushwood, deadwood. **–igbesen,** *see* **–besen. –igbund,** *n.*, **–igbündel,** *n.*, **–igbüschel,** *n.* faggot.

[2]**Reis,** *m.* rice. **–bau,** *m.* cultivation of rice. **–mehl,** *n.* rice flour, ground rice. **–stärke,** *f.* rice starch.

[3]**Reis, –ige(r),** *m.* (*archaic*) mounted soldier, knight on horseback. **–laufen,** *n.* enlistment (of a Swiss) in a foreign army. **–läufer,** *m.* hired (Swiss) soldier, (Swiss) mercenary.

Reise, *f.* (-n) journey, tour, trip, (sea) voyage; *die Hin–,* the outward journey; *die Rück–,* the return journey; *Vergnügungs–,* pleasure-trip; *sich auf die – begeben* or *machen,* set out; *wo geht die – hin?* where are you bound for? *glückliche –!* pleasant journey! **–anzug,** *m.* travelling-clothes. **–apotheke,** *f.* medicine-chest, first-aid outfit. **–bedarf,** *m.* travelling requirements *or* requisites. **–begleiter,** *m.* travelling-companion. **–beschreibung,** *f.* travel book. **–bett,** *n.* camp-bed. **–büro,** *n.* travel agency, tourist office. **–decke,** *f.* travelling-rug. **–fertig,** *adj.* ready to set out. **–flasche,** *f.* travelling-flask. **–führer,** *m.* guide-book. **–gefährte(r),** *m. & f.* fellow-traveller. **–gefolge,** *n.* suite (*of a prince*). **–gepäck,** *n.* luggage. **–geschwindigkeit,** *f.* cruising speed (*Av. & Naut.*). **–gesellschaft,** *f.* party of travellers; travelling companions. **–karte,** *f.* touring-map. **–koffer,** *m.* trunk; *kleiner –koffer,* portmanteau, dressing-case. **–kosten,** *f.pl.* travelling-expenses. **–lustig,** *adj.* fond of travelling.

–marsch, *m.* route-march (*Mil.*). **–marschall,** *m.* (royal) courier. **–n,** *v.n.* (*aux.* h. & s.) travel, journey; go (to); set out (for); go on travels; cruise (*Av.* & *Naut.*); *wir reisten über*, we went by *or* via; *aufs Land –n*, go to *or* leave for the country; *unsre Firma läßt nicht –n*, our firm does not employ travellers. **–nd,** *pr.p.* & *adj.* travelling, itinerant. **–nde(r),** *m.*, **–nde,** *f.* traveller, tourist, passenger; commercial traveller, agent, representative. **–paß,** *m.* passport. **–route,** *f.* itinerary. **–scheck,** *m.* traveller's cheque. **–spesen,** *pl.* travelling-expenses. **–stipendium,** *n.* travelling-scholarship. **–tasche,** *f.* travelling-bag. **–verkehr,** *m.* tourist traffic. **–zeit,** *f.* tourist season. **–ziel,** *n.* destination.

reiß–en, 1. *ir.v.a.* tear, rip, rend, slit; pull, drag; seize, grasp, snatch; (*archaic*) sketch, draw, design, trace, scribe; *an sich* (*Acc.*) *–en*, seize upon, seize hold of, snatch up; monopolize, usurp; *aus der Gefahr –en*, snatch from danger; *einen zu Boden –en*, knock a p. down; *Grimassen –en*, pull a face *or* faces; *Kulissen –en*, rant (*Theat.*); *sich* (*Dat.*) *ein Loch –en* (*in*), tear one's (*coat, etc.*); *eine große Lücke –en*, leave a great gap; *in Stücke –en*, tear to pieces; *Witze –en*, crack jokes; *Zoten –en*, talk obscenely, tell dirty stories. 2. *v.n.* (*aux.* h. & s.) tear, split, burst, break, snap, crack; break loose; *wenn alle Stricke –en*, if all means fail, if the worst come to the worst; *mir –t's in allen Gliedern*, I have rheumatic pains in all my limbs; *da riß mir die Geduld*, at this I lost patience; (*coll.*) *das –t* (*sehr*) *ins Geld*, that runs away with a lot of money. 3. *v.r.* get scratched, scratch o.s.; *sich –en um*, scramble *or* struggle for. 4. *n.* rending; acute pains, rheumatism. **–ahle,** *f.* scriber. **–aus,** *n.* & *m.*; *–aus nehmen*, take to one's heels. **–belastung,** *f.* breaking load. **–blei,** *n.* graphite, blacklead; drawing pencil. **–brett,** *n.* drawing-board. **–end,** *pr.p.* & *adj.* rapid; impetuous; ravening, rapacious, carnivorous; *–ender Strom*, torrent; *–end abgehen*, sell like hot cakes. **–er,** *m.* thriller, box-office success (*Theat.*). **–feder,** *f.* drawing-pen. **–festigkeit,** *f.* breaking *or* tensile strength. **–kohle,** *f.* charcoal crayon. **–leine,** *f.* rip-cord (*parachute*). **–linie,** *f.* perforation. **–nagel,** *m.* drawing-pin, (*Amer.*) thumbtack. **–schiene,** *f.* T-square. **–schnur,** *f.* *see* **–leine. –verschluß,** *m.* zip-fastener. **–zahn,** *m.* canine *or* laniary tooth, fang. **–zeug,** *n.* mathematical instruments, drawing instruments. **–zirkel,** *m.* drawing-compasses. **–zwecke,** *f.* drawing-pin.

reit–en, 1. *ir.v. n.* (*aux.* & s.) ride, go on horseback; *geritten kommen*, come on horseback; *auf einem herum–en*, take advantage of a p.'s good nature; *auf einer S. herum–en*, be always harping on a subject; *auf dem Apostelpferde –en*, go on Shanks's pony; *Galopp, Schritt, Trab –en*, gallop, pace *or* amble, trot; *vor Anker –en*, ride at anchor. 2. *v.a.* ride (a horse); *einen zu Boden* or *über den Haufen –en*, ride a p. down, ride over a p.; *ein Pferd zu Schanden –en*, override, founder a horse; *sich* (*Acc.*) *wund, sich* (*Dat.*) *einen Wolf –en*, gall o.s. in riding; *einen in die Tinte –en*, drive a p. into a corner; *Prinzipien* or *ein Prinzip –en*, have a fad, work an idea to death; *Wechsel –en*, keep o.s. afloat by accommodation bills; *der Teufel muß ihn –en*, he must have the devil in him. 3. *subst. n.* riding, equitation. **–anzug,** *m.* riding-habit. **–bahn,** *f.* riding-school, manège. **–decke,** *f.* saddle-cloth. **–end,** *pr.p.* & *adj.* on horseback; mounted; equestrian; *–ende Artillerie*, horse-artillery. **–er,** *m.* rider, horseman, cavalryman, trooper (*Cavalry*); tab (*of card-index*); slider (*Mach.*); *spanische –er*, chevaux de frise (*Mil.*); *leichte –er*, light horse (*Mil.*). **–erangriff,** *m.* cavalry charge. **–eraufzug,** *m.* cavalcade. **–erei,** *f.* cavalry; riding, equitation. **–erfähnrich,** *m.* cornet. **–erkünste,** *f.pl.* equestrian feats. **–erregiment,** *n.* cavalry regiment. **–ersäbel,** *m.* cavalry sabre. **–erschar,** *f.* troop of horse, cavalcade. **–ersmann,** *m.* horseman. **–erstandbild,** *n.* equestrian statue. **–(er)stiefel,** *m. pl.* riding-boots. **–erwache,** *f.* mounted guard. **–gerte,** *f.* whip, switch. **–gurt,** *m.* saddle-girth. **–handschuh,** *m.* riding-glove. **–hosen,** *f.pl.* riding-breeches. **–kleid,** *n.* ladies' riding-habit. **–knecht,** *m.* groom. **–kunst,** *f.* horsemanship, equitation. **–peitsche,** *f.*; *einem die –peitsche geben*, horsewhip a p. **–pferd,** *n.* riding-horse, saddle-horse, mount. **–post,** *f.* courier. **–sattel,** *m.* riding-saddle. **–schule,** *f.* riding-school, school of equitation, cavalry school; (*Swiss dial.*) merry-go-round. **–schüler,** *m.* pupil at a riding-school, cavalryman in training. **–stunden,** *f.pl.* riding-lessons. **–weg,** *m.* bridle-path. **–zeug,** *n.* riding-equipment.

Reiter, *f.* (-n) (*dial.*) riddle, coarse sieve. **–n,** *v.a.* riddle, sift, screen (*corn*).

Reiz, *m.* (-es, -e) charm, attraction, fascination, attractiveness, allurement; enticement, incentive, stimulus; irritation; impulse (*Phys.*). **–bar,** *adj.* sensitive, susceptible; nervous, irritable; inflammable (*Med.*). **–barkeit,** *f.* susceptibility, sensitiveness; irritability. **–beantwortung,** *f.* response to stimulus. **–empfänglichkeit,** *f.* susceptibility to stimulation. **–en,** *v.a.* excite, stimulate, provoke, stir up, irritate; charm, attract, allure, lure, entice; *–e sie nicht zur Wut*, do not exasperate them. **–end,** *pr.p.* & *adj.* charming, attractive, delightful, delicious, enticing, bewitching, tempting; inflammatory, irritating, irritant, stimulating. **–fähigkeit,** *f.* susceptibility; irritability (*Phys.*). **–gas,** *n.* irritant gas. **–los,** *adj.* non-irritant; unattractive, insipid. **–losigkeit,** *f.* unattractiveness. **–mittel,** *n.* stimulant, irritant; incentive, inducement, stimulus. **–schwelle,** *f.* threshold of sensation (*Physiol.*). **–stoff,** *m.*, *see* **–gas**; stimulant, adjuvant. **–ung,** *f.* irritation, stimulation, excitation; provocation, enticement, inducement; charm, attraction. **–voll,** *adj.* charming, attractive, alluring, exciting. **–wirkung,** *f.* irritant effect.

Reizker, *m.* (-s, –) orange-agaric.

rekel–n, *v.r.* (*dial.*) loll about. **–ei,** *f.* lolling; loutishness.

Reklam–ation, *f.* complaint, protest, objection; claim. **–e,** *f.* (-en) advertisement; advertising; propaganda; window-dressing; *–e machen* (*für eine S.*), advertise (a th.), make propaganda (for a th.), (*coll.*) boost (a th.). **–echef,** *m.* advertising manager. **–efachmann,** *m.* publicity expert. **–ezeichner,** *m.* poster artist. **–ieren,** *v.a.* & *n.* claim; complain, object, protest (*wegen*, about); apply for exemption (*from military service*). **–iert,** *p.p.* & *adj.* exempt from military service, reserved (for essential work). **–ierte(r),** *m.* essential worker.

rekognoszieren, *v.a.* (*archaic*) reconnoitre (*Mil.*); recognize.

rekommandieren, *v.a.* (*archaic* & *dial.*) recommend; register (*a letter, etc.*).

Rekonvaleszen–t, *m.* convalescent. **–z,** *f.* convalescence.

Rekord, *m.* (-s, -e & *Austr. dial.* -s) record (*Sport*); *einen – aufstellen*, establish a record; *den – schlagen*, beat the record. **–versuch,** *m.* attempt on the record.

Rekrut, *m.* (-en, -en) recruit; conscript. **–ieren,** 1. *v.a.* recruit. 2. *v.r.* obtain recruits (*aus*, from). **–ierung,** *f.* recruiting; recruitment.

Rekt–apapier, *n.*, **–awechsel,** *m.* (*C.L.*) bill not to order, direct bill. **–aszension,** *f.* right ascension (*Astron.*).

Rekt–ion, *f.* (-en) complement, agreement, dependence (*Gram.*). **–or,** *m.* (-s, -en) vice-chancellor (*of a university*); rector; headmaster. **–orat,** *n.* office of chancellor. **–oratsrede,** *f.* rectorial address.

Rekurs, *m.* (-es, -e) appeal; redress (*Law*).

Relais, *n.* (–, –) relay (*Elec.* & (*archaic*) *of horses*).

relativ, 1. *adj.* relative, relating (to); respective; approximate. 2. *n.* (-s, -e), *see* **–pronomen. –ität,** *f.* relativity. **–itätstheorie,** *f.* theory of relativity. **–pronomen,** *n.* relative pronoun. **–satz,** *m.* relative clause. **–um,** *n.* (-ums, -a), *see* **–pronomen.**

releg–ieren, *v.a.* expel; send down, rusticate (*a student*). **–ation,** *f.* expulsion; rustication (*Univ.*).

Relief, *n.* (-s, -s & -e) relief, relieve; *Bas–*, bas-relief. **–druck,** *m.* relief *or* embossed printing. **–tapete,** *f.* embossed wallpaper.

Relig–ion, *f.* (-en) religion. **–ionsbekenntnis,** *n.* religious profession. **–ionsduldung,** *f.* religious toleration. **-ionsfreiheit**, *f.* religious liberty. **-ionsgebräuche**, *m.pl.* rites. **-ionsgemeinschaft**, *f.* sect. **-ionslehre**, *f.* doctrine. **-ionslehrer**, *m.* scripture teacher; divine. **-ionslos**, *adj.* irreligious. **-ionssatz**, *m.* dogma. **-ionsschwärmer**, *m.* fanatic. **-ionsstifter**, *m.* founder of a religion. **-ionsstreit**, *m.* religious controversy. **-ionstrennung**, *f.* schism. **-ionsunterricht**, *m.* scripture (teaching *or* lessons). **-ionsverfolgung**, *f.* religious persecution. **-ionswissenschaft**, *f.* theology, divinity. **-iös**, *adj.* religious. **-iosität**, *f.* religiosity.

Reling, *f.* (-e) rail, bulwarks (*Naut.*).

Reliquie, *f.* (-n) relic (*Relig.*). **-ndienst**, *m.* worship of relics. **-nkästchen**, *n.*, **-nschrein**, *m.* reliquary.

Remanenz, *f.* residual magnetism.

Reminiszenz, *f.* (-en) reminiscence, memory.

remis, 1. *adj.* drawn (*Chess*). 2. *n.* (–, – & -en) drawn game. – *machen*, leave the game drawn, agree a draw.

Remise, *f.* (-n) coach-house, shed; cover (*for game*).

Remitt-ende, *f.* remainder, surplus *or* return copy. (*C.L.*) **-ent**, *m.* remitter. **-ieren**, *v.a.* return; remit.

remon-tant, *adj.*, *see* **-tierend**. **-te**, *f.* remount; *eine -te zureiten*, break in *or* train cavalry horses. **-tepferd**, *n.* remount. **-tieren**, *v.a.* remount (*cavalry*); bloom a second time (*Hort.*). **-tierend**, *adj.* perpetual, perennial (*Hort.*). **-toiruhr**, *f.* keyless watch.

Remoulade, *f.* salad-cream, mayonnaise.

rempel-n, *v.n.* jostle, (*sl.*) barge into. **-ei**, *f.* jostling, scuffle.

Rem(p)ter, *m.* (-s, –) refectory; assembly hall (*in castles, monasteries*).

Remulade, *f. see* **Remoulade.**

Rendant, *m.* (-en, -en) treasurer, paymaster, cashier, accountant.

Rendement, *m.* output, yield.

Renegat, *m.* (-en, -en) renegade.

Reneklode, *f.* (-n) greengage.

Renette, *f.* (-n) rennett(-apple).

reniten-t, *adj.* refractory. **-z**, *f.* obstinacy.

Renk, *m.* bayonet lock.

renken, *v.a.* turn, bend, twist, wrench, sprain.

renn-en, 1. *ir.v.n.* (*aux.* h. & s.) run, race, run a race; *-en an* (*Acc.*), *gegen* or *wider*, dash against; *sich ein Loch in den Kopf -en*, injure one's head in a collision; *mit dem Kopfe gegen eine S. -en*, run one's head against a th.; *mit einem um die Wette -en*, race s.o. for a wager; *ins Verderben -en*, rush (headlong) into disaster. 2. *v.a.* & *r.*; *eine Meile in fünf Minuten -en*, run a mile in five minutes; *sich außer Atem -en*, run o.s. out of breath; *einen zu Boden -en*, run s.o. over *or* down; *einem den Degen durch den Leib -en*, run one's sword through a p.'s body. 3. *v.a.* smelt. 4. *n.* running; race; *das -en machen*, win the race, come in first, be the winner; *totes -en*, dead heat. **-bahn**, *f.* racecourse, cinder-track. **-boot**, *n.* racing yacht. **-er**, *m.* runner; race-horse; racing car. **-erei**, *f.* rushing about. **-fahrer**, *m.* racing cyclist *or* motorist. **-pferd**, *n.* race-horse. **-platz**, *m.* race-course. **-schlitten**, *m.* sleigh. **-sport**, *m.* racing, the turf. **-stall**, *m.* (racing) stables. **-strecke**, *f.* distance to be run. **-termin**, *m.* racing fixture. **-wagen**, *m.* racing car. **-ziel**, *n.* winning-post.

Renntier, *n.* (-(e)s, -e) reindeer. **-flechte**, *f.* reindeer-moss *or* lichen.

Renomm-age, *f.* boasting, bragging, big talk; (*Studs. sl.*) good form, proper behaviour. **-ee**, *n.* repute, renown, reputation, name. **-ieren**, *v.n.* *aux.* h.) boast, brag, swagger. **-iert**, *p.p.* & *adj.* renowned, well known, of good repute. **-ist**, *m.* bragger, boaster, braggart.

Renonce, *f.* (-n) revoking (*Cards*).

renovier-en, *v.a.* renew, renovate, redecorate; do up (*a house*). **-ung**, *f.* renovation.

rent-abel, *adj.* profitable, remunerative, lucrative; *eine S. -abel machen*, make a th. pay. **-abilität**, *f.* profitableness. **-amt**, *n.* finance *or* treasurer's office. **-e**, *f.* (-en) income, revenue, interest; annuity, pension; (*pl.*) stocks; *er lebt von seinen -en*, he has a private income, he lives on his means; *jährliche -e*, annuity; *auf -en legen*, invest, put out at interest. **-ei**, *f.*, *see* **-amt**. **-enablösung**, *f.* liquidation of a rent, annuity *or* pension. **-enbank**, *f.* annuity-office. **-enempfänger**, *m.* annuitant. **-engut**, *n.* estate acquired by payment of annual rent. **-enmark**, *f.* (stabilized) mark (based on land values) (1923). **-ier**, *m.* (-s, -s) man of private means. **-ieren**, *v.n.* & *r.* (*aux.* h.) yield a profit *or* revenue, be profitable, pay; (*coll.*) *das -iert sich nicht*, that does not pay; that is not worth while. **-meister**, *m.* treasurer; steward. **-ner**, *m.*, *see* **-ier**. **-nerheim**, *n.* home for old people. **-verwalter**, *m.* trustee; guardian; steward.

Rentrant, *m.* re-entrant angle.

Repar-ation, *f.* (-en) reparation, (war) indemnity. **-ationspflichtig**, *adj.* liable for indemnity. **-atur**, *f.* repair. **-aturbedürftig**, *adj.* in need of repair. **-aturwerkstatt**, *f.* repair shop. **-ieren**, *v.a.* mend, repair.

repassieren, *v.a.* & *n.* repair ladders in stockings; pick up stitches, do invisible mending (*on stockings*).

Repet-ent, *m.* (-en, -en) pupil remaining a second year in a form; *see also* **-itor**. **-ieren**, *v.a.* & *n.* (*aux.* h.) repeat. **-iergewehr**, *n.* repeating rifle. **-ieruhr**, *f.* repeater. **-ition**, *f.* recapitulation, revision. **-itor**, *m.* coach, tutor. **-itorium**, *n.* revision (course) (*on a subject*).

Replik, *f.* (-en) counter-plea, reply.

reponieren, *v.a.* replace, put in its place; set (*a limb*); reduce (*Surg.*).

Report, *m.* (-s, -e) (*C.L.*) contango. **-age**, *f.* eyewitness account, running commentary.

Repositor-ium, *n.* (-iums, -ien) (set of) bookshelves; music-stand, canterbury.

Repräsent-ant, *m.* (-en, -en) representative. **-ationsgelder**, *n.pl.* allowance for representation, upkeep allowance. **-ativverfassung**, *f.* representative *or* constitutional government. **-ieren**, *v.a.* represent, keep up appearances (befitting a position), (*coll.*) make a show.

Repressalie, *f.* (-n) reprisals, retaliation; *-n ergreifen gegen*, make reprisals on.

Reprise, *f.* repeat (*Mus.*); repeat performance (*Theat.*).

Reprodu-ktion, *f.* (-en) reproduction, rendering. **-zieren**, *v.a.* reproduce, render.

Reps, *m.* (*dial.*), *see* **Raps** & **Rips.**

Reptil, *n.* (-s, -ien & *Austr. dial.* -e) reptile.

Republik, *f.* (-en) republic. **-aner**, *m.* (-s, –) republican. **-anisch**, *adj.* republican.

Repunze, *f.* hall-mark.

reputierlich, *adj.* reputable, respectable, (*coll.*) decent; *nicht* –, disreputable.

requi-rieren, *v.a.* demand, request; requisition, confiscate. **-sit**, *n.* (-(e)s, -en & *Austr. dial.* -e) requisite, requirement, indispensable item; (*pl.*) properties (*Theat.*).

resch, *adj.* (*dial.*) crisp, crusty (*bread*); tough (*meat*); acid, tart (*wine*); pithy, lively, gay.

Resed-a, *f.*, **-e**, *f.* (-en) mignonette (*Reseda odorata*) (*Bot.*).

Resektion, *f.* surgical removal.

Reserv-age, *f.* resist, reserve, resist-paste (*Cal. Print.*). **-at**, *n.* reservation, proviso. **-e**, *f.* (-en) reserve, store; relief, reserve (*Mil.*); restraint; *in -e liegen*, be in reserve, be in stock. **-ebett**, *n.* spare bed. **-efonds**, *m.* reserve-fund. **-egut**, *n.* spare sails and stores. **-emannschaft**, *f.* the reserve (*Mil.*). **-eoffizier**, *m.* officer in the reserve. **-erad**, *n.* spare wheel (*Motor.*). **-estücke**, *n.pl.*, **-eteil**, *m.* replacement, spare part. **-ieren**, *v.a.* reserve; *-ierter Platz*, reserved seat; *-iertes Wesen*, retiring manner *or* nature; reserved *or* restrained behaviour. **-ist**, *m.* reservist (*Mil.*). **-oir**, *n.* (-s, -e) reservoir, cistern, tank.

Resid-ent, *m.* (-en, -en) agent on the spot; resident ambassador *or* minister. **-enz**, *f.* (-en) (prince's) residence; seat of the court, capital. **-enzstadt**, *f.* capital town, capital. **-ieren**, *v.n.* (*aux.* h.) reside, be in residence.

Residu-um, *n.* (-ums, -en) residue.

resignieren, *v.n.* & *r.* renounce *or* forgo one's right, give up, be resigned, acquiesce.

Resonanz, *f.* (-en) resonance; (*fig.*) echo, understanding. **–boden,** *m.* sounding-board. **–kreis,** *m.* resonant circuit (*Rad.*).
resorbier–en, *v.a. & n.* reabsorb. **–ung,** *f.* reabsorption.
Respekt, *m.* respect; wide border *or* margin; *mit – zu melden* or *zu sagen,* with all due respect, if I may be allowed to say so, if you will excuse the language. **–abel,** *adj.* estimable, respectable. **–blatt,** *n.* fly-leaf. **–ieren,** *v.a.* respect, esteem; honour (*bills*). **–ierlich,** *adj., see* **–abel.** **–iv,** *adj.* respective. **–ive,** *adv.* respectively; or. **–los,** *adj.* without respect, irreverent. **–losigkeit,** *f.* want of respect. **–sperson,** *f.* person held in respect; notability. (*C.L.*) (*archaic*) **–tage,** *m.pl.* days of grace. **–voll,** *adj.* respectful. **–widrig,** *adj.* disrespectful.
Respiro, *f.* period of grace, respite.
Responsorium, *n.* (-iums, -ien) response; antiphon (*Eccl.*).
Ressort [*pron.* rɛˈsoːr], *n.* (-s, -s) department, sphere, province. **–mäßig,** *adj.* departmental.
Rest, *m.* (-es, -e) rest, residue, dregs, remains, remainder; difference, vestige; balance; (*dial.*) arrears; (*pl.* -er & *Austr.* & *Swiss dial.* –en) remnant (*of cloth, food, etc.*); *sich den – holen,* suffer a relapse; *das wird ihm den – geben,* that will do for him *or* finish him off; *die irdischen –e,* the earthly *or* mortal remains; *der letzte –,* the last vestiges. **–ant,** *m.* defaulter; (*pl.*) arrears. **–auflage,** *f.,* **–bestand,** *m.* remainders, remnants. **–glied,** *n.* residual term, remainder. **–ieren,** *v.n.* (*aux.* h.) (*archaic*) remain, be left; be in arrears; owe. **–lauge,** *f.* residual liquid. **–lich,** *adj.* residual, remaining. **–los,** *adj.* without a remainder, completely, altogether, entirely, absolutely. **–posten,** *m.* remaining stock. **–summe,** *f.* balance.
Restaur–ant, *n.* (-s, -s) restaurant. **–ateur,** *m.* (-s, -e) restaurant proprietor. **–ation,** *f.* (-en) restoration (*Pol., Art*); restaurant. **–ator,** *m.* (-s, -en) restorer (*of pictures*). **–ieren,** *v.a.* restore, repair.
Result–ante, *f.* resultant (*Phys.*). **–at,** *n.* (-(e)s, -e) result, outcome; score (*Sport*).
Resümee, *n.* (-s, -s) summary.
retabl–ieren, *v.a.* re-establish. **–issement,** *n.* re-establishment.
retardier–en, 1. *v.a.* check, impede; *–endes Moment,* retardation in the progress of the (dramatic) action. 2. *v.n.* (*aux.* h.) go slow (*of watches, etc.*).
Retentionsrecht, *n.* lien (*Law*).
Retirade, *f.* (-n) (*archaic*) retreat, withdrawal; latrine.
Retorte, *f.* (-n) retort, alembic (*Chem.*).
retour, *adv.* back. **–en,** *f.pl.* empties; returns. (*C.L.* & *sl.*) **–nieren,** *v.a.* send back, return. **–billet,** *n.* (*Swiss dial.*) return-ticket. (*sl.*) **–kutsche,** *f.* retort in the same form; (*sl.*) *–kutsche selber eins!* same to you! **–waren,** *f.pl.* returns.
Retraite [*pron.* rəˈtrɛːtə], *f.* (*archaic*) retreat; tattoo.
rett–en, 1. *v.a.* save, rescue, recover; deliver, set free, preserve. 2. *v.r.* escape, save o.s.; *seine Ehre –en,* vindicate one's honour; *–e sich wer kann,* everyone for himself; *–ende Tat,* act of deliverance; *–ender Engel,* redeeming angel. **–bar,** *adj.* recoverable, salvageable. **–er,** *m.* rescuer, deliverer; Saviour, Redeemer; *Tauch–er,* (Davis) escape gear (*from submarines*). **–los,** *adj.* unsalvageable (*Naut.*). **–ung,** *f.* saving, preservation; salvage, recovery; deliverance, rescue; escape; *ohne –ung,* past help. **–ungsanker,** *m.* sheet-anchor. **–ungsapparat,** *m.* life-saving apparatus. **–ungsboje,** *f.* rescue-buoy. **–ungsboot,** *n.* life-boat. **–ungsdienst,** *m.* life-boat service. **–ungsgürtel,** *m.* life-belt. **–ungskolonne,** *f.* rescue squad. **–ungsleiter,** *f.* fire-escape. **–ungslos,** *adj.* irremediable, irretrievable, past help, beyond hope. **–ungsmedaille,** *f.* life-saving medal. **–ungsmittel,** *n.* remedy, expedient, resource. **–ungsring,** *m.* life-belt. **–ungsstation,** *f.* first-aid post. **–ungstau,** *n.* lifeline. **–ungsversuch,** *m.* attempted rescue. **–ungswerk,** *n.* rescue work. **–ungswesen,** *n.* life-saving, rescue service.
Rettich, *m.* (-s, -e) radish.
Retusch–e, *f.* (-en) retouching (*Phot.*). **–ieren,** *v.a.* retouch.
Reu–e, *f.* repentance; regret, remorse. **–en,** *v.a.* & *n.* (*aux.* h.) & *imp.* regret, be sorry (for); repent (of); *es –t mich,* I am sorry about it; *es hat ihn gereut,* he was sorry for it, he has repented it; *diese Tat –t mich,* I regret this act. **–(e)gefühl,** *n.* remorse. **–(e)los,** *adj.* impenitent. **–evoll,** *adj.* repentant. **–geld,** *n.,* **–kauf,** *m.* forfeit, penalty. **–ig,** *adj.,* **–mütig,** *adj.* penitent, contrite. **–mütigkeit,** *f.* contrition.
Reuse, *f.* (-n) weir-basket, oyster-basket.
Reut–e, *f.* (*dial.*) clearing. **–en,** *v.a.* root out; plough *or* turn up; clear (*a wood*). **–feld,** *n.* newly reclaimed land; virgin soil. **–hacke,** *f.,* **–haue,** *f.* hoe, mattock.
Revanch–e [*pron.* rəˈvɑ̃ːʃə] *f.* revenge; satisfaction. **–ieren,** *v.r.* have *or* take one's revenge, be revenged; (*coll.*) give a present in return, return a kindness.
Reverenz, *f.* (-en) reverence; courtesy; respect; obeisance, bow, curtsy.
Revers, *m.* (-es, -e) reverse (*of coin, etc.*); lapel; reciprocal bond, declaration (*Law*); *einen – ausstellen,* give a written undertaking.
revi–dieren, *v.a.* revise, check, control, examine, (*C.L.*) audit. **–sion,** *f.* (-en) revision, revisal, review; (*coll.*) check-up; auditing; inspection, examination (*of luggage*); appeal, rehearing (*Law*). **–sor,** *m.* (-s, -en) inspector, examiner, auditor.
Revier, *n.* (-s, -e) quarter, district, precinct, beat (*police*); preserve, hunting ground; sick bay, medical centre (*Mil.*); *– bekommen,* be put on the sick-list (*Mil.*). **–en,** *v.n.* quarter (*hounds, Hunt.*). **–förster,** *m.* gamekeeper. **–kranke(r),** *m.* soldier sick in quarters.
Revolt–e, *f.* (-en) revolt, insurrection. **–ieren,** *v.n.* (*aux.* h.) revolt, rise in revolt.
Revolution, *f.* (-en) revolution. **–är,** *adj.* & *m.* (-s, -e) revolutionary. **–ieren,** *v.a.* revolutionize.
Revolver, *m.* (-s, –) revolver. **–presse,** *f.* yellow press, gutter-press.
Revue, *f.* (-n) revue (*Theat.*); (*archaic*) review; muster; *– passieren,* pass muster; *– passieren lassen,* pass in review.
Rezens–ent, *m.* (-en, -en) critic, reviewer. **–ieren,** *v.a.* criticize, review. **–ion,** *f.* (-en) critique, criticism, review. **–ionsexemplar,** *n.* reviewer's copy.
Rezep–isse, *n.* receipt, acquittance. **–t,** *n.* (-ts, -te) recipe; prescription; formula. **–tor,** *m.* (-s, -en) receiver, collector, receptor organ (*Physiol.*). **–tur,** *f.* receivership; dispensing (*of medicines*).
Rezeß, *m.* (-(ss)es, -(ss)e) compact, treaty.
Rezip–ient, *m.* recipient; receiver (*Chem.*). **–ieren,** *v.a.* receive, admit. **–rok,** *adj.* reciprocal, converse.
Rezit–ativ, *n.* (-s, -e) recitative (*Mus.*). **–ator,** *m.* (-s, -en) reciter. **–ieren,** *v.a.* recite.
Rhabarber, *m.* rhubarb.
Rhapsod–e, *m.* (-en, -en) rhapsodist. **–ie,** *f.* rhapsody. **–isch,** *adj.* rhapsodical.
rhetorisch, *adj.* rhetorical.
Rheuma, *n., see* **–tismus.** **–tisch,** *adj.* rheumatic. **–tismus,** *m.* rheumatism.
Rhinozeros, *n.* (– *or* -ses, -se) rhinoceros.
rhomb–isch, *adj.* rhombic. **–us,** *m.* (-us, -en) rhomb, rhombus.
rhythm–isch, *adj.* rhythmical. **–us,** *m.* (-en) rhythm; *steigender –us,* iambic rhythm; *fallender –us,* trochaic rhythm.
Ribisel, *f.* (-n) & *n.* (-s, –) (*Austr. dial.*) redcurrant.
richt–en, 1. *v.a.* set right, adjust, arrange, put in order, straighten; prepare (*meal, etc.*), settle (*a dispute, etc.*); dress (*Cook., Tan., Mil., etc.*), regulate, set (*a watch, etc.*); direct, turn, point, address; set up, erect; trim (*sails*); lay, sight, aim (*a gun*); *eine Frage an einen –en,* put a question to a p.; *das war auf mich gerichtet,* that was aimed at *or* meant for me; *den Blick gen Himmel –en,* turn one's eyes towards Heaven; *die Segel nach dem Winde –en,* trim the sails to the wind (*also fig.*); be a timeserver; *zugrunde –en,* ruin, destroy. 2. *v.r.* rise, stand erect; dress in line (*Mil.*); *sich in die Höhe –en,* raise o.s. up; *Augen rechts – euch!* eyes right, dress! (*Mil.*);

sich für or *auf eine S. –en*, be prepared for a th.; *sich nach einer S. –en*, be governed by a th., conform to *or* with a th.; depend on a th., be guided by a th.; *der Preis –et sich nach der Güte der Waren*, the price is determined by the quality of the goods; *das Eigenschaftswort –et sich nach dem Hauptwort*, the adjective agrees with its noun. 3. *v.a. & n.* (*aux.* h.) judge, try, pass sentence on, condemn; (*archaic*) execute (*a criminal*). **-antenne,** *f.* directional aerial. **–aufsatz,** *m.* gun sight. **–balken,** *m.* traverse-beam. **–beil,** *n.* executioner's axe. **–blei,** *n.* plumb-line, plummet. **–block,** *m.* executioner's block. **–e,** *f.* straight *or* direct line; shortest distance; normal *or* proper position; *wieder in die –e bringen*, adjust, put straight; *in die –e gehen*, take a short cut, go as the crow flies; *aus der –e kommen*, go astray, get in a muddle. **–er,** *m.* judge; justice; umpire; *sich zum –er aufwerfen*, constitute o.s. a judge. **–eramt,** *n.* judgeship. **–erlich,** 1. *adj.* judicial; judiciary. 2. *adv.* as a judge, judicially. **–erspruch,** *m.* judgement, sentence. **–erstand,** *m.* body of judges, the bench; position of a judge. **–erstuhl,** *m.* tribunal; *das gehört nicht vor seinen –erstuhl*, that is not within his jurisdiction. **–fall,** *m.* required form (*Gram.*). **–feier,** *f.*, *see* **–fest. –fernrohr,** *n.* telescopic sight. **–fest,** *n.* topping-out ceremony. **–funkbake,** *f.* radio beacon. **–gerät,** *n.* laying *or* aiming gear. **–hebel,** *m.* elevating lever. **–hörer,** *m.* sound locator (*Mil.*). **–ig,** *adj.*, *see* **richtig. –kanonier,** *m.* gunlayer. **–kranz,** *m.* garland erected to crown the rafters (*when a house is built*). **–kreis,** *m.* azimuth-circle. **–linie,** *f.* (*usually pl.*) direction, rule, instruction, guiding principle. **–lot,** *n.* plumbline. **–maß,** *n.* standard gauge. **–platz,** *m.* place of execution. **–posten,** *m.* signpost. **–preis,** *m.* standard price. **–punkt,** *m.* aiming point. **–scheit,** *n.* ruler, straight-edge, level; justifier (*Typ.*). **–schmaus,** *m.*, *see* **–fest. –schnur,** *f.* (-en) plumb-line; (*fig.*) rule of conduct, guiding principle. **–schraube,** *f.* elevating screw. **–schwert,** *n.* executioner's sword. **–sendung,** *f.* beam transmission (*Rad.*). **–stätte,** *f.* place of execution. **–strahl,** *m.* directional beam (*Rad.*). **–ung,** *f.* direction, aim; alignment, bearing, course; tendency, line, bent, turn; *neuere –ung*, modern methods; *in jeder –ung*, in all directions; *nach beiden –ungen*, both ways; *in gerader –ung*, in a straight line, straight on; *gerade –ung*, alignment (*Mil.*). **–unggebend,** *adj.* setting the fashion; leading. **–ungshörer,** *m.* sound locator (*Mil.*). **–ungslinie,** *f.* line of direction, base line. **–ungslos,** *adj.* aimless. **–ungsweiser,** *m.* signpost. **–ungswinkel,** *m.* angle of sight. **–ungszeiger,** *m.* direction-indicator (*Motor.*). **–waage,** *f.* level. **–weg,** *m.* short cut. **–weiser,** *m.* radio beacon. **–zahl,** *f.* coefficient.

richtig, 1. *adj.* right, accurate, correct, exact, true; fair, just, genuine, real, regular; in order, settled; *einen – behandeln*, treat a p. in the right way; *geht Ihre Uhr –?* is your watch right? *es ist alles –*, all is well; *–er Londoner*, regular cockney; *es ist hier nicht –*, this place is eerie, eery *or* haunted; *es ist nicht – mit ihm*, or *er ist nicht ganz –*, he is not quite right in the head; *– empfangen* or *erhalten*, duly received. 2. *adv.* (*coll.*) quite right; certainly, just so, sure enough; *er hat es – vergessen*, he has properly forgotten it; *ich sagte, 'er kommt bald' und –! da kam er*, I said he would soon come, and, sure enough, he did. **–gehend,** *adj.* keeping good time (*clocks*); (*coll.*) regular, real. **–machen,** *v.a.* (*coll.*) pay, settle (*a bill*) (but *– machen*, do properly, make in the correct manner). **–keit,** *f.* correctness, accuracy, exactness; justness, rightness, fairness; *in –keit bringen*, adjust, settle, put right *or* in order; *es ist alles in –keit*, everything is in order, settled *or* arranged; *die Sache hat ihre –keit, es hat damit seine –keit*, it is quite true, it is a fact. **–stellen,** *v.a.* put right, rectify (but *– stellen*, place correctly, put in the right place).

Ricke, *f.* (-n) doe.

rieb, rieb(e)st, riebe, *see* **reiben.**

riech–en, *ir.v.a. & n.* (*aux.* h.) smell, scent, (*coll.*) foresee, perceive, find out, (*sl.*) nose *or* smell out; *nach einer S. –en*, smell of *or* like a th.; *an einer S. –en*, smell a th.; *er –t aus dem Munde*, his breath is offensive; *es –t angebrannt*, it smells burnt; *es –t stark*, it gives off a powerful smell; *ich kann es nicht –en*, I cannot stand (the smell of) it; (*coll.*) *ich kann ihn nicht –en*, I cannot stand him; *Lunte –en*, smell a rat; *den Braten –en*, see through it; *er kann kein Pulver –en*, he is a coward; *das kann man nicht –en*, I cannot be expected to know that; (*sl.*) *daran kannst du –en!* put that in your pipe and smoke it! **–end,** *pr.p. & adj.* smelling, perfumed, fragrant, redolent; strong, high (*of meat*). **–er,** *m.* (*coll.*) nose. **–essig,** *m.* aromatic vinegar. **–fläschchen,** *n.* smelling-bottle. **–nerv,** *m.* olfactory nerve. **–salz,** *n.* smelling-salt(s). **–spur,** *f.* scent (*for dogs*). **–stoffe,** *m.pl.* scents, perfumes. **–werkzeuge,** *n.pl.* olfactory organs.

Ried, *n.* (-(e)s, -e) marsh, bog; reed. **–gras,** *n.* sedge.

rief, riefest, riefe, *see* **rufen.**

Riefe, *f.* (-n) groove, chamfer, channel; flute (*of a pillar*). **–ln,** *v.a.*, **–n,** *v.a.* chamfer, channel, flute; groove; rifle (*a gun*); knurl, mill, striate.

Riege, *f.* section, squad (*Gymn.*). **–nführer,** *m.* section leader. **–nturnen,** *n.* section drill.

Riegel, *m.* (-s, –) bolt; rail, bar, cross-bar, tie; bar (*of soap*); *unter Schloß und –*, bolted and barred; *einen – vorschieben*, put an end to (*s.th.*), check (*a p.*), put an obstacle in (*a p.'s*) way. **–n,** *v.a.* bar, bolt. **–fest,** *adj.* (securely) bolted, barred. **–schloß,** *n.* stock-lock.

[1]Riemen, *m.* (-s, –) strap, (rifle) sling; belt; thong, shoelace; *mit – peitschen*, lash; *sich den – enger schnallen*, (*fig.*) tighten one's belt. **–antrieb,** *m.*, *see* **–trieb. –bügel,** *m.* (sling) swivel. **–fett,** *n.* belt dressing. **–scheibe,** *f.* belt-pulley. **–schneider,** *m.*, *see* **Riemer. –schuh,** *m.* sandal. **–trieb,** *m.* belt transmission *or* drive. **–werk,** *n.*, **–zeug,** *n.* straps, harness.

[2]Riemen, *m.* (-s, –) oar; *die – klar machen*, ship the oars. **–schlag,** *m.* stroke (*of an oar*).

Riemer, *m.* (-s, –) saddler, leather-worker, harness-maker.

Ries, *n.* (-es, -e) (*orig.*) ream (*of paper*); (*now* 1,000 sheets).

[1]Ries–e, *m.* (-en, -en) giant, ogre. **–enartig,** *adj.* enormous, gigantic, colossal. **–enerfolg,** *m.* (*sl.*) smash hit. **–enfaultier,** *n.* megatherium. **–engeschlecht,** *n.* race of giants. **–engestalt,** *f.* colossus. **–engroß,** *adj.* colossal. **–enhaft,** *adj.* gigantic; immense, vast, tremendous, colossal. **–en(luft)reifen,** *m.* balloon tyre. **–enmaß,** *n.* gigantic proportions. **–enmäßig,** *adj.*, *see* **–engroß. –enschlange,** *f.* boa-constrictor; python, anaconda. **–enschritt,** *m.* giant stride; *mit –enschritten*, (*go* or *move*) at a rapid pace. **–ig,** 1. *adj.*, *see* **–enhaft.** 2. (*coll.*) immensely, awfully. **–in,** *f.* giantess.

[2]Riese, *f.* timber slide.

riesel–n, *v.n.* (*aux.* h. & s.) ripple; trickle; percolate; *es –t*, it drizzles; *ein Schauer –t mir durchs Gebein*, a shiver goes down my back. **–feld,** *n.* irrigated field, sewage-land. **–jauche,** *f.* sewage (*fertilizer*). **–regen,** *m.* drizzle, drizzling rain. **–schutt,** *m.* shifting scree.

Riester, *m.* (-s, –) patch (*on a shoe, etc.*); (*dial.*) stilt of a plough. **–n,** *v.a.* put on a patch, patch, mend.

riet, rietest, riete, *see* **raten.**

Riff, *n.* (-(e)s, -e) reef, ridge, shelf, ledge, sandbank.

Riffel, *f.* (-n) flax-comb, ripple. **–n,** *v.a.* ripple (*flax*); rib, groove, corrugate, chamfer, flute. **–blech,** *n.* corrugated iron. **–walze,** *f.* fluted roller.

Rigol–e, *f.* (-en) deep furrow. **–en,** *v.a.* trench-plough. **–pflug,** *m.* trench-plough.

rigor–istisch, –os, *adj.* rigorous, severe, strict, **–osum,** *n.* oral examination (*for the doctor's degree*).

Rikoschet(t), *n.* (-s, -s) ricochet. **–(t)ieren,** *v.n.* (*aux.* h.) ricochet, rebound.

Rille, *f.* (-n) rill; furrow; drill (*Agr.*); flute, chamfer; groove (*of gramophone record*); narrow channel (*Naut.*). **–n,** *v.a.* groove.

Rimesse, *f.* (-n) (*C.L.*) remittance; *– machen*, remit.

Rind, *n.* (-es, -er) ox, cow; (*pl.*) (horned) cattle, head of cattle. **-erbraten,** *m.* roast beef. **-erbremse,** *f.* gadfly. **-erfett,** *n.* beef dripping. **-ergalle,** *f.* ox-gall. **-erhirt,** *m.* cow herd, cowboy (*Amer.*). **-erklauenöl,** *n.* neat's-foot oil. **-ern,** *v.n.* desire the bull (*of cows*). **-erpest,** *f.* cattle-plague. **-ertalg,** *m.* beef-suet *or* tallow. **-fleisch,** *n.* beef. **-fleischbrühe,** *f.* beef-tea. **-sbraten,** *m.* (*dial.*) roast beef. **-(s)leder,** *n.* cowhide. **-szunge,** *f.* ox-tongue. **-vieh,** *n.* horned cattle; (*vulg.*) blockhead. **-viehzucht,** *f.* cattle-breeding.

Rind-e, *f.* (-en) rind (*of cheese*); bark (*of a tree*); crust (*of bread*); cortex. **-enartig,** *adj.* cortical. **-enboot,** *n.*, **-enkahn,** *m.* bark canoe. **-engewebe,** *n.* cortical tissue. **-enkoralle,** *f.* fan-coral. **-ig,** *adj.* covered with bark; crusty.

Ring, *m.* (-(e)s, -e) ring; circle; cycle; arena, (prize-)ring (*Boxing*); astragal (*Arch.*); loop, coil (*of wire, etc.*); band, hoop, annulus; (*C.L.*) trust, syndicate, pool; ruff (*in pigeons*); (*pl.*) dark rings (*round the eyes*); *einem den – durch die Nase ziehen,* lead a p. by the nose, have s.o. round one's little finger; *den – betreten,* enter the arena. **-bahn,** *f.* circular railway. **-buch,** *n.* loose-leaf *or* ring-book. **-el,** *n.* small ring; ringlet, curl. **-elblume,** *f.* marigold (*Bot.*). **-elchen,** *n.* ringlet, little ring. **-elig,** *adj.* ringlike, annular. **-ellocke,** *f.* ringlet, curl. **-eln,** 1. *v.a.* curl; ring; girdle; provide with a ring *or* rings. 2. *v.r.* curl; wreathe, wind (*smoke*). **-elnatter,** *f.* grass snake, ring-snake. **-elreigen,** *m.*, **-elreihen,** *m.* round dance. **-elreim,** *m.* refrain, chorus. **-elreiten,** *n.*, *see* **-elstechen.** **-elspiel,** *n.* (*Austr. dial.*) roundabout, merry-go-round. **-elstechen,** *n.* tilting at the ring. **-eltanz,** *m.* round dance. **-eltaube,** *f.* ring-dove. **-elwalze,** *f.* corrugated roller. **-feder,** *f.* annular spring. **-förmig,** *adj.* annular, circular, ringlike, cyclic. **-haube,** *f.* cowling ring (*Av.*). **-hörig,** *adj.* (*Swiss. dial.*) sound-conducting. **-kämpfer,** *m.* pugilist. **-knorpel,** *m.* annular *or* cricoid cartilage. **-lotte,** *f.* (-n) (*Austr. dial.*) greengage. **-mauer,** *f.* town *or* city wall. **-rennen,** *n.* tilting at the ring. **-richter,** *m.* umpire (*Boxing.*) **-s,** *see* **rings.** **-schießen,** *n.* target-shooting. **-sendung,** *f.* nation-wide relay, national hook-up (*Rad.*). **-straße,** *f.* circular road. **-verbindung,** *f.* cyclic compound (*Chem.*). **-wall,** *m.* rampart(s).

ring-en, 1. *ir.v.n.* (*aux.* h.) struggle; wrestle, grapple; (*mit einem*) *um eine S. -en,* contend (with a p.) for a th.; *-en nach einer S.,* strive after *or* for, contend *or* fight for a th.; *nach Atem -en,* gasp for breath. 2. *v.a.* wring, wrench, wrest; *zu Boden -en,* throw (*in wrestling*); *mit dem Tode -en,* be in the throes of death, be in one's last throes. **-er,** *m.* wrestler. **-ergriff,** *m.* wrestling hold. **-kampf,** *m.* wrestling match. **-kämpfer,** *m.*, *see* **-er.**

rings, *adv.* round, around; *-herum, -um, -umher,* round about, all round, all around, on all sides.

Rinn-e, *f.* (-en) gutter, drain, trench; groove, furrow; channel. **-en,** *ir.v.n.* (*aux.* s.) run, flow; trickle, drip; (*aux.* h.) leak, gutter (*of candles*), run (*of nose*). **-sal,** *n.* watercourse, channel, rill, trough; chute. **-stein,** *m.* gutter; sink; sewer, culvert.

Ripp-e, *f.* (-en) rib; vein (*of a leaf*); groin (*Arch.*); (*coll.*) *ich kann es mir nicht aus den -en schneiden,* I cannot do the impossible, you can't squeeze blood from a stone. **-en,** *v.a.* rib, groin; *gerippt,* ribbed, fluted, corded. **-enartig,** *adj. see* **-ig.** **-enbraten,** *m.* roast loin. **-enbruch,** *m.* fracture of a rib. **-enfell,** *n.* pleura (*Anat.*). **-enfellentzündung,** *f.* pleurisy. **-engewölbe,** *n.* rib-vaulting (*Arch.*). **-enknorpel,** *m.* costal cartilage. **-e(n)speer,** *m.* & *n.* (smoked) ribs of pork. **-enstück,** *n.* rib (*of meat*), chop. **-ig,** *adj.* ribbed, costal. **-speer,** *see* **-enspeer.**

Rips, *m.* (-es, -e) rep.

ripsraps, *adv.* & *int.* (*coll.*) in a twinkling.

Ris-iko, *n.* (-ikos, -iken & *Austr. dial.* -ikos) (*C.L.*) risk. **-kant,** *adj.* risky, dangerous. **-kieren,** *v.a.* risk, chance.

Rispe, *f.* (-n) panicle (*Bot.*).

riß, rissest, risse, *see* **reißen.**

Riß, *m.* (-(ss)es, -(ss)e) tear, rent, laceration; cleft, fissure, chink, gap; break, crack, flaw; plan, elevation, design, technical drawing, draft, sketch, outline; schism, breach; *vor dem – stehen,* (*dial.*) step into the breach. **-(ss)ig,** *adj.* torn, rent; cracked, fissured; *-(ss)ig werden,* crack, get brittle, spring (*of wood*).

Rist, *m.* (-es, -e) instep, arch (*of foot*); back of the hand. **-griff,** *m.* hold with fingers upwards (*Gymn.*).

ristorn-ieren, *v.a.* (*C.L.*) transfer (*an item*) from one account to another; cancel. **-o,** *m.* & *n.* (-os, -os) transfer; return premium; cancellation of insurance.

Ritornell, *n.* (-s, -e) ritornello (*Mus.*), triad, triplet (*Metr.*).

Ritratte, *f.* (-n) (*C.L.*) re-exchange, redraft.

ritschratsch! *int.* snip! snap!

ritt, rittest, ritte, *see* **reiten.**

Ritt, *m.* (-(e)s, -e) ride (on horseback); *einen – machen,* take a ride; *in einem -e,* (*coll.*) at one go, without a break. **-ig,** *adj.* broken-in (*of horses*). **-lings,** *adv.* astride. **-meister,** *m.* cavalry captain.

Ritter, *m.* (-s, –) knight; cavalier; *Tempel-,* (Knight) Templar; *Johanniter-,* Knight of St. John, Knight Hospitaller; *fahrender –,* knight-errant; *Deutsch-,* Teutonic Knight; *– ohne Furcht und Tadel,* knight without fear and without reproach (*Bayard*); *– von der traurigen Gestalt,* knight of the woeful countenance (*Don Quixote*); *einen zum – schlagen,* knight a p., dub a p. a knight; *arme – (pl.),* fritters (*Cook.*). **-burg,** *f.* knight's castle. **-dienst,** *m.* gallantry, chivalrous action; *einer Dame -dienste leisten,* act as a lady's cavalier. **-geist,** *m.* spirit of chivalry. **-gut,** *n.* nobleman's estate, manor. **-gutsbesitzer,** *m.* lord of the manor. **-lich,** *adj.* knightly, chivalrous; valiant, gallant. **-lichkeit,** *f.* gallantry, chivalry. **-orden,** *m.* knightly order; *deutscher -orden,* Teutonic order. **-pflicht,** *f.* knight's duty. **-roman,** *m.* romance of chivalry. **-schaft,** *f.* knighthood, body of knights, chivalry. **-schlag,** *m.* dubbing, knighting, accolade. **-smann,** *m.* (-sleute) knight. **-spiel,** *n.* tournament. **-sporn,** *m.* larkspur (*Bot.*). **-stand,** *m.* knighthood. **-tat,** *f.* chivalrous deed of arms. **-treue,** *f.* knightly allegiance. **-tum,** *n.* chivalry. **-wesen,** *n.* chivalry. **-würde,** *f.* knightly rank. **-zeit,** *f.* age of chivalry.

Rit-ual, *n.* (-s, -e) ritual. **-ualismus,** *m.* ritualism. **-uell,** *adj.* ritual. **-us,** *m.* (-us, -en) rite.

Ritz, *m.* (-es, -e) **-e,** *f.* (-en) cleft, fissure, crack, crevice, rift, chink, slit; scratch, chap, abrasion. **-en,** *v.a.* scratch, graze, cut, slit, crack. **-ig,** *adj.* cracked; crannied; scratched.

Ritzel, *n.* pinion (*Mach.*).

Rival, *m.* (-s & -en, -e & *Austr. dial.* -en), **-e,** *m.* (-en, -en), rival. **-isieren,** *v.n.* (*aux.* h.) rival. **-ität,** *f.* rivalry.

Rizinusöl, *n.* castor-oil.

Robbe, *f.* (-n) seal. **-nfell,** *n.* seal-skin. **-nschlag,** *m.* seal-hunting.

Robber, *m.* (-s, –) rubber (*of whist*).

Robot, *m.* (-(e)s, -e), & *Austr. dial. f.* (-e) (*dial.*) villa(i)nage, forced labour. **-er,** *m.* (-s, –) forced labourer, villain; human automaton, robot.

roch, rochest, röche, *see* **riechen.**

Roche, *m.* (-n(s), -n), **-n,** *m.* (-ns, -n) roach, ray, thornback (*Icht.*).

Roch-ade [*pron.* rɔʃ- *or* rɔx-], *f.* castling (*Chess*). **-ieren,** *v.n.* (*aux.* h.) castle (*Chess*).

röcheln, 1. *v.n.* (*aux.* h.) rattle in the throat. 2. *n.* death-rattle.

Rock, *m.* (-(e)s, ⸚e) coat (*for men*), skirt (*for women*); *geteilter –,* divided skirt; *kniefreier –,* knee-length skirt; *des Königs –,* the King's uniform; *der bunte –,* military uniform; *den bunten – anziehen,* join the colours; *ganz ohne ⸚chen,* (*fig.*) naked and unashamed. **-falte,** *f.* pleat of a dress. **-futter,** *n.* lining of a coat. **-schoß,** *m.* coat-tail; *sich einem an die -schöße* or *an jemandes -schöße hängen,* hang on a p.'s coat-tails, follow a p. round, make o.s. a nuisance. **-zipfel,** *m.* lappet of a coat; *der Mutter am -zipfel* or *an Mutters -zipfel hängen,* be tied to one's mother's apron-strings.

Rocken, *m.* (-s, –) distaff; *Werg am – haben,* be mixed up in a th., have one's finger in the pie. **–politik,** *f.* women's wiles, petticoat government. **–stube,** *f.* spinning-room. **–weisheit,** *f.* old wives' tale.

Rod–el, *f.* (-n) & *m.* (-s, –) toboggan. **–elbahn,** *f.* toboggan-run. **–eln,** *v.n.* toboggan. **–elschlitten,** *m.* toboggan. **–elsport,** *m.* tobogganing. **–ler,** *m.* tobogganer.

rödel–n, *v.a.* rack down (*Engin.*). **–balken,** *m.* racking-balk, side-rail, wheel guide.

rod–en, *v.a.* & *n.* (*aux.* h.) root out, clear (*a wood*), make arable. **–eland,** *n.*, **–ung,** *f.* clearing, woodland cleared for cultivation, virgin soil.

Rodomont–ade, *f.* swagger, bragging, bluster. **–ieren,** *v.n.* swagger, brag, (*sl.*) shoot off one's mouth, talk big.

Rog–en, *m.* (hard) roe, spawn. **–enfisch,** *m.* spawner. **–enstein,** *m.* oolite. **–ner,** *m.*, *see* **–enfisch.**

Roggen, *m.* rye. **–bau,** *m.* rye-growing. **–brot,** *n.* rye-bread.

roh, *adj.* raw, unrefined, in native state, unwrought, crude; rough, rude, coarse, gross, vulgar, barbarous, brutal, cruel; *–e Pferde,* untrained horses; *einen behandeln wie ein –es Ei,* treat a p. with the greatest consideration. **–bau,** *m.* bare *or* rough brickwork. **–betrag,** *m.* gross amount. **–eisen,** *n.* pig-iron. **–(h)eit,** *f.* rawness, raw state, roughness, coarseness, crudeness, crudity; rudeness, brutality; piece of rudeness, brutal action. **–ertrag,** *m.* gross yield *or* receipts. **–erzeugnisse,** *n.pl.* raw products. **–formel,** *f.* empirical formula. **–frischen,** *n.* first refining. **–frucht,** *f.* unprocessed produce. **–gar,** *adj.* partly refined. **–gewicht,** *n.* gross weight. **–kost,** *f.* uncooked (vegetarian) food. **–köstler,** *m.* vegetarian. **–leder,** *n.* untanned leather. **–ling,** *m.* brute, coarse lout, ruffian. **–material,** *n.* raw material. **–metall,** *n.* crude metal. **–öl,** *n.* crude oil, naphtha. **–schrift,** *f.* rough copy, first draft. **–schwefel,** *m.* native sulphur. **–seide,** *f.* tussore silk. **–stoffe,** *m.pl.* raw materials, natural products. **–zucker,** *m.* unrefined sugar. **–zustand,** *m.* raw state.

Rohr, *n.* (-(e)s, -e) reed, cane; tube, pipe; flue; barrel (*of guns*); *spanisches –,* Spanish reed, cane; *indisches –,* bamboo; *geschweißtes –,* welded tube; *sich auf ein schwaches – stützen,* trust to a broken reed; (*Prov.*) *wer im – sitzt, hat gut Pfeifen schneiden,* it's all right for you to talk. **–ammer,** *f.* reed-bunting (*Orn.*). **–anschluß,** *m.* pipe-joint. **–bruch,** *m.* burst pipe. **–brunnen,** *m.* artesian well. **–dommel,** *f.* bittern (*Orn.*). **–en,** *adj.* of cane, wicker. **–flöte,** *f.* reed-pipe. **–förmig,** *adj.* tubular. **–geflecht,** *n.* wickerwork, basket work. **–ig,** *adj.* reedy, overgrown with reeds. **–kolben,** *m.* reed-mace (*Bot.*). **–krepierer,** *m.* barrel burst (*Artil.*). **–leger,** *m.* pipe-fitter, plumber. **–leitung,** *f.* pipe-line, conduit. **–matte,** *f.* rush-mat. **–mündung,** *f.* muzzle (*of a gun*). **–netz,** *n.* pipes, conduit. **–post,** *f.* pneumatic post (*in large stores, etc.*). **–rahmen,** *m.* tubular chassis (*Motor.*). **–rücklauf,** *m.* barrel recoil. **–schelle,** *f.* pipe-clip. **–schieber,** *m.* sleeve-valve. **–schlitten,** *m.* barrel slide. **–schmied,** *m.* gun-barrel-maker. **–seele,** *f.* bore (*of a gun*). **–spatz,** *m.*; (*coll.*) *wie ein –spatz schimpfen,* scold like a fishwife. **–stock,** *m.* cane; bamboo. **–stuhl,** *m.* cane, wicker *or* basket-chair. **–weite,** *f.* bore, calibre. **–werk,** *n.* tubing; tube mill; wicker work; reed-stop (*Org.*). **–zange,** *f.* pipe wrench. **–zerspringer,** *m.*, *see* **–krepierer.** **–zucker,** *m.* cane-sugar.

Röhr–e, *f.* (-en) pipe, tube; (wireless) valve; canal, duct, conduit; flue, shaft, tunnel, cylinder; small recess in a stove (*for baking or keeping things warm*). **–en,** *v.n.* (*aux.* h.) fit with tubes; bell (*of stags*). **–enapparat,** *m.* valve-set. **–enempfänger,** *m.* valve-receiver. **–enförmig,** *adj.* fistular, tubular. **–engang,** *m.* conduit, piping. **–enkennlinie,** *f.* valve characteristics (*Rad.*). **–enkessel,** *m.* cylindrical boiler. **–enknochen,** *m.* hollow bone. **–enleitung,** *f.* piping, pipes, tubing. **–ensender,** *m.* valve-transmitter. **–enwasser,** *n.* pipe-water. **–enwerk,** *n.* tubing, piping. **–icht,** *n.* reeds. **–ig,** *adj.* reed-like; tubular; containing pipes.

Rokoko, *n.* (–) rococo. **–mäßig,** *adj.* in rococo style.

Roll–e, *f.* (-en) roll; cylinder, roller; caster, pulley, reel, spool; mangle, calender; twist, bundle, coil, scroll; spiral (*Av.*); role, part (*Theat.*); list of personnel, duty roster (*Mil.*); *auf –en laufend,* moving on rollers *or* casters; *aus der –e fallen,* act out of character, misbehave; *eine –e spielen,* act a part, cut a figure; *keine –e spielen,* be of no importance; *eine große –e spielen,* be of great importance, have considerable influence. **–bahn,** *f.* landing ground, runway, tarmac (*Av.*). **–bewegung,** *f.* rolling (motion). **–brett,** *n.* mangling-board. **–en,** 1. *v.a.* & *n.* (*aux.* h. & s.) roll; revolve, rotate; trundle; taxi (*Av.*); mangle, calender; roar, rumble; *–endes Material,* rolling stock (*Railw.*); *gerolltes r,* trilled r. 2. *v.r.* roll up, curl. **–enbesetzung,** *f.* cast (*Theat.*). **–enförmig,** *adj.* curled, rolled, cylindrical, coiled, convoluted. **–enlager,** *n.* roller-bearing. **–enpresse,** *f.* rolling-press. **–enzug,** *m.* block and tackle. **–er,** *m.* rolling sea (*Naut.*); scooter; canary. **–ern,** *v.n.* play with *or* ride on a scooter. **–feld,** *n.*, *see* **–bahn.** **–film,** *m.* roll-film. **–fuhrwerk,** *n.*, *see* **–wagen.** **–geld,** *n.* cartage; charge for mangling. **–gelenk,** *n.* pivot joint. **–geschäft,** *n.* carter, carrier, transport firm. **–handtuch,** *n.* roller-towel. **–kloben,** *m.* pulley. **–kommando,** *n.* raiding party; organized hecklers (*to break up meetings*). **–kutscher,** *m.* carter, carrier, vanman. **–(l)aden,** *m.* roller-shutter. **–maschine,** *f.* mangle. **–mops,** *m.* pickled herring, soused herring. **–muskel,** *m.* & *f.* trochlear *or* rotator muscle. **–schuh,** *m.* roller-skate. **–schuhlaufen,** *n.* roller-skating. **–sitz,** *m.* sliding seat. **–stein,** *m.* boulder. **–stuhl,** *m.* bath chair, invalid chair, wheel-chair. **–treppe,** *f.* escalator. **–tür,** *f.* sliding door. **–ung,** *f.* curvature, volution. **–verband,** *m.* roller bandage. **–vorhang,** *m.* roller-blind. **–wagen,** *m.* truck, dray. **–wäsche,** *f.* clothes for mangling. **–werk,** *n.* undercarriage (*Av.*); scrollwork (*Arch.*).

Roman, *m.* (-s, -e) novel, work of fiction, romance; *Ritter–,* romance of chivalry. **–haft,** *adj.* fictitious, fanciful, fantastic. **–ist,** *m.* teacher *or* student of Romance languages. **–schriftsteller,** *m.* novelist. **–tik,** *f.* romantic poetry; romantic period, romanticism. **–tiker,** *m.* romantic author *or* poet, romanticist; (*pl.*) the Romantics, Romanticists. **–tisch,** *adj.* romantic. **–ze,** *f.* (-zen) poetic romance; ballad.

Römer, *m.* (-s, –) large drinking-glass, rummer. *See the Index of Names.*

Rond–e, *f.* (-en) round, patrol. **–ell,** *n.* (-s, -e) round plot (*Hort.*); round tower, bastion. **–engang,** *m.*, *see* **–e.**

röntgen, *v.a.* X-ray. **–anlage,** *f.* X-ray plant. **–aufnahme,** *f.*, **–bild,** *n.* X-ray photograph. **–isieren,** *v.a.* (*Austr. dial.*) X-ray. **–ographisch,** *adj.* radiographic. **–strahlen,** *m.pl.* X-rays.

rören, *v.n.*, *see* **röhren.**

rosa, *indecl. adj.* rose-coloured, pink.

Ros–e, *f.* (-en) rose; erysipelas (*Med.*); rose-window; compass-rose; rosette; *wilde –e,* sweet-brier, dog-rose; (*Prov.*) *keine –e ohne Dornen,* no rose without a thorn; *auf –en gebettet,* on a bed of roses. **–enartig,** *adj.* rosaceous; like a rose. **–enbusch,** *m.* rose-bush, rose-tree. **–enessenz,** *f.* attar of roses. **–enfarbig,** *adj.* rose-coloured. **–enholz,** *n.* rosewood. **–enkohl,** *m.* Brussels sprouts. **–enkranz,** *m.* garland of roses; rosary; *seinen –enkranz beten,* tell one's beads. **–enkreuzer,** *m.* Rosicrucian. **–enmontag,** *m.* Monday before Lent. **–enöl,** *n.* attar of roses. **–enstock,** *m.* standard rose-tree; *wilder –enstock,* eglantine. **–enzeit,** *f.* (*fig.*) blossom time, youth. **–enzucht,** *f.* cultivation of roses. **–ette,** *f.* (-n) rosette; centre-piece (*of a ceiling*); rose-diamond. **–ig,** *adj.* rosy, roseate; *in der –igsten Laune,* in the sweetest of tempers; *die Dinge im –igsten Lichte sehen,* look on the brightest side of things, see things through rose-tinted spectacles.

Rosine, *f.* (-n) raisin, sultana; (*coll.*) (*große*) *–n im Kopfe haben,* plan great things, be full of crazy ideas, be full of o.s.

Rosmarin, *m.* rosemary.

Roß, *n.* (-(ss)es, -(ss)e) (*poet.*) steed, charger; (*pl.*

⁻er) (*dial.*) horse; (*coll.*) blockhead; *auf dem hohen – sitzen*, be on one's high horse. **–apfel,** *m.* horse-manure. **–arzt,** *m.* veterinary surgeon. **–bändiger,** *m.*, **–(ss)ebändiger,** *m.* horse-breaker. **–bremse,** *f.* gadfly. **–(ss)en,** *v.n.* desire the stallion (*of mares*). **–haar,** *n.* horsehair. **–händler,** *m.* horse-dealer. **–huf,** *m.* coltsfoot (*Tussilago farfara*) (*Bot.*). **–(ss)ig,** *adj.* desiring the stallion (*of mares*). **–kamm,** *m.* curry-comb; horse-dealer. **–kastanie,** *f.* horse-chestnut. **–kur,** *f.* drastic treatment. **–markt,** *m.* horse-fair. **–schweif,** *m.* horse's tail. **–täuscher,** *m.* horse-dealer, horse-coper. **–wurzel,** *f.* carline thistle.

Rösselsprung, *m.* knight's move (*Chess*).

¹Rost, *m.* (-es, -e) grate, fire-grate; gridiron; duck-board; pilework (*Arch.*). **–braten,** *m.* joint; roast beef.

²Rost, *m.* rust; blight, mildew, smut (*on corn*). **–braun,** *adj.* russet, rusty brown. **–en,** *v.n.* (*aux.* h. & s.) rust, get *or* become rusty. **–fleck(en),** *m.* iron-mould. **–fleckig,** *adj.* rust-stained. **–frei,** *adj.* stainless (*steel*). **–ig,** *adj.* rusty, rusted. **–schutz,** *m.* rust prevention. **–schützend,** *adj.* anti-corrosive. **–schutzfarbe,** *f.* anti-rust paint.

Röst–e, *f.* smelting (*ore*); retting *or* steeping (*of flax*); flax-hole. **–arbeit,** *f.* smelting process (*by affinity*). **–en,** *v.a.* roast, grill, broil; toast; calcine, torrefy; smelt (*ore*); steep, ret (*flax*); *geröstetes Brot*, toast. **–gummi,** *n.* dextrin. **–ofen,** *m.* calcining *or* roasting-furnace, kiln. **–pfanne,** *f.* frying-pan. **–stätte,** *f.* rettery (*flax*).

rot, 1. *adj.* red; ruddy, rubicund; *die –e Erde*, Westphalia; *–er Faden*, (*fig.*) unbroken thread; *den –en Hahn aufs Dach setzen*, set fire to s.o.'s house; *er hat keinen –en Heller*, he hasn't a bean *or* a brass farthing; *–es Kreuz*, Red Cross; *– machen*, make red, redden; cause to blush, put to the blush; *–e Ruhr*, dysentry; (*Prov.*) *heute –, morgen tot*, here today, gone tomorrow; *–es Warnlicht*, (*fig.*) the red light, indication of danger; *– werden*, get red, blush, colour up. 2. *n.* red; redness; rouge. **–auge,** *n.* roach (*Leuciscus*) (*Icht.*). **–äugig,** *adj.* red-eyed. **–backig** *or* **–bäckig,** *adj.* rosy-cheeked, ruddy. **–blond,** *adj.* auburn, sandy. **–braun,** *adj.* & *n.* reddish-brown, russet, bay (*horse*). **–bruch,** *m.* red-shortness (*Metal.*). **–buche,** *f.* copper beech. **–dorn,** *m.* pink hawthorn. **–e(r),** *m.* red-haired *or* -headed person, red-head; communist, bolshevik. **–(e)kreuzschwester,** *f.* Red-Cross nurse. **–fuchs,** *m.* bay *or* sorrel horse. **–gelb,** *adj.* & *n.* orange (coloured). **–gerber,** *m.* tanner. **–gießer** *m.* copper-founder, brazier. **–glühen,** *v.a.* heat to redness. **–glühend,** *adj.* red-hot. **–glühhitze,** *f.*, **–glut,** *f.* red-heat. **–guß,** *m.* red brass, bronze. **–haarig,** *adj.* red-haired. **–haut,** *f.* redskin. **–holz,** *n.* Sappan wood (*Caesalpinia sappa*) (*Bot.*); Brazil wood (*Caesalpinia echinata*); Wellingtonia, Mammoth tree (*Sequoia*); camwood, redwood. **–kabis,** *m.* (*Swiss dial.*) red cabbage. **–käppchen,** *n.* Red Riding Hood, **–kehlchen,** *n.* robin red-breast. **–kohl,** *m.*, **–kraut,** *n.* red cabbage. **–kopf,** *m.* red-haired person, red-head. **–köpfig,** *adj.* red-haired, sandy. **–lauf,** *m.* erysipelas; red murrain (*of pigs*). **–liegende(s),** *n.* lower new red sandstone. **–machend,** *adj.* rubifacient. **–rauschgelb,** *n.* realgar. **–salz,** *n.* sodium acetate. **–schwänzchen,** *n.* redstart (*Orn.*). **–spon,** *m.* (*dial.*) claret. **–stift,** *m.* red pencil. **–spießglanz,** *n.* kermesite. **–tanne,** *f.* spruce-fir (*Picea excelsa*) (*Bot.*). **–verschiebung,** *f.* displacement towards red end of spectrum. **–wangig,** *adj.* rosy-cheeked. **–wein,** *m.* red wine. **–welsch,** *n.* thieves' Latin. **–wild,** *n.* red deer.

Rot–ation, *f.* rotation. **–ationsbewegung,** *f.* rotatory motion. **–ationsmaschine,** *f.* rotary press. **–ationspumpe,** *f.* rotary pump. **–ieren,** *v.n.* (*aux.* h.) rotate.

Röt–e, *f.* redness, red; flush, blush; *die –e steigt ihm ins Gesicht*, the colour rushes to his face, he colours up. **–el,** *m.* ruddle, red ochre; red chalk, red pencil. **–eli,** *n.* (*dial.*) robin. **–eln,** 1. *pl.* German measles, rubella. 2. *v.a.* & *n.* mark with red pencil. **–elstift,** *m.* red (chalk) pencil. **–en,** 1. *v.a.* make *or* colour red, redden. 2. *v.r.* get red, get flushed, flush. **–lein,** *n.* (*dial.*) robin. **–lich,** *adj.* reddish. **–lichbraun,** *adj.* & *n.* russet. **–ling,** *m.* (*dial.*) robin.

Rott–e, *f.* (-en) file (*Mil.*); two aircraft, two ships (*operating together*); band, gang, horde, rabble; *blinde –e*, blank file (*Mil.*). **–en,** *v.a.* & *r.* assemble together; troop, collect in a mob. **–enaufmarsch,** *m.* deployment in file. **–enfeuer,** *n.* volley. **–enführer,** *m.* file-leader; (*Nat. Soc.*) corporal; ganger, foreman. **–enweise,** *adv.* in gangs; in files. **–meister,** *m.* boss, ganger, foreman, overseer.

Rotz, *m.* nasal mucus, (*vulg.*) snot; glanders (*Vet.*). (*vulg.*) **–bube,** *m.*, *see* **–junge.** **–en,** *v.n.* have a running nose, (*vulg.*) blow one's nose. **–ig,** *adj.* (*vulg.*) snotty; glandered (*Vet.*). **–junge,** *m.*, **–löffel,** *m.* impudent young brat. (*vulg.*) **–nase,** *f.* dirty nose; (*fig.*) brat.

Roul–ade, *f.* rolled meat; trill (*Mus.*). **–eau,** *n.* (-s, -s) roller blind.

routiniert, *p.p.* & *adj.* experienced, versed; well trained.

Rüb–e, *f.* rape; *weiße –e*, turnip; *gelbe –e*, carrot; *rote –e*, beetroot; *Mohr–e*, carrot; *Zucker–e*, sugar beet; *durcheinander wie Kraut und –en*, higgledy-piggledy. **–enfeld,** *n.* field of turnips. **–enförmig,** *adj.* turnip-shaped. **–(en)sam(en),** *m.* rape-seed (*Brassica rapus*) (*Bot.*). **–enzucker,** *m.* beet-sugar. **–kohl,** *m.* (*Swiss dial.*) kohlrabi. **–öl,** *n.* rape oil. **–sen,** *m.* rapeseed.

Rubin, *m.* (-s, -e) ruby. **–fluß,** *m.*, **–glas,** *n.* ruby glass. **–rot,** *adj.* ruby-(red).

Rub–rik, *f.* (-en) heading; column, rubric. **–rizieren,** *v.a.* supply headings; arrange in columns.

ruch–bar, *adj.* notorious; known, public; *–bar machen*, noise abroad. *–bar werden*, become known, get about. **–barkeit,** *f.* notoriety. **–los,** *adj.* wicked, nefarious, infamous, impious, profligate, vicious, malicious. **–losigkeit,** *f.* wickedness, profligacy, infamy; wicked act.

Ruck, *m.* (-(e)s, -e) jolt, jerk, tug, sudden push *or* movement, start, shock; *sich einen – geben*, pull o.s. together; *mit* or *in einem –, auf einen –*, all at once, suddenly. **–artig,** *adj.* jerky. **–eln,** *v.n.* (*aux.* h.) edge up. **–en,** *v.n.* (*aux.* h.) 1. (*usually 3rd pers.*) *see* **rücken,** 2; 2. coo (*of doves*). **–weise,** *adv.* by snatches *or* jerks, intermittently.

rück (*prefix normally with nouns*; *for corresponding verbs see* **zurück–.** *As prefix with verbs only in poetry*). **–ansicht,** *f.* rear view. **–antwort,** *f.* reply; *Postkarte mit –antwort*, reply post-card. **–beförderung,** *f.* evacuation to the rear (*Mil.*). **–berufung,** *f.* recall. **–bezüglich,** *adj.* reflexive (*Gram.*). **–bilden,** *v.n.* re-form, undergo involution. **–bildung,** *f.* back-formation (*Philol.*); involution (*Maths.*); reversion to type. **–bleibsel,** *n.* residue, remainder. **–blick,** *m.* backward glance, glance back, retrospect; *einen –blick werfen auf eine S*, pass s.th. in review. **–blickend,** *adj.* retrospective. **–bürge,** *m.*, **–bürgschaft,** *f.* collateral security. **–datieren,** *v.a.* antedate. **–erinnerung,** *f.* reminiscence. **–erstatten,** *v.a.* refund. **–erstattung,** *f.* restitution. **–fahrkarte,** *f.* return-ticket. **–fahrt,** *f.* return journey. **–fall,** *m.* reversion; relapse. **–fällig,** *adj.* revertible; relapsing; *ein –fälliger*, a backslider, recidivist. **–flug,** *m.* homeward *or* return flight. **–forderung,** *f.* reclamation; counter-demand. **–frage,** *f.* query, further inquiry, check-back. **–führung,** *f.* restoring mechanism, follow-up device. **–gabe,** *f.* return, restitution. **–gang,** *m.* back-stroke; (*C.L.*) falling off, decline, relapse, retrogression. **–gängig,** *adj.* retrograde, retrogressive; declining; null and void; *–gängig machen*, cancel, annul, revoke, break off, put an end to. **–gewinnung,** *f.* recovery, salvage. **–grat,** *n.* (-(e)s, -e) backbone, spine, vertebral column. **–grats(ver)-krümmung,** *f.* curvature of the spine. **–gratswirbel,** *m.* spinal vertebra. **–halt,** *m.* prop, stay, support; (*archaic*) restraint, reserve. **–hältig,** *adj.* restrained, reserved. **–haltlos,** *adj.* unreserved, plain, open, frank. **–handschlag,** *m.* backhand stroke (*Tenn.*). **–kauf,** *m.* repurchase; redemption. **–käuflich,** *adj.* redeemable. **–kehr,** *f.*, **–kunft,** *f.* return. **–kopp(e)lung,** *f.* reaction, regeneration, feed-back (*Rad.*). **-lage,** *f.* reserve (fund). **-lauf,** *m.* recoil (*of guns, etc.*). **-laufbremse,** *f.* recoil buffer (*Artil.*). **-läufer,** *m.* dead letter (*Post Office*). **-läufig,** *adj.* retrograde, retrogressive; recurrent; *-läufiger Verband,* figure of eight bandage (*Surg.*); *-läufige Sendung,* postal package addressee unknown. **-läufigkeit,** *f.* reaction. **-lehne,** *f.* (chair-)back. **-leitung,** *f.* return (line) (*of electric circuit*). **-lings,** *adv.* from behind; backwards. **-marsch,** *m.* march back, retreat; return voyage (*Naut.*). **-nahme,** *f.* re-acceptance. **-porto,** *n.* return-postage. **-prall,** *m.* repercussion, rebound; recoil; reaction. **-reise,** *f.* return journey, journey home. **-ruf,** *m.* recall. **-schau,** *f.* review, retrospect. **-schlag,** *m.* recoil, kick (*of a gun*); rebound; (*fig.*) check, set-back, reverse; reaction, atavism, reversion to type. **-schlagventil,** *n.* non-return valve. **-schluß,** *m.* conclusion, inference. **-schritt,** *m.* retrogression, recession; pace back (*Mil.*); relapse, falling off. **-schrittlich,** *adj.* reactionary. **-seite,** *f.* back; reverse, wrong side. **-seitig,** *adj.* on the other side, on the reverse page. **-sendung,** *f.* return (*of goods, etc.*). **-sicht,** *f.* respect, regard, motive, consideration; notice; discretion; *aus -sicht gegen,* in deference to; *in* or *mit -sicht auf* (*Acc.*), with regard to; *ohne -sicht auf,* irrespective of, without regard for; *-sicht nehmen auf* (*Acc.*), take into consideration, have regard (for *or* to), have *or* show consideration for. **-sichtlich,** *adv. & prep.* (*with Gen.* or *auf*); with regard to, considering. **-sichtnahme,** *f.* respect, consideration. **-sichtslos,** *adj.* inconsiderate, unfeeling, ruthless, determined, at all costs, relentless, reckless. **-sichtslosigkeit,** *f.* lack of consideration, disregard. **-sichtsvoll,** *adj.* considerate, thoughtful. **-sitz,** *m.* back seat. **-spiegel,** *m.* driving mirror (*Motor.*). **-spiel,** *n.* return-match. **-sprache,** *f.* conference; discussion, consultation; *-sprache nehmen,* discuss, talk over, confer about. **-stand,** *m.* arrears; remainder; outstanding debt; residue, refuse, scraps, sediment, waste, remains; *im -stand sein,* be behindhand, backward *or* in arrears (*with s.th.*). **-ständig,** *adj.* outstanding, overdue, in arrears, residual; backward, behindhand, behind the times, old-fashioned. **-stelltaste,** *f.* back-spacer (*typewriter*). **-stoß,** *m.* recoil, backstroke; repulsion. **-stoßantrieb,** *m.* jet-propulsion (*Av.*). **-stoßdämpfer,** *m.* muzzle brake (*Artil.*). **-stoßmotor,** *m.* jet engine (*Av.*). **-strahler,** *m.* reflector (*Cycl.*). **-streuung,** *f.* scattering (*of X-rays*). **-tratte,** *f.* redraft. **-trift,** *f.* trail (*Av.*). **-tritt,** *m.* retirement, withdrawal, retreat, retrogression; resignation (*from a post*); *-tritt in den Stand der Mannschaften,* reduction to the ranks (*Mil.*). **-trittbremse,** *f.* back-pedalling brake (*Cycl.*). **-vergütung,** *f.* repayment, reimbursement. **-versicherung,** *f.* reinsurance, guarantee. **-wand,** *f.* back (wall). **-wanderer,** *m.* returning emigrant. **-wärtig,** *adj.* rearward. **-wärts,** *adv.* backward(s), back. **-wärtsbewegung,** *f.* backward movement, retrogression, retrograde motion. **-wärtsgang,** *m.* reverse gear (*Motor.*). **-wärtsgehen,** *v.n.* (*aux.* s.) (*fig.*) decline, go down. **-weg,** *m.* return route, way back. **-widerstand,** *m.* reactance (*Rad.*). **-wirkend,** *pr.p. & adj.* retroactive, reciprocal, retrospective; *-wirkendes Gesetz,* ex post facto law (*Law*). **-wirkung,** *f.* reaction, feedback (*Rad.*), retroaction, repercussion. **-zahlung,** *f.* repayment. **-zieher,** *m.* recantation, abjuration, tergiversation; *einen -zieher machen,* climb down. **-zielend,** *adj.* reflexive (*Gram.*). **-zollgüter,** *n.pl.* debenture goods. **-zollschein,** *m.* certificate of drawback (*C.L.*). **-zug,** *m.* retreat, withdrawal (*Mil.*); (*fig.*) climb-down. **-zündung,** *f.* backfire.

Rücken, 1. *m.* (-s, –) back, rear; ridge; bridge (*of the nose*); chine (*of beef*); saddle (*of mutton*); spine (*of book*); *– an –,* addorsed (*Her.*); *einem den – decken,* cover *or* protect a p.'s rear; *einem den – kehren,* turn one's back upon a p.; *sich* (*Dat.*) *den – frei halten,* cover one's retreat; not commit o.s. absolutely; *einen krummen – machen,* cringe; *in den – fallen,* attack in the rear. **-angriff,** *m.* attack from the rear. **-band,** *n.* dorsal ligament. **-bein,** *n.* backbone, spine. **-blatt,** *n.* reredos. **-deckung,** *f.* cover, backing, support; parados (*Fort.*). **-feuer,** *n.* reverse fire (*Mil.*). **-flosse,** *f.* dorsal fin. **-flug,** *m.* inverted flying. **-kreuz,** *n.* lumbar region. **-lehne,** *f.* back rest, back (*of chair*). **-linie,** *f.* ridge line. **-mark,** *n.* spinal cord. **-naht,** *f.* back seam. **-panzer,** *m.* carapace. **-säule,** *f.* spinal column. **-schmerzen,** *m.pl.* backache. **-schwimmen,** *n.* back-stroke. **-ständig,** *adj.* dorsal. **-stück,** *n.* chine. **-titel,** *m.* spine lettering. **-weh,** *n.* lumbago. **-wehr,** *f.* parados (*Fort.*). **-wind,** *m.* following wind. **-wirbel,** *m.* dorsal vertebra. **-wölbung,** *f.* dorsal curvature. 2. *v.a.* jerk, pull; move, push along, bring nearer; change the place of. 3. *v.n.* (*aux.* h. & s.) move, go along; proceed, advance; *näher –,* get near; *ins Feld –,* take the field, go to war, go into action (*Mil.*); *in ein Land –,* invade a country.

Rucksack, *m.* (-s, ⸚e) knapsack, rucksack.

rucksen, *v.n.* (*aux.* h.) coo (*of pigeons*).

Rüde, *m.* (-n, -n) large hound; male of dogs, foxes, wolves.

rüde, *adj.* rude, coarse, vulgar, low, brutal.

Rudel, *n.* (-s, –) flock, herd, pack (*also Naut. of submarines*). **-n,** *v.r.* assemble in herds. **-weise,** *adv.* in herds.

Ruder, *n.* (-s, –) (*coll.*) oar; rudder, helm; *am – sein,* steer; rule, be at the helm *or* at the head of affairs; *ans – kommen,* come into power; *sich ins – legen,* row hard, (*fig.*) put one's back into. **-bank,** *f.* thwart. **-blatt,** *n.* oar-blade. **-boot,** *n.* rowing boat. **-dolle,** *f.* rowlock, thole-pin. **-er,** *m.* rower, oarsman. **-fuß,** *m.* webbed foot. **-knecht,** *m.* rower. **-kommando,** *n.* steering order (*Naut.*). **-los,** *adj.* without a helm; *-loses Schiff,* disabled ship. **-n,** *v.a. & n.* (*aux.* h. & s.) row, paddle; *lang -n,* pull a long stroke; *rückwärts -n,* back water. **-pinne,** *f.* tiller. **-schlag,** *m.* stroke of the oar. **-schwanz,** *m.* caudal fin. **-sklave,** *m.* galley-slave. **-sport,** *m.* rowing. **-verein,** *m.* rowing club.

Ruf, *m.* (-(e)s, -e) call, shout, cry, hail, summons; exclamation; rumour; repute, reputation, name, standing, fame; *einen in den – bringen,* give a p. the reputation of; *in üblen – bringen,* defame; *der Professor hat einen – nach Berlin erhalten,* the professor has been offered a chair at Berlin; *dem -e nach,* by reputation; *im -e stehen,* be reputed, be considered (to be); *bei einem in gutem -e stehen,* be in a p.'s good books. **-en,** *ir.v.a. & n.* (*aux.* h.) call, summons; cry out, shout, exclaim; *er rief mich,* he called me; *einem etwas ins Gedächtnis -en,* recall a th. to a p., call a th. to a p.'s mind; *ins Gewehr -en,* call to arms; *etwas ins Leben -en,* call a th. into being, start a th.; *einen wieder ins Leben -en,* recall a p. to life; *wie gerufen kommen,* come just at the right moment; *einen -en lassen,* send for a p.; *er rief* (*nach*) *mir,* he called for or to me; *um Hilfe -en,* cry for help; *einen zu sich -en,* summon a p.; *zu Hilfe -en,* call in help *or* assistance. **-name,** *m.* Christian name. **-nummer,** *f.* telephone number. **-strom,** *m.* ringing current (*Tele.*). **-weite,** *f.*; *in -weite,* within call *or* earshot. **-zeichen,** *n.* call-signal, call-sign; exclamation mark.

Rüffel, *m.* (-s, –) (*coll.*) reprimand. **-n,** *v.a.* reprimand sharply; (*sl.*) tear off a strip.

Rüge, *f.* (-n) censure, reprimand. **-n,** *v.a.* reprimand, reprove, censure, blame, find fault with; (*archaic*) punish.

Ruh-e, *f.* rest, repose, sleep; stillness, peace, quiet, silence, calm; *er ist nicht aus seiner -e zu bringen,* nothing disturbs his equanimity; *keine -e haben vor einem,* have no peace with a p.; *-e halten,* keep silent, hold one's tongue; *laß mich in -e!* let *or* leave me alone! *in aller -e,* very calmly; *weder Rast noch -',* neither peace nor quiet; *Störung der öffentlichen -e und Ordnung,* disturbance of the peace; *-e vor dem Sturm,* the quiet before the storm; *einem eine angenehme -e wünschen,* wish s.o. a good night; *zur -e bringen,* hush, calm; put to bed; *zur -e gehen,* go to bed; *zur -e (ein)gehen,* go to one's rest, die; *nicht zur -e kommen,* not get any peace *or* rest; *sich zur -e setzen,* retire (*from office*). **-bett,** *n.* (*Swiss dial.*) sofa. **-ebedürftig,** *adj.* in want of rest. **-egehalt,** *n.* pension. **-ehaltung,** *f.* position at rest. **-elage,** *f.* position of rest (*Mech.*). **-elager,**

n. rest camp (*Mil.*). **–elos,** *adj.* restless. **–elosigkeit,** *f.* restlessness. **–en,** *v.n.* (*aux.* h.) rest, repose, sleep; pause, stand still, come to a standstill; be idle, lie fallow; *auf einer S. –en,* be supported by a th., rest *or* be based on a th.; *hier –t,* here lies; *hier –t sich's* or *es sich gut,* here is a good place to rest *or* good resting place; *wir wollen die S. jetzt –en lassen,* we will now leave the matter, let the matter drop for the present. **–end,** *pr.p.* & *adj.* resting, static, latent; *–endes Kapital,* unused *or* uninvested capital. **–epause,** *f.* pause, interval *or* break for rest. **–epulver,** *n.* sedative powder. **–epunkt,** *m.* rest, pause (*Mus.*); caesura; fulcrum, centre of gravity, point of rest; resting-place. **–equartier,** *n.* rest billets (*Mil.*). **–esessel,** *m.* easy-chair. **–espannung,** *f.* open-circuit voltage. **–estand,** *m.* retirement; *in den –estand versetzen,* superannuate; *in den –estand treten,* retire (*from business*), resign (*a post*). **–estatt,** *f.,* **–estätte,** *f.* place of rest, resting-place. **–estellung,** *f.* at ease position (*Mil.*). **–estörer,** *m.* brawler, rioter. **–estörung,** *f.* breach of the peace, disturbance. **–estunde,** *f.* leisure hour. **–etag,** *m.* day of rest, sabbath; holiday. **–ezeichen,** *n.* pause, rest (*Mus.*). **–ezeit,** *f.* rest, leisure time. **–ezustand,** *m.* state of rest, dormancy. **–ig,** 1. *adj.* quiet, silent, tranquil; still, at rest, motionless; serene, calm, peaceful, composed; *–ig, Kinder!* silence! hush! *–ig(es) Blut bewahren,* keep a cool head; *–ig Blut!* keep cool! steady! *–iges Feuer,* deliberate fire (*Artil.*); *ein –iges Gewissen,* an easy conscience; (*C.L.*) *das Geschäft liegt –ig,* business is dull; *bei –iger Überlegung,* on calm reflection. 2. *adv.* (*coll.*) safely, unhesitatingly; *du kannst –ig mitkommen,* it will be all right for you to come. **–rast,** *f.* half-cock (*of firearms*). **–sam,** *adj.* (*archaic*) restful.

Ruhm, *m.* glory, honour; fame, renown, reputation; *sich mit – bedecken,* win great fame; *den – muß man ihm lassen, daß . . .,* it must be said in his favour *or* to his credit, that . . .; *einem zum –e gereichen,* redound to a p.'s honour. **–bedeckt,** *adj.,* **–bekränzt,** *adj.* crowned with glory. **–begier(de),** *f.* thirst for glory, ambition. **–(be)gierig,** *adj.* thirsting for glory, ambitious. **–esblatt,** *n.* honourable page (*in annals*). **–eshalle,** *f.* temple of fame. **–estitel,** *m.* claim to glory. **–los,** *adj.* inglorious, without fame. **–redig,** *adj.* vainglorious, boastful. **–reich,** *adj.* glorious. **–sucht,** *f.,* **–süchtig,** *adj., see* **–begier, –begierig. –voll,** *adj.* famous, glorious. **–würdig,** *adj.* famous, illustrious, praiseworthy, glorious.

rühm–en, 1. *v.a.* praise, extol, glorify, celebrate, mention with praise; *man –t ihn als tapfer,* he is said to be brave. 2. *v.r.* (*with Gen.*) boast (of), pride o.s. (on), brag (about); *ohne mich zu –en,* without boasting; *ich –e mich, sein Freund zu sein,* I am proud to call myself his friend. 3. *n.*; *viel –ens* (*von einer S.*) *machen,* speak in very high terms (of a th.). **–enswert,** *adj.* praiseworthy. **–lich,** *adj.* laudable, praiseworthy, glorious. **–lichkeit,** *f.* glory, gloriousness.

Ruhr, *f.* dysentery. **–krank,** *adj.* suffering from dysentery.

rühr–en, 1. *v.n.*; *an etwas –en,* finger *or* touch a th., come into contact with a th.; make reference to a th.; *daher –t es, daß . . .,* it follows as a consequence of . . . 2. *v.a.* stir, move; touch, strike, beat; set in motion, agitate; affect, make an impression on; turn up (*the ground*), rake (*hay, etc.*); *keinen Finger –en,* not raise a finger; *kein Glied –en können,* not be able to move *or* stir; *die Trommel –en,* beat the drum; *einen zu Tränen –en,* move a p. to tears; *vom Schlage gerührt,* seized with an apoplectic fit; *vom Donner gerührt,* thunderstruck; *Sahne –en,* whip cream. 3. *v.r.* stir, move; bestir o.s., be active, be up and doing, make a move, take steps; *–t Euch!* stand easy! stand at ease! (*Mil.*); bestir yourselves! be quick! *es –t sein Gewissen,* his conscience pricks him. 4. *n.*; *ein menschliches –en,* a physical need *or* urge; a feeling of sympathy. **–end,** *pr.p.* & *adj.* moving, touching, sentimental, pathetic; *–ender Reim,* identical rhyme. **–ig,** *adj.* stirring, busy, active, bustling, brisk, energetic, eager. **–igkeit,** *f.* activity; agility; nimbleness. **–apparat,** *m.* stirrer, mixer, agitator. **–drama,** *n., see* **–stück. –ei,** *n.* scrambled egg. **–eisen,** *n.* poker, raker, stirrer. **–er,** *m.* stirring rod. **–faß,** *n.* churn. **–löffel,** *m.* stirring-ladle. **–-mich-nicht-an,** *n.* noli me tangere (*Bot.*); (*fig.*) aloof *or* touchy person. **–scheit,** *n.* stirrer, rod, paddle, spatula. **–selig,** *adj.* very emotional, sentimental, lachrymose, touchy. **–seligkeit,** *f.* sentimentality. **–stange,** *f.* rake, poker. **–stück,** *n.* melodrama, (*sl.*) sob-stuff. **–ung,** *f.* compassion, sympathy, feeling, emotion; *unter –ung der Trommeln,* with drums beating.

Ruin, *m.* ruin, downfall, decay. **–e,** *f.* (-en) ruins, ruin. **–enhaft,** *adj.* ruinous, in ruins, dilapidated. **–ieren,** *v.a.* ruin, destroy; spoil.

Rülps, *m.* (-es, -e) eructation, belch; lout. **–en,** *v.n.* (*aux.* h.) belch.

'rum, *adv.* & *sep. prefix, coll. for* **herum.** (*coll.*) **–kriegen,** *v.a.* cajole, prevail upon, (*sl.*) get round.

Rum, *m.* (-s, -s & -e) rum. **–brennerei,** *f.* rum-distillery.

Rummel, *m.* uproar, tumult, hubbub, hullabaloo, row, din; hotch-potch; *see also* **–platz**; (*coll.*) *der ganze –,* the whole lot, bunch, shoot *or* boiling; (*coll.*) *er versteht* or *kennt den –,* he knows what's what, he knows all about it. **–n,** *v.n.* (*aux.* h.) *see* **rumpeln,** 1. **–platz,** *m.* fair-ground, amusement park.

Rumor, *m.* (-s, -e) noise, uproar. **–en,** *v.n.* (*aux.* h.) make a noise, rumble.

Rumpel, 1. *m.* (*dial.*) rubbish, lumber, junk. 2. *f.* (*dial.*) scrubbing board. **–ig,** (**rumplig**) *adj.* bumpy, lumpy, uneven, rugged. **–n,** *v.n.* (*aux.* h. & s.) rumble, jolt; rummage; (*dial.*) scrub (*washing*). **–kammer,** *f.* lumber-room, junk room. **–kasten,** *m.* (*hum.*) bone-shaker; worn-out piano. **–stilzchen,** *n.* hobgoblin.

Rumpf, *m.* (-(e)s, ¨-e) trunk, torso; hull (*of a vessel*); fuselage (*Av.*); *mit – und Stumpf,* root and branch, altogether, completely. **–beuge,** *f.* trunk-bending (*Gymn.*). **–ende,** *n.* tail of fuselage (*Av.*). **–holm,** *m.* longeron (*Av.*). **–kanzel,** *f.* cockpit (*Av.*). **–lastig,** *adj.* tail-heavy (*Av.*). **–spant,** *n.* fuselage frame (*Av.*). **–spitze,** *f.* nose of fuselage (*Av.*). **–stück,** *n.* rump steak.

rümpfen, *v.a.*; *die Nase –* (*über*), sneer, turn up one's nose (at).

rund, 1. *adj.* round; circular, spherical; frank, plain; rotund, fat, plump; about, approximately; *–e Summe,* round sum; *gib mir auf meine –e Frage eine –e Antwort,* give me a plain answer to a plain question; *– heraus,* in plain terms; straight out; out with it! *– und nett,* plainly and bluntly; *– abschlagen,* refuse flatly; *– 10 Meilen,* about 10 miles. 2. *n.* globe, orb, sphere, circle. **–a,** *n.* (-s, -s) (*dial.*) roundelay, chorus, drinking-song. **–bau,** *m.* (-ten) circular building. **–bild,** *n.* panoramic view. **–blick,** *m.* view all round, panorama. **–blickfernrohr,** *n.* panoramic sight. **–blickscheinwerfer,** *m.* revolving beacon. **–bogen,** *m.* Roman arch. **–bogenstil,** *m.* Romanesque style. **–brenner,** *m.* ring-burner. **–dorf,** *n., see* **–ling. –e,** *f.* circle; round dance; company, party; lap (*Racing*), round, heat (*Sport.*); patrol, beat; *eine –e geben,* stand a round of (*drinks*); *die –e machen,* be circulated (*round the table*), go the rounds; *10 Meilen in die –e,* 10 miles round; *rings in der –e,* around, round about. **–eisen,** *n.* iron rod. **–en,** *v.a.* & *r.* make round, round (*lips*). **–erhaben,** *adj.* convex. **–erlaß,** *m.* circular (*notice*). **–fahrt,** *f.* circular tour. **–feile,** *f.* round file. **–flug,** *m.* round flight. **–frage,** *f.* inquiry, questionnaire. **–funk,** *m.* wireless, radio, broadcasting; *–funk hören,* listen-in, listen to the radio. **–funkanlage,** *f.* wireless installation. **–funkansager,** *m.* wireless announcer. **–funkdarbietungen,** *f.pl.* radio programme. **–funken,** *v.a.* & *n.* (-funkte, *p.p.* gerundfunkt) broadcast. **–funkgebühr,** *f.* wireless licence. **–funkgerät,** *n.* wireless set. **–funkgesellschaft,** *f.* broadcasting company, radio corporation. **–funkhörer,** *m.* listener(-in). **–funkrede,** *f.* radio talk. **–funksender,** *m.* wireless transmitter. **–funkstation,** *f.,* **–funkstelle,** *f.* broadcasting station. **–funkteilnehmer,** *m.* owner of wireless set. **-funkübertragung,** *f.* outside broadcast. **-funkwesen** *n.* broadcasting. *See also under* **Funk. -gang,** *m.* round (*Mil., etc.*); stroll. **-gebäude,** *n.* rotunda. **-gesang,** *m.* round, roundelay, glee. **-heit,** *f.* roundness. **-heraus,** *adv.* flatly, bluntly, straight out. **-herum,** *adv.* all around, round about. **-hohl,** *adj.* concave. **-holz** *n.* round timbers, logs. **-keil,** *m.* cylindrical wedge. **-kopfschraube,** *f.* round-headed screw. **-lauf,** *m.* circular motion; giant-stride (*Gymn.*). **-lich,** *adj.* roundish, plump, chubby. **-ling,** *m.* radial form of settlement. **-reim,** *m.* refrain. **-reise,** *f.* circular tour, round trip, circuit. **-reisebillett,** *n.*, **-reisekarte,** *f.* circular ticket. **-schau,** *f.* panorama; review; *literarische -schau,* literary review. **-schreiben,** *n.* circular (letter). **-schrift,** *f.* round-hand (*writing*). **-spruch,** *m.* (*Swiss dial.*), *see* **-funk. -stab,** *m.* astragal (*Arch.*). **-stange,** *f.* rod, round section bar (*Metal.*). **-stück,** *n.* (*dial.*) (breakfast) roll. **-um(her),** *adv.* round about. **-umverteidigung,** *f.* all-round defence. **-ung,** *f.* roundness, curve; labialization (*Phon.*); rounding off. **-weg,** *adv.* flatly, plainly, bluntly. **-zange,** *f.* round-nosed pliers.

Ründ-e, *f.* roundness; rotundity; curve (*of an arch*). **-en,** *v.a., see* **runden.**

Run-e, *f.* (-en) rune, runic letter. **-enschrift,** *f.* runic characters; runic inscription. **-enstein,** *m.* runic stone. **-isch,** *adj.* runic.

Runge, *f.* (-n) upright (*on sides of open goods van*) (*Railw.*). **-nwagen,** *m.* heavy goods van (*Railw.*).

Runk-e, *f.*, **-el,** *f.* (*coll.*) lump, chunk. **-elrübe** *f.* (-n) beet(-root). **-en,** *m.* (*coll.*) thick slice, wad. **-s,** *m.* (-ses, -se), (*coll.*) lout. **-sen,** *v.n.* (*dial.*) behave like a boor, (*sl.*) play dirty (*Sport*).

runter, *adv. & sep. prefix, coll. for* **herunter; -!** jump! **-langen,** *v.a.*; (*sl.*) *einem eine -langen,* land *or* dot a p. one.

Runzel, *f.* (-n) wrinkle, pucker, fold; *-n um die Augen,* crows' feet. **-ig, (runzlig)** *adj.* wrinkled, shrivelled, crumpled, puckered; rugose. **-n,** *v.a. & n.* (*aux.* h.) wrinkle, pucker, shrivel; *die Stirn -n,* knit one's brows, frown.

Rüpel, *m.* (-s, -) coarse fellow, boor, lout. **-ei,** *f.* grossness, boorishness; rudeness, insolence. **-haft,** *adj.* boorish, unmannerly, insolent, impudent.

rupfen 1 *v.a.* pluck, pull, pick; (*coll.*) *einen -,* fleece a p.; (*coll.*) *ein Hühnchen mit einem zu - haben,* have a bone to pick with a p. 2. *m. & n.* hessian (*cloth*).

Rupie, *f.* (-n) rupee.

rupp-ig, *adj.* coarse, unmannerly; (*dial.*) ragged, shabby. **-igkeit,** *f.* meanness. **-sack,** *m.* unmannerly lout; (*dial.*) ragamuffin.

Rusch, *m.* (-es, -e) (*dial.*) rush, reed; *- und Busch,* brake and briar.

Rüsche, *f.* (-n) ruche, frilling.

Ruschel, *f.* (-n) *& m.* (-s, -) (*dial.*) careless *or* slapdash person. **-ig, (ruschlig)** *adj.* careless, slovenly, (*sl.*) slap-happy. (*coll.*) **-kopf,** *m.* harum-scarum. **-n,** *v.n.* (*aux.* h.) rustle; rush, skimp, scamp; do hastily *or* carelessly.

Ruß, *m.* (-es, -e) soot, lamp-black. **-braun,** *adj. & n.* bistre. **-en,** 1. *v.a.* soot, smoke, blacken. 2. *v.n.* get sooty, cake *or* get caked with soot. **-farbe,** *f.* bistre; lamp-black. **-ig,** *adj.* sooty. **-kreide,** *f.* black chalk. **-schwarz,** *n.* lamp-black.

Rüssel, *m.* (-s, -) snout; trunk, proboscis, nozzle. **-ig,** *adj.* snout-like. **-tier,** *n.* proboscidian.

Rüste, *f.* (*dial. & poet.*); *zu* or *zur - gehen,* sink, set (*of the sun*); go to rest, expire.

rüst-en, 1. *v.a.* prepare, equip, fit out, array, arm, mobilize, prepare for war. 2. *v.n.* (*aux.* h. *& r.*) make preparations, prepare, make *or* get ready (*auf* or *zu,* for). **-baum,** *m.* scaffold-pole. **-er,** *m., see* **-mann. -haus,** *n.* arsenal. **-halle,** *f.* assembly hall *or* shed (*in a factory*). **-holz,** *n.* prop, shore (*Min.*). **-kammer,** *f.* armoury, arsenal. **-mann,** *m.* assembly man (*in a factory*). **-meister,** *m.* assembly foreman **-saal,** *m.* armoury. **-ung,** *f.* armaments, arms, munitions; (*fig.*) mobilization, preparation; armour (*Hist. also fig.*), panoply; scaffolding (*Build.*). **-ungsstand,** *m.* state of preparedness (*for war*). **-ungswerk,** *n.* armament *or* munitions factory. **-zeug,** *n.* tools, implements; parts of a scaffold; (*fig.*) knowledge, capacity, (mental) equipment.

Rüster, *f.* (-n) elm. **-n,** *adj.* of elm.

rüstig, *adj.* hale and hearty, vigorous, brisk.

Rute, *f.* (-n) rod, twig, switch, wand, birch (rod); brush (*of foxes*); penis (*Anat.*); (*archaic land measure*; rod, pole *or* perch); *sich die - selbst flechten,* make a rod for one's own back; *einem Kind die - geben,* give a child the stick; *mit eiserner - regieren,* rule with a rod of iron. **-nbündel,** *n.* fasces, bundle of rods. **-nförmig,** *adj.* virgate. **-ngänger,** *m.* dowser, water-diviner. **-nschlag,** *m.*, **-nstreich,** *m.* stroke, lash (*from birch-rod*).

Rutsch, *m.* (-es, -e) slip, fall, slide; landslip. **-bahn** *f.*, **-e,** *f.* slide; chute; **-en,** *v.n.* (*aux.* h. *&* s.) slide, glide, slip, skid, sideslip (*Av.*); (*coll.*) *aufs Land -en,* pop into the country. **-er,** *m.* slider; gallop (*Danc.*). **-ig,** *adj.* slippery. **-pulver,** *n.* talc. **-ung,** *f.* landslide. **-partie,** *f.* sudden short trip.

rütt-eln, *v.a. & n.* (*aux.* h.) shake; jog, jolt, vibrate; winnow (*corn*); (*fig.*) undermine; *daran ist nicht zu -eln,* that remains as it is, you will not change that; *gerüttelt voll,* heaped; *gerüttelt und geschüttelt Maß,* full measure. **-stroh,** *n.* loose straw, litter.

S

S, s, *n.* S, s; **-s** = das, *as* ins = in das, ans = an das, aufs, durchs, *etc.*; **'s** = es, *as* geht's = geht es, ist's, hat's, wenn's, ob's; *for abbreviations see end of German–English Vocabulary.*

Saal, *m.* ((-e)s, Säle) hall, assembly room, large room; ward; *Tanz-,* ballroom, dance-hall; *Empfangs-,* reception-room; *Vorlesungs-,* lecture-room, lecture-theatre; *Speise-,* dining-room. **-bau,** *m.* concert-hall, assembly-rooms. **-einrichtung,** *f.* furnishings and decorations of a hall. **-öffnung,** *f.* opening time (*Theat., etc.*). **-tochter,** *f.* (*Swiss dial.*) waitress.

Saat, *f.* (-en) sowing; seed; standing corn; green crops; *Zeit zur -,* time for sowing; *in - schießen,* run *or* go to seed. **-bestellung,** *f.* sowing. **-egge,** *f.* seed-harrow. **-enstand,** *m.* state of crops. **-erbse,** *f.* field pea (*Pisum arvense*) (*Bot.*). **-feld,** *n.* field of corn. **-getreide,** *n.* **-gut,** *n.* seed-corn. **-kartoffel,** *f.* seed-potato. **-korn,** *n.* (-s, -er) single seed. **-krähe,** *f.* rook. **-reihe,** *f.* drill (*for seed*). **-schule,** *f.* nursery (*Hort.*). **-zeit,** *f.* sowing season.

Sabbat, *m.* (-(e)s, -e) Sabbath (*Jew.*); Sunday (*poet.*); *den - heiligen,* keep the Sabbath; *den - entheiligen,* break the Sabbath. **-jahr,** *n.* Sabbatical year. **-ruhe,** *f.* Sabbath rest *or* quiet, Sunday rest. **-schänder,** *m.* Sabbath-breaker.

Sabbel, *m., see* **Sabber. -n,** *v.n., see* **sabbern.**

Sabber, *m.* (*dial.*) dribble, spittle. **-lätzchen,** *n.* bib. **-n** *v.n.* (*aux.* h.) (*dial.*) dribble, slobber, slaver, drivel.

Säbel, *m.* (-s, -) sabre, broadsword. **-n,** *v.a.* sabre; (*hum.*) hack. **-bajonett,** *n.* sword-bayonet. **-beine,** *n.pl.* bow-legs. **-beinig,** *adj.* bandy-legged, bow-legged. **-fisch,** *m.* sword-fish. **-gehenk,** *n.* sword-belt. **-gerassel,** *n.* sabre rattling, jingoism. **-hieb,** *m.* sword-cut. **-koppel,** *f.* sword-belt. **-rasseln,** *n., see* **-gerassel. -scheide,** *f.* scabbard. **-troddel,** *f.* sword-knot.

Sabot-age, *f.* (-ageakte) sabotage. **-ieren,** *v.a.* sabotage.

Sach-e, *f.* (-en) thing, object, article; cause, action, case (*Law*); subject, matter, affair, business, concern, event; fact, circumstance; (*pl.*) goods, furniture, luggage, clothes, *etc.*; *ich muß wissen, was an der -e ist,* I must know how the matter stands *or* what is the truth of the matter; *bei der -e bleiben,* stick to the point; *nicht bei der -e sein,* not pay attention (to), be absent-minded; *mit ganzer Seele bei der -e sein,* be heart and soul in a th.;

fremde –en, other people's property (*Law*); *eine –e führen*, plead a cause (*Law*); *gemeinsame –e machen*, make common cause (with); *seiner –e gewiß sein*, know what one is about; *seine –e gut machen*, do one's job well, play a part well, (*sl.*) put up a good show; *die –en gehen lassen, die –e laufen lassen wie sie will*, let things slide; (*coll.*) *das ist seine –e*, that is his affair, that is his look-out; *Lügen ist nicht seine –e*, he is not given to lying; *jede –e hat zwei Seiten*, there are two sides to everything; *meine sieben –en*, my belongings, my goods and chattels; *so steht die –e*, that is how the matter stands; *es geht um die –e, nicht die Person*, the issue is above personalities; *kümmere dich um deine (eigenen) –en*, mind your own business; *unverrichteter –e zurückkommen*, return without having accomplished anything; *die –e verhält sich so*, the matter stands thus; *das gehört nicht zur –e*, that has nothing to do with it; *zur –e kommen*, come to the point; *das tut nichts zur –e*, that is beside the point, is insignificant *or* irrelevant. **–bearbeiter,** *m.* official expert. **–beschädigung,** *f.* wilful destruction. **–beweis,** *m.* objective proof. **–bezüge,** *m.pl.* payment in kind. **–dienlich,** *adj.* relevant, pertinent, suitable. **–erklärung,** *f.* factual explanation. **–führer,** *m.* agent; authorized representative. **–gebiet,** *n.* department of knowledge, subject. **–gemäß,** 1. *adj.* relevant, pertinent, appropriate, proper. 2. *adv.* in a suitable manner. **–katalog,** *m.* subject catalogue. **–kenntnis,** *f.*, **–kunde,** *f.* special knowledge, expert knowledge, (professional) experience. **–kundig,** *adj.* experienced (in), expert (in), versed (in), competent; *ein –kundiger*, an expert, a competent judge. **–lage,** *f.* state of affairs, circumstances. **–leistung,** *f.* payment in kind. **–lich,** 1. *adj.* essential, material, pertinent, to the point; objective, unbiased, impartial; technical. 2. *adv.* to the point. **–lichkeit,** *f.* reality, objectivity; impartiality. **–register,** *n.* table of contents, subject index. **–schaden,** *m.* damage to property. **–schadenersatz,** *m.* indemnity. **–verhalt,** *m.* circumstances, state of affairs, facts of a case. **–verständig,** *adj.*, *see* **–kundig. –verzeichnis,** *n.*, *see* **–register. –walter,** *m.* counsel, legal adviser, solicitor, attorney. **–wert,** *m.* real value. **–wörterbuch,** *n.* encyclopaedia.

sächlich, *adj.* neuter (*Gram.*).

sacht(e), 1. *adj.* soft, gentle, easy, light; slow. 2. *adv.* by degrees; cautiously; gradually, slowly, gently.

Sack, *m.* (-(e)s, ⸚e) sack, bag; sac, cyst, pouch; (*dial.*) purse, pocket; *zwanzig – Korn*, twenty sacks of corn; *in – und Asche*, in sackcloth and ashes; *einen im – haben*, have a p. in one's clutches; (*sl.*) *in den – hauen*, throw in one's hand, (*sl.*) chuck it, throw it up; *eine Katze im –e kaufen*, buy a pig in a poke; *eine Faust im –e machen*, bear a secret grudge against s.o.; *einen in den – stecken*, get s.o. under one's thumb; outdo a p.; *mit – und Pack*, with bag and baggage; *wie ein – schlafen*, sleep like a top; *den – schlagen und den Esel meinen*, say one thing and mean another. **–artig,** *adj.* pouch-like, cyst-like. **–bahnhof,** *m.* terminal station. **–band,** *n.* (⸚er) bag-string; purse-string. **–en,** 1. *v.a.* put into sacks, bag, pocket. 2. *v.r.* & *n.* (*aux.* h.) sink, sag, subside, settle, give way; become baggy *or* puckered. **–filter,** *m.* bag-filter. **–garn,** *n.* twine, packing-thread. **–gasse,** *f.* blind alley; dead end; (*fig.*) deadlock. **–geschwulst,** *f.* encysted tumour. **–grob,** *adj.* exceedingly rude. **–grube,** *f.* saphead (*Fort.*). **–hüpfen,** *n.* sack-race. **–ig,** *adj.* baggy. **–landung,** *f.* pancake landing (*Av.*). **leinen,** *n.*, **–leinwand,** *f.* sack-cloth, sacking. **–nadel,** *f.* packing-needle. **–pfeife,** *f.* bagpipe. **–tuch,** *n.* sacking; (*dial.*) pocket-handkerchief **–ung,** *f.* sagging, subsidence. **–weise,** *adv.* by bagfuls. **–zwirn,** *m.*, *see* **–garn.**

Säckel, *m.* purse, money-bag; treasury. **–meister,** *m.*, **–wart,** *m.* cashier, treasurer.

säcken, *v.a.* drown (in a sack).

sacker–lot, –ment, *int.* the deuce! bother(ation)!

sä–en, *v.a.* & *n.* (*aux.* h.) sow. **–er,** *m.*, **–mann,** *m.* sower. **–(e)maschine,** *f.* sowing-machine, drill-plough. **–zeit,** *f.* seed-time, sowing season.

Saffian, *m.* Morocco (leather).

Saflor, Safflor, *m.* (-s, -e) safflower, bastard saffron (*Carthamus tinctorius*) (*Bot.*).

Safran, *m.* (-s, -e) saffron (*Crocus sativus*) (*Bot.*). **–farben,** *adj.*, **–farbig,** *adj.*, **–gelb,** *adj.* saffron-yellow, saffrony.

Saft, *m.* (-(e)s, ⸚e) juice; sap; syrup; gravy; liquor, fluid, liquid, moisture; humour, lymph (*Med.*); *im – stehen*, be in sap; *ohne – und Kraft*, be without strength *or* savour, have no energy *or* backbone, be stale *or* insipid. **–blume,** *f.* nectar-secreting flower. **–grün,** *adj.* sap-green. **–halter,** *m.* nectary (*Bot.*). **–ig,** *adj.* juicy, luscious, succulent; (*vulg.*) spicy, obscene; *eine –ige Ohrfeige*, a sound box on the ear; *eine –ige Anekdote*, a spicy story. **–igkeit,** *f.* juiciness, succulence. **–kanal,** *m.* lymph canal. **–los,** *adj.* sapless; dry, insipid. **–pflanze,** *f.* succulent plant. **–raum,** *m.* cell cavity, vacuole. **–reich,** *adj.* juicy, sappy, succulent. **–röhre,** *f.* lymphatic vessel. **–umlauf,** *m.*, **–verkehr,** *m.* circulation of sap. **–voll,** *adj.* juicy, succulent. **–zeit,** *f.* sap *or* growing season. **–zelle,** *f.* lymph cell.

Sag–e, *f.* (-en) legend, fable, saga, myth, tradition; (*dial.*) tale, rumour; *es geht die –e*, the story goes, it is rumoured. **–en,** 1. *v.a.* say, tell; speak; declare, testify, mean; *Dank –en*, express one's thanks; *wenn ich so –en darf*, if I may be permitted the expression; *es –t mir etwas*, it means s.th. to me, it makes an impression on me; *wenn ich etwas zu –en hätte*, if I had any say in the matter; *auf alles etwas zu –en wissen*, have an answer to everything; *er kann von Glück –en*, he may count himself lucky; *ich kann dasselbe von uns –en*, that applies equally well to us; *jemandem –en lassen*, send a p. word; *ich habe mir –en lassen*, I have been *or* am told; *laß dir das gesagt sein*, let it be a warning to you; *es läßt sich nicht –en*, there is no saying; it is beyond words; *er läßt sich (Dat.) nichts –en*, he will listen to no advice *or* to no one; *ich ließ mir das nicht zweimal –en*, I did not wait to be told twice, I jumped at it; *das sagt man nicht*, that should not be said; *man sagt ihn tot*, they say he is dead; *nun, das muß ich –en*, well, I declare; well, I must say! *was Sie nicht –en!* you don't say! *es hat nichts zu –en*, it does not signify, it is of no great importance, it does not matter; *das will nichts –en*, that is nothing; that is of no consequence; *Sie haben mir nichts zu –en*, you have no right to give me orders; *das –en Sie nur so!* you don't mean it! *wie man (so) zu –en pflegt*, as the saying is *or* goes; *sozu–en*, so to speak, as it were; *mit Verlaub zu –en*, excuse the language; *das will viel –en, das ist viel gesagt*, that is saying a great deal; *das will ich nicht gesagt haben*, I did not mean that, I do not wish it to be thought that I said that; *was ich –en wollte*, as I was about to say, what I was going to say; *er ist reich, wohlhabend, wollte ich –en*, he is rich, I mean comfortably off; *das Gesagte*, what I have said, what has been said; *beiläufig gesagt*, by the way; *gerade heraus* or *offen gesagt*, to put it plainly, in plain language; *richtiger gesagt*, properly speaking; *gesagt, getan*, no sooner said than done; *unter uns gesagt*, between you and me, in confidence; *wie gesagt*, as I said. **–enforschung,** *f.* folklore, investigation of popular legends. **–enhaft,** *adj.* legendary, mythical, fabulous, traditional. **–enkreis,** *m.* legendary cycle, epic cycle. **–enkunde,** *f.* legendary lore; folklore. **–enreich,** *adj.* rich in (popular) legends and traditions. **–enschatz,** *m.* legends; folklore. **–enzeit,** *f.* legendary *or* heroic age; fabulous age.

Säge, *f.* (-n) saw. **–artig,** *adj.* saw-like, serrate(d). **–blatt,** *n.* blade of a saw. **–bock,** *m.* sawing-trestle. **–fisch,** *m.* saw-fish. **–förmig,** *adj.* serrated. **–gatter,** *n.*, **–gestell,** *n.* saw-frame. **–grube,** *f.* saw-pit. **–maschine,** *f.* mechanical saw. **–mehl,** *n.* sawdust. **–mühle,** *f.* saw-mill. **–nblatt,** *n.* saw-blade. **–n,** *v. a.* & *n.* (*aux.* h.) saw; (*coll.*) snore. **–schnitt,** *m.* saw cut. **–späne,** *m.pl.* sawdust. **–werk,** *n.* saw-mill. **–zahn,** *m.* saw-tooth, indentation. **–zähnig,** *adj.* serrate.

Sago, *m.* sago.

sah, sähe, *see* **sehen.**

Sahn–e, *f.* cream. **–en,** 1. *v.a.* skim (*milk*). 2. *r.v.*

form a cream. **–ebonbon,** *m.* & *Austr. dial n.* cream toffee. **–enkäse,** *m.* cream cheese. **–enkuchen,** *m.* cream-tart *or* cake. **–ig,** *adj.* creamy.
Saibling, *m.* (-s, -e) char (*Icht.*).
Saison [sɛ'zɔ̃], *f.* (-s) season; *die tote –*, the off-season. **–arbeiter,** *m.* seasonal worker. **–ausverkauf,** *m.* clearance *or* stock-taking sale. **–gewerbe,** *n.* seasonal trade.
Saite, *f.* (-n) string (*Mus.*); (*fig.*) chord; *andere –n aufziehen,* change one's tone; *eine – anschlagen,* strike a note, touch a chord; *–n auf eine Geige aufziehen,* string a violin; *besponnene –,* silver string, covered string; *gelindere* or *mildere –n aufziehen,* climb down a peg; *die –n zu hoch spannen,* take too much for granted; *schärfere –n aufziehen,* become strict *or* severe; **–nbezug,** *m.* set of strings. **–nhalter,** *m.* tail-piece (*of a violin, etc.*). **–ninstrument,** *n.* stringed instrument. **–nspiel,** *n.* string music; lyre.
Sakko, *m.* & *Austr. dial. n.* (-s, -s) lounge-jacket. **–anzug,** *m.* lounge-suit.
sakra, *int.* damned! **–l,** *adj.* sacral (*Anat.*); sacred. **–ment,** 1. *n.* (-(e)s, -e) sacrament; consecrated Host. 2. *int., see –.* **–mental,** *adj.*, **–mentlich,** *adj.* sacramental.
Sakrist–an, *m.* (-s, -e) sacristan, sexton. **–ei,** *f.* vestry, sacristy.
säkul–ar, *adj.* secular; centennial. **–arfeier,** *f.* centenary. **–arisieren,** *v.a.* secularize **–um,** *n.* (ums, -a) century.
Salamander, *m.* (-s, –) salamander; (*Studs. sl.*) *einen – reiben* (*auf jemanden*), toast a p. with due ceremony.
Sal–är, *n.* (-s, -e) (*Austr.* & *Swiss dial.*) salary. **–arieren,** *v.a.* (*einen*) pay a salary to a p.
Salat, *m.* (-(e)s, -e) salad; lettuce; *den – anmachen,* dress the salad; (*coll.*) *da haben wir den –,* that's a nice mess, a fine *or* pretty how-do-you-do! **–beet,** *n.* bed of lettuce. **–blatt,** *n.* lettuce leaf. **–kopf,** *m.* head of lettuce. **–öl,** *n.* olive oil, salad-oil. **–pflanze,** *f.* salad vegetable.
Salbader, *m.* (-s, –) quack; bore. **–ei,** *f.* quackery; interminable talk, twaddle. **–n,** *v.n.* (*aux.* h.) prate, talk nonsense, bosh *or* twaddle.
Salband, *n.* (-es, ⸚er) selvage.
Salb–e, *f.* (-en) ointment, salve; scented oil, pomade. **–en,** *v.a.* apply ointment, anoint; embalm; (*coll.*) ingratiate; (*fig.*) *einem die Hände –en,* grease a p.'s palm. **–enartig,** *adj.* unctuous. **–enbüchse,** *f.* ointment pot. **–öl,** *n.* anointing oil, consecrated oil. **–ung,** *f.* anointing; unction, pomposity, fulsomeness. **–ungsvoll,** *adj.* unctuous, ingratiating, fulsome, (*sl.*) smarmy, smalmy.
Salbei, *m.* or *f.* sage (*Bot.*).
Salbling, *m.* (-s, -e), *see* **Saibling.**
sald–ieren, *v.a.* pay, balance, settle; strike a balance; *durch Gegenrechnung –iert,* balanced in account, counterbalanced. **–ierung,** *f.* balancing, settlement. **–o,** *m.* (-os *or* -en, -os *or Austr. dial.* -i) balance (of an account); *–o vorgetragen,* balance carried forward; *–o zu unseren Gunsten,* balance in our favour; *–o zu unseren Lasten,* debit balance; *per –o quittieren,* receipt in full; *in –o sein* or *bleiben,* have debts outstanding, be in debt; *den –o ziehen,* strike the balance. **–obetrag,** *m.* amount of balance. **–oguthaben,** *n.* credit balance. **–oübertrag,** *m.* balance brought forward. **–ovortrag,** *m.* balance forward. **–owechsel,** *m.* balance-bill, draft for the balance. **–ozahlung,** *f.* settlement.
Salin–e, *f.* (-en) salt-works, salt-pit. **–isch,** *adj.* saline.
salisch, *adj.* Salic (*Hist.*).
Salizylsäure, *f.* salicylic acid.
Salleiste, *f.*, *see* **Salband.**
[1]**Salm,** *m.* (-s, -e) salmon.
[2]**Salm,** *m.* (*coll.*) *langer –,* rigmarole; *einen langen – machen,* spin a long yarn, be long-winded; (*coll.*) *mache keinen – ! nur keinen – !* come to the point!
Salmiak, *m.* sal-ammoniac, ammonium chloride. **–geist,** *m.* liquid ammonia. **–salz,** *n.* sal volatile.
Salon, *m.* (-s, -s) drawing-room; saloon (*in ships, hairdressing, etc.*); salon. **–bolschewik,** *m.* white-collar socialist. (*sl.*) **–bruch,** *m.* slight damage (*Av.*). **–fähig,** *adj.* fit for (good) society. **–löwe,** *m.* ladies' man. **–musik,** *f.* light music. **–tiroler,** *m.* sham Tyrolese. **–wagen,** *m.* saloon carriage, Pullman car.
salopp, *adj.* slovenly, shabby, (*coll.*) sloppy.
Salpet–er, *m.* nitre, saltpetre, potassium nitrate. **–erartig,** *adj.* nitrous. **–eräther,** *m.* nitrous ether. **–erbildung,** *f.*, **–erblumen,** *f.pl.* nitrous exhalation (*on walls, etc.*). **–erdampf,** *m.* nitric fumes. **–ererde,** *f.* nitrous earth. **–erfraß,** *m.* corrosion by saltpetre. **–ergas,** *n.* nitrous oxide, laughing-gas. **–ergeist,** *m.* spirit of nitre, nitric acid, aquafortis. **–erhaltig,** *adj.* nitrous. **–erhütte,** *f.* saltpetre-works. **–ersalzsäure,** *f.* aqua regia, nitro-hydrochloric acid. **–ersauer,** *adj.* nitric, nitrate of; *–ersaures Salz,* nitrate. **–ersäure,** *f.* nitric acid. **–ersiederei,** *f.* saltpetre-manufactory. **–rig,** *adj.* nitrous; *–rige Säure,* nitrous acid; *–rigsaures Natron,* sodium nitrate.
Salt–o (mortale), *m.* (-o -es *or Austr. dial.* –o –, -o -es & -i -i *or Austr. dial.* -o -i) vault, somersault, break-neck leap.
Salut, *m.* (-(e)s, -e) salute, salutation. **–ieren,** *v.a.* & *n.* (*aux.* h.) salute.
Salve, 1. *int.* hail! welcome! 2. *f.* (-n) salute *or* discharge of guns; burst of fire (*or* of applause); salvo (*Artil.*); volley (*rifle*); round (*of applause*); *eine – abgeben,* fire a volley *or* salvo. **–nfeuer,** *n.* volley firing. **–ngeschütz,** *n.* multiple-barrel gun.
Salweide, *f.* (-n) sallow (*Salix caprea*) (*Bot.*).
Salz, *n.* (-es, -e) salt; *englisches –,* Epsom salts; *basisches –,* subsalt; *weder – noch Schmalz haben,* be without body, be tasteless *or* insipid; *er liegt tüchtig im –,* he is in a pretty pickle; *du hast es noch im –* (*liegen*), you have it in store for you, you have it coming to you. **–abgabe,** *f.* salt-tax. **–ablagerung,** *f.* salt deposit. **–artig,** *adv.* saline. **–äther,** *m.* muriatic ether, ethyl chloride. **–bäder,** *n.pl.* brine *or* sea-water baths. **–bergwerk,** *n.* salt-mine. **–bildend,** *adj.* halogenous. **–bild(n)er,** *m.* halogen. **–bildung,** *f.* salification, halogenation. **–brühe,** *f.* brine, pickle. **–brunnen,** *m.* saline spring. **–en,** *ir.* & *reg. v.a.* salt; pickle; season (*with wit, etc.*); *einem den Buckel –en,* give it s.o. good and hard; *gesalzen,* piquant, spicy, strong; *gesalzener Hering,* salt herring; *gesalzene Preise,* exorbitant prices. **–farbe,** *f.* basic *or* metallic dye. **–faß,** *n.* salt-cellar. **–fleisch,** *n.* salt(ed) meat. **–gehalt,** *m.* saline matter; proportion *or* percentage of salt. **–gehaltsmessung,** *f.* halometry. **–geschmack,** *m.* salty taste; brackishness. **–grube,** *f.* salt-pit. **–gurke,** *f.* pickled cucumber. **–haltig,** *adj.* saline, saliferous. **–haut,** *f.* saline incrustation. **–ig,** *adj.* salt; saline. **–igkeit,** *f.* saltiness, salinity. **–korn,** *n.* grain of salt. **–kote,** *f.* salt refinery. **–lager,** *n.* salt deposits. **–lake,** *f.*, **–lauge,** *f.* brine, pickle. **–lecke,** *f.* salt-lick (*for cattle, etc.*). **–messer,** *m.* salinometer. **–niederschlag,** *m.* saline deposit *or* precipitate. **–pfanne,** *f.* brine-pan. **–pflanze,** *f.* halophyte. **–quelle,** *f.* saline spring. **–rinde,** *f.* crust of salt. **–sauer,** *adj.* (hydro)-chloride of, hydrochlorate, muriatic; *–saures –,* chloride. **–säure,** *f.* hydrochloric *or* muriatic acid. **–siederei,** *f.* salt-works. **–sole,** *f.* brine, salt-spring. **–stange,** *f.* hard-baked white bread (strongly flavoured with salt and caraway seed). **–steuer,** *f.* salt-tax. **–waage,** *f.* salinometer, brine-gauge. **–wasser,** *n.* salt-water, sea-water, brine. **–werk,** *n.* salt-works; salt-mine. **–zoll,** *m.* salt-tax. **–zusatz,** *m.* addition of salt.
Same, *m.*, **–n,** *m.* (-ns, -n) seed, grain; sperm, semen; fry, spawn; (*fig.*) germ, source; (*B.*) descendants. **–nabführungsgang,** *m.* vas deferens (*Anat.*). **–nanlage,** *f.* gemmule, ovule; placenta. **–nbaum,** *m.* tree kept for seed (*Hort.*). **–nbehälter,** *m.* seed-vessel; seminal vesicle. **–nbeständig,** *adj.* true to type, homozygotous. **–ndrüse** *f.* testicle, spermatic gland (*Anat.*). **–neiweiß,** *n.* endosperm, albumen. **–nergießung,** *f.* discharge of semen. **–nfaden,** *m.* spermatozoon. **–nfische,** *m. pl.* young fry. **–nflüssigkeit,** *f.* seminal fluid. **–ngang,** *m.* spermatic duct. **–ngärtner,** *m.* nursery-man. **–ngehäuse,** *n.* pericarp; core. **–ngewächs,** *n.* seedling. **–nhändler,** *m.* seedsman. **–nhülle,** *f.* perisperm, seed-case. **–nhülse,**

f. husk, shell, pod. **-nkapsel,** *f.* capsule, seed-pod. **-nkeim,** *m.* germ embryo. **-nkelch,** *m.* seed cup. **-nkern,** *m.* sperm-nucleus, endosperm, seed kernel. **-nknospe,** *f.* ovule, gemmule. **-nkorn,** *n.* grain of seed, single seed. **-nlappen,** *m.* seed lobe, cotyledon. **-nlehre,** *f.* spermatology. **-nleiter,** *m.* spermatic duct, vas deferens. **-nöl,** *n.* rape-seed oil. **-npflanze,** *f.* seedling. **-nschießen,** *n.* running to seed. **-nschote,** *f.* pod, shell, husk, seed-vessel. **-nschule,** *f.* seed-bed. **-nstaub,** *m.* pollen. **-nstengel,** *m.* seed-stalk. **-nstiel,** *m.* funicle. **-nstrang,** *m.* spermatic cord. **-ntierchen,** *n.* spermatozoon. **-ntragend,** *adj.* seed-bearing, spermatophorous. **-nträger,** *m.* spermatophore (*Bot.*, *Biol.*). **-nzelle,** *f.* sperm-cell. **-nzwiebel,** *f.* seed-bulb.

Säm-erei, *f.* (-en) (*usually pl.*) seeds. **-ereihändler,** *m.* seedsman. **-ling,** *m.* seedling.

sämig, *adj.* (*dial.*) thick, viscid, creamy.

sämisch, *adj.* chamois-dressed, shammy (*Tann.*); fawn, beige (*colour*). **-gerber,** *m.* chamois-dresser. **-leder,** *n.* chamois leather; wash-leather.

samm-eln, 1. *v.a.* gather, collect, pick; amass, accumulate; salvage; assemble, rally, concentrate (*troops, etc.*); *für die Armen -eln*, make a collection for the poor; *Kräuter -eln*, gather herbs, botanize. 2. *v.r.* collect, assemble, rally, flock together; concentrate, collect one's thoughts, regain one's self-possession *or* composure, compose o.s. **-elband,** *m.* omnibus volume. **-elbecken,** *n.* reservoir, receiver, collecting vessel. **-elbuch,** *n.* common-place book, scrap-book. **-elbüchse,** *f.* collecting box. **-eleifer,** *m.*, **-elfleiß** (also **-lerfleiß**) *m.* industry in collecting (*materials*). **-elfahrschein,** *m.* group ticket. **-elfrucht,** *f.* collective fruit, syncarp. **-elgebiet,** *n.* drainage area, watershed. **-elkasten,** *m.* cistern; reservoir. **-ellazarett,** *n.* casualty collecting centre (*Mil.*). **-ellinse,** *f.* convex lens (*Opt.*). **-elmappe,** *f.* portfolio. **-elmeldung,** *f.* situation report (*Mil.*). **-elname,** *m.* collective name. **-elort,** *m.* collecting centre, dump. **-elplatz,** *m.* assembly point, rendezvous (*Mil.*). **-elpunkt,** *m.* rallying-point. **-elschiene,** *f.* busbar (*Elec.*). **-elspiegel,** *m.* concave mirror. **-elstelle,** *f.* collecting centre, salvage depot *or* dump (*Mil.*). **-elsurium,** *n.* medley, jumble, hotch-potch. **-elwort,** *n.* collective noun. **-ler,** *m.* collector; accumulator, storage battery, secondary cell (*Elec.*). **-lerbatterie,** *f.* storage-battery. **-lung,** *f.* collection; collecting; compilation; set; accumulation, concentration; composure, collectedness. **-lungsdatum,** *n.* date of compilation (*on maps*).

Sammet, *m.* (*archaic*), *see* **Samt.**

Samstag, *m.* (-s, -e) Saturday.

Samt, *m.* (-(e)s, -e) velvet; *baumwollener –*, velveteen. **-artig,** *adj.* velvet-like, velvety. **-band,** *n.* velvet ribbon; ribbon velvet. **-en,** *adj.*, **-ig,** *adj.* velvety. **-manchester,** *m.* velveteen. **-pfötchen,** *n.pl.*; *-pfötchen machen*, draw in claws (*of cat*); be all smiles and bows, play the hypocrite. **-tapete,** *f.* velvet hangings. **-weich,** *adj.* velvety.

samt, *adv.* & *prep.* (*Dat.*) with, together with, along with; *– und sonders*, one and all, jointly and severally, all to a man, all without exception.

sämtlich, *adj.* all, all together, all of them, complete, entire; collective.

Samum, *m.* (-s, -s & -e) simoom.

Sand, *m.* sand, grit; *auf den – geraten, auf dem -e sitzen,* (*Naut.*) be aground *or* stranded; (*fig.*) be left in the lurch; *auf den – setzen*, run *or* put (*a ship*) aground; bring (*one's opponent*) to the ground; (*fig.*) place (*s.o.*) in an awkward predicament; *einem – in die Augen streuen*, throw dust in a p.'s eyes, deceive a p.; *etwas in – schreiben*, dismiss a th. from one's mind; *es verlief sich im -e*, it came to nothing, it dried up (*as enthusiasm*). **-bank,** *f.* sandbank; sandy bar; layer *or* bed of sand. **-blatt,** *n.* tobacco-leaf (*used for covering cigars*). **-boden,** *m.* sandy soil. **-dünen,** *f.pl.* sand-dunes. **-en,** *v.a.* (strew *or* sprinkle with) sand. **-fläche,** *f.* (stretch of) sands. **-form,** *f.* sand-mould. **-formerei,** *f.* sand-moulding. **-gegend,** *f.* sandy district. **-grieß,** *m.* grit, fine gravel, coarse sand. **-grube,** *f.* sand-pit. **-guß,** *m.* sand-casting. **-hase,** *m.* (*sl.*), *see* **-latscher**; miss (*at nine-pins*); (*sl.*) foot-slogger (*Amer. sl.*) doughboy (*Mil.*). **-hose,** *f.* sand-spout. **-ig,** *adj.* sandy, gravelly. **-kasten,** *m.* sand tray, sandbox, sand model (*Mil.*). **-korn,** *n.* grain of sand. **-kraut,** *n.* sand wort (*Arenaria*) (*Bot.*). **-kuchen,** *m.*, *see* **-torte.** (*sl.*) **-latscher,** *m.* foot-slogger (*Mil.*). **-(lauf)käfer,** *m.* tiger-beetle (*Cicindelidae*) (*Ent.*). **-mann,** *m.* (*nursery talk*); *der -mann kommt*, the sand-man is coming. **-meer,** *n.* (sandy) desert. **-papier,** *n.* sand- *or* glass-paper (*Carp.*). **-sack,** *m.* sand-bag (*Fort.*), punch-bag (*Boxing*). **-stein,** *m.* sandstone. **-strahlgebläse,** *n.* sand-blasting equipment. **-strahlputzen,** *n.* sand-blasting. **-sturm,** *m.* sand-storm. **-torte,** *f.* Madeira cake. **-uhr,** *f.* hour-glass. **-webe,** *f.*, **-wehe,** *f.* drift of sand. **-wüste,** *f.* (sandy) desert. **-zucker,** *m.* brown sugar.

Sandale, *f.* sandal.

Sandelholz, *n.* sandalwood.

Sander, *m.* (*dial.*), *see* **Zander.**

sandte, *see* **senden.**

sanft, *adj.* gentle, easy; smooth, soft; placid, tender, bland, mild; slight. **-heit,** *f.* softness; mildness, gentleness. **-mut,** *f.* gentleness, meekness, good temper. **-mütig,** *adj.* gentle, mild, meek, good-tempered; (*B.*) *selig sind die -mütigen*, blessed are the meek.

Sänfte, *f.* (-n) sedan chair, litter. **-nträger,** *m.* sedan-chair-man.

sänftigen, *v.a.* (*archaic*) soften, appease, mitigate.

Sang, *m.* (-(e)s, ⁼e) (*Poet.*) song, singing; *mit – und Klang*, with a flourish, with pomp and circumstance; (*coll.*) *ohne – und Klang*, unostentatiously, unceremoniously; *ohne – und Klang abziehen*, sneak off. **-bar,** *adj.* singable, tuneful. **-esbruder,** *m.* member of a glee-club. **-esfroh,** *adj.* fond of *or* given to singing.

sang, sänge, *see* **singen.**

Sänger, *m.* (-s, –) singer; (*archaic*) minstrel, bard, poet; songster (*Orn.*). **-bund,** *m.* choral society. **-fest,** *n.* choral festival. **-schaft,** *f.* glee club, choral society.

Sanguin-iker, *m.* (-s, –) sanguine person. **-isch,** *adj.* sanguine.

sanier-en, *v.a.* cure, reclaim, restore (*depreciated currency*); reorganize. **-ung,** *f.* reorganization, restoration.

sanit-är, *adj.* sanitary, hygienic. **-arisch,** *adj.* (*Swiss dial.*), *see* **-är.** **-ät,** *f.* health, sanitation, hygiene; (*Swiss dial.*) army medical service. **-äter,** *m.* (*coll.*) medical orderly (*Mil.*), ambulance man. **-ätsauto,** *n.* motor ambulance. **-ätsbeamte(r),** *m.* public health officer, medical officer, sanitary inspector. **-ätsbehörde,** *f.* public health department. **-ätsdienst,** *m.* army medical service. **-ätshund,** *m.* first-aid-dog. **-ätskasten,** *m.* first-aid kit. **-ätskolonne,** *f.* first-aid squad, ambulance detachment. **-ätskorps,** *n.* medical corps. **-äts(kraft)wagen,** *m.* motor ambulance. **-ätsoffizier,** *m.* medical officer. **-ätspack,** *n.* first-aid outfit. **-ätspersonal,** *n.* medical personnel. **-ätspflege,** *f.* army nursing (*Mil.*); sanitation. **-ätspolizei,** *f.* sanitary inspectors. **-ätsrat,** *m.* member of the board of health; title conferred on German medical practitioners. **-ätssoldat,** *m.* medical orderly. **-ätsstaffel,** *f.* medical personnel (*at division level*) (*Mil.*). **-ätsunterstand,** *m.* field dressing station. **-ätswache,** *f.* ambulance station; first-aid post. **-ätswesen,** *n.* public health services.

sank, sänke, *see* **sinken.**

Sankt, *indec. adj.* Saint. **-ifizieren,** *v.a.* sanctify. **-ion,** *f.* sanction, ratification; (*pl.*) sanctions, reprisals. **-ionieren,** *v.n.* sanction, ratify. **-issimum,** *n.* consecrated Host (*Rel.*). **-uarium,** *n.* (-s, -ien) sanctuary, reliquary.

sann, sänne, *see* **sinnen.**

Saphir, *m.* (-s, -e) sapphire.

Sapp-e, *f.* (-en) sap trench (*Fort.*). **-enkopf,** *m.* saphead (*Fort.*). **-eur,** *m.* (-s, -e) (*archaic*) sapper, (*Mil.*).

sapper-lot, -ment, *int.* the devil! the dickens!

Sard-elle, *f.* (-n) anchovy. **-ellenbrötchen,** *n.* anchovy sandwich. **-ellenbutter,** *f.* anchovy paste. **-ine,** *f.* sardine.
sardonisch, *adj.* sardonic.
Sarg, *m.* (-(e)s, ⸚e) coffin. **-deckel,** *m.* coffin-lid. **-träger,** *m.* coffin-bearer. **-tuch,** *n.* pall.
Sark-asmus, *m.* (-men) sarcasm. **-astisch,** *adj.* sarcastic.
Sarkom, *n.* (-s, -e) sarcoma (*Med.*).
Sarkophag, *m.* (-s, -e) sarcophagus.
Sarraß, *m.* (-(ss)es, -(ss)e) sabre, broadsword.
Sarsche, *f.* (-n), *see* **Serge.**
Saß, *m.* (-(ss)en, -(ss)en), (*Austr. dial.* **Sasse,** *m.* (-n, -n)) (*archaic*) (*usually as suffix*) settler, tenant, freeholder.
saß, säße, *see* **sitzen.**
säßig, *adj.* (*archaic*) settled, established, resident.
Satan, *m.* (-s, -e) Satan, devil. **-isch,** *adj.* satanic, diabolical.
Satellit, *m.* (-en, -en) satellite (*also fig.*).
Satin, *m.* (-s, -s) satin, sateen. **-age,** *f.* glaze, glazing, finish, gloss. **-ieren,** *v.a.* glaze, gloss, finish, calender (*Pap.*).
Satir-e, *f.* (-en) satire. **-iker,** *m.* satirist. **-isch,** *adj.* satirical.
satt, *adj.* satisfied, full, satiated; saturated; dark, deep, heavy, intensive, rich (*of colour*); *des Lärmes –*, sick of the noise; *sich – essen*, eat one's fill *or* to one's heart's content; *es* (*gründlich*) *– haben, bekommen* or *kriegen*, have had enough of it, get tired of it, (*coll.*) be fed up with it, (*sl.*) be cheesed *or* brassed off; *er hat nicht – zu essen*, he does not get enough to eat; *ich kann mich daran nicht – sehen*, I cannot take my eyes off it; *ich bin –*, I have had sufficient (to eat). **-dampf,** *m.* saturated steam. **-grün,** *adj.* & *n.* dark *or* rich green. **-heit,** *f.* satiety. **-sam,** *adv.* sufficiently, enough.
Satte, *f.* (-n) (*dial.*) milk-pan *or* -bowl.
Sattel, *m.* (-s, ⸚) saddle; bridge (*of nose*), nut (*of violin*); ridge, pass, col (*also Meteor.*); *in allen Sätteln gerecht sein*, be able to turn one's hand to anything, be good at everything; *aus dem – heben*, unhorse; (*fig.*) supplant, supersede; *fest im – sitzen*, have a firm seat; (*fig.*) be firmly established, know one's ground, be master of the situation. **-baum,** *m.* saddle-tree. **-bekleidung,** *f.* saddle trappings. **-bock,** *m.*, *see* **-baum. -bogen,** *m.* saddle-bow. **-dach,** *n.* span-roof, gable roof. **-decke,** *f.* saddle-cloth. **-federn,** *f.pl.* springs (*Cycl.*). **-fertig,** *adj.* ready to mount. **-fest,** *adj.* firm in the saddle, with a good seat; (*fig.*) well up in. **-gurt,** *m.* girth. **-holz,** *n.* transverse beam. **-kammer,** *f.* harness-room. **-knecht,** *m.* groom. **-knopf,** *m.* pommel. **-n,** *v.a.* saddle, (*fig.*) make ready, prepare. **-pausche,** *f.* cantle. **-pferd,** *n.* riding-horse; near (side) horse. **-pistolen,** *f.pl.* horse-pistols. **-riemen,** *m.* girth leather. **-seite,** *f.* near side (*of a horse*). **-steg,** *m.* bridge of a saddle. **-stück,** *n.* saddle (*of mutton, etc.*). **-stütze,** *f.* seat-pillar (*Cycl.*). **-tasche,** *f.* saddle-bag. **-tief,** *adj.* hollow-backed (*of horse*). **-zeug,** *n.* saddle and harness, saddlery.
sättig-en, 1. *v.a.* fill, sate, satisfy, appease, satiate; saturate, impregnate, steep. 2. *v.r.* satisfy one's hunger. **-ung,** *f.* satisfaction, appeasement; satiety, satiation; saturation, neutralization (*Chem.*). **-ungspunkt,** *m.* saturation point.
Sattler, *m.* (-s, –) saddler, harness-maker. **-ahle,** *f.* stitching-awl. **-ei,** *f.* saddlery. **-pech,** *n.* saddler's wax. **-ware,** *f.* saddlery.
saturieren, *v.a.* saturate; satiate.
Satz, *m.* (-es, ⸚e) jump, leap, bound, start, vault; ingredients; composition, matter (*Typ.*); pile, set, nest (*of boxes, etc.*), batch, litter (*of animals*), fry (*of fish*); charge, price, rate; stake, pool, allocation; dregs, grounds, sediment, deposit; sentence, clause, passage, period, phrase (*Mus.*); movement (*Mus.*); proposition, tenet, theme, thesis, theorem, principle; yeast; *seinen – behaupten*, maintain one's point; (*coll.*) *einen – geben*, stand a treat; *in – geben*, send to the printer; *einen – machen* or *tun*, take a leap. **-artig,** *adj.* sedimentary. **-aussage,** *f.* predicate (*Gram.*). **-bau,** *m.*, **-bildung,** *f.* sentence structure *or* construction. **-fehler,** *m.* compositor's *or* printer's error, misprint. **-frei,** *adj.* free from sediment. **-gefüge,** *n.* complex sentence. **-gegenstand,** *m.* subject (*Gram.*). **-glied,** *n.* part of a sentence. **-lehre,** *f.* syntax. **-reif,** *adj.* ready for the press (*Typ.*). **-spiegel,** *m.* face, type area (*Typ.*). **-teich,** *m.* breeding-pond (*for fishes*). **-teil,** *m.*, *see* **-glied. -ung,** *f.* statute, charter (*Law*); law, fixed rule, ordinance, precept, dogma; *-ungen eines Vereins*, articles of an association, rules of a society. **-ungsgemäß,** *adj.*, **-ungsmäßig,** *adj.* statutory. **-weise,** *adv.* sentence by sentence; by sets; by leaps and bounds, intermittently. **-zeichen,** *n.* punctuation mark. **-zeit,** *f.* breeding *or* spawning time.
Sau, *f.* 1. (⸚e) sow; (*fig.*) filthy creature, slut; 2. (-en) wild sow; blot (*of ink*), bad blunder, howler; (*sl.*) *unter aller –*, beneath contempt; (*sl.*) *zur – machen*, smash *or* crack up (*Mil. & Av.*). **-arbeit,** *f.* dirty work, disgusting work, drudgery. **-beller,** *m.* boar-hound. **-bohne,** *f.* fodder bean, vetch. **-borste,** *f.* hog's bristle. (*coll.*) **-dumm,** *adj.* awfully stupid. **-erei,** *f.* beastliness; smuttiness. **-en,** *v.n.* (*aux.* h.) farrow (*of pigs*); (*vulg.*) be filthy; talk obscenely. (*vulg.*) **-essen,** *n.*, **-fraß,** *m.* bad food. **-finder,** *m.*, *see* **-beller. -fleisch,** *n.* boar's flesh. (*vulg.*) **-grob,** *adj.* very rude. **-hatz,** *f.*, **-hetze,** *f.* boar hunting. **-hirt,** *m.* swineherd. **-hund,** *m.* boar-hound; swineherd's dog. **-jagd,** *f.* boar-hunting. (*vulg.*) **-kerl,** *m.* filthy wretch, pig, hog. **-koben,** *m.* pigsty. (*vulg.*) **-mäßig,** *adj.* very bad; very great. (*vulg.*) **-mensch,** *m.* blackguard, rotter, good-for-nothing, bad lot, cur, skunk. **-mutter,** *f.* farrow-sow. **-nest,** *n.* filthy hole. **-rüde,** *m.* boar-hound. **-rudel,** *n.* herd of wild boars. **-stall,** *m.* pigsty. **-trog,** *m.* pig's trough. (*coll.*) **-wetter,** *n.* filthy *or* beastly weather. **-wirtschaft,** *f.* disgusting state of affairs, filthy hole, piggery; bad management (*vulg.*) **-wohl,** *adj.* top-hole, damned well-off.
sauber, *adj.* clean; neat, tidy; (*dial.*) pretty; fine, nice *or* rare (*in irony*); *eine -e Bescherung*, a fine mess! a pretty kettle of fish! *eine -e Abschrift*, a fair copy. **-keit,** *f.* cleanness, cleanliness, neatness, tidiness.
säuber-lich, *adj.* clean; careful, cautious, wary. **-n,** *v.a.* clean, cleanse; purge (*Pol.*), mop up (*Mil.*). **-ung,** *f.* cleansing, cleaning, clearing. **-ungsaktion,** *f.* purge (*Pol.*); mopping-up (*Mil.*).
Sauc-e, *f.*, *see* **Soße. -iere** [*pron.* zosiˈɛ:rə], *f.* (-n) sauce-boat. **-ischen** [*pron.* zoˈsi:sçən], *n.* (-s, –) cocktail sausage.
sauer, 1. *adj.* (*comp.* saurer, *sup.* sauerst) (*when inflected generally* **saur**) sour, acid; acetous; (*as chem. suffix* = bi, e.g. *chrom–*, bichromate; *schweflig–*, bisulphide); (*fig.*) cross, morose, surly, peevish, crabbed; hard, bitter, troublesome, painful; *-e Arbeit*, hard work, grind; (*coll.*) *in den -en Apfel beißen*, swallow a bitter pill; *-er Boden*, marshy land; *– erworbenes Geld*, hard-earned money; *-e Gurken*, pickled cucumbers; *es kommt ihn* or *ihm – an*, he thinks it very hard, he finds it difficult; *einem das Leben – machen*, embitter a p.'s life; *-e Miene*, disgusted expression; *-e Pflicht*, painful duty; *-e Probe*, hard *or* difficult task, trial; *-er Schweiß*, sweat of the brow; *die Milch ist – geworden*, the milk has turned; *das Arbeiten in gebückter Haltung wird ihm –*, he finds working in a stooping posture very irksome *or* trying; *ich lasse es mir – werden*, I take great pains *or* a great deal of trouble (over). 2. *n.* giblets prepared with vinegar; (*dial.*) vinegar; yeast; (*sl.*) *einem Saures geben*, give a p. hell. **-ampfer,** *m.* sorrel (*Rumex acetosa*) (*Bot.*). **-braten,** *m.* stewed pickled beef. **-brunnen,** *m.* mineral water; chalybeate spring. **-egurkenzeit,** *f.* silly season. **-futter,** *n.* ensilage. **-honig,** *m.* oxymel. **-kirsche,** *f.* morello cherry (*Prunus cerasus*) (*Bot.*). **-klee,** *m.* wood-sorrel (*Oxalis acetosella*) (*Bot.*). **-kleesalz,** *n.* salt of lemon, potassium binoxalate. **-kleesäure,** *f.* oxalic acid. **-kohl,** *m.*, **-kraut,** *n.* pickled (white) cabbage. **-machend,** *adj.* acidifying. **-milch,** *f.* curdled milk. **-n,** *v.n.* (*aux.* h.) turn sour, curdle. **-silo,** *m.* trench-silo (*Agr.*). **-stoff,** *m.* oxygen. **-stoffabgabe,** *f.* evolution of oxygen. **-stoffapparat,** *m.*

oxygen-apparatus. **-stoffäther,** *m.* aldehyde. **-stoffatmung,** *f.* oxygen-breathing, aerobic respiration. **-stoffaufnahme,** *f.* oxygenation. **-stoffentzug,** *m.* deoxygenation, reduced oxygen supply. **-stoffhaltig,** *adj.* oxidized, oxygenated. **-stoffion,** *n.* anion. **-stoffmangel,** *m.* oxygen starvation (*Med.*). **-stoffmesser,** *m.* eudiometer. **-stoffpol,** *m.* anode. **-stoffverbindung,** *f.* oxide, oxygen compound. **-stoffzufuhr,** *f.* oxygenation, supply of oxygen. **-süß,** *adj.* bitter-sweet. **-teig,** *m.* leaven, yeast. **-topf,** *m.* morose *or* grumpy fellow. **-töpfisch,** *adj.* peevish, crabbed, cross, sullen. **-wasser,** *n., see* **-brunnen. -wein,** *m.* verjuice. **-werden,** *n.* turning sour, acetification.

säuer-bar, *adj.* acidifiable. **-lich,** *adj.* sourish, tart; acidulous, acidulated, acetous. **-ling,** *m.* medicinal spring; sour wine. **-n,** *v.a.* make sour, acidulate, acidify, leaven (*dough*). **-ung,** *f.* acidification, acidulation, oxydation; leavening (*dough*). **-ungsfähig,** *adj. see* **-bar.**

sauf-en, 1. *ir.v.a. & n.* (*aux.* h.) drink (*of beasts*); (*coll.*) tipple, booze. 2. *n.*; drinking. **-aus,** *m.* (-aus, -aus), **-bold,** *m.* (-s, -e), **-bruder,** *m.* drunkard, sot, toper. **-erei,** *f.*, **-gelage,** *n.* drinking-bout, orgy.

Säufer, *m.* (-s, –) drunkard, toper. **-wahnsinn,** *m.* delirium tremens.

saug-en, *ir.v.a. & n.* (*aux.* h.) suck; absorb; *in sich -en,* imbibe; *an sich -en,* suck up; (*coll.*) *sich* (*Dat.*) *etwas aus den Fingern -en,* invent *or* make up a th.; (*coll.*) *an den Klauen -en,* be hard put to it to make ends meet. **-ader,** *f.* lymphatic vessel. **-er,** *m.* sucker, suckling, suction apparatus, aspirator, nipple, teat (*of feeding bottle*). **-fähig,** *adj.* absorbent, absorptive. **-flasche,** *f.* feeding-bottle. **-füßchen,** *n.pl.* sucker-foot (*Zool.*). **-glas,** *n.* suction bottle, breast pump. **-heber,** *m.* siphon. **-höhe,** *f.* suction head, capillary rise. **-hub,** *m.* intake stroke (*Mach.*). **-klappe,** *f.* suction-valve. **-kolben,** *m.* valve-piston. **-pfropfen** *m.* (rubber) teat. **-pumpe,** *f.* suction-pump. **-rohr,** *n.* induction *or* suction-pipe. **-rüssel,** *m.* proboscis, sucker (*Entom.*). **-ventil,** *n. see* **-klappe. -warze,** *f.* nipple, dug. **-werkzeug,** *n.* suctorial organ (*Zool.*). **-wirkung,** *f.* suction effect. **-wurzel,** *f.* absorbent root, haustorium (*Bot.*). **-zug,** *m.* induced draught.

säug-en, *v.a.* suckle, nurse. **-er,** *m.* mammal. **-amme,** *f.* wet-nurse. **-etier,** *n.* mammal. **-ling,** *m.* infant, suckling. **-lingsausstattung,** *f.* layette. **-lingsfürsorge,** *f.* infant welfare. **-lingsheim,** *n.* crèche. **-lingspflege,** *f.* baby care. **-lingssterblichkeit,** *f.* infant mortality.

säuisch, *adj.* swinish, filthy; (*fig.*) obscene.

Säule, *f.* (-n) column (*also Mil.*), pillar (*also fig.*), post, jamb, upright, pile, prop, support; prism; dry battery. **-nachse,** *f.* prismatic axis. **-nartig,** *adj.* columnar, prismatic. **-nförmig,** *adj., see* **-nartig. -nfuß,** *m.* pedestal (*Arch.*). **-ngang,** *m.* colonnade, arcade, peristyle. **-nhalle,** *f.* colonnade, portico. **-nheilige(r),** *m.* stylite. **-nknauf,** *m.* capital (*Arch.*). **-nlaube,** *f.* portico, piazza. **-nordnung,** *f.* type of column (*Doric, Ionic, etc.*). **-nplatte,** *f.* abacus, plinth (*Arch.*). **-nreihe,** *f.* row of columns. **-nschaft,** *m.* shaft of a column. **-nschluß,** *m.* capital (*Arch.*). **-nweite,** *f.* separation between columns. **-nwerk,** *n.* colonnade. **-nwulst,** *m.* astragal.

¹Saum, *m.* (-s, ⸚e) hem, seam, margin, border, edge, selvage; fillet (*Arch.*); brink; fringe, fimbris (*Bot., Zool.*); – *eines Kleides,* hem of a dress; – *des Waldes,* edge *or* fringe of the forest; – *einer Stadt,* outskirts of a town. **-farn,** *m.* bracken (*Pteris aquilina*) (*Bot.*). **-naht,** *f.*, hem. **-stich,** *m.* hemming stitch.

²Saum, *m.* (-s, ⸚e) (*archaic*) load, burden. **-en,** *v.a., see* **²säumen. -esel,** *m.* sumpter mule. **-pfad,** *m.* mule-track. **-pferd,** *n.* pack-horse. **-sattel,** *m.* pack-saddle. **-tier,** *n.* beast of burden.

¹säum-en, 1. *v.a.* border; hem. **-er,** *m.* hemmer (*person or instrument*).

²säum-en, *v.a.* (*dial.*) convey by beasts of burden; drive pack animals. **-er,** *m.* keeper *or* driver of pack animals; beast of burden.

³säum-en, 1. *v.n.* (*aux.* h.) delay, linger, tarry; defer, put off, hesitate. 2. *n.* delay, tarrying; *ohne -en,* without delay, without hesitation. **-ig,** *adj.* tardy, dilatory, slow; negligent. **-igkeit,** *f.* slowness, tardiness, negligence. **-nis,** *f. & n.* slowness; negligence; delay, postponement.

Saum-sal, *f.* (-e), *& n.* (-a, -e) dilatoriness; negligence. **-selig,** *adj.* dilatory, tardy, slack, negligent, careless. **-seligkeit,** *f.* tardiness, negligence.

Säure, *f.* (-n) acid; sourness, acidity, tartness; moroseness. **-anzug,** *m.* acid-proof clothing. **-äther,** *m.* ester. **-ballon,** *m.* carboy. **-beständig,** *adj.* acid-proof. **-bildend,** *adj.*, **-erzeugend,** *adj.* acidifying. **-dampf,** *m.* acid fumes. **-dichte,** *f.* specific gravity of acid. **-fest,** *adj.* acid resisting. **-frei,** *adj.* non-acid. **-gehalt,** *m.* acidity. **-haltig,** *adj.* acidiferous. **-messer,** *m.* acidimeter. **-rest,** *m.* acid radical. **-widrig,** *adj.* antacid.

Sauregurkenzeit, *f.* silly season.

Saurier, *m.* saurian.

Saus, *m.* (-es) rush, storm, rushing noise; riotous living; *in – und Braus leben,* live riotously. **-en,** *v.n.* (*aux.* h. *&* s.) bluster, blow hard, howl, sough (*as wind*); whistle, whiz (*as arrows*); (*coll.*) rush, dash; *mir -en die Ohren, es -t mir in den Ohren,* I have a ringing in my ears; *es -t mir im Kopf,* my head sings *or* buzzes. **-er,** *m.* (*sl.*) pub-crawl; (*Swiss dial.*) fermented apple juice. **-ewind,** *m.* harum-scarum.

säuseln, *v.a. & n.* (*aux.* h.) rustle, murmur, whisper, sigh.

Saxophon, *n.* (-s, -e) saxophone.

Schabbes, *m.* (–) (*coll.*) Sabbath (*Hebrew*).

¹Schabe, *f.* (-n) cockroach; (*dial.*) moth. **-ngift,** *n.*, **-enpulver,** *n.* insecticide.

²Schab-e, *f.* scraper. **-en,** *v.a.* scrape, grate, scratch, rasp, rub; pare, shave; (*coll.*) *einem Rüben -en,* jeer at *or* make game of a p. **-efleisch,** *n.* (*dial.*) minced meat. **-eisen,** *n.* scraper. **-(e)messer,** *n.* scraping-knife, (vegetable) peeler. **-er,** *m.* scraper, parer, peeler. **-hals,** *m.* (*dial.*) skinflint. **-kunst,** *f.*, **-manier,** *f.* mezzotint. **-sel,** *n.* shavings, scrapings, parings.

Schabernack, *m.* (-(e)s, -e) trick, hoax, practical joke; *jemandem einen – spielen,* play a practical joke on s.o.

schäbig, *adj.* shabby, worn(-out); (*fig.*) mean, stingy. **-keit,** *f.* shabbiness; meanness.

Schablon-e, *f.* (-en) model, mould, form, templet, pattern, stencil; (*fig.*) routine; *nach der -e arbeiten,* work mechanically *or* like a machine. **-enartig,** *adj.*, **-enhaft,** *adj.*, **-enmäßig,** *adj.* stereotyped, mechanical; according to pattern. **-enwesen,** *n.* routine. **-enzeichnung,** *f.* stencil drawing. **-(is)ieren,** *v.a. & n.* stencil, make to pattern.

Schabracke, *f.* (-n) caparison, shabrack, saddle-cloth (*Cavalry*).

Schach, *n.* chess; check; *dem Könige – bieten,* give check to the king; *jemandem – bieten,* defy a p.; *– dem König!* check! *–* (*und*) *matt!* checkmate! *in* or *im – halten,* keep in check. **-aufgabe,** *f.* chess problem. **-brett,** *n.* chess-board. **-brettförmig,** *adj.* chequered; tessellated. **-feld,** *n.* square (*of chess-board*). **-figur,** *f.* chessman; (*fig.*) pawn. **-förmig,** *adj.* chequered, in squares. **-matt,** *adj.* checkmate; (*fig.*) played out, knocked out, worn-out. **-meisterschaft,** *f.* chess championship. **-partie,** *f.* game of chess. **-spiel,** *n.* game of chess; chess-board and men. **-spieler,** *m.* chess-player. **-zug,** *m.* move (*at chess*); (*fig.*) *geschickter -zug,* clever move.

Schacher, *m.*, **-ei,** *f.* chaffering, haggling, higgling; petty dealing, hawking; political jobbery. **-er,** *m.* haggler, petty dealer, broker, vendor. **-n,** *v.n.* (*aux.* h.) barter, chaffer, higgle, haggle; hawk, peddle, carry on petty dealings.

Schächer, *m.* (-s, –) (*B.*) thief, robber, malefactor, felon; (*coll.*) *armer –,* poor devil, poor wretch.

Schacht, *m.* (-(e)s, ⸚e) shaft, well, pit, trench, depression, hollow, tunnel, excavation; gorge, ravine. **-abdeckung,** *f.* manhole-cover. **-arbeiter,** *m.* pitman; navvy. **-einfahrt,** *f.* mouth of a tunnel. **-en,** *v.n.* excavate (*Min.*). **-haspel,** *m.* windlass of a shaft. **-meister,** *m.* pit-overseer; foreman of navvies. **-ofen,** *m.* cupola, kiln, blast-furnace.

-öffnung, *f.* pit-head. **-speicher,** *m.* silo (*Agr.*). **-ung,** *f.* excavation.
Schachtel, *f.* (-n) box, case; (*coll.*) *alte* –, old maid, old frump. **-deckel,** *m.* box-lid. **-halm,** *m.*, **-kraut,** *n.* horse-tail, shave-grass (*Equisetum*) (*Bot.*). **-männchen,** *n.* Jack-in-the-box **-n,** *v.a.* (*coll.*) pack. **-satz,** *m.* involved period (*Gram.*). **-wort,** *n.* portmanteau word.
Schächt-elchen, *n.*, **-elein,** *n.*, little box. **-chen,** *n.*, **-lein,** *n.* small shaft *or* well.
schächt-en, *v.a.* slaughter (*cattle according to Jewish ritual*). **-er,** *m.* Jewish butcher. **-ung,** *f.* kosher butchering.
Schadchen, *m.* (& *n.*) (-s, –) (*Jewish*) match-maker.
schad-e, 1. *int.* unfortunate! a pity! (*coll.*) too bad! *es ist ewig –e!* it is a thousand pities! *–e, daß, ...!* what a pity that . . . ! *–e um die verlorene Zeit,* it is a pity that so much time has been lost; *zu –e für,* too good for. 2. *m.* (-ens, ¨en). **-en,** 1. *m.* (-ens, ¨en) damage, injury, defect, hurt, harm, wrong, mischief; prejudice, detriment, disadvantage, loss; *–en anrichten,* cause damage; *–en bringen,* see *–en tun*; *durch –en klug werden,* learn by experience; (*Prov.*) *durch –en wird man klug,* a burnt child dreads the fire; *fort mit –en!* good riddance; (*Prov.*) *wer den –en hat, braucht für den Spott nicht zu sorgen,* losers are always in the wrong; *innerer –en,* internal disease, canker; *zu –en kommen,* be hurt, sustain losses, come to grief; *–en nehmen,* come to grief, suffer loss; *offener –en,* open sore; *–en tun,* prejudice, damage; *sich* (*Dat.*) *–en tun,* injure *or* hurt o.s.; *mit –en verkaufen,* sell at a loss. **-en,** 2. *v.n.* (*aux.* h.) (*Dat.*) harm, hurt, injure, damage; prejudice; *jemandem bei einem andern –en,* prejudice a p. against another, *was –et es wenn . . .?* what does it matter if . . .? what harm can it do? *das –et dir nicht,* that will not harm *or* hurt you, you will not suffer; *das –et dir nichts,* that serves you right; *das –et nichts,* no matter, never mind. **-enersatz,** *m.* reparation, compensation, damages, indemnification; *einen auf –enersatz verklagen,* sue a p. for damages. **-enersatzklage,** *f.* action for damages. **-enfeuer,** *n.* destructive fire. **-enfreude,** *f.* malicious pleasure, gloating. **-enfroh,** *adj.* gloating over other people's misfortunes. **-enrechnung,** *f.*, **-enschätzung,** *f.* estimate of damage. **-haft,** *adj.* damaged, injured; spoilt, defective, faulty; dilapidated, decayed, wasted. **-haftigkeit,** *f.* damaged condition, defectiveness, dilapidation. **-los,** *adj.* harmless; indemnified; *–los halten,* indemnify, compensate; *sich an einem –los halten,* recoup o.s. from a p. **-losbürgschaft,** *f.* bond of indemnity. **-loshaltung,** *f.* indemnification, compensation.
Schädel, *m.* (-s, –) skull, cranium; *sich den – einrennen,* run one's head against a brick wall. **-bohrer,** *m.* trepan. **-bruch,** *m* fracture of the skull. **-decke,** *f.* scalp. **-form,** *f.* type of skull. **-haut,** *f.* pericranium. **-höhle,** *f.*, **-hohlraum,** *m.* brain cavity. **-ig,** *adj. suff.* -skulled (*e.g.* **lang-ig**). **-lehre,** *f.* phrenology, craniology. **-naht,** *f.* coronal suture. **-stätte,** *f.* Golgotha, Calvary (*B.*).
schäd-igen, *v.a.* harm, injure, damage, wrong, prejudice. **-igung,** *f.* wrong; hurt, damage, prejudice. **-lich,** *adj.* (*Dat.*) detrimental, deleterious, prejudicial, disadvantageous, injurious, obnoxious, noxious, harmful, pernicious, destructive, dangerous. **-lichkeit,** *f.* harm, harmfulness, destructiveness, perniciousness, noxiousness. **-ling,** *m.* (-s, -e) pest, vermin, parasite, weed, noxious plant *or* animal; vile person. **-lingsbekämpfung,** *f.* pest control. **-lingsbekämpfungsmittel,** *n.* insecticide, fungicide.
Schaf, *n.* (-(e)s, -e) sheep, ewe; (*fig.*) stupid p., dolt, *die -e von den Böcken scheiden,* separate the sheep from the goats. **-blattern,** *pl.* chicken-pox; sheep pox, ovinia. **-bock,** *m.* ram. **-bremse,** *f.* sheep-bot(t). **-darmsaite,** *f.* catgut. **-fäule,** *f.* sheep-rot. **-fell,** *n.* sheepskin, fleece. **-fleisch** *n.* mutton. **-garbe,** *f.* yarrow (*Achillea millefolium*) (*Bot.*). **-haut,** *f.* sheepskin; amnion (*Anat.*) **-häutchen,** *n.* amnion. **-herde,** *f.* flock of sheep **-hirt,** *m.* shepherd. **-hürde,** *f.* sheep-pen *or* fold. **-ig,** *adj.* sheep-like, sheepish. **-lamm,** *n.* ewe lamb. **-leder,** *n.* sheepskin; *ausreißen wie –leder,* make o.s, scarce. **-milch,** *f.* ewe's milk. **-mutter,** *f.* ewe. **-pelz,** *m.* fleece; sheepskin fur; *Wolf im –pelz,* wolf in sheep's clothing. **-pocken,** *f.pl.* sheep-pox, ovinia. **-räude,** *f.* scab. **-schere,** *f.* sheep-shears. **-schmiere,** *f.* sheep dip. **-schur,** *f.* sheep-shearing. **-schweiß,** *m.* suint, yolk of wool. **-seuche,** *f.* sheep-rot. **-skopf,** *m.* (*fig.*) blockhead; a card game. (*fig.*) **-sköpfig,** *adj.* silly, stupid. **-stall,** *m.* sheep-fold. **-waschmittel,** *n.* sheep dip. **-wasser,** *n.* amniotic fluid. **-wolle,** *f.* sheep's wool. **-zucht,** *f.* sheep-rearing.
Schäf-chen, *n.* (-s, –) lambkin, lamb; catkin, (*coll.*) pussy-willow; (*pl.*) cirrus (clouds); (*fig.*) *sein –chen ins Trockene bringen,* feather one's nest. **-chen(wolken),** *f.pl.* fleecy clouds, mackerel sky. **-er,** *m.* (-s, –) shepherd; (*hum.*) amorous swain. **-erdichtung,** *f.* pastoral *or* bucolic poetry. **-erei,** *f.* sheep-farm. **-ergedicht,** *n.* pastoral (poem), eclogue, idyll. **-erhund,** *m.* sheep-dog; *deutscher –erhund,* Alsatian. **-erin,** *f.* shepherdess. **-erlied,** *n.* pastoral song. **-erpfeife,** *f.* pastoral pipe. **-erspiel,** *n.* pastoral play. **-erstab,** *m.* shepherd's crook. **-erstunde,** *f.* hour for lovers, time for flirting. **-ertum,** *n.* pastoral life *or* manners. **-erwelt,** *f.* golden age, Arcadia.
Schaff, *n.* (-(e)s, -e) (*dial.*) vat, tub; (*dial.*) cupboard.
schaff-en, 1. *ir.v.a.* & *n.* (*aux.* h.) create; produce; *wie geschaffen für,* made *or* destined for; *er ist für diesen Posten wie geschaffen,* he is the very man for this post, he is cut out for this post. 2. *reg. v.a.* do, make, accomplish; procure, provide, furnish with, let have; bring, convey, transport; (*coll.*) *er hat's ge–t,* he has done it *or* managed it *or* has succeeded; *einen Koffer zur Bahn –en,* convey, bring *or* get a trunk to the station; *beiseite –en,* remove, put aside; kill; hide; embezzle; *ich habe nichts damit zu –en,* that is no concern of mine, I wash my hands of it; *sich* (*Dat.*) *einen vom Halse –en,* shake s.o. off, get rid of a p.; *da werde ich Rat –en,* I shall see to that *or* find a way; *er weiß immer Rat zu –en,* he always knows what to do, he is never at a loss; *etwas aus dem Wege –en,* move a th. out of the way; *einen aus dem Wege* or *der Welt –en,* make away with *or* dispose of a p. 2. *reg. v.n.* (*aux.* h.) do, work, be busy, (*sl.*) eat (*Naut.*); *einem zu –en geben,* give s.o. trouble, give s.o. plenty to do; *zu –en haben,* have s.th. to do; *mit einem zu –en haben,* have business with a p.; *sich* (*Dat.*) *zu –en machen,* occupy o.s., be busy, (*coll.*) potter about. 4. *n.* creating, creative work, creation, production. **-end,** *pr.p. adj.* creative, working. **-ensdrang,** *m.* creative impulse. **-ensfreudigkeit,** *f.* delight in creating. **-enskraft,** *f.* creative power **-enslustig,** *adj.* creative. **-er,** *m.* creator worker; steward (*Nav.*); hard-working man; (*Austr. dial.*) *see* **-ner.** **-erei,** *f.* bread-room (*Nav.*). **-ig,** *adj.* (*Swiss dial.*) busy, industrious. **-ner,** *m.* conductor (*tram, etc.*), guard (*Railw.*); (*archaic*) housekeeper, manager, steward. **-nerin,** *f.* (*archaic*) housekeeper, manageress, stewardess. **-ung,** *f.* production, creation; establishing.
Schäffler, *m.* (-s, –) (*dial.*) cooper.
Schafott, *n.* (-(e)s, -e) scaffold.
Schaft, *m.* (-(e)s, ¨e) shaft, stock (*of a rifle*), handle, shank, leg (*of a boot*); stick, stalk, stem, trunk (*of a tree*); peduncle (*Bot. Zool.*). **-leisten,** *m.* boot-tree, last. **-rein,** *adj.* branchless, clear-boled. **-reinigung,** *f.* self-pruning. **-rinne,** *f.* fluting (*of a column*). **-stiefel,** *m.* top-boot, knee boot.
schäf-ten, *v.a.* fit with a stock, a handle, *etc.*; (*dial.*) give the stick to, cane; splice (*Naut.*); graft (*Hort.*); put new legs to (*boots*). **-tung,** *f.* joint, splice.
Schah, *m.* (-s, -s) shah.
Schakal, *m.* (-s, -e) jackal.
Schake, *f.* (-n) link (of chain) (*Naut.*).
Schäkel, *m.* (-s, –) shackle, link (*Naut.*).
Schäker, *m.* (-s, –) jester, wag, joker; flirt, **-ei,** *f.* badinage, teasing. **-haft,** *adj.* playful, waggish. **-n,** *v.n.* (*aux.* h.) jest, joke; tease; flirt.
Schal, *m.* (-s, -e) shawl; scarf, muffler.
schal, *adj.* stale, flat, dull; insipid, vapid, spiritless; commonplace, trite, hackneyed.

Schal-e, *f.* (-en) skin, peel, rind, bark, crust, shell, pod, husk, carapace (*of crustacea*); outside surface, superficies; capsule, cup (*of acorns*); dish, bowl, basin, vessel; scale (*of a balance*); (*Austr. dial.*) tea *or* coffee cup; cloven hoof; (*pl.*) fishes (*Naut.*); (*B.*) *die -e seines Zornes über einen ausgießen*, pour out the vials of one's wrath on a p.; *die -e senkt sich zu seinen Gunsten*, the scale tipped in his favour. **-brett,** *n.* outside plank of a tree. **-en,** *v.a.* plank, line with timber, revet. **-enbauweise,** *f.* stressed-skin construction (*Av.*). **-enförmig,** *adj.* cup-shaped, shell-like, in layers. **-(en)frucht,** *f.* shell-fruit, caryopsis. **-engehäuse,** *n.* shell (*of snails*). **-enguß,** *m.* chill-casting. **-enhart,** *adj.* chilled (*Metall.*). **-enhaut,** *f.* chorion (*Anat.*). **-enkreuz,** *n.* cup-anemometer, wind gauge. **-enlack,** *m.* shellac. **-enlederhaut,** *f.* chorion (*Anat.*). **-enobst,** *n., see* **-(en)frucht.** **-enwild,** *n.* cloven-hoofed game (*Hunt.*). **-holz,** *n.* barked timber, outer planks. **-ig,** *adj.* scaly, crusted, crustaceous, testaceous, lamellated, foliated. **-tier,** *n.* crustacean, testacean, shell-fish. **-tierkunde,** *f.* conchology. **-tierreste,** *f.* fossil remains. **-ung,** *f.* boarding, sheathing, mould (*for concrete*).

schäl-en, 1. *v.a.* pare, peel (*fruit*), shell (*peas*); blanch (*almonds*); remove bark; *sie ist wie aus dem Ei geschält*, she is as fresh as a daisy *or* looks spick and span. 2. *v.r.* peel *or* scale off; cast the shell, shed the bark. **-hengst,** *m.* stallion. **-messer,** *n.* vegetable knife. **-pflug,** *m.* shallow plough. **-ung,** *f.* peeling, skinning.

Schalk, *m.* (-(e)s, -e, (*dial.*) ⸚e) scoundrel, scamp, rogue, knave; wag; *er hat den –* or *ihm sitzt der – im Nacken*, he is full of roguishness *or* mischief; *der – sieht* or *lacht ihm aus den Augen*, his eyes twinkle with mischief *or* roguish fun. **-haft,** *adj.* roguish, waggish; (*archaic*) wily. **-haftigkeit,** *f.*, **-heit,** *f.* roguishness, mischief; (*archaic*) roguery, guile, villainy. (*B.*) **-sknecht,** *m.* unfaithful servant. **-snarr,** *m.* buffoon.

Schall, *m.* (-(e)s, -e & *Austr. dial.* ⸚e) sound, ring, peal, resonance, noise. **-aufnahme,** *f.* sound recording. **-becken,** *n.* cymbal. **-boden,** *m.* sounding-board. **-dämpfer,** *m.* silencer, muffler. **-deckel,** *m.* sound-board, reflector. **-dicht,** *adj.* sound-proof. **-dose,** *f.* sound-box, pick-up (*Gramophone*). **-en,** *reg.* & (*Austr. dial. ir.*) *v.n.* (*aux.* h. & s.) sound, resound, ring, peal; *-endes Gelächter*, resounding laughter. **-erregung,** *f.* production of sound. **-fenster,** *n.* louvre-board. **-fülle,** *f.* sonority. **-geschwindigkeit,** *f.* velocity of sound. **-glas,** *n.* musical glass. **-kasten,** *m.*, **-körper,** *m., see* **-boden.** **-(l)ehre,** *f.* acoustics. **-(l)och,** *n.* sound-hole (*in violins, etc.*); louvre-window (*in a belfry*). **-mauer,** *f.* sound-barrier (*Av.*). **-messer,** *m.* sonometer. **-meßtrupp,** *m.* sound-ranging section (*Mil.*). **-mine,** *f.* acoustic mine (*Nav.*). **-nachahmend,** *adj.* onomatopoeic. **-nachahmung,** *f.* onomatopoeia. **-platte,** *f.* gramophone record. **-plattenübertragung,** *f.* record programme (*Rad.*). **-quelle,** *f.* source of sound. **-rohr,** *n.* megaphone. **-schwingung,** *f.* sound vibration. **-trichter,** *m.* bell-mouth, horn, trumpet, megaphone. **-welle,** *f.* sound-wave. **-wort,** *n.* onomatopoeic word.

Schalm, *m.* (-(e)s, -e) blaze, mark (*on a tree*). **-en,** *v.a.* blaze (*a tree*).

Schalmei, *f.* (-en) (*obs.*) shawm (*Mus.*).

Schalotte, *f.* (-n) shallot.

schalt, schaltest, *see* **schelten.**

schalt-en, *v.n.* (*aux.* h.) direct, govern, rule; deal with; put in the circuit, insert, connect, switch (*Elec.*); change gear (*Motor.*); *mit* or *über etwas -en* (*und walten*), dispose of *or* do as one likes with a th.; *einen -en und walten lassen*, let a p. do as he likes; *wenn ich frei -en könnte*, if I were my own master, if I could do as I liked. **-ader,** *f.* spurious vein. **-anlage,** *f.* switch gear. **-bild,** *n.* circuit *or* switching diagram. **-brett,** *n.* switchboard, instrument panel; dashboard (*Motor.*). **-dose,** *f.* electric light switch. **-er,** *m.* switch, circuit-breaker, commutator (*Elec.*); counter (*in banks, etc.*); booking-office; *Pakete sind am -er abzuliefern*, parcels must be handed in over the counter. **-erbeamte(r),** *m.* cashier; ticket-clerk. **-erdienst,** *m.* duty at the ticket office, counter-service. **-erraum,** *m.* booking- *or* ticket-office. **-getriebe,** *n.* gearbox. **-hebel,** *m.* gear-lever (*Motor.*); switch (handle). **-jahr,** *n.* leap-year. **-kasten,** *m.* switch box. **-klinke,** *f.* ratchet, latch. **-plan,** *m.* circuit diagram. **-pult,** *n.* switch-board, control-panel. **-schlüssel,** *m.* ignition key (*Motor.*). **-skizze,** *f.* circuit diagram. **-tafel,** *f., see* **-brett.** **-tag,** *m.* intercalary day. **-ung,** *f.* circuit, connexion; gear-change. **-wort,** *n.* interpolated word. **-zelle,** *f.* intercalary cell.

Schaluppe, *f.* (-n) (*archaic*) sloop; long boat.

Scham, *f.* shame, bashfulness, modesty, chastity; genitals, privy *or* private parts, pudenda; (*B.*) nakedness; *vor – erröten*, blush with shame; *vor – vergehen*, die of shame; *aller – bar sein*, be dead to all sense of shame, be past shame. **-bein,** *n.* pubis. **-berg,** *m.* mons pubis *or* mons Veneris, pubes. **-bogen,** *m.* pubic arch. **-erröten,** *n.* blush of shame. **-gang,** *m.* vagina. **-gefühl,** *n.* sense of shame. **-gegend,** *f.* pubic region. **-glied,** *n.* penis. **-haft,** *adj.* modest, bashful, chaste. **-haftigkeit,** *f.* modesty, bashfulness, chastity. **-lippen,** *f.pl.* vulva. **-los,** *adj.* devoid of shame, shameless, impudent, brazen. **-losigkeit,** *f.* shamelessness; impudence. **-rot,** *adj.*, (*coll.*) **-violett,** *adj.* blushing, red with shame; *-rot machen*, put to the blush; *-rot werden*, blush with shame. **-röte,** *f.* blush. **-teile,** *m.pl.* privy *or* private parts, genitals.

Schamade, *f.* parley (*Mil.*); *– schlagen* or *blasen*, sound a parley; (*fig.*) capitulate, give in.

schämen, *v.r.* be ashamed (*über eine S.*, *wegen einer S., also with Gen.*, of a th.); *schäme dich!* for shame! you ought to be ashamed of yourself! *ich brauche mich deshalb* or *dessen nicht zu –*, I have no reason to be ashamed of that; *ich schäme mich deiner*, I am ashamed of you; *sich vor einem –*, feel ashamed in a p.'s presence; *sich vor sich selbst –*, be ashamed of o.s.; *sich zu Tode –*, die of shame.

schamfilen, *v.a.* & *r.* chafe (*of ropes*) (*Naut.*).

schämig, *adj.* (*dial.*) bashful, coy; shamefaced.

Schamotte, *f.* fire-clay. **-stein,** *m.*, **-ziegel,** *m.* fire-brick.

schampunieren, *v.a.* shampoo.

Schampus, *m.* (*coll.*) champagne.

schand-bar, *adj.* infamous, disgraceful; abominable. **-brief,** *m.* slanderous letter. **-bube,** *m.* scoundrel. **-bühne,** *f.* pillory. **-e,** *f.* (-en) shame, disgrace, dishonour; infamy, ignominy; *-e auf sich laden*, bring disgrace upon o.s.; *unempfänglich für -e*, dead to shame; *in -e bringen*, bring disgrace upon, dishonour; *einem -e machen*, be a disgrace to s.o.; *mit Schimpf und -e*, in disgrace, with ignominy; *Schmach und -e*, shame and dishonour; *-e über dich!* shame on you! *einem zur -e gereichen*, be a disgrace to s.o. **-e(n)halber,** *adv.* (*dial.*) for the sake of appearances, for decency's sake. **-fleck,** *m.* stain, blemish. (*coll.*) **-geld,** *n.* scandalous *or* ridiculously low sum. **-kauf,** *m.* disgraceful purchase; (*coll.*) *um einen -kauf*, dirt-cheap. **-leben,** *n.* life of infamy. **-lied,** *n.* obscene song. **-mal,** *n.* brand, stigma. **-maul,** *n.* evil tongue; slanderer. **-pfahl,** *m.* pillory. **-preis,** *m., see* **-geld.** **-tat,** *f.* crime, misdeed; (*hum.*) *zu jeder -tat aufgelegt*, ready for anything.

schänd-en, *v.a.* violate, rape, ravish (*a girl*); profane, defame, desecrate, revile; disfigure, spoil, deface. **-er,** *m.* ravisher, violator; slanderer, traducer; blasphemer; *der -er meiner Ehre*, the defiler of my honour. **-lich,** 1. *adj.* shameful, disgraceful, infamous, dishonourable, scandalous, abominable, despicable, vile, base; *-liches Verbrechen*, foul crime. 2. *adv.* (*coll.*) very much, extremely, intensely; *es ist -lich kalt*, it is dreadfully cold. **-lichkeit,** *f.* infamy, ignominy, disgrace; baseness, disgraceful act *or* conduct. **-ung,** *f.* disfiguring, spoiling, profanation, desecration; violation, rape.

Schank, *m.* sale of liquor. **-bier,** *n.* draught beer. **-gerechtigkeit,** *f.* licence to sell intoxicants. **-gesetz,** *n.* licensing act. **-mädchen,** *n.* barmaid. **-stätte,** *f.* licensed premises, public house. **-stube,** *f.* tap room, bar parlour. **-tisch,** *m.* bar. **-wirt,** *m.* publican. **-wirtschaft,** *f., see* **-stätte.**

Schanker, *m.* (-s, –) chancre (*Med.*).
[1]**Schanz–e,** *f.* (-en) bulwark, trench, entrenchment, field-work, redoubt. **–arbeiten,** *f.pl.* fortifications, entrenchments. **–arbeiter,** *m.* sapper. **–en,** *v.n.* (*aux.* h.) dig in; (*coll.*) work hard, drudge. **–er,** *m.* sapper. **–gerät,** *n.* entrenching tools. **–gräber,** *m.*, *see* **–arbeiter. –korb,** *m.* gabion (*Fort.*). **–pfahl,** *m.* palisade. **–sack,** *m.* sandbag. **–wehr,** *f.* bulwark. **–werk,** *n.* entrenchment. **–zeug,** *n.* entrenching tools.
[2]**Schanze,** *f.* (-n) (*archaic*) chance, hazard; *in die – schlagen,* stake, risk, hazard.
Schar, *f.* (-en) 1. troop, band, (*Nat. Soc.*) squad, platoon; herd, flock; host, multitude, crowd. 2. (plough)share. **–en,** *v.a.* & *r.* collect, assemble, flock together, congregate. **–enweise,** *adv.* in bands *or* troops. **–führer,** *m.* (*Nat. Soc.*) platoon *or* section leader. **–riegel,** *m.* ploughshare-pin. **–wache,** *f.* patrol; watch. **–wächter,** *m.* duty sentry. **–werk,** *n.* (*archaic*) forced *or* statute labour; (*dial.*) jobbing work.
Scharade, *f.* (-n) charade; *–n aufführen,* act charades.
Scharbe, *f.* (-n) cormorant.
scharb–en, schärb–en, *v.a.* (*dial.*) cut into strips (*Cook.*). **–eisen,** *n.* kitchen knife.
Scharbock, *m.* (*archaic*) scurvy. **–heilend,** *adj.* anti-scorbutic. **–skraut,** *n.* fig-wort.
Schären, *f.pl.* cliffs, rocky promontories.
scharf, 1. *adj.* (*comp.* schärfer, *sup.* schärfst) sharp; biting, cutting, pungent, hot, acrid, piquant; acute, pointed, well-focused, keen, strong, severe, rigorous, hard, strict, exact; caustic, corrosive; quick, penetrating, piercing, shrill, harsh; live, armed, primed (*Mil.*); *einen – anlassen,* snap a p. up; *einen – ansehen,* look at a p. hard *or* closely; *–e Antwort,* cutting reply; (*coll.*) *– auf etwas sein,* be keen on a th.; *– aufpassen,* pay close attention; *sich – auswirken,* have a telling effect; *– beschlagen,* rough-shoe (*a horse*); *– betonen,* accentuate strongly; *– bewachen,* guard *or* watch closely; *eine –e Brille,* strong spectacles *or* glasses; *–e Entgegnung,* sharp *or* cutting rejoinder; *– ins Auge fassen,* look at closely *or* intently; *–e Flüssigkeit,* corrosive liquid; *einem – zu Leibe gehen,* attack s.o. vigorously *or* hotly; *–es Gift,* strong poison; *hinter dem Gelde – her sein,* have an eye to the main chance, be keen on making money; *–e Kälte,* biting cold; *–er Kampf,* hotly-contested battle; *–e Kurve,* sharp bend (*Motor.*); *– laden,* load with ball; *–e Linien,* well-defined lines; *–e Luft,* keen air; *etwas – machen,* sharpen, whet *or* grind a th.; *–es Ohr,* quick ear; *–er Protest,* emphatic protest; *– reiten,* ride hard; (*Prov.*) *allzu – macht schartig,* a bow long bent at last grows weak; *–e Stimme,* strident voice; *in –en Umrissen,* with clear outlines; *–e Untersuchung,* searching examination; *–es Urteil,* keen judgement; *–er Verstand,* penetrating mind; *–er Verweis,* severe rebuke; *– vorgehen,* take energetic measures; *–er Widerstand,* bitter resistance; *–e Zunge,* sharp tongue. 2. *n.* tapered end (*of beams, a ship, etc.*). **–blick,** *m.* piercing look, penetrating glance; quick eye, acuteness, penetration. **–eckig,** *adj.* sharp-cornered; acute-angled. **–einstellung,** *f.* (sharp) focusing (*Phot.*). **–kantig,** *adj.* sharp cornered. **–machen,** *v.a.* instigate, excite. **–macher,** *m.* intriguer, agitator, firebrand. **–macherei,** *f.* political agitation. **–macherisch,** *adj.* inflammatory. **–richter,** *m.* executioner. **–salzig,** *adj.* very salty, highly salted. **–schießen,** *n.* firing with live ammunition. **–schmeckend,** *adj.* pungent, acrid, tart. **–schütze,** *m.* sharpshooter, sniper, crack shot. **–schützenfeuer,** *n.* independent fire, accurate rifle fire. **–sicht,** *f.* keen-sightedness, perspicacity. **–sichtig,** *adj.* keen-sighted; clear-sighted, penetrating, subtle. **–sicht(igkeit),** *f.* keenness of vision; perspicacity, penetration. **–sinn,** *m.* sagacity, acuteness, penetration, discernment, acumen. **–sinnig,** *adj.* clear-sighted, sagacious, clever, ingenious, shrewd. **–stellen,** *v.a.* prime (*bombs, etc.*).
Schärf–e, *f.* (-en) edge, sharpness, keenness, fineness; acuteness, trenchancy; point (*of epigrams, etc.*); acidity, pungency, piquancy; severity, rigour; definition (*Phot.*). **–en,** *v.a.* whet, sharpen, grind, set (*razor*); intensify, strengthen, increase, heighten, aggravate; rough-shoe (*a horse*); *einem das Gewissen –en,* appeal to a p.'s conscience; *das Gedächtnis –en,* strengthen the memory; *einem den Blick –en,* widen a p.'s horizon, open a p.'s eyes. **–tiefe,** *f.* depth of focus (*Phot.*). **–ung,** *f.* sharpening, augmenting, strengthening.
Scharlach, 1. *m.* scarlet. 2. *m.* & *n.*, *see* **–fieber. –en,** *adj.* scarlet. **–exanthem,** *n.* scarlet-fever rash. **–farben,** *adj.*, **–farbig,** *adj.* scarlet, vermilion. **–fieber,** *n.* scarlet-fever; scarlatina. **–wurm,** *m.* cochineal insect.
Scharlatan, *m.* (-s, -e) charlatan; quack (doctor). **–erei,** *f.* charlatanism, quackery.
Scharm, *m.* charm. **–ant,** *adj.* charming, engaging. **–ieren,** *v.n.* flirt.
Scharmütz–el, *n.* (-els, -el) skirmish. **–eln,** *v.n.* (*aux.* h.) skirmish. **–ler,** *m.* skirmisher.
Scharnier, *n.* (-s, -e) hinge, joint. **–gelenk,** *n.* rule-joint; hinge-like joint (*Anat.*). **–stift,** *m.* hinge-pin.
Schärpe, *f.* (-n) scarf, sash; sling.
Scharpie, *f.* (-n) lint.
Scharr–e, *f.* (-n) rake, raker, scraper. **–eisen,** *n.* scraper. **–en,** *v.a.* & *n.* (*aux.* h.) scrape, scratch; rake; paw (*of horses*); shuffle the feet; *in die Erde –en,* bury hastily. **–fuß,** *m.* claw of gallinaceous birds; digging claw, (*fig.*) obsequious bow. **–vogel,** *m.* scratcher.
Schar(re)n, *m.*, *see* **Schranne.**
Schart–e, *f.* (-en) notch, crack, nick, slot; gap, fissure, indentation; loophole, embrasure (*Mil.*); *eine –e auswetzen,* make amends (for), (*coll.*) make up (for), make good (*a mistake, etc.*). **–enblende,** *f.* firing-post flap *or* shutter. **–enzeile,** *f.* merlon (*Fort.*). **–ig,** *adj.* jagged, notched.
Scharteke, *f.* (-n) worthless old book; trash; old frump.
Scharwenzel, *m.* (-s, –) knave (*at cards*); busybody, toady. **–n,** *v.n.* be officious *or* obsequious, bow and scrape; toady, fawn; dance attendance (*um,* on).
schassen, *v.a.* (*archaic*) expel (*from school, etc.*).
Schatt–en, 1. *m.* (-ens, -en) shadow, shade; phantom, spirit; *in den –en stellen,* place in the shade, (*fig.*) push into the background; *er macht mir –en,* he stands in my light. 2. *v.n.* (*aux.* h.) (*archaic*) throw a shadow, afford shade. **–enbild,** *n.* silhouette, outline; phantom. **–enblume,** *f.* bifoliate lily of the valley (*Maianthemum bifolium*) (*Bot.*). **–endasein,** *n.* unreal existence. **–engebend,** *adj.* shady, throwing a shadow. **–engestalt,** *f.* phantom. **–enhaft,** *adj.* shadowy, indistinct; ghostly, unreal. **–enindustrie,** *f.* shadow factories. **–enkegel,** *m.* umbra. **–enland,** *n.* the hereafter. **–enlinie,** *f.* outline. **–enlos,** *adj.* without shadow *or* shade. **–enpflanze,** *f.* plant thriving in the shade, heliophobous plant. **–enreich,** 1. *adj.* shady. 2. *n.* realm of the dead, the underworld, Hades. **–enriß,** *m.* silhouette; outline. **–enseite,** *f.* shady side, dark side; drawback; *er sieht an allem nur die –enseite,* he always looks on the dark side of th's. **–enspendend,** *adj.*, *see* **–engebend. –enspiel,** *n.* shadow-play. **–enwesen,** *n.* phantom. **–enzeiger,** *m.* hand of a sun-dial. **–ieren,** *v.a.* & *n.* (*aux.* h.) shade (*of colours, etc.*); tint; hatch (*maps*). **–ierung,** *f.* gradation of colour, shading; hatching (*maps*); shade, tint, hue. **–ig,** *adj.* shady, shaded.
Schatulle, *f.* (-n) cash box, strong-box, jewel case; privy purse (*of a prince*).
Schatz, *m.* (-es, ⸚e) treasure, wealth; store, stock; sweetheart, love, darling. **–amt,** *n.* treasury, exchequer. **–anweisung,** *f.* exchequer bond. **–en,** *v.a.* (*dial.*) tax, impose tax *or* fine on. **–gräber,** *m.* digger for treasure. **–kammer,** *f* treasury; jewel-room; (*fig.*) *–kammer der Natur,* Nature's rich storehouse. **–kanzler,** *m.* chancellor of the exchequer. **–kästchen,** *n.*, **–kästlein,** *n.* collection of gems; casket; treasury (*title of book*). **–meister,** *m.* treasurer; chancellor. **–pflichtig,** *adj.* taxable, ratable. **–schein,** *m.* treasury bill, exchequer bond. **–ung,** *f.* tax, assessment, taxation. **–wechsel,** *m.* treasury bill.
schätz–en, *v.a.* value, appraise, estimate, assess,

reckon (at), consider (to be); esteem, respect, prize; *zu hoch –en*, overrate, overestimate; *es für eine Ehre* or *es sich* (*Dat.*) *zur Ehre –en*, esteem it an honour; *sich glücklich –en*, think o.s. fortunate; *wie alt –en Sie ihn?* how old do you suppose he is? *geschätzt*, *p.p.* & *adj.* esteemed; dear (*friend*); (*C.L.*) *Ihr Geschätztes vom . . .*, your esteemed favour of (*such-and-such a date*). **–bar,** *adj.* valuable, precious, estimable; assessable. **–enswert,** *adj.* estimable, precious. **–ung,** *f.* estimation, valuation, evaluation, computation, estimate, appraisal, assessment; esteem; tax, taxation. **–ungsweise,** *adv.* at a rough estimation, approximately, roughly. **–ungswert,** *m.* estimated value.

Schau, *f.* (-en) show, sight, view; inspection, review; exhibition; *nur zur –*, only for show; *zur – stellen*, exhibit, display; *zur – tragen*, make display of; sham, feign. **–bild,** *n.* diagram, figure, exhibit. **–brot,** *n.* shewbread (*Jew.*). **–bude,** *f.* booth, stall (*at fair*). **–bühne,** *f.* stage, theatre. **–en,** (*coll. in Southern dial., otherwise elev. style*) *v.a.* & *n.* behold, see; look (at), gaze (upon), view; *in die Zukunft –en*, look into *or* scan the future; (*coll.*) *da – mal einer!* look here, now really, I say! **–er,** *m.* spectator; *see* **Schauer.** **–fenster,** *n.* shop-window, show-case. **–fensterdekoration,** *f.* window-dressing. **–fenstergestalter,** *m.* window dresser. **–fliegen,** *n.*, **–flug,** *m.* flying display, aerial pageant. **–gepränge,** *n.* pageantry, pomp. **–gerüst,** *n.* stage; grand-stand. **–haus,** *n.* mortuary. **–herr,** *m.* inspector (*of mines*). **–kasten,** *m.* show-case. **–klappe,** *f.* inspection flap *or* door. **–linie,** *f.* graph, curve, characteristic. **–loch,** *n.* peep-hole. **–lustig,** *adj.* curious (*to see*). **–lustige(r),** *m.* sightseer, onlooker, bystander. **–münze,** *f.* medal, medallion. **–packung,** *f.* dummy (packing) (*for showcases*). **–platz,** *m.* theatre, scene, arena, stage, seat (*of war*). **–raum,** *m.* show-room. **–spiel,** *n.* *n.* (-s, -e) spectacle, sight, scene; play, drama; *ins –spiel gehen*, go to the theatre. **–spielartig,** *adj.* dramatic, theatrical, (*sl.*) stagy. **–spieldichter,** *m.* playwright, dramatist, dramatic poet. **–spieler,** *m.* actor, performer, (*fig.*) play-actor; *herumziehender –spieler*, strolling player. **–spielerei,** *f.* (*fig.*) play-acting; shamming, affectation. **–spielerin,** *f.* actress. **–spielerisch,** *adj.* histrionic, theatrical. **–spiele(r)n,** *v.n.* (*aux.* h.) (*coll.*) act a part, sham, (*sl.*) put it on. **–spielhaus,** *n.* playhouse, theatre. **–spielkunst,** *f.* dramatic art, histrionics, **–stellen,** *v.a.* exhibit, display. **–steller,** *m.* exhibitor; showman. **–stellung,** *f.* exhibition, show. **–stück,** *n.* show-piece, specimen; lavish stage spectacle. **–tafel,** *f.* diagram. **–turnen,** *n.* gymnastic display. **–ware,** *f.*, **–werk,** *n.* specimen, sample, show-goods. **–zeichen,** *n.* line marker (*Typ.*).

Schaub, *m.* (-(e)s, -e & *Austr. dial.* ⸚e) (*dial.*) bundle of straw, sheaf. **–endach,** *n.* thatched roof.

Schaube, *f.* (-n) long cloak *or* mantle open in front (*Hist.*).

Schauder, *m.* (-s, –) shuddering, shivering; shudder, horror, terror, fright; (*Poet.*) awe; *– erregen* (*in* or *bei einem*), cause (*a p.*) to shudder *or* shiver, make (*a p.'s*) flesh creep. **–bar,** *adj.* (*coll.*), **–erregend,** *adj.*, **–haft,** horrible, frightful, terrible, awful, horrifying, atrocious. **–gefühl,** *n.* feeling of dread, (*coll.*) creepy feeling. **–geschichte,** *f.* horrifying tale, gruesome story. **–n,** *v.n.* (*aux.* h. & s.) & *imp.* shudder, shiver; feel dread, be awed; (*coll.*) feel creepy; *mir* or *mich –t bei dem Gedanken*, I shudder at the thought; *vor Kälte –n*, shiver with cold.

Schauer, *m.* (-s, –) 1. shower, downpour; (*dial.*) hail. 2. thrill, shudder, slight tremor. fit, spasm, paroxysm. 3. awe, terror, horror. 4. (*also n.*) (*dial.*) shed, shelter, barn; *unter – gehen*, take shelter. **–(mann),** *m.* (-leute) dock labourer, docker. **–gefühl,** *n.* feeling of terror. **–ig,** *adj.*, **–lich,** *adj.* terrible, horrible, horrid, awful, ghastly, gruesome. **–n,** 1. *v.n.* (*aux.* h.) shudder, shiver, (*coll.*) feel creepy. 2. *imp.*; *es –t*, it is pouring *or* raining; (*dial.*) it is hailing; *mich* or *mir –t bei*, I shudder at. **–roman,** *m.* penny-dreadful; thriller, shocker. **–tat,** *f.* atrocity. **–voll,** *adj.* dreadful, most awful.

Schaufel, *f.* (-n) shovel; scoop, paddle; blade, vane; fluke (*of an anchor*); palm-antler. **–bein,** *n.* sacrum. **–förmig,** *adj.* spade-shaped. **–gehörn,** *n.*, **–geweih,** *n.* palmed antlers. **–hirsch,** *m.* fallow deer over two years old. **–ig,** *adj.* spade-shaped. **–kasten,** *m.* paddle-box. **–n,** *v.a.* shovel, dig. **–pflug,** *m.* moulding-plough. **–rad,** *n.* paddle-wheel. **–weise,** *adv.* by shovelfuls. **–zahn,** *m.* broad incisor.

Schaufler, *m.* shoveller; *see* **Schaufelhirsch.**

Schauk–el, *f.* (-eln) swing. **–elbank,** *f.* see-saw. **–elei,** *f.* pitching and tossing (*Naut.*). **–eln,** *v.n.* (*aux.* h.) & *a.* swing, rock; pitch (*of ship*). **–elpferd,** *n.* rocking-horse. **–elstuhl,** *m.* rocking-chair. **–elwelle,** *f.* rocker-arm.

Schaum, *m.* (-(e)s, ⸚e) foam, froth, spume; scum, skimmings; flurry, lather, bubbles; *zu – schlagen*, beat up, whisk; (*Prov.*) *Träume sind Schäume*, dreams are like bubbles. **–artig,** *adj.* frothy, foamy. **–bedeckt,** *adj.* covered with foam. **–beton,** *m.* aero-concrete. **–blase,** *f.* bubble; (*fig.*) delusion. **–fähig,** *adj.* lathering. **–gold,** *n.* tinsel. **–gummi,** *m.* crêpe rubber. **–haube,** *f.* head (*Brewing*). **–ig,** *adj.* foamy, frothy, lathering. **–kelle,** *f.*, **–löffel,** *m.* skimming-ladle. **–kraut,** *n.* cardamine (*Cardamine pratensis*) (*Bot.*). **–krone,** *f.* white crest (*of waves*), white horses. **–löffel,** *m.* skimmer. **–los,** *adj.* without foam *or* froth; without a head, flat (*of beer*). **–schläger,** *m.* egg-whisk; wind-bag, gas-bag. **–schwimmaufbereitung,** *f.* flotation. **–stand,** *m.*, *see* **–haube.** **–wein,** *m.* sparkling wine, champagne. **–zirpe,** *f.* frog-hopper (*Aphrophora*) (*Entom.*).

schäumen, 1. *v.n.* (*aux.* h.) foam, froth, lather; effervesce, sparkle; (*coll.*) fizz; *vor Wut –*, boil with rage. 2. *v.a.* skim.

schaurig, *adj.*, *see* **schauerlich.**

Schaute, *m.* (-n, -n) (*sl.*) fool.

[1]**Scheck,** *m.* (-en, -en), **–e,** *f.* (-en) piebald *or* dappled animal. **–en,** *v.a.* dapple, spot. **–enbildung,** *f.* piebald spotting, partial albinism. **–ig,** *adj.* pied, piebald; dappled, spotted, mottled, brindled; (*coll.*) *sich –ig lachen*, split one's sides with laughing.

[2]**Scheck,** *m.* (-s, -e & -s) cheque; *ein – (auf* or *über)*, a cheque (for). **–buch,** *n.* cheque-book. **–formular,** *n.* blank cheque. **–inhaber,** *m.* bearer. **–konto,** *n.* current account. **–verkehr,** *m.* business in cheques. **–zahlung,** *f.* payment by cheque.

scheel, *adj.* envious; (*dial.*) cross-eyed, squinting; *– zu etwas sehen*, *etwas mit –en Augen ansehen*, regard a th. askance. **–äugig,** *adj.* jealous; squinting. **–it,** *m.* tungsten. **–sucht,** *f.* envy. **–süchtig,** *adj.* envious, jealous.

Scheffel, *m.* (-s, –) bushel. **–n,** 1. *v.a.* (*coll.*) heap up, rake in; measure by the bushel. 2. *v.n.* (*aux.* h.) yield in abundance. **–weise,** *adv.* by the bushel; abundantly.

Scheg, *m.* (-(e)s, -e) foremost part of the cutwater (*Naut.*); *– des Steuers*, after-piece of a rudder.

Scheib–e, *f.* (-en) disk, washer; orb; slice (*of bread, etc.*); pane (of glass); (honey)comb; target; face (*of a clock, etc.*); quoit; pulley, wheel, potter's wheel, sheave (*of a block*); coil (*of rope*); (*coll.*) *du kannst dir eine –e davon abschneiden*, you can take a leaf out of (his, *etc.*) book; *–e des Kompasses*, compass-card; *–e des Mondes*, disk of the moon; *an der –e vorbeischießen*, (*fig.*) miss the mark. **–en,** *v.n.* (*dial.*), *see* **schieben.** **–enblei,** *n.* glazier's lead. **–en(elektrisier)maschine,** *f.* Wimshurst machine (*Elec.*). **–enförmig,** *adj.* disk-shaped, disk-like. **–engardinen,** *f.pl.* casement-curtain. **–englas,** *n.* window glass. **–enhonig,** *m.* honey in the comb. **–eninstrument,** *n.* astrolabe. **–enkönig,** *m.* best shot at a shooting-match. **–enkupplung,** *f.* plate-clutch (*Motor*). **–enlack,** *m.* shellac. **–enrad,** *n.* disk-wheel. **–enschießen,** *n.* target practice (*Mil.*). **–enspule,** *f.* flanged spool. **–enstand,** *m.* (rifle) butts. **–enweise,** *adv.* in slices. **–enwerfen,** *n.*. quoit-throwing. **–enwischer,** *m.* windscreen-wiper. (*Motor.*). **–ig,** *adj.*, *see* **–enförmig;** *zwei–iger Block*, two-wheeled pulley.

Scheich, *m.* (-s, -e) sheik.

Scheid–e, *f.* (-n) boundry, border, limit, divide;

case, sheath, scabbard; vagina (*Anat.*). **-en,** 1. *ir.v. r.* & *n.* (*aux.* s.) separate, part; depart, go away, leave; *das -ende Jahr*, the closing year; *hier -en sich die Wege*, here the roads part *or* branch off; *so schieden wir*, thus we parted; *hier schieden sie von einander*, here they took leave of one another. 2. *v.a.* separate, divide, pick, sort, sift; part, sever, divorce; analyse, refine, clarify; decompose, defecate; *sich -en lassen*, sue for a divorce; obtain a judicial separation, get divorced; *der* (*die*) *Geschiedene*, divorced person; *wir sind geschiedene Leute*, we have nothing more to do with one another. 3. *n.* parting, separation; *vor seinem -en*, before leaving; previous to his death. **-bar,** *adj.* separable; divisible, decomposable, analysable; that can be analysed (*Chem.*). **-eartig,** *adj.* sheath-like. **-ebank,** *f.* sorting table (*ore*). **-ebrief,** *m.* farewell letter; bill of divorce. **-eerz,** *n.* picked *or* screened ore. **-efeuer,** *n.* refining furnace. **-egefäß,** *n.* decanter. **-egruß,** *m.* farewell (greeting). **-ekunst,** *f.* (*archaic*) analytical chemistry. **-ekuß,** *m.* parting kiss. **-elinie,** *f.* line of demarcation, boundary line. **-emauer,** *f.* partition wall. **-emünze,** *f.* small coin, (small) change. **-enentzündung,** *f.* vaginitis (*Med.*). **-envorfall,** *m.* vaginal prolapsus. **-epunkt,** *m.* point of separation *or* divergence. **-estunde,** *f.* hour of parting *or* death. **-ewand,** *f.* partition, dividing wall; septum (*Anat.*); bulkhead; diaphragm. **-ewasser,** *n.* aqua fortis, nitric acid. **-eweg,** *m.* cross-roads, forked road; *am -ewege stehen*, stand at the parting of the ways *or* at the cross-roads; be in a quandary *or* undecided. **-ing,** *m.* September. **-ung,** *f.* separation; divorce; clarifying; decomposition, defecation; chemical analysis; *-ung von Tisch und Bett*, judicial separation. **-ungserkenntnis,** *n.* decree nisi. **-ungsgrund,** *m.* grounds for divorce. **-ungsklage,** *f.* divorce suit *or* proceedings. **-ungsprozeß,** *m.* divorce-case.

Schein *m.* (-(e)s, -e) shine, light, brilliance, gleam, lustre, bloom, sheen; appearance, air, look, show; pretence, semblance, pretext, illusion; bank-note, receipt, bond, document, paper, ticket, bill, form, licence, certificate; (*fig.*) glory, halo, blaze; *-e und Hartgeld*, notes and coin; *zum -e* or *des -es wegen*, for show, for form's sake; *den bösen – meiden, den – wahren*, keep up appearances; *unter dem -e der Freundschaft*, under the pretence *or* cloak of friendship; *kein – von Hoffnung*, no glimmer of hope; *es hat den –, als ob . . .*, it looks as if . . .; *dem -e nach*, apparently, to all intents and purposes; *sich* (*Dat.*) *den – geben*, pretend, give the impression; *das ist alles nur –*, that is all pretence; *der – spricht gegen ihn*, appearances are against him; (*Prov.*) *der – trügt*, appearances are deceptive. **-angriff,** *m.* feint attack. **-anlage,** *f.* dummy works. **-bar,** *adj.* seeming, apparent, likely, plausible; pretended, fictitious, ostensible; *-barer Horizont*, apparent horizon. **-bewegung,** *f.* feint, apparent movement. **-bild,** *n.* illusion; phantom. **-blüte,** *f.* apparent prosperity. **-christ,** *m.* pretended *or* lip-Christian. **-ding,** *n.* figment of the imagination, chimera. **-ehe,** *f.* mock marriage. **-en,** *ir.v.n.* (*aux.* h.) shine; (*with Dat.*) seem, appear, look; *die Sonne -t warm*, the sun is hot; *sie -en reich zu sein, es -t, als ob sie reich seien*, they seem to be rich; *wie -t dir die Geschichte?* what do you think of the story? **-farben,** *f.pl.* accidental colours (*Opt.*). **-flugplatz,** *m.* decoy airfield. **-friede,** *m.* hollow *or* patched-up peace. **-fromm,** *adj.* hypocritical. **-frucht,** *f.* spurious fruit. **-funk,** *m.* spoof transmission (*Rad.*). **-fuß,** *m.* pseudo-podium. **-gefecht,** *n.* sham fight. **-gelehrsamkeit,** *f.* would-be learning, pretended erudition. **-gelenk,** *n.* false articulation. **-gericht,** *n.* mock trial. **-glück,** *n*, seeming happiness. **-gold,** *n.* artificial gold. **-grund,** *m.* apparent reason; pretext, sophism. **-heilig,** *adj.* hypocritical, sanctimonious. **-heilige(r),** *m.* hypocrite. **-hoffnung,** *f.* delusive hope. **-kampf,** *m.* sham fight. **-krankheit,** *f.* feigned illness. **-leben,** *n.* semblance of life; empty life. **-shalber,** *adv.* to save face, for the sake of appearances. **-tod,** *m.* apparent death, suspended animation, trance. **-tot,** *adj.* seemingly dead, in a trance. **-verkauf,** *m.* pro forma sale, fictitious sale. **-wechsel,** *m.* accommodation bill. **-werfer,** *m.* reflector, projector, searchlight, floodlight; headlight, headlamp (*Motor.*); spot-light (*Theat.*). **-werferkegel,** *m.* searchlight beam. **-wesen,** *n.* imaginary being, phantom. **-widerstand,** *m.* impedance (*Rad.*). **-zwiebel,** *f.* aerial tuber (*Bot.*). **-zwitter,** *m.* pseudo-hermaphrodite.

Scheinergrad, *m.* (-es, -e) photometric unit (*after Julius Scheiner*).

Scheiß-e, *f.* (*vulg.*) shit. **-en,** *ir.v.a.* & *n.* (*aux.* h.) (*vulg.*) shit, crap. (*vulg.*) **-dreck,** *m.*, **-erei,** *f.* trash, piddling *or* piffling stuff. (*vulg.*) **-kerl,** *m.* sorry specimen, lily-livered skunk.

Scheit, *n.* (-(e)s, -e & -er) log, billet, stick (of fire-wood). **-en,** *v.n.* (*Swiss. dial.*) split logs. **-erhaufen,** *m.* funeral pile. **-holz,** *n.* split log(s).

Scheitel, *m.* (-s, –) top, vertex, apex, summit; crown (*of the head*); parting (*of the hair*); origin of co-ordinates (*Math.*); *vom – bis zur Sohle*, from head to foot, from top to toe. **-bein,** *n.* parietal bone. **-fläche,** *f.* vertical plane. **-käppchen,** *n.* skull-cap. **-kreis,** *m.* vertical circle, azimuth. **-lappen,** *m.* parietal lobe. **-linie,** *f.* vertical line. **-n,** *v.a.* & *r.* part (*the hair*). **-punkt,** *m.* vertex, zenith, apex. **-recht,** *adj.* vertical, perpendicular. **-wert,** *m.* peak amplitude. **-winkel,** *m.* vertical *or* opposite angle. **-zelle,** *f.* apical cell.

scheit-ern, 1. *v.n.* (*aux.* h. & s.) run aground, be wrecked, founder, become a wreck; (*fig.*) be frustrated, miscarry, fail, prove unavailing; *daran -ert meine* (*ganze*) *Kunst*, that is beyond me, that beats me. 2. *n.* shipwreck; failure, breakdown.

Schelf-e, *f.* (-en) husk, shell, pod (*of fruits*). **-en, -ern,** *v.n. a.* & *r.* (*aux.* h.) peel (off), scale (off).

Schellack, *m.* shellac. **-politur,** *f.* French polish.

Schell-e, *f.* (-en) 1. (little) bell; diamonds (*Cards*). 2. clamp, clip, collar, manacle, handcuff. 3. (*dial.*) box on the ears; (*B.*) *wie eine klingende -e*, as a tinkling cymbal; (*Prov.*) *der Katze die -e umhängen*, bell the cat. **-en,** *v.a.* & *n.* (*aux.* h.) ring, ring the bell; tinkle; *es hat geschellt*, the bell rang; *ich habe geschellt*, I have rung. **-engeläut(e),** *n.* tinkling; sleigh-bells; bell-harness (*of a horse*). **-enkappe,** *f.* fool's cap and bells. **-enkönig,** *m.* king of diamonds; *einen über den -enkönig loben*, praise a p. to the skies. **-entrommel,** *f.* tambourine; timbrel. **-hengst,** *m.* (-es, -e), *see* **Schälhengst. -kraut,** *n.* (*dial.*) (-(e)s, ⸚er) greater celandine (*Chelidonium majus*) (*Bot.*). **-fisch,** *m,* (-es, -e) haddock (*Icht.*) **-nietung,** *f.* snap-riveting.

Schelm, *m.* (-(e)s, -e) rogue; (*archaic*) rascal, knave, scoundrel; *einen zum – machen*, sully a p.'s good name; (*Prov.*) *ein –, der besser macht* (or *mehr gibt* or *tut*) *als er kann*, you must not expect impossibilities; (*Prov.*) *auf einen – anderthalben setzen*, set a thief to catch a thief; *ein – der Schlechtes dabei denkt*, honi soit qui mal y pense; *ihm sitzt der – im Nacken*, *see* **Schalk. -enroman,** *m.* picaresque novel. **-ensprache,** *f.* thieves' slang. **-enstreich,** *m.*, **-enstück,** *n.* prank. **-enzunft,** *f.* all rogues. **-erei,** *f.* roguishness, roguish ways; (*archaic*) roguery, knavery. **-isch,** *adj.* roguish, teasing, arch.

Schelt-e, *f.* (-n) scolding, rebuke, reprimand; *-e bekommen*, be *or* get scolded. **-en,** *ir.v.a.* & *n.* (*aux.* h.) reproach, scold, chide, reprimand, upbraid, inveigh (against), abuse; (*dial.*) call, nickname; *auf einen -en*, scold a p.; *jemanden einen Dummkopf -en*, call a p. stupid *or* a blockhead. **-name,** *m.* opprobrious name. **-rede,** *f.* philippic, invective, abuse. **-wort,** *n.* invective.

Schema, *n.* (-s, *pl.* -s, -men & -ta) schedule, diagram, model, pattern, scheme, (*coll.*) set-up; *nach – F*, according to rule, without discrimination. **-tisch,** *adj.* diagrammatic, schematic, systematic, reduced to a norm, undifferentiated. **-tisieren,** *v.a.* sketch out, (describe in) outline, (*coll.*) lump together. **-tismus,** *m.* lack of discrimination, formalism.

Schemel, *m.* (-s, –) (foot-)stool.

Schem-en, *m.* (-ens, -en) phantom, shadow, delusion. **-bart,** *m.* false beard, bearded mask. **-enhaft,** *adj.* shadowy, unreal.

Schenk, *m.* (-en, -en) cup-bearer; publican. **-e,** *f.* (-en) inn, tavern, public house. **-bier,** *n.* draught beer. **-en,** *v.a.* 1. give, present, bestow, grant; 2. remit, forgive, acquit; 3. pour out, fill, retail (*liquor*); *etwas zu Weihnachten geschenkt bekommen,* get s.th. as a Christmas present; *etwas beinahe geschenkt bekommen,* buy a th. for next to nothing; *wenn Gott mir das Leben -t,* if God grants me life; *es soll dir geschenkt sein,* I will let you off this time; *das kannst du dir -en,* you can miss *or* cut that out, you can dispense with that; *den Rest der Geschichte -e ich dir,* I will spare you the rest of the story; *ich möchte es nicht geschenkt haben,* I would not have it as a gift. **-er,** *m.* donor. **-gerechtigkeit,** *f.* licence to retail liquor. **-kanne,** *f.* can, tankard. **-mädchen,** *n.* barmaid. **-stube,** *f.* tap-room. **-tisch,** *m.* bar. **-ung,** *f.* donation, gift. **-ungsurkunde,** *f.* deed of gift. **-ungsweise,** *adv.* by way of donation. **-wirt,** *m.* publican. **-wirtschaft,** *f.* public-house.

Schenkel *m.* (-s, -) thigh, shank; side (*of angles, Arch.*); hinged leg, arm, limb, side-piece. **-bein,** *n.* thigh-bone, femur. **-beuge,** *f.* groin, inguinal furrow. **-blutader,** *f.* femoral artery. **-bruch,** *m.* fracture of the thigh. **-gelenk,** *n.* hip joint. **-ig,** *adj.* shanked; *gleich-ig,* isosceles. **-knochen,** *m., see* **-bein. -muskel,** *m.* & *f.* crural muscle. **-recht,** *adj.* tractable (*of horses*). **-zirkel,** *m.* pair of compasses.

Scherbe, *f.* (-n), **-l,** *m.* (-ls, -l), **-n,** *m.* (-ns, -n) fragment (*of glass, earthenware, etc.*), potsherd, shard; (*dial.*) earthenware vessel; flower-pot. **-ngericht,** *n.* ostracism. **-ngewächs,** *n.* pot-plant. **-nhaufen,** *m.* heap of fragments, (*fig.* & *coll.*) shambles.

Scher-e, *f.* (-en) scissors, shears, clippers; shafts (*of a carriage*); claws (*of crabs, etc.*); (*fig.*) reciprocal relationship. **-en,** *reg.* & 1. *ir.v.a.* shear, clip, cut, trim, mow, shave; warp (*Weav.*); reeve (*Naut.*); (*fig.*) *v. imp.* concern. *einem den Bart -en, einen -en,* shave a p.; *sein Schäfchen -en,* feather one's nest; *laß mich ungeschoren!* let me alone! *was -t mich das?* what's that to me? *sich um* (*einen* or *eine Sache*) *-en,* trouble o.s. *or* bother about, be bothered about, be concerned for; *alles über einen Kamm -en,* treat all alike, make no distinction. 2. *v.n.* sheer, yaw (*Naut.*). 3. *v.r.* (*coll.*) go away, clear off, (*sl.*) do a bunk; *-(e)* (or *schier*) *dich weg!* be off with you! you get away! *er mag sich zum Teufel -en,* he can go to the devil. **-enfernrohr,** *n.* stereotelescope. **-enschleifer,** *m.* scissors-grinder. **-enschmied,** *m.* cutler. **-enschnitt,** *m.* silhouette. **-enwerk,** *n.* tenaille (*Fort.*). **-er,** *m.* shearer; barber. (*coll.*) **-erei,** *f.* trouble, bother, worry, vexation, annoyance. **-festigkeit,** *f.* shearing strength. **-gang,** *m.* sheer-strake (*Naut.*). **-garn,** *n.* thread for the warp. **-ling,** *m.* shorn fleece. **-maschine,** *f.* shearing-machine (*for cloth*). **-maus,** *f* mole (*Arvicola scherman*) (*Zool.*). **-messer,** *n.* razor. **-rahmen,** *m.* warping frame; shearing frame. **-spannung,** *f.* shear, shearing stress. **-stift,** *m.* shearing-pin. **-tau,** *n.* sheerline (*Naut.*). **-versuch,** *m.* shearing test. **-winkel,** *m.* angle of yaw (*Naut.*). **-wolle,** *f.* shearings. **-zange,** *f.* wire cutter, cutting pliers. **-zeit,** *f.* shearing time.

Scherflein, *n.* (-s, -) mite; *sein - beitragen,* do one's bit.

Scherge, *m.* (-n, -n) (*archaic*) beadle, constable; myrmidon; executor; *des Gesetzes -n,* myrmidons of the law. **-ndienste,** *m.pl.*; *-ndienste tun,* execute all orders of a tyrant.

Scherwenzel, *m., see* **Scharwenzel.**

Scherz, *m.* (-es, -e) jest, joke, pleasantry, fun, raillery, chaff; *aus -,* for fun; *im -(e),* as a joke; *- beiseite,* joking apart; *er versteht keinen -,* he does not take a joke, he has no sense of humour; *seinen - mit einem treiben,* make fun of a p. **-en,** *v.n.* (*aux.* h.) jest, joke, have fun (with), make fun (of); *Sie -en* or *Sie belieben wohl zu -en,* you are joking, you surely don't mean it; *er läßt nicht mit sich -en,* he is not to be trifled with; *es ist nicht zum -en,* it is no joking matter. **-artikel,** *m.* trick. **-gedicht,** *n.* comic *or* burlesque poem. **-haft,** *adj.* jesting, joking, jocular, facetious, playful, droll, jocose. **-haftigkeit,** *f.* jocularity, facetiousness, playfulness. **-liebend,** *adj.* waggish, fond of a joke. **-lied,** *n.* comic song. **-name,** *m.* nickname. **-rede,** *f.* facetious speech. **-weise,** *adv.* for fun, in jest. **-wort,** *n.* word spoken in jest.

Scherzel, *n.* (-s, -) (*Austr. dial.*) crust (*of bread, etc.*).

scheu, 1. *adj.* shy, timid, timorous; bashful, coy, skittish; shying (*of horse*); *- machen,* startle, frighten; *- werden,* shy, take fright (at) (*of horses*). 2. *f.* shyness, timidity; awe, aversion; (*coll.*) *eine heilige - tragen vor,* have a wholesome dread of; *- vor einem empfinden,* stand in awe of a p. **-en,** 1. *v.a.* fear, dread, shun, avoid, shrink from; (*Prov.*) *tue Recht und -e niemand,* do right and fear no one. 2. *v.r.* (*vor*), be afraid (of); hesitate (at); be shy. 3. *v.n.* (*aux.* h.) be frightened, take fright, shy. **-klappe,** *f.*, **-leder,** *n.* blinker. **-sal,** *n.* horrible creature, monster.

Scheuche, *f.* (-n) scarecrow, (*fig.*) bugbear. **-n,** *v.a.* scare, frighten away.

Scheuer, *f.* (-n) barn, shed, granary.

scheuer-n, *v.a.* scour, scrub, clean, wash; rub, chafe; *das Hemd -t mir den Rücken wund,* the shirt rubs the skin off my back. **-besen,** *m.*, **-bürste,** *f.* scrubbing brush. **-frau,** *f.* charwoman. **-lappen,** *m.* dish-cloth, floor-cloth, mop. **-leiste,** *f.* skirting-board. **-magd,** *f.* scullery-maid. **-papier,** *n.* emery- *or* sandpaper. **-sand,** *m.* scouring sand. **-tuch,** *n., see* **-lappen.**

Scheune, *f.* (-n) barn, granary, hayloft, shed. **-ntenne,** *f.* threshing-floor. **-ntor,** *n.* barn-door; *einem mit dem -ntor winken,* give a p. a broad hint.

scheußlich, *adj.* horrible, frightful, atrocious, abominable, hideous, ugly. **-keit,** *f.* hideousness; atrocity, horrible deed, (*coll.*) horror.

Schi, *m., see* **Ski.**

Schicht, *f.* (-en) & *Austr. dial.* **-e,** *f.* (-en) layer, course, bed, stratum; film, coat, emulsion, coating (*Phot.*); level, class, rank (*in society, etc.*); pile, batch, turn, task; shift, day's work; gang (*of miners, etc.*); *- machen,* knock off (*work*); *in einer -,* uninterruptedly. **-arbeit,** *f.* shift work. **-ebene,** *f.* plane of stratification. **-en,** *v.a.* put into *or* arrange in layers, stratify; pile up, stack; divide, distribute, classify; charge (*the furnace, Min.*). **-enaufbau,** *m.* **-enbildung,** *f.* stratification. **-enfolge,** *f.* geological structure, archaeological sequence. **-enkopf,** *m.* outcrop (*Geol.*). **-enplan,** *m.* relief map. **-enweise,** *adv.*, see **-weise. -gesteine,** *n.pl.* stratified rocks. **-holz,** *n.* stacked wood. **-ig,** *adj.* laminated; *suffix, e.g. viel-ig, adj.* many-layered; *weit-ig, adj.* with widely separated layers; vast, extensive. **-linie,** *f.* contour line. **-lohn,** *m.* pay per shift. **-meister,** *m.* overseer, foreman, ganger. **-seite,** *f.* sensitized side (*of photographic plate or film*). **-ung,** *f.* stratification; classification, separation, arrangement; piling, stacking; second dentition. **-ungsebene,** *f., see* **-ebene. -weise,** *adv.* in layers, stratified; layer by layer; in shifts. **-wolke,** *f.* stratus cloud. **-zahn,** *m.* milk-tooth.

Schick, 1. *m.* taste, elegance; fitness, due order; skill, dexterity; *wieder in - bringen,* put in order again; (*coll.*) *er hat seinen rechten - nicht* he is not quite himself; (*coll.*) *er ist nicht auf dem -,* he is out of sorts, he is seedy. 2. *adj.* elegant, stylish, smart, chic.

schick-en, 1. *v.a.* send, dispatch, remit (*money*); *ins Parlament -en,* return to Parliament; *der Zufall -te es,* it so happened, it chanced; *ein Buch in die Welt -en,* publish a book; *einen in den April -en,* make an April fool of a p.; *Waren ins Haus -en,* deliver goods to the door. 2. *v.r.* come to pass, happen, chance; be adapted (to), suit, be fit (for). be becoming, be proper; agree (*in,* with), conform, accommodate o.s. (*in,* to); *es -t sich nicht für ihn,* it does not become him, it is not suitable for him, it is not the proper thing for him to do; *sich in eine S.* or *darein -en,* become reconciled to a th., be resigned to a th., resign o.s. to a th., submit to a th., (*coll.*) put up with a th.; *sich in die Zeit -en,* move with the times; *sich zu etwas -en,* be fit for a th.; *je nachdem es sich -t,* just as the case may be; *wenn es sich gerade so –t*, if things will turn out that way; *es wird sich schon –en*, it will all come right some day; (*Prov.*) *eines –t sich nicht für alle*, one man's meat is another man's poison. **–lich,** *adj.* proper, correct, becoming, appropriate, fit, suitable, meet; decent, well-bred. **–lichkeit,** *f.* fitness, propriety, decorum, good-breeding. **–lichkeitsgefühl,** *n.* tact, sense of propriety. **–sal,** *n.* destiny, entelechy; fate, fortune, lot. **–salhaft,** *adj.* fateful. **–salreich,** *adj.* chequered. **–salsfrage,** *f.* fateful issue. **–salsfügung,** *f.* act of providence. **–salsgefährte,** *m.*, **–salsgenosse,** *m.* companion in misfortune, fellow-sufferer; *wir sind –salsgefährten*, (*coll.*) we are in the same boat. **–salsglaube,** *m.* fatalism. **–salsgöttinnen,** *f.pl.* the Fates, Destinies, the Parcæ. **–salskampf,** *m.* fateful *or* decisive struggle. **–salsprüfung,** *f.* sore trial, ordeal, visitation. **–salsschlag,** *m.* heavy blow, blow of fate, reverse. **–salsschwanger,** *adj.* portentous. **–salsschwestern,** *f.pl.* weird sisters. **–salstag,** *m.* fateful day. **–salstücke,** *f.* malignant fate, tricks of fortune. **–salswechsel,** *m.* change of fortune, vicissitude(s). **–salswort,** *n.* decree of Providence; oracle. **–ung,** *f.* Providence, fate, dispensation; *Gottes–ung*, divine ordinance, the finger of God.

Schickse, *f.* (-n) (*coll.*) non-Jewish girl (*among Jews*); (*also* **–l,** *n.* (-s, –)) (*coll.*) young Jewess (*among non-Jews*); girl of doubtful repute, (*sl.*) baggage, pick-up.

schieb–en, *ir.v.a.*, *r.* & *n.* (*aux.* h. & s.) shove, push; slide; move; (*coll.*) profiteer; (*coll.*) *wir werden es schon –en*, we'll wangle it somehow; *er muß immer geschoben werden*, he always needs s.o. behind him; *etwas auf die lange Bank –en*, postpone, defer *or* (*coll.*) put off a th.; (*sl.*) *Dienst* (*or Wache*) *–en*, be on (guard) duty (*Mil.*); *einen über die Grenze –en*, get a p. out of the country; *Kegel –en*, play at skittles; (*sl.*) *Kohldampf –en*, be hungry (*Mil.*); *einem etwas in die Schuhe –en*, make a p. appear responsible for a th., (*coll.*) pin s.th. on a p.; *die Schuld auf einen –en*, put *or* lay the blame on s.o.; *einen Stein –en*, make a move (*at draughts*). **–deckel,** *m.* sliding lid. **–(e)fenster,** *n.* sash-window. **–elineal,** *n.* sliding rule. **–er,** *m.* slide, slider, carriage; oven-peel, damper; bar, bolt; running-loop; slide *or* sleeve valve; slide-rule; (*coll.*) racketeer, profiteer. **–erohr,** *n.* sleeve. **–erstange,** *f.* sliding *or* valve-rod. **–ertum,** *n.* profiteering, racketeering. **–erventil,** *n.* slide valve. **–erweg,** *m.* slide-valve travel. **–estange,** *f. see* **–erstange. –esteuerung,** *f.* slide-valve gear. **–(e)tür,** *f.* sliding door. **–eventil,** *n. see* **–erventil. –ewand,** *f.* side scene, movable partition (*Theat.*). **–fach,** *n.*, *see* **–kasten. –karren,** *m.* wheelbarrow. **–kasten,** *m.*, **–lade,** *f.* drawer; till. **–ung,** *f.* profiteering, racketeering, wangling, sharp practice; manœuvre, political jobbery, wangle, put-up job; *spezifische –ung*, shearing strain.

schiech, *adj.* (*dial.*) ugly, terrifying.

schied, schiede, *see* **scheiden.**

schiedlich, *adv.* in – *und friedlich*, amenable to discussion, amicable, reasonable, pacific.

Schieds–gericht, *n.* court of arbitration. **–gerichtlich,** *adj.*, *see* **–richterlich. –gerichtsbarkeit,** *f.*, **–gerichtswesen,** *n.* arbitration. **–richter,** *m.* arbiter, umpire, referee. **–richterlich,** *adj.* by arbitration. **–richtern,** *v.n.* arbitrate, act as arbiter. **–spruch,** *m.* award, decision, arbitration. **–vertrag,** *m.* arbitration treaty.

schief, 1. *adj.* oblique, diagonal, slanting, sloping inclined; bent, crooked, distorted, wry; (*coll.*) lopsided; wrong, false, (*sl.*) cock-eyed; *–e Ebene*, inclined plane; gradient (*Railw.*); *auf die –e Ebene kommen* or *geraten*, go off the straight and narrow path, start on the downward path; *–e Fahrt*, oblique sailing; *in einer –en Lage sein*, be in a false position; *ein –es Gesicht machen*, make a wry face, show one's annoyance *or* disgust; *in ein –es Licht kommen*, be misjudged; *der –e Turm*, the leaning tower; (*coll.*) *– gewickelt sein*, be all wrong, be much mistaken. 2. *adv.* awry, askew, across, cross-wise; amiss; *etwas – anfangen*, set about a th. the wrong way; *– ansehen*, frown upon; *– gehen*, go wrong, turn out badly; (*hum.*) *nur Mut, die Sache wird schon – gehen*, cheer up, there's worse to come; *seine Stiefel – laufen* or *treten*, tread one's boots down at the heels; (*coll.*) *– nehmen*, take amiss; *es steht – darum*, there is something wrong with it. **–blatt,** *n.* begonia, elephant's ear (*Bot.*). **–e,** *f.* inclination, obliquity, obliqueness, crookedness; inclined plane, slope, incline, slant; wrongness, perversity. **–geladen,** *adj.* tipsy. **–heit,** *f. see* **–e. –liegend,** *adj.* sloping, inclined, oblique. **–rund,** *adj.* oval. **–sehen,** *n.* strabismus (*Med.*). **–wink(e)lig,** *adj.* oblique-angled.

Schiefer, *m.* (-s, –) slate, shale, schist; (*dial.*) splinter, (*Scots*) skelp. **–artig,** *adj.* slaty, schistous. **–bedachung,** *f.* slating, slate roof. **–blau,** *adj.* & *n.* slate-coloured. **–bruch,** *m.* slate quarry. **–dach,** *n.* slate roof. **–decker,** *m.* slater. **–griffel,** *m.* slate pencil. **–ig,** (*usually* **schiefrig**), *adj.* slate-like; slaty, schistous; splintery, scaly, flaky, foliated, **–n,** *v.r.* peel off, scale, exfoliate. **–spat,** *m.* schistous spar. **–stein,** *m.* slate, lithographic stone. **–stift,** *m.* slate pencil. **–tafel,** *f.* slate (*school*). **–ton,** *m.* slate clay, shale. **–ung,** *f.* stratification, exfoliation. **–zahn,** *m.* scaly tooth (*Vet.*).

schieg, *adj.* (*dial.*) *see* **schiech. –beinig,** *adj.* (*dial.*) knock-kneed. **–en,** *v.n.* (*dial.*) turn in one's foot, walk on the side of one's foot. **–gen,** *v.n.* (*Swiss dial.*) *see* **–en.**

schiel–en, *v.n.* (*aux.* h.) squint, be cross-eyed; cast a sidelong glance; *–en nach* (*Dat.*) or *auf* (*Acc.*), leer at, cast furtive glances at; have an eye to, hanker after. **–äugig,** *adj.* squint-eyed. **–end,** *pr.p* & *adj.* squint-eyed; leering; (*fig.*) not straightforward, (*sl.*) cock-eyed; (*archaic*) *–ender Vergleich*, inappropriate comparison. **–operation,** *f.* strabotomy.

Schiemann, *m.* (-(e)s, ¨er) sailor, seaman. **–sgarn,** *n.* cordage, (*fig.*) fisherman's story, tall story.

schien, schiene, *see* **scheinen.**

Schien–e, *f.* (-en) splint (*Med.*); iron band, iron rim *or* tyre, rail; greave, slat, strip, rib (*of umbrellas*); *aus den –en springen*, run off the rails, leave the rails; *sein Arm liegt in –en*, his arm is in splints. **–bein,** *n.* shin-bone, tibia. **–en,** *v.a.* put in splints; tyre (*wheels*). **–enkopf,** *m.* rail-head. **–enlasche,** *f.* fish-plate. **–enleger,** *m.* plate-layer (*Railw.*). **–ennetz,** *n.* railway system. **–enräumer,** *m.* cow-catcher (*on engines*). **–enreibung,** *f.* rolling-friction. **–enstrang,** *m.* track, railway line, metals. **–enweg,** *m.* permanent way. **–enweite,** *f.* gauge

[1]**schier,** *see* **scheren.**

[2]**schier,** *adj.* (*rare*) clear, sheer, pure; *–es Fleisch*, meat without fat or bones; *–e Unmöglichkeit*, sheer impossibility. **–tuch,** *n.* canvas.

[3]**schier,** *adv.* (*coll.*) almost, nearly, barely, simply.

Schierling, *m.* (-s, -e) hemlock (*Conium maculatum*) (*Bot.*). **–sbecher,** *m.* cup of hemlock. **–stanne,** *f.* Canadian hemlock, hemlock spruce (*Tsuga canadensis*) (*Bot.*).

schierst, schiert, *see* **scheren.**

schieß–en, 1. *ir.v.n.* (*aux.* s.) shoot (*as stars*), swoop, dart, rush *or* tear along; spring up, burst forth; *das Blut schoß ihm ins Gesicht*, the blood rushed to his face; *in die Höhe –en*, spring up; *ein Gedanke schoß mir durch den Kopf*, a thought flashed through my mind, struck me suddenly, occurred to me *or* crossed my mind in a flash; *ins Kraut –en*, run to leaf; *–en lassen*, let go, let fly, let loose, pay out (*rope*); relinquish, forgo, give up, throw to the wind; *seinen Begierden den* or *die Zügel –en lassen*, give the rein to one's desires, abandon o.s. to one's desires, lose all self-control; *in Samen –en* run to seed. 2. *v.n.* (*aux.* h.) shoot, fire; burst, blast; *blind –en*, shoot with blank cartridges; *das Gewehr –t schlecht*, the rifle fires badly; *gut –en*, be a good shot; *scharf –en*, shoot with live ammunition; *der Schütze –t gut*, the marksman shoots well; *unfehlbar sicher –en*, be an accurate *or* (*coll.*) a dead shot; *weit –en*, carry far; (*coll.*) *es ist zum –en*, it is too funny for words. 3. *v.a.* shoot, fire; *einen Blick auf einen –en*, shoot a glance at s.o.; *einen Bock –en*, (*fig.*) (*coll.*) commit a bloomer; *Brot in den Ofen –en*, bake (*a batch of bread*); *in Grund und Boden –en*, batter down; *Kugeln –en*, fire bullets; *sich*

(*Dat.*) *eine Kugel durch den Kopf –en*, blow one's brains out; *Pfeile –en*, shoot arrows; *einen Purzelbaum –en*, turn a somersault; *sich mit einem –en*, fight a pistol duel with a p.; *die Sonne –en*, take the sun's altitude (*Naut.*); *einen Vogel im Fluge –en*, shoot a bird on the wing. **–ausbildung**, *f.* gunnery *or* musketry-training. **–baumwolle**, *f.* gun-cotton, nitro-cellulose, pyroxylin. **–bedarf**, *m.* ammunition. **–bereich**, *m.* range. **–bude**, *f.* shooting-gallery. **–er**, *m.* shooter; oven-peel. **–erei**, *f.* continuous *or* repeated firing *or* shooting, haphazard firing. **–gerechtigkeit**, *f.* shooting rights. (*hum.*) **–gewehr**, *n.* firearm; *spiele nicht mit dem –gewehr*, don't play with fire. **–hund**, *m.* pointer; (*coll.*) *aufpassen wie ein –hund*, watch like a lynx. **–hütte**, *f.* shooting-box. **–lehre**, *f.* ballistics. **–loch**, *n.* loophole; port-hole. **–patrone**, *f.* cartridge, charge. **–platz**, *m.* rifle-range, artillery-range. (*hum.*) **–prügel**, *m.* firearm. **–pulver**, *n.* gunpowder. **–scharte**, *f.* loophole, embrasure, firing slit *or* port. **–scheibe** *f.* practice target. **–schlitz**, *m.* loophole, embrasure, firing port. **–schule**, *f.* school of musketry *or* gunnery. **–stand**, *m.* rifle-range, butts. **–tabelle**, *f.* range-table. **–übungen**, *f.pl.* musketry, artillery *or* firing practice. **–vorschrift**, *f.* gunnery *or* musketry manual. **–wettbewerb**, *m.* shooting competition. **–zeit**, *f.* shooting season.

Schiff, *n.* (-(e)s, -e) ship, boat, vessel; nave (*of a church*); shuttle (*Weav.*); galley (*Typ.*); *das – befrachten*, load the ship; *das – besteigen*, board ship; *gepanzertes –*, warship, (*archaic*) iron-clad; *klar –*, decks cleared for action; *kleine –e*, small craft; *ein – vom Stapel lassen*, launch a ship; *– voraus*, ship ahoy; *zu –(e) gehen*, go on board *or* aboard, embark (*nach*, for); go by ship; *zu – versenden*, send by water. **–bar**, *adj.* navigable. **–barmachung**, *f.* dredging, opening up (*a waterway*). **–bau**, *m.* shipbuilding. **–bauer**, *m.* shipbuilder. **–baukunst**, *f.* naval architecture. **–baumeister**, *m.* master shipwright; naval architect. **–bein**, *n.* scaphoid bone (*Anat.*). **–beschlag**, *m.*, **–blech**, *n.* sheathing. **–bruch**, *m.* shipwreck (*also fig.*). **–brüchig**, *adj.* shipwrecked. **–brücke**, *f.* pontoon bridge. **–chen**, *n.* little vessel; carina (*Bot.*); scapha (*Anat.*); shuttle (*Weav.*). **–en**, 1. *v.a.* (*rare*) ship (*goods, etc.*). 2. *v.n.* (*aux.* s.) navigate, sail (on), go by water; (*vulg.*) piss, pump ship. **–er**, *m.* (*coll.*) sailor, seaman; skipper, master (*Naut.*). **–erausdruck**, *m.* nautical term. (*hum.*) **–erklavier**, *n.* concertina, accordion. **–erknoten**, *m.* sailor's knot. **–erpatent**, *n.* master's certificate. **–ersprache**, *f.* nautical language. **–erstange**, *f.* boat-hook. **–(f)ahrer**, *m.* seafarer. **–(f)ahrt**, *f.* navigation; shipping. **–(f)ahrtsakte**, *f* navigation act. **–(f)ahrtsausschuß**, *m.* maritime commission. **–(f)ahrtskunde**, *f.* art of navigation. **–(f)ahrtslinie**, *f.* shipping *or* steamship line. **–(f)ahrtssperre**, *f.* embargo. **–(f)ahrtsweg**, *m.* shipping route *or* lane. **–(f)racht**, *f.* freight. **–(f)rachtbrief**, *m.* bill of lading. **–gerippe**, *n.* ribs of a ship, hulk. **–sartillerie**, *f.* naval artillery. **–sarzt**, *m.* ship's surgeon. **–sbau**, *m.* (*Austr. dial.*) *see* **–bau.** **–sbedarf**, *m.* naval stores. **–sbefrachtung**, *f.* freightage, chartering. **–sbekleidung**, *f.* ship's planking. **–sbesatzung**, *f.* crew. **–sbeschlag**, *m.* hull sheathing. **–sbeute**, *f.* maritime prize. **–sbewuchs**, *m.* underwater growth. **–sbreite**, *f.* beam. **–sbrücke**, *f.* pontoon bridge. **–seigentümer**, *m.*, **–seigner**, *m.* shipowner. **–sfrachtbrief**, *m.* bill of lading. **–sfreund**, *m.* part-owner of a ship. **–sführung**, *f.* navigation. **–sgeleit(e)**, *n.* convoy. **–shändler**, *m.* ship's chandler. **–shebewerk**, *n.* ship hoist (*on canals*). **–shinterteil**, *n.* poop, stern. **–sjournal**, *n.* log-book. **–sjunge**, *m.* cabin-boy. **–skapitän**, *m.* captain, master, skipper. **–sklasse**, *f.* (ship's) rating. **–skörper**, *m.*, *see* **–srumpf.** **–sküche**, *f.* galley, caboose. **–skurs**, *m.* steered course. **–sladung**, *f.* cargo. **–slast**, *f.* tonnage. **–slazarett**, *n.* sick bay. **–sleim**, *m.* marine glue. **–sleute**, *pl.* crew, sailors. **–sliste**, *f.* ship's register. **–sluken**, *f.pl.* hatches. **–smaat**, *m.* shipmate. **–smakler**, *m.* shipbroker. **–smannschaft**, *f.* crew. **–sordnung**, *f.* shipboard regulations. **–sortung**, *f.* position finding, dead reckoning. **–spanzer**, *m.* armour-plating. **–spatron**, *m.* ship-master. **–spfandbrief**, *m.* bottomry bond. **–sprediger**, *m.* naval chaplain. **–sraum**, *m.* hold; tonnage, displacement. **–sreeder**, *m.* shipowner. **–srolle**, *f.* sailor's pass. **–srumpf**, *m.* hull. **–srüstung**, *f.* naval armament. **–sschaukel**, *f.* swing-boat. **–sschnabel**, *m.* cutwater, prow. **–sschraube**, *f.* screw. **–ssoldat**, *m.* marine. **–sspiegel**, *m.* stern. **–sspur**, *f.* wake of a ship. **–stagebuch**, *n.* ship's log. **–stau**, *n.* hawser, cable. **–sverkehr**, *m.* shipping traffic. **–svermessung**, *f.* measurement of a vessel. **–svermietung**, *f.* chartering, freighting. **–sverzeichnis**, *n.* shipping-list. **–sverzollung**, *f.* clearance. **–svolk**, *n.* crew. **–svorderteil**, *m.* & *n.* forecastle, prow, bows. **–svorräte**, *m.pl.* naval *or* ship's stores. **–swache**, *f.* look-out; watch. **–swerft**, *f.* ship-yard, dockyard, wharf; dry dock. **–swesen**, *n.* shipping. **–swinde**, *f.* capstan, windlass. **–szeughaus**, *n.* naval arsenal. **–szoll**, *m.* tonnage-duty, freightage. **–szwieback**, *m.* ship's biscuit.

schiften, *v.a.* join, pin (*rafters*).

Schikan–e, . (-en) vexation, annoyance; chicanery, trick, underhand dealing; (*sl.*) *mit allen –en*, with all the frills. **–ieren**, *v.a.* vex, annoy, irritate, torment; play tricks upon. **–ös**, *adj.* annoying, vexatious, tiresome, trying; spiteful.

Schild, 1. *m.* (-(e)s, -e) shield, buckler; escutcheon, coat of arms; shell, carapace, scutum (*Zool.*); *auf den – (er)heben*, choose as leader; *den – der Ehre blank* or *rein erhalten*, maintain one's reputation untarnished, have no blot on one's escutcheon; *einen Eber im –e führen*, bear the wild boar on one's coat of arms; (*fig.*) *etwas im –e führen*, have s.th. up one's sleeve; *Schirm und – sein*, be shield and protector; *zum –e geboren sein*, be of noble birth. 2. *n.* (-(e)s, -er) sign-board, noticeboard; (brass) plate, door-plate, name-plate; badge, label, ticket; peak (*of a cap*); *das – aushängen* (*einziehen*), open (shut up) business *or* a shop. **–abteilung**, *f.* quartering (*Her.*). **–blume**, *f.* aspidistra (*Chelone obliqua*) (*Bot.*). **–bogen**, *m.* arcaded arch. **–bürger**, *m.* stupid bourgeois. **–decke**, *f.* mantle of the shield (*Her.*). **–drüse**, *f.* thyroid gland. **–erhaus**, *n.* sentry-box. **–ermaler**, *m.* sign-painter. **–förmig**, *adj.* shield-shaped, scutiform. **–halter**, *m.* shield-bearer, esquire; (*pl.*) supporters (*Her.*). **–haupt**, *n.* chief (*Her.*). **–jungfrau**, *f.* battle maiden, Valkyrie. **–käfer**, *m.* tortoise-beetle (*Cassididae*) (*Ent.*). **–klappe**, *f.* port cover. **–knappe**, *m.*, **–knecht**, *m.* shield-bearer, squire. **–knorpel**, *m.* thyroid cartilage, shield cartilage, Adam's apple. **–krot**, *n.*, *see* **–patt.** **–kröte**, *f.* tortoise (*land*); turtle (*sea*). **–krötensuppe**, *f.* turtle soup. **–lager**, *n.* trunnion bearing. **–laus**, *f.* shield-louse, scale insect (*Coccidae*) (*Ent.*). **–lehen**, *n.* knight's fief. **–patt**, *n.* tortoise-shell. **–rand**, *m.* bordure (*Her.*). **–teilung**, *f.* quartering (*Her.*). **–träger**, *m.* squire, shield-bearer. **–wache**, *f.* sentinel, sentry; *–wache zu Pferde*, vedette; *–wache stehen*, stand guard. **–wacht**, *f.* sentry-go; sentry. **–zapfen**, *m.* trunnion (*Artil.*).

schilder–n, *v.a.* describe, depict, delineate, portray, draw, sketch, (*dial.*) paint. **–ung**, *f.* description, representation, portrayal.

Schilf, *n.* (-(e)s, -e) reed, rush, bulrush; sedge. **–artig**, *adj.* arundinaceous, reedy. **–dach**, *n.* reed thatch. **–decke**, *f.* rush-mat. **–gras**, *n.* reed-grass. **–en**, *v.a.* clear of reeds. **–ig**, *adj.* reedy, sedgy. **–meer**, *n.* (*B.*) Red Sea. **–rohr**, *n.* reed; reeds, sedge (*Phragmites communis*) (*Bot.*).

Schilfe, *see* **Schelfe.**

Schiller, *m.* (-s, –) play of colours; iridescence. **–falter**, *m.* purple emperor (*Apatura iris*) (*Ent.*). **–ig**, *adj.* iridescent, opalescent, shot, changing. **–n**, *v.n.* (*aux.* h.) fluoresce, scintillate, be iridescent *or* opalescent. **–nd**, *pr.p.* & *adj.* iridescent, fluorescent, opalescent, scintillating, glittering. **–seide**, *f.* shot silk. **–taffet**, *m.*, **–taft**, *m.* shot taffeta. **–wein**, *m.* mixed red and white wine.

Schillerkragen, *m.* (-s, –) open collar.

Schilling, *m.* (-s, -e) shilling.

schilt, schilt(e)st, *see* **schelten.**

Schimäre, *f.* (-n) chimera.

Schimmel, *m.* (-s, –) mould, mildew; grey *or* white horse. **–flecken,** *m.pl.* mildew stains. **–ig,** (*usually* **schimmlig**), *adj.* mouldy, mildewed, musty. **–n,** *v.n.* (*aux.* h. & s.) grow mouldy, moulder; (*hum.*) become grey, get grey hairs; (*coll.*) *das Mädchen –t,* the girl is a wallflower. **–pilz,** *m.* mould fungus, mycoderin.

Schimmer, *m.* (-s, –) glitter, shine, shimmer glimmer, gleam, lustre; (*dial.*) twilight, dusk; (*coll.*) idea, notion; (*coll.*) *ich habe keinen* (*blassen*) – (*davon*), I have not the faintest notion (about it); (*coll.*) *kein – von Aussicht,* not the ghost of a chance; *ein – von Hoffnung,* a spark *or* gleam of hope. **–n,** *v.n.* (*aux.* h.) glitter, glisten, gleam, shine, twinkle, glimmer.

Schimpanse, *m.* (-n, -n) chimpanzee.

Schimpf, *m.* (-(e)s, -e) insult, affront; disgrace; (*dial.*) joke, jest, fun; *jemandem einen – antun,* insult a p.; *einen – auf sich* (*Dat.*) *sitzen lassen,* swallow an insult; *– und Schande,* scorn and contempt; *einem – und Schande nachsagen,* say everything that is bad of a p., disparage, vilify *or* speak ill of a p. **–en,** *v.a.* & *n.* (*aux.* h.) insult, abuse, revile, affront, use bad language, scold; (*dial.*) joke; *jemanden einen Schurken –en,* call a p. a blackguard; *–en auf* (*Acc.*) or *über* (*Acc.*), grumble about. **–erei,** *f.* abusive language; scolding. **–gedicht,** *n.* lampoon. **–ieren,** *v.a.* (*coll.*) insult, malign. **–lich,** *adj.* disgraceful, infamous; (*dial.*) joking. **–name,** *m.* rude name. **–wort,** *n.* term of abuse, insult, invective.

Schinakel, *n.* (-s, –) (*Austr. dial.*) (little) boat, skiff.

Schindel, *f.* (-n) shingle, wooden tile *or* slat; billet (*Her.*). **–dach,** *n.* shingle roof. **–n,** *v.a.* cover *or* roof with shingles; put in splints (*Med.*).

schind–en, 1. *ir.v.a.* & *n.* (*aux.* h.) skin, flay; oppress, ill-treat; (*coll.*) fleece, exploit, try to get (*s.th.*) for nothing; (*sl.*) *Eindruck –en,* be out to impress; (*sl.*) *das Fahrgeld –en* travel without a ticket; (*sl.*) *Kolleg –en,* gatecrash a lecture (*Univ.*); (*sl.*) *Lokal –en,* sit in a restaurant without ordering anything; (*sl.*) *Zeilen –en,* do hack writing. 2. *v.r.* work o.s. to death, drudge, slave. **–aas,** *n. see* **–luder.** **–anger,** *m.* knacker's yard. **–er,** *m.* knacker; sweater, (*coll.*) slave-driver. **–erei,** *f.* knacker's yard; (*fig.*) extortion, ill-treatment, sweating; grind, drudgery. **–ermäßig,** *adj.* cruel, harsh, oppressive. **–ern,** *v.n.* (*aux.* s.) (*dial.*) slide on ice. **–grube,** *f., see* **–anger.** **–luder,** *n.* broken down *or* worn out animal; (*sl.*) *mit einem –luder treiben,* treat a p. abominably. **–mähre,** *f.* miserable jade.

Schinken, *m.* (-s, –) ham; (*sl.*) wretched daub; (*sl.*) old book; *mit der Wurst nach dem – werfen,* use a sprat to catch a mackerel; *– mit Ei,* ham and eggs. **–brot,** *n.,* **–brötchen,** *n.* ham-sandwich, ham-roll. **–schnitte,** *f.* slice of ham.

Schinn, *m.* (-(e)s, –e), **–e,** *f.* (-en) (*usually pl.*) scurf, dandruff. **–en,** *v.r.* scratch one's head.

Schippe, *f.* (-n) shovel, scoop, (child's) spade; spade (*Cards*); (*coll.*) pout; (*coll.*) *eine – machen,* pout. **–n,** 1. *v.a.* & *n.* shovel, scoop. 2. *n.* spade (*Cards*). **–r,** *m.* fatigue man, soldier on fatigues.

Schirm, *m.* (-(e)s, -e) umbrella; screen, shelter, protective cover; peak (*of a cap*); umbel (*Bot.*); *den – neu beziehen lassen,* have one's umbrella re-covered; *Schutz und –,* protection, protector, safeguard; *unter seinem Schutz und –,* under his patronage *or* protection. **–bildverfahren,** *n.* mass radiography. **–dach,** *n.* shelter, shed; tilt. **–en,** *v.a.* screen, shield, shelter, protect, defend, guard. **–er,** *m., see* **–herr.** **–fläche,** *f.* shaded area, covered space. **–förmig,** *adj.* umbellate, umbelliform (*Bot.*). **–gestell,** *n.* umbrella-frame. **–gitter,** *n.* screen grid (*Rad.*). **–gitterröhre,** *f.* tetrode (*Rad.*). **–herr,** *m.* protector, patron. **–mütze,** *f.* peaked cap. **–palme,** *f.* fan-palm, talipot (*Corypha umbraculifera*) (*Bot.*). **–pflanze,** *f.* umbelliferous plant. **–ständer,** *m.* umbrella-stand.

schirr–en, *v.a.* harness. **–kammer,** *f.* harness-room. **–kette,** *f.* pole-chain. **–macher,** *m.* cartwright. **–meister,** *m.* head ostler; M.T. sergeant (*Mil.*).

Schirting, *m.* (-s, -e & (*Austr. dial.*) -s) shirting.

Schisma, *n.* (-mas, -men & (*Austr. dial.*) -mata) schism. **–tisch,** *adj.* schismatic.

Schiß, *m.* (-(ss)es -(ss)e) (*vulg.*) shit; (*coll.*) funk; (*vulg.*) the shits; *–* (*in den Hosen*) *haben,* (*vulg.*) shit o.s. with fright, have the shits.

schlabber–n, *v.n.* (*aux.* h.) (*dial.*) slobber, slaver; overflow; babble, prate, gossip. **–ig,** (**schlabbrig**). *adj.* sloppy, watery. **–rohr,** *n.* overflow-pipe. **–ventil,** *n.* check valve.

Schlacht, *f.* (-en) battle, engagement, fight; *regelrechte –,* pitched battle; *eine – liefern* or *schlagen,* give battle, fight a battle; *– bei,* battle of. **–bar,** *adj.* fit for killing (*of beasts*). **–enbummler,** *m.* camp-follower. **–englück,** *n.* fortune of war. **–engott,** *m.* God of battles, Mars. **–enlenker,** *m.* God of Hosts. **–enmaler,** *m.* painter of battle-scenes. **–feld,** *n.* battlefield; *auf dem –feld bleiben,* fall in battle; *das –feld behaupten,* be victorious. **–fliegerbombe,** *f.* anti-personnel bomb. **–fliegergruppe,** *f.* army-cooperation unit (*Av.*). **–gemälde,** *n., see* **–stück.** **–gesang,** *m.* battle-song. **–geschrei,** *n.* war-cry. **–getöse,** *n.* din of battle. **–getümmel,** *n.,* **–gewühl** *n.* mêlée. **–kreuzer,** *m.* battle-cruiser. **–lied,** *n.* battle-song. **–linie,** *f.* line of battle. **–ordnung,** *f.* order of battle, battle array. **–plan,** *m.* plan of action. **–reihe,** *f.* battle array, line of battle. **–roß,** *n.* charger. **–ruf,** *m.* war-cry. **–schiff,** *n.* battleship. **–schwert,** *n.* broadsword. **–stück,** *n.* battle-scene (*Paint.*).

schlacht–en, 1. *v.a.* slaughter; butcher, slay, immolate (*a sacrifice*). 2. *v.n.* (*aux.* h.) massacre, butcher. **–bank,** *f.* shambles, slaughter-house; *das Opfer zur –bank führen,* lead the lamb to the slaughter. **–beil,** *n.* poleaxe. **–er,** *m.* (*dial.*) butcher. **–erei,** *f., see* **Schlächterei.** **–gewicht,** *n.* dead weight, carcass weight. **–haus,** *n.,* **–hof,** *m.* slaughter-house, abattoir. **–opfer,** *n.* victim, sacrifice. **–tag,** *m.* slaughter-day; day of battle. **–ung,** *f.* slaughtering. **–vieh,** *n.* fat stock.

Schlächt–er, *m.* (-s, –) butcher. **–ei,** *f.* butcher's shop; (*fig.*) butchery. **–ig,** *adj. suff.,* e.g. *halb–ig.* cross-bred, hybrid, mongrel; *ober–ig*; overshot; *unter–ig,* undershot (*of millwheels*).

Schlack, 1. *m.* (*dial.*) sleet, slush, slushy weather. 2. *adj.* (*dial.*), *see* **schlaff.** **–darm,** *m.* rectum. **–e,** *f.* (-en) slag, dross, scoria, cinders, clinker; sediment, dregs, scum; (*dial.*) rectum. **–en,** *v.n.* (*aux.* h.) leave dross, form slag, precipitate sediment; *es –t,* (*dial.*) it is sleeting. **–enbildung,** *f.* scorification. **–enfrei,** *adj.* free from dross. **–enhalde,** *f.* slag-heap. **–ensand,** *m.* ground clinker. **–ensieb,** *n.* clinker screen. **–enstaub,** *m.* coal dust, slack, dross. **–enstein,** *m.* slag-stone. **–enwolle,** *f.* mineral wool. **–erig,** *adj.* (*dial.*) dangling, tottering; sleety, slushy. **–ern,** *v.n.* (*aux.* h.) (*dial.*) slouch, dangle, totter; *es –ert,* it is sleeting. **–(er)wetter,** *n.* (*dial.*) slushy *or* sleety weather. **–ig,** *adj.* slaggy, drossy, scoriaceous; (*dial.*) slushy. **–wurst,** *f.* (fat) North German sausage.

Schlaf, *m.* sleep, slumber; *sie hat einen bleiernen –,* she sleeps like a log; *das wäre mir nicht im –e eingefallen,* I should never have dreamt of such a thing; *fester –,* sound sleep; *die ganze Nacht ist kein – in meine Augen gekommen,* I have not slept a wink all night; *er hat einen leichten –,* he is a light sleeper; *hypnotischer –,* hypnotic trance; *in – sinken* or *fallen,* drop off to sleep; *ein Kind in – wiegen* (*singen*), rock (sing, lull) a baby to sleep. **–abteil,** *n.* & *m.* sleeping-compartment. **–anzug,** *m.* sleeping-suit, pyjamas. **–arznei,** *f.* soporific, narcotic. **–befördernd,** *adj.,* **–bringend,** *adj.* soporific. **–bursche,** *m.* night-lodger. **–decke,** *f.* blanket. **–en,** *ir.v.n.* (*aux.* h.) sleep, be asleep; slumber, rest, repose; be *or* lie dormant; *auswärts –en,* sleep out; *bei einem –en,* sleep with a p., spend the night with s.o.; *–en gehen,* go to bed; *eine Sache –en lassen,* let a matter rest *or* drop; *–en legen,* put to bed; *sich –en legen,* go to bed. **–end,** *pr.p.* & *adj.* sleeping, dormant. **–enszeit,** *f.* bedtime. **–gänger,** *m., see* **–bursche.** **–gast,** *m.* passing traveller, overnight visitor (*in hotel*). **–gefährte,** *m.* bedfellow. **–gemach,** *n., see* **–zimmer.** **–genosse,** *m.,* **–gesell,** *m., see* **–gefährte.** **–ge-**

wand, *n.* night-dress, night-gown. **-haube,** *f.* night-cap. **-kamerad,** *m.* bedfellow. **-kammer,** *f.* (small) bedroom, bed-recess. **-krankheit,** *f.* sleeping sickness, epidemic encephalitis. **-lied,** *n.* lullaby. **-los,** *adj.* sleepless. **-losigkeit,** *f.* insomnia. **-lust,** *f.* drowsiness. **-mittel,** *n.* soporific, narcotic (*Med.*). **-mütze,** *f.* night-cap; (*fig.*) sleepyhead, dull *or* lazy fellow. **-mützig,** *adj.* sleepy, slow. **-ratte,** *f.*, **-ratz,** *m.*, **-ratze,** *f.* sound sleeper; dormouse; slowcoach. **-rock,** *m.* dressing-gown; *Apfel im -rock*, apple-dumpling. **-saal,** *m.* dormitory. **-sack,** *m.* sleeping-bag. **-sofa,** *n.* bed-settee. **-stätte,** *f.*, **-stelle,** *f.* night's lodging, lodging house. **-stellung,** *f.* sleeping *or* nocturnal position. **-stube,** *f.*, *see* **-zimmer.** **-sucht,** *f.* somnolence, lethargy. **-süchtig,** *adj.* somnolent. **-trank,** *m.* sleeping draught. **-trunk,** *m.* drink before retiring, (*coll.*) night-cap. **-trunken,** *adj.* overcome with sleep, very drowsy. **-wachen,** *n.* somnambulism. **-wagen,** *m.* sleeping-car, (*coll.*) sleeper (*Railw.*). **-wandeln,** I. *v.n.* (*aux.* s.) walk in one's sleep. 2. *n.* somnambulism. **-wandelnd,** *adj.* somnambulant. **-wandler,** *m.* sleep-walker, somnambulist. **-wandlerisch,** *adj.* somnambulistic; (*fig.*) in a daze, absent-minded. **-zeug,** *n.* night-things. **-zimmer,** *n.* bedroom; *-zimmer mit einem Bett*, single bedroom; *-zimmer mit zwei Betten*, double bedroom.

Schläf-chen, *n.* (-s, -) doze, nap, (*coll.*) forty winks; *ein -chen machen*, take *or* have a nap. **-er,** *m.* sleeper. **-erig,** *adj.*, *see* **-rig.** **-ern,** *v. imp.* feel sleepy; *es -ert mich*, I feel *or* am sleepy. **-rig,** I. *adj.* sleepy, drowsy; (*fig.*) slow, indolent. 2. *adj. suff. ein-* (*zwei*)*-riges Bett*, single (double) bed. **-rigkeit,** *f.* drowsiness, somnolence; indolence.

Schläfe, *f.* (-n) temple. **-nader,** *f.* temporal vein. **-nbein,** *n.* temporal bone. **-ngegend,** *f.* temporal region.

schlaff, *adj.* slack, loose, flabby, flaccid; feeble, weak, relaxed, limp, soft; (*fig.*) careless, remiss, lax, negligent; indolent; *-es Seil*, slack rope. **-heit,** *f.* looseness, slackness, limpness, flaccidity; atony (*Med.*); (*fig.*) laxity; indolence.

Schlafitt-chen, *n.*, **-ich,** *m.* (*coll.*) coat tails; *einem am* or *beim -chen erwischen, nehmen* or *packen*, (seize by the) collar, seize by the scruff of the neck.

schläfst, schläft, *see* **schlafen.**

Schlag, *m.* (-(e)s, ⁻e) blow, knock, bang, rap, slap, punch, kick; beat (*also Mus.*), oscillation, pulsation, movement; concussion, shock, impact; apoplectic fit, stroke; clap (*of thunder*); striking (*of clocks*), song (*of birds*); stamp, kind, sort, type; carriage-door; pigeon loft, dovecot; parcel (*of land*); (*sl.*) whack (*of food*); plot, strip, tilled field, copse, clearing; tack (*Naut.*); bend, bight (*of rope*) (*Naut.*); lathe, lay (*Weav.*); beat-up (*Weav.*); coinage, stamping; horizontal works (*of a mine*); *von einem andern -e*, cast in a different mould; *auf einen -*, see *mit einem -*; *- auf -*, in rapid succession; *Schläge bekommen*, get a (good) beating; *elektrischer -*, electric shock; *der gewöhnliche -*, the common run (*of men, etc.*); *von gleichem -e*, of the same sort, stamp *or* character; *einen großen - machen*, have great success, make a (great) hit; undertake great things; *zwei Herzen und ein -*, two hearts that beat as one; *kalter -*, flash of lightning that blasts without igniting; *mit einem -e*, at one blow, all at once; *schöner - Pferde*, fine breed of horses; *- 10 Uhr*, on the stroke of 10, at 10 sharp, punctually at 10; *- ins Wasser*, vain attempt, wild-goose chase, (*coll.*) flop. **-ader,** *f.* artery. **-anfall,** *m.* apoplectic fit, stroke. **-artig,** *adj.* sudden, violent, in bursts, at a moment's notice. **-ball,** *m.* rounders. **-band,** *n.* (*Swiss. dial.*) sword knot. **-bar,** *adj.* fit for felling. **-baum,** *m.* turnpike. **-bolzen,** *m.* firing-pin, striker (*Mil.*). **-e,** *f.* hammer. **-en,** I. *ir.v.a.* beat, strike, hit, rap, clap, dash; fell (*trees*); coin, stamp; wrap (*um sich*, around one); defeat, rout (*an enemy*), take (*at draughts, etc.*); toll (*a bell*), touch (*a chord, etc.*); *Alarm -en*, sound the alarm; *-en an* (*Acc.*), fasten to, nail on; *den Feind aufs Haupt -en*, defeat *or* overthrow the enemy; *seine Unkosten auf die Ware -en*, add one's expenses to the price of a th.; *einem etwas aus der Hand -en*, knock s.th. out of a p.'s hand; *sich* (*Dat.*) *etwas aus den Gedanken* or *dem Sinn -en*, dismiss something from one's thoughts *or* mind, not think of a th. any longer; (*Prov.*) *dem Fasse den Boden -en*, knock the bottom out of it, put the lid on it; *die Kugel war durch die rechte Brust geschlagen*, the ball had passed through the right breast; *durch ein Sieb -en*, pass through a sieve; *Eier -en*, beat *or* whisk eggs; *Falten -en*, wrinkle, get creased; *er schlägt zwei Fliegen mit einer Klappe*, he kills two birds with one stone; *die Arme* (*Hände*) *ineinander -en*, cross one's arms (clasp one's hands); *in Fesseln -en*, put in irons; *die Augen in die Höhe -en*, raise one's eyes, look up; *in Papier -en*, wrap up in paper; *sein Leben in die Schanze -en*, risk his life; *in den Wind -en*, cast to the four winds, disregard; *aus einer S. Kapital -en*, make capital out of a th., turn s.th. to account; *die Karten -en*, read the cards, tell fortunes with cards; *kurz und klein -en*, break into small pieces; smash to pieces; *mit Blindheit -en*, smite with blindness; *einen Purzelbaum -en*, turn a somersault; *einen Rekord -en*, break a record (*Sport.*); *Schaum -en*, whip into froth; talk rubbish, (*coll.*) blether; *eine Schlacht -en*, fight a battle, give battle; *jemandem ein Schnippchen -en*, play a trick on s.o.; *den Takt -en*, beat time; *diese Uhr schlägt die Stunden*, this clock strikes the hours; *sich* (*Dat.*) *die Nacht um die Ohren -en*, sit *or* stay up all night, drink *or* carouse the whole night through; *sich* (*Dat.*) *die Welt um die Ohren -en*, go out into the wide world; *Wurzel -en*, take root; *die Augen zu Boden -en*, cast down one's eyes, look down; *einen Zweifel zu Boden -en*, silence a misgiving, overcome a scruple, remove a doubt; *die Zinsen zum Kapital -en*, add the interest to the capital; *einen zum Ritter -en*, dub s.o. a knight, invest a p. with knighthood; *ein geschlagener Mann*, a ruined man; *eine geschlagene Stunde*, a full *or* whole hour; *den ganzen geschlagenen Tag*, the livelong day. 2. *v.r. sich auf die Seite der Verschworenen -en*, take the part of *or* join the conspirators; *sich recht und schlecht durchs Leben -en*, make one's way in the world after a fashion; *sich ins Mittel -en*, interpose, mediate; *sich links -en*, turn to the left; *er schlug sich tapfer*, he fought well, (*coll.*) put up a good show; *sich zu* (*einem*) *-en*, side with, go over to *or* join (a p.); *sich in die Büsche -en*, go into the brushwood. 3. *v.n.* (*aux.* h.) beat; strike (*also of clocks*); sing (*of some birds*); *liebliche Töne schlugen an mein Ohr*, sweet sounds fell upon my ear; *bei einem auf den Busch -en*, tap a p., put out feelers; *der Qualm schlägt ihm auf die Brust* or *Lunge*, the fumes catch his chest *or* make him choke; *mit der Faust auf den Tisch -en*, thump the table, bang one's fist on the table; *aus der Art -en*, be different from the others; *nun schlägt es aber 13!* that's the limit! I can't stand any more! *die Tinte schlägt durchs Papier*, the ink soaks through the paper; *sein Herz schlägt warm für die Armen*, he is full of sympathy for the poor; *die Flammen -en gen* or *zum Himmel*, the flames shoot up toward the sky; *das Gewehr schlägt stark*, the rifle has a strong kick; *das Gewissen schlägt ihm*, his conscience pricks him; *er weiß, was die Glocke geschlagen hat*, he is (well) aware of the situation, state of affairs *or* facts, he has no illusions about the matter; *das Herz schlägt mir*, my heart is pounding *or* thumping; *das schlägt nicht in mein Fach*, that is not in my line; *einer S. ins Gesicht -en*, set s.th. at naught, make a mock of, scoff at *or* deride a th.; *mit den Flügeln -en*, beat one's wings; *die Nachtigall schlägt*, the nightingale is singing; *die Bauern ziehen geradeaus, -en aber schräg*, pawns move forwards but take diagonally (*Chess*); *seine Stunde hat geschlagen*, his hour has come; *dem Glücklichen schlägt keine Stunde*, a happy man is oblivious to time; *über den Strang* or *die Stränge -en*, kick over the traces; *die Uhr schlug*, the clock struck; *heftig um sich -en*, lay *or* set to with one's fists; *wie vor den Kopf geschlagen sein*, be dumbfounded, be at a loss; *der Wagen schlägt*, the carriage jolts. 4. *n.* striking, beating; pulsation; singing, warbling (*of birds*); kicking (*of horses*); fighting; construction (*of a bridge*); felling (*of timber*). **-end,** *pr.p.* & *adj.* striking, impressive; *-ender Beweis*, conclusive or compelling evidence, devastating proof; *–ende Verbindung*, duelling club (*Univ.*); *–ende Wetter* (*pl.*), firedamp. **–er,** *m.* popular song, (*coll.*) hit, box-office draw, (*sl.*) smash hit (*Theat.*); good selling line (*in shops*). **–etot,** *m.* (*coll.*) hulking fellow. **–feder,** *f.* striking spring (*in clocks*); striker spring (*in a gun*). **–fertig,** *adj.* ready with one's tongue, quick-witted, quick at repartee. **–fertigkeit,** *f.* ready wit, quickness of repartee; tactical readiness (*Mil.*). **–festigkeit,** *f.* impact strength (*Metall.*). **–fluß,** *m.* apoplectic fit, apoplexy. **–holz,** *n.* bat (*Crick.*); copse, wood for felling. **–instrument,** *n.* percussion instrument. **–kraft,** *f.* hitting power, striking force, effectiveness. **–licht,** *n.* strong light, glare (*Paint.*). **–loch,** *n.* pot-hole, (*pl.*) bad surface (*of road*). **–lot,** *n.* hard solder. **–mann,** *m.* stroke (*in rowing*). **–mühle,** *f.* crusher (*for ore*). **–obers,** *n.* (*Austr. dial.*) whipped cream. **–pulver,** *n.* fulminating powder. **–rahm,** *m.* whipped cream. **–regen,** *m.* downpour, pelting rain. **–reim,** *m.* rhyme of successive words. **–ring,** *m.* plectrum (*Mus.*); knuckle-duster. **–röhre,** *f.* friction igniter, primer (*Artil.*). **–sahne,** *f.* whipped cream. **–schatten,** *m.* cast shadow; **–schatz,** *m.* brassage. **–seite,** *f.* list (*Naut.*). **–uhr,** *f.* repeater; striking-clock. **–wärter,** *m.* toll-keeper. **–wasser,** *n.* bilge-water. **–weite,** *f.* striking distance, effective range (*Artil.*); spark distance (*Elec.*). **–welle,** *f.* surge, roller; camber. **–werk,** *n.* striking mechanism (*of clock*). **–wetter,** *n.* fire-damp. **–wort,** *n.* catchword, slogan; caption, heading; shibboleth. **–wortkatalog,** *m.* subject-catalogue. **–wunde,** *f.* contused wound. **–zeile,** *f.* headline. **–zeit,** *f.* felling time. **–zeug,** *n.* percussion (instruments). **–zeuger,** *m.* timpanist. **–zünder,** *m.* percussion-fuse.

Schlägel, *m. see* **Schlegel.**

Schläge–r, *m.* (-s, –) hitter, striker; kicker (*said of horses*); batsman; rowdy; sword, rapier; bat, tennis-racket; golf-club; singing-bird, warbler. **–faul,** *adj.* hardened; indolent. **–rei,** *f.* fight, brawl, scuffle. **–rmensur,** *f.* students' duel. **–rn,** *v.a.* (*Austr. dial.*) fell (*trees*).

schlägst, schlägt, *see* **schlagen.**

Schlaks, *m.* (-es, -e) (*dial.*) long, ungainly fellow. (*coll.*) **–ig,** *adj.* lanky.

Schlamassel, *m.* (-s, –) (*sl.*) scrape, fix, mess, jam.

Schlamm, *m.* mud, slime, mire, sludge, silt, ooze. **–bad,** *n.* mud-bath. **–beißer,** *m.* mud-fish (*Cobites fossilis*) (*Icht.*). **–en,** *v.n.* (*aux.* h.) deposit mud. **–herd,** *m.* buddle (*Min.*). **–ig,** *adj.* muddy, slimy, miry, oozy. **–netz,** *n.* drag-net. **–pfütze,** *f.* bog, slough. **–sprudel,** *m.*, **–vulkan,** *m.* mud-volcano. **–werk,** *n.* ore-washing mill.

schlämm–en, *v.a.* cleanse; elutriate, levigate, wash (*ore*). **–apparat,** *m.* elutriating apparatus. **–faß,** *n.* washing tank. **–herd,** *m.* buddle. **–kohle,** *f.* washed coal. **–kreide,** (*usually* **Schlemmkreide**), *f.* whitening, whiting. **–pflanze,** *f.* mud plant. **–schnecke,** *f.* pond snail.

Schlamp, *m.* (-(e)s, -e) (*coll.*) slovenly fellow, bungler. **–ampen,** *v.n.* (*aux.* h.) (*coll.*) gorge o.s., guzzle. **–e,** *f.* (-en) 1. slut, slattern, sloven. 2. slipper, house-shoe (*see also* **Schlempe**). **–en,** 1. *v.n.* (*aux.* h.) be slovenly *or* dirty; (*aux.* s.) slouch, slummock. 2. *m.* (*dial.*) rags, tatters. **–er,** *m.* (*dial.*), *see* **–. –erei,** *f.* slovenliness, untidiness, (*coll.*) mess; carelessness, remissness, unpunctuality. **–ig,** *adj.* slovenly, untidy, (*coll.*) sloppy.

schlang, schlänge, *see* **schlingen.**

Schlange, *f.* (-n) snake, serpent; coil, worm (*of a still*); queue; (*Poet.*) bend, winding; (*coll.*) *– stehen*, queue (up), line up. **–nadler,** *m.* short-toed eagle (*Circaetus gallicus*) (*Orn.*). **–nähnlich,** *adj.*, **–nartig,** *adj.* serpentine, snaky. **–nbalg,** *m.* snake's skin. **–nbeschwörer,** *m.* snake-charmer. **–nbiß,** *m.* snake bite. **–nbohrer,** *m.* spiral drill. **–ngeschlecht,** *n.* ophidians. **–ngift,** *n.* snake venom. **–nhaar,** *n.* serpent locks (*of Medusa*). **–nhaft,** *adj.* snake-like, snaky; spiteful, malicious. **–nhaut,** *f.* snake-skin. **–nkraut,** *n.* marsh calla, bog arum (*Calla palustris*) (*Bot.*). **–nkühler,** *m.* spiral condenser. **–nlinie,** *f.* wavy line. **–nmensch,** *m.* contortionist. **–npfad,** *m.* winding path. **–nrohr,** *n.* worm (*of a still*). **–nstab,** *m.* caduceus (*of Mercury*), Hermes' wand. **–nstein,** *m.* ophite, serpentine. **–nträger,** *m.* Ophiucus (*Astr.*). (*Poet.*) **–nwandelnd,** *adj.* serpentine, winding, meandering. **–nwindung,** *f.* meandering. **–nwurzel,** *f.* snake-root; snake-weed. **–nzunge,** *f.* adder's tongue (*Ophioglossum vulgatum*) (*Bot.*); (*fig.*) malicious *or* wicked tongue. **–nzüngig,** *adj.* backbiting, spiteful.

schlängel–n, 1. *v.a.* twist, wind; *geschlängelter Weg*, winding road. 2. *v.n.* (*aux.* h.) & *r.* twist, coil, meander, wind in and out; *sich aus einer S. –n*, wriggle out of a th.; *sich um etwas –n*, twist, wind *or* coil round a th. **–ig,** *adj.*, **–nd,** *pr.p.* & *adj.* meandering, winding, sinuous, serpentine.

schlank, *adj.* slim, slender; *–e Linie*, slimming line (*fashion*); *– machen*, 1. *v.a.* slim. 2. *v.n.* give a slim appearance, make one look slim (*of clothes*); *see* **–machen. –el,** *m.* (*Austr. dial.*) *see* **Schelm, Schlingel. –heit,** *f.* slimness, slenderness. **–machen,** *v.n.* (*coll.*) dress up, tog up. **–weg,** *adv.* roundly, flatly, downright, without more ado.

schlapp, *adj.* (*coll.*) slack, limp, flabby, tired, spineless. **–e,** *f.* (-en) blow, rebuff, check, reverse, (financial) loss; (*dial.*) slap; (*dial.*) slipper; (*dial.*) fainting fit; *eine –e erhalten* or *erleiden*, be worsted, sustain a reverse. **–en,** 1. *m.* (-s, –) slipper. 2. *v.n.* (*aux.* h.) dangle; slop about (*as ill-fitting shoes*). 3. *v.a.* (*dial.*) swig, swill, guzzle (*liquids noisily*). **–heit,** *f.* indolence, slackness. **–hut,** *m.* slouch hat. (*coll.*) **–machen,** *v.n.* collapse, break down, have a breakdown. **–ohr,** *n.* floppy ear. **–schuhe,** *f.pl.*, *see* **–en,** 1. (*sl.*) **–schwanz,** *m* weakling, coward, (*sl.*) sissy.

Schlaraffe, *m.* (-n, -n) sluggard, idler. **–nland,** *n.* cockaigne, fool's paradise, land of milk and honey.

Schlarfe, *f.* (-n) (*dial.*) slipper.

schlau, *adj.* sly, cunning, crafty; subtle. **–heit,** *f.* **–igkeit,** *f.* slyness, cunning, subtlety. **–berger,** *m.*, **–kopf,** *m.*, **–meier,** *m.* (sly) old fox, sly dog, artful dodger.

Schlaube, *f.* (-n) (*dial.*) husk.

Schlauch, *m.* (-es, ⸚e) tube, tubing, pipe, hose; inner tube (*Cycl.*); leathern bottle *or* skin; ampulla, utricle (*Bot.*); (*sl.*) toper; *er trinkt wie ein –*, he drinks like a drain *or* fish. **–anschluß,** *m.* hose-union. **–balg,** *m.* utricle (*Bot.*, *Zool.*, *Anat.*). **–boot,** *n.* rubber dinghy. **–en,** *v.a.* fill (*barrels, etc.*) by a pipe; (*coll.*) give it a p. hot and strong. **–ventil,** *n.* tyre-valve (*Motor.*, *Cycl.*).

Schlauder, *f.* (-n) brace, iron tie.

Schläue, *f.* (*rare*), *see* **Schlauheit.**

Schlauf, *m.* (-s, -e), **–e,** *f.* (-n), *see* **Schleife.**

schlecht, *adj.* bad, wicked, base; poor, inferior, wretched; (*dial.*) straight, plain, simple; (*coll.*) angry; *–er Absatz*, poor demand *or* sale; *bei einem – angeschrieben sein*, be in a p.'s bad books; *einem – bekommen*, do s.o. no good; *billig und –*, cheap and nasty; *jemandem –en Dank wissen*, give a p. no thanks; *– entzückt von einer S.*, badly pleased with a th.; *–es Haus*, house of ill repute, disorderly house; *– machen*, do *or* make (*s.th.*) badly; *see* **–machen;** *–e Papiere*, worthless papers *or* bills; *– und recht*, after a fashion, as well as one may; *mir ist –*, I feel ill; *es steht – um ihn*, he is in a bad way, he is badly off; *–er Trost*, cold comfort; *– dabei wegkommen*, come off badly; *– werden*, turn sour, go bad; go to the bad; *es kann einem dabei – werden*, it is enough to make one feel sick; *–e Zeiten*, hard times. **–beschaffen,** *adj.*, **–bestellt,** *adj.* ill-conditioned. **–denkend,** *adj.* evil-minded. **–erdings,** *adv.* simply, positively, by all means, utterly, absolutely; *–erdings nicht*, not by any means, by no means. **–gelaunt,** *adj.* in a bad temper. **–heit,** *f.* (*rare*) *see* **–igkeit. –hin,** *adv.* simply, merely, plainly, quite, absolutely. **–hinnig,** *adj.* utter, absolute. **–igkeit,** *f.* badness, baseness, wickedness. **–machen,** *v.a.* speak ill of, run down. **–weg,** *adv. see* **–hin. –wetter,** *n.* bad weather.

Schlecker, *m.* (-s, –) sweet tooth. **–ei,** *f.* daintiness; (*pl.*) sweets, dainties. **–ig,** *adj.* with a sweet tooth, spoiled. **–n,** 1. *v.n.* be dainty *or* pampered, be fond of sweet things. 2. *v.a.* lick; (*coll.*) kiss.

Schleg–el, *m.* (-s, –) mallet, club; beetle; drumstick; clapper (*of bell*); (*dial.*) leg (*of veal, etc.*). **-eln,** I. *v.n.* (*dial.*) (*aux.* h.) limp, hobble; make a bad mistake. 2. *v.a.* beat, stamp.

Schleh-dorn, *m.* sloe-tree, blackthorn (*Prunus spinosa*) (*Bot.*). **-e,** *f.* (-en) sloe, wild plum. **-weiß,** *adj.* snow-white.

Schlei, *f.* (-en) & *m.* (-(e)s, -e), **-e,** *f.* (-en) tench (*Finca vulgaris*) (*Ichth.*).

Schleich-e, *f.* (-n) (*pl.*) anguids. **-en,** *ir.v.r.* & *n.* (*aux.* s.) crawl, creep; slink, sneak, skulk, steal, prowl; *sich in sein Vertrauen -en*, worm o.s. into a p.'s confidence. **-end,** *pr.p.* & *adj.* sneaking, creeping, insidious, furtive; lingering, slow; *-endes Gift*, slow poison; *-endes Fieber*, low *or* slow fever. **-er,** *m.* sneak; intriguer. **-erei,** *f.* sneaking, underhand dealing. **-gut,** *n.* contraband. **-handel,** *m.* smuggling, illicit trade, black market. **-händler,** *m.* smuggler, black-marketeer. **-ware,** *f.*, *see* **-gut. -weg,** *m.* secret ways, underhand means.

Schleier, *m.* (-s, –) veil; pretence, cloak, screen; haze, film; smoke-screen (*Mil.*); *den – nehmen*, take the veil, become a nun; *den – über eine S. ziehen*, draw a veil over s.th., hush s.th. up. **-eule,** *f.* barn-owl. **-flor,** *m.* crape; veiling. **-haft,** *adj.* veiled, mysterious, inexplicable. **-n,** *v.a.* veil; fog (*Phot.*). **-tuch,** *n.*, *see* **-flor.**

Schleif-e, *f.* (-n) slide; sledge, sled; float, dray; slip-knot, noose, bow, loop; curve, S-bend; loop-line (*Railw.*); looping (*Av.*). **-en,** I. *v.n.* (*aux.* h. & s.) slide; glide, skid, slip along; pass (*Cards*); (*sl.*) *einen -en*, put s.o. through his paces. 2. *v.a.* drag, trail; slur (*a note*) (*Mus.*); raze, demolish (*a fortress*); knot, tie in a bow. **-antenne,** *f.* loop aerial (*Rad.*). **-bahn,** *f.* slide. **-enflug,** *m.* looping (*Av.*). **-engalvanometer,** *n.* moving-coil galvanometer. **-er,** *m.* slur (*Mus.*); slow waltz, shuffle (*Danc.*). **-knoten,** *m.* slip-knot, running-knot, noose. **-kohle,** *f.* friction-carbon. **-kontakt,** *m.* sliding contact (*Elec.*). **-ring,** *m.* collecting ring (*Elec.*). **-schritt,** *m.* sliding step (*Danc.*). **-sporn,** *m.* tail skid (*Av.*). **-ung,** *f.* demolition, razing. **-ungszeichen,** *n.* slur (*Mus.*).

schleif-en, *ir.v.a.* grind, polish, smooth, abrade; whet, sharpen (*knives, etc.*); cut, (*gems, glass*); *aus dem Groben -en*, rough-hew; *dieser Mann muß erst* or *noch geschliffen werden*, this young man wants polish; *geschliffenes Glas*, cut glass. **-bank,** *f.* grinding-lathe *or* bench. **-er,** *m.* grinder, polisher; cutter. **-erei,** *f.* grindery. **-lack,** *m.* body *or* flatting varnish. **-mittel,** *n.* abrasive. **-mühle,** *f.* grinding mill. **-papier,** *n.* emery *or* sand-paper. **-rad,** *n.*, **-scheibe,** *f.* grinding *or* polishing wheel. **-stein,** *m.* whetstone, grindstone. **-stoff,** *m.* paper pulp. **-tuch,** *n.* emery-cloth. **-ung,** *f.* grinding, sharpening.

Schleim, *m.* (-(e)s, -e) slime; phlegm, mucus; mucilage (*Bot.*). **-absonderung,** *f.* mucous secretion, blennorrhoea. **-artig,** *adj.* slimy, glutinous, mucoid. **-auswurf,** *m.* expectoration (*of mucus*). **-beutel,** *m.*, *see* **-sack. -drüse,** *f.* mucous gland. **-en,** I. *v.n.* (*aux.* h.) produce phlegm; become slimy (*in boiling*). 2. *v.a.* clear of slime. **-fluß,** *m.*, *see* **-absonderung. -harz,** *n.* gum-resin. **-haut,** *f.* mucous membrane. **-ig,** *adj.* slimy, viscous, mucous, mucilaginous. **-igkeit,** *f.* sliminess. **-sack,** *m.* mucous follicle, fluid vesicle (*Anat.*). **-sauer,** *adj.* mucate of. **-säure,** *f.* mucic acid. **-suppe,** *f.* gruel. **-tier,** *n.* mollusc. **-zucker,** *m.* l(a)evulose.

Schleiß-e, *f.* (-n) (*dial.*) splinter, splint; quill of a feather; lint. **-en,** I. *ir.v.a.* split; slit; *Federn -en*, strip quills. 2. *v.n.* (*aux.* s.) wear out; (*dial.*) slide. **-ig,** *adj.* (*dial.*) cut to pieces, worn out.

Schlemm, *m.* (-s, -e) grand slam (*Cards*).

schlemm-en, I. *v.n.* (*aux.* h.) revel, carouse; gormandize, guzzle. 2. *v.a.*, *see* **schlämmen. -boden,** *m.* diluvial soil. **-kreide,** *f.* whitening. **-er,** *m.* gormandizer, glutton, gourmand, gourmet. **-erei,** *f.* gluttony, feasting.

Schlempe, *f.* (-n) distiller's wash; swill, slops.

Schlend-erer, *m.* (-s, –) lounger. **-ern,** *v.n.* (*aux.* h. & s.) dawdle, lounge, loiter, saunter, stroll about. **-rian,** *m.* (-s, -e) old humdrum way, routine, groove, beaten track.

schlenkern, I. *v.n.* (*aux.* h.) dangle; shamble (*in walking*); *mit den Armen –*, swing one's arms. 2. *v.a.* dangle, swing; (*dial.*) shake off, jerk, toss, sling, fling.

Schlepp-e, *f.* (-n) train (*of a dress*); trail (*Hunt.*); sledge. **-en,** I. *v.a.* drag, trail; tow, haul, tug, (*coll.*) lug. 2. *v.r.* move slowly, drag on; trouble *or* burden o.s. 3. *v.n.* (*aux.* h.) drag, trail. **-end,** *pr.p.* & *adj.* slow, tedious; drawling; shuffling, dawdling. **-antenne,** *f.* trailing aerial (*Rad.*, *Av.*). **-boot,** *n.* tug. **-busch,** *m.* brush harrow (*Agr.*). **-dampfer,** *m.* steam-tug, tug-boat. **-enträger,** *m.* train-bearer. **-er,** *m.* hauler; tractor; tug(-boat); tout (*of customers*); prime mover. **-erei,** *f.* dragging, drudgery. **-flugzeug,** *n.* towing plane. **-geschwindigkeit,** *f.* towing speed. **-kabel,** *n.* tow-rope, hawser **-kahn,** *m.* barge. **-kante,** *f.* trailing edge (*Av.*). **-kleid,** *n.* dress with a train. **-kraft,** *f.* tractive force. **-leine,** *f.*, *see* **-kabel. -netz,** *n.* drag-net. **-schacht,** *m.* inclined gallery (*in mines*). **-scheibe,** *f.* towed target; sleeve, drogue (*Av.*). **-seil,** *n.* drag; drag-rope (*Artil.*); trail-rope (*of a balloon*, *Av.*). **-start,** *m.* towed take-off (*gliders*). **-tau,** *n.* hawser; *ins -tau nehmen*, take in tow. **-versuch,** *m.* towing test. **-wagen,** *m.* trailer. **-winde,** *f.* towing winch. **-zug,** *m.* train of barges.

Schleuder, *f.* (-n) sling, catapult; centrifuge, hydro-extractor, (cream) separator. **-arbeit,** *f.* bungled work. **-artikel,** *m.*, *see* **-ware. -ausfuhr,** *f.* dumping. **-guß,** *m.* centrifugal casting. **-honig,** *m.* extracted honey. **-konkurrenz,** *f.* unfair competition. **-kraft,** *f.* centrifugal force. **-maschine,** *f.* centrifugal machine, hydro-extractor, cream separator. **-mühle,** *f.* disintegrator. **-n,** I. *v.a.* sling, catapult, fling, throw, hurl, toss, project, send, shoot, dart; centrifuge, hydro-extract. 2. *v.n.* (*aux.* h.) shake; skid, side-slip (*Motor.*); roll (*of ship*); undersell, cut prices, dump. **-preis,** *m.* cut price; *zu -preisen*, dirt-cheap. **-pumpe,** *f.* centrifugal pump. **-spur,** *f.* skid marks. **-start,** *m.* catapult take-off (*of gliders*). **-waffe,** *f.* missile. **-ware,** *f.* bargain article.

schleunig, *adj.* quick, speedy, prompt, ready, swift; immediate; *aufs -ste*, in all haste, as soon as possible, with the utmost dispatch. **-keit,** *f.* speed, haste.

Schleuse, *f.* (-n) sluice, lock; sewer. **-n,** *v.a.* tow *or* pass (*ships*) through locks. **-nflügel,** *m.* leaf of a sluice-gate. **-ngas,** *n.* sewer gas. **-ngeld,** *n.* lock-charges. **-nhafen,** *m.* wet dock. **-nkammer,** *f.* lock-basin. **-nmeister,** *m.* lock-keeper. **-ntor,** *n.* sluice-gate, lock-gate. **-ntreppe,** *f.* chain of locks. **-nwärter,** *m.*, *see* **-nmeister. -nwehr,** *n.* lock-weir. **-nzoll,** *m.*, *see* **-ngeld.**

Schlich, *m.* (-(e)s, -e) secret way, by(e)-way; (*pl.*) tricks, dodges, artifices; (*dial.*) *see* **Schlick**; (*coll.*) *alle -e kennen*, be up to all the tricks; (*coll.*) know one's way about.

schlich, schliche, *see* **schleichen.**

schlicht, *adj.* plain, homely, simple, modest, unpretentious, straightforward; sleek, smooth; *-er Menschenverstand*, plain common-sense; *-er Abschied*, unceremonious dismissal (*Mil.*); *-e Erzählung*, plain unvarnished tale; *-es Haar*, smooth hair. **-bar,** *adj.* capable of being settled. **-e,** *f.* dressing, size. **-en,** *v.a.* plane, level, smooth, planish, dress (*yarn*) (*Weav.*); size; arrange, adjust, settle, put right, make up (*quarrels, etc.*). **-er,** *m.* planisher, dresser; mediator, arbitrator. **-hammer,** *m.* planishing-hammer. **-heit,** *f.* plainness, smoothness; simplicity. **-hobel,** *m.* smoothing-plane. **-leim,** *m.* size. **-maschine,** *f.* dressing *or* sizing machine. **-rahmen,** *m.* tanner's stretching-frame. **-ung,** *f.* mediation, arbitration, conciliation, settlement, amicable arrangement. **-ungsausschuß,** *m.*, **-ungsstelle,** *f.* arbitration board. **-ungswesen,** *n.* system of arbitration.

Schlick, *m.* (-(e)s, -e) slime, ooze, silt, mud. **-en,** *v.r.* silt up. **-(e)rig,** *adj.* muddy, slimy. **-ermilch,** *f.* (*dial.*) curdled milk. **-ern,** *v.n.* (*aux.* h.) I. *imp.* sleet. 2. (*dial.*) curdle. **-grund,** *m.* mud bottom. **-ig,** *adj.*, *see* **-(e)rig. -watt,** *n.* mud flat.

schlief, schliefe, *see* **schlafen.**

Schlief, *m.* (-(e)s, -e) sad *or* soggy lump (*in bread, etc.*); (*coll.*) – *backen*, make a hash of. (*dial.*) **–en,** *ir.v.n.* (*aux.* s.) slip, creep into (*Hunt.*). **–er,** *m.* (-s, –) badger-hound. **–ig,** *adj.* sad, soggy (*of bread, etc.*).

Schliere, *f.* (-n) streak *or* flaw in glass *or* negative (*Glassw., Phot.*). **–n,** *v.n.* slip (*of knots, rope, etc.*) (*Naut.*).

Schließ–e, *f.* (-n) catch, latch, clasp, fastening; anchor; shutter (*of a sluice, etc.*). **–en,** 1. *ir.v.a.* shut, close; lock, bolt; contract (*a marriage, etc.*), seal (*a contract*); finish, end, conclude, terminate; balance (*an account*); *hieran –en wir die Bemerkung*, to this we add the remark; *er –t jetzt die dritte Ehe*, he is marrying for the third time; *Freundschaft –en mit*, become friends *or* friendly with; *Frieden –en*, make peace; *in die Arme –en*, embrace; *jemanden in sein Herz –en*, take a fancy to a p.; *einen Kreis –en*, form a circle; *die Reihen –en*, close the ranks; *den Stromkreis –en*, close the circuit; *einen Vergleich –en*, come to an agreement; *geschlossenes Ganze*, complete *or* absolute whole; *geschlossene Gesellschaft*, private party, club; *geschlossene Ortschaft*, built-up area; *geschlossene Persönlichkeit*, rounded *or* harmonious personality; *geschlossene Reihen*, serried ranks (*Mil.*); *geschlossen hinter etwas stehen*, be solid behind a thing; *geschlossen an etwas teilnehmen*, take part as a body; *geschlossene Zeit*, close season (*Hunt.*); *geschlossen zustimmen*, approve unanimously. 2. *v.r.* close, shut; lock; knit (*as wounds*); come to an end; *in sich –en*, include, imply, comprise, comprehend, involve; *sich –en an* (*Acc.*), follow on. 3. *v.n.* (*aux.* h.) shut, close; fit well *or* close, join well; stop, end, conclude; break up (*from school*); come to a conclusion, infer, conclude (*aus*, from), judge (*aus*, by); *da* or *hiermit –t die Geschichte*, here the story ends, that is the end of the story; *der Markt schloß fest*, the market closed firm; *der Schlüssel –t nicht*, the key does not fit (the lock); *von sich* (*Dat.*) *auf andre –en*, judge others by o.s. **–balken,** *m.* iron bar (*for gates; Fort.*). **–bar,** *adj.* closable, lockable; deducible; *–barer Kasten*, box with lock and key. **–baum,** *m.* bar, boom (*of a harbour*). **–end,** *pr.p.* & *adj.* closing, concluding, final. **–er,** *m.* door-keeper, (house) porter; turnkey (*in a prison*); constrictor, sphincter (*Anat.*). **–fach,** *n.* safe deposit, post-office box. **–feder,** *f.* locking-spring, spring-catch; spring-bolt. **–hahn,** *m.* stop-cock. **–haken,** *m.*, *see* **–e. –kappe,** *f.* staple (*of a lock*). **–kopf,** *m.* rivet-head. **–lich,** 1. *adj.* final, definitive, conclusive, ultimate. 2. *adv.* finally, at last, in conclusion, in the long run, eventually. **–muskel,** *m.* & *f.* sphincter, constrictor *or* adductor muscle. **–rahmen,** *m.* chase (*Typ.*). **–riegel,** *m.* dead-bolt. **–rohr,** *n.*, **–röhre,** *f.* sealed tube. **–ung,** *f.* closing, close, conclusion; closure; breaking-up. **–ungsdraht,** *m.* connecting wire (*Elec.*). **–ungsfunke,** *m.* contact spark (*Elec.*).

Schliff, *m.* (-(e)s, -e) grinding, sharpening, smoothing, polishing; polish, good behaviour, style (*manners*); cut, micro-section; grindings (*see also* **Schlief**); *Mensch ohne –*, man without manners *or* refinement. **–bild,** *n.* micrograph. **–stopfen,** *m.* ground-in stopper.

schliff, schliffe, *see* **schleifen.**

schlimm, *adj.* bad, naughty, evil; sad, severe, serious; (*coll.*) ill, sore, unwell; unpleasant, nasty, annoying; *immer –er*, worse and worse; *um so –er*, so much the worse; *im –sten Falle*, see *–stenfalls*; *ich bin – daran*, I am in a bad way; *–e Augen*, sore eyes; *auf das –ste gefaßt sein*, be prepared for the worst; (*coll.*) *– hinter etwas her sein*, be set *or* bent upon s.th. **–stenfalls,** *adv.* if the worst comes to the worst, at the worst.

Schling–e, *f.* (-en) (running) knot, noose, loop; mesh, trap, snare; tendril; sling (*Surg.*); *in die –e gehen*, fall into the trap; *–en legen*, set snares; *den Kopf* or *Hals in die –e stecken*, run one's head into the noose; *sich* or *den Kopf aus der –e ziehen*, get out of a difficulty *or* scrape, get one's head out of the noose; *sich in der eignen –e fangen*, be hoist with one's own petard. **–el,** *m.* (-s, –) rascal; naughty boy. **–elei,** *f.* rascality. **–elhaft,** *adj.* rascally, **–en,** 1. *ir.v.a.* wind, weave, tie, twist, twine, entwine, intertwine; swallow, gulp, devour, engulf; *ein Band in eine Schleife –en*, tie ribbon into a bow. 2. *v.r.* coil, wind, twine, turn. **–beschwerde,** *f.* difficulty in swallowing. **–erbewegung,** *f.* rolling movement (*of ships*). **–erdämpfungsanlage,** *f.* stabilizer (*Naut.*). **–erkiel,** *m.* bilge-keel. **–erkreisel,** *m.* gyroscopic stabilizer (*Naut.*). **–ertank,** *m.* stabilizing tank (*Naut.*). **–ern,** *v.n.* (*aux.* h.) roll (*of ships*), sway, rock (*of vehicles*). **–gewächs,** *n.*, **–pflanze,** *f.* creeper, climber, climbing plant, liana (*Bot.*).

Schlipf, *m.* (-(e)s, -e) (*Swiss dial.*) landslide.

Schlipp–e, *f.* (-n) (*Austr. dial.*) alley, passage; (*dial.*) coat-tail. **–er,** *m.* (*Austr. dial.*), *see* **–ermilch. –erig,** *adj.* curdled. **–ermilch,** *f.* (*dial.*) curdled milk.

Schlips, *m.* (-es, -e) (neck-)tie, cravat; (*coll.*) *einem auf den – treten*, tread on a p.'s corns *or* toes; (*coll.*) *das haut einen auf den –*, that's more than one can swallow.

schliß, schlisse, *see* **schleißen.**

schlitt–eln, *v.n.* (*Swiss dial.*) go sledging. **–en,** *m.* (-ens, -en) sledge, sleigh, sled, toboggan; skid (*Av.*); sliding carriage (*Mach.*); (*coll.*) *unter den –en kommen*, come to grief; (*coll.*) *mit einem –en fahren*, take a p. in, lead s.o. up the garden path; *–en fahren*, go sledging. **–enbahn,** *f.* sledge-run; *es wird bald –enbahn geben*, we shall soon have sledging. **–enfahren,** *n.*, **–enfahrt,** *f.* sledging. **–engeläute,** *n.* sleigh-bells. **–enkufe,** *f.* sledge-runner. **–ern,** *v.n.* (*aux.* h. & s.) (*dial.*) slide. **–schuh,** *m.* skate; *–schuh laufen* or *fahren*, skate. **–schuhbahn,** *f.* skating-rink. **–schuhlaufen,** *n.* skating. **–schuhläufer,** *m.* skater.

Schlitz, *m.* (-es, -e) slit, slot, slash; fly (*in trousers*); split, cleft, notch, aperture, fissure; glyph (*Arch.*). **–auge,** *n.* slit (of an eye) (*Surg.*). **–äugig,** *adj.* narrow-eyed. **–brenner,** *m.* fantail burner. **–bruch,** *m.* longitudinal fracture. **–en,** *v.a.* slit, slash, split, cleave, rip open; *geschlitztes Kleid*, divided skirt. **–flügel,** *m.* slotted wing (*Av.*). **–ig,** *adj.* slashed, having slits. **–ohrig,** *adj.* with slit ears; cunning; roguish. **–verschluß,** *m.* focal-plane shutter (*Phot.*).

schlohweiß, *adj.* snow-white.

Schloß, *n.* (-(ss)es, ⸚(ss)er) castle, palace; lock (*of fire-arms, doors, etc.*); bolt, clasp, snap (*of bracelets, etc.*); hinge (*of shells*); *ins – fallen*, close, snap to (*of a door*); *ein – vor dem Mund haben*, be tongue-tied, not have a word to say; *unter – und Riegel*, under lock and key, behind bars. **–aufseher,** *m.* castellan. **–band,** *n.* hinge ligament. **–beamte(r),** *m.* court official. **–blatt,** *n.*, **–blech,** *n.* lock-plate, key-plate. **–feder,** *f.* spring of a lock. **–fortsatz,** *m.* cardinal process. **–freiheit,** *f.* precincts of a castle. **–graben,** *m.* castle-moat. **–hof,** *m.* castle-yard, courtyard. **–platz,** *m.* palace-yard. **–prediger,** *m.* court-chaplain. **–riegel,** *m.* bolt of a lock. **–verwalter,** *m.*, **–vogt,** *m.* castellan. **–wache,** *f.* palace guard; castle guard-house. **–zirkel,** *m.* reduction-compasses.

schloß, schlösse, *see* **schließen.**

Schloß–e, *f.* (-en) hailstone; (*pl.*) hail. **–en,** *v.n.* (*aux.* h.) hail. **–enwetter,** *n.* hailstorm. **–weiß,** *adj.* (*Austr. dial.*), *see* **schlohweiß.**

Schlosser, *m.* (-s, –) locksmith; fitter, mechanic. **–ei,** *f.* locksmith's trade *or* repair shop; workshop, garage. **–handwerk,** *n.* locksmith's trade.

Schlot, *m.* (-(e)s, -e & ⸚e) chimney, flue; smoke-stack. (*hum.*) **–baron,** *m.*, **–junker,** *m.* factory-owner. **–feger,** *m.*, *see* **–kehrer. –gang,** *m.* neck (*Geol.*). **–kehrer,** *m.* chimney-sweep.

Schlotte, *f.* (-n) hollow stalk, soil pipe (*of lavatories*); *see* **Schlotgang.**

Schlotter, 1. *m.* (*dial.*) trembling, tremors; sediment from boiling. 2. *f.* (*dial.*) child's rattle. **–beinig,** *adj.* unsteady on the legs, shambling. **–gang,** *m.* shuffling *or* unsteady gait. **–ig,** *adj.* loose, shaking, flabby, shaky, tottering, wobbly. **–milch,** *f.* (*dial.*) curdled milk. **–n,** *v.n.* (*aux.* h.) hang loose, fit loosely, flap, shake, tremble, dangle; slouch, totter, wobble; *–nde Knie*, shaking *or* trembling knees.

Schlucht, *f.* (-en & (*poet.*) ⸚e) ravine, defile, gully, gorge, canyon. **-artig,** *adj.* cavernous, deeply excavated.

schluchze-n, 1. *v.n.* (*aux.* h.) sob; (*dial.*) have the hiccups. 2. *n.* sobbing. **-r,** *m.* sob, sobbing.

Schluck, *m.* (-(e)s, -e & ¨-e) sip, gulp, mouthful, draught; *einen – über den Durst trinken,* take a drop too much, have one over the eight. **-akt,** *m.* act of swallowing. **-apparat,** *m.* organs of deglutition. **-auf,** *m.* hiccup. **-en,** 1. *v.a.* swallow, gulp, drink down; pocket (*an insult, etc.*). 2. *v.n.* (*aux.* h.) hiccup. 3. *m.*; *den -en haben,* have the hiccups. **-er,** *m.* hiccup; *armer -er,* poor wretch. **-sen,** *v.n.* have the hiccups. **-ung,** *f.* adsorption. **-weise,** *adv.* by mouthfuls *or* draughts, in gulps.

schluder-n, *v.n.* work carelessly, bungle, botch. **-arbeit,** *f.* botched *or* slapdash work. **-ig (schludrig)** *adj.* botched, bungled, slapdash.

Schluft, *f.* (¨-e) (*dial.*), *see* **Schlucht** & **Schlupfwinkel.**

schlug, schlüge, *see* **schlagen.**

Schlummer, *m.* slumber, nap. **-kissen,** *n.* (soft) pillow. **-körner,** *n.pl.* poppy-seeds. **-lied,** *n.* lullaby. **-n,** *v.n.* (*aux.* h.) slumber, sleep, doze, nap; lie dormant. **-nd,** *pr.p.* & *adj.* slumbering; dormant. **-rolle,** *f.* small bolster.

Schlump-e, *f.* (-en) slut, slattern, sloven. **-en,** *v.n.* (*aux.* h. & s.) be untidy; draggle, hang untidily, dangle. **-er,** *m.* (*dial.*) wrap, shawl. **-ig,** *adj.* slovenly, (*coll.*) draggle-tailed.

Schlund, *m.* (-(e)s, ¨-e) pharynx, throat, œsophagus, gullet; gorge, gulf, abyss, crater; *er jagt sein Geld durch den –,* he squanders his money on drink; *– der Kanone,* mouth of the cannon. **-kopf,** *m.* pharynx. **-kopfschnitt,** *m.* pharyngotomy. **-röhre,** *f.* œsophagus. **-sonde,** *f.*, **-stößer,** *m.* probang.

Schlunz-e, *f.*; **-ig,** *adj.* (*dial.*), *see* **Schlump-e, -ig.**

Schlup, *f.* (-s & -en) sloop (*Naut.*).

Schlupf, *m.* (-(e)s, ¨-e) slip, slipping; running knot, noose; *see* **Unterschlupf. -bluse,** *f.* jumper. **-en,** (*dial.*), *see* **schlüpfen. -er,** *pl.*, *see* **Schlüpfer. -hafen,** *m.* creek. **-hosen,** *pl.* (pair of) knickers. **-jacke,** *f.* sweater. **-loch,** *n.* loophole (*for escape*); hiding-place; fox-hole (*Mil.*). **-pforte,** *f.*, **-tor,** *n.* side gate, postern. **-wespe,** *f.* ichneumon-fly. **-winkel,** *m.* lurking *or* hiding-place, haunt, refuge.

schlüpf-en, *v.n.* (*aux.* s.) slip, slide, glide; *in die Kleider -en,* slip into one's clothes. **-er,** *m.* raglan (coat); sweater, jumper, (*pl.*) pair of knickers. **-rig,** *adj.* slippery; lascivious, equivocal, piquant, racy, indecent, obscene. **-rigkeit,** *f.* slipperiness; lubricity, indelicacy, obscenity, lasciviousness.

Schluppe, *f.* (*dial.*) bow (*of ribbon*).

schlurfen, *v.n.* (*aux.* h. & s.) shuffle, drag one's feet.

schlürfen, 1. *v.a.* sip, lap, quaff, swig; eat *or* drink noisily. 2. *v.n.* (*dial.*), *see* **schlurfen.**

Schlurpen, *m.* (*dial.*) slipper.

Schlurre, *f.* (*dial.*) slipper.

Schluß, *m.* (-(ss)es, ¨-(ss)e) shutting, closing; end, close, finish, termination, conclusion, breaking-up (*of schools, etc.*), winding-up (*of business*); contact, connexion (*Elec., Mech.*); keystone (*of a vault*); cadence (*Mus.*); consequence, inference, deduction, resolution, syllogism (*Log.*); upshot; *Tür und Fenster haben keinen rechten –,* neither door nor window closes properly; *einen guten – haben,* have a good *or* firm seat (*on horseback*); *logischer –,* syllogism; *– machen,* stop, make an end, knock off (*work*), (*coll.*) commit suicide; *– damit!* enough of that! *nach – der Redaktion,* before going to press; *aus einer S. Schlüsse auf etwas ziehen,* draw one's inferences about s.th. from a th.; *zum –,* finally, in conclusion; *eine S. zum – bringen,* terminate *or* settle an affair. **-abrechnung,** *f.* final settlement. **-akt,** *m.* speech-day; final act (*Theat.*). **-antrag,** *m.* motion for closure (*Parl.*). **-bemerkung,** *f.* final observation. **-ergebnis,** *n.* (final) result, upshot. **-fang,** *m.* safety catch (*of rifle*). **-folge,** *f.* chain of reasoning. **-folgerung,** *f.* conclusion, deduction, inference. **-form,** *f.* form of a syllogism. **-formel,** *f.* closing phrase, ending (*of letter*). **-kette,** *f.* chain of reasoning. (*C.L.*) **-kurse,** *m.pl.* closing prices. **-licht,** *n.* tail-light (*Railw.*, *Motor., etc.*). **-note,** *f.* sales-note; broker's note, contract-note. **-notierung,** *f.*, **-preis,** *m.* closing price, final quotation, contract price. **-prüfung,** *f.* final examination. **-punkt,** *m.* full stop, period; last point *or* head. **-rechnung,** *f.* final account; proportion (*Arith.*). **-recht,** *adj.*, **-richtig,** *adj.* conclusive, logically correct. **-rede,** *f.* concluding speech; epilogue. **-rennen,** *n.* final (*Sport.*). **-runde,** *f.* final (*round or match*); *sich in die -runde spielen,* get into the final. **-satz,** *m.* final proposition, conclusion; consequent (*of a syllogism*); finale (*Mus.*). **-schein,** *m.*, *see* **-note. -stand,** *m.* close stand (*of crops*). **-stein,** *m.* keystone, coping-stone. **-strich,** *m.*; *den* or *einen -strich unter eine S. ziehen* or *machen,* draw a line underneath s.th., bring a th. to an end. **-vignette,** *f.* tailpiece (*Typ.*). **-wort,** *n.* summary. **-zeichen,** *n.* sign of conclusion; double-bar, fine (*Mus.*); full stop. **-zettel,** *m.*, *see* **-note.**

Schlüssel, *m.* (-s, –) key; clef (*Mus.*); spanner, wrench; ratio; code, cipher; *falscher –,* skeleton key, picklock. **-bart,** *m.* key-bit. **-bein,** *n.* collar-bone, clavicle. **-blume,** *f.* cowslip, primrose (*Primula officinalis*) (*Bot.*). **-bolzen,** *m.* retaining pin. **-bund,** *n.* & *m.* (-e) bunch of keys, **-fertig,** *adj.* ready for occupation (*of new houses*). **-gewalt,** *f.* the power of the keys (*Eccl.*). **-industrie,** *f.* key-industry. **-loch,** *n.* keyhole. **-n,** *v.a.* & *n.* encode, encipher. **-ring,** *m.* key-ring. **-roman,** *m.* novel in which living persons figure under feigned names. **-soldaten,** *m.pl.* papal soldiers. **-stellung,** *f.* key position. **-ung,** *f.* encoding. **-weite,** *f.* calibre of a spanner, width over flats (*of nuts, etc.*). **-wort,** *n.* key-word, code-word.

schlüssig, *adj.* resolved, determined, decided, sure; *sich* (*Dat.*) *– werden* (*über eine S.*), make up one's mind (about a th.).

Schmach, *f.* insult, outrage, offence; disgrace, humiliation. **-frieden,** *m.* ignominious *or* humiliating peace (treaty). **-voll,** *adj.* humiliating, disgraceful.

schmacht-en, *v.n.* (*aux.* h.) languish, pine; *-en nach,* long for, yearn after. **-blick,** *m.* languishing glance. **-er,** *m.*, **-hans,** *m.*, *see* **-lappen. -korn,** *n.* blighted corn. **-lappen,** *m.* starveling; love-sick swain. **-locke,** *f.* love-lock, kissing-curl. **-riemen,** *m.* (*coll.*) *den -riemen enger schnallen,* tighten one's belt.

schmächtig, *adj.* delicate, slight, slender, slim. **-keit,** *f.* delicate health; slenderness, slimness.

Schmack, *m.* sumac(-tree). **-(e),** *f.* (-en) smack (*Naut.*). **-en,** *v.a.* & *n.* treat with sumac. **-gar,** *adj.* boiled in sumac.

schmackhaft, *adj.* tasty, savoury; palatable, appetizing. **-igkeit,** *f.* savouriness; savour, taste.

Schmadder, *m.* (*dial.*) wet dirt. **-n,** *v.a.* daub, soil; scrawl.

schmäh-en, *v.a.* & *n.* (*aux.* h.) abuse, revile, despise, belittle, insult, slander; *einen -en* or *auf, gegen* or *über einen -en,* rail at, inveigh against, slander *or* insult s.o. **-brief,** *m.* insulting letter. **-lich,** *adj.* ignominious, disgraceful, humiliating; abusive, insulting; (*coll.*) *es ist -lich heiß,* it is frightfully hot; (*coll.*) *er hat sich -lich geärgert,* he was terribly annoyed. **-lied,** *n.* defamatory song. **-rede,** *f.* objurgation, diatribe. **-schrift,** *f.* libel; lampoon. **-sucht,** *f.* slanderous disposition. **-süchtig,** *adj.* slanderous. **-ung,** *f.* (-en, *also used as pl. of Schmach*) abuse, invective, slander, defamation, aspersion; *Klage wegen -ung,* action for libel. **-wort,** *n.* invective.

schmal, *adj.* (*comp.* -er & ¨-er, *sup.* -st & ¨-st) narrow, thin, slim, slender; poor, scanty, meagre; *auf die -e Seite legen,* lay edgewise; *-e Bissen haben,* fare badly, be on short commons. **-brüstig,** *adj.* narrow-chested. **-film,** *m.* 8-mm. film (*Phot.*). **-hans,** *m.*; *heute ist -hans bei uns Küchenmeister,* we are on short commons today. **-heit,** *f.* narrowness; scantiness; poverty. **-leder,** *n.* upper leather (*for shoes*). **-schrift,** *f.* compressed type. **-spur,** *f.* narrow gauge. **-spurbahn,** *f.* narrow-gauge railway, light railway. **-spurig,** *adj.* narrow-gauged. (*sl.*) **-spursoldat,** *m.* short-service soldier. **-tier,** *n.* hind in her second year *or* before calving.

schmälen, *v.a. & n.* (*aux.* h.) scold, abuse; bleat (*of deer*); *auf einen* –, chide *or* scold a p., declaim against a p.
schmäler–n, *v.a.* lessen, diminish, curtail; narrow, reduce in width; detract from, belittle; *jemandes Rechte –n*, encroach upon a p.'s rights. **–ung,** *f.* lessening; narrowing; diminution; retrenchment, curtailment, detraction.
Schmalt, *m.*, *see* **Schmelz** (= enamel). **–e,** *f.*, (*also* **–blau,** *n.*) smalt blue, azure. **–en,** *v.a. & n.* enamel.
Schmalz, *n.* melted fat *or* grease, dripping, lard; (*coll.*) *ohne Salz und* –, wishy-washy. **–birn(e),** *f.* butter-pear. **–brot,** *n.* slice of bread and dripping. **–butter,** *f.* melted butter. **–en,** (*Austr. dial.*) prepare (*food*) with lard, *etc.* **–gebackene(s),** *n.* food fried in lard; *see* **–kuchen. –ig,** *adj.* greasy; (*fig.*) sentimental. **–kuchen,** *m.* dripping- *or* short-cake. **–pfanne,** *f.* frying-pan.
schmälzen, *v.a.* (*p.p. often* geschmalzen) grease, lard, oil.
Schmand, Schmant, *m.* (-(e)s, -e) (*dial.*) cream; slime, ooze, sludge.
schmarotze–n, *v.n.* (*aux.* h.) live as a parasite, sponge (*bei*, upon). **–r,** *m.* parasite; sponger. **–rei,** *f.* parasitism; sponging, toadyism. **–rhaft,** *adj.*, **–risch,** *adj.* parasitic(al). **–rpflanze,** *f.* parasitic plant, parasite. **–rtier,** *n.* animal parasite. **–rtum,** *n.* parasitism.
Schmarr–e, *f.* (-en) slash, cut, scar. **–ig,** *adj.* scarred. **–(e)n,** *m.* (-s, –) (*dial.*) kind of omelette; (*coll.*) worthless object, trash; shocker (*book*).
Schmasche, *f.* (-n) dressed lambskin. **–nleder,** *n.* chamois-leather, shammy(-leather).
Schmatz, *m.* (-es, -e & ¨-e) smack, hearty kiss. **–(e),** *f.* (-en) (*dial.*) tree-stump. **–en,** *v.a. & n.* (*aux.* h.) smack the lips, give a hearty kiss.
Schmauch, *m.* (-(e)s, -e) thick *or* dense smoke. **–en,** *v.a. & n.* (*aux.* h.) smoke, puff at a pipe.
Schmaus, *m.* (-es, ¨-e) feast, banquet; (*fig.*) treat; *jemandem einen – geben*, feast *or* treat a p., give a dinner in a p.'s honour. **–en,** *v.a. & n.* (*aux.* h.) feast, banquet. **–erei,** *f.* feasting; banquet.
schmeck–en, 1. *v.a.* taste; try by tasting; (*fig.*) experience. 2. *v.n.* (*aux.* h.) taste (*bitter, sweet*); taste good, be pleasant to the taste; (*dial.*) smell; *–en nach*, taste, savour *or* smack of; *wie –t es dir?* how do you like it? are you enjoying it? *dieser Wein –t mir*, I like this wine; *ihm will nichts –en*, he has no appetite, nothing is to his taste; *er läßt es sich –en*, he eats it with relish; *es hat mir vortrefflich geschmeckt*, I have thoroughly enjoyed it; *das –t nach mehr*, it is so good that I should like some more of it, (*sl.*) it is morish; (*coll.*) *diese Nachricht –te ihm gar nicht*, he did not relish that piece of news at all. **–zelle,** *f.* gustatory cell.
Schmeiche, *f.* (-n) size, dressing (*Weav.*).
Schmeich–elei, *f.* flattery, adulation; coaxing, cajolery. **–elhaft,** *adj.* flattering, complimentary; coaxing. **–elkatze,** *f.* wheedler, flatterer. **–eln,** *v.n.* (*aux.* h.) (*Dat.*) flatter, compliment; coax, cajole, wheedle; fawn upon; caress, fondle, pet; *sich* (*Dat.*) *in eiteln Hoffnungen –eln*, flatter o.s. with foolish hopes; *das Bild ist geschmeichelt*, the picture is flattering. **–elname,** *m.* flattering name. **–elrede,** *f.*, **–elwort,** *n.* flattering word *or* speech. **–ler,** *m.* flatterer, wheedler. **–lerisch,** *adj.* flattering, adulatory; fawning, wheedling.
schmeidig, *adj.* (*poet. & dial.*), *see* **geschmeidig.**
schmeiß–en, 1. *ir.v.a. & n.* (*aux.* h.) fling, hurl, dash, slam; (*coll.*) stand (*a drink, etc.*). 2. *v.n.* (*aux.* h.) deposit (*eggs*) (*of insects*); *mit Geld um sich –en*, throw one's money about; (*sl.*) *eine S. schon –en*, bring a thing off successfully. **–e,** *f.*, **–fliege,** *f.* blow-fly, bluebottle.
Schmelz, *m.* enamel, glaze, glazing; fusion, melting; (*fig.*) mellowness; *melodischer – einer Stimme*, melting sweetness of a voice. **–e,** *f.* melting, smelting, fusion, thaw; molten *or* fused mass; melt; batch, charge (*of metal*); composition (*of glass*); foundry. **–en,** 1. *ir.v.n.* (*aux.* s.) melt, fuse; diminish, melt away; soften (*of heart*). 2. *reg. & ir.v.a.* melt, liquefy, smelt; fuse, blend. **–arbeit,** *f.* smelting; enamelling. **–bar,** *adj.*, fusible. **–barkeit,** *f.* fusibility. **–blau,** *adj. see* **Schmaltblau. –butter,** *f.* melted butter. **–draht,** *m.* fuse-wire. **–einsatz,** *m.* fuse. **–eisen,** *n.* cast iron. **–end,** *pr. p. & adj.* melting, liquefying, liquescent; touching, sentimental, sweet (*of sound*). **–erei,** *f.* foundry. **–farbe,** *f.* vitrifiable pigment, enamel-colour. **–feuer,** *n.* refinery. **–fluß,** *m.* enamel; fused mass. **–flüssig,** *adj.* molten. **–flußelektrolyse,** *f.* fusion electrolysis. **–glas,** *n.*, **–glasur,** *f.* enamel. **–grad,** *m.*, **–hitze,** *f.* smelting heat. **–hütte,** *f.* smelting-works, foundry. **–ig,** *adj.* fusible. **–koks,** *m.* foundry-coke. **–maler,** *m.* enameller. **–mittel,** *n.* flux. **–ofen,** *m.* furnace, forge. **–perle,** *f.* bugle. **–punkt,** *m.* melting-point, fusing temperature *or* (*Elec.*) load. **–schupper,** *m.* ganoid (*Icht.*). **–sicherung,** *f.* fuse (*Elec.*). **–tiegel,** *m.* crucible. **–ung,** *f.* melting, fusion; liquefaction. **–wärme,** *f.* heat of fusion. **–wasser,** *n.* melting *or* melted snow. **–zement,** *m. & n.* aluminous cement.
Schmer, *n.* fat, grease, suet. **–bauch,** *m.* paunch, (*coll.*) corporation.
Schmergel, *m.*, *see* **Schmirgel.**
Schmerl, *m.* (-(e)s, -e) merlin (*Orn.*). **–e,** *f.* (-en) loach (*Icht.*).
Schmerz, *m.* (-es, -en) pain, ache, smart; (*fig.*) grief, suffering, sorrow. **–bekämpfung,** *f.* alleviation of pain. **–beladen,** *adj.* deeply afflicted. **–betäubend,** *adj.* analgesic. **–empfindlich,** *adj.* sensitive to pain. **–en,** 1. *v.a.* pain, hurt, distress, grieve; *es –t mich, das zu sagen*, it pains me to say so. 2. *v.n.* (*aux.* h.) (*3rd pers. only*) be painful, hurt, smart, ache; *mir* (*mich*) *–t der Kopf*, my head aches. **–ensgeld,** *n.* smart-money, compensation. **–enskind,** *n.* child of sorrow. **–enslager,** *n.* bed of suffering. **–en(s)reich,** *adj.*, **–erfüllt,** *adj.* deeply afflicted. **–frei,** *adj.*, *see* **–los. –gefühl,** *n.* painful sensation. **–haft,** *adj.* painful; *–hafte Stelle*, sore place. **–lich,** *adj.* sad, grievous, painful. **–lindernd,** *adj.* soothing, anodyne. **–los,** *adj.* painless; sluggish (*Med.*). **–stillend,** *adj.* anodyne, deadening, soothing. **–voll,** *adj.* painful, agonizing.
Schmetterling, *m.* (-s, -e) butterfly. **–sblütler,** *m.* papilionaceous flower. **–ssammlung,** *f.* butterfly collection.
schmetter–n, 1. *v.n.* (*aux.* h. & s.) crash; peal, ring, clang; resound, blare; warble (*as birds*). 2. *v.a.* dash, crash, smash, throw down violently. **–schlag,** *m.* smash (*Tenn.*).
Schmicke, *f.* (-n) whip-lash.
Schmied, *m.* (-(e)s, -e) (black)smith; (*Prov.*) *jeder ist seines Glückes* –, every man is the architect of his own fortune. **–bar,** *adj.* malleable. **–barkeit,** *f.* malleability. **–e,** *f.* (-en) smithy, forge; *er kam vor die rechte –e*, he hit upon the right person. **–eamboß,** *m.* anvil. **–earbeit,** *f.* smith's work, wrought-iron work. **–eeisen,** *n.* wrought-iron. **–eeisern,** *adj.* made of wrought-iron. **–eesse,** *f.*, **–eherd,** *m.* forge. **–ehammer,** *m.* sledge-hammer. **–ehandwerk,** *n.* smith's trade. **–en,** *v.a.* forge, hammer; (*fig.*) fabricate, frame, devise, scheme, concoct; *in Eisen –en*, put in irons; *Lügen –en*, concoct lies; *Pläne –en*, devise plans; *Ränke –en*, hatch plots; *Verse –en*, produce, compose, put together *or* pen verses; (*Prov.*) *man muß das Eisen –en, solange es heiß ist*, strike the iron while it is hot; *sein eigenes Unglück –en*, be the author of one's own misfortune. **–estock,** *m.* block of the anvil. **–eware,** *f.* hardware. **–ewerkstätte,** *f.* forge, smithy. **–stück,** *n.* forging.
Schmieg–e, *f.* (-en) bevel; folding rule. **–en,** 1. *v.a.* bend, incline; bevel. 2. *v.r.* bend; cringe; *sich –en an* (*Acc.*), press *or* creep close to, nestle against, cling to; *sich –en und biegen*, give in on every point, climb down. **–sam,** *adj.* pliant, flexible, lithe, supple; (*fig.*) submissive. **–samkeit,** *f.* pliancy, flexibility.
Schmiele, *f.* (-n) hair-grass (*Deschampsia*) (*Bot.*); weal.
Schmier–e, *f.* (-n) grease, lubricant; bribery; small touring theatrical company; (*sl.*) *–e stehen*, keep cave; (*sl.*) *die ganze –e*, the whole shoot *or* boiling **–en,** 1. *v.a.* grease, oil, lubricate; (*coll.*) smear, spread, daub; tip heavily, bribe. 2. *v.n.* (*aux.* h.)

smear, rub off; scribble, scrawl; (*sl.*) *ihm eine –en*, swipe him, give *or* wipe him a fourpenny one; (*coll.*) *einem etwas ins Maul –en*, rub a p.'s nose in s.th.; *einem Honig* or *Brei ums Maul –en*, butter a p. up, soft-soap a p., flatter a p. **–apparat**, *m.* lubricator, oil-feed. **–buch**, *n.* rough notebook. **–büchse**, *f.* axle-box; oil-can, grease cup, lubricator. **–enschauspieler**, *m.* strolling player. **–erei**, *f.* daub, scribble, scrawl. **–fett**, *n.* axle-grease. (*coll.*) **–fink**, *m.* dirty fellow. (*coll.*) **–geld**, *n.* tip, bribe. **–ig**, *adj.* greasy, oily, viscous; (*fig.*) sordid, mean, (*sl.*) smarmy. **–käse**, *m.* soft cheese. **–mittel**, *n.* lubricant; ointment, liniment; (*fig.*) bribe, tip. **–öl**, *n.* lubricating oil. **–plan**, *m.* lubrication chart. **–seife**, *f.* soft soap. **–ung**, *f.* lubrication. **–vorrichtung**, *f.* lubricator, oil-feed. **–wolle**, *f.* dirty greasy wool.

schmilz, schmilzt, *see* **schmelzen**, I.

Schmink–e, *f.* (-n) paint; rouge, cosmetic, make-up. **–en**, *v.a.* & *r.* paint one's face, rouge, make up, use make-up. **–büchse**, *f.*, **–dose**, *f.* rouge-pot. **–läppchen**, *n.* rag for dabbing on colour. **–pflästerchen**, *n.* beauty-patch.

Schmirgel, *m.* emery. **–leinen**, *n.* emery-cloth. **–papier**, *n.* emery-paper. **–n**, *v.a.* rub, polish *or* grind with emery. **–scheibe**, *f.* emery-wheel.

Schmiß, *m.* (-(ss)es, -(ss)e) blow, stroke, cut, lash; duelling scar; (*fig.*) verve, go, dash. (*coll.*) **–(ss)ig**, *adj.* smart, dashing, energetic.

schmiß, schmisse, *see* **schmeißen.**

Schmitz, *m.* (-es, -e) blow, cut, lash; spot, blot, splash, blur. **–e**, *f.* (*dial.*), *see* **Schmicke. –en**, I. *v.a.* (*aux.* h.) lash, whip. 2. *v.a.* & *n.* (*aux.* h.) soil, stain, splash, blur (*Typ.*); (*coll.*) wallop.

Schmöker, *m.* (-s, –) (*coll.*) old book, trashy novel; crib. **–n**, *v.n.* (*aux.* h.) read trash, pore over old books; *herum–n*, ferret about.

schmoll–en, *v.n.* (*aux.* h.) pout, be sulky. **–(l)ippe**, *f.* pouting lip. **–winkel**, *m.* sulking corner.

Schmollis, *n.*; *mit einem – trinken*, have a drink with a p., hobnob with a p.; (*Studs. sl.*) *ein – den Sängern!* a toast to the singers!

schmolz, schmölze, *see* **schmelzen**, I.

schmor–en, I. *v.n.* (*aux.* h.) be stewed; (*coll.*) bake, roast, be suffocated *or* parched with heat; *einen –en lassen*, leave s.o. to *or* let s.o. stew in his own juice. 2. *v.a.* stew, braise. **–braten**, *m.* stewed *or* braised meat. **–pfanne**, *f.*, **–topf**, *m.* stew-pan, stew-pot.

Schmu, *m.* (*coll.*) unfair gain, illicit profit; (*einen*) *– machen*, swindle, diddle.

Schmuck, I. *m.* (-(e)s, -e) ornament, decoration; jewels, jewellery, ornaments, finery, adornment, embellishment. 2. *adj.* spruce, tidy, trim, pretty, nice, handsome. **–anlage**, *f.*, *see* **–platz. –feder**, *f.* plume. **–händler**, *m.* jeweller. **–kästchen**, *n.* jewel-case. **–laden**, *m.* jeweller's shop. **–los**, *adj.* unadorned, plain, simple. **–losigkeit**, *f.* plainness, simplicity. **–nadel**, *f.* shirt-pin, tie-pin, brooch. **–platz**, *m.* ornamental gardens. **–sachen**, *f.pl.* jewels, trinkets, ornaments, finery. **–stück**, *n.* piece of jewellery. **–voll**, *adj.* ornate, ornamental. **–waren**, *f.pl.*, *see* **–sachen. –warenhändler**, *m.* jeweller.

schmück–en, I. *v.a.* decorate; trim, bedeck, set off, embellish, ornament. 2. *v.r.* deck o.s. out. **–ung**, *f.* adorning, decoration, embellishment, ornamentation.

Schmudd–el, *m.* (*coll.*) dirtiness, muckiness. **–elei**, *f.* daub, scribble; slush, muck. **–(e)lig**, *adj.* (*coll.*) dirty, unclean.

Schmugg–el, *m.* (-els, -el), **–elei**, *f.* smuggling. **–eln**, *v.a.* & *n.* (*aux.* h.) smuggle. **–elwaren**, *f.pl.* smuggled goods, contraband. **–ler**, *m.* smuggler.

schmunzeln, *v.n.* (*aux.* h.) smirk, grin, look pleased.

Schmus, *m.* (*sl.*) empty chatter, soft-soap. **–en**, *v.n.* (*aux.* h.) (*coll.*) flatter, soft-soap (*a p.*), gossip, chatter; talk nonsense. **–er**, *m.* chatterbox, lickspittle, toady. **–erei**, *f.* flattery, blarney, honeyed words.

Schmutz, *m.* dirt, filth; smut; mud. **–ärmel**, *m.pl.* sleeve protectors. **–bogen**, *m.* slur, waste sheet (*Typ.*). **–en**, *v.n.* (*aux.* h.) get dirty (easily). **–erei**, *f.* dirty job, filthiness; obscenity. **–farbe**, *f.* dingy *or* drab colour. (*coll.*) **–fink(e)**, *m.* dirty fellow. **–fleck**, *m.* spot, stain. **–ig**, *adj.* dirty, filthy, muddy, soiled; base, sordid, low, mean, shabby; obscene, smutty; *–iger Abdruck*, smudged *or* uneven proof (*Typ.*); *–iger Eigennutz*, sordid self-interest; *–ige Geschichte*, obscene story; *–iger Wucher*, filthy lucre; *–ige Wäsche*, soiled *or* dirty linen. **–kittel**, *m.* overall. **–konkurrenz**, *f.* unfair competition. (*coll.*) **–liese**, *f.* slattern. **–literatur**, *f.* pornography. **–presse**, *f.* gutter press. **–schrift**, *f.* obscene publication. **–seite**, *f.* sham page (*Typ.*). **–titel**, *m.* bastard title, half-title. **–wasser**, *n.* waste water, sewage.

Schnabel, *m.* (-s, ⸚) bill, beak; nozzle, snout; rostrum; prow, cutwater (*of a ship*); (*vulg.*) mouth; (*vulg.*) *halt' den –*, hold your tongue *or* trap; *seinen – an allem wetzen*, poke one's nose into everything; (*coll.*) *er spricht wie ihm der – gewachsen ist*, he speaks according to his lights, he does not mince matters. **–förmig**, *adj.* beak-shaped, rostrate. **–ieren**, *see* **schnabulieren. –kerfe**, *f.* hemiptera (*Ent.*). **–schuhe**, *m.pl.* pointed shoes (*12th–15th centuries*). **–tasse**, *f.* invalid's cup. **–tier**, *n.* duckbill platypus (*Zool.*). **–zange**, *f.* rostrum (*Surg.*).

Schnäbel–ei, *f.* billing and cooing. **–ig**, *adj.* beaked. **–n**, *v.n.* (*aux.* h.) & *r.* bill and coo.

schnabulieren, *v.n.* (*coll.*) eat heartily *or* with relish.

Schnack, *m.* (-(e)s, -e & ⸚e) (*coll.* & *dial.*) chit-chat, stuff and nonsense, fiddlesticks, twaddle. (*dial.*) **–eln**, *v.n.*, *see* **schnalzen.** (*dial.* & *coll.*) **–en**, *v.a.* & *n.* (*aux.* h.) chat, chatter, gossip.

Schnad–ahüpf(e)l, –erhüpfe(r)l, *n.* Alpine folk-song.

Schnak–e, *f.* (-en) I. jest, joke, piece of nonsense; fun. 2. cranefly; (*dial.*) gnat, midge. **–enstich**, *m.* gnat bite. **–ig**, *adj.*, **–isch**, *adj.* funny, amusing, comical.

Schnalle, *f.* (-n) buckle, clasp; latch, catch (*of a door*). **–n**, *v.a.* buckle, strap, fasten. **–ndorn**, *m.* tongue, tooth *or* pin of a buckle. **–nhaken**, *m.* chape. **–nschuh**, *m.* buckled shoe.

schnalz–en, *v.n.* (*aux.* h.) click (*the tongue*); snap (*the fingers*). **–laut**, *m.* click of the tongue.

schnapp, I. *int.* snap! bang! before you can say 'Jack Robinson'! 2. *m.* (-s, -e) (*coll.*) snap, fillip; mouthful. **–en**, I. *v.n.* (*aux.* h. & s.) snap, close with a snap; snatch, grab; *nach Luft –en*, gasp for breath; (*coll.*) *jetzt hat's aber geschnappt*, but now there is an end of it, I will not stand it any longer. 2. *v.a.* get hold of, arrest. **–feder**, *f.* spring-catch. **–hahn**, *m.* highwayman. **–messer**, *n.* clasp-knife. **–sack**, *m.* knapsack. **–schloß**, *n.* spring lock. **–schuß**, *m.* snapshot (*Phot.*).

Schnäpper, *m.* (-s, –) (*dial.*) snap, catch; cupping instrument (*Med.*); flycatcher (*Muscicapa*) (*Orn.*).

Schnaps, *m.* (-(s)es, ⸚e) spirits, liqueur, brandy, gin. (*coll.*) **–bruder**, *m.* toper. **–bude**, *f.* gin-shop, public-house. **–en**, *v.n.* tipple. **–idee**, *f.* (*coll.*) crazy notion, hair-brained scheme. **–ig**, *adj.* (*vulg.*) stupid, fuddled.

schnarch–en, *v.n.* (*aux.* h.) snore. **–erei**, *f.* snoring. **–ventil**, *n.* snifting-valve, sniffle-valve.

Schnarr–e, *f.* (-en) rattle. **–en**, *v.n.* (*aux.* h.) rattle, (speak with a) burr; jar, rasp; *das –en des r*, the burr of the r. **–baß**, *m.* drone (*Mus.*). **–drossel**, *f.* missel-thrush. **–saite**, *f.* snare (*on drums*). **–werk**, *n.* bourdon, reed-stops (*of an organ*).

Schnatter–ei, *f.* (-en) cackle, gabbling. **–gans**, *f.*, **–er**, *m.* chatterer, gabbler. **–haft**, *adj.* babbling, chattering, gabbling. **–n**, *v.n.* (*aux.* h.) chatter (*also of teeth with cold*); gabble; quack, cackle (*of geese*).

schnauben, I. *reg.* & (*archaic except Austr. dial.*) *ir.v.a.* & *n.* (*aux.* h. & s.) pant, puff, blow, breathe heavily, snort. 2. *v.r.* (*dial.*) blow one's nose; (*vor*) *Wut –*, foam *or* fume with rage; *Rache –*, breathe vengeance.

schnäubig, *adj.* (*dial.*) choosy, fussy (*about food*).

schnauf–en, *v.n.* breathe heavily, pant. **–er**, *m.* (*coll.*) breath; *bis zum letzen –er*, to the last gasp. (*dial.* & *hum.*) **–erl**, *n.* tin Lizzie (*for a car*).

Schnauz–e, *f.* (-en) snout, muzzle; spout, nozzle; (*vulg.*) nose, beak, mouth, jaw, snitch; (*sl.*) lip, cheek; (*vulg.*) *die –e halten*, hold one's trap, put a sock in it; (*sl.*) *die –e voll haben*, be fed up to the teeth, have had a bellyful; (*sl.*) *jemandem eins auf die –e geben*, give s.o. a sock on the jaw. (*coll.*) **–en**, *v.n.* (*aux.* h.) shout at, throw one's weight about. **–er**, *m.* rough-haired terrier. **–bart**, *m.* moustache. **–bärtig**, *adj.* moustached; rude, coarse. **–ig**, *adj.* rude, (*sl.*) snorty.

Schnecke, *f.* (-n) snail, slug; cochlea (*of the ear*); spiral, scroll, volute (*Arch.*); fusee (*Horol.*); winding staircase; Archimedes' screw; worm gear. **–nantrieb**, *m.* worm-drive. **–nfeder**, *f.* mainspring (*of a watch*); spiral spring. **–nförmig**, *adj.* helical, spiral. **–nfraß**, *m.* damage done by slugs. **–ngang**, *m.* snail's pace; circuitous path. **–ngehäuse**, *n.* worm-gear housing. **–ngetriebe**, *n.* worm-gear. **–ngewinde**, *n.* helix, whorl. **–nhaus**, *n.* snail-shell. **–nhaft**, *adj.* snail-like; as slow as a snail. **–nhorn**, *n.* feeler, horn (*of a snail*). **–nkegel**, *m.* fusee (*Horol.*). **–nlehre**, *f.* conchology. **–nlinie**, *f.* spiral, helix. **–nmuschel**, *f.* conch-shell. **–npost**, *f.* snail's pace. **–nrad**, *n.* worm-wheel. **–ntempo**, *n.* snail's pace. **–ntreppe**, *f.* spiral *or* winding staircase. **–ntrieb**, *m.* endless screw. **–nwelle**, *f.* worm-shaft.

Schnee, *m.* snow; *Eiweiß zu – schlagen*, beat the white of egg to a froth. **–ammer**, *f.* snow-bunting (*Plectrophenax nivalis*) (*Orn.*). **–ball**, *m.* (*pl.* –bälle) snowball; (*pl.* –ballen) guelder-rose (*Viburnum*) (*Bot.*). **–ballen**, *v.a.* & *r.* (*insep.*) (*aux.* h.) snowball. (*C.L.*) **–ballsystem**, *n.* cumulative returns. **–bedeckt**, *adj.* snow-capped (*of mountains*). **–beere**, *f.* snow-berry (*Symphoricarpus racemosus*) (*Bot.*). **–berg**, *m.* snow-capped mountain. **–blindheit**, *f.* snow-blindness. **–brille**, *f.* dark glasses, snow-goggles. **–eule**, *f.* large white owl (*Nyctea scandiaca*) (*Orn.*). **–flocke**, *f.* snowflake. **–gans**, *f.* snow-goose (*Anser caerulescens*) (*Orn.*); (*fam.*) silly goose. **–gestöber**, *n.* snow flurry. **–glöckchen**, *n.* snowdrop (*Galanthus nivalis*) (*Bot.*). **–grenze**, *f.* snow line. **–hase**, *m.* Alpine hare (*Lepus timidus*) (*Zool.*). **–huhn**, *n.* ptarmigan (*Lagopus lagopus*) (*Orn.*). **–ig**, *adj.* snowy, snow-covered. **–kette**, *f.* non-skid chain (*Motor.*). **–könig**, *m.* (*dial.*) wren; (*coll.*) *sich freuen wie ein –könig*, be as merry as a lark *or* cricket. **–koppe**, *f.*, *see* **–kuppe**. **–kufe**, *f.* landing skid (*Av.*). **–kuppe**, *f.* snow-capped summit. **–lawine**, *f.* avalanche. **–mann**, *m.* snowman. **–pflug**, *m.* snow-plough. **–schipper**, *m.* snow-sweeper. **–schläger**, *m.* whisk (*Cook.*). **–schmelze**, *f.* thaw. **–schuh**, *m.* snow-shoe, ski. **–schüpper**, *m.*, *see* **–schipper**. **–sturm**, *m.*, **–treiben**, *n.* snowstorm, blizzard. **–wächte**, *f.*, *see* **–wehe**. **–wasser**, *n.* melted snow, slush. **–wehe**, *f.* snow-drift. **–weiß**, *adj.* & *n.* snow-white. **–wetter**, *n.* snowy weather; snowstorm. **–wittchen**, *n.* Snow White (*fairy tale*).

Schnegel, *m.* (*dial.*) slug.

Schneid, *m.* (& *dial. f.*) energy, pluck, dash. **–ig**, *adj.* energetic, spirited, dashing, plucky. **–igkeit**, *f.* energy, smartness, dash.

Schneid–e, *f.* (-n) edge (*of a knife, etc.*), cutting edge, knife edge; sharpness, keenness, cut; *auf des Messers –*, at a critical juncture, hanging by a thread. **–en**, 1. *ir.v.a.* & *n.* (*aux.* h.) cut, mow, trim, carve, engrave; interest; *einen –en*, cut a p. (dead); *mit der Dame –en*, finesse the queen (*Cards*); *eine Ecke –en*, cut (off) a corner; *Fleisch –en*, carve meat; *ins lebendige Fleisch –en*, cut to the quick; *Fratzen –en*, pull *or* make faces; *ein Gesicht* or *Gesichter* or *Grimassen –en*, see *Fratzen –en*; *sich die Haare –en lassen*, have one's hair cut; *das –et mir ins Herz*, that cuts me to the heart; *in Holz –en*, carve (in) wood; *einem Mädchen die Kur –en*, pay court to a girl; *sich* (*Dat.*) *die Nägel –en*, cut one's nails; *einem den Stein –en*, operate on a p. for stone (*Surg.*); *ein Tier –en*, castrate an animal; *er ist seinem Vater wie aus den Augen* or *dem Gesicht geschnitten*, he is the very image of his father. 2. *v.r.* intersect, meet; (*fig.*) make a mistake, be mistaken, be disappointed; *sich in den Finger –en*, cut one's finger; *die Linien –en sich*, the lines intersect. **–backen**, *m.pl.* screw-dies. **–ebock**, *m.* chopping-block. **–ebohnen**, *f.pl.* French beans. **–brenner**, *m.* cutting-torch. **–ebrett**, *n.* cutting- *or* chopping-board. **–eisen**, *n.* cutting- *or* edge-tool; die. **–eleder**, *n.* sole-leather. **–eln**, *v.a.* & *n.* prune, lop, trim. **–emühle**, *f.* saw-mill. **–end**, *pr.p.* & *adj.* cutting, sharp, keen, piercing; glaring, biting, penetrating, striking; bitter, sarcastic. **–er**, *m.* tailor; cutter; (*fig.*) poltroon; shepherd-spider (*Ent.*); *aus dem –er heraus kommen*, gain more than half the points (*Bill.*, *Cards*); (*coll.*) *sie ist aus dem –er*, she will not see thirty again; (*coll.*) *wir froren wie die –er*, we were awfully cold. **–erei**, *f.* tailoring (*for men*); dressmaking (*for ladies*). **–erin**, *f.* dressmaker, tailoress. **–ern**, *v.n.* (*aux.* h.) do tailoring *or* dressmaking. **–erpuppe**, *f.* tailor's dummy. **–erseele**, *f.* timorous spirit. **–ervogel**, *m.* tailor-bird (*Orthotomus*) (*Orn.*). **–ewerkzeug**, *n.* cutting tool. **–ezahn**, *m.* incisor. **–ezeug**, *n.* cutting *or* edge-tools. **–kluppe**, *f.* die-stock. **–kopf**, *m.* die-head.

schneien, *v.n.* (*aux.* h. & s.) snow; *es hat viel geschneit*, it has snowed heavily; (*coll.*) *er ist uns ins Haus geschneit*, he dropped in on us.

Schneise, *f.* (-n) cutting, ride, aisle (*in a forest*); lane (*Mil.*); flying-lane (*Av.*).

schneiteln, *v.a.* lop, prune, trim.

schnell, *adj.* rapid, swift, fast, quick, speedy; prompt, sudden, hasty, brisk; presto (*Mus.*); (*C.L.*) *–er Umsatz*, rapid turnover; *–er Strom*, swift stream; *–er Verkauf*, brisk sale; *–e Zahlung*, prompt payment. **–ablaß**, *m.* quick-release. **–bahn**, *f.* high-speed railway. **–binder**, *m.* quick-setting cement. **–bleiche**, *f.* chemical bleaching. **–boot**, *n.* speedboat. **–brücke**, *f.* portable bridge. **–büfett**, *n.* snack-bar. **–drehlegierung**, *f.* high-speed alloy. **–e**, *f.* (-en) rapids; (*no pl.*) *see* **–igkeit**. **–en**, 1. *v.n.* (*aux.* s.) spring, snap, fly back *or* off with a jerk; *in die Höhe –en*, shoot into the air, fly *or* tip up. 2. *v.a.* fling, let fly; toss, flick, jerk, dart; snap one's fingers; (*fig.*) bamboozle, diddle, cheat. **–er**, *m.* snap of the finger; mordant (*Mus.*); trigger (*of crossbow*); (*dial.*) marble (*toy*). **–feuer**, *n.* rapid fire, running fire (*Mil.*). **–feuergeschütz**, *n.* quick-firing gun, pom-pom. **–flüssig**, *adj.* easily *or* readily fusible. **–füßig**, *adj.* swift(-footed), nimble. **–ganggetriebe**, *n.* high-speed gear box (*Motor.*). **–gericht**, *n.* summary court. **–hefter**, *m.* letter-file. **–igkeit**, *f.* velocity, swiftness, speed, dispatch, rapidity, quickness. **–igkeitsmesser**, *m.* speedometer. **–igkeitsprüfung**, *f.* speed trial *or* test. **–käfer**, *m.* click beetle (*Elateridae*) (*Ent.*). **–kochtopf**, *m.* pressure-cooker. **–kraft**, *f.* elasticity. **–(l)ader**, *m.* quick-firing gun, pom-pom. **–(l)auf**, *m.* sprint. **–(l)aufend**, *adj.* high-speed, fast-running. **–(l)ot**, *n.* soft solder. **–post**, *f.* express mail. **–presse**, *f.* mechanical press. **–richter**, *m.* magistrate with power of summary jurisdiction (*Law*). **–schrift**, *f.* (*archaic*) shorthand, stenography. **–schritt**, *m.* quick march (*Mil.*). **–sein**, *n.* promptitude. **–steg**, *m.*, *see* **–brücke**. **–trocknend**, *adj.* quick-drying. **–truppen**, *f.* mobile task force. **–verfahren**, *n.* summary jurisdiction (*Law*). **–waage**, *f.* steelyard. **–zug**, *m.* express train.

Schnepfe, *f.* (-n) snipe, woodcock (*Scolopacidae*) (*Orn.*); (*vulg.*) prostitute. **–ndreck**, *m.* roast giblets (of snipe *or* woodcock). **–nfang**, *m.*, **–njagd**, *f.* snipe-shooting. **–nstrich**, *m.*, **–nzug**, *m.* flight *or* passage of snipe.

Schneppe, *f.* (-n) nozzle, spout, lip; peak (*of a cap*); prostitute; (*dial.*), *see* **Schnepfe**.

Schnepper, *m.* (*Austr. dial.*) *see* **Schnäpper**.

Schnerfer, *m.* (*Austr. dial.*) rucksack.

schneuzen, 1. *v.a.* snuff (*a candle*). 2. *v.r.* blow one's nose.

Schnickschnack, *m.* chit-chat, tittle-tattle.

schniegeln, *v.r.* (*coll.*) dress up, deck o.s. out; *geschniegelt und gebügelt*, spick and span.

Schniepel, *m.* (-s, -) (*coll.*) tailcoat, tails; fop, dandy.

Schnipfel, *m.* (*dial.*) shred, scrap. **–n**, *v.a.* shred, cut up, slice.

schnipp, *int.* snip! flip! flick! **–chen**, *n.* snap of the fingers; *einem ein –chen schlagen*, play a trick on a p., outdo a p. **–el**, *m.* & *n.* (*coll.*) shred, scrap, slice. **–eln**, *v.a.* shred, cut up, slice. **–en**, *v.a.*

& *n.* snap one's fingers; flip, jerk. **–isch,** *adj.* saucy, impertinent, cheeky, pert. **–seln,** *v.a.* (*coll.*), *see* **–en.**

Schnips–el, *n.*, **–eln,** *v.a.* (*coll.*), *see* **Schnipp–el, –eln. –en,** (*dial.*) *see* **schnippen.**

Schnitt, *m.* (-(e)s, -e) cut; cutting, slice, incision, section, intersection; bearing; operation; form, shape, contour, silhouette; reaping, crop, harvest; (paper) pattern, model; edge(s) (*of a book*); (*dial.*) small glass (*of beer*); *der goldene –*, medial section; *seinen – bei* or *an einer S. machen*, make a profit out of a th., get one's cut. **–blumen,** *f.pl.* cut flowers. **–bohne,** *f.* French bean. **–brenner,** *m.* fantail burner. **–dicke,** *f.* thickness of sections. **–e,** *f.* cut, slice (*of bread, etc.*); chop, steak. **–er,** *m.* harvester, reaper, mower. **–fest,** *adj.* firm enough to cut (*as tomatoes*). **–fläche,** *f.* sectional plane *or* area. **–handel,** *m.* drapery-trade. **–holz,** *n.* sawed *or* cut timber. **–kurve,** *f.* intersecting curve. **–ig,** *adj.* racy, streamlined, smart. **–lauch,** *m.* chive (*Bot.*). **–linie,** *f.* secant; intersecting line. **–ling,** *m.* cutting (*Bot.*). **–muster,** *n.* (paper) pattern (*to cut from*). **–punkt,** *m.* point of intersection. **–reif,** *adj.* ready for reaping. **–waren,** *f.pl.* drapery, (*Amer.*) dry goods, haberdashery. **–weise,** *adv.* in slices, cut by cut. **–wunde,** *f.* cut, gash.

schnitt, schnitte, *see* **schneiden.**

Schnitz, *m.* (-es, -e) (*dial.*) slice, cut; chop, cutlet, steak. **–arbeit,** *f.* wood-carving. **–el,** *n.* chip, scrap, shred, slice; (*pl.*) clippings, parings, shavings; *Wiener –el*, fillet of veal, veal cutlet. **–elei,** *f.* cutting, carving. **–eljagd,** *f.* paper-chase. **–elmaschine,** *f.* slicer, shredder. **–eln,** *v.a.* & *n.* (*aux.* h.) carve, whittle, chip, cut finely. **–en,** *v.a.* & *n.* (*aux.* h.) carve, cut. **–er,** *m.* wood-carver; carving-knife; (*coll.*) blunder, mistake, howler. **–erei,** *f.* wood-carving; piece of carved wood. **–ern,** *v.n.* blunder. **–holz,** *n.* wood for carving. **–kunst,** *f.* wood-carving. **–messer,** *n.* wood-carving tool. **–werk,** *n.* wood-carving, carved work.

schnob, schnöbe, *see* **schnauben.**

schnobern, *v.n.*, *see* **schnuppern.**

schnodd(e)rig, *adj.* (*coll.*) pert, cheeky, insolent, **–keit,** *f.* pertness, insolence, cheek.

schnöd–(e), *adj.* base, mean, vile, despicable, iniquitous; insolent, disdainful, scornful, unfriendly; *–es Geld*, filthy lucre; *–er Gewinn*, indecent profit; *–er Undank*, base ingratitude.

Schnorchel, *m.* air inlet, breathing tube, (*sl.*) snort (*on submarines*).

Schnörkel, *m.* (-s, –) florid ornament; flourish (*in writing*); scroll, volute (*Arch.*). **–ei,** *f.* flourishes, superfluous ornamentation. **–haft,** *adj.* full of flourishes, loaded with ornament; (*fig.*) capricious, whimsical. **–n,** *v.n.* (*aux.*) make flourishes; adorn with scrolls, *etc.*

schnorre–n, *v.n.* (*aux.* h.) (*coll.*) cadge. (*coll.*) **–r,** *m.* cadger; tramp.

schnorz, schnurz, *adj.* (*dial.*) *das ist mir ganz –*, much I care! that leaves me cold.

Schnuck–e, *f.* (-en) kind of small sheep. (*coll.*) **–elchen,** *n.*, **–i,** *n.* darling, pet.

schnuffeln, *v.n.* (*aux.* h.) smell, sniff, snuffle.

schnüff–eln, *v.n.* snoop (about); *see also* **schnuffeln. –ler,** *m.* sniffer, snuffler; snooper.

schnull–en, *v.n.* & *a.* (*coll.*) suck. **–er,** *m.* rubber teat, dummy, comforter.

Schnupf–en, 1. *m.* (-ens, -en) cold in the head, catarrh; *den –en bekommen, sich* (*Dat.*) *einen –en holen*, catch cold. 2. *v.a.* & *n.* (*aux.* h.) sniff up, take snuff. **–enfieber,** *n.* feverish cold. **–tabak,** *m.* snuff. **–tuch,** *n.* (*dial.*) pocket-handkerchief.

Schnuppe, 1. *f.* (-n) snuff (*of a candle*); shooting-star. 2. *adj.*; (*coll.*) *das ist mir* (*ganz* or *total*) *–!* it's all the same to me, I don't care a rap. **–rn,** *v.n.* (*aux.* h.) (*dial.*) sniff, smell out, snoop.

[1]**Schnur,** *f.* (⸚e & -en) string, cord, twine; flex (*Elec.*); string of beads; braid, piping; *nach der –*, straight as a die; *nach der – leben*, be strictly methodical; *mit Schnüren besetzen*, lace, braid; trim; *über die – hauen*, overstep the line, kick over the traces. **–besatz,** *m.* braid trimming. **–gerade,** *adj.* dead-straight, as straight as a die. **–lauf,** *m.* groove (*of a pulley*). **–scheibe,** *f.* grooved wheel *or* pulley. **–stracks,** *adv.* straight(way), immediately, directly; at once; *–stracks zuwider*, diametrically opposed.

[2]**Schnur,** *f.* (-en & ⸚e) (*B.*) daughter-in-law.

schnür–en, 1. *v.a.* tie, tie up, tie with string, string, cord, lace, strap, fasten; (*fig.*) tighten, constrict; *das –t mir das Herz zusammen*, that wrings my heart; *sein Bündel –en*, pack up one's traps. 2. *v.r.*; *sich –en*, wear stays. **–band,** *n.* boot-lace; string with a tag. **–boden,** *m.* rigging-loft, grid-iron (*Theat.*); sail-loft (*Naut.*). **–brust,** *f.* *see* **–leib. –bund,** *m.* lashing (*of spars*). **–chen,** *n.*; *wie am* or *nach dem –chen gehen*, go like clockwork; *am –chen haben*, have at one's fingers' ends; *einen am –chen haben*, have s.o. on a bit of string *or* under one's thumb. **–latz,** *m.* stomacher. **–leib,** *m.*, **–leibchen,** *n.* stays, corset. **–loch,** *n.* eyelet. **–nadel,** *f.* bodkin; tag. **–riemen,** *m.* lace, strap. **–schuh,** *m.* lace-up shoe. **–senkel,** *m.* boot-lace. **–stiefel,** *m.* laced boot. **–stift,** *m.* tag.

schnurpsen, *v.n.* (*aux.* h.) (*dial.*) munch noisily, chobble.

Schnurr–ant, *m.* (-en, -en) street-musician. **–bart,** *m.* moustache. **–bärtig,** *adj.* moustached, with a moustache. **–e,** *f.* (-en) funny tale, joke, quip; piece of nonsense; humming-top; old hag. **–en,** 1. *v.n.* (*aux.* h. & s.) hum, buzz, whirr, whizz, purr; go about begging; *Katzen –en*, cats purr. 2. *v.a.* cadge; *Vorlesungen –en*, gate-crash lectures. **–er,** *m.* beggar, tramp. **–ig,** *adj.* droll, funny, quaint, queer, odd. **–pfeiferei,** *f.* (*dial.*) worthless knick-knack, trash, twaddle; prank.

Schnute, *f.* (*dial., coll.*), *see* **Schnauze.**

schob, schöbe, *see* **schieben.**

Schober, *m.* (-s, –) stack, rick; barn; measure = 60 bundles *or* bottles (*of straw, etc.*). **–n** (*also* **schöbern**) *v.a.* stack, pile (*hay*).

[1]**Schock,** *n.* (-(e)s, -e & –) heap, shock; three-score; a (large) quantity; mass, lot; *zwei –*, six-score. **–en,** 1. *v.a.* count by sixties; place in heaps of sixty. 2. *v.n.* (*aux.* h.) yield in abundance. **–schwerenot,** *int.* damn and blast! **–weise,** *adv.* by threescores; in bundles, in heaps *or* masses.

[2]**Schock,** *m.* shock. **–ant,** *adj.* shocking, disgraceful, improper. **–ieren,** *v.a.* shock, offend.

Schof–el, (*vulg.*) 1. *m.* (-s, –) trash, refuse, rubbish. 2. *adj.* **–lig,** *adj.* paltry, worthless, mean; shabby.

Schöffe, *m.* (-n, -n) (*archaic*) juror, juryman. **–ngericht,** *n.* lay assessor's court; court of jurors, judge and jury.

schok–ant, –ieren, *see* **schock–ant, –ieren.**

Schokolade, *f.* (-n) chocolate. **–n,** *adj.* chocolate. **–nfarben,** *adj.* chocolate-coloured. **–ntafel,** *f.* slab of chocolate.

Schol–ar, *m.* (-en, -en) scholar, medieval student. **–arch,** *m.* (-en, -en) school-inspector; headmaster. **–astik,** *f.* scholastic; (*pl.*) the Schoolmen. **–ie,** *f.* (-n), **–ion,** *n.* (-ions, -ien) scholium, comment, annotation.

scholl, schölle, *see* **schallen.**

[1]**Scholl–e,** *f.* (-en) clod, sod; flake, layer, stratum; floe (*of ice*); (*fig.*) soil, homeland; *an der –e haften*, be tied *or* bound to the soil; *Liebe zur –e*, love of the soil. **–ern,** *v.n.* (*aux.* h. & s.) thud, tumble. **–ig,** *adj.* lumpy, cloddy, heavy (*of soil*).

[2]**Scholle,** *f.* (-n) flat fish (*Pleuronectidae*), flounder, plaice.

Schöllkraut, *n.* (-es, ⸚er), *see* **Schellkraut.**

schölte, *see* **schelten.**

schon, *adv.* & *part.* already, as yet, by this time, so far; certainly, surely, indeed, no doubt, after all; *– der Name*, the bare *or* very name; *– den folgenden Morgen*, the very next morning; *es gibt des Elends so – genug*, there is enough misery in the world as it is; *– gut!* all right! very well; *– lange*, long ago; (*coll.*) *mach –!* get a move on! *er mußte – bekennen*, he could not help confessing; *sind Sie – in London gewesen?* have you been in London yet? *das ist – wahr, aber*, that is quite true, but; *– wegen, – weil*, just because; *und wenn – !* even so! and what then? *wenn es – wahr ist*, even though it be true; *wenn –, denn –* or *wenn – dann ordentlich* or *gründlich*, what is worth doing at all is worth doing well; *es wird – gehen*, I am sure it will be all right; *er wird – wissen*, no doubt he will know; *was ist (es) – wieder?* what is it again?

schön, 1. *adj.* beautiful, lovely, fair, handsome; fine, nice; *–e Augen machen*, make sheep's eyes; *eine –e Bescherung*, a pretty kettle of fish, a fine how-do-you-do; *bitte –*, if you please; *danke –! –en Dank!* many thanks; *das –e Geschlecht*, the fair sex; *die –en Künste*, the fine arts; *–e Literatur*, belles lettres; *– machen*, beautify, do up; *see* **–machen**; *sich – machen*, smarten o.s. up, titivate o.s.; *manch –es Mal*, many a time; *das sind (mir) –e Sachen!* (*iron.*) fine goings-on indeed! *–e Seele*, sentimentalist, enthusiast; devotee; *– tun*, do nicely *or* beautifully; *see* **–tun**; *die –e Welt*, the fashionable world; *–e Wissenschaften*, belles lettres; *das wäre ja noch –er*, that would beat everything! impossible! 2. *adv.* very, exceedingly, nicely; *halte dich – warm*, keep yourself nice and warm; *grüßen Sie ihn –stens von mir*, give him my kindest regards; *da sind wir – daran!* well, we are in a nice fix! *das werde ich – bleiben lassen*, I shall take good care not to do that; *Sie haben – lachen*, it is all very well for you to laugh; *er wird sich – erschrecken!* he will get a nice fright. **–e**, 1. *n.* the beautiful; *das –e an diesem Stücke*, what is beautiful in *or* the beauty of this piece; *das ist was –es!* that is fine *or* splendid. *Sie werden was –es von mir denken!* you will have a nice opinion of me! *da haben Sie etwas –es angerichtet*, you have made a fine mess *or* hash of it! 2. *f.* (-en) (*Poet.*) beauty, beautiful woman; (*Poet.*) *see* **–heit**. **–bartspiel**, *see* **Schembartspiel**. **–druck**, *m.* primer (*Typ.*). **–en**, *v.a.* refine, clarify; beautify; brighten, gloss. **–färben**, *v.a.* dye (*clothing*); (*fig.*) gloss over, put in a favourable light. **–färber**, *m.* dyer; (*fig.*) one inclined to a rosy view of things, optimist. **–färberei**, *f.* dyeing; colouring, embellishment; optimism. **–geist**, *m.* bel esprit, aesthete. **–geisterei**, *f.* pretension to wit *or* culture. **–geistig**, *adj.* aesthetic; literary; affecting literary ways. **–heit**, *f.* beauty, fineness; beauty, belle; (*pl.*) compliments. **–heitskonkurrenz**, *f.* beauty contest. **–heitslehre**, *f.* aesthetics. **–heitsmittel**, *n.* cosmetic. **–heitspflästerchen**, *n.* beauty-patch. **–heitspflege**, *f.* beauty treatment *or* culture. **–heitswasser**, *n.* complexion wash, cosmetic. **–machen**, *v.n.* beg, sit up (*of a dog*). **–redend**, *adj.* fine-spoken, flattering. **–redner**, *m.* speechifier, spouter, (*iron.*) fine talker. **–schreiben**, *n.* calligraphy. **–schreiber**, *m.* calligraphist. **–schreibheft**, *n.* copy book. **–tuend**, *adj.* affected; coquettish, flirting. **–tuer**, *m.* poseur, affected p., fop. **–tuerei**, *f.* coquettish ways; affectation. **–tun**, *v.n.* coquet, flirt, flatter; pose, be affected. **–ungsmittel**, *n.* fining *or* brightening agent (*Metall.*). **–wissenschaftlich**, *adj.* belletristic, literary.

schon–en, 1. *v.a.* & (*archaic*) *v.n.* (*aux.* h.) (*Gen.*); treat with consideration *or* indulgence; be sparing of, save, spare, preserve, conserve, husband, economize; take (good) care of, protect, care for; manage, regulate (*woods*); *etwas nicht –en*, be prodigal of, not spare. 2. *v.r.* take care of *or* look after o.s. **–end**, *adj.* careful, considerate, sparing, tender. **–er**, *m.*, *see* **Schoner**. **–ung**, *f.* management, care; consideration, regard; indulgence, forbearance; young plantation, nursery (*for young trees*). **–ganggetriebe**, *n.* high-speed gear, overdrive. **–ungslos**, *adj.* unsparing, pitiless, relentless. **–ungsvoll**, *adj.* sparing; indulgent, considerate. **–zeit**, *f.* close season.

Schoner, *m.* (-s, –) 1. antimacassar. 2. schooner. **–bark**, *f.* barque, barquentine (*Naut.*). **–brigg**, *f.* brigantine (*Naut.*).

Schopf, *m.* (-(e)s, ⸚e) crown, top of the head; tuft of hair, forelock; crest (*of birds*); tree-top; coma (*Bot.*); (*dial.*) shed, shelter; (*coll.*) *die Gelegenheit beim –e fassen*, seize an opportunity, take time by the forelock; *einen beim –e fassen* or *nehmen*, seize s.o. by the scruff of the neck.

schöpf–en, *v.a.* draw (*water*); ladle, dip, scoop out; conceive (*suspicions*); derive, obtain (*information, etc.*); *Atem –en*, take *or* draw breath; *neue Hoffnung –en*, gather fresh hope; *Mut –en*, take courage; *Verdacht –en gegen*, harbour suspicion against a p. **–brett**, *n.* float (*of a mill-wheel*). **–brunnen**, *m.* draw-well. **–bütte**, *f.* pulp-vat (*Pap.*). **–eimer**, *m.* bucket. **–er**, *m.* drawer (*of water*); scoop, ladle, dipper; maker, creator, author, originator. **–erisch**, *adj.* creative, generative, productive. **–ergeist**, *m.* creative genius. **–erhand**, *f.* hand of the creator, creative touch. **–erkraft**, *f.* creative power *or* energy. **–gefäß**, *n.*, **–gelte**, *f.*, **–kelle**, *f.*, **–löffel**, *m.* scoop, dipper, bailer, basting ladle. **–rad**, *n.* bucket *or* well-wheel. **–ung**, *f.* creation; the universe, created things; production; *die Herren der –ung*, (*iron.*) the lords of creation, men. **–ungsgeschichte**, *f.* (**–ungssage**, *f.*) history (myth) of (the) creation, genesis. **–werk**, *n.* hydraulic machine, water-engine.

Schöppe, *m.* (-n, -n) (*dial.*) *see* **Schöffe**.

schöppel–n, *v.n.* (*coll.*) tipple; *er –t gern*, he likes his little drink.

[1]**Schoppen**, *m.* (*dial.*), *see* **Schuppen**.

[2]**Schoppen**, *m.* (-s, –) half a pint; *ein – Bier*, a glass of beer.

Schöps, *m.* (-es, -e) wether, mutton; (*fig.*) simpleton. **–drehe**, *f.* (*coll.*) *da kriegt man die –drehe*, it makes you giddy. **–enbraten**, *m.* roast mutton. **–enfleisch**, *n.* mutton. **–entalg**, *m.* mutton suet. **–ig**, *adj.* (*dial.*) stupid.

schor, schöre, *see* **scheren**.

Schore, *f.* (-n) prop, support, shore (*Naut.*); (*dial.*) spade.

Schorf, *m.* (-(e)s, -e) scab, scurf. **–ig**, *adj.* scabby, scurfy.

Schörl, *m.* (-(e)s, -e) schorl, black tourmaline.

Schorlemorle, *n.* (-s, -s) & *f.* (-n) wine and water mixed.

Schornstein, *m.* (-s, -e) chimney, flue; funnel, smoke-stack; (*coll.*) *eine Schuld in den – schreiben*, dismiss as a bad debt, drop *or* write off a claim. **–aufsatz**, *m.* chimney-pot. **–brand**, *m.* chimney on fire. **–feger**, *m.* chimney-sweep. **–kappe**, *f.* chimney-pot. **–kasten**, *m.* chimney-stack.

schoß, schösse, *see* **schießen**.

[1]**Schoß** [*pron.* ʃɔs] (-(ss)es, -(ss)e(n) & (ss)⸚e(r)) sprig, shoot, sprout, scion; (*archaic*) tax, impost. **–frei**, *adj.* scot-free; immune from taxation. **–kelle**, *f.* driver's seat (*of coach*); luggage rack (*on coach*). **–reis**, *n.*, *see* **Schößling**.

[2]**Schoß** [*pron.* ʃo:s] *m.* (-es, ⸚e) lap; (*poet.*) womb; (*fig.*) bosom; coat-tail; *es ist ihm in den – gefallen*, it fell into his lap; *die Hände in den – legen*, fold one's arms, twiddle one's thumbs, do nothing, be idle; *im –e seiner Familie*, in the bosom of his family; *im –e der Kirche*, within the pale *or* bosom of the Church; *das ruht im –e der Götter*, that lies in the lap of the gods. **–bein**, *n.* os pubis (*Anat.*). **–hund**, *m.* lapdog, pet dog. **–kind**, *n.* pet, darling, spoiled child. **–kissenfallschirm**, *m.* lap-pack *or* -type parachute.

Schößling, *m.* (-s, -e) shoot, sprig, sprout, scion; sucker; stripling.

Schot, *f.* (-e), **–e**, *f.* (-en) sheet (*Naut.*). **–horn**, *n.* clew (*of sail*).

[1]**Schote**, *f.* (-n) pod, husk, shell, cod; (*pl.*) green peas. **–ndorn**, *m.* acacia. **–nerbsen**, *f.pl.* peas in the pod. **–nförmig**, *adj.* pod-shaped. **–nfrucht**, *f.* legume, pod. **–nfrüchtig**, *adj.* leguminous. **–ngewächse**, *n.pl.* leguminous plants. **–npfeffer**, *m.* capsicum, red pepper.

[2]**Schote**, *m.* (-n, -n) (*coll.*) fool.

Schott, *n.* (-(e)s, -e), **–e**, *f.* (-en) bulkhead (*Naut.*). **–(t)üre**, *f.* water-tight doors.

Schotte, *f.*, **–n**, *m.* (*dial.*) whey.

Schotter, *m.* (-s, –) road-metal; ballast (*Railw.*); broken stone, rubble, gravel. **–bahn**, *f.* macadamized *or* metalled road. **–n**, *v.a.* metal (*road*); macadamize. **–ung**, *f.* metalling; broken-stone ballast.

Schraff–e, *f.* *see* **–ur**. (*pl.* –en, hachures). **–en**, *m.* (*dial.*) *see* **Schramme**. **–ieren**, *v.a.* & *n.* (*aux.* h.) hatch, hachure. **–ierung**, *f.*, **–ur**, *f.* hatching (*in drawing, etc.*).

schräg, *adj.* slanting, inclined, sloping; diagonal, oblique, transverse; bevelled; *der –e Durchschnitt eines Kegels*, the oblique conic section; **–e**

Ebene, inclined plane. **-aufnahme,** *f.* oblique photograph. **-balken,** *m.* bar, bend (*Her.*). **-e,** *f.*, *see* **-heit. -en,** *v.a.* slant, slope, bevel. **-entfernung,** *f.* slant range. **-feuer,** *n.* oblique *or* flanking fire, enfilade (*Mil.*). **-heit,** *f.* obliquity, inclination, slope, slant, bevel. **-kante,** *f.* chamfer, bezel. **-kreuz,** *n.* saltire (*Her.*). **-lage,** *f.* sloping position. **-laufend,** *adj.* diagonal. **-linie,** *f.* diagonal. **-maß,** *n.* bevel-rule. **-schrift,** *f.* sloping (style of) writing. **-stellen,** *v.a.* incline, tilt. **-über,** *adv.* almost opposite, across.

Schragen, 1. *m.* (-s, –) trestle, frame, jack; stack (*of wood*). 2. *v.a.* joint (*beams*) slantwise (*Carp.*).

schrak, *see* **schrecken.**

schral, *adj.* weak, unfavourable (*of wind*) (*Naut.*).

Schram, *m.* (-(e)s, ⸚e) holing (*Min.*). **-en,** *v.a.* hole, cut through (*Min.*).

Schramm-e, *f.* (-en) scratch, graze, abrasion, scar. **-en,** *v.a.* scratch, graze, scar. **-stein,** *m.* kerb-(stone).

Schrammel-musik, *f.* popular Viennese music. **-quartett,** *n.* tavern band (*two violins, guitar, and accordion*).

Schrank, *m.* (-(e)s, ⸚e) 1. cupboard, locker, cabinet, bookcase, press, wardrobe; 2. lateral spacing of footprints (*Hunt.*). 3. set (*of a saw*). **-en,** *m.* (*dial.*), *see* **–. -koffer,** *m.* wardrobe-trunk.

Schranke, *f.* (-n) barrier; level-crossing gate, fence, turnpike, toll-bar; limit, boundary, bound; arena, enclosure; (*pl.*) lists; bar (*Law*); *die –n überschreiten*, go beyond (all) bounds; *die –n einhalten, in den –n bleiben*, keep within bounds; *sich in –n halten*, restrain o.s., keep within bounds; *einer S. –n setzen*, set bounds *or* limits to a th.; *in die –n treten*, enter the lists; *in die –n fordern*, defy, provoke, challenge; *vor den –n*, at the bar, before a jury; *–n ziehen*, draw a line, set limits. **-nlos,** *adj.* unbounded, boundless; unbridled, unrestrained. **-nlosigkeit,** *f.* boundlessness; licentiousness. **-nwärter,** *m.* gate-man, signalman (*Railw.*). **-nwerk,** *n.* barrier, railing, fencing.

schränk-en, *v.a.* put crosswise, cross (*one's legs*); fold (*one's arms*); set (*a saw*); *geschränkte Zähne*, cross-cut teeth (*of a saw*). **-eisen,** *n.* saw-set. **-ung,** *f.* setting (*of a saw*); offset; variation in angle of incidence (*Av.*). **-weise,** *adv.* crosswise.

Schranne, *f.* (-n) (*archaic*) (*dial.*) baker's *or* butcher's stall; corn-market. **-nhalle,** *f.* market-hall.

Schranz(e), *m.* (-en, -en), **-e,** *f.* (-en) (*usually* **Hofschranz(e)**) flunkey; parasite, sycophant, lickspittle; (*coll.*) hanger-on. **-en,** *v.n.* be servile, toady, (*sl.*) crawl, creep.

Schrape, *f.* (-n) (*dial.*) scraper. **-n,** *v.a.* scrape.

Schrapnell, *n.* (-s, -e & (*Austr. dial.*) -s) shrapnel.

schrapp-en, *v.a.* & *n.* (*dial.*), *see* **schrapen. -e,** *f.*, **-eisen,** *n.*, *see* **Schrape. -er,** *m.* scraper; niggard, skinflint.

schrat, *adj.* (*dial.*) *see* **schräg. -segel,** *n.* loose-footed sail.

Schrat(t), *m.* (-(e)s, -e) faun, satyr, hobgoblin, imp.

Schrät(t)el, *m.*, *see* **Schrat(t).**

Schraub-deckel, *m.* screw cap, screwed lid. **-e,** *f.* (-en) (screw) bolt, screw (*also Naut.*); airscrew, propeller (*Av.*); (*coll.*) *alte –e*, old maid, gushing female; *Doppel–e*, double-threaded screw; *linksgängige –e*, left-handed screw; *eingelassene –e*, countersunk screw; *–e ohne Ende*, endless screw; (*fig.*) endless business; *bei ihm ist eine –e los*, he has a screw loose. **-en,** *reg.* & *ir.v.a.* screw; *einen –en*, mock, quiz *or* tease a p.; *einen um sein Geld –en*, cheat a p. out of his money; *seine Hoffnungen niedriger –en*, lower one's expectations, come down a peg; *seinen Stil –en*, adopt a high-flown style; *feine Worte –en*, write *or* speak in a stilted way; *den Preis hinauf–en*, force up the price. *geschraubt*, *p.p.* & *adj.* screwed, *etc.*; forced, unnatural, bombastic. **-enachse,** *f.*, *see* **-enwelle. -enartig,** *adj.* spiral, helical. **-enbakterie,** *f.* spirillum. **-enbohrer,** *m.* screw-auger, twist drill; screw-tap. **-enboot,** *n.* screw-driven boat. **-enfeder,** *f.* coil spring. **-enflasche,** *f.* screw-topped bottle. **-enflügel,** *m.* blade (*of propeller or screw*). **-enflugzeug,** *n.* autogyro, helicopter. **-enförmig,** *adj.* screw-shaped, spiral, helical. **-engang,** *m.* pitch of a screw. **-engewinde,** *n.* screw thread. **-enkopf,** *m.* screw-head. **-enmutter,** *f.* female screw, nut. **-enrad,** *n.* worm-wheel. **-enschlüssel,** *m.* spanner, wrench; *englischer –enschlüssel*, monkey-wrench, adjustable spanner. **-enschneidbank,** *f.* screw-cutting lathe. **-enspindel,** *f.* jack-screw. **-ensteigung,** *f.* pitch of a screw. **-enstrahl,** *m.* slipstream (*Av.*). **-enwelle,** *f.* propeller-shaft. **-enwinde,** *f.* screw-jack. **-enwindung,** *f.* spiral turn. **-enzange,** *f.* hand-vice. **-enzieher,** *m.* screwdriver. **-ig,** *adj.* screwed. **-stock,** *m.* (-(es)s, ⸚e) (bench-)vice. **-zwinge,** *f.* screw-clamp, cramp.

Schreber-garten, *m.* (-s, ⸚) allotment, smallholding. **-gärtner,** *m.* allotment holder.

Schreck, *m.* (-(e)s, -e); *see* **-en** 3. **-bar,** *adj.* fearful, easily frightened, timid. **-bild,** *n.*, *see* **-gestalt. -e,** *f.*, *see* **Heuschrecke. -en,** 1. *v.a.* frighten, startle, alarm, terrify; frighten away; chill; (*dial.*) crack. 2. *ir.v.n.* (*aux.* s.) be afraid, become frightened; *see* **erschrecken**; be chilled suddenly; crack. 3. *m.* (-s, –) fright, scare, terror, fear, horror, dread; (*dial.*) crack (*in glass, etc.*); *jemandem einen –en einflößen* or *einjagen*, strike terror into a p.; *in –en setzen*, terrify, dismay; *der –en ist mir in die Glieder gefahren*, I was paralysed with fear. **-ensbleich,** *adj.* pale with fright. **-ensbote,** *m.* bearer of evil tidings. **-ensbotschaft,** *f.* terrible news. **-ensherrschaft,** *f.* reign of terror. **-enskammer,** *f.* Chamber of Horrors. **-enskind,** *n.* enfant terrible. **-enstat,** *f.* atrocity. **-gespenst,** *n.*, **-gestalt,** *f.*, apparition, phantom; bogy, bugbear. **-haft,** *adj.* nervous, frightened, timid. **-haftigkeit,** *f.* timidity, nervousness. **-ladung,** *f.* booby trap. **-lich,** *adj.* frightful, terrible, dreadful, awful, horrible, hideous; (*coll.*) tremendous, excessive. **-lichkeit,** *f.* frightfulness, horror. **-mittel,** *n.* bogy, scarecrow. **-nis,** *n.* (-ses, -se) *see* **-en,** 3. **-platte,** *f.* chill (*Metall.*). **-schuß,** *m.* shot fired in the air; (*fig.*) false alarm. **-stein,** *m.* kerb(stone).

Schrei, *m.* (-(e)s, -e) cry, shout, yell, howl, scream, shriek; *einen – tun* or *ausstoßen*, utter a cry; (*sl.*) *der letzte –*, the latest rage. **-en,** *ir.v.a.* & *n.* (*aux.* h.) cry, shout, shriek, scream; bray (*donkey*); bell (*stag*); hoot, screech (*owl*); *um Hilfe –en*, cry out for help; *aus vollem Halse –en*, call at the top of one's voice; *zum Himmel –en*, cry aloud to heaven; *–en nach* or *um*, cry for; *–en über* (*Acc.*), cry out against; (*coll.*) *das ist zum –en*, that is screamingly funny. **-end,** *pr.p.* & *adj.* crying, *etc.*; clamorous; monstrous, glaring; loud, gaudy, flagrant; *–ende Farbe*, loud colour; *–endes Unrecht*, crying shame, monstrous injustice; *–ender Gegensatz*, flagrant contradiction. **-er,** *m.* crier, bawler, ranter, complainant. **-erei,** *f.* outcry, bawling, howling, cries, clamour, hullabaloo. **-hals,** *m.*, *see* **-er**; screaming *or* howling child. **-vögel,** *m.pl.* Clamatores, screechers.

schreib-en, 1. *ir.v.a.* & *n.* (*aux.* h.) write; write down, record; *einem* or *an einen –en*, write to s.o.; *groß –en*, write with a capital letter; *ins Konzept –en*, jot down, make a rough draft *or* copy of; *zur Last –en*, debit with; (*mit der*) *Maschine –en*, typewrite; *seinen Namen darunter –en*, subscribe *or* put one's name to a th.; *Noten –en*, copy music; (*coll.*) *–en Sie sich das hinter die Ohren* or *hinters Ohr*, take that to heart; *etwas auf Rechnung meiner Dummheit –en*, put s.th. down to my stupidity; *ins reine –en*, make a fair copy, write out; (*coll.*) *sage und –e*, would you believe it, believe it or not; *den wievielten –en wir heute?* what day of the month is it? *die Zeitung –t*, the newspaper says. 2. *v.r. auf diesem Papier –t es sich schlecht*, this paper is no good for writing on; *wie –en Sie sich?* how do you spell your name? what is your name? *es steht ihm auf der Stirne geschrieben*, it is *or* stands written on *or* in his face; *geschriebenes Recht*, statute law; *können Sie Geschriebenes lesen?* can you read writing? 3. *n.* writing; letter, note; (*C.L.*) *Ihr* (*geehrtes* or *geschätztes*) *–en*, your (esteemed) favour; *das –en wird mir sauer*, I am sick of writing, writing becomes a burden to me. **-art,** *f.* manner of writing, style; handwriting. **-bedarf,** *m.* writing materials. **-block,** *m.* scribbling *or* writing-pad. **-büro,** *n.* copying office, typing agency. **-(e)brief,** *m.* (*archaic*) epistle. **–buch,** *n.* copy-book, writing-book, exercise-book. **–eempfänger,** *m.* teletype receiver. **–(e)kunst,** *f.* calligraphy. **–(e)pult,** *n.* writing-desk. **–erseele,** *f.* quill-driver, pen-pusher, pedant. **–faul,** *adj.* lazy about writing (letters); *–faul sein,* be a bad correspondent. **–feder,** *f.* pen, (pen-)nib. **–fehler,** *m.* slip of the pen, typing *or* clerical error. **–fertig,** *adj.* ready to write. **–fertigkeit,** *f.* penmanship. **–gebrauch,** *m.* usual spelling, spelling convention. **–griffel,** *m.* (*Poet.*) pen. **–heft,** *n.* scribbling-jotter, exercise-book, copy-book. **–kalender,** *m.* diary, memorandum-book. **–krampf,** *m.* writer's cramp. **–lehrer,** *m.* handwriting teacher. **–lustig,** *adj.* fond of writing. **–mappe,** *f.* writing-case; blotter. **–maschine,** *f.* typewriter. **–materialien,** *pl.* stationery. **–materialienhändler,** *m.* stationer. **–materialienhandlung,** *f.* stationer's shop. **–papier,** *n.* writing- *or* note-paper. **–selig,** *adj.* fond of writing. **–stube,** *f.* office; orderly-room (*Mil.*). **–stunde,** *f.* writing-lesson. **–tafel,** *f.* slate. **–tinte,** *f.* writing-ink. **–tisch,** *m.* desk, office table. **–ung,** *f.* writing; spelling, orthography; *phonetische –ung,* phonetic script *or* transcription. **–unterlage,** *f.* blotting-pad, desk-pad. **–vorlage,** *f.* copy. **–waren,** *f.pl.* writing materials, stationery. **–warenhandlung,** *f.* stationer's shop. **–weise,** *f.* style. **–zeug,** *n.* pen and ink.

Schrein, *m.* (-(e)s, -e) cupboard; chest, case, cabinet, casket, coffer; shrine; *etwas im – des Herzens* or *der Seele bewahren,* enshrine s.th. in one's heart *or* soul. **–er,** *m.* (*dial.*) joiner, carpenter, cabinet-maker. **–erei,** *f.* (*dial.*) joinery, cabinet making; carpenter's shop. **–ern,** *v.n.* (*dial.*) do joinery.

schreiten, *ir.v.n.* (*aux.* s.) stride, step, stalk; proceed (*to do s.th.*); set about (*doing s.th.*); progress, advance; *zur Abstimmung –,* proceed to a division; *die Erzählung schritt rasch zum Schluß,* the narrative advanced to its close; *zum Äußersten –,* take extreme measures.

schricken, *v.n.* ease away (*Naut.*).

schrie, schriee, *see* **schreien.**

Schrieb, *m.* (-s, -e) (*coll.*) screed.

schrieb, schriebe, *see* **schreiben.**

Schrift, *f.* (-en) writing, handwriting, hand; letters, script, text, type, character(s), fount (*Typ.*); book, publication, paper, review, periodical, pamphlet, composition, work; tails (*on coins*); (*pl.*) writings; *Abdruck vor der –,* proof before letters, proof-impression (*Engr.*); *falsche –,* wrong fount. (*Typ.*); *die Heilige –,* the Holy Scriptures; *Kopf oder –?* heads or tails? *in lateinischer –,* in Roman characters; *Monats–,* monthly; *phonetische –,* phonetic script; *vermischte –en,* miscellaneous writings; *Vierteljahr(s)–,* quarterly; *Wochen–,* weekly. **–absatz,** *m.* paragraph. **–art,** *f.* type, fount. **–auslegung,** *f.* interpretation of the Scriptures, exegesis. **–band,** *n.* label. **–beweis,** *m.* Scriptural proof *or* evidence. **–bild,** *n.* face (*Typ.*). **–deutsch,** *n.* literary German. **–ennachweis,** *m.* list of authorities. **–forschung,** *f.* Scriptural research. **–führer,** *m.* secretary. **–garnitur,** *f.* series of type (*Typ.*). **–gattung,** *f.,* *see* **–art.** **–gelehrte(r),** *m.* (*B.*) scribe; authority on the Scriptures. **–gemäß,** *adj.* according to the Scriptures. **–gießer,** *m.* type-founder. **–gießerei,** *f.* type-foundry. **–gießererz,** *n.,* **–gießermetall,** *n.* type-metal. **–grad,** *m.* size of type. **–guß,** *m.* type-founding; fount of type. **–kasten,** *m.* letter-case (*Typ.*). **–kegel,** *m.* body *or* depth of a letter (*Typ.*). **–kunde,** *f.* Biblical knowledge. **–leiter,** *m.* editor. **–leitung,** *f.* editorship; editorial staff; newspaper-office. **–lich,** *adj.* written, in writing, by letter, in black and white; *–lich abfassen,* put in writing *or* in black and white, write down; *–liche Arbeiten,* written exercise; *–licher (Gerichts)befehl,* writ; *ich gebe es Ihnen –lich,* I will give it you in writing; *–lich mitteilen,* inform by letter; *–liche Überlieferung,* written records; *–liches Zeugnis,* certificate, testimonial. **–liche(s),** *n.* s.th. in writing. **–lichkeit,** *f.* proper legal form. **–malerei,** *f.* lettering. **–mäßig,** *adj.* Scriptural, Biblical. **–material,** *n.* stock of type. **–metall,** *n.* type-metal. **–mutter,** *f.* matrix, type-mould. **–probe,** *f.* specimen of writing *or* type. **–rolle,** *f.* scroll. **–sachverständige(r),** *m.* handwriting expert. **–satz,** *m.* composition (*Typ.*). **–seite,** *f.* page; reverse (*of a coin*). **–setzer,** *m.* compositor, type-setter. **–sold,** *m.* honorarium, fee (*for an article, etc.*). **–sprache,** *f.* written *or* literary language. **–stelle,** *f.* Scriptural passage. **–steller,** *m.* author, writer. **–stellerisch,** *adj.* literary. **–stellern,** *v.n.* write, do literary work. **–stellername,** *m.* pen-name. **–stempel,** *m.* punch (*Typ.*). **–stück,** *n.* document, piece of writing, written deposition; packet (*Typ.*). **–tum,** *n.* literature. **–verfälschung,** *f.* interpolation; forgery of documents. **–verkehr,** *m.* correspondence. **–wart,** *m.* secretary (*to a society*). **–wechsel,** *m.* exchange of letters, correspondence. **–zeichen,** *n.* letter, character. **–zeug,** 1. *m.* type-metal. 2. *n.* worn type. **–zug,** *m.* written character, handwriting; flourish; *deutsche –züge,* German script *or* characters.

schrill, *adj.* shrill. **–en,** *v.n.* (*aux.* h.) sound shrilly, utter a shrill cry. **–ton,** *m.* high pitch.

schrinden, *ir.v.n.* (*dial.*) chap, get chapped, split, crack.

schrinnen, *ir.v.n.* (*aux.* h. & s.) (*dial.*) smart, itch.

Schrippe, *f.* (-n) (*dial.*) breakfast roll.

Schritt, *m.* (-(e)s, -e) step, stride, pace; walk, gait; *einen diplomatischen – tun,* make a démarche; *einen entscheidenden – tun,* take a decisive step; *den ersten – tun,* take the initiative, break the ice, make the first move; *die ersten –e zu . . .,* the preliminary steps to . . .; *– fahren!* 5 m.p.h. max.! dead slow! (*Motor.*); *– für* (or *vor*) *–,* step by step; *im –e gehen,* walk, pace (*of horses*); *gerichtliche –e tun,* take legal proceedings; *– halten (mit),* keep in step, keep abreast (with); *keinen – aus dem Hause tun,* not put one's foot out of doors; *aus dem –(e) kommen,* get out of step; *die nötigen –e tun,* take all necessary steps; *ein paar –e von,* within a stone's throw of; *einem auf – und Tritt nachfolgen,* dog a p.'s steps, shadow a p.; *– um –,* step by step, yard by yard, a step at a time; *den zweiten – vor dem ersten tun,* go about s.th. in the wrong way, put the cart before the horse. **–gänger,** *m.* pacing horse. **–länge,** *f.* length of stride. **–lings,** *adv.* pacing, step by step; straddled, astride; *–lings im Sattel sitzen,* sit astride the saddle. **–macher,** *m.* pace-maker, pacer; (*fig.*) harbinger. **–messer,** *m.* pedometer. (*archaic*) **–schuh,** *m.* skate. **–stein,** *m.* stepping-stone. **–(t)anz,** *m.* step-dance. **–wechsel,** *m.* change of step (*Mil.*). **–weise,** *adv.* step by step, by steps gradually. **–weite,** *f.* length of stride. **–zähler,** *m.* pedometer.

schritt, schritte, *see* **schreiten.**

schrob, schröbe, *see* **schrauben.**

Schröder, *m.* (*dial.*) vanman.

Schrof *m.* (-(e)s & -en, -en), **–e** *f.* (-n) *or* **–en,** *m.* (-s, –) (& *Austr. dial.*) **–f,** *m.* (-(e)s, -en) *or* **–fen,** *m.* (-s, -) crag.

schroff, *adj.* rough, rugged; steep, precipitous; (*fig.*) uncouth, gruff, blunt, abrupt, harsh; *–er Gegensatz,* glaring contradiction, the absolute opposite *or* contrary; *–er Übergang,* abrupt transition. **–heit,** *f.* steepness, ruggedness; roughness, rudeness.

schröpf–en, *v.a.* cup, bleed (*Surg.*); scarify; (*fig.*) fleece, overcharge. **–glas,** *n.* **–kopf,** *m.* cupping-glass; (*einem*) *–köpfe setzen,* bleed (a p.). **–schnäpper,** *m.* cupping-instrument, scarifier (*Surg.*).

Schropphobel, *m.* *see* **Schrupphobel.**

Schrot, *m.* & *n.* (-(e)s, -e) small shot, buck shot, slugs; clump, block; chips, clippings; groats, grist, bruised grain; weight of coin; *see also* **Schrott;** *von echtem* or *gutem (altem) – und Korn,* of standard weight and alloy, (*usually fig.*) of the good old type, of sterling worth; *von gleichem* or *vom selben –,* a chip of the old block. **–axt,** *f.* wood-cutter's axe. **–blatt,** *n.* 15th-century engraving in white on stippled background. **–brot,** *n.* wholemeal bread. **–büchse,** *f.* fowling-piece, shot-gun. **–eisen,** *n.* blacksmith's chisel. **–effekt,** *m.* shot effect (*Rad.*). **–en,** *v.a.* 1. (*p.p.* geschroten & geschrotet) rough-grind (*corn*); bruise (*malt*); saw up (*logs*); gnaw, nibble, eat (*of rats, etc.*). 2. (*p.p.* geschrotet) lower, roll down, load *or* unload (*heavy articles*); parbuckle (*Naut.*); *Münzstücke –en*, clip the edges of coins. **–flinte,** *f.*, *see* **–büchse. –gießerei,** *f.* shot mill. **–hammer,** *m.* blacksmith's hammer. **–käfer,** *m.* stag-beetle. **–kleie,** *f.* coarse bran. **–korn,** *n.* grain of shot, single shot. **–ladung,** *f.* shower of shot. **–lauf,** *m.* smooth barrel. **–leiter,** *f.* drayman's ladder. **–mehl,** *n.* groats, coarse meal. **–mühle,** *f.* grist mill. **–patrone,** *f.* shot-gun cartridge (*Hunt.*). **–säge,** *f.* great saw, pit-saw. **–sägeförmig,** *adj.* runcinate. **–schere,** *f.* plate-shears, tin-snips. **–seil,** *n.* parbuckle. **–silber,** *n.* grains of silver. **–stärke,** *f.* size *or* diameter of shot. **–stück,** *n.* blank, planchet (*Mint.*). **–waage,** *f.* plummet, level.

Schröt–er, *m.* (-ers, -er) stag-beetle; brewer's van-man, drayman. **–ling,** *m.* piece cut off; cutting; minting blank, planchet (*Mint.*).

Schrott, *m.* (-(e)s, -e) scrap-metal. **–eisen,** *n.* scrap iron. **–entfall,** *m.* manufacturing loss (*Metall.*).

schrubbe–n, *v.a.* scrub, scour. **–r,** *m.* scrubber, scourer; swab; scrubbing brush. **–rn,** *see* **–n.**

Schrull–e, *f.* whim, fad, crotchet; (*fig.*) crotchety old woman, crone; *er hat seine –en*, he has his fads; he is in one of his moods. **–enhaft,** *adj.*, **–ig,** *adj.* whimsical.

schrumm, *int.* (*coll.*) done! finished! stop! enough!

Schrump–el, *f.* (-eln) (*dial.*) fold, wrinkle; *alte –el*, withered old crone. **–eln,** *v.n.* (*aux.* s.) (*dial.*) *see* **–fen. –f,** *m.* shrinkage, loss by shrinkage. **–fel,** *f.* (*dial.*), *see* **–el. –fen,** *v.n.* (*aux.* s.) shrivel, shrink, contract; crumple, wrinkle, become wrinkled. **–fend,** *adj.* astringent. **–fgrenze,** *f.* shrinkage limit. **–fig,** *adj.*, **–f(e)lig,** *adj.* wrinkled, shrivelled, creased, crumpled. **–fniere,** *f.* cirrhosis (*Med.*). **–fung,** *f.* shrinking, shrinkage, contraction, shrivel-ing, wrinkling; stricture (*Med.*). **–lig,** *adj.* (*dial.*), *see* **–flig.**

Schrund, *m.* (-(e)s, ¨e & -e), **–e,** *f.* (-en) cleft, crack, chink, crevice, crevasse; (*pl.*) chaps. **–ig,** *adj.* cracked, chapped.

schrund, schründe, *see* **schrinden.**

schrupp–en, *v.a.* (*dial.*, *see* **schrubben**) plane roughly. **–feile,** *f.* rasp. **–hobel,** *m.* jack-plane.

Schub, *m.* (-(e)s, ¨e) shove, push, thrust; throw (*at skittles, etc.*); heap, batch (*of bread*); set (*of skittles*); compulsory conveyance (*of vagrants, etc.*) by the police; thrust (*of a propeller*); shearing (*Mech.*); *ich kam mit dem ersten – hinein*, I entered with the first batch (*of people*); *auf den – bringen*, pass (*paupers, etc.*) to their parish; (*coll.*) give (*a p.*) the push. **–beanspruchung,** *f.* shear-stress. **–deckel,** *m.* sliding lid. **–fach,** *n.* drawer. **–fenster,** *n.* sash-window. **–festigkeit,** *f.* shear-strength. **–karre,** *f.*, **–karren,** *m.* wheelbarrow. **–kasten,** *m.*, **–lade,** *f.* drawer; set *or* chest of drawers. **–lehre,** *f.* sliding callipers. **–paß,** *m.* order for the transport of paupers. **–riegel,** *m.* (sliding) bolt. **–schraube,** *f.* pusher-screw (*Av.*). **–stange,** *f.* connecting-rod. **–ventil,** *n.* slide-valve. **–weise,** *adv.* gradually, little by little, in batches; by com-pulsory conveyance.

schub–ben, *v.a.* (*dial.*) rub, scrub, scour. **–bejack,** *m.* (-s & -en, -s & -e(n)) ragamuffin, scoundrel, dirty wretch. **–bern,** *see* **–ben. –sak,** *see* **–bejack.**

Schubs, *m.* (-es, -e) (*dial.*) push, shove (forward). **–en,** *v.a.* (*dial.*) push.

schüchtern, *adj.* shy, timid, bashful, coy. **–heit,** *f.* shyness, bashfulness, timidity.

Schüdderump, *m.* (*dial.*) rickety cart, bone-shaker.

schuf, schüfe, *see* **schaffen.**

Schuft, *m.* (-(e)s, -e) rogue, scamp, scoundrel, blackguard; *zum – an einem Mädchen werden*, play false with *or* betray a girl, seduce *or* debauch a girl; *ein – wer Böses dabei denkt*, honi soit qui mal y pense. (*coll.*) **–en,** *v.n.* toil, work hard, drudge, slave. **–erei,** *f.* knavery, rascality, villainy, de-pravity; toil, drudgery, slavery, (*coll.*) grind. **–ig,** *adj.* shabby, rascally, blackguardly, base, mean, vile.

Schuh, *m.* (-(e)s, -e *or as measure* –) shoe, boot; foot (*as measure*); shoeing, ferrule, socket (*on lance, car-bine, etc.*); *einem etwas in die –e schieben*, lay (*a fault*) at a p.'s door, put the blame on a p. for s.th.; *das habe ich (mir) längst an den (Kinder)–en abgelaufen*, I knew that long ago; (*Prov.*) *umge-kehrt wird ein – daraus*, you are beginning at the wrong end, you are setting about it in just the wrong way; *Sie wissen nicht, wo der – mich drückt*, you do not know where the shoe pinches. **–absatz,** *m.* heel of a shoe *or* boot. **–ahle,** *f.* shoemaker's awl. **–anzieher,** *m.* shoe-horn. **–band,** *n.* boot-lace. **–bürste,** *f.* boot-brush. **–creme,** *f.*, *see* **–krem. –flicken,** *m.* patch. **–flicker,** *m.* cobbler. **–knöpfer,** *m.* button-hook. **–kratzer,** *m.* (door-)scraper. **–krem,** *m.*, **–kreme,** *f.* boot-polish, shoe-cream. **–leisten,** *m.* last, boot-tree. **–löffel,** *m.* shoe-horn. **–macher,** *m.* shoemaker, boot-maker. **–macherpech,** *n.* cobbler's wax. **–plattler,** *m.* (Bavarian) country dance. **–putzer,** *m.* shoe- *or* boot-black. **–riemen,** *m.* shoe-lace; (*B.*) latchet. **–schmiere,** *f.* dubbin(g). **–schnalle,** *f.* shoe-buckle. **–schwärze,** *f.* blacking. **–span-ner,** *m.* boot- *or* shoe-tree. **–wachs,** *n.* cobbler's wax. **–warenindustrie,** *f.* boot-making industry. **–werk,** *n.* footwear, boots and shoes. **–wichse,** *f.* boot-polish, blacking. **–wichser,** *m.* shoe-black, boots (*in an hotel*). **–zeug,** *n.*, *see* **–werk. –zwecke,** *f.* shoe-tack, brad.

Schuhu, *m.* (-s, -e) (*dial.*) owl.

Schuld, *f.* (-en) debt, indebtedness, obligation; fault, cause, blame; offence, sin, guilt; (*pl.*) debts, liabilities; *eine – abtragen*, pay off a debt; *einem die – geben*, lay the blame on s.o., blame *or* accuse s.o.; (*C.L.*) *– und Gegen–*, debts active and passive; *– haben an einer S.*, see *– tragen*; *–en machen*, run into debt; *er ist – daran*, it is his fault, he is responsible *or* to blame for it; *in –en stecken*, be up to the ears in debt; *ich stehe in Ihrer –*, I am in your debt *or* under an obligation to you, I am indebted to you; *sich in –en stürzen*, see *–en machen*; *– tragen an einer S.*, be guilty of a th.; *die Sühnung der tragi-schen – in einem Stücke*, the Nemesis of a play; *vergib uns unsere –(en)*, forgive us our trespasses; *see also* **zuschulden. –abzahlung,** *f.* liquidation of debts. **–befleckt,** *adj.* disgraced, dishonoured, stigmatized, branded, tarnished, discredited. **–bekenntnis,** *n.* acknowledgement of liabilities. **–beweis,** *m.* proof of guilt. **–bewußt,** *adj.* guilty, with a bad conscience, conscience-stricken. **–bewußtsein,** *n.* guiltiness, bad conscience, acknowledgement of sin. **–brief,** *m.* bond, pro-missory note. **–buch,** *n.* journal, ledger, account-book; *unser –buch sei vernichtet!* let all old scores be wiped out! **–en,** *v.a.* owe; be indebted to (*a p. for a th.*). **–enbelastet,** *adj.* burdened *or* crippled with debts, deep in debt. **–enfrei,** *adj.* free from debt, unencumbered. **–enhalber,** *adv.* on account of debts. **–enlast,** *f.* burden of debt. **–enmasse,** *f.* aggregate liabilities. **–entilgung,** *f.* liquidation of debt; sinking of the (national) debt. **–entil-gungskasse,** *f.* sinking-fund. **–erlaß,** *m.*, **–er-lassung,** *f.* remission of a debt. **–forderung,** *f.* claim, demand for payment. **–frage,** *f.* question of whose responsibility. **–frei,** *adj.*, *see* **–los. –gefängnis,** *n.* debtor's prison. **–haft,** 1. *f.* imprisonment for debt. 2. *adj.* (*archaic except Swiss dial.*) *see* **–ig. –ig,** *adj.* due, owing; indebted, obliged, bound; guilty, culpable, in fault, to blame; *an einer S. –ig sein*, be guilty of (*a crime, etc.*); *sich –ig bekennen*, acknowledge one's guilt, plead guilty (to); *einem die Antwort –ig bleiben*, not answer a p.; *er bleibt einem nichts –ig*, he gives as good as he gets, he is never at a loss for an answer; *sie blieben einander nichts –ig*, they gave each other tit for tat; *das sind wir ihm –ig*, that is due to him, that we owe to him, we have to thank him for that; (*archaic*) *eines Fehlers –ig*, guilty of a fault; (*archaic*) *des Todes –ig sein*, be deserving of death; *–ige Strafe*, just punishment. **–ige(r),** *m.* & *f.* guilty person, person responsible *or* answerable. **–iger,** *m.* (*B.*) culprit; debtor; *wie wir vergeben unsern –igern*, as we forgive them that trespass against us. **–igermaßen,** *adv.* as in duty bound. **–igkeit,** *f.* duty, obligation; debt; *er hat nur seine –igkeit getan*, he has only done his duty. **–igsprechung,** *f.* conviction, condemna-tion, verdict of guilty. **–igst,** *adv.* most duly, as is right and proper. **–klage,** *f.* action for debt. **–los,**

adj. innocent, guiltless, blameless, irreproachable, unimpeachable, immaculate, unsullied, faultless. **-losigkeit,** *f.* innocence, blamelessness. **-ner,** debtor. **-posten,** *m.* amount owing *or* due. **-rest,** *m.* balance due. **-schein,** *m.* statement of liabilities; *see also* **-verschreibung.** **-turm,** *m.* (*archaic*) debtor's prison. **-verschreibung,** *f.* bond, promissory note, debenture. **-voll,** *adj.* guilty.

Schul-e, *f.* (-en) school, college, academy; school of thought; school (*of whales*); *Aufbau–e,* intermediate school; *Fach–e,* technical school; *Fortbildungs–e,* continuation school; *Gewerbe–e,* trade-school, technical school; *Grund–e,* elementary school; *Handels–e,* commercial school; *Handwerker–e,* mechanics' institute; *Hilfs–e,* special school; *höhere –e,* secondary school; *höhere Töchter–e,* high school for girls; *Hoch–e,* (*obs.*) *hohe –e,* university; *Technische Hoch–e,* polytechnic; *Handelshoch–e,* commercial college; *Kleinkinder–e,* infant-school; *konfessionelle –e,* church school; *Mittel–e,* (*Austr. dial.*) secondary school; *Privat–e,* private school; *Simultan–e,* non-confessional school; *Staats–e,* state school; *städtische –e,* municipal school; *Stiftungs–e,* endowed school; *Volks–e,* primary *or* elementary school; *Volkshoch–e,* University Extension; *Vor–e,* preparatory department; *auf der –e,* at school; *aus der –e schwatzen* or *plaudern,* tell tales out of school; *hinter die -e gehen* or *laufen,* see *–e schwänzen*; *Hohe –e reiten,* put a horse through its paces; *in der –e,* see *auf der –e*; *einen in die –e nehmen,* take a p. in hand; *in die –e tun,* send to school; *–e machen,* form a precedent, find followers *or* adherents; *ein Pferd die –e machen lassen,* put a horse through its paces; *neben die – gehen* or *laufen* or *die –e schwänzen,* play truant. **-amt,** *n.* teaching post. **-anstalt,** *f.* school. **-arbeit,** *f.* school-work, home-work. **-arzt,** *m.* school medical officer. **-aufsicht,** *f.* inspection of schools. **-aufsichtsbehörde,** *f.* inspectorate. **-ausflug,** *m.* school outing. **-ausgabe,** *f.* school-edition. **-bank,** *f.,* form, school-bench; *die -bank drücken,* go to school (reluctantly). **-beispiel,** *n.* perfect example, exemplary case, model, pattern. **-besuch,** *m.* attendance at school. **-bube,** *m.* schoolboy. **-buch,** *n.* school-book. **-bücherverlag,** *m.* firm of educational publishers. **-diener,** *m.* school-porter. **-dienst,** *m.* teaching profession. **-direktor,** *m.* headmaster, principal. **-direktorin,** *f.* headmistress. **-drama,** *n.* Latin drama (*of Humanism*). **-en,** *v.a.* school, teach; train (*horses*). **-entlassen,** *adj.* having left school. **-fall,** *m., see* **-beispiel.** **-ferien,** *pl.* (school) holidays, vacation. **-flugzeug,** *n.* training plane. **-frage,** *f.* educational problem. **-frei,** *adj.* no school; *-freier Tag,* day's holiday; *-freier Nachmittag,* half-holiday. **-freund,** *m.* schoolfellow, pal. **-fuchs,** *m.* pedant. **-fuchserei,** *f.* pedantry. **-fuchsig,** *adj.* pedantic. **-funk,** *m.* schools' broadcasts. **-gebrauch,** *m.*; *für den -gebrauch,* for use in schools, for class-use. **-geld,** *n.* school fees. **-gelehrsamkeit,** *f., see* **-weisheit.** **-gemäß,** *adj.,* **-gerecht,** *adj.* according to rule; suited to schools; well-trained (*of horses*). **-gesetz,** *n.* education act. **-haus,** *n.* school premises. **-heft,** *n.* exercise-book. **-heim,** *n.* (country) hostel (attached to a school). **-hof,** *m.* playground. **-isch,** *adj.* scholastic, academic, collegiate. **-jahr,** *n.* scholastic year; (*pl.*) schooldays. **-jugend,** *f.* school-children, juveniles. **-junge,** *m.* schoolboy. **-kamerad,** *m.* schoolfellow. **-kenntnisse,** *f.pl.* scholastic *or* class-room knowledge, rudiments. **-kind,** *n.* school-age child. **-klasse,** *f.* class, form. **-knabe,** *m.* schoolboy. **-kollegium,** *n.* teaching staff. **-konferenz,** *f.* staff *or* teachers' meeting. **-leiter,** *m.* principal, headmaster. **-mädchen,** *n.* schoolgirl. **-mann,** *m.* (-männer) experienced teacher, pedagogue. **-mäßig,** *adj.* scholastic; *see* **-gemäß.** **-meister,** *m.* (*derog.*) schoolmaster. **-meisterlich,** *adj.* pedantic. **-meistern,** *v.a.* & *n.* (*aux.* h.) teach; keep a school; teach pedantically; be pedantic, be censorious, dogmatize; (*coll.*) always know better. **-ordnung,** *f.* school regulations; school discipline. **-pferd,** *n.* trained horse; riding-school horse. **-pflanze,** *f.* nursery seedling. **-pflicht,** *f., see* **-zwang.** **-pflichtig,** *adj.* of school age. **-programm,** *n.* school's annual report. **-ranzen,** *m.* school-bag, satchel. **-rat,** *m.* education authority; school inspector. **-reform,** *f.* educational reform. **-sache,** *f.* scholastic concern. **-sattel,** *m.* manège-saddle. **-schießstand,** *m.* practice rifle-range. **-schiff,** *n.* training-ship. **-schluß,** *m.* end of term, breaking-up. **-schritt,** *m.* short pace (*of a horse*). **-schwänzer,** *m.* truant. **-speisung,** *f.* school meals. **-sprache,** *f.* schoolboy slang. **-system,** *n.* educational system. **-tasche,** *f.* satchel, school-bag. **-ton,** *m.* pedantic *or* dogmatic tone. **-übung,** *f.* school exercise. **-ung,** *f.* training, schooling. **-ungsbrief,** *m.* party directive (*Pol.*). **-ungslager,** *n.* training camp. **-ungswoche,** *f.* short course of instruction, refresher course. **-unterricht,** *m.* school-teaching. **-versäumnis,** *f.* absence from school. **-vorstand,** *m.* school governors. **-wanderung,** *f.* school ramble. **-weg,** *m.* way to school. **-weisheit,** *f.* theoretical *or* book learning, erudition. **-wesen,** *n.* educational system; *das höhere -wesen,* secondary education. **-zahnpflege,** *f.* school dental service. **-zeit,** *f.* school-time, school-days. **-zeugnis,** *n.* class report. **-zimmer,** *n.* classroom, schoolroom. **-zucht,** *f.* school discipline. **-zwang,** *m.* legal obligation to send one's children to school; compulsory education.

Schüler, *m.* (-s, -) schoolboy, pupil, scholar, (*archaic*) student; disciple, follower; tyro; *in dieser Klasse sind zwanzig –,* there are twenty boys in this form; *er ist ein alter – von mir,* he is a former pupil of mine; *ein – Christi,* a disciple of Christ; *fahrender –,* itinerant scholar. **-austausch,** *m.* exchange of visits between schoolchildren of different nations. **-briefwechsel,** *m.* correspondence with a foreign schoolboy (*or* girl). **-haft,** *adj.* schoolboy-like, boyish, juvenile, callow; immature, bungling. **-in,** *f.* schoolgirl. **-mütze,** *f.* school cap.

Schulp, *m.* (-(e)s, -e,), **-e,** *f.* (-en) cuttlebone.

Schulter, *f.* (-n) shoulder; *– an –,* (*fig.*) shoulder to shoulder, side by side; *einen über die – ansehen,* look down upon *or* down one's nose at a p.; *die –n hochziehen,* shrug one's shoulders; *einem die kalte – zeigen,* give s o. the cold shoulder; *etwas auf die leichte – nehmen,* take a th. lightly; *see also* **Achsel.** **-band,** *n.* humeral ligament. **-bein,** *n.* shoulder-bone, humerus. **-blatt,** *n.* scapula, shoulder-blade. **-breite,** *f.* breadth of shoulders. **-decker,** *m.* high-wing monoplane. **-gelenk,** *n.* shoulder-joint. **-höhe,** *f.* height of the shoulders; acromion (*Anat.*); *bis zur -höhe,* up to the shoulder. **-ig,** (*also* **schultrig**), *adj.* shouldered. **-klappe,** *f.* shoulder-strap (*Mil.*). **-maschinengewehr,** *n.* automatic rifle. **-n,** *v.a.* shoulder (*arms, Mil.*). **-riemen,** *m.* cross-strap, cross-belt (*Mil.*). **-stück,** *n.* epaulette; episternum (*Anat.*). **-tuch,** *n.* scapulary (*of monks*). **-verrenkung,** *f.* dislocation of the shoulder. **-wehr,** *f.* epaulement, breastwork (*Fort.*).

Schultheiß, *m.* (-en, -en) (*archaic*) village mayor.

Schulze, *m.* (-n, -n) (*dial.*) *see* **Schultheiß.**

Schum, *m.* (*coll.*) *only in* im –, tipsy, tiddly, fuddled, in one's cups.

schummeln, *v.n.* (*coll.*) diddle, swindle.

Schummer, *m.* (-s, –) (*dial.*) twilight, dusk, gloaming. **-ig,** *adj.* dusky, dim. **-n,** 1. *v.n.* become *or* be dim; sit in the dark. 2. *v.a.* shade, hatch (*maps*). **-ung,** *f.* hatching (*of maps*), hachures. **-stunde,** *f.* gloaming.

Schund, *m.* trash, rubbish, refuse, offal, **-literatur,** *f.* rubbishy *or* trashy literature. **-waren,** *f.pl.* trashy goods.

schund, schünde, *see* **schinden.**

schunkeln, *v.n.* (*coll.*) see-saw.

Schupf, *m.* (-(e)s, -e) (*Austr. & Swiss dial.*) push, shove. **-en,** *v.a.* push, shove.

Schupo, (*coll.*) 1. *f.* the police. 2. *m.* policeman, bobby; *see* **Schutzpolizei** *and* **Schutzpolizist.**

Schupp, *m.* (*dial.*), *see* **Schupf.** **-en,** *see* **schupfen.**

Schupp-e, *f.* (-en) scale; scurf, dandruff; flake, squama (*Bot., Zool.*); *es fielen ihm die -en von den Augen,* the scales have fallen from his eyes, his eyes were opened. **-en,** 1. *v.a.* scale (*fish, etc.*), strip of scales; *see also under* **Schupp.** 2. *v.r.* slough, scale off, peel off, desquamate; form scales, become scaly. **–enartig,** *adj.* scaly, squamous. **–enbaum,** *m.* lepidodendron. **–enbildung,** *f.* flaking. **–eneidechse,** *f.* scaly lizard. **–enflechte,** *f.* psoriasis (*Path.*). **–enförmig,** *adj.* scaly. **–enkette,** *f.* chin-strap (*of helmets*). **–ennaht,** *f.* scaly suture, seam (*of the skull*). **–enpanzer,** *m.* coat of mail. **–entanne,** *f.* monkey-puzzle (*Araucaria imbricata*) (*Bot.*). **–entier,** *n.* scaly ant-eater, pangolin (*Pholidota*) (*Zool.*). **–enweise,** *adv.* in scales, flake by flake. **–enwurz,** *f.* tooth-wort (*Lathraea squamaria*) (*Bot.*). **–ig,** *adj.* scaly, scaled; squamous; scurfy.

Schüppe, *f.* (-n) (*dial.*) shovel, scoop.

Schuppen, *m.* (-s, –) shed, shelter, hangar, coach-house, garage, engine-house (*Railw.*).

Schup(p)s, *m.*, **–er,** *m.* (*dial.*) push, nudge, jolt. **–en,** *v.a.* push, nudge, jolt.

Schur, *f.* (-en) shearing, sheep-shearing, mowing; swath; fleece; clippings; (*coll.*) teasing, raillery.

schür–en, *v.a.* stir, poke, rake (*the fire*); stir up, incite. **–eisen,** *n.* poker. **–er,** *n.* stoker; instigator; poker (*for a furnace*). **–haken,** *m.* poker. **–loch,** *n.* stoke-hole. **–schaufel,** *f.* fire-shovel. **–stange,** *f.* poker. **–werkzeug,** *n.* fire-irons. **–zange,** *f.* tongs.

Schurf, *m.* (-es, ⸚e) opening, pit, hole (*in the ground*); scratch, abrasion; prospector's claim. **–arbeit,** *f.* prospecting. **–schein,** *m.*, **–zettel,** *m.* licence to prospect (*Min.*).

schürf–en, *v.a.* scratch, scrape, rake; burrow, prospect, dig (*for ore*); (*fig.*) *tief –en,* go deeply into, be thorough. **–arbeit,** *f.* prospecting. **–er,** *m.* prospector. **–schein,** *m.*, *see* **Schurfschein.** **–ung,** *f.* prospecting, digging; mining claim; scratch, abrasion.

schurigeln, *v.a.* torment, harass, pester, annoy, vex, worry.

Schurk–e, *m.* (-en, -en) scoundrel, rogue, knave, villain. **–erei,** *f.* rascally *or* (*coll.*) dirty trick, villainy. **–isch,** *adj.* villainous, rascally, base, vile. **–enstreich,** *m.* rascality.

Schurre, *f.* slide, chute. **–n,** *v.n.* (*aux.* s. & h.) glide, slide.

Schurz, *m.* (-es, -e & ⸚e) apron, loin-cloth. **–fell,** *n.* leather(n) apron.

Schürze, *f.* (-n) apron, pinafore; (*coll.*) wench, skirt, petticoat, bit of stuff; *hinter jeder – herlaufen,* run after every skirt. **–nband,** *n.* (⸚er) apron-string; *ans –nband gebunden sein,* be kept in leading-strings, be tied to one's (mother's) apron-strings. **–njäger,** *m.* rip, rake. **–nregiment,** *n.* petticoat government.

schürzen, 1. *v.a.* tie (*a knot, etc.*); tuck *or* fasten up (*one's skirt*); purse (*one's lips*). 2. *v.r.* tuck up one's dress, pick up one's skirts; *sich zu einer S. –,* make ready for a th., (*fig.*) roll up one's sleeves, (*B.*) gird up one's loins; *der Knoten schürzt sich,* the plot thickens.

Schuß, *m.* (-(ss)es, ⸚(ss)e) (live) round; gunshot *or* bullet wound; shot, report (*of a gun*); rapid movement, rush (*of water, etc.*), swing, swoop; rapid growth; blasting charge (*Min.*); woof, weft (*Weav.*); (*pl.* –) batch (*of bread*), dash, swig (*of brandy, etc.*); *einen – abfeuern, abgeben* or *tun,* fire a shot *or* round; *– aufs Geratewohl,* wild shot, blind firing; *es fiel ein –,* a shot was fired, there was a shot; *der – hat gefehlt,* the shot has missed its mark; *sich zum – fertig machen,* make ready to fire; (*coll.*) *den – haben,* have a sudden impulse *or* fit, be in a hurry; *– ins Blaue,* random shot; *in – kommen,* get into working order, get into the spirit of; *einem in den – laufen* or *kommen,* come within shot (*of game*); (*fig.*) *im –(ss)e sein,* be in full swing, be going on well; be running well (*of an engine*); *– ins Zentrum,* bull's-eye; *scharfer –,* live round; *weit vom –,* outside the danger zone; (*fig.*) wide of the mark; *er ist keinen – Pulver wert,* he is not worth a rap. **–beobachtung,** *f.* spotting (*Artil.*). **–bereich,** *m.* zone of fire. **–bereit,** *adj.* ready to fire. **–bremse,** *f.* recoil-brake. **–faden,** *m.*, *see* **–garn.** **–feld,** *n.* field of fire. **–fertig,** *adj.*, *see* **–bereit.** **–fest,** *adj.* bullet-proof, invulnerable; *er ist –fest,* he bears a charmed life. **–folge,** *f.* rate of fire. **–frei,** *adj.* out of range. **–garn,** *n.* woof, weft (*Weav.*). **–gerecht,** *adj.* trained to stand fire (*of horses*); true (*of guns*); within range. **–geschwindigkeit,** *f.* rate of fire. **–ig,** *adj.* (*dial.*) hasty, impetuous. **–linie,** *f.* line of fire, line of sight. **–loch,** *n.*, **–öffnung,** *f.* bullet-hole. **–recht,** *adj.* within range. **–richtung,** *f.* line *or* direction of fire. **–scheu,** *adj.* gun-shy (*of horses*). **–sicher,** *adj.* bullet-proof, shell-proof; *–sicherer Brennstoffbehälter,* self-sealing fuel tank (*Av.*). **–tafel,** *f.* range-table. **–träger,** *m.* shuttle-carrier (*Weav.*). **–verbesserung,** *f.* correction (*Artil.*). **–waffe,** *f.* firearm. **–weise,** *adv.* by jerks, by fits and starts. **–weite,** *f.* range; *in –weite sein,* be within range; *wirksame –weite,* effective range. **–werte,** *m.pl.* firing data. **–wunde,** *f.* gunshot wound; bullet wound. **–zahl,** *f.* number of rounds.

Schussel, *f.* (-n) & *m.* (-s, –) (*coll.*) fidgety, hasty, *or* careless person. **–ig** (*also* **schußlig**) *adj.* careless, restless, fidgety. **–n,** *v.n.* act impetuously; be careless; (*dial.*) slide (*on ice*), go sledging.

Schüssel, *f.* (-n) dish, basin, bowl, tureen (*for soup*); dish (*of food*), course (*of a meal*). **–brett,** *n.* kitchen-dresser; plate-drainer *or* -rack. **–förmig,** *adj.* bowl-shaped. **–glocke,** *f.*, **–stürze,** *f.* dish-cover. **–schrank,** *m.* sideboard. **–tuch,** *n.* dish-cloth. **–wärmer,** *m.* plate-warmer. **–zinn,** *n.* pewter.

Schusser, *m.* (-s, –) (*dial.*) marble, taw. **–n,** *v.n.* play marbles.

Schuster, *m.* (-s, –) shoemaker, cobbler; (*Prov.*) – *bleib' bei deinem Leisten,* cobbler, stick to your last! (*coll.*) *auf –s Rappen,* on Shanks's pony, on foot. **–draht,** *m.* waxed thread, shoemaker's thread. **–junge,** *m.* shoemaker's apprentice. **–n,** *v.n.* (*aux.* h.) mend shoes, cobble; botch, make a botch of; (*coll.*) chum up with. **–pech,** *n.* cobbler's wax, heel-ball. **–pfriem,** *m.* cobbler's awl.

Schute, *f.* (-n) barge, lighter (*Naut.*); (*coll.*) bonnet. **–ngeld,** *n.* lighterage.

Schutt, *m.* ruins; rubble; debris; refuse, rubbish; (*B.*) bank of earth; *eine Stadt in – und Asche legen,* raze a town to the ground. **–abladeplatz,** *m.* refuse-dump. **–halde,** *f.* scree (slope). **–haufen,** *m.* rubbish heap; *in einen –haufen verwandeln,* lay in ruins. **–karren,** *m.* dust-cart.

Schütte, *f.* (-n) (*dial.*) heap, pile (*of straw, etc.*); (*dial.*) truss (*of straw*); (*dial.*) granary; blight (*which attacks pines*).

schüttel–n, 1. *v.a.* shake, agitate, make vibrate; jolt, joggle; churn; *aus dem Ärmel –n,* improvise, do on the spur of the moment, produce from one's sleeve; *einem die Hand* or *Hände –n,* shake a p. by the hand, shake hands with a p.; *es –t mich,* it makes me tremble. 2. *v.r.* tremble, shiver, shudder (*vor,* with). **–frost,** *m.* shivering fit, shivers, chill, ague, rigor. **–reim,** *m.* Spoonerism. **–rinne,** *f.*, **–rutsche,** *f.* shaking-trough, chute. **–rost,** *m.* rocker-grating, raker (*in furnace*).

schütt–en, 1. *v.a.* pour (out), cast, shed, throw, shoot; *leer –en,* empty out; *voll –en,* fill up; *auf einen Haufen –en,* pile up; *Pulver auf die Pfanne –en,* prime a gun; *Öl auf die Wogen –en,* pour oil on troubled waters. 2. *v.n.* yield in abundance; shed leaves (*of pines*); litter, whelp; (*imp.*) pour (*with rain*). **–boden,** *m.* granary, corn-loft. **–enabwurf,** *m.* random bombing (*Av.*). **–enkasten,** *m.* bomb-rack, container for incendiary bombs (*Av.*). **–gelb,** *adj.* & *n.* Dutch pink. **–gewicht,** *n.* loose weight. **–gut,** *n.* loose goods, bulk goods. **–kanal,** *m.* charging chute. **–ofen,** *m.* self-feeding stove. **–stein,** *m.* (*Swiss dial.*) sink, gutter. **–stroh,** *n.* litter.

schütter, *adj.* (*dial.*) thin, sparse.

schüttern, *v.n.* (*aux.* h.) vibrate, rattle, tremble, rock.

Schutz, *m.* shelter, refuge, cover, screen, defence, protection, safeguard, care, keeping; patronage; *– vor* (*einer S.*), protection from (a th.); *– und Schirm,* protection; *im – der Dunkelheit,* under cover of darkness; *unter dem –e der Kanonen,* under cover of the guns; *sich in jemandes – begeben,* seek shelter *or* take refuge with s.o.; *zu – und Trutz,* defensive(ly) and offensive(ly); *– suchen,* take shelter; *in – nehmen*, defend, take under one's protection; (*C.L.*) honour (*a bill*). **-amt,** *n.* protectorship, guardianship. **-anstrich,** *m.* protective coating; dazzle *or* baffle paint (*Mil.*). **-ärmel,** *m.pl.* sleeve-protectors. **-bedürftig,** *adj.* needing protection. **-befohlene(r),** *m.* charge, protégé; ward. **-blech,** *n.* mud-guard, wing (*Motor.*). **-brief,** *m.* (letter of) safe-conduct. **-brille,** *f.* dark spectacles, safety goggles. **-bündnis,** *n.* defensive alliance; *– - und Trutzbündnis*, defensive and offensive alliance. **-dach,** *n.* shed, lean-to, (*fig.*) sheltering roof. **-deckel,** *m.* cardboard box, case, carton. **-engel,** *m.* guardian-angel. **-färbung,** *f.* protective colouring. **-frist,** *f.* term of copyright. **-gebiet,** *n.* protectorate; reservation, nature reserve, sanctuary. **-geist,** *m.* guardian spirit, tutelary genius. **-geländer,** *n.* railing, balustrade. **-geleit,** *n.* safe-conduct, escort, convoy. **-gerät,** *n.* defensive equipment, safety appliances. **-gitter,** *n.* fire-guard; safety *or* protecting screen; grid (*Rad.*). **-glas,** *n.* glass shield. **-glocke,** *f.* bell jar. **-gott,** *m.* tutelary god. **-haft,** *f.* protective custody, preventive arrest. **-heilige,** *f.*, **-heilige(r),** *m.* patron saint. **-heiligtum,** *n.* palladium. **-herr,** *m.* patron, protector. **-herrschaft,** *f.* protectorate. **-hülle,** *f.* casing, armour (*of a cable*); wrapper (*of book*, etc.). **-hütte,** *f.* shelter, refuge (*in the Alps*). **-impfung,** *f.* vaccination, immunization, protective inoculation. **-insel,** *f.* island, refuge (*in the street*). **-kind,** *n.* charge; ward. **-los,** *adj.* defenceless, unprotected; (*coll.*) out in the cold. **-macht,** *f.* protectoral power (*Pol.*). **-mann,** *m.* policeman, constable. **-marke,** *f.* trade-mark. **-masse,** *f.* resist (*of fabrics*). **-maßregel,** *f.* protective *or* precautionary measure, preventative. **-mauer,** *f.* rampart, bulwark. **-mittel,** *n.* preservative, preventative, prophylactic. **-patron,** *m.*, **-patronin,** *f.* patron saint. **-pocken,** *f.pl.* cowpox. **-(pocken)-gift,** *n.* vaccine lymph *or* virus. **-pockenimpfung,** *f.* vaccination. **-polizei,** *f.* (municipal) police. **-polizist,** *m.* policeman. **-raum,** *m.* (air-raid) shelter. **-schiene,** *f.* guard-rail (*Railw.*). **-schild,** *m.* armoured shield (*Mil.*); blast wall. **-staffel,** *f.* (*Nat. Soc.*) S.S., black-shirts. **-stoff,** *m.* antidote, alexin, antibody. **-truppe,** *f.* colonial troops. **-umschlag,** *m.* wrapper, jacket (*of book*). **-verwandte(r),** *m.* stranger enjoying citizen's rights. **-vorrichtung,** *f.* safety-device. **-wache,** *f.* escort. **-waffen,** *f.pl.* defensive arms; means of defence. **-wand,** *f.* safety wall, protecting screen. **-weg,** *m.* pedestrian crossing. **-wehr,** *f.* fence; bulwark, defence work, rampart, mantlet (*Fort.*); defensive weapon. **-zoll,** *m.* protective duty *or* tariff. **-zöllner,** *m.* protectionist. **-zollsystem,** *n.* protectionism.

Schütz, 1. *n.* (-es, -e) remote-control switch (*Elec.*); *see also* **-e,** *f.* 2. *m.*, **-e,** *m.* (-en, -en) marksman, sharpshooter, rifleman, private (*infantry*); member of rifle club, shot; archer; Sagittarius (*Astr.*). **-e,** *f.* (-n) sluice-board, sluice-gate; shuttle (*Weav.*). **-enabzeichen,** *n.* marksman's badge. **-enauftritt,** *m.* fire-step (*Fort.*). **-enbataillon,** *n.* light-infantry battalion. **-enbrigade,** *f.* rifle brigade. **-enbruder,** *m.* fellow member of a rifle-club. **-enfest,** *n.* shooting match. **-enfeuer,** *n.* independent fire (*Mil.*). **-engefecht,** *n.* skirmish. **-engilde,** *f.* rifle club. **-engraben,** *m.* trench (*Mil.*). **-engrabenkrieg,** *m.* trench-warfare. **-enhaus,** *n.* shooting-gallery. **-enkette,** *f.* skirmishing order, extended order, line of skirmishers. **-enkönig,** *m.* champion shot. **-enlinie,** *f.*, *see* **-enkette. -enloch,** *n.* fox-hole (*Mil.*). **-ennest,** *n.* rifle-pit. **-enschleier,** *m.* covering party, infantry screen (*Mil.*). **-ensteuerung,** *f.* remote-control switching (*Elec.*). **-enübung,** *f.* rifle-practice. **-enverein,** *m.* rifle club. **-enzug,** *m.* infantry platoon.

schütz-en, *v.a.* protect, guard, defend; shelter, screen (*vor*, against); dam up; *in dem Besitze -en*, maintain in possession of; *gesetzlich geschützt*, patented. **-er,** *m.* protector. **-ling,** *m.* protégé, protégée, charge.

Schwabbel-ei, *f.* babble; garrulity. **-ig,** *adj.* wobbly, flabby. **-n,** *v.n.* (*aux.* h.) wobble, flop about; babble, gurgle, ripple; (*dial.*) prattle, prate, gossip.

Schwabber, *m.* (-s, -) swab, mop (*Naut.*). **-n,** *v.a.* swab (*the deck*); *see also* **schwabbeln.**

Schwabe, *f.* (-n) cockroach; *see* **Schabe.**

schwäbeln, *v.n.* speak in the Swabian dialect. *See* **Schwabe,** *in the Index of Names.*

schwach, *adj.* (*comp.* schwächer, *sup.* schwächst) weak, feeble, infirm, frail, delicate; mild, slight, thin, poor, meagre, sparse, scanty; faint, dim, dull, low (*of sound, light*); *-er Besuch*, poor attendance; *-es Gedächtnis*, poor *or* bad memory; *das -e Geschlecht*, the weaker sex; *nur -e Hoffnung*, only faint hope; *-e Seite*, weak point; *-e Stelle*, vulnerable spot; *-e Stunde*, moment of weakness, unguarded moment; *-e Stimme*, feeble voice; *-es Zeitwort*, weak verb; *es wurde ihr –*, she felt faint. **-bevölkert,** *adj.* thinly *or* sparsely populated. **-färben,** *v.a.* tint, tinge, tone. **-gläubig,** *adj.* weak in faith. **-heit,** *f.* weakness, feebleness, frailty, debility, debilitated condition; fainting turn *or* fit; weak will; *moralische -heit*, frailty; *sich* (*Dat.*) *-heiten einbilden*, get silly notions into one's head, indulge in false hopes; *bilden Sie sich keine -heiten ein*, do not deceive yourself, do not cherish any delusions! **-herzig,** *adj.* faint-hearted. **-kochen,** *v.a.* boil gently, simmer. **-kopf,** *m.* simpleton, imbecile. **-köpfig,** *adj.* weak-headed, silly. (*hum.*) **-matikus,** *m.* (–, *-kusse & -ker*) weakling; ignoramus. **-sauer,** *adj.* weakly acid. **-sichtigkeit,** *f.* amblyopia, dimness of vision. **-sinn,** *m.* feeble-mindedness, imbecility. **-sinnig,** *adj.* feeble-minded, imbecile. **-strom,** *m.* low-tension current (*Elec.*).

Schwäch-e, *f.* (-en) weakness, faintness, debility, feebleness, frailty, infirmity; foible, failing, weak side; (*männliche*) *-e*, impotence. **-en,** *v.a.* weaken, enfeeble, debilitate, enervate; impair, lessen, diminish, dilute, tone down; (*archaic*) seduce, ravish. **-ezustand,** *m.* feeble condition, asthenia; loss of vital power. **-lich,** *adj.* feeble, weak, weakly, sickly, delicate, frail, infirm. **-lichkeit,** *f.* infirmity, frailty. **-ling,** *m.* weakling. **-ung,** *f.* weakening, debilitation; diminution; (*archaic*) defloration, rape.

Schwad, *m.* (-en, -en), **-e,** *f.* (-n) (*both usually used in pl.*), **-en,** *m.* (-s, –) swath, row of mown corn *or* grass.

Schwaden, *m.* (-s, –) suffocating vapour, exhalation; smoke-screen; fire-damp (*Min.*). **-fang,** *m.* ventilating shaft, ventilator.

Schwadron, *f.* (-en) squadron, troop (of cavalry). **-eur,** *m.* (-s, -e) braggart, blusterer, (*coll.*) gas-bag. **-ieren,** *v.n.* (*aux.* h.) brag, boast, draw the long bow.

Schwafel-ei, *f.* (-en) (*coll.*) silly talk, drivel, piffle. **-n,** *v.n.* talk nonsense, drivel on.

Schwager, *m.* (-s, ¨) brother-in-law; (*archaic*) postilion, coachman.

Schwäger-in, *f.* (-innen) sister-in-law. **-schaft,** *f.* relationship by marriage; brothers- and sisters-in-law, relations by marriage.

Schwäher, *m.* (-s, –) (*archaic & Poet.*) father-in-law; (*rare*) brother-in-law.

schwaien, 1. *v.n.* swing (at anchor) (*Naut.*). 2. *v.a.* swing (*the ship*) round.

Schwaige, *f.* (-n) (*dial.*) dairy-farm. **-n,** *v.n.* make cheese. **-r,** *m.* Alpine herdsman.

schwajen, *see* **schwaien.**

Schwalbe, *f.* (-n) swallow, martin. **-nnest,** *n.* swallow's nest; (*sl.*) blister (*for gunner*) (*Av.*). **-nschwanz,** *m.* swallow-tail; swallow-tail coat; dovetail (*Carp.*); swallowtail (butterfly) (*Papilio machaon*); split-trail (*of gun*).

Schwalch, *m.* (-(e)s, -e) gullet (*of a furnace*). **-en,** *v.n.* smoulder.

schwälen, *v.n. & a.* (*dial.*), *see* **schwelen.**

Schwall, *m.* swell, surge, undulation; deluge, flood; sheet (*of flame*); torrent (*of words*); throng.

Schwalm, *m.* (-(e)s, -e) (*Swiss dial.*), *see* **Schwall.**

Schwamm, *m.* (-(e)s, ¨e) sponge; fungus, mushroom, toadstool; morbid growth (*Path.*); dry-rot, tinder, (*sl.*) *– drüber!* no more of it, let us forget it!

-gewächs, *n.* fungous growth (*Surg.*); fungus (*Bot.*). **-gummi,** *n.* sponge rubber. **-ig,** *adj.* spongy; fungous, fungoid; bloated, puffy. **-igkeit,** *f.* sponginess. **-stein,** *m.* fossil sponge, fungite.

Schwan, *m.* (-(e)s, ⸚e) (*dial.* -en, -en) swan. **-en,** *see* **schwanen.** **-endaunen,** *f.pl.* swan's-down. **-engesang,** *m.* swan-song; death-song. **-enhals,** *m.* swan's neck; jaw (*of a gaff*). **-enjungfrau,** *f.* swan-maiden. **-(en)ritter,** *m.* knight of the swan (*Lohengrin*). **-enteich,** *m.* swannery. **-enweiß,** *adj.* (as) white as a swan.

schwand, *see* **schwinden.**

schwanen, *v.n.* (*imp.*) (*Dat.*) have a foreboding *or* presentiment of.

schwang, *see* **schwingen.**

Schwang, *m.* (*only in*) *im –e, in –e,* in motion, in full swing; in vogue; *in – kommen,* come into fashion.

schwanger, *adj.* pregnant, with child; *hoch–,* far advanced in pregnancy; (*fig.*) *mit etwas – gehen,* brood over a th.; (*fig.*) *mit großen Plänen – gehen,* be full of great projects. **-enfürsorge,** *f.* prenatal care. **-schaft,** *f.* pregnancy.

Schwänger-er, *m.* (-ers, -er) begetter, father. **-n,** *v.a.* make pregnant, get with child, put in the family way; impregnate, fecundate; saturate (*Chem.*). **-ung,** *f.* impregnation, fecundation.

schwank, *adj.* pliable, flexible, supple; slender; loose, wavering, unsteady; vague; (*B.*) *ein –es Rohr im Winde,* a reed shaken by the wind; *–e Schritte,* faltering steps; *–es Seil,* slack rope. **-en,** 1. *v.n.* (*aux.* h.) rock, shake, sway, roll, toss (*as a ship*); totter, reel, stagger; oscillate, fluctuate, vary; be irresolute, vacillate, waver, hesitate, falter. 2. *n.* rocking; staggering; pitching; fluctuation; oscillation; vibration; nutation (*Astr.*); vacillation; perturbation; inconstancy. **-end,** *pr.p.* & *adj.* tottering, unsteady, precarious; fluctuating (*of prices*); uncertain, unsettled, vague. **-ung,** *f.* variation, change; *see* **-en,** 2. **-ungsgrenze,** *f.* limit of variability.

Schwank, *m.* (-(e)s, ⸚e) prank, hoax; funny tale; short anecdote; farce (*Theat.*); *er steckt voller Schwänke,* he is full of fun; he knows a lot of funny stories.

Schwanz, *m.* (-es, ⸚e) tail; end; trail (*of a gun*); queue, string (*of people*); (*dial.*) train (*of dress*); (*sl.*) penis, (*vulg.*) cock, prick; *das Pferd beim – aufzäumen,* place the cart before the horse; *den – einziehen,* draw in one's horns, climb down; (*Studs. sl.*) *einen – machen,* fail in one subject; *den – zwischen die Beine nehmen,* take to one's heels; sneak away; *einem den – streichen,* flatter a p.; *den – eines Pferdes stutzen,* dock a horse; *einem auf den – treten,* hurt s.o.'s feelings, tread on a p.'s corns. **-abschnitt,** *m.* caudal segment. **-blech,** *n.* trail-spade (*Artil.*). **-ende,** *n.* tip of a tail. **-feder,** *f.* tail feather. **-fläche,** *f.* tail-plane (*Av.*). **-flosse,** *f.* caudal fin, tail fin. **-knochen,** *m.* coccyx. **-lastig,** *adj.* tail-heavy (*Av.*) **-meise,** *f.* long-tailed titmouse (*Aegithalos caudatus*) (*Orn.*). **-riegel,** *m.* trail-transom (*Artil.*). **-riemen,** *m.* crupper. **-spitze,** *f., see* **-ende.** **-sporn,** *m.* tail-skid (*Av.*). **-stern,** *m.* comet. **-steuer,** *n.* rudder (*of an aeroplane*). **-stück,** *n.* tail-piece (*of fish*); rump (*of beef*); trail (*Artil.*). **-wirbel** *m.* caudal vertebra (*Zool.*).

schwänz-eln, *v.n.* (*aux.* h.) wag the tail; strut; fawn upon, wheedle, flatter. **-en,** 1. *v.a.* provide with a tail. *geschwänzt p.p.* & *adj.* with a tail, tailed. 2. *v.n.* (*aux.* h.) strut; *die Schule –en,* play truant; *die Kirche* (or *eine Stunde*) *–en,* (*coll.*) cut church (*or* a lesson); *Noten –en,* miss out *or* skip notes (*Mus.*).

schwapp, *int.* splash! smack! whack! **-(e)lig,** *adj.* wobbly. **-eln, -en, -ern,** 1. *v.n.* (*aux.* h.) splash. 2. *v.a.* spill, splash over; *–end voll,* full to overflowing.

schwaps, *see* **schwapp.**

Schwär, *m.* (-(e)s, -e), **-e,** *f.* (-n), **-en,** *m.* (-s, –) abscess, ulcer. **-en,** *ir.v.n.* (*aux.* h. & s.) suppurate, ulcerate, fester. **-ig,** *adj.* covered with sores *or* ulcers.

Schwarm, *m.* (-(e)s, ⸚e) swarm, cluster, colony, troop, herd, flight, flock; host, throng, multitude, crowd; (*coll.*) idol, hero, pet. **-geist,** *m.* enthusiast; (religious) fanatic. **-linie,** *f.* extended order (*Mil.*). **-weise,** *adv.* in swarms.

schwärm-en, *v.n.* (*aux.* h. & s.) swarm, revel, riot; rove, wander, stray, migrate; sprawl, deploy; dream, daydream; rave, adore, be enthusiastic (*für,* about); (*coll.*) enthuse (about), gush (over), have a crush (on); *es –t von Menschen auf der Straße,* the streets are thronged with people; *alles –t für sie,* everybody is in raptures about her; *sie –t für das Theater,* she is mad about the theatre. **-er,** *m.* enthusiast, dreamer, visionary, (religious) fanatic; hawk-moth (*Sphingidae*) (*Ent.*); sharp-shooter (*Mil.*); cracker, squib (*Firew.*). **-erei,** *f.* enthusiasm, rapture, fanaticism; ecstasy, (*coll.*) gush. **-erisch,** *adj.* fanciful, visionary, rapturous, wild, fanatical, enthusiastic, (*coll.*) gushing. **-spore,** *f.* swarm-cell (*Bot.*). **-zeit,** *f.* swarming time (*of bees*).

Schwart-e, *f.* (-en) crust, rind, skin, cortex, crackling (*of pork*); outside plank; *alte –e,* old book; (*coll.*) *daß die –e knackt,* vigorously, till the pips squeak. **-en,** 1. *v.a.* (*coll.*) pommel, pummel, trounce. 2. *v.n.* pore over (*a book*). **-enmagen,** *m.* collared pork (head), smoked brawn. **-ig,** *adj.* thick-skinned.

schwarz, 1. *adj.* (*comp.* schwärzer, *sup.* schwärzest) black; dark, swarthy; sable; gloomy, dismal; *bei einem – angeschrieben sein,* be in a p.'s bad books; *–e Blattern,* malignant smallpox, variola; *–es Brett,* notice-board; *der –e Erdteil,* the dark continent; *–e Liste,* black list; *– machen,* blacken; *der –e Markt,* the black market; *– sehen,* look on the dark side; *es wurde mir – vor den Augen,* everything went black; *–er Star,* amaurosis (*Path.*); *der –e Tod,* Black Death, the (bubonic) plague; *– auf weiß,* in black and white. 2. *n. indec.* black, black colour, blackness; *in – gehen,* wear black, be in mourning. **-arbeit,** *f.* non-union *or* blackleg labour; illegal employment (*i.e. while drawing unemployment benefit*). **-arbeiten,** *sep. v.n.* be a blackleg, work without authority. **-äugig,** *adj.* dark-eyed. **-blau,** *adj.* & *n.* very dark blue. **-blech,** *n.* sheet-iron. **-blei,** *n.* blacklead. **-brot,** *n.* brown bread, rye-bread. **-dorn,** *m.* (*dial.*) sloe (*Prunus spinosa*) (*Bot.*). **-drossel,** *f.* blackbird. **-e,** 1. *m.* (-en, -en) the devil; (*pej.*) Negro; (*sl.*) *ein –er,* a parson; *die –en,* clerical party. 2. *n.* pupil (*of the eye*); bull's-eye (*of a target*); *ins –e treffen,* hit the bull's-eye; hit it off. **-fahren,** *v.n.* drive without a licence, travel without a ticket, go for a joy-ride (*in a stolen car*). **-gallig,** *adj.* melancholic, atrabilious. **-gar,** *adj.* tanned black. **-gelb,** *adj.* & *n.* dark yellow, tawny. **-gestreift,** *adj.* with black stripes. **-grau,** *adj.* dark grey. **-handel,** *m.* black-market(eering). **-hemden,** *n.pl.* (Italian) fascists (*Pol.*). (*coll.*) **-hören,** *n.* listen in illegally. (*coll.*) **-hörer,** *m.* owner of an unlicensed wireless set, secret listener to foreign radio. **-kauf,** *m.* illicit sale. **-kiefer,** *f.* Austrian pine (*Pinus nigricans*) (*Bot.*). **-kunst,** *f.* black art, necromancy; mezzotinto (*Engr.*). **-künstler,** *m.* necromancer, magician. **-pappel,** *f.* black poplar (*Populus nigra*) (*Bot.*). **-rot,** *adj.* & *n.* dark red. **-rotgold(en),** *adj.* & *n.* (German) Republican. **-scheck,** *m.,* **-schecke,** *f.* piebald horse. **-schimmel,** *m.* iron-grey horse. **-schlachtung,** *f.* illicit slaughtering (*of cattle*). **-seher,** *m.* pessimist. **-seherei,** *f.* pessimism. **-sender,** *m.* radio pirate, illegal transmitter. **-stift,** *m.* black crayon. **-weiß,** *adj.* & *n.* black and white. **-weißrot,** *adj.* & *n.* (German) Nationalist. **-weißzeichnung,** *f.* black and white drawing. **-wild,** *n.* wild boars. **-wurz,** *f.* comfrey. (*Symphytum officinale*) (*Bot.*). **-wurzel,** *f.* viper's grass (*Scorzonera*) (*Bot.*).

Schwärz-e, *f.* (-en) blackness, darkness, swarthiness; blacking; blackening; black; printer's ink; baseness, wickedness, atrociousness, heinousness. **-en,** 1. *v.a.* blacken, (make) black; blacklead; ink; darken; slander, defame, vilify; (*dial.*) smuggle in. 2. *v.r.* & *n.* (*aux.* h.) grow black. **-er,** *m.* (*dial.*) smuggler; blackener. **-lich,** *adj.* blackish, darkish, swarthy, tawny; *ins –liche spielen* or *fallen,* incline to black, be very dark. **-ung,** *f.* density (*Phot.*).

Schwatz, *m.* (*coll.*) talk, chatter, twaddle. **-base,** *f.*, *see* **-maul. -en,** *v.n.* (*aux.* h.) chatter, chat, tattle, gossip; *ins Blaue hinein -en,* talk at random *or* foolishly. **-haft,** *adj.* talkative, chatty. **-haftigkeit,** *f.* talkativeness, loquacity. **-maul,** *n.* (*vulg.*) rattletrap, chatterbox, gossip.

schwätz-en, *v.a. & n.* chatter, babble, talk nonsense, (*dial.*) talk, chat. **-er,** *m.* babbler, chatterer, gossip. **-erei,** *f.* gossip, chatter.

Schweb-e, *f.* (state of) suspense; suspension (*Chem.*); *in der -e sein,* be in suspense *or* undecided *or* in abeyance, hang in the balance; *in -e halten,* keep in suspension. **-ebahn,** *f.* suspension-railway. **-ebaum,** *m.* horizontal bar. **-en,** *v.n.* (*aux.* h.) soar; hover, float in the air; be poised *or* suspended, hang; be pending, be in suspense, be undecided; (*B.*) move; *in Gefahr -en,* be in danger; *in Ungewißheit -en,* be kept in suspense; *auf der Zunge -en,* be on the tip of one's tongue; *sein Bild -t mir immer vor Augen,* his image is always before my eyes; *zwischen Leben und Tod -en,* hover between life and death. **-end,** *pr.p. & adj.* floating, gently rising (*of a slope*), suspended, in suspension; (*fig.*) undecided; pending; *-ende Betonung,* fluctuating accent (*Phon.*); *-ende Brücke,* suspension-bridge; *-ende Frage,* pending *or* unsettled question; *-ende Gärten,* hanging-gardens; (*Poet.*) *-ende Pein,* agony of suspense; *-ende Schuld,* floating debt; *-ender Schritt,* light, elastic step. **-eschritt,** *m.* balance-step (*Mil.*). **-estange,** *f.* tightrope walker's pole. **-estoff,** *m.* suspended matter. **-fliege,** *f.* hovering fly (*Syrphidae*) (*Ent.*) **-ung,** *f.* beat, surge (*Rad.*); *-ungen bilden mit,* beat with (*of oscillations*); *um eine -ung hinaufgehen,* rise a shade *or* fraction.

Schwefel, *m.* sulphur; brimstone; *plastischer -,* amorphous sulphur. **-äther,** *m.* sulphuric ether. **-auflösung,** *f.* solution of sulphur. **-bad,** *n.* sulphur-bath; sulphurous springs. (*coll.*) **-bande,** *f.* band of hooligans. **-blei,** *n.* sulphide of lead. **-faden,** *m.* sulphur wick, sulphurated match. **-farbe,** *f.* brimstone colour. **-gang,** *m.* vein *or* lode of sulphur. **-haltig,** *adj.* sulphurous. **-holz,** *n.*, **-hölzchen,** *n.* (*archaic*) lucifer, match. **-ig** (*usually* **schweflig**), *adj.* sulphurous; *-iges Salz,* sulphite; *-ige Säure,* sulphur dioxide, sulphurous acid. **-igsauer,** *adj.* sulphurous, sulphide of. **-kies,** *m.* iron pyrites. **-kohlenstoff,** *m.* carbon disulphide. **-leber,** *f.* potassium sulphide. **-milch,** *f.* flowers of sulphur. **-n,** *v.a.* impregnate with sulphur, sulphurate; treat *or* fumigate with sulphur; vulcanize (*rubber*). *geschwefelt, p.p. & adj.* sulphuretted. **-sauer,** *adj.*; *-saures Salz,* sulphate; *-saurer Kalk,* calcium sulphate. **-säure,** *f.* sulphuric acid, oil of vitriol. **-verbindung,** *f.* sulphur compound, sulphide, sulphuret. **-wasserstoff,** *m.* sulphuretted hydrogen, hydrogen sulphide.

Schweif, *m.* (-(e)s, -e) tail; train (*of a dress*); trail. **-en,** 1. *v.n.* (*aux.* s.) wander *or* roam about, rove, stray; (*aux.* h.) wander, ramble (*of thoughts, etc.*). 2. *v.a.* provide with a tail; curve, cut on the curve; chamfer, bevel; rinse (out); *schön geschweift,* with a handsome tail; finely arched *or* curved. **-haar,** *n.* tail-hair, horsehair. **-riemen,** *m.* crupper. **-säge,** *f.* bow-saw, fretsaw, compass-saw. **-stern,** *m.* comet. **-ung,** *f.* curve, rounding, swell. **-wedeln,** 1. *v.a.* (*coll.*) wag the tail; fawn (*vor,* upon). 2. *n.* fawning, servility.

schweig-en, 1. *ir.v.n.* (*aux.* h.) be silent, keep silence, say nothing, hold one's tongue, be quiet; *er mußte dazu -en,* he had to let it pass without saying a word; *-(e)!* hush! be quiet! silence! *auf eine Frage -en,* not answer a question; *von . . . ganz zu -en,* not to speak of . . .; *-en Sie mir davon,* do not speak to me about it; *-end zuhören,* listen in silence. 2. *n.* silence; *zum -en bringen,* silence, reduce to silence; *-en gebieten,* order *or* impose silence. **-egeld,** *n.* hush-money. **-epflicht,** *f.* professional discretion. **-er,** *m.* taciturn person. **-sam,** *adj.* silent, taciturn; secretive, reserved. **-samkeit,** *f.* taciturnity.

Schwein, *n.* (-(e)s, -e) hog, pig; swine; (*fig.*) filthy wretch; (*coll.*) *- haben,* be in luck, fall on one's feet, strike oil; *wildes -,* wild boar. **-ebraten,** *m.* roast pork. **-efett,** *n.* lard. **-efleisch,** *n.* pork. **-ehals,** *m.* bull-neck. (*coll.*) **-(e)hund,** *m.* scoundrel, blackguard, rapscallion, reprobate, (*sl.*) bad egg, cur, skunk, son of a gun; *der innere -ehund,* cowardice, faint-heartedness, funk. **-ekoben,** *m.* **-ekofen,** *m.* pigsty. **-emast,** *f.* mast for swine. **-emetzgerei,** *f.* pork-butcher's shop. **-epest,** *f.* swine fever. **-epökelfleisch,** *n.* salt-pork. **-erei,** *f.* (*coll.*) filthiness, obscenity, disgusting behaviour, filthy joke. **-erne(s),** *n.* (*dial.*) pork. **-eschmalz,** *n.*, **-eschmer,** *n.* lard. **-estall,** *m.* pigsty. **-etreiber,** *m.* swineherd. (*fig., coll.*) **-ewirtschaft,** *f.* dirty mess, disgusting state of affairs. **-ezucht,** *f.* pig-breeding. **-hund,** *m., see* **-(e)hund. -igel,** *m.* hedgehog; (*fig.*) pig *or* swine. **-igeln,** *v.n.* *aux.* h.) behave in a beastly way; make smutty jokes. **-isch,** *adj.* piggish, swinish, filthy, beastly. **-sborste,** *f.* hog's bristle. **-sbraten,** *see* **-ebraten. -skeule,** *f.* leg of pork. **-skopf,** *m.* hog's (*or* boar's) head. **-sleder,** *n.* pigskin, hogskin. **-srippchen,** *n.* pork-chop. **-srüssel,** *m.* pig's snout. **-srücken,** *m.* loin of pork.

Schweiß, *m.* (-es, -e) sweat, perspiration; moisture; sebaceous secretion, yolk, suint (*of wool*); blood (*Hunt.*); (*fig.*) sweat of one's brow; (*Prov.*) *ohne - kein Preis,* no gains without pains; *in - geraten,* break out into perspiration; *das ist mein saurer -,* that is the fruit of my hard toil. **-bedeckt,** *adj.* perspiring. **-befördernd,** *adj., see* **-treibend. -blätter,** *n.pl.* dress-preservers *or* shields. **-drüse,** *f.* sweat gland. **-erregend,** *adj., see* **-treibend. -fuchs,** *m.* sorrel *or* dark chestnut horse. **-gang,** *m.* sweat *or* sebaceous duct. **-gebadet,** *adj.* bathed in perspiration. **-hund,** *m.* bloodhound. **-ig,** *adj.* perspiring, sweaty. **-loch,** *n.* **-pore,** *f.* pore. **-treibend,** *adj.* sudorific, diaphoretic. **-triefend,** *adj.* dripping with perspiration. **-tropfen,** *m.* bead of perspiration. **-tuch,** *n.* sweat-rag; *das -tuch Christi,* sudarium. (*B.*) **-tüchlein,** *n.* kerchief, napkin.

schweiß-en, 1. *v.n.* (*aux.* h. & s.) bleed (*Hunt.*); leak, (*dial.*) sweat. 2. *v.a.* weld. 3. *n.* welding. **-arbeit,** *f.* welding. **-bar,** *adj.* weldable. **-brenner,** *m.* welding-torch. **-draht,** *m.* welding rod. **-eisen,** *n.* wrought iron. **-er,** *m.* welder. **-erei,** *f.* welding plant. **-hitze,** *f.* welding heat. **-mittel,** *n.* welding flux. **-naht,** *f.* welded joint *or* seam, fillet. **-pulver,** *n., see* **-mittel. -stahl,** *m.* weld steel. **-stelle,** *f.* weld. **-ung,** *f.* welding.

schwel-en, 1. *v.n.* (*aux.* h.) smoulder, char, burn without flame. 2. *v.a.* burn slowly; *Teer -en,* extract *or* distil tar. **-koks,** *m.* carbonization coke. **-ofen,** *m.* distilling oven, carbonizing furnace. **-wasser,** *n.* water of distillation.

schwelg-en, *v.n.* (*aux.* h.) feast, carouse, gormandize; riot, revel, indulge, luxuriate (*in,* in); run riot; (*coll.*) *im Überfluß -en,* live on the fat of the land. **-er,** *m.* sybarite, reveller, epicure, glutton. **-erei,** *f.* revelry, gluttony, feasting, debauchery. **-erisch,** *adj.* luxurious, voluptuous; gluttonous.

Schwelle, *f.* (-n) threshold, doorstep, sill; sleeper, tie (*Railw.*); crossbar, ledge, architrave, joist; (*fig.*) brink, door. **-nreiz,** *m.* threshold of sensation.

schwell-en, 1. *ir.v.n.* (*aux.* s.) swell, rise, increase, grow (fat), grow bigger, swell (*Mus.*); (*fig. coll.*) puff o.s. up, give o.s. airs; *es schwoll ihm der Mut,* his courage rose. 2. *v.a.* swell, inflate, distend, bloat. **-bar,** *adj.* erectile. **-er,** *m.* swell (*Mus.*). **-gewebe,** *n.* erectile tissue. **-rost,** *m.* horizontal pile-work (*Arch.*). **-ton,** *m.* crescendo. **-ung,** *f.* swelling, growth, tumour; tumefaction, tumescence. **-werk,** *n.* swell (*Org.*).

Schwemm-e, *f.* (-n) horse-pond, watering-place (*for cattle*); tavern, taproom; *ein Pferd in die -e reiten,* ride a horse to water; *Vieh in die -e treiben,* water cattle. **-en,** *v.a.* float (*timber, etc.*); wash *or* carry off; rinse, wash (*cattle, etc.*). **-boden,** *m., see* **-land. -gebilde,** *n.* alluvium. **-land,** *n.* alluvial land, delta silt. **-system,** *n.* flushing-system. **-wiese,** *f.* irrigation-meadow.

Schwengel, *m.* (-s, -) clapper (*of a bell*), handle (*of a pump*), swingle (*of a flail*), swingletree, swing-

bar (*of a wagon*); (*coll.*) lout; *Laden–*, counter-jumper.
schwenkbar, *adj.* swivel-mounted, manœuvrable.
schwenk-en, 1. *v.a.* swing; turn, swivel, traverse (*a gun*); shake about, wave to and fro, flourish, brandish, toss (*Cook.*); rinse (*a glass, etc.*); (*coll.*) sling out. 2. *v.r.* & *n.* (*aux.* h.) turn, swivel traverse; wheel (*Mil.*); (*fig.*) change one's mind, change sides; *links –t, marsch!* left wheel, quick march! **–bereich,** *m.* field of traverse (*Artil.*). **–lafette,** *f.* swivelled gun-mounting. (*dial.*) **–er,** *m.* tail coat. **–ung,** *f.* rinsing; turning movement, wheeling, traversing; change of mind; *eine –ung machen*, wheel (*to the right or left*); (*fig.*) change one's mind. **–ungspunkt,** *m.* pivot. **–ungswinkel,** *m.* angle of traverse.
schwer, *adj.* heavy, weighty, ponderous, clumsy; difficult, hard, arduous, severe, oppressive; grave, serious, grievous; strong (*of cigars*); indigestible (*of food*); *–e Angst*, great anxiety; *–e Arbeit*, difficult (piece of) work; *–e Artillerie*, medium artillery (*–ste Artillerie*, heavy artillery); *–er Atem*, shortness of breath; *– von Begriff*, slow *or* dull of comprehension; *– betrunken*, helplessly drunk; *–er Boden*, rich soil; *– büßen*, pay dearly for; *das wird ihm – eingehen*, he will scarcely be able to understand that, he will not easily be reconciled to that; *es fällt mir –*, I find it hard, it is hard for me; *–es Geld kosten*, cost a great deal *or* a lot of money; *–es Geschütz*, heavy guns; *–es Gewitter*, violent storm; *es liegt mir – in den Gliedern*, there is a heaviness in my limbs; *–en Herzens*, reluctantly, with a heavy heart; *sich – hüten*, take good care; (*coll.*) *–er Junge*, professional thief; *es kommt ihn – an*, he finds it hard; *–es Leben*, hard life; *– darniederliegen*, be dangerously ill; *etwas – nehmen*, take a th. to heart; (*coll.*) *er ist – reich*, he is mighty well off; *–e See*, heavy *or* rough sea; *–e Speisen*, heavy *or* solid food; *–e Strafe*, severe punishment, heavy fine; *–e Stunde*, hour of trial; *–e Verantwortung*, grave responsibility; *–es Verbrechen*, serious crime; *er ist – verwundet*, he is severely wounded; *–er Wein*, strong, full-bodied wine; *–e Zunge*, sluggish tongue. **–arbeiter,** *m.* manual labourer, navvy. **–athletik,** *f.* strenuous athletics (*boxing, wrestling, putting the weight, etc.*). **–atmig,** *adj.* asthmatic. **–blütig,** *adj.* phlegmatic. **–e,** *f.* (-en) heaviness, weight, gravity (*Phys.*); severity, difficulty, rigour, hardness; body (*of wine*); full weight (*of a word*). **–enot,** *f.*; *es ist um die –enot zu kriegen*, it's enough to sicken one; (*vulg.*) *–enot noch einmal! daß dich die –enot!* damn your eyes! **–enöter,** *m.* (*coll.*) go-getter, ladies' man, gay Lothario. **–erworben,** *adj.* hard-earned. **–esinnesorgan,** *n.* semicircular canals (*of the ear*), organ of equilibrium. **–fallen,** *v.n.* be difficult *or* a burden. **–fällig,** *adj.* heavy, ponderous, cumbersome, unwieldy; dull, slow, sluggish; clumsy, awkward. **–fälligkeit,** *f.* heaviness, clumsiness, slowness. **–flüssig,** *adj.* difficult to fuse, refractory. **–gewicht,** *n.* heavy weight (*Boxing*); (*fig.*) chief stress, emphasis. **–gewichter,** *m.* heavyweight boxer (*over 80 kg.*). **–gläubig,** *adj.* incredulous. **–halten,** *v.n.* be a hard task; *es wird –halten, daß ich komme*, it will be difficult for me to come. **–hörig,** *adj.* hard of hearing, rather deaf. **–hörigkeit,** *f.* defective hearing, deafness. **–industrie,** *f.* mining and iron and steel industries. **–kraft,** *f.* (force of) gravity. **–kraftstoffe,** *m.pl.* heavy fuels. **–kriegsbeschädigte(r),** *m.* disabled soldier. **–lich,** *adv.* hardly, scarcely, with difficulty. **–mut,** *f.* melancholy, sadness, depression. **–mütig,** *adj.* dejected, sad, melancholy, mournful. **–ölmotor,** *m.* Diesel engine. **–punkt,** *m.* centre of gravity; (*fig.*) point of main effort, crucial point; strong point (*Mil.*). **–punktbildung,** *f.* concentration of forces (*Mil.*). **–spat,** *m.* heavy spar, barytes. **–verbrecher,** *m.* criminal, gangster. **–verdaulich,** *adj.* indigestible. **–verdient,** *adj.* hard-earned. **–verletzt,** *adj.* disabled. **–verständlich,** *adj.* difficult to understand, abstruse. **–verwundete(r),** *m.* major casualty (*Mil.*). **–wiegend,** *adj.* weighty; (*fig.*) grave, serious, important.
Schwert, *n.* (-(e)s, -er) sword; centre-board, lee-board, drop-keel, (*of boats*); (*fig.*) force of arms, military force; *zum –e greifen*, draw one's sword; *zum –e verurteilen*, condemn to be beheaded. **–adel,** *m.* military nobility. **–boot,** *n.* centre-board boat. **–el,** *m.* sword-lily, gladiolus (*Bot.*). **–(er)geklirr,** *n.* clash(ing) of swords. **–(er)tanz,** *m.* sword-dance. **–feger,** *m.* armourer, sword-cutler. **–fisch,** *m.* swordfish (*Xiphias gladius*) (*Ichth.*). **–förmig,** *adj.* sword-shaped, ensiform. **–hieb,** *m.* sword-cut. **–leite,** *f.* inauguration into knighthood (*Hist.*). **–lilie,** *f* iris. **–streich,** *m.*; *ohne –streich*, without striking a blow, without bloodshed. **–schwanz,** *m.* king crab.
Schwester, *f.* (-n) sister; hospital nurse; nun; *leibliche –*, full sister; *barmherzige –*, sister of mercy, hospital nurse. **–art,** *f.* sister-species (*Biol.*). **–kind,** *n.* nephew *or* niece. **–lich,** *adj.* sisterly; sororal. **–(n)liebe,** *f.* sisterly love. **–(n)paar,** *n.* two *or* a couple of sisters. **–schaft,** *f.* sisterhood. **–sohn,** *m.* nephew. **–tochter,** *f.* niece.
Schwibbogen, *m.* flying-buttress, pier-arch.
schwichten, *v.a.* rope together (*Naut.*).
schwieg, schwiege, *see* **schweigen.**
Schwieger, *f.* (-n) (*obs.* & *Poet.*) mother-in-law. **–eltern,** *pl.* parents-in-law. **–mutter,** *f.* mother-in-law. **–sohn,** *m.* son-in-law. **–tochter,** *f.* daughter-in-law. **–vater,** *m.* father-in-law.
Schwiel-e, *f.* (-en) callosity, callous; weal, welt. **–ig,** *adj.* callous, horny; marked with weals.
Schwiem-el, *m.* (*dial.*) giddiness, fainting fit. **–(e)ler,** *m.* (-s, –) rake, tippler. **–elei,** *f.* dissolute behaviour. **–(e)lig,** *adj.* dissolute. **–eln,** *v.n.* (*aux.* h. & s.) (*coll.* & *dial.*) reel, get dizzy; lead a dissolute life.
schwierig, *adj.* difficult, arduous, hard, complicated, (*coll.*) tough, tricky; fastidious, particular; fractious, rebellious; *–e Frage*, knotty question; *–e Verhältnisse*, trying circumstances; *das –ste haben wir hinter uns*, the worst is over. **–keit,** *f.* difficulty, obstacle, trouble; *das macht gar keine –keit*, there is no difficulty about that; *–keiten machen* or *suchen*, raise difficulties *or* objections.
schwiert, *see* **schwären.**
schwill, schwillst, schwillt, *see* **schwellen.**
schwimm-en, *ir.v.n.* (*aux.* h. & s.) swim; float; be bathed in; overflow with, welter, roll; *im Blute* (*in Tränen*) *–en*, be bathed in blood (in tears); *mit dem Strom –en*, go *or* swim with the stream; *der Schauspieler –t*, the actor relies on the prompter; *etwas –en lassen*, give up, forgo, relinquish *or* abandon a th. **–anstalt,** *f.* swimming-baths *or* pool. **–art,** *f.* style of swimming. **–bad,** *n.* swimming-bath. **–bewegung,** *f.* ciliary movement. **–blase,** *f.* air-bladder (*of fish*); water-wings. **–dock,** *n.* floating dock. **–end,** *pr.p.* & *adj.* floating; *–endes Strandgut*, flotsam; *–ende Häuser*, ships; *–ender Tank*, amphibian tank; *–ende Waren*, goods afloat *or* carried by water, goods in transit. **–er,** *m.* swimmer; float (*Mach.* & *Av.*). **–erflugzeug,** *n.* seaplane, hydroplane. **–ergestell,** *n.* float under-carriage *or* landing-gear (*Av.*). **–erventil,** *n.* float-gauge. **–fähig,** *adj.* buoyant. **–fähigkeit,** *f.* buoyancy. **–flosse,** *f.* fin. **–fuß,** *m.* webbed *or* palmated foot. **–gürtel,** *m.* life-belt, water-wings. **–haut,** *f.* web, membrane. **–häutler,** *m.pl.* web-footed animals, palmipeds. **–hosen,** *f.pl.* bathing-trunks. **–käfer,** *m.* water-beetle (*Dytiscidae*) (*Ent.*). **–kampfwagen,** *m.* amphibian tank. **–kasten,** *m.* caisson. **–kraft,** *f.* buoyancy. **–lage,** *f.* trim. **–linie,** *f.* water-line. **–(m)eister,** *m.* champion swimmer. **–panzer,** *m.* amphibian tank. **–sand,** *m.* quick-sand. **–sport,** *m.* swimming. **–stoß,** *m.* stroke. **–vogel,** *m.* web-footed bird, palmiped. **–werk,** *n.* float landing-gear (*Av.*). **–weste,** *f.* life (saving) jacket, (*sl.*) 'Mae West'.
Schwind-el, *m.* (-els, -el) giddiness, dizziness, vertigo, staggers; swindle, fraud, trick, humbug; (*coll.*) *den –el kenn' ich*, I know that trick, I am up to that dodge; (*vulg.*) *der ganze –el*, the whole shemozzle; *den –el bekommen*, turn giddy. **–elanfall,** *m.* attack of giddiness. **–elei,** *f.* swindle, fraud, deceit, trickery. **–elfrei,** *adj* free from giddiness. **–elgefühl,** *n.* vertigo. (*C.L.*) **–elgesellschaft,** *f.*, *see* **–elunternehmen. –elhaft,** *adj.*

fraudulent, deceptive, swindling; dizzy; causing giddiness. **-(e)lig,** *see* **-lig. -elkopf,** *m.* hare-brained *or* giddy person. **-elköpfig,** *adj.* hare-brained. (*coll.*) **-elmeier,** *m.* swindler. **-eln,** *v.n.* (*aux.* h.) swindle, cheat; humbug; *v. imp.* (*Dat.*) be giddy *or* dizzy; *mir -elt,* my head swims, my brain is reeling; I am giddy; *er -elt,* he is not telling the truth. *-elnde Höhe,* dizzy height; **-elunterneh-men,** *n.* bogus company *or* concern. **-ler,** *m.* swindler, fraud, cheat. **-lerisch,** *adj.* fraudulent. **-lig,** *adj.* giddy, dizzy.

schwind-en, 1. *ir.v.n.* (*aux.* s.) become less, contract, wither, shrink, dwindle, fade, atrophy, waste away, vanish, disappear, decline, die away, decay; *die Geschwulst -et,* the swelling is going down; *sein Mut -et ihm,* his courage is dwindling; *die Jahre -en,* the years fly by. 2. *n.* shrinking, shrinkage; drying up, wastage, atrophy. **-lunke,** *f.* shrinkage cavity. **-maß,** *n.* (amount of) shrinkage. **-maßstab,** *m.* scale, reduction factor (*for models*). **-risse,** *m.pl.* shrinkage cracks. **-sucht,** *f.* consumption, phthisis. **-süchtig,** *adj.* consumptive. **-ung,** *f.* shrinkage, contraction. **-ungsloch,** *n., see* **-lunke.**

Schwing-e, *f.* (-en) wing (*of bird*); (*Poet.*) pinion; swingle (*for flax*); winnow, fan. **-en,** 1. *ir.v.a.* swing, whirl round, flourish, brandish, wield, wave; (*Swiss dial.*) wrestle; swingle, winnow, scutch, hydroextract, centrifuge; (*coll.*) *das Tanzbein -en,* foot it, do the light fantastic; *eine Rede -en,* make a speech, hold forth; *sie -t den Pantoffel,* she wears the trousers; (*Swiss dial.*) *den Nidel -en,* whip cream. 2. *v.r.* swing o.s., spring, bound, vault, leap; soar, rise, ascend; *sich in den Sattel -en,* vault *or* jump into the saddle; *sich auf den Thron -en,* usurp the throne. 3. *v.n.* (*aux.* h.) swing, sway, oscillate, vibrate. **-achse,** *f.* independent axle, flexible front-drive axle (*Motor.*). **-blatt,** *n.* membrane. **-brett,** *n.* swingle-board (*for flax*). **-el,** *m.* fescue-grass (*Festuca pratensis*) (*Bot.*). **-end,** *adj.* oscillating, vibrating, vibratory. **-er,** *m.* swing, swinging blow (*Boxing*); (*Swiss dial.*) wrestler. **-fest,** *n.* (*Swiss dial.*) wrestling competition. **-gerät,** *n.* trapeze, swing (*Gymn.*). **-kolben,** *m.* balancer, poiser (*Ent.*). **-messer,** *n.pl.* scutching blades. **-seil,** *n.* slack rope, swing. **-stock,** *m.* flail, swingle. **-ung,** *f.* swinging; oscillation, wave, vibration; *Längs-ung* (*Quer-ung*), longitudinal (transverse) vibration; *in -ung versetzen,* cause to vibrate, set oscillating. **-ungsachse,** *f.* axis of oscillation, nodal line. **-ungsdämpfung,** *f.* attenuation. **-ungsdauer,** *f.* period of oscillation, cycle. **-ungsknoten,** *m.* node. **-ungskreis,** *m.* oscillatory circuit (*Rad.*). **-ungsweite,** *f.* amplitude. **-ungs-welle,** *f.* undulation, travelling wave. **-ungszahl,** *f.* frequency (of oscillations). **-ungszeit,** *f., see* **-ungsdauer. -wanne,** *f.* winnowing fan.

schwipp, 1. *int.* crack! (*as a whip*), splash! 2. *adj.* (*dial.*) nimble, agile; pliant, flexible. **-e,** *f.* (-en) (*dial.*) whip-lash, switch. **-en,** (*dial.*) 1. *v.a.* jerk, throw, fling; lash, (*coll.*) swipe. 2. *v.n.* (*aux.* h. & s.) overflow, spill (over). **-schwager,** *m.,* **-schwäge-rin,** *f.* (*coll.*) brother- (sister-)in-law of one's wife *or* husband; father (mother) of one's son- or daughter-in-law.

schwips, 1. *int.* smack! slap! 2. *m.* (-es, -e), cut, lash *or* flip (*with a whip, etc.*); (*sl.*) *einen – haben,* be tight, tipsy *or* fuddled.

schwirr-en, *v.n.* (*aux.* h. & s.) & *imp.* whiz, whir; buzz, hum; fly (about) (*of rumours*); (*coll.*) buzz off; *es schwirrt mir in den Ohren* (*vor den Augen*), I have a buzzing in my ears (a mist before my eyes); *das -en der Kugeln,* the whizzing of the bullets. **-vogel,** *m.* humming-bird.

Schwitz-e, *f.* thickening (*for soups, etc.*); *in die -e bringen,* sweat (*skins, Tan.*). **-en,** 1 *v.n.* (*aux.* h.) sweat, perspire. 2. *v.a.* (cause to) sweat; *Häute -en,* sweat hides. **-bad,** *n.* Turkish bath. **-ig,** *adj.* sweaty. **-mittel,** *n.* sudorific, diaphoretic. **-wasser,** *n.* condensed water, condensation.

Schwof, *m.* (-(e)s, -e) (*dial.*) (public) dance, (*sl.*) hop. **-en,** *v.n.* go dancing *or* to a dance.

schwoien (*Naut.*), *see* **schwaien.**

schwoll, schwölle, *see* **schwellen.**

[1]**schwor, schwöre,** *see* **schwären.**

[2]**schwor, schwöre,** *see* **schwören.**

schwören, *ir.v.a.* & *n.* (*aux.* h.) swear (on oath); take an oath; (*B.*) swear, curse; *auf einen –,* have absolute confidence in a p., swear by a p.; *ich könnte fast darauf –,* I could almost swear to it; *bei meiner Ehre –,* swear on my honour; *bei Gott –,* swear to God; (*archaic*) *Huld und Treue –,* take the oath of allegiance; *einen – lassen,* administer an oath to a p.; *einem Rache –,* vow vengeance against a p.; *vor Gericht –,* take the oath; *zur Fahne –,* take the military oath.

schwude, *int.* (*dial.*) (to the) left!

schwul, *adj.* (*vulg.*) homosexual.

schwül, *adj.* sultry, close, oppressive; *mir ist – zu Mute, mir wird's – ums Herz,* I feel very uneasy. **-e,** *f.* sultriness, closeness.

Schwulität, *f.* (-en) (*sl.*) trouble, anxiety, embarrassment.

Schwulst, *m.* (-es, ⸚e) & *f.* (⸚e) swelling, tumour; (*usually fig.*) pomposity, bombast, turgidity. **-ig,** *adj.* swollen, puffed up (*not fig*).

schwülstig, *adj.* bombastic, high-flown, turgid. **-keit,** *f.* bombastic style, pomposity.

Schwund, *m.* withering, contraction, shrinkage, disappearance, loss (*of hair, etc.*), falling off, dropping (*of a vowel, etc.*); atrophy (*Med.*), fading (*Rad.*). **-ausgleich,** *m.* automatic volume-control (*Rad.*). **-stufe,** *f.* null-grade (*Philol.*).

Schwung, *m.* (-(e)s, ⸚e) swing, vibration, oscillation; bound, spring, vault; soaring, flight, play (*of imagination, etc.*); energy, imports, verve; animation, warmth, ardour; (*coll.*) go, dash; *einen auf den – bringen,* bring a p. to the point (*of doing s.th.*); *keinen – haben,* fall flat; *in – bringen,* set going; *in – kommen,* get going; *in – sein,* be on *or* in form; *im – sein,* be in full swing. **-bewegung,** *f.* vibratory motion. **-brett,** *n.* spring-board. **-feder,** *f.* pinion (*of birds*). **-flachs,** *m.* scutched flax **-gewicht,** *n.* pendulum. **-haft,** *adj.* soaring, sublime; swinging, full of movement, lively, flourishing, brisk. **-körper,** *m.* swinging body. **-kraft,** *f.* centrifugal force; (*fig.*) energy, liveliness, buoyancy. **-los,** *adj.* dull, commonplace, unimaginative. **-rad,** *n.* fly-wheel; balance-wheel (*Horol.*). **-riemen,** *m.pl.* main-braces, check-braces (*of a carriage*). **-seil,** *n.* slack rope. **-voll,** *adj.* lofty, stirring, full of fire *or* enthusiasm, spirited, animated, energetic.

schwupp, 1. *adv.* & *int.* presto, like a shot, no sooner said than done; got you! 2. *m.* (-es, -e) push, shove, jolt, splash. **-diwupp,** *int., see* – 1. **-er,** *m.* (*dial.*) blunder, howler, bloomer.

schwups, *int.* & *subst. m., see* **schwips.**

Schwur, *m.* (-s, ⸚e) oath, vow; curse; *einen – leisten* or *tun,* take an oath. **-finger,** *m.pl.* the fingers raised in swearing. **-formel,** *f.* wording of an oath. **-gericht,** *n.* assize court.

schwur, schwüre, *see* **schwören.**

Sech, *n.* (-(e)s, -e) ploughshare, coulter.

sechs, 1. *num. adj.* six; *mit -en fahren,* drive a coach and six, drive six in hand; *viertel –,* a quarter past five; *halb –,* half-past five; *drei Viertel –,* (*ein*) *Viertel vor* or *auf –,* a quarter to six; (*sl.*) *meiner – ! see* **Six.** 2. *f.* (-en) number 6. **-achtel-takt,** *m.* six-eight time (*Mus.*). **-blätt(e)rig,** *adj.* hexaphyllous; hexapetalous. **-e,** (*coll.*) *see* – (*only used when not followed by anything*); *wir -e,* we six, the six of us. **-eck,** *n.* hexagon. **-ender,** *m.* stag with 6 points. **-einhalb,** *see* **-undhalb. -er,** *m.* number 6; soldier of the 6th regiment; coin (*denomination varies according to locality*: 5, 10, *or* 20 *Pfennig*); *nicht Verstand für einen -er haben,* not have a ha'porth of sense; **-erlei,** *indec. adj.* of 6 kinds, 6 kinds of. **-fach,** *adj., see* **-fältig. -fache,** *n.* 6 times the amount. **-fältig,** *adj.* sixfold, sextuple. **-flach,** *n.,* **-flächner,** *m.* hexahedron. **-gliedrig,** *adj.* of 6 digits. **-hebig,** *adj.* containing 6 accented syllables (*a verse*). **-hundert,** *num. adj.* six hundred. **-jährig,** *adj.* 6 years old, sexennial. **-kant,** *n.* hexagon. **-kanteisen,** *n.* hexagonal section bar. **-mal,** *adv.* 6 times over. **-malig,** *adj.* 6 times repeated. **-monatig,** *adj.* lasting 6 months. **-monatlich,** 1. *adj.* six-monthly, half-yearly. 2. *adv.* every 6 months.

-seitig, *adj.* hexagonal. **-silbig,** *adj.* of 6 syllables. **-stellig,** *adj.* of 6 digits. **-stern,** *m.* hexagram, six-pointed star. **-stimmig,** *adj.* for 6 voices (*Mus.*). **-t,** *num. adj.* (der, die, das -te) the sixth; *am -ten,* on the 6th; *zum -ten,* sixthly. **-tägig,** *adj.* of *or* lasting 6 days. **-tausend,** *num. adj.* six thousand. **-t(e)halb,** *indec. adj.* five and a half, **-tel** *n.* (*Swiss dial. m.*) one-sixth, sixth part. **-tens,** *adv.* sixthly, in the sixth place. **-(und)einhalb,** *num. adj.* six-and-a-half. **-undsechzig,** 1. *num. adj.* sixty-six. 2. *n.* German card game.

sech-zehn, 1. *num. adj.* sixteen. 2. *f.* the number sixteen. **-zehnfach,** *adj.* 16 times as much. **-zehnjährig,** *adj.* 16 years old. **-zehnlötig,** *adj.* weighing 8 ounces; (*fig.*) pure (*silver*). **-zehnt,** *num. adj.* (der, die, das -zehnte) sixteenth. **-zehntel,** *n.* sixteenth part; semiquaver (*Mus.*). **-zehntelformat,** *n.* sexto-decimo (*Typ.*). **-zehntelnote,** *f.* semiquaver (*Mus.*). **-zehntelpause,** *f.* semiquaver rest (*Mus.*). **-zig,** 1. *num. adj.* sixty. 2. *f.* (-e) the number sixty; *er ist hoch in den -zige(r)n,* he is well advanced in the sixties. **-ziger,** 1. *m.* sexagenarian; pique (*Cards*). 2. *indec. adj.* sixty; *die -ziger Jahre,* the sixties. **-zigst,** *num. adj.* (der, die, das -zigste) sixtieth. **-zigstel,** *n.* sixtieth part. **-zigstens,** *adv.* in the sixtieth place.

Sedez, *n.* (-es, -e) **-format,** *n.* sixteens, 16mo (*Typ.*).

Sediment, *n.* (-s, -e) sediment, deposit, settlings. **-är,** *adj.* sedimentary, result of deposit. **-gestein,** *n.* sedimentary rock.

See, 1. *m.* (-s, -n) lake. 2. *f.* (-n) sea; ocean; *an der -,* by the sea(side); *an die - gehen,* go to the seaside; *auf der -,* at sea; *auf hoher -,* on the high seas, out at sea; *die - ging hoch,* the sea ran high; *in - gehen* or *stechen,* put (out) to sea, set sail; *zur -,* by sea; *zur - gehen,* go to sea, become a sailor; *Kapitän zur -,* naval captain. **-abrüstung,** *f.* naval disarmament. **-adler,** *m.* white-tailed eagle (*Haliaetus albicella*) (*Orn.*). **-alpen,** *m.pl.* maritime Alps. **-amt,** *n.* maritime court, (German) Admiralty Court. **-ausdruck,** *m.* nautical term. **-bad,** *n.* sea-side resort. **-bär,** *m.* (*coll.*) old salt, old sea-dog. **-bataillon,** *n.* marines. **-beben,** *n.* submarine earthquake. **-behörde,** *f.*; *oberste -behörde,* the Admiralty. **-beschädigt,** *adj.* damaged at sea. **-beschreibung,** *f.* hydrography. **-beute,** *f.* prize (*Naut.*). **-brief,** *m.* sailing orders; (*pl.*) ship's papers. **-dienst,** *m.* service afloat. **-fähig,** *adj.* seaworthy, sea-going. **-fahrer,** *m.* sailor; seafarer. **-fahrt,** *f.* seafaring; sea voyage, cruise. **-fahrtbuch,** *n.* seaman's registration book. **-fahrtschule,** *f.* merchant marine school. **-fest,** *adj.* seaworthy; (*coll.*) not subject to seasickness; *-fest sein,* be a good sailor. **-festung,** *f.* fortified naval base. **-fisch,** *m.* salt-water fish. **-flieger,** *m.* naval airman. **-fliegerhorst,** *m.*, **-flugstation,** *f.* seaplane base. **-flugzeug,** *n.* seaplane. **-frachtbrief,** *m.* bill of lading. **-gang,** *m.* heavy sea, swell, seaway; *der -gang nimmt zu,* the sea is getting up. **-gebiet,** *n.* sea area, waters. **-gefecht,** *n.* naval engagement, naval action. **-gefrörne,** *f.* (*Swiss dial.*) closure by ice, state of being icebound. **-geltung,** *f.* naval prestige, mastery of the sea. **-gemälde,** *n.* sea-piece. **-gericht,** *n.* maritime *or* naval court; Court of Admiralty. **-gesetz,** *n.* maritime law. **-gewächs,** *n.* marine plant. **-gras,** *n.* grass weed (*Zostera marina* (*Bot.*). **-gurke,** *f.*, *see* **-walze.** **-hafen,** *m.* seaport. **-hahn,** *m.* seacock. **-handel,** *m.* maritime commerce, shipping trade. **-herrschaft,** *f.* naval supremacy, command of the sea. **-höhe,** *f.* altitude above sea-level. **-hund,** *m.* seal (*Phocidae*) (*Zool.*). **-hundsfell,** *n.* sealskin. **-igel,** *m.* sea-urchin (*Echinoidea*). **-jungfer,** *f.* mermaid; dugong, halicore (*Zool.*). **-kabel,** *n.* submarine cable. **-kadett,** *m.* naval cadet. **-karte,** *f.* (hydrographic) chart. **-klar,** *adj.* ready to sail. **-klima,** *n.* maritime climate. **-klippe,** *f.* shoal, reef. **-kohl,** *m.* sea-kale. **-krank,** *adj.* seasick. **-krankheit,** *f.* seasickness. **-krebs,** *m.* lobster (*Decapoda*) (*Zool.*). **-krieg,** *m.* naval warfare. **-kriegskunst,** *f.* naval strategy. **-kuh,** *f.* sea-cow (*Sirenia*) (*Zool.*). **-kunde,** *f.* hydrography, nautical science, navigation. **-küste,** *f.* seashore, seaboard. **-lachs,** *m.* sea salmon. **-leute,** *pl.* sailors, seamen, mariners. **-licht,** *n.* marine phosphorescence. (*C.L.*) **-liste,** *f.* shipping list. **-löwe,** *m.* sea-lion (*Zalophus*) (*Zool.*). **-macht,** *f.* sea-power, naval forces. **-mann,** *m.* (-leute) seaman, mariner, sailor. **-männisch,** *adj.* seamanlike; seafaring, nautical. **-mannsamt,** *n.* seamen's registration-office. **-mannsheim,** *n.* seamen's hostel. **-mannssprache,** *f.* nautical language. **-marke,** *f.* (marker) buoy. **-meile,** *f.* nautical mile, knot (*1853 metres*). **-nebel,** *m.* sea fog. **-not,** *f.* distress at sea. **-notdienst,** *m.* air-sea rescue service. **-notzeichen,** *n.* SOS. **-nplatte,** *f.* flat country covered with lakes (*Geog.*). **-offizier,** *m.* naval officer. **-pferdchen,** *n.* sea-horse (*Hippocampus*) (*Icht.*). **-pflanze,** *f.* marine plant. **-pocke,** *f.* barnacle. **-polyp,** *m.* octopus. **-rabe,** *m.* cormorant, albatross. (*coll.*) **-ratte,** *f.*, **-ratze,** *f.* old salt, old sea-dog. **-räuber,** *m.* pirate. **-räuberei,** *f.* piracy. **-raum,** *m.*, **-räume,** *f.* sea-room, offing. **-recht,** *n.* maritime law. **-reise,** *f.* (sea) voyage, cruise. **-rose,** *f.* water-lily (*Nymphaea*) (*Bot.*). **-rüstung,** *f.* naval armament. **-schaden,** *m.* loss suffered at sea, average. **-schadenberechnung,** *f.* adjustment of averages. **-schiff,** *n.* sea-going vessel. **-schiffahrt,** *f.* merchant shipping. **-schildkröte,** *f.* turtle (*Cheloniidae*) (*Zool.*). **-schlacht,** *f.* naval engagement *or* battle. **-schlange,** *f.* sea-serpent (*Hydrophiinae*) (*Zool.*); (*fig.*) mare's nest. **-schule,** *f.* naval academy. **-soldat,** *m.* marine. **-sprache,** *f.* nautical language. **-staat,** *m.* maritime nation. **-stadt,** *f.* sea-side *or* coast town. **-stern,** *m.* starfish (*Asteroidea*) (*Zool.*). **-strand,** *m.* strand, beach. **-streitkräfte,** *f.pl.* naval forces. **-stück,** *n.*, *see* **-gemälde.** **-stützpunkt,** *m.* naval base. **-tang,** *m.* sea-weed, brown alga. **-tonne,** *f.* buoy. **-treffen,** *n.*, *see* **-schlacht.** **-trift,** *f.* flotsam and jetsam, jettisoned goods. **-truppen,** *f.pl.* marines. **-tüchtig,** *adj.* seaworthy. **-ufer,** *n.* lakeside. **-ventil,** *n.* sea-cock. **-verbindungslinie,** *f.* (*fig.*) life-line. **-verkehr,** *m.* sea-borne traffic. **-versicherung,** *f.* marine insurance. **-volk,** *n.* maritime people; ship's crews, seamen, seafaring men. **-walze,** *f.* sea-slug, sea-cucumber (*Holothuria*) (*Zool.*). **-warte,** *f.* marine observatory. **-wärts,** *adj.* out to sea, seawards. **-wasser** *n.* sea-water, salt-water; (*Poet.*) brine. **-weg,** *m.* sea-route; *auf dem -wege,* by sea. **-wesen,** *n.* maritime affairs. **-wind,** *m.* sea-breeze. **-wurf,** *m.* jetsam. **-zeichen,** *n.* (marker) buoy, navigational aid. **-zeughaus,** *n.* naval arsenal. **-zunge,** *f.* sole (*Solea vulgaris*) (*Icht.*).

Seel-e, *f.* (-en) soul; mind, spirit, heart; human being; pith (*of a quill*); bore (*of a gun*); sounding-post (*of a violin*); bladder (*of a herring*); central strand (*of shroud-laid rope*); core (*of a cable*) (*Elec.*); *die -e aushauchen,* breathe one's last; *er ist die -e des Ganzen,* he is the very life and soul of (it) all; *sie ist eine -e von einem Mädchen,* she is a dear sweet girl; *es war keine* (*menschliche*) *-e da,* there was not a (living) soul there; *einem etwas auf die -e binden,* enjoin s.th. upon s.o. very earnestly; *das liegt* or *brennt mir auf der -e,* that weighs heavily upon me, that preys on my mind; *Sie sprechen mir aus der -e,* you have read *or* guessed my (inmost) thoughts; (*bei*) *meiner -(e)!* upon my soul! *ein Herz und eine -e sein,* be of one heart and mind; *das ist mir in tiefster -e zuwider,* I detest that from the bottom of my heart; *das tut mir in der -e weh,* that cuts me to the quick; *von ganzer -e,* with all one's heart. **-enachse,** *f.* axis of the bore. **-enadel,** *m.* nobility of soul. **-enamt,** *n.* office for the dead, requiem. **-enangst,** *f.* anguish of soul, mental agony. **-enblindheit,** *f.* visual amnesia. (*Poet.*) **-enbraut,** *f.* mystical bride of Christ, the Church. (*Poet.*) **-enbräutigam,** *m.* Christ. **-endurchmesser,** *m.* calibre (*Artil.*). **-enfreund,** *m.* bosom friend. **-enfriede(n),** *m.* peace of mind. **-enfroh,** *adj.* very glad indeed, delighted. **-engröße,** *f.* magnanimity. **-enhaft,** *adj.*, *see* **-envoll.** **-enheil,** *n.* salvation, spiritual welfare. **-enheilkunde,** *f.* psycho-therapy.

-enhirt, *m.* pastor. **-enkunde,** *f.* psychology. **-enleben,** *n.* inner life, spiritual existence, psyche. **-enlos,** *adj.* soulless, heartless. **-enmesse,** *f.*, *see* **-enamt.** **-ennot,** *f.*, **-enpein,** *f.*, **-enqual,** *f.* anguish of mind, spiritual torment. **-enrohr,** *n.* liner (*Artil.*). **-enruhe,** *f.* peace of mind, tranquillity. **-en(s)gut,** *adj.* thoroughly good; *-enguter Mensch,* dear good soul, kind-hearted person. **-enstärke,** *f.* equanimity, composure, long-sufferance, fortitude. **-entaubheit,** *f.* auditory amnesia. (*sl.*) **-entränke,** *f.* church service. **-envergnügt,** *adj.* heartily glad. **-enverkäufer,** *m.* (*archaic*) kidnapper, slave-dealer; (*coll.*) cranky boat, cockle-shell. **-enverwandt,** *adj.* in harmony *or* unison with, congenial, sympathetic. **-enverwandte,** *pl.* kindred spirits. **-enverwandtschaft,** *f.* congeniality, amity, understanding, harmony. **-envoll,** *adj.* soulful, sentimental, tender. **-enwanderung,** *f.* transmigration of souls, metempsychosis, palingenesis, reincarnation. **-enwärmer,** *m.* (*hum.*) woolly, cardigan. **-enweite,** *f.* calibre (*Artil.*). **-enzustand,** *m.* spiritual condition, psychic state. **-isch,** *adj.* mental, spiritual, emotional, psychic(al). **-sorge,** *f.* care *or* cure of souls; ministerial work, pastoral duties. **-sorger,** *m.* spiritual adviser, clergyman, minister. **-sorgerisch,** *adj.* pastoral, ministerial.

Segel, *n.* (-s, –) sail, canvas; ala, velum (*Bot., Zool. Anat.*); *alle – aufspannen* or *beisetzen,* crowd all sail; *– bergen* or *einziehen,* shorten sail; *das war Wind in seine –,* that was grist to his mill; *lose –,* spare sails; *die – streichen,* strike sail; (*fig.*) give in, climb down; *unter – gehen,* set sail. **-boot,** *n.* sailing boat. **-fertig,** *adj.* ready for sea, ready to sail. **-fliegen,** *n.* gliding. **-flieger,** *m.* glider-pilot. **-flug,** *m.* glide, gliding flight. **-flugzeug,** *n.* glider, sailplane. **-garn,** *n.* sailmaker's thread. **-klar,** *adj.*, *see* **-fertig.** **-klasse,** *f.* rating (*yacht racing*). **-macher,** *m.* sail-maker. **-order,** *f.* sailing orders. **-n,** *v.a.* & *n.* (*aux.* h. & s.) sail; soar (*of glider*). **-schiff,** *n.* sailing ship *or* vessel. **-schlitten,** *m.* ice-yacht. **-sport,** *m.* yachting. **-tuch,** *n.* sailcloth, canvas. **-werk,** *n.* (suit of) sails.

Segen, *m.* (-s, –) blessing, benediction; grace (*at mealtimes*); prosperity, abundance, yield, proceeds; sign of the cross; *den – geben* or *erteilen,* pronounce the benediction; *den – sprechen,* say grace; *Gott gebe seinen – dazu!* God's blessing on it! *das wird Ihnen keinen – bringen,* that will bring you no good luck. **-bringend,** *adj.* **-spendend,** *adj.* beneficial, blessed. **-sreich,** *adj.* prosperous, blessed, lucky. **-sspruch,** *m.* benediction. **-svoll,** *adj.*, *see* **-sreich.** **-swunsch,** *m.* good wish.

Segge, *f.* (-n) sedge, rush (*Carex*) (*Bot.*).

Segler, *m.* (-s, –) yachtsman; sailing vessel, sailer; glider, sailplane; swift (*Micropodidae*) (*Orn.*). **-verein,** *m.* yacht club.

segn-en, 1. *v.a.* bless, give benediction to, make the sign of the cross over, consecrate; *das Zeitliche -en,* depart this life; *gesegneten Andenkens,* of blessed memory; *gesegnete Mahlzeit,* see **Mahlzeit;** *gesegneten Leibes, in gesegneten Umständen,* in the family way, pregnant. 2. *v.r.* cross o.s. **-ung** *f.* blessing, benediction.

Seh-e, *f.* (*archaic*) eyesight; (*dial.*) pupil (*of the eye*); eye (*Hunt.*). **-en,** 1. *ir.v.n.* (*aux.* h.), *a.* & *r.* see, perceive, behold, observe, notice, realize; look, appear; *sieh nur!* just look! *-en Sie mal!* look here! *sieh doch,* would you believe it! (*coll.*) look you now! *siehe oben* (*unten*) (abbr. *s.o., s.u.*) see above (below); *es ist für Geld zu -en,* it can be seen on payment; *einem ähnlich -en,* resemble s.o.; *das sieht ihm ähnlich!* that is just like him! that is just what you would expect of him! *darauf-en,* watch; see *or* look to, be careful about; *einem auf die Finger -en,* watch a p. closely, keep one's eyes on s.o.; *auf Gehalt wird nicht gesehen,* salary is no object; *nur auf seinen Vorteil -en,* have eyes only for one's own advantage, (*coll.*) have an eye to the main chance; *daraus ist zu -en,* hence it appears; *ihm sieht der Schelm aus den Augen,* he looks a rogue; *durch die Finger -en,* connive, pretend not to see; *etwas gern -en,* like *or* be pleased with a th.; *gern* (*bei einem*) *gesehen sein,* be a welcome guest; *Gesellschaft bei sich -en,* receive company; *gut -en,* have good eyes; (*coll.*) *und hast du nicht gesehen!* like a shot, in a flash; *einem ins Gesicht -en,* look a p. in the face; *einem in die Karten -en,* see a p.'s hidden motives; *in die Zukunft -en,* look *or* peer into the future; *etwas -en lassen,* let be seen, show, display, exhibit; *sich -en lassen,* appear, make a show; show o.s., be visible; *sich mit etwas -en lassen können,* have no need to be ashamed of a th.; *-en nach,* look for; look after; *nach dem* (or *zum*) *Rechten -en,* see that everything is in order *or* is done properly; *das Zimmer sieht nach der Straße,* the room faces *or* looks on to the street; *sich satt -en* (*an*), feast one's eyes (on); *ich kann mich an ihm nicht satt -en,* I never get tired of looking at him; *schlecht -en,* have poor eyesight; *sie sieht sich schon als große Schauspielerin,* she pictures herself as a great actress; *mit -enden Augen,* with one's eyes open. 2. *n.* seeing, (eye)sight, vision (*Phys.*); *nur vom -en kennen,* know only by sight; *ihm verging Hören und -en,* he lost all consciousness. **-bahn,** *f.* visual path. **-enswert,** *adj.*, **-enswürdig,** *adj.* worth seeing, remarkable. **-enswürdigkeit,** *f.* object of interest, curiosity, spectacle. **-er,** *m.* seer, prophet. **-erblick,** *m.*, **-ergabe,** *f.* prophetic vision, gift of prophecy. **-erisch,** *adj.* prophetic. **-fehler,** *m.*, *see* **-störung.** **-feld,** *n.* field of vision. **-grübchen,** *n.* optic pit. **-hügel,** *m.* optic thalamus. **-klappe,** *f.* *see* **-schlitz.** **-kraft,** *f.* eyesight. **-lehre,** *f.* optics. **-loch,** *n.* pupil, optic foramen. **-nerv,** *m.* optic nerve. **-organ,** *n.* organ of vision. **-probe,** *f.* eyesight test. **-purpur,** *m.* visual purple. **-rohr,** *n.* telescope; periscope. **-rohrtiefe,** *f.* periscope depth (*of submarine*). **-schärfe,** *f.* focus, clearness of vision, keen eyesight; *auf -schärfe einstellen,* focus. **-schlitz,** *m.* visor, observation port *or* slit (*of a tank*), peep-hole. **-störung,** *f.* defect of vision. **-streifen,** *m.* angle of parallax. **-vermögen,** *n.* visual faculty. **-weite,** *f.* visual range; *in -weite,* within sight; *außer -weite,* out of sight. **-werkzeug,** *n.* organ of sight. **-winkel,** *m.* visual angle. **-zeichen,** *n.* visual signal.

Sehn-e, *f.* (-en) sinew, tendon, fibre; string (*of a bow*); chord (*of an arc*). **-enband,** *n.* ligament, tendon. **-enklapp,** *m.* sprain (*Vet.*). **-enreich,** *adj.* gristly (*of meat*). **-enscheide,** *f.* tendon-sheath. **-enschmiere,** *f.* synovial fluid. **-enschnitt,** *m.* tenotomy. **-enzerrung,** *f.* pulled tendon, strain. **-ig,** *adj.* sinewy, gristly, stringy, fibrous; muscular, (*coll.*) tough.

sehn-en, *v.r.* long, yearn (*nach,* for), desire ardently; *sich nach Hause -en,* long for home, be homesick; *ich sehne mich nach ihr,* I yearn for her; *ich -e mich danach, ihn zu sehen,* I long to see him. **-lich,** *adj.* ardent, passionate, longing. **-sucht,** *f.* longing, yearning, pining, hankering. **-süchtig,** *adj.* longing, yearning; fond, ardent, passionate.

sehr, *adv.* very, much, very well, greatly; *– gern,* most willingly; *– im Rückstand,* very much behind; *– mit Unrecht,* quite wrongly; *recht –,* very much indeed; *wenn er es auch noch so – verlangen sollte,* however much he may wish for it; *– viele,* a great many; *wie – auch . . .,* however much . . ., much as . . .; *zu – verbittert,* too much embittered; *bitte –,* don't mention it! certainly! willingly!

sehren, *v.a.* (*archaic* & *dial.*) hurt, injure.

sei, *see* **[2]sein.**

Seiber, *m.* (*dial.*) dribble. **-n,** *v.n.* dribble, slobber.

Seich, *m.* (*vulg.*) piss; (*coll.*) twaddle, bosh. **-e,** *f.* (*dial.*) urine. **-en,** *v.n.* urinate, (*vulg.*) piss; talk bosh.

seicht, *adj.* shallow; low, flat; superficial; insipid; stupid; *-e Stelle,* shoal; *-e Redensarten,* empty phrases, platitudes. **-gründig,** *adj.* shallow. **-heit,** *f.*, **-igkeit,** *f.* shallowness, insipidity. **-wurzelnd,** *adj.* shallow-rooted.

seid, *see* **[2]sein.**

Seid-e, (-n) silk; *dabei wird er keine -e spinnen,* he will not get much out of that. **-en,** *adj.* silken; *an einem -enen Faden hangen,* hang by a thread. **-enähnlich,** *adj.* silky, silk-like. **-enarbeiter,** *m.* silk-weaver. **-enartig,** *adj.* silky. **-enbast,** *m.* tusser-, tussore-, *or* tussur-silk. **-enbau,** *m.* rearing of silkworms, seri(ci)culture. **-enfabrik,** *f.* silk-mill. **-enfaden,** *m.* silk thread. **-enfadennaht,** *f.* silk suture (*Med.*). **-engarn,** *n.* silk yarn, spun silk. **-engespinst,** *n.* cocoon of the silkworm. **-englanz,** *m.* silky lustre. **-enholz,** *n.* satinwood. **-enpapier,** *n.* tissue paper. **-enraupe,** *f.* silkworm. **-enraupenzucht,** *f.* seri(ci)culture. **-enspinner,** *m.* silk-moth (*Ent.*); silk-spinner *or* -throw(st)er. **-enstickerei,** *f.* embroidery in silk. **-enstoffe,** *m.pl.* silks. **-entüll,** *m.* silk-net. **-enumspinnung,** *f.* silk-covering (*Elec.*). **-enwaren,** *f.pl., see* **-enstoffe. -enweich,** *adj.* (as) soft as silk, silky. **-enwurm,** *m.* silkworm. **-enzüchter,** *m.* rearer of silkworms, silk-grower. **-enzwirnen,** *n.* silk-throwing. **-ig,** *adj.* silky.

Seidel, *n.* (-s, -) (*dial.*) half-litre, pint; tankard; *ein – Bier,* a small (glass of) beer.

Seidelbast, *m. Daphne mezereon* (*Bot.*).

seiet, *see* **sein.**

Seif-e, *f.* (-en) soap; placer, alluvial deposit, silt (*Geol.*); *-e sieden,* boil *or* make soap; *grüne* or *weiche -e,* soft soap; *Stück -e,* cake of soap. **-en,** *v.a.* soap, lather; wash (*alluvial deposits*). **-enbad,** *n.* soap-suds. **-enbildung,** *f.* saponification. **-enblase,** *f.* soap-bubble. **-enbrühe,** *f.* soap-suds. **-enerz,** *n.* alluvial ore. **-enflocken,** *f.pl.* soap-flakes. **-engold,** *n.* alluvial *or* placer gold. **-enhaltig,** *adj.* soapy, saponaceous. **-enkraut,** *n.* soapwort (*Saponaria officinalis*) (*Bot.*). **-enlauge,** *f.* soap-suds. **-enpulver,** *n.* soap-powder. **-enriegel,** *m.* bar of soap. **-enschaum,** *m.* lather. **-ensieder,** *m.* soap-boiler; (*coll.*) *mir geht ein -ensieder auf,* a light dawns, the penny drops. **-ensiederei,** *f.* soap-works. **-enspäne,** *m.pl.* soap-flakes. **-enstein,** *m.* soapstone, saponite, steatite. **-enstoff,** *m.* saponine (*Chem.*). **-entafel,** *f.* cake of soap. **-enton,** *m.* fuller's earth, saponaceous clay. **-enwasser,** *n.* soapy water. **-ig,** *adj.* soapy, saponaceous. **-er,** *m.,* **-ert,** *m.,* **-ner,** *m.* ore-washer.

Seige, *f.* (-n) sump (*Min.*). **-n,** *see* **seihen. -r,** 1. *m.* (-s, -) plumb-line; hour-glass; (*dial.*) pendulum, clock. 2. *adj.* perpendicular (*Min.*). **-rarbeit,** *f.* liquation process. **-rblech,** *n.* cheek (*Metall.*). **-rblei,** *n.* liquation lead. **-rherd,** *m.* refining-hearth. **-rhütte,** *f.* liquation plant. **-rkrätze,** *f.* liquation slag. **-rn,** 1. *v.a., see* **seihen**; sink a shaft; make perpendicular; refine, segregate, liquate (*metals*). 2. *v.n.* (*aux.* s.) drip, trickle. **-rriß,** *m.* vertical section of mine. **-rschaft,** *m.* vertical shaft (*Min.*). **-rteufe,** *f.* perpendicular depth (*of shaft. Min.*). **-rung,** *f.* refining-process, liquation, segregation.

Seih-e, *f.* (-en) strainer, filter; dregs. **-en,** *v.a.* filter, strain, sieve; (*B.*) *Mücken -en und Kamele verschlucken,* strain at a gnat and swallow a camel. **-er,** *m.* filter, strainer. **-(e)papier,** *n.* filter-paper. **-sack,** *m.* filter- *or* straining-bag. **-(e)tuch,** *n.* straining-cloth, strainer.

Seil, *n.* (-(e)s, -e) rope, cord, line; cable; *– und Treil,* rigging; *sich am* (*Narren*)*-e führen lassen,* let o.s. be led by the nose; (*coll.*) *an einem -e ziehen,* be in the same boat. **-bahn,** *f.* cable-railway, funicular. **-draht,** *m.* wire-rope. **-en,** *v.a.* warp (*the yarns*); rig; fasten with rope. **-er,** *m.* rope-maker. **-erarbeit,** *f.* rope-making. **-erbahn,** *f.* rope-walk. **-erei,** *f.* rope-making. **-erwaren,** *f.pl.* cordage. **-schaft,** *f.* roped party (*mountaineering*). **-scheibe,** *f.* rope-pulley. **-springen,** *n.* skipping. **-tanzen,** 1. *v.n.* (*aux.* h.) (*sep.*) walk the tightrope. 2. *n.* tightrope-walking. **-tänzer,** *m.* tightrope-walker. **-trommel,** *f.* cable-drum. **-waren,** *f.pl.* cordage. **-werk,** *n.* rope-work; rigging. **-ziehen,** *n.* tug-of-war. **-zug,** *m.* tackle, towrope.

Seim, *m.* (-(e)s, -e) mucilage; strained honey. **-ig,** *adj.* mucilaginous, viscous, glutinous. **-en,** 1. *v.a.* strain (*honey*). 2. *v.n.* (*aux.* h.) yield a glutinous liquid.

[1]**sein,** (-e, -) 1. *poss. adj. m., f. & n. sing. & pl., referring to 3rd pers. sing. m. & n. antecedents* (*declined as definite article*) his, its, her; one's; *das Mädchen hat -en Schatz verloren,* the girl has lost her sweetheart; *alles zu -er Zeit,* all in good time, all in due course; *in – Haus,* in his house; *für -e Zwecke,* for his purposes; *einer -er Freunde,* one of his friends; (*coll.*) *dem Vater – Stock,* father's stick; (*coll.*) *wem – Hund ist das?* whose dog is that? 2. *archaic & poet. for* -er, (*Gen. sing. of pers. pron.* er & es) of him, of it, of one; *-(er) nicht mehr mächtig sein,* have lost control of o.s.; *ich erinnere mich -(er),* I remember him. 3. *pers. pron. standing alone when antecedent is m. or n. nom. or n. acc.*; *das Haus ist –,* the house is his; *alles was – ist,* everything that is his; *see* **-er,** *etc.* **-er, -e, -es,** *poss. pron.* (*when standing alone*) *wessen Frau ist das? -e,* whose wife is that? his. *But when the antecedent is m. or n. nom. or n. acc.,* sein *remains without ending, see* **–,** 3. (*coll.*) *er macht -s, sie macht ihrs,* he does his part, she does hers. **-erseits,** *adv.* on his side; for his part. **-erzeit,** *adv.* in his *or* its time, at the time, formerly; in due course, one day, in its proper time. **-esgleichen,** *indec. adj. & pron.* of his kind, people like him, such as he, his equals; *einen wie -esgleichen behandeln,* treat a p. as an equal. **-ethalben, -etwegen, um -etwillen,** *adv.* on his account *or* behalf, for his sake, so far as he is concerned. **-(ig)e,** *poss. pron.* his; *das -(ig)e,* his property; his part *or* duty; *das -(ig)e tun,* do one's utmost *or* best; (*Prov.*) *jedem das -e,* to everyone his due; *er hat sie zu der -en gemacht,* he made her his wife; *die -en,* his *or* one's own family *or* people.

[2]**sein,** 1. *ir.v.n.* (*aux.* s.) be; exist, be alive; *sei zufrieden!* be content! *sind Sie es?* is it you? *es ist ein Gott,* there is a God, God exists *or* lives; *alles was war, ist und – wird,* all that was, is, and is to be; *es sind viele Leute angekommen,* many people have come; *es ist ein Jahr, seit er abgereist ist,* it is a year since he left; *es sei!* or *es mag –!* let it pass! granted! *sei es drum!* so be it! *es sei denn, daß,* unless; *dem sei, wie ihm wolle,* be that as it may; *sei es . . ., oder . . .,* whether . . . or . . .; *muß das sein?* is that really necessary; *kann –,* maybe, perhaps; *was soll das –?* what does that mean? *etwas* (*gut*) *– lassen,* leave a thing (well) alone. 2. (*with Gen.*); *der Ansicht –,* hold the view; *des Glaubens –,* believe, hold firmly; *der Meinung –,* be of the opinion; *guten Mutes –,* be of good courage; *tust du es, so bist du des Todes,* if you do it, you are a dead man. 3. (*with Dat. referring to physical condition, health, etc.*) *es ist mir als ob,* I feel as if, it seems to me that; *mir ist warm,* I feel warm; *wie ist Ihnen?* how do you feel? *mir ist schlecht,* I feel unwell; *was ist Ihnen?* what is the matter with you? what ails you? *einem gut –,* like s.o., feel friendly towards a p.; *mir ist nicht nach Feiern zumute,* I don't feel like celebrating; *ihm ist es nur ums Geld,* he is only concerned about money. 4. (*as aux. in compound verbs indicating change of position or state*) *er ist eben abgereist,* he has just left; *er ist vom Dach gesprungen,* he jumped off the roof; *ich bin Schlittschuh gelaufen,* I have been skating; *er ist nach London gereist,* he (has) travelled to London; *er ist viel gereist,* he has been travelling a lot (N.B. *er hat viel gereist,* he has travelled a lot); *er ist eingeschlafen* (*erkrankt, genesen, verarmt*), he has gone to sleep (fallen ill, recovered, become poor); *ich bin gewesen* (*geworden*), I have been (become); (*dial.*) *er ist gesessen,* he (has) sat down. 5. *n.* being, existence; essence, true nature.

Seising, *n.* (-s, -e) seizing, lashing, tie (*Naut.*).

seismisch, *adj.* seismic; *-e Störung,* earthquake.

seit, 1. *prep.* (*Dat.*) since; for; *– alters her,* for ages; *– damals,* since then; *– kurzem,* of late, lately; *– langem,* for some *or* a long time; *– Menschengedenken,* within the memory of man; *– wann?* how long (ago)? *– drei Wochen,* for the last three weeks; *– einiger Zeit,* for some time past; *– undenklicher Zeit,* from time immemorial. 2. *conj. see* **-dem,** 2. **-dem,** 1. *adv.* since, since then *or* that time, ever since; *es sind -dem 20 Jahre vergangen,* 20 years have passed since then. 2. *conj.* since; *es ist lange her -(dem) ich ihn zum letzten Male gesehen habe,* it is a long time since I saw him. **-her,** *adv.* since then, from that time; till now, up till now; *ich habe ihn -her nicht gesehen,* I have not seen him since. **-herig,** *adj.* subsequent.

Seit-e, *f.* (-en) side, face (*Math.*); page; flank (*Mil.*); party; aspect (*of a problem*); member (*of an equation*); *see* **bei-e**; *-e an -e,* side by side; *jemanden* *einem andern an die –e stellen*, compare one p. with another, treat one p. the same as another; *dem ist nichts an die –e zu stellen*, nothing bears comparison with it, (*coll.*) there's nothing to touch it; *auf der einen* (or *anderen*) *–e*, on the one (*or* other) hand; *auf die –e bringen*, see *auf* . . . *schaffen*; (*einen*) *auf seine –e bringen*, bring (a p.) over to one's side; *auf die –e gehen*, step aside; *auf die –e legen*, put on one side, put by, save; *sich auf die –e legen*, turn on one's side (*in bed & of ships*); *sich auf die faule –e legen*, rest in idleness, (*vulg.*) sit on one's bottom; *sich auf die –e machen*, get out of the way; *einen auf die –e nehmen*, take a p. aside; *auf die –e räumen* or *schaffen*, put aside, put out of the way; finish off; make away with; *auf meiner –e stehen*, be on my side *or* of my opinion; *einen bei seiner schwachen –e nehmen*, appeal to a p.'s weakness *or* foible; *in die –e fallen*, attack (*an enemy*) in the flank; *nach allen –en*, in all directions; *nach allen –en hin*, from all points of view; *nach dieser –e hin*, on this side, in this direction; *von –en* (*with Gen.*), on behalf of, on the part of; *von allen –en*, from all sides; *ich habe es von anderer –e*, I have it from another quarter; *von der –e angreifen*, attack (*an enemy*) in the flank; *von der –e ansehen*, look askance at; *zur –e stehen*, support, stand by, help. **–ab,** *adv.* aside, apart. **–enabstand,** *m.* lateral displacement. **–enabweichung,** *f.* lateral deviation, deflexion; error. **–enachse,** *f.* lateral axis. **–enänderung,** *f.* deflexion; correction. **–enangriff,** *m.* flank-attack. **–enansicht,** *f.* side-view; side-elevation; profile. **–enband,** *n.* side-band (*Rad.*). **–enbegrenzer,** *m.* traversing stop. **–enblick,** *m.* side-glance; scornful glance; sneer. **–endeckung,** *f.* flank-guard. **–endruck,** *m.* lateral pressure. **–enerbe,** *m.* collateral heir. **–enfeuer,** *n.* enfilading fire (*Mil.*). **–enflosse,** *f.* vertical fin (*Av.*). **–enflügel,** *m.* side-aisle; transept. **–engang,** *m.* side-path *or* -alley; slip (*Theat.*). **–engebäude,** *n.* wing (*of a building*). **–engewehr,** *n.* side-arm, bayonet; *das –engewehr aufpflanzen*, fix bayonets. **–engleis,** *n.* siding (*Railw.*). **–enhebel,** *m.* traversing lever. **–enhieb,** *m.* side-cut; (*fig.*) sarcastic remark, taunt, innuendo, home-thrust. **–enholm,** *m.* outrigger (*Artil.*). **–enhut,** *f.* flank-guard (*Mil.*). **–enhüter,** *m.* catch-word (*Typ.*). **–enkraft,** *f.* component (force). **–enlampe,** *f.* side-light (*Motor.*). **–enlang,** *adj.* pages long, voluminous. **–enlehne,** *f.* side-rail; arm (*of a chair, etc.*). **–enleitwerk,** *n.* rudder-assembly (*Av.*). **–enlinie,** *f.* collateral line; side (*Geom.*); branch line (*Railw.*). **–enrand,** *m.* margin. **–enrichttrieb,** *m.* traversing mechanism (*Artil.*). **–enriß,** *m.* side-elevation *or* view. **–enruder,** *n.*, *see* **–ensteuer. –enrutsch,** *m.* side-slip (*Av.*). **–ens,** *prep.* (*Gen.*) on *or* from the side (of); on the part of. **–enschiff,** *n.* aisle. **–enschlag,** *m.* branch gallery (*Min.*). **–enschutz,** *m.* flank-protection (*Mil.*). **–enschwimmen,** *n.* side-stroke (*Sport*). **–ensicherung,** *f.*, *see* **–enschutz. –ensprung,** *m.* side-leap, caper; evasion; (amorous) escapade. **–enstechen,** *n.* stitch in the side. **–ensteuer,** *n.* rudder (*Av.*). **–enstraße,** *f.* side-street. **–enstreuung,** *f.* lateral error (*Artil.*). **–enstück,** *n.* side-piece; counterpart, pendant. **–entrieb,** *m.* lateral shoot. **–enverhältnis,** *n.* aspect-ratio (*Av.*). **–enverschiebung,** *f.* lateral deflexion, displacement *or* deviation. **–enverwandschaft,** *f.* collateral relationship. **–envorhalt,** *m.* deflexion lead (*in anti-aircraft gunnery*). **–enwagen,** *m.* sidecar. **–enwand,** *f.* side-wall; cheek (*of press, of gun-carriage*); (*pl.*) side-scenes (*Theat.*). **–enwandbein,** *n.* parietal bone (*Anat.*). **–enweg,** *m.* side-road; (*fig.*) side-track, round-about way; *–enwege gehen*, act surreptitiously; **–enwendung,** *f.* transverse movement. **–enwind,** *m.* side-wind, beam-wind. **–enzahl,** *f.* number of a page; number of pages; *Vieleck von ungerader –enzahl*, inequilateral polygon. **–ig,** *adj. suffix* -sided e.g.; *ein–ig*, *adj.* one-sided, lopsided; *gegen–ig*, *adj.* reciprocal; *wechsel–ig*, *adj.* mutual; *viel–ig*, *adj.* many-sided, multifarious; *zwölf–ig*, *adj.* twelve-sided. **–lich,** 1. *adj.* side, lateral. 2. *adv.* at the side. **–lichgleich,** *adj.* equilateral, symmetrical. **–s,** *adv. suffix* e.g. *meiner–s*, for my part; *mütterlicher–s*, on the mother's side. **–wärts,** *adv.* aside; sideways, edgeways, laterally, on one side.

Sekan–s, *m.* (–, –) secant (*Math.*). **–te,** *f.*, (-n), (**–tenlinie,** *f.*) secant line (*Math.*).

sekk–ant, *adj.* (*Austr. dial.*) vexing, irritating. **–atur,** *f.* (-en) (*Austr. dial.*) teasing, annoyance. **–ieren,** *v.a.* (*Austr. dial.*) tease, plague, torment.

Sekret, *n.* (-(e)s, -e) secretion (*Physiol.*) **–behälter,** *m.* gland. **–ion,** *f.*, *see* **–.**

sekret, *adj.* secret. **–är,** *m.* (-s, -e) secretary, clerical assistant; bureau, writing-desk. **–ariat,** *n.* secretary's office.

Sekt, *m.* (-(e)s, -e) champagne, dry wine.

Sekt–e, *f.* (-en) sect. **–ierer,** *m.* sectarian. **–iererisch,** *adj.* sectarian. **–ion,** *f.* section, department; dissection. **–ionsaufriß,** *m.* sectional elevation. **–ionsbefund,** *m.* findings of post-mortem examination. **–ionschef,** *m.* departmental head. **–ionsfeuer,** *n.* section firing (*Mil.*). **–or,** *m.* (-s, -en) sector (*Geom.*).

Sekund–a, 1. *f.* (-as, -en) fifth form; (*Austr. dial.*) second form. 2. *adj.* (*C.L.*) second grade *or* quality. **–aner,** *m.* fifth-form boy, (*Austr. dial.*) second-form boy. **–ant,** *m.* (-en, -en) second (*in duels, Box., etc.*). **–är,** *adj.* secondary. **–ararzt,** *m.* (*Austr. dial.*) assistant physician. **–ärbahn,** (*archaic*) *f.* branch line. **–ärkreis,** *m.* secondary circuit. **–arschule,** *f.* (*Swiss dial.*) intermediate school. **–ärstrahlung,** *f.* secondary radiation. **–ärstrom,** *m.* secondary circuit (*Elec.*). (*C.L.*) **–awechsel,** *m.* second (bill) of exchange. **–e,** *f.* second (*Mus., Fenc., Chron. & Geom.*). **–enmeter,** *m.pl.* meters a second. **–enuhr,** *f.* watch with a seconds-hand. **–enzeiger,** *m.* seconds-hand. **–ieren,** *v.a.* act as second to (*duel*); second (*a motion*); accompany. **–ogenitur,** *f.* right of the younger son.

sela, *int.* (*B. & coll.*) all right! done! settled! agreed!

selb, 1. *adj.* self, same (*now only in Dat. after certain preps.*); *zur –en Stunde*, at that very hour; *unter –em Dach*, under the same roof. 2. *m.* automaton. **–ander,** *adv.* with *or* and another, we two; (*dial.*) with child. **–dritt,** *adv.* with two others, three together. **–er,** *indec. adj. & pron. see* **–st,** 1; *ich –er*, I myself; *sie –er*, she herself; they themselves. **–ig,** *adj.* the same, the selfsame; *zu –iger Stunde*, at the same hour; immediately. **–st,** 1. *indec. adj. & pron.* self; myself, himself, yourself, *etc. er ist es –st*, it is he himself; *aus sich –st*, of oneself; *sie ist die Güte –st*, she is kindness itself; *mit sich –st reden*, talk to o.s.; *–st getan ist wohl getan*, what one does oneself is well done; *von –st*, of one's own accord, voluntarily; automatically; *das versteht sich von –st*, that goes without saying; *zu sich –st kommen*, come to o.s. *or* to one's senses. 2. *n.* (*indec.*); *sein –st*, his individuality, his own self; *sein ganzes –st*, his whole being. 3. *adv.* even; very; *–st seine Freunde* or *seine Freunde –st*, even his friends; *–st wenn*, even if, even though. **–stachtung,** *f.* self-respect, self-esteem. **–ständig,** *adj.* self-supporting; self-reliant, self-dependent, independent, separate, autonomous; *–ständige Forschung*, original research; *–ständige Stromleitung*, (ionization-, spark- *or* corona-) discharge (*Elec.*). **–ständigkeit,** *f.* independence, self-reliance, autonomy. **–stanklage,** *f.* self-accusation, self-recrimination. **–stanlasser,** *m.* self-starter. **–stanschluß,** *m.* automatic dialling (*of telephone*). **–stanschlußamt,** *n.* automatic exchange (*Phone*). **–stanschlußgerät,** *n.* dial-telephone. **–staufopferung,** *f.* self-sacrifice. **–stauslöser,** *m.* automatic shutter release, self-timer (*Phot.*). **–stbedienung,** *f.* self-service (*restaurant*). **–stbefleckung,** *f.* onanism, self-abuse, masturbation. **–stbefruchtung,** *f.* self-fertilization. **–stbeherrschung,** *f.* self-control. **–stbeobachtung,** *f.* introspection. **–stbesinnung,** *f.* personal considerations. **–stbestäubung,** *f.* self-pollination. **–stbestimmung,** *f.* self-determination. **–stbestimmungsrecht,** *n.* sovereign right (*Pol.*). **–stbewußt,** *adj.* self-assured, self-confident; proud, conceited. **–stbewußtsein,** *n.* self-assurance; self-conceit. **–stbildnis,** *n.* self-portrait. **–stbinder,** *m.* open-end tie; reaper-binder (*Agr.*). **–stbiographie,** *f.* autobiography. **–stdichtend,** *adj.* self-sealing (*of fuel tanks*) (*Av.*). **–steigen,** *adj.* one's very own. **–steinschätzung,** *f.* self-assessment, statement of income. **–stentsagung,** *f.* self-denial. **–stentzündlichkeit,** *f.* spontaneous combustibility. **–stentzündung,** *f.* spontaneous combustion, self-ignition. **–sterhaltung,** *f.* self-preservation. **–sterkenntnis,** *f.* knowledge of oneself *or* one's limitations. **–sterregend,** *adj.* self-excited (*of oscillators*) (*Rad.*). **–stfahrartillerie,** *f.* self-propelled artillery. **–stfahrer,** *m.* owner-driver. **–stgärung,** *f.* spontaneous fermentation. **–stgebacken,** *adj.* home-baked. **–stgefällig,** *adj.* self-satisfied, complacent. **–stgefälligkeit,** *f.* complacency, conceit, vanity. **–stgefühl,** *n.* self-reliance, self-confidence, self-esteem, amour-propre; *–stgefühl haben,* know one's worth. **–stgemacht,** *adj.* home-made. **–stgenügsam,** *adj.* self-sufficient; self-contained, self-satisfied. **–stgenügsamkeit,** *f.* self-sufficiency, self-contentment, self-satisfaction. **–stgerecht,** *adj.* self-righteous. **–gespräch,** *n.* monologue, soliloquy. **–stgezüchtet,** *adj.* home-grown, home-bred. **–stgift,** *n.* autotoxin. **–stherrlich,** *adj.* authoritarian, tyrannical. **–stherrscher,** *m.* autocrat. **–stherrscherisch,** *adj.* autocratic. **–sthilfe,** *f.* self-help, co-operative enterprise; self-defence; *zur –sthilfe schreiten,* take the law into one's own hands. **–stinduktion,** *f.* self-induction (*Elec.*). **–stkante,** *f.* selvage. **–stisch,** *adj.* selfish, egotistic. (*C.L.*) **–stkostenpreis,** *m.* prime cost, cost price. **–stkritik,** *f.* self-criticism. **–stladepistole,** *f.,* **–stlader,** *m.* automatic (pistol). **–stlaut,** *m.* vowel. **–stliebe,** *f.* self-love, self-esteem. **–stlob,** *m.* self-praise. **–stlos,** *adj.* unselfish, disinterested. **–stmord,** *m.* suicide; *–stmord begehen,* commit suicide. **–stmörder,** *m.* suicide; felo-de-se (*Law*). **–stmörderisch,** *adj.* suicidal. **–stmordversuch,** *m.* attempted suicide. **–stöler,** *m.* automatic lubricator. **–stordner,** *m.* card-index. **–stquälerisch,** *adj.* self-tormenting. **–stredend,** *adj.* self-evident, (as a matter) of course, obvious; *das ist –stredend,* that goes without saying. (*C.L.*) **–streflektant,** *m.* principal. **–stregulierend,** *adj.* self-registering, self-adjusting. **–stretter,** *m.* life-saving apparatus; oxygen-apparatus. **–stschmierend,** *adj.* self-lubricating. **–stschreiber,** *m.* self-recording instrument. **–stschuldner,** *m.* debtor in one's own name *or* on one's own account. **–stschuß,** *m.* spring-gun. **–stschutz,** *m.* self-defence, self-protection. **–stsicher,** *adj.* self-assured, self-confident. **–ststeuergerät,** *n.* automatic pilot (*Av.*). **–ststeuerung,** *f.* automatic control. **–ststudium,** *n.* private study. **–stsucht,** *f.* egoism, selfishness. **–stsüchtig,** *adj.* egoistic, selfish. **–sttätig,** *adj.* self-acting, automatic; spontaneous. **–sttätigkeit,** *f.* automatic operation; spontaneity. **–sttäuschung,** *f.* self-deception. **–stteilung,** *f.* fission. **–stüberhebung,** *f.,* **–stüberschätzung,** *f.* overweening opinion of o.s.; presumption. **–stüberwindung,** *f.* self-conquest. **–stumkehr,** *f.* self-reversal. **–stunterbrecher,** *m.* automatic circuit-breaker. **–stunterricht,** *m.* self-instruction. **–stverblendung,** *f.* self-deception. **–stvergessen,** *adj.* self-forgetful, unselfish. **–stvergiftung,** *f.* auto-intoxication. **–stvergötterung,** *f.* self-adulation. **–stverlag,** *m.*; *im –stverlag,* published by the author. **–stverleger,** *m.* author and publisher. **–stverleugnung,** *f.* self-abnegation. **–stverschluß,** *m.*; *mit –stverschluß,* self-locking. **–stverschuldet,** *adj.* brought about by one's own guilt *or* fault. **–stversenkung,** *f.* scuttling (*Naut.*). **–stversorger,** *m.* self-supporter, farmer living on his own produce. **–stverständlich,** 1. *adj.* self-evident, obvious; *das ist –stverständlich,* that goes without saying. 2. *adv.*, *–stverständlich!* of course! **–stverständlichkeit,** *f.* matter of course, foregone conclusion. **–stverstümmelung,** *f.* self-mutilation, mayhem. **–stverteidigung,** *f.* self-defence. **–stvertrauen,** *n.* self-confidence. **–stverwaltung,** *f.* self-government, autonomy. **–stwille,** *m.* obstinacy, self-will. **–stwirkend,** *adj.* self-acting, automatic. **–stzersetzung,** *f.* spontaneous decomposition. **–stzeugung,** *f.* spontaneous generation, abiogenesis. **–stzucht,** *f.* self-discipline. **–stzufrieden,** *adj.* self-satisfied, complacent, self-contented. **–stzufriedenheit,** *f.* self-content, complacency. **–stzündend,** *adj.* self-igniting, pyrophorous. **–stzünder,** *m.* pyrophorus (*Chem.*). **–stzweck,** *m.* end in itself, absence of ulterior motive.

selch–en, *v.a.* & *n.* (*dial.*) smoke, cure (*meats, etc.*). *Geselchtes, n., see* **–fleisch. –er,** *m.* (-s, –) (*dial.*) curer; butcher dealing in sausage, smoked meats, etc.; pork-butcher. **–fleisch,** *n.* smoked meat.

Selekt–a, *f.* (-en) class of senior pupils, special class (of chosen pupils). **–ionstheorie,** *f.* theory of natural selection. **–ivität,** *f.* selectivity (*Rad.*).

Selen, *n.* selenium (*Chem.*). **–ig,** *adj.* selenious. **–igsauer,** *adj.* selenite of. **–it,** *m.* (-s, -e) calcium sulphate, (*archaic*) selenite (*Min.*); (-en, -en) moon-dweller. **–salz,** *n.* selenide. **–sauer,** *adj.* selenate of. **–säure,** *f.* selenic acid. **–zelle,** *f.* selenium cell (*Phot., Tele.*).

selig, *adj.* blessed, happy, blissful, blest; deceased, late; (*coll.*) fuddled, tipsy; *Gott habe ihn –!* God rest his soul! *eines –en Todes sterben,* go to one's rest; *meine –e Mutter,* my deceased *or* late mother; *mein Vater –,* my deceased father; (*coll.*) *meine –e,* my late wife, my wife of blessed memory; (*coll.*) *ihr –er,* her late husband; *–en Andenkens,* of blessed memory; *– werden,* go to heaven, attain salvation; *–e Tage,* blissful days; *die Gefilde der –en,* Elysium. **–keit,** *f.* happiness, bliss; *ewige –keit,* everlasting bliss, salvation. **–gesprochene(r),** *m.* beatified person, canonized saint. **–machend,** *adj.* beatific. **–macher,** *m.* Saviour. **–machung,** *f.* salvation; sanctification. **–preisen,** *v.a.* glorify, beatify. **–preisung,** *f.* (*B.*) Beatitude. **–sprechen,** *v.a.* beatify. **–sprechung,** *f.* beatification.

Sellerie, *m.* & *f.* celeriac (*Apium graveolens*) (*Bot.*). **–stangen,** *f.pl.* celery.

selt–en, 1. *adj.* rare, unusual; infrequent, scarce; *das ist nichts –enes,* that is nothing extraordinary; that happens often. 2. *adv.* rarely, seldom; *nicht eben –en,* not very rarely, pretty frequently; *–en billig,* exceptionally cheap. **–enheit,** *f.* rarity, scarcity, curiosity. **–sam,** *adj.* strange, peculiar, unusual; singular, odd, curious. **–samkeit,** *f.* strangeness, oddness.

Selter(s)wasser, *n.* soda-water.

Semantik, *f.* semantics, science of meanings.

Semaphor, *n.* (& *Austr. dial. m.*) (-s, -e) semaphore.

Semasiologie, *f. see* **Semantik.**

Semester, *n.* (-s, –) half-year; university term, session, semester. **–schluß,** *m.* end of term.

Seminar, *n.* (-s, -e & -ien) training-college (*for teachers*), seminary (*Eccl.*); advanced tutorial class; specialist department, institute (*Univ.*). **–arbeit,** *f., see* **–übung. –bibliothek,** *f.* class *or* departmental library (*Univ.*). **–jahr,** *n.* post-graduate teachers' training course. **–übung,** *f.* tutorial exercise.

Semmel, *f.* (-n) breakfast roll; (*coll.*) *abgehen wie warme –n,* sell like hot cakes. **–blond,** *adj.* flaxen-haired. **–kloß,** *m.* bread dumpling. **–mehl,** *n.* white *or* wheat flour.

Senat, *m.* (-(e)s, -e) senate; university court *or* council (N.B. *not* senate). **–or,** *m.* senator. **–orisch,** *adj.* senatorial.

Send, *m.* (-(e)s, -e) (*archaic*) synod (*Hist.*); (*dial.*) fair. **–gericht,** *n., see* **–.**

send–en, *ir.* & *reg. v.a.* send, dispatch; broadcast, transmit (*Rad.*). **–bote,** *m.* messenger; envoy. **–brief,** *m., see* **–schreiben. –eantenne,** *f.* transmitting aerial (*Rad.*). **–ebereich,** *m.* service area (of a transmitter) (*Rad.*). **–efolge,** *f.* broadcast programme, radio feature. **–eleistung,** *f.* power (of a transmitter) (*Rad.*). **–eleiter,** *m.* radio producer. **–er,** *m.* sender; broadcasting station, transmitter (*Rad.*). **–eranlage,** *f.* transmitting set. **–eraum,** *m.* broadcasting studio. **–erempfänger,** *m.* combined transmitter and receiver, transceiver (*Rad.*). **–eröhre,** *f.* transmitter-valve. **–erwelle,** *f.* carrier wave (*Rad.*). **–espiel,** *n.* radio drama *or* play. **–estation,** *f.,* **–estelle,** *f.* broadcasting *or* transmitting station. **–ling,** *m.* emissary, messenger. **–schreiben,** *n.* open letter, circular. **–ung,** *f.*

sending; mission; transmission, broadcast (*Rad.*); shipment, consignment.
Senf, *m.* mustard; (*coll.*) *einen langen – machen über,* hold forth about s.th.; talk at length on; (*coll.*) *seinen – dazu geben,* have a word to say, put in one's word. **–brühe,** *f.* mustard-sauce. **–büchse,** *f.* mustard-pot. **–gas,** *n.* mustard gas. **–gurke,** *f.* gherkin in piccalilli. **–korn,** *n.* grain of mustard-seed. **–mehl,** *n.* ground mustard. **–öl,** *n.* oil of mustard. **–papier,** *n.*, **–pflaster,** *n.*, **–teig,** *m.*, **–umschlag,** *m.* mustard-plaster. **–saure,** *f.* sinapic acid. **–tunke,** *f. see* **–brühe.**
Senge, *pl.* (*dial.*) sound thrashing.
seng–en, 1. *v.a.* singe, scorch; burn; *–en und brennen,* burn and ravage, lay waste (*a country*). 2. *v.n.* (*aux.*h.) burn, singe, be singed. **–(e)rig,** *adj.* (*smelling or tasting*) burnt; (*fig.*) fishy, suspicious, threatening, dangerous.
senil, *adj.*, senile. **–ität,** *f.*, senility.
Senk–e, *f.* (-n) layering of vines; low ground, depression; countersink; visor (*of helmet*). **–blei,** *n.* plummet, sounding-lead. **–el,** *m.* (boot)lace, string with a tag; (*dial.*) *see* **–blei. –eln,** *v.a.* lace. **–elstift,** *m.* tag. **–en,** 1. *v.a.* sink (*a shaft, etc.*); let down, lower; *Preise –en,* reduce prices; *den Blick –en,* lower *or* cast down one's eyes; *die Fahne –en,* dip the colours; *das Haupt –en,* bow one's head. 2. *v.r.* settle, sink, subside; *die Straße –t sich,* the road dips, drops *or* falls; *die Nacht –t sich,* night falls. **–er,** *m.* layer, shoot (*Hort.*); countersink-bit. **–fuß,** *m.* flat foot, fallen arch (*of foot*). **–fußeinlage,** *f.* arch-support. **–grube,** *f.* cesspool, drain, sump. **–kasten,** *m.* caisson. **–körper,** *m.* sinker, bob. **–lot,** *n.*, *see* **–blei. –niete,** *f.* countersunk *or* flush rivet. **–pfahl,** *m.* prop (*for a young vine*). **–rebe,** *f.* vine-layer. **–recht,** *adj.* perpendicular, vertical; *eine –rechte (Linie) ziehen* (or *fällen*), raise, draw (*or* let fall) a perpendicular; *nicht –recht stehen,* be out of the perpendicular; (*coll.*) *das einzig –rechte,* the only one that is proper, right *or* correct. **–reis,** *n.* layer, shoot. **–rücken,** *m.* sway-back (*Vet.*). **–schacht,** *m.* vertical shaft (*Min.*). **–schnur,** *f.*, **–lot,** *n.* plumb-line. **–spindel,** *f.* hydrometer. **–stück,** *n.*, *see* **–werk. –ung,** *f.* sinking, lowering, reduction (*of wages*); dip, depression, subsidence, hollow, declivity; unaccented syllable, thesis (*Metr.*); prolapsus (*Med.*). **–waage,** *f.* aerometer; hydrometer. **–werk,** *n.* sunken fascine dam.
Senn, *m.* (-(e)s, -e), **–e,** *m.* (-en, -en) Alpine cowherd; cheese-maker. **–e,** *f.* Alpine pasture. **–en,** *v.n.* (*aux.* h.) make cheese. **–er,** *m.* (*dial.*), *see* **–(e). –erei,** *f.* Alpine dairy-farm *or* -farming. **–erin,** *f.* (*dial.*), *see* **–in. –hütte,** *f.* chalet; Alpine dairy. **–in,** *f.* dairy-maid. **–tum,** *n.* (-s, –) (*Swiss dial.*) Alpine herd.
Senne, *f.* (-n) (*archaic*), *see* **Sehne.**
Sennesblätter, *n.pl.* senna-leaves (*Pharm.*).
Sensal, *m.* (-s, -e) licensed broker, agent. **–gebühr,** *f.*, **–ie,** *f.* brokerage.
Sensarie, *f.* (-n) (*Austr. dial.*), *see* **Sensalie.**
Sensation, *f.* (-en) sensation; *– machen,* create a sensation. **–ell,** *adj.* sensational, exciting, thrilling; *–ell wirken,* create a sensation. **–slust,** *f.*, **–ssucht,** *f.* sensationalism.
Sense, *f.* (-n) scythe. **–nmann,** *m.* mower, reaper; (*fig.*) Death. **–nwagen,** *m.* scythed war-chariot (*of the ancients*). **–nwurf,** *m.* handle of a scythe.
sensi–bel, *adj.* sensitive, sensible, sensory. **–bilisieren,** *v.a.* sensitize. **–bilität,** *f.* sensitiveness, sensibility, feeling. **–tiv,** *adj.* (super-)sensitive; (*coll.*) touchy. **–tivität,** *f.* sensitiveness.
Sente, *f.* (-n) centre line (*Naut.*); (*dial.*) thin lath.
Sentenz, *f.* (-en) aphorism, maxim. **–artig,** *adj.*, **–iös,** *adj.* sententious.
sentimental, *adj.* sentimental. (*archaic*) **–isch,** *adj.* subjective, reflective. **–ität,** *f.* sentimentalism.
separ–at, *adj.* separate, detached, special, particular. **–atabdruck,** *m.*, **–atabzug,** *m.* special impression, off-print; reprint. **–ateingang,** *m.* private entrance. **–atist,** *m.* sectarian, seceder. **–atistenbewegung,** *f.* separatist movement (*Pol.*). **–atkonto,** *n.* special account. **–ieren,** *v.a.* & *r.* separate; (*C.L.*) *sich –ieren,* dissolve partnership.
Sepi–a, *f.* (-en) cuttle-fish; sepia. **–aschale,** *f.* cuttle-bone. **–azeichnung,** *f.* sepia-drawing. **–e,** *f.*, *see* **–a.**
Sept–ember, *m.* September. **–ennal,** *adj.* septennial. **–ennat,** *n.* seven-year period. **–ett,** *n.* (-s, -e) septet (*Mus.*). **–ime,** *f.* (-n) seventh, leading note (*Mus.*).
Sequenz, *f.* (-en) sequence (*Cards, Mus.*).
Sequest–er, 1. *n.* (-s, –) sequestration, confiscation, compulsory administration (*of a debtor's estate*) (*Law*); sequestrum (*Med.*). 2. *m.* (-s, –) sequestrator (*Law*). **–rieren,** *v.a.* sequester; sequestrate, confiscate (*Law*).
Serail, *n.* (-s, -s) seraglio.
Seraph, *m.* seraph, angel. **–isch,** *adj.* seraphic, angelic, ecstatic.
Serenissi–mus, *m.* (-mus, -mi) (His) Serene Highness; (*hum.*) petty prince.
Sergeant, *m.* (-en, -en) sergeant, n.c.o. (*Mil.*).
Serie, *f.* (-n) series; (*C.L.*) issue; set (*of periodicals, etc.*). **–nerzeugung,** *f.*, **–nfabrikation,** *f.*, **–nherstellung,** *f.* mass production. **–nfremd,** *adj.* of a different series. **–nschaltung,** *f.* series-connexion (*Elect.*).
seriös, *adj.* serious, responsible.
Sermon, *m.* (-s, -e) diatribe.
serös, *adj.* serous, watery.
Serpentin, *m.* (-s, -e) serpentine(-stone), ophite (*Min.*). **–e,** *f.* (-en) double bend (*in road*), winding road. **–enweg,** *m.* winding path *or* road.
Ser–um, *n.* (-ums, -en & -a) (blood) serum. **–umbehandlung,** *f.* inoculation. **–umeiweiß,** *n.* blood protein.
Serv–ice, 1. *n.* (-s, –) service, set (*of crockery, etc.*). 2. *m.* (-s, –) (*Austr. & Swiss dial.*), *see* **–is. –ieren,** *v.a.* & *n.* (*aux.* h.) serve, wait (*at table*); *es ist –iert,* dinner is on the table. **–ierbrett,** *n.* tray, salver. **–iertisch,** *m.* side-table. **–ierwagen,** *m.* dinner wagon. **–iette,** *f.* table-napkin. **–iettenring,** *m.* napkin-ring. **–il,** *adj.* servile, obsequious. **–ilismus,** *m.*, **–ilität,** *f.* servility. **–is,** *m.* & *n.* billeting allowance (*Mil.*). **–itut,** *f.* (& *Austr. dial. n.*) (*Hist.*) compulsory service; obligation; charge upon an estate. **–us,** *int.* (*Austr. dial.*) hello! greetings!
Sessel, *m.* (-s, –) seat; armchair, easy-chair; (*Austr. dial.*) chair. **–recht,** *n.* right to remain seated in the presence of the sovereign. **–träger,** *m.* sedan-chair bearer.
seßhaft, *adj.* settled, established, sedentary, stationary; resident.
Sestine, *f.* (-n) sextain (*Metr.*).
setz–en, 1. *v.a.* place, set, put; fix, plant, erect, put up; wager, stake (*money*); compose (*Mus., Typ.*); assume, suppose; bring forth young, breed, spawn; *alles daran –en,* stake one's all, risk everything, do one's utmost; *einen Topf ans Feuer –en,* put a pot on the fire; *einem das Messer an die Kehle –en,* hold a pistol to s.o.'s head; *ans Land –en,* put ashore; (*coll.*) *einen an die (frische) Luft –en,* fling *or* sling a p. out; *einen auf freien Fuß –en,* set a p. free; *einem die Pistole auf die Brust –en,* hold a pistol to s.o.'s head; *einen Punkt aufs 'i' –en,* dot one's i's; *alles auf eine Karte –en,* stake everything on one card, put all one's eggs into one basket; *auf seinen Kopf einen Preis –en,* put a price on his head; (*coll.*) *alles auf ein Pferd –en,* put one's shirt on a horse; *den Preis auf eine Mark –en,* fix the price at one mark; *einen auf den Sand –en,* (*coll.*) wipe the floor with s.o.; *aufs Spiel –en,* risk; *auf die Straße –en,* turn out of the house *or* into the street; *auf den Thron –en,* place on the throne; *außer Kraft –en,* invalidate; repeal; *außer Stand –en,* disable; *den Fall –en,* put the case, suppose; *eine Frist –en,* impose a time limit; *Grenzen –en,* set a limit to; *einen in Angst –en,* terrify a p.; *in Bewegung –en,* move, set in motion; *Himmel und Hölle in Bewegung –en,* move heaven and earth, leave no stone unturned; *eine S. mit etwas in Beziehung –en,* relate one th. to *or* with another, establish a relation between one th. and another; *in Brand* or *Flammen –en,* set on fire, set fire to; *in Freiheit –en,* set free, set at liberty, liberate; *in Gang –en,* set going, set in motion; *sich (Dat.) etwas in den Kopf –en,* take s.th. into one's

head; *ein Pferd in Galopp –en*, put one's horse to a gallop; *in Marsch –en*, give orders to march; *in Noten –en*, put to music; *ein Stück in Szene –en*, put a play on the stage; *Kinder in die Welt –en*, bring children into the world; *einen matt –en*, hold in check (*chess & fig.*); *Satzzeichen –en*, put punctuation marks, punctuate; *ich –e keinen Fuß über die Schwelle*, I will not put a foot inside the door; *übers Wasser –en*, take *or* put across the water, ferry across; *unter Wasser –en*, submerge; *einen vor die Tür –en, einem den Stuhl vor die Tür –en*, turn a p. out, show a p. the door; *keinen Fuß vor die Tür –en*, not step (a foot) outside the house; (*Prov.*) *den Bock zum Gärtner –en*, set the fox to keep the geese; *zum Pfande –en*, give as a pledge; pawn; *zum Richter –en*, appoint *or* constitute judge; *einen zur Ruhe –en*, pension a p. off; *gesetzter Herr*, stout middle-aged man; *in gesetzten Jahren*, middle-aged; *gesetzten Falls*, in the given case, suppose; *gesetzt, es wäre so*, supposing it were so, granted that it is so. 2. *v.r.* seat o.s., sit down, take a seat; perch; sink (*of soil, etc.*), subside, settle, precipitate, clarify, be deposited; calm down, become pacified; *sich auf die Hinterbeine –en*, dig one's heels in, be obstinate; (*coll.*) *sich auf die Hosen –en* work hard; (*fig.*) *sich aufs hohe Pferd –en*, ride the high horse; *sich bequem –en*, make o.s. comfortable; *sich gerade –en*, sit up; *ein Geschwulst –t sich*, a swelling goes down; *sich in Besitz –en*, put o.s. in possession of; *sich bei jemandem in Gunst –en*, ingratiate o.s. *or* curry favour with a p.; *sich mit einem in Verbindung –en*, get into communication with s.o.; *sich zu einem –en*, sit down by s.o.; *sich zur Ruhe –en*, retire from business; *sich zu Tische –en*, sit down to a meal; *sich zur Wehr –en*, defend o.s. 3. *v.n.* (*aux* h. & s.) run, spring, leap; pass (over); attack; *an den Feind –en*, fall upon the enemy; *der Gang –t durch das Gebirge*, the lode strikes into the rock; *über einen Fluß –en*, cross a river; *über einen Graben –en*, jump (across) a ditch; *über einen Zaun –en*, take a fence (*in riding*). 4. *v.imp.* (*coll.*) *es wird Schläge –en*, there will be a fight, it will come to blows; you will get into trouble, you will catch it; *was hat es gesetzt?* what is afoot? (*coll.*) what's doing? 5. *n.* composition (*Mus.*), type-setting (*Typ.*). **–arbeit,** *f.* jigging-process (*Metall.*). **–bord,** *m.* washboard (*Naut.*). **–bottich,** *m.* settling vat. **–ei,** *n.* (*dial.*) fried egg, poached egg. **–er,** *m.* compositor (*Typ.*). **–erei,** *f.* composing-room, compositor's room. **–(er)fehler,** *m.* typographical *or* printer's error, misprint. **–ermaschine,** *f. see* **–maschine. –hase** *m.* doe hare (*Hunt.*). **–holz,** *n.* dibble (*Hort.*). **–kartoffel,** *f.* seed-potato. **–kasten,** *m.* type- *or* letter-case (*Typ.*); settling tank. **–kopf,** *m.* round- *or* cheese-head (*of screw*). **–ling,** *m.* cutting, slip, layer, sapling; fry, spawn. **–linie,** *f.* reglet, composing- *or* spacing-rule (*Typ.*). **–maschine,** *f.* type-setting machine (*Typ.*); machine-jigger (*Metall.*). **–rebe,** *f.* vine-layer. **–reis,** *n.* slip, layer, shoot. **–schiff,** *n.* galley (*Typ.*). **–teich,** *m.* fish-(breeding) pond. **–waage,** *f.* level. **–zapfen,** *m.* suppository. **–zeit,** *f.* planting time, breeding time, spawning time.

Seuche, *f.* (-n) contagious disease, epidemic; pestilence. **–nartig,** *adj.* epidemic; contagious, infectious. **–nfest,** *adj.*, **–nfrei,** *adj.* immune. **–ngebiet,** *n.* infested area. **–nhaft,** *adj.* epidemic. **–nherd,** *m.* centre of contagion. **–nlazarett,** *n.* hospital for infectious diseases, isolation hospital.

seufze–n, 1. *v.n.* (*aux.* h.) sigh, heave a sigh. 2. *n.* sighing, groaning. **–r,** *m.* sigh, groan. **–rbrücke,** *f.* Bridge of Sighs. **–rspalte,** *f.* agony-column (*Press*).

Sext–a, *f.* (-en) first form (*school*), (*Austr. dial.*) sixth form. **–aner,** *m.* first- (*or Austr. dial.* sixth-) form boy. **–ant,** *m.* (-en, -en) sextant. **–e,** *f.* sixth (*Mus.*); sequence of six (*Cards*); *kleine* (*große*) *–e*, minor (major) sixth. **–ett,** *n.* (-(e)s, -e) sextet (*Mus.*).

sexu–al, *adj.* sexual. **–alhormon,** *n.* sex-hormone. **–alität,** *f.* sexuality. **–alpädagogik,** *f.* sex-education. **–alzelle,** *f.* germ-cell. **–ell,** *adj.* (*Austr. dial.*), *see* **–al.**

Sezession, *f.* (-en) secession.

sezieren, *v.a.* dissect; (*coll.*) cut up.

sich, (*3rd pers. sing. or pl., m., f. & n. Dat. & Acc. of refl. pron.*) himself, herself, itself, themselves; yourself, yourselves (*where the 3rd pers. is used in address*); one another, each other; oneself (*in infinitives*); *an* (*und für*) –, in itself, on its own, properly considered, in the abstract; *es hat wenig auf* –, it is of little importance; *was hat das auf* – ? what is the point of it? *sie ist nicht bei* –, she is unconscious *or* out of her mind; *Geld bei* – *haben*, have money in one's pocket; *niemand bei* – *sehen*, have no visitors; *das findet* – or *wird* – *finden*, that will be settled later, that will turn *or* work out all right; *es fragt* – *ob*, it is a question whether; *eine S. für* –, a separate matter, a th. apart, a th. to be considered specially; – *etwas zum Muster nehmen*, take s.th. for a model; *das schickt* – *nicht*, that is not proper *or* not nice; *das versteht* – (*von selbst*), that goes without saying, that is self-evident; – *die Hände waschen*, wash one's hands; *sie lieben* –, they love themselves *or* each other; (*Prov.*) *jeder ist* – *selbst der Nächste*, charity begins at home. **–gehenlassen,** *n.* freedom from restraint. **–überheben,** *n.* pride.

Sichel, *f.* (-n) sickle; crescent. **–artig,** *adj.*, **–förmig,** *adj.* crescent- *or* sickle-shaped. **–frone,** *f.* statute-reaping. **–n,** *v.a.* cut with a sickle, reap. *gesichelt*, *p.p. & adj.*; armed with a sickle; sickle-shaped. **–wagen,** *m.* chariot armed with scythes.

sicher, *adj.* secure, safe; sure, certain, positive, assured; trusty, trustworthy, reliable, steady; *–es Auftreten*, self-assured presence; *–er Beweis*, positive *or* certain proof, proof positive; *–e Forderung*, safe demand; – *gehen*, make quite sure, be on the safe side; *–es Geleit*, safe-conduct; – *glauben*, believe confidently, have complete faith; *–e Hand*, sure *or* steady hand; *aus* or *von –er Hand*, on good authority; – *machen*, make (*a place*) secure; reassure (*a p.*), lull (*a p.*) into security; *–e Nachricht*, trustworthy report; definite news; (*coll.*) *er sitzt auf Nummer* –, he is safely locked up, he is behind bars; – *auf einen rechnen*, count confidently upon a p.; *seiner S.* – *sein*, know what one is about; be certain of a th.; be a proficient in a th.; *–es Urteil*, sound *or* reliable judgement; – *vor*, safe from *or* against; – *wissen*, know for certain, be positive, be certain. **–er,** *m.* outpost (*Mil.*). **–heit,** *f.* certainty; trustworthiness; guarantee, safeguard; security, safety; *mit –heit*, confidently, reliably; *–heit im Auftreten*, self-possession, assurance; *–heit leisten*, give security, give as pledge *or* hostage; *in –heit bringen*, secure, make safe. **–heitsausschuß,** *m.* committee of public safety. **–heitsdienst,** *m.* police-duty. **–heitsfach,** *n.* safe, safe-deposit, strong-box. **–heitsfrage,** *f.* question of security (*Pol.*). **–heitsgrad,** *m.* safety-factor. **–heitshalber,** *adv.* for safety. **–heitskette,** *f.* door-chain; guard-chain (*Horol.*). **–heitsklausel,** *f.* safeguard. **–heitskoeffizient,** *m.*, *see* **–heitsgrad. –heitslampe,** *f.* safety-lamp (*Min.*). **–heitsleistung,** *f.* security, bail. **–heitsmaßregel,** *f.* precautionary measure, safeguard. **–heitsnadel,** *f.* safety-pin. **–heitspaß,** *m.* safe-conduct. **–heitspolizei,** *f.* security police. **–heitsschloß,** *n.* safety-lock. **–heitsstift,** *m.* shearing pin. **–heitsventil,** *n.* safety-valve. **–heitszündhölzer,** *n.pl.* safety-matches. **–lich,** *adv.* surely, certainly, undoubtedly. **–n,** 1. *v.a.* secure, ensure; guarantee, safeguard; cover, protect; place at 'safe' (*of a rifle*); belay (*mountaineering*). 2. *v.n.* (*aux.* h.) be watchful *or* on the alert; wind, scent (*Sport*). **–stellen,** *v.a.* secure, place *or* take in custody; make safe, guarantee. **–stellung,** *f.* safeguarding; guarantee. **–ung,** *f.* securing, ensuring; assurance, guarantee; security, safety; protection, defence (*Mil.*); fuse (*Elec.*); safety-catch (*on a rifle*). **–ungsfahrzeug,** *n.* escort vessel. **–ungsflügel,** *m.* protective flank (*Mil.*). (*C.L.*) **–ungsgeschäft,** *n.* covering transaction. **–ungslinie,** *f.* line of defence (*Mil.*).

Sicht, *f.* sight, visibility; *auf* –, at sight; *auf lange* –, with a view to the future, in the long run, (*C.L.*) long term; *7 Tage nach* –, 7 days after sight. **–bar,** *adj.* visible, perceptible, evident; (*coll.*) *ich bin noch nicht –bar*, I am not ready yet (to receive company); *–bar werden*, appear, become visible, manifest itself. **–barkeit,** *f.* visibility. **–barlich,** *adv.* visibly, obviously, evidently. **–en,** *v.a.* sight (*a ship, the enemy*). **–feld,** *n.* field of vision. **–ig,** *adj.* clear (*of the atmosphere*) (*Naut.*); (*in compounds* =) -sighted; e.g. *kurz–ig*, short-sighted. **–igkeit,** *f.* visibility (*Meteor.*). **–lich,** *adj.* visible, apparent, evident, obvious. **–note,** *f.*, *see* **–wechsel.** **–schutz,** *m.* camouflage. **–tage,** *m.pl.* days of grace. **–ung,** *f.* sighting. **–verbindlichkeit,** *f.*, **–vermerk,** *m.* visa (*on passports*). **–wechsel,** *m.* sight-bill, bill payable at sight. **–weite,** *f.* range of sight. **–zeichen,** *n.* ground-signal *or* panel (*Av.*).

sicht–en, *v.a.* sift, sort, winnow; classify, sort over. **–er,** *m.* sorter. **–ung,** *f.* sifting.

sickern, *v.n.* (*aux.* h. & s.) trickle, drip, seep, ooze, percolate, infiltrate.

siderisch, *adj.* siderial.

sie, I. *pers. pron.*; 1. (*3rd sing. f. Nom. & Acc.*) she, her, (it). 2. (*3rd pl. m., f. & n. Nom. & Acc.*) they; them. 3. (*with cap., 2nd pl. Nom. & Acc.*) you. II. *f.* (*coll.*) she, female (*usually of birds*); *dieser Vogel ist eine –*, this bird is a she.

Sieb, *n.* (-es, -e) sieve, filter, colander, riddle, strainer; screen. **–en,** *v.a.* sift, sieve, strain, bolt, riddle, filter (*also Rad.*); (*fig.*) weed *or* pick out. **–band,** *n.* travelling screen. **–boden,** *m.* perforated bottom. **–kette,** *f.* band-pass filter (*Rad.*). **–korb,** *m.* wire basket. **–mehl,** *n.* coarse flour, siftings. **–sel,** *n.*, **–stand,** *m.* siftings. **–trommel,** *f.* revolving screen. **–tuch,** *n.* bolting- *or* straining-cloth.

sieb–en, 1. *num. adj.* seven; *halb –en*, half-past six; *meine –en Sachen*, my belongings, my goods and chattels; *ein Buch mit –en Siegeln*, a sealed book, a complete mystery. 2. *f.* the number 7; *böse –en*, vixen, shrew. **–eneck,** *n.* heptagon. **–eneckig,** *adj.* heptagonal. **–ener,** *m.* soldier of the seventh regiment; the figure 7; one of 7; wine of 1907. **–enerlei,** *indec. adj.* of 7 different kinds. **–enfach,** *adj.*, **–enfältig,** *adj.* sevenfold. **–engescheit,** *adj.* (*dial.*) too clever by half. **–engestirn,** *n.* Pleiades. **–enherrschaft,** *f.* heptarchy. **–enjährig,** *adj.* 7 years old; lasting 7 years; *der –enjährige Krieg*, the Seven Years War (1756–63). **–enjährlich,** *adj.* septennial, occurring every 7 years. **–enmal,** *adv.* 7 times. **–enmalig,** *adj.* 7 times repeated. **–enmeilenschritte,** *m.pl.* giant strides. **–enmeilenstiefel,** *m.pl.* seven-league boots. **–enpunkt,** *m.* lady-bird (*Ent.*). **–ensachen,** *f.pl.* odds and ends, goods and chattels, belongings. **–enschläfer,** *m.* sluggard, lie-abed, lazy-bones; dormouse (*Myoxus glis*) (*Zool.*). **–enstündig,** *adj.* of *or* for 7 hours. **–entägig,** *adj.* 7 days old. **–ente,** *see* **–te.** **–entehalb,** *see* **–tehalb.** **–entel,** *see* **–tel.** **–entens,** *see* **–tens.** **–enundzwanzig,** *num. adj.* twenty-seven. **–enzehn,** *adj.*, *see* **–zehn.** **–t,** (der, die, das -te) *num. adj.* seventh. **–tel,** *n.* (*Swiss. dial. m.*) seventh (part). **–tens,** *adv.* seventhly. **–zehn,** *num. adj.* seventeen. **–zehnt,** *num. adj.* seventeenth. **–zehntel,** *n.* (*Swiss dial. m.*) seventeenth (part). **–zig,** *num. adj.* seventy. **–ziger,** *m.*, **–zigerin,** *f.* septuagenarian; *die –ziger Jahre*, the seventies (*e.g.* 1870–80). **–zigjährig,** *adj.* 70 years old, septuagenarian. **–zigst,** *num. adj.* seventieth. **–zigstel,** *n.* (*Swiss dial. m.*) seventieth (part).

siech, *adj.* ailing, invalid, sickly, infirm. **–bett,** *n.* sick-bed. **–en,** *v.n.* be a confirmed invalid; languish, pine away. **–enhaus,** *n.* infirmary; hospital for incurables. **–tum,** *n.* chronic ill health, (permanent) infirmity, long illness, invalidism.

Sied–e, *f.* boiling; (*dial.*) mash (*for cattle*); *in der –e sein*, be boiling *or* seething. **–en,** 1. *reg. & ir.v. n.* (*aux.* h.) boil; simmer; *mein Blut –ete*, my blood was boiling, I was seething; *–end heiß*, boiling hot. 2. *v.a.* boil, seethe, refine (*sugar*); make (*soap*); *hart gesottene Eier*, hard-boiled eggs. **–eanlage,** *f.* cracking-plant (*oil refinery*). **–ebottich,** *m.* scalding-tub. **–egrad,** *m.*, *see* **–epunkt.** **–eheiß,** *adj.* boiling *or* scalding hot. **–ehitze,** *f.* boiling temperature. **–ig,** *adj.* (*dial.*), *see* **–eheiß.** **–ekessel,** *m.* boiling- *or* evaporating-pan. **–eofen,** *m.* blanching-furnace. **–epunkt,** *m.* boiling-point. **–er,** *m.* boiler, refiner. **–erei,** *f.* refinery. **–erohr,** *n.* boiler-tube. **–etrennung,** *f.* fractional distillation (*oil*). **–everzug,** *m.* delay in boiling.

sied–eln, *v.n.* settle, colonize. **–ler,** *m.* settler, colonist. **–lung,** *f.* settlement, colony; housing estate. **–lungsgelände,** *n.* development area. **–lungsgesellschaft,** *f.* building society. **–lungspolitik,** *f.* housing policy.

Sieg, *m.* (-(e)s, -e) victory, conquest, triumph; *den – davontragen* or *erringen*, carry *or* win the day; *schließlich den – behaupten*, win through; *den – behalten*, be victorious; *– Heil!* (*Nat. Soc.*) hurrah! **–en,** *v.n.* (*aux.* h.) be victorious, triumph, conquer, gain a victory; win (*Sport.*). **–end,** *pr.p. & adj.* victorious, triumphant. **–er,** *m.* conqueror, victor, winner. **–erkranz,** *m.* victor's (laurel) wreath. **–erstaat,** *m.* (*usually pl.*) victorious country. **–es(auf)zug,** *m.* triumphal procession. **–esbahn,** *f.* career of victory. **–esbogen,** *m.* triumphal arch. **–esfeier,** *f.*, **–esfest,** *n.* victory-celebration. **–esgewiß,** *adj.* sure, certain *or* confident of victory. **–eslauf,** *m.*, *see* **–eszug.** **–estaumel,** *m.* flush of victory. **–estrunken,** *adj.* elated with victory. **–eswagen,** *m.* triumphal car. **–eswillen,** *m.* will to victory. **–eszeichen,** *n.* trophy. **–eszug,** *m.* triumphal procession; triumphant progress, victorious advance. **–haft,** *adj.* triumphant. **–reich,** *adj.* victorious.

Siegel, *n.* (-s, –) seal; *geheimes* (*Staats*)–, privy seal; *unter – legen*, seal; *Brief und – über eine S. haben*, have under sign (*or* hand) and seal; *unter dem – der Verschwiegenheit*, under the seal of secrecy, in strict confidence; *das ist für mich ein Buch mit sieben –n*, that is a sealed book to me. **–bewahrer,** *m.* keeper of the seal; Lord Privy Seal. **–erde,** *f.* sealed *or* Lemnian earth. **–gebühr,** *f.* fee paid for affixing a seal. **–lack,** *m.* sealing-wax. **–n,** *v.a.* seal; affix a seal. **–ring,** *m.* signet-ring. **–wachs,** *n.*, *see* **–lack.** **–stecher,** *m.* seal-engraver.

sieht, *see* **sehen.**

Siel, *m. & n.* (-(e)s, -e) (*dial.*) sluice, culvert, drain, sewer. **–wasser,** *n.* sewage.

Siele, *f.* (-n) breast-piece (*of harness*); *in den –n sterben*, die in harness. **–ngeschirr,** *n.* breast-harness.

siezen, *v.a.* be on formal terms with (*a p.*), address (*a p.*) formally with 'Sie' (*and not with* 'Du').

Sigel, *n.* (-s, –) logogram, grammologue (*Shorthand*); sign, symbol.

Sigill, *n.* (*Poet. & archaic*), *see* **Siegel.**

Sigle, *f.* (-n), *see* **Sigel.**

Signal, *n.* (-s, -e) signal; bugle-call. **–apparat,** *m.* signalling apparatus. **–bombe,** *f.* signal-flare. **–buch,** *n.* code of signals. **–ement,** *n.* (-s, -s) description (of a p.). **–feuer,** *n.* beacon. **–flagge,** *f.* signalling flag. **–gast,** *m.* naval signaller. **–glocke,** *f.* warning-bell. **–hupe,** *f.* klaxon horn, siren. **–isieren,** *v.a.* signal; give a summary description. **–lampe,** *f.*, **–laterne,** *f.* signal-light, signalling lamp. **–leine,** *f.* bell-rope, communication cord. **–leuchtkugel,** *f.* star-shell (*Artil.*). **–mast,** *m.* signal post, semaphore (*Railw.*). **–pfeife,** *f.* warning whistle. **–ruf,** *m.* warning cry; bugle-call. **–scheibe,** *f.* disk-signal. **–schuß,** *m.* signal-gun; *–schüsse tun*, fire signals. **–wärter,** *m.* signalman.

Sign–atar, *m.* (-s, -e) signatory. **–atarmacht,** *f.* signatory power (*to treaty*). **–atur,** *f.* (-en) signature (*also Typ.*); sign, mark; stamp, brand; label (*on a medicine-bottle, etc.*); conventional sign (*on maps*); catalogue number (*library books*). **–et,** *n.* (-(e)s, -e) colophon (*Typ.*). **–ieren,** *v.a.* sign; mark, brand.

Sigrist, *m.* (-en, -en) (*Swiss dial.*) sacristan, sexton.

Silb–e, *f.* (-n) syllable; *keine –e davon sagen*, not say a word about it; *–en verschlucken*, swallow one's words; *–en stechen*, quibble, split hairs. **–enmaß,** *n.* metre, quantity. **–enmessung,** *f.* prosody. **–enrätsel,** *n.* charade. **–enstecher,** *m.* stickler, hair-splitter, quibbler. **–enstecherei,** *f.* hair-splitting; quibbling. **–entrennung,** *f.* hyphenation. **–enweise,** *adv.* syllable by syllable. **–ig,** *adj. suff.* syllabic (e.g. *drei–ig*, tri-syllabic); **–isch,** *adj.* syllabic, constituting a syllable.

Silber, *n.* silver; silverplate. **–ader,** *f.* vein of silver (*Min.*). **–arbeiter,** *m.* silversmith. **–artig,**

adj. silvery, argentine. **–ätzstein,** *m.* lunar caustic, silver nitrate. **–barre,** *f.*, **–barren,** *m.* bar *or* ingot of silver. **–bergwerk,** *n.* silver-mine. **–blei,** *n.* argentiferous lead. **–blende,** *f.* galena of silver, pyrargyrite, proustite. **–blick,** *m.* gleam of silver (*in refining process*); bright moment, lucky chance; (*coll.*) slight squint. **–braut,** *f.*, **–bräutigam,** *m.* wife *or* husband celebrating their silver wedding. **–brenner,** *m.* silver-refiner. **–buche,** *f.* white *or* American beech. **–chlorid,** *n.* argentic chloride. **–diener,** *m.* servant *or* official in charge of the plate. **–distel,** *f.* carline thistle (*Carlina acaulis*) (*Bot.*). **–erz,** *n.* silver-ore. **–farben,** *adj.* **–farbig,** *adj.* silvery (*in colour*), silver-coloured. **–fasan,** *m.* silver pheasant (*Phasianus nycthemerus*) (*Orn.*). **–fischchen,** *n.* sugar-mite (*Ent.*). **–gehalt,** *m.* silver content (*of an alloy*). **–geld,** *n.* silver (money). **–geschirr,** *n.* silver (plate). **–glanz,** *m.* silvery lustre; argentine, silver-glance (*Min.*). **–glätte,** *f.* litharge. **–glimmer,** *m.* common mica. **–gold,** *n.* electrum, argentiferous gold. **–grau,** *adj.* silver-grey. **–grube,** *f.* silver-mine. **–hell,** *adj.* (as) bright as silver; *–helle Stimme*, silvery voice. **–hochzeit,** *f.* silver wedding. **–ig,** *adj.* (of) silver. **–kammer,** *f.* plate-room. **–kämmerer,** *m.*, *see* **–diener.** **–klang,** *m.* clear, silvery sound. **–korn,** *n.* grain of silver. **–laden,** *m.* silversmith's shop. **–licht,** *n.* silver light (*of the moon*). **–ling,** *m.* (*B.*) piece of silver, shekel. **–lot,** *n.* silver solder. **–löwe,** *m.* puma. **–möwe,** *f.* herring-gull (*Larus argentatus*) (*Orn.*). **–münze,** *f.* silver coin. **–n,** *adj.* (of) silver; *–ne Hochzeit*, silver wedding. **–nitrat,** *n.* nitrate of silver; lunar caustic. **–oxyd,** *n.* oxide of silver. **–papier,** *n.* silver paper. **–pappel,** *f.* white poplar. **–salpeter,** *m.* nitrate of silver. **–schaum,** *m.* foliated silver. **–scheider,** *m.* silver refiner. **–schein,** *m.* silvery lustre. **–schimmel,** *m.* silver-grey horse. **–schmied,** *m.* silversmith. **–stift,** *m.* silverpoint (*Engr.*). **–stoff,** *m.* silver brocade; silver cloth *or* tissue. **–streif,** *m.* (*fig.*) silver lining, gleam of hope. **–tanne,** *f.* silver fir. **–tresse,** *f.* silver lace. **–verbindungen,** *f.pl.* argentiferous compounds. **–währung,** *f.* silver currency; *Anhänger der –währung*, bimetallist, silverite (*Amer.*). **–waren,** *f.pl.* silver goods; plate. **–weide,** *f.* common white willow. **–weiß,** 1. *adj.* silvery. 2. *n.* shell-silver (*Paint.*). **–zeug,** *n.* silver plate.

silbrig, *adj.*, *see* **silberig.**

Silizium, *n.* silicon.

Sill, *n.* (*dial.*), *see* **Siele.**

Silvester(abend), *m.* (-s, -e) New Year's Eve, (*Scots*) Hogmanay.

Similistein, *m.* (-(e)s, -e) artificial gem, paste diamond.

Simon–ie, *f.* simony. **–isch,** *adj.* simoniacal.

simpel, 1. *adj.* plain, simple, stupid. 2. *m.* (-s, –) (*coll.*) simpleton. **–haft,** *adj.* simple, silly. **–n,** *v.n.* be thoughtless *or* absent-minded; *fach–n*, talk shop.

Sims, *m.* (& *Austr. dial. n.*) (-es, -e) cornice, moulding; mantelpiece, shelf, ledge, (window) sill. **–hobel,** *m.* moulding-plane. **–werk,** *n.* mouldings.

Simul–ant, *m.* (-en, -en) malingerer (*Mil.*); (*sl.*) leadswinger. **–ieren,** *v.a.* & *n.* (*aux.* h.) feign, simulate, sham; malinger (*Mil.*); (*sl.*) swing the lead; (*dial.*) reflect, ponder; *simulierte Rechnung*, pro forma account; (*dial.*) *über eine S. –ieren*, brood over *or* ponder a th.

simultan, *adj.* simultaneous; joint. **–schule,** *f.* undenominational school.

sind, *see* **sein.**

Sinfonie, *f.* (-n) symphony.

sing–en, 1. *ir.v.a.* & *n.* (*aux.* h.) sing, chant, (*Poet.*) carol (*of birds*); *vom Blatte* (*weg*) *–en*, sing at sight; *immer dasselbe Lied –en*, be always harping on the same subject; *falsch –en*, sing out of tune; *davon weiß ich ein Lied zu –en*, I can say s.th. about that; *sein eignes Lob –en*, sing one's own praises, (*coll.*) blow one's own trumpet; *mehrstimmig –en*, sing part songs, sing in parts; *nach Noten –en*, sing from music; *in Schlaf –en*, sing to sleep; *Sopran –en*, have a soprano voice; sing the soprano part; (*coll.*) *das war(d) ihm an der Wiege nicht gesungen*, no one thought he would come to this. 2. *v.r.* & *imp.*; *das Lied –t sich leicht*, this song is easy to sing; *es –t sich schön im Bade*, it is pleasant to sing in the bath; *es –t mir in den Ohren*, there is a singing *or* ringing in my ears; *–ende Säge*, musical saw. **–akademie,** *f.* voice-training school. **–bar,** *adj.* singable. **–drossel,** *f.* song-thrush. **–estunde,** *see* **–stunde.** **–lehrer,** *m.* singing-master. **–sang,** *m.* sing-song. **–spiel,** *n.* operetta; musical comedy. **–stimme,** *f.* singing voice; vocal part (*Mus.*); *Lied für eine –stimme*, song for a single voice, solo song. **–stunde,** *f.* singing lesson. **–vogel,** *m.* song-bird, songster; (*Poet.*) warbler. **–weise,** *f.* style of singing.

Singrün, *n.* periwinkle (*Bot.*).

Singular, *m.* (-s, -e) singular (*number*) (*Gram.*).

singulär, *adj.* singular, unique, strange, peculiar, odd.

sink–en, 1. *ir.v.a.* sink (*a shaft.*) 2. *v.n.* (*aux.* s.) sink, subside, give way; descend, drop, fall; go down, decrease, abate, diminish, decline; *in Ohnmacht –en*, faint, swoon; *die Stimme –en lassen*, lower *or* drop the voice; *in die Knie –en*, fall to one's knees; *bis in die –ende Nacht*, deep into the night; *den Mut nicht –en lassen*, not lose heart *or* courage; *der Mut sank ihm*, his heart failed him. **–kasten,** *m.* street-drain. **–körper,** *m.* sinker. **–stoff,** *m.* sediment, deposit, precipitate.

Sinn, *m.* (-(e)s, -e) sense, faculty, organ of perception, feeling; intellect, mind, understanding, wit, intelligence; consciousness, apprehension, memory; taste, inclination, disposition, tendency, direction; wish, opinion, temper; interpretation, purport, import, meaning, signification; *andern –es werden*, change one's mind; *sich* (*Dat.*) *etwas aus dem –e schlagen*, put *or* get s.th. out of one's mind, dismiss a th. from one's mind; *bei –en sein*, be in one's right mind, have one's wits about one; *es fuhr ihm durch den –*, it suddenly struck him; *eines –es sein*, agree, be of *or* have the same opinion; *seine fünf –e beisammen haben*, have one's wits about one; *– für* (*eine S.*) *haben*, have a taste for, be susceptible to *or* take an interest in (a th.); *– für Humor*, sense of humour; *– für Literatur*, interest in literature, literary taste; *– für Natur*, appreciation of nature; *hoher –*, high-mindedness, magnanimity; *im bildlichen –e*, figuratively; *im eigentlichen –e*, literally, verbally; *in die –e fallen*, appeal to the senses; *in die –e fallend*, striking, conspicuous, manifest, palpable; *in gewissem –e*, in a sense *or* way; *im gleichen –e*, likewise, similarly; *im –e haben*, have in mind, intend, purpose; *in seinem –e handeln*, act as he would, act according to his ideas *or* wishes; *es kam mir in den –, daß*, it occurred to me that; *im übertragenen –e*, metaphorically; *im wahrsten* or *tiefsten –e des Wortes*, in the fullest sense of the word; *im –e wie*, in the way that, just as; *es will mir nicht in den –*, I cannot grasp it *or* make head or tail of it; it does not appeal to me at all; *dem –e nach*, in spirit, according to the intention; *sein – steht nicht nach lauten Freuden*, he has no liking *or* inclination for noisy *or* boisterous pleasures; *weder – noch Verstand*, neither rhyme nor reason; (*Prov.*) *viel Köpfe, viel –e*, many men, many minds; *von –en sein*, be out of one's mind, be crazy. **–bild,** *n.* symbol, emblem. **–bildlich,** *adj.* symbolic(al), emblematic; *–bildliche Darstellung*, allegory. **–en,** 1. *ir.v.n.* (*aux.* h. & s.) think, think over, meditate, reflect, brood, speculate (*über* (*Acc.*), about *or* upon); *–en auf* (*Acc.*), scheme, plan, contrive, devise, plot; *was sinnt ihr?* what are you thinking of? *er –t nichts Gutes*, his intentions are not good; *gesonnen sein*, be inclined, have a mind (to do), intend, purpose. *gesinnt*, *adj.* minded, inclined, disposed; *er war protestantisch gesinnt*, he had Protestant sympathies. 2. *v.a.* think out, plot, invent; *Rache –en*, meditate revenge. 3. *n.* thinking, planning; thoughts, aspirations. **–end,** *pr.p.* & *adj.* musing, pensive, thoughtful, contemplative, reflective. **–engenuß,** *m.* sensual enjoyment. **–enlust,** *f.* sensual pleasure, voluptuousness. **–enmensch,** *m.* sensualist. **–enrausch,** *m.* sensual orgy. **–enreiz,** *m.* sense-stimulus. **–ent-**

stellend, *adj.* falsifying, distorting (*the meaning*). **-enwelt,** *f.* material *or* external world. **-esänderung,** *f.* change of mind; recantation. **-esapparat,** *m.*, *see* **-esorgan. -esart,** *f.* character, disposition. **-eseindruck,** *m.* sense-impression. **-esnerv,** *m.* sensory nerve. **-esorgan,** *n.* sense-organ. **-estäuschung,** *f.* illusion, hallucination. **-eswerkzeug,** *n.*, *see* **-esorgan. -fällig,** *adj.* obvious, apparent, palpable, manifest, conspicuous. **-gedicht,** *n.* epigram. **-gemäß,** *adv.* accordingly, obviously. **-getreu,** *adj.* faithful (*rendering*). **-ieren,** *v.n.* (*dial.*) be lost in thoughts, brood, ponder. **-ig,** *adj.* sensible, judicious; thoughtful; ingenious; (*as suffix*) -minded; *-iges Mädchen*, sensible girl; *-iges Geschenk*, fitting *or* apt gift. **-igkeit,** *f.* thoughtfulness; ingenuity. **-leer,** *adj.* unmeaning, meaningless, devoid of meaning. **-lich,** *adj.* material, physical; sensuous; sensual, voluptuous; sentient (*Phil.*); *-liche Liebe*, sensual love; *-licher Mensch*, sensualist; *-liche Wahrnehmung*, sense, perception. **-lichkeit,** *f.* material nature; sensuality, sensuousness. **-los,** *adj.* senseless, meaningless; thoughtless, foolish. **-losigkeit,** *f.* senselessness; absurdity, foolishness. **-reich,** *adj.* witty, ingenious, clever, talented. **-spruch,** *m.* maxim, epigram, aphorism, motto. **-verwandt,** *adj.* synonymous; *-verwandtes Wort*, synonym. **-voll,** *adj.* significant, pregnant. **-widrig,** *adj.* nonsensical, absurd.

sintemal, *conj.* (*archaic*) since, whereas; (*iron.*) – *und alldieweil*, since, because.

Sinter, *m.* (-s, –) sinter, stalactite, (*dial.*) iron-dross. **-n,** *v.n.* (*aux.* s.) trickle, drip, ooze, percolate; form deposits, petrify; frit together, slag, cake, clinker.

Sintflut, *f.* (*B.*) flood, deluge. **-lich,** *adj.* (*usually* vor-lich) (ante)-diluvian.

Sinus, *m.* (–, – & -se) sine (*Math.*). **-förmig,** *adj.* sinoidal (*Math.*). **-satz,** *m.* sine theorem (*Math.*).

Sipp-e, *f.* (-en) kin, kinship, consanguinity; kindred, relatives, relations, kith and kin; genus, tribe (*Zool.*). **-enforschung,** *f.* (*Nat. Soc.*) genealogical research. **-schaft,** *f.* kinship, kindred; (*coll.*) set, lot, pack, clique; *die ganze -schaft*, (*sl.*) the whole caboodle.

Sirene, *f.* (-n) siren (*Myth., Acoust.*). **-ngeheul,** *n.* hooting of sirens. **-nhaft,** *adj.* seductive, captivating, bewitching.

Sirup, *m.* (-s, -e) syrup; treacle, molasses. **-artig,** *adj.* syrupy.

Sisalhanf, *m.* sisal.

sistier-en, *v.a.* stop, inhibit, check (*a procedure*); arrest. **-ung,** *f.* inhibition; summons (*Law*).

Sitt-e, *f.* (-en) custom, habit, usage; mode, practice, fashion; propriety, etiquette; (*pl.*) manners, morals; *das ist so seine -e*, that is his way *or* habit; *das ist bei uns nicht -e*, that is not the custom here; *feine -en*, good-breeding. **-enbild,** *n.* genre-picture. **-engesetz,** *n.* moral code; moral law. **-enlehre,** *f.* moral philosophy, ethics. **-enlehrer,** *m.* moral philosopher, moralist. **-enlos,** *adj.* immoral, dissolute, profligate. **-enlosigkeit,** *f.* immorality, profligacy. **-enpolizei,** *f.* control of prostitutes, police surveillance (of brothels). **-enprediger,** *m.* moralizer. **-enpredigt,** *f.* moralizing sermon; *jemandem eine -enpredigt halten*, lay down the law to a p. **-enregel,** *f.* rule of conduct; moral precept. **-enrein,** *adj.* (morally) pure, chaste. **-enrichter,** *m.* censor, moralizer. **-enrichterlich,** *adj.* censorious. **-enstreng,** *adj.* puritanical. **-enstrenge,** *f.* austerity (*of morals or manners*). **-enverderbend,** *adj.* demoralizing. **-enverderbnis,** *f.*, **-enverfall,** *m.* deterioration *or* decay of morals; depravity, corruption. **-ig,** *adj.* modest, chaste; polite well-bred. **-lich,** *adj.* moral, ethical. **-lichkeit,** *f.* morality, morals. **-lichkeitsgefühl,** *n.* moral sense. **-lichkeitsverbrechen** *n.*, **-lichkeitsvergehen,** *n.* indecent assault. **-sam,** *adj.* modest; virtuous, chaste; well-behaved, proper. **-samkeit,** *f.* modesty, decency, coyness, bashfulness.

Sittich, *m.* (-(e)s, -e) parakeet.

Situation, *f.* (-en) situation, position, state of affairs; *wir sind in derselben –*, we are in the same position; (*coll.*) we are in the same boat; *auf der Höhe der – stehen, sich der – gewachsen fühlen*, be equal to the occasion; *eine – ausnutzen*, make the most of an opportunity. **-skomik,** *f.* comedy of situation.

situiert, *adj.* placed; *wohl* or *gut –*, well off, well-to-do.

Sitz, *m.* (-es, -e) seat, chair; perch; residence, domicile; place, spot; (episcopal) see; fit (*of a garment*); *– und Stimme im Rate haben*, have a seat and vote in the council; *seinen – an einem Orte aufschlagen*, establish o.s., take up residence *or* settle in a place; *London ist der – der Regierung*, London is the seat of government. **-en,** *ir.v.n.* (*aux.* h. & (*dial.*) s.) sit; perch (*of bird*); stay, be situated, remain; stick fast, adhere; fit (*of clothes*), suit; (*coll.*) be locked up, be in prison; (*coll.*) *er -t*, he is in clink *or* jug; *es -t sich gut hier*, here is a comfortable place to sit; *die Truppen -en am Ufer*, the troops are established on *or* occupy the bank; *einem auf dem Nacken -en*, be a pest *or* (*sl.*) a pain in the neck to a p.; *beim Tanze -en*, sit out (a dance); *da -en wir !* now we're in a mess; *der Hieb -t*, that's a home thrust! (*Fenc.* & *fig.*); (*coll.*) *in Butter -en*, be fine and dandy, (*sl.*) have it jammy; *ihm -t der Schelm im Nacken*, (*hum.*) he is a scamp *or* rascal; *im Rate -en*, have a seat on the council; (*coll.*) *in der Tinte* or *Patsche -en*, be in an awful mess *or* jam *or* fix; *fest im Sattel -en*, have a firm seat, (*fig.*) be firmly in the saddle, be firmly established in power; *da -t der Knoten!* there's the rub! (*einem Maler*) *-en*, sit for a portrait, give a sitting; *der Nagel -t fest*, the nail holds firm; *das Schiff -t fest* (*auf dem Grunde*), the ship is fast aground; *der Schuß saß*, the shot hit the mark; *zu Gericht -en*, hold a council, sit in council, pass judgement. **-arbeit,** *f.* sedentary work. **-bad,** *n.* hip-bath. **-bein,** *n.* ischium. **-enbleiben,** *v.n.* remain seated, keep one's seat; (*fig.*) be a wallflower, be on the shelf; stay down (*at school*); *der Teig bleibt -en*, the dough does not rise. **-end,** *pr.p.* & *adj.* seated, perched; sedentary, fixed, sessile (*Bot.*); *-ende Lebensweise*, sedentary (mode of) life. **-enlassen,** *v.a.* make sit down; (*coll.*) leave in the lurch, jilt, throw over; *auf sich* (*Dat.*) *-enlassen*, put up with *or* pocket (*an affront*). **-er,** *m.* with (*so many*) seats; e.g. *Vier-er*, four-seater. **-fallschirm,** *m.* seat-type parachute. **-fläche,** *f.* seat (*of chair*). **-fleisch,** *n.* (*coll.*) ham, buttock; *er hat kein -fleisch*, (*coll.*) he cannot stick at a job. **-fuß,** *m.* insessorial foot (*Orn.*). **-füßler,** *m.pl.* perchers, insessores (*Orn.*). **-gelegenheit,** *f.* seating-accommodation, (number of) seats (available). **-ig,** *adj. suffix* with (*so many*) seats; e.g. *vier-iger Wagen*, four-seater car. **-platz,** *m.* seat. **-stange,** *f.* perch. **-ung,** *f.* sitting (*also for a portrait*); session, meeting; (*coll.*) *eine lange -ung halten*, sit a long time over one's drink, have a long session (in the pub). **-ungsbericht,** *m.* report of a meeting, proceedings, minutes. **-ungsdauer,** *f.*, **-ungsperiode,** *f.*, **-ungszeit,** *f.* session, term. **-ungszimmer,** *n.* council-room, committee-room, board-room.

Six, *int.*; (*coll.*) *meiner – ! mein -chen !* upon my soul! upon my word!

skabi-ös, *adj.* scabious (*Med.*). **-ose,** *f.*, (-n) scabious (*Bot.*).

Skal-a, *f.* (-en) gamut; scale, graduation. **-enring,** *m.* graduated ring. **-enscheibe,** *f.* tuning-dial (*Rad.*).

Skalde, *m.* (-n, -n) scald, ancient bard. **-ndichtung,** *f.*, **-npoesie,** *f.* old Norse poetry.

Skalp, *m.* (-s, -e) scalp. **-ieren,** *v.a.* scalp.

Skalpell, *n.* (-s, -e) scalpel (*Surg.*).

Skandal, *m.* (-s, -e) scandal; row, uproar. **-geschichte,** *f.* (piece of) scandal. **-ieren,** *v.n.* make a din, kick up a row. **-isieren,** *v.r.* be shocked *or* scandalized (*über*, at). **-ös,** *adj.* scandalous, shocking. **-presse,** *f.* gutter-press.

skandieren, *v.a.* scan (*verses*).

Skat, *m.* (-(e)s, -e) skat (*a German card game*) **-en,** *v.a.* play skat.

Skelett, *n.* (-(e)s, -e) skeleton. **-artig,** *adj.* skeleton-like; reduced to a skeleton, all skin and bones. **-bau,** *m.* skeleton construction (*Arch.*).

Skep-sis, *f.* scepticism, doubt. **-tiker,** *m.* sceptic. **-tisch,** *adj.* sceptical. **-tizismus,** *m.* philosophic scepticism.

Ski, *m.* (-s, -er) ski. **-fahren,** *see* **-laufen.** **-fahrer,** *see* **-läufer.** **-laufen,** 1. *v.n.* ski. 2. *n.* skiing. **-läufer,** *m.* skier. **-springen,** *n.* ski-jumping.

Skizz-e, *f.* (-en) sketch, outline. **-enhaft,** *adj.* sketchy. **-ierblock,** *m.* sketching-pad. **-ieren,** *v.a.* & *n.* sketch; make a rough draught.

Sklav-e, *m.* (-en, -en) slave. **-enarbeit,** *f.* slave-work; (*fig.*) drudgery. **-enbefreiung,** *f.* emancipation of slaves. **-endienst,** *m.* slavery; drudgery. **-enhalter,** *m.* slave-owner. **-enhandel,** *m.* slave-trade. **-enhändler,** *m.* slave-dealer. **-enseele,** *f.* slavish mind, servile disposition. **-enstaaten,** *m.pl.* slave states (*of America*). **-entum,** *n.*, **-erei,** *f.* slavery, servitude, bondage, thraldom. **-in,** *f.* slave (girl), female slave. **-isch,** *adj.* slavish, servile.

skont-ieren, *v.n.* deduct. **-o,** *m.* (& *Austr. dial n.*) discount. **-ration,** *f.* balancing (*accounts*). **-rieren,** *v.a.* check (*cash*), collate. **-rierung,** *f.* settling, balancing, clearing, checking, collating. **-ro,** *n.* settlement, balance; reduction, compensation. **-robuch,** *n.* account-current book. **-rotag,** *m.* settling day.

Skorbut, *m.* scurvy. **-isch,** *adj.* scorbutic.

Skribent, *m.* (-en, -en) writer; scribbler, literary hack.

Skripturen, *f.pl.* papers, documents.

Skrof-el, *f.* scrofula. **-ulös,** *adj.* scrofulous, strumous. **-ulose,** *f.* scrofula.

Skrup-el, *m.* (-s, –) scruple; *sich* (*Dat.*) *-el machen über eine S.*, have one's scruples about a th. **-ellos,** *adj.* unscrupulous. **-ulös,** *adj.* scrupulous.

skull-en, *v.a.* & *n.* scull, row. **-boot,** *n.* skiff.

Skulptur, *f.* (-en) (piece of) sculpture.

skurril, *adj.* ludicrous, farcical, comical.

Smaragd, *m.* (-(e)s, -e) emerald. **-en, -farben, -grün,** *adj.* emerald (green).

Smirgel, *m.* emery.

Smoking, *m.* (-s, -s) dinner-jacket.

so, 1. *adv.* so, thus, in this, that *or* such a way, like this *or* that, as; *er spricht bald –, bald –*, he says now this, now that; *sein Betragen war –, daß*, his conduct was such as (to); *– ein*, such a; *ich habe – eine Ahnung, daß*, I have a sort of notion that; *– etwas*, such a thing, that sort of thing; *– etwas!* would you believe it! well, I never! *er hat nicht – ganz Unrecht*, he is not so far wrong; *ich summte – vor mich hin*, I was just humming to myself (*see also* **-hin**); *– lange (daß)*, so long that (*see also* **-lang**); *Sie sagen das nur –*, you are only saying that, you do not really mean it; *das reicht nur – eben*, that is barely sufficient *or* only just enough and no more (*see also* **-eben**); *– oder –*, one way or another; *– recht!* or *recht –!* quite right! just so! *er ist – schon böse*, he is angry anyhow; *– sehr*, so much, to such a degree; *– sehr auch*, as much as; however much; *– ist es*, that is right, that is so; *– ist das Leben*, such is life; *wenn dem – ist*, if that is so; *es ist mir –, als könnte ich fliegen*, I feel as if *or* though I could fly; *das ist nun einmal –*, that is the way things are; *– bin ich nun einmal*, that is my nature *or* way; *um – besser*, so much the better; *– viel*, so much, so many (*see also* **-viel**); *es waren nicht – viele*, there were not so very many of them; *ich mache mir nicht – viel daraus*, I do not set great store by it; *– wahr ich lebe!* as (sure as) I live! *– . . . wie . . .*, as . . . as . . .; *machen Sie es – wie ich*, do as I do (*see also* **-wie**); *– gut wie keine*, practically none; *– ziemlich*, pretty well, pretty good. 2. *conj.* therefore, for that reason, then; if, in case; *er war nicht zu Hause, – war mein Besuch vergebens*, he was not at home, consequently my visit was in vain; *– wollen Sie nicht?* you won't then? *er ist krank, – daß er nicht kommen kann*, he is too ill to come; *– Gott will*, if it please God; *– groß er auch sein mag*, however great he may be; *– lasset uns gehen*, let us go then; *da du nicht kannst*, (–) *werde ich selbst hingehen*, since you cannot go, (then) I will go myself; *kaum warst du fort*, (–) *kam er zurück*, you were scarcely gone, when he returned. 3. *int.* indeed! really! *ach –!* Oh! I see. 4. (*B.* & *archaic*) *rel. pron.* who, that, which; *diejenigen, – mich lieben*, those who love me. **-bald,** *conj.* as soon as; *-bald es Ihnen bequem ist*, at your earliest convenience. **-dann,** *adv.* & *conj.* then, in that case; after all, afterwards. **-eben,** *adv.* just, just now; *er ist -eben gekommen*, he has just come. **-fern,** *conj.* so far as, inasmuch as; *-fern nur*, if only, as long as. **-fort,** *adv.* immediately, instantly, forthwith, at once. **-fortig,** *adj.* prompt, immediate, instantaneous; ready (*cash*). **-fortmaßnahme,** *f.* urgent measure. **-gar,** *adv.* even; *alle, -gar mein Bruder*, all, even my brother; *ja -gar*, yes, and what is more. **-genannt,** *adj.* so-called; pretended, would-be. **-gleich,** *adv.*, *see* **-fort.** **-hin,** *adv.* (*also* **– hin**) tolerably, passably well, well enough; *das geht noch – hin*, that will just about do. **-lang(e),** *conj.* as *or* so long as, whilst. **-mit,** *adv.*, **-nach,** *adv.* consequently, accordingly, then. **-oft,** *conj.* as often as, whenever, as many times as. **-sehr,** *conj.* much as. **-so,** *adv.* tolerably well, middling, (*coll.*) not bad. **-tan,** (*archaic*) *adj.* such; *unter -tanen Umständen*, as matters stand. **-und-,** 1. *adv.* so-and-so, such-and-such; *Paragraph -und-*, such-and-such a paragraph, paragraph so-and-so. 2. *n.*; *Herr -und-*, Mr. What's-his-name. **-und-viel,** *adj.* so much, a given amount. **-und-vielte(r),** *m.* such-and-such a day of the month. **-viel,** 1. *conj.* so far as, according to. 2. *adv.* so much; *-viel für heute*, so much *or* that is enough for today; *doppelt -viel*, twice as much; *-viel wie ein Eid*, as good as *or* much the same as an oath. **-weit,** 1. *conj. see* **-fern.** 2. *adv.* as *or* so far; *-weit wie* or *als möglich*, as far *or* as much as possible; *es geht ihm -weit gut, nur . . .*, he is so far quite well, only . . . *or* but . . . . **-wenig,** *conj.* as little as. **-wie,** *conj.* as soon as; as well as, as also. **-wie-,** *adv.* anyhow, in any case; *er ist -wie-böse auf mich*, he is angry enough with me as it is. **-wohl,** *conj.* as well as, just the same as; *-wohl er als sie*, he as well as she; *-wohl . . . als auch . . .*, not only . . . but also . . . **-zusagen,** *adv.* so to speak, as it were.

Socke, *f.* (-n) sock; (*coll.*) *sich auf die -n machen*, take to one's heels. **-l,** *m.* base, pedestal, stand, foot, socle, socket. **-lgeschütz,** *n.* pivot-gun. **-lplatte,** *f.* plinth. **-nhalter,** *m.* (sock-) suspender, garter.

Sod, *m.* (-(e)s, -e) boil, boiling, brew; heartburn; (*dial.*) spring, well. **-brennen,** *n.* heartburn, pyrosis.

Soda, *f.* (& *n.*) (carbonate of) soda. **-fabrik,** *f.* soda *or* alkali works. **-haltig,** *adj.* containing soda. **-salz,** *n.* soda salt, sodium carbonate. **-wasser,** *n.* soda-water, aerated *or* mineral water.

sodann, *see under* **so.**

soeben, *see under* **so.**

Sofa, *n.* (-s, -s) sofa, couch, settee.

sofern, *see under* **so.**

Soff, *m. see* **Suff.**

soff, söffe, *see* **saufen.**

Soffitte, *f.* (-n) soffit (*Arch.* & *Theat.*). **-nlampen,** *f.pl.* strip-lighting.

sofort, *see under* **so.**

Sog, *m.* (-(e)s, -e) un dertow; suction (*Av.*); wake (*of a ship*).

sog, söge, *see* **saugen.**

sogar, *see under* **so.**

sogennant, *see under* **so.**

sogge-n, *v.n.*, crystallize out. **-pfanne,** *f.* crystallizing pan.

sogleich, *see under* **so.**

sohin, *see under* **so.**

Sohl-e, *f.* (-n) sole (*of foot or shoe*); face (*of a plane*); bottom (*of a valley*); floor (*of a mine*); (*coll.*) lie, fib; *sich* (*Dat.*) *etwas an den -en abgelaufen haben*, have known s.th. long ago; *sich an meine -en heften*, stick to my heels; *mir brennt es auf* or *unter den -en*, it is getting too hot for me; *auf leisen -en*, (treading) softly *or* gently, on tip-toe; *mach dich auf die -en*, (*coll.*) beat it! *sich die -en wund laufen*, run one's legs off (*nach*, after); *vom Scheitel bis zur -e*, from head to foot, from top to toe. **-bank,** *f.* window-sill. **-en,** 1. *v.a.* sole. 2. *v.n.* (*coll.*) tell fibs. **-enband,** *n.* plantar ligament (*Anat.*). **-engänger,** *m.* plantigrade animal (*Zool.*). **-enleder,** *n.* sole-leather. **-enplatte,** *f.*, bed-plate foundation

söhlig, *adj.* level, horizontal (*Min.*).
Sohn, *m.* (-(e)s, ¨-e) son; *Schmidt* –, Schmidt junior; *Ihr Herr* –, your son; (*B.*) *des Menschen* –, the Son of Man; (*B.*) *der verlorene* –, the prodigal son. **-esliebe,** *f.* filial affection. **-espflicht,** *f.* filial duty. **-schaft,** *f.* filiation (*Law*).
Söhn-erin, *f.* (*dial.*) daughter-in-law. **-lich,** *adj.* filial.
Soiree, *f.* (-n) soirée, dinner-party; evening performance (*Theat., etc.*).
Soja, *f.*, **-bohne,** *f.* soya-bean, soybean (*Bot.*).
solang(e), *see under* **so.**
Solawechsel, *m.* bill (of exchange), promissory note.
solch, 1. *adj. & dem. pron.* (-er, -e, es) such; *ein* -*er Mensch,* – *ein Mensch,* a man like him, such a man; *ich habe* -*e,* I have some like that *or* these. 2. *adv.*; *in* – *schlechter* or – *einer schlechten* or -*er schlechten Lage,* in such a bad position *or* state. **-enfalls,** *adv.* in this case, in such a case. **-ergestalt,** *adv.* in such a way, so, thus, to such a degree. **-erlei,** *indec. adj.* of such a kind, such; (*coll.*) suchlike. **-ermaßen,** *adv.*, **-erweise,** *adv.* in such a manner.
Sold, *m.* (soldier's) pay; *halber* –, half-pay; *der Minne* –, reward *or* guerdon of love; (*B.*) *der Tod ist der Sünde* –, the wages of sin is death. **-buch,** *n.* (soldier's) pay-book. **-truppen,** *f.pl.* hired soldiers, mercenaries.
Soldat, *m.* (-en, -en) soldier; *abgedankter* –, discharged soldier; *alter, erfahrener* –, old campaigner, veteran; *freiwilliger* –, volunteer; – *zu Fuß,* infantryman, foot-soldier; *gedienter* –, time-expired man, ex-service man; *gemeiner* –, private; *gemeine* -*en,* rank and file; – *zu Pferde,* cavalryman, trooper; -*en spielen,* play at soldiers; – *werden,* enlist, join the army. **-enaushebung,** *f.* conscription, levy; recruiting. **-eneid,** *m.* military oath. **-engeist,** *m.* military *or* martial spirit. **-engesindel,** *n.* military rabble, soldiery. **-enhaft,** *adj.*, *see* **-isch. -enhandwerk,** *n.* profession of arms. **-enkost,** *f.* army rations. **-enlied,** *n.* soldier's song, marching song. **-enmütze,** *f.* forage cap. **-enrat,** *m.*; *Arbeiter- und -enrat,* workers' and soldiers' council (1918). **-enrock,** *m.* uniform; *den -enrock anziehen,* enlist; *den -enrock ausziehen,* be demobilized *or* discharged. **-enschenke,** *f.* canteen. **-ensprache,** *f.* military jargon, soldiers' slang. **-entum,** *n.* soldiery; soldierliness, soldierly spirit. **-eska,** *f.* (coarse *or* licentious) soldiery, rabble of soldiers. **-isch,** *adj.* soldier-like, soldierly; martial.
Söld-ling, *m.* (-s, -e), **-ner,** *m.* hired soldier, mercenary, (*fig.*) hireling. **-nerheer,** *n.* (army of) mercenaries. **-nertruppen,** *f.pl.* mercenary troops.
Sol-e, *f.* brine, salt-spring. **-bad,** *n.* salt-water *or* brine bath. **-bohrloch,** *n.* salt-well. **-ei,** *n.* pickled egg. **-quelle,** *f.* salt-well, brine-spring. **-salz,** *n.* pit-salt. **-waage,** *f.* brine-gauge. **-wasser,** *n.* brine.
solenn, *adj.* solemn. **-ität,** *f.* solemnity.
solfeggieren, *v.n.* (*aux.* h.) sing sol-fa.
solid-(e), *adj.* solid, substantial, strong; sterling, thorough, sound, reliable; solvent (*of a firm*); respectable, steady; -*er Mieter,* steady *or* respectable tenant; (*C.L.*) -*e Preise,* reasonable prices, moderate charges. **-arhaftung,** *f.* joint-security. **-arisch,** 1. *adj.* joint, jointly responsible, unanimous; -*arische Verbindlichkeit,* unlimited *or* joint liability; -*arisch trockner Wechsel,* promissory note. 2. *adv.* jointly and severally. **-arität,** *f.* joint-liability, unanimity, solidarity. **-ität,** *f.* solidity, steadiness; trustworthiness, soundness, stability, respectability. **-arschuldner,** *m.* joint-debtor.
Solist, *m.* (-en, -en) soloist.
Solitär, *m.* (-s, -e) brilliant, solitaire; single star.
Soll, *n.* (-(s), -(s)) debit; duty, obligation; *ins* – *eintragen,* debit (*a p.'s account*); (*das*) – *und Haben* debit and credit; *das* – *und das Muß,* obligation and necessity; *ein Mehr gegenüber dem* –, a surplus over and above estimated revenue; *in jedem* – *sieht er ein Muß,* he accepts every obligation as binding. **-bestand,** *m.* presumed assets *or* stock; establishment (*Mil.*). **-bruchlast,** *f.* breaking load. **-einnahme,** *f.* estimated receipts, receipts due. **-en,** *see* **sollen. -etat,** *m.* estimates. **-posten,** *m.* debtor's account. **-stärke,** *f.* establishment (*Mil.*). **-wert,** *m.* theoretical *or* nominal value.
soll-en, 1. *ir.v.n.* (*aux.* h.) be obliged *or* bound to; have to, must; be in debt; mean; be said to, be supposed to, pass for; (*as aux.*) shall, should, ought to, am (is, are) to; *was* – *ich?* what am I (expected) to do? *was* – *das* (*heißen*)? what is the meaning, use *or* purpose of this? *was* – *mir das alles?* what is all that to me? *wir tun nicht immer was wir* -*en,* we do not always do what we ought; *er* – *gelehrt sein,* he is reputed to be very learned; *er* – *es getan haben,* he is said to have done it; (*B.*) *du* -*st nicht töten,* thou shalt not kill; *was* – *ich sagen?* what ought I to *or* shall I say? *er* -*te König werden,* he was (destined) to be king; *ich weiß nicht, was ich tun* –, I do not know what to do; *Ihr Kinder* -*t etwas warten,* you children are *or* have to wait a little; *wie* – *man da nicht lachen?* how can one help laughing? *was* -*te ich dagegen machen?* how could I help it? *man* -*te meinen,* one would think; *es* -*te ein Witz sein,* it was meant for a joke; *nun, er* – *Recht haben,* well, granted that he is right! *wenn es regnen* -*te, sollte es regnen,* if it should rain; -*te es die Katze gewesen sein?* could it have been the cat? -*te er vielleicht krank sein?* can he be ill, do you think he is ill? *was* – *mir das nützen?* what good does *or* will it do me? what is that to me? *ich hätte es nicht tun* -*en,* I ought not to have done it; *der* – *erst noch geboren werden, der . . .,* the man is not yet born who . . . 2. *n.* one's duty, obligations, responsibilities.
Söller, *m.* (-s, –) balcony; loft.
solmisieren, *v.n.* (*aux.* h.) sing sol-fa.
solo, 1. *adv.* alone. 2. *n.* (-s, -s & Soli) solo. **-geiger,** *m.* solo violinist. **-gesang,** *m.* solo (singing). **-partie,** *f.* solo part. **-sänger,** *m.* solo-singer, soloist. **-spieler,** *m.* solo-player, soloist. **-stimme,** *f.* solo part. **-tanz,** *m.* pas seul. **-tänzer,** *m.* principal dancer.
Solözism-us, *m.* (-us, -en) solecism.
somit, *see under* **so.**
Sommer, *m.* (-s, –) summer; (*pl. poet.*) years; *fliegender* –, *see* **-fäden. -birne,** *f.* early pear. **-fäden,** *m.pl.* gossamer. **-fahrplan,** *m.* summer time-table (*Railw.*). **-ferien,** *pl.* summer vacation. **-fleck,** *m.* freckle. **-frische,** *f.* holiday resort, health resort. **-frischler,** *m.* summer visitor, holiday-maker. **-getreide,** *n.* spring wheat. **-grün,** *adj.* deciduous. **-hitze,** *f.* heat of summer. **-kartoffel,** *f.* early potato. **-kleid,** *n.* summer coat (*of animals and birds*). **-leutnant,** *m.* (*sl.*) reserve officer. **-lich,** *adj.* summer-like, summery; *sich* -*lich kleiden,* put on summer clothes. **-n,** 1. *v.n.* (*aux.* h.) & *imp.*; *es* -*t,* summer is drawing on; *der Baum* -*t,* the tree is sprouting. 2. *v.a.* expose to the sun; turn out (*cattle*) to graze; lop, prune (*trees*); sow (*a field*) for early crop. 3. *v.r.*; *die Hühner* -*n sich,* the hens bask in the sun. **-nachtstraum,** *m.* Midsummer Night's Dream. **-obst,** *n.* early fruit. **-saat,** *f.* spring corn. **-semester,** *n.* summer term. **-sonnenwende,** *f.*, summer solstice. **-sprosse,** *f.* freckle. **-sprossig,** *adj.* freckled. **-szeit,** *f.*, *see* **-zeit. -ung,** *f.*, *see* **-getreide. -vogel,** *m.* (*dial.*) butterfly. **-weg,** *m.* fine-weather road, seasonal road. **-weizen,** *m.* spring(-sown) wheat. **-zeit,** *f.* summer-time, summer season; summer time (*advanced by one hour*).
sömmern, *see* **sommern.**
sonach, *see under* **so.**
Sond-e, *f.* (-en) probe; sounding-lead, plummet (*Naut.*). **-ieren,** *v.a.* probe; sound, fathom; (*fig.*) explore the ground. **-ierung,** *f.* probing, sounding. (*fig.*) **-ierungsversuch,** *m.* feeler.
sonder, (*archaic*) *prep.* (*Acc.*) without; – *Zweifel,* without doubt, undoubtedly; – *Zahl,* countless. **-abdruck,** *m.*, **-abzug,** *m.* separate impression; off-print. **-angebot,** *n.* special offer. **-ausgabe,** *f.* special edition. **-bar,** *adj.* singular, peculiar, strange, odd, curious, droll. **-barerweise,** *adv.* strange to say. **-beauftragte(r),** *m.* minister with special responsibilities. **-berichterstatter,** *m.* special correspondent (*to a newspaper*). **-bestrebung,**

f. separatism, particularism. **-bündler,** *m.* separatist. **-druck,** *see* **-abdruck. -fall,** *m.* special *or* particular case, exception. **-gleichen,** *indec. adj.* (*follows noun*) unequalled, unparalleled, incomparable, matchless, unique. **-gut,** *n.* wife's own property. **-heit,** *f.* peculiarity, speciality. **-lich,** *adj.* special, peculiar, particular, remarkable; *nichts -liches*, nothing out of the ordinary; *kein -licher Gelehrter*, no great scholar; *nicht -lich*, not specially, not much. **-ling,** *m.* odd person, oddity, crank, original. **-meldung,** *f.* special announcement. **-n,** 1. *v.a.* separate, segregate, sunder, part, sever; sift, sort; distinguish. 2. *v.r.* separate; *gesonderter Haushalt*, separate (domestic) establishment. **-n,** *conj.* but, on the contrary; *ich werde nicht sterben, -n genesen*, I shall not die, but recover. **-nummer,** *f.* special edition (*of a paper, etc.*). **-recht,** *n.* special privilege. **-s,** *adv.* separately, *only in* samt und -s, one and all, altogether. **-stellung,** *f.* special *or* exceptional position. **-ung,** *f.* separation, division, segregation; *völlige -ung*, isolation. **-urlaub,** *m.* special leave (*Mil.*); *-urlaub aus Familiengründen*, compassionate leave (*Mil.*). **-verband,** *m.* task force (*Mil.*). **-vorführung,** *f.* special performance. **-zug,** *m.* special train. **-zulage,** *f.* special bonus.

Sonett, *n.* (-(e)s, -e) sonnet. **-ist,** *m.* sonnet-writer, sonneteer.

Sonnabend, *see* **Sonn-.**

Sonn-e, *f.* (-en) sun, sunshine; *Platz an der -e*, place in the sun; *die -e meint es gut*, the sun is trying to shine; *die -e schießen*, take bearings on the sun. **-abend,** *m.* Saturday. **-abends,** *adv.* on Saturdays; every *or* each Saturday. **-en,** 1. *v.a.* expose to the sun's rays, air (*beds, etc.*). 2. *v.r.* bask (in the sun); (*fig.*) take delight (*in a th.*). **-enaufgang,** *m.* sunrise. **-enbad,** *n.* sun-bath. **-enbahn,** *f.* ecliptic; orbit of the sun. **-enball,** *m.* orb of the sun. **-enbelichtung,** *f.* exposure to sunlight. **-enbeobachtung,** *f.* bearings on the sun. **-enbeschienen,** *adj.* sunlit, sunny. **-enbeschreibung,** *f.* heliography. **-enbestrahlung,** *f.* solar irradiation, *see* **-enbelichtung. -enblende,** *f.* sun-blind. **-enblick,** *m.* bright, cheerful *or* friendly glance. **-enblume,** *f.* sunflower (*Helianthus annuus*) (*Bot.*). **-enbrand,** *m.* sunburn. **-endach,** *n.* awning, sun-blind. **-endeck** *n.* awning (*Naut.*). **-endienst,** *m.* sun-worship. **-enferne,** *f.* aphelion. **-enfinsternis,** *f.* solar eclipse. **-enfleck,** *m.* sun-spot. **-engeflecht,** *n.* solar plexus (*Anat.*). **-englut,** *f.* blaze of the sun. **-enhaft,** *adj.* sunny, radiant. **-enhell,** *adj.* bright as day, sunny; (*fig.*) clear, evident. **-enhof,** *m.* halo round the sun. **-enhöhe,** *f.* sun's altitude. **-enjahr,** *n.* astronomical year. **-enkäfer,** *m.*, **-enkälbchen,** *n.* lady-bird. **-enklar,** *adj.* (*fig.*) clear as daylight, evident. **-enlicht,** *n.* sunlight. **-enlos,** *adj.* sunless. **-ennähe,** *f.* perihelion. **-enpeilung,** *f.*, *see* **-enbeobachtung. -enprotuberanzen,** *f.pl.* solar prominences (*Astr.*). **-enrose,** *f.*, *see* **-enblume. -enscheibe,** *f.* solar disk. **-enschein,** *m.* sunshine. **-enscheinsdauer,** *f.* hours of sunshine (*Meteor.*). **-enscheu,** *adj.* heliophobic (*Bot.*). **-enschirm,** *m.* sunshade, parasol. **-ensegel,** *n.* awning. **-enseite,** *f.* sunny side, southern aspect. **-enspektrum,** *n.* solar spectrum. **-enspiegel,** *m.* turnsole (*Bot.*). **-enstand,** *m.* position of the sun. **-enstäubchen,** *n.* mote (*in a sunbeam*). **-enstich,** *m.* sunstroke. **-enstillstand,** *m.* solstice. **-enstrahl,** *m.* sunbeam. **-enstrahlung,** *f.* solar radiation. **-ensystem,** *n.* solar system. **-entau,** *m.* sundew (*Drosera*) (*Bot.*). **-entierchen,** *n.* sun-animalcule (*Heliozoa*) (*Zool.*). **-enuhr,** *f.* sundial. **-enuntergang,** *m.* sunset. **-enverbrannt,** *adj.* sunburnt, tanned. **-enwarte,** *f.* solar observatory. **-enwende,** *f.* solstice; heliotrope (*Bot.*). **-enwendepunkt,** *m.* solstitial point. **-enwendfeier,** *f.*, *see* **-wendfeier. -enzeit,** *f.* solar time. **-enzelt,** *n.* awning; (*Poet.*) canopy of the sky. **-ig,** *adj.* sunny, bright, radiant. **-tag,** *m.* (-s, -e) Sunday; *am -*, on Sunday; *-s*, on Sundays, on a Sunday. **-tagabend,** *m.* Sunday evening. **-tägig,** *adj.* Sunday, on Sunday. **-täglich,** *adj.* every Sunday; *sich -täglich anziehen*, put on one's Sunday best. **-tagsanzug,** *m.* Sunday suit. **-tagsausflug,** *m.* week-end excursion. **-tagsbeilage,** *f.* Sunday supplement (*of a newspaper*). **-tagsblatt,** *n.* Sunday paper. **-tagsentheiliger,** *m.* Sabbath-breaker. **-tagsfeier,** *f.* day of rest. **-tagsheiligung,** *f.* keeping the Sabbath. **-tagsjäger,** *m.* holiday *or* week-end sportsman. **-tagskarte,** *f.* week-end *or* day excursion ticket (*Railw.*). **-tagskind,** *n.* Sunday's child; *er ist ein -tagskind*, he was born under a lucky star *or* with a silver spoon in his mouth. **-tagsreiter,** *m.* unskilful rider. **-tagsruhe,** *f.* Sabbath rest, observance of the Sabbath. **-tagsschule,** *f.* Sunday-school. **-tagsstaat,** *m* Sunday best *or* clothes. **-wendfeier,** *f.* midsummer festival.

sonor, *adj.* sonorous.

sonst, *adv.* else, otherwise; besides, moreover; in other respects, at other times; as a rule, usually, formerly; *- sind wir gesund*, otherwise we are all well; *- etwas*, something else *or* besides, anything else; *- jemand*, anybody *or* somebody else; *- keiner*, see *- niemand*; *- nichts*, nothing more *or* else; *- niemand*, no one else; *- nirgendwo*, nowhere else, in no other place; *- habe ich noch zu berichten*, in addition I have to report; *- noch Neues*, any news apart from this, any other *or* further news; *wenn -*, if on the other hand, provided; *- wer*, see *- jemand*; *wie -*, as usual; *sie kommen nicht mehr so häufig wie -*, they no longer come so frequently as they used to. **-ig,** *adj.* other, remaining; former. **-wie,** *adv.* in some other way. **-wo,** *adv.* elsewhere, somewhere (else). **-woher,** *adv.* from some other place. **-wohin,** *adj.* to another place, somewhere else.

sooft, *see under* **so.**

Sophist, *m.* sophist. **-erei,** *f.* (-en) sophistry, subtlety, hair-splitting. **-isch,** *adj.* sophistical.

Sopran, *m.* (-s, -e) treble, soprano.

Sorg-e, *f.* (-en) grief, sorrow; worry, apprehension, anxiety, care, trouble, uneasiness, concern; *Borgen macht -en*, borrowing brings sorrowing; *die -e ertränken* or *ersaufen*, drown one's sorrows (in drink); *sei darum ohne -e*, do not let that worry you; *das ist meine -e*, I shall attend to that, leave that to me, that is my worry; *das ist meine geringste -e*, that is the least of my worries; *ich werde -e tragen, daß . . .*, I will take care that . . ., make it my business that . . . *or* see to it that . . .; *man wird dafür -e tragen, daß . . .*, care will be taken that . . .; *-e um die Zukunft*, concern for the future; *sich* (*Dat.*) *-en machen um, in -e(n) sein um*, be worried about, anxious for. **-en,** 1. *v. r.* be anxious, apprehensive, concerned, solicitous *or* troubled, worry (*um*, about); *-en Sie sich nicht, es geht schon gut*, do not worry *or* be afraid, all is well. 2. *v.n.*; *-en für etwas* or *dafür, daß . . .* attend to *or* look after a th., care for *or* take care of a th., provide for s.th.; *man würde für dich -en*, you would be provided for; *dafür laß mich -en*, leave that to me, let me see to that; *dafür hat er zu -en*, that is his look-out. **-enbrecher,** *m.* (*Poet.*) wine. **-enfrei,** *adj.* free from care(s). **-enkind,** *n.* difficult *or* problem child; delicate child. **-enlos,** *adj.*, *see* **-enfrei. -enstuhl,** *m.* easy-chair. **-envoll,** *adj.* full of care, careworn; anxious, worried, uneasy. **-falt,** *f.* carefulness, care, solicitude, attention; accuracy, neatness, conscientiousness. **-fältig,** *adj.* careful, attentive; painstaking, scrupulous, precise, accurate. **-fältigkeit,** *f.*, *see* **-falt. -lich,** *adj.* careful, anxious; solicitous. **-los,** *adj.* carefree, light-hearted, thoughtless, indifferent, unconcerned, negligent, careless. **-losigkeit,** *f.* light-heartedness, thoughtlessness; unconcern, negligence, carelessness. **-sam,** *adj.* careful, attentive; provident; cautious. **-samkeit,** *f.* carefulness, caution, providence.

sorren, *v.a.* lash, seize (*Naut.*).

Sort-e, *f.* (-en) kind, sort, type, species, quality, grade, variety, brand; (*C.L.*) foreign currency. **-ieren,** *v.a.* classify, arrange, put in order; pick, sort, sift, grade. **-ierung,** *f.* sorting, classifying, grading. **-iment,** *n.* (-s, -e) assortment, range, miscellaneous stock; retail book-trade *or* shop. **-imenter,** *m.* bookseller.

sosehr, *see under* **so.**

soso, *see under* **so.**
Soße, *f.* (-n) sauce, gravy (*from meat*), dressing (*for salad*). **–nschüssel,** *f.* sauce-boat.
sotan, *see under* **so.**
sott, sötte, *see* **sieden.**
Souffl–eur, *m.* (-s, -e), **–euse,** *f.* (-n) prompter. **–eurkasten,** *m.* prompter's box. **–ieren,** *v.a.* prompt.
soundso, *see under* **so.**
Soutane, *f.* (-n) priest's cassock, soutane.
Souterrain, *n.* (-s, -s) basement.
Souverän, I. *m.* (-s, -e) sovereign. 2. *adj.* sovereign, (*fig.*) superior. **–ität,** *f.* sovereignty. **–itätsrechte,** *n.pl.* sovereign rights.
soviel, *see under* **so.**
soweit, *see under* **so.**
sowenig, *see under* **so.**
sowie, *see under* **so.**
sowieso, *see under* **so.**
sowohl, *see under* **so.**
Soz, *m.* (-en, -en), **–i,** *m. & f.* (-is) (*sl.*) red, bolshie. **–ial,** *adj.* social. **–ialbeamte(r),** *m.*, **–ialbeamtin,** *f.* welfare-worker, social worker. **–ialdemokratisch,** *adj.* socialist(ic). **–ialfürsorge,** *f.* welfare-work. **–ialisierung,** *f.* socialization, nationalization. **–ialismus,** *m.* socialism. **–ialist,** *m.* socialist. **–ialistengesetz,** *n.* law against socialists. **–ialistisch,** *adj.* socialist(ic). **–iallasten,** *f.pl.* expenditure for social welfare; employer's contributions to national insurance. **–ialpolitik,** *f.* social betterment, social legislation. **–ialversicherung,** *f.* social insurance. **–ialwissenschaft,** *f.* sociology. **–ietät,** *f.* society; partnership. **–ietätshandel,** *m.* company. **–ietätsvertrag,** *m.* deed of partnership. **–ius,** *m.* (–, -se & Socii) partner; joint-owner; pillion rider; *stiller –ius*, sleeping partner. **–iussitz,** *m.* pillion (seat).
sozusagen, *see under* **so.**
Spachtel *m.* (-s, –) (& *Austr. dial. f.*) (-n) spatula. **–kitt,** *m.* plastic wood. **–masse,** *f.* primer, filler. **–messer,** *n.* putty-knife. **–n,** I. *v.a.* fill *or* smooth (*a surface*). 2. *v.n.* (*dial.*) tuck in.
[1]**Spagat,** *m.* (-s, -e) (*Austr. & Bavar. dial.*) cord, string.
[2]**Spagat,** *m. & n.* splits (*Gymn.*) – *machen*, do the splits.
späh–en, *v.n.* (*aux.* h.) scout, reconnoitre; watch, be on the look out (*nach*, for). **–er,** *m.* scout. **–erblick,** *m.* searching glance. **–trupp,** *m.* patrol (*Mil.*). **–truppwagen,** *m.* reconnaissance (*or coll.*) recce car.
Spakat, *see* [2]**Spagat.**
Spalier, *n.* (-s, -e) espalier, trellis; (*fig.*) lane (*formed by people*); – *stehen*, form a lane. **–en,** *v.a.* trellis; train (*plants*) against a wall. **–obst,** *n.* wall-fruit. **–werk,** *n.* trellis-work.
Spalt, *m.* (-(e)s, -e) cleft, chink, slot, slit, split, crack, fissure, rent, gap, rift, crevice, crevasse. **–bar,** *adj.* cleavable, divisible, fissile. **–barkeit,** *f.* cleavage. **–breite,** *f.* breadth of slot. **–e,** *f.* (-en), *see* **Spalt;** column (*Typ.*). **–en,** (*p.p.* gespalten *and* gespaltet) I. *v.a.* split, cleave, slit, cut open; crack; decompose (*a ray of light*); *Haare* or *Begriffe –en*, split hairs. 2. *v.r. & n.* (*aux.* s.) split off, crack; open, divide, branch off; dissociate; crack (*of oil*). **–enbreite,** *f.* column-width. **–enreich,** *adj.* fissured. **–enweise,** *adv.* in columns. **–enzeile,** *f.* line of the column. **–er,** *m.pl.* schizopoda (*Zool.*). **–fläche** *f.* plane of cleavage (*Min.*). **–flügel,** *m.* slotted wing (*Av.*). **–frucht,** *f.* dehiscent fruit, schizocarp (*Bot.*). **–holz,** *n.* split logs, firewood. **–hufer,** *m.pl.* ruminants (*Zool.*). **–ig,** I. *adj.* split, fissured, full of cracks, divided; easily split *or* cracked; having (*so many*) columns (*to a page, etc.*); e.g. *drei–ig*, three-columned. **–messer,** *n.* grafting-knife; cleaver. **–pfropfung,** *f.* stock-grafting. **–pilz,** *m.* bacteria, fission-fungus. **–ring,** *m.* split-ring. **–stück,** *n.* splinter, detached fragment. **–ung,** *f.* fissure, split, crack, cleavage; splitting, cleaving, division, fission; (*fig.*) dissension, rupture, quarrel, schism.
Span, *m.* (-(e)s, ⸚e) chip, shaving, shred, splinter; (*pl.*) turnings, swarf; (*dial.*) quarrel, squabble; (*dial.*) dug, nipple; *Gedankenspäne*, detached thoughts, aphorisms; *aus einem –*, in one piece; (*coll.*) *einen – mit einem haben*, squabble with a p.; (*coll.*) *mach keine Späne*, don't make a fuss. **–grün,** *n.* verdigris. **–holz,** *n.* matchwood.
spänen, *v.a.* suckle (*animals*); (*also for* **ab–,** wean).
Spanferkel, *n.* (s, –) sucking pig.
Spange, *f.* (-n) clasp, bracelet, brooch; hair-slide; buckle; bar (*military decorations*). **–nschuh,** *n.* buckled shoe, strap shoe.
Spann, *m.* (-(e)s, -e) instep.
spann, *see* **spinnen.**
Spann–e, *f.* (-en) span; stretch; short space of time; margin (*between prices*); *nicht eine –e Boden*, not an inch of ground. **–ader,** *f.* (*archaic*) sinew. **–balken,** *m.* tie-beam. **–dienst,** *m.* statute-labour with teams. **–en,** I. *v.a.* strain, stretch, brace, span; tighten, make tense, subject to tension; bend *or* draw (*a bow*); cock (*a gun*); harness (*an* or *vor*, to); fetter (*grazing cattle*); *Dampf –en*, superheat steam, build up the steam pressure; *auf die Folter –en*, put to the rack; (*fig.*) rouse intense curiosity, keep in suspense; *die Saiten* or *Forderungen zu hoch –en*, demand too much, make excessive demands, pitch one's demands too high; *Gardinen –en*, put up *or* hang curtains; *Neugier aufs höchste –en*, rouse curiosity to white heat; *die Oktave –en können*, be able to stretch an octave; (*Prov.*) *das Pferd hinter den Wagen –en*, put the cart before the horse; *in den Schraubstock –en*, put in the vise; *etwas weit* (or *eng*) *–en*, stretch out (*or* compress, confine, contract) s.th.; *ich bin sehr gespannt, davon zu hören*, I am very anxious *or* curious to hear about it; *jede Muskel gespannt*, all muscles tense; *ich stehe mit ihm auf gespanntem Fuße*, the relations between us are strained. 2. *v.n.* (*aux.* h.) be exciting *or* interesting; fit too tightly; listen eagerly, wait anxiously; *dieser Roman –t sehr*, this novel is most exciting. **–end,** *adj.* exciting, tense, gripping, absorbing, thrilling. **–enlang,** *adj.* brief, fleeting, short-lived. **–er,** *m.* stretcher, press (*for trousers, tennis racket, etc.*); last, boot-tree; tenter (*for cloth*); trigger; gaffle (*of a crossbow*); looper (*Geometridae*) (*Ent.*). **–fähig,** *adj.* able to provide draught-animals. **–feder,** *f.* tension-spring. **–futter,** *n.* mandrel, chuck. **–haken,** *m.* tenter-hook. **–hebel,** *m.* cocking-handle (*Gunn.*). **–kabel,** *n.* bracing-cable. **–kette,** *f.* tether. **–kraft,** *f.* elasticity, spring; strain, tension (*Phys.*); (*fig.*) vigour, tone. **–kräftig,** *adj.* elastic. **–lack,** *m.* stiffening varnish, dope. **–muskel,** *m. & f.* extensor. **–rahmen,** *m.* tenter-frame; stretcher. **–säge,** *f.* frame-saw. **–seil,** *n.* bracing-wire, guy-rope; fetter, tether. **–seite,** *f.* hypotenuse. **–ung,** *f.* stretching, straining, bracing, tightening; tension, stress, strain; span (*of an arch*); pressure, head (*of steam*); voltage, potential (*Elec.*); suspense, close attention, interest, excitement; discord, strained relations; **–ungsabfall,** *m.* voltage- *or* potential-drop. **–ungsapparat,** *m.* tension-regulator (*on sewing-machines*). **–ungsdifferenz,** *f.* potential difference (*Elec.*). **–ungsmesser,** *m.* voltmeter (*Elec.*). **–ungsteiler,** *m.* potentiometer (*Rad.*). **–weite,** *f.* span, spread; wingspread (*Av.*); (*fig.*) range.
-spänn–er; e.g. *Ein–er, m.* one-horse vehicle. **–ig;** e.g. *ein–ig, adj.* with one horse.
Spant, *n.* (-(e)s, -en) rib (*of a ship*), transverse frame (*Av.*).
spar–en, I. *v.a. & n.* (*aux.* h.) economize, cut down expenses; save, lay by, put by, be thrifty; spare, use sparingly. **–er,** *m.* economical *or* thrifty person, saver. **–buch,** *n.* (savings-)bank (deposit-)book. **–büchse,** *f.* money-box. **–einlage,** *f.* deposit in a savings-bank, savings. **–flamme,** *f.* pilot-light. **–flug,** *m.* economical cruising (*Av.*). **–fonds,** *m.*, **–geld,** *n.*, **–gut,** *n.* savings. **–groschen,** *m.*, *see* **–pfennig.** **–herd,** *m.* economical *or* slow-combustion stove. **–kasse,** *f.* savings-bank. **–marke,** *f.* savings-stamp. **–maßnahme,** *f.* economy measure. **–pfennig,** *m.* (small) savings, nest-egg, money laid by for a rainy day. **–sam,** I. *adj.* economical, thrifty; chary, frugal. 2. *adv.* sparingly. **–samkeit,** *f.* economy, thrift, thriftiness, parsimony. **–sinn,** *m.* thrift. **–verein,** *m.* savings-group. **–zwang,** *m.* compulsory saving.
Spargel, *m.* (-s, –) asparagus; *–kohl*, broccoli

(*Brassica oleracea*) (*Bot.*). **–messer,** *n.*, **–stecher,** *m.* asparagus-knife.
spärlich, *adj.* scanty, sparse, thin; bare, meagre, scarce, frugal; beggarly. **–keit,** *f.* scantiness, sparseness, meagreness; scarcity, rareness, rarity.
Sparren, *m.* (-s, –) spar, rafter; chevron (*Her.*); (*coll.*) *einen – (zuviel) haben*, have a screw loose. **–kopf,** *m.* modillion, mutule (*Arch.*), rafter-end. **–werk,** *n.* rafters.
Sparte, *f.* (-n) subject, branch.
Spaß, *m.* (-es, ⸚e) jest, joke; fun, amusement, merriment; *– an etwas haben*, enjoy a thing; *– beiseite!* joking apart! *das ist ein – für ihn*, that is a trifle to him; *es macht mir –*, I think it is good fun; *es wäre ein –, wenn*, it would be good fun *or* a good joke if; *das geht über den –*, that is beyond a joke; *keinen – verstehen*, not understand, appreciate *or* (*coll.*) take a joke; *viel –!* have a good time! enjoy yourself! *zum –*, for fun, for the fun of it. **–en,** *v.n.* (*aux.* h.) joke, jest, make fun; *Sie –en wohl*, you are surely joking; *damit* or *darüber ist nicht zu –en*, that is no joking matter; *mit ihm ist nicht zu –en*, he is not to be trifled with; *Sie belieben zu –en*, you are pleased to be facetious. **–erei,** *f.* jesting, jokes. **–(es)halber,** *adv.* for fun. **–haft,** *adj.* jocular, joking, jocose, funny, facetious. **–ig,** *adj.* funny, amusing, odd, droll, merry. **–liebend,** *adj.* fond of a joke. **–macher,** *m.* wag, joker, clown, buffoon. **–verderber,** *m.* spoil-sport. **–vogel,** *m.*, *see* **–macher.**
spat, *adv.* (*archaic*), *see* **spät.**
Spat, *m.* (-(e)s, -e & ⸚e) spar (*Min.*); (*no pl.*) spavin (*Vet.*). **–ig,** *adj.* sparry; spavined. **–lahm,** *adj.* spavined.
spät, *adj.* & *adv.* late, belated, behindhand, backward, slow; *von früh bis –*, from morning till night; *du kommst –*, you are *or* will be late; (*coll.*) *–es Mädchen*, old maid; *bei –er Nacht*, late at night; *wie – ist es?* what time is it? **–e,** *f.* advanced hour; lateness. **–er,** 1. *adj.* subsequent. 2. *adv.* afterwards, after, later; *–ere Jahreszeit*, end of the season, latter part of the year; *in –eren Jahren*, in after years, in later life; *in –eren Zeiten*, at a later period, in the future. **–erhin,** *adv.* later on. **–estens,** *adv.* at the latest. **–fährte,** *f.* cold scent (*Hunt*). **–geburt,** *f.* delayed birth. **–herbst,** *m.* end of the season, late autumn. **–jahr,** *n.* (*dial.*) autumn. **–ling,** *m.* late arrival; animal born late in the year; late fruit; (*dial.*) autumn. **–reif,** *adj.* late ripe, backward. **–sommer,** *m.* Indian summer. **–zahn,** *m.* wisdom tooth. **–zündung,** *f.* retarded ignition (*Motor.*).
Spatel, *m.* (-s, –) spatula, trowel, slice, scoop (*Med.*). **–förmig,** *adj.* spatulate. **–n,** *v.a.* smooth with a spatula.
Spaten, *m.* (-s, –) spade. **–stich,** *m.* cut with a spade; *den ersten –stich tun*, turn the first sod.
spati–ieren, –nieren, –onieren, *v.n.* space (*Typ.*). **–ös,** *adj.* roomy, broad, spacious, spaced. **–um,** *n.* (-ums, -en) space (*Typ.*); *die –en einsetzen, mit –en durchschießen*, space (*Typ.*).
Spatz, *m.* (-en & *Austr. dial.* -es, -en) (*coll.*) sparrow; *das pfeifen die –en von allen Dächern*, that is all over the town, that is notorious; *mit Kanonen nach –en schießen*, break butterflies on the wheel; (*Prov.*) *besser ein – in der Hand als eine Taube auf dem Dach*, a bird in the hand is worth two in the bush. **–enhaft,** *adj.* cheeky, insolent.
Spätzle, *n.* Swabian dumpling.
spazier–en, *v.n.* (*aux.* s.) go for *or* take a walk *or* stroll. **–enfahren,** *v.n.* go for a drive; go (out) in a boat. **–engehen,** *v.n.*, *see* **–en.** **–fahrt,** *f.* drive; pleasure trip. **–gang,** *m.* walk, stroll; *einen –gang machen*, take a walk. **–gänger,** *m.* walker. **–ritt,** *m.* ride (on horseback). **–stock,** *m.* walking-stick. **–weg,** *m.* pleasant (road for a) walk.
Specht, *m.* (-(e)s, -e) woodpecker. **–meise,** *f.* nuthatch (*Orn.*).
Speck, *m.* (-(e)s, -e) bacon; lard, blubber, fat; paying work; *– auf den Rippen haben*, be well off; *– ansetzen*, put on fat; *den – spicken*, gild the lily; *den – riechen*, be drawn towards a th.; *im – sitzen*, be in clover; (*Prov.*) *mit – fängt man Mäuse*, good bait catches fine fish. **–artig,** *adj.* fatty. **–bauch,** *m.* fat belly, big paunch. **–geschwulst,** *f.* steatoma. **–glanz,** *m.* greasy lustre. **–hals,** *m.* thick(set) neck, bull-neck. **–ig,** *adj.* fat, greasy, fatty; (*coll.*) spotted with grease. **–kuchen,** *m.* cake made with lard. **–schneider,** *m.* blubber-cutter. **–schnitte,** *f.* rasher of bacon. **–schwarte,** *f.* bacon rind. **–seite,** *f.* side *or* flitch of bacon; *die Wurst nach der –seite werfen*, throw a sprat to catch a herring *or* mackerel. **–stein,** *m.* soapstone, talc, steatite.
sped–ieren, *v.a.* forward, dispatch, send (on). **–iteur,** *m.* (-s, -e) forwarding agent, shipping agent, carrier; furniture-remover. **–ition,** *f.* dispatch, delivery, forwarding; forwarding *or* shipping department. **–itionsgebühren,** *f.pl.* charges for delivery. **–itionsgeschäft,** *n.* forwarding agency, furniture-removal business.
Speer, *m.* (-(e)s, -e) spear, lance, javelin. **–en,** *v.a.* spear, pierce, impale. **–förmig,** *adj.* spear-shaped; lanceolate (*Bot.*). **–träger,** *m.* spearman. **–werfen,** *n.* throwing the javelin (*Sport.*). **–wurf,** *m.* throw of the spear, spear-thrust.
Speiche, *f.* (-n) spoke (*of a wheel*); radius, spoke-bone (*Anat.*); *einem in die –n fallen*, put a spoke in s.o.'s wheel; *in die –n greifen*, put one's shoulder to the wheel. **–n,** *v.a.* spoke (*a wheel*). **–nbeuger,** *m.* biceps. **–nblatt,** *n.* inner end of a spoke. **–nnerv,** *m.* radial nerve. **–nrad,** *n.* spoke-wheel. **–nzapfen,** *m.* outer end of a spoke.
Speichel, *m.* (-s, –) spittle, saliva, (*coll.*) spit, dribble. **–absonderung,** *f.* secretion of saliva. **–befördernd,** *adj.* promoting the flow of saliva. **–drüse,** *f.* salivary gland. **–fluß,** *m.* flow of saliva, salivation. **–gang,** *m.* salivary duct. **–lecker,** *m.* toady, sycophant, lickspittle, (*vulg.*) arse-crawler. **–leckerei,** *f.* toadyism. **–leckerisch,** *adj.* toadying, fawning. **–n,** *v.n.* (*aux.* h.) (*dial.*) spit. **–stoff,** *m.* ptyalin (*Chem.*).
Speicher, *m.* (-s, –) granary, silo, (grain) elevator; reservoir, warehouse; (*dial.*) store (room), garret, loft; storage-battery (*Elec.*); hot-water tank. **–anlage,** *f.* barrage for storing water-power. **–geld,** *n.* storage charges. **–gewebe,** *n.* storage tissue. **–kondensator,** *m.* reservoir condenser (*Elec.*). **–n,** *v.a.* store (up); accumulate; warehouse; (*fig.*) hoard, treasure up. **–ung,** *f.* storage, accumulation.
spei–en, *ir.v.a.* & *n.* (*aux.* h.) spit; (*dial.*) spew, vomit; belch forth (*fire*); discharge (*water*); *Feuer und Flamme –en*, fret and fume; *Gift und Galle –en*, vent one's spleen; *es ist mir alles zum –en*, it makes me sick *or* fills me with loathing. **–gatt,** *n.* scupper (*Naut.*). **–napf,** *m.* spittoon. **–röhre,** *f.* gutter-spout, gargoyle.
Speik, *m.*, *see* **Spiek(e).**
Speil, *m.* (-(e)s, -e), **–e,** *f.* (-n), (*Austr. dial.*) **–er,** *m.* (-s, –) skewer. **–en,** (*Austr. dial.*) **–ern,** *v.a.* skewer.
Speis, *m.* (*dial.*) mortar. **–e,** *f.* (-n) food, nourishment, meal, dish; (bell- *or* gun-)metal; mortar; *dem einen ist's –e, dem andern Gift*, one man's meat is another man's poison; (*Prov.*) *verbotene –e schmeckt am besten*, forbidden fruit tastes sweetest. **–en,** 1. *v.a.* give to eat, feed; board, entertain; supply (*a mill or boiler with water, a mill with corn, etc.*); charge (*a battery*) (*Elec.*); *einen mit leeren Hoffnungen –en*, stuff a p. with vain hopes; *durch mehrere Bäche gespeist*, fed by many streams. 2. *v.n.* (*aux.* h.) eat, take food, take one's meals, board, dine, sup; *in diesem Gasthof –t man gut*, the food is good in this inn; *wohl zu –en!* good appetite! *wünsche wohl gespeist zu haben*, I hope you enjoyed your dinner. **–eanstalt,** *f.* eating-house, restaurant. **–ebrei,** *m.* chyme. **–eeis,** *n.* ice (-cream), ices. **–efett,** *n.* edible *or* cooking fat. **–egang,** *m.* alimentary canal, digestive tract. **–egraben,** *m.* feeder (*of a canal*). **–ehahn,** *m.* feed-cock. **–ekammer,** *f.* larder. **–ekarte,** *f.* bill of fare, menu; *nach der –ekarte essen*, dine à la carte. **–ekorb,** *m.* provision-basket, luncheon-basket, hamper. **–eleitung,** *f.* feeder (*Rad.*). **–enaufzug,** *m.* service-lift. **–e(n)folge,** *f.* menu (*at a banquet*). **–eöl,** *n.* salad-oil, olive oil. **–eopfer,** *n.* oblation (*of first fruits, etc.*). **–eordnung,** *f.* diet. **–epumpe,** *f.* feed- *or* supply-pump. **–epunkt,** *m.* input terminals (*Rad.*). **–ereste,** *m.pl.* particles *or*

remains of food. **-erohr,** *n.* feed-pipe. **-eröhre,** *f.* gullet, oesophagus. **-esaal,** *m.* dining-room, dining-hall; dining-saloon (*on steamers*); refectory; mess (*Mil.*). **-esaft,** *m.* chyle. **-esalz,** *n.* table-salt. **-eschrank,** *m.* pantry, meat-safe. **-etrichter** *m.* hopper. **-eventil,** *n.* feed-valve. **-ewagen,** *m.* restaurant-car, dining-car (*Railw.*). **-ewalze,** *f.* feed-roll(er). **-ewasser,** *n.* feed-water (*steam engines*). **-ewein,** *m.* table-wine. **-ewirtschaft,** *f.* (unlicensed) restaurant. **-ewürze,** *f.* condiments. **-ezettel,** *see* **-ekarte. -ezimmer,** *n.* dining-room. **-kobalt,** *m.* arsenic cobalt, smaltite. **-ung,** *f.* feeding, issue of food supply; (*B.*) *-ung der Fünftausend,* feeding of the five thousand.

Spektakel, 1. *m.* (& *Austr. dial. n.*) (-s, –) noise, uproar, row. 2. *n. only* (*archaic*) show, display. (*coll.*) **-n,** *v.n.* (*aux.* h.) make a row. **-macher,** *m.* rowdy. **-stück,** *n.* lavish *or* spectacular show (*Theat.*).

spek-tral, *adj.* spectral, (of the) spectrum. **-tralanalyse,** *f.* spectrum analysis. **-tralanalytisch,** *adj.* spectroscopic. **-trum,** *n.* (-trums, -tren & *Austr. dial.* -tra) spectrum.

Spekul-ant, *m.* (-en, -en) speculator, stock-exchange gambler. **-ation,** *f.* speculation, deliberation, contemplation; (*C.L.*) speculation, gamble, venture, enterprise. **-ationsgeist,** *m.* gambling spirit. **-ationsgeschäft,** *n.* speculative transaction. **-ationspapier,** *n.* speculative stock. **-ationsweise,** *adv.* on speculation. **-atius,** *m.* biscuit of butter and almonds. **-ativ,** *adj.* speculative, venturesome, risky. **-ieren,** *v.n.* (*aux.* h.) speculate, contemplate, meditate, ponder, reflect, cogitate, ruminate, brood; (*C.L.*) speculate, gamble (*auf,* on).

spellen, *v.a.* (*archaic*) split, cleave.

Spelt, *m.* (-(e)s, -e) spelt.

Spelunke, *f.* (-n) low tavern, den, (*sl.*) dive.

Spelz, *m.* (-es, -e) spelt. **-e,** *f.* glume, husk, beard, awn, chaff. **-ig,** *adj.* chaffy, glumaceous. **-enartig,** *adj.* glumaceous.

Spend-e, *f.* (-en) gift, donation, contribution; alms, charity, bounty. **-en,** 1. *v.a.* dispense, distribute; give, bestow, contribute (to). 2. *n.* distribution. **-er,** *m.* distributor, dispenser; donor, benefactor. (*coll.*) **-abel,** *adj.* open-handed, free with one's money. (*coll.*) **-ieren,** *v.a.* give a treat, make a gift of, treat, pay for, (*coll.*) stand; *sich* (*Dat.*) *etwas -ieren,* treat o.s. to a th. **-ung,** *f., see* **-e**; granting, according, conferring, bestowal, presentation; dispensation, administration (*of the Sacrament*).

Spengler, *m.* (-s, –) (*dial.*) tinsmith, sheet-metal worker, plumber.

Sperber, *m.* (-s, –) sparrow-hawk (*Accipiter nisus*) (*Orn.*). **-baum,** *m.* service-tree. **-n,** *v.n.* (*Swiss dial.*) observe closely.

Sperenzchen, Sperenzien, *pl.* (*coll.*) resistance, opposition; *machen Sie keine – !* don't make a fuss! no ceremony, please!

Sperling, *m.* (-s, -e) sparrow. (*coll.*) **-sbeine,** *n.pl.* spindle-shanks. **-skauz,** *m.* pygmy-owl, gnome-owl (*Amer.*) (*Glaucidium passerinum*) (*Orn.*). **-smännchen,** *n.* cock sparrow. **-spapagei,** *m.* love-bird (*Orn.*). **-sschrot,** *n.* small shot. **-svogel,** *m.* passerine (bird); (*pl.*) passerines. **-sweibchen,** *n.* hen sparrow.

Sperm-a, *n.* (-as, -men & -mata) sperm, semen. **-akern,** *m.* sperm-nucleus. **-ien,** *pl.* spermatozoa.

Spermazet, *n.* spermaceti. **-öl,** *n.* sperm oil, whale oil.

Sperr-e, *f.* (-n) shutting, closing (*of gates*); closure, stoppage; block, blockade, barricade, obstruction, barrier, obstacle; ban, prohibition, embargo; quarantine; catch, stop (*Horol.*); drag, skid, shoe (*of a wheel*); *-e verhängen,* ban, block, (apply) closure (to), place an embargo (on). **-angelweit,** *adj.* gaping, wide open. **-ballon,** *m.* barrage balloon. **-bau,** *m.* (-ten) dam. **-druck,** *m.* spaced type. (*Typ.*). **-en,** 1. *v.a.* spread *or* stretch out, sprawl, straddle; space (*a word*) (*Typ.*); bar, block, stop, cut off (*water, gas, etc.*); barricade, obstruct, blockade; confine, lock, trig (*wheels*); (*dial.*) shut, close; *einen Scheck -en,* stop a cheque; *ins Gefängnis -en,* put in prison; *einen aus dem Hause -en,* shut the door in a p.'s face, lock a p. out; *den Seehandel -en,* blockade ports, lay an embargo on commerce; *gesperrte Schrift,* spaced type. 2. *v.n.* not shut, be stuck *or* jammed open; *die Tür -t,* the door will not shut. 3. *v.r.* resist, refuse, oppose; struggle (*wider,* against); bridle up. **-feder,** *f.* retaining-spring. **-feuer,** *n.* barrage, barrage-fire, curtain-fire (*Mil.*); *-feuer legen,* lay down a barrage (*Artil.*). **-filter,** *m.* rejector circuit (*Rad.*). **-flieger,** *m.* interceptor plane, patrol aircraft. **-frist,** *f.* period of closure. **-gebiet,** *n.* prohibited area, blockade zone. **-geld,** *n.* toll, entrance-money; (*coll.*) tip to the porter for opening the door late at night. **-gut,** *n.* bulky goods. **-guthaben,** *n.* blocked account. **-hahn,** *m.* stopcock. **-haken,** *m.* catch; skeleton key, pick-lock. **-hebel,** *m.* locking-lever. **-holz,** *n.* plywood. **-ig,** *adj.* stretched out, spreading, widespread; wide open; loose, unwieldy, cumbersome, bulky. **-kette,** *f.* door-chain; drag-chain. **-klinke,** *f.* safety-catch, pawl. **-kreis,** *m.* rejector circuit, interference filter (*Rad.*). **-mark,** *f.* blocked mark (*currency*). **-maßregeln,** *f.pl.* prohibitive measures. **-(r)ad,** *n.* ratchet-wheel. **-(r)iegel,** *m.* bolt (*of a door*). **-schicht,** *f.* insulating layer. **-schiff,** *n.* ship sunk to block a harbour. **-sitz,** *m.* stall, reserved seat (*Theat.*); *-sitz im Parkett,* orchestra-stall. **-ung,** *f.* spreading out, distension; interspacing; blocking; barricade, stoppage; prohibition, embargo, blockade. **-ventil,** *n.* stop-valve. (*C.L.*) **-vermerk,** *m.* non-negotiability notice. **-vorrichtung,** *f.* ratchet-wheel, stop, catch, locking device. **-weit,** *adj.* wide open. **-wirkung,** *f.* rectifying effect. (*Rad.*). **-zeit,** *f.* closing time. **-zoll,** *m.* prohibitory duty.

Spesen, *f.pl.* charges, expenses, costs; *unter Zurechnung Ihrer –,* plus your expenses. **-frei,** *adj.* expenses paid, free of costs. **-nachnahme,** *f.* charges to follow, expenses (to be) paid on delivery. **-rechnung,** *f.* bill for expenses. **-vergütung,** *f.* reimbursement of expenses.

Spezerei, *f.* (*usually pl.* –en) spices; (*dial.*) groceries. (*dial.*) **-händler,** *m.* grocer. **-handlung,** *f.* grocer's shop.

Spezi, *m.* (-s, –) (*dial.*) *see* **-al,** 2. **-al,** 1. *adj.* (*rare*) special. 2. *m.* (-s, -e) (*dial.*) bosom friend; (*dial.*) choice wine. **-alarzt,** *m.* specialist. **-alfach,** *n.* speciality, special subject. **-fall,** *m.* special case. **-algeschäft,** *n.* one-line shop. **-alien,** *pl.* details, particulars. **-alisieren,** 1. *v.a.* specify, particularize. 2. *v.r.* specialize (*auf,* in). **-alist,** *m.* specialist. **-alität,** *f.* speciality, special subject. **-alkarte,** *f.* local map, large-scale map. **-altruppen,** *f.pl.* technical *or* special-service troops. **-ell,** *adj.* special, specific, particular; *-ell angeben,* specify; *-eller Freund,* particular friend; *auf Ihr -elles!* your health! **-es,** *f.* species; *die 4 -es,* the 4 first rules of arithmetic. **-esfremd,** *adj.* of a different species. **-esgleich,** *adj.* of the same species. (*obs.*) **-estaler,** *m.* specie dollar. **-fisch,** *adj.* specific; *-fischer Bildungstrieb,* automorphosis (*Biol.*); *-fisches Gewicht,* specific gravity; *-fische Wärme,* specific heat. **-fizieren,** *v.a.* specify. **-men,** *n.* (-mens, -mina) specimen, sample.

Sphär-e, *f.* (-en) sphere, range, domain, province; globe. **-isch,** *adj.* spherical. **-enmusik,** *f.* music of the spheres.

spick-en, *v.a.* lard; (*fig.*) garnish; (*dial.*) smoke; (*coll.*) cheat, copy (*in school*); *den Beutel -en,* line one's pocket; (*coll.*) *einen -en,* grease a p.'s palm; *seine Rede mit Zitaten -en,* interlard one's discourse with quotations. **-aal,** *m.* (*dial.*) smoked eel. **-gans,** *f.* smoked goose(-breast). **-nadel,** *f.* larding-pin.

spie, spiee, *see* **speien.**

Spiegel, *m.* (-s, –) looking-glass, mirror; reflector, reflecting surface; speculum (*Surg.*); bull's-eye; tab (*on collar, Mil.*), silk facing (*on evening dress*); medullary rays (*Bot.*); square stern (*Naut.*); white spot on the posterior of roes; *das stecke ich mir hinter den –,* I shall not forget that in a hurry, I will keep that in mind; *einem den – vorhalten,* hold the mirror up to s.o., let a p. see himself as he is; *das Bild ist wie aus dem – gestohlen,* the picture is a wonderful likeness. **-achse,** *f.* axis of symmetry. **-becken,** *n.* barber's sign. **-bild,** *n.* mirror-image. **-blank,** *adj.* highly polished, shining, glassy. **-decke,** *f.* mirrored ceiling. **-ei,** *n.* fried egg. **-eisen,** *n.* specular iron. **-erz,** *n.* specular iron-ore. **-fechter,** *m.* shammer, dissembler. **-fechterei,** *f.* shadow-boxing; pretence, humbug. **-feld,** *n.* mirror-panel. **-fenster,** *n.* plate-glass window. **-fläche,** *f.* smooth *or* glassy surface. **-folie,** *f.* tinfoil, silvering (*of a mirror*). **-frequenz,** *f.* second-channel frequency (*Rad.*). **-gießerei,** *f.* plate-glass factory. **-glanz,** *m.* reflecting lustre. **-glas,** *n.* plate-glass. **-glatt,** *adj.* (as) smooth as a mirror; glassy, slippery (*of ice*). **-glätte,** *f.* perfect smoothness. **-hell,** *adj.* (as) bright *or* clear as a mirror. **-ig,** *adj.* smooth, bright, brilliant, mirror-like; symmetrical. **-klar,** *adj., see* **-hell. -n,** 1. *v. n.* (*aux.* h.) sparkle, glitter, shine. 2. *v.a.* reflect; *das Auge -t Freude,* the eye lights up *or* gleams with joy. 3. *v.r.* be reflected, be revealed; *gespiegeltes Pferd,* dappled horse. **-pfeiler,** *m.* pier (*Arch.*). **-reflexkamera,** *f.* reflex camera (*Phot.*). **-saal,** *m.* hall of mirrors. **-scheibe,** *f.* pane of plate-glass. **-schiefer,** *m.* specular schist. **-schleifer,** *m.* mirror-polisher. **-schrank,** *m.* wardrobe with mirror. **-schrift,** *f.* mirror-writing. **-telegraph,** *m.* heliograph. **-tür,** *f.* plate-glass door. **-ung,** *f.* reflection; mirage. **-visier,** *n.* mirror *or* reflecting sight.

spiegl-ig, *adj.,* **-ung,** *f., see* **spiegel-ig, -ung.**

Spiek, *m.,* **-e,** *f.* (-en) lavender (*Lavandula officinalis*) (*Bot.*); spikenard (*Valeriana spica*). **-öl,** *n.* oil of lavender, spike-oil.

Spieker, *m.* (-s, -) large nail (*Naut.*), spike, brad, peg, tack. **-n,** *v.a.* nail, spike (*Naut.*).

Spiel, *n.* (-(e)s, -e) play, game, sport; playing, acting, performance (*Theat.*); gambling, gaming; set (*of knitting needles, etc.*), pack (*of cards, etc.*); manner of playing, touch (*Mus.*), playing (*of musical instruments*); motion, action, working; plaything; *ich bin am -,* it is my turn to play; *aufs - setzen,* stake; *auf dem - stehen,* be at stake; *aus dem - bleiben,* take no part in *or* have nothing to do with (*a th.*); *aus dem -e lassen,* leave out of the question, let alone; *laß mich aus dem -e,* do not drag me into that; *gute Miene zum bösen - machen,* make the best of a bad job, put a good face on the matter; *dem -e ergeben,* addicted to gambling; *- der Farben,* play of colours; *einem freies - lassen,* leave the field clear for a p., give full scope to s.o.; *ein gewagtes - spielen,* take chances, play a risky game; *gewonnenes - haben,* be sure of the game, have gained the day, (*sl.*) have in one's pocket; *wenn die Katze nicht im Hause ist, haben die Mäuse gewonnenes -,* when the cat's away the mice will play; *Glück im -, Pech in der Liebe,* lucky at cards, unlucky in love; *die Hand im -e haben,* have a finger in the pie; *sich ins - mischen,* interfere with *or* have a hand in (*a matter*); *einem ins - sehen,* look at *or* see a p.'s cards *or* hand; (*fig.*) see through a p.'s game; (*mit*) *im -e sein,* be implicated in *or* involved in a matter; *mit klingendem -e,* with a military band, with martial music; with drums beating and trumpets sounding; *- der Kräfte,* interplay of forces; *leichtes - haben,* have no difficulty (*in doing a th.*), (*coll.*) have a walkover; *- der Muskeln,* action of the muscles; *sein - mit einem treiben,* make fun *or* game of a p.; *das - verloren geben,* throw up the sponge, throw in one's hand; *ein - der Wellen sein,* be at the mercy of the waves; *das - hat sich gewandt,* the tables are turned; *es wird ihm zum -* or *ist ihm ein -,* it comes easy to him. **-art,** *f.* style of play; variety, sport (*Nat. Hist.*). **-ball,** *m.* ball, (*fig.*) sport, plaything; *ein -ball der Winde und Wellen sein,* be at the mercy of the winds and waves. **-bank,** *f.* gaming-table. **-bein,** *n.* leg taking no weight (*Sculp.*). **-brett,** *n* board (*for chess, draughts, etc.*). **-dose,** *f.* musical box. **-en,** *v.a. & n.* (*aux.* h.) play; sport; gamble; act, perform, play *or* take the part of (*Theat.*); trifle, toy, dally *or* coquet (with); feign, simulate, pretend; flash, glitter, sparkle; *die Augen über eine S. -en lassen,* run the eyes over *or* glance at a th.; *vom Blatte -en,* play (music) at sight; *falsch -en,* cheat at cards; play wrong notes (*Mus.*); *eine klägliche Figur -en,* cut a pitiful, sorry, poor *or* wretched figure; *mit dem Gedanken -en,* toy with the idea; *nach Gehör -en,* play (*music*) from ear; *einem etwas in die Hände -en,* slip a th. into s.o.'s hand, help a p. to a th.; *einander in die Hände -en,* play into one another's hands, have a secret understanding; *hoch -en,* play for high stakes; *das Stück spielt in . . .,* the scene is laid *or* takes place in . . .; *ins Loch -en,* pocket a ball (*Bill.*); *ins Rote -en,* incline to red; *im Winde -en,* flutter in the wind; *mit offenen Karten -en,* be open and above board; *mit verdeckten Karten -en,* have underhand dealings, behave in an underhand manner; *Komödie* or *Theater -en,* act a play, make believe, pretend; *er läßt nicht mit sich -en,* he is not to be trifled with, he cannot take a joke; *keine Rolle -en,* count for nothing, carry no weight; *um Geld -en,* play for money. **-end,** 1. *pr.p. & adj.* playing; opalescent. 2. *adv.* easily, with the greatest ease. **-er,** *m.* player, actor, performer; gambler. **-erei,** *f.* play, sport, pastime, childish amusement; dalliance, frivolity; trifle. **-ergebnis,** *n.* score. **-erisch,** *adj.* perfunctory, frivolous; playful, childish; effortless. **-feld,** *n.* playing-field, sports ground, (tennis) court. **-film,** *m.* feature (film). **-gefährte,** *m.* playfellow, playmate. **-gehilfe,** *m.* croupier. **-geld,** *n.* stake(s), pool, card-money. **-genosse,** *m.* playmate. **-gewinn,** *m.* winnings (*at play*). **-grenze,** *f.* (dead-ball) line (*Footb.*). **-hahn,** *m.* heath-cock, black-cock. **-hölle,** *f.* gambling-den *or* hell. **-ig,** *adj.* playful, fond of playing. **-kamerad,** *m., see* **-gefährte. -karte,** *f.* playing card. **-leiter,** *m.* stage-manager, producer. **-leute,** *pl.* musicians, bandsmen; drums and fifes, band. **-mann,** *m.* (-leute) bandsman; troubadour, minstrel, gleeman. **-mannschaft,** *f.* team (*Sport.*). **-mannsdichtung,** *f.* minstrel poesy, minstrelsy. **-marke,** *f.* counter, chip. **-oper,** *f.* comic opera. **-partie,** *f.* card-party; game of cards. **-plan,** *m.* programme; repertory, repertoire. **-platz,** *m.* playground. (*coll.*) **-ratte,** *f.,* **-ratze,** *f.* playful child. **-raum,** *m.* (free) play, full scope, elbow-room; margin, latitude; clearance (*Mech.*); windage (*Artil.*). **-regeln,** *f.pl.* rules of a game. **-sache,** *f.* plaything, toy. **-schar,** *f.* amateur players *or* company (*Theat.*). **-schuld,** *f.* gambling debt. **-schule,** *f.* kindergarten. **-teufel,** *m.* passion for gambling. **-tisch,** *m.* card-table. **-trieb,** *m.* aesthetic sense; play instinct. **-uhr,** *f.* musical box, musical clock. **-verderber,** *m.* spoil-sport, kill-joy, wet-blanket. **-waren,** *f.pl.* toys. **-weise,** 1. *f.* manner of playing *or* acting *or* performing. 2. *adv.* in play. **-werk,** *n.* chime (*of clock*), peal (*of bells*). **-wut,** *f.* passion for gambling. **-zeit,** *f.* playtime; season (*for games* or *performances*); playing time (*Mus., Sport*). **-zeug,** *n.* plaything, toy. **-zimmer,** *n.* play-room; (day-) nursery.

Spier, *m. & n.* (-s, -e) spiraea (*Bot.*); thin stalk, blade of grass. **-chen,** *n.*; (*dial.*) *kein -chen,* not a bit, not in the very least. **-(e),** *f.* (-en) spar, boom (*Naut.*); rib (*Av.*); spiraea (*Bot.*). **-staude,** *f.,* **-strauch,** *m.* spiraea (*Bot.*).

Spieß, *m.* (-es, -e) spear, lance, pike, javelin, harpoon; spit; blot, pick (*Typ.*); first year's antlers; (*sl.*) sergeant-major; *an den - stecken,* spit; *den - umkehren,* turn the tables. **-bock,** *m.* pricket, brocket (*Hunt.*). **-braten,** *m.* meat roasted on a spit. **-bürger,** *m.* narrow-minded townsman, bourgeois, commonplace fellow, philistine. **-bürgerlich,** *adj.* bourgeois, narrow-minded, commonplace, humdrum. **-en,** *v.a.* pierce, spear, impale, transfix. **-er,** *m.* (*coll.*), *see* **-bürger**; *also* **-bock. -erisch,** *adj., see* **-bürgerlich. -gesell(e),** *m.* accomplice. **-glanz,** *m.* antimony. **-glanzhaltig,** *adj.* antimonial. **-glas,** *n., see* **-glanz. -hirsch,** *m., see* **-bock. -ig,** *adj.* spearlike, lance-shaped; (*coll.*) philistine, narrow-minded, uncultured. **-rute,** *f.* rod, switch; *-ruten laufen,* run the gauntlet. **-träger,** *m.* spearman, pikeman, halberdier.

Spill, *n.* (-(e)s, -e) capstan, windlass, winch. **-baum,** *m.* capstan-bar; (*dial.*) *see* **Spindelbaum, -e,** *f.* (*dial.*) *see* **Spindel. -erig,** *adj.* (*dial.*) thin as a rake. **-gelder,** *pl.* (*dial.*) pin-money.

Spilling, *m.* (-s, -e) small yellow plum.
Spinat, *m.* (-(e)s, -e) spinach.
Spind, *n.* (*& dial. m.*) (-(e)s, -e), **–e,** *f.* (-en) locker, wardrobe, press.
Spindel, *f.* (-n) distaff; spindle, shaft; pinion, pivot, arbor, mandrel, axis, axle; pin, peg, skewer; newel (*Arch.*). **–baum,** *m.* spindle-tree (*Evonymus*) (*Bot.*). **–beine,** *n.pl.* spindle-shanks. **–dürr,** *adj.* thin as a rake. **–presse,** *f.* screw-press. **–treppe,** *f.* spiral staircase. **–waage,** *f.* hydrometer. **–welle,** *f.* bobbin. **–zapfen,** *m.* pivot, axis, spindle.
Spinett, *n.* (-(e)s, -e) spinet (*Mus.*).
Spinn–e, *f.* (-en) spider; *ich hasse ihn wie eine –e,* I hate him like poison; (*coll.*) *pfui –e!* disgusting! shocking! *–en sehen,* have spots before one's eyes. **–drüse,** *f.* silk-gland. **–efeind,** *adv.* bitterly hostile; *einem –efeind sein,* hate a p. like poison, be at daggers drawn with a p. **–en,** *ir.v.a. & n.* (*aux.* h.) spin, twist, twirl; purr (*as a cat*); (*sl.*) do a stretch (*in prison*); (*coll.*) be crazy; *ein Garn –en,* spin a yarn (*Naut.*); *Hanf –en,* be on bread and water; *der Kreisel –t,* the top spins; *Verrat –en,* plot treason; *er hat keine Seide dabei gesponnen,* he got nothing out of it, it did not do him much good. **–engewebe,** *n.,* (*coll.*) **–e(n)web,** *n.,* **–e(n)webe,** *f. or n., see* **–gewebe.** **–er,** *m.* spinner; bombycid (*Ent.*). **–erei,** *f.* spinning; spinning-mill. **–erin,** *f.* spinner. **–fäden,** *m.pl.* gossamer. **–faser,** *f.* synthetic fibre. **–gewebe,** *n.* spider's web, cobweb. **–haus,** *n.* (*archaic*) workhouse. **–maschine,** *f.* spinning-machine. **–rad,** *n.* spinning-wheel. **–rocken,** *m.* distaff. **–stoff(waren),** *m.* (*f.pl.*) textiles. **–stube,** *f.* spinning-room. **–warze,** *f.* spinning-orifice (*of spiders*), spinneret. **–web,** *n.,* **–webe,** *f.* (*or n. Austr. dial.*), *see* **–gewebe.**
spinös, *adj.* spiny; (*fig.*) pernickety.
Spint, *n.* (-(e)s, -e) (*archaic*) dry measure (*local variations from ½ gallon to 1½ gallons*).
spintisieren, *v.n.* (*aux.* h.) brood, ruminate; meditate.
Spion, *m.* (-s, -e) spy; looking-glass outside a window. **–age,** *f.* spying, espionage. **–ageabwehr,** *f.* counter-espionage. **–ieren,** *v.n.* (*aux.* h.) spy; pry into, play the spy.
spiral, *adj.* spiral. **–bohrer,** *m.* twist-drill. **–e,** *f.* (-en) spiral (*Math.*); coil, clock-spring. **–feder,** *f.* helical *or* spiral spring; mainspring (*of a watch*). **–förmig,** *adj.* spiral, helical; convolute (*Bot.*). **–ig,** *adj.* spiral, helical. **–linie,** *f.* spiral. **–nebel,** *m.* spiral nebula (*Astr.*).
Spirit–ismus, *m.* spiritualism. **–ist,** *m.* spiritualist. **–istisch,** *adj.* spiritualist(ic). **–ual,** *adj.* spiritual. **–ualismus,** *m.* spiritualism (*Philos.*). **–uell,** *adj.* intellectual, mental. **–uosen,** *pl.* spirits, spirituous liquors. **–us,** *m.* (–, – & –usse) alcohol, spirit, spirits; methylated spirit; (*fig.*) mettle; *denaturierter –us,* methylated spirit; *normalstarker –us,* proof spirit. **–usbrennerei,** *f.* distillery. **–uskocher,** *m.* spirit-stove. **–uslack,** *m.* spirit varnish. **–uslampe,** *f.* spirit-lamp. **–uswaage,** *f.* spirit-level.
Spital, *n.* (-es, ¨er) hospital. **–schiff,** *n.* hospital-ship. **–zug,** *m.* ambulance train.
Spittel, *n.* (*& dial. m.*) (-s, –), *see* **Spital.**
spitz, 1. *adj.* pointed, sharp, tapering, acute; sarcastic, caustic, biting; *–es Kinn,* pointed chin; *–er Wein,* thin, sharp *or* acid wine; *–er Winkel,* acute angle; *–e Zunge,* sharp tongue; *mit –en Fingern angreifen,* handle cautiously; *– auslaufen,* terminate in a point; (*coll.*) *ich kann es nicht – kriegen,* I can't make it out. 2. *m.* (-es, -e) Pomeranian dog; (*Swiss dial.*) see **–e;** (*coll.*) *einen* (*kleinen*) *– haben,* be (somewhat) tipsy. **–ahorn,** *m.* Norway maple (*Acer platanoides*) (*Bot.*). **–axt,** *f.* pickaxe. **–bart,** *m.* pointed beard. **–beutel,** *m.* triangular filter-bag. **–bogen,** *m.* Gothic *or* pointed arch. **–bogenstil,** *m.* Gothic style (*Arch.*). **–bohrer,** *m.* centre-bit. **–bub(e),** *m.* rascal, rogue; swindler, thief; (*fam.*) little rogue *or* rascal. **–bubenstreich,** *m.* piece of rascality, knavish trick. **–büberei,** *f.* rascality. **–bübisch,** *adj.* rascally, roguish. **–e,** *f.* (-en) point, spike; extremity, tip (*of tongue*); nib (*of pen*); mouthpiece (*of a pipe*), (cigarette-)holder; top, summit, peak, head, vertex, apex; cusp; sarcastic remark; (*pl.*) lace; *die –en der Behörden,* the heads of the administration, the authorities; *einem die –e bieten,* defy a p.; *–en klöppeln,* make (pillow-)lace; *an der –e stehen,* be at the head (*of affairs*); *auf die –e treiben,* carry to extremes, carry too far; *auf der –e stehen,* stand on end. **–el,** *m.* secret police-agent, plain-clothes man, informer. **–eln,** *v.n.* spy upon, inform against. **–en,** 1. *v.a.* point, tip, sharpen; (*dial.*) pay attention, look out; *einen Bleistift –en,* sharpen a pencil; *seine Antwort –en,* make a cutting reply; *das ist auf mich gespitzt,* that is aimed at me; *den Mund –en,* purse one's lips; *die Ohren –en,* prick up one's ears. 2. *v.r.*; *sich auf eine S. –en,* look forward to a th., hope for *or* count on a th., set one's heart upon a th. **–enarbeit,** *f.* lace-work. **–enband,** *n.* lace-edging. **–enbelastung,** *f.* peak-load (*Elec.*). **–enbesatz,** *m.* lace-trimming. **–enentladung,** *f.* point-discharge (*Elec.*). **–enfabrikation,** *f.* lace-making. **–enfahrzeug,** *n.* leading vehicle (*of a column*). **–enflieger,** *m.* flying ace. **–englas,** *n.* reticulated glass. **–enkleid,** *n.* dress trimmed with *or* made of lace. **–enklöppel,** *m.* lace-bobbin. **–enklöppelei,** *f.* pillow-lace (making). **–enkompagnie,** *f.* advance party (*Mil.*). **–enleistung,** *f.* first-class *or* outstanding performance, record; maximum output; peak-power (*Elec.*). **–enlohn,** *m.* maximum wages. **–enpapier,** *n.* lace paper. **–enstrom,** *m.* peak current (*Elec.*). **–entanz,** *m.* toe dance. **–enverband** *m.* head *or* central organization. **–enwachstum,** *n.* apical growth (*Bot.*). **–enwirkung,** *f.* needle-effect (*Elec.*). **–er,** *m.* (pencil-, *etc.*) sharpener. **–feile,** *f.* tapered *or* rat-tail file. **–findig,** *adj.* subtle, keen, crafty, shrewd, ingenious; cavilling, hypercritical, hair-splitting. **–findigkeit,** *f.* subtlety; craftiness, sophistry. **–geschoß,** *n.* pointed bullet *or* shell. **–glas,** *n.* conical glass. **–hacke,** *f.* pickaxe. **–hut,** *m.* peaked hat. **–ig,** *adj.* pointed, sharp, tapering, acute; sarcastic; *see* **–.** **–igkeit,** *f.* sharpness; pointedness, piquancy; sarcasm. **–kant,** *m.* (-es, -e) pyramid. **–knospe,** *f.* terminal bud. **–kolumne,** *f.* head-piece (*Typ.*). **–marke,** *f.* heading (*Typ.*). **–maus,** *f.* shrew (*Sorex*) (*Zool.*) **–name,** *m.* nickname. **–nasig,** *adj.* sharp-nosed. **–pfeiler,** *m.* obelisk. **–pocken,** *f.pl.* chicken-pox (*Med.*). **–wegerich,** *m.* ribwort (*Plantago lanceolata*) (*Bot.*).
Spleiß, *m.* (-es, -e) splice (*Naut.*). **–e,** *f.* (*dial.*) splinter; scale (*of iron*). **–en,** *ir.v.a. & n.* (*aux.* s.) splice (*Naut.*); (*rare*) split, splinter, cleave. **–ig,** *adj.* friable, easily split.
splendid, *adj.* splendid, magnificent; liberal, generous; wide, spaced (*Typ.*).
Spließ, *m.* (-es, -e) (*dial.*) shingle, wooden tile.
Splint, *m.* (-(e)s, -e) sap-wood, alburnum (*Bot.*); forelock; peg, securing pin, split-pin (*Mech.*). **–bolzen,** *m.* keyed bolt. **–holz,** *n.* sap-wood.
Spliß, *m.* (-(ss)es, -(ss)e) splice (*Naut.*); *see also* **Splitter.** **–e,** *f.* (-n) chip, shaving; section of a fishing rod. **–(ss)en,** *v.a.* splice (*Naut.*).
spliß, splisse, *see* **spleißen.**
Splitter, *m.* (-s, –) splinter, chip, fragment; scale (*of metal, etc.*); (*B.*) mote. **–bombe,** *f.* fragmentation *or* anti-personnel bomb. **–dicht,** *adj.* splinter-proof. **–(faser)nackt,** *adj.* stark naked. **–frei,** *adj.* non-splintering (*glass*). **–ig.** *adj.* splintery, brittle. **–kohle,** *f.* slaty coal. **–n,** 1. *v.a.* shatter, shiver, splinter, split. 2. *v.n.* (*aux.* s.) splinter, split (up). **–partei,** *f.* fractional party (*Pol.*). **–richten,** *v.a.* criticize minutely; carp, cavil (*at things*). **–richter,** *m.* hair-splitter, caviller, carper, fault-finder. **–sicher,** *adj.* splinter-proof (*glass, etc.*). **–wirkung,** *f.* splinter-effect, fragmentation (*Mil.*).
Spodium, *n.* (-e) bone black.
Spolien, *n.pl.* spoils, booty.
sponde–isch, *adj.* spondaic. **–us,** *m.* (-us, -en), spondee.
spönne, *see* **spinnen.**
Spons–alien, *pl.* betrothal (*Law*), betrothal celebrations. **–ieren,** *v.n.* (*archaic*) court, woo.
spontan, *adj.* spontaneous, autogenous; *–e Änderung* or *Variation,* mutation.
Spor, *m.* (-(e)s, -e) (*dial.*) mildew, mouldiness. **–e,** *f.* (-n) spore, sporule. **–en,** *v.n.* get mouldy,

dry up, rot. **–enbildend,** *adj.* sporular, sporogenous. **–enbildung,** *f.* sporogenesis, sporulation. **–enkapsel,** *f.* spore-capsule, sporangium. **–enpflanzen,** *f.pl.* acotyledons, sporophytes, cryptogamous plants. **–entiere,** *n.pl.* sporozoa. **–fleck,** *m.* mould-stain. **–ig,** *adj.* mildewed, mouldy.

sporadisch, *adj.* sporadic.

Sporn, *m.* (-(e)s, Sporen) spur; tail-skid (*Av.*), trail-spade (*Artil.*); (*pl.* -e) thorn (*Bot.*), spine; (*fig.*) goad, stimulus, incentive; *dem Pferde die Sporen geben,* set spurs to one's horse; *sich* (*Dat.*) *die Sporen verdienen,* win one's spurs. **–en,** *v.a.* spur, set spurs to; goad. **–blume,** *f.* larkspur (*Centranthus*) (*Bot.*). **–halter,** *m.* heel-plate. **–rad,** *n.* tail-wheel (*Av.*). **–rädchen,** *n.* rowel; spur-wheel; mullet (*Her.*). **–stätisch,** *adj.* restive. **–streichs,** *adv.* post-haste, with all speed, at once, immediately.

Sport, *m.* sport; – *treiben,* go in for sport. **–abzeichen,** *n.* (official German) sports-badge. **–anzug,** *m.* sports-suit *or* clothes. **–art,** *f.* type of sport. **–ausrüstung,** *f.* sports-kit. **–(be)kleidung,** *f.* sports-wear. **–eln,** *v.n.* (*coll.*) go in for sport. **–fest,** *n.* sports-day. **–flugzeug,** *n.* sports-plane. **–freund,** *m.* sports-enthusiast. **–funk,** *m.* (radio) sports news *or* commentary. **–ler,** *m.*, **–lerin,** *f.* athlete, athletic type. **–lich,** *adj.* sporting, athletic; *–liche Veranstaltung,* sporting event. **–mäßig,** *adj.* sportsmanlike, sporting, (*sl.*) sporty. **–platz,** *m.* playing-field, sports- (*football, cricket, etc.*) ground. **–smann,** *m.* (-(e)s, ¨er *or* -leute) sportsman. **–swagen,** *m.* folding pram, push-chair. **–verband,** *m.* sports-club. **–welt,** *f.* world of sport.

Sport–eln, *f.pl.* fees, perquisites. **–elfrei,** *adj.* free of cost. **–eltaxe,** *f.* scale of fees. **–ulieren,** *v.n.* (*aux.* h.) collect *or* levy fees.

Spott, *m.* mockery, ridicule, scorn, derision, contumely; butt, laughing-stock; *beißender* –, biting sarcasm; *Schande und* –, shame and disgrace; (*Prov.*) *wer den Schaden hat, braucht für den – nicht zu sorgen,* the laugh is always on the loser; *seinen – treiben mit,* make fun of, turn to ridicule, mock (at), scoff at; *zum – werden,* become the laughing-stock. **–bild,** *n.* caricature. **–billig,** *adj.* dirt-cheap. **–dichter,** *m.* satirical poet. **–drossel,** *f.* mocking-bird (*Mimus polyglottos & Dumetella carolinensis*) (*Orn.*). **–en,** *v.a. & n.* (*aux.* h.) (*über with Acc.*) mock, jeer at, deride, scoff at, ridicule, pillory; (*with Gen.*) disregard, defy; *es –et jeder Beschreibung,* it beggars description. **–enderweise,** *adv.* tauntingly. **–gebot,** *n.* ridiculously low offer. **–geburt,** *f.* monstrosity, abortion. **–gedicht,** *n.* satirical poem, lampoon. **–geist,** *m.* scoffing disposition; scoffer. **–gelächter,** *n.* derisive laughter. **–geld,** *n.* trifling sum, a mere song. **–lied,** *n.* satirical song, lampoon. **–lustig,** *adj.* satirical, sarcastic. **–name,** *m.* abusive name. **–preis,** *m.* ridiculously low price. **–rede,** *f.* gibe, sneer, taunt, satire. **–süchtig,** *adj.* given to mockery, satirical. **–vers,** *m.* lampoon, satirical verse. **–vogel,** *m.* mocking-bird; mocker. **–weise,** *adv.* mockingly, derisively, ironically.

Spött–elei, *f.* banter, raillery, chaff, persiflage. **–eln,** *v.n.* (*aux.* h.) (*über einen* or *eine S.*) laugh, jeer *or* sneer at (a p. *or* a th.). **–er,** *m.* mocker, scoffer, jeerer. **–erei,** *f.* jeering, scoffing, derision, mockery, sarcasm. **–isch,** 1. *adj.* mocking, scoffing, jeering; scornful, derisory, ironical, sarcastic; caustic, biting. 2. *adv.* in mockery, in scorn. **–lich,** *adj.*, *see* **–isch**; shameful.

sprach, spräche, *see* **sprechen.**

Sprach–e, *f.* (-en) speech, diction, parlance; language, tongue, idiom, vernacular; voice, accent, style; discussion; *alte –en,* classical languages; *Berufs–e,* technical jargon, (*coll.*) shop(-talk); *–e der Bibel,* biblical language; *Dichter–e,* poetical language; *–e der Diebe,* thieves' cant; *–e der Kanzel,* pulpit oratory; *Kinder–e,* nursery talk; *neuere –en,* modern languages; *Soldaten–e,* military slang; *Studenten–e,* students' slang; *Umgangs–e,* colloquial language; *–e der Vernunft,* language of common sense; *ich erkenne ihn an der –e,* I know him by his voice *or* by his accent; *einem die –e benehmen,* strike s.o. dumb; *der –e beraubt sein,* be bereft of speech; *blumenreiche –e,* flowery style; *eine dreiste –e führen,* make impudent remarks; *gehobene –e,* elevated diction; *heraus mit der –e!* out with it! speak out! *mit der –e nicht recht herauswollen,* be reluctant to speak, be unwilling to explain o.s. *or* to speak out; *mit der –e herausrücken,* speak freely, (*coll.*) come out with it; *off(e)ne –e,* plain language *or* speech; *die –e verlieren,* not have a word to say; *die –e wiederbekommen,* find one's voice; *zur –e bringen,* broach (*a subject*); *zur –e kommen,* come up for discussion, be mentioned, be touched on. **–bau,** *m.* structure of a language. **–beherrschung,** *f.* command of a language. **–denkmal,** *n.* literary document *or* text. **–ecke,** *f.* correspondence column (*in a newspaper*). **–eigenheit,** *f.*, **–eigentümlichkeit,** *f.* idiomatic peculiarity, idiom; *deutsche* (*englische, amerikanische, französische, lateinische*) *–eigentümlichkeit,* Germanism (Anglicism, Americanism, Gallicism, Latinism). **–engewirr,** *n.* confusion of tongues, babel. **–enkunde,** *f.* linguistics. **–enkundig,** *adj.* proficient in languages. **–(en)verwirrung,** *f.*, *see* **–engewirr. –(en)zwang,** *m.* compulsory use of a language. **–familie,** *f.*, *see* **–stamm. –fehler,** *m.* speech defect, grammatical mistake. **–fertig,** *adj.* fluent, voluble. **–fertigkeit,** *f.* fluency, proficiency in (foreign) languages. **–forscher,** *m.* linguist, philologist. **–forschung,** *f.* philology, linguistics; *vergleichende –forschung,* comparatively philology. **–führer,** *m.* elementary guide (*to a language*), phrase-book. **–gebiet,** *n.* area where a language is spoken; *das gesamte deutsche –gebiet,* all German-speaking countries. **–gebrauch,** *m.* linguistic usage. **–gefüge,** *n.* connected speech. **–gefühl,** *n.* feeling for correct idiom, sense for language, feeling for a language. **–gesellschaft,** *f.* society for promoting the native tongue. **–gesetz,** *n.* linguistic law. **–gewandt,** *adj.* fluent. **–grenze,** *f.* linguistic frontier. **–gut,** *n.* resources of a language. **–ig,** *adj. suff.* e.g. *fremd–ig,* in a foreign language. **–insel,** *f.* district dialectically isolated from its surroundings, isolated dialect. **–kenner,** *m.* linguist; grammarian. **–kenntnis,** *f.* knowledge of a language. **–kunde,** *f.* linguistics. **–kundig,** *adj.* proficient in languages. **–lehre,** *f.* grammar, language primer. **–lehrer,** *m.* teacher of languages. **–lich,** *adj.* linguistic; grammatical. **–los,** *adj.* speechless, dumb, mute, (*coll.*) dumbfounded, flabbergasted. **–neuerer,** *m.* language reformer, neologist. **–pflege,** *f.* fostering the mother tongue. **–regel,** *f.* grammatical rule. **–reinheit,** *f.* purity of speech; purity of a language. **–reiniger,** *m.* purist. **–reinigung,** *f.* elimination of foreign elements from a language. **–richtig,** *adj.* correct, grammatical. **–rohr,** *n.* speaking-tube; megaphone; (*fig.*) mouthpiece; *die –rohre der öffentlichen Meinung,* the organs of public opinion. **–schatz,** *m.* vocabulary. **–schnitzer,** *m.* mistake *or* blunder (*in speech or writing*), solecism, (*coll.*) howler. **–schöpferisch,** *adj.* creative in the use of language, influential on style *or* vocabulary. **–stamm,** *m.* family of languages. **–störung,** *f.* impediment of speech, speech defect. **–studium,** *n.* language study. **–stunde,** *f.* lesson in a (foreign) language; *deutsche –stunden,* German lessons. **–sünde,** *f.* bad grammatical error, howler. **–talent,** *n.* linguistic talent. **–tum,** *n.* (realm of) language. **–unterricht,** *m.* language teaching, teaching of languages; *deutschen –unterricht erteilen,* give lessons in German. **–verbesserung,** *f.* language reform. **–verderber,** *m.* corrupter of a language. **–verein,** *m.* philological society. **–vergleichung,** *f.* comparative philology. **–vermögen,** *n.* faculty of speech; linguistic ability. **–verschandelung,** *f.* corruption of a language. **–werkzeug,** *n.* vocal organs. **–widrig,** *adj.* ungrammatical, incorrect. **–wissenschaft,** *f.* linguistics, philology. **–wissenschaftlich,** *adj.* philological. **–zentrum,** *n.* speech centre.

sprang, spränge, *see* **springen.**

sprech–en, 1. *ir.v.a. & n.* (*aux.* h) speak, talk, converse; discuss, talk over; (*only v.a.*) say, pronounce, declare, utter; *ich möchte ihn –en,* I would like a word with him *or* like to speak to him *or* like to meet *or* see him; *aus seinen Worten spricht Begeisterung,* his words express enthusiasm, enthusiasm is evident from his words; *frei aus dem Kopfe –en*, speak extempore *or* without notes *or* on the spur of the moment; *dafür –en*, support (*a view*), speak in favour of; *ich bin heute für niemand zu –en*, I am not at home to anyone today; *vor Gericht –en*, plead a cause; *auf jemanden gut zu –en sein*, be well *or* kindly disposed towards a p.; *auf jemanden nicht gut zu –en sein*, be ill-disposed towards a p., have no good to say about a p., not have a good word to say about a p.; *einen heilig –en* (also *heilig–en*), canonize a p.; *es spricht sich herum*, it is the talk of (*the town, etc.*); *mit Herrn N. –en*, talk to Mr. N; *er läßt nicht mit sich –en*, he will not listen to reason, it is no use talking to him; *–en wie dir der Schnabel gewachsen ist*, say what you think, give rein to your tongue; *den Segen über einen –en*, pronounce benediction upon a p.; *zu –en sein*, be available, be free (*to see s.o.*); *nicht zu –en sein*, be engaged; *wir werden uns darüber noch –en*, we shall see about that; *unter uns gesprochen*, between ourselves; *man spricht davon*, it is much talked of; *von etwas anderem –en*, change the subject; *zu einem –en*, talk to *or* with s.o.; *ganz allgemein gesprochen*, speaking quite generally. 2. *n.* speaking, talking. **–art**, *f.*, *see* **–weise**. **–bühne**, *f.* living stage. **–end**, *pr.p.* & *adj.* speaking, expressive, eloquent, striking, telling, conclusive; *–end ähnliches Bild*, striking likeness. **–er**, *m.* speaker, spokesman; foreman (*of a jury*); orator, broadcaster, radio announcer. **–film**, *m.* talking picture, (*coll.*) talkie. **–gesang**, *m.* recitative. (*archaic*) **–maschine**, *f.* gramophone, phonograph. **–melodie**, *f.* intonation. **–stelle**, *f.* telephone extension, call-station (*Tele.*). **–stunde**, *f.* time for seeing visitors, consulting hour, surgery-hour (*Med.*); (*C.L.*) office-hour. **–stundenhilfe**, *f.* receptionist. **–trichter**, *m.* mouthpiece (*Phone*). **–übung**, *f.* elocution exercise. **–verbindung**, *f.* telephone line. **–verständigung**, *f.* quality of reception (*Tele.*). **–weise**, *f.* manner of speaking, diction. **–zimmer**, *n.* consulting-room.

Spreißel, *m.* (& *Austr. dial. n.*) (-s, –) (*dial.*) splinter.

Spreit–e, *f.* spread, layer; cover, bed-spread. **–decke**, *f.* counterpane, bed-spread. **–en**, *v.a.* spread out, extend.

Spreiz–e, *f.* (-n) stay, spreader, prop, strut; splits (*Gymn.*); (*sl.*) fag. **–en**, 1. *v.a.* spread, stretch out, force apart, straddle, spread wide (*the legs, wings, etc.*); prop up, support. 2. *v.r.* swagger, strut, boast, be effected; *sich gegen etwas –en*, resist, strive against a th.; *sich mit etwas –en*, boast of *or* plume o.s. on a th. **–beinig**, *adj.* straddle-legged. **–klappe**, *f.* spreader. **–lafette**, *f.* split-trail (*Artil.*).

Sprengel, *m.* (-s, –) diocese, bishopric; sprinkling brush (*for holy water*).

spreng–en, 1. *v.a.* cause to spring, make jump; sprinkle, spray, water; spring, burst, explode, blow up, blast; burst open, rupture (*a blood-vessel*); spring (*a ball*) (*Bill.*); *die Bank –en*, break the bank (*gambling*); *die Fesseln –en*, burst one's chains; break loose, throw over restrictions; *den Garten –en*, water the garden; *in die Luft –en*, blow up; *den Rahmen dieses Aufsatzes –en*, go beyond the limits of this essay; *das Tor –en*, break open a gate; *eine Versammlung –en*, break up a meeting. 2. *v.n.* (*aux.* s.) gallop, ride at full speed; *auf den Feind (los)–en*, charge (at) the enemy. **–arbeit**, *f.* blasting operation. **–bombe**, *f.* high-explosive bomb. **–büchse**, *f.* blasting charge. **–er**, *m.* sprinkler, spray; blaster; started game; *einen –er machen*, spring a ball (*Bill.*). **–falle**, *f.* booby-trap (*Mil.*). **–geschoß**, *n.* projectile, shell. **–granate**, *f.* high-explosive shell. **–höhe**, *f.* height of burst (*of a shell*). **–kanne**, *f.* watering-can. **–kapsel**, *f.* detonator, primer, cap. **–kommando**, *n.* demolition squad, bomb-disposal unit (*Mil.*). **–körper**, *m.* explosive charge (*Mil.*). **–kraft**, *f.* disruptive force. **–ladung**, *f.* explosive charge. **–laut**, *m.* plosive, tenuis (*Phonet.*). **–loch**, *n.* blast-hole (*Min.*). **–mittel**, *n.pl.* explosives. **–öl**, *n.* nitroglycerine. **–patrone**, *f.* blasting-cartridge. **–pulver**, *n.* blasting-powder. **–stoff**, *m.* explosive. **–trichter**, *m.* bomb-crater (*Mil.*). **–ung**, *f.* blasting, explosion; sprinkling, spraying. **–wagen**, *m.* watering-cart. **–wedel**, *m.* sprinkling brush, holy-water sprinkler. **–weite**, *f.* range of burst. **–werk**, *n.* strut-frame. **–wirkung**, *f.* blast-effect.

Sprenk–el, *m.* (-s, –) gin, snare; speckle, spot. **–(e)lig**, *adj.* speckled, spotted. **–eln**, *v.a.* speckle, spot, mottle, dapple.

Spreu, *f.* chaff. **–artig**, *adj.* chaffy; palcaceous (*Bot.*). **–blättchen**, *n.* palea (*Bot.*). **–regen**, *m.* drizzling rain.

sprich, *see* **sprechen.**

Sprich–wort, *n.* saying, proverb, maxim, adage; *zum –wort werden*, become a byword, become proverbial. **–wörtlich**, *adj.* proverbial.

sprichst, spricht, *see* **sprechen.**

Spriegel, *m.* (-s, –) (*dial.*) hoop, strut (*of wagon hood*); frame, rack.

[1]**Sprieß–e**, *f.* (-n) (*dial.*) strut, support. **–en**, *reg.v.a.* (*dial.*) prop, support.

[2]**Sprieß–e**, *f.* (-n) (*dial.*) *see* **Sproß.** **–en**, *ir.v.n.* (*aux.* s.) sprout, germinate, bud.

Spriet, *n.* (-(e)s, -e) sprit, spar (*Naut.*).

Spring, *m.* (-(e)s, -e) spring, source (*of water*); (*also n.* & *f.*) hawser, cable (*Naut.*). **–beine**, *n.pl.* saltatorial legs (*Ent.*). **–bock**, *m.* springbok, Cape antelope. **–bohne**, *f.* jumping-bean. **–brunnen**, *m.* fountain. **–en**, *ir.v.n.* (*aux.* h. & s.) leap, spring, jump, hop, skip, bounce; (*dial.*) run; gush, spout, play (*of fountains*); crack, burst, split, break, explode; copulate (*of animals*); *auf die Seite –en*, leap aside; *aus dem Stand –en*, make a standing jump; *das –t in die Augen*, that leaps to the eye, that is evident *or* obvious; *mir ist, als sollte mein Kopf –en*, my head is fit to split; *–en lassen*, stand a th., treat (*s.o.*) to a th.; *eine Mine –en lassen*, spring *or* detonate a mine; *mit Anlauf –en*, make a running jump; *eine Saite ist gesprungen*, a string has snapped (*violin, etc.*); *über einen Graben –en*, leap a ditch; *über die Klinge –en lassen*, put to the sword; *über die Zunge –en lassen*, let (*a rash statement*) slip out. **–end**, *pr.p.* & *adj.*; *der –ende Punkt*, the salient point. **–er**, *m.* jumper, leaper, vaulter; knight (*Chess*). **–feder**, *f.* spring. **–federmatratze**, *f.* spring-mattress. **–flut**, *f.* spring-tide. **–hart**, *adj.* brittle. **–hengst**, *m.* stallion, stud-horse. **–insfeld**, *m.* harum-scarum, romp, madcap. **–kraft**, *f.* elasticity, resilience. **–kräftig**, *adj.* elastic, springy. **–kraut**, *n.* touch-me-not (*Impatiens noli-me-tangere*) (*Bot.*). **–maus**, *f.* jerboa (*Dipodidae*) (*Zool.*). **–mine**, *f.* anti-personnel mine (*Mil.*). **–quell**, *m.*, **–quelle**, *f.* spring, fountain; (*fig.*) source. **–schloß**, *n.* snap-lock. **–seil**, *n.* skipping-rope. **–stange**, *f.* vaulting- *or* jumping-pole. **–welle**, *f.* tidal wave, bore. **–wurzel**, *f.* mandrake (*Mandragora*) (*Bot.*).

Sprit, *m.* (-s, -e) spirit, alcohol. **–farbe**, *f.* spirit stain. **–ig**, *adj.* alcoholic. **–lack**, *m.* spirit varnish.

Spritz–e, *f.* (-n) syringe, sprayer; (*coll.*) injection; squirt; fire-engine; (*coll.*) trip; *bei der –e sein* or *stehen*, be at one's post; (*coll.*) *erster Mann bei der –e sein*, be cock of the walk. **–apparat**, *m.* spray-gun. **–bad**, *n.* shower-bath, douche. **–bewurf**, *m.* rough-cast, plastering. **–brett**, *n.* dashboard, splash-board. **–düse**, *f.* spraying-nozzle, power jet. **–en**, 1. *v.n.* (*aux.* h. & s.) gush (forth), spurt, splash; splutter (*as a pen*). 2. *v.a.* squirt, syringe, inject; splash, spray, sprinkle, spatter, bespatter; (*coll.*) make an excursion, trip. **–enhaus**, *n.* fire-station. **–enleute**, *pl.* firemen. **–enröhre**, *f.*, **–enschlauch**, *m.* fire-hose. **–er**, *m.* squirter, splasher; syringer; splash, squirt, blob, blot; (*dial.*) shower (*of rain*); (*coll.*) fizzy drink. (*coll.*) **–fahrt**, *f.* flying visit; excursion, trip. **–färbung**, *f.* colour-spraying. **–flasche**, *f.* wash-bottle. **–guß**, *m.* pressure die-casting. **–ig**, *adj.* prickling, fizzy, lively; (*dial.*) impetuous, hot-headed. **–kanne**, (*Swiss dial.*) *f.* watering-can. **–kuchen**, *m.* fritter. **–leder**, *n.* splash-leather (*on carriages*). **–mittel**, *n.* injection (*Med.*). **–nudeln**, *f.pl.* vermicelli. **–pistole**, *f.* spray-gun. **–regen**, *m.* drizzle. **–rohr**, *n.* jet-nozzle. (*coll.*) **–tour**, *f.* trip. **–vergaser**, *m.* spray-carburettor (*Motor.*). **–wand**, *f.* dashboard (*Motor.*). **–wasser**, *n.* spray.

spröd–e, 1. *adj.* brittle, friable, short; hard, inflexible, obstinate; dry, rough, chapped (*of the skin*); coy, prim, reserved, shy, demure; *–er Stoff*, difficult material; *–e tun*, affect shyness, be coy; *–e Tugend*, prim virtue. 2. *f.* (-en) prude. **–igkeit,** *f.* brittleness, friability, hardness, obstinacy, dryness; shyness, demureness, primness, coyness; reserve, coldness.

sproß, sprösse, *see* **sprießen.**

Sproß, *m.* (-(ss)es, -(ss)e) shoot, sprout, spray, sprig; descendant, offspring, scion; tine, branch (*of antlers*); *sein erster –*, his first-born (child). **–(ss)e** *m.* (-en, -en) *see* **Sproß. –en,** *v.n.* (*aux.* h. & s.) sprout, shoot, germinate, bud; spring, come *or* descend from. **–end,** *pr.p.* & *adj.* proliferous. **–enbildung,** *f.* prolification. **–entragend,** *adj.*, **–entreibend,** *adj.* proliferous, prolific. **–enwand,** *f.* wall-bars (*Gymn.*). **–pilz,** *m.* gemmiparous fungus, yeast-fungus. **–silbe,** *f.* excrescent *or* secondary syllable. **–ung,** *f.* germination, budding. **–vokal,** *m.* parasitic vowel.

Sprosse, *f.* (-n) rung (*of ladder*); freckle.

Sprosser, *m.* (-s, –) bastard nightingale (*Luscinia major*) (*Orn.*).

Sprößling, *m.* (-s, -e) sprout, shoot; scion, descendant, offspring.

Sprotte, *f.* (-n) sprat (*Clupea sprattus*) (*Icht.*).

Spruch, *m.* (-(e)s, ⸚e) sentence, decree, judgement, verdict; saying, motto, dictum, aphorism, epigram; passage, text; *Sprüche Salomonis*, Proverbs of Solomon; *zum –e kommen*, come to a decision; *einen – tun* or *fällen*, pass sentence; make an award. **–artig,** *adj.* aphoristic, epigrammatic. **–band,** (⸚er) banderol, scroll (*Arch.*). **–buch,** *n.* book of aphorisms. **–dichter,** *m.* epigrammatic poet. **–dichtung,** *f.* epigrammatic poetry. **–fertig,** *adj.*, *see* **–reif. –haft,** *adj.*, **–mäßig,** *adj.*, *see* **–artig. –reif,** *adj.* ripe for decision; *die S. ist noch nicht –reif*, the matter has not yet been fully investigated, no decision can yet be reached. **–weiser,** *m.* concordance (*to the Bible*). **–weisheit,** *f.* epigrammatic saying *or* truth.

Sprud–el, *m.* (-s, –) bubbling source, spring, well; hot spring; (*coll.*) soda-water; (*fig.*) overflow. **–eln,** (*aux.* s.) bubble, effervesce; (*aux.* h.) bubble *or* boil up, gush, spout; (*fig.*) brim over (with), sparkle (with); *der Witz –elt von seinen Lippen*, he is bubbling over with wit. **–elnd,** *pr.p.* & *adj.* purling, murmuring; *in –elnder Laune*, brimming over with good humour. **–elkopf,** *m.* spitfire, hothead. **–elsalz,** *n.* mineral salt. **–elwasser,** *n.* mineral water. **–ler,** *m.* (*Austr. dial.*) whisk, (egg) beater.

sprüh–en, 1. *v.a.* spray, sprinkle, scatter, spit, emit (*sparks, etc.*). 2. *v.n.* (*aux.* h.) spark, sparkle, scintillate; (*fig.*) flash (*with intellect, etc.*); (*imp.*) shower (*with rain*). **–apparat,** *m.* atomizer. **–elektrode,** *f.* ionizing electrode. **–feuer,** *n.* shower of sparks. **–regen,** *m.* drizzling rain, drizzle, spray. **–teufel,** *m.* squib (*Firew.*).

Sprung, *m.* (-es, ⸚e) crack, fissure, fault, break, discontinuity, split, chink; sheer (*of a deck*); spring, leap, jump, bound, bounce, skip, sudden transition; coition (*of animals*); (*coll.*) short distance, short time; *auf dem – sein zu . . .*, be on the point of . . .; *auf einen – zu dir kommen*, pay you a flying visit, drop in on you (in passing); *einem auf die Sprünge helfen*, help a p. on; *wieder auf seine alten Sprünge kommen*, fall back into one's old ways; *– aus dem Stand*, standing jump; *es ist nur ein – bis dahin*, it is within a stone's throw; *er kann keine großen Sprünge machen*, he cannot go far *or* do much on his income, he cannot afford much; *einem auf die* (or *hinter jemandes*) *Sprünge kommen*, find a p. out; *– ins Ungewisse*, leap in the dark; *Sprünge machen*, frisk, gambol; *mit einem –e*, at a bound; *– mit Anlauf*, running jump, flying leap; *in vollem –e*, at full speed. **–angriff,** *m.* hit-and-run raid (*Av.*). **–bein,** *n.* astragal; saltatorial leg; ankle-bone. **–bildung,** *f.* cracking. **–bock,** *m.* (wooden) horse (*Gymn.*). **–brett,** *n.* spring-board; (*fig.*) stepping-stone. **–feder,** *f.* compression-spring. **–federmatratze,** *f.* spring-mattress. **–geld,** *n.* stud fee. **–gelenk,** *n.* ankle-joint, hock (*of horses*). **–haft,** *adj.* by leaps and bounds; desultory, disconnected, unsteady. **–kasten,** *m.* vaulting-horse (*Gymn.*). **–leine,** *f.* high-jump lath. **–schanze,** *f.* ski-jump. **–schlag,** *m.* half-volley (*Tenn.*). **–stab,** *m.* jumping-pole. **–ständer,** *m.* high-jump stand. **–tuch,** *n.* life-saving *or* jumping sheet. **–turm,** *m.* high-diving board, parachute practice tower. **–weise,** *adv.* by leaps *or* bounds. **–weite,** *f.* length of jump. **–welle,** *f.* tidal wave, bore. **–wellenprobe,** *f.* surge pressure test.

Spuck–e, *f.* (*coll.*) spit, spittle, saliva; (*coll.*) *ihm bleibt die –e weg*, he is dumbfounded *or* flabbergasted; (*Prov.*) *mit Geduld und –e fängt man manche Mucke*, softlee, softlee, catchee monkey. **–en,** *v.a.* & *n.* (*aux.* h.) spit, expectorate. **–napf,** *m.* spittoon.

Spuk, *m.* (-(e)s, -e) (*coll.*) ghost, apparition, spectre, phantom, spook; uproar, mischief; *mach keinen –*, don't make a fuss; *es ist – dabei*, there is something eerie *or* uncanny in that. **–en,** *v.n.* (*aux.* h.) & *imp.* haunt (*a place*); be haunted *or* uncanny; make a row *or* noise; *es –t in diesem Hause*, this house is haunted; *der Wein –t in seinem Kopfe*, the wine has gone to his head; *es –t bei ihm* (*im Kopfe*), he is not quite right in the head. **–geist,** *m.* imp, hobgoblin. **–geschichte,** *f.* ghost-story. **–haft,** *adj.* ghostlike, ghostly, (*coll.*) spooky. **–stunde,** *f.* witching-hour.

Spul–e, *f.* (-en) spool, bobbin; quill; coil (*Elec.*). **–baum,** *m.* spindle-tree. **–eisen,** *n.* bobbin-iron. **–en,** *v.a.* wind, coil, reel; spin. **–engalvanometer,** *m.* & *n.* moving-coil galvanometer. **–er,** *m.* winder; bobbin-winder (*on sewing-machines*). **–maschine,** *f.* bobbin-frame. **–rad,** *n.* spooling-wheel. **–wurm,** *m.* maw-worm.

spül–en, 1. *v.a.* wash, rinse, flush, irrigate; wash (up, away, *etc.*); *die Wogen –ten Trümmer ans Land*, the waves washed up debris on the shore. 2. *v.n.* (*aux.* h.) wash against, lap. **–bad,** *n.* rinsing bath. **–eimer,** *m.* washing-trough. **–faß,** *n.* wash-tub. **–icht,** *n.* dish-water, slops; spent water. **–kammer,** *f.*, **–küche,** *f.* scullery, housemaid's pantry. **–lappen,** *m.* dish-cloth. **–napf,** *m.* slop-basin, rinsing-basin. **–stein,** *m.* sink. **–ung,** *f.* rinsing, washing, flushing. **–wasser,** *n.* washing-up water, slops, dish-water.

Spund, *m.* (-es, ⸚e) bung, plug, stopper, tap; tompion (*Artil.*); bung-hole; feather, tongue (*Carp.*); shutter (*Hydr.*). **–brett,** *n.* tongued board. **–en,** *v.a.*, *see* **spünden. –hobel,** *m.* tonguing- *or* grooving-plane. **–ig,** *adj.*, *see* **spündig. –loch,** *n.* bung-hole. **–messer,** *n.* cooper's hatchet. **–tiefe,** *f.* centre measurement (*of a cask*). **–voll,** *adj.* brimful. **–wand,** *f.* bulkhead, sheet-piling wall (*Hydr.*). **–zapfen,** *m.* bung.

spünd–en, *v.a.* bung; put into casks; tongue and groove (*planks, etc.*). **–ig,** *adj.* doughy, soggy. **–ung,** *f.* bunging; rabbet, rabbeting.

Spur, *f.* (-en) trace, track, footprint, footstep; mark, sign, vestige, remains, clue; gutter, channel, groove, rut (*of a wheel*); wake (*of a ship*); trail, scent; (*coll.*) scrap, bit; *see also* **–weite;** *von der – abbringen*, throw off the scent; *auf die – bringen*, put on the right scent *or* track; *einer S. auf die – kommen*, find a clue to a th., be on the track of a th.; *keine – von*, not the least trace *or* sign, not a bit of, not the faintest notion of, no . . . whatever. **–breite,** *f.*, *see* **–weite. –en,** *v.n.* (*aux.* h.) make a track; follow in the track. **–enhaft, –enweise,** *adv.* sparingly, in traces. **–geschoß,** *n.* tracer (bullet). **–ig,** *adj. suffix*, e.g. *schmal–ig*, narrow-gauge (*Railw.*). **–kranz,** *m.* flange (*of a wheel*). **–los,** *adj.* trackless; without a trace; *–los verschwinden*, disappear without leaving a trace, disappear completely, vanish into thin air. **–weite,** *f.* (width of) track (*of vehicles*); gauge (*of rails*).

spür–en, 1. *v.a.* & *n.* (*aux.* h.) (*nach*) trace, track (down), trail, follow the track of, scent out. 2. *v.a.* perceive, notice, discover, feel, experience, be conscious of. **–er,** *m.*, *see* **–hund. –gang,** *m.* quest of game. **–haar,** *n.* tactile hair, cilium. **–hund,** *m.* bloodhound; pointer; (*fig.*) sleuth, spy. **–nase,** *f.* keen sense of smell, good nose. **–papier,** *n.* gas-detector. **–sinn,** *m.* sagacity, penetration, shrewdness, flair (for).

sputen, *v.r.* make haste, hurry (up).

Staat, *m.* (-(e)s, -en) state, country, government; colony (*of bees, ants, etc.*); (*no pl.*) show, parade, pomp, finery, gala dress; *in vollem –e*, in full dress; *großen – machen*, live in great *or* grand style; *– machen mit*, make a parade of, boast of, show off. **–enbund,** *m.* federal union, confederation. **–engeschichte,** *f.* political history. **–enkunde,** *f.* political geography. **–enlos,** *adj.* without nationality. **–enrecht,** *n.* international law. **–lich,** *adj.* political, national, state; public, civil; *–liche Unterstützung*, state subsidy; *–liche Einrichtung*, public institution. **–sakt,** *m.* state ceremony. **–sakten,** *f.pl.* state-papers, state records. **–saktien,** *f.pl.* government bonds *or* securities. **–saktion,** *f.* government undertaking. **–samt,** *n.* government *or* civil-service appointment, public office. **–sangehörige(r),** *m.* subject, citizen, national. **–sangehörigkeit,** *f.* citizenship, nationality; *–sangehörigkeit erwerben*, become naturalized; *–sangehörigkeit verlieren* or *aufgeben*, become denaturalized; *–sangehörigkeit aberkennen*, deprive of nationality. **–sanleihe,** *f.* government loan. **–sanwalt,** *m.* public prosecutor. **–sanzeiger,** *m.* official gazette. **–sarchiv,** *n.* public-record office. **–saufsicht,** *f.* state control. **–sausgaben,** *f.pl.* public expenditure. **–sbank,** *f.* national bank. **–sbeamte(r),** *m.* civil servant, government official. **–sbehörde,** *f.* government authorities. **–sbürger,** *m.* citizen, subject. **–sbürgerkunde,** *f.* civics, citizenship. **–sbürgerlich,** *adj.* civic, civil; *–sbürgerliche Erziehung*, training in citizenship. **–sdienst,** *m.* civil service. **–seigen,** *adj.* government-owned. **–seigentum,** *n.* government property. **–seinkünfte,** *f.pl.* public revenue. **–sexamen,** *n.* civil-service examination. **–sform,** *f.* form of government. **–sgebäude,** *n.* public building. **–sgefangene(r),** *m.* state-prisoner. **–sgefühl,** *n.* national sentiment. **–sgeheimnis,** *n.* official secret. **–sgerichtshof,** *m.* Supreme Court of Judicature. **–sgesetz,** *n.* law of the land. **–sgewalt,** *f.* supreme *or* executive power. **–sgrundsatz,** *m.* political maxim. **–shandbuch,** *n.* official almanac. **–shaushalt,** *m.* public finance, budget. **–shoheit,** *f.* sovereignty. **–skanzlei,** *f.* chancery. **–skasse,** *f.* public exchequer, treasury. **–skerl,** *m.* (*coll.*) fine fellow. **–skirche,** *f.* established church; *Englische –skirche*, Church of England, Anglican Church. **–skleid,** *n.* gala dress. **–sklug,** *adj.* politic; diplomatic. **–sklugheit,** *f.* political shrewdness; statecraft. **–skörper,** *m.* body politic. **–skosten,** *f.pl.* public expense; *auf –skosten*, at the public expense. **–skredit,** *m.* public credit. **–skunde,** *f.* political science, politics. **–skunst,** *f.* statesmanship, statecraft. **–skutsche,** *f.* state-coach. **–slehre,** *f.* political science. **–smann,** *m.* (*pl.* -smänner) statesman, politician. **–smännisch,** *adj.* statesmanlike. **–smonopol,** *n.* government monopoly. **–soberhaupt,** *n.* head of the state; sovereign. **–sordnung,** *f.* political system. **–spapiere,** *n.pl.* government securities, stocks, consols. **–spolizei,** *f.* state police, political police; *Geheime –spolizei*, (*Nat. Soc.*) Gestapo. **–sprüfung,** *f.* civil-service examination. **–srat,** *m.* council of state; councillor of state; *geheimer –srat*, privy council; privy councillor. **–srecht,** *n.* constitutional law. **–srechtlich,** *adj.* constitutional. **–sruder,** *n.* (*poet.*) helm of the state. **–sschatz,** *m.* exchequer, treasury. **–sschuld,** *f.* national debt; *fundierte –sschuld*, consols, consolidated funds. **–sschuldentilgungskasse,** *f.* sinking-fund. **–sschuldschein,** *m.* government bond. **–ssekretär,** *m.* secretary of state. **–ssiegel,** *n.* official seal; *großes –ssiegel*, Great Seal. **–sstreich,** *m.* coup d'état. **–sverbrechen,** *n.* political crime, sedition. **–sverfassung,** *f.* constitution. **–svertrag,** *m.* international treaty. **–sverwaltung,** *f.* public administration. **–swagen,** *m.* state-coach. **–swesen,** *n.* state *or* public affairs. **–swirtschaft,** *f.* political economy. **–swissenschaft,** *f.* political science. **–swohl,** *n.* common weal. **–szuschuß,** *m.* government subsidy, grant-in-aid.

Stab, *m.* (-(e)s, ⁻e) staff, stick, rod, bar (*of metal*); mace, crosier, baton, (magic) wand, (shepherd's) crook; the staff, headquarters (*Mil.*); *am –e gehen*, walk with the help of a stick; *hinter Stäben*, behind bars; *seinen – weiter setzen*, continue one's journey; *den – über einen brechen*, condemn a p. (to death); *ich stehe nicht unter Ihrem –e*, I am not under your authority *or* jurisdiction. **–antenne,** *f.* dipole (*Rad.*). **–bakterie,** *f.* bacillus. **–eisen,** *n.* wrought iron. **–fußboden,** *m.* parquet floor. **–halter,** *m.*, *see* **–träger.** **–heuschrecke,** *f.* walking-stick insect (*Ent.*). **–hochsprung,** *m.* pole-vault. **–magnet,** *m.* bar-magnet. **–reim,** *m.* alliteration. **–reimend,** *adj.* alliterative. **–sarzt,** *m.* medical officer (*Mil.*); staff-surgeon (*Naut.*). **–sfeldwebel,** *m.* warrant officer, regimental sergeant-major (*Mil.*). **–schef,** *m.* chief of staff (*Mil.*). **–sichtig,** *adj.* astigmatic. **–sichtigkeit,** *f.* astigmatism. **–skompagnie,** *f.* headquarters company (*Mil.*). **–soffizier,** *m.* field-officer. **–springen,** *v.n.* & *subst. n.* pole-vault(ing). **–squartier,** *n.* headquarters. **–swache,** *f.*, *see* **–skompagnie.** **–swagen,** *m.* staff car (*Mil.*). **–tierchen,** *n.* bacillus. **–träger,** *m.* mace-bearer, beadle, sergeant-at-arms.

Stäb-chen, *n.* (-s, –) rod; bacillus; long stitch (*crochet*); (*coll.*) fag. **–chensteif,** *adj.* stiff as a poker. **–eln,** *v.a.* stake (*peas, etc.*).

Stabelle, *f.* (*Swiss dial.*) wooden stool *or* chair.

stabil, *adj.* stable, steady, solid, rugged. **–isieren,** *v.a.* stabilize. **–ität,** *f.* stability, equilibrium. **–isierungsfläche,** *f.*, **–isierungsflosse,** *f.* stabilizer (*Av.*).

stach, stäche, *see* **stechen.**

Stachel, *m.* (-s, -n) thorn, prickle, prick, sting; spine, quill, spike, prong, goad; (*fig.*) sting, spur, stimulus; *ein – im Auge sein*, be a thorn in the flesh; (*B.*) *wider den – lecken* (or *löcken*), kick against the pricks. **–beere,** *f.* gooseberry (*Ribes grossularia*) (*Bot.*). **–beerspanner,** *m.* magpie-moth (*Abraxus grossulariata*) (*Ent.*). **–draht,** *m.* barbed wire. **–flosse,** *f.* spinous dorsal fin. **–flosser,** *m.pl.* acanthopterygians (*Icht.*). **–früchtig,** *adj.* acanthocarpus (*Bot.*). **–halsband,** *n.* spiked dog-collar. **–häuter,** *m.pl.* echinodermata (*Zool.*). **–ig,** *adj.* prickly, thorny, spinous, bristly; stinging, biting, poignant. **–los,** *adj.* without thorns *or* prickles; stingless. **–n,** *v.a.* prick, sting; (*fig.*) stimulate, spur on, prod, goad; *ihn –t Ehrgeiz*, ambition spurs him on. **–raupe,** *f.* prickly caterpillar. **–rede,** *f.* satirical, stinging speech; (*pl.*) sharp words. **–roche,** *m.* thorn-back (*Icht.*). **–schwein,** *n.* porcupine (*Hystrix*) (*Zool.*). **–stock,** *m.* prod, goad. **–zaun,** *m.* barbed-wire fence.

stachlicht, *adj.*, *see* **stachelig.**

Stadel, *m.* (-s, –) (*dial.*) stall, barn, shed.

Staden, *m.* (-s, –) (*dial.*) river-side walk.

Stadi-on, *n.* (-ons, -en) stadium, arena (*Sport.*). **–um,** *n.* (-ums, -en) phase, state, stage (*of development*).

Stadt, *f.* (⁻e) town, city; *die Ewige –*, the Eternal City (*Rome*); *die Heilige –*, the Holy City (*Jerusalem*); *in der – aufgewachsen*, town-bred; *das weiß die ganze –*, that is all over the town. **–adel,** *m.* patricians. **–amt,** *n.* municipal office. **–bahn,** *f.* metropolitan railway. **–bau,** *m.* (-s, -ten) municipal building. **–baukunst,** *f.* town-planning. **–bauplan,** *m.* town-plan. **–behörde,** *f.* municipal authorities. **–bekannt,** *adj.* generally known, notorious; *die Geschichte ist –bekannt*, the story is the talk of the town. **–bewohner,** *m.* townsman. **–bezirk,** *m.* ward, district. **–bild,** *n.* general aspect *or* character of a town. **–brief,** *m.* local letter. **–bürgerrecht,** *n.* civic rights. **–gegend,** *f.*, *see* **–bezirk.** **–gemeinde,** *f.* urban community; municipality. **–gerichtsbarkeit,** *f.* municipal jurisdiction **–gespräch,** *n.* talk of the town; local call (*Phone*). **–graben,** *m.* town-moat. **–haus,** *n.* town-hall, guildhall. **–kern,** *m.* city centre. **–kind,** *n.* town *or* urban dweller, townsman. **–klatsch,** *m.* talk of the town. **–koffer,** *m.* attaché-case. **–kommandant,** *m.* town major (*Mil.*). **–kreis,** *m.* urban district. **–kundig,** *adj.* well acquainted with the town; well known in the town. **–leute,** *pl.* townspeople, townsfolk. **–mauer,** *f.* town wall. **–miliz,** *f.* civic guard. **–neuigkeit,** *f.* local news. **–post,** *f.* local post, local delivery. **–randsiedlung,** *f.* (suburban) housing estate. **–rat,** *m.* town-council; alderman. **–recht,** *n.* municipal law(s); civic rights. **–richter,** *m.* recorder. **–schreiber,** *m.* (*archaic*) town-clerk. **–schule,** *f.* municipal school. **-schulkommission,** *f.* local education committee. **-schulrat,** *m.* local school inspector. **-steuer,** *f.* municipal rates. **-teil,** *m., see* **-bezirk.** **-tor,** *n.* town gate. **-väter,** *m.pl.* city-fathers. **-verordnete(r),** *m.* town-councillor. **-verwaltung,** *f.* municipal government. **-viertel,** *m., see* **-bezirk.** **-wappen,** *n.* municipal arms. **-wohnung,** *f.* town residence.

Städt-ebau, *m.* town-planning. **-ebund,** *m.* league of cities. **-eordnung,** *f.* municipal statutes. **-er,** *m.* (-s, -) town dweller, townsman; (*pl.*) townspeople. **-erin,** *f.* townswoman. **-ewesen,** *n.* civic *or* municipal concerns. **-isch,** *adj.* municipal; urban; *-ischer Beamter*, city *or* civic official; *-ische Schule*, municipal school.

Stafel, *m.* (-s, ¨-) (*Swiss dial.*) Alpine pasture.

Stafette, *f.* (-n) courier, express messenger, dispatch rider. **-nlauf,** *m.* relay race.

Staff-age, *f.* (-n) figures in a landscape, accessories (*Paint.*); decoration, ornamental details. **-ieren,** *v.a.* garnish, dress, trim, decorate; furnish, equip. **-ierer,** *m.* trimmer, dresser; decorator. **-iermalerei,** *f.* decorative painting. **-iernaht,** *f.* garnish-seam.

Staffel, *f.* (-n) rung (*of a ladder*); step (*of a gable, etc.*); (*fig.*) step, stage, degree; relay, lap (*of a race*); echelon, detachment (*Mil.*); squadron (*Av.*). **-ei,** *f.* easel (*Paint.*). **-förmig,** *adj.* in steps; in echelon. **-lauf,** *m.* relay race. **-n,** *v.a.* & *r.* graduate, differentiate; raise in steps, stagger. **-tarif,** *m.* sliding tariff. **-ung,** *f.* gradation, graduation, echelon formation. **-weise,** *adv.* in echelon.

Stag, *n.* (-(e)s, -e(n)) stay (*Naut.*). **-fock,** *f.*, **-segel,** *n.* staysail.

stagnieren, *v.n.* (*aux.* h.) stagnate.

Stahl, *m.* (-s, ¨e & (*Austr. dial.*) -e) steel; (*Poet.*) sword, dagger; steel instrument; heater-bolt (*of a flat iron*). **-bad,** *n.* chalybeate bath *or* spa. **-bandaufnahme,** *f.* steel-tape recording. **-bandmaß,** *n.* steel tape-measure. **-bau,** *m.* steel-girder construction. **-beton,** *n.* ferro-concrete. **-blau,** *adj.* & *n.* steel(y) blue. **-blech,** *n.* sheet-steel. **-brunnen,** *m.* chalybeate spring. **-feder,** *f.* pen-nib; steel spring. **-frischen,** *n.* steel-fining (process). **-gewinnung,** *f.* production of steel. **-guß,** *m.* cast-steel. **-haltig,** *adj.* containing steel, chalybeate. **-hart,** *adj.* (as) hard as steel. **-härtung,** *f.* tempering of steel. **-helm,** *m.* steel helmet; (former) German Association of ex-servicemen (*cf.* British Legion). **-hütte,** *f., see* **-werk.** **-kammer,** *f.* strong-room. **-kassette,** *f.* strong-box. **-kerngeschoß,** *n.* armour-piercing shell. **-panzerung,** *f.* armour-plating. **-quelle,** *f.* chalybeate spring. (*hum.*) **-roß,** *n.* bicycle. **-stecher,** *m.* steel-engraver. **-stich,** *m.* steel-engraving. **-waren,** *f.pl.* cutlery, hardware. **-wasser,** *n.* chalybeate water. **-werk,** *n.* steel-works.

stahl, *see* **stehlen.**

stähl-en, *v.a.* convert into steel; (*fig.*) harden, steel (*the courage, one's heart*). **-ern,** *adj.* steel, steely. **-ung,** *f.* steeling; tempering.

stak, *see* **stecken.**

Stak-e, *f.* (-en), **-en,** *m.* (-s, -) (*dial.*) stake; boathook, pole; wicker-fence; sheaf, stook (*of corn*). **-elig,** *adj.* (*dial.*) stiff, wooden. **-en,** 1. *v.a.* (*aux.* h.) (*dial.*) punt, pole (*a boat*); turn (*sheaves*) with a fork. 2. *v.n.* (*dial.*) walk stiffly. **-et,** *n.* (-s, -e) palisade, fence, rail, railing. **-sig,** *adj.* (*dial.*), *see* **-elig.**

Stall, *m.* (-es, ¨e) stall, stable, sty, kennel. **-dienst,** *m.* stable-work, stable-duty. **-feind,** *m.* (*Swiss dial.*) foot-and-mouth disease. **-fütterung,** *f.* stall-feeding. **-en,** *v.n.* (*aux.* h.) be in a stall *or* stable; urinate (*of animals*); (*dial.*) clean out a stable, *etc.* **-geld,** *n.* stallage; stabling-money. **-hase,** *m.* domestic rabbit. **-hengst,** *m.* stallion. **-junge,** *m.*, **-knecht,** *m.* stable-hand *or* boy, ostler, groom. **-(l)eine,** *f.* picket-line (*Mil.*). **-magd,** *f.* dairy-maid. **-meister,** *m.* equerry, master of the horse; riding-master. **-miete,** *f., see* **-geld.** **-ung,** *f.* stabling, stables, (*pl.*) mews.

Stamm, *m.* (-es, ¨e) stem, trunk, bole; family, clan, tribe, race, stock, breed, strain; stem, root (*of words*); cadre, main body (*of an army, customers, etc.*); *Holz auf dem -e kaufen*, buy standing timber; *einen - Kegel schieben*, play a game of skittles; *die zwölf Stämme*, the twelve tribes; *von königlichem -e*, of royal blood; *- von Kunden*, regular customers; (*Prov.*) *der Apfel fällt nicht weit vom -*, like father, like son. **-aktie,** *f.* original share, founder's share. **-baum,** *m.* genealogical *or* family tree, pedigree. **-besatzung,** *f.* skeleton crew. **-buch,** *n.* album; *sich in ein -buch einschreiben*, write *or* put s.th. in an album. **-burg,** *f.* ancestral castle, family seat. **-eltern,** *pl.* progenitors, first parents. **-en,** *v.n.* (*aux.* s.) be descended, be derived, spring, originate (*aus.* from); *er -t vom Rhein*, he comes from *or* his home is on the Rhine. **-ende,** *n.* stump (*of a tree*). **-erbe,** *m.* lineal descendant. **-eseigenheit,** *f.* racial peculiarity. **-esgeschichte,** *f.* phylogeny. **-eszugehörigkeit,** *f.* inclusion in a race. **-folge,** *f.* line of descent. **-form,** *f.* primitive form (*of a word*); (*pl.*) principal parts (*of a verb*). **-gast,** *m.* regular (guest) (*at an inn, etc.*), regular customer. **-gut,** *n.* family estate. **-haft,** 1. *adj.* radical; racial, tribal. 2. *adv.* in race. **-halter,** *m.* eldest son of the family, son and heir. **-haus,** *n.* ancestral home. **-holz,** *n.* standing timber. **-kapital,** *n.* stock fund. **-kneipe,** *f.* restaurant which a p. frequents regularly, favourite pub. **-kundschaft,** *f.* clientele. **-land,** *n.* mother country. **-lehen,** *n.* family fief, fee-simple. **-leitung,** *f.* trunk line (*Tele.*). **-linie,** *f.* line, lineage. **-lokal,** *n., see* **-kneipe.** **-lösung,** *f.* standard *or* stock solution. **-(m)annschaft,** *f.* cadre, nucleus. **-(m)utter,** *f.* ancestress. **-personal,** *n.* cadre (*Mil.*). **-register,** *n., see* **-baum.** **-rolle,** *f.* nominal roll (*Mil.*). **-silbe,** *f.* radical *or* root syllable. **-sitz,** *m.* ancestral seat. **-tafel,** *f.* genealogical table. **-tisch,** *m.* table reserved for regular customers; regular circle of cronies. **-vater,** *m.* progenitor, ancestor. **-vermächtnis,** *n.* entail. **-vermögen,** *n.* capital. **-verwandt,** *adj.* kindred, cognate. **-verwandtschaft,** *f.* similarity in origin, kinship, affinity. **-vokal,** *m.* root vowel. **-volk,** *n.* aborigines, primitive race; ancestral stock. **-wappen,** *n.pl.* family arms. **-werft,** *f.* parent-yard (*Shipbuilding*). **-wort,** *n.* root-word, stem. **-zeiten,** *f.pl.* principal parts (*Gram.*). **-zuchtbuch,** *n.* herd-book.

stamm-eln, *v.a.* & *n.* (*aux.* h.) stammer, stutter. **-ler,** *m.* stammerer.

stämm-ig, *adj.* full-grown; strong, sturdy, vigorous. **-igkeit,** *f.* strength, sturdiness, robustness.

Stampe, *f.* (*dial.*) tavern. **-rl,** *n.* (*dial.*) small wine- *or* spirits-glass.

Stampf-e, *f.* (-n) stamping, pounding; stamp, pestle, beetle, beater, rammer. **-en,** 1. *v.n.* stamp, trample, trudge; paw (the ground) (*of horses*); pitch (*of ships*). 2. *v.a.* pound, crush, stamp, beat, tamp, mash (*potatoes*), bruise (*corn*), express (*oil*); (*fig.*) *aus dem Boden -en*, conjure up, produce by magic. **-er,** *m.* stamper, pounder, rammer, pestle; pawing *or* stamping horse; pitching ship. **-beton,** *n.* tamped concrete. **-kartoffeln,** *f.pl.* mashed potatoes. **-klotz,** *m.* pile-driver, rammer. **-mühle,** *f.*, **-werk,** *n.* crushing-mill, stamping-mill.

Stampiglie, *f.* (-n) (*Austr. dial.*) stamp, seal.

Stand, *m.* (-es, ¨e) standing *or* upright position, situation, position, station; standing, state, condition; strength (*of army, etc.*); class, rank (*in society*); place to stand, footing; stand, stall, pitch, booth, (*pl.*) estates of the realm; *er ist seines -es Advokat*, he is a lawyer by profession; *- der Aktien*, value of shares; *außer -e, see* **außerstande;** *ehelicher -*, married state; *seinen - einnehmen*, take up one's stand; *geistlicher -*, clergy; *gelehrte Stände*, the learned professions; *einen guten - bei einem haben*, be well thought of by a p.; *ich habe hier keinen guten -*, I am not well placed here; *gut im -e sein*, be in good health *or* in good condition; *mit jemandem einen harten - haben*, have a great deal of trouble with a p.; *im -e, see* **imstande;** *in - setzen, see* **instandsetzen;** *Leute von -e*, men of rank (*or* quality); *von niederem -e*, of low degree; *einen schweren - haben*, be in a difficult position, be badly placed, be awkwardly situated, have very limited opportunities, have a hard fight *or* (*coll.*) tough job; *einen in den – setzen, etwas zu tun*, enable a p. to do a th.; *in –*, see **instand;** *in den vorigen – setzen*, restore to a former condition; *Sprung aus dem –*, standing jump; *– der Sterne*, position of the stars; *– des Wassers*, level of water; *weltlicher –*, laity. **–bein,** *n.* supporting leg (*Sculp.*). **–bild,** *n.* statue. **–e,** *f.* (*dial.*) vat, butt. **–esamt,** *n.* registry office. **–esamtlich,** *adj.*; *–esamtliche Trauung*, civil marriage. **–esbeamte(r),** *m.* registrar of births, marriages, and deaths. **–esdünkel,** *m.* pride of place. **–esehe,** *f.* marriage for position *or* rank. **–esehre,** *f.* professional honour. **–esgebühr,** *f.*; *nach –esgebühr*, with due honour, according to one's rank. **–esgemäß,** *adj.* in accordance with *or* appropriate to one's class *or* rank. **–esgenosse,** *m.* equal in station, compeer; *meine –esgenossen*, people of my own class. **–esherr,** *m.* nobleman, peer, lord. **–esinteresse,** *n.* class-interest. **–esmäßig,** *adj.*, see **–esgemäß.** **–esperson,** *f.* person of quality. **–esregister,** *n.* registrar general's returns. **–esrücksichten,** *f.pl.* considerations of rank. **–esunterschied,** *m.* difference of rank; class distinction. **–esvorurteil,** *n.* class prejudice. **–eswidrig,** *adj.* derogatory to one's rank. **–eswürde,** *f.* dignity of rank *or* position. **–eswürdig,** *adj.* worthy of *or* appropriate to one's rank *or* position. **–fest,** *adj.* firmly placed, steady, firm, stable, steadfast. **–geld,** *n.* stall-rent, stallage. **–gericht,** *n.* summary court of justice; drum-head court-martial. **–glas,** *n.* glass gauge. **–haft,** *adj.* steady, constant, firm, steadfast, unflinching, resolute. **–haftigkeit,** *f.* steadfastness, constancy; resoluteness, firmness. **–halten,** *v.n.* (*Dat.*) withstand, resist, hold one's own (against), stand firm, be steadfast, hold out. **–lager,** *n.*, see **–quartier.** **–licht,** *n.* parking lights (*Motor.*). **–motor,** *m.* stationary engine. **–ort,** *m.* site, location, permanent quarters, station, garrison (*Mil.*), habitat. **–ortälteste(r),** *m.* garrison commander. (*coll.*) **–pauke,** *f.* severe reprimand, (*coll.*) dressing down, telling off. **–platz,** *m.* stand, rank (*for taxis, etc.*). **–punkt,** *m.* point of view, standpoint, viewpoint; *überwundener –punkt*, out-of-date view, exploded notion; *den –punkt vertreten* or *sich auf den –punkt stellen* or *auf dem –punkt stehen*, be of the opinion, hold the view; *einem den –punkt klarmachen*, give a p. a piece of one's mind. **–quartier,** *n.* fixed quarters, base (for operations), base-camp. **–recht,** *n.* summary jurisdiction, martial law. **–rechtlich,** *adj.* summary, according to martial law. **–rede,** *f.*, see **–pauke.** **–rohr,** *n.* stand-pipe. **–scheibe,** *f.* fixed target. **–uhr,** *f.* pendulum-clock, upright clock. **–vogel,** *m.* resident (bird). **–wild,** *n.* game frequenting the same habitat.

stand, stände, see **stehen.**

Standard, *m.* (-s, -s) standard, norm; pattern, sample. **–isieren,** *v.a.* standardize.

Standarte, *f.* (-n) standard, banner; (*Nat. Soc.*) unit *or* regiment (*of S.A. & S.S.*); brush (*of a fox, etc.*).

Ständ–chen, *n.* (-s, –) serenade; *einem ein –chen bringen*, serenade a p. **–e,** see **Stand** (*pl.*). **–er,** *m.* (-s, –) stand; desk for standing at; pillar, post, pedestal, upright; stator (*of dynamo*); (*dial.*) see **Stande.** **–erat,** *m.* (*Swiss dial.*) body representing cantons in federal government. **–estaat,** *m.* corporate state. **–eversammlung,** *f.* assembly of the estates, diet. **–ig,** *adj.* fixed, permanent, established, stationary, constant; *–ige Anstellung*, permanent *or* life appointment; *–iger Begleiter*, constant companion; *–iges Einkommen*, regular income; *–iger Sitz*, permanent seat (*e.g. on a committee*); *–ige Wohnung*, permanent residence. **–isch,** *adj.* belonging to the estates (*of a realm*).

Stander, *m.* (-s, –) pennant (*Naut.*).

Stange, *f.* (-n) pole, post, shaft, perch, stake, stick, staff; bar, rod, ingot (*of iron, etc.*); bridle-bit; *einem die – halten*, take a p.'s part, give a p. a helping hand; *bei der – bleiben*, persevere, stick to it *or* the point; *einen bei der – halten*, not let a p. digress, keep a p. to the point; *einen Anzug von der – kaufen*, buy a suit ready-made *or* off the hook; (*coll.*) *eine – Geld*, amint of money. **–nbesen,** *m.* long-handled broom. **–nbohne,** *f.* runner-bean. **–neisen,** *n.* bar iron, rod iron; trap (*for foxes, etc.*). **–nförmig,** *adj.* rod- *or* bar-shaped. **–ngebiß,** *n.* bridle-bit. **–ngold,** *n.* gold ingots. **–nholz,** *n.* paling; young timber. **–nlack,** *m.* stick of sealing-wax. **–npferd,** *n.* wheeler, pole-horse. **–nreiter,** *m.* wheel-horse rider; wheel-driver. **–nseife,** *f.* soap in bars. **–nsellerie,** *m.* sticks of celery. **–nspargel,** *m.* sticks of asparagus. **–ntabak,** *m.* twist. **–nzaun,** *m.* rail fence.

Stank, *m.* (*dial.*) stench, stink, (*coll.*) dissension, discord.

stank, stänke, see **stinken.**

Stänk–er, *m.* (-s, –) stinker, stinking p. *or* th.; (*coll.*) quarrelsome person, trouble-maker, mischief-maker; nosy-parker. **–erei,** *f.* stink, offensive smell; wrangling, mischief-making, unpleasantness, squabble; prying. **–(e)rer,** *m.*, see **–er.** **–(e)rig,** *adj.* stinking, offensive. **–ern,** *v.n.* (*aux.* h.) have an offensive smell, smell, stink; make trouble, wrangle, make a nuisance of o.s.; pry, rummage (around *or* about).

Stanniol, *n.* (-s, -e) tinfoil, silver paper.

Stanz–e, *f.* (-en) eight-lined stanza; metal stamp, die, punch, matrix, stamping machine, press. **–en,** *v.a.* stamp, punch.

Stapel, *m.* (-s, –) pile, stack, heap; stocks (*shipbuilding*); marketing centre, mart; depot, storehouse; staple (*cotton*); *vom – laufen*, be launched; *vom* or *von – lassen*, launch, (*fig. coll.*) bring out, publish, hold (*a speech*). **–faser,** *f.* artificial silk fibre, rayon. **–holz,** *n.* stacked wood. **–lauf,** *m.* launching. **–n.** 1. *v.a.* pile up, stack, accumulate, store. 2. *v.n.* (*aux.* s.) (*coll.*) stride, stalk, strut. **–platz,** *m.* depot, dump; staple market, trading centre; yard (*Shipb.*).

Stapf, *m.* (-en, -en), **–e,** *f.* (-n) (*Austr. dial.*), **–en,** *m.* (-ens, -en) (*archaic*) footstep. **–en,** *v.n.* (*aux.* h. & s.) trudge, plod.

[1]**Star,** *m.* (-(e)s & -en, -e & -en) starling. **–(en)kasten,** *m.* nesting box (*for starlings*). **–matz,** *m.* (*nursery talk*) starling.

[2]**Star,** 1. *m.* (-(e)s, -e) (*grauer –*) cataract; *grüner –*, glaucoma; *schwarzer –*, amaurosis; (*einem*) *den – stechen*, operate (on a p.) for cataract; (*fig.*) open s.o.'s eyes. 2. *m.* (-s, -s) star (performer), (film) star. **–blind,** *adj.* blind from a cataract. **–operation,** *f.*, **–stechen,** *n.* operation for cataract.

Stär, *m.* (-(e)s, -e) ram.

starb, see **sterben.**

stark, *adj.* (*comp.* stärker, *sup.* stärkst) strong, robust, vigorous; numerous, considerable, voluminous; thick, thickset, stout, portly; intense, violent, severe, heavy (*rain, etc.*), hearty (*as an appetite, etc.*); forte (*Mus.*); *–e Beugung*, strong *or* irregular conjugation; *–e Erkältung*, bad *or* heavy cold; *–er Esser*, hearty eater; *–es Fieber*, high fever; *–er Frost*, hard frost; *–es Gedächtnis*, good memory; *–er Geist*, powerful mind; *das –e Geschlecht*, the stronger sex; *der –e Gott*, the mighty God; *–er Hirsch*, warrantable stag; *–e Kälte*, severe *or* intense cold; *–e Leidenschaften*, violent emotions; *eine –e Meile*, rather more than a mile; *–e Nachfrage*, good demand (*for goods*), (*coll.*) heavy run (on); *–er Regen*, heavy rain; *–er Schachspieler*, good chess-player; *ein –es Stück*, a bold deed, a daring enterprise; (*coll.*) *das ist –er Tabak*, that is vulgar *or* rather near the knuckle; *–e Zeitwörter*, strong *or* irregular verbs; *stärkere Damen*, stout(ish) ladies; *stärker werden*, put on weight *or* flesh; *wie – ist Ihre Familie?* how large is your family? *– auftragen*, boast, exaggerate, (*sl.*) pile it on thick; *man spricht – davon*, it is much talked of; *der Stärkste hat Recht*, might is *or* goes before right; *das ist etwas –! das ist aber (zu) –!* that is the limit, that is a bit thick, that is rather too much! that's too bad! *in –en Tagemärschen*, by forced marches; *darin ist er –*, he is great at that; (*C.L.*) *– gesucht*, in great demand; (*Prov.*) *Einigkeit macht –*, union is strength. **–beleibt,** *adj.* corpulent, stout. **–besetzt,** *adj.* well-attended, crowded. **–gläubig,** *adj.* staunch in faith. **–gliederig,** *adj.* strong-limbed. **–knochig,** *adj.* big-boned. **–leibig,** *adj.* corpulent, stout. **–strom,** *m.* power current (*Elec.*). **–stromleitung,** *f.* power-circuit, high-voltage circuit. **-stromtechnik,** *f.* power-engineering, high-voltage technique.

Stärk-e, *f.* strength, vigour, sturdiness; intensity, violence, stress, energy, force, power; stoutness, corpulence; magnitude, greatness, large number; (*fig.*) strong point, forte; starch. **-efabrik,** *f.* starch-factory. **-egrad,** *m.* degree of strength, intensity. **-ehaltig,** *adj.* containing starch, starchy, amylaceous. **-ekleister,** *m.* starch-paste. **-emehl,** *n.* starch-flour. **-en,** 1. *v.a.* strengthen, fortify, brace, invigorate; corroborate, confirm; starch. 2. *v.r.* take refreshment; (*hum.*) have a quick one. **-ezucker,** *m.* glucose. **-ung,** *f.* strengthening, fortifying, bracing, invigoration; refreshment, tonic; support, corroboration; starching. **-ungsmittel,** *n.* restorative, tonic.

starr, *adj.* stiff, motionless, rigid, benumbed; fixed, staring (*of eyes*); inflexible, obstinate, unbending, stubborn; – *vor Erstaunen*, dumbfounded, transfixed with amazement; – *ansehen*, look at fixedly, stare at. **-äugig,** *adj.* staring, gazing fixedly. **-decker,** *m.* limousine. **-e,** *f.*, *see* **-heit. -en,** *v.n.* (*aux.* h.) stare, look fixedly (*auf*, at); stiffen, be benumbed *or* rigid; stand out, tower up, project; bristle, stand on end; *die Finger -en mir vor Kälte*, my fingers are numb with cold; *von Bajonetten -en*, bristle with bayonets; *seine Hände -en vor Schmutz*, his hands are caked with mud. **-heit,** *f.* stiffness, rigidity, rigor, numbness; inflexibility, obstinacy. **-kopf,** *m.* stubborn person, (*fig.*) mule. **-köpfig,** *adj.* stubborn, obstinate, intractable, (*coll.*) mulish, pig-headed. **-köpfigkeit,** *f.* obstinacy, stubbornness, contumacy, (*coll.*) pig-headednes. **-krampf,** *m.* tetanus, lockjaw. **-sinn,** *m.* obstinacy, inflexibility, obduracy, doggedness, self-will. **-sucht,** *f.* catalepsy.

Start, *m.* (-(e)s, -e & -s) start (*Sport.*); take-off (*Av.*). **-bahn,** *f.* runway (*Av.*). **-en,** *v.n.* start. **-erklappe,** *f.* choke (*Motor.*). **-klar,** *adj.* ready to take off (*Av.*). **-platz,** *m.* start (*Sport*). **-zeichen,** *n.* starting signal.

statarisch, *adj.* standing, progressing slowly; *-e Lektüre*, careful and slow reading.

Stat-ik, *f.* statics. **-isch,** *adj.* static.

Station, *f.* (-en) station, stop; ward (*of hospital*); *freie – haben*, have board and lodging free *or* found; – *machen*, make a halt, break one's journey; *die -en des Kreuzwegs*, the stations of the cross; *wetterkundische –*, weather-station, observatory. **-är,** *adj.* stationary. **-ieren,** *v.a.* station. **-sarzt,** *m.* house physician, resident physician. **-svorsteher,** *m.* station-master.

stätisch, *adj.* restive (*of horses*).

Statist, *m.* (-en, -en) extra, supernumerary, walker-on (*Theat.*).

Statist-ik, *f.* (-en) statistics. **-iker,** *m.* statistician. **-isch,** *adj.* statistical.

Stativ, *n.* (-s, -e) tripod, stand, foot, base, support.

Statt, 1. *f.* (⸚e) place, stead, lieu; *bleibende –*, fixed abode; *an Vaters –*, in the place of a father; *an Kindes – annehmen*, adopt (*a child*); *an Eides –*, in lieu of oath. 2. *prep.* (*Gen.*) (*dial. also dat.*) instead of, in lieu of, in the place of; – *meiner*, instead of me in my place; – *dessen*, in place of that; – *rechts ging er links*, he went to the left instead of to the right; *mit Güte – mit Strenge*, with gentleness instead of with severity; – *mitzuhelfen ging er nach Hause*, he went home instead of helping us; *see also* **anstatt;** *see* **von-en;** *see* **zu-en. -finden,** *ir.v.n.* (*aux.* h.) (*sep.*) (*often imp.*) take place, happen, occur, (*coll.*) come off; *eine Bitte -finden lassen*, grant a request. (*archaic*) **-geben,** *ir.v.n.* (*aux.* h.) (*sep.*) allow, permit, accept, grant (*einem Gesuch*, a request); allow for, bear in mind; *gebt nie dem tollen Wahn des Pöbels –*, never be swayed by the madness of the crowd. **-haben,** *see* **-finden. -haft,** *adj.* admissible, allowable, permissible, valid, legal, legitimate. **-haftigkeit,** *f.* admissibility; validity. **-halter,** *m.* representative, governor. **-halterei,** *f.* **-halterschaft,** *f.* governorship. **-lich,** *adj.* stately, imposing, fine, splendid, majestic, magnificent, grand; solemn, distinguished, commanding; portly. **-lichkeit,** *f.* elegance; magnificence, dignity, stateliness; portliness.

Stätte, *f.* (-n) place, abode; (work)room; *bleibende –* (*poet.*), home, abode.

Statu-e, *f.* (-n) statue; (*pl.*) statuary. **-arisch,** *adj.* statuesque.

stat-uieren, *v.a.* decree, affirm, lay down, establish, ordain, enact; *ein Exempel -uieren*, serve as an example, be a warning. **-ur,** *f.* figure, height, stature. **-us,** *m.* state, amount; (*C.L.*) statement; *die Dinge im -us quo belassen*, leave things as they are; *-us quo ante*, as things were. **-ut,** *n.* (-(e)s, -en) regulation, statute; (*pl.*) articles (of association). **-utarisch, -utenmäßig,** *adj.* statutory, legal.

Stau, *m.* (-(e)s, -e) slack water; *im –*, at the turn of the tide. **-en,** 1. *v.a.* stow (away) (*goods*); dam (up) (*water*). 2. *v.r.* & *n.* be congested, choked *or* obstructed; *das Wasser -t sich*, the water is rising; *der Verkehr -t sich*, there is a traffic jam. **-anlage,** *f.* barrage, dam, reservoir. **-becken,** *n.* reservoir, static-water tank. **-damm,** *m.* dam, dike. **-er,** *m.* stevedore. **-höhe,** *f.* overflow level. **-rohr,** *n.* pressure jet *or* nozzle. **-see,** *m.* reservoir. **-ung,** *f.* stowage, stowing; damming up; backwater; stoppage, obstruction, congestion, block, bottleneck. **-wasser,** *n.* backwater; static water. **-wehr,** *n.* weir. **-werk,** *n.* lock; barrage.

Staub, *m.* dust; powder; pollen; – *aufwirbeln*, (*fig.*) cause a flutter, create a disturbance; *sich aus dem -e machen*, abscond, decamp, make off, (*coll.*) do a bolt; *in den – stürzen, treten* or *werfen*, humble, humiliate; *in den – zerren* or *ziehen*, depreciate, degrade, drag through the mire; *den – löschen*, lay the dust. **-bach,** *m.* waterfall falling in spray. **-bedeckt,** *adj.* dusty, thick with dust. **-besen,** *m.* dust-broom, soft-broom. **-beutel,** *m.* anther (*Bot.*). **-beuteltragend,** *adj.* antheriferous. **-blätter,** *n.pl.* stamens (*Bot.*). **-blüte,** *f.* male flower. **-brand,** *m.* loose smut. **-dicht,** *adj.* dust-proof. **-en,** *v.n.* (*aux.* h.) rise like dust, make a dust; fall in spray; (*as v. imp.*) be dusty. **-faden,** *m.* filament (*of stamens*) (*Bot.*). **-fadenlos,** *adj.* anandrous (*Bot.*). **-fein,** *adj.* fine as dust. **-frei,** *adj.* free from dust. **-geboren,** *adj.* earth-born (*B.*). **-gefäß,** *n.* stamen. **-gehalt,** *m.* pollution (*of atmosphere*). **-ig,** *adj.* dusty, powdery. **-igkeit,** *f.* dustiness. **-kamm,** *m.* small-tooth comb, dust comb. **-kittel,** *m.* smock. **-kohle,** *f.* coal dust, slack. **-korn,** *n.* dust particle. **-lappen,** *m.* duster. **-lawine,** *f.* avalanche of dry snow. **-mantel,** *m.* overall, smock. **-regen,** *m.* fine rain, drizzle, spray. **-same,** *m.* pollen. **-sand,** *m.* very fine sand. **-sauger,** *m.* vacuum-cleaner. **-trocken,** *adj.* bone-dry. **-tuch,** *n.* duster. **-wedel,** *m.* feather duster. **-wolke,** *f.* cloud of dust, dust cloud. **-zucker,** *m.* powdered sugar.

Stäub-chen, *n.* tiny particle, mote. **-en,** 1. *v.n.*, *see* **stauben.** 2. *v.a.* powder, strew with dust; (*usually with prefix* ab-, aus-, *etc.*) dust, do the dusting. **-er,** *m.* (*rare*) duster. **-ling,** *m.* puff-ball.

Stauche, *f.* (-n) *or* *m.* (-ns, -n) thrust, blow; bundle (*of flax*); (*coll.*) muff, mitten. **-n,** *v.a.* bundle (*flax*); upset, compress, shorten by forging; (*coll.*) wrench, jolt, jog; (*sl.*) swipe, pinch. **-r,** *m.* (*coll.*) violent blow; violent exertion; dressing down.

Staud-e, *f.* (-en) shrub, bush; perennial plant; head (*of lettuce, etc.*). **-en,** *v.r.* & *n.* (*aux.* h. & s.) grow bushy, form a head (*as lettuce*). **-enartig,** *adj.*, *see* **-ig. -engewächs,** *n.* shrub. **-ensalat,** *m.* green salad. **-ig,** *adj.* bushy, shrub-like.

Stauf, *m.* (-(e)s, -e) (*dial.*) tankard, beaker.

staunen, 1. *v.n.* (*aux.* h.) be astonished, surprised *or* amazed (*über eine S.*, at a th.). 2. *n.* astonishment, wonder, surprise. **-swert,** *adj.* astonishing, wonderful, amazing.

[1]**Staup-e,** *f.* (-en) public flogging. **-besen,** *m.* birch (rod).

[2]**Staupe,** *f.* (-n) distemper (*of dogs*).

Stäupe, *f.*, *see* [1]**Staupe. -n,** *v.a.* (*rare*) flog, scourge.

Stearin, *n.* stearin. **-kerze,** *f.* **-licht,** *n.* stearin *or* composite candle. **-säure,** *f.* stearic acid.

stech-en, 1. *ir.v.a.* & *n.* (*aux.* h.) prick, pierce; sting, bite (*as fleas*); stab, puncture; tilt, joust; stick (*pigs, etc.*); couch (*a cataract*); play off the tie (*Sport*); burn, scorch (*as the sun*); cut (*turf, peat,* *etc.*); tap, draw *or* rack off (*wine, molten metal, etc.*); engrave; trump (*a card*), take (*a trick*) (*Cards*); *der Hafer sticht ihn*, success has gone to his head, he's getting cocky; *ins Rote –en*, incline to red; *das sticht mir in die Augen*, that takes my fancy; (*aux.* s.) *in See –en*, put to sea; *wie ein gestochenes Kalb*, like a stuck pig; *die Kontrolluhr –en*, clock in; *in ein Wespennest –en*, raise a hornet's nest; *–en müssen*, be forced (*Cards*); *nach dem Ringe –en*, tilt; *Silben –en*, split hairs, (*coll.*) pick holes *or* flies (in); *einem den Star –en*, operate on a p. for cataract, (*fig.*) open a p.'s eyes (to a th.); *um eine S. –en*, cast lots for a th. 2. *n.* jousting, tourney; casting lots; shooting pains. **–apfel,** *m.* thorn-apple. **–bahn,** *f.* tilting-yard. **–becken,** *n.* bed-pan. **–eisen,** *n.* awl, pricker. **–end,** *adj.* penetrating, biting, pungent. **–er,** *m.* pricker; engraver; proof-stick; binoculars; hair-trigger (*of a gun*). **–fliege,** *f.* horse- *or* stable-fly, cleg. **–ginster,** *m.* furze, gorse, whin. **–heber,** *m.* pipette. **–kahn,** *m.* punt. **–karte,** *f.* winning card, trump(-card). **–kunst,** *f.* engraving. **–mücke,** *f.* gnat, midge. **–nelke,** *f.* rose-campion (*Bot.*). **–palme,** *f.* holly (*Ilex aquifolium*) (*Bot.*). **–probe,** *f.* test, sample; touchstone. **–ring,** *m.* tilting-ring. **–sattel,** *m.* jousting-saddle. **–schritt,** *m.* goose-step. **–torf,** *m.* cut peat. **–uhr,** *f.* control-clock. **–zirkel,** *m.* dividers.

steck–en, 1. *reg.* (*&* *ir*) *v.a.* put, place; set, plant; stick, fix; *es einem gehörig –en*, give s.o. a piece of one's mind; *Grenzen –en*, set bounds *or* limits (to); *sich etwas hinter den Spiegel –en*, not forget s.th. in a hurry; *in Brand –en*, set fire to, set on fire; *Geld in ein Geschäft –en*, put money into a business; (*coll.*) *ins Loch –en*, put in prison; *die Nase in alles –en*, poke one's nose into everything; *einen in den Sack –en*, outdo a p., get the better of a p., (*coll.*) have a p. in the bag; *den Degen in die Scheide –en*, sheath one's sword; *das Geld in die Tasche –en*, (*fig.*) pocket the money, put the money in one's pocket; *zu sich –en*, put in one's pocket. 2. *v.r.*; *sich hinter eine S. –en*, get behind a th.; work a th. secretly; *sich hinter einen –en*, make a tool of s.o., let s.o. do one's dirty work. 3. *reg.*(*&* *ir.*) *v.n.* (*aux.* h.) be, stay, remain; stick fast, be fixed *or* stuck; be involved in; hide, be hiding, lie hidden; *da –t's!* there's the rub! *es –t etwas dahinter*, there is more in it than meets the eye, there is something at the bottom of it; (*coll.*) *in dem Kerl –t etwas*, there is something in that fellow; *im Elend –en*, be in great want *or* misery; *im Gefängnis –en*, be in prison; *es –t mir im Halse*, it sticks in my throat *or* gorge; *in seiner Haut –en*, be in his shoes; *noch in den Kinderschuhen –en*, be still in the early stages; *in Schulden –en*, be in debt; *der Schlüssel –t*, the key is left in the door; *den Schlüssel –en lassen*, see **–enlassen;** *mit einem unter einer Decke –en*, have a secret understanding with a p., be hand in glove with a p.; *voll –en von*, be full of; *gesteckt voll*, crammed full; *wo –en Sie denn?* where are you (hiding)? 4. *m.* (-ens, -en) stick, staff, rod; (*B.*) *dein –en und dein Stab*, thy rod and thy staff. **–becken,** *n.* bed-pan. **–bett,** *n.* *see* **–kissen.** **–brief,** *m.* warrant (*for arrest*); *er wird –brieflich verfolgt*, warrants are out against him, he is under a warrant of arrest. **–dose,** *f.* wall-socket (*Elec.*). **–enbleiben,** 1. *v.n.* stick fast, be stuck, come to a standstill; break down (*in a speech*). 2. *n.* stoppage, standstill; break-down (*in a speech*). **–enlassen,** *v.a.* leave (where it is); *den Schlüssel –enlassen*, leave the key in the door; *einen im Schlamm* or *in der Not –enlassen*, leave a p. in the lurch; *laß dein Geld nur –en!* leave it to me! I shall pay. **–enpferd,** *n.* hobby-horse; hobby; fad, whim. **–er,** *m.* plug (*Elec.*). **–garn,** *n.* fowling-net. **–holz,** *n.* dibble. **–hülse,** *f.* adapter-plug (*Elec.*). **–kartoffeln,** *f.pl.* seed potatoes. **–kissen,** *n.* baby's pill w. **–kontakt,** *m.* plug and socket (*Elec.*). **–ling,** *m.* slip, cutting, layer, shoot. **–nadel,** *f.* pin; *eine –nadel fallen hören*, hear a pin drop. **–nadelkissen,** *n.* pin-cushion. **–rübe,** *f.* turnip. **–schlüssel,** *m.* box-spanner.

Steg, *m.* (-(e)s, -e) footpath, narrow path; foot-bridge, plank bridge; gangway, catwalk; crosspiece, strap, bar, stay; bridge (*violin, spectacles*); fillet (*Arch.*); *Weg und – kennen*, know (a place) like the back of one's hand; (*fig.*) know all the ins and outs **–reif,** *m.* (*obs.*) stirrup; *aus dem –reife*, extempore, impromptu, on the spur of the moment, without preparation. **–reifdichter,** *m.* improvisator, extempore poet. **–reifgedicht,** *n.* impromptu poem.

steh–en, 1. *ir.v.n.* (*aux.* h. *&* s.) stand, be upright; be situated; be; stand still, stop; (*coll.*) *da –en die Ochsen am Berge*, that's the difficulty, here's the snag; *die Aktien stehen auf 200%*, the shares are at 200 per cent.; *auf dem Kopf –en*, be topsy-turvy; *es –t der Kopf darauf*, it is a capital crime; *auf einer Liste –en*, figure in a list; *es –t vieles auf dem Spiele*, there is a lot at stake; *auf dem Sprung –en*, be on the point of; *es –t bei Ihnen*, it rests with you; *bei seiner Meinung –en*, hold to one's opinion; *er –t bei den Ulanen*, he serves in the Lancers; *als Bürge –en*, stand *or* go security; *es –t noch dahin ob . . .*, it is not yet decided whether . . .; *dahin –t mein Sinn nicht*, I have no inclination for that, my leanings are not in that direction; *fest –en*, stand firmly *or* solidly, *see* **fest–en;** *das –e Ihnen frei*, you are at liberty to do that; *–en für*, guarantee, stand security for, vouch for; *ich mußte selbst für alles –en*, I had to look after everything myself, I was responsible for everything; *sie –en für einen Mann*, they are jointly responsible; *wie ich gehe und –e*, just as I am; *es –t zu hoffen*, it is to be hoped; *in einem Amte –en*, hold *or* fill an office; *bei einem in Arbeit –en*, be employed by s.o.; *Tränen –en ihr in den Augen*, tears are in her eyes; *im fünften Jahre –en*, be in one's fifth year; *es –t in seinen Kräften*, it lies in his power; *es –t ganz in Ihrer Macht*, the matter rests solely with you; *im Verdachte –en*, be suspected, be under suspicion; *das Kleid –t ihr gut*, the dress suits her; *auf die Füße zu –en kommen*, fall on one's feet, regain one's balance; *es kam ihm teuer zu –en*, he had to pay dearly for it; *ich weiß nicht, wo mir der Kopf –t*, I do not know which way to turn; I am beside myself; *–en lassen*, *see* **–enlassen;** *ich –e gut mit ihm*, I am on good terms with him; *es –t schlecht mit dem Kranken*, the patient's condition is grave, the patient is in a bad way; *ich –e nicht allein mit meiner Meinung*, I am not alone in my opinion *or* in thinking so; *einem Maler Modell –en*, pose for a painter; *–en nach*, aspire to, seek after; *einem nach dem Leben –en*, make an attempt on a p.'s life; *sein Sinn –t nach Geld*, money is his aim; *nahe –en*, stand near *or* close to, *see* **nahe–en;** *Schlange –en*, form a queue, stand in a queue; (*coll.*) *da –t mir der Verstand still*, that is beyond me; *er –t über mir*, he is my superior; *es –t schlecht um ihn*, things go badly with him, he is in a bad way; *er –t unter mir*, he is my subordinate; he is under my care *or* protection; *die Felder –en unter Wasser*, the fields are *or* lie under water; *es –t mir immer vor Augen*, I cannot get it out of my mind; *vor einer vollendeten Tatsache –en*, be faced with a *fait accompli*; *wie –t's?* how are you? how are things? (*coll.*) how's it going? *wie –t's zu Hause?* how are all at home? *wie –en Sie dazu?* what is your view of it? what is your attitude *or* opinion? *er –t zu mir*, he is well disposed towards me; he remains true to me; he gives me his help *or* support; *es –en mir die Haare zu Berge*, my hair stands on end; *die Frage –t nicht zur Debatte*, the question is not up for discussion; *ich –e zu Ihren Diensten*, I am at your service; *einem zur Seite –en*, help a p.; *einem zur Verfügung –en*, be at a p.'s disposal. 2. *v.a.*; *der Hund –t das Wild*, the hound points (the game); *seinen Mann –en*, stand one's ground, hold one's own, be a match for; *einem Rede –en*, answer (to) a p.'s questions; *Rede und Antwort –en*, justify o.s., give an account (of o.s.). 3. *v.r.*; *hier –t es sich besser*, here is a better place to stand; *sich müde –en*, tire o.s. out with standing; (*coll.*) *ich –e mich gut*, I'm in the money; *er –t sich auf 3,000 Mark*, he has *or* gets 3,000 marks (a month *or* a year). 4. *n.* standing, stopping, halting; *das –en fällt ihm schwer*, he cannot stand for long; *im –en schlafen*, sleep on one's feet; *zum –en bringen*, stop, stay, arrest; *das Blut zum –en bringen*, staunch the blood. **–auf,** *m.*, **–aufchen,** *n.*, **–aufmännchen,** *n.* tumbler-doll, kelly. **–bierhalle,** *f.* bar, tap-room. **–en-**

bleiben, *v.n.* remain standing (there), stay (there), stop; remain upright *or* erect. **–end,** *pr.p. & adj.* standing, stationary, upright, vertical; permanent, regular; *–ende Bühne,* permanent theatre; *–enden Fußes,* at once, on the spot; *–endes Gut,* standing rigging (*Naut.*); *–endes Heer,* regular *or* standing army; *–ende Redensart,* hackneyed *or* stock phrase; *–endes Wasser,* stagnant water; *–ende Welle,* standing wave (*Rad.*); *–ender Wind,* settled wind. **–enlassen,** *v.a.* leave there *or* in its place; leave behind, forget (*umbrella, etc.*); leave (untouched), not eat (*as food*); leave (in the bank), not withdraw (*money*). **–er,** *m.* stayer, long-distance racer (*Cycl.*). **–errennen,** *n.* long-distance *or* endurance race (*Cycl.*). **–kolben,** *m.* flat-bottomed flask. **–kragen,** *m.* stand-up collar. **–lampe,** *f.* standard lamp. **–leiter,** *f.* (pair of) steps, step-ladder. **–platz,** *m.* standing-room. **–pult,** *n.* standing-desk, high desk.

stehl–en, 1. *ir.v.a. & n.* (*aux.* h.) steal, rob, pilfer; (*coll.*) *dem lieben Gott die Zeit* or *den Tag –en,* idle away one's time; (*coll.*) *das kann mir gestohlen bleiben,* I do not want to have anything to do with it, that leaves me cold. 2. *v.r.* steal *or* slink away. 3. *n.* stealing, robbery, larceny. **–er,** *m.* (*only in prov.*) *der Hehler ist so schlimm wie der –er,* the receiver is no better than the thief. **–sucht,** *f.* kleptomania.

steif, *adj.* stiff, rigid, inflexible, firm; (*fig.*) unbending, obstinate; awkward, wooden, ungraceful; numb, benumbed; formal, pedantic, strait-laced; taut (*of ropes*) (*Naut.*); starched; *einen –en Daumen haben,* be avaricious; *–er Wind,* strong breeze; *–er Grog,* strong grog; *die Ohren – halten,* keep a stiff upper lip; *– und fest behaupten,* maintain obstinately. **–e,** *f.* stiffness; stiffening, starch, size; starching; prop, buttress, stay, support. **–en,** *v.a.* stiffen, line with buckram; starch; (*dial.*) prop, shore up, stay; *einem den Nacken –en,* inspire a p. with courage. **–halsig,** *adj.* stiff-necked. **–heit,** *f.* stiffness, inflexibility, rigidity; awkwardness; formality. **–igkeit,** *f.*, *see* **–heit. –leinen,** 1. *adj.*; *–leinener Gesell,* strait-laced and pedantic fellow. 2. *n.*, **–leinwand,** *f.* buckram. **–ung,** *f.* stiffening, starching, sizing. **–werden,** *n.* stiffening; erection (*Physiol.*).

Steig, *m.* (-(e)s, -e) path, footpath; mountain track. **–brunnen,** *m.* artesian well. **–bügel,** *m.* stirrup; stirrup-bone (*Physiol.*). **–e,** *f.* (*dial.*), *see* **Stiege. –eisen,** *n.* climbing-irons, crampons. **–en,** 1. *ir.v.n.* (*aux.* s.) climb, mount, ascend, go up; increase, rise; rear, prance; soar; (*coll.*) take place, come off; *auf einen Baum –en,* climb a tree; (*coll.*) *einem aufs Dach –en,* fly at *or* attack a p.; (*vom*) *zu* or *aufs Pferd -en,* (dismount) mount; *aus dem* (*durch das*) *Fenster –en,* go out at (enter by) the window; *aus dem* (*ins*) *Bett –en,* get out of (into) bed; *über den Zaun –en,* climb, step *or* get over the fence; *die Kurse –en,* prices are going up, the market is improving; *der Nebel –t,* the fog comes up; *–en lassen,* fly (*a kite*); (*coll.*) *ein Lied –en lassen,* sing a song; *eine Rede –en lassen,* make *or* give a speech; (*Studs. sl.*) *der Cantus –t,* we now sing the song; *einem in den* or *zu Kopf –en,* go to one's head; *ins Examen –en,* enter for *or* sit an examination; *die Haare –en ihm zu Berge,* his hair stands on end; *in die Schüssel –en,* help o.s. (to more); *Tränen –en ihr in die Augen,* tears come into her eyes; *Waren –en im Preise,* the price of goods is rising; *vom Throne –en,* abdicate; (*coll.*) *das Endspiel wird nächste Woche –en,* the finals come off next week. 2. *n.* rising; rise, advance, increase; *das –en und Fallen,* fluctuation (*of prices*); *im –en sein,* be rising, be on the increase; *Neigung zum –en,* upward tendency (*of prices*). **–end,** *pr.p. & adj.* growing, increasing, rising; *mit –endem Alter,* as one grows older, with increasing years; *–ender Löwe,* lion rampant. **–er,** *m.* mine-inspector. **–erer,** *m.* bidder (*at auctions*). **–ern,** 1. *v.a.* raise, increase, heighten, augment, enhance, advance; intensify, strengthen; (*dial.*) bid for (*auction*), buy at an auction; compare (*Gram.*); *die Miete –ern,* raise the rent. *einen mit der Miete –ern,* raise a tenant's rent; 2. *v.r.* become greater *or* intensified, increase, rise, mount. **–erung,** *f.* increase, augmentation, raising, enhancement, intensification; climax; gradation, comparison (*Gram.*); auction. **–erungsgegenstände,** *m.pl.* articles sold at an auction. **–erungsgrad,** *m.*, **–erungsstufe,** *f.* degree of comparison. **–flug,** *m.* climbing, zooming (*Av.*). **–geschwindigkeit,** *f.* rate of climb (*Av.*). **–höhe,** *f.* ceiling (*Av.*). **–rad,** *n.* balance-wheel (*Horol.*). **–riemen,** *m.* stirrup leather. **–rohr,** *n.* ascending pipe, overflow pipe, standpipe. **–röhre,** *f.* suction pipe (*of a pump*). **–ung,** *f.* ascent, rise, increase; incline, slope, gradient, climb (*Av.*); pitch (*of a screw, etc.*); climax. **–ungswinkel,** *m.* angle of climb *or* ascent.

steil, *adj.* steep, precipitous. **–e,** *f.* steepness; steep place, precipice, declivity. **–feuer,** *n.* high-angle fire (*Mil.*). **–flug,** *m.* climbing (*Av.*). **–hang,** *m.* steep slope, precipice. **–heit,** *f.* steepness. **–kurve,** *f.* sharp curve. **–küste,** *f.* shelving coast, steep shore, bluff (*Geol.*). **–schrift,** *f.* vertical writing.

Stein, *m.* (-(e)s, -e) stone, rock, flint; precious stone, gem; monument, gravestone; man, piece (*Draughts, etc.*); kernel; concretion, calculus (*Med.*); *– des Anstoßes,* stumbling block; *keinen – auf dem andern lassen,* raze to the ground; *behauener –,* hewn stone; *– und Bein frieren,* freeze hard; *– und Bein schwören,* swear by all that is holy *or* all the gods; *bei jemandem einen – im Brett haben,* be in s.o.'s good books; *es hätte einen – erbarmen können,* it was enough to melt a (heart of) stone; *geschnittener –,* gem, intaglio; *es fällt mir ein – vom Herzen,* that is a load *or* a weight off my mind; *über Stock und –,* through thick and thin; *einem -e in den Weg legen,* put obstacles in a p.'s way; *– der Weisen,* philosophers' stone; *zu – machen,* petrify. **–abdruck,** *m.* lithograph(ic) print. **–abfälle,** *m.pl.* stone chips *or* chippings. **–acker,** *m.* stony field. **–adler,** *m.* golden eagle (*Aquila chrysaetos*) (*Orn.*). **–alt,** *adj.* old as the hills. **–art,** *f.* species of stone, mineral. **–artig,** *adj.* rock-like, stony. **–bau,** *m.* stone building. **–beil,** *n.* flint axe. **–beschwerde,** *f.* calculus, the stone (*Med.*). **–beißer,** *m.* loach (*Cobitis taenia*) (*Icht.*). **–bild,** *n.* statue. **–bildung,** *f.* formation of stone; lithiasis (*Med.*). **–bock,** *m.* ibex (*Capra ibex*) (*Zool.*); Capricorn (*Astr.*). **–boden,** *m.* stony soil; stone floor. **–brand,** *m.* stinking smut (*on corn*). **–brech,** *m.* saxifrage (*Bot.*). **–brecher,** *m.* stone crusher. **–bruch,** *m.* quarry. **–butt,** *m.* turbot (*Rhombus maximus*) (*Icht.*). **–druck,** *m.* lithography; lithograph(ic) print. **–drucker,** *m.* lithographic printer. **–eiche,** *f.* oak (*Quercus sessiliflora*) (*Bot.*). **–en,** *v.a.* mark out with stones (*as a boundary*). **–erbarmen,** *n.*, *das ist zum –erbarmen,* it is enough to melt a heart of stone. **–ern,** *adj.* of stone, stony. **–flechte,** *f.* rock lichen. **–frucht,** *f.* stone-fruit. **–galle,** *f.* windgall (*Vet.*). **–garten,** *m.* rock-garden, rockery. **–geröll,** *n.* scree, shingle. **–grieß,** *m.* gravel. **–grube,** *f.* quarry. **–grund,** *m.* stony ground; stony bottom (*of a river*). **–gut,** *n.* stoneware, earthenware, pottery. **–händler,** *m.* lapidary, jeweller. **–hart,** *adj.* hard as stone *or* brick. **–hauer,** *m.*, *see* **–metz. –ig,** *adj.* stony; full of stones, rocky. **–igen,** *v.a.* stone. **–igung,** *f.* death by stoning. **–kauz,** *m.* little owl (*Athene noctua*) (*Orn.*). **–kern,** *m.* stone (*of fruit*). **–klee,** *m.* melilot (*Melilotus officinalis*) (*Bot.*). **–kohle,** *f.* coal, pit-coal, bituminous coal. **–kohlenflöz,** *n.*, **–kohlenlager,** *n.* coal-bed *or* -seam. **–kohlengas,** *n.* coal-gas. **–kohlenteer,** *m.* coal-tar. **–kolik,** *f.*, *see* **–krankheit. –krank,** *adj.* suffering from stone. **–krankheit,** *f.* stone (*Med.*). **–kunde,** *f.* mineralogy; lithology. **–lage,** *f.* layer of stones. **–leiden,** *n.*, *see* **–krankheit. –mann,** *m.* cairn (*Mount.*). **–marder,** *m.* beech marten (*Martes foina*) (*Zool.*). **–meißel,** *m.* stone-mason's chisel. **–metz,** *m.* stone-mason. **–mörtel,** *m.* cement, concrete. **–nelke,** *f.* wood pink (*Bot.*). **–nuß,** *f.* vegetable ivory, corozo nut. **–obst,** *n.* stone-fruit. **–öl,** *n.* petroleum, mineral oil, rock oil. **–operation,** *f.* lichotomy (*Surg.*). **–pappe,** *f.* fire-proof pasteboard, roofing felt. **–pflaster,** *n.* stone pavement. **–pilz,** *m.* edible mushroom

(*Boletus edulis*) (*Bot.*). **–platte,** *f.* stone slab, flagstone. **–reich,** 1. *n.* mineral kingdom. 2. *adj.* stony, full of stones; (*fig.*) enormously rich. **–salz,** *n.* rock-salt. **–salzgrube,** *f.* salt-mine. **–sarg,** *m.* sarcophagus. **–säure,** *f.* lithic acid. **–schlag,** *m.* broken stones, metalling (*for roads*); falling stones (*Mount.*). **–schlaggefährlich,** *adj.* stone-swept (*Mount.*). **–schleifer,** *m.* lapidary, gem-polisher. **–schloßgewehr,** *n.* flint-lock (musket). **–schmätzer,** *m.* wheatear (*Oenanthe oenanthe*) (*Orn.*). **–schneiden,** *n.* gem-carving; engraving on stone; lithotomy (*Surg.*). **–schneider,** *m.* gem cutter, lapidary; stone engraver. **–schnitt,** *m.* stone-cutting; lithotomy (*Surg.*). **–setzer,** *m.* paver, paviour. **–waffen,** *f.pl.* flint weapons. **–ware,** *f.* stoneware. **–weg,** *m.* paved way, causeway. **–werk,** *n.* masonry, stonework. **–wurf,** *m.* stone's throw. **–zeichnung,** *f.* lithograph. **–zeit,** *f.* Stone Age. **–zeitlich,** *adj.* (of the) Stone Age. **–zeug,** *n.* stoneware.

Steiper, *m.* (-s, –) (*dial.*), *see* **Stieper.**

Steiß, *m.* (-es, -e) rump, buttocks (*usually of birds*); (*coll.*) backside. **–bein,** *n.* coccyx (*Anat.*). **–flosse,** *f.* anal fin. **–fuß,** *m.* grebe (*Pygopodes*) (*Orn.*). **–geburt,** *f.* pelvic presentation.

Stellage, *f.* (-n) stand, frame. **–ngeschäft,** *n.* (*C.L.*) dealing in futures.

Stell–e, *f.* (–n) place, position, situation, spot, point; post; department; authority, passage (*in a book, etc.*); figure, digit (*Arith.*); *an meiner –e,* in my place, in place of me, instead of me; *wenn ich an Ihrer –e wäre,* if I were you, if I were in your place; *an jemandes –e treten,* take s.o.'s place, act as s.o.'s substitute, (*coll.*) stand in for s.o.; *an Ort und –e sein,* be on the spot; be delivered (*of goods*); *auf der –e,* on the spot, immediately; *auf der –e treten,* mark time (*Mil.*); *eine –e bekleiden,* hold a post *or* position; *er bewirbt sich um die –e,* he is applying for the post; *offene –e,* vacancy; *schmerzende –e,* sore place *or* spot; *jemandes –e vertreten,* represent s.o., act as s.o.'s representative; *nicht von der –e!* don't stir *or* move! *nicht von der –e kommen,* make no progress, not get on; *zur –e!* here! *zur –e sein,* be present; *zuständige –e,* proper authority. **–en,** 1. *v.a.* put, place, set, lay, arrange; put right, set in order, adjust, regulate; post, station; supply, provide, furnish; *ans Licht –en,* set forth; *einen an den Pranger –en,* pillory a p.; *einen Antrag –en,* bring *or* put forward a motion, move (*Parl.*); *auf den Kopf –en,* turn upside down, upset, bring into disorder, disarrange; *auf die Probe –en,* put to the proof; *er ist ganz auf sich* (*Acc.*) *selbst gestellt,* he is entirely dependent upon himself, he is quite self-dependent; he can look for no one's support; *Bedingungen –en,* impose conditions; *jemandem ein Bein –en,* trip a p. up; *den Feind –en,* challenge, intercept *or* engage the enemy; *Forderungen –en,* make demands; *eine Frage –en,* put *or* ask a question; *ein Gesuch –en,* make *or* submit a petition; *er ist gut gestellt,* he is well-off; *etwas höher –en,* rank a th. *or* consider s.th. higher, give a th. one's preference; *einem das Horoskop –en,* cast a p.'s horoscope; *der Hund –te den Hirsch,* the hound held the stag at bay; *etwas in Abrede –en,* deny a th., dispute (the validity of) a th.; *etwas in Aussicht –en,* hold out the prospect of s.th.; *in Dienst –en,* appoint (*a p.*), put into service (*a ship, etc.*); *etwas in jemandes Belieben* or *Ermessen –en,* leave s.th. to a p.'s pleasure *or* discretion; *etwas in Frage* or *in Zweifel –en,* question the advisability of s.th., have doubts about a th.; *etwas in Rechnung –en,* charge *or* debit to s.o.'s account; *in den Schatten –en,* put into the shade, excel by far, surpass, be pre-eminent in; *den Champagner kalt –en,* put the champagne on ice; *seinen Mann –en,* play one's part, do one's bit; *einem nach dem Leben –en,* seek to kill a p., (make an) attempt (on) a p.'s life; *er ist schlecht gestellt,* he is not at all well-off; *einen Stellvertreter –en,* find a substitute; *die Uhr –en,* regulate a watch *or* clock; *die Uhr auf 12 –en,* set the watch to 12 o'clock; *etwas unter Beweis –en,* support a th. with evidence, supply proof for a th.; (*B.*) *sein Licht unter den Scheffel –en,* hide one's light under a bushel; *einen Verbrecher –en,* arrest a criminal; *das Essen warm –en,* keep the food hot, put the food to keep hot; *Zeugen –en,* produce witnesses; *zur Diskussion –en,* throw open to discussion; *einen zur Rede –en,* call a p. to account, demand an explanation from s.o.; *einem etwas zur Verfügung –en,* place s.th. at a p.'s disposal. 2. *v.r.* place, post *or* station o.s., take one's stand; present o.s.; enlist (*Mil.*); give o.s. up; appear, prove to be; feign, sham, pretend, affect; *der Preis stellt sich auf 8 Mark,* the price is 8 marks; *sich auf eig(e)ne Füße –en,* support o.s., (*coll.*) stand on one's own feet; *sich auf die Hinterbeine –en,* dig one's heels in; *sich auf den Kopf –en,* make every endeavour, set one's mind on, (*sl.*) do one's damnedest; *sich mit einem auf eine Stufe –en,* put o.s. on the same footing as a p.; *der Hirsch –te sich gegen die Hunde,* the stag stood at bay; *sich dem Gerichte –en,* appear in court; *die Sache –t sich günstiger als ich dachte,* the matter is really not so bad as I thought; *sich krank –en,* feign illness; *ich kann mich mit ihm nicht –en,* I cannot get on with him; *der Preis –t sich niedrig,* the price rules low; *er –t sich nur so,* he is only shamming; *vor ein Kriegsgericht gestellt werden,* be tried by court-martial; *wie –en Sie sich dazu?* what is your view of *or* attitude to the matter? **–bar,** *adj.* movable, adjustable. **–bottich,** *m.* fermenting-vat. **–dichein,** *n.* meeting, rendezvous, tryst; *einem ein –dichein geben,* arrange to meet a p., (*coll.*) make a date with a p. **–enangebot,** *n.* offer of a post. **–engesuch,** *n.* application for a post. **–enjäger,** *m.* place-hunter. **–enlos,** *adj.* unemployed. **–ennachweis,** *m.* employment agency. **–ensuche,** *f.* search for a post. **–envermittlung,** *f.* registry-office (*for servants*); Labour Exchange. **–enweise,** *adv.* here and there, in places, sporadically. **–hebel,** *m.* adjusting *or* adjustment lever. **–ig,** *adj.* (*in compounds* =) of (*so many*) digits *or* figures. **–jagd,** *f.* netting (*Hunt.*). **–macher,** *m.* wheelwright. **–mutter,** *f.* adjusting nut, lock-nut. **–ring,** *m.* setting-ring (*of fuse*), damping-collar. **–schlüssel,** *m.* adjustable spanner; setting-ring (*of fuse*). **–schraube,** *f.* adjusting screw, set-screw. **–ung,** *f.* position, situation; disposition, setting, placing, posture, attitude; guard (*Fenc.*); emplacement, line (*Mil.*); (*pl.*) trenches (*Mil.*); post, rank, station; constellation, arrangement, orientation; regulator (*Horol.*); *–ung!* on your guard! *–ung nehmen zu,* express one's view about *or* opinion on; *eine –ung behaupten,* hold a position (*Mil.*). **–ungnahme,** *f.* opinion (expressed), comment (on), attitude (to), point of view. **–ungsbefehl,** *m.* calling-up papers, enlistment order, call-up (*Mil.*). **–ungsgesuch,** *n.* application for a post. **–ungskampf,** *m.*, **–ungskrieg,** *m.* static *or* positional warfare. **–ungslos,** *adj.* unemployed. **–ungspflichtig,** *adj.* liable for military service. **–ungsvermittlung,** *see* **–envermittlung. –ungswechsel,** *m.* change of position *or* job. **–vertretend,** *adj.* vicarious, representative, delegated, acting, deputy, vice-. **–vertreter,** *m.* deputy, representative, delegate, proxy, substitute, second in command. **–vertretung,** *f.* representation, substitution, proxy; *in –vertretung,* by proxy (*C.L.*), per pro(curation). **–vorrichtung,** *f.* adjusting mechanism, regulator (*Mech.*). **–wagen,** *m.* (*Austr. dial.*) coach, motor bus. **–werk,** *n.* signal-box (*Railw.*). **–zeiger,** *m.* regulator index (*Horol.*). **–zirkel,** *m.* adjustable bevel.

Stelz–e, *f.* (-en) stilt; prop, shore (*Min.*); *–en laufen, auf –en gehen,* walk on stilts; (*fig.*) be bombastic *or* stilted. **–bein,** *n.* wooden leg, (*coll.*) peg-leg. **–enläufer,** *m.* oyster catcher (*Haemantopus*) (*Orn.*). **–fuß,** *m.* wooden leg; man with a wooden leg. **–vögel,** *m.pl.* long-legged birds, grallatores. **–wurzel,** *f.* adventitious root.

stemm–en, 1. *v.a.* stem; dam up (*water, etc.*); prop, support, stand firm against; lift heavy weights; prise *or* lever up; chisel, caulk; *die Arme in die Seiten –en,* put one's hands on one's hips, (*coll.*) set one's arms akimbo; *die Arme auf den Tisch –en,* prop one's arms on the table; *die Füße gegen die Wand –en,* plant one's feet firmly against the wall. 2. *v.r.* lean heavily *or* push one's weight against; oppose, resist. **–bogen,** *m.* simple swing *or* curve

(*Skiing*). **-eisen,** *n.* crowbar; paring-chisel. **-(m)eißel,** *m.* caulking-chisel. **-tor,** *n.* sluice-gate.
Stempel, *m.* (-s, -) rubber stamp; mark, imprint, trade-mark, brand, postmark, impress; prop, shore, stemple (*Min.*); pestle, pounder, stamper, punch, stamp, die; piston (*Mach.*); pistil (*Bot.*). **-abgabe,** *f.* stamp-duty. **-eisen,** *n.* stamp; punch. **-farbe,** *f.* stamping *or* marking ink. **-frei,** *adj.* free from stamp-duty. **-kissen,** *n.* ink-pad. **-los,** *adj.* without pistils, male (*Bot.*). **-n,** 1. *v.a.* stamp, mark, brand, hall-mark (*silver, etc.*); cancel (*postage stamps*); prop; (*coll.*) *einen –n,* instruct beforehand, prime. 2. *v.n.* have one's (dole-)card stamped; (*sl.*) *–n gehen,* go on *or* draw the dole. **-pflichtig,** *adj.* liable to stamp-duty. **-presse,** *f.* stamping-press. **-schneider,** *m.* stamp-cutter, die-sinker. **-steuer,** *f.* stamp-duty. **-träger,** *m.* gynophore (*Bot.*).
Stenge, *f.* (-en) topmast. **-l,** *m.* (-els, -el) stalk, stem; (*coll.*) *vom –l fallen,* come a cropper. **-lartig,** *adj.*, **-lförmig,** *adj.* stalk-like, cauliform, **-lbohne,** *f.* climbing bean. **-lglas,** *n.* wine-glass (*with stem*). **-lig,** *adj.* stalked. **-lknolle,** *f.* tuber. **-llos,** *adj.* stemless, acaulose. **-ln,** *v.n.* (*aux.* h.) run to stalk.
Steno-gramm, *n.* (-s, -e) shorthand note, shorthand report; *–gramm aufnehmen,* take down in shorthand. **-graph,** *m.* (-en, -en) shorthand-writer. **-graphie,** *f.* stenography, shorthand. **-graphieren,** *v.a.* write shorthand, take down in shorthand. **-graphisch,** *adj.* stenographic(al), (in) shorthand. **-typist,** *m.* (-en, -en), **-typistin,** *f.* (-innen) shorthand-typist.
Stentorstimme, *f.* stentorian voice, very loud voice.
Steppe, *f.* (-n) steppe, prairie, savannah, grassland. **-nfuchs,** *m.* corsac; caragan. **-nwolf,** *m.* prairie wolf.
stepp-en, 1. *v.a.* quilt. 2. *v.n.* do tap-dancing. **-decke,** *f.* quilt. **-er,** *m.* tap-dancer. **-naht,** *f.* quilting-seam, closing-seam. **-stich,** *m.* back-stitch, lock-stitch. **-(p)tanz,** *m.* tap-dance.
sterb-en, 1. *ir.v.n.* (*aux.* s.) *&* *a.* die (*an with Dat.*, of); die *or* fade away, perish, become extinct; *an der Pest –en,* die of the plague; *am Schlage –en,* die as a result of a stroke; *aus Gram –en,* die of grief; *durch ihn ist sie gestorben,* he was the cause of her death; *durch Mörderhand –en,* die at the hand of an assassin; *den Heldentod –en,* die a hero; *Hungers* or *vor Hunger –en,* die of hunger *or* starvation; *eines natürlichen Todes* or *einen natürlichen Tod –en,* die a natural death; *über seinen Plänen –en,* die before one's plans are carried out; *vor Lange(r)-weile –en,* die of boredom, be bored to death. 2. *n.* dying; death; *im –en liegen,* be dying *or* on the point of death; *es geht um Leben und –en,* it is a matter of life and death; *das große –en,* the plague, the Black Death; *zum –en langweilig,* intolerably boring. **-ebett,** *n.* death-bed. **-efall,** *m.* a death; decease. **-egeld,** *n.* payment in case of death. **-egesang,** *m.* dirge, requiem. **-egewand,** *n.* winding-sheet, shroud; (*pl.*) grave-clothes. **-eglocke,** *f.* funeral bell. **-ehaus,** *n.* house of mourning. **-ejahr,** *n.* year of a p.'s death. **-ekasse,** *f.* burial fund, funeral club. **-ekleid,** *n.* shroud. **-elager,** *n.*, *see* **-ebett.** **-ensangst,** *f.* mortal fear. **-ensbange,** *adj.* mortally afraid. **-enskrank,** *adj.* dangerously ill; (*B.*) sick unto death. **-ensmatt,** *adj.*, **-ensmüde,** *adj.* tired to death. **-ensseele,** *f.*, *keine –ensseele,* not a living soul. **-enswort,** *n.*, *kein –enswort,* not a word *or* syllable. **-esakramente,** *n.pl.* last sacraments *or* unction. **-estunde,** *f.* dying hour. **-etafel,** *f.* mortality tables. **-eziffer,** *f.* number of deaths. **-lich,** *adj.* mortal; *–lich verliebt,* head over heels in love. **-liche(r),** *m.* mortal. **-lichkeit,** *f.* mortality; mortality figures, death-rate; *aus dieser –lichkeit abgefordert* or *abberufen werden,* be called to other realms. **-lichkeitsziffer,** *f.* mortality *or* death-rate.
Stereo-metrie, *f.* solid geometry, stereometry. **-skop,** *n.* (-(e)s, -e) stereoscope. **-skopisch,** *adj.* stereoscopic. **-typ,** *adj.* stereotype, (*fig.*) stereotyped, hackneyed. **-typausgabe,** *f.* stereotype *or* offset edition. **-typie,** *f.* stereotype, offset. **-typieren,** *v.a.* stereotype.

steril, *adj.* barren, sterile, sterilized, antiseptic. **-isieren,** *v.a.* sterilize; *–isierte Watte,* antiseptic cotton-wool. **-isierung,** *f.* sterilization. **-ität,** *f.* sterility, barrenness.
Sterke, *f.* (-n) heifer.
Stern, *m.* (-(e)s, -e) star; asterisk (*Typ.*); white mark (*on horse's face*); *– der Londoner Theaterwelt,* star of the London theatre; *er hat weder Glück noch –,* the fates are against him; *nach den –en greifen,* reach for the stars; *– erster Größe,* star of the first magnitude; *ein* or *sein guter –,* his lucky star; *der Hoffnung letzte –e,* the last rays of hope; *–e schießen,* take bearing on the stars. **-artig,** *adj.* starlike, star-shaped, stellate. **-bild,** *n.* constellation. **-blume,** *f.* star-shaped *or* stellate flower; (*pl.*) Asteraceae. **-chen,** *n.* asterisk. **-deuter,** *m.* astrologer. **-deuterei,** *f.* astrology. **-enbahn,** *f.* orbit of a star. **-enbanner,** *n.* star-spangled banner, Stars and Stripes. **-enförmig,** *adj.*, *see* **-artig.** **-enhell** *adj.*, *see* **-hell.** **-enhimmel,** *m.* (*Poet.*), *see* **-himmel.** **-enlicht,** *n.* star-light. **-(en)stunde,** *f.* sidereal hour; (*fig.*) propitious hour. **-enwelt,** *f.* celestial sphere. **-enzelt,** *n.* (*Poet.*), *see* **-himmel.** **-fahrt,** *f.* motor-rally. **-gucker,** *m.* star-gazer. **-guckerei,** *f.* star-gazing. (*vulg.*) **-hagelvoll,** *adj.* (*sl.*) dead drunk. **-haufe(n),** *m.* multiple star, star cluster. **-hell,** *adj.* starry, star-lit. **-himmel,** *m.* (*Poet.*) starry sky, firmament. **-jahr,** *n.* sidereal year. **-karte,** *f.* astronomical chart. **-klar,** *adj.* starry, star-bright. **-kunde,** *f.* astronomy. **-kundige(r),** *m.* astronomer. **-leuchtpatrone,** *f.* star-shell (*Mil.*). **-miere,** *f.* stitchwort; starwort (*Stellaria*) (*Bot.*). **-motor,** *m.* radial engine. **-physik,** *f.* astrophysics. **-schnuppe,** *f.* shooting star, meteorite. **-sucher,** *m.* astronomical telescope. **-tafel,** *f.* astronomical table. **-tag,** *m.* sidereal day. **-tier,** *n.* starfish (*Asteroida*) (*Zool.*). **-warte,** *f.* observatory. **-wolke,** *f.* nebula. **-zeichen,** *n.* asterisk. **-zeit,** *f.* sideral time.
Sterz, *m.* (-es, -e) plough-handle, tail-end; (*dial.*) tail, rump.
stet, *adj.*, **-ig,** *adj.* constant, continual, continuous, persistent, regular, fixed, perpetual; steady, stable. **-igkeit,** *f.* steadiness, constancy, continuity, stability. **-s,** *adv.* always, regularly, steadily, constantly, continually, (for) ever. **-sfort,** *adv.* (*Swiss dial.*) incessantly, perpetually, continuously.
[1]**Steuer,** *n.* (-s, -) rudder, helm; *das – führen,* be at the helm; *das – an Backbord!* port the helm! *das – herumwerfen,* put the helm over. **-bord,** *n.* starboard (*Naut.*). **-fähigkeit,** *f.* manœuvrability. **-fläche,** *f.* control surface (*Av.*). **-flosse,** *f.* fin (*Av.*). **-flügel,** *m.* fin (*of a bomb*). **-gerät,** *n.* steering gear. **-gitter,** *n.* control grid (*Rad.*). **-hebel,** *m.* control lever. **-knüppel,** *m.* control-column, (*coll.*) joy-stick (*Av.*). **-lastig,** *adj.* trimmed by the stern. **-mann,** *m.* helmsman, coxswain, man at the wheel; mate. **-mannsmaat,** *m.* second mate (*Naut.*). **-n,** 1. *v.a.* steer, control, regulate, pilot, navigate. 2. *v. n.* (*aux.* s.) steer a course for, stand *or* make for (*Naut.*); *hart –n,* not answer the helm readily; *nach London –n,* direct a ship's course to London. **-rad,** *n.* (steering-) wheel. **-ruder,** *n.* rudder, helm. **-säule,** *f.*, *see* **-knüppel.** **-ung,** *f.* steering, driving, piloting; controlling, regulating, distribution, allocation, distributing, control *or* steering gear (*Mach.*); automatic control. **-welle,** *f.* camshaft (*Mach.*); axle of the steering-wheel. **-werk,** *n.* control gear *or* system.
[2]**Steuer,** *f.* (-n) tax, duty, (local) rate; (*archaic*) redress, defence, aid; *Grund–,* land-tax, ground-rent; *indirekte –n,* duties; *städtische –n,* local rates; *die gesamten –n,* rates and taxes; *zur – der Wahrheit,* for the sake or in the interests of truth. **-abzug,** *m.* deduction for (income-)tax. **-amt,** *n.* inland-revenue office, customs house. **-anschlag,** *m.* assessment. **-aufkommen,** *n.* tax yield. **-auflage,** *f.* imposition of a tax. **-bar,** *adj.* liable for tax, taxable, dutiable, rateable; assessable. **-barkeit,** *f.* tax liability. **-beamte(r),** *m.* revenue-officer; tax-collector, inspector of taxes. **-befreiung,** *f.* exemption from taxes. **-behörde,** *f.* inland-revenue

department. **-betrug,** *m.* false return of income. **-einheit,** *f.* basic tax. **-einnehmer,** *m.* tax-collector. **-einschätzung,** *f.* assessment. **-erhebung,** *f.* collection *or* levying of taxes. **-erklärung,** *f.* income-tax return. **-erlaß,** *m.* tax-provision. **-erleichterung,** *f.*, *see* **-nachlaß. -flucht,** *f.* transfer of funds to evade taxation. **-frei,** *adj.* duty-free, tax-free, exempt from taxation. **-gesetz,** *n.* fiscal legislation. **-hinterziehung,** *f.* tax-evasion. **-kasse,** *f.* tax-collector's office. **-kollegium,** *n.* inland-revenue commissioners. **-lich,** *adj.* fiscal. **-marke,** *f.* revenue-stamp. **-n,** 1. *v.a* & *n.* (*aux.* h.) pay (taxes); contribute (to). 2. *v.n.* (*with Dat.*) put a check on, put a stop to. **-nachlaß,** *m.* remission of taxes. **-pferdestärke,** *f.* taxable horse-power (*Motor.*). **-pflichtig,** *adj.* liable for tax, subject to taxation, taxable; dutiable (*goods*). **-politik,** *f.* fiscal policy. **-satz,** *m.* rate of assessment, coding. **-schein,** *m.* tax-collector's receipt. **-schraube,** *f.* (increasingly) oppressive taxation; *-schraube anziehen,* raise taxation. **-schuld,** *f.* tax underpaid. **-verwaltung,** *f.* inland-revenue department. **-verweigerung,** *f.* refusal to pay taxes. **-wesen,** *n.* taxation, taxes. **-zahler,** *m.* taxpayer, ratepayer. **-zettel,** *m.* tax demand, notice of coding. **-zuschlag,** *m.* surtax, supertax.

Steven, *m.* (-s, -) stem; stern-post (*Naut.*).

stibitzen, *v.a.* & *n.* (*coll.*) pilfer, (*sl.*) swipe.

Stich, *m.* (-(e)s, -e & *as measure* -) prick, puncture, stab, thrust; sting, bite (*of an insect*); shooting pain; (*fig.*) gibe, taunt; stitch; engraving, print; cut (*of a spade*); trick (*at cards*); knot, hitch, bend (*Naut.*); tinge; *das ist mir ein – durch die Seele,* that cuts me to the heart; *einen – haben,* turn sour, go bad; (*coll.*) have a screw loose; *– halten,* stand the test, hold good, (*coll.*) hold water; *Hieb und –,* cut and thrust; *– ins Blaue,* tinge, shade *or* touch of blue; *im –(e) lassen,* leave in the lurch. **-bahn,** *f.* branch line (*Railw.*). **-balken,** *m.* half-beam. **-blatt,** *n.* guard (*of a sword*), hilt; winning card, trump; (*fig.*) butt. **-el,** *m.* style, graver, graving tool; burin. **-elei,** *f.* taunt, gibe. **-eln,** *v.a.* & *n.* (*aux.* h.) grave, engrave (*in metal*); stitch, sew; prick, puncture; (*fig.*) taunt, jeer, sneer, gibe; tease. **-elname,** *m.* nickname. **-elrede,** *f.* sarcasm, taunt, gibe. **-entscheid,** *m.* casting vote **-fest,** *adj.* inviolable, unassailable, dependable; *hieb- und -fest,* invulnerable, proof against all danger, immune against all attack. **-flamme,** *f.* jet of flame. **-graben,** *m.* communication trench (*Mil.*). **-halten** (*Austr. dial.*), *see – halten.* **-haltig,** *adj.* (*Austr. dial.* **-hältig**) sound, valid, proof, lasting. **-haltigkeit,** *f.* soundness, validity. **-heber,** *m.* pipette. **-loch,** *n.* tapping-hole (*Metall.*). **-ofen,** *m.* blast-furnace. **-platte,** *f.* needle-plate (*Sew.-Mach.*). **-probe,** *f.* spot-check, random sample. **-säge,** *f.* keyhole-saw. **-tag,** *m.* fixed day, term; key-date. **-torf,** *m.* cut peat. **-waffe,** *f.* pointed weapon, foil. **-wahl,** *f.* second *or* final ballot. **-weise,** *adv.* stitch by stitch. **-wort,** *n.* catch-word, key-word, caption; cue (*Theat.*); party-cry. **-wortverzeichnis,** *n.* index. **-wunde,** *f.* stab. **-zähler,** *m.* tachometer, revolution counter.

stich, stichst, sticht, *see* **stechen.**

Stichling, *m.* (-s, -e) stickleback (*Gasterosteus aculeatus*) (*Icht.*).

[1]**stick-en,** *v.a.* & *n.* embroider. **-arbeit,** *f.*, **-erei,** *f.* embroidery; piece of embroidery. **-erin,** *f.* embroiderer. **-garn,** *n.* embroidery-cotton. **-grund,** *m.* embroidery canvas *or* material. **-häkchen,** *n.* crochet-needle. **-muster,** *n.* embroidery pattern. **-rahmen,** *m.* embroidery-frame.

[2]**stick-en,** *v.n.* choke, suffocate. **-dunst,** *m.*, **-dampf,** *m.* suffocating vapour, choke-damp (*Min.*). **-gas,** *n.* asphyxiating gas, carbon dioxide. **-husten,** *m.* choking cough. **-ig,** *adj.* stifling, suffocating, close, stuffy. **-luft,** *f.* close *or* stuffy air, (*fig.*) oppressive atmosphere. **-oxyd,** *n.*, *see* **-stoffoxyd. -oxydul,** *n.*, *see* **-stoffoxydul. -stoff,** *m.* nitrogen. **-stoffdünger,** *m.* nitrogenous manure *or* fertilizer. **-stoffhaltig,** *adj.* nitrogenous. **-stoffoxyd,** *n.* nitric oxide. **-stoffoxydul,** *n.* nitrous oxide, laughing-gas. **-wetter,** *n.pl.*, *see* **-dampf.**

stickst, stickt, *see* [1]**sticken** & [2]**sticken.**

stieben, *ir. or reg. v.n.* (*aux.* h. & s.) fly about (like dust), rise up, disperse, scatter; drizzle.

Stief-bruder, *m.* stepbrother. **-eltern,** *pl.* step-parents. **-geschwister,** *pl.* stepbrothers and step-sisters. **-kind,** *n.* stepchild; (*usually fig.*) neglected child; *das -kind der Künste,* the Cinderella of the arts. **-mutter,** *f.* stepmother. **-mütterchen,** *n.* pansy (*Viola tricolor*) (*Bot.*). **-mütterlich,** *adj.* like a stepmother; perfunctory, inconsiderate, slighting, unkind, (*coll.*) shabby; *-mütterlich behandeln,* treat shabbily. **-schwester,** *f.* stepsister. **-sohn,** *m.* stepson. **-tochter,** *f.* stepdaughter. **-vater,** *m.* stepfather.

Stiefel, *m.* (-s, -) boot; large tankard; barrel (*of a pump*); (*dial.*) prop, support; (*sl.*) *seinen – arbeiten,* work on in the same old way; (*coll.*) *den alten – weitertragen,* carry on as usual; (*coll.*) *er kann einen guten – vertragen,* he carries his drink well; *hoher –,* knee-boot. **-anzieher,** *m.* shoe-horn. **-appell,** *m.* boot inspection (*Mil.*). **-ette,** *f.* ankle boot. **-holz,** *n.* boot-tree, last; spreader (*on fishing nets*). **-knecht,** *m.* boot-jack. **-lack,** *m.* boot polish. **-n,** 1. *v.a.* provide with boots; *gestiefelt und gespornt,* booted and spurred; *der gestiefelte Kater,* Puss-in-Boots. 2. *v.n.* (*aux.* s.) (*coll.*) walk, march, stride *or* stalk along. **-putzer,** *m.* boots (*at hotels*); shoe-black (*in the streets*). **-schaft,** *m.* leg of a boot. **-schwärze,** *f.* boot-blacking. **-spanner,** *m.*, **-strecker,** *m.* (boot-)tree. **-wichse,** *f.* blacking.

stieg, stiege, *see* **steigen.**

Stieg, *m.* (-(e)s, -e) (*dial.*), *see* **Steig. -e,** *f.* (-n) staircase, (flight of) stairs, steps; crate, hen-house. **-engeländer,** *n.* balustrade.

Stiege, *f.* (-n) score.

Stieglitz, *m.* (-es, -e) goldfinch (*Carduelis*) (*Orn.*).

stiehl, stiehlst, stiehlt, *see* **stehlen.**

Stiel, *m.* (-(e)s, -e) haft, handle, stick (*of a broom*); post, strut; stem, stalk, peduncle, petiole; *mit Stumpf und – ausrotten,* destroy *or* eliminate root and branch. **-augen,** *n.pl.* protruding eyes; *er machte* or *bekam -augen,* his eyes popped out of his head. **-brille,** *f.* lorgnette. **-eiche,** *f.* pedunculate oak. **-en,** *v.a.* furnish with a handle, fit a handle, **-handgranate,** *f.* stick-grenade. **-ig,** *suffix* -stalked, -handled, -pedunculate. **-loch,** *n.* eye (*of a hatchet, etc.*), foramen. **-los,** *adj.* without a handle; sessile, stalkless. **-rippe,** *f.* main rib (*of a leaf*). **-rund,** *adj.* cylindrical. **-ständig,** *adj.* growing on the stem, pedunculate. **-stich,** *m.* stem stitch (*Embroidery*).

Stieper, *m.* (-s, -) short prop, strut, stanchion.

stier, *adj.* fixed, staring; *-er Blick,* fixed stare, vacant look. **-en,** *v.n.* (*aux.* h.) stare, look fixedly at.

Stier, *m.* (-(e)s, -e) bull; Taurus (*Astr.*); *den – an* or *bei den Hörnern fassen* or *packen,* take the bull by the horns. **-artig,** *adj.* bull-like, taurine. **-(en)auge,** *n.* (*Swiss dial.*) fried egg. **-fechter,** *m.* bullfighter. **-gespann,** *n.* team *or* span of oxen. **-kampf,** *m.* bullfight. **-kämpfer,** *m.*, *see* **-fechter. -köpfig,** *adj.* obstinate, stiff-necked, self-willed. **-nackig,** *adj.* bull-necked; *see also* **-köpfig.**

Stiesel, *m.* (-s, -) *see* **Stießel.**

stieß, stieße, *see* **stoßen.**

Stießel, *m.* (-s, -) (*coll.*) boor, clod.

[1]**Stift,** *m.* (-(e)s, -e) spike, pin, peg, rivet, stud, nail, brad, tack; crayon, pencil; quid, plug (*of tobacco*); (*coll.*) apprentice, stripling; (*coll.*) *kleiner –,* little chap. **-halter,** *m.* crayon-holder, pencil-holder. **-kreide,** *f.* (blackboard) chalk. **-schraube,** *f.* set-screw. **-uhr,** *f.* watch with hook-escapement. **-zahn,** *m.* crown, pivot tooth. **-zeichnung,** *f.* pastel-drawing.

[2]**Stift,** *n.* (-(e)s, -e & -er) foundation; charitable institution, home (for old people); religious establishment, seminary, training-college (*for clergymen*); (*dial.*) convent, monastery; (*archaic*) bishopric. **-en,** *v.a.* found, establish, institute; (*coll.*) give, donate, make a present of; bring about, originate, cause, make; *Brand -en,* set on fire, set fire to; *Freundschaft -en,* promote a friendship; *Frieden -en,* make peace; *Gutes -en,* do good; *Ordnung -en,* put in order; *Unfrieden -en,* sow discord. **-er,** *m.* founder, donor; author, originator.

-ler, *m.* member of a seminary, inmate of an institution. **-sdame,** *f.* canoness. **-sgebäude,** *n.* chapter-house. **-sgemeinde,** *f.* congregation of a cathedral. **-sgut,** *n.* chapter property; ecclesiastical endowment. **-sherr,** *m.* canon, prebendary. (*B.*) **-shütte,** *f.* (Jewish) tabernacle. **-skirche,** *f.* collegiate church. **-spfründe,** *f.* prebend. **-sschule,** *f.* school attached to the chapters of collegiate churches. **-sversammlung,** *f.* meeting of a chapter. **-ung,** *f.* founding, establishment; foundation, institution; endowment, bequest; originating, causing, making. **-ungsfest,** *n.* commemoration *or* founder's day. **-ungsurkunde,** *f.* deed of foundation.

Stigma, *n.* (-mas, -mata & -men) mark, stigma; scar (*of plants*); spiracle, stigma (*of insects*). **-tisieren,** *v.a.* stigmatize, brand.

Stil, *m.* (-(e)s, -e) style; manner, way, kind; *nach dem eingeführten –*, according to the established usage, customary. **-art,** *f.* (*Poet.*) genre. **-blüte,** *f.* pun, bull, spoonerism. **-echt,** *adj.* true to style. **-gefühl,** *n.* stylistic sense, feeling for style. **-gerecht,** *adj., see* **-voll.** **-isieren,** *v.a.* compose, word; *er –isiert gut,* he writes good style *or* well, his style is good. **-ist,** *m.* writer with a good style. **-istik,** *f.* art of composition. **-istisch,** *adj.* with regard to style; *in –istischer Hinsicht,* in the matter of style. **-kunde,** *f., see* **-istik.** **-übung,** *f.* exercise in writing, practice in composition. **-voll,** *adj.* in good taste *or* style. **-widrig,** *adj.* in bad taste.

Stilett, *n.* (-(e)s, -e) stiletto.

still, *adj.* silent, quiet, hushed, soft; still, motionless, stagnant, inanimate, calm, peaceful, peaceable; tacit, secret; *–es Beileid,* unspoken sympathy; *wir bitten um –es Beileid,* no visits of condolence desired (*in announcement of a death*); *jemanden – bekommen,* succeed in silencing a p.; *–er Freitag,* Good Friday; *–es Gebet,* silent prayer; *–er Gesellschafter,* see *–er Teilhaber*; *im –en,* quietly, in silence, secretly, privately, (*coll.*) on the quiet; *–e Jahreszeit,* slack season; *–e Liebe,* unavowed love; *jemanden – machen,* kill a p.; *–e Messe,* low mass; *bei –er Nacht,* at dead of night; *–er Ozean,* Pacific (Ocean); *–er Teilhaber,* sleeping partner; *dem –en Trunk ergeben,* addicted to secret drinking; *–e Übereinkunft,* tacit agreement *or* understanding; *sich – verhalten,* not move, keep quiet; *–er Vorbehalt,* mental reservation; *–er Vorwurf,* silent reproach *or* reproof; (*Prov.*) *–e Wasser sind* or *gründen tief,* still waters run deep; *–e Woche,* Passion Week; *–e Wut,* dumb rage; paralytic rabies. **-beglückt,** *adj.* secretly happy. **-bleiben,** *v.n.* be still, remain silent. **-geld,** *n.* insurance money paid to nursing mothers. **-e,** *f.* quiet, stillness, silence; calm, tranquillity, repose, peace; pause, lull; *in der –e, in aller –e,* see *im –en*; *in der –e abziehen,* slink *or* steal away; *in der –e leben,* lead a secluded life; *die –e vor dem Sturm,* the lull before the storm. **-en,** *v.a.* quiet, hush, silence; appease, calm, soothe, mitigate, allay (*pain, etc.*); stay, quench (*thirst, etc.*); staunch (*blood*); gratify, satisfy (*desires*); nurse, suckle (*a child*). **-end,** *pr.p.* & *adj.* soothing, sedative, lenitive. **-gestanden,** *see* **-stehen.** **-halten,** 1. *v.n.* & *a.* keep quiet, pause, stop; *einem –halten,* submit quietly to a p., let a p. do as he likes. 2. *n.* stop, pause, halt. **-halteabkommen,** *n.* moratorium. **-haltung,** *f.* (*C.L.*) respite, delay in payments, moratorium. **-(l)eben,** *n.* still life (*Paint.*). **-(l)egen,** *v.a.* shut down (*a business*). **-(l)egung,** *f.* shutting *or* closing down. **-(l)iegen,** *v.n.* lie quiet; lie down; lie to (*as a ship*); stop; *die Geschäfte liegen –,* trade is dull, business is at a standstill; *der gesamte Verkehr liegt –,* all traffic is suspended. **-schweigen,** 1. *n.* silence. 2. *v.n.* be silent; *zu etwas –schweigen,* pass a th. over in silence. **-schweigend,** *adj.* silent; tacit, implied. **-stand,** *m.* standstill, stop, stoppage, cessation; stagnation, inactivity; deadlock; station (*Astr.*); (*Prov.*) *–stand ist Rückgang,* he who does not advance goes backwards. **-stehen,** 1. *v.n.* stop, stand still; stand at attention; be at a standstill; *da steht mir der Verstand –,* that is beyond me *or* my comprehension; *–gestanden!* (stand at) attention! (*Mil.*). 2. *n.* stop. **-stehend,** *pr.p.* & *adj.* stationary, motionless; inactive, stagnant. **-ung,** *f.* stilling, appeasing; staunching; nursing, breast-feeding, suckling, lactation. **-ungsmittel,** *n.* sedative. **-vergnügt,** *adj.* quietly enjoying o.s., calm and serene.

Stimm-e, *f.* (-en) voice; vote, suffrage; opinion; part (*Mus.*); sound-post (*of a violin*); stop (*of an organ*); *–e abgeben,* vote; *die –en austeilen,* distribute the parts (*Mus.*); (*gut*) *bei –e sein,* in (good) voice; *nicht bei –e,* not in voice; *ohne eine –e dagegen,* without a (single) dissentient voice; *sich der –e enthalten,* withhold one's opinion, abstain from voting; *entscheidende –e,* casting vote; *erste –e,* soprano; *einem seine –e geben,* give one's vote to *or* vote in favour of a p.; *keine –e haben,* have no say in the matter; *–e der Presse,* press comment; *die –en sammeln,* put the matter to the vote; *Sitz und –e haben,* have a seat and vote. **-en,** 1. *v.a.* tune; dispose, incline, prejudice (a p.) (*für,* in favour of); *einen fröhlich –en,* put s.o. in good humour; *die Nachricht hat mich traurig gestimmt,* the news has made me (feel) sad; *seine Forderungen hoch –en,* pitch one's demand high; *er ist schlecht gestimmt,* he is in low spirits *or* in a bad mood. 2. *v.n.* (*aux.* h.) agree (with), tally (with), correspond (to); be correct, be all right; suit, accord, be in tune, be in keeping, harmonize; vote; *gegen einen –en,* vote against a p.; *zu etwas –en,* tone, harmonize, fit in *or* (*coll.*) go with s.th.; (*das*) *–t,* (that is) all right, (*sl.*) O.K. **-abgabe,** *f.* voting, vote. **-band,** *n.* vocal chord. **-berechtigt,** *adj.* entitled to vote. **-berechtigung,** *f., see* **-recht.** **-bildung,** *f.* voice production. **-bruch,** *m.* breaking of the voice. **-bürger,** *m.* (*Swiss dial.*) elector. **-eneinheit,** *f.* unanimity; *mit –eneinheit,* unanimously, with no dissentient vote, nem. con. **-enfang,** *m.* canvassing; *auf –enfang ausgehen,* go round canvassing. **-engewirr,** *n.* confused voices, din of voices. **-engleichheit,** *f.* equality of votes (for and against); *bei –engleichheit den Ausschlag geben,* give the casting vote. **-enmehrheit,** *f.* majority (*of votes*); *einfache –enmehrheit,* bare majority. **-enminderheit,** *f.* minority (*of votes*). **-enprüfung,** *f.* scrutiny *or* recounting of votes. **-enthaltung,** *f.* abstention from voting. **-enverhältnis,** *n.* proportion of votes. **-enzähler,** *m.* teller (*Parl.*). **-er,** *m.* tuner. **-fähig,** *see* **-berechtigt.** **-führer,** *m.* spokesman; leader (*of a choir*). **-gabel,** *f.* tuning-fork. **-haft,** *adj.* voiced (*Phonet.*). **-lage,** *f.* register, pitch. **-lich,** *adj.* vocal. **-los,** *adj.* voiceless (*Phonet.*). **-recht,** *n.* right to vote, franchise, suffrage. **-rechtlerin,** *f.* suffragette. **-ritze,** *f.* glottis. **-ritzendeckel,** *m.* epiglottis. **-ritzenverschluß(laut),** *m.* glottal stop (*Phonet.*). **-saite,** *f., see* **-band.** **-stock,** *m.* sound-post (*of a violin*). **-ung,** *f.* tuning, key, pitch; mood, humour, temper, disposition, state *or* frame of mind, morale (*Mil.*); impression, atmosphere; *–ung machen für,* canvass, make propaganda for; *bei –ung,* in tune, in good humour, in good spirits; *in –ung,* in the mood. **-ungsbericht,** *m.* canvass of opinion. **-ungsbild,** *n.* impressionistic picture. **-ungsmache,** *f.* propaganda. **-ungsmensch,** *m.* moody creature. **-ungsumschwung,** *m.* change of attitude *or* mood. **-ungsvoll,** *adj.* appealing to the emotions; impressive; full of genuine feeling. **-vieh,** *n.* (*coll.*) the fatuous electorate. **-wechsel,** *m., see* **-bruch.** **-werkzeug,** *n.* vocal organs. **-zettel,** *m.* ballot *or* voting-paper.

stimulieren, *v.a.* stimulate.

stink-en, *ir.v.n.* (*aux.* h.) stink, be fetid, smell foul; (*Prov.*) *Eigenlob –t,* self-praise is no recommendation; *er –t nach Geld,* (*vulg.*) he is lousy *or* stiff with money; *der Junge –t vor Faulheit,* that boy is bone idle. **-end,** *pr.p.* & *adj., see* **-ig.** **-adores,** *f.* (*hum.*) cheap cigar, whiff. **-apparat,** *m.* stink gland. **-bombe,** *f.* stink-bomb. **-drüse,** *f., see* **-apparat.** (*sl.*) **-faul,** *adj.* bone idle. **-ig,** *adj.* stinking, fetid, (*fig.*) foul. **-tier,** *n.* skunk. **-wut,** *f.* (*coll.*) filthy temper, towering rage.

Stint, *m.* (-(e)s, -e) smelt (*Osmerus eperlanus*) (*Icht.*).

Stipend-iat, *m.* (-en, -en) scholarship holder, exhibitioner. **-ist,** *m.* (*dial.*), *see* **-iat.** **-ium,** *n.* (-iums, -ien) scholarship, exhibition.

Stipp-e, *f.* (-en) (*dial.*) stigma, mark; pimple,

speck, freckle; gravy, sauce. **–angriff,** *m.* hit-and-run raid. **–el,** *m.* (*dial.*) ladle. **–en,** *v.a. & n.* (*aux.* h.) (*dial.*) steep, dip. (*dial.*) **–visite,** *f.* flying visit, short call.

stipulieren, *v.a.* stipulate.

stirb, stirbst, stirbt, *see* **sterben.**

Stirn, –e, *f.* (-(e)n) forehead, brow; front (*Arch.*); impudence, (*coll.*) cheek, face; *einem etwas an der – ansehen,* read s.th. on a p.'s face; *auf der – geschrieben sein,* be written on one's face; *einem die – bieten,* show a bold front to a p., defy a p.; (*fig.*) *eiserne* or *eherne –,* bold front, brazen-faced impudence; *mit erhobener –,* holding one's head high; *er hatte die –,* he had the cheek; *die – runzeln,* wrinkle one's brow. **–ader,** *f.* frontal vein. **–angriff,** *m.* frontal attack. **–band,** *n.,* **–binde,** *f.* head-band; fillet, frontlet. **–bein,** *n.* frontal bone. **–beinhöhle,** *f.* frontal sinus. **–bogen,** *m.* frontal arch. **–fläche,** *f.* face (*of an arch*), front, end surface. **–hirn,** *n.* frontal lobes. **–höhle,** *f.* frontal cavity, frontal sinus. **–ig,** *adj. suffix*; e.g. *breit–ig,* with a broad forehead. **–krankheit,** *f.* mad staggers (*Vet.*). **–kühler,** *m.* front radiator (*Motor.*). **–leiste,** *f.* leading edge (*of wing*) (*Av.*). **–locke,** *f.* forelock. **–rad,** *n.* spur-gear. **–radgetriebe,** *n.* spur-gearing. **–riemen,** *m.* frontlet, head-piece (*of a bridle*). **–runzeln,** *n.* frown(ing). **–schild,** *m.* frontal bone. **–seite,** *f.* façade, front (*Arch.*). **–welle,** *f.* wave front.

stob, stöbe, *see* **stieben.**

stoben, *v.a.* (*dial.*) stew.

stöber–n, *v.n.* (*aux.* h.) hunt about, search everywhere, rummage; (*dial.*) do spring-cleaning; drift, blow about (*of snow*); drizzle (*of rain*); *in einem Buch –n,* turn over the leaves of a book; *einen aus dem Bett –n,* tumble *or* hustle a p. out of bed. **–ei,** *f.* (*dial.*) spring-clean(ing). **–hund,** *m.* sporting-dog, gun-dog.

Stocher, *m.* (-s, –) poker; toothpick. **–n,** *v.a. & n.* (*aux.* h.) poke about (in); pick (*one's teeth*); poke, rake *or* stir (*the fire*).

Stock, *m.* 1. (-(e)s, ⸗e) stick, staff, rod, pole, wand, baton, cane, walking-stick; stem (*of a plant*), trunk, stump (*of a tree, tooth, etc.*); cue (*Bill.*); stock, block, body (*of an anvil, etc.*); stocks (*for culprits*); (bee)hive; mountain-mass, massif, mass (*of rocks, etc.*); pot plant; (vine-)stock; *in den – legen,* put in the stocks; *im – sitzen,* be (put) in the stocks; *einen Hut über den – schlagen,* put a hat on the block; *über – und Stein,* up hill and down dale; *am – gehen,* walk with the help of a stick; *Regiment des –es,* rule of the rod. 2. (-s, -s) (*C.L.*) capital, stocks, funds. 3. (-(e)s, -(e) *or* -werke) story (*of a house*), floor (*above ground-floor*); *wie viel – hat es?* how many stories has it? *im ersten –,* on the first floor. **–ball,** *m.* hockey. **–blind,** *adj.* stone-blind. **–degen,** *m.* sword-cane. **–dumm,** *adj.* utterly stupid. **–dunkel,** *adj.* pitch-dark. **–dürr,** *adj.* (as) dry as a bone. **–en,** 1. *v.n.* (*aux.* h. & s.) stop, hesitate, falter; stop running, flowing *or* circulating, stand still, stagnate; (*dial.*) curdle, coagulate, cake, thicken; turn mouldy *or* fusty, decay, spoil; *der Handel –t,* trade is dull *or* at a standstill; *die S. –t, es –t mit der S.,* the affair is at a standstill; *im Reden –en,* break down in a speech, falter, hesitate; (*dial.*) *gestockte Milch,* curdled milk. 2. *n.* stopping, cessation; stagnation, interruption; *ins –en geraten,* come to a standstill; *–en der Zähne,* dental caries. **–end,** *adj.* dull, stagnant; stopping. **–ende,** *n.* butt end. **–engländer,** *m.* typical Englishman, John Bull. **–erig,** *adj.* hesitating, faltering. **–erl,** *n.* (*Austr. dial.*) stool. **–erz,** *n.* ore in lumps. **–finster,** *adj.* pitch-dark. **–fisch,** *m.* stockfish, dried cod; (*fig.*) blockhead. **–fleck,** *m.* damp-stain; mildew (*Bot.*). **–fleckig,** *adj.* stained by damp, mouldy; foxed, spotted (*of paper*). **–fremd,** *adj.* entirely strange. **–gelehrt,** *adj.* pedantic. **–griff,** *m.* walking-stick handle. (*archaic*) **–haus,** *n.* jail. **–holz,** *n.* tree stump. **–ig,** *adj.* mildewed, mouldy, musty, fusty; obstinate, stubborn; stocky, stumpy; *–ige Zähne,* decayed teeth. **–makler,** *m.* stock-jobber, stock-broker. (*archaic*) **–meister,** *m.* jailer. **–punkt,** *m.* solidifying point. **–rose,** *f.* hollyhock (*Althaea rosea*) (*Bot.*). **–schirm,** *m.* walking-stick umbrella. **–schnupfen,** *m.* obstinate cold, thick cold. **–steif,** *adj.* (as) stiff as a poker. **–taub,** *adj.* stone-deaf. **–ung,** *f.* stopping, stoppage, cessation, interruption; stagnation; congestion, standstill, (traffic) block *or* jam. **–werk,** *n.* story, floor, tier. **–zahn,** *m.* (*dial.*) molar tooth.

Stöck–el, *m.* (-s, –) (*dial.*) heel (*of shoe*). **–elschuh,** *m.* high-heeled shoe. **–ig,** *adj. suffix* -storied; *zwei–iges Haus,* two-storied house. **–isch,** *adj.* obstinate, pig-headed; thick-headed; taciturn. **–li,** *n.* (*Swiss dial.*) *see* **Altenteil.**

Stoff, *m.* (-(e)s, -e) matter, substance, body; subject, subject-matter, theme, topic; material, stuff, cloth, fabric; pulp (*Pap.*); (*Studs. sl.*) beer; *– zum Lesen,* reading matter. **–bildend,** *adj.* forming tissue. **–en,** *adj.* made of fabric. **–(f)etzen,** *m.* scrap of material. **–(f)ülle,** *f.* wealth of material. **–gebiet,** *n.* range of subjects. **–gewicht** *n.* specific gravity. **–halter,** *m.* foot (*on sewing-machines*). **–haltig,** *adj.* material, substantial. **–lich,** *adj.* material; with regard to the subject-matter. **–los,** *adj.* immaterial, insubstantial, unsubstantial. **–reich,** *adj.* substantial; rich in material. **–teilchen,** *n.* particle of matter. **–umsatz,** *m.* metabolism. **–wahl,** *f.* choice of subject. **–wechsel,** *m.* metabolism, combustion. **–wechselgleichgewicht,** *n.* nutritive equilibrium. **–wechselgröße,** *f.* metabolic rate. **–zerfall,** *m.* decay, decomposition.

Stoff–el, *m.* (-s, –) dolt, lout, booby. **–(e)lig,** *adj.* uncouth, loutish, stupid.

stöhle, *see* **stehlen.**

stöhnen, *v.n.* (*aux.* h.) groan, moan.

Stol–a, –e, *f.* (-en) stole, surplice (*R.C.*).

Stolle, *f.* (-n) (*Austr. dial.*), **–n,** *m.* (-s, –) fruit loaf.

Stollen, *m.* (-s, –) post, prop; dugout, gallery, tunnel (*Min.*); calkin (*of horseshoe*). **–arbeit,** *f.,* **–bau,** *m.* tunnelling. **–hauer, –häuer,** *m.* tunneller. **–holz,** *n.* pit props.

Stolper, *m.* (-s, –) (*dial.*) stumble; blunder. **–draht,** *m.* trip-wire. **–er,** *m.* stumbler, blunderer. **–ig,** *adj.* stumbling, blundering; uneven, rough, bumpy (*as a road*). **–n,** *v.n.* (*aux.* h. & s.) stumble, trip (over); blunder.

stolz, 1. *adj.* proud, haughty, arrogant; splendid, superb, stately; *auf etwas – sein,* be proud of *or* take a pride in a th.; *–es Schiff,* fine ship. 2. *m.* pride, vanity, haughtiness, arrogance; glory, boast; *seinen – in eine S. setzen,* take a pride in a th., make a th. one's boast. **–ieren,** *v.a.* (*aux.* s.) flaunt, strut.

Stöpfel, *m.* (*dial.*), *see* **Stöpsel.**

stopf–en, 1. *v.a.* fill (*a pipe, etc.*), cram; darn, mend (*stockings*); plug, close, stop up, mute (*a wind instrument*); (*dial.*) cork; caulk (*a ship*); cease fire (*Mil.*); (*coll.*) *einem den Mund* (or *das Maul*) *–en,* make a p. shut up; *gestopft voll,* crammed full; *gestopfte Trompete,* muted trumpet. 2. *v.n.* (*aux.* h.) (*coll.*) be filling, bind, cause constipation; *Eier –en,* eggs are binding. 3. *v.r.* stuff o.s., gorge; become blocked *or* jammed. 4. *n.* stuffing, cramming. 5. *m.* (*dial.*) cork, bung, stopper. **–arznei,** *f.* astringent *or* binding medicine. **–büchse,** *f.* stuffing-box; piston-rod collar (*Mach.*). **–end,** *adj.* binding, constipating; astringent, styptic. **–ei,** *n.* darning-mushroom. **–er,** *m.* prodder, prod, filler; cork, bung, plug. **–garn,** *n.* darning-wool. **–mittel,** *n.* astringent, styptic. **–nadel,** *f.* darning-needle. **–naht,** *f.* darn. **–pilz,** *m., see* **–ei. –werg,** *n.* oakum (*for caulking*).

Stopp–el, *f.* (-n) stubble; (*pl.*) pin-feathers, bristles (*of beard*). **–elig,** *adj., see* **–lig. –eln,** *v.a.* glean. **–ler,** *m.* gleaner. **–elbart,** *m.* bristly *or* stubbly beard. **–elfeder,** *f.* pin-feather. **–elfeld,** *n.* stubble-field, field of stubble. **–elmast,** *f.* stubble-grazing. **–elvers,** *m.* halting verse. **–elweide,** *f.* stubble-pasture. **–elwerk,** *n.* patchwork, compilation. **–lig,** *adj.* stubbly, bristly.

stopp–en, *v.a. & n.* stop. **–licht,** *n.* (*pl.* -er) rear light, brake-light (*Motor.*). **–(p)reis,** *m.* ceiling price, price limit. **–straße,** *f.* major road ahead. **–uhr,** *f.* stop-watch.

Stöpsel, *m.* (-s, –) stopper, cork, bung, plug; (*coll.*) little runt. **–automat,** *m.* automatic cut-out (*Elec.*).

–glas, *n.* glass-stoppered bottle. **–n,** *v.a.* cork, stopper, plug.

[1]**Stör,** *m.* (-s, -e) sturgeon (*Acipensidae*) (*Icht.*).

[2]**Stör,** *f.* (*Austr. & Swiss dial.*); *in* or *auf die – gehen, auf der – arbeiten, –en,* work at a customer's house, do job-work; hawk. **–er,** *m.* job-worker; hawker, vagrant.

Storch, *m.* (-(e)s, ⸚e) stork; (*coll.*) *da brat' mir einer einen –,* that beats everything! that's the giddy limit! **–beinig,** *adj.* spindle-shanked. **–(en)nest,** *n.* stork's nest. **–schnabel,** *m.* stork's bill; geranium (*Bot.*); cranesbill (*Surg.*); pantograph (*Draw.*).

Store, *m.* (-s, –s) curtain.

stör–en, 1. *v.a.* disturb, interrupt, inconvenience, trouble, annoy, harass (*the enemy*); disorder, upset, derange; interfere, jam (*Rad.*); (*dial.*) scrape, scratch (*as hens*); *laß dich doch nicht –en*, do not trouble (yourself), do not let me disturb you; *–t Sie mein Rauchen?* do you mind my smoking? *geistig gestört,* mentally deranged. 2. *v.n.* (*aux.* h.) intrude, be in the way; *see also* [2]**Stör.** **–angriff,** *m.*, **–einsatz,** *m.* nuisance raid (*Av.*). **–enfried,** *m.* mischief-maker. **–er,** *m.* troublesome person, meddler; intruder; kill-joy. **–feuer,** *n.* harassing fire (*Mil.*). **–flieger,** *m.* nuisance *or* sneak raider, intruder (*Av.*). **–frei,** *adj.* causing no interference (*of electrical equipment*); free from interference (*of radio reception*). **–funk,** *m.* jamming, interference (*Rad.*). **–schutz,** *m.* interference-filter, screening (*against interference*) (*Rad.*). **–sender,** *m.* jamming station. **–sucher,** *m.*, *see* **–ungssucher.** **–ung,** *f.* disturbance; trouble, upset, annoyance, inconvenience, perturbation; interruption, intrusion, disorder, derangement, break-down; perturbation (*Astr.*); atmospherics, jamming, interference (*Rad.*); *geistige –ung*, mental derangement. **–ungsfrei,** *adj.* undisturbed, uninterrupted, free from interference (*Rad.*). **–ungsstelle,** *f.* fault-section (*Phone, Tele.*). **–ungssucher,** *m.* lineman (*Tele.*).

Storger, *m.* (-s, –) (*dial.*) vagabond, tramp.

storn–ieren, *v.a.* (*C.L.*) correct an entry, annul, cancel. **–o,** *m.* (-s, -i) transfer of account, cancellation.

störr–ig, –isch, *adj.* stubborn, obstinate, headstrong; restive, refractory. **–igkeit,** *f.* stubbornness.

Stoß, *m.* (-es, ⸚e) push, shove, thrust, impulse; knock, blow, hit, stroke; punch, kick, jolt, jerk, nudge, jog; collision, shock, impact, percussion; thrust, pass (*Fenc.*); blast, flourish (*of a trumpet*); swoop; heap, bundle, pile; seam, joint, hem; *stumpfer –,* butt-joint; *– auf Gehrung,* mitre-joint; *der letzte –,* the finishing stroke; *das hat mir einen – gegeben,* that has given me a shock; *seine Gesundheit hat einen empfindlichen – erhalten,* his health suffered a serious setback. **–en,** 1. *ir.v.a.* push, shove, thrust, strike, knock, hit, ram, butt, buffet, punch, nudge, jog, jostle; kick; stab; pound, pulverize, crush, bruise, bray; drive out, expel, oust; *etwas an die Wand –en,* knock a th. against the wall; *einen mit der Nase auf eine S. –en,* place a thing under a p.'s very nose, rub a p.'s nose in s.th.; *einen aus dem Hause –en,* turn *or* fling a p. out; *er stieß ihm den Dolch ins Herz,* he thrust the dagger into his heart; *einen Ball ins Loch –en,* send a ball into a pocket (*Bill.*); *ein Loch ins Papier –en,* punch a hole in the paper; *die Kugel –en,* put the shot (*Sport.*); *einen über den Haufen –en,* throw a p. to the ground; *etwas von sich –en,* push a th. away, reject *or* discard a th., repudiate a th.; *einen vor den Kopf –en,* insult *or* offend a p.; *Zucker –en,* crush sugar. 2. *v.r.* knock (*an,* against); hurt o.s.; take offence at *or* exception to a th. (*an einer S.*); *– dich nicht daran!* do not take it amiss! do not take offence at that! *daran stößt es sich,* that is the difficulty, snag *or* hitch. 3. *v.n.* (*aux.* h.) thrust (*Fenc.*), butt (*as goats*), kick (*of gun*); adjoin, border on (*an*); push, knock, strike (*an* or *gegen,* against); bump, jolt; (*aux.* s.) come across, chance upon, meet with, encounter, pounce upon (*auf*); join up (*zu,* with); *wer stößt?* whose stroke is it? (*Bill., etc.*); *mit dem Fuße an eine S. –en,* stumble against s.th.; *diese Zimmer –en an einander,* these rooms are adjoining; *ans Land –en,* run ashore, land; *wir stießen auf den Feind,* we ran into the enemy; *in das Horn –en,* blow a trumpet; *vom Lande –en,* push off (from shore); *der Wind stößt,* the wind comes in gusts; *das Regiment wird zu Ihrem Korps –en,* the regiment will join (up with) your corps. 4. *n.* pushing, thrusting; trituration; jolting; kick, recoil (*of a gun*). **–balken,** *m.* abutment beam. **–dämpfer,** *m.* shock-absorber (*Motor.*). **–degen,** *m.* rapier, foil. **–empfindlich,** *adj.* sensitive to shock. **–fänger,** *m.* bumper (*Motor.*). **–fechten,** *n.* fencing with foils. **–frei,** *adj.* free, smooth (*of movement*). **–fuge,** *f.* butt-joint. **–gebet,** *n.* short fervent prayer. **–kissen,** *n.*, **–polster,** *n.* (*& Austr. m.*). (spring-)buffer. **–kraft,** *f.* impetus, impact (*Mech.*). **–platte,** *f.* butt-plate (*covering a butt-joint*). **–punkt,** *m.* point of attack. **–rad,** *n.* bogie wheel. **–riemen,** *m.* check-brace (*of a coach*). **–seufzer,** *m.* deep heartfelt sigh. **–sicher,** *adj.* shock-proof. **–stange,** *f.* push-rod (*Motor.*). **–taktik,** *f.* shock tactics (*Mil.*). **–trupp,** *m.* shock troops, assault detachment, raiding party. **–verkehr,** *m.* rush-hour traffic. **–waffe,** *f.* stabbing weapon. **–weise,** *adv.* by jerks, by fits and starts, jerkily. **–wind,** *m.* gust of wind, squall. **–zahn,** *m.* tusk. **–zünder,** *m.* percussion fuse.

Stöß–el, *m.* (-s, –) pestle; rammer, pounder, beetle; tappet (*Motor.*). **–er,** *m.* knocker, kicker, *etc.*; bird of prey; hawk. **–ig,** *adj.* butting, vicious (*of goats, etc.*).

Stotter–er, *m.* (-s, –) stutterer, stammerer. **–ig,** *adj.* stuttering, stammering. **–n,** *v.n.* (*aux.* h.) stammer, stutter; (*coll.*) *auf –n kaufen,* buy on the instalment plan (*or coll.* on the never-never.)

stowen, *v.a.* (*dial.*) steam, stew.

stracks, *adv.* immediately, straightway, directly; direct, straight (ahead), exactly.

Straf–e, *f.* (-en) punishment, penalty, fine; judgement, sentence; *bei –e des Todes,* on pain of death; *bei hoher Geld–e verboten,* forbidden under penalty of a heavy fine; *einen in –e nehmen,* inflict punishment *or* a penalty on a p.; *ihm zur –e,* in order to punish him; *Vorladung bei –e,* subpoena. **–anstalt,** *f.* prison, jail, gaol, penitentiary, house of correction. **–antrag,** *m.* sentence proposed *or* demanded. **–arbeit,** *f.*, **–aufgabe,** *f.* imposition (*at school*). **–arrest,** *m.* detention. **–aufschub,** *m.* deferment of a punishment. **–bar,** *adj.* punishable; culpable. **–barkeit,** *f.* liability to punishment, culpability. **–bataillon,** *n.* delinquent *or* punishment battalion (*Mil.*). **–befehl,** *m.* penal order, penalty. **–befugnis,** *f.* authority to punish, penal authority. **–bestimmung,** *f.* paragraph in the penal code, penal regulation, penalty. **–en,** *v.a.* punish, fine; chastise; (*B.*) blame, reprove, rebuke; *einen an der Ehre –en,* inflict a degrading punishment on a p.; *einen an Geld (und Gut) –en,* fine a p.; *einen an (Leib und) Leben –en,* punish a p. with death; *mit der Rute –en,* inflict corporal punishment; *einen Lügen –en,* give the lie to a p.; *solche Fehler –en sich selbst,* such faults bring their own punishment. **–end,** *pr.p. & adj.* punishing, punitive; revengeful; reproachful (*glance*). **–entlassene(r),** *m.* ex-convict. **–erkenntnis,** *n.* sentence passed on *or* judgement against a p. **–erlaß,** *m.* remission of punishment; amnesty. **–erleichterung,** *f.* mitigation of punishment. **–fall,** *m.*, *see* **–sache.** **–fällig,** *adj.*, *see* **–bar.** **–feuer,** *n.* retaliation fire (*Mil.*). **–frei,** *adj.*, *see* **–los.** **–gefangene(r),** *m.* convict. **–geld,** *n.* fine, forfeit, penalty. **–gericht,** *n.* criminal court; judgement; *ihn traf des Himmels –gericht,* the judgement of God overtook him. **–gerichtsbarkeit,** *f.* criminal justice. **–gerichtsordnung,** *f.* criminal court procedure. **–gesetz,** *n.* penal law. **–gesetzbuch,** *n.* penal code. **–gesetzgebung,** *f.* penal legislation. **–gewalt,** *f.* penal *or* disciplinary authority. **–haft,** *f.* punitive arrest. **–kammer,** *f.* criminal court. **–klage,** *f.* criminal proceedings. **–kolonie,** *f.* penal settlement. **–los,** *adj.* unpunished; exempt from punishment; innocent, guiltless; *–los ausgehen,* get off scot-free. **–losigkeit,** *f.* impunity, immunity. **–mandat,** *n.*, *see* **–befehl.** **–maß,** *n.* degree of punishment; *höchstes –maß,* maximum penalty. **–milderung,** *f.*

mitigation of a penalty, commutation of a sentence. **-milderungsgrund,** *m.* extenuating circumstances. **-mündig,** *adj.* of a responsible age. **-porto,** *n.* surcharge, extra postage. **-predigt,** *f.* reprimand, severe lecture. **-prozeß,** *m.* criminal case. **-prozeßordnung,** *f.* criminal procedure. **-punkt,** *m.* point deducted, penalty (*Sport*). **-raum,** *m.* penalty area (*football*). **-recht,** *n.* criminal *or* penal law. **-rechtlich,** *adj.* penal, criminal. **-rede,** *f.*, *see* **-predigt. -richter,** *m.* criminal court judge. **-sache,** *f.* criminal case. **-satz,** *m.* amount of punishment. **-stoß,** *m.* penalty kick (*football*). **-tat,** *f.* punishable offence. **-urteil,** *n.* penal sentence; *-urteil über einen verhängen*, pass judgement upon a p. **-verfahren,** *n.* criminal procedure. **-verfügung,** *f.* police regulation, penalty. **-versetzung,** *f.* transfer for disciplinary reasons. **-vollstreckung,** *f.*, **-vollziehung,** *f.*, **-vollzug,** *m.* infliction of punishment, execution of sentence. **-weise,** *adv.* as a punishment. **-würdig,** *adj.* deserving punishment; culpable. **-zug,** *m.* punitive expedition.

straff, *adj.* stretched, tense, tight, taut; erect, straight; austere, rigid, strict, stern; – *anliegen*, fit close *or* tightly; *-er Beutel*, well-filled purse; *-er Busen*, firm *or* shapely breasts; *-e Haltung*, erect bearing, stern *or* rigid attitude; *sich – halten*, stand bolt upright; *-e Zucht*, strict *or* rigid discipline. **-en,** *v.a.* & *r.* tighten; stretch; tauten (*Naut.*). **-heit,** *f.* tightness, tension; tautness; (*fig.*) severity, strictness, rigour, strict discipline (*Mil.*). **-ziehen,** *ir. v.a.* tighten, stretch; tauten (*Naut.*).

sträf-lich, 1. *adj.* punishable, wrong, criminal; blamable, unpardonable. 2. *adv.* (*coll.*) severely, enormously; *das tut -lich weh*, that is excruciatingly painful; *er ist -lich faul*, he is awfully lazy. **-lichkeit,** *f.* culpability; wickedness; criminality. **-ling,** *m.* convict. **-lingsfürsorge,** *f.* prison welfare-work.

Strahl, *m.* (-(e)s, -en) ray, beam; jet (*of water, etc.*); (*Poet.*) flash; radius, straight line; frog (*of hoof*) (*Vet.*); – *von Hoffnung*, gleam *or* glimmer of hope; *leuchtende -en*, luminous rays. **-antrieb,** *m.* jet-propulsion (*Av.*). **-düse,** *f.* jet, ejector. **-en,** *v.a.* & *n.* (*aux.* h.) beam, radiate, emit rays, shine; (*fig.*) beam (*as the face*). **-enbehandlung,** *f.* ray-treatment. **-enbrechend,** *adj.* refracting, refractive. **-enbrechung,** *f.* refraction, diffraction. **-enbrechungsmesser,** *m.* refractometer. **-enbündel,** *n.*, **-enbüschel,** *m.* (& *n.*) pencil of rays. **-end,** *pr.p.* & *adj.* radiating; radiant, beaming, shining. **-enförmig,** *adj.* radiate. **-enforschung,** *f.* radiology. **-englanz,** *m.* radiancy; brilliance, lustre. **-enkegel,** *m.* cone of rays. **-enkörper,** *m.* ciliary body. **-enkrone,** *f.* halo, aureole, nimbus, (*fig.*) glory. **-enmesser,** *m.* actinometer, radiometer. **-ensonne,** *f.* astrosphere. **-entierchen,** *n. pl.* wheel-animalcule (*Zool.*). **-enwerfen,** *n.* (ir)radiation. **-enwerfer,** *m.* aerial array, directional aerial (*Rad.*). **-ig,** *adj.* radiant, actinomorphic. **-triebwerk,** *n.* jet-engine (*Av.*). **-ung,** *f.* radiance; radiation. **-ungswärme,** *f.* radiant heat.

Strähl, *m.* (-(e)s, -e), **-e,** *f.* (*dial.*) comb. **-en,** *v.a.* comb.

Strähn, *m.* (-es, -e), *or usually* **-e,** *f.* (-n) lock, strand (*of hair*); skein, hank. **-ig,** 1. *adj.* stranded, in strands; wispy. 2. *adj. suffix*; of (so many) skeins *or* strands, e.g. *drei-ig*, three-skeined.

strakeln, *v.r.* stretch o.s., stretch one's arms.

Stramin, *m.* (-s, -e) fine canvas (*for embroidery*).

stramm, *adj.* tense, tight, rigid; strict; robust, strong, strapping; (*coll.*) snappy, (*sl.*) nifty; *-er Bursche*, strapping youth; – *arbeiten*, work hard, put one's back into it; (*coll.*) *die Hosen – ziehen*, dust the seat of his pants; *-es Mädel*, comely wench; *-er Soldat*, smart soldier; – *stehen*, stand at attention; *-e Zucht*, strict discipline. **-heit,** *f.*, *see* **Straffheit**; fine bearing, smartness.

strampeln, 1. *v.n.* (*aux.* h.) kick about. 2. *v.r.*; *sich bloß–*, kick the bed-clothes off.

Strand, *m.* (-(e)s, -e) shore, seashore, foreshore, beach, strand; *auf* (*den*) – *laufen*, run aground; *auf* (*den*) – *setzen*, beach (*Naut.*). **-ablagerung,** *f.* littoral deposit. **-bad,** *n.* sea-side resort; open-air swimming pool. **-dieb,** *m.* wrecker. **-en,** *v.n.* (*aux.* h. & s.) be stranded; run aground, be shipwrecked; *gestrandete Waren*, cargo washed up on shore; *gestrandetes Mädchen*, girl that has gone to the bad. **-gerechtigkeit,** *f.* prescriptive right over the foreshore. **-gewächse,** *n.pl.* littoral plants. **-gut,** *n.* flotsam, jetsam, wreckage. **-hafer,** *n.* lyme *or* dune grass, bent (*Ammophila arundinacea*) (*Bot.*). **-kanone,** *f.* (*coll.*); *geladen wie eine -kanone*, half-seas over, three sheets in the wind, lit-up. **-korb,** *m.* beach chair. **-läufer,** *m.* redshank (*Totanus calidris*) (*Orn.*). **-linie,** *f.* high-water mark. **-pfeifer,** *m.* family *Charadriidae* (*Orn.*). **-pieper,** *m.* rock pipit (*Anthus spinoletta*) (*Orn.*). **-schuhe,** *m.pl.* beach shoes, sand-shoes. **-schwalbe,** *f.*, *see* **Uferschwalbe. -ung,** *f.* stranding, shipwreck. **-wache,** *f.*, **-wächter,** *m.* coastguard.

Strang, *m.* (-es, ⸚e) rope, cord, line; hank, skein; halter, trace (*of harness*); rail, track; vein, artery; *wenn alle Stränge reißen*, if the worst comes to the worst; *über die Stränge* or *den – schlagen*, kick over the traces; *er verdient den –*, he deserves hanging; *am gleichen – ziehen*, act together *or* in concert, have the same end in view. **-farbig,** *adj.* dyed in the yarn. **-gewebe,** *n.* vascular tissue. **-pressen,** *v.a.* & *n.* extrude (*Metall.*). **-ulieren,** *v.a.* strangle.

Strapaz-e, *f.* (-en) fatigue, exertion, toil, hardship; *an -en gewöhnt*, inured to toil *or* hardship. **-ieren,** *v.a.* tire; (*coll.*) do up, wear out. **-ierfähig,** *adj.* hard-wearing. **-iös,** *adj.* tiring, fatiguing.

Straße, *f.* (-n) street, road, thoroughfare, highway; strait(s), waterway; route; *an der –*, by the wayside *or* roadside; *auf der –*, in the street; *auf die – gehen*, parade the street; *auf die – setzen*, turn out, send packing; *die breit*(*getreten*)*e – des Herkommens*, the well-trodden path of custom; *von der – aufgelesen*, rescued from the gutter; – *von Gibraltar*, Strait(s) of Gibraltar; *seine – wandeln* or *ziehen*, go one's way. **-narbeiter,** *m.* roadman, navvy. **-nausbesserung,** *f.* road repairs. **-nbahn,** *f.* tramway; tramcar, (*Amer.*) street car. **-nbahner,** *m.* tramways employee. **-nbahnhaltestelle,** *f.* tram stop. **-nbahnwagen,** *m.* tramcar. **-nbau,** *m.* road-building *or* construction. **-nbelag,** *m.* road metal, road surface. **-nbeleuchtung,** *f.* street lighting. **-ndamm,** *m.* roadway, causeway. **-ndecke,** *f.*, *see* **-nbelag. -ndieb,** *m.* highwayman. **-ndirne,** *f.* prostitute, street-walker. **-ndisziplin,** *f.* road-sense. **-ndorf,** *n.* village with houses along a single street. **-nfeger,** *m.* scavenger; crossing-sweeper. **-ngraben,** *m.* roadside ditch. **-nhändler,** *m.* street vendor, hawker, costermonger. **-njunge,** *m.* street arab, ragamuffin, guttersnipe. **-nkampf,** *m.* street-fighting. **-nkehrer,** *m.*, *see* **-nfeger. -nkehricht,** *m.* street sweepings. **-nkleid,** *n.* outdoor-dress. **-nkot,** *m.* mud. **-nkreuzung,** *f.* cross-roads. **-nlaterne,** *f.* street-lamp. **-nnetz,** *n.* highway system, network of roads. **-npflaster,** *n.* pavement. **-nräuber,** *m.*, *see* **-ndieb. -nreinigung,** *f.* street-cleaning, scaveng(er)ing. **-nrenner,** *m.* road-racer (*Cycl.*). **-nrinne,** *f.* gutter, ditch. **-nsammlung,** *f.* street collection. **-nschild,** *n.* street-sign. **-nsperre,** *f.*, **-nsperrung,** *f.* barricade, road-block, barrier. **-ntür,** *f.* front door. **-nüberführung,** *f.* viaduct. **-nübergang,** *m.* pedestrian crossing. **-nunfall,** *m.* road *or* traffic accident. **-nunterführung,** *f.* underpass. **-nunterhaltung,** *f.* road maintenance. **-nverkäufer,** *m.*, *see* **-nhändler. -nverkehr,** *m.* (road) traffic. **-nverkehrsordnung,** *f.* traffic regulations. **-nwalze,** *f.* steam-roller.

Strateg-e, *m.* (-en, -en) strategist. **-ie,** *f.* strategy. **-isch,** *adj.* strategic.

sträub-en, 1. *v.a.* ruffle up. 2. *v.r.* stand on end, bristle (up); struggle (against), boggle (at), resist, oppose; *die Feder -t sich zu schildern*, the pen refuses to describe. (*Poet.*) **-ig,** *adj.*, *see* **straubig.**

straubig, *adj.* bristling, stiff, rough, coarse; resisting, rebellious.

Strauch, *m.* (-(e)s, ⸚er & ⸚e) shrub, bush. **-artig,** *adj.* shrub-like. **-birke,** *f.* dwarf birch. **-bündel,** *n.* fascine (*Fort.*). **-dieb,** *m.* footpad, highwayman. **-e,** *f.* (*dial.*) cold in the head. **-eiche,** *f.* scrub oak. **-holz,** *n.* undergrowth, brushwood. **-ig,** *adj.* bushy; covered with shrubs. **-maske,** *f.* screen of shrubbery. **-ritter,** *m.*, *see* **-dieb.** **-werk,** *n.* shrubbery, shrubs; brushwood, undergrowth.

straucheln, *v.n.* (*aux.* h. & s.) stumble, slip; fail, (make a) blunder.

Strauken, *m.* (*dial.*), *see* **Strauche.**

[1]**Strauß,** *m.* (-es, ⁼e) bunch (of flowers), nosegay, bouquet; thyrsus (*Bot.*); (*dial.*) crest, tuft, bush, top-knot; (*Poet.*) strife, struggle, combat, conflict. **-wirtschaft,** *f.* inn kept by a vintner (who sells his own wine).

[2]**Strauß,** *m.* (-es, -e) ostrich; *der Vogel –*, the ostrich. **-enei,** *n.* ostrich-egg. **-(en)feder,** *f.* ostrich feather. **-(en)züchterei,** *f.* ostrich-farming.

Strazze, *f.* (-n) (*C.L.*) scrap-book, rough note-book; day book.

Streb–e, *f.* (-n) support, strut, stay, buttress, prop, brace, shore. **-en,** 1. *v.n.* (*aux.* h.) strive, struggle, strain (*nach*, after); press (towards), aspire (to), aim (at), endeavour (to get); tend, gravitate (towards). 2. *n.* striving, endeavour, effort, aim, aspiration; tendency. **-ebalken,** *m.* prop, shore, buttress, brace. **-ebogen,** *m.* flying-buttress. **-eholz,** *n.*, *see* **-ebalken. -epfeiler,** *m.* buttress, abutment-pier. **-er,** *m.* pushing fellow, place-hunter, careerist. **-ertum,** *n.* place-hunting. **-sam,** *adj.* assiduous, industrious, ambitious, zealous, aspiring. **-samkeit,** *f.* industry, assiduity, perseverance, zeal.

Streck–e, *f.* (-n) space, extent, distance, extension; stretch, tract (*of land*), length (*of trench*), section (*of railway line*), reach (*of a river*); gallery (*Min.*); straight line (*Geom.*); course (*Sport*); bag (*Hunt.*); *auf freie –e*, on the road; on the open track (*Railw.*); *meine –e betrug 20 Hasen*, my bag consisted of 20 hares; *zur –e bringen*, kill, (bring to) bag (*Hunt.*); (*fig.*) destroy, eliminate; *in einer –e*, at a stretch; *eine gute –e Weges*, a good piece of the way, some distance; *eine –e zurücklegen*, cover a distance. **-en,** 1. *v.a.* stretch, extend, elongate; spread, flatten, draw, roll *or* beat out; make (a th.) last *or* go a long way, eke out (*food*); lay low, kill, bag (*Hunt.*); dilute, adulterate, reduce, thin; *Arbeit –en*, go slow (*at work*); *die Hände gegen Himmel –en*, raise one's hands towards heaven; *alle viere von sich –en*, drop down dead, give up the ghost, turn up one's toes; *die Waffen –en*, lay down one's arms, surrender; *zu Boden –en*, fell to the ground; *die Zunge aus dem Munde –en*, put *or* stick one's tongue out; *in gestrecktem Galopp*, at full speed; *gestreckter Winkel*, rectilinear angle. 2. *v.r.* stretch o.s.; *sich nach der Decke –en*, cut one's coat according to one's cloth. **-bar,** *adj.* extensible; ductile, malleable. **-barkeit,** *f.* extensibility; ductility. **-balken,** *m.* strut, stretcher, stringer, cross-beam, road-bearer (*of bridges*). **-bett,** *n.* orthopaedic bed (*Surg.*). **-eisen,** *n.* stretcher (*for hides, etc.*). **-enabschnitt,** *m.* sector. **-enapparat,** *m.* linesman's telephone. **-enarbeiter,** *m.* plate-layer (*Railw.*). **-enbau,** *m.* railway construction, track-laying. **-enblock,** *m.* (signalling) section (*Railw.*). **-endienst,** *m.* supervision of permanent way. **-enflug,** *m.* long-distance flight (*Av.*). **-enförderung,** *f.* underground transport (*Min.*). **-engeschwindigkeit,** *f.* speed of run (*Railw.*, *Av.*, *etc.*). **-ennetz,** *n.* network of airlines. **-enverkehr,** *m.* local traffic (*Railw.*). **-enwärter,** *m.* linesman, permanent way inspector. **-enweise,** *adv.* here and there. **-er,** *m.* stretcher; extensor (-muscle). **-festigkeit,** *f.* tensile strength. **-grenze,** *f.* elastic limit. **-lage,** *f.* extended position (*Gymn.*). **-maschine,** *f.* drawing-frame (*Spin.*). **-mittel,** *n.* adulterant, thinner, diluting medium *or* agent. **-muskel,** *m.* & *f.* extensor-muscle. **-probe,** *f.* tensile test. **-stahl,** *m.* rolled steel. **-stütz,** *m.* resting on one's hands (*Gymn.*). **-ung,** *f.* stretching, extension, tension, elongation, spread; lengthening, adulteration, dilution. **-verband,** *m.* Thomas splint appliance (*Surg.*). **-walze,** *f.* drawing-roller (*Spin.*); rolling press (*Metall.*). **-werk,** *n.* rolling-mill; plate-rollers. **-winkel,** *m.* supplementary angle (*Geom.*).

Streich, *m.* (-(e)s, -e) stroke, blow, stripe, lash; trick, prank, joke; *auf einen –*, at one blow; *einem einen (bösen) – spielen*, play a (nasty) (*coll.* dirty) trick on a p.; (*Prov.*) *von einem –e fällt keine Eiche*, Rome was not built in a day. **-e,** *f.* spatula; direction of strata (*Geol.*). **-eln,** *v.a.* stroke; caress, fondle. **-en,** 1. *ir.v.n.* (*aux.* h. & s.) move *or* rush quickly past; run, fly *or* sweep over, cut *or* plough (*through waves*), wander, stroll, ramble, rove, migrate (*as birds*); graze, rub, touch in passing; spawn; *das Gebirge –t von X nach Y*, the mountain chain runs *or* stretches from X to Y; *der Gang –t*, the lode runs out; *auf dem Boden –en*, trail on the ground (*of dresses*); *mit der Hand über das Gesicht –en*, pass the hand over one's face. 2. *v.a.* stroke, touch gently; spread (*bread*); whet (*a knife*), strop (*a razor*); strike (*a match*); strike out, erase, expunge, cancel, scratch (*Sport*); strike (*a flag*), furl, lower (*sails*); paint, stain, varnish, brush, coat; *den Bogen –en*, resin the bow; *Brot mit Butter –en*, spread butter on the bread; *die Flagge –en*, haul down the flag; (*fig.*) surrender; (*coll.*) *die Geige –en*, scrape on the fiddle; *glatt –en*, smooth, polish; *sich* (*Dat.*) *die Haare aus dem Gesichte –en*, push one's hair out of one's eyes *or* off one's face; (*coll.*) *er ließ einen –en*, he broke wind; *Lerchen –en*, snare larks; *etwas mit Farbe –en*, paint a th.; (*archaic*) *mit Ruten –en*, cane, flog; *die Riemen* or *Ruder –en*, back water (*Naut.*); *den Schweiß von der Stirne –en*, wipe the perspiration from one's brows; *die Segel –en*, furl *or* lower the sails; (*fig.*) give in (*vor*, to); *Wolle –en*, card wool; *Ziegel –en*, make *or* mould tiles; *frisch gestrichen!* wet paint! *gestrichene Note*, ledger-line note; *gestrichen voll*, full to the brim. 3. *n.* passing, moving, roving; grazing, touching; direction of lode *or* strata (*Min.*); pass (*of a conjurer*). **-bar,** *adj.* plastic. **-brett,** *n.* smoothing-board; brick-maker's strike. **-bürste,** *f.* paint *or* paste brush. **-er,** *m.* migratory bird; wool-carder. **-farbe,** *f.* paint, stain. **-feuer,** *n.* flank fire (*Artil.*). **-garn,** *n.*, *see* **-wolle. -holz,** *n.* match. **-holzschachtel,** *f.* match-box. **-instrument,** *n.* string(ed) instrument; (*pl.*) strings (*in an orchestra*). **-kamm,** *m.* carding-comb. **-musik,** *f.* string-music. **-netz,** *n.* drag-net, draw-net, seine. **-ofen,** *m.* reverberating furnace. **-orchester,** *n.* string orchestra. **-quartett,** *n.* string quartette. **-riemen,** *m.* (razor) strop. **-stein,** *m.* hone, whetstone. **-teich,** *m.* breeding pond. **-ung,** *f.* deletion, erasure; cancellation. **-vogel,** *m.* bird of passage. **-wolle,** *f.* carding wool. **-zeit,** *f.* migrating *or* spawning season.

Streif, *m.* (-(e)s, -e) *see* **-en. -e,** *f.* patrol; razzia; raid, sweep. **-en,** 1. *m.* (-ens, -en) stripe, strip, streak, mark; sector, lane (*Mil.*); fillet, band (*Arch.*); plate, sheet (*of metal*); slip (*of paper*); vein (*in marble*); belt (*Astr.*); tape, ribbon (*Tele.*); (*coll.*) in *den –en passen* or *hauen*, see eye to eye with. 2. *v.a.* streak, stripe, striate; channel, flute, rib; touch slightly, touch on, graze, scrape, brush; strip off, take off; *die Ärmel in die Höhe –en*, turn up one's sleeves; *einen Hasen –en*, skin a hare; *den Ring vom Finger –en*, take *or* slip off one's ring. 3. *v.n.* (*aux.* s.) ramble, stroll, wander, rove, roam; reconnoitre, patrol (*Mil.*); *–en an* (*aux.* h.), border on. **-band,** *n.* postal wrapper. **-blick,** *m.* (mere) glance. **-endienst,** *m.* patrolling (*Mil.*). **-enkarte,** *f.* sector map. **-ensaat,** *f.* strip-sowing. **-enweise,** *adv.* in strips. **-erei,** *f.* roaming, ramble, excursion. **-hieb,** *m.* glancing blow. **-ig,** *adj.* striped, streaked, streaky, striated. **-jagd,** *f.* battue. **-kolonne,** *f.*, **-kommando,** *n.* flying column, raiding party. **-kugel,** *f.* grazing bullet. **-licht,** *n.* (-er) side-light, spot-light. **-schuß,** *m.* grazing *or* glancing shot. **-ung,** *f.* streaking, striation. **-wunde,** *f.* scratch, superficial wound. **-zug,** *m.* expedition, excursion; incursion, raid.

Streik, *m.* (-(e)s, -e & -s) strike; *in den – treten*, go on strike. **-brecher,** *m.* strike-breaker; (*coll.*) blackleg, scab. **-en,** *v.n.* strike (*work*), go on strike. **-ende(r),** *m.* striker. **-kasse,** *f.* strike-fund. **-lohn,** *m.* strike-pay. **-posten,** *m.* picket.

Streit, *m.* (-(e)s, -e & -igkeiten) dispute, quarrel, squabble, strife, struggle, lawsuit; contest, combat, fight, conflict, contention; *im –e liegen*, be at variance; *ohne –*, indisputably; *– suchen mit*, pick a quarrel with. **–axt,** *f.* battle-axe; (*fig.*) *die –axt begraben*, bury the hatchet. **–bar,** *adj.* warlike, valiant; pugnacious, quarrelsome, disputatious. **–barkeit,** *f.* warlike spirit, pugnacity. **–en,** 1. *ir.v.n.* (*aux.* h.) quarrel, squabble, dispute, wrangle, disagree; fight, struggle, contend (for), go to law (about); *dieser Umstand –et für uns*, this circumstance tells in our favour; *dagegen will ich nicht –en*, I will not dispute that; *darüber läßt sich –en*, that is a debatable point; *darüber ist nicht zu –en*, that is indisputable. 2. *v.r.* dispute, quarrel; *sich um des Kaisers Bart –en*, quarrel over trifles. **–end,** *pr.p.* & *adj.* fighting; disputing; *–ende Kirche*, Church Militant; *–ende Mächte*, belligerent powers; *–ende Parteien*, opposing parties, litigants. **–er,** *m.* combatant, fighter; disputant, champion. **–fall,** *m.* controversy, point *or* question at issue, matter in dispute. **–frage,** *f.* controversial question, issue, moot point. (*vulg.*) **–hammel,** *m.* quarrelsome fellow. **–hammer,** *m.* club, mace. **–ig,** *adj.* in dispute, disputed, moot, debatable, contestable, questionable; contentious, quarrelsome; *–ige S.*, matter in dispute; *einem etwas –ig machen*, contest *or* dispute a p.'s right to a th.; *die S. ist noch vor Gericht –ig*, the case is *sub judice*. **–igkeit,** *f.* dispute, controversy, difference, quarrel; lawsuit; *–igkeiten beilegen*, settle disputes. **–kolben,** *m.* mace, club. **–kräfte,** *f.pl.* troops, fighting *or* military forces. **–lust,** *f.* pugnacity, quarrelsomeness. **–lustig,** *adj.* quarrelsome, pugnacious; disputatious, litigious. **–macht,** *f.*, *see* **–kräfte. –punkt,** *m.* point at issue, contention, controversial matter. **–roß,** *n.* war-horse, charger. **–sache,** *f.*, *see* **–punkt. –schrift,** *f.* polemic; (*pl.*) controversial writings. **–sucht,** *f.* disputatiousness, quarrelsomeness, combativeness, contentious disposition. **–süchtig,** *adj.* quarrelsome, disputatious, argumentative. **–wagen,** *m.* war-chariot. **–wert,** *m.* sum in dispute (*Law*).

streng(e), 1. *adj.* severe, stern, strict; austere, harsh, rough, stiff, hard, rigorous, stringent; astringent, tart, sharp, acrid; *–er Arrest, –e Haft*, close confinement; *–e Kälte*, bitter cold. *–e Maßregeln*, rigorous measures; *– nach der Vorschrift*, in strict accordance with *or* strictly according to (the) instructions; *–e Prüfung*, stiff examination; *–e Regeln*, stringent rules; *der Schlüssel schließt –*, the key is hard to turn; *im –sten Sinne des Wortes*, in the strictest meaning *or* acceptation of the word; *aufs –ste untersagen*, forbid emphatically; *–(stens) verboten*, strictly prohibited; *– mit einem verfahren*, be severe toward a p.; *–er Winter*, hard winter; *–e Wissenschaft*, exact science. **–e,** 2. *f.* severity, sternness, strictness, austerity, stringency, harshness, bitterness; *–e des Charakters*, austerity of character; *–e des Geschmacks*, sharpness of taste; *–e des Klimas*, rigour of climate. **–en,** *v.a.* stretch, pull tightly. **–flüssig,** *adj.* difficult to fuse, refractory (*of metals*). **–genommen,** *adv.* strictly speaking. **–gläubig,** *adj.* orthodox. **–gläubigkeit,** *f.* orthodoxy. **–lot,** *n.* hard solder, silver solder.

Streu, *f.* (-en) litter; bed *or* layer of straw. **–en,** *v.a.* strew, spread; spray, sprinkle; disseminate; *dem Vieh –en*, litter cattle; *die Flinte –t*, the gun spreads the shot; *sie –ten ihr Blumen* they strewed flowers in her path; *einem Sand in die Augen –en*, throw dust in a p.'s eyes. **–büchse,** *f.*, **–er,** *m.* sprinkler, dredger, (pepper- *or* sugar-) castor. **–feuer,** *n.* searching and sweeping fire (*Mil.*). **–garbe,** *f.* cone of dispersion. **–gold,** *n.* gold dust. **–material,** *n.* bedding material (*for cattle, etc.*). **–mine,** *f.* uncontrolled mine. **–pulver,** *n.* dusting *or* baby powder. **–sand,** *m.* (blotting-) sand. **–sel,** *m.* & *n.* sprinklings, litter, dust; fine crumbs. **–selkuchen,** *m.* cake sprinkled with almonds, etc. **–strahlung,** *f.* scattered radiation. **–ung,** *f.* strewing, scattering, littering, distribution, deviation, variation, dispersion (*Artil.*). **–ungsbereich,** *m.* zone of dispersion. **–ungsgarbe,** *f.*, **–ungskegel,** *m.* cone of dispersion. **–wert,** *m.* extent of scatter, standard deviation (*Stat.*). **–winkel,** *m.* angle of spread *or* scatter. **–zucker,** *m.* granulated sugar.

streun–en, *v.n.* roam about. **–er,** *m.* (*dial.*) tramp, vagabond.

[1]**Strich,** *m.* (-(e)s, -e) stroke, streak, line, dash; hair-line, graticule; notch, stripe; course, way, direction; trend (*Geol.*); (*no pl.*) compass point; migration, flight (*of birds*); grain (*of wood, etc*); region, tract, district; climate, zone; bowing (*Mus.*); (*Swiss dial.*) teat, nipple, dug; *auf den – gehen*, walk the streets, be a prostitute; *jemanden auf dem – haben*, bear s.o. a grudge; *das macht uns einen – durch die Rechnung*, that upsets our calculations; *er hat ihm einen – durch die Rechnung gemacht*, he has frustrated *or* thwarted him; *– fliegen*, fly on a compass course; *das Schiff hält einen guten –*, the ship holds its course well; *in einem –e*, at one stroke, without a break; *– mit der Bürste*, stroke of the brush; *nach – und Faden*, properly, thoroughly; *einen – unter eine S. machen*, put an end to a th.; *unter dem –*, in the feuilleton; *– von Eitelkeit*, touch of vanity; *wider* or *gegen den –*, against the grain. **–ätzung,** *f.* line-etching. **–einteilung,** *f.* graduation (*of a scale*). **–elchen,** *n.* stria. **–eln,** *v.a.* streak, shade, mark, dot, hatch, mark with little lines. **–gitter,** *n.* reticle. **–platte,** *f.* graduated dial. **–punkt,** *m.* semicolon. **–regen,** *m.* local rain. **–scheibe,** *f.*, *see* **–platte. –vogel,** *m.* bird of passage, migratory bird. **–weise,** 1. *adj.* local. 2. *adv.* in certain places, here and there. **–zeit,** *f.* time of migration (*of birds*); spawning time (*of fishes*).

[2]**strich, striche,** *see* **streichen.**

Strick, *m.* (-(e)s, -e) cord, rope, line, string; (*coll.*) scapegrace; good-for-nothing, young rogue; *jemanden –e* or *einen – drehen* or *legen*, lay a trap for s.o., trip a p. up, catch a p. out. **–arbeit,** *f.* knitting. **–beutel,** *m.* knitting-bag. **–en,** *v.a.* knit; *Gestricktes*, knitting, knitted work. **–erin,** *f.* knitter. **–erei,** *f.* knitting. **–garn,** *n.* knitting-wool. **–jacke,** *f.* knitted jacket, cardigan, (*coll.*) woolly. **–leiter,** *f.* rope-ladder. **–masche,** *f.* knitting stitch, stitch of knitting. **–muster,** *n.* knitting pattern. **–nadel,** *f.* knitting-needle. **–naht,** *f.* knitted seam; back seam (*of stockings*). **–strumpf,** *m.* stocking being knitted. **–waren,** *f.pl.* knitted wear *or* goods. **–zeug,** *n.* knitting; knitting things.

Striegel, *m.* (-s, –) (*also f.* (-n)) curry-comb. **–n,** *v.a.* curry, comb; (*fig.*) ill-use, treat roughly; *gestriegelt und gebügelt*, spick and span.

Striem–e, *f.* (-en), **–en,** *m.* (-ens, -en) weal. **–ig,** *adj.* streaked; covered with weals.

[1]**Striezel,** *m.* (-s, –) & *f.* (-n) (*dial.*) form of white loaf.

[2]**Striezel,** *m.* (-s ,–) (*Austr.*) little devil, young rascal.

striezen, *v.a.* (*coll.*) torment, plague (*a p.*), filch, pinch, lift, swipe (*a th.*).

strikt, *adj.* strict, exact. **–ur,** *f.* (-en) stricture (*Med.*).

Strippe, *f.* (-n) (*coll.*) piece of string, string, strap, band, (*coll.*) telephone line; (*coll.*) *dauernd an der – hängen*, be everlastingly on the phone.

stritt, stritte, *see* **streiten.**

strittig, *adj.* questionable, contested, debatable, moot; in dispute.

Strizzi, *m.* (-s, -s) (*Austr. dial.*) idler, lounger, gadabout; pimp.

Strobel, *m.* (-s, –) mop of hair. **–ig,** *adj.*, *see* **struppig.**

Stroh, *n.* (-s) straw; thatch; *eine Schütte –*, a load of straw; *– im Kopfe haben*, be empty-headed; *wie – schmecken*, taste of nothing; (*leeres*) *– dreschen*, waste one's words *or* labour; (*coll.*) beat the air, flog a dead horse. **–blume,** *f.* artificial flower; immortelle (*Bot.*). **–bund,** *n.* truss of straw. **–butter,** *f.* winter butter. **–dach,** *n.* thatched roof. **–decker,** *m.* thatcher. **–ern,** *adj.* of straw; insipid. **–farben,** *adj.*, **–farbig,** *adj.* straw-coloured, beige. **–feuer,** *n.* passing enthusiasm, transient ardour; *–feuer der Liebe*, short-lived passion. **–futter,** *n.* straw fodder. **–gelb,** *adj.*, *see* **–farben. –häcksel,** *m.* chaff, chopped straw. **–halm,** *m.* (single) straw; *sich an einen –halm klammern*, clutch at a straw; *–hälmchen ziehen*, draw lots. **–hut,** *m.* straw hat. **–hütte,** *f.* thatched cottage. **–ig,** *adj.*

straw-like. **-kopf,** *m.* simpleton, blockhead. **-lager,** *n.* straw bed. **-mann,** *m.* scarecrow; man of straw; dummy (*at whist*); lay-figure. **-matte,** *f.* rush mat. **-pappe,** *f.* strawboard. **-puppe,** *f.*, *see* **-mann.** **-sack,** *m.* paillasse, straw mattress; (*coll.*) *ach du gerechter -sack!* good gracious! dear me! **-sitz,** *m.* straw seat *or* bottom (*of chair, etc.*). **-stoff,** *m.* straw pulp. **-teller,** *m.* table-mat. **-wein,** *m.* vin de paille. **-wisch,** *m.* wisp of straw. **-witwe,** *f.* grass-widow. **-witwer,** *m.* grass-widower. **-zeug,** *n.*, *see* **-stoff.**

Strolch, *m.* (-(e)s, -e) idler, lounger; tramp, vagabond. **-en,** *v.n.* (*aux.* h. & s.) stroll about, idle away one's time. **-fahrt,** *f.* (*Swiss dial.*) journey without paying one's fare.

Strom, *m.* (-(e)s, ⸚e) large *or* broad river, stream, current (*also Elec.*); flow, flood (*of words, etc.*); crowd; *in Strömen gießen* (*fließen*), pour (flow) in torrents; *wider* or *gegen den – schwimmen*, swim against the stream; *mit dem -e*, with the stream; *den – öffnen*, break the circuit (*Elec.*); *– von Menschen*, throng of people; *– von Schmähungen*, torrent *or* flood of abuse; *Ströme von Tränen*, flood of tears; *– von Worten*, flow *or* torrent of words; *– der Welt*, hurly-burly of life; *– der Zeit*, passage of time *or* the years. **-ab,** *adv.* downstream. **-abgabe,** *f.* current-output. **-ableitung,** *f.* shunt (*Elec.*). **-abnehmer,** *m.* brush (contact) (*Elec.*). **-abwärts,** *adv.*, *see* **-ab. -anker,** *m.* current-anchor (*bridge-building*). **-atlas,** *m.* hydrographic atlas. **-auf,** *adv.* upstream. **-aufnahme,** *f.* current consumption, charging rate. **-aufwärts,** *adv.*, *see* **-auf. -bett,** *n.* bed of a river. **-einheit,** *f.* unit of current, ampere. **-enge,** *f.* narrows (*of a river*). **-er,** *m.* vagabond, vagrant, tramp. **-ern,** *v.n.* lead a vagabond existence. **-erzeuger,** *m.* dynamo, generator (*Elec.*). **-erzeugung,** *f.* generation of current. **-gebiet,** *n.* river-basin. **-gefälle,** *n.* fall of a river. **-geschwindigkeit,** *f.* speed of current. **-gleichrichter,** *m.*, *see* **-richter. -kreis,** *m.* electric circuit. **-leiter,** *m.* conductor (*Elec.*). **-leitung,** *f.* conduction. **-linienform,** *f.* stream-line shape. **-linienförmig,** *adj.* stream-lined. **-menge,** *f.* quantity of current, coulombs (*Elec.*). **-messer,** *m.* ammeter. **-quelle,** *f.* source of current (*Elec.*). **-richter,** *m.* rectifier, D.C. converter (*Elec.*). **-richtungsanzeiger,** *m.* polarity-indicator. **-sammler,** *m.* storage-battery. **-schiene,** *f.* live rail. **-schnellen,** *f.pl.* rapids. **-schnittig,** *adj.* hydrodynamic. **-schwankung,** *f.* current fluctuation (*Elec.*). **-spannung,** *f.* circuit voltage. **-spule,** *f.* solenoid. **-stärke,** *f.* intensity of current (*Elec.*). **-stärkemesser,** *m.* galvanometer. **-stoß,** *m.* rush *or* surge of current (*Elec.*). (*dial.*) **-tid,** *f.* time of apprenticeship on a farm. **-unterbrecher,** *m.* contact *or* circuit-breaker, cut-out (*Elec.*). **-verbrauch,** *m.* current consumption. **-wache,** *f.* river police. **-wandler,** *m.* current-transformer. **-wärme,** *f.* heating effect of a current (*Elec.*). **-wechsel,** *m.* alternation of current. **-wechsler,** *m.*, *see* **-wender. -weise,** *adv.* in streams *or* torrents. **-wender,** *m.* commutator (*Elec.*).

ström-en, *v.n.* (*aux.* h. & s.) stream, flow, pour, gush, rush, run, flock, crowd; *das Blut -te ihm nach dem Kopfe*, the blood rushed to his head. **-ling,** *m.* small herring (*in the Baltic*). **-ung,** *f.* current, stream, flow, flux, drift, flood; (*fig.*) movement, tendency; *in die -ung geraten*, get caught in the current; *revolutionäre -ung*, revolutionary trend. **-ungskanal,** *m.* wind tunnel. **-ungslehre,** *f.* aerodynamics, hydrodynamics. **-ungsverlauf,** *m.* path of airstream (*Av.*).

Stronti-an, *m.* strontium salt; *kohlensaurer -an*, strontium carbonate, strontianite. **-um,** *n.* strontium (*Chem.*).

Stroph-e, *f.* (-en) stanza, verse; *-e und Gegen-e*, strophe and antistrophe. **-enbau,** *m.* verse structure. **-enform,** *f.* type of stanza. **-ig,** *adj. suffix*; *drei-iges Gedicht*, poem of three stanzas. **-isch,** *adj.* strophic; divided into stanzas; *-ische Gedichte*, poems in stanzas.

Strosse, *f.* (-n) stope (*Min.*). **-nbau,** *m.* stoping.

strotzen, *v.n.* (*aux.* h.) be puffed up, be distended, be swelled up, be swollen; superabound with, abound in, be full of, swarm with, teem; *von Hochmut –*, be puffed up with pride. **-d,** *pr.p.* & *adj.* swollen, distended, turgid, puffed up; exuberant, robust, vigorous; *-d von* or *vor*, abounding in; *-d voll*, full to overflowing.

strub, *adj.* (*Swiss dial.*), *see* **struppig.**

strubbelig, *adj.* shaggy, tousled, unkempt.

Strudel, *m.* (-s, –) eddy, whirlpool, vortex; type of flaky pastry; *– der Vergnügungen*, round of pleasure. **-ig,** *adj.* eddying, bubbling. **-kopf,** *m.* hothead. **-köpfig,** *adj.* hotheaded. **-n,** *v.n.* (*aux.* h.) whirl, swirl, eddy; boil, bubble, spout, gush.

Struktur, *f.* structure; texture (*of metals*). **-ell,** *adj.* structural. **-formel,** *f.* structural formula. **-identisch,** *adj.* structurally identical. **-los,** *adj.* amorphous.

Strumpf, *m.* (-(e)s, ⸚e) stocking, sock, (*pl.*) hose; gas mantle; (*coll.*) *sich auf die Strümpfe machen*, skedaddle, make off. **-band,** *n.* garter. **-halter,** *m.* suspender. **-waren,** *pl.* hosiery. **-weber,** *m.*, **-wirker,** *m.* stocking-weaver. **-wirkerei,** *f.* stocking manufacture. **-wirkerstuhl,** *m.* stocking-loom.

Strunk, *m.* (-(e)s, ⸚e) trunk, stump, stalk, stem; core (*of apple, etc.*).

Strunze, *f.* (*dial.*) slut, slattern.

struppiert, *adj.* (*dial.*) worn out, done up, disabled.

strupp-ig, *adj.* rough, bristly, unkempt, shaggy. **-wuchs,** *m.* stunted undergrowth.

Struw(w)el-bart, *m.* bristly *or* scrubby beard. **-ig,** *adj.*, *see* **strubbelig. -kopf,** *m.* shaggy *or* unkempt hair, mane; shock- *or* shaggy-headed person.

Strychnin, *n.* strychnine.

Stubbe, *f.* (-n), **-n,** *m.* (-ns, -n) tree stump.

Stube, *f.* (-n) room, chamber, apartment; barrack-room (*Mil.*); *gute –*, drawing-room, best room, parlour; *in der – hocken*, hug the fire-place. **-nälteste(r),** *m.* senior soldier (*in a barrack-room*) (*Mil.*). **-narbeit,** *f.* indoor work. **-narrest,** *m.* confinement to quarters (*Mil.*). **-ndienst,** *m.* cleaning barracks (*Mil.*). **-nfarbe,** *f.*; *er hat -nfarbe*, he is pasty-faced. **-nfliege,** *f.* common house-fly. **-ngelehrsamkeit,** *f.* book-learning. **-ngelehrte(r),** *m.* bookworm. **-ngenosse,** *m.* room-mate, fellow-lodger. **-nhocker,** *m.* stay-at-home. **-nluft,** *f.* close *or* stuffy atmosphere. **-nmädchen,** *n.* house-maid, parlour-maid. **-nrein,** *adj.* house-trained (*of dogs*). **-nuhr,** *f.* mantelpiece clock. **-nvogel,** *m.* cage-bird.

Stüber, *m.* (-s, –) stiver (*old coin*); fillip; (*coll.*) biff on the nose.

Stubsnase, *f.*, *see* **Stupsnase.**

Stuck, *m.* stucco. **-arbeit,** *f.* stucco-work. **-decke,** *f.* stuccoed ceiling. **-gips,** *m.* plaster of Paris. **-mörtel,** *m.* plaster, stucco.

Stück, *n.* (-(e)s, -e) piece, bit, part, fragment, lump; play (*Theat.*); piece of music; number (*of a magazine*); passage, extract; point, circumstance, affair; (*no pl.*) head (*of cattle*); butt (*about 1,200 litres*) (*of wine*), *see* **-faß**; pat (*of butter*); slice (*of bread*); lump (*of sugar*); cake, tablet (*of soap*); (*obs.*) field-piece, gun, cannon; (*pl.*) stocks, securities; *6 – Eier*, 6 eggs; *20 – Vieh*, 20 head of cattle; *ein gut(es) – Arbeit*, a hard task, a stiff job; *aus einem -e*, all of a piece; *aus freien -en*, of one's own accord, voluntarily, spontaneously; *– für –*, piece by piece, each piece individually; *man hält große -e auf ihn*, people have a high opinion of him *or* think a lot of him; *sich* (*Dat.*) *große -e einbilden*, think a lot of o.s.; *ein hübsches – Geld*, a nice little sum; *in allen -en*, in every respect, in all respects; *in diesem -e*, in this respect; *in einem -e* (*fort*), continuously, uninterruptedly, the whole (*night, day, etc.*) through; *in -e gehen*, break in *or* fall to pieces; (*coll.*) *ein starkes –*, a bit thick, really too bad *or* much, going too far; *Stoff vom – kaufen*, buy cloth from the piece. **-arbeit,** *f.* piecework. **-chen,** *n.* little piece, particle, morsel, bit, scrap; *einem ein -chen spielen*, play a trick on a p. **-eln, -en,** *v.a.* cut into pieces, cut up; piece together, patch. **-(e)lung,** *f.* dismemberment, disintegration, subdivision. **-(en)zucker,** *m.* lump-sugar. **-farbig,** *adj.* dyed in the piece. **-faß,** *n.* butt, large cask (*of about 8 hogs-*

heads). **–fracht,** *f.* piece of luggage, baled *or* parcelled freight. **–größe,** *f.* size of piece. **–gut,** *n.* piece goods, parcelled goods; (*obs.*) gun-metal. **–holz,** *n.* billets of wood. **–kohle,** *f.* lump-coal. **–lohn,** *m.* wages for piecework. **–metall,** *n.* gun-metal. **–pforte,** *f.* (*archaic*) gun port. **–preis,** *m.* price by the piece. **–verkauf,** *m.* retail sale. **–waren,** *f.pl.*, *see* **–gut.** **–weise,** *adv.* piece by piece, piecemeal. **–werk,** *n.* imperfect, patchy *or* bungled work; *unser Wissen ist –werk*, our knowledge is scrappy, (*B.*) we know in part. **–zahl,** *f.* number of pieces *or* shares. **–zinsen,** *m.pl.* share interest.

stucken, *v.n.* (*Austr. dial.*) swot (*school sl.*).

stuckern, *v.n.* (*aux.* h.) (*dial.*) curdle, congeal; *see also* **stochern.**

Student, *m.* (-en, -en) (university) student, undergraduate; (*Austr. dial.*) secondary school pupil; *– der alten Sprachen*, student of classics, classical student. **–enausschuß,** *m.* students' committee. **–enbund,** *m.* students' association. **–enhaft,** *adj.* student-like (*behaviour, etc.*). **–enhaus,** *n.* students' club. **–enheim,** *n.* students' hostel. **–enhilfe,** *f.* students' self-help organization. **–enleben,** *n.* university life, college life. **–enschaft,** *f.* students, undergraduates, the student body. **–ensprache,** *f.* students' slang. **–entum,** *n.* student life *or* ways. **–enverbindung,** *f.* (German) students' club. **–in,** *f.* woman student. **–isch,** *adj.* student(-like), academic.

Stud–ie, *f.* (-ien) (preparatory) study, sketch, essay. **–ienanstalt,** *f.* girls' secondary school **–ienassessor,** *m.* probationary schoolmaster. **–iendirektor,** *m.* secondary school headmaster. **–ienfreund,** *m.* fellow-student, friend at college. **–iengang,** *m.* course of study. **–iengebühr,** *f.* university fees. **–iengenosse,** *m.* fellow-student. **–ienhalber,** *adv.* for the purpose of studying. **–ienjahre,** *n.pl.* college days, student days. **–ienplan,** *m.* scheme of work. **–ienrat,** *m.* assistant master (*secondary school*); instructor (*Mil.*). **–ienreferendar,** *m.* assistant master on probation. **–ienreise,** *f.* educational journey. **–ienzeit,** *f.* college years, undergraduate days. **–ieren,** *v.a.* & *n.* (*aux.* h) study; be at college; *er läßt seinen Sohn –ieren*, he is sending his son to the university; *er –iert die alten Sprachen*, he is reading classics; *wir –ierten zusammen*, we were at college together. **–ierende(r),** *m.* (university) student. **–ierstube,** *f.*, **–ierzimmer,** *n.* study. **–iert,** *p.p.* & *adj.* studied; premeditated; affected; *ein –ierter*, (*coll.*) a man with a university education, a graduate. **–io,** 1. *n.* (-ios, -ios) (artist's) studio, broadcasting studio. 2. *m.* (-ios, -ios), **–iosus,** *m.* (-iosus, -iosen & *Austr. dial.* -iosi) (*archaic*) student; (*coll.*) *Bruder –io*, student. **–ium,** *n.* (-iums, -ien) study, attendance at a university; university *or* college education; *eifriges –ium*, intensive study.

Stuf–e, *f.* (-en) step, stair, rung (*of ladder*); tuck (*in a dress*); interval (*Mus.*); gradation, shade, nuance; degree, rank, grade, stage; *Achtung, –e!* mind the step! *auf gleicher –e mit*, on a level with, on the same footing as; *erste –e der Handlung*, first stage of the action (*Theat.*); *hohe –e*, high degree; *die höchste –e des Glücks*, the height of happiness, the pinnacle of good fortune; *–en der Steigerung*, degrees of comparison (*Gram.*). **–enartig,** *adj.* step-like; (*fig.*) graduated. **–enfolge,** *f.* gradation; succession of steps *or* stages; gradual development. **–enförmig,** *adj.* graduated, gradual, by steps. **–enleiter,** *f.* step-ladder; (*fig.*) gamut, gradation, scale. **–enschalter,** *m.* step-up switch (*Elec.*). **–enscheibe,** *f.* step-pulley. **–enweise,** *adv.* by steps, by degrees, in stages, gradually. **–ig,** *adj.* graduated, progressing by steps; (*as suffix*) with (*so many*) steps, e.g. *neun–ig*, in nine stages, with nine grades.

Stuhl, *m.* (-(e)s, ⸚e) chair; stool; seat; pew (*in church*); close *or* night stool; (*as suffix*) loom, frame; evacuation of the bowels, faeces; *Gottes –*, God's judgement seat; *keinen – haben*, be constipated, not have been moved; *Heiliger –*, Holy See; *Meister vom –*, Master of the Lodge (*Freem.*); *päpstlicher –*, Holy See; *einem den – vor die Tür setzen*, turn a p. out, break off connexion with a p.; *sich zwischen zwei Stühle setzen*, fall between two stools. **–befördernd,** *adj.* aperient, laxative. **–bein,** *n.* leg of a chair. **–bezug,** *m.* chair-cover. **–drang,** *m.* need to relieve the bowels. **–entleerung,** *f.* bowel movement, stool. **–feier,** *f.* St. Peter's day. **–flechtarbeit,** *f.* cane seating of chairs. **–gang,** *m.* stool, excrement, faeces; action *or* movement of the bowels. **–geld,** *n.* pew-rent. **–gericht,** *n.* secret tribunal. **–lehne,** *f.* back of a chair. **–meister,** *m.* master of a lodge (*Freem.*). **–richter,** *m.* (*archaic*) presiding judge. **–rolle,** *f.* chair-castor. **–sitz,** *m.* seat of a chair. **–verhaltung,** *f.*, **–verstopfung,** *f.* constipation. **–wagen,** *m.* basket-carriage, invalid chair. **–zäpfchen,** *n.* anal suppository. **–zwang,** *m.* tenesmus (*Med.*).

Stukka–teur, *m.* (-s, -e) stucco-worker. **–tur,** *f.* stucco-work.

Stulle, *f.* (-n) (*dial.*) slice of bread and butter.

Stulp, *m.* (-es, -e) turned-back *or* -up flap; sheath, shield, cover, guard. **–e,** *f.* (-en), *see* **–**; boot-top; pot-lid; cuff (*of sleeve*). **–(en)stiefel,** *m.pl.* top-boots. **–handschuh,** *m.* gauntlet (glove).

Stülp, *m.*, *see* **Stulp.** **–en,** *v.a.* turn upside down *or* inside out; turn up, invert; put *or* clap the lid on; *den Hut auf den Kopf –en*, cram one's hat on one's head. **–nase,** *f.* snub *or* turned-up nose.

stumm, *adj.* dumb, mute; silent, speechless; *ein –er*, a mute; *–er Buchstabe*, silent letter; *–er Diener*, dinner wagon; *–e Rolle*, non-speaking *or* walking-on part (*Theat.*); *–es Spiel*, dumb show, byplay. **–heit,** *f.* dumbness.

Stummel, *m.* (-s, –) stump, stub, (fag-)end. **–füße,** *m.pl.* parapodia, prolegs. **–pfeife,** *f.* short-stemmed pipe.

stümmeln, *v.a.* lop, truncate.

Stumpen, *m.* (-s, –) felt hat; (*dial.*) stump; (*Swiss dial.*) small cigar.

Stümper, *m.* (-s, –) bungler, blunderer, dabbler. **–ei,** *f.* bungling, shoddy work. **–haft,** *adj.*, **–mäßig,** *adj.* unskilful, clumsy, bungling. **–n,** *v.a.* & *n.* (*aux.* h.) bungle, botch.

stumpf, 1. *adj.* blunt, obtuse; (*fig.*) dull, matt, dead, flat; insensible, indifferent, apathetic; *–er Kegel*, truncated cone; *–er Reim*, masculine rhyme; *–es Schwert*, blunt sword; *–e Stoßrapiere*, buttoned foils; *für eine S. ganz – sein*, be quite indifferent to a matter; *–er Winkel*, obtuse angle; *die Zähne – machen*, set the teeth on edge. 2. *m.* (-(e)s, ⸚e) stump, stub; *mit – und Stiel*, root and branch; lock, stock, and barrel. **–eckig,** *adj.* obtuse-angled, blunt-cornered. **–heit,** *f.* bluntness, dullness, flatness; obtuseness, apathy, indifference. **–kegel,** *m.* truncated cone. **–nase,** *f.* turned-up *or* snub nose. **–schwanz,** *m.* docked tail. **–sinn,** *m.* stupidity, dullness. **–sinnig,** *adj.* dull, stupid; (*coll.*) thick- *or* bone-headed. **–wink(e)lig,** *adj.* obtuse-angled.

stund, stünde, (*Poet.*), *see* **stehen.**

Stunde, *f.* (-n) hour; period, lesson; distance covered in an hour; *bis auf diese –*, up till this moment; *–n geben*, give lessons; *– halten*, have a class; *in elfter –*, in the nick of time, at the eleventh hour; *in einer schwachen –*, in a weak moment; *eine – lang*, a whole hour, for an hour; *seine – hat geschlagen*, his hour *or* time has come; *von Stund' an*, from that very hour, ever since then; (*dial.*) *was ist die –?* what is the time? *Zeit und – warten nicht*, time and tide wait for no man; *– X*, zero hour; *zur Stund(e)*, now, at once; *zu guter –*, in good time; *zu jeder –*, at any time; *zur rechten –*, at the right moment. **–nbuch,** *n.* prayer-book. **–ndurchschnitt(sgeschwindigkeit),** *f.* speed in (miles *or* kilometres) per hour. **–ngebete,** *n.pl.* the hours (*R.C.*). **–ngeld,** *n.* fee for instruction. **–nglas,** *n.* hour-glass. **–nkilometer,** *m.pl.* kilometre per hour. **–nkreis,** *m.* horary circle (*Astr.*). **–nlang,** *adj.* lasting for hours *or* more than an hour; for hours together. **–nlinie,** *f.* meridian. **–nlohn,** *m.* payment by the hour. **–nplan,** *m.* time-table, schedule. **–ntafel,** *f.* gnomonic table. **–nweise,** *adv.* by the hour. **–nwinkel,** *m.* horary angle(*Astr.*). **–nzeiger,** *m.* hour-hand.

stund–en, *v.a.* allow time to pay, grant a respite.

–ung, *f.* respite, delay of payment. **–ungsfrist,** *f.* days of grace.
stünd–ig, *adj. suffix,* for an hour; e.g. *vier–ig,* lasting four hours. **–lein,** *n.* short hour; *wenn sein –lein kommt,* when his last hour draws nigh; *Gott gebe ihm ein seliges -lein,* God grant him an easy passing. **–lich,** 1. *adj.* hourly, every hour; *vier–lich,* every fourth hour. 2. *adv.* from hour to hour.
Stunk, *m.* (*coll*). squabble; backbiting, slating; (*coll.*) *er macht –,* he is making mischief.
Stupf, *m.*, **–en,** *v.a.* (*dial.*), *see* **Stups, –en.**
stupid(e), *adj.* half-witted, vacuous, fatuous, idiotic, (*N.B. stronger than* stupid).
stup–rieren, *v.a.* rape, violate. **–rum,** *n.* (-rums, -ra), rape, violation.
Stup–s, *m.* (-ses, -se) (*coll.*) nudge, push, shove, jolt. (*dial.*) **–sen,** *v.a.* nudge, jog. **–snase,** *f.* turned-up *or* snub nose.
stur, *adj.* (*dial.*) stubborn, obdurate, (*Scots*) dour. **–heit,** *f.* stubbornness; *–kurs fliegen,* hold to *or* not deviate from one's course.
stürbe, *see* **sterben.**
Sturm, *m.* (-(e)s, ¨-e) storm, gale; strong gale (*Meteor. Beaufort scale* 9); tumult, turmoil, fury; rush, onset, attack, assault (*Mil.*); (*Nat. Soc.*) company, unit; *– blasen,* sound the alarm; *– und Drang,* Storm and Stress (*Liter.*); *im – nehmen,* take by storm; *– laufen,* charge, attack, assault, storm; *sie kamen – gelaufen,* they advanced at the charge; *– läuten,* ring the alarm-bell, (*coll.*) bring the house down; *schwerer –,* storm (*Meteor. Beaufort scale 11*); *voller –,* whole gale (*Meteor. Beaufort scale 10*); *– im Wasserglas,* storm in a teacup; *zum – auf!* charge! (*Mil.*). **–abteilung,** *f.* (*Nat. Soc.*) storm troops *or* detachment, S.A. **–angriff,** *m.* charge, assault, rush. **–band,** *n.* chin-strap (*on helmet*). **–bann,** *m.* (*Nat. Soc.*) battalion of S.A. **–bock,** *m.* battering-ram. **–boot,** *n.* assault boat, landing craft. **–dach,** *n.* testudo (*Hist.*). **–deck,** *n.* hurricane-deck (*Naut.*). **–eseile,** *f.* impetuous haste. **–fahne,** *f.* banner, battle standard. **–fest,** *adj.* storm-proof. **–flut,** *f.* tidal wave. **–frei,** *adj.* unassailable; (*Stud. sl.*) *–freie Bude,* furnished room where there is no objection to lady visitors. **–führer,** *m.* (*Nat. Soc.*) company commander of S.S. **–gasse,** *f.* assault lane. **–glocke,** *f.* tocsin, alarm-bell. **–haube,** *f.* morion (*Mil.*). **–hut,** *m.* monkshood, wolf's bane (*Aconitum napellus*) (*Bot.*). **–kegel,** *m.* (storm) cone. **–laterne,** *f.* storm lantern. **–leiter,** *f.* scaling-ladder. **–möwe,** *f.* common gull (*Larus canus*) (*Orn.*). **–pforten,** *f.pl.* dead lights (*Naut.*). **–reif,** *adj.* easily assailable; *–reif machen,* soften up (*a position*) (*Mil.*). **–riemen,** *m.*, *see* **–band. –schaden,** *m.* damage by storm. **–schritt,** *m.* double-quick step *or* march. **–schwalbe,** *f.* storm(y)-petrel, Mother Carey's Chicken (*Hydrobates pelagicus*) (*Orn.*). **–signal,** *n.* the 'charge' (*Mil.*). **–truppen,** *m.pl.* shock *or* assault troops. **–vögel,** *m.pl.* procellarians, oceanic birds. **–warnung,** *f.* gale warning. **–wetter,** *n.* stormy weather; storm. **–wind,** *m.* heavy gale, high wind.
stürm–en, 1. *v.a.* storm, take by storm, force; *den Himmel –en,* reach for the stars. 2. *v.n.* (*aux.* h.) be stormy, be violent; advance to the attack; storm about, rage; (*aux.* s.) dash, rush along. **–end,** *pr.p. & adj.* attacking; impetuous; violent; *mit –ender Hand erobern,* take by assault. **–er,** *m.* assailant; dare-devil, hothead; forward (*Footb.*); students' cap; *–er und Dränger,* poets of the German Storm and Stress period. **–isch,** *adj.* stormy, turbulent, violent, impetuous, headstrong; *–ischer Beifall,* uproarious *or* tempestuous applause.
Sturz, *m.* (-es, ¨-e) fall, tumble, crash, drop, plunge; waterfall, cataract; downfall, overthrow (*of government, etc.*); ruin, collapse; (*C.L.*) failure; audit (*of accounts*); (*pl.* -e) lintel (*of doors, windows, etc.*); *see also* **Stürze**; *ein Glas auf einen – austrinken,* empty a glass at one draught; *zum – bringen,* overthrow. **–acker,** *m.* newly-ploughed land. **–angriff,** *m.* dive-bombing attack (*Av.*). **–artig,** *adj.* impetuous. **–bach,** *m.* torrent, waterfall. **–bett,** *n.* spillway (*of a dam*). **–bügel,** *m.* safety-stirrup. **–el,** *m.*, *see* **Stürzel. –flug,** *m.* nose-dive (*Av.*). **–furche,** *f.* first ploughing. **–güter,** *n.pl.* goods loaded in bulk (*Naut.*). **–helm,** *m.* crash helmet (*Motor.*). **–kampfflugzeug,** *n.* dive-bomber (*Av.*). **–pflug,** *m.* fallow-plough. **–regen,** *m.* torrential downpour. **–see** *f.* heavy sea. **–spirale,** *f.* spiral dive (*Av.*). **–wellen,** *f.pl.* breakers; *–wellen bekommen,* ship heavy seas.
Stürze, *f.* (-n) cover, lid.
Stürzel, *m.* stub-end, (tree) stump.
stürz–en, 1. *v.a.* hurl, throw (down), plunge, precipitate; overturn, overthrow, ruin; dump, shoot (*rubbish*); check, count over (*cash*); plough up *land*); put on (*a lid, etc.*); toss off (*a drink*); *nicht –en!* with care! do not drop! *einen Minister* (*die Regierung*) *–en,* overthrow a minister (the government); *ins Elend –en,* ruin, plunge into misery. 2. *v.r. & n.* (*aux.* s.) sink; be precipitous, rush, dash, hurry, plunge; crash, smash, fall, tumble down; dive (*Av.*); gush, pour; *sie –te sich von einem Felsen,* she threw herself from a rock; *sich in Schulden –en,* plunge into debt; *Varus –te sich in sein Schwert,* Varus fell upon his sword. 3. *n.* collapse; overthrow; breaking up (*of ground*).
Stuß, *m.* (*coll.*) stuff and nonsense, balderdash.
Stute, *f.* (-n) mare. **–rei,** *f.* (breeding) stud. **–nfüllen,** *n.* foal, filly. **–nknecht,** *m.* stud-groom.
Stuten, *m.* (*dial.*) breakfast roll. **–bäcker,** *m.* pastry-cook.
Stutz, *m.* (-es, -e) (*dial.*) shove, jolt; plume (*on hats*); (*Swiss dial.*) steep slopes; *auf den –, auf – und Blutz,* all of a sudden, suddenly. **–en,** 1. *v.n.* (*aux.* h.) stop short, hesitate; be startled *or* taken aback; prick up the ears (*as horses*). 2. *v.a.* cut short, shorten, curtail, truncate, clip (*wings*), dock (*a tail*), lop (*trees, etc.*), crop (*a dog's ears*), trim. 3. *m.* (-ens, -en) short rifle, carbine; connexion, connecting pipe, socket; footless stocking. **–ärmel,** *m.* sleeve protector. **–bart,** *m.* close-cropped beard. **–degen,** *m.* short sword. **–er,** *m.* fop, dandy, (*coll.*) swell; (*Swiss dial.*) carbine. **–erartig,** *adj.*, **–erhaft,** *adj.* foppish, dandified. **–ertum,** *n.* world of fashionable young men, foppishness, dandyism. **–flügel,** *m.* baby-grand (piano). **–glas,** *n.* short-stemmed glass. **–handschuh,** *m.* mitten. **–ig,** *adj.* startled, puzzled, surprised, perplexed, nonplussed, taken aback; *–ig machen,* disconcert; *–ig werden,* stop short, be taken aback, prick up the ears. **–kopf,** *m.* regulation haircut, short crop. **–nase,** *f.* snub nose. **–ohrig,** *adj.* crop-eared. **–perücke,** *f.* bobtail-wig. **–pflanze,** *f.* lopped *or* truncated plant. **–schere,** *f.* garden *or* pruning shears. **–schwänzig,** *adj.* bobtailed; docked. **–uhr,** *f.* mantelpiece clock.
Stütz, *m.* (-es, -e) resting position (*Gymn.*). **–e,** *f.* (-en) prop, stay, leg, support, joist; (*fig.*) sustainer, pillar; lady help; *im Gesetz keine –e finden,* have no basis in law. **–en,** 1. *v.a.* prop, stay, shore up; sustain, support; rest, lean (*one's arm, etc.*); peg, pin (*a currency*); *gestützt auf sein Recht,* relying on the justice of his cause. 2. *v.r.*; *sich auf eine S. –en,* depend on, rest on, be based on, be founded on *or* rely on a th. **–balken,** *m.* joist, shore, prop, supporting beam, wooden stay *or* support. **–fläche,** *f.* supporting surface. **–ig,** *adj.* (*dial.*), *see* **stutzig. –mauer,** *f.* buttress; retaining wall. **–pfeiler,** *m.* pillar, column; support. **–punkt,** *m.* fulcrum; strong point (*Mil.*); point of support, basis, base; foothold. **–punktlinie,** *f.* line of strong points. **–ungsaktion,** *f.* pegging *or* pinning the market. **–weite,** *f.* span.
Suad–a, –e, *f.* gift of the gab, blarney.
subaltern, *adj.* subordinate, subaltern; *–er Geist,* second-rate mind; *–e Gesinnung,* servile attitude. **–beamte(r),** *m.* subordinate, middle-grade official. **–e(r),** *m.* dependant, underling. **–offizier,** *m.* subaltern (*Mil.*).
Subhast–ation, *f.* (-en) public auction, (*Scots*) public roup. **–ieren,** *v.a.* bring under the hammer.
Subjekt, *n.* (-(e)s, -e) subject (*Gram., Log.*); theme (*Mus.*); (*coll.*) fellow creature; *verkommenes –,* (*coll.*) a bad lot. **–iv,** *adj.* subjective, personal, biased. **–ivismus,** *m.* subjectivism, philosophy of the ego. **–ivität,** *f.* subjectivity, personal attitude.

subkutan, *adj.* sub-cutaneous. **–spritze,** *f.* hypodermic syringe.
sublim, *adj.* sublime. **–at,** *n.* (-(e)s, -e) mercuric chloride, (corrosive) sublimate. **–ieren,** *v.a.* sublimate (*Chem. & Psych.*); *–ierter Schwefel*, flowers of sulphur. **–ierofen,** *m.* subliming furnace. **–ierung,** *f.* sublimation (*Chem. & Psych.*).
submiß, *adj.* submissive, humble(d), resigned, respectful. **–(ss)ion,** *f.* submissiveness, submission, humility; tender (*for a contract*). **–(ss)ionsstrich,** *m.* line drawn lengthwise from the foot of a petition down to the signature(s). **–(ss)ionsweg,** *m.*; *im –(ss)ionswege vorgehen*, offer *or* throw open (*a contract*) to tender.
Subsi–dien, *n.pl.* subsidies; *durch –dien unterstützen*, subsidize. **–stieren,** *v.n.* subsist, maintain o.s.
Subskr–ibent, *m.* (-en, -en) subscriber (*auf eine S.*, to a th.). **–ibieren,** *v.a. & n.* subscribe (*auf eine S.*, to a th.); *ein Buch –ibieren*, order a book in advance (of publication), subscribe to a book. **–iption,** *f.* (-en) subscription. **–iptionsanzeige,** *f.* prospectus (*of a new company*).
substan–tiell, *adj.* substantial, material; sustaining (*of food*). **–tiv,** *n.* (-s, -e), **–tivum,** *n.* (-ums, -a) substantive, noun (*Gram.*) **–tivisch,** *adj.* substantive (*Gram.*). **–z,** *f.* (-zen) substance, matter, stuff, essence; reagent; (*C.L.*) real capital.
substitu–ierbar, *adj.* replaceable. **–ieren,** *v.a.* substitute. **–t,** *m.* (-ten, -ten) substitute, representative. **–tion,** *f.* substitution, replacement; representation.
Substrat, *n.* (-(e)s, -e) base, precipitate; substratum, foundation.
subsum–ieren, *v.a.* ascribe (*unter*, to), impute (to), include (with, among), comprise (within). **–tion,** *f.* inclusion, imputation. **–tiv,** *adj.* presumptive, presumed, imputed, insinuated
subtil, *adj.* subtle, cunning; delicate, fine; *–e Behandlung*, minute and careful treatment; *mit einem sehr – umgehen*, treat a p. with great circumspection, (*coll.*) treat *or* handle a p. gently. **–ität,** *f.* subtlety.
subtra–hieren, *v.a.* subtract, deduct. **–ktion,** *f.* subtraction.
subven–ieren, *v.a.* help, assist, support. **–tion,** *f.* subvention, subsidy. **–tionieren,** *v.a.* subsidize.
Such–e, *f.* (-n) search, quest; scent (*of dogs*); *auf die –e gehen, sich auf die –e machen* (*nach einer S.*), go in search (of a th.), search (for a th.), follow the tracks (of a th.); *auf der –e sein*, be on the look-out *or* hunt (*for a th.*). **–en,** *v.a. & n.* (*aux.* h.) seek, want, desire, try to; trace, search (for), go in quest (of); hunt (for), look for, try to find; *seine Verse –en ihresgleichen*, his verses cannot easily be rivalled; *Händel mit einem –en*, pick a quarrel with a p.; *was hast du hier zu –en?* what do you want here? what business have you here? (*sl.*) what are you nosing about here for? *er –t in allem etwas*, he is very suspicious; *nach Worten –en*, be at a loss for words; *jemandes Verderben –en*, plot a p.'s ruin; *seinen Vorteil –en*, be bent on his own advantage; *das Weite –en*, make o.s. scarce; *gesucht, p.p. & adj.* wanted, in demand, fantastic, elaborate, far-fetched; *das Gesuchte finden*, find what one was looking for; *ein gesuchter Arzt*, a doctor in great demand, (*coll.*) a much-sought-after doctor; *gesuchte Entschuldigung*, far-fetched excuse; *gesuchte Schreibart*, affected style; *eine Stelle* (*ein Schreiber*) *wird gesucht*, wanted a situation (a clerk); *gesuchte Waren*, goods in great demand. **–er,** *m.* seeker, searcher; view-finder (*Phot.*); spot-light; probe. **–gerät,** *n.* sound-detector (*Mil.*).
Sucht, *f.* (¨e *rare*) passion, mania, rage, craze; (*archaic*) sickness, disease, epidemic; *fallende –*, epilepsy.
süchtig, *adj.* having a mania for, passionately desiring, addicted to; diseased, affected with a disease.
suckeln, *v.a.* (*dial.*) go on sucking.
Sud, *m.* (-(e)s, -e) boiling, brewing; decoction, brew. **–el,** *m.* (*dial*) puddle, pool; dirt; rough draft. **–elei,** *f.* dirty work, slovenly work; daubing; scribbling; filth. **–eler,** *m.*, *see* **–ler.** **–(e)lig,** *adj.* dirty, filthy; slovenly, messy. **–elkoch,** *m.* bad *or* slovenly cook. **–eln,** *v.a. & n.* (*aux.* h.) do in a dirty *or* slovenly way, make a mess of, smear, daub; scribble; soil; slur (*Typ.*). **–elwetter,** *n.* dirty weather. **–ler,** *m.* bungler, messy worker. **–seifenbad,** *n.* soap-suds. **–werk,** *n.* brewing plant.
Süd, *m.* south; (-es, -e) (*Poet.*) south wind. **–bahn,** *f.* southern railway. **–en,** *m.* south. **–früchte,** *f.pl.* (semi-)tropical fruit. **–lich,** *adj.* south, southern, southerly, southward; *–liche Breite*, south latitude. *–liche Lage*, southern aspect; *–liche Richtung*, southerly direction; *–lich von Berlin*, (to the) south of B. **–kreuz,** *n.* Southern Cross (*Astr.*). **–länder,** *m.* southerner. **–licht,** *n.* aurora australis. **–ost,** *m.* south-east (wind). **–osten,** *m.* south-east. **–östlich,** *adj.* south-east(ern). **–ostwärts,** *adv.* south-easterly. **–pol,** *m.* South *or* Antarctic pole. **–polarforschung,** *f.* Antarctic exploration. **–polarexpedition,** *f.* Antarctic expedition. **–polarländer,** *n.pl.* south polar regions. **–see** *f.* southern Pacific (Ocean). **–seeinsulaner,** *m.* South Sea islander. **–seeländer,** *n.pl.* South Sea islands. **–wärts,** *adv.* southward(s), to the south. **–western,** *m.* south-west. **–wester,** *m.* south-wester (*Naut.*). **–westlich,** *adj.* south-west(ern). **–wind,** *m.* south wind, southerly breeze.
Suff, *m.* (*sl.*) boozing, tippling; booze; *etwas im – tun*, do a th. when under the influence *or* when sozzled; *sich dem stillen – ergeben*, be a secret drinker.
Süff–el, *m.* drunkard, toper. **–eln,** *v.n.* booze, tipple. **–ig,** *adj.* palatable, delicious, good (*of drinks*).
süffisant, *adj.* self-satisfied, conceited.
sugge–rieren, *v.a.* suggest; influence (*a p.'s mind*) by suggestion. **–stivfrage,** *f.* leading question.
Suhle, *f.* muddy puddle, wallow, slough. **–n,** **sühlen,** *v.n. & r.* wallow in mire.
Sühn–e, *f.* atonement, expiation; reconciliation; propitiation. **–bar,** *adj.* expiable, atonable. **–ealtar,** *m.* altar of expiation. **–en,** *v.a.* expiate, atone for. **–eversuch,** *m.* attempt at reconciliation. **–opfer,** *n.* propitiatory sacrifice, atonement. **–ung,** *f.* propitiation, atonement.
Suite, *f.* (-n) suite, retinue; (*coll.*) prank, lark, trick; *–n reißen*, play tricks.
Sukkurs, *m.* support, succour; reinforcement (*Mil.*).
sukze–dieren, *v.n.* succeed (to), inherit. **–ssion,** *f.* (legal) succession. **–ssionsakte,** *f.* act of settlement (*Pol.*). **–ssionsberechtigt,** *adj.*, **–ssionsfähig,** *adj.* legally entitled to the succession. **–ssiv,** *adj.* gradual, successive.
Sulf–amidsäure, *f.* sulphamic acid. **–at,** *n.* (-(e)s, -e) sulphate. **–hydrid,** *n.*, **–hydrat,** *n.* hydrosulphide. **–id,** *n.* sulphide. **–ieren,** *v.a.* sulphurize, sulphonate. **–obase,** *f.* sulphur base. **–ogruppe,** *f.* sulphonic group. **–ohydrat,** *n.*, *see* **–hydrat.** **–onieren,** *v.a.*, *see* **–ieren.** **–it,** *n.* sulphite. **–ür,** *n.*, *see* **–id.** **–urieren,** *v.a.*, *see* **–ieren.** **–urös,** *adj.* sulphurous.
Sülfmeister, *m.* (*Hist.*) master of a salt-mine; (*dial.*) bungler.
Sulph–, *see* **Sulf–.**
Sultan, *m.* (-s, -e) sultan. **–at,** *n.* sultanate. **–in,** *f.* sultana. **–ine,** *f.* sultana (*raisin*). **–slaune,** *f.* despot's whim.
Sülz–e, *f.*, **Sulz–e,** *f.* (*dial.*) brine; jelly, gelatin; pickled (jellied) meat; brawn; deer-lick. **–en,** *v.a.* pickle in jelly. **–fleisch,** *n.* pickled meat. **–ig,** *adj.* gelatinous.
summ, *int.* buzz. **–en,** *v.a. & n.* (*aux.* h.) buzz, hum; *es –t mir in den Ohren*, my ears are buzzing. **–er,** *m.* buzzer, vibrator (*Phone.*); bluebottle. **–erknopf,** *m.* buzzer key. **–erzeichen,** *n.* buzzing signal (*Phone.*). **–erzusatz,** *m.* buzzer set.
Summ–a, *f.* (-en) (*archaic*) sum; *in –a*, in short, to sum up; *–a –arum*, all in all, sum total, grand total. **–and,** *m.* (-en, -en) term of a sum (*Alg.*); item. **–arisch,** *adj.* summary, succinct; *–arisches Verfahren*, summary proceedings. **–e,** *f.* sum, total, amount; *die –e ziehen*, sum up; *eine fehlende –e ergänzen*, make good a deficit; *höchste –e*, maximum; *–e der Bewegung*, momentum. **–en,** *v.a.*, *see* **–ieren.** **–enwirkung,** *f.* combined effect.

–ieren, 1. *v.a.* add up. 2. *v.r.* amount to, come to; get more and more. **–ierung,** *f.* summing up, summarizing. **–episkopat,** *n.* (& *dial. m.*) supreme Protestant episcopate.
Sümmchen, *n.* (*iron.*) *ein nettes* or *hübsches –,* a pretty penny, a considerable sum *or* amount.
Sumpf, *m.* (-(e)s, ⸗e) swamp, bog, marsh, fen; morass, quagmire; pit, sump (*Min.* & *Motor.*); *– der Schändlichkeit,* sink of corruption, den of iniquity; (*fig.*) *in den – geraten,* go to the bad; *im –e stecken(bleiben),* (*fig.*) stick in the mud, wallow in the mire; *einen – austrocknen* or *trockenlegen,* drain a marsh. **–blüte,** *f.* deplorable exhibition, outrage, indignity, monstrosity, eyesore, vulgarism. **–boden,** *m.* marshy ground. **–dotterblume,** *f.* marsh-marigold (*Caltha palustris*) (*Bot.*). **–en,** *v.n.* be boggy; stagnate; (*Studs. sl.*) lead a dissolute life. **–fieber,** *n.* malaria, marsh-fever. **–gas,** *n.* marsh gas, methane. **–huhn,** *n.* moorhen (*Gallinula chloropus*) (*Orn.*); (*sl.*) dissolute wretch. **–ig,** *adj.* marshy, swampy, boggy. **–meise,** *f.* marsh-tit (*Parus palustris*) (*Orn.*). **–pflanze,** *f.* marsh-plant, uliginose *or* limnodophilous plant. **–schildkröte,** *f.* marsh-turtle (*Emydes*) (*Zool.*). **–schnepfe,** *f.* jack-snipe (*Gallinago gallinula*) (*Orn.*). **–vogel,** *m.* wading-bird, wader. **–wasser,** *n.* stagnant water, marshy pool. **–wiese,** *f.* swampy meadow.
sümpfen, *v.a.* drain (*a mine*); knead (*potter's clay*).
Sums, *m.* (*dial.*) buzzing noise; (*coll.*) empty chatter; (*coll.*) *einen großen – machen über,* make a great fuss about. **–en,** *v.n., see* **summen** *under* **summ.**
Sund, *m.* (-(e)s, -e) sound, strait(s).
Sünd–e, *f.* (-en) sin, transgression, trespass, offence; *Gott verzeih' mir die –e!* Heaven forgive me! *ich hasse ihn wie die –e,* I hate him like poison; *eine –e und Schande,* a sin and a shame, a wicked shame; *der Tod ist der –e Sold,* the wages of sin is death. **–enbahn,** *f.* road to perdition. **–enbekenntnis,** *n.* confession (of sin). **–enbock,** *m.* scapegoat. **–enerlaß,** *m.* remission of sins, absolution. **–enfall,** *m.* the Fall (*of man*). **–engeld,** *n.* ill-gotten gain; (*coll.*) enormous sum of money. **–enleben,** *n.* sinful *or* wicked life, life of sin. **–enlohn,** *m.* wages of sin; starvation-wages. **–(en)losigkeit,** *f.* innocence, sinlessness, blamelessness, righteousness, impeccability. **–enpfuhl,** *m.* sink of corruption. **–enregister,** *n.* list of sins committed. **–envergebung,** *f.* forgiveness of sins; absolution. **–er,** *m.* sinner; culprit; delinquent; *armer –er,* (*fig.*) poor devil *or* wretch; *verstockter –er,* unrepentant sinner; *Gott sei mir –er gnädig!* God forgive me, sinner that I am! **–erschemel,** *m.* stool of repentance. (*coll.*) **–flut,** *f.* the Flood; *see* **Sintflut.** **–haft,** *adj.* sinful, erring, wicked; (*coll.*) *–haft viel,* a mighty lot. **–haftigkeit,** *f.* wickedness, sinfulness. **–ig,** *adj.* sinful, iniquitous, wicked. **–igen,** *v.a.* & *n.* (*aux.* h.) (commit a) sin, trespass, transgress; *was habe ich gesündigt?* what (wrong) have I done? **–lich,** *adj.* sinful, unlawful, impious, infamous, nefarious. (*B.*) **–wasser,** *n.* water of purification.
super–arbitrieren, *v.a.* (*Austr. dial.*) review, revise, reconsider (*a judgement*). **–azidität,** *f.* hyperacidity. **–fein,** *adj.* superfine. **–intendent,** *m.* (Protestant) senior minister. **–iorin,** *f.* Mother Superior. **–iorität,** *f.* superiority, preponderance. **–klug,** *adj.* too clever by half, (*coll.*) cocky. **–lativ,** *m.* superlative. **–oxyd,** *n.* peroxide. **–imponieren,** *v.a.* superimpose. **–revision,** *f.* final revision.
Suppe, *f.* (-n) soup, broth; repast; *die – ausessen müssen,* have to abide by the consequences; *einem eine – einbrocken,* do s.o. a bad turn, make things awkward for a p.; (*coll.*) *das macht die – nicht fett,* that will not do much good, that will not help; *ein Haar in der –,* (*fig.*) a fly in the ointment; *jemanden auf einen Löffel – einladen,* invite s.o. to drop in for a meal; *einem die – versalzen,* (*or vulg.*) *einem in die – spucken,* spoil a p.'s pleasure, spoil things for s.o.; *sein Süppchen am Feuer andrer kochen,* benefit at s.o. else's expense. **–neinlage,** *f.* things added to soup. **–nfleisch,** *n.* gravy-beef. **–nkaspar,** *m.* child who will not eat his meals, s.o. not very fond of soup. **–nkelle,** *f.* soup-ladle. **–nkräuter,** *n.pl.* pot-herbs. **–nlöffel,** *m.* soup-spoon. **–nschüssel,** *f.* soup-bowl. **–nteller,** *m.* soup-plate *or* dish. **–nterrine,** *f.* soup-tureen. **–ntopf,** *m.* stock-pot. **–nwürfel,** *m.* soup-cube, dried soup. **–nwürze,** *f.* seasoning.
Supple–ment, *n.* (-(e)s, -e) supplement, supplementary angle. **–nt,** *m.* (-en, -en) (*Austr. dial.*) assistant master.
Supp–lik, *f.* (-en) petition, plea. **–likant,** *m.* petitioner. **–lizieren,** *v.a.* supplicate, plead, sue. **–onieren,** *v.a.* assume, surmise, presume, suppose, presuppose, impute (to). **–ositorium,** *n.* (-riums, -rien) suppository (*Med.*). **–ositum,** *n.* (-itums, -ita) assumption, surmise, (pre-)supposition, imputation.
surren, *v.n.* (*aux.* h.) hum, buzz, whizz.
Surrogat, *n.* (-(e)s, -e) substitute; makeshift. **–ion,** *f.* substitution, replacement.
suspen–dieren, *v.a.* suspend. **–dierung,** *f.*, **–sion,** *f.* suspension. **–sorium,** *n.* (-riums, -rien) suspensor, suspensory (*Surg.*).
süß, *adj.* sweet, sweetened, fresh; (*fig.*) charming, dear, delightful; *–es Brot,* unleavened bread; *–e Milch,* fresh milk; *–e Speise,* sweets; *–e Tränen,* tears of joy; *–es Wasser,* fresh water; *–e Worte,* soft, smooth *or* winning words. **–brot,** *n.* unleavened bread. **–e,** *f.* sweetness; (*fig.*) darling. **–en,** *v.a.* & *n.* sweeten. **–holz,** *n.* liquorice (*Bot.*); *–holz raspeln,* pay compliments, say sweet nothings; flirt. **–igkeit,** *f.* sweetness; suavity; sweetmeat; (*pl.*) sweets. **–lich,** *adj.* sweetish; mawkish, fulsome; (*sl.*) smarmy. **–liebchen,** *n.* (*archaic*), darling, sweetheart. **–ling,** *m.* spiritless, wishy-washy *or* namby-pamby p., milksop. **–mandelöl,** *n.* oil of sweet almonds. **–maul,** *n.* sweet-tooth. **–most,** *m.* unfermented wine; (*Swiss dial.*) fruit drink. **–sauer,** *adj.* bitter-sweet. **–speise,** *f.* sweet, pudding. **–stoff,** *m.* saccharin, sweetening agent. **–waren,** *f.pl.* sweets, sweetmeats. **–wasser,** *n.* fresh water.
Sust, *f.* (-en) (*Swiss dial.*) shed, shelter.
Susz–eption, *f.* acceptance, taking in hand. **–ipieren,** *v.a.* accept, undertake, take in hand.
Suzerän, 1. *m.* (-s, -e) suzerain, paramount ruler. 2. *adj.* paramount, sovereign. **–ität,** *f.* suzerainty.
Sykomore, *f.* (-n) Egyptian sycamore (*Ficus sycomorus*) (*Bot.*).
Sykophant, *m.* (-en, -en) informer, betrayer, slanderer.
Sylph–e, *m.* (-en, -en) & *Austr. dial. f.* (-en), **–ide,** *f.* (-iden) sylph.
Sylvesterabend, *see* **Silvesterabend.**
Symbasis, *f.* agreement, parallelism.
Symbol, *n.* (-s, -e) symbol. **–haft,** *adj., see* **–isch.** **–ik,** *f.* symbolism. **–isch,** *adj.* symbolical. **–isieren,** *v.a.* symbolize. **–ismus,** *m.* symbolism (*in art*).
Symmet–rie, *f.* symmetry. **–rieachse,** *f.* axis of symmetry. **–risch,** *adj.* symmetrical.
sympath–etisch, *adj.* sympathetic; mysterious, miraculous; *–etische Kur,* faith-healing. **–ie,** *f.* sympathy, fellow-feeling, congeniality; inclination, fondness. **–iestreik,** *m.* strike in sympathy (with). **–isch,** *adj.* congenial, likeable; *sie ist mir –isch,* she appeals to me, I like her; *–isches Nervensystem,* sympathetic nerve ganglia, sympathetic chain. **–isieren,** *v.n.* sympathize, agree, be in agreement (*mit,* with), have similar tastes.
Symphonie, *see* **Sinfonie.**
Symptom, *n.* (-s, -e) symptom. **–atisch,** *adj.* symptomatic, characteristic.
Synagoge, *f.* (-n) synagogue.
synchron, *adj.* synchronous, simultaneous. **–isieren,** *v.a.* synchronize (*sound-film*). **–isierung,** *f.* synchronization. **–ismus,** *m.* synchronism. **–istisch,** *adj.* concurrent, coincident, isochronous.
Syndik–alismus, *m.* trade(s)-union movement, working-class radicalism. **–at,** *n.* (-(e)s, -e) syndicate, cartel, combine, trust. **–us,** *m.* (-us, -en & Syndizi) syndic, trustee, legal representative.
Synkop–e, *f.* (-en) syncope (*Metr., Mus.* & *Med.*), fainting fit. **–ieren,** *v.a.* syncopate (*Metr.* & *Mus.*).
Synod–e, *f.* synod, church council. **–isch,** *adj.* synodal; synodic(al) (*Astr.*).
synonym, 1. *adj.* synonymous, synonymic. 2. *n.* (-s, -e) synonym. **–ik,** *f.* study of synonyms. **–isch,**

adj., *see* –; *–isches Wörterbuch*, dictionary of synonyms.
synoptisch, *adj.* synoptic(al); *die –en Evangelien*, the synoptic gospels.
syntaktisch, *adj.* syntactical.
Synthe–se, *f.* synthesis. **–sieren,** *v.a.* synthesize. **–tisch,** *adj.* synthetic, artificial.
Syringe, *f.* (-n) lilac (*Bot.*).
System, *n.* (-s, -e) system, plan; doctrine, school; (*Nat. Soc. term of reproach*) formal principle (*particularly of the constitution, legal system, etc.*). **–atik,** *f.* taxonomy. **–atiker,** *m.* systematic, methodical *or* dogmatic person. **–atisch,** *adj.* systematic, methodical. **–atisieren,** *v.a.* & *n.* (*aux.* h.) systematize, deal with systematically *or* methodically. **–los,** *adj.* unsystematic, unmethodical. **–zeit,** *f.* (*Nat. Soc.*) Weimar Republic (1918–33). **–zwang,** *m.* force of association, analogy.
Szen–ar, *n.* (-s, -e), **–ario,** *n.*, **–arium,** *n.* (-iums, -ien) scenario. **–e** *f.* (-en) stage, scene (*Theat.* & *fig.*); *eine –e machen*, make a scene *or* fuss, (*coll.*) have a show-down; *in –e setzen*, stage (*a play*), put (*a play*) on the stage; *bei offener –e*, before the curtain falls; *hinter der –e*, behind the scenes; *sich in –e setzen*, show off, make a show, make o.s. felt. **–enwechsel,** *m.* change of scenes. **–erie,** *f.* scenery, decor. **–isch,** *adj.* scenic.
Szepter, *n.*, *see* **Zepter.**

T

Many words were formerly spelt with **Th** which is now archaic, except in some foreign words and proper names.

T, t, *n.* T, t; *for abbreviations see the end of the German–English Vocabulary.* **T–Eisen,** T-section girder. **T–förmig,** *adj.* T-shaped. **T–Schiene,** *f.* T-rail.
Tabak, *m.* (-s, e) tobacco; (*coll.*) *das ist starker* –, that's a bit thick, that is hard to swallow, that is really too bad. **–asche,** *f.* tobacco-ash. **–bau,** *m.* cultivation of tobacco. **–händler,** *m.* tobacconist. **–pflanzung,** *f.* tobacco-plantation. **–regie,** *f.* state tobacco-monopoly. **–(s)beize,** *f.* tobacco-juice, nicotine. **–sbeutel,** *m.* tobacco-pouch. **–sdose,** *f.* snuff-box. **–sorten,** *f.pl.* brands of tobacco, tobaccos. **–spfeife,** *f.* tobacco-pipe. **–steuer,** *f.* duty on tobacco.
Tabatiere [*pron.* -iˈɛːrə], *f.* (-n) snuff-box.
tabell–arisch, *adj.* tabulated, tabular. **–arisieren,** *v.a.* tabulate, summarize. **–e,** *f.* (-n) table, list, chart, index, schedule, synopsis, summary. **–enförmig,** *adj.* tabular.
Tabernakel, *n.* & *m.* (-s, –) tabernacle.
Tabes, *f.* tabes, locomotor ataxia (*Med.*). **–zenz,** *f.* emaciation.
Tablett, *n.* (-s, -e) tray, salver. **–e,** *f.* tablet, lozenge (*Pharm.*).
Tabu, *n.* (-s, -s) taboo. **–ieren,** *v.a.* taboo.
Tabul–ator, *m.* (-s, -en) tabulator rack (*of typewriter*). **–atur,** *f.* tabulature (*Mus.*). **–ett,** *n.* (-es, -e) hawker's *or* pedlar's stand. **–ettkrämer,** *m.* pedlar.
Taburett, *n.* (-(e)s, -e) stool, pouffe.
tach–inieren, *v.n.* (*Austr. dial.*) shirk, (*sl.*) scrimshank; laze, be lazy. **–ometer,** *m.* (-s, –) speedometer (*Motor.*), tachometer (*Engin.*). **–ygraphie,** *f.* shorthand.
Tadel, *m.* blame, censure, reproof, rebuke, reproach, reprimand, bad mark (*in schools*); fault, shortcoming; *an einem keinen – finden*, be unable to find fault with a p.; *ohne* –, blameless, faultless; *Ritter ohne Furcht und* –, knight without fear or reproach (*Bayard*); *ihn trifft kein* –, (*coll.*) there are no flies on him; *sich einen – zuziehen*, lay o.s. open to blame. **–frei,** *adj.*, **–los,** *adj.* irreproachable, flawless, faultless, excellent, splendid, perfect. **–haft,** *adj.* faulty, blameworthy, reprehensible. **–n,** *v.a.* blame, reprove, reprimand, find fault with, criticize, censure; *einen wegen einer S. –n*, rebuke s.o. for a th.; *an allem etwas zu –n finden*, find fault with everything. **–enswert,** *adj.*, **–enswürdig,** *adj.* blameworthy. **–sucht,** *f.* censoriousness. **–süchtig,** *adj.* censorious; nagging.
Tadler, *m.* (-s, –) faultfinder, carper.
Tafel, *f.* (-n), board, blackboard, (school) slate; tablet, slab, cake (*of chocolate, etc.*); plaque, panel; plate (*book illustration*), sheet, table, chart, diagram; index, register; lamina, lamella; (dinner) table, meal, banquet; *die – aufheben*, rise from table; *bei* –, at table, at dinner; *die – decken*, lay the cloth *or* the table; *freie – haben bei* . . ., have free board with . . .; *große – bei Hofe*, court banquet; *mit –n*, with plates (*in books*); *offne – halten*, keep open house; *sich zur – setzen*, sit down to a meal. **–artig,** *adj.* tabular, laminar, lamillar. **–aufsatz,** *m.* table-centre, centre-piece. **–besteck,** *n.* knife, fork, and spoon. **–birne,** *f.* dessert pear. **–blei,** *n.* sheet-lead. **–butter,** *f.* best butter. **–diener,** *m.* waiter (*at table*), footman. **–druck,** *m.* handprinting. **–förmig,** *adj.*, *see* **–artig.** **–gedeck,** *n.* (set of) table-linen. **–gelder,** *n.pl.* living *or* subsistence, allowance. **–geschirr,** *n.* tableware, dinner-service, plate. **–glas,** *n.* plate-glass. **–ig,** *adj.* tabular. **–lack,** *m.* shellac. **–land,** *n.* plateau, tableland. **–leim,** *m.* carpenter's *or* cake glue. **–musik,** *f.* lunch- (tea-, *etc.*) time music. **–n,** *v.n.* (*aux.* h.) dine, feast, banquet. **–obst,** *n.* dessert fruit. **–öl,** *n.* olive oil. **–runde,** *f.* guests, party (*at table*). **–salz,** *n.* tablesalt. **–schiefer,** *m.* slate slabs. **–service,** *n.* table-service, tableware. **–tuch,** *n.* tablecloth. **–waage,** *f.* platform scales. **–wasser,** *n.* table-water, mineral water. **–wein,** *m.* dinner-wine. **–weise,** *adj.* in tabular form; in sheets *or* slabs. **–werk,** *n.* wainscoting (*walls*); inlaying (*floors*), panelling; book with plates. **–zeug,** *n.* table-linen; plate.
täfel–n, *v.a.* floor, inlay (*a floor*); wainscot, panel (*a wall*). **–ung,** *f.* inlaying (*of floors*); panelling, wainscoting. **–holz,** *n.* wainscoting, panelling. **–werk,** *n.*, *see* **–ung.**
Taffet, *see* **Taft.**
Taft, *m.* (-(e)s, -e) taffeta. **–papier,** *n.* satin paper.
Tag, *m.* (-(e)s, -e), day, daylight, broad daylight; open air; life, lifetime; *dem lieben Gott den – stehlen*, idle away one's time; *alle –e*, every day; (*coll.*) (*all*) *mein* –, in all my life, ever; *es ist noch früh am –e*, it is still early; *am –e liegen*, be manifest *or* clear; *an den – bringen*, bring to light, disclose, make manifest; *an den – kommen*, come to light; *auf seine alten –e*, in his old age; *bei –e*, in the daytime, by daylight; *–s darauf*, next day; *zweimal des –es*, twice a day; *dieser –e*, recently, one of these days; *er hat heute seinen dummen* –, he is in a bad mood today; *eines –es*, one fine day; *– für* –, day by day, day after day; *den ganzen* –, the whole *or* all day; *er hat heute seinen guten* –, he is in a good mood today; *sich* (*Dat.*) *einen guten – machen*, enjoy o.s., take it easy; *am hellen*, *lichten* or *hellichten –e*, in broad daylight; *in* or *binnen acht –en*, in *or* within a week; *in diesen –en*, see *dieser –e*; *in den – hinein leben*, live from hand to mouth, live for the present; *vor Jahr und* –, a long time ago; *der jüngste* –, Doomsday; (*Prov.*) *man soll den – nicht vor dem Abend loben*, don't count your chickens before they're hatched; *nächster –e*, shortly, one of these days; *über* –, above ground, on the surface (*Min.*); *heute über acht –e*, this day week; *unter –e arbeiten*, work underground (*Min.*); *es wird* –, day is breaking; *–ein –aus, adv.* day in day out, every day. **–(e)arbeit,** *f.* day-labour; work by the day; daily task. **–(e)arbeiter,** *m.* day-labourer. **–(e)bau,** *m.* opencast working (*Min.*). **–(e)blatt,** *n.* daily paper. **–ebuch,** *n.* daybook, order-book, journal; diary; log (*Naut.*). **–(e)dieb,** *m.* idler, sluggard. **–(e)gelder,** *n.* subsistence *or* travelling allowance. **–elang,** *adj.* for days (on end), all day long. **–elicht,** *n.* (*dial.*) skylight. **–elied,** *n.* morning song, alba (*of the Minnesingers*). **–elohn,** *m.* day's wages, daily wages. **–(e)löhner,** *m.* day-labourer.

–(e)löhnern, *v.a.* (*aux.* h.) work by the day. **–emarsch,** *m.* day's march. **–en,** *v.n.* dawn, get light, (*fig.*) become clear; sit (*in conference*), meet, hold a meeting; deliberate, confer. **–esanbruch,** *m.* break of day, daybreak, dawn. **–esarbeit,** *f.* day's work. **–esbefehl,** *m.* routine order, order of the day. **–esbericht,** *m.* daily report, bulletin. **–eseinflug,** *m.* daylight raid (*Av.*). **–esereignis,** *n.* most notable event of the day. **–esfragen,** *f.pl.* questions of the day. **–esgespräch,** *n.* topic of the day. **–esgrauen,** *n.* dawn. **–eskarte,** *f.* day-ticket. **–eskasse,** *f.* box-office (*for today's performance*) (*Theat.*). **–eskurs,** *m.* day's *or* current rate of exchange, quotation of the day. **–esleistung,** *f.* daily output. **–eslicht,** *n.* daylight; *ans –eslicht kommen,* come to light, become known. **–esliteratur,** *f.* current literature. **–esmarsch,** *m.* day's march. **–esneuigkeiten,** *f.pl.* news of the day. **–esordnung,** *f.* day's programme; agenda; *an der –esordnung sein,* be an everyday occurrence. **–espreis,** *m.* current price. **–espresse,** *f.* daily press. **–eszeit,** *f.* time of day, hour of the day; daytime; *zu jeder –eszeit,* at any hour; *bei guter –eszeit ankommen,* arrive at an early hour. **–eszeitung,** *f.* daily paper. **–ewerk,** *n.* day's work; daily task; (*dial.*) measure of land. **–falter,** *m.* butterfly. **–hell,** *adj.* clear as day. **–hemd,** *n.* shirt (*for men*), chemise (*for women*). **–lohn,** *m.* (*Austr. & Swiss dial.*), *see* **–elohn. –satzung,** *f.* (*Swiss*) Diet; (*Austr. dial.*) fixed day *or* date, term. **–süber,** *adv.* during the day. **–täglich,** *adj.* usual, daily, everyday. **–undnachtgleiche,** *f.* equinox. **–ung,** *f.* (-en) meeting, convention, session, conference. **–wache,** *f.,* **–wacht,** *f.* (*Swiss dial.*) reveille (*Mil.*). **–wasser,** *n.* surface water.

täg–ig, *adj. suffix,* e.g. *drei–ig,* lasting three days; *vierzehn–iges Kind,* child fourteen days old. **–lich,** *adj.* daily, per diem, diurnal, quotidian; ordinary, everyday; *vierzehn–liche Lieferung,* fortnightly delivery; (*C.L.*) *–liches Geld,* call-money; *auf –liche Kündigung,* at call; *dreimal –lich,* three times a day.

Taifun, *m.* (-s, -e) typhoon.

Taill–e [*pron.* ˈtaljə], *f.* (-en) waist, waist-line, bodice. **–ieren,** *v.a.* turn up, lay down (*cards*).

Takel, *n.* (-s, –) block and tackle (*Naut.*). **–age,** *f., see* **–ung. –ing** *f.* (-s, -e) whipping (*Naut.*). **–n,** *v.a.* rig (*a ship*). **–ung,** *f.,* **–werk,** *n.* rigging, tackle.

Takt, *m.* (-(e)s, -e) time, beat, measure (*Mus.*); stroke, cycle (*Mach.*); (*fig.*) tact; *– halten,* keep time; *aus dem –e bringen* (*fig.*) disconcert; *sich aus dem – bringen lassen* (*fig.*), be disconcerted, (*coll.*) be put off one's stroke; *im –e,* in time, in step; *den – angeben* or *schlagen,* beat time. **–art,** *f.* measure, time (*Mus.*). **–bezeichnung,** *f.* time-signature. **–fest,** *adj.* keeping good time; (*coll.*) reliable, sound, consistent. **–gefühl,** *n.* tact, tactfulness. **–ierstab,** *m.,* **–ierstock,** *m.* (conductor's) baton. **–los,** *adj.* tactless, indiscreet, injudicious, ill-advised, in bad taste. **–losigkeit,** *f.* tactlessness, want of tact, bad taste; indiscretion; *eine –losigkeit begehen,* commit an indiscretion. **–mäßig,** *adj.* rhythmical (*Mus., Danc.*); measured. **–messer,** *m.* metronome. **–note,** *f.* semibreve (*Mus.*). **–pause,** *f.* bar-rest. **–schritt,** *m.* measured (*or* dance-) step. **–straße,** *f.* assembly line (*factories*). **–strich,** *m.* bar (*Mus.*). **–voll,** *adj.* tactful, discreet, judicious.

Takt–ik, *f.* (-iken) tactics. **–iker,** *m.* tactician. **–isch,** *adj.* tactical.

Tal, *n.* (-s, ¨er & (*poet.*) -e) valley, vale, dale, glen; *zu – fahren,* go downstream *or* downhill. **–abwärts,** *adv.* downstream, downhill. **–bewohner,** *m.* valley-dweller. **–enge,** *f.* narrow (part of a) valley; (*coll.*) bottle-neck. **–fahrt,** *f.* descent. **–hang,** *m.* valley slope. **–kessel,** *m.,* **–mulde,** *f., see* **–senke. –schaft,** *f.* (*Swiss dial.*) inhabitants of a valley. **–senke,** *f.* basin-shaped valley; hollow, narrow valley. **–sohle,** *f.* bottom of a valley. **–sperre,** *f.* barrage, dam. **–wärts,** *adv., see* **–abwärts. –weg,** *m.* road through a valley; river-bed.

Talar, *m.* (-s, -e) robe (*lawyer*); gown (*clergyman, teacher, etc.*).

Talent [*pron.* -ˈlɛnt], *n.* (-(e)s, -e) talent, (natural) gift, ability, faculty, aptitude, capacity; accomplishments, attainments; gifted *or* talented person; *er hat kein – zu . . .* he has no gift for . . . **–iert,** *adj.* talented, gifted. **–los,** *adj.* without talent *or* ability, not gifted. **–losigkeit,** *f.* lack of talent. **–voll,** *adj., see* **–iert.**

Taler, *m.* (-s, –), (*archaic*) thaler (*coin*).

Talg, *m.* (-(e)s, -e), tallow, grease, sebum; suet. **–artig,** *adj.* tallowy, sebaceous. **–drüse** *f.* sebaceous gland. **–en,** *v.a.* smear *or* grease with tallow. **–fett,** *n.* stearin. **–ig,** *adj.* tallowy; sebaceous; adipose. **–kerze,** *f.,* **–licht,** *n.* tallow candle.

Talje, *f.* (-n) light tackle (*Naut.*), reep, line, halyard.

Talk, *m.* talc(um) (*Min.*) **–artig,** *adj.* talcous, talcose. **–erde,** *f.* magnesia, magnesium oxide. **–gebirge,** *n.,* **–gestein,** *n.* talc rocks. **–ig,** *adj.* (*dial.*) soggy, sad (*of pastry*). **–säure,** *f.* stearic acid. **–spat,** *m.* magnesite. **–stein,** *m.* steatite, soapstone.

Talmi, *n.* pinchbeck; (*fig.*) counterfeit, sham.

Tambour, *m.* (-s, -e & (*Swiss dial.*) -en) drummer; tambour (*Arch., Fort.*); small drum; embroidery frame. **–stab,** *m.* drum-major's baton.

Tambur, *m.* (-s, -e), embroidery frame. **–in,** *n.* (-s, -e) tambourine (*Mus.*). **–ieren,** *v.a.* tambour (*embroidery*).

Tamp, *m.* (-s, -e), end of a rope (*Naut.*).

Tampon, *m.* (-s, -s), swab (*Med.*). **–ieren,** *v.a.* plug (*a wound*).

Tamtam, *m.* (-s, -s), gong, tom-tom, (*fig.*) noise, pother, to-do, palaver.

Tand, *m.* trifle, bauble, trinket, toy, knick-knack, gew-gaw. **–elmarkt,** *m.* (*dial.*), *see* **Tändelmarkt, –ler,** *m.* (*dial.*), see **Tändler.**

Tänd–elei, *f.* (-en) dallying, trifling, toying; flirtation. **–elhaft,** *adj.,* **–elig,** *adj.* trifling, dallying, playful; frivolous. **–eln,** *v.n.* (*aux.* h.) dally, trifle, flirt; dawdle, go slow; (*dial.*) deal in second-hand goods. **–elkram,** *m.* frippery, trifles. **–elmarkt,** *m.* rag-fair, jumble-sale. **–elschürze,** *f.* (small) fancy apron. **–ler,** *m.* trifler; dawdler; (*dial.*) second-hand dealer.

Tang, *m.* (-(e)s, -e), seaweed. **–asche,** *f.* kelp.

Tang–ens, *m.* (–, –) tangent (*Trigonometry*) **–ent,** *m.* (-s, -e) jack (*of a harpsichord*), plectrum. **–ente,** *f.* tangent (*Geometry*). **–entialebene,** *f.* tangent plane. **–ieren,** *v.a.* touch, touch upon; be tangent to.

Tank, *m.* (-(e)s, -e (& *Austr. dial.* -s)) tank (*for liquids & Mil.*). **–abwehr,** *f.* anti-tank defence. **–büchse,** *f.* anti-tank rifle (*Mil.*). **–en,** *v.n.* refuel, fill up. **–fahrer,** *m.* tank driver. **–falle,** *f.* tank trap. **–schiff,** *n.* tanker. **–stelle,** *f.* petrol *or* filling station (*Motor.*). **–wagen,** *m.* tank-car (*Railw.*); tank lorry, petrol tanker (*Motor.*). **–wart,** *m.* petrol-pump attendant.

Tann, *m.* (-(e)s, -e) (*Poet.*) pine forest. **–e,** *f.* (silver) fir (*Abies*) (*Bot.*). **–en,** *adj.* fir. **–enapfel,** *m.* fir-cone. **–enbaum,** *m.* fir-tree. **–enharz,** *n.* resin from fir-trees. **–enholz,** *n.* fir-wood, deal. **–ennadeln,** *f.pl.* fir-needles. **–enzapfen,** *m.* fir-cone. **–icht,** *n.* (*dial.*) fir plantation. **–ig,** *adj.* planted with firs; fir. **–in,** *n.* tannin, tannic acid.

Tantal, *n.* tantalum. **–säure,** *f.* tantalic acid.

Tante, *f.* (-n) aunt; *meine –, deine –,* game of hazard (*Cards or Roulette*); (*coll.*) *bei – Meier,* at the lavatory *or* W.C.

Tantieme [*pron.* tãtiˈɛːmə], *f.* (-n) share, portion, percentage; author's rights, royalty.

Tanz, *m.* (-es, ¨e) dance, dancing, ball; (*coll.*) brawl; *einen – mit einem wagen,* let o.s. in for trouble with a p.; (*coll.*) *da ging der – los,* then the row began; *zum –e auffordern,* request the pleasure of a dance. **–bär,** *m.* dancing bear. **–bein,** *n.* (*coll.*) *das –bein schwingen,* go dancing, have a dance. **–boden,** *m.,* **–diele,** *f.* dance hall. **–en,** *v.a. & n.* (*aux.* h. & s.) dance; be rocked (*on the waves*); *nach der Geige –en,* dance to the fiddle; (*Prov.*) *–en wollen, wenn die Musik aufhört,* come a day after the fair. **–erei,** *f.* dance, (*coll.*) hop. **–fest,** *n.* ball, dance. **–gesellschaft,** *f.* dancing-party, dance. **–kneipe,** *f.* public-house where dancing is allowed. **–kränzchen,** *n.* dancing club. **–kunst,** *f.* dancing. **–lied,** *n.* choral dance. **–lokal,** *n., see* **–boden. –lustig,** *adj.* fond of dancing. **–meister,** *m.* dancing instructor. **–musik,**

f. dance music. **-platz,** *m.* dance-floor, open space for dancing. **-saal,** *m.* ball-room, dance hall. **-stunde,** *f.* dancing lesson. **-unterricht,** *m.* dancing lessons. **-wut,** *f.* dancing mania, rage for dancing.

tänz-eln, *v.n.* (*aux.* h.) trip, skip, hop, caper; amble (*of horses*). **-er,** *m.*, **-erin,** *f.* dancing partner; dancer.

taperig, *adj.* (*dial.*), see **taprig.**

Tapet, *n.* (-(e)s, -e), (*archaic*) carpet; only in *aufs – bringen*, broach *or* introduce a subject; *aufs – kommen*, come under discussion. **-e,** *f.* (-en) wall-paper; tapestry. **-enbahn,** *f.* width of wall-paper. **-entür,** *f.* concealed door.

Tapezier, *m.* (-s, -e), paperhanger, decorator; upholsterer. **-en,** *v.a.* paper, hang with tapestry (*walls*). **-er,** *m.* (-ers, -er), *see* **-.** **-ung,** *f.* papering (*of walls, rooms*).

tapfer, *adj.* brave, gallant, valiant; bold, courageous; *– arbeiten*, work strenuously *or* resolutely; *halte dich –!* be firm! don't flinch! *sich – wehren gegen*, make a bold stand against. **-keit,** *f.* bravery, gallantry, valour.

Tapisserie, *f.* (-n), tapestry-work, embroidery.

Tappe, *f.* (-n) paw; paw mark. **-n,** *v.n.* (*aux.* h. & s.) grope, fumble; *im Dunkeln -n*, grope in the dark.

täppisch, *adj.* awkward, clumsy; ponderous.

tap-rig (*dial.*) *adj.* awkward. **-s,** *m.* (-ses, -se) slap, tap; awkward fellow, clumsy lout. **-sen,** *v.n.* walk clumsily, be awkward.

Tar-a, *f.* (*C.L.*) tare, weight of packing. **-arechnung,** *f.* tare-account. **-avergütung,** *f.* allowance for tare. **-ieren,** *v.a.* allow for *or* ascertain the tare.

Tarantel, *f.* (-n) tarantula (*Ent.*); *wie von der – gestochen*, like a shot.

Tarif, *m.* (-s, -e) price list, table of rates, scale of prices *or* charges; tariff, rate, list of fares (*Railw.*). **-abkommen,** *n.* price settlement, wage agreement. **-ieren,** *v.a.* fix a tariff. **-lohn,** *m.* standard *or* agreed wages. **-mäßig,** *adj.* in accordance with the tariff. **-satz,** *m.* tariff-rate. **-vertrag,** *m.*, *see* **-abkommen.**

tarn-en, *v.a.* mask, screen, disguise, camouflage. **-kappe,** *f.* cloak of invisibility. **-netz,** *n.* camouflage net. **-ung,** *f.* camouflage, dazzle paint, masking, screen.

Tartsche, *f.* (-n) (*archaic*) (small) round shield; target.

Tasch-e, *f.* (-en) pocket; purse, handbag, satchel, wallet, pouch; ventricle; *einem auf der -e liegen*, be a (financial) drain on a p.; *aus jemandes -e leben*, live at another's expense; (*coll.*) live on s.o.; *in die eigne -e arbeiten*, line one's pocket; *etwas schon in der -e haben*, have a th. securely in one's possession, (*coll.*) have s.th. in one's pocket *or* in the bag; *etwas in die -e stecken*, pocket s.th. **-enausgabe,** *f.* pocket-edition. **-enbuch,** *n.* pocket-book, note-book. **-endieb,** *m.* pickpocket; *vor -endieben wird gewarnt*, beware of pickpockets. **-enformat,** *n.* pocket-size. **-engeld,** *n.* pocket-money. **-enkrebs,** *m.* common crab. **-enlampe,** *f.* electric torch, flashlight. **-enmesser,** *n.* pocket-knife, penknife, clasp-knife. **-enspieler,** *m.* juggler, conjurer. **-enspielerei,** *f.* conjuring, sleight of hand, legerdemain. **-entuch,** *n.* (pocket) handkerchief. **-enuhr,** *f.* (pocket) watch. **-ner** (*Austr. dial.*), *see* **Täschner.**

Täschner, *m.* (*dial.*) bag-maker; dealer in leather goods.

Tasse, *f.* (-n) cup. **-nkopf,** *m.* (*dial.*) cup.

Tast-atur, *f.* (-en), **-brett,** *n.* keys, keyboard (*of a piano, typewriter, etc.*). **-bar,** *adj.* palpable, tangible. **-borste,** *f.* tactile bristle. **-e,** *f.* (-en) key (*of a piano, typewriter, etc.*); *eine falsche -e anschlagen*, play a wrong note (*piano*), strike a wrong key *or* letter (*typewriter*). **-empfindung,** *f.* sense *or* sensation of touch. **-en,** 1. *v.a.* & *n.* (*aux.* h.) touch feel, grope, fumble; palpate; *nach einer S. -en*, feel for a th.; *-end gehen*, grope one's way. 2. *v.n.* feel *or* grope one's way. 3. *n.* feeling, touch; groping. **-enwerk,** *n.* key-action. **-er,** *m.* feeler, antenna; callipers; key. **-reiz,** *m.* contact stimulus. **-sinn,** *m.* sense of touch. **-spitze,** *f.* palp. **-versuch,** *m.* tentative experiment, preliminary trial. **-werkzeug,** *n.* organ of touch, feeler.

Tat, *f.* (-en) deed, act, action; fact, feat, achievement; *auf frischer –*, in the very act; *durch die – beweisen*, prove by one's actions; *den guten Willen* or *die gute Absicht für die – nehmen*, take the will for the deed; *in der –*, in reality, actually, truly; indeed, really, in fact, in point of fact, as a matter of fact; *ein Mann der –*, a man of action; *einem mit Rat und – beistehen*, help a p. in every possible way; *zur – schreiten*, proceed to action. **-bericht,** *m.* summary of evidence. **-bestand,** *m.* facts (*of a case*); matter of fact, state of affairs; evidence (*Law*). **-beweis,** *m.* practical *or* factual proof. **-einheit,** *f.* coincidence (*Law*). **-endrang,** *m.*, **-endurst,** *m.* thirst for action, desire to do great things, fervid activity. **-enlos,** *adj.* idle, inactive. **-enreich,** *adj.* active, eventful. **-form,** *f.* active voice (*Gram.*). **-handlung,** *f.* fact; deed of violence. **-kraft,** *f.* energy. **-kräftig,** *adj.* energetic. **-sache,** *f.* fact; (*pl.*) data; *vollendete -sache*, fait accompli; *-sachen sind stärker als Worte*, facts speak louder than words. **-sachenbericht,** *m.* factual *or* first-hand account. **-sachenfrage,** *f.* issue in fact (*Law*). **-sächlich,** 1. *adj.* real, factual, actual; matter-of-fact. *-sächliche Schußweite*, effective range. 2. *adv.* in fact. **-sächlichkeit,** *f.* reality, actuality.

tat, tatest, täte, *see* **tun.**

tatauier-en, *v.a.* & *r.* tattoo. **-ung,** *f.* tattooing.

Tät-er, *m.* (-ers, -er) wrongdoer, culprit; author, perpetrator. **-erisch,** *adj.* warlike, heroic. **-erschaft,** *f.* guilt; perpetration; *er kann die -erschaft nicht leugnen*, he cannot deny having done it. **-ig,** *adj.* active, busy, engaged, employed; energetic; effective; *als Arzt -ig sein*, practise medicine; **-igen,** *v.a.* (*C.L.*) effect (*a sale*); conclude (*a transaction*); carry out (*a project*); *in Goldwährung getätigte Käufe*, purchases effected *or* paid for in gold. **-igkeit,** *f.* activity, action, function; occupation, profession; *in -igkeit setzen*, set going, put into action; *außer -igkeit setzen*, set aside, suspend, put out of action; *in -igkeit treten*, function, become active. **-igkeitsdrang,** *m.* active disposition, appetite for work. **-igkeitsform,** *f.* active voice (*Gram.*). **-igkeitskreis,** *m.* sphere of activity. **-igkeitswort,** *n.* verb. **-lich,** *adj.* violent; *einen -lich angreifen*, commit an assault upon a p.; *-lich werden*, become violent, come to blows. **-lichkeit,** *f.* (act of) violence, assault (and battery).

tätowieren (*archaic, Austr. dial.*), *see* **tatauieren.**

Tatsche *f.* (*dial.*) (podgy) hand; slap. **-n,** 1. *v.a.* slap. 2. *v.n.* talk baby language.

Tätsch-chen, *n.* slap. **-eln,** *v.a.* pet, caress, fondle, stroke.

Tatter-ich, *m.* (*coll.*), trembling, shakiness, tremor (*of old age*). (*coll.*) **-n,** *v.n.* dodder, dither, be shaky.

Tatze, *f.* (-n) paw; claw (*Mach.*); (*coll.*) *einem eine – geben*, give a p. a stroke on the hand with a cane. **-nförmig,** *adj.* claw-like. **-nhieb,** *m.* blow with a paw.

[1]**Tau,** *n.* (-(e)s, -e) rope, cable, hawser; *am – klettern*, rope-climbing (*Gymn.*). **-anker,** *m.* warp anchor. **-en,** *v.a.* tow (*a ship, etc.*). **-ende,** *n.*; *das -ende kosten*, have *or* get a taste of the rope's end, be flogged (*Naut.*). **-enpapier,** *n.* jute paper. **-erei,** *f.* towing, towage. **-kranz,** *m.* coir fender (*Naut.*). **-länge,** *f.* cable's length. **-werk,** *n.* rigging; *laufendes -werk*, running rigging; *stehendes -werk*, standing rigging. **-ziehen,** *n.* tug-of-war (*Sport*).

[2]**Tau,** *m.* dew; *gefrorener –*, hoar-frost; *es fällt –*, the dew is falling; *vor – und Tag*, in the dewy morn; *er hört den – fallen*, he thinks he is mighty clever. **-en,** *v.n.* (*aux.* h. & s.) & *a.* thaw, melt; (*imp.*) fall as dew; *es -t*, the dew is falling; it is thawing. **-feucht,** *adj.* wet with dew, bedewed. **-frisch,** *adj.* dewy, fresh, fresh as a daisy. **-ig,** *adj.* dewy. **-perle,** *f.* dewdrop. **-regen,** *m.* mild rain. **-schlag,** *m.* track (*of game*) in the dew. **-tropfen,** *m.* dewdrop. **-wetter,** *n.* thaw. **-wind,** *m.* warm wind, mild breeze. **-wurzel,** *f.* shallow root.

taub, *adj.* deaf; oblivious, unfeeling, callous; numb;

empty, hollow; dead, sterile, barren; – *machen*, deafen; – *auf einem Ohre*, deaf in one ear; – *sein gegen jemandes Bitten*, be deaf to a p.'s entreaties; *–en Ohren predigen*, cry in the wilderness; *–e Ähre*, empty ear; *–es Ei*, addled egg; *–e Flut*, slack tide; *–er Gang*, exhausted lode; *–es Gestein*, deads, rubble, unproductive rock (*Min.*); *–er Hafer*, wild oats; *–e Nüsse*, empty nuts. **–geboren,** *adj.*, born deaf. **–heit,** *f.* deafness; numbness; barrenness. **–kohle,** *f.* anthracite. **–nessel,** *f.* dead-nettle (*Lamium*) (*Bot.*). **–stumm,** *adj.* deaf and dumb; *ein –stummer*, *m.* a deaf-mute. **–stummenanstalt,** *f.* institute for the deaf and dumb.

Täub–chen, *n.* (-s, –) little dove; sweetheart; *mein –chen!* my poppet *or* pet. **–er, –erich,** *m.*, *see* **Tauber.**

Taube, *f.* (-n), pigeon; dove; *ein Flug –n*, a flight *or* flock of pigeons; *verirrte –*, stray pigeon; *sanft wie eine –*, (as) gentle as a dove; *wo –n sind, fliegen –n hin*, to him that hath shall be given; *Land der gebratenen –n*, fool's paradise; Cockaigne; (*Prov.*) *besser ein Sperling in der Hand als eine – auf dem Dach*, a bird in the hand is worth two in the bush; *ihm fliegen die gebratenen –n in den Mund*, everything falls into his lap. **–nfalk(e),** *m.*, *see* **Wanderfalk(e).** **–nfarbig,** *adj.* dove-coloured. **–nflug,** *m.* flight *or* flock of pigeons. **–nloch,** *n.* pigeonhole. **–npost,** *f.* pigeon-post. **–nschlag,** *m.* dovecote, pigeon loft; *wie in einem –nschlag*, with continual coming and going. **–nstößer,** *m.* goshawk (*Accipiter nisus*) (*Orn.*). **–nzüchter,** *m.* pigeon-fancier. **–r,** *m.*, **–rich,** *m.* cock pigeon.

tauch–en, 1. *v.r.* & *n.* (*aux.* h. & s.) dip *or* plunge (*into water*), dive; remain under water, submerge; *wieder in die Höhe –en*, come to the surface; *die Sonne –t ins Meer*, the sun plunges into the sea. 2. *v.a.* dip, immerse, steep, soak, (*coll.*) duck. **–anlage,** *f.* dipping plant. **–boot,** *n.* submarine. **–er,** *m.* diver; diving-bird. **–eranzug,** *m.* diving-suit. **–erglocke,** *f.* diving-bell. **–erkolben,** *m.* plunger. **–ervögel,** *m.pl.* divers (*Orn.*). **–färbung,** *f.* dip-dyeing. **–klar,** *adj.* ready to submerge (*submarine*). **–korn,** *n.* sinker. **–pflanze,** *f.* submerged plant. **–retter,** *m.* escape apparatus (*from submarines*). **–rohr,** *n.* immersion tube (*of carburettor*). **–sieder,** *m.* immersion-heater (*Elec.*). **–waage,** *f.* hydrometer; aerometer.

Tauf–e, *f.* (-en) baptism, christening; naming ceremony (*ships, etc.*); *aus der –e heben*, be godparent to, (*fig.*) initiate, originate; *einen Verein aus der –e heben*, launch *or* start a society, (*coll.*) get a society going, set a society on its feet; *ein Kind über die –e halten*, present a child at the font. **–en,** *v.a.* baptize, christen, name; (*coll.*) *Wein –en*, water *or* adulterate wine; *ein Kind (auf den Namen) Ernst –en*, christen a child Ernest; *sich –en lassen*, be baptized; **–akt,** *m.* christening ceremony, baptism. **–becken,** *n.* (christening) font. **–buch,** *n.* baptismal, church *or* parish register. **–formel,** *f.* form of baptism. **–gebühr,** *f.* christening fee. **–geschenk,** *n.* christening present. **–gesinnte(r),** *m.* (ana-)baptist, Mennonite. **–handlung,** *f.*, *see* **–akt.** **–kind,** *n.* infant to be baptized. **–name,** *m.* Christian name. **–pate,** *m.* godfather. **–patin,** *f* godmother. **–schein,** *m.* certificate of baptism. **–stein,** *m.* (baptismal) font. **–wasser,** *n.* baptismal water. **–zeuge,** *m.* sponsor, godparent.

Täuf–er, *m.* (-ers, -er) baptizer; *Johannes der –er*, John the Baptist. **–ling,** *m.* infant to be baptized; neophyte, candidate for baptism (*of grown-up persons*).

taug–en, *v.n.* (*aux.* h.) be of use *or* of value, be worth; answer, do, serve, be good *or* fit for; *es –t (zu) nichts*, it is worthless; *er –t nichts*, he is a good-for-nothing fellow; *wozu –t das?* what use is that? what is the good of this? **–enichts,** *m.* (– & -es, -e) good-for-nothing, ne'er-do-well; **–lich,** *adj.* good, able, suitable, qualified, adapted, capable, fit, useful; fit for active service (*Mil.*). **–lichkeit,** *f.* fitness, suitability, usefulness.

Taum–el, *m.* reeling, staggering; giddiness; the staggers (*Vet.*); (*fig.*) intoxication, ecstasy, transport, passion, frenzy, delirium; whirl. **–elgeist,** *m.* harum-scarum, hare-brained crank. **–elig,** *adj.* reeling, giddy. **–elkäfer,** *m.* whirligig beetle (*Gyrinidae*) (*Ent.*) **–eln,** *v.n.* (*aux.* h. & s.) reel, stagger; be giddy; *er kam in das Zimmer getaumelt*, he staggered into the room; *er –elt von diesem unverhofften Glücke*, this unexpected good fortune has turned his head. **–lig,** *adj.*, *see* **–elig.**

Tauner, *m.* (*Swiss dial.*) day-labourer.

Tausch, *m.* (-es, -e) exchange, barter; *in – nehmen*, take in exchange; *einen – machen*, effect an exchange, (*sl.*) do a swop. **–bar,** *adj.* exchangeable. **–en,** *v.a.* & *n.* (*aux.* h.) exchange (*gegen*, for); barter, (*sl.*) swop; *ich möchte nicht mit Ihnen –en*, I would not change places with you, I should not like to be in your place. **–erei,** *f.* (*coll.*) chopping and changing. **–geschäft,** *n.*, **–handel,** *m.* barter; exchange-trade. **–mittel,** *n.* medium of exchange. **–objekt,** *n.* object of value in exchange. **–weise,** *adj.* by *or* in exchange. **–wert,** *m.* exchange value. **–zersetzung,** *f.* double decomposition.

täusch–en, 1. *v.a.* deceive, delude, mislead, cheat, impose upon; disappoint; *der Schein –t*, appearances are deceptive; *in der Liebe getäuscht werden*, be disappointed in love. 2. *v.r.* deceive o.s., be mistaken. **–end,** *pr.p.* & *adj.* deceitful; illusory; *–end ähnlich*, as like as two peas, indistinguishable; *–ende Ähnlichkeit*, striking resemblance; *das ist –end nachgemacht*, that is copied to the life. **–er,** *m.* deceiver, cheat; (*archaic*) (horse)dealer. **–ung,** *f.* deception, fraud; feint; illusion, delusion, mistake. **–ungsangriff,** *m.* feint attack. **–ungsunternehmen,** *n.* diversion (*Mil.*) **–ungsversuch,** *m.* attempt at deception.

tauschieren, *v.a.* inlay (*metals*), damascene.

tausend, 1. *num. adj.* thousand; – *und aber –*, thousands and *or* on *or* upon thousands; *nicht einer unter –*, not one in a thousand; *neun vom –*, nine pro mille, 0·9 per cent.; – *Mann*, a thousand men; *an die – Mann*, getting on for a thousand men. – *und eine Nacht*, the Arabian Nights' (Entertainments). 2. *n.* (-s, -e) thousand; *zu –en*, in (their) thousands; by the thousand; *viele –e*, many thousands; *es geht in die –e*, it runs into thousands; *–e armer Menschen*, thousands of poor people; *–e und aber –e*, *see under* – 1; *neun vom –*, *see under* – 1. 3. *m.* (*archaic*) devil, only in (*ei*) *der –!*, *potz –!* the deuce! **–er,** *m.* thousand (*digit*). **–erlei,** *indec. adj.* of 1,000 kinds; *–erlei Dinge*, thousands of things; ever so many things. **–fach, –fältig,** 1. *adj.* a thousand times, thousandfold. 2. *adv.* in a thousand ways. **–füß(l)er,** *m.* centipede (*Myriapoda*) (*Ent.*). **–güldenkraut,** *n.* centaury (*Erythraea*) (*Bot.*). **–jährig,** *adj.* of 1,000 years, 1,000 years old; millennial; *das –jährige Reich*, the millennium. **–künstler,** *m.* Jack of all trades; conjurer. **–mal,** *adv.* 1,000 times. (*coll.*) **–sackerment,** *int.* the deuce! devil take it! hang it! (*coll.*) **–sappermenter,** *m.*, **–sasa,** *m.* (-s, –; *Austr. dial.* –, -s) devil of a fellow. **–schön(chen),** *n.* daisy (*Bellis perennis*) (*Bot.*). **–st,** *num. adj.* thousandth; *das weiß der –ste nicht*, not one in a thousand knows that. **–stel,** *n.*, (*Swiss dial. m.*) thousandth part. **–stens,** *adv.* in the thousandth place.

Tautolog–ie, *f.* tautology. **–isch,** *adj.* tautological.

Tax–ameter, *m.* (-s, –) taximeter, taxicab. **–ator,** *m.* tax assessor; appraiser, valuer. **–e,** *f.* (-en) official charge, controlled price; valuation, assessment; tax, rate, duty; taxi(cab); *zu fester –e*, at a fixed rate. **–frei,** *adj.* tax-free, exempt from tax. **–i,** *n.* (*Swiss dial. m.*) (-(s), –), taxi(cab). **–ieren,** *v.a.* appraise, value, estimate, assess, rate, tax; fix the price; *zu niedrig –ieren*, rate, assess *or* price too low. **–ifahrer,** *m.* taxi-driver. **–ordnung,** *f.* tariff; scale of fees *or* costs (*in law-courts, etc.*). **–wert,** *m.* assessed value.

Taxus, *m.* (–, –) yew (*Taxus baccata*) (*Bot.*).

Techn–ik, *f.* (-iken) technical *or* applied science; technology, engineering; technique, skill, execution. **–iker,** *m.* technician, engineer, technologist. **–ikum,** *n.* (-ums, -en) technical school. **–isch,** *adj.* technical; *–ische Ausdrücke*, technical terms; *–ische Chemie*, applied chemistry; *–ische Hochschule*, school of technology, polytechnic; *–ische Nothilfe*, first-line repair service; *–ische Störung*, technical hitch *or* breakdown; *–ische Vollendung*, technical perfection. *–isch rein*, commercial (quality). **–izismus,** *m.* (-mus, -men) technicality.

Techtelmechtel, *n.* (-s, –) (*coll.*) flirtation, entanglement, secret understanding.

Teckel, *m.* (-s, –) dachshund.

Tee, *m.* (-s, -s) tea; infusion; tea party; *wollen Sie bei uns – trinken?* will you have tea with us? *im – sein* (*dial.*) drunk; (*dial.*) well in with the teacher; *seinen – kriegen,* (*dial.*) get one's marching orders, be flung *or* kicked out. **–bau,** *m.* tea-growing. **–brett,** *n.* tea-tray. **–büchse,** *f.*, **–dose,** *f.* tea-caddy. **–ei,** *n.*, tea-infuser. **–haube,** *f.* tea-cosy. **–kanne,** *f.* tea-pot. **–kessel,** *m.* tea-kettle; (*coll.*) blockhead. **–kiste,** *f.* tea-chest. **–klatsch,** *m.* (ladies') tea-party. **–kräuter,** *n.pl.* herbs used for infusion. **–löffel,** *m.* tea-spoon. **–maschine,** *f.* tea-urn. **–mischung,** *f.* blend of tea. **–mütze,** *f.* tea-cosy. **–rose,** *f.* tea-rose (*Rosa indica*) (*Bot.*). **–service,** *n.* tea-set *or* service. **–sieb,** *n.* tea-strainer. **–stoff,** *m.* theine. **–strauch,** *m.* tea-plant. **–tasse,** *f.* tea-cup. **–topf,** *m.* tea-pot. **–wagen,** *m.* tea-trolley. **–zeug,** *n.* tea-things.

Teer, *m.* tar, coal-tar, pitch. **–decke,** *f.* tarpaulin. **–en,** *v.a.* tar. **–farben,** *f.pl.* coal-tar *or* aniline dyes. **–faß,** *n.* tar-barrel. **–hütte,** *f.* tar-factory. **–ig,** *adj.* tarred, tarry. (*coll.*) **–jacke,** *f.* Jack Tar. **–pappe,** *f.* roofing felt, tarred paper. **–schwelerei,** *f.* distillation of tar. **–seife,** *f.* coal-tar soap. **–tonne,** *f.* tar-barrel. **–tuch,** *n.* tarpaulin.

Teich, *m.* (-(e)s, -e) pond, pool; *der große –,* the Pond (*Atlantic Ocean*). **–binse,** *f.* bulrush. **–rohr,** *n.*, **–schilf,** *n.* reeds. **–rose,** *f.* (yellow) water-lily (*Nuphar luteum*) (*Bot.*).

Teig, 1. *m.* (-(e)s, -e) dough, paste; pulp, plastic mass. 2. *adj.* (*dial.*) mellow, overripe; soggy, sad (*of pastry*). **–ig,** *adj.* (*coll.*) doughy, pasty; *see also* – 2. **–decke,** *f.* covering *or* crust of pastry. **–holz,** *n.*, **–klöpfel,** *m.* rolling-pin. **–kratze,** *f.*, **–kratzer,** *m.*, *see* **–scharre.** **–mulde,** *f.* baker's trough. **–scharre,** *f.* baker's scraper. **–schüssel,** *f.* kneading-trough. **–waren,** *f.pl.* farinaceous products.

Teil, *m.* (-s, -e) part, portion, piece, component, element, section; (*also n.*) share, division; party (*Law*); *ich an meinem –e,* see *für mein –*; *beide –e,* both parties; *er hat sein – bekommen,* he has got his due; *sich* (*Dat.*) *seinen – denken,* have one's own ideas; *edle –e,* vital parts; *ich für mein –,* I for my part, I for one, as for me; *der größte – der Menschen,* most *or* the majority of people; *ein gut – von etwas,* a good bit *or* a fair share of a th.; *ich halte es mit keinem -e,* I side with neither party; *zum –e,* partly, in part, to some extent; *zum größten –,* for the most part, *see also* **zu–. –bar,** *adj.* divisible, separable. **–besitzer,** *m.* part-owner. **–betrag,** *m.* instalment. **–bruch,** *m.* partial fraction. **–chen,** *n.* particle. **–efertigung,** *f.* manufacture of components. **–en,** 1. *v.a.* divide; share (out), deal out; separate, sever, distribute, graduate. 2. *v.r.* (*mit einem in eine S.*) participate *or* share in; branch off, diverge, divide; *den Unterschied –en,* split the difference; *hier –en sich die Wege,* here the roads divide; *geteilte Gefühle,* mixed feelings; *geteilter Meinung sein,* be of a different opinion. **–er,** *m.* divider; sharer; divisor (*Arith.*); *größter gemeinschaftlicher –er,* greatest common measure. **–erfolg,** *m.* partial success. **–gebiet,** *n.* branch, department. **–haben,** *v.n.* have a share (*an,* in), participate (in), partake (of). **–haber,** *m.* sharer, participant, participator; joint-owner, partner; *stiller –haber,* sleeping-partner. **–haberschaft,** *f.* partnership. **–haft(ig),** *adj.* partaking of, sharing *or* participating in; *sich* (*einer S.*) *–haftig machen,* participate in (s.th.); (*einer S.*) *–haftig werden,* partake of *or* share (s.th.). **–ig,** *adj. suffix,* e.g. *zehn–ig,* in 10 parts. **–kraft,** *f.* component force. **–kreis,** *m.* graduated circle. **–lösung,** *f.* partial solution. **–nahme,** *f.* participation, share; sympathy, interest; complicity, co-operation; *–nahme an einem* (or *für einen*), interest in *or* sympathy for a p.; *–nahme an einer S.,* participation *or* interest in a th. **–nahmlos,** *adj.* (*Austr. dial.*), **–nahmslos,** *adj.*, apathetic, indifferent. **–nahm(s)losigkeit,** *f.* indifference, apathy lack of sympathy. **–nehmen,** *v.n.*; *an einer S. –nehmen,* take part in a th., participate in a th. interest o.s. in a th.; contribute to a th., join in a th.; *jemanden an einer S. –nehmen lassen,* give a p. a share in a th., allow a p. to join in a th. **–nehmend,** *adj.* sympathetic; interested (in). **–nehmer,** *m.* participant, sharer, part-owner, member; subscriber (*Phone*); sympathizer; accomplice. **–pacht.** *f.* share tenancy. **–ring,** *m.*, *see* **–kreis. –schaden,** *m.* part-damage. **–scheibe,** *f.* graduated plate. **–strecke,** *f.* section of a railway (*between stations*). **–streckengrenze,** *f.* fare-stage. **–strich,** *m.* division, graduation mark (*on a scale*). **–strichteilung,** *f.* graduation. **–ung,** *f.* division, separation; partition, distribution; graduation; quartering (*Her.*); sharing; parcelling out (*of lands*). **–ungsartikel,** *m.* partitive article (*Gram.*). **–ungsbruch,** *m.* partial fraction (*Arith.*). **–ungslinie,** *f.* dividing line. **–ungspunkt,** *m.* point of division. **–ungsrecht,** *n.* right of partition. **–ungszahl,** *f.* dividend (*Arith.*). **–ungszeichen,** *n.* division sign (*Arith.*). **–weise,** 1. *adj.* partial, fractional. 2. *adv.* partly, in part, to some extent; in parts *or* numbers. **–zahl,** *f.* quotient. **–zahlung,** *f.* part-payment, instalment; *durch –zahlungen erwerben,* obtain on the instalment plan. **–zeichnung,** *f.* detail drawing.

Tein [*pron.* 'teːiːn], *n.* theine (*Chem.*).

Teint [*pron.* tɛ̃ː] *m.* (-s, -s) complexion.

tektonisch, *adj.* tectonic, structural.

Tele-fon, *n.*, *see* **–phon. –graf,** *m.*, *see* **–graph. –gramm,** *n.* (-s, -e) telegram, (*coll.*) wire. **–grammadresse,** *f.* telegraphic address. **–grammformular,** *n.* telegraph form. **–graph,** *m.* (-en, -en) telegraph; *optischer –graph,* semaphore. **–graphenagentur,** *f.*, **–graphenbüro,** *n.* telegraphic agency. **–graphenbote,** *m.* telegraph-boy. **–graphendraht,** *m.* telegraph-wire. **–graphenstange,** *f.* telegraph-pole. **–graphie,** *f.* telegraphy; *drahtlose –graphie,* wireless telegraphy. **–graphieren,** *v.a.* & *n.* (*aux.* h.) telegraph, cable, (*coll.*) wire. **–graphisch,** *adj.* telegraphic, by telegram. **–objektiv,** *n.* telephoto lens (*Phot.*). **–pathie,** *f.* telepathy. **–phon,** *n.* telephone, (*coll.*) phone; *–phon haben,* be on the telephone. **–phonanruf,** *m.* (tele)phone call. **–phonanschluß,** *m.* telephone extension; *–phonanschluß haben,* be on the telephone. **–phonieren,** *v.a.* & *n.* (*aux.* h.) telephone, (*coll.*) phone. **–phonisch,** *adj.* telephonic, by telephone; *einen –phonisch anrufen,* ring a p. up. **–phonist,** *m.* telephone operator; telephonist (*Mil.*). **–phonleitung,** *f.* telephone circuit. **–phonverbindung,** *f.* telephone connexion. **–phonzelle,** *f.* call-box, phone-box. **–phonzentrale,** *f.* telephone exchange. **–photographie,** *f.* long-distance photography. **–skop,** *n.* (-s, -e) telescope.

Teller, *m.* (*dial. n.*) (-s, –), plate, dish; trencher; (*rare*) palm of the hand. **–bord,** *n.*, **–brett,** *n.* plate-drainer, plate-rack. **–eisen,** *n.* (spring) trap. **–fläche,** *f.* ogive. **–förmig,** *adj.* plate-shaped. **–lecker,** *m.* lickspittle, toady. **–leckerei,** *f.* toadyism. **–mütze,** *f.* flat-peaked cap. **–saat,** *f.* patchy sowing. **–sammlung,** *f.* plate-collection, passing round the plate. **–schrank,** *m.* cupboard, sideboard. **–tuch,** *n.* dish-cloth. **–ventil,** *n.* poppet valve. **–wärmer,** *m.* plate-warmer.

Tellur, *n.* tellurium. **–blei.** *n.* lead telluride. **–ig,** *adj.* tellurous. **–isch,** *adj.* terrestrial. **–ium,** *n.* tellurion (*Astr.*). **–säure,** *f.* telluric acid.

Tempel, *m.* (-s, –) temple, place of worship; synagogue; (*coll.*) *einen zum – hinauswerfen,* turn a p. out. **–diener,** *m.* officer of the temple, priest. **–herr,** *m.* Knight Templar. **–n,** *n.* a game of chance like faro (*cards*). **–orden,** *m.* Order of Knights Templar. **–raub,** *m.* sacrilege. **–räuberisch,** *adj.* sacrilegious. **–ritter,** *m.*, *see* **–herr. –schänder,** *m.* desecrator of a temple. **–weihe,** *f.*; *Fest der –weihe,* (Jewish) Feast of Dedication.

Tempera, *f.*, **–farbe,** *f.* distemper, tempera.

Temper-ament, *n.* (-(e)s, -e) temperament; character, disposition, constitution, humour; temper; spirits; vivacity, liveliness; *seinem –ament die Zügel schießen lassen,* have no control over one's disposition, be carried away by one's high spirits. **-amentlos,** *adj.* spiritless. **-amentvoll,** *adj.* lively, vivacious, high-spirited; ardent, eager. **-atur,** *f.* temperature; *-atur im Freien,* outdoor temperature. **-aturabfall,** *m.* drop in temperature. **-aturbereich,** *m.* range of temperature. **-aturbeständig,** *adj.* unaffected by temperature changes. **-aturerhöhung,** *f.* rise in temperature. **-aturgrad,** *m.* degree of temperature. **-aturkonstanz,** *f.* constant temperature. **-aturmittel,** *n.* mean temperature. **-aturschwankung,** *f.* change of *or* in temperature. **-atursturz,** *m.* sudden fall in temperature. **-enzler,** *m.* (-s, –), teetotaller. **-guß,** *m.* malleable iron casting. **-ieren,** *v.a.* temper, moderate, soften; control the temperature; cool down; *-iertes Wasser,* lukewarm water. **-n,** *v.a.* temper, anneal (*Metall.*).

tempieren, *v.a.* set (*the fuse, Artil.*).

Templer, *m. see* **Tempelherr.**

Temp-o, *n.* (-os, -os & -i) time, tempo, measure, pace, rate, speed; *-o des Angriffs,* pace of the attack; (*coll.*) *-o fahren,* scorch (*Motor.*); *er gab das -o an,* he set the pace. **-oralien,** *pl.* temporalities, secular possessions; (clerical) living. **-orär,** *adj.* temporary. **-orisieren,** *v.n.* (*aux.* h.) temporize; delay. **-us,** *n.* (-us, -ora) tense (*Gram.*).

Tenakel, *n.* (-s, –e) copy-holder (*Typ.*); tenaculum (*Surg.*); filtering frame.

Tend-enz, *f.* (-enzen) tendency, propensity, inclination, trend, intention. **-enziös,** *adj.* tendentious, partisan, biased, prejudiced. **-enzlüge,** *f.* partisan-lie. **-enzmeldung,** *f.* tendentious information. **-enzroman,** *m.*, **-enzstück,** *n.* novel (drama) with a purpose. **-ieren,** *v.n.* tend, be inclined, incline (*nach,* to).

Tender, *m.* (-s, –) supply vessel, tender (*of a railway engine*). **-lokomotive,** *f.*, **-maschine,** *f.* tank locomotive.

Tenne, *f.* (-n), threshing-floor, floor of a barn.

Tennis, *n.* (lawn) tennis. **-meisterschaft,** *f.* **-turnier,** *n.* tennis tournament. **-platz,** *m,* tennis-court. **-schläger,** *m.* tennis-racket.

Tenor, *m.* (-s, -e & ¨-e) tenor (*Mus.*); (*no pl.*) purport, drift, intent, tenor. **-ist,** *m.* (-en, -en) tenor. **-partie,** *f.* tenor part. **-sänger,** *m.* tenor. **-stimme,** *f.* tenor voice *or* part.

Tentamen, *n.* (-mens, -mina) preliminary examination. **-physikum,** pre-medical.

Tenuis, *f.* (-ues), voiceless stop (*Phonet.*).

Tepp, *m.* (-s, -e) (*dial.* & *coll.*) dunce, nincompoop.

Teppich, *m.* (-s, -e) carpet, rug; tapestry; *mit einem – überziehen* or *belegen,* carpet. **-arbeit,** *f.* tapestry-work. **-beet,** *n.* flower-bed. **-kehrmaschine,** *f.* carpet-sweeper. **-pflanzen,** *f.pl.* small plants suited for carpet-gardening. **-schoner,** *m.* drugget. **-sticker,** *m.* tapestry-worker. **-weber,** *m.*, **-wirker,** *m.* carpet-manufacturer.

Termin, *m.* (-s, -e) time, term, date, fixed day; fixture (*Sport*); summons (*Law*); *ich habe morgen –,* I am (summoned) to appear (in court) tomorrow; *in vier -en zahlbar,* payable in four instalments; *seine Miete noch zwei -e schuldig sein,* be two quarters in arrear with one's rent; *äußerster –,* extreme limit, final date. **-geschäft,** *n.* forward transactions, futures. **-handel,** *m.* time-bargain. **-ieren,** *v.a.* terminate, limit; beg alms (*as the mendicant friars*). **-ologie,** *f.* terminology, nomenclature; technical language. **-tag,** *m.* quarter-day. **-us,** *m.* term; *-i technici,* technical terms. **-versicherung,** *f.* term-policy (*life insurance*). **-weise,** *adj.* by instalments; by the term. **-zahlung,** *f.* payment by instalments *or* at fixed terms.

Terpentin, *m.* turpentine. **-öl,** *n.* spirits (*or* oil) of turpentine.

Terr-ain [*pron.* tɛ'rɛ̃:] *n.* (-s, -s) ground, terrain, country (*Mil., etc.*); building site. **-ainaufnahme,** *f.* surveying; *die Idee gewinnt -ain,* the idea gains ground. **-asse,** *f.* terrace; platform, balcony. **-assieren,** *v.a.* terrace, step. **-estrisch,** *adj.* terrestrial. **-ine,** *f.* (-n), tureen, soup-bowl.

Territori-algewalt, *f.* absolute authority (*over independent territory*) (*Hist.*). **-alstaaten,** *m.pl.* (medieval) independent states. **-um,** *n.* (-ums, -en) territory.

terroris-ieren, *v.a.* terrorize, browbeat. **-mus,** *m.* terrorism. **-t,** *m.* (-en, -en) terrorist.

Terti-a, *f.* (-en) fourth form (*school*); (*Austr. dial.*) third form; great primer (*Typ.*). **-aner,** *m.* fourth-(*Austr. dial.* third-) form boy. **-anfieber,** *n.* tertian fever (*Malaria*). **-är,** *adj.* tertiary (*also Geol.*). **-aschrift,** *f.* great primer (*Typ.*).

Terz, *f.* (-en) third (*Mus.*); tierce (*Fenc.*); *kleine –,* minor third; *große –,* major third. **-erol,** *n.* (-s, -e) pocket pistol. **-erone,** *m.* (-n, -n) offspring of a white and a mulatto. **-ett,** *n.* (-s, -e) vocal trio. **-hieb,** *m.* thrust in tierce. (*Poet.*) **-ine,** *f.* terza rima.

Tesching, *n.* (-s, -s) sub-calibre rifle.

Test, *m.* (-(e)s, -s) test, investigation (*Psych.*).

Test-ament, *n.* (-(e)s, -e) testament, will; *Altes* (*Neues*) *-ament,* Old (New) Testament; *ohne -ament sterben,* die intestate *or* without leaving a will; *Anhang zu einem -ament,* codicil to a will. **-amentarisch,** *adj.* testamentary, by will; *-amentarisch hinterlassen* or *vermachen,* leave by will, bequeath. **-amentseröffnung,** *f.* opening *or* reading of the will. **-amentsvollstrecker,** *m.* executor. **-amentszusatz,** *m.* codicil. **-at,** *n.* (-(e)s, -e) certificate, attestation. **-amentator,** *m.* (-s, -en) testator. **-amentieren,** *v.a.* & *n.* (*aux.* h.) make a will, bequeath; testify, issue a certificate; *über eine S. -amentieren,* bequeath s.th.; testify to s.th. **-amentierer,** *m.* testator. **-amentiererin,** *f.* testatrix. **-imonium,** *n.* (-iums, -ien & -ia) certificate, testimonial, testimony.

Tetraed-er, *n.* (-s, –) tetrahedron. **-risch,** *adj.* tetrahedral.

teuer, *adj.* dear, costly, expensive; (*fig.*) dear, beloved, cherished; *ich habe es – bezahlt,* I have paid dearly for it; *– kaufen,* buy at a high price; *hier ist guter Rat –,* not much can be done here; *hoch und – schwören,* swear solemnly, take a solemn oath; *das soll ihm – zu stehen kommen,* that will cost him dear, he shall smart for that; *– verkaufen,* sell for a high price; *wie – ist es?* how much is it? what does it cost? what price is it? **-ung,** *f.* dearth, famine; dearness, high cost of living. **-ungszulage,** *f.* cost-of-living bonus. **-ungszuwachs,** *m.* price increment.

Teufe, *f.* (-n) depth (*Min.*). **-n,** *v.a.* bore (deeper) (*Min.*)

Teufel, *m.* (-s, –) devil, demon, fiend; (*coll.*) deuce, dickens, Old Nick; *armer –,* poor devil *or* wretch, luckless beggar; *eingefleischter –,* devil incarnate; *er fragt den – danach,* he does not care a rap about it; *er hat den – im Leibe,* he is a devil of a fellow; *der – ist los!* hell is loose; *das müßte mit dem – zugehen,* the devil must have his hand in it; *pfui –!* disgusting! *reitet Euch der –?* are you off your head? have you lost control of yourself? *bist du des -s?* are you crazy? *vom – besessen sein,* be possessed of a devil; *den – an die Wand malen,* talk of the devil and he will appear; *der – mag wissen warum,* devil only knows; *er weiß den – davon,* (*sl.*) he knows damn all about it; *was zum –!* what the deuce! *zum – gehen,* go to rack and ruin. **-chen,** *n.* imp, little devil. **-ei,** *f.* devilry, devilment; devilishness, inhumanity. **-in,** *f.* termagant, shrew. **-sabbiß,** *m.* devil's bit (*Succisa pratensis*) (*Bot.*). **-sarbeit,** *f.* devilish *or* tremendously hard work. **-saustreibung,** *f.*, **-sbann,** *m.*, **-sbeschwörung,** *f.* exorcism. **-sbraten,** *m.* villain, rake, thorough scamp. **-sbraut,** *f.* witch. **-sbrut,** *f.* hellish crew, bad lot. **-sdreck,** *m.* asafoetida. **-sfinger,** *m.* belemnite (*Mollusc*). **-sgestank,** *m.* infernal stench. **-sglück,** *n.* devil's own luck. **-sjunge,** *m.* young imp *or* scamp; (*Irish*) broth of a boy. **-skerl,** *m.* devil of a fellow. **-skind,** *n.* hardened sinner. **-skirsche,** *f.* deadly nightshade, belladonna (*Atropa belladonna*) (*Bot.*). **-slärm,** *m.* infernal noise. **-slist,** *f.* diabolical cunning. **-smäßig,** *adj., see* **teuflisch. -sstreich,** *m.* diabolical trick. **-sweib,** *n.* she-devil, shrew. **-swerk,** *n.* piece of devilry.

teuflisch, *adj.* devilish, diabolical, satanic, fiendish, sardonic; infernal.

Teurung, *f., see* **Teuerung.**

Text, *m.* I. (-es, -e) text, letterpress, wording; words (*of a song.*), libretto; (Bible) text. 2. *f.* double pica (*Typ.*); (*coll.*) *weiter im –(e)*, come to the point! (*coll.*) *einem den – lesen*, give s.o. a good talking to; *aus dem – kommen*, lose the thread, get confused, be put out, break down (*in a speech*). **–abbildung**, *f.* illustration in the text. **–ausgabe**, *f.* plain text, edition without notes. **–buch**, *n.* textbook; libretto. **–gemäß**, *adj.*, **–mäßig**, *adj.* in conformity with the text. **–kritik**, *f.* textual criticism. **–lich**, *adj.* textual. **–worte**, *n.pl.* words of the original.

textil, *adj.* textile. **–ien**, *pl.*, **–waren**, *f.pl.* textile goods, textiles.

Textur, *f.* (-en) texture; structure (*Geol.*).

Theat–er, *n.* (-ers, -er) theatre; stage; (*coll.*) hullaballoo, fuss; *ans –er gehen*, see *zum –er gehen*; *ins –er gehen*, go to the theatre; *heute ist kein –er*, there is no performance today; (*coll.*) *–er machen*, dissemble, feign, make believe, sham, (*sl.*) put it on, put on an act; *–er spielen*, go in for amateur theatricals, put on an amateur show; *das reinste –er*, a complete sham, utter humbug; *zum –er gehen*, go on the stage, become an actor (actress), take up acting. **–erbesuch**, *m.* playgoing, theatre-going. **–erbesucher**, *m.* playgoer, theatregoer. **–erbillet**, *n.*, *see* **–erkarte**. **–ercoup**, *m.* *see* **–erstreich**. **–erdichter**, *m.* dramatist, playwright. **–erdirektor**, *m.* theatre manager. **–erfieber**, *n.* stage-fever. **–erheld**, *m.* stage-hero. **–erkapelle**, *f.* theatre orchestra. **–erkarte**, *f.* theatre ticket. **–erkasse**, *f.* box-office. **–erleben**, *n.* theâtrical life *or* profession. **–ermaler**, *m.* scene-painter. **–ermantel**, *m.* opera-cloak. **–ermanuskript**, *n.* acting copy. **–ermaschinist**, *m.* scene-shifter. **–erstreich**, *m.* stage-trick, coup de théâtre. **–erstück**, *n.* stage-play, drama. **–ervorstellung**, *f.* theatrical *or* stage performance. **–erwesen**, *n.* the stage. **–erzensur**, *f.* stage censorship. **–erzettel**, *m.* play-bill. **–ralik**, *f.* staginess, theatricality. **–ralisch**, *adj.* dramatic, scenic, histrionic, theatrical; stagy, unnatural.

Theismus, *m.* theism.

Theke, *f.* (-n) counter (*in a shop*), bar (*in a tavern*); (*Austr. dial.*) notebook.

Them–a, *n.* (-as, -ata & -en) theme, topic, subject. **–atisch**, *adj.* thematic. **–enwahl**, *f.* choice of subject.

Theo–kratie, *f.* theocracy. **–log(e)**, *m.* (-n, -n) theologian. **–logie**, *f.* theology, divinity; *Professor der –logie*, professor of divinity. **–logisch**, *adj.* theological. **–soph**, *m.* theosophist.

Theor–etiker, *m.* theorist. **–etisch**, *adj.* theoretic(al), hypothetical, speculative. **–etisieren**, *v.n.* theorize. **–ie**, *f.* theory, hypothesis; *eine –ie aufstellen*, put forward a theory; *die –ie ist aufgegeben*, the theory is exploded *or* holds good no longer.

Therap–eutik, *f.* therapeutics. **–ie**, *f.* therapy.

Therm–en, **–alquellen**, *f.pl.* hot springs, spa. **–ik**, *f.* thermal, warm up-current of air (*Gliding*). **–isch**, *adj.* thermal, thermic; *–ische Behandlung*, heat treatment. **–oelement**, *n.* thermo-couple (*Elec.*). **–ometer**, *n.* thermometer; *feuchtes –ometer*, wet-bulb thermometer. **–ometerskala**, *f.* thermometric scale. **–ometerstand**, *m.* thermometer reading. **–opaar**, *n.*, *see* **–oelement**. **–osäule**, *f.*, **–ostat**, *m.* thermostat. **–osflasche**, *f.* thermos flask, vacuum flask. **–osyphonkühlung**, *f.* gravity system water cooling (*Motor.*).

thesaurieren, *v.a.* lay up, store, hoard.

Thes–e, *f.* (-en) thesis, postulate, assertion, proposition. **–is**, *f.* (-en) 1. *see* **–e**. 2. unaccented syllable (*Metric*), down-beat (*Mus.*).

Thing, *n.* (-(e)s, -e) (*archaic*) assembly. **–platz**, *m.*, **–stätte**, *f.* (*Nat. Soc.*) arena for national festivals.

Thomas–eisen, *n.* basic (low-carbon) steel. **–mehl**, *n.* artificial fertilizer. **–prozeß**, *m.* Bessemer process (*Metall.*). **–schiene**, *f.* (Thomas) extension splint (*Surg.*). **–stahl** *m.* basic (Bessemer) steel.

Thron, *m.* (-(e)s, -e) throne; *den – besteigen*, ascend the throne; *vom –e stoßen*, dethrone, depose; *auf den – erheben*, raise to the throne; *auf den – verzichten*, renounce the succession. **–anwärter**, *m.* heir apparent. **–besteigung**, *f.* accession (to the throne). **–bewerber**, *m.* pretender to a crown. **–en**, *v.n.*(*aux.* h.) be enthroned; reign; (*coll.*) lord it. **–entsagung**, *f.* abdication. **–erbe**, *m.* heir (to the throne), heir apparent. **–folge**, *f.* succession (to the throne). **–folger**, *m.* successor to the throne. **–himmel**, *m.* canopy. **–räuber**, *m.* usurper. **–rede**, *f.* King's (Queen's) speech (*Parl.*). **–saal**, *m.* throne-room, presence chamber. **–sessel**, *m.* chair of state. **–verzicht**, *m.* abdication. **–wechsel**, *m.* change of sovereign.

Thun, *m.* (-s, -e), **–fisch**, *m.* (-es, -e) tunny (*Thynnus*) (*Icht.*).

Thymian, *m.* (-s, -e), thyme (*Thymus*) (*Bot.*).

Tick, *m.* (-s, -s) wince; (*coll.*) whim, fancy, fad; *einen – haben*, be cracked *or* dotty; be conceited; *einen – auf jemanden haben*, have a grudge against a p. **–en**, *v.n.* (*aux.* h.) tick (*as a clock*). **–tack**, 1. *adv.* tick-tock. 2. *n.* (*nursery talk*) tick-tock, ticker.

tief, 1. *adj.* deep, profound, low, dark; far; (*fig.*) innermost, utmost, extreme, utter; *– atmen*, breathe deeply *or* heavily; *seinen Hut – in die Augen drücken*, pull one's hat low over one's eyes; *etwas –er begründen*, substantiate a th. more fully; *das läßt – blicken*, that gives food for thought; *–e Einsicht*, profound insight; *–es Elend*, utter misery; (*coll.*) *zu – ins Glas gucken*, drink more than is good for one; *aus –stem Herzen*, from the bottom of the heart; *der –ste Himmel*, the blue sky; *der Grund liegt –er*, the reason is not so apparent *or* obvious; *– in der Nacht*, *in –er Nacht*, far into the night; *im –sten Norden*, in the extreme north; (*coll.*) *– in der Patsche sitzen*, be well and truly in a mess; *–es Rot*, dark red; *in –em Schlaf*, in a deep sleep, deep in sleep; *ein Instrument –er stimmen*, lower the pitch of an instrument; *–er Teller*, hollow plate *or* dish; *in der –sten Tiefe*, in the uttermost depths; *in –stem Vertrauen*, in the utmost confidence; *im –en Walde*, in the depths of the wood; *im –sten Winter*, in the depths of winter. 2. *n.* (-(e)s, -s), deep channel of water; (barometric) depression; bass distortion (*Rad.*). **–angriff** *m.* low-level attack (*Av.*). **–aufschlag**, *m.* underhand service (*Tenn.*). **–äugig**, *adj.* hollow-eyed. **–bahn**, *f.* underground railway. **–bau**, *m.* underground *or* deep workings. **–betrübt**, *adj.* deeply grieved. **–bewegt**, *adj.* deeply agitated *or* moved. **–blau**, *adj.* & *n.* dark blue. **–blick**, *m.* penetrating glance, keen insight. **–bohrer**, *m.* auger. **–decker**, *m.* low-wing monoplane (*Av.*). **–druck**, *m.* photogravure printing, heliogravure, intaglio. **–druckgebiet**, *n.* low-pressure area (*Meteor.*). **–e**, *f.* (-en) depth, deepness; profundity; lowness, deep place, abyss, gorge; disposition in depth (*of troops*); *pl.* soundings; *–e des Herzens*, depth *or* bottom of the heart, innermost heart. **–ebene**, *f.* (low-lying) plain, lowland(s). **–eindringend**, *adj.*, **–eingreifend**, *adj.* penetrating. **–en**, *v.a.* deepen, hollow out. **–enanzeiger**, *m.* depth gauge (*submarines*). **–enfeuer**, *n.* searching fire (*Mil.*). **–engestein**, *n.* plutonic rock (*Geol.*). **–engliederung**, *f.* distribution *or* disposition in depth (*Mil.*). **–enlot**, *n.* sounding-lead (*Naut.*). **–enmessung**, *f.* bathymetry. **–enruder**, *n.* elevator, hydroplane (*submarines*). **–ensteuerung**, *f.* hydroplane gear (*submarines*). **–enstreuung**, *f.* dispersion in depth (*Artil.*). **–erlegung**, *f.* lowering (*of level*). **–ernst**, *adj.* deadly serious, very grave. **–flieger**, *m.* low-flying aircraft. **–gang**, *m.* draught (*of vessels*); *ein Schiff von 8 Fuß –gang*, a ship drawing 8 feet of water. **–gebeugt**, *adj.* (*fig.*) deeply afflicted. **–gefühlt**, *adj.* heartfelt. **–gegliedert**, *adj.* organized in depth (*defences*). **–gehend**, *adj.* deep, profound, far-reaching, penetrating; thoroughgoing; deep-drawing (*Naut.*). **–greifend**, *adj.* far-reaching, thoroughgoing; deep-seated, penetrating; fundamental, profound, radical. **–gründig**, *adj.* deep, profound. **–hammer**, *m.* hollowing-hammer. **–kultur**, *f.* subsoil-ploughing. **–ladelinie**, *f.* load-line. **–land**, *n.*, *see* **–ebene**. **–liegend**, *adj.* low-lying; deep-seated; sunken (*of eyes*). **–lot**, *n.* deep-sea lead. **–punkt**, *m.* lowest point, low ebb, rock-bottom. **–rund**, *adj.* concave. **–schlag**, *m.* blow below the belt (*Boxing*). **–schürfend**, *adj.* (*fig.*) profound, exhaustive, thorough. **-seekunde,** *f.* oceanology. **-seelotung,** *f.* deep-sea soundings, bathymetry. **-seeschlamm,** *m.* deep-sea slime *or* ooze. **-sinn,** *m.* thoughtfulness; reverie; melancholy. **-sinnig,** *adj.* thoughtful, pensive, serious; melancholic. **-stand,** *m.* lowest level; nadir; low-water mark, (*C.L.*) depression. **-stehend,** *adj.* low-lying, low; (*fig.*) inferior; **-stellen,** *v.a.* lower. **-stimmig,** *adj.* deep-voiced, deep-mouthed. **-ton,** *m.* secondary accent (*Metr.*). **-unterst,** *adj.* the very deepest, nethermost. **-wurzelnd,** *adj.* deep-rooted.

Tiegel, *m.* (-s, –) saucepan; crucible; platen (*Typ.*). **-druck,** *m.* platen-printing (*Typ.*). **-gußstahl,** *m.* crucible cast steel. **-ofen,** *m.* crucible furnace.

Tiekholz, *n.* teak.

Tiene, *f.* (-n) (*dial.*) little tub *or* cask.

Tier, *n.* (-(e)s, -e) animal, beast, brute; doe, hind; *das – in uns*, the animal side of our nature, the beast in us; (*coll.*) *er ist ein großes* or *hohes* –, he is a big shot. **-art,** *f.* species of animals. **-arzneikunde,** *f.* veterinary science. **-arzt,** *m.* veterinary surgeon. **-ärztlich,** *adj.* veterinary. **-ausstopfer,** *m.* taxidermist. **-bändiger,** *m.* wild-beast tamer. **-bude,** *f.* small menagerie. **-chen,** *n.* animalcule; (*Prov.*) *jedes -chen hat sein Pläsierchen*, every man to his taste, there is no accounting for tastes. **-epos,** *n.* animal epic, beast epic. **-fabel,** *f.* animal fable. **-garten,** *m.* zoological gardens. **-gattung,** *f.* genus of animal. **-haft,** *adj.* animal-like, referring to animals. **-handel,** *m.* trade in livestock. **-heilkunde,** *f.* veterinary science. **-isch,** *adj.* animal; bestial, brutish, beastly. **-kind,** *n.* animal offspring. **-kohle,** *f.* animal charcoal. **-kreis,** *m.* zodiac (*Astr.*). **-kreiszeichen,** *n.* sign of the zodiac (*Astr.*). **-kunde,** *f.* zoology. **-kundige(r),** *m.* zoologist. **-natur,** *f.* animality, brute nature. **-park,** *m.*, *see* **-garten.** **-pflanze,** *f.* zoophyte. **-quälerei,** *f.* cruelty to animals. **-reich,** *n.* animal kingdom, animals. **-sage,** *f.* beast legend, beast epic. **-schau,** *f.* cattle (horse, *etc.*) show. **-schutz,** *m.* protection of animals. **-schutzverein,** *m.* society for the prevention of cruelty to animals. **-stock,** *m.* animal colony. **-stück,** *n.* animal picture. **-versteinerung,** *f.* zoolite. **-wärter,** *m.* keeper (*of animals*). **-welt,** *f.* animal kingdom, animals. **-zucht,** *f.* animal-breeding.

Tiger, *m.* (-s, –) tiger. **-decke,** *f.* tiger-skin (rug). **-farbig,** *adj.* mottled, spotted, striped. **-fell,** *n.*, *see* **-decke.** **-in,** *f.* tigress. **-katze,** *f.* (African) tiger-cat, serval (*Felis serval*) (*Zool.*). **-n,** *v.a.* spot, speckle; *getigert*, speckled, mottled; tabby (*of cats*). **-pferd,** *n.* zebra. **-schlange,** *f.* python (*Python molurus*) (*Zool.*). (*Poet.*) **-tier,** *n.* tiger.

tilg-en, *v.a.* extinguish, blot out, abolish, eradicate, obliterate, efface, erase, extirpate, destroy, exterminate; cancel, annul; amortize, pay off, redeem. **-bar,** *adj.* extinguishable, effaceable; redeemable. **-ung,** *f.* extermination, destruction, eradication; effacement, blotting-out, cancellation, liquidation; repayment, amortization, redemption. **-ungsfonds,** *m.*, **-ungskasse,** *f.* sinking-fund. **-ungsschein,** *m.* bill of amortization. **-ungszeichen,** *n.* delete (*Typ.*).

Tingeltangel, *m.* & *n.* (-s, –) (*coll.*) low music-hall.

tingieren, *v.a.* colour, tinge, dye, stain.

Tinktur, *f.* (-en) tincture, infusion; dye.

Tint-e, *f.* (-en) ink; tint (*Paint.*); (*fig.*) mess, scrape; (*fig.*) *in der -e sitzen*, be in the soup; (*sl.*) *er muß -e gesoffen haben*, he must be cracked. **-enfaß,** *n.* ink-well, inkstand. **-enfisch,** *m.* cuttle-fish, sepia (*Cephalopodae*) (*Icht.*). **-enfleck,** *m.*, *see* **-enklecks.** **-engummi,** *m.* ink-eraser. **-enklecks,** *m.* ink-stain, ink-spot, blot. **-enkleckser,** *m.* scribbler; dauber. **-enstift,** *m.* indelible *or* copying-ink pencil. **-enwischer,** *m.* pen-wiper. **-ig,** *adj.* inky, stained with ink.

Tipp-el, *m.* (-els, -el) (*coll.*) tittle; dot; *bis aufs -elchen wissen*, know down to the last detail. (*dial.*) **-(e)lig,** *adj.* petty, fussy, punctilious. **-eln,** *v.* 1. *a.* dot, stipple. 2. *n.* (*aux.* s.) trip; trudge, tramp. (*coll.*) **-elbruder,** *m.* tramp, beggar. **-en,** *v.a.* touch gently, tap; (*coll.*) type. (*coll.*) **-ler,** *m.*, *see* **-elbruder.** (*coll.*) **-fräulein,** *n.* typist.

Tiraill-eur, *m.* (-s, -s *or* -e) skirmisher. **-ieren,** *v.n.* (*aux.* h.) skirmish (*Mil.*).

tirilieren, *v.n.* warble, chirrup (*of birds*).

Tisch, *m.* (-(e)s, -e) table, board; meal; *den – abdecken*, clear the table; *am – sitzen*, sit at the table; *– zum Ausziehen*, extending table; *Scheidung von – und Bett*, judicial separation; *bei –*, at table; during the meal; *den – decken*, lay the cloth or table; *freien – haben*, have free board; *am grünen –(e)*, in official quarters, at an official level; *Verordnungen vom grünen -e*, red-tape ordinances; *einen guten – führen*, keep a good table; *zum -e des Herrn gehen*, partake of the Lord's Supper; *nach –(e)*, after dinner *or* supper; *reinen – machen*, make a clean sweep (*mit*, of); *über –*, during *or* over the meal; *unter den – fallen*, be ignored, be pushed on one side, come to nothing; *unter den – fallen lassen*, consider unworthy of attention, ignore, let drop; *vor –(e)*, before the meal (dinner, *etc.*); *eine Dame zu –(e) führen*, take a lady in (to dinner); *zu –(e) gehen*, sit down to a meal, dinner, supper, etc.; *zu –(e) laden*, ask to dinner *or* to a meal. **-aufsatz,** *m.* centre-piece, table-centre. **-bein,** *n.* table leg. **-besen,** *m.* crumb-brush. **-blatt,** *n.* table-top; leaf of a table. **-dame,** *f.* lady taken in to dinner. **-decke,** *f.* table-cloth. **-en,** *v.a.* & *n.* (*aux.* h.) lay the cloth *or* the table; *es ist für mich nicht getischt*, there is no cover *or* place laid for me. **-fertig,** *adj.* ready for serving. **-gänger,** *m.* boarder; regular diner. **-gast,** *m.* guest (at dinner). **-gebet,** *n.* grace; *das -gebet sprechen.* say grace. **-geld,** *n.* board-wages (*of servants*); messing allowance (*Mil.*). **-genosse,** *m.* fellow-boarder; messmate. **-gerät,** *n.*, **-geschirr,** *n.* tableware. **-gesellschaft,** *f.* company at dinner, etc. **-gespräch,** *n.* table-talk. **-glocke,** *f.* dinner-bell *or* gong. **-herr,** *m.* gentleman taking a lady in to dinner. **-karte,** *f.* place-card. **-klopfen,** *n.* table-rapping. **-lade,** *f.* table-drawer. **-läufer,** *m.* table-centre *or* runner. **-leindeckdich,** *n.* magic table. **-ler,** *m.*, *see* **Tischler.** **-nachbar,** *m.* neighbour at table. **-platte,** *f.* table-top; stage plate (*of microscope*). **-rede,** *f.* after-dinner speech. **-rücken,** *n.* table-turning. **-tennis,** *n.* table-tennis, ping-pong. **-tuch,** *n.* tablecloth; *das -tuch zwischen sich und ihm zerschneiden*, have nothing more to do with him, break (off all contact) with him. **-wäsche,** *f.* table-linen. **-wein,** *m.* table-wine, dinner wine. **-zeug,** *n.* table-linen and cutlery.

Tischler, *m.* (-s, –) joiner; carpenter; cabinet-maker. **-arbeit,** *f.* carpentry, joinery. **-bank,** *f.* joiner's bench. **-ei,** *f.* carpentry, woodwork, cabinet-making; carpenter's shop. **-leim,** *m.* carpenter's glue. **-meister,** *m.* master joiner. **-n,** *v.a.* & *n.* (*aux.* h.) do carpentry *or* woodwork. **-werkstatt,** *f.* carpenter's shop. **-werkzeug,** *n.* wood-working tools.

Titan, 1. *m.* (-en, -en) Titan. 2. *n.* titanium. **-e,** *m.* (-n, -n) *see* –, 1. **-eisenerz,** *n.* titaniferous *or* titanic iron-ore, ilmenite. **-sauer,** *adj.* titanite of. **-enhaft,** *adj.* **-isch,** *adj.* titanic, gigantic.

Titel, *m.* (-s, –) title; heading; claim; *bloßer –*, mere *or* empty title; *den größten – auf etwas haben*, have the greatest *or* best claim to a th.; *Buch mit aufgedrucktem –*, lettered book; *den – Graf* or *eines Grafen führen*, have *or* bear the title of count. **-auflage,** *f.*, **-ausgabe,** *f.* edition having merely a new title-page. **-bild,** *n.* frontispiece. **-bildchen,** *n.* vignette. **-blatt,** *n.* title-page. **-ei,** *f.* preliminaries (*in a book*). **-halter,** *m.* title-holder (*Sport*). **-kopf,** *m.* heading (*of an article*). **-kupfer,** *n.* frontispiece. **-n,** *v.a.* supply captions (*to films*). **-rolle,** *f.* title-role, name-part. **-sucht,** *f.* craze for titles, tuft-hunting. **-träger,** *m.*, **-verteidiger,** *m.*, *see* **-halter.** **-vignette,** *f.* head-piece. **-wort,** *n.* caption. **-zeile,** *f.* headline.

Titer, *m.* (-s, –) standard strength of solution (*Chem.*).

titrier-en, *v.a.* titrate. **-apparat,** *m.* volumetric *or* titrating apparatus. **-methode,** *f.* titration, volumetric method.

Titsche, *f.* (*dial.*) sauce. **-n,** *v.a.* (*dial.*) dip, soak, sop.

Titte, *f.* (*dial.*) tit, dug.

Titul-ar, 1. *m.* (-s, -e) titular. 2. *adj.* (*in compounds*) titular, nominal, honorary; brevet (*Mil.*). **-atur,** *f.* styling; full title(s). **-ieren,** *v.a.* style; call, give the title of, address with full title.

tja, *int.* (*dial.*) pish!, (*Scots*) hoots!

Tjost, *m.* (-es, -e) *&* *f.* (-en) (*archaic*) joust.

Toast, *m.* (-es, -e) toast, health; toasted bread; *einen – auf jemanden ausbringen*, toast a p., propose a toast to a p.; *auf einen – antworten*, respond to a toast. **-en,** (*Austr. dial.* **-ieren**), *v.a. & n.* (*aux.* h.) toast, propose *or* drink a toast to.

Tobak, *m.* (*archaic*) *see* **Tabak**; (*coll.*) *Anno –*, the year dot.

Tobel, *n. &* (*Austr. dial. m.*) (-s, -e) (*dial.*) wooded gorge, ravine, gully.

tob-en, *v.n.* (*aux.* h.) fume, storm, rage, rave, bluster, roar; romp, be wild. **-sucht,** *f.* frenzy, delirium, mania, madness. **-süchtig,** *adj.* raving mad.

Tochter, *f.* (⸚) daughter; (*Swiss dial.*) girl, servant, waitress; (*hum.*) *höhere –*, high-school girl. **-anstalt,** *f.* branch establishment. **-gesellschaft,** *f.* subsidiary company. **-haus,** *n.*, *see* **-anstalt.** **-kind,** *n.* (*dial.*) daughter's child, grandchild. **-kirche,** *f.* branch church. **-kompaß,** *m.* repeater compass (*Naut.*). **-liebe,** *f.* filial or daughter's love. **-mann,** *m.* (*dial.*) son-in-law. **-sprache,** *f.* derived language. **-staat,** *m.* colony. **-stadt,** *f.* offshoot town.

Töchter-chen, *n.* (-s, –) little daughter, darling daughter. **-heim,** *n.* home for girls. **-lich,** *adj.* daughterly, filial. **-schule,** *f.* high school for girls.

Tod, *m.* (-(e)s, –e (*rare*) *or* -esfälle) death; decease; *sich auf den – erkälten*, catch one's death of cold; *auf den – liegen*, be mortally ill; *auf den – verwundet*, mortally wounded; *bürgerlicher –*, loss of civil rights; *den – finden*, meet one's death; *dem –e geweiht*, doomed; *in den – gehen*, suffer death; (*bis*) *in den – zuwider*, utterly detestable; *du bist ein Kind des –es, wenn . . .*, you are a dead man if . . .; (*Prov.*) *gegen den – ist kein Kraut gewachsen*, there is no remedy against death; *Kampf auf Leben und –*, mortal combat, fight to the death; *mit dem –e abgehen*, die; *nach dem –e*, after death; *nahe am –e* or *dem –e nahe sein*, be at death's door; *eines natürlichen –es sterben*, die a natural death; *das ist mein –*, that will be the death of me; *des –es sein*, be doomed; *es handelt sich um – und Leben*, it is a question of life and death; (*Prov.*) *umsonst ist nur der –*, everything costs money; *sich zu –e ärgern*, fret o.s. to death; *zu –e betrübt*, mortally grieved; *zu –e hetzen*, run down (*Hunt.*); *sich zu –e lachen*, die with laughing; *einen zu –e quälen*, worry a p. to death. **-ähnlich,** *adj.* deathlike, deathly. **-bang,** *adj.* mortally afraid, frightened to death. **-blaß,** *adj.*, **-bleich,** *adj.* deathly pale, pale as death. **-bringend,** *adj.* deadly, fatal, lethal, mortal. **-elend,** *adj.* utterly miserable. **-ernst,** *adj.* deadly serious. **-esahnung,** *f.* foreboding of death. **-esangst,** *f.* mortal terror. **-esanzeige,** *f.* announcement of death, obituary notice. **-esart,** *f.* manner of death. **-esbecher,** *m.* fatal cup. **-esdosis,** *f.* lethal dose. **-eserklärung,** *f.* certification of death. **-esengel,** *m.* Angel of Death. **-esfall,** *m.* (case of) death; casualty (*in war*); (*pl.*) deaths (*used as a plural of* Tod). **-esfurcht,** *f.* fear of death. **-esgabe,** *f.*, *see* **-esdosis.** **-esgefahr,** *f.* deadly peril, peril of one's life; *in –esgefahr schweben*, be in imminent danger; *einen aus –esgefahr retten*, save a p.'s life, rescue a p. from (certain) death. **-eskampf,** *m.* death agony, throes of death. **-eskandidat,** *m.* doomed *or* dying man. **-eskeim,** *m.* seeds of death. **-eskrampf,** *m.* death convulsion. **-esmutig,** *adj.* resolute unto *or* in the face of death. **-esnachweis,** *m.* proof of death. **-esnot,** *f.* peril of death, deadly peril; *in –esnöten*, in the death-throes. **-espatrouille,** *f.* 'death or glory' squad, suicide squad. **-espein,** *f.* pangs of death. **-espforte,** *f.* death's door. **-esqual,** *f.*, *see* **-espein.** **-esröcheln,** *n.* death rattle. **-esschlaf,** *m.* sleep of the dead; deathlike *or* profound sleep. **-esschrecken,** *m.* fear of death; deadly fright. **-esschweiß,** *m.* cold sweat of death. **-esstoß,** *m.* death-blow, finishing stroke, coup de grâce. **-esstrafe,** *f.* death penalty, capital punishment; *bei –esstrafe*, on pain of death. **-esstrahl,** *m.* death-ray. **-esstreich,** *m.* *see* **-esstoß.** **-esstunde,** *f.* hour of death; last, fatal *or* supreme hour. **-essturz,** *m.* fatal fall (*Mount.*) *or* crash (*airmen*). **-estag,** *m.* day of death; anniversary of a p.'s death. **-esursache,** *f.* cause of death. **-esurteil,** *n.* death sentence, sentence of death. **-esverachtung,** *f.* contempt *or* defiance of death. **-esverbrechen,** *n.* capital crime. **-eswunde,** *f.* mortal or fatal wound. **-eswürdig,** *adj.* deserving death. **-fall,** *m.* (*Law*), *see* **-esfall.** **-feind,** 1. *m.* deadly or mortal enemy. 2. *adj.* (*with Dat.*) bitterly hostile. **-feindschaft,** *f.* deadly enmity. **-geweiht,** *adj.* doomed. **-krank,** *adj.* dangerously ill; (*B.*) sick unto death. **-matt,** *adj.*, **-müde,** *adj.* dead tired, completely worn out *or* knocked up. (*sl.*) **-schick,** *adj.* dressed up to the nines. **-schlag,** *m.* manslaughter. (*coll.*) **-sicher,** *adj.* dead certain, sure as fate. **-sünde,** *f.* mortal sin. **-wund,** *adj.* mortally wounded.

tödlich, *adj.* fatal, deadly, lethal, mortal; murderous; *– hassen*, hate like poison; *–er Autounfall*, fatal motor-accident; *er ist – verunglückt*, he has met with a fatal accident; *Unglücksfall mit –em Ausgang*, fatal accident; *sich – langweilen*, be bored to death; *mit –er Sicherheit*, with infallible certainty; *–es Schweigen*, deathly silence.

Toilette, *f.* (-n) toilet, party-dress; dressing-table; lavatory, W.C.; *– machen*, dress, get dressed, make one's toilet; *auf die – gehen*, go to the w.c. **-ngegenstände,** *m.pl.* articles of dress. **-nkasten,** *m.* dressing-case. **-npapier,** *n.* toilet-paper. **-nseife,** *f.* toilet-soap. **-nzimmer,** *n.* dressing-room.

Töle, *f.* (-n) (*dial.*) bitch.

toler-ant, *adj.* tolerant (*gegen*, of). **-enz,** *f.* toleration, tolerance (*also Mach.*). **-ieren,** *v.a.* tolerate.

toll, *adj.* mad, raving, insane; frantic, furious; nonsensical, foolish, senseless, absurd, extravagant, droll, comical; wild, excessive, wanton; *– auf . . .*, mad *or* crazy about *or* after; *das –ste dabei*, the funniest part of it; *–er Einfall*, insane notion; *–er Hund*, mad dog; *einen – machen*, drive a p. out of his mind; *– und voll*, dead drunk; *es ist zum – werden, man möchte – werden*, it is enough to drive one crazy; *–e Wirtschaft*, crazy state of affairs; *–es Zeug*, wild ideas, extravagant views (demands, etc.); *das ist zu –*, that is too bad *or* much *or* (*coll.*) a bit too thick; *er macht* or *treibt es zu –*, he goes too far. **-beere,** *f.*, *see* **-kirsche.** **-en,** *v.n.* (*aux.* h. *&* s.) romp, charge *or* fool about. **-haus,** *n.* lunatic asylum. **-häusler,** *m.* lunatic, madman, maniac. **-heit,** *f.* madness, frenzy; rage, fury; (*coll.*) mad trick, crazy action, piece of folly. **-kirsche,** *f.* deadly nightshade (*Atropa belladonna*) (*Bot.*). **-köpfig,** *adj.* harebrained, hot-headed. **-kühn,** *adj.* foolhardy, rash, daring. **-kühnheit,** *f.* foolhardiness, rashness. **-sucht,** *f.* raving madness, delirium. **-wut,** *f.* hydrophobia, rabies. **-wütig,** *adj.* rabid.

Toll-e, *f.* (-en) (*dial.*) tuft, crest, topknot; frill. **-eisen,** *n.* crimping-iron. **-en,** *v.a.* goffer, crimp.

Tolpatsch, *m.*, *see* **Tölpel.**

Tölp-el, *m.* (-s, –) blockhead, boor, lout; gannet (*Sulidae*) (*Orn.*). **-elei,** *f.* awkwardness, loutishness, boorish manners. **-elhaft,** *adj.* clumsy, doltish, loutish. **-elhaftigkeit,** *f.*, *see* **-elei.** **-eln,** *v.n.* (*aux.* h.) be awkward *or* clumsy. **-isch,** *adj.*, *see* **-elhaft.**

Tomate, *f.* (-n) tomato.

Tombak, *m.* (-s) tombac, pinchbeck (*alloy of zinc and copper*). **-en,** *adj.* of tombac.

[1]**Ton,** *m.* (-(e)s, -e *&* -sorten) clay; kaolin; *feuerfester –*, fire-clay. **-artig,** *adj.*, *see* **-ig.** **-bildnerei,** *f.* ceramics. **-boden,** *m.* clayey soil. **-brennofen,** *m.* clay-kiln. **-erde,** *f.* argillaceous earth; alumina, aluminium oxide; *essigsaure –erde*, aluminium acetate. **-erdeverbindung,** *f.* aluminate. **-gefäß,** *n.* earthen vessel. **-geschirr,** *n.* pottery, earthenware. **-grube,** *f.* clay-pit. **-haltig,** *adj.* argillaceous. **-ig,** *adj.* clayey, clayish, argillaceous. **-lager,** *n.* clay-bed *or* -stratum. **-pfeife,** *f.* clay-pipe. **-rohr,** *n.* earthenware pipe. **-sauer,** *adj.*;

-saures Salz, aluminate. **-schneide,** *f.* potter's knife. **-taube,** *f.* clay pigeon. **-ware,** *f.* (piece of) pottery. **-zelle,** *f.* porous cell.

²**Ton,** *m.* (-(e)s, ⸚e) sound; note (*Mus.*), timbre (*Mus.*); tone (*Mus., Paint., Med., etc.*); tint, shade, colour, tinge, strain; fashion, manners; stress, accent, emphasis; *den – angeben*, set the fashion; *einen andern – anschlagen*, change one's tone; *einfacher –*, simple note; sinusoidal sound wave; *einen – von sich geben*, utter a sound; *Mann von gutem -e*, well-bred man; *das ist kein guter –*, that is not good form, that is not etiquette; *es gehört zum guten –*, good breeding demands it; *halber –*, semitone (*Mus.*); *den – halten*, keep in tune; *keinen – mehr!* not another word! (*coll.*) *hast du Töne!* you don't say! **-abnehmer,** *m.* pick-up (*gramophone*). **-abstand,** *m.* interval (*Mus.*). **-angebend,** *adj.* setting the fashion; *-angebende Kreise*, leading *or* fashionable circles. **-angeber,** *m.* leader of fashion. **-art,** *f.* key (*Mus.*), (*fig.*) tone. **-aufzeichnung,** *f.* sound-recording. **-bad,** *n.* toning bath (*Phot.*). **-blende,** *f.* tone control (*Rad.*). **-dichter,** *m.* composer. **-dichtung,** *f.* musical composition, symphonic poem. **-en,** *v.a.* tone (*Phot.*). **-fall,** *m.* cadence, inflexion, modulation, intonation. **-farbe,** *f.* timbre. **-film,** *m.* sound-film, talking film, (*coll.*) talkie. **-fixierbad,** *n.* toning and fixing bath (*Phot.*). **-folge,** *f.* scale, succession of notes, melodic line. **-frequenz,** *f.* sound frequency (*Rad.*). **-führung,** *f.* tonal quality. **-fülle,** *f.* volume of sound; sonority. **-gebung,** *f.* tone (production) (*Mus.*). **-gemisch,** *n.* composite sound. **-halle,** *f.* concert-hall. **-höhe,** *f.* musical pitch, pitch of a note. **-ig,** *adj. suffix* -toned, e.g. *tieftonig, adj.* deep-toned. **-ika,** *f.* key-note, tonic (*Mus.*). **-isch,** *adj.* tonic (*Med.*). **-kulisse,** *f.* background (*Rad.*). **-kunst,** *f.* music, musical art. **-künstler,** *m.* musician. **-lage,** *f.* compass, pitch. **-leiter,** *f.* gamut, scale. **-los,** *adj.* soundless, voiceless, unaccented. **-malerei,** *f.* onomatopoeia. **-papier,** *n.* tinted paper. **-satz,** *m.* phrase (*Mus.*). **-schöpfung,** *f.* musical creation. **-setzer,** *m.* (musical) composer. **-silbe,** *f.* accented *or* stressed syllable. **-spur,** *f.* track, groove (*of gramophone record*). **-stärke,** *f.* degree of stress; intensity *or* volume of sound. **-stück,** *n.* piece of music, musical composition· **-stufe,** *f.* pitch (*Mus.*); note (*of a scale*). **-übergang,** *m.* change of key, modulation. **-umfang,** *m.* compass, range (*of a voice, etc.*). **-verschiebung,** *f.* shifting of accent. **-verstärker,** *m.* sound-amplifier. **-welle,** *f.* sound-wave. **-zeichen,** *n.* accentuation mark; note (*Mus.*).

tön-en, 1. *v.n.* (*aux.* h.) sound, resound; ring. 2. *v.a.* shade (off); *golden getöntes Haar*, hair with a golden shade. **-ung,** *f.* shade, tint, tone, tinge; shading.

tönern, *adj.* (of) clay, earthen; argillaceous; *-e Füße*, feet of clay; *-es Gefäß*, earthenware vessel.

Tonne, *f.* (-n) cask, barrel, tun, butt; buoy (*Naut.*); tubby person; ton = *1,000 kilograms or 2,205 pounds*; *eine – Heringe*, a cask of herrings. **-nbutter,** *f.* butter in tubs. **-nförmig,** *adj.* barrel-shaped; tubby. **-nfracht,** *f.* freight (charged) by the ton. **-ngehalt,** *m.* (ship's) tonnage, burden. **-ngewölbe,** *n.* barrel-vault (*Arch.*). **-nlager,** *n.* roller bearing. **-nweise,** *adv.* by the barrel; by the ton.

Tonsur, *f.* (-en) tonsure.

Topas, *m.* (-es, -e) topaz. **-gelb,** *adj.* topaz.

Topf, *m.* (-es, ⸚e) pot, jar; chamber (pot); *einen – ansetzen*, put a pot on to boil *or* on the fire; (*Pflanzen*) *in den – einsetzen*, pot (plants); *alles in einen – werfen*, treat all alike, make no distinction(s). **-deckel,** *m.* pot-lid. **-en,** *m., see* **Topfen.** **-erde,** *f.* potting earth. **-flicker,** *m.* mender of pots and pans. **-gewächs,** *n.* pot-plant. **-glasur,** *f.* potter's glaze. **-gucker,** *m.* Nosy Parker. **-haken,** *m.*, **-henkel,** *m.* pot-hook. **-kieker,** *m., see* **-gucker.** **-kuchen,** *m.* large cake. **-lappen,** *m.* kettle-holder; oven-cloth. (*sl.*) **-lecker,** *m.* greedy person. **-macher,** *m.* potter. **-pflanze,** *f.* pot-plant. **-scherbe,** *f.* piece of broken pot, potsherd. **-ständer,** *m.* flowerpot-stand. **-stürze,** *f.* pot-lid.

Topfen, *m.* (*dial.*) curds.

Töpfer, *m.* potter. **-ei,** *f.* pottery, ceramics; pottery-trade. **-erde,** *f.* potter's clay. **-gut,** *n.* earthenware, pottery, crockery. **-handwerk,** *n.* potter's trade. **-n,** 1. *v.a.* & *n.* (*aux.* h.) make pottery. 2. *adj.* earthen, made of pottery. **-scheibe,** *f.* potter's wheel. **-ton,** *m.* potter's clay. **-ware,** *f., see* **-gut.**

Topik, *f.* arrangement of material, theme for discussion, topic (*Log.*).

top-isch, *adj.* local; topical (*Med.*). **-ographie,** *f.* topography.

topp, *int.* done, agreed, (*sl.*) right oh! O.K.

Topp, *m.* (-s, -e) top-mast, head (*Naut.*), (*sl.*) gallery, gods (*Theat.*); *vor – und Takel treiben*, sail under bare poles. **-(e)nant,** *f.* (topping) lift (*Naut.*). **-laterne,** *f.*, **-licht,** *n.* masthead light (*Naut.*). **-reep,** *n.* guy-(line), stay. **-segel,** *n.* topsail.

¹**Tor,** *n.* (-(e)s, -e) gate, gateway; goal (*Footb.*); *ein – machen* or *schießen*, score *or* shoot a goal. **-angel,** *f.* & *m.* hinge of a gate. **-fahrt,** *f.* gateway. **-flügel,** *m.* wing of a gate. **-halle,** *f.* porch (*Arch.*). **-höhe,** *f.* clearance of an archway. **-hüter,** *m.* gate-keeper, porter. **-klappe,** *f.* wicket gate. **-latte,** *f.* crossbar (*Footb.*). **-lauf,** *m.* slalom race (*skiing*). **-linie,** *f.* goal-line. **-pfosten,** *m.* door-post; goal-post (*Footb.*). **-schluß,** *m.* shutting of the gates; closing time; *kurz vor -(es)-schluß*, at the eleventh hour. **-schütze,** *m.* scorer (*Footb., etc.*). **-stoß,** *m.* goal-kick (*Footb.*). **-stube,** *f.* porter's lodge. **-turm,** *m.* gate-tower. **-wächter,** *m.* porter, gate-keeper. **-wart,** *m.* goal-keeper (*Sport*). **-wärter,** *m., see* **-wächter.** **-weg,** gateway, archway. **-weit,** *adj.* very wide.

²**Tor,** *m.* (-en, -en) fool. **-heit,** *f.* (piece of) folly, foolishness, silliness; (*Prov.*) *Alter schützt vor -heit nicht*, age is not proof against folly.

Torf, *m.* (-(e)s, ⸚e (& *Austr. dial.* -e)) peat; *– graben* or *stechen*, cut peat. **-artig,** *adj.* peaty. **-boden,** *m.* peat-soil. **-bruch,** *m.* peat-bog. **-erde,** *f., see* **-boden.** **-feuerung,** *f.* heating with peat. **-geschmack,** *m.* peaty flavour. **-gewinnung,** *f.* turf cutting. **-gräber,** *m.* peat-cutter. **-grube,** *f.* peat-pit. **-haltig,** *adj.* peaty. **-lager,** *n.* peat-bog. **-land,** *n.* moor. **-moor,** *n.* peat-bog. **-mull,** *m.* leaf-mould. **-stecher,** *m.* peat-cutter. **-stich,** *m.* peat-cutting. **-streu,** *f.* peat-litter.

töricht, *adj.* foolish, silly.

Torkel, *m.* (-s, –) *or f.* (-n) (*dial.*) wine press; (*m. only*) (*coll.*) gift from the gods. (*coll.*) **-n,** *v.n.* (*aux.* s.) reel, stagger.

Tornister, *m. or n.* (-s, –) knapsack, rucksack, pack, (*dial.*) satchel, school-bag. **-funk,** *m.* 'walkie-talkie' (*Mil.*).

Torped-er, *m.* (-s, –) officer in charge of torpedoes (*Naut.*). **-ieren,** *v.a.* torpedo. **-ierung,** *f.* torpedoing. **-o,** *m.* (-s, -s) torpedo. **-obomber,** *m.* torpedo-carrying aircraft. **-oboot,** *n.* torpedo-boat, destroyer. **-olaufbahn,** *f.* wake *or* track of a torpedo.

Torsion, *f.* (-en) torsion, torque, twisting. **-sfestigkeit,** *f.* torsional strength, torque. **-swaage,** *f.* torsion-balance. **-swinkel,** *m.* angle of torque.

Tort, *m.* wrong, injury; *einem einen – antun*, play a trick *or* prank on s.o.; *einem zum –*, to spite a p.

Torte, *f.* (-n) flat cake, tart, flan. **-nbäcker,** *m.* pastry-cook. **-nform,** *f.*, baking tin. **-npfanne,** *f.* patty-pan.

Tortur, *f.* (-en) torture; *einen der – unterwerfen*, submit a p. to torture.

tosen, *v.n.* (*aux.* h. & s.) rage, roar; *-der Beifall*, uproarious applause.

tot, *adj.* dead, lifeless, inanimate; stagnant, dull, lustreless; uninvested, idle; exhausted, unprofitable (*Min.*); *-es Fleisch*, proud flesh; *– für etwas sein*, be unreceptive to a th.; *-er Gang*, lost motion, backlash, play (*Mach.*); *aufs -e Gleis fahren*, come to a dead end; *-e Hand*, mortmain; *an die -e Hand verkaufen*, amortize; *-es Kapital*, unemployed capital; *-er Mann*, exhausted *or* worked-out lode (*Min.*); (*coll.*) *-er Ort*, dead-alive hole; *-er Punkt*, dead-centre (*Mach.*); (*fig.*) deadlock; *-es Rennen*, dead heat; *-es Wasser*, slack water; *-er Winkel*, dead arc *or* ground (*Mil., Artil.*); *-es Wissen*, useless knowledge; (*C.L.*) *-e Zeit*, dead *or* silly season; *–e Zone*, skip distance (*Rad.*). **–arbeiten,** *v.r.* kill o.s. with work. **–e(r),** *m.* dead person, deceased, corpse. **–enacker,** *m.* (*dial. poet.*) burying-ground, graveyard. **–enamt,** *n.* burial service, mass for the dead, requiem. **–enbahre,** *f.* bier. **–enbaum,** *m.* (*Swiss dial.*) coffin. **–enbestattung,** *f.* burial. **–enbett,** *n.* death-bed. **–enblaß,** *adj.* pale as death, deathly pale. **–enblässe,** *f.* deathly pallor. **–enbleich,** *adj., see* **–enblaß.** **–enblume,** *f.* marigold (*Calendula officinalis*) (*Bot.*). **–eneule,** *f., see* **–envogel.** **–enfarbe,** *f.* deathly pallor. **–enfeier,** *f.* funeral rites, exequies. **–enfest,** *n.* commemoration *or* memorial ceremony. **–enfleck,** *m.* livid spot (*on corpse*). **–engebeine,** *n.pl.* bones of the dead. **–engeleit,** *n.* funeral cortège. **–engerippe,** *n.* skeleton. **–engeruch,** *m.* cadaverous smell. **–engerüst,** *n.* catafalque. **–englocke,** *f.* passing-bell, knell. **–engottesdienst,** *m.* funeral service. **–engräber,** *m.* grave-digger; burying beetle (*Necrophorus*) (*Ent.*). **–engruft,** *f.* vault, sepulchre. **–enhalle,** *f.* mortuary. **–enhemd,** *n.* shroud, winding sheet. **–enklage,** *f.* dirge, wake. **–enkopf,** *m.* death's head; skull; death's head moth (*Acherontia atropos*) (*Caput mortuum*) (*Ent.*). **–enkranz,** *m.*, **–enkrone,** *f.* funeral wreath. **–enlied,** *n.* funeral chant, dirge. **–enliste,** *f.* list of casualties, death roll. **–enmahl,** *n.* funeral feast, wake. **–enmarsch,** *m.* funeral march. **–enmaske,** *f.* death-mask. **–enmesse,** *f.* mass for the dead, requiem. **–enopfer,** *n.* sacrifice to *or* for the dead. **–enreich,** *n.* Hades, the Underworld. **–enschädel,** *m., see* **–enkopf.** **–enschau,** *f.* coroner's inquest, post-mortem examination. **–enschein,** *m.* death-certificate. **–enschlaf,** *m.*, **–enschlummer,** *m.* trance, sleep of death, last sleep. **–enstarre,** *f.* rigor mortis. **–enstill,** *adj.* as silent as the grave, deathly silent. **–enstille,** *f.* silence of the grave, dead silence. **–entag,** *m.* All Souls Day. **–entanz,** *m.* dance of death, danse macabre. **–enuhr,** *f.* death-watch beetle (*Anobium*) (*Ent.*). **–enurne,** *f.* sepulchral urn. **–envogel,** *m.* little owl (*Carina noctua*) (*Orn.*); (*fig.*) bird of ill omen. **–enwache,** *f.*, **–enwacht,** *f.* wake, death-watch. **–fahren,** *v.a.* kill by running over. **–gar,** *adj.* over-refined (*Metall.*). **–geboren,** *adj.* stillborn. **–gebrannt,** *adj.* overburnt (*lime, etc.*). **–geburt,** *f.* still-birth. **–geglaubt,** *adj.* presumed dead. **–gemahlen,** overshort (*paper pulp*). **–gewalzt,** *adj.* rolled to death (*rubber*). **–hetzen,** *v.a.* work to death. **–küssen,** *v.a.* smother with kisses. **–lachen,** 1. *v.r.* split one's side (with laughter); *sie wollten sich –lachen*, they nearly died with laughter. 2. *n.*; *es ist zum –lachen*, it is enough to make one die with laughing, it is too funny for anything; *Geschichte zum –lachen*, screamingly funny story. **–laufen,** *v.r.* come to a standstill *or* deadlock. **–liegende(s),** *n.*; *das rote –liegende*, the (new) red conglomerate (*Geol.*). **–machen,** *v.a.* scotch, hush up. **–punkt,** *m.* dead-centre (*Mech.*). **–schießen,** 1. *v.a.* shoot dead. 2. *v.r.* blow out one's brains. **–schlag,** *m.* homicide, manslaughter. **–schlagen,** *v.a.* kill; *sein Geld* (or *die Zeit*) *–schlagen*, waste one's money (waste *or* kill time). **–schläger,** *m.* cudgel, life-preserver. **–schweigen,** *v.a.* hush up (*a matter*). **–stellen,** *v.r.* feign death.

total, 1. *adj.* total, whole, entire, complete; *–er Staat*, totalitarian state. 2. *adv.* totally, altogether. **–betrag,** *m.* aggregate. (*C.L.*) **–bilanz,** *f.* final balance. **–isator,** *m.* totalizer, (*sl.*) tote. **–itär,** *adj.* totalitarian. **–ität,** *f.* totality, entirety. **–verkäufe,** *m.pl.* aggregate sales.

töt–en, 1. *v.a.* kill, slay, put to death; destroy; deaden, soften (*colours*); mortify (*the body*). 2. *v.r.* commit suicide. 3. *n.* killing, mortification (*of the flesh*). **–ung,** *f.* homicide; *fahrlässige –ung*, manslaughter.

Tour, *f.* (-en) tour, trip, excursion; set, figure (*Danc.*); toupee; revolution (*Mach.*); round, row, (*of knitting*); *außer der –*, out of one's turn, not according to seniority (*Mil.*); (*coll.*) *in einer –*, at a stretch, without stopping, (*coll.*) in *or* at one go; *auf –en kommen*, pick up, gather speed, (*coll.*) rev up (*Motor.*). **–enrad,** *n.* roadster (*Cycl.*). **–enwagen,** *m.* touring-car. **–enzahl,** *f.* number of revolutions, revolutions per minute. **–enzähler,** *m.* revolution counter, tachometer, speed indicator. **–ist,** *m.* (-en, -en) tourist, excursionist, hiker. **–isten(fahr)karte,** *f.* excursion-ticket. **–istenklasse,** *f.* third *or* tourist class (*on steamers*). **–istenverkehr,** *m.* tourist traffic. **–nee,** *f.* tour (*Theat.*).

Trab, *m.* trot; *im –e*, at a trot; (*fig.*) on the run; *im – reiten*, (ride at a) trot; *in – setzen*, put into a trot; (*coll.*) *einen auf den – bringen*, urge a p. on, make a p. pick up his heels, (*coll.*) make a p. get a move on; get a p. going *or* under way. **–ant,** *m.* (-en, -en) gentleman-at-arms, footman; satellite; (*fig.*) follower, (*coll.*) hanger-on. **–en,** *v.n.* (*aux.* h. & s.) trot; jog along; *hoch –en*, be a high-stepper (*of horses*). **–er,** *m.* trotting horse. **–rennen,** *n.* trotting-race.

Tracht, *f.* (-en) dress, garb, costume, fashion; national costume; load (*as much as one can carry*); pregnancy; litter (*of puppies, etc.*); yield (*of honey, etc.*); *eine – Prügel*, a sound thrashing; *– Wasser*, as much water as can be carried. **–enfest,** *n.* peasant festivity.

trachten, 1. *v.n.* (*aux.* h.); *nach einer S. –*, strive for, endeavour *or* try to get s.th., aspire to a th.; *einem nach dem Leben –*, make an attempt on a p.'s life. 2. *n.* endeavour, aim, aspiration.

trächtig, *adj.* pregnant (*of animals*). **–keit,** *f.* pregnancy, gestation.

traditionell, *adj.* traditional.

träf, *adj.* (*Swiss dial.*) pertinent, to the point.

traf, träfe, *see* **treffen.**

Trafik, *m.* (-s, -s) *or f.* (-en) (*Austr. dial.*) tobacconist's shop. **–ant,** *m.* tobacconist.

Tragant, *m.* (-(e)s, -e) tragacanth (*Astralagus*) (*Pharm.*).

träg(e), *adj.* slow, sluggish, dull, languid; idle, indolent, inactive, inert. **–heit,** *f.* laziness, idleness, indolence; slowness, sluggishness, inactivity, lag, inertia; *natürliche –heit*, phlegm. **–heitsmoment,** *n.* moment of inertia.

trag–en, 1. *ir.v.a.* bear, carry, convey; wear, have on (*clothes, etc.*); support, uphold, sustain; endure, suffer; yield, produce; subtend; *einen auf den Händen –en*, treat s.o. with great consideration; *Bedenken –en*, scruple, hesitate, have one's doubts; *bei sich –en*, have about one *or* on one's person; *seine Haut zu Markte –en*, risk one's skin; *ein Herz im Busen –en*, have one's heart in the right place; *das Herz auf der Zunge –en*, wear one's heart on one's sleeve; *eine Hoffnung zu Grabe –en*, bury one's hopes, abandon all hope; *stets im Herzen –en*, keep in one's heart; *ein Kind* (*unterm Herzen*) *–en*, be with child, be carrying, be pregnant, be expecting, be in the family way; *die Kosten –en*, bear the cost, meet the expenses; *Rechnung –en*, (*with Dat.*) take into account; *die Schuld an etwas –en*, be the cause of *or* be to blame for a th.; *Sehnsucht nach etwas –en*, yearn for s.th.; *den Sieg davon–en*, carry off the victory, be victorious, win the day; *Sorge –en um* or *für*, be anxious about; *die Verantwortung –en*, be responsible for; *Verlangen nach etwas –en*, long for *or* hanker after a th.; *den Verlust –en*, bear the loss; *Waffen –en*, bear *or* carry arms; *Zinsen –en*, bring in *or* yield interest; *zur Schau –en*, expose to view, show off, exhibit publicly. 2. *v.r.*; *sich gut –en*, carry o.s. well, wear well (*of clothes*); *das Zeug trägt sich gut*, that is a good wearing material; *sich mit etwas (herum)–en*, be occupied with, be always thinking of, brood over *or* be intending to do s.th. about a th.; *sich mit der Absicht –en*, have the intention, intend; *sich mit einem Gedanken –en*, entertain an idea; *man trägt sich mit dem Gerücht*, it is rumoured, the rumour goes; *sich mit der Hoffnung –en, daß . . .*, cherish the hope that . . .; *sich nach der letzten Mode –en*, dress in the latest fashion; *das Unternehmen trägt sich* (*selbst*), the enterprise is self-supporting *or* pays its way; *es trägt sich unbequem*, it is awkward to carry *or* uncomfortable in wear. 3. *v.n.* (*aux.* h.) carry, reach; *so weit das Auge trägt*, as far as the eye can reach; *das Geschütz trägt . . .*, the gun has a range of . . .; *der Baum trägt noch nicht*, the tree is not bearing yet; *die Kuh trägt*, the cow is in calf; *eine Stimme trägt gut*, a voice carries well *or* a long way; *die –ende Rolle*, the leading part; *getragene Kleider*, worn clothes; *in einer getragenen Stimmung*, in an elevated *or* solemn frame of mind; *getragene Töne*, sustained notes. **–bahre,** *f.* stretcher, litter. **–balken,** *m.* supporting girder *or* beam, balk, stringer, transom. **–band,** *n.* carrying strap; brace. **–bar,** *adj.* portable, easy to carry; wearable, fit to wear; bearable, endurable, tolerable, supportable, acceptable; *in der Tasche –bar*, pocket-size; *ein noch –bares Kleid*, a dress still good enough to wear; *er ist als Minister nicht –bar*, he is impossible as a Minister; *im Rahmen des –baren*, in so far as is possible. **–baum,** *m., see* **–balken. –bett,** *n.* portable bed. **–beutel,** *m.* suspensor (*Surg.*). **–binde,** *f.* sling. **–bock,** *m.* prop, trestle. **–e,** *f.* (-en) carrying frame, carrier, litter. **–esattel,** *m.* pack-saddle. **–fähig,** *adj.* able to bear the load, capable of standing the load. **–fähigkeit,** *f.* carrying *or* load capacity; load-limit (*of bridge*); productivity. **–fähigkeitstonnen,** *f.pl.* dead-weight tonnage (*Naut.*). **–feder,** *f.* frame *or* main spring (*Motor.*). **–fläche,** *f.* wing (*of aeroplane*); bearing surface. **–flügel,** *m.* aircraft wing. **–himmel,** *m.* canopy. **–holz,** *n.* yoke, bearer, stringer. **–kiepe,** *f.* dosser, pannier. **–(e)kleidchen,** *n.pl.* long clothes (*of a baby*). **–korb,** hamper, basket, pannier. **–kraft,** *f.* transverse strength, *see also* **–fähigkeit. –last,** *f.* peak *or* maximum working load. **–pfeiler,** *m.* pillar. **–pferd,** *n.* sumpter-horse. **–pfosten,** *m.* support, upright. **–räder,** *n.pl.* trailing-wheels. **–riemen** *m.* carrying strap; sling (*Mil.*); (*pl.*) main-braces (*of a coach*). **–rolle,** *f.* bogie wheel. **–sattel,** *m.* pack-saddle. **–schrauber,** *m.* gyroplane. **–seil,** *n.* supporting rope. **–sessel,** *m.* sedan chair. **–stein,** *m.* keystone. **–tier,** *n.* pack-animal. **–vermögen,** *n.* buoyancy. **–weite,** *f.* range; (*fig.*) bearing, significance, importance. **–werk,** *n.* wing assembly (*Av.*), supporting structure (*Arch.*). **–zapfen,** *m.* trunnion. **–zeit,** *f.* period *or* duration of gestation.

Träger, *m.* (-s, –) carrier, porter; stretcher-bearer; supporter; wearer; support bracket, truss, trestle; beam, base, post, pillar; prop, girder; bearer; representative; holder (*of a bill of exchange*); stamen (*Bot.*); atlas (*Anat.*). **–flugzeug,** *n.* carrier-based aircraft. **–lohn,** *m.* porterage, carriage. **–welle,** *f.* carrier-wave (*Rad.*).

Trag–ik, *f.* tragic art; tragedy, calamity. **–iker,** *m., see* **–ödiendichter. –isch,** *adj.* tragic(al); calamitous, sad. *–ische Muse*, tragic muse, muse of tragedy; (*coll.*) *er nimmt alles so –isch*, he takes everything too seriously. **–öde,** *m.* (-n, -n) tragic actor, tragedian. **–ödie,** *f.* tragedy, tragic drama *or* event, calamity. **–ödiendichter,** *m.* writer of tragedies, tragic poet.

Train [*pron.* trɛ̃:], *m.* (-s, -s) vehicle train, army service corps. **–kolonne,** *f.* supply column. **–soldat,** *m.* soldier of a service unit. **–wagen,** *m.* supply truck, ration lorry, baggage-wagon.

Train–er, *m.* (-s, -) trainer, coach. **–ieren (tränieren),** 1. *v.a.* & *n.* train, *sich für* or *auf etwas –ieren*, train *or* go into training for s.th.; *eine Stunde lang –ieren*, do an hour's training. 2. *n.* training, coaching. **–ing,** *n.* training; *im –ing sein*, be in training. **–ingsanzug,** *m.* sports overall, training suit.

Trajekt, *n.* (& *Austr. dial. m.*) (-(e)s, -e) train-ferry.

Trakt, *m.* (-(e)s, -e) tract (*of land*), stretch (*of road*), wing (*of a building*).

Trakt–ament, *n.* -(e)s, -e) treating, entertainment, treatment; (*obs.*) (military) pay. **–andum,** *n.* (-dums, -den) (*Swiss dial.*) subject under discussion *or* of negotiation, object of a transaction. **–at,** *m.* & *n.* (-(e)s, -e) treatise, tract; treaty; (*pl.*) negotiations. **–ätchen,** *n.* tract; short treatise. **–ieren,** *v.a.* & *n.* (*aux.* h.) treat; negotiate (*mit*, with); treat badly *or* roughly; *einen mit dem Stock –ieren*, give a p. a dose of the stick; (*mit etwas*) be generous with, treat to.

Tralje, *f.* (-n) (*dial.* & *Naut.*) bar (*of grating*), rail, banister.

trällern, *v.n.* (*aux.* h.) hum, trill, warble.

Tram, *f.* & *m.* (*Swiss dial. n.*) (*pl.* -s) (*coll.*) tramway, tramcar. **–bahn,** *f.* tramway. **–way,** *m.* (-s, -s) (& *Austr. dial. f.* (*pl.* -s)) tramway, tramcar.

Tramp–el, *n.* (& *Austr. dial. m.*) (-s, –) & *f.* (-n) clumsy lout. **–eln,** *v.n.* (*aux.* h.) trample, stamp. **–eltier,** *n.* Bactrian camel; *see also* **–el. –elweg,** *m.* beaten track. **–en,** **–sen** (*coll.*), *see* **–eln. –olin,** (*Austr. dial.*) *n.* & *m.* (-s, -e), **–oline,** *f.* (-n) spring-board.

Tran, *m.* (-s, -e *or* -sorten) train-oil, fish oil, whale oil, blubber; (*sl.*) *im –e sein*, be inattentive, sleepy *or* drunk. **–ig,** *adj.* smelling *or* tasting of oil; greasy, oily; (*fig.*) indolent, inattentive, sleepy, disinterested, obtuse. **–speck,** *m.* blubber.

tranchier–en, *v.a.* & *n.* (*aux.* h.) carve, cut up. **–besteck,** *n.* pair of carvers. **–messer,** *n.* carving-knife.

Träne, *f.* (-n) tear, teardrop; *in –n schwimmen* or *zerfließen*, be bathed in tears; *in –n aufgelöst sein*, melt into tears; *einem keine –e nachweinen*, not shed a tear of regret for s.o.; *–n vergießen*, shed tears, weep. **–n,** *v.n.* (*aux.* h.) be filled with tears, water (*of eyes*); ooze, weep; *die Augen –n ihm*, his eyes are watering; *mit –nden Augen*, with tears in his (her) eyes; *–ndes Herz*, Dicentra spectabilis (*Bot.*). **–nbenetzt,** *adj.* bedewed with tears. **–ndrüse,** *f.* lachrymal gland. **–nfeucht,** *adj.* wet with tears. **–nfeuchtigkeit,** *f.* lachrymal fluid. **–nfluß,** *m.* flow *or* flood of tears. **–ngang,** *m.* lachrymal duct. **–ngas,** *n.* tear-gas. **–ngrube,** *f.* lachrymal fossa. **–nlos,** *adj.* tearless, dry-eyed. **–nreich,** *adj.* lachrymose. **–nreizend,** *adj.* lachrymatory. **–nsack,** *m.* lachrymatory sac. **–nstrom,** *m.* flood of tears. **–ntal,** *n.* vale of tears. **–nvoll,** *adj.* tearful.

tränieren, *see* **trainieren.**

Trank, *m.* (-(e)s, ⸚e) potion, drink, beverage, draught; *Speise und –*, meat and drink. **–opfer,** *n.* libation. **–same,** *f.* (*Swiss dial.*) drink. **–steuer,** *f.* duty on alcoholic drinks.

trank, tränke, *see* **trinken.**

Tränk–e, *f.* (-n) watering place, drinking trough, horse-pond; *zur –e führen*, water (*cattle*). **–en,** *v.a.* give to drink; water (*cattle, the ground*); soak, saturate, steep, impregnate; (*fig.*) imbue. **–eimer,** *m.*, **–faß,** *n.* drinking tub *or* water bucket (*for horses*); pig's trough. **–stoff,** *m.* liquor, dip, bath. **–trog,** *m.* watering-trough.

trans–atlantisch, *adj.* transatlantic. **–ferieren,** *v.a.* (*C.L.*) transfer. **–formator,** *m.* transformer (station) (*Elec.*). **–fundieren,** *v.a.* & *n.* decant. **–gression,** *f.* submergence, flooding (*by the sea*). **–igieren,** *v.n.* come to an understanding. **–it,** *m.* transit. **–itlager,** *n.* bonded warehouse. **–itverkehr,** *m.* transit trade, through traffic. **–kription,** *f.* transcription (*in phonetic or Latin characters or for another instrument* (*Mus.*). **–lation,** *f.* transposition. **–mission,** *f.* (belt) transmission (*Mach.*). **–ozeanisch,** *adj.* transoceanic. **–parent,** *n.* transparency. **–pirieren,** *v.n.* perspire. **–ponieren,** *v.a.* transpose (*into another key*) (*Mus.*). **–port,** *m.* (-(e)s, -e) transport, transportation, carriage, conveyance, transfer, shipment; (*C.L.*) carrying forward, amount brought forward. **–portabel,** *adj. see* **–portfähig. –porteur,** *m.* (-s, -e) protractor (*Geom.*), feed-dog (*sewing machine*). **–portfähig,** *adj.* transportable, portable, movable. **–portflugzeug,** *n.* troop-carrying *or* transport plane. **–portgeschäft,** *n.* carrying-trade. **–portieren,** *v.a.* transport, convey, carry, ship; (*C.L.*) carry forward, transfer. **–portmakler,** *m.* forwarding agent. **–portpreise,** *m.pl.* transport charges, freight. **–portschiff,** *n.* troopship, (troop) transport. **–portschnecke,** *f.* screw-conveyor (*Mech.*). **–portversicherung,** *f.* insurance against damage in transit. **–versal,** *adj.* transverse, transversal. **–versale,** *f.* transverse (line) (*Geom.*). **–zendent,** *adj.* transcendental.

transchieren, *see* **tranchieren.**

Trapez, *n.* (-es, -e) trapezoid, trapezium (*Math.*); trapeze (*Gymn.*). **–oid,** *n.* (-(e)s, -e) quadrilateral (*Geom.*). **–förmig,** *adj.* quadrilateral, trapezoid(al). **–künstler,** *m.* trapeze artist.

trapp, *int.* clop, clump. **–e,** *f.* (-en) (*dial.*) footstep, (dirty) footmark, track. **–eln,** *v.n.* (*aux.* h.) trot, toddle, patter, trip. **–en,** *v.n.* (*aux.* h. *&* s.), **–sen,** *v.n.* (*coll.*) walk heavily, stride, trudge, stamp, tramp, trample.

Trappe, *f.* (-n) *&* *m.* (-n, -n) bustard (*Otides*) (*Orn.*).

Trara, *n.* (*coll.*) fuss, hullabaloo; bunkum, hanky-panky, flapdoodle.

Trass–ant, *m.* (-en, -en) (*C.L.*) drawer (*of a bill*). (*C.L.*) **–at,** *m.* (-en, -en) drawee. **–e,** *f.* (-en). (*Swiss dial.*) *n.* (-s, -s) line *or* alinement (*of a road, etc.*). **–ieren,** *v.a.* *&* *n.* (*aux*, h.) draw (*a bill*) (*auf einen*, on a p.); mark out, stake out; *–ierter Wechsel*, *see* **Tratte. –ierung,** *f.* drawing *or* issue of a bill.

trat, träte, *see* **treten.**

Tratsch. *m.* (*coll.*) tittle-tattle, silly gossip. **–en,** *v.a.* *&* *n.* (*aux.* h.) chatter, talk nonsense.

trätschen, *v.n.* (*coll. dial.*) splash, drip; rain cats and dogs.

Tratte, *f.* (-n) (*C.L.*) draft, bill of exchange.

Traub–e, *f.* (-en) grape; bunch of grapes; cluster, raceme. **–enabfall,** *m.* husks of grapes. **–enartig,** *adj.* grape-like; in clusters, racemose. **–enbeere,** *f.* grape. **–enblut,** *n.* (*Poet.*) wine. **–engeländer,** *n.* vine-trellis. **–enkamm,** *m.* vine-stalk. **–enkirsche,** *f.* bird-cherry (*Prunus padus*) (*Bot.*). **–enlese,** *f.* grape *or* vine harvest, vintage. **–enmost,** *m.* grape juice, new wine, must. **–enpresse,** *f.* wine-press. **–ensaft,** *m.* juice of the grape; (*poet.*) wine. **–ensauer,** *adj.*; *–ensaurer Zucker*, glucose, grape sugar. **–ensäure,** *f.* racemic acid. **–enstock,** *m.* vine. **–entragend,** *adj.* cluster-bearing. **–enzucker,** *m.* grape-sugar. **–ig,** *adj.*, *see* **–enartig.**

trau–en, 1. *v.n.* (*aux.* h.); *einem –en*, trust (in), believe in, have confidence in *or* rely on a p.; *einer S. nicht –en*, not believe in a th.; *einem nicht über den Weg –en*, not trust a p. out of one's sight; *den Augen kaum –en*, hardly believe one's eyes; *dem Frieden –e ich nicht*, (*fig.*) I have my doubts *or* suspicions; *dem Glück ist nicht zu –en*, fortune is fickle; *restlos –en*, trust unquestioningly, have absolute confidence in; (*Prov.*) *–, schau, wem*, take care in whom you trust. 2. *v.r.* venture, dare, be so bold as. 3. *v.a.* marry, give in marriage, join in wedlock; *sich –en lassen*, get married. **–altar,** *m.* marriage-altar. **–gebühr,** *f.*, **–geld,** *n.* marriage-fee. **–handlung,** *f.* marriage ceremony, wedding. **–lich,** *adj.* familiar, intimate; confidential, cordial; homely, snug, cosy. **–lichkeit,** *f.* familiarity, intimacy, cordiality; cosiness, comfort. **–ring,** *m.* wedding-ring. **–schein,** *m.* certificate of marriage, marriage lines. **–ung,** *f.* marriage ceremony, wedding. **–t,** *adj.*, *see* **traut.** (*coll.*) **–te,** *f.* confidence, courage. **–zeuge,** *m.* witness to a marriage.

Trauer, *f.* mourning, grief, sorrow (*um* or *über*, for); *– anlegen um*, go into mourning for; *in tiefer –*, in deep mourning; *– tragen*, wear *or* go into black *or* mourning. **–anzeige,** *f.* obituary *or* in memoriam notice. **–binde,** *f.* black crape. **–birke,** *f.* weeping birch (*Betula pendula*) (*Bot.*). **–botschaft,** *f.* sad news, mournful tidings; news of a death. **–decke,** *f.* mourning housings (*on horses*). **–fahne,** *f.* half-mast flag. **–fall,** *m.* death, bereavement. **–feier,** *f.* obsequies. **–flor,** *m.* mourning crape. **–geleit,** *n.* funeral procession, mourners. **–geläut(e),** *n.* funeral knell, passing-bell. **–gesang,** *m.* funeral hymn, dirge. **–geschichte,** *f.* sad tale. **–geschrei,** *n.* lamentations. **–gestalt,** *f.* doleful figure. **–gottesdienst,** *m.* funeral service. **–haus,** *n.* house of mourning. **–jahr,** *n.* year of mourning. **–kleid,** *n.*, **–kleidung,** *f.* mourning dress; widow's weeds. (*coll.*) **–kloß,** *m.* spoil-sport, wet blanket. **–leute,** *pl.* mourners. **–mahl,** *n.* funeral repast. **–mantel,** *m.* mourning-cloak; Camberwell Beauty (*Vanessa antiopa*) (*Ent.*). **–marsch,** *m.* funeral march. **–n,** *v.n.* (*aux.* h.) mourn, lament, grieve for; wear mourning; *um einen –n*, mourn for a p.; *über den Tod seines Vaters –n*, mourn his father's death. **–nachricht,** *f.* sad news *or* tidings. **–rand** *m.* black edge (*on notepaper*); (*hum.*) dirty finger-nails. **–rede,** *f.* funeral oration *or* sermon. **–schleier,** *m.* mourning-veil. **–spiel,** *n.* tragedy (*Theat.*). **–voll,** *adj.* sad, mournful. **–weide,** *f.* weeping willow (*Salix babylonica*) (*Bot.*). **–zeit,** *f.* time of mourning. **–zug,** *m.* funeral procession.

Trauf–e, *f.* (-en) drippings (from the roof); gutter, trough, eaves; *aus dem* or *vom Regen in die –e kommen*, out of the frying-pan into the fire. **–en,** *v.n.* (*dial.*), *see* **träufeln** *v.n.* **–faß,** *n.* rain tub, water butt. **–rinne,** *f.* gutter (*of roof*). **–röhre,** *f.* gutter-pipe, spouting. **–wasser,** *n.* rain-water.

träuf–eln, *v.a.* let fall in drops, drop, drip; *Balsam in* or *auf die Wunde –eln*, (*fig.*) pour balm on a wound. **–en,** 1. *v.a.* *see* **–eln.** 2. *v.n.* (*aux* h. *&* s.) (*dial.*) drip, trickle (down).

Traum, *m.* (-(e)s, ⁻e) dream; vision, fancy, illusion; day-dream, daze; *ich habe auch im –e nicht daran gedacht, das ist mir im –e nicht eingefallen*, I never dreamt of such a thing, it never entered my head; *einem aus dem –e helfen*, bring a p. to his senses; *das Kleid ist ein –*, it is a dream of a dress. **–bild,** *n.* vision, phantom, illusion. **–buch,** *n.* dream-book, fortune-book. **–deuter,** *m.* interpreter of dreams, fortune-teller. **–deutung,** *f.* interpretation of dreams. **–gebilde,** *n.*, **–gesicht,** *n.*, **–gestalt,** *f.* vision. **–haft,** *adj.* dreamlike, unreal, illusory. **–leben,** *n.*; *er führt nur ein –leben*, he lives in a dream *or* daze. **–spiel,** *n.* phantasmagoria. **–verloren,** *adj.*, **–versunken,** *adj.* lost in dreams. **–wach,** *adj.* in a trance. **–welt,** *f.* dreamland, world of fancy. **–zustand,** *m.* trance.

träum–en, *v.a.* *&* *n.* (*aux.* h.) *&* *imp.* dream, be lost in thought, day-dream; believe, imagine; *ich –te* or *es –te mir* or *mir –te*, I dreamt; *wachend –en*, go about in a dream *or* daze, be given to day-dreaming; *sich* (*Dat.*) *etwas –en lassen*, believe *or* imagine a th., take a th. for granted; *das hätte ich mir nie –en lassen*, I should never have dreamt of such a thing. **–er,** *m.* dreamer, visionary. **–erei,** *f.* dreaming, musing, fancy, reverie, day-dream, brown study. **–erisch,** *adj.* dreamy, dreaming, musing.

traun, *int.* indeed! to be sure! surely! upon my word! (*archaic*) faith! forsooth!

traurig, *adj.* sad, melancholy, mournful, sorrowful, grieved; depressed, dismal, wretched; *–er Anblick*, deplorable sight; *–er Ausruf*, doleful cry; *Ritter von der –en Gestalt*, Knight of the Doleful Countenance. **–keit,** *f.* sadness, sorrow; depression, melancholy.

traut, *adj.* dear, beloved; cosy, comfortable, intimate; *–es Mädchen*, darling, sweetheart; *–es Plätzchen*, cosy *or* snug corner. (*coll.*) **–e,** *see under* **trau–.**

Travestie, *f.* (-n) travesty, parody, skit. **–ren,** *v.a.* travesty, parody, make ridiculous.

Treber, *pl.* (*Austr. dial.* **–n**) husks *or* skins (of grapes); draff, brewer's grains. **–wein,** *m.* after-wine.

treck–en, *v.a.* (*dial.*) drag, pull, tow (*a ship*). **–er,** *m.* tractor. **–schute,** *f.* canal-boat, barge. **–seil,** *n.* tow-rope. **–weg,** *m.* towing-path.

Treff, 1. *m.* (-(e)s, -e) blow, knock, nudge; winning hit; shrewd *or* cutting remark. 2. *n.* (-s, -s) club (*Cards*); (*coll.*) *er hat einen –*, he is cracked *or* dotty. **–as,** *n.* ace of clubs.

treff–en, 1. *ir.v.a.* *&* *n.* (*aux.* h.) hit, strike; affect, touch, concern; befall, fall in with, come upon, meet (with), encounter, find, light upon; guess, hit upon; *Anstalten –en*, see *Vorkehrungen –en*; *auf einen –en*, meet with *or* encounter a p.; *der Ausdruck trifft*, the remark gets home; *Auslese* or *Auswahl –en*, make a selection; *vom Blitze getroffen*, struck by lightning; (*fig.*) thunderstruck; *eine Entscheidung –en*, come to a decision (about), decide (upon); *sich getroffen fühlen*, feel hurt, take to heart; *wer sich getroffen fühlt, nehme sich bei der Nase*, if the cap fits wear it; *es gut –en*, be successful *or* lucky; *er trifft gut*, he is a good shot; *Sie haben es heute gut getroffen*, it is lucky that you came today; *ins Blaue –en*, miss the mark; *ins Schwarze –en*, hit the mark; *das Los traf ihn*, it fell to his lot; *der Maler hat Sie gut getroffen*, the painter has hit you off well; *Maßnahmen* or *Maßregeln –en*, take steps *or* measures; *den Nagel auf den Kopf –en*, (*fig.*) hit the nail on the head; *nicht –en*, miss; *wen trifft die Schuld?* who is to blame?; *die Reihe trifft dich*, it is your turn; *tödlich –en*, strike a mortal blow; *ein Übereinkommen mit einem –en*, come to an agreement with s.o.; *das Unglück traf mich*, I had the misfortune; *die Verantwortung trifft ihn*, the responsibility rests with him; *Vorkehrungen –en*, make provisions *or* preparations (for); *Vorsichtsmaßregeln* or *Vorsorge –en*, take precautions; *der Vorwurf trifft ihn*, he comes in for the blame; *eine Wahl –en*, make a choice; *getroffen!* right! that's just it! you've got it! 2. *v.r.* happen; *es traf sich, daß*, it so happened that; *sich gut –en*, be lucky. 3. *n.* engagement, action, combat, battle; meeting, encounter, gathering; line of battle (*Mil.*, *Naut.*); *ins –en führen*, bring to bear; *ein –en liefern*, offer battle; *mittleres –en*, centre of an order of battle; *als es zum –en kam*, when it came to the point. **–end,** *pr.p. & adj.* well-aimed, to the point, pertinent, striking; suitable, appropriate; *das –ende Wort*, the right word; *seine Bemerkungen waren –end*, his remarks were to the point. **–er,** *m.* lucky hit; winning ticket, prize; *einen –er haben*, score a hit; *einen –er machen*, be lucky; hold the winning number. **–lich,** *adj.* excellent, choice, exquisite, first-rate, admirable. **–lichkeit,** *f.* excellence, perfection. **–punkt,** *m.* rendezvous, meeting-place; point of impact (*Mil.*). **–sicher,** *adj.* well-aimed, accurate, sound; *–sichere Bemerkungen*, pertinent remarks; *–sicheres Urteil*, sound judgement. **–sicherheit,** *f.* accuracy of fire, unerring aim.

treib–en, 1. *ir.v.a.* drive, push, force; set in motion, propel, impel, urge on, stimulate, promote; refine, sublime, extract (*ore*); hammer, emboss, work, chase, raise (*metals*); put forth (*leaves, branches, etc.*); occupy o.s. with, work at, carry on, practise; *was treibst du da?* what are you doing there?; *er treibt es zu arg* or *zu bunt*, he goes too far; *aufs Äußerste –en* or *zum Äußersten –en*, push to extremes; *etwas auf die Spitze –en*, exaggerate a th.; *aus dem Amte –en*, force out of office; *den Ball –en*, drive the ball (*Golf*); *Blutschande –en*, commit incest; *Deutsch –en*, go in for German, study German; *der Fluß –t Eis*, the river is bringing down ice; *es gemütlich –en*, take things comfortably; *ein Geschäft –en*, follow a (line of) business; *ein Handwerk –en*, follow a trade *or* craft; *einen in die Enge –en*, drive s.o. into a corner; *in die Flucht –en*, put to flight; *Preise in die Höhe –en*, force up prices; *Knospen –en*, bud, come into bud; *Kreisel –en*, play whip and top; *Kühe auf die Weide –en*, drive cattle to pasture; *Kurzweil –en*, amuse o.s., pass one's time; *Musik –en*, devote o.s. to music, study music; *Pflanzen –en*, force plants (*in hothouse*); *Reifen –en*, bowl a hoop; *Schindluder –en mit einem*, treat *or* use a p. badly; *diese Arznei –t den Schweiß*, this medicine promotes perspiration; *seinen Spaß, sein Spiel* or *seinen Spott mit einem –en*, make fun *or* game of s.o.; *Sport –en*, engage in *or* go in for sport; *den Teig –en*, roll out the dough; *–ende Kraft*, driving force, motive power; *getriebene Arbeit*, embossed *or* raised work; *es toll –en*, behave like a fool, act madly; *über das Ziel hinaus –en*, carry *or* push too far; *Unfug* (*Unsinn*) *–en*, play the fool; *ich lasse keinen Unsinn mit mir –en*, I will stand no nonsense; *sein Unwesen –en*, be up to one's tricks; *Unzucht –en*, fornicate; *vor sich her –en*, sweep before one; dribble (*Footb.*); *das Wild –en*, beat game; *einen zur Eile –en*, hurry a p. (up) *or* urge a p. on; *die Gegner zu Paaren –en*, get the better of one's opponents; *zur Verzweiflung –en*, drive to despair. 2. *v.n.* (*aux.* h. & s.) drift, float; sprout, blossom forth; ferment; *vor Anker –en*, drag the anchor; *ans Land –en*, drift *or* be driven ashore; *das Bier –t*, the beer works; *der Saft –t im Holze*, the sap rises in the wood. 3. *n.* driving, drifting; urge, impulse, bursting (*of buds*), germination, gemmation; doings, bustle, life, activity, stir; *das ganze Tun und –en*, all these goings-on; *ein wüstes –en*, riotous scenes. **–anker,** *m.* sea- *or* drag-anchor. **–arbeit,** *f.* cupellation; embossed work. **–beet,** *n.* hotbed. **–eis,** *n.* drift-ice. **–er,** *m.* driver, drover, beater (*Hunt.*); instigator; driving-wheel, propeller; refiner. **–erei,** *f.* hurry, rush, bustle. **–gas,** *n.* motor fuel. **–hammer,** *m.* chasing-hammer. **–haus,** *n.* hothouse, greenhouse, conservatory. **–hauspflanze,** *f.* hothouse plant; (*fig.*) molly-coddle. **–herd,** *m.* cupelling furnace, refining hearth. **–holz,** *n.* drift-wood. **–jagd,** *f.* battue. **–kasten,** *m.* forcing-frame. **–keil,** *m.* wedge, planer (*Typ.*). **–kraft,** *f.* propellant force, motive force, *see* **Triebkraft.** **–ladung,** *f.* propelling charge. **–mine,** *f.* floating mine. **–mittel,** *n.* propellant; raising agent (*baking, etc.*). **–netz,** *n.* drift-net. **–öl,** *n.* fuel oil. **–pflanze,** *f.* forced *or* hothouse plant. **–rad,** *n.* fly-wheel. **–reis,** *n.* sprout. **–riemen,** *m.* driving-belt. **–sand,** *m.* shifting sand, quicksand. **–schwefel,** *m.* native sulphur. **–stange,** *f.* connecting rod, drive-shaft. **–stock,** *m.* embossing anvil. **–stoff,** *m.* (motor) fuel. **–welle,** *f.* drive-shaft.

Treidel, *m.* (-s, –) towline, tow-rope. **–n,** *v.a.* tow (*Naut.*). **–weg,** *m.* tow- or towing-path.

Trekker, *m. see* **Trecker.**

Trema, *n.* (-s, -s & -ta) diaeresis.

tremol–ieren, *v.a. & n.* quaver, shake. **–o,** *n.* (-os, -os) shake, trill, tremolo.

Tremse, *f.* (-n) (*dial.*) cornflower.

Tremul–ant, *m.* (-en, -en) trill, shake, tremolo-stop (*Org.*). **–ieren,** *v.n.* (*aux.* h.) shake (*Mus.*), sing vibrato *or* with a tremolo.

trendeln, *v.a.* (*aux.* h.) dawdle, loiter, temporize.

trenn–en, 1. *v.a.* separate, divide, part, sever, sunder, disconnect; resolve, dissolve, disunite, divorce; detach, undo (*seam, etc.*); break (*the ranks, Mil.*); break up, dissolve (*partnership, a marriage*). 2. *v.r.* part, separate (*von*, from) be(come) divorced; branch off (*as roads*); dissociate, disintegrate, decompose. **–bar,** *adj.* separable, divisible. **–barkeit,** *f.* divisibility. **–punkt,** *m.* point of separation; (*pl.*) diaeresis. **–schalter,** *m.* circuit breaker, cut-out (*Elec.*). **–schärfe,** *f.* selectivity (*Rad.*). **–schnitt,** *m.* cross-section. **–schreibung,** *f.* printed writing, printing. **–ung,** *f.* separation, division, segregation, parting, severing, dissociation, dissolution; disintegration, decomposition; divorce. **–ungsfestigkeit,** *f.* breaking-strength. **–ungsfläche,** *f.* cleavage (*in crystals*). **–ungslinie,** *f.* line of demarcation. **–ungspartikel,** *f.* disjunctive particle (*Gram.*). **–ungspunkte,** *m.pl.* diaeresis. **–ungsschmerz,** *m.* pain of separation. **–ungsstrich,** *m.* dash. **–ungsstunde,** *f.* hour of parting. **–ungszeichen,** *n.* hyphen. **–wand,** *f.* bulk-head.

Trense, *f.* (-n) snaffle, bridoon (*of horses*).

trepanieren, *v.a.* trepan (*Surg.*).

Trepp–e, *f.* (-en) staircase, (flight of) stairs; *die –e hinauf*, upstairs; *man hat ihn die –e hinunter geworfen*, they threw him downstairs; *zwei –en hoch wohnen*, live in the second story *or* on the second floor. **–ab,** *adv.* downstairs. **–auf,** *adv.* upstairs. **–enabsatz,** *m.* landing (*of a staircase*). **–enbaum,** *m.* spindle (*of a winding staircase*). **–enflucht,** *f.* flight of stairs. **–enförmig,** *adj.* rising in steps, stepped, scalariform. **–engeländer,** *n.* railing, banister. **–enhaus,** *n.* hall, well of a staircase. **–enläufer,** *m.* stair-carpet. **–enpodest,** *see* **–enabsatz.** **–enstufe,** *f.* step, stair (*of a staircase*). **–enwitz,** *m.* afterthought, wisdom after the event, esprit de l'escalier.

Tresor, *m.* (-s, -e) treasury; safe, vault, strong-room.

Trespe, *f.* (-en) brome-grass.

Tress–e, *f.* (-en), lace, braid, galloon; (*pl.*) stripes (*Mil.*). **–ieren,** *v.a.* plait, braid (*hair*).

Trester, *pl.* residūe (*of fruit*); grape-skins, husks. **–wein,** *m.* after-wine, poor wine.

tret–en, 1. *ir.v.n.* (*aux.* h. & s.) tread, walk, step; go, pass over to; pedal (*Cycl.*); treadle; *ans Licht–en*, come to light, appear, become known; *an die Spitze –en*, assume the leadership, (take the) lead; *die Endung tritt an den Stamm*, the ending is joined to the stem; *an jemandes Stelle –en*, take a p.'s place, replace a p.; *einem auf den Fuß –en*, tread on a p.'s toes; *auf die Seite –en*, step aside; *auf jemandes Seite –en*, take a p.'s part, side with a p.; *auf der Stelle –en*, mark time (*Mil.*); *kalter Schweiß trat ihm auf die Stirn*, cold perspiration broke out on his brow; *aus dem Dienste –en*, retire from (active) service; *der Mond tritt hinter eine Wolke*, the moon went behind a cloud; *Tränen traten ihm in die Augen*, the tears came into his eyes; *der Saft ist in die Bäume getreten*, the sap has risen in the trees; *in die Bresche –en*, step into the breach; *in den Ehestand –en*, marry, get married; *in Erscheinung –en*, appear, become apparent *or* visible; *in seine*

Fuß(s)tapfen –en, follow a p.'s example *or* in a p.'s footsteps, imitate s.o.; *in den Hintergrund –en*, retire into the background; *sie ist in ihr zehntes Jahr getreten*, she has entered her tenth year; *in Kraft –en*, come into force; *die Sonne tritt in den Löwen*, the sun enters Leo; *in den Militärdienst –en*, enter the army; *in Unterhandlungen –en*, enter into negotiations; *mit einem in Verbindung –en*, enter into association with s.o.; *in den Vordergrund –en*, come into the foreground *or* limelight; *einem in den Weg –en*, oppose *or* obstruct a p., stand in a p.'s way; *in Wirksamkeit –en*, take effect; *leise –en*, go gently, tread softly; be artful; *einem zu nahe –en*, offend *or* insult a p., hurt a p.'s feelings; *ohne der Wahrheit zu nahe zu –en*, without any violation of truth; *ohne ihrer Bescheidenheit zu nahe zu –en*, without offence to her modesty; *–en Sie näher, meine Herren!* walk in, gentlemen! step this way, gentlemen! *über die Ufer –en*, overflow its banks; *tritt mir nie wieder unter die Augen!* never let me see your face again! *ein Wölkchen trat vor den Mond*, a little cloud passed over the moon; *vor den Richterstuhl Gottes –en*, appear before the judgement-seat of God; *zu einem –en*, go up to a p.; take a p.'s side; *zutage –en*, appear, become evident. 2. *v.a.* tread, walk upon; trample, kick; treadle (*a sewing machine, etc.*), work (*a treadle*), push (*a pedal*); treat with contempt; (*sl.*) dun; (*coll.*) *einen –en*, dun, press a p. for payment; *die Bälge –en*, work *or* treadle the bellows; *sich* (*Dat.*) *einen Dorn in den Fuß –en*, run a thorn into one's foot; (*vulg.*) *einen in den Hintern –en*, kick a p.'s bottom; *mit Füßen –en*, trample under foot *or* in the dirt; (*fig.*) ride roughshod over; *sein Glück mit Füßen –en*, act against one's own interest, spurn one's good fortune; *das Pflaster –en*, wander *or* trapse the streets; *seine Schuhe schief –en*, wear one's shoes down at heel; *den Takt –en*, beat time with one's foot; *Trauben –en*, tread grapes; *Wasser –en*, tread water (*swimming*). **–anlasser**, *m.* foot- *or* kick-starter (*Motor.*). **–brief**, *m.* dunning letter. **–butte**, *f.* tub *or* vat in which grapes are trodden. **–er**, *m.* treader; bellows-blower (*Org.*); fuller (*of cloth*); (*pl.*) (*coll.*) boots. **–erei**, *f.* kicking. **–küfe**, *see* **–butte**. **–lager**, *n.* pedal-bearing (*Cycl.*). **–mine**, *f.* contact mine. **–mühle**, *f.* treadmill; *die alte –mühle –en*, work at the old treadmill; *die alte –mühle des Beruf(e)s*, the humdrum daily round. **–rad**, *n.* tread-wheel. **–schalter**, *m.* foot- *or* floor-switch. **–schemel**, *m.* treadle (*of a loom, Weav.*).

treu, 1. *adv.* (*with Dat.*) faithful, loyal, constant; conscientious, staunch, upright, sincere; retentive, accurate, true; (*dial.*) generous; *seinem Charakter – bleiben*, be true to one's character; *seinem Vorsatz – bleiben*, adhere faithfully to one's purpose; *–es Gedächtnis*, reliable *or* retentive memory; (*B.*) *Du –er Gott*, Lord God of Truth; *zu –en Händen übergeben*, entrust, put in trust, place with trustees; *es mit einem – meinen*, mean well by a p.; *sein –es Schwert*, his trusty sword; *–e Übersetzung*, close *or* faithful translation. 2. *f.*, *see* **–e**; *– und Glauben halten*, keep one's word; *auf – und Glauben*, (*Swiss dial.*) *in guten –en*, in good faith; (*bei*) *meiner –!* upon my honour! **–e**, *f.* fidelity, faithfulness, constancy, loyalty; sincerity, honesty; accuracy; *–e brechen* or *verletzen*, break faith; *–e halten* or *bewahren*, keep faith; *den Eid der –e ablegen*, take the oath of allegiance. **–bruch**, *m.* breach of faith; perfidy, disloyalty. **–brüchig**, *adj.* faithless, perfidious, disloyal. **–eid**, *m.* oath of allegiance. **–ergeben**, *adj.*, **–gehorsam**, *adj.* truly devoted. **–gesinnt**, *adj.* loyal. **–händer**, *m.* trustee, executor. **–handgesellschaft**, *f.* trust-company. **–herzig**, *adj.* true-hearted, frank, trusting; candid, simple, naïve, guileless. **–herzigkeit**, *f.* frankness, naïvety. **–lich**, *adv.* truly, faithfully, loyally, conscientiously, reliably. **–liebchen**, *n.* true-love. **–los**, *adj.* faithless, pernicious, disloyal, treacherous, traitorous. **–losigkeit**, *f.* faithlessness, perfidy, treachery. **–schwur**, *m.* plighting of troth.

Tri-angel, *m.* triangle (*Mus.*, *Math.*). **–angulär**, *adj.* triangular, three-cornered. **–angulieren**, *v.a.* triangulate, survey by trigonometry. **–arier**, *m.* triarian (*Roman Hist.*); old campaigner; last hope. **–as**, *f.* triad; trias (*Geol.*). **–nom**, *n.* trinomial. **–nomisch**, *adj.* trinomial. **–ole**, *f.* triplet (*Mus.*). **–pel**, *m.* triple gain. **–plieren**, *v.a.* treble, triplicate. **–plik**, *f.* surrejoinder (*Law*). **–pus**, *m.* (-pus, -poden) tripod.

tribulieren, 1. *v.n.* be importunate. 2. *v.a.* importune, pester.

Trib–un, *m.* (-s, -e & (*Austr. dial.*) -en, -en) tribune. **–unal**, *n.* (-s, -e) tribunal, high court of justice. **–une**, *f.*, **–üne**, *f.* (-n) platform, rostrum, tribune; balcony (*Theat.*); grandstand (*for spectators*); audience. **–ut**, *m.* (-(e)s, -e) tribute, reparations; *den –ut zollen* or *entrichten*, pay tribute (to). **–utär**, **–utpflichtig**, *adj.* tributary.

Trichin–e, *f.* (-en) trichina (*Trichinella spiralis*) (*Zool.*). **–ös**, *adj.* trichinous, trichinosed. **–ose**, *f.* trichinosis.

Trichter, *m.* (-s, –) funnel, cone, hopper; crater, shell-hole; horn (*of a gramophone*); (*fig.*) *einen auf den – bringen*, put a p. on the right way *or* track. **–n**, *v.a.* pour through a funnel. **–feld**, *n.* bombarded area. **–förmig**, *adj.* funnel-shaped, infundibular. **–gelände**, *n.*, *see* **–feld**.

Trick, *m.* (-s, -e & -s) trick, stunt, dodge; trick (*Cards*). **–aufnahme**, *f.* faked *or* trick photo. **–track**, *n.* backgammon.

Trieb, *m.* (-(e)s, -e) sprout, young shoot; driving force, motive power; impetus, urge, spur; instinct, impulse, bent, propensity, inclination, desire, liking; (*dial.*) flock, herd; *aus eignem –e*, instinctively, of one's own accord; *– zum Studieren*, studious bent; *sinnliche –e*, carnal instincts; *den – zu etwas spüren*, feel the urge to do *or* towards a th. **–achse**, *f.* driving shaft. **–artig**, *adj.* instinctive, impulsive; unbridled. **–el**, *m.* (*dial.*) mallet, crank (handle). **–feder**, *f.* main spring (*of clock*); (*fig.*) motive; *die –feder von einer S. sein*, be at the bottom of a th. **–haft**, *adj.*, *see* **–artig**. **–knospe**, *f.* leaf bud. **–kraft**, *f.* impetus, motive power, motivating force; germinating power. **–malz**, *n.* leavening malt. **–mäßig**, *adj.* impulsive. **–rad**, *n.* driving-wheel; pinion. **–sand**, *m.* drift sand, shifting sand, quicksand. **–scheibe**, *f.* knob, dial. **–stange**, *f.* push-rod (*Motor.*). **–stoff**, *m.* motor fuel. **–wagen**, *m.* rail-car. **–welle**, *f.* drive-shaft. **–werk**, *n.* machinery, mechanism; power unit, motor; transmission, driving-gear. **–werksanlage**, *f.* power plant. **–wurzel**, *f.* main *or* tap root. **–zähne**, *m.pl.* drive-gear.

trieb, **triebe**, *see* **treiben**.

trief–en, *ir.v.n.* (*aux.* h. & s.) drop, drip, trickle, gutter, water, run; secrete (*Med.*); *die Augen –en ihm*, his eyes are running, he is blear-eyed; *vor Nässe –en*, be dripping wet. **–äugig**, *adj.* bleary, blear-eyed. **–end**, *pr.p.* & *adj.*, **–ig**, *adj.* dropping, dripping. **–nasig**, *adj.* snivelling. **–naß**, *adj.* sopping *or* dripping wet.

Triel, *m.* (-s, -e) (*dial.*) mouth, maw, muzzle; dewlap. **–en**, *v.n.* (*dial.*) dribble, slaver, slobber. **–er**, *m.* (*dial.*) bib.

triezen, *v.a.* (*coll.*) vex, worry, pester, bother.

triff, **triffst**, **trifft**, *see* **treffen**.

Trift, *f.* (-en) right of pasturage, pasture, common; (*Poet.*) meadow, sward; track, run (*for cattle*); drove, flock, herd; floating, drift (*of timber*); current, drift (*Naut.*). **–en**, *v.a.* float, drift (*timber*); pasture. **–holz**, *n.* driftwood. **–ig**, *adj.* cogent, forcible, weighty, strong, conclusive, convincing, plausible, sound, valid; (*dial.*) drifting, adrift; *aus –igen Gründen*, for weighty reasons. **–igkeit**, *f.* cogency (*of arguments*), validity, soundness. **–strömung**, *f.* glacial current.

Trigonomet–rie, *f.* trigonometry. **–risch**, *adj.* trigonometrical; *–rischer Punkt*, triangulation point (*Surv.*).

Trikot [*pron.* tri'ko:], *m.* & *n.* (-s, -s knitted garment; stockinet; (*pl.*) tights. **–age** [*pron.* triko'ta:ʒə], *f.*, **–waren**, *f.pl.* knitted goods, woollens.

Triller, *m.* (-s, –) trill, shake (*Mus.*); *einen – schlagen*, shake, trill; (*coll.*) *mit einem – über die S. hinweggehen*, pass the matter off *or* over lightly. **–n**, *v.a.* & *n.* (*aux.* h.) shake, trill; warble, twitter (*as birds*).

Trinität, *f.* trinity.

trink–en, *ir.v.a.* & *n.* (*aux.* h.) drink; (*poet.*) imbibe, absorb; *–en auf,* drink to, toast; *mit einem Brüderschaft –en,* pledge one's intimate friendship with a p.; *sich* (*Dat.*) *einen Rausch –en,* get drunk; *der Wein läßt sich gut –en,* the wine is pleasant to drink; *ein Glas leer –en,* empty a glass; *gern einen über den Durst –en,* be fond of the bottle. **–bar,** *adj.* drinkable; ready for drinking. **–becher,** *m.* drinking-cup. **–bruder,** *m.* tippler. **–er,** *m.* heavy drinker, toper, drunkard. **–erheilanstalt,** *f.* hospital for inebriates. **–gefäß,** *n.* drinking-vessel. **–gelag(e),** *n.* drinking-bout, carouse. **–geld,** *n.* gratuity; (*coll.*) tip; (*coll.*) *jemandem ein –geld geben,* tip a p. **–halle,** *f.* pump-room (*of a spa*). **–lied,** *n.* drinking-song. **–schale,** *f.* goblet. **–spruch,** *m.* toast. **–wasser,** *n.* drinking-water.

Trinom, *n. see* **Tri–nom.**

Triole, *f. see* **Tri–ole.**

Tripel, *m.*, **–erde,** *f.* rotten-stone.

triplieren, *see* **tri–plieren.**

Triplik, *f., see* **Tri–plik.**

Tripp, *m.* (-s, -s & -e), **–samt,** *m.* velveteen.

trippeln, *v.n.* (*aux.* h.) trip, patter.

Tripper, *m.* (-s, –) gonorrhoea (*Med.*); (*coll.*) clap.

Tripus, *n. see* **Tri–pus.**

Trischübel, *m.* (-s, –) (*Swiss dial.*) lintel.

Tritt, *m.* (-(e)s, -e) step, pace; tread, trace, footstep, track, footprint; kick; carriage-step; step-ladder, pair of steps; estrade; foothold (*Mountaineering*); *einen falschen – tun,* miss one's step; *einem auf Schritt und – folgen,* follow in a p.'s footsteps; (*coll.*) *einem den – geben,* give s.o. the push; *– vor –,* step by step; *gleichen Schritt und – halten,* keep pace with; *ohne –,* break step! march at ease! *im –e,* get *or* keep in step; *– wechseln!* change step! *– halten,* keep in step; keep pace (with). **–brett,** *n.* treadle (*of a loom*); pedal (*of an organ*); footboard, running-board (*Motor., Railw.*). **–klinke,** *f.* foot-release. **–leiter,** *f.* (pair of) steps, step-ladder. **–wechsel,** *m.* change of step.

tritt, trittst, *see* **treten.**

Triumph, *m.* (-(e)s, -e) triumph, victory; *einem den – gönnen,* not grudge a p. his victory. **–ator,** *m.* (-s, -en) conquering hero, victor. **–bogen,** *m.* triumphal arch. **–ieren,** *v.n.* (*aux.* h.) triumph (*über,* over), vanquish, conquer; exult (in), boast. **–wagen,** *m.* triumphal car. **–zug,** *m.* triumphal procession.

trivial, *adj.* trivial, trite, hackneyed. **–ität,** *f.* triviality.

trochä–isch, *adj.* trochaic. **–us,** *m.* (-us, -en) trochee.

trock–en, *adj.* dry, dried up, arid, parched, barren; (*fig.*) dull, uninteresting, tedious, boring; *auf dem –nen,* high and dry, stranded, stuck fast; *auf dem –nen sitzen,* be on one's beam-ends, be in a fix *or* hole, be in low water, be at the end of one's tether, not know which way to turn; *–ner Empfang,* cool reception; *–ene Fäulnis,* dry-rot; *–enen Fußes,* dry-shod; *–enes Gedeck,* dinner without wine; *noch nicht –en hinter den Ohren,* still wet behind the ears; *ins –ne bringen,* rescue, save, bring into safety; *sein Schäfchen ins –ne bringen,* line one's pocket, feather one's nest; *–ener Mensch,* prosaic fellow, dry stick; *–ene Messe,* mass without the Sacrament; *einen mit –enem Munde* (or *einen –en*) *sitzen lassen,* offer a guest no refreshment; *auf dem* or *im –(e)nen sein,* be out of danger, be safe; *–ene Wahrheit,* plain truth; *–ener Wechsel,* promissory note, bill drawn on o.s. **–enanlage,** *f.* drying plant. **–enapparat,** *m.* drying apparatus *or* frame, drier. **–enbagger,** *m.* excavator. **–enboden,** *m.* drying-room *or* loft. **–endampf,** *m.* dry steam. **–endock,** *n.* graving-dock, dry-dock. **–enelement,** *n.* dry cell, dry battery. **–enfäule,** *f.* dry-rot. **–enfutter,** *n.* fodder, provender. **–enfütterung,** *f.* dry-feeding *or* fodder. **–engehalt,** *m.* amount of solid matter. **–engestell,** *n.* drying-frame, clothes-horse. **–engewicht,** *n.* dry weight. **–enheit,** *f.* dryness, drought, aridity; (*fig.*) dullness. **–enkammer,** *f.* drying-room. **–enlegen,** *v.a.* drain (*a marsh*); change (*a baby*). **–enlegung,** *f.* draining, drainage; prohibition (*in U.S.A.*). **–enmaß,** *n.* dry measure. **–enmilch,** *f.* milk-powder, dried milk, dehydrated milk. **–enmittel,** *n.* drier, drying agent, siccative. **–enobst,** *n.* dried fruit. **–enofen,** *m.* drying-stove *or* kiln. **–enperiode,** *f.* dry spell (*weather*). **–enpflanze,** *f.* xerophyte. **–enplatte,** *f.* dry-plate (*Phot.*). **–enplatz,** *m.* drying-ground. **–enrahmen,** *m.* drying-frame, stenter. **–enreiben,** *v.a.* rub dry. **–enreinigung,** *f.* dry-cleaning. **–enrückstand,** *m.* dry residue. **–enschleuder,** *f.* centrifugal drier. **–enschwund,** *m.* shrinkage through drying. **–enstand,** *m., see* **–engestell. –enstange,** *f.* drying-pole. **–enstoff,** *m.* drier, drying agent, siccative. **–enstube,** *f.* drying-room. **–enverfahren,** *n.* drying-process. **–enwäsche,** *f.* dried laundry. **–ne,** *n.* dry land; dryness. **–nen,** 1. *v.n.* (*aux.* s.) dry, dry up, become dry. 2. *v.a.* dry; air; desiccate; drain; *getrocknete Feigen,* dried figs. 3. *n. see* **–nung;** *zum –nen aufhängen,* hang up to dry. **–ner,** *m.* drier (*Chem.*). **–nung,** *f.* drying; desiccation.

Troddel, *f.* tassel, bob; swordknot.

Trödel, *m.* (-s, -) rubbish; (*fig.*) vexation, nuisance, bother; lumber, second-hand goods, bric-à-brac; (*rare*) fun, pleasantry; (*coll.*) lark, spree. **–ei,** *f.* dawdling, loitering, dilatoriness, negligence. **–kram,** *m.* lumber, old clothes, second-hand goods. **–markt,** *m.* second-hand market, rag-fair. **–n,** *v.n.* (*aux.* h.) deal in second-hand goods; dawdle, loiter, waste one's time; (*coll.*) go slow (*at work*). **–waren,** *f.pl. see* **–kram.**

troff, tröffe, *see* **triefen.**

Trog, *m.* (-(e)s, ⸗e) trough; *schwingender –,* cradle (*for washing ore*).

trog, tröge, *see* **trügen.**

Troll, *m.* (-(e)s, -e) hobgoblin, gnome. **–blume,** *f.* globe-flower (*Trollius europaeus*) (*Bot.*).

trollen, 1. *v.n.* (*aux.* s.) trot, trundle. 2. *v.r.* go away, toddle off, stroll away; *trolle dich!* be off! get away! away with you!

Trombe, *f.* (-n) water (*or* sand) spout.

Trommel, *f.* (-n) drum; tympanum; ear-drum (*Anat.*); cylinder, barrel (*Mach.*); (tin) canister, specimen box (*Bot.*); *auf der – wirbeln,* give a roll on the drum. **–ei,** *f.* drumming, din. **–fell,** *n.* drumskin, drumhead; drum of the ear, tympanic membrane (*Anat.*). **–fellerschütternd,** *adj.* deafening, ear-splitting. **–feuer,** *n.* drum-fire, barrage, intense *or* heavy bombardment. **–klöppel,** *m.* drumstick. **–n,** *v.a.* & *n.* (*aux.* h.) drum, beat the drum; *es –t,* the drum is beating; *einen Marsch –n,* beat a march on the drum; *mit den Fingern –n,* drum with one's fingers; *ich lasse nicht auf mir –n,* I will not stand for it, (they, *etc.*) cannot do as (they, *etc.*) please with me. **–schlag,** *m.* beat on the drum; *unter –schlag,* with drums beating; *bei gedämpftem –schlag,* with muffled drums. **–schläger,** *m.* drummer. **–schlegel,** *m.* drumstick. **–sucht,** *f.* tympanitis (*Med.*). **–wirbel,** *m.* roll of the drum.

Trommler, *m.* (-s, –) drummer.

Trompete, *f.* (-n) trumpet; Fallopian (*or* Eustachian) tube (*Anat.*); *die –* or *auf der – blasen, in die – stoßen,* blow *or* sound the trumpet; *die – bläst* or *schmettert,* the trumpet is sounded, the trumpet blares. **–n,** *v.n.* blow (on the trumpet); (*fig.*) trumpet forth; *einen aus dem Schlafe –n,* sound the reveille; *der Elefant –t,* the elephant trumpets. **–nbaum,** *m.* snake-wood (*Bot.*). **–nbläser,** *m.* trumpeter. **–ngeschmetter,** *n.* blare of trumpets. **–nregister,** *n., see* **–nzug. –nschall,** *m.* sound of trumpets; *unter –nschall bekannt machen,* announce with a flourish of trumpets. **–nzug,** *m.* trumpet stop (*of an organ*). **–r,** *m.* trumpeter. **–rkorps,** *n.* brass band.

Trop–e, *f.* (-en) trope (*Rhet.*); (*pl.*) the tropics. **–enausführung,** *f.* tropical finish (*Motor.*). **–enausrüstung,** *f.* tropical kit. **–enfestigkeit,** *f.* resistance to tropical conditions, suitability for the tropics. **–enhelm,** *m.* pith *or* sun-helmet, topee. **–enkoller,** *m.* tropical frenzy. **–enkrankheit,** *f.* tropical disease. **–isch,** *adj.* tropical; metaphorical, figurative. **–us,** *m.* (-us, -en) (*Austr. dial.*), *see* **–e.**

Tropf, *m.* (-(e)s, ⸗e) simpleton, ninny, booby; *armer –,* poor wretch! **–bar, –barflüssig,** *adj.*

liquid. **-bernstein,** *m.* liquid amber. **-brett,** *n.* draining board. **-en,** 1. *m.* (-ens, -en) drop, spot, tear, bead (*of perspiration*); (*pl.*) drops (*Med.*); *haben Sie einen -en Milch*, have you a drop *or* spot of milk; *-en auf einen heißen Stein*, a drop in the bucket *or* ocean; *er trinkt gern seinen -en*, he is fond of his drink. (*Prov.*) *steter -en höhlt den Stein*, constant dripping wears the stone. 2. *v.a.* & *n.* drop, drip, trickle; *es -t*, it is spotting with rain; *dir -t die Nase*, your nose is running. **-enfänger,** *m.* drip-catcher. **-enförmig,** *adj.* bead-like. **-enmesser,** *m.* burette, pipette. **-enweise,** *adj.* in drops, drop by drop. **-naß,** *adj.* dripping wet. **-öler,** *m.* drop-oiler. **-pfanne,** *f.* drip-pan. **-rinne,** *f.* gutter. **-stein,** *m.* stalactite.

tröpf-eln, 1. *v.n.* (*aux.* h. & s.) drop, drip, trickle, fall in *or* form drops; spot with rain. 2. *v.a.* drip, pour drop by drop.

Trophäe, *f.* (-n) trophy.

[1]**Troß,** *m.* (-(ss)es, -(ss)e) supply lines, baggage train (*Mil.*); heavy baggage; camp followers; crowd, followers, hangers-on. **-knecht,** *m.* man in charge of baggage; camp-follower. **-schiff,** *n.* supply ship. **-wagen,** *m.* baggage wagon.

[2]**Troß, Trosse** *f.* (-(e)n) cable, hawser, warp.

Trost, *m.* comfort, consolation, solace; *einem - zusprechen*, comfort *or* console a p.; *schlechter -*, cold *or* poor comfort; *es gereicht mir zum -e, daß . . .*, it is a comfort to me to think that . . .; (*coll.*) *du bist wohl nicht bei -e?* you are off your head *or* (*sl.*) rocker *or* you are not in your right mind. **-bedürftig,** *adj.* in need of consolation. **-brief,** *m.* letter of condolence. **-bringend,** *adj.* comforting, consolatory. **-bringer,** *m.* comforter. **-los,** *adj.* hopeless, cheerless, bleak, desolate; disconsolate, inconsolable, desperate. **-losigkeit,** *f.* despair, hopelessness; cheerlessness, dreariness. **-preis,** *m.* consolation prize. **-rede,** *f.* words of consolation. **-reich,** *adj.* consoling, comforting. **-wort,** *n.* comforting word.

tröst-en, 1. *v.a.* comfort, console, solace; *jemanden über eine S.* or *wegen einer S. -en*, console a p. for a thing. 2. *v.r. sich mit . . . -en*, take comfort *or* find consolation in . . ., console o.s. with . . ., be consoled *or* comforted by . . . **-bar,** *adj.* consolable. **-er,** *m.* comforter, consoler; child's comforter *or* dummy; (*B.*) the Comforter; (*coll.*) cane; consolation of the bottle; favourite book. **-lich,** *adj.* consoling, comforting; pleasant, cheering; (*dial.*) cheerful, merry, gay. **-ung,** *f.* consolation, comfort; *die letzten -ungen*, the last unction.

Trott, *m.* (-(e)s, -e) trot, jog-trot; *der gewöhnliche -*, the daily round, the old jog-trot. **-eln, -en,** *v.n.* (*aux.* s.) jog along. **-oir** [*pron.* trɔto'a:r], *n.* (-s, -e (& *Austr. dial.* -s)) pavement, footpath; sidewalk (*Amer.*).

Trottel, *m.* (-s, -) cretin, (*coll.*) idiot, fool. **-haft,** *adj.* imbecile, idiotic, half-witted, block-headed, fatuous.

Trotz, 1. *m.* defiance, insolence; stubbornness, obstinacy, intrepidity (*gegen*, to *or* in the face of); *- bieten*, set at defiance, defy; weather (*a storm*); *einem etwas zum -e tun*, do a th. in spite *or* in defiance of a p., do a th. to spite a p. 2. *prep.* (*Dat. or now less good Gen.*) in spite of, despite, notwithstanding; *- des schlechten Wetters*, in spite of the bad weather; *- allem* or *alledem*, in spite of *or* for all that *or* notwithstanding everything. **-dem,** 1. *adv.* in spite of it, nevertheless, notwithstanding. 2. *conj.* notwithstanding that, although, even though, albeit. **-en,** *v.n.* (*aux.* h.) (*Dat.*) bid defiance to, defy; be obstinate (about), oppose, brave; *auf eine S. -en*, *see under* **pochen**; *mit einem -en*, be sulky with a p. **-ig,** *adj.* defiant, refractory, obstinate; sulky; (*einen*) *-ig ansehen*, look at (a p.) disdainfully, defiantly *or* haughtily. **-iglich,** *adj.* (*archaic*) boldly. **-kopf,** *m.* stubborn *or* pig-headed person. **-köpfig,** *adj.* obstinate, pig-headed; defiant.

trüb-(e), *adj.* muddy, cloudy, opaque, turbid, thick; (*fig.*) gloomy, dreary, cheerless, sad, melancholy; overcast, dull, dim, dead, flat; clouded (*of gems, etc.*), tarnished (*of metal*); *die Lampe brennt -*, the lamp burns dimly; *im -en fischen*, fish in troubled waters; *es sieht - damit aus*, things are looking black. **-e,** *see* **-heit.** **-en,** 1. *v.a.* make thick *or* muddy, darken, dim, cloud, tarnish; disturb, ruffle, upset, trouble, sadden, cast a gloom over; (*iron.*) *er sieht aus, als ob er kein Wässerchen -en könnte*, he looks the picture of innocence, he looks as if butter would not melt in his mouth; *einem die Freude -en*, spoil a p.'s pleasure. 2. *v.r. der Himmel -t sich*, the sky becomes overcast; *das Verhältnis -t sich*, relations become strained. **-heit,** *f.* muddy *or* turbid state; dimness, opaqueness; gloom. **-nis,** *f.* (-nisse), **-sal,** *f.* (-sale) & *n.* (-sals, -sale) affliction, distress, misery, sorrow, woe; (*coll.*) *-sal blasen*, mope, be in the dumps. **-selig,** *adj.* troubled, afflicted, sad, woeful, miserable. **-seligkeit,** *f.* sadness, dolefulness, despondency, gloom. **-sinn,** *m.* melancholy, dejection, depression, gloom. **-sinnig,** *adj.* low-spirited, dejected, gloomy, sad, melancholy, sombre. **-ung,** *f.* darkening, cloudiness, turbidity, dimness.

Trubel, *m.* confusion, turmoil, excitement, hubbub, hurly-burly.

Truch-seß, *m.* (-(ss)en, -(ss)e & (*Austr. dial.*) -(ss)es, -(ss)e) (*obs.*) lord high steward.

trudeln, 1. *v.a.* & *n.* (*aux.* s.) saunter, drift, roll; go into a spin (*Av.*); (*coll.*) roll *or* play dice. 2. *n.* ambling, sauntering; *das Flugzeug geriet ins -*, the aeroplane developed a spin.

Trüffel, *f.* (-n) truffle. **-n,** *v.a.* garnish *or* flavour with truffles.

trug, trüge, *see* **tragen.**

Trug, *m.* deceit, imposture, deception, fraud; delusion, illusion; *ohne -*, open and above board; *ein Mann ohne -*, a straightforward *or* an upright man; *Lug und -*, deceit and lying. **-bild,** *n.* phantom, vision, mirage, optical illusion. **-dolde,** *f.* cyme (*Bot.*). **-gebilde,** *n.*, **-gestalt,** *f.* phantom. **-gewebe,** *n.* tissue of lies. **-los,** *adj.* artless, guileless. **-mine,** *f.* booby-trap (*Mil.*). **-schluß,** *m.* sophism, (intentional) false conclusion *or* fallacy.

trüg-en, *ir.v.a.* & *n.* (*aux.* h.) deceive, delude, be deceitful, mislead, be deceptive; prove fallacious; *Gottes Wort kann nicht -en*, the word of God cannot fail; (*Prov.*) *der Schein -t*, appearances are deceptive. **-erisch,** *adj.*, **-lich,** *adj.* deceptive, misleading, deceitful, delusive; insidious, treacherous (*as ice*).

Truhe, *f.* (-n) trunk, chest; (clothes-)press; (*dial.*) coffin.

Trulle, *f.* (-n) (*dial.*) trollop, wench, hussy.

Trumm, *n.* & (*Austr. dial.*) *m.* (-(e)s, -e & ⸗er) (*dial.*) (stub-)end, stump, lump, clod; thrum (*Weav.*); *ein - Arbeit*, a pile of work; *ein - von einem Kerl*, a great lump of a fellow; *den - verlieren*, unthread one's needle, lose the end (*of thread*).

Trümmer, *pl.* wreckage, ruins, remains; broken pieces, fragments, debris, wreck; *zu -n* or *in - gehen*, go to rack and ruin; *zu -n schlagen*, smash to pieces, wreck. **-feld,** *n.* expanse of ruins. **-gestein,** *n.* rubble (*Geol.*). **-haft,** *adj.* in ruins, decayed. **-haufe(n),** *m.* heap of ruins *or* rubble. **-mine,** *f.* fragmentation mine.

Trumpf, *m.* (-(e)s, ⸗e) trumps, trump-card (*Cards*); *was ist - ?* what are trumps? *Herz ist -*, hearts are trumps; *letzter -*, last resource; *einen - darauf setzen*, play one's trump-card; make it one's special business *or* concern; *seine Trümpfe ausspielen*, exploit every *or* push home one's advantage; *einem zeigen, was - ist*, show a p. what is what; *kariert ist jetzt -*, checks are now the last word. **-en,** *v.a.* & *n.* (*aux.* h.) trump, play trumps; **-farbe,** *f.* trump (-suit). **-karte,** *f.* trump-card.

Trunk, *m.* (-(e)s, ⸗e) drink, potion; draught, gulp; drunkenness, alcoholism; *dem - ergeben*, addicted to drink; *an den - kommen*, take to drink; *auf einen -*, at one draught *or* gulp. **-en,** *adj.* (*Poet.*) drunk, intoxicated; *sie waren -en vor Freude*, they were wild *or* elated with joy. **-enbold,** *m.* drunkard. **-enheit,** *f.* drunkenness, intoxication. **-sucht,** *f.* drunkenness, dipsomania. **-süchtig,** *adj.* given to drink(ing), dipsomaniac.

Trupp, *m.* (-s, -s & *Austr. dial.* -e) troop, band; flock, drove, herd; section, party, group; squad, detail (*Mil.*). **-e,** *f.* (-en) unit (*Mil.*); troupe, company (*of actors*); (*pl.*) the troops, the army, military forces, soldiers; *–en zusammenziehen*, mass troops. **–enabteilung,** *f.* unit, detachment (*Mil.*). **–enansammlung,** *f.* concentration of forces, massing of troops. **–enaushebung,** *f.* levy of troops. **–enbetreuung,** *f.* troops' welfare. **–enbewegung,** *f.* troop movements *or* manœuvres. **–eneinteilung,** *f.* disposition of forces (*Mil.*). **–enfahrzeug,** *n.* troop carrier. **–enführer,** *m.* commander. **–enführung,** *f.* leadership (*Mil.*). **–engattung,** *f.* arm of the service. **–enkörper,** *m.* corps (*Mil.*). **–ennachschub,** *m.* reinforcements. **–enschau,** *f.* military review, parade. **–enteil,** *m.* body of troops; unit; arm of the service; *vom –enteil zurückbleiben*, straggle. **–enübung,** *f.* manœuvres, field exercise. **–enübungsplatz,** *m.* training area. **–enverband,** *m.* formation, unit, task force. **–enverbandplatz,** *m.* advanced dressing-station (*Mil.*). **–enverschiebung,** *f.* change in disposition of troops. **–führer,** *m.* section leader. **–verband,** *m.* unit (*Mil.*). **–weise,** *adv.* in troops, in bands.

Trut–hahn, *m.* turkey(-cock). **–henne,** *f.* **–huhn,** *n.* turkey-hen. **–hühner,** *n.pl.* turkeys (*Meleagris*) (*Orn.*).

Trutschel, *f.* (-n) (*dial.*) buxom wench *or* lass; fat woman.

Trutz, *m.* (*archaic*) defiance; offensive; *zu Schutz und –*, offensively and defensively. **–bündnis,** *n.* offensive alliance. **–en,** *v.a.*, **–ig,** *adj.*, *see* **trotzen, trotzig.** **–waffen,** *f.pl.* weapons for attack.

Tschako, *m.* (-s, -s) shako.

Tschapka, *f.* (*pl.* -s) lancer's helmet.

Tub–a, *f.* (-en) tuba (*Mus.*); Eustachian *or* Fallopian tube (*Anat.*). **–e,** *f.* tube (*paint, tooth-paste, etc.*), *see also* **–a** (*Anat.*).

Tuber–kel, *m.* (-s, –) & *f.* tubercle. **–kulös,** *adj.* tubercular, tuberculous. **–kulose,** *f.* tuberculosis.

Tuch, *n.* 1. (-(e)s, -e) cloth, fabric, stuff, material. 2. (-es, ¨er) kerchief, shawl, scarf; *das bunte –*, soldiers, the military; *die Herren von zweierlei –*, the officers. **–arten,** *f.pl.* cloths. **–en,** *adj.* cloth, fabric. **–fühlung,** *f.* shoulder to shoulder, (*fig.*) close touch *or* contact. **–halle,** *f.* drapers' hall. **–händler,** *m.* draper. **–lager,** *n.* cloth-warehouse. **–nadel,** *f.* shawl-pin, breast-pin, brooch. **–rahmen,** *m.* tenter. **–rauhmaschine,** *f.* cloth-dressing machine. **–rest,** *m.* remnant (*of cloth*). **–schrot,** *n.*, **–streifen,** *m.* list (*of cloth*). **–walker,** *m.* fuller. **–waren,** *f.pl.* drapery. **–zeichen,** *n.* ground- *or* strip-panel, ground-signal (*for aeroplanes, Mil.*).

tüchtig, *adj.* fit, able, capable, qualified; sound, strong, hearty, good, excellent, thorough; clever, skilful, proficient, efficient; *– sein in einer S.*, be good at a th.; *er wurde – geneckt*, he was thoroughly teased; *er wurde – durchgeprügelt*, he got a sound thrashing; *– essen*, eat heartily. **–keit,** *f.* ability, fitness; solidity, soundness, excellence; proficiency, efficiency.

Tuck, *m.* (-(e)s, ¨e) (*dial.*) spiteful trick. **–tuck,** *int.* cluck, chuck (*of hen*).

Tück–e, *f.* (-en) prank, trick; malice, malignity, spite, knavery. **–isch,** *adj.* malicious, spiteful; artful, insidious; *–ische Krankheit*, malignant disease; *–ischer Hund*, vicious dog. (*hum.*) **–ebold,** *m.* mischievous imp. **–schen,** *v.n.* (*dial.*) be aggrieved.

Tuder, Tüder, *m.* (-s, –) tether, hobble.

Tuerei, *f.* humbug, make-believe, lip-service, dissimulation, dissembling.

Tuff, *m.* (-s, -e) tufa, tuff; volcanic rock. **–kalk,** *m.*, **–stein,** *m.* tufaceous *or* volcanic limestone.

Tüffel, *m.* (*dial.*) slipper.

Tüfte, *f.* (-n) (*dial.*) potato.

Tüft–elei, *f.* (-en) hair-splitting, subtlety. **–(e)ler,** *m.* punctilious person. **–(e)lig,** *adj.* very fussy, pernickety. **–eln,** *v.a.* split hairs, draw overnice distinctions; go in for subtleties.

Tugend, *f.* (-en) virtue; female virtue, chastity, purity; *aus der Not eine – machen*, make a virtue of necessity; *arme – ist besser als reiche Schande*, virtuous poverty is better than shameful riches; (*Prov.*) *Jugend hat keine –*, boys will be boys. **–bild,** *n.* model of virtue. (*iron.*) **–bold,** *m.* one of the elect. **–haft,** *adj.* virtuous. **–haftigkeit,** *f.* respectability, goodness, righteousness, rectitude. **–held,** *m.* paragon of virtue. **–lehre,** *f.* moral philosophy, morals, ethics. **–pfad,** *m.* path of virtue. **–richter,** *m.* moralist, censor. **–sam,** *adj.* virtuous, chaste. **–spiegel,** *m.*, *see* **–bild.**

Tukan, *m.* (-s, -e) toucan (*Rhamphastidae*) (*Orn.*).

tulich, *adj.* (*archaic*), *see* **tunlich.**

Tulipane, *f.* (-n) (*archaic*), *see* **Tulpe.**

Tüll, *m.* (-(e)s, -e) tulle; net. **–gardine,** *f.* net *or* lace curtain.

Tülle, *f.* (-n) spout, nozzle; socket.

Tulpe, *f.* (-n) tulip; beer-glass; name of several molluscs. **–nbaum,** *m.* tulip-tree (*Liriodendron tulipifera*) (*Bot.*). **–nzucht,** *f.* tulip-growing. **–nzwiebel,** *f.* tulip-bulb.

tumm–eln, 1. *v.a.* exercise (*horse, etc.*), keep a p. moving; wheel (*a horse*) round. 2. *v.r.* move, keep moving, bustle about, romp; hurry, make haste; (*rare*) *sich mit einem –eln*, wrestle, scuffle with s.o. **–elplatz,** *m.* exercise-ground; riding-school; playground. **–ler,** *m.* (glass) tumbler.

Tümmler, *m.* tumbler-pigeon; dolphin, porpoise.

Tümpel, *m.* (-s, –) pond, pool; puddle.

Tumult, *m.* (-(e)s, -e) uproar, tumult, hubbub, commotion, riot, disturbance. **–uant,** *m.* (-en) rioter. **–uarisch,** *adj.* riotous, tumultuous, noisy, excited. **–uieren,** *v.n.* (*aux.* h.) create a disturbance, be noisy.

tun, 1. *ir.v.a.* do, perform, execute; make; put; *Abbitte –*, apologize, make an apology; *einer S. Abbruch –*, injure *or* damage a th., do a th. harm; *eine Bitte –*, make a request; *einen Blick – (in)*, cast a glance (at); *Buße –*, do penance; *jemandem einen Dienst –*, do s.o. a service; *einen Eid –*, take an oath; *dem Unfug Einhalt –*, put a stop to the mischief *or* nonsense; *Einspruch –*, protest; *einer S. Eintrag –*, affect a th. adversely, militate against a th.; *einer S. Erwähnung –*, make mention of *or* mention a th.; *einen Fall –*, have a fall, fall; *einen Fehltritt –*, commit a faux-pas *or* (*coll.*) a bloomer, (*coll.*) put one's foot in it; *eine Frage –*, ask a question; *einen Gang –*, take a walk; *ein Gebet –*, offer up a prayer; *Genüge –*, give satisfaction, satisfy; *in den Bann –*, excommunicate; *in die Schule –*, put *or* send to school; *Salz in die Suppe –*, put salt in the soup; *das können Sie – und auch lassen*, you can do that or not as you please; *mein möglichstes –*, do all I can, do whatever is in my power; *tue ihm nichts!* do not hurt him! *er tut nichts*, he does nothing, he is idle; he does no harm; it does not bite (*of a dog*); *das tut nichts zur S.*, that is not to the purpose, that does not advance matters *or* alter things, that is of no significance; *es tut not*, there is need; *einen Schluck –*, take a drink *or* (*sl.*) a swig; *einen Schritt –*, take a step; *seine Schuldigkeit –*, do one's duty, repay one's obligations; *das Seinige –*, play one's part, (*coll.*) do one's bit; *einen Spruch –*, pronounce sentence; *ein Übriges –*, do more than necessary; *einem Unrecht –*, wrong a p., do a p. wrong; *von sich –*, put away; *was habe ich dir getan?* what harm have I done you? *etwas hat seine Wirkung getan*, s.th. has had the effect; *das hat Wunder getan*, that has worked miracles; *einem etwas zuleide* (*or poet. ein Leides*) *–*, hurt, harm *or* injure a p.; *des Guten zu viel –*, go too far, overdo a th. 2. *v.n.* (*aux.* h.) act, do; pretend, affect; *– Sie, als ob Sie zu Hause wären*, make yourself at home; *ich habe zu –*, I am busy; *es zu – haben mit einer S.*, deal with a th., have to do with a th.; (*archaic*) *einem etwas kund und zu wissen –*, give a p. notice, inform a p. of s.th.; *es tut mir leid*, I am sorry, I regret; *sich* (*Dat.*) *etwas zu – machen*, busy o.s., find s.th. to do; *es mit der Angst zu – bekommen*, be overcome with fear; *jetzt haben nur wir beide mit einander zu –*, now it rests with you and me; *es ist damit nicht getan*, the matter does not end there, that does not settle it; *Sie haben recht getan*, you did well *or* right; *das will getan sein*, that wants doing; *er tut nur so*, he only pretends; *er tat (so) als ob er uns nicht sähe*, he pretended not to see us; *spröde –*, play the prude; *es ist mir sehr darum zu –*, I attach great importance to it; *es ist mir nur darum zu –*, my only concern is, I am only concerned about; *es ist mir um mein Geld zu –*, I am anxious about my money; *alle Hände voll zu – haben*, have one's hands full; *Sie täten besser zu gehen*, you had better go; (*coll.*) (*pres.* & *imperf.* (*often archaic* tät) *with inf. instead of simple verb*) *rechnen tue ich gut*, I am good at sums; *lesen tat* (or *tät*) *er das nicht*, he did not read it; (*Poet.*) *die Augen täten ihm sinken*, he lowered his eyes. 3. *v.r.* (*coll.*) *sich dicke – mit etwas*, brag *or* boast of, give o.s. airs about a th.; *sich gütlich –*, eat heartily, enjoy *or* relish one's food, (*coll.*) do o.s. well; (*coll.*) *das tut sich leicht*, that's easy; *sich – lassen*, be practicable, feasible; *das läßt sich –*, that can be done *or* is possible; (*coll.*) *man tut sich leicht daran*, that won't give much trouble; *er tut sich schwer damit*, he meets with great difficulties. 4. *n.* doings, proceeding(s); conduct; dealings, action; *sein – und Lassen* or *– und Treiben*, his dealings, actions *or* conduct; *Sagen und – ist zweierlei*, promise and performance are two different things. **–ichtgut**, *m.* (-(e)s, –) ne'er-do-well, good-for-nothing. **–lich**, *adj.* feasible, practicable, possible, advisable, expedient, convenient. **–lichkeit**, *f.* feasibility, practicability, expediency, convenience. **–lichst**, *adv.* as far as possible *or* practicable; *–lichst kurz*, as short *or* brief as possible; (*C.L. archaic*) *in –lichster Bälde*, at the earliest opportunity.

Tünch–e, *f.* lime-wash, whitewash, distemper; (*fig.*) varnish, veneer. **–en**, *v.a.* whitewash, distemper. **–farbe**, *f.* distemper. **–pinsel**, *m.* white-wash brush.

Tunke, *f.* (-n) sauce, gravy. **–n**, *v.a.* dip, soak, steep; sop (*bread, etc.*).

Tunnel, *m.* (-s, -s & *Austr. dial.* –) tunnel; subway. **–bau**, *m.* tunnelling. **–ieren**, *v.a.* & *n.* (*aux.* h.) tunnel, excavate.

Tupf, *m.* (-es, -e) (*Austr. dial.*), **–en**, 1. *m.* (-ens, -en) dot, spot. 2. *v.a.* dab. **–er**, *m.* tampon, swab (*Surg.*).

Tüpf–el, *m.* & *Austr. dial. n.* (-s, –) dot, spot, speck, point, pit; iota, jot, tittle; *etwas bis aufs –elchen wissen*, know the minutest details of a th. **–(e)lig**, *adj.* dotted, spotted, speckled. **–eln**, *v.a.* dot, spot, speckle, mottle, stipple. **–elfarn**, *m.* polypodium (*Bot.*). **–elgewebe** *n.* pitted tissue.

Tür(–e), *f.* (-n) door; *offene –en einrennen*, assert the obvious, carry coals to Newcastle; *mit der – ins Haus fallen*, blurt out; *die – fiel ins Schloß*, the door slammed; *vor seiner eigenen – kehren*, mind one's own business; *einen vor die – setzen*, show a p. the door, turn a p. out; (*fig.*) *vor der – stehen*, be imminent *or* near at hand; *einem die – vor der Nase zuschlagen*, slam the door in a p.'s face; *zwei –en von hier*, the next door but one; *zwischen – und Angel*, on the point of leaving; in a dilemma. **–angel**, *f.* & *m.* hinge of a door. **–einfassung**, *f.* door-frame. **–falle**, *f.* (*Swiss dial.*), *see* **–griff**. **–feld**, *n., see* **–füllung**. **–flügel**, *m.* leaf *or* wing of a door. **–füllung**, *f.* door-panel. **–giebel**, *m.* pediment (*of a door*). **–griff**, *m.* door-handle. **–hüter**, *m.* door-keeper, porter; pylorus (*Anat.*). **–klinke**, *f.* latch, door-handle. **–klopfer**, *m.* (door-)knocker. **–pfosten**, *m.* door-post. **–rahmen**, *m.* door-frame. **–riegel**, *m.* bolt. **–schild**, *n.* door-plate, brass plate. **–schließer**, *m.* door-closing spring; door-keeper. **–schwelle**, *f.* threshold. **–steher**, *m. see* **–hüter**; usher (*Law*). **–stock**, *m.* door-jamb. **–sturz**, *m.* lintel.

Turbine, *f.* (-n) turbine. **–nantrieb**, *m.* turbine-drive. **–nleitschaufel**, *f.* guide-blade.

Türkis, *m.* (-es, -e) turquoise. **–blau**, *adj.* turquoise (blue).

Turm, *m.* (-(e)s, ⸚e) tower, spire, steeple, belfry; turret (*of tank*), conning tower (*of submarine*); (*archaic*) dungeon, prison; rook, castle (*Chess*). **–artig**, *adj.* tower-like, towering; turreted. **–bau**, *m.* building of a tower; tower-like structure. **–fahne**, *f.* vane. **–falk(e)**, *m.* kestrel (*Falco tinnunculus*) (*Orn.*). **–geschütz**, *n.* turret-gun. **–hoch**, 1. *adj.* towering, very high. 2. *adv.* beyond, far above. **–höhe**, *f.* height of a tower. **–lafette**, *f.* turret-mounting. **–luke**, *f.* louvre-window, turret hatch (*Naut.*). **–schwalbe**, *f.* swift (*Micropus apus*) (*Orn.*). **–spitze**, *f.* spire. **–springen**, *n.* high diving. **–uhr**, *f.* tower-clock, church-clock. **–verließ**, *n.* dungeon, keep. **–wächter**, *m.* **–wart**, *m., see* **Türmer**. **–wagen**, *m.* tramways-department servicing vehicle. **–zinne**, *f.* battlement(s) of a tower.

Turmalin, *m.* (-s, -e) tourmaline (*Min.*).

türm–en, 1. *v.a.* pile up. 2. *v.r.* (*aux.* h.) be piled high, tower up, rise high. 3. *v.n.* (*sl.*) clear off, do a bunk, vamose. **–er**, *m.* (-s, –) watchman, look-out.

Turn, *m.* (*archaic*) *for* **Turm**.

Turnei, *m.* (*archaic*), *see* **Turnier**.

turn–en, 1. *v.n.* (*aux.* h.) do gymnastics *or* drill; (*coll.*) wriggle out of a difficulty, wangle through. 2. *n.* gymnastics, drill, physical training (P.T.). **–anzug**, *m.* gym-dress *or* clothes. **–er**, *m.* gymnast. **–erei**, *f.* gymnastics. **–erisch**, *adj.* gymnastic. **–erschaft**, *f.* group *or* squad of gymnasts, athletic club. **–fest**, *n.* gymnastic display. **–gerät**, *n.* gymnastic apparatus. **–halle**, *f.* gymnasium. **–hose**, *f.* P.T. shorts. **–ier**, *n.* (-s, -e) tournament, contest. **–ieren**, *v.n.* (*aux.* h.) hold a tournament *or* contest; tilt, joust. **–ierbahn**, *f.*, **–ierplatz**, *m.* the lists. **–ierrichter**, *m.* marshal of the lists. **–ierschranken**, *f.pl.*, *see* **–ierbahn**. **–ierspiel**, *n.* tournament. **–lehrer**, *m.* gym(nastic) instructor. **–riege**, *f.*, *see* **–erschaft**. **–schuh**, *m.* gym(nasium) shoe, pump. **–spiele**, *n.pl.* indoor games. **–übung**, *f.* gymnastic exercise. **–unterricht**, *m.* P.T. lesson. **–üre**, *f.* (-n) bustle (*of dress*); deportment. **–us**, *m.* (-us, -usse) turn, cycle, rotation, sequence. **–vater**, *m.* the Old Man of gymnastics (Ludwig Jahn). **–verein**, *m.* gymnastic *or* athletic club. **–wart**, *m.* squad leader, supervisor (*at gymnastics*). **–wesen**, *n.* gymnastics.

Turteltaube, *f.* (-n) turtle-dove (*Streptopelia turtur*) (*Orn.*).

Tusch, *m.* (-(e)s, -e) fanfare, flourish of trumpets; (*Stud. sl.*) challenge, affront. **–e**, *f.* (-en) water-colour; (waterproof) drawing-ink; *schwarze* or *chinesische –*, Indian ink. **–eln**, *see under* **tusch**. **–en**, *v.a.* draw in Indian ink. colour-wash; *see also under* **tusch**. **–farbe**, *f.* watercolour; waterproof ink. **–ieren**, *v.a.* (*archaic*) affront, insult, challenge. **–kasten**, *m.* watercolour paint-box. **–zeichnung**, *f.* watercolour drawing; sketch in Indian ink.

tusch, *int.* hush! **–eln**, *v.n.* mutter, whisper. **–en**, *v.a.* quell, suppress, silence, smother (*revolt, etc.*); hush, (*coll.*) shush.

Tütchen–dreher, *m.*, **–krämer**, *m.* huckster.

Tut–e, *f.* (-en) (*dial.*) *see* **Tüte**; *see* **–horn**. **–en**, *v.a.* blow (a horn), (*coll.*) toot, honk. **–horn**, *n.* watch-man's horn.

Tüte, *f.* (-n) paper bag; (*coll.*) (ice-cream) cone; candle extinguisher; (*coll.*) *er muß –n kleben*, he is doing time; (*coll.*) *das kommt nicht in die –!* not on your life!

Tutel, *f.* (-en) guardianship.

Tütte, **(Tutte)**, *f.* (*dial.*) nipple, teat, pap, dug; (*sl.*) tit. **–lchen**, *n.* dot; tittle, jot.

Twiete, *f.* (*dial.*) narrow side-street, alley.

Twing, *m.*, **Twinger**, *m.* (*dial.*), *see* **Zwing, Zwinger**.

Typ, *m.* (-s, -e(n)) type, standard, model, prototype. **–e**, *f.* (-en) type (*for printing*); (*coll.*) crank, eccentric, queer fish, (queer) card. **–endruck**, *m.* type-printing. **–enhaft**, *adj.*, *see* **–isch**. **–enhebel**, *m.* type-bar (*typewriter*). **–enmetall**, *n.* type-metal. **–enmuster**, *n.* standard sample. **–isch**, *adj.* typical; *das –ische*, the typical character. **–isieren**, *v.a.* typify; standardize. **–ograph**, *m.* typographer. **–ographisch**, *adj.* typographic. **–us**, *m.* (–, -en) *see* **–**.

typh–ös, *adj.* typhoid. **–us**, *m.* (–) typhoid (fever). **–uskranke(r)**, *m.* typhoid patient.

Tyrann, *m.* (-en, -en) tyrant, despot. **–ei**, *f.* tyranny, despotism. **–enmord**, *m.* tyrannicide. **–isch**, *adj.* tyrannical, despotic, power-loving. **–isieren**, *v.a.* tyrannize over, oppress, enslave.

U

U, u, *n.* U, u; *einem ein X für ein U machen*, deceive, humbug, cheat *or* dupe a p., (*coll.*) take a p. in, pull a p.'s leg; *for abbreviations see end of German-English Vocabulary.*
U-bahn, *see* **Untergrundbahn.**
übel, 1. *adj. & adv.* (übler, üble, übles; *comp.* übler) evil, bad, wrong; sick, ill; – *angebracht*, misplaced, inappropriate; – *ankommen*, catch a Tartar; *bei einem – angeschrieben sein*, be in s.o.'s bad books; *eine S. – aufnehmen*, take a th. amiss *or* in bad part; – *auslegen*, misconstrue; *mir bekam es* –, I came off badly; *es wird ihm – bekommen*, he will have to suffer for that; – *daran sein*, be in a bad way; *Übles von einem denken*, think ill of a p., not have a good word to say for s.o., have a poor opinion of s.o.; – *deuten*, put a wrong construction on; *jemandem Übles gönnen*, wish s.o. ill; *einem – mitspielen* or *jemandem einen üblen Dienst erweisen*, do s.o. a bad turn, treat a p. badly *or* shabbily, (*coll.*) play a dirty trick on s.o.; *einen in üble Nachrede bringen*, slander a p., give a p. a bad name; *nicht* –, rather nice, not bad; *das wäre nicht* –, that is not a bad *or* is quite a good idea *or* plan; *nicht – Lust zu einer S. haben*, be inclined *or* have a good mind to do a th.; *in üblem Ruf stehen*, have a bad name, be in bad odour; *mir ist* or *wird* –, *es ist mir* –, I do not feel well, I feel sick; *auf einen – zu sprechen sein*, not have a good word to say of a p.; *es steht – mit ihm* or *um ihn*, his affairs are *or* he is in a bad way; *dabei kann einem – werden*, it is enough to make one sick, it is sickening; *wohl oder* –, willy-nilly, cost what it may, at all costs, in any case; *mir ist – zumute*, I am ill at ease, I feel uncomfortable. 2. *n.* (-s, –) evil; wound, injury; complaint, ailment, malady, disease; inconvenience, misfortune; (*B.*) *was darüber ist, das ist vom* –, whatsoever is more cometh of evil. **-befinden,** *n.* indisposition. **-beraten,** *adj.* ill-advised. **-berüchtigt,** *adj.* ill-famed. **-gelaunt,** *adj.* ill-humoured, cross, grumpy. **-gesinnt,** *adj.* evil-minded. **-keit,** *f.* sickness, nausea; (*fig.*) disgust; *-keit verursachen*, make one feel sick, turn the stomach. **-nehmen,** *v.a.* take amiss; *nehmen Sie es mir nicht – !* pardon me, no offence, I hope! **-nehm(er)isch,** *adj.* easily offended, touchy. **-riechend,** *adj.* fetid, foul, offensive, malodorous. **-stand,** *m.* disadvantage, drawback, nuisance, inconvenience, (*pl.*) abuses. **-tat,** *f.* misdeed, misdemeanour. **-täter,** *m.* wrongdoer, evil-doer, miscreant. **-tun,** *n.* wrong-doing. **-wollen,** 1. *v.a.*; *einem -wollen*, bear a grudge against a p., bear s.o. ill-will. 2. *n.* ill-will, malevolence, enmity. **-wollend,** *adj.* malevolent, ill-disposed, spiteful.
üb-en, 1. *v.a. & n.* exercise, drill, train; practise; use, exert; do military training; *Barmherzigkeit an einem -en*, show a p. mercy; *Betrug -en*, practise deceit; *Geduld -en (mit)*, have patience, be patient (with); *Gerechtigkeit -en*, exercise justice; *Gewalt -en*, use violence; *ein Handwerk -en*, pursue *or* carry on a trade; *Nachsicht -en*, show consideration; *Rache an einem -en*, take *or* wreak vengeance on a p. 2. *v.r.* (in *with Dat.*) practise, do exercise. *geübt*, *p.p. & adj.* skilled, skilful, practised, experienced, well versed; *eine im Schreiben wohl geübte Hand haben*, be skilled in writing, be a clever writer. **-lich,** *adj.* usual, customary, common, in use; *das Wort ist nicht mehr -lich*, the word has gone out of use *or* is obsolete. **-lichkeit,** *f.* usage; customariness. **-ung,** *f.* exercising, exercise, practice, use; dexterity; training (*Mil.*); (*Prov.*) *-ung macht den Meister*, practice makes perfect; *aus der -ung kommen*, get out of practice; *sich in der -ung erhalten*, keep in training; *diese Sitte ist schon lange außer -ung*, this custom has long fallen into disuse; *von der -ung abweichen*, deviate from the usual practice. **-ungsflug,** *m.* practice flight. **-ungslager,** *n.* practice *or* training-camp. **-ungsmarsch,** *m.* route-march. **-ungsmunition,** *f.* blank *or* practice ammunition. **-ungsplatz,** *m.* drill-ground. **-ungsstück,** *n.* exercise.

über, 1. *prep.* (*a*) *with Dat. when implying rest or limited motion*; (*b*) *with Acc. when implying transfer or motion across, to, past or over, and in figurative uses without reference to motion*; over, above, on top of, higher than, superior to, more than; in the process of, during, while; across, beyond, on the other side of; upon, on, about, concerning, with regard to; *einen – die Achsel ansehen*, look askance at s.o., (*coll.*) look down one's nose at s.o.; *das geht – alles*, that beats everything; *das geht mir – alles andere*, I prefer that to everything else; *die Wahrheit – alles lieben*, love truth more than anything; *ein Mal – das andere*, time after time, time and again, again and again; – *der Arbeit einschlafen*, fall asleep over one's work; – *der Arbeit sein*, be at work; – *alle Begriffe*, beyond all conception; – *alle Berge sein*, be gone, be far away; – *Berg und Tal*, up hill and down dale; – *Bord werfen*, jettison; *Briefe – Briefe*, letter after letter, one letter after another; – *den Büchern hocken*, pore over one's books; *eins – den Durst trinken*, drink one over the eight; – *etwas entrüstet sein*, be indignant about a th.; – *sich ergehen lassen*, bear, endure, tolerate, (*coll.*) put up with, swallow; – *alles Erwarten glücklich*, happy beyond all expectation; *sich – eine S. freuen*, rejoice at *or* over s.th.; – *Gebühr*, more than was due *or* right; – *die Straße gehen*, cross the street; *Zufriedenheit geht – Reichtum*, contentment is better than riches; *es – sich gewinnen*, bring o.s. to, find it in one's heart to; *einen – den Haufen rennen*, knock s.o. over, run s.o. down; – *das Knie hinab reichen*, reach below the knee; – *einen herfallen*, take a p. by surprise, attack a p. without warning, fall (up)on a p. unawares; *sich – etwas hermachen*, fall upon a th., (*coll.*) make a dive at a th.; *Herr – etwas sein*, have s.th. under (one's) control, have mastery over s.th.; *Herr – etwas werden*, master a th., get a th. under (one's) control; – *ein Volk herrschen*, rule over a people; *ich bin – die Neugierde hinaus*, I am past *or* above curiosity; – *die Vierzig(e) hinaus sein*, have passed *or* be over forty; *er ist – etwas hinausgewachsen*, he has grown too big for his boots; *sich – etwas hinwegsetzen*, not allow o.s. to be influenced by a th., rise above a th.; – *Ungerechtigkeit klagen*, complain of injustice; *Hals – Kopf*, head over heels; *einem – den Kopf gewachsen sein*, be head and shoulders above s.o. (*also fig.*); – *die Kräfte gehen*, be beyond one's strength; – *Kreuz binden*, cross and tie, tie crosswise *or* crossed; – *kurz oder lang*, sooner or later; – *Leichen gehen*, ride rough-shod over; *alles – einen Leisten schlagen*, treat everything the same; – *alles Lob*, beyond praise; *sich – einen lustig machen*, make fun of a p.; – *Macht verfügen* or *gebieten*, have power in one's hands; *das geht – das Maß des Erlaubten*, that goes beyond what is permissible, that goes too far; – *alle Maßen schön*, incomparably beautiful; *man vergaß den Dichter – dem Menschen*, one forgot the poet in the man; *von Aachen – Köln nach Berlin*, from Aix-la-Chapelle via Cologne to Berlin; *es geht nichts – ein Glas Rheinwein*, there is nothing like a glass of hock; *bis – die Ohren in Schulden*, up to one's ears in debt; *bis – den Ohren verliebt*, head over heels in love; – *den Parteien stehen*, be above party, be impartial; *es lief ihm eiskalt – den Rücken*, a cold shudder ran down his back; – *die Schnur hauen*, see – *die Stränge*; *den Sommer* –, the whole summer; *das geht – den Spaß*, that is beyond a joke; – *Stock und Stein*, through thick and thin; – *die Stränge schlagen*, kick over the traces; *Bier – die Straße verkaufen*, sell beer outdoor; *der Übergang – die Donau*, the crossing of the Danube; *Tränen flossen ihr – die Wangen*, tears trickled down her cheeks. 2. (*elliptically*) *O, – den Narren !* oh! what a fool! *Fluch – dich !* a curse upon you! *O, – die Jugend!* oh, youth! youth! 3. *with expressions of time or quantity*; *heute – acht Tage*, this day week; *heute –s Jahr*, a year from today; *es ist noch – ein Meter davon vorrätig*, there is still more than a metre in stock; – *mittag*, during the lunch-hour; – *Nacht*, all night, during the night; – *dem Essen*, during the meal, while eating; – *100 Studenten*, more than 100 students. 4. *adv.* over, above, too much, in excess; – *und* –, through and through, out and out, completely, thoroughly, entirely; *die ganze Zeit* –, all along; *Gewehr –!* shoulder arms! (*Mil.*); *see also* **überhaben** *and* **übersein;** *as a prefix to nouns and adjs.*; over-, super-, supra-, per-, hyper-; *see the alphabetical list following.* 4. *verb prefix. Intransitive verbs compounded with* über *are generally insep.; most transitive verbs may be both sep. & insep.; when sep.* über *carries the accent and its meaning is more or less literal, when insep. and unstressed the meaning is more or less figurative. See the alphabetical list following.*

überall, 1. *adv.* everywhere; all over, throughout; at all times. **–her,** *adv.*; *von –her,* from all sides. **–hin,** *adv.* everywhere, in every direction.

überaltert, *p.p. & adj.* grown too old, superannuated.

Überangebot, *n.* (-(e)s, -e) excessive supply.

überanstreng–en, *v.a. & r.* (*insep.*) (*p.p.* überanstrengt) overwork, over-exert, strain. **–ung,** *f.* over-exertion, overstrain.

überantworten, *v.a.* (*insep.*) deliver up, surrender, consign.

überarbeit–en, 1. *v.n.* (*aux* .h.) (*sep.*) work overtime. 2. *v.a.* revise, go over, retouch, touch up. 3. *v.r.* (*insep.*) overwork, work too hard. **–ung,** *f.* revision, retouching, touching up; overwork, exhaustion.

überaus, *adv.* exceedingly, extremely, excessively.

Überbau, *m.* (-(e)s, -e & -ten) superstructure; projecting part. **–en,** 1. *v.a.* (*insep.*) build over *or* on top of, raise above (*s.th.*). 2. *v.a. & n.* (*sep.*) (*aux.* h.) build a projection (*over another building*); build above; build higher. **–ung,** *f.* raising (*a structure*); addition of another story.

Überbein, *n.* (-s, -e) exostosis (*Surg.*); ganglion (*in the sinews*); node; bone-spavin (*Vet.*).

überbelicht–en, *v.a.* (*sep.*) over-expose (*Phot.*). **–ung,** *f.* over-exposure (*Phot.*).

überbiegen, 1. *ir.v.a.* (*insep.*) bend too much. 2. *v.a. & r.* (*insep.*) bend over.

überbieten, 1. *ir.v.a.* (*insep.*) outbid; outdo, excel, surpass; *den Plan* –, be ahead of schedule; *den Rekord* –, break the record. 2. *v.r.*; *sie – sich in Höflichkeit,* they vie with each other in civilities.

überbild–en, *v.a.* (*insep.*) over-educate, over-refine. **–ung,** *f.* over-refinement.

überbleib–en, *ir.v.n.* (*aux.* s.) (*sep. p.p.* übergeblieben) remain (over), be left over; (*insep.*) (*only in p.p.*) *überblieben,* surviving. **–sel,** *n.* remainder, remains, relic, residue; vestige, remnant, (*pl.*) ruins, debris, waste.

Überblick, *m.* survey, view, prospect; general view, conspectus, review, synopsis, summary (*über with Acc.*, of). **–en,** *v.a.* (*insep.*) glance over, survey, take in at a glance.

Überbliebene(r), *m.* survivor (*see* **überbleiben**).

überborden, *v.n.* (*Swiss dial.*) overflow (*the banks*).

Überbrettl, *n.* (-s, –) cabaret, variety theatre.

überbring–en, 1. *ir.v.a.* (*insep.*) (*einem etwas*) bring, deliver, convey, carry. 2. *n.* delivery. **–er,** *m.* bearer. **–ung,** *f.* delivery, transmission, conveyance.

überbrück–en, *v.a.* (*insep.*) bridge, span; (*fig.*) bridge over, reconcile, settle (*a difference*). **–ung,** *f.* spanning; settlement; jumper (*Elec.*). **–ungskredit,** *m.* short-term *or* emergency loan.

überbürd–en, *v.a.* (*insep.*) overload, overburden. **–ung,** *f.* overburdening, excessive work.

überchlorsauer, *adj.* perchlorate of.

überdachen, *v.a.* (*insep.*) roof (over).

Überdampf, *m.* surplus *or* excess steam.

überdauern, *v.a.* (*insep.*) outlast, outlive, survive.

überdeck–en, *v.a.* (*sep.*) stretch over, spread out over; (*insep.*) cover up, veil, shroud; make a ceiling over; overlap. **–ung,** *f.* covering, cover, shelter; overlap.

überdem, *adv.* besides, moreover.

überdenken, *ir.v.a.* (*insep.*) think over, reflect *or* meditate on, consider.

überdies, *adv.* besides, moreover.

überdrehen, *v.a.* (*insep.*) overwind (*a watch*).

Überdruck, *m.* (-(e)s, -e) overprint; surcharge (*postage stamps*); excess pressure; transfer, transfer printing. **–anzug,** *m.* high-pressure diving suit. **–en,** *v.a.* (*insep.*) overprint. **–höhenkabine,** *f.* pressurized cabin (*Av.*).

Über–druß, *m.* boredom, ennui; satiety, disgust; *zum –druß werden,* become boring *or* a bore; *Überfluß bringt –druß,* abundance begets indifference. **–drüssig,** *adj.* (*Acc. or Gen.*) sick, tired *or* weary of; satiated, disgusted *or* bored with.

übereck, *adv.* (*dial.*) across, diagonally.

Übereifer, *m.* over-great zeal.

übereign–en, *v.a.* (*insep.*) (*einem etwas*) transfer, assign, convey. **–ung,** *f.* assignment, conveyance (*Law.*).

Übereil–e, *f.*, *see* **–ung. –en** (*insep.*) 1. *v.a.*; hurry (too much), press forward; precipitate (*a decision, etc.*), scamp (*work*); *die Nacht –te uns,* night overtook us. 2. *v.r.* be in too much of *or* too great a hurry, be precipitate, act rashly *or* inconsiderately. **–t,** *p.p. & adj.* premature, rash, over-hasty, unguarded, thoughtless. **–ung,** *f.* precipitancy, hastiness, rashness; overhaste, heedlessness.

überein, *adv.* in agreement, accord *or* accordance; conformably, alike. **–ander,** *adv.* one upon another, superimposed. **–andergreifen,** *v.n.* overlap. **–anderlagern,** *v.a.* superimpose. **–anderlegen,** *v.a.* lay one upon another, pile up. **–anderschlagen,** 1. *v.a.*; *die Beine –anderschlagen,* cross one's legs. 2. *v.n.*, *see* **–andergreifen. –anderschweißung,** *f.* lap-weld. **–andersetzung,** *f.* superposition. **–anderstehen,** *v.n.*, **–andertreffen,** *v.n.*, *see* **–andergreifen. –kommen,** 1. *ir.v.n.* (*aux.* s.) come to an agreement *or* terms, reach an agreement; *über eine S. –kommen,* agree on *or* about a th. 2. *n.*, **–kunft,** *f.* agreement, arrangement, settlement; contract, pact, treaty; *ein –kommen treffen,* make *or* reach an agreement; *laut –kunft mit,* by agreement with, as arranged with; *gegenseitige –kunft,* mutual consent; *stillschweigende –kunft, stillschweigendes –kommen,* tacit agreement. **–stimmen,** *v.n.* (*aux.* h.) agree, concur, be in agreement; (*mit*) accord, harmonize (with), coincide, correspond (to); *ich stimme damit* –, I agree to that. **–stimmend,** 1. *pr.p. & adj.* in accordance, agreeing, harmonious; (*fig.*) corresponding, conformable, congruous. 2. *adv.* universally. **–stimmung,** *f.* agreement, conformity, accord, concord, harmony, unison, correspondence, synchronization. **–treffen,** *ir.v.n.* (*aux.* s.) (*mit etwas*) agree (with a th.).

übereisen, *v.a.* (*insep.*) cover with ice *or* hoarfrost. *übereist, p.p. & adj.* covered with ice, frozen over.

überempfindlich, *adj.* hypersensitive.

überessen, 1. *ir.v.r.* (*insep.*) overeat. 2. *v.a.* (*sep.*); *sich* (*Dat.*) *etwas* –, have a surfeit of a th.

überfahr–en, 1. *ir.v.n.* (*sep.*) (*aux.* s.) pass over, cross. 2. *v.a.* (*insep.*) traverse, pass over, stroke, smear; run over (*a person*); pass, overrun (*a certain point*); (*sep.*) convey over, ferry across. **–t,** *f.* passage, crossing (*by ship*). **–tsgeld,** *n.* passage-money, fare; ferry-charges.

Überfall, *m.* surprise attack, raid; inroad, invasion; overfall, weir. **–en,** 1. *ir.v.a.* (*insep.*) fall upon suddenly, attack, surprise; invade; overtake (*as nightfall, illness, etc.*); *sie wurden vom Regen überfallen,* they were caught in the rain; *der Schlaf überfiel mich,* sleep stole upon me; *Schrecken überfiel uns,* we were seized with terror. 2. *imp.* (*fig.*) have suddenly the feeling that . . ., imagine; *plötzlich überfiel es ihn,* suddenly he fancied, it came to him suddenly. 3. *v.n.* (*sep.*) (*aux.* s.) fall over (*to the other side*). **–kommando,** *n.* raiding party, flying squad. **–krieg,** *m.* undeclared war. **–rohr,** *n.* overflow pipe.

überfällig, *adj.* overdue.

überfein, *adj.* over-refined, superfine.

überfliegen, 1. *ir.v.n.* (*sep.*) (*aux.* s.) fly over (*to the other side*). 2. *v.a.* (*insep.*) fly over, pass swiftly across; glance quickly over, skim through; *den Kanal* –, fly (over) the Channel; *ihr Antlitz überflog ein roter Schein,* the colour mounted to her face.

überfließen, 1. *ir.v.n.* (*sep.*) (*aux.* s.) flow over, overflow; be overflowing (*vor Freude, usw.*, with joy, etc.). 2. *v.a.* (*insep.*) flow over, inundate.

überflügeln, *v.a.* (*insep.*) outflank (*Mil.*); surpass, outstrip, outdo.

Über-fluß, *m.* superabundance, profusion, plenty, abundance, surplus, superfluity, exuberance; *-fluß haben an* or *in einer S.*, have plenty of a th., abound in a th.; *zum -fluß*, unnecessarily, needlessly; (*Prov.*) *-fluß bringt Überdruß*, abundance begets indifference. **-flüssig,** *adj.* superfluous, unnecessary, in excess, surplus, left over; (*B.*) running over; *-flüssig machen*, render unnecessary *or* superfluous, supersede.
überflut-en, 1. *v.n.* (*sep.*) (*aux.* s.) overflow. 2. *v.a.* (*insep.*) inundate, flood, swamp. **-et,** *adj.* awash (*Naut.*). **-ung,** *f.* flooding, inundation, overflow.
überforder-n, *v.a.* & *n.* (*insep.*) (*aux.* h.) demand too much, overcharge. **-ung,** *f.* exorbitant demand, excessive charge, overcharge.
Überfracht, *f.* overweight, overload; (charge for) excess luggage.
überfragen, *v.a.* & *n.* (*aux.* h.) (*insep.*) (*Swiss dial.*) overwhelm with questions.
überfremd-en, *v.a.* (*insep.*) overwhelm with foreigners *or* foreign influence. **-ung,** *f.* foreign influence *or* penetration, infiltration of foreigners *or* foreign goods.
Überfuhr, *f.* (*Austr. dial.*) ferry.
überführ-en, *ir.v.a.* (*sep.*) conduct across, transfer, transport, convey, ferry across; convert, bring over (*to an opinion*); convert, transform (*in with Acc.*, into) (*Chem.*); (*insep.*) convince; convict (*Gen.*, *of a crime, etc.*); transport (*a corpse*) in state. **-bar,** *adj.* transferable, convertible. **-ung,** *f.* conviction; transference, conversion; transport, conveying, transportation, ferrying, transfer; crossing, viaduct.
Überfüll-e, *f.* superabundance, excess, repletion, plethora; exuberance (*of spirits, etc.*). **-en,** *v.a.* (*insep.*) overfill, overload, surfeit, overstock, glut (*a market*); crowd, cram. (*C.L.*) **-t,** *p.p.* & *adj.* overstocked. **-ung,** *f.* overfilling, overloading, overcrowding; cramming, surfeiting, repletion; oversupply, (*C.L.*) glut.
überfüttern, *v.a.* (*insep.*) overfeed; *überfüttert, p.p.* & *adj.* gorged.
Übergabe, *f.* delivery, conveyance, transfer; handing over, surrender, capitulation.
Übergang, *m.* (-s, ⸚e) passage, crossing, level crossing (*Railw.*), foot-bridge, viaduct, ford; reorganization (*Mil.*), change of tactics; transition, changeover, conversion; desertion, going over (*to the enemy*); (*pl.*) shades, nuances, blending (*Paint.*, *Mus.*). **-sbestimmungen,** *f.pl.* provisional *or* temporary arrangements. **-sgebirge,** *n.* transition *or* secondary rocks (*Geol.*). **-spunkt,** *m.* crossing place, passage. **-sstadium,** *n.* transition stage. **-sstelle,** *f.* crossing place (*Mil.*). **-szeit,** *f.* transition period. **-szustand,** *m.* state of transition; temporary arrangement.
übergeben, 1. *ir.v.a.* (*sep.*); *einem eins -*, cane *or* beat a p., (*coll.*) give a p. one; (*insep.*) (*einem etwas*) deliver up (to), hand over (to); give up (to), remit; give in charge, leave *or* commit to; surrender; *dem Druck -*, have printed; *eigenhändig -*, deliver personally; *eine Eisenbahnlinie dem Verkehr -*, open a railway for traffic; *eine S. den Gerichten -*, bring a matter before the courts. 2. *v.r.* (*insep.*) vomit, be sick. 3. *n.* vomiting.
Übergebot, *n.* higher bid.
Übergebühr, *f.* surcharge, postage due.
übergeh-en, 1. *ir.v.n.* (*sep.*) (*aux.* s.) flow *or* run over, overflow; cross, go *or* pass over; desert; change *or* turn (*in*, into); change over (to), pass on, turn *or* proceed to; be transient; *die Augen gingen ihm über*, his eyes filled with tears; *in Fäulnis -en*, become rotten; *eine Farbe geht in eine andere über*, one colour merges into another; *der Druckfehler ist in alle folgenden Ausgaben übergegangen*, the misprint has been retained in all subsequent editions; *zur Gegenpartei -en*, change sides. 2. *v.a.* (*insep.*) skip, pass over, pass by, neglect, omit, overlook, ignore; run one's eye over, run *or* go over, revise, retouch; *mit Stillschweigen -en*, pass over in silence. 3. *v.r.* walk o.s. off one's feet. 4. *n.*, **-ung,** *f.* omission, neglect; passing over (*in silence*); pretermission (*Rhet.*).
übergenug, *adv.* more than enough, ample; *- haben*, have enough and to spare.
übergerollt, *adj.* convolute.
Übergewicht, *n.* overweight, excess weight; loss of balance, top-heaviness; predominance, preponderance, ascendancy, superiority; *das - bekommen*, get top-heavy; *das - behaupten*, have the upper hand, maintain one's superiority; *das - haben*, predominate; *diese Meinung gewann das -*, this view prevailed.
übergießen, *ir.v.a.* (*sep.*) pour over, spill; sprinkle, douche, irrigate, water (*flowers*); pour (*from one vessel into another*); (*insep.*) pour on *or* over (*a th.*); transfuse; *mit Licht -*, bathe in light; *mit Zucker -*, ice with sugar, glaze; *es übergoß ihn purpurrot*, he grew crimson.
überglasen, *v.a.* (*insep.*) glaze, ice (*cakes*).
überglücklich, *adj.* extremely happy, overjoyed.
übergolden, *v.a.* (*insep.*) gild (*also fig.*).
über-greifen, *ir.v.n.* (*sep.*) (*aux.* h.) overlap; shift, glide (*on a violin*); (*fig.*) spread (*auf*, to), encroach *or* infringe (upon). **-griff,** *m.* encroachment, infringement.
übergroß, *adj.* too large; huge, enormous, colossal.
Überguß, *m.* (-(ss)es, ⸚(ss)e) pouring over; crust, covering, icing (*on cakes*).
überhaben, *ir.v.a.* (*sep.*) have on (*over other things*); have remaining, have left over; (*coll.*) *eine S. -*, be weary *or* sick of a th.
Überhand, *f.* (*archaic*) the upper hand. **-nahme,** *f.* rapid growth *or* increase, prevalence. **-nehmen,** 1. *v.n.* gain ground, get the upper hand, become too powerful; prevail, spread, grow large, increase. 2. *n.* increase, spread, growth, prevalence.
Überhang, *m.* projection (*Arch.*); curtain, hangings, cover; cornice (*of snow*); overhang, overhanging rock. **-en,** *ir.v.n.* (*sep.*) (*aux.* h.) hang over, overhang, project over.
überhängen, (*sep.*) 1. *v.a.* hang (*a th.*) over, cover over; put on; sling over one's shoulder. 2. *v.n.* (*aux.* h.), *see* **überhangen.**
überhapps, *adv.* (*Austr. dial.*) approximately, roughly, about.
überhasten, *v.a.* & *n.* (*aux.* h.) (*insep.*) hurry *or* race through, take too quickly (*Mus., etc.*).
überhäufen, *v.a.* (*insep.*) load (with), overwhelm (with); overload, overstock, glut (*the market, etc.*).
überhaupt, *adv.* generally, in general; really, on the whole, after all, altogether, at all; *du hättest es - nicht tun sollen*, you should not have done it at all; *gibt es - eine Möglichkeit?* is there any chance whatever? *wenn -*, if at all; *- kein*, none at all; *und -*, (*coll.*) as things stand, if you think about it.
überheb-en, 1. *ir.v.a.* (*sep.*) lift over; (*insep.*) *jemanden einer S.* (*Gen.*) *-en*, exempt *or* excuse from, relieve from, spare, save. 2. *v.r.* (*insep.*) strain o.s. (*by lifting*); (*fig.*) be overweening *or* overbearing, boast (of), presume too much. **-lich,** *adj.* overbearing, presumptuous. **-lichkeit,** *f.*, **-ung,** *f.* presumption, arrogance.
überheizen, *v.a.* (*insep.*) overheat (*a room*).
überhin, *adv.* superficially, sketchily; *ein Buch nur - lesen*, skim (through) a book; (*dial.*) *see* **überdies.**
überhitzen, *v.a.* (*insep.*) overheat (*a room*); superheat (*an engine*); *überhitztes Gemüt*, impassioned soul, highly strung temperament.
überhöh-en, *v.a.* command, surmount; increase (*Geometry*). **-ung,** *f.* banking, camber (*of a bend in the road*); super-elevation (*Railw.*).
überhol-en, 1. *v.a.* (*sep.*) bring across (*sails*); take over to the other side, ferry across; (*insep.*) overhaul, bring up to date, put in order; overtake, overhaul, out-distance; (*fig.*) outstrip, surpass. 2. *v.n.* (*sep.*) heel (over) (*Naut.*). **-t,** *adj.* antiquated, out of date. **-ungsgleis,** *n.* loop line, siding (*Railw.*).
überhören, *v.a.* (*insep.*) not pay attention to, miss, ignore; *einem seine Aufgabe -*, hear a p. say *or* repeat a lesson, hear a p.'s lesson.
überirdisch, *adj.* super-terrestrial, unworldly; spiritual, celestial, divine; supernatural, unearthly.
überjährig, *adj.* more than a year old; last year's; too old, superannuated.
überkippen, 1. *v.n.* (*sep.*) (*aux.* s.) tip over, tilt over, lose one's balance. 2. *v.a.* overturn, upset.
Überkleid, *n.* outer garment; overall. **-ung,** *f.* patching, plastering up holes (*in a wall*).

überklug, *adj.* too clever (by half), conceited, pert, cheeky.
überkochen, 1. *v.n.* (*sep.*) (*aux.* s.) boil over, (*fig.*) boil, seethe (*with rage, etc.*). 2. *v.a.* (*insep.*) boil (up).
überkommen, (*insep.*) *ir.v.a.* & *n.* (*aux.* s.) (*with Dat.*) get, receive; have handed down; seize, befall; overcome; *eine plötzliche Angst überkam sie,* they were gripped in *or* by a sudden fear; *wir haben es von den Vorfahren –,* it has come down to us from our forefathers. 3. *adj.* traditional, handed down.
überladen, 1. *ir.v.a.* (*sep.*) tranship, trans-ship; (*insep.*) overload, overburden, surfeit, overdo. 2. *adj.* florid, ornate, flamboyant, pretentious, bombastic.
Überlager–er, *m.* superheterodyne (receiver) (*Rad.*). **–n,** *v.a.* (*insep.*) superimpose, overlap, overlie; heterodyne (*Rad.*). **–ungsempfänger,** *m., see* **–er.** **–ungsröhre,** *f.* baretter (*Rad.*).
Überland–bahn, *f.* overland route, transcontinental railway. **–flug,** *m.* cross-country flight. **–leitung,** *f.* overhead supply (*Elec.*). **–zentrale,** *f.* power-station supplying the grid.
überlang, *adj.* too long. **–e,** *adv.* too *or* ever so long; *–e ausbleiben,* be slow in coming, not come when expected.
überlass–en, 1. *ir.v.a.* (*sep.*) leave (remaining); (*insep.*) (*einem etwas*) leave (*to someone else*); give up, relinquish, abandon, cede, make over, let have; *zur Miete –en,* let; *käuflich –en,* sell; *–en Sie das mir,* leave that to me; *–en Sie mich meinem Schicksal,* leave *or* abandon me to my fate; *das muß man der Beurteilung des Lesers –en,* this must be left to the reader's discretion; *es ist ihm –en, was er tun will,* he is at liberty to do as he pleases; *ihn sich selbst –en,* leave him to his own resources *or* devices. 2. *v. r.*; *sich einer S.* (*Dat.*) *–en,* give way to a th., give o.s. up to a th., abandon o.s. to a th. **–ung,** *f.* leaving, abandonment, yielding up, cession.
überlasten, *v.a.* (*insep.*) overload; overburden, overstrain.
Überlauf, *m.* overflow, spillway; flash-over; net profit. **–en,** 1. *ir.v.a.* (*insep.*) run all over, run down, spread over, run too far, overrun; (*fig.*) overwhelm, deluge *or* besiege with, importune; *einen mit Besuchen –en,* pester a p. with visits; *es überläuft mich,* I shudder, my blood runs cold; *es überlief ihn ein kalter Schauer,* a cold shudder seized him. 2. *v.n.* (*sep.*) (*aux.* s.) run *or* flow over, overflow; boil over; desert, go over to (*Mil.*); *die Augen laufen ihm über,* the tears run down his cheeks; *die Galle läuft ihm über,* his blood boils; *die Farben laufen ineinander über,* the colours run (into one another). **–rohr,** *n.* overflow(-pipe).
Überläufer, *m.* (-s, –) deserter (*Mil.*); apostate (*Rel.*); turncoat (*Pol.*).
überlaut, *adj.* too loud; (too) noisy, uproarious.
überleb–en, 1. *v.a.* (*insep.*) outlive, survive; *das –e ich nicht,* that will be the death of me; *die Ansicht ist –t,* that view is out of date, obsolete *or* outmoded. 2. *v.r.* get out of fashion, become out-of-date, be antiquated; *das hat sich –t,* that has had its day, that has gone out of fashion. **–ende(r),** *m.* survivor. **–ensgroß,** *adj.* more than life-size; larger than life. **–ensrente,** *f.* dependant's pension. **–sel,** *n.* (-s, –) vestige.
¹**überlegen,** *adj.* (*Dat.*) superior to, excelling, surpassing, more than a match for. **–heit,** *f.* superiority, dominance, ascendancy, preponderance.
²**überleg–en,** (*sep.*) 1. *v.a.* (*über with Acc.*) lay over *or* upon, cover; (*coll.*) *ein Kind –en,* put a child over one's knee; *einem Pferd eine Decke –en,* cover a horse with a blanket. 2. *v.r.* lean *or* bend over, heel over (*of a ship*). (*insep.*) *v.a.* reflect on, ponder over, weigh, consider; *mit jemandem etwas –en,* consult with s.o. about a th.; *ich werde es mir –en,* I shall think the matter over, I shall think about it. **–sam,** *adj.* deliberate, prudent, circumspect, discreet, guarded, judicious. **–t,** *p.p.* & *adj.* well weighed, deliberate; *alles wohl –t,* taking everything into account. **–theit,** *f.* deliberation, care, premeditation, circumspection, discretion, studied demeanour, guarded manner. **–ung,** *f.* reflection, consideration, deliberation; *nach reiflicher –ung,* upon mature consideration; *bei nochmaliger –ung,* on second thoughts; *mit –ung verübtes Verbrechen,* premeditated crime; *ohne –ung,* inconsiderate, unpremeditated, indiscreet, injudicious.
überlei, *adv.* (*dial.*), *see* **übrig.**
überleiten, *v.a.* (*sep.*) lead *or* conduct over *or* across; form a transition, lead (*from one argument to another*); transfuse (*blood*).
überlesen, 1. *ir.v.a.* (*sep.*) read *or* run through, run over; overlook in reading; *einem zu(m) – geben,* give to s.o. to read over.
überliefer–n, *v.a.* (*insep.*) (*einem etwas*) deliver up, hand over; transmit, hand down, pass on. **–ung,** *f.* delivery, surrender; tradition.
überlist–en, *v.a.* (*insep.*) outwit; deceive, dupe. **–ung,** *f.* outwitting; deception, fraud.
überm, *for* **über dem.**
übermach–en, *v.a.* (*insep.*) (*einem etwas*) make *or* hand over, bequeath; transmit; consign, remit; *Geld* (*durch Wechsel*) *–en,* remit money (by cheque); *–te Summe* remittance. **–ung,** *f.* transmission, remittance (*of money*).
Übermacht, *f.* superior strength, superiority, predominance.
übermächtig, *adj.* overwhelming, paramount; too powerful.
übermalen, *v.a.* (*insep.*) paint over *or* out, cover up with paint.
übermangansauer, *adj.* permanganate of.
übermannen, *v.a.* (*insep.*) overcome, overpower, subdue, master.
Übermantel, *m.* overcoat, greatcoat.
Über–maß, *n.* excess; abundance, superfluity; *im –maß,* to excess, excessively. **–mäßig,** *adj.* extravagant, excessive; exorbitant, extreme, immoderate.
Übermensch, *m.* superman, demi-god. **–lich,** *adj.* superhuman; godlike; (*coll.*) excessive, enormous; *sich –lich anstrengen,* make superhuman efforts.
übermitt–eln, *v.a.* (*insep.*) (*einem etwas*) convey; deliver, hand over, transmit. **–(e)lung,** *f.* conveyance; delivery, transmission.
übermorgen, *adv.* & *n.* the day after tomorrow; *morgen oder –,* tomorrow or the day after.
übermüd–en, 1. *v.a.* (*insep.*) overtire; (*usually only*) *übermüdet,* overtired, tired out. **–ung,** *f.* over-fatigue, great weariness.
Über–mut, *m.* high spirits; wantonness; arrogance; presumption; bravado; (*Prov.*) *–mut tut selten gut,* look before you leap. **–mütig,** *adj.* high-spirited, playful, wanton; arrogant, presumptuous.
übern, *for* **über den.**
übernächst, *adj.* the next but one; *–e Woche,* the week after next; *am –en Tage,* the day after tomorrow.
übernacht, *adv.* overnight. **–en,** 1. *v.n.* (*insep.*) (*aux.* h.) stay overnight, pass the night. 2. *v.a.* (*archaic*) take in for the night, give a night's lodging. **–ung,** *f.* spending *or* staying the night; lodging for the night.
übernächtig, *adj.* tired out, fatigued (from lack of sleep), worn out, heavy- *or* bleary-eyed, (*coll.*) with the bed on one's back; (*coll.*) *– aussehen,* look tired to death.
Übernahm–e, *f.* taking over, acceptance, taking possession *or* charge of, taking in hand, undertaking, taking upon o.s., assumption; negotiation (*of a loan*); *–e eines Amtes,* entering upon an office; *–e einer Arbeit,* undertaking a task; *–e einer Erbschaft,* acceptance of a legacy, entering upon an inheritance. **–ebedingungen,** *f.pl.* conditions of acceptance. **–skurs,** *m.* negotiation price; transfer-rate. **–sschein,** *m.* receipt, acknowledgement of acceptance, bill of lading.
Übername, *m.* (-ns, -n) (*dial.*) nickname.
übernatürlich, *ad*. supernatural, miraculous, *–es Ereignis,* miracle.
übernehm–en, 1. *ir.v.a.* (*sep.*) take over *or* across, transfer; cover over with; ship (*a sea*); *ein Gewehr –en,* shoulder a rifle; (*insep.*) take possession of, receive; take over, take charge of, take upon o.s.; undertake (*work*); accept, assume (*responsibility, etc.*); *sich vom Zorne –en lassen,* allow o.s. to be overcome with rage; *Bürgschaft –en,* stand security. 2. *v.r.* (*insep.*) undertake too much; over-exert o.s.; overwork, overeat; (*C.L.*) *übernommene Gefahr,*

risk subscribed; *übernommene Sendung*, outside broadcast, (*Amer.*) hook-up (*Rad.*). **-er,** *m.* receiver; transferee; contractor, drawee.
überordnen, *v.a.* (*sep.*) place above, set over, superpose.
Überort, *adv.* (*dial.*) *see* **übereck.**
Überoxyd, *n.* (su)peroxide.
Überpflanzung, *f.* (-en) grafting, transplantation (*Surg.*).
Überproduktion, *f.* overproduction.
überprüf-en, *v.a.* (*insep.*) examine, test, scrutinize, check, revise. **-ung,** *f.* examination, scrutiny, check.
überquellen, *v.n.* (*aux.* s.) (*sep.*) overflow (*usually fig.*).
überquer, *adv.* (*archaic*) across, crosswise, crossways, diagonally; *es geht mir* –, all my efforts come to nothing, everything goes wrong. **-en,** *v.a.* cross, traverse. **-ung,** *f.* crossing.
überragen, 1. *v.a.* (*insep.*) overtop, rise *or* tower above; extend beyond; overlook; hang over; (*fig.*) exceed, surpass, excel, transcend. 2. *v.n.* (*aux.* h.) (*sep.*) project.
überrasch-en, *v.a.* (*insep.*) surprise, take unawares, startle. **-end,** *adj.* astonishing, amazing, surprising, unexpected, startling. **-ung,** *f.* surprise.
überrechnen, *v.a.* (*insep.*) calculate, reckon up; compute; run through *or* check (*an account*).
überred-en, *v.a.* (*insep.*) persuade, (*coll.*) talk over; *einen -en, etwas zu tun* or *einen zu einer S. -en,* persuade s.o. to do a th.; *sich durch Gründe -en lassen,* allow o.s. to be persuaded *or* convinced by reasons. **-end,** *pr.p.* & *adj.* persuasive. **-ung,** *f.* persuasion.
überreich, *adj.* too rich; extremely rich; – (*an*), abounding (in), teeming *or* overflowing (with). **-lich,** 1. *adj.* superabundant. 2. *adv.* in profusion.
überreich-en, *v.a.* (*insep.*) (*einem etwas*) hand over, present, deliver. **-ung,** *f.* handing over; presentation.
überreif, *adj.* overripe; overdue; (*fig.*) decadent. **-e,** *f.* overripeness.
überreiten, *ir.v.a.* (*insep.*) ride over, run down (*a child, etc.*).
Überreiz, *m., see* **-ung. -en,** *v.a.* (*insep.*) overexcite, overstimulate; overstrain; outbid (*Cards*); *-tes Gehirn,* overtasked brain. **-theit,** *f.*, **-ung,** *f.* overexcitement, excessive stimulation.
überrennen, *ir.v.a.* (*insep.*) run over, run down; overrun; pester, importune.
Überrest, *m.* (-(e)s, -e) rest, remains, remnant; residue, remainder; (*pl.*) fragments, ruins, relics, scraps, shreds; *sterbliche -e,* mortal remains, (*Poet.*) ashes.
überrieseln, 1. *v.a.* (*sep.*) irrigate. 2. *v.n.* (*aux.* s.) (*insep.*) trickle over.
Überrock, *m.* overcoat, top-coat; frock coat; top skirt.
überrumpel-n, *v.a.* (*insep.*) (take by) surprise, take *or* catch unawares. **-ung,** *f.* surprise, sudden attack.
übers, *for* **über das.**
übersäen, *v.a.* (*insep.*) scatter seeds over; (*usually fig.*) dot *or* strew with; *mit Sternen übersät,* studded with stars.
über-satt, *adj.* surfeited, gorged; *einer S. -satt,* sick and tired of a th. **-sättigen,** *v.a.* (*insep.*) surfeit, satiate; pamper; supersaturate (*Chem.*). **-sättigung,** *f.* supersaturation (*Chem.*); satiation, satiety.
übersäuern, *v.a.* (*insep.*) make too acid, overacidify.
Überschall, *m.* supersonic.
überschatten, *v.a.* overshadow.
überschätz-en, *v.a.* (*insep.*) think too highly of, overrate, overestimate; assess too heavily (*a house*). **-ung,** *f.* over-estimate; over-estimation.
Überschau, *f., see* **Übersicht, Überblick. -en,** *v.a.* (*insep.*) overlook, survey, command a view of; (*fig.*) comprehend, grasp.
überschäumen, *v.n.* (*aux.* s.) (*sep.*) froth over; *-de Lust,* exuberant mirth.
Überschein, *m.* overtone.
überschicken, *v.a.* (*insep.*) (*einem etwas*) transmit, send; remit (*money*).
überschießen, 1. *ir.v..a.* (*insep.*) fire across *or* over; shoot too high; overshoot (*the mark*); shoot better than. 2. *v.n.* (*sep.*) (*aux.* s.) shoot, fly, gush *or* fall over; exceed; *Wasser überschießt,* water begins to freeze *or* is covered with a film of ice; *die -de Summe,* the balance left, the surplus.
überschlächtig, *adj.* overshot (*of a water-wheel*).
Überschlag, *m.* somersault; turn (*of the scale*); poultice; rough calculation, estimate; – *in der Luft,* loop (*Av.*); – *über den Flügel,* barrel roll (*Av.*). **-en,** 1. *ir.v.a.* (*sep.*) throw, lay *or* spread over; apply (*a poultice*); fold over; cross (*one's legs*); (*insep.*) skip, miss, pass over, omit, leave out; estimate, make a rough calculation; drown (*a sound*). 2. *v.r.* go head over heels, capsize, (turn a) somersault; follow each other in quick succession (*events*); crack *or* break (*of the voice*); loop the loop (*Av.*). 3. *v.n.* (*aux.* s.) (*sep.*) turn over; tumble over; fall backwards; jump *or* spring over; go over into; be too loud; *der elektrische Funken schlägt über,* the electric spark leaps *or* flashes across; (*insep.*) become covered *or* coated (*with mildew, etc.*); *-en lassen,* take the chill off. 4. *p.p.* & *adj.* lukewarm, tepid. **-sdecke,** *f.* rug; horse-cloth. **-slaken,** *n.* top sheet. **-srechnung,** *f.* rough estimate.
überschnappen, *v.n.* (*sep.*) (*aux.* s.) snap, slip *or* jerk over; (*fig.*) become crazy, lose one's head; *die Stimme schnappte über,* (his, *etc.*) voice cracked; *das Schloß ist übergeschnappt,* the lock snapped to *or* shut; *er ist übergeschnappt,* he is cracked, he has gone crazy.
überschneiden, *v.a.* & *r.* (*insep.*) intersect, cross, cut, overlap.
überschreib-en, *ir.v.a.* (*sep.*) write (*something left out*) above *or* over the line; (*insep.*) entitle, label, address; dedicate; superscribe, inscribe; (*C.L.*) (*einem etwas*) carry over, transfer, remit. **-ung,** *f.* transfer, remittance.
überschreien, 1. *ir.v.a.* (*insep.*) shout louder than, cry down. 2. *v.r.* shout o.s. hoarse, strain one's voice.
überschreit-en, 1. *ir.v.a.* (*insep.*) step *or* stride over, pass over, cross; ford (*a stream*); (*fig.*) overstep, go beyond, exceed; transgress, infringe; overdraw (*one's account*); *das -en der G(e)leise ist verboten,* it is forbidden to cross the lines; *das -et alles Maß,* that oversteps all bounds *or* goes too far; *ein Gesetz -en,* infringe a law. **-ung,** *f.* crossing; transgression, infringement; excess.
Überschrift, *f.* superscription, inscription, heading, title.
Überschuh, *m.* overshoe, golosh (*usually pl.*).
überschuld-et, *p.p.* & *adj.* involved in debt, greatly encumbered. **-ung,** *f.* heavy indebtedness.
Über-schuß, *m.* surplus, excess; (*C.L.*) balance, profit. **-schüssig,** *adj.* projecting; surplus, remaining.
überschütten, *v.a.* (*sep.*) pour over suddenly, upset, spill; (*insep.*) pour over *or* on, cover (with); load, overwhelm.
Überschwang, *m.* superabundance; rapture, exuberance.
überschwappen, (*sep.*) *v.n.* (*aux.* h.) & *v.a.* (*coll.*) spill, overflow, slop *or* splash over.
überschwemm-en, *v.a.* (*insep.*) inundate, flood, submerge; (*fig.*) deluge; (*C.L.*) overstock, flood (*the market*). **-te(r),** *m.* flood casualty. **-ung,** *f.* inundation, submersion, flooding, flood. **-ungsangriff,** *m.* saturation raid (*Av.*).
überschwenglich, *adj.* superabundant, boundless, excessive; exuberant, high-flown, rapturous, extravagant. **-keit,** *f.* excess, exuberance; extravagance.
Übersee, *f.* overseas; *nach – gehen,* go overseas; *Bestellungen aus* –, oversea orders. **-isch,** *adj.* transoceanic, oversea (*route*). **-dampfer,** *m.* ocean liner. **-handel,** *m.* overseas trade. **-markt,** *m.* colonial market.
übersegeln, 1. *v.a.* (*insep.*) sail faster than, run foul of, run down (*a ship*). 2. *v.a.* & *n.* (*sep.*) (*aux.* s.) sail over (to).
überseh-en, 1. *ir.v.a.* (*insep.*) take in at a glance, perceive, survey, run the eye over, glance over; overlook, omit, miss, not see *or* notice, take no notice of, wink at, shut one's eyes to, connive at (*a*

fault), make allowances for. **-bar,** *adj.* visible at a glance, comprehensible; in full view.
übersein, *ir.v.n.* (*sep.*) remain over; excel, surpass; be tiresome, be too much for; *das ist mir über*, I am sick and tired of it; *darin ist er dir über*, there he has the better of you, there he beats you.
übersend–en, *ir.v.a.* (*insep.*) (*einem etwas*) send, transmit; consign, ship, remit. **–er,** *m.* consignor, sender, remitter; forwarding agent. **–ung,** *f.* consignment.
übersetz–en, 1. *v.n.* (*aux.* s.) & *a.* (*sep.*) leap *or* jump over, cross, pass over; ferry across, transport. 2. *v.a.* (*insep.*) translate, adapt (*for the stage, etc.*); (*archaic*) crowd, overstock, overload; (*dial.*) get the better of; *ihn in der Miete –en*, raise his rent; *wörtlich* or *wortgetreu –en*, translate literally; *frei –en*, give a free rendering; *falsch –en*, mistranslate. **–er,** *m.* translator. **–ung,** *f.* translation (*aus*, from; *in*, into); version; gear, transmission (ratio) (*Mech.*); *kleine –ung*, bottom gear; *doppelte –ung*, two-speed gear (*Cycl.*); *größte –ung*, top gear. **–ungsgetriebe,** *n.* transmission gearing. **–ungsverhältnis,** *n.* gear-ratio (*Mech.*).
Übersicht, *f.* view, sight, prospect; survey, review, abstract, summary, synopsis, digest, abridgement; overtone (*Dye.*); control, supervision. **–ig,** *adj.* long-sighted. **–igkeit,** *f.* long-sightedness, hypermetropia. **–lich,** *adj.* clear, distinct, clearly arranged; synoptical. **–lichkeit,** *f.* clearness, clarity, lucidity; perspicuity. **–skarte,** *f.* general map, index map. **–stabelle,** *f.* tabular summary. **–stafel,** *f.* synopsis.
übersied–eln, 1. *v.n.* (*sep.*) (*aux.* s.) emigrate (*nach*, to); remove, move, shift (*to new quarters*). 2. *v.a.* (*insep.*, *rare*) colonize, settle (*territory*). **–(e)lung,** *f.* emigration; removal.
übersieden, *v.a.* & *n.* (*sep.*) distil.
übersinnlich, *adj.* supernatural, spiritual, immaterial; supersensual; transcendental.
übersommern, (*insep.*) 1. *v.a.* keep through the summer. 2. *v.n.* (*aux.* s.) spend *or* pass the summer (*in a place*).
überspann–en, *v.a.* (*sep.*) stretch over; (*insep.*) spread over, cover, span; overstrain, over-excite, over-exert; stretch too far; (*fig.*) exaggerate, carry *or* push too far (*one's demands, etc.*); (*fig.*) *den Bogen –en*, go too far, force the issue. **–t,** *p.p.* & *adj.* overstrained, exaggerated, extravagant, high-flown, fantastic, crazy, eccentric. **–theit,** *f.* exaltation, excitement, enthusiasm; extravagance, exaggeration, eccentricity. **–ung,** *f.* over-tension; excess-voltage (*Elec.*); overexcitement; exaggeration.
überspinnen, *ir.v.a.* (*insep.*) wind over *or* round, enclose (*as in a cocoon*), cover; *übersponnene Saiten*, silver (covered) strings; *übersponnener Kupferdraht*, covered copper wire.
überspitzt, *adj.* too subtle, (*coll.*) footling.
übersprechen, *v.a.* (*insep.*) supply synchronized speech to (*a film*); *ein englischer Film deutsch übersprochen*, an English film with German dialogue.
überspringen, 1. *ir.v.a.* (*insep.*) leap (across) (*a ditch, etc.*); pass over, jump over; omit, miss, skip; *einen im Amte –*, be promoted over the head of a p.; (*dial.*) strain, sprain (*an ankle, etc.*). 2. *v.n.* (*sep.*) (*aux.* s.) leap over; pass over (to); flash across *or* over (*Elec.*); dart *or* flit from one (*subject*) to another.
übersprudeln, *v.n.* (*sep.*) (*aux.* s.) bubble over, gush over; *–der Witz*, sparkling wit; *–de Freude*, exuberant mirth.
überstaatlich, *adj.* international, cosmopolitan.
überständig, *adj.* that has stood too long, old, outworn, stale, flat, vapid, decrepit; *–e Frucht*, over-ripe fruit.
überstark, *adj.* exceedingly strong *or* powerful, too much.
überstechen, *ir.v.a.* & *n.* (*sep.* & *insep.*) (*aux.* h.) play a higher card, trump higher.
überstehen, 1. *ir.v.a.* (*insep.*) endure, overcome, support, surmount, stand; weather, survive, go through, get over; *er hat (es) überstanden*, he is gone to rest, he has died. 2. *v.n.* (*sep.*) (*aux.* h.) stand out, project, hang over; overlap.
übersteig–en, 1. *ir.v.a.* (*insep.*) step *or* get over; climb *or* pass over, cross, traverse (*a mountain*); scale; surmount, overcome; exceed, surpass, go beyond; *es –t seinen Verstand (alle Begriffe)*, it passes his understanding (all belief); *der Erfolg –t alle Erwartungen*, the success exceeds all expectations. 2. *v.n.* (*aux.* s.) (*sep.*) step over *or* across; overflow. **–bar,** *adj.* surmountable, passable. **–ern,** *v.a.* (*insep.*) push *or* force up (*prices*); outbid (*a p.*); exaggerate, bolster up.
überstellen, *v.a.* (*insep.*) (*Austr. dial.*) transfer (*an official to another post*).
überstimmen, *v.a.* (*insep.*) tune too high *or* above concert-pitch (*Mus.*); out-vote, overrule.
überstrahlen, *v.a.* (*insep.*) shine all over, irradiate; outshine, eclipse.
überstreichen, *ir.v.a.* (*insep.*) paint *or* put colour over; *mit Firnis –*, varnish; (*mit*) *schwarz –*, black(en) out.
überström–en, 1. *v.a.* (*insep.*) inundate, deluge. 2. *v.n.* (*sep.*) (*aux.* s.) flow *or* run over; overflow, abound; (*fig.*) exult; *sein Mund strömte über von ihrem Lobe*, he was loud in praise of her. **–kanal,** *m.* transfer port (*Motor.*). **–rohr,** *f.* waste-pipe, overflow-pipe.
Überstrumpf, *m.* gaiter.
überstudiert, *p.p. as adj.* worn out with study, stale with overwork, mentally exhausted.
überstülpen, *v.a.* (*sep.*) put on, cover over with.
Überstunden, *f.pl.* overtime; *– machen*, work overtime. **–gelder,** *n.pl.* overtime pay.
überstürz–en, 1. *v.a.* (*sep.*) cover over; (*insep.*) precipitate, hurry, do rashly *or* in a hurry, carry (*s.th.*) out hastily. 2. *v.n.* (*sep.*) (*aux.* s.) capsize, upset, tumble *or* topple over *or* backwards. 3. *v.r.* (*insep.*) act hastily, rashly *or* precipitately; press on each other; talk nineteen to the dozen. **–t,** *p.p.* & *adj.* hasty, precipitate; headlong. **–ung,** *f.* hurry, precipitation, rashness; *nur keine –ung!* do not act rashly! do not (be in a) hurry! take it easy!
übertäuben, *v.a.* (*insep.*) drown (*one sound by another*); deafen; stifle.
überteu–ern, *v.a.* (*insep.*) charge too much for; raise, push up (*price*). **–(e)rung,** *f.* rise in prices, overcharging.
übertölp–eln, *v.a.* (*insep.*) deceive, cheat, dupe, take (*a p.*) in, bamboozle. **–(e)lung,** *f.* imposition, duplicity, double-dealing, trickery.
Überton, *m.* supersonic (wave).
übertönen, *v.a.* (*insep.*) drown, rise above, be louder than (*a sound*).
Übertrag, *m.* (-(e)s, ¨-e) (*C.L.*) amount brought forward, balance. **–bar,** *adj.* transferable, negotiable; infectious, contagious; translatable. **–barkeit,** *f.* transferability; (*C.L.*) negotiability; infectiousness (*Med.*). **–en,** 1. *ir.v.a.* (*sep.*) carry over *or* across; transport; (*insep.*) transfer, (*C.L.*) carry over, bring forward; transmit, communicate, spread (*a disease*), infect with; convey, give up to, assign, entrust with; transmit, broadcast, relay (*Rad.*); translate, transcribe; *etwas auf einen –en*, leave s.o. to do a th., consign *or* entrust a th. to a p.; *einen Artikel in das Hauptbuch –en*, enter an item in the ledger; (*aus einer Sprache in die andere*) *–en*, translate; *eine Oper im Rundfunk –en*, relay *or* broadcast an opera; *sein Eigentum –en*, cede *or* make over one's property; *–ene Bedeutung*, figurative sense, metaphorical meaning. 2 *v.r.* (*insep.*); *die Krankheit hat sich auf mich –en*, I have caught the disease. **–er,** *m.* transferrer; endorser (*of a bill*); transmitter, transporter, vehicle, carrier (*Med.*); transformer (*Elec.*). **–ung,** *f.* transfer, transference, carrying over, communication, spreading; (*C.L.*) transfer (*of book-debts*); conveyance, transmission, propagation, relaying, relay, broadcast; endorsement (*of a bill of exchange*); cession, assignment; conferring (*of an office*); translating, translation, transcription. **–ungsbrief,** *m.*, *see* **–ungsurkunde. –ungspapier,** *n.* transfer-paper. **–ungsstation,** *f.* relay-station (*Tele.*). **–ungsurkunde,** *f.* deed of conveyance; bill of sale (*of shares*).
übertreff–en, 1. *ir.v.a.* (*insep.*) surpass, exceed, excel, outdo. 2. *v.r.* (*insep.*) do better than usual. **–bar,** *adj.* surpassable.
übertreib–en, 1. *ir.v.a.* (*insep.*) overdrive; carry

too far, carry to excess, exaggerate; overact, overdo (*a part*). 2. *v.n.* (*insep.*) (*aux.* h.) exaggerate, be given to exaggeration; *–ende Gerüchte*, exaggerated reports; *see* **übertrieben.** **–ung,** *f.* exaggeration, over-statement; excess, extravagance.

übertret–en, 1. *ir.v.a.* (*insep.*) overstep, trespass, transgress, violate, infringe, break (*the law*); *sich* (*Dat.*) *den Fuß –en* or *sich* (*Acc.*) *–en*, strain one's ankle. 2. *v.n.* (*sep.*) (*aux.* s.) step *or* pass over, run over, overflow (*of rivers*); go over, change over to, join (*a party, etc.*); *zur christlichen Kirche –en*, become Christian; *er ist zum Katholizismus übergetreten*, he has turned Catholic. **–er,** *m.* trespasser, transgressor. **–ung,** *f.* transgression, trespass; infringement, breach, violation (*of a law*), misdemeanour; *sich* (*Acc.*) *einer –ung schuldig machen*, be guilty of a misdemeanour *or* breach of the law. **–ungsfall,** *m.*; *im –ungsfalle*, in case of infringement.

übertrieben, *p.p.* & *adj.* exaggerated, excessive, overdone, boundless, extravagant, immoderate, exorbitant; *leicht –*, mildly *or* slightly exaggerated; *in –em Maße*, to an exaggerated degree; *aus übertriebenem Eifer*, through excessive zeal. **–heit,** *f.* extravagance, excess, lack of moderation.

Übertritt, *m.* (-(e)s, -e) passage, going over to, joining (*a party*); change (*of religion*), conversion; stile.

übertrumpfen, *v.a.* (*insep.*) trump higher; (*fig.*) surpass, outdo.

übertun, *v.r.* (*insep.*), *see* **übernehmen,** *v.r.*

übertünch–en, *v.a.* (*insep.*) whitewash; (*fig.*) gloss over; *die Wahrheit –en*, veil the truth; *–te Höflichkeit*, veneer of civility.

übervölker–n, *v.a.* (*insep.*) over-populate. **–t,** *adj.* over-populated, crowded. **–ung,** *f.* over-population.

übervoll, *adj.* brimful; overcrowded; *– von*, brimming with.

übervorteilen, *v.a.* (*insep.*) take advantage of, cheat, defraud, take in.

überwach–en, 1. *v.a.* (*insep.*) watch over, control, inspect, supervise, superintend. **–t,** *adj.*, *see* **übernächtig.** **–ung,** *f.* supervision, surveillance, superintendence. **–ungsausschuß,** *m.* control commission. **–ungsstelle,** *f.* control board *or* point.

überwachsen, 1. *ir.v.a.* (*insep.*) overgrow. 2. *v.r.* outgrow one's strength (*of children*). 3. *v.n.* (*sep.*) (*aux.* s.) grow over.

überwallen, 1. *v.n.* (*sep.*) (*aux.* s.) boil over; heal over, be occluded. 2. *v.a.* (*insep.*) allow to grow over (*Gard.*).

überwältig–en, *v.a.* (*insep.*) overcome, subdue, vanquish, conquer, subjugate, overpower, overwhelm. **–end,** *adj.* imposing, overwhelming; (*iron.*) *nicht –end*, (*coll.*) nothing to write home about. **–ung,** *f.* overwhelming, subjugation.

Überwasser–fahrt, *f.* travelling on the surface (*submarines*). **–fahrzeug,** *n.* surface craft (*Nav.*).

überweis–en, *ir.v.a.* (*insep.*) (*einem etwas* or *etwas an einen*) transfer, make over, remit, refer, send; (*dial.*) *jemanden eines Irrtums –en*, convince a p. of his error. **–ung,** *f.* conviction; allotment, assignment, transfer, remittance; devolution. **–ungsgrund,** *m.* convincing proof *or* argument. **–ungsscheck,** *m.* transfer-cheque.

überwend–lich, *adj.* whipped, overcast; *–liche Naht*, overhand seam. **–lings,** *adv.*; *–lich* or *–lings nähen*, oversew.

überwerfen, 1. *ir.v.a.* (*sep.*) throw over; cover over; *einen Mantel –*, throw a coat round one's shoulders. 2. *v.r.* (*mit*) fall out (with).

Überwert, *m.* superiority. **–en,** *v.a.* (*insep.*) overrate, overesteem. **–ig,** *adj.* superior.

überwiegen, 1. *ir.v.a.* (*insep.*) outweigh, weigh down; preponderate, surpass, exceed; prevail, predominate. 2. *v.n.* (*sep.*) (*aux.* h.) be overweight. **–d,** 1. *pr.p.* & *adj.* predominant, preponderant, dominant, dominating, paramount; *–de Mehrzahl*, vast *or* overwhelming majority. 2. *adv.* mainly, chiefly.

überwind–en, 1. *ir.v.a.* (*insep.*) overcome, prevail over, conquer, subdue, vanquish, surmount (*obstacles*). 2. *v.r.*; *ich kann mich nicht –en*, I cannot prevail on myself *or* bring myself to. 3. *v.n.* (*aux.* h.) (*insep.*) die; *überwundener Standpunkt*, outmoded *or* obsolete viewpoint. **–er,** *m.* conqueror. **–lich,** *adj.* superable, surmountable. **–ung,** *f.* overcoming; conquest, victory; self-control; *das hat mich –ung gekostet*, it cost me an effort, I did it with great reluctance.

überwinter–n, (*insep.*) 1. *v.a.* keep through the winter. 2. *v.n.* (*aux.* h.) winter, pass the winter; hibernate (*of animals*). **–ung,** *f.* wintering; hibernation.

überwölben, *v.a.* (*insep.*) arch *or* vault over.

überwölk–en, *v.r.* (*insep.*) cloud over, grow cloudy. **–t,** *p.p.* & *adj.* overcast, cloudy (*sky*).

überwucher–n, 1. *v.a.* (*insep.*) overgrow, overrun; (*fig.*) stifle. 2. *v.n.* (*sep.* & *insep.*) (*aux.* s. & h.) grow luxuriantly. **–ung,** *f.* hypertrophy.

Überwuchs, *m.* luxurious growth.

Überwurf, *m.* cloak, shawl, wrap; rough-cast; hasp; infantile rupture.

Überzahl, *f.* surplus, majority; superior numbers *or* forces (*Mil.*), numerical superiority; *große* or *starke –*, heavy odds (*Mil.*).

überzähl–en, *v.a.* (*insep.*) count over; *ich habe das Geld zweimal –t*, I have twice recounted *or* checked the money. **–ig,** *adj.* surplus, spare, supernumerary.

überzeichn–en, *v.a.* (*insep.*) over-subscribe; *die Anleihe ist fünfmal –et*, the loan has been subscribed five times over. **–ung,** *f.* over-subscription.

Überzeitarbeit, *f.* (*Swiss dial.*) overtime.

überzeug–en, 1. *v.a.* (*insep.*) convince, persuade. 2. *v.r.*; *sich selbst* or *sich mit eignen Augen von etwas –en*, satisfy o.s. about a th.; *man –e sich selbst!* go and see for yourself! **–end,** *pr.p.* & *adj.* convincing, conclusive. **–t,** *adj.* convinced, certain, sure. **–ung,** *f.* persuasion; conviction, belief; *er ist der festen –ung*, he is thoroughly convinced: *seiner –ung treu bleiben*, hold firm to one's convictions. **–ungskraft,** *f.* persuasive power. **–ungstreue,** *f.* fidelity to one's convictions.

überzieh–en, 1. *ir.v.a.* (*sep.*) put *or* draw over; put on; clothe, coat, cover, line, case, encrust; *jemandem eins* or *einen Hieb –en*, give s.o. a blow, (*sl.*) swipe s.o. one; (*insep.*) cover (over with), overlay, spread over; invade, overrun; suffuse (*with blushes, etc.*); overdraw (*an account*); *das Bett –en*, change the bed-clothes; *Ihr Konto ist um . . . überzogen*, your account is overdrawn by . . .; *mit Zucker –en*, ice (*a cake*); *mit Gips –en*, plaster; *einen Stuhl –en*, cover a chair; *ein Land mit Krieg –en*, carry war into a country. 2. *v.r.*; *der Himmel überzieht sich mit Wolken*, the sky becomes overcast. 3. *v.n.* (*sep.*) (*aux.* s.) move, remove (*into a new house, etc.*). 4. *n.* covering; plating; overlaying; stall (*Av.*). **–ärmel,** *m.* sleeve protector. **–er,** *m.* overcoat, great-coat, top-coat; sweater, jersey.

überzuckern, *v.a* (*insep.*) (cover with) sugar, sugar (over); candy (*fruit*); ice (*cakes*).

Überzug, *m.* cover; coverlet, pillow-case, pillow slip, cushion cover, bed tick; coat, coating; plating; crust (*Min.*); fur *or* coating on the tongue (*Med.*); *galvanischer –*, electroplating. **–slack,** *m.* finishing coat.

überzwerch, *adv.* (*dial.*) awry; athwart, across, aslant, cross-wise, diagonally.

üblich, *adj.* **–keit,** *f.*, *see under* **üben.**

U-boot, *see* **Unterseeboot.**

übrig, *adj.* (left) over, remaining, to spare, residual; *mein –es Geld*, the rest of my money, the money I have left; *– haben*, have over, have more than enough; (*coll.*) *nichts – haben für*, not care for, not think much of; *keine Zeit – haben*, have no time to spare; *ein –es tun*, do more than is necessary; go out of one's way to show a kindness; *die –en*, the others, the rest; *im –en*, for the rest, in other respects. **–ens,** *adv.* moreover, besides, after all; however, furthermore, by the way. **–bleiben,** *v.n.* remain over. **–lassen,** *v.a.* leave over *or* behind, leave a remainder (*Arith.*); *viel* (*wenig*) *zu wünschen –lassen*, leave much (little) to be desired.

Ufer, *n.* (-s, –) bank (*of river*); beach, shore; edge, brink; *ans – gehen*, go ashore; *am – sein*, be ashore. **–bau,** *m.* embankment construction *or* repairs. **–brücke,** *f.* cantilever bridge. **–damm,** *m.* embankment, quay. **–hin,** *adv.* shorewards. **–lie-**

bend, *adj.* frequenting river banks, riparious. **–los,** *adj.* boundless, leading nowhere, extravagant. **–nah,** *adj.* inshore. **–schutzbauten,** *m.pl.* embankment, dikes, sea-walls. **–schwalbe,** *f.* sandmartin (*Riparia*) (*Orn.*).

Uhr, *f.* (-en) clock, watch; timepiece; time of the day, o'clock, hour; meter; (*Poet.*) *seine – ist abgelaufen*, his time has come, his sands have run; *nach der – sehen*, have one's eye on the clock; *wie nach der –*, like clockwork; *Mann nach der –*, punctual man; *eine – stellen (nach)*, set a watch, regulate a timepiece (by); *um wieviel –?* at what time? when? *wieviel – ist es?* what is the time? what time is it? *können Sie mir sagen, wieviel – es ist?* can you tell me the time? *es ist halb drei –*, it is half-past two. **–armband,** *n.* watch-bracelet. **–band,** *n.* watch-guard. **–enfabrikation,** *f.* watch- (*or* clock-) making industry. **–feder,** *f.* watch-spring. **–gehänge,** *n.* trinkets on a watch-chain. **–gehäuse,** *n.* clock *or* watch case. **–gewicht,** *n.* clock-weight. **–glas,** *n.* watch-glass. **–kette,** *f.* watch-chain *or* -guard. **–macher,** *m.* watch- (*or* clock-)maker. **–macherei,** *f.* watch-(*or* clock-)making. **–schrank,** *m.* clock-case. **–tasche,** *f.* watch-pocket. **–werk,** *n.* clockwork, clockwork motor; works (*of a clock*). **–zeiger,** *m.* hand of a watch *or* clock. **–zeigergegensinn,** *m.* counter-clockwise direction. **–zeigersinn,** *m.* clockwise direction.

Uhu, *m.* (-s, -s & *rare* -e) eagle owl (*Bubo bubo*) (*Orn.*).

Ulan, *m.* (-en, -en) uhlan, lancer.

Ule, *f.* (-n) (*dial.*) hair-broom. (*dial.*) **–n,** *v.a.* & *n.* sweep.

Ulk, *m.* (-(e)s, -e) fun, trick, joke, (*sl.*) lark, spree. **–en,** *v.n.* (*aux.* h.) (*coll.*) lark (about), play practical jokes. **–erei,** *f.* skylarking. **–ig,** *adj.* funny, amusing; (*coll.*) *das war –ig*, that was really comic. **–bild,** *n.* caricature.

Ulme, *f.* (-n) elm (*Ulmus*) (*Bot.*). **–n,** *adj.* (made of) elm(-wood).

Ultimo, *m.* (-s, -s) (*C.L.*) last day of the month, end of the month; *per –*, for the monthly settlement; *– August*, at the end of August. **–abschluß,** *m.* monthly settlement. **–geld,** *n.* money due end of this month. **–geschäft,** *n.* business (done) for the (monthly) settlement. **–liquidation,** *f.*, **–regulierung,** *f.*, *see* **–abschluß.**

Ultra–lampe, *f.* ultra-violet lamp. **–marin,** *n.* ultramarine, lazulite blue. **–rot,** *adj.* infra-red. **–schall,** *m.* supersonic. **–strahlung,** *f.* cosmic radiation. **–violett,** *adj.* ultra-violet.

um, 1. *prep.* (*with Acc.*) (see – . . . *herum*) about, round, around; approximately, round about, near, toward(s); (see – . . . *willen*) for, because of; (in exchange) for; by (*so much*); at; alternately with, after; *– alles in der Welt nicht*, not for (all) the world; *einen Tag – den andern*, every other day; day by day, every day; *– ein bedeutendes, beträchtliches* or *erkleckliches*, by a great deal, very much, considerably; *einen –s Leben bringen*, cause a p.'s death, kill a p.; *– bares Geld kaufen*, buy for cash; *es ist – ihn geschehen*, he is done for *or* is lost; *– sich greifen*, spread, get out of hand; *– einen Kopf größer*, taller by a head, a head taller; *– ein Haar*, by a hair's breadth; *– die Hälfte mehr*, half as much again; *– uns herum*, round about us; *– 100 Mark herum*, round about 100 marks; *Sie wissen nicht, wie mir –s Herz ist*, you have no idea how (sad, anxious, *etc.*) I feel; *– etwas kommen*, lose a th.; *–s Leben kommen*, lose one's life, die, perish; *– Lohn arbeiten*, work for money; *– ein Mehrfaches*, many times over; *– nichts gebessert*, no better in any way, showing no improvement; *es ist schade – den Verlust!* it is a pity about the loss; *– so besser!* all the better! so much the better! *– so mehr*, so much the more; *– so viel mehr ist er zu beklagen*, all the more is he to be pitied; *– so weniger müssen Sie hingehen*, so much less reason for your going there; *je mehr . . . – so . . .*, the more . . . the . . .; *wie steht's – euch?* how are you going *or* getting on? how are you? *– die sechste Stunde*, about the sixth hour; *es ist mir nur –s Lesen zu tun*, all I care for is reading; *– 6 Uhr*, at 6 o'clock; *– die Wette*, for a wager; *– Gottes willen!* for God's sake! *–s (– des) Himmels willen*, for Heaven's sake! *– meinetwillen*, for my sake; *– eine S. wissen*, be privy to *or* informed of a th.; *Woche – Woche*, week after week. 2. *conj.*; *– zu (with inf.)* so as to, in order to, to; *– Ihnen zu beweisen*, in order to prove to you. 3. *adv.* past, out, ended, over; upset; around, enclosing, surrounding; round about; *– und –*, round about, everywhere, from *or* on all sides; *– mit diesem Baume!* down with this tree! *rechts –!* right turn! (*Mil.*); *– sein*, be over *or* gone, have expired, have come to a close; *das Jahr ist –*, the year has come to an end; *seine Zeit ist –*, his time is up. 4. *prefix, either sep. or insep. implying* (*a*) round, round about; (*b*) over again, repeatedly; (*c*) in another way; (*d*) to the ground, down, over. *When sep. the prefix is stressed, when insep. the root is stressed.*

umackern, 1. *v.a.* (*sep.*) plough up.

umadressieren, *v.a.* (*sep.*) redirect (*letters*).

umänder–n, *v.a.* (*sep.*) alter, convert, change, transform. **–ung,** *f.* change, modification, transformation, conversion, metamorphosis.

umarbeiten, *v.a.* (*sep.*) do over again, work over, remodel, recast, rewrite, revise.

umarm–en, *v.a.* (*insep.*) embrace, hug. **–ung,** *f.* embrace, hug.

Umbau, *m.* (-s, -ten) rebuilding, reconstruction, building alterations; (*fig.*) transformation. **–en,** *v.a.* (*insep.*) surround with buildings; (*sep.*) rebuild, reconstruct; make alterations (in).

umbehalten, *ir.v.a.* (*sep.*) keep on (*a wrap, shawl, etc.*).

[1]**Umber,** *m.*, **–erde,** *f.* umber.

[2]**Umber,** *m.* (-s, -n), **–fisch,** *m.* (-es, -e) grayling (*Sciaenidae*) (*Icht.*).

umbiegen, *ir.v.a.* (*sep.*) bend back *or* over, turn *or* double back *or* down.

umbild–en, *v.a.* (*sep.*) remould; remodel, recast, transform; reform, reconstruct. **–ung,** *f.* change, transformation; modification, metamorphosis.

umbinden, *ir.v.a.* (*sep.*) tie *or* bind round; *sich* (*Dat.*) *eine Schürze –*, put on an apron.

umblasen, *ir.v.a.* (*sep.*) blow down *or* over; (*insep.*) *von den Winden –*, exposed to every wind that blows.

umblättern, *v.a.* & *n.* (*sep.*) (*aux.* h.) turn over leaves (*of a book*).

Umblick, *m.* panorama, survey; backward glance. **–en,** *v.r.* & *n.* (*sep.*) (*aux.* h.) look about one; look back *or* round.

Umbra, *f.*, *see* [1]**Umber.**

umbrechen, *ir.v.a.* (*sep.*) break down; plough up, turn (*a field*); (*insep.*) make up into pages (*Typ.*).

umbringen, 1. *ir.v.a.* (*sep.*) kill, murder, destroy, make away with, slay. 2. *v.r.* commit suicide.

Umbruch, *m.* (-s, ⸚e) revolutionary *or* radical change, complete changeover *or* reorganization (*Pol.*); page-proof; making up into pages (*Typ.*).

umdämmen, *v.a.* (*insep.*) embank, surround with a dike.

umdecken, *v.a.* (*sep.*) recover, retile (*a roof*); lay (*a table-cloth*) over again.

umdeuten, *v.a.* (*sep.*) give a new interpretation *or* meaning to.

umdreh–en, 1. *v.a.* (*sep.*) turn *or* twist round; turn, rotate, revolve, roll; *einem den Hals –en*, wring a p.'s neck; *einem das Wort im Munde –en*, twist a p.'s words; *wie man die Hand –t*, in a twinkling; *den Spieß –en*, turn the tables (upon a p.). 2. *v.r.* turn round, rotate, revolve; *sich im Grabe –en*, turn (over) in one's grave. **–end,** *adj.* rotatory, revolving. **–ung,** *f.* turning round; turn, rotation, revolution. **–ungsachse,** *f.* axis of rotation. **–ungsbewegung,** *f.* rotary motion. **–ungsgeschwindigkeit,** *f.* rotary velocity. **–ungszähler,** *m.* revolution counter, tachometer. **–ungszeit,** *f.* period of revolution.

Umdruck, *m.* reprint, transfer(-printing), manifolding. **–en,** *v.a.* (*sep.*) reprint, transfer. **–papier,** *n.* transfer-paper.

umdüstert, *adj.* gloomy, overshadowed.

Umerziehung, *f.* re-education, indoctrinization.

umfahr–en, 1. *ir.v.a.* (*sep.*) run down *or* over; (*insep.*) drive round; (sail) round, double (*a headland, etc.*). 2. *v.n.* (*sep.*) (*aux.* s.) drive a roundabout way, make a detour. **–t,** *f.* circular tour, round trip; *eine –t halten*, go upon circuit (*of judges*);

make the round (*of a parish, etc.*). **-ung,** *f.* circumnavigation.

Umfall, *m.* fall, tumble; (*coll.*) sudden change of mind. **-en,** *ir.v.n.* (*sep.*) (*aux.* s.) fall down *or* over, be overturned *or* upset, tumble, overturn; (*fig.*) give in, give way.

Umfang, *m.* (-(e)s, ⸚e) circumference, circuit, periphery, perimeter; girth, bulk, size; volume (*of sound*); compass (*of instruments*); extent (*of a business*); range (*of interests*); radius, sphere (*of activity*; *im großen* –, to a great extent; *in vollem* –, in its entirety; – *des Körpers*, girth. **-en,** *ir.v.a.* (*insep.*) enclose, embrace, surround, encircle, encompass. **-reich,** *adj.* extensive, comprehensive; bulky, voluminous, spacious. **-slinie,** *f.* periphery.

umfänglich, *adj.*, *see* **umfangreich.**

umfass-en, *v.a.* (*sep.*) put one's arm round; reset (*jewels*); (*insep.*) clasp; contain, include, comprise, comprehend; embrace, enclose, span; surround, envelop, outflank (*Mil.*); *in einem Blick -en*, take in at a glance. **-end,** *pr.p. & adj.* far-reaching; extensive, broad, comprehensive. **-ung,** *f.* resetting; embrace; enclosure, fence, enceinte (*Fort.*); outflanking movement, investment, envelopment (*Mil.*).

umflattern, *v.a.* (*insep.*) flutter round, flow loosely round.

umflechten, *ir.v.a.* (*sep.*) re-plait, plait anew; (*insep.*) weave round, cover with wickerwork.

umfliegen, 1. *ir.v.a.* (*insep.*) fly round. 2. *v.n.* (*sep.*) (*aux.* s.) (*coll.*), *see* **umfallen.**

umfließen, *ir.v.a.* (*insep.*) flow (a)round, encircle; *von Licht umflossen*, bathed in light.

umflor-en, *v.a.* (*insep.*) cover with crape; veil; *-te Augen*, eyes dim with tears; *-te Stimme*, muffled voice.

umfluten, *v.a.* (*insep.*) wash on all sides (*waves, etc.*), surround with water.

umform-en, *v.a.* (*sep.*) remodel, recast, reshape, transform, convert (*Elec.*). **-er,** *m.* rotary converter (*Elec.*).

Umfrage, *f.* (-n) inquiry. – *halten*, **-n,** *v.n.* (*sep.*) (*aux.* h.) inquire everywhere, make general inquiries.

umfried(ig)-en, *v.a.* (*insep.*) enclose, fence in. **-ung,** *f.* enclosure, fence.

umfüllen, *v.a.* (*sep.*) transfuse, decant.

Umgang, *m.* (social) intercourse, intimate acquaintance, intimacy, connexion, (business, *etc.*) relations, association; society, acquaintances; round, circuit, rotation, loop, turn (*of a spiral*), volution (*of a shell*); procession; passage, gallery, ambulatory (*Arch.*); breeching (*harness*); *mit einem* – *haben*, be on visiting terms with a p., see a great deal of a p., associate with a p.; *durch vielen* –, by mixing much with people; *wir haben hier wenig* –, we have few acquaintances here, we do not see many people here; *geschlechtlicher* –, sexual intercourse; *guten* (*schlechten*) – *haben* or *pflegen*, keep good (bad) company. **-sformen,** *f.pl.* (good) manners, deportment. **-ssprache,** *f.* colloquial speech.

umgänglich, *adj.* sociable, companiable; affable. **-keit,** *f.* sociability, pleasant ways, affability.

umgarn-en, *v.a.* (*insep.*) ensnare, enmesh, trap. **-ung,** *f.* entanglement, maze.

umgaukeln, *v.a.* (*insep.*) hover, flit *or* flutter around, (*fig.*) delude.

umgeändert, *p.p.*, *see* **umändern.**

umgearbeitet, *p.p.*, *see* **umarbeiten.**

umgeb-en, *ir.v.a.* (*sep.*) put on (*a cloak*); (*insep.*) surround, encircle. **-ung,** *f.* surroundings, environs, neighbourhood; environment, background; acquaintances, associates, company, society.

umgebogen, *adj.*, *see* **umbiegen**; resupinate (*Bot.*).

Umgegend, *f.* surroundings, vicinity, environs, neighbourhood.

umgehängt, *p.p.*, *see* **umhängen.**

umgeh-en, 1. *ir.v.n.* (*aux.* s.) (*sep.*) go round, revolve, circulate; make a circuit *or* detour, go a roundabout way; (*mit*) associate, have to do (with) deal, be occupied *or* have intercourse (with); handle, manage, have in mind; haunt (*of ghosts*); *einen Brief -en lassen*, let a letter circulate pass a letter round; *in diesem Schlosse geht es um*, this castle is haunted; *gern mit einem -en*, like a p.'s company; *er weiß mit Menschen umzugehen*, he knows how to get on with people, he know the (ways of the) world; *mit etwas umzugehen wissen*, know how to manage *or* handle a th.; *du gehst nicht recht damit um*, you set about it the wrong way; *mit einem Gedanken -en*, turn an idea over in one's mind; *mit einem Plane -en*, plan s.th., have s.th. in mind; *mit Betrug -en*, practise deceit; *mit Mord -en*, meditate murder; *mit Verrat -en*, contemplate treachery; *damit -en, sich zu verheiraten*, think of *or* toy with the idea of marrying; (*Prov.*) *sage mir, mit wem du -s , und ich will dir sagen, wer du bist*, a man is known by the company he keeps, birds of a feather flock together; *mit einem hart -en*, treat a p. harshly. 2. *v.a.* (*insep.*) walk round; elude, evade, (*coll.*) dodge; outflank, turn (*the enemy's flank. Mil.*). **-end,** *adj.* immediate; *mit -ender Post* or *-end antworten*, reply by return; *-ende Antwort dringend erbeten*, an answer by return is urgently requested; *wir bitten um -ende Mitteilung*, kindly inform us by return (of post). **-ung,** *f.* going round, detour; avoidance, evasion; turning movement, flanking movement, envelopment (*Mil.*). **-ungsstraße,** *f.* by-pass (road).

umgekehrt, 1. *p.p. & adj.* opposite, contrary, reverse, inverse, reciprocal; *see* **umkehren.** 2. *adv.* on the other hand, conversely, vice versa.

umgestalt-en, *v.a.* (*sep.*) transform, metamorphose; reorganize, remodel. **-ung,** *f.* alteration, transformation, metamorphosis, adaptation.

umgießen, *ir.v.a.* (*sep.*) pour from one vessel into another, decant; recast.

umgliedern, *v.a.* (*sep.*) reorganize, regroup, redistribute (*forces*) (*Mil.*).

umgraben, *ir.v.a.* (*sep.*) dig (up), dig over, break up (*soil*).

umgrenz-en, *v.a.* (*insep.*) encircle, enclose, bound; circumscribe, limit, define. **-ung,** *f.* boundary; enclosure; circumscription, limitation.

umgruppieren, *v.a.* (*sep.*) regroup, redistribute (*Mil.*).

umgucken, *v.r.* glance round, look around one.

umgürten, *v.a.* (*sep.*) gird, gird o.s. with; buckle on (*a sword*); (*insep.*); *seine Lenden* –, gird up one's loins.

Umguß, *m.* transfusion; recasting; recast.

umhaben, *ir.v.a.* (*sep.*) have round (one), have (*a cloak, etc.*) on.

umhals-en, *v.a.* (*insep.*) embrace, hug. **-ung,** *f.* embrace.

Umhang, *m.* (-(e)s, ⸚e) wrap, shawl, cloak, mantle, cape.

umhäng-en, *v.a.* (*sep.*) put on (*a shawl, etc.*); sling (*arms*); re-hang (*a picture*); *der Katze die Schelle -en*, bell the cat, call a spade a spade; *einer S. ein Mäntelchen -en*, wrap s.th. up in fine words, hide the truth about a th.; (*insep.*) hang round (*mit*, with). **-etasche,** *f.* shoulder-bag. **-etuch,** *n.* shawl, wrap.

umhauen, *ir.v.a.* (*sep.*) hew *or* cut down, fell (*trees, etc.*).

umher, *adv. & sep. prefix*, about, around, up and down, all round, here and there, on all sides. **-blicken,** *v.n.* look around, glance round, have *or* take a look round. **-fahren,** *ir.v.n.* (*aux.* s.) drive about; *mit der Hand -fahren*, gesticulate. **-führen,** *v.a.* lead *or* conduct round (*a building, etc.*). **-gehen,** *ir.v.n.* (*aux.* s.) stroll about. **-irren,** *v.n.* (*aux.* s.) be lost, wander about trying to find the way. **-laufen,** *v.n.* (*aux.* s.) rush around, run about, (*coll.*) chase about. **-liegen,** *v.n.* lie about. **-schweifen,** *v.n.* (*aux.* s.) roam about; *seine Blicke -schweifen lassen*, let one's eyes wander. **-treiben,** wander about, loaf about. **-ziehend,** *pr.p. & adj.* wandering, strolling, itinerant.

umhinkönnen, *v.n.* (*sep.*); *ich kann nicht umhin, zu . . .*, I cannot help (doing), I have no choice but (to do), I cannot but (do), I cannot refrain from (doing).

umhören, *v.r.*; *sich nach einer S.* –, inquire *or* make inquiries about a th., (*coll.*) keep one's ear to the ground.

umhüll-en, *v.a.* (*sep.*) *sich mit einem Tuch -en*,

wrap o.s. up in a shawl; (*insep.*) envelop, cover, wrap up, veil, clothe. **-ung,** *f.* envelopment; cover, covering, wrapping, envelope, case, casing, jacket.

Umkehr, *f.* turning back, return; change, revulsion (*of feeling*); conversion; reversal (*Elec.*). **-en,** (*sep.*) 1. *v.n.* (*aux.* s.) turn back, turn round, return, retrace one's steps, (*fig.*) reform, turn over a new leaf. 2. *v.a.* turn (round, about, back, over, up, inside out, upside down, *etc.*); overturn, reverse, subvert, invert, convert, throw into disorder; *einen Bruch -en*, invert a fraction; *wie man die Hand -t*, in a twinkling; *mit umgekehrter Hand*, with the back of the hand; *einen Satz -en*, invert a proposition; *den Spieß -en* (*gegen*), turn the tables (upon); *die Taschen -en*, turn one's pockets inside out; *die Reihenfolge der Wörter -en*, invert the order of the words; *see* **umgekehrt.** 3. *v.r.* turn round, turn over in bed; *mir kehrt sich das Herz um*, it makes my heart bleed; *bei dem Anblick kehrt sich der Magen um*, it is a sickening sight, the sight turns one's stomach. **-bar,** *adj.* reversible, convertible. **-feld,** *n.* reversing field (*Elec.*). **-motor,** *m.* reversible engine. **-ung,** *f.* overturning; inversion; reversion; reversal, subversion.

umkippen, *v.a.* & *n.* (*sep.*) (*aux.* s.) tip over, upset, overturn, lose one's balance; change one's mind.

umklammer-n, *v.a.* (*insep.*) clasp, clutch (at), embrace; clinch (*Boxing*); encircle (*Mil.*). **-ung,** *f.* clinch (*Box.*), pincer-movement (*Mil.*).

umkleid-en, 1. *v.a.* (*sep.*) change the dress of; (*insep.*) clothe, cover, drape, adorn; (*fig.*) surround, invest. 2. *v.r.* (*sep.*) change (one's clothes *or* dress). **-eraum,** *m.* changing- *or* dressing-room.

umknicken, *v.n.* & *a.* (*sep.*) (*aux.* s.) snap off; *der Fuß ist mir umgeknickt*, I have twisted my foot.

umkommen, *ir.v.n.* (*sep.*) (*aux.* s.) perish, die, succumb; fall (*in battle*); spoil, go bad; be lost *or* wasted; *vor Langweile –*, die of boredom.

Umkreis, *m.* circle, circumference; circuit; zone, area, vicinity; extent, range, radius, circumscribed circle (*Geom.*). **-en,** *v.a.* (*insep.*) turn on, revolve *or* circle round, encircle. **-ung,** *f.* encirclement.

umkrempeln, 1. *v.n.* (*sep.*) (*aux.* s.) turn *or* tuck up; disturb, disarrange; (*coll.*) *das ist zum –*, that is enough to make one die with laughter *or* to drive one silly. 2. *v.r.* (*coll.*) change one's entire nature.

umlad-en, *ir.v.a.* (*sep.*) reload, transfer a load; tranship. **-ebahnhof,** *m.* reloading station. **-ungskosten,** *f.pl.* reloading charges, cost of transhipment.

Umlage, *f.* (-n) assessment (*of taxes*), rating; contribution, apportionment.

umlager-n, *v.a.* (*insep.*) enclose, surround closely, besiege; *einen -n* or *-t halten*, assail, beset; (*sep.*) transpose, rearrange; re-store (*goods*); move camp. **-ung,** *f.* transposition, rearrangement.

Umlauf, *m.* turn, cycle, revolution, rotation, circulation, circular; whitlow (*Path.*); *in – bringen* or *setzen*, put into circulation, issue, circulate; spread (*a rumour*); *außer – setzen*, withdraw from circulation; *im – sein*, circulate. **-en,** (*sep.*) 1. *ir.v.a.* run over, run *or* knock down. 2. *v.n.* (*aux.* s.) rotate, revolve; circulate (*as blood, reports, money, etc.*); go a roundabout way, make a detour; (*insep.*) *v.a.* (*aux.* h.) run round (*a circuit, course, etc.*). **-getriebe,** *n.* planetary gear. **-motor,** *m.* rotary engine (*Av.*). **-skapital,** *n.* floating capital. **-smittel,** *n.* currency. **-szeit,** *f.* time of rotation, circulation period.

Umlaut, *m.* (-(e)s, -e) modification (*of a vowel*) (*Phonet.*). **-en,** (*sep.*) 1. *v.a.* modify (*the vowel*), cause modification. 2. *v.n.* (*aux.* s.) modify, become modified, take modification; *die Plurale auf "... er" lauten gewöhnlich um*, plurals in "... er" usually modify; *dieser Diphthong lautet um*, this diphthong is modified.

umleg-en, *v.a.* (*insep.*) surround (with); garnish; (*sep.*) lay *or* put round; lay down, turn up (*Cards*); put on (*a cloak, etc.*); shift, change the position of; remove to other quarters (*Mil.*); careen (*a ship*); lower (*a funnel on passing bridges*); turn down (*an edge*); apportion; (*sl.*) kill; *sich im Bette -en*, turn over in bed; *die Kosten -en*, divide *or* apportion the expenses. **-bar,** *adj.* reversible, inclinable. **-(e)kragen,** *m.* turn-down collar. **-ung,** *f.* division *or* allocation of land.

umleit-en, *v.a.* (*sep.*) divert (*traffic, etc.*); turn aside; lead a roundabout way. **-ung,** *f.* (traffic) diversion.

umlenken, *v.a.* & *n.* (*sep.*) (*aux.* h. & s.) turn *or* steer round.

umlernen, *v.a.* & *n.* (*sep.*) (*aux.* h.) learn afresh change one's views, readjust one's ideas.

umleuchten, *v.a.* (*insep.*) (*aux.* h.) bathe in light throw *or* shed light on.

umliegend, *pr. p.* & *adj.* surrounding, neighbouring; circumjacent.

ummauern, *v.a.* (*insep.*) wall in *or* round.

ummodeln, *v.a.* (*sep.*) remodel, reshape, alter.

umnacht-en, *v.a.* (*insep.*) shroud in darkness. **-et,** *p.p.* & *adj.* benighted, deranged. **-ung,** *f.* mental derangement, insanity.

umnebeln, *v.a.* (*insep.*) (*fig.*) cloud, fog, confuse.

umnehmen, *ir.v.a.* (*sep.*) put on, wrap round o.s.

umpacken, *v.a.* (*sep.*) repack, pack over again; (*insep.*) *see* **umhüllen.**

umpflanzen, *v.a.* (*sep.*) transplant, replant; (*insep.*) plant all round (*with trees, etc.*).

umpflügen, *v.a.* (*sep.*) plough up, turn (*soil*); (*insep.*) encircle with furrows.

umquartieren, *v.a.* (*sep.*) (*p.p.* umquartiert) remove to other quarters, re-billet (*troops*).

umrahmen, *v.a.* (*insep.*) frame, surround.

umrand-en, *v.a.* (*insep.*), **umrändern,** *v.a.* (*insep.*) surround, border, edge. **-ungsfeuer,** *n.* boundary *or* perimeter lights.

umranken, *v.a.* (*insep.*) twine round; (*fig.*) entwine; *efeuumrankt*, ivy-clad.

umrechn-en, *v.a.* (*sep.*) reduce (*in*, to), convert (into). **-ung,** *f.* reduction, conversion. **-ungsgrößen,** *f.pl.* conversion data. **-ungskurs,** *m.* rate of exchange. **-ungstafel,** *f.* conversion table.

umreisen, *v.a.* (*insep.*) travel round, take a trip round.

umreißen, *ir.v.a.* (*sep.*) pull, tear *or* throw down; blow down (*trees, etc.*); demolish; (*insep.*) outline, sketch (*usually fig.*).

umreiten, 1. *ir.v.a.* (*insep.*) ride round (*the track*); (*sep.*) ride down. 2. *v.n.* (*sep.*) (*aux.* s.) make a detour (*on horseback*).

umrennen, (*sep.*) 1. *ir.v.a.* run down, knock over (*an obstacle*). 2. *v.n.* rush *or* race round.

Umrichter, *m.* frequency-changer (*Rad.*).

umringen, *reg.* & *ir.v.a.* (*insep.*) encircle, enclose, close in on, encompass, surround, beset.

Umriß, *m.* (-(ss)es, -(ss)e) outline, sketch, contour; *in kräftigen -(ss)en*, in bold outlines; *in groben -(ss)en*, in broad outline; *-(ss)e des Gesichts*, outline of the face. **-karte,** *f.* outline *or* skeleton-map.

umrühren, *v.a.* (*sep.*) stir, agitate; puddle, rake (*Metall.*).

ums = um das; um's (*coll.*) **= um des.**

umsatteln, (*sep.*) 1. *v.a.* resaddle (*a horse*). 2. *v.n.* (*aux.* h. & s.) (*fig.*) change one's studies *or* profession; change one's ideas *or* opinion.

Umsatz, *m.* (-es, ⸚e) turnover, exchange, returns, sale, business; reaction, conversion, transformation, decomposition; (*C.L.*) *geringer –*, small turnover, slow returns; (*C.L.*) *rascher –*, quick returns; *großer –, kleiner Nutzen*, small profits and quick returns. **-betrag,** *m.* total turnover. **-kapital,** *n.* working capital. **-produkt,** *n.* product of metabolism. **-steuer,** *f.* purchase tax, sales tax.

umsäumen, *v.a.* (*sep.*) hem, edge, fringe; (*insep.*) surround, hem in.

umschaff-en, *ir.v.a.* (*sep.*) transform; remodel. **-ung,** *f.* transformation, regeneration.

umschalt-en, *v.a.* (*sep.*) switch over; reverse the current. **-bar,** *adj.* interchangeable. **-er,** *m.* change-over switch, commutator, shift-key (*typewriter*). **-erbrett,** *n.* switch-board. **-hebel,** *m.* switch-lever. **-stöpsel,** *m.* switch-plug. **-tafel,** *f.* switch-board. **-ung,** *f.* switching, commutation. **-ungsschlüssel,** *m.* reversing-key.

umschatten, *v.a.* (*insep.*) shade, overshadow.

Umschau, *f.* survey, review; backward glance; *– halten*, look out *or* round (*nach einer S.*, for a th.).

-en, *v.r.* & *n.* (*sep.*) (*aux.* h.) look round, take a look around; look *or* glance back.

umschaufeln, *v.a.* (*sep.*) turn over with a shovel.

Umschicht, *f.* (-en) shift (*Min.*). **-en,** *v.a.* (*sep.*) pile anew, rearrange in layers; (*fig.*) shift, regroup. **-ig,** *adv.* (*fig.*) in turns, alternately. **-ung,** *f.* shifting, regrouping, reshuffle.

umschiff-en, *v.a.* (*insep.*) sail round, circumnavigate; round *or* double (*a cape*); (*sep.*) tranship (*cargo*), transfer (*passengers*). **-ung,** *f.* circumnavigation; transhipment; *-ung der Erde,* circumnavigation of the globe.

Umschlag, *m.* (-(e)s, ⸚e) revulsion, sudden change (*of the weather, of opinions*), turn, alteration; cover, covering, wrapper, jacket (*of a book*), envelope; facing, hem, cuff, collar, flap, turn-up, rim; compress, poultice; reshipment, transfer (*of goods*); sale, turnover; *einen – machen um,* apply a poultice to. **-en,** (*sep.*) 1. *ir.v.a.* knock down *or* over, fell (*a tree*), turn over (*a page, etc.*), turn up (*a hem, cuff*), turn down (*a collar*), roll up (*sleeves*); wrap round, wrap up, poultice. 2. *v.n.* (*aux.* s.) turn over, overturn, capsize, upset, fall over; (*Swiss dial. aux.* h.) turn, change suddenly; shift, change, grow worse, go sour (*of milk*); break (*of the voice*); *zum Guten -en,* take a favourable turn; *das Boot schlägt um,* the boat capsizes; *in etwas* (*Acc.*) *-en,* change into s.th. else; *das Wetter schlug um,* the weather changed; *der Wind schlug um,* the wind shifted. **-bogen,** *m.* sheet of wrapping-paper. **-epapier,** *n.* wrapping-paper. **-platz,** *m.*, **-stelle,** *f.* place *or* port of reshipment, reloading point. **-(e)tuch,** *n.* shawl, wrap. **-shafen,** *m.* port of transhipment.

umschleichen, *ir.v.a.* (*insep.*) & *n.* (*sep.*) (*aux.* s.) sneak *or* prowl round.

umschließ-en, *ir.v.a.* (*insep.*) (*aux.* h.) enclose, surround; invest, besiege; (*fig.*) include, comprise; *mit seinen Armen -en,* clasp in one's arms, embrace.

umschlingen, *ir.v.a.* (*sep.*) twist *or* wind round; (*insep.*) embrace, entwine in, enclose tightly, cling to.

umschlossen, *p.p.*, *see* **umschließen.**

umschmeißen, *ir.v.a.* & *n.* (*sep.*) (*aux.* h. & s.) (*vulg.*), *see* **umwerfen.**

umschmelz-en, *ir.v.a.* (*sep.*) re-melt, recast, refound; (*fig.*) alter completely. **-ung,** *f.* (*fig.*) melting-pot.

umschnallen, *v.a.* (*sep.*) buckle on (*a sword*).

umschnüren, *v.a.* (*sep.*) lace, bind *or* strap round; lace again *or* differently; (*insep.*) rope, tie up.

umschreib-en, *ir.v.a.* (*sep.*) rewrite, transcribe; transfer, make over; *einen Wechsel -en,* reindorse a bill; *ein Recht auf einen -en,* transfer *or* make over a right to a p.; (*insep.*) circumscribe; (*fig.*) (*usually p.p. only*) localize (*Med.*); paraphrase; *ein Dreieck mit einem Kreise -en,* describe a circle round a triangle. **-ung,** *f.* transcription, transcript; paraphrase; (circular) inscription, legend (*on a coin*).

Umschrift, *f.* (-en) *see* **Umschreibung.**

umschuld-en, *v.a.* (*sep.*) convert a debt. **-ung,** *f.* conversion of a debt.

umschulen, *v.a.* (*sep.*) remove from one school to another, (re-)train (*black-coated workers for industry, etc.*).

umschütten, *v.a.* (*sep.*) spill, upset; pour into another vessel, decant.

umschwärmen, *v.a.* (*insep.*) swarm, buzz *or* crowd round, beset; (*usually passive*) adore.

Umschweif, *m.* (-s, -e) circumlocution, digression; (*coll.*) falderal; *ohne -e,* bluntly, point-blank; *-e machen,* digress, beat about the bush.

umschwenken, *v.a.* & *n.* (*sep.*) (*aux.* h.) turn round, wheel about; (*fig.*) change one's mind.

umschwirren, *v.a.* (*insep.*) buzz round.

Umschwung, *m.* (-s, ⸚e) rotation, revolution, turn, wheeling; sudden change, reaction, revulsion (*of feeling, etc.*); swing (*round the bar. Gymn.*); (*pl.*) vicissitudes (of fortune); (*Swiss dial. sing. only*) land round *or* immediate surroundings of a house.

umsegeln, *v.a.* (*sep.*) run foul of, run down; (*insep.*) sail round, circumnavigate (*the world*); double (*a cape*).

umsehen, *ir.v.r.* (*sep.*) look back, look round; look about one; *im –,* in a twinkling *or* flash; *sich in der Stadt –,* take a look round the town; *er hat sich viel in der Welt umgesehen,* he has seen a great deal of the world; *sich nach einem –,* look out for s.o.

umsein, *ir.v.n.* (*sep.*) be over, have come to an end.

umseitig, *adj.* on the next page, overleaf.

umsetz-en, 1. *v.a.* (*sep.*) place otherwise, transplant, transfer, transpose (*Mus.*); convert, permutate, transform; (*C.L.*) sell, dispose of, realize, convert into cash; *etwas in die Tat -en,* carry out s.th. 2. *v.r.* (*sep.*) change, become transformed. **-bar,** *adj.* convertible, negotiable; saleable, marketable; exchangeable. **-ung,** *f.* change of place; transposition; conversion, permutation, reaction (*Chem.*); transplantation; *see* **Umsatz.**

Umsichgreifen, *n.* progress; spreading, spread.

Umsicht, *f.* circumspection, discretion, caution, wariness, prudence, tact. **-ig,** *adj.* circumspect, prudent, cautious, open-eyed. **-igkeit,** *f.*, *see* **-.**

umsied-eln, *v.n.* (*sep.*) settle somewhere else, change one's quarters. **-(e)lung,** *f.* change of home *or* country, resettlement.

umsinken, *ir.v.n.* (*sep.*) (*aux.* s.) sink down, drop, fall to the ground.

umsonst, *adv.* for nothing, without pay, gratuitously, gratis, free of charge; to no purpose, in vain; *er gibt nichts –,* he gives nothing away (free); *er sagte das nicht –,* he meant what he said; *sich – bemühen,* work to no purpose, waste one's labour; (*Prov.*) *– ist nur der Tod,* nothing for nothing; no pay, no work; *das soll er nicht – getan haben,* he will not have done that in vain; he will pay for that.

umspann-en, *v.a.* (*sep.*) change (*horses*); transform (*Elec.*); (*insep.*) surround, encompass, comprise. **-er,** *m.* transformer (*Elec.*).

umspinnen, *ir.v.a.* (*insep.*) wrap in a web, entwine, entangle; braid (*a wire*).

umspringen, 1. *ir.v.a.* (*insep.*) jump round (*a p.*). 2. *v.n.* (*sep.*) (*aux.* s.) jump about; change, shift (*of wind*); *mit einem* (*einer S.*) *umzuspringen wissen,* know how to deal with a p. (a th.).

umspülen, *v.a.* (*insep.*) wash round (*a rock*).

Umstand, *m.* (-(e)s, ⸚e) circumstance, case, fact; condition, situation; (*pl.*) particulars, details, circumstances, state of affairs; formalities, ceremonies; fuss, bother, trouble, difficulty; *mildernder –,* redeeming feature, extenuating circumstance; *in andern* (or *in gesegneten*) *Umständen sein,* be with child, be in the family way; *große Umstände machen,* make a lot of fuss; go to great trouble; *in guten Umständen,* well-to-do, well off; *machen Sie keine Umstände,* do not put yourself out, do not go to any special trouble; *die kleinsten Umstände,* minutiae; *die näheren Umstände,* further particulars; *ohne* (*viele*) *Umstände,* without much ado, without (standing on) ceremony; *unter Umständen,* in certain cases, under certain circumstances, circumstances permitting; *unter allen Umständen,* in any case, at all events; *unter diesen Umständen,* in these circumstances; *unter keinen Umständen,* on no account. **-sbestimmung,** *f.* adverbial modification. (*dial.*) **-sbrötchen,** *n.* sandwich. **-shalber,** *adv.* owing to circumstances. **-skleid,** *n.* maternity dress. **-skasten,** *m.*, **-skrämer,** *m.* fussy person, (*coll.*) fuss-pot. **-ssatz,** *m.* adverbial clause. **-swort,** *n.* adverb.

umständ-ehalber, *adv.* owing to circumstances. **-lich,** *adj.* circumstantial; minute, detailed, intricate, involved; ceremonious, formal, fussy, troublesome, laborious, (*coll.*) long-winded; *-lich erzählen,* particularize, go into all the details of, narrate at great length; *das ist mir viel zu -lich,* that is far too much bother *or* trouble. **-lichkeit,** *f.* circumstantiality; ceremoniousness, formality, fussiness; (*pl.*) formalities.

umstehend, 1. *pr. p.* & *adj.*; *-e Seite,* next page; *die -en* the bystanders. 2. *adv.* on the next page; *wie –,* as stated overleaf.

umsteig-en, *ir.v.n.* (*sep.*) (*aux.* s.) change (*trains, etc.*). **-(e)fahrschein,** *m.*, **-(e)karte,** *f.* through-ticket, transfer-ticket.

umstell-en, 1. *v.a.* (*sep.*) place differently, put in a different place, rearrange; transpose, invert (*Gram.*); convert, change over (*auf,* to); *auf Kraft-(fahr)betrieb -en,* motorize; *auf Maschinenbetrieb*

–en, mechanize; (*insep.*) surround, encompass. 2. *v.r.* (*sep.*) adapt *or* accommodate o.s. (*to changed conditions*), change one's attitude, assume a different attitude (to). **–ung,** *f.* change of position, inversion, transposition, conversion, adaptation; change of face; *politische –ung*, change of political attitude.

umstimm–en, *v.a.* (*sep.*) retune, tune to another pitch (*Mus.*); *einen –en*, make a p. change his opinion *or* mind, bring *or* talk a p. round, talk a p. over. **–ung,** *f.* conversion, change of mind.

umstoß–en, *ir.v.a.* (*sep.*) overturn, upset, overthrow, knock down; subvert, abrogate, abolish, cancel, revoke, annul, void, quash, invalidate. **–ung,** *f.* upsetting, overthrow, cancelling, revocation, rescission, abolition, abrogation, subversion, invalidation, annulment, reversal.

umstößlich, *adj.* reversible, subvertible, revocable, annullable.

umstrahlen, *v.a.* (*insep.*) irradiate, bathe in light.

umstricken, *v.a.* (*insep.*) ensnare, entangle; (*sep.*) re-knit.

umstritten, *adj.* controversial, disputed.

umstülpen, *v.a.* (*sep.*) turn upside down, invert, overturn.

Umsturz, *m.* (-es, ⸚e) fall, downfall, ruin, overthrow; revolution; subversion. **–bestrebungen,** *f.pl.*, revolutionary aims. **–ideen,** *f.pl.* subversive ideas. **–partei,** *f.* anarchists, revolutionary party (*Pol.*).

umstürz–en, (*sep.*) 1. *v.a.* throw down, overthrow, upset, overturn; subvert; demolish, destroy. 2. *v.n.* (*aux.* s.) fall down, collapse, tumble. **–ler,** *m.* revolutionary, anarchist. **–lerisch,** *adj.* revolutionary.

umtaufen, *v.a.* (*sep.*) rechristen, rename.

Umtausch, *m.* (-es, -e) exchange. **–en,** *v.a.* (*sep.*) exchange, change (for).

umtreib–en, *ir.v.a.* (*sep.*) drive round, rotate, revolve, turn, spin. **–er,** *m.* rotator muscle (*Anat.*).

Umtrieb, *m.* (-(e)s, -e) cycle, circulation, cycle of cultivation (*forestry*); (*pl.*) agitation; intrigues, plots, machinations. **–szeit,** *f.* rotation period.

umtun, (*sep.*) 1. *ir.v.a.* put on (*a shawl, etc.*). 2. *v.r.* bestir o.s.; *sich nach einer S. –*, go to a lot of trouble to find a th., look around for a th.; *sich bei einem –*, make inquiries of a p.

umwachsen, *ir.v.a.* (*insep.*) grow round, overgrow, surround; *efeuumwachsen*, ivy-clad.

umwälz–en, *v.a.* (*sep.*) rotate, revolve, roll over, whirl round; (*usually fig.*) overturn, overthrow, revolutionize. **–ung,** *f.* upheaval; revolution.

umwand–eln, 1. *v.a.* (*sep.*) change, turn, metamorphose, transform, convert; conjugate, inflect (*Gram.*). 2. *v.r.* become assimilated (*Physiol.*). 3. *v.n.* (*insep.*) saunter round. **–elbar,** *adj.* convertible. **–ler,** *m.* transformer, converter (*Elec.*). **–lung,** *f.* change, transformation, metamorphosis; (*C.L.*) conversion. **–lungsfähig,** *adj.* convertible.

umwechs–eln, *v.a.* (*sep.*) exchange (for), change (*money*). **–(e)lung,** *f.* exchange, money changing.

Umweg, *m.* (-(e)s, -e) roundabout way, detour; (*fig.*) subterfuge, wile, ruse, (*coll.*) dodge; *auf –en*, indirectly, in a roundabout way, underhand, stealthily, by subterfuge; *–e machen*, go a roundabout way, take a circuitous route; shuffle, fence, hedge, practice double-dealing, employ evasions; *ohne –e*, straightforward, ingenuous, plain-spoken, without mincing matters *or* the matter, in plain English, straight to the point; *auf –en erfahren*, get to know by roundabout *or* devious means.

umwehen, *v.a.* (*sep.*) blow down; (*insep.*) blow around, fan (*with breezes*).

Umwelt, *f.* world around us, (social) surroundings, milieu, environment. **–seinflüsse,** *m.pl.* environmental factors.

umwend–en, (*sep.*) 1. *reg. & ir.v.a. & r.* turn, turn round *or* over; reverse, invert; *wie man eine Hand –et*, in a twinkling; *mit umgewandter Hand*, with the back of the hand; *es wendet mir das Herz um*, it wrings my heart; *umgewandte Seite*, wrong side (*of cloth, etc.*); *bitte umwenden!* please turn over! 2. *ir.v.n.* (*aux.* h. & s.), *see* **umkehren.** **–bar,** *adj.* reversible. **–ung,** *f.* veering (*of wind*).

umwerben, *ir.v.a.* (*insep.*) court, woo; *sie ist viel umworben*, she has many suitors, she is much sought after.

umwerfen, (*sep.*) 1. *ir.v.a.* overturn, upset, overthrow, subvert; throw round, throw *or* put on; reverse (*a judgement*). 2. *v.n.* (*aux.* h.) overturn, break down.

umwert–en, *v.a.* (*sep.*) ascribe a different value to, revalue, reassess. **–ung,** *f.* revaluation.

umwickeln, *v.a.* (*sep.*) wrap round, bind; cover, case, lap; (*insep.*) *mit etwas –*, wrap up in.

umwinden, *ir.v.a.* (*insep.*) twine *or* wind around, encircle; (*sep.*) twist around.

umwohn–end, *pr.p. & adj.*, neighbouring. **–er,** *m.pl.* inhabitants of the same latitude on the opposite side of the world.

umwölken, *v.a. & r.* (*insep.*) cloud (over), become overcast, darken.

umzäun–en, *v.a.* (*insep.*) enclose, hedge round, fence in. **–ung,** *f.* enclosing; enclosure, hedge, fence.

umziehen, 1. *ir.v.a.* (*sep.*) change (*clothes*), put fresh clothes on (*a child, etc.*); *die Schuhe –*, change one's shoes; *die Kleider –*, change one's clothes; (*insep.*) walk round, surround; draw the outlines of; cover, hang with, envelop. 2. *v.r.* (*sep.*) change (one's clothes); *er hat sich bei mir umgezogen*, he changed at my place; (*insep.*) *der Himmel hat sich umzogen*, the sky has become overcast. 2. *v.n.* (*sep.*) (*aux.* s.) remove, move (to), change one's dwelling; *er ist gestern umgezogen*, he moved (house) yesterday; (*Prov.*) *dreimal umgezogen ist einmal abgebrannt*, three removals are as bad as a fire.

umzing–eln, *v.a.* (*insep.*) surround, encompass, encircle, envelop, invest (*Mil.*). **–(e)lung,** *f.* investment, encirclement.

umzogen, *p.p.* overcast, *see* **umziehen** 1 (*insep.*).

Umzug, *m.* (-(e)s, ⸚e) change of dwelling, removal; procession. **–shalber,** *adv.* owing to removal *or* change of address. **–skosten,** *f.pl.* cost of removal, moving expenses.

umzüngeln, *v.a.* (*insep.*) play around, surround, envelop (*as flames*).

un-, *negative prefix* = un-, in-, im-, dis-, ir-, not, non-. *The principal meanings of* un- *are*: 1. *absolute negation, e.g.* **Unglück, unwahr;** 2. *a bad sort of, e.g.* **Unmensch, Untier;** 3. *excessive amount, e.g.* **Unmenge, Unsumme.** *Of the numberless compounds with* un- *only those are given in which the English equivalent is not also merely* un-. *In the case of compounds from nouns and adjectives formed from them, and of negative adjectives, the stress is usually on the prefix. In the case of verbal and participial negatives the position of stress may vary, depending on the emphasis desired on the negation.*

unabänderlich, *adj.* unalterable, unchangeable, everlasting, irrevocable, immutable. **–keit,** *f.* unchangeableness, immutability.

unabdingbar, *adj.* unalterable, irrevocable, final.

unabhängig, *adj.* independent, autonomous; unrelated, absolute (*Gram.*). **–keit,** *f.* independence, autonomy.

unabkömmlich, *adj.* indispensable, essential; reserved (*Mil.*). **–keit,** *f.* indispensability.

unablässig, *adj.* incessant, uninterrupted, unremitting, unceasing, interminable.

unablöslich, *adj.* irredeemable (*mortgage*), perpetual (*loan*); *–e Anleihe*, consolidated fund.

unabsehbar, *adj.* immense, unbounded, boundless, incalculable, immeasurable, unlimited, limitless, unfathomable.

unabsetzbar, *adj.* irremovable, immutable.

unabsichtlich, *adj.* unintentional, accidental, fortuitous, adventitious; involuntary, unintended.

unabweisbar, unabweislich, *adj.* unavoidable, inescapable, inevitable, irrevocable; pressing, urgent, imperative.

unabwendbar, *adj.*, *see* **unabweisbar.**

unachtsam, *adj.* inattentive, careless, negligent; thoughtless, mindless, unmindful, heedless, inadvertent. **–keit,** *f.* inattention, carelessness, heedlessness, negligence, inadvertence, inadvertency.

unähnlich, *adj.* unlike, dissimilar. **–keit,** *f.* unlikeness, dissimilarity, diversity.

unanfechtbar, *adj.* incontestable, indisputable, undeniable, incontrovertible.

unangebracht, *adj.* unsuitable, inapt, inappropriate, inopportune, inexpedient, unseemly, out of place.
unangefochten, *adj.* undisputed, undoubted, indubitable; unhampered, unhindered, unmolested; *laß mich – !* let me alone! let me be!
unangemessen, *adj.* inadequate, unfit, unfitting, unsuited, unsuitable, unseemly, improper, incompatible, incongruous.
unangenehm, *adj.* unpleasant, disagreeable, distasteful, displeasing, unwelcome.
unangesehen, 1. *adj.* not looked at; disregarded, unheeded. 2. *prep.* (*Gen. or Acc.*) (*archaic*) irrespective of.
unangreifbar, *adj.* unassailable; unimpeachable, secure, safe (*from attack*).
Unannehmlichkeit, *f.* (-en) unpleasantness, disagreeableness, vexatiousness, irksomeness, inconvenience; annoyance, trouble, nuisance.
unansehnlich, *adj.* poor-looking, plain, unattractive, unsightly, ill-favoured, unprepossessing, inconsiderable, mean, ordinary, paltry, insignificant. **–keit,** *f.* plainness, homeliness, smallness, paltriness, insignificance.
unanständig, *adj.* improper, indecent, indecorous, immodest, unseemly, indelicate, unmannerly, coarse, loose, gross, shocking. **–keit,** *f.* impropriety, immodesty, indelicacy, indecency, coarseness, grossness, unmannerliness.
unanstellig, *adj.* awkward, clumsy, unskilful, unhandy, bungling, maladroit.
unanstößig, *adj.* inoffensive, harmless, innocuous, unobjectionable.
unantastbar, *adj.* inviolable, incontestable, inassailable, inalienable, unimpeachable, prescriptive, sacrosanct.
unanwendbar, *adj.* inapplicable; inapposite, unsuitable, unbefitting, unadapted. **–keit,** *f.* inapplicability.
unappetitlich, *adj.* not appetizing; uninviting; disgusting, repellent.
Unart, 1. *f.* ill breeding, bad manners, rudeness, incivility; bad habit; bad behaviour, naughtiness (*of children*). 2. *m.* (-s, -e) (*coll.*) naughty child. **–ig,** *adj.* badly behaved, naughty; ill-bred, rude; vicious (*of horses*). **–igkeit,** *f.*, *see* – 1.
unartikuliert, *adj.* inarticulate.
unästhetisch, *adj.* repellent, odious, horrid; unrefined, coarse, vulgar.
unauffällig, *adj.* unobtrusive, inconspicuous.
unauffindbar, *adj.* not to be found, undiscoverable, impenetrable.
unaufgefordert, *adj.* uncalled for, unasked, unbidden, of one's own accord, voluntarily, freely, spontaneously.
unaufgeschnitten, *adj.* uncut (*of books*).
unaufhalt–bar, –sam, *adj.* without stopping, incessant; irresistible; impetuous.
unaufhörlich, *adj.* incessant, constant, continuous, unceasing, unending, perpetual, endless.
unauflös–bar, –lich, *adj.* insoluble, impenetrable, inscrutable, undecipherable; inexplicable.
unaufmerksam, *adj.* inattentive; absent-minded. **–keit,** *f.* inattention, absent-mindedness, daydreaming, wool-gathering.
unaufrichtig, *adj.* insincere, deceitful, disingenuous, underhand, double-faced, shady, shifty.
unaufschiebbar, *adj.* pressing, urgent, vital.
unausbleiblich, *adj.* unfailing, certain; inevitable, inexorable, ineluctable.
unausführbar, *adj.* impracticable, not feasible, impossible.
unausgemacht, *adj.* undecided, uncertain, not settled, questionable.
unausgesetzt, 1. *adj.* continual, perpetual, uninterrupted, unending, constant. 2. *adv.* continually, without interruption.
unausgesprochen, *adj.* unspoken, tacit; (*fig.*) implied, inferred, implicit.
unauslöschlich, *adj.* inextinguishable, indelible, unquenchable, imperishable, indestructible; *–e Dankbarkeit,* undying gratitude; *–e Tinte,* permanent ink; *–e Erinnerung,* ineffaceable memory.
unaussprech–bar, *adj.* unpronounceable. **–lich,** *adj.* inexpressible, indefinable; unspeakable, unutterable, stupendous, ineffable.
unausstehlich, *adj.* insufferable, unbearable, unendurable, insupportable, intolerable; hateful, odious.
unaustilgbar, *adj.* ineradicable, indelible, ineffaceable.
unausweichlich, *adj.* inevitable, unavoidable, inescapable.
Unband, *m.* (-(e)s, ⸚e & -e) unruly child.
unbändig, *adj.* unruly, intractable, wayward, headstrong, refractory; (*coll.*) excessive, tremendous; (*coll.*) *er hat sich – gefreut,* he was mighty *or* mightily pleased.
unbarmherzig, *adj.* unmerciful, merciless, pitiless, relentless, unrelenting, ruthless, hard, cruel, inhuman. **–keit,** *f.* harshness, cruelty.
unbeachtet, 1. *adj.* unnoticed, neglected, unheeded, disregarded. 2. *adv.* notwithstanding; – *lassen,* ignore, disregard, overlook, pay no regard to.
unbeanstandet, *adj.* not objected to, unexceptionable, unopposed, unhampered, uncensured, unimpeached.
unbearbeitet, *adj.* unwrought, undressed, unformed, in the raw *or* native state, rough, crude, raw; not treated before (*of a subject*).
unbedacht, –sam, *adj.* inconsiderate, unthinking, remiss, thoughtless, careless, imprudent, improvident, indiscreet, rash. **–samkeit,** *f.* negligence, remissness, inadvertency (*aus,* through).
unbedenklich, 1. *adj.* unhesitating, unswerving; unobjectionable, harmless, inoffensive. 2. *adv.* unhesitatingly, resolutely, without hesitation *or* scruples.
unbedeutend, *adj.* insignificant, unimportant, immaterial, of no account *or* consequence, trifling, trivial. **–heit** (*Austr. also* **Unbedeutenheit**) *f.* insignificance, unimportance, paltriness.
unbedingt, 1. *adj.* unconditional, unquestioning, unqualified, absolute; implicit. 2. *adv.* whatever happens, without fail.
unbefähigt, *adj.* incompetent, untalented, ill-qualified, unqualified.
unbefahr–bar, *adj.* impracticable, impassable. **–en,** *adj.* untraversed, untrodden, pathless, trackless; *–enes Volk,* inexperienced sailors; green hands.
unbefangen, *adj.* unprejudiced, unbiased, impartial, disinterested; calm, dispassionate, unembarrassed, unabashed; unconstrained, free and easy; artless, natural, unaffected, ingenuous. **–heit,** *f.* impartiality, freedom from bias; ease, unreservedness, ingenuousness, openness, simplicity, naivete, naïveté, candour.
unbefestigt, *adj.* unfortified, open (*town, etc.*).
unbefiedert, *adj.* without feathers, unfledged.
unbefleckt, *adj.* spotless, undefiled, unblemished, unsullied, unspotted, blameless, pure, virgin; immaculate; *–te Empfängnis,* immaculate conception.
unbefrachtet, *adj.* unfreighted, empty.
unbefriedig–end, *adj.* unsatisfying, unsatisfactory, disappointing, insufficient. **–t,** *adj.* unsatisfied, dissatisfied, discontented, disappointed; unappeased. **–theit,** *f.* dissatisfaction.
unbefugt, *adj.* unauthorized, unwarranted, incompetent. **–e(r),** *m.* trespasser; *–en ist der Eintritt untersagt!* no admittance except on business! **–erweise,** *adv.* without authority.
unbegabt, *adj.* not gifted *or* clever, untalented. **–heit,** *f.* lack of talent.
unbegreiflich, *adj.* inconceivable, incredible, incomprehensible; inexplicable. **–keit,** *f.* incomprehensibility, incredibility; incredible thing; mystery.
unbegrenz–bar, *adj.* illimitable. **–t,** *adj.* boundless, unbounded, limitless, unlimited, infinite. **–theit,** *f.* boundlessness, infinitude.
unbegründet, *adj.* unfounded, groundless; spurious, factitious.
unbegütert, *adj.* without landed property; not rich, not well off, badly off.
unbehaart, *adj.* hairless, bald; smooth; smooth-leaved (*Bot.*); glabrous (*Anat.*).
Unbehag–en, *n.* discomfort, uneasiness, malaise; disquiet, displeasure. **–lich,** *adj.* unpleasant; un-

comfortable, uneasy, ill at ease. **–lichkeit,** *f.* uneasiness.
unbehelligt, *adj.* unmolested, undisturbed.
unbehilflich, *adj.* helpless.
unbehindert, *adj.* unrestrained, unimpeded, unencumbered, untrammelled, unhindered.
unbeholfen, *adj.* clumsy, awkward, bungling; ungainly, brusque, blunt, bluff; embarrassed. **–heit,** *f.* clumsiness, awkwardness, brusqueness, ungraciousness.
unbeirr–bar, *adj.* imperturbable, unruffled, composed. **–t,** *adj.* unperturbed, unflinching, unconcerned.
unbekannt, 1. *adj.* unknown, unheard of, obscure; ignorant, unaware (*mit,* of); unacquainted, unconversant (with), a stranger (to), unversed (in); *er ist mir –,* I do not know him; *es wird dir nicht – sein, daß . . .,* you know, of course, that . . .; *ich bin hier –,* I am a stranger here; *–e Größe,* unknown quantity (*Math.*). 2. *n.* person or persons unknown (*Law*). **–erweise,** *adv.* unwittingly, without personal knowledge. **–heit,** *f.* unfamiliarity; ignorance.
unbekehrbar, *adj.* inconvertible, confirmed.
unbekümmert, *adj.* untroubled, carefree; unconcerned, careless. **–heit,** *f.* unconcern, carelessness.
unbelaubt, *adj.* leafless, bare, without foliage, aphyllous.
unbelebt, *adj.* lifeless, inanimate; dull, dead, slack, inactive, torpid, sluggish; unfrequented, empty (*streets*). **–heit,** *f.* lifelessness; dullness, torpidity.
unbeleckt, *adj.*; (*coll.*) *von der Kultur –,* without any trace of culture, uncultured, uncivilized, barbarous.
unbelesen, *adj.* unlettered, unread, illiterate.
unbeliebt, *adj.* disliked, unpopular. **–heit,** *f.* unpopularity.
unbemerk–bar, *adj.* imperceptible, undiscernible, unapparent. **–t,** *adj.* unperceived, unnoticed, unobserved, unseen.
unbemittelt, *adj.* poor, needy, poverty-stricken.
unbenannt, *adj.* nameless, unnamed, anonymous; *–e Zahl,* abstract number.
unbenommen, *adj.* permitted; *es ist* (*bleibt*) *Ihnen – zu . . .,* you are (still) free *or* at liberty to. . . .
unbenutzt, *adj.* unused, unemployed; idle (*of money*); *das wird er nicht – lassen,* he will make good use of it.
unbequem, *adj.* uncomfortable, inconvenient, irksome, troublesome, disagreeable, embarrassing, inopportune. **–lichkeit,** *f.* inconvenience, discomfort.
unberechenbar, *adj.* incalculable, unfathomable; *er ist ganz –,* there is no telling what he will do.
unberechtigt, *adj.* unauthorized, unjustified, unlawful, unwarranted, without authority; not entitled (to); unqualified.
unberitten, *adj.* not broken in (*of horses*); unmounted (*of cavalry*).
unberücksichtigt, *adj.* unconsidered, unheeded, disregarded, overlooked, not taken into account.
unberufen, *adj.* unauthorized, unjustified, uncalled for, unwarrantable, gratuitous, officious; (*coll.*) *–!* touch wood!
unberührt, *adj.* untouched, unused, intact; innocent, chaste; virgin (*forest, soil*); unmoved (by), proof (against), inured (to); unnoticed, passed over in silence.
unbeschadet, *prep.* (*Gen.*) without detriment to, without prejudice to.
unbeschädigt, *adj.* uninjured, undamaged, unhurt, intact, safe and sound; (*C.L.*) in good condition.
unbeschaffen, *adj.* (*dial.*) sickly, poorly, ailing.
unbescheiden, *adj.* unabashed, unblushing, self-opiniated, arrogant, presumptuous, impudent, overweening, forward; (*coll.*) stuck up, bumptious; unreasonable, exorbitant (*demands*). **–heit,** *f.* presumptuousness, arrogance, bumptiousness, assurance, effrontery; (*coll.*) brass, cheek, lip, side, nerve.
unbeschnitten, *adj.* uncircumcised; unshorn, untrimmed; unclipped (*of coin*); uncut (*of books*).
unbescholten, *adj.* irreproachable, blameless; of good reputation. **–heit,** *f.* integrity, good name, blamelessness.
unbeschränkt, *adj.* boundless, unlimited, infinite; absolute, unconditional, uncontrolled; discretionary. **–heit,** *f.* limitlessness; absoluteness.
unbeschreiblich, *adj.* indescribable, inexpressible, unutterable, unaccountable; stupendous, prodigious, wondrous, monstrous, beggaring description.
unbeschrieben, *adj.* blank; unwritten, undescribed.
unbeschwert, *adj.* unburdened, easy, light (*conscience*).
unbeseelt, *adj.* soulless, spiritless, lifeless, inanimate.
unbesehen, *adv.* without examination *or* inspection; unseen; just as it is; (*dial.*) suddenly; *etwas – kaufen,* buy a pig in a poke.
unbesetzt, *adj.* unoccupied, empty, free, vacant, disengaged; *dieser Stuhl ist –,* this chair is vacant *or* free.
unbesieg–bar, –lich, *adj.* invincible, unconquerable.
unbesonnen, *adj.* thoughtless, inconsiderate, ill-advised, heedless, reckless, rash; indiscreet, imprudent. **–heit,** *f.* imprudence, thoughtlessness, indiscretion, rashness, recklessness.
unbesorgt, *adj.* unconcerned; carefree; *seien Sie* (*deswegen*) *–!* do not trouble yourself (about), do not worry, make your mind easy (about that)!
Unbestand, *m.* instability, impermanence, fugitiveness, changeableness, inconstancy.
unbeständig, *adj.* inconstant, unstable, unsteady, changeable, unsettled, fluctuating, variable, erratic, shifting, fickle, labile. **–keit,** *f.* inconstancy, inconsistency, instability, variability.
unbestellbar, *adj.* 'addressee unknown', dead (*letter*).
unbestimm–bar, *adj.* indeterminable, undefinable; equivocal, problematic, vague, nondescript. **–t,** *adj.* indeterminate, undetermined, undefined, ambiguous, indefinite, uncertain, indecisive, undecided, doubtful; vague; unlimited; *–tes Zahlwort,* indefinite numeral; *auf –te Zeit vertagen,* put off indefinitely, adjourn sine die. **–theit,** *f.* indefiniteness, uncertainty, vagueness; indecision, lack of determination.
unbestreitbar, *adj.* incontestable, indisputable, undeniable, unquestionable, acknowledged.
unbestritten, *adj.* undisputed, uncontested; absolutely certain, positive, categorical.
unbeteiligt, *adj.*; *bei etwas –,* not interested *or* concerned in, indifferent to *or* not participating in a th.
unbeträchtlich, *adj.* trifling, trivial, scant, inconsiderable, inappreciable, of little importance.
unbeugsam, *adj.* inflexible, unbending, stubborn, obstinate, firm. **–keit,** *f.* inflexibility, stubbornness, obstinacy.
unbewaffnet, *adj.* unarmed, defenceless; thornless (*Bot.*); *mit –em Auge,* with the unaided *or* naked eye.
unbewandert, *adj.* inexperienced; unskilled, unversed.
unbeweg–lich, *adj.* immovable, immutable, fixed, motionless; real (*property*); apathetic, impassive, unimpressionable, unresponsive; resolved, determined; unbending, uncompromising, inflexible. **–lichkeit,** *f.* immutability, stability, permanence, fixedness, inflexibility. **–t,** *adj.* motionless; unflinching, unwavering, unmoved, unshaken, inflexible.
unbeweibt, *adj.* unmarried, single, bachelor.
unbewohn–bar, *adj.* uninhabitable. **–t,** *adj.* uninhabited, deserted, vacant.
unbewußt, *adj.* unconscious, unaware; involuntary; instinctive; *sich* (*Dat.*) *einer S. – sein,* not be aware of a th.; *es ist mir nichts weniger als –,* I know it all too well; *Philosophie des –en,* philosophy of the unconscious. **–heit,** *f.* unawareness, unconsciousness.
unbezahlbar, *adj.* priceless.
unbezähmbar, *adj.* untamable; unyielding, indomitable.
unbezwing–bar, –lich, *adj.* invincible, indomitable, unconquerable, unassailable, impregnable.
unbiegsam, *adj.* inflexible, unbending, stiff, rigid. **–keit,** *f.* inflexibility, rigidity.
Unbilden, *f.pl.* injury, hardship; wrong, injustice; *see* **Unbill;** *– der Witterung,* inclemency of the weather; *– des Winters,* rigour of winter.

Unbildung, *f.* lack of education *or* culture.
Unbill, *f.* (**Unbilden,** *q.v.*) iniquity, wrong, injustice; insult; inclemency (*of weather*). **–ig,** *adj.* unfair, unjust; unreasonable; iniquitous. **–igkeit,** *f.* iniquity; injustice, unfairness.
unblutig, *adj.* bloodless, unbloody (*R.C.*).
unbotmäßig, *adj.* insubordinate, unruly, refractory, contumacious. **–keit,** *f.* insubordination, unruliness, contumacy.
unbrauchbar, *adj.* useless, unserviceable, of no use. **–keit,** *f.* uselessness.
unbußfertig, *adj.* impenitent, unrepentant.
unchristlich, *adj.* unchristian, uncharitable.
und, *conj.* and; *an dem – dem Platze* or *da – da,* at such-and-such a place; – *?* and then? and afterwards? well! *er – Furcht haben!* he afraid! – *wenn,* even if; – *ich auch nicht,* nor I either; *fort – fort,* on and on; *für – für,* continually, incessantly; – *zwar,* that is; – *desgleichen* (*mehr*), and so forth.
Undank, *m.* ingratitude. **–bar,** *adj.* ungrateful, thankless (*task*). **–barkeit,** *f.* ingratitude.
undefinierbar, *adj.* indefinable.
undehnbar, *adj.* inextensible; inelastic, nonductile.
undeklinierbar, *adj.* indeclinable.
undenk–bar, *adj.* inconceivable, incredible, unthinkable, out of the question. **–lich,** *adj.* immemorial, long past; *seit –licher Zeit,* for ages, from time out of mind.
undeutlich, *adj.* indistinct, blurred, hazy; obscure, vague, confused, unintelligible; inarticulate. **–keit,** *f.* indistinctness, haziness, vagueness; obscurity, confusion, lack of clarity.
undicht, *adj.* not watertight, leaky, unsound, pervious. **–igkeit,** *f.* leakage, leak.
Unding, *n.* (-(e)s, -e) impossibility, absurdity, nonsense.
unduldsam, *adj.* intolerant, impatient. **–keit,** *f.* intolerance.
undurchdringlich, *adj.* impenetrable, impermeable, impervious, watertight, waterproof.
undurchführbar, *adj.* impracticable, not feasible.
undurchlässig, *adj.* impermeable, impervious (*für,* to), waterproof, light-tight.
undurchsichtig, *adj.* non-transparent, opaque. **–keit,** *f.* opaqueness, opacity.
uneben, *adj.* uneven, rough, rugged; (*coll.*) *nicht –,* not bad, rather good. **–bürtig,** *adj.* of inferior rank. **–heit,** *f.* unevenness, irregularity, roughness, ruggedness.
unecht, *adj.* not genuine, false, sham, spurious, counterfeit(ed), imitation, artificial; not fast (*of colours*), affected (*gegen,* by), fugitive (to) (*light, etc.*); improper (*Arith.*). **–heit,** *f.* artificiality; spuriousness.
unedel, *adj.* ignoble, vulgar, base; inert, electronegative.
unehelich, *adj.* illegitimate, natural (*child*), unmarried (*mother*).
unehr–bar, *adj.* disgraceful, improper, immodest, indecent. **–barkeit,** *f.* indecency. **–e,** *f.* dishonour, disgrace, discredit. **–enhaft,** *adj.* dishonourable, discreditable. **–erbietig,** *adj.* disrespectful, irreverent. **–erbietigkeit,** *f.* irreverence, want of respect. **–lich,** *adj.* dishonest, insincere, underhand, false, (*coll.*) shady, shifty, double-faced. **–lichkeit,** *f.* dishonesty, insincerity, duplicity, double-dealing.
uneigennützig, *adj.* disinterested, unselfish, magnanimous, altruistic.
uneigentlich, *adj.* not literal, figurative.
uneinbringlich, *adj.* irretrievable, irrecoverable.
uneingedenk, *adj.* (*Gen.*) forgetful *or* unmindful of; regardless of.
uneinig, *adj.* disunited, disagreeing, at variance (with); – *sein,* disagree (with), be at variance *or* odds (with), dissent (from), differ (from); – *werden,* quarrel, wrangle, squabble, fall out, disagree; *ich bin mit mir selber noch* – or *uneins,* I have not quite made up my mind yet. **–keit,** *f.* disunion; disagreement, dissension, discord, misunderstanding, dispute.
uneinnehmbar, *adj.* impregnable, invulnerable.
uneins, *adv.*; – *sein,* disagree (with), be at odds *or* variance (with), join issue (with), fall foul (of); *see* **uneinig.**
unempfänglich, *adj.* unreceptive, insusceptible (*für,* to), unimpressionable.
unempfindlich, *adj.* insensible (*gegen,* to), insensitive (to), indifferent (to), unaffected (by), resistant (to); (*fig.*) cold, unfeeling, apathetic. **–keit,** *f.* coldness, indifference, insensibility, stability (*Chem.*).
unendlich, *adj.* infinite, endless, unlimited, illimitable, immense; – *klein,* infinitesimal; *ins –e,* ad infinitum; *das geht ins –e,* there is no end to it; **–keit,** *f.* infinity, endlessness.
unentbehrlich, *adj.* indispensable, essential, absolutely necessary. **–keit,** *f.* absolute necessity.
unentgeltlich, *adj.* free (of charge), for nothing, gratis, gratuitous, (*sl.*) buckshee.
unenthaltsam, *adj.* incontinent, intemperate, self-indulgent.
unentschieden, *adj.* undecided, in dispute, uncertain, drawn (*game*); indecisive, irresolute; *–e Frage,* open question. **–heit,** *f.* indecision, uncertainty.
unentschlossen, *adj.* undecided, irresolute, wavering, vacillating, indecisive. **–heit,** *f.* indecision, irresolution, vacillation.
unentschuldbar, *adj.* inexcusable, unpardonable, indefensible.
unentwegt, *adj.* firm, steadfast, unflinching; staunch; *die –en,* the die-hards.
unentwickelt, *adj.* undeveloped, immature, in embryo.
unentwirrbar, *adj.* inextricable, involved, tangled.
unentzifferbar, *adj.* indecipherable, inscrutable.
unentzündbar, *adj.* non-inflammable.
unerachtet, *prep.* (*archaic*), *see* **ungeachtet 2.**
unerbittlich, *adj.* inexorable, relentless, unrelenting, inflexible, unbending, pitiless.
unerbrochen, *adj.* intact, unopened (*letter*), unbroken (*seal*).
unerfahren, *adj.* inexperienced; inexpert, unskilled; (*coll.*) raw, green.
unerfindlich, *adj.* undiscoverable, incomprehensible, impenetrable, unknowable, bewildering, baffling, mysterious; *es ist mir –,* it is a mystery to me, it baffles me.
unerforschlich, *adj.* impenetrable, inexplicable, inscrutable.
unerfreulich, *adj.* unpleasant, displeasing, unwelcome, distasteful, vexatious, unsatisfactory, thankless, tiresome, irksome.
unerfüllbar, *adj.* unrealizable, impossible of fulfilment.
unergiebig, *adj.* unproductive, unfruitful, unprofitable; sterile, barren.
unergründlich, *adj.* unfathomable, bottomless; impenetrable.
unerheblich, *adj.* insignificant, unimportant, inconsiderable, trivial, trifling; immaterial, irrelevant.
unerhört, *adj.* unheard, not granted, disallowed, turned down; unheard of, unprecedented; shocking, scandalous; exorbitant.
unerkenntlich, *adj.* ungrateful, unmindful. **–keit,** *f.* ingratitude, thanklessness.
unerklär–bar, –lich, *adj.* inexplicable, unaccountable, puzzling, enigmatical, abstruse, obscure.
unerläßlich, *adj.* indispensable; essential, requisite.
unerlaubt, *adj.* unlawful, illicit, forbidden, unauthorized.
unerledigt, *adj.* unfinished, unaccomplished, left undone, not disposed of.
unermeßlich, *adj.* immense, immeasurable, boundless, unbounded; vast, huge, untold.
unermüdlich, *adj.* indefatigable, unflagging, untiring, unremitting.
unerquicklich, *adj.* unpleasant, unedifying; uncomfortable, disagreeable.
unerreich–bar, *adj.* unattainable, inaccessible, out of reach, unprocurable, unobtainable, impracticable. **–t,** *adj.* unequalled, unrivalled, unparalleled, record (*performance*).
unersättlich, *adj.* insatiable, ravenous, rapacious, avid.
unerschlossen, *adj.* undeveloped (*of territory, etc.*), not opened up.
unerschöpflich, *adj.* inexhaustible.

unerschrocken, *adj.* fearless, intrepid, undaunted, undismayed. **-heit,** *f.* fearlessness, intrepidity.
unerschütterlich, *adj.* immovable, unshakeable, imperturbable, unflinching, firm as a rock.
unerschwinglich, *adj.* unattainable; beyond one's means, exorbitant, unreasonably dear; *das ist mir –*, I cannot afford it, it is too dear for me.
unersetzlich, *adj.* irreparable, irretrievable, irrecoverable, irreplaceable.
unersprießlich, *adj.* unpleasant, displeasing, distasteful; unprofitable, fruitless.
unerträglich, *adj.* intolerable, unbearable, insupportable, insufferable, overpowering (*heat, etc.*).
unerwartet, *adj.* unexpected, unlooked for, unforeseen; sudden, abrupt.
unerweis-bar, -lich, *adj.* indemonstrable.
unerwidert, *adj.* unanswered (*letter*); unreturned, unrequited (*love*).
unerwiesen, *adj.* not proved, unconfirmed; not proven (*Scottish Law*).
unerzogen, *adj.* unmannerly, ill-bred, churlish.
unfähig, *adj.* incapable (of), unable (to), unfit (for); incompetent, disabled. **-keit,** *f.* unfitness, incompetence, incapacity, inability, disability.
Unfall, *m.* (-(e)s, ⸗e) accident, mishap, misadventure; misfortune, mischance; disaster, calamity, catastrophe; *– mit tödlichem Ausgang*, fatal accident. **-station,** *f.* first-aid post. **-versicherung,** *f.* accident insurance.
unfaßbar, *adj.* unintelligible, inconceivable, incomprehensible.
unfehlbar, 1. *adj.* inevitable, unavoidable, unfailing, infallible, unerring. 2. *adv.* certainly, surely. **-keit,** *f.* infallibility.
unfein, *adj.* coarse, indelicate, unmannerly, impolite, rude, tactless.
unfern, 1. *adv.* not far off, near. 2. *prep.* (*with Gen., Dat. or* von) near, not far from.
unfertig, *adj.* unfinished, incomplete, immature.
Unflat, *m.* filth, dirt; riff-raff.
Unflät-er, *m.* (-s, –) filthy beast. **-ig,** *adj.* filthy, dirty; nasty, beastly, lewd. **-igkeit,** *f.* dirtiness, filthiness, nastiness, lewdness, beastliness.
unfolgsam, *adj.* disobedient, unruly, wilful, wayward (*of children*). **-keit,** *f.* disobedience.
Unform, *f.* deformity, monstrosity.
unförm-ig, *adj.* misshapen, deformed; shapeless, unwieldy, clumsy. **-igkeit,** *f.* shapelessness. **-lich,** *adj.* unwieldy, shapeless, clumsy; informal, unceremonious.
unfrankiert, *adj.* not prepaid, unstamped (*letter*).
unfrei, *adj.* constrained, embarrassed; dependent, subject, subjugated, in bondage *or* thrall to, feudatory; *see also* **unfrankiert. -gebig,** *adj.* illiberal, niggardly, parsimonious, ungenerous, close-fisted, (*coll.*) mean, stingy. **-willig,** *adj.* involuntary, compulsory.
unfreund-lich, *adj.* unfriendly, unkind, disobliging, ungracious, uncharitable; ill-disposed, spiteful, churlish, cold; harsh, unpleasant, cheerless (*as a room*), inclement (*weather*). **-lichkeit,** *f.* unfriendliness, unkindness, ill will, ill feeling; cheerlessness (*of a room*); inclemency (*of the weather*). **-schaftlich,** *adj.* unfriendly.
Unfried-e(n), *m.* discord, dissension, strife, enmity, friction. **-lich,** *adj.* discordant, dissentient, factious, quarrelsome.
unfruchtbar, *adj.* unfruitful, unprofitable, unproductive; barren, sterile; *auf -en Boden fallen*, fall upon stony ground, produce no effect (*bei einem*, on a p.). **-keit,** *f.* barrenness, sterility. **-machung,** *f.* sterilization.
Unfug, *m.* disorder, disturbance; offence, misdemeanour; misconduct, nuisance; nonsense, mischief; *grober –*, gross misconduct; *großer –*, sheer nonsense; *– treiben*, be up to mischief.
unfühlbar, *adj.* impalpable, intangible, imperceptible.
ungangbar, *adj.* impassable, impracticable; not current (*of coins*); unsaleable (*of wares*).
ungastlich, *adj.* inhospitable, unsociable. **-keit,** *f.* inhospitality.
ungattlich, *adj.* (*Swiss dial.*) clumsy, massive, misshapen.
ungeachtet, 1. *adj.* disregarded, unnoticed, overlooked, snubbed. 2. *prep.* (*with Gen. or rarely Dat.*) notwithstanding, in spite of; *des–* (*Austr. dial.*), *dessen–* or *dem–*, in spite of that, for all that. 3. *conj.* though, although, nevertheless.
ungebärdig, *adj.* wild, unruly, boisterous, rowdy.
ungebeten, *adj.* uninvited; unasked, unbidden; *-er Gast*, intruder; (*sl.*) gate-crasher.
ungebildet, *adj.* rude, ill-bred, discourteous, unmannerly; uneducated, uncultured, unrefined.
Ungebühr, *f.* indecency, impropriety; abuse, excess; *zur –*, unduly, to excess. **-end,** *adj.*, **-lich,** *adj.* undue, excessive; unbecoming, unsuitable, unseemly, improper, indecorous, indecent. **-lichkeit,** *f.* impropriety, indecency.
ungebunden, *adj.* unbound, in sheets; free and easy, unrestrained, unbridled; licentious, dissolute, (*coll.*) loose; free, unlinked, uncombined; *-e Rede*, prose. **-heit,** *f.* freedom, liberty; lack of restraint, licence, dissoluteness, licentiousness, profligacy.
ungedeckt, *adj.* uncovered, dishonoured (*cheque*); open, exposed, unprotected; *der Tisch ist noch –*, the table is not yet laid.
Ungedeih, *m.* only in *auf Gedeih und –*, in success or failure, in sickness or in health.
Ungeduld, *f.* impatience. **-ig,** *adj.* impatient.
ungeeignet, *adj.* unsuitable, unsuited, unfit (*zu*, for), inappropriate, incongruous, inopportune. **-heit,** *f.* unsuitableness, unfitness, inappropriateness, incongruity.
ungefähr, 1. *adj.* casual, vague, accidental; approximate; *-er Stoß*, chance blow; *-e Berechnung*, approximate calculation. 2. *adv.* casually, by chance; about, nearly, almost, approximately; *vor – einem Monat*, about a month ago; *das war –, was er mir sagte*, that was pretty much what he said to me. 3. *n. von –*, by chance, by accident. **-det,** *adj.* safe, secure, unharmed, out of harm's way, in safety. **-lich,** *adj.* not dangerous, harmless, safe, innocuous.
ungefällig, *adj.* discourteous, ungracious, uncivil, churlish, unaccommodating, disobliging, disagreeable, unkind; ungraceful, ungainly, brusque. **-keit,** *f.* unkindness, discourtesy, incivility.
ungeflügelt, *adj.* wingless, apterous.
ungefrierbar, *adj.* non-freezing, uncongealable.
ungefüg-e, *adj.* misshapen, clumsy, huge, massive, monstrous. **-ig,** *adj.* inflexible, unbending, unyielding; unwieldy, unmanageable; disobedient.
ungehalten, *adj.* angry, indignant (*über*, about; *auf with Acc.*, with).
ungeheißen, 1. *adj.* unbidden, unasked, uninvited. 2. *adv.* voluntarily, of one's own accord, spontaneously.
ungeheuer, 1. *adj.* huge, colossal, enormous, monstrous; atrocious, frightful. 2. *adv.* exceedingly, (*coll.*) mighty, mightily. 3. *n.* (-s, –) monster. **-lich,** *adj.* monstrous, atrocious, shocking. **-lichkeit,** *f.* monstrosity, atrocity, enormity.
ungehobelt, *adj.* unplaned, (*fig.*) rude, rough, uncouth, boorish, without polish *or* manners.
ungehörig, *adj.* undue, unmerited; unseemly, improper; impertinent, impudent. **-keit,** *f.* impropriety, unseemliness; impertinence; incongruity.
ungehorsam, 1. *adj.* disobedient, refractory, intractable; insubordinate. 2. *m.* disobedience, insubordination, non-compliance; default (*Law*).
ungekocht, *adj.* uncooked, raw.
ungekränkt, *adj.* unhurt, uninjured, unimpaired, untouched; *der Vorwurf läßt mich –*, that reproach leaves me cold.
ungekünstelt, *adj.* unaffected, artless, naïve, ingenuous, simple, natural, frank. **-heit,** *f.* artlessness, naïveté, ingenuousness, candour, simplicity.
ungeladen, *adj.* unloaded, not loaded; uninvited, unbidden.
Ungeld, *n.* (*dial.*) a mint of money.
ungeleg-en, *adj.* inconvenient, inexpedient, inopportune, unwelcome, unseasonable, unsuitable. **-enheit,** *f.* inconvenience, inexpediency, inopportuneness, unseasonableness; *einem -enheiten machen*, inconvenience a p., give a p. trouble.
ungelegt, *adj.* unlaid; *kümmere dich nicht um -e*

Eier, don't count your chickens before they're hatched.

ungelehrig, *adj.* unteachable, incapable of learning, dull, unintelligent.

ungelenk-(ig), *adj.* stiff, ungainly, uncouth, awkward, clumsy. **-heit,** *f.*, **-igkeit,** *f.* stiffness; awkwardness.

ungelernt, *adj.* unskilled (*workman*).

ungelogen, *adj.* (*coll.*) without a word of a lie.

ungelöscht, *adj.* unquenched; *-er Kalk*, unslaked lime, quicklime.

Ungemach, *n.* discomfort, privation, hardship, trouble, toil.

ungemächlich, *adj.* unpleasant, disagreeable, uncomfortable; troublesome, tiresome, irksome, annoying. **-keit,** *f.* unpleasantness, irksomeness, discomfort.

ungemein, 1. *adj.* extraordinary, unusual, uncommon. 2. *adv.* greatly, extremely, exceedingly, intensely, supremely, acutely, inordinately, extraordinarily, unspeakably, particularly, remarkably, singularly, profoundly.

ungemessen, *adj.* boundless, immense, unlimited; *ins -e gehen* or *wachsen*, go beyond all limits, know no bounds. **-heit,** *f.* excess, boundlessness.

ungemütlich, *adj.* cheerless, uncomfortable, unpleasant; (*coll.*) *- werden*, get awkward, turn nasty.

ungenannt, *adj.* anonymous; nameless, unnamed.

ungenau, *adj.* inaccurate, inexact. **-igkeit,** *f.* inaccuracy, inexactitude.

ungeneigt, *adj.* disinclined, unwilling (to), averse (from), reluctant; unfriendly. **-heit,** *f.* disinclination, reluctance; ill will.

ungeniert, 1. *adj.* unembarrassed, unabashed, free and easy. 2. *adv.* unhesitatingly, without let or hindrance. **-heit,** *f.* lack of constraint, free and easy way(s); unceremoniousness.

ungenießbar, *adj.* unpalatable, uneatable, inedible; dull, tedious, boring, unbearable; (*coll.*) *- sein*, be in a bad humour, be sullen *or* surly, (*coll.*) be grumpy.

ungenüg-end, *adj.* insufficient; below standard, unsatisfactory. **-sam,** *adj.* exacting; insatiable. **-samkeit,** *f.* greediness, avidity, insatiability.

ungenutzt, ungenützt, *adj.* unused, not made use of, not taken advantage of.

ungeordnet, *adj.* disorganized, disorderly, disarranged, deranged, unregulated, incoherent; *-er Lebenswandel*, dissolute life.

ungepflegt, *adj.* untidy, neglected, unkempt.

ungerade, *adj.* not straight, uneven; odd (*number*).

ungeraten, *adj.* abortive, stultified, unavailing, ineffectual, unsuccessful, ruined, spoiled, (*coll.*) done for; (*dial.*) dirty; *-e Kinder*, spoiled *or* undutiful children.

ungerechnet, *adj.* not counted; not included, not taken into account.

ungerecht, *adj.* unjust, unfair, inequitable, unrighteous. **-igkeit,** *f.* injustice, unfairness.

ungerechtfertigt, *adj.* unjustified, unwarranted, unauthorized.

ungereimt, *adj.* unrhymed; (*fig.*) nonsensical, absurd. **-heit,** *f.* absurdity, nonsense, inanity.

ungern, *adv.* unwillingly, reluctantly, regretfully, grudgingly, perforce, (*coll.*) against the grain; *ich sehe -*, I am sorry to see; *gern oder -*, willy-nilly, whether you like it or not.

ungerochen, *adj.* (*archaic*), *see* **ungerächt.**

ungerupft, *adj.* unplucked; *- davonkommen*, get off lightly, not be fleeced.

ungesäuert, *adj.* unleavened, azymous.

ungesäumt, 1. *adj.* seamless. 2. *adv.* without delay, at once, immediately, straightway, forthwith.

ungeschehen, *adj.* undone; rectified, redressed, remedied; *man kann das nicht - machen*, it cannot be undone.

ungescheut, *adj.* fearless, undaunted, unabashed.

Ungeschick, *n.* incompetence, bungling, awkwardness, clumsiness; *- läßt grüßen!* clumsy fool! (*iron.*) that's clever! **-lichkeit,** *f.* awkwardness, clumsiness; gaucherie, ineptitude. **-t,** *adj.* awkward, clumsy, unskilful; gauche, inept.

ungeschlacht, *adj.* uncouth, ungainly, boorish, lubberly, rude, coarse.

ungeschlechtlich, *adj.* asexual, agamic, neuter, unsexed.

ungeschliffen, *adj.* unpolished, uncut (*jewels*), unground, blunt (*knives*); ill-bred, uncouth, crude, rude, coarse, unrefined. **-heit,** *f.* roughness, lack of manners, coarseness, boorishness.

Ungeschmack, *m.* (*archaic*) tastelessness; bad taste.

ungeschmälert, *adj.* undiminished; whole, intact.

ungeschmeidig, *adj.* rigid, firm, inflexible; unbending, unyielding, obdurate, self-opiniated, intractable, (*coll.*) stiff-necked.

ungeschminkt, *adj.* without rouge, (*fig.*) unadorned, unvarnished, plain (*truth*).

ungeschoren, *adj.* unshorn; unmolested; *lassen Sie mich -!* let me alone! leave me in peace!

ungesellig, *adj.* unsociable, unsocial, (*coll.*) standoffish; shy, retiring, unneighbourly, misanthropic.

ungesetz-lich, *adj.* illegal, unlawful, illicit. **-lichkeit,** *f.* illegality, unlawfulness. **-mäßig,** *adj.* lawless, illegitimate, injudicial, unauthorized, contraband.

ungesittet, *adj.* unmannerly, uncivil, ungracious, ungenteel, ill-bred; rude, uncivilized, uncultured. **-heit,** *f.* rudeness, unmannerliness, incivility.

ungesprächig, *adj.* taciturn, reserved, silent.

ungestalt, 1. *adj.* shapeless, misshapen, deformed. 2. *f.* deformity, shapelessness. **-et,** *adj.* defaced, mutilated, disfigured. **-heit,** *f.* deformity, disfigurement, defacement, mutilation.

ungestört, *adj.* untroubled, undisturbed, uninterrupted, peaceful, tranquil. **-heit,** *f.* tranquillity, quietude.

ungestraft, 1. *adj.* unpunished, absolved. 2. *adv.* with impunity. **-heit,** *f.* impunity.

ungestüm, 1. *adj.* stormy, turbulent, blustering, raging, fierce, furious, violent, vehement, boisterous, obstreperous, impetuous. 2. *m.* & *n.* impetuosity, violence, vehemence, turbulence.

ungesucht, *adj.* unsought, unaffected, natural, artless. **-heit,** *f.* artlessness, naturalness, simplicity, homeliness.

ungesund, *adj.* unhealthy, unsound, sickly, poorly, (*coll.*) seedy; insanitary, unwholesome, deleterious, noxious, injurious to health.

ungeteilt, *adj.* undivided, unanimous; general; ungraduated (*as a dial*).

ungetreu, *adj.* disloyal, unfaithful, faithless.

ungetrübt, *adj.* untroubled, unruffled, serene, placid; unclouded, clear. **-heit,** *f.* serenity.

Ungetüm, *n.* (-(e)s, -e) monster, monstrosity.

ungewandt, *adj.* unskilful, clumsy, awkward.

ungewaschen, *adj.* unwashed, unclean, soiled, dirty; *-es Zeug!* stuff and nonsense! cock-and-bull story; *-es Maul*, scurrilous tongue; (*vulg.*) foul-mouthed p.

ungewiß, *adj.* uncertain, doubtful, dubious, indecisive; hazardous, precarious, problematic, (*coll.*) chancy; contingent, undecided, indeterminate, depending on circumstances; *aufs -(ss)e*, at random; *einen im -(ss)en lassen*, leave a p. in the dark; *ins -(ss)e leben*, live from hand to mouth. **-(ss)enhaft,** *adj.* unconscientious. **-heit,** *f.* doubt, suspense, uncertainty, chance; perplexity, hesitation, misgiving, qualm.

Ungewitter, *n.* (-s, -) storm, thunder-storm, cloudburst.

ungewöhnlich, *adj.* unusual, uncommon, exceptional, abnormal, odd, extraordinary, rare, strange.

ungewohnt, *adj.* unusual, unaccustomed, unfamiliar, unwonted. **-heit,** *f.* strangeness, unfamiliarity, novelty.

ungezählt, *adj.* unnumbered, uncounted; untold, innumerable, unlimited, endless.

ungezähnt, *adj.* imperforate (*of postage stamps*).

Ungeziefer, *n.* (-s, -) vermin, noxious *or* parasitic insect.

ungezogen, *adj.* ill-bred, ill-mannered, rude, uncivil, impudent; *-es Kind*, naughty *or* disobedient child. **-heit,** *f.* naughtiness; rudeness, impertinence, piece of impudence.

ungezwungen, *adj.* unconstrained, free, spontaneous, unbridled; natural, unaffected, unforced, easy. **-heit,** *f.* naturalness, spontaneity, ease.

ungiftig, *adj.* non-poisonous, non-toxic, innocuous.
Unglaub–e(n), *m.* incredulity, unbelief, disbelief, scepticism. **–lich,** *adj.* incredible, unbelievable, unheard of, staggering; (*coll.*) *–licher Kerl*, astonishing, incredible *or* impossible fellow. **–lichkeit,** *f.* incredibility, unlikelihood. **–würdig,** *adj.* untrustworthy, unreliable; unauthenticated.
ungläubig, *adj.* incredulous, sceptical, doubting; dubious, suspicious, unbelieving, irreligious, undevout, freethinking, lacking faith. **–e(r),** *m.* unbeliever, atheist, freethinker, agnostic, sceptic, infidel.
ungleich, 1. *adj.* unequal, unlike, different, varying, dissimilar, disparate, diverse, diversified; uneven, odd; disproportionate, not level. 2. *adv.* incomparably, a great deal, much; – *besser*, far better; – *schöner*, much more beautiful. **–artig,** *adj.* different, dissimilar, multifarious, polymorphic, heterogeneous. **–artigkeit,** *f.* diversity, divergence, differentiation, heterogeneity. **–erbig,** *adj.* heterozygous. **–förmig,** *adj.* not uniform, unequal, unlike, dissimilar. **–heit,** *f.* inequality, disparity, dissimilarity, diversity, variation, difference, unlikeness, disproportion. **–mäßig,** *adj.* disproportionate, unsymmetrical, asymmetrical. **–seitig,** *adj.* scalene (*of triangles*). **–stoffig,** *adj.* inhomogeneous. **–stoffigkeit,** *f.* inhomogeneity.
Unglimpf, *m.* rigour, stringency, sternness, harshness; wrong, injustice, unfairness; insult, affront, indignity, outrage. **–lich,** *adj.* unfair; harsh; insulting; *einen –lich behandeln*, deal harshly with a p.
Unglück, *n.* (*no pl.*) misfortune, ill *or* bad luck; distress, misery, affliction, woe; (*pl.* Unglücksfälle) accident, mishap, piece of ill luck, misadventure, mischance, calamity, catastrophe, disaster; *zum* –, unfortunately; (*Prov.*) *kein – so groß, es hat ein Glück im Schoß*, it is an ill wind that blows no one any good; (*Prov.*) *ein – kommt selten allein*, it never rains but it pours. **–lich,** *adj.* unfortunate, unlucky, luckless, hapless; unhappy, miserable, sad, woebegone; unsuccessful, disastrous, calamitous; ill-fated, ill-starred, unrequited (*love*); *–lich ablaufen*, turn out badly, miscarry, end disastrously, come to nothing. **–licherweise,** *adv.* unluckily, unfortunately, as ill luck would have it. **–sbote,** *m.* bringer of bad tidings; bird of ill omen. **–selig,** *adj.* unhappy, miserable; unfortunate, distressing, grievous, lamentable, deplorable, disastrous, calamitous. **–seligkeit,** *f.* unhappiness, misery, wretchedness, affliction. **–sfall,** *m.* accident, casualty, mishap. **–skind,** *n.*, **–smensch,** *m.* victim of misfortune, child of woe. **–srabe,** *m.* croaker, prophet of evil, Jeremiah. **–sschwanger,** *adj.* ominous, inauspicious, threatening, fraught with danger. **–sstifter,** *m.* mischief-maker. **–sstunde,** *f.* unlucky hour. **–stag,** *m.* fatal day. **–svogel,** *m.* Jeremiah, (*coll.*) dismal Jimmy. (*coll.*) **–swurm,** *m.* & *n.* wretched *or* miserable creature.
Ungnade, *f.* disgrace, displeasure; *in – fallen*, incur displeasure, fall out of favour; *sich* (*Dat.*) *jemandes – zuziehen*, incur a p.'s displeasure, get into a p.'s bad books; *auf Gnade und* or *oder* –, unconditionally.
ungnädig, *adj.* ungracious, uncivil, unaccommodating, churlish, unkind, ill-humoured, cross; up in arms, unfavourable, antagonistic, adverse, harsh; – *aufnehmen*, take amiss.
ungrade, (*coll.*), *see* **ungerade.**
Ungrund, *m.* invalidity, speciousness, groundlessness, baselessness; (*archaic*) *see* **Abgrund.**
ungründlich, *adj.* superficial, shallow, (*coll.*) skin-deep. **–keit,** *f.* superficiality, shallowness.
ungültig, *adj.* invalid, invalidated, refuted, rebutted, disproved; void, worthless, not current, cancelled, inadmissible; not available (*as a ticket*); *für – erklären, – machen*, annul, invalidate, abrogate, cancel, countermand, repudiate, revoke, rescind, nullify, repeal, quash, declare null and void. **–keit,** *f.* invalidity, nullity. **–machung,** *f.* invalidation, abrogation, cancellation, repudiation, revocation, annulment, nullification, repeal.
Ungunst, *f.* (-en) disfavour, ill-will, malignity, malice, unkindness; inauspiciousness, unpropitiousness; – *des Wetters*, inclemency of the weather; *zu seinen –en*, to his disadvantage; *es fiel zu seinen –en aus*, it went against him.
ungünstig, *adj.* unfavourable, adverse, disadvantageous, detrimental, deleterious; *einem – sein*, be ill-disposed towards s.o.
ungut, *adj.* (only in) *für – nehmen*, take amiss *or* ill; *nichts für – !* no offence! no harm meant!
unhaltbar, *adj.* not durable, impermanent, fugitive, evanescent; untenable, indefensible (*of a position*); that cannot be kept (*of promises*).
unhandlich, *adj.* unwieldy.
unharmonisch, *adj.* inharmonious, discordant.
Unheil, *n.* harm, mischief, trouble; disaster, calamity; – *stiften* or *anrichten*, cause mischief. **–bar,** *adj.* incurable, irreparable. **–bringend,** *adj.* mischievous, pernicious, detrimental, baneful, baleful, hurtful; unlucky, ominous, fatal. **–drohend,** *adj.* boding ill, ominous, portentous. **–sam,** *adj.* unwholesome, noxious. **–schwanger,** *adj.* fraught with danger. **–stifter,** *m.* mischief-maker. **–voll,** *adj.* harmful, pernicious, calamitous, disastrous.
unheilig, *adj.* unholy, unhallowed, profane.
unheim–isch, (*rare*); **–lich,** 1. *adj.* uncanny, sinister; uncomfortable, uneasy; gloomy, dismal, weird. 2. *adv.* (*coll.*) awfully, tremendously, mighty; *es ward ihm –lich zu Mute*, he grew uneasy.
unhöflich, *adj.* rude, impolite, uncivil, unmannerly, discourteous. **–keit,** *f.* rudeness, discourtesy, bad manners, incivility, impoliteness.
unhold, 1. *adj.* unfriendly, disobliging, unkind, ungracious, ill-disposed, churlish, malevolent. 2. *m.* (-(e)s, -e) monster, demon, fiend.
unhörbar, *adj.* inaudible.
unhygienisch, *adj.* insanitary, unhygienic.
uni [*pron.* 'yni:] *adj.* of one colour, plain.
unier–en, *v.a.* unite. **–te,** *pl.* United Protestants; Greek Catholics.
uni–form, 1. *adj.* uniform, homogeneous. 2. *f.* (-en) uniform, regimentals; livery. **–formiert,** *p.p.* reduced to uniformity; uniformed, in uniform. **–formierung,** *f.* levelling. **–formität,** *f.* uniformity, homogeneity, regularity, conformity. **–kum,** *n.* (-kums, -kums & -ka) unique instance, unique example; original (*person*).
uninteress–ant, *adj.* uninteresting, dull, boring, tedious, devoid of interest. **–iert,** *adj.* (*an with Dat.*) disinterested (in), impartial (about), with no personal interest (in).
universal, *adj.* universal. **–erbe,** *m.* sole heir, residuary legatee. **–mittel,** *m.* sovereign *or* universal remedy, panacea, cure-all. **–schraubenschlüssel,** *m.* monkey-wrench.
universell, *adj.*, *see* **universal.**
Universität, *f.* (-en) university. **–sdozent,** *m.* university lecturer. **–srektor,** *m.* vice-chancellor of the university. **–sstudium,** *n.* study at a university. **–svorlesung,** *f.* university lecture.
Universum, *n.* universe.
Unke, *f.* (-n) orange-speckled toad (*Bombinator*) (*Zool.*); (*coll.*) croaker, grumbler, prophet of evil, Jeremiah. **–n,** *v.n.* croak; (*coll.*) prophesy evil, (*sl.*) belly-ache. **–nruf,** *m.* ominous croaking, ominous cry.
unkennt–lich, *adj.* unrecognizable, irrecognizable, indiscernible; *–lich machen*, disguise. **–lichkeit,** *f.* irrecognizable condition; *bis zur –lichkeit entstellt*, past recognition. **–nis,** *f.* ignorance, unawareness, incognizance; *einen in –nis über eine S. (er)halten*, keep a p. in the dark about a th.; *–nis schützt vor Strafe nicht*, ignorance of the law is no excuse.
unkeusch, *adj.* unchaste, impure, immodest, lecherous, salacious. **–heit,** *f.* unchastity, impurity, immodesty.
unklar, *adj.* not clear, muddy, thick, turbid; hazy, misty, foggy, indistinct; unintelligible, obscure, abstruse; vague, confused, uncertain; fouled, not ready, out of action; *im –en sein*, be in doubt; – *laufen* or *kommen von*, run *or* get foul of (*Naut.*). **–heit,** *f.* obscurity, vagueness, confusion.
unklug, *adj.* thoughtless, silly, senseless, idiotic; unwise, misguided, imprudent, ill-advised, impolitic. **–heit,** *f.* imprudence, indiscretion, silliness.
unkollegial, *adj.* unfriendly, disobliging, unaccommodating, unneighbourly, stand-offish, uncooperative.

unkontrollierbar, *adj.* unverifiable, unable to be vouched for.
unkörperlich, *adj.* incorporeal, disembodied, immaterial; spiritual.
Unkosten, *pl.* expense(s), costs, charges; *auf meine –*, at my expense; *sich in – stürzen*, go to great expense.
Unkraut, *n.* (-(e)s, ⸚er) weed, weeds; parasite (*of a person*); (*Prov.*) *– vergeht* or *verdirbt nicht*, ill weeds grow apace.
unkristallinisch, *adj.* non-crystalline, amorphous.
unkündbar, *adj.* irredeemable, irreclaimable, irreversible, irrevocable, incommutable, immutable; permanent (*post*); *–e Papiere*, consolidated stocks, consols; *–er Vertrag*, binding agreement. **–keit,** *f.* immutability, irrevocableness, permanence.
unkundig, *adj.* (*Gen.*) ignorant, unaware *or* incognizant (of); unacquainted *or* not conversant (with), uninformed (about); unversed (in); a stranger (to); *des Griechischen –*, knowing *or* having no Greek.
unkünstlerisch, *adj.* inartistic.
Unland, *n.* (-(e)s, ⸚er) waste land.
unlängst, *adv.* not long ago, recently, the other day, of late.
unlauter, *adj.* impure; ignoble, mean, sordid, self-interested; *–er Wettbewerb*, unfair competition.
unleid-ig, *adj.* irritable, impatient, moody. **–lich,** *adj.* intolerable, insufferable, unbearable; (*dial.*) *see* **–ig.**
unlenksam, *adj.* unruly, unmanageable, intractable. **–samkeit,** *f.* unruliness.
unles-bar, –erlich, *adj.* illegible, unreadable; *–erlich schreiben*, scrawl. **–erlichkeit,** *f.* illegibility.
unleugbar, *adj.* undeniable, unquestionable, indisputable.
unlieb, *adj.* (*only with* zu *& inf.*) displeasing, disagreeable; *es ist mir nicht – zu hören*, I am rather glad to hear that. **–enswürdig,** *adj.* unfriendly, disobliging, churlish, surly. **–sam,** *adj.* disagreeable, unpleasant.
unliniert, *adj.* without lines, unruled.
unlogisch, *adj.* illogical.
unlös-bar, *adj.* indissoluble; inextricable, unsolvable, not admitting solution. **–barkeit,** *f.* indissolubility. **–lich,** *adj.* insoluble (*Chem.*).
Unlust, *f.* dislike, disinclination, aversion, repugnance, disgust; (*C.L.*) dullness, slackness. **–ig,** *adj.* listless, disinclined, averse; reluctant.
Unmacht, *f.* (*dial.*) *see* **Ohnmacht.**
Unmanier, *f.*, *see* **Unart,** 1. **–lich,** *adj.* unmannerly, boorish, uncouth; *sich –lich aufführen*, behave abominably. **–lichkeit,** *f.* unmannerliness, ill-breeding, bad behaviour.
unmännlich, *adj.* unmanly, effeminate, cowardly.
Unmaß, *n.*, *see* **Unmasse**; *im –*, *see* **unmäßig,** *adv.* **–geblich,** *adj.* not authoritative, open to correction; *nach meiner –geblichen Meinung*, speaking without authority *or* subject to correction, in my humble opinion.
Unmasse, *f.* enormous number, vast quantity, no end of; *in –n*, *see* **unmäßig,** *adv.*
unmäßig, 1. *adj.* immoderate, intemperate, excessive. 2. *adv.* extremely, exceedingly, extraordinarily. **–keit,** *f.* excess, intemperance, etc.
Unmenge, *f.*, *see* **Unmasse.**
Unmensch, *m.* (-en, -en) inhuman creature, hard-hearted wretch, monster, brute; (*hum.*) *ich bin kein –*, I will not say no, I am open to persuasion. **–lich,** *adj.* inhuman, barbarous, fiendish; (*coll.*) vast, prodigious, tremendous, exorbitant; *–liche Kraft*, superhuman strength. **–lichkeit,** *f.* inhumanity, hardness of heart, cruelty, brutality, barbarity, ferocity.
unmerklich, *adj.* imperceptible, inappreciable, insensible.
unmeßbar, *adj.* immeasurable, incommensurable.
unmitteil-bar, *adj.* incommunicable; unfit for publication. **–sam,** *adj.* uncommunicative, secretive, close, reserved, taciturn. **–samkeit,** *f.* reserve, taciturnity.
unmittelbar, *adj.* immediate, direct; *–er Sinn*, literal sense (*of a passage*); *sich – an einen wenden*, apply directly to a p.; *– darauf*, immediately afterwards. **–keit,** *f.* directness.
unmod-ern, –isch, *adj.* old-fashioned, out of date, antiquated, unfashionable.
unmöglich, *adj.* impossible; *ich kann es – tun*, it is out of the question *or* impossible for me to do that; *sich – machen*, compromise o.s.; *–es leisten*, do the impossible. **–keit,** *f.* impossibility; *es ist ein Ding der –keit*, that can never be.
unmoralisch, *adj.* immoral.
unmotiviert, *adj.* without motive *or* reason, unmotivated, unfounded, groundless.
unmündig, *adj.* under age, not of age; *–es Kind*, dependent child. **–e(r),** *m.* minor. **–keit,** *f.* minority.
Unmut, *m.* ill humour, bad temper; displeasure. **–ig,** *adj.* displeased, annoyed, indignant, angry. **–svoll,** *adj.* disgruntled.
unnachahmlich, *adj.* inimitable, matchless.
unnachgiebig, *adj.* inflexible, hard, unyielding, relentless, uncompromising; stubborn.
unnachsicht-ig, *adj.*, **–lich,** *adj.* unrelenting, strict, severe.
unnahbar, *adj.* inaccessible, unapproachable. **–keit,** *f.* inaccessibility.
Unnatur, *f.* unnaturalness, abnormality; abnormity, monstrosity.
unnatürlich, *adj.* unnatural, abnormal; outlandish, grotesque, out of the ordinary, monstrous; affected, stilted, pretentious, forced. **–keit,** *f.* unnaturalness, anomaly; affectation, preciosity.
unnennbar, *adj.* unutterable, inexpressible, ineffable.
unnötig, *adj.* unnecessary, needless, superfluous. **–erweise,** *adv.* unnecessarily, needlessly.
unnütz, *adj.* useless, unprofitable, vain, idle, superfluous; good-for-nothing, naughty; *–es Geschwätz*, idle talk; *–es Zeug*, trash, nonsense; *den Namen Gottes – im Munde führen*, take the name of God in vain; *sich – machen*, make o.s. a nuisance. **–lich,** *adj.* useless, worthless, unavailing. **–lichkeit,** *f.* uselessness, fruitlessness.
unord-entlich, *adj.* disorderly; irregular, confused; untidy; dissolute. **–entlichkeit,** *f.* dissoluteness, profligacy. **–nung,** *f.* disorder, confusion; litter, untidiness; *in –nung bringen*, throw into confusion, disarrange, disorder, confuse, disorganize.
unorganisch, *adj.* inorganic.
unorthographisch, *adj.* wrongly spelt, misspelt.
unpaar, –ig, *adj.* not even, odd (*number*); not paired, odd, without a fellow (*gloves, etc.*); azygous (*Bot., etc.*). **–igkeit,** *f.* oddness. **–wertig,** *adj.* of odd valence (*Chem.*). **–zeher,** *m.* perissodactyl (*Zool.*).
unpartei-isch, –lich, *adj.* impartial, disinterested, unprejudiced, unbiased, neutral. **–ische(r),** *m.* umpire. **–lichkeit,** *f.* impartiality.
unpaß, 1. *adv.* inopportunely. 2. *adj.* (*only predicative*), *see* **unpäßlich.**
unpassend, *adj.* unsuitable, unfit, unbecoming; improper, indiscreet; misplaced; out of place, inopportune.
unpassierbar, *adj.* impracticable, impassable; unfordable (*of rivers*).
unpäßlich, *adj.* unwell, ailing, off-colour, indisposed, ill. **–keit,** *f.* indisposition.
unpersönlich, *adj.* impersonal (*also Gram.*), objective. **–keit,** *f.* objectivity.
unpolitisch, *adj.* non-political, unpolitical; (*fig.*) impolitic, injudicious, ill-advised, ill-judged.
unpraktisch, *adj.* unpractical, inexpert, unskilful; impracticable, unmanageable.
unproportioniert, *adj.* ill-proportioned, unshapely; disproportionate.
unqualifizierbar, *adj.* unspeakable, indescribable (*esp. of behaviour*).
Unrast, 1. *f.* restlessness. 2. *m.* (-es, -e) (*coll.*) restless *or* fidgety child.
Unrat, *m.* rubbish, refuse, garbage, ordure; excrement, dirt; *– merken* or *wittern*, (*coll.*) smell a rat.
unrationell, *adj.* wasteful, extravagant; misapplied.
unrätlich, *adj.*, **unratsam,** *adj.* unadvisable, inadvisable, inexpedient.
unrecht, 1. *adj.* wrong, false, incorrect, not right; unsuitable, inopportune, bad, improper; unjust, unfair; *das geht mit –en Dingen zu*, there is

s.th. uncanny *or* queer about it; (*Prov.*) – *Gut gedeiht nicht*, ill-gotten gain never thrives; *es ist in –e Hände gekommen*, it has fallen into the wrong hands; *es ist mir etwas in die –e Kehle gekommen*, something has gone down the wrong way; *komme ich –?* have I come at the wrong *or* at a bad time? *an den –en kommen*, catch a Tartar; *seine Bemerkungen waren ganz am –en Orte*, his remarks were quite out of place; *–e Seite*, wrong *or* reverse side (*of stuff*). 2. *n.* wrong, injustice; error, fault; *bei dir bekommt er nie –*, in your opinion he is never wrong; *einem – geben*, decide against a p.; *es geschieht ihm –*, he has been wronged; *– haben*, see *im – sein*; *mit –*, unjustly; *im – sein*, be (in the) wrong, be mistaken; *einem – tun*, wrong a p.; *zu –*, illegally, unlawfully. **–lich,** *adj.* unjust, wrongful, illegal; dishonest, unrighteous. **–lichkeit,** *f.* injustice, illegality; dishonesty. **–mäßig,** *adj.* unlawful, illegal. **–mäßigerweise,** *adv.* unlawfully, illegally. **–mäßigkeit,** *f.* illegality.

unredlich, *adj.* dishonest. **–keit,** *f.* dishonesty.

unreell, *adj.* (*C.L.*) dishonest, fraudulent; unfair; unsound, unreliable.

unregelmäßig, *adj.* irregular, anomalous, abnormal; erratic, aperiodic, zygomorphic. **–keit,** *f.* irregularity; anomaly; (*pl.*) (*C.L.*) irregularities.

unreif, *adj.* unripe, raw, green; immature. **–e,** *f.*, **–heit,** *f.* unripeness, immaturity.

unrein, *adj.* unclean, dirty, impure, foul, smutty, obscene; out of tune (*Mus.*); *im –en* (*ins –e*) *schreiben*, jot down, make a rough copy; *–e Luft*, foul air; *–er Stil*, bad style; *–er Ton*, false note. **–heit,** *f.* uncleanness; impurity, foulness, pollution. **–igkeit,** *f.* (*pl. only*) impurities, dross, dirt. **–lich,** *adj.* unclean, dirty, unwashed, unkempt, squalid. **–lichkeit,** *f.* dirtiness, uncleanliness, slovenliness, squalor.

unrentabel, *adj.* unprofitable, unremunerative.

unrettbar, 1. *adj.* irrecoverable, irretrievable, past help, saving *or* recovery. 2. *adv.* infallibly, definitely; *– verloren*, irretrievably lost, lost for good.

unrichtig, *adj.* false, wrong, incorrect, erroneous; *diese Uhr geht –*, this watch does not keep time. **–keit,** *f.* incorrectness, falsity, error, inaccuracy.

Unruh, *f.* (-en) balance wheel (*of watch*). **–e,** *f.* (-en) unrest, commotion, disturbance, restlessness; uneasiness, disquiet, anxiety, alarm, agitation, excitement; (*coll.*) *see* **–**; (*pl.*) disturbances, tumult, rising, outbreaks of violence, riot. **–ig,** *adj.* unsettled, uneasy, restless, agitated, excited, troubled, unquiet, turbulent, restive (*of horses*). **–(e)stifter,** *m.* mischief-maker, agitator. **–voll,** *adj.* restless, unsettled, much troubled.

unrühmlich, *adj.* inglorious, abject, shameful, infamous, discreditable, reprehensible **–keit,** *f.* ingloriousness, shame, disgrace, obloquy, opprobrium, infamy.

uns, *pers. pron.* (*Acc. & Dat. of* wir) us; to us; ourselves; to ourselves; *ein Freund von –*, a friend of ours, one of our friends; *er gehört zu –*, he is one of us; *unter – gesagt*, between ourselves; *von – beiden*, from both of us. **–er,** *see* **unser.**

unsachgemäß, *adj.* improper, inappropriate, unapt.

unsachlich, *adj.* subjective, personal; not to the point.

unsagbar, unsäglich, 1. *adj.* unspeakable, unutterable. 2. *adv.* immensely.

unsanft, *adj.* harsh, rough, violent.

unsauber, *adj.* unclean, dirty, filthy; unfair, (*coll.*) shady; *–e Mittel*, underhand dealings. **–keit,** *f.* uncleanliness, dirtiness.

unschädlich, *adj.* harmless, safe, innocuous; *– machen*, render innocuous, prevent from doing harm; disarm, (*coll.*) hamstring; (*coll.*) clip the wings of; neutralize (*a poison*). **–keit,** *f.* harmlessness. **–machung,** *f.* neutralization (*of a poison*).

unscharf, *adj.* blurred, hazy, not sharp; *–e Trennung*, poor selectivity (*Rad.*).

unschätzbar, *adj.* invaluable, inestimable. **–keit,** *f.* pricelessness.

unscheinbar, *adj.* dull, plain, insignificant, inconsiderable, homely, unpretentious; *– werden*, tarnish, lose brightness. **–keit,** *f.* humbleness, insignificance.

unschicklich, *adj.* unbecoming, improper, unseemly, indecent; out of place, inapt, inadmissible. **–keit,** *f.* impropriety, unseemliness, unsuitability, inappropriateness.

Unschlitt, *n.* tallow, suet.

unschlüssig, *adj.* wavering, irresolute, undecided, vacillating, indecisive. **–keit,** *f.* indecision, lack of resolution, vacillation, hesitancy.

unschmackhaft, *adj.* tasteless, insipid.

unschön, *adj.* unlovely, ungracious, unpleasant, plain, ugly; (*fig.*) unfair.

Unschuld, *f.* innocence; purity, chastity; *ich wasche meine Hände in –*, I wash my hands of it; *in aller –*, quite innocently, with no evil intent; *die – vom Lande*, simple innocent country girl; *gekränkte –*, injured innocence. **–ig,** *adj.* innocent, guiltless, guileless; pure, chaste (*girl*); harmless (*remark*). (*hum.*) **–sengel,** *m.* little innocent. **–smiene,** *f.* air of innocence.

unschwer, *adj.* not difficult, easy; *ich errate es –*, I can guess it without difficulty.

Unsegen, *m.* adversity, misfortune; evil genius.

unselbständig, *adj.* dependent, helpless; unoriginal. **–keit,** *f.* dependence, helplessness; lack of originality.

unselig, *adj.* unhappy, unlucky, unfortunate, fatal, accursed, wretched. **–keit,** *f.* misery, wretchedness.

unser, 1. *pers. pron.* (*Gen. of* wir) of us; *wir* (or *es*) *waren – vier*, there were four of us; (*B.*) *Vater –, der Du bist im Himmel*, Our Father which art in heaven; *– aller Wunsch*, the wish of all of us. 2. *poss. adj.* (unser, uns(e)re, unser) our; *die Schriftsteller –er Zeit*, the writers of our time. **–einer,** *pron.*, **–eins,** *indec. pron.* one of us; such as we, people like us. **unserer, unsere, unseres,** (der, die, das –e *or* –ige), *poss. pron.* ours; our property; our duty; *die –igen* or *Unsrigen*, our people, part *or* soldiers. **–(er)seits,** *adv.* as for us, for our part. **–(e)sgleichen,** *adj.* the like of us, people like us. **–thalben,** *adv.*, **–twegen,** *adv.*, **(um) –twillen,** *adv.* for our sake, on our behalf, because *or* on account of us.

unsicher, *adj.* unsafe, insecure, unstable, unsteady, precarious; uncertain, doubtful, dubious; *–es Gedächtnis*, unreliable *or* shaky memory. **–heit,** *f.* insecurity, precariousness, uncertainty.

unsicht–bar, *adj.* invisible, imperceptible, lost to view. **–barkeit,** *f.* invisibility. **–ig,** *adj.* hazy, misty (*of the atmosphere*).

Unsinn, *m.* nonsense, absurdity, (*coll.*) rigmarole, twaddle, piffle; folly, senselessness, madness; *barer* or *blühender –*, utter *or* downright nonsense; *– treiben*, play the fool, fool about. **–ig,** *adj.* nonsensical, absurd, crazy, senseless, foolish; mad, insane; *–ig verliebt sein in*, be madly in love with. **–lich,** *adj.* spiritual, supersensual; *–liche Liebe*, platonic love.

Unsitt–e, *f.* bad habit; abuse. **–lich,** *adj.* immoral; immodest, indecent. **–lichkeit,** *f.* immorality; indecency, immoral act.

unsolid, *adj.* (*C.L.*) unreliable; (*fig.*) loose, dissipated.

unsozial, *adj.* anti-social; unsociable.

unsre, unsrige, *etc., see* **unser.**

unständig, *adj.* impermanent; casual (*worker*).

unstarr, *adj.* non-rigid (*of airships*).

unstät, *adj.* (*dial.*) *see* **unstet.**

unstatthaft, *adj.* inadmissible; forbidden, illicit, illegal.

unsterblich, *adj.* immortal; *sich – blamieren*, disgrace o.s. for all time; *sich – machen*, gain immortality. **–keit,** *f.* immortality.

Unstern, *m.* unlucky star, evil genius; misfortune, adversity.

unstet, *adj.* changeable, inconstant; unsteady, fluctuating, variable; restless, wandering, not fixed. **–ig,** *adj., see* **–**; *–ige Größe*, discrete quantity. **–igkeit,** *f.* unsteadiness, instability, inconstancy, changeableness; unsettled condition, restlessness.

unstillbar, *adj.* insatiable, unappeasable, unquenchable.

Unstimmigkeit, *f.* (-en) discrepancy, inconsistency; difference of opinion, disagreement.

unstörbar, *adj.* imperturbable, impassive; – *im Besitze,* in incommutable possession (*Law*).
unstrafbar, unsträflich, *adj.* irreproachable, blameless, impeccable. **-keit,** *f.* integrity, correctness, rectitude, probity.
unstreckbar, *adj.* non-ductile.
unstreitig, 1. *adj.* incontestable, indisputable, unquestionable. 2. *adv.* doubtless, certainly.
unsühnbar, *adj.* inexpiable.
Unsumme, *f.* (-n) enormous *or* immense sum.
unsymmetrisch, *adj.* asymmetrical, unsymmetrical.
unsympathisch, *adj.* unpleasant, disagreeable, distasteful; *er ist mir –,* I do not like him.
untadel-haft, -ig, *adj.* irreproachable, blameless, unexceptionable.
Untat, *f.* (-en) crime, outrage.
Untät-chen, *n.* (*dial.*) spot, blemish. **-ig,** *adj.* inactive, indolent, idle, unemployed, non-productive; indifferent, inert, dormant. **-igkeit,** *f.* inactivity, inaction, idleness, indolence, inertness.
untauglich, *adj.* unfit, unserviceable, disabled, useless, unsuitable. **-keit,** *f.* uselessness, unfitness.
unteil-bar, *adj.* indivisible. **-barkeit,** *f.* indivisibility. **-haftig,** *adj.* (*Gen.*) having no part *or* share in, not partaking of, not sharing *or* participating in.
unten, *adv.* below, beneath, under(neath); at the bottom *or* foot; downstairs; – *am Berge,* at the foot of the hill; – *auf der Erde,* here below; down on the ground; (*coll.*) – *durch sein,* be lost, abandoned, sacrificed, ruined *or* despised, count for nothing; – *im Fasse,* at the bottom of the cask; *nach –,* downwards; *von oben bis –,* from top to bottom; (*coll.*) – *wie oben sein,* be much of a muchness, be no great shakes; *kaum noch wissen was oben und was – ist,* not know whether a th. is on its head or its feet; *siehe –* (*abbr.* s.u.) see below; *von – an* or *auf,* right up from below; *von – auf dienen,* rise from the ranks (*Mil.*); *weiter –,* farther down; farther on, later on (*in the text*). **-an,** *adv.* at the foot *or* bottom; *-an gehen,* go last. **-her,** *adv.* from (down) below. **-hin,** *adv.* downwards, down to the bottom. **-stehend,** *adj.* undermentioned, mentioned below.
unter, 1. *prep.* (*with Acc. or Dat.*) (*with Dat. in answer to* **wo?** where? in which place? *With Acc. in answer to* **wohin?** whither? to which place?) under, below, beneath, underneath, among, amongst; (*with Dat. only*) during, by; **(a)** (*with Dat.*) (*sl.*) – *allem Affen,* see – *aller Kritik;* – *anderem,* moreover, besides, furthermore; – *dieser Bedingung,* on this condition; – *jeder Bedingung,* on any terms; – *dem dreißigsten Breitengrade,* latitude 30°; (*C.L.*) – *dem heutigen Datum,* under today's date; *mit jemandem – einer Decke stecken,* be hand in glove with a p.; *einem den Boden – den Füßen wegziehen,* cut the ground from under a p.'s feet; – *dem Gesetze stehen,* be subject to the law; – *diesem Gesichtspunkt,* from this point of view; – *Glockengeläute,* with bells ringing; – *der Hand,* secretly, on the quiet; *etwas – den Händen* or *der Hand haben,* have a th. in hand; *ein Kind – dem Herzen haben,* be pregnant, be in the family way; – *freiem Himmel,* in the open air; (*sl.*) *das ist – aller Kanone, das ist – aller Kritik,* that is beneath criticism; *nicht – 50 Mark,* not less than 50 marks; – *3 Monaten,* in less than 3 months; – *dem Namen bekannt sein,* be known by the name of; – *Null,* below zero; – *seinen Papieren,* amongst his papers; – *Pari,* below par; – *der Presse,* in the press; – *Quarantäne,* in quarantine; – *der Regierung von,* in *or* during the reign of; – *dem Schutz der Nacht,* under cover of night; – *seinem Stande heiraten,* marry beneath o.s.; – *dem Strich,* in the feuilleton; – *Tage,* below ground (*Min.*); – *Tränen,* with tears in (his, her, *etc.*) eyes, weeping; – *zwei Übeln das kleinere wählen,* of two evils choose the less; – *Umständen,* under certain conditions, in certain circumstances; – *allen Umständen,* in any case; – *diesen* or *solchen Umständen,* in these circumstances, this being the case, in this case; – *uns,* among *or* between ourselves; *der Größte – uns,* the tallest of us; – *uns gesagt,* between ourselves, it must go no farther: – *Verschluß,* under lock and key; *was verstehst du – diesem Ausdruck?* what do you understand by this expression? – *vier Augen,* face to face, tête à tête, in private; – *Vorbehalt aller Rechte,* all rights reserved; – *üblichem Vorbehalt,* with the usual reservations; – *dem Vorwand,* under the pretext; – *Waffen,* under arms, in the field; *er wohnt – mir,* he lives in the room below mine; – *meiner Würde,* beneath my dignity. **(b)** (*with Acc.*) *einem – die Augen treten,* come into s.o.'s sight, be seen by a p.; *bis – das Dach voll,* full right up to the roof; *einen – die Erde bringen,* be the death of s.o.; – *die Haube kommen,* find a husband; *alle – einen Hut bringen,* make them all agree upon the same thing, reconcile conflicting opinions; *wenn es – die Leute kommt,* if it is talked about, if it gets around *or* about; *einem etwas – die Nase halten* or *reiben,* rub a p.'s nose in a th.; – *die Räuber geraten,* fall among thieves; – *die Soldaten gehen,* enlist; *etwas – Strafe stellen,* impose a penalty on a th.; – *den Tisch fallen,* fall under the table; (*fig.*) be pushed on one side, be set aside; be forgotten; – *Wasser setzen,* flood, inundate. 2. *adj.* under, underneath; lower, inferior; *-st,* the lowest, the last; *zu -st,* at the bottom; *der -ste in der Klasse,* the bottom of the class; *das -ste zu oberst kehren,* turn everything topsy-turvy *or* upside down, upset everything. 3. *m.* (-s, –) knave (*Cards*). 4. *adv. & sep. & insep. prefix,* below, beneath, under; among; amid. *In general, when the prefix has a literal meaning it is separable and carries the accent; when the prefix has a figurative meaning it is inseparable and the accent is on the root of the verb. See entries below, from which in most cases the obvious literal* (*sep.*) *meanings are omitted.*
Unterabteilung, *f.* subdivision; (*C.L.*) branch, department.
Unterarm, *m.* forearm.
Unterart, *f.* subspecies, variety.
Unterarzt, *m.* junior surgeon; surgeon ensign (*navy*), medical N.C.O. (*Mil.*).
Unteraugenlid, *n.* lower (eye)lid.
Unterbau, *m.* substructure; foundation; formation level (*Railw.*); (*fig.*) *gemeinsamer –,* common basis. **-en,** *v.n.* (*insep.*) undermine; lay a foundation for; found, establish, underpin.
Unterbauch, *m.* hypogastrium (*Anat.*).
Unterbeamte(r), *m.* subordinate official.
Unterbeinkleider, *n.pl.* knickers, pants.
unterbelichten, *v.a.* (*insep.*) under-expose (*Phot.*).
Unterbett, *n.* feather bed, mattress.
unterbewußt, *adj.* subconscious. **-sein,** *n.* subconsciousness.
unterbieten, *v.a.* (*insep.*) undercut, undersell; lower (*a record*).
Unterbilanz, *f.* deficit.
unterbind-en, 1. *ir.v.a.* (*sep.*) tie underneath; (*insep.*) tie up *or* off; apply a ligature to (*a vein*); neutralize (*an attack*); (*fig.*) cut off, check, thwart, paralyse. 2. *n.,* **-ung,** *f.* ligature; (*fig.*) prevention.
unterbleiben, 1. *ir.v.a.* (*insep.*) not take place, not occur, be left undone, be omitted; cease, be discontinued. 2. *n.* cessation, discontinuance.
Unterboden, *m.* subsoil; base plate (*of a watch*), base.
unterbrech-en, *ir.v.a.* (*insep.*) interrupt; discontinue, suspend, cut short, stop; break (*a journey*). **-er,** *m.* interrupter; circuit-breaker, cut-out (*Elec.*). **-ung,** *f.* interruption, intermission, cessation, suspension, stop, break, disconnexion. **-ungsstrom,** *m.* interrupted current, contact current (*Elec.*).
unterbreiten, *v.a.* (*sep.*) spread underneath; (*insep.*) (*einem etwas*) present, lay before, submit to.
unterbring-en, *ir.v.a.* (*sep.*) shelter, house, accommodate, lodge; billet, quarter (*troops*); provide *or* arrange (*a place*) for; store; dispose of, sell, invest (*money*); negotiate (*bills*); *Pferde -en,* stable horses; *einen -en,* get a p. a situation; lodge *or* find accommodation for a p. **-ung,** *f.* accommodation, quarters; storage; investment.
unterbrochen, *adj.* intermittent, interrupted, broken.
Unterbruch, *m.* (*Swiss dial.*), *see* **Unterbrechung.**
unterchlorigsauer, *adj.* hypochlorite of (*Chem.*).

Unterdeck, *n.* lower deck, below decks.
unterderhand, *adv.* secretly, in secret, on the quiet; as occasion arises.
unterdes, -sen, *adv. & conj.* meanwhile, in the meantime.
Unterdruck, *m.* partial vacuum, negative pressure, sub-atmospheric pressure; depression (*Meteor.*).
unterdrück-en, *v.a.* (*insep.*) suppress, oppress, crush, quell, repress, restrain, stifle. **-er,** *m.* oppressor, tyrant. **-ung,** *f.* oppression; suppression, repression.
untereinander, 1. *adv.* between *or* with each other; among themselves; together, mutually, reciprocally; *alles* –, higgledy-piggledy, topsy-turvy. 2. *n.* mix-up, jumble, hugger-mugger.
Untereinheit, *f.* sub-unit.
Untereinteilung, *f.* subdivision.
unterernähr-t, *p.p. & adj.* underfed, undernourished. **-ung,** *f.* underfeeding, malnutrition.
unterfahren, *ir.v.a.* (*insep.*) pass (*one's hand*) under s.th.; excavate, reach by tunnelling; underpin.
unterfangen, 1. *ir.v.r.* (*insep.*) (*Gen.*) attempt, venture on; (zu *with inf.*) venture (to), dare (to), presume (to). 2. *n.* enterprise, undertaking, venture.
unterfassen, 1. *v.a.* (*sep.*) put one's hand under, hold up; (*coll.*) *sie gehen untergefaßt*, they go arm in arm.
Unterfeldwebel, *m.* sergeant.
unterfertig-en, *v.a.* (*C.L.*) undersign. **-t(er),** *m.* the undersigned.
unterführ-en, *v.a.* (*insep.*) carry down (*a word, etc.*) with the ditto mark (*Typ.*). **-ung,** *f.* subway. **-ungszeichen,** *n.* ditto mark (*Typ.*).
Unterfuß, *m.* sole of the foot.
Unterfutter, *n.* inner lining.
Untergang, *m.* going down; setting, sinking, decline, downfall, fall, failure, ruin, destruction.
Untergärung, *f.* bottom fermentation.
Untergattung, *f.* subspecies.
untergeben, 1. *ir.v.a.* (*sep.*) lay *or* place under; (*insep.*) (*Poet.*) commit, submit *or* entrust to; subordinate, subject. 2. *p.p. & adj.* inferior, subordinate, subject. **-e(r),** *m.* subordinate, underling; subject. **-heit,** *f.* subordination, subjection.
untergehen, *ir.v.n.* (*sep.*) (*aux.* s.) set (*of sun, etc.*), sink, be wrecked, founder; go to ruin, perish, be lost *or* annihilated, become extinct; *mit Mann und Maus* –, go down with all hands.
untergeordnet, *p.p. & adj.* subordinate, inferior, minor, secondary.
untergeschoben, *adj.* counterfeit, spurious, forged; substituted, interpolated.
Untergeschoß, *n.* ground-floor.
Untergestell, *n.* under-carriage (*Av.*); chassis (*Motor.*).
Untergewicht, *n.* short weight.
Unterglied, *n.* lower limb; minor proposition (*Log.*).
untergrab-en, *ir.v.a.* (*sep.*) dig in (*as manure*); (*insep.*) undermine, sap; (*fig.*) destroy, shatter, ruin, corrupt, eat away. **-ung,** *f.* destruction; undermining.
Untergrund, *m.* subsoil, lower stratum; (back)-ground; undercoat (*of paint*). **-bahn,** *f.* underground (railway); *coll.*) tube, (*Amer.*) subway. **-pflug,** *m.* subsoil-plough.
Untergruppe, *f.* sub-unit.
unterhaken, *v.a.* (*coll.*) take a p.'s arm.
unterhalb, *prep.* (*Gen.*) below; at the lower end of; under.
Unterhalt, *m.* maintenance, support, livelihood, sustenance; *seinen – verdienen*, earn one's living *or* livelihood. **-en,** 1. *ir.v.a.* (*insep.*) sustain, support, maintain, keep; keep up (*a correspondence*); entertain, amuse. 2. *v.r.* (*insep.*); *sich mit einem (über eine S.) -en*, converse with a p. (about a th.); *sich mit etwas -en*, amuse o.s. with s.th., pass the time with s.th.; *sich gut -en*, enjoy o.s., have a good time. **-sam,** *adj.* amusing, entertaining. **-sbeitrag,** *m.* maintenance grant. **-skosten,** *pl.* cost of maintenance. **-spflichtig,** *adj.* responsible for maintenance. **-ung,** *f.* (*no pl.*) keeping up, maintenance, support, keep; (*pl.* -en) conversation; entertainment, amusement. **-ungsbeilage,** *f.* recreational *or* humorous supplement (*of newspaper*). **-ungslektüre,** *f.*, **-ungsliteratur,** *f.* light reading *or* fiction.
unterhand-eln, *v.a. & n.* (*insep.*) (*aux.* h.) negotiate (*a peace, etc.*); treat (with), parley; *mit einem wegen einer S.* or *über eine S. -eln*, confer with s.o. about s.th., discuss a th. with s.o. **-lung,** *f.* negotiation, transaction; mediation; *in -lungen stehen*, carry on negotiations (with).
Unterhändler, *m.* negotiator, mediator, agent, intermediary, contact-man, go-between.
unterhauen, *ir.v.a.* (*insep.*) undercut, underwork (*Min.*); (*sl.*) sign, endorse.
Unterhaus, *n.* lower part of a house, ground floor; Lower Chamber *or* House, House of Commons.
Unterhaut, *f.* hypodermis.
Unterhemd, *n.* vest.
unterhöhlen, *v.a.* (*insep.*) tunnel; undermine, wear away.
Unterholz, *n.* undergrowth, brushwood; copse.
Unterhosen, *pl.* (under) pants.
unterirdisch, *adj.* underground, subterraneous, subterranean.
Unterjacke, *f.* waistcoat, vest.
unterjochen, *v.a.* (*insep.*) subjugate, subdue; enslave.
Unterkäufer, *m.* middle-man.
unterkellern, *v.a.* excavate for a cellar.
Unterkiefer, *m.* lower jaw, mandible. **-gebiß,** *n.* the lower teeth.
Unterkinnlade, *f.* inferior maxilla (*Anat.*).
Unterklassen, *f.pl.* lower school.
Unterkleid, *n.* undergarment. **-ung,** *f.* underwear, underclothing.
unterkommen, 1. *ir.v.n.* (*sep.*) (*aux.* s.) find shelter, refuge *or* accommodation; find employment *or* a situation, be taken on. 2. *n.*, *see* **Unterkunft.**
Unterkörper, *m.* lower part of the body, abdomen.
unterkötig, *adj.* (*dial.*) festering.
unterkriegen, *v.a.* (*sep.*) conquer, get the better of; (*coll.*) *laß dich nicht* –, hold your ground, do not give in.
unterkühlen, *v.a.* (*insep.*) supercool.
Unterkunft, *f.* (¨e) shelter, lodging, accommodation; barracks, billet; situation, employment. **-slager,** *n.* rest camp (*Mil.*).
Unterlag-e, *f.* support; bracket, stand, rest; basis, base, foundation; ground, bottom, bed, substratum, subsoil; foil (*Jewellery*); blotting-pad; under-blanket; pattern, model; evidence, voucher, record, document; (*pl.*) particulars, data; *-e eines Hebels*, fulcrum. **-scheibe,** *f.* washer. **-splatte,** *f.* sole plate (*Railw.*).
Unterland, *n.* lowland(s), low-lying *or* flat country.
Unterlaß, *m.* (*only in*) *ohne* –, without intermission, unceasingly, incessantly, continuously. **-(ss)en,** *ir.v.a.* (*insep.*) leave off, discontinue; fail (*to do*), omit (*to do*), neglect (*doing*), forbear, abstain (*from doing*). **-(ss)ung,** *f.* omission, neglect, default, oversight. **-(ss)ungsfall,** *m.* case of neglect *or* oversight. **-(ss)ungsklage,** *f.* action for default. **-(ss)ungssünde,** *f.* sin of omission.
Unterlauf, *m.* lower course (*of a river*). **-en,** 1. *ir.v.n.* (*sep.*) (*aux.* s.) occur, creep in (*of mistakes*); (*insep.*) be suffused; *mit Blut -en*, bloodshot, extravasated. 2. *v.a.* (*insep.*) run *or* get in under s.o.'s guard (*Fenc.*).
unterleg-en, 1. *v.a.* (*sep.*) put underneath; attribute *or* impute (*to a person*); credit (*a p.*) with; *einem Kinde frische Windeln -en*, change a baby's napkin; *einer Melodie Worte -en*, put (new) words to a tune; *einem Worte einen anderen Sinn -en*, put a new construction upon *or* give *or* attach another meaning to a word; (*insep.*) trim, back, stiffen, *or* line with. 2. *p.p.* inferior, *see* **unterliegen.** **-scheibe,** *f.* washer.
Unterleib, *m.* abdomen, belly. **-sbeschwerde,** *f.* abdominal trouble *or* complaint. **-sentzündung,** *f.* peritonitis. **-shöhle,** *f.* abdominal cavity. **-sschmerzen,** *m.pl.* abdominal pains. **-styphus,** *m.* enteric *or* typhoid (fever).
Unterlieferer, *m.* sub-contractor.
unterlieg-en, *ir.v.n.* (*insep.*) (*aux.* s.) (*with Dat.*) succumb, be overcome, overthrown *or* defeated; (*also aux.* h.) *es -t einem Rabatt*, it is subject to

discount; *das –t keinem Zweifel*, that admits of no doubt; (*sep.*) (*aux.* h.) be at the bottom of, serve as a basis for.

Unterlippe, *f.* lower-lip.

unterm = unter dem.

untermalen, *v.a.* (*insep.*) prepare the canvas, apply the ground colour, supply the background (*Mus., etc.*); (*fig.*) make clear the underlying motives.

untermauern, *v.a.* (*insep.*) build a foundation to, underpin.

untermengen, *v.a.* (*sep.*) mix with; (*insep.*) mingle, intermix.

Untermensch, *m.* gangster, thug.

Untermieter, *m.* subtenant.

untermischen, *v.a.* (*insep.*) intermingle, intermix.

unternehm–en, 1. *ir.v.a* (*insep.*) undertake, attempt. 2. *n. see* **–ung. –end,** *pr.p. & adj.* enterprising, bold, venturesome. **–er,** *m.* contractor, entrepreneur; (*Amer.*) undertaker. **–erverband,** *m.* employers' combine. **–ung,** *f.* undertaking, enterprise, venture. **–ungsgeist,** *m.* spirit of enterprise. **–ungslustig,** *adj.* enterprising, venturesome.

Unteroffizier, *m.* non-commissioned officer (*Mil.*), petty officer (*Nav.*).

unterordn–en, *v.a. & r.* (*sep.*) subordinate (o.s.), submit to. **–ung,** *f.* subordination.

Unterpfand, *n.* pledge, security, mortgage.

Unterprima, *f.* lower sixth (form).

unterred–en, *v.r.* (*insep.*) converse, confer (*mit*, with). **–ung,** *f.* conversation, talk, discussion, conference; parley (*Mil.*).

Unterricht, *m.* instruction, teaching, tuition, lessons. **–en,** 1. *v.a.* (*insep.*) teach, instruct, educate, train; (*von* or *in with Dat., über with Acc.*) inform of, acquaint with, apprise of. 2. *v.r. sich von einer S.* or *über eine S. –en*, obtain information about s.th. **–sanstalt,** *f.* educational establishment. **–sbriefe,** *m.pl.* correspondence course. **–sfach,** *n.* special subject, subject in which a p. is qualified to teach. **–sminister,** *m.* Minister of Education. **–swesen,** *n.* education, educational affairs, public instruction. **–ung,** *f.* instruction, briefing, apprisal.

Unterrock, *m.* petticoat; (*sl.*) petticoat, skirt (*for woman*).

unters = unter das.

untersagen, *v.a.* (*insep.*) (*einem etwas*) forbid, prohibit.

Untersatz, *m.* support, base, stand, trestle, socle (*Arch.*); saucer; table-mat; minor proposition (*Log.*).

unterschätz–en, *v.a.* (*insep.*) undervalue, underrate; depreciate. **–ung,** *f.* underestimate, undervaluation.

unterscheid–bar, *adj.* distinguishable, discernible. **–en,** 1. *ir.v.a.* (*insep.*) distinguish, discern, discriminate, separate, differentiate. 2. *v.r.* differ (from). **–end,** *pr.p. & adj.* distinctive, characteristic. **–ung,** *f.* distinction, discrimination. **–ungsgabe,** *f.*, **–ungskraft,** *f. see* **–ungsvermögen. –ungsmerkmal,** *n., see* **–ungszeichen. –ungsvermögen,** *n.* power of discrimination, discernment, **–ungszeichen,** *n.* distinctive mark, characteristic, criterion.

Unterschenkel, *m.* tibia, shin-bone; shank; gaskin.

unterschieben *ir.v.a.* (*sep.* (*& Austr. dial. also insep.*) (*einem etwas*) substitute, interpolate; forge; (*fig.*) impute to, insinuate, foist *or* father upon; *Worten einen falschen Sinn –*, put a wrong construction on words.

Unterschied, *m.* (-e) distinction, difference, discrimination, variation, dissimilarity; *einen – machen*, make *or* draw a distinction; *zum –e von*, in contradistinction to, unlike; *ohne –*, without distinction, irrespective of, indiscriminately. **–en,** *p.p. & adj.*, **–lich,** *adj.* different, distinct, differential, variable; divers, sundry, several; *–liches*, many a thing, various things. **–slos,** *adv.* indiscriminately, without exception. **–sschwelle,** *f.* threshold of perceptibility.

unterschlächtig, *adj.* undershot (*of a mill-wheel*), succubous (*Bot.*).

unterschlag–en, *ir.v.a.* (*sep.*) cross (*the arms, etc.*); *einem ein Bein –en*, trip a p. up; (*insep.*) embezzle; intercept (*a letter, etc.*); suppress (*a will, etc.*). **–ung,** *f.* suppression, interception, embezzlement, conversion (*Law*).

Unterschleif, *m.* embezzlement, fraud.

Unterschlupf, *m.* shelter, dug-out, refuge, (*coll.*) hide-out.

unterschreiben, *ir.v.a.* (*insep.*) sign; subscribe *or* put one's name to; (*fig.*) approve of.

unterschreiten, *v.a.* (*insep.*) not come up to the estimate, work out cheaper than (*prices*).

Unterschrift, *f.* signature; inscription, caption (*under a picture, etc.*).

unterschwef–elsauer, *adj.* hyposulphate of. **–ligsauer,** *adj.* hyposulphite of.

Untersee–boot (U-Boot), *n.* submarine. **–isch,** *adj.* submarine.

Untersekunda, *f.* lower fifth (form).

untersetz–en, *v.a.* (*insep.*) mix (with), intermix; gear down. **–er,** *m.* stand, support (*for flower-pots, etc.*), table-mat. **–t,** *p.p. & adj.* square-built, thick-set, dumpy, squat. **–ung,** *f.* (gear) reduction. **–ungsgetriebe,** *n.* reduction gear.

Unterstaatssekretär, *m.* Under-Secretary of State.

Unterstand, *m.* dug-out, fox-hole (*Mil.*).

unterstehen, 1. *ir.v.n.* (*sep.*) (*aux.* h. & s.) be *or* stand under; shelter under. 2. *v.r.* (*insep.*) dare, presume, venture, be so bold as to; *–steh' dich nicht, das zu tun!* do not dare to do that! 3. *v.n.* (*insep.*) (*with Dat.*) be (placed) under, be subordinate to.

unterstell–en, 1. *v.a.* (*sep.*) put *or* place under; put under cover *or* shelter; (*insep.*) insinuate, impute; subordinate, put under the command of, attach (*Mil.*); *einem –t sein*, be under s.o. 2. *v.r.* subordinate o.s. (*Dat.*, to), acknowledge the authority (of). **–ung,** *f.* imputation, insinuation; subordination, attachment (*Mil.*).

unterstreichen, *ir.v.a.* (*insep.*) underline; (*fig.*) emphasize.

Unterstufe, *f.* lower grade; lower (forms of a) school.

unterstütz–en, *v.a.* (*insep.*) prop up, support; sustain, aid, assist, patronize. **–er,** *m.* supporter, patron. **–ung,** *f.* propping, support, help, aid, assistance, relief; patronage, subsidy. **–ungsgelder,** *n. pl.* subsidies. **–ungsgesuch,** *n.* application for relief. **–ungskasse,** *f.* benevolent fund, friendly society. **–ungsmauer,** *f.* supporting wall. **–ungspunkt,** *m.* point of support, fulcrum. **–ungstrupp,** *m.* reinforcements, supporting troops.

Untersuch, *m.* (*Swiss dial.*) *see* **–ung. –en,** *v.a.* (*insep.*) inquire into, examine, investigate, test, analyse, probe, explore, inspect. **–ung,** *f.* examination, inquiry, investigation, inspection, probing, research. **–ungsausschuß,** *m.* commission of inquiry. **–ungsbescheid,** *m.* award of a court of inquiry (*Law*). **–ungsgericht,** *n.* court of inquiry, magistrate's court. **–ungsgefangene(r),** *m.* prisoner on trial. **–ungshaft,** *f.* imprisonment on remand, detention pending investigation; *in –ungshaft nehmen* (*wegen*), commit for trial (on a charge of). **–ungsrichter,** *m.* examining magistrate.

Untertaille, *f.* bodice.

untertan, 1. *p.p. & adj.* (*Dat.*) subject (to); dependent (on); *sich* (*Dat.*) (*einen* or *etwas*) – *machen*, subdue (a p. *or* a th.), get (a p. *or* a th.) into one's power. 2. *m.* (-s *or* -en, -en) subject, vassal. **–enpflicht,** *f.* allegiance. **–entreue,** *f.* loyalty, fealty. **–enverstand,** *m.* short-sightedness of the common herd.

untertänig, *adj.* submissive, obedient, humble; subject; *–ster Diener*, (your) most humble and obedient servant. **–keit,** *f.* submission; submissiveness, humility.

Untertasse, *f.* saucer.

untertauchen, (*sep.*) *v.a. & n.* (*aux.* h. & s.) plunge, dip, (*coll.*) duck; dive, submerge (*of submarines*); (*fig.*) disappear, be lost.

Unterteil, *m. & n.* lower part, base. **–en,** *v.a.* (*insep.*) subdivide, split up, classify.

Untertertia, *f.* lower fourth (form).

Untertitel, *m.* subtitle, subhead(ing) (*of a book*).

untertreten, (*sep.*) *ir.v.n.* (*aux.* s.) step under; take shelter under.

untertunneln, *v.a.* (*insep.*) excavate *or* tunnel under.

untervermiet-en, *v.a.* & *n.* (*insep.*) sublet. **-er,** *m.* subletter.
unterwachsen, *adj.* overgrown, thick with undergrowth, (*dial.*) streaky (*of bacon, etc.*); interlarded.
unterwärts, *adv.* (*dial.*) downwards, underneath.
Unterwäsche, *f.* underclothing, underwear.
unterwaschen, *ir.v.a.* (*insep.*) wash away, erode.
Unterwasser, *n.* subsoil water; tail-race (*of a mill*). **-bombe,** *f.* depth charge. **-horchgerät,** *n.* hydrophone.
unterweg-en, (*Swiss dial.*) see *unterwegs lassen.* **-s,** *adv.* on the way, en route; *-s lassen,* leave undone *or* alone; *-s bleiben,* be passed over; not take place.
unterweilen, *adv.* (*dial.*) from time to time.
unterweis-en, *ir.v.a.* (*insep.*) (*in with Dat.*) instruct, teach. **-ung,** *f.* instruction; (*Swiss dial.*) preparation for confirmation; *-ung abwarten,* await instructions.
Unterwelt, *f.* underworld (*also of criminals*); lower regions, Hades.
unterwerf-en, 1. *ir.v.a.* (*insep.*) (*einen jemandem* or *einer S.*) subjugate, subject (to); *einer S. unterworfen sein,* be subject *or* exposed to s.th. 2. *v.r.* submit, yield, resign o.s. to. **-ung,** *f.* subjection, submission, resignation (to), acquiescence (in).
unterwertig, *adj.* below value; *-e Qualität,* inferior quality.
unterwinden, *ir.v.r., see* **unterfangen.**
Unterwuchs, *m.* brushwood, undergrowth.
unterwühlen, *v.a.* (*insep.*) excavate, undermine.
unterwürfig, *adj.* subject, submissive; obsequious, subservient, servile. **-keit,** *f.* submissiveness, subservience, obsequiousness, servility.
unterzeichn-en, 1. *v.a.* (*insep.*) sign; ratify, underwrite. 2. *v.r.* sign one's name. **-er,** *m.* signatory (*of a treaty*). **-ete(r),** *m.* undersigned. **-ung,** *f.* signing; signature, ratification.
Unterzeug, *n.* underclothing, undergarments, underwear.
unterziehen, 1. *ir.v.a.* (*sep.*) draw *or* put under; put on (underneath) (*as a petticoat*). 2. *v.a.* (*insep.*) submit *or* subject (*Dat.*, to). 3. *v.r.* (*insep.*) submit to, undergo, undertake; *sich der Mühe –,* take the trouble; *sich einer Operation –,* undergo an operation; *sich einer Prüfung –,* go in *or* sit for an examination; *sich einer S. –,* undertake (to do) a th.
Unterzug, *m.* support, prop, beam, girder.
untief, *adj.* shallow. **-e,** *f.* shallow water; shallow place; shoal, sand-bank; (*coll.*) bottomless pit, abyss.
Untier, *n.* (-(e)s, -e) monster, brute.
untilgbar, *adj.* inextinguishable; indelible; indestructible; irredeemable.
untragbar, *adj.* unwearable; unbearable, intolerable, insufferable.
untrennbar, *adj.* inseparable.
untreu, *adj.* unfaithful, faithless, disloyal; *einen seiner Pflicht – machen,* turn a p. from the path of duty; *seinen Schwüren – werden,* break one's oath(s). **-e,** *f.* unfaithfulness, faithlessness, disloyalty, inconstancy, infidelity, breach of trust, malfeasance (*Law*); (*Prov.*) *-e schlägt ihren eignen Herrn,* treachery comes back on the traitor.
untröstlich, *adj.* disconsolate, inconsolable, forlorn. **-keit,** *f.* disconsolateness.
untrüglich, *adj.* unerring, infallible, certain, sure; unmistakable, indubitable. **-keit,** *f.* infallibility, certainty.
untüchtig, *adj.* incapable, unfit, incompetent, inefficient; good-for-nothing. **-keit,** *f.* unfitness, incapacity, incompetence.
Untugend, *f.* vice, bad habit.
untunlich, *adj.* impracticable, not feasible, impossible. **-keit,** *f.* impracticability.
unüberbrückbar, *adj.* irreconcilable.
unüberlegt, *adj.* inconsiderate, ill-advised, unthinking, thoughtless, careless, heedless, rash.
unüberschreitbar, *adj.* insurmountable, insuperable.
unübersehbar, *adj.* immense, vast; incalculable, illimitable, boundless, unbounded. **-keit,** *f.* immensity, vastness, magnitude.
unübersichtlich, *adj.* obscure, unintelligible, involved, tortuous; blind (*corner*).
unübersteig-bar, -lich, *adj.* insurmountable, insuperable.
unübertragbar, *adj.* incommunicable (*of diseases*); not negotiable, not transferable, unassignable (*Law*); untranslatable.
unübertrefflich, *adj.* unequalled, unrivalled, incomparable.
unübertroffen, *adj.* unsurpassed, unexcelled, unparalleled, matchless.
unüberwindlich, *adj.* unconquerable, invincible, indomitable, impregnable; insurmountable, insuperable (*difficulties*).
unumgänglich, *adj.* indispensable, absolutely necessary, unavoidable, inevitable, ineluctable; *-e Notwendigkeit,* absolute necessity. **-keit,** *f.* inevitableness, absolute necessity.
unumschränkt, *adj.* unlimited; unconditional, absolute, arbitrary. **-heit,** *f.* absoluteness; despotic authority.
unumstößlich, *adj.* irrefutable, indisputable, unanswerable, irrevocable, incontrovertible, incontestable, irrefragable; *-e Gewißheit,* dead certainty. **-keit,** *f.* incontestableness, irrevocableness, conclusiveness.
unumwunden, 1. *adj.* open, plain, candid, frank, unreserved. 2. *adv.* point-blank. **-heit,** *f.* candour, frankness.
ununterbrochen, *adj.* uninterrupted, unbroken, consecutive, continuous; incessant, unremitting.
ununterscheidbar, *adj.* indistinguishable.
unveränder-lich, *adj.* unchangeable, unalterable, constant, invariable, immutable, incorruptible. **-lichkeit,** *f.* constancy, immutability. **-t,** *adj.* unchanged, unaltered, invariable.
unverantwortlich, *adj.* irresponsible; unjustifiable, inexcusable. **-keit,** *f.* irresponsibility; inexcusable action.
unverarbeitet, *adj.* not worked up, raw, in the native state.
unveräußerlich, *adj.* inalienable, unsaleable. **-keit,** *f.* inalienability.
unverbesserlich, *adj.* incorrigible, irredeemable, irreclaimable; perfect, unimpeachable, indefectible, faultless; *-er Junggesell,* confirmed bachelor. **-keit,** *f.* incorrigibility; perfection.
unverbindlich, *adj.* not binding *or* obligatory; without guarantee; without obligation; disobliging, impolite, uncivil.
unverblümt, *adj.* plain, blunt, direct, point-blank.
unverbrenn-bar, -lich, *adj.* fire-proof, incombustible.
unverbrüchlich, *adj.* inviolable; firm, steadfast, lasting, absolute.
unverbunden, *adj.* unconnected, uncombined; without obligation; not dressed (*of wounds*).
unverbürgt, *adj.* unwarranted, unconfirmed, not authenticated.
unverdau-lich, *adj.* indigestible, heavy (*of food*). **-t,** *adj.* undigested; crude.
unverderblich, *adj.* incorruptible, unspoilable. **-keit,** *f.* incorruptibility.
unverdichtbar, *adj.* incompressible.
unverdient, *adj.* unmerited, undeserved; unjust. **-ermaßen,** *adv.*, **-erweise,** *adv.* undeservedly, unjustly.
unverdrossen, *adj.* indefatigable, untiring, unflagging, unwearied, persistent, persevering, unremitting, assiduous; patient. **-heit,** *f.* assiduity, indefatigableness, perseverance, persistence, patience; good spirits.
unverehelicht, *see* **unverheiratet.**
unvereinbar, *adj.* incompatible, irreconcilable, incongruous inconsistent (with), repugnant (to). **-keit,** *f.* incompatibility, discrepancy, incongruity, inconsistency.
unverfälscht, *adj.* unadulterated, pure; real, genuine. **-heit,** *f.* genuineness.
unverfänglich, *adj.* natural, simple; harmless.
unverfroren, *adj.* unabashed, imperturbable, impudent, bold, pert, audacious, (*coll.*) cheeky. **-heit,** *f.* imperturbability; boldness, impudence, (*coll.*) cheek, face.

unvergänglich, *adj.* imperishable, everlasting, ageless, deathless, undying, immortal. **-keit,** *f.* imperishableness, persistence, permanence, immortality.
unvergeßlich, *adj.* unforgettable, memorable; *das wird mir – bleiben,* I shall never forget that.
unvergleich-bar, -lich, *adj.* incomparable, inimitable, unrivalled, matchless, peerless, unique. **-lichkeit,** *f.* perfection, superiority.
unverhältnismäßig, *adj.* disproportionate, incongruous. **-keit,** *f.* disproportion, incongruity.
unverheiratet, *adj.* unmarried, single.
unverhofft, *adj.* unhoped (for); unexpected, unforeseen; (*Prov.*) – *kommt oft,* the unexpected always happens.
unverhohlen, *adj.* unconcealed, open, frank, candid, unreserved.
unverkäuflich, *adj.* unsaleable, unmarketable, not negotiable; not for sale; *-e Ware,* a drug on the market; (*coll.*) white elephant.
unverkennbar, *adj.* unmistakable, unambiguous, unequivocal; obvious, evident, manifest, palpable; (*coll.*) glaring, plain as a pikestaff, clear as day.
unverletz-lich, *adj.* invulnerable, unassailable, inviolable; sacred, sacrosanct. **-lichkeit,** *f.* invulnerability, inviolability, sanctity. **-t,** *adj.* unhurt, uninjured, unimpaired, safe; inviolate, intact.
unverlierbar, *adj.* safe; unforgettable; immortal.
unvermählt, *adj., see* **unverheiratet.**
unvermeid-lich, *adj.* inevitable, unavoidable, inexorable, ineluctable , irresistible. **-lichkeit,** *f.* inevitableness, stern necessity.
unvermerkt, *adj.* unperceived, unnoticed, unobserved.
unvermischt, *adj.* unmixed, unalloyed, pure.
unvermittelt, *adj.* sudden, abrupt, unexpected, unheralded.
Unvermögen, *n.* powerlessness, inability, incapacity, ineptitude, impotence; insolvency; – *zu bezahlen,* insolvency. **-d,** *adj.* unable, incapable, incompetent, inept, feeble, powerless, impotent; poor, penniless, impecunious.
unvermutet, *adj.* unthought (of), unlooked (for), unexpected, unforeseen.
unvernehm-bar, -lich, *adj.* indiscernible; dim, indistinct; inaudible; unintelligible, inscrutable.
Unvernunft, *f.* unreasonableness, irrationality, senselessness, absurdity, folly, silliness; *das ist die höhere – !* that is the height of absurdity!
unvernünftig, *adj.* irrational, unreasonable, senseless, foolish, silly, nonsensical, ridiculous, absurd; *-e Tiere,* dumb animals.
unverpfändbar, *adj.* not subject to distraint.
unverrichtet, *adj.* unaccomplished, left undone, not completed. **-erdinge,** *adv.*, **-ersache,** *adv.* unsuccessfully, without having achieved one's purpose.
unverrück-bar, *adj.* immovable, fixed. **-t,** 1. *adj.* unmoved, in its place; steady, fixed. 2. *adv.* fixedly, immovably; uninterruptedly, steadily.
unverschämt, *adj.* shameless, impudent, brazen; exorbitant (*price*); (*coll.*) cheeky; *-e Lüge,* barefaced lie. **-heit,** *f.* impudence, insolence, effrontery; (*coll.*) cheek, face.
unverschuldet, *adj.* unmerited, undeserved; not in debt, unencumbered. **-erweise,** *adv.* undeservedly, innocently.
unversehens, *adv.* unexpectedly, suddenly, unawares, in less than no time; unintentionally, accidentally, fortuitously, casually, by chance.
unversehrt, *adj.* undamaged, uninjured, intact, safe, entire. **-heit,** *f.* entirety.
unversieg-bar, -lich, *adj.* inexhaustible; everflowing.
unversöhnlich, *adj.* irreconcilable; implacable, intransigent.
unversorgt, *adj.* unprovided (for); without means, destitute.
Unverstand, *m.* lack of understanding *or* judgement, irrationality, senselessness, imprudence, folly. **-en,** *adj.* not understood; misunderstood, misinterpreted, misconstrued.
unverständ-ig, *adj.* unwise, injudicious, foolish, silly, stupid, imprudent. **-lich,** *adj.* unintelligible, incomprehensible, inconceivable, inexplicable, inscrutable, impenetrable; obscure, enigmatic, recondite, indistinct. **-lichkeit,** *f.* unintelligibility, incomprehensibility; obscurity.
unversucht, *adj.* untried, unattempted; *nichts – lassen,* leave no stone unturned.
unvertilgbar, *adj.* indelible, ineffaceable, ineradicable, indestructible, imperishable. **-keit,** *f.* indelibility.
unverträglich, *adj.* irreconcilable, incompatible; unsociable; intolerant; quarrelsome, irritable. **-keit,** *f.* unsociability, quarrelsomeness, irritability; incompatibility.
unverwandt, *adj.* unmoved, fixed, resolute, steadfast, immovable; unflinching, unwavering, undeterred; constant, ceaseless, unceasing, incessant; unrelated (*mit,* with).
unverwehrt, *adj.* permitted, conceded, vouchsafed; *es ist Ihnen – zu . . .,* you are quite free *or* at liberty to . . .
unverweilt, *adv.* without delay, directly, promptly, immediately, at once, forthwith.
unverweslich, *adj.* incorruptible.
unverwischbar, *adj.* ineffaceable, ineradicable, indelible.
unverwundbar, *adj.* invulnerable, impregnable, inexpugnable. **-keit,** *f.* invulnerability.
unverwüstlich, *adj.* indestructible, imperishable, inexhaustible; indefatigable, irrepressible.
unverzagt, *adj.* undaunted, undismayed, unabashed; fearless, intrepid, bold, stout-hearted, resolute, indomitable. **-heit,** *f.* intrepidity, boldness, courage, fearlessness, valour, fortitude.
unverzeihlich, *adj.* unpardonable, inexcusable, indefensible, reprehensible.
unverzins-bar, -lich, *adj.* paying no interest; *-bares Darlehen,* free loan.
unverzollt, *adj.* duty unpaid, in bond.
unverzüglich, 1. *adj.* immediate, instant, prompt, sudden, summary. 2. *adv.* without delay, at once, immediately, straightway, forthwith, at short notice.
unvollendet, *adj.* unfinished, incomplete; *etwas – lassen,* leave a th. half finished.
unvollkommen, *adj.* incomplete, imperfect; defective, deficient, wanting. **-heit,** *f.* imperfection, defectiveness, deficiency, defect.
unvollständig, *adj.* incomplete, deficient; defective, imperfect. **-keit,** *f.* incompleteness; defectiveness.
unvorbereitet, *adj.* unprepared, unready, not ready; unpremeditated, extemporaneous, extempore; *-e Übersetzung,* unseen (translation); – *sprechen,* extemporize.
unvordenklich, *adj.* in *seit -er Zeit,* from time immemorial, time out of mind.
unvoreingenommen, *adj.* impartial, unbiased, fair, scrupulous.
unvorgreiflich, *adj.* disinterested, impartial; with diffidence, subject to correction.
unvorhergesehen, *adj.* unforeseen, unexpected; *-er Schicksalsschlag,* bolt from the blue.
unvorsichtig, *adj.* careless, negligent; unwary, incautious; inconsiderate, improvident, unwise, imprudent. **-keit,** *f.* lack of foresight, improvidence, imprudence; carelessness, negligence; *aus -keit,* inadvertently, by mistake, through negligence.
unvorteilhaft, *adj.* disadvantageous, unbecoming (*of a dress*); inexpedient; unprofitable, unremunerative.
unwägbar, *adj.* imponderable. **-keit,** *f.* imponderability.
unwahr, *adj.* false, untrue, fictitious, invented, illusory; insincere, hypocritical, lying. **-haftig,** *adj.* untrue, false, spurious, untruthful, insincere, disingenuous, not reliable. **-haftigkeit,** *f.* insincerity, dissimulation, inaccuracy, falsification, falseness, mendacity. **-heit,** *f.* falsehood, untruth, lie, inaccuracy, falsity, misstatement, misrepresentation, false assertion, perjury, fiction. **-scheinlich,** *adj.* unlikely, improbable. **-scheinlichkeit,** *f.* unlikelihood, improbability.
unwandelbar, *adj.* immutable, invariable, un-

shakable, undeviating, unchangeable; constant, permanent, durable, stable, lasting; indeclinable (*Gram.*). **-keit,** *f.* immutability, stability, unchangeableness, permanence, durability, constancy.

unwegsam, *adj.* impracticable, impassable, pathless. **-keit,** *f.* difficult terrain, impracticable condition (*of roads*).

Unweib, *n.* virago, shrew, vixen, termagant. **-lich,** *adj.* unwomanly.

unweigerlich, 1. *adj.* unhesitating, unquestioning; *-er Gehorsam,* unquestioning *or* implicit obedience. 2. *adv.* without fail.

unweit, *adv.* not far off, near, close by. 2. *prep.* (*Gen.*) not far from, close to, near; *– von hier,* in the immediate vicinity *or* neighbourhood, close by, close at hand.

unwert, 1. *adj.* unworthy; worthless. 2. *m.* unworthiness, worthlessness.

Unwesen, *n.* disorder, confusion; mischief, nuisance, abuse; excess; *sein – treiben,* be up to one's tricks; haunt (*a place*). **-tlich,** *adj.* unessential, non-essential, immaterial, unimportant, insignificant; accidental, accessory, beside the point. **-tlichkeit,** *f.* unimportance, insignificance, triviality, paltriness.

Unwetter, *n.* stormy weather, violent storm.

unwichtig, *adj.* unimportant, insignificant, trifling, trivial, slight; (*coll.*) footling, fiddling, piffling. **-keit,** *f.* insignificance, unimportance, triviality, paltriness; *eine -keit,* a trifle, bagatelle; (*coll.*) flea-bite, brass farthing, fig.

unwiderleg-bar, -lich, *adj.* unanswerable, irrefutable.

unwiderruflich, *adj.* irrevocable, irretrievable, irreversible; *die S. ist –,* the affair is past recall; *– letzte Aufführung,* positively the last performance (*Theat.*).

unwidersprechlich, *adj.* incontestable, incontrovertible, undeniable.

unwidersprochen, *adj.* uncontradicted, unquestioned, undisputed, approved, agreed.

unwiderstehlich, *adj.* irresistible; *-er Wunsch,* overpowering desire.

unwiederbringlich, *adj.* irreparable, irremediable, irretrievable, irrecoverable, irredeemable; *– dahin* or *verloren,* irretrievably lost, gone for ever.

Unwill-e(n), *m.* (-ens, -en) resentment, displeasure, animosity; indignation, anger, annoyance, vexation, bitterness; reluctance. **-ig,** *adj.* indignant, resentful, exasperated, angry (*über,* about); (*coll.*) nettled, riled, sore; reluctant, unwilling. **-fährig,** *adj.* disobliging, uncomplying, grudging, contumacious. **-fährigkeit,** *f.* contumacy, insubordination, non-compliance. **-kommen,** *adj.* unwelcome; unpleasant, disagreeable; troublesome. **-kürlich,** *adj.* involuntary, unintentional, unintended; instinctive, automatic, mechanical. **-kürlichkeit,** *f.* involuntariness.

unwirk-lich, *adj.* unreal, non-existent. **-sam,** *adj.* ineffectual, ineffective, inefficient, inefficacious; inoperative, inactive, neutral, null, void. **-samkeit,** *f.* inefficacy, invalidity, inefficiency, incapacity, incapability, inaptitude.

unwirsch, *adj.* morose, surly, churlish, brusque, uncivil; (*coll.*) grumpy. **-heit,** *f.* bad temper, brusqueness, incivility, churlishness.

unwirt-lich, -sam, *adj.* uninhabited, waste, barren; dreary, uninviting, inhospitable.

unwissen-d, *adj.* ignorant (of), unacquainted (with), unconversant (with), unaware (of), not cognizant (of), ill informed (about); uninformed, inexperienced, ignorant, stupid; *-der Mensch,* ignoramus. **-heit,** *f.* ignorance, incomprehension; inexperience. **-tlich,** *adv.* unwittingly, unknowingly, unconsciously, unawares.

unwohl, *adj.* unwell, indisposed; (*coll.*) poorly, off colour, out of sorts, seedy; *mir ist –, ich bin –, ich fühle mich –,* I don't feel well; I feel unwell; *sie ist –,* she has her period. **-sein,** *n.* indisposition; monthly period.

unwohnlich, *adj.* uninhabitable; cheerless, uncomfortable.

unwürdig, *adj.* unworthy, discreditable, disgraceful; despicable, disreputable, shameful, mean, base, (*coll.*) shabby; *Lobes –,* undeserving of praise. **-keit,** *f.* unworthiness, worthlessness; discredit, disgrace.

Unzahl, *f.* immense number.

unzählig, *adj.* innumerable, countless, numberless. **-emal,** *adv.* times without number.

unzähmbar, *adj.* untameable, unyielding, recalcitrant, indomitable. **-keit,** *f.* recalcitrance.

unzart, *adj.* ungracious, rough, rude, bluff, **blunt,** unceremonious, tactless. **-heit,** *f.* rudeness, **bluntness,** bluffness, incivility, ungraciousness.

[1]**Unze,** *f.* (-n) ounce (= *approx. 30 gr.*).

[2]**Unze,** *f.* (-) jaguar (*Felis uncia*) (*Zool.*).

Unzeit, *f.* wrong time; (*only in*) *zur –,* unseasonably, inopportunely; prematurely. **-gemäß,** *adj.* out-of-date, behind the times, old-fashioned, unfashionable; out of season, inopportune. **-ig,** *adj.* untimely, inopportune, unpropitious, inauspicious, unseasonable, ill-timed; out of season, immature, unripe, premature.

unzerbrechlich, *adj.* unbreakable, infrangible.

unzerlegbar, unzersetzbar, *adj.* indivisible, elementary, simple.

unzerstörbar, *adj.* indestructible, imperishable.

unzertrenn-lich, *adj.* inseparable; *-liche Eigenschaften,* inherent qualities. **-lichkeit,** *f.* inseparableness, tenacity, cohesiveness.

unziem-end, -lich, *adj.* unbecoming, unseemly, improper, indecorous, indecent, unmentionable. **-lichkeit,** *f.* impropriety, indecorum, unseemliness, indecency, immodesty, indelicacy.

Unzucht, *f.* unchastity, lechery, lewdness, incontinence, fornication; *gewerbsmäßige –,* prostitution.

unzüchtig, *adj.* unchaste, bawdy, lewd, lecherous, obscene, indecent, lascivious, salacious, meretricious. **-keit,** *f.* unchastity, immodesty, concupiscence, obscenity, bawdiness, lewdness.

unzufrieden, *adj.* dissatisfied, discontented. **-heit,** *f.* discontent, dissatisfaction.

unzugänglich, *adj.* inaccessible, unapproachable, intractable; reserved; incorruptible. **-keit,** *f.* inaccessibility.

unzukömmlich, *adj.* unfit, unfitting, inappropriate; ill-assorted, incongruous. **-keit,** *f.* incongruity, unfitness.

unzulänglich, *adj.* insufficient, inadequate; unavailing. **-keit,** *f.* insufficiency, inadequacy, shortcoming.

unzulässig, *adj.* inadmissible, ineligible, forbidden. **-keit,** *f.* inadmissibility, ineligibility.

unzurechnungsfähig, *adj.* not responsible (for), not accountable (for), not answerable (for) (*one's actions*); certifiable, feeble-minded. **-keit,** *f.* feeble-mindedness; irresponsibility.

unzureichend, *adj.* insufficient, inadequate.

unzusammenhängend, *adj.* unconnected, disconnected, disjointed; incoherent.

unzuständig, *adj.* incompetent (*Law*).

unzuträglich, *adj.* disadvantageous, prejudicial, not good for; unhealthy, unwholesome. **-keit,** *f.* unwholesomeness, failure.

unzutreffend, *adj.* false, incorrect, erroneous; unfounded, groundless (*of news*).

unzuverlässig, *adj.* unreliable, untrustworthy, treacherous, (*coll.*) crooked, slippery; uncertain, fallible, dubious, (*coll.*) fishy. **-keit,** *f.* untrustworthiness, unreliability.

unzweckmäßig, *adj.* unsuitable, inopportune, inexpedient; inappropriate, inapt, inapposite, not pertinent. **-keit,** *f.* unsuitableness, inappropriateness, inexpediency.

unzweideutig, *adj.* unequivocal, unambiguous, explicit, clear, precise. **-keit,** *f.* perspicuity, precision, clarity.

unzweifelhaft, *adj.* undoubted, indubitable, unquestionable; *-e Tatsache,* established fact, certainty; *es ist – (wahr),* it is beyond question, there is no doubt about it, (*coll.*) sure as fate, depend upon it.

üppig, *adj.* abundant, plentiful, rich, sumptuous, luxuriant, rank, exuberant, voluptuous, well-developed (*woman's figure*); supercilious, pompous, haughty, arrogant, lordly; (*coll.*) uppish, high and mighty; *-er Haarwuchs*, exuberant growth of hair; *-es Mahl*, sumptuous repast; *-es Unkraut*, rank weeds. **-keit,** *f.* luxuriant growth, exuberance, plenty, richness; voluptuousness, luxury; haughtiness, pomposity, arrogance, uppishness.

Ur, *m.* (-(e)s, -e), **-ochs,** *m.*, **-stier,** *m.* aurochs (*Bos primigenius*) (*Zool.*).

ur-, *prefix added to many nouns & adj.s indicating*: (1) origin, source; (2) very old, primitive; (3) *intensification. See examples below.*

Urahn, *m.* (-en, -en) great-grandfather; ancestor. **-e,** *f.* (-en) great-grandmother; ancestress.

ur-alt, *adj.* very old, aged; ancient, primeval, as old as the hills. **-alter,** *n.* great age; earliest times. **-alters,** *adv.* in ancient times; *von -alters her*, from time immemorial.

Uran, *n.* uranium.

Uran-fang, *m.* the very beginning, prime origin. **-fänglich,** 1. *adj.* primordial, primeval, primitive; original. 2. *adv.* in the very beginning.

Uranlage, *f.* original disposition; rudiment, vestige, primordium.

uraufführ-en, *v.a.* (*p.p. uraufgeführt*) play *or* perform for the first time. **-ung,** *f.* first performance, first night; release (*Films*).

urban, *adj.* urbane, polite, civil, suave, bland. **-ität,** *f.* urbanity, suavity.

urbar, 1. *adj.* arable, capable of cultivation; cultivated. 2. *n.* (*archaic*) land register. **-isierung,** *f.* (*Swiss dial.*), **-machung,** *f.* clearing, tilling, cultivating; reclamation, cultivation.

Urbestandteil, *m.* ultimate constituent.

Urbewohner, *m.* original inhabitant, native, (*pl.*) aborigines.

Urbild, *n.* original; archetype, prototype. **-lich,** *adj.* original, archetypal. **-ungsstoff,** *m.* protoplasm.

Urblatt, *n.* primordial leaf.

Urboden, *m.* virgin soil.

urchig, *adj.* (*Swiss dial.*) genuine, primitive.

Urchrist, *m.* early Christian. **-entum,** *n.* primitive Christianity, the early Church.

urdeutsch, *adj.* thoroughly German, German to the core.

Urei, *n.* primitive ovum.

ureigen, *adj.* original; innate, inherent, peculiar (to); (one's) very own. **-heit,** *f.* characteristic, particularity, specific peculiarity. **-tümlich,** *adj.*, *see* **-. -tümlichkeit,** *f.*, *see* **-heit.**

Ureinwohner, *m.* original inhabitant.

Ureltern, *pl.* ancestors; first-parents.

Urenkel, *m.* great-grandson, great-grandchild. **-in,** *f.* great-granddaughter.

Urfarbe, *f.* primitive colour.

Urfehde, *f.* oath to keep the peace, oath of truce.

urfidel, *adj.* (*coll.*) very jolly.

Urform, *f.* original form, prototype, archetype.

Urgebirge, *n.*, *see* **Urgestein.**

urgemütlich, *adj.* exceedingly comfortable.

Urgeschicht-e, *f.* early history, pre-history. **-lich,** *adj.* prehistoric.

Urgestalt, *f.*, *see* **Urform.**

Urgestein, *n.* primitive rock.

Urgewicht, *n.* original weight.

Urgroß-eltern, *pl.* great-grandparents. **-mutter,** *f.* great-grandmother. **-vater,** *m.* great-grandfather.

Urheber, *m.* author, creator, founder, originator. **-recht,** *n.* copyright. **-schaft,** *f.* authorship, parentage.

urig, *adj.* (*dial.*) original, odd, eccentric, whimsical, ludicrous.

Urin, *m.* urine. **-glas,** *n.* urinal. **-ieren,** *v.n.* (*aux.* h.) urinate, pass *or* make water. **-stein,** *m.* urinary calculus. **-treibend,** *adj.* diuretic.

Urkirche, *f.* primitive *or* early church.

urkomisch, *adj.* very *or* screamingly funny.

Ur-kraft, *f.* original force, elementary power; moving principle. **-kräftig,** *adj.* very *or* most powerful, with primitive strength.

Urkund-e, *f.* (-en) deed, document, charter, title (deed); voucher, record, attestation; (*archaic*) *zu - dessen*, in witness whereof. **-ei,** *f.* archive. **-enbeweis,** *m.* documentary proof. **-enbuch,** *n.* record, register. **-enforscher,** *m.* palaeographer. **-enlehre,** *f.* palaeography. **-ensammlung,** *f.* archives. **-lich,** *adj.* documentary; authentic; *-lich dessen*, in proof of which. **-sbeamte(r),** *m.* registrar.

Urlaub, *m.* (-(e)s, -e), leave (of absence), furlough, vacation; *wilder -*, absence without leave. **-er,** *m.* soldier on leave. **-sgesuch,** *n.* application for leave. **-sverlängerung,** *f.* extension of leave.

Urlehre, *f.* master gauge.

Urmensch, *m.* primitive man.

Urne, *f.* (-n) urn, casket; ballot-box.

Urning, *m.* (-s, -e) homosexual.

Urochs, *m.*, *see* [1]**Ur.**

urplötzlich, 1. *adj.* very sudden. 2. *adv.* quite suddenly, all of a sudden.

Urpreis, *m.* manufacturer's price.

Urquell, *m.* (-(e)s, -e), **-e,** *f.* (-en) fountain-head; primary source, origin.

Ursache, *f.* (-n) cause, reason, origin, motive, ground, occasion; *keine -*, don't mention it; *man hat - zu glauben*, there is reason to believe; *gleiche -n, gleiche Wirkungen*, like causes produce like effects; (*Prov.*) *kleine -n, große Wirkungen*, important developments often come from small beginnings.

ursächlich, *adj.* causal, causative. **-keit,** *f.* causalty.

Ursatz, *m.* axiom.

Urschleim, *m.* protoplasm.

Urschrift, *f.* original text, original. **-lich,** *adj.* (in the) original.

Ursprache, *f.* primitive language; original speech.

Ursprung, *m.* source, origin, inception, derivation, provenance, starting-point, beginning, cause; *seinen - haben* or *nehmen von*, take its rise from, descend from; *deutschen -s*, native of Germany; made in Germany. **-szeichen,** *n.* **-szeugnis,** *n.* trade mark certifying country of origin.

ursprünglich, *adj.* primitive, primordial; initial, primary, original; natural, spontaneous, impulsive. **-keit,** *f.* primitiveness; originality, impulsiveness.

Urstier, *m.*, *see* [1]**Ur.**

Urstoff, *m.* original substance, primary matter; element.

Urteer, *m.* crude tar.

Urteil, *n.* (-s, -e) judgement, decision; sentence, verdict; view, opinion; *sich ein - bilden über*, form an opinion about, pass judgement on; *ein - über eine S. fällen*, pass sentence upon *or* express a considered opinion about a th.; *meinem -(e) nach*, in my opinion; *sich dem -(e) unterwerfen*, submit to a decision; *einem das - sprechen*, pass judgement *or* sentence on a p.; *darüber enthalte ich mich jedes -s*, I refuse to express any opinion about it, I have no views on the subject. **-en,** *v.n.* (*aux.* h.) judge, pass sentence, give one's opinion, form an opinion; *nach seinen Reden* or *seiner Sprache nach zu -en*, according to his expressed opinion; *darüber kann er nicht -en*, he is no judge of such matters; *dem Schein nach -en*, judge by *or* from appearances. **-seröffnung,** *f.* publication of a judgement, pronouncement of sentence. **-sfähig,** *adj.* competent to judge, judicious. **-sfällung,** *f.* passing of sentence. **-skraft,** *f.* (power of) judgement; reasoning faculty; discernment. **-slos,** *adj.* injudicious. **-sspruch,** *m.* judgement, sentence, verdict. **-svermögen,** *n.*, *see* **-skraft. -svollstreckung,** *f.* execution of a sentence.

Urtel, *m.* (-s, -) *dial. & Poet. for* **Urteil.**

Urtext, *m.* original text.

Urtier, *n.* primitive *or* antediluvian animal; protozoon. **-e,** *n.pl.*, **-chen,** *n.pl.* protozoa.

urtümlich, *adj.* original, native.

Urur-ahn, *m.* progenitor, great-great-grandfather. **-eltern,** *pl.* forefathers, first parents, early ancestors. **-enkel,** *m.* great-great-grandson, great-great-grandchild. **-enkelin,** *f.* great-great-granddaughter.

Urvater, *m.* first parent, forefather.

urväter-lich, *adj.* primitive; ancestral. **-zeit,** *f.* olden times, days of yore.

urverwandt, *adj.* of the same origin, cognate (*of words*). **-schaft,** *f.* primitive affinity, cognation (*Philol.*).

Urvolk, *n.* primitive people, aborigines.
Urwahl, *f.* preliminary election (*of electors*).
Urwald, *m.* primeval *or* virgin forest, tropical forest.
Urwelt, *f.* primeval world. **-lich,** *adj.* primeval, antediluvian.
urwüchsig, *adj.* original, native; (*fig.*) racy; blunt, rough.
Urzeit, *f.* primitive times, prehistory. **-lich,** *adj.* prehistoric, primeval, primordial.
Urzelle, *f.* ovem.
Urzeugung, *f.* spontaneous generation, abiogenesis.
Urzustand, *m.* primitive state, original condition.
Us-ance, *f.* (*pl.* -n) (*C.L.*) usage, custom, practice; *nach -ance,* **-ancenmäßig,** *adv.* as is customary (in the trade), according to (stock exchange) practice. **-o,** *m.* (-os, -os) time which a bill has to run, usance; *see also* **-ance.** (*C.L.*) **-owechsel,** *m.* bill at usance.
Usurp-ator, *m.* (-s, -en) usurper. **-ieren,** *v.a.* usurp.
Usus, *m.* (-, -) usage, tradition, custom, habit, rule.
Utensilien, *pl.* utensils, tools, implements.
Utilit-arier, *m.* (-s, -) utilitarian. **-aristisch,** *adj.* utilitarian. **-ät,** *f.* utility. **-ätslehre,** *f.* doctrine of utilitarianism. **-ätsrücksichten,** *f.pl.* considerations of utility.
Utop-ie, *f.* (-ien) utopia, utopian scheme. **-isch,** *adj.* utopian.
Uviollicht, ultra-violet rays.
Uz, *m.* (-es, -e) (*coll.*) chaffing, leg-pulling, teasing, quizzing; fun. **-en,** *v.a.* (*coll.*) mock, tease, chaff. **-erei,** *f.*, *see* **-.**

V

V, v, *n.* V, v; *for abbreviations see Index at end. In German words it is pronounced as f; in foreign borrowings usually as w.*
vag, *adj.* vague, indeterminate. **-abund,** *m.* (-en, -en) vagabond, vagrant, tramp. **-abundentum,** *n.* vagabondage, vagrancy; (*coll.*) tramps, vagabonds. **-abundieren,** *v.n.* (*aux.* h. & s.) rove, wander, roam, lead a vagrant life; *-abundierender Strom,* stray current (*Elec.*). **-ant,** *m.* (-en -en) medieval wandering scholar. **-ieren,** *v.n.* stroll about.
vakant, *adj.* vacant, void, unoccupied. **-z,** *f.* (-zen) vacancy, vacant post; vacation, recess (*Law*).
Vakuum, *n.* (-ums, -ua) vacuum (*Phys.*). **-pumpe,** *f.* air suction pump. **-röhre,** *f.* vacuum-tube.
Vakzin-ation, *f.* vaccination. **-ieren,** *v.a.* vaccinate.
Valand, *m.* (*dial.*) devil, evil fiend.
Valenz, *f.* valence, valency.
Valet, *n.* (-s, -s) farewell, adieu, valediction; - *geben,* dismiss; - *sagen,* bid farewell *or* adieu, take leave. **-schmaus,** *m.* farewell banquet, valedictory celebration.
val-idieren, 1. *v.a.* (*C.L.*) make valid; effect (*an insurance, etc.*). 2. *v.n.* be valid; *eine Summe -idieren lassen gegen,* place a sum against. **-idierung,** *f.* validation, ratification. **-orisieren,** *v.a.* peg prices. **-uta,** *f.* (-ten) value, rate (of exchange), currency, monetary standard. **-utaschwach,** (**-utastark**), *adj.* with a low (high) rate of exchange. **-utieren,** *v.a.* value, valuate. **-vieren,** *v.a.* (*archaic*), *see* **-utieren.**
Vampir, *m.* (-s, -e) vampire.
Vanadin, *n.* vanadium.
Vanille, *f.* vanilla.
Vari-a, *pl.* sundries, odds and ends, miscellaneous items. **-ante,** *f.* variant (reading); sport (*Biol.*). **-antenapparat,** *m.* synopsis of all the various readings. **-ationsfähig,** *adj.* variable. **-ationsrechnung,** *f.* calculus of variations. **-ationsreihe,** *f.* frequency distribution. **-etät,** *f.* variety. **-eté,** *n.* variety theatre, music hall. **-ieren,** *v.a.* & *n.* (*aux.* h.) vary; *ein Thema -ieren,* compose *or* play variations of an air.
Varizen, *pl.* varicose veins.
Vasall, *m.* (-en, -en) vassal, retainer. **-enstaat,** *m.* tributary (state).
Vaselin, *n.* (-s) -e, *f.* vaseline.
Vater, *m.* (-s, ⸚) father; (male) parent; (*Poet.* & *Zool.*) sire; *unsre Väter,* our forefathers *or* ancestors; *die Väter der Stadt,* the civic dignitaries. **-haus,** *n.* paternal house *or* roof, home (of one's childhood). **-land,** *n.* native country *or* land, mother-country, fatherland; *fürs -land sterben,* die for one's country; *für König und -land,* for king and country; *der Prophet gilt nichts in seinem -land,* a prophet is without honour in his own country. **-ländisch,** *adj.* native, national; patriotic. **-landsliebe,** *f.* patriotism. **-landslos,** *adj.* without a fatherland; unpatriotic. **-landsverräter,** *m.* traitor. **-los,** *adj.* fatherless. **-mord,** *m.* parricide. **-mörder,** *m.* parricide; (*obs.*) (old-fashioned) stand-up collar. **-name,** *m.*, *see* **-sname.** **-pflicht,** *f.* parental duty. **-sbruder,** *m.* paternal uncle. **-schaft,** *f.* paternity, fatherhood; *Nachforschung über die -schaft,* affiliation case (*Law*). **-schaftsklage,** *f.* affiliation case. **-(s)name,** *m.* family name, surname. **-sschwester,** *f.* paternal aunt. **-stadt,** *f.* native town. **-stelle,** *f.*; *-stelle vertreten* (*an* or *bei einem*), be a father to (a p.). **-unser,** *n.* (-s, -) the Lord's Prayer; paternoster (*R.C.*).
Väter-chen, *n.* (-s, -) papa, daddy. **-gruft,** *f.* ancestral vault. **-lich,** *adj.* paternal, fatherly; *er hat sich meiner -lich angenommen,* he has taken a fatherly interest in me; *-liches Erbteil,* patrimony. **-licherseits,** *adv.* on the father's side. **-sitte,** *f.* manners of our forefathers.
Veget-abilien, *pl.* vegetables, herbs, greenstuff. **-abil,** *adj.*, **-abilisch** (*Austr. dial.*), vegetable. **-ari(an)er,** *m.* vegetarian. **-arisch,** *adj.* vegetarian. **-arismus,** *m.* vegetarianism. **-ation,** *f.* vegetation, growth. **-ativ,** *adj.* vegetative. **-ieren,** *v.n.* (*aux.* h.) vegetate.
Vehemenz, *f.* vehemence, impetuosity.
Vehikel, *n.* (-s, -) vehicle; medium.
Veilchen, *n.* (-s, -) violet (*Bot.*). **-blau,** *adj.* violet. (*dial.*) **-fresser,** *m.* lady-killer, ladies' man.
Veitstanz, *m.* St. Vitus's dance.
Velin, *n.*, **-papier,** *n.* vellum.
Velo, *n.* (-s, -s) (*Swiss dial.*) bicycle.
Ven-e, *f.* (-en) vein (*Anat.*). **-ös,** *adj.* venous; veined. **-enentzündung,** *f.* phlebitis.
Venerabile, *n.* (*R.C.*) the consecrated wafer, the host.
venerisch, *adj.* venereal, syphilitic.
Venisektion, *f.* phlebotomy.
Ventil, *n.* (-s, -e) valve, air-valve, vent; ventilator (*Mach.*). **-ation,** *f.* ventilation, airing, weathering. **-ator,** *m.* (-s, -en) ventilator; fan, blower. **-führung,** *f.* valve-guide. **-ieren,** *v.a.* ventilate, air (*also fig.*). **-kolben,** *m.* valve-piston. **-leine,** *f.* rip-cord (*Av.*). **-röhre,** *f.* rectifier valve (*Rad.*). **-sitz,** *m.* valve seating. **-steuerung,** *f.* valve timing, mechanism *or* gear. **-stößel,** *m.* valve rocker. **-trompete,** *f.* key-bugle.
ver-, *insep. and unstressed prefix to verbs and to nouns and adjectives derived from them, with the idea of* (1) removal, loss; (2) stoppage, reversal, opposite; (3) using up, expenditure, continuation to the end; (4) alteration (*usually* deterioration); (5) *to form verbs from nouns or adjs. without any change of the root meaning. See entries below.*
verabfolg-en, *v.a.* (*einem etwas*) deliver, send, consign, remit, let (*a p.*) have, give up, hand over, surrender, serve (*food*); *nicht -en* (*lassen*), retain, keep back. **-ung,** *f.* delivery, consignment.
verabred-en, 1. *v.a.* agree upon, fix, appoint, stipulate; conspire (*Law*). 2. *v.r.* agree, come to an understanding; make an appointment. **-etermaßen,** *adv.* according to arrangement, as agreed upon. **-ung,** *f.* agreement, arrangement, appointment; conspiracy (*Law*).
verabreichen, *v.a.* (*einem etwas*), hand over, deliver, tender, furnish; dispense (*medicine*); *einem eine Ohrfeige -,* give a p. a box on the ear.

verabsäumen, *v.a.* (*usually used negatively*) neglect, omit, fail (to do).
verabscheu-en, I. *v.a.* abhor, abominate, detest. 2. *n.*, **-ung,** *f.* abhorrence, detestation. **-ungswert,** *adj.*, **-ungswürdig,** *adj.* abominable, detestable, execrable.
verabschied-en, I. *v.a.* dismiss, discharge, send away; disband (*troops*); *ein Gesetz -en*, pass *or* dispose of a bill. 2. *v.r.* (*von* or *bei einem*) take leave of, say good-bye to; retire (*from service*). **-ung,** *f.* dismissal; discharge.
veracht-en, *v.a.* despise, scorn, disdain, look down upon; *nicht zu -en*, (*coll.*) not to be sneezed at. **-ung,** *f.* disdain, contempt, scorn.
Verächt-er, *m.* (-s, -) scorner, despiser. **-lich,** *adj.* contemptuous, scornful, disdainful; despicable, contemptible. **-lichkeit,** *f.* contemptuousness, disdainfulness; despicableness.
veralbern, *v.a.* hold to ridicule, mock, make a fool of; (*coll.*) play up.
verallgemeiner-n, *v.a.* & *n.* generalize. **-ung,** *f.* generalization.
veralt-en, *v.n.* (*aux.* s.) grow old *or* stale; go out of use, become obsolete. **-et,** *p.p.* & *adj.* old, antiquated, obsolete; *-eter Ausdruck*, archaism.
Veranda, *f.* (-den) veranda.
veränder-lich, *adj.* changing, changeable, variable; unsettled, unsteady, unstable, inconstant, fickle, vacillating, fluctuating. **-lichkeit,** *f.* variability, changeableness; instability, inconstancy, fickleness. **-n,** I. *v.a.* change, alter, vary, transform, modify. 2. *v.r*, change, alter, vary; take another situation (*of servants*); *er hat sich zu seinem Vorteil* (*Nachteil*) *verändert*, he has changed for the better (worse). **-ung,** *f.* change, alteration, transformation, variation, modification.
verängstigt, *adj.* cowed, intimidated.
veranker-n, *v.a.* anchor, moor; (*fig.*) establish firmly. **-ung,** *f.* anchorage, mooring.
veranlag-en, *v.a.* assess (*fur eine* or *zu einer Steuer*, for taxation). **-t,** *adj.* (*fig.*) *gut -t*, talented, cut out for; *künstlerisch -t*, artistically gifted. **-ung,** *f.* assessment; talent, gift, turn (for).
veranlass-en, *v.a.* cause, occasion, bring about, effect, call forth, give rise to; instigate, induce, motivate; *das -te ihn zu denken*, that made him think *or* gave him cause to think; *das hat mich zu dem Glauben -t*, that has led me to believe. **-er,** *m.* author, cause. **-ung,** *f.* cause, occasion; motive, instigation, suggestion, inducement, order, request; *-ung geben*, cause, give rise *or* occasion to; *auf -ung von*, at the instance *or* instigation of; *aus dienstlicher -ung*, in line of duty.
veranschaulich-en, *v.a.* make clear, illustrate, be illustrative of; visualize. **-ung,** *f.* demonstration. **-ungsmittel,** *n.pl.* visual aids.
veranschlag-en, *v.a.* value, rate, estimate, appraise, assess, make an estimate (of). **-ung,** *f.* valuation, estimate, assessment, appraisal.
veranstalt-en, *v.a.* contrive, arrange, organize, bring about; (*coll.*) get up. **-er,** *m.* organizer. **-ung,** *f.* arrangement, organization, management; performance, entertainment, show, fête, (sporting) event; *-ungen treffen*, arrange, prepare, make arrangements (for).
verantwort-en, I. *v.a.* answer for, account for, be responsible for; defend, vindicate; *das kann ich schon -en*, I can explain that, leave that to me; *er hat viel zu -en*, he has much to answer for. 2. *v.r.* justify o.s., vindicate o.s.; *sich vor einem für etwas* or *wegen einer S. -en*, justify one's action with s.o. **-lich,** *adj.* responsible, accountable, answerable; *gegenseitig -lich*, mutually *or* jointly responsible; *ihn dafür -lich machen*, hold him responsible for; *-liches Amt*, responsible post. **-lichkeit,** *f.* responsibility. **-ung,** *f.* responsibility; justification, vindication, excuse; *die -ung auf sich laden*, incur the responsibility; *auf seine -ung*, at his (own) peril, on his own responsibility; *einen zur -ung ziehen*, call a p. to account. **-ungsbewußtsein,** *n.* sense of duty. **-ungsfreudig,** *adj.* willing to accept responsibility. **-ungslos,** *adj.* irresponsible. **-ungsschrift,** *f.* apology; defence (*Law*). **-ungsvoll,** *adj.* involving great responsibility; responsible.
verarbeit-en, *v.a.* manufacture; manipulate, work up, process; wear out with hard work; ponder over, assimilate, digest inwardly; (*coll.*) *einen gehörig -en*, pitch into a p., pull s.o. to pieces; *-ete Hände*, hands worn with work; *-etes Silber*, wrought silver. **-ung,** *f.* manufacturing; treatment, processing, working up; digestion, thorough study; elaboration, working out.
verargen, *v.a.* take amiss, blame, reproach; *einem etwas -*, blame a p. for a th.; *ich verarge es Ihnen gar nicht*, I do not hold it against you at all; *das kann mir niemand -*, no one can take me up about that.
verärgern, *v.a.* make angry, irritate, annoy, exasperate.
verarm-en, *v.n.* (*aux.* s.) become poor *or* impoverished, be reduced to poverty. **-ung,** *f.* impoverishment, pauperization.
veraschen, *v.a.* & *n.* incinerate, reduce to ashes.
veräst-eln, *v.r.* branch out, ramify. **-(e)lung,** *f.* ramification.
verauktionier-en, *v.a.* put up for sale, sell by auction; *-t werden*, come under the hammer, be sold by auction.
verausgab-en, I. *v.a.* spend, expend, pay out. 2. *v.r.* spend all one's money, (*coll.*) spend o.s. out, run short of money; (*fig.*) wear o.s. out. **-ung,** *f.* paying out, payment; *-ung falschen Geldes*, passing *or* uttering counterfeit money.
veräußer-lich, *adj.* alienable, saleable. **-lichen,** *v.n.* & *a.* grow *or* make superficial. **-n,** *v.a.* alienate; sell. **-ung,** *f.* alienation; sale.
Verb, *n.* (-s, -en), **-um,** *n.* (-ums, -a) verb. **-al,** *adj.* verbal; terminological. **-alinjurie,** *f.* insult, slander.
verbalhornen, (*dial.*) **verballhornen,** *v.a.* bowdlerize.
Verband, *m.* (-(e)s, ⸚e) assemblage; bonding, bond, joint; bandage, surgical dressing; union, association, league, alliance, combine; unit, formation (*Mil.*). **-kasten,** *m.* ambulance-box, medicine chest. **-päckchen,** *n.* field-dressing, first-aid kit. **-platz,** *m.* dressing-station (*Mil.*). **-schere,** *f.* surgical scissors. **-sfliegen,** *n.* formation flying (*Av.*). **-skasse,** *f.* funds of a society. **-smitglied,** *n.* member of a society *or* an association. **-stelle,** *f.* dressing station. **-stoff,** *m.*, **-zeug,** *n.* dressing, bandage.
verbann-en, *v.a.* banish, exile; (*fig.*) dispel. **-te(r),** *m.* exile. **-ung,** *f.* banishment, exile. **-ungsort,** *m.* place of exile.
verbarrikadieren, I. *v.a.* barricade; block. 2. *v.r.* intrench o.s.
verbau-en, I. *v.a.* shut out, obstruct, block up, build up; use up in building (*materials*); spend in building (*money*); build badly; *einem Hause die Aussicht -en*, spoil the view from a house. **-ung,** *f.* obstruction (*of view*); building up.
verbauern, *v.n.* (*aux.* s.) become countrified.
verbeißen, I. *ir.v.a.* clench one's teeth on; (*fig.*) swallow, stifle, suppress; *sich* (*Dat.*) *das Lachen -*, stifle (one's) laughter; *seinen Ärger -*, conceal one's annoyance; put a brave face on matters; *mit schlecht verbissenem Grimm*, with ill-concealed wrath. 2. *v.r.* stick obstinately (*in etwas*, to a th.), be set (on a th.).
Verbene, *f.* (-n) verbena (*Bot.*).
verberg-en, I. *ir.v.a.* hide, conceal; *etwas einem* (or *vor einem*) *-en*, hide a th. from a p. 2. *v.r.* hide. **-ung,** *f.* concealment; (*B.*) covert, shelter.
Verbesser-er, *m.* (-s, -) improver; reformer. **-lich,** *adj.* improvable, reparable. **-n,** *v.a.* improve, ameliorate, amend, revise, correct, rectify, repair, reform, perfect; *seine Umstände haben sich -t*, his circumstances have improved; *ein zu -nder Fehler*, an error (which ought) to be corrected. **-ung,** *f.* improvement, amendment, correction, adjustment, emendation, reform, reformation, amelioration. **-ungsantrag,** *m.* amendment. **-ungsfähig,** *adj.* capable of improvement. **-ungsmittel,** *n.* corrective.
verbeug-en, *v.r.* bow, make a bow. **-ung,** *f.* bow, reverence, obeisance.
verbeul-t, *adj.* battered. **-ung,** *f.* dent, bulge.
verbiegen, I. *ir.v.a.* bend, twist; bend out of shape, distort. 2. *v.r.* twist, warp, get bent.

verbiestern, *v.r.* (*coll. & dial.*) become confused *or* annoyed.
verbiet–en, *ir.v.a.* (*einem etwas*) forbid, prohibit; *das –et sich von selbst,* that obviously cannot be allowed; *du hast mir nichts zu –en,* you have no authority over me; *streng verboten,* strictly prohibited.
verbild–en, *v.a.* spoil; train *or* educate badly. **–lichen,** *v.a.* symbolize, typify. **–ung,** *f.* malformation; bad training.
verbillig–en, *v.a.* cheapen, make cheaper, reduce in price. **–ung,** *f.* reduction in price, cheapening.
verbind–en, 1. *ir.v.a.* bind, unite, join, connect, link, combine, amalgamate (*Chem.*); dress (*wounds*), tie, bind up; pledge, engage; *einen zu etwas –en,* bind *or* pledge a p. to s.th.; *eng verbunden mit,* closely bound up with; *mit verbundenen Augen,* blindfolded; *durch Heirat verbunden,* connected by marriage; *mit Gefahr* or *mit einem gewissen Risiko verbunden,* involving a certain amount of danger *or* risk; *mit einander verbunden,* united; *ich bin Ihnen sehr verbunden,* I am greatly obliged *or* indebted to you. 2. *v.r.*, *sich geschäftlich mit einem –en,* go into partnership with a p.; *sich chemisch –en,* combine (*chemically*); *sich ehelich –en* (*mit einem Mädchen*), marry (a girl). **–lich,** *adj.* binding, obligatory, compulsory, bound, obliged; obliging, courteous; *sich –lich machen zu,* bind o.s. to . . ., undertake *or* engage to . . .; *sich gerichtlich –lich machen,* enter into recognizances; *das ist für mich nicht –lich,* that does not bind me; *einem etwas –liches sagen,* pay a p. a compliment; *danke –lichst,* many thanks, very much obliged! **–lichkeit,** *f.* binding force (*of treaties*); obligation, liability; civility, courtesy, favour, kindness, compliment; *mit gegenseitiger –lichkeit,* mutually binding; *gegen einen eine –lichkeit haben,* be under an obligation to a p.; *mündliche –lichkeit,* verbal promise; *seinen –lichkeiten nachkommen,* fulfil one's engagements, pay one's way; *ohne –lichkeit,* without liability *or* responsibility; *die –lichkeit, womit er es mir sagte,* the polite way in which he said it to me. **–ung,** *f.* binding, joining, connecting, blending; union, club association, league, alliance; connexion (*Tele.*); bond, joint, junction; relation, combination, compound; bandaging, dressing (*Surg.*); inosculation (*Anat.*); communication, contact, liaison (*Mil.*); *–ung aufnehmen,* establish contact *or* communications; *chemische –ungen,* chemical compounds; *in eine –ung eintreten,* join a students' association, become a member of a students' club; *lösbare –ung,* detachable connexion, soluble combination; *in –ung mit,* in conjunction with; *rückwärtige –ungen,* lines of communication (*Mil.*); *in –ung stehen,* be connected (with), correspond (with), be in touch *or* communication (with); *sich in –ung setzen mit,* get into touch with; *schlagende –ung,* duelling association (*of students*); *studentische –ung,* students' corporation; *in –ung treten,* enter into connexion *or* correspondence (with); *eine –ung herstellen,* make contact, get a connexion (*Phone*). **–ungsbahn,** *f.* branch- *or* junction-line. **–ungsfähigkeit,** *f.* affinity (*Chem.*). **–ungsgang,** *m.* connecting passage *or* duct. **–ungsglied,** *n.* connecting link. **–ungsgraben,** *m.* communication trench. **–ungskabel,** *n.* trunk line (*Tele.*) **–ungsleute,** *pl.* connecting files (*Mil.*). **–ungslinie,** *f.*, **–ungsweg,** *m.* line of communication. **–ungsmann,** *m.* liaison officer; mediator, go-between. **–ungsmittel,** *n.* means of communication. **–ungsmütze,** *f.* students' cap. **–ungspunkt,** *m.* juncture, junction. **–ungsrohr,** *n.*, **–ungsröhre,** *f.* connecting tube *or* pipe. **–ungsschraube,** *f.* assembling screw. **–ungsstange,** *f.* connecting rod. **–ungsstrich,** *m.* hyphen. **–ungsstück,** *n.* tie, joint, coupling (*Arch.*). **–ungsstudent,** *m.* member of a students' club. **–ungswort,** *n.* copula; conjunction. **–ungszeichen,** *n.*, *see* **–ungsstrich.**
verbissen, *p.p.* (*of* verbeißen) *& adj.* obstinate, dogged, grim; morose, sullen; *–er Gegner,* grim opponent; *mit –er Hartnäckigkeit,* with dogged obstinacy. **–heit,** *f.* obstinacy, doggedness, sullenness.
verbitt–en, *ir.v.a.* refuse to tolerate, not permit, deprecate, object to, decline; (*coll.*) not stand for, not put up with; *das –e ich mir,* I will not stand that; *ich –e mir die Ehre,* I beg to decline the honour; *solche Bemerkungen –e ich mir,* I will not tolerate such remarks; *das –e ich mir für die* or *in Zukunft!* do not do that again! that must not occur again! *Beileid dankend verbeten,* no cards and no flowers by request.
verbitter–n, 1. *v.a.* (*einem etwas*) embitter. 2. *v.r. & n.* (*aux.* s.) grow bitter, become soured; *sich –n lassen,* become soured. **–ung,** *f.* embitterment, bitterness (*of heart*).
verblassen, *v.n.* (*aux.* s.) grow *or* turn pale, lose colour, fade.
verblättern, *v.a.* lose one's place (*of a book*).
Verbleib, *m.* (storage) place; abode, whereabouts; *dabei muß es sein – haben,* that must be the end of the matter. **–en,** 1. *ir.v.n.* (*aux.* s.) remain, continue, stay the same, abide; *bei seiner Meinung –en,* persist in *or* hold to one's opinion; *lassen wir es dabei –en,* let the matter rest there; *ich –e hochachtungsvoll,* Yours faithfully.
verbleichen, *ir.v.n.* (*aux.* s.) grow pale, fade; (*Poet.*) expire, pass away.
verbleien, *v.a.* line *or* coat with lead, affix a lead seal.
verblend–en, *v.a.* blind, dazzle; delude, beguile, infatuate; face (*a wall*) with brick, plaster *or* roughcast; mask, screen (*a light*); *einen über eine S. –en,* delude a p. with regard to a th.; *durch sein Glück –et,* dazzled by his good fortune. **–er,** *m.*, **–klinker,** *m.* facing brick *or* tile. **–ung,** *f.* facing (*Build.*); delusion.
verbleuen, *v.a.* (*coll.*) beat (*a p.*) black and blue.
verblichen, *adj.* (*cf.* verbleichen) ashy-pale, faded; (*fig.*) dead, deceased. **–e(r),** *m.* deceased (person).
verblüff–en, 1. *v.n.* (*aux.* h. *&* s.) startle, disconcert, bewilder, amaze, stagger, flabbergast. **–end,** *pr.p. & adj.* startling, staggering, amazing, stupendous. **–t,** *p.p. & adj.* amazed, nonplussed, dumbfounded, flabbergasted; *er machte eine sehr –te Miene,* he looked quite taken aback. **–theit,** *f.*, **–ung,** *f.* stupefaction, bewilderment, amazement.
verblüh–en, 1. *v.n.* (*aux.* h. *&* s.) fade, wither, decay; *die Rosen sind –t,* the roses are over; *–te Schönheit,* faded beauty. (*coll.*) *–e!* be off! clear off! 2. *n.*; *im –en sein,* begin to fade, be fading away.
verblümt, *adj.* figurative, allusive, veiled, covert, indirect; *etwas – zu verstehen geben,* hint at a th., make insinuations.
verblut–en, *v.r. & n.* (*aux.* s.) bleed to death; *–en lassen,* allow to bleed (to death). **–ung,** *f.* bleeding to death; severe haemorrhage.
verbogen, *p.p. & adj.*, *see* **verbiegen.**
verbohr–t, *adj.* (*fig.*) stubborn, obstinate, obdurate, pig-headed. **–theit,** *f.* obstinacy, stubbornness, pig-headedness.
verbolzen, *v.a. & n.* bolt together.
[1]**verborgen,** *v.a.* lend (out), make a loan of.
[2]**verborgen,** *p.p.* (*of* verbergen) *& adj.* hidden, concealed, secret, clandestine; obscure; occult; inconspicuous; latent (*Phys.*); *im –en,* in secret, unnoticed; (*B.*) in wait; *–e Befruchtung,* cryptogamy; *–e Wärme,* latent heat. **–erweise,** *adv.* secretly, by stealth. **–heit,** *f.* concealment, secrecy; privacy, retirement, seclusion, obscurity; *in –heit leben,* live in retirement *or* obscurity.
Verbot, *n.* (-(e)s, -e) prohibition; inhibition (*Law*); suppression (*of a book, etc.*); veto. **–en,** *p.p.* (*of* verbieten) & *adj.* forbidden, prohibited, illicit; *–ene Waren,* contraband goods; *streng –en,* strictly forbidden. **–szeit,** *f.* close season.
verbracht, verbrachte, *see* **verbringen.**
verbräm–en, *v.a.* border, edge, trim, garnish, embellish. **–ung,** *f.* border, edging, trimming.
verbrannt, *p.p. & adj.*, *see* **verbrennen.**
Verbrauch, *m.* consumption, expenditure (*an,* of). **–en,** *v.a.* use (up), consume, spend, expend; wear out, exhaust. **–er,** *m.* consumer. **–ergas,** *n.* generator gas. **–sartikel,** *m.*, **–sgegenstand,** *m.* article of consumption, commodity. **–sskala,** *f.* maintenance scale, vitamin requirements (*Physiol.*). **–ssteuer,** *f.* indirect tax, excise duty. **–t,** *p.p. & adj.* worn out, used, spent, exhausted; *–te Luft,* stale air.

verbrausen, *v.n.* (*aux.* h. & s.) cease fermenting; (*fig.*) subside, calm down, sober down.
verbrech-en, 1. *ir.v.a.* commit a crime *or* an offence, do s.th. wrong, perpetrate; *was habe ich verbrochen?* what have I done wrong? 2. *n.* crime, felony, offence, misdeed; *leichtes -en,* venial offence. **-er,** *m.* criminal, felon, wrongdoer, delinquent, offender; *überführter -er,* convicted felon. **-eralbum,** *n.* thieves' gallery. **-ergesicht,** *n.* guilty look. **-erisch,** *adj.* criminal. **-erkneipe,** *f.* thieves' kitchen. **-erkolonie,** *f.* convict *or* penal settlement.
verbreit-en, 1. *v.a.* & *r.* spread, disseminate, diffuse, disperse, distribute; circulate, spread abroad, propagate; *weit -ete Ansichten,* widespread *or* very common views; *-eter Gebrauch,* common usage, general custom. 2. *v.r.* (*über eine S.*) expatiate *or* enlarge upon *or* elaborate (a matter). **-ern,** *v.a.* broaden, widen. **-erung,** *f.* widening, broadening. **-ung,** *f.* expansion, spreading, diffusion, propagation, dissemination, dispersal, circulation; distribution, range, spread. **-ungsbezirk,** *m.* habitat. **-ungsgebiet,** *n.* range of distribution. **-ungsweise,** *f.* method of dissemination.
verbrenn-en, 1. *ir.v.a.* burn, scorch, singe; cremate (*the dead*); *zu Asche -en,* reduce to ashes; (*fig.*) *sich* (*Dat.*) *die Finger -en,* burn one's fingers; *verbrannte Erde,* scorched earth; *alle Schiffe hinter sich -en,* burn one's boats. 2. *v.r.* & *n.* (*aux.* s.) burn, be scorched, be burnt up. **-bar,** *adj.* combustible. **-lich,** *adj.* inflammable. **-ung,** *f.* burning, combustion, incineration, cremation (*of the dead*); burn, scald. **-ungs(kraft)maschine,** *f.*, **-ungsmotor,** *m.* internal-combustion engine. **-ungsnarbe,** *f.* burn scar. **-ungsofen,** *m.* cremating furnace. **-ungsprobe,** *f.* ignition test. **-ungsprodukt,** *n.* combustion product. **-ungsraum,** *m.* combustion chamber. **-ungsvorgang,** *m.* (process of) combustion.
verbrief-en, 1. *v.a.* (*einem etwas*) acknowledge *or* confirm in writing; mortgage *or* pledge by document. 2. *v.r.* give a written undertaking, bind o.s. by deed; *sich für einen -en,* stand security for a p. **-t,** *p.p.* & *adj.* chartered, documented; *-te Rechte,* vested rights; *-te Schulden,* obligations; *versiegelt und -t,* positive, categorical, indisputable. **-ung,** *f.* written acknowledgement *or* pledge, bond, confirmation in writing, charter.
verbringen, *ir.v.a.* spend, pass (*time*).
verbrüder-n, *v.r.* become intimate, fraternize, get on good terms (*mit einem,* with a p.). **-ung,** *f.* fraternization.
verbrühen, *v.a.* scald.
verbuchen, *v.a.* (*C.L.*) book (*an order, etc.*).
verbuhlt, *p.p.* & *adj.* amorous, wanton, debauched. **-heit,** *f.* debauchery, wantonness.
Verbum, *n.*, *see* **Verb.**
verbum-feien, -fiedeln, *v.a.* (*sl.*) botch, bungle, make a hash of.
verbummel-n, *v.a.* spend, waste, squander, idle away (*time*). **-t,** *adj.* come down in the world.
Verbund, *m.* (-(e)s, ⸗e) compound (*Engin.*). **-en,** *p.p.* (*of* verbinden) & *adj.* united, connected, combined; obliged, indebted. **-enheit,** *f.* agreement, relationship, association; obligation, bond; tie, connexion. **-glas,** *n.* laminated glass. **-lokomotive,** *f.*, **-maschine,** *f.* compound engine. **-stück,** *n.* connector, coupling.
verbünd-en, *v.r.* ally o.s. (with); enter into, make *or* form an alliance, join up with. **-ete(r),** *m.* ally, confederate. **-ung,** *f.* alliance, confederation.
verbürg-en, *v.a.* & *r.* guarantee, vouch for, answer for. **-t,** *p.p.* & *adj.* authentic(ated), well-founded.
verbüß-en, *v.a.* atone for, pay the penalty of; *seine Strafzeit -en,* serve one's sentence, (*coll.*) do one's time. **-ung,** *f.* atonement, punishment.
verbutt-en, *v.n.* (*dial.*) become dwarfed *or* stunted. **-et,** *p.p.* & *adj.* stunted, dwarfed.
verbuttern, *v.a.* (*coll.*) bungle, botch; waste, squander.
verchrom-en, *v.a.* & *n.* plate with chromium. **-ung,** *f.* chromium plating.
Verdacht, *m.* suspicion, distrust; *einen in - bringen,* bring s.o. under suspicion; *einen* (*wegen einer S.*) *in - haben,* suspect s.o. (of a th.); *in - kommen* or *geraten,* incur suspicion; *im -e stehen,* be suspected; *- schöpfen* or *hegen,* become suspicious. **-sgrund,** *m.* grounds for suspicion.
verdächtig, *adj.* (*with Gen.*) suspected; suspicious, questionable, doubtful; *- sein,* be suspected (of); *- machen* or **-en,** *v.a.* throw suspicion on, be suspicious of, distrust; (*with Gen.*) accuse (of), inculpate (in). **-keit,** *f.* suspiciousness, suspicion, mistrust. **-ung,** *f.* inculpation, accusation, insinuation.
verdamm-en, *v.a.* condemn, damn, curse, anathematize. **-enswert,** *adj.* damnable, execrable. **-nis,** *f.* damnation, perdition. **-t,** *p.p.* & *adj.* condemned, damned, accursed; (*coll.*) *-t!* damn it! damnation! (*sl.*) *es ist -t kalt,* it is damnably cold; (*sl.*) *das ist seine -te Schuldigkeit,* that is his bounden duty. **-ung,** *f.* condemnation, damnation; *ewige -ung,* eternal damnation. **-ungswürdig,** *adj.*, *see* **-enswert.**
verdampf-en, *v.a.* & *n.* (*aux.* s.) vaporize; evaporate. **-er,** *m.* vaporizer. **-ung,** *f.* evaporation, vaporization.
verdanken, *v.a.* owe (*einem etwas,* s.th. to a p.), be indebted *or* obliged (to a p. for a th.); *seinem Rate ist es zu -, daß . . .* it is owing *or* due to his advice that . . .; *ich hatte ihm alles zu -,* I was indebted to him for everything, I owed everything to him; (*Swiss dial.*) give *or* return thanks for; *wir - Ihren Brief,* we thank you for your letter.
verdarb, *see* **verderben.**
verdattert, *adj.* (*coll.*) flabbergasted.
verdau-en, *v.a.* & *r.* digest; (*fig.*) understand; tolerate, (*coll.*) stand, swallow, get over; *diese Speisen -en sich leicht,* these foods are easily digested *or* digestible. **-lich,** *adj.* digestible; *schwer -lich,* indigestible, rich, heavy (*of food*). **-lichkeit,** *f.* digestibility. **-ung,** *f.* digestion. **-ungsbeschwerden,** *f.pl.* indigestion, digestive trouble. **-ungsdrüse,** *f.* digestive gland. **-ungsferment,** *n.* pepsin. **-ungsflüssigkeit,** *f.*, *see* **-ungssaft.** **-ungskanal,** *m.* alimentary canal, digestive tract. **-ungsmittel,** *n.* stomachic, digestive remedy. **-ungssaft,** *m.* gastric juice. **-ungsschwäche,** *f.* weak digestion, dyspepsia. **-ungsspaziergang,** *m.* constitutional. **-ungsstoff,** *m.* pepsin. **-ungsstörung,** *f.* indigestion; bilious attack.
Verdeck, *n.* (-(e)s, -e) covering, awning; hood, tilt (*of a carriage*); deck (*Naut.*). **-en,** *v.a.* cover, hide, conceal; camouflage, mask, veil, screen. **-t,** *p.p.* & *adj.* hidden, covered; covert; camouflaged, screened, masked. **-ung,** *f.* covering, concealment, occultation.
verdenken, *v.a.* (*einem etwas*) blame, take amiss, find fault with; *es ist keinem zu -, wenn er . . .,* nobody is to be blamed, if he . . .
Verderb, *m.* ruin, destruction; decay; *sie ist ein - für ihn,* she is his undoing; *auf Gedeih und -,* in success or adversity, come what may. **-en,** 1. *reg.* & *ir.v.a.* (*einem etwas*) spoil, damage, ruin; corrupt, demoralize, drag down; *an ihm ist ein Schauspieler verdorben,* a good actor is lost in him, he was cut out to be an actor; *sich* (*Dat.*) *die Augen -en,* ruin one's eyes; *einem die Freude -en,* spoil a p.'s pleasure; *einem das Konzept -en,* put a spoke in a p.'s wheel; *sich* (*Dat.*) *den Magen -en,* upset one's stomach; *es mit einem -en,* fall out *or* quarrel with a p., incur s.o.'s displeasure; *er will es mit keinem -en,* he tries to please everybody, he wishes to keep in with everybody; *die Preise -en,* bring down prices; (*Prov.*) *böse Beispiele -en gute Sitten,* evil communications corrupt good manners. 2. *ir.v.n.* (*aux.* s.) be spoilt, decay, deteriorate, go bad, perish; fail. 3. *n.* corruption, destruction, ruin, perdition; *einen ins -en stürzen,* ruin a p.; *sich ins -en stürzen,* rush into destruction; *der Weg des -ens,* the road to ruin; *einem zum -en gereichen,* prove a p.'s ruin. **-lich,** *adj.* corruptible, easily spoiled, perishable; pernicious, ruinous, destructive, injurious; unfortunate, fatal. **-lichkeit,** *f.* corruptibility; perniciousness, destructiveness. **-nis,** *f.* corruption, decay; destruction, deterioration; depravity, perversion. **-t,** *p.p.* & *adj.* corrupt(ed), depraved, vicious, dissolute, dissipated. **-theit,** *f.* corruption, depravity, vice.

verdeutlichen, *v.a.* elucidate, make clear.
verdeutschen, *v.a.* translate into German.
Verdicht-barkeit, *f.* condensability, compressibility. **-en,** 1. *v.a.* thicken, condense, compress, solidify; concentrate, consolidate; liquefy (*a gas*). 2. *v.r.* become thick, condensed, concentrated, solid (*of a liquid*) *or* liquid (*of a gas*); (*fig.*) take shape (*in one's mind*). **-er,** *m.* condensor, compressor. **-ung,** *f.* compression, condensation, solidification, consolidation, concentration, liquefaction. **-ungshub,** *m.* compression stroke (*Motor.*). **-ungszahl,** *f.* compression ratio.
verdick-en, *v.a.* thicken, boil down, inspissate (*Chem., etc.*); solidify, condense, concentrate, coagulate, congeal, clot, curdle. **-ung,** *f.* thickening; thickening agent, thickener. **-ungsmittel,** *n.* thickening agent.
verdien-en, *v.a.* earn; gain, get, win; deserve, merit; *mehr Glück -en als haben*, be more deserving than lucky; *er hat seinen -ten Lohn*, he has only got what he deserves, he has got no more than he deserves; *-ter Mann*, deserving man; *man -t dabei nicht das Salz zur Suppe*, that brings in next to nothing; *das habe ich um Sie nicht -t*, I have not deserved that from you; *er hat sich um das Vaterland -t gemacht*, he has deserved well of his country. **-st,** 1. *m.* gain, profit; earnings, wages; *das ist mein ganzer -st dabei*, that is all I get out of it. 2. *n.* (*with* um, *or* an (*with Dat.*)) merit, deserts; *das -st wird selten belohnt*, merit seldom receives its due reward; *darin liegt kein -st*, there is no merit in that; *die -ste dieses Mannes*, the services which this man has rendered; *man wird ihn nach -st behandeln*, he will be treated according to his deserts; *wie das -st, so der Ruhm*, honour (is given) to whom honour is due; *es ist hauptsächlich sein -st, daß . . .*, to him the credit is principally due that . . .; *sich* (*Dat.*) *etwas zum -ste anrechnen*, take credit for s.th. **-stausfall,** *m.* loss of wages. **-stkreuz,** *n.* distinguished service medal, order of merit. **-stlich,** *adj.*, *see* **-stvoll.** **-stlos,** *adj.* undeserving; unprofitable. **-stmöglichkeit,** *f.* chance to earn money. (*C.L.*) **-stspanne,** *f.* margin of profit. **-stvoll,** *adj.* meritorious, deserving, creditable. **-termaßen,** *adv.*, **-terweise,** *adv.* deservedly, according to one's deserts.
Verdikt, *n.* (-(e)s, -e) verdict, decision, judgement.
Verding, *n.* (-(e)s, -e) *see* **-ung;** *auf – übernehmen*, contract for. **-en,** 1. *reg. & ir.v.a.* hire out, contract for; put out (*to board*); *seinen Sohn als Diener bei einem -en*, put one's son to service with a p.; *Arbeiten -en*, let out work under contract; *den Bau eines Hauses -en*, contract for the building of a house. 2. *v.r.*; *sich* (*als Diener*) (*bei*) *einem -en*, go into service *or* take a situation with s.o. **-ung,** *f.* hiring out, agreement, contract.
verdirb, verdirbst, verdirbt, *see* **verderben.**
verdolmetschen, *v.a.* translate, interpret, expound.
verdonner-n, *v.a.* (*coll.*) scold, condemn. **-t,** *p.p. & adj.* thunderstruck, dumbfounded.
verdoppel-n, *v.a. & r.* double, duplicate, redouble. **-ung,** *f.* doubling, duplication.
verdorben, *p.p.* (*of* verderben) *& adj.* tainted, spoilt, rotten, depraved; *see* **verderbt;** *-es Fleisch*, tainted meat. **-heit,** *f.* spoiled *or* ruined condition, rottenness, depravity.
verdorren, *v.n.* (*aux.* s.) dry up, wither.
verdräng-en, *reg. & ir.v.a.* drive out, dislodge, supplant, oust, push aside, displace, expel, crowd out; suppress, repress, inhibit. **-ung,** *f.* removal; displacement (*of a ship*); dispossession; suppression; repression, inhibition (*Psych.*).
verdreh-en, *v.a.* twist, roll (*one's eyes*), contort (*one's limbs*); wrench, sprain, dislocate; force, distort, misrepresent, warp, pervert; *sich* (*Dat.*) *den Arm -en*, sprain one's arm; *das Gesicht -en*, make a grimace; (*sich*) *den Hals -en*, crane one's neck; *einem den Kopf -en*, turn a p.'s head; *das Recht -en*, pervert justice. **-t,** *p.p. & adj.* twisted, distorted; forced; (*fig.*) cracked, crazy, (*coll.*) dotty, barmy. **-theit,** *f.* craziness. **-ung,** *f.* twisting, torsion; sprain; contortion; distortion, misrepresentation, prevarication; perversion. **-ungsfestigkeit,** *f.* torsional strength. **-ungsversuch,** *m.* torsion test.
verdreifachen, *v.a.* treble.
verdreschen, *v.a.* (*coll.*) thrash, give (*a p.*) a good thrashing.
verdrieß-en, *ir.v.a.* grieve, vex, annoy, displease; *sich etwas -en lassen*, shrink from, be discouraged by, (*coll.*) be put off by; *sich keine Mühe -en lassen*, spare no pains. **-lich,** *adj.* vexed, annoyed, grieved, peevish, cross, bad-tempered, out of humour; vexatious, annoying, irksome, tiresome, unpleasant, disagreeable. **-lichkeit,** *f.* bad temper, peevishness, crossness; unpleasantness, irksomeness, vexation, annoyance, bother; *einem -lichkeiten bereiten*, cause a p. bother.
verdroß, verdrösse, *see* **verdrießen.**
verdrossen, *p.p. & adj.* cross, peevish, vexed, annoyed; sulky, sullen; *see* **verdrießen.** **-heit,** *f.* peevishness, sulkiness, bad temper.
verdrucken, *v.a.* misprint.
verdrücken, 1. *v.a. dial. for* **zerdrücken;** (*sl.*) devour, polish off. 2. *v.r.* (*sl.*) slink away.
Verdruß, *m.* ill humour, irritation, displeasure, dismay, chagrin, vexation, discontent, annoyance; *einem etwas zum – tun*, do a th. in order to spite *or* vex a p.; *allen Menschen zum –*, to everyone's annoyance; *einem – machen*, vex, annoy *or* irritate s.o.; *zu meinem – finde ich*, I am annoyed to find; (*sl.*) *einen – haben*, be humpbacked.
verduften, *v.r. & n.* (*aux.* s.) evaporate; (*coll.*) vanish, slip away, make off.
verdumm-en, 1. *v.a.* make stupid, stupefy. 2. *v.n.* (*aux.* h.) become stupid.
verdunk-eln, 1. *v.a.* darken, black out, obscure, cloud; eclipse, throw into the shade. 2. *v.r.* grow dim; *der Himmel -elt sich*, the sky becomes clouded *or* overcast. **-(e)lung,** *f.* darkening; eclipse; black-out. **-(e)lungsgefahr,** *f.* danger of prejudicing the course of justice (*Law*).
verdünn-en, *v.a.* thin, weaken, dilute; attenuate, rarefy; reduce, temper (*colours*); *-te Lösung*, dilute solution (*Chem.*). **-bar,** *adj.* dilutable; rarefiable. **-ung,** *f.* thinning, dilution, rarefaction, attenuation. **-ungsmittel,** *n.* diluting agent, thinner, reducer.
verdunst-en, *v.n.* (*aux.* s.) evaporate, vaporize, volatilize. **-ung,** *f.* evaporation, vaporization, volatilization. **-ungskälte,** *f.* cold due to evaporation.
verdünst-en, *v.a.* evaporate. **-ung,** *f.*, *see* **Verdunstung.**
verdürbe, *see* **verderben.**
verdursten, *v.n.* (*aux.* s.) die of thirst.
verdüster-n, 1. *v.a.* darken, cloud, wrap in gloom. 2. *v.r. & n.* (*aux.* s.) grow dark *or* gloomy.
verdutz-en, *v.a.* startle, bewilder, nonplus, disconcert. **-theit,** *f.* bewilderment, stupefaction.
verebben, *v.n.* die down, die away.
vered-eln, *v.a.* ennoble, improve, refine, purify, enrich, cultivate, graft (*Hort.*); finish (*goods*). **-(e)lung,** *f.* ennobling; improvement; refinement, cultivation; finishing (*of goods*); budding, grafting.
verehelich-en, *v.a. & r.* marry; *eine Tochter -en*, give one's daughter in marriage. **-ung,** *f.* marriage.
verehr-en, *v.a.* revere, worship, venerate, reverence; admire, respect, honour, adore; *einem etwas -en*, present s.o. with a th. **-er,** *m.* reverer; devoted admirer, lover; *er ist ein großer -er Schillers*, he is a great admirer of Schiller. **-lich,** *adj.* honourable, esteemed, venerable. **-ung,** *f.* respect, veneration, reverence, devotion, worship, adoration. **-ungswürdig,** *adj.* respected, worthy, honourable, illustrious.
vereid(ig)-en, *v.a.* put on oath, administer an oath to, swear in. **-ung,** *f.* attestation, swearing-in, taking the oath.
Verein, *m.* (-s, -e) association, society, club, union, alliance, syndicate; *im – mit meinen Freunden*, together *or* jointly with my friends; *– für neuere Sprachen*, modern language association. **-bar,** *adj.* reconcilable, compatible, consistent. **-baren,** *v.a.* agree (*mit einem*, with s.o.), come to an understanding, make compatible, reconcile; *-bartes Vorgehen*, concerted action; *-barte Regelungen*, agreed ruling; *zu -bartem Lohn*, for *or* at a negotiated wage. **-barkeit,** *f.* compatibility. **-bartermaßen,** *adv.*

as agreed, according to the terms of the agreement. **-barung,** *f.* agreement, arrangement, reconciliation; *-barungen mit einem treffen*, come to an agreement *or* arrangement with a p. **-en,** *v.a.* (*archaic & poet.*) *see* **-igen**; (*still used in p.p.*) *mit -ten Kräften*, with all (our, your, *etc.*) *or* united strength. **-fachen,** *see* **vereinfachen. -heitlichen,** *see* **vereinheitlichen. -igen,** *v.a. & r.* unite, join, ally (o.s.) with, combine, blend, coalesce; concentrate, collect, assemble, rally (*Mil.*); reconcile (with); *zwei Ämter in sich -igen*, unite *or* combine two offices in one's own person; *ich kann es mit seinem Charakter nicht -igen*, I cannot reconcile it with his character; *sich -igen lassen mit* . . ., be compatible *or* consistent with. . . . *-igte Staaten*, United States (of America). **-igung,** *f.* union, combination, alliance; accord, agreement; meeting, connexion, junction, confluence, fusion; concentration, incorporation, amalgamation; anastomosis. **-igungsort,** *m.* assembly *or* meeting place. **-igungspunkt,** *m.* point of union, junction, focus (*Phys.*); rallying-point, rendezvous (*Mil.*). **-igungsrecht,** *n.* right of assembly *or* association. **-nahmen,** *see* **vereinnahmen. -sabend,** *m.* club night. **-samen,** *see* **vereinsamen. -sfreiheit,** *f.* freedom of association. **-sgesetz,** *n.* law concerning societies. **-shaus,** *n.* club(-house). **-skasse,** *f.* funds of a society. **-sleitung,** *f.* executive committee of a society. **-slokal,** *n.* club rooms. **-s-und-Versammlungsrecht,** *n. see* **Vereinigungsrecht. -swesen,** *n.* co-operative system *or* movement; trade-unionism. **-zeln,** *see* **vereinzeln.**

vereinfach-en, *v.a.* simplify, reduce. **-ung,** *f.* simplification, reduction.

vereinheitlich-en, *v.a.* unify, standardize. **-ung,** *f.* unification, standardization.

vereinnahmen, *v.a.* take, receive (*money*).

vereinsam-en, *v.n.* grow lonely, become isolated, become more and more cut off from society. **-t,** *p.p. & adj.* solitary, lonely. **-ung,** *f.* isolation.

vereinzel-n, *v.a.* isolate, separate, segregate; sever, detach, dismember; take separately; *Zusammengehöriges -n*, separate *or* break up a pair *or* set. **-t,** *p.p. & adj.* single, solitary, isolated; scattered, sporadic. **-ung,** *f.* isolation, segregation, detachment, separation, individualization.

vereis-en, *v.n.* (*aux.* h.) turn to ice, freeze (*of rivers*), be covered with ice (*of roads*), ice up (*of aircraft*). **-t,** *p.p. & adj.* frozen, covered with ice. **-ung,** *f.* freezing, ice formation, icing-up (*Av.*).

vereitel-n, *v.a.* thwart, frustrate, balk, baffle, bring to naught; *Hoffnungen -n*, disappoint hopes; *eine Absicht -n*, defeat a purpose; *das Unternehmen ist -t*, the undertaking has miscarried. **-ung,** *f.* frustration, disappointment, defeat.

vereiter-n, *v.r. & n.* (*aux.* s.) fester, suppurate. **-ung,** *f.* suppuration.

verekeln, *v.a.* (*coll.*) (*einem etwas*) make loathsome, disgust (*a p.*) with, spoil (*a th.*) for.

verelend-en, 1. *v.a.* make miserable *or* wretched. 2. *v.n.* become wretched *or* miserable, sink into poverty *or* very low. **-ung,** *f.* progressive deterioration; pauperization.

verenden, *v.n.* (*aux. &* s.) die, perish (*of animals*).

verenge(r)n, *v.a. & r.* narrow, contract, constrict; become narrow(er).

vererb-en, 1. *v.a.* (*einem etwas* (*legally*) *or etwas auf einen* (*genetically*)) leave, bequeath, hand down (s.th. to a p.); transmit (*diseases, etc.*). 2. *v.r. & n.* (*aux.* s.) devolve (*auf*, upon); be hereditary, run in the family. **-bar,** *adj.*, **-lich,** *adj.* inheritable; transmissible, hereditary. **-t,** *p.p. & adj.* hereditary, inherited, bequeathed, handed down. **-ung,** *f.* inheritance, heredity, transmission. **-ungsfähigkeit,** *f.* right to bequeath inheritance. **-ungsforschung,** *f.* genetics. **-ungsgesetz,** *n.* law of succession. **-ungslehre,** *f.* law of heredity (*Physiol.*).

verewig-en, 1. *v.a.* perpetuate, immortalize. 2. *v.r.* (*coll.*) carve *or* scratch one's name (*on benches, stones, etc.*). **-t,** *p.p. & adj.* (*Poet.*) deceased, departed, late.

verfahr-en, 1. *ir.v.n.* (*aux.* h. & s.) act, behave, proceed; handle, manage, deal (*mit*, with), use; *redlich -en*, deal honestly; *mit Nachsicht -en*, act with leniency, be indulgent; *gerichtlich gegen einen -en*, take legal proceedings against a p.; (*C.L.*) *womit Sie nach Bericht zu -en belieben*, of which you will dispose according to advices. 2. *v.a.* spend (*time or money*) driving *or* travelling about; convey, transport; *einen Gang -en*, work a mine; *der Karren* or *die Sache ist gründlich -en*, the matter is in hopeless confusion. 3. *v.r.* lose one's way, take the wrong road; (*fig.*) be on the wrong tack *or* track, be barking up the wrong tree. 4. *n.* proceeding, procedure, treatment, process, method; dealing, management, conduct; *gerichtliches -en*, legal proceedings; *das -en einleiten* (*gegen*), take proceedings (against); *das -en einstellen*, quash proceedings. 5. *adj.* hopeless, bungled, (*coll.*) in a mess. **-ungsart,** *f.*, **-ungsweise,** *f.* procedure, method, process. **-ungslehre,** *f.* methodology.

Verfall, *m.* decay, dilapidation, deterioration; decadence, decline, fall, downfall, ruin; (*C.L.*) maturity (*of a bill*), foreclosure; *in - geraten* or *kommen*, go to ruin, decay, become dilapidated; decline, deteriorate; *- der Kräfte*, decline of vital powers; *- der Sitten*, corruption of morals, moral decay, depravity; *- des Reiches*, downfall of the empire; (*C.L.*) *bei -*, when due; (*C.L.*) *bis -*, till maturity, till due; *- einer Klage*, nonsuit; *- eines Rechtes*, forfeiture *or* loss of a right. **-datum,** *n.* due-date (*of a bill*). **-en,** *ir.v.n.* (*aux.* s.) decay decline, deteriorate, go to ruin; expire, elapse, fall due, be forfeited, lapse; (*with Dat.*) fall to, come into the power *or* possession of; (*auf etwas*) hit *or* chance upon; (*in etwas*) fall, sink *or* slip back into; *auf den wäre ich nicht -en*, I should never have thought of him; *einem Laster -en*, addicted to a vice; *dem Staate -en*, become the property of the state; *dem Teufel -en*, fall into the hands of the devil; *-enes Gebäude*, dilapidated premises; *-e Gesichtszüge*, worn features; *-e Güter*, confiscated property; *in die alten Fehler -en*, slip back into one's old ways; *in eine Geldstrafe -en*, incur a penalty, be fined; *die Klage ist -en*, the plaintiff has been non-suited; *das Pfand ist -en*, the pledge is forfeited *or* has lapsed; *ein Pfand für -en erklären*, foreclose a mortgage; *-enes Vermächtnis*, lapsed legacy. **-erklärung,** *f.* confiscation. **-frist,** *f.*, *see* **-zeit. -serscheinung,** *f.* symptom of decline. **-(s)recht,** *n.* right of confiscation. **-(s)zeit,** *f.*, **-tag,** *m.*, **-termin,** *m.* day of payment, maturity; *zur -zeit*, when due; *bis zur -zeit*, until maturity, till due.

verfälsch-en, *v.a.* adulterate; falsify, counterfeit, debase (*coin*). **-er,** *m.* adulterator, falsifier, counterfeiter. **-ung,** *f.* falsification; adulteration. **-ungsmittel,** *n.* adulterant.

verfangen, 1. *ir.v.r.* be caught, become entangled; get caught up, become involved; *sich im Reden -*, become confused, contradict o.s. 2. *v.n.* (*aux.* h.) & *imp.* (*usually negative*) operate, take effect, be of avail, (*coll.*) tell; *nichts -*, avail nothing, be of no avail, be thrown away on.

verfänglich, *adj.* insidious, fallacious, captious; artful, deceitful; risky, (*coll.*) tricky; awkward, embarrassing. **-keit,** *f.* insidiousness, captiousness.

verfärben, 1. *v.a.* discolour. 2. *v.r. & n.* (*aux.* h.) fade, grow pale.

verfass-en, *reg. & ir.v.a.* compose, write (*a book*), draw up (*a document*). **-er,** *m.* author, writer, composer. **-erin,** *f.* authoress. **-erschaft,** *f.* authorship. **-ung,** *f.* composition, writing (*of a book*); condition, disposition, situation, state; frame of mind; system of government, constitution. **-ungsbruch,** *m.* violation of the constitution. **-ungsgebend,** *adj.* constituent (*as an assembly*). **-ungsmäßig,** *adj.* constitutional. **-ungsrecht,** *n.* constitutional law. **-ungsurkunde,** *f.* charter of the constitution. **-ungswidrig,** *adj.* unconstitutional.

verfaul-en, *v.n.* (*aux.* s.) rot, decay, putrefy, decompose. **-bar,** *adj.* putrescible, corruptible.

verfecht-en, *ir.v.a.* fight for, stand up for, advocate, defend, champion (*a cause*). **-er,** *m.* defender, advocate, champion. **-ung,** *f.* advocacy, defence.

verfehl-en, 1. *v.a.* fail (*to do*), miss; *kein Wort -t den Eindruck*, every word tells; *diese Nachricht wird* *nicht –en, Aufsehen zu machen*, this news will not fail to make a sensation; *ich werde nicht –en, Sie zu besuchen*, I shall be sure to call on you. *es –te seine Wirkung*, it produced no effect, was of no avail, failed to carry any weight *or* (*coll.*) missed fire; *er hat seinen Beruf* (or *Zug*) *–t*, he has missed his vocation (*or* train); *sich* or *einander –en*, miss each other, fail to meet. 2. *v.r.* offend, trespass (*gegen*, against). **–t,** *adj.* unsuccessful, misplaced, wrong, false; *ihre Stellung war –t*, she was in a false position. **–ung,** *f.* lapse, mistake, (*coll.*) slip.

verfeinden, *v.a.* (*& usually*) *r.* (*mit*) make an enemy of, fall out with.

verfeiner–n, 1. *v.a.* refine, improve, polish, purify, bolt (*flour*). 2. *v.r.* become *or* grow (more) refined, become (more) polished, improve. **–ung,** *f.* refinement; improvement; polish.

verfemen, *v.a.* proscribe, outlaw.

verfertig–en, *v.a.* make, manufacture, construct. **–er,** *m.* maker, manufacturer, fabricator. **–ung,** *f.* making, manufacture, preparation, fabrication.

verfestigen, *v.a. & n.* harden, solidify, strengthen, stabilize, consolidate.

Verfettung, *f.* fatty degeneration (*Path.*).

verfeuern, *v.a.* burn, use as fuel; use up (*powder or ammunition*); burn up, consume, waste (*coal, etc.*).

verfilmen, *v.a.* film, make a film of.

verfilz–en, *v.a.* clog up, mat (together). **–t,** *p.p. & adj.* matted, clogged.

verfinster–n, 1. *v.a.* darken, obscure, eclipse. 2. *v.r.* grow dark. **–ung,** *f.* darkening; eclipse; darkness, gloom.

verfitzen, 1. *v.a.* entangle. 2. *v.r.* get tangled up.

verflachen, 1. *v.a.* flatten, level. 2. *v.n. & r.* (*aux.* s.) become flat, become shallow; become superficial (*mentally*).

verflecht–en, *ir.v.a.* entwine, interlace, interweave; (*fig.*) involve, implicate. **–ung,** *f.* interlacing, interweaving; (*fig.*) entanglement, involvement, implication; *–ung von Umständen*, (strange) coincidence.

verflieg–en, *ir.v.n. & r.* (*aux.* s.) fly away; evaporate, volatilize; (*fig.*) vanish, disappear; *die Zeit* or *Stunde –t*, time flies; *sich –en*, get lost (*in flight*); *verflogene Tauben* or *Bienen*, stray pigeons *or* bees. **–end,** *adj.* volatile, evanescent.

verfließen, *ir.v.n.* (*aux.* s.) flow away; blend, run into, run (*as ink*); subside; elapse, pass; *verflossen sein*, be past *or* over; *das verflossene Jahr*, the past year; *in der verflossenen Woche*, last week.

verflixt, *adj.* (*coll.*) confounded; *–e Geschichte*, nice mess, pretty kettle of fish; *–er Kerl*, devil of a fellow.

verflossen, *see* **verfließen.**

verfluch–en, *v.a.* curse, damn, execrate. **–t,** *p.p. & adj.* accursed, confounded; *–t!* confound it! curse it!; (*coll.*) *seine –te Schuldigkeit*, no more than his duty, his bounden duty; (*sl.*) *–ter Bengel*, devil of a fellow. **–ung,** *f.* curse, malediction; anathema.

verflüchtig–en, *v.a. & r.* volatilize, evaporate, sublime, sublimate. **–ung,** *f.* volatilization, evaporation, sublimation.

verflüssig–en, *v.a.* liquefy; condense, fuse (*by heat*). **–ung,** *f.* liquefaction.

Verfolg, *m.* course, progress; sequel; *in* or *im – der Arbeit*, in the course of the work; *im –e Befehls*, in pursuance of orders. **–en,** *v.a.* pursue, follow (up); trail; persecute, prosecute; *heimlich –en*, shadow. **–er,** *m.* pursuer; persecutor. **–ung,** *f.* pursuit, chase; persecution, prosecution; pursuance, continuation. **–ungskampf,** *m.* rearguard engagement (*Mil.*). **–ungswahn,** *m.* persecution mania.

Verformung, *f.* deformation.

verfracht–en, *v.a.* charter (*a ship*), hire out; pay the freight *or* carriage; load *or* ship (*goods*). **–er,** *m.* consigner, shipper, carrier. **–ung,** *f.* chartering, freighting, shipping, transport; shipment, consignment.

verfranzen, *v.r.* (*sl.*) get off course, lose one's way (*Av.*).

verfressen, *p.p. & adj.* (*coll.*) greedy.

verfroren, *p.p.* (*of* verfrieren) *& adj.* frozen, chilly, icy; *–er Mensch*, a p. sensitive to cold.

verfrüh–en, *v.a.* precipitate, anticipate. **–t,** *p.p. & adj.* premature.

verfüg–en, 1. *v.a.* dispose, order, arrange; prescribe, decide, ordain, decree, enact. 2. *v.r.* (*nach einem Orte* or *zu einem Menschen*) proceed (to), betake o.s. (to). 3. *v.n.* (*aux.* h.) (*über eine S.*) dispose of, have at one's disposal; *–en Sie über mich*, I am at your disposal, command me. **–bar,** *adj.* at one's disposal, available; *–bares Geld*, available funds, cash in hand; *–bares Kapital*, uninvested capital; *-bare Waren*, spot goods. **–ung,** *f.* disposal; disposition, arrangement; order, instruction, decree, enactment; *weitere –ungen abwarten*, await further orders *or* instructions; *–ungen über* (*eine S.*) *treffen*, take steps about, give orders with regard to (a th.); *zu meiner –ung*, at my disposal; *zur besonderen –ung*, seconded for special duty (*Mil.*); *ich stehe Ihnen ganz zur –ung*, I am quite at your disposal; *zur –ung stellen*, place at s.o.'s disposal. **–ungstruppen,** *pl.* reserves (*Nat. Soc.*).

verführ–en, *v.a.* lead astray, entice, tempt, seduce; induce, prevail upon, suborn (*witnesses*); (*coll.*) *einen fürchterlichen Lärm –en*, make a dreadful noise, kick up a terrible row; *–tes Mädchen*, fallen girl. **–er,** *m.* tempter, seducer. **–erisch,** *adj.* tempting, seductive, fascinating, alluring. **–ung,** *f.* temptation, seduction; subornation. **–ungskünste,** *f.pl.* art of deception, wiles, artifice.

verfuhrwerken, *v.a.* (*Swiss dial.*) botch, bungle.

verfünffachen, *v.a.* increase fivefold.

verfüttern, *v.a.* use as fodder; overfeed (*cattle, etc.*).

vergab–en, *v.a.* (*Swiss dial.*) present, bequeath. **–ung,** *f.* gift, donation, legacy, bequest.

vergaffen, *v.r.* fall in love (*in with Acc.*, with), be smitten (with).

vergällen, *v.a.* embitter, mar, make loathsome; denature (*Chem.*), methylate (*alcohol*); *sich* (*Dat.*) *das Leben –*, make one's life a burden, become embittered; *die ganze Welt ist mir vergällt*, I have lost all joy in life.

vergaloppieren, *v.r.* (*coll.*) make a bad blunder, overshoot the mark.

vergangen, *p.p.* (*of* vergehen) *& adj.* past, gone, bygone; last; *–e Woche*, last week. **–heit,** *f.* the past; preterite *or* past tense, (*Gram.*); *dunkle –heit*, shady past; *der –heit angehören*, be a th. of the past, belong to the past.

vergänglich, *adj.* fleeting, passing, transient, ephemeral, transitory; perishable. **–keit,** *f.* perishableness, instability, transitoriness.

verganten, *v.a.* (*dial.*) sell by auction.

vergas–en, *v.a.* vaporize; carburet (*Motor.*); gas (*Mil.*). **–er,** *m.* carburettor. **–ung,** *f.* vaporization, carburetion; gassing.

vergaß, vergäße, *see* **vergessen.**

vergatter–n, *v.a.* enclose with trellis-work *or* a grating; assemble (*troops*). **–ung,** *f.* lattice-work; grating; assembly; changing of the guard; *die* or *zur –ung schlagen*, call out the guard.

vergeb–en, 1. *ir.v.a.* (*etwas an einen*) give away *or* dispose of (to), confer *or* bestow (on). 2. (*einem etwas*) forgive, pardon. 3. (*also v.r.*) misdeal (*Cards*); *ein Amt an einen –en*, appoint a p. to an office, bestow an office on a p.; *einen Auftrag –en*, give *or* place an order; *die Stelle ist noch nicht –en*, the place is still vacant; *die Hand seiner Tochter –en*, give one's daughter in marriage; *ihre Hand ist schon –en*, she is engaged to be married; *sein Recht –en*, cede one's rights; *ich habe den nächsten Tanz schon –en*, I have already promised the next dance. 4. *sich* (*Dat.*) *etwas –en*, forget o.s., degrade o.s., compromise o.s.; *sich* (*Dat.*) or *seiner Ehre nichts –en*, be jealous of one's honour, maintain one's dignity; *sich* (*Dat.*) *von seinem Rechte etwas –en*, allow one's rights to be infringed; 5. *p.p.*, *see* **–lich**; *–ene Liebesmüh*, wasted effort; *–enes Hoffen*, vain hopes. **–ens,** *adv.* in vain, vainly, to no purpose. **–lich,** *adj.* vain, idle, fruitless, futile; *sich* (*Dat.*) *–liche Mühe machen*, go to a lot of trouble for nothing. **–lichkeit,** *f.* uselessness, fruitlessness. **–ung,** *f.* giving, granting, bestowal, appointing (*to an office*); collation (*to a benefice*), allocation (*of work*), placing (*of an order*); misdeal (*Cards*); forgiveness, pardon, remission; (*ich bitte*) *um –ung!* excuse me! I beg your pardon! pardon me!

vergegenwärtig–en, *v.a.* represent, bring to mind;

imagine *or* realize a th.; *sich* (*Dat.*) *etwas –en*, picture a th. to o.s. **–ung,** *f.* representation, graphic picture, realization.

vergeh–en, 1. *ir.v.n.* (*aux.* s.) pass, cease, slip by, elapse, subside, vanish, disappear, be lost; pine, waste away, perish, die (*vor*, of); *vor Scham –en*, die of shame; *vor Gram –en*, pine away; (*B.*) *meine Tage sind vergangen wie ein Rauch*, my days are consumed like smoke; (*Prov.*) *Unkraut –t nicht*, ill weeds grow apace; *es verging ihm Hören und Sehen*, it took his breath away; *der Appetit ist mir vergangen*, I have lost my appetite. 2. *v.r.* go astray, go wrong, err, offend, transgress, trespass, commit a fault; *sich an einem, wider* or *gegen einen –en*, insult *or* injure a p.; *sich gegen das Gesetz –en*, offend *or* transgress against *or* infringe the law; *sich tätlich an einem –en*, assault a p. 3. *n.* disappearance, passing, lapse (*of time*); offence, petty crime, misdemeanour, fault, transgression, trespass, sin.

vergeistig–en, *v.a.* spiritualize, etherealize. **–ung,** *f.* spiritualization.

vergelt–en, *v.a.* (*einem etwas*) requite, return, repay, pay back, reward, recompense; retaliate; *Gott –e es Ihnen* or *–s Gott!* Heaven bless you! (*coll.*) *Gleiches mit Gleichem –en*, give tit for tat; *Böses mit Gutem –en*, return good for evil. **–er,** *m.* recompenser, remunerator; revenger. **–ung,** *f.* requital, return, reward, recompense; retaliation, reprisal; *zur –ung für*, in return for. **–ungsfeuer,** *n.* retaliating fire (*Mil.*). **–ungsmaßregel,** *f.* retaliatory measure. **–ungsrecht,** *n.* right of reprisal *or* retaliation, lex talionis. **–ungstag,** *m.* day of retribution, day of judgement.

vergesellschaft–en, *v.a.* & *r.* associate, combine, unite with, form into a public company; socialize, nationalize. **–ung,** *f.* socialization, nationalization.

vergess–en, *ir.v.a.* forget; neglect; (*Austr. dial.*) *auf sein Versprechen hatte er –en*, he had forgotten his promise; *ja, daß ich nicht vergesse . . .*, oh! in case I should forget . . .; *etwas bei einem –en*, leave a th. behind at a p.'s house; *vergiß mich nicht*, (*B.* & *Poet.*) *vergiß mein nicht*, do not forget me! *so etwas vergißt sich leicht*, such things are easily forgotten. **–enheit,** *f.*, **–ensein,** *n.* oblivion; *in –enheit geraten*, fall (*or* sink) into oblivion. **–lich,** *adj.* forgetful, oblivious; easily forgotten. **–lichkeit,** *f.* forgetfulness, negligence.

vergeud–en, *v.a.* squander, dissipate, waste, fritter away. **–er,** *m.* spendthrift. **–ung,** *f.* squandering, waste, wastefulness, extravagance.

vergewaltig–en, *v.a.* use force, offer violence (to), rape, violate. **–ung,** *f.* assault, violation, rape.

vergewisser–n, *v.a.* & *r.* confirm, make sure (of), ascertain; (re)assure, convince; *sich einer S.* (*Gen.*) or *über eine S. –n*, assure o.s. *or* make sure of a th., ascertain s.th. **–ung,** *f.* confirmation; assurance.

vergieß–en, 1. *ir.v.a.* spill, shed, pour out; (*coll.*) drown (*plants by watering too much*). 2. *n.*, **–ung,** *f.* spilling, shedding (*of blood, etc.*).

vergift–en, *v.a.* poison, contaminate; (*fig.*) taint, infect; embitter (*one's life*). **–ung,** *f.* poisoning, contamination.

vergilben, *v.n.* turn yellow.

vergiß, vergissest, vergißt, *see* **vergessen.**

Vergißmeinnicht, *n.* (-(e)s, -e & *Austr. dial.* -) forget-me-not (*Myosotis*) (*Bot.*).

vergitter–n, *v.a.* enclose with lattice-work, a trellis *or* bars, grate (up), wire in. **–ung,** *f.* lattice-work, trellis; grating, bars.

verglas–en, 1. *v.a.* vitrify; glaze (*a window*). 2. *v.n.* (*aux.* h.) turn into glass, become glazed. **–t,** *p.p.* & *adj.* glazed (*also fig. of eyes*).

Vergleich, *m.* (-(e)s, -e) comparison, parallel, simile; agreement, arrangement, compromise; composition (*with creditors*); *einen – schließen*, conclude an agreement, come to terms; *gütlicher –*, amicable arrangement *or* settlement; *über allen –*, beyond comparison, incomparably; *im – mit* or *zu*, compared *or* in comparison with; *einen – anstellen* or *machen*, make a comparison; *den – aushalten*, bear comparison. **–bar,** *adj.* comparable. **–en,** 1. *r.v.a.* compare, check, collate, draw *or* make a comparison (*between ths.* or *with a th.*); adjust, settle (*disputes*), reconcile (*enemies*), compensate, equalize; *etwas Strittiges –en*, settle a quarrel, compose a difference; *niemand ist mit ihm zu –en*, no one is comparable with him *or* can be compared with him; *Handschriften mit einander –en*, collate manuscripts. 2. *v.r.* come to an arrangement, agreement *or* to terms; become reconciled; *sich mit einem über eine S.* or *wegen einer S. –en*, come to an agreement with a p. about a th.; *sich mit einem –en*, compare o.s. with a p.; *diese Dinge lassen sich nicht –en*, these things are not comparable *or* cannot be compared. **–end,** *pr.p.* & *adj.* comparative. **–lich,** *adj.*, *see* **–bar.** **–slösung,** *f.* standard solution. **–smäßig,** *adj.* according to agreement, stipulated. **–spunkte,** *m.pl.* articles of an agreement. **–stag,** *m.*, **–stermin,** *m.* day of settlement. **–summe,** *f.* compensation, indemnity. **–sversuch,** *m.* attempt to reach a settlement. **–sweise,** *adv.* comparatively, by way of comparison. **–swert,** *m.* relative value. **–ung,** *f.* comparison, parallel; collation; *in –ung mit*, in comparison with. **–ungsgrad,** *m.*, **–ungsstufe,** *f.* degree of comparison (*Gram.*); *erster, zweiter, dritter –ungsgrad*, positive, comparative, superlative degree. **–ungspunkt,** *m.* point of comparison. **–ungsversuch,** *m.* comparative test.

vergletscher–n, *v.n.* (*aux.* s.) form a glacier. **–ung,** *f.* glacier formation.

verglimmen, *ir.v.n.* (*aux.* s.) cease glowing, die out *or* away, go *or* burn out.

verglüh–en, 1. *v.n.* (*aux.* s.) cease glowing, cool down; die out *or* down. 2. *v.a.* fire, bake (*porcelain*). **–er,** *m.* brick- *or* porcelain-burner.

vergnüg–en, 1. *v.a.* amuse, please, delight; (*dial.*) divert, entertain, content, satisfy, gratify. 2. *v.r.* enjoy o.s., delight in. 3. *n.* pleasure, fun, joy, delight, enjoyment; amusement, diversion, entertainment. *–en an einer S. finden*, find pleasure *or* delight in a th.; *sein –en an einer S. haben*, delight in a th.; *mit –en!* with pleasure, willingly; *viel –en!* enjoy yourself! have a good time! *es macht mir viel –en*, it gives me much pleasure; *zu meinem –en*, to my delight; *etwas zum –en tun*, do a thing for pleasure *or* for fun. **–enshalber,** *adv.* for the sake of enjoyment. **–lich,** *adj.* amusing, diverting, light-hearted. **–t,** *p.p.* & *adj.* pleased, glad, delighted, joyous, cheerful, gay. **–ung,** *f.* (*usually pl.*) pleasure, amusement, recreation, entertainment, pastime, diversion. **–ungshalber,** *adv.* (*Austr. dial.*), *see* **–enshalber.** **–ungslokal,** *n.* fun-fair, amusement-arcade. **–ungsreise,** *f.* pleasure-trip, excursion. **–ungsreisende(r),** *m.* tourist, excursionist, (*coll.*) tripper. **–ungssteuer,** *f.* entertainment-tax. **–ungssucht,** *f.* love of pleasure, craze for amusement. **–ungssüchtig,** *adj.* pleasure-seeking *or* -loving. **–ungszug,** *m.* excursion-train.

vergold–en, *v.a.* gild. **–er,** *m.* gilder. **–et,** *p.p.* & *adj.* gilt, gilded, gold-plated. **–ung,** *f.* gilding, gold-plating; *trockene –ung*, leaf-gilding; *nasse –ung*, water-gilding; *galvanische –ung*, electro-gilding.

vergönnen, *v.a.* (*einem etwas*) permit, allow, grant, not grudge *or* (*coll.*) begrudge.

vergott–en, 1. *v.n.* be deified, become god-like. 2. *v.a.*, *see* **vergöttern.** **–ung,** *f.* apotheosis.

vergötter–n, *v.a.* deify; (*fig.*) idolize, worship, adore. **–ung,** *f.* deification; adoration, worship, idolatry.

vergraben, 1. *ir.v.a.* bury, hide. 2. *v.r.* burrow (*of animals*); (*fig.*) hide o.s., bury o.s. (*in books*).

vergräm–en, *v.a.* grieve, vex, anger (a p.), give trouble to (a p.); start (*game*). **–t,** *p.p.* & *adj.* careworn, woebegone.

vergrasen, *v.n.* (*aux.* s.) be overgrown *or* covered with grass.

vergreif–en, 1. *ir.v.a.* *sich* (*Dat.*) *die Hand* (*den Finger*) *–en*, sprain one's hand (finger). 2. *v.r.* seize wrongly *or* by mistake; (*fig.*) go about a th. in the wrong way, play the wrong note; (*an with Dat.*) attack, violate, appropriate, make off with; *sich an einem –en*, lay violent hands upon a p., seize hold of a p.; *sich an einer S. –en*, misappropriate a th.; *sich an den Gesetzen –en*, violate *or* infringe the law; *sich an dem Namen Gottes –en*, take the name of God

in vain; *sich an einer Kasse -en*, embezzle money; *sich an einem Mädchen -en*, rape, violate *or* seduce a girl, commit an indecent assault; *sich an geheiligten Sachen -en*, profane holy things. **-ung,** *f.* violent seizure; violation; profanation; outrage.
vergriffen, *adj.* sold out, out of print.
vergreisen, *v.n.* become old *or* senile, age (*of population*).
vergröbern, 1. *v.a.* make coarse(r) *or* crude(r). 2. *v.r.* become coarse(r) *or* rude(r).
vergrößer-n, 1. *v.a.* enlarge, magnify; increase, augment, raise, extend; (*fig.*) aggravate, exaggerate; *in -tem Maßstabe zeichnen*, draw on a larger scale. 2. *v.r.* grow larger, aggrandize o.s., extend one's power. **-ung,** *f.* enlargement, increase, augmentation, magnification, exaggeration. **-ungsapparat,** *m.* enlarger (*Phot.*). **-ungsglas,** *n.* magnifying glass. **-ungskraft,** *f.* magnifying power. **-ungslaterne,** *f.* magic lantern, projector. **-ungsplan,** *m.* programme of aggrandizement. **-unsspiegel,** *m.* concave mirror.
vergucken, *v.r.* (*coll.*) make a mistake, see wrong; (*coll.*) *sich in einen -en*, be smitten by a p.
vergülden, (*Poet.*), *see* **vergolden.**
Vergunst, *f.* only in *mit* –, by your leave.
Vergünstigung, *f.* (-en) permission; privilege, favour, concession; (*C.L.*) price reduction, deduction, rebate, allowance.
vergüt-en, *v.a.* (*einem etwas*) make amends, make good, pay back, refund, indemnify, compensate; temper, heat-treat, refine (*metals*); *einem die Auslagen -en*, reimburse a p.; *ich werde Ihnen Ihre Mühe -en*, I shall make it worth your while. **-ung,** *f.* compensation, amends, indemnification, reimbursement, allowance; refining, heat treatment (*Metall.*).
Verhack, *m.* (-(e)s, -e) abatis (*Fort.*).
Verhaft, *m.* arrest, custody, imprisonment; *in* –, under arrest, in custody; *in – nehmen*, seize, arrest, take into custody; – *auf eine S. legen*, lay an embargo on a th. **-en,** *v.a.* arrest, apprehend, take into custody, give in charge, imprison; *einem -et sein*, be closely bound up with *or* dependent on a p.; *der Scholle -et*, bound to the soil; *einer Idee -et*, dominated by an idea. **-ung,** *f.* arrest, imprisonment, capture. **-(ungs)befehl,** *m.*, **(-ungs)brief,** *m.* warrant of arrest; *einen -(ungs)-brief gegen einen erlassen*, issue a warrant for the arrest of a p.
verhageln, *v.n.* (*aux.* s.) be destroyed *or* damaged by hail; (*coll.*) *ihm ist die Petersilie verhagelt*, he has had (a stroke of) bad luck, his plan did not come off.
verhallen, *v.n.* (*aux.* s.) die *or* fade away (*of sounds*), become attenuated, become fainter and fainter.
Verhalt, *m.* state of affairs, condition; behaviour. **-en,** 1. *ir.v.a.* keep *or* hold back; stop, check; hold (*one's breath*); retain (*urine*); repress, suppress, restrain; *Schritte -en*, check one's step, shorten step (*Mil.*). 2. *v.r.* be, be the case; be in the ratio of, have a certain relation to; act, behave, conduct, comport *or* demean o.s.; *die S. verhält sich so*, the matter stands thus, the facts of the matter are; *wenn es sich so verhält*, if that be the case; *sich -en zu*, be in proportion to; *a verhält sich zu b, wie 5 zu 2*, a is to b as 5 is to 2; *sich umgekehrt -en zu*, be in inverse ratio to; *sich ruhig -en*, keep quiet; *-en Sie sich passiv*, maintain a passive attitude; *-et Euch brav!* behave yourselves! be good! *mit -enem Atem*, with bated breath; *mit -enem Gähnen* (*Lächeln*), suppressing a yawn (smile); *-ene Stimmung*, tense atmosphere, suppressed excitement; *schlecht -ener Zorn*, barely concealed anger. 4. *n.* conduct, behaviour; procedure; attitude, approach (*to a problem*), *see also* **-ung.** **-enheit,** *f.* restraint. **-ensmuster,** *n.* behaviour pattern, socially determined attitude. **-ung,** *f.* suppression, retention, repression. **-ungsbefehl,** *m.* **-ungsmaßregeln,** *f.pl.* rules of conduct; directions, rules, orders, instructions, precautions.
Verhältnis, *n.* (-(ss)es, -(ss)e) relation, proportion, rate, ratio; (*generally pl.*) (economic) situation, condition, circumstances; love-affair, liaison; (*coll.*) mistress; *er lebt in angenehmen -(ss)en*, he lives in easy circumstances, he is comfortably off; *in freundschaftlichem -(ss)e zu einem stehen*, be on a friendly footing *or* on friendly terms with a p.; *in umgekehrtem* –, in inverse ratio; *im – von 2 zu 4*, in the ratio of 2 to 4; *im – zu*, in comparison with; *im* or *nach* –, accordingly, in keeping, in proportion, proportionately, relatively; *ein sträfliches – mit einem haben* or *unterhalten*, have illicit intercourse with a p.; *nach – der Bevölkerung*, in proportion to the population; *über seine -(ss)e leben*, live beyond one's means; *unter solchen -(ss)en*, such being the case, in these circumstances. **-anteil,** *m.* quota, share; dividend. **-anzeiger,** *m.* exponent (*Math.*). **-los,** *adj.* without relation (to). **-mäßig,** 1. *adj.* proportionate, proportional, relative, commensurate, pro rata. 2. *adv.* in proportion, comparatively (speaking). **-regel,** *f.* rule of three *or* proportion (*Arith.*). **-wahl,** *f.* election by proportional representation. **-widrig,** *adj.* disproportionate, out of all proportion. **-wort,** *n.* preposition, **-zahl,** *f.* proportional number, ratio, coefficient, factor.
verhand-eln, 1. *v.n.* (*aux.* h.) negotiate (*über with Acc.*), treat, parley, discuss, debate, deliberate; (*über*) *den Frieden -eln*, negotiate a peace; *gerichtlich -eln*, try (a case). 2. *v.a.* transact, discuss; sell, dispose of, barter away. **-lung,** *f.* negotiation, transaction, discussion, deliberation, debate, parley, conference; proceedings, trial, hearing. **-lungsbericht,** *m.*, **-buch,** *n.* record of proceedings, minutes, minute-book. **-lungsfriede,** *m.* negotiated peace. **-ungsführer,** *m.* clerk of sessions. **-lungspapiere,** *n.pl.* records, acts, minutes. **-lungssaal,** *m.* court, chamber, debating hall. **-lungstag,** *m.* **-lungstermin,** *m.* day fixed for trial.
verhäng-en, *v.a.* cover (with), veil, conceal; hang up in a wrong way *or* place; decree, ordain, pronounce (*judgement*); inflict (*a punishment*); impose (*a penalty*) (*über with Acc.*, on); *einem Pferde den Zügel -en*, give a horse his head; *mit -tem Zügel*, with reins flying, at full gallop; *den Belagerungszustand -en*, proclaim martial law; *wie es Gott -t*, as God ordains. **-nis,** *n.* fate, destiny; doom, misfortune; *durch ein sonderbares -nis*, by strange ill luck; *einem zum -nis werden*, be one's doom, be fatal for one; *sie wurde sein -nis*, she was his undoing. **-nisvoll,** *adj.* fatal, unhappy; fateful, disastrous, ominous, portentous. **-ung,** *f.* decree, pronouncement; imposition, infliction.
verhärmt, *adj.* care-worn, woebegone.
verharren, *v.n.* (*aux.* h. & s.) remain, abide; continue *or* persist (in), remain unchanged, hold out, persevere; *in, auf*, or *bei seiner Ansicht* –, persist in *or* (*coll.*) stick to one's opinion.
verharsch-en, *v.n.* (*aux.* s.) form a scab, cicatrice; heal up, close (*of wounds*); form a crust (*of snow*). **-ung,** *f.* scabbing over (*of wounds*); crusting (*of snow, etc.*).
verhärt-en, 1. *v.a.* harden, make hard; indurate. 2. *v.n.* (*aux.* s.) harden, grow hard; become obdurate. **-et,** *p.p.* & *adj.* (*fig.*) obdurate, callous. **-ung,** *f.* hardness, hardening; induration, callosity; obduracy.
verharzen, 1. *v.a.* impregnate *or* smear over with resin. 2. *v.r.* & *n.* (*aux.* s.) become resinous, turn to resin.
verhasp-eln, *v.* 1. *a*, entangle, get (*thread*) into a tangle. 2. *r.* become tangled (up); (*coll.*) break down *or* become confused, muddled *or* embarrassed (*in speaking*). **-(e)lung,** *f.* entanglement, tangle, muddle.
verhaßt, *adj.* detested, hated; (*coll.*) hateful, odious.
verhätscheln, *v.a.* over-indulge, spoil, coddle, pamper.
Verhau, *m.* (-(e)s, -e) abatis, entanglement (*Fort.*).
verhauchen, *v.a.* (*das Leben*), give up (the ghost), breathe one's last; give off (*scent*).
verhauen, 1. *ir.v.a.* mutilate, hack, spoil by cutting; (*coll.*) thrash soundly; bungle, make a mess *or* hash of (*a job*); squander, run through (*one's money*); *einem den Weg* –, put obstacles in a p.'s way; (*coll.*) *das Spiel* –, spoil the game. 2. *v.r.* make a false cut, chop in the wrong place; (*coll.*) make an awful blunder, perpetrate a howler.

verheben, *v.r.* strain o.s. in lifting.
verheddern, *v.r.* (*coll. & dial.*) get muddled *or* confused.
verheer-en, *v.a.* ravage, devastate, lay waste. **-end,** *adj. & p.p.* devastating, catastrophic; (*coll.*) awful. **-ung,** *f.* devastation.
verhehl-en, *v.a.* (*einem etwas*) hide, conceal (from s.o.). **-t,** *see* **verhohlen.** **-ung,** *f.* concealing, hiding; concealment.
verheil-en, *v.n.* heal up, get better. **-ung,** *f.* healing process.
verheimlich-en, *v.a.* conceal, hide, secrete, keep secret; receive (*stolen goods*). **-ung,** *f.* concealment; dissimulation; receiving (*stolen goods*).
verheirat-en, 1. *v.a.* marry, give in marriage; perform the marriage ceremony. 2. *v.r.* marry, get married; *sich mit einem -en,* marry a p.; *sich günstig -en,* make a good match; *sich unter einander -en,* intermarry. **-ung,** *f.* marriage; *-ung unter verschiedenen Rassen,* racial intermarriage.
verheiß-en, *ir.v.a.* (*einem etwas*) promise; *das -ene Land,* the Promised Land. **-ung,** *f.* promise. **-ungsvoll,** *adj.* promising.
verhelfen, *ir.v.n.* (*aux.* h.); *einem zu einer S. -,* help *or* assist s.o. to a th. *or* to get a th., procure a th. for a p.
verherrlich-en, *v.a.* glorify, extol, exalt. **-ung,** *f.* glorification.
verhetz-en, *v.a.* instigate, incite, stir up; goad on, exasperate, irritate. **-ung,** *f.* setting on; incitement, instigation.
verheuern, *v.a.* sign on (*ship's crew*) (*Naut.*).
verhexen, *v.a.* bewitch, enchant.
verhimm-eln, *v.a.* praise *or* laud to the skies. *-elt sein,* be in raptures. **-(e)lung,** *f.* extravagant praise, adulation, rapture, ecstasy.
verhinder-n, *v.a.* hinder, prevent, impede; *jemanden an einer S. -n,* make a th. impossible for a p.; *am Kommen -t,* prevented from coming; *den Umlauf des Blutes -n,* stop the circulation of the blood. **-ung,** *f.* hindrance, prevention, obstacle, impediment. **-ungsfall,** *m.* (in) case of impediment. **-ungsmittel,** *n.* preventative.
verhoffen, 1. *v.n.* (*aux.* h.) (*archaic*), *see* **hoffen;** scent the air (*of game*) (*Hunt.*). 2. *n.* only in *wider alles -,* contrary to all expectations.
verhohlen, 1. *p.p.* (*of* verhehlen) hidden, concealed. 2. *adj.* secretive, underhand, clandestine.
verhöhn-en, *v.a.* scoff (at), mock, jibe (at), jeer (at), laugh (at), deride; make game of, expose to ridicule. **-er,** *m.* mocker, scoffer, jeerer. **-ung** *f.* derision, mockery.
verhol-en, *v.a.* tow, haul, warp (*Naut.*).
Verhör, *n.* (-(e)s, -e) judicial examination, hearing, trial; *ein - anstellen,* institute an inquiry; *einen zum - ziehen,* bring a p. up for cross-examination; *ins - nehmen,* question closely, cross-examine; (*fig.*) take to task. **-en,** hear, try, question, interrogate, examine (*an accused person*); hear say *or* repeat (*lessons of school-children*); not hear. 2. *v.r.* hear wrongly, misunderstand a p.'s words. **-ung,** *f.* cross-examination.
verhudeln, *v.a.* (*coll.*) bungle, botch.
verhüll-en, 1. *v.a.* cover, veil, wrap up; disguise; *in -enden Worten,* in veiled language, euphemistically; *unser Schicksal ist in Dunkelheit -t,* our fate is wrapped in obscurity. 2. *n.,* **-ung,** *f.* covering, wrapping, veil, disguise.
verhundertfachen, *v.a.* multiply a hundredfold, centuple.
verhunger-n, *v.n.* (*aux.* s.) die of hunger, starve; *-t,* wretched, famished, half-starved. **-ung,** *f.* starvation.
verhunzen, *v.a.* spoil, bungle, botch; disfigure; *die englische Sprache -,* murder the Queen's English.
verhüt-en, *v.a.* prevent, obviate, avert, ward off, preserve (from); *das -e Gott!* God forbid! **-end,** *adj.* preventive. **-ung,** *f.* prevention, prophylaxis. **-ungsmaßregel,** *f.* preventive measure. **-ungsmittel,** *n.* prevent(at)ive, prophylactic.
verhütten, *v.a.* work, smelt (*ore*).
verhutzelt, *adj.* shrivelled (up), wizened.
verinnerlich-en, *v.a. & n.* (*aux.* s.) intensify, deepen. **-ung,** *f.* intensification.
verirr-en, *v.r. & n.* (*aux.* s.) go astray, lose one's way, err; *-te Kugel,* stray bullet. **-ung,** *f.* aberration, error, mistake.
verjag-en, *v.a.* drive away *or* out, expel, put to flight, dispel. **-ung,** *f.* expulsion; dislodgement.
verjähr-en, *v.n.* (*aux.* s.) grow old, become superannuated, go out of date *or* fashion; become obsolete; become rooted *or* inveterate; (*also v.r.*) fall under the statute of limitations, lapse, become null and void. **-bar,** *adj.* prescriptible (*Law*). **-t,** *p.p. & adj.* inveterate, deep-rooted; prescriptive (*Law*); old, obsolete, superannuated; *-tes Recht,* prescriptive right; *-te Schuld,* prescriptive debt. **-ung,** *f.* prescription, limitation (*Law*). **-ungsfrist,** *f.* term of limitation *or* prescription. **-ungsgesetz,** *n.,* **-ungsrecht,** *n.* statute of limitations.
verjubeln, *v.a.* pass *or* waste (*one's time, etc.*) squander, (*sl.*) blow (*one's money*); (*coll.*) frivol away.
verjud-en, *v.a. & n.* (*aux. s.*) become *or* make Jewish, come *or* bring under Jewish influence. **-ung,** *f.* increasing Jewish influence.
verjüng-en, 1. *v. a.* rejuvenate, renovate, regenerate; reduce to a smaller scale; lessen, diminish, constrict, narrow, taper; *in -tem Maßstabe,* on a small(er) *or* reduced scale, in miniature; *-te Probe,* small assay (*Smelting*). 2. *v.r.* be rejuvenated *or* regenerated; taper. **-ung,** *f.* rejuvenation, regeneration; reduction, diminution, attenuation; tapering. **-ungszeitraum,** *m.* regeneration cycle (*For.*). **-ungsmaßstab,** *m.* reduced scale. **-ungsquelle,** *f.* fountain of youth.
verjuxen, *v.a.* (*coll.*) *see* **verjubeln.**
verkalben, *vn.* (*aux.* h.) calve prematurely.
verkalk-en, *v.a., r. & n.* (*aux.* s.) calcine, calcify, turn to chalk; (*coll.*) grow old, become decrepit, ossify. **-ung,** *f.* calcination, calcification, arteriosclerosis (*Path.*).
verkannt, *p.p.* (*of* verkennen) *& adj.* mistaken, misunderstood.
verkapp-en, 1. *v.a.* muffle up, envelop; cloak, mask, disguise, hoodwink (*a hawk*). 2. *v.r.* disguise o.s. **-t,** *p.p. & adj.* masked, veiled, disguised; secret, insidious, surreptitious; *-ter Schriftsteller,* writer under an assumed name; *-ter Freidenker,* under-cover free-thinker. **-ung,** *f.* concealment, disguise, incognito, mystification; duplicity, pretence; mask, cloak, veil.
verkaps-eln, *v.r.* become encysted (*Med.*). **-(e)lung,** *f.* encystation.
verkatert, *adj.* (*coll.*) having a hang-over.
Verkauf, *m.* (-(e)s, ⸚e) sale; selling, disposal; *zum -,* on sale, for sale. **-en,** 1. *v.a.* (*einem etwas* or *etwas an einen*) sell, dispose of; *mit Schaden -en,* sell at a loss; *zu -en sein,* to be for sale *or* to be sold; (*coll.*) *verraten und -t,* sold, done, finished, helpless; *sein Leben teuer -en,* sell one's life dearly. 2. *v.r.* sell, sell o.s. (*of prostitutes or traitors*); *es -t sich gut,* it sells well, has a ready sale *or* finds ready buyers; *das -t sich schwer,* that is a drug in the market *or* is difficult to dispose of. **-sabteilung,** *f.* sales department. **-sautomat,** *m.* automatic *or* penny-in-the-slot machine. **-sbedingungen,** *f.pl.* terms *or* conditions of sale. **-sbuch,** *n.* salesbook, daybook. **-sbude,** *f.* stall, booth (*of a vendor*). **-slokal,** *n.* shop, saleroom. **-spreis,** *m.* selling-price. **-swert,** *m.* market-value.
Verkäuf-er, *m.* (-s, -) seller, vendor, salesman, shop-assistant. **-erin,** *f.* shop-assistant, shop-girl, saleswoman. **-lich,** 1. *adj.* for sale, saleable, marketable; venal, mercenary; negotiable (*of bills*); *leicht -lich,* commanding a ready sale; *schwer -lich,* difficult to dispose of, drug in the market. 2. *adv.* by sale; *einem etwas -lich überlassen,* sell a th. to a p. **-lichkeit,** *f.* saleableness; venality.
Verkehr, *m.* (-(e)s traffic; commerce, business, trade, (train, *etc.*) service, communication; (sexual *or* social) intercourse; circulation (*of money*); *brieflicher -,* correspondence; *freier -,* unrestricted communication *or* trade; *geselliger* or *gesellschaftlicher -,* social intercourse; *Handel und -,* trade and commerce; *inniger - mit der Natur,* communings with nature; *das ist kein - für dich,* that is poor company for you; *mit einem - haben, in - mit*

einem stehen, have intercourse *or* dealings with a p. **–en,** 1. *v.a.* turn the wrong way, turn upside down, invert, turn topsy-turvy; turn *or* change (into), transform, convert into; reverse, pervert; *Freude in Leid –en*, change joy into sadness; *jemandes Worte –en*, put a wrong construction upon a p.'s words. 2. *v.r.* change into its opposite, become reversed. 3. *v.n.* (*aux.* h.) come and go, frequent, visit; *regelmäßig* (*zwischen zwei Orten*) *–en*, run regularly *or* ply between two places; *Lokal, in dem* (*viele Schiffer*) *–en*, tavern frequented by (sailors); *mit einem –en*, cohabit *or* have (sexual) intercourse with a p.; associate with *or* see a good deal of a p.; *bei einem* or *in einem Hause –en*, be a frequent visitor at a p.'s house. **–sader,** *f.* arterial road. **–sampel,** *f.* traffic-light. **–samt,** *n.* tourist office. **–sbureau,** *n.* travel-agency. **–seinrichtungen,** *f.pl.* communications, traffic arrangements. **–sflugzeug,** *n.* passenger *or* commercial aeroplane, air-liner, civil aircraft. **–sinsel,** *f.* island, refuge. **–skarte,** *f.* road *or* rail map. **–sknotenpunkt,** *m.* railway junction. **–sminister,** *m.* Minister of Transport. **–smittel,** *n.pl.* means of communication, conveyance, passenger vehicle; currency. **–sordnung,** *f.*, *see* **–sregelung.** **–spolizist,** *m.*, **–sposten,** *m.*, *see* **–sschutzmann.** **–sregelung,** *f.* traffic control. **–sreich,** *adj.* congested, crowded. **–sschrift,** *f.* commercial shorthand. **–sschutzmann,** *m.* traffic policeman, point-duty policeman. **–sschwach,** *adj.* slack. **–ssicherheit,** *f.* road safety. **–ssignale,** *pl.* traffic signals, road signs. **–sstark,** *adj.* busy; *–sstarke Zeit*, rush hours. **–sstockung,** *f.*, **–sstörung,** *f.* traffic jam *or* block. **–sstraße,** *f.* main road, highway, thoroughfare; trade-route. **–sturm,** *m.* traffic control tower. **–sunfall,** *m.* street accident. **–sverein,** *m.* association for promoting tourist traffic. **–swerbung,** *f.* tourist-traffic propaganda. **–swesen,** *n.* traffic, (train) service. **–szeichen,** *n.* traffic *or* road sign. **–szucht,** *f.* road sense. **–t,** *p.p. & adj.* turned the wrong way, reversed, inside out, upside down, inverted; wrong, perverted, perverse, wrongheaded, absurd, preposterous; *–te Seite*, wrong side; *mit –tem Gewehr*, arms reversed (*Mil.*); *Kaffee –t*, coffee with a lot of milk, white coffee, (*coll.*) coffee dash; *–te Welt*, topsy-turvy *or* crazy world; *–t anfangen*, go the wrong way to work, set about s.th. the wrong way, put the cart before the horse. **–theit,** *f.* perversity, wrongheadedness, absurdity, folly. **–ung,** *f.* overturning, reversal, inversion; perversion; inverse proposition; misstatement (*of facts*).

verkeilen, *v.a.* wedge tight, fasten with a wedge; drive up the quoins (*Typ.*); (*sl.*) thrash (a p.); (*sl.*) sell a th. at any price; (*fig.*) *ihm den Kopf –*, daze, stupefy *or* stun a p.

verkenn–en, *ir.v.a.* mistake, fail to recognize, take for another; misunderstand, misjudge, misconstrue, have a false idea of, fail to appreciate, undervalue; *nicht zu –en*, unmistakable; *verkanntes Genie*, unrecognized genius. **–bar,** *adj.* mistakable, easily mistaken *or* misunderstood. **–ung,** *f.* mistaking; misunderstanding, lack of appreciation.

verkett–en, *v.a.* chain *or* link together, (*usually fig.*) connect, unite. **–et,** *adj.* interlinked. **–ung,** *f.* chaining, linking, linkage, union, chain, concatenation, coincidence.

verketzer–n, *v.a.* accuse of heresy; (*fig.*) disparage, calumniate, slander. **–ung,** *f.* charge of heresy; calumniation, disparagement, slander, abuse.

verkiesel–n, *v.a. & n.* silicify. **–t,** *adj.* silicated.

verkirchlichen, *v.a.* bring under ecclesiastical control.

verkitt–en, *v.a.* cement, lute, seal with putty. **–ung,** *f.* cementing, luting, puttying.

verklag–en, *v.a.* sue, bring an action against, accuse, inform against; *einen wegen einer Schuld –en*, sue a p. for debt; *einen des Hochverrats –en*, arraign *or* indict s.o. on a charge of high treason. **–bar,** *adj.* actionable, indictable. **–te(r),** *m.* accused, defendant; respondent. **–ung,** *f.* accusation, prosecution, suit, indictment.

verklammen, *v.n.* (*dial.*) grow stiff *or* numb with cold.

verklammern, *v.a.* clamp, fasten with cramp-irons.

verklär–en, *v.a.* make bright *or* radiant; transfigure; glorify. **–t,** *adj.* transfigured, glorified, radiant, effulgent; *die –ten*, the blessed ones, the blest. **–ung,** *f.* transfiguration, glorification, radiance, effulgence, ecstasy.

Verklarung, *f.* (-en) sea-protest (*Law*).

verklatschen, *v.a.* waste (*time*) gossiping; defame, inform against, slander, backbite, tell tales about.

verklaus–eln, (*Austr. dial.*) **–ulieren,** *v.a.* stipulate, limit by provisos. **–elt, –uliert,** *p.p. & adj.* specially provided *or* stipulated. **–elung, –ulierung,** *f.* proviso, stipulation.

verkleb–en, *v.a.* plaster up, glue, lute, cement, paste over, gum up, stick together; apply a plaster. **–ung,** *f.* sticking together, agglutination.

verklecksen, *v.a.* cover with blots *or* smudges, make a mess of (*book, tablecloth, etc.*), spill ink on.

verkleid–en, 1. *v.a.* cover, face *or* case (with); revet, plank; board, wainscot; disguise, mark; camouflage, veil (*an insult, etc.*). 2. *v.r.* make up (*Theat.*); dress up (as). **–ung,** *f.* covering, facing, lining, casing, cowling, wainscoting, panelling, revetment (*Fort.*), fairing (*Av.*).

verkleiner–n, *v.a.* make smaller, diminish, reduce; (*fig.*) disparage, depreciate, belittle; detract from; *einen Bruch –n*, reduce a fraction; *den Wert –n*, depreciate the value; *einen* or *jemandes Verdienst –n*, belittle a p., disparage a p.'s services. **–er,** *m.* (-s, –) belittler, detractor. **–ung,** *f.* diminution, reduction, detraction, depreciation, disparagement. **–ungsglas,** *n.* concave lens, diminishing glass. **–ungswort,** *n.* diminutive (*Gram.*).

verkleistern, *v.a.* paste up; (*fig.*) patch up (*a difference*); cover up (*faults, mistakes*).

Verklicker, *m.* (-s, –) burgee (*Naut.*).

verklingen, *ir.v.n.* (*aux.* s.) die *or* fade away (*of sounds*).

verklommen, p.p., *see* **verklammen.**

verklopfen, (*dial.* **verkloppen**) *v.a.* (*coll.*) beat soundly, thrash; (*Stud. sl.*) sell, dispose of.

verknack–en, *v.a.* (*coll.*) sentence (*a p.*), play a trick on (*a p.*), pull (*a p.'s*) leg. **–sen,** *v.a.* (*coll.*) *sich* (*Dat.*) *den Fuß –sen*, sprain one's foot.

verknall–en, 1. *v.n.* (*aux.* s.) explode, go off with a bang; (*sl.*) *in sie –t*, badly smitten with *or* head over heels in love with her. 2. *v.a.* fire off, use up (*all one's ammunition*).

verknapp–en, *v.r.* become scarce, (*coll.*) get tight *or* short. **–ung,** *f.* scarcity, shortage.

verkneifen, 1. *ir.v.a.* stifle; (*sl.*) *sich* (*Dat.*) *etwas –*, deny o.s. a th., forgo s.th.; *verkniffenes Gesicht*, pinched, hardbitten *or* grim expression.

verknistern, *v.n.* decrepitate.

verknittern, *v.a.* crumple, crease.

verknöcher–n, 1. *v.a.* ossify; make hard. 2. *v.n.* (*aux.* s.) ossify, (*coll.*) grow stiff with age; grow narrow-minded *or* pedantic. **–ung,** *f.* ossification, bone-formation; hardening.

verknorpeln, *v.r. & n.* (*aux.* s.) become cartilaginous.

verknoten, *v.a.* knot, knit together, tie up (in knots), entangle. .

verknüllen, *v.a. see* **verknittern.**

verknüpf–en, *v.a.* knot, tie, bind, join, link, knit, connect, combine, unite, attach to; involve, entail; *mit Übelständen –t sein*, be attended with *or* accompanied by drawbacks; *logisch –te Ideen*, logically connected ideas; *mit wenig Kosten –t*, involving *or* entailing little expense. **–ung,** *f.* knotting *or* tying together, linkage, unification, combination, connexion, bond, link.

verknusen, *v.a.* (*dial., usually negative*) stomach; put up with, stand; *ich kann ihn nicht –*, (*coll.*) I can't stick him.

verkochen, *v.a. & n.* (*aux.* s.) overboil, boil into the water; boil down *or* away, concentrate, evaporate; *sein Zorn verkochte bald*, his anger soon cooled down.

verkohl–en, *v.a. & n.* (*aux.* s.) char, carbonize; (*coll.*) hoax, pull (*a p.'s*) leg, pull the wool over (*a p.'s*) eyes. **–ung,** *f.* carbonization.

verkok–en, *v.a.* coke, carbonize, char. **–ung,** *f.* carbonization. **–ungsmeiler,** *m.* coking-mound .

verkomm-en, 1. *ir.v.n.* (*aux.* s.) decay, go bad; be ruined, come down in the world; become demoralized; die (*vor*, of). 2. *p.p. & adj.* decayed, ruined, degenerate, depraved, gone to the bad. **-enheit,** *f.* depravity, demoralization, degeneracy. **-nis,** *n.* (-nisses, -nisse) (*Swiss dial.*) agreement, treaty.

verkoppeln, *v.a.* couple, link, join together, combine.

verkork-en, *v.a.* cork (up). **-sen,** *v.a.* (*coll.*) spoil, bungle, botch; *sich* (*Dat.*) *den Magen verkorksen*, upset one's stomach.

verkörnen, *v.a.* granulate.

verkörper-n, *v.a.* embody, personify, clothe in flesh and blood, incarnate, materialize. **-ung,** *f.* embodiment, personification, incarnation.

verkost-en, *v.a.* taste, test, try (*food*). **-gelden,** *v.a.* (*Swiss dial.*) put out to board.

verköstig-en, *v.a.* feed, board **-ung,** *f.* board, food.

Verköterung, *f.* mongrelization, **racial degeneration.**

verkrach-en, *v.n.* (*coll.*) go bankrupt, go smash *or* broke; fall out (with, *mit*); *eine -te Existenz*, ne'er-do-well, failure.

verkraften, *v.a.* supply electricity to; (*coll.*) cope with.

verkrampft, *adj.* cramped, clenched, rigid; unnatural (*style*).

verkriechen, *ir.v.r.* crawl away, sneak off, hide o.s.; *sich in das Bett* -, creep into one's bed; *er verkriecht sich vor jedem*, he shuns everyone; *er muß sich vor Wilhelm* -, he is no match for William.

verkrümel-n, 1. *v.a. & n.* (*aux.* s.) crumble away, fritter away, dissipate; *sein Geld -n*, fritter away one's money. 2. *v.r.* disappear gradually; slink away, make off; *das Geld -t sich*, the money dribbles away; *die Gäste -n sich*, the guests depart one by one.

verkrümm-en, 1. *v.a.* make crooked, bend, spoil by bending. 2. *v.r.* grow crooked. **-ung,** *f.* crookedness, curvature, bend; *-ung der Wirbelsäule*, curvature of the spine.

verkrüppeln, 1. *v.a.* stunt, deform, mutilate. 2. *v.n.* (*aux.* s.) become deformed, mutilated *or* stunted.

verkühlen, *v.r.* (*dial.*) catch cold.

verkümmer-n, 1. *v.a.* (*einem etwas*) spoil; *jemandes Freude -n*, spoil a p.'s pleasure; *jemandes Rechte -n*, encroach *or* infringe upon another's rights. 2. *v.n.* (*aux.* s.) become stunted, atrophy, shrink, shrivel up; pine away, languish, perish. **-t,** *adj.* stunted, rudimentary, vestigial. **-ung,** *f.* stunted growth, vestige; dwarfing, atrophy; curtailment, encroachment.

verkünd-en, -igen, *v.a.* (*einem etwas*) announce, make known, publish, proclaim; preach (*the Gospel*); pronounce (*a judgement*); *im voraus -(ig)en*, foretell, forwarn, prophesy; (*dial.*) *ein Brautpaar -igen*, publish the banns. **-(ig)er,** *m.* messenger, harbinger, herald, prophet. **-(ig)ung,** announcement, publication, proclamation; preaching (*of the Gospel*); prophecy, prediction; pronouncing (*of a sentence*); *Mariä -igung*, the Annunciation, Lady Day.

verkupfer-n, *v.a.* plate *or* line with copper, copper-plate, copper-face (*Typ.*). **-t,** *p.p. & adj.* copper-sheated *or* -bottomed (*of ships*), copper-plate(d).

verkuppeln, *v.a.* couple, connect (*coaches, shafts, etc.*); bring together, pair off; pander, procure.

verkürz-en, 1 *v.a.* shorten, abridge, curtail, cut; lessen, diminish, foreshorten (*Paint., etc.*); *einen -en*, encroach upon a p.'s rights; *die Zeit -en*, beguile *or* while away the time. 2. *v.r.* become shorter, diminish, contract, shrink; *-te Arbeitszeit*, short time. **-ung,** *f.* shortening, abridgement, curtailment; retrenchment, stinting, cutting down; foreshortening (*Paint., etc.*); abbreviation, contraction, syncope (*Gram.*).

verlachen, *v.a.* laugh at, deride.

Verlad, *m.* (*Swiss dial.*) *see* **-ung. -en,** *ir.v.a.* load (*goods*), ship, entrain (*troops*); dispatch, forward (*goods by train, etc.*); *lose -en*, ship in bulk; **-er,** *m.* shipping-agent; carrier; exporter. **-estelle,** *f.* loading point, entraining point, point of embarkation. **-ung,** *f.* loading, entraining, embarkation; shipping, shipment; carriage, forwarding. **-ungsgebühren,** *f.pl.*, **-ungskosten,** *f.pl.* loading- *or* shipping-charges. **-ungspapiere,** *n.pl.*, **-ungsschein,** *m.* bill of lading.

Verlag, *m.* (-s, -e & *Austr. dial.* ⸚e) publication (*of a book*); publishing house, (firm of) publishers; publications; stock on show; *in - nehmen*, undertake the publication of, publish; *er hat nur einen juristischen* -, only law books are published by him. **-sartikel,** *m.pl.*, **-sbücher,** *n.pl.* publications, books published. **-s(buch)handel,** *m.* publishing business *or* trade. **-s(buch)handlung,** *f.* publishing house *or* firm. **-skatalog,** *m.* publisher's catalogue. **-srecht,** *n.* copyright. **-srechtlich,** *adj.* pertaining to copyright; *-srechtliche Ausgabe*, copyright edition. **-szeichen,** *n.* publisher's mark *or* monogram.

Verläge, *pl.* outlay, estimated expenses, advance.

verlager-n, *v.a. & r.* shift. **-ung,** *f.* shifting, displacement (*statics, Geol., etc.*).

verlang-en, 1. *v.a.* demand, claim, ask for, require, desire; *Genugtuung -en*, demand satisfaction; *was -en Sie von mir?* what do you want of me? *wieviel -en Sie dafür?* how much do you want for it? *man -t zu wissen*, information is desired; *du hast gar nichts zu -en*, you are in no position to make demands; *das ist zu viel -t*, that is asking too much; *mehr kann man nicht -en!* one cannot wish for more; (*imp.*) *mich -t zu wissen*, I am anxious *or* I want to know; *es soll mich -en*, I ask myself. 2. *n.* (*aux.* h.) (with *nach*) desire, wish for, long for, hanker after, crave. 3. *n.* request, demand, desire, wish, longing (*nach*, for); claim (*Law*); *auf -en*, on demand, by request; at call. **-enswert,** *adj.* desirable. **-termaßen,** *adj.* as desired. **-zettel,** *m.* order-form.

verlänger-n, 1. *v.a.* lengthen, extend, elongate; protract, prolong, delay, (*coll.*) spin out; renew (*bills*); produce (*Geom.*); eke out, dilute (*paint, soup, etc.*). 2. *v.r.* grow longer, lengthen, stretch. **-ung,** *f.* lengthening, extension, elongation, prolongation; production (*Geom.*); process (*Anat.*). **-ungsfähig,** *adj.* extensible, extensile, protractile. **-ungspunkt,** *m.* dot (*Mus.*). **-ungsstück,** *n.* extension piece; rider, allonge (*of a bill*). **-ungstrieb,** *m.* terminal shoot (*Bot.*). **-ungszettel,** *m.* rider (*to a bill of exchange*).

verlangsam-en, *v.a.* slacken, slow down, retard, delay. **-ung,** *f.* delay(ing); slackening, retardation.

verläppern, *v.a.* (*coll.*) waste (*money*) on trifles; trifle away, squander, fritter away.

verlarv-en, *v.a. & r.* disguise, wear a mask; enter the larval state (*Ent.*). **-ung,** *f.* masking, masquerade, mummery.

Verlaß, *m.* trustworthiness, trust, dependence, reliability; *auf den ist kein* -, there is no relying on him, there is no dependence on him, he cannot be trusted, he cannot be relied on. **-(ss)en,** 1. *ir.v.a.* leave, quit, vacate; relinquish, give up; leave behind, forsake, abandon, desert, leave in the lurch; *seine Kräfte -(ss)en ihn*, his strength fails him. 2. *v.r.* (*auf etwas*) rely on, trust to, depend upon; *darauf kannst du dich -(ss)en*, you may rely on it! (*coll.*) sure as fate!, (*sl.*) you can bet your bottom dollar on that! *Sie können sich (fest) darauf verlassen, daß* . . ., you may rest assured *or* depend upon it, that . . . 3. *p.p. & adj.* deserted, forsaken, abandoned, forlorn, lonely, derelict; *von aller Welt -en*, forsaken by everyone. **-(ss)enheit,** *f.* loneliness, solitude, isolation; abandonment; destitution **-(ss)enschaft,** *f.* (*dial.*) bequest, legacy.

verläss-ig, (*dial.*), (*usually*) **-(ß)lich,** *adj.* reliable, trustworthy, to be depended on. **-(ß)lichkeit,** *f.* reliability, trustworthiness, dependence.

verläster-n, *v.a.* slander, defame, malign, calumniate, traduce. **-ung,** *f.* defamation, calumny, slander.

Verlaub, *m.* only in *mit Verlaub*, with your permission, by your leave.

Verlauf, *m.* lapse, expiration; course, process (*of time*); progress, development (*of a matter*); outcome; *nach - einiger Tage*, in the course of a few days, after (the lapse of) some days; – *einer Krankheit*, course of a disease; *der ganze – der S.*, the whole history of the affair; *einen schlimmen – nehmen*, take a turn for the worse. **–en,** 1. *v.n.* (*aux.* s.) pass, elapse, proceed, take its course, turn out, develop; *die Zeit verläuft*, time passes quickly, time flies; *die Krankheit verläuft normal*, the disease is taking its normal course; *wie ist die S. –en?* how has the affair turned out? *alles ist sehr gut –en*, everything has gone off very well. 2. *v.r.* (*aux.* h.) & *n.* (*aux.* s.) lose one's way, get lost, go astray; scatter, be dispersed; flow away, subside, blend *or* flow into, run (*of colours*); *wir haben uns –en*, we have lost our way, we have taken the wrong road *or* turning; *die Menge verlief sich*, the crowd dispersed; *die S. verlief im Sand*, nothing came of the affair. 3. *adj.* stray, lost; *–ener Kerl*, vagrant, vagabond; *–enes Mädchen* abandoned girl; *ein –ener*, a runaway, a refugee.

Verläufer, *m.* (-s, –) straggler.

verlaut-baren, 1. *v.a.* make known, divulge, publish, notify. 2. *v.n.* (*aux.* h.) become *or* be made known *or* public. **–barung,** *f.* announcement, notification, promulgation. **–en,** *v.n.* (*aux.* h. & s.) & *imp.* be said *or* rumoured, transpire; (*Swiss dial.*) *see* **–baren;** *–en lassen*, give to understand, hint; *nichts von der S. –en lassen*, let nothing leak out, not breathe a word; *sie ließen (sich) –en*, they were heard to say; *es –et, daß . . .*, it is said that . . .; *wie –et*, according to report, as the story goes.

verleb-en, *v.a.* pass, spend (*time*); overtask, overtax (*one's constitution*) (*usually p.p.*). **–endigen,** *v.a.* vivify. **–t,** *p.p.* & *adj.* worn out, broken down, spent, debilitated, jaded, decrepit. **–theit,** *f.* debility, exhaustion, decrepitude.

[1]**verleg-en,** 1. *v.a.* transfer, shift, remove to another place; mislay, put in the wrong place; delay, postpone, adjourn, put off; lay (*pipes, cables, etc.*); locate (*the scene of a story*); (*einem etwas*) stop, hinder, obstruct, bar (him from doing it); *einem den Rückzug –en*, block his retreat; publish, bring out (*a book*); (*archaic*) (*einem etwas*) settle (*a debt*), advance (*a sum of money*); *sein Geschäft nach London –en*, transfer one's business to London; *auf einen andern Tag –en*, postpone to another day; *seinen Schwerpunkt nach. . . –en*, shift the centre of gravity to . . .; *den Schauplatz nach Deutschland (ins Mittelalter) –en*, locate the scene in Germany (in the Middle Ages); *einem den Weg –en*, throw obstacles in a p.'s way. 2. *v.r.* (*auf etwas*) apply *or* devote o.s. to a th., (*coll.*) go in for a th., take a th. up; *er –te sich aufs Leugnen*, he turned to denials. 3. *p.p. of* verliegen, *see* [2]**verlegen.** 4. *n., see* **–ung. –er,** *m.* publisher; (*dial.*) retailer, distributor (*liquor trade particularly*). **–ung,** *f.* shift, change of position, transfer, removal; postponement, adjournment; mislaying, temporary loss; laying; barricading; publication.

[2]**verlegen,** *p.p.* (*of* verliegen) & *adj.* spoiled through lying *or* keeping, stale (*of goods*); embarrassed, confused, self-conscious, disconcerted; *um eine S. – sein*, be at a loss for a th.; *um Geld – sein*, be short of cash, be financially embarrassed. **–heit,** *f.* embarrassment, difficulty, perplexity, dilemma, straits; *in –heit bringen* or *(ver)setzen*, embarrass, make (*s.o.*) embarrassed; *einem –heit(en) bereiten*, embarrass a p., cause a p. some embarrassment; *einem aus der –heit helfen*, help a p. over his (*etc.*) embarrassment; *sich aus der –heit ziehen*, get out of a difficulty.

verleiden, *v.a.* (*einem etwas*) spoil (a th. for s.o.), disgust (s.o. with a th.); *das Landleben war ihm verleidet*, he had taken a dislike to life in the country; *es ist mir alles verleidet*, I am sick of everything.

Verleih, *m.* (-s, -e), **–e,** *f.* lending department (*of a library, etc.*); loan office, loan society; hire service. **–bar,** *adj.* loanable, hirable; conferable. **–en,** *ir.v.a.* (*einem etwas*) lend, let out, hire out; give, grant, endow, bestow, confer, invest with (*a fief, etc.*); *Geld auf Zinsen –en*, lend *or* loan money at interest; *einem eine Pfründe –en*, endow a p. in a living; *einem ein Amt –en*, appoint a p. to an office; *einem Hilfe –en*, render s.o. assistance; *Gott –e uns seinen Segen*, may God grant us His blessing! **–ung,** *f.* lending, loan; investiture, conferment, granting, bestowal.

verleit-en, *v.a.* lead astray, induce, mislead, lure, seduce, suborn; *einen Soldaten zur Fahnenflucht –en*, induce a soldier to desert. **–ung,** *f.* misleading; temptation, seduction, subornation (*of witnesses*); *–ung zum Bösen*, incitement *or* instigation to wrong (doing); *–ung zum Meineid*, inducement to perjury (*Law*).

verlernen, *v.a.* unlearn, forget (what one has learnt).

verles-en, 1. *ir.v.a.* read out, call out (*names*), call (*a register*); (*dial.*) pick out, select. 2. *v.r.* make a mistake in reading, misread. 3. *n.*; *das –en der Namen*, calling of the roll. **–ung,** *f.* roll-call.

verletz-en, *v.a.* hurt, wound; damage, injure; insult, offend; offend (against), violate; encroach (upon) (*rights*), infringe (*laws*); *jemandes guten Namen –en*, injure *or* damage a p.'s reputation; *eine Regel –en*, break a rule; *jemandes Ehre –en*, wound a p.'s honour; *jemandes Interessen –en*, wrong a p., damage a p.'s interest(s). *er fühlte sich –t*, he felt (himself) aggrieved. **–end,** *adj.* offensive, insulting. **–lich,** *adj.* vulnerable, easily damaged; susceptible, (*coll.*) touchy. **–ung,** *f.* hurt, damage, injury, wound; violation, infringement, encroachment; offence, insult.

verleugn-en, 1. *v.a.* deny, disown, disavow, renounce; not follow suit, revoke (*Cards*); act contrary to, act against; *seinen Glauben –en*, renounce one's belief; *sich –en lassen*, refuse to see visitors; *sie ließ sich für ihre Freunde –en*, she was not 'at home' to her friends. 2. *v.r.* (*with nicht*) reveal itself, become clear; *sein Geiz –ete sich nicht*, his meanness showed itself; *sich selbst –en*, belie o.s., be untrue to o.s., give a wrong impression of o.s. **–ung,** *f.* denial, disavowal, renunciation; revoking (*Cards*).

verleumd-en, *v.a.* calumniate, slander, defame, traduce, accuse wrongfully. **–er,** *m.* calumniator, slanderer, libeller. **–erisch,** *adj.* slanderous, libellous, defamatory. **–ung,** *f.* libel, calumny, slander, defamation, wrongful accusation. **–ungsprozeß,** *m.* action for defamation of character, action for libel.

verlieb-en, *v.r.* fall in love (*in, with Acc.*, with). **–t,** *p.p.* & *adj.* in love (with), enamoured (of); amorous, love-sick; *närrisch –t*, madly in love, infatuated; *–te Augen machen*, cast amorous glances, make sheep's eyes (at), (*coll.*) give the glad eye. **–theit,** *f.* amorousness (*of disposition*).

verliegen, *ir.v.n.* (*aux.* s.) deteriorate through standing *or* keeping (*of goods*); crease (*a th.*) by lying on it.

verlier-en, 1. *ir.v.a.* lose, forfeit, let slip; *Sie haben an ihm einen guten Freund verloren*, you have lost a good friend in him; *an ihm ist Hopfen und Malz verloren*, he is incorrigible, one might as well give him up as a bad job; *einen aus den Augen –en*, lose sight of a p.; *bei einem –en*, sink in a p.'s estimation; *alle Bitten waren bei ihm verloren*, all entreaties were lost on him; *Blätter –en*, shed leaves; *den Boden unter den Füßen –en*, get out of one's depth; *etwas verloren geben*, give a th. up for lost *or* as a bad job; *ich gebe das Spiel verloren*, I throw my hand in, I acknowledge defeat, I give in; *verloren gehen*, be lost, get lost, go astray, disappear, vanish; miscarry (*of letters*); founder, go down (*of ships*); *see also* **verloren,** *adj.*; *an ihm ist ein Diplomat verloren gegangen*, he was cut out for a *or* would have made a good diplomat; *Hoffnung –en*, give up hope; *den Kopf –en*, lose all self-control, lose one's head; *kein Wort –en*, not waste a word; *Zeit –en*, waste time; *da ist keine Zeit zu –en*, there is no time to be lost. 2. *v.n.* (*an*) fall off, decline (*in value*), suffer loss (of); *die Blume hat etwas an Duft verloren*, the flower has lost something of its fragrance. 3. *v.r.* get lost, lose o.s., lose one's way, go astray; disperse; disappear; *diese Farbe –t sich ins Grüne*, this colour melts into green; *sich in Gedanken –en*, be lost in thought; *die Menge –t sich*, the crowd disperses; *die Schmerzen –en sich*, the pains are subsiding; *die Töne –en sich*, the sounds die away. **–er,** *m.* loser.

Verlies (*Austr. dial. also* **Verließ**), *n.* (-(s)es, -(s)e) dungeon, keep.

verlob–en, 1. *v.a.* affiance, betroth (to); *–t sein mit . . .*, be engaged to. . . . 2. *v.r.*; *sich –en*, (*mit*), become engaged (to). **–te(r),** *m.* fiancé. **–te,** *f.* fiancée; *die –ten*, the engaged couple. **–ung,** *f.* engagement, betrothal; *eine –ung aufheben*, break off an engagement; *die –ung ist rückgängig gemacht*, the engagement has been broken off. **–ungsanzeige,** *f.* announcement of an engagement. **–ungsring,** *m.* engagement-ring.

Verlöbnis, *n.* (-ses, -se), *see* **Verlobung.**

verlock–en, *v.a.* entice, mislead, tempt, allure, seduce. **–end,** *adj.* enticing, tempting. **–ung,** *f.* enticement, allurement, temptation, seduction.

verlogen, *adj.* mendacious, untruthful. **–heit,** *f.* untruthfulness, mendacity.

verlohnen, *v. imp.* (*usually with Gen.*) *es verlohnt die* or *sich der Mühe*, it is worth the trouble, it is worth while.

verlor, verlöre, *see* **verlieren.** **–en,** *p.p.* (*of* verlieren) & *adj.* lost, forlorn; *–ene Arbeit*, wasted labour; *–ene Eier*, poached eggs; *in Gedanken -en*, lost in thought; *–ene Hoffnung*, vain hope; *das –ene Paradies*, Paradise Lost; *–ener Kopf*, blind riser (*Metall.*); *–ener Posten*, forlorn hope; *–ener Schuß*, random shot, stray bullet; (*B.*) *der –ene Sohn*, the Prodigal Son. *–en gehen, see under* **verlieren.**

verlösch–en, 1. *v.a.* extinguish; obliterate, efface. 2. *ir.v.n.* (*aux.* s.) be extinguished; go out, become extinct, expire, die out; *verloschene Kohlen*, dead coals; *verloschene Inschriften*, obliterated inscriptions. 3. *n.*; *im –en sein*, be on the point of going out *or* dying away. **–bar,** *adj.* extinguishable, effaceable. **–ung,** *f.* extinction, obliteration.

verlos–en, *v.a.* raffle, cast lots for. **–ung,** *f.* lottery, raffle.

verlöten, *v.a.* solder.

verlottern, verludern, verlumpen, 1. *v.a.* (*coll.*) waste in riotous living, squander. 2. *v.n.* come down in the world, go to the dogs, go to rack and ruin.

Verlust, *m.* (-es, -e) loss, damage, privation, bereavement; detriment, disadvantage, forfeiture; leak, escape (*of gas*); (*pl.*) casualties (*in war*); *bei –*, with loss of, with forfeiture of, under pain of; *mit – verkaufen*, sell at a loss. **–bringend,** *adj.* involving loss, detrimental; prejudicial. **–ig,** *adj.* (*with Gen.*) deprived of, without; *einer S. –ig gehen*, incur the loss of a th., lose or forfeit a th.; *jemanden einer S. für –ig erklären*, declare a p., devoid of all claims to a th. **–liste,** *f.* list of casualties, casualty returns (*Mil.*). **–träger,** *m.* loser. **–vortrag,** *m.* debit balance, carried forward. **–winkel,** *m.* phase angle (*Elec.*).

vermachen, *v.a.* (*einem etwas*) bequeath.

Vermächtnis, *n.* (-(ss)es, -(ss)e) will, testament; legacy, bequest; *ohne – sterben*, die intestate. **–erbe,** *m.* **–nehmer,** *m.* legatee. **–geber,** *m.* legator.

vermag, *see* **vermögen.**

vermahlen, *ir.v.a.* grind (down).

vermähl–en, 1. *v.a.* marry, give in marriage; (*fig.*) unite. 2. *v.r.* marry, get married (to), wed; *die –ten*, the bride and bridegroom, the bridal pair, newly-married couple. **–ung,** *f.* marriage, wedding. **–ungsfeier,** *f.* marriage *or* wedding ceremony.

vermahn–en, *v.a.* admonish, warn, exhort. **–ung,** *f.* admonition, exhortation.

vermaledei–en, *v.a.* curse, execrate.

vermasseln, *v.a.* (*sl.*) spoil beyond repair, do (*s.th.*) wrong, play the deuce with.

vermauern, *v.a.* wall in *or* up.

vermehr–en, *v.a.* & *r.* increase, multiply, augment, enlarge; propagate; *dies –t meinen Kummer*, this adds to my grief; *–te Auflage*, enlarged edition; *sich rasch –en*, breed rapidly. **–ung,** *f.* increase, augmentation, multiplication, propagation, reproduction. **–ungsorgane,** *n.pl.* reproductive organs. **–ungstrieb,** *m.* procreative instinct. **–ungszahl,** *f.* multiplier, factor (*Arith.*).

vermeid–en, *ir.v.a.* avoid, shun, evade, elude, escape (from), (*coll.*) shirk; *es läßt sich nicht –en*, it cannot be helped. **–bar, –lich,** *adj.* avoidable. **–ung,** *f.* avoidance, evasion; *bei –ung unserer Ungnade*, under pain of (incurring) our displeasure.

vermein–en, *v.a.* think, believe, consider, be of the opinion; imagine, suppose, presume, deem. **–tlich,** *adj.* supposed, presumed, alleged; presumptive, would-be, pretended, imaginary.

vermelden, *v.a.* (*einem etwas*) announce, notify, inform, send (*a p.*) word; *mit Respekt zu –*, with all due deference to you, saving your presence.

vermeng–en, 1. *v.a.* mingle, mix, blend; mix up, confuse; *er ist mit darein –t*, he is involved in *or* mixed up with that affair. 2. *v.r.* meddle (*mit*, with), be *or* get mixed up (with) a matter. **–ung,** *f.* mixture, medley; confusion.

vermenschlichen, *v.a.* represent in a human form; humanize; *die Gottheit –*, clothe Divinity with a human form.

Vermerk, *m.* (-(e)s, –e) observation, notice, note, entry. **–en,** *v.a.* observe, remark, note down, make *or* take a note of; *einem etwas übel –en*, take a th. amiss, take offence *or* umbrage at a th.

vermess–en, 1. *ir.v.a.* measure, take the measurement of; survey. 2. *v.r.* make a mistake in measuring; (*with Gen. or inf. with* zu) presume, venture, dare, have the audacity (to); *sich einer S.* (*Gen.*) *–en*, *sich –en etwas zu tun*, venture on a th., dare to undertake a th.; *sich zu viel –en*, be cocksure, take too much upon oneself. 3. *p.p.* & *adj.* daring, bold, presumptuous, rash, arrogant, impudent. **–enheit,** *f.* boldness, daring, audacity, overconfidence, presumptuousness, arrogance, impudence, insolence. **–entlich,** *adv.* audaciously, presumptuously, arrogantly. **–er,** *m.* surveyor. **–ung,** *f.* measuring; measurement; survey; mistake in measuring. **–ungskarte,** *f.* ordnance-survey map. **–ungskunde,** *f.* **–ungskunst,** *f.* surveying, geodesy.

vermiet–en, 1. *v.a.* let, lease, hire out; *Haus zu –en*, house to let; *Boot zu –en*, boat for hire. 2. *v.r.* (*bei einem*) enter (a p.'s) service; *solche Häuser –en sich leicht*, houses like these are easy to let. **–er,** *m.* landlord; hirer. **–ung,** *f.* letting, leasing, hiring (-out).

verminder–n, 1. *v.a.* lessen, diminish (*also Mus.*), decrease, reduce, abate; impair; *an Zahl –n*, reduce *or* decrease in number; *um die Hälfte –n*, reduce by half; *seine Kräfte –n*, impair one's strength. 2. *v.r.* grow less, decrease, decline, abate; *sein Eifer –t sich*, his zeal is abating. **–t,** *p.p.* & *adj.* lessened, decreased, reduced; *–te Terz*, diminished third (*Mus.*). **–ung,** *f.* lessening, diminution, decrease, reduction, abatement; decrement, depreciation.

verminen, *v.a.* & *n.* lay mines; mine (*a harbour, etc.*).

vermisch–en, 1. *v.a.* mix, mingle, blend; cross, interbreed; adulterate, alloy; *sich gut –en lassen*, blend well, amalgamate easily, go well together. 2. *v.r.* mix, mingle, blend with, breed, interbreed. **–t,** *p.p.* & *adj.* mixed, miscellaneous. **–ung,** *f.* mixture, blend, intermixture, adulteration, alloy(ing) (*of metals*); crossing *or* interbreeding (*of races*).

vermiss–en, 1. *v.a.* miss; *man –(ß)t ihn*, he is missing, he is missed, his absence is (greatly) felt. 2. *n.* missing; *schmerzliches –en*, deep regret. **–(ß)t,** *adj.* missing. **–(ß)te(r),** *m.* missing man.

vermitt–eln, 1. *v.n.* (*aux.* h.) mediate, intervene. 2. *v.a.* adjust, arrange (*a difference, etc.*); negotiate (*a peace, a loan, etc.*); establish; (*einem etwas*) bring about, facilitate, secure, procure (*for a p.*); *widerstreitende Ideen –eln*, reconcile conflicting ideas; *einen Widerspruch –eln*, reconcile a (seeming) contradiction; *–elnd eintreten*, intercede. **–els,** (*Austr. dial.*) **–elst,** *prep.* (*Gen.*) (*rare*) by means of, with the help of, through. **–(e)lung,** *f.* supplying, providing, procuring; mediation, agency, intercession, intervention, negotiation, adjustment (*of differences*); conveyance, transmission (*of sound*), exchange (*Tele.*); *durch jemands freundliche –(e)lung*, by a p.'s good offices *or* kind intervention. **–ler,** *m.* mediator, agent, go-between. **–(e)lungsbureau,** *n.* registry-office (*for servants*), **–(e)lungsgeschäft,** *n.* (commission)-agency. **–lungsklinke,** *f.* switchboard jack (*Tele.*). **–(e)lungsstelle,** *f.* (telephone) exchange; agency. **–(e)lungsvorschlag,** *m.* offer of mediation; proposal for a settlement. **–leramt,** *n.*, **–lerrolle,** *f.* task of an arbitrator *or* arbiter.

vermöbeln, (*coll.*) *v.a.* sell, turn s.th. into cash; sell at any price; waste; (*sl.*) thrash.
vermodern, *v.n.* (*aux.* s.) moulder, (fall into) decay, rot.
vermöge, *prep.* (*Gen.*) in *or* by virtue of, by dint of, in pursuance of, according to.
vermögen, 1. *ir.v.a.* be able (*to do*) *or* capable (*of doing*), have the power *or* capacity (*to do*); have influence (over), induce, prevail (upon); *ich will tun, was ich kann und vermag*, I will do all that lies in my power; *viel bei einem* –, have great influence with a p.; *viel über einen* –, have great influence over a p.; *wenn er es über sich vermag*, if he can bring himself to do it. 2. *n.* ability, power, capacity, faculty; means, fortune, wealth, riches, property; – *erwerben*, make a fortune; *alles, was in meinem* – *steht*, all that lies in my power; *nach bestem* –, to the best of my ability; *das geht über mein* –, that is beyond me *or* my power; *zu* – *kommen*, ccme into a fortune. **–d,** *pr.p. & adj.* capable, able; rich, well off, well-to-do, wealthy, affluent; powerful, influential. **–dheit,** *f.* affluence, wealth. **–sabgabe,** *f.* capital levy. **–sanfall,** *m.* succession to property. **–sbestand,** *m.*, **–sbetrag,** *m.* amount of property, assets. **–slos,** *adj.* impecunious. **–slosigkeit,** *f.* want of fortune, indigence. **–smasse,** *f.* estate. **–srecht,** *n.* law of property. **–srechtlich,** 1. *adj.* in right of one's fortune *or* property; *–srechtliche Ansprüche*, action for recovery of one's property. 2. *adv.* in money matters. **–ssteuer,** *f.* property-tax. **–sumstände,** *m.pl.*, **–sverhältnisse,** *n.pl.* financial position, means, resources. **–sverwalter,** *m.* administrator of an estate, trustee.
vermorscht, *adj.* mouldy, mouldering, rotten.
vermottet, *adj.* moth-eaten.
vermumm–en, *v.a.* wrap *or* muffle up; mask, disguise. **–ung,** *f.* masquerade, mummery.
vermut–en, 1. *v.a.* suppose, surmise, presume, imagine, conjecture, suspect; *nichts Arges –en*, suspect no harm *or* nothing wrong. 2. *n.* supposition, expectation; *meinem –en nach*, in my opinion, as I imagine, I suppose, (*coll.*) my guess is. **–lich,** *adj.* presumable, probable, likely. **–ung,** *f.* presumption (*Law*), supposition, conjecture, surmise, suspicion, guess(-work), (*sl.*) hunch; *gegen alle –ung*, contrary to all expectation; *aller –ung nach*, to all appearances; *das brachte ihn auf die –ung*, that gave him the idea. **–ungsweise,** *adv.* presumably, supposedly.
vernachlässig–en, *v.a.* neglect, disregard, ignore; slight. **–ung,** *f.* negligence; neglect (*einer S.* or *von einer S.*, of a th.).
vernageln, *v.a.* nail, nail up (*a crate*), nail down (*a lid*); *eine Kanone* –, spike a gun (*Mil.*); (*coll.*) (*wie*) *vernagelt sein*, be wooden-headed, dense, stupid *or* obtuse.
vernarben, *v.r. & n.* (*aux.* s.) heal up, scar over.
vernarr–en, *v.r.* become infatuated (*in*, with), (*coll.*) become crazy (over); *sie ist in das Kind –t*, she dotes on the child. **–theit,** *f.* infatuation.
vernaschen, *v.a.*; *sein Geld* –, spend *or* waste one's money on sweets.
vernebel–n, 1. *v.a.* cover with a smoke-screen, screen with smoke (*Mil.*). 2. *v.n.* (*aux.* s.) become wreathed in mist. **–ung,** *f.* (laying a) smoke-screen.
vernehm–en, 1. *ir.v.a.* perceive, become aware of; understand, learn, hear; examine, interrogate (*Law*); *vernimm mein Gebet!* hearken to my prayer!; *sich –en lassen*, express one's opinion, intimate, declare. 2. *v.r.*; *sich mit einem –en*, come to an understanding with a p. 3. *n.*; *dem –en nach*, according to report, from what one hears; *gutem –en nach ist er schon fort*, we have it on good authority that he is already gone; *das gute –en*, friendly terms, good understanding. **–bar,** *adj.*, *see* **–lich. –lassung,** *f.* (*Swiss dial.*) notification, promulgation. **–lich,** *adj.* audible, perceptible; distinct, clear, intelligible. **–lichkeit,** *f.* audibility, clarity, intelligibility. **–ung,** *f.* hearing, trial (*Law*); examination, interrogation, questioning. **–ungsfähig,** *adj.* fit to plead (*Law.*).
verneig–en, *v.r.* bow, curtsy. **–ung,** *f.* bow, curtsy, obeisance.
vernein–en, 1. *v.a.* deny, disavow, answer (*a question*) in the negative; contradict. 2. *v.n.* (*aux.* h.) reply in the negative, say no. **–end,** *pr.p. & adj.* negative; *–ende Antwort*, negative answer *or* reply. **–ung,** *f.* denial, contradiction, negation; negative (*Gram.*). **–ungssatz,** *m.* negative clause. **–ungswort,** *n.* negative.
vernicht–en, *v.a.* annihilate, destroy, demolish, exterminate, overthrow; disappoint (*hopes*); annul, cancel, nullify, declare null and void, revoke, abolish, quash, abrogate (*Law*). **–end,** *pr.p. & adj.* destructive, devastating; crushing, scathing. **–ung,** *f.* destruction, annihilation, extermination, demolition; abrogation, abolition. **–ungskampf,** *m.*, **–ungskrieg,** *m.* war of extermination, war to the knife. **–ungslager,** *n.* (*Nat. Soc.*) extermination camp.
vernickeln, *v.a.* nickel-plate.
Vernunft, *f.* reason, intellect, intelligence; understanding, judgement, discernment, common *or* good sense; – *annehmen*, listen to reason; *bei guter* – *sein*, be in one's senses; *die Jahre der* – *erreichen*, come to years of discretion; *gesunde* –, common sense; *einem* – *predigen*, plead with a p. to be reasonable; *das geht über die* or *alle* –, that goes beyond the bounds of reason; *einen zur* – *bringen*, bring a p. to his senses, make a p. listen to reason; *zur* – *kommen*, come to one's senses. **–begabt,** *adj.* reasonable, sensible. **–begriff,** *m.* rational idea. **–beweis,** *m.* rational proof. **–ehe,** *f.* prudential match, mariage de convenance. **–gemäß,** *adj.* reasonable, rational, logical. **–glaube,** *m.* rationalism. **–grund,** *m.* rational argument; *aus –gründen*, a priori (*Log.*). **–heirat,** *f.*, *see* **–ehe. –los,** *adj.* irrational, unreasonable, senseless, unreasoning. **–losigkeit,** *f.* irrationality. **–schluß,** *m.* syllogism. **–wesen,** *n.* rational being. **–widrig,** *adj.* unreasonable, irrational, illogical, ridiculous.
Vernünft–elei, *f.* (-en) sophistry, chicanery, casuistry, subtlety, quibbling, hair-splitting. **–eln,** *v.n.* (*aux.* h.) reason speciously, subtilize, (*coll.*) split hairs. **–ig,** *adj.* reasonable, sensible, rational, logical; wise, judicious; *–ige Wesen*, rational beings; *–iger Mann*, sensible *or* reasonable man; *–ig handeln*, act sensibly, reasonably, judiciously *or* wisely; *–ig reden*, talk sense. **–igerweise,** *adv.* from a rational point of view. **–igkeit,** *f.* reasonableness, rationality; good sense. **–ler,** *m.* sophist, casuist, quibbler, hair-splitter.
veröd–en, 1. *v.a.* lay waste, devastate. 2. *v.n.* (*aux.* s.) become waste, desolate *or* deserted. **–ung,** *f.* desolation; devastation; *–ung des Verkehrs*, stagnation of the market.
veröffentlich–en, *v.a.* publish, announce, advertise, make public; *ein Gesetz –en*, promulgate a law. **–ung,** *f.* publication; public announcement, promulgation.
verordn–en, *v.a.* order, prescribe; decree, enact; ordain, establish, institute; *einem Ruhe –en*, order a p. to rest *or* to take things easy, prescribe rest for s.o. (*Med.*). **–ete(r),** *m.* delegate, commissioner. **–ung,** *f.* prescription (*Med.*); decree, ordinance, regulation, order, enactment, precept; ordination, nomination, appointment, establishment, institution. **–ungsblatt,** *n.* official list, gazette. **–ungsgemäß,** *adj.*, **–ungsmäßig,** *adj.* as decreed *or* prescribed, by order *or* appointment.
verpacht–en, *v.a.* let, lease, farm out. **–ung,** *f.* farming out, letting (out) on lease.
verpack–en, *v.a.* pack (up), wrap up; (*coll.*) *hart –t*, dull of comprehension, thick- *or* block-headed. **–er,** *m.* packer. **–ung,** *f.* packing, wrapping; loading; packing (material), wrapping (paper). **–ungsgewicht,** *n.* tare.
verpäppeln, *v.a.* pamper, spoil (*a child*), (*coll.*) (molly-)coddle.
verpassen, *v.a.* let slip (*an opportunity*), miss (*a train*), pass (*cards, etc.*); try on, fit on (*clothes, etc.*), adjust; (*sl.*) *einem eins* or *eine* (*Ohrfeige*) –, give s.o. a box on the ears.
verpatzen, *v.a.* (*sl.*) spoil, bungle, botch, make a mess of.
verpest–en, *v.a.* pollute, contaminate, taint, defile, infect, poison. **–ung,** *f.* pollution, defilement, infection.

verpetzen, *v.a.* inform against, tell tales (*in school*).
verpfänd–en, *v.a.* pledge, pawn, mortgage; raise money by bottomry (*Naut.*); *sein Wort –en*, give *or* pledge one's word, promise faithfully. **–ung,** *f.* pawning, mortgaging, pledging; pledge.
verpflanz–en, *v.a.* transplant. **–ung,** *f.* transplanting, transplantation.
verpfleg–en, *v.a.* feed, cater for, provide for, board (*a p.*), provision (*an army*); tend, nurse (*an invalid*). **–ung,** *f.* feeding, board, food, food-supply; maintenance, support, alimentation; provisioning, messing, rations (*Mil.*); nursing, diet (*Med.*); *gute –ung*, good table *or* food; *Wohnung mit –ung*, board and lodging. **–ungsamt,** *n.* food office; commissariat (*Mil.*). **–ungsbeamte(r),** *m.* commissariat officer (*Mil.*), Ministry of Food official. **–ungsentschädigung,** *f.* maintenance allowance, board-wages (*of servants*). **–ungsgeld,** *n.pl.* cost of maintenance, charge for board, maintenance allowance. **–ungskolonne,** *f.* supply-column (*Mil.*). **–ungsmittel,** *n.pl.* victuals, provisions. **–ungsstärke,** *f.* ration strength (*Mil.*). **–ungszuschuß,** *m.* cost of living bonus.
verpflicht–en, 1. *v.a.* bind, pledge, engage, oblige; *einen eidlich –en*, bind a p. on oath; *zu Dank –en*, lay under an obligation; *wir sind Ihnen sehr zu Dank –et*, we are greatly indebted to you; *zu pünktlicher Zahlung –et*, liable for prompt payment. 2. *v.r.* (*zu etwas*) bind *or* commit o.s., engage (*to do a th.*). **–ung,** *f.* obligation, duty, responsibility; engagement, commitment; *seinen –ungen nachkommen*, fulfil one's obligations, (*C.L.*) meet one's liabilities; *–ung(en) haben gegen*, be under an obligation to.
verpfuschen, *v.a.* bungle, botch, make a mess of, wreck (*one's life, etc.*).
verpich–en, *v.a.* (coat with) pitch *or* tar, stop with pitch; (*coll.*) *auf etwas –t sein*, be intent *or* bent on a th., (*sl.*) be stuck on a th.
verpimpeln, *v.a.* & *r.* (*coll.*) coddle, pamper; muffle up (*in too many clothes*).
verplappern, *v.r.* (*coll.*) betray, o.s., give o.s. away, blab, let the cat out of the bag.
verplaudern, 1. *v.a.* chatter (*time, etc.*) away. 2. *v.r.*, *see* **verplappern.**
verplempern, 1. *v.a.* fritter away, squander, waste foolishly. 2. *v.r.* waste one's opportunities, make a mess of one's life, throw o.s. away on a (*socially inferior or worthless*) woman, marry beneath o.s.
verpön–en, *v.a.* (*archaic*) forbid, prohibit. **–t,** *adj.* taboo(ed), despised, in bad taste.
verprassen, *v.a.* waste in riotous living, dissipate.
verproviantieren, *v.a.* supply, victual, provision.
verprozessieren, *v.a.* squander in litigation.
verprügeln, *v.a.* thrash soundly.
verpuffen, 1. *v.a.* throw away, scatter to the winds, waste. 2. *v.n.* (*aux.* s.) detonate, explode, fulminate, deflagrate, decrepitate; (*coll.*) peter out, be lost (upon), have no effect (on), fall flat (*as a joke*).
verpulvern, *v.a* (*coll.*) squander, waste.
verpumpen, *v.a.* (*sl.*) lend, give on credit.
verpupp–en, *v.r.* & *n.* pupate, change into a chrysalis; (*coll.*) retire into one's shell. **–ung,** *f.* pupation.
verpusten, *v.r.* (*sl.*) recover one's breath, get one's wind back.
Verputz, *m.* plaster, roughcast. **–en,** *v.a.* plaster, rough-cast; squander on finery; (*coll.*) gobble up, polish off; *das kann ich nicht –en*, I cannot stomach *or* stand that.
verqualmt, *p.p.* & *adj.* filled *or* thick with smoke.
verquasen, *v.a.* (*dial.*) squander.
verquellen, *v.n.* (*aux.* s.) swell with the damp, warp, get warped.
verquer, *adv.* (*coll.*) *mir geht das –*, that upsets my plans *or* puts a spoke in my wheel.
verquick–en, *v.a.* amalgamate (with), mix up with. **–ung,** *f.* amalgamation, fusion.
verquisten, *v.a.* (*dial.*), *see* **verquasen.**
verquollen, *p.p.* (*of* verquellen) & *adj.* swollen, bloated (*of a face*), warped (*of wood*).
verramm–eln, –en, *v.a.* ram tight; bar, barricade, block up. **–(e)lung, –ung,** *f.* barricading.
verramschen, *v.a.* (*sl.*) sell dirt-cheap.
verrannt, *p.p.* (*of* verrennen) & *adj.* stubborn, obstinate, prejudiced; – *sein in etwas*, be stubbornly attached to a th. *or* (*sl.*) stuck to a th.; be wedded to (*an opinion.*) **–heit,** *f.* stubbornness, bigotry.
Verrat, *m.* treason; treachery; betrayal (of); – *an einem begehen*, betray a p.; – *militärischer Geheimnisse*, disclosure of military secrets. **–en,** 1. *ir.v.a.* betray, divulge, disclose, reveal; give evidence of, manifest; *das Vaterland dem Feind –en*, betray one's country to the enemy; *es verrät eine Meisterhand*, it reveals *or* betrays the hand of a master; *seine Bücher –en große Belesenheit*, his books give evidence of wide reading; *ein Geheimnis –en*, betray *or* divulge a secret. 2. *v.r.* betray *or* commit o.s.
Verräter, *m.* (-s, –) traitor, betrayer, informer; *er ist ein – an seinem Vaterlande*, he is a traitor to his country. **–ei,** *f.* treason; treachery. **–isch,** *adj.* treacherous, treasonable, traitorous; faithless, perfidious; revealing. **–ischerweise,** *adv.* treacherously, traitorously.
verrauch–en, 1. *v.a.* spend (*time, etc.*) in smoking *or* (*money*) on tobacco. 2. *v.n.* (*aux.* s.) evaporate, go up in smoke; (*fig.*) subside, pass away, blow over. **–t,** *p.p.* & *adj.* smoky, thick with smoke; smoke-dried, black with smoke. **–ung,** *f.* evaporation.
verräuchern, *v.a.* cure, smoke; fill *or* blacken with smoke; *ein Zimmer –*, fumigate a room.
verrauschen, *v.n.* (*aux.* s.) (*fig.*) die away, subside; pass away, roll on (*of time*).
verrechn–en, 1. *v.a.* reckon up, charge (to account). 2. *v.r.* make a mistake in one's accounts; be mistaken, miscalculate; *er hat sich um 20 Mark –et*, he is 20 marks out in his accounts. **–ung,** *f.* charging to account, settlement of an account; reckoning up, calculation; compensation (*Law*); error in calculation, miscalculation. **–ungsabkommen,** *n.* clearing. **–ungsscheck,** *m.* crossed cheque, non-negotiable cheque. **–ungsstelle,** *f.* clearing-house.
verrecken, *v.n.* (*aux.* s.) (*vulg.*) die, turn up one's toes, kick the bucket; (*vulg.*) *nicht ums –*, not on your life.
verred–en, 1. *v.a.* (*usually neg.*) gainsay, disdain, forswear, abjure; *ich will das nicht –en*, I will not gainsay that. 2. *v.r.* make a slip of the tongue; betray o.s., let s.th. slip out indiscreetly. **–ung,** *f.* slip of the tongue, indiscreet remark.
verregnen, *v.a.* spoil by rain.
verreiben, *ir.v.a.* grind *or* rub well; rub away; rub *or* grind down, triturate.
verreisen, 1. *v.n.* (*aux.* s.) go on a journey, set out (*nach*, for); *wie lange ist er verreist?* how long has he been away (from home)? 2. *v.a.* spend (*money or time*) travelling.
verreißen, *v.a.* (*coll.*) criticize harshly, pull to pieces, pick holes (in), run down.
verrenk–en, *v.a.* dislocate, sprain, put out of joint; *sich* (*Dat.*) *den Hals –en*, crane one's neck (*with curiosity*). **–ung,** *f.* dislocation, sprain.
verrennen, *v.r.* (*in with Acc.*) be prejudiced, be obstinately wrong-headed (about); *sich in eine Sackgasse –*, run one's head against a brick wall.
verricht–en, *v.a.* do, perform, execute, achieve, accomplish, acquit o.s. of; *seine Andacht –en*, perform one's devotions; *Arbeit –en*, do a job, carry out a task; *einen Auftrag –en*, execute *or* carry out a commission; *seine Dienste –en*, officiate, be on duty (*of persons*); work well, answer the purpose (*of things*); *sein Gebet –en*, say one's prayers; *Geschäfte –en*, transact business; *seine Notdurft –en*, ease nature, relieve o.s. **–ung,** *f.* doing, performance, execution; accomplishment, achievement, discharge (*of business*); work, action; function, *tägliche –ungen*, daily work, routine jobs; *ich wünsche Ihnen gute –ung*, I wish you much success, I hope everything goes off well; *ich bin mit seiner –ung zufrieden*, I am satisfied with his achievement.
verriegeln, *v.a.* bolt, bar, lock, latch; cut off, encircle (*Mil.*).
verringer–n, 1. *v.a.* diminish, lessen, reduce, attenuate; mitigate, extenuate, (*coll.*) cut down. 2. *v.r.* diminish, decrease, grow less. **–ung,** *f.* decrease, reduction, attenuation; extenuation.

verrinnen, *ir.v.n.* (*aux.* s.) run off *or* out, run *or* pass away, elapse, fly (*of time*).
verröcheln, *v.a.* (*aux.* h.) breathe one's last, expire.
verroh–en, *v.n.* become brutal *or* savage. **–ung,** *f.* brutalization.
verrollen, 1. *v.n.* roll away, die away. 2. *v.r.* (*coll.*) toddle off.
verrost–en, *v.n.* (*aux.* s.) rust. **–et,** *p.p.* & *adj.* rusty, rusted. **–ung,** *f.* rusting; rust.
verrotten, *v.n.* (*aux.* s.) rot, corrode, decay.
verrucht, *adj.* infamous, vile, atrocious, heinous, rascally, wicked, nefarious. **–heit,** *f.* infamy, atrociousness, wickedness, villainy, atrocity.
verrück–en, *v.a.* displace, shift, remove; disarrange, derange, disturb, confuse, unsettle; *jemandes Plan* or *einem den Plan –en,* upset *or* frustrate a p.'s plan; *einem den Kopf –en,* turn a p.'s head. **–t,** *p.p.* & *adj.* mad, insane, deranged, crazy, (*coll.*) cracked, foolish; *er ist –t auf sie,* he is crazy *or* dotty over her; *du bist wohl –t,* you're off your head. **–te(r),** *m.* lunatic, madman. **–theit,** *f.* mental derangement, madness; crazy, mad *or* foolish action. **–ung,** *f.* displacement, shift; derangement.
Verruf, *m.* (-(e)s, -e) obloquy, boycott; ill repute; *in – bringen,* bring into discredit; *in – sein* (*kommen*), be in (fall into) disrepute, get into bad odour, be boycotted. **–en,** 1. *ir.v.a.* decry, disparage, condemn; give a bad name to; withdraw (*coin*) from circulation; discredit. 2. *p.p.* & *adj.* notorious, infamous, disreputable, in disrepute. **–ung,** *f.* defamation, depreciation, disparagement, disapproval, censure, contumely, odium.
verrühren, *v.a.* whip, beat up (*eggs, etc.*).
verrußen, *v.a.* & *n.* become sooty, sooted *or* smoked.
Vers, *m.* (-es, -e) verse, poetry; line (*of verse*); strophe, stanza; verse (*of the Bible*); *in –e bringen,* put into verse; *ich kann mir keinen – daraus* (or *darauf*) *machen,* I cannot make head or tail of it; *–e schmieden,* hammer out verses, versify. **–abschnitt,** *m.* hemistich. **–art,** *f.* metre, verse form. **–bau,** *m.* versification, metrical structure. **–einschnitt,** *m.* caesura. **–fuß,** *m.* (metrical) foot. **–kunst,** *f.* (art of) versification; poetic art. **–künstler,** *m.* versifier, rhymester, poetaster. **–lehre,** *f.* prosody, metrics. **–machen,** *n.* versification, rhyming. **–macher,** *m.*, *see* **–künstler. –maß,** *n.* metre; rhythm; *nach dem –maße lesen,* scan. **–messung,** *f.* scanning, scansion. **–überschreitung,** *f.* enjambement. **–weise,** *adv.* in verse; verse by verse. **–zeile,** *f.* metrical line, line of poetry, verse.
versacken, *v.n.* (*aux.* s.) sink, go down (*of a ship*); become blocked, make no headway; be ditched, get bogged down; be overdue.
versag–en, 1. *v.a.* (*einem etwas*) deny, refuse; (*in past tense*) have promised *or* granted, be engaged (*i.e. implying refusal now*); *ihm den nächsten Tanz –en,* refuse (to grant) him the next dance; *sie hat den nächsten Tanz bereits –t,* she has already promised the next dance, she is engaged for the next dance; *die Beine –en mir den Dienst,* my legs fail me *or* refuse to carry me; *dieses Glück ist mir –t,* this happiness is denied to me; *sich* (*Dat.*) *eine S. –en,* deny o.s. a th., deprive o.s. of a th., forgo a th.; *ich bin schon* (*anderwärts*) *–t,* I am engaged already (elsewhere); *die Stelle war schon –t, als er sich meldete,* the appointment had been made when he applied for it; *sie ist* (*bereits*) *–t,* she is (already) promised in marriage, she is engaged. 2. *v.n.* (*aux.* h.) fail, fail to work, break down, miss fire; *sie haben –t,* they have failed *or* disappointed, they have not come up to expectations. 3. *n.* failure, breakdown. **–er,** *m.* misfire, breakdown; failure, unsuccessful person; blank (*lottery ticket*); (*sl.*) flop. **–ung,** *f.* refusal, denial.
Versalbuchstabe, *m.* (-n. -n *or* Versalien) capital letter, initial (*Typ.*).
versalzen, *v.a,* (*p.p.* versalzt) oversalt; (*fig.*) (*p.p.* versalzen) *einem ein Vernügen –,* spoil *or* mar a p.'s pleasure; *einem die Suppe –,* I will make it hot for him, I will spoil his little games.
versamm–eln, 1. *v.a.* assemble, bring together, gather, collect; convoke, convene; *die Truppen –eln,* rally the troops; *zu seinen Vätern –elt werden,* be gathered to one's fathers. 2. *v.r.* meet, assemble, come together. **–lung,** *f.* assembly, gathering, meeting, congress, convention, convocation; company, collection, congregation, concourse; *eine –lung sprengen,* break up a meeting. **–lungsfreiheit,** *f.* right of assembly. **–lungshaus,** *n.* assembly rooms, meeting-house. **–lungsort,** *m.*, **–lungsplatz,** *m.* meeting-place, assembly point, rendezvous. **–lungsrecht,** *n.*, *see* **–lungsfreiheit, –lungsschutz,** *m.* (guard for the) protection of a meeting. **–lungszimmer,** *n.* assembly hall; greenroom (*Theat.*).
Versand, *m.* dispatch, forwarding, conveyance; shipping, shipment, export(ation). **–artikel,** *m.* article for export, (*pl.*) export goods, exports. **–bereit,** *adj.* ready for dispatch. **–bier,** *n.* beer for export. **–fertig,** *adj.*, *see* **–bereit. –geschäft,** *n.* mail-order house. **–kosten,** *f.pl.* forwarding costs, delivery charges. **–rechnung,** *f.* bill for delivery. **–spesen,** *f.pl.*, *see* **–kosten. –vorschriften,** *f.pl.* forwarding-instructions.
versand–en 1. *v.a.* cover *or* fill up *or* choke with sand. 2. *v.r.* & *n.* (*aux.* s.) become covered *or* choked up with sand, silt up; (*fig.*) get stuck, break down, make no headway. **–ung,** *f.* silting, choking with sand.
Versatz, *m.* pledging, pawning; rubble, refuse (*Min.*); *in – geben,* pledge, pawn. **–amt,** *n.*, **–haus,** *n.* pawn-shop, loan-bank. **–mauer,** *f.* partition-wall, embankment (*Min.*). **–stück,** *n.* movable scenery, set (*Theat.*). **–ung,** *f.* pledge.
versauern, 1. *v.n.* (*aux.* s.) turn sour; (*fig.*) get rusty *or* stale (*of the mind*), vegetate; become moody *or* morose.
versäuern, *v.a.* acidify, sour; spoil, embitter.
versaufen, 1. *ir.v.a.* (*vulg.*) waste (*time, etc.*) drinking, squander (*money*) on drink. 2. *v.n.* (*aux.* s.) (*coll.*) drown (*cf.* ersaufen). *versoffen, p.p.* & *adj,* drunken, given to hard drinking, beery (*nose, voice, etc.*); (*vulg.*) *versoffner Kerl,* drunkard, toper.
versäum–en, *v.a.* neglect, omit, miss, let slip; *den Appell –en,* be absent at roll-call; *ich habe keine einzige Stunde –t,* I have not missed a single lesson; *den Zug –en,* miss the train. **–nis,** *f.* (-se) & *n.* (-ses, -se) neglect, omission; failure to appear, late arrival; loss of time, delay. **–nisurteil,** *n.* judgement by default (*Law*). **–ung,** *f.* neglect, omission, absence.
verschachern, *v.a.* sell off, barter away.
verschaff–en, *v.a.* (*einem etwas*) get, obtain, secure, procure (s.th. for s.o.); supply, provide (s.o. with s.th.); *sich* (*Dat.*) *Arbeit –en,* find work; *was –t mir die Ehre Ihres Besuches?* to what do I owe the pleasure of your visit? *sich* (*Dat.*) *Gehör –en,* obtain a hearing; *sich* (*Dat.*) *Geld –en,* raise money; *sich* (*Dat.*) *Geltung –en,* secure recognition; *sich* (*Dat.*) *Genugtuung –en,* obtain satisfaction; *sich* (*Dat.*) *Gewißheit –en,* reassure o.s.; *dies wird Ihnen Linderung –en,* this will give you relief; *einem Recht –en,* see that justice is done to a p.; *sich* (*Dat.*) *selbst Recht –en,* take the law into one's own hands. **–ung,** *f.* supply, provision.
verschal–en, *v.a.* case (in), board, plank *or* box in, fish (*a mast*) (*Naut.*), cover with boards *or* planks. **–ung,** *f.* planking, boarding, revetment; covering, casing, form, mould, fairing, cowling.
verschallen, *ir.v.n.* (*aux.* s.) die away (*of sound*); be forgotten, sink into oblivion. *verschollen, p.p.* & *adj.* lost sight of, forgotten missing; *er ist verschollen,* he has disappeared *or* never been heard of again, he is presumed dead; *verschollenes Schiff,* missing vessel; *in verschollenen Jahrhunderten,* in time long past.
verschämt, *adj.* bashful, modest; ashamed, shamefaced, abashed, confused; *–e Arme,* deserving poor. **–heit,** *f.* bashfulness, modesty, confusion.
verschandel–n, *v.a.* (*coll.*) ruin, disfigure. **–ung,** *f.* vandalism.
verschanz–en, 1. *v.a.* entrench, fortify. 2. *v.r.* entrench o.s., (*fig.*) shelter *or* take up a position (behind), **–t,** *p.p.* & *adj.* secure, dug in. **–ung,** *f.* entrenchment, fortification, earthworks, trenches.

verschärf-en, *v.a.* heighten, sharpen, intensify, aggravate, make worse; tighten up (*regulations, etc.*). **-ung,** *f.* increase, intensification, sharpening, tightening up.

verscharren, *v.a.* bury secretly *or* hurriedly, cover with earth.

verschäumen, *v.n.* (*aux.* s.) turn into foam, vanish in spray.

verscheiden, 1. *ir.v.n.* (*aux.* s.) (*Poet.*) pass away, die, expire. 2. *n.* death, decease; *am – sein, im – liegen,* be on the point of death.

verschenken, *v.a.* give away, make a present of; *sein Herz –,* give one's heart, bestow one's affections; *Bier –,* sell *or* serve beer.

verscherz-en, 1. *v.a.* spend *or* pass (*time*) in joking; *sich* (*Dat.*) *etwas -en,* lose *or* forfeit a th. (frivolously); *sein Glück -en,* frivolously throw away one's chance of happiness; *-te Jugend,* youth spent in frivolity. 2. *n.,* **-ung,** *f.* loss, forfeiture.

verscheuchen, *v.a.* chase *or* drive off, scare away; (*fig.*) banish.

verschick-en, *v.a.* send out (*invitations, etc.*), evacuate, send away (*into the country, etc.*); forward, dispatch, transport; deport (*a criminal*). **-ung,** *f.* evacuation; forwarding, dispatch; transportation, deportation.

verschieb-en, 1. *ir.v.a.* move out of place, remove, shift, displace, disarrange; postpone, defer, delay, (*coll.*) put off; shunt (*Railw.*); sell on *or* through the black-market; *verschobenes Viereck,* lozenge (*Math.*). 2. *v.r.* get out of place. **-bar,** *adj.* sliding, displaceable. **-ebahnhof,** *m.* shunting *or* marshalling yard (*Railw.*). **-egleis,** *n.* siding (*Railw.*). **-ung,** *f.* displacement, shifting; slip, shift, fluctuation, dislocation; delay, procrastination; illicit sale; transference (*Psych.*). **-ungsstrom,** *m.* displacement current (*Elec.*).

verschieden, 1. *p.p.* (*of* verscheiden) (*Poet.*) deceased, dead, departed. 2. *adj.* different, differing, distinct (from); diverse, unlike; (*pl.*) sundry, various, divers; *himmelweit –,* as different as day from night *or* as chalk from cheese; *die Anlagen sind –,* dispositions differ; *-es zu tun haben,* have various jobs to do; (*coll.*) *da hört* (*sich denn*) *doch -es auf!* that is really too much. **-artig,** *adj.* varied, various; heterogeneous, dissimilar. **-erlei,** *indec. adj.* of various kinds, sundry, divers. **-farbig,** *adj.* variegated, parti-coloured, motley. **-heit,** *f.* difference, diversity, disparity, variation, variety, dissimilarity, discrepancy. **-tlich,** 1. *adj.* different, several, repeated. 2. *adv.* at (different) times, repeatedly, more than once, occasionally.

verschießen, 1. *ir.v.a.* fire off, discharge, use up, expend (*ammunition*); (*dial.*) forget, do wrong; *sein Pulver –,* (*fig.*) try everything in vain, come to the end of one's tether. 2. *v.r.* use all *or* exhaust one's ammunition; (*coll.*) *sich in einen –,* fall madly in love with a p. 3. *v.n.* (*aux.* s.) fade, discolour, become discoloured, lose colour; *nicht -d,* non-fading, fast.

verschiff-en, *v.a.* ship, send *or* transport by water; export. **-ung,** *f.* shipping, shipment, exportation.

verschimmel-n, *v.n.* (*aux.* s.) get *or* go mouldy. **-ung,** *f.* mould, mouldiness.

verschimpfieren, *v.a.* (*coll.*) revile, disparage (*a p.*); disfigure (*a th.*).

Verschiß, *m.* (*Studs. sl.*) ill-repute, bad odour.

verschlacken, *v.r.* & *n.* (*aux.* s.) scorify, be reduced to dross *or* slag.

verschlafen, 1. *ir.v.a.* spend *or* pass in sleeping, miss *or* lose by sleeping; sleep off (*effects of alcohol, etc.*). 2. *v.r.* oversleep o.s. 3. *p.p.* & *adj.* sleepy, drowsy. **-heit,** *f.* sleepiness, drowsiness.

Verschlag, *m.* (-(e)s, ⸚e) wooden partition; compartment, room partitioned off, shed; (*dial.*) crate, box. **-en,** 1. *ir.v.a.* fasten with nails, nail up, board up, board off, partition off; nail badly, spoil with hammering; mishit, knock too far; make cowed (*by punishment*); drive (*a ship*) off *or* out of its course *or* on to the shore *or* ashore; take the chill off; *viele Nägel -en,* waste many nails; *mit Nägeln -en,* stud with nails, nail; *mit Brettern -en,* board (up); *ein Zimmer -en,* partition off a room; *den Ball -en,* lose a ball, knock a ball out of bounds; *ein Pferd -en,* shoe a horse badly; *der Sturm verschlug uns nach Indien,* the storm drove us to the coast of India; *eine Stelle in einem Buche -en,* lose one's place in a book; *sich* (*Dat.*) *etwas -en,* lose *or* miss through error *or* carelessness; *sich* (*Dat.*) *die Kunden -en,* drive away customers; *es verschlägt mir die Rede* or *Sprache,* words fail me; *es verschlug mir die Luft* or *den Atem,* I caught my breath. 2. *v.n.* (*aux.* s.) be *or* become lukewarm. 3. *impers.* (*aux.* h.) (*with Dat.*) (*only in negative and interrogative sentences*) avail, be of use, matter; *was verschlägt's?* what does it matter? *das verschlägt nichts,* that does not matter (at all *or* in the least); *was verschlägt Ihnen das?* what is that to you? *nichts will bei ihm -en,* nothing has any effect on him; *es will nichts -en,* it will be no good, it will be of no use, it will not do. 4. *p.p.* & *adj.* cunning, crafty, sly; tepid, lukewarm. **-enheit,** *f.* slyness, craftiness, subtlety, cunning. **-wagen,** *m.* crate car, cattle truck.

verschlammen, *v.n.* (*aux.* s.) get filled *or* choked with mud, silt up, become bogged up.

verschlämmen, 1. *v.a.* fill, choke *or* cover with mud. 2. *v.r.* get filled with mud, become blocked with sludge.

verschlampen, 1 *v.a.* (*coll.*) lose, forget, ruin through neglect, take no care of. 2. *v.n.* become slovenly, neglect o.s.

verschlechter-n, 1. *v.a.* impair, make worse, spoil. 2. *v.r.* get worse, worsen, deteriorate, degenerate. **-ung,** *f.* deterioration, degradation, degeneration; exacerbation.

verschleier-n, *v.a.* veil, mask conceal; palliate, gloss over; screen (*an attack*); (*coll.*) cook, doctor (*an account*). **-t,** *adj.* hazy, overcast (*sky*), husky (*voice*), veiled. **-ung,** *f.* veiling, masking, screening; camouflage, concealment.

verschleifen, *reg.* & *ir.v.a.* slur (*notes*) (*Mus.*).

verschleim-en, 1. *v.a.* choke with phlegm *or* mucus; coat, fur (*the tongue*); *ein Gewehr -en,* foul *or* choke up a gun. 2. *v.r.* & *n.* (*aux.* s.) be choked with slime *or* phlegm, become slimy *or* congested; foul (*of guns*); *-te Zunge,* foul *or* coated tongue.

[1]**Verschleiß,** *m.* (-es, -e) (*Austr. dial.*) retail trade. **-en,** *v.a.* retail. **-er,** *m.* retailer, retail dealer. **-spanne,** *f.* margin of profit. **-stelle,** *f.* retail shop *or* stall, (*usually*) newspaper *or* tobacco kiosk.

[2]**Verschleiß,** *m.* abrasion, wear and tear. **-en,** 1. *ir.v.n.* & *r.* wear out, get worn out. 2. *v.a.* wear (out). **-festigkeit,** *f.* abrasion resistance, resistance to wear and tear.

verschlemmen, *v.a.* squander on food and drink.

verschlepp-en, 1. *v.a.* carry off, deport; spread (*disease*); protract, draw out, delay, postpone, put off. **-ung,** *f.* removing, carrying off, deportation; spreading, spread (*of disease*); delay, procrastination, obstruction. **-ungspolitik,** *f.* policy of obstruction (*Parl.*), (*Amer.*) filibuster.

verschleuder-n, *v.a.* waste, squander, throw away, dissipate; sell below cost, sell at a loss, sell off (dirt) cheap, flood the market with, dump. **-ung,** *f.* squandering, selling below cost, dumping.

verschließ-en, 1. *ir.v.a.* close, shut, lock, put under lock and key; plug, block, obstruct, blockade (*a port, etc.*); hide (*feeling*); *ein Geheimnis in sich -en,* keep a secret to o.s.; *gegen jemanden sein Herz -en,* hide one's feelings from a p., steel one's heart against a p. 2. *v.r.*; *sich in sich selbst -en,* turn in on o.s., become wrapped up in o.s.; *sich einer S. -en,* refuse to have anything to do with a th., stand *or* keep aloof from a th. **-muskel,** *m.* sphincter muscle (*Anat.*).

verschlimmbessern, *v.a.* make worse instead of better.

verschlimmer-n, 1. *v.a.* make worse, do harm to, aggravate. 2. *v.r.* & *n.* (*aux.* s.) deteriorate, get worse. **-ung,** *f.* change for the worse, aggravation, deterioration, exacerbation.

[1]**verschling-en,** *ir.v.a.* swallow (down *or* up), gulp down, devour; (*fig.*) drink in; *das -t viel Geld,* that swallows up *or* runs away with a lot of money; *ich wollte, die Erde verschlänge ihn,* I wish the earth would open and swallow him; *ein Buch begierig -en,*

devour a book greedily; *einen mit den Augen –en*, stare at a p. open-mouthed.

[2]**verschling-en,** 1. *ir.v.a.* twist, interlace, (inter-) twine, entwine, entangle; *verschlungene Pfade*, tortuous paths; *verschlungene Buchstaben*, intertwined *or* interwoven letters. 2. *v.r.* become interlaced *or* entangled, be inextricably mixed, blend. **–ung,** *f.* entwining, interlacing; festoon; intricacy, maze.

verschlissen, p.p. (*of* verschleißen) & *adj.* worn (out), threadbare.

verschlossen, *p.p.* (*of* verschließen) locked up, closed, shut; (*fig.*) reserved, uncommunicative, taciturn; *das bleibt mir –*, that remains a mystery to me; *–er Brief*, sealed letter; *–er Mensch*, reserved *or* taciturn person; *hinter –en Türen*, behind closed doors. **–heit,** *f.* reserve, taciturnity.

verschlucken, 1. *v.a.* swallow, imbibe, absorb (*Chem.*); slur over (*one's words*). 2. *v.r.* swallow the wrong way, choke; *ich habe mich –t*, something has gone down the wrong way.

verschlungen, *see* **verschlingen.**

Verschluß, *m.* (-(ss)es, ⸚(ss)e) closing, locking, occlusion; closure; lock, clasp, seal, stopper, plug, fastener, fastening; breech (mechanism) (*Artil.*), lock, bolt, breech-block (*of gun*); locker, cover; shutter (*Phot.*); *unter –*, under lock and key; *Waren in – legen*, bond goods; *aus dem – nehmen*, take out of bond. **–hahn,** *m.* stopcock. **–laut,** *m.* stop, plosive (*Phonet.*). **–schraube,** *f.* locking screw. **–stück,** *n.* plug, stopper, lid, operculum (*Bot.*, *Zool.*), breech-block. **–vorrichtung,** *f.* locking device.

verschlüsseln, *v.a.* encode, encipher.

verschmacht-en, *v.n.* (*aux.* s.) languish, pine away, faint, die (*vor*, of); *vor Durst –en*, be parched with *or* dying of thirst; *ich –e vor Hitze*, I am suffocated with (the) heat; *einen –en lassen*, let a p. die of thirst. **–ung,** *f.* languishing existence, slow death.

verschmäh-en, *v.a.* disdain, scorn, despise, reject; *–te Liebe*, unrequited love.

verschmälern, *v.a.* narrow, constrict, diminish.

verschmausen, *v.a.* (*coll.*) eat up with relish.

verschmelz-en, 1. *reg.* & *ir.v.a.* melt, smelt, fuse; blend, merge, amalgamate; *mit etwas* or *in etwas –en*, blend *or* run into one another; *gut verschmolzene Farben*, well-blended colours. 2. *v.n.* (*aux.* s.) melt, fuse; blend, coalesce, merge. **–ung,** *f.* melting, fusion, smelting, blending, coalescence, (*fig.*) merging, merger, amalgamation.

verschmerzen, *v.a.* console o.s. for, get over; put up with, make the best of.

verschmieren, 1. *v.a.* smear over, daub, stop up, lute, glue up; *Papier –en*, cover paper with scribble. 2. *v.r.* fog, become blurred.

verschmitzt, *adj.* wily, artful, cunning, crafty, sly. **–heit,** *f.* craftiness, cunning, slyness, wiliness.

verschmutzen, *v.n.* dirty, soil.

verschnappen, *v.r.* make a slip of the tongue, say a word too many, let the cat out of the bag, give the show away.

verschnauben, verschnaufen, *v.r.* & *n.* (*aux.* s.) recover one's breath.

verschneiden, *ir.v.a.* cut away, cut off, cut down; cut badly, spoil in cutting; clip, prune, lop; castrate, geld; reduce, dilute, adulterate, blend, mix; *einem die Flügel –*, clip a p.'s wings; *6 Meter Stoff zu einem Kleide –*, use *or* cut up 6 metres of material for a dress.

verschneien, *v.n.* be(come) covered with snow *or* snowed up.

Verschnitt, *m.* blend, adulteration. **–en,** *p.p.* & *adj.* castrated; badly cut; *–ener Hahn*, capon; *–ener Stier*, bullock; *–enes Tier*, gelding; *–enes Kleidungsstück*, misfit (*article of clothing*); *–enes Öl*, blended oil. **–ene(r),** *m.* eunuch, *see* **verschneiden. –mittel,** *n.* adulterant, diluent, reducing agent. **–wein,** *m.* blended *or* adulterated wine.

verschnörkeln, *v.a.* adorn *or* disfigure with flourishes.

verschnupf-en, *v.a.* have a cold in the head *or* a thick cold, be stuffed up with a cold; (*fig.*) *das –t ihn*, that annoys, rattles *or* nettles him; (*coll.*) *das hat mich –t*, I was put out by it.

verschnüren, *v.a.* cord, lace *or* tie up.

verschollen, *p.p.* (*see* **verschallen**) & *adj.* missing, lost, forgotten. **–heit,** *f.* disappearance; prolonged absence. **–heitserklärung,** *f.* presumption of death.

verschon-en, *v.a.* spare, exempt (from); *–t bleiben*, be spared, be exempt *or* exempted, remain immune (*Path.*); *ich bitte Sie, mich mit diesem Auftrage zu –en*, I beg you will excuse me from carrying out this instruction. **–ung,** *f.* forbearance, exemption.

verschön-en, –ern, *v.a.* beautify, embellish, adorn. **–erung,** *f.* embellishment. **–erungsverein,** *m.* society for the preservation of local amenities.

verschossen, *p.p.* (*of* verschießen) & *adj.* faded, discoloured; (*coll.*) *er ist in sie –*, he is madly in love with her.

verschränk-en, *v.a.* cross, fold (*like arms, etc.*), entwine, interlace; *mit –ten Armen*, with folded arms, (*fig.*) with one's hands in one's pockets, without raising a finger. **–barkeit,** *f.* lock (*of steering axle*) (*Motor.*).

verschraub-en, *reg.* & *ir.v.a.* screw up, on *or* in; overscrew, get the thread crossed, screw wrong. **–ung,** *f.* screwing; screw cap, screw joint.

verschreib-en, 1. *ir.v.a.* use up in writing; spend (*time*) in writing; (*einem etwas*) order, write for, prescribe (*Med.*); assign, make over to (*Law*); *ein Wort –en*, miswrite a word, write a wrong word. 2. *v.r.* make a mistake in writing, make a slip of the pen; give a written pledge; *sich dem Teufel –en*, sell o.s. to the devil. 3. *n.* error in writing, slip of the pen. **–ung,** *f.* order, prescription, assignment; written promise *or* undertaking, bond.

verschreien, *ir.v.a.* decry, cry down, give a bad name to, cast a slur on. *verschrien*, *p.p.* & *adj.* in ill repute, in bad odour.

verschroben, *p.p.* (*of* verschrauben) & *adj.* intricate, confused; eccentric, odd, queer; wrong-headed perverse. **–heit,** *f.* perverseness, wrong-headedness; eccentricity, oddity.

verschroten, *v.a.* grind coarsely.

verschrotten, *v.a.* break up, scrap.

verschrumpfen, (*coll.*) **verschrumpeln,** *v.a.* & *n.* (*aux.* s.) shrink, contract, shrivel up, wither.

verschüchtern, *v.a.* intimidate, scare.

verschuld-en, 1. *v.a.* be guilty of, incur (*blame*), be the cause of. 2. *v.r.* (*an einem* or *wider einen*) act wrongly (towards a p.). 3. *n.* fault, blame, *ohne mein –en*, through no fault of mine. **–et,** *p.p.* & *adj.* indebted, in debt, encumbered, under obligation; *was habe ich –et?* what (wrong) have I done? **–etermaßen,** *adv.* deservedly. **–ung,** *f.* encumbering, mortgaging; error, guilt, sin.

verschütt, *adv.*; *– gehen*, (*sl.*) be lagged, be run in; (*coll.*) go off the rails, come unstuck. **–en,** *v.a.* fill *or* choke up with earth *or* rubble; spill, upset; bury (alive), overwhelm; (*coll.*) *er hat es bei ihm –et*, he has got into his bad books *or* has fallen out with him; *sich* (*Dat.*) *alles –en*, make a complete mess of everything.

verschwäger-n, *v.r.* become related by marriage (*mit*, to). **–t,** *p.p.* & *adj.* related by marriage. **–ung,** *f.* relationship by marriage.

verschwatzen, verschwätzen, 1. *v.a.* pass in chatting *or* gossiping, chatter away. 2. *v.r.* give o.s. away, let the cat out of the bag, put one's foot in it.

verschweig-en, *ir.v.a.* (*einem etwas*) keep secret, conceal (from); pass over in silence, suppress; *ich habe nichts zu –en*, I have nothing to conceal. **–ung,** *f.* silence (*regarding a th.*), suppression, concealment.

verschwend-en, *v.a.* waste, squander, lavish (*an*, *with Acc.*, on); *an ihn ist alle Mühe –et*, it is a waste of effort to bother about him, all effort is wasted on him. **–er,** *m.* spendthrift. **–erisch,** *adj.* wasteful, extravagant, lavish, prodigal; *–erisch mit etwas umgehen*, be lavish *or* prodigal of a th.. **–ung,** *f.* wastefulness, lavishness, prodigality; waste; *sündhafte –ung*, sinful waste. **–ungssucht,** *f.* extravagance, prodigality.

verschwiegen, *p.p.* (*of* verschweigen) & *adj.* discreet, reserved, reticent, taciturn, (*coll.*) close; quiet, secluded; – *wie das Grab*, silent as the grave. **–heit,** *f.* secrecy, discretion, reserve, reticence; silence, seclusion; *unter dem Siegel der –heit*, under the seal of secrecy.

verschwimmen, *ir.v.n.* (*aux.* s.) grow hazy, become blurred; merge *or* melt into one another; *in einander* –, blend, mingle.

verschwind–en, 1. *ir.v.n.* (*aux.* s.) vanish, disappear; be lost, pass away; *–en neben* or *im Vergleich mit* (*with Dat.*) or *gegen* (*with Acc.*), sink into insignificance by the side of; *auf Nimmerwiedersehen –en*, disappear never to be seen again. 2. *n.* disappearance, loss. **–end,** *adv.* negligible, infinitesimal. **–epunkt,** *m.* vanishing point. **–fahrwerk,** *n.* retractable undercarriage (*Av.*).

verschwister–t, *adj.* like brothers *or* sisters, (*fig.*) closely united, intimately connected; *–te Seelen*, congenial souls, kindred spirits; *–te Tugenden*, sister virtues. **–ung,** *f.* brotherly *or* sisterly union, close relationship, intimate connection.

verschwitzen, *v.a.* wet through *or* soak with perspiration; (*coll.*) forget.

verschwommen, *p.p* (*of* verschwimmen) & *adj.* indistinct, hazy, blurred, indefinite, vague, (*coll.*) woolly (*as ideas*). **–heit,** *f.* haziness, vagueness, uncertainty.

verschwör–en, 1. *ir.v.a.* forswear, abjure, renounce. 2. *v.r.* conspire, form a conspiracy, plot; swear, protest on oath, bind o.s. by an oath; *sich zu etwas –en*, plot s.th. **–er,** *m.* conspirator, plotter. **–ung,** *f.* conspiracy, plot; abjuration, renunciation.

Verschworene(r), *m.* conspirator, plotter.

versehen, 1. *ir.v.a.* provide, furnish, equip *or* supply with; discharge *or* perform (*a duty*); administer the Sacrament; do wrong, make a mistake (about); (*C.L.*) *mit Akzept* –, accepted, honoured; *er versah das Amt des Lehrers*, he filled the post as *or* acted as teacher; *es bei einem* –, be in *or* get into a p.'s bad books; *den Dienst eines andern* –, discharge another man's duties; take another man's place, (*coll.*) stand in for s.o. else; *Geschäfte* –, transact business, look after the business; (*C.L.*) *den Wechsel mit dem Giro* –, endorse a bill *or* a cheque; *den Gottesdienst* –, hold divine service; *die Küche* –, do the cooking; *wohl –es Lager*, well-equipped store, good supply *or* stock; *sich – lassen*, receive the Last Sacrament; *mit Mitteln reichlich* –, with ample means *or* resources; *einen Sterbenden* –, administer the Last Sacrament to a p.; *ein Schriftstück mit seiner Unterschrift* –, affix *or* append one's signature to a document; *einen Mann mit Vollmacht* –, invest a p. with full power(s); *die Wirtschaft* –, keep house, look after the house, do the housekeeping. 2. *v.r.* equip, supply *or* furnish o.s. (with); make a mistake, be mistaken, be in error, go wrong (*in with Dat.*, about); *er hatte sich vermutlich* –, very likely he made a mistake; (*Prov.*) – *ist auch verspielt*, a miss is as good as a mile; *sich eines Dinges zu jemandem* –, look (confidently) to a p. for a th., expect s.th. of a p.; *ich versehe mich eines Bessern zu euch*, I expect better things of you; *wes* or *wessen soll man sich zu euch –?* what is one to expect from you? *ehe er sich's* or *sich dessen versah*, before he was aware of it, in the twinkling of an eye; *ehe man sich's versieht*, suddenly, unexpectedly, all of a sudden, (*coll.*) before you can say Jack Robinson; *wer hätte sich das* –, who would have looked for, expected *or* anticipated that; (*an einer S.*) be frightened *or* scared (by a th.), take fright (at a th.), have a shock (from a th.) (*used of pregnant women*). 3. *n.* oversight, error, mistake, blunder, slip; *aus* –, through oversight *or* inadvertence, in error, by mistake. **–tlich,** *adv.* inadvertently, in error, by mistake, erroneously.

versehr–en, *v.a.* (*Poet.*) wound, hurt, injure, damage, disable. **–te(r),** *m.* disabled soldier. **–tengeld,** *n.* disability pension. **–theit,** *f.* disability.

verseif–en, *v.a.* saponify; soap (*all over*), lather thoroughly; (*sl.*) thrash. **–ung,** *f.* saponification.

verselbständigen, *v.a.* render independent, grant autonomy (to).

versend–en, *reg.* & *ir.v.a.* send out, off *or* away, dispatch, forward, transmit; *ins Ausland –en*, export, ship. **–er,** *m.* consigner, forwarder, exporter, shipper. **–ung,** *f.* consignment, conveyance, forwarding, dispatch, transport, transmission, exportation, shipping. **–ungsanzeige,** *f.* dispatch note. **–ungsfähig,** *adj.* transportable, consignable. **–ungsgüter,** *n.pl.* goods for dispatch, forwarding *or* exportation. **–ungskosten,** *pl.* cost of transport, forwarding charges.

versengen, *v.a.* singe, scorch, parch.

versenk–en, 1. *v.a.* sink, lower, let down; submerge, send to the bottom, scuttle; countersink (*screws*); *die Hände in die Taschen –en*, stick *or* thrust one's hands in one's pockets; *tief in Gedanken –t*, deeply absorbed *or* deep in thought. 2. *v.r.* become absorbed (*in with Acc.*, in). **–er,** *m.* countersink *or* rose bit (*Carp.*). **–ung,** *f.* sinking, depression, hollow; submersion, scuttling; lowering, dropping; trap-door (*Theat.*); *in der –ung verschwinden*, disappear from sight, disappear off the face of the earth, cease to exist.

versessen, *adj.* (*coll.*) (*auf, with Acc.*) bent on, mad about. **–heit,** *f.* craze.

versetz–en, 1 *v.a.* transfer, remove, transplant, move up (*at school*), advance, promote (*an officer, etc.*), displace; transpose (*Typ.*), permute (*Math.*); put, place (*into a certain condition*); give, deal (*a blow, etc.*); obstruct, block, bar, put an obstacle in the way of, dam up; pledge, mortgage, pawn; (*with mit*) compound, treat, mix, temper, alloy *or* prepare (with); (*coll.*) leave in the lurch; *–te Betonung*, shifting of the accentuation; *–ter Rhythmus*, transposed rhythm; *er wurde von W. nach P. versetzt*, he was transferred from W. to P.; *in den Ruhestand –en*, pension off; *das –t mich in die Notwendigkeit*, that reduces me to the necessity (*of doing*); *einen in große Angst –en*, alarm *or* terrify a p. greatly; *seine Uhr –en*, pawn one's watch; *Wein mit Wasser –en*, add water to wine; *jemandem einen Schlag –en*, give a p. a blow; *das –t mir den Atem*, that takes my breath away; *der Glaube –t Berge*, faith removes mountains; *den Eingang mit Steinen –en*, block up the entrance with stones. 2. *v.r.* change its place, shift; curdle; *–en Sie sich in meine Lage* or *an meine Stelle*, put, place *or* imagine yourself in my position. 3. *v.a* & *n.* (*aux.* h.) answer, (say in) reply, rejoin. **–bar,** *adj.* removable, movable, transposable, transplantable; acceptable as a pledge. **–ung,** *f.* displacing, transplantation, removal, transfer, transference; putting, placing (*in a certain condition*); pawning, pledging; transposition, inversion (*of words*), metathesis; moving up, promotion; permutation (*Math.*); metastasis (*Med.*); drift, deviation from course (*Naut., Av.*); mixing, dilution, alloy; reply, rejoinder, repartee; *–ung eines Bischofs*, translation of a bishop. **–ungsprüfung,** *f.* examination for promotion (*to a higher form*). **–ungszeichen,** *n.* accidental (*Mus.*).

verseuch–en, 1. *v.a.* infect, infest; contaminate (*with gas*) (*Mil.*). 2. *v.n.* become infected. **–ung,** *f.* infection, contamination.

versicher–n, 1. *v.a.* insure, assure, make sure (of), certify; (*einem etwas*) protest, affirm, aver, assert; *einem etwas* or *einen einer S.* (*Gen.*) *–n*, assure *or* convince s.o. of a th.; *ich –e dir* or (*coll.*) *dich*, I assure you; *er –te mir das Gegenteil* or *–te mich des Gegenteils*, he assured me of *or* to the contrary; *seien Sie –t, daß*, you may depend *or* rely upon it that; *an Eidesstatt –n*, pledge one's word. 2. *v.r.* make sure of, assure o.s. of, ascertain; insure one's life; *sich einer Person* (*Gen.*) *–n*, make sure of a p., get a p. under one's control, take s.o. into one's custody. **–bar,** *adj.* insurable. **–er,** *m.* insurer, underwriter. **–ung,** *f.* insurance (*against fire, etc.*); assurance (*of life*); assurance, affirmation, protestation; guarantee, security; *eine –ung abschließen* or *besorgen*, effect an insurance, take out a policy; *–ung gegen Einbruch*, insurance against burglary. **–ungsanstalt,** *f.* insurance company. **–ungsbetrag,** *m.* amount insured. **–ungsfonds,** *m.* benefit fund. **–ungsmathematisch,** *adj.* actuarial. **–ungsnehmer,** *m.* insured *or* assured per-

son, policy holder. **–ungspolice,** *f.*, *see* **–ungsschein. –ungsprämie,** *f.* insurance premium. **–ungsschein,** *m.* insurance policy. **–ungsstatistiker,** *m.* actuary.
versicker–n, *v.n.* (*aux.* s.) ooze, seep *or* trickle away, percolate. **–ung,** *f.* seepage, percolation.
versieg–eln, *v.a.* seal (up), affix one's seal to, (*coll.*) pawn. **–(e)lung,** *f.* sealing.
versieg–en, *v.n.* (*aux.* s.) dry up; be exhausted. **–bar,** *adj.* exhaustible, liable to run dry.
versiert, *adj.* versed (*in* (*Dat.*), in).
versifizieren, *v.a.* versify, put into verse.
versilber–n, *v.a.* silver-plate; *galvanisch –n*, electroplate; (*coll.*) realize, turn into cash; (*coll.*) pawn; *einem die Hände –n*, cross a p.'s palm with silver. **–ung,** *f.* silvering, silver-plating; (*coll.*) selling, realization.
versimpel–n, *v.n.* (*aux.* s.) become childish *or* simple. **–t,** *p.p. & adj.* half-witted, fatuous, drivelling, addle-pated, (*sl.*) half-baked, dim.
versinken, 1. *ir.v.n.* (*aux.* s.) sink, be swallowed up; founder, go down (*of ships*); *in einen Abgrund –*, become engulfed; *in Gedanken versunken sein*, be lost *or* absorbed in thought. 2. *n.* sinking; foundering; immersion, submersion.
versinnbild(lich)–en, *v.a.* symbolize, represent. **–ung,** *f.* symbolization, symbolic representation.
versinnlichen, 1. *v.a.* render tangible *or* perceptible to the senses, materialize; convey a clear idea of, illustrate. 2. *v.n.* (*aux* s.) become sensual.
versinter–n, *v.a.* incrust, sinter. **–ung,** *f.* incrustation.
versipp–en, *v.r.*, *see* **verschwägern. –t,** *adj.* closely related.
versittlichen, *v.a.* improve the morals of, civilize.
versklaven, *v.a.* enslave.
verso, 1. *adv.* overleaf. 2. *n.* reverse (*of the sheet*).
versoffen, *p.p. & adj.* (*vulg.*) drunk, drunken.
versohlen, *v.a.* (*coll.*) thrash; (*sl.*) beat the hide off, tan.
versöhn–en, 1. *v.a.* reconcile, conciliate, propitiate, appease. 2. *v.r.* become reconciled, make one's peace (with). **–lich,** *adj.* forgiving, conciliatory. **–ung,** *f.* reconciliation, propitiation, appeasement. **–ungsbund,** *m.* covenant of peace. **–ungsfest,** *n.*, *see* **–ungstag. –ungslehre,** *f.* doctrine of atonement. **–ungsopfer,** *n.* expiatory sacrifice; scapegoat; expiatory victim. **–ungspolitik,** *f.* appeasement policy. **–ungstag,** *m.* Day of Atonement, (*Jew.*) Jom Kippur.
versonnen, *adj.* lost in thought, day-dreaming, pensive.
versorg–en, *v.a.* (*einem etwas* or *einen mit etwas*) provide, supply, furnish (with); provide for, establish, settle (*in life*); take care of, look after, care for, nurse, maintain; *er ist lebenslänglich –t*, he is provided for for the rest of his life. **–er,** *m.* mainstay, support, supporter, bread-winner. **–t,** *adj.* careworn. **–ung,** *f.* maintenance, care, provision, supply; provisioning; appointment, post, situation; public assistance. **–ungsanlagen,** *f.pl.* public utilities. **–ungsanspruch,** *m.* claim for maintenance. **–ungsbetrieb,** *m.* public utility. **–ungslage,** *f.* supply situation *or* position. **–ungstruppen,** *f.pl.* army service corps, supply services. **–ungswesen,** *n.* public assistance, poor-relief.
verspann–en, *v.a.* stay, guy, brace. **–ung,** *f.* stays, struts, bracing.
versparen, *v.a.* (*sich* (*Dat.*) *etwas*) postpone, defer, (*coll.*) put off (*a th.*).
verspät–en, 1. *v.a.* delay, make late, keep back. 2. *v.r.* be late, come too late, be behind time; *er hat sich um einen Tag –et*, he arrived a day too late. **–et,** *p.p. & adj.* late, behind time, belated, delayed, overdue. **–ung,** *f.* delay, lateness; *der Zug hat 20 Minuten –ung*, the train is 20 minutes late.
verspeisen, *v.a.* eat up, consume.
verspekulieren, *v.r.* make a bad speculation, lose by speculation; (*fig.*) be out in one's reckoning.
versperr–en, *v.a.* bar, barricade, obstruct, block, shut, close, lock up; *einem die Aussicht –en*, obstruct a p.'s view. **–ung,** *f.* barring, blocking, obstruction, barricading; barricade, obstruction, blockage, blockade (*of a port*).
verspielen, 1. *v.a.* lose, gamble away, pass (*an evening, etc.*) in playing. 2. *v.r.* play wrong; lead badly (*Cards*); *du hast verspielt*, you have lost your chance; *er hat (es) bei ihr verspielt*, he has lost her favour *or* got into her bad books.
Verspillern, *n.* etiolation (*Bot.*).
verspinnen, 1. *ir.v.a.* use up in spinning. 2. *v.r.* get wrapped up (*in an idea*), get mixed up (*in an affair*).
verspott–en, *v.a.* scoff, mock *or* jeer at, deride, ridicule. **–er,** *m.* scoffer, mocker. **–ung,** *f.* scoffing, derision, ridicule.
versprech–en, 1. *ir.v.a.* (*einem etwas*) promise (a p. a th. *or* s.th. to a p.); bind o.s., give one's word; give promise of (*s.th.*), bid fair (*to do*); *sich* (*Dat.*) *etwas –en von einer S.*, expect much of a th., have one's hopes *or* expectations of a th.; *ich versprach ihm, es zu tun* or *daß ich es tun wollte*, I promised him I would do it; *er war ein junger Mensch, der viel versprach*, he was a very promising youth; *er verspricht ein großer Maler zu werden*, he has the makings of *or* he promises to be a great painter; *sie sind miteinander versprochen*, they are engaged (to be married); *das Unternehmen verspricht etwas*, the undertaking shows promise; *ich –e mir nicht viel davon*, I do not expect much from it, I have no great hopes of it; *hoch und teuer –en*, promise faithfully; *auf Treu und Glauben –en*, pledge one's word; *das Blaue vom Himmel –en*, promise the earth. 2. *v.r.* make a slip of the tongue, say the wrong thing; be *or* become engaged; *ich habe mich schon für den nächsten Tanz versprochen*, I am already engaged for the next dance. 3. *n.* slip of the tongue; *see also* **–ung;** *einem das –en abnehmen*, exact a promise from a p.; *schriftliches –en*, written promise, promissory note; *einen seines –ens entbinden*, release a p. from his promise; *auf dein –en hin*, on the strength of your promise; *gebrochenes –en, gesprochenes Verbrechen*, a promise broken is a bad deed spoken. **–ung,** *f.* promise, undertaking, engagement; *einem große –ungen machen*, hold out great hopes to a p.
versprengen, *v.a.* scatter, disperse (*troops, etc.*); strike (*a ball*) off the table (*Bill.*); *–te Truppen*, troops cut off from the main body. **–te(r),** *m.* straggler (*Mil.*); (air raid) casualty reported missing. **–ung,** *f.* dispersal; isolation (*Mil.*).
verspritzen, *v.a.* spatter, splash, spurt, squirt, spill, shed; *sein Blut –*, shed one's blood.
versprochenermaßen, *adv.* as promised.
Versprossung, *f.* proliferation, prolification.
Verspruch, *m.* (-(e)s, ⸗e) (*archaic*) betrothal.
verspunden, (*Austr. dial.*) **verspünden,** *v.a.* bung up (*a cask*).
verspüren, *v.a.* feel, perceive, notice, be *or* become aware of.
verstaatlich–en, *v.a.* nationalize, bring under public ownership. **–ung,** *f.* nationalization, public ownership.
verstädter–n, 1. *v.a.* urbanize. 2. *v.n.* become urbanized. **–ung,** *f.* urbanization.
verstadtlichen, *v.a.* take over by the municipality, bring under municipal control.
Verstand, *m.* understanding, mind, intellect, intelligence, (common) sense, (*coll.*) wits, brains; discernment, comprehension, judgement, (*sl.*) nous; (*archaic*) sense, meaning; *er ist nicht* (*recht*) *bei –*, he is not in his right mind; *der Kranke blieb bei –e*, the patient retained his mental faculties; (*Prov.*) *– kommt mit den Jahren*, reason comes with years; *nach meinem geringen –e*, in my humble opinion; *ohne Sinn und –*, without rhyme or reason; *ihm steht der – still*, he is at his wits' end; *das geht über meinen –*, that is beyond me; *einen um den – bringen*, drive a p. out of his senses *or* wits; *den – verlieren*, go out of one's mind; *zu –e kommen*, arrive at the age of discretion; *wieder zu – kommen*, come to one's senses; (*coll.*) *man muß seinen – zusammennehmen*, you must have all your wits about you; (*archaic*) *im eigentlichen –*, in its literal meaning, in the true sense; *in jedem –e*, in every sense *or* respect. **–en,** *p.p. of* verstehen; *–en?* is that clear? (*coll.*) you get me? *wohl –en*, let it be understood. **–esbegriff,** *m.* mental concept, (abstract) idea. **–esgemäß** *see* **–esmäßig. –es-**

kraft, *f.* intellectual power. **-esmäßig**, *adj.* reasonable, sensible, rational. **-esmensch**, *m.* matter-of-fact person. **-esschärfe**, *f.* penetration, sagacity; acumen, sound judgement. **-eswesen**, *n.* rational *or* intelligent being.

verständ-ig, *adj.* intelligent; sensible, reasonable, rational; wise, prudent, cautious, judicious; *-iges Alter*, years of discretion; *-iger Einfall*, sensible idea. **-igen**, 1. *v.a.* (*einen von etwas*) inform (a p.) of (a th.), give (a p.) notice of (s.th.), acquaint (s.o.) with (a th.); *einen über eine S. -igen*, enlighten a p. about s.th. 2. *v.r.* (*mit einem*) come to an understanding (with s.o.) (*über eine S.*, about a th.); *sich mit Deutschen -igen können*, be able to make o.s. understood with Germans. **-igkeit**, *f.* good sense wisdom, prudence, insight. **-igung**, *f.* agreement, understanding, arrangement; information; (quality of) reception (*Tele.*, *Rad.*). **-igungsfriede**, negotiated peace. **-lich**, *adj.* intelligible, clear, distinct; understandable, comprehensible; *allgemein -lich*, within everybody's grasp; *sich -lich ausdrücken*, express o.s. clearly; *sich -lich machen*, make o.s. understood; *einem etwas -lich machen*, make a th. clear to a p. **-lichkeit**, *f.* intelligibility, clarity, clearness, lucidity. **-nis**, *n.* comprehension, understanding, intelligence; appreciation, sympathy; *-nis für eine S. haben*, appreciate *or* be capable of appreciating a th., have a proper understanding of a th.; *einem -nis beibringen*, bring s.o. to understand, render intelligible to a p.; *einem -nis entgegenbringen*, show understanding *or* sympathy for a p. **-nisinnig**, *adj.* with profound understanding, with deep insight; *-nisinniger Blick*, knowing glance; *-nisinnige Worte*, appreciative words. **-nislos**, *adj.* devoid of understanding, unappreciative; imbecile. **-nislosigkeit**, *f.* lack of comprehension. **-nisvoll**, *adj.* understanding, sympathetic, appreciative; (*coll.*) knowing.

verstänkern, *v.a.* fill with stench, (*sl.*) stink (*a room, etc.*) out.

verstärk-en, *v.a.* strengthen, fortify, reinforce; augment, increase, enlarge; intensify (*Phot.*); concentrate (*liquids*); amplify (*sound*). **-er**, *m.* repeater (*Phone*), amplifier (*Rad.*), magnifier (*lens*), intensifier (*Phot.*), activator, reinforcing agent. **-erröhre**, *f.* amplifying valve (*Rad.*). **-ung**, *f.* strengthening, reinforcement(s); support, corroboration; increase, concentration, amplification, magnification, gain (*Rad.*); *-ung pro Stufe*, stage gain (*Rad.*). **-ungsfaktor**, *m.* amplification factor (*Rad.*). **-ungsflasche**, *f.* Leyden jar. **-ungsmaß**, *n.* amplification, gain (*Rad.*). **-ungstruppen**, *f.pl.* reinforcements (*Mil.*). **-ungswort**, *n.* augmentative *or* intensifying word.

verstatt-en, *v.a.* (*archaic*) allow, permit, grant. **-ung**, *f.* permission, concession.

verstauben, *v.n.* (*aux.* s.) be covered with dust, become dusty.

verstäub-en, 1. *v.a.* atomize, reduce to dust *or* powder; (cover with) dust *or* powder. 2. *v.n.* (*aux.* s.) fly off as dust. **-er**, *m.* atomizer, spray, sprayer.

verstauchen, *v.a.* (*sich* (*Dat.*) *die Hand, etc.*) sprain, strain (one's hand, *etc.*), (*coll.*) put (one's hand, *etc.*) out.

verstauen, *v.a.* stow away.

verstechen, *ir.v.a.* fine-draw (*Sewing*); adulterate (*wine*); *seine Trümpfe -*, play out one's trumps.

Versteck, *n.* (-(e)s, -e) hiding-place; ambush, ambuscade (*Mil.*), (*dial.*) hide-and-seek. **-en**, 1. *v.a.* hide, conceal, secrete. 2. *v.r.* hide, get hidden; (*fig.*) *sich vor einem -en müssen*, hide one's face with shame, not be a match for a p. 3. *n.*, **-enspiel**, *n.*, **-enspielen**, *n.*, **-ensspiel**, *n.*, **-spiel**, *n.* hide-and-seek. **-t**, *p.p.* & *adj.* hidden, concealed; (*fig.*) veiled, covert, indirect; reserved; obscure, (*coll.*) deep, sly, secretive; *-te Absichten*, ulterior motives; *-te Anspielung*, obscure hint, indirect reference; *-ter Vorwurf*, veiled reproach.

verstehen, 1. *ir.v.a.* understand, comprehend, grasp, know well, know (how); *was - Sie darunter?* what do you mean by it? *or* understand by that? what does that mean to you? *Sie - mich falsch*, you misunderstand me; *einem etwas zu - geben*, give a p. to understand, intimate to a p.; *von Grund aus -*, know thoroughly; (*Prov.*) *jeder macht's wie er's versteht*, everyone acts according to his lights; (*sl.*) *den Rummel -*, know what's what, be up to all the tricks; *er versteht keinen Spaß*, he does not see *or* cannot take a joke; *sie versteht es, einen Brief zu schreiben*, she knows how to write a letter. 2. *v.r.* understand one another, agree; *sich auf eine S. -*, understand a th., know a thing well; be skilled in *or* an expert at a th.; *sich auf seinen Vorteil -*, know where one's own interest lies, know which side one's bread is buttered; *sich mit einem -*, come to an understanding with a p.; *das versteht sich* (*von selbst*), that goes without saying, that is a matter of course, that is obvious; *sich zu einer S. -*, consent, accede *or* agree to, lend o.s. to *or* condescend to do a th.

versteif-en, 1. *v.a.* stiffen, harden; strut, stay, prop, brace, reinforce. 2. *v.n.* (*aux.* s.) become stiff, stiffen. 3. *v.r.*; *sich auf eine S. -en*, stick obstinately to a th., insist upon *or* make a point of a th.; harden (*of the market*). **-er**, *m.* stiffening (agent). **-ung**, *f.* bracing, reinforcement, prop, stiffening.

versteigen, *ir.v.r.* climb too high, lose o.s. in the mountains; (*fig.*) (*zu etwas*) fly high, go too far, attempt too much, go so far as to, have the presumption to; *so hoch habe ich mich nie verstiegen*, I have never ventured *or* aspired as high as that; *er verstieg sich zur Behauptung . . .*, he went so far as to maintain, he had the presumption to assert. . .

versteiger-n, *v.a.* sell by auction. **-ung**, *f.* auction; *es kam zur -ung*, it came under the hammer.

versteiner-n, *v.a.*, *r.* & *n.* (*aux.* s.) turn (in)to stone, petrify. **-ung**, *f.* petrification; fossil. **-ungskunde**, *f.* palaeontology.

verstell-en, 1. *v.a.* put one thing in the place of another, transpose, shift, adjust; remove, change the position *or* order of, put in the wrong place, misplace, disarrange; (*einem etwas*) bar, block (up), obstruct; feign, sham, disguise, counterfeit; *man hat mir alle Bücher -t*, all my books have been disarranged; *die Handschrift -en*, disguise one's handwriting. 2. *v.r.* dissemble, feign, pretend, sham; *sich zu -en wissen*, know how to dissemble, be a good dissembler; *sich gut -en*, play one's part well. 3. *n.* displacement, disarrangement, removal. **-bar**, *adj.* movable, adjustable, controllable. **-(l)uftschraube**, *f.* variable pitch airscrew (*Av.*). **-t**, *p.p.* & *adj.* pretended, disguised, feigned, sham. **-ung**, *f.* adjustment; pretence, make-believe, disguise, dissimulation, hypocrisy. **-ungskunst**, *f.* dissimulation, hypocrisy.

versterben, *ir.v.n.* (*aux.* s.) (*Poet.*) *only past tense*, breathe one's last; expire; *see* **verstorben.**

versteu-ern, *v.a.* pay duty on. **-ert**, *adj.* duty-paid. **-(e)rung**, *f.* payment of duty.

verstieben, *ir.v.n.* (*aux.* s.) be scattered as dust; fly off as dust; fly away, disappear.

verstiegen, *p.p.* (*of* versteigen) & *adj.* (*fig.*) high-flown, extravagant, eccentric. **-heit**, *f.* extravagance, eccentricity.

verstimm-en, 1. *v.a.* put out of sorts, upset; put into a bad temper, annoy. 2. *v.r.* get out of tune. **-t**, *adj.* out of tune; in a bad temper *or* mood, annoyed, cross; upset (*as stomach, etc.*). **-ung**, *f.* discord, upset, disorder; ill humour, bad temper; ill feeling (*between*).

verstock-en, *v.n.* (*aux.* s.) become mildewed; grow hard, obdurate *or* impenitent. **-t**, *adj.* stubborn, obdurate; impenitent, hardened; stained with damp, marked with iron-mould. **-theit**, *f.* obduracy, stubbornness, hardness of heart, callousness, insensibility.

verstohlen, *adj.* stealthy, furtive, secret, clandestine, surreptitious. **-erweise**, *adv.* stealthily, on the sly.

verstopf-en, 1. *v.a.* stop up, plug up, choke, block, clog, obstruct; constipate (*Med.*). 2. *v.r.* become stopped up, obstructed *or* choked. **-ung**, *f.* choking, clogging, stopping, obstructing; stoppage, obstruction; constipation; *an -ung leiden*, be constipated.

verstorben, *p.p.* (*of* versterben) & *adj.* dead, deceased, late. **-e(r)**, *m.* & *f.* the deceased.

verstör–en, *v.a.* disturb, interfere (with), trouble, disquiet, confuse, upset. **–t,** *p.p. & adj.* troubled, confused, disconcerted, agitated; *ein –tes Gesicht haben* or *–t aussehen*, have a haggard, wild look, have an air of consternation, look troubled *or* agitated. **–theit,** *f.* haggard appearance; agitation, consternation, confusion.

Verstoß, *m.* (-es, ⸚e) offence, mistake, error, fault, blunder, slip; *einen – gegen etwas machen*, offend against a th., violate a th. **–en,** 1. *ir.v.n.* (*aux.* h.) (*gegen*) give offence to, offend against, transgress, violate (*a regulation, etc.*). 2. *v.a.* push away, cast off; repel, repulse, reject, repudiate; divorce (*a wife*); disown, disinherit (*a son, etc.*); dispossess, turn out, expel. **–ene(r),** *m. & f.* outcast. **–ung,** *f.* expulsion, banishment, rejection, repudiation; *see also* **–.**

verstreben, *v.a.* brace, support, strut, stay.

verstreich–en, 1. *ir.v.a.* spread, smear with; fill in (*cracks*), grout (*joints*); *eine Mauer mit Mörtel –en*, plaster up *or* parget a wall; *verstrichene Fugen*, filled joints. 2. *v.n.* (*aux.* s.) slip by, pass (*of time*); expire, elapse; *der Termin ist verstrichen*, the term has expired. **–ung,** *f.* flight of time; expiration (*of a term*); pargetting, rough-casting (*of a wall*).

verstreu–en, *v.a.* scatter, disperse, strew about, litter; *–te Felsblöcke*, erratic blocks (*Geol.*).

verstricken, 1. *v.a.* use up (*wool, etc.*) in knitting; ensnare, entangle; *in einer S. verstrickt sein*, be involved in an affair; *in eine S. verstrickt werden*, get mixed up *or* entangled in a th. 2. *v.r.* get entangled, be caught.

verstümm–eln, *v.a.* mutilate, maim, mangle; curtail, truncate; garble; *–elter Bericht*, garbled account; *–elter Schwanz*, docked tail. **–(e)lung,** *f.* mutilation, truncation, curtailment.

verstumm–en, *v.n.* (*aux.* s.) grow dumb; become silent; *vor Erstaunen –en*, be struck dumb with astonishment; *–en machen, zum –en bringen*, silence. **–ung,** *f.* loss of speech.

Versuch, *m.* (-(e)s, -e) attempt, trial, endeavour, test, experiment; assay, proof; *es kommt auf einen – an*, it depends upon how it stands the test; *–e anstellen*, experiment, try, attempt; *einen – mit einer S. machen*, give s.th. a trial, experiment upon a th.; *ein – kann nicht schaden*, it can do no harm to try; *strafbarer –*, attempted felony. **–en,** 1. *v.a.* attempt, try; test, put to the test, experiment on; tempt, entice; sample, taste; *sein Äußerstes –en*, do one's utmost; *sein Heil* or *sein Glück –en*, seek one's fortune; *den Kaffee –en*, taste *or* try the coffee; *das letzte –en*, make a final attempt; *es mit etwas –en*, give a th. a trial, put a th. to the test; *es mit ihm –en*, try him, (*sl.*) see if he will play; *die Vorsehung –en*, tempt Providence. 2. *v.r.*; *sich in etwas –en*, have experience of a th., (*coll.*) have a shot at a th.; *sich in der Welt –en*, see life, (*coll.*) get around, know one's way around. **–er,** *m.* tempter; seducer; (*B.*) the devil. **–sanstalt,** research institute, experimental station *or* plant. **–sarbeit,** *f.* experimental work. **–sballon,** *m.* (*fig.*) attempt to gauge public opinion, kite. **–sbedingungen,** *f. pl.* test *or* experimental conditions. **–sfehler,** *m.* experimental error. **–sflug,** *m.* test flight. **–sgut,** *n.* experimental farm. **–skaninchen,** *n.* (*fig.*) (experimental) guinea-pig. **–sladung,** *f.* proof-charge (*Artil.*). **–smodell,** *n.* working model. **–smuster,** *n.* trial *or* experimental model. **–sraum,** *m.* test room, laboratory. **–sreihe,** *f.* series of tests. **–srennen,** *n.* trial stakes. **–sstadium,** *n.* experimental stage, **–sstand,** *m.* testing-stand. **–sstation,** *f.*, **–sstelle,** *f.* testing *or* experimental station. **–sweise,** *adv.* by way of experiment, as an experiment, tentatively; *–sweise nehmen*, take on trial *or* on approval. **–ung,** *f.* temptation; *in –ung führen*, lead into temptation; *in –ung fallen, geraten* or *kommen*, be tempted, fall into temptation.

versumpf–en, *v.n.* (*aux.* s.) become marshy *or* boggy; (*sl.*) come down in the world, go to the bad, become dissolute. **–ung,** *f.* swampiness, bogginess.

versündig–en, *v.r.* sin (*an, with Dat.*, against), do wrong. **–ung,** *f.* sin, offence; *–ung an Gott*, sin against God.

versunken, *p.p.* (*of* versinken) *& adj.* sunk, lost; engrossed, absorbed. **–heit,** *f.* (*fig.*) absorption (*in thought*), preoccupation, reverie, thoughtfulness, intentness.

versüßen, *v.a.* sweeten, oversweeten, sugar.

vertag–en, 1. *v.a.* adjourn, prorogue (*parliament*); *–ter Wechsel*, bill that has fallen due. 2. *v.r.* adjourn. **–ung,** *f.* adjournment, prorogation.

vertändeln, *v.a.* fritter away.

vertäuen, *v.a.* moor (*a boat*).

vertausch–en, *v.a.* (with *für, gegen, mit* or *um*) exchange, barter; interchange; change (*places*); substitute, permute (*Math.*); mistake, take *or* leave by mistake *or* in mistake for (*umbrella, hat, etc.*); *Berlin mit Leipzig –en*, move from B. to L., leave B. for L. **–bar,** *adj.* exchangeable, permutable. **–barkeit,** *f.* interchange, barter; permutation, substitution, interchangeability. **–ung,** *f.* exchange, (*Math.*); substitution *or* removal by mistake.

vertausend–fachen, –fältigen, *v.a.* increase a thousandfold; multiply by a thousand.

verteidig–en, 1. *v.a.* defend; justify, vindicate, stand up for, uphold, support; *einen Satz –en*, maintain a proposition. 2. *v.r.* stand up for one's rights, defend, justify *or* vindicate o.s. **–er,** *m.* defender; advocate, counsel for the defence; full back (*Footb.*). **–ung,** *f.* defence; vindication, advocacy, justification, case for the defence (*Law*); *in die –ung gedrängt*, forced on to the defensive, compelled to adopt a defensive attitude; *zur –ung meiner Ehre*, in defence of my honour. **–ungsanlagen,** *f.pl.* defence works, defences. **–ungsbündnis,** *n.* defensive alliance. **–ungsgrund,** *m.* ground for defence, justification. **–ungskrieg,** *m.* defensive war. **–ungslos,** *adj.* defenceless. **–ungsmittel,** *n.pl.* means of defence; defence (*Law*). **–ungsrede,** *f.* plea, counsel's speech, speech for the defence. **–ungsschrift,** *f.* vindication in writing, written defence. **–ungsstand,** *m.* state of defence. **–ungsstellung,** *f.* defensive position (*Mil.*). **–ungswaffen,** *f.pl.* defensive weapons. **–ungsweise,** 1. *f.* method of defence. 2. *adv.* by way of defence; on the defensive. **–ungszustand,** *m.*, *see* **–ungsstand.**

verteien, verteuen, *v.a.*, *see* **vertäuen.**

verteil–en, 1. *v.a.* distribute, disperse, disseminate, divide, spread; assign, apportion, allot, dispense; *milde Gaben an die Armen –en*, distribute money *or* dispense charity among the poor; *Steuern –en*, assess taxes; *die Rollen –en*, assign *or* allot the parts (*Theat.*). 2. *v.r.* spread, disperse; *die Kosten –en sich auf alle*, the cost is spread among everyone, everyone shares the cost. **–er,** *m.* divider, distributor. **–erfinger,** *m.* distributor arm. **–erkasten,** *m.* junction box. **–erscheibe,** *f.* distributor-plate (*Tele.*). **–ung,** *f.* distribution, dispersion, diffusion; division, apportionment, allotment, assessment (*of taxes*). **–ungskurve,** *f.* distribution curve (*Statistics*). **–ungsschlüssel,** *m.* ratio of distribution.

verteu–ern, *v.a.* raise in *or* the price, make dearer. **–(e)rung,** *f.* rise *or* increase in price.

verteufelt, 1. *adj.* devilish. 2. *adv.* (*coll.*) deuced, infernally, awfully; *was für ein –es Geschäft!* what a confounded nuisance! *–er Kerl*, devil of a fellow; *einem – mitspielen*, play the very devil with a p.

vertief–en, 1. *v.a.* deepen, sink deeper; *den Eindruck –en*, heighten the impression; *in Gedanken –t*, lost *or* absorbed in thought; *eine Schüssel –en*, hollow out a vessel; *der –te halbe Ton zu C*, the half-tone lower than C (*Mus.*). 2. *v.r.* become deeper, deepen; (*in with Acc.*) busy o.s. in, become engrossed in; *sich in seine Gedanken –en*, be wrapped up in one's thoughts. **–ung,** *f.* deepening; cavity, hollow, indentation, depression, recess, niche; (*fig.*) absorption, preoccupation.

vertier–en, *v.n.* (*aux.* s.) become brutalized *or* brutish. **–t,** *p.p. & adj.* brutish, bestial.

vertilg–en, *v.a.* destroy, annihilate, extirpate, exterminate, eradicate, uproot, efface, blot out, extinguish; (*coll.*) devour, consume; (*sl.*) finish off, polish off. **–bar,** *adj.* eradicable, destructible. **–ung,** *f.* extermination, extirpation, destruction. **–ungskrieg,** *m.* war of extermination, war to the death.

vertippen, *v.a. & r.* (*coll.*) make a typing error, type wrong.

vertoben, *v.a.* (*coll.*) miss, overlook.

verton–en, *v.a.* set to music. **–er,** *m.* composer. **–ung,** *f.* musical composition, musical arrangement; coastal outline (*on charts*) (*Naut.*).

vertönen, *v.n.* (*aux.* s.) die away (*of sounds*).

vertrackt, *adj.* (*coll.*) distorted, contorted, twisted; vexatious, awkward, difficult, confounded; *–e Gebärden*, contortions.

Vertrag, *m.* (-(e)s, ⸗e) treaty, contract, agreement, covenant, compact, settlement, accord; *leoninischer –*, one-sided bargain, settlement by which one party has the lion's share. **–en,** 1. *ir.v.a.* bear, stand, endure, suffer, tolerate, brook; digest; wear out; carry away *or* off, displace; *das kann ich nicht –en*, I cannot bear that; this does not agree with me; (*Prov.*) *Pack schlägt sich, Pack verträgt sich*, thieves may squabble, but they stick together; *er kann einen Puff –en*, he has a thick skin *or* (*coll.*) tough hide; *einen Spaß –en*, understand *or* take a joke; *diese Speise kann ich nicht –en*, this food does not agree with me; *er kann nicht viel –en*, he cannot stand much; *er kann keinen Widerspruch –en*, he cannot tolerate contradiction. 2. *v.r.* get on well together; agree, harmonize, be compatible *or* consistent; *sich mit einem* (*wieder*) *–en*, be reconciled to s.o., settle one's differences with a p., (*coll.*) make it up with a p.; *sie –en sich wie Hund und Katze*, they live a cat-and-dog life; *Grün und Blau –en sich nicht*, green and blue do not go well together *or* do not match; *es verträgt sich nicht mit meiner Pflicht*, it is incompatible with my duty. **–lich,** 1. *adj.* contractual, according to the terms of the contract *or* treaty; *–licher Anspruch*, claim by virtue of treaty. 2. *adv.* as stipulated, agreed (upon) *or* fixed by treaty. **–sartikel,** *m.* article *or* term of contract. **–sbrüchig,** *adj.* defaulting (*in a contract*). **–schließende(r),** *m.* party to a contract. **–sentwurf,** *m.* draft treaty. **–serbe,** *m.* heir under settlement. **–shafen,** *m.* treaty-port. **–smäßig,** *adj.* stipulated, agreed (upon). **–srecht,** *n.* contractual right. **–sstrafe,** *f.* penalty for breach of contract. **–swidrig,** *adj.* contrary to the terms of an agreement *or* to the provisions of a treaty. **–swidrigkeit,** *f.* contravention of an agreement.

verträglich, *adj.* friendly, peaceable, good-natured, sociable; tractable, accommodating, conciliatory; compatible *or* consistent (with). **–keit,** *f.* sociability, good nature, easy temper, peaceable disposition, conciliatory spirit, tolerant attitude; compatibility.

vertrau–en, 1. *v.n.* (*aux.* h.) (*Dat. or auf with Acc.*) trust *or* confide (in), have confidence (in), put one's trust (in), rely upon; *–e mir*, trust me. 2. *v.a.* (*rare*) (*einem etwas*) confide, entrust. 3. *v.r.* (*with Dat.*) confide (in), open one's heart *or* unbosom o.s. (to). 4. *n.* confidence, trust; reliance; *im –en*, in confidence, confidentially, between ourselves; *im –en auf*, relying on, trusting to; *sein –en in einen setzen*, have confidence in a p., place one's trust in a p.; *einen ins –en ziehen*, take a p. into one's confidence; *einem sein –en schenken*, trust, place one's trust in a p., bestow one's confidence on a p.; *–en zu einem haben* or *fassen*, trust, rely on *or* have faith in a p.; *das –en zu einem verlieren*, lose one's faith *or* confidence in a p. **–enerweckend,** *adj.* inspiring trust, trustworthy; (*fig.*) promising. **–ensamt,** *n.* confidential post, position of trust. **–ensbruch,** *m.* breach of confidence *or* faith. **–ensfrage,** *f.*; *die –ensfrage stellen*, ask for a vote of confidence (*Parl.*). **–ensmann,** *m.* confidant, trusted person; shop steward (*in factories*). **–ensposten,** *m.*, *see* **–ensamt. –enssache,** *f.* confidential matter. **–ensselig,** *adj.* gullible, too trusting. **–ensseligkeit,** *f.* blind faith, gullibility. **–ensvoll,** *adj.* full of confidence, confident. **–enswürdig,** *adj.* trustworthy, reliable. **–lich,** *adj.* familiar, intimate; confidential, private; *etwas –lich behandeln*, deal with a th. in confidence; *auf einem –lichen Fuß mit einem leben*, be on familiar terms *or* on terms of intimacy with s.o.; *–liche Mitteilung*, confidential communication; *–liche Sitzung*, session in camera, private meeting; *–licher Stil*, familiar style; *streng –lich!* private and confidential; *er tut sehr –lich*, he is rather familiar; *–lich mit einem umgehen*, see *auf einem –lichen Fuß*. **–lichkeit,** *f.* familiarity, intimacy; confidence; *sich* (*Dat.*) *–lichkeiten herausnehmen*, permit o.s. liberties, become too familiar. **–t,** *adj.* friendly, intimate; familiar (with), conversant (with), versed (in); *mit einem –t sein, auf –tem Fuße mit einem stehen*, be very familiar *or* on terms of intimacy with s.o.; *mit einer S. wohl –t sein*, be well acquainted *or* fully conversant with a th., be well versed in a th.; *sich mit etwas –t machen*, make o.s. (thoroughly) familiar with a th.; *–ter Freund*, intimate friend. **–te(r),** *m. & f.* confidant, confidante. **–theit,** *f.* intimacy, familiarity; thorough knowledge (of), acquaintance (with).

vertrauern, *v.a.* pass (*one's life, etc.*) in mourning.

verträum–en, *v.a.* dream away; *–te Augen*, dreamy eyes; *–tes Dörfchen*, sleepy village.

vertreib–en, *ir.v.a.* drive away, expel, banish; disperse, dispel, scatter, dislodge; soften, blend, shade down (*colours*); kill, beguile (*time*); distribute, sell, retail (*goods*); *einen aus seinem Besitze –en*, dispossess a p.; *einen aus dem Lande –en*, banish *or* exile a p.; *einen aus seiner Wohnung –en*, eject a p., turn a p. out of house and home; *Gewalt mit Gewalt –en*, repel force by force; *einem den Kitzel –en*, knock the nonsense out of a p.'s head; *die Umrisse –en*, soften the outlines; *sich* (*Dat.*) *die Zeit –en*, while away *or* beguile the time, kill time. **–ung,** *f.* expulsion, banishment; dispersion; dispossession, eviction; sale, disposal; softening (*Paint.*).

vertret–en, *ir.v.a.* replace, represent, deputize for, act as substitute (for); appear for, plead *or* intercede for (*a p.*); defend, advocate, champion (*a th.*); tread down, trample; bar, block, obstruct; *sich* (*Dat.*) *den Fuß –en*, sprain one's foot; (*coll.*) *sich* (*Dat.*) *die Beine –en*, stretch one's legs (*by walking*); *einem den Weg –en*, stand in a p.'s way, stop s.o.; *eine Ansicht –en*, support *or* adopt a view; *vor Gericht –en*, defend in court; *jemandes Interessen –en*, look after a p.'s interests; *die Kinderschuhe –en haben*, have outgrown childish things; *er vertritt den Staat nach außen*, he represents the country abroad, he is his country's representative for foreign affairs; *einen Wahlbezirk –en*, sit for a constituency, represent a constituency (*in parliament*). **–bar,** *adj.* replaceable, fungible (*Law*). **–er,** *m.* representative, substitute, deputy, proxy, locum (tenens); intercessor, advocate, champion; agent. **–erschaft,** *f.* representative body. **–ung,** *f.* representation, substitution, replacement; intercession, advocacy, defence; agency; sprain; *die –ung übernehmen*, deputize (for), take the place (of), act as substitute (for); (*C.L.*) *in –ung des . . .*, representing . . ., signed for . . . **–ungskosten,** *pl.* expenses of representation. **–ungsvollmacht,** *f.* power of attorney. **–ungsweise,** *adv.* as a substitute *or* representative, by proxy, per pro.

Vertrieb, *m.* (-(e)s, -e) sale, distribution, retail trade. **–sgenossenschaft,** *f.*, **–sgesellschaft,** *f.* trading company. **–sleiter,** *m.* sales manager.

vertrieben, *p.p. of* vertreiben.

vertrinken, *v.a.* spend *or* squander on drink.

vertrocknen, 1. *v.n.* (*aux.* s.) dry up, wither. 2. *v.a.* desiccate.

vertrödeln, *v.a.* idle away, fritter away, waste (*one's time*); (*archaic*) hawk.

vertröst–en, *v.a.* (*auf with Acc.*) console, give hope to, feed with hope, put (*s.o.*) off (with); *einen auf eine S. –en*, console a p. with the prospect of s.th.; *seine Gläubiger von einem Tage auf den andern –en*, put off one's creditors from day to day; *auf später –en*, put off for the time being. **–ung,** *f.* consolation, vain promise.

vertrusten, *v.a. & r.* (*C.L.*) corner, pool.

Vertu–er, *m.* (-s, –) spendthrift. **–erisch,** *adj.*, **–lich,** *adj.* extravagant; prodigal. **–n,** 1. *ir.v.a.* waste, squander. 2. *v.n.* (*aux.* h.) do one's share *or* bit, do what one can. 3. *v.r.* (*dial.*) (*mit einer S.*) waste time (on *or* with s.th.).

vertusch–eln, –en, *v.a.* hide, conceal, keep secret *or* (*coll.*) dark, hush up. **–(el)ungsversuch,** *m.* attempt to hush (*s.th.*) up *or* keep (*s.th.*) secret.

verübeln, *v.a.* (*einem etwas*) take amiss, blame (*s.o.*) for.
verüb-en, *v.a.* commit, perpetrate. **-er,** *m.* perpetrator, author. **-ung,** *f.* perpetration, commission (*of a crime*).
verulken, *v.a.* make fun of, tease, pull (*s.o.'s*) leg.
Verumständung, *f.* (*Swiss dial.*) *see* **Umstand.**
verunedeln, 1. *v.a.* degrade, debase. 2. *v.r.* deteriorate, become poor (*Min.*).
verunehren, *v.a.* dishonour, disgrace; profane.
veruneinig-en, 1. *v.a.* set at variance. 2. *v.r.* fall out, quarrel. **-ung,** *f.* disunion, discord.
verunglimpf-en, *v.a.* bring into discredit, dishonour, defame, disparage, revile, blacken, calumniate, traduce. **-ung,** *f.* defamation, disparagement, calumny.
verunglück-en, *v.n.* (*aux.* s.) meet with an accident *or* misfortune; perish, be killed; fail, miscarry, come to grief; *er -te beim Radeln,* he was killed in a cycling accident; *das Schiff ist -t,* the vessel has been lost; *der Plan -te,* the scheme failed. *er ist tödlich -t,* he has met with a fatal accident; *-ter Versuch,* abortive attempt. **-te(r),** *m.* victim, injured person. **-ung,** *f.* failure, miscarriage; (fatal) accident.
verunmöglichen, *v.a.* (*Swiss dial.*) render *or* make impossible.
verunreinig-en, *v.a.* dirty, soil, contaminate, defile, pollute, taint, vitiate. **-ung,** *f.* soiling, contamination, pollution, defilement.
verunschicken, *v.a.* (*Swiss dial.*) lose *or* forfeit through one's own fault *or* by one's own mistake.
verunstalt-en, *v.a.* disfigure, deface, deform. **-et,** *p.p. & adj.* misshapen, disfigured, deformed, ugly. **-ung,** *f.* deformity, disfigurement, ugliness.
veruntreu-en, *v.a.* embezzle, misappropriate; *Gelder -en,* embezzle money, defalcate. **-ung,** *f.* embezzlement, misappropriation; *-ung öffentlicher Gelder,* defalcation *or* embezzlement of public money.
verunzieren, *v.a.* disfigure, deface, mar.
verursach-en, *v.a.* cause, occasion, bring about, produce, give rise to, entail. **-er,** *m.* author, originator. **-ung,** *f.* cause, occasion.
verurteil-en, *v.a.* condemn, convict, sentence; *einen zum Tode -en,* sentence a p. to death; *einen zu einer Geldstrafe von 20 Mark -en,* fine a p. 20 marks, impose a fine of 20 marks on a p. **-te(r),** *m.* condemned person. **-ung,** *f.* condemnation, conviction, sentence.
verviel-fachen, *v.a.* multiply. **-fachung,** *f.* multiplication. **-fältigen,** *v.a.* copy, reproduce, duplicate, mimeograph; *see also* **-fachen. -fältiger,** *m.* multiplier. **-fältigung,** *f.* multiplication; reproduction, duplication, copying. **-fältigungsapparat,** *m.* duplicator, hectograph, mimeograph. **-fältigungsverfahren,** *n.* copying process, duplication.
vervierfachen, 1. *v.a.* quadruple. 2. *v.r.* increase *or* multiply fourfold.
vervollkommn-en, *v.a.* perfect, improve. **-ung,** *f.* perfection, improvement, completion. **-ungsfähig,** *adj.* perfectible.
vervollständig-en, *v.a.* complete; replenish. **-ung,** *f.* completion.
verwachs-en, 1. *ir.v.a.* outgrow, grow out of (*one's clothes, etc.*); lose in growing (*as scars*). 2. *v.r.* grow crooked; heal up *or* over. 3. *v.n.* (*aux.* s.) close, heal up, grow over, fill up, grow together, coalesce; be tied (to), be engrossed (in); grow crooked *or* deformed. 4. *p.p. & adj.* grown together, healed up; deformed, crooked, misshapen; intimately bound up with, engrossed in; *innig -en sein mit,* be as one with. **-ung,** *f.* fusion, coalescence, concrescence; healing up, cicatrization; defective growth, deformity.
verwackeln, *v.a.*; *eine Aufnahme -,* move the camera, spoil a picture by moving (*Phot.*).
Verwahr, *m.* (-(e)s, -e), *see* **-ung;** *in - geben* (*nehmen*), give (take) into custody. **-en,** 1. *v.a.* keep, secure, preserve, put away safely; *vor* or *gegen etwas -en,* guard, preserve from, secure against s.th; *einem Geld zu -en geben,* give money into a p.'s safe-keeping; *trocken -en,* keep dry. 2. *v.r.* (*gegen*) take precautions (against), secure o.s. (against), (make a) protest against, resist; *sich* or *sein Recht -en,* reserve the right (to). **-er,** *m.* keeper, guardian, trustee. **-losen,** 1. *v.a.* neglect. 2. *v.n.* be spoiled by neglect, degenerate; (*coll.*) go to the bad. **-lost,** *adj.* neglected, unkempt; degenerate, depraved. **-losung,** *f.* neglect; injury caused by neglect; degeneration, demoralization. **-sam,** *m.,* **-ung,** *f.* keeping, guard, care, custody, preservation; *etwas in -ung nehmen,* take charge of a th., take a th. under one's care; *einen in -ung nehmen,* take a p. into custody; *einem etwas in -ung geben,* give a th. into s.o.'s care, give a th. to s.o. to look after; *in -ung liegen,* be deposited, be well looked after, be in safe keeping; *-ung gegen eine S. einlegen,* protest, enter *or* make a protest against a th. **-ungsmittel,** *n.* preservative; protest (*Law*). **-ungsort,** *m.* place of safe-keeping, repository, depot.
verwais-en, *v.n.* (*aux.* s.) become an orphan, lose one's parent(s); (*fig.*) be deserted, be abandoned. **-t,** *p.p. & adj.* orphan(ed); fatherless; (*fig.*) deserted, destitute.
verwalken, *v.a.* (*coll.*) beat, thrash.
verwalt-en, *v.a.* administer, manage, conduct, superintend, supervise; fill (*a post*), hold (*an office*); *übel -en,* mismanage, maladminister, misgovern; *jemandes Vermögen -en,* act as trustee to a p.'s property *or* estate. **-er,** *m.* administrator, manager, steward, superintendent, trustee, curator. **-ung,** *f.* administration, government, management, stewardship trusteeship. **-ungsabteilung,** *f.* administrative branch. **-ungsamt,** *n.* managership, post in the administration. **-ungsausgaben,** *f.pl., see* **-ungskosten. -ungsausschuß,** *m.* committee of management, administrative body. **-ungsbeamte(r),** *m.* administrative official. **-ungsbehörde,** *f.* the administration; government office; board of management. **-ungsbezirk,** *m.* administrative area. **-ungsdienst,** *m.* civil service. **-ungsfach,** *n.* branch of the administration. **-ungskosten,** *pl.* administrative expenses, costs of management. **-ungsmaßregel,** *f.* administrative measure. **-ungsrat,** *m.* administrative board, committee of management; managing director. **-ungsweg,** *m.*; *auf dem -ungswege,* administratively, through administrative channels. **-ungswesen,** *n.* administration, management. **-ungszweig,** *m. see* **-ungsfach.**
verwamsen, *v.a.* (*coll.*) beat, thrash.
verwand-eln, 1. *v.a.* change, convert, turn (into), transform, transmute, transfigure, metamorphose; commute (*penalties, etc.*); reduce (*Arith.*); *in einen Trümmerhaufen -eln,* reduce to (a heap of) rubble; *in Geld -eln,* turn into money, realize; *in den Leib und das Blut Christi -eln,* change into the body and blood of Christ. 2. *v.r.* change, alter, turn, be converted, transformed, transmuted, transfigured *or* reduced. **-elbar,** *adj.* transformable, transmutable, convertible. **-elbarkeit,** *f.* transmutability, convertibility. **-lung,** *f.* alteration, change, modification; conversion, transformation, metamorphosis, transubstantiation; commutation (*of a punishment*). **-lungskünstler,** *m.* quick-change artist. **-lungsszene,** *f.* transformation scene (*Theat.*).
verwandt, *adj.* related, kindred, cognate (*word*); analogous, like, similar, allied; sympathetic, congenial; *er ist mit mir -,* he is a relative of mine; *wir sind nahe -,* we are near relations; *wie sind Sie mit ihm - ?* in what way are you related to him? *Malerei und Dichtkunst sind mit einander -,* painting and poetry are kindred arts. **-e(r),** *m.,* **-e,** *f.* relative, relation; *der nächste -e,* the next of kin. **-enehe,** *f.* consanguineous marriage. **-schaft,** *f.* relationship, kinship, consanguinity; sympathy, congeniality; connexion; (chemical) affinity; (*coll.*) relations, relatives; *-schaft der Stämme und Sprachen,* affinity of race and language; *-schaft von Begriffen,* affinity of ideas. **-schaftlich,** *adj.* kindred, allied, as among relatives; congenial. **-schaftsbegriffe,** *m.pl.* cognate ideas. **-schaftsbeziehung,** *f.* (points of) relationship. **-schaftsgrad,** *m.* degree of relationship, affinity. **-schaftskraft,** *f.* force of affinity (*Chem.*). **-schaftskreis,**

m. family, relations. **–schaftslinie,** *f.* line of descent. **–schaftsverhältnis,** *n.* hereditary relationship, family relationship.
verwanzt, *adj.* bug-ridden, (*coll.*) buggy.
verwarn–en, *v.a.* warn, caution, admonish. **–ung,** *f.* warning, admonition, reprimand, caution.
verwaschen, 1. *v.a.* wash away *or* wash out (*stains, etc.*); wear out *or* spoil through washing. 2. *p.p.* & *adj.* washed-out, faded, indistinct; pale, vague, undecided, characterless, (*coll.*) wishy-washy. **–heit,** *f.* paleness, vagueness, indistinctness, (*fig.*) indecision.
verwässer–n, *v.a.* water, dilute, weaken; (*fig.*) make vapid *or* insipid, water down; *–te Schreibart,* vapid style.
verweben, *reg.* & *ir.v.a.* weave up (*all the thread*); weave into, interweave; (*usually p.p.*) intertwine, intermingle; *Wahrheit mit Dichtung –,* mingle truth inextricably with fiction.
verwechs–eln, *v.a.* confuse, mix up, take for, mistake for; change by mistake; *er –elt stets die Namen,* he is always mixing up *or* confusing names; *wir haben unsere Hüte –elt,* we have taken the wrong hats. **–elbar,** *adj.* easily confused *or* mistaken. **–(e)lung,** *f.* confusion, mistake, (*coll.*) mix-up; permutation; *sie sehen einander zum –eln ähnlich,* they are confusingly alike.
verwegen, *adj.* bold, daring, audacious; rash, foolhardy; presumptuous, insolent, (*coll.*) cheeky, saucy. **–heit,** *f.* boldness, daring, (*coll.*) dash; temerity, audacity, rashness, foolhardiness; presumption, insolence, (*coll.*) cheek, face, nerve. **–tlich,** *adj.* (*rare*) *see* **–**.
verweh–en, 1. *v.a.* blow away *or* about, scatter; *der Wind hat den Weg mit Schnee –t,* the wind has covered the path with snow. 2. *v.n.* (*aux.* s.) blow about *or* away, drift, be scattered; *seine Hoffnungen sind –t,* his hopes are dead *or* are blighted. **–ung,** *f.* snow-drift.
verwehren, *v.a.* (*einem etwas*) hinder, prevent, restrain (a p. from doing a th.), forbid, prohibit.
verweiblicht, *adj.* effeminate.
verweichlich–en, 1. *v.a.* coddle, pamper, enervate. 2. *v.n.* become effeminate, flabby *or* soft. **–t,** *adj.* pampered, coddled, effeminate. **–ung,** *f.* coddling, pampering; effeminacy.
verweiger–n, *v.a.* (*einem etwas*) refuse, deny (s.o. s.th.), decline, reject; *Annahme –n,* refuse acceptance, decline to accept; *Dienst –n,* refuse *or* withhold one's service; *Gehorsam –n,* refuse *or* decline to obey. **–ung,** *f.* denial, refusal; *–ung der Annahme,* non-acceptance. **–ungsfall,** *m.*; *im –ungsfalle,* in case of refusal, if refused.
verweilen, 1. *v.n.* & (*rare*) *r.* (*aux.* h.) stay, remain, tarry, linger (*bei,* with). 2. *v.a.* (*dial.*) delay, hold back; *bei einem Gegenstande –,* dwell on a subject.
verweint, *adj.* ruined with weeping; *–e Augen,* eyes red with tears; *–es Gesicht,* tear-stained face.
Verweis, *m.* (-es, -e) 1. reprimand, rebuke, reproof, censure. 2. reference (*to a book*); *einem wegen einer S. einen – geben,* reprove, rebuke *or* censure a p. for a th. **–en,** 1. *ir.v.a.* (*einem etwas*) reprove, rebuke, reprimand, upbraid (for), reproach (with). 2. (*an with Acc.,* a p.; *auf with Acc.,* a. th) refer (to). 3. (*aus, or Gen.*) banish, exile, expel (from); *einen des Landes* or *aus dem Lande –en,* banish a p. (from the country); *er ist verwiesen worden,* he has been expelled (*from school*) *or* exiled (*from the country*); *einen von der Bahn –en,* warn a p. off the track (*Sport*). **–ung,** *f.* 1. reference (*auf,* to); 2. banishment, exile; proscription; relegation. **–ungszeichen,** *n.* reference mark (*Typ.*).
verwelk–en, *v.n.* (*aux.* s.) fade, wither, wilt, droop. **–ung,** *f.* withering, wilting.
verwelschen, *v.a.* frenchify, italianize.
verweltlich–en, 1. *v.a.* secularize. 2. *v.n.* (*aux.* s.) become worldly. **–ung,** *f.* secularization.
verwend–en, 1. *reg.* & *ir.v. a.* (*auf with Acc., zu,* or *für*) use, make use of, employ, utilize (in *or* for); apply (to); bestow, spend, expend (upon); (*usually neg.*) turn aside *or* away; *er verwandte kein Auge von ihr,* he never moved *or* turned his eyes from her; *viel Sorgfalt auf eine S. –en,* bestow much care upon a th.; *etwas zu einem besonderen Gebrauch –en,* assign a th. to a particular use; *seine Zeit zu . . . –en,* employ one's time in . . .; *die nötige Zeit auf eine S. –en,* give the necessary time to a th.; (*etwas*) *nützlich* or *zu seinem Nutzen –en,* turn s.th. to account. 2. *v.r.* use one's influence *or* intercede (*für,* on behalf of). **–bar,** *adj.* available (for), applicable (to), adapted (to), suitable (for). **–barkeit,** *f.* availability, applicability, suitability. **–ung,** *f.* use, utilization, application, employment, expenditure, appropriation; intercession; *auf seine –ung hin,* as a result of *or* following his intervention; *zur –ung kommen,* come into use, be used; *zur besonderen –ung,* (seconded) for special duty (*Mil.*). **–ungsfähigkeit,** *f.* employability, applicability, usefulness. **–ungsgebiet,** *n.* field of application. **–ungsstoffwechsel,** *m.* metabolism.
verwerf–en, 1. *ir.v.a.* throw away, discard; (*usually fig.*) reject, disallow, refuse, disavow, condemn, repudiate, spurn; wear our *or* spoil by throwing; throw into the wrong place *or* in the wrong direction; *eine Klage –en,* dismiss a summons; *die Anklage wurde verworfen,* the indictment was quashed; *eine Einwendung als ungültig –en,* overrule an objection. 2. *v.r.* throw badly, miss (the mark); throw out wrongly, play the wrong card (*Cards*); warp, become warped (*of wood*); (show a) fault (*Geol.*). 3. *v.n.* (*aux.* h.) bear (young) prematurely, miscarry (*of animals*). **–lich,** *adj.* objectionable, reprehensible, thoroughly bad. **–ung,** *f.* rejection, refusal, repudiation; reprobation, censure, condemnation; exception (*Law*); fault (*Geol.*).
verwert–en, *v.a.* utilize, turn to (good) account, make use of; sell, realize, turn into cash; *Papiere –en,* convert stock; *sich gut –en lassen,* fetch a good price; be most useful, come in handy. **–bar,** *adj.* realizable; utilizable. **–ung,** *f.* utilization; sale, disposal, realization; *ich habe keine –ung dafür,* I have no use for it, I cannot use it, do anything with it *or* make any use of it.
verwes–en, 1. *v.a.* administer, manage, deal with on s.o.'s behalf. 2. *v.n.* (*aux.* s.) putrefy, decompose, decay, moulder, rot. **–er,** *m.* administrator, manager, regent. **–lich,** *adj.* perishable, corruptible, liable to decay. **–ung,** *f.* decay, decomposition, putrefaction; management, administration.
verwetten, *v.a.* gamble away, stake.
verwettert, *adj.* ravaged by the weather, weather-beaten.
verwichen, *adj.* (*archaic*) former, past, late; *–es Jahr,* last year.
verwichsen, *v.a.* (*sl.*) thrash soundly; (*vulg.*) squander on frivolity.
verwick–eln, 1. *v.a.* entangle, implicate, involve. 2. *v.r.* (*in with Acc.*) get entangled in, be involved *or* implicated in; *sich in seine eigenen Worte –eln,* get tied up in one's own words. **–elt,** *adj.* complicated, intricate, involved, entangled. **–(e)lung,** *f.* complication, complexity, intricacy; embarrassment, confusion; tangle, entanglement.
verwiegen, *v.a.* weigh out.
verwiesen, *p.p.* (*of* verweisen) referred to; *es sei – auf,* reference should be made to. **–e(r),** *m.* exile, outlaw.
verwilder–n, *v.r.* & *n.* (*aux.* s.) grow wild *or* savage, become depraved *or* brutalized (*of a p.*); run wild, run to seed (*of plants*); be neglected, (*coll.*) become a wilderness (*of a garden*); *–n lassen,* let run wild, neglect. **–t,** *p.p.* & *adj.* wild, savage, unruly, brutal; uncultivated, overgrown with weeds. **–ung,** *f.* return to a wild *or* savage state; degeneration; wildness, unruliness, barbarism.
verwilligen, *v.a.* (*archaic*), *see* **einwilligen.**
verwind–en, *ir.v.a.* overcome, get the better of; get over, recover from; warp, twist (*Av.*); *er wird es nie –en,* he will never get over it. **–ung,** *f.* torsion. **–ungsklappe,** *f.* aileron (*Av.*).
verwirk–en, *v.a.* forfeit, lose (*through one's own fault*); merit, incur (*a punishment*); use up, consume. **–ung,** *f.* loss, forfeiture.
verwirklich–en, 1. *v.a.* realize, embody, materialize. 2. *v.r.* be realized, come true. **–ung,** *f.* realization, materialization.
verwirr–en, *ir.v.a.* tangle, entangle, disorder, dis-

arrange; complicate, make involved *or* intricate; confuse, embarrass, disconcert, bewilder, perplex. **–t,** *adj.* complicated; confused, perplexed; *einen –t machen*, embarrass *or* bewilder a p.; *einem den Kopf –en*, make s.o. quite confused, make a p.'s head spin. **–ung,** *f.* entanglement, complication, confusion, disorder; embarrassment, perplexity; *in –ung bringen*, throw into disorder, confuse; *in –ung geraten*, become confused, get mixed up.

verwirtschaften, *v.a.* squander through bad management, dissipate one's resources.

verwisch–en, 1. *v.a.* wipe away, efface, blot out, obliterate; stump, soften (*an outline, Draw.*). 2. *v.r.* become effaced *or* obliterated. **–ung,** *f.* effacement, obliteration.

verwitter–n, *v.n.* (*aux.* s.) weather, crumble away, disintegrate, decay, decompose; become dilapidated, be weather-beaten; effloresce (*Chem.*). **–t,** *adj.* weather-beaten *or* -worn, weathered, dilapidated; *–ter Kalk*, air-slaked lime. **–ung,** *f.* weathering (*Geol.*), decomposition, decay, disintegration; efflorescence (*Chem.*).

verwitw–en, *v.n.* (*aux.* s.) become a widow(er). **–et,** *p.p.* & *adj.* widowed; *–ete Königin*, Queen dowager, dowager queen. **–ung,** *f.* widowhood; *seit ihrer –ung*, since she became a widow, since she lost her husband.

verwogen, *adj.* (*archaic* & *dial.*) bold, audacious, rash, foolhardy; *see* **verwegen.**

verwöhn–en, 1. *v.a.* spoil, pamper, coddle. 2. *v.r.* (over)indulge o.s., allow o.s. to be pampered. **–t,** *p.p.* & *adj.* spoiled, pampered; fastidious. **–theit,** *f.* bad habits, evil results of pampering; fastidiousness. **–ung,** *f.*, *see* **–theit;** pampering, spoiling, indulgence.

verworfen, 1. *p.p.* (*of* verwerfen) cast off, abandoned, rejected. 2. *adj.* depraved, vile, infamous; reprobate (*Theol.*). **–heit,** *f.* depravity, baseness, vileness, infamy; reprobation.

verworren, *adj.* entangled, intricate, confused, muddled; *der –e Bericht eines verwirrten Menschen*, the confused *or* muddled account of a bewildered *or* muddle-headed person. **–heit,** *f.* entanglement, confusion, muddled state, disorder.

verwund–en, 1. *p.p.*, *see* **verwinden.** 2. *v.a.* wound, injure, hurt; *auf das Schmerzlichste –en*, cut to the quick. **–bar,** *adj.* vulnerable; *–bare Stelle*, weak *or* sore point. **–barkeit,** *f.* vulnerability. **–et,** *p.p.* & *adj.* wounded, injured, hurt. **–ete(r),** *m.* injured person, wounded soldier, casualty. **–etenabschub,** *m.* evacuation of wounded (*Mil.*). **–etenabzeichen,** *n.* wound-stripe (*Mil.*). **–etennest,** *n.* advanced aid post (*Mil.*). **–etensammelstelle,** *f.* casualty clearing-station. **–ung,** *f.* wound, injury; *tödliche –ung.* mortal wound, fatal injury.

verwunder–n, 1. *v.a.* surprise, astonish. 2. *v.r.* be astonished, be surprised, wonder (*über with Acc.*, at); *er –te sich, mich dort zu sehen*, he was surprised to see me there. 3. *v.imp. es –t mich*, it surprises me, I wonder; *sich –t stellen*, feign *or* affect surprise; *es ist nicht zu –n*, it is not to be wondered at. **–lich,** *adj.* astonishing, surprising, wondrous, strange. **–ung,** *f.* astonishment, surprise, wonder. **–ungsausruf,** *m.* exclamation of surprise. **–ungsbrille,** *f.*; (*coll.*) *die –ungsbrille aufsetzen*, affect astonishment, pretend to be surprised.

verwunschen, *adj.* (*Poet.*) bewitched, enchanted.

verwünsch–en, *v.a.* deplore (*a th.*), wish (*a p.*) ill, curse, execrate, bewitch, cast a spell on. **–t,** 1. *p.p.* & *adj.* cursed, confounded, damned, execrable; *das –te Geld*, that confounded money; *–ter Spaß*, joke in bad taste; (*coll.*) *–t gescheit*, confoundedly *or* damned clever. 2. *int.*; *–t!* confound it! curse! damn! **–ung,** *f.* curse, imprecation, malediction; *–ungen gegen einen ausstoßen*, curse a p., hurl imprecations at a p.

verwurmt, *adj.* worm-eaten.

verwurz–eln, *v.n.* & *r.* be *or* become rooted. **–(e)lung,** *f.* (*mit* or *in*) close attachment (to), intimate contact (with).

verwüst–en, *v.a.* lay waste, devastate, ruin, destroy. **–ung,** *f.* devastation, destruction.

verzag–en, *v.n.* (*aux.* s.) despair (*an einer S.*, of a th.) lose heart *or* courage, be despondent. **–t,** *p.p.* & *adj.* discouraged, despondent, dejected, disheartened; faint-hearted, timorous, pusillanimous; *–t machen*, dishearten, discourage; *–t werden*, despond, lose heart, give up hope. **–theit,** *f.* despair, despondency, faint-heartedness, cowardice.

verzähl–en, *v.r.* make a mistake in counting, count wrong, miscount. **–ung,** *f.* error in counting.

verzahn–en, 1. *v.a.* tooth, cog (*a wheel, etc.*), dovetail (*a joint*) (*Carp.*); mesh together; (*fig.*) link together, supply with cross-references. 2. *v.r.* (*ineinander*) engage, mesh (*as gears*), dovetail (*Carp.* & *fig.*); become closely connected with. **–ung,** *f.* notch, dovetailing; gear, gearing.

verzapf–en, *v.a.* sell (*beer, etc.*) on draught; join by mortise (*Carp.*); (*sl.*) say, talk (*nonsense, etc.*). **–ung,** *f.* draught sale; mortise and tenon joint.

verzärtel–n, *v.a.* spoil, coddle, pamper, pet. **–t,** *p.p.* & *adj.* pampered, spoilt, petted. **–ung,** *f.* over-indulgence, pampering, coddling; effeminacy.

verzauber–n, *v.a.* charm, bewitch, put a spell on; *–n in* (*Acc.*), transform, change (into); *–ter Prinz*, enchanted prince. **–ung,** *f.* enchantment, magic spell.

verzehn–fachen, *v.a.* increase *or* multiply tenfold. **–ten,** *v.a.* (*archaic*) pay tithe on.

Verzehr, *m.* consumption (*of food*). **–en,** 1. *v.a.* consume, eat up; use up, waste, spend, expend (*money*); *was habe ich –t?* what have I to pay? what does my bill come to? 2. *v.r.* be consumed (*vor*, with); fret, waste *or* pine away. **–end,** *pr.p.* & *adj.* (all-)consuming, burning (*passion*). **–ung,** *f.* (*coll.*) consumption, tuberculosis. **–zwang,** *m.* obligation to order (*food, drink, etc., at an inn*).

verzeichn–en, 1. *v.a.* write *or* note down, book, enter, record, register, mark, specify, make a list of, take an inventory of; draw badly; (*C.L.*) *zu dem –eten Kurs*, at the price quoted. 2. *v.r.* make a mistake in drawing. **–is,** *n.* list, catalogue, inventory, index, register; statement, specification, bill, invoice, price-list; *–is der Anmerkungen*, index of notes; *–is der Druckfehler*, list of errata; *–is der Einkünfte*, rent-roll; *–is des Inhalts*, table of contents; *–is der Verstorbenen*, obituary. **–ung,** *f.* error in drawing; distortion (*Opt.*); noting down, specification. **–ungsfrei,** *adj.* orthoscopic (*Opt.*).

verzeigen, *v.a.* (*Swiss dial.*), *see* **anzeigen.**

verzeih–en, *ir.v.a.* (*einem etwas*) forgive, pardon, excuse; remit (*sins*); pass over (*a fault*); *–en Sie!* excuse me! pardon me! I beg your pardon!; *nicht zu –en*, inexcusable. **–lich,** *adj.* pardonable, excusable, venial. **–ung,** *f.* pardon, forgiveness, remission (*of sins*); *einen um –ung bitten*, beg a p.'s pardon; (*um*) *–ung!* I beg your pardon! excuse me! please forgive me!

verzerr–en, 1. *v.a.* distort, deform, twist *or* pull out of shape. 2. *v.r.* get out of shape; pull a face, make a grimace, roll one's eyes; *etwas ins Lächerliche –en*, make s.th. appear ridiculous; *den Mund –en*, make a wry mouth; *–t darstellen*, caricature. **–ung,** *f.* distortion, contortion, grimace.

verzetteln, 1. *v.a.* scatter, disperse, dissipate, fritter away; make a card index of, enter on cards, catalogue. 2. *v.r.* dissipate one's energies, (*coll.*) spread o.s. too much.

Verzicht, *m.* renunciation, resignation; *auf eine S. – leisten*, renounce a th. **–en,** *v.n.* (*aux.* h.) (*auf eine S.*) renounce, resign, waive, relinquish, give up all claim to, forgo (a th.); *auf einen Anspruch –en*, waive a claim. **–leistung,** *f.* renunciation, abandonment.

verzieh–en, 1. *ir.v.a.* distort, twist (up), drag, pull, warp, contract; train badly, spoil (*children*); delay; *den Mund –en*, make a wry mouth, pull a face; *er verzog keine Miene*, he did not move a muscle, (*sl.*) he did not bat an eyelid; *den Mund zum Lächeln –en*, twist one's mouth into a smile; *sich* (*Dat.*) *eine Sehne –en*, strain a sinew; *einen Stein –en*, move the wrong piece, make a false move (*in draughts, etc.*). 2. *v.r.* (*coll.*) draw away, withdraw, make off slowly, disperse, be dispersed, vanish, pass away, disappear; warp, be twisted, hang badly, pucker; *das Gewitter –t sich*, the storm is passing over. 3. *n.* (*aux.* s.) move, remove, go away; *in die Stadt –en*, move into town; *von M. nach O. –en*, remove from M. to O.; *falls verzogen*, in case of change of address. 4. *v.n.*

(*aux.* h.) & *r.* (*archaic*) delay, go slow, hesitate. **-ung,** *f.* distortion, contortion; spoiling, bad bringing up (*of children*); change of address.

verzier-en, *v.a.* adorn, ornament, decorate, beautify, embellish; *ein Buch mit Kupferstichen -en*, illustrate a book with copperplate engravings; *-ter Kontrapunkt*, figured counterpoint. **-end,** *pr.p.* & *adj.* decorative, ornamental. **-ung,** *f.* decoration, ornamentation, ornament, embellishment, flourish, illustration; *musikalische -ungen*, flourishes, grace-notes.

verzimmern, *v.a.* fit the woodwork, do the carpentry in *or* of; line with a planking, revet (*Mil.*).

verzink-en, *v.a.* coat *or* line with zinc, galvanize; (*coll.*) denounce, inform against. **-ung,** *f.* galvanization.

verzinn-en, *v.a.* tin, tin-plate, coat *or* line with tin; *-tes Eisenblech*, tin-plate. **-ung,** *f.* tinning, tin-plating.

verzins-en, 1. *v.a.* pay interest on; *ihm das Geld zu 3% -en*, pay him 3% interest on the money. 2. *v.r.* yield *or* bear interest; *es -t sich nicht*, it yields no interest. **-bar,** *adj.* liable for *or* subject to interest. **-lich,** *adj.* bearing interest; *-lich anlegen*, put out at interest, invest; *-liches Darlehen*, loan on interest; *-lich vom ersten Oktober*, interest payable from October 1. **-ung,** *f.* interest; payment of interest; *zur -ung ausleihen*, put out at interest.

verzogen, *p.p.* (*of* verziehen) & *adj.* warped, distorted; spoiled (*of a child*).

verzöger-n, 1. *v.a.* defer, delay, put off, postpone; retard, slow down, protract, spin out. 2. *v.r.* be delayed, come later; be protracted *or* deferred. **-er,** *m.* restrainer, retarder. **-ung,** *f.* delay, postponement, adjournment; retardation, time-lag, delay(ed)-action.

verzoll-en, *v.a.* pay duty on; *haben Sie etwas zu -en?* have you anything to declare? *Waren -en*, pay duty on goods, clear goods at the custom-house. **-bar,** *adj.* liable to duty, dutiable, excisable. **-t,** *adj.* duty-paid. **-ung,** *f.* payment of duty, clearance (*by customs officer*).

verzück-t, *p.p.* & *adj.* enraptured, ecstatic, rapt, in raptures, in transports, in ecstasy, (*coll.*) beside o.s. (with enthusiasm). **-theit,** *f.*, **-ung,** *f.* ecstasy, rapture, transport, trance, convulsion.

verzuckern, *v.a.* sweeten, sugar (over), ice, (*fig.*) gild *or* sugar (*the pill*).

Verzug, *m.* (-(e)s, ¨-e) delay, postponement; darling, pet, spoilt child; *bei – der Zahlung*, in the case of arrears of *or* in payment; *bei – neue Anschrift angeben!* notify any change of address; *es ist Gefahr im -e*, there is danger imminent *or* imminent danger, delay is dangerous; *in –*, in arrears, in default; *ohne –*, without delay, at once, immediately, forthwith. **-saktien,** *f.pl.* deferred shares. **-sklausel,** *f.* clause relating to default. (*C.L.*) **-stage,** *m.pl.* days of grace. **-szinsen,** *m.pl.* interest payable on arrears.

verzwatzeln, *v.n.* (*dial.*) despair, lose one's patience.

verzweif-eln, 1. *v.n.* (*aux*, s. & h.) despair (*an ihm*, of him; *über eine S.*, of a th.); give up hope, be despondent. **-elt,** *adj.* despairing, desperate; *eine -elte Geschichte*, a desperate *or* hopeless case, (*coll.*) a dreadful business. 2. *n.*; *es ist zum -eln*, it is enough to drive one mad, crazy *or* to despair. **-(e)lung,** *f.* despair, desperation; *einen in* or *zur -lung bringen*, reduce a p. to despair, drive s.o. mad; *in -lung geraten*, become despondent, give up hope; *aus, in* or *vor -lung tun*, do in desperation; *die Kraft der -lung*, the strength of despair; *-lung an Gott*, despair about *or* over (the existence of) God. **-(e)lungsmut,** *m.* courage of despair.

verzweig-en, *v.r.* branch (out), ramify. **-ung,** *f.* branching, ramification.

verzwerg-en, *v.n.* (*aux.* s.) become dwarfed, grow stunted. **-t,** *p.p.* & *adj.*, dwarf, dwarfed, dwarfish, stunted.

verzwick-en, *v.a.* entangle, confuse; fill up with rubble *or* packing (*Mas.*); *den Weinstock -en*, prune the vine. **-t,** *p.p.* & *adj.* puzzling, confused, awkward, complicated, intricate, difficult; *-te Geschichte*, (*coll.*) tricky business. **-theit,** *f.* awkwardness, difficulty.

Vesper, *f.* (-n) vespers, evensong; afternoon tea; *die – schlägt*, the evening bell tolls. **-bild,** *n.* pietà, Virgin with dead body of Christ. **-brot,** *n.* afternoon tea. **-gesang,** *m.* evensong. **-glocke,** *f.* vesper-bell. **-n,** *v.n.* (*aux.* s.) take afternoon-tea. **-stunde,** *f.* **-zeit,** *f.* evening-time, afternoon; vespers.

Vestalin, *f.* (-nen) vestal (virgin).

Vestibül, *n.* (-s, -e) vestibule, hall.

Veteran, *m.* (-en, -en) veteran (soldier), (*sl.*) old sweat.

Veterinär, 1. *m.* (-s, -e) veterinary surgeon. 2. *adj.* veterinary.

Veto, *n.* (-s (*or Austr. dial.* -n), -s) veto; *aufschiebendes –*, suspensive veto; *gegen eine S. sein – einlegen*, veto a th., protest against a th.

Vettel, *f.* (-n) slut, slattern, trollop, drab.

Vetter, *m.* (-s (*or Austr. dial.* –), -n) (male) cousin. **-lich,** *adj.* cousinly, cousin-like. **-liwirtschaft,** *f.* (*Swiss dial.*), *see* **-nwirtschaft. -n,** *v.a.* & *r.* treat as a cousin. **-schaft,** *f.* cousinship; (*collect.*) cousins, kinsmen. **-(n)straße,** *f.*; *die -nstraße ziehen*, do *or* go the round of one's relations. **-nwirtschaft,** *f.* nepotism.

vexier-en, *v.a.* vex, tease, trick, puzzle, mystify, hoax, (*coll.*) take in. **-bild,** *n.* picture-puzzle. **-schloß,** *n.* puzzle- *or* combination-lock. **-spiegel,** *m.* distorting mirror. **-spiel,** *n.* Chinese puzzle.

Vezier, *m.* (-s, -e) vizier.

Viatikum, *n.* (-kums, -ka & -ken) viaticum, alms; extreme unction (*R.C.*).

Vibr-ation, *f.* (-en) vibration. **-ationsmassage,** *f.* vibro-massage (*Med.*). **-ieren,** *v.n.* (*aux.* h.) vibrate.

vidimieren, *v.a.* pass for press, sign as correct.

Viech, *n.* (-s, -er) (*dial.*), *see* **Vieh**; (*vulg.*) beast, swine, cow (*as abuse*).

Vieh, *n.* cattle, beast, livestock; dumb animal; *zwei Stück –*, two head of cattle; *eine Herde* or *Trift –*, a drove of cattle; *Menschen und –*, men and beasts. **-arzt,** *m.* veterinary surgeon. **-bestand,** *m.* cattle population, livestock. **-diebstahl,** *m.* cattle-stealing. **-dünger,** *m.* stable manure. **-futter,** *n.* fodder, forage. **-haltung,** *f.* cattle-breeding *or* rearing. **-händler,** *m.* cattle-dealer. **-herde,** *f.* herd of cattle. **-hof,** *m.* stockyard. **-hürde,** *f.* cattle-pen. **-isch,** *adj.* brutal, bestial. **-knecht,** *m.* farmhand, cattle-hand, herdsman. **-magd,** *f.* farm-servant, dairy-hand, dairymaid. **-markt,** *m.* cattle- *or* stock-market. **-mast,** *f.* fattening of cattle. **-salz,** *n.* rock *or* block salt (*for cattle*). **-schlag,** *m.* breed of cattle. **-schwemme,** *f.* watering-place for cattle, horse-pond. **-seuche,** *f.* cattle-pest, murrain, foot-and-mouth disease. **-stall,** *m.* cow-house, cattle-shed, stable. **-stamm,** *m.*, *see* **-schlag. -stand,** *m.*, **-stapel** *m.*, *see* **-bestand. -tränke,** *f.*, *see* **-schwemme. -treiber,** *m.* drover. **-trift,** *f.* cattle-run, pasturage. **-wagen,** *m.* cattle-truck; stock-car (*Amer.*). **-weide,** *f.* pasture, cattle-range; (*pl.*) pasturage. **-zählung,** *f.* cattle-census. (*coll.*) **-zeug,** *n.* animals. **-zucht,** *f.* stock-farming, cattle-breeding. **-züchter,** *m.* stock-farmer, cattle-breeder.

viel, 1. *adj.* (*comp.* mehr, *sup.* meist) much, a great deal, (*coll.*) a lot; *pl.* many, *see* **-e**; *-es andere*, many other things; *– Geld*, much money, a lot of money; *das -e Geld*, all that money; *trotz seines -en Geldes*, in spite of all his riches; *ein bißchen –, etwas –*, rather *or* a little too much; *gar –*, a great deal; *wir haben gleich –*, we have equal amounts, we have each the same amount, (*coll.*) we have just as much as each other; (N.B. *gleich– ob*, all the same *or* immaterial whether); (*Prov.*) *mit -em hält man Haus, mit Wenigem kommt man aus*, the more you have, the more you want; *in -em*, in many respects; *er hat – gelesen*, he has read a great deal, he is widely read; *– mehr als*, much *or* far more than (N.B. *-mehr*); *nicht –*, not much; *nicht -es, sondern –*, non multa, sed multum; *es hätte nicht – gefehlt, so hatte er . . .*, a little more and he would have . . .; *recht –*, see *sehr –*; *das will – sagen*, that is saying a great deal;

sehr –, very much, a great deal; *wenn es (sehr) viel ist*, at the most; *eben so* –, just as much; *noch einmal so* –, as much again; *so* – *weiß ich*, this *or* that much I know (N.B. *so– ich weiß*, as far as I know); *soundso* –, so much (and no more), neither more nor less (N.B. *am soundso–ten März*, on March the so-and-so *or* the something or other, on such-and-such day in March; *zu soundso– Prozent*, at such-and-such a percentage); *um –es größer*, larger by far; *ein wenig* –, see *etwas* –; *ohne ihn würde ich –es nicht wissen*, without him I should be ignorant of many things; *ziemlich* –, a good deal; *zu* –, far *or* much too much (N.B. *zu–*, too much); – *zu* –, much *or* far too much; *mehr als zu* –, more than enough. 2. *n.*; *viele Wenig machen ein* –, many a little makes a mickle *or* muckle. **–artig,** *adj.* manifold, multifarious, various. **–ästig,** *adj.* with many branches, much branched, ramose. **–bändig,** *adj.* of many volumes. **–bedeutend,** *adj.* very significant. **–beschäftigt,** *adj.* much occupied, very busy. **–besprochen,** *adj.* much talked of. **–betreten,** *adj.* well-trodden. **–blätt(e)rig,** *adj.* many-leaved, polyphyllous, polypetalous. **–deutig,** *adj.* ambiguous. **–deutigkeit,** *f.* ambiguity. **–e,** *pl. adj.* many; *die –en*, the many; *es kamen ihrer –e*, many of them came; *die –en Menschen, welche . . .*, the number of people who . . .; *gar –e*, very many; *sehr –e*, very many, a great many; *seine –en Liebschaften*, his numerous *or* many affairs. **–eck,** *n.* polygon. **–eckig,** *adj.* many-cornered, polygonal. **–ehe,** *f.* polygamy. **–ehig,** *adj.* polygamous. **–enorts,** *adv.* in many places. **–erfahren,** *adj.* much experienced. **–erlei,** 1. *adj.* various, divers, multifarious, many kinds of, different. 2. *n.* great variety. **–erörtert,** *adj.*, *see* **–besprochen. –erorts,** *adv.*, *see* **–enorts. –fach,** 1. *adj.* manifold, multifarious, various; multitudinous; repeated, reiterated. 2. *adv.* often, frequently; in many cases *or* ways. **–fache,** *n.* the multiple; *um ein –faches*, many times over. **–fächerig,** *adj.* many-celled, multilocular (*Bot.*). **–fachschaltung,** *f.*, **–fachumschalter,** *m.* multiple switch (*Phone*). **–fältig,** *adj.* abundant, frequent, manifold, various. **–fältigkeit,** *f.* diversity, variety, multiplicity. **–farbig,** *adj.* multi-coloured, variegated, polychromatic. **–fingrig,** *adj.* polydactylous. **–flach,** *n.* polyhedron. **–flächig,** *adj.* polyhedral. **–flächner,** *m.* polyhedron. **–flüg(e)lig,** *adj.* polypterous (*Ent.*). **–förmig,** *adj.* multiform, polymorphous. **–fraß,** *m.* glutton (*also* Gula gulo (*Zool.*)); voracious eater. **–früchtig,** *adj.* polycarpous (*Bot.*). **–fuß,** *m.* polypod, centripede, millepede (*Ent.*). **–gebraucht,** *adj.* much *or* constantly used. **–geliebt,** *adj.* well-beloved. **–genannt,** *adj.* often-named, much discussed, renowned. **–gereist,** *adj.* widely travelled. **–gerühmt,** *adj.* much praised. **–geschäftig,** *adj.* much occupied; bustling; *–geschäftiger Mensch*, busybody. **–geschmäht,** *adj.* much abused. **–gestaltig,** *adj.* of many shapes, polymorphic, multiform. **–glied(e)rig,** with *or* composed of many members, polynomial (*Math.*). **–götterei,** *f.* polytheism. **–griffelig,** *adj.* polygynous, polystylous (*Bot.*). **–heit,** *f.* plurality, multiplicity; multitude, large *or* great number *or* quantity. **–jährig,** *adj.* many years old; *–jähriger Freund*, friend of many years standing. **–kantig,** *adj.* many-sided, polygonal. **–köpfig,** *adj.* many-headed, polycephalous, (*fig.*) numerous. (*obs.*) **–lieb,** *adj.* very dear, darling. **–liebchen,** *n.* darling, sweetheart; philippina. **–linig,** *adj.* multilinear. **–malig,** *adj.* often-repeated, reiterated, frequent. **–mal(s),** *adv.* often, frequently, many times, (*archaic*) oftentimes; *ich danke Ihnen –mals*, I thank you very much, many thanks; *einen –mals grüßen lassen*, send one's kind regards to a p. **–männerei,** *f.* polyandry (*also Bot.*). **–mehr,** 1. *adv.* rather, much more. 2. *conj.* rather, on the contrary. **–motorig,** *adj.* multi-engined (*Av.*). **–reihig,** *adj.* multiserial. **–sagend,** *adj.* expressive, significant, highly suggestive, full of meaning. **–saitig,** *adj.* many-stringed. **–schichtig,** *adj.* many-layered, stratified. **–schreiber,** *m.* prolific writer, quill-driver, scribbler. **–seitig,** *adj.* multilateral; polygonal, polyhedral; many-sided, versatile; *–seitiger Wunsch*, widespread desire. **–seitigkeit,** *f.* many-sidedness, versatility. **–silbig,** *adj.* polysyllabic. **–sprachig,** *adj.* polyglot. **–sprecher,** *m.* great talker, (*vulg.*) windbag, gasbag. **–staaterei,** *f.* tendency towards decentralisation, separatism. **–stimmig,** *adj.* for many voices, many-voiced, polyphonic. **–tätigkeit,** *f.* many-sided activity. **–tausendmaltausend,** many many thousands, very many thousands, thousands and *or* upon thousands. **–teilig,** *adj.* multipartite; multinominal (quantity); multifid, multisect, polytomous (*Bot.*, *Zool.*). **–tuer,** *m.* fussy person, busybody. **–tuerei,** *f.* fussiness, officiousness. **–umfassend,** *adj.* vast, comprehensive. **–umstritten,** *adj.* much discussed. **–umworben,** *adj.* much wooed, eagerly sought after. **–verheißend,** *adj.*, *see* **–versprechend. –vermögend,** *adj.* very influential, powerful. **–verschlungen,** *adj.* highly complex. **–versprechend,** *adj.* very promising, of great promise. **–weiberei,** *f.* polygamy. **–weibig,** *adj.* polygynian (*Bot.*). **–wertig,** *adj.* polyvalent. **–wertigkeit,** *f.* polyvalance, multivalence. **–wink(e)lig,** *adj.* with many angles. **–wissen,** *n.* wide knowledge, great learning. **–wisser,** *m.* erudite man, man of great learning (*coll.*) pundit, walking encyclopaedia. **–wisserei,** *f.* smattering of many things, broad superficial knowledge, sciolism. **–zellig,** *adj.* multicellular.

vielleicht, *adv.* perhaps, possibly, maybe, perchance; *wenn er – kommen sollte*, should he chance to come; *Sie haben – Recht*, you may be right.

vier, 1. *num. adj.* (*coll. when used predic. Nom. & Acc.* -e; *Dat.* -en) four; *auf allen –en gehen*, go on all fours; *alle –e von sich strecken*, stretch o.s. out, lie sprawling, (*coll.*) turn up one's toes, give up the ghost; *unter – Augen*, tête-à-tête, privately, confidentially; *setz dich auf deine – Buchstaben !* (*vulg.*) find somewhere to sit; *sich in seine – Ecken* or *Pfähle begeben*, be off home; *um halb* –, at half-past three; *mit –en fahren*, drive four-in-hand; *in seinen – Wänden*, at home; *in alle – Winde*, to the four winds; *wir waren zu –en*, there were four of us; *zu je –en*, in fours. 2. *f.* (-en) the number 4, the figure 4. **–ballspiel,** *n.* foursome (*Golf*). **–beinig,** *adj.* four-legged. **–blatt,** *n.* four comradcs; quatrefoil (*Arch.*); quadrifolium (*Bot.*). **–blattschraube,** *f.* four-bladed propeller. **–blätt(e)rig,** *adj.* four-leaved, tetrapetalous. **–bund,** *m.* quadruple alliance. **–dimensional,** fourth-dimensional; (*coll.*) unreal, spooky. **–eck,** *n.* square, rectangle, quadrilateral; *verschobenes –eck*, rhomb, rhombus; *rechtwinkliges –eck*, rectangle. **–eckig,** *adj.* square, quadrilateral, rectangular, quadrate, four-cornered. **–einhalb,** *num. adj.* four and a half. **–elektrodenröhre,** *f.* tetrode (*Rad.*). **–er,** *m.* one of four; soldier of the fourth regiment; wine of the year '04; four (*Rowing*), foursome (*Golf*). **–erlei,** *indec. adj.* of four different kinds. **–erreihe,** *f.* column of four (*Gymn.*). **–errennen,** four-man relay-race. **–erzug,** *m.* four-in-hand. **–fach,** *adj.* quadruple, fourfold; *um das –fache vermehren*, multiply by four, quadruple. **–falt,** *adj.*, **–fältig,** *adj.* fourfold, quadruple. **–farbendruck,** *m.* four-colour printing. **–felderwirtschaft,** *f.* four-strip cultivation. **–flach,** *n.* tetrahedron. **–flächig,** *adj.* tetrahedral. **–flächner,** *m.* tetrahedron. **–fürst,** *m.* tetrarch. **–füßer,** *m.* quadruped, tetrapod. **–füßig,** *adj.* four-footed. **–füßler,** *m.*, *see* **–füßer. –gesang,** *m.* four-part song, quartette. **–gespann,** *n.* four-in-hand, quadriga. **–gestrichen,** *adj.* four-tailed (note); (note) in altissimo; *–gestrichenes F*, F in altissimo, F of the sixth octave; *das Klavier geht bis ins –gestrichene F*, it is a six-octaved piano. **–gliederig,** *adj.* with 4 members *or* parts; quadrinomial (*Alg.*). **–händig,** *adj.* four-handed; *–händiges Tonstück*, piece arranged as a piano duet *or* for four hands; *–händig spielen*, play a duet. **–heber,** *m.* tetrameter (*Metr.*). **–hundert,** *adj.* four hundred. **–jährig,** *adj.* of four years; lasting four years, quadrennial; *–jähriges Kind*, four-year-old child. **–jährlich,** *adj.* recurring every fourth year, occurring once every four years; quadrennial. **–kant,** 1. *n.* square. 2. *adj.* level, on an even keel (*Naut.*), **–kantholz,** *n.* squared timber.

-kantig, *adj.* square, four-sided. **-kantstange**, *f.* bar of rectangular section. **-linge**, *m.pl.* quadruplets. **-lingsturm**, *m.* four-gun turret. **-mal**, *adv.* four times. **-malig**, *adj.* repeated four times. **-mals**, *adv.*, *see* **-mal**. **-mächtepakt**, *m.* four-power agreement. **-paß**, *m.* quatrefoil (*Arch.*). **-pfünder**, *m.* four-pounder. **-plätzer**, *m.*, **-plätzig**, *adj.* (*Swiss dial.*), *see* **-sitzer**, **-sitzig**. **-pol**, *m.*, **-polschaltung**, *f.* network (*Elec.*). **-radantrieb**, *m.* four-wheel drive (*Motor.*). **-radbremse**, *f.* four-wheel brake (*Motor.*). **-raumwohnung**, *f.* four-room(ed) flat. **-röhrenverstärker**, *m.* four-valve amplifier (*Rad.*). **-ruderer**, *m.* four (*Rowing*). **-schrötig**, *adj.* square-built; thick-set, stocky. **-seitig**, *adj.* four-sided, quadrilateral, rectangular. **-silbig**, *adj.* four-syllabled, tetrasyllabic. **-sitzer**, *m.* four-seater (*car*). **-sitzig**, *adj.* with four seats. **-spänner**, *m.* carriage and four, four-in-hand. **-spännig**, *adj.* drawn by four horses; *-spännig fahren*, drive in a carriage and four, drive four-in-hand. **-spiel**, *n.* quartet(te) (*Mus.*), quadrille (*Cards*); foursome (*Golf*). **-stellig**, *adj.* of four places *or* digits. **-stimmig**, *adj.* for four voices *or* parts; *-stimmiges Stück*, four-part song; quartet(te). **-stöckig**, *adj.* four-storied. **-stündig**, *adj.* lasting four hours. **-stündlich**, *adj.* every four hours. **-tägig**, *adj.* of four days, lasting four days; *-tägiges Fieber*, quartan ague. **-täglich**, *adj.* recurring *or* happening every fourth day. **-taktmotor**, *m.* four-stroke engine. **-te**, *num. adj.* fourth; *das -te Gebot*, the fourth commandment; *der -te Stand*, the fourth estate, the working class, the proletariat. **-t(e)halb**, *num. adj.* three and a half. **-teilen**, *v.a.* (*p.p.* geviertelt) divide into four parts; draw and quarter (*a criminal*). **-teilig**, *adj.* quadripartite; quadrinomial; quartered (*Her.*). **-tel**, *see* **Viertel**. **-tens**, *adv.* fourthly, in the fourth place. **-tletzt**, *adj.* last but three, fourth from the end. **-undeinhalb**, *num. adj.*, see **-einhalb**. **-undsechzigstel**, *n.* one sixty-fourth. **-undsechzigstelnote**, *f.* hemidemisemiquaver. **-ung**, *f.* intersection of the nave (*Arch.*); quadrature (*of the circle*). **-ungskuppel**, *f.* central cupola (*Arch.*). **-vierteltakt**, *m.* common time (*Mus.*). **-wertig**, *adj.* tetravalent, quadrivalent. **-zahl**, *f.* quaternary number. **-zählig**, *adj.* quaternary. **-zehig**, *adj.* four-toed. **-zehn**, *see* **vierzehn**. **-zeiler**, *m.* quatrain, four-lined stanza. **-zeilig**, *adj.* four-lined. **-zig**, *see* **vierzig**.

Viertel, *n.* (*& Swiss dial. m.*) (-s, -) fourth (part), quarter; ward (*of a town*), district; *ein – (auf) vier*, a quarter past three; *drei – (auf) vier*, a quarter to four; *fünf Minuten vor drei –*, twenty minutes to; *ein – Wein*, a quarter (of a litre) of wine; *akademisches –*, 15 minutes after the time announced (*Univ.*). **-größe**, *f.* quarto. **-jahr**, *n.* quarter (of a year); three months. **-jahr(es)schrift**, *f.* quarterly (*journal*). **-jahrhundert**, *n.* quarter century. **-jährig**, *adj.* three months old, lasting three months. **-jährlich**, *adj.* every three months, once in three months, quarterly; *-jährliche Kündigung*, three months notice. **-jahrsgehalt**, *n.* quarter's salary. **-kreis**, *m.* quadrant. **-meile**, *f.* quarter of a mile. **-n**, 1. *v.a.* quarter (*also Her.*). 2. *v.n.* (*aux.* h.) strike *or* sound the quarters. **-note**, *f.* crotchet. **-pause**, *f.* crotchet-rest. **-stunde**, *f.* quarter of an hour; *drei -stunden*, three-quarters of an hour (N.B. *eine halbe bis drei – Stunden*, half to three quarters of an hour, between half an hour and three-quarters). **-stündig**, *adj.* lasting a quarter of an hour, fifteen minute (*break, etc.*). **-stündisch**, *adj.* every 15 minutes. **-ton**, *m.* half a semitone; *durch -töne fortschreitend*, enharmonic.

vierzehn, 1. *num. adj.* fourteen; *– Tage*, a fortnight; *alle – Tage*, every fortnight; *heute über – Tage* or *in – Tagen*, this day fortnight; *vor – Tagen*, a fortnight ago. 2. *f.* the number 14. **-ender**, *m.* stag with 14 tines. **-er**, *m.* soldier of the fourteenth regiment; wine of (19)14 vintage. **-fach**, 1. *adj.* fourteenfold. 2. *adv.* 14 times. **-t**, *adj.* fourteenth. **-tägig**, *adj.* lasting a fortnight. **-täglich**, *adj.* (recurring) every fortnight, fortnightly. **-tel**, *n.* fourteenth part. **-tens**, *adv.* in the fourteenth place.

vierzig, 1. *num. adj.* forty. 2. *f.* the number 40. **-er**, *m.* man in the forties, man of forty, wine of (19)40 vintage, soldier of the fortieth regiment; *in den -ern, in den -er Jahren*, in the forties. **-erin**, *f.* woman in the forties. **-fach**, *adj.*, **-fältig**, *adj.* fortyfold. **-st**, *num. adj.* fortieth. **-stel**, *n.* fortieth part. **-stens**, *adv.* in the fortieth place.

vigil-ant, 1. *adj.* (*coll.*) watchful, vigilant. 2. *m.* (-en, -en) (police) spy *or* agent. **-ie**, *f.* vigil; eve (*of a feast*) (*R.C.*). **-ieren**, *v.n.* (*aux.* h.) (*dial.*) (*auf with Acc.*) watch out *or* search for (*a p.*), keep an eye on (*a p.*) *or* open for (*a p.*)

Vignette, *f.* (-n) vignette (*Typ.*) (*Phot.*).

Vikar, *m.* (-s, -e) curate; substitute. **-iat**, *n.* (-(e)s, -e) curacy; temporary office.

Viktoria, *f.* acclamation of victory; *– rufen*, acclaim victory. *– schießen*, fire a victory salute.

Viktualien, *pl.* victuals, provisions.

Vill-a, *f.* (-en) villa, country house. **-enbesitzer**, *m.* house-owner, owner-occupier. **-enbewohner**, *m.* suburban dweller, (*coll.*) suburbanite. **-enkolonie**, *f.*, **-enviertel**, *n.* residential suburb, garden-city.

vindizieren, *v.a.* claim, lay claim to, assert *or* vindicate one's right to.

Viol-a, *f.* (-en) viola (*Mus.*). **-e**, *f.* (-en) violet, viola. **-ett**, *adj.* & *n.* violet. **-ine**, *f.* violin. **-inist**, *m.* violinist. **-inkasten**, *m.* violin-case. **-inschlüssel**, *m.* treble clef (*Mus.*). **-instimme**, *f.* violin-part. **-oncell(o)**, *n.* (-(o)s, -(o)s) violoncello, cello.

Viper, *f.* (-n) viper, adder.

virtuell, *adj.* virtual.

virtuos, 1. *adj.* masterly. 2. *m.*, **-e**, *m.* (-en, -en) virtuoso, masterly (*usually* musical) performer; artist; star (*Theat.*). **-enhaft**, *adj.* masterly, technically perfect (*often implying superficiality*). **-entum**, *n.* professional skill; (*often*) superficial finesse, airs of a virtuoso; (*collect.*) virtuosi. **-ität**, *f.* virtuosity, (musical) skill.

Visage, *f.* (*vulg.*) face, dial, fizz.

Visier, *n.* (-s, -e) visor (*of helmet*); gun-sight, back-sight (*of a gun*); *im – anpeilen*, sight, get a fix on; *das – aufschlagen*, lift one's visor; *– einstellen*, adjust the sight; (*fig.*) *mit offnem –*, fearlessly, in the face of the world. **-en**, 1. *v.a.* aim, adjust, gauge; examine (*passport*), endorse, visé. 2. *v.n.* (*aux.* h.) (*auf with Acc.*) take aim at, look out for (*a th.*), **-fernrohr**, *n.* telescopic sight. **-kimme**, *f.* notch of back-sight. **-schuß**, *m.* sighting shot. **-(schuß)-linie**, *f.* line of sight. **-winkel**, *m.* elevation setting.

Vision, *f.* dream, vision. **-är**, *m.* & *adj.* visionary.

Visit-ation, *f.* (-en) (visit of) inspection, search, examination, inquiry. **-ationsrecht**, *n.* right of search. **-ator**, *m.* inspector, excise-officer. **-e**, *f.* visit, (social) call. **-enkarte**, *f.* visiting card. **-entag**, *m.* at-home day; visiting day. **-enzimmer**, *n.* drawing-room, reception-room. **-ieren**, *v.a.* inspect, search; *eine Wunde -ieren*, probe a wound.

viskos, *adj.* viscous, viscid. **-e**, *f.* artificial silk, rayon.

Vista, *f.* (-sten) view, vista; sight (*Mus.*); (*C.L.*) *a –*, at sight. (*C.L.*) **-wechsel**, *m.* sight-bill.

Visum, *n.* (-sums, -sa) visa, endorsement.

Vitamin, *n.* (-s, -e) vitamin. **-mangel**, *m.* vitamin deficiency.

Vitrine, *f.* (-n) glass case, show case. **-npuppe**, *f.* display model, tailor's dummy.

Vitriol, *m.* & (*coll.* & *Austr. dial.*) *n.* (-s, -e) vitriol. **-flasche**, *f.* carboy. **-haltig**, *adj.* vitriolic, vitriolated. **-öl**, *n.*, **-säure**, *f.* oil of vitriol, sulphuric acid. **-sauer**, *adj.* sulphuric; *-saures Salz*, sulphate.

Vivat, 1. *n.* (-s & *Austr. dial.* –, -s) cheer, shout of acclamation; *einem ein – bringen*, give three cheers for a p. 2. *int.* hurrah! *– der König!* long live the king!

Vize-admiral, *m.* vice-admiral. **-kanzler**, *m.* vice-chancellor. **-könig**, *m.* viceroy, lord-lieutenant. **-präsident**, *m.* vice-president.

Vizinal-bahn, *f.* branch *or* local line (*Railw.*). **-straße**, *f.* country road.

Vlies (*Austr. dial.* **Vließ**) *n.* (-es, -e) fleece; *goldenes –*, golden fleece (*Hist.*), toison d'or (*Her.*).

Vogel, *m.* (-s, ⸚) bird; (*coll.*) fellow, chap, customer; *den – abschießen*, carry off the prize, hit the mark; *– Bülow* (*dial.*), golden oriole; (*Prov.*) *friß – oder stirb*, sink or swim, devil take the hindmost; (*Prov.*) *einem jeden – gefällt sein Nest*, there is no place like home; *einen – haben*, have a bee in one's bonnet, be off one's head; *gerupfter –*, one who has been fleeced (*at gaming*); *es ist ihm so wohl, wie dem – im Hanfsamen*, he is in clover; *lockerer* or *loser –*, loose fish, good-for-nothing scamp; *lustiger –*, gay dog; (*Prov.*) *ein schlechter –, der sein eigen Nest beschmutzt*, it is an ill bird that fouls its own nest; (*Prov.*) *jeder – singt wie ihm der Schnabel gewachsen ist*, every bird is known by its song; *– Strauß*, ostrich; (*coll.*) *seltener –*, strange fellow, queer bird *or* fish (*of a p.*). **–art,** *f.* species of bird. **–artig,** *adj.* birdlike. **–bauer,** *n.* bird-cage. **–beerbaum,** *m.* mountain-ash, rowan (*Sorbus aucuparia*) (*Bot.*). **–beere,** *f.* mountain-ash berry. **–beize,** *f.* falconry. **–deuter,** *m.* augur. **–deuterei,** *f.* divination by the flight of birds, augury. **–dunst,** *m.* small shot. **–ei,** *n.* bird's egg. **–er,** *m.*, *see* **Vogler.** **–fang,** *m.* fowling, bird-catching. **–fänger,** *m.*, *see* **–steller.** **–flinte,** *f.* fowling-piece. **–flug,** *m.* flight *or* flock of birds. **–frei,** *adj.* outlawed; *für –frei erklären*, outlaw. **–fuß,** *m.* bird's-foot (*Ornithopus*) (*Bot.*). **–futter,** *n.* bird-seed. **–garn,** *n.* fowler's net. **–(ge)sang,** *m.* bird-song. **–händler,** *m.* bird-dealer. **–haus,** *n.* aviary. **–hecke,** *f.* breeding-cage *or* -place. **–herd,** *m.* fowling-place. **–kenner,** *m.* ornithologist, bird-fancier. **–kirsche,** *f.* bird-cherry; common wild cherry (*Prunus avium*) (*Bot.*). **–klaue,** *f.* talon, bird's claw. **–kunde,** *f.* ornithology. **–kundig,** *adj.* ornithological. **–leicht,** *adj.* light as a feather. **–leim,** *m.* bird-lime. **–miere,** *f.* chickweed (*Stellaria*) (*Bot.*). **–mist,** *m.* bird's droppings, guano. **–n,** *v.n.*, *see* **vögeln.** **–napf,** *m.* seed-box *or* drawer. **–nest,** *n.* bird's nest. **–netz,** *n.*, *see* **–garn.** **–perspektive,** *f.*, **–schau,** *f.* bird's-eye view. **–schauer,** *m.*, *see* **–deuter.** **–scheuche,** *f.* scarecrow. **–schlecht,** *adj.* (*dial.*) horizontal, level. **–schutz,** *m.* protection of birds. **–stange,** *f.* perch (*in a bird-cage*). **–stellen,** 1. *v.n.* (*aux.* h.) catch *or* snare birds. 2. *n.* fowling, bird-catching. **–steller,** *m.* bird-catcher, fowler. **–Strauß-Politik,** *f.* ostrich-like attitude; *–Strauß-Politik treiben*, shut one's eyes to facts, hide one's head in the sand. **–strich,** *m.* flight of migratory birds. **–wahrsager,** *m.*, *see* **–deuter.** **–warte,** *f.* ornithological station, bird sanctuary. **–weibchen,** *n.* hen bird. **–welt,** *f.* feathered world. **–wicke,** *f.* bird's-tares (*Vicia cracca*) (*Bot.*). **–wildbret,** *n.* wildfowl. **–zucht,** *f.* breeding of birds; bird-fancying. **–züchter,** *m.* bird-fancier. **–zug,** *m.*, *see* **–strich.**

Vög–elchen, *n.* (-s, –) little bird, birdie; *ich habe ein –elchen singen hören*, a little bird told me. **–eln,** *v.n.* (*aux.* h.) mate (*of birds*); (*vulg.*) fornicate. **–lein,** *n.*, *see* **–elchen.**

Vogler, *m.* fowler, bird-catcher.

Vogt, *m.* (-(e)s, ⸚e) overseer, bailiff, steward, warden; prefect, magistrate, governor, administrator; provost, constable, beadle; (*Swiss dial.*) guardian. **–ei,** *f.* office, duties, jurisdiction, residence *or* income of a Vogt; prefecture, bailiwick; (*dial.*) prison. **–eilich,** *adj.* belonging to a bailiwick; relating to the office *or* jurisdiction of a bailiff. **–en,** *v.a.* (*Swiss dial.*) act as guardian to.

Vokab–el, *f.* (-n) word, vocable. **–elbuch,** *n.* word list, vocabulary. **–elschatz,** *m.* vocabulary. **–ular,** (*Austr. dial.* **–ularium**) *n.* (-s, -e (& *Austr. dial.*) -ularien), vocabulary.

Vokal, 1. *m.* (-s, -e) vowel. 2. *adj.* vocal. **–ablaut,** *m.* (vowel) gradation. **–anlaut,** *m.* initial vowel. **–auslaut,** *m.* final vowel. **–inlaut,** *m.* medial vowel. **–isch,** *adj.* vocalic; *–ischer Laut*, vowel sound; *–ischer Auslaut*, vowel ending, word *or* syllable ending with a vowel. **–isieren,** *v.n.* (*aux.* h.) vocalize. **–isierung,** *f.* vocalization. **–ismus,** *m.* vowel-system. **–merkmale,** *n.pl.* vowel points (*Stenography*). **–musik,** *f.* vocal music. **–partie,** *f.* vocal *or* voice part. **–resonanz,** *f.* pitch. **–schwund,** *m.* vowel atrophy (*Philol*). **–steigerung,** *f.* gradation of vowels. **–umlaut,** *m.* (vowel) mutation.

Vokation, *f.* (-en) nomination to an office, call.

Vokativ, *m.* (-s, -e) vocative (*Gram.*). **–us,** *m.* (*coll.*) sly dog, rogue.

Voland, *m.* (*Poet.*) evil fiend.

Volant [*pron.* vɔ'la:], *m.* (-s, -s) flounce, frill; (*archaic*) steering-wheel (*Motor.*).

Volk, *n.* (-(e)s, ⸚er) people, nation, tribe, race; soldiery, troops, men, crew; herd (*of beasts*), flock (*of birds*), covey (*of partridges, etc.*), swarm (*of bees*); the common people, the lower classes, the crowd; *das arbeitende –*, the working classes; *das gemeine –*, the common herd, the rabble, the mob; *das junge –*, young people, youngsters; *das kleine –*, little folk, children; *der Mann aus dem –*, the man in the street; *viel –*, a lot *or* crowd of people, a great multitude; *ein – Bienen*, a swarm of bees; *ein – Rebhühner*, a covey of partridges; *ein – Sperlinge*, a flock of sparrows; *ein – Wachteln*, a bevy of quails. **–arm,** *adj.* thinly peopled *or* populated. **–haft,** *adj.* national, racial. **–heit,** *f.*, *see* **–stum.** **–leer,** *adj.* deserted. **–lich,** *adj.*; *–liche Minderheiten*, national minorities. **–reich,** *adj.* populous, thickly populated. **–saberglaube,** *m.* popular superstition. **–sabstimmung,** *f.* plebiscite, referendum. **–saufklärung,** *f.* education of the masses. **–saufruhr,** *m.*, **–saufstand,** *m.* popular rising, insurrection. **–saufwiegler,** *m.* agitator, demagogue. **–sausgabe,** *f.* popular edition. **–sbeauftragte(r),** *m.* people's delegate (*Pol.*). **–sbegehren,** *n.*, *see* **–sabstimmung.** (*iron.*) **–sbeglücker,** *m.* public benefactor. **–sbeliebt,** *adj.* popular. **–sbelustigung,** *f.* popular amusement. **–sbeschluß,** *m.*, *see* **–sabstimmung.** **–sbewaffnung,** *f.* mobilization of the whole people. **–sbewegung,** *f.* national movement. **–sbewußtsein,** *n.* national consciousness. **–sbibliothek,** *f.* public library, free library. **–sbildung,** *f.* popular education. **–sbildungswerk,** *n.* (*Nat. Soc.*) adult education programme. **–sbrauch,** *m.* national custom. **–sbuch,** *n.* popular prose romance; chapbook. **–sbücherei,** *f.*, *see* **–sbibliothek.** **–sdeutsche,** *m.pl.* (members of the) German ethnic group, Germans abroad. **–dichte,** *f.* density of population. **–sdichter,** *m.* popular poet; national poet. **–sdichtung,** *f.* popular poetry; national poetry. **–seinkommen,** *n.* national income. **–sempfänger,** *m.* utility radio set. **–sentscheid,** *m.*, *see* **–sabstimmung.** **–sepos,** *n.* national epic. **–serziehung,** *f.*, *see* **–sbildung.** **–setymologie,** *f.* popular etymology. **–sfeindlich,** *adj.* inimical to the national interests, unpatriotic. **–sfest,** *n.* national festival. **–sführer,** *m.* popular leader, demagogue. **–sganze,** *n.* the whole nation, all the people. **–sgebrauch,** *m.* popular usage. **–sgeist,** *m.* national spirit. **–sgenosse,** *m.* (fellow) countryman, (*Nat. Soc.*) fellow German. (*Nat. Soc.*) **–sgericht,** *n.* people's court. **–sgesundheit,** *f.* the nation's health. **–sglaube,** *m.* popular belief. **–sgunst,** *f.* popularity. **–shaufe,** *m.* mob, crowd. **–sheer,** *n.* conscript army, people's army. **–sherrschaft,** *f.* democracy. **–shochschule,** *f.* adult education classes, evening school, extramural studies, university extension. **–shymne,** *f.* national anthem. **–sjustiz,** *f.* mob-justice; lynch-law. **–sklasse,** *f.* class of people, social stratum; *die höheren –sklassen*, the upper classes. **–sküche,** *f.* soup-kitchen, feeding centre. **–skunde,** *f.* folklore. **–skundler,** *m.* folklorist. **–skundlich,** *adj.* regarding folklore. **–släufig,** *adj.* common, current, popular. **–slied,** *n.* folksong. **–smärchen,** *n.* popular legend *or* fairy story. **–smäßig,** *adj.* popular; *–smäßig machen*, popularize. **–smeinung,** *f.* public opinion *or* feeling. **–smelodie,** *f.* popular air. **–smenge,** *f.* crowd, throng; mob. **–smund,** *m.* vernacular. **–snah,** *adj.* rooted in *or* responsive to popular sentiment, popular. **–spartei,** *f.* National Liberal Party, People's Party, the Moderates. **–spoesie,** *f.*, *see* **–sdichtung.** **–sredner,** *m.* popular speaker, soap-box orator, agitator. **–sregierung,** *f.* popular government; democracy. **–ssage,** *f.* national legend, popular tradition. **–sschädling,** *m.* (*Nat. Soc.*) anti-social parasite.

-sschicht, *f.* social class, social stratum. **-sschlag,** *m.* race, racial group. **-sschrift,** *f.* popular work. **-sschule,** *f.* elementary *or* primary school. **-sschüler,** *m.* elementary school pupil. **-sschullehrer,** *m.* primary teacher, elementary teacher. **-sschulwesen,** *n.* primary education. **-ssitte,** *f.* national custom. **-ssouveränität,** *f.* sovereignty of the people. **-ssprache,** *f.* vernacular, popular speech. **-sstaat,** *m.* republic. **-sstamm,** *m.* tribe, race. **-sstimme,** *f.* public opinion. **-sstimmung,** *f.* public temper, popular feeling. **-stanz,** *m.* folk-dance. **-stracht,** *f.* national costume *or* dress. **-strauertag,** *m.* day of national mourning. **-stum** *n.* (-s, ¨-er), nationality, nationhood, national characteristics; *sein -stum bewahren,* preserve one's national characteristics. **-stümeln,** *v.a.* court popularity. **-stümlich,** *adj.* national, popular; *-stümliche Dichtung,* popular national poetry. **-stümlichkeit,** *f.* nationality; national trait *or* characteristic; popularity. **-süberlieferung,** *f.* popular tradition. **-sunterricht,** *m.* national system of education. **-sverbunden,** *adj.* rooted in one's national soil. **-sverbundenheit,** *f.* national solidarity. **-svermögen,** *n., see* **-seinkommen. -sversammlung,** *f.* national assembly. **-sversicherung,** *f.* national insurance. **-svertreter,** *m.* deputy, elected representative. **-svertretung,** *f.* representation of the people. **-swagen,** *m.* people's car, cheap popular car. **-sweise,** *f.* popular air. **-swirt,** *m.* political economist. **-swirtschaft,** *f.*, **-swirtschaftslehre,** *f.* political economy. **-swirtschaftler,** *m. see* **-swirt. -swirtschaftlich,** *adj.* economic. **-swohl,** *n.* common weal *or* good. **-swohlfahrt,** *f.* (*Nat. Soc.*) social welfare. **-swohlstand,** *m.* standard of living of the masses, national wealth. **-szählung,** *f.* census. **-swerdung,** *f.* emergence as a nation, growth of national consciousness.

Völk-chen, *n.* (-s, -) tribe; set (of people); young people, the young generation; *mein -chen,* my little ones; *lustiges -chen,* merry party. **-erbeschreibung,** *f.* ethnography. **-erbund,** *m.* League of Nations. **-erkunde,** *f.*, **-erlehre,** *f.* ethnology. **-erkundlich,** *adj.* ethnological. **-errecht,** *n.* international law. **-erschaft,** *f.* (*pl.* -en) people, tribe, nation. **-erschlacht,** *f.* the battle of Leipzig (1815). **-erstamm,** *m.* race. **-erwanderung,** *f.* mass migration. **-isch,** *adj.* national, (*Nat. Soc.*) pure German, anti-Semitic.

voll, 1. *adj.* (*comp.* -er, *sup.* -st) (*with Gen. or von*) full, filled, replete; complete, whole, entire; rounded; (*sl.*) drunk; *der Saal ist* – or *-er* or – *mit* or – *von Menschen,* the hall is full of *or* filled with people; *des Lobes* –, full of praise; *ein Glas – Wein,* a glassful of wine; *einen für – ansehen,* take a p. seriously; *in -er Arbeit,* in the midst of work; *mit -en Backen sprechen,* speak with one's mouth full; *-e Börse,* well-filled purse; *zum Brechen* –, enough to make one sick; *aus -er Brust,* heartily, lustily; *einem den Buckel – schlagen,* thrash a p. soundly; *die Aktien sind – eingezahlt,* the shares are fully paid up; *sich recht – gegessen haben,* have eaten one's fill, have gorged o.s.; *in -er Fahrt,* at full *or* top speed; *-es Gesicht,* round *or* chubby face; *alle Hände – zu tun haben,* have one's hands full; *see* **vollhaben**; *das Herz ist* –, the heart is overflowing; *aus -em Herzen,* from the bottom of one's heart, heartily; *er ist -e 40 Jahr(e alt),* he is quite 40 years (old); *aus -er Kehle,* at the top of one's voice; *-e Kraft voraus,* full steam ahead, at full throttle; *im -en leben,* live in the lap of luxury; (*coll.*) *das Kind macht sich* –, the child soils itself (its trousers, napkin, etc.); *das Maß ist* –, that is the limit; *für – nehmen,* take seriously; *see* **vollnehmen**; *einem die Ohren – schreien,* din (a th.) in a p.'s ears; *mit -em Recht,* with perfect right; *die Uhr hat – geschlagen,* the clock has struck the hour; *aus dem -en schöpfen,* draw freely on lavish resources; *die -e Summe,* the entire sum; *in -em Trabe,* at full trot; *um das Unglück – zu machen,* to crown everything, as the last straw; *-es Vertrauen,* complete confidence; *die -e Wahreit sagen,* tell the whole truth; *aus dem -en wirtschaften,* not be sparing, not stint o.s.; *in -en Zügen trinken,* drink off at a gulp. 2. *verb prefix signifying completion, accomplishment, etc.* (*a*) *insep. & unstressed,* (*b*) *sep. & stressed* = full, to the top, *etc. In the latter case, words should be sought under the stem inf. if not found here.*

Vollaktie, *f.* fully paid-up share.

Vollanstalt, *f.* secondary school with sixth form.

vollauf, *adv.* abundantly, plentifully; – *zu tun haben,* have one's hands full, have plenty to do.

vollaufen, *v.n.* (*sep.*) (*aux.* s.) be filled to overflowing.

vollautend, *adj.* sonorous.

Vollbad, *n.* bath, plunge-bath.

Vollbahn, *f.* standard gauge railway.

Vollbart, *m.* beard.

vollberechtigt, *adj.* fully entitled *or* authorized.

vollbeschäftig-t, *adj.* fully employed. **-ung,** *f.* full employment.

Vollbesitz, *m.*, full possession.

Vollbild, *n.* full-page illustration.

Vollblut, *n.*, **-pferd,** *n.* thoroughbred (horse).

Vollblüt-er, *m., see* **Vollblut. -ig,** *adj.* full-blooded, plethoric; sanguine. **-igkeit,** *f.* full-bloodedness, plethora.

vollbring-en, *ir.v.a.* (*insep.*) accomplish, achieve, execute, fulfil, carry out, complete, consummate; perform fully, perpetrate; *es ist vollbracht,* it is finished, completed *or* carried out. **-ung,** *f.* accomplishment, achievement, performance, execution; consummation, perpetration.

Vollbürger, *m.* fully enfranchised citizen.

vollbürtig, *adj.* of the same parents, whole-blood; *-e Geschwister,* full brothers and sisters.

vollbusig, *adj.* full-bosomed, (*coll.*) bosomy.

Volldampf, *m.* full (steam) pressure; – *voraus* full steam ahead!

Volldruck, *m.* full pressure. **-höhe,** *f.* rated altitude (*Av.*).

volleibig, *adj.* corpulent, stout. **-keit,** *f.* stoutness, corpulence, obesity.

vollend-en, 1. *v.a.* (*insep.*) (*aux.* h.) bring to a close, finish, terminate; achieve, accomplish, complete, consummate, perfect. 2. *v.r. & n.* (*aux.* h.) die. **-et,** *p.p. & adj.* finished, accomplished, achieved; consummate, perfect; (*high style*) *er hat -et,* he has passed away; *die früh -eten,* those who died young; *-eter Blödsinn,* sheer, perfect *or* utter nonsense; *-ete Tatsache,* accomplished fact, fait accompli. **-s,** *adv.* wholly, completely, entirely, altogether, quite; finally, moreover. **-ung,** *f.* completion, finishing, termination, ending; perfecting, consummation, perfection.

voller, 1. *comp. adj.* fuller. 2. *indec. adj.* full of, *see* **voll.**

Vollerbe, *m.* sole heir.

Völlerei, *f.* intemperance, gluttony.

vollführ-en, *v.a.* (*insep.*) carry out, execute. **-ung,** *f.* execution.

vollfüllen, *v.a.* (*sep.*) fill up.

Vollgas, *n.* open *or* full throttle (*Motor.*); – *geben,* open the throttle, (*coll.*) put one's foot down.

vollgefahren, *adj.* able-bodied (*seaman*).

Vollgefühl, *n.* (full) consciousness.

vollgehalt, *m.* good alloy, full weight and value. **-ig,** *adj.* of good alloy, of full weight and value; of sterling value, standard.

vollgelaufen, *adj.* swamped, filled to overflowing.

Vollgenuß, *m.* full enjoyment.

vollgepfropft, *adj.* crammed (full), packed tight, crowded.

vollgeschlagen, *adj., see* **vollgelaufen.**

vollgestopft, *adj., see* **vollgepfropft.**

Vollgewalt, *f.* full power, absolute power; power of attorney.

Vollgewicht, *n.* full weight.

vollgießen, *v.a.* (*sep.*) *see* **vollfüllen.**

vollgültig, *adj.* of full value, sterling; valid, unexceptionable.

Vollgummireifen, *m.* solid (rubber) tire.

vollhaben, *v.a.*; (*coll.*) *die Nase* –, be fed up to the teeth, (*vulg.*) have had a bellyful.

vollhaltig, *adj., see* **vollgehaltig.**

Vollheit, *f.* fullness, completeness.

vollhauen, *v.a.*; *ihm die Jacke* –, give him a good hiding.

Vollholz, *n.* log.

völlig, 1. *adj.* full, total, entire, complete, undiminished, thorough; circular (*of cross-section*). (*usually*) 2. *adv.* quite, utterly; *–er Ablaß*, plenary indulgence; (*einem etwas*) *– abschlagen*, give a flat refusal (to a p.); *–e Gewißheit*, dead certainty; *ich bin nicht – Ihrer Meinung*, I do not quite agree with you; *–er Narr*, downright fool; *–e Unwahrheit*, utter falsehood. **–keit,** *f.* circular cross-section.
volljährig, *adj.* of (full) age. **–keit,** *f.* majority, full age; *seine –keit erlangen*, come of age, attain one's majority.
vollkantig, *adj.* full square.
Vollkettenfahrzeug, *n.* full-track vehicle (*Mil.*).
Vollklang, *m.* full chord.
vollkommen, *adj.* perfect, consummate, full, complete, entire, finished; full, easy (*of clothes*); big, fat, stout (*of people*); *–e Gewalt*, absolute power; *–e Zahl*, perfect number. **–heit,** *f.* perfection, completeness.
Vollkornbrot, *n.* wholemeal bread.
vollkörnig, *adj.* full-grained.
Vollkraft, *f.* full strength *or* vigour, energy, prime (*of life*).
Vollkugel, *f.* round shot.
vollmachen, (*sep.*) 1. *v.a.* fill up, complete; *die Summe –*, pay the remainder *or* deficit. 2. *v.r.* (*coll.*) dirty *or* soil o.s., get dirty.
Vollmacht, *f.* full power of authority; fullness of power; power of attorney; warrant; proxy; procuration; (*C.L.*) *in –*, per pro; *einem – geben*, empower *or* authorize a p. **–brief,** *m.* warrant, (written) authority, permit; procuration. **–haber,** *m.* mandatory; proxy, procurator.
vollmast, *adj.* at full mast (*of flags*).
Vollmatrose, *m.* able-bodied seaman.
Vollmensch, *m.* complete *or* rounded personality.
Vollmilch, *f.* full-cream milk.
Vollmond, *m.* full moon; *wir haben –*, the moon is full. **–sgesicht,** *n.* round *or* plump face.
vollmundig, *adj.* strong, full-bodied (*of beer*).
vollnehmer, *v.a.*; *den Mund –*, brag, boast, blow one's own trumpet, draw the long bow.
vollpfropfen (*sep.*) 1. *v.a.* stuff. 2. *v.r.* stuff o.s., gorge, eat too much.
Vollreifen, *m.* solid tire.
Vollrohr, *n.* one-piece barrel (*of gun*).
Vollsein, *n.* (*coll.*) drunkenness, tipsiness.
vollsaftig, *adj.* very juicy, succulent.
Vollschiff, *n.* full-rigged ship.
vollschwenkbar, *adj.* fully *or* completely traversable.
Vollsichtkanzel, *f.* cabin with all-round visibility (*Av.*).
Vollsitzung, *f.* plenary session.
Vollspur–bahn, *f.*, *see* **Vollbahn. –ig,** *adj.* standard gauge (*Railw.*).
vollst, *sup. of* voll.
vollständig, 1. *adj.* complete, entire, total, whole, integral. 2. *adv.* perfectly, quite, utterly; *das Unglück – machen*, crown everything, (*coll.*) put the lid on it. **–keit,** *f.* completeness, entirety, totality, integrity.
Vollstange, *f.* (solid) bar.
vollstimmig, *adj.* for full orchestra *or* chorus.
vollstock, *adv.*, *see* **vollmast.**
vollstopfen, *v.a.* (*sep.*), *see* **vollpfropfen.**
vollstreck–en, *v.a.* (*insep.*) execute, discharge, put into effect, carry out. **–bar,** *adj.* executable, dischargeable. **–er,** *m.* executor. **–ung,** *f.* execution, discharge. **–ungsbeamte(r),** *m.* executory officer (*Law*). **–ungsbefehl,** *m.* writ of execution, warrant.
volltön–end, *adj.*, **–ig,** *adj.* full-sounding, full-toned, sonorous, rich.
Volltraghöhe, *f.* ceiling with full load (*Av.*).
Volltreffer, *m.* direct hit (*Artil.*).
Vollversammlung, *f.* plenary session.
vollwertig, *adj.* of full value, sterling, up to standard, of high quality; valid.
vollwichtig, *adj.* of full weight, weighty, forcible, very important. **–keit,** *f.* full weight.
Vollwort, *n.* (-(e)s, -e) consent.
vollwüchsig, *adj.* full-grown.
vollzählig, *adj.* complete, in full strength. **–keit,** *f.* completeness, fullness.
vollzieh–en, 1. *ir.v.a.* (*insep.*) *see* **vollstrecken**; accomplish, execute, carry out, fulfil, discharge, consummate, ratify; *ein Urteil –en*, execute a sentence; *–ende Gewalt*, executive (power); *eine Heirat –en*, consummate a marriage. 2. *v.r.* be effected, take place, come to pass. **–ung,** *f.* execution, discharge, accomplishment, fulfilment.
Vollzug, *m.*, *see* **Vollziehung. –sgewalt,** *f.* executive power.
Volont–är, *m.* (-s, -e) volunteer, voluntary helper unsalaried clerk, unpaid assistant. **–ieren,** *v.n.* volunteer, give voluntary help, do voluntary work.
Volt, *n.* (-s & –, –) volt (*Elec.*). **–aisch,** *adj.* galvanic, voltaic. **–ameter,** *n.* ammeter. **–ampere,** *n.* watt (*Elec.*). **–messer,** *m.* voltmeter. **–zahl,** *f.* voltage.
Volt–e, *f.* (-en) volte (*Fenc.*, *Equestrianism*); sleight of hand; *die –e schlagen*, make the pass (*Cards*). **–igeur,** *m.* (-s, -e) vaulter, tumbler, equestrian acrobat. **–igieren,** *v.n.* (*aux.* h.) perform equestrian acrobatics. **–igierkunst,** *f.* equestrian acrobatics.
Volubilität, *f.* volubility.
Volum–en, *n.* (-ens, -en (& *Austr. dial.* –ina)) volume, content; capacity, size, bulk; tome, bulky volume. **–eneinheit,** *f.* unit of volume. **–engewicht,** *n.* specific gravity. **–enmessung,** *f.* measurement of volume. **–enregler,** *m.* volume control (*Rad.*). **–inös,** *adj.* bulky, voluminous.
vom = von dem.
vom–ieren, *v.n.* & *a.* (*aux.* h.) vomit. **–itiv,** *n.* (-s, -e) (*Austr. dial.*), **–itorium,** *n.* (-riums, -rien) emetic.
von, *prep.* (*Dat.*) of; from; by; in; on, upon; about; concerning. **1.** = of. 1. *possession or instead of genitive*; *die Ausfuhr – Kohlen*, the export of coal; *der Bau – Häusern*, the erection of houses; *die Belagerung – Paris*, the siege of Paris; *ein Freund – mir*, a friend of mine; *der Herr vom Hause*, the master of the house; *die Lage – Paris*, the situation of Paris; *das Unglück – Millionen*, the misfortune of millions. 2. *partitive genitive*; *zwei – uns*, two of us; *– allem nichts mehr übrig*, nothing left of it all; *trinken Sie – diesem Weine*, drink some of this wine. 3. *to denote quality or material*; *ein Mann – edlem Sinne*, a man of noble mind; *ein Geschäft – Wichtigkeit*, an affair of importance; *Lehre – der Buße*, doctrine of repentance; *klein – Gestalt*, small of stature; *ein Engel – einem Weibe*, an angel of a woman; *– gutem Schrot und Korn*, of sterling worth; *ein Denkmal – Marmor*, a monument of marble. 4. *before a proper name which is part of a title*; *Königin – England*, Queen of England; *Herzog Johann – Schwaben*, Duke John of Swabia. *Before family names* von *is part of title and should be left unchanged or rendered by* de. (N.B. *a capital* V (Von Bismarck) *is a common mark of ignorance among British writers.*) 5. *to denote the subject treated of*; *– wem sprechen Sie?* of whom are you speaking? *also to denote various other relations*; *es ist nicht recht – ihm*, it is not right of him. **2.** = from. 1. *used with an adv. or prep. following*; *– da an*, onwards from there; *– heute an*, from this day on *or* forward; *– nun an*, henceforth; *– klein auf*, from childhood upwards *or* onwards, from earliest childhood; *– Hause aus*, originally, in its origins; *– mir aus*, as far as I am concerned *or* care, if you like, I do not mind *or* care, from my point of view; *– wo aus*, whence; *– außen*, from without; *– alters her*, from time immemorial; *– oben herab*, down from above, from on high; *– der Kanzel herab*, from the pulpit; *– hinnen*, hence; *– hinten*, from behind; *– hinten hervor*, (out) from behind; *– jeher*, at all times, from time immemorial; *– neuem*, afresh, anew, all over again; *– oben*, from above; *– Rechts wegen*, by rights, according to (the) law; *– ungefähr*, by chance *or* accident; *– vornherein*, from the outset, from the first, from the beginning; *– weitem*, from afar. 2. *to denote motion or separation from*; *– Berlin kommen*, come from Berlin; *ich behalte 2 Mark – dieser Summe*, I am keeping 2 marks out of this sum; *etwas – jemandes Gehalt abziehen*, deduct something from a p.'s

salary; *nehmen Sie das – dem Tische weg*, take that off the table; *was wollen Sie – mir?* what do you want with, of, *or* from me? – *wem haben Sie das Geld geliehen?* from whom did you borrow that money? *etwas – einem Original abschreiben*, copy s.th. from the original; *es – etwas trennen* or *unterscheiden*, separate *or* distinguish it from s.th.; – *Sinnen sein*, be off one's head; – *der Arbeit ruhen*, rest from work; – *einem abfallen*, break faith with s.o., desert a p.; *keinen Ton – sich geben*, not utter a sound. **3.** = by, *incl. use with agent of passive verb or participial forms; with some other idioms*; – *Gottes Gnaden*, by the grace of God; – *allen geliebt*, beloved of *or* by all; – *ganzem Herzen*, with all one's heart; – *Person kennen*, know personally, know at first hand; – *Seiten der Regierung*, on the part of the government, as far as the government is concerned; – *selbst*, automatically, of its own accord, of itself, spontaneously; *Kinder – der zweiten Frau*, children by the second wife; *gedruckt und im Verlage –*, printed and published by; *ein Deutscher – Geburt*, a German by birth; – *deutschen Eltern geboren*, born of German parents; – *seinen Einkünften leben*, live on one's income; – *allen Seiten*, from all sides, from every side; *er ist nicht – heute*, he was not born yesterday; *er kann – Glück sagen*, he can consider himself lucky *or* thank his lucky stars. **–einander,** *adv.* apart, separate, asunder; from *or* of each other. **–einandergehen,** *v.n.* part (company), separate. **–nöten,** *adv.*; *–nöten haben*, be *or* stand in need of; *–nöten sein*, be needful *or* necessary; *ich habe es –nöten*, I need it badly. **–statten,** *adv.*; *–statten gehen*, proceed, progress, go (well), prove (a success). (*obs. & coll.*) **–wegen,** *prep.* because, on account of, for the sake of.

vor, 1. *prep.* (*a*) (*with Dat.*), *though in referring to place only when it indicates condition or rest* (*if it answers the question* 'where?') before, previous *or* prior to, ere, antecedent to (*in time*); before, in front of, ahead of (*in place*); in presence of; for, on account of, through, because of, with (*joy, etc.*); from *or* against (*with verbs of protection, warning, etc.*); in preference to, more than, above; (*Prov.*) *man soll den Tag nicht – dem Abend loben*, don't count your chickens until they are hatched, don't halloo till you're out of the wood; – *allem*, above all; – *alters*, of yore; – *Angst*, with fear; – *Anker gehen*, ride at anchor; – *Augen haben*, have before one's eyes, have in view, intend, purpose; – *seinen Augen*, before his very eyes; – *allen Augen verborgen*, hidden from all eyes; *sich – einem auszeichnen*, distinguish o.s. above another; *er steht – dem Bankerott*, he is on the verge of bankruptcy; (*Prov.*) *er sieht den Wald – lauter Bäumen nicht*, he cannot see the wood for trees: – *sich hin brummen*, mutter to o.s.; – *Christi Geburt*, B(efore) C(hrist); – *allen Dingen*, above all; – *Freude*, with joy; *sich – einem* or *einer S. fürchten*, fear *or* be afraid of s.o. *or* s.th.; *ich habe keine Geheimnisse – Ihnen*, I have no secrets from you; – *sich gehen*, occur, take place; *Achtung – dem Gesetz*, respect for the law; – *Gott*, in the presence of God, in the eyes of God; – *sich* (*Dat.*) *haben*, be face to face with, (*fig.*) have s.th. clearly in mind; *heute – einem Jahr*, a year ago today; – *vielen Jahren*, many years ago; – *Kälte zittern*, shiver with cold; – *kurzem*, recently; *einem die Tür – der Nase zuschlagen*, shut the door in a p.'s face; (*Prov.*) *Gewalt geht – Recht*, might is stronger than right; *Gnade – Recht ergehen lassen*, be moved by compassion rather than by justice; *Schritt – Schritt*, step by step; *Schutz – dem Winde*, shelter from the wind; – *einer S. sicher* or *in Sicherheit sein*, be safe *or* secure from a th.; – *einem da sein*, exist *or* be there before somebody else; – *Hunger sterben*, die of hunger *or* starvation; *der Tag – dem Feste*, the day before the festival; – *dem Tore wohnen*, live outside the gates; *der Wagen hält – der Tür*, the carriage stops at the door; – *der Türe sein* or *stehen*, be at the door, (*fig.*) be close at hand; *sein Herz – einer S. verschließen*, shut one's heart to *or* against s.th.; *sich – einem verstecken*, hide from a p.; *sie hat – ihrer Schwester den Vorrang*, she takes precedence over her sister; – *einem warnen*, warn against a p.; – *der Zeit*, prematurely, in advance (*as payment*); – *Zeiten*, formerly, in time gone by; – *alten Zeiten*, in old(en) times, in times of old *or* yore; *das Subjekt steht – dem Zeitwort*, the subject precedes the verb. (*b*) (*with Acc.*); *when, referring to place, it indicates movement or change of condition* (*if it answers the question* 'whither?'); *das Subjekt stellt man – das Zeitwort*, the subject is placed before the verb; *sich* (*Dat.*) *eine Kugel – den Kopf schießen*, blow out one's brains, put a bullet through one's head; – *das Tor gehen*, go out of the gate; *einen – die Tür werfen*, throw s.o. out. **2.** *adv.*; only in *nach wie –*, as always, as ever, still, now as before. **3.** *sep. prefix*, before, ahead of, formerly, front.

vorab, *adv.* first of all, to begin with, tentatively; (*rare*) above all, especially.

Vorabend, *m.* eve, evening before.

vorahn–en, *v.a.* have a presentiment *or* foreboding of. **–ung,** *f.* presentiment, foreboding.

voran, *adv. & sep. prefix.* before, on, onwards, forward; at the head, in front, foremost, first; *nur –!* go on! go ahead! **–gehen,** *ir.v.n.* (*aux.* s.) go before, precede; take the lead, go at the head of, lead the way; *die Arbeit geht gut –*, the work is making good progress *or* is getting on nicely; *mit gutem Beispiel –gehen*, set a good example; *das –gehende*, the foregoing. **–kommen,** *v.n.* get on, (make) progress. **–schicken,** *v.a.* send on ahead *or* before; put at the head of, premise. **–schreiten,** *v.n.* (*aux.* s.) (*Dat.*) go on ahead of.

Voranmeldung, *f.* preliminary announcement, advance notice.

Voranschlag, *m.* preliminary estimate, estimated cost.

Voranzeige, *f.*, *see* **Voranmeldung.**

Vorarbeit, *f.* preliminary *or* preparatory work, preparation; (*pl.*) preliminary studies. **–en,** *v.a. & n.* (*aux.* h.) work in preparation, prepare (work); show (*einem*, a p.) the way to work, prepare the ground for, pave the way for; forge ahead, work one's way up; *ich habe auf morgen vorgearbeitet*, I have done my preparation for tomorrow's work. **–er,** *m.* foreman.

vorauf (*archaic*), *see* **voran.**

voraus, 1. *adv. & sep. prefix* in advance, forward, before, in front, on ahead; previously; in preference; *er ging –*, he went on in front; *er ist* (*vor*) *seinem Alter –*, he is in advance of his age *or* years; *im* or *zum –*, in advance, beforehand; *vielen Dank im –*, many thanks in anticipation (*of your favour*). 2. *m.* advantage, greater *or* extra share, inalienable portion (*of a legacy*) (*Law*). **–bedingen,** *reg. & ir.v.a.* stipulate; *sich* (*Dat.*) *etwas –bedingen*, reserve to o.s. (*a right, etc.*). **–bedingung,** *f.* stipulation, understanding. **–bestellen,** *v.a.* order in advance, subscribe to. **–bestimmung,** *f.* predetermination, predestination. **–bezahlen,** *v.a.* pay in advance, prepay. **–datieren,** *v.a.* antedate. **–eilen,** *v.n.* (*Dat.*) hurry on ahead (of), anticipate. **–gegangen,** *adj.* previous, preliminary. **–gehen,** *ir.v.n.* (*aux.* s.) go before, walk in front, lead the way, go on ahead, go in advance, precede. **–gehend,** *adj.* previous, preceding. **–haben,** *v.a.*; *etwas* (*vor*) *einem –haben*, have an advantage over s.o. in a th., excel a p. in s.th. **–nahme,** *f.* anticipation, forestalling. **–nehmen,** *ir.v.a.* anticipate, forestall. **–sage,** *f.* prediction, prophecy, forecast; (*coll.*) tip, selections (*horse racing*); *ärztliche –sage*, prognosis. **–sagen,** *v.a.* prophesy, predict, forecast, foretell. **–schauen,** 1. *v.n.* look forward, anticipate. 2. *n.* anticipation. **–schicken,** *v.a.*; send in advance, send on ahead; say beforehand, premise; *dies –geschickt, gehen wir zur S. über*, with this introduction, let us pass on to the matter in hand. **–sehen,** *ir.v.a.* foresee. **–setzen,** *v.a.* presuppose, suppose, assume, surmise, presume; *vorausgesetzt, daß*, provided that. **–setzung,** *f.* supposition, presupposition, assumption, postulate, hypothesis, provision, prerequisite; *zur –setzung haben*, presuppose; *zur –setzung machen*, make the basis of, take for granted. **–setzungslos,** *adj.* unconditional, unqualified, absolute. **–sicht,** *f.* foresight, forethought, prudence; provision; *in der –sicht, daß*, on the assumption that.

–sichtlich, *adj.* probable, presumable, expected prospective. **–wissen,** *v.a.* know beforehand, know already.
Vorbau, *m.* front (*of building*), projecting structure. **–en,** 1. *v.a.* build in front of, build out beyond. 2. *v.n.* (*Dat.*) obviate, prevent, preclude, guard against, take precautions against, provide for (*the future*).
Vorbedacht, *m.* forethought, premeditation; *mit –*, deliberately, on purpose.
vorbedächtig, *adj.* cautious, deliberate, prudent.
vorbedeut–en, forebode, presage. **–ung,** *f.* foreboding, omen, augury.
vorbeding–en, *ir.v.a.* stipulate beforehand. **–ung,** *f.* inescapable condition (*zu*, of *or* for).
Vorbefehl, *m.* warning order (*Mil.*).
Vorbehalt, reservation, proviso; *mit – meiner Rechte*, without prejudice to my rights; *unter – aller Rechte*, all rights reserved; *ohne –*, without reserve *or* restriction, unconditionally; *unter dem üblichen –*, with the usual proviso; *geistiger* or *stiller –*, mental reservation. **–en,** *ir.v.a.* (*einem etwas*) hold *or* keep in reserve, withhold, reserve (to), make reservations. **–lich,** *prep.* (*Gen.*) with the proviso *or* reservation that, on condition that, dependent on. **–los,** *adj.* without reservation, unconditional. **–sklausel,** *f.* proviso clause.
Vorbehandlung, *f.* preliminary treatment, pretreatment, preparations.
vorbei, *adv. & sep. prefix,* along, by, past; past, over, done (with), gone; *es ist mit ihm –*, it is all over *or* up with him; *– ist –*, what is done, is done, it is no good crying over spilt milk; *vier Uhr –*, past 4 o'clock; *an ihm –*, past him, beyond him, over his head· *drei Schüsse –!* missed three times (*the target*). **–gehen,** 1. *ir.v.n.* (*aux.* s.) (*an einem*) go *or* pass by, go past, pass (*a p.*); *daran –gehen*, take no notice of it, overlook *or* ignore it, pass over it in silence. 2. *n.*; *im –gehen*, in passing. (*sl.*) **–gelingen,** *v.n.* (*Dat.*) not be successful, miss the mark, go wrong, miscarry, (*sl.*) come unstuck. **–marsch,** *n.* march past. **–marschieren,** *v.n.* (*aux.* s.) march past. **–reden,** *v.n.* (*an with Dat.*) be at cross-purposes (with); *an den Dingen –reden*, talk round the subject, not get to grips with the matter. **–schießen,** *ir.v.n.* (*aux.* s.) shoot past, dart quickly past; (*aux.* h.) miss (*in shooting*). **–ziehen,** *ir.v.n.* (*aux.* s.) pass; march past.
Vorbemerkung, *f.* preliminary remark, prefatory notice, preamble.
Vorbenutzung, *f.* prior use.
vorbereit–en, 1. *v. a.* prepare, get ready beforehand, make ready; *auf eine S. –et sein*, be prepared for a th. 2. *v.r.* (*auf with Acc.*, *für* or *zu*) prepare o.s., make one's preparations, get ready; train (for); *es bereitet sich etwas vor*, there is s.th. brewing (*or sl.* cooking), there is s.th. in the air. **–end,** *pr.p. & adj.* preparatory, preliminary; predisposing. **–ung,** *f.* preparation, preparatory training; (*pl.*) preparations, arrangements, preliminaries.
Vorberg, *m.* mountain spur, foothill.
Vorbericht, *m.* introduction, preface; preliminary *or* advance report.
Vorbescheid, *m.* preliminary decree, interlocutory judgement (*Law*). **–en,** *v.a.* summon (*before a court*).
Vorbesprechung, *f.* preliminary discussion.
vorbestraft, *adj.* previously convicted.
vorbet–en, *v.a. & n.* (*aux.* h.) repeat *or* recite (a prayer), lead in prayer. **–er,** *m.* prayer leader.
vorbeug–en, 1. *v. a. & r.* bend forward. 2. *v. n.* (*aux.* h.) (*Dat.*) hinder, prevent, obviate, guard against. **–end,** *pr.p. & adj.* preventive, prophylactic (*Med.*). **–ung,** *f.* bending forward; preventing, prevention; prophylaxis. **–ungsmaßregel,** *f.*, **–ungsmittel,** *n.* preventive (measure), preventative; preservative; prophylactic (*Med.*).
Vorbild, *n.* model, example, pattern, standard, prototype, original. **–en,** *v.a.* prepare, train (*zu*, for), represent, typify. **–lich,** *adj.* typical, representative (*für*, of); model, ideal, exemplary. **–ung,** *f.* preparation, preliminary instruction; basic education *or* training; *allgemeine –ung*, general education in the rudiments.
vorbinden, *ir.v.a.* tie *or* put on; show how to tie; *dem Buche das Inhaltsverzeichnis –*, put the table of contents at the beginning of a book.
Vorblatt, *n.* bract.
Vorbleiche, *f.* preliminary bleach.
Vorbohrer, *m.* auger, gimlet.
Vorbote, *m.* precursor, forerunner, harbinger, herald; early sign, indication, symptom, presage.
Vorbramsegel, *n.* fore-topgallant-sail.
vorbringen, *ir.v.a.* bring forward *or* up, produce, propose, adduce, allege; advance, put forward (*an opinion*), state, utter, express, make (*excuses*); *Beweise –*, produce proofs; *er konnte kein Wort –*, he could not utter *or* say a word; *er wußte nicht, was er zu seiner Entschuldigung – sollte*, he did not know what excuse to offer; *eine Anklage –* (*gegen*), prefer a charge (against).
vorbuchstabieren, *v.a.* (*einem etwas*) spell out (s.th.) for *or* to (a p.).
Vorbühne, *f.* proscenium (*Theat.*).
vorchristlich, *adj.* pre-Christian.
Vordach, *n.* projecting roof, overhanging eaves.
vordatieren, *v.a.* antedate.
vordem, *adv.* (*archaic*) formerly, in former times, of old.
vorder, *adj.* fore, forward, anterior, front, foremost. **–achse,** *f.* front axle (*Motor.*). **–achsenantrieb,** *m.* front-wheel drive. **–ansicht,** *f.* front view. **–arm,** *m.* forearm. **–bauch,** *m.* epigastrium. **–bein,** *n.* foreleg, front leg. **–deck,** *n.* fore-deck. **–decke,** *f.* front cover (*of books*). **–fläche,** *f.* anterior surface. **–fuß,** *m.* fore-foot, front part of the foot, metatarsus. **–gaumen,** *m.* hard palate. **–gaumenlaut,** *m.* palatal sound. **–giebel,** *m.* front gable (*Arch.*). **–glied,** *n.* fore-limb, anterior member; front rank; antecedent, first term (*Arith.*); major (*Log.*), antecedent (*Log.*). **–grund,** *m.* foreground, (*fig.*) forefront; *in den –grund rücken* or *stellen*, place in the foreground, place in the forefront, put first, emphasize, throw into relief. **–hand,** 1. *adv.* for the present, in the meantime, for the while, just now. 2. *f.* fore-part of the hand; metacarpus; fore-paw; lead (*at cards*). **–hang,** *m.* forward slope (*Mil.*). **–haupt,** *n.* fore-part of the head, forehead, sinciput. **–kante,** *f.* leading edge (*Av.*). **–kopf,** *m.*, *see* **–haupt.** **–lader,** *m.* muzzle-loader (*Gun.*). **–lage,** *f.* anterior position. **–lastig,** *adj.* nose-heavy (*Naut.*, *Av.*). **–lauf,** *m.* fore-leg (*Hunt.*), fore-end (*of the barrel*). **–leute,** *pl.* front-rank men; *ich habe noch zehn –leute*, there are still ten ahead *or* before me. **–lich,** *adj.*; *–liche See*, head-sea (*Naut.*). **–mann,** *m.* front-rank man, man ahead *or* in front; (*C.L.*) preceding endorser; *–mann halten*, keep in line *or* file. **–mast,** *m.* foremast. **–mund,** *m.* peristome. **–pferd,** *n.* leader, leading horse. **–pfote,** *f.* forepaw. **–radantrieb,** front-wheel drive (*Motor.*). **–radgabel,** *f.* front fork (*Cycl.*). **–radschutzblech,** *n.* front mudguard (*Motor.*, *Cycl.*). **–reihe,** *f.* front rank. **–satz,** *m.* protasis (*Gram.*); antecedent, premise (*Log.*). **–seite,** *f.* front, façade (*Arch.*); obverse (*Typ.*); face (*of a coin*); recto (*in manuscripts*). **–sitz,** *m.* front seat. **–st,** *sup. adj.* first, foremost. **–steven,** *m.* stem (*of a ship*), prow, cutwater (*Naut.*). **–stich,** *m.* running stitch (*Semp.*). **–teil,** *n.* front; prow (*of a ship*). **–treffen,** *n.* first line (*of battle*). **–tür,** *f.* house-door, front door. **–wagen,** *m.* limber (*Artil.*). **–wand,** *f.* front wall. **–zahn,** *m.* incisor, (*pl.*) front teeth.
vordrängen, *v.r.* press *or* push forward, thrust o.s. forward.
vordring–en, *ir.v. n.* (*aux.* s.) push on, press forward, advance, forge ahead, gain ground. **–lich,** *adj.* pressing, urgent, importunate, (*coll.*) pushing, forward.
Vordruck, *m.* first *or* original impression (*Typ.*), (printed) form.
vorehelich, *adj.* prenuptial, premarital.
voreil–en, *v.n.* (*aux.* s.) (*Dat.*) hurry on ahead (of), hasten on before. **–ig,** *adj.* hasty, precipitate, rash; premature. **–igkeit,** *f.* precipitancy, rashness, overhaste. **–ung,** *f.* lead (*in time*).
voreingenommen, *adj.* prejudiced, biased (*für*, in favour of; *gegen*, against). **–heit,** *f.* prejudice, bias.

Voreltern, *pl.* ancestors, forefathers.
vorempfind–en, *ir.v.n.* have a presentiment of; anticipate. **–ung,** *f.* presentiment, foreboding.
vorenthalt–en, *ir.v.a. sep. & insep.* (*but inf. only sep. & p.p. only insep.*) (*einem etwas*) withhold, keep back (from a p.); detain (*Law*). **–ung,** *f.* withholding; detention.
Vorentscheidung, *f.* prior decision, previous judgement.
vorerst, *adv.* first of all, in the meantime, for the time being.
vorerwähnt, *adj.* before-mentioned, aforesaid.
vorerzählen, *v.a.* (*einem etwas*) relate, recount (*s.th.*) to (*a p.*).
voressen, 1. *ir.v.a. das ist vorgegessenes Brot,* that is counting one's chickens before they are hatched. 2. *n.* entrée.
Vorfahr, *m.* (-en & *archaic* -s, -en), ancestor, forefather, progenitor.
vorfahr–en, *ir.v.n.* (*aux.* s.) (*bei*) drive up to, stop at (*a p.'s door*); overtake (*in traffic*); *den Wagen –en lassen,* have the car brought round; *an einem Hause –en,* drive up to a house. **–tsrecht,** *n.* right of way (*Motor.*).
Vorfall, *m.* occurrence, event, incident, case; prolapsus (*Med.*); detent (*of a clock*). **–en,** *ir.v.n.* (*aux.* s.) happen, occur, come to pass, take place; fall (down) before, fall forward; become misplaced, prolapse (*Med.*).
vorfärben, *v.a.* pre-dye, ground, bottom.
Vorfechter, *m.* pioneer, champion, advocate.
Vorfeier, *f.* preliminary celebration, eve of a festival.
Vorfeld, *n.* approaches, perimeter.
vorfinden, 1. *ir.v.a.* find, meet with, come *or* light upon. 2. *v.r.* be found, be met with; be forthcoming.
vorflunkern (*coll.*) *v.a.* (*einem etwas*) tell a fib.
Vorfluter, *m.* main drainage channel.
vorfordern, *v.a.* summon to appear, cite.
Vorfrag–e, *f.* preliminary *or* previous question. **–en,** *reg. & ir.v.a.* (*bei*), call (*at a p.'s house*) to inquire.
Vorfreude, *f.* pleasure of anticipation.
Vorfrucht, *f.* early crop, preceding crop (*in rotation*).
Vorfrühling, *m.* early spring.
vorfühlen, *v.a.* have a foreboding of; (*fig.*) feel one's way forward *or* towards.
vorführ–en, *v.a.* bring forward *or* up, bring to the front; produce, demonstrate, present, (*coll.*) trot out; *dem Richter –en,* bring before the court. **–dame,** *f.* mannequin. **–er,** *m.* operator (*Films*). **–ung,** production, demonstration, presentation. **–ungsbefehl,** *m.* warrant to appear in court. **–ungsraum,** *m.* demonstration room.
Vorgabe, *f.* points *or* odds given *or* allowed; start, handicap (*Sport*). **–rennen,** *n.* handicap (race).
Vorgang, *m.* (-(e)s, ⸚e) proceeding, procedure, process, reaction, transaction; occurrence, incident, event; example, model, precedent; *einem den – lassen,* yield precedence to a p.; *nach seinem –,* following his example.
Vorgäng–er, *m.* forerunner, predecessor. **–ig,** *adj.* preliminary, preparatory, preceding, foregoing, previous.
Vorgarten, *m.* front garden.
vorgaukeln, *v.a.* (*einem etwas*) buoy up (*a p.*) with false promises *or* hopes, lead (*s.o.*) to believe that, (*coll.*) lead a p. up the garden path.
Vorgebäude, *n.* fore-part of a building; porch, vestibule.
vorgeb–en, *ir.v.a.* (*einem etwas*) give handicap, give points to, allow points; assert, advance, allege, pretend; *wieviel wollen Sie mir –en?* how many points will you allow *or* give me? **–lich,** *adj.* pretended, supposed, ostensible; so-called, would-be.
Vorgebirge, *n.* promontory, cape, headland; mountain spur, foothills.
vorgeburtlich, *adj.* prenatal.
vorgedacht, *adj., see* **vorerwähnt.**
vorgefaßt, *adj.* preconceived; *–e Meinung,* preconceived idea, prejudice, bias.
Vorgefühl, *n.* presentiment, foreboding, anticipation.
vorgehen, 1. *ir.v. n.* (*aux.* s.) go too fast (*of watches, etc.*); go before, precede, lead, go first, take the lead; advance, go forward, march (*auf,* upon); proceed, act, take steps *or* measures; (*with Dat.*) take precedence (over), excel, outstrip, transcend; happen, occur, go on, take place; *meine Uhr geht 5 Minuten vor,* my watch is 5 minutes fast; *gehen Sie vor, ich folge,* lead the way, I will follow; *rücksichtslos –,* act ruthlessly; *deine Schularbeiten gehen jetzt allem andern vor,* your homework is more important than anything else, your homework must come first; *gerichtlich* (*gegen einen*) *–,* proceed (against a p.) (*Law*); *was geht hier vor?* what is going on here? *ich weiß nicht, was in mir vorging,* I do not know what came over me. 2. *n.* advance; procedure, proceedings, (concerted) action.
Vorgelege, *n.* gearing, connecting-rod, transmission (*Mach.*). **–welle,** *f.* counter-shaft (*Mech.*).
vorge–meldet, *adj.,* **–nannt,** *adj.* aforementioned.
vorgerückt, *adj.* advanced (*in time*), late; *ein Mann –en Alters,* an elderly man, a man of advancing *or* advanced years; *wegen der –en Zeit,* owing to the lateness of the hour, season, *etc.*
Vorgeschicht–e, *f.* prehistory, early history, prehistoric times; history of the preceding period, previous history; antecedents. **–lich,** *adj.* prehistoric.
Vorgeschmack, *m.* foretaste.
vorgeschoben, *adj.* forward, advanced (*sentries, etc.*).
Vorgesetzt–e(r), *m.* chief, superior, principal, employer, master. **–enverhältnis,** *n.* authority (*Mil.*).
vorgest–ern, *adv.* the day before yesterday. **–rig,** *adj.* of two days ago.
vorgetäuscht, *adj.* simulated.
Vorgraben, *m.* avant-fosse, outer *or* forward trench.
vorgreif–en, *ir.v.n.* (*aux.* h.) (*with Dat.*) anticipate, forestall; encroach *or* entrench upon; *den Ereignissen –en,* anticipate (the) events; *einer Frage –en,* prejudge a matter. **–lich,** *adv.* in anticipation. **–ung,** *f.* anticipation, forestalling; encroachment.
vorhaben, 1. *ir.v.a.* have before one; have on, wear (*as an apron*); have in mind *or* in view, design, propose, intend; be engaged on *or* in, be busy *or* occupied with, be about, (*coll.*) have on; (*coll.*) call to account, rebuke, chide, reprimand; *sie hatte eine blaue Schürze vor,* she had on a blue apron; *ich habe ihn schon vorgehabt,* I have already taken him to task, rebuked *or* reprimanded him; *was hat er vor?* what is he about *or* after? *er hat etwas Böses vor,* he is plotting some mischief; *haben Sie für morgen etwas vor?* have you anything on tomorrow? *was hast du mit ihm vor?* what do you intend to do with him? what are your plans with him? 2. *n.* intention, design, plan, project, purpose, intent (*Law*), *er mußte von seinem – ablassen,* he had to abandon his purpose.
Vorhafen, *m.* outer harbour.
Vorhalle, *f.* vestibule, (entrance) hall.
Vorhalt, *m.* (*Swiss dial.*), *see* **–ung;** suspended note (*Mus.*); lead (*Av., etc.*). **–emaß,** *n.* allowance for speed (*of aircraft in A.A. fire & bombing*), lead. **–en,** 1. *ir.v. a.* (*einem etwas*) hold (s.th.) up to, out to, out for, before *or* in front of (a p.); charge *or* reproach (s.o.) with (a th.), remonstrate with (s.o.) about (a th.). 2. *v.n.* (*aux.* h.) hold out, wear well, endure, stand, last; *solange das Geld vorhält,* as long as the money holds out. **–ewinkel,** *m.* **–swinkel,** *m.* angle of lead, bombing angle. **–ung,** *f.* reproach, rebuke, remonstrance.
Vorhand, *f., see* **Vorderhand;** (*C.L.*) precedence, lead (*Cards*); *einem die – lassen* or *geben,* give a p. the lead; give *or* allow a p. the refusal (*of a th.*); *wer hat die –?* who has the lead?
vorhanden, *adj.* on hand, in stock; present, available, existing, existent, extant; *– sein,* be, exist, be on hand, be in stock; *es ist nichts mehr davon –,* there is no more of it (left). **–sein,** *n.* existence, presence.
Vorhang, *m.* curtain; *eiserner –,* fire-proof curtain (*Theat.*), iron curtain (*Pol.*).
vorhäng–en, 1. *v.n.* (*aux.* s.) hang in front, project. 2. *v.a.* hang before *or* in front of. **–eschloß,** *n.* padlock.
Vorhaut, *f.* foreskin, prepuce.

Vorhemd, *n.* shirt-front; (*coll.*) dickey.
vorher, *adv.* & *sep. prefix*, beforehand, in front, in advance; before, previously; *am Abend –*, (on) the previous evening; *kurz –*, a short *or* little time *or* while before. **–bestimmen,** *v.a.* determine *or* settle beforehand; preordain; predestine. **–bestimmung,** *f.* predetermination, predestination. **–dasein,** *n.* pre-existence. **–empfinden,** *ir.v.a.* have a presentiment (of). **–gehen,** *ir.v.n.* (*aux.* s.) (*Dat.*) precede; *ohne –gegangene Warnung*, without previous notice. **–gehend,** *pr.p.* & *adj.* preceding, anterior, previous, prior; *aus dem –gehenden folgt, daß . . .*, it follows from what has already been said that . . .; *die –gehenden Seiten*, the foregoing pages. **–geschehen,** *ir.v.n.* (*aux.* s.) take place previously, precede. **–ig,** *adj.* previous, preceding, former, antecedent. **–sage,** *f.*, **–sagung,** *f.* prediction, prophecy, prognosis, forecast. **–sagen,** *v.a.*, *see* **voraussagen. –sehen,** *ir.v.a.* foresee. **–verkündigen,** *v.a.* predict, foretell, announce beforehand. **–wissen,** *ir.v.a.* know beforehand *or* already.
Vorherrsch–aft, *f.* predominance, ascendancy. **–en,** *v.n.* (*aux.* h.) prevail, dominate, predominate. **–end,** *adj.* dominant, predominant, prevailing, prevalent.
vorheucheln, *v.a.* (*einem etwas*) pretend, feign, sham; *einem Treue –*, simulate fidelity to a p.
vorhin, *adv.* before, heretofore; a short time ago; *erst –*, only just now. **–ein,** only in *im –ein* (*Austr. dial.*) from the beginning *or* outset.
Vorhof, *m.* outer court, forecourt, vestibule, porch; auricle (*of the heart*).
vorhol–en, *v.a.* haul home (*Naut.*). **–er,** *m.* counter-recoil mechanism (*Artil.*).
Vorhölle, *f.* limbo.
Vorhut, *f.* advance guard, vanguard (*Mil.*).
vorig, *adj.* former, preceding, previous, last; *die –en*, the same (*in stage directions*); *das –e*, the foregoing; *–en Monats*, of last month, (*C.L.*) ult(imo).
Vorjahr, *n.* preceding year.
vorjährig, *adj.* of last year, last year's; *–e Kartoffeln*, old potatoes.
vorkämpf–en, *v.n.* (*aux.* h.) (*Dat.*) lead the attack, be an example to other combatants. **–er,** *m.* champion, pioneer.
vorkauen, *v.a.* (*einem* (*Kinde*) *etwas*) chew previously (for); *usually fig.* (*coll.*) spoon-feed.
Vorkauf, *m.* pre-emption, option on purchase, first refusal. **–en,** *v.a.* buy before others, forestall, buy for future delivery. **–spreis,** *m.* pre-emption price. **–srecht,** *n.* right of pre-emption; *das –srecht auf eine S. haben*, have the (first) refusal of a th.
Vorkehr, *f.* (*Swiss dial.*), *see* **–ung. –en,** *v.a.*, *see* **vorbauen. –ung,** *f.* provision, precaution, preventive *or* precautionary measure; *–ungen treffen*, make arrangements *or* provision, take precautions, provide for (a contingency).
Vorkenntnis, *f.* previous knowledge, basic knowledge, necessary grounding, rudiments.
vorkiefrig, *adj.* prognathous. **–keit,** *f.* prognathism.
vorklönen, *v.a.* (*dial.* & *coll.*) (*einem etwas*) blether (*about s.th.*), unburden o.s.
vorknöpfen, *v.r.* (*coll.*) take to task; *den knöpfe ich mir ordentlich vor*, I will give him a good dressing-down.
vorkomm–en, 1. *ir.v.n.* (*aux.* s.) come forth, forward *or* out; (*bei*) visit, call (on), look in (on), (*coll.*) drop in (on); (*with Dat.*) seem, appear, be found, present itself, happen, occur, take place, (*coll.*) crop up; get ahead of, outstrip, surpass; *kommen Sie nächsten Sonntag bei mir vor*, give me a call, look in on me *or* drop in next Sunday; *dergleichen kommt nicht alle Tage vor*, such things do not occur every day; *so etwas ist mir noch nicht vorgekommen*, I have never heard *or* come across such a thing before; *er kommt sich* (*Dat.*) *recht gelehrt vor*, he fancies himself as a great scholar, he believes himself to be *or* thinks he is very learned; *es kam mir recht seltsam vor*, it seemed very strange to me; (*coll.*) *wie kommst du mir eigentlich vor?* who do you think you are? *das kommt mir spanisch vor*, that strikes me as odd; *ich weiß nicht, wie du mir heute vorkommst*, I do not know what to make of you *or* I cannot make you out today. 2. *n.* presence, existence. **–endenfalls,** *adv.* should the case arise, in the eventuality of. **–nis,** *n.* occurrence, event; *see also* **–en** 2. (*of minerals, etc.*).
Vorkost, *f.* hors d'œuvres, entrée.
Vorkriegszeit, *f.* pre-war years.
Vorlack, *m.* primer, priming lacquer.
vorlad–en, *ir.* & *reg. v.a.* summon (*a witness*). **–egewehr,** *n.*, *see* **Vorderlader. –eschein,** *m.*, **–ung,** *f.*, **–ungsbefehl,** *m.*, **–ungsschreiben,** *n.*, **–ungszettel,** *m.* summons, warrant, citation.
Vorlage, *f.* proposal, subject *or* matter (*for discussion, etc.*), bill (*Parl.*); copy, model, pattern, prototype; receiver (*in distilleries*), receiving vessel (*Chem.*); bedside carpet; flash hider (*on guns*); forward kick (*Footb.*).
Vorlager, *n.* front; prothallus (*Bot.*); advance camp (*Mil.*). **–n,** 1. *v.r.* sit down *or* pitch one's tent before (*s.th.*). 2. *v.n.* & *a.* extend before, stretch out in front of.
Vorland, *n.* foreland, foreshore; mud-flat; land outside a dike.
vorlängst, *adv.* (*archaic*) long ago, long since.
vorlass–en, *ir.v.a.* let come forward, give precedence to; admit, show in; *ich wurde* (*bei ihm*) *vorgelassen*, I was shown in *or* admitted (to his presence). **–ung,** *f.* admission, admittance.
Vorlauf, *m.* heat (*Sport*); first runnings, heads (*Distilling, etc.*). **–en,** *ir.v.n.* (*aux.* s.) run forward, run out in front; (*with Dat.*) outstrip, pass, surpass.
Vorläuf–er, *m.* forerunner, precursor, harbinger; early symptom (*Med.*). **–ig,** *adj.* preliminary, preparatory, introductory, provisional, temporary. 2. *adv.* for the present, for the time being, provisionally, in the meantime.
vorlaut, *adj.* forward, cheeky, saucy, pert; *– sein*, be badly trained (*of dogs*).
vorleben, 1. *v.a.* (*aux.* h.) (*einem etwas*) hold (*a th.*) up as *or* set (*a th.*) as an example (*to s.o.*). 2. *n.* former life, previous career *or* history, early life, antecedents; *sie hat kein einwandfreies –*, she has a doubtful past.
vorleg–en, 1. *v.a.* put *or* lay before, serve (*food*), put on, apply; (*einem etwas*) display, show, exhibit, produce, offer, submit. 2. *v.n.* (*aux.* h.) eat heartily; *dem Vieh Heu –en*, give the cattle hay; *Waren zum Verkauf –en*, expose goods for sale; *etwas weiter –en*, push a th. forward; *ein Tempo –en*, put on a spurt (*Sport*); *Punkte –en*, be leading on points (*Sport*); *Schloß und Riegel –en*, bolt and bar, barricade, make o.s. secure against intrusion. **–ebesteck,** *n.* (pair of) carvers. **–egabel,** *f.* carving-fork. **–ekelle,** *f.* fish-slice. **–elöffel,** *m.* serving spoon; soup-ladle. **–emesser,** *n.* carving knife. **–er,** *m.* carpet, mat, rug. **–eschloß,** *n.* padlock. **–ung,** *f.* submission, proposal; exhibition, production; carving, serving.
Vorlese, *f.* early vintage.
vorles–en, *ir.v.a.* read aloud, read to. **–ung,** *f.* reading aloud, recital, (university) lecture, course of lectures; *–ungen halten über* (*Acc.*), lecture (on), give a course of lectures (on); *–ungen hören*, attend lectures; *–ungen belegen*, register for a course of lectures; join a class (on); *–ungen schwänzen*, cut lectures; *–ungen schinden*, gate-crash lectures. **–ungsgebühr,** *f.* lecture-fee. **–ungsverzeichnis,** *n.* university prospectus.
vorletzt, *adj.* last but one, penultimate.
Vorlieb–e, *f.* predilection, preference, partiality; *eine – haben für*, have a special liking for. **–nehmen,** *v.n.* (*mit*), put up (with), make do (with), have to be satisfied (with).
vorliegen, *ir.v.n.* (*aux.* h.) be in front of; be put forward *or* submitted; be in hand, be under discussion *or* consideration; be (present); *das Haus liegt vor*, the house is at the *or* faces the front; *es liegt heute nichts vor*, there is nothing to do today, (*coll.*) nothing doing today; *hier muß ein Irrtum –*, there must be some mistake here; *–der Fall*, case in question.
vorlügen, *v.a.* (*einem etwas*) tell a p. lies, lie to s.o. (*about a th.*).
Vorluke, *f.* fore- or forward hatch (*Naut.*).
vorm = **vor dem.**

vormach-en, *v.a.* put *or* place before; (*einem etwas*) demonstrate, show how to do; impose upon (*a p.*), take (*a p.*) in, humbug (*a p.*); *einem (einen) blauen Dunst -en*, throw dust in a p.'s eyes; *mir kannst du nichts -en*, you cannot impose on me *or* take me in. **-t,** *f.* supremacy. **-tstellung,** *f.* hegemony.
Vormagen, *m.* omasum, crop (*Zool.*).
vormal-ig, *adj.* former. **-s,** *adv.* formerly, once upon a time.
Vormann, *m., see* **Vordermann.**
Vormars, *m. or f.* foretop (*Naut.*).
Vormarsch, *f.* advance, push (*Mil.*). **-ieren,** *v.n.* (*aux.* s.) advance.
vormärzlich, *adj.* reactionary, obscurantist (*characterizing political attitude*) before 1848 (revolution).
Vormast, *m.* foremast.
Vormauer, *f.* outer wall, bulwark; claustrum.
Vormeldung, *f.* preliminary report.
Vormensch, *m.* early *or* primitive man.
vormerk-en, *v.a.* note *or* take down, make *or* take a note of, book, bespeak; *seine Fahrkarte -en lassen*, book one's ticket; *sich -en lassen (für)*, put one's name down (for). **-ung,** *f.* rough note, memorandum; reservation, booking.
Vormilch, *f.* colostrum.
Vormittag, *m.* (-s, -e) morning, forenoon. **-s,** *adv.* in the morning. **-sstunde,** *f.* morning hour; morning lesson.
vormittäg-ig, *adj.* (in the) morning, matutinal; *-ige Kirche*, morning service. **-lich,** *adj.* each *or* every morning.
Vormund, *m.* (-(e)s, ⸚er) guardian, trustee; *ich brauche keinen -*, (*coll.*) I will not stand any interference. **-schaft,** *f.* guardianship, trusteeship, tutelage; *unter -schaft stehen*, (*stellen*), be (place) under the care of a guardian. **-schaftlich,** *adj.* tutelary. **-schaftsgelder,** *n.pl.* trust-money, property of a ward. **-schaftsgericht,** *n.* Court of Chancery. **-schaftsordnung,** *f.* order in chancery. **-schaftsrechnung,** *f.* account of guardianship, of a ward's estate *or* trust-money.
vornächtig, *adj.* last night's.
Vorname, *m.* first name, Christian name.
vorn, 1. *adv.* in front; in the front; at the beginning, before; *ganz -*, right at the *or* in front; *nach - heraus wohnen*, live at *or* in the front (of the house); *- im Buche*, at the beginning of the book; *- und hinten*, before and behind, fore and aft; *er ist überall, hinten und -*, he is here, there and everywhere; *von -*, from the front, opposite, facing; *ich sah sie von -*, I saw her to her face; *von - anfangen* start afresh, anew *or* at the beginning; *nach -*, forward. 2. *n.*; *das - und Hinten*, the front and the back. **-(e)an,** *adv.* in front; *-an sitzen*, sit at the *or* in front. **-(e)hin,** *adv.* to the front. **-(e)weg,** *adv.* from the start, to begin with; *mit dem Mundwerk -eweg*, (*vulg.*) shooting off his mouth. **-herein** *adv.*; *von* or *im -herein*, from the first *or* beginning, from *or* at the outset, to start *or* begin with; a priori, as a matter of course. **-hinein,** *adv.* in by the front. **-über,** *adv.* bent *or* leaning forward.
vornehm, *adj.* of high rank, aristocratic, noble, grand, elegant, fashionable, genteel, refined; distinguished, eminent, principal, chief; *-er Anstrich*, aristocratic air *or* bearing; *-es Äußere*, distinguished appearance; *-er Besuch*, distinguished visitor; *- denken*, be high-minded *or* high-principled, behave like a gentleman, (*coll.*) act very decently; *dies ist das -ste und größte Gebot*, this is the first and greatest commandment; *- und gering*, high and low, all and sundry; *-e Gesinnung*, high-mindedness; *die -en (Leute)*, people of rank, distinguished people; *- tun*, give o.s. *or* put on airs; *die -e Welt*, the fashionable high (class) society; *-es Wesen*, air of superiority. **-heit,** *f.* distinction, superiority, high rank; distinguished bearing, refined manners. **-lich,** *adv.* particularly, especially, principally, mainly, chiefly, above all. **-tuerei,** *f.* airs and graces, superciliousness, (*sl.*) swank, cockiness, side.
vornehmen, 1. *ir.v.a.* put on (*as an apron*); take in hand, undertake; *sich (Dat.) etwas -*, intend, resolve, propose *or* make up one's mind to do a th.; occupy *or* busy o.s. with a th., (*coll.*) take a th. up; *ich habe mir vorgenommen (es zu tun)*, I have made up my mind (to do it); *sich (Dat.) einen -*, call a p. to account, take a p. to task, (*coll.*) take a p. up (about). 2. *n.* undertaking, project, proposal, intention.
Vorort, *m.* suburb; administrative headquarters *or* central offices (*of an association*). **-verkehr,** *m.* suburban traffic. **-zug,** *m.* suburban *or* local train.
Vorplatz, *m.* esplanade, forecourt; landing (*of a staircase*).
Vorposten, *m.* outpost, advance post (*Mil.*); *auf -*, on outpost duty; *- ausstellen*, place outposts, throw out pickets. **-boot,** *n.* patrol vessel. **-dienst,** *m.* outpost duty. **-gefecht,** *n.* outpost skirmish.
Vorpress-e, *f.*, **-(ß)walze,** *f.* baby press, dandy-roll.
Vorprobe, *f.* preliminary trial.
Vorprüfung, *f.* preliminary examination; trial (*Sport*).
vorquellen, *v.n.* (*aux.* s.) ooze out *or* forth; bulge.
Vorrang, *m.* pre-eminence, superiority, precedence, priority; *den - vor einem haben*, have *or* take precedence over s.o.
Vorrat, *m.* (-(e)s, ⸚e) store, stock, provision, supply, reserve; *zu viel - haben*, be overstocked; *in - halten*, store, keep in stock; *im -*, in stock, in store, in reserve; *auf - kaufen*, buy into stock; *- auf Lager*, stock in hand; *sich (Dat.) einen - verschaffen*, take in a supply *or* stock (of). **-skammer,** *f.* storeroom, larder, pantry. **-sverzeichnis,** *n.* inventory.
vorrätig, *adj.* in stock, on hand, in reserve, in store; *- haben*, stock (*an article*), have *or* keep in stock; *eine S. nicht mehr - haben*, not have a th. in stock, be out of a th.; *nicht mehr - sein*, be out of stock.
vorrech-nen, *v.a.* compute, reckon up, calculate; give details *or* an account of one's figures, enumerate. **-t,** *n.* special right, privilege, prerogative, priority.
Vorred-e, *f.* words of introduction, opening speech, introduction, preface, preamble, prologue; (*Prov.*) *-e spart Nachrede*, a word before is worth two after. **-en,** *v.a.* (*einem etwas*) tell a plausible tale, talk (a p.) into (s.th.) *or* over; *sich (Dat.) etwas -en lassen*, let o.s. be talked into (a th.) *or* over, let the wool be pulled over one's eyes. **-ner,** *m.* last *or* previous speaker.
Vorreiber, *m.* window catch.
vorreit-en, 1. *ir.v.a.* put (*a horse*) through its paces; (*einem etwas*) make a parade *or* show of a th. *or* show a th. off before a p. 2. *v.n.* (*aux.* s.) (*einem*) ride before; ride forward; outride; show (*a p.*) how to ride. **-er,** *m.* outrider.
vorricht-en, *v.a.* prepare, make *or* get ready, put in order, fit up; put on, advance (*a watch, etc.*). **-ung,** *f.* preparation, arrangement; apparatus, contrivance, appliance, device, attachment, mechanism.
vorrücken, 1. *v.a.* put, move *or* push forward, put (*a clock*) on; (*einem etwas*) reproach *or* charge (a p. with a th.). 2. *v.n.* (*aux.* s.) advance, move forward, progress, move *or* push on; *Truppen - lassen*, order troops to advance, push the troops forward; *die Zeit rückt vor*, time is getting on.
Vorrunde, *f.* preliminary *or* elimination round, heat (*Sport*).
vors = **vor das.**
Vorsaal, *m.* (-(e)s, -säle) entrance hall, vestibule, ante-room, antechamber, waiting-room.
vorsagen, *v.a.* (*einem etwas*) say to *or* tell; rehearse *or* recite (*what one has to say*); prompt, dictate to; *einem viel Schönes -*, make pretty speeches to a p.; *du sagst mir das wohl nur so vor*, you are only saying that, there is not a word of truth in it, I do not believe a word of it.
Vorsänger, *m.* leader of a choir, precentor, officiating minister (*in a synagogue*).
Vorsatz, *m.* (-es, ⸚e) design, project, purpose, resolution, plan, intention; premeditation; (*also n.*) endpaper (*Bookb.*); *aus* or *mit -*, on purpose, purposely, deliberately, intentionally, with premeditation; *mit - lügen*, tell a deliberate lie; (*Prov.*) *der Weg zur Hölle ist mit guten Vorsätzen gepflastert*, the road to hell is paved with good intentions. **-blatt,** *n.*, **-papier,** *n.* end-paper (*Bookb.*).

vorsätzlich, 1. *adj.* intentional, deliberate, wilful. 2. *adv.* purposely, designedly, premeditatedly.

Vorschein, *m.* appearance; (only in) *zum – bringen,* produce; *zum – kommen,* appear.

vorschicken, *v.a.* send forward *or* to the front.

vorschieb-en, *ir.v.a.* push *or* shove forward; slip (*a bolt*); pretend, plead as an excuse; *vorgeschobene Befestigungen,* advanced forts, outlying fortifications; *vorgeschobene Person,* man of straw. **-er,** *m.* slide-bolt; sliding door. **-ung,** *f.* feed (*Sew. mach.*).

vorschießen, 1. *ir.v.a.*; *einem Geld –,* advance, provide with, loan *or* lend a p. money; *einen Saum –,* turn up *or* make a hem. 2. *v.n.* (*aux.* s.) shoot *or* dart forth; (*aux.* h.) (*with Dat.*) show how to shoot; shoot first.

Vorschiff, *n.* forecastle.

Vorschlag, *m.* (-(e)s, ⸚e) proposition, proposal, suggestion, motion, offer; appoggiatura, grace-note (*Mus.*); anacrusis (*Metr.*); first blow *or* stroke; blank space on the first page of a book (*Typ.*); amount added to the price; *Vorschläge machen* or *tun,* make proposals; *in – bringen,* propose, move; *auf einen – eingehen,* agree to a proposal; *– zur Güte,* conciliatory proposal; good way out of the difficulty. **-en,** *ir.v.a.* put forward, nominate, propose, propound, offer, suggest, move (*a resolution*); overcharge; *einem etwas –,* propose s.th. to a p.; *einen zu einem Amte –,* propose *or* nominate a p. for an office; *auf eine Ware 3 Mark –,* put 3 marks on to the price of s.th.; *einem den Ton* or *eine Note –,* give s.o. the note (*Mus.*); *den Takt –,* beat time; *der -ende,* the proposer, mover, presenter; *der Vorgeschlagene,* the nominee. **-hammer,** *m.* sledge hammer. **-snote,** *f.* appoggiatura (*Mus.*). **-srecht,** *n.* right of nominating (*to an office*). **-ssilbe,** *f.* anacrusis (*Metr.*).

Vorschlußrunde, *f.* semi-final (*Sport*).

Vorschmack, *m.* (*archaic*) foretaste, foreboding.

vorschneide-n, *ir.v.a.* carve, cut up (*at table*). **-brett,** *n.* trencher. **-messer,** *n.* carving-knife.

vorschnell, *adj., see* **voreilig.**

vorschreiben, *ir.v.a.* (*einem etwas*) set as a copy, write out (for s.o.); dictate, prescribe (to s.o.), lay down (for s.o.), command, order, direct (s.o. to do); *ich lasse mir nichts –,* I will not be dictated to; *Sie haben mir nichts vorzuschreiben,* (*coll.*) you have no say over me.

vorschreiten, *ir.v.n.* (*aux.* s.) step forth *or* forward, advance, march on, go on ahead; *vorgeschrittenes Stadium,* advanced stage; *vorgeschrittene Jahreszeit,* advanced season, late in the year *or* season.

Vorschrift, *f.* (–, -en) copy; recipe, formula; prescription; direction, provision, precept, rule; order, instruction, regulation; *nach –,* as prescribed. **-enbuch,** *n.* manual of instructions. **-sgemäß,** *adv.*, **-smäßig,** *adj.* according to instructions *or* regulations, as ordered, as prescribed. **-swidrig,** *adj.* contrary to instructions, against orders, against the rules.

Vorschub, *m.* (unfair) help, assistance, aid *or* support, furtherance; feed (*Mech.*); *einem – leisten,* help, support *or* abet a p., afford a p. assistance, lend a p. a hand; *einer S. – leisten* or *tun,* further *or* promote a matter, support a th. **-leistung,** *f.* aiding and abetting (*Law.*)

Vorschuh, *m.* vamp, upper leather (*of a boot*). **-en,** *v.a.* new-foot, re-vamp (*shoes*).

Vorschule, *f.* preparatory department *or* school; elementary course.

Vorschuß, *m.* (-(ss)es, ⸚(ss)e) advance (of money), payment in advance; *Vorschüsse leisten, machen* or *tun,* advance money; make loans. **-kasse,** *f.* loan-fund. **-weise,** *adv.* as an advance, by way of a loan. **-zahlung,** *f.* payment in advance.

vorschütten, *v.a.* (*einem etwas*) throw down, strew, give (*provender*).

vorschütz-en, *v.a.* throw up as a defence, shelter behind; pretend; plead (*as excuse*); *Unwissenheit -en,* plead ignorance. **-ung,** *f.* pretext, excuse, hollow pretence.

vorschweben, *v.n.* (*aux.* h.) (*with Dat.*) swim, float *or* hover before; be in s.o.'s mind, have a recollection of.

vorschwindeln, *v.a.* (*einem etwas*) try to make (*a p.*) believe (*s.th.*), humbug (*a p.*), tell lies (*to s.o.*) about (*a th.*).

Vorsegel, *n.* foresail.

vorseh-en, 1. *ir.v.a.* consider, provide for; *der Fall ist im Gesetze nicht vorgesehen,* this case is not provided for by the law. 2. *v.r.* take care, be cautious *or* careful, be mindful of, be on one's guard, mind, beware (of); (*mit etwas*) lay in stock (*of a th.*); provide *or* supply o.s. (with); *vorgesehen!* look out! take care! *sich vor einem Menschen -en,* be on one's guard against a p.; *vorgesehen ist besser als nachgesehen,* better be careful than sorry, prevention is better than cure. **-ung,** *f.* providence.

vorsetz-en, *v.a.* set, place *or* put before; (*einem etwas*) **serve** (*food*); offer; set over (*s.o. else*); prefix (to); *darf ich Ihnen etwas -en?* may I offer you anything (to eat)? *sich* (*Dat.*) *einen Zweck -en,* propose to do s.th., aim at s.th., intend, resolve *or* determine to do a th., determine upon s.th.; *jemanden einem andern –,* set a p. over another, prefer a p. to another; *jemanden einem Amte -en,* appoint a p. to an office; *einer Note ein Kreuz* (*ein B*) *-en,* prefix a note with a sharp (a flat) (*Mus.*); *vorgesetzte Behörde,* appointed authorities, those in authority; *seine Vorgesetzten,* his superior officers, his superiors. **-er,** *m.* fire-screen, fire-guard, fender. **-blatt,** *n.* fly-leaf (*of a book*). **-fenster,** *n.* outer window (*of double windows*). **-(ungs)-zeichen,** *n.* accidental (*Mus.*).

Vorsicht, *f.* foresight, precaution, care, prudence; caution, discretion, circumspection; (*archaic*) providence; *–!* look out! have a care! take care! beware! *mit vieler – zu Werke gehen,* act very cautiously; (*Prov.*) *– ist die Mutter der Weisheit* or (*coll.*) *der Porzellanschüssel,* caution is the mother of wit; *– Stufe!* mind the step! **-ig,** *adj.* cautious, careful, prudent, wary, guarded, circumspect, discreet; *-ig sein,* be cautious, take care, go carefully; *-igen Gebrauch machen,* use with discretion. **-shalber,** *adv.* as a precaution. **-smaßnahme,** *f.*, **-smaßregel,** *f.* precautionary measure, precaution.

Vorsilbe, *f.* prefix.

vorsingen, 1. *ir.v.a.* (*with Dat.*) sing to. 2. *v.n.* lead the singing.

vorsintflutlich, *adj.* antediluvian.

Vorsitz, *m.* presidency, chairmanship; the chair; *den – haben* or *führen,* preside, be in the chair; *den – übernehmen,* take the chair, act as chairman. **-en,** *ir.v.n.* (*aux.* h.) (*with Dat.*) preside (over). **-ende(r) -er,** *m.* president, chairman.

vorsohlen, *v.a.* (*einem etwas*) (*coll.*), *see* **vorlügen.**

Vorsorg-e, *f.* foresight, care, attention, precaution, provision; *-e tragen* or *treffen, daß . . .,* make provision for . . . , take care that . . . , (*coll.*) see to it that . . . **-en,** *v.n.* (*aux.* h.) take precautions; provide for, take care that. **-lich,** 1. *adj.* provident, careful. 2. *adv.* as a precaution.

Vorspann, *m.* (extra) team of horses; *– leisten* or *stellen,* help, give a hand. **-en,** *v.a.* harness to. **-pferd,** *n.* relay-horse, additional horse. **-ung,** *f.* grid potential (*Rad.*), initial stress.

Vorspeise, *f.* hors-d'œuvre.

vorspiegel-n, *v.a.* (*einem etwas*) dazzle (s.o.) with (a th.); present (s.th.) in a clear *or* favourable light (to a p.); deceive (s.o.), delude (s.o.), raise false hopes (in s.o.'s mind). **-ung,** *f.* illusion, delusion, pretence, sham, shamming; misrepresentation, false pretences; *unter -ung falscher Tatsachen,* under false pretences.

Vorspiel, *n.* (-(e)s, -e) prelude, overture (*Mus.*), curtain-raiser (*Theat.*); prologue. **-en,** *v.a.* (*einem etwas*) play before *or* to (a p.).

vorspinn-en, *n.* roving (*Spin.*). **-maschine,** *f.* roving-frame.

vorsprechen, 1. *ir.v.a.* (*einem etwas*) pronounce to *or* for (s.o.), demonstrate how to pronounce. 2. *v.n.* (*aux.* h. & s.) (*bei*) call on *or* drop in on (*s.o.*).

vorspringen, *ir.v.n.* (*aux.* s.) leap forward; jut out, project. *-des Fenster,* bay-window, projecting window; *-der Winkel,* salient.

Vorsprung, *m.* projection, prominence, protrusion; ledge; salient; start, lead, advantage; *den – gewinnen, einem den – abgewinnen,* get a start *or* lead over a p.

Vorstadt, *f.* suburb, outskirts.

Vorstädt-er, *m.* suburban dweller, (*coll.*) suburbanite. **-isch,** *adj.* suburban.

Vorstand, *m.* (-(e)s, ⸚e) board of directors, directorate, managing *or* executive committee, governing body. **-smitglied,** *n.* director, manager, member of the governing body.

vorstechen, 1. *ir.v.a.* prick an outline, mark out with holes. 2. *v.n.* (*aux.* h.) stand out, be prominent, catch the eye.

vorsteck-en, 1. *reg. & ir.v.a.* pin *or* fasten on; poke *or* stick out; *den Kopf -en,* put *or* poke out one's head; *sich* (*Dat.*) *ein Ziel -en,* set o.s. a goal, aim at s.th.; *das vorgesteckte Ziel erreichen,* attain *or* achieve one's object, reach one's goal. **-ärmel,** *m.* oversleeve, sleeve-protector. **-blume,** *f.* buttonhole (*flower*). **-er,** *m.* pin, peg, stake, fastener, fastening. **-keil,** *m.* block, chock (*for a wheel*). **-latz,** *m.*, **-lätzchen,** *n.* bib, pinafore, stomacher. **-nadel,** *f.* scarf-ring. **-schlips,** *m.* bow (*as neckwear*).

vorsteh-en, *ir.v.n.* (*aux.* h.) jut out, project, protrude, overhang; (*with Dat.*) superintend, preside over, oversee, be at the head of, manage, direct, administer; *der Hund steht vor,* the dog points *or* sets (*Hunt.*); *einem Amte -en,* hold *or* administer an office. **-end,** *pr.p. & adj.* projecting, protruding; preceding; *im -enden,* in the foregoing, see above. **-er,** *m.* principal, chief, administrator, director, manager, superintendent, supervisor, foreman, inspector; headmaster; superior (*of a convent*); warden, master (*of a college*). **-erdrüse,** *f.* prostate gland (*Anat.*). **-erin,** *f.* manageress, forewoman, mother-superior. **-hund,** *m.* pointer, setter.

vorstell-en, 1. *v.a.* place before, put in front of; put forward, advance, put on (*a clock*); (*einem etwas*) present, introduce; demonstrate, represent, personate, pose (as); mean, signify; make clear, explain; remonstrate, protest, expostulate; (*with Dat.* sich) imagine, fancy, suppose, conceive; *darf ich Sie meiner Schwester -en?* may I introduce you to my sister? *eine Rolle -en,* play a part, act the character; *etwas -en, was man nicht ist,* set up to be what one is not; *etwas Großes -en wollen,* wish to be thought somebody, try to make a show; *was stellt das vor? was soll das -en?* what is that supposed to be? what is the meaning of that? *stellen Sie sich meine Freude vor,* imagine my delight; *ich kann mir kein geeigneteres Denkmal -en,* I can think of no more fitting memorial. 2. *v.r.* go *or* come forward *or* to the front; introduce o.s., make o.s. known. **-ig,** *adj.* (only in) *-ig werden,* present a case *or* petition (to), protest (to), lodge a complaint (with) (*the authorities*). **-ung,** *f.* introduction, presentation (*at court, etc.*); performance, representation; complaint, remonstrance, expostulation; imagination, idea, notion, conception, mental image; *das geht über alle -ung,* the imagination boggles at it; *etwas in seine -ung aufnehmen,* get some idea of a th., get a grasp of a th., get s.th. into one's head; *-ungen erheben,* raise *or* take up a point, lodge a complaint; *erste -ung,* first performance; first night (*of a play*); *sich* (*Dat.*) *eine -ung machen von . . .,* form an idea *or* some notion of . . . **-ungsfähigkeit,** *f.*, **-ungskraft,** *f.*, **-ungsvermögen,** *n.* (power of) imagination. **-ungsweise,** *f.* way of looking at things; way of putting things.

Vorstoß, *m.* (-es, ⸚e) push forward, forward movement, attack, advance, drive, thrust (*Mil.*); projection, ledge; beak, spout (*of a vessel*); piping, edging, braid, binding, raised seam (*Semp.*). **-en,** 1. *ir.v.a.* push forward; *einen Saum -en,* make a raised seam. 2. *v.n.* (*aux.* s.) push *or* thrust forward, attack, march against; project, protrude.

Vorstrafe, *f.* (–, -en) previous conviction.

vorstrecken, *v.a.* stretch forward *or* out, stick out, poke out, extend; advance, lend (*money*).

vorstreich-en, *ir.v.a. & n.* (*aux.* h.) apply an undercoat. **-farbe,** *f.* undercoat, priming colour.

Vorstufe, *f.* first step, first stage, preliminary stage; (*pl.*) rudiments, elements.

vorstürmen, *v.n.* rush forward.

vortanzen, 1. *v.a.* demonstrate a dance. 2. *v.n.* (*aux.* h.) lead the dance.

Vortänzer, *m.* leader, opener (*of a dance*); dancing demonstrator.

vortäuschen, *v.a.* feign, simulate.

Vorteil, *m.* (-(e)s, -e) advantage, benefit, interest, profit, emolument, gain; *einem den – abgewinnen,* get the better of a p.; *seinen – ausnützen,* exploit one's advantage; *zu seinem – ausschlagen,* turn out to his advantage; *– bringen,* be advantageous *or* of advantage; (*Prov.*) *jeder – gilt,* all's fair in love and war; *ihm zum – gereichen,* see *– ausschlagen; davon keinen – haben,* derive no benefit from it; *einer S. einen – herausholen* or *herausschlagen,* turn a th. to (one's) advantage; *auf seinen – sehen* or *bedacht sein,* have an eye to one's own interests; *im – sein* (*vor einem*), be at an advantage *or* have the advantage (of *or* over a p.); *es wird zu Ihrem – sein,* it will be in your interest *or* to your advantage; *mit – verkaufen,* sell at a profit; *sich einen unerlaubten – verschaffen,* take an unfair advantage; *von* or *aus einer S. – ziehen,* derive benefit *or* advantage from a th., turn s.th. to account; *sich zu seinem – von einem andern unterscheiden,* show up to advantage in comparison with s.o. else; *sich zu seinem – verändern,* change for the better. **-bringend,** *adj.*, **-haft,** *adj.* profitable, lucrative, remunerative, advantageous, favourable; *-haft aussehen,* look one's best; *-hafte Gelegenheit,* favourable opportunity. **-suchend,** *adj.* self-seeking.

Vortrab, *m.* vanguard, advance guard.

Vortrag, *m.* (-(e)s, ⸚e) diction, delivery, utterance, enunciation; elocution; execution (*Mus.*); lecture, address, discourse, recital, recitation, report, statement; (*C.L.*) balance carried forward; *einen – halten über* (*Acc.*), lecture *or* give a lecture on; *der Redner hat einen deutlichen –,* the speaker has a clear delivery; *zum – bringen,* sing (*a song*), play (*a piece of music*), recite (*a poem*), deliver (*a speech*), express (*one's views*); *– auf neue Rechnung,* balance (*of an account*) carried forward. **-en,** *ir.v.a.* carry *or* bring forward (*also C.L.*); carry before *or* in front of; explain, expound, report on; propose, speak (of); recite, declaim, perform, execute, play (*piece of music*), express (*one's opinion*), discourse *or* lecture (on); give *or* deliver (*a speech, etc.*); *eine Bitte -en,* make a request, solicit a favour; *den Saldo auf neue Rechnung -en,* carry forward the balance. **-ekreuz,** *n.* processional cross (*R.C.*). **-ende(r),** *m.* speaker, lecturer; performer. **-ieren,** *v.n.* (*iron.*) rant. **-sart,** *f.* manner of speaking, delivery. **-sfolge,** *f.* series of lectures. **-skunst,** *f.* declamation, elocution. **-skünstler,** *m.* elocutionist, executant, (musical) performer. **-sweise,** *f.*, *see* **-art.**

vortrefflich, *adj.* excellent, admirable, splendid, fine, capital. **-keit,** *f.* excellence.

Vortrieb, *m.* propulsion.

Vortritt, *m.* precedence; *den – vor einem haben,* take precedence over a p.; *einem den – lassen,* give precedence to a p.

vortrocknen, *v.a.* pre-dry.

Vortrupp, *m.* vanguard. **-en,** *f.pl.* advance troops.

Vortuch, *n,* (*dial.*) apron, bib.

vortun, 1. *ir.v.a.* put on (*as an apron*); do rashly *or* prematurely; show how to do; *ein Taschentuch –,* hold a handkerchief in front of one's mouth; *es einem –,* surpass a p. in doing; (*Prov.*) *vorgetan und nachgedacht, hat manchem schon groß Leid gebracht,* it's no use shutting the stable door after the horse is gone, look before you leap. 2. *v.r.* push o.s. forward, be pushing.

vorturn-en, *v.n.* (*aux.* h.) lead *or* take a squad of gymnasts. **-er,** *m.* squad leader (*Gymn.*), gymnastics demonstrator.

vorüber, *adv. & sep. prefix.* along, by, past, gone (by); over, finished, done with; *der Regen ist –,* the rain is over; *sein Ruhm war schnell –,* his fame soon passed away; *er ging an mir –,* he went past me, he passed me (by). **-gehen,** 1. *ir.v.n.* (*aux.* s.), pass, pass by, go past *or* by; pass over, neglect; pass away, be over, (*coll.*) blow over; *an einem -gehen,* go past a p., pass by a p. *or* a p. by, pass over a p. *or* a p. over; *eine Gelegenheit -gehen lassen,* miss a chance, let a chance slip by. 2. *n.*; *im -gehen,* in passing

(*also fig.*); by the way, incidentally. **-gehend,** *pr.p. & adj.* passing, temporary, transient, transitory; *sich -gehend aufhalten*, make a short stay, stay for the time being; *die -gehenden*, the passers-by. **-ziehen,** *ir.v.n.* (*aux.* s.) pass (by).
Vorübung, *f.* previous practice; preparatory exercise.
Voruntersuchung, *f.* preliminary inquiry *or* investigation.
Vorurteil, *n.* (-s, -e) prejudice, bias, prepossession; *sich von seinen -en freimachen*, get the better of one's prejudices; *einem -e einflößen*, prejudice a p.; *einem - entgegentreten*, make allowances for bias. **-sfrei,** *adj.*, **-slos,** *adj.* unprejudiced, unbiased. **-slosigkeit,** *f.* freedom from prejudice, open-mindedness, impartiality. **-svoll,** *adj.* prejudiced, biased.
Vorvater, *m.* (-s, ¨-) forefather, ancestor, progenitor.
Vorverdichter, *m.* (-s, -) supercharger (*Mech.*).
Vorvergangenheit, *f.* pluperfect (*Gram.*).
Vorverkauf, *m.* advance sale *or* booking (*Theat.*); *im - zu haben*, bookable.
vorverlegen, *v.a.* lift (*a barrage*); increase range (*Artil.*).
Vorverstärker, *m.* input amplifier (*Rad.*).
vorvorgestern, *adv.* three days ago.
vorvorig, *adj.* last but one, penultimate.
Vorwähler, *m.* preselector (*Elec.*).
Vorwall, *m.* outer rampart.
vorwalten, *v.n.* (*aux.* h.) predominate, prevail; (*archaic*) be, exist.
Vorwand, *m.* (-(e)s, ¨-e) pretext, pretence, subterfuge, excuse, plea; *unter dem -*, on the pretext, with the plea; *einen - suchen*, look for an excuse.
vorwärmen, *v.a.* preheat, warm up.
vorwärts, *adv. & sep. prefix*, forward, onward, (further) on; to the front, towards the front, forwards; *-!* forward! march! move on! go on! get on! go ahead!; *sich - bewegen*, move forward, advance; *- gehen*, go forwards *or* to the front; *see* **-gehen;** *sich* (*Dat.*) *- helfen*, make one's way in the world; *- kommen* come forwards *or* to the front; *see* **-kommen;** (*Prov.*) *langsam kommt man auch -*, slow and sure wins the race, more haste less speed. **-beuge,** *f.* forwards bend (*Gymn.*). **-bringen,** *v.a.* promote, advance, further, foster, abet, expedite. **-gang,** *m.* forward speed (*Motor.*). **-gehen,** improve, get on, advance, progress; *es will* (*mit ihm*) *nicht -gehen*, he makes no headway *or* progress. **-kommen,** 1. *v.n.* proceed, get on, get ahead, make headway, prosper, advance. 2. *n.*, **-schreiten,** *n.* progress, advance. **-treiben,** *v.a.* propel.
vorweg, *adv.* before, beforehand, to begin with, from the beginning; *- genießen*, enjoy in anticipation; (*coll.*) *-* (*mit der Zunge*) *sein*, be too free with one's tongue, let one's tongue run away with one. **-nahme,** *f.* anticipation, forestalling. **-nehmen,** *ir.v.a.* anticipate, forestall.
vorweis-en, *ir.v.a.* show, produce (for inspection), display, exhibit. **-ung,** *f.* production, showing.
Vorwelt, *f.* former ages, antiquity, primitive *or* prehistoric world *or* times. **-lich,** *adj.* primeval, prehistoric, primitive.
vorwerfen, *ir.v.a.* cast before, throw to; (*einem etwas*) reproach a p. with (*a th.*), cast (*s.th.*) in a p.'s teeth; *sie haben einander nichts vorzuwerfen*, the one is as bad as the other, six of one and half-a-dozen of the other.
Vorwerk, *n.* farm steading; outworks (*Fort.*).
Vorwiderstand, *m.* compensating resistance (*Elec.*)
vorwiegen, *ir.v.n.* (*aux.* h.) outweigh, preponderate, prevail, predominate, dominate. **-d,** 1. *adj.* preponderant, predominant, prevalent. 2. *adv.* mostly, mainly, chiefly, principally.
Vorwind, *m.* head wind.
Vorwissen, *n.* foreknowledge, (previous) knowledge; *es geschah mit meinem -*, it happened with my full knowledge and consent; *ohne mein -*, without my knowledge, unknown to me.
Vorwitz, *m.* curiosity, inquisitiveness; forwardness, impertinence, pertness. **-ig,** *adj.* inquisitive, prying; forward, pert, impertinent.
Vorwort, *n.* (*pl.* -e) foreword, preface, preamble; (*pl.* ¨-er) preposition.
Vorwurf, *m.* reproach, reproof, rebuke, blame, remonstrance; subject, theme, motif. **-sfrei,** *adj.*, **-slos,** *adj.* irreproachable, blameless. **-svoll,** *adj.* reproachful.
vorzählen, *v.a.* (*einem etwas*) count out to, enumerate.
Vorzahn, *m.* projecting tooth.
Vorzeich-en, *n.* previous indication, symptom, omen, prognostic; sign (*Math.*); signature (*Mus.*). **-enwechsel,** *m.* change of sign (*Math.*). **-nen,** *v.a.* (*einem etwas*) draw *or* sketch (*a th.*) for (*s.o.*), show (*s.o.*) how to draw (*s.th.*), prescribe, point out, mark, indicate; trace out, sketch. **-nung,** *f.* sign, indication, prescription; signature (*Mus.*).
vorzeig-en, *v.a.* show, display, expose, exhibit; produce, present (*a bill*). **-er,** *m.* bearer (*of a bill*). **-ung,** *f.* production, exhibition.
Vorzeit, *f.* (-en) antiquity, past ages, olden times; *die graue -*, remote antiquity, days of yore. **-en,** *adv.* (*Poet.*) formerly, once upon a time. **-ig,** *adj.* premature, untimely, all too soon; precocious. **-lich,** *adj.* prehistoric.
vorziehen, 1. *ir.v.a.* draw forward *or* forth, draw in front of; (*einem etwas*) prefer, give preference to; *den Vorhang -*, draw the curtain. 2. *v.n.* (*aux.* s.) march before, go on, advance, move up, move to the front.
Vorzimmer, *n.* anteroom, antechamber.
Vorzug, *m.* (-(e)s, ¨-e) preference, precedence, priority; excellence, superiority; prerogative, privilege; pilot train (*Railw.*); (*pl.*) good qualities, merit(s), advantage; *den - vor einem haben*, be preferred to a p., have the advantage over a p.; surpass *or* excel a p. **-saktien,** *f.pl.* preference shares. **-sbehandlung,** *f.* preferential treatment. **-sdruck** *m.* de-luxe edition. **-spreis,** *m.* special (reduced) price. **-srecht,** *n.* privilege. **-sweise,** *adv.* preferably, by preference, pre-eminently, chiefly.
vorzüglich, 1. *adj.* superior, excellent, choice. first-rate; (*archaic*) chief, principal, pre-eminent, 2. *adv.* above all, particularly; very well *or* much, (*coll.*) immensely. **-keit,** *f.* superiority, excellence, superior quality.
Vorzündung, *f.* premature ignition (*Motor.*).
vot-ieren, *v.n.* (*aux.* h.) vote; *die -ierenden*, the voters *or* electors. **-ivbild,** *n.*, **-ivgemälde,** *n.* votive picture. **-um,** *n.* (-ums, -en & -a) vote, suffrage.
vulg-är, *adj.* vulgar, common, base, coarse. **-ata,** *f.* Vulgate. **-o,** *adv.* commonly, usually, normally.
Vulkan, *m.* (-s, -e) volcano; *auf einem - tanzen*, sit on a volcano. **-fiber,** *f.* vulcanized fibre. **-isch,** *adj.* volcanic; Plutonic. **-isieren,** *v.a.* vulcanize (*india-rubber*). **-isierung,** *f.* vulcanization.

W

W, w, *n.* W, w; *for abbreviations see Index at end.*
Waag-e, *f.* (-en) scales, balance, weighing-machine; Libra (*Astr.*); (spirit) level, levelling bubble; horizontal position (*on parallel bars*) (*Gymn.*); *in die -e fallen*, be of weight, import *or* importance; *einem die -e halten*, be a match for s.o.; *sich* or *einander die -e halten*, counterbalance each other; *auf die -e legen*, weigh; *das Zünglein an der -e bilden*, turn *or* tip the scale. **-(e)amt,** *n.* public weighbridge. **-(e)balken,** *m.* beam of a balance. **-(e)geld,** *n.* weighbridge-toll *or* -fee. **-emeister,** *m.* official in charge of a weighbridge, inspector of weights and measures. **-(e)recht,** *adj.* horizontal, level. **-(e)zunge,** *f.*, **-(e)zünglein,** *n.* pointer, finger *or* needle of a balance. **-schale,** *f.* pan of the scales; *schwer in die -schale fallen*, weigh heavily, carry great weight (*in a decision*); *seine Worte auf die -schale legen*, weigh one's words; *etwas in die -schale werfen*, tip the scales with s.th., use s.th. to

add weight (*to a conclusion, in a point at issue, etc.*).
wabb(e)lig, *adj.* flabby, wobbly.
Wabe, *f.* (-n) honeycomb. **–nartig,** *adj.* honeycombed, alveolar. **–nhonig,** *m.* honey in the comb.
waber–n, *v.n.* flicker. **–lohe,** *f.* (*Poet.*) flickering flame, magic fire.
wach, *adj.* awake; on the alert, wide-awake, brisk, astir, (*fig.*) (a)live (*interest, etc.*); – *werden*, awake, wake up. **–dienst,** *m.* guard-duty. **–e,** *f.* guard, watch, watchman, sentinel, sentry; guard-house; guard-room; police station; *–e ablösen*, relieve the guard, change guard; *–e haben, –e stehen, auf –e sein,* (*sl.*) *–e schieben*, be on guard; *auf –e ziehen*, mount guard; *–e halten*, keep guard, be on the watch *or* look-out. **–en,** *v.n.* (*aux.* h.) sit up; be awake, be on guard, keep watch; *bei einem –en*, sit up with a p.; *–en über* (*with Acc.*), keep an eye on, watch over. **–gänger,** *m.* look-out (man). **–habend,** *adj.* on guard, on duty. **–habende(r),** *m.* guard commander; *–habender Offizier*, officer of the watch (*Naut.*). **–mann,** *m.* (*dial.*) policeman. **–rufen,** *v.a.* wake, rouse; (*usually fig.*) call forth, bring back (*a memory, etc.*). **–sam,** *adj.* vigilant, watchful, wide-awake, attentive, alert; *ein –sames Auge auf eine S. haben*, keep a sharp *or* watchful eye on a th. **–samkeit,** *f.* vigilance. **–t,** *f.* (-en) watch (*Naut.*), guard (*Mil.*); *die –t am Rhein*, the watch on the Rhine. **–tdienst,** *m., see* **–dienst. –(t)feuer,** *n.* watch-fire. **–thabend,** *see* **–habend. –(t)hund,** *m.* watchdog. **–(t)mannschaft,** *f.* picket, guard, watch. **–tmeister,** *m.* sergeant-major (*of artillery & cavalry*). **–tparade,** *f.* changing of the guard. **–tposten,** *m.* sentry, sentinel. **–traum,** *m.* day-dream. **–(t)stube,** *f.* guard-room. **–tturm,** *m.* watch-tower. **–zustand,** *m.* waking state.
Wacholder, *m.* (-s, –) juniper. **–branntwein,** *m.* geneva gin. **–geist,** *m.* juniper-spirit. **–harz,** *n.* gum-juniper.
Wachs, *n.* (-es, -e) wax. **–abdruck,** *m.* wax impression. **–artig,** *adj.* waxy, wax-like; waxen. **–bild,** *n.* wax figure *or* image. **–blume,** *f.* wax flower; honey-wort (*Cerinthe minor*) (*Bot.*). **–bohner,** *m.* floor-polish. **–en,** *v.a.* (*Austr. dial.*), *see* **wächsen. –figurenkabinett,** *n.* waxworks. **–haut,** *f.* cere (*of a bird's bill*). **–kerze,** *f.* wax candle, taper. **–leinen,** *n.* **–leinwand,** *f., see* **–tuch. –papier,** *n.* grease-proof paper. **–salbe,** *f.* cerate. **–sonde,** *f.* bougie (*Surg.*). **–stock,** *m.* taper. **–streichholz,** *n.* wax-vesta. **–tafel,** *f.* cake of beeswax; wax tablet (*ancient writing*). **–tuch,** *n.* oilcloth, American cloth. **–weich,** *adj.* soft as wax. **–zieher,** *m.* wax-chandler.
wachs–en, 1. *ir.v.n.* (*aux.* s.) grow, sprout, come up (*of plants*); extend, increase, thrive, (*archaic*) wax; *einer S. gewachsen sein*, be equal to s.th., be able to cope with a th.; *einem an Körperkraft nicht gewachsen sein*, be no match for a p. in physical strength; *ans Herz –en*, become attached to, grow fond of; *an Weisheit –en*, grow in wisdom; *er ist aus den Kleidern gewachsen*, he has outgrown his clothes; *in die Breite –en*, grow broad, extend, stretch out; *in die Höhe –en*, grow tall, shoot up; *sehr ins Kraut –en*, run to leaf; *der Mond wächst*, the moon is on the increase *or* is waxing; *darüber keine grauen Haare –en lassen*, not get grey hairs on that account; (*fig.*) *einem über den Kopf –en*, get too much for s.o.; *das Wasser wächst*, the water is rising. 2. *n.* growing, growth, increase, development. **–end,** *pr.p. & adj.* growing; increasing; crescendo (*Mus.*). **–tum,** *n.* growth; increase; *Wein, mein eignes –tum*, wine of my own growing.
wächs–en, *v.a.* coat *or* smear with wax. **–ern,** *adj.* waxen, wax-like, wax-coloured.
wächst, *see* **wachsen.**
Wacht, *see under* **wach–.**
Wächte, *f.* (-n) snow-cornice.
Wachtel, *f.* (-n) quail (*Coturnix*) (*Orn.*). **–hund,** *m.* spaniel. **–könig,** *m.* landrail, corn-crake (*Crex*) (*Orn.*). **–weizen,** *m.* (meadow) cow-wheat (*Melampyrum pratense*) (*Bot.*).
Wächter, *m.* (-s, –) watchman, guard, caretaker, attendant, keeper, warder; look-out man (*Naut.*). **–lied,** *n.* aubade. **–ruf,** *m.* (night) watchman's call.
wack–(e)lig, *adj.* shaky, unsteady, tottering; loose, wobbly, rickety; (*coll.*) on the verge of bankruptcy, tottering on the brink. **–eln,** *v.n.* (*aux.* h.) shake, rock; stagger, reel, totter; wobble, be loose; *mit dem Kopfe –eln*, shake *or* wag one's head; (*coll.*) *es –elt mit seiner Gesundheit*, his health is rather shaky. **–elkontakt,** *m.* loose connexion (*Elec.*).
wacker, 1. *adj.* valiant, brave, gallant, stout (-hearted). 2. *adv.* bravely; well, soundly, thoroughly; (*coll.*) heartily, lustily.
Wade, *f.* (-n) calf (*of the leg*). **–nbein,** *n.* fibula; splint-bone. **–nkrampf,** *m.* cramp in the leg. **–nstrumpf,** *m.* long *or* knee-length stocking.
Waff–e, *f.* (-en) weapon, arm; *bei welcher –e hast du gedient?* which branch of the service were you in? *einen mit seinen eigenen –en schlagen*, beat s.o. at his own game; *die –en strecken*, lay down one's arms, surrender; *unter den –en*, under arms; *zu den –en greifen*, take up arms (against). **–enamt,** *n.* ordnance department. **–enbeistand,** *m.* armed support *or* assistance. **–enbruder,** *m.* comrade in arms; comrade, ally. **–endienst,** *m.* military service. **–enfarbe,** *f.* arm-of-service flash. **–enfähig,** *adj.* capable of bearing arms. **–engang,** *m.* passage of arms; armed conflict. **–engattung,** *f.* branch *or* arm of the service. **–engeklirr,** *n.* clash of arms. **–engewalt,** *f.* force of arms, armed force. **–englück,** *n.* fortune of war. **–enkammer,** *f.* armoury. **–enkundig,** *adj.* skilled in the use of arms. **–enlos,** *adj.* unarmed. **–enplatz,** *m.* (*Swiss dial.*) garrison town. **–enrock,** *m.* tunic, battle-dress. **–enruf,** *m.* call to arms. **–enruhe,** *f.* truce, suspension of hostilities. **–enruhm,** *m.* military glory. **–enrüstung,** *f.* armour; armament; warlike preparation. **–enschein,** *m.* gun-licence. **–enschmied,** *m.* armourer. **–enschmuck,** *m.* full armour, warlike accoutrements; (*hum.*) full war-paint. **–enschmuggel,** *m.* gun-running. **–enstillstand,** *m.* armistice. **–enstreckung,** *f.* capitulation, surrender. **–enstück,** *n.* feat of arms. **–entanz,** *m.* war-dance. **–entat,** *f.* feat of arms, military exploit, warlike achievement. **–enträger,** *m.* armour-bearer, esquire. **–enübung,** *f.* military exercise. **–nen,** 1. *v.a.* arm; *mit gewaffneter Hand*, by force of arms. 2. *v.r.* take up arms.
Waffel, *f.* (-n) wafer, waffle, (*dial.*) chatterbox. **–eisen,** *n.* waffle-iron.
wäg, *adj.* (*Swiss dial.*) good, fine, splendid; *die –sten und Besten*, the élite, the cream.
Wage, *f.* (-n), *former spelling of* **Waage.**
wag–en, 1. *v.a. & n.* venture, risk, dare, hazard, presume, attempt; *es mit einem –en*, cross swords with *or* measure one's strength with a p.; *ich –e (es) nicht, dies zu behaupten*, I do not *or* would not venture *or* presume to assert this; *alles –en*, risk everything; *ich will es darauf –en*, I will risk it. *gewagt*, *p.p. & adj.* risky, hazardous, dangerous, perilous, daring; *frisch gewagt!* take a chance! (*Prov.*) *frisch gewagt ist halb gewonnen*, well begun is half done; fortune favours the brave. 2. *v.r.*; *sich an eine S. –en*, venture upon s.th.; *sich auf das Eis –en*, trust o.s. to the ice, venture on the ice; *sich unter die Leute –en*, venture into society. **–(e)hals,** *m.* dare-devil. **–(e)halsig,** *adj.* daring, bold, reckless, rash, foolhardy. **–(e)halsigkeit,** *f.* recklessness, foolhardiness. **–emut,** *m.* daring, gallantry. **–espiel,** *n.* game of chance. **–(e)stück,** *n., see* **–nis. –nis,** *n.* hazardous enterprise, bold venture, risky undertaking, hazard, chance, risk.
Wagen, *m.* (-s, – & *dial.* ¨) vehicle, conveyance; van, truck, car, lorry; wagon, cart, carriage (*also of typewriters*), coach, chariot; *der Große –*, the Great Bear, the Plough, Charles's Wain (*Astr.*); *die Pferde hinter den – spannen*, put the cart before the horse; *– erster Klasse*, first-class carriage; (*coll.*) *unter den – kommen*, be worsted. **–abteil,** *m.* compartment (*of a railway carriage*). **–achse,** *f.* axle-tree. **–bauer,** *m.* cartwright, coach-builder. **–burg,** *f.* barricade of wagons, laager. **–decke,** *f.* tilt, cover, tarpaulin. **–deichsel,** *f.* carriage-pole; cart-shaft. **–er, (Wagner),** *m.* (*dial.*), *see* **–bauer;** (*dial.*) wheelwright. **–führer,** *m.* wagoner, coachman, driver, charioteer. **–geleise,** *n., see* **–spur. –gestell,** *n.* frame, chassis (*Motor.*). **–heber,** *m.*

(lifting-)jack. **-kasten,** *m.* vehicle body. **-lack,** *m.* coach varnish. **-ladung,** *f.* cart-load. **-lenker,** *m.* driver, wagoner. **-material,** *n.* rolling-stock (*Railw.*). **-park,** *m.* car-park, carriage-stand. **-pferd,** *n.* coach-horse. **-rennen,** *n.* chariot racing. **-schlag,** *m.* coach-door. **-schmiere,** *f.* cart-grease, axle-grease. **-spur,** *f.* wheel-rut *or* track. **-verkehr,** *m.* vehicular traffic. **-winde,** *f.*, *see* **-heber.**

wäg-en, *ir.v.a.* weigh; poise, balance, (*fig.*) ponder, consider; *er wog das Schwert in der Hand*, he poised the sword in his hand; *seine Worte wohl -en*, weigh *or* consider one's words well; (*Prov.*) *erst -en, dann wagen*, look before you leap. **-bar,** *adj.* weighable, ponderable.

Waggon, *m.* (-s, -s & -e) railway carriage, luggage *or* goods van, truck; (*Amer.*) freight car. **-weise,** *adv.* by the truck-load.

Wagner, *see* **Wagener.**

Wahl, *f.* (-en) choice, selection; option, election; alternative; *sich zur – aufstellen lassen*, put up for election; *jemandes – billigen*, approve (of) a p.'s choice; *mir bleibt keine –*, I have no choice; *direkte -en*, elections by direct suffrage; *in (die) engere – kommen*, be on the short list (*or Scottish* leet); *die – fällt mir schwer*, I find it hard to choose; *aus freier –*, of one's own (free) choice; *einem die – lassen*, leave the choice to a p., leave a p. to please himself; *seine – treffen*, make one's choice, come to a decision; *einen vor die – stellen*, let a p. choose, give s.o. the option, leave the decision to s.o.; *Waren dritter –*, goods of third quality, grade three goods. **-abstimmung,** *f.* polling, balloting. **-agitation,** *f.* electioneering. **-akt,** *m.* election. **-akten,** *f.pl.* election returns (*Parl.*). **-alter,** *n.* voting age. **-amt,** *n.* elective office. **-aufruf,** *m.* election manifesto. **-berechtigt,** *adj.* entitled to vote, enfranchised. **-bezirk,** *m.* ward, constituency. **-bude,** *f.* polling-booth. **-bühne,** *f.* hustings. **-eltern,** *pl.* (*Austr. dial.*) foster parents. **-ergebnis,** *n.* election result. **-fach,** *n.* optional subject. **-fähig,** *adj.* eligible for election; *also see* **-berechtigt. -fähigkeit,** *f.* elegibility; electoral qualification; franchise. **-frei,** *adj.* optional; *-freie Fächer*, optional subjects. **-fürst,** *m.* princely elector. **-handlung,** *f.* election; the poll. **-heimat,** *f.* adopted country. **-kampf,** *m.* election campaign. **-kasten,** *m.* ballot-box. **-kind,** *n.* (*Austr. dial.*) adopted child, foster child. **-kommissar,** *m.* returning officer. **-kreis,** *m.*, *see* **-bezirk. -liste,** *f.* register of electors. **-lokal,** *n.* polling-centre. **-los,** *adj.* indiscriminate, without consideration. **-mann,** *m.* delegate (*electing a deputy*). **-männerwahl,** *f.* election of delegates. **-prüfung,** *f.* scrutiny of the poll. **-recht,** *n.* right to vote, suffrage, franchise; *passives -recht*, elegibility; *allgemeines -recht*, universal suffrage; *Entziehung des -rechts*, disfranchisement. **-rede,** *f.* election address. **-reform,** *f.* electoral reform. **-spruch,** *m.* device, motto. **-stimme,** *f.* vote. **-tag,** *m.* election day. **-umtriebe,** *m.pl.* electioneering. **-urne,** *f.* ballot-box. **-verfahren,** *n.* electoral system, system of voting. **-versammlung,** *f.* election meeting. **-verwandt,** *adj.* congenial, like-minded, akin; *-verwandte Seelen*, kindred spirits. **-verwandtschaft,** *f.* congeniality; elective affinity (*Chem.*). **-weise,** *adv.* by choice. **-zelle,** *f.* polling booth. **-zettel,** *m.* ballot *or* voting-paper.

wähl-en, *v.a.* choose, select, pick out; elect, vote; dial (*Phon.*); *-en Sie!* make your choice! dial your number! *einen in den Ausschuß -en*, elect s.o. to the committee; *ins Parlament -en*, return to parliament; *das kleinere Übel -en*, choose the lesser of two evils; *sie -ten ihn zu ihrem Führer*, they chose him as their leader; *zum Präsidenten -en*, elect as president, vote into the chair; *gewählte Gesellschaft*, select company; *gewählte Sprache*, well-chosen words, choice language, high style. **-bar,** *adj.* eligible (for election). **-er,** *m.* voter, elector; selector (*Elec.*); dial (*Phone*). **-erisch,** *adj.* particular, fussy, fastidious, difficult to please, (*coll.*) choosy. **-erschaft,** *f.* body of electors, constituency. **-(er)scheibe,** *f.* dial (*Phone*). **-ig,** *adj.*, *see* **-erisch.**

Wahn, *m.* illusion, hallucination; delusion, error, erroneous impression, fancy; madness, folly. **-bild,** *n.* hallucination, delusion, chimera, vision, phantom. **-glaube,** *m.* superstition, false belief. **-haft,** *adj.* illusory. **-hoffnung,** *f.* vain hope. **-idee,** *f.* delusion, mania. **-korn,** *n.* (*dial.*) empty ear of corn. (*dial.*) **-schaffen,** *adj.* misshapen, deformed. **-sinn,** *m.* madness, insanity, craziness, frenzy; *es wäre -sinn, so zu handeln*, it would be madness to act so; *dichterischer -sinn*, poetic frenzy; *religiöser -sinn*, religious mania; *stiller -sinn*, melancholia. **-sinnig,** *adj.* mad, insane, crazy, frantic, (*coll.*) terrific; *es ist zum -sinnig werden*, it is enough to drive one mad. **-sinnige(r),** *m.* madman, lunatic. **-vorstellung,** *f.* crazy notion. **-witz,** *m.* madness, absurdity. **-witzig,** *adj.* mad, senseless, foolish, absurd; reckless, irresponsible.

wähnen, *v.a. & n.* (*aux.* h.) think, believe, imagine, fancy, suppose, presume.

wahr, *adj.* true, real, genuine, sincere, correct, veritable, proper; *das -e an der S. ist*, the fact of the matter is; *-er Gesichtskreis*, rational horizon; *etwas für – halten*, believe a th. to be true, believe in a th.; *so – mir Gott helfe!* so help me God! *der -e Jakob*, just the man; *so – ich lebe!* as sure as I am here *or* alive; *– machen*, make come true, carry out, bring about, realize, fulfil; *nicht –?* isn't it? don't you think? *eine -e Null*, a mere cipher; *– werden*, come true; *es ist kein -es Wort daran*, there is not a word of truth in it. **-en,** *v.a.* watch over, look after, take care of, keep safe; keep up, maintain, preserve; *ein Geheimnis -en*, keep a secret; *seine Interessen -en*, look after one's interests; *seine Würde -en*, maintain one's dignity. **-haben,** *v.a.* admit, accept, acknowledge (the truth of); *etwas nicht -haben wollen*, not (be ready to) admit s.th. **-haft,** *adj.* true, actual, genuine, real, truthful, sincere, veracious. **-haftig,** 1. *adj.* *see* **-haft.** 2. *adv.* truly, really, surely, actually, indeed. **-haftigkeit,** *f.* veracity. **-heit,** *f.* truth; reality, fact; *in -heit*, truly, in fact; *einem derb die -heit sagen*, tell a p. the plain truth, speak plainly to s.o., give a p. a piece of one's mind; *der -heit gemäß*, faithfully, in accordance with the facts *or* truth. **-heitsbeweis,** *m.* factual evidence. **-heitseifer,** *m.* zeal for truth. **-heitsgemäß,** *adj.*, **-heitsgetreu,** *adj.* faithful, true, truthful, in accordance with the truth. **-heitsliebe,** *f.* love of truth. **-heit(s)liebend,** *adj.* truthful, veracious. **-heit(s)sucher,** *m.* seeker after truth. **-lich** *adv.* truly, surely, verily, indeed. **-machung** *f.* verification, realization, fulfilment. **-nehmbar,** *adj.* perceptible, noticeable, visible. **-nehmen,** *ir.v.a.* (*sep.*) notice, observe, perceive; look after, protect, give attention to; profit by *or* from, make use of, avail o.s. of; *die Gelegenheit -nehmen*, take the opportunity, make the most of the chance; *einen Termin -nehmen*, appear on the appointed day; *seinen Vorteil -nehmen*, look after one's interests. **-nehmung,** *f.* perception, observation; maintenance; protection. **-nehmungsbild,** *n.* perceptual image. **-nehmungskraft,** *f.* **-nehmungsvermögen,** *n.* power of perception *or* observation. **-sagen,** *v.a. & n.* (*aux.* h.) (*sep. & insep.*) (*with Dat.*) prophesy, predict, foretell; tell fortunes; *aus Kaffeesatz -sagen*, tell fortunes in coffee-grounds (*usually* tea leaves); *sich* (*Dat.*) *-sagen lassen*, have one's fortune told. **-sager,** *m.* soothsayer, fortune-teller, prophet. **-sagerei,** *f.* soothsaying, divination; fortune-telling. **-sagung,** *f.* prophecy, prediction; *see also* **-sagerei. -scheinlich,** *adj.* probable, likely, plausible. **-scheinlichkeit,** *f.* probability, likelihood, plausibility; *aller -scheinlichkeit nach*, in all probability, very probably. **-scheinlichkeitsrechnung,** *f.* theory of probabilities. **-spruch,** *m.* verdict (*of a jury*). **-traum,** *m.* prophetic dream, dream destined to come true. **-ung,** *f.* maintenance, preservation, protection, support. **-zeichen,** *n.* distinctive mark, token, sign; landmark.

währ-en, *v.n.* (*aux.* h.) last, continue, endure, hold out; (*Prov.*) *ehrlich -t am längsten*, honesty is the best policy; *die Erinnerung an ihn wird ewig -en*, his memory will remain undimmed; *es –te nicht lange, so . . .*, it was not long before . . . **–schaft,** (*Swiss dial.*) 1. *adj.* lasting, permanent, enduring, sound, genuine. 2. *f.* guarantee, surety, security, bail. **–ung,** *f.* fixed value, standard; currency; *in deutscher –ung*, in German currency; *von echter –ung*, of sterling value. **–ungskrise,** *f.* monetary crisis.

während, 1. *prep.* (*with Gen., or sometimes Austr. dial. Dat.*) during, in the course of, pending; *– der Regierung* (*Gen.*), during, in the reign (of); *– eines Jahres*, for a year. 2. *conj.* while, whilst, during the time that, whereas. **–dem,** *adv.* (*Austr. dial.*), **–des,** *adv.* **–dessen,** *adv.* meanwhile.

Waid, *m.* (-(e)s, -e) woad (*Isatis tinctoria*) (*Bot.*).

Waid–mann, *m.*, **–werk,** *n. see* **Weid–mann, –werk.**

Waise, *f.* (-n) orphan; *zum –n machen*, orphan. **–nhaus,** *n.* orphanage. **–nknabe,** *m.* orphan boy; (*coll., fig.*) *ein –nknabe sein gegen*, not to be compared with, not able to hold a candle to. **–nmutter,** *f.* matron of an orphanage. **–nvater,** *m.* superintendent of an orphanage.

Wake, *f.* (-n) hole in the ice.

[1]**Wal,** *m.* (-s, -e) whale. **–fahrer,** *m.* whaler (*ship and man*). **–fang,** *m.* whaling. **–fänger,** *m.* whale fisher. **–fisch,** *m.* (*coll.*) *see* –. **–fischbarte,** *f.*, **–fischbein,** *n.* whalebone. **–fischfett,** *n.*, **–fischspeck,** *m.* blubber. **–fischtran,** *m.* train-oil, sperm oil. **–rat,** *n.* (*& Austr. dial. m.*), **–ratfett,** *n.*, **–ratöl,** *n.* spermaceti. **–roß,** *n.* walrus. **–tier,** *n.* cetacean.

[2]**Wal,** *f.*, **–feld,** *n.*, **–platz,** *m.*, **–statt,** *f.* (*archaic & Poet.*) battlefield.

Wald, *m.* (-(e)s, ¨er) wood, forest, woodland; (*Prov.*) *wie man in den – hinein ruft, so schallt's heraus*, as you make your bed, so you must lie in it; (*coll.*) *er sieht den – vor (lauter) Bäumen nicht*, he cannot see the wood for the trees. **–ahorn,** *m.* sycamore (*Acer pseudoplatanus*) (*Bot.*). **–ameise,** *f.* red ant. **–arm,** *adj.* sparsely wooded. **–aufseher,** *m.* forest ranger. **–bau,** *m.* afforestation. **–baum,** *m.* woodland tree. **–baumschule,** *f.* young plantation. **–bauschule,** *f.* school of forestry. **–bedeckt,** *adj.* well-wooded. **–beere,** *f.* cranberry (*Vaccinium myrtillus*) (*Bot.*). **–blume,** *f.* woodland flower. **–brand,** *m.* forest fire. **–ein,** *adv.* into the forest. **–einsamkeit,** *f.* silvan solitude. **–erdbeere,** *f.* wild strawberry (*Fragaria vesca*) (*Bot.*). **–erholungsstätte,** *f.* woodland sanatorium. **–esdunkel,** *n.* forest gloom. **–frevel,** *m.* vandalism, spoliation, wanton damage (*to trees*). **–gegend,** *f.* woodland, wooded country. **–gehege,** *n.* plantation, forest-preserve. **–geist,** *m.* woodland spirit; faun, satyr. **–gott,** *m.*, *see* **–geist. –göttin,** *f.* wood-nymph, dryad. **–grenze,** *f.* timber line. **–horn,** *n.* French horn; (*Poet.*) bugle, hunting horn. **–hüter,** *m.* keeper, forest-ranger. **–ig,** *adj.* wooded, woody. **–kauz,** *m.* wood, brown *or* tawny owl (*Strix aluco*) (*Orn.*). **–kultur,** *f.* forestry, silviculture. **–landschaft,** *f.* woodland scenery. **–lichtung,** *f.* glade, clearing. **–männchen,** *n.* sprite, goblin; *see* **–geist. –meister,** *m.* woodruff (*Asperula odorata*) (*Bot.*) **–ohreule,** *f.* long-eared *or* horned owl (*Asio otus*) (*Orn.*). **–ordnung,** *f.* forest laws. **–rebe,** *f.* traveller's joy (*Clematis vitalba*) (*Bot.*). **–reich,** *adj.* well-wooded. **–revier,** *n.* preserve. **–saum,** *m.* forest fringe. **–schaden,** *m.*, *see* **–frevel. –schneise,** *f.* forest aisle, vista. **–schnepfe,** *f.* woodcock (*Scolopax rusticola*) (*Orn.*). **–schrat,** *m.*, *see* **–männchen. –schule,** *f.* open-air school, children's sanatorium. **–schütze,** *m.* forest-ranger. **–stätte,** *pl.* (*Swiss dial.*) Forest Cantons. **–ung,** *f.* wood; woodland, wooded expanse. **–wärts,** *adv.* forestward. **–weg,** *m.* woodland path. **–wiese,** *f.* forest *or* woodland glade. **–wirtschaft,** *f.* forestry. **–wolle,** *f.* pine-needle wool.

wälger–n, *v.a. & n.* (*dial.*) roll (*pastry*). **–holz,** *n.* rolling-pin.

walk–en, *v.a.* full (*cloth*); felt (*hats*); (*coll.*) pummel, cudgel. **–erdistel,** *f.* fuller's teazle *or* teasel. **–erei,** *f.* fulling; fulling-mill. **–(er)erde,** *f.* fuller's earth. **–mittel,** *n.* fulling agent. **–mühle,** *f.* fulling-mill. **–müller,** *m.* fuller.

[1]**Wall,** *m.* (-(e)s, ¨e) rampart, mound, bank, embankment, dam, dike. **–beine,** *pl.* (*dial.*) bow *or* bandy legs. **–bruch,** *m.* breach in a dike. **–gang,** *m.* path along the ramparts. **–graben,** *m.* rampart-ditch, moat. **–meister,** *m.* inspector of dikes and defence works. **–schild,** *n.* ravelin (*Fort.*).

[2]**Wall,** *m.* (-(e)s, –) fourscore (*of fish*).

Wallach, *m.* (-(e)s & -en, -e (& *Austr. dial.* -en)) gelding.

[1]**wall–en,** *v.n.* (*aux.* h.) undulate, flutter, float, flow, wave; bubble, simmer, boil, seethe, effervesce; be agitated; *ihm –t das Blut*, his blood boils, his blood is up. **–ung,** *f.* boiling, bubbling, ebullition; undulation, flutter, flow; undue excitement, emotion, agitation; *sein Puls ist in –ung*, his pulse is high; *in –ung geraten*, become agitated, fly into a passion.

[2]**wall–en,** *v.n.* (*aux.* s.) (*Poet.*) travel, wander; go on a pilgrimage. **–er,** *m.* (*archaic*) pilgrim; (*Poet.*) wanderer. **–fahrer,** *m.* pilgrim. **–fahrt,** *f.* pilgrimage. **–fahr(t)en,** *v.n.* (*insep.*) (*aux.* s.) go on *or* make a pilgrimage. **–fahrtsort,** *m.* place of pilgrimage.

wällen, *v.a.* (*dial.*) boil, steam, simmer.

Walm, *m.* (-(e)s, -e) slope (*of roof*), hip (*Arch.*). **–dach,** *n.* hiproof.

Walnuß, *f.* (¨) walnut (*Juglans regia*) (*Bot.*).

Wal–rat, –roß, *see* [1]**Wal.**

Walstatt, *f.*, *see* [2]**Wal.**

walte–n, 1. *v.n.* (*aux.* h.) rule, govern, hold sway, hold the reins of government; (*with Gen.*) carry out, execute; (*über with Dat. or Acc.*) control, dispose of, manage; *schalten und –n*, have complete authority, rule, command; *einen –n lassen*, let a p. do as he pleases; *Gnade –n lassen*, show mercy; *– deines Amtes!* discharge the duties of your office! *das – Gott!* God grant it! amen! 2. *n.* rule, government; management, working.

Walz–e, *f.* (-en) roll, roller, barrel, cylinder, drum, platen, squeegee; (*coll.*) *auf der –e sein*, be on the road; (*coll.*) *immer die alte –e!* the same old song, the usual complaint. **–blech,** *n.*, **–eisen,** *n.* rolled (sheet) iron. **–en,** 1. *v.a.* roll, roll out (*dough, etc.*). 2. *v.n.* (*aux.* s. *or* h.) waltz, dance the waltz; (*coll.*) tramp. **–endruck,** *m.* cylinder printing. **–enförmig,** *adj.* cylindrical. **–enkessel,** *m.* cylindrical boiler. **–enpresse,** *f.* rolling-mill. **–er,** *m.* waltz. **–hütte,** *f.* rolling-mill. **–stahl,** *m.* rolled steel. **–werk,** *n.* rolling-mill.

wälz–en, 1. *v.a.* roll, turn about, rotate, trundle; *Bücher –en*, pore over books; *Gedanken –en*, turn over in one's mind; *von sich –en*, exonerate o.s. from, shift (the blame) from o.s.; *die Schuld –en (auf einen)*, throw the blame (on a p.). 2. *v.r.* roll, wallow, welter; revolve; *er –t sich vor Lachen*, he shakes *or* is convulsed with laughter. 3. *n.* rolling; (*coll.*) *das ist zum –en*, it is enough to make a cat laugh. (*coll.*) **–er,** *m.* ponderous tome, heavy volume. **–lager,** *n.* roller bearing (*Mech.*).

Wamme, *f.* (-n) dewlap; (*dial.*) belly, paunch.

Wams, *n. & m.* (-(s)es, ¨er & ¨e) jacket, doublet, jerkin, jersey. (*coll.*) **–en,** *v.a.* (*coll.*) thrash, give a good hiding.

Wand, *f.* (¨e) wall (*of a room*), partition, screen; septum (*Bot., Anat., etc.*); side, cheek, coat, (rock) face; *einen an die – drücken*, push s.o. to the wall; (*coll.*) *es ist um an den Wänden* or (*die Wände*) *hinaufzulaufen* or *emporzuklettern*, it is exasperating beyond measure *or* enough to drive one mad; (*Prov.*) *der Horcher an der – hört seine eigne Schand*, listeners never hear good of themselves; (*Prov.*) *man soll den Teufel nicht an die – malen*, talk of the devil and he will appear; (*coll.*) *mit dem Kopfe durch die – wollen*, run one's head against a wall; *die Wände haben Ohren*, walls have ears; *spanische –*, folding screen; *in seinen vier Wänden*, at home; (*zu*) *leeren Wänden reden*, waste one's breath, beat the air. **–bein,** *n.* parietal bone (*Anat.*). **–bekleidung,** *f.* wainscot(ing), panelling. **–bewurf,** *m.* plastering. **–fest,** *adj.* fixed to the wall. **–gemälde,** *n.* fresco, mural painting. **–gestell,** *n.* wall-bracket. **–getäfel,** *n.* wainscoting. **–karte,** *f.* wall-map. **–leuchter,** *m.* bracket, sconce. **–malerei,** *f.*, *see* **–gemälde. –nachbar,** *m.* dweller in the adjoining room, person in the next room. **-pfeiler,** *m.* pilaster. **-platte,** *f.* tile. **-putz,** *m.* parget, plaster. **-schirm,** *m.* folding screen. **-schrank,** *m.* built-in cupboard. **-spiegel,** *m.* hanging mirror, pier-glass. **-ständig,** *adj.* marginal, parietal. **-stärke,** *f.* thickness of a wall. **-tafel,** *f.* blackboard, wall chart. **-teppich,** *m.* tapestry. **-uhr,** *f.* wall-clock, hanging clock. **-ung,** *f.* wall, partition, lining. **-verkleidung,** *f.* wainscot(ing), (*paper*) hangings.

wand, wände, *see* **winden.**

Wand-el, *m.* change, alteration, mutation; mode of life, conduct, behaviour, habits; traffic, trade (*only in*) *Handel und -el*, trade, commerce; *einen tugendhaften -el führen*, lead a virtuous life; *-el schaffen in* (*Dat.*), bring about a change in; (*B.*) *Gottes Wege sind ohne -el*, God's way is perfect. **-elbar,** *adj.* changeable, variable, fickle; fragile, perishable. **-elbarkeit,** *f.* changeability, fickleness. **-elgang,** *m.*, **-elhalle,** *f.* corridor; lounge; lobby, foyer. **-ellos,** *adj.* unalterable. **-eln,** 1. *v.a.* & *v.r.* change, convert, turn (in, into). 2. *v.n.* (*aux.* h. & s.) go, walk, saunter, amble, wander, travel; (*B.*) live; *handeln und -eln*, trade, traffic; *unsträflich -eln*, lead an irreproachable life; *-elndes Lexikon*, walking encyclopaedia. **-elobligation,** *f.* convertible bond (*C.L.*). **-elstern,** *m.* planet. **-ler,** *m.* wanderer, ambler, saunterer; pilgrim. **-lung,** *f.* change, alteration, transformation, metamorphosis; transubstantiation; transformer (*Elec.*).

wander-n, *v.n.* (*aux.* s.) travel (*on foot*), go, walk, wander, ramble, hike, roam; migrate (*of birds*); walk (*of ghosts*); be shifting (*of sand, etc.*); (*coll.*) *ins Gefängnis -n*, go to prison; *seines Weges -n*, go one's way; *seine Uhr -te aufs Leihhaus*, his watch has found its way to the pawn-shop. **-nd,** *pr.p.* & *adj.* itinerant, strolling, nomadic, migratory, circulating (*of a library*); erratic, (*Geol.*); floating (*kidney*); shifting (*sand*). **-arbeiter,** *m.* itinerant workman. **-auftrag,** *m.* roving commission. **-ausstellung,** *f.* touring exhibition. **-blöcke,** *m.pl.* erratic blocks (*Geol.*). **-bühne,** *f.* travelling theatre. **-bursch,** *m.* travelling journeyman. **-er,** *m.* (-s, -) wanderer, pedestrian, traveller, hiker. **-fahrt,** *f.*, *see* **-ung.** **-falk(e),** *m.* peregrine falcon (*Falco peregrinus*) (*Orn.*). **-geschütz,** *n.* mobile gun. **-gesell,** *m.*, *see* **-bursch.** **-gewerbe,** *n.* hawking, peddling. **-heuschrecke,** *f.* migratory locust. **-jahre,** *n.pl.* (journeyman's) years of travel. **-lager,** *n.* itinerant vendor's stall *or* booth. **-leben,** *n.* wandering, nomadic *or* roving life. **-lust,** *f.* call of the open (air). **-niere,** *f.* floating kidney. **-prediger,** *m.* itinerant preacher, evangelist. **-preis,** *m.* challenge trophy. **-ratte,** *f.* brown *or* sewer rat (*Epimys norvegicus*) (*Zool.*). **-schaft,** *f.* travelling; travels, tour, journey, trip, migration; *auf die -schaft gehen*, leave home, set out on one's travels; *auf der -schaft sein*, be on one's travels (*of journeymen*). **-smann,** *m.* (-sleute) traveller, wayfarer. **-stab,** *m.* pilgrim's staff; walking stick; *den -stab ergreifen, zum -stabe greifen*, set out (*on one's travels*), leave home; *den -stab weiter setzen*, continue on one's way. **-stamm,** *m.* nomadic tribe. **-trieb,** *m.* migratory instinct; restlessness. **-ung,** *f.* travelling, travels; trip, walking tour, excursion, hike; migration. **-vogel,** *m.* bird of passage (*also fig.*); German youth movement; (*pl.*) ramblers, hikers. **-zeit,** *f.*, *see* **-jahre.**

Wandrer, *see* **Wanderer.**

wandte, *see* **wenden.**

Wang-e, *f.* (-en) cheek; side-piece. **-enbein,** *n.* cheek-bone. **-ig,** *adj. suffix* -cheeked; e.g. *rotwangig*, rosy-cheeked.

Wank, 1. only in *ohne -*, unwavering, unflinchingly. 2. *adj.* **-el,** *adj.* (*dial.*), *see* **-end.** **-elmut,** *m.* vacillation, fickleness, inconsistency. **-elmütig,** *adj.* fickle, changeable, inconstant, inconsistent. **-en,** *v.n.* (*aux.* h. & s.) stagger, reel, totter; waver, vacillate, be irresolute, hesitate, flinch; *den Feind zum -en bringen*, break the enemy's ranks; *weder weichen noch -en*, stand firm, not waver *or* flinch. **-end,** *pr.p.* & *adj.* unsteady, wavering; *in der Treue -end machen*, shake (*a p.'s*) allegiance.

wann, 1. *adv.* when; *seit* ? since when? how long? *dann und -*, now and then. 2. *conj.* (*dial.*) when; *es sei - es wolle*, whenever *or* whatever time it may be; *- immer*, whenever; *von -en*, (*archaic*) whence.

Wanne, *f.* (-n) tub, vat, trough, tank, bath; hull (*of a tank*) (*Mil.*); (*dial.*) winnow, swingle. **-n,** 1. *v.a.* (*dial.*) winnow. 2. *v.n.* (*dial.*) hover (*of birds*). **-nbad,** *n.* bath.

Wanst, *m.* (-es, ⸚e) belly, paunch.

Wanten, (*pl.*) shrouds (*Naut.*). **-tau,** *n.*, **-troß,** *f.* shroud.

Wanz-e, *f.* (-en) bug (*Heteroptera*) (*Ent.*). **-ig,** *adj.* bug-ridden *or* infested, (*coll.*) buggy.

Wappen, *n.* (-s, -) (coat of) arms, escutcheon, armorial bearings; *- ohne Beizeichen*, plain coat of arms; *- im Siegel*, crest, signet; *im - führen*, bear. **-ausleger,** *m.* herald. **-auslegung,** *f.*, *see* **-erklärung.** **-balken,** *m.* fesse (*Her.*). **-berechtigt,** *adj.* authorized to bear a coat of arms. **-bild,** *n.* heraldic figure. **-buch,** *n.* book of heraldry. **-erklärung,** *f.* blazonry, heraldry. **-feld,** *n.* field, quarter. **-halter,** *m.* supporter (*Her.*). **-könig,** *m.* king-at-arms. **-kunde,** *f.* heraldry. **-mantel,** *m.* mantling (*Her.*). **-schild,** *n.* escutcheon. **-schmuck,** *m.* blazonry. **-spruch,** *m.* heraldic motto, device. **-zierde,** *f.* accompaniment (*Her.*).

wappnen, *v.a.* (*obs.* & *Poet.*) arm.

war, ward, wardst, wäre, *see* **sein.**

warb, *see* **werben.**

Ward-ein, *m.* (-s, -e) assayer, mint warden. **-ieren,** *v.a.* (*dial.*) value, test, check.

Ware, *f.* (-n) article, commodity; (*pl.*) goods, wares, merchandise; *grüne -*, vegetables, greenstuff, greens; *gute - lobt sich selbst*, good wine needs no bush; *irdene -*, pottery, crockery; *kurze -*, small wares; hardware; *ordinäre -*, rough, low-class goods; *schwimmende -*, flotsam; *verbotene -*, contraband goods; *das ist teure -*, that is a luxury. **-nabsatz,** *m*, sale of goods. **-nabschluß,** *m.* contract in goods. **-nbedarf,** *m.* demand. (*C.L.*) **-nbestand,** *m.* stock on hand. **-nbezieher,** *m.* importer. **-nbörse,** *f.* commodity exchange. **-neinsender,** *m.* consigner. **-nempfänger,** *m.* consignee. **-nhaus,** *n.* department stores. **-nkonto,** *n.* current-account book, goods account. **-nkredit,** *m.* credit (allowed) on goods. **-nkunde,** *f.* market research. **-nlager,** *n.* stock in trade; warehouse. **-nlieferant,** *m.* contractor, purveyor of goods. **-nmakler,** *m.* broker, commission-agent. **-nmarkt,** *m.* produce-market. **-nniederlage,** *f.* warehouse, magazine. **-npreis,** *n.* current price of goods. **-nprobe,** *f.* sample, pattern. **-nsendung,** *f.* consignment *or* shipment of goods. **-nstempel,** *m.* trade-mark, manufacturer's *or* factory mark. **-nsteuer,** *f.* duty, excise. **-numsatzsteuer,** *f.* purchase tax. **-nverkaufsbuch,** *n.* sales-book. **-nverzeichnis,** *n.* list of goods; specification; inventory. (*C.L.*) **-nvorrat,** *m.* stock in hand. **-nzeichen,** *n.* trade-mark.

warf, *see* **werfen.**

warm, *adj.* (*comp.* wärmer, *sup.* wärmst) warm; hot; *- auftragen*, serve up hot; *- baden*, take hot baths; *-er Bruder*, homosexual; (*Prov.*) *man muß das Eisen schmieden, solang es noch - ist*, strike while the iron is hot; *- essen*, have a hot meal; *sich - halten*, keep (o.s.) warm, dress warmly; *einen - halten*, cultivate a p.'s acquaintance, do all one can to oblige a p., keep in a p.'s good books; *nicht - nicht kalt*, neither one thing nor another; *einem - machen*, make it hot *or* unpleasant for a p.; *einem den Kopf - machen*, provoke a p., stir a p. up; *mir ist -*, I am warm; *wie -e Semmeln abgehen*, go *or* sell like hot cakes; *- stellen*, keep (*food*) hot; *- sitzen*, be in easy circumstances; *- werden*, get hot *or* excited (over), get into a passion (*für*, about); *bei einem - werden*, feel at home *or* at one's ease with a p. **-bad,** *n.* thermal springs. **-blüter,** *m.* warm-blooded animal. **-blütig,** *adj.* warm-blooded. **-brunnen,** *m.* hot spring. **-halter,** *m.* hot-plate, plate-warmer; tea-cosy. **-haus,** *n.* hothouse, conservatory. **-herzig,** *adj.* warm-hearted. **-laufen,** *v.n.* warm up, heat up; get *or* run hot. **-(luft)-front,** *f.* warm front (*Meteor.*). **-luftheizung,** *f.* hot-air heating (installation). **-wasserheizung,** *f.* central heating. **-wasserspeicher,** *m.* geyser,

hot-water tank. **-wasserversorgung,** *f.* hot-water supply.
Wärm-e, *f.* warmth, warmness, heat; ardour; *-e durchlassen,* transmit heat; *freie -e,* sensible heat (*Phys.*); *gebundene -e,* latent heat; *12 Grad -e,* 12 degrees of heat; *strahlende -e,* radiant heat. **-eabgabe,** *f.* loss of heat. **-eäquator,** *m.* thermal equator. **-eaufnahme,** *f.* absorption of heat. **-eausstrahlung,** *f.* heat radiation. **-ebeständig,** *adj.* heat-proof, heat-resistant. **-edurchlässig,** *adj.* heat conducting, diathermic. **-eeinheit,** *f.* thermal unit, unit of heat, calory. **-eelektrizität,** *f.* thermo-electricity. **-eerzeugend,** *adj.* calorific. **-egrad,** *m.* degree of heat; temperature. **-ejahresmittel,** *n.* mean annual temperature. **-ekonstanz,** *f.* constant heat. **-kraftlehre,** *f.* thermodynamics. **-ekraftmaschine,** *f.* heat-engine. **-elehre,** *f.* theory of heat. **-eleitend,** *adj.* heat-conducting. **-eleiter,** *m.* conductor of heat. **-eleitung,** *f.* heat conduction. **-emenge,** *f.* quantity of heat. **-emesser,** *m.* thermometer, calorimeter. **-emessung,** *f.* calorimetry. **-en,** 1. *v.a.* warm, heat; make warm *or* hot; *sich* (*Dat.*) *die Hände -en,* warm one's hands. 2. *v.r.* warm o.s., bask. **-e-quelle,** *f.* source of heat, heat supply. **-er,** *m.* heater, stove, hot-plate; warming-pan, (tea-)cosy. **-eregler,** *m.* thermostat. **-eschutz,** *m.* lagging (*of pipes, etc.*). **-estrahl,** *m.* heat-ray. **-estrahler,** *m.* radiator. **-estrahlung,** *f.* heat radiation. **-etechnik,** *f.* heat technology. **-eübertragung,** *f.* heat convection. **-evergütung,** *f.* artificial ageing (*of metals*). **-ewert,** *m.* calorific value. **-ewirkungsgrad,** *m.* thermal efficiency. **-flasche,** *f.* hot-water bottle. **-kraft,** *f.* heating power. **-pfanne,** *f.* warming-pan; chafing-dish.
warn-en, *v.a.* (*vor with Dat.*) warn, caution (against). **-dienst,** *m.* warning service. **-ruf,** *m.* warning cry. **-ung,** *f.* warning; caution, admonition; *laßt euch das zur -ung dienen,* let this be a warning to you. **-ungslaterne,** *f.* danger-light. **-ungsruf,** *m.* warning cry. **-ungssignal,** *n.* danger signal. **-ungstafel,** *f.* danger notice.
Warp, *m.* & *n.* (-s, -e) warp (*Naut.* & *Weav.*). **-anker,** *m.* kedge (anchor). **-en,** *v.a.* tow, kedge (*Naut.*).
Wart, *m.* (-(e)s, -e) (*archaic*) keeper, warder; *now only in compounds,* e.g. *Kassenwart, Schriftwart, Turnwart.* **-e,** *f.* (-en) look-out, watch-tower; observatory; *alles von hoher -e sehen,* adopt a lofty standpoint toward everything. **-efrau,** *f.* nurse, attendant. **-egeld,** *n.* half-pay. **-en,** 1. *v.n.* (*aux.* h.) wait, stay, bide; be on the look-out, (*auf with Acc., or rarely Gen.*) await, wait for, wait on; (*coll.*) *da können Sie lange -en,* you will wait till the cows come home, you may whistle for it; (*coll.*) *-e nur!* you just wait! *er läßt auf sich -en,* he is a long time coming; *einen -en lassen,* keep a p. waiting; *mit dem Essen auf einen -en,* keep dinner waiting for s.o.; *seines Amtes, seiner Arbeit -en,* (*archaic*) discharge one's duties, attend to one's work; *eine schlimme Nachricht -et seiner,* there is bad news in store for him. 2. *v.a.* attend to, look after, tend, nurse; mind (*children*); groom (*horses*). 3. *n.* waiting; tending; *ich bin des -ens müde,* I am tired of waiting. **-esaal,** *m.* waiting-room (*Railw.*). **-estand,** *m.* provisional retirement. **-ezeit,** *f.* demurrage, time of waiting; (*C.L.*) gap. **-ezimmer,** *n.* (doctor's) waiting room. **-turm,** *m.* watch *or* look-out tower. **-ung,** *f.* nursing, tending; attendance, maintenance, servicing, grooming.
Wärt-el, *m.* (*archaic*), **-er,** *m.* (-s, -) keeper, caretaker, (prison) warder, attendant, male nurse; signalman. **-erhaus,** *n.* signal box. **-erin,** *f.* attendant; nurse.
-wärts, *adv. suffix* -wards, e.g. *vorwärts,* forward.
warum, *adv.* & *conj.* why, for what reason? wherefore; *- nicht gar?* you don't say so! surely not!
Warz-e, *f.* (-en) wart; nipple, teat; tubercle (*Bot.*); knob, stud, lug, pin. **-enartig,** *adj.* warty, wart-like, papillary, mammillary; mastoid. **-enbein,** *n.* mastoid bone. **-enfortsatz,** *m.* papillary tubercle; mastoid process. **-engewebe,** *n.* papillary tissue. **-enhof,** *m.,* **-enring,** *m.* areola of the nipple. **-enschwein,** *n.* wart-hog (*Phacochoerus aethiopicus*) (*Zool.*). **-ig,** *adj.* warty.
was, 1. *inter. pron.* what; whatever; *ach -!* rubbish! stuff and nonsense! *- bekommen Sie?* how much is it? the bill, please; *- dann?* what then? is that all? *- ist Ihnen denn?* what is wrong? what is the matter (with you)? what is the trouble? *- für ein,* what a; *- für ein?* what sort of a? *- für ein Unglück!* what a misfortune! *- hilft's?* what use is it? *- haben wir gelacht!* how we laughed! *- rennt das Volk?* why are the people running? *- Sie nicht sagen!* you don't say so! really! *- weiter?* see *- dann?* 2. *rel. pron.* what, that which; whatever; *alles, was du siehst,* all that you can see; *nimm dir, was du willst,* take whatever you want; *er läuft - er (nur) kann,* he runs as hard as he can; *- mich anlangt or betrifft,* as for me; *- auch immer,* whatever, no matter what. 3. *coll. for* etwas; *ich will dir mal - sagen,* I will tell you something; *das ist auch - Rechtes!* I do not think much of that! *nein, so -!* well, I never! *so - lebt nicht!* such a thing has never been heard of; *zu - Bessern sind wir geboren,* man is born for better things. 4. (*coll. for* - meinen Sie?); *ein bißchen kalt heute, -?* rather cold today, don't you think?
Wäsch-e, *f.* (-en) washing, wash, laundry; linen, underclothing; *morgen haben wir (große) -e,* tomorrow is washing-day; *das Hemd ist in der -e,* the shirt is being washed *or* is in the wash; *in die -e geben, tun or schicken,* send to the laundry; *schmutzige -e,* dirty linen (*also fig.*); *die -e wechseln,* change one's underclothes; *-e zeichnen,* mark linen. **-ebeutel,** *m.* soiled-linen *or* dirty clothes bag. **-erei,** *f.* washing; laundry. **-egeschäft,** *n.* lingerie *or* draper's shop. **-egestell,** clothes-horse. **-erin,** *f.* washerwoman, laundress. **-eklammer,** *f.* clothes-peg. **-ekorb,** *m.* dirty clothes basket. **-eleine,** *f.* clothes line. **-emangel,** *f.,* **-erolle,** *f.* mangle, wringer. **-erollen,** *n.* mangling. **-eschrank,** *m.* linen-cupboard, linen-press. **-eständer,** *m., see* **-egestell.** **-ezettel,** *m.* laundry-list.
Wascheln, *f.pl.* (*dial.*) ears, (*sl.*) lugs.
wasch-en, *ir.v.a.* & *n.* (*aux.* h.) wash, launder; (*coll., dial.*) gossip, chatter; (*Prov.*) *eine Hand wäscht die andere,* one good turn deserves another; *wir -en heute,* this is washing-day; *sich -en lassen,* bear *or* stand washing, wash well; *sich* (*Dat.*) *das Gesicht* or *die Hände -en,* wash one's face *or* hands; *ich -e meine Hände in Unschuld,* I wash my hands of it; (*coll. fig.*) *einem den Kopf -en,* give s.o. a dressing down; (*coll.*) *das hat sich gewaschen!* that is capital *or* A 1!; *mit allen Wassern gewaschen,* artful, cunning. **-anstalt,** *f.* laundry. **-bar,** *adj.* washable, fast (*of colours*). **-bär,** *m.* raccoon (*Procyon lotor*) (*Zool.*). **-becken,** *n.* washing- *or* hand-basin. **-beständig,** *adj.* washable, fast (*of colours*). **-blau,** *n.* washing-blue. **-brett,** *n.* wash-board. **-echt,** *adj.* washable, fast (*in colour*); (*fig.*) genuine, real, true, thorough. **-erde,** *f.* fuller's earth. **-faß,** *n.* wash-tub. **-flasche,** *f.* washing bottle (*Chem.*). **-frau,** *f.* washerwoman, laundress. **-gelegenheit,** *f.* lavatory, toilet. **-geschirr,** *n.* washstand set. **-gold,** *n.* placer gold. **-handschuhe,** *m.pl.* wash-leather gloves. **-haus,** *n.* wash-house. **-kessel,** *m.* copper, boiler. **-kleid,** *n.* washable dress, cotton frock. **-korb,** *m.* clothes-basket. **-küche,** *f.* wash-house. **-lappen,** *m.* face-cloth; (*fig.*) milksop, (*sl.*) sissy. **-leder,** *n.,* **-ledern,** *adj.* wash-leather, chamois, (*coll.*) shammy; *-lederne Handschuhe,* wash-leather gloves. **-maschine,** *f.* washing-machine. **-mittel,** *n.* lotion, detergent. **-raum,** *m.* lavatory, toilet. **-schüssel,** *f. see* **-becken.** **-seife,** *f.* washing soap. **-tisch,** *m.,* **-toilette,** *f.* wash-stand. **-topf,** *m.* washing-up bowl. **-trog,** *m.* wash-tub; standing-buddle; wash-cradle (*Min.*). **-ung,** *f.* washing, ablution, lavation; wash, lotion. **-wasser,** *n.* washing water; wash, cosmetic, lotion; dish-water. **-weib,** *n.* washerwoman, gossip, chatterbox (*also used of men*). **-zettel,** *m.* (*sl.*) publisher's blurb.
Wasen, *m.* (-s, -) sod, turf, grass; lawn; (*dial.*) bundle of brushwood; (*dial.*) steam, vapour. **-meister,** *m.* knacker.
Wasser, *n.* (-s - & (Mineral)¨-) water; *voll -,*

waterlogged (*of ships*); *gebranntes* –, brandy, liqueur; *fließendes* –, running water; *stehendes* –, stagnant water; *Kölnisches* –, eau-de-Cologne; *sein – abschlagen*, make *or* pass water; *mit allen –n gewaschen*, cunning; (*Prov.*) – *hat keine Balken*, water is a treacherous element; *bei – und Brot sitzen*, be on bread and water; – *lassen*, see – *abschlagen*; *ins – fallen*, see *zu – werden*; *das – lief mir vom Leibe herunter*, I was in a bath of perspiration; *das – läuft ihm im Munde zusammen*, his mouth waters; *das ist – auf seine Mühle*, that is grist to his mill; *einem nicht das – reichen können*, be far inferior to, not to be compared with *or* not able to hold a candle to a p.; *von reinstem* –, of the first water; (*Prov.*) *stille – sind tief*, still waters run deep; (*Prov.*) – *ins Meer tragen*, carry coals to Newcastle; *sich über – halten*, keep one's head above water; *unter – setzen*, inundate, submerge; – *ziehen*, let in water, leak; *zu – und zu Lande*, by land and sea; *zu – machen*, bring to naught, frustrate; *zu – werden*, end in smoke, come to naught, fall to the ground. **–abfluß,** *m.* drain, scupper. **–abfuhr,** *f.* draining, drainage. **–abgabe,** *f.* elimination of water, transpiration. **–ablaufrinne,** *f.* gutter, spouting (*on a roof*). **–abspaltung,** *f.* dehydration. **–ader,** *f.* underground watercourse. **–anziehend,** *adj.* hygroscopic. **–arm,** *adj.* parched, arid. **–armut,** *f.* scarcity of water. **–ball,** *m.* water-polo. **–bau,** *m.* dike construction *or* maintenance. **–becken,** *n.* natural reservoir, basin. **–behälter,** *m.* reservoir, cistern, tank. **–beize,** *f.* water-stain. **–berieselung,** *f.* irrigation. **–beschreibung,** *f.* hydrography. **–beständig,** *adj.* waterproof. **–bewohner,** *m.* aquatic (animal *or* plant). **–blase,** *f.* vesicle, pustule, bubble. **–blau,** *adj.* & *n.* sea-blue. **–blume,** *f.* aquatic flower. **–bombe,** *f.* depth-charge (*Mil.*). **–bruch,** *m.* hydrocele (*Med.*). **–dampf,** *m.* steam. **–dicht,** *adj.* watertight; waterproof. **–druck,** *m.* hydrostatic pressure. **–dunst,** *m.* water vapour. **–durchlässig,** *adj.* permeable. **–enthärtung,** *f.* water softening. **–entziehung,** *f.* dehydration. **–fahrt,** *f.* trip by water, boating excursion. **–fall,** *m.* waterfall, cascade, cataract. **–fang,** *m.* cistern, reservoir, catchment. **–farbe,** *f.* water-colour, distemper. **–fläche,** *f.* surface of water; water-level; sheet of water. **–flasche,** *f.* water bottle, carafe. **–flugzeug,** *n.* seaplane. **–frei,** *adj.* free from water, anhydrous; *–freier Alkohol*, absolute alcohol. **–gang,** *m.* aqueduct, canal; drain, scupper. **–geflügel,** *n.* waterfowl. **–gehalt,** *m.* moisture *or* water content. **–geist,** *m.* water-sprite. **–geschwulst,** *f.* oedema. **–gewächs,** *n.* aquatic plant. **–gierig,** *adj.* hygroscopic. **–glas,** *n.* tumbler, drinking-glass; waterglass, sodium silicate; *Sturm im –glase*, storm in a tea-cup. **–gott,** *m.* Neptune. **–hahn,** *m.* water-cock, water-tap. **–haft,** *adj.* aqueous. **–haltig,** *adj.* containing water, watery; aqueous, hydrous, hydrated (*Chem.*). **–hart,** *adj.* air-dried (*of pottery*). **–haushalt,** *m.*, *see* **–wirtschaft.** **–heilanstalt,** *f.* hydropathic. **–heilkunde,** *f.* hydropathy. **–heizung,** *f.* central heating. **–hell,** *adj.* pellucid, clear as water. **–hose,** *f.* waterspout. **–huhn,** *n.* coot (*Fulica atra*) (*Orn.*). **–jungfer,** *f.* water-nymph, mermaid; dragon-fly (*Odonata*) (*Ent.*). **–käfer,** *m.* water-beetle (*Hydrophilidae*) (*Ent.*). **–kanne,** *f.*, *see* **–krug.** (*dial.*) **–kante,** *f.* seaboard (of N. Germany). **–kessel,** *m.* cauldron, copper, kettle, boiler. **–kitt,** *m.* hydraulic cement. **–kläranlage,** *f.* water purifying plant. **–klee,** *m.* marsh trefoil (*Menyantus trifoliata*) (*Bot.*). **–klosett,** *n.* W.C. **–kopf,** *m.* hydrocephalus. **–kraft,** *f.* water-power, hydraulic power. **–kraftlehre,** *f.* hydrodynamics. **–kraftwerk,** *n.* hydro-electric plant. **–kresse,** *f.* watercress (*Nasturtium amphibium*) (*Bot.*). **–krug,** *m.* water jug, ewer, pitcher. **–kunde,** *f.* hydrology. **–kunst,** *f.* fountain; hydraulic engine. **–kur,** *f.* hydropathic treatment. **–lache,** *f.* pool, puddle. **–lauf,** *m.* watercourse. **–läufer,** *m.* pond skater (*Gerridae*) (*Ent.*). **–leer,** *adj.* dry, parched, arid. **–leitung,** *f.* aqueduct, canal, conduit; water main, water piping, water supply; *–leitung ins Haus bekommen*, have the water laid on; *die –leitung abschneiden*, cut off the water at the main. **–leitungshauptrohr,** *n.* water main. **–leitungsröhre,** *f.* water-pipe, conduit. **–leitungswasser,** tap water. **–lilie,** *f.* water lily (*Nymphaea alba*) (*Bot.*). **–linie,** *f.* waterline, load line (*Naut.*). **–linse,** *f.* duckweed (*Lemna minor*) (*Bot.*). **–löslich,** *adj.* water-soluble. **–mangel,** *m.* scarcity of water, drought. **–mann,** *m.* Aquarian (*Astr.*). **–mantel,** *m.* water-jacket (*Mach.*). **–maschine,** *f.* hydraulic engine. **–menge,** *f.* amount of water; plenty of water. **–messer,** *m.* hydrometer, water-gauge. **–meßkunst,** *f.* hydrometry. **–mühle,** *f.* watermill. **–n,** *v.n.* (*aux.* h. & s.) alight on water (*Av.*). **–nixe,** *f.*, **–nymphe,** *f.* water-nymph *or* sprite, naiad. **–not,** *f.* scarcity of water, water-famine, drought. **–partie,** *f.*, *see* **–fahrt.** **–paß,** 1. *adj.* level with the water; horizontal. 2. *m.* level of the water. **–perle,** *f.* imitation pearl. **–pest,** *f.* water-weed (*Elodea canadensis*) (*Bot.*). **–pfahl,** *m.* underwater pier *or* pile. **–pfeife,** *f.* narghile, hookah. **–pflanze,** *f.* aquatic plant, hydrophyte. **–pocken,** *f.pl.* chicken-pox (*Path.*). **–polizei,** *f.* river *or* harbour police. **–prüfung,** *f.* water analysis. **–pumpe,** *f.* water-pump. **–rabe,** *m.* cormorant (*Phalacrocorax carbo*) (*Orn.*). **–rad,** *n.* waterwheel; *ober*(or *unter*)*schlägiges –rad*, overshot (undershot) water-wheel. **–ratte,** *f.* water-rat (*Arvicola scherman*) (*Zool.*); (*coll.*) good swimmer; old salt, seadog. **–recht,** *n.* law of waters. **–reich,** *adj.* well watered; of high humidity. **–rinne,** *f.* gutter (*Build.*). **–röhre,** *f.* water-pipe. **–rose,** *f.* water-lily. **–rübe,** *f.* turnip (*Brassica rapa*) (*Bot.*). **–rutschbahn,** *f.* water-chute. **–sack,** *m.* watery cyst; water trap (*of pipe*); canvas bucket. **–schacht,** *m.* draining-shaft (*in a mine*). **–schaden,** *m.* flood damage. **–scheide,** *f.* watershed, (*Amer.*) divide. **–scheu,** 1. *adj.* shunning water. 2. *f.* hydrophobia. **–schlange,** *f.* sea-serpent; Hydra (*Astr.*). **–schlauch,** *m.* water-hose; bladder-wort (*Utricularia*) (*Bot.*). **–schwalbe,** *f.* sandmartin (*Riparia*) (*Orn.*). **–schwebegesellschaften,** *f.pl.* plankton. **–schwere,** *f.* specific gravity of water. **–semmel,** *f.* plain roll. **–snot,** *f.* floods, inundation. **–speicher,** *m.* tank, reservoir. **–speier,** *m.* gargoyle. **–sperre,** *f.* water obstacle. **–spiegel,** *m.* surface of the water; water level; expanse of water. **–sport,** *m.* aquatic sports. **–spritze,** *f.* squirt, syringe, sprinkler. **–stand,** *m.* state of the tide, water-level. **–standsanzeiger,** *m.*, **–standsglas,** *n.*, **–standsmesser,** *m.* water-gauge. **–staub,** *m.* spray. **–stein,** *m.* incrustation, scale. **–stiefel,** *m.* gum-boot, thigh boot. **–stoff,** *m.* hydrogen. **–stoffblond,** *adj.* peroxide blond, bleached. **–stoffhaltig,** *adj.* hydrogenous. **–stoff(hy)peroxyd, –stoffsuperoxyd,** *n.* hydrogen peroxide. **–strahl,** *m.* jet of water. **–straße,** *f.* channel (*of a river*), navigable river, waterway, canal; ocean highway. **–sucht,** *f.* dropsy. **–süchtig,** *adj.* dropsical, hydrophillic. **–suppe,** *f.* gruel. **–teilchen,** *n.* aqueous particle, molecule of water. **–tier,** *n.* aquatic animal. **–tor,** *n.* flood-gate. **–tracht,** *f.* (*ship's*) draught (*Naut.*). **–träger,** *m.* water-carrier. **–tragesack,** *m.* canvas bucket. **–transport,** *m.* carriage, transportation *or* conveyance by water. **–treibend,** *adj.* diuretic. **–treten,** *n.* treading water (*Swimming*). **–triebwerk,** *n.* hydraulic machine. **–trog,** *m.* water-trough. **–uhr,** *f.* water gauge. **–umschlag,** *m.* cold-water bandage. **–verdrängung,** *f.* displacement (*of water*). **–versorgung,** *f.* water supply. **–vögel,** *m.pl.* water-fowl, aquatic birds. **–wa(a)ge,** *f.* water-level (*Surv.*), hydrometer, water gauge. **–weg,** *m.* waterway; *auf dem –wege*, by water. **–welle,** *f.* water-wave (*Hairdressing*). **–werk,** *n.* water works. **–wirtschaft,** *f.* water conservation, water supply. **–wüste,** *f.* watery waste. **–zeichen,** *n.* watermark (*in paper*); *mit –zeichen*, watermarked. **–zement,** *m.* & *n.* hydraulic cement. **–zins,** *m.* water-rate. **–zuleitungsrohr,** *n.* water-pipe.

Wässer–chen, rivulet, brook; (*coll.*) *er sieht aus, als könne er kein –chen trüben*, he looks as if butter would not melt in his mouth. **–ig,** *adj.* watery, aqueous; serous; insipid; diluted, weak; *einem den Mund* (*nach etwas*) *–ig machen*, make a p.'s mouth water (for a th.). **–n.** 1. *v.a.* water, irrigate, wash

(*Phot.*); soak, steep, macerate; dilute, hydrate (*Chem.*). 2. *v.n.* (*aux.* h.) water; *ihr –ten die Augen*, tears came into her eyes; *der Mund –t mir darnach*, it makes my mouth water. **–ung,** *f.* watering, irrigation; maceration, soaking; dilution, hydration. **–ungskasten,** *m.* washing-tank (*Phot.*).

Wat, *f.* (*archaic & Poet.*) garment, garb, raiment.

Wate, *f.* (-n) (*dial.*) drag-net.

wat–en, *v.n.* (*aux.* h. & s.) wade, paddle. **–vogel,** *m.* wading bird (*Limicolae*) (*Orn.*).

Watsch–e, *f.* (*dial.*) box on the ear, (*sl.*) clout. **–(e)lig,** *adj.* (*coll.*) waddling. **–eln,** *v.n.* (*aux.* h. & s.) (*coll.*) waddle.

[1]**Watt,** *n.* (-(e)s, -e), **–e,** *f.* (-en) (*usually pl.*) sandbank, shoal, mud flat, shallows. **–enfahrer,** *m.* shallow-draught coasting vessel. **–enfischerei,** *f.* shoal *or* inshore fishing. **–enmeer,** *n.* shoals, shallows. **–enschlick,** *m.* shoal mud.

[2]**Watt,** *n.* (-s, –) watt (*Elec.*).

Watt–e, *f.* (-en) wadding, cotton-wool (*Med.*). **–ebausch,** *m.* wad *or* swab of cotton-wool. **–ieren,** *v.a.* wad, line with wadding, pad, quilt with cotton-wool; (*coll.*) *einem die Backen –ieren*, slap a p.'s face.

Wau, *m.* (-(e)s, -e) dyer's weed (*Reseda luteola*) (*Bot.*). **–gelb,** *n.* luteolin.

wauwau, 1. *int. & m.* (-(e)s, -e & -s) (*nursery talk*) bow-wow.

Web–e, *f.* (-en) piece of weaving, web, tissue. **–en,** 1. *reg. &* (*poet. & Swiss dial.*) *ir.v.a. & n.* weave. 2. *reg. v.n.* (*aux.* h.) (*Poet.*) move, be active; wave, float; (*B.*) *in Ihm leben, –en und sind wir*, in Him we live and move and have our being; *alles lebt und –t*, everything is full of life *or* activity. **–ekante,** *f.* selvage. **–eleine,** *f.* ratline (*Naut.*). **–er,** *m.* weaver. **–erbaum,** *m.* weaver's beam, warp-beam, yarn-roller. **–erdistel,** *f.* fuller's teasel (*Dipsacus fullonum*) (*Bot.*). **–erei,** *f.* weaving; texture; tissue, woven material; weaving-mill. **–ereinschlag,** *m.*, **–ereintrag,** *m.* woof, weft. **–ergesell,** *m.* journeyman weaver. **–erkamm,** *m.* weaver's reed. **–erknecht,** *m.* daddy-long-legs (*Phalangium*) (*Ent.*). **–erlade,** *f.* batten, lathe of the loom. **–(er)schiffchen,** *n.* shuttle. **–ervogel,** *m.* weaver-bird (*Ploceidae*) (*Orn.*). **–(e)stoff,** *m.* textile, fabric. **–garn,** *n.* yarn, thread. **–stuhl,** *m.* weaver's loom. **–waren,** *f.pl.* woven *or* textile goods, textiles.

Wechsel, *m.* (-s, –) change, alteration; succession, turn, alternation, rotation (*of crops, etc.*); variation, fluctuation, vicissitude; relay (*of horses*), interchange; oscillation (*Elec.*); exchange, bill of exchange, draft; (*Stud. sl.*) allowance; run, runway, haunt (*Hunt.*), joint, junction; (*dial.*) points (*Railw.*); *einen – ausstellen auf* (*Acc.*), draw a bill on; *eigener –*, note of hand, promissory note; *gezogener –*, bill, draft; *indossierter –*, endorsed bill (of exchange); *keinen – in Kleidern haben*, have no change of clothes; *kurzer –*, bill at short date; *langer –*, long-dated *or* -sighted bill of exchange; *offener –*, letter of credit; *– auf Sicht*, sight bill; **–agent,** *m.* bill-broker. **–agio,** *n.* exchange. **–akzept,** *n.* acceptance of a bill. **–balg,** *m.* changeling. **–bar,** *adj.* changeable, convertible. **–beanspruchung,** *f.* alternating stress. **–bewegung,** *f.* intermittent motion, reciprocal movement. **–beziehung,** *f.* correlation, interrelation. **–brief,** *m.* (*archaic*) bill of exchange. **–bureau,** *n.* exchange-office. **–diskont,** *m.* bill-discount. **–fähig,** *adj.* entitled to draw bills of exchange. **–fall,** *m.* alternative (case). **–fälle,** *m.pl.* vicissitudes, (*coll.*) ups and downs. **–fälschung,** *f.* forgery of bills. **–farbig,** *adj.* iridescent. **–fieber,** *n.* intermittent fever, malaria. **–folge,** *f.* alternation. (*C.L.*) **–frist,** *f*, usance. **–geber,** *m.* drawer (of a bill). **–gebrauch,** *m.* usance. **–gebühr,** *f.* commission; discount. **–geld,** *n.* exchange, agio. **–gesang,** *m.* antiphony. **–geschäft,** *n.* banking transaction; banking *or* exchange business. **–gespräch,** *n.* dialogue. **–getriebe,** *n.* variable gear. **–gläubiger,** *m.* creditor holding a bill of exchange. **–handel,** *m.* bill-broking. **–händler,** *m.* bill-broker. **–inhaber,** *m.* holder of a bill of exchange. **–jahre,** *n.pl.* climacteric, change of life. **–konto,** *n.* account of exchange, bill account. **–kurs,** *m.* rate of exchange. **–makler,** *m.* bill-broker. **–n,** 1. *v.a. & n.* (*aux.* h. & s.) change, vary, alternate (with), change places (with); draw bills; *die Kleider –n*, change one's clothes; *die Zähne –n*, cut one's new teeth. 2. *v.a.* exchange, interchange; *Worte mit einem –n*, bandy words with a p.; *Briefe mit einem –n*, correspond *or* be in correspondence with a p.; *–n Sie mir diese Note*, give me change for this note; *seinen Wohnort –n*, move (house). **–nehmer,** *m.* taker *or* buyer of a bill of exchange. **–note,** *f.* appoggiatura (*Mus.*). **–ordnung,** *f.* law regarding bills of exchange. (*fig.*) **–pfennig,** *m.* nest-egg. **–protest,** *m.* bill-protest. **–rechnung,** *f.* exchange account. **–recht,** *n.* right of exchange; laws regarding exchange. **–rede,** *f.* dialogue, discussion. **–reiten,** *n.*, **–reiterei,** *f.* bill-jobbing; speculation in accommodation bills, (*sl.*) kite-flying. **–richter,** *m.* inverter (*Elec.*). **–satz,** *m.* converse (*Math. & Log.*). **–schaltung,** *f.* alternating switch, alternate switching (*Elec.*). **–seitig,** *adj.* mutual, reciprocal, alternate. **–spiel,** *n.* fluctuation. **–ständig,** *adj.* alternate, alternating. **–stellung,** *f.* alternative position. **–streit,** *m.* dispute, conflict. **–strom,** *m.* alternating current (*Elec.*). **–stube,** *f.* exchange-office. **–tierchen,** *n.* amoeba. **–verjährung,** *f.* prescription of a bill of exchange. **–warm,** *adj.* with variable temperature. **–weide,** *f.* temporary pasture. **–weise,** *adv.* mutually, reciprocally, alternately. **–wild,** *n.* migratory game. **–winkel,** *m.pl.* adjacent angles. **–wirkung,** *f.* reciprocal action, mutual effect. **–wirtschaft,** *f.* rotation-system in farming. **–zahn,** *m.* milk tooth. **–zersetzung,** *f.* double decomposition. **–zustand,** *m.* reciprocity. **–verkehr,** *m.* two-way communication (*Tele.*). **–voll,** *adj.* changeable, subject to change.

Wechsler, *m.* (-s, –) money-changer.

Weck, *m.* (-(e)s, -e), **–e,** *f.* (-en), **–en,** *m.* (-ens, -en) (*dial.*) (breakfast-)roll.

weck–en, 1. *v.a.* wake, waken, awaken, rouse. *geweckt, p.p. & adj.*; *also fig.* mentally alert, intelligent. 2. *n.* waking, awakening, reveille (*Mil.*). **–er,** *m.* knocker-up; alarm clock; buzzer. **–ruf,** *m.* call (to rise); reveille (*Mil.*). **–uhr,** *f.* alarm clock.

Wedel, *m.* (-s, –) fan; feather-duster; tail, brush (*of foxes, etc.*); frond (*Bot.*). **–förmig,** *adj.* fan-shaped; fronded. **–n,** *v.a. & n.* (*aux.* h.) wag (*the tail*); fan, brush.

weder, *conj.* neither; *– er noch ich*, neither he nor I.

Weg, *m,* (-(e)s, -e) way, road, path, course, direction, route, passage; process, manner, method, means; walk, errand, business; *am –e*, by the roadside; *auf dem –e*, on the way; approaching, in a fair way; *sich auf den – machen* or *begeben*, set off *or* out, start; *Glück auf den –!* good luck! a pleasant journey to you! *die S. ist auf gutem –e*, the matter is making satisfactory progress; *auf gütlichem –e*, amicably, in a friendly way; *auf halbem –e stehen bleiben*, stop half-way *or* midway; *einem auf halbem –e entgegenkommen*, meet a p. half-way; *auf den rechten – bringen*, put in the right way; *einer S. aus dem –e gehen*, make way for s.th., get out of the way of s.th.; stand aside from a th., (*fig.*) shirk, evade; *aus dem –e räumen*, remove, kill, liquidate, (*sl.*) bump off; *bedeckter –*, covert-way (*Fort.*); *geht Eures –es!* be off! go your way! have nothing more to do with it! get *or* be about your business! *lassen Sie ihn seiner –e gehen!* let him alone! let him go his own way; (*Prov.*) *der gerade – ist der beste*, honesty is the best policy; *es hat damit gute –e!* there is no hurry for that! there is plenty of time; *einem in den – laufen* or *kommen*, get in a p.'s way; befall, occur; thwart, oppose; *einem etwas in den – legen*, put s.th. in a p.'s way, embarrass *or* oppose a p. with s.th.; *etwas in die –e leiten*, prepare s.th., pave the way *or* arrange for s.th.; *im –e Rechtens*, by law; *sich* (*Dat.*) *selbst im –e stehen*, stand in one's own light; *einem in den – treten*, *sich einem in den – stellen*, thwart *or* oppose a p.; *–(e) und Steg(e) kennen*, know one's way well, know all the ins and outs; *–e machen*, go errands, do the shopping; *er weiß Mittel und –e*, he has ways and means; *seinen ruhigen – fortgehen*, go on in one's own quiet way; *ich traue ihm nicht über den –*, I do not trust him out of my sight; *verbotener – !* no thoroughfare! private! *einem seine –e weisen*, send a p. about his business; *woher des –s?* whence do you come? *zu –e bringen*, bring about, accomplish; *mit etwas zu –e kommen*, complete *or* finish s.th. **–bereiter,** *m.* pioneer, forerunner. **–eabgabe,** *f.* highway toll. **–eamt,** *n.* office of works. **–ebau,** *m.* road-making. **–edorn,** *m.* buckthorn (*Rhamnus catharticus*) (*Bot.*). **–egabel,** *f.* fork in a road. **–egeld,** *see* **–eabgabe.** **–ekreuzung,** *f.* crossroads; road crossing. **–elagerer,** *m.* highwayman. **–emesser,** *m.* odometer. **–enetz,** *n.* road network *or* system. **–enge,** *f.* narrow defile. **–erecht,** *n.* right of way. **–erich,** *see* **Wegerich.** **–espinne,** *f.* road junction. **–genosse,** *m.* fellow traveller. **–kreuz,** *n.* wayside crucifix. **–kundig,** *adj.* familiar with the road. **–leitung,** *f.* (*Swiss dial.*) direction, instruction. **–los,** *adj.* pathless, trackless. **–müde,** *adj.* footsore, weary. **–rand,** *m.* verge. **–recht,** *n.* right of way. **–sam,** *adj.* passable, practicable, penetrable, accessible. **–scheid,** *m.* crossroads. **–schnecke,** *f.* slug (*Arionidae*) (*Zool.*). **–sperre,** *f.* road block. **–strecke,** *f.* distance, stretch of road; *eine lange –strecke*, a long way. **–stunde,** *f.* league. **–überführung,** *f.* road bridge. **–unterführung,** *f.* road tunnel, subway. **–warte,** *f.* chicory (*Cichorium intybus*) (*Bot.*). **–weiser,** *m.* signpost, road sign, finger-post; guide (book). **–zehrung,** *f.* food for the journey; viaticum (*R.C.*).

weg, 1. *adv., part. & sep. prefix*, away, gone, lost, far off, off; *– ist er*, he is gone; *der Reiz ist –*, the charm has gone; *das Haus liegt weit – von der Straße*, the house stands *or* lies far back from the street; (*coll.*) *ganz* or *rein – sein*, be quite beside o.s. (*vor*, with), be in raptures (about); *über eine S. – sein*, be beyond *or* have passed s.th.; *– wie der Blitz*, off like a shot; *in einem –*, without stopping, continually; (*coll.*) *frisch von der Leber –*, straight out, without frills. 2. *int.*; *– da!* be off! get out! *Hände – !* hands off! *Kopf – !* mind your head!

wegätzen, *v.a.* remove by caustics, cauterize, burn off, corrode.

wegbegeben, *ir.v.r.* go away, set off, withdraw, retire.

wegbekommen, *ir.v.a.* (*coll.*) succeed in removing, get off *or* away; bring about, accomplish, get; learn to do, (*coll.*) get the hang *or* knack of; *eins –*, (*sl.*) stop one.

wegbleiben, *ir.v.n.* (*aux.* s.) stay away; be omitted *or* left out; *bleiben Sie davon weg!* do not meddle with it! leave it alone! *ihm blieb die Spucke weg*, (*vulg.*) he was flabbergasted.

wegbrennen, 1. *ir.v.a.* burn away *or* off, cauterize. 2. *v.n.* (*aux.* s.) be burnt down.

wegbringen, *ir.v.a.* bring, take *or* carry away, remove; *mit Zitronensaft bringt man Tintenflecke weg*, lemon-juice takes out ink-stains.

wegdenken, *ir.v.a.* imagine as absent *or* non-existent.

wegeilen, *v.n.*; (*aux.* s.) hasten away, hurry off; *– über*, hurry over, touch on.

wegen, *prep.* (*with preceding or following Gen. or dial. Dat.*) because of, on account of, in consequence of, owing to; for the sake of, on behalf of; with regard to, regarding, in consideration of; *von –*, (*coll.*) *see* **–**; (*von*) *meinet–*, for my sake; *der Kürze –*, for the sake of brevity, to be short; *von Amts –*, by virtue of one's office; *von Polizei –*, by order of the police; *von Rechts –*, by right.

Wegerich, *m.* (-s, -e) plantain (*Plantago*) (*Bot.*).

wegessen, *ir.v.a.* eat up; (*coll.*) *einen –essen*, give a p. a farewell dinner.

wegfahren, 1. *ir.v.a.* cart away. 2. *v.n.* (*aux.* s.) drive away *or* off; sail away.

Wegfall, *m.* cessation, suppression, omission, abolition; *in – bringen*, abolish, suppress; *in – kommen*, be omitted, abolished *or* suppressed. **–en,** *ir.v.n.* (*aux.* s.) fall away *or* off; be omitted, be suppressed; cease, come to nothing, not take place.

wegfieren, *v.n.* lower away boats (*Naut.*).

wegfischen, *v.a.*; *einem etwas –*, snatch s.th. from under a p.'s nose.

wegfressen, *v.a.* (*vulg.*) eat up, devour, polish off.

wegführ-en, *v.a.* lead away, carry off. **–ung,** *f.* carrying off; abduction.

Weggang, *m.* departure.

weggeben, *ir.v.a.* give away; let go; send away (*to school, etc.*).

weggehen, *ir.v.n.* (*aux.* s.) go away, leave, depart; *einen – heißen*, bid a p. be gone; *über eine S. –*, pass over a th.; *geh mir weg damit!* drop the subject! *im –*, on leaving *or* departure.

weghaben, *ir.v.a.* have received (one's share), (*coll.*) have got the knack of; *er hat es gleich weg*, he sees it *or* the point at once; *der hat aber einen weg*, he has had one over the eight.

wegheben, *ir.v.a.* lift off, carry away; (*archaic*) *hebe dich weg!* begone!

weghelfen, *ir.v.n.* (*aux.* h.) (*einem*) help (a p.) get away.

wegjagen, 1 *v.a.* drive *or* chase away; expel. 2. *v.n.* gallop off.

wegkapern, *v.a.* (*coll.*), *see* **wegfischen.**

wegkommen, *ir.v.n.* (*aux.* s.) get away; get lost, be missing; *gut –* come off well (*bei* or *über*, in); *am schlimmsten –*, get the worst of it; *über eine S. –*, get over a trouble.

wegkratzen, *v.a.* scratch off *or* out.

wegkriegen, *v.a. coll. for* **wegbekommen.**

weglassen, *ir.v.a.* leave out, omit; let go.

weglegen, *v.a.* put away *or* aside, lay down.

wegleitend, *adj.* efferent.

wegleugnen, *v.a.* deny, disavow.

wegloben, *v.a.* (*coll.*) get rid of (*as result of flattery*).

wegmachen, 1. *v.a.* take away *or* off, remove, take out (*stains*), obliterate. 2. *v.r.* (*coll.*) get off.

Wegmarsch, *m.* marching off, departure.

Wegnahme, *f.* taking away, elimination; seizure, confiscation; capture.

wegnehmen, *ir.v.a.* take away, remove, take out (*stains, etc.*); carry off, seize, confiscate; take up, occupy (*space, etc.*).

wegpacken, 1. *v.a.* pack *or* put away. 2. *v.r.* (*vulg.*) pack off, make o.s. scarce.

wegputzen, *v.a.* brush *or* wipe away; (*coll.*) shoot (*sl.*) rub *or* wipe out (*a.p.*).

wegradieren, *v.a.* erase, scratch out.

wegraffen, *v.a.* carry off (*a p. by disease*).

wegräumen, *v.a.* clear away, tidy up, remove.

wegreisen, *v.n.* (*aux.* s.) depart, set out on a journey.

wegreißen, *ir.v.a.* tear down, demolish, pull down; snatch away.

wegrücken, 1. *v.a.* move away, remove. 2. *v.n.* (*aux.* s.) make way, move aside, withdraw.

wegsacken, *v.n.* sink, sag.

wegschaben, *v.a.* scrape away *or* off.

wegschaffen, *v.a.* clear away, carry off, remove, get rid of; make away with; eliminate (*Math.*).

wegscheren, *v.r.* (*imper. only*) (*coll.*) be off, decamp, (*sl.*) do a bunk.

wegschließen, *v.a.* lock up, lock away, put under lock and key.

wegsehen, *ir.v.n.* (*aux.* h.) look away; *über eine S. –*, overlook (*a th.*), shut one's eyes to a th.

wegsehnen, *v.r.* long to depart.

wegsetzen, 1. *v.a.* lay aside. 2. *v.r.* think o.s. superior (*über*, to); *sich über eine S. –*, not trouble about a th. 3. *v.n.* (*aux.* s.) jump (*über*, over).

wegsickern, *v.n.* ooze away.

wegspülen, *v.a.* wash *or* swill away.

wegstehlen, *v.r.* steal away, slink off.

wegstoßen, *ir.v.a.* push away; knock off, repel.

wegstreichen, 1. *ir.v.a.* smooth away *or* off; erase, strike out. 2. *v.n.* (*aux.* s.) fly away, depart (*of birds*).

wegtreiben, 1. *v.a.* drive away. 2. *v.n.* drift away.

wegtreten, 1. *ir.v.a.* tread down. 2. *v.n.* (*aux.* s.) step aside, retire; dismiss, fall out (*Mil.*). *weggetreten!* dismiss! fall out! (*Mil.*).

wegtun, *ir.v.a.* put away, set *or* lay aside; remove, throw away, cast aside.

wegweis-en, *ir.v.a.* send away, direct to another place. **–er,** *see under* **Weg.**

wegwenden, *ir.v.a.* turn away, off *or* aside; *mit weggewandtem Gesichte*, with averted face.

wegwerfen, 1. *ir.v.a.* threw away, cast off, jettison, reject; throw down *or* away (*Cards*). 2. *v.r.* throw o.s. away, degrade o.s. **-d,** *pr.p.* & *adj.* disparaging, disdainful, contemptuous.

wegwischen, *v.a.* wipe away *or* off, efface.

wegziehen, 1. *ir.v.a.* draw *or* pull away *or* off; draw aside, withdraw. 2. *v.n.* withdraw (from), depart, move, change one's home, go somewhere else.

Wegzug, *m.* removal; migration; departure.

weh(-e), 1. *int.* alas! oh dear! – *mir!* woe is me! – *ihm, wenn er . . .!* woe betide him if he . . .! *ach und – schreien,* make a loud outcry. 2. *adj.* painful, sore, aching; sad, woeful; *-er Finger,* sore finger; *-es Gefühl,* feelings of sorrow; *mit -em Herzen,* with heavy *or* aching heart; *es ist mir – zumute* or *ums Herz,* my heart aches, I am sore of heart; *mir tut der Kopf –,* my head hurts *or* is aching; *einem – tun,* hurt a p., give pain to a p., offend *or* wrong a p.; *ihm tut kein Zahn mehr –* he is beyond the reach of pain. 3. *n.* (-e *Austr.*) pain, ache; misery, misfortune, woe, grief; *Ach und –,* plaint, lament; *Wohl und –,* weal and woe. **-en,** *pl.* labour-pains, travail. **-enmittel,** *n.* ecbolic. **-gefühl,** *n.* feeling of grief *or* pain. **-geheul,** *n.*, **-geschrei,** *n.* howl, wailing, screams of pain. **-klage,** *f.* lamentation, wail. **-klagen,** *v.a.* & *n.* (*insep.*) (*aux.* h.) lament (*über,* about), bewail. **-leidig,** *adj.* plaintive, woebegone, sorry for o.s. **-mut,** *f.* sadness, melancholy. **-mütig,** *adj.*, **-mutsvoll,** *adj.* sad, melancholy. **-mutter,** *f.* midwife. **-wehchen,** *n.* (*nursery talk*) sore place.

Weh-e, *f.* (-en) snow-drift, sand-drift. **-en,** 1. *v.a.* blow away *or* along. 2. *v.n.* (*aux.* h.) blow; flutter, wave; *wissen woher der Wind -t,* (*fig.*) know which way the wind blows.

Wehl, *n.* (-(e)s, -e), **-e,** *f.* (-n) (*dial.*) bay, bight.

[1]**Wehr,** *f.* (-en) arm, weapon, military equipment; defence, resistance; bulwark; *schimmernde –,* shining armour; *sich zur – setzen* or *stellen,* resist, offer resistance, show fight; *mit – und Waffen,* fully armed. **-bereitschaft,** *f.* military preparedness. **-bewußt,** *adj.* military *or* defence-minded. **-bezirk,** *m.* recruiting district. **-dienst,** *m.* military service. **-dienstbeschädigung,** *f.* disability due to military service. **-drüse,** *f.* defensive scent gland (*Zool.*). **-en,** 1. *v.n.* (*aux.* h.) (*Dat.*) restrain, arrest, control, check. 2. *v.a.* (*einem etwas*) hinder, prevent *or* keep (a p. from doing s.th.); forbid (s.o. to do a th.); *dem Feuer -en,* arrest the spread of the fire; *wer will es -en?* who is to prevent it? 3. *v.r.* defend o.s.; resist (*Gen.* or *gegen,* against); *sich mit Hand und Fuß -en,* put up a fierce resistance; *sich seines Lebens* or *seiner Haut -en,* fight for one's life. **-ertüchtigung,** *f.* pre-military training. **-fähig,** *adj.* fit for military service, able-bodied. **-fliegertauglich,** *adj.* fit for flying duties (*Av.*). **-gehenk,** *n.* sword-belt. **-gesetz,** *n.* national defence regulations. **-haft,** *adj.* strong, valiant, militant, full of fight. **-haftigkeit,** *f.* valiant *or* militant bearing; valour. **-haftmachung,** *f.* arming, preparation for defence, establishment on a military footing. **-industrie,** *f.* armament industry. **-kraft,** *f.* military potential. **-kreis,** *m.* army corps area. **-los,** *adj.* unarmed, defenceless, weak; *-los machen,* disarm. **-losigkeit,** *f.* defencelessness. **-macht,** *f.* armed forces. **-machtakademie,** *f.* senior staff college. **-machtbericht,** *m.* army communiqué. **-machteigentum,** *n.* W.D. property. **-machtgefängnis,** *n.* military prison. **-mann,** *m.* (¨er) warrior, soldier; conscript, militiaman. **-minister,** *m.* Defence Minister. **-mittelbeschädigung,** *f.* sabotage. **-ordnung,** *f.*, *see* **-gesetz.** **-paß,** *m.* service man's papers. **-pflicht,** *f.* liability for military service; *allgemeine -pflicht,* compulsory military service, universal conscription. **-pflichtig,** *adj.* liable for military service. **-politik,** *f.* national defence policy. **-sold,** *m.* basic pay (*Mil.*). **-sport,** *m.* para-military physical training. **-stand,** *m.* military profession, the military, army. **-tüchtigung,** *f.* pre-military training. **-verein,** *m.* national defence league. **-vorlage,** *f.* army bill. **-wesen,** *n.* military *or* defence matters. **-wille,** *m.* desire for military preparedness. **-wirtschaft,** *f.* organization for total war. **-wissenschaft,** *f.* military science. **-würdig,** *adj.* eligible for service.

[2]**Wehr,** *n.* (-(e)s, -e) weir, spillway; dam, dike. **-bau,** *m.* dam, dike. **-baum,** *m.* sluice gate. **-gatter,** *n.* weir grate.

Weib, *n.* (-(e)s, -er) woman; (*Poet.* & *dial.*) wife; *er nimmt sie sich* (*Dat.*) *zum -e,* he takes her for his wife; *zum -e geben,* give in marriage. **-chen,** *n.* female (animal), she-, hen (bird); (*coll.*) wifie. **-erart,** *f.* woman's (silly) ways. **-erfeind,** *m.* woman-hater, misogynist. **-ergeklatsch,** *n.*, **-ergeschwätz,** *n.*, **-ergewäsch,** *n.* women's gossip *or* cackle. **-erhaß,** *m.* misogyny. **-erheld,** *m.* lady-killer, ladies' man. **-erherrschaft,** *f.* petticoat government. **-erlist,** *f.* woman's wiles. **-ermännig,** *adj.* gynandrian (*Biol.*). **-ernarr,** *m.*, *see* **-erheld.** **-erregiment,** *n.*, *see* **-erherrschaft.** **-erstamm,** *m.* female line. **-ertoll,** *adj.* crazy about women. **-ervolk,** *n.* women(folk). **-ig,** *adj. suffix* -pistilled, e.g. *drei-ig,* having three pistils. **-isch,** *adj.* womanish, effeminate. **-lich,** *adj.* womanly, feminine; female, pistillate (*Bot.*); *-liche Keimzelle,* megaspore; *-licher Vorkern,* egg nucleus. **-licherseits,** *adv.* on the female side, in the female line. **-lichkeit,** *f.* womanhood, womanliness; feminine nature, ways *or* weakness; *die holde -lichkeit,* the fair sex. **-sen,** *n.* (*dial.*), **-sbild,** *n.* female, (*sl.*) skirt. (*coll.*) **-sleute,** *pl.* womenfolk, females. **-sperson,** *f.*, **-sstück,** *n.* (*vulg.*), *see* **-sbild.** **-svolk,** *n.* women(folk).

Weibel, *m.* (-s, –) (*dial.*) bailiff, (*archaic*) sergeant. **-n,** *v.n.* (*Swiss dial.*) make propaganda for.

weich, *adj.* soft, smooth, mellow; gentle, mild, tender, delicate; effeminate, weak, yielding; sensitive, impressible, soft(-hearted); ductile, pliant, supple; – *gesottene* or *gekochte Eier,* soft-boiled eggs; *Fleisch – kochen,* boil meat until tender; *mir wird ganz – ums Herz,* I feel deeply touched *or* moved. **-blei,** *n.* refined lead. **-bottich,** *m.* steeping vat. **-e,** *f.* (-en) (*Poet.*) softness; flank, side; weak part *or* side; (*pl.*) groin, *see also* **Weiche** *below.* **-eisen,** *n.* pure iron, soft iron. **-en,** 1. *v.a.* make soft, soften, steep, soak. 2. *v.n.* (*aux.* h. & s.) become soft, grow tender *or* mellow, *see also* **weichen** *below.* **-enband,** *n.* inguinal ligament. **-engegend,** *f.* groin. **-haarig,** *adj.* soft-haired, pilose, pubescent. **-häutig,** *adj.* soft-skinned. **-herzig,** *adj.* tender-hearted. **-heit,** *f.* softness, suppleness, plasticity; tenderness, mellowness, mildness, gentleness, sensibility; permeability. **-käse,** *m.* cream-cheese. **-lich,** *adj.* soft, flabby, weak, feeble, effeminate, (*sl.*) sloppy; delicate, tender; inactive, tame, spiritless, insipid. **-lichkeit,** *f.* softness, flabbiness, weakness, delicacy, effeminacy. **-ling,** *m.* weakling, molly-coddle, milksop, (*sl.*) sissy, sap. **-teile,** *m.pl.* abdomen, belly, underside. **-tier,** *n.* mollusc. **-macher,** *m.* softener, softening agent, plasticizer.

Weichbild, *n.* municipal area, outskirts (of a town), precincts.

Weiche, *f.* (-n) points, switch, shunt (*Railw.*); *die -n stellen,* shift the points. **-n,** 1. *ir.v.n.* (*aux.* s.) (*Dat.* or *von*) yield, give in; give way, give ground; fall back, withdraw, retire, retreat (*Mil.*); fall (*of prices*), sag; *nicht von der Stelle – n,* not budge an inch; *aus dem Wege -n,* make room, give way; *von einem -n,* leave, abandon, desert a p. 2. *n.*; *zum -n bringen,* push back, repel; *die Kurse sind im -n,* the rate of exchange is falling; *die Kurse kommen ins -n,* prices are sagging *or* falling. **-nbock,** *m.* switch-box. **-nschiene,** *f.* switch-rail. **-nsignal,** *n.* switch-signal. **-nsteller,** *m.*, **-nwärter,** *m.* points-man.

Weichsel, *f.* (-n), **-kirsche,** *f.* morello, mahaleb *or* perfumed cherry (*Prunus cerasus*) (*Bot.*). **-rohr,** *n.* cherry-wood pipe. **-zopf,** *m.* elf-lock, Polish plait.

Weid, *f.* (*archaic*) hunt, chase (*now only in compounds*). **-gerecht,** *adj.* skilled in hunting *or* woodcraft; broken-in, trained to the chase. **-geschrei,** *n.*, *see* **-ruf.** **-lich,** 1. *adj.* brave, lusty; *usually* 2. *adv.* very much, thoroughly, to one's heart's content. **-loch,** *n.* anus of game. **-mann,** *m.* (-männer) huntsman. **-männisch,** *adj.* sportsmanlike. **-mannssprache,** *f.* language of the chase. **-messer,** *n.* hunting-knife. **-ruf,** *m.* tally-ho, hue and cry. **–sack,** *m.* **–tasche,** *f.* game-bag. **–werk,** *n.* chase, hunt, hunting, venery, woodcraft; game; *niederes –werk,* small game; *edles –werk,* noble sport of hunting. **–wund,** *adj.* shot in the belly.

[1]**Weide,** *f.* (-n) pasture, meadow, pasturage; *auf die – treiben,* turn out to grass, drive to pasture. **–gang,** *m.* grazing. **–koppel,** *f.* grazing paddock. **–land,** *n.* pasture land. **–n,** 1. *v.a.* lead *or* drive to pasture; tend, feed (*a flock*). 2. *v.n.* graze. 3. *v.a. & r.* (*an with Dat.*) feast one's eyes (on), delight (in), gloat (over). **–platz,** *m.* grazing-place; pasturage. **–recht,** *n.* pasture rights.

[2]**Weid–e,** *f.* (-en) willow, osier (*Salix*) (*Bot.*). **–en,** *adj.* willow. **–engeflecht,** *n.* wickerwork. **–engerte,** *f.* willow twig, osier-switch. **–enkätzchen,** *n.* willow catkin. **–enkorb,** *m.* wicker basket. **–enröschen,** *n.*; *Wald–enröschen,* rose-bay (*Epilobium angustifolium*); *Zottiges –enröschen,* willow-herb (*Epilobium hirsutum*) (*Bot.*). **–enrute,** *f., see* **–engerte. –erich,** *m.* purple loosestrife, (*Lythrum salicaria*) (*Bot.*). **–icht,** *n.* willow-plantation *or* thicket.

Weife, *f.* (-n) reel. **–n,** *v.a. & n.* (*aux.* h.) wind, reel (*yarn*).

weiger–n, 1. *v.a.* (*rare*) (*einem etwas*) refuse, deny (a p. s.th.); *see* **verweigern;** *usually* 2. *v.r.* (*with inf.*) refuse, decline (to do). **–ung,** *f.* refusal. **–ungsfall,** *m.*; *im –ungsfalle,* in case of refusal or non-acceptance.

Weih, *m.* (-en, -en), *usually* **–e,** *m.* (-en, -en) & *f.* (-en) kite (*Milvus*) (*Orn.*).

Weih–e, *f.* (-en) consecration, dedication, ordination; inauguration, initiation; solemn mood, solemn festivity; *einem die –e(n) erteilen,* ordain a p., consecrate a p. in holy orders. **–el,** *m.* nun's veil. **–en,** 1. *v.a.* consecrate, dedicate, ordain; sanctify, bless; *einen zum Priester –en,* ordain s.o. as a priest; *dem Untergang geweiht,* doomed to destruction. 2. *v.r.* devote o.s. (to); *sich –en lassen,* take (holy) orders. **–altar,** *m.* holy *or* consecrated altar. **–becken,** *n., see* **–wasserbecken. –bischof,** *m.* suffragan (bishop). **–brot,** *n.* consecrated bread, host. **–eakt,** *m.* solemn dedication, ceremony of ordination *or* consecration. **–elos,** *adj.* without solemnity; profane. **–estunde,** *f.* hour of commemoration. **–evoll,** *adj.* solemn, hallowed, holy. **–(e)gabe,** *f.* **(e)geschenk,** *n.* votive offering, oblation. **–kessel,** *m., see* **–wasserbecken. –nacht,** *f.*, **–nachten,** *f. or n.* Christmas; *fröhliche –nachten!* a merry Christmas! *ein trauriges -en,* a sad Christmas; *es –nachte(l)t sehr,* it is very Christmasy. **–nachtlich,** *adj.* characteristic of Christmas; *–nachtliches Wetter,* Christmasy weather. **–nachtsabend,** *m.* Christmas Eve. **–nachtsbaum,** *m.* Christmas-tree. **–nachtsfest,** *n.* festival of Christmas; Christmas festivities **–nachtsgeschenk,** *n.* Christmas present, box *or* gift. **–nachtskind,** *n.* the child Jesus. **–nachtslied,** *n.* Christmas carol. **–nachtsmann,** *m.* Father Christmas, Santa Claus. **–nachtsrose,** *f.* Christmas *or* Lenten rose (*Helleborus niger*) (*Bot.*). **–nachtssänger,** *m.pl.* waits. **–nacht(s)spiel,** *n.* nativity play. **–nachtsstollen,** *m.* Christmas cake. **–nachtstag,** *m.*; *erster –nachtstag,* Christmas Day; *zweiter –nachtstag,* Boxing Day. **–nachtszeit,** *f.* Christmas-time, Yule-tide. **–rauch,** *m.* incense, frankincense; *einem –rauch streuen,* laud a p. to the skies, overwhelm a p. with flattery; (*sl.*) boost a p. **–räuchern,** *v.n.* (*aux.* h.) (*einem*) extol, flatter (a p.). **–rauchfaß,** *n.* censer. **–ung,** *f., see* **–e. –wasser,** *n.* holy water. **–wasserbecken,** *n.* font, aspersorium. **–wedel,** *m.* aspergillum.

Weiher, *m.* (-s, –) (fish)pond.

weil, *conj.* because, since; (*archaic & dial.*) while, as long as; *freut euch des Lebens – noch das Lämpchen glüht,* enjoy life while you may. **–and,** *adv.* (*archaic*) formerly, of old, quondam; late, deceased.

Weil–e, *f.* a while, a (space of) time; leisure; (*Prov.*) *eile mit –e,* more haste less speed; *lange –e,* leisure; *geraume –e,* long time; *über eine kleine –e,* a short time afterwards; *damit hat es gute –e,* there is no hurry, we shall see; *Zeit und –e mit etwas verlieren,* lose time *or* waste one's time over a thing; (*Prov.*) *gut Ding will –e haben,* nothing good is done in a hurry, haste makes waste; (*bei*) *nächtlicher –e,* during the night. **–en,** *v.n.* (*aux.* h.) (*Poet.*) stay stop, abide, sojourn, tarry, linger; *er –t nicht mehr unter uns,* he is no longer with us, he has passed away.

Weiler, *m.* (-s, –) hamlet.

Weimutskiefer, *f.* (-n) Weymouth pine.

Wein, *m.* (-(e)s, -e) wine; fermented fruit juice; vine; *– bauen,* cultivate the vine; (*coll.*) *einem klaren* or *reinen – einschenken,* tell a p. the whole truth, speak plainly; *– keltern,* press the grapes; *den – lesen,* gather the grapes; *beim – sitzen,* sit over one's wine; *Wasser in seinen – gießen,* pour cold water on his enthusiasm; *Wasser predigen und – trinken,* not practice what one preaches; *wilder –,* Virginia creeper (*Parthenocissus quinquefolia*) (*Bot.*). **–artig,** *adj.* vinous, vinaceous. **–bau,** *m.* wine-growing. viniculture. **–bauer,** *m.* wine-grower. **–becher,** *m.* goblet. **–beere,** *f.* grape. **–berg,** *m.* vineyard. **–bergschnecke,** *f.* edible snail. **–blatt,** *n.* vine-leaf. **–blattlaus,** *f.* phylloxera. **–blume,** *f.* bouquet (*of wine*). **–brand,** *m.* brandy, cognac. **–ernte,** *f* vintage. **–essig,** *m.* wine vinegar. **–faß,** *n.* wine-cask; (*hum. & fig.*) wine-bibber, toper. **–flasche,** *f* wine-bottle. **–gar,** *adj.* fermented. **–garten,** *m.* vineyard. **–gärtner,** *m.* vine-dresser. **–gehalt,** *m.* wine content. **–geist,** *m.* spirits of wine; ethyl alcohol. **–geisthaltig,** *adj.* alcoholic, spirituous. **–geländer,** *n.* trellis for vines. **–haft,** *adj., see* **–artig. –haltig,** *adj.* vinous. **–händler,** *m* vintner, wine-merchant. **–hauer,** *m.* (*Austr. dial.*), *see* **–bauer. –hefe,** *f.* dregs *or* lees of wine, wine yeast **–jahr,** *n.* year's wine crop, vintage. **–karaffe,** *f.* decanter. **–karte,** *f.* wine-list. **–kauf,** *m.* glass of wine to seal a bargain. **–keller,** *m.* wine-cellar, vaults. **–kelter,** *f.* wine-press. **–kenner,** *m.* connoisseur of wine. **–krug,** *m.* wine-jug. **–laub,** *n.* vine-leaves. **–laune,** *f.* expansive mood; *in –laune sein,* be in one's cups. **–lese,** *f.* vintage; *–lese halten,* gather the grapes. **–leser,** *m.* vintager. **–met,** *m.* vinous hydromel (*Pharm.*). **–monat,** *m.*, **–mond,** *m.* October. **–most,** *m.* must. **–palme,** *f.* toddy-palm. **–panscher,** *m.* adulterator of wine. **–probe,** *f* tasting of wine; sample of wine. **–ranke,** *f.* vine-branch *or* tendril. **–rebe,** *f.* grape vine. **–reis,** *n.* vine-shoot. **–reisende(r),** *m.* traveller for a wine-firm. **–rose,** *f.* eglantine, sweet-brier (*Rosa rubiginosa*) (*Bot.*). **–rot,** *adj.* ruby- *or* claret-coloured. **–sauer,** *adj.* tartrate of. **–säure,** *f.* tartaric acid. **–schank,** *m., see* **–schenke. –schenk,** *m.* cup-bearer, butler. **–schenke,** *f.* wine-tavern. **–schlauch,** *m.* wine-skin; (*hum. & fig.*) wine-bibber. **–selig,** *adj.* in one's cups. **– -und Speisewirt,** *m.* licensee. **–stein,** *m.* (cream of) tartar, potassium bitartrate. **–steinsauer,** *adj., see* **–sauer. –steinsäure,** *see* **–säure. –stock,** *m.* grape vine. **–stube,** *f.* tavern, wine-cellar. **–tragend,** *adj.* wine-producing. **–traube,** *f.* grape, bunch of grapes. **–treber,** *pl.*, **–trester,** *pl.* skins *or* husks of pressed grapes. **–umrankt,** *adj.* vine-clad. **–verfälschung,** *f.* adulteration *or* doctoring of wine. **–waage,** *f.* wine-gauge. **–wirtschaft,** *f.* licensed house. **–zeche,** *f.* wine-bill. **–zierl,** *m.* (*Austr. dial.*), *see* **–bauer. –zoll,** *m.* duty on wine. **–zwang,** *m.* obligation to take wine with one's meal.

wein–en, 1. *v.a. & n.* (*aux.* h.) weep, cry; *um einen –en,* shed tears over s.o.; *über etwas –en,* weep about *or* lament s.th.; *vor Freude –en,* weep for joy; *sich* (*Dat.*) *die Augen rot –en,* make one's eyes red with weeping; *sich* (*Acc.*) *blind –en* or *sich* (*Dat.*) *die Augen aus dem Kopfe –en,* cry one's eyes out. 2. *n.* weeping, tears; *zum –en bringen,* move to ears; *ihr war das –en näher als das Lachen,* she was nearer to tears than to laughter. **–erlich,** *adj.* inclined to weep, given to tears, lachrymose, tearful; whining, crying; (*coll.*) weepy; *ihm ist –erlich zu Mute,* he is in a crying mood; *in –erlichem Tone,* in a whimpering *or* whining tone; *–erliches Lustspiel,* comédie larmoyante, (*coll.*) sob-stuff drama. **–krampf,** *m.* crying fit, convulsive sobbing.

weis–e, *adj.* wise; prudent, judicious; *–e Frau,* midwife; fortune-teller; *–e anordnen,* make sensible arrangements. **-e(r)**, *m.* wise man, sage, philosopher; *Stein der -en*, philosophers' stone; *die -en aus dem Morgenlande*, the (three) wise men from the East. **-heit**, *f.* wisdom, knowledge; prudence; *-heit Salomos*, Psalms of Solomon; *er denkt, er hat die -heit mit Löffeln gegessen*, he thinks he is very clever; *behalte deine -heit für dich!* keep your ideas *or* views to yourself; *mit seiner -heit zu Ende sein*, be at one's wits' end. **-heitsdünkel**, *m.* intellectual arrogance. **-heitskrämer**, *m.* wiseacre. **-heitszahn**, *m.* wisdom-tooth; *die -heitszähne bekommen*, cut one's wisdom-teeth. **-lich**, *adv.* wisely, prudently, well-considered.

Weise, 1. *f.* (-n) manner, way, method; style, fashion, mode, habit, custom; mood (*Gram.*); melody, air, tune (*Mus.*); *Art und -*, way, manner; *das ist doch keine Art und -*, that is no way to behave; *in der - daß*, in such a way that, so that; *in derselben -*, likewise, similarly; *auf diese -*, *in dieser -*, in this way, like this; *auf folgende -*, as follows; *auf jede* (or *alle*) *-*, in every way; in any case; *auf keine -*, *in keiner -*, by no means, not at all; *jeder nach seiner* or *auf seine -*, everyone in his own way; *auf welche -?* in what way? *Wort und -*, words and melody. 2. *adv. suffix* (*a*) *of adj.*, e.g. *glücklicher-*, happily, fortunately; *irrtümlicher-*, by mistake; *natürlicher-*, naturally, of course; (*b*) *of a noun*, e.g. *haufen-*, by heaps; *kreuz-*, in the form of a cross, crosswise; *massen-*, in large numbers, plentifully; *teil-*, partly, partially, in part.

Weisel, *m.* queen bee. **-wiege**, *f.* queen cell.

weis-en, 1. *ir.v.a.* (*einem etwas* (*usually direction or place*)) show, direct, indicate, point out; send (*a p.*) to *or* from (*a place*); *-en an* or *auf*, refer to; *-en aus*, expel *or* banish (from), exile; *von sich* or *von der Hand -en*, decline, refuse, reject, dismiss, set aside; *einen in seine Schranken -en*, put a p. in his place; *einem die Tür -en*, show a p. the door. 2. *v.n.* point (*nach*, at *or* towards); *mit den Fingern auf eine S. -en*, point out a th.; *mit Fingern auf einen -en*, point at a p. (derisively); *das wird sich bald -en*, it will soon be seen, we shall soon see. **-er**, *m.* pointer, indicator, finger, hand (*of a clock, etc.*). **-ung**, *f.* direction, instruction, order.

weis-machen, *v.a.* (*sep.*); (*einem etwas*) make (*a p.*) believe (*a. th*). hoax (*a p.*); *das machen Sie andern -!* don't try that one on me! tell that to the marines *or* to your grandmother! **-sagen**, *v.a.* & *n.* (*insep.*) foretell, predict, prophecy. **-sagend**, *pr.p.* & *adj.* prophetic. **-sager**, *m.*, **-sagerin**, *f.* prophet(ess), fortune-teller. **-sagung**, *f.* prophecy, prediction. **-tum**, *n.* (-s, ⁼er) precedent, prescription (*Law.*).

[1]**weiß**, 1. *adj.* white, clean, blank; argent (*Her.*); *- sieden*, blanch; *- lassen*, leave blank; *- machen*, blanch, bleach; *ein -es Blatt Papier*, a clean sheet of paper; *sich - brennen*, clear o.s., assert one's innocence; *-er Fluß*, leucorrhoea; *die -e Frau*, the Woman in White; *- kleiden*, dress in white; *-e Kohle*, water power; *-er Leim*, gelatine; *ein -er Rabe*, a white crow; *etwas schwarz auf - haben*, have a th. in black and white; *-er Sonntag*, Sunday after Easter, Low Sunday; *der -e Tod*, freezing to death; *-er Ton*, china clay, kaolin; *die -e Wand*, the screen (*cinema*); *einen - waschen wollen*, try to whitewash a p.; *eine -e Weste haben*, be entirely blameless, have clean hands; *-e Woche*, white sale (*in large stores*); *das -e*, the white (*of the eye*; *of an egg*); *die -en*, white men, the white races. **-bäcker**, *m.* baker and confectioner. **-bier**, *n.* light *or* pale ale. **-binder**, *m.* (*dial.*) cooper, decorator, house-painter. **-birke**, *f.* silver birch (*Betula alba*) (*Bot.*). **-blech**, *n.* tin-plate. **-blechwaren**, *f.pl.* tinware. **-bleiche**, *f.* full bleaching. **-bluten**, *n.* last extremity; *eine Firma zum -bluten bringen*, bring a business to the verge of ruin; *einen zum -bluten auspressen*, extort the last penny from a p., (*sl.*) squeeze s.o. till the pips squeak. **-blütigkeit**, *f.* leucemia (*Path.*). **-brennen**, *n.* blanching, bleaching. **-brot**, *n.* white bread *or* loaf. **-buch**, *n.* white paper (*Pol.*). **-buche**, *f.* hornbeam (*Carpinus betulus*) (*Bot.*). **-dorn**, *m.* hawthorn, may (*Crataegus oxyacantha*) (*Bot.*). **-e**, *f.* whiteness; whitewash; *eine -e*, a white woman; *eine* (*Berliner*) *-e*, (*dial.*) a (glass of) wheaten ale. **-en**, *v.a.* & *n.* (*aux.* s.) whiten; whitewash; blanch; refine (*cast iron*). **-er**, *m.* white man. **-fichte**, *f.* white spruce (*Picea canadensis*) (*Bot.*). **-fisch**, *m.* silver-scaled fish (*e.g.* bleak (*Alburnus lucidus*), bream (*Sparus pagrus*), chub (*Leuciscus rutilus*), roach (*Leuciscus cephalus*) (*Icht.*). **-fluß**, *m.* leucorrhoea (*Med.*). **-fuchs**, *m.* silver fox (*Vulpes lagopus*) (*Zool.*); light sorrel horse. **-gar**, *adj.* tawed. **-gerben**, *v.a.* taw. **-glühend**, *adj.* white-hot, incandescent. **-glühhitze**, *f.*, **-glut**, *f.* white heat, incandescence. **-gold**, *n.* artificial platinum. **-grau**, *adj.* & *n.* light grey. **-güldenerz**, *n.*, **-guldigerz**, *n.* argentiferous tetrahedrite. **-haarig**, *adj.* white-haired. **-käse**, *m.* cream cheese. **-kohl**, *m.* white cabbage. **-köpfig**, *adj.*, *see* **-haarig**. **-kraut**, *n.*, *see* **-kohl**. **-kupfer**, *n.* German silver. **-lich**, *adj.* whitish. **-ling**, *m.* Pieridae (*white butterfly*) (*Ent.*). **-lot**, *n.* soft solder. **-mehl**, *n.* wheat(en) flour. **-nähen**, *v.n.* (*sep.*) do plain needlework. **-näherin**, *f.* seamstress, needlewoman. **-ofen**, *m.* refining furnace. **-papp**, *m.* white resist (*Paperm.*). **-sieden**, *ir.v.a.* blanch, whiten. **-spießglanzerz**, *n.* white antimony. **-sucht**, *f.* albinism. **-sud**, *m.* blanching solution. **-tanne**, *f.* silver fir (*Abies alba*) (*Bot.*). **-tüncher**, *m.* whitewasher. **-waren**, *f pl.* linens, cottons, linen goods, drapery. **-warenhändler**, *m.* draper. **-wäsche**, *f.* (household) linen. **-wein**, *m.* white wine, hock. **-wurz**, *f.* Solomon's Seal (*Polygonatum multiflora*) (*Bot.*). **-zeug**, *n.*, *see* **-wäsche**.

[2]**weiß, weißt**, *see* **wissen**.

weit, 1. *adj.* wide, broad; large, vast extensive, spacious, ample, capacious, loose (*of clothes*); long, far, distant, remote; *-er Begriff*, all-embracing concept; *das steht noch in -em Felde*, that is still a very remote possibility; *-es Gewissen*, elastic conscience; *-e Hosen*, baggy trousers; *-e Reise*, long journey; *-er Umweg*, long way round; *-er Unterschied*, vast difference; *in die -e Welt gehen*, go out into the world. 2. *adv.* off, far, far off, much, greatly, by far, additional, further, moreover; *- aus*(or *von*)*einander*, far apart, widely separated, at long intervals; *bei -em nicht*, by no means, not nearly; *- besser*, much *or* far better; *- und breit*, far and wide; *es - bringen*, get on (well); *- gefehlt!* far from it! not at all! quite wrong! *- nach Hause haben*, be a long way from home; *nicht - her sein*, be of little value, not be worth much, (*coll.*) not be up to much; (*Prov.*) *mit der Zeit kommt man auch -*, many a little makes a mickle; *die Zeit ist nicht mehr -*, the time is drawing near; *eine Meile -*, a mile off; *wenn es so - ist*, if *or* when it is ready; *ist es so - gekommen?* is it reduced *or* has it come to this? *es ist noch nicht so -*, the moment has not yet arrived, it has not come to that yet; *von -em*, from afar, from a distance; *4 Fuß - von der Wand*, 4 feet from the wall; *- davon entfernt sein, etwas zu glauben*, be far from believing a th.; (*Prov.*) *- davon ist gut vorm Schuß*, prudence is the better part of valour; *wie - sind Sie mit Ihrer Arbeit?* how far have you got with your work? *es zu - treiben*, go too far; *das -e suchen*, take to one's heels, make o.s. scarce; *die S. liegt noch ganz im -en*, the matter is still quite uncertain; *des -en und Breiten etwas erzählen*, relate in detail *or* at length. 3. *n.* beam (*Naut.*). **-ab**, *adv.* far away. **-ästig**, *adj.* with spreading branches. **-aus**, *adv.* by far, much. **-ausgebreitet**, *adj.* expanded, widespread, effuse. **-aussehend**, *adj.*, *see* **-gehend**. **-bekannt**, *adj.*, **-berühmt**, *adj.* well-known, far-famed. **-bewundert**, *adj.* much admired. **-blick**, *m.* far-sightedness, foresight. **-blickend**, *adj.* far-seeing, far-sighted. **-e**, 1. *f.* width, breadth, wideness; size, capacity, extent, diameter, amplitude (*Astr.*); length, distance; fullness, comprehensiveness, range; *lichte -e*, width in the clear, inside *or* internal diameter, bore; *in die -e ziehen*, go out into the world. **-en**, 1. *v.a.* widen, expand, enlarge, extend, stretch (*shoes, etc.*). 2. *v.r.* become broader, broaden out. **-er**, 1. *compar. adj.* farther, further, wider; additional. 2. *adv.* farther, furthermore; on, forward; else; *bis auf -eres*, for the present, until further notice; *-er entfernt*, more distant, farther away; *hören Sie -er!* hear what follows! *immer -er*, on and on; *immer –er!* see *nur –er! in –eren Kreisen*, widely; *–er hat es keinen Zweck*, it serves no other purpose, that is all it is good for; *nicht –er*, not any further, no further; *nichts –er, –er nichts*, nothing more, nothing further; *das hat –er nichts zu sagen*, that (after all) carries no weight *or* is of no consequence; *–er niemand*, no one else; *nur –er!* continue! go on! proceed! *ohne –eres* (*Austr. dial. ohne –ers*) without more ado, immediately, directly, readily; *ohne –eren Aufschub*, without further delay; *ohne –ere Umstände*, without further *or* more ado, unceremoniously; *und –er?* and then? *und so –er*, and so on; *was –er?* what after that? what else? *und wer –er?* and who else? *das –ere*, what follows, the remainder *or* rest; further particulars *or* details; *des –ern*, moreover, furthermore; *–eres mündlich*, further details by word of mouth, more when I see you. **–erbefördern,** *v.a.* transport forward, send on, post on. **–erbeförderung,** *f.* transport, forwarding, transmission, dispatch; *zur –erbeförderung an Herrn. M.*, to be forwarded to Mr. M. **–erbegeben,** *v.a.* negotiate (*bills*). **–erbestehen,** *v.n.* continue to exist, go on. **–erbewegen,** *v.n.* move forward, advance, proceed. **–erbildung,** *f.* development, improvement; further education; derivation (*Gram.*). **–erbringen,** *v.a.* (*sep.*) promote, help on; *das bringt mich nicht –er*, that is not much help; *es –erbringen*, make progress, get on. **–erentwicklung,** *f.* further development. **–ererzählen,** *v.a., see* **–ersagen. –erführen,** *v.a.* carry on, continue. **–ergeben,** *v.a.* (*sep.*) pass on (*to others*). **–ergehen,** *v.n.* (*sep.*) walk on, go on, continue. **–erhelfen,** *v.a.* (*sep.*) (*Dat.*) help (*a p.*) on. **–erhin,** *adv.* for the *or* in future, from now on, furthermore. **–erkommen,** *v.n.* (*sep.*) get on, progress, advance. **–erkönnen,** *v.n.* (*sep.*); *nicht –erkönnen*, be brought to a standstill *or* forced to stop; (*coll.*) get stuck. **–erleiten,** *v.a., see* **–erbefördern. –erlesen,** *v.a.* & *n.* (*sep.*) go on *or* continue reading. **–ermarsch,** *m.* continuation of the march. **–ern,** *v.a.* & *r.* (*rare*), *see* **erweiten. –erreise,** *f.* continuation of the journey. **–ersagen,** *v.a.* tell others, repeat (*what one has heard*). **–erschicken,** *v.a.* send on. **–erschreiten,** *v.n.* advance. **–erungen,** *f.pl.* difficulties, complications, formalities. **–erverbreiten,** *v.a., see* **–ersagen. –ervermieten,** *v.a.* sub-let. **–erwursteln,** *v.n.* (*coll.*) muddle along. **–gehend,** *adj.* (*superl.* –gehendst *or* –estgehend) vast, far-reaching, extensive; exceptional; much, largely. **–gereist,** *adj.* widely travelled. **–her,** *adv.* from afar. **–hergeholt,** *adj.* far-fetched. **–hin,** *adv.*, **–hinaus,** *adv.* far off, in the distance. **–läuf(t)ig,** *adj.* copious, spacious, roomy; vast, widespread, extensive, wide, scattered; rambling, diffuse, prolix, long-winded, lengthy, detailed, circumstantial; distant; *sie sind –läufig verwandt*, they are distantly related; *die S. ist sehr –läufig*, the matter is very complicated. **–läuf(t)igkeit,** *f.* wideness, vast extent; diffuseness, prolixity, copiousness; (*pl.*) formalities, difficulties. **–maschig,** *adj.* wide-meshed. **–reichend,** *adj.* far-reaching, very extensive. **–schichtig,** *adj.* widely spaced, far apart; extensive, large, vast. **–schweifig,** *adj.* wide, vast; long-winded, tedious, detailed, circumstantial, diffuse, verbose, prolix. **–schweifigkeit,** *f.* verbosity, prolixity. **–sichtig,** *adj.* long-sighted; far-seeing, far-sighted, clear-sighted. **–sichtigkeit,** *f.* long-sightedness; perspicacity. **–sprung,** *m.* long jump (*Sport*). **–spurig,** *adj.* wide-tracked, broad-gauged. **–tragend,** *adj.* of long range (*of fire-arms*); (*fig.*) very important, far-reaching. **–umfassend,** *adj.* comprehensive, extensive. **–ung,** *f.* enlargement, extension, widening; distance, space, width; *–ung einer Treppe*, room under a staircase; (*pl.*) hollows, excavations (*Min.*). **–verbreitet,** *adj.* widespread, prevalent, general, widely known. **–verzweigt,** *adj.* widely ramified *or* spread, very extensive.

Weizen, *m.* wheat; corn; *türkischer –*, maize, Indian corn; (*coll.*) *mein – blüht*, I am in luck's way, I am in clover; (*coll.*) *mein – blüht nicht*, my ship has not come home. **–acker,** *m.* wheat field. **–artig,** *adj.* frumentaceous. **–bau,** *m.* cultivation of wheat. **–brand,** *m.* black rust. **–brot,** *n.* white bread. **–flugbrand,** *m.* loose smut (*of wheat*). **–grieß,** *m.* grits, middlings (*of wheat*). **–mehl,** *n.* wheaten flour. **–steinbrand,** *m.*, **–stinkbrand,** *m.* bunt (*of wheat*).

welch, 1. *indec. pron.* – (*ein*) *Erfolg!* what (a) success! *hast du gelesen, – ein Erfolg er gehabt hat?* have you read what a success he had? *da sieht man, – (ein) großer Tor er gewesen ist*, you see what a fool he has been. 2. *inter. adj.* which? what? *–er Mann?* which man? *–e Frau?* which woman? *–es Ding gefällt dir?* which of the things pleases you? 3. (-er, -e, -es) *inter. pron.* which? what? who? *–e von euch Damen?* which of you ladies? *einer meiner Brüder; –er?* one of my brothers; which one? *–es sind ihre Kinder?* which are her children? *–e schöne Tage*, what lovely days, *see also* – 1. 4. *rel. pron.* (*Gen. sing. m.* & *n.* dessen; *Gen. sing. f.* deren; *Gen. pl.* deren, *Dat. pl.* denen) which, what, that, who, whom; *derjenige –er*, he who; *die Dame, –er wir geschrieben haben*, the lady to whom we wrote; *die Bücher, ohne –e ich meine Arbeit nicht vollenden kann*, the books, without which I cannot finish my work; *–er auch* (*immer*), who(so)ever, whichever; *–es auch immer Ihre Ansprüche sein mögen*, whatever your claims may be, let your claims be what they may. 5. *rel. adj.*; *100 Mark, –e Summe Sie einliegend finden*, 100 marks, which (sum) I enclose; *–e Tugenden er auch haben mag*, whatever virtues he may possess; *von –er Art auch*, of whatever kind, whatsoever. 6. *indef. pron.* (*coll.*) some, any; *haben Sie Zucker? ich habe –en*, have you sugar? yes, I have some; *ich brauche Zucker, haben Sie –en?* I need some sugar, have you any? *es sind schon –e da*, there are some (people) here already; *eine Menge Menschen, –e zu Pferde und –e zu Fuß*, a lot of people, some on horseback and some on foot. **–erart,** *adv.*, **–ergestalt,** *adv.* in what form *or* manner; in consequence of which, by what means, how. **–erlei,** *indec. adj.* of what kind *or* sort; *–erlei Gründe er auch haben mag, –erlei Art seine Gründe auch sein mögen*, whatever sort of reasons he may have, whatever his reasons may be.

Welf, *n.* (-(e)s, -er) & *m.* (-(e)s, -e) whelp, cub (*Hunt.*). **–en,** *v.n.* (*aux.* h.) cub, have young (*Hunt.*).

welk, *adj.* withered, faded; shrivelled, wrinkled, parched; limp, flabby, flaccid; languid. **–en,** *v.a.* & *n.* (*aux.* s.) wilt, wither, fade (away), decay, shrivel *or* dry (up). **–heit,** *f.* faded *or* withered state; flabbiness, flaccidity.

Well–e, *f.* (-en) wave, billow, ripple, surge; wave-length, undulation; axle-shaft, spindle, arbor (*Mach.*); (*dial.*) faggot, bundle of brushwood; bottle (*of straw*); circling *or* revolution round the horizontal bar, grinder (*Gymn.*); *liegende –e*, horizontal shaft; *gekröpfte –e*, crank-shaft; *stehende –e*, vertical shaft, capstan; stationary wave (*Elec.*); *gedämpfte –e*, damped wave; *ungedämpfte –e*, undamped oscillation; *–en schlagen*, rise in waves, surge; *die –en durchschneiden*, plough the waves; *eine –e machen*, revolve round the bar (*Gymn.*). **–baum,** *m.* shaft, axle-tree, arbor. **–blech,** *n.* corrugated (sheet) iron; (*sl.*) *–blech reden*, talk rot *or* bilge. **–en,** *v.a.* wave (*hair*); corrugate (*iron*). **–enantrieb,** *m.* shaft drive. **–enartig,** *adj.* waved, wavy, wave-like, undulating, rolling, undulatory. **–enausbreitung,** *f.* wave propagation. **–enbad,** *n.* sea-bath, swimming-bath with artificial waves. **–enband,** *n.* wave-band (*Rad.*). **–enbaum,** *m., see* **–baum. –enbereich,** *m.* wave-range *or* band (*Rad.*). **–enberg,** *m.* wave crest, crest of a wave. **–enbewegung,** *f.* undulatory motion, undulation. **–enbrecher,** *m.* breakwater, groyne. **–enecho,** *n.* second-channel interference (*Rad.*). **–enförmig,** *adj., see* **–enartig. –enholz,** *n.* (*dial.*) brushwood. **–enlager,** *n.* shaft-bearing. **–enlänge,** *f.* wave-length (*Rad., etc.*). **–enlinie,** *f.* wavy line. **–enmesser,** *m.* wavemeter (*Rad.*). **–enreiten,** *n.* surf-riding. **–enschaltung,** *f.* wave-change switch (*Rad.*). **–enschlag,** *m.* breaking of the waves; *kurzer –enschlag*, choppy sea. **–enschlucker,** *m.* wave-trap, interference filter (*Rad.*). **–enschwingung,** *f.* undulation. **–ensit-**

tich, *m.* budgerigar (*Melopsittacus undulatus*) (*Orn.*). **-ental,** *n.* wave trough; trough of the sea. **-entheorie,** *f.* wave theory (*of light, etc.*). **-enübertragung,** *f.* shaft transmission. **-enwiderstand,** *m.* surge resistance (*Elec.*). **-fleisch,** *n.* boiled pork. **-ig,** *adj.* wavy, undulating. **-papier,** *n.*, **-pappe,** *f.* corrugated paper. **-rad,** *n.* winding drum *or* spindle, arbor wheel. **-sand,** *m.* shifting sand. **-zapfen,** *m.* pivot.

Weller, *m.* daub. **-n,** *v.a.* build with wattle and daub.

Welpe, *m.* (-n, -n), *see* **Welf.**

Wels, *m.* (-es, -e) catfish (*Silurus glanis*) (*Icht.*).

Welt, *f.* (-en) world, earth; people, society, humanity; universe; *alle –*, all the world, everyone, everybody; *auf der –*, on earth; *auf die – kommen*, come into the world, be born; *aus der – schaffen* or *räumen*, put out of the way, do away with, put to death; *nicht aus der – sein*, not be all that far away; (*coll.*) *da ist die – mit Brettern vernagelt*, that is beyond the wit of man (to find out); *sich durch die – schlagen*, make one's way in the world; *die große –*, high society, the upper ten; *warum in aller – ?* why on earth? why in the world? *in aller – nicht*, not for all the world, not on your life; *das geht mich in aller – nichts an*, I have no earthly concern with that; *um alles in der –*, for all the world; (*coll.*) *so geht es in der –*, that is the way of the world; *nichts in der –*, nothing on earth; *in die – setzen*, see *zur – bringen*; *die junge –*, young people; *ein Mann von –*, a man of good breeding; *zur – bringen*, give birth to, bring into the world. **-abgeschieden,** *adj.*, *see* **-entrückt.** **-achse,** *f.* earth's axis. **-all,** *n.* universe, cosmos. **-alter,** *n.* age, period in history. **-anschaulich,** *adj.* ideological. **-anschauung,** *f.* philosophy of life, world outlook, views, creed, ideology. **-ausstellung,** *f.* international exhibition; World Fair. **-ball,** *m.* globe. **-bau,** *m.* cosmic system, the universe; the world. **-bekannt,** *adj.* known everywhere, world-famous, generally known, notorious. **-berühmt,** *adj.* world-renowned, of world-wide fame. **-berühmtheit,** *f.* (person of) world-wide fame. **-beschreibung,** *f.* cosmography. **-bewegend,** *adj.* world-shaking *or* -shattering. **-bild,** *n.* view of life; theory of life. **-bummler,** *m.* globe-trotter. **-bund,** *m.* international union. **-bürger,** *m.* cosmopolitan; *ein kleiner -bürger ist angekommen*, a little visitor has arrived. **-bürgerlich,** *adj.* cosmopolitan. **-bürgersinn,** *m.*, **-bürgertum,** *n.* cosmopolitanism. **-dame,** *f.* woman of the world, fashionable lady. **-eislehre,** *f.* glacial cosmogony. **-enall,** *n.*, *see* **-all.** (*coll.*) **-(en)bummler,** *see* **-bummler.** **-ende,** *n.* end of the world. **-(en)-fern,** *adj.*, *see* **-fern.** **-enlehre,** *f.* cosmology. **-enraum,** *m.* (immensity *or* infinity of) space. **-entrückt,** *adj.* isolated, secluded. **-entstehung,** *f.* creation of the world, origin of the universe; *Lehre von der -entstehung*, cosmography. **-ereignis,** *n.* event of world-wide importance. **-erfahren,** *adj.*, *see* **-klug.** **-erfahrung,** *f.* experience of the world. **-erschütternd,** *adj.* world-shaking. **-flucht,** *f.* withdrawal from life, seclusion; escapism. **-fremd,** *adj.* secluded, solitary; awkward, gauche; ignorant of the world. **-früh,** *adj.* primeval. **-geist,** *m.* spirit of the age. **-geistliche(r),** *m.* secular priest. **-geistlichkeit,** *f.* secular clergy. **-gericht,** *n.* last judgement. **-gerichtshof,** *m.* international court of justice. **-geschichte,** *f.* universal history. **-gewandt,** *adj.*, *see* **-klug.** **-gürtel,** *m.* zone. **-handel,** *m.* international trade, world commerce. **-händel,** *m.pl.* political struggles. **-herrschaft,** *f.* universal empire, world dominion. **-karte,** *f.* map of the world. **-kenntnis,** *f.* knowledge of the world, savoir vivre. **-kind,** *n.* worldling, voluptuary, opportunist, hedonist. **-klug,** *adj.* worldly-wise, prudent, astute. **-klugheit,** *f.* worldy wisdom, prudence. **-körper,** *m.* heavenly body, sphere. **-krieg,** *m.* world war. **-kugel,** *f.* globe. **-lage,** *f.* general political situation, condition of affairs. **-lich,** *adj.* worldly, mundane; lay, civil, secular, temporal, profane; *-liche Güter*, temporal possessions, temporalities; *am -lichen hängen*, be fond of the things of this world; *-lich machen*, secularize; *-liche Schulen*, independent *or* undenominational schools. **-lichkeit,** *f.* secular state; civil power; worldliness, worldly-mindedness; (*pl.*) temporal rights *or* possessions. **-lichmachung,** *f.* secularization. **-ling,** *m.* worldling. **-macht,** *f.* world power. **-mann,** *m.* man of the world. **-männisch,** *adj.*, *see* **-klug.** **-markt,** *m.* the world market, international trade. **-meer,** *n.* ocean. **-meister,** *m.* world champion (*Sport*). **-meisterschaft,** *f.* world championship (*Sport*). **-müde,** *adj.* tired of life. **-politik,** *f.* world-policy, global politics. **-postverein,** *m.* Postal Union. **-priester,** *m.* secular priest. **-produktion,** *f.* world supply *or* production. **-rätsel,** *n.* riddle of the universe. **-raum,** *m.* space; universe. **-reich,** *n.* empire. **-rekord,** *m.* world record. **-ruf,** *m.* world-wide reputation. **-scheu,** *adj.* misanthropic, retiring. **-schmerz,** *m.* weariness of life, pessimistic outlook, romantic discontent. **-spannend,** *adj.*, *see* **-umfassend.** **-sprache,** *f.* international *or* world language. **-staat,** *m.* world state, great power. **-stadt,** *f.* metropolis. **-städtisch,** *adj.* metropolitan. **-stellung,** *f.* position of great importance in the world. **-teil,** *m.* continent; quarter of the globe. **-umfassend,** *adj.* world-wide, universal. **-umseg(e)lung,** *f.* circumnavigation of the globe; journey round the world. **-untergang,** *m.* end of the world. **-vergessen,** *adj.* cut off from the world, solitary. **-verkehr,** *m.* international commerce, world trade. **-verlassen,** *adj.*, **-verloren,** *adj.* solitary, lonely, isolated. **-weise(r),** *m.* philosopher. **-weisheit,** *f.* worldly wisdom. **-wende,** *f.* turning-point in world history. **-wirtschaft,** *f.* international commerce, world trade, world economic relations. **-wunder,** *n.* wonder of the world; prodigy.

wem, *Dat. of* wer; (to) whom? **-fall,** *m.* dative case.

wen, *Acc. of* wer; whom; *– man auch wählen mag*, whoever may be chosen; (*coll.*) *ich höre – rufen*, I hear someone calling. **-fall,** *m.* accusative case.

Wend-e, *f.* (-n) turning, turn; face vault (*Gymn.*); turning-point, change, new epoch *or* era. **-en,** 1. *reg. & ir.v.a. & v.n.* (*aux.* h.) turn, turn round, turn over (*hay*); turn up (*earth*); change; turn away; *viel Geld an eine S. -en*, spend a lot of money on a th.; *seine Kräfte auf eine S. -en*, apply one's strength *or* direct one's energies to a th.; *viele Mühe auf etwas -en*, devote a lot of care to s.th.; *seine Zeit auf eine S. -en*, devote one's time to s.th.; *die Augen auf eine S. -en*, glance at a th.; *bitte -en*, please turn over; *mit -ender Post*, by return of post; *ein Schiff -en*, put a ship about; *ein gewendetes Kleidungsstück*, a garment that has been turned; *see* **gewandt**; *das Segelboot -et*, the yacht goes about; *sich an einen -en*, turn *or* apply to s.o., have recourse to a p.; *um nähere Auskunft -e man sich an*, for particulars apply to; *das Gespräch -ete* or *wandte sich auf den Gegenstand*, the conversation turned upon *or* came round to the subject; *sich gegen einen -en*. turn to *or* towards a p.; turn against *or* on a p.; *sich von etwas -en*, turn away from a th., turn one's back on a th.; *sich zum Guten -en*, take a turn for the better, turn out for the best. **-egetriebe,** *n.* reversing gear. **-ehals,** *m.* wryneck (*Jynx torquilla*) (*Orn.*). **-ekreis,** *m.* tropic; turning circle (*Motor.*) **-el,** *f.* spiral, helix. **-elbaum,** *m.* axle-tree, winch. **-elsteig,** *m.* winding path. **-eltreppe,** *f.* winding stairs, spiral staircase; *Scalaria pretiosa* (*Mollusc.*). **-epflug,** *m.* swivel-plough. **-epunkt,** *m.* turning-point, critical moment, crisis; solstitial point (*Astr.*), point of inflexion (*Geom.*). **-er,** *m.* turnspit; commutator (*Elec.*), rotator (muscle) (*Anat.*). **-ewinkel,** *m.* angle of yaw (*Naut.*) **-ig,** *adj.* manœuvrable, manageable, easily managed; nimble, agile; (*fig.*) versatile; *ein -iges Boot*, a handy boat. **-igkeit,** *f.* manœuvrability, adaptability, manageableness. **-ung,** *f.* turn, sinuosity, turning, winding, volte (*Fenc.*); change, turning-point, crisis; turn of expression, phrase, saying, idiomatic expression; wheeling (*Mil.*); going about (*Naut.*); *einer S. eine andere -ung geben*, give a new turn *or* twist to a matter; *eine andere –ung nehmen*, take a new turn, (*coll.*, *fig.*) go off on another tack; *glückliche –ung*, favourable turn; *–ung zur Besserung*, change *or* turn for the better.

wenig, *adj.* little, not much; slightly; (*pl.*) few, a few; (*usually undecl. in sing.*; *may be undecl. even in pl. when not preceded by art. or pron.*, *and esp. when governed by prep.*); *ein –*, a little, some; *mit ein – Geduld*, with a little patience; *mit ein – gutem Willen*, with a little good will; *ein klein –*, a tiny bit, just a little; *mein –es* or *das –e, was ich habe*, the little I have; *– Gutes*, not much that is good; *– Geld*, little *or* not much money; *ein – Geld*, some *or* (just) a little money; *sein –(es) Geld*, the little money he has; *die –en*, the few (*persons*, *etc.*); *die –en Male, daß*, the few times that; *in –(en) Worten*, in a few words; *in diesen –en Worten*, in these few words; *in nicht –(en) andern Ländern*, in not a few *or* in many other countries; *in den –en andern Ländern*, in few remaining countries; *einige –e*, a few, some few, a small quantity; *um einiges –e*, by a small amount; *ein – schneller*, a little quicker; *eine – bekannte Tatsache*, a little-known fact; *es fehlte –, so wäre ich*, I was nearly; *eben so – als*, as little as; *so – auch*, however little; *– gut*, not very good; *ich war nicht – überrascht*, I was not a little surprised; *er ist so – arm, daß . . .*, so far from being poor. . . . **–er,** *compar. adj.* less, fewer; *nichts –er als*, anything but, nothing less than; *nicht –er als*, no less than; *um so –er*, all the less; *sechs –er eins*, six minus one. **–keit,** *f.* the few, the little, small quantity; littleness, smallness, trifle; *meine –keit*, my humble self, your humble servant. **–st,** *super. adj.* least; *nicht zum –sten*, last not least; *die –sten*, only very few (people). **–stens,** *adv.* at least, at all events.

wenn, 1. *conj.* when, whenever; if, in case, provided; *– die Zeit da ist, müssen wir fort*, when the time comes we must be off; *– Fritz vor mir stirbt, so wird mir das Haus gehören*, if Fred should die before me, the house will be mine; *– ich es wüßte, würde ich es Ihnen sagen*, if I knew it, I should tell you; *– man ihn hört, sollte man glauben . . .*, to hear him, one would think . . .; *– ich Ihnen die Wahrheit sagen soll*, to tell you the truth; *allemal –*, whenever; *als –*, as if; *nicht als – das nicht häufig vorkäme*, it is not as if it were a rare occurrence; *– auch*, although, even if; *– es auch noch so wenig ist*, little though it be, if it be ever so little; *außer –*, unless, except when *or* if; *– etwa*, if by chance; *– gleich*, see *– auch*; *– ich es gleich gesehen habe*, although I have seen it; *– man kein Narr ist*, unless one is a fool; *– nicht*, if not, unless, except when *or* if, but that; *– schon*, even so; what of it! what does it matter? see also *– auch*; *– er schon nicht viel gelernt hat*, even if he has not learned much; (*coll.*) *– schon, denn schon*, what must be, must be; it cannot be helped; *selbst –*, even if *or* though, although, supposing that, granted that; *selbst – ich es könnte*, even if I could; *und –*, see *selbst –*; *wie –*, see *als –*. 2. *n. ohne – und Aber*, without 'ifs' or 'buts', without shilly-shally, hesitation, indecision *or* vacillation, unreservedly. **–gleich, –schon,** *conj.*, though, although.

Wenzel, *m.* (-s, –) knave, jack (*Cards*).

wer, 1. *inter. pron.* who? which? *– ist größer, er oder sein Bruder?* which is the taller, he or his brother? *– von euch?* which of you? *– ist da?* who is there? *– da?* who goes there? *– ander als*, who else but; *– bist du, der du . . .?* who are you that . . .? (*coll.*) *– kommt denn alles?* who are all these people? 2. *rel. pron.* who, he who *or* that; *– auch*, who(so)ever; *– es auch sei*, whoever it may be; *– nur* or *auch immer*, whoever. 3. *indef. pron.* (*coll.*) somebody, some one, anyone; *ist –, der's leugnen will*, is there anyone who will deny it; *es ist – an der Tür*, there is somebody at the door. **–da,** *n.*, **–daruf,** *m.* sentry's challenge. **–fall,** *m.* nominative case.

werb-en, 1. *ir.v.a.* recruit, enlist, levy, enrol. 2. *v.n.* (*aux.* h.) (*um einen* or *etwas*) sue (for), solicit, woo, court, aspire (to), strive (after); *um ein Mädchen –en*, seek a girl's hand (in marriage), woo, court, propose to a girl; *für eine S. –en*, canvass *or* make propaganda for a th.; *einen zu* or *für etwas –en*, enlist a p.'s sympathies for a th., win a p. over to a th.; *zum Soldatendienst –en*, recruit for the army; *–endes Kapital*, productive capital. **–eabteilung,** *f.* publicity department. **–eamt,** *n.* recruiting-office. **–ebrief,** *m.* (*C.L.*) sales letter. **–efilm,** *m.* advertising film. **–egewohnheit,** *f.* courting habit (*of animals or birds*). **–ekosten,** *pl.* advertising expenses. **–ekräftig,** *adj.* of great publicity value. **–eleiter,** *m.* advertising manager. **–emittel,** *n.* means of propaganda, publicity resources. **–enummer,** *f.* complimentary copy. **–eoffizier,** *m.* recruiting-officer. **–er,** *m.* recruiting-officer; wooer, suitor; proselytizer, propagandist. **–eredner,** *m.* propagandist. **–eschrift,** *f.* advertising pamphlet. **–etätigkeit,** *f.* propaganda. **–etrommel,** *f.*; *die –etrommel rühren*, rouse enthusiasm (for), make propaganda (for), (*coll.*) push, boost. **–ewesen,** *n.* publicity. **–ung,** *f.* courtship, wooing; solicitation, propaganda, publicity; levying, recruiting. **–ungskosten,** *f.pl.* outlay on publicity, advertising expenses.

werde-n, 1. *ir.v.n.* (*aux.* s.) (*imp.* wurde *or* (*Poet.*) ward) (*p.p.* geworden *or* (*Poet.*) worden) become; come to be, grow, get, turn out, prove; come into existence; *alt –n*, grow old; *es muß anders –n*, there must be a change, things must change; *Arzt –n*, become a doctor; *daraus wird nichts*, nothing will come of it, it will come to nothing; *aus ihm wird nichts*, he will not amount to much, he will come to no good; *aus nichts wird nichts*, nothing comes from nothing; (*coll.*) *glaubst du, daß aus der S. was wird* or *was –n wird?* do you think anything will come of it? *was soll aus ihm –n?* what will become of him; *was würde daraus –n?* what would be the consequence? *wird's bald?* will you soon be done? will it soon be ready? hurry up, I am waiting; *mir wurde bange*, I began to feel afraid; *bekannt –n*, become well-known *or* notorious; *mit einem bekannt –n*, make a p.'s acquaintance; *blind –n*, go blind; *böse –n*, grow angry; *einig –n*, agree, come to an understanding; *wie wird die Ernte –n?* how will the harvest turn out? *frech –n*, get cheeky; *was wird mir dafür?* what shall I get out of *or* by it? *etwas gewahr –n*, become aware of s.th.; *es wird hell*, it is getting light; *er ist katholisch geworden*, he has turned Catholic; *klug –n*, grow wise; *was nicht ist, kann noch –n*, what is not yet may yet be; *er ist krank geworden*, he has fallen ill; *alle Tage, die Gott –n läßt*, every day which God grants us; (*B.*) *es – Licht! und es ward Licht*, let there be light! and there was light; *man weiß nicht, was noch –n soll*, there is no knowing what might happen; *Mutter –n*, be going to have a child; *Recht soll euch –n*, justice shall be done you; *satt –n*, eat one's fill; *es wird mir schwach*, I feel faint; *mir wird schwer ums Herz*, my heart grows heavy; *die Tage –n länger*, the days grow longer; *man möchte des Teufels –n*, it is enough to drive one mad; *es wird schon –n*, it will surely turn out all right; *die S. wird –n*, the matter will be all right *or* is getting on nicely; *das Wetter wird kalt*, the weather turns cold; (*coll.*) *der Kranke wird wieder –n*, the patient will recover; *was will er –n?* what is he going to be *or* does he want to be? *es wird Zeit*, the time is drawing near, it will soon be time; *die Zeit wird mir lang*, time hangs heavy with *or* on me; *zu etwas –n*, change, turn (in)to; *zum Gelächter –n*, become a laughing-stock; *es wird mir zur Last*, it becomes a burden to me; *zum Mann –n*, grow into a man; *die Ausnahme wird zur Regel*, the exception is becoming the rule; *es wird mir zum Rätsel*, it gets mysterious, it begins to puzzle me; *der Schnee wird zu Wasser*, the snow is turning to water; *alle seine Pläne sind zu Wasser geworden*, all his plans have fallen through, gone up in smoke *or* come to nothing; *alle seine Pläne wurden zuschanden*, all his cunning plans were foiled. 2. *As auxiliary* **(a)** (*forming the future and conditional tenses*) shall, will; should, would; *ich – es ihm gleich sagen*, I shall tell him at once; *er würde es mir gesagt haben*, he would have told me; *wo – ich nur den Schlüssel haben?* where can I have put the key? *es wird ihm doch nichts passiert sein?* I hope nothing has happened to him, he surely will not have come to any harm; *wart! euch werd' ich (kommen)!* wait! you will catch it! **(b)** (*forming the passive voice, p.p.* worden) be, is, are, *etc.*; *ich – geliebt*, I am loved; *ich bin geliebt worden*, I have been loved; *das Haus wird eben gebaut*, the house is just being built; *die Glocke wurde geläutet*, the bell was rung; *–nde Mutter*, expectant mother. 3. *n.* growing, developing, development; evolution, genesis, origin, rise, growth, formation; *noch im –n sein*, be in embryo; *große Dinge sind im –n*, great things are in preparation. **–gang,** *m.* development, evolution, growth, process.

Werder, *m.* (-s, –) river island, islet, eyot, ait, holm.

werf–en, 1. *ir.v.a.* & *n.* (*aux.* h.) throw, cast, fling, toss, pitch, hurl, project; bring forth young; *Anker –en*, cast anchor; *die Augen auf eine S. –en*, cast a glance at a th.; *etwas beiseite –en*, toss *or* fling a th. aside; *Blasen –en*, give off bubbles; *durcheinander –en*, see *untereinander –en*; *Falten –en*, pucker, wrinkle, hang in folds; *einen Gegner –en*, throw one's opponent; *den Feind über den Haufen –en*, overthrow the enemy; *alle Pläne über den Haufen –en*, upset all the plans; *einen aus dem Hause –en*, throw *or* fling a p. out; *Junge –en*, bring forth young; *ein Kalb –en*, calve; *ich warf mich in meine Kleider*, I threw my clothes on; *einem etwas an den Kopf –en*, fling s.th. in a p.'s teeth; *die Fl'nte ins Korn –en*, throw up the sponge, lose heart; *das Los –en*, cast lots (*über eine S.*, for a th.); *Schatten –en*, cast a shadow; *mit dem Schinken* or *der Wurst nach der Speckseite –en*, throw good money after bad; *Strahlen –en*, emit rays, beam forth; *alles in einen Topf –en*, treat all things alike, make no distinctions; *mit Geld um sich –en*, throw one's money about; *mit Beleidigungen um sich –en*, insult people right and left; *mit französischen Brocken um sich –en*, show off by using French phrases; *untereinander –en*, jumble up, throw into disorder *or* confusion; *einen Verdacht auf einen –en*, throw suspicion on a p.; *Wellen –en*, break in waves; *Sie –en zuerst*, you have the first throw (*Dice*). 2. *v.r.* warp, get warped, become distorted; throw o.s. (into), apply o.s. (to); *sich auf etwas –en*, give o.s. up to, fling o.s. into, apply o.s. to a th., take up s.th. energetically *or* vigorously; *sich in die Brust –en*, swagger, strut; *sich ins Zeug –en*, exert o.s.; *sich im Bett hin und her –en*, toss about in bed. **–er,** *m.* mortar, rocket projector (*Mil.*).

[1]**Werft,** *f.* (-en), (*dial.*) **–e,** *f.* (-en), (*Austr. dial.*) **–,** *n.* (-(e)s, -e) wharf, dock, dockyard; ship(-building)-yard, aerodrome workshops. **–arbeiter,** *m.* dock labourer, docker. **–besitzer,** *m.* wharfinger. **–geld,** *n.* wharfage.

[2]**Werft,** *m.* (-(e)s, -e) warp (*Weav.*).

Werg, *n.* tow; oakum. **–en,** *adj.* hempen.

Wergeld, *n.* (*archaic*) mulct for homicide, weregeld.

Werk, *n.* (-(e)s, -e) work, labour; action, act, deed, performance; job, undertaking, enterprise; production, workmanship, composition; mechanism, works, clockwork; workshops, works, factory; publication, book, opus; (*pl.*) forts, fortifications; *am – sein*, be at work, be on the job; *ans – gehen*, *sich ans – machen*, *ans – schreiten*, (*coll.*) go to it, set to work; *Hand ans – legen*, set about a job, take a job in hand; *es ist etwas im –e*, there is something in the wind *or* s.th. going on; *ins – setzen*, set going, bring about, put into practice, effect, accomplish; *das – lobt den Meister*, a man is known by his work; *zu –e gehen*, set about (a th.), begin (a th.). **–abteilung,** *f.* shop, bay (*in a factory*). **–bank,** *f.* work-bench. **–blei,** *n.* crude lead. **–eltag,** *m.* (*archaic*), see **–tag. –en,** *v.n.* & *a.* work perfunctorily. **–führer,** *m.* foreman, overseer. **–gemeinschaft,** *f.* working-party. **–heilige(r),** *m.* sanctimonious person, hypocrite. **–heiligkeit,** *f.* sanctimoniousness, outward piety; hypocrisy. **–holz,** *n.* building timber. **–küche,** *f.* factory canteen. **–leute,** *pl.* workpeople, workmen, (*coll.*) hands. **–meister,** *m.*, see **–führer**; (*dial.*) master builder. **–sanlage,** *f.* factory buildings, industrial plant. **–satz,** *m.* set of type for book-work (*Typ.*). **–seide,** *f.* floss silk. **–sgemeinschaft,** see **–gemeinschaft. –skamerad,** *m.* fellow workman. **–sleiter,** *m.* factory manager. **–spionage,** *f.* industrial espionage. **–statt,** *f.*, **–stätte,** *f.*, **–stelle,** *f.* workshop, place of work. **–stein,** *m.* freestone. **–stellig machen,** accomplish, effect, bring about. **–stoff,** *m.* raw material. **–stoffprüfung,** *f.* material-testing. **–stück,** *n.* worked article; dressed stone. **–student,** *m.* a student who earns his living. **–sverband,** *m.* company union. **–tag,** *m.* working day, week-day. **–täglich,** *adj.* week-day, everyday, commonplace. **–tags,** *adv.* on week-days. **–tätig,** *adj.* active, working, practical; *–tätige Bevölkerung*, working classes; *–tätige Liebe*, charity; *–tätige Unterstützung*, active support. **–tätigkeit,** *f.* activity, industry. **–unterricht,** *m.* practical instruction. **–zeug,** *n.* tool, implement, (*fig.*) instrument, organ. **–zeugmaschinen,** *f.pl.* machine-tools.

Wermut, *m.* wormwood; vermouth; absinthe; (*fig.*) bitterness, gall.

Werre, *f.* (-n) (*dial.*) mole-cricket (*Gryllotalpa*) (*Ent.*); sty(e) (*in one's eye*).

wert, 1. *adj.* (*with Dat.*) dear, valued, honoured, esteemed, estimable; (*with Gen.*) worth, valuable; worthy; *er ist mir lieb und –*, he is very dear to me; *Sie und Ihre –e Familie*, you and your family; *wie ist Ihr –er Name?* may I ask your name? to whom have I the honour of speaking? (*C.L.*) *Ihr –es Schreiben*, your esteemed favour; *nichts – sein*, be worthless, be no good; *das ist nicht der Rede –*, that is not worth speaking of; (*coll.*) don't mention it; *das ist nicht der Mühe –*, that is not worth the trouble; *er ist es nicht –, daß man . . .*, he does not deserve . . .; *keinen Schuß Pulver –*, *keinen* (*roten*) *Heller –*, not worth a straw, pin *or* fig; *einer ist so viel – wie der andre*, one is as good as the other; *ebensoviel – wie*, equivalent to; *das ist viel –*, that is of great use, that is very valuable; *er ist seine 100,000 Mark –*, he is worth 100,000 marks. 2. *m.* worth, use, value; price, rate; appreciation, merit, importance, stress; standard (*of coin*); valence, atomicity (*Chem.*); *pl.* data; *– erhalten*, value received (*on bills of exchange*); *fester –*, fixed quantity (*Math.*); (*C.L.*) *der – in Faktura*, value as per invoice; *gleicher –*, equivalent; (*C.L.*) *in gleichem –e*, at par; *großen – auf eine S. legen*, set great value on *or* store by a th., attach great importance to a th.; *größter* (*kleinster*) *–*, maximum (minimum) value; *im –e von*, at a price of, to the value of; (*C.L.*) *– bei Verfall*, value when due; (*C.L.*) *– in Waren*, value received in goods. **–achten** *v.a.* (*sep.*), see **–schätzen. –angabe,** *f.*, **–betrag,** *m.* declaration of value, declared value. **–bemessung,** *f.* standardization. **–beständig,** *adj.* stable, of fixed value. **–bestimmung,** *f.* determination of value *or* valence. **–brief,** *m.* letter containing valuables, registered letter. **–en,** *v.a.* value, estimate, appraise, appreciate. **–ermittelung,** *f.* tax assessment. **–ersatz,** *m.* equivalent. **–gegenstände,** *m.pl.* valuables. **–geschätzt,** *adj.* esteemed, valued. **–ig,** *adj. suffix* of . . . value; valent, atomic (*Chem.*); e.g. *gleich–ig*, of equal value, equivalent; *minder–ig*, of inferior quality. **–igkeit,** *f.* atomicity, valence (*Chem.*) **–los,** *adj.* worthless; undeserving. **–losigkeit,** *f.* worthlessness. **–marke,** *f.*, see **–zeichen. –maß,** *n.* standard. **–messer,** *m.* standard of value, criterion. **–minderung,** *f.* depreciation. **–paket,** *n.* (registered) parcel containing valuables. **–papier,** *n.* bond, security; scrip. **–sachen,** *f.pl.* valuables. **–schätzen,** *v.a.* value *or* esteem highly. **–schätzung,** *f.* esteem, estimation, appreciation, regard. **–schrift,** *f.* (*Swiss dial.*), see **–papier. –sendung,** *f.* consignment of valuables. **–ung,** *f.* valuing, appraising; valuation, estimation, appreciation. **–urteil,** *n.* value judgement. **–verhältnis,** *n.* comparative *or* relative value, ratio of values. **–verringerung,** *f.* diminution in value. **–voll,** *adj.* valuable, precious. **–zeichen,** *n.* paper money; postage-stamp; coupon, voucher. **–zoll,** *m.* ad valorem duty. **–zuwachssteuer,** *f.* increment-value tax.

Werwolf, *m.* werewolf.

wes, (*archaic*) see **wessen**; (*B.*) *– das Herz voll ist, des gehet der Mund über*, out of the abundance of the heart the mouth speaketh. **–fall,** *m.* genitive case. **–halb, –wegen,** *adv.* & *conj.* why, wherefore, on account of which; therefore, so; *ich traf ihn nicht, –halb ich weiter reiste*, I did not meet him, so I went on.

Wesen, 1. *n.* (-s, –) reality, substance, essence; being, creature, living thing, organism; state, condition; nature, character, property, intrinsic virtue; conduct, demeanour, air, way, bearing; (*coll.*) bustle, fuss, bother, noise, row; (*often in compounds*) organization, system, arrangement, disposition, concern; e.g. *Finanz–*, financial affairs *or* matters; *Rettungs–*, rescue service; *das gelehrte –*, the learned world; *gesetztes –*, quiet bearing; *gezwungenes –*, affected air; *das höchste –*, the Supreme Being; *sein – mißfällt mir*, his manner displeases me; *das gehört zum – der S.*, that is the essence of the th.; (*coll.*) *sein – treiben*, go on in one's own way, be up to one's mischief; (*coll.*) *viel –s von etwas machen*, make a fuss about s.th.; (*coll.*) *nicht viel –s mit einem machen*, treat a p. unceremoniously. 2. *v.n.* (*Poet.*) live, work, be. **–haft,** *adj.* real, substantial; characteristic. **–heit,** *f.* spirit, essence, substance, decisive *or* significant factors. **–los,** *adj.* incorporeal, unsubstantial, unreal, shadowy; insignificant, trivial. **–losigkeit,** *f.* unreality. **–sähnlich,** *adj.*, *see* **–sgleich. –seigen,** *adj.* characteristic. **–seinheit,** *f.* consubstantiality (*Relig.*). **–seins,** *adj.*, *see* **–sgleich. –sfremd,** *adj.* incompatible. **–sgleich,** *adj.* homogeneous, identical, consubstantial. **–sgleichheit,** *f.* identity. **–slehre,** *f.* ontology. **–sschau,** *f.* phenomenology. **–szug,** *m.* characteristic feature. **–tlich,** *adj.* essential, real, substantial, material, important, vital, significant, fundamental, intrinsic, principal; *das –tliche*, that which is essential, the vital point, the essential thing *or* factor; *–tlicher Inhalt eines Buches*, the substance of a book; *im –tlichen*, essentially.

weshalb, *see under* **wes.**

Wesir, *m.* (-s, -e) vizier.

Wespe, *f.* (-n) wasp. **–nbein,** *n.* sphenoid bone. **–nnest,** *n.* (*coll.*) *in ein –nnest stechen* or *greifen*, put one's foot into it, stir up a hornet's nest. **–nstich,** *m.* wasp sting.

wessen, *Gen. sing. of* wer *and* was, whose, of which; *in – Hause wohnst du?* in whose house do you live? *– klagt man dich an?* what are you charged with? *– er mich anklagt*, what he accused me of.

West, *m.* west; (*Poet.*) (*pl.* -e) west wind. **–en,** *m.* the west, the Occident; *nach –en zu, gegen –en*, westward, towards the west. **–europäisch,** *adj.* Western European; *–europäische Zeit*, Greenwich time. **–isch,** *adj.* Mediterranean (*Ethn.*). **–lich,** 1. *adj.* west(ern), westerly, occidental. 2. *adv.* westward; *–lich von*, to the west of. **–mächte,** *f.pl.* Western Powers. **–wärts,** *adv.* westward. **–wind,** *m.* west(erly) wind.

Weste, *f.* (-n) waistcoat, vest; *er hat eine reine, saubere* or *weiße –*, he has not a blot on his scutcheon; (*coll.*) *feste auf die –!* let him have it. **–ntasche,** *f.* vest- *or* waistcoat-pocket.

weswegen, *see under* **wes.**

wett, *adj.* (*only used with* sein *or* werden) equal, even; *nun sind wir –*, now we are quits. **–bewerb,** *m.* competition, contest. **–bewerber,** *m.* competitor, contestant. **–e,** *f.* (-n) bet, wager; rivalry; *eine –e eingehen*, make a bet; *was gilt die –e?* what do you bet? *die –e gilt!* done! agreed! *um die –e*, in emulation, in rivalry; *sie boten mir um die –e ihre Dienste an*, they vied with one another in their offers of assistance; *um* (*Austr. dial. also* in) *die –e laufen*, race (against) s.o., run a race. **–eifer,** *m.* emulation, rivalry, competition. **–eiferer,** *m.* rival, competitor. **–eifern,** *v.n.* (*insep.*) (*aux.* h.) emulate, vie (with), contend (with); *mit einem um etwas –eifern*, compete with s.o. for s.th. **–en,** *v.a. & n.* (*aux.* h.) bet, wager, stake, bet on, back (*a horse, etc.*); *es läßt sich Hundert gegen Eins –en, daß* . . ., it is a hundred to one that . . .; *auf eine S. –en*, bet on s.th.; *für einen –en*, back a p.; *so haben wir nicht gewettet*, we did not bargain for that. **–fahren,** 1. *ir.v.n.* (*sep.*) (*aux.* s.) race. 2. *n.* racing. **–fahrt,** *f.* motor-race, cycle-race, boat-race. **–fliegen,** *n.*, **–flug,** *m.* air-race. **–kampf,** *m.* contest, match; prize-fight. **–kämpfer,** *m.* champion, athlete; antagonist, rival; prize-fighter. **–lauf,** *m.* race. **–laufen,** *ir.v.n.* (*sep.*) (*aux.* s.) run a race, race. **–läufer,** *m.* runner. **–machen,** *v.a.* (*sep.*) square *or* balance (*a th.*), make good, make up for make amends for; *wie soll ich ihm das je –machen?* how am I ever to make it up to him? **–rennen,** *n.* racing, race. **–rudern,** 1. *v.n.* (*sep.*) (*aux.* s.) row in a race. 2. *n.* boat-race. **–rüsten,** *n.* armaments race. **–schwimmen,** *n.* swimming contest. **–segeln,** *n.* regatta. **–spiel,** *n.* match; tournament. **–streit,** *m.* emulation; contest, competition, match.

Wetter, *n.* (-s, –) weather; bad weather, storm; air, atmosphere, firedamp (*Min.*); *ein – zieht sich zusammen*, a storm is gathering; *es ist schönes –*, it is a fine day, the weather is fine; *alle –! – noch* (*ein*)*mal!* good gracious! good heavens! my word! by Jove! confound it! damnation! *die Grube hat böse –*, the mine is badly ventilated; *schlagende –*, firedamp. **–ansage,** *f.* weather report (*on the radio*). **–beobachter,** *m.* meteorologist. **–bericht,** *m.* meteorological report; weather-forecast. **–beständig,** *adj.*, *see* **–fest. –dach,** *n.* canopy, eaves, shelter (*Build.*). **–dienst,** *m.* meteorological *or* weather service. **–fahne,** *f.* weather-vane. **–fest,** *adj.* weather-proof, hardened *or* immune to exposure. **–führung,** *f.* ventilation of mines. **–funk,** *m.* radio weather-forecasts. **–glas,** *n.* barometer. **–hahn,** *m.* weather-cock. **–karte,** *f.* meteorological chart. **–kunde,** *f.* meteorology. **–kundig,** *adj.* weather-wise. **–lage,** *f.* weather conditions, atmospheric conditions. **–leuchten,** 1. *v.n. & imp.* (*insep.*) (*aux.* h.); *es –leuchtet*, it lightens, there is summer lightning. 2. *n.* summer lightning. **–loch,** *n.* storm-centre. **–mantel,** *m.* cape, raincoat. **–maschine,** *f.* mine-ventilator. **–meldung,** *f.*, **–nachrichten,** *f.pl.* weather report. **–n,** 1. *v.n.* (*aux.* h. & s.) & *imp.* thunder and lightning, be stormy; curse and swear, storm, bluster. **–prognose,** *f.* weather-forecast. **–säule,** *f.* whirlwind, tornado, cyclone. **–schacht,** *m.* air-shaft (*Min.*). **–schaden,** *m.* storm damage; damage from exposure. **–scheide,** *f.* area over which storms break. **–schutz,** *m.* protection against exposure. **–seite,** *f.* weather-side. **–stein,** *m.* belemnite (*Geol.*). **–stelle,** *f.* weather station. **–strahl,** *m.* flash of lightning. **–sturz,** *m.* sudden fall of temperature, change in the weather. **–tür,** *f.* ventilation trap (*Min.*). **–umschlag,** *m.*, *see* **–wechsel. –voraussage,** *f.*, **–vorhersage,** *f.* weather-forecast. **–wart,** *m.* meteorological observer. **–warte,** *f.* meteorological *or* weather station. **–wechsel,** *m.* change of weather. **–wendisch,** *adj.* fickle, capricious, changeable. **–winkel,** *m.* storm-centre. **–wolke,** *f.* storm-cloud, thunder-cloud. **–zeichen,** *n.* sign of approaching storm.

wetz-en, 1. *v.a.* whet, grind, sharpen. 2. *v.n.* (*aux.* h.) brush (against). **–stahl,** *m.* honing steel. **–stein,** *m.* whetstone, hone.

wich, wiche, *see* **weichen.**

Wichs, *m.* (-es, -e) (German) students' garb; (*sl.*) glad rags; *sich in – werfen*, deck o.s. out; *in vollem* (*höchstem*) *–*, decked out, in full dress, in one's best clothes. **–bürste,** *f.* blacking-brush. **–e,** *f.* blacking, boot-polish; (*sl.*) thrashing, tanning. **–en,** *v.a.* black, polish (*boots, etc.*); (*dial.*) wax (*thread, a floor, etc.*); (*sl.*) thrash, tan; *gewichst*, *adj.* (*coll.*) sly, cunning. **–er,** *m.* bootblack; (*coll.*) awkward situation, jam, hole, tricky matter. (*coll.*) **–ier,** *m.* bootblack. **–lappen,** *m.* polishing cloth. **–zeug,** *v.n.* shoe-cleaning utensils.

Wicht, *m.* (-(e)s, -e) creature, little child, urchin, brat, chit, wight; *armer –*, poor wretch; *grober –*, rough customer. **–el,** *m. & n.* (-els, –), **–elmännchen,** *n.* brownie, pixie, goblin.

Wichte, *f.* specific gravity.

wichtig, *adj.* weighty; important, significant, momentous, serious; *– tun, sich – machen*, give o.s. airs. **–keit,** *f.* weight, weightiness; importance, significance, moment, consequence. **–tuer,** *m.* braggart, pompous ass. **–tuerei,** *f*, bragging, boasting, self-importance, pomposity.

Wicke, *f.* (-n) vetch (*Vicia*) (*Bot.*); *in die –n gehen*, (*coll.*) get lost; come down in the world.

Wickel, *m.* (-s, –) & *s.* (-n) roll; wrapping, wrapper; curl-paper; distaff-full (*of flax*); hair, wig; wet compress, ice-pack, hot fomentation (*Med.*); (*sl.*)

einen beim – kriegen, catch hold of *or* collar a p. **–band,** *n.* baby's binder, swaddling-band. **–bär,** *m.* kinkajou (*Potus flavus*) (*Zool.*). **–blatt,** *n.* wrapper, outside leaf (*of cigars*). **–gamaschen,** *f.pl.* puttees. **–kind,** *n.* baby in swaddling *or* long clothes. **–maschine,** *f.* winder (*for wool, etc.*); lap-machine (*Spin.*). **–n,** *v.a.* roll, roll up, coil, wind, twist; wrap (up), put (*hair*) in curlers; dress (*a baby*); roll *or* make (*cigarettes*); *zu einem* or *in ein Knäuel –n*, roll into a ball; *man kann ihn um den Finger –n*, you can twist him round your little finger; *sich aus dem Handel –n*, wriggle out of the difficulty; (*sl.*) *schief gewickelt*, in error, much mistaken. **–puppe,** *f.* baby-doll. **–ranke,** *f.* tendril, runner, cirrus. **–rankig,** *adj.* cirrate (*Bot.*). **–schwanz,** *m.* prehensile tail (*Zool.*) **–tuch,** *n.* wrapper; baby's binder. **–zeug,** *n.* baby-clothes, swaddling-clothes.

Wick–ler, *m.* (leaf-)roller moth (*Tortricidae*) (*Ent.*). **–lung,** *f.* wrapping, casing, winding, envelopment.

Widder, *m.* (-s, –) ram; battering-ram; Aries (*Astr.*). **–chen,** *n.*, **–schwärmer,** *m.* burnet-moth (*Zygaenidae*) (*Ent.*).

wider, 1. *prep.* (*Acc.*) against, contrary to, in opposition to, versus; – *Willen*, against one's will, unwillingly; *das Für und –*, the pros and cons; *hin und –*, there and back again, to and fro. 2. *insep. or sep. prefix*, counter-, contra-, anti-, re-, with-. **–borstig,** *adj.* (*coll.*) obstinate, perverse. **–druck,** *m.* counter-pressure, reaction (*Phys.*); counter-proof (*Engr.*). **–fahren,** *ir.v.n.* (*insep.*) (*3rd pers. only, with Dat.*) (*aux.* s.) happen, occur, befall, fall (*to a p.*); *mir ist viel Ehre –fahren*, great honour has been done me; *das kann Ihnen auch –fahren*, the same may happen to you; *einem –fahren lassen*, mete out to a p.; *jedem sein Recht –fahren lassen*, give everyone his due. **–haarig,** *adj.* (*dial.*) cross-grained; stubborn, perverse, refractory. **–haken,** *m.* barb. **–hakig,** *adj.* barbed, glochidiate. **–hall,** *m.* (-(e)s, -e) echo, reverberation; (*fig.*) response. **–hallen,** *v.n.* (*sep.* & *insep.*) echo, resound (*von*, with). **–halt,** *m.* support, prop, hold. **–haltig,** *adj.* resisting, resistant. **–handlung,** *f.* (*Swiss dial.*) contravention. **–klage,** *f.* counter-plea (*Law*). **–lager,** *n.* abutment, buttress, pier. **–legbar,** *adj.* refutable. **–legen,** *v.a.* (*insep.*) refute, confute, disprove, negative; *seine eignen Worte –legen*, give the lie to one's own words. **–legung,** *f.* refutation. **–lich,** *adj.* offensive, repugnant, loathsome, unsavoury, nauseous, nauseating, obnoxious, disgusting, repulsive. **–lichkeit,** *f* loathsomeness, repulsiveness. **–n,** *v.imp.* (*aux.* h.); *es widert mich*, it is repugnant to me, I loathe it. **–natürlich,** *adj.* unnatural, artificial, monstrous. **–part,** *m.* (-(e)s, -e) adversary, opponent; opposition; *einem –part halten*, oppose a p. **–prall,** *m.* rebound, reflection. **–raten,** *ir.v.a.* (*insep.*) (*einem etwas*) dissuade (a p.) from (*a th.*), advise (*s.o.*) against (*s.th.*). **–rechtlich,** *adj.* unjust, unlawful, unrighteous; illegal; *sich* (*Dat.*) *–rechtlich aneignen*, misappropriate, usurp. **–rede,** *f.* contradiction, objection; *ohne –rede*, unquestionably. **–reden,** *v.n.* (*insep.*), *see* **–sprechen.** **–rist,** *m.* (-es, -e) withers (*Vet.*). **–ristschaden,** *m.* saddle gall (*Vet.*). **–ruf,** *m.* recantation, revocation, disavowal, countermand, disclaimer (*Law*); *bis auf –ruf*, until recalled, countermanded *or* cancelled. **–rufbar,** *adj.*, *see* **–ruflich.** **–rufen,** *ir.v.a.* (*insep.*) revoke, recant, retract, withdraw, countermand, disavow. **–ruflich,** *adj.* revocable; uncertain (*tenure of office, etc.*). **–sacher,** *m.* adversary, opponent. **–schein,** *m.* reflection. **–scheinen,** *ir.v.n.* (*aux.* h.) (*sep.*) be reflected. **–see,** *f.* backwash. **–setzen,** *v.r.* (*insep.*) (*Dat.*) oppose, resist, combat, act in opposition (to), disobey (*the law*). **–setzlich,** *adj.* refractory, insubordinate; disobedient. **–setzlichkeit,** *f.* insubordination, recalcitrance. **–sinn,** *m.* opposite sense; contradiction, paradox, absurdity, nonsense. **–sinnig,** *adj.* contrary to common-sense, flying in the face of reason, absurd, nonsensical, paradoxical, contradictory. **–spenstig,** *adj.* refractory, recalcitrant, rebellious, unmanageable, restive, unruly, stubborn, obstinate; *die –spenstige*, shrew. **–spenstigkeit,** *f.* recalcitrance, refractoriness, obstinacy. **–spiegeln,** 1. *v.a.* (*sep.*) reflect, mirror. 2. *v.r.* be reflected. **–spiel,** *n.* reverse, contrary, opposite, opposition; *einem das –spiel halten*, act in opposition to a p. **–sprechen,** *ir.v.a.* & *n.* (*insep.*) (*aux.* h.) (*Dat.*) contradict; be at variance with, conflict with, gainsay, oppose; *diese Sätze –sprechen einander*, these propositions are contradictory. **–sprechend,** *adj.* contradictory, conflicting, contrary (to). **–spruch,** *m.* contradiction; opposition; disagreement, conflict; *einen –spruch beseitigen*, reconcile a contradiction; *im –spruch stehend mit* or *zu*, incompatible with. **–spruch(s)voll,** *adj.* (self-)contradictory; inconsistent. **–stand,** *m.* opposition, resistance; rheostat (*Elec.*); *–stand leisten*, offer resistance, resist; *hinhaltender –stand*, delaying action (*Mil.*); *induzierter –stand*, induced drag (*Av.*); *schädlicher –stand*, parasitic drag (*Av.*). **–standsbewegung,** *f.* resistance movement (*Pol.*). **–standsfähig,** *adj.* hardy, resistant. **–standsfähigkeit,** *f.*, **–standskraft,** *f.* hardiness, power of resistance, stability; load-bearing capacity. **–standsherd,** *m.*, **–standskessel,** *m.* pocket of resistance (*Mil.*). **–standsmesser,** *m.* ohm meter, megger. **–standsnest,** *n.*, *see* **–standsherd.** **–standsschaltung,** *f.* resistance (box), shunt (*Elec.*). **–stehen,** *ir.v.n.* (*insep.*) (*aux.* h.) (*Dat.*) oppose, resist, withstand; be repugnant to, (*coll.*) go against the grain; *nicht –stehen*, succumb to. **–streben,** 1. *v.n.* (*insep.*) (*aux.* h.) (*Dat.*) resist, oppose, struggle against, be repugnant to (*a p.*). 2. *n.* opposition, resistance, reluctance, repugnance; *mit –streben*, reluctantly, against one's will; *ohne –streben*, readily, with a good grace. **–strebend,** *adj.* reluctant. **–streit,** *m.* opposition, conflict. **–streiten,** *ir.v.n.* (*insep.*) (*aux.* h.) (*Dat.*) conflict (with), clash (with), be antagonistic (with), be contrary (to), militate (against). **–streitend,** *pr.p.* & *adj.* antagonistic, conflicting. **–strom,** *m.* reverse- *or* counter-current. **–wärtig,** *adj.* disagreeable, annoying, vexatious, offensive, disgusting, repugnant, hateful. **–wärtigkeit,** *f.* disagreeableness, loathsomeness, offensiveness, nuisance, bother; adversity, accident, calamity. **–wille(n),** *m.* repugnance, antipathy, aversion, disgust; *mit –willen*, reluctantly, with a bad grace. **–willig,** *adj.* reluctant, unwilling.

widm–en, *v.a.* & *r.* (*Dat.*) dedicate; devote (o.s.); consecrate. **–ung,** *f.* dedication. **–ungsschrift,** *f.* dedicatory epistle.

widrig, *adj.* adverse, hostile, untoward, contrary, inimical, unfavourable; disgusting, repugnant; *–e Umstände*, adverse circumstances. **–enfalls,** *adv.* (*C.L.*) failing which, in default whereof. **–keit,** *f.* unpleasantness; untoward event, adversity; *allerlei –keiten*, all sorts of unpleasantnesses.

wie, 1. *adv.* how; in what way; to what extent; – *geht's?* how are you? how are things getting on? – *kommt es, daß . . . ?* how is it that. . . . ? – *denn anders?* how else? how could it be otherwise? *und – sie alle heißen mögen*, whatever their names may be; *ich weiß nicht, – ich handeln soll*, I don't know how to act; – *schwer es mir auch ankommt*, however much it may cost me; – *bitte?* I beg your pardon? what did you say? – *wäre es, wenn . . . ?* what if . . . ? – *leicht läßt man sich täuschen!* how easily one is deceived! *–! hat sie es wirklich gesagt?* what! did she really say so? 2. *conj.* as, just as, such as, like; as if; *so – ich bin*, such as I am; *ein Mann – er*, such a man as he; – *sich's gebürt* or *gehört*, as is proper; *schön – ein Engel*, beautiful as an angel; – *gesagt*, as stated, as has been said; – *man mir gesagt hat*, as I have been told; – *die Sachen jetzt stehen*, as matters now stand; – *du mir, so ich dir*, as you treat me so I shall treat you, tit for tat; (*Prov.*) – *man's treibt, so geht's*, as you make your bed, so you must lie; (*Prov.*) – *die Saat, so die Ernte*, like father, like son; – *er dies hörte, ging er weg*, on hearing this, he went away; – *gesagt so getan*, no sooner said than done; – *dem auch sei*, be that as it may; – (*auch*) *immer*, in whatever way, howsoever. 3. *n.*; *das – und das warum*, the why and the wherefore; *auf das – kommt es an*, it all depends on the way (in which it is done *or* said). **–fern,** *adv.*; *in –fern?* in what respect? to what extent. **–so,** *adv.* why? but why? *–so weißt du* *das?* how is it that you know that? **–viel,** *adv.* how much, (*pl.*) how many; *um –viel mehr wird er es jetzt tun!* how much rather will he do it now! *–viel unnütze Mühe geben Sie sich!* what needless trouble you give yourself! *der –vielte ist er in seiner Klasse?* what is his position in class? *den –vielten haben wir heute?* what is the date today? **–weit,** *see* **–fern. –wohl,** *conj.* although, albeit.

Wiede, *f.* (-n) (*dial.*) withe, willow-twig.

Wiedehopf, *m.* (-(e)s, -e) hoopoe (*Upupa epops*) (*Orn.*).

wieder, 1. *adv.* again, anew, once more, afresh; *– und –*, time and again, over and over again; *hin und –*, now and then, from time to time; *immer –*, again and again. 2. *prefix* (*sep. except when stated, when the accent is on the root*) = re-, back (again), in return (for). **–abdruck,** *m.* reprint, new impression. **–anfang,** *m.* recommencement; reopening (*of school, etc.*). **–anziehung,** *f.* reattraction (*Phys.*). **–aufbau,** *m.* reconstruction, rebuilding. **–aufbauen,** *v.a.* rebuild, reconstruct. **–auffinden,** *v.a.* recover, find. **–aufforstung,** *f.* reforesting, reafforestation. **–aufheben,** *v.a.* annul, rescind. **–aufleben,** *n.* resurrection; revival (*of learning, etc.*). **–aufnahme,** *f.* resumption. **–aufnahmeverfahren,** *n.* retrial, appeal (*Law*). **–aufnehmen,** *ir.v.a.* resume, take up again. **–aufrichtung,** *f.* re-erection; re-establishment. **–aufsuchen,** *v.a.* look up (*a p.*). **–auftauchen,** *v.n.* (*aux.* s.) come to light again. **–ausbruch,** *m.* fresh outbreak; renewal (*of hostilities*). **–ausgrabung,** *f.* disinterment. **–beginn,** *m.* recommencement. **–bekommen,** *ir.v.a.* recover, get back. **–beleben,** *v.a.* reanimate, reactivate, resuscitate, call back to life, revive, revivify. **–belebung,** *f.* resuscitation. **–beschaffungspreis,** *m.* cost of replacement. **–brauchbarmachen,** *n.* regeneration (*of materials*). **–bringen,** *ir.v.a.* bring back; restore, return to. **–druck,** *m.* reprint, new impression. **–einfallen,** *v.n.* (*aux.* s.) (*with Dat.*) come to (one's) mind, occur (*to a p.*). **–einsetzen** *v.a.* replace; reinstate, reinstall. **–einsetzung,** *f.* reinstatement. **–erhalten,** *v.a., see* **–bekommen. –erkennen,** *ir.v.a.* recognize. **–eröffnen,** *v.a.* reopen, resume. **–ersetzen,** *v.a.*, **–erstatten,** *v.a.* return, restore; refund. **–erstattung,** *f.* restitution, repayment. **–fordern,** *v.a.* demand the return of, recall. **–gabe,** *f.* restitution, return; reproduction, rendering; response, reply. **–geben,** *ir.v.a.* give back, return, restore; reproduce; render. **–geboren,** *adj.* reborn, regenerated. **–geburt,** *f.* rebirth, regeneration, palingenesis. **–gewinnen,** *v.a.* recover, regain, reclaim, regenerate. **–gutmachen,** *v.a.* compensate, make amends for, make good; reclaim (*used materials*). **–gutmachung,** *f.* reparation; reclaiming. **–herrichten,** *v.a.*, **–herstellen,** *v.a.* restore, revive, cure; re-establish, repair, rebuild. **–herstellung,** *f.* thorough repair, restoration, recovery, readjustment, reinstatement. **–herstellungsmittel,** *n.* restorative. **–herstellungszeichen,** *n.* (*Mus.*) natural (♮); quadrant. **–holen,** 1. *v.a.* (*sep.*) bring *or* fetch back; (*insep.*) repeat, reiterate, say again, do again; *kurz –holen,* sum up, briefly recapitulate. 2. *v.r.* repeat o.s., recur, occur over and over again; *das läßt sich nicht –holen,* that won't bear repeating. 3. **–holt,** *adv.* repeatedly, again and again. *n.*, **–holung,** *f.* repeat, repetition; reiteration; recapitulation; *im –holungsfall,* if it should occur again. **–holungskurs,** *m.* (*Swiss dial.*) annual military training. **–holungsspiel,** *n.* re-play. **–holungszeichen,** *n.* dittomarks (*Typ.*), repeat (*Mus.*). **–hören,** *v.n.*; *auf –hören!* good-night, everybody! (*on the radio*), good-bye (*on the phone*). **–instandsetzen,** *v.a.* recondition, overhaul, repair. **–instandsetzung,** *f.* thorough overhaul, reconditioning. **–kauen,** *v.a. & n.* (*aux.* h.) ruminate, chew the cud; (*coll.*) repeat over and over. **–käuer,** *m.* ruminant. **–kauf,** *m.* repurchase; redemption. **–kehr,** *f.* return, reappearance, recurrence, repetition; *die 25jährige –kehr,* the 25th anniversary. **–kehren,** *v.n.*, **–kommen,** *v.n.* (*aux.* s.) come back, return, recur, reappear, repeat. **–kunft,** *f.* return. **–schein,** *m.* reflection. **–sehen,** 1. *ir.v.a.* see again. 2. *n.* reunion, subsequent meeting; *auf –sehen!* good-bye! au revoir! (*coll.*) so long! **–spiegeln,** *v.a.* reflect, mirror. **–strahl,** *m.* reflected ray. **–täufer,** *m.* anabaptist. **–tun,** *ir.v.a.* do again, repeat; *daß du das nicht –tust!* don't do that again! **–um,** *adv.* again, anew, afresh; on the other hand; on the contrary; in return, in (his, her, their) turn. **–vereinigung,** *f.* reunion, reconciliation; recombination. **–vergelten,** *v.a.* requite, retaliate. **–vergeltung,** *f.* retaliation. **–verkaufen,** *v.a.* resell; retail. **–verkäufer,** *m.* retailer. **–wahl,** *f.* re-election. **–wählbar,** *adj.* eligible for re-election.

Wieg–e, *f.* (-n) cradle (*also Artil.*); *von der –e bis zum Grabe,* from cradle to grave. **–(e)messer,** *n.* chopping-knife. **–en,** 1. *ir.v.a. & n.* (*aux.* h.) weigh; *wieviel –st du?* how heavy are you? what is your weight? *sein Urteil –t am schwersten,* his judgement carries most weight. 2. *reg. v.a.* rock (*a cradle*); move gently; shake, sway; chop, mince (*meat, etc.*); *in (den) Schlaf –en,* rock to sleep; *–ender Gang,* rolling gait: *in einer S. gewiegt,* well versed in *or* skilled in a th.; *gewiegter Kaufmann,* experienced merchant. 3. *reg. v.r.* (*with in* (*Dat.*)) lull *or* delude o.s. with, indulge in (*vain hopes, etc.*). **–endruck,** *m.* incunabulum (*Typ.*); early printed book. **–enfest,** *n.* birthday (celebrations) (*high style*). **–enkind,** *n.* young baby, infant. **–enkorb,** *m.* bassinet. **–enlied,** *n.* cradle-song, lullaby. **–evorrichtung,** *f.* weighing-machine.

wiehern, 1. *v.n.* (*aux.* h.) neigh; *–des Gelächter,* horse-laugh, (*vulg.*) belly-laugh. 2. *n.* neighing.

Wiek, *f.* (-en) (*dial.*) creek, bay, cove.

Wieling, *f.* (-e) fender (*Naut.*).

Wiemen, *m.* (-s, –) (*dial.*) perch, roost; drying frame.

Wiepe, *f.* (-n) (*dial.*) wisp (*of straw*).

wies, wiese, *see* **weisen.**

Wies–e, *f.* (-en) meadow, field, pasture-land, (*Poet.*) greensward, mead. **–baum,** *m.* binder, beam (*over a load of hay*). **–enbau,** *m.* cultivation of pasture. **–enfeld,** *n.* grassland, meadow. **–engras,** *n.* meadow-grass. **–engrund,** *m.* meadow-land; grassy valley. **–enklee,** *m.* red clover (*Trifolium pratense*) (*Bot.*). **–enknarrer,** *m.* corn-crake (*Crex pratensis*) (*Orn.*). **–enknopf,** *m.* great burnet (*Sanguisorba*) (*Bot.*). **–enralle,** *f. see* **–enknarrer. –enschaumkraut,** *n.* cuckoo-flower, lady's smock (*Cardamine pratensis*) (*Bot.*). **–(en)wachs,** *m.* herbage; grass-crop, hay-crop.

Wiesel, *n.* (-s, –) weasel (*Mustela vulgaris*) (*Zool.*).

wieviel, wiewohl, *see under* **wie.**

wild, 1. *adj.* wild, uncultivated, in the natural state; growing naturally, rough, unkempt, dishevelled; savage, uncivilized, ferocious, fierce; unruly, impetuous, intractable, noisy, turbulent, furious; unrestrained, angry; *– auf etwas sein, coll.*) be crazy about s.th.; *–er Boden,* virgin soil, *–e Ehe,* unrecognized marriage, concubinage; *–es Fleisch,* proud flesh; *–e Flucht,* headlong flight, rout; *–e Gegend,* rugged country; *–es Geflügel,* wild fowl; *–es Gestein,* dead *or* non-ore-bearing rock; *–es Haar,* dishevelled *or* unkempt hair; *–e Jagd,* Wotan's horde, wild chase; uproar; *–es Leben,* disorderly life; *– machen,* enrage, exasperate; *ein Tier –machen,* make an animal shy; *den –en Mann machen,* get wild, go berserk; *–es Pferd,* runaway horse, ungovernable *or* unmanageable horse; *–er Streik,* illegal strike; *–es Volk,* savage tribe; *–er Wein,* Virginia creeper; *– werden,* shy (*of horses*); *seid nicht so –!* don't make so much noise! 2. *n.* game, a head of game; deer, venison; *hohes –,* large game, deer. **–acker,** *m.* game preserve. **–bach,** *m.* mountain torrent. **–bad,** *n.* natural springs. **–bahn,** *f.* hunting-ground. **–bann,** *m.* exclusive right of chase; preserve; game regulations. **–braten,** *m.* roast venison. **–bret,** *n.* game, venison. **–dieb,** *m.* poacher. **–dieben,** *v.n.* (*insep.*) (*aux.* h.) poach. **–dieberei,** *f.* poaching. **–e,** 1. *f., see* **–nis.** 2. *n.* wildness. 3. **–e(r),** *m. & f.* savage; (*coll.*) freelance. **–enzen,** *v.n.* taste of *or* like venison; smell *or* taste high *or* gamy; (*coll.*) have a beastly smell; behave like a beast. **–erei,** *f.* poaching. **–erer,** *m., see* **–deib. –ern,** *v.n.* (*aux.*

h.) poach; run wild, revert to the wild *or* savage state. **–fang,** *m.* unruly child; madcap, romp; tomboy (*of girls*). **–fraß,** *m.* damage (*to crops*) done by game. **–fremd,** *adj.* utterly strange; *ein –fremder*, an utter *or* perfect stranger. **–frevel,** *m.*, *see* **–dieberei. –gans,** *f.* wild goose. **–garten,** *m.*, **–gehege,** *n.* game preserve. **–geschmack,** *m.* gamy taste. **–heit,** *f.* wildness, savagery, barbarity, ferocity; anger, fury; barbarous act. **–hüter,** *m.* gamekeeper. **–kalb,** *n.* fawn. **–knecht,** *m.* gamekeeper's man. **–leder,** *n.* deerskin, buckskin, doeskin. **–ling,** *m.* parent stock, wild seedling *or* tree; wild beast; animal in the wild state; *see also* **–fang. –nis,** *f.* wilderness; desert; jungle; savage state. **–park,** *m.*, *see* **–garten. –pret,** *n.*, *see* **–bret. –schaden,** *m.*, *see* **–fraß. –schur,** *f.* heavy fur, travelling cloak. **–schütz(e),** *m.* poacher. **–schwein,** *n.* wild boar (*Sus scrofa*) (*Zool.*). **–spur,** *f.* scent *or* track of game. **–stock,** *m.* head of game; covert. **–taube,** *f.* wood-pigeon. **–wachsend,** *adj.* growing wild *or* naturally, run wild, self-sown. **–wasser,** *n.* torrent. **–zaun,** *m.* deer fence.

will, willst, *see* **wollen.**

Will–e, *m.* (-ens, -en) will, volition, determination; design, purpose, intent, intention, wish, inclination; *aus freiem –en*, voluntarily, of one's own accord; *guter –e*, benevolent intention; *mit dem guten –en vorlieb nehmen*, take the will for the deed; *ich ließ ihm seinen –en*, I let him have his (own) way; *letzter –e*, last will and testament; *mit –en*, on purpose, intentionally, designedly; *nach –en*, as one pleases; *es ging ihm nach –en*, he had his wish; *ohne meinen –en*, without my consent, against my will; *wider –en*, unwillingly, involuntarily, unintentionally, in spite of o.s.; *einem zu –en sein*, do as s.o. wishes, humour a p.; *das Mädchen war ihm zu –en*, the girl gave herself to him. **–en,** 1. *m.* (*Austr. dial.*) *see* **–e.** 2. *prep.* (*Gen.*) (*always preceded by* um) *um meinet–*, for my sake; *um Gottes (Himmels) –en*, for God's (Heaven's) sake. **–enlos,** *adj.* involuntarily, having no will of one's own, irresolute, weak-minded, characterless. **–enlosigkeit,** *f.* lack of will-power, indecision. **–ensakt,** *m.* act of volition, voluntary action. **–ens,** *adv.*; *–ens sein*, be willing, ready *or* disposed (to), have a mind (to). **–ensänderung,** *f.* change of mind. **–ensbestimmung,** *f.* testamentary disposition, will. **–enserklärung,** *f.* declaratory act (*Law*). **–ensfreiheit,** *f.* free will, freedom of will. **–enskraft,** *f.* will power, strength of will *or* mind. **–ensmeinung,** *f.* will, pleasure. **–ensschwäche,** *f.* weak will. **–ensstärke,** *f.*, *see* **–enskraft. –enstätigkeit,** *f.* function of the will, voluntary action. **–entlich,** *adj.* intentional, wilful; *wissentlich und –entlich*, consciously and deliberately. **–fahren,** *v.n.* (*aux.* h.) (*p.p.* willfahrt *&* gewillfahrt) (*Dat.*) accede to, comply with, gratify, grant (*a wish*); humour, please (*a p.*); *einem in einer S. –fahren*, concede *or* grant a th. to a p. **–fährig,** *adj.* (*Dat.*) obliging, accommodating, complaisant, compliant. **–fährigkeit,** *f.* compliancy, complaisance. **–ig,** *adj.* willing, voluntarily; ready; docile; *sich zu einer S. –ig finden lassen*, show o.s. willing to do s.th.

Willkomm, *m.* (-s, -e) (*Austr. dial.*), **–en,** 1. *n.* (*& Austr dial. m.*) welcome, reception. 2. *adj.* (*with Dat.*) welcome, acceptable, opportune, gratifying; *seien Sie –en!* welcome! *einen –en heißen*, bid a p. welcome, welcome a p.; *–ene Kunde*, welcome news.

Willkür, *f.* free will, option, choice; decree (*Law*); discretion; caprice; inconsiderate, reckless *or* arbitrary action; despotism; *ich lasse das in Ihre – gestellt, handeln Sie nach Ihrer –* I leave that to you, act according to your own discretion; *nach –*, at will, as one pleases; in an arbitrary manner; *er ist ihrer – preisgegeben*, he is at their mercy **–herrschaft,** *f.* despotism; tyranny. **–lich,** *adj.* optional, voluntary; arbitrary, despotic. **–lichkeit,** *f.* arbitrariness; arbitrary act. **–verfahren** *n.* arbitrary proceedings.

wimmeln, *v.n.* (*aux.* h. *&* s.) swarm, be crowded, abound, teem, be filled (*von*, with).

wimm–en, *v.n.* (*Swiss dial.*) harvest grapes. **–er,** 1. *f.* vintage. 2. *m.* vintager.

Wimmer, *m.* 1. gnarled branch, tree stump. 2.; **–chen,** *n.*, (*dial.*) **–l,** *n.* birthmark, mole.

wimmer–n, *v.n.* (*aux.* h.) whimper, whine, moan, (*coll.*) grizzle. (*coll.*) **–holz,** *n.* screechy fiddle. (*coll.*) **–kasten,** *m.* twangy piano.

Wimpel, *m.* (-s, –) pennon, pennant, burgee. **–fall,** *m.* pennon-halyards.

Wimper, *f.* (-n) eyelash; (*pl.*) cilia (*Bot., Zool.*); *ohne mit der – zu zucken*, without turning a hair. **–ig** *adj.* ciliate. **–n,** *v.n.* (*aux.* h.) wink.

Wimperg, *m.* (-(e)s, -e), **–e,** *f.* (-en) Gothic gable (*Arch.*).

Wind, *m.* (-(e)s, -e) wind, breeze; blast; scent; emptiness, humbug; flatulence, belch, wind; *dicht beim* or *hart am –e segeln*, sail close to the wind, hug the wind; *bei – und Wetter*, in all weathers; *– davon bekommen*, get wind of it; *frischer –*, fresh breeze (Beaufort 5); *gegen den – segeln*, sail against the wind, go right in the wind's eye; *guten – haben*, have a fair wind; *halber –*, side wind; *harter –*, moderate gale (Beaufort 7); *in den – schlagen*, disregard, set at nought, make light of, pay no heed to; *der – kommt von Osten*, the wind is in the east; (*einem*) *– (vor)machen*, bluster, talk hot-air; *mäßiger –*, moderate breeze (Beaufort 4); *den Mantel nach dem –e hängen*, trim one's sails to the wind; *in den – reden*, beat the air, talk in vain; *schwacher –*, gentle breeze (Beaufort 3); *das ist – in seine Segel*, that is grist to his mill; *starker –*, high wind; *steifer –*, strong breeze (Beaufort 6); *stürmischer –*, fresh gale (Beaufort 8); *über den – kommen*, gain the wind; *unter dem –e*, under the lee; *die Inseln unter dem –e*, the Leeward Isles; *vom –e abkommen*, fall to leeward; *woher weht der –?* in what quarter is the wind? *sich den – um die Nase wehen lassen*, see the world; *zwischen – und Wasser*, awash. **–beutel,** *m.* cream puff, éclair; windbag, braggart. **–beutelei,** *f.* idle boasting, humbug, hot air. **–blattern,** *f.pl.*, *see* **–pocken. –blume,** *f.* anemone. **–blütler,** *m.pl.* anemophilae (*Bot.*). **–bruch,** *m.* windfall, windfallen wood; pneumatocele (*Med.*). **–brüchig,** *adj.* windfallen. **–büchse,** *f.* air-gun. **–darm,** *m.* colon. **–dicht,** *adj.* airtight. **–dürr,** *adj.* air-dried; lean. **–ei,** *n.* addled egg; wind-egg; soft-shelled egg. **–en,** *v.n.* (*aux.* h.) catch the scent; *es –et*, it is windy, there is a high wind. (*fig.*) **–eseile,** *f.* lightning-speed. **–fahne,** *f.* weather-vane. **–fang,** *m.* porch, wind-breaker. **–flaute,** *f.* lull. **–flügel,** *m* fan, vane, fan blade (*Motor.*). **–frei,** *adj.* sheltered. **–geschwulst,** *f.* emphysema. **–hafer,** *m.* wild oats (*Avena fatua*) (*Bot.*). **–harfe,** *f.* Aeolian harp. **–hetze,** *f.*, **–hetzen,** *n.* coursing. **–hose,** *f.* whirlwind, cyclone, tornado. **–hund,** *m.* greyhound, whippet; (*fig.*) windbag. **–ig,** *adj.* windy, breezy; vain, empty, thoughtless, heedless, frivolous, giddy, light-hearted; (*dial.*) *es sieht –ig um ihn* (*mit ihm*) *aus*, he seems in a bad way. **–jacke,** *f.* wind-proof jacket *or* jerkin. **–kanal,** *m.* wind tunnel. **–kappe,** *f.* chimney-cowl. **–kessel,** *m.* air-regulator (*of a pump*). **–klappe,** *f.* air-valve. **–lade,** *f.* wind-chest, sounding-board. **–laden,** *m.* window-shutter. **–lehre,** *f.* anemology. **–licht,** *n.* storm lantern. **–loch,** *n.* air-hole; draughty place. **–macher,** *m.* braggart, humbug, charlatan. **–macherei,** *f.* charlatanry; empty bluster. **–mantel,** *m.* windbreak. **–messer,** *m.* anemometer, wind indicator. **–mühle,** *f.* windmill. **–mühlenflugzeug,** *n.* autogyro, gyroplane (*Av.*). **–ofen,** *m.* blast-furnace, draught-furnace. **–pocken,** *f.pl.* chicken-pox, varicella. **–richtung,** *f.* direction of the wind. **–röschen,** *n.* wood-anemone (*Anemone silvestris*) (*Bot.*). **–rose,** *f.* rhumb-card, compass-card. **–rücken,** *m.* windward side. **–sack,** *m.* wind sleeve (*Av.*). **–sbraut,** *f.* gale, whirlwind, hurricane. **–schacht,** *m.* air-shaft. **–schatten,** *m.* lee side. **–schief,** *adj.* twisted, warped, awry, skew; *–schief werden*, warp; *–schiefe Ansichten*, warped views. **–schirm,** *m.* wind-breaker, screen. **–schnell,** *adj.* quick as lightning. **–schnittig,** *adj.* streamlined, aerodynamic. **–(schutz)scheibe,** *f.* windscreen (*Motor.*). **–seite,** *f.* exposed side, weather-side. **–spiel,** *n.* whippet. **–sprung,** *m.* change of *or* shift in the wind. **–stärke,** *f* velocity *or* strength of the wind. **–still,** *adj.* calm. **–stille**

f. calm (Beaufort o). **–stoß,** *m.* gust of wind. **–strich,** *m.* direction of the wind, point of the compass, rhumb. **–strom,** *m.*, **–strömung,** *f.* current of air, blast. **–sucht,** *f.* flatulence, tympanitis. **–tür,** ventilation door *or* trap (*Min.*). **–wärts,** *adv.* windward. **–wehe,** *f.* snowdrift. **–winkel,** *m.* angle of drift (*Av.*). **–wirbel,** *m.* whirlwind. **–zeiger,** *m.* wind indicator. **–zug,** *m.* draught, current of air.

Wind–e, *f.* (-n) 1. bindweed, wild convolvulus. 2. reel, winder, windlass, winch, capstan, lifting-jack. 3. (*Swiss dial.*) attic, loft. **–ebaum,** *m.* beam (*of a windlass, etc.*). **–en,** 1. *ir.v.a.* wind, twine, reel, twist, coil; wring, wrest, wrench; *in die Höhe –en,* hoist; *einem etwas aus den Händen –en,* wrest s.th. out of a p.'s hands. 2. *v.r.* writhe, wriggle; wind, twist, turn; meander (*of streams, rivers*); coil round; *sich vor Schmerz –en,* writhe with pain. **–enartig,** *adj.* of the convolvulus family (*Bot.*). **–enschwärmer,** *m.* convolvulus hawk-moth (*Protopare convolvuli*) (*Ent.*). **–ung,** *f.* winding, twisting; twist, turn; spiral, coil, convolution, sinuosity; meandering (*of a stream*); whorl (*of a shell*); worm (*of a screw*); torsion.

Windel, *f.* (-n) baby's napkin; *noch in den –n stecken,* be still in the early stages. **–band,** *n.* baby's binder. **–bohrer,** *m.* wimble, centrebit. **–kind,** *n.* new-born baby. **–n,** *v.a.* swaddle. **–weich,** *adj.* very soft, yielding, compliant; *–weich schlagen,* beat to a jelly.

Windung, *see* **Wind-ung.**

Wingert, *m.* (-s, -e) (*dial.*) vineyard.

Wink, *m.* (-(e)s, -e) sign, wink, wave (*with the hand*); hint, suggestion; (*coll.*) tip; (*dial.*) twinkling, jiffy; *einem einen – geben,* sign *or* beckon to a p.; (*fig.*) drop a hint; *einen – verstehen,* take a hint; *– mit dem Laternenpfahl* or *Zaunpfahl,* broad hint. **–en,** *v.a. & n.* (*aux.* h.) (*Dat.*) wave, sign, make signs, beckon, nod, wink, signal, semaphore (*Mil.*); *dem Kellner –en,* beckon the waiter; *einem Stillschweigen –en,* make signs to a p. to keep silent. **–er,** *m.* (-s, –) trafficator (*Motor.*), flag *or* semaphore signaller, flag-man. **–erflagge,** *f.* signalling flag. **–zeichen,** *n.pl.* manual signals.

Winkel, *m.* (-s, –) angle, corner, nook; stripe, chevron (*Mil.*); (*dial.*) business, shop, workshop; *ausspringender –,* salient (*Fort.*); *einspringender –,* re-entrant (*Fort.*); *rechter –,* right angle; *spitzer* (*stumpfer*) *–,* acute (obtuse) angle; *vorspringender* or *vorstehender –,* see *ausspringender –.* **–advokat,** *m.* shady lawyer, unqualified lawyer. **–blatt,** *n.* (*coll.*) local rag. **–bogen,** *m.* arc subtending an angle. **–börse,** *f.* unlicensed exchange, outside broker's business, (*coll.*) bucket-shop. **–börsenspekulant,** *m.* sham stock-broker. **–druckerei,** *f.* clandestine printing press. **–ehe,** *f.* clandestine marriage. **–eisen,** *n.* angle-iron. **–förmig,** *adj.* angular. **–funktion,** *f.* trigonometrical ratio. **–gasse,** *f.* back lane. **–geschwindigkeit,** *f.* angular velocity. **–größe,** *f.* size of an angle. **–halbierende,** *f.* bisector of an angle. **–haken,** *m.* justifier (*Typ.*); composing-stick (*Typ.*). **–ig,** *adj.* angular; full of angles *or* corners; bent, cornered, crooked, twisted. **–kneipe,** *f.* back-street pub, low haunt. **–lineal,** *n.* set-square. **–linie,** *f.* diagonal. **–makler,** *m.* outside broker. **–maß,** *n.* set- *or* T-square. **–messer,** *m.* goniometer, clinometer, protractor, theodolite. **–naht,** *f.* lambdoidal suture (*Anat.*). **–recht,** *adv.* rectangular, right-angled. **–scheibe,** *f.* astrolabe (*Astr.*). **–schenke,** *f. see* **–kneipe.** **–schule,** *f.* unrecognized school, dame-school. **–spiegel,** *m.* optical square (*Surg.*). **–ständig,** *adj.* axillary. **–stück,** *n.* angle-plate. **–treue,** *f.* congruity. **–züge,** *m.pl.* subterfuge, evasions, shifts, pretexts, dodges, tricks.

winklig, *adj.*, *see* **winkelig.**

winseln, *v.n.* (*aux.* h.) whine, whimper, moan.

Winter, *m.* (-s, –) winter; *mitten im –,* in the depth of winter. **–festigkeit,** *f.* winter hardiness. **–frische,** *f.* winter resort. **–frucht,** *f.* winter *or* spring crop. **–garten,** *m.* conservatory. **–getreide,** *n., see* **–frucht.** **–grün,** *n.* wintergreen (*Pirola*) (*Bot.*); periwinkle (*Vinca*) (*Bot.*). **–hart,** *adj.* hardy (*of plants*). **–hilfswerk,** *n.* (*Nat. Soc.*) compulsory charity (*ostensibly for relieving hardship during cold weather*). **–kleid,** *n.* winter-coat *or* -plumage. **–kleidung,** *f.* winter clothes *or* clothing. **–kohl,** *m.* spring cabbage. **–korn,** *n., see* **–frucht.** **–(kur)ort,** *m.* winter (health) resort. **–lagerung,** *f.* winter storage. **–lich,** *adj.* wintry. **–ling,** *m.* winter aconite (*Eranthus hiemalis*) (*Bot.*). **–n,** 1. *v.n.* (*aux.* h.); *es –t,* winter is coming, it grows wintry. 2. *v.a.* lay by for the winter. **–öl,** *n.* non-freezing oil. **–punkt,** *m.* winter solstice. **–saat,** *f.* autumn sowing, seed for autumn sowing. **–schlaf,** *m.* hibernation. **–schläfer,** *m.* hibernating animal. **–seite,** *f.* northern aspect. **–semester,** *n.* winter term (*October to March*). **–sonnenwende,** *f., see* **–punkt.** **–sport,** *m.* winter sports. **–sportler,** *m.* winter sports addict. **–süber,** *adv.* through(out) the winter. **–vorrat,** *m.* winter stocks. **–weizen,** *m.* autumn-sown wheat.

Winzer, *m.* (-s, –) vine-grower, vine-dresser; vintager. **–fest,** *n.* vintage festival. **–lied,** *n.* vintager's song.

winzig, *adj.* tiny, minute, diminutive; petty, scanty, trifling, paltry, puny. **–keit,** *f.* diminutiveness, tininess, minuteness, pettiness.

Wipfel, *m.* (-s, –) (tree-)top. **–n,** 1. *v.a.* lop (*trees*). 2. *v.r. & n.* (*aux.* h.) tower, rise aloft.

Wippchen, *n.* (-s, –) (*coll.*) trick, shift, evasion; (*coll.*) *mache mir keine – vor,* don't try your tricks with me, none of your nonsense!

Wipp–e, *f.* (-n) see-saw; brink; critical point; strappado; (*dial.*) whip; (*dial.*) tip-wagon; balancing (exercise) (*Gymn.*). (*coll.*) *auf der –e sein* or *stehen,* be on the point of falling *or* turning back. **–en,** *v.a. & n.* (*aux.* h.) rock, move up and down, see-saw; tip over, tilt up, overturn; swipe; strappado (*criminals*); *Münzen kippen und –en,* clip coin. **–galgen,** *m.* strappado. (*coll.*) **–sterz,** *m.* wagtail (*Motacilla*) (*Orn.*).

wir, *pers. pron.* (1st *pers. pl.*) we.

wirb, wirbst, wirbt, *see* **werben.**

Wirbel, *m.* (-s, –) whirl, swirl; whirlpool, vortex, eddy; whirlwind; wreath, curl (*of smoke*); giddiness, vertigo, intoxication, turmoil, hurly-burly; crown (*of the head*); vertebra; peg (*of violins, etc.*); window catch; drum roll; warbling (*of birds*); *einen – schlagen,* sound a roll (on the drum); *vom – bis zur Zehe,* from top to toe. **–balken,** *m.*, **–stock,** *m.* screw-plate of a piano. **–bein,** *n.* vertebra. **–förmig,** *adj.* whirling, vertebral; spindle-shaped. **–gelenk,** *n.* swivel-joint. **–haft,** *adj.*, **–ig,** *adj.* whirling, eddying, swirling. **–kasten,** *m.* neck for the pegs (*violin*). **–knochen,** *m., see* **–bein.** **–los,** *adj.* invertebrate, spineless. **–n,** *v.a. & n.* (*aux.* h. & s.) whirl, eddy, turn, whirl *or* swirl round; warble; trill; roll (*of drums*); *der Kopf –t mir,* my head is in a whirl, my head is swimming; *gewirbelt,* *p.p. & adj.* vertebrate. **–säule,** *f.* spine, vertebral column. **–strom,** *m.* eddy current (*Elec.*). **–sturm,** *m.* cyclone, tornado, typhoon, hurricane. **–tier,** *n.* vertebrate (animal). **–wind,** *m.* whirlwind.

wird, *see* **werden.**

wirf, wirfst, wirft, *see* **werfen.**

wirk–en, 1. *v.a.* effect, do, work, operate; bring about, produce; weave, knit (*stockings, etc.*); (*archaic*) knead (*dough*). 2. *v.n.* (*aux.* h.) work, operate, act, have an effect; *an einer Schule –en,* teach in a school, be employed as a teacher; *auf einen –en,* have an influence on, impress *or* influence a p.; *auf die Sinne –en,* affect the senses; *gut auf Schüler –en,* have a good influence on pupils; *nachhaltig auf die Gemüter –en,* produce a lasting impression on the minds; *nachteilig auf eine S. –en,* have a bad *or* prejudicial effect upon a th., tell upon a th.; *jedes Wort –te,* every word told *or* counted. **–bank,** *f.*, **–brett,** *n.* pastry board. **–end,** *pr.p. & adj.* acting, active, causative, operating; efficacious, efficient, effective, operative, telling, drastic. **–er,** *m.* knitter, stocking-maker, weaver. **–erei,** *f.* weaving, knitting. **–leistung,** *f.* output (*Mach.*), overall efficiency. **–lich,** 1. *adj.* actual, real; substantial, true, genuine; effective, effectual. 2. *adv.* exactly, quite, indeed, really; *–lich vorhanden,* effective (*Mil.*); *–licher Bestand,* effective force; *–licher geheimer Rat* (a title in imperial times bestowed on Under Secretaries, etc., and carrying the form of address 'Exzellenz'); *-liche Schuld*, real debt; *-lich machen*, realize; *-lich werden*, be *or* become realized. **-lichkeit,** *f.* reality, actuality, actual fact, truth; *in -lichkeit*, in reality. **-lichkeitsform,** *f.* indicative mood (*Gram.*). **-lichkeitsnahe,** *adj.* realistic. **-lichkeitssinn,** *m.* sense of reality; matter-of-fact outlook. **-sam,** *adj.* effective, efficacious; active, working, operative; efficient, powerful (*Med.*); *gegen eine S. -sam*, effective against *or* good for a th. (*Med.*). **-samkeit,** *f.* efficacy, effectiveness, efficiency virtue; effect, agency; *in -samkeit sein*, be in operation; be in working order; *außer -samkeit setzen*, suspend (*a law*), put out of action (*Mach.*); *in -samkeit setzen*, start, set going; put into gear; *in -samkeit treten*, come into force, take effect. **-stoff,** *m.* hormone. **-strom,** *m.* effective current (*Elec.*). **-stuhl,** *m.* loom. **-ung,** *f.* working, operation, action, reaction; force, efficacy; result, consequence, effect, impression produced, influence; *auf jemanden eine -ung ausüben*, produce an effect upon a p.; *ohne -ung bleiben*, prove ineffectual, produce no effect; (*Prov.*) *keine -ung ohne Ursache*, no effect without cause, no smoke without a fire. **-ungsbereich,** *m.* radius of action, zone of fire, effective range (*Artil.*). **-ungsdauer,** *f.* persistency, effective duration. **-ungsfähig,** *adj.* effective, efficient. **-ungsgehalt,** *m.* active principle. **-ungsgrad,** *m.* efficiency (*of a machine*). **-ungskraft,** *f.* efficacy, efficiency, virtue, active force. **-ungskreis,** *m.* field *or* sphere of action *or* activity; province, domain. **-ungslos,** *adj.* ineffectual, futile, inefficient; ineffective, without effect; *-ungslos bleiben*, produce no effect, be lost (*bei*, upon). **-ungslosigkeit,** *f.* inefficacy; inefficiency inactivity. **-ungsvoll,** *adj.* efficacious, effective, striking, telling. **-ungswert,** *m.* effective strength *or* value. **-waren,** *f.pl.* woven goods, knitted ware, knitwear. **-widerstand,** *m.* effective resistance (*Elec.*). **-zeit,** *f.* reaction time.

wirr, *adj.* confused, bewildered; tangled, disorderly, wild, chaotic; dishevelled; *-es Durcheinander*, chaos, confusion. **-e,** *f.* (*usually pl.*) tangle, disorder, confusion, chaos; disturbances, troubles. **-en,** *v.a.* (*archaic*) entangle, jumble, mix up, confuse. **-kopf,** *m.* (*fig.*) muddle-headed thinker. **-nis,** *f.* (-se), **-sal,** *n.* (-s, -e) entanglement, confusion, disorder, disturbance, trouble, perplexity. **-seide,** *f.* silk-waste. **-warr,** *m.* jumble, chaos, disorder or confusion, hubbub.

wirsch, *adj.* abrupt, gruff, disobliging.

Wirsing(kohl), *m.* savoy (cabbage).

wirst, *see* **werden.**

Wirt, *m.* (-(e)s, -e) host; landlord; innkeeper, restaurant proprietor, lodging-house keeper; (*dial.*) head of the household; *den - machen*, do the honours; *die Rechnung ohne den - machen*, overlook the most vital factor. **-in,** *f.* hostess, innkeeper's wife, landlady. **-lich,** *adj.* hospitable; habitable. **-lichkeit,** *f.* hospitality. **-schaft,** *see* **Wirtschaft.** **-shaus,** *n.* inn, public-house. **-sleute,** *pl.* host and hostess, landlord and landlady, innkeeper and his wife. **-spflanze,** *f.* plant attacked by parasites, host plant (*Bot.*). **-sstube,** *f.* private bar, inn parlour. **-stafel,** *f.*, **-stisch,** *m.* table d'hôte.

Wirtel, *m.* (-s, -) distaff fly-wheel; whorl, verticil (*Bot.*). **-ig,** *adj.* verticillate.

Wirtschaft, *f.* housekeeping, domestic economy, husbandry; management of affairs, administration, economic system; public house, inn; household, establishment; (*coll.*) doings, goings-on, todo, row, mess; *die - führen*, keep house; (*coll.*) *die ganze -*, the whole show, shoot *or* boiling; (*coll.*) *was ist das für eine -?* how do you explain this mess? what do you (does he, *etc.*) mean by going on like this? (*iron.*) *eine schöne -!* nice goings-on! (*coll.*) *eine schreckliche* or *polnische -*, a shocking state of affairs, a terrible mess. **-en,** *v.n.* (*aux.* h.) keep house; manage *or* run (*a house, farm, business*); keep an inn *or* a public-house; administer (*property*); economize; (*coll.*) rummage about; *arg* or *übel -en*, make havoc; *gut -en*, manage well, husband (*one's income*), economize; *toll -en*, make a great to-do, turn everything upside down; *etwas zugrunde -en*, ruin a th. by bad management. **-er,** *m.* manager; housekeeper; steward. **-ler,** *m.* (political) economist, economic expert. **-lich,** *adj.* economical, thrifty; orderly, efficient, regular; economic; belonging to a farm, agricultural; self-supporting, profitable. **-lichkeit,** *f.* economy, thrift, husbandry, good management; profitableness. **-samt,** *n.* department of economic affairs. **-saufseher,** *m.* manager; steward, bailiff. **-sbetrieb,** *m.* management of a household, inn *or* farm; *mit -sbetrieb*, fully licensed. **-sbuch,** *n.* housekeeping book. **-sgebäude,** *n.* farm-buildings, outhouses. **-sgeld,** *n.* housekeeping-money. **-sgeographie,** *f.* economic geography. **-sgerät,** *n.* household utensils. **-sgruppe,** *f.* trust, corporation. **-shilfe,** *f.* economic support. **-sinspektor,** *m.* steward; overseer of an estate. **-sjahr,** *n.* financial year. **-skonferenz,** *f.* economic conference. **-skörper,** *m.* co-operative enterprise; self-help organization. **-skrieg,** *m.* economic warfare. **-skrise,** *f.* economic crisis. **-slage,** *f.* economic situation. **-slehre,** *f.* economics, political economy. **-splan,** *m.* working plan. **-spolitik,** *f.* economic policy. **-spolitisch,** *adj.* economic. **-sprüfer,** *m.* chartered accountant. **-srat,** *m.* advisory economic council. **-srechnung,** *f.* household account. **-sregel,** *f.* working rule. **-sstelle,** *f.* economic board, planning board. **-sverwalter,** *m.* steward, manager. **-swesen,** *n.* economic system.

Wisch, *m.* (-(e)s, -e) wiper, rag, wisp, (*coll.*) scrap of paper, note, chit. **-en,** *v.a.* wipe, rub. **-er,** *m.* wiper, cloth; windscreen-wiper (*Motor.*); (*coll.*) rebuff, rebuke, telling-off. **-gold,** *n.* gold leaf. **-iwaschi,** *n.* (*coll.*), *see* **-wasch.** **-lappen,** *m.* duster, cleaning-rag, dish-cloth. **-stock,** *m.* cleaning-rod (*Artil.*). **-tuch,** *n.*, *see* **-lappen.** **-wasch,** *m.*, (*coll.*) twaddle, bosh.

Wisent, *m.* (-(e)s, -e) bison.

Wismut, *n.* (& *Austr. dial. m.*) (-s) bismuth. **-en,** *v.a.* solder with bismuth. **-butter,** *f.* bismuth richloride. **-oxyd,** *n.* bismuth trioxide. **-säureanhydrid,** bismuth pentoxide.

Wispel, *m.* (-s -) (*obs.*) corn measure (*about* 24 *bushels*).

wispeln, wispern, *v.a.* & *n.* (*aux.* h.) whisper.

Wißbegier-(de), *f.* thirst for knowledge, (intellectual) curiosity. **-ig,** *adj.* curious, anxious to know, inquisitive.

wissen, 1. *ir.v.a.* know, have knowledge of, be aware *or* informed of, be acquainted with; understand, know how to, be able to; *ich weiß nicht anders als daß . . .*, all I know is that. . .; *ich weiß Bescheid*, I know for certain; *einem Dank -*, be grateful to a p.; *aus Erfahrung -*, know from experience; *weiß Gott!* God (only) knows! (*Prov.*) *was ich nicht weiß, macht mich nicht heiß*, what the eye does not see the heart does not grieve about; *kund und zu - sei hiemit*, (*archaic*), be it known by these presents; *einen etwas - lassen*, let a p. know, send a p. word, tell s.o.; *nicht aus noch ein -*, not know which way to turn; *nicht daß ich wüßte*, not that I am aware of; *weißt du noch?* do you remember? *sich* (*Dat.*) *keinen Rat -*, be at a loss, not know what to do; *ich weiß nicht recht*, I don't rightly know; *soviel ich weiß*, so *or* as far as I know, for all I know; *einem etwas* (*kund und*) *zu - tun*, see *- lassen*; *mit um eine S. -*, be privy to a th.; *er weiß von keiner Sorge*, he knows no care; *was weiß ich?* (*sl.*) search me! *- Sie was?* I'll tell you what; *er tut, als wäre er wer weiß was*, he acts as if he were the Lord Almighty; *der kann mir wer weiß was sagen*, I don't believe a word he says; *woher weißt du das?* how do you know that? *ich will von ihm nichts -*, I will have nothing to do with him; *davon will er nichts -*, he will not hear of it; *er will ihn glücklich -*, he wishes him to be happy; *er weiß zu reden*, he knows how to talk. 2. *n.* knowledge, learning, scholarship, erudition; *meines -s*, so *or* as far as I know, to the best of my knowledge; *mit seinem - ist es nicht weit her*, his learning is not great; *mit - und Willen*, intentionally, on purpose; *nach bestem - und Gewissen*, most conscientiously; *ohne mein -*, unknown to me, without my knowledge; *wider besseres* –, against one's better judgement. **–d,** *pr.p.* & *adj.* knowing, initiated. **–de(r),** *m.* & *f.* s.o. in the know, party to a secret. **–schaft,** *f.* learning, knowledge, scholarship, science; *die schönen –schaften,* belles lettres; *exakte –schaften,* the exact sciences; *philologisch-historische –schaften,* arts, humanities. **–schaftler,** *m.* learned man, scholar, scientist, man of science. **–schaftlich,** *adj.* scholarly, learned, scientific; *–schaftlich gebildet,* academically *or* scientifically trained, scholarly. **–schaftlichkeit,** *f.* scientific *or* scholarly method *or* character. **–schaftslehre,** *f.* theory of knowledge, philosophy. **–sdrang,** *m.*, **–sdurst,** *m.* thirst for knowledge. **–sgebiet,** *n.* field *or* branch of knowledge. **–strieb,** *m.*, *see* **–sdrang. –swert,** *adj.* worth knowing, interesting. **–swürdigkeit,** *f.* thing worth knowing; interesting fact. **–szweig,** *m.*, *see* **–sgebiet. –tlich,** 1. *adj.* conscious, wilful, deliberate. 2. *adv.* on purpose, deliberately, intentionally, knowingly.

Wit-frau, *f.*, *see* **–we.** (*archaic*) **–ib** (*Austr. dial.* **–tib**), *f.*, *see* **–we. –tum,** *n.* (-tume, -tümer & *Austr. dial.* -tume) (*archaic*) widow's jointure, estate *or* settlement. **–we,** *f.* (-n) widow; *zur –we gemacht* or *geworden,* widowed; *Königin–we,* queen dowager. **–wengehalt,** *n.*, **–wengeld,** *n.* widow's jointure, allowance *or* pension. **–wenjahr,** *n.* year of mourning. **–wenkasse,** *f.* widows' pension fund. **–wenkleid,** *n.* widow's weeds. **–wenschaft,** *f.* widowhood. **–wensitz,** *m.* dowager's estate. **–wenstand,** *m.* widowhood. **–wentracht,** *f.*, **–wentrauer,** *f.* widow's weeds. **–wentum,** *n.*, *see* **–wenstand. –wenverbrennung,** *f.* suttee. **–wer,** *m.* widower.

witter-n, *v.a.* & *n.* (*aux.* h.) scent, smell; perceive, suspect, (*coll.*) nose out; *nach einer S. –n,* nose s.th. out; *etwas –n,* scent s.th. out, get wind of s.th.; *er –t überall nur Sünde,* he is always suspecting evil; *ich –e Morgenluft,* I scent the morning air; *Unrat –n,* smell a rat. **–ung,** *f.* weather, weather *or* atmospheric conditions; scent, trail; *bei günstiger –ung,* weather permitting; *bei jeder –ung,* in all weathers; *von einer S. –ung bekommen,* get scent *or* wind of a th.; *eine gute* or *feine –ung haben,* have a good nose (*of dogs* & *fig.*). **–ungsbeständig,** *adj.* resistant to exposure. **–ungseinfluß,** *m.*, **–ungseinwirkung,** *f.* influence of the weather, atmospheric effect, exterior ballistics (*Artil.*). **–ungskunde,** *f.*, **–ungslehre,** *f.* meteorology. **–ungsumschlag,** *m.* atmospheric change, change in the weather. **–ungsverhältnisse,** *n.pl.* atmospheric conditions. **–ungsversuch,** *m.* weathering test (*Metall.*). **–ungswechsel,** *m.*, *see* **–ungsumschlag.**

Witz, *m.* (-es, -e) wit, wittiness; witticism, joke; (*archaic*) esprit, mother wit, common sense; *faule –e machen,* make *or* crack weak jokes; play silly practical jokes; *alter –,* stale joke, (*coll.*) chestnut; *beißender –,* caustic wit, sarcasm; *das ist ja eben der –, das ist der (ganze) –,* that is the (whole) point of it; *weder – noch Verstand,* neither rhyme nor reason. **–blatt,** *n.* comic paper. **–bold,** *m.* (-(e)s, -e) witty fellow, wit, wag, joker, clown. **–elei,** *f.* chaffing, leg-pulling. **–eln,** *v.n.* (*aux.* h.) poke fun (at), make a joke (of); *über einen –eln,* be witty at another's expense; *über eine S. –eln,* mock *or* ridicule a th. **–ig,** *adj.* witty, funny, facetious, (*coll.*) smart, bright; *–iger Einfall,* witty *or* clever idea. **–igen,** *v.a.* (*archaic*) teach a lesson. **–igung,** *f.* (*archaic*) warning, example, lesson.

wo, 1. *inter. adv.* where, in which; (*sl.*) how; *das Haus, – ich wohne,* the house in which I live; *– anders als hier,* in some place apart from here, not here but somewhere else; *– auch immer,* wherever; *– immer er auch sein mag,* wherever he may be; (*sl.*) *i – !* what are you thinking of? what nonsense! *von –,* whence, from which; (*sl.*) *– werd' ich so dumm sein?* do you think I'm a fool! 2. *ind. pronominal adv.* (*dial.*) somewhere; *ich habe es – gefunden,* I found it somewhere. 3. *conj.* when; *es gab Zeiten wo,* there were times when; *– nicht . . ., so doch . . .,* if not . . ., then certainly . . . 4. *n.*; *es kommt auf das – an,* it depends on where it is *or* on its whereabouts. **–anders,** *adv.* somewhere or other, elsewhere. **–bei,** *inter.* & *rel. adv.* (= **bei welchem,** *inter. or rel. pron. with prep.*) whereby, whereat, near, at *or* during which; in doing so, in the course of which, by doing which, in connexion with which, as well as; *es geschieht nichts, –bei sein Name nicht genannt würde,* nothing is done without his name appearing; *–bei mir einfällt,* and that brings to my mind; *–bei es sein Bewenden hatte,* and there the matter ended.

wob, wöbe, *see* **weben.**

Woche, *f.* (-n) week; *von – zu –,* week in, week out; *– für* or *um –,* week by week; *heute in* or *über einer –,* today week; *stille –,* Passion Week; *Weiße –,* white sale. *pl.* childbed, lying-in period; *in den –n sein* or *liegen,* be confined, be in childbed; *in die –n kommen mit einem Sohne,* be delivered of a son, be brought to bed with a son. **–nausgabe,** *f.* weekly edition. **–nbett,** *n.* childbed. **–nbettfieber,** *n.* puerperal fever. **–nblatt,** *n.* weekly paper. **–neinnahme,** *f.* week's receipts. **–nend(e),** *n.* weekend. **–nfluß,** *m.* lochia (*Med.*). **–nhilfe,** *f.* maternity benefit. **–nkind,** *n.* new-born child. **–nkleid,** *n.* everyday dress. **–nlang,** *adv.* for weeks. **–nlohn,** *m.* weekly wage. **–nrechnung,** *f.* weekly bill. **–nschau,** *f.* news-reel (*Cinema*). **–nschrift,** *f.* weekly publication *or* magazine. **–nstube,** *f.* lying in room. **–ntag,** *m.* weekday. **–ntags,** *adv.* on weekdays.

wöch-entlich, *adj.* weekly; every week; by the week; *dreimal –entlich,* three times a week, three times weekly. **–ig,** *adj. suffix* of . . . weeks, e.g. *vier–ig,* lasting 4 weeks; 4 weeks old. **–nerin,** *f.* woman in childbed; maternity case.

Wocken, *m.* (-s, –) (*dial.*) distaff.

wodurch, *inter.* & *rel. adv.* (= **durch welches** *or* **was,** *inter. or rel. pron. with prep.*) whereby, through *or* by means of which.

wo-fern, *conj.* if, in case, provided that, (in) so far as; *–fern nicht,* unless. **–für,** *inter.* & *rel. adv.* (= **für welches** *or* **was,** *inter. or rel. pron. with prep.*) wherefore; for which, for what, what for? *–für ist das gut?* what is that good for? what good is that? *–für halten Sie mich?* what do you take me for? *er ist das nicht, –für er angesehen sein will,* he is not what he pretends to be.

wog, wöge, *see* **wägen; wiegen.**

Wog-e, *f.* (-en) wave, billow. **–en,** *v.n.* (*aux.* h.) surge, heave, roll, wave, undulate, fluctuate. **–ig,** *adj.* wavy, billowy; surging.

wo-gegen, 1. *inter.* & *rel. adv.* (= **gegen welches** *or* **was,** *inter. or rel. pron. with prep.*) against which, in return *or* exchange for which. 2. *conj.* whereas, whilst, on the other hand. **–her,** *inter.* & *rel. adv.* whence, from where, from which *or* what place; how; *–her wissen Sie das?* how do you know that? *–her er auch kommen mag,* wherever he may come from; (*coll.*) *ach –her!* such nonsense! where do you get that from? **–hin,** *inter.* & *rel. adv.* whither, where, which way, to what *or* which place; *–hin gehen Sie,* (*coll.*) *– gehen Sie hin?* where are you going to? *der Ort –hin ich gehe,* the place I am going to. **–hinaus,** *inter.* & *rel. adv.* to what place, which way; *–hinaus das führen soll, weiß ich nicht,* I don't know where that will lead to *or* end. **–hingegen,** *conj.* while, whilst, whereas. **–hinter,** *inter.* & *rel. adv.* (= **hinter welchem** *or* **was,** *inter. or rel. pron. with prep.*) behind *or* after which.

wohl, 1. *adv.* (*comp.* -er & besser, *sup.* am -sten & am besten) (*accented*) well; *– dem, der . . .,* happy he, who . . .; *– ihm, daß er das nicht erlebt hat!* good for him that he missed that; *– !* aye, aye, sir! (*Naut.*); *– bekomm's (Ihnen)!* your health! *sich wieder – finden,* be well again, be recovered; *–er habe ich mich nie gefühlt,* I never felt better; *ich fühle mich hier am –sten,* I am happiest here, it suits me best here; *leben Sie – !* farewell! good-bye! (*ich*) *wünsche – geruht zu haben!* I hope you slept well, did you have a good night? (*ich*) *wünsche (Ihnen) – zu schlafen,* I wish you a good night, sleep well! *sich's (Dat.) – sein lassen,* enjoy o.s., have a good time; (*ich*) *wünsche – gespeist zu haben!* I hope you enjoyed your meal, I hope the meal was to your satisfaction; *das tut –,* that's nice, comforting *or* soothing (*see* **–tun**); *es tut mir –, wenn,* it does me good when, I feel happy when; – *oder übel*, willy-nilly, come what may. **2.** *part.* (*unaccented*) indeed, to be sure, no doubt; perhaps, probably, I shouldn't wonder, I daresay; (*archaic*) forsooth; *es heißt – . . ., aber . . .*, it is said indeed . . ., but . . .; *heute nicht, – aber morgen*, not today, but perhaps tomorrow; *er hat – Geld, aber . . .*, it is true that *or* to be sure he has money, but . . .; *das habe ich mir – gedacht*, I thought as much; *er wird – noch kommen*, he will probably come; *du hättest – kommen können*, you might very well have come; *das könnte – sein, es kann – sein*, that may well be, that is very possible; *ich möchte – wissen*, I should like to know; *das ist – möglich*, that is indeed possible; *es ist – möglich, daß*, quite possibly; *das kann er – nicht tun*, he cannot very well do that; *siehst du nun –, daß ich Recht habe?* now do you see that I am right? *ob er mich – noch kennt!* I wonder whether he still knows me! *es sind – drei Jahre, daß . . .*, I suppose it is three years since . . . **3.** *n.* welfare, well-being, prosperity; good health, (*archaic*) weal; *auf Ihr* or *zum –!* your health! here's to you! *das gemeine –*, the common weal, the common good; – *und Wehe*, weal and woe. **–achtbar,** *adj.* right honourable; worshipful. **–an,** 1. *adv.* boldly. 2. *int.* come on! well! now then! *–an, es sei darum!* all right! good, that's settled. **–angebracht,** *adj.* well-timed, opportune. **–anständigkeit,** *f.* decorum, propriety. **–auf,** 1. *adv.* well, in good health. 2. *int.* cheer up! come on! now then! **–bedacht,** 1. *adj.* well-considered, deliberate. 2. *m.*; *mit –bedacht*, after mature reflection. **–bedächtig,** 1. *adj.* deliberate. 2. *adv.* advisedly. **–befinden,** *n.* good health; well-being. **–befugt,** *adj.* well qualified, quite competent, justly entitled. **–begabt,** *adj.* richly endowed, highly gifted. **–begütert,** *adj.* well-off, rich. **–behagen,** *n.* comfort, ease. **–behalten,** *adj.* safe and sound; in good condition. **–bekannt,** *adj.* well-known, familiar, notorious. **–beleibt,** *adj.* corpulent, stout, fat. **–belesen,** *adj.* well-read. **–beschaffen,** *adj.* in good condition. **–bestallt,** *adj.* duly installed *or* appointed. **–bewußt,** *adj.* conscious. **–durchdacht,** *adj.* well-considered. **–ergehen,** 1. *v.n.* (*aux.* s.) (*sep.*) (*with Dat.*) go well (with), prosper. 2. *n.* well-being, welfare, health and happiness, prosperity. **–erzogen,** *adj.* well-bred, well brought up. **–fahrt,** *f.* welfare, weal; *–fahrt beziehen* or *erhalten, in die –fahrt kommen*, receive public assistance; *der –fahrt zur Last fallen*, be a burden on the rates; *öffentliche –fahrt*, public welfare, common weal. **–fahrtsamt,** *n.* welfare centre. **–fahrtsausschuß,** *m.* Committee of Public Safety (*Hist.*). **–fahrtspflege,** *f.* welfare work. **–fahrtspflegerin,** *f.* woman welfare-worker. **–fahrtsstaat,** *m.* welfare state. **–feil,** *adj.* cheap. **–feilheit,** *f.* cheapness. **–gebaut,** *adj.* well-made. **–gebildet,** *adj.* well-shaped, well-formed, fine, handsome. **–geboren,** *adj.* (*archaic*) Esquire; Sir *or* Madam. **–gefallen,** *n.* liking, pleasure, satisfaction, (*B.*) goodwill; *sich in –gefallen auflösen*, be settled to everyone's satisfaction; (*coll.*) slip into oblivion; *Friede auf Erden und den Menschen ein –gefallen*, (*B.*) peace on earth and goodwill to all men. **–gefällig,** *adj.* pleasant, agreeable, satisfactory, complacent. **–gefühl,** *n.* pleasant feeling. **–gelitten,** *adj.* much liked, popular. **–gemeint,** *adj.* well-intentioned, well-meant. **–gemerkt,** *adv.*, *see* **–verstanden** (2). **–gemut,** *adj.* cheerful, cheery, joyous, gay. **–genährt,** *adj.* well-fed, well-nourished. **–geneigt,** *adj.* well-disposed, favourably inclined. **–geruch,** *m.* pleasant odour, scent, aroma, fragrance, perfume. **–geschmack,** *m.* pleasant taste *or* flavour. **–gesinnt,** *adj.* well-disposed (*einem*, to a p.). **–gesittet,** *adj.* well-mannered, well brought up. **–gestalt,** *see* **–gebildet. –gestaltet,** *adj., see* **–gebaut. –gewogen,** *adj., see* **–geneigt. –gewogenheit,** *f.* kindness, affection. **–habend,** *adj.* wealthy, well-to-do, well-off. **–habenheit,** *f.* easy circumstances, affluence, opulence, wealth. **–ig,** *adj.* happy, cheerful, content; nice, pleasant, comfortable, (*coll.*) cosy, snug. **–klang,** *m.* pleasing sound; euphony, harmony, melody. **–klingend,** *adj.* harmonious, melodious, musical; sonorous; euphonious, pleasing to the ear. **–laut,** *m., see* **–klang. –lautend,** *adj.* euphonious. **–leben,** *n.* life of pleasure; luxury, good living. **–meinend,** *adj.* well-meaning, friendly. **–redenheit,** *f.* eloquence. **–riechend,** *adj.* scented, fragrant, perfumed, aromatic; *–riechende* or *spanische Wicken*, sweet-peas (*Lathyrus odoratus*) (*Bot.*). **–schmeckend,** *adj.* tasty, palatable, savoury, nice. **–sein,** *n.* good health, well-being; (*auf*) *Ihr* or *zum –sein!* your health! **–stand,** *m.* prosperity, fortune, wealth, easy circumstances, well-being. **–tat,** *f.* benefit, blessing; kindness, favour; good deed, benefaction, charity; *eine –tat annehmen* (*erweisen*), accept (do) a favour. **–täter,** *m.* benefactor. **–täterin,** *f.* benefactress. **–tätig,** *adj.* beneficent, salutary; charitable. **–tätigkeit,** *f.* charity, beneficence. **–tuend,** *adj.* beneficial, pleasant, comforting. **–tun,** *ir.v.n.* (*sep.*) (*aux.* h.) do good, give pleasure, be comforting, be pleasing *or* pleasant; dispense charity; (*Prov.*) *–tun bringt Zinsen*, he who gives to the poor lends to the Lord. **–unterrichtet,** *adj.* well-informed. **–verdient,** *adj.* just, well-deserved, well-merited. **–verhalten,** *n.* good conduct. **–verleih,** *m.* arnica (*Bot.*). **–verstanden,** 1. *adj.* well-known, generally understood. 2. *p.p. used as imper.* mark my words! **–weise,** *adj.* most wise. **–weislich,** *adv.* prudently, wisely. **–wollen,** 1. *ir.v.n.* (*sep.*) (*aux.* h.) (*einem*) wish (a p.) well, be well-disposed to (a p.). 2. *n.* goodwill, kindness, benevolence, kind feeling(s); good opinion; *einem –wollen entgegenbringen* or *bezeigen*, show goodwill towards s.o., be well disposed to s.o. **–wollend,** *adj.* kind, benevolent.

wohn–en, 1. *v.n.* (*aux.* h.) dwell, live, reside, (*Scots*) stay; *er –t bei meinem Bruder*, he lives at my brother's *or* with my brother; *zur Miete –en*, lodge; *so wahr ein Gott im Himmel –t*, as true as there is a God in Heaven; *die Hoffnung –t in seinem Herzen*, hope lives in his heart. **–bar,** *adj.* habitable, fit for habitation. **–bau,** *m.* domestic architecture. **–bezirk,** *m.* locality, habitat. **–gebiet,** *n., see* **–bezirk. –grube,** *f.* cave dwelling. **–haft,** *adj.* living, dwelling, resident; *sich an einem Orte –haft niederlassen*, settle *or* take up residence in a place. **–haus,** *n.* dwelling-house. **–haushalt,** *m.* ecology. **–küche,** *f.* living room-cum-kitchen. **–lich,** habitable, comfortable, convenient, pleasant to live in, (*coll.*) cosy, snug. **–lichkeit,** *f.* habitableness; comfort. **–ort,** *m.* place of residence, home, domicile. **–raum,** *m.* living-room, quarters (*Naut.*, *Mil.*). **–schlafzimmer,** *n.* bed-sitting-room. **–sitz,** *m., see* **–ort. –stätte,** *f., see* **–ort. –stube,** *f.* living-room. **–tier,** *n.* host (*of parasites*). **–ung,** *f.* dwelling, residence, habitation; house, flat; *Kost und –ung*, board and lodging. **–ungsamt,** *n.* lodgings-office. **–ungsgeldzuschuß,** *m.* lodging allowance. **–ungslos,** *adj.* homeless. **–ungsnachweis,** *m.* house-agency. **–ungsnot,** *f.* housing shortage *or* problem. **–ungssuche,** *f.* house-hunting. **–ungs(ver)änderung,** *f.*, **–ungswechsel,** *m.* change of address *or* residence. **–ungswesen,** *n.* housing. **–viertel,** *n.* residential district. **–wagen,** *m.* caravan. **–zimmer,** *n.* living-room.

Woilach, *m.* (-s, -e) saddle-blanket.

wölb–en, *v.a. & r.* vault, arch; camber; *sich –en*, arch, vault; *gewölbter Gang*, arched passage; *gewölbter Keller*, vault. **–ung,** *f.* arch, dome, vault; camber, curvature, bow; *–ung des Gaumens*, roof of the mouth. **–fläche,** *f.* (äußere) extrados; (innere) intrados. **–stütze,** *f.* centring (*Arch.*).

Wolf, *m.* (-(e)s, ⸗e) wolf; chafing (*of the skin*); pig, bloom (*of metal*); mincing machine, devil, willow (*Spin.*); (*Prov.*) *mit den Wölfen heulen*, do at Rome as the Romans do; *sich* (*Dat.*) *einen – laufen*, rub o.s. sore by walking; (*Prov.*) *wenn man den – nennt, so kommt er gerennt*, or *wenn man vom –e spricht, ist er nicht weit*, speak of the devil and he appears; *reißende Wölfe*, ravening wolves; – *und Schaf*, fox and geese (*game*); – *im Schafspelz*, wolf in sheep's clothing. **–en,** 1. *v.a.* clean (*cotton or wool*) with the willow, willow. 2. *v.n.* whelp (*of wolves*); (*dial.*) cut teeth (*of children*). **–sbohne,** *f.* lupin(e) (*Bot.*)

-seisen, *n.* wolf-trap, caltrop; bloom-iron (*Metall.*). **-sgrube,** *f.* pit *or* trap for catching wolves; pitfall; covered pit, tank trap (*Mil.*). **-shund,** *m.* wolf-hound, Alsatian (dog). **-shunger,** *m.* ravenous hunger. **-skirsche,** *f.* deadly nightshade, belladonna (*Bot.*). **-slager,** *n.* wolf's haunt *or* lair. **-smilch,** *f.* spurge (*Euphorbia*) (*Bot.*). **-srachen,** *m.* cleft palate (*Med.*). **-(s)schlucht,** *f.* den of wolves. **-ssucht,** *f.* lycanthropy.

Wölfi-n, *f.* she-wolf. **-sch,** *adj.* wolfish.

Wolfram, *n.* tungsten, wolframite (*Chem.*). **-sauer,** *adj.* tungstate of. **-säure,** *f.* tungstic acid.

Wolk-e, *f.* (-en) cloud; flaw (*in gems*); swarm; (*fig.*) *in die -en erheben,* exalt to the skies; (*wie*) *aus den* or *allen -en fallen,* be thunderstruck, be taken aback; *die -en ziehen,* the clouds are drifting. **-enachat,** *m.* clouded agate. **-enan,** *adv.* up to the clouds. **-enartig,** *adj.* cloud-like. **-enbildung,** *f.* cloud formation. **-enbruch,** *m.* cloudburst, violent downpour. **-endecke,** *f.* pall of cloud. **-enhaft,** *adj.* cloud-like. **-enhimmel,** *m.* cloudy sky, welkin. **-enhoch,** *adj.* (as) high as the clouds. **-enkratzer,** *m.* skyscraper. **-enkuckucksheim,** *n.* Cloud-Cuckoo-Land, castles in the air. **-enleer,** *adj.,* **-enlos,** *adj.* cloudless. **-enschäfchen,** *n. pl.* fleecy clouds. **-enschicht,** *f.* cloud layer *or* stratum. (*coll.*) **-enschieber,** *m.* scene-shifter (*Theat.*). **-enstufe,** *f.* cloud level. **-enwand,** *f.* bank of clouds. **-ig,** *adj.* clouded, cloudy.

wölken, *v.a., n. & r.* (*aux.* h.) cloud (over), become cloudy *or* overcast.

Woll-e, *f.* (-arten *or* -en) wool; down; hair (*of rabbits, goats, camels, etc.*); *einen in die -e bringen,* make a p. angry; *in der -e gefärbt,* dyed in the wool (*also fig.*); *in die -e geraten,* get angry; *-e lassen müssen,* come off a loser, be fleeced; *in der -e sitzen,* be on velvet, be in clover; *-e spinnen,* (*fig.*) make a nice profit; (*Prov.*) *viel Geschrei und wenig -e,* great boast, small roast; much ado about nothing. **-abgang,** *m.* wool waste. **-baum,** *m.* silk-cotton-tree, kapok (*Ceiba & Bombax*) (*Bot.*). **-bereiter,** *m.* wool-dresser. **-decke,** *f.* blanket. **-endecke, -engarn, -enstoff, -enwaren,** *see* **-decke, -garn, -stoff, -waren. -färber,** *m.* wool-dyer. **-farbig,** *adj.* dyed in the wool. **-faser,** *f.* wool fibre. **-fett,** *n.* lanoline. **-garn,** *n.* woollen yarn, wool. **-gras,** *n.* cotton-grass (*Eriophorum*) (*Bot.*). **-haar,** *n.* woolly hair; strand of wool. **-ig,** *adj.* woolly, fleecy, downy; curly; cotton-bearing, lanate, laniferous. **-industrie,** *f.* woollen industry. **-kamm,** *m.* carding-comb. **-kratze,** *f.* wool-card. **-kraut,** *n.* mullein (*Verbascum*) (*Bot.*). **-markt,** *m.* wool mart. **-pulver,** *n.* flock. **-reißer,** *m.* wool-carder. **-schur,** *f.* sheep-shearing. **-schweiß,** *m.* suint. **-staub,** *m., see* **-pulver. -stoff,** *m.* woollen material. **-waren,** *f.pl.* woollens. **-zeug,** *n.* woollen material.

woll-en, 1. *ir.v.a.* will, be willing; wish, want, desire, like, choose; ordain, intend, have a mind (to), be about (to), be on the point (of); **(a)** (*ellipt.*) *was -en Sie von mir?* what do you want of me? *wo willst du hin?* where do you wish to go? where are you going to? *er -te nach England,* he wished to go to England; (*coll.*) *sie -te ihn nicht,* she refused him; *zu wem -en Sie?* whom do you wish to see? *die Sache will nicht recht vom Flecke* or *will nicht vorwärts,* the affair does not progress; *der Deckel will nicht ab,* the lid won't come off; (*coll.*) *wart! dir will ich,* just wait! you'll catch it! *einem zu Leibe -en,* fall upon, attack a p.; *hoch hinaus -en,* have extravagant aims; **(b)** *macht was Ihr -t,* do what you like, do your worst; (*das*) *-e Gott,* would to God! *Gott will es,* it is God's will; *das -e Gott nicht!* God forbid! *so Gott will,* please God; *ich will nur hoffen, daß er . . .,* I do hope he . . .; *lieber -en,* prefer; *ich will lieber, ich -te lieber,* I would rather, I should prefer; *er mag -en oder nicht,* whether he likes it or not; **(c)** *ohne es zu -en,* unintentionally; *wir -en gehen,* let us go; *ich -te eben ausgehen, als . . .* I was on the point of going *or* about to go out when . . .; *hier ist nichts zu -en,* there is nothing to be had here; (*coll.*) *mit ihm ist nichts zu -en,* there is nothing to be done with him; *was willst du damit sagen?* what do you mean by that? *das will nicht viel sagen,* that is of little account *or* of no consequence; *es will Nacht werden,* night is coming on; **(d)** *er will alles wissen,* he claims to know everything; *ich will nicht hoffen, daß er . . .,* I hope he won't . . .; *ich will es nicht gehört haben,* I shall pretend *or* maintain I haven't heard it; *ich will nichts gesagt haben,* I take back my words *or* what I said; *dieser Baum will fetten Boden,* this tree requires a rich soil; *das will ich meinen,* I should think so indeed; **(e)** (= **mögen**) *ich will mich gern geirrt haben,* I should be glad to think I was mistaken; *ich will gern glauben, daß Sie . . .,* I am ready to believe that you . . .; *das will etwas heißen,* that means something, there's s.th. in that; *es geschehe was da -e,* whatever happens *or* may happen; come what may; *dem sei wie ihm -e,* be that as it may; *es sei, wo es -e,* wherever it may be; **(f)** (= **können**) *mir will scheinen,* it seems to me; *das will mir nicht in den Sinn,* I can't understand that; *es will mir nicht aus dem Sinn,* I can't forget it, I can't get it out of my mind; **(g)** (= **müssen;** *with negative* = **dürfen**) *er -e sofort kommen,* he is to come immediately; *das Werkzeug will so angefaßt sein,* the tool must be held thus; *eine solche Arbeit will Zeit haben.* such work demands time; *weitere Auskunft -e man einholen bei . . .,* for (further) particulars apply to . . .; *das will nicht übereilt sein,* it must not be hurried; *was -en wir sagen wenn,* what are we (going) to say if; **(h)** *after an inf.* = *p.p.* **gewollt;** *er hat nicht kommen -en,* he didn't want to come; *ich habe nur scherzen -en,* I only intended it as a joke, I was only joking. 2. *n.* will, volition, intention, inclination.

Woll-ust, *f.* (⸚e) sensual pleasure, voluptuousness; lasciviousness, lust, debauchery; (*archaic*) delight, bliss; *höchste -ust,* orgasm; *der -ust nachhängen,* be given to pleasures of the flesh. **-üstling,** *m.* sensualist, voluptuary; debauchee, libertine.

wo-mit, *inter. & rel. adv.* (= **mit welchem,** *inter. or rel. pron. with prep.*) wherewith, with *or* by which *or* what, by what means; *das ist's -mit ich nicht zufrieden bin,* that is what I am not satisfied with. **-möglich,** *adv.* if possible; perhaps, possibly. **-nach,** *inter. & rel. adv.* (= **nach welchem,** *inter. or rel. pron. with prep.*) whereafter, whereupon, after *or* towards *or* according to which; *-nach fragt er?* what is he asking for *or* about?

Wonn-e, *f.* (-en) joy, delight, rapture, ecstasy, bliss; *in -e schweben* or *schwimmen,* be enraptured. **-egefühl,** *n.* delightful sensation. **-emonat,** *m.,* **-emond,** *m.* month of May. **-erausch,** *m.* transport of delight. **-ereich,** *adj.* blissful. **-esam,** *adj.* (*Poet.*), *see* **-ig. -eselig,** *adj.* in ecstasy. **-etaumel,** *m.* rapture, ecstasy of delight. **-etränen,** *f. pl.* tears of joy. **-etrunken,** *adj.* enraptured. **-ig,** *adj.,* **-iglich,** *adj.* (*Poet.*) delightful, delicious, blissful.

wor-, *prefix* (= **wo**) *before prep. beginning with vowel;* = *case of inter. or rel. pron.* wer, was, welcher, der, *governed by the prep.* **-an,** *inter. & rel. adv.* whereon, whereat, on, of, against *or* by which *or* what; *das Buch, -an ich arbeite,* the book I am working on; *ich weiß nicht, -an ich mit ihm bin,* I don't know what to make of him; *-an bin ich?* where have I got to? how far did I reach? where did I leave off? *der Kasten, -an er sich mit dem Kopfe gestoßen,* the chest against which he struck his head; *-an liegt es, daß . . .?* how is it that . . .? *-an hat er mich erkannt?* by what did he recognize me? *-an war es befestigt?* what was it fastened to? **-auf,** *inter. & rel. adv.* whereupon, upon, to *or* at which *or* what; *-auf sinnst du?* what are you meditating on? *-auf alle fort gingen,* whereupon everyone went away. **-aus,** *inter. & rel. adv.* whence, by, out of *or* from which *or* what. **-ein,** *inter. & rel. adv.* (*rare for* wohinein, in was, in den) whereinto, into which *or* what; *das ist etwas -ein ich mich nicht mische,* that is a thing I don't meddle with. **-in,** *inter. & rel. adv.* wherein, in which *or* what. **-nach** (*Austr. dial.*), *see* **wonach. -über,** *inter. & rel. adv.* whereat, whereof, of, about *or* over which *or* what; *-über lachst du?* what are you laughing at? *das ist es, -über ich mich wundere,* that is what astonishes me; *-über ich sehr ärgerlich war,* at which

I was very angry. **-um,** *inter. & rel. adv.* for *or* about which; *-um handelt es sich?* what is it about? what is the matter? **-unter,** *inter. & rel. adv.* in, under *or* among which *or* what; *-unter hatte er sich versteckt?* what did he hide under? *die verbotenen Bücher, -unter auch dieses gehört,* the prohibited books, of which this is one.

worden, *p.p. of* werden *in compound tenses.*

Worf-el, *f.* (-n) (*dial.*) winnowing-shovel. **-eln,** *v.a.* fan, winnow. **-ler,** *m.* winnower. **-maschine,** *f.* fan, winnowing-machine. **-tenne,** *f.* winnowing floor.

Wort, *n.* (-(e)s, ⸚er = *unconnected words, vocables; in all other cases* -e) word, vocable, term, expression, saying; promise, pledge, word of honour; *einem die -e vom Munde ablesen,* see *das - aus dem Munde nehmen*; *einem das - abschneiden,* see *ins - fallen*; *das - abtreten,* allow another p. to speak; *am -e sein,* have leave to speak, have the ear of the House (*Parl.*); *aufs -,* to the letter, implicitly; *auf ein -!* just a word! *auf mein -,* on my word of honour; *einem aufs - glauben,* believe a p. implicitly, take a man's word for it; *auf seine -e hin,* on the strength of his remarks; *ich komme nur auf ein paar -e,* may I have a few words; *auf jemandes - schwören,* pin one's faith on a p.'s words; *er hielt mich beim -,* he held me to my word; *er nahm mich beim -e,* he took me at my word; *in - und Bild,* with text and illustrations; *dein - in Ehren,* with all deference to you; *einem das - entziehen,* refuse a p. permission to continue, stop a p. (speaking); *das - ergreifen,* (begin to) speak; *das - erhalten,* be allowed to speak (*Parl.*); *einem das - erteilen,* see *einem das - geben*; *nicht das leiseste - fallen lassen,* not drop *or* let fall the slightest hint; *das - führen,* be spokesman, speak for *or* on behalf of (s.o.); *das große - führen,* swagger, brag, boast, draw the long bow; *einem das - geben,* allow a p. to speak; *ein - gab das andere,* one word led to another; *geflügelte -e,* household words, familiar quotations; *mit wenig -en,* in a few words, briefly; *einem gute -e geben,* speak a p. fair; *nicht für Geld und gute -e zu haben,* not to be had for love or money; *das - haben,* see *am -e sein*; (*coll.*) *hast du -e!* my word! goodness gracious! *er will es nicht - haben,* he denies *or* will not admit (the truth of) it *or* acknowledge it as true; *- halten,* keep one's word; *nicht - halten,* break one's word; *man kann sein eigenes - nicht hören,* one can't hear one's own voice; *in die -e . . . ausbrechen,* burst out with the words . . .; *einem ins - fallen,* interrupt a p., cut a p. short; *kein - mehr!* not another word! *er läßt ein - mit sich reden,* he listens to reason; *jedes - auf die Goldwaage legen,* see *jedes - zählen*; *seinen Gedanken -e leihen,* clothe one's thoughts in words; *ohne viel(e) -e zu machen,* to cut a long story short; *er macht nicht viel(e) -e,* he is a man of few words; *viel -e um nichts machen,* make a fuss *or* a great to-do *or* much ado about nothing; (*Prov.*) *ein Mann, ein -!* word of honour! honour bright! *mit ausdrücklichen -en,* in express terms; *mit dürren -en,* dryly; *mit einem -e,* in a word; *es war mit keinem - davon die Rede,* not a word of it was mentioned; (*Prov.*) *ein gutes - findet eine gute Statt,* a good (*or* kind) word is never out of place; *den -en nach verstehen,* take literally; *einem das - aus dem Munde nehmen,* take the words out of a p.'s mouth; *einem* (or *einer S.*) *das - reden,* speak for *or* in favour of a p. (*or* a th.), take a p.'s part; *große -e reden,* make rash promises, brag, (*sl.*) talk big; *spare dir deine -e,* save your breath; *ums - bitten,* beg permission *or* ask leave to speak (*Parl.*); *einem das - im Munde umdrehen,* misinterpret what s.o. says, twist a p.'s words; *kein - über eine S. verlieren,* waste no words about a matter; *er ist ein Mann von -,* he is as good as his word *or* is a man of his word; *- und Weise,* words and music; *jedes - zählen,* weigh every word; *nicht zu -e kommen,* not get a chance to speak; *einen zu -e kommen lassen,* let a p. have his say; *einen nicht zu -e kommen lassen,* not allow a p. to get a word in edgeways; *sich zum -e melden,* see *ums - bitten*; *ein - zu seiner Zeit,* a word spoken in season. **-arm,** *adj.* deficient in vocabulary. **-armut,** *f.* poverty of language. **-art,** *f.* part of speech (*Gram.*). **-aufwand,** *m.* verbosity. **-bau,** *m.* structure of words. **-bedeutungslehre,** *f.* semantics. **-biegung,** *f.* inflection. **-biegungslehre,** *f.* accidence. **-bildung,** *f.* word-formation. **-bruch,** *m.* treachery, breach of faith. **-brüchig,** *adj.* having broken one's word, treacherous, disloyal, false; *-brüchig werden,* break one's word. **-emacher,** *m.* idle talker. **-erklärung,** *f.* verbal explanation; definition. **-fechter,** *m.* stickler for words. **-folge,** *f.* word order. **-forscher,** *m.* philologist, etymologist. **-forschung,** *f.* etymology. **-fügung,** *f.* syntax, sentence structure. **-führer,** *m.* spokesman; foreman (*of a jury*). **-fülle,** *f.* verbosity. **-gefecht,** *n.* dispute, altercation. **-gepränge,** *n.* bombast. **-geschichte,** *f.* etymology. **-gestalten,** *v.a.* (*sep.*) put into words. **-getreu,** *adj.* word for word, literal. **-habend,** *adj.* presiding. **-held,** *m., see* **-emacher. -kampf,** *m., see* **-gefecht. -karg,** *adj.* laconic, taciturn. **-kargheit,** *f.* taciturnity. **-klauber,** *m.* quibbler, hair-splitter. **-klauberei,** *f.* hair-splitting. **-kram,** *m.* verbiage, idle talk. **-krämer,** *m.* phrase-monger. **-kunde,** *f.* philology. **-laut,** *m.* wording, text. **-lehre,** *f.* accidence. **-macherei,** *f.* verbiage, empty talk. **-mangel,** *m., see* **-armut. -rätsel,** *n.* rebus. **-register,** *n.* vocabulary. **-reich,** *adj.* fluent; wordy, verbose. **-reichtum,** *m.* verbosity; wordiness, verbiage. **-reiz,** *m.* verbal stimulus. **-schatz,** *m.* vocabulary, words in use. **-schwall,** *m.,* **-schwulst,** *m.* torrent of words, rigmarole, verbosity, bombast, fustian. **-sinn,** *m.* literal sense, meaning of a word. **-spiel,** *n.* play upon words, pun. **-stammkunde,** *f.* etymology. **-stellung,** *f., see* **-folge. -streit,** *m.* dispute, controversy. **-stummheit,** *f.* motor aphasia. **-taubheit,** *f.* sensory aphasia. **-tarif,** *m.* charge per word (*Tele.*). **-treue,** *f.* fidelity to the text. **-verdrehung,** *f.* distortion of the meaning. **-versetzung,** *f.* transposition of words, inversion. **-verstand,** *m.* literal sense **-verzeichnis,** *n., see* **-register. -wechsel,** *m.* high words, dispute, altercation. **-wechseln,** *v.n.* (*insep.*) make a slip in words, confuse terms. **-wörtlich,** *adv.* literally, word for word, exactly. **-zeichen,** *n.* trade name, catch-word.

Wört-chen, *n.* (-s, -) little *or* trivial word; *unveränderliches -chen,* particle; *ein -chen mitzureden haben,* have a say in the matter. **-eln,** *v.n.* (*dial.*) quarrel, squabble, haggle, bicker. **-erbuch,** *n.* dictionary; vocabulary; glossary. **-erverzeichnis,** *n.* list of words, vocabulary. **-lich,** *adj.* literal, verbal, word for word, verbatim; *-liche Beleidigung,* verbal insult, slander. **-lichkeit,** *f.* literalness, literal character.

woselbst, *adv.* where, in the very place where *or* that.

wo-von, *inter. & rel. adv.* (= **von welchem,** *inter. or rel. pron. with prep.*) whereof, of, about *or* concerning which. **-vor,** *inter. & rel. adv.* (= **vor welchem,** *inter. or rel. pron. with prep.*) of, from *or* before which *or* what; *-vor fürchtest du dich?* what are you afraid of? **-zu,** *inter. & rel. adv.* (= **zu welchem** *or* **was,** *inter. or rel. pron. with prep.*) whereto, to what purpose; why; to, for, at *or* in addition to what *or* which; *-zu das?* what is that for? why that? *-zu man Lust hat,* what one is inclined for.

wrack, 1. *adj.* wrecked, derelict (*Naut.*); unserviceable, beyond repair; (*C.L.*) unusable, discarded. 2. *n.* (-(e)s, -e & -s) wreck, wreckage, derelict, hulk (*Naut.*). **-gut,** *n.* jetsam; *treibendes -gut,* flotsam.

Wrasen, *m.* (-s, -) (*dial.*) steam, hot exhalation.

wricken, wriggen, *v.a.* scull (*a boat over the stern*).

wring-en, *v.a.* twist; wring. **-maschine,** *f.* wringer, mangle.

Wruke, *f.* (-n) (*dial.*) Swedish turnip.

Wucher, *m.* (-s, -) usury; profiteering, (*B. & dial.*) gain, profit; interest; *- treiben,* practise usury, make excessive profit; *mit - vergelten,* repay *or* return with interest. **-blume,** *f.* (ox-eye) daisy (*Chrysanthemum leucanthemum*) (*Bot.*). **-ei,** *f.* usury, profiteering. **-er,** *m.* money-lender, usurer; profiteer. **-frei,** *adj.* without interest *or* usury. **-geschäft,** *n.,* **-handel,** *m.* usurious trade. **-gewinn,** *m.* inordinate profit. **-isch,** *adj.*

usurious, profiteering; *-isch aufkaufen*, forestall. **-miete,** *f.* rack-rent. **-n,** *v.n.* (*aux.* h.) grow rapidly, luxuriantly *or* rankly, be rampant, proliferate, produce abundantly; give a good return; practise usury, profiteer; make the most of; *mit dem Gelde -n*, lend money at usurious interest; *mit seinen Gaben -n*, exploit one's resources. **-nd,** *adj.* rank (*growth*); (*fig.*) prolific, rampant. **-preis,** *m.* exorbitant charge. **-stier,** *m.* (*dial.*) bull. **-ung,** *f.* rank growth, proliferation, exuberance; growth, tumour, proud flesh (*Path.*). **-zins,** *m.* extortionate interest.

Wuchs, *m.* (-es, ⸚e) growth, development; form, figure, shape, stature, height; plantation. **-haft,** *adj.* organic. **-kräftig,** *adj.* having vigorous growth (*of plants*).

wuchs, wüchse, *see* **wachsen.**

-wüchsig, (*suffix*) growing well; of . . . growth *or* stature; *hoch-*, tall-growing.

Wucht, *f.* (-en) weight, pressure, burden; force, impetus, kinetic energy, fulcrum; (*dial.*) load; (*coll.*) *eine - Prügel*, a sound thrashing. **-baum,** *m.* lever. **-en,** 1. *v.n.* (*aux.* h.) (*Poet.*) weigh heavy, lie *or* press heavily upon; *-ende Last*, heavy *or* oppressive burden. 2. *v.a.* lift with difficulty, lever *or* prise up; (*coll.*) work like a horse. **-ig,** *adj.* weighty, heavy; vigorous, powerful.

wühl-en, *v.a., v.n. & v.r.* (*aux.* h.) root, dig *or* grub up (*the ground*); burrow, turn up the ground; rummage, rake about (in); (*fig.*) agitate, stir up, foment (*discontent, etc.*); (*fig.*) gnaw (*as pain*); *sich* (*Dat.*) *in den Haaren -en*, run one's hands through one's hair; *in einer Wunde -en*, probe a wound; *der Schmerz -t mir in den Eingeweiden*, pain is gnawing at my vitals; *-ender Schmerz*, gnawing pain. **-arbeit,** *f.* subversive activity. **-er,** *m.* agitator; (*pl.*) rooting animals. **-erei,** *f.* rummaging, raking about; underground activity. **-erisch,** *adj.* inflammatory, subversive. **-gang,** *m.* run, burrow (*of mole, etc.*). **-maus,** *f.* vole (*Microtus*) (*Zool.*).

Wuhne (*Austr. dial.*), *see* **Wune.**

Wulst, *m.* (-es, ⸚e) & *f.* (⸚e) swelling, tuberosity; bulge, hump; fold, pad, roll, convolution; chignon (*for hair*); torus (*Arch.*). **-ig,** *adj.* stuffed, padded, swollen, puffed up, swelled, tumid, protruding, pouting; *-ige Lippen*, thick *or* puffy lips. **-haar,** *n.* chignon, hair-roll. **-ling,** *m.* death angel (*Amanita*) (*Bot.*).

wund, *adj.* sore, galled, chafed, chapped; wounded, injured; *sich* (*Dat.*) *die Füße - laufen*, get sore feet; *sich - liegen*, get bedsores; *-er Punkt*, (*fig.*) sore point; *-e Stelle*, sore *or* tender place *or* spot. **-arz(e)neikunst,** *f.* (*archaic*) surgery. **-arzt,** *m.* (*archaic*) surgeon. **-balsam,** *m.* vulnerary balsam. **-brand,** *m.* mortification, necrosis (*Med.*). **-e,** *f.* wound, injury, sore; (*fig.*) hurt. **-enfrei,** *adj.* unwounded, unhurt; (*Poet.*) unscathed. **-fieber,** *n.* wound-fever. **-gedrückt,** *adj.* galled. **-gelaufen,** *adj.* footsore. **-heit,** *f.* soreness, tenderness. **-klammer,** *f.* suture clip (*Med.*). **-klee,** *m.* kidney vetch (*Anthyllis vulnararia*) (*Bot.*). **-mal,** *n.* scar; stigma (*Eccl.*). **-rose,** *f.* erysipelas. **-schere,** *f.* probe-scissors. **-sein,** *n.* soreness, excoriation. **-starrkrampf,** *m.* tetanus.

Wunder, *n.* (-s, -) marvel; miracle; wonder, surprise, astonishment; *sein blaues - an, bei* or *mit einer S. erleben*, marvel *or* be amazed at a th.; *das ist kein -*, that is not surprising; (*es ist*) *kein -* or *was -, daß . . .*, (it is) no wonder that . . .; *es nimmt mich -*, I wonder at it; *- tun*, work wonders *or* miracles; *er denkt - was getan zu haben*, he thinks he has done something wonderful; *ich dachte - was es wäre*, I had expected far more, I was bitterly disappointed with *or* at it; *er bildet sich - was ein*, he thinks a lot *or* no end of himself, is full of conceit *or* (*sl.*) is cocky; *er bildet sich - was darauf ein*, he prides himself ever so much on it; *ich hielt sie für - wie klug*, I thought her wonderfully clever. **-bar,** *adj.* amazing, surprising, strange, marvellous, wondrous, miraculous; (*coll.*) wonderful, splendid, great, (*sl.*) ripping, spiffing, wizard. **-barerweise,** *adv.* strange to say. **-baum,** *m.* castor-oil plant (*Riccinus communis*) (*Bot.*). **-baumöl,** *n.* castor-oil. **-bild,** *n.* wonder-working image. **-ding,** *n.* wonderful thing, marvel, prodigy, phenomenon. **-doktor,** *m.* quack (doctor). **-erscheinung,** *f.* miraculous phenomenon. **-glaube,** *m.* belief in miracles. **-groß,** *adj.* colossal. **-hold,** *adj.* exceptionally charming; most gracious. **-horn,** *n.* enchanted *or* magic horn. **-hübsch,** *adj.* extremely lovely, wonderfully pretty. **-kerze,** *f.* sparkler. **-kind,** *n.* infant prodigy. **-kraft,** *f.* magic *or* miraculous power. **-kur,** *f.* faith healing. **-lich,** *adj.* strange, odd, singular, peculiar, queer, curious; whimsical, wayward, eccentric; *-licher Kauz*, odd fish, queer chap; *es ist ihm -lich ergangen*, strange things happened to him; *mir wurde -lich zu Mute*, I felt very queer. **-lichkeit,** *f.* oddness, strangeness; whimsicality; eccentricity. **-märe,** *f.* wonderful *or* wondrous news, fantastic story. **-mittel,** *n.* panacea. **-n,** 1. *v.a. & imp.* surprise, astonish; *das -t mich*, I am astonished at it; *es -t mich daß . . .*, I am surprised that; *es soll mich doch -n, ob . . .*, I wonder if . . . 2. *v.r.* (*aux.* h.) be surprised (*über*, at); *ich -e mich zu hören*, I am astonished to hear; *ich -e mich über ihn*, I am surprised at him. **-nehmen,** *v.a.* (*sep.*) astonish, surprise; *es nimmt mich -, daß . . .*, I am astonished that . . .; *es sollte mich nicht -nehmen, wenn . . .*, I should not be at all surprised if . . . **-sam,** *adj.* (*Poet.*), *see* **-bar.** **-schön,** *adj.* very beautiful, lovely, exquisite. **-tat,** *f.* miracle; wonderful exploit, (*Poet.*) doughty deed. **-täter,** *m.* miracle-worker. **-tätig,** *adj.* wonder-working, miraculous. **-tier,** *n.* monster; (*coll.*) prodigy; *einen wie ein -tier anstaunen*, stare at a p. as if he were a strange animal. **-voll,** *adj.* wonderful; marvellous; splendid, admirable, wondrous. **-werk,** *n.* phenomenal achievement, wonder, miracle. **-zeichen,** *n.* miraculous sign, portent.

Wune, *f.* (-n) (*dial.*) vent-hole in ice, ice-hole.

Wunsch, *m.* (-es, ⸚e) wish, desire; desideratum (*pl.* desiderata), felt want; (*pl.*) good wishes, congratulations; *einem jeden - von den Augen ablesen*, anticipate a p.'s every wish; *auf -*, if desired; *einen - ausdrückend*, desiderative, optative (*Gram.*); (*C.L.*) *hätten Sie noch einen -?* is there anything else you require? can I serve you with anything else? *je nach -*, as desired *or* required; *mir geht alles nach -*, everything is going on as well as I could wish; *mein sehnlichster -*, my dearest wish. **-bild,** *n.* ideal. **-erfüllung,** *f.* realization of one's desires. **-form,** *f.* optative form (*Gram.*). **-gemäß,** *adv.* according to one's wishes. **-los,** *adj.* contented, satisfied; resigned, unrepining; blasé. **-mädchen,** *n.*, **-maid,** *f.* (*Poet.*) Valkyrie. **-partikel,** *f.* optative particle. **-satz,** *m.* optative clause. **-programme,** *n.* request programme. **-traum,** *m.* wish-fulfilment. **-weise,** *adv.* in the form of a wish. **-zettel,** *m.* list of things one would like, letter to Santa Claus.

wünsch-en, *v.a.* wish, desire (*einem etwas*, a th. for s.o.); (*sich* (*Dat.*)) long for, wish for; *ich -e* (*Ihnen*) *von* (*ganzem*) *Herzen*, I wish it (for you) with (all) my heart; *ich -te mir einige tausend Mark mehr*, I wish I had a few thousand marks more; *einem* (*zu etwas*) *Glück -en*, congratulate a p. (on a th.), wish s.o. luck; *nichts sehnlicher -en als*, wish nothing better than; *es läßt* (*viel*) *zu -en übrig*, it is not satisfactory, it leaves much to be desired; (*ich*) *-e wohl geruht zu haben*, I hope you have slept well. **-bar,** *adj.* (*Swiss dial.*), *see* **-enswert.** **-ding,** *n.* desirable object. **-elrute,** *f.* wishing-wand; divining-rod. **-enswert,** *adj.* (*with Dat.*) desirable; *es wäre mir -enswert zu wissen*, I should very much like to know.

wupp-(s), *int. & adv.* like a shot, in a flash, here goes! pop! **-dich,** *m.* (-s, -s) jerk; (*dial.*) noggin, shot (*of brandy, etc.*). **-tizität,** *f.* (*sl.*) speed, agility.

würbe, *see* **werben.**

wurde, würde, *see* **werden.**

Würd-e, *f.* dignity, majesty; propriety; (*pl.* -en) post (of honour), rank, office, honour, title, (academic) degree; *akademische -e*, academic degree; *in Amt und -en*, holding (high) office; *nach -en*, worthily; *unter aller -e*, beneath contempt; *unter meiner -e*, beneath my dignity; *seiner -e etwas vergeben*, compromise one's dignity; *zu den höchsten -en erheben*, raise to the highest position of honour. **-elos,** *adj.* undignified. **-enträger,** *m.* dignitary. **-evoll,** *adj.* dignified. **-ig,** *adj.* worthy, deserving (*Gen.*, of); estimable, respectable, dignified; *er ist dessen nicht -ig*, he does not deserve it. **-igen,** *v.a.* (*Acc. of p. & Gen. of th.*) deem worthy, deign, vouchsafe; value, appreciate, rate, estimate; *er -igte mich seiner Freundschaft*, he honoured me with his friendship; *nach seinem Werte -igen*, rate at its true value, value at its true worth; *er -igte mich keiner Antwort*, he vouchsafed no answer; *zu -igen wissen*, know how to appreciate. **-igkeit,** *f.* merit, worth. **-igung,** *f.* appreciation, estimation, valuation, assessment.

Wurf, *m.* (-es, ⸚e) throw, cast, projection, line, direction, style; brood, litter; *Sie sind am -e*, it is your throw; *alles auf einen - setzen*, stake all on one throw, put all one's eggs in one basket; *auf den ersten -*, at the first shot; *der - der Falten*, the way the folds hang; *glücklicher -*, lucky shot; *einem in den - kommen, laufen* or *rennen*, come within a p.'s field, just suit s.o., (*sl.*) be just up s.o.'s street; *einen - tun*, (have a) throw; *zum - aufholen*, get ready to throw. **-bahn,** *f.* trajectory. **-bewegung,** *f.* projectile motion. **-bild,** *n.* projected picture, projection. **-feuer,** *n.* (trench) mortar fire (*Mil.*). **-geschoß,** *n.* projectile, missile. **-geschütz,** *n.* mortar, howitzer. **-granate,** *f.* mortar shell *or* bomb. **-größe,** *f.* size of litter. **-holz,** *n.* throwing stick. **-kraft,** *f.* projectile force. **-lehre,** *f.* ballistics. **-linie,** *f.*, *see* **-bahn. -maschine,** *f.* catapult. **-messer,** *n.* throwing knife, boomerang. **-mine,** *f.* thrown explosive. **-netz,** *n.* casting-net. **-pfeil,** *m.* dart. **-riemen,** *m.* leash (*Falconry*). **-ring,** *m.*, **-scheibe,** *f.* quoit; discus. **-schaufel,** *f.* winnowing-shovel *or* -fan. **-schlinge,** *f.* lasso. **-sendungen,** *f.pl.* mass distribution of pamphlets. **-speer,** *m.*, **-spieß,** *m.* javelin, dart. **-taube,** *f.* clay-pigeon (*Sport*). **-waffe,** *f.* missile. **-weise,** *adv.* in lots *or* heaps. **-weite,** *f.* stone's throw; range (*Artil.*).

würfe, *see* **werfen.**

Würfel, *m.* (-s, -) cube; hexahedron; die (*pl.* dice); *der - ist* or *die - sind gefallen*, the die is cast; *falsche -*, cogged *or* loaded dice; *die - kneipen*, cog the dice; *- spielen*, play at dice. **-becher,** *m.* dice-box. **-bein,** *n.* cuboid bone (*Anat.*). **-förmig,** *adj.* cubic, in the form of a cube, cube-shaped. **-ig,** *adj.* cubical; checkered; tessellated. **-inhalt,** *m.* cubic content. **-kapitell,** *n.* cubiform capital (*Arch.*). **-kohle,** *f.* small coal; (*pl.*) nuts. **-muster,** *n.* checkered pattern. **-n,** 1. *v.n.* (*aux.* h.) play at dice, throw dice; *um eine S. -n*, throw dice for s.th. 2. *v.a.* checker, (*dial.*) throw *or* toss about, winnow (*grain*). **gewürfelt,** *p.p. & adj.*, *see* **-ig.** 3. *n.* dice-playing. **-spiel,** *n.* game of dice; dice-playing. **-stein,** *m.* boracite. **-zahl,** *f.* cubic number, cube. **-zucker,** *m.* lump-sugar.

würg-en, 1. *v.n.* (*aux.* h.) & *r.* choke, gulp, retch; wreak havoc; *er -t* (*sich*) *an diesem Bissen, dieser Bissen -t ihn im Halse*, this mouthful has stuck in his throat; *an einer Arbeit -en*, struggle hard at a task; (*coll.*) *mit Hängen und -en*, with no end of trouble, with the greatest difficulty. 2. *v. a.* choke; strangle, throttle; take by the throat; (*Poet. & B.*) slaughter, slay, massacre. **-engel,** *m.* angel of destruction *or* death. **-er,** *m.* (*Poet.*) destroyer, slayer, murderer; butcher-bird, red-backed shrike (*Lanius collurio*) (*Orn.*).

Wurm, *m.* (-(e)s, ⸚er) worm, grub, maggot; (*Poet.*) (*pl. also* ⸚*e*) serpent, snake, dragon, reptile, vermin; fancy, whim, crotchet; whitlow; farcy (*Vet.*); (*also n.*) helpless little child, little mite, poor little creature; *auch der - krümmt sich*, even a worm will turn; (*coll.*) *einem die Würmer aus der Nase ziehen*, draw a p. out, worm secrets out of a p.; *du armes -* (or *Würmchen*)! poor little mite! *den - haben*, be maggoty (*Hort.*). **-abtreibend,** *adj.* anthelmintic; *-abtreibendes Pulver*, worm-powder, vermifuge. **-artig,** *adj.* vermiculate. **-en,** *v.a. usually imp.*; *es -t mich*, it rankles, I am vexed at it; *das -t und frißt so weiter*, that keeps on eating at me, it is gall and wormwood (to me). **-farn,** *n.* shield-fern (*Dryopteris*) (*Bot.*). **-förmig,** *adj.* vermicular, worm-shaped. **-fortsatz,** *m* appendix (*Med.*). **-fraß,** *m.* damage by maggots; *das Holz hat -fraß*, the wood is worm-eaten. **-fräßig,** *adj.* worm-eaten. **-ig,** *adj.* worm-eaten; wormy, maggoty, worm-like; annoyed, vexed. **-krank,** *adj.* suffering from worms. **-krankheit,** *f.* (intestinal) worms. **-kraut,** *n.* anthelmintic herb. **-loch,** *n.* worm-hole. **-mehl,** *n.* worm(-hole) dust. **-mittel,** *n.* vermifuge, anthelmintic, worm-medicine. **-nudeln,** *f.pl.* vermicelli. **-pille,** *f.*, **-plättchen,** *n.*, **-pulver,** *n.* worm-pill, -powder. **-samen,** *m.* worm-seed (*Artemsia* & *Chenopodium*) (*Bot.*). **-stich,** *m.* worm-hole. **-stichig,** *adj.* worm-eaten, maggoty. **-treibend,** *adj.*, **-widrig,** *adj. see* **-abtreibend.**

Würm-chen, *n.* (-chens, *pl.* -chen) (*coll.*) poor little mite. **-erkunde,** *f.* vermeology.

Wurst, *f.* (⸚e) sausage; *die - nach dem Manne braten*, treat a p. according to his deserts; *du willst immer eine besondere - gebraten haben*, you always expect special consideration; (*Prov.*) *bratst du mir die -, so lösch' ich dir den Durst*, one good turn deserves another; (*sl.*) *das ist mir* (*ganz*) -, it is all one *or* all the same to me, it leaves me cold; (*coll.*) *es geht um die -*, it's a question of now or never; *die -* or *mit der - nach der Speckseite werfen*, a sprat to catch a mackerel; *- wider -*, tit for tat. **-brühe,** *f.* water in which sausages were boiled. **-darm,** *m.* sausage gut *or* skin. **-eln,** (*sl.*) muddle through *or* along; *es wird so weiter gewurstelt*, it goes on in the same way. **-elprater,** *m.* (*Austr. dial.*) fun-fair (*Prater in Vienna*). **-eltheater,** *n.* (*Austr. dial.*) Punch and Judy show. **-en,** *v.n.* (*aux.* h.) make sausages. **-fleisch,** *n.* sausage-meat. **-förmig,** *adj.* sausage-shaped. **-händler,** *m.* pork-butcher. **-ig,** *adj.* (*sl.*) quite indifferent. **-igkeit,** *f.* indifference. **-igkeitsgefühl,** *n.* mood of utter indifference. **-kessel,** *m.* sausage-maker's copper; (*coll.*) *jetzt sitze ich im -kessel*, now I am in the soup. **-kraut,** *n.* marjoram (*Majorana hortensis*) (*Bot.*). **-laden,** *m.* pork-butcher's shop. **-reiter,** *m.* parasite. **-suppe,** *f.*, *see* **-brühe. -vergiftung,** *f.* sausage-poisoning, botulism, allantiasis (*Med.*). **-waren,** *f.pl.* sausages. **-warenhandlung,** *f.*, *see* **-laden.**

Wurz, *f.* (-en) (*only as suffix*) = **Wurzel.**

Würz-e, *f.* (-en) spice; seasoning, flavouring, dressing; wort (*Brew.*); (*fig.*) zest; (*Prov.*) *in der Kürze liegt die -e*, brevity is the soul of wit. **-elchen,** *n.* radicle, rootlet. **-en,** *v.a.* spice, season; (*fig.*) give zest (to). **-fleisch,** *n.* spiced meat. **-haft,** *adj.*, **-ig,** *adj.* spicy; piquant, well-seasoned; fragrant, aromatic. **-kräuter,** *m.pl.* aromatic herbs. **-los,** *adj.* flavourless, insipid, unseasoned, unspiced; (*fig.*) flat. **-näg(e)lein,** *n.*, **-nelke,** *f.* clove (*Eugenica aromatica*) (*Bot.*). **-stoff,** *m.* seasoning, condiment. **-wein,** *m.* spiced *or* mulled wine; medicated wine.

Wurzel, *f.* (-eln) root (*Bot.*, *Gram.*, *Math.*); *mit der - ausreißen* or *ausrotten*, uproot, pull up by the root(s); (*fig.*) eradicate; *die - aus einer Zahl ziehen*, find the (square) root of a number; *- schlagen, treiben* or *fassen*, take *or* strike root; *gelbe -n*, carrots. **-artig,** *adj.* root-like. **-ausläufer,** *m.* stolon. **-ausschlag,** *m.* sucker. **-auszieher,** *m.* stump-forceps (*Dentistry*). **-brand,** *m.* root rot (*of sugar beet*). **-echt,** *adj.* ungrafted; genuine. **-exponent,** *m.* radical index (*Math.*). **-faser,** *f.* root fibril. **-fest,** *adj.* root-bound. **-fressend,** *adj.* root feeding. **-füß(l)er,** *m.pl.* rhizopoda (*Zool.*). **-gemüse,** *n.* root vegetable. **-gewächse,** *n.pl.* root crops. **-größe,** *f.* radical quantity (*Maths.*). **-haft,** *adj.* rooted, radical. **-ig,** *adj.* rooty, full of roots (*of the ground*). **-keim,** *m.* radicle. **-knollen,** *m.* root nodule, tubercle, tuber. **-knospe,** *f.* turion (*Bot.*). **-locker,** *adj.* not firmly rooted. **-los,** *adj.* rootless, without roots. **-n,** 1. *v.n.* (*aux* h. & s.) take *or* strike root, become rooted, send out roots; *in einer S. -n*, have its root *or* origin in a th. 2. *v.r.*; *sich fest -n*, become firmly established. **-ranke,** *f.* runner (*Bot.*). **-schoß,** *m.*, **-schößling,** *m.* sucker, runner, layer. **-silbe,** *f.* root syllable, stem (*Gram.*). **-sprosse,** *f.* sucker. **-sprossend,** *adj.* putting forth suckers, soboliferous. **-ständig,** *adj.* radical; growing from the root.

-stock, *m.* rootstock, rhizome. **-stoff,** *m.* radical principle. **-vokal,** *m.* radical *or* root vowel. **-werk,** *n.* root system. **-zahl,** *f.* root (*of a number*). **-zeichen,** *n.* root *or* radical sign (*Math.*).

wusch, wüsche, *see* **waschen.**

wuschel-ig, *adj.* tousled. **-kopf,** *m.* (*dial.*) mop of hair.

wußte, wüßte, *see* **wissen.**

Wust, *m.* confusion, chaos, mess, rubbish, lumber; (*Austr. & Swiss dial.*) (*abbr. for* **Warenumsatzsteuer**) purchase-tax. **-feld,** *n.* (*dial.*) fallow land.

wüst, *adj.* desert, waste, desolate, deserted, uncultivated, fallow; confused, wild, disorderly; dissolute; (*dial.*) filthy, ugly, vulgar, coarse, rude; – *stehen* or *liegen*, lie fallow; – *durcheinander*, in utter confusion; *der Kopf ist mir ganz* –, my head is quite muddled; *ein -es Leben führen*, lead a dissolute life. **-e,** *f.* desert, wilderness; (*B.*) *Prediger in der -e*, voice crying in the wilderness; (*einen*) *in die -e schicken*, (*fig.*) send into the wilderness *or* to Coventry, remove from office, deprive of influence (*Pol.*). **-en,** *v.n.* (*aux.* h.) (*with* mit) waste, squander, spoil, ruin; lead a dissolute life. **-enei,** *f.* barren place, wilderness. **-enschiff,** *n.* ship of the desert (*camel*). **-heit,** *f.* wilderness, desolation; disorderliness; dissoluteness. **-ling,** *m.* libertine, dissolute person. **-ung,** *f.* derelict area *or* site, (abandoned) site.

Wut, *f.* rage, fury, frenzy, madness, mania; rabies, hydrophobia; *in – geraten*, fly into a rage; *in – setzen*, enrage; *seine – an einem auslassen*, vent one's fury on a p. **-anfall,** *m.* fit of rage. **-ausbruch,** *m.* outburst of fury. **-entbrannt,** *adj.* infuriated, furious, enraged. **-schäumend,** *adj.*, **-schnaubend,** *adj.* foaming with rage, in a towering rage, infuriated, furious. **-seuche,** *f.* rabies, hydrophobia.

wüt-en, *v.n.* (*aux.* h.) rage, rave, be furious. **-end,** *pr.p. & adj.* raging, enraged, frantic, fanatical, furious, raving, frenzied, mad. **-erich,** *m.* ruthless tyrant; bloodthirsty villain. **-ig,** *adj.*, *see* **-end;** rabid (*of dogs*).

X

X, x, *n.* X, x; unknown quantity, *x* (*Math.*); *Herr* –, Mr. what's his name? *jemandem ein – für ein U vormachen*, throw dust in a p.'s eyes, take a p. in, bamboozle a p.; dupe a p.; *ich lasse mir kein – für ein U vormachen*, I was not born yesterday; *see Index of Abbreviations.* **-t,** *adj.*; *die -te Potenz*, the *n*th power; (*coll.*) *zum -ten Male*, for the hundredth time. **--achse,** *f.* axis of the abscissa (*Math.*). **--beine,** *n.pl.* knock-knees. **--beinig,** *adj.* knock-kneed. (*coll.*) **--beliebig,** *adj.* any (whatever), whatever *or* whoever (you like); *eine --beliebige Linie*, any line you please; *eine --beliebige Person*, anyone you like. (*coll.*) **--mal,** *adv.* ever so often, any number of times; (*coll.*) umpteen; *ich habe es ihm --mal gesagt*, I have said it to him times without number, I don't know how many times, umpteen times; *ich habe ihn --mal gewarnt*, I have warned him, I have said it to him *or* I've told him over and over again.

Xanthippe, *f.* (*coll.*) shrewish wife, (*sl.*) 'trouble and strife'.

Xenie, *f.* (-n) satirical epigram.

Xereswein, *m.* sherry.

Xylograph, *m.* (-en, -en) wood-engraver. **-ie,** *f.* wood-engraving. **-ieren,** *v.a.* engrave on wood. **-isch,** *adj.* xylographic.

Xylophon, *n.* (-s, -e) xylophone.

Y

Y, y, *n.* Y, y; ypsilon; *Noctua gamma* (*Ent.*). **--achse,** *f.* axis of the ordinate (*Math.*).

Yperit, *n.* mustard gas.

Ypsiloneule, *f. Agrotis ypsilon* (*Ent.*).

Ysop, *m.* (-s, -e) hyssop (*Hyssopus officinalis*) (*Bot.*).

Ytter-binerde, *f* ytterbium earth. **-erde,** *f* yttrium earth. **-spat,** *m.* xenotime.

Z

See also under C.

Z, z, *n.* Z, z; *von A bis Z*, from beginning to end; *see Index of Abbreviations.*

Zabel, *m.* (-s, –) (*obs.*) chess-board.

Zack-e, *f.* (-en), **-en,** *m.* (-ens, -en) point, peak, jag, spike; prong (*of a fork*); tooth (*of a comb*); scallop, scalloping (*dressmaking*), crenature (*Bot.*). **-en,** *v.a.* fix spikes to, tooth, notch; pink (*Dressm.*). **-enförmig,** *adj.* notched, jagged. **-enkrone,** *f.* indented crown. **-enlinie,** *f.* notched *or* serrated line; line of a redan; line of peaks. **-enmuster,** *n.* toothed pattern. **-enwalze,** *f.* notched roller, clod-crusher. **-enwerk,** *n.* scalloping, pinking; redan (*Fort.*). **-ig,** *adj.* pointed, jagged, toothed, pronged; notched, indented, scalloped; crenate, dentated, serrate (*Bot.*); (*coll.*) smart, snappy, glamorous.

zäckeln, *v.a.* cut notches in, notch, indent, scallop, pink.

zackern, *v.a.* (*dial.*) plough.

zag, -(e), *adj.*, *see* **-haft. -en,** *v.n.* (*aux.* h.) be afraid, be faint-hearted *or* timorous, hesitate; *mit Zittern und -en*, with great trepidation, (*coll.*) quaking in one's shoes. **-haft,** *adj.* faint-hearted, fearful, timorous, afraid, timid, cautious, irresolute. **-haftigkeit,** *f.*, **-heit,** *f.* timidity, fear, timorousness; irresolution.

Zagel, *m.* (-s, –) (*dial.*) tail, pigtail; penis.

zäh(e), 1. *adj.* tough, tenacious; stubborn; viscous, sticky, glutinous, gluey; ductile; *-e Beharrlichkeit*, stubborn perseverance; *ein -es Leben haben*, be tenacious of life. 2. *f.* tenacity, **-eit,** *f.*, **-igkeit,** *f.* tenacity, toughness; stickiness, viscosity. **-festig,** *adj.* tenacious. **-flüssig,** *adj.* viscous, sticky. **-flüssigkeit,** *f.* viscosity, sluggishness. **-lebig,** *adj.* tenacious of life, difficult to kill.

Zahl, *f.* (-en) number, numeral, figure, digit, cipher; *wenig an der* –, few in number; *benannte* –, denominate quantity, concrete number; (*Prov.*) *-en beweisen*, numbers are conclusive *or* convincing; *ganze* –, whole *or* integral number; *gebrochene* –, fraction; *gerade* –, even number; *in großer* –, in large numbers; *ohne* –, numberless, countless, innumerable; *runde* –, round number; *-en sprechen*, numbers talk; *unbenannte* –, abstract number; *ungerade* –, odd number; *vierstellige* –, number of four digits; *die volle* –, the full number, the total, all of them. **-abverb(ium),** *n.* numeral adverb. **-bar,** *adj.* payable, due; *-bar werden*, fall due; *-bar auf* or *bei Sicht*, a vista, payable at sight. **-buchstabe,** *m.* numeral letter, Roman numeral. **-en,** *v.a.* (*einem etwas*) pay; pay for, atone for; *Kinder -en die Hälfte*, children half-price; *Kellner, -en!* waiter! the bill, please; *einen Wechsel -en*, meet a bill. **-enangabe,** *f.* numerical data. **-enbeispiel,** *n.* numerical example. **-enbruch,** *m.* numerical fraction. **-enfolge,** *f.* numerical order. **-engröße,** *f.* number, numerical quantity. **-enlotterie,** *f.* lottery with numbers, lotto. **-enmäßig,** *adj.* numerical. **-enmystik,** *f.* magic of numbers. **-enreihe,** *f.* numerical series *or* progression. **-enschloß,** *n.* combination lock. **-entafel,** *f.* table of figures. **-entheorie,** *f.* theory of numbers.

–enverhältnis, *n.* numerical proportion. **–enwert,** *m.* numerical value. **–er,** *m.* payer; *säumiger –er*, one who is slow *or* behind in his payments; *schlechter –er*, defaulter, bad customer. **–fähig,** *adj.* solvent. **–karte,** *f.* money-order form. **–kellner,** *m.* head-waiter. **–los,** *adj.* numberless, innumerable, countless. **–meister,** *m.* paymaster (*Mil.*), purser (*Naut.*). **–meisterei,** *f* paymaster's *or* purser's office. **–pfennig,** *m.* counter (*for indoor games*). **–pult,** *n.* pay- *or* cash-desk. **–reich,** *adj.* numerous. **–schein,** *m.* promissory note. **–stelle,** *f.* pay-office, cashier's office. **–tag,** *m.* pay-day, settling-day. **–tisch,** *m.*, *see* **–pult.** **–unfähig,** *adj.* insolvent. **–ung,** *f.* payment; acquittance; *einen zur –ung anhalten*, enforce payment on a p.; *gegen bar(e) –ung*, for cash; *um –ung bitten*, solicit payment, solicit the favour of a cheque; *die –ung einstellen*, suspend payment; *–ung erhalten*, paid, settled (*at the foot of bills*); *–ung leisten*, (*C.L.*) make a payment, effect payment; *eine –ung in Raten leisten*, pay by instalments; *mangels –ung*, in default of payment; *Mangel an –ung*, non-payment; *in –ung nehmen*, take in part-payment; *an –ungs Statt*, in lieu of cash. **–ungsabkommen,** *n.* economic agreement. **–ungsanweisung,** *f.* order, draft, cheque, money *or* postal order. **–ungsaufschub,** *m.* moratorium. **–ungsbedingungen,** *f.pl.* terms (of settlement). **–ungsbefehl,** *m.* writ of execution. **–ungsbilanz,** *f.* balance of payments. **–ungseinstellung,** *f.* suspension of payment. **–ungsempfänger,** *m.* payee. **–ungsfähig,** *adj.* solvent. **–ungsfähigkeit,** *f.* solvency. **–ungsfrist,** *f.* date of payment. **–ungsmittel,** *n.* (legal) tender. **–ungsunfähig,** *adj.* insolvent. **–ungsunfähigkeit,** *f.* insolvency. **–ungsverbindlichkeit,** *f.* liability to pay. **–ungsverkehr,** *m.* financial transactions. **–ungsweise,** *f.* mode of payment. **–wort,** *n.* numeral (*Gram.*).

zähl–en, *v.a.* & *n.* (*aux.* h.) count, reckon, number, compute; (*with* zu) belong to, be classed with, be among; *die Stadt –t 100,000 Einwohner*, the town numbers 100,000 inhabitants; *meine Tage sind gezählt*, my days are numbered; *auf jemanden –en*, count *or* rely on a p.; *die Bevölkerung –en*, take the census of the population; *er sieht aus, als könnte er nicht bis drei –en*, he looks as if he could not say boo to a goose; *einem die Bissen in den Mund –en*, grudge s.o. everything; *wenn ich mich zu Ihren Freunden* or *unter Ihre Freunde –en darf*, if I may consider myself one of your friends; *er –t zu den Besten*, he is reckoned among the best. **–apparat,** *m.* automatic counter. **–bar,** *adj.* computable, assessable. **–er,** *m.* counter, indicator; teller, (billiard-) marker; numerator (*Arith.*); meter, speedometer. **–reim,** *m.* children's rhyme for counting out. **–rohr,** *n.* Geiger counter (*Phys.*). **–stab,** *m.* counter (*Cards.*). **–strich,** *m.* tally. **–tisch,** *m.* counter. **–ung,** *f.* count, counting, calculation, computation, enumeration, census. **–zettel,** *m.* census-form.

zahm, *adj.* tame, domestic cultivated, tractable, docile, gentle, peaceable; *einen – kriegen*, bring s.o. to heel. **–heit,** *f.* tameness.

zähm–en, *v.a.* tame, domesticate, break in (*a horse*); subdue, check, curb, control, master, restrain. **–bar,** *adj.* tameable, controllable, restrainable. **–ung,** *f.* taming; domestication.

Zahn, *m.* (-(e)s, ⸚e) tooth, fang, tusk; tine, cog, prong; *einem auf den – fühlen*, sound a p., try a p. out; *Haare auf den Zähnen haben*, be a Tartar, be well able to look after o.s.; *einem etwas aus den Zähnen reißen*, snatch a th. out of a p.'s grip; *sich* (*Dat.*) *an etwas die Zähne ausbeißen*, break one's teeth on s.th.; *Zähne bekommen*, cut one's teeth; *bis an die Zähne bewaffnet*, armed to the teeth; *die Zähne fletschen*, show *or* bare one's teeth; *die Zähne klapperten, mir klapperten die Zähne* or *ich klapperte mit den Zähnen*, my teeth chattered; *mit den Zähnen knirschen*, gnash one's teeth; *die Zähne stumpf machen*, set one's teeth on edge; (*einem*) *die Zähne zeigen*, (*fig.*) show one's teeth, threaten, show fight; *der – der Zeit*, the ravages of time; *die Zähne zusammenbeißen*, set *or* clench one's teeth (*also fig.*). **–arm,** *adj.* having few teeth. **–artig,** *adj.* tooth-shaped, tooth-like. **–arzt,** *m.* dentist, dental surgeon. **–ärztlich,** *adj.* concerning dental surgery; *–ärztliche Behandlung*, *see* **–behandlung.** **–ausbruch,** *m.* dentition. **–behandlung,** *f.* dental treatment. **–bein,** *n.* dentine. **–belag,** *m.* film (on teeth). **–bildung,** *f.* formation *or* growth of teeth. **–bogen,** *m.* dental arch. **–bürste,** *f.* tooth-brush. **–durchbruch,** *m.*, *see* **–ausbruch.** **–email,** *n.* dental enamel. **–en,** *v.n.* (*aux.* h.) teethe, be teething, cut one's teeth. (*but cf. pp.* **gezähnt,** toothed, notched, denticular). **–ersatz,** *m.* artificial teeth, denture. **–fach,** *n.* alveolus. **–fäule,** *f.*, **–fäulnis,** *f.* dental caries. **–fistel,** *f.* fistula in the gum. **–fleisch,** *n.* gum(s). **–fleischerkrankung,** *f.* gingivitis. **–förmig,** *adj.* tooth-shaped, dentiform; odontoid. **–füllung,** *f.* stopping, filling. **–geschwür,** *n.* gum-boil, abscess. **–heilkunde,** *f.* dentistry. **–höhle,** *f.* socket of a tooth, dental cavity. **–ig,** *adj.* toothed, indented, jagged (*only as suffix, e.g.* **scharf–ig,** sharp-toothed). **–kitt,** *m.* dental cement *or* filling. **–kranz,** *m.* spur-gear. **–krone,** *f* crown of a tooth. **–künstler,** *m.* (*archaic*), *see* **–techniker.** **–laut,** *m.* dental (consonant). **–lehre,** *f.* odontology. **–lippenlaut,** *m.* labiodental (sound). **–los,** *adj.* toothless; *–lose Tiere*, edentata. **–lücke,** *f.* gap between teeth. **–paste,** *f.* tooth-paste, dentifrice. **–pflege,** *f.* care of the teeth. **–plombe,** *f.* stopping, filling. **–pulver,** *n.* dental powder; dentifrice. **–rad,** *n.* cogged *or* toothed wheel; cog wheel, gear(-wheel). **–radbahn,** *f.* rack-railway. **–räderwerk,** *n.* gearing. **–radgetriebe,** *n.* gear drive. **–reihe,** *f.* set of teeth, denture; row of indentations. **–reinigung,** *f.* cleaning of teeth. **–reißen,** *n.*, *see* **–schmerz.** **–schmelz,** *m.* dental enamel. **–schmerz,** *m.* toothache. **–schnitt,** *m.* denticulation; row of dentils (*Arch.*). **–stange,** *f.* rack; cog-rail. **–stangengetriebe,** *n.* rack and pinion. **–stein,** *m.* tartar. **–steinansatz,** *m.* tartar deposit. **–stocher,** *m.* toothpick. **–techniker,** *m.* dental mechanic. **–trommel,** *f.* sprocket. **Zahn- und Triebbewegung,** coarse and fine adjustment. **–ung,** *f.* dentition; serration. **–wasser,** *n.* tooth-wash, mouth-lotion. **–wechsel,** *m.* second dentition. **–weh,** *n.*, *see* **–schmerz.** **–weinstein,** *m.* tartar. **–wurzel,** *f.* root of a tooth. **–zange,** *f.* dentist's forceps.

Zähne–fletschen, 1. *n.* showing *or* baring one's teeth. 2. *v.n.* (*insep.*) bare one's teeth. **–klappern,** *n.* chattering of teeth. **–knirschen,** *n.* grinding of teeth. **–ln,** *v.a.* indent, denticulate, notch, tooth. **–lung (Zähnung),** *f.* serration, perforation (*of postage-stamps*). **–n,** *v.a.*, *see* **–ln.**

Zähre, *f.* (-n) (*Poet.*) tear.

Zain, *m.* (-(e)s, -e) ingot, bar, fillet, slip (*Mint.*); willow switch. **–e,** *f.* (*dial.*) basketwork, wickerwork, wicker basket.

Zander, *m.* (-s, –) pike-perch.

Zange, *f.* (-n) pliers, tongs, pincers; tweezers, forceps; palp (*Ent.*); maxilla, forcipated claw (*Zool.*). **–nförmig,** *adj.* pincer-like, claw-like. **–nbewegung,** *f.* pincer-movement (*Mil.*). **–nentbindung,** *f.*, **–ngeburt,** *f.* delivery with forceps. **–nschanze,** *f.*, **–nwerk,** *n.* tenail. **–nwinkel,** *m.* flanking angle.

zäng–en, *v.a.* shingle (*Metall.*). **–e(l)maschine,** *f.* metal-shingler.

Zank, *m.* (-es, (*rare*) ⸚e) quarrel, wrangle, brawl: (*coll.*) row; *einen – vom Zaune brechen*, go out of one's way to pick a quarrel; *mit jemandem – suchen*, pick a quarrel with a p. **–apfel,** *m.* bone of contention. **–en,** 1. *v.r.* & *n.* (*aux.* h.) quarrel, wrangle, fall out, have words (with). 2. *v.a.* scold; *sie –en sich über* (*Acc.*) *Kleinigkeiten* or *um des Kaisers Bart*, they quarrel over trifles. **–erei,** *f.* wrangling, bickering. **–haft,** *adj.* quarrelsome. **–lust,** *f.* quarrelsomeness. **–lustig,** *adj.* quarrelsome, bickering. **–stifter,** *m.* mischief-maker. **–sucht,** *f.*, *see* **–lust.** **–süchtig,** *adj.*, *see* **–lustig.** **–teufel,** *m.* wrangler; shrew.

Zänk–er, *m.* (-ers, -er) quarrelsome person, squabbler, bickerer, shrew. **–erei,** *f.*, *see* **Zankerei.** **–isch,** *adj.*, *see* **zankhaft.**

Zapf, *m.* (*dial.*), *see* **–en;** tap-room; hydrant; toper.

-en, 1. *m.* (-s, –) plug, bung, spigot, cock, tap; peg, pin, pivot, gudgeon, journal, trunnion; tenon (*Carp.*); fir-cone; fruit of the hop. 2. *v.a.* tap (*a cask*); join (*timber*) with mortise and tenon; *stehender -en*, pivot; *-en vom Tropfstein*, stalactite. **-artig,** *adj.*, **-enähnlich,** *adj.* pluglike; cone-shaped. **-enbäume,** *m.pl.* conifers. **-enbohrer,** *m.* tap-bore. **-enfrucht,** *f.* cone. **-enkorn,** *n.* ergot. **-enlager,** *n.* bush, socket, trunnion seat, journal bearing. **-enloch,** *n.* bung-hole; mortise. **-enlochmaschine,** *f.* mortising-machine. **-enstreich,** *m.* tattoo, retreat (*bugle-call*) (*Mil.*); *den -enstreich schlagen*, beat the tattoo. **-entragend,** *adj.* coniferous. **-enträger,** *m.pl.* conifers. **-enzieher,** *m.* (*dial.*) corkscrew. **-säule,** *f.* petrol-pump (*Motor.*). **-stelle,** *f.* (petrol-)filling station. **-wart,** *m.* petrol-pump attendant.

Zäpfchen, *n.* (-s, –) uvula (*Anat.*). **Zäpfchen-R,** *n.* uvular *or* guttural r. **-schnitt,** *m.* staphylotomy.

zapp-eln, *v.n.* (*aux.* h.) kick, struggle, wriggle, fidget (about), make convulsive movements; *einen -eln lassen*, keep a p. in suspense, (*coll.*) keep a p. dangling. **-(e)ler,** *m.* restless person. (*coll.*) **-elfritz(e),** *m.* fidget. **-(e)lig,** *adj.* struggling; fidgetty, restless.

Zar, *m.* (-en, -en) tsar. **-in,** *f.* tsarina.

Zarge, *f.* (-en) top rail (*of chairs, tables, etc.*); surround (*of doors, windows, etc.*); side (*of a flat box or case*), ribs (*of a violin, etc.*).

zart, *adj.* (*comp.* -er, *sup.* -est) delicate, fragile, frail; slender, slight; tender, soft, fine, sensitive; subdued, pale (*of colours*); *-es Fleisch*, tender meat; *das -e Geschlecht*, the weaker sex; *-e Gesichtsfarbe*, delicate complexion; *-e Gesundheit*, delicate health; *-er Wink*, gentle hint. **-besaitet, -fühlend,** *adj.*, sensitive; with fine feelings; tactful, considerate. **-gefühl,** *n.* delicacy of feeling, tactfulness, considerateness. **-heit,** *f.* tenderness, delicacy, softness; weakness, delicateness, frailty; morbidezza (*Paint.*). **-rosa,** *adj.* pale pink. **-sinn,** *m.*, *see* **-gefühl. -sinnig,** *adj.*, *see* **-fühlend.**

Zärt-elei, *f.* (-en) affectation of sensitiveness, exaggerated fondness. **-eln,** *v.n.* fondle, caress; flirt. **-lich,** *adj.* affectionate, tender, loving, fond; *-liches Geflüster* or *Getue*, billing and cooing, sweet nothings. **-lichkeit,** *f.* affection, tenderness, fondness; amourousness; caresses. **-ling,** *m.* (-s, -e) weakling, milksop, (*sl.*) pansy, cissy.

Zaser, *f.*, **-ig,** *adj.* (*dial.*), *see* **Faser, faserig.**

Zaspel, *f.* (-n) skein, hank.

Zäsur, *f.* (-en) caesura; *klingende –*, feminine caesura; *stumpfe –*, masculine caesura.

Zauber, *m.* (-s, –) spell, charm; magic, enchantment, glamour, fascination; (*coll.*) *fauler –*, lame excuse, tall story; (*coll.*) *der ganze –*, the whole concern; (*coll.*) *den – kennen wir*, we are up to those tricks; *– treiben* or *ausüben*, do magic, cast spells; *den – lösen* or *bannen*, break the spell. **-buch,** *n.* book of charms. **-ei,** *f.* magic, sorcery, witchcraft; spell, enchantment. **-er,** *m.* magician, sorcerer, wizard, conjurer, juggler. **-flöte,** *f.* magic flute. **-formel,** *f.*, *see* **-spruch. -garten,** *m.* enchanted garden. **-haft,** *adj.* magical, enchanted; bewitching, enchanting. **-in,** *f.* sorceress, witch. **-insel,** *f.* enchanted isle. **-isch,** *adj.*, *see* **-haft. -kasten,** *m.* box of conjuring tricks. **-kraft,** *f.* magic power. **-kräftig,** *adj.* magical. **-kunst,** *f.* magic art, black magic, witchcraft, sorcery; (*pl.*) conjuring tricks, sleight-of-hand. **-künstler,** *m.* magician, conjurer, illusionist, juggler. **-kunststück,** *n.* conjuring trick. **-land,** *n.* fairy-land. **-laterne,** *f.* (*archaic*) magic lantern. **-macht,** *f.*, *see* **-kraft. -mittel,** *n.* charm. **-n,** 1. *v.a.* conjure up, charm, cast a spell on *or* over; *sich* (*Dat.*) *etwas aus dem Ärmel -n*, produce from one's sleeve. 2. *v. n.* (*aux.* h.) practise magic *or* witchcraft, do by magic; conjure, do conjuring tricks; *ich kann doch nicht -n*, I can't work miracles. **-spiegel,** *m.* magic mirror. **-spruch,** *m.* incantation, charm, spell. **-stab,** *m.* magic wand. **-trank,** *m.* magic potion, philtre. **-werk,** *n.*, *see* **-ei. -wort,** *see* **-spruch. -wurzel,** *f.* mandrake (*Mandragora officinarum*) (*Bot.*).

zauder-n, 1. *v.n.* (*aux.* h.) hesitate, delay, procrastinate, temporize; waver, dally; *mit etwas -n*, hesitate about a th. 2. *n.*, **-ei,** *f.* hesitation, procrastination, delay; slackness. **-er,** *m.* **(Zaudrer)** dilatory *or* irresolute person; temporizer, procrastinator. **-haft,** *adj.* hesitating, irresolute, vacillating, dilatory. **-haftigkeit,** *f.* hesitation, irresolution, dilatoriness.

Zaum, *m.* (-(e)s, ⸚e) bridle, rein; *einem den – anlegen*, or *einen im -e halten*, keep a tight rein on a p., keep a p. in check, curb *or* restrain a p. **-los,** *adj.* unbridled. **-zeug,** *n.* horse's bridle.

zäum-en, *v.a.* bridle, curb, restrain, keep in check.

Zaun, *m.* (-(e)s, ⸚e) fence, railing; hedge; *lebendiger –*, quickset hedge; *eine Gelegenheit vom -e brechen*, make an opportunity; *einen Streit vom -e brechen*, take the first opportunity to pick a quarrel; *hinter jedem – zu finden*, to be found at every street corner; *das ist nicht hinter jedem – zu finden*, that is not to be met with every day; *einem über den – helfen*, (*fig.*) help s.o. over a stile; *hinterm -e sterben*, die in a ditch. **-gast,** *m.* looker-on, intruder. **-grasmücke,** *f.* lesser whitethroat (*Sylvia curruca*) (*Orn.*). **-könig,** *m.* wren (*Troglodytes*) (*Orn.*). **-latte,** *f.*, *see* **-pfahl. -lilie,** *f.* St. Bernard's lily, spiderwort (*Anthericum liliago*) (*Bot.*). **-(s)pfahl,** *m.* stake, pale; *einem mit dem -pfahl winken*, give a p. a broad hint. **-rebe,** *f.* Virginia creeper (*Parthenocissus quinquefolia*) (*Bot.*). **-rübe,** *f.* bryony (*Bryonia*) (*Bot.*). **-schlüpfer,** *m.*, *see* **-könig;** *großer -schlüpfer*, hedge-sparrow. **-tritt,** *m.* stile. **-wicke,** *f.* vetch (*Vicia sepium*) (*Bot.*). **-winde,** *f.* bearbine, bindweed (*Convolvulus sepium*) (*Bot.*).

zäunen, *v.a.* fence in, provide with a fence.

zausen, *v.a.* pull (about), tug; tousle, ruffle.

Zebra, *n.* (-s, -s) zebra.

Zebu, *m.* (-(s), -s) Indian bull, zebu.

Zech-e, *f.* (-en) 1. bill, score, reckoning (*at an inn*); 2. mine, mining company; *die -e bezahlen*, foot the bill, (*fig.*) suffer the consequences; *die -e machen*, make up the bill, present the bill; *die -e ohne den Wirt machen*, overlook the most important factor; *die -e prellen*, leave without paying the bill. **-bruder,** *m.* boon companion. **-en,** *v.a.* & *n.* (*aux.* h.) drink, tipple, carouse; run up a bill at an inn. **-enkoks,** *m.* foundry *or* furnace coke. **-enpreis,** *m.* pithead price. **-enrevier,** *n.* mining district *or* area. **-er,** *m.* (hard) drinker; toper; reveller. **-erei,** *f.* hard drinking; drinking-bout. **-frei,** *adj.* free of expense, scot-free; *einen -frei halten*, stand a p.'s drinks. **-gelage,** *n.* drinking party, spree. **-genosse,** *m.* *see* **-bruder. -gesellschaft,** *f.* drinking-party. **-kumpan,** *m.*, *see* **-bruder. -preller,** *m.* one who evades paying his bill. **-prellerei,** *f.* evading payment of one's bill. **-stein,** *m.* zechstein (*Min.*).

Zechine, *f.* (-n) sequin.

Zeck, *n.* (*dial.*) tick, tag (*game*). **-en,** *v.n.* (*dial.*) play tick *or* tag; (*dial.*) tease. **-spiel,** *n.*, *see* **-.**

Zecke, *f.* (-n) tick (*Ixodes*) (*Ent.*).

Zed-ent, *m.* (-en, -en) assigner, transferrer. **-ierbar,** *adj.* transferable, negotiable. **-ieren,** *v.a.* cede, surrender, transfer, assign.

Zeder, *f.* (-n) cedar (*Pinus cedrus*) (*Bot.*). **-n,** *adj.* of cedar. **-nholz,** *n.* cedar-wood.

Zedrat, *n.* candied (lemon) peel.

Zeh, *m.* (*rare*) -(e)s, -en), **-e,** *f.* (-en) toe; root (*of ginger*), stick (*of celery*); *auf den -en gehen*, walk on tiptoe *or* on one's toes; *sich auf die -en stellen*, stand on one's toes *or* on tiptoe; *einem auf die -en treten*, (*fig.*) tread on a p.'s toes *or* corns; *vom Wirbel bis zur -e*, from top to toe. **-engänger,** *m.pl.* Ungulata (*Zool.*). **-ennagel,** *m.* toe-nail. **-enspitze,** *f.* tip of the toe, tiptoe. **-enstand,** *m.* standing on tiptoe (*Gymn.*). **-gängig,** *adj.* digitigrade (*Zool.*). **-ig,** *adj.* (*only as suffix*) with (*so many*) toes.

zehn, *num. adj.* ten; *es ist dreiviertel –*, it is a quarter to 10; *es ist halb –*, it is half-past 9. **-(e),** *f.* the figure 10; the number 10, the ten (*at cards*). **-eck,** *n.* decagon. **-eckig,** *adj.* decagonal. **-einhalb,** *num. adj.* ten-and-a-half. **-ender,** *m.* stag of ten points. **-er,** *m.* a ten, half a score; a ten-pfennig piece; wine of the year 1910; soldier of the tenth regiment; *in den -ern stehen*, be in one's teens. **–erlei,** *adv.* of ten kinds. **–erreihe,** *f.* column of tens (*Arith.*). **–fach,** *adj.*, **–fältig,** *adj.* tenfold. **–flach,** *n.*, **–flächner,** *m.* decahedron (*Geom.*). **–füßer,** *m.* decapoda (*Zool.*). **–füßig,** *adj.* ten-footed, decapod. **–herrschaft,** *f.* decemvirate. **–jährig,** *adj.* 10 years old, of 10 years. **–jährlich,** *adj.* decennial. **–kampf,** *m.* decathlon (*Sport.*). **–mal,** *adv.* 10 times. **–malig,** *adj.* 10 times repeated. **–männ(er)ig,** *adj.* decandrian. **–pfennigstück,** *n.* ten-pfennig piece, (German) penny piece. **–silbig,** *adj.* decasyllabic. **–t,** 1. *num. adj.* (der, die, das -te) tenth; *der –te August*, August 10th, the tenth of August; *im –ten Kapitel*, in the tenth chapter; *die –te Muse*, variety (stage); *das kann der –te nicht vertragen*, not one in ten can stand it; *das weiß der –te nicht*, nine out of ten don't know it. 2. *m. see* **–te. –tablösung,** *f.* commutation of tithes. **–te,** *m.* (-en, -en) tithe; *mit –en belegen*, tithe; *den –en entrichten*, pay tithe (*von*, on). **–t(e)halb,** *num. adj.* nine-and-a-half. **–teinnehmer,** *m.* tithe-collector. **–tel,** *n.* (*& Swiss dial. m.*) a tenth ($\frac{1}{10}$). **–ten** *v.a.* tithe; pay tithe; decimate. **–tens,** *adv.* tenthly, in the tenthplace. **–tfrei,** *adj.* exempt from paying tithe. **–therr,** *m.* tithe-owner. **–tpflichtig,** *adj.* tithable, subject to pay tithe. **–trecht,** *n.* right to levy tithe.

zehr–en, *v.n.* (*aux.* h.) (*with* von) live on, consume, feed on; (*with* an) (*fig.*) gnaw at, prey upon; waste, make thin; (*aux.* h. *&* s.) grow thin, shrink, become less; *vom eignen Fett –en*, live on one's fat; *von Vorräten –en*, live on one's reserves, consume one's stocks; *Seeluft –t*, sea air gives you an appetite; *Kummer –t an ihr*, she wastes away with worry; *von seinen Zinsen –en*, live on one's revenue *or* proceeds; *wir haben drei Wochen an diesem Schinken gezehrt*, we have been eating at this ham for three weeks. **–end,** *pr.p. & adj.* wasting, consumptive, hectic; *–ende Krankheit*, wasting disease. **–fieber,** *n.* hectic fever. **–frei,** *adj.* with free board. **–geld,** *n.*, **–pfennig,** *m.* travelling expenses *or* allowance, subsistence. **–ung,** *f.* consumption; expenses bill (*at an inn*); provisions, victuals; waste, loss through shrinkage; *die letzte –ung*, viaticum, extreme unction. **–ungssteuer,** *f.* duty on articles of food.

Zeichen, *n.* (-s, –) sign, symbol, mark, token; indication, proof, testimony, evidence, symptom (*Med.*); brand, stamp, badge; signal, call-sign; omen, portent; *ich bin meines –s ein Tischler*, I am a joiner by trade; *als* or *zum – der Freundschaft*, as a mark of friendship; *ein – geben*, (give a) signal, (make a) sign; *das – des Kreuzes*, the sign of the cross; *– setzen*, punctuate, put in punctuation marks; *wenn nicht alle – trügen*, if all indications are not deceptive; *unter einem glücklichen – geboren*, born under a lucky star; *die – der Zeit verstehen*, understand the signs of the times; *zum –, daß . . .*, as a proof that. . . . **–block,** *m.* sketching block. **–brett,** *n.* drawing-board. **–deuter,** *m.* astrologer, augur, prophet. **–deutung,** *f.* divination, astrology. **–erklärung,** *f.* list of conventional signs, key to the symbols used. **–rolle,** *f.* register of trade-marks. **–schrift,** *f.* hieroglyphics. **–heft,** *n.* drawing-book, sketch-book. **–kreide,** *f.* crayon. **–kunst,** *f.* drawing, designing, sketching. **–lehrer,** *m.* art master. **–mappe,** *f.* portfolio. **–papier,** *n.* drawing-paper. **–saal,** *m.* drawing-office, art room (*at school*). **–setzung,** *f.* punctuation. **–sprache,** *f.* sign language. **–stärke,** *f.* signal strength (*Rad. Tele.*); *Verhältnis der –stärke zur Geräuschstärke*, signal-to-noise ratio (*Rad.*). **–telegraph,** *m.* visual telegraph, semaphore. **–stift,** *m.* crayon. **–stunde,** *f.* **–unterricht,** *m.* drawing *or* painting lesson, art (*at school*). **–tinte,** *f.* marking-ink. **–vorlage,** *f.* drawing-copy.

zeich–nen, 1. *v.a. & n.* (*aux.* h.) draw, sketch, delineate, design, mark, brand; sign, put one's signature to, subscribe; *nach dem Leben –nen*, draw from life; *Wäsche –nen*, mark the laundry; *der Hund –net die Fährte*, the dog draws on the scent; *das Wild –net*, the quarry leaves a trail; *eine Schrift –nen*, sign a paper; *ich –ne hochachtungsvoll* or *ergebenst*, I have the honour to remain, Sir (*or* Madam), your obedient servant *or* yours faithfully; *zu etwas 100 Mark –nen*, subscribe 100 marks towards a th.; *vom Tode gezeichnet*, with the mark of death, touched *or* marked with the hand of death; *vom Schicksal gezeichnet*, marked out by fate. 2. *n.* drawing, sketching, designing, graphic art; *–nen aus freier Hand*, freehand drawing. **–ner,** *m.* designer, draughtsman; signatory, subscriber. **–nerisch,** *adj.* graphic, diagrammatic; *–nerische Begabung*, gift for drawing. **–nung,** *f.* drawing, design, sketch, diagram, signature.

zeid–eln, *v.a. & n.* (*aux.* h.) cut honeycombs (from the hives). **–elbär,** *m.* sloth *or* honey bear (*Melurses ursinus*) (*Zool.*). **–elmeister,** *m.* (*archaic*) bee-keeper. **–ler,** *m.* (-s, –) (*archaic*) bee-keeper.

zeig–en, 1. *v.a.* (*einem etwas*) *& n.* (*aux.* h.) show, point at *or* out, exhibit, display, indicate; manifest, demonstrate, prove; *einem den Herrn –en*, show a p. who is master *or* (*coll.*) the boss; *einem den Rücken –en*, turn one's back on a p.; *einem die kalte Schulter –en*, give a p. the cold shoulder; *das Thermometer –t 20 Grad*, the thermometer stands at 20°; *die Uhr –t (auf) 12*, the clock points to 12; *einem –en was eine Harke ist*, (*coll.*) show s.o. where he gets off; *ich werde dir –en wo der Zimmermann das Loch gelassen hat*, (*coll.*) you'll get thrown out on your neck. 2. *v.r.* appear, be found, make one's appearance, emerge, become evident, come to light, show itself, be found to be, turn out, prove to be; *das wird sich bald –en*, it will soon appear *or* be seen, we shall soon see; *es –t sich, daß . . .*, it appears that . . .; we see that . . .; *seine Unschuld wird sich zuletzt –en*, his innocence will become apparent at last; *er –t sich dumm*, he shows his stupidity *or* how stupid he is, he proves to be stupid; *er –te sich freundlich zu mir*, he was friendly towards me; *er –te sich unfreundlich gegen mich*, he showed animosity towards me; *er kann sich überall –en*, he can show himself anywhere; *da hat er sich recht gezeigt*, there he has shown what he could do; *er will sich nur –en*, he is only trying to show off. **–efinger,** *m.* forefinger, index finger. **–er,** *m.* one who demonstrates, exponent; pointer, needle, indicator; finger, hand (*of clocks, watches*); index (*Math.*); (*C.L.*) *–er dieses*, the bearer of this (note, paper); *der große –er*, the big hand (*of a clock*). **–erausschlag,** *m.* needle deflexion. **–erblatt,** *n.* dial. **–ergalvanometer,** *n.* needle galvanometer. **–erstange,** *f.* style, gnomon (*of a sun-dial*). **–ertelegraph,** *m.* needle telegraph. **–ervisier,** *n.* dial sight. **–estock,** *m.* pointer. **–etisch,** *m.* demonstration table.

zeihen, *ir.v.a.* (*high style*); *einen – einer S.*, accuse a p. of a th., charge a p. with a th.

Zeil–e, *f.* (-n) line, row, furrow; lane; *–e für –e*, line by line; *ein paar –en*, a short note; *zwischen den –en lesen*, read between the lines; *zwischen zwei –en geschrieben*, interlinear. **–enbreite,** *f.* measure (*Typ.*). **–engetreu,** *adj.* line for line. **–engießmaschine,** *f.*, **–engußmaschine,** *f.* linotype machine. **–enlänge,** *f.* length of line; justification (*Typ.*). **–enschreiber,** *m.* penny-a-liner. **–enweise,** *adv.* in lines, line by line. **–ig,** *adj. suffix*, *e.g.* **vier–ig,** four-lined.

Zein, *see* **Zain.**

zeise(l)n, 1. *v.a.* (*dial.*) lure, entice. 2. *v.n.* (*dial.*) hurry.

Zeisig, *m.* (-s, -e) siskin (*Carduelis*) (*Orn.*); (*coll.*) *lockerer –*, dissolute fellow, loose fish. **–grün,** *adj. & n.* canary-green.

Zeising, *f.* seizing, lashing (*Naut.*).

Zeit, 1. *f.* (-en) time; epoch; period, age, era; season, term, space of time, duration; tense (*Gram.*); (*dial.*) (*pl.*) tides; *seine – abwarten*, bide one's time; *es ist an der –*, it is time, the moment has come; *es ist früh an der –*, it is too early; (*Prov.*) *andre –en, andre Sitten*, manners change with the times; *die – arbeitet für uns*, time is on our side; (*C.L.*) *auf –*, on account, on credit; *auf ewige –en*, for ever and ever, in perpetuity; *auf eine kurze* or *einige –*, for a short *or* certain time; *außer der –*, out of season; *eine – festsetzen*, appoint a date, fix a time; *er kam für die – zu Boden*, he went down for the count (*Boxing*); *die (ganze) – her, durch or über*, all along, ever since; *es ist – genug*, there is time enough *or* plenty of time; *hast du – ?* have you time? can you spare the time? *hast du genaue – ?* have you the right *or* exact time? *sie hat ihre –*, she has her (monthly) period; *alles hat seine –*, there's a right time for everything; *das hat –, damit hat es –*, there is no hurry; *es ist die höchste –*, it is high time; *in – von acht Tagen*, within a week; *in früherer –*, formerly; *in jüngster* or *neuester –*, quite recently; (*Prov.*) *spare in der –, so hast du in der Not*, waste not, want not; *in der –* or *in den –en der römischen Herrschaft*, at the time of the Roman domination; *in der nächsten –*, in the near future; *in alten –en*, in days gone by; (*Prov.*) *kommt –, kommt Rat*, time brings wisdom; *seine – ist gekommen*, he is about to die; *ihre – ist gekommen*, her child is about to be born; *das kostet –*, that takes time; *lange – vorher*, long before this; *eine* (*kurze*) *– lang*, for a time *or* a little while *or* a short space of time; *längere –*, for a fairly long time; *laß dir nur –*, give yourself time; *die – wird es lehren*, time will tell; (*coll.*) *O du liebe – !* good heavens! *mit der –*, in (the course of) time, in the end, gradually; *mit der – gehen*, march *or* keep pace with the times; *mit der – geizen*, not waste a minute *or* second; *nach einiger –*, after some time, some time afterwards; *wo nimmst du die – her?* where do you find the time? *die – ist noch nicht reif*, the time has not come; *er hat bessere –en gesehen*, he has seen better days; *er war seiner – . . .*, he was . . . in his day; *seit längerer* or *langer –*, for a long time; (*coll.*) *dem lieben Gott die – stehlen*, idle one's time away; *es sind schon zwei Tage über die –*, it is now two days past the time; *um die –*, about that time; *vor der –*, prematurely; *vor –en*, once upon a time, formerly, in olden times; *vor grauen –en*, in days of yore; *vor kurzer –*, a short time ago; *vor langer –*, long ago, a long time ago; *von – zu –*, from time to time; (*Prov.*) *jedes Ding währt seine –*, every dog has his day; *während der –, daß . . .*, whilst . . .; *mir wird die – lang*, time hangs heavy on my hands; *der Zahn der –*, the ravages of time; *zur –*, at present, now, for the time being; *zu meiner –*, in my time *or* day; (*Prov.*) *alles zu seiner –*, in all good time; *zur – der Römer*, in the age of the Romans; *zu gleicher –*, at the same time; *zu rechter –*, at the right moment; à propos; *zur rechten –*, in (the nick of) time; (*Prov.*) *wer nicht kommt zur rechten –, der muß essen was übrig bleibt*, first come, first served; *zu –en*, now and then, at times; *zu allen –en, zu jeder –*, at any time, always; *zu –en Schillers, zu Schillers –en*, in the time of Schiller. 2. *prep.* (*with Gen.*) *– seines Lebens*, during his lifetime, as *or* so long as he lives. **–abschnitt,** *m.* period, epoch. **–abstand,** *m.* time interval. **–alter,** *n.* age, generation, era. **–angabe,** *f.* date, day and hour; *ohne –angabe*, undated. **–aufnahme,** *f.* time exposure (*Phot.*). **–aufwand,** *m.* sacrifice *or* loss of time, time spent (on). **–ball,** *m.* tide indicator (*in harbours*). **–bedürfnis,** *n.* needs of the time. **–behelf,** *m.* temporary expedient. **–berechnung,** *f.*, **–bestimmung,** *f.* chronology. **–dauer,** *f.* space of time, period. **–dehnung,** *f.* time yield (*Metall.*). **–einheit,** *f.* unit of time. **–einteilung,** *f.* schedule, time-table, timing. **–(en)folge,** *f.* sequence of tenses. **–epoche,** *f.* chronological era. **–ersparend,** *adj.* time-saving. **–ersparnis,** *f.* saving of time. **–folge,** *f.* chronological order. **–form,** *f.* tense. **–frage,** *f.* question of time; topic of the day. **–gebunden,** *adj.* transient, fleeting, passing, evanescent. **–geist,** *m.* spirit of the age. **–gemäß,** *adj.* timely, seasonable, opportune; up to date, modern. **–genosse,** *m.*, **–genössisch,** *adj.* contemporary. **–geschäft,** *n.* time-purchase *or* bargain; option business; call (*of stocks*). **–geschmack,** *m.* prevailing taste, fashion. **–gewinn,** *m.*, *see* **–ersparnis.** **–hafen,** *m.* tidal harbour. **–ig,** 1. *adj.* early; ripe, mature; coming at the right time, opportune, timely, seasonable. 2. *adv.* early, in *or* on time. **–igen,** 1. *v.a.* mature, ripen, bring to maturity; bring to a head, effect, produce. 2. *v. n.* (*aux.* s.) mature, grow ripe. **–igung,** *f.* ripening, maturing, maturity, maturation. **–karte,** *f.* season-ticket. **–kauf,** *m.* credit sale, sale on account. **–kürzend,** *adj.* amusing, entertaining. **–lage,** *f.* juncture, state of affairs. **–lang,** *f.* while; *eine –lang*, a while, for a *or* some time. **–lauf,** *m.* (-s, ⸚e *or* ⸚te) (*usually pl.*) course of time, course of events; lapse of time. **–läuf(t)e,** *m.pl.*, *see* **–lauf;** (occurrences of the) times, conjunctures. **–lebens,** *adv.* for life, during life; all his (her) life, all their lives. **–lich,** *adj.* temporal, secular, earthly; passing, temporary, transient, periodic; per unit time; *das –liche segnen*, depart this life (*high style*); *–licher Verlauf*, progress within a given time. **–lichkeit,** *f.* this life, earthly life, life on earth; temporal power; (*pl.*) temporalities. **–lohn,** *m.* time-work system of wages. **–los,** *adj.* lasting, permanent, timeless, valid at all times. **–lose,** *f* meadow saffron (*Colchicum autumnale*) (*Bot.*). **–lupe,** *f.* slow-motion camera (*Films*). **–mangel,** *m.* lack *or* shortage of time. **–maß,** *n.* measure of time; time, tempo (*Mus.*); measure, quantity (*Metr.*). **–messer,** *m.* chronometer; metronome (*Mus.*). **–meßkunde,** *f.*, **–messung,** *f.* measurement of time; timing; prosody. **–nahe,** *adj.* with contemporary appeal, of interest to our age. **–nehmer,** *m.* time-keeper (*Sport.*). **–ordnung,** *f.* chronological order. **–punkt,** *m.* moment, point of time; *von dem –punkt an*, from that point on. **–raffer,** *m.* quick-motion apparatus (*Films*). **–raubend,** *adj.* time-wasting *or* consuming; tedious, wearisome, protracted. **–raum,** *m.* period, interval, space of time. **–rechnung,** *f.* chronology; era; *neue –rechnung*, new style; *Verstoß gegen die –rechnung*, anachronism. **–rente,** *f.* annuity. **–schrift,** *f.* periodical (publication), journal, magazine. **–schriftenaufsatz,** *m.* magazine article. **–schriftenwesen,** *n.* periodical literature. **–sichtwechsel** *m.* (*C.L.*) after-sight bill. **–sinn,** *m.* sense of time *or* timing. **–spanne,** *f.* period of time. **–tafel,** *f.* chronological table. **–umstände,** *m.pl.*, **–verhältnisse,** *n.pl.* circumstances (of the time), times, juncture(s); *bei den augenblicklichen –umständen*, in the present state of affairs. **–verlauf,** *m.* course *or* lapse of time. **–verlust,** *m.* loss of time. **–verschwendung,** *f.* waste of time. **–vertreib,** *m.* pastime, amusement; *zum –vertreib*, to pass the time, for amusement. **–weilig,** *adj.* temporary, for the time being; at times, occasionally; actual, current, present. **–weise,** *adv.* temporarily, for a time, at times, from time to time. **–widrig,** *adj.* unseasonable. **–wort,** *n.* verb. **–zeichen,** *n.* time-signal (*Rad.*). **–zünder,** *m.* time-fuse, delayed action fuse (*Artil.*).

Zeitung, *f.* (-en) newspaper, (*archaic*) news, intelligence; *sich* (*Dat.*) *eine – halten*, take in a newspaper; *in die – setzen*, insert in a newspaper, advertise. **–sabonnement,** *n.* subscription to a paper. **–sanzeige,** *f.* newspaper advertisement, announcement in the press. **–sartikel,** *m.* newspaper article. **–sausschnitt,** *m.* press cutting. **–sbeilage,** *f.* supplement. **–sberichterstatter,** *m.* newspaper correspondent, reporter. **–sdeutsch,** *n.* journalese. **–sente,** *f.* canard, newspaper hoax. **–sexpedition,** *f.* newspaper office. **–sinserat,** *n.* *see* **–sanzeige.** **–sjunge,** *m.* paper-boy. **–skiosk,** *m.* newspaper stall. **–smache,** *f.* puff. **–spapier,** *n.* old newspapers. **–sreklame,** *f.* newspaper advertising; puff. **–srubrik,** *f.* newspaper column. **–sschreiber,** *m.* journalist. **–sstil,** *m.* journalese. **–sverkäufer,** *m.* news-vendor, newsagent, paper-boy. **–swesen,** *n.* journalism; the press.

zekeln, *v.n.* (*aux.* h.) (*coll.*) stand on tiptoe.

Zelebr–ant, *m.* (-en, -en) officiating priest (*at Mass*); celebrant. **–ieren,** *v.a.* celebrate, officiate at. **–ität,** *f.* celebrity.

Zell–e, *f.* (-en) cell, segment, compartment, vesicle, alveolus (*Anat.*); bucket (*of water-wheels*); phone-box; air-frame (*Av.*). **–enartig,** *adj.* cellular, cell-like. **–enbildung,** *f.* cell-formation. **–enförmig,** *adj.* cellular, alveolate. **–engang,** *m.* cellular duct (*Anat.*); corridor (*in prisons, etc.*). **–engefangene(r),** *m.* prisoner in solitary confinement. **–engewebe,** *n.*, *see* **–gewebe.** **–enkunde,** *f.*, **–enlehre,** *f.* cytology. **–enleib,** *m.* protoplasm. **–enpflanzen,** *f.pl.* vascular plants. **–enrad,** *n.* bucket-wheel. **–ensystem,** *n.* system of solitary confinement. **–faser,** *f.* cellular fibre. **–faserstoff,**

m. cellulose. **–gewebe,** *n.* cellular tissue. **–haut,** *f.* cellophane. **–horn,** *n.* celluloid. **–ig,** *adj.* cellular, vesicular, honeycombed. **–kern,** *m.* cytoplast, nucleus (*Zool.*, *Bot.*). **–masse,** *f.* cellular substance. **–ophan,** *n.*, *see* **–haut.** **–stoff,** *m.* cellulose, wood pulp *or* fibre. **–uloid,** *n. see* **–horn.** **–ulose,** *f.* (-n), *see* **–stoff.**

Zelot, *m.* (-en, -en) zealot; fanatic. **–entum,** *n.*, **–ismus,** *m.* fanaticism. **–isch,** *adj.* fanatical.

[1]**Zelt,** *n.* (-(e)s, -e) tent; marquee; awning; (*B.*) tabernacle; (*Poet.*) vault *or* canopy of heaven. **–bahn,** *f.* ground-sheet. **–bett,** *n.* canopy bed. **–dach,** *n.* awning, canvas roof. **–e,** *f.* **–en,** *m.* (*dial.*) small flat. **–en,** *v.n.* camp (out), sleep under canvas. **–hering,** *m.*, *see* **–pflock.** **–lager,** *n.* camp. **–leben,** *n.* camping (out), living under canvas. **–leinwand,** *f.* tent-cloth. **–pflock,** *m.* tent-peg. **–schnur,** *f.* guy-rope *or* -line. **–stock,** *m.* tent-pole. **–stuhl,** *m.* camp-stool.

[2]**Zelt,** *m. see* **–gang.** **–en,** *v.n.* amble, pace. **–er,** *m.* palfry. **–gang,** *m.* ambling pace, amble.

Zeltchen, *n.* (-s, –) (*dial.*) lozenge, pastille.

Zement, *m.* & *n.* (-(e)s, -e) cement. **–ieren,** *v.a.* cement; convert (*iron*) into steel; precipitate. **–ierofen,** *m.* converting furnace. **–ierung,** *f.* cementation; converting. **–metall,** *n.* precipitated metal. **–stahl,** *m.* converted *or* cementation steel.

Zenit (*Austr. dial.* **–h**) *m.* & *n.* zenith, vertical point, (*fig.*) climax, height.

zens–ieren, *v.a.* censor, examine before publication; criticize, censure; give marks (*school-work*). **–or,** *m.* (-s, -en) censor (*of films, press*). **–ur,** *f.* (-en) censorship; marks (*at school*), school report, certificate.

Zent, *f.* (-en) hundred (*Hist.*). **–enarfeier,** *f.* (-n) centenary. **–esimal,** *adj.* centesimal, hundredth. **–ifolie,** *f.* (-n) centifolious rose, cabbage-rose. **–igramm,** *n.* (-(e)s, -e) centigram. **–imeter,** *n.* (& *coll.* & *Swiss dial. m.*) (-s, –) centimetre. **–ner,** *m.* (-s, –) hundredweight, fifty kilograms. **–nerlast,** *f.* (*fig.*) heavy burden. **–nerschwer,** *adj.* (*fig.*) very heavy.

zentral, *adj.* central. **–amt,** *n.* directorate. **–e,** *f.* control room; telephone exchange; power plant; chief office; line joining two *or* more centres (*Geom.*). **–gewalt,** *f.* federal government, central authority. **–heizung,** *f.* central-heating. **–isieren,** *v.a.* centralize. **–isierung,** *f.* centralization. **–mächte,** *f.pl.* Central Powers (*Germany and Austria-Hungary*). **–stelle,** *f.* central office, coordinating office. **–verband,** *m.* industrial federation.

zentri–eren, *v.a.* centre. **–erbohrer,** *m.* centre-bit. **–fuge,** *f.* centrifuge, hydroextractor, separator. **–winkel,** *m.* angle at the centre.

Zentrum, *n.* (-trums, -tren & *Austr. dial.* -tra) centre; centre party; bull's-eye. **–spartei,** *f.* Roman-Catholic party in German Parliament.

Zephir, *m.* (-s, -e) zephyr.

Zepter, *n.* & *m.* (-s, –) sceptre, mace; *das – tragen, schwingen* or *führen*, wield the sceptre.

Zer, *n.* cerium (*Chem.*).

zer–, *insep. verbal prefix denotes* to pieces, asunder, *etc.*, *also* to spoil by. *For verbs not given see the simple verbs.*

zerarbeiten, *v. a.* & *v.r.* destroy by working; *sich –*, overwork, work o.s. to death; *zerarbeitete Hände*, hands ruined *or* roughened by work.

zerbeißen, *ir.v.a.* crunch, bite through, break with the teeth *or* beak.

zerbersten, *ir.v.n.* (*aux.* s.) burst, split asunder.

zerbrech–en, *ir.v.a.* & *n.* (*aux.* s.) break in *or* to pieces, shatter, smash; *sich* (*Dat.*) *den Kopf –en*, rack one's brains. **–lich,** *adj.* brittle, fragile, breakable. **–lichkeit,** *f.* fragility, brittleness.

zerbröckeln, *v.a.* & *n.* (*aux.* s.) crumble away *or* to pieces.

zerdrücken, *v.a.* crush, squash, squeeze flat, crumple.

Zerealien, *f.pl.* cereals.

Zeremon–ie, *f.* (-ien) ceremony, formality. **–iell,** 1. *n.* ceremonial. 2. *adj.* formal, precise, ceremonial. **–ienmeister,** *m.* master of ceremonies. **–iös,** *adj.* ceremonious, punctilious.

zerfahren, 1. *ir.v.a.* destroy by driving over; cut (*roads*) to pieces with traffic. 2. *v. n.* (*aux.* s.) burst, fly asunder. 3. *p.p.* & *adj.*; (*fig.*) confused, inattentive, scatter-brained, distracted, absent-minded. **–heit,** *f.* carelessness, absent-mindedness.

Zerfall, *m.* ruin, decay, decomposition, disintegration, destruction, dissociation; (*fig.*) decadence. **–en,** 1. *ir.v.n.* (*aux.* s.) fall apart *or* to pieces, crumble away, fall into ruin, decay, decompose; disintegrate, dissociate; break down, come to grief; (*fig.*) quarrel; *in zwei Teile –en*, fall under two heads; *in Stücke –en*, fall to pieces; *mit einem –en*, quarrel with a p. 2. *p.p.* & *adj.* in ruins, dilapidated; on bad terms *or* at variance (with). **–enheit,** *f.* ruinous state, dilapidation. **–grenze,** *f.* dissociation limit. **–produkt,** *n.* product of decomposition. **–sreihe,** *f.* stage of radio-active disintegration. **–wärme,** *f.* heat of dissociation.

zerfasern, *v.a.* (reduce to) pulp, disintegrate, break up; unravel, fray (out).

zerfetzen, *v.a.* tear up, tear to rags, shred, slash, hack to pieces; mangle, mutilate.

zerflattern, *v.n.* (*aux.* s.) be scattered, flutter away, (*fig.*) be ineffective.

zerfleischen, *v.a.* lacerate, tear to pieces, mangle.

zerfließ–en, *ir.v.n.* (*aux.* s.) melt, dissolve, liquefy, deliquesce, run (out); disperse; *in Tränen –en*, melt into tears. **–end,** *adj.*, **–lich,** *adj.* deliquescent. **–ung,** *f.* liquefaction, deliquescence.

zerfress–en, *ir.v.a.* eat *or* gnaw away; corrode, cauterize. **–ung,** *f.* corrosion.

zerfurcht, *adj.* furrowed, wrinkled.

zergehen, *ir.v.n.* (*aux.* s.) melt, dissolve, liquefy, deliquesce; dwindle away, vanish; *der Nebel zergeht*, the mist disperses; *in Nichts –*, dwindle to nothing.

zergen, *v.a.* (*dial.*) tease, pester.

zerglieder–n, *v.a.* dissect, dismember, cut up; analyse (*also Gram.*). **–er,** *m.* dissector, analyst. **–ung,** *f.* dissection; dismemberment; analysis. **–ungskunde,** *f.* anatomy.

zerhacken, *v.a.* hack, chop *or* cut in pieces; mince.

zerhauen, *ir.v.a.* cut in pieces; chop *or* cut up; *den* (*gordischen*) *Knoten –*, cut the Gordian knot.

zerkauen, *v.a.* masticate *or* chew thoroughly.

zerkleinern, *v.a.* break up, reduce to small pieces, disintegrate; crush, grind, shred, pulverize, triturate, comminute.

zerklopfen, *v.a.* beat, pound, knock to pieces, smash.

zerklüft–en, *v.a.* cleave, split, divide. **–et,** *p.p.* & *adj.* cleft, riven, fissured, rugged. **–ung,** *f.* cleft, cleavage, fissure; disruption, fragmentation.

Zerknall, *m.* (-(e)s, -e) explosion. **–en,** *v.a.* & *n.* burst, blow up, explode.

zerknautschen, *v.a.* (*coll.*) crush, crumple.

zerknick–en, *v.a.* break, crack, crush. **–ungsfestigkeit,** *f.* thrust resistance.

zerknirsch–en, *v.a.* crush, crunch; bruise; overwhelm with remorse *or* sorrow. **–t,** *p.p.* & *adj.* contrite. **–theit,** *f.*, **–ung,** *f.* broken-heartedness, remorse, contrition.

zerknistern, *v.a.* & *n.* decrepitate.

zerknittern, *v.a.* crumple, rumple, crease, wrinkle.

zerknüllen, *v.a.*, *see* **zerknautschen.**

zerkörnen, *v.a.* granulate.

zerkratzen, *v.a.* scratch, spoil with scratches.

zerlassen, *ir.v.a.* melt, dissolve; liquefy.

zerleg–en, *v.a.* decompose, resolve, reduce; analyse (*also Gram.*); split up, cut up, dissect, carve (*a joint*); disperse, divide; dismantle, take to pieces, strip (*a weapon*); (*sl.*) shoot up (*Mil.*). **–bar,** *adj.* divisible, decomposible, collapsible. **–ung,** *f.* dismantling, dissection; decomposition; analysis; *–ung der Kräfte*, resolution of forces (*mechanics*).

zerlesen, *adj.* well-thumbed (*of a book*).

zerlöchert, *adj.* full of holes.

zerlumpt, *adj.* in rags, ragged, tattered; *–er Mensch*, ragamuffin.

zermahlen, *ir.v.a.* grind, crush, pulverize.

zermalm–en, 1. *v.a.* bruise, crush, dash in pieces; grind, crunch, powder, pulverize; (*fig.*) cast down, depress. 2. *n.*, **–ung,** *f.* bruising, crushing, crunching; pulverization.

zermartern, *v.a.* torment, torture; *sich* (*Dat.*) *das Gehirn* –, rack one's brains.
zermürb–en, *v.a.* crush, grind down, wear down (*also the enemy*). **–t,** *p.p.* & *adj.* broken(-down), exhausted, worn-out. **–erscheinung,** *f.* fatigue (*Mech.*). **–ungskrieg,** *m.* war of attrition. **–versuch,** *m.* fatigue test. **–widerstand,** *m.* resistance to fatigue.
zernagen, *v.a.* gnaw *or* eat away; erode; corrode.
zernier–en, *v.a.* invest, besiege, encircle, blockade. **–ung,** *f.* investment, siege.
zerpflücken, *v.a.* pluck to pieces, pull apart.
zerplatzen, *v.n.* burst asunder *or* in pieces.
zerpulvern, *v.a.* pulverize.
zerquetschen, *v.a.* crush, squash, pulp, mash.
Zerrbild, *n.*, *see* **zerren.**
zerreib–en, *ir.v.a.* rub away; crush, grind down; pulverize, triturate, pound. **–bar,** *adj.*, **–lich,** *adj.* friable, triturable.
zerreiß–en, 1. *ir.v.a.* tear *or* rip up, tear to pieces, rend; break up, dismember; split, rupture; lacerate, mutilate, mangle; worry; break (*an alliance, a p.'s heart, etc.*); *ich werde mich nicht darum –en,* I shan't break my neck over it; *ich kann mich nicht –en,* I cannot do two things *or* be in two places at once. 2. *v.n.* (*aux.* s.) break, tear, split, wear out. **–diagramm,** *n.* stress-strain diagram (*Metall.*). **–festigkeit,** *f.* tensile strength. **–versuch,** *m.* tensile test. **–ung,** *f.* rending, breaking, tearing; laceration; rupture.
zerr–en, 1. *v.a.* pull, tug, drag; stretch; tear; haul about; tease, worry; *etwas in den Kot –en,* drag a th. through the mud. 2. *v.n.* (an *with Dat.*) pull, tug *or* tear at. **–bild,** *n.* caricature. **–ung,** *f.* pulling, stretching, strain (*of a muscle*). (*sl.*) **–wanst** *m.* squeeze-box.
zerrinn–en, *ir.v.n.* (*aux.* s.) melt, dissolve; disappear, come to nothing; *Geld –t ihm unter den Fingern,* money runs through his fingers like water; (*Prov.*) *wie gewonnen, so zerronnen,* easy come, easy go.
zerrissen, *p.p. see* **zerreißen. –heit,** *f.* raggedness; want of union, disunion, inner strife.
zerrühren, *v.a.* stir to a pulp.
zerrütt–en, *v.a.* disarrange, derange, unsettle, disturb, disorganize, throw into confusion; ruin, destroy; unhinge (*the mind*); *eine –ete Ehe,* a marriage that has gone to pieces. **–ung,** *f.* disorder, confusion; ruin; derangement.
zerschellen, 1. *v.a.* dash in pieces, smash, shatter, shiver. 2. *v.n.* (*aux.* s.) go to pieces, be dashed to pieces, be shattered *or* smashed.
zerschießen, *ir.v.a.* shoot to pieces; riddle with shot.
zerschlagen, 1. *ir.v.a.* dash to pieces; batter, bruise; beat unmercifully; destroy, (*sl.*) wipe out; parcel out (*an estate*). 2. *p.p.* & *adj.* broken, battered, shattered; *ich bin an allen Gliedern* (*wie*) –, *alle Glieder sind mir* (*wie*) –, I feel as if I had been beaten black and blue, I am all in. 3. *v.r.* break off, break up, be dispersed, be broken off; come to nothing, be disappointed (*hopes, etc.*). **–heit,** *f.* physical depression *or* weakness.
zerschleißen, *ir.v.n.* be worn to shreds *or* into holes, become tattered.
zerschlitzen, *v.a.* slit, slash, lacerate, rip up.
zerschmettern, 1. *v.a.* shatter, smash, crush, destroy, overwhelm, confound. 2. *v.n.* (*aux.* s.) be shattered *or* smashed.
zerschneiden, *ir.v.a.* cut in pieces, cut into shreds, cut up, carve, dissect; *einem das Herz* –, break a p.'s heart; *das* (*Tisch*)*Tuch ist* (*zwischen ihnen*) *zerschnitten,* it is all over between them.
zersetz–en, *v.a.* & *v.r.* decompose, break up; (*fig.*) disintegrate, undermine. **–bar,** *adj.* decomposable. **–end,** *adj.* destructive, deleterious; decomposing; demoralizing. **–ung,** *f.* decay, decomposition, disintegration, dissolution. **–ungsgase,** *n.pl.* gases *or* gaseous products of decomposition. **–ungsliteratur,** *f.* seditious pamphlets. **–ungsvorgang,** *m.* process of decomposition.
zersingen, *v.n.* garble (*a song*).
zerspalten, *v.a.* & *n.* (*aux.* s.), **zerspellen,** *v.a.*, **zerspleißen,** *v.a.* cleave, split up, slit.
zersplitter–n, 1. *v.a.* & *r.* splinter, split, break up, disperse, scatter, dissipate; *seine Zeit –n,* fritter away one's time; *sich* or *seine Kräfte –n,* have too many irons in the fire. 2. *v.n.* (*aux.* s.) burst, fly into bits, splinter, split. **–ung,** *f.* comminuted fracture (*Surg.*); violent rupture, splintering, dissipation, waste; disunion (*Pol.*).
zersprengen, *v.a.* burst, blow up, blast, explode; rout, disperse; *–ende Kraft,* disruptive force.
zerspringen, *ir.v.n.* (*aux.* s.) fly to pieces, break, burst, split, crack; explode, *der Kopf will mir* –, my head is splitting; *das Herz wollte ihr* (*vor Aufregung*) –, she was beside herself (with excitement).
zerstampfen, *v.a.* trample *or* tread down, pound; *zu Pulver* –, reduce to powder.
zerstäub–en, 1. *v.a.* pulverize, atomize, reduce to dust *or* spray; disperse, scatter. 2. *v.n.* (*aux.* s.) turn to dust. **–er,** *m.*, **–ungsapparat,** *m.* pulverizer, atomizer, sprayer, spray-diffuser, spray-gun.
zerstieben, *ir.v.n.* (*aux.* s.) turn to dust; be scattered as dust, disperse, scatter; vanish.
zerstör–en, *v.a.* destroy, demolish, ruin, devastate, ravage, disrupt, disorganize, overthrow; *–te Gesundheit,* broken, ruined *or* shattered health; *–te Gebiete,* devastated areas; *–te Hoffnungen,* blighted hopes. **–bar,** *adj.* perishable, destructible. **–er,** *m.* destroyer (*also Nav.*); fighter-bomber, light bomber, long-range fighter (*Av.*). **–lich,** *adj.* (*Swiss dial.*) unconditional, absolute, final. **–ung,** *f.* destruction, demolition; disorganization, overthrow, ruin. **–ungsarbeiten,** *f.pl.* demolitions. **–ungsfeuer,** *n.* devastating fire. **–ungslust,** *f.* destructiveness. **–ungswerk,** *n.* work of destruction.
zerstoßen, *ir.v.a.* knock *or* beat to pieces; bruise, pound, crush, pulverize, levigate.
zerstreu–en, 1. *v.a.* disperse, dissipate, diffuse, spread, scatter, disseminate, dispel, banish (*fear, etc.*); distract, divert, amuse. 2. *v.r.* disperse, scatter; break up; amuse o.s. **–t,** *p.p.* & *adj.* dispersed, scattered; loose; detached; wandering; sporadic; *–tes Licht,* diffused light; *–t sein,* be preoccupied, absent-minded *or* distracted; *sich –en lassen,* allow one's attention to be distracted. **–theit,** *f.* distraction; absent-mindedness, preoccupation. **–ung,** *f.* dispersion, diffusion, dissipation, dissemination; distraction, diversion, amusement. **–ungslinse,** *f.* diverging *or* dispersing lens (*Opt.*). **–ungspunkt,** *m.* point of dispersion, focus of divergence. **–ungsspiegel,** *m.* convex mirror. **–ungssucht,** *f.* craze for amusements.
zerstück–eln, *v.a* cut into little pieces, chop up, cut up, mangle, dismember; divide, parcel out, partition. **–(e)lung,** *f.* dismemberment; parcelling out, partition.
zerteil–en, *v.a.* divide, separate; cut, split *or* break up, disintegrate, dissolve; disperse; resolve. **–bar,** *adj.* divisible. **–barkeit,** *f.* divisibility. **–ung,** *f.* division, dismemberment, separation; decomposition, dissolution; resolution (*Med.*). **–ungsmittel,** *n.* resolvent (*Med.*).
zertrampeln, zertreten, *v.a.* trample under foot, trample down.
zertrümmer–n, 1. *v.a.* smash, crush, shatter, split (*the atom*); wreck, break in pieces, destroy, lay in ruins, demolish, overthrow. 2. *v.n.* (*aux.* s.) shatter, be wrecked *or* ruined. **–ung,** *f.* ruin, destruction; disintegration, demolition, splitting (*of atoms*).
Zervelatwurst, *f.* smoked sausage; Saveloy.
Zerwürfnis, *n.* (-ses, -se) difference (of opinion), disagreement, dissension, quarrel, dispute, strife.
zerzausen, *v.a.* tumble, crumple; dishevel (*hair*); pull to pieces; *einen tüchtig* –, treat a p. roughly *or* (*coll.*) rough.
zerzupfen, *v.a.* pull *or* pick to pieces.
Zession, *f.* (-en) cession, transfer, assignment; abandonment (*of claims*). **–ar,** *m.* assignee, transferee.
Zeter, 1. *n.*, **–mordio,** *n.* cry of murder, cry for help. 2 *int.* (*archaic*) help! murder! – *schreien,* cry murder, cry for help; – *über einen schreien,* raise an outcry about *or* a hue and cry after a p. **–geschrei,** *n.* shout for help; cry of murder; outcry. **–n,** *v.a.*, see – *schreien.*
[1]**Zettel,** *m.* (-s, –) (scrap of) paper; slip, note;

ticket, (hand-)bill, poster, placard, label, docket. **-ankleber,** *m.*, **-anschläger,** *m.* bill-sticker, bill-poster. **-anschlagen,** *n.* bill-sticking; *das -anschlagen ist verboten,* stick no bills! **-bank,** *f.* bank of issue. **-kartei,** *f.*, **-kasten,** *m.* filing-cabinet. **-katalog,** *m.* card-index. **-n,** *v.a. & n.* catalogue, card-index. **-wahl,** *f.* card-vote.

[2]**Zettel,** *m.* (-s, -) chain, warp (*Weav.*).

zeuch, zeuchst, zeucht, (*archaic & Poet.*) *see* **ziehen.**

Zeug, *n.* (-(e)s, -e) stuff, material; cloth, fabric, textiles, textile goods; clothes; implements, tools, equipment; utensils, pots and pans, crockery; dough; yeast, baking powder; type-metal, (paper) pulp; (*archaic*) arms, ordnance; (*coll.*) matter, things; (*coll.*) rubbish, bosh, nonsense, trash; *allerhand -(s),* all sorts of things; *einem etwas am -e flicken,* pick holes *or* a hole in a p., pull s.o. to pieces; *dummes -,* (stuff and) nonsense; *mach' kein dummes -,* don't play the fool! *das - haben zu,* have it in one (to), be cut out (for); *was das - hält* or (*nur*) *halten will,* with might and main; *ins - gehen, sich ins - legen,* set to work with a will. (*archaic*) **-amt,** *n.* ordnance department. **-bütte,** *f.* pulp-vat (*Pap.*). **-druck,** *m.* calico printing. **-druckerei,** *f.* textile printing. **-haus,** (*archaic*) arsenal, armoury. **-meister,** *m.* (*archaic*) master of ordnance. **-probe,** *f.* sample of material. **-schmied,** *m.* (*archaic*) armourer. **-schuhe,** *m.pl.* canvas shoes. **-waren,** *f.pl.* fabrics.

Zeug-e, *m.* (-en, -en) witness; *als -e auftreten,* appear as a witness; *einen -en stellen,* produce evidence *or* a witness; *als -e vorgeladen werden,* be called as a witness. **-en,** *v.n.* (bear) witness, testify, depose, give evidence (of); (*von*) show, prove, be evidence of. **-enaussage,** *f.* evidence, deposition, testimony. **-enbank,** *f.* witness-box. **-enbestechung,** *f.* suborning of witnesses. **-enbeweis,** *m.* first-hand proof. **-eneid,** *m.* oath administered to witnesses. **-eneidlich,** *adj.*; *-eneidliche Vernehmung,* deposition made on oath. **-enschaft,** *f.* the witnesses. **-enverhör,** *n.*, **-envernehmung,** *f.* hearing of witnesses. **-nis,** *n.* testimony, evidence, proof; certificate, testimonial, character, school-report; *-nis ablegen,* bear witness (to), give evidence (of), testify (to), vouch (for); *einem ein -nis ausstellen,* write a p. a testimonial; *ein hinreichendes -nis von . . .* satisfactory evidence *or* proof of . . .; *Du sollst kein falsch -nis reden wider Deinen Nächsten,* thou shalt not bear false witness against thy neighbour. **-nisablegung,** *f.* deposition. **-nisverweigerungsrecht,** *n.* right of refusal to give evidence. **-niszwang,** *m.* obligation to give evidence.

zeug-en, *v.a.* beget, procreate, generate, produce, engender. **-er,** *m.* procreator, generator, begetter, father. **-ung,** *f.* generation, begetting, procreation, reproduction. **-ungsfähig,** *adj.* capable of begetting, procreative. **-ungsflüssigkeit,** *f.* seminal fluid. **-ungsglied,** *n.* penis. **-ungskraft,** *f.*, *see* **-ungsvermögen. -ungsmittel,** *n.* aphrodisiac. **-ungsorgane,** *n.pl.* reproductive, sexual *or* genital organs. **-ungsstoff,** *m.* semen. **-ungstrieb,** *m.* procreative instinct. **-ungsunfähig,** *adj.* impotent; sterile. **-ungsunfähigkeit,** *f.* impotence, sterility. **-ungsvermögen,** *n.* procreative power, virility, potency.

Zibbe, *f.* (-n) (*dial.*) ewe (*of rabbit, hare, goat*).

Zibebe, *f.* (-n) (*dial.*) raisin.

Zibet, *m.* civet (*secretion*). **-katze,** *f.*, **-tier,** *n.* civet cat (*Viverra civetta*) (*Zool.*).

Zichorie, *f.* (-n) chicory, succory (*Cichorium intybus*) (*Bot.*).

Zick-e, *f.* (-en) (*dial.*), *see* **Ziege;** (*sl.*) *mach' keine -en,* don't be funny. **-el,** *n.* (*dial.*), *see* **-lein. -eln,** *v.n.* (*aux.* h.) kid. **-lein,** *n.* kid.

Zickzack, *m.* (-s, -e) & *adv.* zigzag; *im - fahren,* zigzag, follow a zigzag course. **-förmig,** *adj.* zigzag.

Zider, *m.* cider.

Zieche, *f.* (-n) (*dial.*) coverlet, quilt.

Ziege, *f.* (-n) goat; she-goat; *Pelecus cultratus* (*Icht.*). **-nartig,** *adj.* goat-like, goatish. **-nbart,** *m.* goatee. **-nbock,** *m.* he-goat, billy goat. **-nfell,** *n.* goatskin. **-nhainer,** *m.* knobkerrie. **-nhirt,** *m.* goatherd. **-nkäse,** *m.* goat's milk cheese. **-nlamm,** *n.* kid. **-nleder,** *n.* kid (*leather*). **-nmelker,** *m.* goatsucker (*Orn.*). **-nmilch,** *f.* goat's milk. **-npeter,** *m.* mumps (*Med.*).

Ziegel, *m.* (-s, -) brick; tile; *- brennen,* bake *or* fire bricks; *mit -n decken,* tile, roof with tiles. **-bau,** *m.* bricklaying; brick structure. **-brenner,** *m.* brickmaker; owner of a brick-kiln. **-brennerei,** *f.* brickworks, brickyard. **-dach,** *n.* tiled roof. **-decker,** *m.* tiler, roofer. **-ei,** *f.* brickworks, brick-yard, brick-kiln. **-erde,** *f.* brick-clay. **-farbig,** *adj.* brick red. **-hütte,** *f.* brick-kiln. **-mehl,** *n.* brick-dust. **-n,** *v.n.* makes bricks. **-ofen,** *m.* brick-kiln. **-rohbau,** *m.* rough brickwork. **-rot,** *adj. & n.* brick-red. **-stein,** *m.* brick; tile. **-streichen,** *n.* brick-making. **-streicher,** *m.* brickmaker. **-ton,** *m.*, *see* **-erde.**

Zieger, *m.* (-s, -), **-käse,** *m.* (*dial.*) soft, milk *or* cream cheese.

Ziegler, *m.* (-s, -) brickmaker.

zieh, ziehe, *see* **zeihen.**

zieh-en, 1. *ir.v.a.* draw, pull, drag, haul, tug; tow (*a boat, etc.*); take off *or* raise (*one's hat*); move (*at draughts, etc.*); draw out (*iron, etc.*); pull out, extract (*teeth*); bring up, rear, cultivate, grow, breed, nurture, train, educate; erect (*a perpendicular*); describe (*a circle, etc.*); rifle (*a gun*); dig (*a trench*); make (*a comparison*); *an sich* (*Acc.*) *-en,* attract, draw to o.s., collect; engross, monopolize, absorb, win over to one's side; *einen am Ärmel -en,* pluck a p. by the sleeve; *ein Boot ans Land -en,* haul a boat ashore; *etwas ans Licht* or *Tageslicht -en,* bring s.th. to light, make a th. known; *einen an den Ohren -en,* pull s.o.'s ears; *Perlen auf einen Faden -en,* string pearls, thread pearls; *Wein auf Flaschen -en,* bottle wine; *alle* or *aller Augen* or *Aufmerksamkeit auf sich -en,* attract universal attention; *Saiten auf eine Geige -en,* string a violin; *auf die Seite -en,* draw aside; *auf seine Seite -en,* win over to one's side; *einen Wechsel auf einen -en,* draw a bill on s.o.; *einen aus der Klemme* or *Patsche -en,* get s.o. out of a jam *or* scrape; *eine Lehre aus einer S. -en,* learn a lesson from a th.; *einem Würmer aus der Nase -en,* worm secrets out of s.o.; *Nutzen aus einer S. -en,* derive profit *or* advantage from a th.; turn s.th. to one's own account; *den Kopf aus der Schlinge -en,* slip the collar, make one's escape, extricate o.s.; *Schlüsse aus etwas -en,* draw conclusions from a th.; *Öl aus Samen -en,* extract oil from seeds; *wie aus dem Wasser gezogen,* drenched; *die Wurzel aus einer Zahl -en,* extract the root of a number; (*C.L.*) *die Bilanz -en,* draw up the balance-sheet; *Blasen -en,* raise blisters; *durch den Schmutz* or (*coll.*) *Kakao -en,* drag s.o.'s name in the dirt; *der Leim -t Fäden,* the gum is getting tacky; *Flachs -en,* pull flax; *Flachs durch die Hechel -en,* hackle flax; (*coll.*) *einen Flunsch* or *Fratze -en,* see *ein Gesicht -en*; *Folgerungen -en,* see *Schlüsse -en*; *einen Gewinn -en,* draw a winner; *ein Gesicht -en,* make faces, pull a face; *ein schiefes Gesicht -en,* pull a long face; *einen Graben -en,* dig a ditch, throw up trenches; *Grenzen -en,* set limits; *den Hut vor einem -en,* raise one's hat to a p.; *in Betracht* or *Erwägung -en,* take into consideration; *die Stirn in Falten -en,* frown; *ins Geheimnis -en,* take *or* let into the secret; *in die Höhe -en,* pull up, raise; *etwas ins Lächerliche -en,* make s.th. look ridiculous; *in die Länge -en,* draw, drag *or* spin out; *in Verdacht -en,* suspect; *in Zweifel -en,* call in question, doubt; *den kürzeren -en,* come off a loser, get the worst of it; *das Los -en,* draw lots; *ein schiefes Maul -en,* make a wry face; *nach sich -en,* entail, involve, be attended with, have as a consequence; *eine Niete -en,* draw a blank; *Parallelen -en,* see *Vergleiche -en*; *alle Register -en,* (*fig.*) show what one can do; *einen Strich -en,* draw a line; *einem das Fell über die Ohren -en,* fleece s.o.; *Vergleiche -en,* draw *or* make a comparison; *Gewinn* or *Vorteil von etwas -en,* derive profit from a th.; *vor Gericht -en,* summon before a magistrate, bring to justice; *Wasser -en,* leak, absorb water; *sich* (*Dat.*) *etwas zu Gemüte -en,* take a th. seriously; *einen zu Rate -en,* consult (with) a p.; *zur Rechenschaft* or *Verantwortung -en,* call to account;

einen zur Strafe –en, punish a p., inflict a penalty on a p.; *einen zur Tafel –en*, invite s.o. to dinner, *etc.* **2.** *v. r.* move, draw (toward), march (toward); stretch, extend; be elastic; warp, distort; penetrate, soak in; *das Gebirge –t sich weit ins Meer*, the mountains run far out into the sea; *der Wald –t sich längs den Bergen hin*, the wood extends along the mountains; *die Strümpfe –en sich nach dem Fuße*, the stockings give to the feet; *sich in die Länge –en*, go on and on, drag on for a long time, be protracted; *sich ins Blaue –en*, have a tinge of blue; *das Brett hat sich gezogen*, the board has warped. **3.** *v. n.* **1.** (*aux.* h.) prove attractive, make an impression, have a strong appeal, attract, draw; (*imp.*) be draughty; ache; *der neue Professor –t*, the new professor draws large audiences; *dieser Grund –t bei mir nicht*, this reason does not weigh with me; *es –t mich nach Hause*, I am drawn towards home; *vom Leder –en*, draw one's sword; *es –t hier*, there is a draught here; *der Tee hat jetzt genug gezogen*, the tea has stood long enough; *–en, wer Karten gibt*, cut *or* draw for deal; *der Ofen –t gut*, the stove draws well; *die Bremse –t nicht*, the brake does not hold; *an einem Stricke* or *am gleichen Strange –en*, have the same aim, play the same game; *an einer Zigarre –en*, draw at a cigar; *an der Glocke –en*, pull *or* ring the bell; *mit dem König –en*, move *or* play the king (*Chess*); *du mußt –en*, your move (*Chess*); *–en lassen*, allow to fill *or* empty, allow to steep, draw *or* infuse (*tea, etc.*). 2. (*aux.* s.) move, stroll, wander, advance slowly; grow (*of flowers, plants*); march, go, advance; change one's residence, move (to), remove, migrate; *das Gewitter ist südwärts gezogen*, the storm has passed over to the south; *gezogen kommen*, come along, arrive; *in ein anderes Zimmer –en*, change one's room; *die Wolken –en aus dem Süden*, the clouds come from the south; *der Rauch –t ins Zimmer*, the smoke is coming into the room; *durch die Stadt –en*, pass through the town; *in die Fremde –en*, go abroad; *in den Krieg –en*, go to the war; *übers Meer –en*, cross the sea, go across the sea; *laß mich –en*, let me go, let me free; *in die Stadt –en*, go and live in the town; *aufs Land –en*, move to the country; *in ein Haus –en*, move into a house; *zu einem –en*, go to live with a p.; *zu Felde* or *ins Feld –en*, take the field; *gezogene Lichte*, dips, tallow candles; *gezogenes Rohr*, rifled barrel. **4.** *n.* drawing, pulling; cultivation, rearing; draught, traction; removal, move, migration; attraction, appeal; rheumatic pain, twinges in the limbs. **–arm,** *m.* crank, handle. **–band,** *n.* draw-thread *or* -string. **–bank,** *f.* wire-drawing frame. **–bar,** *adj.* ductile. **–barkeit,** *f.* ductility. **–brücke,** *f.* drawbridge. **–brunnen,** *m.* draw-well, bucket-well. **–e,** *f.* (*dial.*) nursing, rearing; *in die –e geben*, put with foster-parents. **–harmonika,** *f.* accordion, concertina. **–hund,** *m.* draught dog. **–kind,** *n.* foster-child. **–klimmen,** *n.* hanging climb (*Gymn.*). **–kraft,** *f.* traction-power; (*fig.*) attraction, (*coll.*) draw (*Theat.*). **–leine,** *f.* tow-rope. **–maschine,** *f.* wire-drawing machine; stretcher. **–mutter,** *f.* foster-mother. **–pferd,** *n.* draught-horse. **–pflaster,** *n.* blistering-plaster. **–tag,** *m.* moving day. **–topf,** *m.* steeping pot. **–ung,** *f.* drawing, draw (*of lots, etc.*). **–ungsliste,** *f.* list of prizewinners (*in a lottery*). **–ungstag,** *m.* day of the draw (*lottery*). **–vermögen,** *n.* affinity. **–weg,** *m.* towing-path, towpath. **–werk,** *n.* hauling engine.

Ziel, *n.* (-(e)s, -e) goal, end, object, objective, destination, winning-post (*Sport.*); target, aim; limit, extremity, boundary, scope; *der erste am – sein*, be the first at the winning-post; *am – seiner Wünsche angelangt sein*, have attained *or* reached the object of one's desire; *auf kurzes –*, at short date; *auf 3 Monate –*, with 3 months to pay *or* to run, at 3 months date, with 3 months' grace; *das – aufsitzen lassen*, aim; *begrenztes –*, limited objective; *das – fehlen*, miss one's aim; *Maß und – halten*, keep within reasonable limits *or* bounds; *am –e seines Lebens sein*, be at the end of one's life; *ohne Zweck und –*, without aim or purpose; *über – schießen*, (*fig.*) see *das – überschreiten*; *einem ein – setzen*, put a stop to (*a th.*), check, curb (*a p.*); *seinem Ehrgeize ein – setzen*, set limits to one's ambition; *sich ein – setzen* or *stecken*, aim at, have as one's aim; *sich* (*Dat.*) *ein hohes – stecken* or *setzen*, aim high; *das – treffen*, hit the mark; *das – überschreiten*, overstep the mark, go too far; (*fig.*) *er ist weit vom –e*, he is quite beside the mark; *weitgestecktes –*, unlimited objective; *zum – gelangen*, achieve one's object, attain one's end. **–abschnitt,** *m.* target sector (*Mil.*). **–anflug,** *m.* bombing run (*Av.*). **–ansprache,** *f.* fire-order (*Mil.*). **–aufnahme,** *f.* reconnaissance photograph. **–band,** *n.* tape (*Sport*). **–beleuchter,** *m.* pathfinder (*Av.*). **–bewußt,** *adj.* with an aim in view, resolute, clear-sighted; systematic, methodical. **–bezeichnung,** *f.* target designation. **–bild,** *n.* aerial photograph. **–en,** *v.n.* (*aux.* h.) (*with* nach) aim (at); take aim (at); *auf eine S. –en*, (*fig.*) aim at, drive at, allude *or* refer to a th.; *–endes Zeitwort*, transitive verb. **–er,** *m.* aimer, gun-layer; target marker. **–fernrohr,** *n.* telescope-sight, sighting telescope. **–gelände,** *n.* target area (*Av.*). **–genauigkeit,** *f.* accuracy of aim. **–gerade,** *n.* the straight (*Sport*). **–gerät,** *n.* sighting *or* aiming mechanism. **–hafen,** *m.* port of destination. **–karte,** *f.* fighting-chart, range-table. **–landung,** *f.* precision landing (*Av.*). **–linie,** *f.* line of sight. **–los,** *adj.* aimless, purposeless. **–punkt,** *m.* aiming point, aim, mark, goal; bull's eye. **–reaktion,** *f.* purposive behaviour. **–richter,** *m.* judge (*Sport*). **–scheibe,** *f.* (practice) target; *–scheibe des Spottes* or *Witzes*, laughing-stock, butt. **–schiff,** *n.* target-ship. **–setzung,** *f.* fixing of an aim; object in view. **–sicher,** *adj.* sure of one's aim. **–strebigkeit,** *f.* purposeful behaviour, resoluteness.

Ziem, *m.* (-s, -e) rump (steak).

ziem-en, *v.r.* & *n.* (*aux.* h.) (*imp. with Dat.*) beseem, be seemly, become, suit, be suitable, be fitting *or* proper; *es –t sich nicht, das zu tun*, it is not the proper thing to do it; *es –t sich nicht, daß du ...*, or *nicht für dich, zu ...*, it is not becoming *or* seemly for you to.... **–lich,** 1. *adj.* becoming, fit, suitable; passable, fair, middling, tolerable, moderate, pretty considerable; *eine –liche Strecke*, a considerable distance; *eine –liche Anzahl Leute*, a fair *or* good number of people. 2. *adv.* fairly, rather, tolerably, (*coll.*) pretty; *–lich gut*, pretty good, fair; *–lich natürlich*, natural enough; *–lich spät*, rather late; *–lich weit*, rather a long way; *–lich viel*, a good deal; *er ist so –lich fertig*, he is almost *or* pretty well ready *or* done.

Ziemer, *m.* (-s, –) buttock, hind quarter (*of animals*), haunch (*of venison*); penis (*of large animals*), pizzle.

ziepen, 1. *v.a.* (*dial.*) tug, pluck, pull. 2. *v.n.* squeak, cheep. 3. *v. imp.* itch, prick.

Zier, *f.* (-en), *see* **–de.** **–äffchen,** *n.*, **–affe,** *m.* fop, coxcomb; affected person, dressy woman. **–at,** *m.* (-(e)s, -e) *or f.* (-en) ornament, ornamentation, decoration, embellishment, finery, flourish. **–bengel,** *m.* fop. **–de,** *f.* ornament, decoration; *die –de der Familie*, a credit to the family. **–druck,** *m.* ornamental type. **–en,** 1. *v.a.* adorn, grace, be an ornament to; decorate, embellish, set off; garnish. 2. *v.r.* be affected, behave affectedly, put on airs; mince (*one's words*); refuse out of politeness; *–en Sie sich nicht so!* do not be so affected! do not give yourself airs! *nehmen Sie es nur und –en Sie sich nicht!* just take it and do not stand upon ceremony; *sich beim Essen –en*, not help o.s. **–erei,** *f.* airs (and graces), affectation. **–garten,** *m.* ornamental garden, flower-garden. **–leiste,** *f.* edging, border, frieze; vignette, tail-piece (*Typ.*). **–lich,** *adj.* graceful, dainty, neat, elegant, pretty, nice, fine, smart; decorative, ornamental. **–lichkeit,** *f.* grace, elegance; daintiness, neatness. **–pflanze,** *f.* ornamental plant. **–puppe,** *f.* dressy woman. **–schrift,** *f.* ornate type, fancy letters. **–stab,** *m.* beading. **–strauch,** *m.* ornamental shrub. **–vogel,** *m.* cage-bird. **–werk,** *n.* fancy-work.

Ziesel, *m.* (-s, –), **–maus,** *f.* ground-squirrel (*Citellus*) (*Zool.*).

Ziest, *m.* (-es, -e) hedge-nettle (*Stachys*) (*Bot.*).

Ziestig, *m.* (*dial.*) Tuesday.

Ziffer, *f.* (-n) figure, numeral, digit, cipher, number; *mit* or *in –n schreiben*, write in cipher. **–blatt,**

n. clock-face, face, dial. **–ig** (*also* **ziffrig**) *adj. suffix, e.g.* **vier–ig,** of 4 digits *or* figures. **–(n)-kasten,** *m.* figure-case (*Typ.*). **–n,** *v.a. & n.* (*aux.* h.) cipher. **–(n)mäßig,** *adj.* numerical, in figures; *etwas –nmäßig beweisen,* prove a th. by figures. **–schlüssel,** *m.* key to cipher. **–schrift,** *f.* cipher, code. **–system,** *n.* numerical notation. **–telegramm,** *n.* code telegram, cipher telegram.

Zigar–ette, *f.* (-n) cigarette. **–ettenetui,** *n.* cigarette-case. **–ettenschachtel,** *f.* cigarette packet. **–ettenspitze,** *f.* cigarette-holder. **–re,** *f.* (-n) cigar; (*coll.*) snub, wigging; *die –re hat keine Luft,* the cigar does not draw. **–rendeckblatt,** *n.* wrapper. **–renhändler,** *m.* tobacconist. **–renkiste,** *f.* cigar-box. **–renspitze,** *f.* cigar-holder. **–renstummel,** *m.* cigar-end.

Ziger, (*Swiss dial.*), *see* **Zieger.**

Zigeuner, *m.* (-s, –) gipsy. **–in,** *f.* gipsy woman *or* girl. **–haft,** *adj.* **–isch,** *adj.* gipsy-like, gipsy; vagrant. **–kapelle,** *f.* gipsy *or* Tzigane band. **–lager,** *n.* gipsy encampment. **–leben,** *n.* Bohemianism, roaming *or* vagrant life. **–n,** *v.n.* (*aux.* h.) (*dial.*) rove, wander about; lead a vagrant life. **–sprache,** *f.* Romany. **–tum,** *n., see* **–leben.** **–volk,** *n.* the gipsies. **–wagen,** *m.* gipsy caravan.

Zikade, *f.* (-n) grasshopper.

Zille, *f.* (-n) barge.

Zimbel, *f.* (-n) cymbal (*Mus.*).

Zimmer, *n.* (-s, –) room, apartment, chamber; – *mit zwei Betten* or *zweibettiges* –, double-bedded room; *Haus mit elf –n,* eleven-roomed house; *das – hüten,* keep to one's room; *möblierte* –, furnished apartments; – *nach hinten hinaus,* back room; – *nach vorn hinaus,* front room; – *nach der Straße hinaus,* room facing *or* overlooking the street; *unmöbliertes* –, unfurnished room. **–arbeit,** *f.* carpentry, timber-work. **–bekleidung,** *f.* wainscoting, panelling. **–bock,** *m.* joiner's trestle. **–decke,** *f.* ceiling. **–einrichtung,** *f.* furnishings (of a room). **–er,** *m., see* **–mann.** **–flucht,** *f.* suite of rooms *or* apartments. **–gesell(e),** *m.* journeyman carpenter. **–handwerk,** *n.* carpentry; carpenter's trade. **–herr,** *m.* gentleman lodger. **–holz,** *n.* timber, building material. **–ling,** *m.,* (*Min.*). *see* **–mann.** **–mädchen,** *n.* chambermaid, housemaid. **–mann,** *m.* (-männer & -leute) carpenter, joiner; shipwright (*Naut.*); (*coll.*) *einem zeigen, wo der –mann das Loch gelassen hat,* show a p. the door. **–meister,** *m.* master carpenter; master builder. **–n,** *v.a. & n.* (*aux.* h.) frame, joint, build; carpenter; make, fabricate. **–nachweis,** *m.* letting agency, lodgings bureau. **–pflanze,** *f.* pot *or* indoor plant. **–platz,** *m.* timber *or* lumber yard. **–polier,** *m.,* **–polierer,** *m.* foreman carpenter. **–spiel,** *n.* indoor game, parlour-game. **–tanne,** *f.* Norfolk Island pine (*Araucaria excelsa*) (*Bot.*). **–ung,** *f.* timbers, revetment, revetting (*Min.*). **–vermieter,** *m.* landlord. **–vermieterin,** *f.* landlady. **–werk,** *n.* timber-work.

Zimmet, *m.* (*archaic*), *see* **Zimt.**

zimper–lich, *adj.* prim, prudish; affected; super- *or* hypersensitive. **–lichkeit,** *f.* primness, prudery; affectation, super-sensitiveness. **–liese,** *f.* prude.

Zimt, *m.* cinnamon; (*sl.*) nonsense, rubbish. **–blüte,** *f.* cinnamon-flower, cassia bud. **–rinde,** *f.* cinnamon bark. **–stange,** *f.* stick of cinnamon. **–säure,** *f.* cinnamic acid.

Zindel, *m.* (-s, –), **–taft,** *m.* light taffeta.

Zingulum, *n.* girdle (*of a R.C. priest*).

Zink, *n.* (& *Austr. dial. m.*) zinc; spelter. **–asche,** *f.* dross of zinc. **–ätzung,** *f.* zinc etching, zincography. **–blech,** *n.* sheet-zinc. **–blumen,** *f.pl.* zinc bloom, hydrozincile. **–en,** *adj.* of zinc. **–haltig,** *adj.* containing zinc. **–kalk,** *m., see* **–asche.** **–salbe,** *f.* zinc ointment. **–vitriol,** *m. & n.* sulphate of zinc, white copperas. **–wasser,** *n.* zinc lotion.

Zink–e, *f.* (-en), **–en,** *m.* (-ens, -en) prong, tine; spike; tooth (*of a comb*); tenon, dovetail (*Carp.*); cornet (*Mus.*); card-sharper's *or* beggar's secret mark; (*sl.*) beak, boko. **–en,** *v.a.* play the cornet; furnish with prongs; join by means of mortise and tenon; mark (*Cards*). **–enbläser,** *m.* cornet player, bugler. **–enist,** *m.* (*dial.*), *see* **–enbläser.** **–enregister,** *n.,* **–enzug,** *m.* cornet-register (*Org.*). **–ig,** *adj.* spiked, pronged.

Zinn, *n.* tin; pewter; tinware. **–asche,** *f.* tin-ashes, (tin-)putty. **–bergwerk,** *n.* tin-mine. **–ern,** *adj.* of tin, pewter; stannic. **–folie,** *f.* tin-foil. **–geschirr,** *n.* pewter vessel. **–gießer,** *m.* tinfounder. **–haltig,** *adj.* stanniferous. **–kies,** *m.* tin-pyrites, sulphuret of tin. **–kraut,** *n.* horse-tail, Dutch rush (*Equisetum hyemale*) (*Bot.*). **–krug,** *m.* pewter mug. **–lot,** *n.* soft solder. **–oxyd,** *n.* stannic oxide. **–oxydul,** *n.* stannous oxide. **–säure,** *f.* stannic acid. **–soldat,** *m.* tin soldier. **–stufe,** *f.* tin ore. **–waren,** *f.pl.* tinware, pewter.

Zinne, *f.* (-n) pinnacle; battlement, rocky crag; *mit –n versehen,* crenel(l)ated, embattled. **–n,** *v.a.* crenelate. **–nförmig,** *adj.* crenel(l)ated. **–nlücke,** *f.* loophole, crenelle. **–nwerk,** *n.* embattled work, crenel(l)ated wall.

Zinnober, *m.* cinnabar, red mercury sulphide; (*sl.*) fuss, business, poppycock. **–farbig,** *adj.,* **–rot,** *adj.* vermilion.

Zins, *m.* (-es, -e) tax, duty, rent, (*B.*) tribute; (*pl.* -en), *see* **–en,** 1. **–abzug,** *m.* discount. **–bar,** *adj. see* **–pflichtig.** **–bauer,** *m.* tenant farmer, copyholder. **–brief,** *m.* copyhold deed. **–bringend,** *adj.* bearing interest; *–bringend anlegen,* put out at interest. **–en,** 1. *m.pl.* interest; *auf –en geben* or *(aus)leihen,* lend on interest; *die –en zum Kapital schlagen,* allow the interest to accumulate; *von seinen –en leben,* live on one's private income; *4 Prozent –en tragen,* bear 4 per cent. interest. 2. *v.n.* (*with Dat.*) pay rent *or* interest. **–enberechnung,** *f.* calculation of interest. **–eszins,** *m.* compound interest; *mit – und –eszins,* (*fig.*) in full measure. **–frei,** *adj.* free of interest; rent-free; freehold; *Kapital –frei leihen,* lend money free of interest; *–freies Gut,* freehold. **–fuß,** *m.* rate of interest. (*B.*) **–groschen,** *m.* tribute-money. **–gut,** *n.* leasehold. **–herr,** *m.* lord of the manor. **–knechtschaft,** *f.* (*Nat. Soc.*) dominance of invested capital (in the economic system). **–lehen,** *n.* copyhold fief. **–mann,** *m.* (-leute), **–ner,** *m.* (*archaic*) copyholder; feudatory. **–pächter,** *m.* copyholder. **–pflichtig,** *adj.* subject to tax, tributary. **–rechnung,** *f.* calculation of interest. **–satz,** *m.* rate of interest. **–schein,** *m.* coupon; dividend-warrant. **–tabelle,** *f.* table of interest. **–tag,** *m.,* **–termin,** *m.* rent-day; quarter-day. **–weise,** *adj.* as rent; as interest.

Zipfel, *m.* (-s, –) tip, point, end; lobe, tongue; corner (*of a kerchief, etc.*); lappet; *eine S. beim rechten – anfassen,* set the right way to work, set about a th. in the right way; *etwas bei allen vier –n anfassen,* get a good hold of a th. **–ig,** *adj.* pointed, peaked. **–klappen,** *f.pl.* tricuspid and mitral valves (*of the heart*). **–mütze,** *f.* peaked cap, nightcap.

Zipolle, *f.* (-n) (*dial.*) onion, shallot, scallion.

Zipp–e, *f.* song-thrush (*Turdus ericetorum*) (*Orn.*). **–ammer,** *f.* foolish bunting (*Emberiza cia*) (*Orn.*). **–drossel,** *f., see* **–e.**

Zipperlein, *n.* (*coll.*) twinges (*gout or rheumatism*).

Zirbe, *f.* (-n), **–l,** *m.* (-ls, -l) & *f.* (-ln) stone-pine (*Pinus cembra*) (*Bot.*). **–ldrüse,** *f.* pineal gland (*Anat.*). **–lkiefer,** *f., see* **–.**

zirka, *adv.* about, approximately.

Zirkel, *m.* (-s, –) (pair of) compasses *or* dividers; circle, group, gathering, company; cycle, circulation; (*Poet.*) *der goldne* –, the crown; *alles mit dem – abmessen,* do everything by rule *or* most precisely. **–n,** *v.a.* draw with compasses. **–schluß,** *n.* vicious circle (*Log.*). **–zug,** *m.* flourish, scroll.

Zirkon, *m.* (-s, –e) zirconium silicate, zircon (*precious stone*). **–erde,** *f.* zirconia.

Zirkul–ar, *n.* (-s, -e) circular, brochure, pamphlet, fly-sheet. **–ieren,** *v.n.* circulate; *–ieren lassen,* pass *or* send round. **–ierpumpe,** *f.* circulating pump.

Zirkus, *m.* (–, -se) circus, (*coll.*) hurly-burly.

Zirpe, *f.* (-n) cricket; grasshopper, Cicadidae. **–n,** *v.n.* (*aux.* h.) chirp, cheep.

zisch–eln, *v.a. & n.* (*aux.* h.) speak in an undertone, whisper. **–en,** 1. *v.a. & n.* (*aux.* h. & s.) hiss, sizzle, fizz, fizzle, whiz. 2. *n.* hiss(ing), whiz(zing), hisses (*in theatre, etc.*). **–laut,** *m.* hissing sound, sibilant (*Phonet.*).

ziselier–en, *v.a.* engrave, chisel, chase. **–arbeit,** *f.* chased *or* chiselled work.
Zisterne, *f.* (-n) cistern, (water-)tank.
Zitadelle, *f.* (-n) citadel.
Zit–at, *n.* (-at(e)s, -ate) quotation, citation. **–atenlexikon,** *n.*, **–atenschatz,** *m.* dictionary of quotations. **–ation,** *f.* citation, summons. **–ieren,** *v.a.* quote, cite; call up, summon; invoke (*spirits*).
Zither, *f.* (-n) zither, cithara (*of the ancients*).
Zitron–at, *n.* (-at(e)s, -ate) candied (lemon) peel. **–e,** *f.* (-en) lemon. **–enfalter,** *m.* brimstone butterfly (*Gonopteryx rhamni*) (*Ent.*). **–engelb,** *adj.* & *n.* lemon-yellow. **–enholz,** *n.* candlewood. **–enlimonade,** *f.* lemon-squash. **–enpresse,** *f.* lemon-squeezer. **–ensaft,** *m.* lemon-juice; lemon-squash. **–ensauer,** *adj.* citrate of. **–ensäure,** *f.* citric acid. **–enschale,** *f.* lemon-peel. **–enscheibe,** *f.* slice of lemon. **–enwasser,** *n.* still lemonade.
zitter–n, *v.n.* (*aux.* h.) tremble, shiver, shudder, shake, quiver, flutter, quake, waver, vibrate; *mit –n und Zagen*, with fear and trembling, shaking with fear; *mir –n alle Glieder*, I am shaking in every limb; *er –t an allen Gliedern*, he is trembling *or* shaking all over; *es –t alles vor ihm*, all tremble before him. **–aal,** *m.* electric eel (*Gymnotus electricus*) (*Icht.*). **–gras,** *n.* quaking-grass (*Briza media*) (*Bot.*). **–ig,** *adj.* trembling, shaky, shaking; shivery. **–lähmung,** *f.* shaking paralysis, Parkinson's disease (*Path.*). **–pappel,** *f.* aspen (*Populus tremula*) (*Bot.*). **–roche(n),** *m.* torpedo fish, electric ray (*Icht.*). **–spiel,** *n.* spillikins. **–stimme,** *f.* quaking voice. **–wels,** *m.* electric catfish, thunder-fish (*Icht.*).
Zitwer, *m.* zedoary (*Curcuma zedoaria*) (*Bot.*).
Zitz, *m.* (-es, -e) chintz, printed calico. **–en,** *adj.* (of) chintz.
Zitze, *f.* (-n) nipple, teat, dug. **–ntiere,** *n.pl.* mammals, mammalia.
zivil [*pron.* –ˈviːl], 1. *adj.* civil; moderate, reasonable (*prices*). 2. *n.* civil body, civilians; *in –*, in plain-clothes, (*coll.*) in civvies *or* mufti. **–beamte(r),** *m.* civil servant; government official. **–bevölkerung,** *f.* civilians, population, non-combatants. **–courage,** *f.* courage of one's convictions. **–ehe,** *f.* civil marriage. **–gericht,** *n.* civil court. **–gerichtsbarkeit,** *f.* civil jurisdiction. **–gesetzbuch,** *n.* code of civil law. **–isation,** *f.* civilization. **–isatorisch,** *adj.* civilizing. **–isieren,** *v.a.* civilize, humanize, refine. **–ist,** *m.* (-en, -en) civilian, non-combatant. **–klage,** *f.* civil action. **–kleidung,** *f.* civilian *or* plain-clothes. **–liste,** *f.* civil list. **–luftfahrt,** *f.* civil aviation. **–prozeß,** *m.* civil suit. **–recht,** *n.* civil law. **–rechtlich,** *adj.* according to civil law; *einen –rechtlich verfolgen*, bring a civil action against a p. **–stand,** *m.* citizenship. **–standsamt,** *n.* (*Swiss dial.*) registry office. **–standsbeamte(r),** *m.* (*Swiss dial.*) registrar for births, deaths and marriages. **–trauung,** *f.* marriage at a registry office. **–versorgung,** *f.* guarantee of civil employment for ex-service men. **–verwaltung,** *f.* civil *or* government service.
Zobel, *m.* (-s, –) sable (*Mustela zibellina*) (*Zool.*). **–pelz,** *m.* sable fur.
Zober, *m.* (-s, –) (two-handled) tub; firkin (*for butter*).
zock–eln, *v.n.* (*aux.* s.) (*dial.*) saunter, dawdle. **–en,** *v.n.* (*aux.* s.) (*dial.*) amble, toddle.
Zodiakus, *m.* zodiac.
Zofe, *f.* (-n) lady's-maid.
zog, zöge, *see* **ziehen.**
zöger–n, 1. *v.n.* (*aux.* h.) hesitate, linger, loiter, tarry, delay, defer; *ich werde nicht –n, Ihre Bitte zu erfüllen*, I shall lose no time in complying with your request. 2. *n.* delay; hesitation; *ohne –n*, without delay, unhesitatingly. **–nd,** *pr.p.* & *adj.* hesitating, hesitant, dilatory. **–ung,** *f.*, *see* **–n** 2.
Zögling, *m.* (-s, -e) pupil.
Zohe, *f.* (*dial.*) bitch.
Zölestin, *m.* celestine, celestite, strontium sulphate (*Min.*).
Zölibat, *m.* & *n.* celibacy; bachelordom.
[1]**Zoll,** *m.* (-(e)s, –) inch; digit (*Astr.*); *auf – und Linie*, exactly, in every respect; *jeder – ein König*, every inch a king; *– für –*, inch by inch. **–breit,** *adj.* inch-wide; *auf keinen –breit Landes verzichten*, surrender not an inch of territory. **–ig,** (*Austr.* **-zöllig**) *adj. suffix* (*with figures*) measuring . . . inches. **–stock,** *m.* rule; yard-stick. **–weise,** *adv.* by inches, inch by inch.
[2]**Zoll,** *m.* (-(e)s, ⸚e) tariff, customs, duty, toll, dues; (*fig.*) tribute; debt (*of nature, of gratitude*); *– bezahlen für*, pay duty on; *etwas beim – angeben*, declare a th. at the customs, enter a th. at the custom-house; *den – der Dankbarkeit entrichten*, show one's thanks; *der Natur den – entrichten*, pay one's debt to nature. **–abfertigung,** *f.* clearing of the customs. **–abfertigungsstelle,** *f.* custom-barrier. **–amt,** *n.* custom-house. **–amtlich,** *adj.*; *–amtliche Untersuchung*, examination by the customs; *unter –amtlichem Verschluß*, in bond. **–angabe,** *f.* declaration at the custom-house. **–aufschlag,** *m.* increase in duty, additional duty. **–aufseher,** *m.* customs-officer. **–ausschließzone,** *f.* free territory. **–bar,** *adj.*, *see* **–pflichtig. –beamte(r),** *m.* customs officer; revenue-officer. **–begleitschein,** *m.* bond-note. **–behörde,** *f.* inland revenue authority. **–einfuhrschein,** *m.* bill of entry. **–einnehmer,** *m.* toll collector. **–fahrzeug,** *n.* revenue vessel. **–en,** 1. *v.n.* (*aux.* h.) impose a tax, charge duty. 2. *v.a.* (*einem etwas*), render what is due; *Achtung –en*, show due respect; *Beifall –en*, applaud; *Dank –en*, thank; *Tränen –en*, shed tears for. **–frei,** *adj.* duty free; (*Prov.*) *Gedanken sind –frei*, thought is free; *–freier Verkehr*, free trade. **–freiheit,** *f.* exemption from duty; freedom of trade. **–freilager,** *n.* bond, bonded warehouse. **–gebühr,** *f.* duty, customs dues. **–gefälle,** *n.* inland revenue. **–gesetz,** *n.* tariff law. **–grenze,** *f.* customs-boundary. **–haus,** *n.* custom-house, (*archaic*) toll-booth. **–hinterziehung,** *f.* evasion of the customs. **–krieg,** *m.* tariff-war. **–pflichtig,** *adj.* liable to duty, dutiable. **–politik,** *f.* customs policy. **–quittung,** *f.* clearance (bill). **–revision,** *f.* customs examination. **–rückgabeschein,** *m.* customs-drawback. **–satz,** *m.* rate of duties; tariff-rate. **–schein,** *m.* customs receipt, certificate of clearance. **–schiff,** *n.* revenue-cutter. **–schranke,** *f.* customs-barrier. **–schutz,** *m.* (tariff-) protection. **–straße,** *f.* turnpike *or* toll road. **–tarif,** *m.* tariff, list of dues. **–union,** *f.*, **–verein,** *m.* customs-union, tariff-union. **–vergünstigungen,** *f.pl.* preferential tariff. **–verschluß,** *m.* customs seal, leads, bond; *unter –verschluß lassen*, leave in bond. **–verwaltung,** *f.* customs administration. **–wesen,** *n.* tariff system.
zöll–ig, *adj.* inch-thick; *drei–ig*, three-inch. **–ner,** *m.* toll collector; (*B.*) publican.
Zönakel, *n.* (-s, –) monastery refectory.
Zone, *f.* (-n) zone, region; *die heiße, kalte, gemäßigte –*, the torrid, frigid, temperate zone. **–nkarte,** *f.* railway ticket (*valid within prescribed zones*). **–nlinsen,** *f.* echelon lens (*lighthouse*).
Zoolog–(e), *m.* (-en, -en) zoologist. **–ie,** *f.* zoology. **–isch,** *adj.* zoological.
Zopf, *m.* (-(e)s, ⸚e) pigtail, plait, tress; tuft; tree-top; pedantry, red tape, pettifoggery; (*coll.*) *einem auf den – spucken*, give s.o. a dressing down. **–band,** *n.* hair-ribbon. **–ende,** *n.* top (of a tree). **–holz,** *n.* top branches. **–ig,** *adj.* (*fig.*) antiquated, old-fashioned; pedantic, pettifogging. **–stil,** *m.* mid-18th century *or* late rococo style (*art, etc.*). **–zeit,** *f.* mid-18th century.
Zorn, *m.* anger, wrath, rage, (*Poet.*) ire, choler; passion, temper; *seinen – an einem auslassen*, *die Schale seines –s über einen ausgießen*, vent one's anger, pour out the vials of one's wrath upon a p.; *einen in – bringen*, enrage *or* anger a p. **–entbrannt,** *adj.*, *see* **–glühend. –(es)ader,** *f.* frontal vein. **–(es)anfall,** *m.*, **–(es)ausbruch,** *m.* fit of anger. **–(es)röte,** *f.* flush of anger. **–glühend,** *adj.* furious, boiling with rage. **–ig,** *adj.* angry, irate, in a temper, rage *or* passion; *–ig werden*, get angry, fly into a passion.
Zot–e, *f.* (-en) obscenity, indecent *or* filthy expression, dirty *or* smutty joke; *–en reißen*, tell dirty stories. **–en,** *v.n.* talk smut. **–enhaft,** *adj.* obscene, filthy, smutty, lewd, indecent, bawdy.

-enlied, *n.* bawdy song. **-enreißen,** *n.* obscene talk, obscenity. **-enreißer,** *m.* obscene talker, retailer of dirty jokes. **-ig,** *adj.*, *see* **-enhaft.**

Zott-e, *f.* (-en) villus (*Anat.*); lock, tuft; matted *or* shaggy hair; (*dial.*) spout; rose (*of watering can*); (*dial.*) tassel. **-el,** *f.* (*dial.*), *see* **-e.** **-elbär,** *m.* shaggy bear. **-(e)lig,** *adj.*, *see* **-ig.** **-eln,** *v.n.* (*aux.* s.) shuffle along, dawdle; *sich* (*Dat.*) *etwas -eln*, get with great difficulty. **-elwicke,** *f.* hairy vetch (*Vicia villosa*) (*Bot.*). **-enanhang,** *m.* villous appendage. **-enhaut,** *f.* chorion (*Anat.*). **-ig,** *adj.* shaggy, matted, tufted, downy, hairy (*Bot.*); villous.

Zötus, *m.* (–, -ten) division (*of a school form*), (parallel) set or form.

zu, 1. *prep.* (*Dat.*) to, towards, up to, unto; in addition to, along with; at, on, in, by; for, in order to; – *Abend*, in the evening; – *allerletzt*, last of all; – *Anfang*, at the *or* as a beginning; *-m Beispiel* (*z.B.*), for instance; *e.g.*; *Verein -r Bekämpfung . . .*, society for combating . . .; – *Berg fahren*, go uphill; go up-stream *or* against the stream; – *Berlin*, in at, *or* of Berlin; *-m besten*, for the best; *es geriet nicht -m besten*, it did not succeed as well as was expected; *es geschieht – deinem Besten*, it is for your good; *-m besten haben*, make game of; *Gott schuf den Menschen ihm -m Bilde*, God created man in his own image; – *Boden fallen*, fall to the ground, fall down; *-r Bühne gehen*, go on the stage; – *Deutsch*, in German; – *Dritt*, three of us; three of them; – *ebener Erde*, on the ground floor; *einem -r Ehre gereichen*, redound to a p.'s honour; *einen – etwas ermuntern*, exhort *or* encourage a p. to do a th.; – *Ende sein*, be at an end, be over, have done *or* finished; *-m ersten*, in the first place; *-r Fährte kommen*, get the scent; *sich* (*Dat.*) *einen -m Feinde machen*, make an enemy of a p.; – *Felde ziehen*, take the field; *-m Fenster hinaus*, out of *or* through the window; *Brot -m Fleisch essen*, eat bread with one's meat; *-r Folge haben*, have as a result *or* consequence; *-r Frau nehmen*, take as one's wife; *einen -m Freunde haben*, have s.o. for a friend; – *Fuß*, on foot; *aus Freundschaft – ihm*, out of friendship for him; *einem – Füßen fallen*, throw o.s. at a p.'s feet; *einen – Gaste bitten*, invite a p. as one's guest; *-m Dichter geboren*, born (to be) a poet; *mir – Gefallen*, to please me, for my sake; *einem etwas – Gemüte führen*, impress a th. on a p.; *etwas -r Genüge haben*, have sufficient of a th.; *über einen – Gericht sitzen*, pass judgement on a p.; – *Gesicht bekommen*, catch sight *or* a glimpse of; *-m Glück*, fortunately, happily; – *Grunde gehen*, be ruined, be lost; *sich -m Guten wenden*, take a turn for the better, show signs of improvement; *-r Hälfte*, by half, half of it; *-r Hälfte machen*, half do *or* finish; – *einem halten*, stand by a p.; *ein Musikstück – vier Händen*, a piece arranged for four hands, a pianoforte duet; *-r Hand sein*, be at hand; *-r rechten Hand*, on *or* at the right hand (side); – *Händen* (*z. H.*) *des Herrn N.*, into the hands of Mr. N., to Mr. N. personally; – *Hause sein*, be at home, be in; *-r Tür herein*, in at, by *or* through the door; – *Hunderten*, by hundreds, in their hundreds; *Milch -m Kaffee*, milk in *or* with one's coffee; – *Kreuze kriechen*, humble o.s., eat humble pie, (*coll.*) climb down; *es ist -m Lachen*, it is laughable; *mir ist nicht -m Lachen*, I am in no laughing mood; – *Lande*, by land; on the land; *einem – Leibe gehen*, attack a p.; – *guter Letzt*, finally, last of all, to finish up with; *Ihnen – Liebe, aus Liebe – Ihnen*, out of love for you; *-r linken Hand heiraten*, marry morganatically; *-m Lohne für*, in return for, as a reward for; *Lust – einer S. haben*, find pleasure in a th., have a liking for a th.; *-m König machen*, make a king, put on the throne; *-m letzten Male*, for the last time; – *6 Mark das Stück*, at 6 marks each; *das Pfund – 2 Mark*, a pound for 2 marks, 2 marks a pound; *sich* (*Dat.*) *-m Muster nehmen*, take as a model; *ihm ist schlecht – Mute*, he is in a bad mood; – *Nacht*, by night, in the night-time, at night; *einen -m Narren haben* or *halten*, make a fool of a p.; *-r Not*, in case of necessity, if necessary, if need be; *-r Ordnung rufen*, call to order; – *Ostern*, at Easter; – *Paaren*, in couples; – *Paaren treiben*, rout (*Mil.*); *etwas – Papier bringen*, put s.th. (down) in writing *or* in black and white; – *Rate ziehen*, consult; – *Recht bestehen*, be valid; *-r Rechten*, on the right hand (side); *-(r) Rede stellen*, call to account; – *Schaden kommen*, meet with an accident, sustain an *or* suffer injury; *-r Schau tragen*, make a show of; *-m Scherz*, as a joke, jokingly, in fun; *-m Schmuck*, as ornament; – *einer S. schweigen*, take no notice of a th., be silent about s.th.; *-r See*, at sea; *einem -r Seite*, at a p.'s side; *-m Spaß*, see *-m Scherz*; *das Spiel steht 'zu'*, the game is a draw *or* tie; – *Tage bringen*, bring to light, make known; – *Tage ausgehen*, crop out, lie on the surface (*Min.*); – *Tal fahren*, go downhill, go downstream *or* with the stream; – *nichts taugen*, be good for nothing, be no use at all; *-m Teil*, in part, partly, partially; *-m größten Teil*, for the most part; – *Tisch gehen* (*führen*), go (take) in to dinner; *-m Theater gehen*, see *-r Bühne gehen*; *Wasser -m Trinken*, drinking-water; *einem -m Trotz*, in spite *or* defiance of a p.; *-r Unterhaltung der Gesellschaft*, for the entertainment of the company; *-r Unzeit*, at an unsuitable time, inopportunely, unseasonably, prematurely; *einen -r Verantwortung ziehen*, hold a p. responsible; *-r Verfügung stehen*, be at (one's) disposal, be available; *im Vergleich* –, in comparison with; – *seiner Verteidigung*, in his defence; *im Verhältnis* –, in proportion to; *kein Geld -m Verspielen*, no money to lose; – *Wagen*, in a *or* by car *or* coach; – *Wasser und – Lande*, by sea and land; – *Wasser werden*, melt, turn to water; (*fig.*) come to nothing; *-m wenigsten*, at least; – *Staub werden*, turn to dust; – *Werke gehen*, set to work; *-r Zeit*, at the time, at present; – *rechter Zeit*, at the right time; – *Zeiten*, at times; – *welchem Zwecke?* for what purpose? – *zweien*, in *or* by twos, in couples; – *zweit*, two of us *or* them. **2.** *particle* (*with the infinitive*) *ich habe – arbeiten*, I have to work, I have work to do; *anstatt selbst – gehen*, instead of going oneself; *ich erinnere mich, ihn gesehen – haben*, I remember seeing *or* having seen him; *es steht – hoffen*, it is to be hoped; *eine gute Ernte ist – hoffen*, a good harvest may be hoped for; *es ist schwer – tun*, it is hard to do; *was ist – tun?* what is to be done? *das ist – erwarten*, that is to be expected; *um mich – täuschen*, in order to deceive me; *es ist – unterscheiden*, a distinction must be made; *das ist – kaufen*, that may be purchased, that is for sale; *das Haus ist – verkaufen*, the house is for sale *or* is to be sold; *ohne – wissen*, without knowing (it). (*with pr.p. used as adj.*) *ein – verbessernder Fehler*, an error to be corrected *or* requiring correction; *ein – erwartendes Ereignis*, an event that may be expected; *ein – verkaufendes Haus*, a house for sale; *eine nicht – ertragende Hitze*, an unendurable heat. **3.** *adv. & sep. prefix*, to, towards; closed, shut; *der Küste* or *auf die Küste* –, towards the shore, shorewards; *die Tür ist nicht* –, *mach sie* –, the door is not closed, shut it. (*preceding an adj. or adv.*) too, overmuch; – *neugierig*, over-inquisitive; – *sehr*, too much; *gar* –, far too; *er ist ein gar – ehrgeiziger Mann*, he is much too ambitious (a man); – *schön um wahr – sein*, too good to be true; *ab und* –, at times, now and then; *geh –! immer –!* go on! get on! keep on! *Glück –!* good luck! *schreibe nur –!* go on writing!

zualler-erst, *adv.* first of all. **-letzt,** *adv.* last of all.

zuäußerst, *adv.* outermost.

zuballern, *v.a.* (*coll.*) slam (*a door*).

Zubau, *m.* annex(e); extension *or* addition (*to a building*). **-en,** *v.a.* build up, block up; add to (*by building*), extend (*a building*).

Zubehör, *m.* (*& Austr. dial. n.*) (-s, -e *& Swiss dial.* -den) belongings, appurtenances, accessories, appendages, fittings, trimmings; *Wohnung von sechs Zimmern mit* –, six-roomed house with offices *or* all conveniences; – *zu den Speisen*, dressing, seasoning. **-teile,** *m.pl.* accessories.

zubeißen, *ir.v.a. & n.* (*aux.* h.) snap at, (have *or* take a) bite at; (*coll.*) *tüchtig* –, eat away heartily, tuck in.

zubenam(s)t, zubenannt, *adj.* surnamed.

Zuber, *m.*, *see* **Zober.**

zubereit-en, *v.a.* prepare, get ready, dress, finish; cook, mix (*a drink*) season; *-etes Pelzwerk*, dressed

furs. **-ung,** *f.* preparation; dressing; cooking (*of food*).
zubillig-en, *v.a.* (*einem etwas*) grant, allow, concede. **-ung,** *f.* acknowledgement, acquiescence, compliance; *-ung mildernder Umstände*, allowing for extenuating circumstances, making allowances.
zubinden, *ir.v.a.* bind *or* tie up, bandage; *einem die Augen* –, blindfold a p.
zu-blasen, 1. *ir.v.n.* (*aux.* h.) go on blowing. 2. *v.a.* close by blowing; (*einem etwas*) whisper, suggest, prompt. **-bläser,** *m.* (-s, –) prompter; tell-tale.
zubleiben, *ir.v.n.* (*aux.* s.) remain shut *or* closed.
zublin-ken, -ze(l)n, *v.n.* (*aux.* h.) (*einem etwas*) wink at; make a sign to, intimate with one's eyes.
zubring-en, *ir.v.a.* (*einem etwas*) bring, carry, convey *or* take to; pass *or* spend (*time*); *einem eins* or *einen Trunk -en*, pledge a p., drink a p.'s health, drink a toast to a p.; *das Zugebrachte*, separate personal estate, dowry; *zugebrachte Kinder*, children by a previous marriage; *die Zeit mit Lesen -en*, pass one's time reading; *sie hat 3 Jahre damit zugebracht*, she has spent 3 years at it, it has taken her 3 years to do it. **-er,** *m.* follower (*Gun.*); feed mechanism; tell-tale; pimp, pander. **-erdienst,** *m.* feeder *or* ferry service. **-erlinie,** *f.* auxiliary railway.
Zubrot, *n.* s.th. spread on bread.
Zu-buße, *f.* (-en) (additional) contribution, new *or* additional payment. **-büßen,** *v.a.* contribute, pay (*one's share*); spend *or* lose over and above (*one's estimate*).
Züchen, *m.* (*dial.*) ticking, tick (*for bedding*).
Zucht, *f.* (-en) breeding, rearing (*cattle, etc.*); cultivation growing (*plants, etc.*), culture (*bacteria*); breed, stock, race, brood; education, training; discipline, drill; propriety, decorum, good breeding *or* manners, modesty; *zur – halten*, keep for breeding; *Mangel an* –, lack of discipline *or* good breeding; *einen an – und Ordnung gewöhnen*, accustom a p. to discipline; *in – halten*, keep good *or* strict discipline; *er nimmt keine – an*, he is not amenable to discipline, (*coll.*) you can do nothing with him; *unter jemandes – stehen*, be in a p.'s charge; *in – und Ehre(n), in allen Züchten*, with due propriety, in all modesty; (*coll.*) *das ist ja eine nette –!* a fine way to go on, fine goings-on! *was ist das für eine –?* what sort of behaviour is this? **-buch,** *n.* stud-book, pedigree. **-garten,** *m.* nursery. **-gesetz,** *n.* disciplinary law. **-gestüt,** *n.* stud. **-haus,** *n.* convict prison, penitentiary; *er erhielt 10 Jahre -haus*, he got 10 years' penal servitude. **-häusler,** *m.* convict. **-hausstrafe,** *f.* penal servitude. **-hengst,** *m.* stallion. **-huhn,** *n.* brood-hen. **-hund,** *m.* stud-dog. **-los,** *adj.* insubordinate; undisciplined; dissolute, licentious. **-losigkeit,** *f.* want of discipline; insubordination; licentiousness, loose-living. **-meister,** *m.* taskmaster; disciplinarian. **-mittel,** *n.* disciplinary measure, corrective. **-perle,** *f.* culture pearl. **-rasse,** *f.* improved breed. **-rute,** *f.* (*fig.*) scourge, punishment. **-sorte,** *f.* breed. **-stier,** *m.* bull. **-stute,** *f.* brood-mare. **-tiere,** *n.pl.*, **-vieh,** *n.* beasts kept for breeding, breeding cattle. **-wahl,** *f.* natural selection.
zücht-en, *v.a.* breed, raise, rear, (*coll.*) keep (*animals, etc.*); cultivate, grow; train, bring up. **-er,** *m.* breeder, grower, cultivator. **-ig,** *adj.* chaste, modest, bashful, coy; proper, discreet. **-igen,** *v.a.* chastise, punish; discipline, correct; *körperlich -igen*, flog, thrash; *mit Worten -igen*, lash with one's tongue; *sein Fleisch -igen*, mortify one's flesh. **-igkeit,** *f.* chastity, propriety, modesty; bashfulness. **-igung,** *f.* punishment, chastisement, correction. **-igungsrecht,** *n.* right to inflict corporal punishment. **-ling,** *m.* convict. **-ung,** *f.* breeding, rearing (*animals*); growing, cultivation (*plants*); culture (*of bacteria*), selection.
Zuck, 1. *m.* (-(e)s, -e) short and quick movement, twitch, start; *in einem* (*Ruck und*) –, in one jerk, in one rush, all at once, in a trice. 2. *int.* quick! (*coll.*) put a jerk in it! (*coll.*) **-eln,** *v.n.* (*aux.* s.) (*dial.*) move on in fits and starts; meander, dawdle. **-en,** 1. *v.n.* (*aux.* h.) move convulsively, jerk, start, twitch, wince; palpitate, quiver, thrill; *der Blitz -te*, the lightning flashed; *mit den Augen -en*, blink; *er -t mit den Augenlidern*, his eyelids quiver; *ohne mit der Wimper zu -en*, without turning a hair *or* blinking (*or coll.* batting) an eyelid; *das -te ihm in allen Gliedern*, he was itching to do it; *es -te ihm durch alle Glieder*, he started with pain. 2. *v.a.*; *die Achseln* or *mit den Achseln -en*, shrug one's shoulders. **-end,** *pr.p. & adj.* jerky, convulsive, spasmodic; palpitating, quivering. **-ung,** *f.* jerk, spasm, convulsion, convulsive movement, twitch, thrill, quiver; palpitation; *letzte -ungen*, death throes.
zücken, *v.a.* draw (*one's sword*); (*coll.*) *den Geldbeutel* –, put one's hand in one's pocket.
Zucker, *m.* sugar; *ein Stück* –, a lump of sugar; *in – einmachen*, preserve, candy; *er hat* –, he is diabetic *or* has diabetes; *seinem Affen – geben*, pander his whims. **-abbau,** *m.* breaking down of sugar. **-ahorn,** *m.* sugar maple (*Acer saccharinum*) (*Bot.*). **-anreicherung,** *f.* increase in sugar content. **-arten,** *f.pl.* sugars. **-ausbeute,** *f.* sugar yield. **-bäcker,** *m.* confectioner. **-bäckerei,** *f.* confectionery; confectioner's shop. **-backwerk,** *n.* confectionery, sweetmeats. **-bau,** *m.* cultivation of the sugar-cane. **-bildung,** *f.* formation of sugar, saccharification. **-bonbon,** *n.* sweet. **-büchse,** *f.* sugar-basin. **-couleur,** *f.* caramel. **-dicksaft,** *m.* molasses, treacle. **-dose,** *f.*, *see* **-büchse.** **-erbse,** *f.* small green pea. **-fabrik,** *f.* sugar-refinery. **-fabrikant,** *m.* sugar-refiner. **-früchte,** *f.pl.* candied fruit. **-gärung,** *f.* saccharine fermentation. **-gast,** *m.* sugar-mite (*Ent.*). **-gebäck,** *n.*, **-geback(e)ne(s),** *n.*, *see* **-backwerk.** **-gehalt,** *m.* sugar content. **-guß,** *m.* icing. **-haltig,** *adj.* containing sugar, sugary, saccharine. **-harnruhr,** *f.*, *see* **-krankheit.** **-honig,** *m.* old *or* crystallized honey. **-hut,** *m.* sugar-loaf. **-ig,** *adj.* sugary. **-kand(is),** *m.* sugar-candy. **-krank,** *adj.*, **-kranke(r),** *m.* diabetic. **-krankheit,** *f.* diabetes (mellitus). **-l,** *n.* (*Austr. dial.*) sweet, bonbon. **-mandeln,** *f.pl.* sugared almonds. **-mäulchen,** *n.* sweet-tooth. **-mehl,** *n.* powdered sugar. **-melone,** *f.* sweet melon. **-messung,** *f.* saccharometry. (*coll.*) **-mund,** *m.* honeyed lips. **-n,** *v.a.* sugar, sweeten. **-pflanzung,** *f.* sugar-plantation. **-plätzchen,** *n.* sweet. **-puppe,** *f.* (*coll.*) honey-child, sweetie. **-rohr,** *n.* sugar-cane. **-rübe,** *f.* sugar-beet. **-rübenzucker,** *m.* beet sugar. **-ruhr,** *f.*, *see* **-krankheit.** **-saft,** *m.* syrup, molasses. **-satz,** *m.* molasses. **-sauer,** *adj.* saccharic; *-saures Salz*, saccharate. **-säure,** *f.* saccharic acid. **-schale,** *f.*, *see* **-büchse.** **-schote,** *f.*, *see* **-erbse** (*Pisum sativum*) (*Bot.*). **-sieden,** *n.* sugar-refining. **-sieder,** *m.* sugar-refiner. **-siederei,** *f.*, *see* **-fabrik.** **-sirup,** *m.* molasses, treacle. **-steuer,** *f.* duty on sugar. **-stoff,** *m.* saccharine matter. **-stoffhaltig,** *adj.* saccharine. **-streubüchse,** *f.* sugar-castor *or* sprinkler. **-süß,** *adj.* sweet as sugar, sugary; (*fig.*) honeyed. **-überzug,** *m.* coating of sugar, icing. **-umwandlung,** *f.* sugar metabolism. **-verbindungen,** *f.pl.* saccharates, sucrates. **-waren,** *f.pl.* confectionery, sweetmeats, sweets. **-werk,** *n.* confectionery, sweets, candy. **-zange,** *f.* sugar-tongs. **-zeltchen,** *n.* (*Austr. dial.*) sweet.
zuckrig, *adj.*, *see* **zuckerig.**
zudämmen, *v.a.* stop *or* close a hole.
Zudecke, *f.* quilt, coverlet. **-n,** *v.a.* cover up; put a lid on; cloak, conceal; *durch Artillerie zugedeckt*, pinned *or* held down by artillery fire.
zudem, *adv.* besides, moreover, in addition.
zudenken, *ir.v.a.* (*einem etwas*) (*usually p.p. only*) destine, intend for; *dies hatte ich dir zum Geschenk zugedacht*, I had intended this as a present for you.
Zu-drang, *m.* crowding; crowd, throng, press, rush (*to*), run (*on*). **-drängen,** *v.r.* throng *or* crowd to; press forward; thrust o.s. into, intrude.
zudrehen, *v.a.* shut *or* turn off, turn towards: *einem den Rücken* –, turn one's back on a p.
zudringlich, *adj.* importunate, intruding, forward, pushing; obtrusive. **-keit,** *f.* importunity, forwardness, obtrusiveness.
zudrücken, *v.a.* shut, close; *ein Auge bei einer S.* –, connive *or* wink at a th., overlook a th., let a th. pass.

zueign–en, *v.a.* (*einem etwas*) dedicate (*a book*); *sich* (*Dat.*) *etwas –en*, appropriate (to o.s.), claim as one's own; *sich* (*Dat.*) *widerrechtlich –en*, arrogate to o.s., usurp. **–ung,** *f.* dedication; appropriation; *rechtswidrige –eignung*, misappropriation. **–ungsschrift,** *f.* dedicatory epistle.

zueilen, *v.n.* (*aux.* s.) (*Dat. or* auf *with Acc.*) run towards *or* up to, hasten towards; *seinem Verderben –*, rush headlong into ruin *or* to destruction.

zueinander, *adv.* to each other.

zuerkenn–en, *ir.v.a.* (*einem etwas*) grant, award, confer, decree; acknowledge, adjudge, adjudicate; *einem eine Ehre –en*, confer an honour on s.o.; *einem einen Preis –en*, award a p. a prize; *einem den Vorzug –en*, give the preference to a p.; *einem das Recht –en*, acknowledge *or* admit a p.'s right; *einem eine Strafe –en*, sentence a p. to be punished. **–ung,** *f.* award, adjudication.

zuerst, *adv.* first, firstly, in the first place, at first, first of all; above all, especially; *gleich –*, at the very beginning; *der – Angekommene*, the first comer.

zuerteilen, *v.a.* confer *or* bestow (on), apportion (to).

zufächeln, *v.a.* (*einem etwas*) fan *or* waft towards; *sich* (*Dat.*) *Luft –*, fan o.s.

zufahr–en, *ir.v.n.* (*aux.* h. & s.) drive *or* go on; approach, drive towards; rush at; *fahr zu, Kutscher!* drive on, coachman! *dem Dorfe –en*, drive to *or* in the direction of the village; *auf die Kirche –en*, drive up to the church; (*fig.*) *auf einen –en*, fly, rush at *or* fall upon a p.; *blind auf eine S. –en*, rush blindly *or* headlong at *or* upon a th.; *gut –en*, drive at a brisk pace; *die Tür ist zugefahren*, the door has slammed. **–t,** *f.* drive; approach. **–tsweg,** *m.* approach road.

Zufall, *m.* (-(e)s, ⸚e) chance, accident; contingency, casual event, incident, occurrence; *der – wollte, daß . . .*, as good (*or* bad) luck would have it . . .; *den Launen des –s unterworfen*, subject to the caprice of fortune; *bloßer –*, mere accident; *glücklicher –*, lucky chance, piece of good luck; *widriger –*, misfortune, piece of ill-luck; *durch –*, accidentally, by accident *or* chance. **–sgesetz,** *n.* law of probability. **–skurve,** *f.* probability curve. **–streffer,** *m.* chance hit.

zufallen, *ir.v.n.* (*aux.* s.) close, fall to; (*with Dat.*) fall to one's lot, devolve (up)on; *die Augen fallen ihm zu*, his eyes are closing with sleep; *die Schuld fällt ihm zu*, the blame rests with him; *der Beweis hiervon fällt ihm zu*, the burden of proof is his; *viel Geld ist ihm zugefallen*, much money has fallen to his share, he has come in for a lot of money; *ihm ist eine Erbschaft zugefallen*, he has inherited some property.

zufällig, 1. *adj.* accidental, fortuitous, chance, random, casual, contingent, non-essential, incidental. 2. *adv.* by chance; *–e Ausgaben*, incidental expenses; *–er Kunde*, chance customer; *wir waren – da*, we happened to be there; *ich traf ihn –*, I chanced to meet him, I met him accidentally *or* by chance. **–erweise,** *adv.* by chance, by accident, as chance would have it. **–keit,** *f.* fortuitousness, contingency, chance; unforeseen occurrence, accident. **–keitsfehler,** *m.* accidental error.

zufassen, *v.n.* seize, jump at; set to work, lend a hand.

zufertigen, *v.a.* (*einem etwas*) (*C.L.*) forward, deliver *or* send (*s.th. to a p.*).

zuflicken, *v.a.* mend, patch, repair.

zufliegen, *ir.v.n.* (*aux.* s.) (*with Dat.*) fly to *or* towards; *die Tür flog zu*, the door slammed *or* shut with a bang; *ihm fliegt alles nur so zu*, he learns easily, he picks things up without difficulty.

zufließen, *ir.v.n.* (*aux.* s.) flow to *or* towards, flow into; *einem etwas – lassen*, bestow s.th. upon a p., give *or* grant s.th. to a p.; *die Worte fließen ihm* (*nur so*) *zu*, words come readily to him, he is never at a loss for words; *ein Gewinn fließt ihm zu aus . . .*, he derives (a) profit from. . . .

Zuflucht, *f.* (-en) refuge, shelter; recourse; *zu einem* or *einer S. seine – nehmen*, have recourse to *or* take refuge with a p. *or* in a th.; *seine – zu den Waffen nehmen*, appeal to arms. **–sort,** *m.*, (-s, -e & ⸚er), **–sstätte,** *f.* place of refuge, retreat, asylum, sanctuary; retirade (*Fort.*).

Zufluß, *m.* (-(ss)es, ⸚(ss)e) flowing in, influx, inflow; feed, tributary; supply (*of goods*); *die Zuflüsse des Rheins*, the tributaries of the Rhine; *Abfluß und – des Meeres*, ebb and flow of the tide; *– von Blut nach dem Kopfe*, flow of blood to the head; *– von Fremden*, influx of foreigners. **–behälter,** *m.* feed tank. **–graben,** *m.* feeder (*of a pond*). **–röhre,** *f.* feed-, service- *or* supply-pipe.

zuflüster–n, *v.a.* (*einem etwas*) whisper, prompt; insinuate. **–ung,** *f.* prompting, insinuation.

zufolge, *prep.* (*with Dat. when following, with Gen. when preceding*) in consequence of; by *or* in virtue of, owing to, according to, in pursuance of.

zufrieden, *adj.* content, pleased, satisfied; *sich – geben* (*mit*), rest content (with), acquiesce (in); *ich bin damit* or *mit etwas –*, I am satisfied with it; *ich bin es –*, all right, well and good, I have no objections; *laß ihn –!* let him alone! leave him in peace! **–heit,** *f.* contentment, satisfaction. **–stellen,** *v.a.* (*sep.*) content, satisfy, give satisfaction. **–stellend,** *adj.* satisfactory. **–stellung,** *f.* satisfaction.

zufrieren, *ir.v.n.* (*aux.* s.) freeze up *or* over, get frozen, be covered with ice.

zufügen, *v.a.* add to; (*einem etwas*) do, cause, inflict; *einem* (*ein*) *Leid –*, grieve a p.; *jemandem Schaden –*, harm *or* injure a p.

Zufuhr, *f.* (-en) conveying, conveyance, bringing up (*of supplies*); importation; imports, supply, feed, stock, store; supplies, provisions; *starke – von Waren*, large supply of goods; *die – abschneiden*, cut off supplies. **–straße,** *f.* supply road.

zuführ–en, *v.a.* (*einem etwas*) conduct, lead to, bring to; supply, procure, convey, transport; introduce (*customers*); lead in; feed (*Mech.*); *einem künstlich Nahrungsmittel –en*, feed s.o. artificially; *eine Sache ihrer Bestimmung –en*, devote s.th. to its proper purpose; *einem eine Braut –en*, procure a bride for a p.; *einen seinem Untergang –en*, lead a p. to ruin, be the cause of a p.'s ruin; *einem Heere Lebensmittel –en*, provision an army. **–end,** *pr.p.* & *adj.* conducting, afferent; *–ende Gefäße*, deferents (*Anat.*); ducts (*Bot.*). **–er,** *m.* procurer; duct; feeder (*Mech.*); belt pawl (*of machine gun*). **–schlauch,** *m.* supply pipe. **–ung,** *f.* conveyance, importation, provision, supply, feed, lead (*Elec.*); *–ung von Lebensmittel*, victualling, food-supply. **–ungsdraht,** *m.* lead (*Elec.*). **–ungsrohr,** *n.* feed *or* supply pipe. **–ungswalzen,** *f.pl.* feeding-rollers.

zufüllen, *v.a.* fill up, fill in.

Zug, *m.* (-(e)s, ⸚e) drawing, pulling; stretch, pull, tension; tug; stroke (*rowing*), move (*chess*); draught, traction (*Mech.*); (railway) train; march, marching, passage, progress, procession, expedition, migration; flight, flock, herd, shoal; drift (*of clouds*); range (*of mountains*); row (*of houses*); draught, current (*of air*); train, retinue, band, gang, troop, platoon, squad, section (*Mil.*); span, yoke (*of oxen, etc.*); stroke (*of a pen*), line, outline; feature, characteristic, trait, lineament; attraction, sympathy, bent, disposition, inclination, bias, drawing power, impulse; gulp, draught (*in drinking*); whiff, puff (*of smoke*); pull (*at a pipe*); set (*of strings, chords, etc.*); draw-thread, grip (*for pulling*); (bell-)pull; rifling (*gun-barrels*); *ankommender* (*abgehender*) *–*, train arriving (departing); *wer ist am –e?* whose move is it? who has the next move? (*chess, etc.*); *auf einen –*, at one draught *or* gulp; (*coll.*) *einen auf dem –e haben*, be dead set against a p.; *ein – seines Charakters*, a feature of his character; *durchgehender –*, through-train; *– der Ereignisse*, train of events; *es ist kein – im Handel*, trade is very dull; *dem –e des Herzens folgen*, follow the promptings of one's heart; *im –e von*, in the course of; *in – bringen*, set going, start, give an impetus to; *in einem –e*, at one pull, stroke *or* (*coll.*) go, straight off, uninterruptedly; *in großen Zügen*, along general lines, in broad outline, generally; *gut im – haben*, have well under control; *in kräftigen Zügen*, in bold outlines; *in den letzten Zügen liegen*, be at one's last gasp, be dying; *im* (*besten*) *–e sein*, be (well) under way, be (well) in hand, be in full swing; be in the (right) vein; *im –e stehen*, stand in a draught; *im vollen –e*, in full march, on the march; *in vollen Zügen*, fully, thoroughly, deeply, to the full; *seinen – nehmen* *durch*, pass through, make one's way through; *einen – tun*, (make a) move (*chess, etc.*); *– um –*, without delay, uninterruptedly, without a break; *ein – der Zeit*, a sign of the times. **-abteil,** *n. & m.* railway compartment. **-artikel,** *m.* popular article, (*coll.*) draw. **-band,** *n.* tie-rod. **-beanspruchung,** *f.* tensile stress. **-brücke,** *f.* drawbridge. **-brunnen,** *m.* draw-well. **-entgleisung,** *f.* derailment. **-feder,** *f.* tension spring. **-festigkeit,** *f.* tensile strength. **-fisch,** *m.* migratory fish. **-führer,** *m.* platoon *or* section commander; guard (*of train*). **-garn,** *n., see* **-netz. -haken,** *m.* trace-hook, pintle. **-haspel,** *m. & f.* windlass, pulley. **-ig,** *adj.* draughty. **-kanal,** *m.* air duct, flue. **-klappe,** *f.* damper, register (*of furnace*). **-kraft,** *f.* tractive *or* pulling power, propelling force, thrust (*of a propeller*), (force of) attraction, suction. **-kräftig,** *adj.* in vogue, attractive. **-leine,** *f.* drag-rope, tow-rope. **-linie,** *f.* line of march (*Mil.*); column (*Mil.*). **-luft,** *f.* current of air, draught. **-maschine,** *f.* prime mover; (traction-)engine, tractor. **-material,** *n.* rolling-stock. **-mittel,** *n.* attraction, draw, means of attracting (*a crowd, etc.*); vesicatory (*Med.*). **-netz,** *n.* drag-net. **-ochse,** *m.* draught-ox. **-ofen,** *m.* air-furnace, blast-furnace. **-personal,** *n.* crew of a train. **-pferd,** *n.* draught-horse. **-pflaster,** *n.* blister, vesicatory (*Med.*). **-riemen,** *m.* trace, tug-strap (*of horses*). **-rohr,** *n.*, **-röhre,** *f.* air-pipe; air-vent. **-rolle,** *f.* pulley. **-schalter,** *m.* pull-switch (*Elec.*). **-schnur,** *f.* string, draw-thread. **-schraube,** *f.* tractor airscrew (*Av.*). **-seil,** *n.* towing-line, tow-rope, hawser. **-sicherung,** *f.* automatic safety device (*on trains*). **-spannung,** *f.* tensile stress. **-stange,** *f.* swipe (*of a pump*). **-stiefel,** *m.* elastic-sided boot. **-straße,** *f.* route of migration (*birds*). **-stück,** *n.* popular play, (*coll.*) draw (*Theat.*). **-tau,** *n.* drag-rope. **-tier,** *n.* draught-animal, beast of burden. **-verkehr,** *m.* railway traffic. **-versuch,** *m.* tensile test. **-vogel,** *m.* bird of passage. **-vorhang** *m.* draw curtain. **-wagen,** *m.* tractor. **-weise,** *adv.* in flocks *or* troops; in squads, by platoons. **-wind,** *m., see* **-luft. -winde,** *f.* draw-winch.

Zugabe, *f.* (-n) addition, extra; overweight; make-weight; adjunct, supplement, repetition, encore; *als –*, into the bargain. **-wesen,** *n.* use of free gifts (*for advertisement*).

Zugang, *m.* (-(e)s, ⸚e) admittance, access, entry, entrance, approach; increase; *– zum Meere*, access to the sea. **-sgraben,** *m.* approach-trench, communication-trench (*Mil.*).

zugäng-ig, *adj.* accessible (*only with* sein, werden *or* machen). **-lich,** *adj.* (*with Dat.*) accessible, approachable, open (to), susceptible (to); affable; *-lich machen*, render accessible, throw open; popularize; *er ist vernünftigen Gründen stets -lich*, he is always open to conviction (by reasonable arguments). **-lichkeit,** *f.* accessibility, susceptibility; affability.

zugeben, *ir.v.a.* add; give into the bargain, (*einem etwas*) grant, concede, admit, allow; agree to, accede to, acknowledge, own, confess, follow suit (*Cards*); *klein –*, follow suit with a low card. **zugegeben,** *p.p. & adj.* granted, admitting. **zugegebenermaßen,** *adv.* as already acknowledged, admittedly.

zugegen, *indec. adv.* present.

zugehen, *ir.v.n.* (*aux.* s.) close, shut, meet, fasten; (*with* auf) go up to, move towards, go on *or* faster; come to pass, take place, happen; *wie geht es zu, daß . . .*, how is that . . ., how does it come about *or* to pass that . . .? *hier geht es bunt zu*, there's plenty of excitement here; *der Brief ist mir eben zugegangen*, the letter has just reached me; *gut –*, go on well; *es müßte komisch* or *mit dem Teufel –, wenn . . .*, it would be strange if . . .; *einem etwas – lassen*, forward *or* send s.th. to a p.; *dort geht es lustig zu*, there are merry goings-on there; *mit rechten Dingen –*, come about naturally; *es geht nicht mit rechten Dingen zu*, there is something uncanny about it; *es geht sonderbar zu in dieser Welt*, queer things are happening in the world; *spitz –* ,end in a point.

Zugeh-erin, -frau, *f.* (*dial.*) charwoman, daily help.

Zugehör, *n.* (*archaic*), *see* **Zubehör. -en,** *v.n.* (*aux.* h.) (*with Dat.*) belong *or* appertain to. **-ig,** *adj.* appertaining, belonging to, accompanying; proper, pertinent; *-ige Briefumschläge*, envelopes to match. **-igkeit,** *f.* membership, relationship, forming part of.

zugeknöpft, *adj.* uncommunicative, reserved.

Zügel, *m.* (-s, –) rein, reins; bridle; check, curb; *einem den* or *die – kurz halten*, keep a tight rein on s.o.; *die – der Regierung*, the reins of government; *dem Pferde die – schießen lassen*, give the horse his head; *einem den – (schießen) lassen*, let a p. do as he likes; *seinen Leidenschaften die – schießen lassen*, give full rein *or* free vent to one's passions; *mit verhängtem –*, at full speed. **-hand,** *f.* bridle-hand, left hand. **-los,** *adj.* unbridled, unrestrained, licentious. **-losigkeit,** *f.* impetuosity, licentiousness. **-n,** *v.a. & r.* bridle, curb, check; (*Swiss dial.*) move (house), move one's quarters.

Zugemüse, *n.* vegetables served with a dish, side dish of vegetables.

zugenannt, *adj.* surnamed.

zugesellen, *v.a. & r.* associate with, join.

Zugeständnis, *n.* (-ses, -se) concession, admission, compromise, (*pl.*) allowances.

zugestehen, *ir.v.a.* (*einem etwas*) grant, concede, admit; **zugestanden,** see *zugegeben.*

zugetan, *p.p. & adj.* (*with Dat.*) (*usually with* sein) attached *or* devoted to.

zugewandt, *p.p. & adj.* (*with Dat.*) sympathetic towards, *die -en Orte*, cantons affiliated to the old Swiss Confederation (*Hist.*).

zugießen, 1. *ir.v.a.* pour in, fill up; *darf ich Ihnen Tee – ?* may I fill your cup? 2. *v.n.* keep on pouring; *gieß zu!* pour away!

zügig, *adj.* unbroken, uninterrupted; (*Swiss dial.*), *see* **zugkräftig.**

zugleich, *adv.* at the same time, together, along (with), also, conjointly (with).

zugreifen, *ir.v.n.* (*aux.* h.) lay *or* take hold of, lay hands on, seize, grab, grasp at; fall to; help, lend a hand, take a hand, take the opportunity; help o.s. (*at table*); (*allzu*) *leicht –*, be lightfingered; *der Anker greift zu*, the anchor bites *or* holds.

Zugriff, *m.* grip, clutch(es).

zugrunde, *adv.*; *– gehen*, perish, be ruined; *– legen*, (*einem etwas*) base upon, take as a basis; *– liegen*, underlie, be based upon, be at the root of, be at the bottom of; *– richten*, ruin, destroy. **-gehen,** *n.* destruction, ruin. **-legung,** *f.*; *unter -legung von . . .*, taking . . . as a basis.

zugunsten, *prep.*(*Gen.*) for the benefit of, in favour of.

zugute, *adv.* to the benefit *or* advantage of; *etwas – halten*, take s.th. into consideration, allow for a th.; *einem etwas – halten*, take a lenient view of s.th., be forbearing with a p. *or* (*coll.*) let a p. down gently over a th.; *einem – kommen*, be for the benefit *or* to the advantage of a p.; stand a p. in good stead; *– kommen lassen*, give the benefit of; *einem eine Sache – tun*, treat a p. to a th.; *sich* (*Dat.*) *etwas – tun*, indulge, pamper o.s.; *sich* (*Dat.*) *auf eine S. etwas – tun*, pride o.s. on a th., be proud of s.th.

zuhaben, *ir.v.a.* be *or* stay shut; *der Bäcker hat am Montag zu*, the baker's does not open on Monday; *den Rock –*, have one's coat buttoned up; *er will noch Geld –*, he wants money besides *or* in addition.

zuhalt-en, 1. *ir.v.a.* keep shut; close (*one's eyes, etc.*); clench (*one's fist*); *sich* (*Dat.*) *die Nase -en*, hold one's nose. 2. *v.n.* (*aux.* h.) (auf *with Acc.*) make for, proceed towards, go straight for; *mit einem -en*, have an understanding *or* (illicit) relations with a p. 3. *v.r.* hurry, make haste. **-ung,** *f.* tumbler (*of lock*).

Zuhälter, *m.* (-s, –) souteneur. **-ei,** *f.*, **-wesen,** *n.* dependence (*of a man*) on a prostitute's earnings.

zuhanden, *adv.* (*with* sein *or* kommen) close at hand, ready, to hand; *einem –*, (to be) delivered to a p. personally.

zuhängen, *v.a.* cover with a curtain *or* drapery; hang, drape.

zuhauen, 1. *ir.v.a.* rough-hew; dress, trim (*stones*); cut to shape, cut up (*meat*). 2. *v.n.* (*aux.* h.) persist in striking; *auf einen* –, strike a p.
zuhauf, *adv.* (*Poet.*) together.
Zuhause, *n.* home.
zuheilen, *v.n.* (*aux.* s.) close *or* heal up, cicatrize.
Zuhilfenahme, *f.*; *unter* (*ohne*) – *von*, by *or* with (without) the aid *or* help of, with (without) having recourse to.
zuhinterst, *adv.* at the very end, last of all.
zuhöchst, *adv.* topmost, uppermost, highest of all.
zuhorchen, *v.n.* (*aux.* h.) (*with Dat.*) listen secretly to, eavesdrop.
zuhöre–n, *v.n.* (*aux.* h.) (*Dat.*) listen (to); attend (to). **–r,** *m.* listener, auditor; member of the audience; (*pl.*) (members of the) audience. **–rraum,** *m.* auditorium, lecture-room *or* -hall. **–rschaft,** *f.* audience.
zuinnerst, *adv.* innermost, in the very heart, right inside, in the interior.
zujauchzen, zujubeln, *v.a. & n.* (*aux.* h.) (*with Dat.*) cheer, hail, shout to.
zukehren, *v.a.* (*einem etwas*) turn to(wards), face; stop (*a hole*) by sweeping (*sand, etc., into it*); *einem das Gesicht* –, turn one's face toward a person; *einem den Rücken* –, turn one's back on a p.
zuklappen, 1. *v.a.* close, slam, bang. 2. *v.n.* (*aux.* s.) close with a snap, slam to.
zuklatschen, *v.a. & n.* (*aux.* h.) (*einem*) applaud (a p.), clap (a p.).
zukleben, zukleistern, *v.a.* paste *or* glue up, fasten *or* gum down.
zuknöpfen, *v.a.* button up; **zugeknöpft,** *p.p. & adj.* buttoned up; (*fig.*) reserved.
zuknüpfen, *v.a.* tie up, knot, fasten with a knot.
zukommen, *ir.v.n.* (*aux.* s.) (*with* auf) come up to, approach; (*with Dat.*) arrive, come to hand, reach; belong to, be due to, befit, fall to (*one's share* or *lot*); cover (*of horses*); *auf einen* –, come to *or* approach a p.; *einem etwas – lassen*, let a p. have a th., accommodate *or* furnish s.o. with a th., make a p. a present of a th., pass *or* send s.th. to a p.; *einem ärztliche Behandlung – lassen*, let a p. receive medical attention; *es ist mir zugekommen*, it reached me, I received it; *es kommt dir nicht zu, so zu sprechen*, it is not for you to speak like that; *das kommt ihm nicht zu*, he has no right to that; *es kommt mir nicht zu*, it is not within my province; *jedem, was ihm zukommt*, to everyone his due.
zukorken, *v.a.* cork (up).
Zukost, *f.* something eaten with bread *or* served with meat.
Zukunft, *f.* future, life hereafter, future tense; *in* –, in future, henceforth, from this time onwards; *in nächster* –, in the immediate future; *das muß die – lehren*, that remains to be seen; *Mann der* –, coming man, rising star. **–sfreudig,** *adj.* optimistic. **–shoffnung,** *f.* hopes for the future. **–smusik,** *f.* (*fig.*) future aims, plans for the future, castles in the air. **–spläne,** *m.pl.* future plans. **–sstaat,** *m.* utopia.
zukünftig, 1. *adj.* future, to come; *–e Zeit*, time to come; future tense; *mein –er, meine –e*, (*coll.*) my intended, my husband *or* wife to be. 2. *adv.* in future, for the future.
zulächeln, *v.a. & n.* (*aux.* h.) (*with Dat.*) smile at; *einem Beifall* –, smile on a p.
Zulad–egewicht, *n.*, **–ung,** *f.*, **–ungsgewicht,** *n.* useful load.
Zulage, *f.* (-n) addition, increase (of salary); extra pay; allowance; scaffolding.
zulande, *adv.*; *bei uns* –, in my country.
zulangen, 1. *v.a.*; (*einem etwas*) –, hand to. 2. *v.n.* (*aux.* h.) stretch out the hand for, reach out for, help o.s. (*at table*); suffice, be sufficient; reach; *es langt nicht zu*, it is not enough, it won't reach.
zulänglich, *adj.* sufficient, adequate. **–keit,** *f.* sufficiency; adequacy.
Zulaß, *m.*, *see* **–(ss)ung.** **–(ss)en,** 1. *ir.v.a.* leave closed, not open; grant, concede, allow, permit, admit of; let cover (*of horses*); *einen zu einer Stelle –(ss)en*, admit s.o. to a position; *sie sind zugelassen*, they are admitted *or* accepted; *diese Erklärung läßt zwei Deutungen zu*, this explanation admits of two interpretations. **–(ss)ung,** *f.* admission; permission, concession; *um –(ss)ung zum Examen nachsuchen*, make application for admission to an examination. **–(ss)ungsgesuch,** *n.* application for admission. **–(ss)ungsprüfung,** *f.* entrance *or* qualifying examination. **–(ss)ungsschein,** *m.* ticket of admission, pass, permit, licence.
zulässig, *adj.* admissible, allowable, permissible; *nicht* –, inadmissible, objectionable.
Zulauf, *m.* crowd, rush, throng, concourse, influx, inflow; *einen – von Kunden haben*, have a rush of customers; *großen – haben*, be sought after, be popular, be in vogue; draw large crowds. **–en,** 1. *ir.v.n.* (*aux.* s.) (auf *with Acc.*) run to, run towards *or* up to; run faster; (*with Dat.*) crowd *or* flock to; *lauf zu!* be quick, hurry there! *spitz –en*, run *or* come to a point, taper (off).
zulegen, 1. *v.a.* add (to), put more (to), increase (*a salary*); attribute, assign; close, cover up; *es wurden ihm 300 Mark zugelegt*, his salary was increased by 300 marks; *Sie müssen noch etwas* –, you must raise your offer; (*coll.*) *sich* (*Dat.*) –, provide *or* procure for o.s., get o.s. 2. *v.n.* (*aux.* h.) continue adding to; get fatter, put on weight *or* flesh.
zuleid (*Austr. dial.*), **–e,** *adv.*; *einem etwas –e tun*, hurt, harm, do harm to a p.; *niemandem zuliebe niemandem –e*, without fear or favour.
zuleit–en, *v.a.* lead in *or* to; conduct direct to; bring before. **–ung,** *f.* feed pipe, lead (*Elec.*); supply. **–ungsdraht,** *m.* lead-in-wire, input lead (*Elec.*). **–ungskanal,** *m.* feeder. **–ungsrohr,** *n.* feed *or* inlet pipe.
zuletzt, *adv.* finally, at last, ultimately, eventually, after all, in the end; last, for the last time; (*Prov.*) *wer – lacht, lacht am besten*, who laughs last, laughs longest.
zulieb (*Austr. dial.*), **–e,** *adv.*; *einem etwas –e tun*, do a th. to please, oblige *or* help a p.; *niemandem –e niemandem zuleide*, without fear or favour.
Zulk, *m.*, **Zuller,** *m.*, **Zulp(er),** *m.* (*dial.*) dummy, comforter (*for a child*).
Zuluft, *f.* air supply *or* intake.
zum = zu dem.
zumachen, 1. *v.a.* close, shut, fasten, put down (*an umbrella*); button *or* do up (*a coat*); stop (up) (*a hole*); seal (*a letter*); *er mußte* (*die Bude*) –, he had to pack up (shop). 2. *v.n.* (*aux.* h.) (*coll.*) make haste, be quick, hurry.
zumal, 1. *adv.* above all, particularly, especially, chiefly. 2. *conj.*; – (*da*) . . ., especially since, particularly because, all the more so as . . .
zumauern, *v.a.* enclose with brickwork, wall up.
zumeist, *adv.* mostly, generally, for the most part, in most cases.
zumessen, *ir.v.a.* (*einem etwas*) measure out, mete out, allot, assign, apportion, allocate; *eine sehr kurze Zeit wurde uns zugemessen*, a very short time was allowed us *or* was allotted to us; *der zugemessene Teil*, the portion allocated.
zumindest, *adv.* at least.
zumisch–en, *v.a.* admix. **–ung,** *f.* admixture.
zumut–e, *adv.*; *mir ist schlecht* (*gut*) *–e*, I am in low (good) spirits. **–en,** *v.a.* (*einem etwas*) demand, expect (s.th. of a p.), require, exact (*s.th. from a p.*); *er mutet mir viel zu*, he demands (expects) a great deal from (of) me; *einem zu viel –en*, expect *or* ask too much of a p.; *sich* (*Dat.*) *zu viel –en*, attempt *or* take on too much. **–ung,** *f.* (unreasonable) demand *or* expectation; imputation; *an einen eine starke –ung stellen*, ask too much of a p.
zunächst, 1. *adv.* first (of all), above all, chiefly, to begin with, in the first instance. 2. *prep.* (*Dat.*) next *or* close to. **–liegende(s),** *n.* the obvious.
zunageln, *v.a.* nail up, nail down.
zunähen, *v.a.* sew up *or* together.
Zunahme, *f.* (-n) increase, advances, rise, growth, increment; augmentation, advancement, improvement, progress.
Zuname(n), *m.* (-ns, -n) family name; surname.
zünd–en, 1. *v.n.* (*aux.* h.) catch fire, kindle, ignite, (*dial.*) (*with Dat.*) shine *or* hold a light for. 2. *v.a.* set on fire, set fire to, set alight, ignite, kindle, (*fig.*) inflame; stir up, arouse enthusiasm. **–ap-**

parat, *m.* ignition device; magneto. **–bar,** *adj.* inflammable. **–end,** *pr.p.* & *adj.* inflammable; inflammatory, stirring, rousing, electrifying; *–ende Ansprache*, rousing *or* stirring speech. **–er,** *m.*lighter, fuse, detonator. **–fertig,** *adj.* primed. **–flamme,** *f.* pilot light. **–folge,** *f.* order of firing (*of engines*). **–holz,** *n.*, **–hölzchen,** *n.* match. **–holzmasse,** *f.* match-head. **–holzschachtel,** *f.* match-box. **–hütchen,** *n.* percussion-cap. **–kanal,** *m.* flash-hole; priming. **–kapsel,** *f.* detonator. **–kerze,** *f.* sparking plug (*Motor.*). **–kraut,** *n.*, *see* **–pulver.** **–ladung,** *f.* detonating *or* firing-charge. **–loch,** *n.* touch-hole (*Min.*); flash vent (*of a gun*). **–magnet,** *m.* magneto. **–masse,** *f.*, *see* **–holzmasse.** **–mittel,** *n.* means of ignition. **–nadel,** *f.* priming needle. **–nadelgewehr,** *n.* needle-gun. **–papier,** *n.* slow match, touch-paper. **–patrone,** *f.* priming-cartridge. **–pfanne,** *f.* touch-pan. **–pulver,** *n.* priming-powder. **–punkt,** *m.* ignition point. **–regelung,** *f.* ignition control (*Motor.*). **–rute,** *f.* linstock, match. **–satz,** *m.* detonating powder. **–schalter,** *m.* ignition switch (*Motor.*). **–schlüssel,** *m.* ignition key (*Motor.*). **–schnur,** *f.* (-en & ⸗e) match, fuse. **–schwamm,** *m.* tinder. **–spannung,** *f.* discharge *or* sparking voltage. **–spule,** *f.* spark coil. **–stoff,** *m.* inflammable matter, fuel; (*fig.*) seeds of discontent. **–ung,** *f.* kindling; priming, detonation; ignition. **–ungsstörung,** *f.* ignition trouble (*Motor.*).

Zund–el, *m.*, **–er,** *m.* (-s, –) tinder, touchwood, punk; (*coll.*) blows, punishment; heavy punishment (*by gunfire*); dross, scale (*Metall.*). **–erbüchse,** *f.* tinder-box.

zunehmen, 1. *ir.v.a.* take in addition, take more; increase (*the number of stitches in knitting*). 2. *v.n.* (*aux.* h.) increase, augment, grow (larger *or* heavier); rise, swell; improve, advance, thrive, prosper; grow worse (*of an evil*); get stouter, put on weight, flesh *or* fat, get longer (*of the days*); *an Kräften –*, grow stronger; *an Jahren –*, advance in years; *an Zahl –*, increase in number; get more; **–d,** 1. *adj.* increasing, growing; *nach und nach –d*, progressing, progressive; *–de Geschwindigkeit*, acceleration; *bei –den Jahren*, with advancing years; *–der Mond*, waxing moon. 2. *adv.* increasingly, progressively, more and more; *der Mond ist im –*, the moon is waxing.

zuneig–en, *v.a.* & *n.* (*with Dat.*) lean towards; incline to; *sich dem Ende –en*, draw to a close. **–ung,** *f.* (*with* zu) liking (for), affection (for), attachment (to), partiality (for), inclination (for *or* towards); sympathy (with); *–ung zu einem fassen*, take a liking to a p.

Zunft, *f.* (⸗e) guild, corporation, company, craft; (*iron.*) fraternity, clique, gang, band, tribe; *die – der Gelehrten*, the learned fraternity; *– der Handwerker*, craft guild. **–brief,** *m.* charter of a guild *or* city company. **–geist,** *m.* party-spirit; sectarianism. **–gemäß,** *adj.* according to the statutes *or* practice of the guild. **–haus,** *n.* guildhall. **–mäßig,** *adj.*, *see* **–gemäß.** **–meister,** *m.* master of a guild. **–wesen,** *n.* system of guilds, guild matters *or* affairs.

zünft–ig, *adj.* belonging to a guild; incorporated, skilled; competent; (*coll.*) proper, thorough; *–ig werden*, receive the freedom of a company.

Zunge, *f.* (-n) tongue; (*Poet.*) language; tongue (*of shoe*); languet (*Org.*); reed (*of wind instruments*); switch-tongue (*Railw.*); catch (*of a buckle, etc.*); slide (*of slide rule*), blade (*of T-square*), pointer, finger (*of scales*); sole (*Icht.*); *mit der – anstoßen*, lisp; *belegte –*, coated *or* dirty tongue; *eine feine – haben*, be a gourmand; *einem die – herausstrecken*, put one's tongue out at s.o.; *das Herz auf der – tragen*, wear one's heart on one's sleeve; *die – klebt mir am Gaumen*, my tongue cleaves to the roof of my mouth; *der – freien Lauf lassen*, let one's tongue run away with one; *einem das Wort von der – nehmen*, take the words out of a p.'s mouth; *es schwebt mir auf der –*, I have it on the tip of my tongue; *eine schwere – haben*, have an impediment in one's speech, be slow *or* awkward of speech; *seine – im Zaum halten*, keep a rein *or* check on his tongue. **–nband,** *n.* frenulum of the tongue. **–nbein,** *n.* hyoid bone (*Anat.*). **–nbelag,** *m.* fur on the tongue. **–nblüte,** *f.* ligulate flower. **–nblütig,** *adj.* ligulate (*Bot.*). **–ndrescher,** *m.* babbler, chatterbox, wind-bag. **–ndrescherei,** *f.* clap-trap, jabber, prattle, gab. **–ndrüse,** *f.* lingual gland. **–nfaul,** *adj.* tongue-tied. **–nfehler,** *m.* slip of the tongue, lapsus linguae. **–nfertig,** *adj.* glib, fluent, voluble, flippant. **–nfertigkeit,** *f.* volubility, verbosity, garrulity, glibness; *–nfertigkeit besitzen*, have a ready tongue, have the gift of the gab. **–nförmig,** *adj.* tongue-shaped. **–nhaut,** *f.* epithelium of the tongue. **–nhieb,** *m.* bitter *or* harsh remark, thrust, cut. **–nkrebs,** *m.* cancer of the tongue, glossanthrax. **–nlaut,** *m.* lingual sound; (*pl.*) linguals. **–npfeife,** *f.* reed-pipe (*Org.*). **–nregister,** *n.* flute-stop (*Org.*). **–nrücken,** *m.* dorsal surface *or* (*coll.*) back of the tongue. **–nschiene,** *f.* switch-point (*Railw.*). **–nschlag,** *m.* thick speech (*when drunk*). **–nspitze,** *f.* tip of the tongue. **–n(spitzen)-R,** *n.* lingual r, trilled r. **–nvorfall,** *m.* glossocele (*Med.*). **–nwurzel,** *f.* root *or* base of the tongue.

züng–eln, *v.n.* (*aux.* h.) shoot out, dart, leap up, *or* lick (*as flames*); *Schlangen –eln*, snakes hiss. **–ig,** *adj. suffix* -tongued. **–lein,** *n.*; *das –lein an der Wa(a)ge sein*, tip the scale.

zunicht (*Austr. dial.*), **–e,** *adv.* ruined, destroyed; *–e machen*, ruin, destroy, frustrate; *–e werden*, come to nothing.

zunicken, *v.a.* & *n.* (*aux.* h.) (*einem*) nod (to a p.) (*a greeting, etc.*).

zunutze, *adv.*; *sich eine S. – machen*, make use of a th., put a th. to use, turn a th. to account, profit by a th.

zuoberst, *adv.* at the very top, uppermost.

zuordn–en, *v.a.* adjoin, coordinate, associate with, attach *or* appoint to; *zugeordnet*, allied, co-ordinate (*Math.*). **–ung,** *f.* co-ordination, association, relation.

zupacken, *v.n.* grasp at, set to (work); *etwas –des*, s.th. arresting.

zupaß, –(ss)e, *adv.* (*with Dat.*). *– kommen*, come at the right time *or* moment, come in the nick of time; suit admirably.

zupf–en, *v.a.* pull, tug, pluck; pick, unravel; *Leinwand zu Charpie –en*, prepare lint; (*coll.*) *–en Sie sich doch an Ihrer eigenen Nase*, sweep before your own door, consider your own faults. **–geige,** *f.* guitar. **–leinwand,** *f.* lint.

zupfropfen, *v.a.* cork, stopper *or* bung up.

zur = zu der.

zuraten, 1. *ir.v.a.* & *n.* (*with Dat.*) advise, persuade, council, recommend; *ich will dir weder zu- noch abraten*, I don't wish to advise (*or* persuade) you one way or the other. 2. *n.*; *auf sein –*, on his advice, at his suggestion.

zuraunen, *v.a.*, *see* **zuflüstern.**

Zurdispositionstellung, *f.* relegation on half-pay.

zurechn–en, *v.a.* (*einem etwas*) add in *or* to; put to (*a p.'s account*); include *or* class with, ascribe, attribute to, impute. **–ung,** *f.* addition, attribution; *mit –ung aller Kosten*, including all charges. **–ungsfähig,** *adj.* accountable, responsible (*for one's actions*), of sound mind. **–ungsfähigkeit,** *f.* soundness of mind, sound judgement, responsibility.

zurecht, *adv.* & *sep. prefix*, right, in (good) order, to rights, rightly, with reason; in the right place; in (good) time, as it ought to be. **–finden,** *ir.v.r.* find one's way (about). **–kommen,** *ir.v.n.* arrive in good time; (*mit etwas*) get on well (with a th.), succeed in doing (s.th.), manage (s.th.); *ich kann mit ihm nicht –kommen*, I cannot get on with him. **–legen,** *v.n.* arrange, get *or* put ready, lay in order, put out; *sich* (*Dat.*) *eine S. –legen*, account for *or* explain a th. to s.o., (*coll.*) figure s.th. out *or* out s.th. **–machen,** 1. *v.a.* get ready, prepare, arrange, organize; *den Salat –machen*, dress the salad. 2. *v.r.* dress, get (o.s.) ready, make (o.s.) up, (*coll.*) put on one's face (*of ladies*); *er hat sich eine Ausrede –gemacht*, he has an excuse *or* story ready. **–rücken,** *v.a.* put right, straight *or* in order; put in the right place; *einem den Kopf –rücken*, bring a p. to his senses. **–setzen,** *v.a.*; *einem den Kopf*

–*setzen*, bring s.o. to reason. **–stellen,** *v.a., see* **–rücken. –weisen,** *ir.v.a.* show the way, direct; set right *or* to rights, reprimand, rebuke. **–weisung** *f.* correction; reprimand, reproof. **–zimmern,** put *or* knock into shape.

zureden, 1. *v.n.* (*aux.* h.) (*einem*) advise, urge, persuade, encourage *or* exhort a p. (*to do s.th.*); *er läßt sich* (*Dat.*) *nicht* –, he is not to be persuaded, he will not listen to anyone. 2. *n.* persuasion; encouragement, exhortation; entreaties; *auf vieles* –, at the urgent request.

zureichen, 1. *v.n.* (*aux.* h.) suffice, reach; *es reicht nicht zu*, it is not enough, it won't do; –*d*, sufficient (just) enough; –*der Grund*, sufficient *or* conclusive reason. 2. *v.a.* (*einem etwas*) pass or hand to, hold out to.

zureite–n, 1. *ir.v.a.* break in (*a horse*); *nicht zugeritten*, unbroken. 2. *v.n.* (*aux.* s.) ride on, press on; *einem Orte –n*, ride (up) to a place. **–r,** *m.* horse-breaker.

zuricht–en, *v.a.* prepare, make *or* get ready, finish, do up; dress (*leather, cloth, etc.*); cook, leaven (*dough*), convert, shape, trim, square (*timber, stone*). **zugerichtet,** *p.p. & adj.* in good register (*Typ.*); *übel –en*, use badly, ill-treat, maltreat, handle roughly; *übel* or *arg zugerichtet worden*, badly knocked about. **–(e)bogen,** *m.* register-sheet (*Typ.*). **–(e)hammer,** *m.* paviour's dressing-hammer. **–er,** *m.* feeder (*Typ.*); dresser, finisher; (leather-)currier. **–ung,** *f.* preparation, conversion, dressing; finish (*of fabrics*).

zürnen, *v.n.* (*aux.* h.); *auf eine S.* or *wegen einer S.* –, be annoyed *or* angry about s.th.; (*mit*) *einem* or *auf einen* –, be angry with a p.

zurren, *v.a.* seize, lash (*Naut.*).

Zurruhesetzung, *f.* (-en) pensioning, retirement.

Zurschaustellung, *f.* exhibition, display, parading.

zurück, 1. *int.* stand back! back there! 2. *adv. & sep. prefix* back, backward(s), behind(hand), in the rear, in arrears, late. *See also* **rück–.**

zurückarten, *v.n.* revert to type.

zurückbeben, *v.n.* (*aux.* s.) start back; recoil (*vor*, from).

zurückbegeben, *v.r.* return (*an einen Ort*, to a place).

zurückbehalt–en, *ir.v.a.* keep back, detain; reserve, retain. **–ung,** *f.* retention; detention. **–ungsrecht,** *n.* right of reservation *or* retention.

zurückbekommen, *ir.v.a.* get back; recover.

Zurückbeugemuskel, *m. & f.* supinator (*Anat.*).

zurückbezahlen, *v.a.* pay back, repay, refund.

zurückbeziehen, *ir.v.r.* refer back; be reflexive (*Gram.*). *See* **rückbezüglich.**

zurückbleiben, *ir.v.n.* (*aux.* s.) remain, stay *or* lag behind; fall behind *or* back, be left behind; survive, be left over; lose, be slow (*of clocks*); be backward, retarded *or* late, stay *or* be kept down (*at school*); remain *or* be left as a residue; *hinter einer S.* –, fall short of *or* not come up to s.th.; *auf der Rennbahn* –, be out-distanced in the race; *meine Uhr bleibt zurück*, my watch is slow; *geistig zurückgeblieben*, mentally retarded. **–d,** *adj.* residual, surviving. *See* **Rückbleibsel.**

zurückblicken, *v.n.* (*aux.* h.) look back; *auf* or *in die Vergangenheit* –, recall *or* review the past. **–d,** *pr.p. & adj.* retrospective. *See* **Rückblick.**

zurückbringen, *ir.v.a.* bring back, recall; restore, put back; *von Irrtümern* –, convince of error, undeceive; *zum Gehorsam* –, reduce to obedience; *einen ins Leben* –, bring a p. back to life; *diese Verluste haben ihn sehr zurückgebracht*, these losses have put him back a great deal.

zurückdatieren, *v.a.* antedate.

zurückdenken, 1. *ir.v.n.* (*aux.* h.) (*with* an) reflect (on), think back (on), recall to memory; *an seine Jugend* –, recall one's youth. 2. *v.r.* (*with* in) carry one's thoughts back (to).

zurückdrängen, *v.a.* press, push, roll, force *or* drive back; repel, repress.

zurückerhalten, *ir.v.a., see* **zurückbekommen.**

zurückerinner–n, *v.r.* (*with* an) remember, recollect; *so weit ich mich –n kann*, as far as I can recall *or* remember. *See* **Rückerinnerung.**

zurückerobern, *v.a.* reconquer.

zurückfahr–en, 1. *ir.v.n.* (*aux.* s.) drive, come *or* travel back; return; recoil, fly back, rebound; (*fig.*) start back (in surprise). 2. *v.a.* drive *etc.* (*a vehicle*) back. *See* **Rückfahrt.**

zurückfallen, *ir.v.n.* (*aux.* s.) fall back, revert, relapse; be reflected; *die Schande davon ist auf ihn zurückgefallen*, the disgrace redounds upon him; *an einen* –, revert to a p., fall to a p. by reversion. *See* **Rückfall, rückfällig.**

zurückfinden, *ir.v.r. & n.* (*aux.* h. & s.) find the way back.

zurückfließen, *ir.v.n.* (*aux.* s.) flow back, recede, *die Wohltat fließt auf den Wohltäter zurück*, a good deed comes home to the benefactor.

zurückfordern, *v.a.* demand back, claim back, reclaim. *See* **Rückforderung.**

zurückführ–en, *v.a.* (*with* zu) lead back, reconduct; (*with* auf) trace back (to), reduce (to), attribute (to). **–bar,** *adj.* traceable, reducible. **–ung,** *f.* attribution; reduction (*Arith.*); –*ung auf das Unmögliche*, reductio ad absurdum (*Log.*); –*ung des Heeres auf den Friedensstand*, reduction of the army to a peace footing. *See* **Rückführung.**

Zurückgabe, *f.* returning, return, restoration; surrender.

zurückgeben, *ir.v.a.* give back, return, restore, deliver up, surrender.

zurückgebogen, *adj.* reflexed.

zurückgehen, *ir.v.n.* (*aux.* s.) go back, return, revert; recede, subside, go down, fall; retire, fall back, retreat (*Mil.*); get smaller, decline, deteriorate, retrograde; be broken off, be cancelled, not take place, come to nothing; (*with* auf) be traced back (to), originate (in *a th.*; with *or* from *a p.*), have its origin *or* source (in); *Waren – lassen*, return goods; *auf den Ursprung* –, trace to its source; *seine Geschäfte gehen zurück*, his business is going down; *die Verlobung ist zurückgegangen*, the engagement has been broken off. *See* **Rückgang, rückgängig.**

zurückgestellt, *adj.* exempted, deferred.

zurückgewinnen, *v.a.* reclaim, recover.

zurückgezogen, *adj.* retired, secluded; – *leben*, lead a retired life. **–heit,** *f.* privacy, seclusion, retirement, solitude.

zurückgreifen, *ir.v.n.* (*aux.* h.) reach *or* extend back, refer to; *weiter* –, begin farther back.

zurückhalt–en, 1. *ir.v.a.* hold *or* keep back, retain; detain, delay, stop, retard, curb, prevent, hold in, repress, check; keep in (*detention*); hold (*one's breath*); suppress (*cries, etc.*); restrain (*tears, etc.*); reserve, suspend (*one's opinion, etc.*); *einen –en, etwas zu tun*, keep a p. from doing s.th.; *seine Gefühle –en*, keep to o.s., be reserved, repress one's feelings. 2. *v.r.* restrain o.s., hold back, keep a rein on o.s. 3. *v.n.* (*aux.* h.); (*mit einer S.*), keep back, conceal, hide; reserve (*judgement*), refrain from; *die Käufer halten sehr zurück*, customers are holding back. **–end,** *pr.p. & adj.* reserved, cautious, discreet, uncommunicative, (*coll.*) cool, distant. **–ung,** *f.* reserve, caution, discretion, modesty, propriety; retention (*Med.*); retardation (*Mus.*). *See* **Rückhalt, rückhaltlos.**

zurückkehren, *v.n.* (*aux.* s.) return, go *or* come back, revert. *See* **Rückkehr.**

zurückkommen, *ir.v.n.* (*aux.* s.) come back, return; become reduced in circumstances; get behind hand (*with work*), (*fig.*) change (*one's mind or opinion*); (*auf eine S.*) revert to; *ich komme auf diesen Punkt wieder zurück*, I shall return *or* revert to (*or* deal with) this subject (again). *See* **Rückkunft.**

Zurückkunft, *f.* *See* **Rückkunft.**

zurücklassen, *ir.v.a.* leave behind; allow to return.

zurücklaufen, *ir.v.n.* (*aux.* s.) run back; ebb, flow back; recoil, recur, retrogade. *See* **Rücklauf, Rückläufer, rückläufig.**

zurücklegen, 1. *v.a.* place behind; put back; shelve; (*also with* sich (*Dat.*)) lay aside, hold in reserve, lay *or* put by, save (*money*); travel, traverse, complete, go over, pass; *einen Weg* or *eine Strecke* –, walk *or* cover a distance; *nach zurückgelegtem achtzehnten Lebensjahre*, after having completed one's eighteenth *or* attained one's nineteenth year. 2. *v.r.* lie back, recline. *See* **Rücklage.**

zurückleiten, *v.a.* lead back; (*with* zu) trace back (to).
zurücklenken, *v.a.* turn *or* guide back; *seine Schritte* –, retrace one's steps.
zurückliegen, *v.n.* belong to the past.
zurückmelden, 1. *v.a.* send a reply. 2. *v.r.* report back (*Mil.*).
Zurücknahme, *f.* reacceptance, *see* **Rücknahme;** resumption; withdrawal, recantation, revocation; *ich hoffe, daß Sie die – nicht beanstanden,* I hope you won't object to take it back.
zurücknehmen, *ir.v.a.* take back, withdraw, retract, revoke, cancel; *sein Wort* –, go back on one's word *or* promise, withdraw what one has said.
zurückprallen, *v.n.* (*aux.* s.) rebound, recoil; be reflected, reverberate; start back (*vor,* from). *See* **Rückprall.**
zurückreichen, 1. *v.a.* hand *or* give back. 2. *v.n.* reach *or* go back (*bis,* to).
zurückruf–en, *ir.v.a.* call back; (*einem* or *sich* (*Dat.*) *etwas*) recall, call to mind. **–ung,** *f.* recall.
zurückschallen, *v.n.* (*aux.* s.) resound, re-echo.
zurückschau–dern, *v.n.,* **–ern,** *v.n.* (*aux.* s.) (*with* vor) recoil, shrink back in horror (from).
zurückscheuchen, *v.a.* scare, frighten away.
zurückschicken, *v.a.* send back, return (*by post, etc.*).
zurückschieben, *ir.v.a.* push back, repulse; reduce (*a dislocation*), pass over (*in appointing to an office*).
zurückschlagen, 1. *ir.v.a.* strike, beat *or* drive back; repel, repulse, throw off; *den Mantel* –, throw open one's coat; *zurückgeschlagener Wagen,* open carriage; *einen Ball* –, return a ball (*Tenn.*). 2. *v.n.* (*aux.* s.) fall backwards; relapse violently; *die Preise sind zurückgeschlagen,* prices have fallen (still lower); *auf die Lunge* –, attack the lungs. 3. *n.* backfiring (*of a gas jet*). *See* **Rückschlag.**
zurückschließen, *ir.v.n.* (*aux.* h.) reason a posteriori. *See* **Rückschluß.**
zurückschneiden, *ir.v.a.* lop, prune.
zurückschnellen, 1. *v.a.* fling back. 2. *v.n.* (*aux.* s.) fly back, rebound, recoil.
zurückschrecken, 1. *v.a.* (*reg.*) frighten away; discourage, deter from. 2. *v.n.* (*irreg.*) (*aux.* s.); (*vor einer S.*) shrink, start back (from).
zurücksehen, *ir.v.n.* (*aux.* h.) look back, look behind; reflect on, review (*the past, etc.*). *See* **Rücksicht.**
zurücksein, *ir.v.n.* be back, have returned *or* come back; be behind(hand), be too slow, be backward, be behind the times, be in arrears; *in der Schule* –, be backward at school.
zurücksetz–en, put back, replace; (*fig.*) push into the background; neglect, slight; degrade, reduce, lower (*price, etc.*), set aside (*s.th. for a p.*); reject (*as useless, unsaleable, etc.*); *das Datum eines Briefes –en,* antedate a letter; *zurückgesetzte Waren,* rejects; *sich zurückgesetzt fühlen,* feel o.s. slighted *or* snubbed. **–ung,** *f.* slight, snub, disregard, neglect.
zurücksinken, *ir.v.n.* (*aux.* s.) sink *or* fall back; *in Laster* –, relapse into evil ways.
zurückspiegeln, *v.a.* reflect. *See* **Rückspiegel.**
zurückspringen, 1. *ir.v.n.* (*aux.* s.) leap, spring *or* jump back; run back, rebound, recoil, re-enter (*of an angle*); be reflected; recede (*Arch.*). 2. *n.* resilience. **–d,** *pr.p.* & *adj.* rebounding; resilient, re-entrant; receding.
zurückstecken, *v.a.* put *or* place farther back; *einen Pflock* –, come down a peg.
zurückstehen, *ir.v.n.* (*aux.* s.) not come up to, be inferior to; (*coll.*) – *müssen,* be pushed into the background, be passed over, have to stand down *or* wait. *See* **Rückstand, rückständig.**
zurückstell–en, *v.a.* put back, replace; return; set back, put aside (*goods to be called for later*); put back (*a watch*); adjourn, postpone, hold over, stop, abandon; *einen Militärpflichtigen –en,* defer a conscript's military service. **–ung,** *f.* replacement, postponement; deferment (*Mil.*). *See* **Rückstelltaste.**
zurückstoß–en, *ir.v.a.* push *or* thrust back; repel, repulse. **–end,** *pr.p.* & *adj.* repulsive, repellent, revolting. **–ung,** *f.* repulsion (*Phys. etc.*); (*fig.*) repulse. **–ungskraft,** *f.* repulsive force. *See* **Rückstoß.**
zurückstrahl–en, 1. *v.n.* (*aux.* s.) be reflected, shine back. 2. *v.a.* reflect. **–ung,** *f.* reflexion, reverberation. *See* **Rückstrahler.**
zurückstreifen, *v.a.* turn up *or* back (*sleeves, etc.*).
zurückstürzen, *v.n.* (*aux.* s.) rush back.
zurücktaumeln, *v.n.* (*aux.* s.) reel back.
zurücktreiben, *ir.v.a.* drive back, drive home; check.
zurücktreten, *ir.v.n.* (*aux.* s.) step back; (*with* von) resign, withdraw (from); return (to), recede; subside (*of a river*); diminish, be insignificant *or* unimportant (*gegenüber,* in comparison with); be checked; *ins Privatleben* –, return to private life; *von einer Bewerbung* –, withdraw from a candidature; *von seinem Amte* –, resign (from) one's post *or* office. **–d,** *pr.p.* & *adj.* receding, retreating (*forehead*). *See* **Rücktritt.**
zurücktun, *ir.v.a.* put back, replace; *einen Schritt* –, (take a) step back.
zurückübersetzen, *v.a.* retranslate, translate back (*into the original*).
zurückverlegen, *v.a.* shorten (*range*) (*Artil.*).
zurückversetz–en, *v.a.* put back; restore, relegate to a lower class, put down; degrade (*Mil.*); *sich in eine Zeit –en,* go back (in imagination) to a former time.
zurückverweisen, *v.a.* refer back (*an,* to).
zurückweichen, 1. *ir.v.n.* (*aux.* s.) (*with* vor) give way, fall back, give ground, recede (before); retreat, withdraw, shrink back (from); yield, give in. 2. *n.* recoil (*of a gun*); withdrawal, recession, retreat.
zurückweis–en, *ir.v.a.* refer back to, send (*a p.*) back *or* away; refuse, decline, reject; repulse, repel, (*an attack*); retort. **–ung,** *f.* repulse; rejection, refusal.
zurückwerfen, *ir.v.a.* throw back; reflect (*rays*); repel, repulse (*an enemy*).
zurückwirken, *v.n.* (*aux.* h.) react (*auf,* upon). *See* **Rückwirkung.**
zurückzahl–en, *v.a.* pay back; repay, refund, reimburse. **–ung,** *f.* repayment, refund, reimbursement. *See also* **Rückzahlung.**
zurückzieh–en, 1. *ir.v.a.* draw back, withdraw; retract, recant; take back (*move at chess, etc.*); redeem (*a pledge*). 2. *v.r.* retire, retreat, withdraw; (*with* von) give up, quit, leave, take no more part in, be no longer interested in; *sich auf* (or *in*) *sich selbst –en,* retire into o.s., become self-absorbed; *sich auf . . . –en,* fall back upon . . . (*prepared positions, etc.*). 3. *v.n.* (*aux.* s.) return, retire, retreat, move *or* march back. **–end,** *adj.* retractive. **–er,** *m.* screw-back (*Bill.*); *see* **Rückzieher. –ung,** *f.* withdrawal (*money, promise, etc.*). *See* **Rückzug.**
Zuruf, *m.* (-(e)s, –e) shout, call, cheer, acclamation; *durch – gewählt,* elected by acclamation. **–en,** *ir.v.a.* & *n.* (*einem etwas*) call *or* shout to; *jemandem Beifall –en,* cheer *or* applaud a person.
zurüst–en, *v.a.* fit out, equip; prepare, make *or* get ready. **–ung,** *f.* fitting out, equipment; preparation; *–ungen treffen,* make preparations.
Zusage, *f.* (-n) assent, acceptance, promise, pledge. **–n,** 1. *v.a.* (*einem etwas*) promise; *einem etwas auf den Kopf –n,* tell a p. s.th. plainly *or* to his face. 2. *v.n.* (*aux.* h.) (*with* Dat.) accept (*an invitation*); meet a p.'s wishes, suit a p., be to s.o.'s taste; agree with a p. (*of food*); *das sagt mir nicht zu,* that is not my taste; *ich habe zugesagt.* I have promised; I have accepted (*an invitation*). **–nd,** *pr.p.* & *adj.* pleasant, suitable, agreeable; affirmative.
zusammen, *adv.* & *sep. prefix* together; jointly, (all) in all, all together, all told, in a body (*as adv. written separately when meaning* '*jointly*', '*at the same time*'; *as prefix when meaning* '*joined*', '*united*').
Zusammenarbeit, *f.* co-operation, collaboration. **–en,** *v.n.* (*aux.* h.) work together, collaborate, co-operate.
zusammenbacken, *v.n.* cake, stick together, agglomerate.
zusammenball–en, *v.a.* roll into a ball, concentrate, mass; agglomerate, conglomerate, condense, gather (*of clouds*); *die Fäuste –en,* clench one's fists. **–ung,** *f.* agglomeration; conglomerate.
Zusammenbau, *m.* montage, assembly.
zusammenbeißen, *v.a.* clench, set (*one's teeth*).

zusammenbetteln, *v.a.* get together *or* collect by begging.
zusammenbinden, *ir.v.a.* tie together; tie up, link together.
zusammenbrechen, *ir.v.n.* (*aux.* s.) break, crumble, collapse, break down, go to pieces, smash; *seine Knie brechen unter ihm zusammen*, his knees give way under him.
zusammenbringen, *ir.v.a.* bring together, join, unite; collect, gather together, raise (*money*), amass (*a fortune*), rally (*troops*); *seine Gedanken* –, collect one's thoughts; *keine drei Sätze* –, not have a sensible word to say; *zusammengebrachtes Vermögen*, joint property; *zusammengebrachte Kinder*, half-brothers and sisters.
Zusammenbruch, *m.* collapse, débâcle, failure, breakdown.
zusammendräng–en, *v.a.* & *v.r.* crowd *or* press together; compress, concentrate, condense. **–ung,** *f.* condensation, concentration.
zusammendrück–en, *v.a.* compress. **–bar,** *adj.* compressible. **–barkeit,** *f.* compressibility.
zusammenfahren, *ir.v.n.* (*aux.* s.) come into collision, collide; start back (*vor*, in), wince (*vor*, with).
zusammenfallen, *v.n.* fall down, collapse, shrink, crumble away; lose strength; *in sich* –, (*fig.*) fall to the ground; converge (*Opt.*); coincide (*mit*, with); concur; synchronize. **–d,** *adj.* coincident.
zusammenfalten, *v.a.* fold (up); furl (*sails*).
zusammenfass–en, *v.a.* embrace, include, combine, comprise, comprehend, unite, collect (*one's thoughts, etc.*); summarize, condense, sum up, recapitulate; *um es kurz zusammenzufassen*, to sum up. **–end,** *adj.* comprehensive, summary. **–ung,** *f.* summary, compilation, summing up, recapitulation, synopsis.
zusammenfinden, *ir.v.r.* come together, meet.
zusammenfließen, 1. *ir.v.n.* flow together, meet (*of rivers*); fuse.
Zusammenfluß, *m.* confluence, junction (*of two rivers*); fusion.
zusammenfrier–en, *ir.v.n.* (*aux.* s.) freeze together, congeal. **–ung,** *f.* congelation.
zusammenfügen, *v.a.* join (together), unite, combine; fit into one another, articulate; pair, match.
zusammenführen, *v.a.* bring together.
zusammengedrängt, *adj.* crowded.
zusammengehen, *ir.v.n.* (*aux.* s.) go together, suit one another, match; shrink, get smaller, diminish; be attended with.
zusammengehör–en, *v.n.* (*aux.* h.) belong together, be correlated, match, be fellows, form a pair. **–ig,** *adj.* belonging together, correlated, congruous, homogeneous, homologous. **–igkeit,** *f.* correlation, congruity, intimate connexion, unity; solidarity (*of persons*).
zusammengeraten, *ir.v.n.* (*aux.* s.) fall out, quarrel.
zusammengerollt, *adj.* convulate.
zusammengesetzt, *p.p.* & *adj.* composed, composite, compounded, compound, complex, complicated.
zusammengewürfelt, *adj.* motley.
Zusammenhalt, *m.* holding together; consistence, consistency, coherence, cohesion, cohesiveness, unity. **–en,** 1. *ir.v.a.* hold together; compare; maintain, keep going, support. 2. *v.n.* (*aux.* h.) hold *or* stick together; be firm friends; cohere. **–end,** *adj.* cohesive.
Zusammenhang, *m.* connexion, association; relationship, relation, correlation; cohesion, continuity, coherence; context; *Mangel an* –, incoherence; *aus dem – kommen*, lose the thread (of one's discourse); *aus dem – gerissene Wörter*, words separated from their context; *– der Begriffe*, association of ideas; *der ganze – der Sache*, the whole story, the ins and outs of the matter; *dieser Gedanke steht nicht im – mit . . .*, this idea has no connexion with . . .; *ohne* –, incoherent disconnected. **–en,** *ir.v.n.* (*aux.* h.), *see* **zusammenhängen. –slos,** *adj.* disconnected, incoherent, inconsistent, disjointed, loose, rambling. **–slosigkeit,** *f.* incoherence, disconnectedness, inconsistency.
zusammenhängen, *v.n.* (*aux.* h.) adhere, cohere, be connected, hang together. **–d,** *pr.p.* & *adj.* connected, continuous, coherent, cohesive.
zusammenhauen, *ir.v.a.* cut to pieces; thrash soundly; (*coll.*) knock together.
zusammenhäuf–en, *v.a.* heap *or* pile up, accumulate. **–ung,** *f.* heaping up, accumulation; aggregation; heap, pile.
zusammenheilen, *v.n.* (*aux.* s.) heal up.
zusammenkauern, *v.r.* cower; roll o.s. up.
zusammenkitten, *v.a.* cement, lute.
Zusammenklang, *m.* accord, consonance, harmony.
zusammenklapp–en, 1. *v.a.* fold together; fold up; close (*a knife, fan, etc.*). 2. *v.n.* (*aux.* h.) (*coll.*) collapse, go to pieces, break down, have a (nervous) breakdown. **–bar,** *adj.* folding, collapsible.
zusammenkleben, *v.a.* & *n.* stick together.
zusammenkleistern, *v.a.* glue, paste together.
zusammenklingen, *v.n.* harmonize; *mit den Gläsern* –, clink one's glasses.
zusammenkommen, *ir.v.n.* (*aux.* h.) come together; assemble; meet; *scharf mit einem* –, have a clash with a p., quarrel.
Zusammenkunft, *f.* meeting, reunion, conference, assembly, convention; interview, rendezvous; conjunction (*Astr.*).
Zusammenlagerung, *f.* assemblage.
zusammenlassen, *ir.v.a.* leave together, let (come) together.
Zusammenlauf, *m.*, *see* **Zusammenfluß. –en,** *ir.v.n.* (*aux.* h.) run together; congregate, collect, meet; converge, tend to meet in a point; blend, run (into one another) (*Paint.*); shrink; curdle, coagulate; *auf* or *in einen Punkt –en*, meet in a point, converge; *das Wasser lief ihm im Munde zusammen*, his mouth watered.
zusammenleben, 1. *v.n.* live together; cohabit (*sexually*); *mit einem* –, live with a p. 2. *n.* living together, association; companionship; social life; cohabitation.
zusammenleg–en, *v.a.* place, lay *or* put together; pile up; fold up, close (*a penknife*); collect, club together, contribute; combine, consolidate, unite, merge; *auf einen Haufen –en*, put into a pile, make a heap of. **–bar,** *adj.* folding, collapsible. (*C.L.*) **–ung,** *f.* consolidation, merger, fusion.
zusammenleimen, *v.a.*, *see* **zusammenkleistern.**
zusammenlesen, *ir.v.a.* gather together, collect.
zusammennehmen, 1. *ir.v.a.* take together, gather; husband (*one's strength, etc.*), economize *or* be economical with (*money, etc.*); *seine Gedanken* –, collect one's thoughts; *alles zusammengenommen*, all in all, all things considered; *alle Umstände* –, take all the circumstances into consideration. 2. *v.r.* collect o.s., control o.s.; make an effort, summon all one's strength; pluck up courage; be on one's best behaviour, look out; take care; *nimm dich zusammen!* be a man! pull yourself together!
zusammenpacken, *v.a.* pack up.
zusammenpassen, 1. *v.n.* (*aux.* h.) be well matched, go well together; agree. 2. *v.a.* fit, adapt, adjust, match, assort.
zusammenpferchen, *v.a.* pack, crowd *or* squeeze together; pen up (*cattle*).
zusammenprasseln, *v.n.* (*coll.*) collide.
zusammenpressen, *v.a.* press together, compress.
zusammenraffen, 1. *v.a.* seize; sweep *or* snatch up; collect hurriedly, amass (*a fortune*). 2. *v.r.* pull o.s. together, make an effort.
zusammenrechnen, *v.a.* & *n.* (*aux.* h.) reckon up; add up, compute; *alles zusammengerechnet*, taking everything into account, all in all.
zusammenreimen, 1. *v.a.* understand, make out. 2. *v.n.* rhyme (with each other). 3. *v.r.* make sense (of), fit in; *reimen Sie das zusammen, wenn Sie können*, make sense of that if you can; *ich kann es mir nicht* –, I cannot make head or tail of it.
zusammenreißen, *v.r.* make a desperate effort.
zusammenrott–en, *v. r.* band together, form a gang; plot, conspire. **–ung,** *f.* unlawful assembly.
zusammenrücken, *v.a.* & *n.* (*aux.* s.) draw *or* move nearer, draw closer *or* together; *nach rechts* –, move to the right (*Mil.*).

zusammenrufen, *ir.v.a.* call together, convoke, summon.
zusammenrühren, *v.a.* stir *or* mix up.
zusammenschichten, *v.a.* pile, heap up; pile up in layers.
zusammenschießen, 1. *ir.v.a.* shoot down; *eine Summe* –, club together to raise a sum. 2. *v.n.* (*aux.* s.) crystallize.
zusammenschlagen, 1. *ir.v.n.* (*aux.* s.) strike against one another; close with a bang *or* crash; *die Wellen schlugen über ihm zusammen,* the waves closed over *or* engulfed him. 2. *v.a.* strike together; clap (*one's hands*); click (*one's heels*); smash (up) (*a hostile force*); combine, merge, unite; fold (up); gather (*Typ.*); *vor Verwunderung die Hände über dem Kopf* –, throw up one's hands in astonishment. 3. *v.r.* (*aux.* h.) unite, join forces, amalgamate; close (*ranks*) (*Mil.*).
Zusammenschluß, *m.* union, federation, amalgamation, alliance, merger.
zusammenschmelz–en, 1. *v.n.* (*aux.* s.) melt, dissolve, fuse; melt away. 2. *v.a.* melt down, fuse. **–ung,** *f.* fusion.
zusammenschmieden, *v.a.* weld together.
zusammenschmieren, *v.a.* (*coll.*) scribble, jot down hurriedly.
zusammenschnüren, *v.a.* lace *or* tie up, cord; strangle, choke; *das schnürt mir das Herz zusammen,* that wrings my heart.
zusammenschreiben, *ir.v.a.* compile; write in *or* as one word; earn by writing; *sich* (*Dat.*) *ein Vermögen* –, make a fortune by one's books *or* out of writing.
zusammenschrumpfen, *v.n.* (*aux.* s.) shrivel up, shrink, contract, wrinkle; run short.
zusammenschütteln, *v.a.* shake up well.
zusammenschütten, *v.a.* pour together, mix up together.
zusammenschweißen, *v.a.* weld (together) (*zu*, into).
Zusammensein, *n.* meeting, gathering.
zusammensetz–en, 1. *v.a.* put together, pile, stack; compose, make up, piece together; compound, combine, construct, assemble; *die Gewehre* –, pile arms; *zusammengesetztes Wort,* compound (word). 2. *v.r.* sit (down) together; be composed of; consist of. **–spiel,** *n.* jigsaw puzzle. **–ung,** *f.* composition, combination; construction, assembly, formation; union, compound, mixture, structure, synthesis.
zusammensinken, *ir.v.n.* (*aux.* s.) sink down, collapse.
zusammensparen, *v.a.* save up, accumulate, amass by saving.
Zusammenspiel, *n.* playing together, acting in unison; ensemble (*Mus. & Theat.*); teamwork (*Theat. & Sport*).
zusammenstecken, 1. *v.a.* stick *or* put together, fasten *or* pin together; *die Köpfe* –, put one's heads together. 2. *v.n.* (*aux.* h.); (*coll.*) conspire together, be hand in (*or* and) glove with one another.
zusammenstehen, *ir.v.n.* (*aux.* h.) stand together *or* side by side; stand shoulder to shoulder; side with one another, unite for a common cause, (*coll.*) stick together.
zusammenstell–en, *v.a.* place *or* put together; compare, collate; group, compile, make up (*a list*), summarize, assemble (*a train*). **–ung,** *f.* combination, compilation, list, synopsis, summary, grouping, inventory, classification; juxtaposition.
zusammenstimmen, *v.n.* (*aux.* h.) agree, accord, harmonize; suit, be congruous.
zusammenstoppel–n, *v.a.* patch up, piece together. **–ung,** *f.* patchwork, medley.
Zusammenstoß, *m.* shock, collision, impact; hostile encounter, engagement, conflict, clash. **–en,** 1. *ir.v.a.* bang *or* knock against one another; join; *die Gläser –en,* clink *or* touch glasses. 2. *v.n.* (*aux.* h. & s.) collide, smash, clash, conflict; meet, encounter; adjoin, abut; effect a junction (*Mil.*). **–end,** *pr.p. & adj.* contiguous, adjacent, adjoining.
zusammenströmen, *v.n.* (*aux.* s.) flow together, come *or* crowd together, assemble.
zusammenstücke(l)n, *v.a.,* *see* **zusammenstoppeln.**
zusammensuchen, *v.a.* gather together *or* up, collect.
zusammentragen, *ir.v.a.* bring together, gather, collect, compile.
zusammentreffen, 1. *ir.v.n.* (*aux.* s.) meet (each other), encounter; coincide, concur; *zu etwas* –, co-operate in, work together at; *mit etwas* –, agree *or* coincide with s.th.; *es trifft nicht mit unseren Erwartungen zusammen,* it does not meet *or* answer our expectation. 2. *n.* meeting, gathering, encounter; concurrence, coincidence, identity; engagement (*with the enemy*); inosculation (*of veins*).
zusammentreiben, *ir.v.a.* drive together; beat up (*game*); (*fig.*) bring together, get hold of, raise.
zusammentreten, 1. *ir.v.a.* tread down *or* underfoot. 2. *v.n.* (*aux.* s.) meet, join, unite, combine; appear together.
Zusammentritt, *m.* coalition; meeting (*of parliament, creditors, etc.*).
zusammentun, 1. *v.a.* put together, mix. 2. *v.r.* come together; associate, combine, join, unite.
zusammenwachsen, *v.n.* (*aux.* s.) grow together, coalesce.
zusammenwerfen, *ir.v.a.* throw together, throw into a heap; mix *or* jumble up, confuse, confound.
zusammenwirken, 1. *v.n.* (*aux.* h.) act *or* work together; co-operate, collaborate. 2. *n.* combined efforts, collaboration, co-operation. **–d,** *pr.p. & adj.* co-operative.
Zusammenwuchs, *m.* coalescence.
zusammenwürfeln, *v.a.* throw together, jumble up.
zusammenzählen, *v.a.* count *or* add up.
zusammenzieh–en, 1. *ir.v.a.* draw together, tighten, contract, concentrate; abridge, epitomize; gather, assemble; *Zahlen –en,* add up figures, reduce figures to a total; *die Augenbrauen –en,* knit one's brows; *die Lippen –en,* purse one's lips; *zusammengezogene (Wort)Formen,* contracted forms, contractions. 2. *v.r.* collect, gather; draw to a head contract, shrink; *es zieht ein Gewitter zusammen,* a storm is gathering *or* brewing; *–ende Mittel,* astringents. 3. *v.n.* (*aux.* s.) move into the same rooms; share rooms. **–bar,** *adj.* contractible. **–barkeit,** *f.* contractibility, contractility. **–ung,** *f.* contraction, constriction, shrinking; mustering, concentration (*of troops, etc.*); contracted word.
Zusatz, *m.* (-es, ¨e) addition, adjunct, admixture; appendix, postscript, supplement, corollary, codicil (*to a will*); alloy (*Chem.*). **–abkommen,** *n.* supplementary agreement. **–antrag,** *m.* amendment. **–artikel,** *m.* further clause, rider. **–batterie,** *f.* booster battery. **–behälter,** *m.* spare tank (*Motor.*). **–gerät,** *n.* auxiliary *or* ancillary apparatus. **–legierung,** *f.* hardener (*Metall.*). **–steuer,** *f.* supplementary tax.
zusätzlich, *adj.* additional, extra, supplementary.
zuschanden, *adv.*; *sich – arbeiten,* wear o.s. out by work; kill o.s. with work; – *gehen* go to rack and ruin; – *machen,* spoil, ruin, destroy, foil, thwart, frustrate, confound, overthrow; – *reiten,* override, founder (*a horse*); – *werden,* come to nothing, be ruined *or* confounded.
zuschanzen, *v.a.* (*coll.*) (*einem etwas*) procure, secure; (*sl.*) wangle.
zuschärfen, *v.a.* point, sharpen, taper off.
zuscharren, *v.a.* cover, fill up (*a hole*).
zuschau–en, *v.n.* (*aux.* h.) (*Dat.*) look on, watch. **–er,** *m.* spectator, onlooker, bystander, witness; (*pl.*) spectators, audience, the public. **–erplätze,** *m.pl.* seats, standing-room (*for spectators*). **–erraum,** *m.* auditorium, house (*Theat.*).
zuschaufeln, *v.a.* shovel in, fill up *or* in.
zuschicken, *v.a.* (*einem etwas*) send on, forward transmit, remit (*money*), consign (*goods*).
zuschieben, *ir.v.a.* shove *or* push towards, shut (*a drawer*); (*einem etwas*) put (the blame) on; make over to, pass *or* (*coll.*) shove (it) on to; *den Riegel* –, shoot the bolt, put the bolt on; *einem den Eid* –, put a p. on oath.
zuschießen, 1. *ir.v.n.* (*aux.* h.) shoot (away), fire; (*aux.* s.) (auf *with Acc.*) rush at. 2. *v.a.* (*einem etwas*) supply, add to, furnish with, contribute; subsidize; *einem einen Blick* –, give *or* throw a p. a rapid look, dart a glance at s.o.

Zuschlag, *m.* (-(e)s, ⸚e) extra *or* additional charge; addition, increase (*in price*), bonus, surtax; knocking down (*to a bidder*); flux (*Metall.*); *der – erfolgte an . . .*, it was knocked down to. **–en**, 1. *ir.v.a.* slam (*a door*); nail up *or* down; knock down to (*a bidder*); give as bonus; put on, add (*surcharge*); serve (*the ball*) (*Tennis*); add as a flux; *einem die Tür vor der Nase –en*, bang the door in a p.'s face. 2. *n.* (*aux.* h.) strike, hit hard; strike away, hit out, lay on; (*aux.* s.) bang, slam. **–(s)gebühr**, *f.* extra charge, excess fare, additional fee. **–(s)karte**, *f.* additional ticket, excess fare ticket. **–(s)pflichtig**, *adj.* liable to additional payment. **–(s)porto**, *n.* excess postage, surcharge, postage due.

Zuschläger, *m.* (-s, –) beater, (blacksmith's) striker.

zuschleifen, *ir.v.a.* sharpen, whet; polish.

zuschließen, *ir.v.a.* lock (up).

zuschmeißen, *ir.v.a.* (*vulg.*) throw to; slam, bang (to).

zuschmelzen, *ir.v.a.* close by fusion; seal hermetically.

zuschmieren, *v.a.* smear *or* daub on *or* over, daub *or* plaster up.

zuschnallen, *v.a.* buckle, fasten, strap up.

zuschnappen, 1. *v.a. & n.* (*aux.* s.) close with a snap, snap to *or* shut. 2. *v.n.* (*aux.* h.) snap at.

zuschneid–en, *ir.v.a.* cut up; cut out (*a dress, etc.*); *einem das Brot* (*kärglich*) *–en*, keep a p. on short allowance; *eine Rolle auf einen –en*, write a part for a p. (*Theat.*). **–ekunst**, *f.* art of cutting out. **–emaschine**, *f.* cutting-out machine. **–er**, *m.* tailor's cutter. **–erei**, *f.* cutting-out room.

Zuschnitt, *m.* (-(e)s, -e) cut (*of clothes*); style, arrangement, ways; *der häusliche –*, style of living, household arrangements; *der – seines Lebens*, his way of life; *es schon im – versehen*, go wrong *or* make a mistake at the very outset, (*coll.*) start on the wrong foot.

zuschnüren, *v.a.* lace (up); *einem die Kehle –*, strangle *or* choke a p.; *mir war die Kehle wie zugeschnürt*, I could not speak, a lump came into my throat.

zuschrauben, *reg. & ir.v.a.* screw down *or* up.

zuschreiben, 1. *ir.v.a.* add (a few words) (*to a letter, etc.*); assign, attribute, blame, impute to, (*coll.*) put down to; owe (it) to, thank; (*C.L.*) place to (*a p.'s*) credit; transfer to, confer on by a deed, charter, *etc.*; (*archaic*) dedicate, inscribe; *einem eine Summe –*, credit a p. with a sum; *das müssen Sie sich selbst –*, you have yourself to blame for this; *das schreibe ich seiner Unwissenheit zu*, I attribute that *or* (*coll.*) put that down to his ignorance. 2. *v.a.* send a written acceptance, write and accept.

zuschreien, *ir.v.a. & n.* (*aux.* h.) cry out; (*einem etwas*) shout *or* call out to.

zuschreiten, *ir.v.n.* (*aux.* s.); (auf *with Acc.*) step towards *or* up to; walk along, step out, walk on briskly.

Zuschrift, *f.* (-en) letter, communication; (*archaic*) address, dedication, inscription. **–lich**, *adv.* by letter.

zuschulden, *adv.*; *sich etwas – kommen lassen*, be guilty of a th., do s.th. wrong.

Zuschuß, *m.* (-(ss)es, ⸚(ss)e) additional supply, extra allowance, subsidy, contribution, rise (*in salary*). **–betrieb**, *m.* subsidized undertaking. **–bogen**, *m.* extra sheet (*Typ.*). **–steuer**, *f.* surtax. **–summe**, *f.* additional sum. **–tage**, *m.pl.* epact (*Astr.*). **–wirtschaft**, *f.* policy of (economic) subsidies.

zuschütten, *v.a.* fill up *or* in, pour on, add to.

zuschwören, *ir.v.a.* (*einem etwas*) swear to, give a solemn assurance (about *or* on).

zusehen, 1. *ir.v.n.* (*aux.* h.) (*with Dat.*) look on, watch, witness; wait and see, stand by, tolerate, overlook, stand for it; look out for, take care *or* heed, see to (it), look after *or* to; *einer S. ruhig –*, look on at a th. unmoved, tolerate, connive at *or* wink at a th.; *noch ein wenig –*, be patient, wait a little longer; *da kann ich nicht länger –*, I cannot put up with *or* stand this any longer; *sieh zu, daß du nicht fällst*, take care not to fall; *da muß er –*, that is his look out. 2. *n.* view; the rôle of spectator; *bei genauerem –*, on closer examination *or* inspection; *das – haben*, get nothing for one's trouble, (*coll.*) get no change. **–ds**, *adv.* visibly, obviously, noticeably.

zusenden, *ir.v.a.*, *see* **zuschicken.**

zusetz–en, 1. *v.a.* add to, replenish; put on *or* over (*the fire*); contribute; mix up with, admix, alloy with; stake higher; lose, sacrifice (*money, etc.*); block up, close, obstruct; *er hat sein Vermögen dabei zugesetzt*, he lost everything by it; *er hat dabei zugesetzt*, he was the loser by it. 2. *v.n.* (*aux.* h.) (*with Dat.*) press, importune, pester; pursue closely, attack vigorously; *einem mit Bitten –*, overwhelm s.o. with entreaties. **–ung**, *f.* addition; contribution.

zusicher–n, *v.a.* (*einem etwas*) assure of, promise. **–ung**, *f.* assurance, promise.

zusiegeln, *v.a.* seal up.

Zuspeise, *f.* (-n) (*dial.*) side dish, vegetables served with meat.

zusperren, *v.a.* block up, close, bar, lock.

zuspielen, *v.a.* (*einem etwas*) play *or* pass (*the ball*) to, serve (*Tenn.*); (*fig.*) play into a p.'s hands.

zuspitz–en, 1. *v.a.* point, sharpen, cut to a point, taper; toe off, graft (*a stocking in knitting*); *epigrammatisch –en*, give an epigrammatic turn to, turn into an epigram. 2. *v.r.* taper off; (*fig.*) come to a crisis, get critical. **–ung**, *f.* pointing, sharpening; tapering off; point (*of an epigram*); *die –ung der politischen Lage*, the increasing gravity of the political situation.

Zusprache, *f.* (-n) consolation, encouragement.

zusprechen, 1. *ir.v.a.* (*einem etwas*) impart by word of mouth; award, grant, adjudge; *einem Mut –*, cheer s.o. up, encourage a p.; *einem Trost –*, comfort *or* console a p.; *dem Amt ein Telegramm –*, hand in a telegram by phone, phone a telegram. 2. *v.n.* (*aux.* h.) (*Dat.*) address, accost; exhort, encourage, console, comfort; *der Flasche fleißig –*, partake freely of the bottle; *einer Speise wacker –*, do ample justice to a dish, eat heartily of a dish; *sprich zu!* go on speaking, speak away!

zuspringen, *ir.v.n.* (*aux.* s.) spring *or* run towards, jump at, snap *or* spring to (*of locks*); *auf einen –*, rush towards a p.

Zuspruch, *m.* ((-(e)s, ⸚e) exhortation; praise, encouragement, consolation; customers, custom, clientele; *– finden*, be in demand, be much sought after, (*coll.*) go down well.

Zustand, *m.* ((-e)s, ⸚e) condition, state, situation, position; lot, state of affairs *or* things; *in elendem –e*, in wretched condition *or* plight; *in gutem –e*, in good condition *or* order; in good repair (*of buildings*); *– des Gemüts*, frame of mind; *mobiler –*, on a war footing. **–e**, *adv.*; *–e bringen*, achieve, accomplish, bring about; *–e kommen*, occur, happen, come to pass, take place; *nicht –e kommen*, not come off *or* to pass, fail to materialize. **–ebringen**, *n.* accomplishment, realization, achievement. **–ekommen**, *n.* occurrence; *das –ekommen des Kongresses ist gesichert*, the congress is sure to meet. **–sänderung**, *f.* change of state. **–schaubild**, *n.* phase diagram, constitution diagram.

zuständ–ig, *adj.* belonging to, appertaining to, appropriate; duly qualified, authorized, responsible, competent; *von –iger Seite hören wir*, we are informed from a responsible quarter. *–ige Stelle* or *Behörde*, competent authority; *mir –ig*, (*dial.*) belonging to me, mine. **–igkeit**, *f.* competence. **–lich**, *adj.* neutral, objective.

zustatten, *adv.*; *einem – kommen*, come in *or* prove useful to a p.

zustechen, 1. *ir.v.a.* (*aux.* h.) stitch up. 2. *v.n.* (auf *with Acc.*) thrust at.

zustecken, *v.a.* (*einem etwas*) slip into a p.'s hand *or* pocket, give *or* hand a p. secretly; pin up, fix with pins.

zustehen, *ir.v.n.* (*aux.* h.) (*with Dat.*) belong to, pertain, behove, be the duty of, be due to, be incumbent upon; become, suit; *das steht dir nicht zu*, it is not for you, that is none of your business, you have no right to (do) this, it is not yours by right.

zustell–en, *v.a.* close, block up, barricade; (*einem etwas*) hand to, forward to, deliver to; *einem eine Klage –en*, serve a writ on a p. **–postamt**, *n.* district post-office. **–ung**, *f.* delivery, forwarding, sending on; writ. **–ungsgebühr**, *f.* charge for delivery. **–ungsurkunde**, *f.* writ.

zusteuern, 1. *v.a.* (*with Dat. or* zu) contribute,

make a contribution. 2. *v.n.* (*aux.* s.) (*with Dat. or with* auf *and Acc.*) steer *or* make for, set a course for; *immer* –, steer straight ahead.
zustimm-en, *v.n.* (*aux.* h.) (*with Dat.*) assent, consent *or* agree to, concur with. **-ung,** *f.* agreement, assent, consent, concurrence; *unter –ung von,* with the consent of.
zustopfen, *v.a.* stop *or* fill up, stuff, close, stop (*the ears*); darn (*a hole*).
zustöpseln, *v.a.* cork *or* stopper up.
zustoßen, 1. *ir.v.a.* push to, close, shut (*the door*). 2. *v.n.* (*aux.* h.) push *or* thrust forward *or* on; give a push, lunge; (*aux.* s.) (*with Dat.*) befall, happen to, meet with (*misfortune, evil, etc. only*); *falls mir etwas – sollte,* in case of anything happening to me.
zustreb-en, *v.n.* (*aux.* h.) (*with Dat.*) strive for *or* after, try to reach, tend towards, make for, hurry towards. **-ekraft,** *f.* centripetal force.
zustricken, *v.a.* cast off (*knitting*), toe off, graft (*a stocking*).
Zustrom, *m.* (-(e)s, ⸚e) influx; crowd, throng, multitude, run (*on the bank*).
zuströmen, *v.n.* (*aux.* s.) (*with Dat.*) pour, flood *or* stream in *or* towards, flow into, throng to(wards).
zustürzen, *v.n.* (*aux.* s.) (auf *with Acc.*) rush upon *or* towards.
zustutzen, *v.a.* fashion, adapt, put into shape, trim, cut, lop; *ein Stück für die Bühne* –, adapt a piece for the stage.
zutage, *adv.* to light, open to view; – *bringen,* bring to light; – *fördern, v.a.* extract (*Min.*), unearth, bring to light; – *liegen,* be evident *or* manifest, be on the surface (*Min.*). – *kommen,* – *treten, v.n.* come to light, become evident. **-streichen,** *n.* cropping-out (*of strata*).
zutappen, *v.n.* (*aux.* h.) grope, fumble, blunder.
Zutat, *f.* (*usually pl.* –en) trimming, ornamentation; seasoning, garnishing; addition.
zuteil, *adv.*; *einem – werden,* fall to a p.'s share *or* lot; *einem etwas – werden lassen,* allot a p. a th. *or* a th. to a p. **-en,** *v.a.* (*einem etwas*) assign, allot, allocate, distribute, apportion (to); attach, post, appoint (*Mil.*); *die ihm zugeteilte Rolle,* the part allotted *or* allocated to him; *in reichem Maße –en,* lavish upon. **-ung,** *f.* distribution, apportioning; attachment, appointment, posting (*Mil.*).
zutiefst, *adv.* at bottom, deeply.
zutragen, 1. *ir.v.a.* carry *or* bring to; carry (*tales*) to, tell, repeat, report. 2. *v.r.* happen, take place, come to pass.
Zuträg-er, *m.* (-ers, -er) informer, tale-bearer, tell-tale; scandalmonger, gossip. **-erei,** *f.* tale-bearing, informing; tittle-tattle, gossip. **-lich,** *adj.* conducive to, beneficial, profitable, advantageous, useful; salutary, wholesome; *der Gesundheit –lich,* healthful, salubrious. **-lichkeit,** *f.* usefulness, advantageousness; wholesomeness, salubrity.
zutrau-en, 1. *v.a.* (*einem etwas*) believe capable of, give credit for, credit with; *ich traue ihm nicht viel zu,* I do not expect much of him; *sich* (*Dat.*) *zuviel –en,* over-estimate o.s., be over-confident, take too much on o.s. 2. *n.* trust, confidence, reliance (*zu,* in). **-enerweckend,** *adj.* inspiring confidence. **-ens-voll,** *adj.* full of confidence. **-enswert,** *adj.* trustworthy. **-lich,** *adj.* confiding, trusting, friendly; tame (*of animals*). **-lichkeit,** *f.* trust, confidence, trustfulness, friendliness; tameness (*of animals*).
zutreffen, *ir.v.n.* (*aux.* s.) come true, prove right, true *or* correct; happen, occur, take place; *es traf alles zu,* it all turned out to be true; *dies trifft auf seinen Charakter zu,* this is in keeping with his character; *auf ein Haar* –, be exactly correct *or* right to a T. **-d,** *pr.p.* & *adj.* to the point, right, correct, striking, decisive, suitable, pertinent; *–de Bemerkung,* apt remark; *das –de unterstreichen,* underline what is applicable. **-denfalls,** *adv.* if this should be the case.
zutreten, 1. *ir.v.a.* trample *or* tread down *or* in. 2. *v.n.* (*aux.* s.) (auf *with Acc.*) approach, come up to; (*aux.* h.) intervene, interpose, take steps.
zutrinken, *ir.v.n.* (*aux.* h.) (*with Dat.*) drink to, pledge.
Zutritt, *m.* (-(e)s, -e) access, entrance, admission, admittance; – *haben,* be received, have access (*to a p.*); *einem freien – verschaffen,* secure admittance for s.o., get s.o. a free *or* complimentary ticket.
zutulich, *adj., see* **zutunlich.**
zutun, 1. *ir.v.a.* add to; close, shut; *ich habe kein Auge zugetan,* I have not slept a wink. 2. *n.* assistance, help, co-operation; *es geschah ohne mein* –, I had nothing to do with it, it was none of my doing.
zutunlich, *adj.* confiding, friendly, obliging; engaging, assiduous, complaisant.
zuungunsten, *adv.* to the detriment *or* disadvantage (of).
zuunterst, *adv.* right at the bottom, below all the others.
zuverlässig, *adj.* reliable, trustworthy, dependable, certain, positive, authentic; *er ist nicht* –, he is not to be trusted *or* relied on. **-keit,** *f.* reliability, trustworthiness; certainty, authenticity. **-keits-fahrt,** *f.* reliability trial (*Motor.*).
Zuversicht, *f.* confidence, trust, faith (*auf,* in), reliance, dependence (on); certainty, conviction; – *zu Gott,* trust in God; *ich hege die* –, I trust; *er hat die feste* or *ist der festen* –, he confidently expects, he is confident. **-lich,** *adj.* confident, assured, positive, certain, undoubting, hopeful. **-lichkeit,** *f.* trust, confidence; certainty, assurance, self-assurance.
zuviel, 1. *adv.* too much; *mehr als* –, more than enough; – *des Guten,* more than is good for one, too much of a good thing; *des Guten – tun,* go too far; *viel* –, much *or* far too much; (*Prov.*) *was – ist, ist* –, more than enough is too much. 2. *n.* excess.
zuvor, *adv.* before, previously, beforehand, first, formerly. **-derst** (*or* **zuvörderst**), *adv.* in the front rank, foremost; first of all, in the first place, first and foremost, to begin with.
zuvorkommen, *ir.v.n.* (*aux.* s.) (*sep.*) (*with Dat.*) come first, get in front of, forestall, anticipate; prevent; *einem mit* or *in einer S.* –, steal a march on a p. with a th.; *einer S.* –, prevent *or* obviate s.th. **-d,** *pr.p.* & *adj.* friendly, obliging, polite, charming, civil, **-keit,** *f.* politeness, civility, kindness.
zuvortun, *ir.v.a.* (*sep.*); *es einem in einer S.* –, surpass, excel *or* outdo a p. in s.th.
Zuwaage, *f.* (-n) (*dial.*) makeweight.
Zuwachs, *m.* growth, increase, expansion, increment, accretion, accession, augmentation; – *in der Familie bekommen,* have an addition to the family; *einen Rock auf – machen,* make a coat allowing for growth *or* so as to allow for growing. **-en,** *ir.v.n.* (*aux.* h.) heal up, close up, grow together, encrust, become overgrown; accrue. **-ring,** *m.* growth ring (*Bot.*). **-steuer,** *f.* increment-tax.
zuwägen, *ir.v.a.* weigh out, distribute by weight; (*fig.*) mete out.
Zuwahl, *f.* (-en) co-option.
zuwählen, *v.a.* co-opt.
zuwälzen, *v.a.* roll towards; throw, put *or* lay (*the blame, etc.*) upon; *den Eingang der Höhle mit einem Stein* –, block up the mouth of the cave with a stone.
zuwander-n, *v.n.* (*aux.* s.) immigrate; *ein Zugewanderter,* an immigrant. **-ung,** *f.* immigration.
zuwarten, 1. *v.a.* (*aux.* h.) wait patiently *or* quietly; *sich –d verhalten,* play the waiting game. 2. *n.* patient waiting; *Politik des –s,* laissez-faire policy.
zuwege, *adv.*; – *bringen,* bring about, effect, bring to pass, accomplish; *gut* –, (*dial.*) in good condition; quite well.
zuweilen, *adv.* sometimes, at times, occasionally, now and then.
zuweis-en, *ir.v.a.* (*einem etwas*) attribute, assign *or* allot (to); *einem einen Kunden –en,* send *or* recommend a customer to a p. **-ung,** *f.* assignment, allotment.
zuwend-en, 1. *reg.* & *ir.v.a.* (*einem etwas*) turn to(wards), give, bestow (upon), make a present (of), let have, devote (to). 2. *v.r.* (*with Dat.*) devote o.s. (to), apply o.s. (to); *einem das Gesicht –en,* turn one's face toward a p.; *einem seine Liebe –en,* give one's love to a p.; *seine Freundlichkeit wandte ihm alle Herzen zu,* his kindliness won him all hearts; *seine ganze Kraft einem Gegenstande –en,* expend all one's strength on an object, apply . . . to an object; *sich*

einer anderen Arbeit –*en*, change *or* switch over to other employment. **–ung,** *f.* gift, donation.
zuwerfen, *ir.v.a.* (*einem etwas*) throw to(wards); fill up (*with earth*); slam (*a door*); *einem Blicke* –, cast glances at s.o.; *ihr eine Kußhand* –, throw a kiss to her; *die Tür* –, slam the door.
zuwider, 1. *prep.* (*Dat. following*) contrary to, against. 2. *adv.* (*only with* sein) repugnant, odious, offensive; *das Glück war uns* –, fortune was against us; *Gefühle, die ihrer Pflicht – waren*, feelings which conflicted with her duty; *das ist mir* –, I loathe *or* hate that; *er ist mir in den Tod* –, I hate the very sight of him; *einem etwas – machen*, disgust a p. with a th.; *es wird Ihnen nicht – sein, wenn* . . ., you will have no objection if. . . . **–handeln,** *v.n.* (*sep.*) (*with Dat.*) offend against, disobey, contravene, infringe, violate; *er suchte meinem Plane –zuhandeln*, he tried to oppose my plan. **–handelnde(r),** *m.* offender, trespasser. **–handlung,** *f.* contravention, infringement, violation. **–laufen,** *v.n.* (*sep.*) (*aux.* s.) (*with Dat.*) run counter *or* be contrary to.
zuwinken, *v.n.* (*aux.* h.) (*with Dat.*) wave, make signs, nod *or* beckon to.
Zuwuchs, *m.*, *see* **Zuwachs.**
zuzahlen, *v.a.* pay in addition, pay over and above, make an extra *or* further payment.
zuzählen, 1. *v.a.* add (to), include; (*einem etwas*) count out to. 2. *v.n.* be among.
zuzeiten, *adv.* at times.
zuzieh-en, 1. *ir.v.a.* draw together, draw tight, tighten, tie, draw (*curtains, etc.*); admit, invite, call in, consult; cause, incur; *einen Knoten –en*, pull a knot tight; *die Vorhänge –en*, draw the curtains (to); *zur Beratung –en*, consult; *sich* (*Dat.*) *Händel –en*, involve o.s. in a squabble; *sich* (*Dat.*) *einen Tadel –en*, incur blame; expose o.s. to criticism; *sich* (*Dat.*) *eine Krankheit –en*, contract a disease, catch an illness; *sich* (*Dat.*) *einen Verdacht –en*, bring suspicion upon o.s., lay o.s. open to suspicion. 2. *v.n.* (*aux.* s.) (*with Dat.*) drag *or* move towards; remove to, move in (*a house, etc.*), come into (*a district, etc.*); march to (*the aid of*); go to a new place (*of servants*); migrate; (*aux.* h.) pull on; *kräftig –en*, pull hard, pull away. **–ung,** *f.* drawing together; tying; incurring; aid, assistance; *unter –ung Ihrer Spesen*, including your expenses; *mit* or *unter –ung eines Arztes*, a doctor having been consulted, on doctor's orders.
Zuzug, *m.* immigration, increase in population; reinforcements, contingent.
Zuzüg–er, *m.* (*Swiss dial.*), **–ler,** *m.* (-s, –) volunteer; newcomer, recent settler. **–lich,** *prep.* (*Gen.*) with the addition of, in addition to, including, plus.
zwacken, *v.a.* pinch, pull, tease, pester, torment.
Zwang, *m.* force, coercion, compulsion, constraint, control, restraint; (moral) obligation, pressure; constriction, tenesmus (*Med.*); *ohne* –, unconstrained(ly); *einem – antun*, use violence to, compel *or* constrain a p.; *dem Sinn einer Stelle – antun*, twist the meaning of a passage; *sich* (*Dat.*) – *antun*, check *or* restrain o.s.; *sich* (*Dat.*) *keinen – antun*, be quite free and easy; *dem Gesetze – antun*, pervert the law. **–läufig,** *adj.* direct *or* fixed drive (*Mach.*). **–lauflehre,** *f.* transmission theory (*Mach.*). **–los,** *adj.* unconstrained, unrestricted, free; irregular, indefinite, at random, occasional; unconventional, informal, free and easy; *in –loser Folge*, in irregular sequence, as a random series; *in –losen Heften*, appearing in occasional numbers and at no fixed dates. **–losigkeit,** *f.* freedom, unconstraint, informality; lack of regularity. **–sanleihe,** *f.* forced loan. **–sarbeit,** *f.* forced labour, hard labour. **–senteignung,** *f.* compulsory expropriation. **–sernährung,** *f.* forcible feeding. **–serscheinung,** *f.*, *see* **–sneurose.** **–serziehung,** *f.* education in a reformatory. **–sgesetz,** *n.* coercive law. **–sgestellt,** *p.p.* & *adj.* in custody. **–sjacke,** *f.* strait-jacket. **–skurs,** *m.* legal rate. **–slage,** *f.* embarrassing situation; *in einer –slage*, under the necessity (of doing), hard pressed. **–släufig,** 1. *adj.* obligatory, enforced, necessary. 2. *adv.* necessarily, automatically, inevitably. **–slieferung,** *f.* enforced delivery. **–smaßregel,** *f.* coercive measure; *–smaßregeln anwenden*, use force. **–smittel,** *n.* violent means, means of coercion, force. **–sneurose,** *f.* compulsion, obsession. **–spreise,** *pl.* fixed *or* controlled prices. **–srecht,** *n.* right of coercion. **–(s)schiene,** *f.* check-rail. **–sschlaf,** *m.* hypnosis. **–sstellung,** *f.* constrained position. **–sverfahren,** *n.* coercive measures. **–svergleich,** *m.* enforced settlement. **–sversteigerung,** *f.* compulsory *or* bankrupt sale (*by auction*). **–sverwaltung,** *f.* sequestration. **–svollstreckung,** *f.* distraint, legal execution. **–svorstellung,** *f.* hallucination. **–sweise,** *adv.* compulsorily, forcibly, by (main) force. **–swirtschaft,** *f.* government control, economic control, controlled economy.
zwang, zwänge, *see* **zwingen.**
zwängen, *v.a.* force, constrain, coerce, press, squeeze; *das Recht* –, do violence to the law.
zwanzig, 1. *num. adj.* twenty. 2. *f.* (-en) the number twenty, a score; *in den –en*, see *in den –ern*; *sie ist über die – hinaus*, she is over *or* turned 20. **–er,** *m.* 20-year-old man; wine of the year '20; soldier of the 20th regiment; *in den –ern sein*, be in one's twenties. **–erlei,** *indec. adj.* of 20 different kinds; *auf –erlei Art*, in 20 (different) ways. **–fach,** *adj.*, **–fältig,** *adj.* twentyfold. **–flach,** *n.*, **–flächner,** *m.* icosahedron. **–flächig,** *adj.* icosahedral. **–st,** *num. adj.* twentieth. **–stel,** *n.* (*Swiss dial. m.*) twentieth part; *drei –stel*, three-twentieths. **–stens,** *adv.* in the 20th place.
zwar, *adv.* (*with* aber *or* doch *in the following clause*) indeed, certainly, of course, to be sure, I admit; *und* –, that is, in fact, namely, specifically; *er schwimmt, und – gut*, he swims, and very well in fact.
Zweck, *m.* (-(e)s, -e) aim, end, object, objective, purpose, design, goal; *seinen – erreichen*, attain one's goal *or* object, carry one's point; *der – heiligt die Mittel*, the end justifies the means; *keinen – haben*, be (of) no use, be pointless; *mit dem –e*, with a view to, with the object of, with this end in view; (*coll.*) *das ist der – der Übung*, that is the whole point; *– und Ziel*, aim and purpose; *zu welchem –e?* what for? for what purpose? why? **–bau,** (-bauten) utilitarian *or* functional structure. **–bewußt,** *adj.* clear-sighted, purposeful. **–dienlich,** *adj.* to the point, suitable, appropriate, useful, serviceable, efficient, efficacious. **–dienlichkeit,** *f.* utility, suitability, efficacy, efficiency, fitness. **–entsprechend,** *adj.* appropriate, expedient. **–essen,** *n.* banquet on some special occasion. **–gemäß,** *adv.*, **–haft,** *adj.*, *see* **–mäßig.** **–los,** 1. *adj.* aimless, pointless, purposeless, useless. 2. *adv.* to no purpose, at random. **–losigkeit,** *f.* aimlessness, pointlessness, uselessness. **–mäßig,** *adj.* appropriate, expedient, practical, useful. **–mäßigkeit,** *f.* suitability, expediency, appropriateness, fitness, opportuneness, functionalism (*Phil.*). **–mäßigkeitslehre,** *f.* teleology. **–s,** *prep.* (*Gen.*) for the purpose of. **–widrig,** *adj.* inappropriate, unsuitable, injudicious, inexpedient. **–widrigkeit,** *f.* unsuitableness.
Zwecke, *f.* (-n) tack, brad, drawing-pin, peg, hobnail, sprig (*for shoes*). **–n,** *v.a.* peg, tack, fasten with drawing-pins *or* brads.
Zwehle, *f.* (-n) (*dial.*) towel.
zwei, 1. *num. adj.* two; *es ist halb* –, it is half-past one; *aus –(en) bestehend, in – zerfallend*, binary; *zu –(en) stehend*, double (*Bot.*); *zu –en*, two by two, in twos; *das Spiel läßt sich zu –en spielen*, two can play at that game; *Tagebuch –er Kinder*, diary of two children. 2. *f.* (-en) two; deuce. 3. *n.* pair, couple. **–achsig,** *adj.* biaxial. **–aktig,** *adj.* of two acts (*play*). **–armig,** *adj.* two-armed. **–astig,** *adj.* bifurcate(d). **–atomig,** *adj.* diatomic. **–äugig,** *adj.* binocular. **–bändig,** *adj.* two-volume (*edition*). **–basisch,** *adj.* bibasic, dibasic (*Chem.*). **–beinig,** *adj.* two-legged. **–bettig,** *adj.* with two beds; *–bettiges Zimmer*, double-bedded room. **–blätt(e)rig,** *adj.* two-leaved, bifoliate; bipetalous. **–blattschraube,** *f.* two-bladed propeller. **–blumig,** *adj.*, **–blütig,** *adj.* biflorate. **–brüderig,** *adj.*, **–bündelig,** *adj.* diadelphous (*Bot.*). **–bund,** *m.* dual alliance. **–decker,** *m.* biplane. **–deutig,** *adj.* ambiguous, equivocal, doubtful; suggestive, un-

seemly, improper, ribald, smutty, risqué; *–deutig reden*, equivocate. **–deutigkeit,** *f.* ambiguity, suggestiveness, unseemliness, impropriety. **–doppelt,** *adj.* binate (*Bot.*). **–dritteltakt,** *m.* two-three time. **–ehig,** *adj.* digamous (*Bot.*). **–eiig,** *adj.* biovular, dizygotic. **–elektrodenröhre,** *f.* diode (*Rad.*). **–en,** *v.r.* (*Poet.*) go together in pairs, pair off; select a partner. **–er,** *m.* the figure 2; a two (mark, *etc.*) piece; a two (pfennig, *etc.*) stamp; a soldier of the 2nd regiment; a boat for two. **–erlei,** *indec. adj.* of two kinds; twofold, different; *das ist –erlei*, those are two very different things. **–fach,** *adj.* double, twofold; binate; *in –facher Ausführung*, in duplicate. **–fächerig,** *adj.* two-celled, bilocular (*Bot.*). **–fachgeteilt,** *adj.* bipartite. **–fachkohlensaures Natron,** bicarbonate of soda. **–fältig,** *adj.* twofold. **–farbendruck,** *m.* two-colour print(ing). **–farbig,** *adj.* two-coloured, dichromatic; fluorescent. **–felderwirtschaft,** *f.* two-crop rotation (*Agriculture*). **–flügelig,** *adj.* two-winged; dipterous. **–flügler,** *m.pl.* diptera (*Ent.*). **–frontenkrieg,** *m.* war on two fronts. **–füßig,** *adj.* biped. **–füß(l)er,** *m.* biped. **–gabelig,** *adj.* dichotomous. **–gesang,** *m.* (vocal) duet. **–geschlechtig,** *adj.* hermaphrodite, bisexual, androgynous. **–gespann,** *n.* carriage with two horses; *ein –gespann führen*, drive a (carriage and) pair. **–gespräch,** *n.* dialogue. **–gestaltig,** *adj.* dimorphous. **–gestrichen,** *adj.* twice marked *or* accented; *–gestrichene Note*, semiquaver. **–geteilt,** *adj.* bipartite. **–gipf(e)lig,** *adj.* double-peaked; *–gipfliger Akzent*, intermittent accent. **–gitterröhre,** *f.* screen-grid valve (*Rad.*). **–gleisig,** *adj.* double-tracked (*Railw.*). **–glied(e)rig,** *adj.* two-membered; binomial (*Alg.*); biarticulate (*Zool.*); in two ranks (*Mil.*). **–händer,** *m.* two-handed sword. **–händig,** *adj.* two-handed (*of a sword*); *–händiges Stück*, piece for two hands (*Mus.*). **–häusig,** *adj.* diœcious (*Bot.*). **–heit,** *f.* duality, dualism. **–herr,** *m.* duumvir. **–herrschaft,** *f.* duumvirate. **–höckerig,** *adj.* two-humped; *–höckeriges Kamel*, Bactrian camel. **–hufer,** *m.* cloven-footed animal. **–hufig,** *adj.* cloven-footed, bisulcate. **–hundert,** *num. adj.* two hundred. **–hundertjährig,** *adj.* lasting 200 years; bicentennial; *–hundertjährige Feier*, bicentenary. **–jährig,** *adj.* of 2 years, 2 years old; lasting 2 years, biennial. **–jährlich,** *adj.* occurring every 2 years, biennial. **–kammersystem,** *n.* (legislative) system with upper and lower houses *or* chambers. **–kampf,** *m.* duel. **–kämpfer,** *m.* duellist. **–klappig,** *adj.* bivalvular, bivalvous. **–kontentheorie,** *f.* theory of double entry (*Bookkeeping*). **–köpfig,** *adj.*; *–köpfiger Muskel*, biceps. **–lappig,** *adj.* two-lobed (*Bot.*). **–lebig,** *adj.* amphibious. **–mächtig,** *adv.* didynamian (*Bot.*). **–mal,** *adv.* twice; double; *er wird sich das nicht –mal sagen lassen*, he will need no second telling. **–malig,** *adj.* done twice, repeated. **–männig,** *adj.* diandrian (*Bot.*). **–master,** *m.* two-masted vessel. **–monatig,** *adj.* lasting 2 months; *–monatiger Urlaub*, 2 months' leave. **–monatlich,** *adj.* occurring every 2 months; *–monatliche Lieferung*, delivery every second month. **–motorig,** *adj.* twin-engined. **–pasch,** *m.* double-two (*dominoes*). **–pfünder,** *m.* two-pounder (*Artil.*). **–phasig,** *adj.* two-phase (*Elec.*). **–polig,** *adj.* bipolar. **–polröhre,** *f.* diode (*Rad.*). **–rad,** *n.* bicycle. **–räd(e)rig,** *adj.* two-wheeled; *–rädriger Wagen*, two-wheeler, hansom. **–reihig,** *adj.* having two rows; bifarious, distichous (*Bot.*); double-breasted (*jacket*). **–röhrenempfänger,** *m.* two-valve receiver (*Rad.*). **–schalig,** *adj.* bivalve, bivalvular. **–schenk(e)lig,** *adj.* branched, forked. **–schläfig,** *adj.*, **–schläfrig,** *adj.*; *–schläf(r)iges Bett*, double bed, bed for two persons. **–schneidig,** *adj.* two-edged; *die Bemerkung ist –schneidig*, that observation cuts both ways. **–schraubendampfer,** *m.* twin-screw vessel. **–schürig,** *adj.* that is shorn *or* mown twice a year; *–schürige Wiese*, meadow for second mowing; *–schürige Wolle*, wool of the second shearing. **–seitig,** *adj.* bilateral, duplex, double-sided, two-sided. **–silbig,** *adj.* two-syllabled, disyllabic. **–sitzer,** *m.* two-seater (*motor-car*); tandem (*bicycle*). **–spaltig,** *adj.* forked, bifid (*Bot.*); in double columns (*Typ.*). **–spänner,** *m.* coach drawn by two horses; farmer who works two horses. **–spännig,** *adj.* drawn by two horses. **–sprachig,** *adj.* bilingual. **–sprachigkeit,** *f.* bilingualism. **–spurig,** *adj.* double-tracked. **–ständig,** *adj.* dichotomous. **–stärkenglas,** *n.* bifocal lens. **–stimmig,** *adj.* for two voices. **–stöckig,** *adj.* two-storied. **–stoff,** *m.* two-component alloy. **–stufig,** *adj.* two-stage. **–stündig,** *adj.* lasting 2 hours; 2 hours old. **–stündlich,** *adj.* every second hour. **–t,** *num. adj.*, second; next; *der –te Mai*, May the 2nd; *den –ten Tag darauf*, the next day but one; *mein –tes Ich*, my other self, my alter ego; *–tes Gesicht*, second-sight; *zu –t*, two of (us, them, *etc.*). **–tägig,** *adj.* lasting 2 days, 2 days old. **–taktmotor,** *m.* two-stroke engine. **–tälteste(r),** *m.* second-eldest, eldest but one. **–tausend,** *num. adj.* two thousand. **–tausfertigung,** *f.* duplication; duplicate. **–tbest,** *adj.* second-best. **–tdruck,** reprint, second impression. **–teilig,** *adj.* bipartite; two-piece (*suit*). **–teilung,** *f.* bisection, binary fission, dichotomy, bifurcation. **–tens,** *adv.* secondly, in the second place. **–tfrucht,** *f.* second crop. **–tgeboren,** *adj.* second, younger. **–tjüngste(r),** *m.* youngest but one. **–tklasswagen,** *m.* (*Swiss dial.*) second-class compartment. **–tkommandierende(r),** *m.* second-in-command. **–tletzt,** *adj.* last but one, penultimate. **–tling,** *m.* runner-up. **–tmädchen,** *n.* second maid. **–tnächst,** *adj.* next but one. **–unddreißigstelformat,** *n.* 32mo. **–unddreißigstelnote,** *f.* demisemiquaver. **–unddreißigstelpause,** *f.* demisemiquaver rest. **–viertelnote,** *f.* minim. **–viertelpause,** *f.* minim rest. **–vierteltakt,** *m.* two-four time (*Mus.*). **–weiberei,** *f.* bigamy. **–wellig,** *adj.*, *see* **–phasig.** **–wertig,** *adj.* bivalent, divalent (*Chem.*); *–wertiges Element*, dyad (*Chem.*). **–wöchentlich,** *adj.* fortnightly. **–wöchig,** *adj.* 2 weeks old; lasting 2 weeks. **–zackig,** *adj.* two-pronged; bifurcated. **–zahn,** *m.* bur marigold (*Bidens cernua*) (*Bot*). **–zeiler,** *m.* couplet, distich. **–zeilig,** *adj.* two-lined, double-spaced, distichous; *–zeilige Gerste*, two-rowed barley. **–zipfelig,** *adj.* bicuspidate. **–züngig,** *adj.* double-tongued; double-faced, two-faced, shifty, insincere, hypocritical.

Zweifel, *m.* (-s, –) doubt, uncertainty, hesitation, misgiving, suspicion; *außer –*, beyond (a) doubt; *in – stellen* or *ziehen*, call in question, doubt; *ohne –*, without doubt, doubtless, unquestionably; *über allen* or *jeden – erhaben*, beyond all doubt. **–geist,** *m.* scepticism; *see also* **Zweifler.** **–haft,** *adj.* doubtful, uncertain, undecided, equivocal, irresolute; doubting, dubious, questionable, suspicious; *etwas –haft lassen*, leave a th. in suspense; *etwas –haft machen*, cast a doubt upon, throw suspicion on a th. **–los,** 1. *adj.* undoubted, unquestionable, indubitable, certain. 2. *adv.*, *see* **–sohne.** **–mut,** *m.* irresolution, uncertainty. **–mütig,** *adj.* irresolute, wavering. **–n,** *v.n.* (*aux.* h.) doubt, question, be distrustful, suspect, be in doubt (about), waver; *an einer S.* or *an einem –n*, have one's doubts about *or* doubt a th. *or* mistrust *or* distrust a p.; *ich zweifle nicht daran*, I do not doubt it; *er –te, was er tun sollte*, he was in doubt as to what he should do; *ich zweifle, ob es passend ist*, I doubt *or* question whether it is proper. **–nd,** *pr.p.* & *adj.* doubting; sceptical. **–sfall,** *m.* doubtful case; *im –sfall*, in case of doubt. **–sohne,** *adv.* doubtless, undoubtedly, without doubt, decidedly. **–sucht,** *f.* scepticism. **–süchtig,** *adj.* sceptical.

Zweifler, *m.* (-s, –) doubter, sceptic.

Zweig, *m.* (-(e)s, -e) branch, bough, twig; scion; department, section; (*coll.*) *er kommt auf keinen grünen –*, he will never get on in the world, he will never come to anything *or* never amount to much. **–bahn,** *f.* branch railway. **–en,** *v.r.* branch, divide. **–geschäft,** *n.* branch (business *or* office). **–lager,** *n.* branch depot. **–leitung,** *f.* branch pipe *or* wire. **–stelle,** *f.* branch office; branch exchange (*Phone*). **–strecke,** *f.* branch line. **–verein,** *m.* affiliated society, local branch (*of a society*).

zweit, *see under* **zwei.**

zwerch, *adj.* (*dial.*) athwart, across. **–fell,** *n.* diaphragm, midriff. **–fellerschütternd,** *adj.* side-splitting.

Zwerg, *m.* (-(e)s, -e) dwarf, pygmy, midget. **–apfel,** *m.* dwarf apple. **–apfelsine,** *f.* tangerine. **–bildung,** *f.*, *see* **–wuchs.** **–bohne,** *f.* dwarf kidney-bean. **–enhaft,** *adj.*, **–ig,** *adj.* diminutive, undersized, tiny, stunted, dwarfish. **–haftigkeit,** *f.*, **–heit,** *f.* dwarfishness. **–huhn,** *n.* bantam. **–hund,** *m.* toy dog, lap dog. **–kiefer,** *f.* dwarf-pine. **–ling,** *m.* pygmy. **–maus,** *f.* harvest-mouse (*Micromys domesticus*) (*Zool.*). **–mensch,** *m.* pygmy. **–pferd,** *n.* pony (*under* 1.36 *metres*). **–wuchs,** *m.* stunted growth, nanism. **–wüchsig,** *adj.* dwarfish, stunted.

Zwetsch–(g)e, *f.* (-n), (*Austr. dial.*) **–ke,** *f.* (-ken) damson (*Prunus domestica*) (*Bot.*).

Zwick, *m.* (-(e)s, -e) pinch, nip; twinge; whip-lash; cut with a whip; *see also* **Zwecke.** **–bohrer,** *m.* g mlet. **–e,** *f.* peg, spike; pincers. **–el,** *m.* wedge; gusset, gore; clock (*of a stocking*); spandrel (*Arch.*). **–elbart,** *m.* twirled moustaches. **–eln,** *v.a.* put in a gore *or* gusset. **–en,** 1. *v.a.* pinch, nip, tweak. 2. *v.n.* twinge, gripe; *es –t mich im Leibe,* I have the gripes. **–er,** *m.* eye-glasses, pince-nez. **–mühle,** *f.* double row of pieces (*in a game*); dilemma, predicament; *in einer –mühle sein,* be in a fix *or* jam. **–nagel,** *m.* tack, brad. **–zange,** *f.* shoemaker's pincers.

Zwie–back, *m.* (-(e)s, -e & ⸚e) rusk. **–brache,** *f.* double ploughing. **–brachen,** *v.a.* (*insep.*) plough a second time, twifallow (*a field*). **–erbig,** *adj.* heterozygous. **–fach,** *adj.*, **–fältig,** *adj.* twofold, double. **–gespräch,** *n.* dialogue, colloquy, private talk. **–laut,** *m.* diphthong. **–licht,** *n.* twilight, dusk. **–metall,** *n.* bimetal, dual alloy. **–spalt,** *m.* discord, dissension; schism. **–spältig,** *adj.* disunited, divided, conflicting, schismatic. **–spältigkeit,** *f.* disunity, division, conflict (*of aims, etc.*). **–sprache,** *f.* dialogue, conversation, discussion. **–tracht,** *f.* discord, dissension. **–trächtig,** *adj.* discordant, at variance. **–trachtstifter,** *m.* mischief maker.

Zwiebel, *f.* (-n) onion; bulb; (*sl.*) turnip (*big watch*). **–artig,** *adj.* bulbous. **–fische,** *m.pl.* pie (*Print.*). **–förmig,** *adj.* bulbous. **–gewächs,** *n.* bulbous plant. **–knollen,** *m.* bulbous tuber. **–n,** *v.* season with onion; (*coll.*) *einen –n,* treat a p. roughly, give a p. a bad time. **–tragend,** *adj.* bulbiferous. **–turm,** *m.* bulbous spire (*as of Bavarian and Russian churches*).

Zwiesel, 1. *m.* (-s, –); *Hinter–,* cantle; *Vorder–,* pommel. 2. *f.* (-n) fork, bifurcation; forked branch. **–bart,** *m.* forked beard. **–ig,** *adj.* forked, bifurcate. **–n,** *v.n.* & *r.* fork, bifurcate.

Zwil–(li)ch, *m.* (-ches, -che) ticking, drill (*material*). **–(li)chen,** *adj.* of ticking.

Zwilling, *m.* (-s, -e) twin; (*pl.*) Gemini (*Astr.*). **–sbereifung,** *f.* double tyres. **–sbildung,** *f.* twinning, congemination. **–sbruder,** *m.* twin-brother. **–sgeburt,** *f.* birth of twins, twin birth. **–sgeschwister,** *pl.* twins. **–sgestirn,** *n.* Gemini, Castor and Pollux (*Astr.*). **–skristalle,** *m.pl.* twinned crystals. **–smaschine,** *f.* twin-cylinder engine. **–smuskeln,** *m.* & *f.pl.* gemelli (*Anat.*). **–spaar,** *n.* twins. **–sschwester,** *f.* twin-sister.

Zwinge, *f.* (-n) clamp, cramp, (hand-)vice, hold-fast; ferrule (*on sticks*).

zwing–en, 1. *ir.v.a.* force, compel, constrain; master, overcome, get the better of; finish, complete, bring to an end, cope with; *einen zu etwas –en,* compel a p. to (*do, etc.*), force a p. into (*doing, etc.*); *sich zu nichts –en lassen,* not submit to force; *durch Hunger –en,* reduce by starvation. 2. *v.r.* (*with* zu) force o.s. to (*do, etc.*) with difficulty, make a great effort; *man braucht ihn nicht dazu zu –en,* he will do it of his own accord; *das läßt sich nicht –en,* violence *or* force will not do any good; *er läßt sich nicht –en,* he won't give way to force, force won't move him; *sich zum Lachen –en,* force o.s. to laugh, laugh with difficulty; *sich zur Freundlichkeit –en,* make an effort to appear pleasant, be pleasant with an effort. **–burg,** *f.* fortified castle, fortress, stronghold. **–end,** *pr.p.* & *adj.* forcible, coercive; cogent, compelling, convincing, conclusive. **–er,** *m.* outer courtyard; enclosure; den, bear-pit, arena; donjon, keep, fort. **–herr,** *m.* despot, tyrant. **–herrschaft,** *f.* despotism, tyranny.

zwinke(r)n, *v.n.* (*aux.* h.) wink, blink, twinkle.

zwirbel–ig, *adj.* (*Swiss dial.*) giddy, dizzy. **–n,** *v.a.* twirl, twist.

Zwirn, *m.* (-(e)s, -e) thread, sewing cotton, twine; (*sl.*) ideas, notions, fancies; (*coll.*) *sie hat – im Kopfe,* she's no fool; (*coll.*) *der – ging ihm aus,* he came to the end of what he had to say, he had nothing more to say. **–en,** 1. *adj.* of thread. 2. *v.a.* (double and) twist (*yarn*), twine (*thread*); throw (*silk*); *gezwirnte Seide,* silk twist. **–haspel,** *m.* & *f.*, *see* **–winde.** **–knäuel,** *n.* & *m.* ball of thread. **–maschine,** *f.*, **–mühle,** *f.* twisting-frame, doubler; spinning-mill. **–seide,** *f.* thrown silk. **–(s)faden,** *m.* piece of cotton *or* thread; *über einen –sfaden stolpern,* strain at gnats. **–spitze,** *f.* thread-lace. **–(s)rolle,** *f.* reel of cotton *or* thread.

zwischen, *prep.* (*with Dat. in answer to* wo? *with Acc. in answer to* wohin?) between, among, amongst; *– Himmel und Erde,* between *or* (*poet.*) 'twixt heaven and earth; *Unkraut – den Weizen säen,* sow tares among the wheat; *er setzte sich – sie und mich,* he seated himself between her and me; *sich – zwei Stühle setzen,* fall between two stools; *er saß – ihr und mir,* he sat between her and me; *– mir und dir soll kein anderer stehen,* no one shall come between us; *– Tür und Angel sagen,* say hurriedly when leaving, add as a final word; *Wettrudern – den Universitäten,* inter-university boat-race; *wählen Sie – diesen Büchern,* choose from among these books. **–abschluß,** *m.* interim balance. **–akt,** *m.* interval, entr'acte. **–aktsmusik,** *f.* musical entr'acte. **–balken,** *m.* mid-beam. **–bahnhof,** *m.* intermediate station. **–band,** *n.* intervertebral ligament; copula. **–bemerkung,** *f.* incidental remark; digression, aside. **–bescheid,** *m.* provisional decree. **–bilanz,** *f.* interim statement. **–blatt,** *n.* interleaved blank sheet *or* page. **–deck,** *n.* lower deck, steerage. **–ding,** *n.* combination, mixture, cross, hybrid. **–drein, –drin,** *adv.* in among; *–drein legen,* lay in among; *–drin liegen,* be *or* lie (in) among. **–durch,** *adv.* through, in the midst, in between; at times, between whiles, at intervals; for *or* as a change. **–ergebnis,** *n.* provisional result. **–fall,** *m.* (untoward) incident, episode. **–farbe,** *f.* half-tint, secondary colour, intermediate shade. **–frage,** *f.* interpolated question. **–gebläse,** *n.* supercharger (*Mech.*). **–gelände,** *n.*; *neutrales –gelände,* No-Man's-Land (*Mil.*). **–gericht,** *n.* side-dish, entrée. **–geschäft,** *n.* incidental business. **–geschoß,** *n.*, *see* **–stock.** **–gewinn,** *m.* middleman's profit. **–glied,** *n.* connecting link. **–glühung,** *f.* intermediate annealing. **–handel,** *m.* middleman's business, carrying trade; commission business. **–händler,** *m.* (commission-) agent, intermediary, middleman. **–handlung,** *f.* episode, incident. **–haut,** *f.* diaphragm. **–her,** *adv.* in the interval, in the meantime, meanwhile. **–hin,** *adv.* right in(to) the *or* their midst. **–hirn,** *n.* mid-brain. **–inne,** *adv.* in the midst of, right among. **–kiefer(knochen),** *m.* intermaxillary bone. **–klage,** *f.* interpleader. **–kreis,** *m.* aerial *or* input circuit (*Rad.*). **–lage,** *f.* intermediate position. **–landung,** *f.* touch-down (*Av.*); *Flug ohne –landung,* non-stop flight. **–legierung,** *f.* hardener (*Metall.*). **–liegend,** *adj.* intermediate. **–lösung,** *f.* interim solution. **–mahl,** *n.* **–mahlzeit,** *f.* snack. **–mauer,** *f.* partition wall. **–pause,** *f.* interval, interlude, break. **–person,** *f.* agent, intermediary, middleman; go-between. **–prüfung,** *f.* intermediate examination. **–raum,** *m.* intermediate space, gap, interstice, interval, space (*Typ.*); *in langen –räumen,* at long intervals; *Anordnung der –räume,* spacing. **–regierung,** *f.* interregnum, interim government. **–rippenraum,** *m.* intercostal space (*Anat.*). **–ruf,** *m.* interruption, exclamation. **–satz,** *m.* insertion; interpolation, parenthesis. **–schaltung,** *f.* intermediate switch position (*Elec.*). **–scheibe,** *f.* intervertebral disk (*Anat.*). **–sender,** *m.* relay station (*Rad.*). **–spiel,** *n.* intermezzo, interlude; incident. **–staat,** *m.* buffer state. **–staatlich,** *adj.* international. **–stadium,** *n.* intermediate stage. **–ständig,** *adj.*

intermediate. **-station,** *f.* intermediate station, wayside station. **-stecker,** *m.* adapter plug (*Elec.*). **-stock(werk),** *n.* mezzanine, entresol. **-streifen,** *m.* insertion (*embroidery*). **-stück,** *n.* insertion, inset, intermediate piece; interlude, entr'acte, intermezzo (*Theat.*). **-stufe,** *f.* intermediate stage *or* grade. **-stufig,** *adj.* intermediate, intermediary. **-stunde,** *f.* interval, pause, break (*between lessons*). **-ton,** *m.* intermediate shade. **-träger,** *m.* go-between, tale-bearer, scandal-monger. **-trägerei,** *f.* tale-bearing. **-urteil,** *n.* interlocutory judgement. **-völkisch,** *adj.* international. **-vorhang,** *m.* drop-scene; drop-curtain. **-wand,** *f.* partition (wall), bulkhead, baffle. **-weite,** *f.* interval, separation, space. **-welle,** *f.* main drive shaft (*Mach.*). **-zaun,** *m.* boundary fence. **-zeile,** *f.* space between lines; space-line (*Typ.*). **-zeilig,** *adj.* interlinear. **-zeit,** *f.* intervening time, interval, interim; *in der -zeit,* in the meantime, meanwhile. **-ziel,** *n.* interim goal. **-zustand,** *m.* intermediate state.

Zwist, *m.* (-es, -e) dissension, discord, quarrel. **-ig,** *adj.* discordant, disagreeing, dissentient; in dispute, questionable. **-igkeit,** *f.* difference, discord, dissension, quarrel.

zwitschern, *v.a. & n.* (*aux.* h.) twitter, chirp; (*Prov.*) *wie die Alten sungen, so – die Jungen,* like father, like son; a chip off the old block.

Zwitter, *m.* (-s, –) mongrel, hybrid, bastard; hermaphrodite; gynandromorph. **-artig,** *adj., see* **-haft.** **-bildung,** *f.* hybridization, hermaphroditism. **-blume,** *f.*, **-blühte,** *f.* hermaphroditic flower. **-fahrzeug,** *n.* half-track vehicle. **-geschlecht,** *n.* hybrid stock; mongrel *or* bastard race. **-haft,** *adj.* hybrid, mongrel, hermaphroditic, androgynous, bisexual. **-haftigkeit,** *f.* mongrelism, hybrid character. **-ig (zwittrig),** *adj., see* **-haft.** **-igkeit (Zwittrigkeit)** *f.*, **-tum,** *n.*, **-wesen,** *n., see* **-haftigkeit.** **-wort,** *n.* hybrid (word).

zwo (*archaic*), *num. adj.* two; (*commonly used now on the telephone, etc., to avoid confusion with* drei). **-te,** second.

zwölf, 1. *num. adj.* twelve; *um dreiviertel* (*auf*) –, at a quarter to 12; *nun hat es aber – geschlagen,* that's really too much, that's really the limit; *die – Nächte,* see *die -ten.* 2. *f.* the number 12; a dozen. **-achteltakt,** *m.* twelve-eight time. **-eck,** *n.* dodecagon. **-eckig,** *adj.* twelve-sided, dodecagonal. **-ender,** *m.* stag of twelve points. **-er,** *m.* the figure twelve; wine of the year '12; soldier of the twelfth regiment. **-erausschuß,** *m.* committee of twelve. **-erlei,** *indec. adj. or adv.* of twelve different kinds; in twelve different ways. **-fach,** *adj.*, **-fältig,** *adj.* twelvefold. **-fingerdarm,** *m.* duodenum (*Anat.*). **-flach,** *n.* dodecahedron. **-flächig,** *adj.* dodecahedral. **-flächner,** *m., see* **-flach.** **-jährig,** *adj.* 12 years old; lasting 12 years. **-jährlich,** *adj.* every 12 years. **-malig,** *adj.* repeated 12 times. **-pfünder,** *m.* twelve-pounder (*Artil.*). **-seitig,** *adj., see* **-eckig.** **-stündig,** *adj.* lasting 12 hours; of *or* in 12 lessons. **-stündlich,** *adj.* every 12 hours. **-t,** *num. adj.* twelfth; *Karl der Zwölfte,* Charles the Twelfth; *der -te des Monats,* the 12th of the month; *die -ten,* the period between Christmas and Twelfth-night (Epiphany); *in -ter Stunde,* at the eleventh hour; *zum -ten, see* **-tens.** **-tägig,** *adj.* of 12 days, lasting 12 days. **-teilig,** *adj.* of *or* in twelve parts; duodecimal. **-tel,** *n.* (*Swiss dial., m.*) twelfth part; *sieben -tel,* seven twelfths. **-telformat,** *n.* duodecimo (*Typ.*). **-tens,** *adv.* in the twelfth place.

Zyan, *n.* cyanogen (*Chem.*). **-kali(um),** *n.* cyanide of potassium. **-metall,** *n.* metallic cyanide. **-wasserstoffsäure,** *f.* hydrocyanic *or* prussic acid.

Zyane, *f.* cornflower, bluebottle, batchelor's button (*Centaurea cyanus*) (*Bot.*).

zykl-isch, *adj.* cyclic. **-us,** *m.* (–, -len) cycle; series, course (*of lectures*).

Zyklon, *m.* (-s, -e) cyclone, tornado. **-e,** *f.* (-en) depression (*Meteor.*).

Zyklop, *m.* (-en, -en) Cyclops. **-isch,** *adj.* cyclopean, gigantic.

Zylind-er, *m.* (-s, –) cylinder, drum, roll; chimney (*of a lamp*); top-hat, silk hat. **-erbohrung,** *f.* cylinder bore (*Mech.*). **-erbüro,** *n.* roll-top desk. **-erdecke,** *f.* cylinder jacket. **-erförmig,** *adj.*, see **-risch.** **-erhemmung,** *f.* cylinder escapement (*Horol.*). **-erhut,** *m.* top-hat, silk hat. **-erinhalt,** *m.* cylinder *or* cubic capacity (*Motor.*). **-erkopf,** *m.* cylinder head (*Mech.*). **-erpresse,** *f.* roller-press, revolving-press. **-n,** *v.a., see* **-rieren.** **-erschreibtisch,** *m., see* **-büro.** **-eruhr,** *f.* lever watch. **-erzahl,** *f.* number of cylinders (*Mech.*). **-rieren,** *v.a.* calender. **-rig,** *adj. suffix, e.g.* **vier-rig,** with four cylinders (*Motor.*). **-risch,** *adj.* cylindrical.

Zyn-iker, *m.* (-s, –) cynic. **-isch,** *adj.* cynical; sneering, shameless, impudent. **-ismus,** *m.* cynicism; impudence, shamelessness.

Zyper-gras, *n.* Cyperus (*Bot.*). **-wein,** *m.* Cyprian wine.

Zypresse, *f.* (-n) cypress (*Cupressus*) (*Bot.*). **-n,** *adj.* of cypress. **-nhain,** *m.* cypress grove. **-n-Wolfsmilch,** *f.* cypress spurge (*Euphorbia cyparissias*) (*Bot.*).

Zyste, *f.* (-n) cyst (*Med.*).

INDEX OF NAMES

GEOGRAPHICAL AND PROPER NAMES

FROM this list the following classes of words have, as a rule, been omitted:

1. Those in which the German and English forms correspond exactly: e.g. *Alfred*, Alfred; *Richard*, Richard; *London*, London; *Hamburg*, Hamburg, etc.
2. Those names of countries in which the German terminations *-ien*, *-ika*, correspond to the English *-ia*, *-ica*: e.g. *Asien*, Asia; *Indien*, India; *Skandinavien*, Scandinavia; *Attika*, Attica, etc.

It should also be noticed that where the difference between the English and German forms is very slight, the names usually occur in the English–German part only. Names of rivers which are the same in both languages appear in the English–German part, where the German gender is shown.

A

Aachen, *n.* Aix-la-Chapelle.
Aargau, *m.* Argau, Argovia. **–er,** *m.* Argovian.
Abderit, *m.* Abderite; Gothamite.
Abessin–ien, *n.* Abyssinia. **–ier,** *m.* **–isch,** *adj.* Abyssinian.
Abraham, *m.* Abraham; *in –s Schoß sitzen,* be in the lap of luxury.
Abruzzen, *pl.* the Abruzzi Mountains.
Achä–er, *m.* Achaean, Greek. **–isch,** *adj.* Achaean.
Achill, *m.*, Achilles. **–esferse,** *f.* heel of Achilles.
Adalbert, *m.* Albert, Ethelbert.
Adam, *m.*, (*fig.*) *den alten – ausziehen,* mend one's ways, turn over a new leaf; *nach – Riese,* according to Cocker *or* the rules of arithmetic. **–sapfel,** *m.* Adam's apple. **–sbiß,** *m.*, *see* **–sapfel.** **–sfeige,** *f.* sycamore.
Adana, *n.* Adowa.
Adelbert, *m.*, *see* **Adalbert.**
Adele, *f.* Adela.
Adelheid, *f.* Adelaide.
Admiralitätsinseln, *pl.* (the) Admiralty Islands.
Adolf, *m.* Adolphus.
Adonai, *m.* Adonijah (*B.*).
Adria, *f.*, **Adriatisches Meer,** *n.* Adriatic (Sea).
Adrianopel, *n.* Adrianople.
Afghane, *m.* Afghan.
Afrikan–er, *m.*, **–isch,** *adj.* African.
Ägäisches Meer, *n.* Aegean Sea.
Agathe, *f.* Agatha.
Ägatische Inseln, *pl.* (the) Aegates; Egadi Islands.
Ägidius, *m.* Giles.
Ägypt–en, *n.* Egypt. **–er,** *m.*, **–isch,** *adj.* Egyptian.
Ahasver, *m.* Ahasuerus.
Akadien, *n.* Acadia.
Akka, *n.*, **Akkon,** *n.* Acre.
Aladin, *m.* Aladdin.
Alarich, *m.* Alaric.
Alb, *f.*; *die rauhe –,* the Swabian Alb.
Alban–ier, –ese, *m.*, **–isch,** *adj.* Albanian.
Albertine, *f.* Alberta.
Albigenser, *pl.* Albigensians, Albigenses.
Albrecht, *m.* Albert.
Alcide, Alcides, *m.* Hercules.
Alemann–e, *m.* Aleman. **–isch,** *adj.* Alemannic.
Alexandriner, *m.* Alexandrian; Alexandrine (verse).
Alexie, Alexia, *f.* Alice, Alison.
Alfons, *m.* Alphonso.
Al(l)gäu, *n.* Algau.
Algier, *n.* Algeria (*country*); Algiers (*town*). **–er,** *m.*, **–isch,** *adj.* Algerian.
Alkoran, *m.* Alcoran, Koran.
Alois, *m.* Aloysius.
Alpen, *pl.* (the) Alps.
alpinisch, *adj.* Alpine.
Älpler, *m.* Alpine dweller.
Alt–englisch, *adj.* Old English, Anglo-Saxon. **–griechisch,** *adj.* Ancient Greek. **–hochdeutsch,** *adj.* Old High German. **–nordisch,** *adj.* Old Norse. **–russe,** *m.*, **–russisch,** *adj.* Muscovite. **–sächsisch,** *adj.* Old Saxon, Old Low German.
Alwine, *f.* Albina.
Amalie, Amalia, *f.* Amelia.
Amazon–as, *m.* River Amazon. **–e,** Amazon **–enhaft,** *adj.* Amazonian. **–enstrom,** *m.* Amazon River.
Ambrosi–us, *m.* Ambrose. **–anisch,** *adj.* Ambrosian.
Amelie, *f.*, *see* **Amalie.**
Amerikan–er, *m.*, **–isch,** *adj.* American. **–ismus,** *m.* (-ismen), Americanism (*in language*).
Anakreont–iker, *m.* Anacreontic poet. **–isch,** *adj.* Anacreontic.
Anden, *pl.* Andes.
Andreas, (*dial.*) **Andres,** *m.* Andrew. **–kreuz,** *n.* St. Andrew's cross. **–nacht,** *f.* St. Andrew's eve. **–tag,** *m.* St. Andrew's day (*Nov. 30*).
Äne–as, *m.* Aeneas. **–ide, –is,** *f.* Aeneid.
Angel, *m.* Angle. **–sachse,** *m.*, **–sächsisch,** *adj.* Anglo-Saxon.
angl–ikanisch, *adj.* Anglican; *die –ikanische Kirche,* the Anglican Church, Church of England. **–onormanne,** *m.* Anglo-Norman. **–ophobie,** *f.* Anglophobia.
Anna, *f.* Anna, Anne, Ann.
annamitisch, *adj.* Annamese.
Ännchen, *n.* Annette, (*dim. of* **Anna**), Annie, Nancy.
Ansbach, *n.* Anspach.
Antarktis, *f.* the Antarctic. **–ch,** *adj.* antarctic, south-polar.
Antillen, *pl.* (the) Antilles; *die kleinen –,* the Leeward Islands.
antioch–enisch, *adj.* Antiochian. **–ien,** *n.* Antioch.
Anton, –ius, *m.* Anthony, Antony. **–ie,** *f.* Antonia. **–iusfeuer,** *n.* St. Anthony's fire, erysipelas.
Antwerpen, *n.* Antwerp.
Äol–us, *m.* Aeolus. **–isch,** *adj.* Aeolian. **–sharfe,** *f.* Aeolian harp.
Apennin, *m.* (-en) (the) Apennine Mountains.
apollinisch, *adj.* Apollonian (*Nietzsche's term*).
Appalachen, *pl.* (the) Appalachian Mountains.
Appische Straße, *f.* Appian Way.
apulisch, *adj.* Apulian.
Äquator, *m.* Equator.
Aquitanie–n, *n.* Aquitaine. **–r,** Aquitanian.
Arab–er, *m.* Arab. **–isch,** *adj.* Arabian (*culture, etc.*); Arab (*people*); Arabic (*language*).
Aragon–ien, *n.* Aragon. **–isch,** *adj.* Aragonese.
Aramä–a, *n.* Aram. **–er,** *m.* Aramaean. **–isch,** *adj.* Aramaic.
archimedisch, *adj.* Archimedean.
Ardenn–erwald, *m.* Forest of Ardennes. **–en,** *pl.* the Ardennes.
Areopag, *m.* Areopagus.
Argentin–ien, *n.* Argentina, the Argentine. **–(i)er,** *m.*, **–isch,** *adj.* Argentinian.
Argiv–er, *m.* (*pl.* -en), **–isch,** *adj.* Argive, (ancient) Greek.
Argonauten, *pl.* Argonauts.
Arian–er, *m.*, **–isch,** *adj.* Arian.
Ari–er, *m.*, **–sch,** *adj.* Aryan; non-Jew (*Nat. Soc.*). **–erparagraph,** *m.* clause excluding non-Aryans from public service (*Nat. Soc.*).
Ariovist, *m.* Ariovistus.

Aristotel–es, *m.* Aristotle. **–iker,** *m.* Aristotelian.
Arkadien, *n.* Arcadia.
Ärmelkanal, *m.* English Channel.
Armen–ier, *m.*, **–isch,** *adj.* Armenian.
Arminian–er, *m.*, **–isch,** *adj.* Arminian.
Armorikan–er, *m.*, **–isch,** *adj.*, Armorican.
artesisch, *adj.* Artesian.
Artur, *m.* Arthur.
Artus, *m.* **(König –),** King Arthur. **–ritter,** *m.* Knight of the Round Table. **–sage,** *f.* Arthurian legend.
Aschanti, *n.* Ashanti.
Aschen–brödel, –puttel, *n.* Cinderella.
Asiat–e, *m.*, **–isch,** *adj.* Asiatic. **Halb–e,** *m.*, **halb–isch,** *adj.* Eurasian.
Äskulap, *m.* Aesculapius.
Äsop, *m.*, Aesop. **–isch,** *adj.* Aesopian.
Asowsches Meer, *n.* Sea of Azov.
assam–esisch, *adj.*, **–it,** *m.* Assamese.
Assur, *m.* Asshur.
Assyr–(i)er, *m.*, **–isch,** *adj.* Assyrian.
Astarte, *f.* As(h)taroth.
Asturie–n, *n.* Asturias. **–r,** *m.* Asturian.
athanasianisch, *adj.* Athanasian.
Athen, *n.* Athens. **–er,** *m.*, **–isch,** *adj.* Athenian; *Eulen nach – tragen,* carry coals to Newcastle.
Äthiop–ien, *n.* Ethiopia. **–ier,** *m.* Ethiop(ian).
Atlant–ik, *m.* Atlantic. **–isch,** *adj.*; *–isches Meer,* the Atlantic (Ocean).
Ätna, *m.* Mt. Etna.
Augias, *m.* Augeas. **–stall,** *m.* Augean stable.
August, *m.* Augustus, August (*month*). **–e,** *f.* Augusta. **–eisch,** *adj.* Augustan.
Augustin–(us), *m.* Augustine, Austin. **–er,** *m.* Augustine friar. **–erkloster,** *n.* Augustine monastery.
Austral–ier, *m.*, **–isch,** *adj.* Australian.
Avaren, *pl.* (the) Avarsi.
Aventin, *m.* Mt. Aventine.
Azoren, *pl.* (the) Azores.
Azteke, *m.* Aztec.

B

Babylon–ier, *m.*, **–isch,** *adj.* Babylonian.
Bacchus, Bachus *m.* Bacchus. **–feste,** *n.pl.*, **Ba(c)chanalien,** *pl.* Bacchanalian feasts, Bacchanalia. **–stab,** *m.* thyrsus.
Baden, *n.* Baden (*the grand-duchy*). **– -Baden,** *n.* Baden (*the town*).
Baier, *m.*, *see* **Bayer.**
Bajuvar(e), *m.* (*poet.*) Bavarian; (*also coll. as term of abuse*).
Baktr–er, *m.*, **–isch,** *adj.* Bactrian. **–ien,** *n.* Bactria.
Balduin, *m.* Baldwin.
Baldur, *m.* Balder.
Balearen, *pl.* (the) Balearic Islands.
Balkan, *m.*, **–länder,** *n.pl.* the Balkans. **–staaten,** *m.pl.* Balkan States, Balkans.
Ballhausplatz, *m.* the Austrian Foreign Office at Vienna.
Balt–e, *m.* inhabitant of the Baltic provinces. **–enland,** *n.*, **–ikum,** *n.* Baltic provinces. **–isch,** *adj.*; *–isches Meer,* the Baltic. *See* **Ostsee.**
Balthasar, *m.* Balthazar.
Barbar–ei, *f.*, *see* **Berberei. –eskenstaaten,** *pl.* the Barbary States.
Bärbel, *f.*, **–chen,** *n.* (*dim. of* **Barbara**).
Barfüßer, *m.* Franciscan friar.
Barnabas, *m.* Barnaby.
Bart(h)el, *m.*, *see* **Bartholomäus**; (*coll.*) *er weiß wo – den Most holt,* he knows what's what, he knows a thing or two.
Bartholomäus, *m.* Bartholomew. **–nacht,** *f.* (Massacre of) St. Bartholomew('s Eve) (*Aug. 23–24, 1572*).
Baschkire, *m.* Bashkir. **–nland,** *n.* Bashkiria.
Basel, *n.* Basle.
Basilius, *m.* Basil.
Bask–e, *m.*, **–isch,** *adj.* Basque. **–enmütze,** *f.* beret.
Batav(i)er, *m.* Batavian.
Bathseba, *f.* Bathsheba.
Bay–er, *m.*, **–(e)risch,** *adj.* Bavarian. **–ern,** *n.* Bavaria.
Beate, *f.* (*dim. of* **Beatrix.**)
Beatrix, *f.* Beatrice.
Beda, *m.* (the Venerable) Bede.
Beduin–e, *m.*, **–isch,** *adj.* Bedouin.
Beg(h)ine, *f.* Beguine (*member of a female order in Holland and Germany*).
Beirut, *n.* Beyrout.
Belg–ien, *n.* Belgium. **–(i)er,** *m.*, **–isch,** *adj.* Belgian.
Belgrad, *n.* Belgrade.
Belisar, *m.* Belisarius.
Belle-Alliance; *Schlacht bei –,* Battle of Waterloo.
Belsazar, *m.* Belshazzar.
Belutschistan, *n.* Baluchistan.
Benedikt, *m.* Benedict, Benedick, Bennet. **–iner,** *m.* Benedictine friar; Benedictine (*liqueur*).
Bengal–e, *m.* Bengali, Bengalese. **–en,** *n.* Bengal. **–isch,** *adj.* Bengal(ese), Bengali.
Berber–ei, *f.* Barbary. **–isch,** *adj.* Berber. **–pferd,** *n.* Barbary horse.
Bergschotte, *m.* (Scottish) Highlander.
Bering(s)–meer, *n.* Bering Sea. **–straße,** *f.* Bering Strait.
Berliner, *m.* inhabitant of Berlin. **–blau,** *n.* Prussian blue.
Bern, *n.* Berne; (*Poet.*) Verona; *Dietrich von –,* Theodoric of Verona. **–er,** *m.*, **–(er)isch,** *adj.* Bernese; *–er Oberland,* Bernese Alps.
Bernhard, *m.* Bernard. **–iner(hund),** *m.* St. Bernard dog. **–iner(mönch),** *m.* Bernadine (monk).
Bersaba, *n.* Beersheba.
Berthel, *see* **Bar(th)el.**
Bethania, *n.* Bethany.
Betschuanaland, *n.* Bechuanaland.
Bileam, *m.* Balaam.
Birma, *n.* Burma. **–ne,** *m.*, **–nisch,** *adj.* Burman, Burmese.
Biskayischer Meerbusen, Bay of Biscay.
Blanka, *f.* Blanche.
Blasius, *m.* Blaise.
Blaubart, *m.* Bluebeard.
Blindheim, *n.* Blenheim.
Blocksberg, *m.* the Brocken.
Bodensee, *m.* Lake of Constance.
Boheme, *f.* (*fig.*) Bohemia (*of artists, etc.*).
Böhm–en, *n.* Bohemia. **–erbrüder,** *m.pl.*, or *–ische Brüder,* Moravian Brethren. **–erwald,** *m.* Bohemian Forest. **–isch,** *adj.* Bohemian; (*coll.*) *das sind ihm –ische Dörfer,* that's all Greek to him; *–isch-mährische Höhe,* Bohemian chain (*Geog.*).
Bojar, *m.* Boyard.
Bolognes–er, *m.*, **–isch,** *adj.* of Bologna, Bolognese, Bononian.
Bolschew–ismus, *m.* Bolshevism. **–ist,** *m.*, **–istisch,** *adj.* Bolshevik, Bolshevist.
Bonifa–tius, –z, *m.* Boniface.
Böot–ien, *n.* Boeotia. **–isch,** *adj.* Boeotian.
Bord–eaux, *m.* claret. **–elese,** *m.* inhabitant of Bordeaux.
Bosn–iake, *m.*, **–ier,** *m.*, **–isch,** *adj.* Bosnian.
Bosporus, *m.* Bosphorus.
bott–nisch, *adj.* Bothnian; *–nischer Meerbusen,* Gulf of Bothnia. **–en,** *n.* Bothnia.
Brahm–ane, –ine, *m.*, **–anisch, –inisch,** *adj.* Brahmin. **–a(n)ismus,** *m.* Brahminism.
Brasil–ien, *n.* Brazil. **–ianer,** *m.*, **–ianisch,** *adj.*, **–ier,** *m.*, **–isch,** *adj.* Brazilian.
Braun, *m.* Bruin (*the Bear in the Beast Epic*).
Braunschweig, *n.* Brunswick.
Brem–er, *m. & adj.*, **–isch,** *adj.* of Bremen.
Bret–agne, *f.* Brittany. **–agner,** *m.*, **–one,** *m.*, **–onisch,** *adj.* Breton.
Brigitt–a, –e, *f.* Bridget.
Brit–annien, *n.* Britain; Britannia. **–annisch, –isch,** *adj.* British; Britannic; Brythonic. **–e,** *m.* Briton.
Brügge, *n.* Bruges.
Brüssel, *n.* Brussels; *–er Kohl,* Brussels sprouts; *–er Spitzen,* Brussels lace.
Buchar–ei, *f.* Bokhara (*district*). **–a,** *n.* Bokhara (*town*).

buddhistisch, *adj.* Buddhist.
Bukarest, *n.* Bucharest.
Bulgar-e, *m.*, **-isch,** *adj.* Bulgarian. **-ien,** *n.* Bulgaria.
Buren, *pl.* Boers. **-krieg,** *m.* Boer War.
Burgund, *n.* Burgundy. **-er,** *m.* Burgundian; Burgundian wine, Burgundy. **-isch,** *adj.* Burgundian.
Buschmänner, *pl.* Bushmen.
Byzan-z, *n.* Byzantium, Constantinople. **-tiner,** *m.*, **-tinisch,** *adj.* Byzantine.

C

See also under **K, Z**

Cäcilie, *f.* Cecilia, Cicely.
Calais, *n.*; *Straße von –*, Straits of Dover.
Capuletti, *pl.* the Capulets.
Cäsar, *m.* Caesar. **-isch,** *adj.* Caesarean.
Cevennen, *pl.* Cevennes Mountains.
Chaldä-a, *n.* Chaldaea. **-er,** *m.*, **-isch,** *adj.* Chaldee, Chaldaean.
Champagne, *f.* Champagne (*province*). **-r,** *m.* Champagne (*wine*).
Charybde, *f.* Charybdis.
Chersones, *m.* the Chersonese (peninsula).
Chilen-e, *m.*, **-isch,** *adj.* Chilian.
Chin-a, *n.* China. **-ese,** *m.* Chinaman, Chinese. **-esisch,** *adj.* Chinese.
Chlodwig, *m.* Clovis.
Christ, *m.* Christian. **-lich,** *adj.* Christian. **-us,** (*Acc.* -um; *Gen.* -i; *Dat.* -o; *or all cases in* -us) *m.* Christ; *vor* (*nach*) *–i Geburt*, before (after) Christ (*B.C., A.D.*) *see list of abbreviations*; *–i Himmelfahrt*, the Ascension; Ascension Day. **-baum,** *m.* Christmas-tree. **-kind,** *n.* baby Jesus. **-mond,** *m.* December. **-woche,** *f.* Christmas week.
Christel, *f.* (*dim. of* **Christiane**) Chrissie.
Christiane, *f.* Christiana.
Christoph, *m.* Christopher.
ciceroni(ani)sch, *adj.* Ciceronian.
Comer See, *m.* Lake Como.

D

Dahome, *n.* Dahomey.
Dalmat-iner, *m.*, **-inisch,** *adj.*, **-isch,** *adj.* Dalmatian.
Damaszen-er, 1. *m.* inhabitant of Damascus. 2. *adj.*, **-isch,** *adj.* Damascene, damask.
Danaer, *pl.* Danai, primitive Greeks. **-geschenk,** *n.* double-edged gift.
Dän-e, *m.* Dane. **-isch,** *adj.* Danish. **-emark,** *n.* Denmark. **-ensteuer,** *f.* Danegeld.
Danzig, *n.* Dantzig.
Dardanellen(straße), *f.* (Straits of) the Dardanelles.
Darwinsche Lehre, Darwinian Theory.
Däumling, *m.*; *der kleine –*, Tom Thumb.
Dazien, *n.* Dacia.
Delfter Geschirr, *n.* Delft (*or* Dutch) ware.
Delila, *f.* Delilah.
delphisch, *adj.* Delphic; *–e Weisheit*, Delphic oracle.
Derwisch, Dervish.
deutsch, *adj.* German; *die –e Bucht*, the Bay of Heligoland; *der –e Bund*, the Germanic Confederation (1815–66); *der Nord–e Bund*, the North-German Confederation (1866–71); *der –e Gruß*, Hitler salute; *der –e Michel*, see *Michel*; *das heilige römische Reich –er Nation*, the Holy Roman Empire (962–1806); *der –e Orden*, the Teutonic Order (*established* 1198); *groß–*, pan-German; *klein–*, 'little'-German (*the policy opposing pan-German, and excluding Austria*); *Nieder–*, Low German, North German; *Ober–*, Upper German, South German; *Platt–*, Low German; *kann er –?* does he know German? *auf –*, in German; *– reden*, speak plainly *or* candidly; *das heißt auf* (*gut*) *–*, that is, to put it plainly, *or* in plain English; *er spricht ein schlechtes –*, he speaks bad German; *aus dem –en übersetzen*, translate from German. **-e,** *f.* German woman. **-e(r),** *m.* German. **-freundlich,** *adj.* Germanophile. **-heit,** German character *or* nationality. **-herr,** *m.*, **-ritter,** *m.* Knight of the Teutonic Order. **-kunde,** *f.* study of German life and customs. **-land,** *n.* Germany. **-landlied,** *n.* German national anthem (*Deutschland, Deutschland über alles*). **Hoch- und -meister,** *m.* Grand Master of the Teutonic Order. **-ordensland,** *n.* territories colonized by the Teutonic Order, East Prussia. **-schweizer,** *m.* German(-speaking) Swiss. **-tum,** German nationality. **-tümelei,** *f.* Germanomania; exaggerated emphasis on German ways and customs.
Dietrich, *m.* Theodoric, Derrick; *– von Bern*, Theodoric (the Great) of Verona.
Dionys, Dionysius, *m.* Dionysius; Dennis, Denis.
Dioskuren, *pl.* (the) Dioscuri (Castor and Pollux), Gemini (*Astr.*).
Dnjepr, *m.* River Dnieper.
Dnjestr, *m.* River Dniester.
Dolomiten, *pl.* Dolomites.
Dominik-us, (*der heilige –us*) *m.* Saint Dominic. **-aner,** *m.* Dominican, Black friar.
Don Quichotte, Don Quijote, *m.* Don Quixote. **Quichotterie,** *f.* quixotic behaviour.
Donau, *f.* Danube. **-monarchie,** *f.* Austria-Hungary.
Dor-chen, *n*, **-ette,** *f.*, **-is,** *f.*, (*dial.*) **-teken,** *n.* (*dim. of* **Dorothea**), Doris, Dorrit, Dora, Doll(y), Dot.
dorisch, *adj.* Dorian, Doric; *–e Tonart*, Dorian mode; *–er Stil*, Doric style (*Arch.*).
Dornröschen, *n.* Sleeping Beauty.
Dorothea, *f.* Dorothea, Dorothy.
Drau, *f.* River Drave.
Druid-e, *m.*, Druid. **-entum,** *n.* Druidism. **-isch,** *adj.* Druidical.
Duero, *m.* River Douro.
Dummerjan, Dummrian, *m.* Simple Simon.
Düna, *f.* (Southern) River Dwina.
Dünkirchen, *n.* Dunkirk.
Dwina, *f.* (Northern) River Dwina.

E

Eberhard, *m.* Everard.
Ebräer, *m.*, *see* **Hebräer.**
Eduard, *m.* Edward.
Eismeer, *n.* Polar Sea; *Nördliches –*, Arctic Ocean; *Südliches –*, Antarctic Ocean.
Eleonore, *f.* Eleanor.
eleusinisch, *adj.* Eleusinian.
Elia(s), *m.* (*B.*) Elias, Elijah.
Elisa, *m.* (*B.*) Elisha.
Elisabeth, *f.* Elizabeth.
Elise, *f.* Eliza, Elsa, Elsie.
Elsaß, *n.* Alsace. **–-Lothringen,** *n.* Alsace-Lorraine. **Elsäss-er,** *m.* **-isch,** *adj.* Alsatian.
Elsbeth, *f.* (*dim. of* **Elisabeth**), Elsie, Lizzie.
elys-äisch, *adj.*, **-isch,** *adj.* Elysian.
Emanuel, *m.* Emmanuel.
Emil, *m.* Emile. **-ia, -ie,** *f.* Emily.
Enak, *m.* Anak.
Engländer, *m.* Englishman. **-ei,** *f.* Anglomania. **-freundlich,** *adj.* Anglophile. **-scheu,** *f.* Anglophobia.
englisch, *adj.* English; *–e Krankheit*, rickets; *–es Pflaster*, court-plaster; *–(es) Salz*, Epsom salts.
Ephes-er, *m.*, **-isch,** *adj.* Ephesian; *der –erbrief*, Epistle to the Ephesians.
Epikur, *m.* Epicurus. **-äer,** *m.* Epicure(an). **-(ä)isch,** *adj.* Epicurean.
Erich, *m.* Eric.
Erinnyen, *f.pl.* Furies, Erinnys.
Erlkönig, *m.* the Elf-king.

Ermelind, *f.* Vixen, wife of Reynard the Fox.
Ernst, *m.* Ernest.
ersisch, *adj.* Erse.
Erzjude, *m.* Hebrew Jew.
Esaias, *m.* Isaiah.
Esra, *m.* Ezra.
Est–e, *m.*, **–länder,** *m.*, **–ländisch,** *adj.*, **–nisch,** *adj.* Est(h)onian. **–land,** *n.* Est(h)onia.
Esther, *f.* Esther, Hester.
Etrusk–er, *m.*, **–isch,** *adj.* Etruscan, Etrurian.
Etsch, *f.* River Adige.
Etzel, *m.* Attila.
Eugen, *m.* Eugene. **–ie,** *f.* Eugenia.
Euklid(es), *m.* Euclid.
Eulenspiegel, *m.* Owlglass, Howleglass. **–ei,** practical joke, tomfoolery.
Euphrat, *m.* River Euphrates.
Europ–a, *n.* Europe. **–äer,** *m.*, **–äisch,** *adj.* European. **Halb–äer,** *m.*, **halb–äisch,** *adj.* Eurasian.
Eusta–chius, –sius, *m.* Eustace.
Ev–a, –e, *f.* Eva, Eve. **–askind,** *n.* human being, mortal. **–askostüm,** *n.* nakedness, nudity, birthday suit. **–astochter,** *f.* daughter of Eve, woman.
Evchen, *n.* (*dim. of* Eva), Evelyn, Evy.
Ezechiel, *m.* Ezekiel.

F

Fabier, *pl.* the Fabians, Fabii.
Färinger, *m.*, *see* **Färöer.**
Färöer, Faroese, *m.*; – *Inseln, f.pl.* Faroe Islands.
Fasch–ismus, *m.* Fascism. **–ist,** *m.*, **–istisch,** *adj.* Fascist.
Faust, *m.* Faustus.
Fellachen, *pl.* Fellaheen.
Felsengebirge, *n.* Rocky Mountains.
Fen–ier, *m.*, **–isch,** *adj.* Fenian. **–iertum,** *n.* Fenian movement, Fenianism.
Fernambuk, *see* **Pernambuko. –holz,** *n.* Brazil wood.
Feuer–land, *n.* Tierra del Fuego. **–länder,** *m.*, **–ländisch,** *adj.* Fuegian, Patagonian.
Fidschi-Inseln, *pl.* Fiji Islands.
Finn–e, *m.* Finn; *–ischer Meerbusen,* Gulf of Finland. **–land,** *n.* Finland. **–länder,** Finlander.
Flam–e, *m.*, **–länder,** *m.* Fleming. **–ländisch,** *adj.* Flemish.
Fläm–in, *f.* Flemish woman. **–isch,** *adj.* Flemish.
Florentin–e, *f.* Florence (*girl's name*). **–er,** *m.*, **–isch,** *adj.* Florentine.
Florenz, *n.* Florence (*town*).
Fortunat, *m.* Fortunatus.
Frank–e, *m.* Frank, Franconian. **–en(land),** *n.* Franconia. **–enreich,** *n.* the Frankish kingdom. **–reich,** *n.* France; (*coll.*) *wie der Herrgott in –reich leben,* live like a fighting cock.
Frankfurt, *n.* Frankfurt; – **a/M** *or* **a/O,** Frankfurt on the Main *or* on the Oder.
fränkisch, *adj.* Frankish, Franconian.
Franz, *m.* Francis, Frank; – *von Assisi,* St. Francis of Assisi. **–band,** *m.* calf-binding; calf-bound book. **–iska,** *f.* Frances. **–iskaner,** *m.* Franciscan friar.
Fränzchen, *n.* (*dim. of* **Franz** *and* **Franziska**) Frank, Fanny, Frankie.
Franz–ose, *m.* (-osen, -osen) Frenchman. **–öseln,** *v.n.* (*aux.* h.) ape the French. **–ösieren,** *v.a.* Frenchify. **–ösin,** *f.* Frenchwoman. **–ösisch,** *adj.* French. **–osenfreundlich,** *adj.* Francophile, Gallophile. **–osenhaß,** *m.* Gallophobia. **–osensucht,** *f.* Gallomania.
Freundschafts-Inseln, *f.pl.* Friendly Islands.
Friaul, *n.* Friuli.
Frida, *f.* (*dim. of* **Friederike**) Freda.
Fried–el, *m.* (*dim. of* **Gottfried**) Geoff, Jeff.
Friederike, *f.* Frederica, Freda.
Friedrich, *m.* Frederic, Frederick.
Fries–e, *m.*, **–isch,** *adj.*, **–länder,** *m.*, **–ländisch,** *adj.* Frisian.
Fritz, *m.*, (*dim. of* **Friedrich**) Freddy, Fred; (*coll.*) *der alte–,* Frederick the Great.
Fünen, *n.* Fyen.

G

Galater, *pl.* (the) Galatians.
Gäl–e, *m.* Gael. **–isch,** *adj.* Gaelic.
Galilä–a, *n.* Galilee. **–er,** *m.*, **–isch,** *adj.* Galilean.
Galizien, *n.* Galicia (*in Spain & Poland*).
Gallen, St., *n.* St. Gall (*Swiss town and canton*).
Gall–ien, *n.* Gaul (*territory*). **–ier,** *m.* Gaul (*inhabitant*). **–ikanisch,** *adj.* French Catholic. **–isch,** *adj.* Gallic, Gaulish. **–izismus,** *m.* Gallicism.
Gallus, *m.*; *der heilige* –, St. Gall (*saint*).
Ganymed, *m.* Ganymede.
Gaskogn–e, *f.* Gascony. **–er,** *m.* Gascon; (*fig.*) braggart.
Gdingen, *n.* Gdynia.
Geldern, *n.* G(u)eldern (*the town*); G(u)elderland (*the district*).
Generalstaaten, *m.pl.* States General (*of Holland*).
Genf, *n.* Geneva. **–er,** *m.*, **–erisch,** *adj.* Genevese; *–er See,* Lake of Geneva.
Genoveva, *f.* Genevieve.
Gent, *n.* Ghent.
Genu–a, *n.* Genoa. **–ese(r),** *m.*, **–esisch,** *adj.* Genoese.
Georg, *m.* George. **–ia,** *n.* Georgia (*U.S.A.*). **–ien,** *n.* Georgia (*U.S.S.R.*). **–ier,** *m.*, **–isch,** *adj.* Georgian (*U.S.S.R.*).
Georgine, *f.* Georgina, Georgiana.
Gerhard, *m.* Gerard, Gerald.
German–e, *m.* Teuton. **–entum,** *n.* Teutonism. **–isch,** *adj.* Germanic, Teutonic. **–ismus,** *m.* Germanism (*style*). **–ist,** *m.* student of Germanic philology *or* literature. **–istik,** *f.* study of German philology, literature, etc.
Gerold, *m.* Gerald.
Gertrud(e), *f.* Gertrude.
Geusen, *pl.* the Gueux.
Glarner, *pl.* inhabitants of Glarus.
Golfstrom, *m.* the Gulf Stream.
gordisch, *adj.* Gordian.
Gorgon(e), *f.* Gorgon.
Gosen, *n.*; (*B.*) *das Land* –, the land of Goshen.
Got–e, *m.* Goth. **–ik,** *f.* Gothic style; Gothic architecture. **–isch,** *adj.* Gothic; *–ische Schrift,* Gothic *or* black-letter type.
Gottfried, *m.* Godfrey, Geoffrey.
Gotthard, *m.* Goddard; *St.* –, St. Gothard.
Gott–hold, *m.*, **–lieb,** *m.* Theophilus.
Götz, *m.* (*dim. of* **Gottfried**).
Grachen, *pl.* (the) Gracchi.
Gral, *m.* (the) Sangreal, Holy Grail.
Graubünd–en, *n.* the Grisons. **–ner,** *m.* inhabitant of the Grisons. **–nerisch,** *adj.* Grison.
Gravelingen, *n.* Gravelines.
Grazien, *f. pl.* Graces.
Gregor, *m.*, **–ius,** *m.* Gregor, Gregory. **–ianisch,** *adj.* Gregorian.
Gret–e, *f.*, **–el,** *n.*, **–chen,** *n.* Madge, Margery, Meg, Peggy.
Griech–e, *m.* Greek. **–enland,** *n.* Greece. **–entum,** *n.* Hellenism. **–isch,** *adj.* Greek, Grecian, Hellenic. **–isch-katholisch,** *adj.* Greek Orthodox.
Griseldis, *f.* Griselda.
Grönland, *n.* Greenland. **–fahrer,** *m.* whaler.
Groß–britannien, *n.* Great Britain. **–deutschland,** *n.* Greater Germany.
Großer Ozean, *m.* Pacific (Ocean).
Grünes Vorgebirge, *n.* Cape Verde.
Guido, *m.* Guy.
Günther, *m.* Gunther.
Gust–av, *m.* Gustavus, Guy. **–ave,** *f.* Gustava, Augusta.

H

(Den) Haag, *m.* The Hague; *im Haag,* at The Hague.
Habakuk, *m.* Habakkuk.
Habichtsinseln, *f.pl.* the Azores.
Habsburg, *n.* Hapsburg. **–er,** *m.* a member of the Hapsburg family; *die –er,* the Hapsburg dynasty.

Hadrian, *m.* Hadrian, Adrian.
Hallenser, *m.* native of Halle.
Hameln, *n.* Hamelin; *der Rattenfänger von –*, the Pied Piper of Hamelin.
Hann–chen, *n.*, **–e,** *f.*, **–ele,** *n.* (*dim. of* **Johanna**) Hannah, Jane, Jenny.
Hannover, *n.* Hanover. **–aner,** *m.*, **–sch, hannöversch,** *adj.* Hanoverian.
Hans, *m.* (*pl.* Hansen, Hänse) Jack, Johnnie; (*coll.*) *der blanke –*, the North Sea; (*Prov.*) *– bleibt –*, you cannot make a silk purse from a sow's ear; *die großen –en*, the big-wigs; *– Guckindieluft*, Johnnie Head-in-the-air; *oder ich will – heißen*, or I am a Dutchman; *– Huckebein, – in allen Gassen*, Nosey Parker, Jack of all trades, busybody, Paul Pry; *– im Glück*, lucky dog *or* devil; *– Liederlich*, libertine, scapegrace; *– Sachte*, slowcoach; (*Prov.*) *was Hänschen nicht lernt, lernt – nimmermehr*, you can't teach an old dog new tricks. **–dampf,** *m.* blusterer, bombastic fellow, windbag. **–narr,** *m.*, **–wurst,** *m.* merry-andrew, clown.
Hanse, *f.*, **–bund,** *m.* Hansa, Hanseatic League. **–(at)isch,** *adj.* Hanseatic. **–stadt,** *f.* Hanseatic town.
Hansel, Hänsel, *m* **Hänschen,** *n.* Jack, Johnnie.
Havanna, *f.* Havana.
Hebrä–er, *m.* Hebrew. **–isch,** *adj.* Hebrew, Hebraic.
Hebriden, *pl.* (the) Hebrides.
Hedschas, *n.* Hedjaz.
Hedschra, *f.* Hegira, Hejira.
Hegelianer, *m.* Hegelian.
Heiduck, *m.* (-en, -en) Hungarian foot-soldier; Hungarian manservant.
Hein, *m.*; (*coll.*) *Freund –*, Death.
Hein–i, *m.*, **–z,** *m.* (*dim. of* **Heinrich**) Harry, Hal.
Heinrich, *m.* Henry.
Helena, *f.*, **Helene,** *f.* Helen.
Helgoland, *n.* Heligoland.
Hellen–e, *m.* Hellene, Greek. **–isch,** *adj.* Hellenic.
Helsingör, *n.* Elsinore.
Helvet–ier, *m.* Swiss; (*pl.*) Helvetii. **–isch,** *adj.* Helvetian, Swiss.
Hennegau, *m.* Hainault.
Henning, *m.* Chanticleer (*the Cock in the Beast Epic*).
Henoch, *m.* Enoch.
Henriette, *f.* Henrietta, Harriet.
Herakles, *m.* Hercules.
Heraklit, *m.* Heraclitus.
herkulisch, *adj.* Herculean.
Herman(n), *m.* Hermann; Arminius. **–sschlacht,** *f.* battle of the Teutoburg Forest.
Hermandad, *f.* fraternity; *die heilige –*, the police.
Hermine, *f.* Hermione.
Herodes, *m.* Herod.
Herrnhuter, *m.pl.* Moravian brethren.
Herzegowina, *f.* Herzegovina.
Hesekiel, *m.*, *see* **Ezechiel.**
Hess–e, *m.* Hessian; (*coll.*) *blinder –e*, person as blind as a bat; stupid fellow. **–en,** *n.* Hesse. **–isch,** *adj.* Hessian.
Hieronymus, *m.* Jerome.
Hilarius, *m.* Hilary.
Hilde, *f.*, **–gard,** *f.* Hilda.
Hindostan, *n.* Hindustan.
Hinter–indien, *n.* Further India, Indo-China. **–pommern,** *n.* Further Pomerania. **–rhein,** *m.* Upper Rhine.
Hinz, *m.* (*dim. of* **Heinrich**) Hal; *– und Kunz*, Tom, Dick, and Harry.
Hiob, *m.* Job. **–sbote,** *m.* bringer of bad news. **–spost,** *f.* bad news.
Hiskia(s), *m.* (*B.*) Hezekiah.
Hochheimer, *m.* hock (*Rhine wine*).
Hohe Pforte, *f.*, *see* **Pforte.**
Holländ–er, *m.*, **–erin,** *f.* Dutchman, Dutchwoman; (*pl.*) the Dutch. **–erei,** *f.* Dutch farm, dairy farm. **–isch,** *adj.* Dutch.
Horaz, *m.* Horace. **–isch,** Horatian.
Hospitaliter, *m.* Knight of St. John, Hospitaller (of St. John).
Hottentott–(e), *m.*, **–isch,** *adj.* Hottentot.
Hugenott–e, *m.*, **–isch,** *adj.* Huguenot.
Hugo, *m.* Hugh.
Hunne, *m.* Hun. **–nschlacht,** *f.* battle of the Catalaunian fields (451 A.D.).
Hunsrück, *m.* Hundsruck.
Huronensee, *m.* Lake Huron.
Hussit, *m.* Hussite.

I

Iberer, *m.* Iberian.
Ignaz, *m.* Ignatius.
Iliade, *f.*, **Ilias,** *f.* the Iliad.
Illyr–ier, *m.*, **–isch,** *adj.* Illyrian.
Ilse, *f.* Elsie, Lizzie.
Immanuel, *m.*, *see* **Emanuel.**
Ind–er, *m.* Indian, Hindu. **–ianer,** *m.*, **–ianisch,** *adj.* American Indian, Red Indian. **–ien,** *n.* India; the Indies. **–ienfahrer,** *m.* East-Indiaman (*ship*). **–ier,** *m.* (East) Indian. **–isch,** *adj.* (East) Indian. *–ische Kompanie*, East India Company.
Innozenz, *m.* Innocent.
ionisch, *adj.* Ionian, Ionic; *–es Meer*, Ionian Sea.
Iphigenie, *f.* Iphigenia.
Irak, *m.* Iraq. **–er,** *m.*, **–isch,** *adj.* Iraqi, Iraki.
Ir–e, –länder, *m.* Irishman. **–in,** *f.*, **–länderin,** *f.* Irishwoman. **–isch,** *adj.*, **–ländisch,** *adj.* Irish; Erse (*language*). **–land,** *n.* Ireland, Eire.
Irokese, *m.* Iroquois.
Isaak, *m.* Isaac.
Isabella, *f.* Isabel, Isobel.
Ischarioth, *m.* Iscariot.
Isebel, *f.* Jezebel.
Isegrim, *m.* Isengrim (*the Wolf in the Beast Epic*).
Is–land, *n.* Iceland. **–länder,** *m.* Icelander. **–ländisch,** *adj.* Icelandic.
Ismael, *m.* Ishmael. **–it,** *m.* Ishmaelite.
Israelit, *m.*, **–isch,** *adj.* Israelite.
Itali–en, *n.* Italy. **–ener,** *m.*, **–enisch,** *adj.* Italian. **–sch,** *adj.* Italic.
Itzig, *m.* (*pej.*) Jew.

J

Jakob, *m.* James, Jacob; (*coll.*) *das ist der wahre –*, that is the real McCoy! **–ine,** *f.* Jacqueline, Jemima. **–iner,** *m.* Jacobin (*Hist.*). **–it,** *m.* Jacobite. **-(it)isch,** *adj.* Jacobean, Jacobite. **–sleiter,** *f.* Jacob's ladder. **–sstab,** *m.* quadrant (*Naut.*). **–sstraße,** *f.* Milky Way. **–us,** *m.* (*B.*) Jacob.
Jakute, *m.* Yakut.
Jan, *m.*, *see* **Johann.**
Jangtsekiang, *m.* Yangtse-Kiang.
Japan–er, *m.*, **–isch,** *adj.* Japanese.
Javan–er, *m.*, **–isch,** *adj.* Javanese.
Jehova, *m.* Jehovah.
Jemen, *n.* Yemen.
Jenenser, *m.* inhabitant of Jena.
Jenissej, *m.* Yenisei River.
Jeremias, *m.* Jeremiah, Jeremy.
Jerez(wein), *m.* sherry.
Jerobeam, *m.* Jeroboam.
Jesaia(s), *m.* Isaiah.
Jett–chen, *n.*, **–e,** *f.* (*dim. of* **Henriette**) Hetty.
Jiddisch, *n.* & *adj.* Yiddish.
Jodok, –us, *m.* Jocelyn.
Johann, *m.* John.
Johanna, *f.* Johanna, Joan; *die Päpstin –*, Pope Joan.
Johann–es, *m.* John; *der heilige –es*, St. John; *–es der Täufer*, John the Baptist. **–isbeere,** *f.* currant. **–isbrot,** *n.* carob-bean, locust bean. **–isfeuer,** *n.* St. John's fire. **–iskäfer,** *m.*, **–iswurm,** *m.* glow-worm. **–iskraut,** *n.* St. John's wort. **–istag,** *m.* Midsummer Day. **–istrieb,** *m.* second bloom. **–iter,** *m.* (-iters, -iter) Knight of St. John of Jerusalem; knight hospitaller. **–iterorden,** *m.* Order of the Knights of St. John.
Jona, *m.*, (*B.*) Jonah.
Jörg, *m.* (*dim. of* **Georg**) Georgie.
Jörn, *m.*, *see* **Jürgen.**
Josaphat, *m.* Jehoshaphat.

Jose–f, –ph, *m.* Joseph. **–fa, –pha, –phine,** *f.* Josephine.
Josias, *m.* Josiah.
Jost, *m.* Jocelyn.
Josua, *m.* Joshua.
Juda, *m.* Judah. **–ismus,** *m.* Judaism.
Judäa, *n.* Judea, Judaea.
Jude, *m.* Jew; *Erz–,* Hebrew Jew; *der ewige –,* the Wandering Jew; (*coll.*) *haust du meinen –n, hau ich deinen –n,* tit for tat. **–n,** *v.n.,* **jüdeln,** *v.n.* speak *or* act like a Jew. **–nbart,** *m.* Wandering Jew, saxifrage (*Bot.*). **–nchrist,** *m.* Christian Jew. **–ndeutsch,** *adj.* & *n.* Yiddish. **–ngasse,** *f.* ghetto. **–nhetze,** *f.* Jew-baiting. **–nkirsche,** *f.* winter-cherry. **–ntum,** *n.* Jewry, Judaism.
Jüd–in, *f.* Jewess. **–isch,** *adj.* Jewish.
Jugoslaw–e, *m.* Yugoslav. **–ien,** *n.* Yugoslavia.
Jul–chen, *n.* (*dim. of* **–ia(ne)**), Julie, Jill, Jenny. **–ia(ne),** *f.* Julia(na).
Julische Alpen, *pl.* Julian Alps.
junonisch, *adj.* Juno-like.
Jürg(en), *m.* Georg(i)e.
Jüt–e, *m.,* **–länder,** *m.* Jutlander. **–land,** *n.* Jutland.
Jutt–a, –e, (*dim. of* **Johanna**) Janet, Joan.

K

Kadmus, *m.* Cadmus.
Kaffer, *m.* Kaffir.
Kain, *m.* Cain. **–szeichen,** *n.* mark of Cain.
Kaiphas, *m.* Caiaphas.
Kalabres–e, *m.,* **–isch,** *adj., see* **Kalabr–ier, –isch.** **–er,** *m.* broad-brimmed hat, slouched hat.
Kalabr–ien, *n.* Calabria. **–ier,** *m.,* **–isch,** *adj.* Calabrian.
kaledonisch, *adj.* Caledonian.
Kalif, *m.* Caliph. **–at,** *n.* Caliphate.
Kaliforn–ien, *n.* California. **–ier,** *m.,* **–isch,** *adj.* Californian.
Kalliope, *f.* Calliope.
Kalmücken, *f. pl.* Kalmucks.
Kalvarienberg, *m.* Mount Calvary.
Kalvin, *m.* Calvin. **–ismus,** *m.* Calvinism. **–ist,** *m.* Calvinist. **–(ist)isch,** *adj.* Calvinist(ic).
Kamerun, *n.* the Cameroons.
Kamtschadal–e, *m.,* **–in,** *f.* inhabitants of Kamchatka.
Kana, *n.*; *Simon von –,* Simon the Canaanite.
Kan–aan, *n.* Canaan. **–aaniter,** *m.,* **–aanitisch,** *adj.,* **–(a)anäisch,** *adj.* Canaanite.
Kanad–a, *n.* Canada. **–ier,** *m.,* **–isch,** *adj.* Canadian.
Kanal, *m.* the English Channel. **–inseln,** *pl.* Channel Islands.
Kanar–ienvogel, *m.* canary (*bird*). **–isch,** *adj.*; *die –ischen Inseln,* the Canary Islands.
Kap–kolonie, *f.,* **–land,** *n.* Cape Colony, Cape Province. **–stadt,** *f.* Cape Town. **–verdische Inseln,** Cape Verde Islands. **–wein,** *m.* South African wine.
Kapetinger, *pl.* Capetians.
Kar(a)ib–e, *m.* Carib. **–isch,** *adj.* Caribbean.
Karl, *m.* Charles; *– der Große,* Charlemagne. **–mann,** *m.* Carloman.
Karmeliter, *m.* Carmelite, White friar. **–in,** *f.* Carmelite nun.
Kärnt–en, *n.* Carinthia. **–isch,** *adj.,* **–ner,** *m.,* **–nerisch,** *adj.* Carinthian.
Karoline, *f.* Caroline. **–n,** *pl.* Caroline Islands.
Karoling–er, *m.,* **–isch,** *adj.* Carolingian, Carlovingian.
Karpat(h)en, *pl.* Carpathian Mountains.
Kart–ause, *f.* (-en) Carthusian friar. **–äuserlikör,** *m.* Chartreuse.
Karthag–o, *n.* Carthage. **–er,** *m.,* **–isch,** *adj.* Carthaginian.
Kaschmir, *n.* Cashmere.
Kasp–ar, *m.,* **–er,** *n.* Jasper. **–erletheater,** *n.* Punch and Judy show.
Kaspi–sches Meer, *n.,* **–see,** *m.* Caspian Sea.
Kassel, *n.* Cassel.
Kastil–ien, *n.* Castile. **–ier,** *m.,* **–isch,** *adj.* Castilian.
Katalaunisch, *adj., die –en Felder,* the Catalaunian fields (*battle* 451 A.D.).
Katalon–ien, *n.* Catalonia. **–ier,** *m.,* **–isch,** *adj.* Catalan.
Kät–chen, *n.,* **–e,** *f.* (*dim. of* **Katharine**) Cathie, Katie, Cathleen, Kitty.
Käte, *f.* Kate, Kitty.
Kath–arina, –arine, *f.* Katharine, Katherine, Catharine, Catherine. **–rine,** *f.* (*dim. of* **–arine**) Cathie, Katie, Cathleen.
Kaukas–ien, *n.* Caucasus. **–ier,** *m.,* **–isch,** *adj.* Caucasian.
Kelt–e, *m.* Celt, Kelt. **–isch,** *adj.* Celtic, Keltic.
Kiew, *n.* Kiev.
Kimbern, *see* **Zimbern.**
Kirgis–e, *m.,* **–isch,** *adj.* Kirghiz.
Klara, *f.* Clara.
Kla(u)s, *m.* (*abbr. of* **Nikola(u)s**) Nick.
Klein–asien, *n.* Asia Minor. **–rußland,** *n.* Little Russia, Ukraine.
Klemens, *m.* Clement.
Kleopatra, *f.* Cleopatra.
Kleve, *n.* Cleves.
Klio, *f.* Clio, Muse of History.
Kluniazenser, *m.* Cluniac monk.
Knut, *m.* Canute, Cnut.
Koblenz, *n.* Coblenz.
Köln, *n.* Cologne. **–er,** *m.* inhabitant of Cologne. **–isches** or **–isch Wasser,** eau-de-Cologne.
Kolosser, *pl.* the Colossians.
Kolumbi–a, *n.* Columbia (*U.S.A.*). **–en,** *n.* Colombia (*S. Amer.*).
Kolumbus, *m.* Columbus.
Konfu–tse, *m.* Confucius. **–zianisch,** *adj.* Confucian.
Königgrätz, *n.* Sadowa.
Konrad, *m.* Conrad.
Konstantza, *f.* Constanta (*Rumania*).
Konstantin–(us), *m.* Constantine. **–opel,** *n.* Constantinople.
Konstanz, *n.* Constance (*the town*). **–e,** *f.* Constance (*girl's name*).
Kopt–e, *m.,* **–isch,** *adj.* Coptic.
Kord–ova, *n.* Cordova. **–uanisch,** *adj.* Cordovan. **–uan,** *m.,* **–uanleder,** *n.* Spanish leather, cordovan.
Korinth–er, *m.,* **–isch,** *adj.* Corinthian.
Kornelie, *f.* Cornelia.
Kors–ar, *m.* Corsair. **–e,** *m.* Corsican.
Kosak, *m.* Cossack.
Krain, *n.* Carniola.
Krakau, *n.* Cracow. **–er,** *m.,* **–isch,** *adj.* Cracovian.
Kreml, *m.* the Kremlin.
Kret–a, *n.* Crete. **–er,** *m.,* **–enser,** *m.,* **–isch,** *adj.* Cretan.
Krethi und Plethi, *pl.* the Cherethites and Pelethites (*David's bodyguard*); (*coll.*) rag, tag, and bobtail.
Krim, *f.* Crimea. **–mer,** *m.* Persian lamb(-skin), astrakhan. **–krieg,** *m.* Crimean war (1853–6).
Kroat–(e), *m.* Croatian. **–ien,** *n.* Croatia. **–isch,** *adj.* Croatian.
Krösus, *m.* Croesus.
Kunz, *m.* (*dim. of* **Konrad**).
Kupido, *m.* Cupid.
Kur–bayern, *n.* Electorate of Bavaria. **–hessen,** *n.* Electorate of Hesse. **–isch,** *adj.* of Courland. **–land,** *n.* Courland. **–länder,** *m.* Courlander. **–pfalz,** *f.* the Palatinate. **–sachsen,** *n.* Electorate of Saxony.
Kurt, *m.* (*dim. of* **Konrad**).

L

Lambrecht, Lamprecht, *m.* Lambert.
Langobard–e, *m.,* **–isch,** *adj.* Lombard, Longobard.
Lapp–e, *m.,* **–isch,** *adj.* Lapp, Laplandish, **–land,** *n.* Lapland. **–länder,** *m.,* **–ländisch,** *adj.* Lapp.
latein–(isch), *adj.* & *n.* Latin; *–ische Buchstaben,*

Roman characters; *–isches, Segel*, lateen sail; *–ische Volkssprache*, Vulgar Latin, Low Latin. **–er,** *m.* inhabitant of Latium, Latin; Latin scholar. **–schule,** *f.* grammar-school.
Latiner, *m.* inhabitant of Latium.
Lätitia, *f.* Letitia.
Laurentius, *m.* Laurence, Lawrence.
Lausitz, *f.* Lusatia. **–er,** *m.*, **–isch,** *adj.* Lusatian.
Lazedämon–ier, *m.*, **–isch,** *adj.* Lacedaemonian.
Lea, *f.* Leah.
Len–a, *f.*, **–chen,** *n.* (*dim. of* **Helene, Magdalene**) Nellie.
Lenore, Leonore, *f.* Leonora, Eleanor.
Leonhard, *m.* Leonard.
Lett–e, *m.* Lett, Latvian. **–isch,** *adj.* Latvian. **–land,** *n.* Latvia.
Levant–e, *f.* the Levant. **–inisch, –isch,** *adj.* Levantine.
Levit, *m.* Levite. **–isch,** *adj.* Levitical.
Libanon, *m.* Mount Lebanon.
Liby–en, *n.* Libya. **–sch.** *adj.* Libyan.
Lies–chen, *n.* **–e, –el,** *f.* (*dim. of* **Elisabeth**) Lizzie.
Lilli, *f.* Lilian, Lil(y).
Lin–a, *f.*, **–chen,** *n.*, **–e,** *f.* (*dim. of* **Karoline**) Carrie.
Liparische Inseln, *pl.* Lipari Islands.
Lis–beth, *f.*, **–(s)ette,** *f.* (*dim. of* **Elizabeth**) Lizzie.
Lissabon, *n.* Lisbon.
Litau–en, *n.* Lithuania. **–er,** *m.*, **–isch,** *adj.* Lithuanian.
Livius, *m.* Livy.
Liv–land, *n.* Livonia. **–länder,** *m.*, **–ländisch,** *adj.* Livonian.
Livorno, *n.* Leghorn
Lollardentum, *n.* Lollardry.
Lombard–e, *m.* Lombard. **–ei,** *f.* Lombardy. **–isch,** *adj.* Lombard, Lombardic.
Lor–chen, *n.*, **–e,** *f.* (*dim. of* **Leonore**), Laura.
Lorenz, *m.* Lawrence, Laurence. **–strom,** *m.* St. Lawrence River.
Lothar, *m.* Lothario, Lothair.
Lothring–en, *n.* Lorraine. **–er,** *m.*, **–isch,** *adj.* (*inhabitant*) of Lorraine.
Lott–chen, *n.*, **–e,** *f.* (*dim. of* **Charlotte**) Lottie.
Löwen, *n.* Louvain.
Löwenherz, *m.* Richard Lion-Heart, Cœur de Lion.
Ludwig, *m.* Lewis, Louis.
Luise, *f.* Louisa, Louise.
Luitpold, *m.* Leopold.
Lukas, *m.* Lucas, Luke; *der heilige* –, St. Luke. **–evangelium,** *n.* Gospel according to St. Luke.
Lukretia, *f.* Lucrece, Lucretia.
Lukrez, *m.* Lucretius.
Luther–aner, *m.*, **–isch,** *adj.* Lutheran.
Lüttich, *n.* Liége.
Luzern, *n.* Lucerne.
Luzie, *f.* Lucy.
Luzifer, *m.* Lucifer.
Lyd–er, –ier, *m.*, **–isch,** *adj.* Lydian.
Lykurg, *m.* Lycurgus.
Lyon, *n.* Lyons. **–er,** *m.*, **–eser,** *m.* inhabitant of Lyons.

M

Mäander, *m.* River Meander.
Maas, *f.* River Meuse.
Maastricht, *n.* Maestricht.
macchiavellistisch, *adj.* Macchiavellian.
Madegasse, *m.* Malagasy, Madagascan.
Madjar, *m.*, *see* **Magyar.**
Magdalen–a, –e, *f.* Magdalen(e), Madeleine.
Magier, *m.pl.* the Magi.
Magyar, *m.* (-en, -en) Magyar. **–isch,** *adj.* Magyar.
Malstrom, *m.* Maelstrom.
Mähr–e, *m.* Moravian. **–en,** *n.*, Moravia. **–isch,** *adj.* Moravian.
Mai–land, *n.* Milan. **–länder,** *m.*, **–ländisch,** *adj.* Milanese.
Mainz, *n.* Mayence.
Makkabä–er, *m.* Maccabee. **–isch,** *adj.* Maccabean.
Malai–e, *m.*, **–isch,** *adj.* Malay, Malayan.
Malchen, *n.* (*dim. of* **Amalie**) Amelia.
Maleachi, *m.* (*B.*) Malachi.
Malediven, *pl.* Maldive Islands, the Maldives.
Maltes–er, *m.*, **–isch,** *adj.* Maltese.
Mamelu(c)k, *m.* Mameluke.
Mandschur–ei, *f.* Manchuria. **–isch,** *adj.* Manchurian.
Manichäer, *m.* Manichee.
Margarete, *f.* Margaret, Margery, Marjory.
Maria, *f.*, *see* **Marie.**
Marianne, *f.* Marian, Marion, Mary Ann.
Marie, *f.* Mary. **–nbild,** *n.* image of the Virgin Mary. **–nblume,** *f.* daisy. **–ndienst,** *m.* Mariolatry. **–ndistel,** *f.* milk thistle (*Silybum marianum* (*Bot.*). **–nfäden,** *m.pl.*, *see* **–ngarn.** **–nflachs,** *m.* toadflax (*Linaria*) (*Bot.*). **–nfest,** *n.* Lady Day. **–ngarn,** *n.* gossamer. **–nglas,** *n.* mica, selenite. **–nglöckchen,** *n.* Canterbury bell. **–ngras,** *n.* feather-grass. **–nkäfer,** *m.* ladybird (*Coccinellidae*) (*Ent.*). **–nkapelle,** *f.* Lady Chapel. **–nwürmchen,** *n.* lady-bird.
Mark, *f.* (the) March(es); – *Brandenburg*, Brandenburg Marches.
Märk–er, *m.* inhabitant of Brandenburg. **–isch,** *adj.* of Brandenburg.
Markus, *m.* Mark. **–evangelium,** *n.* Gospel according to St. Mark.
Marmarameer, *n.* Sea of Marmora.
Marokk–aner, *m.*, **–anisch,** *adj.* Moroccan. **–o,** *n.* Morocco.
Marsbewohner, *pl.* Martians.
Martin–i, *m.*, **–sfest,** *n.* Martinmas.
Mathilde, *f.* Matilda.
Matthäus, Matthias, *m.* Matthew. **–evangelium,** *n.* Gospel according to St. Matthew.
Maur–e, *m.* Moor, Morisco. **–isch,** *adj.* Moorish, Moresque, Morisco.
Mazedon–ien, *n.* Macedonia. **–ier,** *m.*, **–isch,** *adj.* Macedonian.
Mäzen, *m.* Maecenas.
Mechel–n, *n.* Mechlin, Malines. **–er,** *adj.*; *–er Spitzen*, Mechlin lace.
Meder, *m.* Mede.
Mediceische Venus, *f.* Venus of Medici.
Meduse, *f.* Medusa.
Meißen, *n.* Meissen, Misnia. **–er (Meißner),** *m.* Misnian; *–er Porzellan*, Dresden china.
Mekka, *n.* Mecca.
Melanes–ier, *m.*, **–isch,** *adj.* Melanesian.
Merkur, *m.* Mercury.
Merowing–er, *m.*, **–isch,** *adj.* Merovingian.
Merten, *m.* Martin.
Messias, *m.* Messiah.
Meta, *f.* (*dim. of* **Margareta**) Peggy.
Methusalem, *m.* Methuselah.
Micha, *m.* (*B.*) Micah.
Michaelis, *n.*, (**–tag,** *m.*) Michaelmas (day).
Michel, *m.*; *der deutsche* –, the average German.
Min–a, *f.*, **–chen,** *n.*, **–e, –na,** *f.* (*dim. of* **Hermine** *or* **Wilhelmine**) Minnie.
Mittel–asien, *n.* Central Asia; **–europäische Zeit,** Central European time. **–meer** *n.* Mediterranean (Sea).
Mohikaner, *m.* Mohican.
Mohr, *m.* Moor.
Mokka, *n.* Mocha; Mocca (coffee).
Moldau, *f.* Moldavia. **–er,** *m.*, **–isch,** *adj.* Moldavian.
Molukken, *pl.* the Moluccas.
Mongol–e, *m.* Mongolian. **–ei,** *f.* Mongolia. **–isch,** *adj.* Mongolian.
Montenegrin–er, *m.*, **–isch,** *adj.* Montenegrin.
Morgen–land, *n.* East, Orient. **–ländisch,** *adj.* Oriental.
Moritz, Moriz, *m.* Maurice, Morris.
Mormone, *m.* (-en, -en) Mormon.
mos–aisch, *adj.* Mosaic. **–es,** *m.* Moses; *die fünf Bücher –es* or *–is*, the Pentateuch; *das 1. Buch –is*, Genesis; *das 2. Buch –is*, Exodus; *das 3. Buch –is*, Leviticus; *das 4. Buch –is*, Numbers; *das 5. Buch –is*, Deuteronomy.

Mosel, *f.* Moselle.
Mosk-au, *n.* Moscow. **-owit(er),** *m.*, **-owitisch,** *adj.* Muscovite.
Moslem, *m.* (-s -s & -in), Moslem, Mussulman.
Mülhausen, *n.* Mulhouse.
Münch-en, *n.* Munich. **-ner,** 1. *n.* inhabitant of Munich. 2. *adj.*; *-ner Bier*, Munich beer.
Musel-man, (-en, -en), **-mann,** *m.* (-s, -männer), **-manisch,** *adj.*, **-männisch,** *adj.* Moslem, Mussulman.
Myken-ä, -e, *n.* Mycenae. **-isch,** *adj.* Mycenaean.

N

Nann-erl, *n.*, **-ette,** *f.*, **-i,** *f.* (*dim. of* **Anna**) Nancy, Annie.
Nasiräer, *m.* Nazarite.
Nathaniel, *m.* Nathaniel.
Nazar-äer, *m.*, **-ener,** *m.*, **-enisch,** *adj.* Nazarene.
Neapel, *n.* Naples.
Nebuchadnezar, *m.* Nebuchadnezzar.
Neger, *m.* Negro. **-in,** *f.* Negro (woman, girl).
nemeisch, *adj.* Nemean.
Nepomuk, *m.*; *der heilige* –, St. John of Nepomuk.
Neptun, *m.* Neptune.
Nervier, *pl.* the Nervii.
Nett-chen, *n.*, **-i,** *f.* (*dim. of* **Annette**) Nancy.
Neuenburg, *n.* Neuchâtel.
Neu-fundland, *n.* Newfoundland. **-schottland,** *n.* Nova Scotia. **-seeland,** *n.* New Zealand. **-südwales,** *n.* New South Wales. **-york,** *n.* New York.
Nieder-lande, *pl.* Netherlands; Low Countries. **-länder,** *m.* Dutchman. **-ländisch,** *adj.* Dutch.
Nikola(u)s, *m.* Nicholas.
Nil, *m.* River Nile.
Nimwegen, *n.* Nimeguen.
Ninive, *n.* Nineveh.
Nizä-a, *n.* Nicea. **-isch, -nisch,** *adj.*; *-isches* or *-nisches Glaubensbekenntnis*, **-um, -num,** *n.* Nicene Creed.
Nizza, *n.* Nice.
nord-isch, *adj.* Nordic, Norse. **-kap,** *n.* North Cape. (*Poet.*) **-mann,** *m.* Norseman. **-see,** *f.* North Sea.
Norman-die, *f.* Normandy. **-ne,** *m.*, **-nisch,** *adj.* Norman; *die -nischen Inseln*, the Channel Islands.
Norne, *f.* Norn.
Norweg-en, *n.* Norway. **-er,** *m.*, **-isch,** *adj.* Norwegian.
Nub-ier, *m.*, **-isch,** *adj.* Nubian.
Numid-(i)er, *m.*, **-isch,** *adj.* Numidian.
Nürnberg, *n.* Nuremberg.

O

Obadja, *m.* (*B.*) Obadiah.
Ober-ägypten, *n.* Upper Egypt. **-bayern,** *n.* Upper Bavaria. **-italien,** *n.* North Italy. **-land,** *n.* Highlands, uplands; *Berner -land*, Bernese Alps. **-österreich,** *n.* Upper Austria. **-pfalz,** *f.* Upper Palatinate. **-schlesien,** *n.* Upper Silesia.
Oder, *f.* River Oder.
Odyssee, *f.* Odyssey.
Ofen, *n.* Buda. **-pest,** Budapest.
Ölberg, *m.* Mount of Olives.
Olymp, *m.* Mount Olympus. **-iade,** *f.* Olympiad. **-ische Spiele,** Olympic Games.
Oranien, *n.* Orange.
Oranjefreistaat, *m.* Orange Free State.
Orest, *m.* Orestes.
orphisch, *adj.* Orphic.
Osman-e, *m.*, **-isch,** *adj.* Ottoman.
Ost-asien, *n.* Eastern Asia, the Far East. **-elbien,** *n.* land east of the Elbe. **-ende,** *n.* Ostend. **-friese,** *m.*, **-friesisch,** *adj.* East Frisian. **-friesland,** *n.* East Frisia. **-gote,** *m.* Ostrogoth. **-indien,** *n.* the East Indies. **-indisch,** *adj.* East Indian; *-indischer Archipel*, Malay Archipelago; *-indische Kompanie*, East India Company. **-mark,** *f.* Eastern frontier districts of Germany. **-see,** *f.* Baltic (Sea).
Österreich, *n.* Austria. **-er,** *m.*, **-isch,** *adj.* Austrian. **-isch-ungarisch,** *adj.* Austro-Hungarian. **- -Ungarn,** *n.* Austria-Hungary.
Ottoman-e, *m.*, **-isch,** *adj.* Ottoman.
Ozeanien, *n.* South Sea Islands.

P

Palästin-a, *n.* Palestine. **-er,** *m.*, **-isch,** *adj.* Palestinian.
Pandschab, *n.* Punjab.
Pankraz, *m.* Pancras.
parisch, *adj.* Parian (*marble*), of Paros.
Parm-aer, *m.*, **-aisch,** *adj.*, **-esaner,** *m.*, **-esanisch,** *adj.* Parmesan.
Parnaß, *m.* Parnassus.
Pars-e, *m.*, **-isch,** *adj.* Parsee.
Parth-er, *m.*, **-isch,** *adj.* Parthian.
Parzen, *f.pl.* (the) Parcae, Fates.
Parzival, *m.* Percival.
Passah, *n.* Passover.
Patagon-ier, *m.*, **-isch,** *adj.* Patagonian.
Paul-(us), *m.* Paul. **-inisch,** *adj.*; *die -inischen Briefe*, Epistles of St. Paul.
Pauline, *f.* Paulina, Pauline, Paula.
Peking, *n.* Pekin.
Pelasger, *pl.* the Pelasgians.
Peloponnes, *m. or f.* Peloponnesus.
Pendschab, *see* **Pandschab.**
Pepi, *m.* & *f.* (*dim. of* **Joseph, Josephine,** *or* **Sophie**) Joe, Josey.
Pernambuko, *n.* Pernambuco.
Pers-er, *m.* Persian. **-ien,** *n.* Persia. **-isch,** *adj.* Persian.
Peruan-er, *m.*, **-isch,** *adj.* Peruvian.
Peter, *m.* Peter; *dummer* –, Simple Simon. **-skirche,** *f.* St. Peter's (*Rome*). **-spfennig,** *m.* Peter's pence.
Petrarka, *m.* Petrarch.
Petr-us, *m.* (*B.*) Peter the Apostle. **-ikirche,** *f.* St. Peter's (Church).
Pfalz, *f.* the Palatinate; *Kurfürst von der* –, Elector Palatinate. **-graf,** *m.* Count Palatine. **-grafschaft,** *f.* Palatinate.
Pfälz-er, *m.* inhabitant of the Palatinate. **-isch,** *adj.* of the Palatinate.
Pforte, *f.*; *die Hohe* –, the (Sublime) Porte.
Phäak-e, *m.* Phaeacian. **-ien,** *n.* Phaeacia. **-isch,** *adj.* Phaeacian.
Pharao, *m.* Pharaoh.
Pharisä-er, *m.* Pharisee. **-isch,** *adj.* Pharisaical.
Philipp, *m.* Philip. **-er,** *pl.* Philippians. **-erbrief,** *m.* Epistle to the Philippians. **-ika,** *f.* Philippic. **-ine,** *f.* Philippa. **-iner,** *m.* Philippian. **-opel,** *n.* Philippopolis.
Philister, *m.* Philistine; philistine.
Philomele, *f.* Philomela.
Phinchen, *n.* (*dim. of* **Josephine**).
Phöb-e, *f.* Phoebe. **-us,** *m.* Phoebus Apollo.
Phöniz-ier, *m.*, **-isch,** *adj.* Phoenician.
Piemont, *n.* Piedmont. **-ese,** *m.*, **-(es)isch,** *adj.* Piedmontese.
Pikte, *m.* Pict.
Pilatus, *m.* Pilate; Pilatus (*a Swiss mountain*).
Pippin, *m.* Pepin.
Platoni-ker, *m.* Platonist. **-sch,** *adj.* Platonic.
Plattdeutsch, 1. *adj.* Low German. 2. *n.* Low German language.
Plejaden, *pl.* Pleiades.
Plinius, *m.* Pliny.
Polack, *m.* (-en, -en) Pole (*disdainful*); Polish horse. **-ei,** *f.* Poland.
Polarkreis, *m.*; *nördlicher* –, Arctic Circle; *südlicher* –, Antarctic Circle.
Pol-e, *m.* Pole. **-en,** *n.* Poland. **-nisch,** *adj.* Polish; *der -nische Korridor*, the Polish Corridor.
Policinello, *m.* (*Austr. dial.*) Punchinello.

Polynes–(i)er, *m.*, **–isch**, *adj.* Polynesian.
Pommer, *m.* Pomeranian. **–ellen**, *n.* eastern Pomerania. **–n**, *n.* Pomerania. **–(i)sch**, *adj.* Pomeranian.
Pompej–aner, *m.*, **–anisch**, *adj.* Pompeian. **–i**, *n.* Pompeii. **–us**, *m.* Pompey.
Pontinisch, *adj.* Pontine.
Portugies–e, *m.*, **–isch**, *adj.* Portuguese.
Posen, *n.* Posnania (*province*); Posnan (*town*).
Prag, *n.* Prague. **–er**, *m.* inhabitant of Prague.
Preßburg, *n.* Bratislava.
Preuß–e, *m.* Prussian. **–en**, *n.* Prussia. **–entum**, *n.* Prussianism. **–isch**, *adj.* Prussian.
Priamus, *m.* Priam.
Prokop, *m.* Procopius.
prometheisch, *adj.* Promethean.
Properz, *m.* Propertius.
proteisch, *adj.* Protean.
Provenzal–e, *m.*, **–isch**, *adj.* Provençal.
Ptolemäus, *m.* Ptolemy.
Puritan–er, *m.* Puritan. **–isch**, *adj.* Puritan(ical).
Pyrenäen, *pl.* Pyrenees.
Pyrrussieg, *m.* Pyrric victory.
Pythisch, *adj.* Pythian.

Q

Quäker, *m.* Quaker, Friend. **–tum**, *n.* Quakerism. **–bund**, *m.* Society of Friends. **–speisung**, Society of Friends' Relief Organization.

R

Raben, *n. obs. & poet. for* Ravenna.
Radschpute, *m.* Rajput.
Rahel, *f.* Rachel.
Raimund, *m.* Raymond.
Raubstaaten, *m.pl.* Barbary States.
Rebekka, *f.* Rebecca.
Reformierte(r), *m.* Reformed Protestant, Calvinist.
Regensburg, *n.* Ratisbon.
Rehabeam, *m.* (*B.*) Rehoboam.
Reichslande, *n.pl.* Alsace and Lorraine.
Reims, *n.* Rheims.
Rein–eke, *m.*, **–hard**, *m.* Re(y)nard (*the Fox*). **–hold**, *m.* Reginald.
R(h)ätoromanisch, *n. & adj.* Rhaeto-Romanic, Romansh (*dialect*).
Rhein, *m.* River Rhine. **–bund**, *m.* Confederation of the Rhine (1806–13). **–franken**, *n.* Rhenish Franconia. **–fränkisch**, *adj.* Rheno-Franconian. **–hessen**, *n.* Rhenish Hesse. **–isch**, *adj.* Rhenish. **–land**, *n.* Rhineland. **–länder**, *m.* Rhinelander. **–pfalz**, *f.* Rhenish Palatinate. **–provinz**, *f.* Rhineland. **–wein**, *m.* Rhenish wine, hock.
Rhod–ier, *m.* inhabitant of the Island of Rhodes. **–us**, *n.* Rhodes.
Richard, *m.* Richard; – *Löwenherz*, Richard Cœur de Lion.
Rik–chen, *n.*, **–e**, *f.* (*dim. of* **Friederike**) Freda.
ripuarisch, *adj.* Ripuarian.
Roderich, *m.* Roderick.
Roland, *m.* Roland, Rowland.
Rom, *n.* Rome.
Roman–en, *pl.* the Romance nations, the Neo-Latin peoples. **–isch**, *adj.* Romance; Norman, Romanesque (*style. Arch.*). **–ist**, *m.* Romance philologist; student of Roman law.
Rom–aunsch, **–ontsch**, *n. & adj.*, *see* **Rhätoromanisch.**
Röm–er, *m.*, **–isch**, *adj.* Roman. **–erbrief**, *m.* Epistle to the Romans. **–isch-katholisch**, *adj.* (Roman-)Catholic; *das heilige –ische Reich* (*deutscher Nation*), the Holy Roman Empire.
Rosa, *f.* Rose. **–linde**, *f.* Rosalind. **–munde**, *f.* Rosamond.
Röschen, *n.* (*dim. of* **Rosa**) Rosie.
Rosenkreuzer, *m.* Rosicrucian.
Rotbart, *m.* Barbarossa.
Rot–häute, *pl.* redskins. **–käppchen**, *n.* Little Red-Riding-Hood. **–kehlchen**, *n.* Robin Redbreast.
Ruben, *m.* Reuben.
Rübezahl, *m.* Rape-tail, Old Nip.
Rud–i, *m.* (*dim. of*) **–olf**, Rudolph(us), Ralph.
Rüdiger, *m.* Roger.
Rumän–e, *m.* Rumanian. **–ien**, *n.* Rumania. **–isch**, *adj.* Rumanian.
Ruprecht, *m.* Rupert; *Knecht* –, Santa Claus, St. Nicholas.
Russ–e, *m.*, **–isch**, *adj.* Russian; *–isch-Asien*, Russia in Asia. **–ifizieren**, *v.a.* Russianize. **–land**, *n.* Russia.
Ruthen–e, *m.*, **–isch**, *adj.* Ruthenian.

S

Saba, *n.* Sheba.
Sacharja, *m.* (*B.*) Zachariah.
Sachse, *m.* Saxon. **–n**, *n.* Saxony. **–n-Koburg**, *n.* Saxe-Coburg. **–n-Meiningen**, *n.* Saxe-Meiningen. **–n-Weimar**, *n.* Saxe-Weimar.
sächsisch, *adj.* Saxon.
Sadduzäer, *m.* Sadducee.
Salier, *m.* Salian.
Salmanassar, *m.* Shalmaneser.
Salomo, *m.* Solomon; *das hohe Lied –nis*, the Song of Songs; *Prediger –nis*, Ecclesiastes; *Sprüche –nis*, Proverbs. **–ninseln**, *pl.* Solomon Islands.
Samariter, *m.*; *der barmherzige* –, the Good Samaritan.
Sambesi, *m.* Zambezi River.
Samiel, *m.* (*B.*) Zamiel.
Samnit–er, *m.*, **–isch**, *adj.* Samnite.
Samoaner, *m.* Samoan.
Samojede, *m.* Samoyed.
Sanherib, *m.* Sennacherib.
Sansibar, *n.* Zanzibar.
Sanskrit, *n.*, **–isch**, *adj.* Sanskrit.
Sara, *f.* Sarah.
Sarazen–e, *m.*, **–isch**, *adj.* Saracen.
Sardanapal, *m.* Sardanapalus.
Sard–e, *m.*, **–inier**, *m.*, **–inisch**, *adj.*, **–isch**, *adj.* Sardinian. **–inien**, *n.* Sardinia.
Sau, *f.* River Save.
Sauerland, *n.* Southern Westphalia.
Savoy–arde, *m.*, *see* **–er.** **–en**, *n.* Savoy. **–er**, *m.*, **–isch**, *adj.* Savoyard.
Schah, *m.* (-s) Shah.
Schanghai, *n.* Shanghai.
Schelde, *f.* River Scheldt.
Schild–a, *n.* Gotham. **–bürger**, *m.* Gothamite, wise man of Gotham.
Schlesi–en, *n.* Silesia. **–er**, *m.*, **–sch**, *adj.* Silesian.
Schleswig, *n.* Sleswig.
Schneewittchen, *n.* Snow-White.
Schonen, *n.* Scania.
Schott–e, **–länder** *m.* Scot, Scotsman. **–isch**, *adj.* Scottish (*history, etc.*); Scots (*law, etc.*); Scotch (*whisky, etc.*). **–land**, *n.* Scotland.
Schwabe, *m.* Swabian, Suabian. **–n**, *n.* Swabia, Suabia. **–nalter**, *n.* 40 years; the age of discretion.
schwäbisch, *adj.* Swabian, Suabian; *–e Kaiser*, Hohenstaufen emperors.
Schwarzwald, *m.* Black Forest.
Schwed–e, *m.* Swede. **–en**, *n.* Sweden. **–isch**, *adj.* Swedish; *hinter –ischen Gardinen*, behind bars.
Schweiz, *f.* Switzerland; *in der* –, in Switzerland. **–er**, *m.* Swiss. **–erbund**, *m.* Swiss Confederation. **–erdeutsch**, *n.* Swiss dialect. **–ergarde**, *f.* Papal bodyguard. **–erisch**, *adj.* Swiss.
Sebadja, *m.* (*B.*) Zebadiah.
Seeland, *n.* Zealand.
Seldschucke, *m.* Seljuk (Turk).
Sem, *m.* (*B.*) Shem. **–it(e)**, *m.* Semite. **–itisch**, *adj.* Semitic.
Sepp, *m.*, **Seppe(r)l**, *m.*, **Seppi**, *m.* (*dim. of* **Joseph**) Joe.
Serb–e, *m.* Serb. **–isch**, *adj.* Serbian.
Seschellen, *pl.* the Seychelles.

Sevennen, *pl.* the Cevennes.
Sevilla, *n.* Seville.
Siames–e, *m.*, **–isch,** *adj.* Siamese.
Sibiri–en, *n.* Siberia. **–er,** *m.*, **–sch,** *adj.* Siberian.
Sibyll–a, –e, *f.* Sibyl.
Siebenbürg–en, *n.* Transylvania. **–er,** *m.*, **–isch,** *adj.* Transylvanian.
Siegmund, *m.*, **Sigismund,** *m.* Sigismund.
Simson, *m.* Samson.
Singapur, *n.* Singapore.
Sirach, *m.* Ecclesiasticus.
Sitten, *n.* Sion (*Switzerland*).
Sixtinisch, *adj.* Sistine.
Sizil–ien, *n.* Sicily. **–ier,** *m.*, **–isch,** *adj.* Sicilian.
Skagerrak, *n.* Skager Rak. **–schlacht,** *f.* battle of Jutland.
Skandinavi–er, *m.*, **–sch,** *adj.* Scandinavian.
Skythe, *etc.*, *see* **Szythe.**
Slaw–e, *m.* Slav. **–isch,** *adj.* Slav, Slavonic. **–onien,** *n.* Slavonia (*in Yugoslavia*). **–onier,** *m.*, **–onisch,** *adj.* Slavonian.
Slowak–e, *m.*, **–isch,** *adj.* Slovak. **–ei,** *f.* Slovakia.
Slowen–e, *m.* Slovene. **–isch,** *adj.* Slovene, Slovenian. **–ien,** *n.* Slovenia (*in Yugoslavia*).
sokratisch, *adj.* Socratic.
Sophie, *f.* Sophia, Sophy.
Söul, *n.* Seoul.
Sowjet, *m.* Soviet. **–rußland,** *n.* Soviet Russia.
Spani–en *n.* Spain. **–er,** *m.*, **–sch,** *adj.* Spanish; (*coll.*) *das kommt mir –sch vor,* it is all Greek to me; *–sche Fliege,* Spanish fly, cantharis; *–scher Stiefel,* boot (*torture*); *–sche Reiter,* chevaux-de-frise; *–sches Rohr,* Bengal cane; *–sche Wand,* folding screen.
Spart–aner, *m.*, **–anisch,** *adj.* Spartan (*also fig.*). **–iat,** *m.* Spartan (*in antiquity*).
Stambul, *n.* Istanbul, Constantinople.
Stauf–er, *m.* member of the Hohenstaufen dynasty. **–isch,** *adj.* Hohenstaufen. **–erzeit,** *f.* the Hohenstaufen period (1138–1254).
Steffen, *m.*, *see* **Stephan.**
Steier–er, *m.*, **–isch,** *adj.*, *see* **–märker, –märkisch. –mark,** *f.* Styria. **–märker,** *m.*, **–märkisch,** *adj.* Styrian.
Steir–er, *m.*, **–isch,** *adj.*, *see* **Steiermärk–er, –isch.**
Stephan, *m.* Stephen, Steven.
Stiller Ozean, *m.* Pacific (Ocean).
Stoffel, *m.* (*dim. of* **Christoph**) Chris.
Stoi–ker, *m.* Stoic. **–sch,** *adj.* stoic(al).
Straßburg, *n.* Strasbourg.
Stru(w)welpeter, *m.* Shockheaded Peter.
Süd–afrika, *n.* South Africa. **–afrikanisch,** *adj.* South African. **–see,** *f.* Oceania, the South Seas. **–slawien,** *n.* Yugoslavia. **–slawisch,** *adj.* Yugoslav.
Sudan–er, –ese, *m.*, **–isch,** *adj.* Sudanese.
Sudeten, *pl.* Sudetes Mountains. **–deutsche(r),** *m.* member of German minority in Czechoslovakia. **–land,** *n.* German-speaking parts of Czechoslovakia.
Südsee, *f.*, *see under* **Süd–.**
Sueven, *pl.* (the) Suevi.
Suleika, *f.* Zuleikah.
Sumer–(i)er, *m.*, **–isch,** *adj.* Sumerian.
Sund, *m.* (the) Sound.
Sus–anna, –anne, *f.* Susannah, Susan. **–e, –i,** (*dim.*) Susie, Sue.
Syrakus, *n.* Syracuse.
Syr–ien, *n.* Syria. **–(i)er,** *m.*, **–isch,** *adj.* Syrian, Syriac.
Syrte, *f.* the Syrtis.
Szylla, *f.* Scylla.
Szyth–e, *m.*, **–isch,** *adj.* Scythian.

T

Taborit, *m.* Taborite.
Tafel–berg, *m.* Table Mountain. **–runde,** *f.* the Round Table.
Tajo, *m.* River Tagus.
Tamerlan, *m.* Tamerlane, Tamburlaine.
Tamul–e, *m.* **–isch,** *adj.* Tamil.
Tanger, *n.* Tangier(s).
Tarent, *n.* Taranto.
Tarpejisch, *adj.* Tarpeian.
Tarser, *m.* inhabitant of Tarsus.
Tatar, *m.* Tartar, Tatar. **–ei,** *f.* Tartary. **–isch,** *adj.* Tartar, Tatar.
Taurische Halbinsel, *f.*, **Taurien,** *n.*, **Tauris,** *n.* Tauric Chersonese.
Teerjacke, *f.* Jack Tar.
Tejo, *m. see* **Tajo.**
Telemach, *m.* Telemachus.
Tempel–herr, *m.* (Knight) Templar. **–orden,** *m.* Order of the Templars.
Templer, *m.*, *see* **Tempelherr. –orden,** *m.*, *see* **Tempeorden.**
Terenz, *m.* Terence.
Tessin, *m.* Ticino.
Teuton–e, *m.* Teuton. **–isch,** *adj.* Teutonic.
Teutsch, *adj.*, *archaic for* Deutsch.
Theb–ais, *n.* Thebaid (*district*). **–aner,** *m.*, **–anisch,** *adj.* Theban. **–en,** *n.* Thebes.
Themse, *f.* River Thames.
Theoderich, *m.* Theodoric.
Theodor, *m.* Theodore. **–ich,** *m.*, *see* **Theoderich.**
Theokrit, *m.* Theocritus.
Theres–e, –ia, *f.* Theresa.
Thermopylen, *pl.* the pass of Thermopylae.
Thessal–ien, *n.* Thessaly. **–ier,** *m.*, **–isch,** *adj.* Thessalian. **–onicher,** *m.* (*B.*) Thessalonian. **–oniki,** *n.* Salonika, Thessalonica, Thessalonike.
Thilde, *f.* (*dim. of* **Mathilde**) Tilly.
Thrak–, Thraz–ien, *n.* Thrace. **–ier,** *m.*, **–isch,** *adj.* Thracian.
Thüring–en, *n.* Thuringia. **–er,** *m.*, **–isch,** *adj.* Thuringian.
Tilde, *f.*, *see* **Thilde.**
Timotheus, *m.* Timothy.
Timur, *m.*, *see* **Tamerlan.**
Tin–chen, *n.*, **–e,** *f.* (*dim. of* **Christine**) Tina, Chrissie.
Tirol, *n.* the Tyrol. **–er,** *m.* **–isch,** *adj.* Tyrolese.
Titan, *m.* Titan (*sun-god*). **–e,** *m.* (-n, -n) Titan (*giant*). **–isch,** *adj.* Titanic.
Tizian, *m.* Titian.
Tobias, *m.* Tobias, (*B.*) Tobit; *das Buch Tobiä,* Book of Tobit.
Toffel, Töffel, *m.* (*dim. of* **Christoph(el)**) Chris; (*sl.*) blockhead.
Toka–ier, –jer, *m.* Tokay (wine).
Toni, *m. & f.* (*dim. of* **Anton, Antonie**) Tony.
Toskan–a, *n.* Tuscany. **–er,** *m.*, **–isch,** *adj.* Tuscan.
transpadanisch, *adj. & adv.* of *or* in Italy north of the River Po.
Trapezunt, *n.* Trebizond.
tridentin–isch, *adj.*, **–er,** *adj.* of Trento *or* Trentino; *–isches Konzil,* Council of Trent.
Trient, *n.* Trento; *–er Konzil,* Council of Trent.
Trier, *n.* Treves.
Triest, *n.* Trieste.
Trin–e, *f.* (*dim. of* **Katharine**) Katy, Kitty; *dumme –e,* silly goose.
Tripoli–s, *n.* Tripoli. **–tanisch,** *adj.* Tripolitan.
Tristan, *m.* Tristram.
Tro–as, *n.* the Troad. **–er,** *m.*, **–janer,** *m.*, **–janisch,** *adj.* Trojan. **–ja,** *n.* Troy.
Trud–e(l), *f.*, **–chen,** *n.* (*dim. of* **Gertrud**) Gertie.
Tschech–e, *m.*, **–isch,** *adj.* Czech. **–oslowakei,** *f.* Czechoslovakia. **–oslowakisch,** *adj.* Czechoslovakian.
Tscherkess–e, *m.*, **–isch,** *adj.* Circassian.
Tscherokese, *m.* Cherokee (Indian).
Tullius, *m.* Tully.
Tun–eser, *m.*, **–iser,** *m.*, **–esisch, –isisch,** *adj.* Tunisian. **–esien,** *n.* Tunisia. **–is,** *n.* Tunis.
Turk–estan, *n.*, **–istan,** *n.* Turkestan.
Türk–e, *m.* (-en), Turk. **–ei,** *f.* Turkey. **–enbund,** *m.* Turk's cap (*Lilium martagon*) (*Bot.*). **–isch,** *adj.* Turkish. **–ischrot,** *n. & adj.* Turkey red.
Turkmene, *m.* Turcoman.
Turko, *m.* (-s) Turco, Zouave.
Tyr–ier, *m.*, **–isch,** *adj.* Tyrian. **–us,** *n.* Tyre.

U

Ulrike, *f.* Ulrica.
Umbr–ier, *m.,* **–isch,** *adj.* Umbrian.
Ungar, *m.,* **–isch,** *adj.* Hungarian. **–n,** *n.* Hungary.
Unterfranken, *n.* Lower Franconia.
Uria(s), *m.* Uriah. **–sbrief,** *m.* evil tidings.
Urian, *m.* Old Nick.
Ursel, *f.* (*dim. of* **Ursula).**
Ursulinerin, *f.* Ursuline nun.
Utopi–en, *n.* Utopia. **–sch,** *adj.* Utopian.
Utraquist, *m.* (-en, -en) Hussite.

V

Valand, *m.* (*archaic*), *see* **Voland.**
Valentin, *m.* Valentine.
Vandale, *n., see* **Wandale.**
Vatikan, *m.* Vatican. **–isch,** *adj.* Papal, curial. **–stadt,** *f.* Vatican City.
Veda, *m., see* **Weda.**
Veit, *m.* Vitus. **–stanz,** *m.* St. Vitus' dance.
Velten, *m.* (*dim. of* **Valentine**); (*coll.*) *potz* –, good gracious.
Veltlin, *n.* Valtellina.
Vendeer, *m.* inhabitant of the Vendee.
Vene–dig, *n.* Venice. **–diger,** *m.,* **–disch,** *adj.,* **–zianer,** *m.,* **–zianisch,** *adj.* Venetian.
venezuelisch (*less correctly* **venezolanisch**), *adj.* Venezuelan.
Vereinigte Staaten, *m.pl.* United States (of America) (*sing. construction*).
Vergil, *m.* Virgil, Vergil.
Vesuv, *m.* Mt. Vesuvius.
Vierwaldstätter See, *m.* Lake of Lucerne.
Vinzenz, *m.* Vincent.
Virginie, *f.* Virginia (*girl's name*). **–n,** *n.* Virginia (*U.S.A.*).
Vlame, *m., see* **Flame.**
Vlissingen, *n.* Flushing.
Vogesen, *pl.* Vosges Mountains.
Voland, *m.*; *Junker* –, the Devil, Satan.
Völkerschlacht, *f.* Battle of Leipzig.
Voralpen, *pl.* the lower Alps.
vorderasi–atisch, *adj.* Near Eastern. **–en,** *n.* the Near East.
Vroni, *f.* (*dim. of* **Veronika**) Veronica.

W

Waadt–(land), *n.* Vaud. **–länder,** *m.,* **–ländisch,** *adj.* Vaudois.
Waal, *f.* River Vaal.
Wagnerianer, *m.* Wagnerite, Wagner enthusiast.
Waibling(er), *m.* Ghibelline, Hohenstaufen.
Walach–e, *m.,* **–isch,** *adj.* Wallachian. **–ei,** *f.* Wallachia.
Wal–hall(a), *f.* Valhalla. **–küre,** *f.* Valkyrie. **–kürenritt,** *m.* ride of the Valkyries.
Walis–er, *m.* Welshman. **–isch,** *adj.* Welsh, Cambrian.
Wall–is, *n.* Valais. **–iser,** *m.,* **–isisch,** *adj.* Valaisan.
Wallon–e, *m.,* **–isch,** *adj.* Walloon.
Walpurgisnacht, *f.* eve of May day.
Walther, Walter, *m.* Walter.
Wandal–e, *m.,* **–isch,** *adj.* Vandal (*also fig.*).
Waräger, *m.* Viking.
Warschau, *n.* Warsaw.
Wasgau, *n.,* **Wasgenwald,** *m.* see **Vogesen.**
Wed–a, *m.* (-as & -en) Veda.
Weichsel, *f.* River Vistula.
Welfe, *m.* Guelph.
welsch, *adj.* Italian, French; Romance; foreign; (*Swiss dial.*) French-speaking (*people or district of Switzerland*); *–e Bohne,* French bean; *–e Nuß,* walnut. **–kraut,** *n.* Savoy cabbage. **–land,** *n.* Italy; (*Swiss dial.*) the French-speaking cantons. **–tum,** *n.* foreign (*esp. French*) ways.
Wend–e, *m.,* **–isch,** *adj.* Wend.
Wenz–el, *m.* Wenceslas; knave (*at cards*). **–eslaus,** *m.* Wenceslas.
West–falen, *n.* Westphalia. **–fale,** *m.,* **–fälisch,** *adj.* Westphalian. **–gote,** *m.* Visigoth. **–indien,** *n.* the West Indies. **–indienfahrer,** *m.* West-Indiaman (*ship*).
Wieland der Schmied, *m.* Wayland Smith.
Wien, *n.* Vienna. **–er,** *m.,* **–erisch,** *adj.* Viennese; *–er Kongreß,* Congress of Vienna.
Wiking, *m.* (-s, -e & -er), Viking.
Wilfried, *m.* Wilfred.
Wilhelm, *m.* William; – *der Eroberer,* William the Conqueror; – *der Rote,* William Rufus. **–ine,** *f.* Wilhelmina. **–inisch,** *adj.* of William II, Wilhelmian (*of Germany*); *–inisches Zeitalter* (*late Victorian & Edwardian age in England*).
Willi, *m.* (*dim. of* **Wilhelm**) Bill, Will, Billie, Willie, Billy, Willy.
Wischnu, *m.* Vishnu.
Wladis–laus, –law, *m.* Ladislaus.
Wodan, *m.* Odin, Woden.
Wolga, *f.* River Volga.
Wotan, *m., see* **Wodan.**
Wulfila, *m.* Ulfilas.

X

Xaver, *m.* Xavier.
Xeres, *m., see* **Jerez.**

Y

Ypern, *n.* Ypres.

Z

Zabern, *n.* Saverne.
Zacharias, *m.* Zachariah.
Zachäus, *m.* (*B.*) Zaccheus.
Zar, *m.* (-en, -en), Tsar, Czar. **–in,** *f.* Tsarina, Czarina. **–istisch,** *adj.* Tsarist, Czarist.
Zebaoth, *m.* (*B.*) Sabaoth.
Zebedäus, *m.* (*B.*) Zebedee.
Zendawesta, *n.* Zend-Avesta.
Zephanja, *f.* Zephaniah.
Zilli, *f.* (*dim. of* **Cäcilie**), Cissie.
Zimb–ern, *pl.* Cimbri. **–risch,** *adj.* Cimbrian; *–rische Halbinsel,* Jutland.
Zirkass–ier, *m.,* **–isch,** *adj., see* **Tscherkesse,** etc.
zisalpin(isch), *adj.* Cisalpine.
Zisterzienser, *m.* Cistercian.
Zölestin, *m.* Celestine (*man's name*). **–e,** *f.* Celestine (*girl's name*).
Zuave, *m.* (-n, -n) Zouave.
Zuidersee, *f.* or *m.* Zuyder Zee.
Zür–cher, –cherisch, *adj.* (*Swiss dial.*), *see* **–icher, –icherisch.** (*Swiss dial.*) **–chersee,** *m.,* see *–icher See.* **–icher, –icherisch,** *adj.* of Zurich; *–icher See,* (*Swiss dial.*) **–ichsee,** Lake of Zurich.
Zykladen, *pl.* the Cyclades.
Zyp–ern, *n.* Cyprus. **–rer,** *m.,* **–risch,** *adj.* Cypriot.
zyrill–isch, *adj.* Cyrillic. **–(us),** *m.* Cyril.

THE MOST COMMON GERMAN ABBREVIATIONS

(For the symbols of chemical elements see separate list)

A

a, *Ar* (= 100 sq. m.).
a., 1. *aus.* 2. *an, am* (*before names of rivers*).
A, *Ampere* (*Elec.*)
A., *akzeptiert* (*on bills of exchange*).
A. A., *Auswärtiges Amt.*
a. a. O., 1. *am angeführten Orte* (= loc. cit.). 2. *an andern Orten.*
Abb., *Abbildung.*
ABC–Staaten, Argentinien, Brasilien, Chile.
abds., *abends.*
Abf., *Abfahrt.*
Abg., *Abgeordnete(r).*
Abh., *Abhandlung.*
abh., *abhängig.*
Abk., *Abkürzung.*
Abs., 1. *Absatz.* 2. *Absender.*
abs., *absolut.*
Abschn., *Abschnitt.*
Abt., *Abteilung.*
a. c., *anni currentis.*
A. Ch., *ante Christum* (= B.C.).
a d., *a dato.*
a. d., *an der* (*before names of rivers*).
a. D., *außer Dienst* (*Mil.*).
A. D., *anno domini.*
ADB., *Allgemeine Deutsche Biographie.*
ADGB., *Allgemeiner Deutscher Gewerkschaftsbund.*
AEG, *Allgemeine Elektrizitäts-Gesellschaft.*
a. G., *auf Gegenseitigkeit.*
A.-G. 1. *Aktiengesellschaft.* 2. *Atomgewicht.*
Agfa, *Aktiengesellschaft für Anilinfabrikation.*
A. H., *alter Herr*; *pl.* **AA. HH.**, *alte Herren.*
ahd., *althochdeutsch.*
Akt.-Ges., *see* **A.-G.** (1).
a./L., *an der Lahn*; *e.g.* **Marburg a./L.**
allg., *allgemein*
a./M., *am Main*; *e.g.* **Frankfurt a./M.**
Amp., *Ampere* (*Elec.*).
anerk., *anerkannt.*
Anfr., *Anfrage.*
Ang., **Angeb.**, *Angebot.*
Angekl., *Angeklagte(r).*
angew., *angewandt.*
Anh., *Anhang.*
Ank., *Ankunft.*
Anl., *Anlage.*
Anm., *Anmerkung.*
Ann., *Annalen.*
anorg., *anorganisch.*
Anz., *Anzeigen* or *Anzeiger.*
a./O., *an der Oder*; *e.g.* **Frankfurt a./O.**
A. O., *Auslandorganisation* (*Nat. Soc.*).
a. o. Prof., *außerordentlicher Professor.*
Arch., *Archiv.*
a./Rh., *am Rhein*; *e.g.* **Bonn a./Rh.**
Art., *Artikel.*
a./S., *an der Saale*; *e.g.* **Halle a./S.**
A. S., *Ampere-Stunde.*
ASKI., *Ausländersonderkonten für Inlandszahlungen.*
a. St., *alten Stils* (*of dates*).
A. T., *Altes Testament.*
At, At-G(ew)., see **A.-G.** (2).
Atm., *Atmosphäre* (*Phys.*).
Aufl., *Auflage.*
Ausl., *Ausland.*
ausschl., *ausschließlich.*
Ausspr., *Aussprache.*
autom., *automatisch.*
ä. W., *äußere Weite* (=o.d.).

B

b., *bei, beim, bei dem*; *e.g.* **Gohlis b. Leipzig.**
-b., final, as the second part of a word, stands for *-bau, e.g.* **Bergb.**, *Bergbau.*
B, *Brief* (*C.L.*) (*in opposition to* **G** (Geld)).
bayr., *bayrisch.*
Bd., *Band*; *pl.* **Bde.**, *Bände.*
BDM., *Bund deutscher Mädchen* (*Nat. Soc.*).
Bdtg., *Bedeutung.*
Bearb., *Bearbeiter* or *Bearbeitung.*
bed., *bedeutet*; **Bed.**, *Bedeutung.*
Beibl., *Beiblatt.*
beif., *beifolgend.*
Beih., *Beiheft.*
beil., *beiliegend.*
Bem., *Bemerkung.*
Ber., *Bericht.*
bes., *besonders.*
Best., 1. *Bestimmung.* 2. *Bestellung.* 3. *Bestand.*
best., *bestimmt.*
betr., *betreffend, betreffs.*
bev., *bevollmächtigt.*
bez., 1. *bezahlt.* 2. *bezüglich.* 3. *beziehungsweise.*
Bez., *Bezirk.*
Bf., *Brief* (*C.L.*).
Bg., *Bogen.*
BGB., *Bürgerliches Gesetzbuch.*
BHE, *Bund der Heimatvertriebenen und Entrechteten.*
Bhf., *Bahnhof.*
bibl., *biblisch.*
bildl., *bildlich.*
bisw., *bisweilen.*
Bl., *Blatt*; *pl.* **Bll.**, *Blätter.*
BMW, *Bayerische Motorenwerke.*
B. P., *beschleunigter Personenzug.*
br., 1. *breit.* 2. *broschiert.* 3. *brutto.*
Br., 1. *Bruder.* 2. *Breite* (*Geog.*).
BRT, *Bruttoregistertonnen.*
b. w., *bitte wenden* (= P.T.O.).
Bz., *Bestellzettel.*
bzw., *beziehungsweise.*

C

ca., *circa.*
cand. phil., *candidatus philosophiae, Student kurz vor seiner Doktor- oder Staatsprüfung.*
cbm, *Kubikmeter.*
cca., see **ca.**
ccm, *Kubikzentimeter.*
CDU, *Christlich-Demokratische Union.*
cg, *Zentigramm.*
chem., *chemisch.*
Chem., *Chemiker.*
Chr., 1. *Christus.* 2. *Chronik.*
cm, *Zentimeter.*
corr., *korrigiert.*
Cos., *Kosinus.*
crt., *currentis.*
CSU, *Christlich-Soziale Union.*
c.t., *cum tempore* (i.e. 15 minutes after the time announced) (*Univ.*).
C.V.J.M., *Christlicher Verein Junger Männer.*

D

d., *der, des, dem, den, die, das.*
D., 1. *Deutschland.* 2. *Dichte*; D^{16} = spec. grav. at

16°; D_4^{16} = spec. grav. at 16° with reference to water at 4°. 3. *Doktor theologiae.*
d. Ä., *der Ältere.*
das., *daselbst.*
dass., *dasselbe.*
DAF., *Deutsche Arbeitsfront* (*Nat. Soc.*).
DB, *Deutsche Bundesbahn.*
d. Bl., *dieses Blattes.*
DBP, *Deutsche Bundespost.*
d. d., *de dato.*
DDR, *Deutsche Demokratische Republik.*
D. E., *Dielektrizitätskonstante* (*Elec.*).
Dego, *Deutsche Golddiskontbank.*
Dekl., *Deklination.*
Delag, *Deutsche Elektrizitäts-Aktiengesellschaft.*
ders., *derselbe.*
D.G.B., *Deutscher Gewerkschaftsbund.*
dgl., *dergleichen, desgleichen*; **u. dgl.**, *und dergleichen.*
d. Gr., *der Große.*
d. h., *das heißt* (= viz.).
d. i., *das ist* (= i.e.).
DIN, *Deutsche Industrie-Norm.*
Dipl.-Ing., *Diplomingenieur.*
Dipl.-Kaufm., *Diplomkaufmann.*
Diss., *Dissertation.*
d. J., 1. *dieses Jahres.* 2. *der Jüngere.*
DJ., *Deutsches Jungvolk* (*Nat. Soc.*).
DJH, *Deutsche Jugendherberge.*
DKW, *Deutsche Kraftwagen-Werke.*
d. M., *dieses Monats* (= inst.).
Dm., *Durchmesser.*
DM, *Deutsche Mark.*
DNB, *Deutsches Nachrichtenbüro.*
d. O., *der Obige* (*often in place of a signature*).
do., *detto, ditto.*
DPA, *Deutsche Presse-Agentur.*
DR(B), *Deutsche Reichsbahn* (*pre-1918*)
DRGM, *Deutsches Reichs-Gebrauchsmuster* (*pre-1918*).
Dr. Ing., *Doktor der Ingenieurwissenschaft.*
Dr. j. u., *doctor juris utriusque* (= LL.D.).
Dr. med., *doctor medicinae* (= M.D.).
DRP, 1. *Deutsche Reichspost.* 2. *Deutsches Reichspatent.*
Dr. phil., *doctor philosophiae* (= Ph.D.).
Dr. rer. nat., *doctor rerum naturalium* (= D.Sc. *or* Sc.D.).
Dr. rer. pol., *doctor rerum politicarum.*
Dr. theol., *doctor theologiae* (= D.D.).
DSG, *Deutsche Schlafwagen-Gesellschaft.*
dtsch., *deutsch.*
Dtzd., *Dutzend.*
d.u., *dienstuntauglich* (*Mil.*) (= C. 3).
Durchl., *Durchlaucht.*
Dutz., see **Dtzd.**
d. Vf., *der Verfasser.*
D-Wagen, *Durchgangswagen.*
dz., *derzeit.*
D-Zug, *Durchgangszug.*

E

E., 1. *Erstarrungspunkt.* 2. *Elektromotorische Kraft* (= EMF) (*Elec.*).
ea., *einander.*
ebd., *ebenda, ebendaselbst.*
edul., *entgegengesetzt dem Uhrzeiger laufend.*
E.G.m.b.H., *Eingetragene Genossenschaft mit beschränkter Haftpflicht.*
e.h., *ehrenhalber* (*of degree*).
Ehape, *Einheitspreisgeschäft.*
ehm., *ehemals.*
eidg., *eidgenössisch* (*Swiss*).
eigtl., *eigentlich.*
eing., *eingegangen.*
Einl., *Einleitung.*
einschl., *einschließlich.*
Einw., 1. *Einwirkung.* 2. *Einwohner.*
einz., *einzeln.*
Einz., *Einzahl.*
E. K., *Eisernes Kreuz.*
em., *emeritus.*
EMK, see E. (2).
engl., *englisch.*
enth., *enthaltend.*
Entschl., *Entschließung.*
entspr., *entsprechend.*
Entsteh., *Entstehung.*
entw., *entweder.*
E. P., *englisches Patent.*
erg., *ergänze.*
Erg.-Bd., *Ergänzungsband*
Erl., *Erläuterung.*
etw., *etwas.*
ev., 1. *evangelisch.* 2. *eventuell.*
Ev., *Evangelium.*
E. V., *Eingetragener Verein.*
event., *eventuell.*
EVG. *Europäische Verteidigungs-Gemeinschaft* (= EDC).
ev.-luth., *evangelisch-lutherisch.*
evtl., *eventuell.*
Ew., *Euer, Eure, Eurer* (*in titles*).
EWG, *Europäische Wirtschaftsgemeinschaft* (= EEC, Common Market).
exkl., *exklusive.*
Expl., *Exemplar.*
Exz., *Exzellenz.*
E-Zug, *Eilzug.*

F

f., 1. *für.* 2. *folgende.*
F., *Fusionspunkt.*
F, 1. *Farad* (*Elec.*). 2. *Fahrenheit.*
FAD, *Freiwilliger Arbeitsdienst* (*Nat. Soc.*).
Fam., *Familie.*
farbl., *farblos.*
f. d. D., *für den Dienstgebrauch* (*Mil.*).
FDJ, *Freie Deutsche Jugend.*
FDP, *Freie Demokratische Partei.*
FD-Zug, *Fern-D-Zug.*
ff., *folgende.*
F. f., *Fortsetzung folgt.*
Fil., *Filiale.*
fl., *Florin, Gulden.*
Flak, *Flieger-Abwehr-Kanone.*
Flugschr., *Flugschrift.*
F.O., *Felddienstordnung.*
Fol., *Folio.*
folg., *folgend.*
Forts., *Fortsetzung*; **Forts. f.**, *Fortsetzung folgt.*
F. P., **Fr. P.**, *französisches Patent.*
fr., *franko, frei.*
Fr., *Frau*; **Fr. v.**, *Frau von.*
franz., *französisch.*
frbl., see **farbl.**
frdl., *freundlich.*
Frh., **Frhr.**, *Freiherr.*
Frl., *Fräulein*: **Frl. v.**, *Fräulein von.*
Frzbd., *Franzband.*
F-Schlüssel, *Baßschlüssel* (*Mus.*).
F. T., *Funktelegraphie* (= R.T.).

G

g, *Gramm.*
G, 1. *Geld* (*on bills of exchange*). 2. *Gauß* (*Magnet.*).
geb., 1. *geboren.* 2. *gebunden.*
gebr., *gebräuchlich, gebraucht.*
Gebr., *Gebrüder.*
gef., *gefälligst.*
Gef. P., *Gefrierpunkt.*
geg., *gegen.*
Gegenw., *Gegenwart.*
gegr., *gegründet.*
geh., *geheftet.*
Geh. Rat, *Geheimrat.*
geistl., *geistlich.*
gek., *gekürzt.*
gem., 1. *gemäß.* 2. *gemischt.*
gen., 1. *genannt.* 2. *geneigt.*
Ge. N., *geographischer Nord.*
Ges., 1. *Gesang.* 2. *Gesellschaft.*
geschr., *geschrieben.*

ges. gesch., *gesetzlich geschützt.*
gespr., *gesprochen.*
gest., *gestorben.*
Gestapo, *Geheime Staatspolizei* (*Nat. Soc.*).
gew., *gewöhnlich.*
Gew., *Gewicht.*
Gew.-O., *Gewerbeordnung.*
gez., *gezeichnet.*
Ggs., *Gegensatz.*
Gldr., *Ganzleder.*
gleichbd., *gleichbedeutend.*
gl. N., *gleichen Namens.*
glz., *gleichzeitig.*
G. m. b. H., **GmbH**, *Gesellschaft mit beschränkter Haftung.*
GPU, *Russische Geheimpolizei* (= Ogpu).
gr., 1. *groß.* 2. *Gramm.*
Grdr., *Grundriß.*
gr.-kath., *griechisch-katholisch.*
Grp., *Gruppe* (*Mil.*).
gründl., *gründlich.*
G-Schlüssel, *Sopranschlüssel* (*Mus.*).

H

h. 1. *hoch.* 2. *heiß.*
-h., final, as the second part of a compound, stands for: 1. *–handwerk*, e.g. **Schmiedeh.**, *Schmiedehandwerk.* 2. *–hütte*, e.g. **Eisenh.**, *Eisenhütte.*
H, *Höhe.*
H., *Haben* (*Guthaben*).
ha, *Hektar.*
Hapag, *Hamburg-Amerikanische Paketfahrt-Aktiengesellschaft.*
Hbf., *Hauptbahnhof.*
hd., *hochdeutsch.*
H(d)b., *Handbuch.*
Hekt., *Hektoliter.*
herg., *hergestellt.*
hfl., *holländischer Gulden.*
Hfrzbd., *Halbfranzband.*
hg., *herausgegeben.*
HGB., *Handelsgesetzbuch.*
H.H., *Handelshochschule.*
HJ., *Hitlerjugend* (*Nat. Soc.*).
HK, *Hefner-Kerze* (*Phys.*).
hl, *Hektoliter.*
Hldr., *Halbleder.*
HO, *Handelsorganisation.*
holl., *holländisch.*
Hpt., *Haupt.*
Hptm., *Hauptmann* (*Mil.*).
Hptw., *Hauptwort.*
Hr., *Herr*; *pl.* **HH.**, *Herren.*
hrsg., *herausgegeben.*
Hrsg., *Herausgeber.*
Hs., *Handschrift* (= MS.); *pl.* **Hss.** (= MSS.).

I

i., *in, im*; *e.g.* **Freiberg i. Sachsen.**
I, *elektrische Stromstärke.*
I., *Ihre.*
i. A., *im Auftrage.*
I. A. A., *Internationales Arbeitsamt.*
i. allg., *im allgemeinen.*
i. b., *im besonderen.*
i. D., *inklusive Dividende.*
i. Durchschn., *im Durchschnitt.*
i. e. R., *im einstweiligen Ruhestand.*
I. G., *Interessengemeinschaft*; *e.g.* **I. G. Farben.**
i. J., *im Jahre.*
I. K. H., *Ihre Königliche Hoheit.*
I. M., *Ihre Majestät.*
Imp., *Imperator.*
inakt., *inaktiv.*
Ind., *Industrie.*
Ing., *Ingenieur.*
Inh., *Inhalt.*
inkl., *inklusive.*
insb., *insbesondere.*
Inst., *Institut.*
i. P., *in Preußen.*
i. R., *im Ruhestand.*
I. R., *Imperator Rex.*
i. Sa., *in Sachsen.*
i. V., 1. *in Vertretung* 2. *im Vakuum.*
i. W., 1. *in Westfalen.* 2. *in Worten.* 3. *innere Weite* (= i.d.).
i. W. v., *im Werte von.*

J

J., *Jahr.*
Jahrh., *Jahrhundert.*
Jb., 1. *Jahrbuch.* 2. *Jahresbericht.*
Jg., *Jahrgang* (*of a periodical*).
Jh., *Jahrhundert.*
JH, *Jugendherberge.*
J.-Nr., *Journalnummer* (*C.L.*).
jr., **jun.**, *junior.*

K

k., 1. *kaiserlich.* 2. *königlich.* 3. *kalt.*
-k., final, as the second part of a word, stands for: 1. *–keit*, e.g. **Ewigk.**, *Ewigkeit.* 2. *–kunde*, *–kunst*, e.g. **Heilk.**, *Heilkunde*; **Bauk.**, *Baukunst, Baukunde.*
K., 1. *Kap.* 2. *Kapitel.* 3. *Konstante.* 4. *Kalorie.*
Ka., *Kathode* (*Rad.*).
kais., *kaiserlich.*
Kal, *Kilogramm-Kalorie.*
kal, *Gramm-Kalorie.*
Kap., *Kapitel.*
kart., *kartoniert.*
kath., *katholisch.*
KdF, *Kraft durch Freude* (*Nat. Soc.*).
kg, *Kilogramm.*
K.-G. (a.A.), *Kommanditgesellschaft* (*auf Aktien*).
kgl., *königlich.*
kHz, *Kilohertz* (*Rad.*).
k.J., *kommenden* or *künftigen Jahres.*
k.k., **K.K.**, **k.u.k.**, *kaiserlich* (*und*) *königlich* (*title of Austrian royalty*).
kl., *klein.*
Kl., *Klasse.*
km, *Kilometer.*
k. M., *künftigen Monats* (= prox.).
kn, *Knoten* (*Naut.*).
KO, *Konkursordnung.*
k.o., *knockout* (*Boxing*). (*coll.*) *erledigt, fertig.*
Koeff., **Koeffiz.**, *Koeffizient.*
Komp., *Kompanie* (*Mil.*).
kompr., *komprimiert.*
Konj., *Konjunktiv.*
kons., *konservativ.*
konst., *konstant.*
konz., *konzentriert.*
kor(r)., *korrigiert.*
Kp., *Kochpunkt.* **Kp. 10**, *Kochpunkt bei 10 mm Quecksilberdruck.*
KPD, *Kommunistische Partei Deutschlands.*
Kr., 1. *Krone* (*Scandinavian currency*). 2. *Krystallographie.*
krist., *kristallisiert, kristallinisch.*
k. T., *konkreter Tatbestand.*
kub., *kubisch.*
Kub.-Gew., *Kubikgewicht* (= density).
k.v., *kriegsverwendungsfähig* (= A 1) (*Mil.*).
kV, *Kilovolt.*
kVA, *Kilovolt-ampere.*
kW, **kw**, *Kilowatt.*
kWh, *Kilowattstunde.*
KZ, *Konzentrationslager.*
K. Z., *Kurszettel.*

L

l, *Liter.*
l., 1. *lies.* 2. *links.* 3. *löslich.*
-l., final, as the second part of a word, stands for: 1. *-lich, e.g.* **jährl.,** *jährlich*; **frdl.,** *freundlich.* 2. *-lung, e.g.* **Handl.,** *Handlung.*
L., 1. *Länge (also Geogr.).* 2. *Selbstinduktionskoeffizient (Elec.).*
lab., *labil.*
L.A.G., *Lastenausgleichgesetz.*
landw., *landwirtschaftlich.*
langj., *langjährig.*
Ldr., 1. *Louis d'or.* 2. *Leder.*
Ldrb., *Lederband.*
Ldrr., *Lederrücken.*
Lebensl., *Lebenslauf.*
Legg., *Legierungen.*
leichtl., *leichtlöslich.*
lfd., *laufend*; **lfde. Nr.,** *laufende Nummer.*
Lfg., Lfrg., *Lieferung.*
lg., *lang.*
Lit., *Literatur.*
l. J., *laufenden Jahres.*
LKW., Lkw., *Lastkraftwagen.*
l. l., see **leichtl.**
l. M., *laufenden Monats* (= inst.).
Ln., *Leinen(band).*
log, *Logarithmus.*
lösl., *löslich.*
Lösl., *Löslichkeit.*
LPG, *Landwirtschaftliche Produktionsgenossenschaft.*
L. S., *lange Sicht (C.L.).*
Lsg., *pl.* **Lsgg.,** *Lösung(en).*
lt., *laut.*
luth., *lutherisch.*
Lw., *Lehnwort.*
l. w., *lichte Weite* (= i. d.).
Lw(d)., *Leinwand.*
Lwdb., *Leinwandband.*
L-Zug, *Luxuszug.*

M

m, *Meter.*
m., 1. *merke.* 2. *mit.* 3. *männlich.* 4. *Minute.*
-m., final, as the second part of a compound, stands for: *-macher, e.g.* **Schuhm.,** *Schuhmacher.*
M., 1. *Mark.* 2. *Meile.* 3. *Monat.* 4. *Masse.* 5. *Molekulargewicht.*
mA, *Milliampere.*
M. A., *Miniaturausgabe.*
MA, *Mittelalter.*
magn(et)., *magnetisch.*
m. A. n., *meiner Ansicht nach.*
m. a. W., *mit anderen Worten.*
m. b. H., *mit beschränkter Haftung (C.L.).*
M. d. B., *Mitglied des Bundestags.*
M. d. L., *Mitglied des Landtags.*
M. d. R., *Mitglied des Reichstags (cf.* M.P.).
m. E., *meines Erachtens.*
mechan., *mechanisch.*
Mehrz., *Mehrzahl.*
Meth., *Methode.*
MEZ, *Mitteleuropäische Zeit (one hour in advance of Greenwich time but corresponding to the English summer time).*
mg, *Milligramm.*
m. G., *mit Goldschnitt.*
M. G., 1. *Maschinengewehr.* 2. see **M. (5).**
mhd., *mittelhochdeutsch.*
m. HH., *meine Herren*; **m. Hr.,** *mein Herr.*
Min., *Minute(n).*
Mitropa, *Mitteleuropäische Schlaf- und Speisewagen-Aktiengesellschaft (Railw.).*
mitt., *mittels.*
Mitt., *Mitteilung(en).*
Mitw., *Mitwirkung.*
Mk., *Mark.*
mk(r)., *mikroskopisch.*
m.l., *mein lieber, meine lieben.*
mm, *Millimeter.*
möbl., *möbliert.*
mögl., *möglich.*
mol., *molekular.*
Mol., *Molekül(e).*
Monatsh., *Monatsheft.*
mot., *motorisiert (Mil.).*
m./R., *meine Rechnung.*
Mschr., *Monatsschrift.*
MS., Mskr., *Manuskript.*
mul., *mit dem Uhrzeiger laufend.*
m. W., *meines Wissens.*
mx., *Maximum.*
Mz., *Mehrzahl.*
m.Z., *mangels Zahlung (C.L.).*

N

n., 1. *nach.* 2. *neu.* 3. *nächst.* 4. *nördlich.* 5. *normal.* 6. *Nutzeffekt, Wirkungsgrad.*
N, 1. *Nord(en) (wind and direction).* 2. *Leistung (Mech.).*
N., *Name.*
N. A., *neue Ausgabe* or *Auflage.*
Nachf., *Nachfolger.*
nachm., *nachmittags.*
Nachn., *Nachnahme (C.L.).*
nat.-soz., *nationalsozialistisch.*
n. B., *nördliche(r) Breite (Geog.).*
Nchf., see **Nachf.**
n. Chr., *nach Christo, nach Christi Geburt* = A.D.)
N.D., *Niederdruck (Meteor.).*
ndrd., *niederdeutsch (Philol., Geog.).*
Ne., *effektive Leistung (Mech.).*
neb., *neben.*
neutr., *neutralisiert.*
N. F., *neue Folge.*
nhd., *neuhochdeutsch.*
n. J., *nächsten Jahres.*
NK, *Normalkerze.*
n. l., *nicht löslich.*
Nm., 1. *nachmittags* (= p.m.). 2. *mechanischer Wirkungsgrad (Mech.).*
n. M., *nächsten Monats* (= prox.).
NN, *Normalnull.*
no., ntto., *netto.*
No., *Numero.*
NO, *Nordost, Nordosten (wind and direction).*
Norm., *Normen.*
Norw. P., *norwegisches Patent.*
N.P., *Nullpunkt.*
Nr., *Nummer* (= No.).
NS., 1. *Nachschrift* (= P.S.). 2. *Nationalsozialistisch.*
N.S., *Nach Sicht (C.L.).*
NSDAP, *Nationalsozialistische deutsche Arbeiterpartei.*
n. St., *neuen Stils (of dates).*
N.T., *Neues Testament.*
Nt., *thermischer Wirkungsgrad.*
Ntzl., *Nutzlast.*
NW, *Nordwest, Nordwesten (wind and direction).*
Nw., *wirtschaftlicher Wirkungsgrad*
NWDR, *Nordwestdeutscher Rundfunk.*
N.Z., *Normalzeit.*

O

o., 1. *oben.* 2. *ohne.* 3. *oder.*
O., 1. *Order.* 2. *Ort.*
O, *Osten.*
ö., österr., *österreichisch.*
o. ä., *oder ähnliches.*
o. B., *ohne Befund (Med.).*
Obb., *Oberbayern.*
obh., *oberhalb.*
Obus, *Oberleitungsomnibus.*
od., *oder.*
o. D(b)., *ohne Dividende(nbogen).*
o. dgl., o. drgl., *oder dergleichen.*
OEZ, *osteuropäische Zeit.*

OHL, *Oberste Heersleitung* (*1st World War*).
o. J., *ohne Jahr* (= n.d.).
OKH, *Oberkommando des Heeres* (*2nd World War*).
OKW, *Oberkommando der Wehrmacht* (*2nd World War*).
ö. L., *östliche(r) Länge* (*Geogr.*).
o. O. u. J., *ohne Ort und Jahr* (*of publication*).
opt., *optisch.*
Ord., *Ordnung.*
org., *organisch.*
Ostpr., *Ostpreußen.*
o. V., 1. *ohne Verzögerung* (*C.L.*). 2. *ohne Verpflegung* (*Mil.*).

P

p., 1. *pro.* 2. *para.*
P, 1. *Papier* (*C.L.*). 2. *Parkplatz* (*Motor.*).
pa., *prima* (*C.L.*).
p.a., *pro anno.*
p.A., *per Adresse* (*on letters*) (= c/o).
p. c., *Prozent, pro Cent.*
p. Chr. (n.), *post Christum* (*natum*) (= A.D.).
Pf., *Pfennig.*
Pfd., *Pfund*; **Pfd. St.**, *Pfund Sterling.*
Pg., *Parteigenosse* (*Nat. Soc.*).
Pkt., *Punkt.*
PKW, Pkw., *Personenkraftwagen.*
p. m., 1. *post mortem.* 2. *pro mille.* 3. *pro Minute.*
p. p., *per procura.*
P. P., p.p., *praemissis praemittendis* (*on business letters*); *der p. p. Müller*, the (afore)said Miller.
Ppbd., *Pappband.*
Pr., 1. *Presse.* 2. *preußisch.*
pr. pa., pr. pr., *see* **p. p.**
prim., *primär.*
Prof., *Professor.*
Progr., *Programm.*
Prov., *Provinz.*
Proz., *Prozent*; **proz.**, *prozentig.*
PS, *Pferdestärke* (= H.P.).
p. t., *pro tempore.*
P. T., *praemisso titulo.*

Q

q, *Quadrat.*
qcm, *Quadratzentimeter.*
qkm, *Quadratkilometer.*
qm, *quadratmeter.*
qmm, *Quadratmillimeter.*
Q. S., *Quecksilberstand* or *Quecksilbersäule.*

R

r., *rund.*
R, 1. *Réaumur.* 2. *rechter Winkel.* 3. *Rechnung.* 4. *Widerstand* (*Elec.*).
RA, *Rechtsanwalt.*
Rab., *Rabatt.*
RAB, *Reichsautobahn.*
RAD, *Reichsarbeitsdienst* (*Nat. Soc.*).
rd., see **r.**
Rdfk., *Rundfunk.*
Ref., 1. *Referent.* 2. *Referate.*
Reg.-Bez. *Regierungsbezirk.*
resp., *respektive.*
rglm., *regelmäßig.*
Rh., *Rhein, rheinisch.*
RIAS, *Rundfunk im Amerikanischen Sektor.*
Rk., *Reaktion*; *pl.* **Rkk.**, *Reaktionen* (*Chem.*).
rm, *Raummeter* (*of timber, etc.*).
RM, Rmk., *Reichsmark.*
R. M., *Reichsmarine.*
röm., *römisch*; **röm.-kath.**, *römisch-katholisch.*
Rp., *Rappen* (*Swiss*).
R.P., *Reichspatent.*
Rpf., *Reichspfennig.*
Rtm., *Rittmeister.*
RWD., *Reichswetterdienst.*

S

s., *siehe.*
S, 1. *Süd, Süden* (*wind and direction*). 2. *Schilling* (*Austrian currency*).
S., *Seite* (= p.).
s. a., *siehe auch.*
Sa., 1. *summa.* 2. *Sachsen.*
SA, *Sturmabteilung* (*Nat. Soc.*).
S.A., *Sonderabdruck.*
s. a. S., *siehe auch Seite.*
Sächs., *Sächsisch.*
s. B, *südliche(r) Breite* (*Geogr.*).
SBB, *Schweizer Bundesbahnen.*
Schmp., Sch.P., Schmpt., *Schmelzpunkt.*
Schupo, *Schutzpolizist.*
schw., 1. *schwach.* 2. *schwer.*
Schw., 1. *Schwester.* 2. *Schweizerisch.* 3. *Schwedisch.*
s. d., *siehe dies, siehe dort* (= q.v.).
Sd., Sdp., *Siedepunkt.*
S(e)., *Seine, Seiner.*
SED, *Sozialistische Einheitspartei Deutschlands.*
Sek., *Sekunde.*
sel., *selig* (*in all cases, genders, and numbers*).
selbst., *selbständig.*
seq., seqq., *sequens, sequentes.*
Ser., *Serie.*
s. G., *spezifisches Gewicht.*
S. K. H., *Seine Königliche Hoheit.*
Skt., *Sankt.*
sm, *Seemeile.*
SM., *Sekundenmeter.*
S. M., *Seine Majestät.*
S. M. S., *Seiner Majestät Schiff* (= H.M.S.).
SO, *Südost, Südosten* (*wind and direction*).
s. o., *siehe oben.*
sof., *sofort.*
sog., sogen., *sogenannt.*
soz., *sozialistisch.*
Soz., *Sozialdemokrat.*
Sp., *Spalte.*
S.P., *Siedepunkt.*
SPD, *Sozialdemokratische Partei Deutschlands.*
spez. Gew., see **s. G.**
spr., *sprich.*
sp. W., *spezifische Wärme.*
Sr., see **S(e).**
SS, *Schutzstaffel* (*Nat. Soc.*).
SS. *Sante, Santi.*
s. S., *siehe Seite.*
S. S., *Sommersemester.*
st., *stark.*
St., 1. *Stück.* 2. *Stamm.* 3. *Sankt.* 4. *Stil.* 5. *Stunde.*
s. t., *sine tempore* (*i.e.* at the time announced).
Std., *Stunde(n).*
StGB., *Strafgesetzbuch.*
Str., *Straße.*
s. u., *siehe unten.*
s. W., see **sp. W.**
SW, *Südwest, Südwesten* (*wind and direction*).
s. w. u., *siehe weiter unten.*
s. Z., *seinerzeit.*

T

t, *Tonne* (= *1000 kilogrammes*).
t°, Celsius.
T., 1. *Tausend.* 2. *Tage* (*C.L.*).
T°, *absolute Temperatur.*
T. A., *Taschenausgabe.*
Tbc, *Tuberkulose* (= T.B.).
techn., *technisch.*
Tel.-Adr., *Telegrammadresse.*
teilw., *teilweise.*
term. techn., *terminus technicus.*
T. F., *Taschenformat.*

Tfg., *Tiefgang.*
tg., *Tangente.*
T. H., *Technische Hochschule.*
Th., *Thema.*
Thlr., *Thaler.*
Titl., *Titel.*
Tl., *Teil.*

U

u., 1. *und.* 2. *unter.* 3. *unten.*
U., 1. *Uhr.* 2. *Umdrehung.*
u. a., 1. *unter anderem.* 2. *und andere.*
u. a. m., 1 *und andere mehr.* 2. *und anderes mehr.*
u. ä. (m.), *und ähnliches (mehr).*
u. A. w. g., *um Antwort wird gebeten* (= R.S.V.P.).
übers., *übersetzt.*
U-Boot, *Unterseeboot.*
u. dgl. (m.), *und dergleichen (mehr).*
u. d. M., *unter dem Meeresspiegel.*
ü. d. M., *über dem Meeresspiegel.*
u. E., *unseres Erachten .*
u.e.a., *und einige andere.*
Ufa, *Universum-Film-Aktiengesellschaft.*
Uffz., *Unteroffizier* (= N.C.O.)
u. ff., *und folgende.*
u.k., *unabkömmlich (Mil.).*
UKW, *Ultra-Kurzwellen (Rad.).*
U.L.F., *Unsere Liebe Frau (R.C.).*
ü. M., see **ü. d. M.**
U./M., *Umdrehungen in der Minute.*
Umg., *Umgebung.*
unbest., *unbestimmt.*
unfl., *unflektiert.*
ung., *ungefähr.*
unr., **unreg.**, *unregelmäßig.*
u. ö., *und öfter.*
U. p. M., see **U./M.**
ursp., *ursprünglich.*
usf., *und so fort* (= etc.).
usw., *und so weiter* (= etc.).
u. U., *unter Umständen.*
u. ü. V., *unter üblichem Vorbehalt.*
u. v. a., *und viele andere.*
u. W., *unseres Wissens.*
u .zw., *und zwar.*

V

v., *von, vom.*
V, 1. *Volt.* 2. *Volumen (Phys., Chem.).*
V., *Vers.*
VA, *Voltampere.*
Vak., *Vakuum.*
v. Chr. (G.), *vor Christi (Geburt)* (= B.C.).
VEB, *Volkseigener Betrieb.*
verb., *verbessert.*
Verf., *Verfasser*; *pl.* **Verff.**, *Verfasser.*
verfl. J., *verflossenen Jahres.*
Vergl., *Vergleich.*
verk., *verkürzt.*
verl., *verlängert.*
Verl., *Verleger, Verlag.*
verm., 1. *vermehrt.* 2. *vermählt.*
versch., *verschieden.*
verst., *verstorben.*
Ver. St., *Vereinigte Staaten (von Amerika).*
verw., 1. *verwitwet.* 2. *verwandt.*
Vf., see **Verf.**
Vfg. v., *Verfügung vom.*
vgl., 1. *vergleiche* (= cp.). 2. *vergleichend*; **vgl. a.**, *vergleiche auch*; **vgl. o.**, *vergleiche oben.*
v., g., u., *vorgelesen, genehmigt, unterschrieben.*
v. H., *vom Hundert.*
viell., *vielleicht.*
v. J., 1. *vorigen Jahres.* 2. *vom Jahre.*
Vjs., *Vierteljahrschrift.*
v. M., *vorigen Monats* (= ult.).
Vm., *vormittags* (= a.m.).
v. o., *von oben.*
VO, *Verordnung.*
Vol.-Gew., *volumetrisches Gewicht.*
vollst., *vollständig.*
Vopo, *Volkspolizei.*
vor., *vorig.*
vorm., 1. *vormals.* 2. *vormittags* (= a.m.).
Vors., *Vorsitzende(r).*
v. R. w., *von Rechts wegen.*
V. St. A., *Vereinigte Staaten von Amerika* (= U.S.A.).
v.T., *vom Tausend.*
v. u., *von unten.*

W

-w., final, as the second part of a compound, stands for: 1. *-weise*, *e.g.* **teilw.**, *teilweise*; see **bezw.** 2. *-wesen*, *e.g.* **Finanzw.**, *Finanzwesen.* 3. *-wort*, *e.g.* **Bindew.**, *Bindewort.*
W., 1. *Währung.* 2. *Wechsel.*
W, 1. *Watt.* 2. *West, Westen (wind and direction).* 3. *Widerstand.*
Wbl., *Wochenblatt.*
W.E., *Wärmeeinheit.*
weil., *weiland.*
Westf., *Westfalen.*
Wewa., *Wetterwarte.*
WEZ, *westeuropäische Zeit* (= G.M.T.).
willk., *willkürlich.*
wiss., *wissenschaftlich.*
w. L., *westliche(r) Länge (Geogr.).*
WO, *Wechselordnung.*
WPV, *Weltpostverein.*
W. S., *Wintersemester.*
W. S. g. u., *Wenden Sie gefälligst um* (= P.T.O.).
Württ., *Württemberg.*
WUSt., *Warenumsatzsteuer.*
Wwe., *Witwe.*

Z

z., *zu, zum, zur.*
Z., 1. *Zahl.* 2. *Zeile.* 3. *Zeit.* 4. *Zoll.*
zahlr., *zahlreich.*
z. B., *zum Beispiel* (= e.g.).
z. b. V., *zur besonderen Verwendung (Mil.).*
z.D., *zur Disposition (Mil.).*
z. E., *zum Exempel* (= e.g.).
zgl., *zugleich.*
z. H., *zu Händen, zuhanden.*
Zs., *Zeitschrift*; *pl.* **Zss.**, *Zeitschriften.*
z. S., *zur See.*
z. s. Z., *zu seiner Zeit.*
Zszg., *Zusammensetzung.*
Zt., *Zeit.*
z. T., *zum Teil.*
Ztg., *Zeitung.*
Ztr., *Zentner* (= cwt.).
Ztschr., see **Zs.**
ztw., *zeitweise.*
Ztw., *Zeitwort.*
zul., *zuletzt.*
zus., *zusammen.*
Zus., 1. *Zusatz.* 2. *Zusammensetzung.*
Zuschl., *Zuschlag.*
Zus.-P., *Zusatzpatent.*
zuw., *zuweilen.*
zw., 1. *zwischen.* 2. *zwar.*
z. Z., **z. Zt.**, *zur Zeit.*

CHEMICAL ELEMENTS

Only those elements are listed of which the German name or symbol differs from the English.

Atomic Number (Ordnungszahl)	*English Name*	*German Name*	*German Symbol*
1	Hydrogen	*Wasserstoff*	H
4	Beryllium (Glucinum)	*Beryllium*	Be
5	Boron	*Bor*	B
6	Carbon	*Kohlenstoff*	C
7	Nitrogen	*Stickstoff*	N
8	Oxygen	*Sauerstoff*	O
9	Fluorine	*Fluor*	F
11	Sodium	*Natrium*	Na
14	Silicon	*Silizium*	Si
15	Phosphorus	*Phosphor*	P
16	Sulphur	*Schwefel*	S
17	Chlorine	*Chlor*	Cl
18	Argon	*Argon*	Ar
19	Potassium	*Kalium*	K
20	Calcium	*Kalzium*	Ca
22	Titanium	*Titan*	Ti
24	Chromium	*Chrom*	Cr
25	Manganese	*Mangan*	Mn
26	Iron	*Eisen*	Fe
27	Cobalt	*Kobalt*	Co
29	Copper	*Kupfer*	Cu
30	Zinc	*Zink*	Zn
33	Arsenic	*Arsen*	As
34	Selenium	*Selen*	Se
35	Bromine	*Brom*	Br
40	Zirconium	*Zirkon*	Zr
41	Columbium	*Niobium*	Nb
42	Molybdenum	*Molybdän*	Mo
47	Silver	*Silber*	Ag
50	Tin	*Zinn*	Sn
51	Antimony	*Antimon*	Sb
52	Tellurium	*Tellur*	Te
53	Iodine	*Jod*	J
55	Caesium	*Cäsium (Zäsium)*	Cs
57	Lanthanum	*Lanthan*	La
59	Praseodymium	*Praseodym*	Pr
60	Neodymium	*Neodym*	Nd
71	Lutecium	*Lutetium*	Lu
73	Tantalum	*Tantal*	Ta
74	Tungsten	*Wolfram*	W
78	Platinum	*Platin*	Pt
80	Mercury	*Quecksilber*	Hg
82	Lead	*Blei*	Pb
83	Bismuth	*Wismut*	Bi
85	Astatine	*Astaton*	At
86	Radon (Niton)	*Radon Emanation*	Rn (Em)
89	Actinium	*Aktinium*	Ac
92	Uranium	*Uran*	U

LIST OF GERMAN IRREGULAR VERBS

INCLUDING ALL VERBS OF THE STRONG AND ANOMALOUS CONJUGATION AS WELL AS THOSE OF THE WEAK WHICH ARE CONJUGATED IN ANY WAY IRREGULARLY

¶ Plural forms *of the* imperative *correspond in form to the* 3rd person present indicative *unless otherwise stated.*

‖ *The* past participle *of an auxiliary verb of mood* (dürfen, mögen, müssen, wollen, etc.) *is replaced by its* infinitive *in the past compound tenses when immediately preceded by an infinitive; this is also the case with* lassen *used as an auxiliary, as well as with the verbs* heißen, helfen, hören, lehren, lernen, sehen.

(*a*) = not so good acc. to Duden. (*b*) = obsolete or poetical. (*c*) = dialect.

Letter *e* enclosed in parentheses may be included or omitted.

For compounds with *be-, ent-, er-, ge-, miß-, ver-, voll-, zer-*, and other prefixes, see the simple verbs where not otherwise given.

INFINITIVE	PRESENT INDIC.	IMPERF. INDIC.	IMPERF. SUBJ.	IMPERATIVE ¶	PAST PART.
(*b*) **auslöschen** (*also v.a. & weak; weak forms also used for v.n.*) (*see* **erlöschen, verlöschen**)	(das Licht) lischt aus	(das Licht) losch aus	lösche aus	S lisch aus! P löscht aus!	ausgeloschen
backen (*also weak in the meaning* 'to stick to', 'to clot', *and* (*Austr.*) 'to bake')	2 bäckst 3 bäckt	buk *or* backte	büke *or* backte	S backe! P backt!	gebacken
befehlen	2 befiehlst 3 befiehlt	befahl	beföhle (*c*) befähle	S befiehl! P befehlt!	befohlen
(sich) befleißen (*rare*)	2 befleißest *or* befleißt (dich) 3 befleißt (sich)	befliß (sich)	beflisse (sich)	S befleiß(e) (dich)! P befleißt (euch)!	beflissen
beginnen	2 beginnst 3 beginnt	begann	begönne, (*c*) begänne	beginn(e)!	begonnen
beißen	2 beißest *or* beißt 3 beißt	biß	bisse	beiß(e)!	gebissen
bergen	2 birgst 3 birgt	barg	bürge, (*c*) bärge	S birg! P bergt!	geborgen
bersten	2 birst, (*a*) & (*c*) berstest 3 birst, (*a*) & (*c*) berstet	barst, (*c*) borst	börste, (*a*) bärste	S birst! P berstet!	geborsten
betrügen (*see* **trügen**)					
bewegen (=to induce anyone to do anything. *In the meaning* 'to move' *physically or when used metaphorically, the verb is weak*)	2 bewegst 3 bewegt	bewog	bewöge	beweg(e)!	bewogen
biegen	2 biegst 3 biegt	bog	böge	bieg(e)!	gebogen
bieten	2 biet(e)st, (*b*) beutst 3 bietet, (*b*) beut	bot	böte	biet(e)! (*b*) beut!	geboten
binden	2 bindest 3 bindet	band	bände	bind(e)!	gebunden
bitten	2 bittest 3 bittet	bat	bäte	bitte!	gebeten
blasen	2 bläst *or* bläses 3 bläst	blies	bliese	S blas(e)! P blast!	geblasen
bleiben	2 bleibst 3 bleibt	blieb	bliebe	bleib(e)!	geblieben
(*b*) **bleichen** (= to grow pale, to fade. *In the meaning* 'to bleach' *the verb is weak*) (*see* **erbleichen**)	2 bleichst 3 bleicht	blich	bliche	S bleich(e) P bleicht	geblichen

INFINITIVE	PRESENT INDIC.	IMPERF. INDIC.	IMPERF. SUBJ.	IMPERATIVE ¶	PAST PART.
braten	2 brätst 3 brät	briet	briete	S brat(e)! P bratet!	gebraten
brechen	2 brichst 3 bricht	brach	bräche	S brich! P brecht!	gebrochen
brennen	2 brennst 3 brennt	brannte	brennte	brenne!	gebrannt
bringen	2 bringst 3 bringt	brachte	brächte	bring(e)!	gebracht
denken	2 denkst 3 denkt	dachte	dächte	denk(e)!	gedacht
dingen	2 dingst 3 dingt	dang *or* dingte	dingte, (*a*) dänge, (*a*) dünge	ding(e)!	gedungen *or* gedingt
dreschen	2 drisch(e)st 3 drischt	drasch*, (*c*) drosch	drösche, (*c*) dräsche	S drisch! P drescht!	gedroschen
dringen	2 dringst 3 dringt	drang	dränge	dring(e)!	gedrungen
dünken (*imp.*)	3 mich (*or* mir) dünkt (*b*) deucht	deuchte *or* dünkte	deuchte *or* dünkte		mich hat gedeucht *or* gedünkt
dürfen	S 1 & 3 darf 2 darfst,	durfte	dürfte		‖gedurft
empfangen	2 empfängst 3 empfängt	empfing	empfinge	S empfang(e)! P empfangt!	empfangen
empfehlen	2 empfiehlst 3 empfiehlt	empfahl	empföhle, (*c*) empfähle	S empfiehl! P empfehlt!	empfohlen
empfinden	2 empfindest 3 empfindet	empfand	empfände	empfind(e)!	empfunden
erbleichen	2 erbleichst 3 erbleicht	erbleichte *or* erblich	erbleichte *or* erbliche	erbleiche!	erbleicht *or* erblichen (= gestorben)
erkiesen (*see* kiesen)					
erlöschen (to become extinguished). *Weak forms are found, but Duden condemns them as bad.*	2 erlisch(e)st 3 erlischt	erlosch	erlösche	S erlisch! P erlöscht!	erloschen
erschrecken (*v.n.*) (*weak when v.a.* = to frighten)	2 erschrickst 3 erschrickt	erschrak	erschräke	S erschrick! P erschreckt!	erschrocken
erwägen	2 erwägst 3 erwägt	erwog	erwöge	erwäg(e)!	erwogen
essen	2 ißt *or* issest 3 ißt	1, 3 aß 2 aßest	äße	S iß! P eßt!	gegessen
fahren	2 fährst 3 fährt	fuhr	führe	S fahr(e)! P fahrt!	gefahren
fallen	2 fällst 3 fällt	fiel	fiele	S fall(e)! P fallt!	gefallen
fangen	2 fängst 3 fängt	fing	finge	S fang(e)! P fangt!	gefangen
fechten	2 ficht(e)st 3 ficht	focht	föchte	S ficht! P fechtet!	gefochten
finden	2 findest 3 findet	fand	fände	find(e)!	gefunden
flechten	2 flicht(e)st 3 flicht	flocht	flöchte	S flicht! P flechtet!	geflochte
fliegen	2 fliegst, (*b*) fleugst 3 fliegt, (*b*) fleugt	flog	flöge	flieg(e)! (*b*) fleug!	geflogen
fliehen	2 fliehst, (*b*) fleuchst 3 flieht, (*b*) fleucht	floh	flöhe	flieh(e)! (*b*) fleuch!	geflohen
fließen	2 fließest *or* fließt 3 fließt, (*b*) fleußt	floß	flösse	fließ(e)! (*b*) fleuß!	geflossen

* Archaic, in spite of what Duden says: now ousted by the dialect form.

INFINITIVE	PRESENT INDIC.	IMPERF. INDIC.	IMPERF. SUBJ.	IMPERATIVE ¶	PAST PART.
fragen	2 fragst, (*c*) frägst* 3 fragt, (*c*) frägt*	fragte, (*c*) frug*	fragte, (*c*) früge*	frag(e)!	gefragt
fressen	2 frißt *or* frissest 3 frißt	fraß	fräße	S friß! P freßt!	gefressen
frieren	2 frierst 3 friert	fror	fröre	frier(e)!	gefroren
gären (*weak when used figuratively*)	2 gärst 3 gärt	gor, (*a*) gärte	göre (*a*) gärte	gäre!	gegoren, (*a*) gegärt
gebären	2 gebierst 3 gebiert	gebar	gebäre	S gebier! P gebärt!	geboren
geben	2 gibst 3 gibt	gab	gäbe	S gib! P gebt!	gegeben
gedeihen	2 gedeihst 3 gedeiht	gedieh	gediehe	gedeih(e)!	gediehen
geh(e)n	2 gehst 3 geht	ging	ginge	geh(e)!	gegangen
gelingen (*imp.*)	3 (mir) gelingt	gelang	gelänge	geling(e)!	gelungen
gelten	2 giltst 3 gilt	galt	gölte *or* gälte	S gilt! P geltet!	gegolten
genesen	2 genes(es)t 3 genest	genas	genäse	genese!	genesen
genießen	2 genieß(es)t 3 genießt	genoß	genösse	genieß(e)!	genossen
geraten (*see* **raten**)					
geschehen (*imp.*)	3 (mir) geschieht	geschah	geschähe	—	geschehen
gewinnen	2 gewinnst 3 gewinnt	gewann	gewönne *or* gewänne	gewinn(e)!	gewonnen
gießen	2 gieß(es) 3 gießt	goß	gösse	gieß(e)!	gegossen
gleichen	2 gleichst 3 gleicht	glich	gliche	gleich(e)!	geglichen
gleiten	2 gleit(e)st 3 gleitet	glitt (*a*) gleitete	glitte	gleit(e)!	geglitten (*a*) gegleitet
glimmen	2 glimmst 3 glimmt	glomm *or* glimmte	glömme *or* glimmte	glimm(e)!	geglommen *or* geglimmt
graben	2 gräbst 3 gräbt	grub	grübe	S grab(e)! P grabt!	gegraben
greifen	2 greifst 3 greift	griff	griffe	greif(e)!	gegriffen
haben	2 hast 3 hat	hatte	hätte	S habe! P habt!	gehabt
halten	2 hältst 3 hält	hielt	hielte	S halt(e)! P haltet!	gehalten
hangen, *v.n.* (*In Pres. Ind. & Imper., forms of* hängen, *v.a., have practically replaced the correct forms.*)	2 hängst 3 hängt	hing	hinge	häng(e)!	gehangen
hauen	2 haust 3 haut	hieb, (*a*) haute	hiebe	hau(e)!	gehauen, (*a*) gehaut
heben	2 hebst 3 hebt	hob, (*c*) hub	höbe, (*c*) hübe	hebe!	gehoben
heißen	2 heiß(es)t 3 heißt	hieß	hieße	heiß(e)!	‖geheißen
helfen	2 hilfst 3 hilft	half	hülfe, (*c*) hälfe	S hilf! P helft!	‖geholfen
kennen	2 kennst 3 kennt	kannte	kennte	kenn(e)!	gekannt
(*b*) **(er)kiesen** (*see* **küren**)	2 (er)kies(es)t 3 (er)kiest	(er)kor, (*a*) (er)kieste	(er)köre, (*a*) (er)kieste	(er)kies(e)!	(er)koren
(*b*) **klieben**	2 kliebst 3 kliebt	klob *or* kliebte	klöbe *or* klieb(e)te	klieb(e)!	gekloben *or* gekliebt
klimmen	2 klimmst 3 klimmt	klomm *or* klimmte	klömme *or* klimm(e)te	klimm(e)!	geklommen *or* geklimmt

* These forms are not properly speaking dialectal. They used to be common in North Germany, due to the misunderstanding of High German conjugation by Low German speakers.

Infinitive	Present Indic.	Imperf. Indic.	Imperf. Subj	Imperative¶	Past Part.
klingen	2 klingst 3 klingt	klang	klänge	kling(e)!	geklungen
kneifen	2 kneifst 3 kneift	kniff	kniffe	kneif(e)!	gekniffen
kommen	2 kommst, (*b*) & (*c*) kömmst 3 kommt, (*b*) & (*c*) kömmt	kam	käme	S komm(e) P kommt!	gekommen
können	1 & 3 kann 2 kannst	konnte	könnte	—	‖gekonnt
kreischen	2 kreisch(e)st 3 kreischt	kreischte, (*a*) krisch	kreischte, (*a*) krische	kreisch(e)!	gekreischt, (*a*) gekrischen
kriechen	2 kriechst, (*b*) kreuchst 3 kriecht, (*b*) kreucht	kroch	kröche	kriech(e)! (*b*) kreuch!	gekrochen
(*b*) **küren** (*see* **kiesen**)	2 kürst 3 kürt	kürte *or* kor	kür(e)te *or* köre	kür(e)!	gekoren
laden (= auf-laden)	2 lädst 3 lädt	lud	lüde	S lad(e)! P ladet!	geladen
laden (= ein-laden) (*orig. only weak*)	2 ladest *or* lädst 3 ladet *or* lädt	lud *or* ladete	lüde *or* ladete	lad(e)!	geladen
lassen	2 läßt *or* lässest 3 läßt	ließ	ließe	S laß! P laßt!	‖gelassen
laufen	2 läufst 3 läuft	lief	liefe	S lauf(e)! P lauft!	gelaufen
leiden	2 leidest 3 leidet	litt	litte	leid(e)!	gelitten
leihen	2 leihst 3 leiht	lieh	liehe	leih(e)!	geliehen
lesen	2 lies(es)t 3 liest	las	läse	S lies! P lest!	gelesen
liegen	2 liegst 3 liegt	lag	läge	lieg(e)!	gelegen
(*b*) **löschen** (*v.n.* = to be extinguished) (*see* **erlöschen**); löschen, *v.a. is weak.*					
lügen	2 lügst 3 lügt	log	löge	lüg(e)!	gelogen
mahlen (*weak except p.p.*)	2 mahlst 3 mahlt	mahlte	mahlte	mahle!	gemahlen
meiden	2 meidest 3 meidet	mied	miede	meid(e)!	gemieden
melken	2 melkst, (*c*) milkst 3 melkt, (*c*) milkt	melkte, (*c*) molk	mölke, (*c*) melkte	melk(e)! (*b*) & (*c*) milk!	gemelkt; gemolken (*as adj. only*)
messen	2 mißt *or* missest 3 mißt	maß	mäße	S miß! P meßt!	gemessen
mißlingen (*imp.*)	3 (mir) mißlingt	mißlang	mißlänge	—	mißlungen
mögen	1 & 3 mag 2 magst	mochte	möchte	—	‖gemocht
müssen	1 & 3 muß 2 mußt	mußte	müßte	—	‖gemußt
nehmen	2 nimmst 3 nimmt	nahm	nähme	S nimm! P nehmt!	genommen
nennen	2 nennst 3 nennt	nannte	nennte	nenne!	genannt
pfeifen	2 pfeifst 3 pfeift	pfiff	pfiffe	pfeif(e)!	gepfiffen
pflegen	2 pflegst 3 pflegt	pflegt, *pflog	pflegte, *pflöge	pflege! *pfleg(e)!	gepflegt, *gepflogen
preisen	2 preis(es)t 3 preist	pries	priese	preis(e)!	gepriesen
quellen, *v.n.* (*v.a. is weak*)	2 quillst† 3 quillt	quoll	quölle	S quill! P quellt!	gequollen

* These forms are only used in certain stock phrases: *Rat pflegen, Ruhe pflegen*, etc.
† The forms *ich quille, wir quillen* also occur, but are not approved.

Infinitive	Present Indic.	Imperf. Indic.	Imperf. Subj.	Imperative ¶	Past Part.
(ge)raten	2 (ge)rätst* 3 (ge)rät*	(ge)riet	(ge)riete	S (ge)rat(e)! P (ge)ratet!	geraten
reiben	2 reibst 3 reibt	rieb	riebe	reib(e)!	gerieben
reißen	2 reiß(es)t 3 reißt	riß	risse	reiß(e)!	gerissen
reiten	2 reit(e)st 3 reitet	ritt	ritte	reit(e)!	geritten
rennen	2 rennst 3 rennt	rannte	rennte	renn(e)!	gerannt
riechen	2 riechst 3 riecht	roch	röche	riech(e)!	gerochen
ringen	2 ringst 3 ringt	rang	ränge	ring(e)!	gerungen
rinnen	2 rinnst 3 rinnt	rann	rönne, (*c*) ränne	rinn(e)!	geronnen
rufen	2 rufst 3 ruft	rief	riefe	ruf(e)!	gerufen
salzen	2 salz(es)t 3 salzt	salzte	salz(e)te	salze!	gesalzt *or* gesalzen (*used fig. only* gesalzen)
saufen	2 säufst 3 säuft	soff	söffe	sauf(e)!	gesoffen
saugen	2 saugst 3 saugt	sog, (*a*) saugte	söge	saug(e)!	gesogen, (*a*) gesaugt
schaffen (= to create. *In the meaning* 'to do, be busy' *the verb is weak*)	2 schaffst 3 schafft	schuf	schüfe	schaff(e)!	geschaffen
schallen	2 schallst 3 schallt	schallte, (*c*) scholl	schallete *or* schölle	schall(e)!	geschallt, (*b*) geschollen (*but* erschollen, verschollen)
scheiden	2 scheidest 3 scheidet	schied	schiede	scheid(e)!	geschieden
scheinen	2 scheinst 3 scheint	schien	schiene	schein(e)!	geschienen
scheißen	2 scheiß(es)t 3 scheißt	schiß	schisse	scheiß(e)!	geschissen
schelten	2 schiltst 3 schilt	schalt, (*c*) scholt	schölte, (*c*) schälte	S schilt! P scheltet!	gescholten
scheren	2 schierst, (*c*) scherst 3 schiert, (*c*) schert	schor *or* scherte	schöre *or* scherte	schier! (*c*) scher(e)!	geschoren *or* geschert
schieben	2 schiebst 3 schiebt	schob	schöbe	schieb(e)!	geschoben
schießen	2 schieß(es)t 3 schießt	schoß	schösse	schieß(e)!	geschossen
schinden	2 schindest 3 schindet	schund, (*a*) schand	schünde	schind(e)!	geschunden
schlafen	2 schläfst 3 schläft	schlief	schliefe	schlaf(e)!	geschlafen
schlagen	2 schlägst 3 schlägt	schlug	schlüge	schlag(e)!	geschlagen
schleichen	2 schleichst 3 schleicht	schlich	schliche	schleich(e)!	geschlichen
schleifen (= to grind, polish, slide. *In the meaning* 'to drag, to dismantle' *the verb is weak*)	2 schleifst 3 schleift	schliff	schliffe	schleif(e)!	geschliffen
schleißen	2 schleiß(es)t 3 schleißt	schliß, (*c*) schleißte	schlisse	schleiß(e)!	geschlissen, (*c*) geschleißt
schliefen	2 schliefst 3 schlieft	schloff	schlöffe	schlief(e)!	geschloffen

* N.B. The following stock phrases: *du ratest und tatest*, or *er ratet und tatet*, and *wer nicht mitratet, auch nicht mittatet* or *wer will mitraten, soll auch mittaten.*

Infinitive	Present Indic.	Imperf. Indic.	Imperf. Subj.	Imperative¶	Past Part.
schließen	2 schließ(es)t 3 schließt (*b*) schleußt	schloß	schlösse	schließ(e)! (*b*) schleuß!	geschlossen
schlingen	2 schlingst 3 schlingt	schlang	schlänge	schling(e)!	geschlungen
schmeißen	2 schmeiß(es) 3 schmeißt	schmiß	schmisse	schmeiß(e)!	geschmissen
schmelzen (*v.n.*)	2 schmilz(es)t 3 schmilzt	schmolz	schmölze	S schmilz! P schmelzt!	geschmolzen
schnauben	2 schnaubst 3 schnaubt	schnaubte, (*b*) schnob	schnaubte, (*b*) schnöbe	schnaub(e)!	geschnaubt, (*b*) ge- schnoben
schneiden	2 schneid(e)st 3 schneidet	schnitt	schnitte	schneid(e)!	geschnitten
schrauben	2 schraubst 3 schraubt	schraubte, (*b*) schrob	schraubte, (*b*) schröbe	schraub(e)!	geschraubt, (*b*) geschroben (*fig.* = tortu- ous *only the* *former*)
schrecken (*v.n.*)	2 schrickst 3 schrickt	schrak	schräke	S schrick! P schreckt!	(*b*) geschrocken (*only used now* *in compounds as* zusammenge- schrocken; *re-* *placed by* erschrocken)
schreiben	2 schreibst 3 schreibt	schrieb	schriebe	schreib(e)!	geschrieben
schreien	2 schreist 3 schreit	schrie	schriee	schrei(e)!	geschrie(e)n
schreiten	2 schreit(e)st 3 schreitet	schritt	schritte	schreit(e)!	geschritten
(*b*) **schrinden**	2 schrind(e)st 3 schrindet	schrund	schründe	schrind(e)!	geschrunden
schroten	2 schrotest 3 schrotet	schrotete	schrotete	schrote!	geschrotet, (*b*) ge- schroten
schwären (*imp.*)	3 schwärt *or* schwiert	schwor	schwöre	S schwier! *or* schwär(e)! P schwär(e)t!	geschworen
schweigen (= 'to be silent' *is v.n. & strong*; = 'to silence' *is v.a. & weak*)	2 schweigst 3 schweigt	schwieg	schwiege	schweig(e)!	geschwiegen
schwellen	2 schwillst 3 schwillt	schwoll	schwölle	S schwill! P schwellt!	geschwollen
schwimmen	2 schwimmst 3 schwimmt	schwamm	schwömme, (*c*) schwämme	schwimm(e)!	geschwommen
schwinden	2 schwindest 3 schwindet	schwand	schwände	schwind(e)!	geschwunden
schwingen	2 schwingst 3 schwingt	schwang	schwänge	schwing(e)!	geschwungen
schwören	2 schwörst 3 schwört	schwur, (*b*) schwor	schwüre	schwör(e)!	geschworen
seh(e)n	2 siehst 3 sieht	sah	sähe	S sieh! (*as int.*, siehe!) P seht!	‖gesehen
sein	S 1 bin 2 bist 3 ist P 1 sind 2 seid 3 sind	war	wäre	S sei! P seid!	gewesen
senden	2 sendest 3 sendet	sandte *or* sendete	sendete	send(e)!	gesandt *or* ge- sendet (*the* *latter form* *alone used in* *sense of* 'broad- cast by radio').
sieden	2 siedest 3 siedet	sott *or* siedete	sötte *or* siedete	sied(e)!	gesotten
singen	2 singst 3 singt	sang	sänge	sing(e)!	gesungen
sinken	2 sinkst 3 sinkt	sank	sänke	sink(e)!	gesunken

INFINITIVE	PRESENT INDIC.	IMPERF. INDIC.	IMPERF. SUBJ.	IMPERATIVE¶	PAST PART.
sinnen	2 sinnst 3 sinnt	sann	sänne, (*a*) sönne	sinn(e)!	gesonnen (= have the intention; gesinnt (= be of the opinion)
sitzen	2 sitz(es)t 3 sitzt	saß	säße	sitz(e)!	gesessen
sollen	1 & 3 soll, 2 sollst	sollte	sollte	—	‖gesollt
spalten	2 spalt(e)st 3 spaltet	spaltete	spaltete	spalt(e)!	gespalten *or* gespaltet
speien	2 speist 3 speit	spie	spiee	spei(e)!	gespie(e)n
spinnen	2 spinnst 3 spinnt	spann	spönne, (*c*) spänne	spinn(e)!	gesponnen
spleißen	2 spleiß(es)t 3 spleißt	spliß, (*a*) spleißte	splisse *or* spleißte	spleiß(e)!	gesplissen, (*a*) gespleißt
sprechen	2 sprichst 3 spricht	sprach	spräche	S sprich! P sprecht!	gesprochen
sprießen	2 sprieß(es)t 3 sprießt	sproß	sprösse	sprieß(e)!	gesprossen
springen	2 springst 3 springt	sprang	spränge	spring(e)!	gesprungen
stechen	2 stichst 3 sticht	stach	stäche	S stich! P stecht!	gestochen
stecken (= to be in a place)	2 steckst 3 steckt	steckte *or* stak	steckte *or* stäke	steck(e)!	gesteckt
steh(e)n	2 stehst 3 steht	stand, (*b*) & (*c*) stund	stände *or* stünde	steh(e)!	gestanden
stehlen	2 stiehlst 3 stiehlt	stahl	stöhle, (*c*) stähle	S stiehl! P stehlt!	gestohlen
steigen	2 steigst 3 steigt	stieg	stiege	steig(e)!	gestiegen
sterben	2 stirbst 3 stirbt	starb	stürbe	S stirb! P sterbt!	gestorben
stieben	2 stiebst 3 stiebt	stob *or* stiebte	stöbe *or* stiebte	stieb(e)!	gestoben *or* gestiebt
stinken	2 stinkst 3 stinkt	stank	stänke	stink(e)!	gestunken
stoßen	2 stöß(es)t 3 stößt	stieß	stieße	S stoß(e)! P stoßt!	gestoßen
streichen	2 streichst 3 streicht	strich	striche	streich(e)!	gestrichen
streiten	2 streitest 3 streitet	stritt	stritte	streit(e)!	gestritten
tragen	2 trägst 3 trägt	trug	trüge	S trag(e)! P tragt!	getragen
treffen	2 triffst 3 trifft	traf	träfe	S triff! P trefft!	getroffen
treiben	2 treibst 3 treibt	trieb	triebe	treib(e)!	getrieben
treten	2 trittst 3 tritt	trat	träte	S tritt! P tretet!	getreten
triefen	2 triefst 3 trieft	troff *or* (*also c*) triefte	tröffe *or* (*also c*) triefte	treif(e)!	getrieft, (*a*) getroffen
trinken	2 trinkst 3 trinkt	trank	tränke	trink(e)!	getrunken
(be)trügen	2 (be)trügst 3 (be)trügt	(be)trog	(be)tröge	(be)trüg(e)!	getrogen (betrogen)
tun	S 1 tue 2 tust 3 tut P 1 & 3 tun 2 tut	tat, (*b*) tät P 1 & 3 taten, (*b*) täten	täte	tu(e)!	getan
verbleichen (*see* **erbleichen**)					
verderben (*v.n.*); (*the active verb is weak, but the forms are, apart from p.p., archaic & superseded by irr. forms.*)	2 verdirbst 3 verdirbt	verdarb	verdürbe	S verdirb! P verderbt!	verdorben (*but as adj.* verderbt)

INFINITIVE	PRESENT INDIC.	IMPERF. INDIC.	IMPERF. SUBJ.	IMPERATIVE ¶	PAST PART.
verdrießen	2 verdrieß(es)t 3 verdrießt	verdroß	verdrösse	verdrieß(e)!	verdrossen
vergessen	2 vergißt *or* vergissest 3 vergißt	vergaß	vergäße	S vergiß! P vergeßt!	vergessen
verhehlen	2 verhehlst 3 verhehlt	verhehlte	verhehlte	verhehle!	verhehlt *or* verhohlen
verlieren	2 verlierst 3 verliert	verlor	verlöre	verlier(e)!	verloren
verlöschen (*v.n. see* **erlöschen**) (*v.a. is weak*)					
verschallen (= become forgotten)	3 verschillt (*rare*)	verscholl	verschölle	S verschalle! P verschallet!	verschollen
verschallen (= diminish *or* (*of sound*) become attenuated)	3 verschallt	verschallte, (*b*) verscholl	verschallte, (*b*) verschölle	verschalle!	verschallt
verwirren	2 verwirrst 3 verwirrt	verwirrte	verwirrte	verwirre!	verwirrt *or* verworren (*latter form alone as adj.*)
wachsen (= to grow); (*v.a.* = to wax *is weak*)	2 wächs(es)t 3 wächst	wuchs	wüchse	S wachs(e)! P wachst!	gewachsen
wägen	2 wägst 3 wägt	wog *or* wägte	wöge *or* wägte	wäg(e)!	gewogen
waschen	2 wäsch(e)st 3 wäscht	wusch	wüsche	S wasch(e)! P wascht!	gewaschen
weben	2 webst 3 webt	webte, (*b*) & (*c*) wob	webte, (*b*) & (*c*) wöbe	web(e)!	gewebt, (*b*) & (*c*) gewoben
weichen (= yield) (*v.a.* = soften *is weak*)	2 weichst 3 weicht	wich	wiche	weich(e)!	gewichen
weisen	2 weis(es)t 3 weist	wies	wiese	weis(e)!	gewiesen
wenden	2 wendest 3 wendet	wandte *or* wendete	wendete	wend(e)!	gewandt *or* gewendet
werben	2 wirbst 3 wirbt	warb	würbe	S wirb! P werbt!	geworben
werden	2 wirst 3 wird	wurde, (*b*) ward	würde	S werde! P werdet!	geworden (*b*) worden*
werfen	2 wirfst 3 wirft	warf	würfe	S wirf! P werf(e)t!	geworfen
wiegen ('to weigh' is *v.n.* & strong; 'to rock' is *v.a.* & weak)	2 wiegst 3 wiegt	wog	wöge	wieg(e)!	gewogen
winden (*v.a.*)	2 windest 3 windet	wand	wände	wind(e)!	gewunden
wissen	1 & 3 weiß 2 weißt	wußte	wüßte	S wisse! P wißt! *or* wisset!	gewußt
wollen	1 & 3 will 2 willst	wollte	wollte	S wolle! P wollt!	‖gewollt
zeihen	2 zeihst 3 zeiht	zieh	ziehe	zeih(e)!	geziehen
zieh(e)n	2 ziehst (*b*) zeuchst 3 zieht, (*b*) zeucht	zog	zöge	zieh(e)! (*b*) zeuch!	gezogen
zwingen	2 zwingst 3 zwingt	zwang	zwänge	zwing(e)!	gezwungen

* Also in compound tenses after another p.p.

COMMON WEIGHTS AND MEASURES AND THEIR APPROXIMATE EQUIVALENTS

Ar, *n.* = 120 sq. yds., or 0·025 acre.
Atmosphäre, *f.* = 29/30ths of the British unit.
Gramm, *n.* = 15 grains troy, *or* 0·03 ounce avoir.
Hektar, *n.* = 2·5 acres.
Kilogramm, *n.* = 2·2 lb.
Kilometer, *n.* = 0·6 mile.
Kubikzentimeter, *n.* = 0·06 cu. in.
Liter, *n.* & *m.* = 60 cu. in., *or* 1·7 Imp. pint. (2·1 U.S. pints).
Meter, *n.* & *m.* = 39·5 in.
Millimeter, *n.* & *m.* = 0·04 in.
Pferdestärke, *f.* = a fraction less than British horse power.
Quintal, *m.* = 220 lb. (a fraction less than 2 cwt.).
Tonne, *f.* = 2,200 lb. (40 lb. less than 1 ton).
Zentimeter, *n.* & *m.* = 0·4 in.

Acre = 40 Are (4,000 Quadratmeter).
Atmosphere = 1·033 of Metric unit.
Bushel = 36 Liter.
Cubic Inch = 17 Kubikzentimeter.
Foot = 0·3 Meter.
Horse Power = a fraction more than Metric H.P.
Hundredweight = 50 Kilogramm.
Inch = 2·5 Zentimeter.
Mile = 1,600 Meter.
Ounce = 28 Gramm.
Pint = 0·6 Liter.
Pound = 0·45 Kilogramm.
Quart = 1·2 Liter.
Square Mile = 2·6 Quadratkilometer (260 Hektar).
Ton = a fraction over 1,000 Kilogramm.
Yard = 0·9 Meter.

Temperature: Celsius (Centigrade) ÷ 10 = (Fahrenheit − 32) ÷ 18.
(Fahrenheit − 32) ÷ 18 = (Centigrade) ÷ 10.

$$F = \frac{18\,C}{10} + 32 \qquad C = \frac{10\,(F - 32)}{18}$$

CLOTHING SIZES
(approx. equivalents)

Shoes:

German	36	37	38	39	41	42	43	44
English	3	4	5	6	7	8	9	10

Hats:

German	53	54	55	56	57	58	59	60	61
Engl. & Amer.	$6\frac{1}{2}$	$6\frac{5}{8}$	$6\frac{3}{4}$	$6\frac{7}{8}$	7	$7\frac{1}{8}$	$7\frac{1}{4}$	$7\frac{3}{8}$	$7\frac{1}{2}$

GERMAN-ENGLISH APPENDIX

Abbildungsvermögen, *n.* resolving power (*lens*).
abbuchen, *v.a.* write off (*debt, loss, etc.*), debit (*amount*).
Abbuchung, *f.* debit-entry.
Abgabekurs, *m.* issue price (*C.L.*).
Abgabepreis, *m.* selling price, tariff, charge (*electricity, etc.*).
Abgleichkondensator, *m.* trimming condenser (*Rad.*).
Abhorchgerät, *n.* anti-submarine sound-detector (ASDIC) (*Nav.*).
Abhördienst, *m.* monitoring service (*Tele. & Mil.*).
Abhörraum, *m.*, **Abhörzelle,** *f.* control *or* monitoring room.
abklappern, *v.a.* (*coll.*) traipse round.
abknutschen, *v.r.* (*sl.*) smooch.
Abmeldeformular, *n.* form for registration of change of address.
Abnäher, *m.* dart (*Dressm.*).
Abraumdecke, *f.* overburden (*Min.*).
abreagieren, *v.n.* abreact.
Abrißpunkt, *m.* bench-mark (*Surv.*).
Absatzkosten, *pl.* distribution costs.
absäugeln, *v.a.* inarch (*Hort.*).
Abschirmvorrichtung, *f.* interference suppressor.
Abschleudermaschine, *f.* centrifuge, hydro-extractor.
Abschlußborte, *f.* frieze.
Abschußrampe, *f.* launching pad *or* platform.
Abseit, *n.* (-s, –) offside (*Sport*).
Abseiter, *m.* outsider.
abservieren, 1. *v.n.* clear the table. 2. *v.a.* (*coll.*) give (*s.o.*) the push.
Absonderungsanspruch, *m.* preferential claim (*Law*).
Absonderungsberechtigte(r), *m. & f.* preferential *or* secured creditor (*Law*).
Absprenger, *m.* glass cutter.
Absprunghafen, *m.* operational base (*Mil., etc.*).
Absprungtisch, *m.* take-off platform (*skiing*).
Absteige, *f.* temporary lodging.
Abstelltisch, *m.* side table; dumb waiter.
Abtastdose, *f.* pick-up (*gramophone*).
Abtaster, *m.* scanner (*T.V.*).
Abtastperiode, *f.* time-base (*T.V.*).
abwerten, *v.a.* 1. devalue, devaluate, depreciate (*currency*); 2. estimate, appraise, value (*goods*).
Abwertung, *f.* devaluation, depreciation; valuation, estimation (of the value).
abwuchern, *v.a.* wring *or* extort (*Dat.*, from).
abyssisch, *adj.* abysmal; plutonic (*Geol.*).
Abzweigmuffe, *f.* junction box (*Elec.*).
Abzweigstrom, *m.* shunt current (*Elec.*).
Achsengeld, *n.* transport charges; toll (*on bridge, etc.*).
Achsschenkelbolzen, *m.* kingpin.
Achsschenkelträger, *m.* steering head.
Achtgroschenjunge, *m.* (*sl.*) copper's nark.
addieren, *v.a.* add (up).
Addiermaschine, *f.* adding machine.
Addierung, *f.* addition.
Affentanz, *m.*, **Affentheater,** *n.* utter *or* sheer farce.
Agamie, *f.* cryptogamy (*Bot.*).
agamisch, *adj.* cryptogamic, cryptogamous.
Agenda, *f.* (-den) memorandum; price-list (*C.L.*).
Agens, *n.* (–, Agenzien) active *or* motive force, agency, agent.
Agrarkommunismus, *m.* collective farming.
Akribie, *f.* extreme precision, (over-)exactness.
Aktentasche, *f.* dispatch-case, briefcase.
Aktivbilanz, *f.* favourable balance of trade.
Aktivmasse, *f.* (bankrupt's) estate.
Aktualität, *f.* actuality, topicality, contemporary reality *or* importance, (*coll.*) up-to-dateness; question of the moment, (*pl.*) current events, items of topical interest.
Aktualitätenkino, *n.* news theatre.
Akupunktur, *f.* acupuncture.
Alkoholnachweis, *m.* blood-test (for alcohol).
Alkoholteströhrchen, *n.* breathalyser.
Alkoholvergiftung, *f.* alcoholism.
Alleingang, *m.* single-handed *or* lone effort, solo attempt; *im* –, on one's own.
Alleinverkauf, *m.* exclusive sale, sales monopoly.
Alleinvertrieb, *m.* sole agency *or* distributing rights.
allergisch, *adj.* allergic.
Allmenge, *f.* universal set (*Math.*).
Allonge, *f.* extension, lengthening-piece; allonge (*C.L.*); longe, lunge (*horsemanship*).
Allüre, *f.* gait, action (*of a horse*); (*pl.*) mannerisms, grand airs.
Altsteinzeit, *f.* Palaeolithic Age.
Ambiente, *f.* ambience (*Art*).
ambulant, *adj.* ambulatory, peripatetic, itinerant; *–e Behandlung*, out-patient treatment (*Med.*).
Ambulanz, *f.* (-en) out-patient treatment (*Med.*); ambulance (*Mil., etc.*).
Amtsfreizeichen, *n.* (*phone*) dialling tone.
Amtsstunden, *pl.* office hours.
Amtsuntersagung, *f.* suspension from duty.
Amtsunterschlagung, *f.* embezzlement, malversation.
Amtsweg, *m.* official channels.
Amtswidrigkeit, *f.* dereliction of duty.
Anbaumöbel, *pl.* unit furniture.
Anbindezeit, *f.* setting-time (*cement, etc.*).
Anbindezettel, *m.* tie-on label.
Anbrennholz, *n.* kindling, firewood.
Anciennität, *f.* seniority.
andienen, *v.a.* make (*land*), put into (*a port*) (*Naut.*); offer (*immediate delivery*), deliver (*goods, etc.*), notify (*intentions*) (*C.L.*).
angelfest, *adj.* securely *or* firmly fixed.
anhimmeln, *v.a.* (*coll.*) go into raptures over (*a p.*).
Anken, *m.* (*Swiss dial.*) butter.
ankörnen, *v.a.* mark the centre (with a punch).
Ankörner, *m.* centre-punch.
Anlaufstreifen, *m.* leader (*film*).
Anleihschein, *m.* bond (*C.L.*).
Anliegerverkehr, *m.* access only for residents.
Anmeldefrist, *f.* (interval before the) closing date; *– bis zum . . .*, closing date for applications. . . .
Anmeldegebühr, *f.* registration *or* entrance fee.
Anmeldepflicht, *f.* obligation to register (with the police).
Anorak, *m.* (-s, -s) anorak, windcheater.
Anschlagfaden, *m.* tacking thread.
Anschlagschiene, *f.* T-square.
Anschlagschraube, *f.* locking- *or* set-screw.
Anschlagwinkel, *m.* try-square.
Anschlagzünder, *m.* percussion-fuse.
anschließend, 1. *adj.* adjacent; following. 2. *adv.* subsequently, (immediately) afterwards *or* following.
Anschreibeblatt, *n.* score-card (*Sport*).
Ansitz, *m.* hide, hiding-place.
anstrengend, *adj.* exacting, trying, arduous, strenuous, laborious.
Antibiotikum, *n.* (-s, -ka) antibiotic (*Med.*).
[1]**Antiphon,** *n.* (-s, -e) ear-plug.
[2]**Antiphon,** *f.* (-en) antiphon (*Mus.*).
Aparte, *n.* aside, stage-whisper (*Theat.*).
apfelbraun, *adj.* dappled bay (*horse*).
Arbeitslosigkeit, *f.* unemployment.
Arbeitsstreckung, *f.* short-time working.
Arrestat, *m.* (-en, -en) distrainee (*Law*).
arrivieren, *v.n.* (*aux.* s.) succeed, (*coll.*) get on (in the world).
Ärztekammer, *f.* = General Medical Council.
Asoziale(r), *m. & f.* (*coll.*) drop-out.
Astronaut, *m.* (-en, -en) astronaut.
Astronautik, *f.* astronautics.

Astrophysik, *f.* astrophysics.
Atomabfall, *m.* atomic waste *or* fallout.
Atomantrieb, *m.* nuclear propulsion.
atomar, *adj.* atomic; *–e Abschreckung,* nuclear deterrent; *–e Waffen,* nuclear weapons.
Atombatterie, *f.* atomic pile.
atomisieren, *v.a.* reduce to atoms, atomize.
Atomkernforschung, *f.* nuclear research.
Atomkraftanlage, *f.,* **Atomkraftwerk,** *n.* nuclear power station.
Atomkrieg(führung), *m.* (*f.*) atomic *or* nuclear war *or* warfare.
Atommeiler, *m.* reactor, atomic pile.
Atomsprengkopf, *m.* nuclear warhead.
attrappieren, *v.a.* take (*s.o.*) in, catch *or* (*coll.*) do (*s.o.*).
Aufbausalze, *pl.* nutrient salts (*Physiol.*).
Aufkömmling, *m.* (-s, -e) upstart, parvenu, self-made man.
aufmöbeln, 1. *v.a.* (*coll.*) buck up. 2. *v.r.* put on one's glad rags, doll o.s. up.
aufmutzen, *v.a. einem etwas –,* tax *or* reproach s.o. with s.th.
Aufnäharbeit, *f.* appliqué work.
aufpulvern, *v.a.* (*coll.*) pick *or* buck up, pull together.
aufrauchen, *v.a.* finish (smoking) (*a cigarette*), smoke all (*one's cigarettes*).
Aufsage, *f.* cancellation, withdrawal.
Auftragsüberhang, *m.* orders on hand (*C.L.*).
Aufwandsentschädigung, *f.* entertainment allowance.
aufwendig, *adj.* expensive, extravagant, sumptuous, lavish; involving great expense (*of a project*).
Aufzieherei, *f.* chaff, banter, teasing.
auseinanderjagen, *v.a.* scatter, disperse, break up.
Ausfallschwung, *m.* telemark (*skiing*).
ausgefallen, *adj.* strange, queer, curious, unusual, extraordinary, striking, out of the way *or* the ordinary.
ausgeleiert, *adj.* hackneyed, trite.
Ausgleichskapazität, *f.* neutrodyne capacitance (*Elec.*).
Ausgleichskonto, *n.* suspense account.
Ausgleichsrennen, *n.* handicap race.
Ausgleichsverfahren, *n.* partial satisfaction of creditors (*C.L.*), procedure for settling international debts (*Pol.*).
Auskehricht, *m. or n.* sweepings.
ausklammern, *v.a.* remove the brackets from (*Math.*); (*fig.*) ignore, push on one side (*a p.*).
auslasten, *v.a.* balance, equalize (*loads*); employ (*s.o.*) fully, make (*a firm, a p.*) work to capacity (*C.L.*); *ausgelastet sein,* (*of a p.*) be fully employed *or* occupied, (*of a firm*) be working at full capacity.
Auslaufmodell, *n.* discontinued model *or* line (*C.L.*).
Ausschnittarbeit, *f.* fretwork.
Außenläufer, *m.* wing-half (*Footb.*).
Außenstürmer, *m.* wing-forward (*Footb.*).
Ausspielung, *f.* raffle, lottery.
Aussteuerung, *f.* modulation (*Rad.*); (*of tape-recorder*) level control.
austufteln, *v.a.* (*coll.*) puzzle out.
Ausweichklausel, *f.* escape clause (*in contract*).
Ausweichstraße, *f.* by-pass.
Auswertestelle, *f.* plotting *or* computing centre (*Mil.*).
auswringen, *ir. v.a.* wring (out).
Auswringmaschine, *f.* wringer.
Auswürfling, *m.* (-s, -e) piece of ejected material (*Geol.*).
Auszählung, *f.* counting (out); count-down (*rocketry*).
Auszeichnungsschrift, *f.* bold type (*Typ.*).
Auszeichnungszettel, *m.* price tag *or* ticket.
Autarch, *m.* (-en, -en) autocrat.
Autobox, *f.* (-en) lock-up (garage).
Autoempfänger, *m.* car-radio.
Autofähre, *f.* car-ferry.
Autoführer, *m.* taxi-driver, bus-driver, chauffeur.
autogen, *adj.* autogenous; *–e Schweißung,* oxy-acetylene welding.
Autogenapparat, *m.* oxy-acetylene welder.
[1]**Autograph,** *m.* (-en, -en) copying machine.
[2]**Autograph,** *m.* (-(e)s, -e(n)) autograph (manuscript).
Autographie, *f.* autolithography; dermographia (*Med.*).
Autohaltestelle, *f.* taxi-rank.
Autokolonne, *f.* motorcade.
Automatenbüfett, *n.* automat (*Amer.*).
automatisieren, *v.a.* mechanize.
Automatisierung, *f.* automation, mechanization.
Autoschlepp, *m.* (-s, -) auto-tow (*for gliders*).
Autostopp, *m.* hitch-hiking; *mit* or *per – fahren,* hitch-hike.
Autostunde, *f.* hour's drive, hour by car.
Autotaxe, *f.* taxi.
Avantageur [*pron.* avɑ̃tɑˈʒøːr], *m.* (-s, -s *or* -e) ensign (*Mil.*).
Avantgarde [*pron.* ɑˈvɑ̃gɑrdə], *f.* vanguard (*of movement*).
Avantgardist, *m.* (-en, -en) avant-garde artist.
Aversalsumme, *f.* sum (paid) in settlement.
avertieren, *v.a.* warn, notify, advise.
Avertissement [*pron.* ɑvɛrtiːs(ə)ˈmɑ̃], *n.* warning, notification, advice.
Azetatlack, *m.* cellulose varnish.
Azet(yl)säure, *f.* acetic acid.

B

Badenixe, *f.* bathing-beauty.
Badezelle, *f.* cubicle.
baen, *v.n.* bleat, baa (*of sheep*).
Bafel, *m.* silk waste; (*sl.*) hot air.
Bahnreiten, *n.* show-jumping.
Bahnsteigüberführung, *f.* footbridge (*between platforms*).
Bahnsteigunterführung, *f.* subway (*between platforms*).
Bahnüberführung, *f.* railway bridge.
Bahnübergang, *m.* level crossing.
Bahnunterführung, *f.* railway tunnel.
Baiser, *m. or n.* (-s, -s) meringue (*Cul.*).
Baissegeschäft, *n.* bear transaction.
Baissespekulant, *m.* bear (*stock-exchange*).
Baissestimmung, *f.* downward tendency, bear tone.
Bakterienkrieg, *m.* bacteriological *or* (*coll.*) germ warfare.
Balancement [*pron.* bɑlɑ̃səˈmɑ̃], *n.* tremolo (*Mus.*).
Balkenüberschrift, *f.* banner headline (*Typ.*).
Bambusbär, *m.* giant panda (*Zool.*).
Bandaufnahme, *f.* tape-recording.
Bandscheibe, *f.* intervertebral disc (*Anat.*).
Bandscheibenvorfall, *m.* (*coll.*) slipped disc.
Bandtransport, *m.* (belt-)conveyor, assembly line.
Bang, *m.* Indian hemp, bhang (*Bot.*).
Bardame, *f.* barmaid.
Bareme, *m.* (–, -n) ready-reckoner; price-schedule.
Barras, *m.* army; army bread; *beim –,* in the forces.
Basisbruch, *m.* fracture of the base of the skull.
Basküle, *f.* fastening, catch, snib (*of window, etc.*).
Bastardwechsel, *m.* dummy bill (*C.L.*).
Bauernfrühstück, *n.* bacon and potato omelet.
Baufachmann, *m.* quantity surveyor.
baufähig, *adj.* arable (*land*).
Baukostenzuschuß, *m.* (tenants') contribution to the building costs.
Baurat, *m.* (local government) planning officer.
Bauvergebung, *f.* allocation of building contracts.
Bauzaun, *m.* hoarding.
Bazillenausscheider, *m.* chronic carrier.
Bazillenkrieg, *m.* bacterial *or* germ warfare.
beatmen, *v.a.* apply artificial respiration to (*a p.*).
bebildern, *v.a.* illustrate (*a book*).
Bedienungszuschlag, *m.* service charge.
Beerenwein, *m.* home-made wine.
Befeuerung, *f.* lights, markers, beacons.
begönnern, *v.a.* patronize, treat condescendingly *or* in a patronizing manner.
Begrenzungslicht, *n.* side-light (*on vehicle*).
Begriffsinhalt, *m.* connotation.

Beingeschwür, *n.* varicose ulcer (*Med.*).
Beisel, *n.* (*Austr. dial.*) tavern.
Beitöne, *pl.* overtones (*Mus.*).
Bekennermut, *m.* courage of one's convictions, unshakeable faith.
Belastungsanzeige, *f.* debit note (*C.L.*).
Belastungstal, *n.* minimum load.
beliebäugeln, *v.a.* cast a covetous eye on, (*coll.*) have an eye on.
Bemalung, *f.* coat of paint; daubing.
Bemessung, *f.* rating (*of a motor, etc.*).
benachteiligt, *adj.* handicapped (*child, etc.*).
bene, *adv.* (*coll.*) well.
Bene, *n.* (*coll.*) good turn.
Benimm, *m.* (-s, -) (*hum.*) manners; *er hat keinen* –, he has no manners *or* polish.
Benzedrin, *n.* amphetamine.
Berichtigungskonto, *n.* suspense account.
Berieselungsfeld, *n.* sewage farm.
Berliner, *m.* doughnut.
Beschäftigungsbehandlung, *f.* occupational therapy.
Beschäftigungsspiele, *pl.* creative *or* active play (*in kindergarten*).
beschildern, *v.a.* label (*luggage*), signpost (*a road*), mark (*streets*) with street-names.
Beschiß, *m.* (-(ss)es, –) (*coll.*) swindle, dirty trick.
Beschleunigungsabnahme, *f.* retardation, deceleration, negative acceleration.
Besetzplatte, *f.* paving stone, flagstone.
Besetzteich, *m.* breeding pond.
Besitzstörung, *f.* trespass (*Law*).
Besitztitel, *m.* title-deed (*Law*).
Besorgungszettel, *m.* shopping list.
Bestandgeber, *m.* (*Austr. dial.*) landlord, lessor.
Bestandnehmer, *m.* (*Austr. dial.*) tenant, leaseholder, lessee.
bestimmungswidrig, *adj.*, *adv.* against the rules, contrary to *or* in contravention of regulations.
Bestreuung, *f.* sand, gravel (*for paths*).
Beteiligungsgesellschaft, *f.* holding company (*C.L.*).
Betise, *f.* stupidity, folly, silliness.
Bettcouch, *f.* sofa-bed.
Bettelhandwerk, *n.* professional begging.
Bettschuh, *m.* bed-sock.
Beuschel, *n.* (*Austr. dial.*) lights (*Cul.*).
Beutelmelone, *f.* cantaloup.
Bevölkerungsstatistik, *f.* vital statistics.
Bewährungseinheit, *f.* rehabilitation unit (*Mil.*).
Bewährungshelfer, *m.* probation officer.
Beweisnachholung, *f.* introduction of new evidence (*Law*).
Bewußtseinsinhalt, *m.* conscious experience.
Bewußtseinskunst, *f.* stream-of-consciousness technique (*in writing*).
Bibelforscher, *m.* Jehovah's Witness.
Biegeeisen, *n.* tyre-lever.
Bilanzjahr, *n.* financial year.
Bildabtaster, *m.* scanner (*T.V.*).
Bildabzug, *m.* (photographic) copy, photostat.
Bildausschnitt, *m.* detail.
Bildband, *n.* book of illustrations, volume of plates; video tape (*T.V.*).
Bildberichterstatter, *m.* press photographer; news cameraman.
Bildbetrachter, *m.* (slide) viewer (*for colour films*).
Bildebene, *f.* focal plane (*Phot.*).
Bildfrequenz, *f.* camera speed (*Film*); frame *or* picture speed (*T.V.*); videofrequency.
Bildraum, *m.* field of vision.
Bildröhre, *f.* television *or* cathode-ray tube.
Bildschirm, *m.* (television) screen.
Bildsucher, *m.* view finder (*Phot.*).
Bildtreiben, *n.* embossing.
Bildverzerrung, *f.* distortion (of the image).
Bildwerfer, *m.* projector, epidiascope.
Bildzeile, *f.* (scanning) line (*T.V.*).
Bildzerleger, *m.* scanner (*T.V.*).
Bildzuschrift, *f.* letter (of application) enclosing a photograph.
Billiarde, *m.* a thousand billions, (*Amer.*) quadrillion.
Binge, *f.* surface depression, crater (*Min.*).
Bingenbau, *m.* opencast working (*Min.*).
Binnenklima, *n.* continental climate.
Binnenmauer, *f.* party wall.
Bircht, *m. or n.* (*Swiss dial.*) hoar-frost.
Bittage, *pl.* Rogation days (*Eccl.*).
Bittgottesdienst, *m.* Rogation service.
Bittwoche, *f.* Rogation week.
Blasengrind, *m.* impetigo (*Med.*).
Blasenspiegel, *m.* cystoscope (*Med.*).
Blauzwecke, *f.* tintack.
Bleier, *m.* roach (*Ichth.*).
Bleiglätte, *f.* yellow lead oxide, litharge.
Bleizinn, *n.* pewter.
Blindmuster, *n.* (showcase) dummy.
blindschlagen, *ir. v.a.* leave blank (*Typ.*).
Blockflöte, *f.* recorder (*Mus.*).
Blonde, *f.* (*coll.*) (glass of) light ale.
Blutdruckmesser, *m.* sphygmomanometer.
Blutentnahme, *f.* blood-sample.
Bluterkrankheit, *f.* haemophilia.
Blutführung, *f.* pedigree.
Blutgeräusch, *n.* harmic murmurs (*Med.*).
Blutharnen, *n.* haematuria (*Med.*).
Blutpfropf, *m.* thrombus (*Med.*).
Bockleiter, *f.* step-ladder, pair of steps.
Bockmotor, *m.* underslung vertical engine.
bocksteif, *adj.* mulish, stubborn; awkward, clumsy.
Bockwurst, *f.* sausage (*for boiling*).
Bodenschnelle, *f.* push-up (*Gymn.*).
Bodenwaage, *f.* weigh-bridge.
Böenlinie, *f.* cold front (*Meteor.*).
Bogenlaufen, *n.* figure-skating.
Bohnermasse, *f.* (floor) polish.
Bombage [*pron.* bɔmˈbɑːʒə], *f.* dishing, flanging (*of sheet-metal, etc.*).
Bombenräumtrupp, *m.* bomb-disposal squad.
Bordmechaniker, *m.* flight engineer.
Bordmonteur, *m.* flight mechanic.
Bordmuster, *n.* ribbing (*knitting*).
Bosse, *f.* boss, umbo; roughly blocked-out figure (*Sculp.*).
Boulevardpresse, *f.* gutter press.
Boulevardstück, *n.* kitchen-sink drama.
Boxe, *f.* lock-up (garage); (*submarine*) pen; pit (*motor-racing*); loose box (*in stable*).
Boxermotor, *m.* horizontally-opposed engine.
Boxerohr, *n.* cauliflower ear.
Branchenverzeichnis, *n.* (*phone*) classified directory.
Bratensoße, *f.* gravy.
Bravour, *f.* bravado, gusto.
Bravourstück, *n.* act of daring.
Bremsklappe, *f.* wing-flap (*Av.*).
Bremslänge, *f.* braking distance.
Bremsmittel, *n.* moderator (*atomic physics*).
Bremsrakete, *f.* retro-rocket.
bremssicher, *adj.* skid-proof (*tyres*), with reliable brakes (*vehicle*).
Bremsträger, *m.* back-plate of brake.
Brennschluß, *m.* burn-out.
Brenzgallussäure, *f.* pyrogallic acid (*Chem.*), pyro (*Phot.*, *coll.*).
Brestling, *m.* (-s, -e) (*dial.*) strawberry.
Briefkurs, *m.* selling-price (*stock-exchange*).
Briefsendung, *f.* (small) postal package.
Brillengestell, *n.* spectacle frame.
brillieren, *v.n.* shine, sparkle (*of a p.*).
Broschierung, Broschur, *f.* stitching, sewing (*of books*), binding in paper covers; paper cover.
Brossage [*pron.* brɔˈsɑːʒə], *f.* carding (*textiles*).
brossieren, *v.a.* card.
Bruchbildung, *f.* herniation (*Med.*).
Brucheinklemmung, *f.* strangulation of a hernia.
Bruchschrift, *f.* Gothic *or* black-letter type.
Brustleier, *f.* brace and bit.
Bruststärker, *m.* chest expander.
Buchse, *f.* bush(ing) (*Tech.*); liner (*of cylinder*), sleeve (*of shaft*); socket (*Elec.*).
Buchstabenbild, *n.* type-face (*Typ.*).
Buchstabenglaube, *m.* literalism, strict adherence to the letter.
Buchstabenschloß, *n.* combination lock.
Buddel, *f.* (-n) (*dial.*) bottle.
Budenangst, *f.* (*coll.*) claustrophobia.

Bulette, *f.* meat-ball, rissole.
Bummelstreik, *m.* go-slow strike, working to rule.
Buntmetall, *n.* non-ferrous metal.
Buntwaren, *pl.* printed cottons.
Burse, *f.* grant, scholarship; students' hostel, (*archaic*) college.
Buschaffe, *m.* oran(g)-utang (*Zool.*).
Büschelnelke, *f.* sweetwilliam (*Bot.*).
Butterstulle, *f.* slice of bread and butter.

C

Chargenspieler, *m.* character-actor.
Chemiefaser, *f.* man-made fibre.
Chemotechniker, *m.* laboratory technician.
chlorsauer, *adj.* chlorite of; *–es Salz*, chlorite.
Chlorsäure, *f.* chlorous acid.
Chlorür, *n.* (-s, -e) chloride.
Chlorwasser, *n.* chlorine water.
Chlorwasserstoff, *m.* hydrochloric acid, hydrogen chloride.
chokant [*pron.* ʃ], *adj.* shocking.
Comment, *m.* (-s, –) students' drinking ritual.
Cord, *m.* (-(e)s, -e), **Cordsamt,** *m.* corduroy.
coulant, *adj.* obliging.
Coupage [*pron.* kuˈpɑːʒə], *f.* blending, mixing (*wine, etc.*).
Croisé [*pron.* krwɑˈze], *n.* (-s, -s) twill (*Weav.*).
croisiert, *adj.* twilled.

D

Dämmstoff, *n.* insulation material.
Dampfkocher, Dampfkochtopf, *m.* pressure-cooker.
Dampfungsfläche, *f.* stabilizer (*Av.*).
Dampfungsflosse, *f.* tailplane (*Av.*).
Datenverarbeitung, *f.* data processing (*computers*).
Dauerauftrag, *m.* standing order (*C.L.*).
Dauerflamme, *f.* pilot light.
Dauerlutscher, *m.* (*coll.*) gob-stopper.
Debent, *m.* (-en, -en) debtor.
Deckenvorgelege, *n.* overhead transmission gear.
Deckgeld, *n.* stud-fee.
Decklinie, *f.* line of defence.
Deckungsbestände, *pl.* cover of notes in circulation.
Deckungsforderungen, *pl.* assets.
Defektenprotokoll, *m.* statement of deficit.
Dehnlänge, *f.* linear expansion.
deinsen, *v.n.* make stern way; fall *or* drop astern (*Nav.*).
Dekupiersäge, *f.* fret-saw machine.
Demarche, *f.* diplomatic step, démarche.
demarkieren, *v.a.* demarcate, delimit; mark the boundaries of.
Demerit, *m.* (-en, -en) delinquent priest.
Demonstration, *f.* (practical) demonstration; show of force (*Mil.*).
Demonstrationszug, *m.* protest march.
Dependance [*pron.* depɑ̃ˈdɑ̃s(ə)], *f.* annex(e) (*of hotel, etc.*).
deplacieren, *v.a.* displace (*water*); displace, shift, change the position of (*a th.*).
deplaciert, *adj.* out of place (*of a p.*), out of place, misplaced (*as a remark*).
Derivationsrechnung, *f.* differential calculus.
Derivationswinkel, *m.* angle of drift (*Naut.*).
Dezibel, *n.* decibel.
Dezimeterwelle, *f.* ultra-short wave, ultra-high frequency.
Dia, *see* **Diapositiv.**
Diagonalkraft, *f.* resultant (force).
Diagrammpapier, *n.* graph-paper.
Diatetiker, *m.* nutritionist, dietician.
Dienst nach Vorschrift, *m.* work to rule.
diffizil, *adj.* difficult, delicate, awkward, (*coll.*) ticklish; (*of a p.*) hard to please.
diffundieren, 1. *v.n.* diffuse, mix. 2. *v.a.* diffuse, scatter, spread (*rays, etc.*).
digen, *adj.* digenous (*Bot.*).
Dikotyle, *f.* dicotyledon (*Bot.*).
Diopter, *n.* sight (*of optical instrument*), view-finder (*of camera*).
Direktaufnahme, *f.* live programme (*Rad. & T.V.*).
Direktorialversammlung, *f.* directors' *or* board meeting.
diskriminieren, 1. *v.a.* discriminate against, treat unfairly. 2. *v.n.* discriminate, differentiate.
dissolut, *adj.* dissolute (*behaviour*); disjointed, disconnected, unconnected, incoherent.
Dollbord, *n.* gunwale (*Naut.*).
Dolle, *f.* rowlock, thole-pin (*Naut.*).
Doppelanschluß, *m.* party-line (*phone*).
Doppelboot, *n.* catamaran.
Doppelfenster, *n.* double-glazed window.
Doppelmeister, *m.* doubles champion (*Tenn.*).
Doppelschalter, *m.* two-way switch (*Elec.*).
Doppelschlußmotor, *m.* compound-wound motor (*Elec.*).
Doppelstecker, *m.* two-way adaptor (*Elec.*).
Doppelvierer, *m.* sculling-four.
Doppelweggleichrichtung, *f.* full-wave rectification (*Rad.*).
Doppelwertigkeit, *f.* ambivalence.
Dornschuhe, *pl.* spiked, track *or* running shoes, (*coll.*) spikes.
Double, *m.* understudy (*Theat., etc.*), (*coll.*) stand-in.
doublieren, *v.a.* plate (*metal*).
Drachenanker, *m.* grapnel, grappling anchor (*Naut.*).
Drahtanweisung, *f.* telegraphic money-order.
drallieren, *v.a.* twist tightly.
Drehbuchautor, *m.* script writer.
Dreiecksaufnahme, *f.* triangulation (*Surv.*).
Dreieckschaltung, *f.* delta connection (*Elec.*).
Dreifachstecker, *m.* three-way (plug) adaptor.
Dreikäsehoch, *m.* (-s, –) (*coll.*) whippersnapper, nipper, (little-)titch.
Drops, *m.* boiled sweet(s).
Druckanzug, *m.* pressurized *or* space suit (*Av.*).
Druck (ausgleichs)kabine, *f.* pressurized cabin (*Av.*).
Druckbrand, *m.* bed-sore, decubitus (*Med.*).
druckdicht, *adj.* pressurized (*Av.*).
druckfest, *adj.* resistant to compression; pressurized (*Av.*).
Druckflasche, *f.* siphon.
Druckförderung, *f.* pressure feed (*Mech.*).
Druckhub, *m.* compression stroke (*Motor.*).
Druckjahr, *n.* date of publication.
Druckkammer, *f.* caisson; air-lock.
Druckkessel, *m.* autoclave.
Druckkugelschreiber, *m.* retractable ball-point pen.
Drucklinie, *f.* axis of thrust *or* compression.
Druckluftkrankheit, *f.* caisson disease, (*coll.*) the bends.
Druckposten, *m.* (*coll.*) soft *or* cushy job.
druckreif, *adj.* ready for publication.
Druckschmierpresse, *f.* grease-gun.
Drucktopf, *m.* pressure-cooker.
Druckzwang, *m.* obligation to print (*a thesis*).
Duble, *see* **Double.**
Dublee, *n.* (-s, -s) rolled gold, gold-plate; stroke off the cushion (*Bill.*).
Duktus, *m.* lines (*of a building*), flow (*of handwriting*).
duplieren, *v.a.* plate (*metal*), line (*a garment*).
Durchbruchstaktik, *f.* shock tactics.
durchformen, *v.a.* (*sep.*) develop fully, work out thoroughly; *durchgeformt*, fully worked out *or* developed, mature.
Durchgabe, *f.* 1. transmission, broadcast (*of radio programme*), announcement, release, circulation (*of news*), dictation, delivery by telephone (*of a telegram*); 2. (service) hatch.
Durchleuchtungsschirm, *m.* fluorescent screen.
Durchleuchtungsverfahren, *n.* radioscopy.
Durchreiche, *f.* (service) hatch.

durchreichen, *v.a.* (*sep.*) hand round; pass through.
Durchschlupf, *m.* way through, (*coll.*) bolt-hole; (*fig.*) way out (*of difficulties*).
Durchschrift, *f.* carbon copy.
Durchstoß, *m.* break-through (*Mil.*); mechanical punch, punching machine (*Mech.*).
durchwetzen, *v.a.* (*sep.*) wear through, wear a hole in (*trousers, etc.*).

E

ebauchieren [*pron.* ebɔˈʃiːrən], *v.a.* outline, sketch, make a rough draft *or* skeleton of.
Echozeichen, *n.* echo signal, (*coll.*) blip.
Eckstoß, *m.* corner(-kick) (*Footb.*).
Edelbeere, *f.* choice grape.
Edelbeerenauslese, *f.* (superior) wine from choice grapes.
Edelpilz, *m.* field mushroom.
Effektenbestand, *m.* holdings.
Effektenkurs, *m.* quotation, market price.
Eheanbahnung, *f.* (introduction by) marriage bureau.
Ehrenabzeichen, *n.* medal, decoration.
Ehrenakzept, *n.* acceptance supra protest (*C.L.*).
Ehrensalve, *f.* (gun) salute.
Ehrenschutz, *m.* (*Austr. dial.*) patronage.
Eichordnung, *f.* regulations for the standardization of weights and measures.
Eichpfahl, *m.* calibration mark.
Eichzeichen, *n.* official stamp (*after standardization, calibration, etc.*).
Eidesbelehrung, *f.* caution (*before administering oath*).
Eidesversicherung, *f.* affidavit, sworn statement, statement on oath.
Eierapfel, *m.* aubergine, egg-plant.
Eierlaufen, *n.* egg-and-spoon race.
Eierlikör, *m.* egg-flip.
Eierschläger, *m.* egg-whisk, egg-beater.
Eierspiegel, *m.* ooscope.
Eierstein, *m.* oolite (*Geol.*).
Eigenwechsel, *m.* note of hand, promissory note (*C.L.*).
einbahnig, *adj.* single-line *or* lane (*traffic*), one-way (*street*).
Einbauküche, *f.* ready-fitted kitchen.
Einbaumöbel, *pl.* unit furniture.
einbekennen, *ir. v.a.* admit, acknowledge; (*Austr. dial.*) declare *or* return one's income.
Einbekennung, *f.* (*Austr. dial.*) income-tax return.
einblenden, *v.a.* focus, concentrate (*rays*); – *in* (*Acc.*), blend with (*colours*), fade in (*Rad. & Films*).
Einbrennsoße, *f.* brown sauce.
eineiig, *adj.* uniovular, (*coll.*) identical (*twins*).
einfärben, *v.a.* dye (*fabric*), ink (*type*).
einglasen, *v.a.* glaze, put new glass in.
eingleisen, 1. *v.a.* put on the rails (again) (*Railw.*), (*fig. & coll.*) put right. 2. *v.r.* (*coll.*) come (out all) right.
Einheitsbewegung, *f.* movement towards unity.
Einheitsboot, *n.* one-design (racing) boat.
Einheitskurs, *m.* adjusted rate (*C.L.*).
Einheitsspiel, *n.* bogey play (*Golf*).
Einheitswert, *m.* taxable value (*of property*).
einlangen, (*Austr. dial.*) 1. *v.a.* submit, hand in (*application*). 2. *v.n.* (*um*) apply, make application, submit *or* hand in an application (for).
Einlaßgrund, *m.* primer (paint).
Einlaßhub, *m.* induction stroke (*Motor.*).
Einlegeplatte, *f.* extension leaf (*of table*).
Einlegestück, *n.* inset, lining, reinforcement.
Einmalpackung, *f.* disposable wrapper *or* package.
einmotten, *v.a.* put in mothballs; (*coll.*) mothball (*a ship*).
einrasten, 1. *v.a.* lock in position, engage (*a catch, etc.*). 2. *v.n.* (*aux.* s.) lock, catch, snap into position.
Einsprengling, *m.* (-s, -e), **Einsprengung,** *f.* scattered deposit, xenolith (*Geol.*).
einvernehmen, *ir. v.a.* (*Austr. & Swiss dial.*) interrogate, question.
einweisen, *ir. v.a.* (*in*) instruct (in), introduce (to) (*duties*); install; induct (in) (*office*) (*Eccl.*); direct, assign, allocate, send (to) (*appropriate place*).
Einzel, *m.* singles (*Tenn.*).
Einzelanfertigung, *f.* job-work.
Einzelaufhängung, *f.* independent suspension.
Einzüger, *m.* (*Swiss dial.*) (tax) collector.
Eisenblausäure, *f.* ferrocyanic acid (*Chem.*).
Eisenblauspat, *m.* vivianite.
Eisenglanz, *m.* haematite.
Eisennährpräparat, *n.* iron blood-tonic (*Med.*).
Eisenschwärze, *f.* black-lead, graphite, plumbago.
Ekart, *m.* (-s, -s) margin of profit (*C.L.*).
Eklat [*pron.* eˈklaː], *m.* (-s, -s) stir, commotion; *mit* –, splendidly, (*coll.*) famously; (*ironic*) *mit* – *durchfallen,* fail dismally, be a resounding failure, (*coll.*) be an utter flop.
Elektrodose, *f.* electro-magnetic pick-up (*gramophone*).
Elektronenschleuder, *m.* bekatron.
Elektronik, *f.* electronics.
eloxieren, *v.a.* anodize.
Emballage [*pron.* ɑ̃baˈlaːʒə], *f.* (cost of) packing.
emballieren, *v.a.* pack.
Emd(e), *n.* (*Swiss dial.*) aftermath.
emeritieren, *v.a.* discharge, retire, relieve of duties.
Eminenz, *f.* Eminence (*title*); *die graue* –, the power behind the throne.
Emittent, *m.* (-en, -en) issuing authority (*C.L.*).
Empfangschef, *m.* reception *or* (*Amer.*) room clerk.
Endel, *n.* (*Austr. dial.*) selvedge.
endeln, *v.a.* (*Austr. dial.*) oversew.
Endröhre, *f.* output valve (*Rad.*).
Engagement [*pron.* ɑ̃gaʒəˈmɑ̃], *n.* (-s, -s) engagement (*Theat.*); commitment (*C.L.*).
Enquete [*pron.* ɑ̃ˈkeːtə], *f.* (official) inquiry *or* investigation.
Entfesselungskünstler, *m.* escapologist.
Entlastungsanzeige, *f.* credit note (*C.L.*).
Entlastungswehr, *n.* spill-way.
Entlastungszug, *m.* relief train.
entpersönlichen, 1. *v.a.* make impersonal, deprive of individuality. 2. *v.r.* become impersonal, surrender one's individuality *or* personality.
Entrepot [*pron.* ɑ̃trəˈpoː], *n.* (-, -s) store, bonded warehouse.
entschärfen, *v.a.* render harmless (*bomb, etc.*).
entstaatlichen, *v.a.* denationalize (*industry*), disestablish (*Church*).
Entwicklungsfähigkeit, *f.* viability.
Entwicklungsland, *n.* underdeveloped country.
Entzug, *m.* withdrawal, cancellation; deprivation, stopping, (*coll.*) docking; extraction (*Chem.*).
Epidermistransplantation, *f.* skin-grafting.
epizön, *adj.* hermaphrodite (*Biol.*); epicene (*Gram.*).
Erbabweichung, *f.* mutation (*Biol.*).
Erbanfall, *m.* inheritance, reversion of an estate (*Law*).
Erbbiologie, *f.* genetics.
Erbfaktor, *m.* gene (*Biol.*).
Erder, *m.* earth *or* (*Amer.*) ground connection (*Rad.*).
Erdgas, *n.* natural gas.
Erdvermessung, *f.* geodesy.
Erfolgsanteilsystem, *n.* profit sharing *or* bonus system (*C.L.*).
Erfolgskonto, *n.* profit and loss account (*C.L.*).
Erkennungsdienst, *m.* (police) records department.
Erkennungstuch, *n.* ground strip *or* panel (*Av.*).
Erklärungstag, *m.* contango(settlement) day (*C.L.*).
Ernährungssachverständige(r), *m.* nutritionist.
Ersatzanspruch, *m.* claim for indemnity *or* damages.
Ersatzkasse, *f.* recognized private sickness benefit.
Ersatzwahl, *f.* by-election.
Ersatzwesen, *n.* recruitment (*Mil.*).
Ersatzwiderstand, *m.* equivalent resistance (*Elec.*).
erstechen, *v.a.* stab to death.
Erstmeldung, *f.* exclusive news, (*coll.*) scoop.
eruieren, *v.a.* elicit (*facts*); (*Austr. dial.*) establish the identity of.

Estampe, *f.* print, engraving.
Europäische Wirtschaftsgemeinschaft, *f.* Common Market.
Eventualforderung, *f.* contingent claim (*C.L.*).
eventualiter, *adv.* alternatively, as an alternative (*Law*).
Eventualverbindlichkeit, *f.* contingent liability (*C.L.*).
Evolvente, *f.* involute.
exekutionsfrei, *adj.* immune from distraint (*Law*).
Exekutionskauf, *m.* buying-in (*stock-exchange*).
Exekutionsverkauf, *m.* selling-out (*stock-exchange*).
exigieren, *v.a.* demand (*payment, etc.*).
Exmission, *f.* eviction, ejection (*Law*).
exogam, *adj.* exogamous.
exogen, *adj.* exogenous.
exspoliieren, *v.a.* despoil, plunder.
extern, *adj.* external; *–e Schüler*, day-pupils.
Externat, *n.* (-(e)s, -e) day school.
Externe(r), *m.* & *f.* day-pupil; external candidate (*for examination*).
Externist, *m.* (-en, -en) specialist for external diseases; (*Austr. dial.*) *see* **Externe(r).**
Extradividende, *f.* bonus.
Extrahent, *m.* (-en, -en) p. making a statement *or* abstract of account (*C.L.*); p. issuing a writ (*Law*).
Extraordinariat, *n.* (-en, -en) (supernumerary) professorship, (*Amer.*) associate professorship.
Extraordinarium, *n.* supplementary budget (*Parl.*).
Extraordinarius, *m.* (supernumerary) professor, (*Amer.*) associate professor.
Extrastrom, *m.* self-induction current (*Elec.*).
Exulant, *m.* (-en, -en) exile.
Exzedent, *m.* (-en, -en) transgressor, evildoer, malefactor.
exzidieren, *v.a.* excise (*Surg.*).
exzipieren, *v.a.* except, make an exception of.
exzitieren, *v.a.* excite, stimulate.

F

fabrikneu, *adj.* brand-new.
Fächerfenster, *n.* fanlight.
Fackelzug, *m.* torchlight procession.
Fahrerflucht, *f.* hit-and-run offence.
Fahrpraxis, *f.* driving experience.
Fahrschule, *f.* driving school.
Fahrvorschrift, *f.* rule(s) of the road.
Fallbeschleunigung, *f.* acceleration due to gravity.
fallweise, *adv.* case by case, (taking) each case in turn.
Fama, *f.* fame, (good) repute.
fantasieren, *v.n.* improvize (*Mus.*).
Farbbrühe, *f.* dye.
farbenfreudig, farbenfroh, *adj.* colourful, gaily coloured.
Farbengebung, *f.* colouring (*of a painting*).
Farinade, *f.*, **Farinzucker,** *m.* powdered *or* caster sugar.
Fassonarbeit, *f.* profiling, shaping (*Engin.*).
fassonieren, *v.a.* profile, form, shape (*Engin.*).
febril, *adj.* feverish.
Federmotor, *m.* clockwork motor.
Federspannung, *f.* spring tension; *unter* –, spring-loaded.
Fehldisposition, *f.* blunder, (*coll.*) bloomer.
Fehlfarbe, *f.* cigar of imperfect appearance.
Fehlrechnung, *f.* miscalculation.
Fehwerk, *n.* furs, furriery.
Feinstruktur, *f.* microstructure.
Feldflur, *f.* arable (land).
Ferch, *m.* fire-damp (*Min.*).
Fergger, *m.* (*Swiss dial.*) carrier, haulage contractor, (forwarding) agent.
fernher, *adv.* from afar.
Fernkurs(us), *m.* correspondence course.
Fernlaster, *m.* (*coll.*) long-distance lorry.
Fernlastverkehr, *m.* long-distance road haulage.
Fernmeldedienst, *m.* telecommunications.
Fernmeldetechnik, *f.* telecommunication engineering.
Fernschuß, *m.* long-range shot; long shot (*Footb.* & *fig.*).
Fernsehsprecher, *m.* telecaster.
Fernsehübertragung, *f.* telecast.
Fernsprechbuch, *n.* telephone directory, (*coll.*) phone book.
fernstehen, *ir. v.n.* (*Dat.*) have no contact(s) with, be a stranger to.
Fernstudium, *n.* correspondence course.
Fernweh, *n.* wanderlust.
Fertigbauweise, *f.* prefabrication.
Festkraftstoff, *m.* solid fuel.
Festlandsockel, *m.* continental shelf.
Feststeller, *m.* shift lock (*typewriter*).
festverzinslich, *adj.* bearing fixed interest (*C.L.*).
Festwert, *m.* standard value; coefficient, constant (*Phys.*).
Fettpolster, *n.* subcutaneous fatty layer.
Fettpresse, *f.* grease-gun.
Feuilleton [*pron.* føjəˈtɔ̃], *n.* (-s, -s) feuilleton, light literature.
feuilletonistisch, *adj.* belletristic.
Fez, *m.* (*coll.*) lark, joke.
Filmbearbeitung, *f.* screen adaptation.
Filmvorschau, *f.* preview (*for critics*), trailer (*advertisement*).
Finanzausgleich, *m.* allocation of revenue between central and local authorities.
Finanzwechsel, *m.* paper transaction; accommodation bill.
fipsig, *adj.* (*coll.*) paltry, footling, fiddling.
Firmenwert, *m.* intangible assets, good will.
florieren, *v.n.* flourish, prosper, thrive.
Flötentöne, *pl.* (*fig.*) good manners *or* behaviour.
Flugball, *m.* volley (*Tenn.*).
Fluse, *f.* frayed edge *or* ends, loose ends (*of thread*).
flusig, *adj.* frayed, fuzzy.
Flußsäure, *f.* hydrofluoric acid.
Fördergerüst, *n.* pithead rig (*Min.*).
Förderleistung, *f.* output, production; delivery (*of a pump*).
Förderleitung, *f.* pipe-line, feed-pipe.
fortmachen, *v.n.* (*coll.*) carry on; (*coll.*) make off, clear out.
fötal, *adj.* foetal, intra-uterine.
Fragekasten, *m.* correspondence column (*in newspapers*).
Fraktionsführer, *m.* party whip (*Parl.*), floor leader (*Amer.*).
Fraktionszwang, *m.* party line *or* discipline; *Abstimmung ohne* –, non-party voting.
Fregattenkapitän, *m.* commander (*navy*).
Freibad, *n.* open-air baths, outdoor swimming pool.
Freibetrag, *m.* sum (of money) exempt from tax.
freihaben, *ir. v.n.* have time off, have a holiday.
Freihand, *f.* open access (*library*).
Freiheitsberaubung, *f.* false imprisonment.
Freiverkehr, *m.* unofficial *or* kerb market (*stock-exchange*); *im* –, in *or* on the open market, (*coll.*) over the counter.
Freizeichen, *n.* dialling tone (*phone*).
Freizeichnung, *f.* exoneration (*Law*), public subscription (*of shares*) (*C.L.*).
Frequenztreue, Frequenzwiedergabe, *f.* frequency response.
Frischhaltepackung, *f.* sealed *or* vacuum-packed container.
Fristablauf, *m.* lapse of time; expiry, maturity (*C.L.*).
Fristversäumnis, *f.* default.
Frivolitätenarbeit, *f.* tatting.
Frontneurose, *f.* battle-fatigue, shell-shock.
Frottee, *n.* terry towelling.
Früchtchen, *n.* (*coll.*) scamp, rascal, scapegrace.
Frühgesang, *m.* dawn chorus (*Orn.*).
Frühstart, *m.* false start (*Sport*).
Füller, *m.* (*coll.*) fountain-pen.
Funkentstörung, *f.* interference suppression (*Rad.*).
funkferngesteuert, *adj.* radio *or* remote controlled.
Funkfernpeilung, *f.* long-range navigation (LORAN) (*Naut.* & *Av.*).

Funkstille, *f.* radio silence.
Futterkrippenjäger, *m.* (*coll.*) placeman; spoilsman (*Amer.*).
Futterkrippensystem, *n.* (*coll.*) spoils system.
Futtertisch, *m.* bird-table.

G

Gamet, *m.* (-s, -e) gamete (*Biol.*).
Gammler, *m.* beatnik, lay-about.
Ganzaufnahme, *f.* full-length portrait.
Gasbenzin, *n.* natural gas(oline).
Gebärmutterbruch, *m.* hysterocele.
Gebärmutterentfernung, *f.* hysterectomy.
Gebärmutterschmerz, *m.* hysteralgia.
Gebrauchsdiebstahl, *m.* (*of a car*) joy-riding.
Gedankenverbindung, *f.* association of ideas.
Gefasel, *n.* (*coll.*) twaddle, tosh, bosh.
Gegenbuchung, *f.* cross-entry (*C.L.*).
Gegengerade, *f.* back straight (*Sport*).
Gegengetriebe, *n.* differential (gear) (*Mech.*).
Gegenlicht, *n.* light in one's eyes.
Gegenlichtblende, *f.* lens shade (*Phot.*), anti-dazzle screen (*Motor.*).
Gegenschlag, *m.* counterblow, counterattack.
Gegentakt, *m.* push-pull (*Rad.*).
Gehbahn, *f.* pavement, (*Amer.*) sidewalk.
Gehirnwäsche, *f.* brainwashing.
Gehstörung, *f.* locomotor disturbance.
Gehwerk, *n.* movement, works (*of clock*), clock-work mechanism.
Geißklee, *m.* broom (*Cytisus*) (*Bot.*).
Geländewagen, *m.* cross-country vehicle.
Gelbbleierz, *n.* wulfenite.
Gelbkali, *n.* potassium ferrocyanide (*Chem.*).
Geldflüssigkeit, *f.* money turnover.
Geldforderung, *f.* outstanding debt, money due *or* owing.
Geldleihsatz, *m.* bank rate.
Gelegenheitsdieb, *m.* sneak-thief.
Gelöstheit, *f.* relaxed mood.
Gemeinschaftsanschluß, *m.* party line (*Tele.*).
Gemeinschaftsbetrieb, *m.* joint enterprise.
Gemeinschaftsküche, *f.* canteen.
Gemeinschaftskunde, *f.* social studies.
Generalbevollmächtigte(r), *m.* plenipotentiary; agent with full powers of attorney (*Law*).
Generalbilanz, *f.* annual balance.
geradestehen, *ir. v.n.* stand erect; (*fig.*) – *für*, accept *or* acknowledge responsibility for, answer for.
Geräteschalter, *m.* plug (*Elec.*).
Gerätestecker, *m.* adaptor plug (*Elec.*).
Geräuschkulisse, *f.* background noise (*Rad.*).
gesellschaftsfähig, *adj.* presentable; gentlemanly, ladylike; acceptable in good society, (*coll.*) drawing-room.
Gesellschaftskapital, *n.* joint *or* capital stock, share capital (*C.L.*).
Gesellschaftssatzungen, *pl.* articles of association.
Gesellschaftssteuer, *f.* corporation tax.
Gesichtsschnitt, *m.* cast of features.
Gesichtsspannung, *f.* face-lifting.
Gewinnabführungsgesetz, *n.* excess profits tax.
Gewinnschere, Gewinnspanne, *f.* profit margin.
Gittergleichrichter, *m.* grid-leak detector (*Rad.*).
Gitterkapazität, *f.* (grid) input capacity (*Rad.*).
Gitternetz, *n.* (*on maps*) grid (co-ordinates).
Gittersteuerung, *f.* grid control (*Rad.*).
Gitterwiderstand, *m.* grid-leak resistance (*Rad.*).
Gleitbrett, *n.* surfboard.
Gleiter, *m.* glider (*Av.*).
Glockenrock, *m.* pleated *or* gored skirt.
Glypte, *f.* gem.
Glyptothek, *f.* collection of gems; museum of antique sculpture.
Gottesanbeterin, *f.* praying mantis.
Grabung, *f.* excavation.
Gradierwaage, *f.* areometer, hydrometer.
Grammophonanschluß, *m.* gramophone pick-up.
Gratismuster, *n.* free sample.
Gremium, *n.* (-s, -mien) board, panel, body (of experts).
Grenzgänger, *m.* illegal emigrant, refugee, escapee (*Pol.*); worker whose home and employment are on different sides of a frontier.
Grenzkohlenwasserstoff, *m.* saturated hydro-carbon (*Chem.*).
Grenzkonzentration, *f.* threshold concentration (*Chem.*).
Grenznachbar, *m.* next-door neighbour.
Grenzverbindung, *f.* saturated compound (*Chem.*).
Grobschnitt, *m.* rough-cut tobacco.
Groschenroman, *m.* penny dreadful, (*Amer.*) dime novel.
Großabnehmer, *m.* bulk purchaser.
Großverbraucher, *m.* bulk consumer.
Großversandgeschäft, *n.* mail-order house *or* firm.
Großverteiler, *m.* wholesaler, wholesale distributor.
Großvertrieb, *m.* wholesale distribution.
Großvieh, *n.* horned cattle.
Grünanlage, *f.* ornamental gardens, park; lawn, green.
grundanständig, *adj.* upright, high-principled.
Grundpeilung, *f.* sounding (*Naut.*).
Grundstufe, *f.* lower classes of elementary school; positive mood (*Gram.*).
Gründungsurkunde, *f.*, **Gründungsvertrag,** *m.* articles of association *or* incorporation.
grundverkehrt, *adj.* totally *or* utterly mistaken *or* wrong.
Grüngürtel, *m.* green belt (*round town*).
Grünstreifen, *m.* centre strip (*of motorway*).
Gruppenmord, *m.* mass murder.
Grützbeutel, *m.* wen, atheroma (*Med.*).
Gummihaut, *f.* rubberized fabric.
Gummilinse, *f.* (*coll.*) zoom lens.
Gummischlüpfer, *m.* (*coll.*) roll-on.
Gurtbogen, *m.* transverse arch (*Arch.*).
Gütermakler, *m.* estate *or* land agent, (*Amer.*) realtor.
Gütermarkt, *m.* commodity market.
Gütertrennung, *f.* antenuptial contract (*Law*).

H

Haarnest, *n.* chignon.
Haarschneidemaschine, *f.* hair clippers.
Haarwaschen, *n.* shampoo.
Hackbraten, *m.* minced meat, mince.
Haftgläser, *pl.* contact lenses.
Haftlokal, *n.* guard-room, detention room (*Mil.*).
Haftpflichtversicherung, *f.* third-party insurance.
Haftschale, *f.* contact lens.
Halbblüter, *m.* half-breed (horse).
Halblinke(r), *m.* inside left (forward) (*Footb.*).
Halbstarke(r), *m.* Teddy boy.
Halbwertzeit, *f.* half-life (period) (*Phys.*).
Halbwolle, *f.* linsey-woolsey.
halbwüchsig, *adj.* adolescent, teen-age.
Halbwüchsige(r), *m.* adolescent, juvenile, teen-ager.
Halterung, *f.* support, fixture, mounting (*Tech.*).
Handharmonika, *f.* accordion (*Mus.*).
Handlungsbevollmächtigte(r), *m.* head-clerk, authorized representative.
Handlungsvollmacht, *f.* power of attorney *or* procuration.
Handstandüberschlag, *m.* handspring (*Gymn.*).
Handwechsel, *m.* change of hands.
Hangwind, *m.* up- *or* anabatic current.
Hangwinkel, *m.* gradient of a slope.
Hartfloß, *n.* specular iron (*Metall.*).
Hartplatz, *m.* hard court (*Tenn.*).
Hartpost, *f.* typing *or* bank paper.
hauptamtlich, 1. *adj.* full-time (*occupation*). 2. *adv.* on a full-time basis.
Hauptberuf, *m.*, **Hauptbeschäftigung,** *f.* regular *or* full-time occupation.

Hauptgeschäftsstunden, *pl.* rush hours.
Hauptmannsrang, *m.* captaincy (*Mil.*).
Hauptschlager, *m.* theme song (*in film, etc.*); special bargain, main selling line (*C.L.*).
Hauptstrommotor, *m.* series-wound *or* direct-current motor (*Elec.*).
Hauptversammlung, *f.* general business meeting.
Häuserviertel, *n.* residential quarter.
Haushaltsvoranschlag, *m.* the estimates (*Pol.*).
Haushaltszuweisung, *f.* appropriation (*Pol.*).
Hausmacht, *f.* dynastic power (*Pol.*).
Haussekauf, *m.* bull purchase (*C.L.*).
Haussespekulant, *m.* bull, (*Amer.*) long (*C.L.*).
Haussestimmung, *f.* rising trend, lively tone (*of the market*).
Haussier, *m.* (-s, -s) (*C.L.*) *see* **Haussespekulant.**
Heckantrieb, *m.* rear drive (*Motor.*).
Heckbauer, *m.* breeding-cage.
Heftmaschine, *f.* stapling machine, stapler.
Heftnaht, *f.* tacking.
heftweise, *adv.* in (serial) parts.
Heimzahlung, *f.* (*coll.*) pay-off.
Heißluftdusche, *f.* hair-dryer.
Heißstrahltriebwerk, *n.* thermojet engine (*Av.*).
Heizkörper, *m.* heating element; heater, radiator.
Herrengesellschaft, *f.* male gathering, (*coll.*) stag-party.
Herrenkonfektion, *f.* men's ready-to-wear clothing.
Herrenzimmer, *n.* study; smoking room.
Hertz, *n.* cycles per second (*Phys.*).
Heulton, *m.* high-frequency hum (*Rad.*).
heutzutage, *adv.* today, nowadays, in our times, in these days.
Hexenjagd, *f.* witch-hunt (*Pol.*).
Hilfsaktion, *f.* relief work.
Hilfsphase, *f.* split phase (*Elec.*).
hinhauen, 1. *ir. v.a.* (*coll.*) knock off, do in a slapdash manner. 2. *v.r.* (*coll.*) turn in, hit the hay. 3. *v.n.* (*coll.*) *das haut hin,* that's done the trick.
hinhören, *v.n.* prick up one's ears.
hinzuwählen, *v.a.* co-opt.
hochgezüchtet, *adj.* high-compression (*Motor.*).
hochrappeln, *v.r.* struggle to one's feet.
Hochsaison, *f.* height of the season.
Hochschulkursus, *m.* extramural classes.
Höhenangabe, *f.* altitude reading.
Höhenkabine, *f.* pressurized cabin (*Av.*).
Höhenleitwerk, *n.* elevator unit (*Av.*).
Höhenschreiber, *m.* barograph, altigraph.
Holzschwamm, *m.* dry-rot.
Holzzellstoff, *m.* ligno-cellulose.
Holzzucker, *m.* xylose.
Honigbrot, *n.* gingerbread.
Hubvolumen, *n.* piston displacement (*Motor.*).
Hubweg, *m.* piston travel (*Motor.*); (height of) valve lift.
Hubzahl, *f.* number of strokes (*Motor.*).
Hüfthalter, *m.* suspender belt, girdle.
Hüfthose, *f.* (*usu. pl.*) jeans, hipsters.
Hüttenindustrie, *f.* iron and steel industry.
Hüttentechnik, *f.* metallurgical engineering.
Hypophyse, *f.* pituitary gland (*Anat.*); hypophysics.

I

Idiotenhügel, *m.* (*coll.*) nursery slopes (*skiing*).
Impedanz, *f.* impedance (*Rad.*).
Impedanzspule, *f.* reactance (coil).
Industrieberater, *m.* management consultant.
Infarkt, *m.* (-(e)s, -e) infarct(ion) (*Med.*).
Infragestellung, *f.* casting doubts (up)on, questioning; endangering, imperilling.
Inlandabsatz, *m.* sales in the home market.
Intarsia, *f.* inlay, inlaid work, marquetry.
Interessengruppe, *f.* pressure group (*Pol.*).
Inzahlungsnahme, *f.* trading-in.

J

Jackenkleid, *n.* (ladies') costume, two-piece.
Jackett, *n.* (-(e)s, -e *or* -s) (short) coat, jacket (*for men*).
Jackettanzug, *m.* lounge suit.

K

Kabelschacht, *f.* manhole.
Kälteanlage, *f.* refrigeration plant.
Kälteeinbruch, *m.* cold snap.
Kälteschutzmittel, *n.* antifreeze mixture (*Motor.*).
kaltschnäuzig, 1. *adj.* cool, (*coll.*) snooty. 2. *adv.* coolly, as cool as you please.
Kampfeinsatz, *m.* commitment (*of troops*); combat, action.
Kannvorschrift, *f.* permissive *or* discretionary provision (*Law*).
Kapitalbilanz, *f.* net capital movement.
Kapitaleinkommen, *n.* unearned income.
Kapitalertragssteuer, *f.* capital gains tax.
Kapitalverkehr, *m.* turnover of capital.
Kapitalvermögen, *n.* capital assets.
kariös, *adj.* decayed, carious (*Med.*).
karitativ, *adj.* charitable, benevolent.
kaschieren, *v.a.* line; cover, conceal.
Kassakurs, *m.* spot price.
Kassenpatient, *m.* panel patient.
Kassenraub, *m.* pay-roll robbery.
Kassenscheck, *m.* open *or* uncrossed cheque.
Kaufunlust, *f.* sales resistance.
Keilhose, *f.* (*usu. pl.*) close-fitting (ski) trousers.
Keilriemen, *m.* V-belt (*Tech.*).
Keimblatt, *n.* cotyledon.
Kellerwirtschaft, *f.* basement restaurant.
Kennmarke, *f.* identification label *or* tag.
Kennummer, *f.* reference number, (*newspapers*) box number.
Kernabstand, *n.* inter-nuclear distance.
Kernaufbau, *m.* nuclear synthesis.
Kernforschung, *f.* nuclear research.
Kernfrage, *f.* crucial question.
Kernspaltung, *f.* nuclear fission.
Kernwaffe, *f.* nuclear weapon.
kernweich, *adj.* soft-boiled (*egg*).
Kernwolle, *f.* prime wool.
kettenförmig, *adj.* aliphatic (*Chem.*).
Kettengeschäft, *n.* chain- *or* multiple-store.
Kilometerstand, *m.* mileage reading.
Kinderheilkunde, *f.* pediatrics.
Kindsmutter, *f.* unmarried *or* natural mother (*Law*).
Kintopp, *m.* (*sl.*) the flicks, the movies.
Klacks, *m.* (*coll.*) blob.
Klapperkiste, *f.* (*coll.*) boneshaker, jalopy, rattletrap, crate.
Kleiderhaken, *m.* coat-hook, hat and coat peg.
Kleinbus, *m.* minibus.
Klo, *n.* (-s, -s) (*coll.*) lav, loo, john (*toilet*).
Knäckebrot, *n.* crispbread.
Knalldämpfer, *m.* silencer (*Motor.*).
Knipszange, *f.* ticket-punch.
Knobelbecher, *m.* dice-box.
knockentrocken, *adj.* dry as a bone.
Knopfsteuerung, *f.* push-button control.
Kochnische, *f.* kitchenette.
Kochplatte, *f.* hotplate.
Kolbenverdichter, *m.* reciprocating compressor.
Kolchose, *f.* collective farm.
Kolchosenwirtschaft, *f.* collective farming.
Kollaps, *m.* (-es, -e) collapse, fainting fit (*Med.*).
Kolloquium, *n.* (-s, -quien) colloquy, discussion (group).
Kolonnensteller, *m.* tabulator (*typewriter*).
Kombinationsgabe, *f.* acumen, perspicacity, discernment, (*coll.*) gumption, mother-wit.
Kombinationsschloß, *n.* combination lock.
Kombinationsspiel, *n.* good combination, teamwork.

Kombiwagen, *m.* (*coll.*) estate car, station wagon.
Kommandogerät, *n.* (anti-aircraft) predictor.
Kommandostand, *m.* (anti-aircraft) command post.
Kommandotrupp, *m.* task force, raiding party (*Mil.*).
Kommandotruppe, *f.* Commandos (*Mil.*).
Kommerz, *m.* commerce.
kommerzialisieren, *v.a.* convert into a negotiable loan.
kommerziell, *adj.* commercial.
Konföderation, *f.* confederacy.
Kontrollampe, *f.* pilot light (*Tech.*).
Kontrollgang, *m.* (police) beat.
Kontrollgerät, *n.* monitoring device, monitor.
Kontrollkarte, *f.* time-sheet.
Kontrollkasse, *f.* cash-register.
Kontrollversuch, *m.* control test, spot check.
Konuskupplung, *f.* cone clutch.
konziliant, *adj.* conciliatory.
Koordinate, *f.* coordinate.
Koordinatenpapier, *n.* graph paper.
Kopfstoß, *m.* header (*Footb.*), butt (*Box.*), masse (*Bill.*).
koronar, *adj.* coronary.
Koronarthrombose, *f.* coronary (thrombosis).
Körpermaße, *pl.* vital statistics.
Kotze, *f.* (*vulg.*) spew, vomit.
Kraftstück, *n.* stunt.
Kranzarterie, *f.* coronary artery (*Anat.*).
Kriegseinwirkung, *f.* enemy action.
Kriegsneurose, *f.* shell-shock, battle fatigue.
Kriminalbeamte(r), *m.* detective, plainclothes man.
krumpfen, *v.a.* pre-shrink.
Kuchenheber, *m.* cake-slice, pastry server.
Kulturschaffende(r), *m.* intellectual; creative artist; performing artist (*the approved Communist word for workers outside production or organization*).
Kundendienst, *m.* (after-sales) service.
Kundendienststelle, *f.* service depot.
Kundenkreis, *m.* clients, clientele, customers; good will (*C.L.*).
Kundenwerber, *m.* tout, canvasser.
Kunstdarm, *m.* synthetic sausage-skin.
Kunstfahrer, *m.* trick cyclist.
Kunstflieger, *m.* stunt flyer.
Kupon [*pron.* kuˈpɔ̃], *m.* (-s, -s) coupon, counterfoil.
Kurswagen, *m.* through carriage (*Railw.*).
Kurvenradius, *m.* half turning-circle (*Motor.*).
Kurvenscheibe, *f.* cam.
Kurvenvorgabe, *f.* staggered start (*Sport*).
Kurznachricht, *f.* news flash; (*pl.*) news summary, news in brief.
Kurzschlußhandlung, *f.* (*fig.*) panic action.
Kurzschlußkontakt, *m.* arcing contact (*Elec.*).

L

Lackel, *m.* (*coll.*) boor, oaf, yokel.
Lackschuhe, *pl.* patent-leather shoes, dress shoes.
Lagebesprechung, *f.* briefing (*Mil.*).
Lagerfähigkeit, Lagerfrist, *f.* shelf-life.
Langsamtreten, *n.* (*coll.*) go-slow (strike), working to rule.
Langspielplatte, *f.* long-playing record.
läppen, *v.a.* lap (*Tech.*).
Lärmbekämpfung, *f.* noise-abatement campaign.
latent, *adj.* latent; dormant, potential; *-e Kraft,* latent force, (*fig.*) potentiality.
Latenz, *f.* latency.
Latenzstadium, *n.*, **Latenzzeit,** *f.* incubation period (*Med.*).
Laufdisziplinen, *pl.* track events (*Sport*).
Läuferreihe, *f.* half-back line (*Footb.*), three-quarter line (*Rugby Footb.*).
Läuferstoff, *m.* (stair-)carpeting.
Laufgitter, *n.*, **Laufstall,** *m.* playpen.
Leibesvisitation, *f.* bodily search.
Leihgebinde, *n.* returnable container (*C.L.*).
Leistungsabgabe, *f.* power output (*Elec.*).
Leistungsaufnahme, *f.* power input (*Elec.*).
Leistungseinheit, *f.* unit of power.
Leistungsgesellschaft, *f.* meritocracy.
Leistungsprämie, *f.* efficiency bonus.
Leistungssoll, *n.* output target.
Leistungssteigerung, *f.* increased efficiency.
Leistungssystem, *n.* piecework system.
Leistungswettbewerb, *m.* efficiency drive.
Leitungsmast, *m.* pylon (*Elec.*).
Leitungsplan, *m.* wiring diagram.
Lendenschnitte, *f.* rumpsteak.
Letternkasten, *m.* lower case.
Letternsetzmaschine, *f.* monotype machine.
Leuchtfleck, *m.* (*coll.*) blip (*radar*).
Leuchtreklame, *f.* neon lights *or* signs.
Leuchtskala, *f.* luminous dial.
Leuchtstofflampe, *f.* fluorescent lamp.
Leuchtstoffröhre, *f.* fluorescent tube.
Leukämie, *f.* leukaemia (*Med.*).
Leukoplast, *n.* adhesive tape.
Leukozyten, *pl.* leucocytes (*Anat.*).
lichtelektrisch, *adj.* photo-electric.
Lichtfarbendruck, *m.* photomechanical colour-print(ing) (*Typ.*).
Lichtpausverfahren, *n.* heliographic printing.
Lichtquant, *n.* photon (*Phys.*).
Lichtsignal, *n.* traffic light; flare (*Naut.*).
Lichtzelle, *f.* photo-electric cell.
Liegenschaften, *pl.* real estate, landed property, immovables (*Law*).
Liegestütz, *m.* push-up (*Gymn.*).
Liegewiese, *f.* space for sun-bathing (*in open-air baths*).
Lift, *m.* (-(e)s, -e *or* -s) lift, (*Amer.*) elevator.
linksgerichtet, *adj.* leftist (*Pol.*).
Linkspartei, *f.* left-wing party.
Linksradikale(r), *m.* (extreme) left-winger.
Linksstricken, *n.* purl (stitches) (*knitting*).
Lohnabbau, *m.* reduction in wages, wage-cut.
Lohnabrechnung, *f.* statement of earnings, pay-slip.
Lohnkellner, *m.* day-waiter.
Lohnsteuerabzug, *m.* pay-as-you-earn.
Lokaltermin, *m.* investigation on the spot (*Law*).
Luftbrücke, *f.* air-lift (*Av.*).
Luftparade, *f.* fly-past (*Av.*).
Luftschleuse, *f.* air-chamber.
Luftspalt, *m.* air-gap.
Luftstrahlantrieb, *m.* jet propulsion.
Luftverunreinigung, *f.* air pollution.
Lulatsch, *m.* (-es, -e) (*coll.*) bag of bones, bean-pole.
Lutschbonbon, *m.* lolly.
Luxusausführung, *f.* de-luxe model.
Luxusausgaben, *pl.* luxury spending.
Luxuswagen, *m.* de-luxe model (*Motor.*).

M

Macher, *m.* maker, manager; wire-puller (*Pol., etc.*).
Magendarmkatarrh, *m.* gastro-enteritis.
Magnetbildband, *n.* videotape.
Magnetophon, *n.* (-s, -e) tape recorder.
Magnetregler, *m.* rheostat.
managen [*pron.* ˈmɛnɪdʒən], *v.a.* (*coll.*) have under one's thumb; bring off, wangle, work.
Managerkrankheit [*pron.* ˈmɛnɪdʒər–], *f.* (*coll.*) thrombosis, stress disease.
Manchester [*pron.* ˈmɛntʃɛstər], *m.* corduroy, (*coll.*) cord; velveteen.
Mängelrüge, *f.* (dissatisfied customer's) complaint.
Marionettenregierung, *f.* puppet government.
Marktanalyse, *f.* market research.
Marktfähigkeit, *f.* sal(e)ability.
Marktforschung, *f., see* **Marktanalyse.**
Maroquin [*pron.* marɔˈkɛ̃], *m.* Marocco leather.
Maschinenpark, *m.* machinery, mechanical equipment.
Maschinensetzer, *m.* machine compositor (*Typ.*).

Maßabteilung, *f.* custom-made department.
Massenabwurf, *m.* mass bombing (*Av.*).
Massenanziehung, *f.* gravitation.
Massenträgheit, *f.* moment of inertia (*Phys.*).
Massenmedien, *pl.* mass media.
Massenpublikum, *n.* (*coll.*) admass.
Maturant, *m.* (-en, -en) (*Austr. dial.*) school-leaver.
maturieren, 1. *v.a.* mature. 2. *v.n.* (*Austr. dial.*) sit *or* take the school-leaving examination.
Meckerei, *f.* grousing, nagging.
Medianwert, *m.* median (*Stat.*).
Megahertz, *n.* megacycles per second (*Rad.*).
Mehrwertsteuer, *f.* added-value tax.
Meldeblock, *m.* message pad.
Meldekopf, *m.* message centre (*Mil.*).
Meldeliste, *f.* list of entries (*Sport*).
Mensa, *f.* (-sen) students' refectory (*Univ.*).
Mief, *m.* (*sl.*) fug.
Mietwaschsalon, *m.* laundrette.
miezeln, *v.n.* (*coll.*) canoodle, bill and coo.
Milchreis, *m.* rice pudding.
milieugestört, *adj.* uprooted, maladjusted.
Minusglas, *n.* concave lens (*Opt.*).
Mischpult, *n.* control desk (*Rad., etc.*).
Mixbecher, *m.* cocktail shaker.
modal, *adj.* modal.
Modalität, *f.* modality; proviso, arrangement.
Modekünstler, *m.* couturier.
Mogler, *m.* (*coll.*) cheat.
Monatsbinde, *f.* sanitary napkin.
Moped, *n.* (-s, -s) motor scooter.
Mordsgeschichte, *f.* (*coll.*) cock-and-bull story.
Motivforschung, *f.* motivation research (*C.L.*).
Motorroller, *m.* motor scooter.
Müllfahrer, *m.* dustman, (*Amer.*) garbageman.
Müllschlucker, *m.* waste disposer.
Muni, *f.* (*coll.*) ammo.
Münzeinwurf, *m.* coin slot (*on slot-machines*).
Museumstück, *n.* period piece.
Musikautomat, *m.*, **Musikbox,** *f.* juke-box.
Mutti, *f.* (*coll.*) mummy, mama.
Myelomatose, *f.* osteomyelitis.
Myxomatose, *f.* myxomatosis.

N

nachfassen, *v.a.* & *v.n.* have a second helping (of).
nachfeilen, *v.a.* (*fig.*) retouch, put the finishing touches to.
nachfordern, *v.a.* charge extra, claim subsequently.
Nachfrist, *f.* respite, extension (of time).
Nachhang, *m.* postscript, addendum.
Nachholbedarf, *m.* backlog.
nachreichen, *v.n.* serve second helpings.
nachsenden, *ir. v.a.* re-address, forward, send on (*letters*); *bitte –!* please forward!
nachsteigen, *ir. v.n.* (*aux.* s.) (*Dat.*) (*coll.*) go *or* be after, chase (*girls*).
Nachtstromtarif, *m.* off-peak tariff.
Nachzugsaktie, *f.* deferred share (*C.L.*).
Nadelpunktierung, *f.* acupuncture.
Nadelstreifen, *m.* pin-stripe.
Naheinstellung, *f.* short focus, close-up (*Phot.*).
Nährkrem, *f.* skin-food.
Nährmittelchemie, *f.* chemistry of food.
Nährmittelfabrik, *f.* food-processing plant.
Nährsorgen, *pl.* difficulty in making a living.
Nahsender, *m.* local transmitter (*Rad.*).
Naturalbezüge, *pl.* remuneration in kind.
nebenamtlich, *adj.* part-time.
nebenberuflich, 1. *attrib. adj.* part-time, spare-time. 2. *adv.* in one's spare time, as a side-line.
Nebenhöhlenentzundung, *f.* sinusitis.
Nennkurs, *m.* par value (*C.L.*).
nennwertlos, *adj.* no-par (*C.L.*).
Neonlampe, *f.* neon light *or* lamp.
Nepplokal, *n.* (*sl.*) gyp-joint.
nervenaufreibend, *adj.* nerve-racking.
Nervenbündel, *n.* nerve-fascicle (*Anat.*); (*coll.*) bag of nerves.
Nervenkitzel, *m.* sensation, thrill.
Netzkarte, *f.* unrestricted season ticket.
Neubeurteilung, Neubewertung, *f.* reappraisal.
Neufassung, *f.* revised text, revision; amendment (*Law, Pol.*).
Neurotiker, *m.* neurotic.
nichttropfend, *adj.* non-drip.
niederknallen, *v.a.* shoot down, (*sl.*) bump off.
niederstimmen, *v.a.* outvote, vote down.
Normenvorschrift, *f.* standard specifications.
Notlager, *n.* makeshift *or* shakedown bed.
nuscheln, *v.n.* mumble, slur one's words.
Nutzungsgüter, *pl.* consumer goods.

O

obengesteuert, *adj.* overhead (*valve*) (*Motor.*).
oben ohne, *adj.* (*coll.*) topless (*dress*).
Oberregierungsrat, *m.* senior civil servant, senior government official.
Oberschwester, *f.* (ward) sister.
Objektivverschluß, *m.* instantaneous shutter (*Phot.*).
O-Bus, *m.* (*coll.*) trolley bus.
Offertsteller, *m.* tenderer.
Originalaufnahme, *f.* master tape.
Originalsendung, *f.* live transmission (*Rad.*).
Originaltreue, *f.* high fidelity.
ostentativ, *adj.* explicit, (*of a p.*) ostentatious.
Ostflüchtling, *m.* refugee from the East.
Ostvertriebene(r), *m.* displaced p. from eastern territory.
Overall, *m.* boiler-suit.

P

Päckchen, *n.* (postal) package, parcel.
Papageialk, *m.* paraquet, (*Amer.*) parakeet.
Papageitaucher, *m.* puffin.
Papierkrieg, *m.* red-tape.
Paradeflug, *m.* fly-past.
Paradepferd, *n.* (*fig.*) showpiece (*of a p.*).
Parallelversammlung, *f.* overflow meeting.
Parallelwährung, *f.* dual currency.
Parikurs, *m.* par (*C.L.*).
Parkuhr, *f.* parking meter.
Parkwache, *f.* car-park attendant.
Parteiapparat, *m.* party machine.
Parteigrundsätze, *pl.* party-line.
Parteigruppe, *f.* faction, splinter-party.
Partizipationsgeschäft, *n.* business on joint account (*C.L.*).
Passatströmung, *f.* equatorial current.
Paßbild, *n.* passport photograph.
Paßform, *f.* fit (*of clothes*).
Paßsitz, *m.* (*of clothes*) good *or* snug fit.
Paßstück, *n.* adapter, fitting (*Mech.*).
Peiltisch, *m.* plotting board *or* table.
Pendelzug, *m.* commuter train.
Pendler, *m.* commuter.
penibel, *adj.* (*of a p.*) difficult, fussy, (*coll.*) pernickerty.
Persiflage [*pron.* –ˈflɑːʒə], *f.* persiflage, satire.
persiflieren, *v.a.* satirize, burlesque.
Personalaufwendungen, *pl.* wages and salaries (*C.L.*).
Petent, *m.* (-en, -en) petitioner.
Pfeifkonzert, *n.* hissing, cat-calls.
Pfeilflügel, *m.* swept-back wing (*Av.*).
Pfeilmotor, *m.* V-type engine.
Pfennigabsatz, *m.* stiletto heel.
Pflichtübung, *f.* set figure (*skating*).
Phon, *n.* (-s, -s) decibel.
pikfein, *adj.* (*coll.*) tiptop, posh, (*sl.*) slap up, snazzy.

Pinakothek, *f.* art *or* picture gallery.
Pionierarbeit, *f.* (*fig.*) spadework.
placieren, 1. *v.a.* place, negotiate (*C.L.*). 2. *v.r.* be placed.
placiert, *adj.* well-placed (*Sport*).
Planetengetriebe, *n.* planetary *or* epicyclic gear(ing) (*Mech.*).
Plansoll, *n.* quota, target.
Planspiel, *n.* map-reading exercise (*Mil.*).
Planstärke, *f.* establishment (*Mil.*).
Planvorschub, *m.* transverse feed (*Mech.*).
Planziel, *n.* planned output, output target.
plätschern, *v.n.* splash *or* paddle about; (*of water*) ripple, babble.
Platzherren, *pl.* home team (*Sport*).
Platzmeister, *m.* groundsman (*Sport*).
Platzpatrone, *f.* blank cartridge.
Plexiglas, *n.* (*trade name*) perspex.
Podiumgespräch, *n.* panel discussion.
Polende, *n.* electrode (*Elec.*).
Polyeder, *n.* polyhedron.
Postbezug, *m.* mail order(ing).
Postenjägerei, *f.* (*coll.*) rat-race.
postenweise, *adv.* in lots *or* parcels (*C.L.*); item by item; – *aufführen*, itemize.
Postleitzahl, *f.* postal zone (prefix) number.
postum, *adj.* posthumous.
Postversandhaus, *n.* mail-order firm.
Postwurfsendung, *f.* mail circular.
Postzustellbezirk, *m.* postal district.
Präjudizrecht, *n.* case-law (*Law*).
Pratze, *f.* paw.
Preisauftrieb, *m.* upward trend (of prices).
Preisdruck, *m.* downward trend (of prices).
Preisgefüge, *n.* price-structuring.
Preisschild, *n.*, **Preiszettel,** *m.* price-tag *or* label.
Pressetribüne, *f.* press gallery (*Parl.*).
Presseverlautbarung, *f.* news *or* press release.
Pressevertreter, *m.* pressman, reporter; public relations officer.
Priese, *f.* neckband (*of shirt*).
Privatier, *m.* (-s, -s) man of independent means.
Privatinitiative, *f.* private venture; personal initiative.
Probeaufnahme, *f.* screen test (*films*).
programmieren, *v.a.* programme (*computer*).
Protoplasma, *n.* protoplasm.
Prototyp, *m.* (-(e)s, -e) prototype.
Protozoen, *pl.* protozoa.
Protuberanz, *f.* protuberance; (solar) prominence (*Astr.*).
Prüffeld, *n.* test-bay (*Tech.*).
Prünelle, *f.* prune.
pulen, *v.n.* pick, finger (*dial.*).
Pulk, *m.* (-s, -e) group, formation (*Av.*).
Punktmuster, *n.* polka-dot pattern.
Punktniederlage, *f.* defeat on points (*Box.*).
Punktrichter, *m.* (ringside) judge (*Box.*).
Punktzahl, *f.* score (*Sport*).

Q

Qualifikationsfreilos, *n.* bye (*Sport*).
Querlage, *f.* (*of birth*) transverse presentation (*Med.*).
Querlager, *n.* radial bearing (*Tech.*).
Querlatte, *f.* cross-bar (*Footb.*).

R

Radabstand, *m.* wheel-base.
Radar, *n.* radiolocation, radar.
Radarnavigationsgerät, *n.* plan position indicator.
Radarwarnnetz, *n.* radar warning network.
Radaukomödie, *f.* slapstick comedy.
Radiogrammophon, *n.* radiogram.
Radiologe, *m.* (-n, -n) radiologist.
Radiopeilgerät, *n.* (radio) direction finder.
Raffinesse, *f.* finesse, subtlety, cleverness; polish, elegance, refinement, discrimination.
Raketenabschußbasis, *f.* launching ramp *or* pad.
Raketenabwehrakete, *f.* anti-missile missile.
Raketenbombe, *f.* guided missile.
Raketenbrennkammer, *f.* rocket-motor.
Raketenforschung, *f.* rocketry.
Raketenstart, *m.* rocket-assisted take-off.
Raketentechnik, *f.* rocketry.
Raketenversuchsgelände, *n.* rocket range.
Rassenschranke, *f.* colour bar.
Rassentheorie, *f.* racialism.
Rassentrennung, *f.* racial segregation.
Rasterlinien, *pl.* scanning lines (*T.V.*).
Raststelle, *f.* lay-by, rest area (*Motor.*).
Rauchnebel, *m.* smog.
Raumfahrer, *m.* cosmonaut.
Raumflug, *m.* space-flight.
Raumgestalter, *m.* interior decorator.
Raummessung, *f.* stereometry.
Raumschiff, *n.* space-ship.
Raumschiffahrt, *f.* space-travel.
Raumtonne, *f.* freight ton (*Naut.*).
Raumtonwirkung, *f.* stereoscopic effect (*Rad.*).
Räumtrupp, *m.* demolition party.
Räumungsbefehl, *m.* eviction order.
Rauschfaktor, *m.* signal-to-noise ratio (*Rad.*).
Rauschgiftsüchtige(r), *m.* drug-addict, (*sl.*) junkie.
reagibel, *adj.* sensitive.
reaktionsschnell, *adj.* susceptible, impressionable, responsive; lively, mettlesome, highly-strung.
Recherchen [*pron.* rɛˈʃɛrʃən], *pl.* inquiries, investigation.
rechtsradikal, *adj.* (extreme) right wing (*Pol.*).
Reduktionsteilung, *f.* meiosis (*Biol.*).
Reformhaus, *n.* health-food shop.
Regelausführung, *f.* standard design *or* model.
Regiefehler, *m.* (*coll.*) bad management.
Regiepult, *n.* mixing desk (*Rad., etc.*).
Regierungsumbildung, *f.* cabinet changes.
Reifendruckmesser, *m.* tyre gauge.
Reifenprofil, *n.* tread (*of a tyre*).
Reihenhaus, *n.* terrace-house.
Reinigungsanstalt, *f.* dry-cleaners.
reinlegen, *v.a.* (*coll.*) double-cross.
reinweg, *adv.* flatly, completely, absolutely, altogether.
Reiteration, *f.* stereotypy (*Med.*).
Reklamefeldzug, *m.* advertising drive *or* campaign.
Reklamesendung, *f.* commercial programme (*Rad.*).
Reklamestück, *n.* (*coll.*) show-piece.
Reklamezettel, *m.* handbill.
rekonstruieren, *v.a.* reconstruct, re-enact (*a crime*) (*Law*).
Relaisender, *m.* relay *or* repeater station (*Rad.*).
Remanenzspannung, *f.* residual voltage.
Rembours, *m.* (–, –) remittance (*C.L.*).
Repertoire, *n.* (-s, -s) repertoire, repertory (*Theat.*).
Repertoirestück, *n.* stock-play.
Ressentiment, *n.* resentment, grudge, rancour, ill-will.
restituieren, *v.a.* restore.
Revierdienst, *m.* light duties (*Mil.*).
Revolverblatt, *n.* (*coll.*) scandal-sheet, rag.
Revolverheld, *m.* (*coll.*) gunman, thug, hoodlum.
revozieren, 1. *v.a.* revoke, retract, recall. 2. *v.n.* retract one's words.
Revuegirl, *n.* showgirl.
rezeptieren, *v.a.*, *v.n.* prescribe.
Rippchen, *n.* cutlet, chop (*Cul.*).
Robinsonade, *f.* far-fetched adventure story; full-length save (*Footb. coll.*).
Rohbilanz, *f.* trial balance.
Rohblock, *m.* ingot (*Metall.*).
Roheinnahme, *f.* gross receipts.
rückenfrei, *adj.* backless (*dress*).
Rückgriff, *m.* recourse, resort.
Rückkaufswert, *m.* redemption *or* surrender value; resale price.
Rückstoßrakete, *f.* retro-rocket.
Rückumwandlung, *f.* reconversion.

Rührstäbchen, *n.* swizzle-stick.
Rüstungsbeschränkung, *f.* restriction of military expenditure.
Rüstungswettbewerb, *m.* armament race.
rutschfest, *adj.* skid-proof.

S

Sachanlagevermögen, *n.* tangible fixed assets (*Law*).
Sachbuch, *n.* non-fiction work.
Sachentscheidung, *f.* decision on the merits of the case (*Law*).
Sachverständigengutachten, *n.* expert opinion.
Safe [*pron.* ze:f], *m.* (-s, -s) safe, strong-room; safe-deposit box.
saisonbedingt, saisonmäßig, *adj.* seasonal.
Salzbrezel, *f.* pretzel.
Sammelaktion, *f.* salvage drive (*for goods*), fund-raising campaign (*for money*).
Sammelschule, *f.* comprehensive school.
Sammeltag, *m.* flag-day.
samtschwarz, *adj.* black as night.
Sandbahn, *f.* dirt-track (*Motor.*).
sanforisiert, *adj.* pre-shrunk.
satisfaktionsfähig, *adj.* (*of a p.*) of the sort who may be expected to make amends *or* from whom one may expect satisfaction (*partic. duelling, also fig.*).
Sattelkissen, *n.* pillion.
Sattelschlepper, *m.* articulated lorry *or* truck.
sauigeln, *v.n.* (*coll.*) talk smut.
Schälerzeugnisse, *pl.* prepared cereals.
Schallgrenze, Schallmauer, *f.* sound barrier.
Schanzentisch, *m.* jump-off platform (*skiing*).
Schauerdrama, *n.* blood-and-thunder melodrama.
Schaufensterbummel, *m.* window-shopping.
Schaufenstereinbruch, *m.* smash-and-grab raid.
Schaumgebäck, *n.* meringue(s).
scheppern, *v.n.* (*coll.*) clatter, rattle; (*sl.*) (have a) crash (*Motor.*).
Schichtstoff, *m.* laminated plastic.
Schienbeinschützer, *m.* shin-guard, (shin-)pad (*Sport*).
Schirokko, *m.* sirocco.
Schirting, *m.* (-s, -e (*Austr.* -s)) shirting.
schizophren, *adj.* schizophrenic.
Schizophrenie, *f.* schizophrenia.
Schlafcouch, *f.* studio couch.
Schlagerkomponist, *m.* pop(ular)-song writer.
Schlagermelodie, *f.* pop-song, (*pl.*) pop-music.
Schlagerparade, *f.* hit-parade, top of the pops.
Schlagerpreis, *m.* rock-bottom *or* give-away price.
Schlagersänger, *m.* pop-singer, crooner.
Schlechtgestellten, die, *pl.* (the) underprivileged (classes).
Schleudersitz, *m.* ejector seat (*Av.*).
Schlingenfalle, *f.* gin-trap.
Schlundspiegel, *m.* pharyngoscope.
Schmelzkäse, *m.* process(ed) cheese.
Schneebesen, *m.* egg-beater, whisk.
Schnellgang, *m.* overdrive (*Mech.*).
Schnellgaststätte, *f.* self-service restaurant, cafeteria.
Schnellimbißstube, *f.* snack-bar.
Schnellreinigung, *f.* express dry-cleaning.
Schnelltriebwagen, *m.* express diesel train.
Schnellverband, *m.* adhesive dressing, Band Aid (*trade name*) (*Med.*).
Schnellwäscherei, *f.* self-service laundry, laundrette.
Schnittmeister, *m.* cutter, editor (*films*).
Schnittmesser, *n.* scalpel (*Surg.*).
Schnulze, *f.* sentimental ditty, (*sl.*) tear-jerker, (*coll.*) pop-song.
Schonbezug, *m.* (protective) covering, seat cover.
Schongang, *m.* overdrive (*Motor.*).
Schonkost, *f.* diet (*Med.*).
schrankfertig, *adj.* (*of laundry*) ironed and ready for use.
Schrecksekunde, *f.* reaction time (*of driver*).
Schreibarbeit, *f.* clerical work.
Schreiberei, *f.* scribbling, (endless) paperwork.
schrumpffest, *adj.* shrink-proof, non-shrinking.
Schulbildung, *f.* (statutory) education.
Schuldversprechen, *n.* acknowledgement of liabilities.
Schülerlotsendienst, *m.* (system of) traffic wardens.
Schußfahrt, *f.* downhill run (*skiing*).
Schwangerschaftsunterbrechung, *f.* interruption of pregnancy, abortion.
schwangerschaftsverhütend, *adj.* contraceptive.
Schwarzmarkthändler, *m.* black marketeer.
Schweigemarsch, *m.* (silent) protest march.
Schwenk, *m.* (-(e)s, -e) pan-shot (*Film*).
Schwule(r), *m.* nancy-boy, queer.
Schwundzone, *f.* area of no reception (*Rad.*).
Sedativum, *n.* (-s, -va) tranquillizer.
Seesack, *m.* kitbag.
Seidenaffe, *m.* marmoset (*Zool.*).
Sektkühler, *m.* ice-pail.
Sektquirl, *m.* swizzle-stick.
Selbstbespiegelung, *f.* self-conceit, self-importance, self-admiration, self-esteem.
Selbstfahrerdienst, *m.* drive-yourself car-hire service.
Selbstreflektant, *m.* prospective buyer *or* customer (*C.L.*).
Selbstwähler, *m.* (*phone*) dial.
Selbstwählerfernverkehr, *m.* subscriber trunk dialling, (*Amer.*) direct distance dialling.
Senior, *m.* (-s, -en) chairman, spokesman.
Senkrechtstart, *m.* vertical take-off (*Av.*).
Senkrechtstarter, *m.* vertical take-off plane.
Serienarbeit, *f.* serial work.
Serienartikel, *m.* mass-produced article.
serienmäßig, 1. *adj.* mass-produced. 2. *adv.* – *herstellen,* mass-produce.
Serienrennen, *n.* stock-car race *or* racing.
Serienwagen, *m.* mass-produced, production-line *or* standard-model car.
Servolenkung, *f.* servo-control, power (assisted) steering.
Sicherheitsfonds, *m.* guarantee fund (*C.L.*).
Sicherheitsgurt, *m.* safety belt (*Motor.*).
Sicherungsverwahrung, *f.* preventive detention (*Law*).
Sichtgeschäft, *n.* forward transaction, (*pl.*) futures (*stock-exchange*).
Siebenmonatskind, *n.* premature child.
Siedlungsbau, *m.* (suburban) housing development.
Siegespokal, *m.* challenge-cup (*Sport*).
Silikat, *n.* (-(e)s, -e) silicate (*Chem.*).
Silikose, *f.* silicosis (*Med.*).
sinnenfreudig, *adj.* sensuous.
Sitzstreik, *m.* sit-down strike.
Sommertheater, *n.* open-air theatre.
Sonnenbräune, *f.* (sun-)tan.
Sonnenwende, *f.* solstice; heliotrope (*Bot.*).
Sozialabgaben, *pl.* national insurance contributions.
sozialdenkend, *adj.* public-spirited.
Sozialeinrichtungen, *pl.* social services.
Sozialprodukt, *n.* gross national product.
Sozialrentner, *m.*, **Sozialrentnerin,** *f.* national insurance *or* (*coll.*) old-age pensioner.
Sozialunterstützung, *f.* national assistance.
Spaltprodukt, *n.* product of (atomic) fission.
Spankorb, *m.* chip-basket.
Spannbeton, *m.* pre-stressed concrete.
spannungsführend, *adj.* live (*Elec.*).
spannungslos, *adj.* (*fig.*) unexciting, dull, dead.
Sparanleihe, *f.* savings certificate.
Sparbrenner, *m.* pilot light.
Sparprämienlos, *n.* premium bond.
Speicherkraftwerk, *n.* hydro-electric scheme *or* power-station.
Spezialkräfte, *pl.* specialists, skilled workers.
spiegelgleich, *adj.* symmetrical (*Geom.*).
Spiegeltisch, *m.* glass-topped table.
Spielanzug, *m.* playsuit, rompers.
Spielautomat, *m.* one-armed bandit, pin-table.
Spielmannszug, *m.* (military) band.
Spielverbot, *n.* suspension (*Sport*).

Spielverlängerung, *f.* extra time (*Sport*).
Spitzenfilm, *m.* star production.
Sportgeist, *m.* sportsmanship.
Sportgeschäft, *n.* sports-shop.
Sportkabriolett, *n.* roadster, sports car.
Sportskanone, *f.* (*coll.*) top-ranking athlete, star performer.
Sporttaucher, *m.* skin-diver.
Sprechband, *n.* sound-track (*Film, etc.*).
Sprechfunk, *m.* radio-telephony.
Sprechmuschel, *f.* (*phone*) mouthpiece.
Sprechprobe, *f.* audition (*Theat., etc.*).
Sprengkopf, *m.* warhead.
Spruchkammer, *f.* (denazification) tribunal (*Pol.*).
Sprungbalken, *m.* springboard (*Sport*).
Sprunggrube, *f.* (landing) pit (*Sport*).
Sprungnetz, *n.* life-saving net.
Sprungrevision, *f.* direct appeal (*Law*).
Sprungriemen, *m.* (*harness*) martingale.
Spulenanlage, *f.* tape deck.
Spurhaltigkeit, *f.* steering stability (*Motor.*).
Stadtsyndikus, *m.* town-clerk.
Stahlfach, *n.* safe-deposit *or* strong-box.
Ställchen, *n.* (*coll.*) playpen.
Stammgericht, *n.* speciality of the house.
Standesbewußtsein, *n.* class-consciousness; caste-allegiance *or* feeling.
Starkstrom-Steckdose, *f.* power point.
Startgeld, *n.* entry-fee (*Sport*).
Starthilfe, *f.* assisted take-off (*Av.*).
Startknopf, *m.* starter-button (*Motor.*).
Startkommando, *n.* starter's order (*Sport*).
Startrakete, *f.* launching rocket (*Av.*).
Startschleuder, *f.* catapult launching device (*Av.*).
Startschuß, *m.* starting-signal, starter's gun.
Startstrecke, *f.* take-off run (*Av.*).
Startverbot, *m.* disqualification, suspension (*Sport*); grounding (*Av.*).
Stationärbehandlung, *f.* hospitalization, in-patient treatment.
Stationskala, *f.* tuning dial (*Rad.*).
Statistin, *f.* (female) stand-in, extra *or* walker-on.
Staublunge, *f.* pneumoconiosis.
Staudruckmesser, *m.* pressure gauge, airspeed indicator.
Stehbild, *n.* still (*Phot.*).
Stehhöhe, *f.* standing headroom.
Stehimbiß, *m.* stand-up snack.
Stehvermögen, *n.* staying-power, stamina (*Sport*).
Steinholz, *n.* xylolith.
Steinpflanze, *f.* lithophyte.
Steinwerkzeug, *n.* eolith.
Steißlage, *f.* breech presentation (*Med.*).
Stellgeld, *n.* premium for put and call *or* (*Amer.*) for spread (*C.L.*).
Stelling, *m.* gangway (*Naut.*).
Stellungsbau, *m.* construction of defences (*Mil.*).
Stellungsspiel, *n.* positional play (*Footb.*).
Sterbehilfe, *f.* mercy killing, euthenasia (*Med.*).
Stereoaufnahme, *f.* stereoscopic photograph.
Stereographie, *f.* descriptive geometry.
Sternkreuzung, *f.* (*on roads*) multiple crossing.
Sternschreiber, *m.* (*radar*) plan position indicator.
Sternstunde, *f.* sidereal hour, (*fig.*) fateful *or* auspicious hour.
Steuerautomatik, *f.* automatic pilot.
Steuerdruck, *m.* burden of taxation.
Steuermeßzahl, *f.* (income-tax) code number *or* coding.
Steuerwert, *m.* taxable value.
Stewardeß, *f.* (-(ss)en) stewardess; air-hostess (*Av.*).
Stillgeld, *n.* insurance payment for nursing mothers.
Stilmöbel, *pl.* period furniture.
Stimmenwerber, *m.* canvasser.
Stopp, *m.* ban, prohibition; freeze (*prices, incomes*).
Stoppschild, *m.* halt sign (*Motor.*).
Störanzeigelampe, *f.* warning light, fault indicator lamp (*Motor., etc.*).
Störungstrupp, *m.* (*phone*) repair gang.
Stoßarbeiter, *m.* shock-worker.
Stoßkeil, *m.* spearhead (*Mil.*).
Stoßwelle, *f.* percussion wave, shock-wave.
Strafmaßnahme, *f.* sanction.
Strahlendosis, *f.* radiation dosage.
Strahleneinfall, *m.* incidence of rays.
Strahler, *m.* emitter, radiator, heater; aerial array, directional *or* beam aerial *or* (*Amer.*) antenna (*Rad.*).
Strahlmotor, *m.* jet-engine.
Strahlofen, *m.* radiator.
Strahlsender, *m.* directional *or* beam transmitter (*Rad.*).
Strahlungsquant, *n.* photon.
Strampelhöschen, *n.* rompers.
Straßenanzug, *m.* lounge suit.
Straßenbeschaffenheit, *f.* road conditions.
Straßeneinmündung, *f.* road junction.
Straßenfalle, *f.* speed trap.
Straßenlage, *f.* road-holding qualities (*Motor.*).
Straßenordnung, *f.* traffic regulations, rules of the road, Highway Code.
Straßenplanum, *n.* street-level.
Straßenschreck, *m.*, (*coll.*) **Straßenschwein,** *n.* road-hog.
Straßenspinne, *f.* multiple intersection *or* road junction.
Straßentransport, *m.* road-haulage.
Straßenverstopfung, *f.* traffic congestion *or* (*coll.*) jam.
Streckentauchen, *n.* underwater swimming.
Streichkäse, *m.* soft *or* spreading cheese.
Streichmasse, *f.* plastic compound, filler, coating.
Streifenwagen, *m.* (police) patrol *or* squad car.
Strohbedeckung, *f.* mulch.
Stromnetz, *n.* power supply.
Strompolizei, *f.* river police.
stufenlos, *adj.* infinitely variable (*Mech.*).
Stufenrakete, *f.* multi-stage rocket.
Stufentransformator, *m.* step-up *or* step-down transformer (*Elec.*).
Submittent, *m.* (-en, -en) tenderer.
substanzieren, *v.a.* particularize (*a claim*) (*Law*).
Suchaktion, *f.* search.
Suchanzeige, *f.* wanted advertisement.
Suchbüro, *n.* department for tracing missing persons.
Suchmannschaft, *f.*, **Suchtrupp,** *m.* search-party.
sukzessive, *adv.* gradually, little by little, (*coll.*) bit by bit.
Superkaftstoff, *m.* high-octane fuel.
Szenenaufnahme, *f.* shot (*Film*); shooting.

T

tafelfertig, *adj.* ready-to-eat *or* to-serve.
Tafelziffer, *f.* reading (*on a dial*).
Tagesablauf, *m.* daily routine.
Tagessatz, *m.* daily rate; today's *or* current rate (*C.L.*); (*of food*) daily ration, one day's supply.
Tagesschau, *f.* news (on television).
tailliert, *adj.* close-fitting, fitted to the waist.
Tanksäule, *f.* petrol pump.
Tarifordnung, *f.* wage-scale.
Tarifverhandlungen, *pl.* collective bargaining.
Tarnbezeichnung, *f.* code-word.
Taschenapotheke, *f.* pocket first-aid kit.
Taschenkalender, *m.* pocket diary.
Tatarennachricht, *f.* canard, alarmist report.
Tatumstände, *pl.* circumstances surrounding the case.
Tatverdacht, *m.* suspicion (of being the culprit).
Taucherlunge, *f.* aqualung.
Technologe, *m.* (-n, -n) technologist, engineer.
Technologie, *f.* technology, engineering.
Teilbild, *n.* frame, (*Amer.*) field (*T.V.*).
Teilstaat, *m.* constituent state.
Teilzieher, *m.* partial migrant (*Orn.*).
Telekolleg, *n.* University of the Air, Open University.
termingemäß, termingerecht, *adv.* on the appointed day, (*coll.*) to schedule, on time.

Terminkalender, *m.*, **Terminliste,** *f.* case list (*Law*).
testen, *v.a.* (submit to a) test, submit to investigation.
testieren, 1. *v.a.* bequeath, dispose of by will; certify, testify, attest. 2. *v.n.* make a will.
Teuerungszuschlag, *m.* price rise due to rising costs.
Texter, *m.* copywriter.
Tiefbunker, *m.* deep *or* underground shelter.
Tiefenschärfe, *f.* depth of focus (*Phot.*).
Tiefenwirkung, *f.* effect in depth, (*of sound*) stereophonic effect, (*of pictures*) stereoscopic effect.
tiefgekühlt, *adj.* in deep-freeze.
Tiefkühltruhe, *f.* deep-freeze tray *or* compartment.
Tiefseetauch(er)kugel, *f.* bathysphere.
Tip, *m.* (-s, -s) hint, warning; tip (*Sport*); *einem einen – geben,* tip s.o. off.
Tippfehler, *m.* typing error.
tipptopp, *adj.* (*coll.*) tip-top, first-class *or* -rate, (*sl.*) posh, swell.
Tohuwabohu, *n.* hubbub, confusion, hullabaloo, (*sl.*) racket.
Toilettengarnitur, *f.* toilet-set, dressing-case.
Tonaufnahme, *f.* sound-recording.
Tonbandaufnahme, *f.* tape-recording.
Tonbandgerät, *n.* tape-recorder.
Tonschwund, *m.* fading (*Rad.*).
Tonstreifen, *m.* sound-track (*Film*).
Tonüberwacher, *m.* sound monitor.
Tonwiedergabe, *f.* sound reproduction (*Rad.*); fidelity.
Torraum, *m.* goal area (*Footb.*).
Torschlußpanik, *f.* (*coll.*) last-minute panic.
Torschuß, *m.* kick *or* shot at goal; goal.
Totalausverkauf, *m.* clearance sale.
Toto, *m.* (-s, -s) football pools; *im – spielen,* bet on *or* (*coll.*) do the pools; *im – gewinnen,* win on the pools.
Totogewinn, *m.* win on the pools; pools premium.
Totozettel, *m.* pools coupon.
Tourenfahrt, *f.* reliability trial (*Motor.*).
Tragflächenprofil, *n.* airfoil.
transistorisieren, *v.a.* transistorize.
Transmissionskette, *f.* driving-chain.
Transmissionswelle, *f.* connecting-rod *or* shaft.
Transportband, *n.* conveyor (belt).
Transportkolonne, *f.* motor convoy (*Mil.*).
Trefferbild, *n.* (*target shooting*) group (*of hits*).
Tresorfach, *n.* safe-deposit (box).
Trichterwagen, *m.* hopper-truck.
Trickfilm, *m.* cartoon.
Trödler, *m.* secondhand *or* junk dealer.
Turbinenflugzeug, *n.* turbo-jet plane.
Turbinenstrahltriebwerk, *n.* turbo-jet engine.
turbulent, *adj.* turbulent, (*fig.*) hectic.
Twist, *m.* (-es, -e) darning-thread.

U

Überbett, *n.* quilt, coverlet.
Übergangsfarbe, *f.* half-tone, intermediate shade.
Übergangskleidung, *f.* between-seasons wear.
übergeordnet, *adj.* superior, higher.
Übernahmeangebot, *n.* take-over bid.
überparteilich, *adj.* non-party (*Pol.*).
Überraschungsmoment, *n.* element of surprise.
überrunden, *v.a.* (*insep.*) lap (*Sport*).
Überschall-Knall, *m.* sonic boom.
Überschicht, *f.* overtime *or* extra shift.
überschlafen, *v.a.* (*insep.*) sleep on (*an idea*).
überspielen, *v.a.* (*insep.*) out-manœuvre (*also Sport & fig.*); over-play, over-act (*Theat.*); dub (*film*).
überspitzen, *v.a.* (*insep.*) exaggerate, overdo.
Ulkbild, *n.* caricature.
Ultrahochfrequenz, *f.* ultra-high frequency.
umbuchen, *v.a.* (*sep.*) transfer to another account (*C.L.*).
Umbuchung, *f.* book-transfer (*C.L.*).
umdisponieren, 1. *v.a.* (*sep.*) rearrange, redispose. 2. *v.n.* (*sep.*) change one's plans, make new arrangements.
Umsatzziffer, *f.* turnover rate.
umspielen, *v.a.* (*sep.*) play back (*a recording*); (*insep.*) dribble round (*Footb.*).
umspulen, *v.a.* (*sep.*) rewind.
unaufgeschlossen, *adj.* reserved; narrow-minded, (*coll.*) blinkered.
Unbedenklichkeitsbescheinigung, *f.* clearance (certificate).
unbeglichen, *adj.* unpaid, outstanding (*debt*).
unbelastet, *adj.* unencumbered; (*of a p.*) carefree, light-hearted; with a clean record, not incriminated (*Pol.*), uncompromised (*Law*); with no load (*Elec.*); – *von,* free of, unencumbered by.
Unfallverhütungsvorschrift, *f.* safety precautions.
ungewollt, *adj.* unintentional, involuntary.
Uni, *f.* (*coll.*) varsity.
Unruhstifter, *m.* trouble-maker, disturber of the peace (*Law*), agitator (*Pol.*).
unterbesetzt, *adj.* understaffed, shorthanded.
Unterdruckkammer, *f.* decompression chamber.
Unterfunktion, *f.* subnormal functioning.
Untermenge, *f.* sub-set (*Math.*).
unterschwellig, *adj.* subliminal.
unterwandern, *v.a.* (*insep.*) infiltrate.
Unterwanderung, *f.* infiltration.
Unterwassergleitfarbe, *f.* anti-fouling paint.
unverausgabt, *adj.* unexpended (*C.L.*).
unverjährbar, *adj.* not subject to prescription, imprescriptible (*Law*); not subject to a period of limitation.
unvorstellbar, *adj.* unimaginable, incredible.
Urkoks, *m.* low-temperature coke.

V

Vaku-Blitz, *m.* flashlight, photo-flash (*Phot.*).
Valutanotierung, *f.* foreign-exchange quotation.
Varioptik, *f.* zoom lens.
Verbrauchergas, *n.* generator gas.
Verbrauchergenossenschaft, *f.* co-operative society.
Verbrauchsgüter, *pl.* commodities, consumer goods.
Verbrauchssatz, *m.* rate of consumption.
Verhandlungsweg, *m. auf dem –e,* by negotiation, (*coll.*) round the table.
Verkaufsbüro, *n.* distribution centre.
Verkaufsförderung, *f.* sales promotion.
Verkaufsleiter, *m.* sales manager.
Verkaufsschlager, *m.* popular line.
Verkaufsstelle, *f.* (retail) outlet, retail shop.
Verkehrserziehung, *f.* road-safety campaign.
Verkehrsspitze, *f.* rush-hour, peak-traffic period.
Verkehrssünder, *m.* traffic offender, (*pedestrian*) jay-walker.
Vermögensanlage, *f.* capital asset.
Vermögensaufstellung, *f.* financial statement.
Vermögensgegenstand, *m.* asset.
Vermögenszuwachssteuer, *f.* capital gains tax.
Versandhaus, *n.* mail-order firm.
Verschleif, *m.* disposal, sale (*of goods*) (*C.L.*); abrasion, wear (and tear) (*Tech.*).
Verständigungspolitik, *f.* policy of appeasement.
verstofflichen, *v.a.* materialize.
Vertreiber, *m.* distributor (*of goods*).
Verzichterklärung, *f.* waiver, disclaimer (*Law*).
Verzögerungstaktik, *f.* delaying action.
Vogelbeobachtung, *f.* bird watching.
Vogelschutzgebiet, *n.* bird sanctuary.
Vogeltränke, *f.* bird-bath.
Völkermord, *m.* genocide.
Vollbildfrequenz, *f.* picture frequency (*T.V.*).
vollschlank, *adj.* (*coll.*) not-so-slim.
Voralarm, *m.* preliminary *or* early warning.
Vorfertigung, *f.* prefabrication.
Vorkampf, *m.* semifinal (*Sport*), preliminary bout (*Box.*).
vorschalten, *v.a.* connect in series (*Elec.*).

Vorschaltwiderstand, *m.* series resistance (*Elec.*).
Vorschau, *f.* forecast, preview (*auf*, of); trailer (*Films, etc.*).
Vorstrafen(register), *n.* criminal record.
Vorwarnung, *f.* preliminary *or* early warning.
Vorwahl, *f.* preliminary *or* (*Amer.*) primary election; preselection (*Rad.*).
Vorwählnummer, *f.* (*phone*) dialling prefix.
Vorwählschalter, *m.* preselector gear-change (*Motor.*).

W

Wachstumsfähigkeit, *f.* viability.
Wahlbericht, *m.* election returns.
Wahlbeteiligung, *f.* percentage of votes cast, (*coll.*) turnout.
Wählerbetrieb, *m.* (*phone*) automatic dialling (system).
Wahlgang, *m.* ballot, poll.
Wahlstatistik, *f.* psephology.
Wahlstatistiker, *m.* psephologist.
Währungspolitik, *f.* monetary *or* currency policy.
währungspolitisch, *adj.* monetary, currency.
Warenausfall, *m.* loss of production (*C.L.*).
Wärmespeicher, *m.* storage-heater.
Wartungsmonteur, *m.* maintenance man.
Wäscheschleuder, *f.* spin-dryer.
Wasserbaukunst, *f.* hydraulic engineering.
Wechselabrechnung, *f.* discount liquidation.
Wechselbürgschaft, *f.* collateral acceptance on a bill.
Wechsellager, *n.* double-thrust bearing (*Mech.*).
wehrfreudig, *adj.* military-minded.
weltabgewandt, *adj.* detached from the world, remote from reality.
Weltfirma, *f.* firm of international importance.
Weltgeltung, *f.* international reputation *or* standing.
Weltgeschehen, *n.* world affairs.
Weltraumfahrer, *m.* cosmonaut, astronaut, (*coll.*) spaceman.
Weltraumflug, *m.* space travel.
Weltraumzeitalter, *n.* space-age.
Weltrekordler, Weltrekordmann, *m.* world-record holder.
Werbeagent, *m.* canvasser, sales-promotion agent.
Werbeartikel, *m.* (free) advertising offer.
Werbeberater, *m.* advertising *or* publicity agent.
Werbeblatt, *n.* advertising leaflet.
Werbebüro, *n.* advertising agency; recruiting office (*Mil.*).
Werbefeldzug, *m.* publicity *or* advertising campaign *or* (*coll.*) drive.
Werbefläche, *f.* advertising space.
Werbegraphik, *f.* commercial art.
Werbemuster, *n.* trial *or* free sample.
Werbesendung, *f.* commercial (radio *or* T.V. programme).
Werknummer, *f.* production (serial) number.
Werksnorm, *f.* standard specification.
Werkstückzeichnung, *f.* component drawing.
Werkswohnung, *f.* company-owned house.
Werkszeichnung, *f.* working drawing.
wertmäßig, *adj.*, *adv.* ad valorem (*C.L.*).
Wettkurs, *m.* (betting) odds.
Wettspringen, *n.* ski-jumping competition.
Wiederbekehrung, *f.* reconversion (*Rel.*).
Wiedereingliederung, *f.* reintegration; (*of workers*) resettlement.
wiedereinlösen, *v.a.* redeem.
Wiedereinlösung, *f.* redemption.
Wiedereinreiseerlaubnis, *f.* re-entry permit.
Wiedergabegüte, *f.* fidelity, quality of reproduction (*Rad.*).
Wiedergaberöhre, *f.* (picture-)tube (*T.V.*).
Wiegebrett, *n.* chopping-board.
Wiegebrücke, *f.* weigh-bridge.
Wiegemesser, *n.* chopping-knife.
Wimperntusche, *f.* mascara.
Wirbelbildung, *f.* turbulence (*Av., etc.*).
Wirtschaftsberater, *m.* business consultant.
Wirtschaftsführer, *m.* captain of industry, (*coll.*) business tycoon.
Wirtschaftslenkung, *f.* government control (of trade and industry).
Wirtschaftszweig, *m.* sector of the economy.
wischfest, *adj.* spongeable.
Wochenbeihilfe, *f.* maternity benefit.
Wohngebäude, *n.* residential premises, dwelling-house, block of flats, apartment house.
Wohnkultur, *f.* style of living.
Wohnpartei, *f.* tenant(s).
Wohnsiedlung, *f.* housing estate.
Wolkenhöhe, *f.* (cloud) ceiling (*Av.*).
Wolkenkunde, *f.* nephology.
wummern, *v.n.* (*coll.*) boom.
Wunschkonzert, *n.* (musical) request programme.
Wurfgerät, *n.* projector, (rocket) launcher (*Mil.*).
wuseln, *v.n.* (*coll.*) swarm, crawl, be swarming *or* crawling (*von*, with).

Z

Zackenschere, *f.* pinking scissors.
zaddrig, *adj.* sinewy, stringy (*as meat*).
Zahlgrenze, *f.* fare-stage.
Zahlkarte, *f.* census form; score *or* scoring card (*Sport*); money-order form.
Zahlungserleichterungen, *pl.* credit facilities, deferred terms.
Zahlungsplan, *m.* instalment plan, deferred payment; (*of debt*) terms of redemption.
Zaster, *m.* (*sl.*) lolly, brass, dough (*money*).
Zehnfingersystem, *n.* touch-typing.
Zeichenfilm, *m.* animated cartoon.
Zeichensystem, *n.* code.
zeitbedingt, *adj.* under the current circumstances.
Zeitwert, *m.* current value (*C.L.*).
Zellwolle, *f.* rayon.
Zentimeterwelle, *f.* ultra-high frequency (wave) (*Rad.*).
zentrisch, *adj.* (con)centric.
zerbeulen, *v.a.* dent, crumple.
zerstörend, *adj.* destructive, devastating.
Zielflug, *m.* homing (flight) (*Av.*).
Zielkamera, *f.* photo-finish camera (*Sport*).
Zielpeilung, *f.* homing (*Av.*).
Zielphotographie, *f.* photo-finish (*Sport*).
Zinsmehraufwand, *m.* net interest paid.
Zinsmehrertrag, *m.* net interest earned.
Zonengrenze, *f.* zone boundary (*usu. the frontier between Federal Germany and the Democratic Republic*).
Zufallsauswahl, *f.* random sample.
Zufallsmoment, *n.* chance factor.
Zukunftsroman(e), *m.*(*pl.*) science fiction.
Zulieferer, *m.* supplier, purveyor; sub-contractor.
Zulieferungsindustrie, *f.* ancillary *or* supply industry.
Zulieferungsteile, *pl.* manufactured components.
zurückblenden, *v.n.* (*film*) flash back.
zurückerstatten, *v.a.* hand back, return (*look, etc.*), restore, refund (*money*).
zurückschalten, *v.n.* change down (*Motor.*).
zurücksehnen, *v.r.* long to be back *or* to return.
zurückspulen, *v.a.* rewind.
zusammengeben, *ir. v.a.* join in marriage *or* wedlock.
Zusammenschau, *f.* synoptic presentation.
zusammenschrecken, *v.n.* (give a) start (*bei*, at).
Zwangsbewirtschaftung, *f.* economic control.
Zwangshandlung, *f.* compulsive act(ion).
Zwangsherrschaft, *f.* despotism, absolute rule.
Zweckbestimmung, *f.* (*of money*) appropriation (*for a purpose*), application (*to an end*).
zweckentfremdet, *adj.* used for purposes other than originally intended.
zweckgebunden, *adj.* appropriated, earmarked.

Zweckmöbel, *pl.* functional furniture.
Zwischenentscheidung, *f.* interlocutory decree (*Law*).
Zwischenraumtaste, *f.* space-bar (*typewriter*).
Zwischenverkauf, *m.* – *vorbehalten,* subject to prior sale (*C.L.*).
zytogen, *adj.* cytogenous.
Zytologie, *f.* cytolysis.

ENGLISH-GERMAN DICTIONARY

KEY TO PRONUNCIATION

WHERE examples are given in both languages, it should not be assumed that the pronunciations are identical. In many cases the similarity is no more than approximate. In the case of the letters *l* and *r* no attempt is made to distinguish between the characteristic English and German treatments of the sounds.

Vowels—Vokale

	ENGLISH	GERMAN
[æ]	man	hängen (*South Germ.*)
[ɑ]	—	Antwort, flach
[ɑ:]	half, father, harbour	Ader, Haar, Jahr
[ɑ̃]	—	Chance (*French*, en)
[ɛ]	very, head	Ente, besser
[ɛ:]	fairy	Fähre, Käse
[ɛ̃]	—	Bassin (*French*, vin)
[e:]	—	Ehre, Teer, Ekel
[ə]	perhaps, idea, mother, honour, horror	Ehre, beantworten
[ə:]	sir, her, fur, word, earn, adjourn	—

	ENGLISH	GERMAN
[ɪ]	bit, hymn	ich, nisten
[ɪ:]	be, beat, see, field	ihre, Liebe
[ɔ]	not, want	Rock
[ɔ:]	for, ward	—
[ɔ̃]	—	Bonbon (*French*, bon)
[o]	molest, obey	—
[o:]	—	Hose, Boot, Sohn
[ʌ]	but, son, flood	—
[ʊ]	foot, pull, could	Futter, Pult
[ʊ:]	do, boot, soup	Mut, Kuh
[y]	—	Hütte, füllen
[y:]	—	Hüte, fühlen
[ø]	—	Hölle
[ø:]	—	Höhle
[œ̃]	—	Parfum (*French*, brun)

Diphthongs Diphthonge

	ENGLISH	GERMAN
[ɑɪ]	my, wife, high	mein, Mai
[ɑɪə]	fire, higher	Feier, Reihe
[ɑj]	—	Email (*French*)
[ɑʊ]	house, how	Haus
[ɑʊə]	hour	Bauer
[ɛə]	bare, bear, hair, their	—
[eɪ]	same, day, they, remain	—
[ɪə]	here, hear, pierce, interior	—

	ENGLISH	GERMAN
[ɔɪ]	boy, noise	neu, Bäume
[ɔɪə]	royal	Feuer
[oʊ]	go, slow	—
[oʊə]	goer, slower	—
[ʊə]	sure, poor, doer	—
[ʊɪ]	—	pfui
[ju:]	few, view, duty deuce, suit, beauty, Tuesday	—

Consonants—Konsonanten

The sounds represented by the symbols [b], [d], [f] [g], [h], [k], [m], [n] [p], [t] are more or less identical in English and German.

	ENGLISH	GERMAN
[ç]	—	ich, nicht
[χ]	(*Scots*) loch	Loch
[dʒ]	just, German, ridge	—
[kw]	quite	—
[ŋ]	hanging, thing	Ring
[ŋk]	sink	sinken
[ŋg]	finger	jonglieren
[s]	see, scent, receive	das, daß, Wasser
[ʃ]	shoe, bush, sugar, session, special, lotion	Schuh, Busch
[ts]	hats	trotz, Zaun, Nation

	ENGLISH	GERMAN
[tʃ]	chin, patch, mixture	Patsche
[θ]	thick, path	—
[ð]	that, father, paths	—
[v]	van, vine, of, gravy	wann, Wein, ewig, Vase
[w]	well, doughy, persuade	—
[j]	yes, battalion	ja
[z]	his, zone, faces	Sohn, Sonne, reisen, Sense
[ʒ]	measure, garage	Journal, Garage

absolut–e ['æbsəl(j)u:t], *adj.* unumschränkt, unbeschränkt, unabhängig, eigenmächtig, absolut; vollkommen, vollständig, vollendet; wasserfrei, rein (*Chem.*); unbedingt, wirklich, tatsächlich; an und für sich bestehend (*Phil.*); *–e fool*, völliger Narr; *–e space*, absoluter Raum; *–e vacuum*, luftleerer Raum. **–ely**, *adv.* unumschränkt; wirklich, tatsächlich, unbedingt; (*coll.*) durchaus, ganz, völlig. **–eness**, *s.* das Absolute. **–ion** [–'l(j)u:ʃən], *s.* der Sündenerlaß, die Absolution (*Theol.*). **–ism**, *s.* der Absolutismus, unbeschränkte Regierung.

absolve [əb'zɔlv], *v.a.* lossprechen, freisprechen (*from*, von), (einem) Absolution erteilen (*Theol.*).

absorb [əb'sɔ:b], *v.a.* ansaugen, einsaugen, aufsaugen, anziehen, in sich ziehen, verschlingen, einverleiben; (*fig.*) beschäftigen, in Anspruch nehmen, fesseln; federn (*shocks*); annehmen, aufnehmen, absorbieren (*Chem.*); *be –ed*, angehen, aufziehen (*of colours, etc.*); (*fig.*) in Anspruch genommen, gefesselt (*in*, von); *–ed in thought*, in Gedanken vertieft; *–ing power*, das Aufsaugevermögen. **–ency**, *s.* die Saugfähigkeit. **–ent**, 1. *adj.* aufsaugend, einsaugend, aufnahmefähig, absorbierend, saugfähig; *–ent paper*, das Saugpapier. 2. *s.* das Einsaugmittel. Absorptionsmittel (*Chem.*). **–ing**, *adj.* fesselnd, höchst interessant.

absorption [əb'sɔ:pʃən], *s.* das Einsaugen; die Einsaugung, Aufsaugung, Ansaugung, Aufnahme, Absorption (*Chem.*); (*fig.*) das Vertieftsein, die Versunkenheit.

abstain [əb'steɪn], *v.n.* sich enthalten (*from* (*Gen.*)), abstinent leben. **–er**, *s.* der Abstinenzler, Temperenzler.

abstemious [æb'stɪ:mɪəs], *adj.* enthaltsam, mäßig. **–ness**, *s.* die Enthaltsamkeit, Mäßigkeit.

abstention [æb'stɛnʃən], *s.* die Enthaltung (*from*, von).

abstergent [əb'stə:dʒənt], **abstersive**, 1. *adj.* reinigend (*Bot.*); abführend (*Med.*). 2. *s.* das Reinigungsmittel, Abführmittel.

abstinen–ce ['æbstɪnəns], *s.* die Enthaltsamkeit, Enthaltung; *day of –ce*, der Fasttag. **–t**, *adj.* enthaltsam, mäßig.

abstract 1. [æb'strækt], *v.a.* (= *withdraw*) abziehen, ablenken; (= *separate*) absondern, ausziehen, abstrahieren; für sich *or* abgesondert betrachten; destillieren (*Chem.*); (*coll.*) entwenden, stehlen. 2. ['æbstrækt], *adj.* abgezogen; abstrakt, theoretisch, rein begrifflich (*Log.*); dunkel, tiefsinnig, schwer verständlich; *– noun*, das Begriffswort, Abstraktum (*Gram.*); *– number*, unbekannte Zahl. 3. ['æbstrækt], *s.* das Abstrakte; Abstraktum (*Gram.*); der Abriß, Auszug; *in the –*, an und für sich, rein begrifflich, theoretisch betrachtet. **–ed** [æb'stræktɪd], *adj.* abgesondert, abgezogen; (*fig.*) geistesabwesend, unaufmerksam, zerstreut. **–edly**, *adv.* getrennt, abgesehen (*from*, von); zerstreut. **–edness**, *s.* die Zerstreutheit. **–ion**, *s.* die Begriffsbildung, Verallgemeinerung; Abziehung, Abstraktion; abstrakter Begriff, das bloß Gedachte; die Entwendung, Wegnahme; (*fig.*) Geistesabwesenheit, Zerstreutheit; Absonderung (*Chem.*) **–ly**, *adv.* abstrakt, an sich. **–ness**, *s.* das Abstrakte, die Abstraktheit, Unwirklichkeit.

abstruse [æb'strʊ:s], *adj.* dunkel, schwerverständlich, unklar, verworren, verborgen, tief, tiefsinnig. **–ness**, *s.* die Dunkelheit, Unklarheit, Unverständlichkeit, Schwerverständlichkeit.

absurd [əb'sə:d], *adj.* absurd, sinnwidrig; albern, lächerlich, abgeschmackt; *that's –!* das ist Unsinn! **–ity**, *s.* die Sinnwidrigkeit, Absurdität; Albernheit, Abgeschmacktheit.

abund–ance [ə'bʌndəns], *s.* die Fülle, Menge, der Überfluß, die Ausgiebigkeit (*of*, an); *in –ance*, vollauf; *live in –ance*, im Überfluß leben. **–ant**, *adj.* reich (*in* or *with*, an (*Dat.*)); reichlich (versehen mit), übergenug, genugsam. **–antly**, *adv.* vollauf; *this will –antly show*, dies wird völlig *or* zur Genüge beweisen.

abus–e 1. [ə'bjʊ:z], *v.a.* mißbrauchen (*one's position, etc.*); beschimpfen, schmähen, heruntermachen; mißhandeln, schänden; täuschen (*a p.'s hopes, confidence, etc.*); verraten (*a confidence*). 2. [ə'bjʊ:s], *s.* der Mißbrauch, Übergriff, Mißstand; die Mißhandlung, Mißachtung, Beschimpfung; Schändung; Schimpfworte, Beleidigungen; *crying –*, grober Mißbrauch. **–ive** [–sɪv], *adj.* schimpfend, schmähend; *–ive language*, Schimpfworte. **–iveness**, *s.* das Beleidigende, grobe Beleidigung.

abut [ə'bʌt], *v.n.* angrenzen, anstoßen, auslaufen (*upon*, an *or* auf (*Acc.*)). **–ment**, *s.* das Angrenzen (*upon*, an); der Strebepfeiler, Stützpfeiler (*Arch.*); das Widerlager (*of a bridge*); *–ment beam*, der Stoßbalken. **–ter**, *s.* der Anlieger, angrenzender Besitzer (*of land, etc.*).

abys–m [ə'bɪzm], *s.* (*poet.*) = **abyss**. **–mal** [–məl], *adj.* abgrundtief, bodenlos, unergründlich. **–s** [ə'bɪs], *s.* der Abgrund, Schlund.

acacia [ə'keɪʃə], *s.* die (falsche) Akazie.

academ–ic(al) [ækə'dɛmɪk(l)], *adj.* akademisch, gelehrt, wissenschaftlich; theoretisch, pedantisch, unpraktisch; *–ic dress* or *robe(s)*, akademische Tracht; *a purely –ic discussion*, eine nutzlose Auseinandersetzung *or* theoretische Erörterung. **–ically**, *adv.* (*usually*) theoretisch, *etc.* **–ician** [əkædə'mɪʃən], *s.* das Mitglied einer Akademie. **–y** [ə'kædəmɪ], *s.* die Akademie; Hochschule; literarische *or* gelehrte Gesellschaft.

acanthus [ə'kænθəs], *s.* die Bärenklau (*Bot.*); das Laubwerk, der Akanthus (*Arch.*).

acatalectic [ə'kætə'lɛktɪk], *adj.* vollzählig, akatalektisch (*Metr.*).

acatalepsy [ə'kætəlɛpsɪ], *s.* die Unbegreiflichkeit (*Phil.*).

accede [æk'sɪ:d], *v.n.* einwilligen (*to*, in), nachkommen, beistimmen (*to* (*Dat.*)); besteigen (*a throne*); *– to an office*, ein Amt antreten; *– to a treaty*, einem Vertrage beitreten.

accelerat–e [æk'sɛləreɪt], *v.a.* beschleunigen. **–ion** [–'reɪʃən], *s.* die Beschleunigung; *–ion due to gravity*, die Erdbeschleunigung. **–or**, *s.* der (Fuß)-Gashebel, Beschleuniger (*Motor.*); Treibmuskel (*Anat.*).

accent 1. [æk'sɛnt], *v.a. see* **–uate**. 2. ['æksənt], *s.* der Ton, die Betonung; der Tonfall, fremde Aussprache, der Akzent; das Tonzeichen (*Gram.*); *acute –*, der Hochton; *grave –*, der Tiefton. **–uate** [–'sɛntjʊeɪt], *v.a.* betonen, akzentuieren; (*fig.*) hervorheben. **–uation** [–jʊ'eɪʃən], *s.* die Betonung.

accept [ək'sɛpt], *v.a.* annehmen, entgegennehmen; gelten lassen; hinnehmen, auf sich nehmen; akzeptieren (*C.L.*); (*B.*) gnädiglich ansehen; *– defeat*, (eine) Niederlage hinnehmen; *– the terms*, die Bedingungen annehmen, auf die Bedingungen eingehen; *– £30*, nehme £30 (*C.L.*). **–ability** [–ə'bɪlɪtɪ], *s.* die Annehmlichkeit, Annehmbarkeit. **–able** [–'sɛptəbl], *adj.*, **–ably**, *adv.* annehmbar (*to*, für); angenehm, willkommen. **–ableness**, *s. see* **–ability**. **–ance**, *s.* die Annahme; günstige Aufnahme, der Empfang (*with*, bei); die Billigung, Genehmigung; das Akzept (*of a bill*); *qualified –ance*, bedingtes Akzept; *–ance under protest*, das Interventionsakzept; *–ance of a bid*, der Zuschlag; *find –ance*, angenommen werden, Annahme *or* Geltung finden; *my proposals did not meet with –ance from him*, er ging nicht auf meine Vorschläge ein. **–ation** [–'teɪʃən], *s.* anerkannte Bedeutung (*of a word, etc.*), günstige Aufnahme. **–ed**, *adj.* angenommen, gebilligt; *–ed before God*, Gott angenehm. **–er**, *s.* der Annehmer. **–or**, *s.* der Akzeptant; *–or circuit*, durchlässiger Kreis (*Rad.*).

access ['æksɛs], *s.* der Zugang, Zutritt; die Zugänglichkeit; Audienz (*to*, bei); der Anfall, Eintritt (*Med.*); *easy of –*, zugänglich; *difficult of –*, schwer zugänglich; *– hatch* (*of a tank, etc.*), die Einsteigluke. **–ary** [æk'sɛsərɪ], 1. *s.* der Mitschuldige, Helfershelfer (*to*, an); Nebenumstand, Begleitumstand; *–ary after the fact*, der Hehler; *–ary before the fact*, der Anstifter. 2. *pred. adj.* mitschuldig, teilhabend (*to*, an). **–ibility** [–ɪ'bɪlɪtɪ], *s.* die Zugänglichkeit (*to*, für). **–ible**, *adj.* zugänglich (*to*, für); erreichbar, ersteigbar. **–ion** [æk'sɛʃən], *s.* der Zuwachs, die Zunahme, Vermehrung, Vergrößerung, das Hinzukommen (*of property, etc.*); die Annäherung; der Beitritt, Eintritt (*to*, in), Antritt (*to* (*Dat.*)); *–ion to the throne*, die Thronbesteigung; *–ion to knowledge*, die Bereicherung *or* der Gewinn für das Wissen. **–ions**, *pl.* Neuanschaffungen, Neuerwerbungen. **-ory,** 1. *adj.* hinzugefügt, hinzukommend, zusätzlich, akzessorisch; Extra–, Ersatz–; beiläufig, nebensächlich, untergeordnet; Neben–, Bei–, Begleit–; *-ory parts,* das Beiwerk; *-ory phenomenon,* die Begleiterscheinung; *be -ory to,* beitragen zu. 2. *s.* der Nebenumstand, die Begleiterscheinung; der *or* die Mitschuldige(r) (*Law*); (*pl.*) die Staffage, das Beiwerk (*Paint.*); Zubehör, die Zubehörteile, Zubehörstücke.

accidence ['æksɪdəns], *s.* die Formenlehre, Flexionslehre (*Gram.*).

accident ['æksɪdənt], *s.* der Unfall; Unglücksfall; Zufall, die Zufallserscheinung, zufällige Eigenschaft, die Nebensache, das Unwesentliche, Zufällige; die Akzidenz (*Log., etc.*); *by –,* zufällig(erweise), von ungefähr; *it was by mere – that . . .,* es war der reine Zufall daß . . .; *he met with an –,* ihm stieß ein Unfall zu; *in an –,* bei einem Unfall; *the – of life,* die Zufälligkeiten des Lebens. **-al** [–'dɛntl], 1. *adj.* zufällig; unwesentlich, nebensächlich; *-al death,* der Tod durch Unfall; *-al error,* der Zufälligkeitsfehler; *-al sharp,* das Erhöhungszeichen (*Mus.*). 2. *s.* das Zufällige; Unwesentliche, die Nebensache; das Versetzungszeichen (*Mus.*); die Unebenheit, Ungleichmäßigkeit (*Geog. & Astr.*). **-ally,** *adv.* zufällig, durch Zufall, unbeabsichtigt.

acclaim [ək'leɪm], 1. *s.* (*poet.*) *see* **acclamation.** 2. *v.n.* zujubeln, zujauchzen (*Dat.*). 3. *v.a.* Beifall zurufen; *– a p. king,* einen als König begrüßen.

acclamat-ion [æklə'meɪʃən], *s.* jauchzender Beifall; der Zuruf; *elected by -ion,* durch Zuruf gewählt; *with -ion,* unter Beifall. **-ory** [ək'læmətərɪ], *adj.* zurufend, zujauchzend.

acclimat-ization [əklaɪmətaɪ'zeɪʃən], *s.* die Akklimatisierung, Eingewöhnung, Einbürgerung. **-ize** [ə'klaɪmətaɪz], *v.a. & n.* akklimatisieren, eingewöhnen, einbürgern; *become -ized,* sich akklimatisieren *or* gewöhnen (*to,* an).

acclivity [ə'klɪvɪtɪ], *s.* (steile) Anhöhe, die Böschung.

accolade ['ækoleɪd], *s.* der Ritterschlag; (geschweifte) Klammer (*Mus.*).

accommodat-e [ə'kɔmədeɪt], *v.a.* (= *adapt*) anpassen (*to* (*Dat.*)); schlichten, beilegen (*a quarrel*); beherbergen, unterbringen, einquartieren; *-e a p. with s.th.,* einen mit etwas versehen *or* versorgen; einem mit etwas aushelfen *or* eine Gefälligkeit erweisen; *-e o.s. to circumstances,* sich in die Umstände fügen *or* schicken, sich den Verhältnissen anpassen; *be well -ed,* bequem wohnen, gut untergebracht sein. **-ing,** *pr.p. & adj.* gefällig, entgegenkommend. **-ion** [–'deɪʃən], *s.* die Anpassung (*to,* an); Beilegung, Schlichtung (*of a dispute*); Bequemlichkeit, Räumlichkeit, der Platz; das Darlehn, die Aushilfe (*with money*); Unterkunft, Unterbringung, Versorgung; Gefälligkeit; *have good -ion,* gut untergebracht sein, behaglich wohnen; bequem eingerichtet sein (*as a hotel*); *-ion for cyclists,* Unterkunft für Radfahrer; *find -ion,* unterkommen; *seating -ion,* die Sitzgelegenheit. **-ion-bill,** *s.* der Reitwechsel, das Gefälligkeitsakzept (*C.L.*). **-ion-ladder,** die Fallreeptreppe (*Naut.*).

accompani-ment [ə'kʌmpənɪmənt], *s.* die Begleitung (*Mus. etc.*); die Begleiterscheinung. **-st,** *s.* der (die) Begleiter(in) (*Mus.*).

accompany [ə'kʌmpənɪ], *v.a. & n.* begleiten (*also Mus.*); geleiten (*Acc.*), Gesellschaft leisten (*Dat.*). **-ing,** *adj.* begleitend, mitgehend.

accomplice [ə'kɔmplɪs], *s.* der *or* die Mitschuldige, der Helfershelfer (*in,* an), Mittäter.

accomplish [ə'kɔmplɪʃ], *v.a.* vollenden, durchführen, ausführen, vollführen, zustandebringen; erlangen, erreichen, erfüllen. **-ed,** *adj.* vorzüglich, vollendet, feingebildet. **-ment,** *s.* die Ausführung, Durchführung, Erfüllung; Vollendung, Vollkommenheit; (*pl.*) vielseitige Ausbildung, Talente, Fertigkeiten, Kenntnisse; *she has many -ments,* sie ist vielseitig gebildet.

accord [ə'kɔ:d], 1. *s.* die Übereinstimmung; Eintracht, Einigkeit, der Einklang; Akkord (*Mus.*); Vergleich (*Law*); *with one –,* einstimmig, einmütig; *of one's own –,* aus eigenem Antriebe, freiwillig; *of its own –,* von selbst; *in – with,* in Einklang mit. 2. *v.a.* (einem etwas) gewähren, bewilligen, zuteil werden lassen. 3. *v.n.* übereinstimmen (*with,* mit). **-ance,** *s.* die Übereinstimmung; *be in -ance with,* übereinstimmen mit; *in -ance with,* gemäß. **-ant,** *adj.* im Einklang, übereinstimmend (*with,* mit); gemäß, entsprechend (*with* (*Dat.*)). **-ing,** 1. *conj.*; *-ing as,* je nachdem wie, insofern wie. 2. *prep.*; *-ing to,* gemäß, zufolge, nach, laut; *-ing to circumstances,* nach Lage der Dinge, den Umständen gemäß; *cut one's coat -ing to one's cloth,* sich nach der Decke strecken; *-ing to Cocker,* nach Adam Riese; *-ing to law,* gesetzmäßig, dem Rechte nach; *-ing to report,* laut Meldung; *-ing to the latest intelligence,* den letzten Nachrichten zufolge. **-ingly,** *adv.* danach, demnach, demgemäß, folglich, also, somit.

accordion [ə'kɔ:dɪən], *s.* die Ziehharmonika.

accost [ə'kɔst], 1. *v.a.* anreden, ansprechen. 2. *s.* der Gruß, die Anrede.

accouche-ur [æku:'ʃə:], *s.* der Geburtshelfer. **-use,** *s.* die Hebamme. **-ment,** *s.* die Entbindung.

account [ə'kaʊnt], **1.** *s.* die Berechnung, der Rechnungsauszug; das Konto, die Rechnung, Note; der Bericht, die Erzählung, Darstellung; Liste, das Verzeichnis, die Rechenschaft; Verantwortung, der Grund, die Ursache; der Vorteil, Gewinn, Nutzen; die Wichtigkeit, Bedeutung, Geltung, das Ansehen, der Wert, die Schätzung, Berücksichtigung; (*C.L.*) der Liquidationstermin (*stock exchange*); *bank –,* das Bankkonto; *cash –,* das Kassenkonto; *current –, – current,* laufende Rechnung, das Kontokorrent; *open –,* offenes Konto, laufende Rechnung; *– sales,* Verkauf auf Rechnung. 1. (*after preps.*) *by all -s,* wie man hört; (*C.L.*) *for – and risk,* für Rechnung und Gefahr; *from the latest -s,* nach den neuesten Berichten; (*C.L.*) *in – with,* in Rechnung mit; *of no –,* unbedeutend, ohne Bedeutung; (*C.L.*) *on –,* a conto *or* Konto, als Akontozahlung, auf Abschlag; *payment on –,* die Abschlagszahlung; *on his –,* um seinetwillen *or* seinetwegen; *on – of,* wegen; *on another –,* zudem; *on one's own –,* aus eigener Kraft, aus sich; *each on his own –,* jeder für sich; *on no –,* auf keinen Fall; *on that –,* darum, deswegen; (*C.L.*) *to – rendered,* laut eingeschickter Sendung. 2. (*after verbs*) *balance an –,* ein Konto *or* eine Rechnung saldieren; *call to –,* zur Rechenschaft ziehen; *carry to a new –,* auf neue Rechnung übertragen; *debit s.th. to a p.'s –,* einen belasten mit etwas; *give an – of,* Rechenschaft ablegen von (*or* über), Bericht erstatten über; *he gave a good – of himself,* er bewährte sich, er tat sich hervor; *have an – with a p.,* mit einem in Rechnung stehen; *keep -s,* Bücher führen, buchhalten; *keep an – of,* Rechnung führen über (*Acc.*); *leave out of –,* außer Betracht lassen; *make out a p.'s –,* einem die Rechnung ausstellen; *open an –,* ein Konto eröffnen; *overdraw one's –,* sein Konto überziehen; *pay on –,* auf Abschlag bezahlen; *place s.th. to a p.'s –,* einem etwas in Rechnung stellen, einem etwas gutschreiben; *render an –,* eine Rechnung einsenden; *settle an –,* eine Rechnung bezahlen *or* begleichen; *settle -s with,* (*fig.*) abrechnen mit; *take a th. into –* or *take – of a th.,* eine Sache berücksichtigen *or* beachten, in Betracht *or* Rechnung ziehen *or* in Anschlag bringen, einer Sache Rechnung tragen; *take no – of,* nicht beachten; *turn to –,* sich (*Dat.*) zunutze machen, (gut) ausnützen. **2.** *v.n.* Rechnung ablegen; Rechenschaft ablegen (*for,* über), einstehen für, verantwortlich sein für; genügenden Grund angeben für, erklären; (*coll.*) *– for,* erledigen (*sport*); *that -s for it,* das erklärt die Sache; *there is no -ing for taste,* über den Geschmack läßt sich nicht streiten. **3.** *v.a.* betrachten *or* ansehen als, halten für; *– o.s. lucky,* sich glücklich schätzen. **-ability** [–ə'bɪlɪtɪ], *s.* die Verantwortlichkeit (*to a p.,* einem gegenüber; *for a th.,* für etwas). **-able,** *adj.* verantwortlich (*to a p. for a th.,* einem für etwas), erklärlich. **-ancy,** *s.* die Buchführung, das Rechnungswesen. **-ant,** *s.* der Rechnungsführer, Wirtschaftsprüfer, Bücherrevisor, Buchhalter; *chartered -ant,* geprüfter Bücherrevisor. **-ant-general,** *s.* der Hauptrechnungsführer. **-ant officer,** der Marinezahlmeister

(*Naut.*). **--book,** *s.* das Rechnungsbuch, Kontobuch. **-ing,** *s.* die Abrechnung, Berechnung; Buchführung.
accoutre [ə'ku:tə], *v.a.* ausrüsten, ausstatten, ausstaffieren. **-ment,** *s.* die Ausstaffierung (*usually pl.*), der Anzug, Anputz; die Ausrüstung (*Mil.*).
accredit [ə'krɛdɪt], *v.a.* beglaubigen, akkreditieren; bevollmächtigen; – *a p. with a th.*, einem etwas zuschreiben.
accretion[ə'krɪ:ʃən], *s.* das Wachstum; der Zuwachs, die Zunahme, Hinzufügung; das Zusammenwachsen; der Zuwachs durch Akkreszenz (*Law*).
accrue [ə'krʊ:], *v.n.* zukommen, zufallen, zufließen, zulaufen (*to* (*Dat.*)); entstehen, erwachsen (*from*, aus).
accumulat-e [ə'kju:mjʊleɪt], 1. *v.a.* aufhäufen, anhäufen, anlagern, aufspeichern, ansammeln. 2. *v.n.* sich anhäufen, sich ansammeln, zunehmen, anreichern. **-ion** [–'leɪʃən], *s.* die (An)Häufung, Anlagerung, Anreicherung, Ansammlung; der Haufe(n). **-ive** [–lətɪv], *adj.* sich häufend, wachsend, zusammenhäufend. **-or,** *s.* der Ansammler, Anhäufer; Akkumulator, (*coll.*) Akku (*Elec.*); Sammler (*Tech.*).
accuracy ['ækjʊrəsɪ], *s.* die Genauigkeit, Sorgfalt; Richtigkeit, Pünktlichkeit (*in time*); (*of aim*) Zielsicherheit, Treffsicherheit.
accurate ['ækjʊrət], *adj.* genau, sorgfältig, pünktlich; fehlerfrei, richtig, getreu.
accurs-ed [ə'kə:sɪd], **-t** [–'kə:st], *adj.* verflucht, verdammt, verwünscht, (*coll.*) verflixt; fluchwürdig, abscheulich.
accusation [ækjʊ'zeɪʃən], *s.* die Anklage, Anschuldigung, Beschuldigung; *bring an – against a p.* einen anklagen.
accusative [ə'kju:zətɪv], *s.* der Akkusativ, Wenfall (*Gram.*).
accusatory [ə'kjʊ:zətərɪ], *adj.* anklagend.
accuse [ə'kjʊ:z], *v.a.* anklagen, anschuldigen (*of*, wegen); beschuldigen (*of a th.* (*Gen.*); *of doing*, getan zu haben). **-d,** *s.* der (die) Angeklagte. **-r,** *s.* der Ankläger.
accustom [ə'kʌstəm], *v.a.* gewöhnen (*to*, an); – *o.s. to a th.*, sich an eine S. gewöhnen. **-ed,** 1. *pred. adj.* gewohnt (*to doing*, zu tun); *get -ed to*, sich gewöhnen an. 2. *attr. adj.* gewohnt, gewöhnlich; *be -ed to do*, pflegen zu tun.
ace [eɪs], *s.* das As; die Eins; der Spitzenflieger, (*sl.*) die Fliegerkanone (*Av.*); *be within an – of* (*falling, being killed, etc.*), um ein Haar, um eine Haaresbreite *or* beinahe (fallen, getötet werden, *etc.*).
acephalous [ə'sɛfələs], *adj.* kopflos, ohne Kopf.
acerb-ate ['æsəbeɪt], *v.a.* bitter machen; (*fig.*) verbittern. **-ity** [ə'sə:bɪtɪ], *s.* die Herbheit; (*fig.*) Härte, Strenge, Rauheit.
acet-ate ['æsɪteɪt], *s.* das Azetat, die Essigsäureverbindung, essigsaures Salz; *aluminium -ate*, essigsaure Tonerde. **-ic** [ə'sɪ:tɪk, ə'sɛtɪk], *adj.* essigsauer; *-ic acid*, die Essigsäure. **-ify** [ə'sɛtɪfaɪ], *v.a. & n.* sauer machen *or* werden, Essig bilden, in Essig verwandeln. **-one** ['æsɪtoʊn], *s.* das Azeton, der Essiggeist. **-ose, -ous** ['æsɪtəs], *adj.* essigsauer. *-ous fermentation*, die Essiggärung. **-ylene** [ə'sɛtɪlɪ:n], *s.* das Azetylen; *-ylene lamp*, die Karbidlampe.
ache [eɪk], 1. *s.* der Schmerz, das Weh. 2. *v.n.* schmerzen, wehe tun; *my head -s*, ich habe Kopfweh *or* Kopfschmerzen; *my heart -s for her*, ich sehne mich schmerzlich *or* ich verlange schmerzlich nach ihr.
achiev-able, *adj.* erreichbar, ausführbar. **-e** [ə'tʃɪ:v], *v.a.* ausführen, zustandebringen, vollenden, vollbringen, leisten; gewinnen, erlangen, erreichen (*a goal, etc.*). **-ement,** *s.* die Ausführung, Vollendung; das vollendete Werk; die Leistung, Errungenschaft; der Erfolg, die Heldentat; das Wappenschild (*Her.*).
aching ['eɪkɪŋ], *adj.* schmerzhaft, schmerzlich.
achromatic [ækro'mætɪk], *adj.* achromatisch, farblos (*Opt.*).
acicular [ə'sɪkjʊlə], *adj.* nadelförmig (*Bot.*)
acid ['æsɪd], 1. *adj.* sauer, herb, scharf; (*fig.*) bitter; – *drops*, saure Bonbons. 2. *s.* die Säure; *the – test* (*fig.*), der Prüfstein, die Feuerprobe. **-ify** [ə'sɪdɪfaɪ], 1. *v.a.* säuern, in Säure verwandeln (*Chem.*). 2. *v.n.* sauer werden. **-imeter** [–'dɪmətə], *s.* der Säuremesser. **-ity,** *s.* die Schärfe, Herbheit; Magensäure. **-ulate,** *v.a.* säuern. **-ulous,** *adj.* säuerlich; *-ulous water*, der Sauerbrunnen.
ack-ack ['æk'æk], *s. & attr. adj.* (*coll.*) die Flak; Flak–.
acknowledg-e [ək'nɔlɪdʒ], *v.a.* anerkennen; zugeben, eingestehen, bestätigen; dankbar anerkennen, erkenntlich sein für; *I -e the truth of this*, ich erkenne die Wahrheit hiervon an; *-e the receipt of a letter*, den (richtigen) Empfang eines Briefes bestätigen; *-e the receipt of a remittance*, den Empfang einer Rimesse bescheinigen *or* bestätigen. **-ment,** *s.* die Anerkennung; das Bekenntnis, Zugeständnis, Eingeständnis; die Bestätigung, Empfangsbescheinigung, Quittung, der Empfangsschein. **-ments,** *pl.* die Anerkennung, Erkenntlichkeit.
acme ['ækmɪ], *s.* der Gipfel, der Höhepunkt, die Spitze.
acne ['æknɪ], *s.* der Hautausschlag, der Pickel.
acolyte ['ækolaɪt], *s.* der Altardiener, Meßgehilfe (*Eccl.*).
aconite ['ækonaɪt], *s.* der Eisenhut (*Bot.*); das Akonit (*Pharm.*); (*poet.*) tödliches Gift.
acorn ['eɪkɔ:n], *s.* die Eichel, Ecker.
acoustic [ə'kaʊstɪk, ə'kʊstɪk], *adj.* akustisch; – *effect*, die Schallwirkung, Klangwirkung; – *mine*, die Schallmine; – *nerve*, der Gehörnerv. **-al,** *adj.* *see* –; Schall–, Hör–. **-ally,** *adv.* in akustischer Hinsicht. **-s,** *pl.* die Akustik, Lehre vom Schall.
acquaint [ə'kweɪnt], *v.a.* bekannt machen; mitteilen, berichten, melden (*a p. with a th.*, einem etwas); *be -ed with s.th.*, etwas kennen; *become -ed with*, kennen lernen; – *o.s. with . . .*, sich mit . . . bekannt machen, sich in . . . einarbeiten; *we are -ed*, wir sind Bekannte, wir kennen uns. **-ance,** *s.* die Bekanntschaft; die Kenntnis; der (die) Bekannte; *on closer -ance*, bei näherer Bekanntschaft; *make a p.'s -ance*, Bekanntschaft mit einem machen; *have -ance with a th.*, Kenntnis von einer S. haben; *an -ance of mine*, eine(r) meiner Bekannten. **-ances,** *pl.* der Bekanntenkreis. **-anceship,** *s.* die Bekanntschaft.
acquiesce [ækwɪ'ɛs], *v.n.* es ruhig hinnehmen; einwilligen (in eine S.), sich (*Dat.*) gefallen lassen, sich beruhigen, sich (in eine S.) fügen. **-nce,** *s.* die Ergebung (in); die Einwilligung (in). **-nt,** *adj.* ergeben, fügsam.
acquirable [ə'kwaɪərəbl], *ad*. erlangbar, erreichbar, erwerbbar.
acquire [ə'kwaɪə], *v.a.* erlangen, gewinnen, erwerben; (er)lernen; *-d taste*, anerzogener Geschmack. **-ment,** *s.* die Erwerbung, Erlangung; das Erworbene; erworbene Fertigkeit. **-ments,** Kenntnisse, erworbene Bildung.
acquisit-ion [ækwɪ'zɪʃən] *s.* die Erwerbung; Erlernung; der Erwerb, das Erworbene, die Errungenschaft (*to*, für); (*coll.*) Bereicherung, Eroberung. **-ive** [ə'kwɪzɪtɪv], *adj.* gewinnsüchtig, habsüchtig, erwerbslustig. **-iveness,** *s.* der Erwerbstrieb, Erwerbssinn, die Gewinnsucht.
acquit [ə'kwɪt], *v.a.* freisprechen, lossprechen, entlasten (*a p.*); abtragen, quittieren (*a debt*); – *s.o. of a duty, etc.*, einen einer Pflicht *etc.* entbinden; – *o.s. of a duty, etc.*, sich einer Pflicht *etc.* entledigen; – *o.s. well*, sich gut machen. **-tal,** *s.* die Lossprechung, Freisprechung, der Freispruch; die Erfüllung, Erledigung (*of duty, etc.*). **-tance,** *s.* die Bezahlung, Abtragung; Befreiung (*from duty, etc.*); die Empfangsbescheinigung, Empfangsbestätigung, Quittung.
acre ['eɪkə], *s.* der Morgen Landes (= *4840 Quadrat-Yards or 0·40467 Hektar*); *God's –*, der Gottesacker. **-age,** *s* der Flächeninhalt.
acrid ['ækrɪd], *adj.* scharf, beißend, ätzend.
acrimonious [ækrɪ'moʊnjəs], *adj.* (*fig.*) scharf, beißend, bitter, verletzend.
acrimony ['ækrɪmənɪ], *s.* die Bitterkeit, Schärfe.
acrobat ['ækrobæt], *s.* der Akrobat, Seiltänzer. **-ic** [–'bætɪk], *adj.* akrobatisch. **-ics,** *pl.* die Akrobatik.

across [əˈkrɔs], 1. *adv.* kreuzweise, quer hinüber, quer herüber. 2. *prep.* quer durch, quer über, mitten durch; jenseits, über. – *country*, querfeldein, querbeet(ein); *a short cut – the fields*, ein Richtweg durch die Felder; *I have come – him*, ich bin ihm zufällig begegnet, habe ihn zufällig getroffen *or* bin auf ihn gestoßen; *it flashed – my mind*, es fiel mir plötzlich ein.

acrostic [əˈkrɔstɪk], *s.* das Akrostichon.

act [ækt], **1.** *s.* die Handlung, Tat; Leistung, Ausführung; der Aufzug, Akt (*Theat.*); das Gesetz, der Beschluß, Erlaß (*Law*); die Akte, das Aktenstück (*Law*); *one-– play*, der Einakter; – *of parliament*, die Parlamentsakte, das Reichsgesetz; *the –s* (*of the Apostles*), die Apostelgeschichte; – *of God*, höhere Gewalt, das Naturereignis; *in the – of doing*, im Begriff zu tun; *in the* (*very*) –, auf frischer Tat. **2.** *v.a.* – *a part*, eine Rolle spielen *or* darstellen; sich verstellen; – *the part of*, fungieren als; – *a play*, ein Stück aufführen; *he –ed the part of Hamlet*, er spielte *or* gab den Hamlet. **3.** *v.n.* wirken, einwirken, wirksam sein, tätig sein, funktionieren; sich betragen, sich verhalten, sich benehmen, handeln; spielen (*on the stage, etc.*); – *cautiously*, vorsichtig zu Werke gehen; *the play –s well*, das Stück läßt sich gut spielen; – *well by a p.*, an einem gut handeln; – *on*, wirken auf (*Acc.*), Einfluß haben auf; – *upon*, sich richten nach; – *up to*, handeln gemäß, entsprechen. **–ing,** 1. *s.* das Handeln; das Spiel; die Darstellung, Schauspielkunst. 2. *adj.* handelnd, wirkend; stellvertretend, diensttuend, amtierend, geschäftsführend; *self-–ing*, selbstwirkend, selbsttätig; *–ing copy*, das Bühnenmanuskript; *–ing manager*, stellvertretender Direktor.

actin–ic [ækˈtɪnɪk], *adj.* aktinisch, chemisch wirksam; *–ic power of light*, chemische Wirksamkeit des Lichts; *–ic screen*, der Leuchtschirm. **–ism** [ˈæktɪnɪzm], *s.* chemische Wirkung der Sonnenstrahlen. **–ometer** [–ˈnɔmətə], *s.* der Strahlenmesser.

action [ˈækʃən], *s.* die Tätigkeit, Bewegung; das Unternehmen, die Handlung, Tat; Wirkung, Einwirkung, der Einfluß; das Funktionieren; der Gang, die Haltung, Gangart (*of a horse*); die Handlung (*of a play, etc.*); der Rechtshandel, das Rechtsverfahren, der Prozeß, die Klage (*Law*); das Treffen, Gefecht, die Kampfhandlung, Aktion, der Einsatz (*Mil.*); das Werk, der Mechanismus; *double –*, doppelte Wirkung; *bring an – against*, eine Klage anstrengen gegen; *an – for debt*, eine Schuldklage; *be in –*, in Bewegung *or* tätig sein, wirken; im Gefecht sein (*Mil.*); *put* (*troops, etc.*) *into –*, einsetzen; *ready for –*, kampfbereit, einsatzbereit; klar zum Gefecht (*Naut.*); *readiness for –*, die Einsatzbereitschaft; *fight an –*, eine Schlacht liefern; *go into –*, eingreifen, ins Gefecht kommen; *killed in –*, gefallen; *man of –*, Mann der Tat; *put into –*, in die Tat umsetzen; *out of –*, außer Betrieb; *put out of –*, außer Gefecht setzen, kampfunfähig *or* bewegungsunfähig machen; – *station*, die Gefechtsstation; – *stations!* klar zum Gefecht! (*Navy*). **–able,** *adj.* klagbar, strafbar.

activ–ate, *v.a.* aktivieren. **–e** [ˈæktɪv] *adj.* tätig; emsig, rührig, geschäftig; wirkend, wirksam; behend, flink, mobil, energisch, lebhaft; belebt (*C.L.*); aktiv (*Mil.*); aktiv, tätig (*Gram.*); *–e bonds*, selbstverzinsliche Obligationen; *–e debts*, die Außenstände; *an –e life*, ein tätiges Leben; *an –e part in*, aktive Teilnahme an; *–e partner*, tätiger Teilhaber; *on –e service*, an der Front, im Krieg; *–e service allowance*, die Frontzulage; *–e service pay*, der Wehrsold. **–ity** [–ˈtɪvɪtɪ], *s.* die Tätigkeit, Betätigung; Wirksamkeit; Behendigkeit, Rührigkeit; *in full –ity*, in vollem Gange *or* Betrieb; *sphere of –ity*, der Wirkungskreis.

act–or [ˈæktə], *s.* der Täter, Handelnde; handelnde Person; der Schauspieler. **–ress** [ˈæktrɪs], *s.* die Schauspielerin.

actual [ˈæktjuəl], *adj.* wirklich, tatsächlich; jetzig, gegenwärtig, vorliegend; – *price*, der Tagespreis; – *state of affairs*, die wirkliche Sachlage; – *strength*, die Iststärke, der Iststand (*Mil.*). **–ity** [æktjuˈælɪtɪ], *s.* die Wirklichkeit, Tatsächlichkeit.

actuary [ˈæktjuərɪ], *s.* der Aktuar, Urkundsbeamte(r), Gerichtsschreiber; Statistiker (*insurance*).

actuat–e [ˈæktjueɪt], *v.a.* in Bewegung setzen, in Gang bringen, antreiben; *–ed by the purest motives*, von den reinsten Absichten beeinflußt. **–ion** [–ˈeɪʃən], *s.* der Antrieb.

acuity [əˈkjuːɪtɪ], *s.* (*fig.*) die Schärfe.

acumen [əkˈjuːmɛn], *s.* der Scharfsinn.

acute [əˈkjuːt], *adj.* spitz(ig); scharf, stechend (*of pain*); fein, klar (*of the senses*); scharfsinnig, klug; innerst, tiefst; – *accent*, der Akut; – *angle*, spitzer Winkel; – *disease*, heftige *or* akute Krankheit. **–ness,** *s.* die Spitze, Schärfe; Klugheit, der Scharfsinn, die Schlagfertigkeit; Feinheit (*of the hearing*); Heftigkeit (*of a disease*).

ad [æd], *s.* (*sl.*) die Reklame, Annonce.

adage [ˈædɪdʒ], *s.* das Sprichwort.

adagio [əˈdɑːdʒɪou], 1. *adv.* adagio, langsam (*Mus.*). 2. *s.* das Adagio.

adamant [ˈædəmənt], 1. *s.* sehr harter Stein; (*poet.*) außerordentliche Härte. 2. *adj.* unerbittlich, felsenfest. **–ine** [–ˈmæntaɪn], *adj.* diamantenhart, demanten; (*fig.*) unerschütterlich.

adapt [əˈdæpt], *v.a.* anpassen (*to* (*Dat.*)), einrichten (*to*, nach), zurechtmachen; bearbeiten (*from*, nach) (*Theat.*); – *o.s. to circumstances*, sich nach den Verhältnissen richten. **–ability** [–əˈbɪlɪtɪ], *s.* die Anwendbarkeit; die Anpassungsfähigkeit (*to*, an). **–able** [əˈdæptəbl], *adj.* anwendbar; anpassungsfähig. **–ation** [–ˈteɪʃən], *s.* die Anwendung; Herrichtung, Umarbeitung, Bearbeitung. **–er,** *s.* die Verbindungsröhre; die (Filmpack)Kassette (*Phot.*); der Bearbeiter (*Theat.*); *–er* (*plug*), die Steckhülse (*Elect*). **–ive,** *adj.* anpassungsfähig.

add [æd], *v.a.* & *n.* hinzutun, hinzusetzen, hinzufügen (zu); beifügen, beimengen, verbinden, versetzen (mit); beitragen (zu), vermehren, erhöhen, nachsetzen; zusammenzählen, addieren (*Arith.*); – *fuel to the fire*, (*fig.*) Öl ins Feuer gießen; – *in*, hinzurechnen, einschließen; – *insult to injury*, etwas noch verschlimmern; – *the interest to the capital*, die Zinsen zum Kapital schlagen; *–ed to this*, dazu kommt noch, zuzüglich; *–ed to which*, wozu kommt noch; – *up* or *together*, zusammenzählen, addieren. **–ed,** *adj.* erhöht, verstärkt. **–endum** [əˈdɛndəm], *s.* (pl. *–enda*), der Zusatz, Nachtrag. **–ing-machine,** *s.* die Rechenmaschine.

adder [ˈædə], *s.* die Natter.

addict 1. [əˈdɪkt], *v.n.* & *r.*; – *o.s.*, sich ergeben; *–ed to drink*, dem Trunke ergeben. 2. [ˈædɪkt], *s.* der *or* die Süchtige. **–ion** [əˈdɪkʃən], *s.* (*to*), die Hingabe (an); Neigung, der Hang (zu).

addition [əˈdɪʃən], *s.* die Beifügung, Hinzusetzung, Beimengung; der Zusatz, Anhang, die Zugabe, Zutat; die Vermehrung, Anlagerung, der Zuwachs; die Zusammenzählung, Addition (*Arith.*); *in* – (*to this*), noch dazu, außerdem. **–al,** *adj.* hinzukommend, beigefügt; nachträglich, ergänzend, neu; weiter; vermehrt; *–al charge*, der Zuschlag; *–al charges*, Mehrkosten; *–al clause*, die Zusatzklausel; *–al duty*, der Steuerzuschlag; *–al payment*, die Nachzahlung. **–ally,** *adv.* als Zusatz, in verstärktem Maße.

addle [ˈædl], 1. *v.a.* unfruchtbar machen; (*fig.*) verwirren (*the brains*). 2. *v.n.* faul werden; *–d egg*, faules Ei, das Windei. **--brained,** *adj.*, **--pated,** *adj.* dumm, hohlköpfig.

address [əˈdrɛs], 1. *s.* die Anrede, Ansprache, Rede, der Vortrag; die Anschrift, Aufschrift, Adresse (*on a letter*); (= *dexterity*) die Gewandtheit, Geschicklichkeit; (= *manner*) das Benehmen, die Manier, Haltung; das Dankschreiben, die Bittschrift; *in case of change of –*, falls verzogen; *pay one's –es to a lady*, einer Dame den Hof machen, um eine Dame anhalten. 2. *v.a.* anreden; adressieren, überschreiben (*a letter*); sprechen (zu), richten (*words*) (*to*, an (*Acc.*)); – *a meeting*, in *or* zu einer Versammlung sprechen, an eine Versammlung eine Ansprache halten; – *o.s. to* (*a task, etc.*), sich zu (einer Aufgabe, *etc.*) anschicken *or* bereit machen; (*coll.*) – *the ball*, ansprechen (*golf*). **–ee,** *s.* der (die) Empfänger(in), Adressat(in).

adduc-e [əˈdjuːs], *v.a.* anführen, beibringen (*proofs, witnesses, etc.*). **-ible,** *adj.* anführbar.
adductor [æˈdʌktə], *s.* der Anziehmuskel.
ademption [əˈdɛmʃən], *s.* die Entziehung, Wegnahme (*Law*).
adenoid [ˈædɪnɔɪd], *s.* (*usually pl.*) die Wucherung *or* Polypen in der Nase (*Path.*).
adept 1. [əˈdɛpt], *adj.* erfahren; geschickt; eingeweiht. 2. [ˈædɛpt] *s.* Eingeweihte(r), *m.*, der Kenner, Könner, Meister; Goldmacher, Alchimist; (*coll.*) *be an – at a th.*, gut *or* geschickt in einer Sache sein.
adequacy [ˈædɪkwəsɪ], *s.* die Zulänglichkeit, Angemessenheit.
adequate [ˈædɪkwət], *adj.* angemessen, genügend, ausreichend, hinreichend, zureichend (*to*, für), entsprechend (*to* (*Dat.*)). **-ness,** *s.*, *see* **adequacy.**
adhere [ədˈhɪə], *v.n.* kleben, haften (*to*, an (*with Dat.*)); *– together*, zusammenhängen; *– to an opinion*, bei einer Meinung bleiben, an einer Ansicht festhalten; *– to a party*, einer Partei zugetan sein; *– to orders*, Vorschrift(en) befolgen. **-nce** [-rəns], *s.* das Festhalten; die Teilnahme (*to*, an (*with Dat.*)), Anhänglichkeit (*to*, an (*with Acc.*)). **-nt** [-rənt], 1. *adj.* anhaftend, verbunden mit, festhaltend an (*Dat.*). 2. *s.* der Anhänger.
adhesi-on [ədˈhɪːʒən], *s.* das Anhaften, Anhangen; die Adhäsion, Adhäsionskraft, Haftfähigkeit, Bindefestigkeit (*Phys.*); das Verwachsen (*Med.*); die Bindung, Reibung; (*fig.*) die Anhänglichkeit; der Anschluß, Beitritt; *the -on to an opinion*, das Festhalten an einer Meinung; *give one's -on to a th.*, sich für etwas erklären. **-ve** [-sɪv], 1. *adj.* anhaftend, festhaftend, klebend, klebrig. 2. *s.* das Bindemittel, Klebemittel, der Klebestoff; *-ve envelope*, gummierter Briefumschlag; *-ve force*, die Adhäsionskraft; *-ve plaster*, das Heftpflaster; *-ve power*, das Haftvermögen. **-veness,** *s.* die Klebrigkeit, Klebefähigkeit, das Anhaften.
adieu [əˈdjuː], 1. *int.* lebewohl! 2. *s.* das Lebewohl; *bid* or *say –*, *make one's -x*, Abschied nehmen.
adipose [ˈædɪpoʊs], *adj.* fett, fettig, fetthaltig, talgig, feist; *– tissue*, das Fettgewebe.
adit [ˈædit], *s.* der Zugang, Stollen (*Min.*).
adjacency [əˈdʒeɪsənsɪ], *s.* das Angrenzen, Naheliegen; das Anliegende.
adjacent [əˈdʒeɪsənt], *adj.* anliegend, angrenzend, anstoßend (*to*, an); *– angles*, Nebenwinkel.
adjectival [ædʒɛkˈtaɪvəl], *adj.* adjektivisch.
adjective [ˈædʒɪktɪv], 1. *s.* das Eigenschaftswort, Adjektiv. 2. *adj.* adjektivisch.
adjoin [əˈdʒɔɪn], *v.a. & n.* aneinandergrenzen, anliegen (*Dat.*), angrenzen, anstoßen (an (*with Acc.*)); anfügen, hinzufügen (*to*, zu). **-ing,** *adj.* Neben-, anstoßend, angrenzend, benachbart.
adjourn [əˈdʒəːn], 1. *v.a.* vertagen, aufschieben, verschieben. 2. *v.n.* sich vertagen, die Sitzung vertagen; sich (an einen andern Ort) begeben, den Sitzungsort nach . . . verlegen. **-ment,** *s.* die Vertagung, Verschiebung, der Aufschub.
adjudge [əˈdʒʌdʒ], *v.a.* entscheiden; zuerkennen, zusprechen; erklären; *– a p.* (*to be*) *guilty*, einen schuldig erklären; *the prize was -d to the victor*, der Preis wurde dem Sieger zuerkannt.
adjudicat-e [əˈdʒuːdɪkeɪt], 1. *v.a. & n.* gerichtlich erklären (*to be*, für), (richterlich) entscheiden. 2. *v.n.* richten, urteilen (*on*, über (*with Acc.*)); als Schiedsrichter tätig sein (*at*, bei). **-ion** [-ˈkeɪʃən] *s.* die Zuerkennung, Zusprechung; Entscheidung, der Entscheid, Rechtsspruch, das Urteil. **-or,** *s.* der Schiedsrichter.
adjunct [ˈædʒʌŋkt], *s.* der Zusatz, die Beigabe; der Nebenumstand; das Attribut (*Gram.*); der (Amts)Gehilfe, Beigeordnete.
adjuration [ædʒʊəˈreɪʃən], *s.* die Beschwörung, inständige Bitte; die Beschwörungsformel.
adjure [əˈdʒʊə], *v.a.* beschwören, inständig bitten.
adjust [əˈdʒʌst], *v.a.* zurechtmachen, ordnen; regulieren, regeln; anpassen, einstellen, aufstellen, justieren; berichtigen, begleichen (*accounts*); ausgleichen, abmachen, schlichten (*disputes*); (ab)eichen (*a measure*); *– the average*, die Havarie berechnen (*Naut.*). **-able,** *adj.* verschiebbar, regulierbar, einstellbar, verstellbar; *-able-pitch airscrew*, einstellbare *or* verstellbare Luftschraube, die Verstelluftschraube. **-ment,** *s.* die Anordnung, Einrichtung, Einstellung; Neueinstellung, Ordnung, Anpassung; Abrichtung, Eichung, Justierung; Berichtigung, Ausgleichung; Schlichtung, Beilegung (*of a quarrel*); *-ment of average*, die Havarieberechnung (*Naut.*); *bracket -ment*, das Gabelschießen (*Artil.*); *-ment of fire*, das Einschießen (*Artil.*). **-ing-balance,** *s.* die Justierwage. **-ing-screw,** *s.* die Einstellschraube.
adjut-ancy [ˈædʒʊtənsɪ], *s.* das Amt eines Adjutanten, die Adjutantur. **-ant,** *s.* der Adjutant (*Mil.*).
admeasurement [ædˈmɛʒəmənt], *s.* die Zumessung (*Law*); das Abmessen; das Maß, der Umfang; *bill of –*, der Meßbrief.
administ-er [ædˈmɪnɪstə], 1. *v.a.* verwalten; handhaben, vollstrecken (*justice*); austeilen, spenden (*the sacraments*); *-er an oath*, (einem) einen Eid abnehmen; *-er the law*, Recht sprechen; *-er medicine*, Arznei eingeben. 2. *v.n.* behilflich sein; dienen; als Administrator walten. **-ration** [-ˈtreɪʃən], *s.* die Verwaltung, Verwaltungsbehörde; Regierung, das Ministerium; die Handhabung; Austeilung, Darreichung, Spendung; *local -ration*, der Ortsvorstand; *-ration of the oath*, die Eidesabnahme, Vereidigung. **-rative** [-trətɪv], *adj.* verwaltend; administrativ; *-rative difficulties*, Verwaltungsschwierigkeiten. **-rator** [-reɪtə], *s.* der Verwalter, Verweser; Spender; Verwaltungsbeamte, Administrator; Nachlaßverwalter. **-ratorship,** *s.* das Amt eines Verwalters. **-ratrix,** *s.* die Verwalterin.
admirabl-e [ˈædmərəbl], *adj.*, **-y,** *adv.* bewunderungswürdig, (vor)trefflich. **-eness,** *s.* die Trefflichkeit.
admiral [ˈædmərəl], *s.* der Admiral (*also Ent.*); *rear--*, der Konteradmiral; *vice--*, der Vizeadmiral; *– of the fleet*, der Flottenadmiral, Großadmiral. **-ty,** *s.* das Marineamt, die Admiralität; das Oberkommando der Marine; *High Court of -ty*, das Admiralitätsgericht; *First Lord of the -ty*, der Marineminister.
admiration [ædmɪˈreɪʃən], *s.* die Bewunderung (*of* or *for*, für); *to –*, in bewundernswerter Weise; *be* or *become the – of*, bewundert werden von.
admir-e [ədˈmaɪə], *v.a.* bewundern, verehren. **-er** [ədˈmaɪərə], *s.* der Bewunderer; Anbeter, Verehrer.
admissib-ility [ədmɪsɪˈbɪlɪtɪ], *s.* die Zulässigkeit. **-le** [ədˈmɪsɪbl], *adj.* zulässig, erlaubt, annehmbar.
admission [ədˈmɪʃən], *s.* die Zulassung, der Zugang, Eintritt, Zutritt, Einlaß, die Aufnahme; das Zugeständnis, die Einräumung; *– free!* Eintritt *or* Zutritt frei!; *--ticket*, die Einlaßkarte, Eintrittskarte.
admit [ədˈmɪt], 1. *v.a.* einlassen, zulassen (*to* or *into*, zu); einweihen, aufnehmen (in); gestehen, einräumen, zugeben (*to a p.*, einem gegenüber); Raum haben für, Raum geben (*with Dat.*); *– into one's confidence*, ins Vertrauen ziehen; *I will – that*, das gebe ich zu, lasse ich gelten; *this ticket -s two*, diese Karte ist gültig für zwei Personen. 2. *v.n.* erlauben, gestatten; *it -s of no excuse*, es läßt sich nicht entschuldigen; *the words do not – of this construction*, die Worte lassen diese Auslegung nicht zu; *this ticket -s to the evening performance*, diese Karte ist gültig für die Abendvorstellung. **-tance,** *s.* der Einlaß, Eintritt, Eingang, Zutritt, die Zulassung; *no -tance!* verbotener Eingang! Zutritt verboten! **-tedly,** *adv.* anerkanntermaßen, zugestandenermaßen.
admix [ədˈmɪks], *v.a.* beimengen, zusetzen. **-ture** [-tʃə], *s.* die Beimischung, Beimengung; der Zusatz.
admoni-sh [ədˈmɒnɪʃ], *v.a.* ermahnen; warnen (*against* or *of*, vor (*with Dat.*)). **-tion** [-məˈnɪʃən], *s.* die Ermahnung; Warnung; der Verweis; die Vermahnung (*Law*). **-tory** [-nɪtərɪ], *adj.* ermahnend, warnend.
ado [əˈduː], *s.* das Tun, Treiben, Getue, Aufheben, Aufsehen, der Lärm; *much – about nothing*, viel Lärm um nichts; *without more –*, ohne weitere Umstände.
adobe [æˈdoʊb(ɪ)], *s.* luftgetrockneter Ziegelstein.

adolescen–ce [ædo'lɛsəns], *s.* die Jugend(zeit), das Jünglingsalter. **–t** [–ənt], 1. *adj.* jugendlich, heranwachsend. 2. *s.* der Jüngling; junges Mädchen.

adopt [ə'dɔpt], *v.a.* an Kindes Statt annehmen, adoptieren; (*fig.*) sich aneignen, annehmen; – *an attitude*, eine Haltung annehmen; – (*a p. as*) *a candidate* (*Parl.*), einen (als) Kandidaten aufstellen; – *a course*, einen Weg einschlagen; *–ed child*, angenommenes Kind; *his –ed country*, seine Wahlheimat. **–er,** *s.* der Adoptivvater. **–ion** [–ʃən], *s.* die Annahme an Kindes Statt, Adoption; (*fig.*) Annahme; *country of* –, die Wahlheimat; *brother by* –, der Adoptivbruder. **–ive,** *adj.* angenommen; Adoptiv–.

adora–ble [ə'dɔ:rəbl], *adj.*, **–bly,** *adv.* anbetungswürdig, verehrungswürdig. **–tion** [ædo'reɪʃən], *s.* die Anbetung, Verehrung (*of* or *for*, für).

ador–e [ə'dɔ:], *v.a.* anbeten, verehren; (*coll.*) sehr gern haben. **–er** [–rə], *s.* der Anbeter, Verehrer. **–ing,** *adj.* Liebes–.

adorn [ə'dɔ:n], *v.a.* schmücken, zieren, putzen; (mit Worten) ausschmücken, verschönern. **–ment,** *s.* der Schmuck, Zierrat; die Schmückung, Verzierung.

adrenal glands [ə'drɪ:nəl glændz], (*pl.*) die Nebennieren.

adrift [ə'drɪft], *adv.* treibend, schwimmend, Wind und Wellen preisgegeben; *set* or *cut* –, treiben lassen; *I was turned* –, ich wurde fortgejagt; *cut o.s. – from*, sich absondern von.

adroit [ə'drɔɪt], *adj.* geschickt, gewandt. **–ness,** *s.* die Geschicklichkeit, Gewandtheit.

adsorb [əd'zɔ:b], *v.a.* adsorbieren. **–ent,** *s.* das Absorbens.

adulat–ion [ædjʊ'leɪʃən], *s.* die Lobhudelei, Speichelleckerei, Schmeichelei. **–or** [–leɪtə], *s.* der Speichellecker, Schmeichler. **–ory** [–lətərɪ], *adj.* schmeichlerisch, servil.

adult [ə'dʌlt], 1. *adj.* erwachsen, reif. 2. *s.* der (die) Erwachsene; – *education*, die Erwachsenenbildung.

adulter–ant [ə'dʌltərənt], *s.* das Fälschungsmittel, Verfälschungsmittel; Streckmittel, Verschnittmittel. **–ate** [–reɪt], *v.a.* fälschen, verfälschen, vermischen, mischen, strecken, verschneiden, verdünnen; (*fig.*) verderben. **–ation** [–'reɪʃən], *s.* die Verfälschung, Mischung, Streckung, der Verschnitt; *–ation of food*, die Nahrungsmittelfälschung. **–ator,** *m.* der (Ver)Fälscher.

adulter–er [ə'dʌltərə], *s.* der Ehebrecher. **–ess,** *s.* die Ehebrecherin. **–ous,** *adj.* ehebrecherisch. **–y** [–tərɪ], *s.* der Ehebruch.

adumbrat–e ['ædʌmbreɪt], *v.a.* andeuten; flüchtig entwerfen, skizzieren. **–ion** [–'breɪʃən], *s.* die Andeutung, Skizze, der Umriß, flüchtiger Entwurf.

advance [əd'vɑ:ns], 1. *v.n.* vorrücken, vorgehen, vordringen, anrücken, vorwärts gehen; Fortschritte machen, fortschreiten; vorwärts kommen, zunehmen (*in*, an (*Dat.*)); steigen (*in price*); befördert werden, aufrücken, avancieren (*in rank, etc.*); *–d sentry*, vorgeschobener Posten. 2. *v.a.* vorausbezahlen, vorschießen (*money*); befördern, beschleunigen, erhöhen; vorwärts bringen, fördern; vorrücken; aufstellen, vorbringen, vortragen, äußern (*an opinion*); – *a claim*, auf eine S. Anspruch machen; – *a p.'s interests*, jemandes Interesse fördern *or* jemandes Interessen Vorschub leisten; – *a p. in office*, einen befördern. 3. *s.* der Vormarsch, das Vorrücken, Anrücken, Vorschreiten; der Fortschritt, die Vervollkommnung; Beförderung (*in office*); der Vorschuß (*of money*); die Erhöhung (*in price*); das Mehrgebot (*on an offer*); *in* –, vorn, voraus (*in position*), im voraus (*in time*); *payment in* –, die Vorauszahlung; *prices are on the* –, die Preise sind im Steigen begriffen; *be in – of a p.*, einem voraus sein. 4. *adj.*; – *guard*, die Vorhut, Avantgarde; – *party*, die Spitzenkompanie, der Vortrupp (*Mil.*); – *sale*, der Vorverkauf. **–d,** *adj.* vorgeschoben; vorgeschritten, modern, emanzipiert, extrem; *–d thinker*, vorgeschrittener Denker; *–d age*, vorgerücktes Alter. **–ment,** *s.* die Verbreitung, Förderung; der Fortschritt, das Emporkommen; die Beförderung. **–s,** *pl.* Annäherungsversuche.

advantage [əd'vɑ:ntɪdʒ], 1. *s.* der Vorteil (*also Tennis*), Vorzug, Nutzen; die Überlegenheit, das Übergewicht; *gain the* –, Vorteil gewinnen; *have the – of a p.*, einem überlegen sein, einem gegenüber im Vorteil sein; *take – of a th.*, etwas ausnutzen, Vorteil aus einer S. ziehen, sich (*Dat.*) etwas zunutze machen; *take – of s.o.*, einen übervorteilen; *turn s.th. to* –, sich (*Dat.*) etwas zunutze machen; *to the best* –, auf das Vorteilhafteste; *to his* –, ihm zum Nutzen, zu seinem Vorteil; *personal –s*, körperliche Vorzüge. 2. *v.a.* (einem) Vorteil gewähren, (einem) nützen; (eine S.) fördern. **–ous** [ædvən'teɪdʒəs], *adj.* vorteilhaft, günstig.

advent ['ædvənt], *s.* der Advent (*Eccl.*); die Ankunft; – *to power*, das Zurmachtkommen, Emporkommen zur Macht. **–itious** [–'tɪʃəs], *adj.* zufällig, fremd, hinzukommend.

adventur–e [əd'vɛntʃə], 1. *s.* das Abenteuer; Erlebnis; das Wagnis, Wagestück; unerwartetes Ereignis; die Spekulation. 2. *v.a. & n.* wagen, riskieren. **–er** [–rə], *s.* der Abenteurer, Glücksjäger, Spekulant. **–ous** [–rəs], *adj.* abenteuerlich; kühn, waghalsig, unternehmungslustig; riskant.

adverb ['ædvə:b], *s.* das Adverb(ium), Umstandswort. **–ial** [–'və:bjəl], *adj.* adverbial.

adversary ['ædvəsərɪ], *s.* der Gegner, Feind, Widersacher.

advers–e [æd'və:s], 1. *adj.* ungünstig, nachteilig (*to*, für); gegenüberstehend, gegenüberliegend, gegnerisch, feindlich (gesinnt) (*to* (*Dat.*)); widrig (*as fate, etc.*). 2. *pred. adj.* zuwider; *be –e to a th.*, gegen etwas sein; *–e balance*, die Unterbilanz; *–e fate*, das Mißgeschick; *–e majority*, Mehrheit gegen einen Antrag; *–e party*, die Gegenpartei; *–e winds*, widrige Winde. **–ely,** *adv.* zuwider. **–ity,** *s.* das Elend, die Not, das Unglück, Mißgeschick.

advert [æd'və:t], *v.n.* hinweisen, anspielen (*to*, auf); berühren, erwähnen.

advertis–e ['ædvətɑɪz], *v.a & n.* öffentlich anzeigen *or* bekanntmachen; ankündigen, annoncieren, inserieren, Reklame machen; (*archaic*) in Kenntnis setzen, benachrichtigen; *–e for*, durch Reklame suchen, annoncieren nach. **–ement** [əd'və:tɪzmənt], *s.* die Anzeige, Bekanntmachung, Ankündigung, das Inserat, die Annonce, Reklame; *put* or *insert an –ement in a paper*, ein Inserat in einer Zeitung aufgeben. **–er,** *s.* der Anzeiger, Inserent; das Anzeigeblatt. **–ing,** 1. *s.* das Bekanntmachen, Ankündigen; die Reklame, das Reklamewesen. 2. *attr. adj.* Anzeige–, Reklame–, Inseraten–; *–ing agency*, das Annoncenbüro; *pictorial –ing*, die Bildwerbung.

advice [əd'vɑɪs], *s.* (*sing. only*) der Rat, Ratschlag; (*with pl.*) die Nachricht, Meldung, Mitteilung, der Bericht; Avis (*C.L.*); *on my* –, auf meinen Rat; *on* or *by the – of*, auf Rat von; *ask, take* or *seek – from*, Rat holen von, sich raten lassen; *take my – !* folge meinem Rate! *follow* or *take his* –, seinen Rat befolgen; *take medical* –, einen Arzt konsultieren; *he will not take any* –, er läßt sich nicht raten; *as per* –, laut Bericht; *a piece of* –, ein (guter) Rat; *according to –s from Rome*, nach Berichten aus Rom; *until further* –, bis auf weitere Nachricht; *letter of* –, der Avisbrief. **– –boat,** *s.* der Aviso, das Depeschenschiff.

advisa–bility [ədvɑɪzə'bɪlɪtɪ], *s.* die Ratsamkeit, Zweckmäßigkeit. **–ble,** *adj.* ratsam, rätlich; nützlich.

advis–e [əd'vɑɪz], 1. *v.a.* raten (*with Dat.*); beraten (*a p.*); empfehlen (einem etwas); benachrichtigen, melden, avisieren (*C.L.*); *–e against*, warnen, ermahnen; *I – you not to go out* or *against going out*, ich warne dich auszugehen; *be –ed by me*, laß dir von mir raten; *he –ed me*, er riet mir, er beriet mich, er gab mir seinen Rat; *she –ed them to go*, sie gab ihnen den Rat *or* riet ihnen zu gehen; *–e s.o. to the contrary*, einem (von etwas) abraten; *as –ed*, laut Bericht. 2. *v.n.* (sich) beraten (*with*, mit); *–e with one's pillow*, etwas beschlafen; *–e with o.s.*, mit sich zu Rate gehen. **–ed,** *adj.* überlegt, absichtlich; *ill –ed*, unbedachtsam, schlecht beraten; *well –ed*, wohl überlegt, wohlerwogen. **–edly** [–ɪdlɪ], *adv.* mit Vorbedacht *or* Überlegung. **–er,** *s.* der Ratgeber, Berater. **–ory,** *adj.* beratend, ratgebend; *–ory council*, technischer Beirat.

advocacy [ˈædvokəsɪ], *s.* die Verteidigung, Befürwortung; das Eintreten (für); *in – of*, zur Verteidigung von.
advocate 1. [ˈædvokət], *s.* (*Scots*) der Anwalt, Rechtsanwalt, Rechtsbeistand, Advokat; (*fig.*) der Verteidiger, Verfechter, Fürsprecher, Befürworter; *I am a great – of*, ich halte viel von *or* große Stücke auf (*Acc.*). 2. [–keɪt], *v.a.* verteidigen, verfechten, befürworten; eintreten (für); *– a th*, einer S. (*Dat.*) das Wort reden, eine S. befürworten.
advowson [ədˈvɑuzən], *s.* das Pfründenbesetzungsrecht (*Law*).
adze [ædz], 1. *s.* das Breitbeil, die Krummaxt. 2. *v.a.* mit dem Breitbeil bearbeiten.
aegis [ˈɪːdʒɪs], *s.* die Ägis; (*fig.*) die Ägide, der Schutz.
Aeolian [ɪˈoʊljən], *adj.*; *– harp*, die Äolsharfe, Windharfe.
aeon [ˈɪːən], *s.* der Äon, die Ewigkeit.
aerated [ˈɛəreɪtɪd], *adj.* kohlensauer; *– water*, kohlensaures Wasser.
aerial [ˈɛərɪəl], 1. *s.* die Antenne (*Rad.*); *directional –*, die Richtantenne. 2. *adj.* luftig; atmosphärisch; in der Luft; (*fig.*) ätherisch, wesenslos; *– camera*, die Fliegerkamera; *– combat*, der Luftkampf; *– defence*, der Luftschutz; *– escort*, Begleitflugzeuge (*pl.*); *– navigation*, die Luft(schif(f))fahrt; *– photograph*, die Luftaufnahme; *– survey*, die Luftvermessung; *– transport*, der Lufttransport; *– warfare*, der Luftkrieg.
aerie [ˈɛərɪ], *s.* der (Adler)Horst, das Nest eines Raubvogels; erhöhter Standpunkt *or* Wohnort; junge Brut.
aero– [ˈɛəro], *prefix*, Aero–, Flug–, Luft–. **–batics,** *pl.* das Kunstfliegen. **–drome,** *s.* der Flughafen, Flugplatz; der Fliegerhorst (*Mil.*). **–dynamic,** *adj.* aerodynamisch; *–dynamic centre*, der Druckpunkt (*Av.*). **–dynamics,** *s.* die Aerodynamik. **–foil,** *s.* der Flügel, die Tragfläche; *–foil section*, die Profildicke. **–lite,** *s.* der Meteorstein, Aerolith. **–meter** [–ˈrɔmətə], *s.* der Luftmesser, Dichtemesser, Dichtigkeitsmesser, die Senkwage. **–naut,** *s.* der Luftfahrer, Flieger. **–nautic(al),** *adj.* aeronautisch, Luftfahrts–. **–nautics,** *pl. used as sing.* die Luftschiffahrt, das Flugwesen. **–plane,** *s.* das Flugzeug. **–static,** *adj.* aerostatisch. **–statics,** *pl. used as sing.* die Aerostatik, Luftgleichgewichtslehre.
aeruginous [ɛˈruːdʒɪnəs], *adj.* grünspanartig.
aesthet–e [ˈɪːsθɪːt], *s.* der Ästhetiker; der ästhetisch Gebildete, Ästhet. **–ic** [–ˈθɛtɪk], *adj.* ästhetisch; Kunst–; geschmackvoll. **–icism,** die Schöngeistelei. **–ics** [ɪːsˈθɛtɪks], *s.* die Schönheitslehre, Ästhetik.
aestivat–e [ˈɛstɪveɪt, ˈɪːstɪveɪt], *v.n.* übersommern, Sommerschlaf halten. **–ion** [–ˈveɪʃən], *s.* der Sommerschlaf (*Zool.*); die Knospenlage (*Bot.*).
aetiology [ɪːtɪˈɔlədʒɪ], *s.* die Lehre von Ursachen (*Phil. & Med.*).
afar [əˈfɑː], *adv.* (*poet.*) fern, weit, entfernt; *from –*, aus weiter Ferne, weit her.
affability [æfəˈbɪlɪtɪ], *s.* die Leutseligkeit, Freundlichkeit.
affabl–e [ˈæfəbl], *adj.*; **–y,** *adv.* leutselig, freundlich (*to*, zu *or* gegen).
affair [əˈfɛə], *s.* die Angelegenheit; Sache; das Geschäft, der Handel, die Affäre; das Treffen, Gefecht (*Mil.*); *family –s*, Familienverhältnisse; *minister for foreign –s*, der Minister des Auswärtigen, Außenminister; *at the head of –s*, an der Spitze des Unternehmens; *– of honour*, die Ehrensache, das Duell; *love –*, (*coll.* –) der Liebeshandel; die Liebelei; (*coll.*) *that's your –*, das ist Ihre Sache; *as –s stand*, wie die Dinge liegen *or* stehen; *– of state*, Staatsangelegenheit; *state of –s*, die Lage der Dinge, die Sachlage.
affect [əˈfɛkt], *v.a.* 1. angreifen (*the eyes, etc.*), beeinträchtigen, schädlich wirken auf, auf (eine S.) wirken, einwirken *or* Eindruck machen, beeinflussen; (*fig.*) (be)rühren, bewegen. 2. gern haben, Gefallen finden an, mit Vorliebe tun. 3. vorgeben, (er)heucheln; tun als ob (*to do*, man tut); *that will – your health*, das wird Ihre Gesundheit angreifen; *that does not at all – my assertion*, das entkräftet meine Behauptung keineswegs; *– modesty*, Bescheidenheit heucheln. **–ation** [–ˈteɪʃən], *s.* gezwungenes Wesen, übertriebene Vorliebe (*of*, für), die Zimperlichkeit, Geziertheit, Affektiertheit, Künstelei; Heuchelei, Verstellung. **–ed,** *adj.* 1. gerührt, bewegt; beeinträchtigt, behaftet (mit), befallen, angegriffen (von). 2. geziert, gezwungen, unnatürlich, affektiert; verstellt, erheuchelt; gesinnt, geneigt; *a fashion –ed by silly girls*, eine Mode beliebt bei albernen Backfischen; *–ed style*, gekünstelte Art; *we were –ed by the decision*, durch die Entscheidung wurden wir betroffen. **–edly,** *adv.* gezwungen, geziert, affektiert. **–ing,** *adj.* rührend, ergreifend. **–ive,** *adj.* Affekt–, Gefühls–.
affection [əˈfɛkʃən], *s.* die Gemütsbewegung, das Gefühl, die Stimmung, der Affekt; die Neigung, Zuneigung, Liebe (*for* or *towards*, zu); Erkrankung, das Leiden, die Affektion (*Med.*); *have an – for s.o.*, eine(n) lieb haben; *set one's –s upon a p.*, sein Herz an eine(n) hängen. **–ate** [–ət], *adj.* liebevoll, zärtlich, herzlich; *your –ate cousin*, Dein Dich liebender Vetter. **–ately,** *adv.*; *yours –ately*, innigst, herzlichst *or* in Liebe dein. **–ateness,** *n.* die Zärtlichkeit.
afferent [æˈfɛrənt], *adj.* zuführend.
affiance [əˈfɑɪəns], 1. *v.a.* verloben; *–d bride*, die Verlobte. 2. *s.* die Verlobung; das Vertrauen (*in*, in (*with Acc.*)).
affidavit [æfɪˈdeɪvɪt], *s.* eidliche Erklärung, schriftliche Zeugenaussage; *make an – of*, eidlich erhärten, eidesstattlich erklären.
affiliat–e [əˈfɪlɪeɪt], *v.a.* als Mitglied aufnehmen, anschließen, angliedern (*to*, an); (*fig.*) beigesellen, zugesellen (*Dat.*); verbinden (*with*, mit); *–ed church*, die Schwesterkirche; *–e a child on a p.*, einem die Vaterschaft eines Kindes zuschreiben *or* zuschieben (*Law*); *–ed company*, die Tochtergesellschaft; *–ed institution*, die Zweiganstalt. **–ion** [–ˈeɪʃən], *s.* die Angliederung, Anschließung; Aufnahme als Mitglied; Annahme an Kindes Statt; Feststellung der Vaterschaft (*Law*).
affinity [əˈfɪnɪtɪ], *s.* die Verwandtschaft, Verschwägerung; Verbindungsfähigkeit, das Ziehvermögen, die Affinität (*Chem.*); Ähnlichkeit; *elective –*, die Wahlverwandtschaft (*Chem.*).
affirm [əˈfəːm], *v.a.* bestätigen, versichern, feierlich erklären; behaupten, bekräftigen; bejahen, bezeugen. **–ation** [æfəˈmeɪʃən], *s.* die Behauptung, Bestätigung, Versicherung, Bejahung, Bekräftigung; eidliche Erklärung. **–ative,** 1. *adj.* bejahend; positiv (*Math.*). 2. *s.* das Jawort, die Bejahung; *answer in the –ative*, bejahen; *in the –ative*, bejahend.
affix [əˈfɪks], 1. *v.a.* anheften, anhängen, aufkleben, befestigen (*to*, an); (*fig.*) (hin)zufügen, beifügen; *– one's signature*, unterschreiben; *– one's seal*, sein Siegel aufdrücken. 2. *s.* das Affix (*Gram.*), der Anhang.
afflatus [əˈfleɪtəs], *s.* die Eingebung; Begeisterung.
afflict [əˈflɪkt], *v.a.* betrüben; quälen, plagen, peinigen, kränken, heimsuchen. **–ed,** *adj.* betrübt, niedergeschlagen (*at*, über); leidend, krank (*with*, an). **–ion** [–ʃən], *s.* die Betrübnis, Niedergeschlagenheit, Trauer; das Leiden, Gebrechen; der Kummer, das Leid, die Not.
affluen–ce [ˈæfluəns], *s.* der Überfluß, Zufluß; der Reichtum. **–t** [–ənt], 1. *adj.* reichlich (fließend); wohlhabend, reich (*in*, an). 2. *s.* der Nebenfluß.
afflux [ˈæflʌks], *s.* der Zufluß, Andrang; das Herbeiströmen.
afford [əˈfɔːd], *v.a.* geben, liefern, bieten; bewilligen, gewähren, ermöglichen; (with *can*, *etc.*) sich (*Dat.*) erlauben *or* leisten, die Mittel haben, erschwingen, aufbringen; *– a good view*, einen weiten Ausblick bieten; *– satisfaction*, Befriedigung gewähren; *– a new suit*, sich einen neuen Anzug leisten.
afforest [ˈfærɪst], *v.a.* aufforsten. **–ation** [–ˈteɪʃen], *s.* die Aufforstung.
affranchise [əˈfræntʃɑɪz], *v.a.* befreien; freigeben.
affray [əˈfreɪ], *s.* die Schlägerei, das Handgemenge, Geplänkel; der Aufruhr, (*coll.*) Krawall.
affright [əˈfrɑɪt], 1. *v.a.* (*poet.*) erschrecken. 2. *s.* (*poet.*) der Schrecken.
affront [əˈfrʌnt], 1. *s.* die Beleidigung, Beschimp-

fung, der Schimpf; *swallow an –*, eine Beleidigung einstecken. 2. *v.a.* beleidigen, beschimpfen; (*fig.*) trotzen, die Stirn bieten (*Dat.*).

affusion [əf'ju:ʒən], *s.* das Begießen, Übergießen.

afield [ə'fi:ld], *adv.* im Felde; ins Feld; in die *or* der Schlacht; auf das *or* dem Schlachtfeld; *go far –*, weit hinaus gehen, in die Ferne schweifen; *look far –*, sich weit umtun *or* umschauen.

afire [ə'faɪə], *pred. adj. & adv.* in Feuer, in Flammen, brennend.

aflame [ə'fleɪm], *pred. adj. & adv. see* **afire**; (*fig.*) glänzend.

afloat [ə'floʊt], *pred. adj. & adv.* schwimmend, flott; auf See, auf dem Meere, zu Wasser, an Bord; (*fig.*) im Umlauf, in Kurs, zirkulierend; in Gang; (*C.L.*) ohne Schulden; *the rumour is –*, das Gerücht geht um; *be –*, schwimmen; *keep –*, sich über Wasser halten (*also fig.*); *set –*, in Gang setzen *or* bringen; in Umgang setzen.

afoot [ə'fʊt], *pred. adj. & adv.* zu Fuße; (*fig.*) in Bewegung, im Gange.

afore [ə'fɔ:], 1. *adv.* vorn, vorwärts (*Naut.*). 2. *prep.* vor (*Naut.*). **–mentioned,** *adj.*, **–named,** *adj.*, **–said,** *adj.* vorher erwähnt, vorgenannt, obig. **–thought,** *adj.* vorbedacht, vorsätzlich; *with malice –thought*, in böser Absicht. **–time,** *adv.* ehemals, ehedem, früher.

afraid [ə'freɪd], *pred. adj.* ängstlich, besorgt, bange, erschrocken; *be – of a th.*, sich vor einer S. fürchten, Angst haben vor einer S.; *be – that* or *lest*, fürchten daß; *be – to do* or *of doing*, sich scheuen zu tun. (*coll.*) *I am – I am late*, es tut mir leid, daß ich zu spät komme.

afresh [ə'frɛʃ], *adv.* von neuem, aufs neue, wieder, abermals.

aft [ɑ:ft], *adv.* achtern (*on board ship*), achteraus (*behind the ship*); *fore and –*, vorn und achtern; *right –*, recht achteraus.

after ['ɑ:ftə], 1. *prep.* nach (*of time*); hinter (. . . her) (*in sequence*); (= *according to*) nach, zufolge, entsprechend, gemäß; *– all*, am Ende, letzten Endes, übrigens, bei alledem, doch, schließlich, trotz, infolge; *– this fashion*, auf diese Weise; *one – another*, nacheinander; *one – the other*, einer nach dem andern; *day – day* Tag für Tag; *the day – tomorrow*, übermorgen; *the week – next*, die übernächste Woche; *– that*, darauf, hierauf; *– hours*, nach der Polizeistunde, nach Ladenschluß; (*coll.*) *what are you – ?* was machst *or* willst du da? (*coll.*) *I'll go – him*, ich will ihm nach; (*coll.*) *be – a th.*, hinter etwas her sein. 2. *adv.* hinterher; nachher, später; *shortly –*, kurz darauf; *the day –*, den Tag darauf; *the year –*, im folgenden Jahr. 3. *adj.* achter, hinter (*Naut.*); folgend, später; *– ages*, die Nachwelt; *in – years*, in späteren Jahren, im späteren Leben. 4. *conj.* nachdem; *– having said so, he went away*, nachdem er dies gesagt hatte, ging er fort. **–birth,** *s.* die Nachgeburt. **– -care,** *s.* die Fürsorge nach der Entlassung. **– -compartment,** *s.* der Heckraum (*Naut.*). **–damp,** *s.* die Nachschwaden (*pl.*). **– -dinner,** *adj. – -dinner nap*, der Nachmittagsschlaf; *– -dinner speech*, die Tischrede. **– -effect,** *s.* die Nachwirkung. **–glow,** *s.* das Nachglühen, Abendrot; (*fig.*) der Nachglanz. **– -grass,** *s.*, **–math,** *s.* zweite Grasernte, das Grummet; (*fig.*) die Nachwirkungen, Folgen (*pl.*). **– -hold,** *s.* der Achterladeraum. **– -life,** *s.* späteres Leben; zukünftiges Leben. **–noon,** *s.* der Nachmittag; *good –noon*, guten Tag; *in the –noon*, am Nachmittag, nachmittags; *–noon-tea*, der Fünfuhrtee. **– -pains,** *pl.* die Nachwehen. **– -part,** *s.* das Hinterteil (*Naut.*). **–piece,** *s.* das Nachstück (*Theat.*). **– sail,** das Hintersegel. **– season,** *s.* stille Zeit (*C.L.*). **– -sight bill,** *s.* der Zeitsichtwechsel, Vistawechsel (*C.L.*). **– -taste.** *s.* der Nachgeschmack. **–thought,** *s.* nachträglicher Einfall. **– -times,** *pl.* die Folgezeit. **– -treatment,** *s.* die Nachbehandlung, Nachkur **–wards,** *adv.* später, nachher, hernach, darauf, in der Folge.

again [ə'geɪn, ə'gɛn], 1. *adv.* wieder, wiederum, schon wieder, noch einmal, von neuem; *– and –*, *time and –*, immer wieder; *ever and –*, see *now and –*; *as much –*, noch einmal soviel; *now and –*, ab und zu, dann und wann. 2. *conj.* ferner, außerdem.

against [ə'geɪnst], *prep.* gegen, wider; an, bei; *– the grain*, gegen den Strich, wider Willen, ungern; *a crime – the state*, ein Verbrechen gegen den Staat; *it hangs – the wall*, es hängt an der Wand; *– my arrival*, auf mein Kommen; (*Prov.*) *– death there is no remedy*, gegen den Tod ist kein Kraut gewachsen; *over –*, nahe an, gegenüber. (*coll*) *be up – it*, in Schwierigkeit sein; (*coll.*) *run up – a person*, einen zufällig treffen.

agape [ə'geɪp], *adj. & adv.* gaffend, mit offnem Munde.

agaric ['ægərɪk], *s.* der Blätterpilz, Blätterschwamm.

agate ['ægət], *s.* der Achat.

age [eɪdʒ], 1. *s.* (*a*) das Alter, Lebensalter; die Reife, Volljährigkeit; *old –*, das hohe Alter, Greisenalter; *old- -pension*, die Altersrente; *be of –*, volljährig *or* mündig sein; *come of –*, mündig werden; *under –*, minderjährig, unmündig; *at an early –*, frühzeitig; *at the – of 16*, im Alter von 16 Jahren; *6 years of –*, 6 Jahre alt; *he is my –*, er ist so alt wie ich, er ist in meinem Alter. (*b*) das Zeitalter, Menschenalter, die Generation; (*coll.*) lange Zeit, eine Ewigkeit; *down the –s*, durch die Jahrhunderte hindurch; *the – of Goethe*, das Zeitalter Goethes; *the Ice –*, die Eiszeit. 2. *v.n.* altern, alt werden. 3. *v.a* alt machen, ausreifen. **–d,** 1. *p.p.* [–d] alt, im Alter von. 2. *adj.* [–ɪd] alt, bejahrt, betagt; *the –d*, die Bejahrten. **–less,** *adj.* zeitlos. **– -limit,** *s.* die Altersgrenze. **– -old,** *adj.* uralt. **–s,** *pl.* (*coll.*) *wait for –s*, eine Ewigkeit warten; *the Middle –s*, das Mittelalter; *–s yet unborn*, noch ungeborene Geschlechter; *former –s*, frühere Zeiten.

agenc–y ['eɪdʒənsɪ], *s.* die Wirkung, Wirksamkeit, Tätigkeit; (*C.L.*) Vertretung, Vermittlung, Agentur, Vermittlungsstelle; *–y business*, das Kommissionsgeschäft; *by the –y of*, mit Hilfe von, vermittels (*with Gen.*).

agenda [ə'dʒɛndə], die Tagesordnung; das Notizbuch.

agent ['eɪdʒənt], *s.* der *or* die Handelnde; die Ursache, das Werkzeug; (*Chem*) das Agens; wirkende Kraft; der Agent, Vertreter, Vermittler; Geschäftsträger, Gutsverwalter, Gutsinspektor; (*C.L.*) Kommissionär; *physical –s*, Naturkräfte.

agglomerat–e [ə'glɒməreɪt], 1. *v.a.* (*& n.* sich) zusammenballen, häufen. [–ət], 2. *adj.* zusammengeballt, aufgehäuft. 3. *s.* das Agglomerat (*Geol.*). **–ion** [–'reɪʃən], *s.* die Ansammlung, Anhäufung; (*coll.*) das Durcheinander.

agglutinat–e [ə'glu:tɪneɪt], 1. *v.a.* zusammenkleben, verbinden; **agglutinieren** (*Med.*, *Gram.*). 2. *v.n.* sich verbinden. 3. *adj.* zusammengeklebt, verbunden; agglutinierend (*Gram.*). **–ion** [–'neɪʃən], *s.* das Zusammenkleben, Festkleben, die Verklebung; Agglutination (*Gram.*). **–ive,** *adj.* zusammenklebend; agglutinierend (*Gram.*).

aggrand–ize, –ise ['ægrəndaɪz], *v.a.* vergrößern, erweitern (*power, etc.*); (*fig.*) erhöhen, erheben, verherrlichen. **–izement** [ə'grændɪzmənt], *s.* die Vergrößerung, Erweiterung, Erhöhung, Zunahme, Beförderung.

aggravat–e ['ægrəveɪt], *v.a.* erschweren, verschlimmern; (*coll.*) ärgern, reizen. **–ing,** *adj.* erschwerend; (*coll.*) ärgerlich, verdrießlich. **–ion** [–'veɪʃən], *s.* die Erschwerung, Verschlimmerung; (*coll.*) der Ärger, die Erbitterung.

aggregat–e ['ægrɪgeɪt], 1. *v.a.* aufhäufen, verbinden, vereinigen. 2. *v.n.* sich anhäufen, sich belaufen (*to*, auf (*Acc.*)). [–gət], 3. *adj.* angehäuft, vereint, gesamt; vereinigt (*Zool.*); aggregiert (*Bot.*); zusammengesetzt (*Geol.*); *–e amount*, der Gesamtbetrag. 4. *s.* das Aggregat, die Anhäufung, Masse, Menge, Summe; *in the –e*, im ganzen, insgesamt, als Ganzes. **–ion** [–'geɪʃən], *s.* die Ansammlung, Anhäufung.

aggress–ion [ə'grɛʃən], *s.* der Angriff, Überfall. **–ive** [–sɪv], *adj.* angreifend, kampflustig, aggressiv; *take the –ive*, aggressiv werden; *–ive war*, der Angriffskrieg. **–iveness,** *s.* die Angriffslust. **–or,** *s.* der Angreifer.

aggrieve [ə'gri:v], *v.a.* kränken, betrüben; *feel –d*, sich gekränkt fühlen.

aghast [ə'gɑ:st], *adj.* entsetzt, bestürzt (*at*, über).

agil–e ['ædʒaɪl], *adj.* beweglich, behend(e), flink,

hurtig, gelenkig. **-ity** [əˈdʒɪlɪtɪ], *s.* die Behendigkeit, Beweglichkeit.
agio [ˈædʒɪoʊ], *s.* (*C.L.*) das Aufgeld, Agio. **-tage** [-tɪdʒ] *s.* (*C.L.*) das Wechselgeschäft, die Agiotage.
agitat-e [ˈædʒɪteɪt], 1. *v.a.* bewegen, in Bewegung bringen, schütteln, aufrühren; erregen, aufregen, beunruhigen, stören; erörtern, verhandeln, zur Diskussion stellen, debattieren (*a question*). 2. *v.n.* wühlen, agitieren (*for*, für). **-ion** [-ˈteɪʃən], *s.* die Bewegung, das Schütteln; die Erschütterung, Erregung, Aufregung; Gemütsbewegung; Unruhe, der Aufruhr, die Agitation; Erörterung. **-or,** *s.* der Aufwiegler, Agitator, Hetzredner.
aglow [əˈgloʊ], *adv.* glühend, gerötet; (*fig.*) erregt (*with*, von *or* vor (*Dat.*)).
agnate [ˈægneɪt], *adj.* väterlicherseits verwandt, agnatisch. **-s,** *pl.* die Agnaten, Verwandten väterlicherseits.
agnostic [ægˈnɔstɪk], 1. *adj.* agnostisch. 2. *s.* der Agnostiker. **-ism** [-tɪsɪzm], *s.* der Agnostizismus.
ago [əˈgoʊ], *adv.*; *a year* –, vor einem Jahre; *a little while* –, vor kurzem; *some time* –, vor einiger Zeit; *long* –, lange her, vor langer Zeit; *not long* –, vor kurzem, vor kurzer Zeit; *how long – is that?* wie lange ist das her? *no longer – than yesterday*, erst gestern noch *or* erst noch gestern; *it is but a few days – since* . . ., es ist erst ein paar Tage her, daß . . .
agog [əˈgɔg], *pred. adj.* & *adv.* (*coll.*) neugierig, erpicht (*about* or *for*, auf (*Acc.*)); *set a p.* –, jemandes Neugierde erregen.
agon-ize, -ise [ˈægənaɪz], 1. *v.a.* quälen, martern. 2. *v.n.* mit dem Tode ringen *or* kämpfen, Qual erleiden. **-izing,** *adj.* qualvoll. **-y** [ˈægənɪ], *s.* der Todeskampf; die Pein; *-y of mind*, die Seelenangst, Seelenqual; (*coll.*) *-y column*, die Seufzerspalte.
agoraphobia [ægərəˈfoʊbɪə], *s.* die Platzangst (*Med.*).
agrarian [əˈgrɛərɪən], *adj.* agrarisch, Agrar-, landwirtschaftlich; – *law*, das Agrargesetz, Ackergesetz; – *party*, die Bauernpartei; – *question*, die Landfrage.
agree [əˈgrɪ:], *v.n.* übereinstimmen, zusammenpassen; übereinkommen, einig werden, sich einigen (*about* or *on*, über (*Acc.*)); sich vertragen, miteinander in Eintracht leben; (= *suit*) stimmen, passen (zu); – *to a th.*, etwas annehmen *or* genehmigen, auf eine S. eingehen, einer S. zustimmen *or* beipflichten; – *on* or *upon a th.*, etwas vereinbaren, sich über eine S. verständigen, über eine S. einig werden, einwilligen in eine S., sich einigen auf eine S.; *as -d upon*, wie vereinbart *or* verabredet; *I have -d to act*, ich habe mich bereit erklärt zu handeln; *let us – to differ*, streiten wir nicht mehr darüber; – *with*, einig sein *or* übereinstimmen mit (*also Gram.*), (*of food*) bekommen (*Dat.*); *wine does not – with me*, Wein bekommt mir nicht, ich kann keinen Wein vertragen; *they all -d that*, sie vereinbarten, daß . . . *or* kamen alle überein, daß; *they are -d*, sie sind einig; *it is -d that*, man ist sich einig daß; *-d!* abgemacht! **-able,** *adj.*, **-ably,** *adv.* liebenswürdig; angenehm (*to a p.*, einem *or* für einen), gefällig (einem); *I am -able to it*, ich gehe darauf ein, ich bin damit einverstanden; (*coll.*) *I am -able*, es ist mir recht. **-ableness,** *s.* die Freundlichkeit, Annehmlichkeit. **-ment,** *s.* die Übereinstimmung (*to* or *with*, mit) (*with*: *also Gram.*), Zustimmung (*to*, zu), Vereinbarung, Verständigung, das Übereinkommen, Abkommen, der Vertrag; Einklang, die Eintracht; *come to an -ment*, ein Übereinkommen treffen, sich verständigen; *by mutual -ment*, durch gütliches Abkommen (über eine S.); *be in -ment*, übereinstimmen; *make an -ment*, übereinkommen.
agricultur-al [ægrɪˈkʌltʃərəl], *adj.* landwirtschaftlich, Landwirtschafts-, Land-, Ackerbau-; *-al labourer*, der Landarbeiter; *-al wages*, ländliche Arbeitslöhne. **-alist** [-əlɪst], *s.* der Landwirt. **-e** [ˈægrɪkʌltʃə], *s.* die Landwirtschaft; *Ministry of -e*, das Landwirtschaftsministerium. **-ist,** *s. see* **-alist.**
agronomy [əˈgrɔnəmɪ], *s.* die Ackerbaukunde.
aground [əˈgraʊnd], *adv.* & *pred. adj.* gestrandet (*Naut.*); *run* –, auflaufen, stranden, auf Strand *or* an Grund laufen; *run a ship* –, ein Schiff auf Strand *or* an Grund setzen.
agu-e [ˈeɪgjʊ:], *s.* das Wechselfieber, der Fieberfrost, Schüttelfrost; das Zittern, Beben; *-e fit*, der Fieberanfall. **-ish,** *adj.* fieberhaft; kalt, frostig.
ah [ɑ:], *int.* ah! ha! ei! ach! **-a** [ɑˈhɑ:], *int.* aha! (*Scots coll.*) ja.
ahead [əˈhɛd], *pred. adj.* & *adv.* vorwärts, voraus, voran, vorn, nach vorn zu; *straight* –, geradeaus; *go on* –, vorausgehen; *full steam* –, Volldampf voraus; *right* –, recht voraus (*Naut.*); *wind* –, vorlicher Wind (*Naut.*).
ahoy [əˈhɔɪ], *int.* ahoi! ho! (*Naut.*).
aid [eɪd], 1. *s.* die Hilfe, der Beistand; das Hilfsmittel; *by* or *with the – of*, mit Hilfe (*with Gen.*); *come to a p.'s* –, einem zu Hilfe kommen; *give – to*, unterstützen; *in – of*, zum Besten, zugunsten (*with Gen.*). 2. *v.a.* helfen, beistehen (*Dat.*), unterstützen (*Acc.*), fördern (*digestion, etc.*); – *and abet*, Vorschub *or* Beistand leisten (*Dat.*) (*Law*). **-er,** *s.* der Gehilfe, Helfer, Beistand; *-er and abettor*, der Helfershelfer (*Law*).
aide-de-camp [ˈeɪddəˈkɑ̃:], *s.* der Adjutant (eines Generals).
aigrette [ˈeɪgrɛt], *s.* der Federbusch, Reiherbusch; die Reiherfeder; weißer Reihe (*Orn.*).
aiguillette [eɪgwɪˈlɛt], *s.* Schnüre (*f.pl.*), die Achselschnur (*Mil.*).
ail [eɪl], 1. *v.n.* unwohl *or* unpäßlich sein. 2. *v.imp.* weh tun, schmerzen; *what -s him?* was fehlt ihm? **-ing,** *pr.p.* & *adj.* unwohl, leidend, kränklich. **-ment,** *s.* das Leiden, die Unpäßlichkeit.
aileron [[ˈeɪlərən], *s.* das Querruder (*Av.*).
aim [eɪm], 1. *s.* die Richtung; das Ziel; (*fig.*) der Zweck, die Absicht, das Vorhaben; *take – at a th.*, zielen auf eine S. *or* nach einer S.; *miss one's* –, das Ziel verfehlen, fehlschießen; seinen Zweck verfehlen. 2. *v.n.* zielen (*at*, nach *or* (*fig.*) auf (*with Acc.*)); streben (*at* or *for*, nach); – *to do s.th.*, etwas erstreben; *that was -ed at me*, das galt mir *or* war auf mich abgesehen; *he -s too high*, er spannt die Saiten zu hoch, er steckt sich (*Dat.*) ein zu hohes Ziel. 3. *v.a.* (*a weapon, blow, etc.*) richten (*at*, auf). **-less,** *adj.* ohne Ziel, ziellos, zwecklos.
air [ɛə], 1. *s.* (*a*) die Luft; der Luftzug; (*b*) die Melodie, Weise, Arie, das Lied (*Mus.*); (*c*) das Aussehen, die Miene, der Anschein; *by* –, per Flugzeug; (*fig.*) *beat the* –, sich erfolglos bemühen, Lufthiebe hauen; (*fig.*) *in the* –, unsicher, im Ungewissen; *there 's s.th. in the* –, es liegt etwas in der Luft; *castles in the* –, Luftschlösser (*n.pl.*); *war in the* –, der Luftkrieg; *in the open* –, im Freien, unter freiem Himmel, an der frischen Luft; *open-- school*, die Freiluftschule, Waldschule; *open- – theatre*, die Freilichtbühne; *take the* –, (frische) Luft schöpfen; abfliegen, aufsteigen (*Av.*); *go off the* –, die Sendung einstellen (*Rad.*); *on the* –, im *or* durch Rundfunk; *be on the* –, senden (*Rad.*); *put on the* –, im Radio übertragen; *without a breath of* –, ohne ein Lüftchen, ohne daß sich ein Lüftchen regt; – *of assurance*, dreistes Betragen; *there is an – of sadness about him*, er sieht so traurig aus; *Secretary of State for* –, der Luftfahrtminister; *give o.s. -s*, vornehm tun, sich in die Brust werfen; *-s* (*and graces*), vornehmes Getue. 2. *v.a.* lüften, an die Luft bringen, trocknen; (*fig.*) bekanntmachen, an die Öffentlichkeit bringen; sich groß tun mit. **--base,** *s.* der Fliegerstützpunkt. **--bladder,** *s.* die Luftblase; Schwimmblase (*Icht.*). **-borne troops**, Luftlandetruppen. **– bubble,** *s.* die Luftblase. **--conditioning,** *s.* die Klimaanlage. **-craft,** *s.* & (*usually pl.*) das Luftfahrzeug. **-craft-carrier,** *s.* der Flugzeugträger, das Flugzeugmutterschiff. **-crew,** *s.* fliegendes Personal. **– current,** *s.* der Luftzug, die Zugluft; Luftströmung. **– exhaust,** *s.* die Abluft. **-flow,** der Luftstrom. **--force,** die Luftflotte, die Luftstreitkräfte (*pl.*). **-frame,** *s.* die Zelle, das Gerippe (*of aircraft*). **-graph letter,** *s.* der Photobrief. **-gun,** *s.* das Luftgewehr, die Windbüchse. **--gunner,** *s.* der Bordschütze. **--hole,** *s.* das Luftloch (*Av.*); die Wetterleitung (*Min.*); das Zugloch (*Arch.*). **-iness,** *s.* die Luftigkeit; Leichtigkeit; (*fig.*) Leichtfertigkeit, Munterkeit, Lebhaftigkeit. **-ing,** *s.* das Lüften, die Lüftung, das Trocknen; der Spaziergang, Spazierritt, die Spazierfahrt. **--jacket,** *s.* die Schwimmweste.

--lock, *s.* der Luftabschluß. **-line,** *s.* die Luftverkehrslinie, Flugstrecke. **--liner,** *s.* das Verkehrsflugzeug. **-mail,** die Luftpost, Flugpost. **-man,** *s.* der Flieger. **--mechanic,** *s.* der Bordmonteur. **--mindedness,** *s.* die Flugbegeisterung. **- ministry,** das Luftfahrtministerium. **-plane,** *s.* das Flugzeug. **--pocket,** *s.* das Luftloch, die Fallbö (*Av.*). **-port,** *s.* der Flughafen. **--pump,** *s.* die Luftpumpe. **--raid,** der Fliegerangriff. **--raid precautions,** der Luftschutz. **--raid shelter,** der Luftschutzbunker, -raum, -keller. **--raid warden,** der Luftschutzwart. **- route,** der Luftweg (*Av.*). **-screw,** *s.* die Luftschraube, der Propeller. **--shaft,** *s.* der Wetterschacht. **-ship,** *s.* das Luftschiff. **--sick,** *adj* luftkrank. **- speed,** die Eigengeschwindigkeit. **--speed indicator,** der Fahrtmesser. **- supply,** die Zuluft. **-tight,** *adj.* luftdicht, hermetisch. **--tube,** *s.* die Luftröhre, der Luftschlauch. **--vessel,** *s.* das Luftgefäß (*Bot., Zool.*). **-way,** *s.* der Wetterschacht (*Min.*); die Luftverkehrslinie, Flugstrecke. **-woman,** *s.* die Fliegerin. **-worthy,** *adj.* lufttüchtig. **-y,** *adj.* luftig; leicht, zierlich zart, ätherisch; nichtig, eitel; sorglos, leichtfertig, lebhaft, munter.

aisle [ɑɪl], *s.* das Seitenschiff, der Chorgang (*in a church*); die Schneise (*in a forest*).

aitch [eɪtʃ], *s.* der Buchstabe h; *drop one's -es,* das h (im Anlaut) nicht aussprechen. **--bone,** das Lendenstück.

ajar [əˈdʒɑ:], *adv* halb offen, angelehnt.

akimbo [əˈkɪmboʊ], *adv.*; *with arms -,* die Arme in die Seiten gestemmt.

akin [əˈkɪn], *adj.* verwandt (*to,* mit); ähnlich (*to* (*Dat.*)).

alabaster [ælәbɑ:stə], 1. *s.* der Alabaster. 2. *adj.* alabastern; (*fig.*) schimmernd weiß.

alack [əˈlæk], *int.* (*archaic*) o weh! ach! **--a-day,** *int.* (*archaic*) ach Gott!

alacrity [əˈlækrɪtɪ], *s.* die Munterkeit, Lebhaftigkeit; Bereitwilligkeit, Dienstfertigkeit.

alarm [əˈlɑ:m], 1. *s.* der Alarm (*Mil.*); Alarmruf. Warnungsruf, die Warnung; der Schreck, die Unruhe, Bestürzung; der Wecker (*in a clock*); der Appell (*Fenc.*); *cause -,* Unruhe erregen; *false -,* blinder Alarm; *give* or *raise the -,* Lärm schlagen, das Alarmzeichen geben; *take -,* in Angst geraten, unsicher *or* unruhig werden (*at,* über). 2. *v.a.* Lärm blasen *or* schlagen; erschrecken, in Furcht setzen, beunruhigen, in Aufregung versetzen; aufschrecken, alarmieren. **--bell,** *s.* die Sturmglocke. **--clock,** *s.* der Wecker, die Weckuhr. **- cord,** *s.* die Notleine. **-ing,** *adj.* beunruhigend, beängstigend. **-ist,** 1. *s.* der Bangemacher, Schwarzseher. 2. *adj.* beunruhigend. **--post,** *s.* der Sammelplatz (*Mil.*).

alarum [əˈlɑ:rəm], (*archaic*) *see* **alarm** 1; die Alarmglocke, das Läutwerk.

alas [əˈlɑ:s], *int.* leider! ach! o weh! *- the day!* o Unglückstag!

alb [ælb], *s.* das Chorhemd, Priestergewand.

albacore [ˈælbəkɔ:], *s.* der Thunfisch.

albatross [ˈælbətrɔs], *s.* der Albatros, Sturmvogel.

albeit [ɔ:lˈbɪ:ɪt], *conj.* (also *- that*) obgleich, obwohl, ungeachtet, wiewohl.

albin-ism [ˈælbɪnɪzm], *s.* der Albinismus. **-o** [ælˈbɪ:noʊ], *s.* der Albino.

album [ˈælbəm], *s.* das Stammbuch, Album; (*Amer.*) Fremdenbuch.

albumen [ælˈbjʊ:mɪn], *s.* der Eiweißstoff, das Weiße des Eies.

albumin-ate [ælˈbjʊ:mɪnət], *s.* die Eiweißverbindung. **-ous** [-nəs], *adj.* eiweißhaltig.

alburnum [ælˈbə:rnəm], *s.* der Splint, das Splintholz.

alchem-ical [ælˈkɛmɪkl], *adj.* alchimistisch. **-ist** [ˈælkɪmɪst], *s.* der Alchimist. **-y** [ˈælkɪmɪ], *s.* die Alchimie.

alcohol [ˈælkəhɔl], *s.* der Alkohol, Spiritus, Weingeist. **-ic** [-ˈhɔlɪk], 1. *adj.* alkoholisch; *non--ic,* alkoholfrei; *-ic liquor,* geistige Getränke. 2. *s.* der Alkoholiker. **-ism** [-ɪzm], *s.* der Alkoholismus, die Trunksucht; die Alkoholvergiftung. **-ization** [-həlɑɪˈzeɪʃən], *s.* die Spiritusrektifikation; die Sättigung mit Alkohol. **-ometer** [-həlˈɔmətə], *s.* der Alkoholometer.

alcove [ˈælkoʊv], *s.* der Alkoven; die Nische; Laube.

aldehyde [ˈældɪhɑɪd], *s.* der Aldehyd (*Chem.*).

alder [ˈɔ:ldə], 1. *s.* die Erle. 2. *adj.* erlen.

alderman [ˈɔ:ldəmən], *s.* der Stadtrat, Ratsherr. **-ic** [-ˈmænɪk], *adj.* ratsherrlich; (*fig.*) würdevoll.

ale [eɪl], *s.* englisches Bier, das Ale; *pale -,* helles Bier. **--bench,** die Bierbank. **--house,** *s.* das Bierhaus, die Schenke. **--house keeper,** der Schenkwirt.

alee [əˈlɪ:], *adv.* leewärts, in Lee, unter dem Winde (*Naut.*).

alembic [əˈlɛmbɪk], *s.* der Destillierkolben, Stehkolben.

alert [əˈlə:t], 1. *adj.* wachsam, vorsichtig; munter, flink; *on the -,* auf der Hut. 2. *s.* die Alarmbereitschaft; der Alarmruf; *air-raid -,* der Fliegeralarm. **-ness,** *s.* die Wachsamkeit, Vorsicht; Munterkeit, Flinkheit.

alexandrine [ælɪgˈzændrɑɪn], *s.* der Alexandriner (*Metr.*).

alfresco [ælˈfrɛskoʊ], *adv. & attr. adj.* im Freien.

algae [ˈældʒɪ:], *pl.* die Algen, das Seegras.

algebra [ˈældʒɪbrə], *s.* die Algebra, Buchstabenrechnung. **-ic(al)** [-ˈbreɪɪk(l)], *adj.* algebraisch. **-ist** [-breɪɪst], *s.* der Algebraiker.

algid [ˈældjɪd], *adj.* kalt, kühl (*Med.*). **-ity** [ælˈdʒɪdɪtɪ], *s.* die Kühle, Kälte.

alias [ˈeɪlɪəs], 1. *adv.* anders, sonst (. . . genannt). 2. *s.* angenommener Name; *under an -,* unter falschem Namen.

alibi [ˈælɪbɑɪ], *s.* das Alibi (*Law*); *establish* or *prove an -,* sein Alibi beibringen (*Law*).

alien [ˈeɪljən], 1. *adj.* fremd, ausländisch; unangemessen (*to,* für *or* (*Dat.*)); *it is - to my purpose,* es entspricht nicht meiner Absicht *or* ist meiner Absicht zuwider. 2. *s.* der (die) Ausländer(in), Fremde; *-s' act,* das Einwanderungsgesetz; *undesirable -,* lästiger Ausländer. **-able** [-nəbl], *adj.* übertragbar, veräußerlich. **-ate** [-neɪt], *v.a.* übertragen, veräußern (*property*); entfremden (*from a p.,* einem); *-ate a p.,* sich (*Dat.*) einem entfremden. **-ation** [-ˈneɪʃən], *s.* die Übertragung, Veräußerung; Entfremdung (*from,* von); *mental -ation, -ation of mind,* die Geistesgestörtheit. **-ator** [-neɪtə], *s.* der Übertrager, Veräußerer (*Law*). **-ist** [-nɪst], *s.* der Psychiater, Irrenarzt.

[1]**alight** [əˈlɑɪt], *v.n.* sich niederlassen, sich setzen (*on,* auf); niedergehen, landen, wassern (*Av.*); absteigen (von), aussteigen (aus); (*fig.*) *- on;* stoßen auf.

[2]**alight,** *pred. adj.* in Flammen, brennend; (*fig.*) erleuchtet.

align, aline [əˈlɑɪn], 1. *v.a.* in eine gerade Linie bringen; abmessen, abstecken; (aus)richten (*Artil.*); (*fig.*) *- o.s. with,* sich anschließen an. 2. *v.n.* sich richten, eine Linie bilden (*with,* mit). **-ment,** *s.* das Ausrichten, Abmessen, Abstecken; die Richtung, aufgestellte Linie, Verlängerungslinie; Absteck-linie, Trasse (*Surv.*); *out of -ment,* nicht gerade.

alike [əˈlɑɪk], 1. *adj.* gleich, ähnlich. 2. *adv.* gleich, in gleicher Weise, ebenso; *for you and me* - or - *for you and me,* sowohl für dich wie mich.

aliment [ˈælɪmənt], *s.* die Nahrung, Speise, das Futter, Nahrungsmittel, der Unterhalt. **-al** [-ˈmɛntl], *adj.* nährend, nahrhaft. **-ary** [-ˈmɛntərɪ], *adj.* nährend, Nahrungs-, Ernährungs-; *-ary canal,* der Verdauungskanal. **-ation** [-mɛnˈteɪʃən], *s.* die Ernährung, Beköstigung, der Unterhalt; die Ernährungsart.

alimony [ˈælɪmənɪ], *s.* der Unterhaltsbeitrag; (*pl.*) Alimente.

aliqu-ant [ˈælɪkwənt], *adj.* nicht aufgehend (*Arith.*). **-ot** [-kwɔt], *adj.* (ohne Rest) aufgehend (*Arith.*).

alive [əˈlɑɪv], *adj.* (*usually pred.*) lebend, lebendig, am Leben; lebhaft, munter; in voller Kraft; unter Spannung (*Elec.*); *- to,* empfänglich für; *be - to a th.,* sich einer S. bewußt sein, etwas würdigen; (*coll.*) *look - !* beeile dich! mach nur zu! *he is still -,* er lebt noch, er ist noch am Leben; *there's not a man - who can . . .,* niemand auf der Welt *or* kein Sterblicher kann; *be - with,* wimmeln von.

alizarin [əˈlɪzərɪn], *s.* das Krapprot.

alkal-i [ˈælkəlɑɪ], *s.* das Alkali, Laugensalz. **-ify,**

[–ˈkælifɑɪ], *v.a.* & *n.* (sich) in Alkali verwandeln. **–ine,** *adj.* laugensalzig; *–ine salts,* alkalische Salze. **–oid,** 1. *adj.* alkaliartig, laugenhaft. 2. *s.* das Alkaloid.

all [ɔ:l], **1.** *adj.* & *pron.* ganz, alle (*pl.*), sämtliche (*pl.*), all, jed-er, –es, –e, *etc.*, alles; (*a*) (*before nouns*) *lose – contact,* jede Art von Kontakt verlieren; *– day,* den ganzen Tag; *– Europe,* ganz Europa; *– kinds* or *sorts of,* allerlei; *– my life,* mein ganzes Leben lang; *– men,* alle Menschen; *– good men,* alle guten Menschen; *– the men who,* alle (die) Männer, die; *he is – things to – men,* er ist allen alles; *– the world,* die ganze Welt, alle Welt; *– the world over,* in der ganzen Welt; (*b*) *– and everyone, one and –,* alle miteinander, alle zusammen; *– in –,* im ganzen; *– but,* beinahe, fast; *each and – of,* jeder einzelne von; *it's – one to me,* es ist mir ganz gleich *or* einerlei, es ist mir alles eins; *– over,* ganz vorbei, fertig *or* aus; *– and sundry,* all und jeder; *– of us,* wir alle; *that is –,* das ist alles; das genügt, genug, (*coll.*) damit basta; *– that,* alles was; *and – that,* und dergleichen; *if that is –,* wenn's weiter nichts ist; (*coll.*) *that's – very well but,* das ist alles ganz schön aber; (*c*) (*after prepositions*) *above –,* vor allem, vor allen Dingen; *after –,* bei alledem, trotz allem, schließlich, am Ende, übrigens; *at –,* überhaupt, durchaus; *not at –,* keineswegs, ganz und gar nicht; *nothing at –,* gar nichts; *nowhere at –,* nirgends; *at – events,* auf alle Fälle; *by – means,* gewiß, auf jeden Fall; *for – I know,* soviel ich weiß; *for good and –,* gänzlich, für immer; *once for –,* ein für allemal; *for – that,* dessenungeachtet, trotzdem; (*coll.*) *for – the world* (*like*), durchaus *or* gerade (wie); (*coll.*) *not for – the world,* nicht um alles in der Welt; *he looked for – the world as if,* er sah gerade so aus, als ob; *in –,* im ganzen, in allem; *on – fours,* auf allen vieren; *till – hours of the night,* sehr spät, lange; *to – intents and purposes,* in jeder Hinsicht; *with – my heart,* von ganzem Herzen; *with – speed,* in aller Eile. **2.** *adv.* (*when compounded with adjs. see compounds below*) ganz, gar, gänzlich, völlig; *– along,* die ganze Zeit über; *– at once,* auf einmal, plötzlich; *– the better,* umso besser, desto besser; *be – ears,* ganz Ohr sein; *– over the town,* durch die ganze Stadt, in der ganzen Stadt; *that's Richard – over,* das ist ganz Richard *or* Richard, wie er leibt und lebt; *have pains – over,* überall Schmerzen haben; *tremble – over,* am ganzen Leibe zittern; *– right!* ganz richtig! recht! gut! schön! sehr wohl! einverstanden! alles in Ordnung! *I am – right,* es geht mir gut, ich bin ganz gesund; *– round,* rings umher; *taking it – round,* ohne Unterschied, im großen und ganzen; *– the same,* nichtsdestoweniger, ganz gleich; *– the same whether . . .,* gleichgültig ob . . .; (*coll.*) *be – there,* bei Sinnen sein; (*coll.*) *not quite – there,* nicht ganz gescheit; *– too dear,* nur zu teuer; (*coll.*) *it's – up with him,* es ist aus mit ihm; *– in vain,* vergebens. **3.** *s.* das Ganze, Alles, der Gesamtbesitz; *my –,* mein Alles; *I lost my –,* ich habe all mein Hab und Gut verloren; *you are – in – to him,* Sie gelten (bei) ihm (über) alles; (*Prov.*) *–'s well that ends well,* Ende gut, alles gut. **–-absorbing,** *adj.* völlig in Anspruch nehmend. **–-admiring,** *adj.* allbewundernd. **–-bounteous, –-bountiful,** *adj.* allgütig. **–-destroying,** *adj.* alles zerstörend. **–-devouring,** *adj.* alles verschlingend. **–-efficient,** *adj.* allwirksam. **–-embracing,** *adj.* allumfassend. **–-Fools' Day,** der erste April. **–-Hallows,** das Allerheiligen. **–-in,** *adj.* alles einschließend, Gesamt–; (*sl.*) (*pred. only*) erschöpft, erledigt, geschlagen, kaput; *–-in cost,* die Gesamtkosten, Gestehungskosten; *–-in insurance,* die Versicherung gegen alle Gefahren. **–-merciful,** *adj.* allbarmherzig. **–-oblivious,** *adj.* alles vergessend. (*coll.*) **–-out,** *adj.* mit voller Stärke, mit größter Geschwindigkeit, hundertprozentig, konzentriertest; *–-out war,* der Totalkrieg. **–-red,** *adj.* rein britisch (*Tele.*). **–-round,** *adj.* vielseitig, allgemeingültig; *–-round price,* der Pauschalpreis. **– Saints' Day,** *see* **–-Hallows. – Souls,** (das Fest) Allerseelen. **–-sufficient,** *adj.* völlig genugsam. **–-sustaining,** *adj.* alles unterhaltend.

allay [əˈleɪ], *v.a.* lindern, mildern, dämpfen, mäßigen, unterdrücken, stillen, beruhigen, beschwichtigen.

allegation [æləˈgeɪʃən], *s.* (unerwiesene) Behauptung, die Angabe, Anführung.

allege [əˈlɛdʒ], *v.a.* anführen, angeben, vorbringen, aussagen, (Unerwiesenes) behaupten, versichern *or* erklären. **–d,** *p.p.* angeblich.

allegiance [əˈlɪ:dʒəns], *s.* die Untertanenpflicht, Untertanentreue, Lehnspflicht; *oath of –,* der Huldigungseid, Untertaneneid, Treueid.

allegor–ical [æləˈgɔrɪkl], *adj.* (sinn)bildlich, allegorisch. **–ize** [ˈælɪgərɑɪz], 1. *v.a.* (sinn)bildlich darstellen. 2. *v.n.* Allegorien brauchen. **–y** [ˈæləgərɪ], *s.* die Allegorie, sinnbildliche Darstellung, das Sinnbild, Gleichnis.

allegro [əˈleɪgroʊ], 1. *s.* das Allegro. 2. *adv.* allegro, lebhaft.

allelujah, alleluia [ælɪˈlu:jə], *s.* das Hallelujah, Loblied.

allevia–te [əˈlɪ:vɪeɪt], *v.a.* erleichtern, mindern, lindern, mildern. **–tion** [–ˈeɪʃən], *s.* die Erleichterung, Linderung.

alley [ˈælɪ], *s.* die Allee, der Gang; die Gasse, Seitenstraße; *blind –,* die Sackgasse; *skittle –,* die Kegelbahn.

alli–ance [əˈlɑɪəns], *s.* das Bündnis, der Bund; die Verbindung, Verwandtschaft, Verschwägerung, Gemeinschaft; *Dual –ance,* der Zweibund; *Triple –ance,* der Dreibund; *offensive and defensive –ance,* das Schutz- und Trutzbündnis; *enter into, form* or *make an –ance,* sich verbinden, ein Bündnis schließen. **–ed, –es,** *see* **ally.**

alligation [ælɪˈgeɪʃən], *s.* die Verbindung; Mischung; *the rule of –,* die Mischungs- *or* Alligationsrechnung.

alligator [ˈælɪgeɪtə], *s.* der Alligator, Kaiman.

alliterat–e [əˈlɪtəreɪt], *v.n.* alliterieren, mit demselben Buchstaben anfangen. **–ion** [–ˈreɪʃən], *s.* der Stabreim, die Alliteration. **–ive,** *adj.* stabreimend, alliterierend; *–ive poetry,* die Stabreimdichtung.

allocat–e [ˈælokeɪt], *v.a.* zuteilen, anweisen. **–ion** [–ˈkeɪʃən], *s.* die Verteilung, Zuteilung, Anweisung.

allocution [æləˈkju:ʃən], *s.* die Anrede, Ansprache.

allod–ial [əˈloʊdɪəl], *adj.* allodial, erbeigen, lehnzinsfrei; *–ial lands,* Allodialgüter. **–ium** [–dɪəm], *s.* das Allod, Freigut, freies Erbgut.

allopath [ˈælopæθ], *s.*, **–ist** [æˈlɔpəθɪst], *s.* der Allopath. **–y** [–θɪ], *s.* die Allopathie.

allot [əˈlɔt], *v.a.* anweisen, zuteilen, zumessen (*s.th. to a p.,* einem etwas); austeilen, verteilen. **–ment,** 1. *s.* der Anteil, das Los; die Zuteilung, Abtretung, Zuweisung, Verteilung, Ausgabe; Parzelle; der Schrebergarten; (*C.L.*) *on –ment,* bei Zuteilung der Aktien; *–ment holder,* der Kleingärtner.

allotropy [əˈlɔtrəpɪ], *s.* die Allotropie (*Chem.*).

allow [əˈlɑʊ], 1. *v.a.* (*a. th.*), (etwas) gestatten, (einer S.) stattgeben; (*a p. to do*), (einem) erlauben *or* gestatten (zu tun *or* daß er tut); zugeben, einräumen, gelten lassen; gewähren, gönnen, bewilligen, zukommen lassen; ansetzen, anrechnen, in Anschlag bringen (*for,* für); (*coll.*) glauben, behaupten; *I – her to go,* ich erlaube ihr zu gehen, ich erlaube *or* gestatte, daß sie geht; *they were not –ed out,* sie durften nicht ausgehen; *– me,* gestatten Sie mir bitte; *I – him £30 a year,* ich lasse ihm jährlich 30 Pfund zukommen; *he –ed 3 hours for the work,* er setzte 3 Stunden für die Arbeit an; *– me one word,* gestatten Sie mir ein Wort; *they would not – that he . . .,* sie wollten nicht zugeben *or* einräumen, daß er. . . . 2. *v.n.*; *– for,* in Betracht ziehen, Rücksicht nehmen auf (*Acc.*); *–ing for,* wenn man berücksichtigt; *his conduct –s of no excuse,* sein Betragen läßt sich nicht entschuldigen *or* läßt keine Entschuldigung zu. **–able,** *adj.* zulässig, erlaubt, rechtmäßig. **–ance,** 1. *s.* die Einräumung, Zulassung; Genehmigung, Anerkennung, Billigung; Einwilligung, Erlaubnis; ausgesetzte Summe *e.g.* das Taschengeld, die Rente, jährliches Gehalt; zugeteilte Ration; die Nachsicht, Schonung, Rücksicht(nahme) (auf (*Acc.*)); Entschädigung, Vergütung, der Zuschuß, die Zulage, der Abzug, Rabatt (*C.L.*); die Toleranz (*Tech.*); *education –ance,* die Erziehungsbeihilfe; *field –ance,* die Feldzulage (*Mil.*); *mileage –ance,* Kilometergelder (*pl.*); *monthly –ance,* das Monatsgeld, der Wechsel (*of a student*); *short –ance,* knappe Ration; *make*

–ance (for), Nachsicht üben (bei), in Anschlag bringen, in Betracht ziehen, Rücksicht nehmen (auf), zugute halten; *make s.o. an –ance*, einem eine Summe, ein Taschengeld, Monatsgeld, *etc.*, aussetzen *or* zukommen lassen. 2. *v.a.* portionsweise austeilen, rationieren *(goods)*; auf Rationen setzen *(a p.)*.

alloy [ə'lɔɪ], 1. *s.* die Legierung; das Zusatzmetall; der Feingehalt; *(fig.)* die Mischung; *– of gold*, die Goldlegierung. 2. *v.a.* legieren, mischen; *(fig.)* verschlechtern. 3. *v.n.* sich vermischen.

allspice ['ɔ:lspaɪs], *s.* der Nelkenpfeffer.

allude [ə'l(j)u:d], *v.n.* anspielen *(to*, auf *(Acc))*; sprechen *(to*, von); *the person –d to*, der– (die–)jenige, den (die) man meint, der *or* die Betreffende.

allur–e [ə'ljuə], *v.a.* anlocken, verlocken, ködern; *(fig.)* anziehen, reizen, bezaubern. **–ement,** *s.* die Lockung, Verlockung, Reizung; der Reiz, das Lockmittel, der Köder; die Anziehungskraft. **–ing,** *adj.* reizend, verlockend, verführerisch.

allusi–on [ə'l(j)u:ʒən], *s.* die Anspielung, Andeutung, Hinweisung *(to*, auf *(Acc.))*; *make an –on to*, anspielen auf; *in –on to*, anspielend auf. **–ve** [–sɪv], *adj.* anspielend *(to*, auf), verblümt. **–veness,** *s.* die Anspielung; anspielende Manier.

alluvi–al [ə'lu:vɪəl], *adj.* angeschwemmt, angespült; Alluvial– *(Geol.)*. **–on** [–vɪən], *s.* die Anschwemmung, Ablagerung; das Alluvium, die Landeszunahme durch Anschwemmung. **–um** [–vɪəm], *s. see* **–on**; *(fig.)* der Überrest, das Überbleibsel.

ally, 1. *v.a.* [ə'laɪ], verbünden, vereinigen, alliieren; *allied to* or *with*, verbündet *or* verwandt mit. 2. *s.* ['ælaɪ] der Verbündete, Bundesgenosse; *(pl.)* die Alliierten.

almanac ['ɔ:lmənæk], *s.* der Almanach, Kalender, das Jahrbuch.

almight–iness [ɔ:l'maɪtɪnɪs], *s.* die Allmacht. **–y,** 1. *adj.* allmächtig. 2. *s.* der Allmächtige.

almond ['ɑ:mənd], *s.* die Mandel; der Mandelbaum. **– –shaped,** *adj.* mandelförmig.

almoner ['ælmənə], *s.* der Almosenpfleger; Almosenier.

almost ['ɔ:lmoust], *adv.* fast, beinahe, nahezu, geradezu.

alms [ɑ:mz], *s.* *(also used as pl.)* das Almosen, die Armenhilfe, Liebesgabe, milde Gabe. **– –box,** *s.* die Almosenbüchse, Opferbüchse. **– –giver,** *s.* der Almosenspender. **– –giving,** *s.* das Almosenspenden, die Armenpflege. **– –house,** *s.* das Armenhaus, Spital. **– –people,** *pl.* die Almosenempfänger, Hausarmen.

aloe ['ælou], *s.* die Aloe *(Bot.)*. **–s,** *pl.* das Aloeholz *(B.)*; der Aloesaft *(Pharm.)*. **–tic** [ælo'ɛtɪk], *adj.* aloehaltig.

aloft [ə'lɔft], *adv.* hoch oben, droben, empor; in die *or* der Takelung *(Naut.)*; *(fig.)* nach oben, gen Himmel.

alone [ə'loun], *pred. adj. & adv.* allein; *he –*, nur *or* bloß er; *leave –*, allein lassen, verlassen; *leave* or *let a p. –*, einen in Frieden lassen; *leave* or *let a th. –*, eine Sache (bleiben) lassen; *let –*, geschweige (denn), abgesehen von *or* davon; *not – . . . but also*, nicht nur . . . sondern auch; *he is not – in it*, er ist hierin nicht der Einzige.

along [ə'lɔŋ], 1. *adv.* entlang, der Länge nach; weiter, fort, geradeaus; einher–, dahin–; *all –*, der ganzen Länge nach, überall; die ganze Zeit (hindurch), durchweg, fortwährend; *move – !* weiter! vorwärts! *come – with (me)*, komm mit (mir); *he drove –*, er fuhr dahin; *get* or *go – with you!* packe dich! fort mit dir! *go – !* geh doch! *let me go – with you*, laß mich mit dir gehen; *as we go –*, unterwegs; *take that – with you*, nimm das mit; *– with*, zugleich *or* zusammen mit, nebst, samt. 2. *prep.* entlang *(Dat. & Acc.)*; längs *(Gen.)*; an . . . vorbei; *– the road*, die Straße entlang; *– the forest*, am Walde hin; *we strolled – the river*, wir gingen den *or* am Fluß entlang. **–side,** 1. *adv.* nebenan, Seite an Seite; Bord an Bord, längsseits *(Naut.)*. 2. *prep.* längsseit(s) *(Gen.)*, neben *(Dat.)*.

aloof [ə'lu:f], *pred. adj. & adv.* fern, weitab; *hold, keep* or *stand – from*, sich fernhalten von, neutral bleiben. **–ness,** *s.* die Abgeschlossenheit.

aloud [ə'laud], *pred. adj. & adv.* laut, vernehmlich.

alp [ælp], *s.* die Alm, Alpe. **–s,** die Alpen.

alpaca [æl'pækə], *s.* das Alpaka, Pako *(Zool.)*; die Alpakawolle; der Alpakastoff.

alphabet ['ælfəbɛt], *s.* das Alphabet, Abc. **–ical** [–'bɛtɪkl], *adj.* alphabetisch

alpin–e ['ælpaɪn], *adj.* alpin(isch); Alpen–, Hochgebirgs–; *–e boots*, die Bergschuhe, Nagelschuhe; *–e club*, der Alpenklub *or* –verein; *–e dweller*, der Älpler, Alpenbewohner; *–e plant*, die Alpenpflanze; *–e rope*, das Bergseil; *–e sun*, die Höhensonne. **–ist** [–pɪnɪst], *s.* der Bergsteiger.

already [ɔ:l'rɛdɪ], *adv.* bereits, schon

also ['ɔ:lsou], *adv.* auch, ebenfalls, gleichfalls; ferner, außerdem. **– ran,** *s.* *(sl.)* einer der zurückbleibt.

altar ['ɔ:ltə], *s.* der Altar. **– –cloth,** *s.* die Altarbekleidung, Altardecke. **– –piece,** *s.* das Altargemälde. **– –screen,** *s.* der Altarschrein.

alter ['ɔ:ltə], 1. *v.a.* ändern, verändern, umändern. 2. *v.n.* anders werden, sich (ver)ändern; *it does not – the fact*, es ändert nichts an der Tatsache. **–able** [–rəbl], *adj.* veränderlich, wandelbar. **–ation** [–'reɪʃən], *s.* die Änderung *(to*, an), Veränderung; Neuerung. **–ative** [–rətɪv], *adj.* verändernd; alterierend *(Med.)*.

altercation [ɔ:ltə'keɪʃən], *s.* der Streit, Zank, Wortwechsel.

alternat–e ['ɔ:ltəneɪt], 1. *v.a.* wechselweise verrichten *or* verändern, wechseln *or* abwechseln lassen. 2. *v.n.* abwechseln; abwechselnd folgen; *–ing current*, der Wechselstrom. 3. *adj.* [ɔ:l'tə:nət], abwechselnd; wechselseitig; wechselständig *(Bot.)*; *–e angles*, Wechselwinkel; *on –e days, on each –e day*, einen Tag um den andern. **–ely,** *adv.* abwechselnd, nacheinander, bald . . ., bald . . .; wechselweise. **–ion** [–'neɪʃən], *s.* die Abwechs(e)lung, der Wechsel, die Permutation *(Math.)*; das Abwechseln (beim Chorgesang). **–ive** [ɔ:l'tə:nətɪv], 1. *s.* die Wahl (zwischen zwei Dingen); Möglichkeit, der Ausweg, die Alternative; *have no –ive*, keine Wahl haben, es bleibt *(with Dat.)* nichts anderes übrig als. 2. *adj.* abwechselnd, alternativ, einander ausschließend; *–ive target*, das Ausweichziel *(Mil.)*. **–or** ['ɔ:ltəneɪtə], *s.* die Wechselstrommaschine *(Elec.)*.

although [ɔ:l'ðou], *conj.* obgleich, obwohl, obschon, obzwar, wenn . . . schon, wenn . . . gleich, wenn.

altimeter [æl'tɪmɪtə], *s.* der Höhenmesser.

altitude ['æltɪtju:d], *s.* die Höhe; hochgelegener Ort; *take the sun's –*, die Sonnenhöhe messen.

alto ['æltou], *s.* der Alt; *– key*, der Altschlüssel; *– voice*, die Altstimme. **– –relievo,** *s.* das Hochrelief.

altogether [ɔ:ltə'gɛðə], *adv.* zusammen, im Ganzen, allesamt; gänzlich, ganz und gar, völlig, durchaus.

altruis–m ['æltruɪzm], *s.* die Selbstlosigkeit, Uneigennützigkeit. **–t,** *s.* uneigennütziger Mensch. **–tic** [–'ɪstɪk], *adj.* selbstlos, uneigennützig.

alum ['æləm], *s.* der Alaun *(Chem.)*; *– earth*, die Alaunerde. **–ina** [ə'lju:mɪnə], *s.* die Tonerde *(Chem.)*. **–inate** [–neɪt], *s.* das Aluminat, die Tonerdeverbindung. **–inium** [ælju'mɪnjəm], *s.* das Aluminium; *–inium acetate*, essigsaure Tonerde. **–inous** [ə'lju:mɪnəs], *adj.* alaunhaltig. **–inum** [æ'lu:mɪnəm], *s.* *(Amer.) see* **–inium.**

alumnus [ə'lʌmnəs], *s.* *(Amer.)* Alter Herr *(University, etc.)*.

alveol–ar [æl'vɪ:olə], *adj.* alveolar *(Anat.)*; *–ar sound*, der Alveolarlaut. **–us** [–oləs], *s.* die Bienenzelle; das Zahnfach *(Anat.)*.

always ['ɔ:lweɪz], *adv.* immer, stets, ständig, allezeit.

am [æm, əm, m *acc. to emphasis*], *first pers. sing pres. indic. of* to be; *I – to go, – I not?* ich soll gehen, nicht wahr? *I – going to see him tomorrow*, ich werde ihn morgen sehen; *I – told*, es wird mir gesagt, man sagt mir.

amain [ə'meɪn], *adv.* *(archaic)* mit voller Kraft, heftig, auf einmal.

amalgam [ə'mælgəm], *s.* das Amalgam; *(fig.)* die Mischung. **–ate,** 1. *v.a.* amalgamieren, vermischen, verschmelzen 2. *v.n.* sich vereinigen, sich zusammenschließen; *(fig.)* sich vermischen. **–ation** [–'meɪʃən], *s.* die Amalgamierung, Vermischung,

Verschmelzung; (*fig*) Vereinigung, der Zusammenschluß, die Fusion (*C.L*).
amanuensis [əmænjuˈɛnsɪs], *s.* der Sekretär, Famulus.
amaranth [ˈæmərænθ], *s.* der Amarant, das Tausendschön (*Bot.*); (*fig.*) unverwelkliche Blume. **–ine** [–ˈrænθɑɪn], *adj.* amaranten, amarantfarben; (*fig.*) unverwelklich.
amaryllis [æməˈrɪlɪs], *s.* die Belladonnalilie (*Bot.*).
amass [əˈmæs], *v.a.* (an)sammeln, (auf)häufen, zusammenscharren. **–ment,** *s.* die Anhäufung.
amateur [ˈæmətəː, –tjuə], 1. *s.* der Liebhaber (der Kunst), Amateur, Dilettant; – *rider*, der Herrenreiter; – *theatricals*, das Liebhabertheater. **–ish** [–ˈtəːrɪʃ, –tjuərɪʃ], *adj.* dilettantisch; stümperhaft. **–ishness,** *s.* die Liebhaberei, der Dilettantismus; die Stümperhaftigkeit.
amative [ˈæmətɪv], *adj.* sinnlich, verliebt. **–ness,** *s.* die Sinnlichkeit, Leidenschaftlichkeit.
amatory [ˈæmətərɪ], *adj.* erotisch, verliebt, sinnlich, Liebes–.
amaz–e [əˈmeɪz], *v.a.* erstaunen, überraschen, in höchstes Erstaunen setzen; *be –ed at a th.*, erstaunt sein *or* erstaunen über eine S. **–ement,** *s.* größtes Erstaunen, höchste Verwunderung. **–ing,** *adj.* höchst erstaunlich, wunderbar, verblüffend. **–ingly,** *adv.* erstaunlich, außerordentlich.
amazon [ˈæməzən], *s.* die Amazone; das Mannweib. **–ian** [–ˈzounjən], *adj.* amazonenhaft.
ambassad–or [æmˈbæsədə], *s.* der Botschafter, Gesandte(r), *m.* **–orial** [–ˈdɔːrɪəl], *adj.* gesandtschaftlich, Botschafts–. **–ress,** *s.* die Gemahlin des Gesandten.
amber [ˈæmbə], 1. *s.* der Bernstein. 2. *adj.* Bernstein–, bernsteinfarbig. **––seed,** *s.* die Bisamkörner (*pl.*). **––tree,** *s.* der Ambrastrauch.
ambergris [ˈæmbəgrɪs], *s.* die Ambra, der graue Amber.
ambidext–erity [æmbɪˈdɛkstɛrɪtɪ], *s.* gleiche Geschicklichkeit mit beiden Händen; (*fig.*) die Unaufrichtigkeit, Achselträgerei. **–rous** [–strəs], *adj.* beidhändig, mit beiden Händen gleich geschickt; (*fig.*) hinterhältig, achselträgerisch.
ambient [ˈæmbɪənt], *adj.* umgebend, umfließend.
ambigu–ity [æmbɪˈgjuːɪtɪ], *s.* die Zweideutigkeit; der Doppelsinn; die Ungewißheit, (*fig.*) Dunkelheit. **–ous** [–ˈbɪgjuəs], *adj.* zweideutig, doppelsinnig; (*fig.*) ungewiß, unklar, dunkel. **–ousness,** *s. see* **–ity.**
ambit [ˈæmbɪt], *s.* der Umkreis, Umfang.
ambitio–n [æmˈbɪʃən], *s.* die Ehrsucht, der Ehrgeiz (*for*, nach); Gegenstand des Ehrgeizes. **–us,** *adj.* ehrgeizig, ehrsüchtig, hochstrebend; begierig (*of*, nach); *be –us of*, streben *or* trachten nach. **–usness,** *s.* die Ruhmsucht, Ehrsucht.
amble [ˈæmbl], 1. *s.* der Paßgang. 2. *v.n.* den Paßgang gehen, im Paßgang reiten; (*fig.*) gemächlich gehen.
ambo [ˈæmbou], *s.* die Kanzel, das Lesepult (*Eccl.*).
ambrosia [æmˈbrouzɪə], *s.* die Götterspeise, Ambrosia. **–l,** *adj.* ambrosisch; (*fig.*) köstlich.
ambulance [ˈæmbjuləns], 1. *s.* das Feldlazarett, der Krankenwagen, Sanitätswagen; *motor* –, das Krankenauto. **––man,** *s.* der Krankenträger. **––station,** *s.* die Unfallstation. **––train,** *s.* der Lazarettzug.
ambula–nt [ˈæmbjulənt], *adj.* ambulant (*Med.*), umherwandernd. **–tory** [–lətərɪ], 1. *adj.* herumziehend, vorübergehend, Wander–, Geh–, beweglich. 2. *s.* der Wandelgang, gedeckter Bogengang (*Eccl.*).
ambus–cade [æmbəsˈkeɪd], 1. *s.* der Hinterhalt, das Versteck. 2. *v.a.* im Hinterhalt verstecken. **–h** [ˈæmbuʃ], *s.* 1. der Hinterhalt; *lie in –h*, im Hinterhalt liegen, auf der Lauer liegen. 2. *v.a.* aus dem Hinterhalt überfallen. 3. *v.n.* im Hinterhalt liegen, auflauern.
ameer [əˈmɪːə], *s.* der Emir.
ameliorat–e [əˈmɪːlɪəreɪt], 1. *v.a.* verbessern. 2. *v.n.* sich bessern, besser werden. **–ion** [–ˈreɪʃən], *s.* die Verbesserung. **–ive,** *adj.* (ver)bessernd.
amen [ɑːˈmɛn], 1. *int.* amen! 2. *s.* das Amen.
amenable [əˈmɪːnəbl], *adj.* willfährig, leitsam, zugänglich (*to*, für); abhängig (*to*, von), unterworfen (*to a p.* (*Dat.*)); – *to law*, verantwortlich. **–ness,** *s.* die Zugänglichkeit (*to*, für), Verantwortlichkeit (*to*, gegenüber).
amend [əˈmɛnd], 1. *v.a.* verbessern, berichtigen, ergänzen; – *one's conduct*, sein Betragen bessern. 2. *v.n.* sich bessern, besser werden. **–able,** *adj.* verbesserungsfähig. **–ment,** *s.* die Verbesserung, Besserung (*conduct*), Genesung (*health*); der Zusatzantrag, Verbesserungsantrag, Abänderungsantrag (*Parl.*); *move an –ment*, einen Zusatzantrag stellen *or* einbringen. **–s,** *s.* (*also pl.*) der Schadenersatz, die Entschädigung, Vergütung, Genugtuung; *make –s for a th.*, etwas ersetzen, wieder gutmachen; *make –s*, Schadenersatz leisten.
amenity [əˈmɪːnɪtɪ], *s.* die Annehmlichkeit, Lieblichkeit, Anmut; (*pl.*) die Vorzüge, Reize.
amerc–e [əˈməːs], *v.a.* mit einer Geldstrafe belegen, eine Geldstrafe auferlegen (*Dat.*), bestrafen. **–ement,** *s.* die Geldstrafe. **–iable,** *adj.* straffällig, strafbar.
amethyst [ˈæmɪθɪst], 1. *s.* der Amethyst. 2. *adj.* amethystartig, amethystfarben.
amiab–ility [eɪmjəˈbɪlɪtɪ], *s.* die Liebenswürdigkeit, Freundlichkeit. **–le** [ˈeɪmjəbl], *adj.* liebenswürdig, liebenswert, holdselig, leutselig, freundlich. **–leness,** *see* **–ility.**
amianthus [æmɪˈænθəs], *s.* der Amiant.
amicabl–e [ˈæmɪkəbl], *adj.* freundschaftlich, gütlich, friedlich; *–e settlement*, gütlicher Vergleich. **–eness,** *s.* die Freundlichkeit, Freundschaftlichkeit.
amice [ˈæmɪs], *s.* das Achseltuch eines Meßpriesters.
amid–(st) [əˈmɪd(st)], *prep.* mitten in, mitten unter (*Dat.*), inmitten (*Gen.*). **–ships,** *adv.* mittschiffs (*Naut.*).
amir, *s. see* **ameer.**
amiss [əˈmɪs], *pred. adj. & adv.* verkehrt, schlecht, übel, unrecht, (*coll.*) schief, nicht in Ordnung; *do* –, unrecht handeln, Übles tun; *if anything should happen* –, wenn etwas schief gehen sollte; *it would not be – for you to do, etc.*, es könnte dir nicht schaden, wenn, *etc.*; *not* –, nicht schlecht *or* übel; *nothing comes – to him*, ihm ist alles recht; *not come* –, nicht ungelegen kommen, nicht unlieb *or* unbequem sein; *nothing* –, nichts für ungut; *take* – übelnehmen.
amity [ˈæmɪtɪ], *s.* die Freundschaft, gutes Einvernehmen.
ammeter [ˈæmɪːtə], *s.* das Amperemeter, der Strommesser (*Elec.*).
ammoni–a [əˈmounɪə], *s.* das Ammoniak; *liquid –a*, der Salmiakgeist. **–ac, –acal** [–æk(l)], *adj.* Ammoniak–, ammoniakalisch; *sal –ac*, der Salmiak. **–ated** [–eɪtɪd], *adj.* mit Ammoniak gemischt. **–um** [əˈmounɪəm], *s.* das Ammonium; *–um chloride*, der Salmiak.
ammunition [æmjuˈnɪʃən], *s.* die Munition, der Kriegsvorrat. **––boots,** *pl.* die Kommißstiefel. **––bread,** *s.* das Kommißbrot. **––wagon,** *s.* der Munitionswagen.
amnesia [æmˈnɪːzɪə], *s.* die Amnesie, der Gedächtnisverlust.
amnesty [ˈæmnɛstɪ], 1. *s.* der Straferlaß, die Amnestie, Begnadigung. 2. *v.a.* begnadigen, amnestieren.
amnion [ˈæmnɪən], *s.* die Embryohülle (*Anat.*).
amoeba [əˈmɪːbə], *s.* die Amöbe.
amok [əˈmʌk], *see* **amuck.**
among(st) [əˈmʌŋ(st)], *prep.* (mitten) unter, zwischen, bei; *from* –, aus, aus . . . hervor, mitten heraus; *be* –, gehören zu; *he is – the best*, er ist mit der beste.
amoral [eɪˈmɔrəl], *adj.* amoralisch.
amor–ist [ˈæmorɪst], *s.* der Buhler, Liebhaber. **–ous** [ˈæmərəs], *adj.* verliebt (*of*, in), Liebes–; *–ous ditty*, das Liebesliedchen; *of an –ous nature*, (von) verliebter Natur. **–ousness,** *s.* die Verliebtheit.
amorphous [əˈmɔːfəs], *adj.* unkristallinisch, amorph (*minerals*); mißgestaltet, anomal (*Anat.*); (*fig.*) formlos.
amortiz–able [əˈmɔːtɪzəbl], *adj.* tilgbar, amortisierbar. **–ation** [–ˈzeɪʃən], *s.* die (Schulden)Tilgung, Amortisation, Veräußerung an die tote Hand; *bill of –ation*, der Tilgungsschein. **–e** [əˈmɔːtɑɪz], *v.a.* tilgen, amortisieren, an die tote Hand veräußern.

amount [əˈmɑʊnt], 1. *s.* der Betrag; die (Gesamt)-Summe, Masse, Menge, der Bestand; *what is the – ?* wieviel macht *or* beträgt es? *to the – of*, im Betrage von, bis zur Höhe von; *any –*, jede beliebige Menge; (*coll.*) *any – of nonsense*, nichts als Unsinn. 2. *v.n.* sich belaufen (*to*, auf (*Acc.*)), betragen; (*fig.*) hinauslaufen (auf (*Acc.*)); *not – to much*, belanglos sein; *it all –s to the same thing*, es kommt *or* läuft auf dasselbe *or* eins hinaus.

amour [əˈmʊə], *s.* die Liebschaft.

ampere [ˈæmpɛːə], *s.* das Ampere.

ampersand [ˈæmpəsænd], *s.* das Zeichen für 'und' (&).

amphibi–an [æmˈfɪbɪən], *s.* die Amphibie (*Zool.*); das Land- und Wasserflugzeug. **–ous** [–ɪəs], *adj.* amphibisch, beidlebig; *–ous tank*, der Schwimmkampfwagen (*Mil.*).

amphitheatre [ˈæmfɪθɪətə], *s.* das Amphitheater.

ampl–e [ˈæmpl], *adj.*, **–y**, *adv.* weit, breit, geräumig, groß, weitläufig, reichlich, genügend; *–e means*, reichliche Mittel; *–e satisfaction*, völlige Genugtuung; *it 's –e*, es genügt vollständig. **–itude**, *s.* der Umfang, die Größe, Weite; die Schwingungsweite, Amplitude (*Physics*); (*fig.*) der Reichtum, die Fülle.

amplif–ication [æmplɪfɪˈkeɪʃən], *s.* die Erweiterung, Vergrößerung, Ausdehnung (*Gram.*), weitere Ausführung (*Rhet.*); die Verstärkung (*Rad.*). **–ier**, *s.* der Verstärker (*Rad.*). **–y**, *v.a.* vergrößern, erweitern, ausdehnen; weiter ausführen, ausführlich darstellen; verstärken (*Rad.*).

ampulla [æmˈpʊlə], *s.* das Gefäß, die Phiole.

amputat–e [ˈæmpjʊteɪt], *v.a.* abschneiden, abnehmen, amputieren (*Med.*). **–ion**, *s.* die Amputation, Absetzung (*Med.*).

amuck [əˈmʌk], *adv.*; *run –*, amoklaufen, wütend *or* tobend herumlaufen.

amulet [ˈæmjʊlɪt], *s.* das Amulett.

amus–e [əˈmjuˑz], *v.a.* unterhalten, vergnügen, amüsieren, belustigen, ergötzen, die Zeit vertreiben (*Dat.*); *be –ed by*, Spaß haben an (*Dat.*), sich ergötzen an (*Dat.*); *it –es me*, es macht mir Spaß. **–ement**, *s.* die Unterhaltung, der Zeitvertreib, das Vergnügen, die Belustigung; *for –ement*, zum Vergnügen; *place of –ement*, der Vergnügungsort. **–ing**, *adj.* unterhaltend, belustigend, ergötzlich, amüsant.

amyloid [ˈæmɪlɔɪd], *adj.* stärkehaltig, mehlartig

[1]**an** [æn, ən *acc. to emphasis*], *indef. art. used before a vowel or silent h*, ein, *etc.*

[2]**an**, *conj.* (*archaic*) wenn.

Anabaptist [ænəˈbæptɪst], *s.* der Wiedertäufer.

anachronism [əˈnækrənɪzm], *s.* der Anachronismus, Zeitverstoß.

anaconda [ænəˈkɔndə], *s.* die Riesenschlange (*Zool.*).

Anacreontic [ænəkreˈɔntɪk], *adj.* anakreontisch.

anaemi–a [əˈnɪːmɪə], *s.* die Blutarmut, Anämie. **–c**, *adj.* blutarm, bleichsüchtig, anämisch.

anaesthe–sia [ænɪsˈθɪːzɪə], *s.* die Unempfindlichkeit, Empfindungslosigkeit. **–tic** [–ˈθɛtɪk], 1. *adj.* unempfindlich, betäubend. 2. *s.* das Betäubungsmittel. **–tize** [əˈnɪːsθətɑɪz], *v.a.* anästhetisieren.

anaglyph [ˈænəglɪf], *s.* flacherhabene Arbeit, das Bas-Relief.

anagog–e, *see* **–y.** **–ical** [ænəˈgɔdʒɪkl], *adj.* mystisch. **–y** [ˈænəgɔdʒɪ], *s.* mystische *or* sinnbildliche Auslegung.

anagram [ˈænəgræm], *s.* das Anagramm. **–matical** [–ˈmætɪkl], *adj.* anagrammatisch.

anal [ˈeɪnəl], *adj.* Steiß–, After– (*Anat.*).

analect–a [ænəˈlɛktə], **–s** [ˈænəlɛkts], *pl.* Auszüge, ausgewählte Stücke, die Blumenlese.

analeptic [ænəˈlɛptɪk], 1. *adj.* stärkend. 2. *s.* das Kräftigungsmittel (*Med*).

analgesia [ænəlˈdʒɪːsɪə], *s.* die Schmerzbetäubung.

analog–ical [ænəˈlɔdʒɪkl], *adj.* ähnlich, verwandt. **–ous** [əˈnæləgəs], *adj.* entsprechend, analog. **–ue** [ˈænəlɔg], *s.* etwas Ähnliches, das Seitenstück. **–y** [əˈnælədʒɪ], *s.* die Analogie, Übereinstimmung, Ähnlichkeit; *by –y with*, *on the –y of*, analogisch nach; *bear –y to*, Ähnlichkeit zeigen mit.

analy–se [ˈænəlɑɪz], *v.a.* analysieren, auflösen; (*fig*) zergliedern, zerlegen, genau untersuchen. **–ser**, *s.* der Analysator. **–sis** [əˈnæləsɪs], *s.* die Analyse (*Chem.*); Analysis (*Math.*), Zerlegung, Zergliederung, Untersuchung, Darlegung, der Abriß; *in the last –sis*, letzten Endes; *volumetric –sis*, die Maßanalyse. **–st**, *s.* der Analytiker; *public –st*, der Gerichtschemiker. **–tic(al)** [ænəˈlɪtɪk(l)], *adj.* analytisch.

anapaest [ˈænəpɪˑst], *s.* der Anapäst. **–ic**, *adj.* anapästisch.

anarch–ical [æˈnɑːkɪkl], *adj.* anarchisch, anarchistisch, zügellos. **–ist** [ˈænəkɪst] *s.* der Anarchist. **–y** [ˈænəkɪ], *s.* die Anarchie, Zügellosigkeit, Gesetzlosigkeit, der Umsturz.

anathema [əˈnæθəmə], *s.* der Kirchenbann, Bannfluch; (*fig.*) der Fluch, die Verwünschung; verwünschte Person *or* Sache. **–tize**, *v.a.* verfluchen, mit dem Bann belegen, in den Bann tun.

anatom–ic(al) [ænəˈtɔmɪk(l)], *adj.* anatomisch. **–ist** [əˈnætəmɪst], *s.* der Anatom. **–ize** [əˈnætəmɑɪz], *v.a.* zergliedern, (anatomisch) zerlegen. **–y** [əˈnætəmɪ], *s.* die Anatomie, (anatomische) Zergliederung; (*fig.*) das Skelett, Gerippe.

ancest–or [ˈænsəstə], *s.* der Vorfahr; (*poet.*) Ahn(herr); (*pl.*) Vorfahren, Ahnen, Väter. **–ral** [–ˈsɛstrəl], *adj.* angestammt, Stamm–, Ahnen–, Ur–, altererbt; *–ral castle*, die Stammburg, das Ahnenschloß; *–ral estate*, das Erbgut; *–ral right*, das Erbrecht. **–ress**, *s.* die Stammutter; die Ahnfrau, (*poet.*) Ahne. **–ry**, *s.* die Ahnen, Vorfahren (*pl.*); die Abstammung, das Geschlecht.

anchor [ˈæŋkə], 1. *s.* der Anker; (*fig.*) die Zuflucht, der Rettungsanker, fester Grund; *bower-–*, der Buganker; *kedge-–*, der Warpanker; *sheet-–*, der Notanker; *cast* or *drop –*, ankern, vor Anker gehen; *drag the –*, vor Anker treiben; *weigh –*, den Anker lichten; *lie* or *ride at –*, vor Anker liegen. 2. *v.n.* ankern, vor Anker gehen. 3. *v.a.* verankern, vor Anker legen; (*fig.*) befestigen; *be –ed to*, verankert sein in. **–age**, *s.* der Ankergrund, Ankerplatz; das Ankergeld; (*fig.*) fester Grund *or* Halt, die Verankerung.

anchor–et [ˈæŋkərɛt], **–ite** [–ɑɪt], *s.* der Einsiedler, Klausner.

anchovy [ˈæntʃəvɪ], *s.* die Anschovis, Sardelle; *– paste*, die Sardellenpaste.

ancient [ˈeɪnʃənt], 1. *adj.* alt, uralt, ehemalig, vormalig, aus alter Zeit *or* alten Zeiten; (*fig.*) (alt)-ehrwürdig; *that is – history*, das ist eine altbekannte Geschichte. 2. *s.* (*archaic*) der Alte; (*archaic*) der Fähnrich; die Fahne; (*B.*) *– of Days*, Gott der Vater; *the –s*, die Alten (Griechen und Römer). **–ly**, *adv.* ehemals, von alters. **–ness**, *s.* hohes Alter.

ancillary [ænˈsɪlərɪ], *adj.* untergeordnet, ergänzend, dienend, Hilfs–.

and [ænd, ənd, ən, n *acc. to emphasis*], *conj.* und; *bread – butter*, das Butterbrot; *both . . . –. . .*, sowohl . . . als auch . . .; *a coach – four*, eine Kutsche mit vier Pferden; *there are dogs – dogs*, es gibt solche und solche; *good – loud*, schön laut; *a little more – he would*, es fehlte nicht viel, so wäre er; *how can you go out – not take him with you?* wie können Sie ausgehen ohne ihn mitzunehmen? *later – later*, immer später; *soap – water*, das Seifenwasser; *a hundred – one*, hunderteins; *she wept – wept*, sie weinte in einem fort; *both you – I*, Sie sowohl wie ich; *try – come*, versuchen Sie zu kommen; *walk two – two*, zu zweien *or* je zwei und zwei gehen; *go* or *look – see*, sehen Sie nach; *nice – warm*, hübsch warm; *years – years*, viele Jahre; *write – ask*, fragen Sie mal an.

andante [ænˈdæntɪ], 1. *adv.* langsam. 2. *s.* das Andante.

andiron [ˈændɑɪən], *s.* der Feuerbock, Kaminbock.

androgynous [ænˈdrɔdʒɪnəs], *adj.* zwitterartig, zweigeschlechtig.

anecdot–al [ænɪkˈdoutl], *adj.* anekdotisch; anekdotenhaft. **–e**, *s.* das Geschichtchen, die Anekdote. **–ical** [–ˈdɔtɪkl], *adj. see* **–al.**

anemometer [ænɪˈmɔmɪtə], *s.* der Windmesser.

anemone [əˈnɛmənɪ], *s.* das Windröschen, die Anemone (*Bot.*); *sea –*, die Seeanemone.

anemoscope [ˈænɪmoskoup], *s.* die Windfahne.

anent [əˈnɛnt], *prep.* (*archaic*) betreffs, bezüglich.

aneroid ['ænərɔɪd], *adj.*; – *barometer*, das Aneroidbarometer.
aneurysm ['ænjuərɪzm], *s.* die Pulsadergeschwulst.
anew [ə'njuː], *adv.* von neuem, aufs neue; wieder, noch einmal.
angel ['eɪndʒəl], *s.* der Engel; Gottesbote; (*coll.*) *join the –s*, in den Himmel kommen. **–ic(al)** [æn'dʒɛlɪk(l)], *adj.* engelgleich, engelhaft, Engel–. **– -fish**, *s.* der Meerengel. **– -noble**, *s.* (*archaic*) der Engeltaler.
angelica [æn'dʒɛlɪkə], *s.* die Brustwurz, Engelwurz, Angelika (*Bot.*).
angelus ['ændʒɪləs], *s.* das Angelus(geläut); die Angelusglocke; das Angelus(gebet).
anger ['æŋgə], 1. *s.* der Zorn, Unwille, die Wut, der Ärger; *fit of* –, der Zornesausbruch, Wutanfall. 2. *v.a.* erzürnen, aufbringen; böse machen.
angina ['ændʒɪnə, æn'dʒɑɪnə], *s.* die Hals-, Rachen- *or* Mandelentzündung; – *pectoris*, die Herzbräune.
[1]**angle** ['æŋgl], *s.* der Winkel; Knick, das Knie (*Mech.*); *right, acute, obtuse, adjacent, alternate, exterior* or *external, vertical* –, rechter, spitzer, stumpfer, Neben–, Wechsel–, Außen–, Scheitel-Winkel; – *of elevation*, der Erhöhungswinkel; – *of incidence*, der Einfallswinkel; – *of reflection*, der Reflexions– *or* Ausfallswinkel; – *of refraction*, der Brechungswinkel; – *of sight, visual* –, der Sehwinkel; *at right –s to*, im rechten Winkel zu; *at an – to*, in einem Winkel stehend zu; – *iron*, das Winkeleisen; (*fig.*) *from a new* –, von einem neuen Standpunkt *or* Gesichtspunkt, von einer neuen Seite. **–d**, *adj. suffix* –wink(e)lig, –eckig.
[2]**angle**, 1. *s.* (*archaic*) die Angel. 2. *v.n.* angeln (*for*, nach); (*fig.*) zu bekommen suchen. **–r**, *s.* der Angler.
Anglican ['æŋglɪkən], 1. *adj.* anglikanisch; staatskirchlich. 2. *s.* der (*or* die) Anglikaner(in).
anglic-e ['æŋglɪsɪː], *adv.* auf Englisch. **–ism**, *s.* der Anglizimus. **–ize** ['æŋglɪsɑɪz], *v.a.* anglisieren, englisch machen; *become –ized*, englisch werden.
angling ['æŋglɪŋ], *s.* das Angeln, die Angelei.
Anglo- ['æŋglou], *prefix*; *see the Index of Names.*
angrily ['æŋgrɪlɪ], *adv. see* **angry.**
angry ['æŋgrɪ], *adj.* zornig, böse, aufgebracht, ärgerlich (*at* or *about a th.*, über etwas; *with a p.*, auf *or* über einen); entzündet (*of a wound*); (*fig.*) heftig, stürmisch, aufgeregt; *get* –, in Zorn geraten; *have an – look*, böse aussehen; *make a p.* –, einen ärgern *or* böse machen; *the – sea*, die stürmische See.
anguish ['æŋgwɪʃ], *s.* der Schmerz, die Pein, Qual; – *of mind*, die Seelenangst, Seelenqual.
angular ['æŋgjulə], *adj.* winklig, eckig, spitzig; (*fig.*) steif, ungelenk, eckig, formell; – *point*, der Scheitelpunkt; – *velocity*, die Winkelgeschwindigkeit. **–ity** [–'lærɪtɪ], *s.* die Winkligkeit, Eckigkeit; Ungelenkheit, Steifheit.
anhydr-ide [æn'hɑɪdrɑɪd], *s.* das Anhydrid (*Chem.*). **–ite**, *s.* der Anhydrit (*Min.*). **–ous** [–drəs], *adj.* wasserfrei.
anigh [ə'nɑɪ], *adv.* nahe.
anile ['ænɑɪl], *adj.* altweiberhaft.
aniline ['ænɪlɑɪn], *s.* das Anilin; – *dyes*, Anilinfarbstoffe.
animadver-sion [ænɪmæd'vəːʃən], *s.* der Tadel, Verweis, die Rüge, Kritik (*on*, an). **–t** [ænɪməd'vəːt], *v.n.* rügen, tadeln, kritisieren (*on* or *upon* (*Acc.*)).
animal ['ænɪməl], 1. *s.* das Tier, Lebewesen. 2. *adj.* animalisch, tierisch; (*fig.*) sinnlich, fleischlich; – *charcoal*, die Knochenkohle; – *food*, die Fleischnahrung; – *functions*, tierische Verrichtungen; – *kingdom*, das Tierreich; – *magnetism*, tierischer Magnetismus; – *spirits*, Lebensgeister; *full of – spirits*, voller Lebenskraft. **–cule** [–'mælkjuːl], *s.* mikroskopisches Tierchen. **–ism** [–ɪzm], *s.* der Animalismus, Lebenstrieb; (*fig.*) die Sinnlichkeit. **–ity**, *s.* die Tierheit. **–ize**, *v.a.* vertieren.
anim-ate ['ænɪmeɪt], 1. *v.a.* beleben, beseelen; (*fig.*) anregen, ermuntern, aufmuntern. 2. *adj.*, **–ated**, *p.p.* & *adj.* belebt; beseelt (*with* or *by*, von); lebhaft, munter. **–ating**, *adj.* belebend, beseelend. **–ation** [–'meɪʃən], *s.* die Belebung, Beseelung; (*fig.*) das Leben, die Lebhaftigkeit, Munterkeit, das Feuer. **–ism**, *s.* die Naturbeseelung.
anim-osity [ænɪ'mɔsɪtɪ], *s.* der Unwille, die Abneigung, Feindseligkeit, der Haß, Groll. **–us** ['ænɪməs], *s. see* **–osity**; die Absicht (*Law*).
anis-e ['ænɪs], *s.* der Anis (*Bot.*). **–eed** ['ænɪsɪːd], *s.* der Anissamen.
ankle ['æŋkl], *s.* der Fußknöchel, Enkel; *sprain one's* –, sich (*Dat.*) den Fuß verstauchen. **– -bone**, *s.* der Fußknöchel, das Sprungbein. **– -deep**, *adv.* & *adj.* fußtief, bis über die Knöchel. **–t** [–ɪt], *s.* die Fußspange.
ankylos-is [æŋkɪ'lousɪs], *s.* die Ankylose, Gelenkversteifung. **–tomiasis** [–tə'mɑɪəsɪs], *s.* die Hakenwurmkrankheit (*Med.*).
annal-ist ['ænəlɪst], *s.* der Chronist, Annalenschreiber. **–s**, *pl.* die Annalen, Jahrbücher, die Chronik, Geschichte.
anneal [ə'nɪːl], *v.a.* ausglühen, anlassen, tempern, kühlen (*glass*). **–ing-furnace**, *s.* der Kühlofen(*for glass*).
annelid ['ænəlɪd], *s.* der Ringelwurm (*Zool.*).
annex 1. *v.a.* [ə'nɛks], anhängen, beifügen (*to*, an), sich (*Dat.*) aneignen, einverleiben, annektieren; (*fig.*) vereinigen, verbinden (*to*, mit); *as –ed*, laut Anlage (*C.L.*); *at the –ed cash-prices*, zu beigefügten *or* beigesetzten Barpreisen; *we – a report for your perusal*, wir schließen Ihnen einen Bericht zur Durchsicht bei. 2. *s.* ['ænɛks], das Beigefügte, die Beilage, der Anhang, Zusatz, Nachtrag; das Nebengebäude, der Anbau. **–ation** [–'eɪʃən], *s.* die Beifügung, Anhängung; Vereinigung, Verknüpfung, Verbindung; Annexion, Einverleibung, gewaltsame Aneignung.
annihilat-e [ə'nɑɪəleɪt], *v.a.* vernichten, zerstören, aufheben, ausrotten. **–ion** [–'leɪʃən], *s.* die Vernichtung, Abschaffung, Aufhebung.
anniversary [ænɪ'vəːsərɪ], *s.* der Jahrestag, die Jahresfeier; *15th* –, fünfzehnjährige Wiederkehr; – *of his death*, sein Todestag.
annotat-e ['ænouteɪt], *v.a.* mit Anmerkungen versehen, kommentieren; *–ed edition*, Ausgabe mit Anmerkungen. **–ion** [–'teɪʃən], *s.* das Kommentieren, Glossieren; die Anmerkung, Glosse. **–or**, *s.* der Kommentator.
announce [ə'nɑuns], *v.a.* ankündigen, anzeigen, verkündigen, in Aussicht stellen, melden, bekanntmachen, ansagen (*Rad.*); – *an arrival*, einen Besuch anmelden; – *o.s.*, sich anmelden; *have one's name –d*, sich (an)melden lassen. **–ment**, *s.* die Anzeige, Ankündigung, Veröffentlichung, Nachricht, Bekanntmachung, Meldung, Anmeldung. **–r**, *s.* der Ankündiger, Ansager (*Rad.*).
annoy [ə'nɔɪ], *v.a.* beunruhigen; (= *disturb*) stören; belästigen, plagen, ärgern, behelligen; *be –ed*, sich ärgern (*at a th.*, *with a p.*, über). **–ance**, *s.* der Ärger, Verdruß; die Störung, Beunruhigung, Plage, der Unfug. **–ing**, *pr.p.* & *adj.* ärgerlich, lästig, verdrießlich, störend.
annual ['ænjuəl], 1. *adj.* jährlich; einjährig (*Bot.*); – *balance*, die Schlußbilanz, Jahresbilanz; – *report*, der Jahresbericht. 2. *s.* einjährige Pflanze (*Bot.*); die Jahresschrift, das Jahrbuch.
annuit-ant [ə'njuːɪtənt], *s.* der Leibrentner. **–y** [–ɪtɪ], *s.* die Jahresrente, Lebensrente, das Jahreseinkommen, Jahresgeld, die Jahresrate, die Jahreszinsen (*pl.*); *government –y*, die Staatsrente; *life –y*, die Leibrente; *–y bond*, der Rentenschein, Rentenbrief; *settle an –y*, ein Jahresgehalt aussetzen (*on, Dat.*).
annul [ə'nʌl], *v.a.* für ungültig erklären, kündigen, abschaffen, aufheben; vernichten, tilgen. **–ment**, *s.* die Vernichtung, Abschaffung, Aufhebung, Tilgung, Ungültigkeitserklärung.
annul-ar ['ænjulə], *adj.* ringförmig. **–ated**, *adj.* geringelt. **–et**, *s.* kleiner Ring, das Ringlein (*Her.*); die Ringverzierung (*Arch.*). **–us**, *s.* der Ring (*Bot.*), Lichtring (*Astr.*).
annunciation [ənʌnsɪ'eɪʃən], *s.* die Verkündigung (*Eccl.*).
anode ['ænoud], *s.* die Anode (*Elec.*); – *circuit*, der Anodenkreis; – *current*, der Anodenstrom; – *potential*, die Anodenspannung.
anodyne ['ænodɑɪn], 1. *adj.* schmerzstillend, lindernd. 2. *s.* schmerzstillendes Mittel.
anoint [ə'nɔɪnt], *v.a.* einölen, einreiben, ein-

schmieren; salben; (*B.*) *Lord's -ed*, Gesalbte des Herrn. **-ing,** *s.* die Salbung.
anomal-ous [ə'nɔmələs], *adj.* unregelmäßig, ungewöhnlich, abweichend, anomal, abnorm, von der Regel abweichend. **-y** [ə'nɔməlɪ], *s.* die Unregelmäßigkeit, Abweichung; Anomalie, Ungereimtheit; der Winkelabstand von der Sonnennähe (*of a planet*) (*Astr.*).
anon [ə'nɔn], *adv.* gleich, sogleich, sofort, auf der Stelle; bald; nachher; *ever and –*, immer wieder, dann und wann; *of this more –*, hiervon bald mehr.
anonym-ity [æno'nɪmɪtɪ], *s.* die Anonymität. **-ous** [ə'nɔnɪməs], *adj.* namenlos, ungenannt, anonym.
anopheles [ə'noufəlɪ:z], *s.* die Fiebermücke.
another [ə'nʌðə], *adj. & pron.* ein anderer, *etc.*, ein verschiedener, *etc.*; noch ein(e), *etc.*; *– and –*, immer noch mehr; *give me – (= different) cup*, geben Sie mir eine andere Tasse; *give me – (= one more) cup*, geben Sie mir noch eine Tasse; *just such –*, gerade so einer; *many –*, manch andere(r); *not – word*, kein Wort mehr; *one –*, einander; gegenseitig; *one after –*, einer nach dem anderen; *we are often taken for one –*, wir werden oft miteinander verwechselt; *one from –*, *from one –*, von einander; *one with –*, miteinander, zusammengerechnet; *it is one thing to promise, – to perform*, Versprechen und Halten sind zweierlei; *– place*, das Haus der Lords (*Parl.*); *– time*, ein anderes Mal; *that's – thing entirely*, das ist etwas völlig anderes; *one upon –*, eins aufs andere; *I am of – way of thinking*, ich denke anders; *yet – ?* noch einer? *one thing with –*, eins ins andere gerechnet; *– Hitler*, ein zweiter Hitler; (*Sport*) *A. N. Other*, ungenannter Spieler.
anserine ['ænsəraɪn], *adj.* gänseartig, Gänse–; (*fig.*) albern.
answer ['ɑ:nsə], 1. *s.* die Antwort, Erwiderung, Entgegnung, der Bescheid (*to*, auf (*Acc.*)); die Lösung, das Resultat (*Math.*); die Gegenschrift, Verteidigung, Replik (*Law*); der Gegengruß (*Naut.*); der Gegenhieb, Gegenstoß (*Fenc.*); *– in the affirmative* (*negative*), eine bejahende (verneinende) Antwort; *in – to*, als Antwort auf; *give* or *make an –*, eine Antwort geben; (*C.L.*) *the favour of an – is requested*, um Antwort wird gebeten; (*C.L.*) *in – to your letter*, in Beantwortung Ihres Schreibens. 2. *v.a.* beantworten, antworten auf, entgegnen; erwidern (*a p.* (*Dat.*)); erfüllen; dienen, entsprechen (*Dat.*); genügen, befriedigen, gehorchen, Folge leisten, sich richten nach; *– the door* or (*door*) *bell*, auf das Klingeln hören, dem Klingelnden öffnen; *– a bill of exchange*, einen Wechsel decken *or* einlösen *or* honorieren; *– a debt*, eine Schuld abtragen; *– a p.'s expectations*, jemandes Erwartungen entsprechen; *– the helm*, dem Ruder gehorchen; *– a prayer*, ein Gebet erhören; *– the purpose*, dem Zwecke entsprechen; *it -s no purpose*, es hilft zu nichts; *– a riddle*, ein Rätsel lösen *or* herausbekommen; *he -ed my question in the affirmative*, er bejahte meine Frage; *– a summons*, einer Vorladung Folge leisten (*Law*). 3. *v.n.* antworten (*a p.* (*Dat.*)); erwidern, entgegnen (*to*, auf (*Acc.*)); gelingen, passen, taugen; *– back*, frech antworten; *– for*, Rede stehen für, eintreten für, gutsagen, Rechenschaft geben von, haften *or* bürgen für; *he -ed in the negative*, er verneinte es; *this plan will never –*, dieser Plan eignet sich nicht *or* gelingt nicht, schlägt nicht an *or* geht nicht; *– to*, reagieren auf; *– (to) the description*, mit der Beschreibung übereinstimmen; *he -s to the name of Charles*, er hört auf den Namen Karl **-able,** *adj.* beantwortbar; verantwortlich, haftbar (*for*, für); *be -able for*, haften, bürgen, einstehen *or* verantwortlich sein für.
ant [ænt], *s.* die Ameise. **--eater,** *s.* der Ameisenbär, Ameisenfresser **--hill,** *s.* der Ameisenhaufen.
antacid [ænt'æsɪd], 1. *adj.* gegen Magensäure wirkend. 2. *s.* gegen Magensäure wirkendes Mittel.
antagon-ism [æn'tægənɪzm], *s.* der Widerstreit, das Widerstreben; die Feindschaft, der Antagonismus (*to*, gegen), Gegensatz (*between*, zwischen). **-ist,** *s.* der Gegner, Widersacher. **-istic** [–'nɪstɪk], *adj.* widerstreitend, entgegengesetzt. **-ize** [–naɪz], *v.a.* sich (*Dat.*) einen zum Gegner machen.
antarctic [ænt'ɑ:ktɪk], *adj.* antarktisch; *– circle*, südlicher Polarkreis; *– expedition*, die Südpolexpedition; *the – Ocean*, das Südliche Eismeer; *the –* or *the – regions*, Südpolarländer (*pl.*).
anteceden-ce [æntɪ'si:dəns], *s.* das Vorhergehen, der Vortritt, Vorrang; die Rückläufigkeit (*Astr.*). **-t,** 1. *adj.* vorhergehend, vorig; früher (*to*, als). 2. *s.* das Vorhergehende; vorhergehender Umstand; das Beziehungswort (*Gram.*); der Vordersatz (*Log.*); erstes Glied (*Math.*); (*pl.*) frühere Ereignisse, das Vorleben.
antechamber ['æntɪtʃeɪmbə], *s.* das Vorzimmer.
antechapel ['æntɪtʃæpəl], *s.* die Vorhalle einer Kapelle (*Arch.*).
antedate ['æntɪ'deɪt], *v.a.* zurückdatieren, vordatieren (*a letter*); vorwegnehmen, vorempfinden; vorhergehen (*Dat.*).
antediluvian [æntɪdɪ'lu:vɪən], 1. *adj.* vorsintflutlich, antediluvianisch; (*fig.*) altmodisch. 2. *s.* vorsintflutliches Tier; altmodischer Mensch.
antelope ['æntɪloup], *s.* die Antilope.
antemeridian ['æntɪmə'rɪdɪən], *adj. & adv.* vor Mittag, vormittägig.
antenatal ['æntɪ'neɪtəl], *adj.* vor der Geburt, vorgeburtlich.
antenna [æn'tɛnə], *s.* das Fühlhorn, der Fühler (*Zool.*); die Antenne (*Amer.*, *Rad.*).
antenuptial ['æntɪ'nʌpʃəl], *adj.* vorehelich, vor der Hochzeit.
antepenultimate ['æntɪpə'nʌltɪmət] 1. *adj.* drittletzt. 2. *s.* drittletzte Silbe.
anterior [æn'tɪ:ərɪə] *adj.* (*in time*) vorhergehend, vorangehend; früher, älter (*to*, als); (*in space*) vorder; voranstehend (*to*, vor).
anteroom ['æntɪru:m], *s.* das Vorzimmer, der Vorraum.
anthelion [æn'θɪ:lɪən], *s.* die Gegensonne.
anthem ['ænθəm], *s.* der Wechselgesang, die Hymne; *national –*, die Nationalhymne.
anther ['ænθə], *s.* der Staubbeutel.
anthology [æn'θɔlədʒɪ], *s.* die Anthologie, Gedichtsammlung, Blumenlese.
anthracite ['ænθrəsaɪt], *s.* der Anthrazit, die Glanzkohle.
anthrax ['ænθræks], der Karbunkel; der Milzbrand (*Vet.*).
anthropo- ['ænθropo], *prefix*, Menschen–. **-id,** 1. *s.* menschenähnliches Tier. 2. *adj.* menschenähnlich; *-id ape*, der Menschenaffe. **-logist** [–'pɔlədʒɪst], *s.* der Anthropolog. **-logy,** *s.* die Menschenkunde, Anthropologie. **-morphism** [–po'mɔ:fɪzm], *s.* die Vermenschlichung (Gottes) (*Theol.*). **-morphous,** *adj.* menschenähnlich, von menschenähnlicher Gestalt. **-phagous** [–'pɔfəgəs], *adj.* menschenfressend. **-phagy** [–'pɔfədʒɪ], *s.* die Menschenfresserei.
anti- ['æntɪ], *prefix*, entgegen, gegen, Gegen–, Wider–, Anti–. **--aircraft,** *adj.* Flugabwehr–, Flak–, Luftschutz– **-body,** *s.* der Immunkörper.
antic ['æntɪk], 1. *adj.* (*archaic*) grotesk, phantastisch, fratzenhaft, possierlich. 2. *s.* (*usually plural*) die Posse, Fratze.
antichrist ['æntɪkraɪst], *s.* der Antichrist. **-ian** [–'krɪstjen], *adj.* christenfeindlich.
anticipat-e [æn'tɪsɪpeɪt], *v.a.* vorwegnehmen, im voraus tun (*s.th.*); vorgreifen, zuvorkommen (*a p.*, einem); voraussehen, vorhersagen, ahnen; erhoffen, erwarten; im voraus *or* vor der Zeit bezahlen *or* einlösen (*a bill*); *-ing your early arrival*, in Erwartung Ihrer baldigen Ankunft; *she always -es my wishes*, sie kommt meinen Wünschen immer zuvor; *-ed bill of exchange*, vor der Verfallzeit eingelöster Wechsel. **-ion** [–'peɪʃən], *s.* die Vorwegnahme, Vorausnahme; das Zuvorkommen, Vorgreifen; das Vorgefühl, der Vorgeschmack, die Vorempfindung, der Vorgenuß; die Voraussicht, Erwartung; Verfrühtheit; Vorauszahlung, Abschlagszahlung; *by -ion*, vorweg, im voraus; (*C.L.*) auf Abschlag; *contrary to -ion*, wider Erwarten; *in -ion of s.th.*, etwas vorwegnehmend, in Erwartung einer S., in der Voraussicht auf etwas; *thanking you in -ion*, Ihnen im voraus dankend. **-ory** [–pətərɪ], *adj.* vorgreifend, vorwegnehmend; erwartend, zuvorkommend.
anti--climax [æntɪ'klaɪmæks], *s.* die Antiklimax;

(*fig.*) das Abfallen, Absteigen, der Niedergang. **--clockwise,** *adv.* dem Uhrzeiger entgegen. **-cyclone,** *s.* das Hochdruckgebiet, Hoch. **-dote** ['æntɪdout], *s.* das Gegenmittel, Gegengift (*against* or *to*, gegen). **-febrile,** *s.* fieberstillendes Mittel. **--freeze,** *s.* das Frostschutzmittel (*Motor.*). **--gas,** *adj.* Gasabwehr–, Gasschutz– (*Mil.*). **--knock,** *adj.* klopffest (*as petrol*) (*Motor.*). **-macassar,** *s.* der Sofaschoner, Überzug. **--monarchical,** *adj.* antimonarchisch. **--monarchist,** *s.* der Gegner der Monarchie.

antimon-ial [æntɪ'mounɪəl], *adj.* Antimon–, antimonhaltig. **-y** ['æntɪmənɪ], *s.* das Antimon, der Spießglanz.

antinomian [æntɪ'noumɪən], *adj.* gesetzwidrig; Antinomisten–.

antinomy [æn'tɪnəmɪ], *s.* der Widerspruch (*Law*), das Paradoxon (*Log.*).

antipath-etic(al) [æntɪpə'θetɪk(l)], 1. *adj.* antipathisch. 2. *pred. adj.* zuwider. **-y** [æn'tɪpəθɪ], *s.* die Abneigung, der Widerwille, die Antipathie (*to* or *against*, gegen).

anti-phon ['æntɪfən], *s.* das Antiphon. **-phony** [æn'tɪfənɪ], *s.* kirchlicher Wechselgesang, der Wechselchor; (*fig.*) das Echo, die Antwort.

antipod-al [æn'tɪpədəl], *adj.* antipodisch, entgegengesetzt, gegenfüßlerisch. **-e,** *s.* (*fig.*) der Gegensatz, genaues Gegenteil; die Gegensätzlichkeit; *pl.* [–pədɪ:z] die Gegenfüßler.

antipope ['æntɪ'poup], *s.* der Gegenpapst.

antipyr-etic [æntɪpaɪ'retɪk], *s.* das Fiebermittel. **-in** [æntɪ'paɪərɪn], *s.* das Antipyrin.

antiqu-arian [æntɪ'kweərɪən], 1. *adj.* altertümlich; *-arian society*, Verein der Altertumsfreunde. 2. *s.* **-ary** ['æntɪkwərɪ], der Altertumsforscher, Altkunstsammler. **-arianism** [–ɪzm], *s.* die Altertümelei **-ated** ['æntɪkweɪtɪd] *adj.* veraltet, überlebt. **-e** [æn'tɪ:k], 1. *adj.* alt, antik; altmodisch. 2. *s.* die Antike, antikes *or* altes Kunstwerk. **-e-dealer,** *s.* der Antiquitätenhändler. **-e-shop,** *s.* der Antiquitätenladen. **-ity** [æn'tɪkwɪtɪ], *s.* das Altertum, die Vorzeit; klassisches Altertum. **-ities,** (*pl.*) die Altertümer, Antiquitäten; das Alter.

anti--religious ['æntɪrɪ'lɪdʒəs], *adj.* religionsfeindlich. **--rust,** *adj.* Rostschutz–. **--Semite,** *s.* der Antisemit. **--semitic,** *adj.* judenfeindlich. **-septic,** 1. *adj.* fäulnisverhindernd, keimtötend, antiseptisch. 2. *s.* keimtötendes Mittel. **-social,** *adj.* antisozial. **--submarine,** *adj.* U-Bootabwehr–. **--tank,** *adj.* Panzerabwehr–.

antithe-sis [æn'tɪθəsɪs], *s.* (*pl.* –ses) die Antithese, der Gegensatz. **-tic(al)** [–'θetɪk(l)], *adj.* gegensätzlich.

anti-toxin [æntɪ'təksɪn], *s.* das Gegengift. **-type,** *s.* das Gegenbild.

antler ['æntlə], *s.* die Sprosse am Geweih; (*pl.*) das Geweih; *stag with 10 –s*, der Zehnender.

antonym ['æntənɪm], *s.* das Wort von entgegengesetzter Bedeutung, entgegengesetzter Begriff.

anus ['eɪnəs], *s.* der After (*Anat.*); die Mündung, der Ausgang (*Bot.*).

anvil ['ænvɪl], *s.* der Amboß; *be on the –*, in Arbeit *or* Vorbereitung sein; (*fig.*) erörtert *or* behandelt werden.

anxi-ety [æŋ'zaɪətɪ], *s.* die Angst, Besorgnis, das Bangen (*for*, um); die Unruhe, Beängstigung; eifriges Verlangen (*for*, nach); die Beklemmung (*Med.*); *causing –ety*, besorgniserregend; *in great –ety*, ängstlich, besorgt. **-ous** ['æŋkʃəs], *adj.* ängstlich, bange, bekümmert, besorgt (*about*, um, wegen); eifrig bemüht, bestrebt (*for*, um (*Acc.*)), bedacht (auf (*Acc.*)); begierig (nach); beunruhigend, beängstigend; *I am –ous to see him*, ich bin begierig, ihn zu sehen; *I am very –ous about the result*, um das Ergebnis bin ich sehr besorgt.

any ['enɪ], 1. *adj. & pron.* (*a*) *in affirmative clauses.* jed-er, –es, –e, *etc.*, irgendein(e) (beliebige(r, –s)); *as good as –*, so gut wie nur einer; *take – you please*, nehmen Sie, was Ihnen beliebt; *in – case, at – rate*, auf jeden Fall; (*b*) *in negative clauses. not –*, (überhaupt) kein(–er, –s, –e); *never –*, (überhaupt) nie; (*c*) *in interrogative or conditional clauses.* irgendein, irgendwelch, ein, *etc.*, einige, etwas; *have you – ?* hast du welche? *have you – sugar?* hast du Zucker? *is there – hope?* ist noch Hoffnung vorhanden? *are – of you coming?* kommt einer von Ihnen? *is there – more?* ist noch etwas da? *not more than one, if –*, nicht mehr als einer, wenn überhaupt. 2. *adv.* (*before compar.*) irgend; *not – better for it*, keineswegs besser daran; *– longer*, (noch) länger; *not – longer*, nicht länger, nicht mehr; *will you have – more?* wollen Sie noch mehr *or* noch ein wenig haben? *not – more*, nicht(s) mehr, nicht wieder; *not – more than*, ebenso wenig wie. **-body,** *s. & pron.* irgendeiner, irgend jemand, jeder; *–body can do that*, jedermann kann das tun; *not –body*, niemand; *scarcely –body*, fast niemand, kaum jemand; *everybody who is –body*, alle die etwas sind. **-how,** 1. *adv.* irgendwie, auf irgendeine Weise; *not . . . –how*, auf keinen Fall; *do s.th. –how*, etwas nachlässig *or* nur so obenhin tun. 2. *conj.* gleichviel, gleichwohl, immerhin, jedenfalls; *–how I will try it*, probieren will ich es auf jeden Fall. **-one,** *s. see* **-body. -thing,** *s.* irgend etwas, alles, jedes beliebige; *–thing at all*, überhaupt etwas; *–thing but*, nichts weniger *or* weiter als, alles andere als; *never –thing but trouble*, immer nur Sorge; *capable of –thing*, zu allem fähig; *for –thing I know*, so viel ich weiß; *if –thing*, womöglich, nur noch; *that is if –thing a little better*, das ist eher etwas besser; *not –thing*, nichts; *not for –thing*, um keinen Preis; *not –thing so good*, nicht im entferntesten so gut; *–thing rather than*, alles eher als; *scarcely –thing*, fast nichts, kaum etwas; *–thing will do for him*, er ist mit allem zufrieden. **-way,** 1. *adv.* irgendwie, auf irgendeine Weise. 2. *conj.* jedenfalls, immerhin; *–way, he would not . . .*, wie dem auch sei, er wollte nicht . . . . **-where,** *adv.* irgendwo(hin), überall; *not –where*, nirgendwo(hin); *scarcely –where*, fast nirgends. **-wise,** *adv.* auf irgendeine Weise, irgendwie.

aorta [eɪ'ɔ:tə], *s.* die Hauptschlagader, Aorta.

apace [ə'peɪs], *adv.* geschwind, schnell, eilig; eilends, flink, zusehends.

apanage ['æpənɪdʒ], *s.* das Leibgedinge, Jahrgeld; abhängiges Gebiet (*Pol.*).

apart [ə'pɑ:t], *adv.* abseits, beiseite; für sich, getrennt, abgesondert, einzeln; *– from*, abgesehen von; *joking –*, Scherz beiseite; *keep –*, getrennt halten; *set –*, bestimmen, aufbewahren. **-ment,** *s.* das Zimmer, (*Amer.*) die Etagenwohnung; *pl.* die Wohnung; *suite of –ments*, die Zimmerflucht.

apath-etic(al) [æpə'θetɪk(l)], *adj.* teilnahmslos, gleichgültig, apathisch (*towards*, gegen). **-y** ['æpəθɪ], *s.* die Unempfindlichkeit, Apathie (gegen), Gefühllosigkeit (für); Teilnahmslosigkeit, Gleichgültigkeit (gegen).

ape [eɪp], 1. *s.* der Affe. 2. *v.a.* nachäffen, vortäuschen, vorgeben.

apeak [ə'pɪ:k], *adv. & pred. adj.* auf der Spitze; auf und nieder, senkrecht (*Naut.*).

aperient [ə'pɪərɪənt], 1. *adj.* abführend. 2. *s.* das Abführmittel.

aperture ['æpətjuə], *s.* die Öffnung.

ap-ex ['eɪpeks], *s.* (*pl.* –ices *or* –exes) die Spitze, der Gipfel; der Scheitelpunkt (*Geom.*).

aphasia [ə'feɪzɪə], *s.* die Aphasie.

aphelion [æ'fɪ:lɪən], *s.* die Sonnenferne.

aphesis ['æfəsɪs], *s.* der Vokalschwund im Anlaut (*Phon.*).

aphis ['æfɪs], *s.* (*pl.* –ides) die Blattlaus.

aphoris-m ['æfərɪzm], *s.* kurzer Denkspruch *or* Lehrspruch, der Gedankensplitter, Aphorismus. **-tic,** *adj.* aphoristisch.

aphrodisiac [æfrə'dɪzɪək], *adj.* (*or s.*) Geschlechtstrieb erregend(es Mittel).

aphta ['æftə], *s.* die Schleimhautentzündung.

apiar-ist ['eɪpɪərɪst], *s.* der Imker, Bienenzüchter. **-y,** *s.* der Bienenstand, das Bienenhaus.

apic-al ['æpɪkl], *adj.* gipfelständig, an der Spitze befindlich, apikal (*Phonet.*). **-es,** *pl. see* **apex.**

apiculture ['eɪpɪkʌltʃə], *s.* die Bienenzucht.

apiece [ə'pɪ:s], *adv.* (für) jedes Stück, pro Stück; pro Person, pro Kopf.

apish ['eɪpɪʃ], *adj.* affenartig; (*fig.*) äffisch, närrisch.

aplomb [ə'pləm], *s.* selbstbewußtes Auftreten.

Apo-calypse [ə'pəkəlɪps], *s.* die Offenbarung; *the four horsemen of the –calypse*, die vier apokalyp-

tischen Reiter. **-cope** [-kɔpɪ], *s.* die Endverkürzung (eines Wortes), Apokope (*Phonet.*). **-crypha** [-krɪfə], *s.* die Apokryphen (*pl.*). **-cryphal,** *adj.* apokryph, unecht, verdächtig, zweifelhaft.
apodal ['æpoudl], *adj.* fußlos (*Zool.*).
apo-dictic [æpə'dɪktɪk], *adj.* unwiderleglich, apodiktisch. **-dosis** [ə'pɔdəsɪs], *s.* der Nachsatz (*Gram.*). **-gee** ['æpodzɪ:], *s.* das Apogäum, die Erdferne des Mondes; (*fig.*) der Höhepunkt, Gipfel.
apolo-getic(al) [əpɔlə'dʒɛtɪk(l)], *adj.* entschuldigend, verteidigend, rechtfertigend, reumütig, apologetisch. **-getics,** *s.* die Apologetik. **-gist** [ə'pɔlədʒɪst], *s.* der Verteidiger, Apologet; (*fig.*) der Ehrenretter. **-gize** [ə'pɔlədʒɑɪz], *v.n.* sich entschuldigen; um Entschuldigung *or* Vergebung bitten, Abbitte tun (*for s.th.*, wegen; *to s.o.* (*Dat.*)). **-gy** [ə'pɔlədʒɪ], *s.* die Entschuldigung, Abbitte, Verteidigungsrede *or* Verteidigungsschrift; (*coll.*) der Notbehelf, kaum annehmbarer Ersatz; *make an -gy*, sich entschuldigen (*to a p.*, bei; *for s.th.*, für); *in -gy for*, als *or* zur Entschuldigung für.
apologue ['æpəlɔg], *s.* der Apolog, die Lehrfabel.
apophthegm, *s.* ['æpoθɛm], *s.* der Kernspruch, Denkspruch.
apople-ctic [æpo'plɛktɪk], *adj.* apoplektisch, Schlaganfall-; *an -ctic habit of body*, eine zu Schlaganfällen geneigte Körperbildung. **-xy** ['æpoplɛksɪ], *s.* der Schlagfluß, Schlaganfall, Schlag.
aposta-sy [ə'pɔstəsɪ], *s.* der (Glaubens)Abfall, die Abtrünnigkeit. **-te** [ə'pɔstɪt], 1. *s.* der Apostat, Abtrünnige. 2. *adj.* abtrünnig. **-tize** [-tɑɪz], *v.n.* abtrünnig werden, abfallen, untreu werden.
a posteriori [ə'pɔstərɪɔ:rɪ], *adv.* von Wirkung auf Ursache schließend; induktiv, empirisch.
apost-le [ə'pɔsl], *s.* der Apostel, Jünger (*of Christ*); (*fig.*) der Verfechter; *-les' Creed*, Apostolisches Glaubensbekenntnis. **-olic(al)** [-'tɔlɪk(l)] *adj.* apostolisch.
apostroph-e [ə'pɔstrəfɪ], *s.* der Apostroph (*Typ.*); die Anrede (*Rhet.*); der Apostroph, das Auslassungszeichen (*Gram.*). **-ize** [-fɑɪz], *v.a.* anreden (*Acc.*).
apothecary [ə'pɔθɪkərɪ], *s.* (*archaic*) der Apotheker; *-'s shop*, die Apotheke.
apotheosis [əpɔθɪ'ousɪs], *s.* die Vergötterung, Apotheose; (*fig.*) Verherrlichung; Auferstehung.
appal [ə'pɔ:l], *v.a.* erschrecken, entsetzen. **-ling,** *pr.p. & adj.* entsetzlich, erschreckend, schrecklich.
appanage ['æpənɪdʒ], *s. see* **apanage.**
apparatus [æpə'reɪtəs], *s.* der Apparat, das Gerät, die Vorrichtung, Ausrüstung, Hilfsmittel (*pl*); *critical -*, kritischer Apparat, *wireless -*, der Radioapparat.
apparel [ə'pærəl], 1. *s.* (*archaic*) die Kleidung, Tracht, das Gewand, der Anzug. 2. *v.a.* bekleiden, schmücken; ausrüsten, ausstatten (*Naut.*).
apparent [ə'pærənt], *adj.* sichtbar (*to*, für), offenbar (*to* (*Dat.*)), einleuchtend; scheinbar, anscheinend, augenscheinlich, ersichtlich; zweifellos, klar; *heir -*, rechtmäßiger Erbe, der Erbprinz.
apparition [æpə'rɪʃən], *s.* die Erscheinung; das Gespenst, der Geist; das Sichtbarwerden (*Astr.*).
appeal [ə'pɪ:l], 1. *v.n.* appellieren, sich wenden (*to*, an), sich berufen (*to*, auf); Berufung einlegen (*against*, gegen) (*Law*); sich beschweren, Beschwerde führen (*to*, bei); dringend ersuchen; werben, bitten (*for*, um); gefallen, zusagen (*to*, (*Dat.*)), Anklang finden (*to*, bei); *this does not - to me*, dies sagt mir nicht zu; *- to arms*, zu den Waffen greifen; *- to the country*, zur Neuwahl aufrufen (*Parl.*). 2. *s.* die Berufung, Verweisung (*to*, an), Appellation (*Law*), das Berufungsrecht; dringende Bitte (*for*, um), der Appell (*to*, an); der Anklang, die Anziehung(skraft); *an - to the people*, ein Aufruf an das Volk; *action upon -*, die Appellationsklage; *give notice of -*, Berufung einlegen; *the - was allowed*, die Berufung wurde zugelassen; *the court of -*, das Berufungsgericht; *High Court of -*, das Oberberufungsgericht; *make an - to*, appellieren *or* sich wenden an; *it makes no - to me*, es findet bei mir keinen Anklang. **-ing,** *adj.* flehend. **-ingly,** *adv.* flehentlich.
appear [ə'pɪ:ə], *v.n.* erscheinen, sichtbar werden, zum Vorschein kommen, sich zeigen, sich stellen, auftreten; scheinen; den Anschein haben; *it now -s that*, es stellt sich jetzt heraus, daß; *it -s to me*, mir scheint; *it would -*, es scheint; *- in print*, im Druck erscheinen; *- against a p.* (*in court*), gegen einen (vor Gericht) auftreten; *make -*, beweisen, zeigen, dartun; *he -ed as Othello* (*Theat.*), er trat als Othello auf. **-ance** [-rəns], *s.* das Erscheinen, Auftreten, Sichtbarwerden; die Erscheinung, der Anschein, Schein; Anblick, das Aussehen, Äußere; *-ances are against you*, der Schein spricht gegen Sie; *to all -ance(s)*, allem Anschein nach; *-ances are deceptive*, der Schein trügt; *there is every -ance of an improvement*, es hat ganz den Anschein, als ob eine Besserung eintritt; *in -ance*, dem Anschein nach, anscheinend; *judge by -ances*, nach dem Schein urteilen; *to keep up -ances*, um den Schein zu wahren; *make one's -ance*, erscheinen, sich zeigen; *non- -ance*, das Nichterscheinen; *she thinks a great deal of her personal -ance*, sie hat eine hohe Meinung von ihrer äußeren Erscheinung; *put in an -ance*, sich zeigen, erscheinen; *for the sake of -ances*, des Scheines *or* guten Aussehens wegen.
appease [ə'pɪ:z], *v.a.* beruhigen, besänftigen, beschwichtigen, versöhnen, mildern, beilegen, stillen (*hunger, etc.*). **-ment,** *s.* die Beruhigung, Stillung; *-ment policy*, die Befriedungspolitik.
appell-ant [ə'pɛlənt], 1. *adj.* appellierend. 2. *s.* der Appellant, Berufungskläger (*Law*), Bittsteller. **-ation** [-'leɪʃən], *s.* die Benennung, der Name. **-ative** [-lətɪv], 1. *adj.* benennend. 2. *s.* der Gattungsname, die Benennung, das Appellativum. **-ee,** *s.* der Appellat, Berufungsbeklagte(r) (*Law*).
append [ə'pɛnd], *v.a.* anhängen, befestigen (*to*, an); hinzufügen, beifügen (*to*, zu). **-age** [-ɪdʒ], *s.* der Anhang, Anhänger, das Anhängsel; die Zugabe, das Zubehör.
appendicitis [əpɛndɪ'sɑɪtɪs], *s.* die Blinddarmentzündung.
appendix [ə'pɛndɪks], *s.* (*pl.* -dices) der Anhang, das Anhängsel, Zubehör; der Fortsatz (*Anat.*); der Blinddarm (*Med.*); *vermiform -*, der Wurmfortsatz (*Anat.*).
appercepti-on [æpə:'sɛpʃən], *s.* die Apperzeption. **-ve,** *adj.* apperzipierend.
appertain [æpə:'teɪn], *v.n.* zugehören, zustehen (*to* (*Dat.*)); *things -ing to this life*, die zeitlichen Güter.
appetenc-e ['æpɪtəns], **-y,** *s.* die Begierde, das Gelüst(e), Verlangen, der Trieb (*for, after*, nach).
appeti-te ['æpɪtɑɪt], *s.* der Appetit, Hunger (*for*, auf), die Begierde, das Verlangen, der Trieb, die Neigung (*for*, nach). **-zer,** *s.* pikante Vorspeise. **-zing,** *adj.* appetitlich, appetitreizend, lecker.
applau-d [ə'plɔ:d], 1. *v.a. & n.* Beifall klatschen (*Dat.*); (*fig.*) zustimmen, billigen, loben, preisen. **-se,** *s.* der Beifall, Applaus, das Beifallklatschen, Händeklatschen; (*fig.*) die Billigung; *round of -se*, lauter Beifall.
apple [æpl], *s.* der Apfel; *- of discord*, der Zankapfel; *- of the eye*, der Augapfel, Liebling. **--cart,** *s.* der Apfelkarren; *upset the* or *a p.'s --cart*, jemandes Pläne zunichte machen. **--dumpling,** *s.* der Apfelkloß. **--fritters,** *pl.* die Apfelschnitten. **--pie,** *s.* die Apfelpastete; (*coll.*) *--pie order*, peinliche Ordnung. **--sauce,** *s.* die Apfeltunke, das Apfelmus. **--tart,** *s.* die Apfeltorte.
appliance [ə'plɑɪəns], *s.* die Anwendung, das Hilfsmittel, der Apparat, das Gerät, die Vorrichtung.
applica-bility [æplɪkə'bɪlɪtɪ], *s.* die Anwendbarkeit. **-ble** ['æplɪkəbl], *adj.* anwendbar (*to*, auf (*Acc.*)); verwendbar, angängig. **-nt** ['æplɪkənt], *s.* der Bittsteller, Bewerber. **-tion** [-'keɪʃən], *s.* die Auflegung, Anlegung; der Verband, Umschlag (*Med.*); die Verwendung, Anwendung (*to*, auf (*Acc.*)); der Gebrauch, die Bedeutung (*to*, für); die Bewerbung, das Gesuch, der Antrag, die Bitte (*to a p.*, an; *for a th.*, um); der Fleiß, die Aufmerksamkeit, Hingabe; *for external -tion*, äußerlich (zu gebrauchen); *make (an) -tion for*, sich bewerben um; *-tion to a case*, die Anwendung auf einen Fall; *on -tion*, auf Wunsch *or* Ersuchen; *on the -tion of ...*, auf das Gesuch *or* auf Ansuchen von ...; *close -tion is necessary*, großer Fleiß ist erforderlich; *point of -tion*, der Angriffspunkt (*Phys.*).

applied [ə'plaɪd], *adj.* angewandt; – *mathematics*, angewandte Mathematik.

appliqué work [ə'plɪ:keɪ wɔ:k], *s.* die Applikationsstickerei.

apply [ə'plaɪ], 1. *v.a.* anwenden, gebrauchen, verwenden (*to*, zu); anlegen, auflegen (*Med.*); – *colours*, Farben auftragen; – *one's mind to a th.*, den Sinn auf etwas lenken *or* richten; – *a th. to a certain use*, eine Sache zu einem gewissen Zwecke anwenden *or* verwenden. 2. *v.r.*; – *o.s. to*, sich (einer S.) widmen, sich (einer S.) befleißigen, sich auf (etwas) legen. 3. *v.n.* passen, sich schicken (*to*, zu); sich beziehen, sich anwenden lassen (*to*, auf), zur Anwendung kommen; sich bewerben (*for*, um), beantragen (*for a th.*, (*Acc.*)); – *to a p.* (*for assistance, etc.*), sich an einen (um Hilfe, *etc.*) wenden, sich bei einem (wegen Hilfe) melden; – *for an increase in salary*, eine Gehaltszulage beantragen; *does that – to me?* gilt das mir? geht das mich an? – *at the office*, Meldungen im Büro.

appoint [ə'pɔɪnt], *v.a.* bestimmen, festsetzen, verabreden, anberaumen (*a day, etc.*); vorschreiben, anordnen; ernennen; bestellen, anstellen; *I –ed to meet him today*, ich habe mit ihm verabredet, ihn heute zu treffen; *he was –ed guardian*, er wurde zum Vormund bestellt *or* ernannt; *well –ed*, gut eingerichtet, wohl ausgerüstet. **–ment,** *s.* die Bestimmung, Festsetzung; Verabredung; das Stelldichein; die Stelle, das Amt; die Ernennung, Anstellung; Anordnung, Verordnung, der Befehl, Beschluß; *make an –ment*, eine Stelle besetzen; *make an –ment with*, sich verabreden mit, eine Verabredung treffen mit; *keep* (*break*) *an –ment*, zur verabredeten Zeit (nicht) erscheinen; *have an –ment*, eine Verabredung haben; *by –ment*, verabredetermaßen, laut Verabredung; *purveyor by royal –ment*, königlicher Hoflieferant; *hold an –ment*, eine Stelle innehaben. **–ments,** *pl.* die Ausrüstung, Einrichtung, Ausrüstungsgegenstände (*pl.*).

apportion [ə'pɔ:ʃən], *v.a.* verhältnismäßig *or* richtig verteilen, zuteilen, zumessen. **–ment,** *s.* die Verteilung, Zuteilung.

apposit–e ['æpozɪt], *adj.* passend, treffend, angemessen. **–eness,** *s.* die Schicklichkeit, Angemessenheit. **–ion** [–'zɪʃən], *s.* die Nebeneinanderstellung, Beifügung; Apposition (*Gram.*).

apprais–al [ə'preɪzəl], *s. see* **–ement. –e** [ə'preɪz], *v.a.* abschätzen; anschlagen, taxieren. **–ement,** *s.* die Abschätzung; Bewertung. **–er,** *s.* der Taxator.

appreciabl–e [ə'prɪ:ʃɪəbl], *adj.*, **–y,** *adv.* abschätzbar, taxierbar; merklich, beträchtlich.

appreciat–e [ə'prɪ:ʃɪeɪt], 1. *v.a.* (hoch– *or* wert–) schätzen, richtig schätzen, würdigen, zu würdigen wissen; einsehen, gewahr werden, wahrnehmen. 2. *v.n.* an Wert zunehmen, im Preise steigen. **–ion** [–'eɪʃən], *s.* die Würdigung, Schätzung, Wertschätzung; das Verständnis (*of*, für); die Preiserhöhung. **–ive** [–ʃɪətɪv], **–ory** [–ʃɪətərɪ], *adj.* verständnisvoll, anerkennend; *–ive of*, empfänglich für.

apprehen–d [æprɪ'hɛnd], *v.a.* anfassen, ergreifen; verhaften (*a prisoner, etc.*); (er)fassen, begreifen, verstehen, einsehen (*an idea, etc.*); voraussehen, befürchten. **–sible,** *adj.* wahrnehmbar, faßlich, begreiflich. **–sion** [–ʃən], *s.* das Ergreifen, die Festnahme, Verhaftung, das Auffassungsvermögen, die Auffassung, Wahrnehmung; der Begriff, die Vorstellung; Furcht, Befürchtung, Besorgnis, Angst; *be quick of –sion*, leicht fassen *or* schnell begreifen; *dull of –sion*, schwer von Begriff(en), langsam auffassend; *be under –sion of*, (etwas) befürchten. **–sive,** *adj.* besorgt (*for*, um), furchtsam; *be –sive of*, sich fürchten vor, befürchten.

apprentice [ə'prɛntɪs], 1. *s.* der Lehrling; (*fig.*) Anfänger, Neuling. 2. *v.a.* in die Lehre geben (*to*, bei); *be –d to*, in der Lehre sein *or* in die Lehre kommen bei. **–ship,** *s.* die Lehrzeit, die Lehrjahre (*pl.*); die Lehre, Lehrlingsausbildung; *serve one's –ship*, seine Lehrzeit durchmachen, in der Lehre sein.

apprise [ə'praɪz], *v.a.* benachrichtigen, in Kenntnis setzen (*of*, von).

appro ['æproʊ] (*abbr. of* **approval**); *on* –, zur Ansicht (*C.L.*).

approach [ə'proʊtʃ], 1. *v.n.* & *a.* sich nähern (*Dat.*); (*fig.*) sich wenden an, herantreten an, angehen; nahekommen, ähnlich sein (*to* (*Dat.*)). 2. *v.n.* nahen, näherkommen. 3. *s.* das Herannahen, die Annäherung; der Anmarsch (*Mil.*); der Zutritt, Zugang (*to*, zu); die Auffahrt; der Annäherungsversuch; die Stellungnahme (*to*, gegenüber). **–es,** *pl.* das Vorfeld; *method of* –, die Annäherungsmethode (*Math.*); *easy of* –, leicht zugänglich; *make the first* –, die ersten Schritte tun; – *shot*, der Annäherungsschlag (*Golf*). **–able,** *adj.* erreichbar; zugänglich. **– –trench,** *s.* der Laufgraben.

approbat–e ['æprobeɪt], *v.a.* (*Amer.*) die Erlaubnis geben, die Genehmigung erteilen (*to*, zu); anerkennen, billigen (*Acc.*). **–ion** [–'beɪʃən], *s.* die Billigung, Genehmigung, Zustimmung; *on –ion*, zur Ansicht (*C.L.*).

appropriat–e 1. [ə'proʊprɪeɪt], *v.a.* sich aneignen; bestimmen, verwenden; *–e s.th.* (*to o.s.*), sich (*Dat.*) etwas aneignen. 2. [rɪət] *adj.* zuständig, zugehörig, eigen; zweckmäßig, angemessen, passend. **–eness,** *s.* die Angemessenheit. **–ion** [–'eɪʃən], *s.* die Aneignung, Besitznahme; Anwendung, Verwendung, Anweisung, Zuweisung, Bestimmung, Bewilligung (*Parl.*). **–or,** *s. see* **impropriator;** einer der sich etwas aneignet.

approv–able [ə'pru:vəbl], *adj.* löblich. **–al** [ə'pru:vəl], *s.* die Billigung, Zustimmung, Bewilligung, Genehmigung, Gutheißung, der Beifall; *meet with –al*, Beifall finden; *give –al to*, billigen; *with the –al of the senate*, mit Genehmigung des Senates; *on –al*, zur Ansicht (*C.L.*). **–e** [ə'pru:v], 1. *v.a.* & *n.* (with *of*) billigen, genehmigen, gutheißen; anerkennen, bestätigen; empfehlen. 2. *v.r.* sich erweisen (*to be*, als); *be –ed of*, Anklang finden (*by*, bei). **–ed,** *adj.* anerkannt, bewährt, erprobt. **–er,** *s.* der Billiger; Kronzeuge (*Law*).

approximat–e 1. [ə'prɔksɪmət], *adj.* annähernd: nahe, dicht (*to*, bei, an (*Dat.*)). **–ely,** *adv.* etwa, ungefähr. 2. [–eɪt] *v.n.* & *a.* sich nähern *or* nahen, nahekommen (*to* (*Dat.*)); nahebringen, ähnlich machen. **–ion** [–'meɪʃən], *s.* die Näherung, Annäherung (*to*, an), der Näherungswert (*Math.*); *by –ion*, annähernd. **–ive,** *adj.* annähernd.

appurtenan–ce [ə'pə:tɪnəns], *s.* das (*or* der) Zubehör, das (Besitz)Recht (*Law*). **–t,** *adj.* zugehörig, gehörend (*to*, zu).

apricot ['eɪprɪkɔt], *s.* die Aprikose.

April ['eɪprɪl], *s.* der April. **– –fool,** *s.* der Aprilnarr; *I made an – –fool of him*, ich habe ihn in den April geschickt; *– –fool(s) day*, der erste April.

a priori ['æprɪɔ:rɪ], *adj.* & *adv.* von Ursache auf Wirkung schließend, von aller Erfahrung unabhängig.

apron ['eɪprən], *s.* die Schürze; das Schurzfell (*of a smith*); der Schurz (*Eccl.*); das Spritzleder, Schutzleder (*on carts, etc.*); der Pfannendeckel (*of a gun*); die Vorbühne (*Theat.*); Binnenvorsteven (*Shipb.*); Landebahn (*Av.*). **– –string,** *s.* das Schürzenband; (*coll.*) *he is tied to his mother's – –strings*, er ist ein Muttersöhnchen.

apropos ['æprəpoʊ], 1 *adv.* nebenbei, beiläufig. 2. *pred. adj.* gelegen, angemessen, passend. 3. *prep.*; – *of*, anläßlich, hinsichtlich, in betreff (*Gen.*).

aps–e [æps], *s.* die Apsis, Altarnische. **–is,** *s.* (*pl.* -ides) die Apside (*Astron.*).

apt [æpt], *adj.* tauglich, angemessen, geeignet, geschickt, fähig, gewandt (*at*, in (*Dat.*)); geneigt; (*Amer.*) voraussichtlich, wahrscheinlich; – *scholar*, fähiger Schüler, ein Schüler, der leicht faßt; *he is – to forget*, er vergißt leicht; – *to quarrel*, streitsüchtig. **–itude,** *see* **aptitude. –ness,** *s.* die Angemessenheit, Geeignetheit.

apter–a ['æptərə], *pl.* Flügellose (Insekten). **–ous,** *adj.* flügellos. **–yx,** *s. see* **Kiwi.**

aptitude ['æptɪtju:d], *s.* die Angemessenheit; Geneigtheit, Neigung, der Hang; die Fähigkeit, Begabung, Tauglichkeit, Eignung, Befähigung (*in*. zu, in (*Dat.*)). **– –test,** die Eignungsprüfung.

aqua– –fortis [ækwə'fɔ:tɪs], *s.* das Scheidewasser, Ätzwasser. **–marine,** 1. *s.* der Aquamarin, Beryll. 2. *adj.* blaugrün. **– –regia** [–'rɪ:dʒɪə], *s.* das Königswasser, Goldscheidewasser, die Salpetersäure. **–relle** [ækwə'rɛl], *s.* die Aquarellmalerei.

–rium [ə'kwɛərɪəm], *s.* das Aquarium. **–rius** [ə'kwɛərɪəs], *s.* der Wassermann (*Astron.*). **–tic** [ə'kwætɪk], *adj.* Wasser–; *–tic plant,* die Wasserpflanze. **–tics,** *pl.* der Wassersport. **–tint** ['ækwətɪnt], *s.* die Aquatintamanier, Tuschmanier (*Engr.*); der Aquatintadruck. **--vitae,** *s.* der Aquavit, Branntwein.
aque–duct ['ækwɪdʌkt], *s.* die Wasserleitung; der Kanal (*Anat.*). **–ous** ['eɪkwɪəs], *adj.* wässerig, wasserhaft, wasserhaltig, Wasser–; *–ous humour,* wässerige Feuchtigkeit (*of the eye*) (*Med.*); *–ous rocks,* das Sediment– *or* Schichtgestein; *–ous vapour,* der Wasserdampf, Wasserdunst.
aquiline ['ækwɪlaɪn], *adj.* dem Adler gehörig, adlerartig; (*fig.*) krumm, gebogen; – *nose,* die Adlernase.
arabesque [ærə'bɛsk], 1. *s.* die Arabeske. 2. *adj.* arabisch, maurisch, arabesk.
arable ['ærəbl], 1. *adj.* pflügbar, bestellbar, urbar, anbaubar, kulturfähig. 2. *s.* das Ackerland.
arachn–id [ə'ræknɪd], *s.* das Spinnentier. **–oid** [–nɔɪd], *adj.* spinnenartig, spinnwebartig; *–oid tunic,* die Spinnwebenhaut (*of the brain*) (*Anat.*).
arbit–er ['ɑ:bɪtə], *s.* der Schiedsrichter; (*fig.*) Gebieter, Herr. **–ral,** *adj.* schiedsrichterlich. **–rament** [ɑ:'bɪtrəmənt], *s.* der Schiedsspruch, die Entscheidung.
arbitrar–ily ['ɑ:bɪtrərəlɪ], *adv. see* **–y. –iness,** *s.* despotische Gewalt, die Willkür. **–y,** *adj.* willkürlich, launenhaft; eigenmächtig, unumschränkt, despotisch.
arbitrat–e ['ɑ:bɪtreɪt], *v.a. & n.* schiedsrichterlich entscheiden, durch Schiedsspruch schlichten, einen Schiedsspruch fällen, Schiedsrichter sein; entscheiden, festsetzen. **–ion** [–'treɪʃən], *s.* schiedsrichterliches Verfahren, schiedsrichterliche Entscheidung *or* Schlichtung; *court of –ion,* der Schlichtungsausschuß; *submit a disputed point to –ion,* einen Streitpunkt einem Schiedsgericht unterwerfen; *settle by –ion,* durch Schiedsspruch *or* schiedsgerichtlich schlichten; *–ion of exchange,* die Wechselarbitrage (*C.L.*). **–or** [–treɪtə], *s.* der Schiedsrichter, Schlichter.
arbor ['ɑ:bə], *s.* die Spindel, Welle, Achse, der Drehbaum (*Mech.*). **–aceous** [–'reɪʃəs], *adj.* Baum–, baumartig, bewaldet. **–eal** [ɑ:'bɔ:rɪəl], *adj.* Baum–, auf Bäumen lebend. **–escent** [–'rɛsnt], *adj.* baumförmig, baumartig, verzweigt. **–iculture,** *s.* die Baumzucht. **–ization,** *s* baumförmige Gestaltung (*of crystals, etc.*) (*Chem.*). **– vitae** [–'vaɪtɪ], *s.* der Lebensbaum.
arbour ['ɑ:bə], *s.* die Laube.
arbutus [ɑ:'bju:təs], *s.* der Erdbeerbaum.
arc [ɑ:k], *s.* der Bogen (*Geom.*); der Lichtbogen (*Elec.*); *describe an –,* einen Kreisbogen schlagen. **–ade** [ɑ:'keɪd], *s.* der Bogengang, die Arkade, der Durchgang. **--lamp,** *s.* die Bogenlampe (*Elec.*). **--light,** *s.* das Bogenlicht.
arcan–um [ɑ:'keɪnəm], *s.* (*usually pl.* –a) das Geheimnis.
[1]**arch** [ɑ:tʃ], 1. *s.* der Bogen, die Wölbung, das Gewölbe; *triumphal –,* der Triumphbogen. 2. *v.a.* wölben, überwölben; bogenförmig machen. **–ed,** *p.p. & adj.* gewölbt, geschweift, bogenförmig, Bogen–. 3. *v.a.*; *– one's back,* einen Buckel machen. 4. *v.n.* sich wölben. **--buttress,** *s.* der Strebebogen. **--stone,** *s.* der Schlußstein. **– support,** *s.* die Senkfußeinlage. **–way,** *s.* der Bogengang, überwölbter Torweg.
[2]**arch,** 1. *prefix,* oberst, erst, hauptsächlich, führend, Haupt–, Erz–. 2. *adj.* schlau, durchtrieben; schalkhaft, schelmisch (*see* **–ness**). **–angel** ['ɑ:k–], *s.* der Erzengel. **–bishop,** *s.* der Erzbischof. **–bishopric,** *s.* das Erzbistum. **–deacon,** *s.* der Archidiakonus. **–ducal,** *adj.* erzherzoglich. **–duchess,** *s.* die Erzherzogin. **–duchy,** *s.* das Erzherzogtum. **–duke,** *s.* der Erzherzog. **--enemy,** *s.* der Erzfeind. **--fiend,** *s.* Satan, der Teufel. **--see,** *s* die Erzdiözese.
archaean [ɑ:'kɪ:ən], *adj.* azoisch (*Geol.*).
archaeolog–ical [ɑ:kɪə'lɔdʒɪkl], *adj.* archäologisch, Altertums–. **–ist** [–'ɔlədʒɪst], *s.* der Altertumsforscher, Archäolog. **–y** [–'ɔlədʒɪ], *s.* die Altertumswissenschaft, Archäologie.
archai–c [ɑ:'keɪɪk], *adj.* altertümlich, veraltet, altmodisch. **–sm,** *s.* veralteter Ausdruck, der Archaismus.
archangel, *see* [2]**arch–.**
archbishop–ric, *see* [2]**arch–.**
archdeacon, *see* [2]**arch–.**
archdu–cal, –chess, –chy, –ke, *see* [2]**arch–.**
archer ['ɑ:tʃə], *s.* der Bogenschütze; Schütze (*Astron.*). **–y** [–rɪ], *s.* das Bogenschießen.
archetyp–al ['ɑ:kɪtaɪpl], *adj.* urbildlich. **–e,** *s.* das Urbild, Vorbild, die Urform.
archi–diaconal [ɑ:kɪdaɪ'ækənl], *adj.* archidiakonisch. **–episcopal** [–ɛ'pɪskəpl], *adj.* erzbischöflich.
archipelago [ɑ:kɪ'pɛləgoʊ], *s.* der Archipel, die Inselgruppe, das Inselmeer.
architect ['ɑ:kɪtɛkt], *s.* der Baumeister, Architekt; (*fig.*) Begründer, Urheber, Schöpfer; *the – of his own fortune,* seines eignen Glückes Schmied. **–onic** [–'tɔnɪk], *adj.* architektonisch. **–ural** [–'tɛktʃərəl], *adj.* baulich, baukünstlerisch, Bau–, Architektur–. **–ure** [–tʃə], *s.* die Baukunst, Architektur; der Baustil, die Bauart; der Bau (*also fig.*); *school of –ure,* die Bauschule; *naval –ure,* der Schiffsbau, die Schiffsbaukunst.
architrave ['ɑ:kɪtreɪv], *s.* der Architrav.
archiv–al [ɑ:'kaɪvəl], *adj.* Archiv–, archivalisch **–es** ['ɑ.kaɪvz], *pl.* das Archiv, die Urkundensammlung; *keeper of the –es,* **–ist** ['ɑ:kɪvɪst], *s.* der Archivar.
archivolt ['ɑ:kɪvəlt], *s* die Archivolte, Bogeneinfassung.
archness ['ɑ:tʃnɪs], *s.* die Schelmerei, Schalkhaftigkeit, der Mutwille, die Schlauheit.
archway, *s see* [1]**arch–.**
arctic ['ɑ:ktɪk], *adj.* arktisch, nördlich, Polar–; *– circle,* nördlicher Polarkreis; *– expedition,* die Nordpolexpedition; *– fox,* der Polarfuchs; *– Ocean,* Nördliches Eismeer; *– regions,* die Nordpolarländer (*pl.*).
arden–cy ['ɑ:dənsɪ], *s.* die Hitze, Glut; Inbrunst. **–t** ['ɑ:dənt], *adj.* heiß, glühend, feurig, innig, inbrünstig, eifrig; *–t spirits,* geistige Getränke.
ardour ['ɑ:də], *s.* die Hitze, Glut, Heftigkeit; Inbrunst, der Eifer.
arduous ['ɑ:djʊəs], *adj.* schwierig, mühsam; (*archaic*) jäh, steil; ausdauernd, eifrig, tätig, emsig (*of persons*). **–ness,** *s.* die Schwierigkeit, Mühseligkeit.
are [ɑ:, ə *acc. to emphasis*], *see* **be.**
area ['ɛərɪə], *s.* die (Grund)Fläche; der Raum, freier Platz; das Gebiet, die Zone; (*fig.*) der Bereich, Spielraum; Flächeninhalt, Flächenraum; Vorplatz, Souterrainvorhof; *the – of a circle,* der Flächeninhalt eines Kreises; *covered –,* bestrichener Raum (*Artil.*); *prohibited –,* das Sperrgebiet. **--bell,** *s.* die Dienstbotenglocke. **– steps,** *pl.* die Außentreppe zum Souterrain.
arena [ə'rɪ nə], *s.* die Arena, der Kampfplatz. **–ceous,** *adj.* sandig.
areola [ə'rɪ:ələ], *s.* die Areole, Zelle (*Bot.*); der Brustwarzenring (*Anat.*). **–r,** *adj.* netzförmig, zellig; *–r tissue,* das Zellengewebe (*Anat.*).
areometer [ærɪ'ɔmɪtə], *s.* die Senkwaage, der Aräometer.
arête ['æreɪt], *s.* der Bergkamm.
argent ['ɑ:dʒənt], *adj.* silberfarbig, glänzend, silbern; silberweiß (*Her.*). **–iferous** [–'tɪfərəs], *adj.* silberhaltig. **–ine** [–taɪn], *adj.* silbern, silberartig.
argill–aceous [ɑ:dʒɪ'leɪʃəs], *adj.* tonig, tonartig, tönern. **–iferous** [–'lɪfərəs], *adj.* tonhaltig.
argon ['ɑ:gən], *s.* das Argon.
argosy ['ɑ:gəsɪ], *s.* das Handelsschiff.
argu–able, *adj.* diskutierbar, bestreitbar. **–e** ['ɑ:gju:], 1. *v.a. & n.* beweisen, erweisen; erörtern, diskutieren; bekunden, verraten, deuten (auf (*Acc.*)); *–e sagacity,* Scharfsinn verraten; *–e the point,* die Sache bestreiten; *–e a p. into a th.,* einen zu etwas überreden; *I won't be –ed out of that,* davon lasse ich mich nicht abbringen. 2. *v.n.* Schlüsse ziehen (auf (*Acc.*)), schließen, folgern (*from,* von, aus); Einwendungen machen (*against,* gegen), Gründe anführen (*for,* für; *against,* gegen); streiten, disputieren (*about,* über (*Acc.*)). **–ment,** *s.*

der Beweis(grund), das Beweismittel, die Beweisführung, Schlußfolgerung; das Argument, der Streit, die Streitfrage, der Streitpunkt, Einwand, die Erörterung, Auseinandersetzung; das Disputieren; der Schluß (*Log.*); Gegenstand, das Thema, der Hauptinhalt; *clinch an –ment*, triftige Beweisgründe anführen; *hold an –ment*, diskutieren; *lame* or *weak –ment*, schwacher Beweis; *strong –ment*, stichhaltiger Beweis, wichtiges Argument. **–mentation** [–mɛn'teɪʃən], *s.* die Beweisführung, Schlußfolgerung, Erörterung. **–mentative** [–'mɛntətɪv], *adj.* streitsüchtig. **–mentativeness,** *s.* die Streitlust.

aria ['ɑ:rɪə], *s.* die Arie.

arid ['ærɪd], *adj.* dürr, trocken; wasserlos, unfruchtbar; (*fig.*) reizlos, schal, trocken. **–ity** [–'rɪdɪtɪ], *s.* die Dürre, Trockenheit.

Aries ['ɛərɪi:z], *s.* der Widder (*Astr.*).

aright [ə'raɪt], *adv.* recht, richtig; zurecht.

arise [ə'raɪz], *ir.v.n.* sich erheben, aufstehen; entstehen, erscheinen; hervorgehen, entspringen (*from*, aus); herrühren (*from*, von); auferstehen (*from the dead*); *the question doesn't –*, es kommt gar nicht in Frage.

aristocra–cy [ærɪs'tɔkrəsɪ], *s.* die Aristokratie, Adelsherrschaft, der Adel; (*fig.*) die Elite. **–t** ['ærɪstəkræt], *s.* der Aristokrat, Adelige(r). **–tic** [–'krætɪk], *adj.* aristokratisch, adlig, edel, vornehm.

arithmetic [ə'rɪθmətɪk], *s.* die Rechenkunst, Arithmetik; *mental –*, das Kopfrechnen. **–(al)** [–'mɛtɪk(l)], *adj.* arithmetisch; *– mean*, arithmetisches Mittel; *–al progression*, arithmetische Reihe. **–ian** [–mə'tɪʃən], *s.* der Arithmetiker, Rechner.

ark [ɑ:k], *s.* die Lade, der Kasten; *Noah's –*, die Arche Noah; *– of the covenant*, die Bundeslade.

¹arm [ɑ:m], *s.* der Arm; (*fig.*) die Macht, Stärke; der Ast, Zweig; die Seitenlehne (*of a chair*); der Flügel (*of a windmill*); *at –'s length*, auf Armlänge; *hold at –'s length*, vor sich ausgestreckt halten; *keep a p. at –'s length*, sich (*Dat.*) einen vom Leibe halten; *distributor –*, der Verteilerfinger (*Mech.*); *fold one's –s*, die Arme kreuzen; *go – in –*, Arm in Arm gehen; *child in –s*, das Tragkind, kleines Kind; *take s.o. in one's –s*, einen in die Arme schließen; *with a girl on his –*, mit einem Mädel am Arm; *with open –s*, mit offenen Armen; *– of the sea*, der Meeresarm; *the secular –*, die weltliche Macht, die Obrigkeit; *– of service*, die Waffengattung (*Mil.*); *within –'s reach*, im Machtbereich, in unmittelbarer Nähe. **–band,** *s.* die Armbinde. **–chair,** *s.* der Lehnstuhl, Sessel. **–ed,** *adj. suffix* –armig. **–ful,** *s.* der Armvoll. **––hole,** *s.* das Armloch. **–let,** *s.* die Armbinde, das Armband; die Armspange. **–pit,** *s.* die Achselhöhle. **–rest,** *s.* die Armlehne.

²arm, 1. *s.* (*usually pl.*) *see* **–s;** die Waffe, Waffengattung. 2. *v.a.* bewaffnen, (aus)rüsten; armieren (*a magnet*); *– a grenade*, eine Granate scharf machen. 3. *v.n.* aufrüsten, sich rüsten *or* bewaffnen; *–ed to the teeth*, bis an die Zähne bewaffnet; *–ed assistance*, der Waffenbeistand; *–ed forces*, die Wehrmacht, die Streitkräfte (*pl.*).

armada [ɑ:'meɪdə], *s.* die Kriegsflotte, Armada.

armadillo [ɑ:mə'dɪloʊ], *s.* das Armadill, Gürteltier.

armament ['ɑ:məmənt], *s.* die Kriegsrüstung; Kriegsmacht; Bewaffnung; schweres Geschütz, Schiffsgeschütze (*pl.*); die Bestückung (*of a ship*); *– race*, das Wettrüsten.

armature ['ɑ:mətjʊə], *s.* die Armatur, der Anker (*Elec.*); *– winding*, die Ankerwicklung.

armchair, *see* **¹arm;** *– politician*, der Bierbankpolitiker.

armful ['ɑ:mfʊl], *see* **¹arm.**

armillary [ɑ:'mɪlərɪ], *adj.* ringförmig.

armistice ['ɑ:mɪstɪs], *s.* der Waffenstillstand, die Waffenruhe; *– day*, der Heldengedenktag.

armlet ['ɑ:mlɪt], *see* **¹arm.**

armorial [ɑ:'mɔ:rɪəl], *adj.* heraldisch, Wappen–; *– bearings*, das Wappen(schild).

armour ['ɑ:mə], 1. *s.* die Rüstung, der Harnisch, Panzer; die Bepanzerung; Panzerung, Schutzdecke (*Zool.*); Bewehrung (*of a cable*); der Taucheranzug; *suit of –*, die Rüstung; *chain-–*, der Kettenpanzer. 2. *v.a.* panzern, bewaffnen. **––bearer,** *s.* der Waffenträger, Schildknappe. **––clad,** *see* **––plated.** **–ed,** *p.p. & adj.* gepanzert; *–ed cable*, armiertes *or* bewehrtes Kabel; *–ed car*, der Panzerwagen; *–ed train*, der Panzerzug. **–er** [–rə], *s.* der Waffenschmied, Büchsenmacher; der Waffenmeister. **––piercing,** *adj.* panzerbrechend; *––piercing bullet*, das Kerngeschoß; *––piercing gun*, die Panzerabwehrkanone; *––piercing shell*, die Panzergranate. **––plate,** *s.* der Panzer. **––plated,** *adj.* gepanzert; *––plated ship*, das Panzerschiff. **–y,** *s.* die Rüstkammer, das Zeughaus.

arms [ɑ:mz], *pl.* die Waffen, Bewaffnung. 1. (*with nouns & adjectives*) *coat of –*, das Wappen; *companion in –*, der Waffenbruder; *fire-–*, Feuerwaffen; *man-at-–*, der Soldat; *passage of –*, der Waffengang; *profession of –*, der Soldatenstand; *serjeant-at-–*, der Parlamentsbeamte; *side-–*, das Seitengewehr; *small-–*, Handfeuerwaffen; *stand of –*, volle Ausrüstung. 2. (*with verbs*) *be under –*, unter den Waffen stehen *or* sein; *bear* or *carry –*, Waffen führen; *capable of bearing –*, waffenfähig; *call to –*, zu den Waffen rufen; *ground* or *order –!* Gewehr ab! *lay down one's –*, die Waffen strecken, sich ergeben; *pile –!* setzt die Gewehre zusammen! *present –!* präsentiert das Gewehr! *rise in –*, die Waffen ergreifen, sich erheben; *shoulder –!* Gewehr an Schulter! *slope –!* Gewehr über! *stand to your –!* an die Gewehre! *the men stood to their –*, die Mannschaft trat unters Gewehr; *take up –*, zu den Waffen greifen. 3. (*with prepositions*) *by force of –*, mit Waffengewalt; *up in –*, unter Waffen; (*fig.*) in hellem Zorn, in hellem Aufruhr.

army ['ɑ:mɪ], *s.* das Heer, die Armee; (*fig.*) der Schwarm, die Schar; *enter* or *go into the –*, ins Heer eintreten (*as an officer*); *join the –*, Soldat werden (*in the ranks*). **– bill,** die Wehrvorlage (*Parl.*). **––chaplain,** *s.* Feldgeistliche(r), *m.* **––contractor,** *s.* der Heereslieferant. **––corps,** *s.* das Armeekorps. **––list,** *s.* die Rangliste. **––school,** *s.* die Heeresfachschule. **– service corps,** Nachschubtruppen, Versorgungstruppen, Fahrtruppen (*pl.*), der Train. **– welfare,** die Heeresbetreuung.

arnica ['ɑ:nɪkə], *s.* die Arnika.

aroma [ə'roʊmə], *s.* der Duft, Geruch, Wohlgeruch, das Aroma; die Würze; das Bukett, die Blume (*of wine*). **–tic** [æro'mætɪk], *adj.* duftig, würzig, wohlriechend, aromatisch.

arose [ə'roʊz], *see* **arise.**

around [ə'raʊnd], 1. *adv.* rundherum, ringsherum, rundum; (*coll.*) um, etwa, ungefähr; (*sl.*) *stick –!* bleib in der Nähe! 2. *prep.* um . . . herum; *they danced – the Maypole*, sie tanzten um den Maibaum (herum).

arouse [ə'raʊz], *v.a.* (auf)wecken; (*fig.*) aufregen, erregen, aufrütteln.

arquebus ['ɑ:kwɪbəs], *s.* die Arkebuse.

arrack ['ærək], *s.* der Arrak.

arraign [ə'reɪn], *v.a.* (*fig.*) anklagen, beschuldigen; vor Gericht ziehen *or* stellen; anfechten. **–ment,** *s.* die Anklage, Beschuldigung, gerichtliche Belangung.

arrange [ə'reɪndʒ], *v.a. & n.* ordnen, arrangieren; in Ordnung bringen; (ein)richten, Anstalten treffen, veranstalten, anordnen, gliedern; festsetzen, abmachen, vereinbaren, verabreden; beilegen, erledigen, schlichten; bearbeiten (*music*); *– a quarrel*, einen Streit schlichten; *the matter has been –d*, die Sache ist abgemacht *or* beigelegt; *I will – for it* (*to be done*), ich will dafür sorgen (daß . . . *etc.*). **–ment,** *s.* die Ordnung, Anordnung, Einrichtung; Einteilung, Gliederung, Aufstellung; der Vergleich, die Erledigung, Beilegung; Übereinkunft, Verabredung, Abmachung; Bearbeitung (*of music*); *–ments, pl.* Vorkehrungen, Vorbereitungen; *come to an –ment*, sich vergleichen, zu einem Vergleich kommen; *enter into* or *make an –ment with*, ein Übereinkommen treffen mit; *make –ments*, Vorkehrungen treffen. **–r,** *s.* der Anordner, Bearbeiter.

arrant ['ærənt], *adj.* durchtrieben, abgefeimt, Erz–; *– knave*, der Erzbösewicht; *– nonsense*, ausgesprochener Unsinn.

arras ['ærəs], *s.* gewirkter Teppich, gewirkte Tapete.

array [ə'reɪ], 1. *v.a.* kleiden, schmücken; ordnen, aufstellen; in Ordnung bringen; – *o.s.*, sich putzen; – *a panel*, die Geschworenen einweisen (*Law*). 2. *s.* die Ordnung (in Reih' und Glied); Truppenmacht, Mannschaften (*pl.*); Schar, das Aufgebot, die Menge, stattliche Reihe, Aufstellung; Kleidung, Tracht; Geschworenenliste (*Law*), Einsetzung der Geschworenen (*Law*); *aerial* –, das Richtantennennetz (*Rad.*); *battle*- –, die Schlachtordnung; *in rich* –, in prächtigen Gewändern.

arrear [ə'rɪ:ə], *s.* der Rückstand; *pl.* rückständige Summe, Rückstände (*pl.*), Schulden (*pl.*); *in –s*, im Rückstand; *–s of rent*, rückständige Miete.

arrest [ə'rɛst], 1. *s.* die Verhaftung, Festnahme; Inhaftnahme, der Arrest; die Haft; Beschlagnahme (*of goods*); Hemmung, Stockung; Aufschiebung, das Aufhalten, der Einhalt, die Unterbrechung; – *of judgement*, die Urteilssistierung (*Law*); *close* –, der Stubenarrest (*Mil.*); *lay – on*, mit Beschlag belegen (*Acc.*); *open* –, der Garnisonarrest (*Mil.*); *preventive* –, die Schutzhaft; *under* –, in Haft *or* Gewahrsam; in Beschlag; *place under* –, *see* **–**, 2. 2. *v.a.* in Haft nehmen, verhaften, festnehmen; mit Beschlag belegen; aufhalten, zurückhalten, anhalten, hemmen; – *s.o.'s attention*, jemandes Aufmerksamkeit fesseln; – *judgement*, das Verfahren aussetzen (*Law*). **–ing**, *adj.* fesselnd. **–ment**, *s.* die Hemmung; (*Scots*) Verhaftung, Festnahme (*Law*).

arrière–-ban ['ærɪɛ:'bæn], *s.* der Landsturm, Heerbann. **–-pensée** ['–'pɑ̃se], *s.* der Hintergedanke.

arrival [ə'raɪvl], *s.* die Ankunft, das Ankommen, Eintreffen, Erscheinen; der Ankömmling; *new* –, der Neuangekommene, (*coll.*) neugeborenes Kind; *on my* –, bei meiner Ankunft, gleich nach meiner Ankunft; – *platform*, der Ankunftsbahnsteig. **–s**, *pl.* die Zufuhren (*C.L.*), ankommende Personen, Züge, *etc.*; *list of –s*, die Fremdenliste.

arrive [ə'raɪv], *v.n.* ankommen, eintreffen (*at*, an *or* in); (*fig.*) gelangen (zu), erreichen; *it has just –d*, es ist soeben eingelaufen; – *at a conclusion*, zu einem Schlusse gelangen; – *on the scene*, auftreten.

arroga–nce ['ærəgəns], *s.* die Anmaßung, der Dünkel, Hochmut, die Vermessenheit, Unverschämtheit. **–nt**, *adj.* anmaßend, vermessen; hochmütig; unverschämt. **–te** ['ærogeɪt], *v.a.* (*usually with* to o.s.) sich (*Dat.*) anmaßen, für sich beanspruchen *or* verlangen, sich (*Dat.*) unrechtmäßig aneignen; *–te to s.o.*, für einen verlangen *or* fordern, einem zusprechen. **–ation**, *s.* die Anmaßung.

arrow ['ærou], *s.* der Pfeil; der Zählstab, Markierstab (*Surv.*); *shower of –s*, der Pfeilhagel; *straight as an* –, pfeilgerade; *swift as an* –, pfeilgeschwind. **–-grass**, *s.* der Dreizack (*Bot.*). **–-head**, *s.* die Pfeilspitze. **–root**, *s.* die Pfeilwurz (*Bot.*), das Pfeilwurzelmehl. **–y**, *adj.* pfeilförmig.

arse [ɑ:s], *s.* (*vulg.*) der Arsch, Steiß.

arsenal ['ɑ:sənl], *s.* das Zeughaus.

arsen–ate ['ɑ:sɪnɪt], **–iate** [ɑ:'sɪ:nɪɪt], *s.* arsen(ik)-saures Salz; *–iate of lead*, arsensaures Blei, das Arsenblei. **–ic** ['ɑ:snɪk], *s.* das Arsen, Arsenik. **–ical** [ɑ:'sɛnɪkl], *adj.* arsen(ik)haltig. **–ious** [–'sɪ:nɪəs], *adj.* arsenig; *–ious oxide*, die Arsenikblume. **–ite** [–naɪt], *s.* arsenigsaures Salz.

arsis ['ɑ:sɪs], *s.* die Hebung (*Metr.*).

arson ['ɑ:sn], *s.* die Brandstiftung.

[1]**art** [ɑ:t], 1. *s.* die Kunst; Kunstfertigkeit, Geschicklichkeit; der Kniff, die List, Verschlagenheit, Schlauheit; *applied* –, angewandte Kunst, das Kunstgewerbe; *–s and crafts*, Kunst und Gewerbe; *commercial* –, die Gebrauchskunst; *the –s*, die Geisteswissenschaften; *an –s degree*, ein Grad in der philosophischen Fakultät (*Univ.*); *faculty of –(s)*, philosophische Fakultät (*Univ.*); *the fine –s*, die schönen Künste; *the liberal –s*, die freien Künste; *master of –s*, Magister der philosophischen Fakultät (*Univ.*); *work of* –, das Kunstwerk. **–-gallery**, *s.* die Kunsthalle, Gemäldegalerie. **– master**, der Zeichenlehrer. **–s ball**, der Künstlerball.

[2]**art**, (*archaic & poet.*) *see* **be.**

arter–ial [ɑ:'tɪ:ərɪəl], *adj.* Pulsader–, Arterien–; *–ial blood*, das Arterienblut; *–ial road*, die Verkehrsader, Hauptverkehrsstraße, Autobahn. **–iosclerosis** [–rɪoʊsklə'roʊsɪs], *s.* die Arterienverkalkung. **–iotomy** [–'ɔtəmɪ], *s.* die Pulsaderöffnung. **–y** ['ɑ:tərɪ], *s.* die Arterie, Pulsader, Schlagader; (*fig.*) *main –ies of trade*, die Hauptverkehrsadern, Haupthandelswege.

artesian [ɑ:'tɪ:zɪən], *adj.*; *–well*, artesischer Brunnen.

artful ['ɑ:tful], *adj.* listig, schlau, verschlagen, gerissen, verschmitzt, gerieben; geschickt, kunstvoll. **–ness**, *s.* die List, Schlauheit, Verschlagenheit, *etc.*

arthrit–ic [ɑ:'θrɪtɪk], *adj.* gichtisch. **–is** [ɑ:'θraɪtɪs], *s.* die Gelenkentzündung; Gicht.

arthropoda [ɑ:'θrɔpədə], *pl.* die Gliederfüßler.

artichoke ['ɑ:tɪtʃoʊk], *s.* die Artischocke; *Jerusalem* –, die Erdartischocke.

article ['ɑ:tɪkl], 1. *s.* der Abschnitt, Teil; Artikel (*of faith, etc.*); die Klausel, Bedingung (*usually pl.*); der Aufsatz; (*C.L.*) der Gegenstand, die Ware; der Posten, Punkt; das Geschlechtswort, der Artikel (*Gram.*); *–s of agreement*, Übereinkunftsbedingungen (*pl.*); *–s of apprenticeship*, der Lehrvertrag; *–s of association*, Vereinsstatuten (*pl.*); – *of clothing*, das Kleidungsstück; – *of commerce*, der Handelsposten; – *of faith*, der Glaubensartikel; *leading* –, der Leitartikel; *serve one's –s*, als Lehrling dienen; *ship's –s*, der Heuervertrag (*Naut.*); *–s of war*, die Kriegsartikel (*pl.*). 2. *v.a.* schriftlich anklagen (*for*, wegen); kontraktlich binden, in die Lehre geben (*to*, bei); *–d clerk*, der Buchhalter– *or* Kontorlehrling.

articulat–e 1. [ɑ:'tɪkjʊleɪt], *v.a.. & n.* zusammenfügen, verbinden, gliedern; deutlich aussprechen, deutlich sprechen, artikulieren. 2. [–ət] *adj.* gegliedert; deutlich, vernehmlich, klar erkenntlich, scharf ausgeprägt. **–eness**, *s.* die Deutlichkeit. **–ion** [–'leɪʃən], *s.* die Aneinanderfügung, Verbindung, Gliederung, Gelenkfügung; das Gelenk; deutliche Aussprache, die Artikulation.

artifact, ['ɑ:tɪfækt], *s.* das Kunsterzeugnis.

artifice ['ɑ:tɪfɪs], *s.* der Kunstgriff, Kniff; die Kunstfertigkeit; List, Schlauheit. **–r** [ɑ:'tɪfɪsə], *s.* der Mechaniker, Handwerker; Artillerietechniker (*Mil.*), Maschinistenmaat (*Naut.*); (*fig.*) Stifter, Urheber.

artificial [ɑ:tɪ'fɪʃl], *adj.* künstlich; erkünstelt, nachgemacht, unecht, Schein–; geziert (*of persons*); – *flowers*, Kunstblumen; – *limb*, die Prothese; – *person*, juristische Person, die Körperschaft; – *silk*, die Kunstseide; – *smile* gekünsteltes Lächeln; – *tears*, erheuchelte Tränen; – *teeth*, falsche Zähne. **–ity** [–fɪʃɪ'ælɪtɪ], *s.* die Künstlichkeit.

artillery [ɑ:'tɪlərɪ], *s.* die Artillerie, das Geschütz; *under – fire*, unter Beschuß; *horse*- –, reitende Artillerie. **–man**, *s.* der Artillerist.

artisan [ɑ:tɪ'zæn], *s.* der Handwerker, Mechaniker.

artist ['ɑ:tɪst], *s.* der Künstler; (*fig.*) Könner. **–e**, der Artist. **–ic(al)**, [ɑ:'tɪstɪk(l)], *adj.* künstlerisch, kunstvoll, artistisch. **–ry**, *s* der Kunstsinn, das Künstlertum, künstlerisches Können.

artless ['ɑ:tlɪs], *adj.* kunstlos, ungekünstelt; natürlich, einfach, schlicht; naiv, arglos. **–ness**, *s.* die Kunstlosigkeit; Einfachheit, Natürlichkeit, Schlichtheit; Arglosigkeit, Naivität.

arum ['ærəm], *s.* die Zehrwurz (*Bot.*).

Aryan ['ɛərɪən], *adj. & s. see Index of Names.*

as [æz], 1. *adv.* so, ebenso; – . . . –, (eben)so . . wie; – *big again*, noch einmal so groß; – *clear – crystal*, kristallhell; (–) *cold – ice*, eiskalt; *twice – far*, noch einmal so weit; – *long* –, so lange wie; – *quiet – a mouse*, mäuschenstill; *I thought – much*, das dachte ich mir; – *soon* –, sobald als; – *soft – butter*, butterweich; – *well*, ferner, außerdem, noch dazu; *he might – well help me*, er könnte mir wirklich helfen; – *yesterday so today*, wie gestern so heute; – *yet*, bis jetzt, noch; *not – yet*, noch nicht. 2. *conj.* (*a*) (*comparison*) wie; – . . . –, (eben)so . . . wie; *it's – broad – it is long*, es ist so lang wie es breit ist, es läuft auf eins hinaus; – *clear – day*, sonnenklar; – *far – Africa*, so weit wie Afrika, bis (nach) Afrika; – *far – I am concerned*, was mich betrifft, meinetwegen; – *far – I know*, soviel ich weiß; – *large – life*, in Lebensgröße, lebensgroß; – *like – two peas*, zum Verwechseln ähnlich, wie ein Ei dem anderen; – *little – you please*, so wenig Sie wollen; – *much – you* *like*, soviel Sie wollen; – *sure – I live*, so wahr ich lebe; – *well – I*, ebensogut wie ich; *this – well – that*, sowohl dies als auch jenes; – *for example*, wie zum Beispiel; *great men – Caesar*, große Männer wie Cäsar; *he loves her – a father*, er liebt sie wie ein Vater; *they rose – one man*, sie standen wie ein Mann auf. (*b*) (*concession*) da; wenn auch, obgleich; *old – I am*, so alt ich auch bin, wenn ich auch alt bin, obgleich ich alt bin, da ich alt bin; *try – he would*, soviel er auch versuchte; – *you will not come, we must go without you*, da Sie nicht kommen wollen, müssen wir ohne Sie gehen. (*c*) (*time*) als, während; – *I go by*, im Vorbeigehen; – *he was reading*, beim Lesen; *he trembled – she spoke*, er zitterte während sie sprach. (*d*) (*in the capacity of*) – *if*, – *though*, als ob; *his election – chairman*, seine Wahl zum Vorsitzenden; *let me tell you – a friend*, lassen Sie mich Ihnen als Freund sagen; *she loves him – a father*, sie liebt ihn als Vater. (*e*) (*manner*) *do – I say*, tue was *or* wie ich sage; *do – I do*, machen Sie's wie ich; *according – things fall out*, je nachdem die Sachen ausfallen; – *good luck would have it*, glücklicherweise; – *you like*, wie es Euch gefällt; – *you were!* zurück! (*Gymn.*). (*f*) (*condition*) – *you love me*, wenn Du mich liebst, so wahr Du mich liebst. (*g*) (*insertion*) – *is the case*, wie es der Fall ist; – *compared with*, im Vergleich mit, gegenüber; – *follows*, wie folgt, folgendermaßen; – *it is*, wie die Dinge liegen, ohnehin, sowieso; – *regards* . . ., was . . . anbetrifft; – *requested*, wunschgemäß; – *a rule*, in der Regel; – *usual*, wie gewöhnlich; – *it were*, sozusagen, gleichsam. (*h*) (*with prepositions*) – *for me*, was mich betrifft, in Bezug auf mich; – *per bill of lading*, laut Verladungsschein; *I was mistaken – to the day*, ich hatte mich in dem *or* in Bezug auf den Tag *or* hinsichtlich des Tages geirrt. (*i*) (*before inf.*) *be so good – to tell him*, seien Sie so gut, ihm zu sagen; *do it so – not to offend him*, tun Sie es so, daß er sich nicht verletzt fühlt; *I did not so much – see him*, ich sah ihn überhaupt nicht. **3.** *rel. pron. such a fool – to believe*, ein solcher Esel der glaubt; *his conduct was such – to deserve punishment*, sein Betragen war derart, daß es Strafe verdiente; *such – I like*, die, welche mir gefallen; *such* (*people*) – *are homeless*, diejenigen, die heimatlos sind; *he was a Russian, – we perceived from his accent*, er war Russe, was wir an seiner Sprache hörten.

asafœtida [æsə'fɛtɪdə], *s.* der Stinkasant, Teufelsdreck.

asbestos [æz'bɛstɔs], *s.* der Asbest, Steinflachs, das Bergleder.

ascen–d [ə'sɛnd], **1.** *v.n.* hinaufsteigen, aufsteigen, auffahren, auffliegen; sich erheben, in die Höhe fliegen; (*of time*) zurückgehen, hinaufreichen (*to*, bis *or* an); aufgehen (*Astron.*); in die Höhe gehen (*Mus.*). **2.** *v.a.* besteigen, ersteigen; hinauffahren (*a river*); *–d* (*to*) *the throne*, den Thron besteigen. **–dancy, –dency,** *s.* das Übergewicht, die Überlegenheit (über (*Acc.*)); bestimmender Einfluß (auf (*Acc.*)); *gain the –dency over*, bestimmenden Einfluß gewinnen über; *rise to –dency*, die Oberhand gewinnen, zur Macht *or* ans Ruder kommen. **–dant, –dent,** **1.** *adj.* aufsteigend, aufgehend (*Astr.*); sich erhebend; vorwiegend; *–dant over*, überlegen (*Dat.*). **2.** *s.* see **–dency;** der Aufgangspunkt (*Astr.*), das Horoskop, der Geburtsstern; der Aszendent; Verwandte in aufsteigender Linie; (*pl.*) die Voreltern; *his star is in the –dant*, sein Glück ist im Steigen. **–sion** [ə'sɛnʃən], *s.* das Aufsteigen, die Besteigung; Aufsteigung (*Astr.*); Auffahrt; *–sion of Christ*, die Himmelfahrt Christi; *–sion Day*, der Himmelfahrtstag, (*Swiss dial.*) Auffahrtstag; *right –sion*, die Rektaszension (*Astr.*). **–t,** *s.* das Aufsteigen, Ansteigen, der Aufflug (*Av.*); der Aufstieg, die Auffahrt, Rampe; Anhöhe; Steigung (*Surv.*).

ascertain [æsə'teɪn], *v.a.* ermitteln, feststellen, nachweisen, in Erfahrung bringen; bestimmen (*a target* (*Artil.*)); *–ed fact*, festgestellte Tatsache. **–able,** *adj.* ermittelbar, nachweisbar. **–ment,** *s.* die Feststellung, Vergewisserung, Ermitt(e)lung.

ascetic [ə'sɛtɪk], **1.** *adj.*, **–ally,** *adv.* asketisch. **2.** *s.* der Asket. **–ism** [–tɪsɪzm], *s.* die Askese.

ascrib–able [ə'skraɪbəbl], *adj.* zuzuschreiben(d), zuschreibbar; *it is –able to him*, es ist ihm zuzuschreiben. **–e** [ə'skraɪb], *v.a.* zuschreiben, beimessen, beilegen (*to*, (*Dat.*)).

asep–sis [æ'sɛpsɪs], *s.* keimfreie Behandlung (*Med.*). **–tic** [–tɪk], *adj.* keimfrei.

[1]**ash** [æʃ], **1.** *s.* die Esche; das Eschenholz; *mountain–*, die Eberesche.

[2]**ash,** *s.*, **–es,** *pl.*, die Asche; (*always pl.*) die sterblichen Überreste, der Staub; (*always pl.*) das Symbol des Sieges im australisch-englischen Kricket-Wettkampf; *in sackcloth and –es*, in Sack und Asche; *burn to –es*, einäschern; *lay in –es*, niederbrennen; *reduce to –es*, veraschen. **–-can,** (*Amer.*) der Abfalleimer. **–-colour,** *s.* das Aschgrau. **–-coloured,** *adj.* aschgrau, aschfarben. **–en,** *adj.* aschig; aschgrau, aschfarben, (*fig.*) totenbleich. **–-pan,** *s.* der Aschkasten. **–-pit,** *s.* die Aschengrube. **–-tray,** *s.* der Asch(en)becher. **–-Wednesday,** *s.* der Aschermittwoch. **–y,** *adj. see* **–en.**

ashamed [ə'ʃeɪmd], *pred. adj.* beschämt, verschämt; *make a p.* –, einen beschämen; *be* or *feel – of o.s.*, sich schämen; *be* or *feel – of a th.*, sich einer S. schämen; *you ought to be – of yourself*, schäme dich!

ashen ['æʃən], *see* [2]**ash.**

ashlar ['æʃlə], *s.* der Bruchstein, Quaderstein. **–-work,** die Quadermauer.

ashore [ə'ʃɔ:], *adv.* ans Ufer *or* Land; am Ufer, zu Lande, an(s) Land: gestrandet (*of a ship*); *bring* –, ans Land bringen; *get* –, landen, ans Land schaffen; *go* –, an Land gehen; *run* or *be driven* –, auf Strand laufen, stranden, auflaufen; *run* or *cast a ship* –, ein Schiff auf Strand setzen *or* ans Land werfen.

ashy, *see* [2]**ash.**

aside [ə'saɪd], **1.** *adv.* seitwärts, abseits, auf der *or* die Seite, beiseite; leise, für sich (*Theat.*); (*Amer.*) außerdem; *put* (*money*) –, auf die hohe Kante legen; *she has laid – her mourning*, sie hat die Trauer abgelegt; *set – a judgment*, ein Urteil aufheben; *he took him* –, er nahm ihn beiseite; *turn – from the path of virtue*, vom Pfade der Tugend abweichen. **2.** *s.* beiseite gesprochenes Wort, die Aparte (*Theat.*).

asinine ['æsɪnaɪn], *adj.* eselartig, Esels–; (*fig.*) eselhaft, dumm.

ask [ɑ:sk], **1.** *v.a.* & *n.* fragen nach, erfragen; fragen (*a p.*) (*about*, über); bitten (*for*, um), erbitten, verlangen, fordern; einladen; – *about a th.*, sich nach einer S. erkundigen; – *a p.'s advice*, einen um seinen Rat fragen; – *after a p.*('*s health*), sich nach jemandes Befinden erkundigen; – *a p. a favour*, von einem einen Gefallen erbitten; – *for*, bitten um, erbitten, verlangen; *how much do you – for it?* wieviel fordern Sie dafür? *has anybody –ed for me?* hat jemand nach mir gefragt? *it is often –ed for*, es wird oft erbeten; – *a p.'s hand in marriage*, um jemandes Hand anhalten; *there's no harm in –ing*, eine Frage schadet nichts; – *a p. home*, einen zu sich einladen; – *a p. in*, einen hereinbitten; – *a p.'s name*, nach jemandes Namen fragen; – *s.o. his name*, einen nach seinem Namen fragen; *may I – you to pass me the bread?* darf ich Sie um das Brot bitten? *be –ed out*, eingeladen sein; – *a p.'s permission*, einen um Erlaubnis bitten; – *a p. a question*, eine Frage an einen stellen; – *of a p. that* . . ., – *a th. of a p*, von einem verlangen, daß . . ., etwas von einem verlangen; – *for trouble* (or sl. *for it*), herausfordernd wirken; – *the gentleman upstairs*, bitten Sie den Herrn, sich heraufzubemühen; – (*a p.*) *the way*, (einen) nach dem Wege fragen, sich (bei einem) nach dem Wege erkundigen. **–er,** *s.* der Bittsteller, Bittende; Frager. **–ing,** *s.* die Bitte, das Bitten, Aufgebot; *it can be had for the –ing*, es kostet nur eine Frage, es ist umsonst zu haben; *second time of –ing*, zweites Aufgebot.

askan–ce [əs'kæns], **–t,** *adv.* seitwärts; *look –ce at a p.*, einen von der Seite ansehen, einen mißtrauisch betrachten, einen scheel *or* schief ansehen.

askew [ə'skju:], *adv.* & *pred. adj.* schief, quer, schräg.

aslant [ə'slɑ:nt], **1.** *adv. see* **askew. 2.** *prep.* quer-über (*Acc.*), -durch.

asleep [ə'sli:p], *adv.* & *pred. adj.* schlafend, im Schlafe, in den Schlaf; *be* –, schlafen, eingeschlafen sein; *be fast* –, in tiefem Schlafe liegen, fest eingeschlafen sein, fest schlafen; *fall* –, einschlafen; *my foot has fallen* –, der Fuß ist mir eingeschlafen; – *in the Lord*, im Herrn entschlafen.
aslope [ə'sloup], *adv.* & *pred. adj.* schief, schräg, abschüssig.
asp [æsp], *s. see* **aspen;** (*poet.*) die Natter.
asparagus [əs'pærəgəs], *s.* der Spargel.
aspect ['æspɛkt], *s.* der Anblick; die Erscheinung, das Aussehen, die Miene; Aussicht, Lage; (*fig.*) der Gesichtspunkt, das Licht, die Seite; der Aspekt (*Astr.*); *in all its* –*s*, in jeder Hinsicht; *southern* –, die Lage nach Süden; *in its true* –, vom richtigen Gesichtspunkt aus, im richtigen Lichte; – *ratio*, das Seitenverhältnis (*Av.*).
aspen ['æspən], 1. *s.* die Espe. 2. *adj.* espen. **--leaf,** *s.*; *tremble like an --leaf*, wie Espenlaub zittern.
asperity [æs'pɛrɪtɪ], *s.* die Rauheit, Unebenheit (*of surface*); Härte (*of sound*); Strenge (*of climate, etc.*); Schroffheit (*of character, etc.*), Schärfe, Herbheit (*of taste*).
aspers-e [əs'pə:s], *v.a.* bespritzen, besprengen; (*fig.*) verleumden, beschmutzen, in üblen Ruf bringen. **-ion** [-'pə:ʃən], *s.* die Besprengung, Bespritzung, Benetzung; (*fig.*) Verleumdung, Anschwärzung, Schmähung; *cast -ions on a p.*, einen anschwärzen, jemandes Ehre beflecken.
asphalt ['æsfælt], 1. *s.* der Asphalt, das Erdharz. 2. *adj.* Asphalt-. 3. *v.a.* asphaltieren.
asphodel ['æsfodɛl], *s.* der Affodill; *bog* –, der Beinbrech.
asphyxia [əs'fɪksɪə], *s.* die Erstickung, Asphyxie (*Med.*). **-te** [-ɪeɪt], *v.a.* & *n.* ersticken. **-tion,** *s.* die Erstickung.
aspic ['æspɪk], *s.* die Sülze, der Aspik.
aspir-ant [əs'pɑɪərənt], *s.* der Bewerber, Anwärter, Kandidat; Emporstrebende; *-ant to an office*, der Bewerber um ein Amt, Amtsanwärter. **-e** [əs'pɑɪə], *v.n.* verlangen, trachten, streben (*after, to*, nach); emporstreben. **-ing** [-ərɪŋ], *adj.* trachtend, strebend, aufstrebend, hochstrebend, strebsam, streberhaft, ehrgeizig (*see* **aspiration**).
aspirat-e ['æspəreɪt], 1. *v.a.* aspirieren (*Phon.*); aufsaugen, abziehen (*liquid*) (*Chem.*). 2. *adj.*, **-ed,** *p.p.* aspiriert. 3. *s.* die Aspirata, der Hauchlaut; Spiritus asper (*in Greek*). **-ion** [-'reɪʃən], *s.* die Aspiration (*Phon.*); der Atemzug, Hauch; die Aufsaugung, Einsaugung; das Streben, Trachten, der Wunsch, die Sehnsucht (*for* or *after*, nach).
aspirin ['æspərɪn], *s.* das Aspirin.
aspiring [əs'pɑɪərɪŋ], *see* **aspir-ing.**
ass [æs], *s.* der Esel; (*fig.*) Dummkopf, Narr; *she--*, die Eselin; *silly* –*!* dummer Esel! *make an* – *of o.s.*, sich blamieren, sich lächerlich machen; *make an* – *of a p.*, einen zum Narren halten.
assail [ə'seɪl], *v.a.* angreifen, anfallen, überfallen, bestürmen. **-able,** *adj.* angreifbar; (*fig.*) anfechtbar. **-ant,** *s.* der Angreifer, Gegner.
assassin [ə'sæsɪn], *s.* der Meuchelmörder. **-ate,** *v.a.* meuchlerisch umbringen, ermorden. **-ation** [-'neɪʃən], *s.* der Meuchelmord, die Ermordung.
assault [ə'sɔ:lt], 1. *v.a.* angreifen, anfallen; stürmen, bestürmen (*a position*) (*Mil.*); tätlich beleidigen (*Law*). 2. *s.* der Angriff (*on* or *upon*, auf (*Acc.*)); Sturm, die Bestürmung (*Mil.*); tätlicher Angriff, die Gewalttätigkeit, körperliche *or* tätliche Beleidigung (*Law*); – *and battery*, tätliche Beleidigung (*Law*); – *of* or *at arms*, das Kontrafechten; die Fechtübung; *carry by* –, im Sturm nehmen (*Mil.*); – *detachment*, der Stoßtrupp (*Mil.*); *indecent* –, der Notzuchtversuch; *take by* –, erstürmen.
assay [æ'seɪ], 1. *s.* die Erzprobe, Metallprobe; Analyse, Probe, Prüfung, Erprobung; *mark of* –, das Probezeichen. 2. *v.a.* prüfen, proben, eichen (*Metall., Chem.*). 3. *v.a.* & *n.* (*fig.*) probieren, versuchen; sich bemühen; – *by the cupel*, abtreiben. **--balance,** *s.* die Probewaage. **-er,** *s.*, **--master,** *s.* der Münzwardein; **--office,** *s.* das Probeamt.
assembl-age [ə'sɛmblɪdʒ], *s.* die Versammlung, Vereinigung, das Zusammenbringen; die Verbindung, das Zusammenfügen, die Montage (*Mech.*). **-e** [ə'sɛmbl], 1. *v.a.* versammeln; zusammenberufen (*parliament, etc.*); zusammenziehen, bereitstellen (*troops, etc.*); zusammenstellen, zusammenbauen, zusammensetzen, (auf)montieren (*Mech.*). 2. *v.n.* sich versammeln, sich sammeln, zusammenkommen, zusammentreten (*parliament, etc.*). **-er,** *s.* der Monteur. **-y,** *s.* die Versammlung; Gesellschaft, beratende Körperschaft, das Plenum; Zusammensetzen, die Montage (*Mech.*); das Sammelsignal (*Mil.*); Repräsentantenhaus (*Amer.*); *General -y* (*of the Church of Scotland*), die Generalsynode (der schottischen Staatskirche); *place of -y*, der Treffpunkt, Versammlungsplatz. **-y area,** *s.* der Bereitstellungsraum (*Mil.*). **-y belt,** *s.* das Fließband. **-y line,** *s.* die Montagerampe. **-y-room,** *s.* der Versammlungssaal, Festsaal. **-y shop,** *s.* die Montagehalle.
assent [ə'sɛnt], 1. *s.* die Zustimmung, Genehmigung, Billigung; *royal* –, königliche Genehmigung (*Parl.*); *she nodded* –, sie nickte ein 'ja'; *with one* –, einmütig, einstimmig. 2. *v.n.* einwilligen (*to*, in), beistimmen, beipflichten, zustimmen (*Dat.*); genehmigen, billigen, zugeben (*Acc.*).
assert [ə'sə:t], *v.a.* behaupten, erklären, bestehen auf; verfechten, verteidigen; geltend machen, Ansprüche machen auf; – *o.s.*, sich geltend machen, sich zur Geltung bringen, fest auftreten, sich durchsetzen; – *one's rights*, sein(e) Recht(e) verteidigen. **-ion** [-ʃən], *s.* die Behauptung, Erklärung, Aussage, Versicherung; *make an -ion*, eine Behauptung aufstellen. **-ive,** *adj.* bestimmt, zuversichtlich, ausdrücklich, positiv, bejahend. **-or,** *s.* der Behaupter, Verteidiger, Verfechter.
assess [ə'sɛs], *v.a.* besteuern; auferlegen (*upon a p.* (*Dat.*)) (*taxes*); abschätzen, einschätzen, veranschlagen; – *damages*, die Entschädigungssumme festsetzen; *I am -ed at £25*, ich zahle 25 Pfund Steuer. **-able,** *adj.* steuerpflichtig. **-ment,** *s.* die Einschätzung, Schätzung; Steuer, Abgabe; der Steuertarif, die Steuerveranlagung, Festlegung (einer Summe). **-or,** *s.* der Assessor, Syndikus, Beisitzer, Steuerabschätzer, Steuereinschätzer.
asset ['æsɛt], *s.* der Posten auf der Aktivseite; (*coll.*) Wert, Vorzug. **-s,** *pl.* der Nachlaß, die Fallitmasse, Konkursmasse, der Vermögensstand, die Aktiva (*pl.*); *-s and liabilities*, Aktiva und Passiva, Aktiv- und Passivbestände; *no -s*, kein Guthaben (*on cheques*).
asseverat-e [æ'sɛvəreɪt], *v.a.* beteuern, feierlich versichern *or* behaupten. **-ion** [-'reɪʃən], *s.* die Beteuerung, Versicherung.
assidu-ity [æsɪ'dju:ɪtɪ], *s.* die Emsigkeit, Beharrlichkeit, ausdauernder Fleiß; die Aufmerksamkeit. **-ous** [ə'sɪdjuəs], *adj.* emsig, fleißig; unverdrossen, ausdauernd, unablässig; *-ous attentions*, unablässige Aufmerksamkeiten. **-ousness,** *s. see* **-ity.**
assign [ə'sɑɪn], 1. *v.a.* anweisen, zuweisen, überweisen, zuteilen, zuschreiben (*to a p.* (*Dat.*)); festsetzen (*a time*); angeben (*a reason*); übermachen, abtreten, zedieren (*Law*); ernennen, bestellen. 2. *s.* der Rechtsnachfolger, Zessionar (*Law*). **-able,** *adj.* bestimmbar, angebbar, anweisbar, zuzuschreiben(d); übertragbar (*Law*). **-ation** [æsɪg'neɪʃən], *s.* die Bestellung, Bestimmung; Anweisung, Zuweisung; Verabredung, das Stelldichein; die Übertragung, Abtretung (*Law*). **-ee** [æsɪ'nɪ:], *s.* Bevollmächtigte(r), *m.*, der Zessionar (*Law*); *-ee in bankruptcy*, der Konkursverwalter. **-ment,** *s.* die Anweisung, Zuteilung, Zuweisung, Übertragung, Abtretung, Zession (*Law*); Angabe (*of reasons, etc.*); das Aufgabengebiet (*allotted to reporter*); *deed of -ment*, die Abtretungsurkunde. **-or** [æsɪ'nɔ:], *s.* Anweisende(r), *m.*; Abtretende(r), *m.*, der Zedent.
assimilat-e [ə'sɪmɪleɪt], 1. *v.a.* ähnlich machen, assimilieren (*to, with*, (*Dat.*)); angleichen (an), vergleichen (mit); einverleiben (*nourishment*) (*Physiol.*); sich aneignen, in sich aufnehmen. 2. *v.n.* ähnlich werden, sich assimilieren. **-ion** [-'leɪʃən], *s.* die Assimilation, Angleichung (*to*, an); Assimilierung, Einverleibung, Verwandlung (*Physiol.*).
assist [ə'sɪst], *v.a.* beistehen, helfen (*Dat.*), unterstützen (*Acc.*) (*in a th.*, bei einer S.); förderlich sein (*Dat.*); fördern, mitwirken; beiwohnen,

zugegen sein (*at*, bei), teilnehmen (*in*, an). **-ance,** *s.* der Beistand, die Hilfe, Unterstützung; Mitwirkung; *afford -ance*, Hilfe gewähren; *lend* or *render -ance*, Hilfe leisten. **-ant,** 1. *s.* der Gehilfe, Beistand; *shop -ant*, der (die) Verkäufer(in). 2. *adj.* Hilfs–; *-ant editor*, der Hilfsredakteur; *-ant librarian*, der Unterbibliothekar; *-ant manager*, stellvertretender Direktor; *-ant master*, der Lehrer, Studienrat; *-ant secretary*, zweiter Sekretär, der Ministerialdirektor (*civil service*).

assize [ə'sɑɪz], *s.* die Gerichtssitzung, der (Urteils)-Spruch; (*pl.*) das Geschwor(e)nengericht, die Assisen; *hold the -s*, die Assisen abhalten.

associat-e [ə'souʃɪeɪt], 1. *v.a.* zugesellen, verbünden, vereinigen, verbinden. 2. *v.n.* sich gesellen (*with*, zu); sich verbinden (mit), Umgang haben (mit), verkehren (mit), assoziieren (*C.L.*); *-e o.s. with a th.*, sich einer S. anschließen. 3. *s.* der Genosse, Kollege, außerordentliches Mitglied; der Gesellschafter, Teilhaber, Teilnehmer (*C.L.*). 4. *adj.* verbunden, verbündet, Mit–; nicht vollamtlich; *-e professor* (*Amer.*), außerordentlicher Professor. **-eship,** *s.* die Teilhaberschaft, Amtsgenossenschaft. **-ion** [–sɪ'eɪʃən], *s.* die Verbindung, Vereinigung; der Verein, Bund, die Gesellschaft, Genossenschaft, der Verband, das Bündnis; die Assoziation; *Modern Language -ion*, der Neuphilologenverband; *articles of -ion*, Statuten der Handelsgesellschaft; *-ion of ideas*, die Ideenassoziation, Gedankenverbindung; (*coll.*) *pleasant -ions*, angenehme Erinnerungen. **-ion-football,** *s.* das Fußballspiel.

assonan-ce ['æsənəns], *s.* der Anklang, vokalischer Gleichklang, die Assonanz. **-t,** 1. *adj.* vokalisch gleichlautend, anklingend, assonierend. 2. *s.* assonierendes Wort.

assort [ə'sɔ:t], 1. *v.a.* passend zusammenstellen, ordnen, sortieren, (*C.L.*) assortieren. 2. *v.n.* übereinstimmen (mit), passen (zu); *ill- -ed couple*, schlecht zueinander passendes Ehepaar. **-ment,** *s.* das Sortieren, Ordnen, die Sammlung; (*C.L.*) das Sortimentlager, die Auswahl.

assuage [ə'sweɪdʒ], *v.a.* mildern, erleichtern, lindern (*pain*), stillen (*thirst*); besänftigen, beruhigen, mäßigen. **-ment,** *s.* die Milderung, Linderung.

assum-e [ə'sjuː:m], *v.a.* annehmen, auf sich (*Acc.*) nehmen, übernehmen (*responsibility, etc.*); sich (*Dat.*) anmaßen, anlegen, ergreifen, (als wahr) annehmen, voraussetzen, gelten lassen; *-e a haughty air*, eine hochmütige Miene anlegen; *-e the reins of government*, die Regierung übernehmen; *-ed address* (*name, etc.*), angenommene, Schein– *or* Deckadresse. **-ing,** *adj.* vermessen, anmaßend; *-ing that*, angenommen *or* vorausgesetzt daß, unter der Annahme daß. **-ption** [ə'sʌmpʃən], *s.* das Annehmen, Aufnehmen; die Übernahme; Anmaßung, Aneignung; Annahme, Voraussetzung, das Postulat, logischer Untersatz; *the -ption of the Blessed Virgin*, Mariä Himmelfahrt; *Christ's -ption of our flesh*, Christi Menschwerdung; *-ption of power*, die Machtübernahme; *on the -ption that*, unter der Voraussetzung daß.

assurance [ə'ʃuərəns], *s.* die Versicherung, Beteuerung; Zusage, Sicherstellung, Bürgschaft; Sicherheit, Zuversicht, das (Selbst)Vertrauen; die Anmaßung, Dreistigkeit, Unverschämtheit; (Lebens)Versicherung, Assekuranz (*C.L.*); *– of manner*, sicheres Benehmen; *air of –*, dreiste Miene; *with –*, mit Nachdruck; *– company*, die Versicherungsgesellschaft.

assure [ə'ʃuə], *v.a.* sichern, sicher machen, sicher stellen; versichern, zusichern, ermutigen; assekurieren, versichern (*one's life*) (*C.L.*); *he -d me that . . .*, er versicherte mir daß . . . . **-d,** *adj.* versichert, gewiß, unzweifelhaft; gesichert, gefestigt; selbstbewußt, dreist; *be -d of a th.*, einer S. sicher sein, von einer S. fest überzeugt sein; (*you may*) *be* or *rest -d that . . .*, Sie können sich darauf verlassen, daß . . .; *his position is -d*, seine Stellung ist gesichert. **-dly** [–rɪdlɪ], *adv.* sicherlich, gewiß, unzweifelhaft. **-dness** [–rɪdnɪs], *s.* die Sicherheit, Zuversichtlichkeit, Gewißheit; das Selbstvertrauen, die Selbstbewußtheit. **-r** [–rə], (*C.L.* **assuror**) *s.* der Versicherer; Versicherte(r), *m.*

assurgent [æ'sə:dʒənt], *adj.* aufsteigend, emporstrebend; nach oben gebogen (*Bot.*); (*fig.*) herrschsüchtig.

astatic [æ'stætɪk], *adj.* astatisch, unstet.

aster ['æstə], *s.* die Aster (*Bot.*).

asterisk ['æstərɪsk], *s.* das Sternchen (*Typ.*).

astern [ə'stə:n], *adv.* achtern, achteraus (*of*, von); nach hinten, rückwärts; *drop* or *fall –*, achteraus sacken; *wind –*, achterlicher Wind.

asteroid ['æstərɔɪd], 1. *s.* der Planetoid, Asteroid (*Astr.*). 2. *adj.* sternartig.

asthma ['æsθmə], *s.* die Atemnot, das Asthma; *he suffers from –*, (*coll.*) er hat es auf der Brust. **-tic** [æsθ'mætɪk], 1. *adj.* engbrüstig, kurzatmig, asthmatisch. 2. *s.* der Asthmatiker.

astigmat-ic [æstɪg'mætɪk], *adj.* astigmatisch. **-ism** [æs'tɪgmətɪzm], *s.* der Astigmatismus.

astir [ə'stə:], *pred. adj. & adv.* in Bewegung, auf (den Beinen), aus dem Bett; aufgeregt, rege; *be –*, wimmeln (*with*, von).

astonish [əs'tɔnɪʃ], *v.a.* in Erstaunen setzen; befremden, verblüffen, überraschen; *be -ed*, erstaunen, sich wundern (*at*, über). **-ing,** *pr.p. & adj.* erstaunlich, wunderbar. **-ment,** *s.* das Erstaunen, die Bestürzung, Verwunderung, das Staunen (*at*, über); *cause -ment*, Staunen erregen; *fill with -ment*, in Staunen versetzen.

astound [əs'taʊnd], *v.a.* in Staunen *or* Schrecken versetzen, verblüffen. **-ing,** *adj.* verblüffend, überraschend.

astraddle [ə'strædl], *pred. adj. & adv.* rittlings; *– of*, rittlings auf, reitend auf.

astragal ['æstrəgəl], *s.* der Rundstab (*Arch.*); das Sprungbein (*Anat.*); Band (*on fire-arms*).

astral ['æstrəl], *adj.* gestirnt, Stern(en)–, sternig, sternartig; *– body*, der Astralleib; *– lamp*, die Astrallampe.

astray [ə'streɪ], *pred. adj. & adv.* vom rechten Wege ab, irre, verirrt; *go –*, irregehen, sich verirren, sich verlieren, verlorengehen; (*fig.*) abschweifen; *lead –*, verleiten, verführen, irreführen.

astride [ə'strɑɪd], 1. *pred. adj. & adv.* rittlings, mit gespreizten Beinen; *– of*, rittlings auf (*Dat.*); *ride –*, im Herrensattel reiten. 2. *prep.*; *– a horse*, zu Pferd.

astringen-cy [əs'trɪndʒənsɪ], *s.* zusammenziehende Kraft, die Adstringenz; (*fig.*) Strenge, der Ernst. **-t,** 1. *adj.* zusammenziehend, adstringierend; (*fig.*) streng, ernst. 2. *s.* zusammenziehendes Mittel.

astro-labe ['æstroleɪb], *s.* das Astrolabium, der Winkelmesser. **-loger** [əs'trɔlədʒə], *s.* der Sterndeuter, Astrolog(e). **-logical** [–'lɔdʒɪkl], *adj.* astrologisch. **-logy** [əs'trɔlədʒɪ], *s.* die Sterndeuterei, Astrologie. **-naut** ['æstrənɔ:t], *s.* der Astronaut. **-nomer** [əs'trɔnəmə], *s.* der Astronom, Sternforscher. **-nomic(al)** [–'nɔmɪk(l)], *adj.* astronomisch; *-nomical tables*, astronomische Tafeln; *-nomical year*, siderisches Jahr, das Sternjahr. **-nomy,** *s.* die Sternkunde, Astronomie.

astute [əs'tju:t], *adj.* listig, schlau; scharfsinnig. **-ness,** *s.* der Scharfsinn; die Schlauheit.

asunder [ə'sʌndə], *adv.* auseinander, voneinander, entzwei, getrennt; *tear –*, zerreißen.

asylum [ə'sɑɪləm], *s.* das Asyl, die Zufluchtsstätte; das Heim; (*coll.*) (*lunatic*) –, die Irrenanstalt.

asymmet-ric(al) [æsɪ'metrɪk(l)], *adj.* unsymmetrisch, ungleichförmig. **-ry** [æ'sɪmətrɪ], *s.* die Asymmetrie, Ungleichförmigkeit.

asymptote ['æsɪmptout], *s.* die Asymptote (*Math.*).

at [æt, ət *acc. to emphasis*], *prep.* **1.** (*place*) in, an, bei; *it happened – Oxford*, es geschah in Oxford; *he is – school*, er ist in der Schule; *he spent 3 years – Oxford* (*i.e. at the university*), er verbrachte 3 Jahre in Oxford; *he was killed – the battle of Hastings*, er fiel in der Schlacht bei Hastings; *– court*, am Hof; *– the mouth of the river*, an der Mündung des Flusses; *– the top*, an der Spitze; *– the baker's*, beim Bäcker; *– my uncle's*, bei meinem Onkel; *– table*, bei Tisch. **2.** (*time*) um, zu; *– 2 o'clock*, um 2 Uhr; *– midnight*, um Mitternacht; *– Christmas*, zu Weihnachten; *– the same time*, zur selben Zeit; *– the same hour*, um dieselbe Stunde, zur selben Stunde. **3.** (*condition*) in, bei; *– the age of 16*, im Alter von 16 Jahren; – *fault*, im Irrtum; – *large*, im Freien, in Freiheit; – *liberty*, in Freiheit; – *peace*, im Frieden; – *the point of death*, im Sterben; – *my time of life*, in meinem Alter; – *work*, bei der Arbeit. **4.** (*number, price, etc.*) zu, auf; – *my expense*, auf meine Kosten; *I estimate them – 20*, ich schätze sie auf 20; – *a low price*, zu einem niedrigen Preis; – *half-price*, zum halben Preis; – *reduced prices*, zu herabgesetzten Preisen. **5.** (*origin*) aus, von; *receive s.th. – his hands*, etwas von ihm empfangen; – *second-hand*, aus zweiter Hand. **6.** (*various idioms not conforming to the above classification*) – *the beginning*, am *or* zu Anfang, anfangs; – *daybreak*, bei Tagesanbruch; – *a distance*, in einiger Entfernung, von ferne; – *the door*, an *or* vor der Tür; *drink – one draught*, auf einen Zug trinken; – *an end*, zu Ende, aus; – *his feet*, ihm zu Füßen; – *home*, zuhause, daheim; – *any moment*, jeden Augenblick; – *the right moment*, im richtigen Augenblick; – *the very moment when*, gerade (in dem Augenblick) als; – *night*, nachts, bei Nacht; – *about 2 o'clock*, gegen 2 Uhr; *they were – one*, sie waren einig *or* einer Meinung; – *your* (*his, etc.*) *pleasure*, nach Belieben; – *any price*, um jeden Preis; – *sea*, zur See; – *your service*, zu Ihren Diensten; – *stake*, auf dem Spiel; *be – a standstill*, stocken; *two – a time*, zwei auf einmal; – *no time*, niemals; – *times*, zuweilen, manchmal, bisweilen, mitunter; – *the university*, auf der Universität; – *one's wits end*, in der größten Verlegenheit. **7.** (*other idioms*); – *all*, überhaupt; *not – all*, durchaus nicht; – *best*, bestenfalls; – *one blow*, mit einem Schlag; *out – elbows*, schäbig; – *all events*, auf alle Fälle; – *first*, zuerst; – *hand*, zur Hand; *close – hand*, nahe bei der Hand; – *last*, zuletzt, endlich; – *least*, wenigstens, zum wenigsten; das heißt, jedoch, freilich; – *length*, endlich; – *great length*, ausführlich, weitläufig; – *arm's length*, vom Leibe; *you are – liberty* (*fig.*), es steht Ihnen frei; – *his mercy*, in seiner Gewalt; – (*the*) *most*, höchstens; – *once*, sofort, auf einmal; *all – once*, plötzlich; – *sight*, auf Sicht (*C.L.*); – *the sight of*, beim Anblick (*with Gen.*); *take him – his word*, ihn beim Wort nehmen. **8.** (*after verbs*); *aim* –, zielen auf (*Acc.*); streben nach; (*coll.*) *be – a th.*, mit etwas beschäftigt sein; (*coll.*) *be always – a p.*, einen fortwährend belästigen; *what are you –?* was machst du da? (*coll.*) *what are you driving –?* worauf zielst du hin? was willst du überhaupt? *laugh* –, lachen über; *be laughed* –, ausgelacht werden; *point* –, zielen nach, zeigen; *surprised* –, erstaunt über. **9.** (*after adjectives*); *angry* –, zornig auf (*Acc.*), erzürnt über; *good* –, gut *or* geschickt in; *hard – work*, fleißig bei der Arbeit; (*coll.*) *hard – it*, tüchtig hinterher, vollauf beschäftigt; (*coll.*) *and stupid – that*, und dumm noch dazu. **--home**, *s.* zwangloser Empfangstag.

atavism ['ætəvɪzm], der Atavismus, Entwicklungsrückschlag, die Rückartung.

ataxia [ə'tæksɪə], *s.* die Bewegungsstörung, Ataxie (*Med.*).

ate [ɛt], *see* **eat.**

atheis-m ['eɪθɪɪzm], *s.* die Gottesleugnung, der Atheismus. **-t**, *s.* der Gottesleugner, Atheist. **-tic(al)** [eɪθɪ:'ɪstɪk(l)], *adj.* atheistisch.

athirst [ə'θə:st], *pred. adj.* (*poet.*) durstig; (*fig.*) begierig (*for*, nach).

athlet-e ['æθlɪ:t], *s.* der Athlet, Wettkämpfer, Sportsmensch. **-ic** [əθ'lɛtɪk], *adj.* athletisch; stark, muskulös; *-ic form*, kräftige Gestalt; *-ic sports*, athletische Wettspiele; die Leichtathletik. **-ics**, *pl.* (*used as sing.*) die Leichtathletik, der Sport.

athwart [ə'θwɔ:t], **1.** *prep.* querüber, durch, über; *lie – the waves*, dwars See liegen. **2.** *adv.* schräg, schief, quer; dwars, dwarsüber (*Naut.*); – *the beam*, vorlicher als dwars (*Naut.*). **--hawse**, *adv.* quer vor dem Bug eines vor Anker liegenden Schiffes. **--ships**, *adv.* querschiffs, dwarsschiffs.

atilt [ə'tɪlt], *adv.* mit gefällter Lanze; vorwärts gebeugt; kippend; *set a cask* –, ein Faß kippen.

atlas ['ætləs], *s.* der Atlas (*Myth., Geog.*); Träger (*Arch.*); oberster Halswirbel (*Anat.*); das Atlasformat, Großfolio (*Bookb.*).

atmospher-e ['ætməsfɪ:ə], *s.* die Atmosphäre, der Luftkreis; (*fig.*) die Stimmung, Umwelt, Umgebung, der Wirkungskreis, Einfluß. **-ic(al)** [–'fɛrɪk(l)], *adj.* atmosphärisch, luftförmig, luftartig; *-ic conditions*, die Wetterlage, Wetterverhältnisse (*pl.*), die Witterung; *-ic pressure*, der Luftdruck. **-ics**, *pl.* Ätherwellen (*pl.*); atmosphärische Störungen, Nebengeräusche (*Rad.*).

atoll ['ætəl, ə'təl], *s.* ringförmige Koralleninsel, das Atoll.

atom ['ætəm], *s.* das Atom; (*fig.*) kleinstes Teilchen, das Bißchen, der Deut, die Spur, Kleinigkeit; *not an – of truth*, keine Spur von Wahrheit; *smash* (*in*)*to –s*, in tausend Stücke *or* kurz und klein schlagen. **--bomb**, *s.* die Atombombe. **-ic** [ə'təmɪk], *adj.* atomistisch, atomartig, Atom–; *-ic bomb, see* **- -bomb**; *-ic fission*, die Atomspaltung; *-ic nucleus*, der Atomkern; *-ic power*, die Atomenergie; *-ic scientist*, der Atomforscher; *-ic theory*, die Atomtheorie; *-ic weight*, das Atomgewicht. **-ism**, *s.* die Atomlehre. **-ize**, *v.a.* zerkleinern, zerstäuben. **-izer**, *s.* der Zerstäuber, Zerstäubungsapparat.

atone [ə'toun], *v.n.* (with *for*) büßen, sühnen, wieder gut machen, Ersatz leisten für; *he -d for his faults by his death*, er büßte seine Fehler mit dem Tode. **-ment**, *s.* die Buße, Sühne; (*B.*) das Sühnopfer (Christi); die Versöhnung, Genugtuung, der Ersatz (für); *make -ment for s.th.*, etwas abbüßen, sühnen *or* wieder gut machen, Genugtuung für etwas leisten.

aton-ic [æ'tənɪk], *adj.* unbetont, tonlos (*Gram.*); schlaff, abgespannt, kraftlos (*Med.*). **-y** ['ætənɪ], *s.* die Schlaffheit, Schwäche, Kraftlosigkeit.

atop [ə'təp], **1.** *adv.* obenauf, zu oberst. **2.** *prep.* (oben) auf.

atrabilious [ætrə'bɪlɪəs], *adj.* schwarzgallig, schwermütig, melancholisch.

atrip [ə'trɪp], *adv.* gelichtet (*anchor*) (*Naut.*).

atrium ['eɪtrɪəm], *s.* die Vorhalle; Vorkammer (*of the heart*) (*Anat.*).

atroc-ious [ə'trouʃəs], *adj.* gräßlich, entsetzlich, scheußlich, schauderhaft, abscheulich, grausam; (*coll.*) sehr schlimm. **-iousness**, *s.* die Abscheulichkeit, Scheußlichkeit. **-ity** [ə'trəsɪtɪ], *s.* die **Greueltat**; *see also* **-iousness;** (*coll.*) grober Verstoß, der Schnitzer.

atrophy ['ætrəfɪ], **1.** *s.* die Abzehrung, Verkümmerung, Abmagerung; der (Muskel)Schwund, die Atrophie. **2.** *v.n.* absterben, auszehren.

attach [ə'tætʃ], **1.** *v.a.* anheften, anknüpfen, anbinden (*to*, an (*Dat. & Acc.*)); festmachen, befestigen (*to*, an); beifügen, beilegen (*to* (*Dat.*)); angliedern, zuteilen (*Mil.*); an sich ziehen, gewinnen, fesseln, für sich einnehmen; verhaften, mit Beschlag belegen (*Law*); – *blame to a p.*, einem Schuld geben, einen tadeln (wegen einer S.); *I – no value to his remarks*, ich lege seinen Äußerungen keinen Wert bei; *deeply -ed to*, innig ergeben, zugetan sein (*Dat.*), hängen an; *he was -ed to the regiment*, er wurde dem Regiment zugeteilt; – *o.s. to*, sich anschließen an; *become -ed to*, liebgewinnen. **2.** *v.n.* haften (an), sich knüpfen (an), verknüpft sein (mit); *no blame -es to him*, ihn trifft keine Schuld. **-able**, *adj.* verknüpfbar; mit Beschlag belegbar, verhaftbar (*Law*). **-ed**, *adj.* gehörig (zu), angetan, ergeben (*Dat.*); fest; unbeweglich; eingebaut (*Arch.*). **-ment** [ə'tætʃmənt], *s.* die Befestigung, Anbringung, Verknüpfung, Anknüpfung, Anfügung (*to*, an); das Anhängsel, Beiwerk, Zusatzgerät; die Anhänglichkeit, Ergebenheit (*to*, an), Zuneigung, Neigung (*to*, zu); Angliederung, Zuteilung (*Mil*); Verhaftung, Beschlagnahme (*Law*); *foreign -ment*, Beschlagnahme des Eigentums eines Ausländers (*Law*).

attaché-case [ə'tæʃekeɪs], *s.* der Stadtkoffer.

attack [ə'tæk], **1.** *v.a.* angreifen, anfallen, überfallen; in Angriff nehmen, anpacken (*work*); anfressen (*metal*); befallen (*Med.*). **2.** *s.* der Angriff, Anfall (*Med.*), Einsatz (*Mus.*); *feigned* or *feint* – der Scheinangriff; *surprise* –, der Überfall. **-able**, *adj.* angreifbar. **-er**, *s.* der Angreifer; angreifender Teil.

attain [ə'teɪn], *v.a. & n.* (with *to*) erreichen, gewinnen, erlangen, gelangen zu; – *one's end*, seinen Zweck erreichen, zum Ziele gelangen.

-able, *adj.* erreichbar. **-ment** [əˈteɪnmənt], *s.* die Erlangung, Erwerbung, Erreichung; das Erreichte, die Errungenschaft; (*pl.*) Kenntnisse, Fertigkeiten, Errungenschaften. **-der** [əˈteɪndə], *s.* der Verlust der bürgerlichen Ehrenrechte, Ehr- und Eigentumsverlust; *bill of -der*, der Parlamentsbeschluß zur Bestrafung des Hochverrats (*Hist.*). **-t** [əˈteɪnt], *v.a.* eines Kapitalverbrechens überführen, zum Tode verurteilen, dem Verlust der bürgerlichen Ehrenrechte aussetzen; anstecken, befallen (*of disease*); (*fig.*) entehren, schänden, beflecken.

attar [ˈætə], *s.* die Blumenessenz; – *of roses*, das Rosenöl.

attemper [əˈtɛmpə], *v.a.* durch Mischung verändern, tempern (*metals*), regulieren (*temperature*); (*fig.*) mildern, lindern, mäßigen, dämpfen; in Anklang bringen (*to*, mit), anpassen (*to*, an (*Acc.*)).

attempt [əˈtɛmpt], 1. *v.a.* versuchen, unternehmen; anpacken, angreifen; *don't – it!* wagen Sie es nur nicht! – *a p.'s life*, einen Mordversuch auf einen machen. 2. *s.* der Versuch; Angriff, das Attentat (*upon*, auf *with Acc.*).

attend [əˈtɛnd], 1. *v.a.* beiwohnen, besuchen, zugegen sein (bei), aufwarten (*Dat.*), bedienen (*Acc.*), seine Aufwartung machen (*Dat.*); behandeln (*of doctors*); pflegen; begleiten; *be -ed with difficulties*, mit Schwierigkeiten verknüpft sein, Schwierigkeiten nach sich ziehen; *she -ed me in my illness*, sie pflegte mich in meiner Krankheit; *success -ed his undertaking*, Erfolg krönte sein Unternehmen; – *a lecture*, eine Vorlesung besuchen *or* hören; – *school*, die Schule besuchen; – *divine service*, dem Gottesdienste beiwohnen; *have you been -ed to?* werden Sie schon bedient? *the theatre was poorly -ed*, das Theater war schlecht besetzt. 2. *v.n.* (auf)merken, achtgeben, aufpassen; zugegen sein (*at* bei); – *on a p.*, einen pflegen; einen bedienen, einem dienen *or* aufwarten; – *to*, besorgen, nachsehen, sich befassen mit; achten auf, achtgeben auf, hören auf; – *to one's devotions*, seine Andacht verrichten; – *to the children*, auf die Kinder achten, nach den Kindern sehen; *I will – to it myself*, ich will es selbst besorgen. **-ance,** *s.* die Bedienung, Aufwartung; Dienerschaft, das Gefolge; die Zuhörerschaft; Anwesenheit (*at*, bei), der Besuch; *be in -ance at*, anwesend sein bei, teilnehmen an; *the doctor is in daily -ance*, der Arzt kommt täglich; *medical -ance*, ärztliche Behandlung; *-ance at church*, der Kirchenbesuch; *-ance at lectures*, der Besuch der Vorlesungen; *be in -ance on a p.*, einem aufwarten; *dance -ance (up)on a p.*, einem den Hof machen, um einen herumscharwenzeln; *hours of -ance*, die Dienststunden; *-ance list*, die Präsenzliste, das Verzeichnis der Anwesenden. **-ant,** 1. *adj.* begleitend; anwesend; abhängig; aufwartend, folgend; *-ant circumstances*, die Begleitumstände. 2. *s.* Aufwartende(r), *m.*, der Begleiter; Diener; Wärter (*in hospitals, etc.*); (*pl.*) die Dienerschaft, das Gefolge; die Begleitung.

attenti-on [əˈtɛnʃən], *s.* die Aufmerksamkeit, Achtung; (*pl.*) Höflichkeitsbezeugungen; *-on!* stillgestanden! Achtung!; *be all -on*, ganz Ohr sein; *attract -on*, Aufmerksamkeit erregen; *arrest a p.'s -on*, jemandes Aufmerksamkeit fesseln; *call* or *draw -on to*, die Aufmerksamkeit lenken (auf (*Acc.*)); *come to -on*, Front machen (*Mil.*); *with close -on*, mit angespannter Aufmerksamkeit; *focus one's -on on*, seine Aufmerksamkeit richten auf; *pay -on to*, achtgeben auf (*Acc.*), Aufmerksamkeit schenken (*Dat.*); *pay -ons to a p.*, einem den Hof machen; *stand at -on*, stramm stehen. **-ve** [-tɪv], *adj.* aufmerksam, bedacht (*to*, auf (*Acc.*)); gefällig.

attenuat-e [əˈtɛnjʊeɪt], *v.a.* verdünnen, verringern, vermindern, verkleinern; verjüngen, verflüchtigen. **-ed,** *p.p.* & *adj.* verdünnt; abgemagert; vermindert. **-ion** [-ˈeɪʃən], *s.* die Verdünnung, Verminderung, Abmagerung, Abnahme, Schwächung; Verjüngung; Verwitterung (*of stone*); Dämpfung (*of waves, sound, etc.*).

attest [əˈtɛst], *v.a.* beglaubigen, bezeugen, bescheinigen; beweisen, bestätigen, darlegen; vereidigen (*soldiers, etc.*). **-ation** [-ˈteɪʃən], *s.* das Zeugnis; der Schein, die Bescheinigung, Bestätigung; Bezeugung, Eidesleistung, Vereidigung, Beeidigung, Aussage unter Eid. **-or,** *s.* der Zeuge.

[1]**Attic** [ˈætɪk], *adj.* attisch, klassisch; – *order*, attische Säulenordnung; – *salt* or *wit*, geistreicher Witz.

[2]**attic,** *s.* die Dachstube; (*pl.*) das Dachgeschoß.

attire [əˈtaɪə], 1. *s.* die Kleidung, Tracht, der Anzug, Schmuck, Putz; das Geweih (*of stags*). 2. *v.a.* ankleiden, kleiden, putzen, schmücken (mit).

attitud-e [ˈætɪtjuːd], *s.* die Stellung, Körperhaltung; Haltung, Stellungnahme, das Benehmen, Verhalten; *-e of mind*, die Geisteshaltung; *strike an –*, sich in Positur setzen. **-inize** [-ˈtjuːdɪnaɪz], *v.n.* posieren, sich zieren.

attorney [əˈtəːnɪ], *s.* der Anwalt; der Rechtsbeistand; Vertreter, Bevollmächtigte(r), *m.*, der Sachwalter; – *-at-law*, der Rechtsanwalt, Rechtsbeistand; – *in fact*, der Rechtswahrer, Bevollmächtigte(r), *m.*; *power of –*, die (gerichtliche) Vollmacht; *prosecuting –*, der Staatsanwalt. **--general,** *s.* der Kronanwalt.

attract [əˈtrækt], *v.a.* anziehen; an sich ziehen, auf sich (*Acc.*) ziehen, locken, fesseln, reizen; *be -ed to*, hingezogen werden zu; *the magnet -s iron*, der Magnet zieht das Eisen an; – *attention*, Aufmerksamkeit erregen. **-ion** [-ʃən], *s.* die Anziehung, Anziehungskraft, der Reiz; das Reizende, Lockende; die Zauberkraft; *-ion of gravity*, die Schwerkraft; *the great -ion of the evening*, die Hauptzugnummer des Abends; *exert -ion*, Anziehung ausüben; *capillary -ion*, die Haarröhrchenanziehung. **-ive** [-tɪv], *adj.* anziehend; reizend, fesselnd; *-ive force*, die Zugkraft; *-ive power*, die Ziehkraft, Anziehungskraft. **-iveness,** *s.* der Reiz, das Anziehende.

attribut-able [əˈtrɪbjʊtəbl], *adj.* zuzuschreiben, beizulegen. **-e** 1. [əˈtrɪbjuːt], *v.a.* beilegen, zuschreiben, beimessen (*to* (*Dat.*)), zurückführen (*to*, auf). 2 [ˈætrɪbjʊt] *s.* charakteristische Eigenschaft, das Kennzeichen, Merkmal; Attribut (*Gram.*). **-ion** [ætrɪˈbjuːʃən], *s.* die Zuschreibung, Beimessung; beigelegte Eigenschaft. **-ive** [-jʊtɪv], 1. *adj.* attributiv (*Gram.*). 2. *s.* das Attribut (*Gram.*).

attrition [əˈtrɪʃən], *s.* das Abreiben, die Reibung, Abreibung, Abnutzung; (*fig.*) die Zermürbung; die Reue (*Theol.*); *war of –*, der Zermürbungskrieg.

attune [əˈtjuːn], *v.a.* (ab)stimmen (*to*, auf (*Acc.*)), in Einklang bringen (*to*, mit), anpassen (*to*, an (*Acc.*)); *-d to*, eingestellt auf (*Acc.*).

auburn [ˈɔːbən], *adj.* rotbraun, kastanienbraun, nußbraun.

auction [ˈɔːkʃən], 1. *s.* die Versteigerung, Auktion; *sell by –, put up for –* or 2. *v.a.* versteigern, verauktionieren. **-eer** [-ˈnɪːə], *s.* der Versteigerer, Auktionator.

audaci-ous [ɔːˈdeɪʃəs], *adj.* kühn, verwegen, keck, dreist, vermessen, unverschämt, frech. **-ty** [-ˈdæsɪtɪ], *s.* die Kühnheit, Verwegenheit, Dreistigkeit, Frechheit, Unverschämtheit.

audib-ility [ɔːdɪˈbɪlɪtɪ], *s.* die Hörbarkeit, Vernehmbarkeit. **-le** [ˈɔːdɪbl], *adj.* hörbar, vernehmbar, vernehmlich.

audience [ˈɔːdjəns], *s.* die Audienz, der Zutritt, Empfang; das Gehör, die Anhörung; das Publikum, die Zuhörerschaft, Zuhörer (*pl.*), der Leserkreis (*of a book*), die Hörerschaft (*radio*); *receive in –*, (in Audienz) empfangen; *grant* or *give an –*, eine Audienz erteilen. **--chamber,** *s.* der Audienzsaal.

audio-frequency [ˈɔːdɪo-ˈfrɪːkwənsɪ], *s.* die Tonfrequenz, Hörfrequenz (*Rad.*).

audion [ˈɔːdɪɔn], *s.* die Kathodenröhre, das Audion (*Rad.*).

audit [ˈɔːdɪt], 1. *s.* die Rechnungsabnahme *or* -prüfung, Bücherrevision. 2. *v.a.* Rechnungen prüfen, amtlich revidieren. **- ale,** starkes Bier. **--office,** *s.* das Rechnungsamt, die Rechnungskammer. **-or** [ˈɔːdɪtə], *s.* der Rechnungsrevisor.

audit-ion [ɔːˈdɪʃən], *s.* das Gehör, Anhören; die Probe, Hörprobe (*Rad.*). **-orium** [ɔːdɪˈtɔːrɪəm], *s.* der Hörsaal, Zuhörerraum, Zuschauerraum, das Auditorium. **-ory** [ˈɔːdɪtərɪ], 1. *adj.* Gehör-; *-ory nerves*, Gehörnerven. 2. *s.* die Zuhörerschaft.

auger [ˈɔːgə], *s.* großer Bohrer.

aught [ɔːt], *s.* & *pron.* (*archaic* & *poet.*) (irgend)-

etwas; *for – I care*, meinetwegen; *for – I know*, soviel ich weiß.
augment [ɔ:gˈmɛnt], 1 *v.a.* vermehren; vergrößern, steigern. 2. *v.n.* zunehmen, sich vergrößern, sich vermehren. 3. [ˈɔ:gmənt], *s.* das Augment (*Gram.*). **–ation** [–ˈteɪʃən], *s.* die Vermehrung, Vergrößerung, Zunahme, Erhöhung, das Wachstum; der Zusatz, Zuwachs; die Augmentation, Themenverlängerung (*Mus.*). **–ative** [–ˈmɛntətɪv], 1. *adj.* vermehrend, vergrößernd, verstärkend. 2. *s.* die Verstärkungsform (*Gram.*).
augur [ˈɔ:gə], 1. *s.* der Augur, Wahrsager. 2. *v.a.* weissagen, prophezeien, ankündigen. 3. *v.n.*; – *ill* (or *well*), ein schlechtes (*or* gutes) Zeichen sein, böses (*or* gutes) versprechen. **–y** [ˈɔ:gjʊrɪ], *s.* die Wahrsagung; das Anzeichen, Vorzeichen, die Vorbedeutung, Vorahnung.
[1]**august** [ɔ:ˈgʌst], *adj.* erhaben, erlaucht, hehr. **–ness,** *s.* die Hoheit, Erhabenheit.
[2]**August** [ˈɔ:gəst], *s.* der August; *in* –, im August.
auk [ɔ:k], *s.* der Alk (*Orn.*).
auld lang syne [ˈɔ:ldˈlæŋˈsaɪn], *s.* (*Scots*) die gute alte Zeit.
aulic [[ˈɔ:lɪk], *adj.* Hof–, fürstlich.
aunt [ɑ:nt], *s.* die Tante, (*poet.*) Muhme; *great-–*, die Großtante; – *Sally*, das Knüttelwerfen. **–ie, –y,** *s.* das Tantchen.
aura [ˈɔ:rə], *s.* der Hauch, Duft, das Aroma; (*fig.*) die Atmosphäre, das Fluidum.
aural [ˈɔ:rəl], *adj.* Ohr–, Ohren–.
aureole [ˈɔ:rɪoʊl], *s.* die Strahlenkrone, der Heiligenschein; (*fig.*) der Nimbus, Ruhmeskranz; Hof (*Astr.*).
auric [ˈɔ:rɪk], *adj.* Gold–.
auricle [ˈɔ:rɪkl], *s.* äußeres Ohr, die Ohrmuschel; – *of the heart*, die Vorkammer des Herzens.
auricula [ɔ:ˈrɪkjʊlə], *s.* die Aurikel.
auricular [ɔ:ˈrɪkjʊlə], *adj.* Ohren–, Ohr–, ohrförmig; Hör–, heimlich; – *confession*, die Ohrenbeichte; – *tradition*, mündliche Überlieferung.
auriferous [ɔ:ˈrɪfərəs], *adj.* goldhaltig; – *quartz*, der Goldquarz.
aurochs [ˈɔ:rəks], *s.* der Auerochs.
aurora [əˈrɔ:rə], *s.* die Morgenröte; – *borealis*, das Nordlicht.
auscultat–e [ˈɔ:skəlteɪt], *v.a.* auskultieren, abhorchen, behorchen (*Med.*). **–ion,** *s.* die Auskultation, Abhorchung, Behorchung (*Med.*).
auspic–es [ˈɔ:spɪsɪz], *pl.* die Vogelschau; die Anzeichen, Vorzeichen, Auspizien (*pl.*); der Schutz, Beistand; *under favourable –es*, unter günstigen Anzeichen; *under the –es of*, unter dem Schutze *or* der Leitung von. **–ious** [ɔ:sˈpɪʃəs], *adj.* günstig, glücklich, glückverheißend.
auster–e [ɔ:sˈtɪ:ə], *adj.* nüchtern, ernst, einfach; streng, hart, herb, rauh; *–e look*, strenger Blick; *–e style*, schmuckloser Stil. **–ity** [–ˈtɛrɪtɪ], *s.* die Strenge, Härte, Nüchternheit, Einfachheit; der Ernst.
austral [ˈɔ:strəl], *adj.* südlich.
autarchy [ˈɔ:tɑkɪ], *s.* die Autarchie, Selbstherrschaft.
autarky [ˈɔ:tɑkɪ], *s.* die Autarkie, (wirtschaftliche) Unabhängigkeit.
authentic [ɔ:ˈθɛntɪk], *adj.* echt, wirklich, verbürgt, zuverlässig, glaubwürdig, authentisch, quellenmäßig, maßgebend, rechtskräftig. **–ate** [ɔ:ˈθɛntɪkeɪt], *v.a.* als echt erweisen, verbürgen, beglaubigen, rechtskräftig machen. **–ation** [–ˈkeɪʃən], *s.* die Beglaubigung; Glaubwürdigkeit. **–ity** [–ˈtɪsɪtɪ], *s.* die Echtheit, Glaubwürdigkeit, Rechtsgültigkeit.
author [ˈɔ:θə], *s.* der Stifter, Urheber, Schöpfer, (*fig.*) die Ursache; der Verfasser, Autor, Schriftsteller; *he is the – of*, er ist der Verfasser von; *the – of my being*, mein Schöpfer; *his profession as an –*, sein Schriftstellerberuf; *–'s copy*, das Handexemplar. **–ess,** *s.* die Verfasserin, Schriftstellerin. **–ship,** *s.* die Urheberschaft; Autorschaft; der Schriftstellerberuf.
authorit–arian [ɔ:θɔrɪˈtɛərɪən], *adj.* autoritär; *–arian principle*, das Führerprinzip; *–arian state*, der Obrigkeitsstaat. **–ative** [ɔ:ˈθɔrɪteɪtɪv], *adj.* autoritativ, Autorität habend, maßgebend, maßgeblich, bevollmächtigt; gebieterisch, herrisch. **–ativeness.** *s.* gebieterisches Wesen, das Bevollmächtigtsein. **–y** [ɔ:ˈθɔrɪtɪ], *s.* die Autorität, rechtmäßige Macht, die Amtsgewalt, Vollmacht; Behörde; der Einfluß, das Gewicht, Ansehen, die Glaubwürdigkeit (*with*, bei); das Zeugnis; Befugnis, der Auftrag, die Ermächtigung; der Gewährsmann, die Quelle, der Beleg; die Fachgröße, der Fachmann, Sachverständige(r), *m.*, die Autorität; *civil –y*, die Zivilbehörden (*pl.*); *confirming –y*, die Bestätigungsinstanz (*Law*); *convening –y*, der Gerichtsherr (*Law*); *delegation of –y*, die Übertragung von Amtsgewalt; *enforcement of –y*, die Gehorsamserzwingung; *reviewing –y*, die Revisionsinstanz (*Law*); *the –ies*, die Behörde(n), Obrigkeit; *local –ies*, die Ortsbehörde; *be in –y*, Vollmacht haben, die Gewalt in Händen haben; *by –y*, mit Befugnis der Obrigkeit; *he has no –y over them*, er hat keine Macht über sie; *he is an –y on philology*, er ist ein Fachmann auf dem Gebiet der Philologie; *on the –y of*, im Auftrage von; *on one's own –y*, aus eigener Machtbefugnis; *on good –y*, aus guter Quelle; *on the –y of St. Paul*, Paulus ist ein Gewährsmann dafür daß . . .; *have –y to do*, berechtigt *or* autorisiert sein zu tun, die Vollmacht haben zu tun.
authoriz–ation [ɔ:θəraɪˈzeɪʃən], *s.* die Ermächtigung. **–e** [ˈɔ:θəraɪz], *v.a.* bevollmächtigen, ermächtigen, autorisieren (*a p.*); rechtfertigen, genehmigen, billigen, gutheißen (*an action*); *–ed agent*, Bevollmächtigte(r), *m.*, Beauftragte(r), *m.*, rechtsverbindlicher Vertreter; *–ed capital*, registriertes Kapital; *–ed Version*, die englische Bibel von 1611.
autobiograph–ical [ɔ:tobaɪoˈgræfɪkl], *adj.* autobiographisch. **–y** [ɔ:tobaɪˈɔgrəfɪ], *s.* die Selbstbiographie.
autochthon [ɔ:ˈtɔkθən], *s.* (*usually pl.* [–z] *or* –es [–ɪ:z]) der Ureinwohner. **–al, –ic** [–ˈθɔnɪk], **–ous,** *adj.* ureingesessen.
autocra–cy [ɔ:ˈtɔkrəsɪ], *s.* die Selbstherrschaft, Autokratie. **–t** [ˈɔ:təkræt], *s.* der Selbstherrscher, Autokrat. **–tic** [–ˈkrætɪk], *adj.* selbstherrlich, unumschränkt, autokratisch.
auto-da-fé [ɔ:todɑ:ˈfeɪ], *s.* das Ketzergericht.
autogiro [ɔ:toˈdʒaɪroʊ], *s.* das Windmühlenflugzeug, Drehflügelflugzeug, der Tragschrauber (*Av.*).
autograph [ˈɔ:təgrɑ:f], *s.* das Autograph, die Originalhandschrift, Urschrift; eigenhändige (Unter)Schrift; – *letter*, eigenhändig geschriebener *or* unterzeichneter Brief. **–ic** [–ˈgræfɪk], *adj.* eigenhändig geschrieben, autographisch.
autogyro, *see* **autogiro.**
automatic [ɔ:təˈmætɪk], 1. *adj.* selbsttätig, selbstbeweglich, automatisch; mechanisch, unwillkürlich; – *gun*, das Selbstladegewehr; – *machine*, der Automat; – *telephone*, das Telephon mit Selbstanschluß; – *telephone-exchange*, das Selbstanschlußamt; – *volume control*, der Schwundausgleich (*Rad.*). 2. *s.* der Revolver.
automat–on [ɔ:ˈtɔmətən], *s.* (*pl.* –a *or* –ons) der Automat; die Gliederpuppe.
automobile [ˈɔ:təmoʊbi:l], *s.* das Auto, der Kraftwagen.
autonom–ous [ɔ:ˈtɔnəməs], *adj.* selbstregierend, unabhängig, selbständig. **–y** [–mɪ], *s.* die Selbstregierung, Selbständigkeit; Willensfreiheit, Autonomie (*Phil.*).
autopsy [ˈɔ:tɔpsɪ], *s.* die Selbstschau, der Augenschein; die Leichenöffnung, Leichenschau, Autopsie (*Med.*); (*fig.*) Sezierung, Zergliederung.
auto-–suggestion [ɔ:tosəˈdʒɛstʃən], *s.* die Autosuggestion, Selbstbeeinflussung. **–type** [ˈɔ:totaɪp], 1. *s.* die Autotypie, der Faksimileabdruck (*Typ.*); die Netzätzung (*Phot.*). 2. *v.a.* durch Autotypie vervielfältigen, autotypieren.
autumn [ˈɔ:təm], *s.* der Herbst. **–al** [ɔ:ˈtʌmnəl], *adj.* herbstlich.
auxiliary [ɔ:gˈzɪlɪərɪ], 1. *adj.* helfend, zusätzlich, Hilfs–; mitwirkend (*Gram.*); – *engine*, der Hilfsmotor; – *forces* or *troops*, die Hilfstruppen; – *verb*, das Hilfszeitwort. 2. *s.* Verbündete(r), *m.*, der Helfer; das Hilfszeitwort (*Gram.*); (*pl.*) Hilfstruppen.
avail [əˈveɪl], 1. *v.a.*; – *o.s. of a th.*, sich einer S. bedienen, eine S. benutzen, Gebrauch von einer

S. machen; *I – myself of the opportunity*, ich benutze die Gelegenheit. 2. *v.n.* **nützen**, helfen; *what –s it?* was nützt es? 3. *s.* der Nutzen; *all was of no –*, es half alles nichts; *without –*, vergeblich, ohne Erfolg. **–ability,** *s.* die Verwendbarkeit, Verfügbarkeit, das Vorhandensein, die Gültigkeit. **–able,** *adj.* vorhanden, vorrätig, verfügbar, zugänglich, statthaft; verwendbar, brauchbar; gültig (*by*, für); *return ticket –able for 3 days*, Rückfahrkarte mit dreitägiger Gültigkeit; *be –able*, zur Verfügung stehen.

avalanche ['ævəlɑ:nʃ], *s.* die Lawine.

avaric–e ['ævərɪs], *s.* die Habsucht, der Geiz. **–ious** [–'rɪʃəs], *adj.* habsüchtig, geizig.

avast [ə'vɑ:st], *int.* genug! halt! (*Naut.*)

avatar ['ævətɑ.], *s.* das Herabsteigen einer Gottheit (*Indian myth.*).

avaunt [ə'vɔ:nt], *int.* (*archaic*) hinweg! fort!

avenge [ə'vɛndʒ], *v.a.* rächen; *– o.s.* or *be –d on a p.*, sich an einem rächen; *– a murder*, einen Mord rächen (*or poet.* ahnden). **–r,** *s.* der Rächer.

avenue ['ævɪnju:], *s.* die Allee; große breite Straße; die Anfahrt, der Zugang, Weg.

aver [ə'və:], *v.a.* behaupten, als Tatsache hinstellen, versichern; beweisen, bekräftigen. **–ment,** *s.* die Behauptung, Versicherung; der Beweis (*Law*).

average ['ævərɪdʒ], 1. *adj.* durchschnittlich; *the – man*, der Durchschnittsmensch; *– price*, der Mittelpreis. 2. *v.n. & a.* im Durchschnitt betragen; den Durchschnitt berechnen *or* nehmen. 3. *s.* der Durchschnitt, die Havarie (*Naut.*); *at an – of*, durchschnittlich um; *general –*, allgemeiner Durchschnittswert; große Havarie (*Naut.*); *particular –*, partikuläre Havarie (*Naut.*); *petty –*, kleine *or* ordinäre Havarie (*Naut.*); *on an –*, im Durchschnitt, durchschnittlich; *rough –*, mittleres Verhältnis.

avers–e [ə'və:s], *adj.* abgeneigt (*to*, gegen), abhold (*to* (*Dat.*)); *I am –e to it*, es ist mir zuwider; *my father was –e to my going*, mein Vater war nicht geneigt mich gehen zu lassen. **–eness,** *s.* die Abgeneigtheit (*to*, gegen). **–ion** [–ʃən], *s.* die Abneigung, der Widerwille (*to*, *for*, gegen; *from*, vor (*Dat.*)); der Gegenstand des Abscheus, Greuel; (*coll.*) *it is my pet –ion*, es ist mir ein ausgesprochener Greuel.

avert [ə'və:t], *v.a.* abwenden, ablenken, verhüten, vorbeugen.

aviary ['eɪvɪərɪ], *s.* das Vogelhaus.

aviat–ion [eɪvɪ'eɪʃən], *s.* das Flugwesen, Fliegen. **–or,** *s.* der Flieger.

avid ['ævɪd], *adj.* begierig (*of* or *for*, nach). **–ity** [ə'vɪdɪtɪ], *s.* die Gier, Begierde (*of*, *for*, nach).

avocation [ævo'keɪʃən], *s.* die Nebenbeschäftigung, der Nebenberuf; das Berufsgeschäft; (*archaic*) die Abhaltung, Abberufung, Zerstreuung.

avoid [ə'vɔɪd], *v.a.* meiden (*a p.*); vermeiden, entgehen (*Dat.*) (*a. th.*); ausweichen (*Dat.*) (*a duty, etc.*); aufheben, ungültig machen, umstoßen (*Law*); *he –s me*, er geht mir aus dem Wege; *in order to – delay*, um Verzögerungen zu vermeiden. **–able,** *adj.* vermeidlich, vermeidbar. **–ance,** *s.* das Meiden (*of a p.*), die Vermeidung (*of a th.*); das Freiwerden, die Vakanz; der Widerruf, die Aufhebung (*Law*).

avoirdupois [ævədə'pɔɪz], *s.* gewöhnliches englisches Handelsgewicht; (*coll.*) das Gewicht.

avouch [ə'vautʃ], 1. *v.a.* behaupten, bekennen, anerkennen, versichern, bekräftigen, verbürgen. 2. *v.n.* einstehen (*for*, für), garantieren.

avow [ə'vau], *v.a.* offen bekennen, anerkennen, eingestehen. **–al** [–əl], *s.* die Erklärung, das Bekenntnis, Geständnis. **–ed** [–d], *adj.* anerkannt; offen erklärt, ausgesprochen. **–edly** [–ɪdlɪ], *adv.* offen, unverhohlen, eingestandenermaßen.

avuncular [ə'vʌŋkjulə], *adj.* einen Onkel betreffend, dem Onkel zukommend, onkelhaft.

await [ə'weɪt], *v.a.* erwarten (*Acc.*), entgegensehen (*Dat.*); *–ing your answer*, in Erwartung Ihrer Antwort; *– instructions*, Anweisung abwarten! (*C.L.*).

awake [ə'weɪk], 1. *ir.v.a.* wecken, erwecken, aufwecken; erregen (*suspicion*). 2 *ir v.n.* erwachen, aufwachen; *– to s.th.*, sich einer S. bewußt werden, sich über eine S. klar werden. 3. *pred. adj.* wach, wachend, munter; *be wide –* ganz wach sein; (*fig.*) auf der Hut sein, schlau sein; *be – to a th.*, einer S. bewußt sein, etwas wohl wissen *or* kennen. **–n,** *v.a. & n. see* **–.** **–ning,** *s.* das Erwachen; Erwecken; religiöse Erweckung.

award [ə'wɔ:d], 1. *v.a.* zuerkennen, zusprechen; verleihen. 2. *s.* das Urteil, die Entscheidung, der Urteilsspruch; der Preis, die Auszeichnung, Prämie; Belohnung (*or* Strafe).

aware [ə'wɛə], *pred. adj.* gewahr; unterrichtet, wissend; *be –*, wissen; *become – of a th.*, etwas merken, etwas zur Kenntnis nehmen, eine(r) S. gewahr werden; *he is – of it*, er weiß es, es ist ihm bekannt, er hat Kenntnis davon; *before I was –*, ehe ich mich's versah. **–ness,** *s.* die Bewußtheit, Erkenntnis.

awash [ə'wɔʃ], *adj.* überspült, überflutet; zwischen Wind und Wasser (*Naut.*).

away [ə'weɪ], *adv.* weg, hinweg, fort; fern von, entfernt, abwesend, auswärts, nicht da; *be –*, verreist sein; *come –!*, komm nur her! *do – with*, vernichten, abschaffen, beseitigen; *explain –*, beseitigen, wegerklären (*difficulties, etc.*); *fall –*, abfallen; *far and –*, bei weitem; (*coll.*) *fire –!* schieß los! mach zu! (*coll.*) *give a p. –*, einen verraten; *go –*, weggehen; *laugh –!* lacht nur zu! *make – with*, umbringen (*a p.*), beiseitebringen, (*sl.*) verduften mit (*a th.*); (*coll.*) *right –*, sofort; fertig! abfahren! (*of trains, etc.*); *run –*, weglaufen; *send –*, wegsenden, fortschicken; *throw –*, wegwerfen, vergeuden; *trifle –*, vertändeln; *waste –*, verfallen, abnehmen, vergehen, verschwendet werden, dahinschwinden; (*coll.*) *work –*, drauflos arbeiten.

awe [ɔ:], 1. *s.* die Furcht, Scheu, Ehrfurcht; *in – of* aus Ehrfurcht vor; *fill, inspire* or *strike a p. with –* (*of a th.*), einem Ehrfurcht einflößen (vor einer S.). 2. *v.a.* Scheu *or* Ehrfurcht einflößen (*Dat.*); einschüchtern (*Acc.*); *– s.o. into silence*, einen durch Furcht zum Stillschweigen bringen. **– –inspiring,** *adj.* einschüchternd. **–some,** *adj.* erschreckend, schrecklich, furchtbar. **– –struck,** *adj.* von Ehrfurcht *or* Scheu ergriffen.

awful ['ɔ:ful], *adj.* ehrfurchterregend, erhaben; furchtbar, schrecklich, ungeheuer, entsetzlich, verheerend. **–ly,** *adv.* (*coll.*) äußerst, höchst; *–ly cold day*, schrecklich kalter Tag. **–ness,** *s.* die Ehrwürdigkeit; Furchtbarkeit, Schrecklichkeit.

awhile [ə'waɪl], *adv.* eine Weile, eine Zeitlang.

awkward ['ɔ:kwəd], *adj.* ungeschickt, linkisch, unbeholfen, verlegen; ungünstig, ungelegen, peinlich, unangenehm, mißlich. **–ness,** *s.* unbeholfenes Wesen; die Ungeschicklichkeit; *the –ness of the situation*, das Unangenehme, Peinliche *or* Heikle an der Lage.

awl [ɔ:l], *s.* die Ahle, der Pfriemen.

awn [ɔ:n], 1. *s.* die Granne. 2. *v.a.* entgrannen.

awning ['ɔ:nɪŋ], *s.* die Wagendecke *or* –plane Markise; das Sonnensegel, Sonnenzelt (*Naut.*).

awoke [ə'wouk], *see* **awake.**

awry [ə'raɪ], *adv. & pred. adj.* schief, krumm, verkehrt, irre–; *go –*, schiefgehen (*of things*), sich irren (*of persons*).

axe [æks], 1. *s.* die Axt, Hacke, Haue, das Beil; (*coll.*) der Beamtenabbau; *headman's –*, das Henkersbeil; *have an – to grind*, eigennützige Zwecke verfolgen. 2. *v.a.* (*coll.*) beschneiden (*expenses*), abbauen (*officials*). **– –head,** *s.* das Eisen der Axt.

axial ['æksiəl], *adj.* achsenförmig, Achsen–.

axil ['æksɪl], *s.* die Blattachsel, der Astwinkel (*Bot.*). **–la** [–ə], *s.* die Achselhöhle. **–lary** [–ərɪ], *adj.* Achsel–; achselständig (*Bot.*).

axiom ['æksɪəm], *s.* das Axiom, der Grundsatz. **–atic(al),** [–'mætɪk(l)], *adj.* axiomatisch, grundsätzlich, unumstößlich, von vornherein erwiesen, allgemein anerkannt, zweifellos, sicher, gewiß.

axis ['æksɪs], *s.* (*pl.* axes) die Achse, Mittellinie, Hauptlinie; *longitudinal –*, die Längsachse; *– of the earth*, die Erdachse; *transverse –*, die Querachse; *vertical –*, die Höhe (*Geom.*).

axle ['æksl], *s.* die Achse, Welle; *driving –*, die Antriebachse; *independent –*, die Schwingachse; *wheel and –*, das Rad an der Welle. **– –base,** *s.* der

Achsabstand. **--bearing,** das Achslager. **--bed,** *s.* das Achsenfutter. **--box,** *s.* die Lagerschale, Nabenbüchse. **- load,** der Achsdruck. **--pin,** *s.* der Achsennagel, die Lünse. **--tree,** *s.* die Welle, Radachse.

¹ay, -e [ɑɪ], 1. *adv.* ja, freilich; –, – *!* zu Befehl! (*Naut.*). 2. *s.*; *the -es and the Noes,* die Stimmen für und wider; *the -es have it,* die Mehrheit ist für den Antrag, der Antrag ist angenommen.

²ay(e) [eɪ], *adv.* (*Scots*) ewig, immer; *for ever and –,* auf immer und ewig.

ayah [ˈɑɪə], *s.* das Kindermädchen (*Anglo-Indian*).

azalea [əˈzeɪlɪə], *s.* die Azalie.

azimuth [ˈæzɪməθ], *s.* der Azimut, Scheitelkreis (*Astr.*).

azoic [æˈzoʊɪk], *adj.* ohne Leben, azoisch (*Geol.*); – *period,* das Azoikum (*Geol.*).

azote [əˈzoʊt], *s.* der Stickstoff.

azure [ˈæz(j)ə], 1. *adj.* himmelblau, (*poet.*) azurn; blau (*Her.*). 2. *s.* das Himmelblau, der Azur; blaues Feld (*Her.*); (*poet.*) das Himmelszelt.

azyme [ˈæzɑɪm], *s.* ungesäuertes Brot.

B

B, b [bɪː], *s.* das B, b; das H (*Mus.*); *B flat,* das B; *B major,* H-Dur; *B minor,* H-Moll; *B sharp,* His. *See Index of Abbreviations.*

baa [bɑː], 1. *s.* das Blöken, Geblök. 2. *v.n.* blöken.

babbl-e [ˈbæbl], 1. *v.n.* schwatzen, plappern; plätschern, murmeln (*of brooks*); stammeln, lallen. 2. *v.a.* ausschwatzen, nachschwatzen. 3. *s.* das Geschwätz, Plappern, Nachschwatzen; Murmeln, Plätschern. **-er,** *s.* der Schwätzer. **-ing,** *s.* das Geschwätz, Geplapper; Geplätscher.

babe [beɪb], *s.* (*B., poet.*) kleines Kind, das Kindchen *or* Kindlein.

babel [ˈbeɪbl], *s.* der Lärm, die Verwirrung, das Durcheinander, der Wirrwarr.

baboon [bəˈbuːn], *s.* der Pavian.

baby [ˈbeɪbɪ], 1. *s.* kleines Kind, das Kindlein, Kindchen; der Säugling, das Baby; (*coll.*) *carry* or *hold the –,* das Unangenehme tun müssen *or* übertragen bekommen. 2. *attrib.* klein. **--clothes,** *pl. see* **--linen. --farm,** *s.* das Säuglingsheim. **--farmer,** *s.* jemand der Kinder in Pflege nimmt; der Engelmacher. **- grand,** der Stutzflügel (*Mus.*). **-hood,** *s.* frühe Kindheit, das Säuglingsalter. **-ish,** *adj.* kindisch. **--linen,** *s.* das Kinderzeug, Kinderwäsche. **--snatcher,** *s.* der Kinderräuber.

baccalaureate [bækəˈlɔːrɪɪt], *s.* das Bakkalaureat.

bacchanal [ˈbækənl], 1. *s.* der Bacchant; Bacchuspriester. 2. *adj.* bacchantisch, schwelgerisch. **-ia** [–ˈneɪlɪə], *pl.* die Bacchanalien; Orgie. **-ian,** *adj.* bacchantisch; *-ian song,* das Trinklied. **-s,** *pl. see* **-ia.**

baccy [ˈbækɪ], *s.* (*coll.*) der Tabak.

bachelor [ˈbætʃələ], *s.* der Junggeselle, lediger Mann; der Bakkalaureus (*Univ.*); *knight –,* der Ritter (*as title*); *old –,* alter Hagestolz; *-'s button,* der Patentknopf; Scharfer Hahnenfuß (*Bot.*). **--girl,** *s.* alleinstehendes Mädchen, die Junggesellin. **-hood,** *s.* der Junggesellenstand; das Bakkalaureat.

bacill-us [bəˈsɪləs], *s.* (*pl.* -i) der Bazillus.

back [bæk], 1. *s.* der Rücken; das Kreuz (*of a horse*); die Rückseite, Hinterseite; der Hintergrund; Verteidiger (*Footb.*); die Kehrseite (*of a coin*); die Rückenlehne (*of a chair*); linke Seite (*of cloth*); (*a*) (*with nouns*) *in the – of the car,* auf dem Rücksitz des Wagens; *– of the chimney,* die Kaminplatte; *the -s* (*of the Colleges*), die Parkseite der Cambridger Colleges; *– of the hand,* der Handrücken, die Rückseite der Hand; *– of the head,* der Hinterkopf; *at the – of the house,* hinter dem Haus; *– of the neck,* der Nacken, das Genick; *– of a sword,* der Rücken eines Schwertes; (*b*) (*with verbs*) *break a p.'s –,* einem das Rückgrat brechen, (*fig.*) einen zu Grunde richten; *break the – of a th.,* das Schwerste *or* Schlimmste erledigen *or* hinter sich haben; *give* or *make a –,* sich bücken; *put one's – into a th.,* sich hinter eine S. (*or* sich dahinter) setzen; *put* or *get a p.'s – up,* einen reizen *or* ärgern; *the cat puts up her –,* die Katze krümmt den Rücken; *turn one's –,* sich umwenden; *turn one's – upon a p.,* einem den Rücken kehren; (*fig.*) einen im Stich lassen; (*c*) (*with prepositions*) *at his –,* hinter ihm *or* seinem Rücken; *at the – of,* hinter; *be at the – of a p.,* hinter einem stehen, einen unterstützen; *behind a p.'s –,* hinter jemandes Rücken, insgeheim; *be* or *lie on one's –,* bettlägerig sein, auf dem Krankenbett liegen; *he hasn't a shirt to his –,* er hat kein Hemd auf dem Leibe; *– to –,* Rücken an Rücken; *with one's – to the wall,* (*fig.*) in die Enge getrieben, in großer Bedrängnis, hart bedrängt. **2.** *adj.* Hinter–, Rück–; fern, abgelegen; (*see comps. below*); *– pay,* rückständiges *or* rückläufiges Gehalt; *take a – seat,* in den Hintergrund treten, eine untergeordnete Stellung einnehmen, zurückgedrängt werden. **3.** *adv.* zurück, rückwärts; früher, zurückliegend; hinten; – (*again*), wieder, wiederum, wieder zurück; *– and forth,* hin und her; *a few years –,* vor einigen Jahren; *I shall be –* (*again*) *directly,* ich bin gleich wieder da; *come –,* zurückkommen, wiederkommen; *get one's own –,* sich an einem rächen; (*coll.*) *get – at,* den Spieß umkehren gegen, sich rächen an, sich schadlos machen an; *go –,* zurückgehen; *go – on one's word,* sein Versprechen nicht erfüllen, vom gegebenen Wort abweichen; *keep –,* zurückbehalten, see also *stand –*; *lie –,* sich rückwärts legen; *pay –,* zurückbezahlen; (*fig.*) vergelten; *stand – !* zurück! *there and –,* hin und zurück. **4.** *v.a.* stützen, den Rücken decken (*Dat.*), unterstützen, beistehen, begünstigen; (*C.L.*) gegenzeichnen, indossieren; wetten auf; mit einem Rücken *or* einer Lehne versehen; rückwärts gehen *or* fahren lassen; *– a horse,* (*poet.*) ein Pferd besteigen; (*coll.*) *– a horse* (*to win*), auf ein Pferd wetten; *– the oars,* see *– water*; *– the sails,* die Segel backlegen; (*coll.*) *– up,* unterstützen; beistehen (*Dat.*); *– water,* rückwärtsrudern. **5.** *v.n.* sich zurückbewegen, zurücktreten, rückwärts gehen; *– on to,* hinten anstoßen an, nach hinten blicken auf (*rooms, etc.*); *– out,* sich zurückziehen (*of,* von *or* aus), zurücktreten, (*coll.*) kneifen, klein beigeben. **-ache,** *s.* Rückenschmerzen (*pl.*). **-band,** *s.* der Rückengurt, Kreuzriemen. **--basket,** *s.* der Tragkorb, die Kiepe. **--bencher,** *s.* der Abgeordnete der nicht Kabinettsmitglied ist. **-bite,** 1. *v.a.* verleumden. 2. *v.n.* afterreden. **-biter,** *s.* der Verleumder. **-biting,** 1. *pr.p. & adj.* verleumderisch. 2. *s.* das Verleumden, die Verleumdung. **--board,** *s.* das Rückenbrett; der Geradehalter (*for improving the posture*) (*Med.*). **-bone,** *s.* das Rückgrat; (*fig.*) die Willenskraft, Charakterstärke, Festigkeit; *to the -bone,* eingefleischt, durch und durch; *he has no -bone,* er ist ein Waschlappen. **--chat,** *s.* gegenseitige Unverschämtheiten, unverschämte Antwort. **--cloth,** *s.* der Prospekt, die Kulisse (*Theat.*). **--coupling,** *s.* die Rückkopplung (*Rad.*). **-door,** die Hintertür. **-er,** *s.* der Helfer; Wettende(r), *m.*; (*C.L.*) der Hintermann, Indossierer. **-fire,** *s.* die Fehlzündung (*Gunn.*), Frühzündung (*Motor.*). **--formation,** *s.* die Rückbildung (*Philol.*). **-gammon,** *s.* das Puffspiel. **-ground,** *s.* der Hintergrund; *keep in the -ground,* im Hintergrund bleiben; *-ground noise,* das Störgeräusch (*Rad.*). **-hand,** *s.* die Rückhand (*sport*); *-hand drive,* der Rückhandtriebschlag (*Tenn.*). **-handed,** *adj.* Rückhand–; (*fig.*) spöttisch; zweifelhaft, doppelsinnig; indirekt, unerwartet. **-hander,** *s.* der Schlag mit dem Handrücken. **-ing,** *s.* die Hilfe, Unterstützung; Deckung, Indossierung (*C.L.*); Rückenschicht, Unterlage, das Futter. **-lash,** *s.* toter Gang (*Mech.*). **- number,** alte Nummer (*of newspaper*); (*fig.*) rückständiger Mensch. **--pedal,** *v.n.* rückwärtstreten (*Cycl.*); *--pedalling brake,* die Rücktrittbremse. **--settlement,** *s.* entlegene Siedlung. **-side,** die Rückseite, Hinterseite, (*vulg.*) Hintere(r), *m.*, das Gesäß, der Popo. **--sight,** *s.* das Visier, die Kimme (*on a gun*); *-sight notch,* *s.* die Visierkimme. **-slide,** *v.n.* abfallen, abtrünnig werden. **-slider,** *s.* Abtrünnige(r), *m.* **--spacer,** *s.* die Rücktaste (*Typewriter*). **-stairs,** die Hintertreppe, Dienstbotentreppe; *–stairs influence*, geheimer Einfluß. **–stay,** *s.* die Pardune (*Naut.*). **--stitch,** *s.* der Steppstich. **--stroke,** *s.* der Gegenschlag; das Rückenschwimmen. **--talk,** *s.* (*Amer.*) *see* **--chat. –wash,** *s.* die Kielwasserströmung. **–water,** *s.* das Stauwasser; (*fig.*) der Stillstand. **--wheel,** das Hinterrad. **–woods,** *pl.* die Hinterwälder. **–woodsman,** *s.* der Hinterwäldler. **--yard,** der Hinterhof.

backward [ˈbækwəd], 1. *adj.* spät eintretend *or* reifend, spätreif, zurückgeblieben, rückständig; zurückhaltend, schwerfällig; abgeneigt, widerwillig; rückwärtswirkend, verkehrt, Rück–; *– children*, zurückgebliebene Kinder; *– course*, der Rücklauf; *be – in doing one's duty*, seine Pflicht nur mit Abneigung erfüllen; *he is – in learning*, das Lernen fällt ihm schwer; *he is rather – at school*, er ist in der Schule ziemlich zurück. 2. *adv.*, **–s,** *adv.* rückwärts, zurück, von hinten; rückgängig, rücklings, verkehrt; *–s and forwards*, hin und her; *go –s*, rückwärts gehen. **–ation,** *s.* der Deport, Kursabschlag (*C.L.*). **–ness,** *s.* das Zurücksein, Zurückbleiben; die Abgeneigtheit, der Widerwille, das Widerstreben; die Langsamkeit, Spätreife, Rückständigkeit.

bacon [ˈbeɪkən], *s.* der Speck; *flitch of –*, die Speckseite; *gammon of –*, der Schinken; *rasher of –*, die Speckschnitte; *fried eggs and –*, Spiegeleier und Schinken; (*coll.*) *save one's –*, sich in Sicherheit bringen, sich sicherstellen *or* retten. **--rind,** *s.* die Speckschwarte.

bacter–ial [bækˈtɪːərɪəl], *adj.* Bakterien–. **–iology** [bæktɪərɪˈɔlədʒɪ], *s.* die Bakterienkunde, Bakteriologie. **–ium** [–rɪəm], *s.* (*usually pl.* –ia) die Bakterie.

bad [bæd], *adj.* schlecht, schlimm, böse, ungezogen; übel, schädlich, verdorben, faul; krank, unwohl; (*a*) (*with nouns*) *– arm*, kranker Arm; *– blood*, (*fig.*) böses Blut; *in his – books*, schlecht bei ihm angeschrieben; *– coin*, falsche Münze; *– cold*, starke Erkältung, heftiger Schnupfen; *– debts*, nicht einziehbare Außenstände; *– egg*, faules Ei, (*fig. coll.*) unzuverlässiger Kerl; *it's – form*, das schickt sich nicht; *with a – grace*, widerwillig, unfreundlich; *– headache*, übles Kopfweh; (*sl.*) *– hat*, unzuverlässiger Mensch; *– heart*, angegriffenes Herz; *– job*, schlimmer Handel; *– language*, Flüche, unanständige Worte (*pl.*); *– life*, schlechter Lebenswandel; *– luck*, das Unglück, (*coll.*) Pech; *– news*, schlechte Nachricht(en); (*coll.*) *– shot*, falsche Vermutung; *– surface*, das Plattengeräusch (*gramophone*); (*coll.*) *in a – way*, in schlechten Verhältnissen; sehr krank; *– ways*, schlechte Angewohnheiten; (*b*) (*with verbs*) *he is too –*, er treibt es zu bunt; *that is too –*, das ist zu dumm; *that is –*, das ist arg; (*coll.*) *that is not –*, das ist nicht übel; *it was too – of you*, es war nicht schön von dir; *feel – about*, sich ärgern über; *go –*, verderben, verfallen; (*c*) (*as a subst.*) *be £100 to the –*, hundert Pfund Verlust haben; *from – to worse*, schlimmer und schlimmer, immer schlimmer; (*coll.*) *go to the –*, auf Abwege geraten, in schlechte Gesellschaft kommen; *take the – with the good*, das Unangenehme hinnehmen. **–ly,** *adv.* ernstlich, dringend, sehr; *–ly wanted*, dringend erforderlich; *be –ly in want of food*, Nahrung dringend benötigen; *be –ly off*, übel daran sein; *things go –ly with me*, es geht mir schlecht. **–ness,** *s.* die Schlechtigkeit, Bösartigkeit; schlechter Zustand, die Schädlichkeit; Bosheit.

bade [bæd], *see* **bid.**

badge [bædʒ], *s.* das Abzeichen, Rangabzeichen, Dienstabzeichen; die Marke, das Merkzeichen.

badger [ˈbædʒə], 1. *s.* der Dachs (*Zool.*). 2. *v.a.* hetzen, plagen, quälen, belästigen.

badinage [bædɪˈnɑːʒ], *s.* der Scherz, die Neckerei, Schäkerei.

badminton [ˈbædmɪntən], *s.* das Federballspiel.

baffl–e [ˈbæfl], 1. *v.a.* vereiteln; verwirren, täuschen; *it –es description*, das spottet aller Beschreibung; *–e his designs*, seine Pläne durchkreuzen; *–e pursuit*, die Verfolgung verhindern; *he was –ed*, es war ihm ein Rätsel. 2. *s.* der Dämpfer (*of loudspeaker*). **–e paint,** *s.* der Tarnanstrich. **–e plate,** *s.* die Ablenkplatte. **–ing,** *pr.p.* & *adj.* vereitelnd, verwirrend, hinderlich; unverständlich, täuschend; *–ing winds*, unstete *or* widrige Winde.

bag [bæg], 1. *s.* der Beutel, Sack, die Tasche, Tüte; Jagdbeute; (*pl.*) (*coll.*) die Hosen; *– and baggage*, mit Sack und Pack, Hab und Gut; *– of bones*, das Knochengerippe; *let the cat out of the –*, die Katze aus dem Sack lassen; *Gladstone –*, die Herrenreisetasche; *make a good –*, viel Wild erlegen, viel Jagdglück haben; *lucky –*, die Glückstüte; (*coll.*) *the whole – of tricks*, der ganze Kram; (*coll.*) *it's in the –*, es ist so gut wie sicher; *– of wool*, der Ballen (*240 Pfd.*) Wolle. 2. *v.a.* einsacken, einstecken; (*sl.*) beanspruchen, an sich nehmen. 3. *v.n.* sich bauschen, aufschwellen; schlecht sitzen, lose hängen (*of clothes*). **–ful,** *s.* der Sackvoll; *in –fuls*, sackweise. **–ging,** 1. *adj.* herabhängend, ausbauschend. 2. die Packleinwand. **–gy,** *adj.* bauschig, sackartig. **–man,** *s.* der Handlungsreisende(r). **–pipe,** *s.* die Sackpfeife, der Dudelsack.

bagasse [bæˈgæs], *s.* Zuckerrohrrückstände (*pl.*).

bagatelle [bægəˈtɛl], *s.* die Kleinigkeit, Lappalie; das Tivolispiel.

baggage [ˈbægɪdʒ], *s.* das Gepäck, (*Amer.*) Reisegepäck; der Troß, die Bagage (*Mil.*); (*sl.*) das Frauenzimmer, Weibsbild; *bag and –*, *see under* **bag. – car,** (*Amer.*) der Gepäckwagen.

bagnio [ˈbænjoʊ], *s.* das Badehaus; (*obs.*) Bordell; Gefängnis.

bagpipe [ˈbægpaɪp], *see* **bag–.**

[1]**bail** [beɪl], 1. *s.* der Bürge; Bürgschaft; Kaution (*C.L.*); *allow –*, Bürgschaft zulassen; *be out on –*, gegen Kaution entlassen; *give –*, einen Bürgen stellen; *go* or *stand – for a p.*, Bürgschaft für einen leisten, für einen bürgen; *refuse –*, Bürgschaft ablehnen. 2. (*archaic*) *v.a.* Bürgschaft leisten für, bürgen für; deponieren, hinterlegen (*goods*); (*usually v.n.*) *– out*, durch Bürgschaft befreien. **–able,** *adj.* gegen Bürgschaft freizulassen(d); Bürgschaft zulassend. **–ee,** *s.* der Bewahrer, Depositar. **–iff,** *s.* der Amtmann, Gerichtsdiener; Landvogt; (Guts)Verwalter. **–iwick,** *s.* der Amtsbezirk, die Vogtei. **–ment,** *s.* die Freilassung gegen Bürgschaft. **–or,** *s.* der Hinterleger, Deponent (*Law*).

[2]**bail,** *s.* der Henkel, Bügel, Griff, Reifen; das Querholz (*Crick.*).

[3]**bail,** *v.a.* & *n.* Wasser ausschöpfen (*from a boat*); *– (out) a boat*, ein Boot ausschöpfen; (*coll.*) *– out*, mit Fallschirm abspringen; (also **bale**).

bailey [ˈbeɪlɪ], *s.* der Außenhof (*of a castle*).

bairn [bɛːrn], *s.* (*Scots*) das Kind.

bait [beɪt], 1. *s.* der Köder, die Lockspeise; die Rast, der Imbiß; (*fig.*) die Lockung, der Reiz; *live –*, der Köderfisch; *–ing place*, der Ausspann, die Einkehr; *take the –*, sich ködern lassen, (*fig.*) auf den Leim *or* in die Falle gehen. 2. *v.a.* ködern, (*fig.*) (an)locken, reizen; mit Hunden hetzen, (*fig.*) quälen; füttern und tränken (*horses*). 3. *v.n.* futtern, fressen (*of horses*); (*fig.*) Rast *or* Halt machen.

baize [beɪz], *s.* der Boi, Fries.

bak–e [beɪk], 1. *v.a.* backen (*Cul.*); brennen (*bricks*); *half-–ed*, (*fig.*) blöde, unreif. 2. *v.n.* backen, sich härten. **–e-house,** *s.* das Backhaus. **–er,** *s.* der Bäcker; *–er's dozen*, dreizehn; *–er's shop*, der Bäckerladen. **–ery,** *s.* die Bäckerei. **–ing,** 1. *s.* das Backen; Brennen; der Schub; *at one –ing*, auf einen Schub; *bread of the first –ing*, Brot vom ersten Schub. **–ing-plate,** *s.* das Backblech. **–ing-powder,** *s.* das Backpulver. **–ing-tin,** *s.* die Backform.

bakelite [ˈbeɪkəlaɪt], *s.* das Bakelit.

balanc–e [ˈbæləns], 1. *s.* die Waage (*also Astr.*); das Gleichgewicht; die Entscheidung, der Ausschlag; Ausgleich, die Ruhe, der Gleichmut; Rechnungsabschluß, Saldo, die Bilanz (*C.L.*); der Überschuß, Rest; die Unruhe (*Horol.*); (*a*) (*with nouns & adjectives*) *–e of accounts*, der Rechnungsabschluß; *assay-–e*, die Probierwaage; *–e at the bank*, das Bankguthaben; *–e carried forward*, der Saldovortrag; *–e due*, der Debitsaldo; *–e (in favour of a p.)*, das Guthaben (einer Person); *–e in hand*, der Kassenbestand; *hydrostatic –e*, die Senkwaage; *–e of mind*, seelisches Gleichgewicht, der Gleichmut; *–e of power*, politisches *or* internationales Gleichgewicht; *–e of trade*, die Handelsbilanz; (*b*) (*with verbs*) *adjust the –e*, das Gleichgewicht herstellen; *have a –e in one's favour*, eine Summe guthaben; *hold the –e*, das Gleichgewicht bewahren; *lose one's –e*, das Gleichgewicht verlieren; (*fig.*) die Fassung verlieren; *strike a –e*, die Bilanz ziehen; (*fig.*) das Ergebnis ziehen; *throw s.o. off his –e*, einen aus dem Gleichgewicht bringen; *tip* or *turn the –e*, den Ausschlag geben; (*c*) (*with prepositions*) (*fig.*) *in the –e*, in der Schwebe; *on –e*, nach gründlicher Überlegung. 2. *v.a.* wägen, abwägen, erwägen; im Gleichgewicht halten, ins Gleichgewicht bringen, aufwiegen, ausgleichen; begleichen, abschließen, saldieren (*accounts*) (*C.L.*); *–e an account*, eine Rechnung begleichen; *–e accounts with a p.*, mit einem abrechnen; *–e one th. against another*, eine S. gegen die andere abwägen; *–e the ledger*, das Hauptbuch saldieren; *more than –ed by*, überwogen durch; *the expenses –e the receipts*, die Ausgaben balancieren mit den Einnahmen *or* stehen mit den Einnahmen gleich. 3. *v.n.* im Gleichgewicht sein, sich das Gleichgewicht halten; sich ausgleichen, balancieren. **–ers,** *pl.* die Schwingkölbchen (*Ent.*). **–e-sheet,** *s.* der Rechnungsabschluß, Bilanzbogen, Kassenbericht. **–e-weight,** *s.* das Gegengewicht. **–e-wheel,** *s.* das Steigrad (*Horol.*). **–ing-pole,** *s.* die Balancierstange.

balcony ['bælkənɪ], *s.* der Balkon, Söller, Altan; die Achtergalerie (*Naut.*); zweiter Rang (*Theat.*).

bald [bɔ:ld], *adj.* kahl, unbehaart; (*fig.*) nackt, schmucklos, armselig, dürftig; nüchtern (*of style*); – *buzzard*, der Fischadler; – *eagle*, weißköpfiger Seeadler; – *translation*, dürftige *or* trockene Übersetzung; – *truth*, nackte Wahrheit. **–head,** *s.* der Kahlkopf, die Glatze. **– -headed,** *adj.* kahlköpfig; (*coll.*) *go – -headed for s.th.*, sich ohne Besinnen auf etwas stürzen. **–ly,** *adv.* (*fig.*) schmucklos, deutlich, ungeschminkt. **–ness,** *s.* die Kahlheit; (*fig.*) Dürftigkeit, Nüchternheit. Schmucklosigkeit. **–pate,** *s.* (*coll.*) *see* **–head.**

baldachin ['bældəkɪn], *s.* der Baldachin, Thronhimmel.

balderdash ['bɔ:ldədæʃ], *s.* (*coll.*) das Geschwätz.

baldric ['bɔ:ldrɪk], *s.* der Gürtel; das Wehrgehänge.

[1]**bale** [beɪl], 1. *s.* der Ballen; – *of cotton*, der Ballen Baumwolle; – *goods*, Güter in Ballen. 2. *v.a.* in Ballen verpacken; *see also* [3]**bail.** (*coll.*) – *out*, *v.n.* abspringen, aussteigen (*parachutes*).

[2]**bale,** *s.* (*archaic*) das Elend, die Qual, Not. **–ful,** *adj.* unheilvoll, verderblich.

balefire ['beɪlfɑɪə], *s.* das Signalfeuer, Freudenfeuer; der Scheiterhaufen.

balk [bɔ:k], 1. *s.* der Furchenrain (*Agr.*); der Balken, Tragbalken (*Arch.*); der Kessel, das Quartier (*Bill.*); (*fig.*) Hindernis; *miss-in- –*, absichtlicher Fehlstoß (*Bill.*). 2. *v.a.* aufhalten, hemmen, hindern, vereiteln, durchkreuzen, enttäuschen; ausweichen, umgehen, meiden. 3. *v.n.* anhalten, stocken, stutzen; scheuen (*at*, vor (*Dat.*)) (*of horses*). **– -line,** *s.* der Strich (*Bill.*). **–y,** *adj.* störrisch (*of horses*).

[1]**ball** [bɔ:l], *s.* der Ball; die Kugel (*Artil.*); der Ballen (*Typ.*, *etc.*); Knäuel (*of wool*, *etc.*); (*a*) (*with nouns*) – *of the eye*, der Augapfel; – *of the foot*, der Fußballen; – *of the thumb*, der Handballen; (*b*) (*with verbs*) *have the – at one's feet*, Herr der Situation sein, etwas in seiner Macht haben; *have a game at –*, Ball spielen; (*fig.*) *keep the – rolling*, das Gespräch im Gang halten; *load with –*, scharf laden; *miss the –*, einen Kicks machen (*Bill.*); *no –*, spielwidriger Wurf (*Cricket*); (*sl.*) *be on the –*, auf Draht sein; *pocket a –*, einen Ball machen, ins Loch spielen (*Bill.*); (*fig.*) *set the – rolling*, etwas in Gang bringen. **– and socket joint,** das Nußgelenk, Kugelgelenk. **– -bearings,** *s.* das Kugellager, Walzlager. **– -cartridge,** *s.* scharfe Patrone, die Kugelpatrone. **– -cock,** *s.* der Zulaß- und Absperrhahn. **– game,** *s.* das Ballspiel. **– -race,** die Laufrille (*Mech.*). **– -valve,** *s.* das Kugelventil.

[2]**ball,** *s.* der Ball, die Tanzgesellschaft; *fancy-dress –*, der Maskenball, das Kostümfest.

ballad ['bæləd], *s.* die Ballade. **– concert,** der Liederabend. **– -monger,** *s.* der Bänkelsänger.

ballast ['bæləst], 1. *s.* der Ballast, Schotter; die Bettung (*Railw.*); *in –*, nur mit Ballast beladen; *mental –*, innere Festigkeit, sittlicher Halt; – *tank*, die Tauchzelle (*submarine*). 2. *v.a.* ballasten, mit Ballast beladen; beschottern; (*fig.*) im Gleichgewicht halten.

ballet ['bæleɪ], *s.* das Ballett.

ballist-a [bə'lɪstə], *s.* die Wurfmaschine. **–ic,** *adj.* ballistisch. **–ics,** *pl. used as sing.* die Ballistik, Schießlehre.

balloon [bə'lu:n], 1. *s.* der Ballon, Luftballon; Rezipient (*Chem.*); die Kugel (*Arch.*). 2. *v.n.* aufschwellen, sich aufblähen; *barrage –*, der Sperrballon; *captive –*, der Fesselballon; *pilot –*, der Registrierballon; – *ascent*, der Ballonaufstieg; – *barrage*, die Ballonsperre; – *tyre*, der Ballonreifen.

ballot ['bælət], 1. *s.* die Wahlkugel, der Wahl- *or* Stimmzettel; geheime Abstimmung; *by –*, durch Abstimmung; *second* (or *final*) –, die Stichwahl. 2. *v.n.* abstimmen, wählen, ballotieren; – *for*, abstimmen über, losen um. **– -box,** *s.* die Wahlurne. **– -paper** der Stimmzettel.

bally ['bælɪ], *adj.* (*sl.*) verdammt, verflixt. **–hoo,** *s.* (*sl.*) das Getue, Reklamegeschrei.

balm [bɑ:m], *s.* der Balsam; die Melisse (*Bot.*); (*fig.*) der Trost, die Linderung. **–y,** *adj.* balsamisch, lindernd

balsam ['bɔ:lsəm], *s.* der Balsam; das Springkraut, die Balsamine (*Bot.*). **–ic** [–'sæmɪk], *adj.* lindernd, erquickend, balsamisch.

balust-er ['bæləstə], *s.* die Geländersäule. **–rade** [–'reɪd], *s.* die Brüstung, das Geländer.

bamboo [bæm'bu:], *s.* der Bambus, das Bambusrohr; – *cane*, der Bambusstock.

bamboozle [bæm'bu:zl], *v.a.* (*coll.*) betrügen, beschwindeln; verwirren, verblüffen.

ban [bæn], 1. *s.* die Bekanntmachung, Aufforderung; der Bann, die Acht, der Fluch; die Ächtung, das Verbot, die Verbannung; *the – of the church was pronounced against him*, der Kirchenbann wurde über ihn ausgesprochen; *he was laid* or *placed under the – of the empire*, er wurde in die Reichsacht erklärt *or* getan. 2. *v.a.* in den Bann tun; verfluchen, bannen, ächten; verbieten; – *a p. from a place*, einem den Ort verbieten. **–ned,** *adj.* verboten (*by the censor*).

banal ['beɪnəl], *adj.* abgedroschen, alltäglich, banal. **–ity** [bə'nælɪtɪ], *s.* die Alltäglichkeit, Banalität.

banana [bə'nɑ:nə], *s.* die Banane.

[1]**band** [bænd], 1. *s.* das Band, die Binde; Schnur; Heftschnur (*Bookb.*); Borte, Leiste, der Reifen, Streifen; Lauf- *or* Treibriemen (*Mech.*); *rubber –*, das Gummiband, der Gummistreifen. 2. *v.n.*; – *together*, sich vereinigen, sich zusammentun, sich verbinden. **–box,** die Hutschachtel; *look as if one had come out of a –box*, wie aus der Lade genommen aussehen. **– -pass filter,** der Bandfilter, die Siebkette (*Rad.*). **– -saw,** die Bandsäge. **–width,** die Bandbreite (*Rad.*).

[2]**band,** *s.* die Bande, Schar, Kompagnie, Truppe; (Musik)Kapelle, Regimentsmusik; *German –*, umherziehende Musikanten; *military –*, *regimental –*, die Militärkapelle, Regimentsmusik; – *of robbers*, die Räuberbande. **– instruments,** das Blech- und Schlagzeug. **– -leader, –master,** *s.* der Kapellmeister, Musikmeister (*Mil.*). **–sman** [–zmən], *s.* der (Militär)Musiker. **–stand,** *s.* der Musikpavillon. **– -wagon,** *s.* (*coll. Amer.*) die Woge der Volksgunst; *jump on the – -wagon*, sich dem Sieger anschließen, zum Sieger übergehen.

bandage ['bændɪdʒ], 1. *s.* die Binde, der Verband, die Bandage. 2. *v.a.* verbinden.

bandanna [bæn'dænə], *s.* buntes Kopftuch.

banderol(e) ['bændərəl, –roul], *s.* das (Lanzen)-Fähnchen; der Wimpel (*Her.*); das Inschriftband, Spruchband (*Arch.*).

bandit ['bændɪt], *s.* der Bandit, Räuber; (*sl.*) feindlicher Flieger (*Av.*). **–ti** [–'dɪtɪ], *pl.* die Räuberbande.

bandog ['bændɔg], *s.* der Kettenhund, Bullenbeißer.

bandol-eer, –ier [bændə'lɪ:ə], *s.* der Patronengurt; das Wehrgehenk, Bandelier.

bandy ['bændɪ], 1. *v.a.* wechseln, austauschen, sich

zuwerfen; – *words with s.o.*, Worte mit einem wechseln, hin und her streiten; *her name was freely bandied about*, ihr Name war in aller Leute Munde. 2. *adj.* (*coll.*) krumm(beinig), O-beinig. **--legged,** *see* –, 2.

bane [beɪn], *s.* das Gift (*only in comps. e.g.* rats–, Rattengift); (*fig.*) das Verderben; *he was the – of her existence*, er war der Fluch ihres Lebens. **–ful,** *adj.* verderblich, tödlich; giftig.

bang [bæŋ], 1. *s.* der Schlag, Schall, Knall; (*coll.*) die Ponyfrisur; – *on the head*, der Schlag auf dem Kopf; *it went off with a* –, es knallte los. 2. *int.* bums! paff! – *went the door*, bums flog die Tür zu. 3. *v.a.* schlagen; – *the table with one's fist*, – *one's fist on the table*, mit der Faust auf den Tisch schlagen; – *the door to*, die Tür zuschlagen; – *about*, unsanft behandeln; herumstoßen; – *the hair*, das Haar an der Stirn abschneiden. 4. *v.n.* schallen, knallen; zuschlagen; *the door -ed* (*to*), die Tür schlug zu.

bangle [ˈbæŋgl], *s.* der Arm– *or* Fußring, das Armband; die Spange.

banian [ˈbænjən], *s.* indischer Kaufmann, der Händler. **--days,** *pl.* fleischlose Tage, Fasttage (*Naut.*).

banish [ˈbænɪʃ], *v.a.* verbannen, ausweisen, vertreiben; – *sorrow*, die Sorgen bannen; – *the thought of s.th.*, sich (*Dat.*) etwas aus dem Sinne schlagen. **–ment,** *s.* die Verbannung, Vertreibung.

banister [ˈbænɪstə], *s.* der Geländerstab; (*pl.*) das Treppengeländer.

banjo [ˈbændʒoʊ], *s.* der Banjo, die Negerguitarre.

[1]**bank** [bæŋk], 1. *s.* der Damm, Deich, die Böschung, der Erdwall; das Ufer, Gestade; die Anhöhe, der Abhang; Kurvenflug; die Querlage, Schräglage (*Av.*); – *of sand*, die Sandbank; – *of clouds*, die Wolkenbank, Wolkenwand. 2. *v.a.* eindämmen, aufhäufen; in Schräglage legen (*Av.*). 3. *v.n.* in die Schräglage gehen (*Av.*). **– indicator,** *s.* der (Quer)Neigungsmesser (*Av.*).

[2]**bank,** 1. *s.* die Bank (*C.L., cards, etc.*); *branch* –, die Filialbank; *break the* –, die Bank sprengen (*cards, etc.*); – *of circulation*, die Girobank; – *of deposit*, die Depositenbank; *deposit money in the* –, Geld auf einer Bank deponieren; – *of England*, die Bank von England; *go* –, Bank setzen (*cards*); – *of issue*, die Notenbank; *joint-stock* –, die Aktienbank; *savings* –, die Sparkasse. 2. *v.a. & n.* deponieren, auf die Bank bringen; in der Bank hinterlegen; Bankgeschäfte machen; – *on*, (*coll.*) Hoffnung setzen auf, sich verlassen auf, bauen auf. **–able,** *adj.* diskontierbar, zahlbar. **--account,** *s.* das Bankkonto; *open a --account*, ein Konto aufmachen. **--bill,** *s.* der Bankwechsel; (*Amer.*) die Banknote. **--book,** *s.* das Bankbuch. **--clerk,** *s.* Bankbeamte(r), *m.* **–er,** *s.* der Bankier (*C.L.*); Bankhalter (*cards*); *–er's order*, der Zahlungsauftrag an die Bank. **– holiday,** *s.* der Bankfeiertag. **–ing,** *s.* das Bankwesen, Bankgeschäft, der Bankverkehr; *–ing-house*, *s.* die Bank; *–ing transaction*, das Wechselgeschäft. **--note,** *s.* die Banknote. **--paper,** *s.* das Bankpostpapier. **--rate,** *s.* der Bankdiskont, Diskontsatz, Zinsfuß. **--roll,** *s.* (*Amer.*) der Stoß Banknoten. **--share,** *s.* die Bankaktie. **--stock,** *s.* das Bankkapital, die Aktien der Staatsbank. **--transfer,** *s.* die Banküberweisung.

bankrupt [ˈbæŋkrʌpt], 1. *s.* der Bankrotteur, Zahlungsunfähige(r), *m.*; *declare o.s. a* –, sich als zahlungsunfähig angeben; *–'s estate*, die Konkursmasse. 2. *adj.* bankrott, zahlungsunfähig, (*coll.*) pleite; (*fig.*) arm (*in*, an); *go* –, Konkurs machen, (*coll.*) Pleite machen; – *in health*, am Ende mit seiner Gesundheit. 3. *v.a.* bankrott machen, zugrunde richten (*a p.*). **–cy** [–rəpsɪ], *s.* die Zahlungseinstellung, der Bankrott, Konkurs; (*fig.*) Schiffbruch; *fraudulent –cy*, betrügerischer Bankrott; *court of -cy*, das Konkursgericht; *file a petition in –cy*, den Konkurs anmelden.

banner [ˈbænə], 1. *s.* die Fahne; das Banner, Panier (*also fig.*); das Fähnchen (*Bot.*). 2. *attrib.* (*Amer.*) Haupt–, führend. **–et** [–rɛt], *s.* der Bannerherr. **--line,** (*Amer.*) die Schlagzeile. **- screen,** der Ofen– *or* Kaminschirm.

bannock [ˈbænək], *s.* (*Scots*) der Haferkuchen.

banns [bænz], *pl.* das Heiratsaufgebot; *their – have been published*, sie sind aufgeboten worden; *forbid the* –, gegen die Heirat Einspruch erheben.

banquet [ˈbæŋkwɪt], 1. *s.* das Gastmahl, Festessen, Bankett. 2. *v.n.* schmausen, bankettieren. **–er,** *s.* der Schmauser, Festteilnehmer. **–ing,** *s.* das Schmausen; *–ing-hall*, *–ing-room*, der Festsaal, Speisesaal.

banquette [bæŋˈkɛt], *s.* der Auftritt, die Grabenstufe, der Schützenstand; die Bahnböschung; (*Amer.*) der Bürgersteig.

banshee [ˈbænʃiː], *s.* (*Scots & Irish*) die Fee (die einen Todesfall vorhersagt).

bantam [ˈbæntəm], 1. *s.* das Bantamhuhn, Zwerghuhn; (*fig.*) der Zwerg, Knirps. 2. *adj.* winzig. **--weight,** *s.* das Bantamgewicht (*Sport*).

banter [ˈbæntə], 1. *s.* die Neckerei, der Scherz. 2. *v.a. & n.* necken, hänseln, aufziehen; (*Amer.*) auffordern, herausfordern. **–er** [–rə], *s.* der Necker; der Spaßvogel.

bantling [ˈbæntlɪŋ], *s.* kleines Kind, der Balg.

banyan [ˈbænjən], *s.*, **--tree,** *s.* indischer Feigenbaum.

bapti–sm [ˈbæptɪzm], *s.* die Taufe; *certificate of –sm*, der Taufschein; *–sm of fire*, die Feuertaufe; *private –sm*, die Haustaufe. **–smal** [–ˈtɪzməl], *adj.* Tauf–; *–smal font*, der Taufstein, das Taufbecken; *–smal service*, die Taufhandlung. **–st,** *s.* der Täufer; Baptist; *John the –st*, Johannes der Täufer. **–stery** [–tɪstrɪ], *s.* die Taufkapelle; der Taufstein. **–ze** [–ˈtaɪz], *v.a.* taufen.

bar [bɑː], 1. *s.* die Stange, Barre, der Stab; Riegel, Querbalken, die Barriere, Schranke; (*fig.*) das Hindernis, der Querstrich; Anwaltsstand, die Gerichtsschranke, das Gericht; die (Rechts)-Anwaltschaft, Advokatur; der Streifen, Strich; Takt, Taktstrich (*Mus.*); Querbalken *or* Querstreifen (*Her.*); die Ordensspange (*to a medal*); der Schenktisch, das Büfett, die Schenke, der Ausschank; *–s, pl.* das Gitter; (*a*) (*with nouns*) *the bench and the* –, Richter und Advokaten; – *of chocolate*, die Stange *or* der Riegel Schokolade; *colour* –, der Ausschluß von Farbigen; *the – of God*, Jüngstes Gericht; – *of gold*, die Goldbarre; – *of a grate*, der Roststab; *harbour* –, die Hafenbarre; – *of iron*, die Eisenstange; – *of rest*, die Pause (*Mus.*); *sand* –, die Barre, Sandbank; *torsion* –, der Drillstab (*Motor.*); – *of wood*, der Holzstab; (*b*) (*with verbs & prepositions*) *the prisoner at the* –, der Gefangene vor den Schranken; *he is at the* –, er ist Anwalt; *bring before the – of public opinion*, vor die Schranken der Öffentlichkeit bringen; *he was called to the* –, er wurde als Anwalt zugelassen; *cross the* –, an der Barre vorbeikommen (*Naut.*); *he was educated for the* –, er hat Jura studiert; (*c*) (*with adjectives*) *horizontal* --(*s*), das Reck (*Gymn.*); *parallel –s*, der Barren (*Gymn.*); – *sinister*, das Zeichen der Illegitimität (*Her.*); *window –s*, Fensterstäbe (*pl.*), das Fenstergitter. 2. *v.a.* verriegeln, verrammeln, vergittern; sperren, versperren, verhindern; (*fig.*) hemmen, hindern (*from*, an), aufhalten; verbieten, untersagen, ausschließen, ausnehmen, absehen von; (*coll.*) beanstanden. 3. *prep.*; – *one*, außer einem; – *none*, niemand ausgenommen. **--bell,** *s.* die Hantel (*Gymn.*). **--gold,** *s.* das Barrengold. **--iron,** *s.* das Stangeneisen, Stabeisen. **--keeper,** *s.* der Schenkwirt. **–maid,** *s.* die Kellnerin, Schenkmamsell. **–man,** *s.* der Kellner (in einer Schenke). **--parlour,** *s.* die Schenkstube. **–ring,** *prep.* abgesehen von, ausgenommen. **--shot,** *s.* die Stangenkugel (*Naut.*). **--silver,** *s.* das Barrensilber. **--stool,** *s.* der Barhocker. **–tender,** *s. see* **--keeper.**

[1]**barb** [bɑːb], 1. *s.* der Bart (*Bot.*); der Widerhaken (*of a hook, arrow, etc.*); die Fahne (*of a feather*). 2. *v.a.* mit Widerhaken versehen; *–ed wire*, der Stacheldraht; *–ed-wire entanglement*, der *or* das Drahtverhau.

[2]**barb,** *s.* (*poet.*) das Berberroß.

barbar–ian [bɑːˈbɛərɪən], 1. *adj.* barbarisch; roh, ungesittet. 2. *s.* der Barbar, roher Mensch, der Unmensch. **–ic** [bɑːˈbærɪk], *adj. see* **–ian;** ausländisch, fremd. **–ism** [ˈbɑːbərɪzm], *s.* die Roheit, Wildheit, Unkultur; Sprachwidrigkeit, der Barbarismus. **–ity** [bɑːˈbærɪtɪ], *s.* die Grausamkeit.

Unmenschlichkeit, Roheit. **–ous** [ˈbɑːbərəs], *adj.* barbarisch, unmenschlich, roh, grausam, unkultiviert, ungesittet, ungebildet.
barbate [ˈbɑːbeɪt], *adj.* bärtig.
barbecue [ˈbɑːbɪkjuː], 1. *s.* der Bratrost, gebratenes Tier; das Volksfest im Freien (*Amer.*); der Röstboden (*for coffee beans*) (*Amer.*). 2. *v.a.* unzerlegt braten (*animals*); (Kaffebohnen) rösten (*Amer.*).
barbel [ˈbɑːbəl], *s.* die Barbe (*Icht.*).
barber [ˈbɑːbə], 1. *s.* der Friseur, Frisör, Barbier; *surgeon* –, (*archaic*) der Bader. 2. *v.a.* (*Amer.*) barbieren.
barberry [ˈbɑːbərɪ], *s.* die Berberitze, Berbesbeere.
barbette [bɑːˈbɛt], *s.* die Geschützlafette, der Geschützstand, die Kasematte.
barbican [ˈbɑːbɪkən], *s.* das Außenwerk; der Wachtturm.
bard [bɑːd], *s.* der Barde, Sänger; (*poet.*) Dichter. **–ic,** *adj.* bardisch.
bare [bɛə], 1. *adj.* nackt, bloß, entblößt, blank, kahl, unbehaart, entlaubt; (*fig.*) bar, leer; arm; *the – facts,* die nackten Tatsachen; *the – idea,* die bloße Idee; *lay –,* offen darlegen, bloßlegen, aufdecken; *at the – mention of it,* bei der bloßen Erwähnung davon; *the – necessities of life,* das Nötigste zum Leben; *under – poles,* vor Topp und Takel (*Naut.*). 2. *v.a.* entblößen, bloßlegen, enthüllen, entkleiden; *he –d his breast,* er entblößte seine Brust; *– one's heart to a p.,* einem sein Herz erschließen. **–back(ed),** *adj.* ungesattelt (*of horses*); *ride –back,* ohne Sattel reiten. **–faced,** *adj.* frech, unverschämt, schamlos; *–faced lie,* schamlose Lüge. **–facedness,** *s.* die Schamlosigkeit, Frechheit. **–foot(ed),** *adj.* barfuß. **– -headed,** *adj.* barhäuptig, mit bloßem Kopfe, unbedeckt(en Hauptes). **– -legged,** *adj.* nacktbeinig. **–ly,** *adv.* nackt; offen; bloß, gerade, kaum; *–ly 3 feet,* knapp 3 Fuß, kaum 3 Fuß. **– -necked,** *adj.* mit bloßem Halse. **–ness,** *s.* die Nacktheit, Blöße; Armut, Dürftigkeit.
baresark [ˈbɛːəsɑːk], 1. *s.* der Berserker. 2. *adv.* unbewaffnet.
bargain [ˈbɑːgɪn], 1. *s.* der Handel, Kauf, das Geschäft; der Vertrag; billiger Einkauf, der Gelegenheitskauf; das Gekaufte; *a –'s a –,* Kauf ist Kauf! ein Mann ein Wort! *it's a (good) –,* es ist spottbillig; *it's a –!* abgemacht! *bad –,* böser (*or* unvorteilhafter) Handel; *make* or *strike a –,* einen Handel abschließen, handelseinig werden; *make the best of a bad –,* sich so gut wie möglich aus einem schlimmen Handel *or* aus einer bösen Angelegenheit herausziehen; *chance –,* der Gelegenheitskauf; *drive a hard –,* um den Pfennig feilschen; *into the –,* obendrein, noch dazu, in den Kauf, als Zugabe. 2. *v.n.* handeln; feilschen; *by –ing I got it cheaper,* ich habe vom Preise etwas abgehandelt; *– away,* im Handel verlieren; *– for,* (*usually neg.*) rechnen mit; *this was more than I –ed for,* dieses habe ich nicht erwartet; *I didn't – for that,* damit habe ich nicht gerechnet. **– -sale,** *s.* der (Ramsch)Ausverkauf.
barge [bɑːdʒ], 1. *s.* der Lastkahn, Schleppkahn, die Schute, Barke, der Leichter, Fahrprahm, die Zille; das Vergnügungsboot, Galaruderboot. 2. *v.n.* rennen, torkeln. **–e** [bɑːˈdʒiː], *s.* der Bootsmann. **– -pole,** *s.* die Bootstange; (*coll.*) *I wouldn't touch it with a – -pole,* ich möchte es nicht mit der Feuerzange berühren.
baritone [ˈbærɪtoun], *s.* der Bariton.
[1]**bark** [bɑːk], 1. *s.* die Rinde, Borke; *tanner's –,* die Lohe. 2. *v.a.* abrinden, entrinden (*trees, etc.*); *– one's shin,* sich (*Dat.*) das Schienbein abstoßen *or* abschürfen.
[2]**bark,** *s. see* **barque;** (*poet.*) das Schiff.
[3]**bark,** 1. *v.n.* bellen, kläffen; *– at,* anbellen; *– when one cannot bite,* den Mond anbellen. 2. *s.* das Bellen, Gebell; *his – is worse than his bite,* er kläfft nur (aber beißt nicht), bellende Hunde beißen nicht; *– up the wrong tree,* sich an die falsche Stelle *or* Adresse wenden. **–er,** *s.* der Kläffer; Ausrufer.
barley [ˈbɑːlɪ], *s.* die Gerste; *French* or *pot –,* Graupen (*pl.*); *pearl –,* Perlgraupen (*pl.*). **– -broth,** *s.* die Graupensuppe. **–corn,** *s.* das Gerstenkorn (*Bot.*); *John –corn,* der Gerstensaft, Whisky.
– -sugar, *s.* der Gerstenzucker. **– -water,** *s.* der Gerstenschleim.
barm [bɑːm], *s.* die Hefe, Bärme. **–y,** *adj.* hefig, schaumig; (*coll.*) verrückt, verdreht, blöd.
barn [bɑːn], *s.* die Scheune, Scheuer, (*Amer.*) der Stall. **– -door,** *s.* das Scheunentor; *– -door fowl,* gewöhnliches Huhn. **– floor,** die Tenne. **– -owl,** *s.* die Schleiereule. **– -stormer,** *s.* der Schmierenspieler. **–yard,** *s.* der Bauernhof, Scheunenhof.
[1]**barnacle** [ˈbɑːnəkl], *s.* die Bernikel– *or* Ringelgans; Entenmuschel; (*fig.*) Klette.
[2]**barnacle,** *s.* die Bremse, der Nasenknebel (*for unruly horses*); (*pl. coll.*) der Kneifer, Klemmer, Zwicker.
baromet–er [bəˈrɔmɪtə], *s.* das Barometer, Wetterglas. **–ric(al)** [–ˈmɛtrɪk(l)], *adj.* barometrisch; *–ric level,* der Barometerstand; *–ric pressure,* der Luftdruck.
baron [ˈbærən], *s.* der Baron, Freiherr; (*fig.*) Magnat; *– of beef,* das Lendenstück des Rinds. **–age** [–ɪdʒ], *s.* die Freiherrschaft; die Barone (*pl.*). **–ess,** *s.* die Baronin, Freifrau, Freiin. **–et** [–ɛt], *s.* der Baronet. **–etcy** [–ɛtsɪ], *s.* die Baronetswürde. **–ial** [bəˈrounɪəl], *adj.* freiherrlich, Barons–; (*fig.*) prunkvoll. **–y,** *s.* die Baronie, der Freiherrnstand.
baroque [bəˈrouk], *adj.* barock; wunderlich, verschroben; schiefrund (*of pearls*); *– style,* der Barockstil.
barouche [bəˈruːʃ], *s.* viersitziger Landauer.
barque [bɑːk], *s.* die Bark, das Barkschiff.
barrack [ˈbærək], 1. *s.* die Baracke, Hütte; (*pl. with sing. constr.*) Kaserne (*Mil.*); *confined to –s,* unter Kasernenarrest (*Mil.*); *– yard, – square,* der Kasernenhof. 2. *v.a. & n.* (*coll.*) verhöhnen, verspotten, Zwischenrufe machen (*Cricket*).
barrage [ˈbærɑːʒ], *s.* der Damm, die Sperre, das Wehr, Stauwerk; Sperrfeuer (*Mil.*); *– balloon,* der Sperrballon; *box –,* das Abriegelungsfeuer (*Artil.*); *creeping –,* die Feuerwalze (*Artil.*).
barrel [ˈbærəl], 1. *s.* das Faß, die Tonne; der Lauf, das Rohr, Geschützrohr, der Gewehrlauf (*Artil.*); das Federgehäuse (*Horol.*); die Walze, Trommel, der Zylinder (*Mech.*); Rumpf, Leib (*of cattle*); *by the –,* faßweise; *built-up –,* das Ringrohr; *one-piece –,* das Vollrohr; *smooth –,* der Schrotlauf, das Glattrohr; *sub-calibre –,* der Einstecklauf, das Einlegerohr. 2. *v.a.* (*– off, – up*) eintonnen, auf Fässer füllen. **–led,** *adj.* in ein Faß abgefüllt; *double- -led gun,* zweiläufiges Gewehr. **– -maker,** *s.* der Faßbinder. **– -organ,** *s.* die Drehorgel, der Leierkasten. **– -organ-grinder,** *s.* der Orgeldreher, Leier(Kasten)Mann. **– ring,** *s.* die Faßdaube; der Laufring (*Artil.*). **– roll,** *s.* der Überschlag über den Flügel (*Av.*). **– -vault,** *s.* das Tonnengewölbe (*Arch.*).
barren [ˈbærən], *adj.* unfruchtbar, steril, dürr; leer, arm (*of,* an (*Dat.*)); unproduktiv, wertlos; taub (*Min.*); tot (*capital*). **–ness,** *s.* die Unfruchtbarkeit, Dürre; Leere, Armut, der Mangel (*an einer S.*).
barretter [ˈbærətə], *s.* die Überlagerungsröhre (*Rad.*).
barricade [bærɪˈkeɪd], 1. *s.* die Barrikade, Verschanzung, Sperre, das Hindernis. 2. *v.a.* verrammeln, sperren, verschanzen.
barrier [ˈbærɪə], *s.* die Schranke, Sperre, das Schutzgatter, der Schlagbaum.
barring, *see* **bar.**
barrister [ˈbærɪstə], *s.,* **– -at-law,** *s.* der Rechtsanwalt, Advokat.
[1]**barrow** [ˈbærou], *s.* die Trage, Bahre; der Schubkarren. **–man,** *s.* der Karrenschieber, Höker.
[2]**barrow,** *s.* der Grabhügel, das Hünengrab.
barter [ˈbɑːtə], 1. *s.* der Tausch, Tauschhandel. 2. *v.a.* vertauschen, austauschen, eintauschen (*for,* gegen). 3. *v.n.* Tauschhandel treiben. **–er,** *s.* der Tauschhändler.
baryt–a [bəˈrɑɪtə], *s.* die Baryterde. **–es** [–ˈrɑɪtiːz], *pl.* der Schwerspat.
barytone [ˈbærɪtoun], *see* **baritone.**
bas–al [ˈbeɪsəl], *adj.* fundamental, Grund–. **–e** [beɪs], 1. *adj.* niedrigstehend, niedriggeboren; niederträchtig, gemein, verächtlich; unedel (*of metals*); falsch, unecht (*of coin*). 2. *s.* die Grund-

lage, Basis, der Grund; Fuß, das Fußgestell, der Sockel, das Postament, Fundament, der Träger, die Unterlage, Bettung; Grundfläche, Grundlinie, Ausgangslinie (*Geom. & Surv.*); Grundzahl (*Arith.*); der Stützpunkt, die Etappe, Operationsbasis (*Mil.*): der Einsatzhafen (*Naut.*); Horst (*Av.*); das Mal (*in games*); die Base, der Grundstoff (*Chem.*); *naval* –, der Flottenstützpunkt; *prisoner's* –*e*, das Barlaufspiel. 3. *v.a.* gründen, begründen; *be* –*ed on*, beruhen auf, basieren auf. **–eball,** *s.* der Baseball (amerikanisches Nationalspiel). **–e-born,** *adj.* von niedriger Geburt; unehelich. **–e-burner,** *s.* der Füllofen. **–e camp,** das Hauptlager, Ausgangslager. **–e-court,** *s.* äußerer Hof (*of a castle*). **–e-hearted,** *adj.* gemein, treulos, verräterisch. **–eless,** *adj.* grundlos. **–eline,** *s.* die Standlinie (*Surv.*); Grundlinie (*Tenn.*). **–ement,** *s.* das Erdgeschoß, Souterrain; der Sockel, das Fundament (*Arch.*). **–e-minded,** *adj.* von unedler Gesinnung. **–eness,** *s.* die Niedrigkeit, Gemeinheit, Niederträchtigkeit; Unechtheit. **–eplate,** *s.* die Bodenplatte, Lagerplatte, der Untersatz. (*sl.*) **–e-wallah** [–wɔlə], *s.* das Etappenschwein (*Mil.*). **–ic** [ˈbeɪsɪk], *adj.* grundlegend, fundamental, Grund–; basisch (*Chem.*); –*ic industry*, die Grundindustrie, Hauptindustrie; –*ic iron*, das Thomaseisen; –*ic material*, der Ausgangswerkstoff; –*ic pay*, der Wehrsold (*Mil.*); –*ic steel*, der Siemens-Martin-Stahl; –*ic wage*, der Grundlohn. **–ically,** *adv.* im Grunde. **–is,** *see* **basis.**

basalt [bəˈsɔːlt], *s.* der Basalt. **–ic,** *adj.* basaltisch, Basalt–.

basan [ˈbæzən], *s.* gegerbtes Schaffell.

bascule-bridge [ˈbæskjuːl ˈbrɪdʒ], *s.* die Fallbrücke, Zugbrücke.

bash [bæʃ], *v.a.* (*sl.*) heftig schlagen, schmeißen.

bashful [ˈbæʃful], *adj.* verschämt; schüchtern, blöde. **–ness,** *s.* die Schüchternheit, Blödigkeit.

basil [ˈbæzl], *s.* das Basilienkraut (*Bot.*).

basilica [bəˈsɪlɪkə], *s.* die Basilika.

basilisk [ˈbæzɪlɪsk], *s.* der Basilisk (*Myth.*); die Kroneidechse (*Zool.*).

basin [ˈbeɪsn], *s.* das Becken; die Schüssel, Schale; der Wasserbehälter, das Bassin; das Stromgebiet (*of a river*); die Mulde, das Talbecken (*Geol.*); das Hafenbecken, der Binnenhafen (*Naut.*); *wash* –, das Waschbecken. **– -shaped,** *adj.* beckenförmig.

basinet [ˈbæsɪnət], *s.* die Kesselhaube.

basis [ˈbeɪsɪs], *s.* die Grundlage, Basis.

bask [bɑːsk], *v.n.* sich sonnen, sich wärmen.

basket [ˈbɑːskɪt], *s.* der Korb; die Ballongondel (*Av.*); *the pick of the* –, das beste vom Ganzen; *put all one's eggs in one* –, alles auf eine Karte setzen. **– -ball,** *s.* das Korbballspiel. **– -carriage,** *s.* der Korbwagen. **–ful,** *s.* der Korbvoll; *by* –*fuls*, korbweise, in Körben. **– -handle,** *s.* der Korbhenkel. **– -hilt,** *s.* der Säbelkorb. **– -stitch,** der Korbstich (*Embroid.*). **–work,** *s.* das Flechtwerk; Korbwaren (*pl.*).

bas-relief [ˈbæsrɪlɪːf], *s.* das Basrelief, Flachbildwerk (*Sculp.*).

[1]**bass** [beɪs], 1. *s.* der Baß, die Baßstimme, der Bassist; Baßschlüssel, das Baßregister (*Mus.*). 2. *adj.*; – *clef*, der Baßschlüssel; – *singer*, der Bassist; – *string*, die Baßsaite; – *voice*, die Baßstimme. **– -bar,** *s.* der Balken (*of violin*). **– -viol,** *s.* die Baßgeige, das Cello.

[2]**bass** [bæs], *s.* der (Linden)Bast; die Bastmatte. **– -broom,** *s.* der Bastbesen. **– -mat,** *s.*, **– -matting,** *s.* die Bastmatte.

[3]**bass** [bæs], *s.* der Seebarsch (*Icht.*).

bassinet [bæsɪˈnɛt], *s.* der Kinderwagen; die Korbwiege.

bassoon [bəˈsuːn], *s.* das Fagott; *double* – das Kontrafagott. **–ist,** *s.* der Fagottist.

bast [bæst], *s.* der Bast; das Bastseil; *see* [2]**bass.**

bastard [ˈbæstəd], 1. *s.* der Bastard. 2. *adj.* unehelich; unecht, falsch; – *branch*, der Seitentrieb (*Bot.*); – *file*, die Bastardfeile; – *title*, der Schmutztitel (*Typ.*). **–ize,** *v.a.* als Bastard erklären. **–y,** *s.* uneheliche Geburt, die Bastardschaft.

[1]**bast-e** [beɪst], *v.a.* mit Fett begießen; (*coll.*) verprügeln. **–ing-ladle,** *s.* der Fettlöffel.

[2]**baste,** *v.a.* lose nähen, (an)heften.

bastinado [bæstɪˈneɪdoʊ], 1. *s.* die Bastonade, Prügelstrafe. 2. *v.a.* einem die Bastonade geben.

bastion [ˈbæstɪən], *s.* die Bastion, Bastei, das Bollwerk.

[1]**bat** [bæt], *s.* die Fledermaus (*Zool.*); *as blind as a* –, stockblind; (*coll.*) *he has* –*s in the belfry*, er hat Raupen im Kopf, er ist nicht recht gescheit.

[2]**bat,** 1. *s.* das Schlagholz (*Crick.*); der Schläger; (*sl.*) das Tempo; (*sl.*) *at a good* –, mit raschem Schritt; (*coll.*) *off one's own* –, auf eigne Faust. 2. *v.n.* schlagen; am Schlagen sein (*Crick.*); *without* –*ting an eyelid*, ohne mit der Wimper zu zucken. **–man,** *s.* der (Offiziers)Bursche (*Mil.*). **–sman,** (**–ter**), *s.* der Schläger (*Crick.*).

batch [bætʃ], *s.* der Schub (*Bak.*); Satz (*Pott.*); die Schicht, Partie (*of things*); der Stoß (*of books, letters*); die Menge, der Trupp (*of persons*).

bate [beɪt], *v.a. & n.* herabsetzen, vermindern; nachlassen; *with* –*d breath*, mit verhaltenem Atem.

bath [bɑːθ], 1. *s.* das Bad; die Badewanne; Waschung (*Chem.*); *take a* –, ein Bad nehmen. *pl. see* **–s;** *Order of the* –, der Bathorden; *Commander of the* –, der Komtur des Bathordens; *initial* –, das Ansatzbad (*Dyeing*); *standing* –, laufendes Bad (*Dyeing*); *charge* or *prepare a* –, ein Bad ansetzen (*Dyeing*); *reinforce the* –, die Flotte ergänzen (*Dyeing*). 2. *v.a. & n.* baden. **– -chair,** *s.* der Rollstuhl. **–e** [beɪð], 1. *v.n.* baden (im Freien); *be* –*ed in tears*, in Tränen schwimmen. 2. *s.* das Bad im Freien. **–er** [ˈbeɪðə], *s.* der & die Badende. **–ing** [ˈbeɪðɪŋ], 1. *adj.* badend, Bade–. 2. *s.* das Baden; *mixed* –*ing*, das Familienbad. **–ing-costume,** *s.*, der Badeanzug, das Badekostüm. **–ing-drawers,** *pl.* die Badehose. **–ing-machine,** *s.* der Badewagen. **–ing-place,** *s.* der Badeplatz; Badeort. **–ing-season,** *s.* die Badezeit, Badesaison. **–ing-wrap,** *s.* der Bademantel. **– -robe,** *s.* (*Amer.*) der Schlafrock. **–room,** *s.* das Badezimmer. **–s,** *pl.* die Badeanstalt, das Badehaus; –*s attendant*, der Badewärter. **– -sheet,** *s.* das Badelaken. **– -towel,** *s.* das Badetuch. **– -tub,** *s.* die Badewanne.

bathos [ˈbeɪθɔs], *s.* der Übergang vom Erhabenen zum Lächerlichen; die Trivialität, der Gemeinplatz.

bating [ˈbeɪtɪŋ], *pr.p.* (*rare*) ausgenommen, abgerechnet.

batiste [bəˈtɪːst], *s.* der Batist.

batman, *see* [2]**bat.**

baton [ˈbætən], *s.* der Stock, Stab; Taktstock; Querstab (*Her.*); *marshal's* –, der Feldherrnstab, Marschallstab.

batrachian [bəˈtreɪkɪən], 1. *adj.* Frosch–. 2. *s.* das Froschtier.

batsman, *see* [2]**bat.**

battalion [bəˈtæljən], *s.* das Bataillon, die Abteilung.

battels [ˈbætlz], *pl.* die Rechnung für Verpflegung (*in Oxford colleges*).

[1]**batten** [ˈbætn], 1. *s.* die Latte, Leiste; (Weber)-Lade (*of looms*). 2. *v.a.* mit Latten versehen, bekleiden, verschalen (*a wall*); – *down*, zunageln (*Naut.*); –*ed door*, die Leistentür.

[2]**batten,** 1. *v.n.* sich mästen, fett werden (*on*, an); (*fig.*) gedeihen; sich weiden (*on*, an), schwelgen (*on*, in). 2. *v.a.* mästen.

batter [ˈbætə], 1. *s.* geschlagener Teig, der Eierteig (*Cook.*); *see also* [2]**bat.** 2. *v.a.* schlagen; zerschlagen; beschießen (*Mil.*); abnutzen, beschädigen, entstellen, böse zurichten; – *down*, zusammenschießen; niederreißen; – *in*, einschlagen. **–ed,** *adj.* beschädigt, abgenutzt, mitgenommen. **–ing-ram,** *s.* der Sturmbock, Mauerbrecher. **–ing-train,** *s.* der Belagerungstrain. **–y** [ˈbætərɪ], *s.* tätliche Beleidigung, die Mißhandlung (*Law*); Batterie (*Mil., Phys.*), der Sammler, das Element (*Elec.*); das Linsen– *or* Prismensystem (*Opt.*); *action for assault and* –*y*, Klage wegen Tätlichkeiten; *dry* –*y*, das Trockenelement; –*y eliminator*, die Netzanode (*Rad.*); –*y of field-artillery*, fahrende Batterie; –*y of horse-artillery*, reitende Batterie; *floating* –*y*, schwimmende Batterie. **–y-charger,** *s.* die Lademaschine (*Elec.*). **–y-charging,** *adj.*; –*y-charging station*, die Ladestation (*Elec.*). **–y-operated,** *adj.* mit Batterieanschluß (*Rad.*).

battle [ˈbætl], 1. *s.* die Schlacht, der Kampf, das Gefecht, die Kampfhandlung; *drawn* –, unentschiedene Schlacht; *do – for*, kämpfen um; *a good start is half the –*, frisch gewagt ist halb gewonnen; *that is half the –*, das ist schon ein großer Vorteil; *fight one's own –*, sich ohne fremde Hilfe durchschlagen; *give* or *join –*, eine Schlacht liefern, sich zum Kampfe stellen; *pitched –*, regelrechte Schlacht; *– royal*, allgemeine Schlägerei; *the – is to the strong*, der Sieg liegt bei den Starken; *– of Waterloo*, die Schlacht bei Belle-Alliance; *– of words*, das Wortgefecht. 2. *v.n.*; *– against*, bekämpfen; *– for*, kämpfen, fechten *or* streiten um *or* für; (*coll.*) *– it out*, es auskämpfen. **--area,** *s.* der Kampfraum. **--array,** *s.* die Schlachtordnung. **--axe,** *s.* die Streitaxt. **--cruiser,** *s.* der Schlachtkreuzer. **--cry,** *s.* der Schlachtruf, das Kriegsgeschrei. **–field,** *s.* das Schlachtfeld. **--fleet,** *s.* die Hochseeflotte. **–formation,** *s.* die Gefechtsgliederung. **–ground,** *s.* das Schlachtfeld, der Kriegsschauplatz, (*fig.*) die Streitursache. **--maiden,** *s.* die Schlachtjungfrau, Walküre. **–ment,** *s.* (*usually pl.*) die Brustwehr, Zinnen (*pl.*). **--piece,** *s.* das Schlachtgemälde. **–ship,** *s.* das Schlachtschiff, Kriegsschiff, Linienschiff. **--stations,** *pl.* die Gefechtsstation (*Naut.*).

battledore ['bætldɔ:], *s.* das Rakett, der Federballschläger; *– and shuttlecock*, das Federballspiel.

battue [bæ'tu:], *s.* die Treibjagd, (*fig.*) das Gemetzel.

batty ['bætɪ], *adj.* (*sl.*) verrückt, toll.

bauble, bawble ['bɔ:bl], *s.* das Spielzeug; der Tand; (*fig.*) die Kleinigkeit; (*archaic*) der Narrenstab.

baulk [bɔ:k], *see* **balk.**

bauxite ['bɔ:ksaɪt], *s.* das Bauxit.

bawd [bɔ:d], *s.* die Kupplerin. **–ry,** *s.* die Unflätigkeit, Zoten (*pl.*); die Unzucht. **–y,** *adj.* unzüchtig, unflätig; *talk –y*, Zoten reißen. **–y-house,** *s.* (*coll.*) das Bordell.

bawl ['bɔ:l], *v.a.* & *n.* schreien; brüllen; plärren (*as children*); *– at*, anbrüllen; *– out*, ausrufen; *– a p. out*, (*Amer. sl.*) einen schelten *or* anschnauzen.

[1]**bay** [beɪ], 1. *adj.* rötlichbraun, kastanienbraun. 2. *s.* der Braune, Fuchs (*horse*).

[2]**bay,** *s.* (**–tree**) der Lorbeer(baum) (*Bot.*). **--leaf,** *s.* das Lorbeerblatt. **–rum,** *s.* der Bayrum.

[3]**bay,** *s.* die Bai, Bucht; der Meerbusen; das Fach, die Abteilung (*Build.*); die Banse (*of a barn*); der Zwischenraum, die Lücke, Nische, der Erker. **–roof,** *s.* das Sägedach, Scheddach. **--salt,** *s.* das Seesalz. **–window,** *s.* das Erkerfenster.

[4]**bay,** *s.* die Bedrängnis, Not, Notwehr; das Stellen (*of game*); *at –*, gestellt, (*fig.*) sich zur Wehr setzend, in Bedrängnis; *keep at –*, hinhalten, in Schach halten; *stand at –*, sich zur Wehr setzen.

[5]**bay,** *v.n.* bellen; anschlagen. **–ing,** *s.* das Gebell.

bayonet ['beɪənɪt], 1. *s.* das Seitengewehr, Bajonett; *at the point of the –*, mit dem Bajonett; *with fixed –s*, mit aufgepflanztem Seitengewehr. 2. *v.a.* mit dem Bajonett erstechen.

bayou ['baɪju:], *s.* (*Amer.*) die Sumpfstelle an See *or* Fluß.

bazaar [bə'zɑ:], *s.* (orientalischer) Basar; der Wohltätigkeitsbasar; billiges Warenhaus.

bazooka [bə'zu:kə], *s.* das Panzergeschütz, der Panzerbrecher, die Panzerfaust.

be [bi:, bɪ], **1.** *ir.v.n.* sein, existieren, bleiben; sich befinden, vorhanden sein; **(a)** *there is, there are*, es gibt (*Acc.*); es ist, es sind (*Nom.*); *there is plenty to eat*, es gibt eine Menge zu essen; *there is no bread on our table*, es ist kein Brot auf dem Tisch; *as it is*, so wie die Dinge liegen; *as you were!* in die Stellung zurück! herstellt euch! (*Mil. & Gymn.*); *let it –!* laß es bleiben! *how is it that . . .?* wie kommt es daß . . .? *what is it now?* was willst du nun? *how are you?* wie geht es dir?; *how have you been?* wie ist es dir ergangen? *– that as it may*, das mag sein wie es will; *twice two is four*, zweimal zwei macht vier; *are you coming? of course I am*, kommst du? Jawohl, natürlich; *are you coming? I am not*, kommst du? Keineswegs; *he lived to be 70*, er wurde 70 Jahre alt; **(b)** (*with adjectives & adverbs*) *– about to do*, im Begriffe sein zu tun; *I will – along soon*, ich komme bald; *there you are!* da hast du es! (*coll.*) *how much is it?* wieviel kostet das? wieviel macht das? *to – ill* or *well*, sich übel *or* wohl befinden; *do not – long!* bleiben Sei nicht lange; *– a long time doing*, lange gebrauchen um zu tun; *– off!* fort mit dir! packe dich!; *I must – off*, ich muß fort; **(c)** (*with prepositions*) *– about*, handeln von; *I will – after you*, ich will hinter dir her sein; *– at*, zugegen sein bei; *what is she at?* was hat sie vor? (*coll.*) *they are at it again*, sie sind wieder dabei; *I am for the former suggestion*, ich erkläre mich für den ersten Vorschlag; *is this the train for London?* fährt dieser Zug nach London? *it is for him to apologize*, es kommt ihm zu sich zu entschuldigen; *she was not of the party*, sie gehörte nicht zur Gesellschaft; *what is that to you?* was macht das Ihnen aus? was bedeutet das für Sie? was gilt es Ihnen? *it is just the same with me*, es geht mir genau so; **(d)** (*in questions*) *he is not dead, is he?* er lebt doch noch, nicht wahr? *the weather is fine today, is it not?* nicht wahr, das Wetter ist heute schön? **2.** *ir.v.aux.* **(a)** (*with present participle expressing continuous action*) *I am reading*, ich bin am *or* beim Lesen, ich lese gerade; *the house is being built*, das Haus ist im Bau; *I have just been drinking tea*, ich habe eben Tee getrunken; *I shall – writing soon*, ich werde bald schreiben; **(b)** (*with infinitive expressing necessity or obligation*) *he is to come today*, er soll heute kommen; *he is to die*, er muß sterben; *if I were to die*, wenn ich sterben sollte; *his wife that is to –*, seine zukünftige Frau; *it was not to –*, es sollte nicht sein; *what am I to do?* was soll ich tun?; *it is to – hoped*, es ist zu hoffen; *the house is to – sold*, das Haus ist zu verkaufen; *that is to say*, das heißt; **(c)** (*aux. of the passive*) werden; *I am told*, mir wurde gesagt; *I shall – loved*, ich werde geliebt werden. **3.** (*in compounds*) **--all,** *s.* das Ganze; *the --all and end-all*, das Ein und Alles; *he is a has-been*, er hat seine Glanzzeit hinter sich; *the might-have-beens*, die verpaßten Gelegenheiten; *the to-be*, die Zukunft; *a would-be poet*, ein Dichterling.

beach [bi:tʃ], 1. *s.* der Strand, das Gestade, flaches Ufer. 2. *v.a.* auf den Strand setzen *or* ziehen, stranden lassen. **–comber,** *s.* die Strandwelle; der Strandguträuber. **--head,** *s.* der Brückenkopf, Landekopf. **--wear,** *s.* die Strandkleidung.

beacon ['bɪ:kən], *s.* die Bake; der Leuchtturm, das Leuchtfeuer, Signalfeuer; (*fig.*) der Leitstern, die Leuchte; *mark by –s*, abbaken; *landing –*, das Ansteuerungsfeuer (*Av.*); *radio –*, der Funkmeßturm; *traffic –*, das Verkehrs(warn)zeichen. **–age,** *s.* das Bakengeld. **--buoy,** *s.* die Bakenboje.

bead [bɪ:d], *s.* die Perle (*of glass, etc.*), das Kügelchen, Knöpfchen; (*fig.*) der Tropfen (*of liquid*); das Korn (*of a gun*); (*pl.*) die Perlschnur, das Halsband, der Rosenkranz; (*sl.*) *draw a – on*, zielen auf; *string –s*, Perlen (auf eine Schnur) aufreihen; *tell one's –s*, den Rosenkranz beten. **–ing,** *s.* die Perlstickerei; Perlstabverzierung (*Arch.*). **–work,** *s.* die Perlarbeit. **–y,** *adj.* perlartig. **–y-eyed,** kleinäugig.

beadle ['bɪ:dl], *s.* der Kirchendiener, Gerichtsdiener, Büttel (*Law*), Pedell (*Univ.*).

beagle ['bɪ:gl], *s.* der Spürhund.

beak [bɪ:k], *s* der Schnabel (*of birds*); die Schnauze, der Ausguß, die Schneppe, Tülle (*of vessels, etc.*); (*sl.*) der Polizeirichter; Lehrer. **–ed,** *adj.* mit einem Schnabel; schnabelförmig, spitz.

beaker ['bɪ:kə], *s.* der Becher, Humpen; das Becherglas (*Chem.*).

beam [bɪ:m], 1 *s.* der Balken, Träger, Holm, die Schwelle, der Tragbaum (*Build.*); Ketten- *or* Weberbaum (*of a loom*); Pflugbaum (*of a plough*); Arm, Waagebalken (*of a balance*); Balancier, Ausgleichshebel (*of steam-engines*); die Breite (*of a ship*); der Strahl, Lichtstrahl, Lichtkegel (*of light, etc.*); Glanz (*of the eye*); *cantilever –*, der Kraftträger; *cross –*, der Querbalken, die Ducht; *header –*, der Unterzug (*Bridgeb.*); *kick the –*, zu leicht sein; *main –*, der Hauptträger, Hängebalken, Spannbalken; *–s of the moon*, die Mondstrahlen; *– of the roof*, der Dachbalken; *radio –*, die Funkbake, der Peilstrahl; *rectangular –*, das Kantholz; *searchlight –*, der Lichtkegel; *supporting –*, der Tragbalken; *– of a windlass*, der Haspelbaum; *wing –*, der Flügelholm (*Av.*); *off the –*, dwars, querab (*Naut.*); *right on the –*, dwars ein (*Naut.*); *– wind*, der Dwarswind, Seitenwind, halber Wind; *wind on the starboard –*, der Steuerbordwind. 2. *v.n.* strahlen, Strahlen werfen, anstrahlen; *–ing countenance*, strahlendes Gesicht. **– -compasses,** *pl.* der Stangenzirkel. **– -ends,** *pl.* die Querbalkenköpfe, *the ship is on her – -ends*, das Schiff liegt auf der Seite; (*sl.*) *he is on his – -ends*, er ist in einer schlimmen Lage, er ist in Verlegenheit, er pfeift auf dem letzten Loch, er sitzt in der Klemme, er ist pleite. **– -engine,** *s.* die Balanciermaschine. **– sea,** die Dwarssee. **– -station,** *s.*, **– -transmitter,** *s.* der Richtstrahler (*Rad.*).

bean [bɪ:n], *s.* die Bohne; (*sl.*) der Kopf, *broad –*, die Saubohne, Puffbohne; *French dwarf-–*, die Zwerg–, Busch–, *or* Zuckerbohne; *kidney –*, *haricot –*, die Schmink–, Veits– *or* Steigbohne; *scarlet runner* (–), die Stangen– *or* Feuerbohne; (*coll.*) *old –*, alter Junge, mein Lieber. (*coll.*) *be full of –s*, springlebendig *or* lebensprudelnd sein; (*coll.*) *give s.o. –s*, einen tüchtig prügeln; einen gehörig schlagen; (*coll.*) *spill the –s*, ein Geheimnis verraten. **– -feast,** *s.*, **–o,** *s.* das Fest, die Lustbarkeit, die Zecherei. **–stalk,** *s.* die Bohnenranke.

[1]**bear** [bɛə], 1. *s.* der Bär; ungeschliffener Mensch; der Baissier, Baissespekulant (*C.L.*). 2. *v.n.* auf Baisse spekulieren (*C.L.*). 3. *v.a.* drücken (*the market*) (*C.L.*); *she-–*, die Bärin; *the Great and Little –*, der große und der kleine Bär (*Astr.*). **– -baiting,** *s.* die Bärenhetze. **– -garden,** *s.* (*fig.*) lärmende Versammlung. **–ish,** *adj.* bärenhaft; plump, täppisch; flau, Baisse– (*C.L.*). **–'s-ear,** *s.* die Aurikel (*Bot.*). **–'s-foot,** stinkende Nieswurz (*Bot.*). **–skin,** *s.* die Bärenmütze (*of a grenadier*).

[2]**bear, 1.** *ir.v.a.* (*p.p.* borne) tragen, bringen, überbringen; hegen (*ill will, etc.*); führen (*a name, etc.*); vertragen, ertragen, aushalten (*a p., etc.*); dulden, leiden (*pain, etc.*); (*p.p.* born) zur Welt bringen, gebären (*children*); *– o.s. well*, sich gut betragen *or* halten; *born and bred*, von Geburt und Erziehung; **(a)** (*with nouns*) *– the blame*, es auf sich nehmen, die Schuld tragen; *– the brunt*, der Wucht ausgesetzt sein; *– s.o. company*, einem Gesellschaft leisten; *– comparison with*, Vergleich aushalten mit; *– a date*, datiert sein; *– false witness*, falsches Zeugnis ablegen; *– fruit*, Frucht tragen (*also fig.*); *– a p. good will*, einem gewogen sein; *– s.o. a grudge*, *– a grudge against s.o.*, Groll gegen einen hegen; *the text will not – such an interpretation*, die Stelle kann nicht so ausgelegt werden; *– a loss*, einen Verlust tragen *or* leiden; *not – repeating*, sich nicht wiederholen lassen; *– no relation to*, in keinem Verhältnis stehen zu; *– a resemblance to*, Ähnlichkeit haben mit; **(b)** *bring to –*, geltend machen; ausüben (*pressure*); **(c)** (*with prepositions or adv.*) *– away*, fort– *or* davontragen; hingerissen werden; *– down*, niederdrücken; niederschlagen, niederwerfen, überwinden; *it was borne in upon me that . . .*, es drängte sich mir auf, es wurde mir klar, daß . . .; *– s.th. in mind*, sich etwas merken, einer S. gedenken; (*coll.*) sich (*Dat.*) eine Sache hinters Ohr schreiben; *–ing in mind the conditions*, wenn man die Bedingungen bedenkt; *– off*, wegtragen, entführen; *– out*, hinaustragen; (*fig.*) unterstützen, verteidigen; bestätigen, bekräftigen, erhärten; *she bore him out*, sie gab ihm recht; *– up*, stützen, unterstützen, aufrechterhalten. **2.** *ir.v.n.* (*p.p.* borne) tragen; fruchtbar werden, tragfähig sein (*as ice, etc.*); sich halten (*direction*); leiden, dulden; *this tree will – next year*, dieser Baum wird nächstes Jahr tragen; *– and forbear*, leide und meide; (*with prepositions or advs.*) *– against*, angreifen, losgehen auf (*with Acc.*); *– against the wind*, kreuzen, lavieren (*Naut.*); *– away*, abfahren, davonsegeln (*Naut.*); *– down upon*, losgehen *or* zusteuern auf (*with Acc.*); zuhalten auf (*Acc.*); *– on*, Bezug haben *or* sich beziehen auf; *bring to – on*, zur Geltung bringen, einwirken lassen, anwenden auf; *– to the right* (*left*), sich rechts (links) halten; *– up*, standhaft sein, festbleiben, nicht verzagen; *– up against*, widerstehen (*Dat.*); standhalten *or* sich behaupten gegen; *– up towards*, zusegeln auf (*Acc.*); *– upon*, lasten, ruhen auf (*Dat.*); *– with*, geduldig ertragen, auskommen mit, Nachsicht haben mit. **–able** [–rəbl], *adj.* erträglich, zu ertragen(d). **–er** [ˈbɛərə], *s.* der Träger, Überbringer (*of a letter*); Inhaber (*of a bill or title*); Sargträger (*at a funeral*); Schildhalter (*Her.*). **–ing** [–rɪŋ], *s.* das Tragen; Betragen, die Haltung; das Ertragen, Erdulden; die Beziehung, der Bezug, das Verhältnis; die Richtung, Lage, der Anschnitt (*Surv., etc.*); die Peilung; Tragweite, Spannweite (*Arch.*); das Lager, die Unterlage (*Mach.*); das Wappenbild; *armorial –ings*, das Wappen; *ball –ings*, das Kugellager; *friction –ing* das Gleitlager; *journal –ing*, das Zapfenlager, Radlager; *lose one's –ings*, sich verlaufen, sich verirren; *it has no –ing on this matter*, es steht in keinem Zusammenhang mit der Sache; *obtain a –ing on*, peilen, orten anschneiden (an); *radio –ing*, die Funkpeilung, Funkortung; *reciprocal –ings*, die Gegenpeilung; *roller –ing*, das Rollenlager; *his arrogance is past –ing*, sein Hochmut ist unerträglich *or* unausstehlich; *take –ings*, sich orientieren, (an)peilen; *trunnion –ing*, das Zapfenlager, Schildlager. **–ing-rein,** *s.* der Aufsatzzügel. **–ing-seat,** *s.* die Lagerschale. **–ing spring,** *s.* die Tragfeder. **–ing surface,** *s.* die Arbeitsfläche. **–ing wall,** *s.* die Mittelwand, Scheidemauer.

beard [bɪ:əd], 1. *s.* der Bart, Vollbart; die Granne (*Bot.*). 2. *v.a.* trotzen (*Dat.*), kühn entgegentreten. **–ed,** *adj.* bärtig; mit Grannen. **–less,** *adj.* bartlos.

beast [bɪ:st], *s.* das Tier, Vieh; (*coll.*) die Bestie, das Biest; der Antichrist; roher Mensch; *– of burden*, das Lasttier; *– of prey*, das Raubtier; *– epic*, das Tierepos. **–liness,** *s.* die Bestialität, Gemeinheit, Roheit, das Gemeine, die Schweinerei. **–ly,** *adj.* tierisch; viehisch, bestialisch, gemein, brutal; (*coll.*) ekelhaft, garstig, scheußlich; (*sl.*) *–ly shame*, die Affenschande, Gemeinheit; (*sl.*) *–ly weather*, das Sauwetter.

beat [bɪ:t], **1.** *ir.v.a.* schlagen, prügeln, klopfen; stoßen, zerstoßen; mahlen, stampfen (*Paperm.*); schmieden (*metal*); schwingen (*flax*); (aus)klopfen (*clothes, etc.*); schlagen, rühren (*the drum*); abpelzen (*skins*); bahnen, betreten (*a path*); aufjagen (*game*); schlagen, besiegen (*an enemy*); übertreffen (*a rival*); **(a)** (*with nouns*) *– the air*, umsonst reden; (*sl.*) *– the band*, alles übertreffen; *– the bounds*, die (Kreis)Grenzen bezeichnen; *– one's breast*, sich an die Brust schlagen; *– eggs*, Eier schlagen *or* rühren; *– a retreat*, zum Rückzuge trommeln (*also fig.*); (*fig.*) sich zurückziehen, klein beigeben; *– a tattoo*, (den) Zapfenstreich schlagen; *– time*, den Takt schlagen; *– a wood*, einen Wald durchstöbern; *– the wings*, mit den Flügeln schlagen; **(b)** (*with pronouns*) *that –s everything!* da hört alles auf! (*sl.*) *– it*, ausreißen, abhauen, verduften; (*coll.*) *can you – it!* so eine Unverschämtheit! *there is nothing to – it*, darüber geht nichts; *that –s me*, ich kann nicht mehr mit; **(c)** (*with adv. or prep.*) *– back*, zurückschlagen, abschlagen, zurücktreiben; *– down*, niederschlagen; (*fig.*) überwinden; herabsetzen, drücken (*prices*); *– into*, hineintreiben; *– a th. into s.o.'s head*, einem etwas einhämmern *or* einbleuen; (*coll.*) *– into a cocked hat*, vernichtend schlagen; *– off*, abschlagen, zurückschlagen; *– out*, aushämmern, aushauen; (*fig.*) herausarbeiten; *– up*, zusammentrommeln, auftreiben; *– up recruits*, Rekruten werben; (*sl.*) durchprügeln; rühren (*eggs, dough, etc.*); **(d)** (*with adverbs*) *– hollow*, bei weitem übertreffen, vollständig schlagen. **2.** *ir.v.n.* schlagen, klopfen, pochen; lavieren, kreuzen (*Naut.*); *the drum –s*, es wird getrommelt; *my heart –s*, mein Herz schlägt, klopft *or* pocht; *– about the bush*, wie die Katze um den heißen Brei herumgehen; *– about for a th.*, (eine Lösung *or* einen Ausweg) suchen; *– to quarters*, Klarschiff zum Gefecht blasen; *– up against the wind*, gegen den Wind segeln. **3.** *s.* das Schlagen, Pochen, Klopfen, der Schlag, Pulsschlag; Taktschlag (*Mus.*); die Schwebung (*between two notes*); das Revier, die Runde (*of a policeman, etc.*); der Nichtsnutz, Schmarotzer (*Amer.*); *– of the drum*, der Trommelschlag. **–en,** *adj.* geschlagen; gehämmert; (*fig.*) abgedroschen, breitgetreten; *–en gold*, das Blattgold; *–en path*, gebahnter *or* vielbegangener Weg; *–en track*, herkömmliche Art und Weise; *weather-–en face*, wettergebräuntes Gesicht. **–er,** *s.* der Schläger (*a p.*); Treiber (*Sport*); Schlegel, Klöpfel, die Ramme, das Schlageisen, die Stoffmühle (*Paperm.*). **–ing,** *s.* das Schlagen, Klopfen, Pochen,

Hämmern; die Schläge (*pl.*), die Züchtigung, Besiegung; das Treiben (*Sport*); *get a sound –ing*, eine Tracht Prügel bekommen.

beati–fic [bɪːəˈtɪfɪk], *adj.* selig, beseligend, glückstrahlend. **–fication** [bɪːætɪfɪˈkeɪʃən], *s.* die Seligsprechung. **–fy** [bɪːˈætɪfaɪ], *v.a.* seligmachen, seligsprechen (*R.C.*). **–tude** [bɪːˈætɪtjuːd], *s.* die Seligkeit, Glückseligkeit; (*pl.*) die Seligpreisungen (*pl.*) (*B.*).

beau [bou], *s.* (*pl.* –x) der Stutzer, Geck; Verehrer, Courmacher. **– -ideal,** *s.* das Ideal, Vorbild, Muster.

beaut–eous [ˈbjuːtjəs], *adj.* sehr schön. **–eousness,** *s.* die Schönheit. **–ician,** *s.* (*Amer.*) der Schönheitsspezialist. **–ification** [bjuːtɪfɪˈkeɪʃən], *s.* die Verschönerung. **–iful** [ˈbjuːtɪful], *adj.* schön; (*coll.*) eindrucksvoll. **–ify** [ˈbjuːtɪfaɪ], *v.a.* verschönern, schön machen, ausschmücken. **–y** [ˈbjuːtɪ], *s.* die Schönheit, das Schöne; die Schöne, Schönheit (*a p.*); der Reiz; *the –y of it*, das Schönste daran; (*coll.*) *it is really a –y*, es ist eine wahre Pracht; *–y and the Beast*, die Schöne und das Tier; *–y is but skin-deep*, man kann nach dem Äußeren nicht urteilen; *Sleeping –y*, Dornröschen; *Camberwell –y*, der Trauermantel (*Ent.*). **–y contest,** der Schönheitswettbewerb. **–y-culture,** *s.* die Schönheitspflege. **–y parlour,** der Schönheitssalon. **–y-sleep,** *s.* der Schlaf vor Mitternacht. **–y-spot,** *s.* das Schönheitspflästerchen; schöne Gegend.

beaver [ˈbɪːvə], *s.* der Biber (*Zool.*); das Visier (*of a helmet*); der Biberpelz; (*sl.*) der Bart; *– hat*, der Kastorhut. **– -dam,** *s.*, **– -lodge,** *s.* der Biberbau.

becalm [bɪˈkɑːm], *v.a.* beruhigen, besänftigen, stillen; bekalmen (*Naut.*); *be –ed*, von einer Windstille überfallen werden, eine Flaute haben.

became [bɪˈkeɪm], *see* **become.**

because [bɪˈkɔz], *conj.* weil; *– of*, wegen; *– of you*, Ihretwegen; um Ihretwillen.

bechamel [ˈbɛʃæməl], *s.* weiße Rahmsoße.

[1]**beck** [bɛk], *s.* (*dial., poet.*) das Bächlein.

[2]**beck,** *s.* der Wink, das Kopfnicken; *be at his – and call*, auf seinen Wink und Ruf bereit sein. **–on,** 1. *v.a. & n.* (heran)winken, nicken; *–on to s.o.*, einem zuwinken.

becloud [bɪˈklaud], *v.a.* umwölken (*also fig.*).

becom–e [bɪˈkʌm], 1. *ir.v.n.* werden; *they became acquainted*, sie wurden miteinander bekannt; *he became a doctor*, er wurde Arzt; *it became a fashion*, es wurde zur Mode; *they became friends*, sie wurden Freunde; *what is to –e of her?* was soll aus ihr werden? 2. *ir.v.a.* geziemen; sich ziemen or schicken für; anstehen (*Dat.*); stehen, kleiden (*of clothes*) (*Dat.*); *it ill –es you*, es steht Ihnen übel an, es paßt sich schlecht für Sie; *the hat –es you*, der Hut steht Ihnen *or* kleidet Sie. **–ing,** 1. *s.* das Werden. 2. *adj.* geziemend, passend, schicklich; kleidsam; *he was treated with –ing respect*, man behandelte ihn mit gehöriger Ehrerbietung; *such conduct is not –ing*, solches Benehmen ist unschicklich; *it is –ing to his station*, es geziemt seinem Stande.

bed [bɛd], 1. *s.* das Bett (*also of a river*); Lager (*of animals*); die Unterlage, Bettung (*Mach., Arch.*); Lage, Schicht (*of a wall*); das Lager, die Schicht, das Flöz (*Geol.*); Beet (*of flowers*); der Unterbau (*Railw.*); (*a*) (*with nouns*) *– of clay*, die Tonschicht; *– of ease*, das Faulbett; *– of a mountain torrent*, der Graben; *– of the ocean*, der Meeresgrund; *– of a river*, das Flußbett; *– of roses*, rosige Lage; *– of sickness*, das Krankenlager; *– of state*, das Paradebett; *– of straw*, das Strohlager; (*b*) (*combinations*) *double –*, das Doppelbett, Ehebett, zweischläfriges Bett; *flower-–*, das Blumenbeet; *sick-–*, das Krankenlager; *– and board*, Tisch und Bett; (*c*) (*with verbs*) *be brought to –*, niederkommen, entbunden werden; *be confined to one's –*, bettlägerig sein; *get into –*, ins Bett gehen, sich zu Bett legen; *get out of –*, aufstehen; (*coll.*) *get out of – on the wrong side*, mit dem linken *or* verkehrten Fuß aus dem Bett steigen; *go to –*, schlafen *or* zu Bett gehen; (*prov.*) *early to – and early to rise, makes a man healthy, wealthy and wise*, Morgenstunde hat Gold im Munde; *keep one's –*, darniederliegen, das Bett hüten; (*prov.*) *as one makes one's –, so one must lie*, wie man sich bettet so liegt man; *put to –*, schlafen legen, zu Bett bringen; *take to one's –*, sich legen, bettlägerig werden; *turn down a –*, die Bettdecke zurückschlagen. 2. *v.a.* betten (*beasts*); pflanzen, einbetten (*plants, etc.*); *– down*, 1. *v.a.* mit Streu versorgen (*cattle, etc.*). 2. *v.n.* (*coll.*) sich schlafen legen, zu Bett gehen, sich ein Lager bereiten; *– out*, verpflanzen. **– -bug,** *s.* die Wanze. **–chamber,** *s.* das Schlafgemach; *Lord of the King's –chamber*, königlicher Kammerherr; *Lady of the Queen's –chamber*, königliche Hofdame. **–clothes,** *pl.* das Bettzeug, die Bettwäsche. **– -curtains,** *pl.* die Bettvorhänge. **–ding,** *s.* das Bettzeug; die Streu (*for cattle*). **–fellow,** *s.* der Schlafkamerad; (*fig.*) der Genosse. **– -head,** *s.* das Kopfende. **– -linen,** *s.* die Bettwäsche. **–maker,** *s.* die Bettmacherin; Aufwärterin (*Univ.*). **– -pan,** *s.* die Leibesschüssel, Stechbecken. **– -plate,** *s.* die Grundplatte, Bettung. **– -post,** *s.* der Bettpfosten, die Bettsäule. **–ridden,** *adj.* bettlägerig. **–rock,** *s.* der Untergrund (*Geol.*), (*fig.*) das Fundament, die Grundlage; *–rock truth*, die Grundwahrheit; *–rock price*, niedrigster *or* äußerster Preis. **–room,** *s.* das Schlafzimmer. **–side,** *s.* die Bettseite; *by her –side*, an ihrem Bette; *–side carpet*, der Bettvorleger; *have a good –side manner*, mit den Patienten gut umzugehen wissen, sich taktvoll benehmen (*of doctors*). **– -sitting-room,** *s.* das Wohnschlafzimmer. **–sore,** *s.* der Dekubitus; *get –sores*, sich wund liegen. **–spread,** *s.* die Bettdecke. **–stead,** *s.* die Bettstelle. **– -tick,** *s.* der (Bett)Überzug. **–time,** *s.* die Schlafenszeit.

bedaub [bɪˈdɔːb], *v.a.* beschmieren, bemalen.

bedeck [bɪˈdɛk], *v.a.* schmücken, zieren.

bedevil [bɪˈdɛvl], *v.a.* behexen, quälen. **–ment,** *s.* die Besessenheit; Verwirrung.

bedew [bɪˈdjuː], *v.a.* betauen, benetzen.

bedizen [bɪˈdaɪzn], *v.a.* herausputzen, ausstaffieren.

bedlam [ˈbɛdləm], *s.* das Irrenhaus; (*fig.*) das Tollhaus, toller Lärm. **–ite,** *s.* Verrückte(r), Wahnsinnige(r), *m.*

bedraggle [bɪˈdrægl], *v.a.* beschmutzen, ramponieren (*clothes*).

bee [bɪː], *s.* die Biene; (*fig.*) arbeitsamer Mensch; (*coll.*) das Arbeitskränzchen; (*coll.*) *have a – in one's bonnet*, eine Grille haben; *queen –*, die Bienenkönigin; *spelling-–*, das Buchstabierspiel; *swarm of –s*, der Bienenschwarm. **– -bread,** *s.* das Bienenbrot. **– -culture,** *s.* die Bienenzucht, Imkerei. **– -eater,** *s.* der Bienenfresser, Spint. **– -glue,** *s.* das Bienenharz, Stopfwachs. **–hive,** *s.* der Bienenstock, Bienenkorb. **–keeper,** *s.* der Bienenmeister, Bienenvater, Imker. **– -line,** *s.* gerader Weg, die Luftlinie; *make a – -line*, schnurstracks losgehen (*for*, auf (*Acc.*)) **– -master,** *s. see* **–keeper. –sting,** *s.* der Bienenstich. **–swax** [–zwæks], 1. *s.* das Bienenwachs. 2. *v.a.* bohnern, wachsen.

beech [bɪːtʃ], *s.* die Buche; *common –*, die Rotbuche; *copper –*, die Blutbuche. **–en,** *adj.* buchen. **– -forest,** *s.* der Buchenwald. **– -mast,** *s.* die Buchmast. **– -nut,** *s.* die Buchecker. **– -oil,** *s.* das Bucheckernöl. **– -tree,** *s.* die Buche.

beef [bɪːf], *s.* das Rindfleisch; das Rind; (*coll.*) die Muskelkraft; *boiled –*, gekochtes Rindfleisch; *corned –*, das Büchsenfleisch; *roast –*, der Rindsbraten, Rostbraten; *round of* (*salt*) *–*, das Hinterschenkelstück, Pökelfleisch; *sirloin of –*, der Lendenbraten. **– cube,** der Bouillonwürfel. **–eater,** *s.* königlicher Leibgardist, der Wärter im Tower von London. **–steak,** *s.* das Beefsteak. **– stew,** *s.* der Rindsgulasch. **– suet,** *s.* das Rinderfett, der Rindertalg. **– -tea,** *s.* die Fleischbrühe, Kraftbrühe. **–y,** *adj.* (*coll.*) kräftig, muskulös.

been [bɪːn], *see* **be.**

beer [bɪə], *s.* das Bier; *life is not all – and skittles*, das Leben ist nicht eitel Freude; *small –*, das Dünnbier; (*coll.*) *think no small – of a th.*, sehr viel von etwas halten. **– -barrel,** *s.* das Bierfaß. **– -engine,** *s.* der Bierdruckapparat. **– -house,** *s.* das Bierhaus, die Bierhalle, Kneipe, Schenke. **– -mug,** *s.* der Bierkrug, das (Bier)Seidel. **–y,** *adj.* nach Bier riechend, (*coll.*) versoffen.

beestings [ˈbɪːstɪŋz], *pl.* die Biestmilch.

beet [bɪːt], *s.* die Runkelrübe, Bete; *red –*, rote

Rübe; *sugar* –, die Zuckerrübe. **–root,** *s.* rote Rübe. **– -sugar,** *s.* der Rübenzucker.

[1]**beetl–e** [ˈbɪ:tl], 1. *s.* der Schlegel, die Ramme, Stampfe. 2. *v.a.* rammen, stampfen. **–ing-mill,** *s.* der Stampfkalander.

[2]**beetle,** *s.* der Käfer (*Ent.*); *black–*, die Küchenschabe. (*sl.*) **– -crusher,** sehr großer Fuß.

[3]**beetle,** *v.n.* überhängen, vorstehen, hervorragen. **– -browed,** *adj.* mit überhängenden Augenbrauen.

beeves [bɪ:vz], *pl.* das Rindvieh, die Rinder (*pl.*).

befall [bɪˈfɔ:l], 1. *ir.v.a.* befallen (*Acc.*), zustoßen, widerfahren (*Dat.*). 2. *v.n.* sich ereignen, sich zutragen.

befit [bɪˈfɪt], *v.a.* sich schicken für, sich ziemen für, passen (*Dat.*), anstehen (*Dat.*). **–ting,** *adj.* geziemend, passend.

befog [bɪˈfɔg], *v.a.* in Nebel hüllen, umnebeln, verdunkeln; (*fig.*) verwirren.

befool [bɪˈfu:l], *v.a.* betören, anführen, zum Narren *or* besten haben.

before [bɪˈfɔ:], 1. *adv.* vorn, voran, voraus (*in place*); vorher, früher, vormals, ehemals, ehedem, eher, bereits, schon (*in time*); *an hour* –, eine Stunde vorher; *he is gone on*–, er ist vorausgegangen; *that was never known* –, ehemals wußte man das nicht; *I have told him* –, ich habe ihm schon gesagt. 2. *prep.* vor; – *all*, vor allem; – *his arrival*, vor seiner Ankunft; – *the door*, vor der Tür; – *my very eyes*, gerade vor meinen Augen; *swear* – *God*, vor Gott schwören; *the week* – *last*, vorvorige Woche; – *the mast*, als gewöhnlicher Matrose (*Naut.*); *he carries everything* – *him*, er hat in allem Erfolg; *the question* – *us*, die (uns) vorliegende Frage; *sail* – *the wind*, vor dem Wind segeln; *the day* – *yesterday*, vorgestern. 3. *conj.* bevor, ehe, bis; – *you know where you are*, im Handumdrehen; *he knew* – *I told him*, bevor ich es ihm sagte, wußte er es; *I guessed it* – *he had told me*, ich ahnte es, ehe er es mir noch gesagt hatte; *I would die* – *I would behave so*, lieber stürbe ich, als daß ich mich so aufführte; *it will not be long* – *you repent of it*, es dauert nicht lange, bis Sie es bereuen *or* so bereuen Sie es. **–hand,** *adv.* vorher, zuvor, im voraus; *I think it necessary to observe –hand*, ich halte es für notwendig, von vornherein zu bemerken; *be –hand with a p.*, einem zuvorkommen. **– -mentioned,** *adj.* vorhererwähnt, obenerwähnt.

befoul [bɪˈfaʊl], *v.a.* besudeln, beschmutzen.

befriend [bɪˈfrɛnd], *v.a.* als Freund behandeln, (einem) Freundschaft erzeigen; unterstützen, begünstigen; *she –ed him*, sie nahm sich seiner an.

beg [bɛg], 1. *v.a.* bitten um, erbitten, ersuchen (etwas von einem), betteln um; – *a p. to come*, einen bitten zu kommen; *I* – *your pardon*, verzeihen Sie! wie bitte? – *the question*, eine *petitio principii* machen. 2. *v.n.* betteln; flehen (*for*, um); – *for mercy*, um Gnade flehen; – *of a p. not to go*, einen dringend bitten nicht zu gehen; *I* – *to differ*, ich erlaube mir anderer Ansicht zu sein; *I* – *to remain yours respectfully*, ich verbleibe mit vorzüglicher Hochachtung Ihr sehr ergebener; *I* – *to inform you*, ich gestatte mir Ihnen mitzuteilen. **–ging,** *s.* das Betteln; Bitten; *go a-–ging*, betteln gehen; *–ging letter*, das Bittschreiben.

began [bɪˈgæn], *see* **begin.**

begat [bɪˈgæt], (*obs.*) *see* **beget.**

beget [bɪˈgɛt], *ir.v.a.* zeugen; (*fig.*) hervorbringen, erzeugen. **–ter,** *s.* der Erzeuger, Vater; (*fig.*) Urheber.

beggar [ˈbɛgə], 1. *s.* der Bettler; (*coll.*) Bursche, Kerl; (*prov.*) *–s must not be choosers*, einem geschenkten Gaul sieht man nicht ins Maul; (*coll.*) *lucky* –, der Glückspilz. 2. *v.a.* zum Bettler machen, an den Bettelstab bringen; berauben, entblößen; (*fig.*) übersteigen; *it –s description*, es spottet jeder Beschreibung, es geht über alle Beschreibung. **– -boy,** der Betteljunge. **–liness,** *s.* die Bettelarmut; Armseligkeit; Erbärmlichkeit, Dürftigkeit. **–ly,** *adj.* bettelhaft; armselig, erbärmlich; *–ly price*, der Bettelpreis. **– -man,** *see* –. **– -my-neighbour,** *s.* der Bettelmann (*Cards*). **–'s opera,** die Dreigroschenoper. **– -woman,** das Bettelweib, die Bettlerin. **–y,** *s.* die Bettelarmut; *reduce to –y*, an den Bettelstab bringen.

begging, *see* **beg.**

begin [bɪˈgɪn], *ir.v.a. & n.* anfangen, beginnen; – *a journey*, eine Reise antreten; – *again*, von neuem anfangen; – *by doing s.th.*, damit anfangen, etwas zu tun; – *on a th.*, etwas in Angriff nehmen; – *with a th.*, mit einer S. anfangen; *to* – *with*, erstens, vorerst, zunächst; *I* – *to see*, es geht mir ein Licht auf; (*prov.*) *well begun is half done*, wohl begonnen ist halb gewonnen. **–ner,** *s.* der Anfänger. **–ning,** *s.* der Anfang, Beginn; Ursprung; das Anfangen, Beginnen; *at the –ning*, bei Beginn; *the –ning of the end*, der Anfang vom Ende; *from the –ning*, von Anfang an; *from –ing to end*, von Anfang bis zu Ende; *in the –ning*, im Anfang. **–nings,** *pl.* die ersten Anfänge, das Anfangsstadium. *small –nings*, ein kleiner Anfang.

begird [bɪˈgə:d], *ir.v.a.* umgürten; (*fig.*) umgeben, einschließen.

begirt [bɪˈgə:t], *p.p. of* **begird.**

begone [bɪˈgɔn], *int.* hinweg! fort! weg (mit dir)! packe dich!

begonia [bɪˈgoʊnjə], *s.* die Begonie (*Bot.*).

begot [bɪˈgɔt], **begotten** [bɪˈgɔtn], *see* **beget;** *the only begotten Son of God*, Gottes eingeborener Sohn.

begrime [bɪˈgraɪm], *v.a.* beschmieren, besudeln.

begrudge [bɪˈgrʌdʒ], *v.a.* mißgönnen (einem etwas), beneiden (einen um etwas).

beguil–e [bɪˈgaɪl], *v.a.* betrügen (*of*, um), verleiten (*into doing*, zu tun); bestricken, bezaubern, locken, reizen; hinbringen, verkürzen (*time*); *–e away the time*, die Zeit vertreiben. **–ement,** *s.* der Betrug, die Täuschung, Hintergehung; der Zeitvertreib. **–er,** *s.* der Betrüger. **–ing,** *adj.* verführerisch, betrügerisch, täuschend; lockend, bezaubernd, berückend.

begum [ˈbɪ:gəm], *s.* die Begum, indische Prinzessin.

begun [bɪˈgʌn], *see* **begin.**

behalf [bɪˈhɑ:f], *s.* (*archaic*) der Behuf, Vorteil, Nutzen; (*only in phrases*) *on* – *of myself*, für mich; in meinem Namen, in meinem Interesse, um meinetwillen, meinetwegen; *on* – *of the poor*, zugunsten *or* zum Besten der Armen.

behav–e [bɪˈheɪv], 1. *v.n.* handeln, sich benehmen, sich betragen; sich gut betragen (*of persons*); sich verhalten, fungieren (*of things*); *well-–ed*, wohlerzogen, artig. 2. *v.r.* sich artig *or* anständig benehmen. **–iour** [–jə], *s.* das Betragen, Verhalten, Auftreten, die Führung, der Anstand; *he is on his good* or *best –iour*, er achtet sehr auf sein Benehmen. **–iorism,** *s.* der Behaviorismus (*Psych.*).

behead [bɪˈhɛd], *v.a.* enthaupten, köpfen. **–ing**, *s.* die Enthauptung.

beheld [bɪˈhɛld], *see* **behold.**

behest [bɪˈhɛst], *s.* (*poet.*) das Geheiß, der Befehl.

behind [bɪˈhaɪnd], 1. *adv.* hinten, zurück, dahinter, hinterher; *be* –, zurück sein, im Rückstande sein (*in* or *with*, mit); *fall* –, zurückbleiben; *get up* –, hinten aufsteigen; *leave* –, zurücklassen, hinter sich lassen. 2. *prep.* hinter; – *his back*, hinter seinem Rücken; ohne sein Wissen, heimlich; *she is not* – *him in zeal*, sie steht ihm an Eifer nicht nach; *she looked* – (*her*), sie sah hinter sich *or* sah sich um; *the groom rode* – *him*, der Diener ritt hinter ihm her; – *the house*, hinter dem Hause; (*go, etc.*, gehen, *etc.*) hinter das Haus; – *the scenes*, hinter der Szene, im geheimen; *be* – *time*, sich verspätet haben; *be* – *the times*, rückständig sein; *there is something* – *all that*, es steckt etwas dahinter. 3. *s.* (*coll.*) der Hintere. **–hand,** *adv. & pred. adj.* im Rückstande, zurück (*with*, mit); spät, verspätet; (*fig.*) rückständig.

behold [bɪˈhoʊld], 1. *ir.v.a.* ansehen, betrachten; sehen, erblicken. 2. *int.* sieh (da)! **–en** [–dn], *pred. adj.* verpflichtet, verbunden. **–er** [–də], *s.* der Zuschauer, Beobachter.

behoof [bɪˈhu:f], *s.* (*archaic*) der Behuf; Vorteil, Nutzen, (*only in*) *on my* (*etc.*) –, um meinetwillen.

behove [bɪˈhoʊv], *v.a. & imp.* gebühren, frommen, sich ziemen *or* schicken; *it –s me*, es geziemt mir, es liegt mir ob.

beige [beɪʒ], 1. *s.* ein Wollstoff. 2. *adj.* gelbgrau.

being [ˈbɪ:ɪŋ], 1. *see* **be.** 2. *s.* das Sein, Dasein, die Existenz; das Wesen; *in* –, tatsächlich vorhanden, in Wirklichkeit; *call into* –, ins Leben rufen; *come into* –, entstehen; *human* –, der Mensch; *the Supreme* –, das höchste Wesen.

belabour [bɪˈleɪbə], *v.a.* tüchtig prügeln, durchprügeln.

belated [bɪˈleɪtɪd], *adj.* verspätet; von der Nacht überrascht.

belay [bɪˈleɪ], *v.a.* festmachen, befestigen, anbinden, belegen (*Naut.*); sichern (*Mount.*); – *the rope!* belegt das Ende! (*Naut.*). **–ing-pin,** *s.* das Befestigungsholz (*Naut.*).

belch [bɛltʃ], *v.n.* rülpsen; (*fig.*) ausstoßen, ausspeien.

beldam(e) [ˈbɛldəm], *s.* (*archaic*) altes Weib, alte Hexe.

beleaguer [bɪˈlɪ:gə], *v.a.* belagern.

belemnite [ˈbɛləmnaɪt], *s.* der Donnerkeil, Belemnit.

belfry [ˈbɛlfrɪ], *s.* der Glockenturm, Glockenstuhl.

belie [bɪˈlaɪ], *v.a.* nicht entsprechen (*Dat.*); Lügen strafen; täuschen (*hopes*).

belief [bɪˈlɪ:f], *s.* der Glaube (*in*, an), die Meinung; das Glaubensbekenntnis; *to the best of my* –, nach meiner besten Überzeugung; *past all* –, unglaublich. **–s,** *pl.* Glaubensanschauungen.

believ–able [bɪˈlɪ:vəbl], *adj.* glaublich, glaubhaft. **–e** [bɪˈlɪ:v], *v.a.* & *n.* glauben, meinen; *he is not to be –ed*, man darf ihm keinen Glauben schenken; *I –e him to be an honest man*, ich halte ihn für einen ehrlichen Menschen; *I –e so*, das glaube ich, ich glaube ja; *I –e not*, das glaube ich nicht, ich glaube nein; *–e in God*, an Gott glauben; *make –e*, vorgeben, vorschützen; *make a p. –e*, einen glauben lassen, einem weismachen. **–er,** *s.* Gläubige(r), *m.*; *be a great –er in*, fest glauben an, viel halten von; *true –er*, der Rechtgläubige. **–ing,** *adj.* glaubend, gläubig.

belike [bɪˈlaɪk], *adv.* (*archaic*) wahrscheinlich, vermutlich.

belittle [bɪˈlɪtl], *v.a.* verkleinern, schmälern, herabsetzen.

bell [bɛl], 1. *s.* die Glocke, Schelle, Klingel; der Kelch (*Bot.*, *Arch.*); Schalltrichter (*of a trumpet*); das Glas (*Naut.*); (*pl.*) das Geläut, Schellengeläut (*on harness*); *eight –s*, acht Glasen (*Naut.*); *answer the* (*door*) –, auf die Klingel hören; *carry off the* –, den Preis davon tragen, der Erste sein; *cap and –s*, die Schellenkappe; *chime* or *peal of –s*, das Glockenspiel; *curse by* –, *book and candle*, in Grund und Boden verfluchen; *ring the* –, klingeln; *as sound as a* –, kerngesund; *toll the* –, läuten. 2. *v.a.*; – *the cat*, der Katze die Schelle umhängen. **––bottomed,** *adj.* unten weit (*of trousers*). **––button,** *s.* der Klingelknopf. **––clapper,** *s.* der Glockenklöppel. **––crank,** *s.* das Glockengelenk. **–flower,** *s.* die Glockenblume. **––founder,** *s.* der Glockengießer. **––founding,** *s.* der Glockenguß. **––foundry,** *s.* die Glockengießerei. **––glass,** *s.* die Glasglocke. **––hop,** (*coll. Amer.*) der Hotelpage. **––jar,** *s.* die Glocke (*Chem.*). **––metal,** *s.* die Glockenspeise. **––mouth,** *s.* der Schalltrichter. **––mouthed,** *adj.* trichterförmig. **––pull,** *s.* der Klingelzug. **––punch,** *s.* der Billettknipser mit Glocke. **––ringer,** *s.* der Glöckner. **––rope,** *s.* die Klingelschnur, der Glockenstrang, das Glockenseil. **––shaped,** *adj.* glockenförmig. **––tent,** *s.* das Rundzelt. **––tower,** *s.* der Glockenturm, Bergfried. **––wether,** *s.* der Leithammel; (*fig.*) Anführer. **––wire,** *s.* der Klingeldraht.

belladonna [bɛləˈdɔnə], *s.* die Tollkirsche, Belladonna.

belle [bɛl], *s.* die Schöne, Schönheit. **–s-lettres** [bɛlˈlɛtr], *pl.* schöne Literatur. **–tristic** [bɛlɛˈtrɪstɪk], *adj.* Unterhaltungs–, schöngeistig.

bellicos–e [ˈbɛlɪkoʊs], *adj.* kriegslustig, kriegerisch. **–ity** [–ˈkɔsɪtɪ], *s.* die Kriegslust.

bellied [ˈbɛlɪd], *adj.* geschwollen, bauchig; (*in compounds* =) –bäuchig.

belligeren–t [bəˈlɪdʒərənt], 1. *adj.* kriegführend. 2. *s.* Kriegführende(r), *m.* **–ce, –cy,** *s.* die Kriegführung, der Kriegszustand.

bellow [ˈbɛloʊ], 1. *v.n.* brüllen; heulen; (*coll.*) laut schreien. 2. *s.* das Gebrüll.

bellows [ˈbɛloʊz], *pl.* der Blasebalg; das Gebläse; die Bälge (*of an organ*); der Balgen (*Phot.*); *a pair of* –, das Gebläse. **––blower,** *s.* der Bälgetreter.

belly [ˈbɛlɪ], 1. *s.* der Bauch, Unterleib; (*vulg.*) der Magen; Wanst, Schmerbauch; Kasten (*of a violin*). 2. *v.n.* bauchig werden, (an)schwellen; *the –ing canvas*, die schwellenden Segel. (*vulg.*) **––ache,** *s.* die Leibschmerzen (*pl.*), das Bauchweh. **––band,** *s.* der Bauchgurt (*harness*). **––flop,** *s.* (*sl.*) der Bauchklatscher. **–ful,** *s.* der Bauchvoll, (*vulg.*) die Genüge. (*vulg.*) **––worship,** *s.* die Schlemmerei.

belong [bɪˈlɔŋ], *v.n.* gehören, zugehören, zu eigen sein, angehören (*to* (*Dat.*)); zukommen, gebühren (*to* (*Dat.*)); *it –s to me*, es gehört mir; *essays of Schiller which – to this period*, Aufsätze Schillers, welche dieser Zeit angehören; *this town –s to Hessen*, diese Stadt gehört zu Hessen; *it –s here*, es gehört hierher; *I – here*, ich bin von hier *or* bin hier ansässig. **–ings,** *pl.* die Habe, der Besitz, das Eigentum, Habseligkeiten (*pl.*), das Zubehör; *with all his –ings*, mit seinem ganzen Gepäck.

beloved, 1. [bɪˈlʌvd], *adj.* geliebt (*of* or *by*, von). 2. [bɪˈlʌvɪd], *s.* Geliebte(r), *m.*; *dearly –!* liebe Gemeinde.

below [bɪˈloʊ], 1. *adv.* unten; auf Erden; *down* –, in der Hölle; *here* –, hienieden; *it will be noticed* –, es wird später *or* unten davon die Rede sein. 2. *prep.* unter, unterhalb; – *the belt*, unehrlich, unfair; – *ground*, unter Tage (*Min.*); – *par*, unter Pari; (*fig.*) mittelmäßig; – *stairs*, bei den Dienstboten.

belt [bɛlt], 1. der Gürtel; das Kranzgesims (*Arch.*); der (Treib)Riemen (*Mach.*); das Fließband, laufendes Band; das Gehenk, Gehänge, Koppel; der Panzergürtel (*Naut.*); Belt (*Geog.*); die Zone, das Gebiet, der Bereich; die Gürtellinie (*Boxing*); *ammunition* –, der Patronengurt; Gurt (*of machine gun*); *blow below the* –, unerlaubter Schlag (*Boxing*); (*fig.*) die Unehrlichkeit; – *of fire*, der Feuergürtel; *–s of Jupiter*, die Streifen des Jupiter. 2. *v.a.* (um-) gürten; (*coll.*) schlagen, prügeln. **––drive,** *s.* der Riemenantrieb. **––feed,** *s.* die Gurtenzuführung; der Zuführer (*machine gun*). **––pulley,** *s.* die Riemenscheibe.

bemoan [bɪˈmoʊn], *v.a.* betrauern, beweinen, beklagen, bejammern.

bemuse [bɪˈmju:z], *v.a.* benebeln, verwirren.

bench [bɛntʃ], *s.* die Bank, Werkbank, der Arbeitstisch; die Richterbank, Richter (*pl.*), das Richterkollegium, der Gerichtshof, das Gericht; *the – and the bar*, Richter und Advokaten, alle Rechtsgelehrten; *carpenter's* –, die Hobelbank; *the Queen's* –, das Oberhofgericht; *Queen's – division*, höchster Gerichtshof in Strafsachen; *be on the* –, Richter sein; *the opposition –es*, die Reihen der Opposition. **–er,** *s.* das Vorstandsmitglied eines Gerichtshofs (*Inn of Court*). **––mark,** *s.* der Lattenpunkt, die Höhenmarke, das Nivellierungszeichen (*Surv.*). **––plane,** *s.* der Bankhobel. **––warrant,** *s.* der Verhaftungsbefehl.

bend [bɛnd], 1. *ir.v.a.* biegen, krümmen, beugen; spannen (*a bow*); befestigen (*a rope*) (*Naut.*); anschlagen, anreihen, anmarlen (*sails*) (*Naut.*); (*fig.*) unterwerfen, zwingen (*to*, unter); richten, lenken, wenden (*to* or *on*, auf) (*one's thoughts, etc.*); *he bent his head*, er beugte den Kopf hinunter *or* nieder; – *the knee*, das Knie beugen; – *one's steps towards home*, die Schritte heimwärts lenken. 2. *ir. v.n.* sich biegen, sich krümmen, sich neigen, sich beugen (*to*, vor (*Dat.*)); überhängen; – *back*, sich zurückbeugen; – *down*, sich niederbeugen; – *forward*, sich bücken, sich neigen; *he is bent on mischief*, er führt Böses im Schilde; *he is bent on his work*, er geht seiner Arbeit eifrig nach; *he is bent upon doing it*, es ist ihm sehr daran gelegen *or* er ist darauf erpicht es zu tun; *he bent to her will*, er beugte sich ihrem Willen. 3. *s.* die Biegung, Krümmung, Kurve; der Schrägbalken (*Her.*); Knoten (*Naut.*). **–able,** *adj.* biegsam. **–ed,** *adj.* (*archaic, except in*) *on –ed knee*, kniefällig. **–er,** *s.* (*Amer. sl.*) das Zechgelage. **–ing strength,** *s.* die Knickfestigkeit (*Metal.*).

beneath [bɪˈnɪ:θ], 1. *adv.* unten. 2. *prep.* unter, unterhalb; – *contempt*, unter aller Würde; – *me*, unter meiner Würde.

benedick [ˈbɛnɪdɪk], *s.* (*coll.*) neuverheirateter Ehemann.

benediction [bɛnɪˈdɪkʃən], *s.* der Segen, Segensspruch, das Dankgebet; die Weihe, Segnung (*R.C.*).

benefact–ion [bɛnɪˈfækʃən], *s.* die Wohltat; Wohltätigkeit. **–or,** *s.* der Wohltäter. **–ress,** *s.* die Wohltäterin.

benefic–e [ˈbɛnɪfɪs], *s.* die Pfründe. **–ed,** *adj.* mit einer Pfründe bedacht. **–ence** [bɪˈnɛfɪsəns], *s.* die Wohltätigkeit. **–ent,** *adj.* wohltätig, mildtätig. **–ial** [bɛnɪˈfɪʃəl], *adj.* heilsam, zuträglich (*to* (*Dat.*)), vorteilhaft, nützlich (*to*, für), nutznießend (*Law*). **–iary,** *s.* der Pfründner; Almosenempfänger; Nutznießer, Erbberechtigte(r), *m.*

benefit [ˈbɛnɪfɪt], 1. *s.* die Wohltat, das Vorrecht, der Vorteil, das Privileg, der Nutzen, Gewinn; das Benefiz (*Sport or Theat.*); – *of clergy*, das Vorrecht der Geistlichen; *for the – of*, zum Nutzen von; *derive – from*, Vorteil ziehen aus; *give a p. the – of the doubt*, einem im Zweifelsfalle recht geben; (*Law*) *in dubio pro reo*, genießen lassen. 2. *v.a.* begünstigen, fördern (*Acc.*); Nutzen bringen, nützen, zugutekommen, heilsam *or* vorteilhaft sein (*Dat.*). 3. *v.n.* Vorteil haben *or* Nutzen ziehen (*by*, aus); *he –ed by this*, dies kam ihm zugute; *I –ed by the mistake*, der Irrtum hat mir genützt. **– -match,** das Benefizspiel (*Sport*). **– -performance,** die Benefizvorstellung (*Theat.*). **– -society,** der Wohltätigkeitsverein; Versicherungsverein auf Gegenseitigkeit.

benevolen–ce [bɪˈnɛvələns], *s.* das Wohlwollen; die Güte; Wohltat, Wohltätigkeit. **–t,** *adj.* wohlwollend; gütig; *–t fund*, der Unterstützungsfonds.

benighted [bɪˈnaɪtɪd], *adj.* von der Nacht überfallen; (*fig.*) umnachtet, unwissend.

benign [bɪˈnaɪn], *adj.* gütig, mild, liebevoll; wohltuend, heilsam, nicht bösartig (*Med.*); günstig, zuträglich (*climate*). **–ant** [bɪˈnɪgnənt], *see* **–.** **–ity** [–ˈnɪgnɪtɪ], *s.* die Güte, Milde; das Wohlwollen.

bent [bɛnt], 1. *adj.* gebogen; krumm, gekrümmt; *see* **bend.** 2. *s.* die Richtung, Neigung, der Hang (*for*, zu); *to the top of one's –*, bis zum äußersten, mit höchster Kraftanstrengung. **–(-grass),** *s.* das Straußgras (*Bot.*).

benumb [bɪˈnʌm], *v.a.* erstarren; betäuben, lähmen. **–ed,** *adj.* erstarrt. **–ing,** *adj.* erstarrend, betäubend.

benz–ene [bɛnˈziːn], *s.* das Benzol, Kohlenbenzin. **–ine,** *s.* das Benzin. **–oic** [–ˈzouɪk] *adj.*; *–oic acid*, die Benzoesäure. **–ol(e)** [ˈbɛnzəl], *s.* das Kohlenbenzin, Handelsbenzol. **–olize, –olise,** *v.a.* mit Benzol sättigen *or* behandeln.

bequ–eath [bɪˈkwiːð], *v.a.* testamentarisch vermachen; hinterlassen. **–eather,** *s.* der Erblasser, Testator. **–est** [bɪˈkwɛst], *s*, das Vermächtnis, Erbteil.

berate [bɪˈreɪt], *v.a.* ausschelten, ausschimpfen.

bereave [bɪˈriːv], *v.a.* berauben (*of a th.*, einer S.). **–d,** *adj.* durch Tod beraubt, verwaist. **–ment,** *s.* die Beraubung; schmerzlicher Verlust; *in their –ment*, in ihrer Verlassenheit.

bereft [bɪˈrɛft], *see* **bereave.**

beret [ˈbɛreɪ], *s.* die Baskenmütze.

bergamot [ˈbəːgəmət], *s.* die Bergamottenbirne; *essence of –*, das Bergamottöl.

berm [bəːm], *s.* die Grabenstufe, der Böschungsabsatz (*Mil.*).

berry [ˈbɛrɪ], *s.* die Beere. **– -bearing,** *adj.* beerentragend. **– -shaped,** *adj.* beerenförmig.

berserk [ˈbəːsəːk], *s.* der Berserker, Wüterich.

berth [bəːθ], 1. *s.* die Koje, das Kajütenbett; der Liegeplatz, Ankerplatz (*Naut.*); (*fig.*) die Stelle, Anstellung, Unterkunft; *loading –*, die Ladestelle; *give* (*a p.* or *a th.*) *a wide –*, (einem *or* einer S.) weit aus dem Wege gehen. 2. *v.a.* vor Anker gehen, ankern lassen; (einem) eine Koje anweisen, (einen) unterbringen.

beryl [ˈbɛrɪl], *s.* der Beryll (*Min.*). **–line,** *adj.* beryllartig; hellgrün.

beseech [bɪˈsiːtʃ], *ir.v.a.* ersuchen, anflehen, dringend bitten. **–ing,** *adj.* flehend, flehentlich.

beseem [bɪˈsiːm], *v.a.* & *n.* (*archaic*) sich ziemen, sich schicken, sich passen für.

beset [bɪˈsɛt], *v.a.* besetzen, umringen, einschließen, umgeben, umlagern; bedrängen, bestürmen; *she was hard –*, sie war hart bedrängt; – *with difficulties*, von Schwierigkeiten umgeben; *he was – with entreaties*, man bestürmte ihn mit Bitten; *–ting sin*, die Gewohnheitssünde.

beshrew [bɪˈʃruː], 1. *v.a.* (*archaic*) verwünschen, verfluchen. 2. *int.* zum Teufel mit, der Teufel hol . . .

beside [bɪˈsaɪd], *prep.* neben, nahe *or* dicht bei; *he is – himself with rage*, er ist außer sich *or* aus dem Häuschen vor Wut; *he sat – me*, **er** saß neben mir; – *the point*, nebensächlich, belanglos; – *the purpose*, unzweckmäßig. **–s,** 1. *adv.* überdies, außerdem, zudem, abgesehen davon, noch dazu; *nobody –s*, sonst niemand. 2. *prep.* außer, neben, abgesehen von; *–s all this*, außer allem diesem.

besiege [bɪˈsiːdʒ], *v.a.* belagern; (*fig.*) bedrängen bestürmen. **–r,** *s.* der Belagerer.

beslaver [bɪˈslævə], *v.a.* begeifern.

beslobber [bɪˈslɔbə], *v.a.* begeifern; (*coll.*) abküssen.

besmear [bɪˈsmɪə], *v.a.* beschmieren, besudeln, beschmutzen.

besmirch [bɪˈsməːtʃ], *v.a.* besudeln.

besom [ˈbɪːzəm], *s.* der Besen.

besot [bɪˈsɔt], *v.a.* betören; berauschen; betäuben. **–ted,** *adj.* betört, berauscht; vernarrt (*on*, in (*Acc.*)).

besought [bɪˈsɔːt], *see* **beseech.**

bespatter [bɪˈspætə], *v.a.* bespritzen.

bespeak [bɪˈspiːk], *ir.v.a.* bestellen; ankündigen, kundgeben, anzeigen; verraten; – *a book* (*at a library*), ein Buch vormerken lassen; – *a p.'s favour*, jemandes Gunst zu gewinnen suchen; *his manners – the gentleman*, sein Benehmen verrät den Mann von Bildung.

bespoke [bɪˈspouk], *adj.*; – *tailor*, der Maßschneider; – *work*, die Maßarbeit. **–n,** *see* **bespeak.**

besprinkle [bɪˈsprɪŋkl], *v.a.* besprengen, bestreuen.

best [bɛst], 1. *adj.* best, feinst, vornehmst; *he was on his – behaviour*, er achtete sehr auf sein Benehmen; *put the – construction on a th.*, etwas aufs beste deuten; *put one's – foot forward*, tüchtig ausschreiten; *his – girl*, sein Schatz; *the – man*, der Beistand des Bräutigams; *the – man in the world*, der beste Mensch von der Welt; *the – part*, der größere *or* größte Teil, das meiste; – *seller*, vielverlangtes Buch. 2. *adv.* am besten, aufs beste; *as – he could*, so gut er konnte; *what had I – do?* was sollte ich wohl tun, was täte ich am besten? *I think it – not to go*, ich halte es für das beste, nicht zu gehen. 3. *s.* das Beste; die Besten (*pl.*); (*a*) (*with verbs*) (*coll.*) *the – of it is that* . . ., der Witz der Sache ist daß . . .; *do one's* (*level*) *–*, sein Möglichstes tun; *the –* (*thing*) *you can do is to go away*, das Beste, was Sie tun können, ist fortzugehen; *did he get* or *have the – of it?* hat er gewonnen? schnitt er am besten ab? *get the – of a p.*, einem überlegen sein, einen in die Enge treiben, einem einen Streich spielen; *make the – of a th.*, jeden erdenklichen Vorteil aus einer Sache ziehen, etwas nach Kräften ausnutzen, tun was man kann (mit); *make the – of a bad job*, gute Miene zum bösen Spiel machen; *his Sunday –*, sein Sonntagsanzug; *the very –*, der, das *or* die Allerbeste; (*b*) (*with prepositions*) *at* (*the*) *–*, bestenfalls, im günstigsten Falle; *be at one's –*, sich am besten zeigen; *for the –*, zum Besten, in der besten Absicht; *to the – of my knowledge*, nach bestem Wissen, soviel ich weiß; *to the – of my power*, so gut ich kann; *to the – of my recollection*, soviel ich mich erinnere; *with the –*, so gut wie nur einer. 4. *v.a.* (*coll.*) übervorteilen, übertreffen. **– -hated,** *adj.* bestgehaßt.

bested [bɪˈstɛd], *adj.* (*archaic, only in*) *well-* (*ill-*) *–*, gut (schlecht) situiert.

bestial [ˈbɛstjəl], *adj.* tierisch, viehisch. **–ity** [–ɪˈælɪtɪ], *s.* viehisches Wesen, die Bestialität. **–ize,** *v.a.* vertieren.

bestir [bɪˈstəː], *v.r.* sich rühren, sich regen; – *yourself!* streng dich doch an!

bestow [bɪˈstou], *v.a.* geben, schenken, erteilen, verleihen (*on* or *upon* (*Dat.*)); (*archaic*) anwenden.

verwenden; (*archaic*) unterbringen, aufbewahren. **–al** [–əl], *s.* die Schenkung, Verleihung (*of a th. on a p.*, einer S. an einen).
bestrew [bɪ'stru:], *ir.v.a.* bestreuen.
bestride [bɪ'straɪd], *ir.v.a.* besteigen, reiten (*a horse*); mit gespreizten Beinen stehen über *or* auf; (*fig.*) beschreiten, durchschreiten.
bestrode [bɪ'stroʊd], *see* **bestride.**
bet [bɛt], *s.* die Wette; *even –*, Wette mit gleichen Chancen; *heavy –*, hohe Wette; *lay* or *make a –*, eine Wette machen; *take a –*, eine Wette annehmen. 2. *v.a. & n.* wetten; setzen; *what do you –?* was gilt die Wette? *I will – (you) five to one*, ich wette (mit Ihnen) fünf gegen eins; (*sl.*) (*you can*) *– your life* (*on it*), darauf können Sie schwören *or* Gift nehmen; (*sl.*) *you –!* ganz gewiß! sicherlich! **–ter,** *s. see* **–tor. –ting,** *s.* das Wetten. **–ting slip,** *s.* der Wettzettel. **–tor,** *s.* Wettende(r), *m.*
betake [bɪ'teɪk], *ir.v.r.* sich begeben *or* verfügen (*to*, nach); (*fig.*) seine Zuflucht nehmen zu, sich wenden an.
bethink [bɪ'θɪŋk], *ir.v.r.* sich besinnen (*of*, auf (*Acc.*)); sich erinnern (*of*, an (*Acc.*)); sich bedenken (*Gen.*).
betide [bɪ'taɪd], 1. *v a.* zustoßen, begegnen (*Dat.*); *woe – him!* wehe ihm! 2. *v.n.* geschehen, sich ereignen.
betimes [bɪ'taɪmz], *adv.* beizeiten, (recht)zeitig, bald.
betoken [bɪ'toʊkn], *v.a.* bezeichnen, andeuten, anzeigen, verkünden.
betook [bɪ'tʊk], *see* **betake.**
betray [bɪ'treɪ], *v.a.* verraten (*a p. to s.o.*, einen an einen; *s.th. to a p.*, einem etwas); enthüllen (einem etwas); verführen, verleiten (*a woman*); (*fig.*) an den Tag legen. **–al,** *s.* der Verrat, Treubruch (*of*, an (*Dat.*)); *–al of confidence*, der Vertrauensbruch. **–er,** *s.* der Verräter; Verführer.
betroth [bɪ'troʊð], *v.a.* (*usually passive*) verloben. **–al,** *s.* die Verlobung. **–ed** [–d], *s.*; *your –ed*, Ihre Braut, Ihre Verlobte; Ihr Bräutigam, Ihr Verlobter.
better ['bɛtə], 1. *adj.* besser, geeigneter, passender, günstiger, vorteilhafter; gesünder; *upon – acquaintance*, bei näherer Bekanntschaft; *the – the day, the – the deed*, je heiliger der Tag, desto besser *or* heiliger die Tat; (*coll.*) *his – half*, seine Frau; *the – part of an hour*, fast eine ganze Stunde; *his – self*, seine bessere Seite. 2. *adj. & adv.* (*with aux. verbs*) *he is –*, es geht ihm besser, er befindet sich wohler; *be – as one is*, so besser daran sein, lieber bleiben wie man ist; *be – off*, besser daran sein, in besseren Umständen sein; *he is no – than he should be*, man kann nichts besseres von ihm erwarten; *she is no – than she should be*, sie ist ein lockeres Mädchen, sie führt einen unsittlichen Lebenswandel; *I am none the – for it*, es hat mir nichts genützt, ich bin nicht besser daran; *you had – (sl. you –) go*, es wäre besser Sie gingen, Sie täten besser zu gehen; *you (had) – not!* das will ich dir nicht raten; *be – than one's word*, mehr halten als man versprochen hat. 3. *adv.* besser, wohler, mehr; *– and –*, immer besser; *get –*, sich erholen; (*coll.*) *go one –*, übertrumpfen; *all the –, so much the –*, um so besser, desto besser; *he knows –*, er weiß es besser; *he always knows –*, er läßt sich nichts vormachen; *I like her – than him*, ich habe sie lieber als ihn; *I like it none the – for it*, deswegen liebe ich es nicht mehr; *I thought – of it*, ich habe mich eines Besseren besonnen, ich habe es mir genauer überlegt. 4. *s.* das Bessere; *his –*, der ihm Überlegene; *my –s*, meine Vorgesetzten, die Höhergestellten; *for – for worse*, in Freud und Leid; auf Gedeih und Verderb; *change for the –*, sich bessern; *a change for the –*, eine Wendung zum Besseren; *get the – of a p.* or *a th.*, einen *or* etwas überwinden *or* besiegen, die Oberhand gewinnen über einen. 5. *v.n.* sich bessern, besser werden. 6. *v.a.* bessern, verbessern, vervollkommnen; *o.s.*, sich *or* seine Lage verbessern, vorwärtskommen; *– up*, *v.a.* veredeln (*raw materials*). **–ment,** *s.* die Besserung, Verbesserung, Melioration (*Agric.*).
betting ['bɛtɪŋ], *see* **bet.**
between [bɪ'twi:n], 1. *adv.* dazwischen; *few and far –*, selten; *in –*, mitten darin; *space –*, dazwischenliegender Raum, der Zwischenraum. 2. *prep.* zwischen; *in –*, mitten in; *– the devil and the deep sea*, unrettbar verloren, in einer hoffnungslosen Klemme; *– ourselves* or *you and me*, unter uns, unter vier Augen, im Vertrauen; *– stations*, auf freier Strecke (*Railw.*); *there is nothing – them*, sie stehen in keinem besonderen Verhältnis zueinander; *– two and three o'clock*, zwischen zwei und drei Uhr; *– two and three years ago*, vor etwa zwei bis drei Jahren; *we bought it – us*, wir kauften es zusammen. **––decks,** *s.* das Zwischendeck. **––maid,** *s* das Aushilfsmädchen. **times, – whiles,** *adv.* zuweilen, von Zeit zu Zeit.
betwixt [bɪ'twɪkst], *prep. & adv.* (*archaic & poet.*); *– and between*, weder eins noch das andere in der Mitte.
bevel ['bɛvl], 1. *adj.* schräg(kantig), schief. 2. *s.* schiefe *or* schräge Richtung, schräger Anschnitt, die Fase, Abgratung, Schräge, Gehrung; der Winkelpasser, die Schmiege (*Carp.*); *on a –*, schräg, schiefwinklig. 3. *v.a.* schräg abschneiden, abschrägen, abschleifen, abkanten. 4. *v.n.* schräg sein, eine schräge Richtung haben. **––edge,** *s.* schräge Kante, die Facette. **––gear(ing),** *s.* das Kegelrad(getriebe). **–led,** *p.p. & adj.* schräg geschnitten, abgeschrägt, abgeschliffen; *–led glass*, facettiertes Glas. **–ling,** *s.* die Abschrägung. **––wheel,** *s.* das Kegelrad, konisches Zahnrad.
beverage ['bɛvərɪdʒ], *s.* das Getränk, der Trank, das Gebräu.
bevy ['bɛvɪ], *s* der Flug, Trupp (*of birds*); das Rudel, die Herde; Schar, der Schwarm, Flor (*of girls*).
bewail [bɪ'weɪl], 1. *v.a.* beklagen, beweinen, betrauern. 2. *v.n.* (weh)klagen, trauern (um).
beware [bɪ'wɛə], *v.n.* (*only inf. & imper.*) sich hüten, sich in Acht nehmen, sich vorsehen (*of*, vor); *– lest you fall*, nimm dich in Acht, daß du nicht fällst; *– how you step out*, hüte dich beim Aussteigen. *– of pickpockets!* vor Taschendieben wird gewarnt!
bewilder [bɪ'wɪldə], *v.a.* verwirren, irreführen, irremachen. **–ed,** *adj.* verwirrt, bestürzt; *get –ed*, sich verirren, sich verblüffen lassen. **–ing** [–rɪŋ], *adj.* verwirrend, verblüffend, irreführend. **–ment,** *s.* die Verwirrung, Bestürzung.
bewitch [bɪ'wɪtʃ], *v.a.* behexen; (*fig.*) bezaubern. **–ing,** *adj.* bezaubernd, reizend. **–ment,** *s.* die Bezauberung.
bey [beɪ], *s.* (*Hist.*) der Bei, hoher türkischer Beamter.
beyond [bɪ'jɔnd], 1. *adv.* darüber hinaus; jenseits. 2. *prep.* jenseits, über (. . . hinaus), weiter als, außer; *– belief*, unglaublich; *– all blame*, über jeden Tadel erhaben; *she is – my control*, sie ist mir über den Kopf gewachsen; *go – one's depth*, den Boden verlieren (*in water*), (*fig.*) den Grund unter den Füßen verlieren; *– dispute*, außer allem Zweifel, zweifellos, unstreitig; *– doubt*, einwandfrei; *– endurance*, unerträglich; *– human aid*, nicht mehr zu retten; *that is – me*, das geht über meine Begriffe; *live – one's means*, über sein Vermögen *or* seine Mittel leben; *– measure*, maßlos, über die Maßen; *– memory*, seit Menschengedenken; *– possibility*, unmöglich; *– all praise*, über alles Lob erhaben; *– all price*, unbezahlbar; *that is – my reach*, das kann ich nicht erreichen; (*fig.*) das ist außer meinem Bereiche; *– recognition*, bis zur Unkenntlichkeit; *– recovery*, unrettbar, nicht mehr wiederherzustellen; *– reproach*, tadellos, einwandfrei; *– what is sufficient*, mehr als genug; *– one's time*, über die Zeit, zu lange. 3. *s.* das Jenseits; (*coll.*) *the back of the –*, das Ende der Welt.
bezel ['bɛzl], *s* der Kasten (*of a ring*); die Kante, Schneide (*of a chisel*); Schrägfläche (*of a jewel*).
bezique [bəzɪ:k], *s.* das Besik (*Cards*).
bhang [bæŋ], *s.* das Haschisch.
bi– [baɪ], *prefix* zwei(mal), doppelt, zweifach *e g.* **–angular,** *adj.* zweiwinklig. **–annual,** *adj.* halbjährlich; *for other examples see below.*
bias ['baɪəs], 1. *adj. & adv.* schräg. 2. *s.* schiefe *or* schwere Seite; schräger Schnitt, der Keil (*Tail.*); schiefer Lauf (*Bowls*), der Überhang; (*fig.*) die Neigung der Hang; die Zuneigung, Vorliebe; das

Vorurteil; *cut on the –*, schräg schneiden; *– against*, Vorurteil gegen; *– in favour of*, Neigung zu; *free from* or *without –*, vorurteilsfrei, unvoreingenommen, unbefangen. 3. *v.a.* eine (gewisse) Richtung geben; (*fig.*) beeinflussen, bestimmen; *be –ed by self-interest*, durch Eigennutz voreingenommen sein; *she was –ed in his favour*, sie war für ihn eingenommen.

[1]**bib** [bɪb], *s.* das (Kinder– *or* Geifer)Lätzchen; der Schürzenlatz; (*coll.*) *in best – and tucker*, im Sonntagsstaat.

[2]**bib**, *v.a. & n.* gern und oft trinken. **–ber,** *s.* der Trinker. **–ulous,** *adj.* trunksüchtig.

bibl–e [ˈbaɪbl], *s.* die Bibel; *–e oath*, heiliger Schwur. **–e-society,** *s.* die Bibelgesellschaft. **–ical** [ˈbɪblɪkl], *adj.* biblisch.

biblio–grapher [bɪblɪˈɔgrəfə], *s.* der Bücherkenner, Bibliograph. **–graphic(al)** [–oˈgræfɪk(l)], *adj.* bibliographisch. **–graphy,** *s.* die Bücherkunde, Bibliographie; gesamte *or* einschlägige Literatur (*on a subject*). **–latry** [–ˈɔlətrɪ], *s.* die Bibelverehrung, der Buchstabenglaube. **–mania,** *s.* die Bücherwut, Bibliomanie. **–maniac,** *s.* der Büchernarr. **–phile** [–oˈfaɪl], *s.* der Bücherfreund.

bibulous [ˈbɪbjʊləs], *see* [2]**bib.**

bicarbonate [baɪˈkɑːbənɪt], *s.* das Bikarbonat, doppel(t)kohlensaures Salz; *– of soda*, doppel(t)kohlensaures Natron.

bicenten–ary [baɪsɛnˈtɪːnərɪ], 1. *adj.* zweihundertjährig. 2. *s.* die Zweihundertjahrfeier. **–nial** [–ˈtɛnɪəl], 1. *adj.* zweihundertjahrelang. 2. *s.* der Zeitraum von zweihundert Jahren.

biceps [ˈbaɪsɛps], *s.* der Bizeps, zweiköpfiger Armmuskel.

bichloride [baɪˈklɔːraɪd], *s.* das Bichlorid.

bichromate [baɪˈkroumɪt], *s.* das Bi– *or* Dichromat; doppeltchromsaures Salz (*Chem.*); *– of potash*, doppeltchromsaures Kali.

bicker [ˈbɪkə], *v.n.* zanken, streiten, hadern; (*fig.*) rasseln, plätschern. **–ing** [–rɪŋ], *s.* der Hader, Zwist, Streit, Zank.

bicuspid [baɪˈkʌspɪd], *adj.* zweispitzig.

bicycl–e [ˈbaɪsɪkl], 1. *s.* das Fahrrad, Zweirad, Rad; *ride a –e*, radfahren. 2. *v.n.* radfahren, radeln. **–ist,** *s.* der Radfahrer.

bid [bɪd], 1. *ir.v.a.* heißen (*Acc.*), befehlen, gebieten (*Dat.*); bieten (*at auctions, etc.*); reizen (*Cards*); (*archaic*) ankündigen; (*archaic*) bitten, einladen; *– up*, in die Höhe treiben (*prices*); *– him come in*, heiß ihn eintreten; *do as you are –*, tue was man dir sagt; *– defiance*, Trotz bieten; *– (a p.) farewell*, (einem) Lebewohl sagen; *– s.o. good morning*, einem einen guten Morgen wünschen; *– a p. welcome*, einen willkommen heißen. 2. *ir.v.n.* bieten (*at auctions*), reizen (*at cards*); *– for an article*, auf einen Artikel bieten; *– for safety*, vorsichtig zu Werke gehen; *– against a p.*, einen reizen; *– fair*, zu Hoffnungen berechtigen, versprechen, auf dem besten Wege sein. 3. *s.* das Angebot; *make a – for*, sich bewerben um. (*coll.*) **–dable,** *adj.* folgsam, gehorsam, willig. **–der,** *s.* der Bieter; *highest –der*, Meistbietende(r), *m.* **–ding,** *s.* der Befehl, das Gebot, Geheiß; die Einladung; das Bieten (*at auctions*); *do a p.'s –ding*, tun was einem geheißen wird.

bide [baɪd], 1. *ir.v.n.* (*Scots*) bleiben. 2. *ir.v.a.* abwarten; (*only in*) *– one's time*, seine Zeit abwarten.

biennial [baɪˈɛnɪəl], *adj.* zweijährig.

bier [bɪə], *s.* die Bahre; Totenbahre.

biff [bɪf], 1. *s.* (*sl.*) der Schlag. 2. *v.a.* schlagen.

bifurcat–e [ˈbaɪfəːkeɪt], 1. *adj.* zweizackig, zweizinkig, zweiästig, gabelförmig. 2. *v.n.* sich gabeln, sich abzweigen (*of a way*). **–ion** [–ˈkeɪʃən], *s.* die Spaltung, Gabelung.

big [bɪg], *adj. & adv.* groß; dick; schwanger, trächtig; hoch, erwachsen; (*sl.*) *– bug*, see *– pot*; *– business*, die Großindustrie; *– drum*, große Trommel; (*coll.*) *get too – for one's boots*, eingebildet werden; *– game*, das Hochwild; (*sl.*) *the – idea*, die Absicht, der Zweck; *– man*, großer Mann, wichtige Persönlichkeit; dicker Herr; (*sl.*) *– noise*, große Kanone; (*sl.*) *– pot*, großes Tier; (*coll.*) *talk –*, großsprechen, aufschneiden, prahlen; (*coll.*) *– talk*, die Prahlerei; *– toe*, große Zehe; *– wheel*, das Riesenrad; *woman – with child*, schwangere Frau; *– with misfortune*, unheilschwanger; *– with pride*, aufgeblasen, hochmütig; *– with significance*, voll von Bedeutung. **– -bellied,** *adj.* dickbäuchig. **– -boned,** *adj.* starkknochig, vierschrötig. **–ness,** *s.* die Größe, Dicke, der Umfang. (*coll.*) **–wig,** *s.* der Bonze.

bigam–ist [ˈbɪgəmɪst], *s.* der in Doppelehe Lebende, Bigamist. **–ous,** *adj.* der Bigamie schuldig. **–y** [–mɪ], *s.* die Doppelehe, Bigamie.

bight [baɪt], *s.* die Bucht (*Geog., Naut.*), Einbuchtung.

bigot [ˈbɪgət], *s.* der Frömmler, Eiferer, Fanatiker, blinder Anhänger. **–ed** [–ɪd], *adj.* frömmelnd, bigott, blind ergeben. **–ry,** *s.* die Frömmelei, Blindgläubigkeit, Bigotterie.

bike [baɪk], *s. coll. for* **bicycle;** *push–*, das Fahrrad.

bilabial [baɪˈleɪbɪəl], *adj.* zweilippig, mit beiden Lippen gesprochen.

bilateral [baɪˈlætərəl], *adj.* zweiseitig; (*C.L.*) gegenseitig, beiderseitig.

bilberry [ˈbɪlbərɪ], *s.* die Heidelbeere, Blaubeere.

bilbo [ˈbɪlbou], *s.* (*poet.*) das Schwert, die Klinge. **–es,** *pl.* die Fußfesseln.

bil–e [baɪl], *s.* die Galle; (*fig.*) der Ärger, die Bitterkeit. **–e-duct,** *s.* der Gallengang. **–iary,** *adj.* Gallen–. **–ious,** *adj.* gallsüchtig, Gallen–; (*fig.*) gallig, reizbar.

bilge [bɪldʒ], *s.* der Bauch (*of a cask, etc.*); die Bilge, Kimm, der Schiffsboden (*Naut.*); (*sl.*) Quatsch, Unsinn. **– -keel,** *s.* der Kimmkiel, Schlingerkiel. **– -pump,** *s.* die Lenzpumpe, Sodpumpe. **– -water,** *s.* das Schlagwasser, Schmutzwasser. **–ways,** *s.* die Schlittenbalken (*Naut.*).

biliary [ˈbɪlɪərɪ], *see* **bile.**

bilingual [baɪˈlɪŋgwəl], *adj.* zweisprachig. **–ism,** *s.* die Zweisprachigkeit.

bilious [ˈbɪljəs], *see* **bile.**

bilk [bɪlk], 1. *v.a.* betrügen, prellen. 2. *v.n.* (*coll.*) durchbrennen mit; (*coll.*) *– one's fare*, schwarzfahren.

[1]**bill** [bɪl], *s.* (*archaic*) die Pike. **– -hook,** *s.* die Hippe, das Gartenmesser.

[2]**bill,** 1. *s.* der Schnabel (*of a bird*), die Spitze (*of a ship*). 2. *v.n.* sich schnäbeln (*of birds*); (*fig.*) *– and coo*, liebkosen.

[3]**bill, 1.** *s.* das Schriftstück, der Schein, Zettel, die Liste, das Verzeichnis, Inventar; der Gesetzentwurf, die Gesetzvorlage, Bill (*Parl.*); Anklageschrift, Klageschrift (*Law*); der Wechsel, die Rechnung (*C.L.*); (*Amer.*) Banknote; **(a)** (*with adjectives & nouns*) *accommodation –*, das Gefälligkeitsakzept; *– of costs*, die Spesenrechnung; *– of credit*, der Kreditbrief; *– of entry*, die Zolldeklaration; *– of exchange*, der Wechsel, die Tratte; *– of fare*, die Speisekarte; *– of health*, der Gesundheitspaß, das Gesundheitsattest; *clean – of health*, gesund, ohne Krankheit; *– of indictment*, die Anklageschrift; *– of lading*, der Frachtbrief; Verladungsschein, das Konnossement; *–s and money*, Brief und Geld; *– of mortality*, die Sterbeliste; *private –*, der Gesetzantrag in privatem Interesse; *–s receivable*, Wechselforderungen (*pl.*); *– of Rights*, die Freiheitsurkunde (*1689*); *– of sale*, der Kaufbrief, die Übertragungsurkunde, Mobiliarschuldverschreibung; *– of sight*, der Zollgutbesichtigungsschein; **(b)** (*with verbs*) *accept a –*, einen Wechsel akzeptieren; *bring in a –*, eine Gesetzvorlage einbringen; *bring in a true –*, see *find a true –*; *the – was carried*, die Vorlage ging durch; (*coll.*) *fill the –*, allen Anforderungen genügen; *draw a – on*, einen Wechsel ziehen *or* trassieren auf; *find a true –*, die Anklage annehmen, die Anklage für begründet erklären; (*coll.*) *foot a –*, eine Rechnung bezahlen; *give a –*, einen Wechsel ausstellen; *ignore a –*, die Anklage für unbegründet erklären, die Anklage verwerfen; *make out a –*, see *give a –*; *pass a –*, einen Gesetzentwurf annehmen; *post –s*, Zettel ankleben; *protest a –*, einen Wechsel protestieren; *stick no –s!* Zettelankleben verboten; *table the –*, die Vorlage vertagen; *take up a –*, einen Wechsel honorieren; *throw out a –*, einen Gesetzentwurf ablehnen. **2.** *v.a.* anzeigen; *–ed to appear*, auftretend

(*Theat.*). **--book,** *s.* das Wechselbuch. **--broker,** *s.* der Wechselmakler. **--brokerage,** *s.* die Wechselcourtage. **--business,** *s.* das Wechselgeschäft. **--holder,** *s.* der Wechselinhaber. **--jobber,** *s.* der Wechselreiter. **--head,** *s.* der Kopf einer Rechnung. **--poster,** *s.*, **--sticker,** *s.* der Zettelankleber, Plakatanschläger. **--posting,** *s.*, **--sticking,** *s.* das Zettelankleben, Plakatanschlagen. **--stamp,** *s.* der Wechselstempel.

[1]billet ['bɪlɪt], 1. *s.* der Quartierzettel; das Quartier, die Unterkunft (*Mil.*); (*coll.*) *good* –, gute Stellung. 2. *v.a.* einquartieren, unterbringen (*on*, bei). **-ee,** *s.* der Einquartierte. **-ing,** *s.* die Einquartierung. **-ing officer,** *s.* der Quartiermacher. **-ing party,** *s.* der Quartiermachertrupp.

[2]billet, *s.* das Scheit (*of wood*).

billhook, *see* **[1]bill.**

billiard-s ['bɪljəd3], *pl.* (*sing. constr.*) das Billard; *game of -s*, die Partie Billard. **--ball,** *s.* die Billardkugel. **--cue,** *s.* der Billardstock, das Queue. **--marker,** *s.* der (Billard)Markör. **--table,** *s.* das Billard.

Billingsgate ['bɪlɪŋzgeɪt], *s.* (*sl.*) die Pöbelsprache.

billion ['bɪljən], *s.* die Billion (*Eng. = 1,000,000 millions*); die Milliarde (*Amer., French = 1,000 millions*).

billow ['bɪlou], 1. *s.* die Woge, Welle. 2. *v.a.* wogen. **-y,** *adj.* schwellend, wogend.

billy ['bɪlɪ], *s.* der Kochkessel; (*Amer.*) die Keule. **-can,** *s.* der Kochkessel. **-cock** [-kɔk], *s.* (*coll.*) die Melone (*hat*). **--goat** [-gout], *s.* der Ziegenbock.

bimetallis-m [baɪ'mɛtəlɪzm], *s.* der Bimetallismus, die Doppelwährung. **-t,** *s.* der Anhänger des Doppelwährungssystems.

bi-monthly ['baɪ'mʌnθlɪ], *adj.* vierzehntägig, halbmonatlich; zweimonatlich.

bin [bɪn], 1. *s.* der Kasten, Behälter; *dust-*, der Kehrichtkasten; *wine--*, der Weinschrank. 2. *v.a.*; – *wine*, Wein lagern.

bina-ry ['baɪnərɪ], *adj.* binär, zweiteilig; *-ry compound*, binäre Verbindung (*Chem.*); *-ry measure*, gerader Takt (*Mus.*); *-ry stars, pl.* Doppelsterne. **-te,** *adj.* gepaart (*Bot.*).

bind [baɪnd], 1. *ir.v.a.* binden, befestigen, festmachen; (ein)binden (*books*), einfassen (*a dress, etc.*), beschlagen (*a wheel*); (*fig.*) verbinden, verpflichten; verstopfen (*the bowels*); – *a p. as apprentice*, einen in die Lehre geben; *be bound to do*, verpflichtet sein zu tun; (*coll.*) *I'll be bound*, ohne Zweifel, ich bürge dafür, ich stehe dafür ein; *bound by a promise*, durch ein Versprechen gebunden; – *over*, (einen) unter Bürgschaft verpflichten; *bound over for a year in the sum of £100*, eine Bewährungsfrist von einem Jahr unter Kaution von £100 erhalten; – *up*, verbinden (*a wound*); zusammenbinden (*pamphlets, etc.*); *his interests are bound up with mine*, seine Interessen hängen mit meinen aufs engste zusammen, seine Interessen sind mit meinen aufs engste verknüpft; *see also* **[1]bound.** 2. *ir.v.n.* steif *or* hart werden; binden; stopfen (*Med.*); verpflichten. **-er,** *s.* der Binder, Buchbinder; das Bindemittel, die Binde, das Band; der Garbenbinder (*Agr.*); Zugbalken (*Building*); *-er's board*, die Buchbinderpappe. **-ing,** 1. *adj.* bindend; verbindlich (*on*, für). 2. die Bindung; Binde, der Verband; Einband (*of a book*); Besatz, die Einfassung (*of a dress*). **-ing agent,** *s.* das Bindemittel. **-ing-screw,** *s.* die Klemmschraube. **-weed,** *s.* die Winde (*Bot.*).

binge [bɪnd3], *s.* (*sl.*) die Bierreise, der Saufabend.

binnacle ['bɪnəkl], *s.* die Kompaßhaube, das Kompaßhäuschen, Nachthaus (*Naut.*).

bino-cular [baɪ'nɔkjulə], 1. *s.* (*usually pl.*) der Feldstecher; Feldgläser (*pl.*); das Operngias. 2. *adj.* zweiäugig, für beide Augen. **-mial** [-'noumɪəl], 1. *s.* das Binom. 2. *adj.* binomisch, zweigliedrig (*Math.*). **-minal,** *adj.* zweinamig.

bio-chemist [baɪo'kɛmɪst], *s.* der Biochemiker. **-chemistry** [baɪə'kɛmɪstrɪ], *s.* die Biochemie. **-grapher** [baɪ'ɔgrəfə], *s.* der Biograph. **-graphic-(al)** [-'græfɪk(l)], *adj.* biographisch. **-graphy** [-'ɔgrəfɪ], *s.* die Biographie, Lebensbeschreibung. **-logic(al)** [-'lɔd3ɪk(l)], *adj.* biologisch; *-logical warfare*, der Bazillenkrieg (*Mil.*). **-logist** [-'ɔləd3ɪst], *s.* der Biolog. **-logy** [-'ɔləd3ɪ], *s.* die Biologie. **-metry** [-'ɔmətrɪ], *s.* die Biometrie.

bipartite [baɪ'pɑ:taɪt], *adj.* zweiteilig (*Bot.*); in doppelter Ausfertigung (*of documents, etc.*) (*Law*).

biped ['baɪpɛd], *s.* der Zweifüßler.

biplane ['baɪpleɪn], *s.* der Doppeldecker, Zweidecker (*Av.*).

bipod ['baɪpɔd], *s.* das Zweifußgestell.

birch [bə:tʃ], 1. *s.* die Birke; – (*rod*), die Rute. 2. *v.a.* mit der Rute züchtigen. 3. *adj.*, **-en,** *adj.* birken. **-ing,** *s.* die Züchtigung.

bird [bə:d], *s.* der Vogel; (*coll.*) der Bursche; (*sl.*) das Mädchen; *cock* –, das Männchen; (*prov.*) *the early – catches the worm*, Morgenstund' hat Gold im Mund'; *-s of a feather*, (*fig.*) gleiche Brüder; *-s of a feather flock together*, gleich und gleich gesellt sich gern; *fine feathers make fine -s*, Kleider machen Leute; (*sl.*) *give a p. the* –, einen auszischen *or* auspfeifen; (*prov.*) *a – in the hand is worth two in the bush*, ein Sperling in der Hand ist besser als eine Taube auf dem Dache; *hen* –, das Weibchen; – *of paradise*, der Paradiesvogel; – *of passage*, der Zugvogel; – *of prey*, der Raubvogel; (*coll.*) *queer* –, seltsamer Mensch; *a little – told me*, ich habe ein Vögelchen singen hören; *kill two -s with one stone*, zwei Fliegen mit einer Klappe schlagen; (*coll.*) *wise old* –, schlauer Bursche. **--cage,** *s.* der *or* das Vogelbauer. **--call,** *s.* der Vogelruf, die Lockpfeife. **--catcher,** *s.* der Vogelfänger, Vogelsteller. **--fancier,** *s.* der Vogelliebhaber, Vogelzüchter. **--lime,** *s.* der Vogelleim. **--seed,** *s.* das Vogelfutter. **-'s egg,** das Vogelei. **-'s-eye,** *s.* das Adonisröschen (*Bot.*); *-'s eye tobacco*, fein geschnittener Tabak; *-'s-eye view*, die Vogelperspektive, (der Blick aus der) Vogelschau, das Luftbild; (*fig.*) allgemeiner Überblick. **-'s-nest,** 1. *s.* das Vogelnest; der Ausguck, Mastkorb (*Naut.*). 2. *v.n.* Vogelnester ausnehmen; *they went -('s)-nesting*, sie gingen auf die Suche nach Vogelnestern.

birth [bə:θ], *s.* die Geburt; Herkunft, Abstammung; (*fig.*) Abkunft, der Ursprung, die Entstehung; *at a* –, bei einer Geburt, auf einmal geboren; *by* –, von Geburt; *give – to*, gebären, zur Welt bringen; (*fig.*) Veranlassung geben zu, hervorbringen; *monstrous* –, die Mißgeburt; *new* –, die Wiedergeburt, Neugeburt; *of noble* –, von adliger Abkunft; *untimely* –, die Frühgeburt. **--certificate,** die Geburtsurkunde, der Geburtsschein. **--control,** *s.* künstliche Geburtenbeschränkung, die Empfängnisverhütung. **-day,** *s.* der Geburtstag; *-day present*, das Geburtstagsgeschenk; (*coll.*) *in one's -day suit*, splitternackt. **--mark,** *s.* das Muttermal. **-place,** *s.* der Geburtsort. **--rate,** *s.* die Geburtenziffer; *falling --rate*, der Geburtenrückgang. **-right,** *s.* das Geburtsrecht, angestammtes Recht.

biscuit ['bɪskɪt], *s.* der Zwieback, der *or* das Biskuit *or* Keks; *ship's* –, der Schiffszwieback (*Naut.*); – (*china*), das Biskuitporzellan.

bisect [baɪ'sɛkt], 1. *v.a.* halbieren (*Math.*), zweiteilen, in zwei teilen. 2. *v.n.* sich teilen, sich gabeln. **-ion,** *s.* die Halbierung. **-or,** *s.* die Mittellinie, Halbierungslinie.

bisexual [baɪ'sɛksjuəl], *adj.* zweigeschlechtig, zwitterig.

bishop ['bɪʃəp], *s.* der Bischof; Läufer (*Chess*); **-ric,** *s.* das Bistum.

bismuth ['bɪzməθ], *s.* der *or* das Wismut.

bison ['baɪsn], *s.* amerikanischer Auerochs, der Bison.

bissextile [bɪ'sɛkstaɪl], 1. *adj.* Schalt-; – *day*, der Schalttag; – *year*, das Schaltjahr. 2. *s.* das Schaltjahr.

bistoury ['bɪsturɪ], *s.* der Bistouri, das Klappmesser (*Surg.*).

bistre ['bɪstə], 1. *s.* der *or* das Bister, das Nußbraun. 2. *adj.* nußbraun, bisterfarben.

bisulph-ate [baɪ'sʌlfeɪt], *s.* doppeltschwefelsaures Salz; *-ate of potash*, doppeltschwefelsaures Kalium. **-ite,** *s.* das Bisulfit, doppeltschwefligsaures Salz.

bit [bɪt], 1. *s.* der Bissen, das Stück; Stückchen, Bißchen; Gebiß (*of a bridle*); der Bohrer, das Bohreisen, die Schneide (*Carp., etc.*); der Bart (*of a key*); *a – of a fool*, so etwas wie ein Narr; – *by* –, stückweise, nach und nach; *not care a* –, sich gar nichts daraus machen; *centre* –, der Herzbohrer; *curb* –, das Stangengebiß; (*coll.*) *do one's* –, das Seine tun, sein Scherflein beitragen; *every* –, ganz und gar, gänzlich, in jeder Beziehung; *give a p. a – of one's mind*, einem gehörig die Meinung sagen; *a good* –, ein ordentliches Stück; *a little* or *tiny* –, ein ganz klein wenig; *not a* –, ganz und gar nicht, nicht im geringsten, keine Spur; *snaffle* –, das Trensengebiß; *take the – in* or *between his teeth*, störrisch *or* widerspenstig werden; durchgehen (*of a horse*); (*coll.*) *wait a* –, warte einen Augenblick. 2. *see* **bite.**

bitch [bɪtʃ], *s.* die Hündin, Petze; (*vulg.*) böses Weib; die Hure, Metze.

bite [baɪt], 1. *ir.v.a.* beißen; stechen (*of insects*); zerfressen, ätzen, beizen (*metals*); (*a*) (*with nouns*) – *the dust*, ins Gras beißen; – *one's lip*, sich (*Dat.*) auf die Lippe beißen; – *one's nails*, an den Nägeln kauen; (*b*) (*with adverbs & prepositions*) – *at*, anbeißen, schnappen nach; – *in*, ätzen (*as an acid*); eingreifen (*of a wheel*); – *into*, tief einschneiden in; – *off*, abbeißen; *see* **nose** 1; (*coll.*) – *off more than one can chew*, zu viel unternehmen, mehr auf sich nehmen als man schaffen kann, sich zuviel zumuten; (*c*) (*passive*) (*coll.*) *be bitten*, betrogen werden, hereinfallen; *once bitten twice shy*, das gebrannte Kind scheut das Feuer; (*coll.*) *be bitten by*, angesteckt werden von, sich begeistern für. 2. *v.n.* beißen; stechen, brennen (*as mustard, etc.*); eingreifen (*of wheels*); fassen, halten (*of the anchor*); anbeißen (*of a fish*). 3. *s.* das Beißen, der Biß, die Bißwunde; der Stich (*of insects*); das Anbeißen (*of fishes*); Fassen, Eingreifen (*Mech.*); Ätzen; der Bissen, Happen; *give me a* –, laß mich mal abbeißen. **–r,** *s.* der Beißer; *the –r bit*, der betrogene Betrüger; wer anderen eine Grube gräbt, fällt selbst hinein.

biting ['baɪtɪŋ], *adj.* beißend, scharf, schneidend; sarkastisch; – *jest*, beißender Scherz; – *wind*, scharfer *or* schneidend kalter Wind.

bitt [bɪt], *s.* (*usually pl.*) der Poller (*Naut.*); *mooring –s*, der Vertäupoller; *towing –s*, der Schleppoller.

bitten ['bɪtn], *see* **bite.**

bitter ['bɪtə], 1. *adj.* bitter, scharf, herb, beißend, schneidend, heftig, schmerzhaft; erbittert, verbittert; – *beer*, helles Bier; – *blast*, schneidender Wind; *to the – end*, bis aufs letzte, bis zum äußersten, bis zum Tode; – *enemy*, der Todfeind; *as – as gall*, gallenbitter; – *principle*, der Bitterstoff (*Chem.*); – *quarrel*, heftiger Streit; – *sorrow*, herber Schmerz; – *words*, verbitterte Worte. 2. *s.* das Bittere, die Bitterkeit; helles Bier. **--gourd,** die Koloquinte. **–ness,** *s.* die Bitterkeit, Herbheit; Strenge, Verbitterung, Härte. **–s,** *pl* der Magenbitter, Bittertropfen (*pl.*). **–sweet,** 1. *adj.* bittersüß. 2. *s.* das Bittersüß (*Bot.*).

bittern ['bɪtə:n], *s.* die Rohrdommel (*Orn.*).

bitum-en [bɪ'tju:mən], *s.* das Erdpech, der Bergteer, Asphalt. **–inous** [–ɪnəs], *adj.* bituminös; asphalthaltig; *–inous cement*, der Asphaltkitt; *–inous coal*, die Fettkohle.

bivalen-ce [baɪ'veɪləns], *s.* die Zweiwertigkeit. **–t,** *adj.* zweiwertig.

bivalv-e ['baɪvælv], *s.* zweischalige Muschel; zweiklappige Frucht. **–ular** [baɪ'vælvjʊlə], *adj.* zweischalig; zweiklappig (*Bot.*).

bivouac ['bɪvʊæk], 1. *s.* das Biwak, Feldlager, Nachtlager (*Mil.*). 2. *v.n.* biwakieren.

bizarre [bɪ'zɑ:], *adj.* wunderlich, phantastisch, grotesk, bizarr.

blab [blæb], 1. *s.* (*coll.*) der Schwätzer, Angeber; das Geschwätz, die Klatsche. 2. *v.a.*; – (*out*), ausschwatzen, ausplaudern, verraten. 3. *v.n.* ein Geheimnis verraten.

black [blæk], 1. *adj.* schwarz; dunkel, finster, düster; mürrisch; abscheulich (*as a crime*); (*a*) (*with nouns*) *the – art*, schwarze Kunst; *I am in his – books*, ich bin bei ihm schlecht angeschrieben; – *cap*, schwarze Kappe (*of a judge*); – *and white drawing*, die Schwarzweißzeichnung; – *eye*, blaues *or* blaugeschlagenes Auge; – *frost*, trockener Frost; – *heart*, böses Herz; – *look*, drohender *or* mißmutiger Blick; *get a – mark*, in üblen Ruf kommen; – *Monday*, der Unglückstag; erster Schultag; – *pudding*, die Blutwurst; – *sheep*, räudiges Schaf; der Taugenichts; (*b*) (*with verbs & prepositions*) *beat – and blue*, grün und blau schlagen; *look – at a p.*, einen mißmutig ansehen; *go – in the face*, blau werden (*through choking*); *not so – as he is painted*, besser als sein Ruf. 2. *s.* das Schwarz, die Schwärze; das Trauerkleid; die Trauerkleidung; *bone* –, die Knochenkohle, das Beinschwarz; *shoe*–, der Schuhputzer; *speck of* –, der Rußfleck, Schmutzfleck; *wear* –, in Trauer gekleidet sein; *have a th. in – and white*, etwas schriftlich *or* schwarz auf weiß haben. 3. *v.a.* schwärzen, wichsen. **–amoor,** *s.* (*pej.*) der Neger, Mohr. **–ball,** 1. *s.* schwarze Wahlkugel. 2. *v.a.*; *–ball a p.*, gegen seine Aufnahme stimmen, (*fig.*) einen ausschließen *or* zurückweisen. **--beetle,** *s.* die Küchenschabe. **–berry,** *s.* die Brombeere. **–bird,** *s.* die Amsel. **–board,** *s.* die Wandtafel. **–cap,** *s.* die Mönchsgrasmücke, das Schwarzplättchen (*Orn.*). (*coll.*) **--coated,** *adj.* *--coated worker*, Büroangestellte(r), *m.*, der Kontorarbeiter. **--cock,** *s.* der Birkhahn (*Orn.*). **--currant,** *s.* die Johannisbeere. **–en,** 1. *v.a.* schwarz machen, schwärzen; (*fig.*) anschwärzen, verleumden. 2. *v.n.* schwarz werden. **--eyed,** *adj.* schwarzäugig. **–guard** ['blægɑ:d], 1. *s.* der Schuft, Lump, Spitzbube. 2. *v.a.* beschimpfen. **–guardly,** *adv.* roh, gemein. **–head,** *s.* der Mitesser. **--hearted,** *adj.* bösartig. **– hole,** finsteres Loch, das Hundeloch. **–ing** ['blækɪŋ], *s.* das Schwärzen, Wichsen; die Schwärze, Wichse; *–ing brush*, *s.* die Wichsbürste. **–ish,** *adj.* schwärzlich. **–lead,** 1. *s.* der Graphit, das Reißblei; die Ofenwichse, Ofenschwärze; *–lead pencil*, der Bleistift. 2. *v.a.* schwärzen (*a stove, etc.*). **–leg,** *s.* der Streikbrecher. **--leg,** *s.* die Klauenseuche (*Vet.*). **--letter,** *s.* die Fraktur, gotische Schrift. **--list,** *s.* schwarze Liste. **–mail,** 1. *s.* die Erpressung; das Erpressergeld. 2. *v.a.* Geld erpressen (*a p.*, von einem). **--market,** *s.* schwarzer Markt. **--marketeer,** *s.* der Schwarz– *or* Schleichhändler. **--marketeering,** *s.* der Schwarzhandel, Schleichhandel. **–ness,** *s.* die Schwärze; (*fig.*) Abscheulichkeit, Verderbtheit. **–out,** *s.* die Verdunkelung; (*fig.*) die Ohnmacht, Bewußtlosigkeit. **– out,** *v.a. & n.* verdunkeln; (*fig.*) bewußtlos werden. **–shirt,** *s.* das Schwarzhemd, der Faschist. **–smith,** *s.* der Grobschmied, Hufschmied. **–thorn,** *s.* der Schwarzdorn, Schlehdorn (*Bot.*).

bladder ['blædə], *s.* die Blase; Schwimmblase; (Harn)Blase (*Anat.*). **--fern,** *s.* der Blasenfarn. **--wort,** *s.* der Wasserschlauch, Wasserfenchel (*Bot.*). **--wrack,** *s.* der Blasentang (*Bot.*).

blade [bleɪd], *s.* das Blatt, der Halm (*of grass, etc.*); die Klinge (*of a knife, etc.*); (*fig.*) der Degen; *fan* –, der Windflügel; *oar* –, das Riemenblatt; *propeller* –, das (Luft)Schraubenblatt, der (Luft)Schraubenflügel; *razor* –, die Rasierklinge; *saw*–, das Sägeblatt; *shoulder*–, das Schulterblatt; – *of grass*, der Grashalm; *in the* –, auf dem Halm (*Agric.*).

blain [bleɪn], *s.* die Beule, das Geschwür.

blam-able ['bleɪməbl], *adj.* tadelnswert, strafbar. **–e** [bleɪm], 1. *s.* der Tadel; die Schuld, Verantwortung; *bear* or *take the –e*, die Schuld auf sich nehmen; *lay, put* or *throw the –e on s.o.*, einem die Schuld geben. 2. *v.a.* tadeln (*for*, wegen); *–e a p. for*, einem Schuld geben an (*Dat.*); *be to –e for*, schuld an (einer S.) sein, die Schuld an (einer S.) tragen; *I have only myself to –e*, die Schuld habe ich allein, es ist meine eigne Schuld; *no one can –e you for it*, das kann Ihnen niemand verargen; *–e a th. upon s.o.*, einen für etwas verantwortlich machen. **–eless,** *adj.* untadelig, schuldlos (*of*, an (*Dat.*)). **–elessness,** *s.* die Tadellosigkeit, Makellosigkeit, Unschuld. **–eworthiness,** *s.* die Tadelnswürdigkeit. **–eworthy,** *adj.* tadelnswert.

blanch [blɑ:ntʃ], 1. *v.a.* weißen, weiß machen, bleichen; beizen, weiß sieden (*metals*); abhülsen, schälen (*almonds*); (*fig.*) bleich machen; – *over*, beschönigen. 2. *v.n.* erbleichen, bleich werden.

blancmange [blə'mɔnʒ], *s.* der Flammeri, die Mandelsüßspeise.

bland [blænd], *adj.* (ein)schmeichelnd; mild, sanft. **–ish** ['blændɪʃ], *v.a.* schmeicheln (*Dat.*), liebkosen. **-ishment,** *s.* die Schmeichelei; (*pl.*) schmeichelhafte Worte. **-ness,** *s.* die Milde, Sanftmut.

blank [blæŋk], 1. *adj.* unbeschrieben, leer (*of paper, etc.*); reimlos (*of verse*); (*fig.*) verblüfft, bestürzt; (*archaic*) blank, weiß; (*a*) (*with nouns*) – *acceptance*, das Blankoakzept; – *ammunition*, die Exerziermunition; *in – astonishment*, in sprachlosem Erstaunen; – *cartridge*, die Platzpatrone; – *cheque*, der Blankoscheck, unausgefüllter Wechsel; (*fig.*) unbeschränkte Vollmacht; – *endorsement*, das Blankoindossement; *point-–*, schnurgerade, direkt; rundweg, klipp und klar, offen heraus; *point-–refusal*, glatte *or* offene Ablehnung; *point-– shot*, der Kernschuß; – *space*, leerer Raum; – *verse*, der Blankvers, reimloser Vers; – *window*, blindes Fenster; (*b*) (*with verbs*) *leave –*, leer *or* unbeschrieben lassen; *leave a line –*, eine Zeile frei lassen; *look –*, verblüfft aussehen; *his mind went –*, er verlor sein Gedächtnis. 2. *s.* die Platzpatrone; der Vordruck, unbeschriebenes Blatt; das Blindmaterial (*Typ.*), die Münzplatte (*Mint.*); der Rohling, das Werkstück (*Manuf.*); die Niete (*lottery*); Lücke; *his mind became a –*, er hat sein Gedächtnis verloren; *in –*, in Blanko; *drawn in –*, unausgefüllt; *draw a –*, eine Niete ziehen; (*coll.*) *what the* (*–ety*) *– . . . ?* was zum Teufel . . .? **-ness,** *s.* die Öde, Leere; Verwirrung.

blanket [ˈblænkɪt], 1. *s.* die Wolldecke, Bettdecke, Schlafdecke; (*fig.*) *wet –*, der Dämpfer, kalte Dusche; der Miesmacher, Spaß- *or* Spielverderber; *saddle –*, die Satteldecke, der Woilach. 2. *v.a.* verdecken, unterdrücken, verheimlichen; den Wind abfangen (*Dat.*) (*Naut.*); der Sicht entziehen, verschleiern. 3. *attr. adj.* Gesamt-, alles umfassend. **-ing,** *s.* das Wollzeug zu Bettdecken.

blare [blɛə], 1. *v.n.* schmettern; – *forth*, ausschmettern. 2. *s.* das Geschmetter.

blarney [ˈblɑːnɪ], *s.* (*coll.*) grobe Schmeichelei, die Flunkerei (*Irish*).

blasé, [ˈblɑːzeɪ], *adj.* blasiert.

blasphem-e [blæsˈfiːm], *v.a.* & *n.* lästern; *-e against*, fluchen. **-er,** *s.* der Gotteslästerer. **-ous** [ˈblæsfɪməs], *adj.* lästernd, lästerlich. **-y** [ˈblæsfəmɪ], *s.* die (Gottes)Lästerung.

blast [blɑːst], 1. *s.* der Windstoß, Sturm; Schall, Stoß, das Geschmetter (*of trumpets*); die Sprengladung, Explosion, Druckwelle; der Meltau, Brand (*Bot.*); Pesthauch; das Gebläse (*Metall.*); *muzzle –*, der Mündungsknall; (*coll.*) *in full –*, in vollem Betrieb *or* Schwung, mit Volldampf, im Gange, in Tätigkeit. 2. *v.a.* sprengen; versengen, vernichten, verderben; verdammen, verfluchen; erblasen (*metals*); – *a p.'s reputation*, einen um seinen guten Namen bringen. (*vulg.*) **-ed,** *adj.* verdammt; *-ed hopes*, vereitelte Hoffnungen; *-ed corn*, verbranntes Getreide. **--furnace,** *s.* der Hochofen. **--hole,** *s.* das Bohrloch, Sprengloch. **-ing,** *s.* das Sprengen; die Sprengung; Vernichtung, das Verderben; *-ing-cartridge* or *-charge*, die Bohrpatrone, Bohrladung, Sprengladung, der Sprengkörper (*Min.*). **-ing-powder,** *s.* das Sprengpulver. **--pipe,** *s.* das Dampfrohr.

blastoderm [ˈblɑːstədəːm], *s.* die Keimhaut.

blatan-cy, *s.* anmaßendes Benehmen. **-t** [ˈbleɪtənt], *adj.* blökend, plärrend; lärmend, dreist.

[1]**blaz-e** [bleɪz], 1. *s.* der Schein, Glanz (*of light*); die Flamme, das Feuer, der Brand, die Glut; das Auflodern, (*poet.*) die Lohe; *-e of colour*, das Farbenmeer; *it went up in a -e*, es ging in Flammen auf; (*sl.*) *go to -es*, zum Teufel gehen; *what the -es?* was zum Teufel? *like -es*, Gott weiß wie; (*sl.*) *run like -es*, laufen was das Zeug hält. 2. *v.n.* aufflammen, lodern, leuchten, glänzen; *the fire was -ing away*, das Feuer brannte lichterloh; (*coll.*) *-e away at*, drauflos schießen, (*fig.*) herangehen an.

[2]**blaze,** 1. *s.* die Blesse (*on a horse's forehead*); Wegmarkierung, der Einschnitt (*on a tree*). 2. *v.a.* markieren, anschalmen (*a tree*); – *the trail*, den Weg bahnen, (*fig.*) Pionierarbeit leisten, Bahn brechen.

blazer [ˈbleɪzə], *s.* bunte Sportjacke.

blazon [ˈbleɪzn], 1. *s.* die Wappenkunde; das Wappen(schild), Panier; (*fig.*) die Verkündigung. 2. *v.a.* beschreiben (*Her.*); heraldisch verzieren *or* schmücken; (*fig.*) verkünden; – *abroad* or *forth*, verherrlichen, ausposaunen; *-ed windows*, wappengeschmückte Fenster. **-ment,** *s.* die Verkündigung; Ausschmückung. **-ry,** *s.* die Wappenkunde; heraldische Kunst; (*fig.*) pomphafte Hervorhebung.

bleach [bliːtʃ], 1. *v.a.* & *n.* bleichen. 2. *s.* das Bleichmittel, der Chlorkalk. **-er,** *s.* der Bleicher; (*pl.*) unbedeckte Zuschauersitze (*Amer.*). **-ing,** 1. *adj.* bleichend. 2. *s.* das Bleichen, die Bleiche. **-ing-agent,** das Bleichmittel. **-ing-powder,** *s.* das Bleichpulver; der Chlorkalk.

[1]**bleak** [bliːk], *adj.* öde, kahl, rauh, ungeschützt; trübe, unfreundlich, freudlos. **-ness,** *s.* die Öde, Kahlheit, Ungeschütztheit, Rauheit, Kälte; Unfreundlichkeit.

[2]**bleak,** *s.* der Ukelei, die Albe (*Icht.*).

blear-(y) [ˈblɪə(rɪ)], *adj.* trüb(e), umnebelt; **--eyed** [ˈblɪəraɪd], *adj.* triefäugig.

bleat [bliːt], 1. *v.n.* blöken. 2. *s.*; **-ing,** *s.* das Blöken.

bleb [blɛb], *s.* kleine Blase, das Bläschen; die Pustel.

bled [blɛd], *see* **bleed.**

bleed [bliːd], 1. *ir.v.n.* bluten; – *to death*, sich verbluten; *my heart -s for you*, mir blutet das Herz um dich. 2. *ir.v.a.* bluten lassen, zur Ader lassen; abzapfen (*sap*); ausfließen lassen (*liquid*); (*fig. coll.*) schröpfen, rupfen; – *a p. white*, einen um sein Letztes bringen. **-er,** *s.* der Bluter (*Path.*). **-ing,** 1. *adj.* blutend; (*vulg.*) verflucht. 2. *s.* die Blutung; das Bluten; der Aderlaß (*Surg.*); das Abzapfen (*of trees*); *-ing at* or *from the nose*, das Nasenbluten.

blemish [ˈblɛmɪʃ], 1. *s.* der Makel, Flecken; Fehler, Mangel, das Gebrechen; (*fig.*) der Schandfleck. 2. *v.a.* verunstalten, entstellen; schänden, brandmarken; verleumden (*Law*).

blench [blɛntʃ], *v.n.* zurückschrecken, zurückfahren, zurückbeben, zurückweichen, stutzen.

blend [blɛnd], 1. *v.a.* (ver)mischen, (ver)mengen, melieren, verschneiden (*wine*). 2. *v.n.* ineinander übergehen, sich verbinden, sich vermischen. 3. *s.* die Mischung, das Gemisch, der Verschnitt (*of wine*).

blende [blɛnd], *s.* die Blende, Zinkblende (*Min.*).

blennorrhoea [blɛnəˈrɪə], *s.* der Schleimfluß (*Med.*).

bless [blɛs], *v.a.* segnen, weihen; beglücken, glücklich machen; preisen, loben, verherrlichen; – *me!*, – *my soul!* verflixt! du meine Güte! *I haven't a penny to – myself with*, ich habe nicht einen roten Heller. **-ed** [*as pred.* blɛst; *as attr.* ˈblɛsɪd], *adj.* glücklich, selig; gesegnet; (*coll.*) verwünscht, verflixt; *-ed Virgin*, Jungfrau Maria; *of -ed memory*, seligen Angedenkens; (*coll.*) *be -ed with*, beglückt sein mit. **-edness,** [-ɪdnəs], *s.* die Glückseligkeit, das Glück, der Segen; die Seligkeit, das Heil; *single-edness*, die Unvermähltheit, lediger Stand. **-ing,** *s.* der Segen, die Segnung; Wohltat, Gnade; das Glück; *by the -ing of God*, durch Gottes Segen *or* Huld; *ask a -ing*, das Tischgebet sprechen; (*coll.*) *that's a -ing!* das ist ein Glück! *-ing in disguise*, das Glück im Unglück.

blest [blɛst], (*poet.*) *adj.* glücklich, selig.

blether [ˈblɛðə], 1. *s.* das Geschwätz, Gequassel. 2. *v.n.* Unsinn schwatzen.

blew [bluː], *see* **blow.**

blight [blaɪt], 1. *s.* der Meltau, Brand; (*fig.*) Gifthauch, Dunst; (*coll.*) schädlicher Einfluß. 2. *v.a.* durch Meltau verderben; am Gedeihen hindern; (*fig.*) vernichten, vereiteln; *-ed hopes*, im Keime erstickte Hoffnungen. (*sl.*) **-er,** *s.* der Nichtsnutz, Schuft, Lump.

Blighty [ˈblaɪtɪ], *s.* (*sl.*) die Heimat (*England*); *a – wound*, der Heimatschuß.

blimey [ˈblaɪmɪ], *interj.* (*vulg.*) potztausend!

blimp [blɪmp], *s.* kleines unstarres Luftschiff.

blind [blaɪnd], 1. *adj.* blind; unbesonnen, verständnislos; verborgen, unsichtbar; – *drunk*, besoffen; *stone-–*, stockblind; *strike –*, blenden; (*a*) (*with nouns*) – *alley*, die Sackgasse; (*fig.*) totes Gleis; *–-alley occupation*, der Beruf ohne Aussichten; – *coal*, der Anthrazit; – *corner*, unübersichtliche Straßenecke; *turn a – eye to a th.*, tun als ob man etwas nicht sieht, etwas absichtlich übersehen; – *flying*, der Blindflug, das Blindfliegen; – *-flying instrument*, das Blindfluggerät; *in a – fury*, in blinder Wut; – *letter*, der Brief mit mangelhafter Anschrift; – *man*, Blinde(r), *m.*; – *-man's-buff*, die Blindekuh; – *-man's holiday*, das Zwielicht, die Dämmerung; – *shell*, der Blindgänger (*Artil.*); *a p.'s – side*, jemandes schwache Seite; – *wall*, blinde Mauer; (*b*) (*with prepositions*) – *of one eye*, auf einem Auge blind; – *to one's own failings*, gegen die eigenen Fehler blind; – *with rage*, blind vor Wut. 2. *s.* die Blende, der Schirm; Vorhang, die Jalousie, das Rouleau (*at a window*); die Scheuklappe (*of harness*); (*fig.*) der Vorwand, die Bemäntelung; *Venetian* –, die Jalousie. 3. *v.a.* blind machen, blenden; verblenden, täuschen (*to*, gegen) (*also v.r.*). 4. *v.n.* (*sl.*) unvorsichtig fahren. **-fold,** 1. *adj. & adv.* mit verbundenen Augen; (*fig.*) blind. 2. *v.a.* die Augen verbinden (*a p.*, einem); (ver)blenden. **-ly,** *adv.* blind, (*fig.*) blindlings, unbesonnen, ins Blaue hinein. **-ness,** *s.* die Blindheit (*also fig.*) (*to*, gegen). **--tooling,** *s.* die Blindpressung (*Bookb.*). **--worm,** *s.* die Blindschleiche.

blink [blɪŋk], 1. *s.* das Blinzeln; der Schimmer, das Blinken. 2. *v.a.* absichtlich übersehen, nicht sehen wollen; – *the facts*, die Wahrheit ignorieren. 3. *v.n.* blinken, blinzeln, mit den Wimpern zucken; schimmern (*of light*). **-er,** *s.* die Klappe, Scheuklappe; *-er apparatus*, das Blinkgerät. **-ing,** *adj.* (*vulg.*) verflixt.

bliss [blɪs], *s.* die Seligkeit, Wonne. **-ful,** *adj.* (glück)selig, wonnig, wonnevoll. **-fulness,** *s.* die Glückseligkeit, Wonne.

blister [ˈblɪstə], 1. *s.* die Blase, Hautblase; Pustel; das Zugmittel, Blasenpflaster (*Med.*); Schwalbennest (*on aircraft*). 2. *v.a.* Blasen ziehen (auf (*Dat.*)); Zugpflaster auflegen (*Dat.*); 3. *v.n.* Blasen bekommen. **-ed** [-d], *adj.* voller Blasen, blasig. **--steel,** *s.* der Blasenstahl, Zementstahl.

blithe [blaɪð], *adj.* (*poet.*) munter, froh, fröhlich, lustig heiter, vergnügt, wohlgemut. **-ness,** *s.* die Fröhlichkeit, Munterkeit. **-some** [-səm], *adj. see* **-.**

blizzard [ˈblɪzəd], *s.* der Schneesturm, das Schneegestöber.

bloat [bloʊt], *v.n.* aufblasen, aufschwellen; – *herrings*, Heringe räuchern. **-ed,** *adj.* aufgedunsen, aufgeschwollen, aufgeblasen. **-er,** *s.* geräucherter Hering, der Bück(l)ing.

blob [blɔb], *s.* das Klümpchen, der Tropfen, Klecks.

block [blɔk], 1. *s.* der Block, Klotz; die Flasche, Rolle (*Mach.*, *Naut.*); der Häuserblock; die Hutform, der Hutstock; Farbstein, Bildstock (*Typ.*); das Lochholz (*Shoem.*); der Richtblock (*of the executioner*); Perückenstock (*of wigmakers*); die Blockstrecke (*Railw.*); (*fig.*) Sperre, das Hindernis; die Stockung, Lahmlegung (*Parl.*); (*fig.*) der Tölpel, Klotz, Dummkopf; – *and tackle*, der Flaschenzug; *a chip of the old* –, ganz der Vater; – *of houses*, der Häuserblock; – *of marble*, der Marmorblock; *pulley* –, der Flaschenzug; *put on the* –, (auf dem Stock) formen; *road* –, die Straßensperre; *traffic* –, die Verkehrsstockung. 2. *v.a.* (– *up*) (ver)sperren; einschließen, blockieren; blocken, aufhalten (*Railw.*); verschleppen, hemmen, hindern, hinausschieben (*a bill*) (*Parl.*); stoppen (*a ball*) (*Crick.*); aus freier Hand bedrucken (*Typ.*); *be no longer -ed*, entblockt sein (*of a railway line*); – *in* or *out*, entwerfen, skizzieren; – *a hat*, einen Hut pressen *or* formen; **-ade** [blɔˈkeɪd], 1. *s.* die Blockade, Sperre; *run the -ade*, die Blockade brechen. 2. *v.a.* blockieren, sperren; *-aded area*, das Sperrgebiet. **-ade-runner,** *s.* der Blockadebrecher. (*sl.*) **--buster,** *s.* die Bezirksbombe. **– calendar,** *s.* der Abreißkalender. **-head,** *s.* der Dummkopf. **-headed,** *adj.* dumm. **-house,** *s.* das Blockhaus (*Fort.*). **--letters,** *pl.* große Druckschrift. **--making,** das Klischieren (*Typ.*). **--printing,** *s.* der Holzdruck; Handdruck. **--trail,** *s.* der Lafettenschwanz (*Artil.*).

bloke [bloʊk], *s.* (*sl.*) der Bursche, Kerl, Geselle.

blond-e [blɔnd], *s.* die Blondine. **-(e),** *adj.* blond, hell. **-e-lace,** *s.* die Blonde, geklöppelte Spitze.

blood [blʌd], 1. *s.* das Blut; die Abstammung, Herkunft, Rasse, das Geblüt; die Blutsverwandtschaft; das Leben; der Saft; (*a*) (*with nouns*) *loss of* –, der Blutverlust; *princes of the* –, Prinzen von königlichem Geblüt; – *and thunder*, 1. *s.* Mord und Totschlag; 2. *attr. adj.* Mord–, Schauer–, sensationell; (*b*) (*with adjectives*) *blue* –, edles Blut, adeliges Blut; *in cold* –, mit kaltem Blute; *fresh* –, neues Blut (*in a family*); *full* –, das Vollblut(pferd); *half*-–, das Halbblut(pferd); halbbürtige Geschwister (*of persons*); *in hot* –, im Zorn; *next of* –, am nächsten verwandt; (*coll.*) *young* –, junges Blut, der Hitzkopf, Geck, Draufgänger; (*c*) (*with verbs*) *his – is up*, sein Blut ist in Wallung; (*prov.*) – *is thicker than water*, Blut ist dicker als Wasser; *breed bad* –, böses Blut machen; *get – from a stone*, Geld vom Geizigen bekommen; *let*–, zur Ader lassen; *make his – run cold*, sein Blut gerinnen machen; *it runs in the* –, es steckt im Blute ; *spill* –, Blut vergießen. 2. *v.a.* an Blut gewöhnen (*a dog*). **--brother,** *s.* leiblicher Bruder; (*fig.*) der Blutsbruder. **--corpuscle,** *s.* das Blutkörperchen. **– count,** *s.* die Blutkörperchenzählung. **--curdling,** *adj.* haarsträubend, grausig. **--donor,** *s.* der Blutspender. **--feud,** *s.* die Blutfehde. **--guilt(iness),** *s.* die Blutschuld. **--guilty,** *adj.* mit Blutschuld beladen. **--heat,** *s.* die Blutwärme, Körperwärme. **-hound,** *s.* der Blut– *or* Schweißhund; (*fig.*) Verfolger. **-less,** *adj.* blutlos, blutleer; unblutig; farblos, leblos. **-letting,** *s.* der Aderlaß. **--money,** *s.* das Blutgeld, Sühnegeld. **--orange,** *s.* die Blutapfelsine. **--poisoning,** *s.* die Blutvergiftung. **--pressure,** *s.* der Blutdruck. **--red,** *adj.* blutrot. **--relation,** *s.* der (die) Blutsverwandte. **--relationship,** *s.* die Blutsverwandtschaft. **-shed,** *s.* das Blutvergießen. **-shot,** *adj.* blutunterlaufen. **--stain,** *s.* der Blutfleck. **-stained,** *adj.* blutbefleckt. **--stock** *s.* das Vollblut(pferd). **-stone,** *s.* der Blutstein, Roteisenstein. **-sucker,** *s.* der Blutigel; (*fig.*) Blutsauger. **--test,** die Blutprobe. **-thirstiness,** *s.* der Blutdurst, die Blutgier. **-thirsty,** blutdürstig, blutrünstig. **--transfusion,** *s.* die Blutübertragung. **--vessel,** *s.* das Blutgefäß. **-y,** *adj.* blutig; blutrot, blutbefleckt; grausam, blutdürstig; (*vulg.*) sehr, verdammt, verflucht; *-y flux*, der Blutfluß; *-y sweat*, blutiger Schweiß; *-y tyrant*, blutrünstiger Tyrann. **-y-minded,** *adj.* blutgierig, mordsüchtig; (*fig. vulg.*) widerborstig, trotzig. **--wort,** *s.* der Hainampfer (*Bot.*).

[1]**bloom** [blu:m], 1. *s.* die Blüte, Blume; der Flor, die Jugendfrische, Jugendblüte; Blütenpracht, Fülle; der Flaum, Hauch (*on peaches, etc.*); *in* (*full*) –, in Blüte, blühend; – *of youth*, die Jugendblüte; *take the – off s.th.*, etwas der Frische, des Glanzes *or* des Zaubers berauben. 2. *v.n.* blühen (*also fig.*). **-ing,** *adj.* blühend, blütenreich; (*sl.*) verflixt.

[2]**bloom,** *s.* die Luppe (*Metall.*). **-ery** [ˈblu:mərɪ], *s.* das Frischfeuer (*Metall.*).

bloomer [ˈblu:mə], *s.* (*sl.*) der Schnitzer, Bock. **-s,** *pl.* (*archaic*) die Schlupfhose.

blossom [ˈblɔsəm], 1. *s.* die Blüte. 2. *v.n.* blühen, Blüten treiben; – *out into*, sich entwickeln zu.

blot [blɔt], 1. *v.a.* beflecken, beklecksen; ablöschen; – *out*, (*fig.*) tilgen, löschen, vernichten. 2. *s.* der Fleck, Klecks, Tintenfleck; (*sl.*) die Sau; (*fig.*) der Makel, Schandfleck; *make a* –, einen Klecks machen; *a – on his character*, ein Makel seines Charakters; *a – on the landscape*, Verunstaltung der Landschaft. **-ter,** *s.* der Tintenlöscher; das Löschpapier, Fließpapier. **-ting-pad,** *s.* die Schreibunterlage. **-ting-paper,** *s.* das Löschpapier.

blotch [blɔtʃ], *s.* die Pustel, der Hautfleck; der Klecks. **-y,** *adj.* fleckig, gefleckt.

blotto [ˈblɔtoʊ], *adj.* (*sl.*) betrunken.

blouse [blaʊz], *s.* die Bluse.

[1]**blow** [bloʊ], *s.* der Schlag, Streich, Hieb, Stoß; das Unglück; *come to* or *exchange -s*, handgemein werden; *without striking a* –, ohne Mühe, ohne Kampf; *strike a – for*, sich einsetzen für; *strike a – against*, sich (einer S.) entgegenstellen; *at a single* or *one* –, auf einmal.

[2]**blow,** 1. *v.n.* (*poet.*) blühen; (*fig.*) erblühen, sich entfalten. 2. *s.* (*poet.*) die Blüte.

[3]**blow,** 1. *ir.v.n.* blasen, wehen (*as wind*); keuchen, schnaufen (*of persons*); (er)schallen, ertönen (*of

trumpets); durchbrennen (*of a fuse*) (*Elec.*); *it is –ing*, es ist windig; *he knows which way the wind –s*, er weiß wie der Hase läuft; – *hot and cold*, unbeständig sein; bald so bald anders sein, sich in einem Atem widersprechen; (*sl.*) *I'm –ed if I will!* zum Teufel wenn ich's täte! (*sl.*) – *in*, eintreffen, hereingeschneit kommen; – *out*, ausgehen, (v)erlöschen (*of light, etc.*); (*coll.*) – *over*, vorüberziehen, vorübergehen, verfliegen; (*fig.*) sich legen; – *up*, in die Luft fliegen, explodieren; sich erheben (*of wind*); – *upon*, herabsetzen, bloßstellen, verunglimpfen. 2. *ir.v.a.* blasen; wehen, treiben; anblasen, anfachen (*the fire, etc.*); aufblasen, aufblähen (*also fig.*); – *the bellows*, die Bälge treten; – *an egg*, ein Ei ausblasen; (*sl.*) – *the gaff*, das Spiel verraten; – *a person a kiss*, einem einen Handkuß zuwerfen; – *one's nose*, sich die Nase putzen, sich schneuzen; – *the tanks*, anblasen (*submarine*); – *one's own trumpet*, sich selbst loben, prahlen; – *away*, wegblasen; – *down*, umwehen, umblasen; – *in*, eintreiben (*a window*); (*sl.*) vergeuden (*money*); – *off steam*, Dampf ablassen; (*fig.*) Zorn verrauchen lassen, Energie loswerden; abreagieren; – *out*, ausblasen, auslöschen (*light*); – *one's brains out*, sich erschießen, sich (*Dat.*) eine Kugel durch den Kopf jagen; – *one's cheeks out*, – *out one's cheeks*, seine Wangen aufblasen; – *up*, aufblasen; anblasen; (in die Luft) sprengen, explodieren; aufwirbeln (*dust*); (*coll.*) – *a p. up*, einem einen Krach machen, einen heruntermachen *or* tüchtig ausschelten. 3. *s.* der Luftzug. **–er,** *s.* der Bläser; Glasbläser, Schmelzer; das Schiebeblech (*of a furnace*); das Gebläse; *organ-–er*, der Bälgetreter. **–fly,** *s.* die Schmeißfliege. **–-hole,** *s.* das Luftloch, Zugloch; Atemloch (*of a whale*). **–lamp,** *s.* die Gebläselampe. **–-off,** *attrib.*; *–-off cock*, der Ablaßhahn; *–-off pipe*, das Ablaßrohr. **–-out,** *s.* (*sl.*) das Durchbrennen (*of a fuse*); (*sl.*) Platzen (*of a tire*), die Panne; (*sl.*) das Gelage, reiches Essen. **–pipe,** das Blasrohr; Lötrohr; die Pfeife (*of glass-blowers*); **–pipe flame,** *s.* die Stichflamme. **–-torch,** *s.* (*Amer.*) das Lötrohr. **–y,** *adj.* (*coll.*) windig, luftig.

blowzy [ˈblɑuzɪ], *adj.* pausbäckig, hochrot; zerzaust, nachlässig, unordentlich, schlampig.

blubber [blʌbə], 1. *s.* der (Braun)Tran, Walfischspeck; – *cheeks*, dicke *or* aufgeschwollene Backen. 2. *v.n.* (*coll.*) flennen, plärren, heulen, weinen.

bludgeon [ˈblʌdʒən], 1. *s.* der Knüttel, Knüppel, die Keule. 2. *v.a.* niederknüppeln.

blue [bluː], 1. *adj.* blau; (*coll.*) ängstlich, mutlos; (*coll.*) niedergeschlagen, schwermütig; (*coll.*) unanständig, obszön; *–-black*, dunkelblau; – *blood*, adliges Blut; – *devils*, (*coll.*) Spukgestalten (*of the drunkard*) *feel* –, in gedrückter Stimmung sein; (*coll.*) – *funk*, die Mordsangst; *be in a – funk*, einen Bammel, Dampf *or* (*vulg.*) Schiß haben; *look* –, ängstlich aussehen; *once in a – moon*, höchst selten; – *Peter*, die Abfahrtssignalflagge (*Naut.*); – *pill*, die Quecksilberpille; – *ribbon*, der Hosenbandorden, (*fig.*) höchste Auszeichnung, Blaues Band; *true* –, treu, unwandelbar. 2. *s.* das Blau; Waschblau, die Bläue (*Laundry*); blauer Himmel; offenes Meer; die Mitgliedschaft der ersten Mannschaft (*school or university*); das Mitglied der ersten Mannschaft; *bolt from the* –, der Blitz aus heiterm Himmel; *dark* –, die Oxforder Farbe; *light* –, die Cambridger Farbe; *fire into the* –, drauflosknallen; *navy* –, das Marineblau; *Prussian* –, das Berlinerblau; *rowing* –, das Mitglied der ersten Rudermannschaft (*of school or university*); *get one's* –, als Mitglied der ersten Mannschaft erwählt werden; *true* –, der Konservative; *the –s*, die englischen königlichen Gardereiter; (*coll.*) der Trübsinn, die Melancholie; *have a fit of the –s*, in gedrückter Stimmung sein. 3. *v.a.* blau färben, bläuen, anbläuen; (*sl.*) vergeuden, verschleudern. **–beard,** *s.* Ritter Blaubart. **–bell,** *s.* blaue Hyazinthe (*England*), die Glockenblume (*Scotland*). **– book,** *s.* das Blaubuch, staatliche Veröffentlichung (*in Germany usually* das Weißbuch, *in France* das Gelbbuch). **–berry,** *s.* die Blaubeere (*Amer. Bot.*). **–bottle,** *s.* die Schmeißfliege (*Ent.*); Kornblume (*Bot.*). **–-coat boy,** der Schüler von Christ's Hospital; **–-coat school,** Christ's Hospital. **–-eyed,** *adj.* blauäugig. **–-grass,** *s.* (*Amer.*) das Riedgras. (*coll.*) **–jacket,** *s.* die Blaujacke, der Matrose. (*Amer.*) **– law,** *s.* strenges Sittengesetz. **–ness,** *s.* die Bläue. **–-pencil,** *s.* (*coll.*) die Zensur, das Zensuramt. **–print,** *s.* die Blaupause, der Blaudruck; (*fig.*) Plan, Vorschlag. **–-stocking,** *s.* der Blaustrumpf. **–stone, –-vitriol,** *s.* das Kupfervitriol. **–-tit,** *s.* die Blaumeise (*Orn.*).

[1]**bluff** [blʌf], 1. *adj.* plump, derb, grob, freimütig (*of manner*); breit, offen, steil, schroff (*coast*); breit (*Naut.*). 2. *s.* steiles Felsenufer. **–ness,** *s.* die Freimütigkeit, Plumpheit, Geradheit (*of manner*).

[2]**bluff,** 1. *s.* der Bluff, Einschüchterungsversuch, die Spiegelfechterei, Irreführung, Täuschung, der Schreckschuß; *call a p.'s* –, jemanden zwingen Farbe zu bekennen. 2. *v.n.* & *a.* bluffen, einschüchtern, täuschen, irreführen. **–er,** *s.* der Bluffer.

bluish [ˈbluːɪʃ], *adj.* bläulich.

blunder [ˈblʌndə], 1 *s.* der Schnitzer, Fehler, Mißgriff. 2. *v.a.* & *n.* einen Schnitzer machen einen Bock schießen; (*coll.*) vermasseln, verkorksen, verpfuschen; straucheln, stolpern; – *about*, umhertappen; – *along*, blindlings weitergehen; immer weiter Fehler machen; – *out*, herausplatzen (mit etwas); – *upon*, durch Zufall treffen auf. **–er,** *s.* der Tölpel. **–ing,** *adj.* ungeschickt, taktlos.

blunderbuss [ˈblʌndəbʌs], *s.* die Donnerbüchse.

blunt [blʌnt], 1. *adj.* stumpf; plump, grob, barsch, derb, unverblümt, unbeholfen, ungeschliffen; unempfindlich; *grow* –, sich abstumpfen; *be – with a p.*, einem offen heraus sagen. 2. *v.a.* stumpf machen, abstumpfen (*also fig.*). 3. *s.* (*sl.*) das Geld. **–-edged,** *adj.* stumpf. **–ness,** *s.* die Stumpfheit; Plumpheit, Derbheit, Offenheit. **–-witted,** *adj.* stumpfsinnig, schwer von Begriffen.

blur [bləː], 1. *s.* der Fleck; Schleier, die Unklarheit, Verschwommenheit; (*fig*) der Makel. 2. *v.a.* beflecken; trüben, verwischen; auslöschen. **–red,** *adj.* verschwommen, verwischt.

blurb [blə.b], *s.* (*sl.*) die Reklame; der Reklamestreifen, Waschzettel (*of a book*).

blurt [bləːt], *v.a.*; – *out*, unbesonnen heraussagen, (mit einer Sache) herausplatzen.

blush [blʌʃ], 1. *s.* das Erröten; die Schamröte; (*fig.*) rosiger Glanz; *put s.o. to the* –, einen schamrot machen *or* beschämen; *at the first* –, auf den ersten Blick. 2. *v.n.* erröten (*at*, über (*Acc.*)), rot werden; (*fig.*) sich schämen. **–ing,** 1. *pr.p.* & *adj.* errötend. 2. *s.* das Erröten. **–-rose,** *s.* blaßrote Rose.

bluster [ˈblʌstə], 1. *s.* das Brausen, Toben; Getöse, der Lärm, die Prahlerei. 2. *v.n.* brausen, tosen; lärmen, toben, drohen; prahlen, aufbegehren, den Mund voll nehmen. **–er** [–rə], *s.* der Prahlhans, das Großmaul. **–ing,** *adj.* tobend, stürmisch; drohend, prahlend.

bo [bou], 1. *int.* buh! huh! *he cannot say – to a goose*, er kann den Mund nicht auftun. 2. **–-peep,** *s.* **das Guckguckspiel.**

boa [ˈbouə], *s.* die Riesenschlange; Boa (*lady's fur*). **–-constrictor,** *s.* die Königs– *or* Abgottschlange.

boar [bɔː], *s.* der Eber, Keiler; *wild* –, das Wildschwein; *young wild* –, der Frischling; *–'s head*, der Schweinskopf. **–-spear,** *s.* der Sauspieß.

board [bɔːd], 1. *s.* das Brett, die Diele; der Tisch, die Tafel; der Bord (*Naut.*); die Pappe, der Pappdeckel, Karton (*Bookb.*); (*fig.*) die Kost, der Unterhalt, die Beköstigung, Pension; der Ausschuß, das Kollegium, die Körperschaft, Behörde; der Rat, das Amt; *–s*, der Pappband (*Bookb.*); *the –s*, die Bühne, die Bretter (*pl.*) (*Theat.*); *above* –, offen, ehrlich, einwandfrei; *accommodation and* –, Verpflegung und Unterkunft; *bed and* –, Tisch und Bett; *bound in –s*, kartoniert (*Bookb.*); *chess* –, das Spielbrett; – *of control*, die Aufsichtsbehörde; – *of directors*, der Aufsichtsrat, Verwaltungsrat, das Direktorium; *diving-–*, das Sprungbrett; *drawing* –, das Reißbrett; *duck-–*, das Laufbrett; – *of examiners*, die Prüfungskommission; *floor* –, das Fußbodenbrett; *free* –, freie Kost; *go by the* –, über Bord gehen; fehlschlagen, scheitern; – *and lodging*, freie Station, Kost und Logis; *medical* –, die Sanitätskommission; *on* –, an Bord (*Naut.*); *free on* –, frachtfrei bis an Bord (*C.L.*); *on the –s*, am Theater; *plotting* –, der Meßtisch; – *of Revenue*, die Finanzkammer; *statutory* –, gesetzlich genehmigte Körperschaft; *–s of study*, die Fakultätsausschüsse; – *of Trade*, das Handelsministerium; – *of Trade unit*, die Kilowattstunde; *put to* –, in Kost geben; – *of trustees*, der Treuhänderausschuß, das Kuratorium. 2. *v.a.* täfeln, dielen, verschalen; entern (*Naut.*); an Bord gehen, (ein)steigen in, besteigen; in Kost nehmen, beköstigen; (*coll.*) vor einem Ausschuß prüfen (*a p.*); – *out*, in Kost geben; – *up*, mit Brettern verschlagen, mit Pappdeckel vermachen *or* vernageln (*a window, etc.*). 3. *v.n.* in Kost sein; einschiffen, einsteigen; – *out*, auswärts essen. **–er,** *s.* der Kostgänger, Pensionär; Internatsschüler. **–ing,** *s.* die Holzverschalung, Bretterverkleidung, Täfelung; der Verschlag; die Beköstigung, Verpflegung; das Entern, die Enterung (*Naut.*). **–ing-house,** *s.* die Pension. **–ing-party,** *s.* die Entermannschaft (*Naut.*). **–ing-pike,** *s.* die Enterpike. **–ing-school,** *s.* das Internat, Pensionat, die Heimschule. **--meeting,** *s.* die Vorstandssitzung. **--room,** *s.* das Sitzungszimmer. **--school,** *s.* (*archaic*) die Volksschule. **--wages,** *pl.* das Kostgeld.

boast [boust], 1. *v.n.* sich rühmen (*of, about* (*Gen.*)), prahlen, großsprechen, großtun mit. 2. *v.a.* sich rühmen (*Gen.*); *that is all he can* –, das ist alles, dessen er sich rühmen kann. 3. *s.* die Prahlerei, das Großtun; der Stolz; (*prov.*) *great –, small roast*, viel Geschrei und wenig Wolle; *make great – of*, sich etwas einbilden auf. **–er,** *s.* der Prahler, Prahlhans, Wichtigtuer, Großsprecher. **–ful,** *adj.* prahlerisch, großsprecherisch, ruhmredig. **–fulness,** *s.* die Prahlsucht, Ruhmredigkeit.

boat [bout], 1. *s.* das Boot, der Kahn, Nachen; das Schiff, der Dampfer; *be in the same* –, in der gleichen (schlechten) Lage sein; *burn one's –s*, alle Brücken hinter sich abbrechen; *sauce*-–, die Sauciere. 2. *v.n.* in einem Boote fahren, rudern, segeln. **--building,** *s.* der Bootsbau. (*coll.*) **–er,** *s.* steifer Strohhut. **--hook,** *s.* der Bootshaken. **–ing,** *s.* das Bootfahren, die Bootfahrt; *go –ing*, rudern, segeln, *etc.* gehen; *–ing excursion*, die Bootfahrt, Wasserfahrt. **–man,** *s.* der Jollenführer. **--race,** *s.* das Wettrudern, der Ruderwettkampf. **--shaped,** *adj.* kahnförmig, nachenförmig. **–swain** ['bəsn], *s.* der Hochbootsmann; *–swain's mate*, der Bootsmannsmaat. **--train,** *s.* der Sonderzug mit Dampferlinieverbindung.

bob [bɔb], 1. *s.* die Quaste, das Gehänge; der Haarknoten; Knicks; Stoß, Ruck; das Gewicht, die Linse (*Horol.*), das Senkblei (*on plumb-line*); der Bubikopf; (*sl.*) Schilling. 2. *v.n.* baumeln, springen; einen Knicks machen; – *about*, umherspringen; – – *up*, emporschnellen, (*fig.*) plötzlich auftauchen; – *up and down*, sich auf- und abbewegen. 3. *v.a.* ruckweise bewegen; stutzen (*tail*); kurz schneiden (*hair*); – *a curtsy*, einen Knicks machen; – *one's head up*, plötzlich aufblicken; *have one's hair –bed*, sich die Haare kurz schneiden lassen; *–bed hair*, der Bubikopf. **–bish,** *adj.* (*sl.*) lebhaft, munter.

bobbin ['bɔbɪn], *s.* die Spule, der Klöppel; die Induktionsrolle (*Elec.*). **–et,** *s.* Englischer Tüll. **--frame,** *s.* die Spindelbank, Spulmaschine. **--lace,** *s.* geklöppelte Spitzen (*pl.*).

bobby ['bɔbɪ], *s.* (*sl.*) der Polizist. **--soxer,** *s.* (*Amer. sl.*) der Backfisch.

bob--run ['bɔbrʌn], *s.* die Bobbahn. **–sleigh** [–sleɪ], *s.* der Bob(sleigh), Rennschlitten.

bobtail ['bɔbteɪl], *s.* der Stutzschwanz; *rag, tag and* –, Krethi und Plethi, das Lumpenpack, das Gesindel.

[1]**bode** [boud], *v.a. & n.* vorhersagen, vorbedeuten, ahnen (lassen); – *ill for*, von schlechter Vorbedeutung sein.

[2]**bode,** *see* **bide.**

bodice ['bɔdɪs], *s.* das Leibchen, Schnürleibchen; Mieder, die Taille.

-bodied ['bɔdɪd], *adj. suffix* –leibig, –gestaltet; *able*-–, gesund, stark, handfest; dienstfähig (*of sailors*); *full*- –, voll, stark (*of wine*).

bodi-less ['bɔdɪləs], *adj.* unkörperlich, körperlos. **–ly,** 1. *adj.* Körper–, körperlich. 2. *adv.* persönlich, leiblich; wirklich; gänzlich, als Ganzes; *–ly exercise*, die Leibesübung.

bodkin ['bɔdkɪn], *s.* die Schnürnadel, Haarnadel; der Pfriem (*Bookb.*); die Ahle (*Typ.*).

body ['bɔdɪ], *s.* der Körper, Leib; Rumpf, Hauptteil; Kasten (*of a cart*); die Karosserie (*of a motor-car*); (*coll.*) Person, der Mensch; das Leibchen, Mieder (*Dressm.*); die Leiche, der Leichnam; die Substanz, der Stoff, die Materie; das Wesentliche, der Gehalt; die Masse, Menge, das Ganze, die Gesamtheit; Körperschaft, Gesellschaft; der Körpergehalt; *any*–, irgend einer; *every*–, jedermann, (ein) jeder; *keep – and soul together*, Leib und Seele zusammenhalten; (*Scots*) *what is a – to do?* was soll man tun? (*a*) (*with adjectives*) *advisory* –, der Beirat; *compound* –, die Verbindung (*Chem.*); – *corporate*, die Körperschaft, juristische Person; *heavenly* –, der Himmelskörper; *legislative* –, gesetzgebende Körperschaft; – *politic*, der Staat; *solid* –, fester Körper; (*b*) (*with nouns*) *main – of an army*, das Gros, der Hauptteil des Heeres; *main – of a building*, das Hauptgebäude; – *of a church*, das Schiff; *the – of the clergy*, die gesamte Geistlichkeit; *the – of civil law*, das Corpus Juris; *colour with good* –, Farbe von guter Dichtigkeit; – *of a letter*, der Text eines Briefes; – *of troops*, die Mannschaft, der Truppenkörper; (*c*) (*with prepositions*) *in a* –, zusammen; auf einmal, in Masse. **--belt,** *s.* die Leibbinde, der Leibgurt. **--cloth,** *s.* die Pferdedecke, Schabracke. **--colour,** *s.* die Deckfarbe. **-guard,** *s.* die Leibwache. **--snatcher,** *s.* der Leichenräuber.

bog [bɔg], 1. *s.* der Sumpf, Morast, das Moor; (*usually pl.*) (*vulg.*) der Abort; (*vulg.*) *go to the –s*, austreten. 2. *v.a.* in Schlamm versenken, verschlammen; *be –ged* (*down*), im Schlamme versinken *or* stecken bleiben. **--berry,** *s.* die Moosbeere, Preiselbeere. **–gy,** *adj.* sumpfig. **–land,** *s.* das Marschland. **--oak,** *s.* das Sumpfholz. **--trotter,** *s.* (*coll.*) der Irländer.

bogey ['bougɪ], *s.* die Norm für gute Spieler, guter Durchschnitt (*Golf*); *see also* **bogy.**

boggle ['bɔgl], *v.n.* stutzen, zurückweichen (*at*, vor); unschlüssig sein, zögern, schwanken (*at*, bei).

bogie ['bougɪ], 1. *s.* das Drehgestell; *see also* **--engine.** **--engine,** *s.* der Blockwagen mit Drehgestell (*Railw.*). **--wheel,** *s.* das Rad des Drehgestells.

bogus ['bougəs], *adj.* (*coll.*) falsch, unecht, Schwindel–; – *bank*, die Schwindelbank.

bogy ['bougɪ], *s.* der Kobold, Teufel, das Schreckgespenst; – *man*, der Butzemann, das Gespenst.

Bohemian [bo'hɪ:mɪən], *s.* der Bohemien; leichtlebiger Literat *or* Künstler; *see the Index of Names.*

[1]**boil** [bɔɪl], *s.* der Furunkel, das Blutgeschwür.

[2]**boil,** 1. *s.* das Sieden, Kochen. 2. *v.a. & n.* sieden, kochen; (*fig.*) wallen, brausen; – *away* or *down*, einkochen, verdicken; verdampfen; (*coll.*) *it –s down to this*, es kommt auf folgendes heraus; – *gently*, schwach kochen; – *off*, abkochen, auskochen; – *over*, überkochen, überwallen; – *over with rage*, rasend werden, vor Wut schäumen; – *up*, aufsieden, wallen; *–ed oil*, trocknendes Öl; (*coll.*) *–ed shirt*, steifes Hemd; (*coll*) *hard-–ed*, *adj.* abgebrüht; *bring to the* –, ankochen. **–er,** *s.* der Sieder, Kocher; Kessel, Dampfkessel. **–er-maker,** *s.* der Kesselschmied. **–er scale,** *s.* der Kesselstein. **–ing,** 1. *adj.*; *–ing hot*, siedend heiß; *–ing point*, der Siedepunkt. 2. *s.* das Kochen, Sieden; das (auf einmal) Gekochte; *fast to –ing*, kochfest; (*sl.*) *the whole –ing*, die ganze Sippschaft.

boisterous ['bɔɪstərəs], *adj.* ungestüm, heftig, laut, lärmend, rauh. **–ness,** *s.* das Ungestüm.

boko ['boukou], *s.* (*sl.*) die Nase, Schnauze.

bold [bould], *adj.* kühn, mutig; verwegen, dreist, keck, frech, unverschämt; hervortretend, hervorragend, in die Augen fallend; *as – as brass*, frech, mit einer eisernen Stirn; – *face*, fetter Druck (*Typ.*); *put a – face on s.th.*, sich über etwas kühn hinwegsetzen; – *outline*, deutlicher Umriß; *make* –, sich erkühnen *or* erdreisten, sich (*Dat.*) die Freiheit nehmen; *make so – as to do*, so frei sein zu tun. **--faced,** *adj.* unverschämt; fett (*Typ.*). **–ness,** *s.* die Kühnheit, Verwegenheit; Dreistigkeit, Frechheit, Unverschämtheit.

[1]**bole** [boul], *s.* der Stamm (*of a tree*).

[2]**bole,** *s.* der Bolus, die Siegelerde.
boletus [bo'lɪ:təs], *s.* der Röhrenpilz, Röhrling (*Bot.*).
boll [boʊl], *s.* die Samenkapsel, Schote; runder Knopf.
bollard ['bɔləd], *s.* der Poller, Pfahl.
boloney [bə'lounɪ], *s.* (*sl.*) der Quatsch.
bolster ['boulstə], 1. *s.* das Polster, Kissen, die Unterlage. 2. *v.a.* polstern; (*coll.*) – *up*, unterstützen.
[1]**bolt** [boʊlt], 1. *s.* der Bolzen, Pfeil; die Schraube; der Riegel, Schließhaken, die Sperrklaue; der Verschluß (*of a gun*); die Rolle, das Bündel, das Bund (*of cloth*); – *from the blue*, der Blitz aus heiterm Himmel; (*coll.*) *make a* – (*for*), stürzen (nach), Reißaus nehmen; *screw*– –, der Schraubenbolzen; *shoot the* –, den Riegel vorschieben; (*coll.*) *shoot one's* –, sein Pulver verschießen; – *upright*, kerzengerade. 2. *v.a.* verbolzen, mit Bolzen befestigen; verriegeln, zuriegeln, abriegeln; (*coll.*) hastig hinunterschlingen, hinunterwürgen. 3. *v.n.* durchbrennen, ausreißen, davonstürzen (*of persons*); durchgehen (*of horses*). **–er,** *s.* (*coll.*) der Ausreißer, Durchgänger. **– –head,** *s.* der Bolzenkopf; Destillierkolben (*Chem.*). **– –rope,** *s.* der Liek, Segelsaum.
[2]**bolt,** *v.a.* beuteln, sieben; prüfen, sichten. **–er,** *s.*, **–ing-cloth,** *s.* das Beutelsieb, Siebtuch.
bolus ['bouləs], *s.* große Pille (*Med.*).
bomb [bɔm], 1. *s.* die Bombe; Handgranate. 2. *v.a.* mit Bomben belegen, Bomben abwerfen auf (*Acc.*); **– –aimer,** *s.* der Bombenschütze (*Av.*). **– –disposal squad,** die Sprengtruppe. **– –door,** *s.* die Bombenklappe. **–ed,** *adj.* verbombt; *–ed out*, ausgebombt. **–er** ['bɔmə], *s.* der Bomber, das Bombenflugzeug (*Av.*). **–ing,** *s.* der Bombenabwurf; *–ing run*, der Zielanflug. **–ing up,** *s.* das Laden der Bomben. **– –proof,** *adj.* bombenfest, bombensicher. **– –rack,** *s.* der Bombenträger. (*fig.*) **–shell,** *s.* die Bombe. **– –sight,** *s.* das Bombenzielgerät, Bombenvisier.
bombard [bɔm'bɑ:d], *v.a.* bombardieren, beschießen; (*fig.*) – *with*, bestürmen mit. **–ier** [–bə'dɪə], *s.* der Artillerieunteroffizier, (*Amer.*) Bombenschütze (*Av.*). **–ment,** *s.* die Beschießung.
bombast ['bɔmbæst], *s.* der Wortschwall, Schwulst. **–ic** [–'bæstɪk], *adj.* schwülstig, hochtrabend.
bona fide ['bounə 'faɪdɪ], *adj.* & *adv.* in gutem Glauben, gutgläubig; echt, zuverlässig, ehrlich. **– –s** [– –dɪ:z], *pl.* ehrliche Absichten, die Treuherzigkeit, Geradheit, der Geradsinn.
[1]**bond** [bɔnd], 1. *s.* die Bindung, Verbindung, das Bündnis; die Verschreibung, Schuldverschreibung, der Pfandbrief, die Obligation (*C.L.*); das Abkommen, Übereinkommen, die Bürgschaft (*Law*); der Verband (*Archit.*); der Zollverschluß. **–s,** *pl.* die Fesseln, Bande; – *of friendship*, das Freundschaftsbündnis; *goods in* –, Waren unter Zollverschluß; *take goods out of* –, Waren vom Zollamt abholen. 2. *v.a.* in Zollverschluß legen; verpfänden; verbinden (*masonry*). **– –creditor,** *s.* Obligationsgläubige(r), *m.* **– –debts,** *pl.* Obligationsschulden. **–ed,** *adj.* mit Obligationen belastet; unter Zollverschluß; *–ed debt*, die Obligationsschuld; *–ed goods*, Waren unter Zollverschluß; *–ed warehouse*, das Freilager, der Zollspeicher. **– –holder,** der Obligationsinhaber.
[2]**bond,** *adj.* (*archaic*) leibeigen. **–age,** *s.* die Leibeigenschaft, die Knechtschaft; die Sklaverei, Gefangenschaft, Haft. **–(s)man,** *s.*, **– –servant,** *s.* Leibeigene(r), *m.*
bone [boun], 1. *s.* der Knochen, das Bein; die Gräte (*of fish*); – *of contention*, der Zankapfel; *I have a* – *to pick with you*, ich habe mit Ihnen ein Hühnchen zu pflücken *or* rupfen; (*prov.*) *what is bred in the* –, *will come out in the flesh*, Art läßt nicht von Art; *cut to the* –, bis auf den Knochen schneiden, (*fig.*) auf das alleräußerste herabsetzen (*prices*). 2. *adj.* beinern. 3. *v.a.* die Knochen *or* Gräten entfernen von; Fischbein einsetzen (*in a dress, etc.*); (*sl.*) klauen, stiebitzen. **– black,** das Beinschwarz, die Knochenkohle. **–d,** *suffix* –knochig. **– dry,** knochentrocken. **– –dust,** *s.* das Knochenmehl. **– –earth,** *s.* die Knochenerde. **–head,** *s.* (*sl.*) der Dummkopf. **– –lace,** *s.* geklöppelte Spitze. **–less,** *adj.* knochenlos, (*fig.*) haltlos. **– –manure,** *s.* das Knochenmehl, der Knochendünger. **–s,** *pl.* die Knochen, die Gebeine, (*poet.*) das Gebein; (*coll.*) die Kastagnetten (*Mus.*); (*sl.*) die Würfel; *my poor old –s*, meine armen Knochen; *bag of –s*, der Haufen Knochen, das Gerippe; *feel s.th. in one's –s*, ein ganz sicheres Gefühl haben; (*coll.*) *make no –s about*, keine Umstände machen über, kein Bedenken tragen betreffs, sich (*Dat.*) kein Blatt vor den Mund nehmen. **–setter,** *s.* der Knocheneinrichter. **– –spavin,** *s.* der (Huf)Spat. **–yard,** *s.* (*Amer.*) die Abdeckerei.
bonfire,' ['bɔnfaɪə], *s.* das Freudenfeuer, Feuer.
bonhomie [bɔnə'mɪ:], *s.* die Gutartigkeit.
bonnet ['bɔnɪt], *s.* *die* Damenmütze, Haube; Mütze, Kappe (*Scots*) (*for men*); Haube (*Motor*); Kappe (*of a chimney*); *have a bee in one's* –, einen Vogel haben.
bonny ['bɔnɪ], *adj.* hübsch, anmutig, drall; (*Scots*) schön, fein, nett.
bonus ['bounəs], *s.* die Prämie, Extradividende, Tantieme, Zulage, der Zuschlag, die Gratifikation; *cash* –, bar ausgezahlte Dividende; – *share*, die Gratisaktie.
bony ['bounɪ], *adj.* knöchern, beinern; grätig (*of fish*), knochig; starkknochig, mager, skelettartig.
boo [bu:], 1. *interj.* buh! 2. *v.n.* & *a.* muhen; auszischen, auspfeifen.
boob [bu:b], *s.* (*sl.*) *see* **–y.** **–y,** *s.* der Tölpel (*also Orn.*), Einfaltspinsel. **–y-hatch,** *s.* die Achterlukenkappe (*Naut.*). **–y-prize,** *s.* der Trostpreis. **–y-trap,** *s.* derber Streich; die Schreckladung, Minenfalle, Trugmine (*Mil.*).
book [buk], 1. *s.* das Buch; (*a*) (*with nouns*) – *of commission*, das Auftragsbuch; – *for complaints*, das Beschwerdebuch; – *of reference*, das Nachschlagebuch; – *of sales*, das (Waren)Verkaufsbuch; (*b*) (with *to be*) *be at one's –s*, beim Studieren sein; *he is deep in our –s*, er ist uns viel schuldig; *be in a p.'s good* (*bad*) *–s*, bei einem gut (schlecht) angeschrieben sein; *be upon the –s*, eingetragenes Mitglied sein; (*c*) (*with verbs*) *bring to* –, zur Rechenschaft *or* Verantwortung ziehen, zur Rede stellen; *keep –s*, Bücher führen; *kiss the* –, auf die Bibel schwören; *make a* –, Wetten eintragen; *repeat* or *say without the* –, auswendig hersagen; *speak without the* –, ohne Autorität reden; (*coll.*) *suit one's* –, einem passen; *swear on the* –, see *kiss the* –; *take a leaf out of a p.'s* –, einem nachahmen; *talk like a* –, wie ein Buch *or* wie gedruckt reden. 2. *v.a.* aufschreiben, eintragen, buchen (*an entry in a book*); bestellen, belegen (*a seat, room, etc.*); lösen (*a ticket*); im Vorverkauf besorgen (*a theatre ticket*); engagieren (*a performer*); vormerken (*a library book*); anmelden (*a phone call*); *all rooms are –ed*, alle Zimmer sind besetzt *or* reserviert; *all the seats have been –ed*, das Haus ist ausverkauft. 3. *v.n.*; – *to*, eine Karte lösen nach; – *through to Basle*, eine direkte Karte bis Basel lösen; *be –ed up*, besetzt *or* ausverkauft sein; (*coll.*) vorläufig beschäftigt sein; (*coll.*) *be –ed to do*, verpflichtet sein zu tun; (*coll.*) *I am –ed to see him tomorrow*, ich habe mich auf morgen mit ihm verabredet. **–able,** *adj.* im Vorverkauf zu haben. **–binder,** *s.* der Buchbinder. **–binding,** *s.* das Buchbinden, die Buchbinderei. **–case,** *s.* der Bücherschrank. **– –club,** *s.* der Lesezirkel. **– –ends,** *pl.* die Bücherstützen. **–ing,** *s.* das Buchen; der Vorverkauf; bestellter Platz, gelöste Karte; *cancel a –ing*, Karten abbestellen; *advance –ing*, der Vorverkauf. **–ing clerk,** der Fahrkartenverkäufer. **–ing-office,** *s.* der (Fahrkarten)Schalter (*Railw.*); die (Theater)-Kasse. **–ish,** *adj.* (*coll.*) den Büchern ergeben, auf Bücher versessen; pedantisch. **–ishness,** *s.* die Stubengelehrsamkeit, das Buchwissen; die Bücherliebhaberei. **– –keeper,** *s.* der Buchhalter, Rechnungsführer. **– –keeping,** *s.* die Buchhaltung, Buchführung. **– –learning,** *s.* die Buchgelehrsamkeit. **–let,** *s.* die Broschüre, das Büchlein. **–maker,** *s.* der Buchmacher (*Sport*). **–man,** *s.* Buchgelehrte(r), *m.* **–marker,** *s.* das Lesezeichen. **– –muslin,** *s.* feiner Musselin. **– plate,** *s.* das Exlibris. **– –post,** *s.* die Drucksachenpost; *by – –post*, unter Kreuzband. **– –rack,** *s.* das Büchergestell, Bücherbort. **–seller,** *s.* der Buchhändler, Sorti-

menter. **-selling,** *s.* der Buchhandel. **-shelf,** *s.* das Bücherbrett, Bücherregal. **-shop,** *s.* die Buchhandlung. **-stall,** *s.* der Bücherverkaufsstand; *railway -stall,* die Bahnhofsbuchhandlung, der Zeitungsstand. **-stand,** *s.* das Büchergestell. **--trade,** *s.* der Buchhandel. **-worm,** *s.* der Bücherwurm (*also fig.*). **--wrapper,** *s.* die Buchhülle.

[1]**boom** [bu:m], *s.* der Baum; die Spiere (*Naut.*); der Schnabel (*of a crane*); Galgen (*for camera or microphone*) (*Cinema*); die Hafensperre, der Hafenbaum.

[2]**boom,** 1. *v.n.* dröhnen, schallen, brummen, brausen, summen; schreien (*as a bittern*); mit vollen Segeln fahren (*Naut.*). 2. *s* das Dröhnen, Gebrumme.

[3]**boom,** 1. *s.* der Aufschwung, die Konjunktur, Hausse; Stimmungsmache. 2. *v.n.* rasch in die Höhe kommen, sich schnell entwickeln, einen Aufschwung nehmen. 3. *v.a.* in die Höhe treiben; Reklame machen für (*C.L.*); *business is -ing,* das Geschäft geht flott.

boomerang ['bu:məræŋ], *s.* der *or* das Bumerang.

[1]**boon** [bu:n], *s.* die Wohltat, Gunst, Gnade, der Segen; die Gabe, Gefälligkeit.

[2]**boon,** *adj.* fröhlich, munter; *- companion,* der Zechbruder.

boor [buə] *s.* der Lümmel, Grobian. **-ish** [-rɪʃ], *adj.* bäurisch, grob, ungeschliffen. **-ishness,** *s.* die Grobheit, Ungeschliffenheit.

boost [bu:st], 1. *v.a.* unterstützen, nachhelfen (*Dat.*), anpreisen, Reklame machen für; verstärken (*Elec*); hinauftreiben (*prices*). 2. *s.* der Ladedruck, Auftrieb (*Mech.*); die Reklame, Propaganda; der Aufschwung. **-er,** *s.* der Zusatzdynamo.

[1]**boot** [bu:t], 1. *s.* (*archaic*) der Vorteil, Nutzen (*only in*) *to -,* obendrein, noch dazu, in den Kauf, überdies, außerdem. 2. *v.a.* (*archaic*) nutzen, frommen (*only in*) *what -s it?* was hilft es? **-less,** *adj.* nutzlos, zwecklos, unnütz, vergeblich.

[2]**boot,** 1. *s.* der Stiefel, hoher Schuh; Wagenkasten, Kutschkasten, Hinterkasten; spanischer Stiefel (*torture*); *elastic -s,* die Zugstiefel (*pl.*); *fishing -s,* die Wasserstiefel (*pl.*); (*sl.*) *get the -,* entlassen werden; (*sl.*) *give s.o. the -,* einen entlassen; (*sl.*) *give s.o. a good -,* einem einen guten Stoß (mit dem Fuß) geben; *in -s,* gestiefelt; *die in one's -s, die with one's -s on,* einen plötzlichen Tod finden; *he had his heart in his -s,* er hatte große Angst; *the - is on the other foot,* die Sache *or* Wahrheit liegt genau umgekehrt; *- and saddle!* das Signal zum Aufsitzen (*Mil.*). *top --s, pl.* die Stulpenstiefel, Langschäfter (*pl.*). 2. *v a.* (*coll.*) (mit dem Fuß) wuchtig stoßen, kräftig kicken (*Footb.*); (*sl.*) *- a p. out,* einen hinauswerfen, einen entlassen. **--black,** *s.* der Schuhputzer. **-ed,** *adj.* gestiefelt. **-ee,** *s.* der Damenhalbstiefel, (wollener) Kinderschuh. **--jack,** *s.* der Stiefelknecht. **--lace,** *s.* der Schuhriemen Schnürsenkel. **--last,** *s.* der Schuhleisten, das Stiefelholz. **-legger,** *s.* der Alkoholschmuggler (*Amer.*). **-maker,** *s.* der Schuster, Schuhmacher. **--polish,** *s.* die Schuhcreme. **--trees,** *pl.* der Stiefelspanner.

booth [bu.ð], *s.* die Bude, der Marktstand; die Zelle (*telephone or voting*).

bootless ['bu:tlɪs], *see* [1]**boot.**

boots [bu:ts], *s.* (*coll.*) der Stiefelputzer, Hausdiener (*in a hotel*).

booty ['bu:tɪ], *s* die Beute, Kriegsbeute, der Raub.

booz-e [bu:z], 1. *v.n.* (*vulg.*) zechen, saufen. 2. *s.* alkoholisches Getränk; *go on the -e,* zechen, saufen. **-ed,** *adj.* angeheitert, betrunken. **-y,** *adj.* trunksüchtig.

bora-cic [bo'ræsɪk], *see* **boric.** **-te** [bɔreɪt], *s.* das Borat, borsaures Salz. **-x** ['bɔræks], *s.* der Borax, das Natriumborat.

bord-er ['bɔ·də], 1 *s* der Rand, Saum, die Borte, Einfassung; Rabatte, das Schmalbeet (*Hort.*); der Rain (*of a wood, etc.*); die Grenze (*often pl.*) (*of a country*); Randleiste, Randverzierung (*Typ.*); *-erline case,* der Grenzfall. 2. *v.a.* einfassen, einsäumen, besetzen (*dresses, etc.*). 3. *v.n.* grenzen (*cn,* an (*with Acc.*)), nahekommen (*Dat.*). **-erer** [-rə], *s.* der Grenzbewohner. **-erland,** *s.* das Grenzland, (*fig.*) Grenzgebiet. **-ure** [-djuə], *s.* der Schildrand (*Her.*).

[1]**bor-e** [bɔ:], 1. *v.a.* bohren, ausbohren, durchbohren, aushöhlen; verdrängen (*Racing*). 2. *v.n.* bohren, schürfen (*for,* nach) (*Mining*). 3. *s.* das Bohrloch; die Höhlung, Bohrung (*of a cylinder*); Seele, das Kaliber, Rohr (*of a gun*); lichte Weite; *smooth* (*rifled*) *-e,* glatte (gezogene) Bohrung. **-er,** *s* der Bohrer; Bohrwurm (*Entom.*). **-ing,** *s.* das Bohrloch; die Bohrung, das Bohren. **-ings,** *pl.* die Bohrspäne.

[2]**bore,** 1. *v.a.* langweilen, belästigen; (*coll.*) *be -d stiff,* sich zu Tode langweilen. 2. *s.* langweilige *or* lästige Sache; langweiliger Mensch; *what a -,* wie ärgerlich! **-dom,** *s.* die Langeweile, Lästigkeit.

[3]**bore,** *see* **bear.**

[4]**bore,** *s.* brandende Flutwelle.

borea-l ['bɔ:rɪəl], *adj.* nördlich. **-s** [-s], *s.* der Nordwind, Boreas.

boredom ['bɔ:dəm], *see* [2]**bore.**

boric ['bɔ:rɪk] *adj.* Bor-, boraxhaltig; *- acid,* die Borsäure.

born [bɔ:n], *adj. see* [2]**bear;** geboren; *be a - actor,* zum Schauspieler geboren sein; *- blind,* blind geboren; (*coll.*) *in all my - days,* mein Lebtag, in meinem ganzen Leben; *Dante was - and bred a Guelph,* Dante war seiner Geburt und Erziehung nach ein Welfe; *a nobleman -,* ein geborener Edelmann; *- fool,* vollkommener Narr; *- to renown,* zum Ruhme bestimmt; *be - with a silver spoon in one's mouth, be - under a lucky star,* ein Glückskind *or* Sonntagskind sein. **-e,** *see* [2]**bear.**

boron ['bɔ:rən], *s.* das Bor (*Chem.*).

borough ['bʌrə], *s.* der Stadtbezirk, die Stadtgemeinde, städtischer Wahlbezirk; *- council,* der Stadtrat, *- councillor,* der Stadtrat.

borrow ['bɔroʊ], *v a.* borgen, (ent)leihen, sich (*Dat.*) leihen; (*fig.*) entlehnen, entnehmen (*from a p.,* (von) einem); *he has -ed of me,* er hat mich angeborgt; *-ed plumes,* fremde Federn. **-er,** *s.* der Borger, Entleiher; (*fig.*) der Entlehner.

boscage ['bɔskɪdʒ], *s.* das Gebüsch, Gehölz, Unterholz, Dickicht.

bosh [bɔʃ], *s.* (*sl.*) der Unsinn, Quatsch.

bosky ['bɔskɪ], *adj.* buschig, waldig.

bosom ['buzəm], *s.* die Brust, der Busen; (*fig.*) das Herz, Innere, die Tiefe, der Schoß; *in the - of his family,* im Schoße seiner Familie; *the - of the sea,* die Tiefe des Meeres; *come to my -,* komm an mein Herz; *- friend,* der Busenfreund, Herzensfreund. **-ed,** 1. *suffix* -busig, -brüstig. 2. *adj.* (*poet.*) verborgen, (ein)gebettet.

[1]**boss** [bɔs], *s.* der Buckel (*of a shield*), Knopf. Knauf, Beschlag; die Nabe (*of a wheel*); die Bosse (*Arch.*). **-age,** *s.* das Bossenwerk (*Arch.*). **-y,** *adj.* mit Buckeln verziert.

[2]**boss,** 1. *s.* (*sl.*) der Meister, Chef, Arbeitgeber, Vorgesetzte(r), *m.,* tonangebender Mann; (*sl.*) der Bonze. 2. *v.a.* (*sl.*) arrangieren, dirigieren, leiten; *- the show,* der Hauptmacher sein, das entscheidende Wort zu sprechen haben. **- rule,** *s.* die Bonzenwirtschaft. **-y,** *adj.* (*sl.*) herrisch, despotisch.

bosun ['bɔsn], *s.* (*coll.*) *see* **boatswain.**

bot [bɔt], *s.* die Dassellarve, *the -s,* die Dasselplage. **--fly,** *s.* die Dasselfliege.

botan-ic [bo'tænɪk], (*in certain phrases, e.g. -ic* gardens, *otherwise*) **-ical,** *adj.* botanisch. **-ist** ['bɔtənɪst], *s.* der Botaniker. **-ize** ['bɔtənaɪz], *v.n.* Pflanzen sammeln, botanisieren. **-y** ['bɔtənɪ], *s.* die Botanik, Pflanzenkunde.

botch [bɔtʃ], 1 *s.* die Beule, das Geschwür; Flickwerk; *make a - of a job,* eine Arbeit verhunzen. 2. *v.a.* flicken; verhunzen, *-ed work,* das Flickwerk, die Pfuscherei. **-er,** *s.* der Flickschneider, Flickschuster; (*fig*) Pfuscher.

both [bouθ], 1. *adj. & pron.* beide, beides; *I will take them* - or - *of them,* ich will sie alle beide mitnehmen; *make - ends meet,* sich nach der Decke strecken; *- her sisters,* ihre beiden Schwestern; *- are true,* beides ist wahr. 2. *conj.*; *- . . . and,* sowohl . . . als (auch); *- by day and by night,* bei Tag wie bei Nacht; *- in word and deed,* in *or* mit Wort und Tat.

bother ['bɔðə], 1. *v.a.* plagen, belästigen, beunruhigen; – *the boys!* die verflixten Jungen! (*coll.*) – *it!* zum Henker *or* Kuckuck; – *one's head about*, sich den Kopf zerbrechen über. 2. *v.n.* sich bemühen, sich aufregen (*about*, über); sich (*Dat.*) Gedanken machen (über (*Acc.*)). 3. *s.* der Verdruß, die Belästigung, Mühe, Schererei. (*coll.*) **–ation** [–ˈreɪʃən], *interj.* verflixt! wie ärgerlich! **–some,** *adj.* lästig, ärgerlich.

[1]**bottle** [ˈbɔtl], 1. *s.* die Flasche; *bring up* (*a child*) *on the* –, mit der Flasche nähren; *by the* –, flaschenweise; *crack a – together*, eine Flasche zusammen trinken; *be fond of the* –, gern trinken; *hot-water* –, die Wärmflasche; *chat over a – of beer*, beim Glase Bier plaudern; *stone* –, der Steinkrug, Tonkrug; *water*-–, die Feldflasche. 2. *v.a.* auf Flaschen ziehen *or* füllen; – *up one's wrath*, seinen Zorn zurückhalten *or* unterdrücken; *–d beer*, das Flaschenbier. **–-fed,** *adj.* mit der Flasche genährt; **–-feeding,** *s.* die Ernährung mit der Flasche. **–-glass,** *s.* grünes Flaschenglas. **–-gourd,** *s.* der Flaschenkürbis. **–-holder,** *s.* (*sl.*) der Sekundant (*Sport*). **–-label,** das Flaschenetikett. **–-neck,** *s.* der Flaschenhals; (*fig.*) Engpaß, die Enge, Stauung; Straßenverengung, enge Straßenmündung. **–-nose,** *s.* die Schnapsnase. **–-nosed,** *adj.* mit aufgedunsener Nase; *–-nosed whale*, *s.* der Butzkopf (*Zool.*). **–-washer,** *s.* (*coll.*) das Faktotum.

[2]**bottle,** *s.* das Bund, das Bündel (*of hay*).

bottom [ˈbɔtəm], 1. *s.* der Boden (*of a cask, cup, etc.*), Grund (*of water*); (*fig.*) die Tiefe, Grundlage, Basis, Ursache, Triebfeder, der Ursprung; das Schiff, der Schiffsboden (*Naut.*); die Unterlage, der Fond (*of colour*); (*usually pl.*) der Bodensatz, die Hefe (*of beer, etc.*); (*vulg.*) Hintere(r), *m.*, das Gesäß; (*coll.*) die Ausdauer, Stärke (*of a horse, etc.*); *at* –, im Grunde, in Wirklichkeit; *at the* –, ganz unten; *be at the – of a th.*, einer S. zugrunde liegen; – *of the bed*, unteres Ende des Bettes; – *coat*, erster Auftrag (*of colour*); *he is at the – of his form*, er ist der Letzte *or* Unterste (in) seiner Klasse; *get to the – of a th.*, einer S. auf den Grund gehen; *go to the* –, sinken, untergehen; *from the – of my heart*, aus tiefstem Herzen; – *of a hill*, der Fuß eines Berges; *knock the – out of a th.*, einer S. den Boden entziehen; *at the – of the street*, am Ende der Straße; *from top to* –, von oben bis unten; *touch* –, auf Grund geraten; (*fig.*) den tiefsten Stand erreichen; – *up*(*wards*), kieloben, das Unterste zu oberst; (*sl.*) *–s up!* Prosit! Trink zu!; *valley* –, die Talsohle. 2. *adj.* unterst, tiefst, niedrigst; – *gear*, erster Gang (*Motor.*); (*sl.*) *bet one's – dollar*, den letzten Pfennig darauf setzen, darauf Gift nehmen; *rock-– price*, alleräußerster Preis. 3. *v.a.* einen Boden einsetzen; (*fig. usually passive*) gründen, stützen, bauen (*on*, auf (*Acc.*)); grundieren, vorfärben (*painting*); *double-–ed*, mit doppeltem Boden; *flat-–ed boat*, der Prahm; *full-–ed wig*, die Allongeperücke; *leather-–ed chair*, der Lederstuhl. (*coll.*) **–-drawer,** *s.* der Hamsterkasten für die Aussteuer. **–-fishing,** *s.* das Grundangeln. **–less,** *adj.* bodenlos, grundlos; unergründlich; *the –less pit*, die tiefste Tiefe, die Hölle. **–most,** *adv.* ganz zu unterst. **–ry** [ˈbɔtəmrɪ], 1. *s.* die Bodmerei (*Naut.*). 2. *v.a.* verpfänden (*a ship*).

botulism [ˈbɔtjulɪzm], *s.* die Wurstvergiftung.

boudoir [ˈbuːdwɑː], *s.* das Boudoir, Damenzimmer.

bough [bɑu], *s.* der Zweig, Ast.

bought [bɔːt], *see* **buy.**

bougie [ˈbuːʒɪː], *s.* die Wachskerze, das Wachslicht; die (Harnröhren)Sonde.

bouillon [buˈjõː, bulˈjõː], *s.* die Fleischbrühe, Kraftbrühe.

boulder [ˈbouldə], *s.* der Uferkiesel; Felsblock; *erratic* –, erratischer Block (*Geol.*). **–-clay,** *s.* eiszeitlicher Geschiebelehm (*Geol.*). **–-period,** *s.* die Eiszeit.

bounc–e [bɑuns], 1. *v.n.* springen, aufschlagen, aufprallen; (*coll.*) großsprechen, aufschneiden, prahlen; *the ball –es high*, der Ball springt hoch in die Luft; *–e about*, herumspringen; *–e into a room*, ins Zimmer hineinplatzen *or* hineinstürzen; *–ing girl*, lebhaftes, dralles *or* strammes Mädel. 2. *v.a.* aufschlagen lassen (*a ball*); (*coll.*) *–e a p. into doing*, einen einschüchtern zu tun. 3. *s.* der Sprung, Rückprall, Aufprall; die Sprungkraft; (*sl.*) Prahlerei. **–er,** *s.*; *the ball is a good –er*, der Ball springt gut; (*sl.*) unverschämte Lüge; (*sl.*) der Aufschneider.

[1]**bound** [bɑund], *see* **bind;** gebunden; verpflichtet; *fog-–*, vom Nebel gehindert; *ice-–*, von Eis umgeben *or* im Eis eingeschlossen; *I will be* –, ich stehe dafür ein; *he is – to go*, er wird auf jeden Fall *or* unbedingt gehen. **–en,** *adj.* (*archaic, only in*) *it is your –en duty*, es ist Ihre Pflicht und Schuldigkeit *or* Ihre heilige Pflicht.

[2]**bound,** *adj.* bestimmt unterwegs nach; *ship – for London*, das nach London bestimmte Schiff; *London-– train*, der nach London fahrende Zug; *where are you – for?* wo geht die Reise hin? wohin gehts? wo wollen Sie hin? *homeward-–*, auf der Heim– *or* Rückreise; *outward-–*, auf der Ausreise.

[3]**bound,** 1. *s.* der Sprung, Satz; Prall, Anprall, Aufprall, Rückprall; *at a* –, mit einem Satze; *by leaps and –s*, in gewaltigen Sätzen, in raschem Tempo. 2. *v.n.* springen, hüpfen, (auf)prallen.

[4]**bound,** 1. *s.* (*usually* –s, *pl.*) die Grenze; Schranke, das Maß; (*a*) (*with verbs*) *overstep the –s*, die Grenze überschreiten; *set –s to one's desires*, seine Wünsche in Schranken halten; (*b*) (*with prepositions*) *beyond all –s*, übermäßig, außer Rand und Band; *out of –s*, verboten; *put out of –s*, verbieten; *within –s*, mit Maß, in Schranken, mäßig; *it is within the –s of possibility*, es liegt im Bereich des Möglichen; *keep within the –s of propriety*, sich in den Grenzen des Anstands halten. 2. *v.a.* begrenzen, beschränken, einschränken, in Schranken halten. **–ary,** *s.* die Grenze, Grenzlinie. **–ary-line,** *s.* die Grenzlinie. **–less,** *adj.* grenzenlos, unbegrenzt, unbeschränkt. **–lessness,** *s.* die Grenzenlosigkeit.

bounder [ˈbɑundə], *s.* (*coll.*) unartiges Kind; unfeiner Kerl, der Prolet, Plebejer.

bount-eous [ˈbɑuntɪəs], **–iful,** *adj.* freigebig, gütig (*of persons*); reichlich (*of things*). **–y,** *s.* die Freigebigkeit, Großmut, Wohltätigkeit; Wohltat, Gabe; Prämie (*C.L.*); das Handgeld (*Mil.*).

bouquet [buˈkeɪ], *s.* der (Blumen)Strauß, das Bukett; der Duft, die Blume (*of wine*).

bourdon [ˈbuːədən], *s.* der Brummbaß (*organ*).

[1]**bourgeois** [ˈbuəʒwɑː], 1. *s.* der Bürger, Philister. 2. *adj.* bürgerlich, philisterhaft. **–ie** [–ˈzɪː], *s.* der Bürgerstand.

[2]**bourgeois** [bəːˈdʒɔɪs], *s.* die Borgis(schrift) (*Typ.*).

bourn(**e**) [buːən], *s.* (*poet.*) der Bach; die Grenze; das Ziel.

bout [bɑut], *s.* die Reihe, Wechselfolge, der Gang, die Tour; *drinking* –, das Zechgelage, der Schmaus; – *of illness*, der (Krankheits)Anfall.

bovine [ˈbouvaɪn], *adj.* Ochsen–, Rinder–; träge.

[1]**bow** [bɑu], *s.* (*often pl.*) der Bug (*of a ship*); vorderster Ruderer; *on the port* –, an Backbord voraus (*Naut.*). **–sprit,** *s.* das Bugspriet.

[2]**bow** [bɑu], 1. *s.* die Verbeugung, Verneigung; *make one's* –, abtreten, sich zurückziehen; *make one's first* –, zum ersten Male auftreten. 2. *v.a.* biegen, beugen, neigen; *–ed with*, niedergedrückt von; *–ed down by*, niedergedrückt *or* gebeugt von; – *one's assent*, seine Genehmigung durch eine Verbeugung ausdrücken; – *the ear to s.o.*, einem Gehör schenken; – *the knee to*, sich in Ehrfurcht beugen vor; – *a p. out*, einen hinauskomplimentieren; – *one's thanks*, sich dankend verneigen. 3. *v.n.* sich verbeugen, sich bücken, sich verneigen; eine Verbeugung machen (*to*, vor); (*fig.*) sich fügen, sich unterwerfen, sich beugen, sich demütigen; – *and scrape*, Kratzfüße machen; – *down*, sich niederbeugen, sich unterwerfen (*to s.o.*, einem); *have a –ing acquaintance with*, auf dem Grußfuße stehen mit, nur flüchtig kennen; – *to the inevitable*, sich ins Unvermeidliche schicken.

[3]**bow** [bou], 1. *s.* der Bogen, die Kurve; Schleife (*of ribbons*); *cross*–, die Armbrust; *draw a* –, einen Bogen spannen; *draw the long* –, aufschneiden; *draw a – at a venture*, auf den Busch klopfen; *rain*–, der Regenbogen; *saddle-–*, der Sattelbogen; – *tie*, die Fliege, Schleife; *have two strings to one's* –, mehrere Eisen im Feuer haben; *tie a* –, eine Schleife

knüpfen; *violin* –, der (Geigen)Bogen. 2. *v.a.* den Bogen führen (*violin*). **--arm,** *s.* rechter Arm (*of violinist*). **--compasses,** *pl.* der Nullenzirkel, Bogenzirkel. **--drill,** *s.* der Bogenbohrer. **-ing,** *s.* die Bogenführung, der Strich (*of violinist*). **--legged,** *adj.* o-beinig. **-man,** *s.* der Bogenschütze. **--saw,** *s.* die Bügelsäge. **--shaped,** *adj.* bogenförmig. **-shot,** *s.*; *within -shot,* in Bogenschußweite. **--string,** 1. *s.* die Bogensehne. 2. *v.a.* (mit der seidenen Schnur) erdrosseln. **--window,** *s.* das Erkerfenster.

bowdleri-ze [ˈbaudləraɪz], *v.a.* von anstößigen Stellen reinigen, verballhornen, verschlimmbessern. **-zation** [–ˈzeɪʃən], *s.* die Verballhornung, Verschlimmbesserung.

bowel [ˈbauəl], *s.* der Darm (*Med.*); *pl.* das Eingeweide; (*fig.*) Innere; (*archaic*) *-s of compassion,* das Mitleid; *action of the -s,* der Stuhlgang; *have your -s moved?* hatten Sie Stuhlgang?

[1]**bower** [ˈbauə], *s.* die Laube; (*archaic*) das Damengemach.

[2]**bower,** *s.* der Buganker.

bowie-knife [ˈbouɪnaɪf], *s.* das Jagdmesser.

[1]**bowl** [boul], *s.* der Napf, Becher, das Becken, die Schale, Schüssel; Kuvette (*Chem.*); Bowle; der Pfeifenkopf; die Höhlung (*of a spoon*); *– fire,* die Heizsonne (*Elec.*).

[2]**bowl,** 1. *s.* die Holzkugel. 2. *v.a.* rollen, kugeln, schieben, werfen; treiben, schlagen (*a hoop*); *– down,* umwerfen, niederwerfen; *– out,* absetzen (*Crick.*), (*fig.*) besiegen, schlagen; *– over,* umwerfen, (*fig.*) überraschen, niederschmettern, erledigen. 3. *v.n.* rollen, kegeln; den Ball werfen (*Crick.*); *– along,* dahinrollen. **-er** [ˈboulə], *s.* 1. der Bowlingspieler; Ballmann, Werfer (*Crick.*). 2. (**-er hat**) steifer Filzhut. **-ing,** *s.* das Bowlingspiel; Kegeln; Werfen (*Crick.*). **-ing-alley,** *s.* die Kegelbahn. **-ing-green,** *s.* der Rasen zum Bowlingspiel. **-s,** *pl.* das Bowlingspiel.

bowline [ˈboulɪn], *s.* die Buleine, Buline (*Naut.*).

bowse [bauz], *v.a.* auftaljen, anholen (*Naut.*).

bowsprit [ˈbausprɪt], *see* [1]**bow.**

bow-wow [ˈbauˈwau], 1. *int.* wauwau! 2. *s.* (*nursery talk*) der Hund.

bowzer [ˈbauzə], *s.* (*sl.*) der Tankwagen.

[1]**box** [bɔks], 1. *s.* der Buchsbaum (*Bot.*). 2. *adj.* Buchsbaum–. **--thorn,** *s.* der Teufelszwirn (*Bot.*). **-wood,** *s.* das Buchsbaumholz.

[2]**box,** 1. *s.* die Büchse, Schachtel, Dose; der Kasten, die Kiste, das Kästchen; der (Kutsch)Bock; die Loge (*Theat.*); das Gehäuse (*Mech.*); Fach des Schriftkastens (*Typ.*); Häuschen; der Stand, die Abteilung (*stable, etc.*); *axle--,* die Radbüchse; *ballot –,* die Wahlurne; *– of bricks,* der Baukasten; *cardboard –,* die Pappschachtel, der Karton; *– of chocolates,* die Schachtel Schokolade; *Christmas –,* das Weihnachtsgeschenk; *cigar –,* die Zigarrenkiste; *junction –,* die Abzweigdose (*Elec.*); *letter--,* der Briefkasten; *– of matches,* die Schachtel Streichhölzer; *money –,* die Sparbüchse; *musical –,* die Spieldose; *– of paints,* der Tuschkasten; *sentry –,* das Schilderhaus; *signal –,* die Blockstelle (*Railw.*); *shooting –,* das Jagdhäuschen; *strong –,* die Kassette; (*coll.*) *the whole – of tricks,* der ganze Kram; *witness –,* der Zeugenstand; *be in the wrong –,* auf dem Holzwege sein. 2. *v.a.* in Büchsen verschließen, einpacken, einschachteln; mit Büchsen versehen (*a wheel*); anzapfen (*trees*); *– the compass,* die Kompaßpunkte in der Ordnung hersagen, (*fig.*) sich gänzlich umstellen; *– off,* in Fächer abteilen; abriegeln (*Artil.*); *– up,* einschließen; zusammenschachteln. **– barrage,** *s.* das Abriegelungsfeuer (*Artil.*). **--bed,** *s.* der Bettschrank. **--car,** *s.* (*Amer.*) der Güterwagen. **-ful,** *s.* die Büchsevoll, der Kastenvoll. **--iron,** *s.* das Bügeleisen mit Einsteckheizer. **--keeper,** *s.* der Logenschließer. **--kite,** *s.* der Rahmendrache. **--number,** *s.* das Schließfach. **--office,** *s.* die Theaterkasse (*Theat.*); (*coll.*) *--office success,* der Erfolg beim Publikum, Kassenerfolg (*Theat.*); (*coll.*) *--office life,* die Spieldauer; (*coll.*) *--office attraction,* die Anziehungskraft (*of film, etc.*). **--spanner,** *s.* der Steckschlüssel.

box, 1. *s.*; *– on the ear,* die Ohrfeige; (*B.*) der Backenstreich. 2. *v.n.* (sich) boxen. 3. *v.a.*; *– s.o.'s ears,* einen ohrfeigen. **-er,** *s.* der Boxer. **-ing,** *s.* der Boxsport; *-ing day,* zweiter Weihnachtstag; *-ing gloves, pl.* die Boxhandschuhe; *-ing match,* der Boxkampf.

box-haul [ˈbɔkshɔːl], *v.a* halsen, vor dem Winde umwenden (*Naut.*).

boy [bɔɪ], *s.* der Knabe, Junge, (*dial.*) Bub(e); eingeborener Diener; *day--,* der Extraner; *old –,* früherer Schüler, alter Herr; (*coll.*) lieber Freund, alter Knabe; (*prov.*) *-s will be -s,* Jugend kennt keine Tugend. **--friend,** der Liebste. **-hood** [ˈbɔɪhud], *s.* das Knabenalter, die Jugend. **-ish,** *adj.* knabenhaft. **-ishness,** *s.* knabenhaftes Wesen, die Knabenart. **– scout,** *s.* der Pfadfinder.

boycott [ˈbɔɪkɔt], 1. *v.a.* boykottieren, in Verruf tun *or* erklären, verfemen, kaltstellen. 2. *s.* der Boykott, die Boykottierung, Verrufserklärung.

brac-e [breɪs], 1. *s.* das Band, die Binde, der Gurt, Gürtel, Riemen; die Strebe, Stütze, das Tragband, der Stützbalken (*Arch., etc.*); (*-e and bit*) die Brustleier, Bohrwinde (*Carp.*); Spannschnur (*of a drum*); geschweifte Klammer (*Mus., Typ.*); (*no pl.*) das Paar (*game, etc.*); die Brasse (*Naut.*); *pair of -es,* die Hosenträger (*pl.*); *a -e of pistols,* ein Paar Pistolen; (*coll.*) *splice the main -e,* Besanschot an! (*Naut.*); (*coll.*) Grog trinken (*Naut.*). 2. *v.a.* straff ziehen, spannen, verspannen, stützen, festigen, absteifen; brassen (*Naut.*); abstreben (*Av.*); (*fig.*) stärken, kräftigen; *-e o.s. for,* die Kräfte zusammennehmen für; *-e o.s. up to,* sich aufraffen *or* anspannen zu. **-er,** *s.* die Armschiene; (*coll.*) der Nervenstärker, Schluck Schnaps. **-ing,** 1. *s.* die Versteifung, Verspannung, Verstrebung. 2. *adj.* stärkend, erfrischend; *-ing air,* erfrischende Luft.

bracelet [ˈbreɪslɪt], *s.* das Armband; die Armspange; *pl.* (*sl.*) die Handschellen.

brach [brætʃ], *s.* die Bracke; (Spür)Hündin.

brachia-l [ˈbreɪkɪəl], *adj.* Arm–; *-l nerves,* die Armnerven. **-te,** *pred. adj.* gegenständig (*Bot.*).

bracken [ˈbrækən], *s.* das Farnkraut.

bracket [ˈbrækɪt], 1. *s.* der Kragstein, Träger (*Arch.*); das Wandbrett, die Konsole, der (Wand) Arm; die Gabel (*Artil.*); Klammer (*Typ.*). *– mounting, s.* der Drehkranz (*of guns*); *corner –,* das Eckbrett; *in -s,* in Klammern; *lamp –,* der Lampenarm; *spring –,* der Federbock (*of a vehicle*); *wall –,* der Mauerbügel; Wandarm. 2. *v.a.* einklammern (*Typ.*); eingabeln (*Artil.*); (*fig.*) gleichstellen, in dieselbe Rubrik *or* Klasse bringen; *they were -ed together,* sie wurden in eine Linie gestellt; sie wurden gleich gut erklärt; *he was -ed sixth in the class list,* in der Rangliste wurde er zusammen mit einem andern an sechster Stelle genannt. **-ing,** *s.* die Gabelbildung; das Gabelschießen (*Artil.*).

brackish [ˈbrækɪʃ], *adj.* (etwas) salzig; brackig; *– water,* das Brackwasser.

bract [brækt], *s.* das Deckblatt, die Braktee (*Bot.*). **-eate** [ˈbræktɪɪt], 1. *adj.* mit Brakteen. 2. *s.* der Brakteat (*coin*).

brad [bræd], *s.* kopfloser Nagel, der Bodennagel; die Schuhzwecke. **-awl,** *s.* der Vorstechbohrer.

brae [breɪ], *s.* der Abhang, Hügel (*Scots*).

brag [bræg], 1. *s.* die Prahlerei. 2. *v.n.* prahlen (*about,* über); sich rühmen (*with Gen.*). **-gart,** *s.* der Prahler, Aufschneider. **-gadocio** [–əˈdouʃɪou], *s.* die Prahlerei; (*archaic*) der Prahler.

braid [breɪd], 1. *s.* die Borte, Schnur, Litze, Tresse; (Haar)Flechte. 2. *v.a.* flechten (*the hair*); mit Borten *or* Litzen besetzen. **-ing,** *s.* die Litzen (*pl.*), der Besatz.

brail [breɪl], 1. *s.* das Geitau. 2. *v.a.*; *– up,* aufgeien (*Naut.*).

Braille [breɪl], *s.* die Blindenschrift.

brain [breɪn], 1. *s.* das Gehirn (*Anat.*); (*fig. usually pl.*) der Verstand, Kopf, die Intelligenz; *blow a p.'s -s out,* einem eine Kugel durch den Kopf jagen; *dash one's -s out,* sich (*Dat.*) den Schädel einschlagen; *he hasn't much -s,* er ist keiner von den Klügsten; *have s.th. on the –,* fortwährend an etwas denken müssen, einen Gedanken nicht loswerden können; *cudgel, puzzle* or *rack one's -s,* sich (*Dat.*) den Kopf zerbrechen; (*sl.*) *pick a p.'s -s,* einen ausquetschen; *softening of the –,* die Gehirner-

weichung; *turn a p.'s* –, einem den Kopf verdrehen. 2. *v.a.* (einem) den Schädel einschlagen. **-ed,** *adj. suffix*; *crack--ed*, verrückt; *scatter--ed*, gedankenlos. **--fag,** *s.* geistige Überanstrengung. **--fever,** *s.* die Gehirnentzündung, Hirnhautentzündung. **-less,** *adj.* hirnlos; ohne Verstand, dumm. **--pan,** *s.* die Hirnschale. **--storm,** *s.* geistige Umnachtung. **--twister,** *s.* schwer lösbares Rätsel. **-wave,** *s.* geistreicher Einfall. **--worker,** *s.* der Kopfarbeiter. **-y,** *adj.* geistreich, gescheit.
braise [breɪz], *v.a.* schmoren.
[1]**brake** [breɪk], *s.* das Farnkraut (*Bot.*); das Dickicht, Gebüsch, Gestrüpp.
[2]**brake,** 1. *s.* die Bremse, Hemmvorrichtung; (*fig.*) der Einhalt, Zügel; vierrädriger Wagen; *external contraction* –, die Außenbackenbremse; *four-wheel* –, die Vierradbremse; *internal expanding* –, die Innenbackenbremse; *put on* or *apply the* –, bremsen. 2. *v.n.* (ab)bremsen. **--block,** *s.* der Bremsklotz. **--cable,** *s.* die Bremstrosse. **--lever,** *s.* der Bremshebel. **- power,** *s.* die Bremsleistung. **-(s)man,** *s.* der Bremser. **--shoe,** *s.* die Bremsbacke. **--van,** *s.* der Bremswagen (*Railw.*). **--wheel,** *s.* das Bremsrad.
[3]**brake,** 1. *s.* die (Flachs)Breche; schwere Egge, die Harke. 2. *v.a.* brechen (*flax*); harken.
brambl-e ['bræmbl], *s.* der Brombeerstrauch; Dornbusch. **-ing,** *s.* der Bergfink (*Orn.*).
bran [bræn], *s.* die Kleie.
branch [brɑːntʃ], 1. *s.* der Ast, Zweig (*of a tree*); Arm (*of a candlestick*; *of a river, etc.*); die Zweigstelle, Filiale, das Zweiggeschäft (*of a business*); der Zweig, die Linie (*of a family*); das Fach (*of knowledge*); der Teil, die Unterabteilung, der Abschnitt (*of a whole*); – *of service*, die Waffengattung (*Mil.*); – *establishment*, das Zweiggeschäft, die Zweigstelle, Filiale; – *line*, die Zweigbahn, Seitenlinie (*Railw.*); Abzweigleitung (*Elec.*); Seitenlinie (*of a family*); *local* –, die Ortsgruppe; – *post-office*, das (Neben)-Postamt; *root and* –, gründlich. 2. *v.n.* Zweige treiben (*Bot.*); – *off*, (sich) abzweigen; – *out*, sich verzweigen, sich ausbreiten. **-less,** *adj.* zweiglos. **-y,** *adj.* zweigig, ästig.
brand [brænd], 1. *s.* der (Feuer)Brand, Kien; das Brandmal, der Makel; das (Waren)Zeichen, die Marke, Sorte, Warengattung (*C.L.*); der Brand (*of corn*); (*poet.*) das Schwert, die Fackel. 2. *v.a.* brandmarken; Zeichen einbrennen (*Dat.*). **-ing,** *s.* das Einbrennen, Brandmarken. **-ing-iron,** *s.* das Brenneisen. **--new,** *adj.* (*coll.*) funkelnagelneu.
brandish ['brændɪʃ], *v.a.* schwingen.
brandy ['brændɪ], *s.* der Kognak, Weinbrand, Branntwein; *cherry--*, das Kirschwasser. **--snap,** der Pfefferkuchen.
brash [bræʃ], 1. *s.* das Sodbrennen; Trümmergestein, die Eistrümmer (*pl.*). 2. *adj.* brüchig, morsch, bröckelig; (*coll.*) unverschämt, keck, dreist.
brass [brɑːs], *s.* das Messing; die Blasinstrumente (*pl.*); (*sl.*) die Unverschämtheit, eherne Stirn; (*sl.*) = *money*) die Pinke, der Draht; die Grabplatte; *bold as* –, frech wie Oskar. **- band,** das Blasorchester, die Blechmusik. **- farthing,** roter Heller, der Deut. **--founder,** *s.* der Gelbgießer. (*sl.*) **- hat,** der Stabsoffizier, hohes Tier. **- plate,** das Namenschild. (*sl.*) **--tacks,** die Hauptsache; *get down to --tacks*, zur Sache kommen. **-y,** *adj.* messingartig; (*fig.*) frech, unverschämt; grell, blechern (*of sound*).
brassard [brə'sɑːd], *s.* die Armbinde, das Armband.
brassie ['bræsɪ], *s.* eine Art Golfschläger (mit Messingbeschlag).
brassiere ['bræsɪɛː], *s.* der Büstenhalter.
brat [bræt], *s.* (*sl.*) der Balg, Knirps, Fratz, die Range.
bravado [brə'vɑːdoʊ], *s.* die Prahlerei.
brave [breɪv], 1. *adj.* tapfer, mutig; brav, rechtschaffen; prächtig, stattlich. 2. *v.a.* mutig entgegentreten (*Dat.*); trotzen (*Dat.*); herausfordern; standhalten; – *it out*, etwas trotzig durchsetzen. 3. *s.* indianischer Krieger. **-ry,** *s.* der Mut, die Tapferkeit; Pracht, der Putz.
bravo ['brɑːvoʊ], 1. *s.* der Bandit, Räuber, Meuchelmörder. 2. *int.* bravo!
brawl [brɔːl], 1. *v.n.* laut zanken, lärmen; *-ing brook*, murmelnder *or* rauschender Bach. 2. *s.* der Streit, Zank; Aufruhr; *street* –, der Straßenauflauf. **-er,** *s.* der Lärmer, Zänker.
brawn [brɔːn], *s.* die Schweinesülze; (*coll.*) das Muskelfleisch; (*fig.*) die Muskelkraft. **-iness,** *s.* die Muskelfülle. **-y,** *adj.* sehnig, muskulös.
[1]**bray** [breɪ], 1. *v.n.* schreien (*of donkeys*); schmettern (*as trumpets*). 2. *v.a.*; – *out*, ausposaunen, laut verkünden. 3. *s.* das Eselgeschrei; Schmettern.
[2]**bray,** *v.a.* zerstoßen, zerreiben.
braze [breɪz], *v.a.* hart löten, schweißen.
braz-en ['breɪzən], 1. *adj.* ehern, messingen; (*fig.*) frech, unverschämt; *-en-faced*, mit eherner Stirn, frech. 2. *v.a.*; *-en it out*, sich unverschämt durchsetzen. **-ier** [-ʒɪə], *s.* der Kupferschmied, Gelbgießer; die Kohlenpfanne, Feuerschale.
breach [briːtʃ], *s.* der Bruch, Riß, Sprung, die Lücke; Bresche, Einbruchstelle (*Mil.*); (*fig.*) die Übertretung, Verletzung, der Verstoß; die Uneinigkeit, Trennung, der Zwist; *stand in the* –, den Angriff aushalten; *step into the* –, in die Bresche springen; – *of close*, unbefugtes Betreten (*Law*); – *of a covenant*, der Vertragsbruch; – *of honour*, die Verletzung der Ehre; – *of the peace*, die Friedensstörung; – *of privilege*, die Übertretung der Privilegien; – *of promise* (*of marriage*), der Bruch des Eheversprechens; – *of trust*, die Veruntreuung, die Wortbrüchigkeit, der Vertrauensbruch.
bread [brɛd], *s.* das Brot; *black* –, das Roggenbrot; *brown* –, das Weizenschrotbrot; (*a piece* or *slice of*) – *and butter*, das Butterbrot; (*fig.*) der Lebensunterhalt, tägliches Brot; *--and-butter business*, das Geschäft das seinen Mann ernährt; *quarrel with one's – and butter*, aus Unzufriedenheit seine Stellung aufgeben; (*prov.*) *he knows on which side his – is buttered*, er versteht sich auf seinen Vorteil, er weiß, wo Barthel den Most holt; – *and cheese*, das Käsebrot; *consecrated* –, die Hostie; *loaf of* –, das (*or* der Laib) Brot; *piece* or *slice of* –, die Scheibe Brot; (*coll.*) – *and scrape*, dünn geschmiertes Brot; (*fig.*) knappe Nahrung; *take the – out of a p.'s mouth*, einem den Lebensunterhalt rauben; *be* (*put*) *on – and water*, nur Wasser und Brot bekommen. **--basket,** *s.* der Brotkorb; (*sl.*) Magen. **--bin,** der Brotkasten. **--crumb,** *s.* die Brotkrume. **--cutter,** *s.* die Brotschneidemaschine. **--fruit,** *s.* die Frucht des Brot(frucht)baumes. **-knife,** *s.* das Brotmesser. **--line,** *s.* (*coll.*) (*Amer.*) die Schlange der Bedürftigen bei Verteilungen von Speisen. **--stuffs,** *pl.* das Brotgetreide. **--winner,** *s.* der Ernährer, Brotverdiener; das Mittel zum Lebensunterhalt.
breadth [brɛdθ], *s.* die Breite, Weite, Ausdehnung, das Ausmaß; die Bahn (*of cloth*); Fülle, Größe; Großzügigkeit (*of mind*). **-ways, -wise,** *adv.* der Breite nach, in der Breite.
break [breɪk], **1.** *s.* der Bruch, die Lücke, der Riß, Zwischenraum, Einschnitt (*in* (*Gen.*)); die Unterbrechung, Pause; Abwechs(e)lung; der (Gedanken)-Strich (*Typ.*); Absatz (*Typ.*); Vorsprung, die Vertiefung (*Arch.*); Lichtung, der Durchhau (*in woods*); die Serie, Tour (*Bill.*); das Effet (*Crick.*); der Anbruch (*of day*); *at* –, in der Pause (*at schools*); (*sl.*) *bad* –, der Schnitzer; (*sl.*) *give s.o. a* –, einem eine Chance geben; *a – in the weather*, ein Witterungsumschwung; *without a* –, ohne Unterbrechung. **2.** *ir.v.a.* brechen; zerbrechen, zerschlagen, zersprengen; aufreißen (*the surface*); umbrechen (*the ground*); aufbrechen, durchbrechen, erbrechen (*locks, doors, letters, etc.*); bankrott machen, zugrunde richten (*a p. financially*); degradieren (*an officer*); unterbrechen (*a circuit*); ausschalten (*the current*) (*Elec.*); mahlen (*Paperm.*); **(a)** (*with nouns*) *that will – his back*, das wird ihm den Hals brechen *or* ihn zugrunde richten; (*coll.*) – *the back of s.th.*, das Schwerste einer S. hinter sich haben; – *the bank*, die Bank sprengen; – *the blow*, den Schlag mildern *or* abschwächen; – *bounds*, über die erlaubte Grenze hinausgehen; – *bulk*, zu löschen anfangen (*Naut.*); – *camp*, das Lager abbrechen; – *cover*, aus dem Lager hervorbrechen, ins Freie gehen (*of game*); – *the engagement*, die Verlobung auflösen; – *a fall*, den Fall aufhalten *or* schwächen; – *a flag*, eine Flagge aus-

breiten; – *one's fast*, etwas zu sich nehmen; – (*new*) *ground*, (ein Brachfeld) (um)pflügen; (*fig.*) ein neues Gebiet erschließen; *broken in health*, mit geschwächter Gesundheit; – *a p.'s heart*, einem das Herz brechen; – *the ice*, (*fig.*) das Eis brechen; – *a horse to harness*, ein Pferd einfahren; – *one's journey*, die Reise unterbrechen; – *the law*, das Gesetz übertreten; – *a matter to a p.*, einem etwas schonend mitteilen; – *o.s. of a habit*, sich (*Acc.*) von einer Gewohnheit abbringen *or* einer S. (*Gen.*) entwöhnen; sich (*Dat.*) etwas abgewöhnen; – *a promise*, ein Versprechen nicht halten; – *a p.'s pride*, jemandes Stolz demütigen; – *ranks*, wegtreten (*Mil.*); – *a record*, den Rekord schlagen; – *the silence*, das Schweigen brechen; *her sleep was broken*, ihr Schlaf wurde gestört; – *the spell*, den Zauber brechen; – *step*, ohne Tritt (marschieren); – *stones*, Steine klopfen; – *water*, an die Oberfläche kommen; – *wind*, Winde lassen; *they broke his windows*, sie warfen ihm die Fenster ein; – *one's word*, see – *a promise*; (**b**) (*with adverbs*) – *down*, abbrechen, niederreißen; – *down opposition*, Widerstand *or* Widerspruch beseitigen; – *in*, aufbrechen (*a door*); bändigen, abrichten, zureiten (*a horse*); – *off* abbrechen, losbrechen, lösen, unterbrechen (*conversation, etc.*); – *open*, aufbrechen, erbrechen; – *to pieces*, zerschlagen, zertrümmern; – *up*, zerkleinern, zerteilen, zerfasern, aufspalten, auflösen, zersprengen, zerschmettern; abwracken (*a ship*); auseinandertreiben (*a gathering*). **3.** *ir.v.n.* brechen, zerbrechen, zerspringen, reißen (*of rope, etc.*), zerreißen, bersten, platzen, in Stücke gehen, entzweigehen; schlagen, stürzen (*over*, über) (*as waves*); anbrechen, grauen (*of day*); wechseln, umschlagen (*of the voice*); sich zum Schlechten verändern (*of weather*); abspringen (*of a ball*); *my heart is ready to* –, mir will das Herz zerspringen; (*with adv. and preps.*) – *away*, sich losmachen, sich lossagen, abfallen, sich losreißen (*from*, von); sich davonmachen; abspringen; – *down*, zusammenbrechen, zerfallen; versagen, steckenbleiben; eine Panne haben (*Motor.*); ausgehen, zu Ende gehen, abnehmen, aussetzen; –*forth*, ausbrechen, hervorbrechen; – *in*, einbrechen, eindringen; unterbrechen; – *into*, einbrechen in; *the house was broken into*, in das Haus wurde eingebrochen; ausbrechen in (*laughter, etc.*); plötzlich anfangen (*a run*, zu laufen); – *in upon*, unterbrechen, einfallen in; – *loose*, sich losreißen, ausbrechen; – *off*, aufhören, abbrechen; – *out*, ausbrechen; geraten (*into*, in); – *out of*, ausbrechen aus; – *through*, durchbrechen, durchdringen (durch); – *to pieces*, in Trümmer gehen; – *up*, sich auflösen, auseinanderfallen, auseinandergehen, in Stücke gehen; für die Ferien schließen (*of school*); *he is –ing up*, es geht zu Ende mit ihm; *school –s up on Tuesday*, die Schule schließt am Dienstag; – *with a p.*, sich mit einem überwerfen, mit einem brechen *or* zerfallen. **–able,** *adj.* zerbrechlich; **–ables,** *pl.* zerbrechliche Waren. **–age,** *s.* das Brechen; der Bruch; *payment for –age*, die Refaktie. **–down,** *s.* der Zusammenbruch, das Versagen, die Zerrüttung (*of health*); *nervous –down*, der Nervenzusammenbruch, (*coll.*) Nervenklaps; die Betriebsstörung; technische Störung, der Versager (*Mech.*); die Panne (*of motor-cars, etc.*); *–down crane*, der Bergungskran; *–down gang*, die Hilfskolonne; *–down lorry*, der Abschleppwagen; *–down of negotiations*, das Scheitern der Verhandlungen. **–er,** *s.* der Brecher, Zerstörer; Übertreter (*Law*); die Sturzsee. **–ers,** *pl.* die Brandung, die Sturzwellen (*pl.*); *–ers ahead!* Gefahr in Sicht. **–ing,** *s.* das Brechen, Abreißen; *–ing and entering*, der Einbruch (*Law*); **–ing-in,** *s* der Einbruch; das Zureiten, Abrichten (*of animals*). **–ing-load,** *s.* die Bruchbelastung, Reißbelastung. **–ing-off,** *s.* der Abbruch. **–ing-out,** *s.* der (Haut)Ausschlag (*Med.*); der Ausbruch. **–ing-point,** *s.* der Bruchpunkt, die Festigkeitsgrenze. **–ing-strength,** *s.* die Reißfestigkeit, Zugfestigkeit. **–ing-stress,** *s.* **die** Bruchbeanspruchung. **–ing-up,** *s.* der (Schul)-Schluß. **– –neck,** *adj.* halsbrecherisch. **– –through,** *s.* der Durchbruch (*Mil.*). **– –up,** *s.* der Aufbruch, die Auflösung. **–water,** *s.* der Wellenbrecher, die Buhne.

breakfast [ˈbrɛkfəst], **1.** *v.n.* frühstücken. **2.** *s.* das Frühstück; – *things*, das Frühstücksgeschirr.

[1]**bream** [briːm], *s.* der Brassen (*Icht.*).

[2]**bream,** *v.a.* reinbrennen, abflammen (*Naut.*).

breast [brɛst], **1.** *s.* die Brust; der Busen; das Herz; *a child at her* –, ein Kind an der Brust; *make a clean* – *of it*, es offen bekennen, eingestehen *or* heraussagen, reinen Wein einschenken. **2.** *v.a.* trotzen, Trotz bieten (*Dat.*); gerade losgehen auf (*Acc.*); – *a hill*, einen Hügel hinaufsteigen; – *the waves*, sich gegen die Strömung stemmen; *double–ed*, zweireihig; *narrow-–ed*, engbrüstig. **–bone,** *s.* das Brustbein. **– –high,** *adj.* brusthoch. **– –pin,** *s.* die Vorstecknadel, Schlipsnadel. **–plate,** *s.* der Brustharnisch, Brustpanzer (*of armour*); das Vorderzeug (*of harness*); der Bauchschild (*of tortoises*). **– –strap,** *s.* das Blatt (*of harness*). **– –stroke,** *s.* das Brustschwimmen. **–work,** *s.* die Brustwehr, Schulterwehr (*Fort.*); das Schanzkleid, die Reeling (*Naut.*).

breath [brɛθ], *s.* der Atem; Hauch; Atemzug; die Stimmlosigkeit (*Phonet.*); (*a*) (*with nouns*) – *of air*, das Lüftchen; – *of scandal, suspicion, etc.*, eine Spur *or* leiseste Andeutung von Verleumdung, Verdacht, *etc.*; *shortness of* –, die Kurzatmigkeit; (*b*) (*with verbs*) *draw* –, Atem schöpfen *or* holen; *draw a deep* –, tief aufatmen; *give me time to draw* –, laß mich ein wenig zu Atem kommen; *gasp for* –, nach Luft schnappen; *get one's* – (*back*), Atem holen, verschnaufen; *hold one's* –, den Atem anhalten; (*coll.*) *keep your* – *to cool your porridge*, spare deine Worte, behalte deinen Rat für dich; *that knocks the* – *out of me* or *takes my* – *away*, das benimmt, raubt *or* versetzt mir den Atem; *waste one's* –, in den Wind reden; (*c*) (*with prepositions*) *at every* –, bei jedem Atemzuge; *in one* –, in einem Atem; *in the same* – *with*, in demselben Augenblicke wie, zugleich mit; *out of* –, außer Atem; *to one's dying* –, bis zum letzten Atemzuge; *under one's* –, leise flüsternd; *with bated* –, mit verhaltenem Atem. **–e** [briːð], **1.** *v.n.* atmen, Atem holen, Luft einholen; *–e in*, einatmen; *–e out*, ausatmen; *–e again* or *freely*, wieder frei aufatmen; *–e on a p.*, einen anhauchen; *–e upon a p.'s reputation*, jemandes Ruf beflecken *or* besudeln. **2.** *v.a.* atmen, einatmen, ausatmen; hauchen, flüstern; verlauten lassen, verraten; verschnaufen lassen (*horses*); *–e one's last*, den letzten Atemzug tun, in den letzten Zügen liegen; *–e vengeance*, Rache schnauben; *–e a wish*, einen Wunsch äußern *or* an den Tag legen; *not –e a word of* or *about it*, kein Wort davon erwähnen. **–ed,** *adj.* stimmlos (*Phonet.*). **–er** [ˈbriːðə], *s.* Atmende(r), *m.*; (*coll.*) die Atempause; *go for the –er*, Luft schöpfen gehen; *take a –er*, Ruhepause machen. **–ing** [ˈbriːðɪŋ], **1.** *adj.* lebenswahr, sprechend (*as a portrait*). **2.** *s.* das Atmen, die Atmung, das Hauchen; der Hauchlaut (*Phonet.*); *deep-–ing exercise*, die Atemgymnastik. **–ing-hole,** *s.* das Luftloch. **–ing-pipe,** *s.* der Schnorchel (*submarines*). **–ing space,** *s.* die (Atem)Pause. **–less** [ˈbrɛθlɪs], *adj.* atemlos, außer Atem; außer sich (*with*, vor); schwül (*weather*). **–lessness,** *s.* die Atemlosigkeit. **– –taking,** *adj.* atemberaubend.

bred [brɛd], *see* **breed;** *cross-– dog*, Hund gekreuzter Rassen; *high-–*, vornehm; *ill-–*, ungebildet, ungezogen, unerzogen; *low-–*, gemein, ungebildet; *pure-–*, reinrassig; *thorough–* (*horse*), das Vollblut; *well-–*, wohlerzogen, gebildet.

breech [briːtʃ], **1.** *s.* Hintere(r), *m.*, das Gesäß; der Boden (*of trousers*); das Verschlußstück, der Laderaum (*of a gun*); – *leather*, das Hinterleder, Fahrleder (*of miners*). **2.** *v.a.* einem Jungen die ersten Hosen anziehen. **– –block,** *s.* der Verschluß, Verschlußblock, Blockverschluß; Verschlußkeil. **–ed,** *adj.* hosentragend. **–es** [ˈbrɪtʃɪz], *pl.* die Reithosen, Kniehosen; (*coll.*) *wear the –es*, die Hosen anhaben. **–es-buoy,** *s.* die Hosenboje. **–ing** [ˈbriːtʃɪŋ], *s.* das Hinterzeug, der Umgang (*Saddl.*). **– –loader,** *s.* der Hinterlader. **– –loading,** die Hinterladung. **– –plate,** *s.* das Bodenstück (*Gun.*). **– –pin,** *s.*, **– –plug,** *s.* der Verschlußkeil.

breed [briːd], **1.** *ir.v.n.* sich vermehren, sich fortpflanzen; zeugen, brüten, erzeugt werden; – *in and in*, sich durch Inzucht fortpflanzen; – *true*, rein weitervererben (*Biol.*) 2. *ir.v.a.* erzeugen, gebären; aufziehen, züchten; (*fig.*) hervorbringen, fortpflanzen, ausbrüten, aushecken; – *ill blood*, böses Blut machen; *bred in the bone*, angeboren. 3. *s.* die Brut, Zucht, Rasse, Art. **-er,** *s.* der Erzeuger; Züchter (*of cattle*); das Zuchttier. **-ing,** *s.* das Züchten, Aufziehen; Erzeugen, Brüten; die Erziehung, Bildung; *good -ing*, feine Lebensart. **-ing ground,** (*fig.*) der Nährboden. **-ing-pond,** *s.* der Laichteich.

[1]**breez-e** [brɪ:z], *s.* die Brise, leichter Wind; (*coll.*) der Zank, Streit; *light -e*, leichte Brise; *gentle -e*, schwacher Wind; *moderate -e*, mäßiger Wind; *fresh -e*, frischer Wind; *strong -e*, steifer Wind (*the above are Beaufort Scale 2 to 6*). **-y,** *adj.* windig, luftig; (*coll.*) munter, flott.

[2]**breeze,** *s.* die Bremse, Biesfliege (*Ent.*).

[3]**breeze,** *s* das Kohlenklein, die Lösche.

brehon [ˈbrɪ:hən], *s.* irischer Landrichter.

brent-goose [ˈbrɛntgʊ:s], *s* die Wildgans.

brethren [ˈbrɛðrɪn], *pl.* (*archaic*) die Brüder; (*Eccl.*) *my* –, liebe Brüder.

breve [brɪ:v], *s.* doppelte Taktnote (*Mus.*); das Kürzezeichen (*Phonet.*).

brevet [ˈbrɛvɪt], *s.*; – (*rank*), der Titularrang (*of*, als); – *major*, der Hauptmann mit Rang eines Majors.

breviary [ˈbrɪ·vɪərɪ], *s.* das Brevier (*R.C.*).

brevier [brəˈvɪ:ə], *s.* die Petit(schrift) (*Typ.*).

brevity [ˈbrɛvɪtɪ], *s.* die Kürze, (*prov.*) – *is the soul of wit*, Kürze ist des Witzes Würze.

brew [brʊ:], 1. *v.a.* brauen; kochen, bereiten; schmieden, ausbrüten, anzetteln (*mischief*). 2 *v.n.* im Anzug sein, sich zusammenziehen, heranziehen (*as a storm, etc.*); *a storm is -ing*, ein Gewitter zieht auf *or* ist im Anzuge. 3. *s.* das Gebräu, Bräu. **-er,** *s.* der Brauer, Bierbrauer. **-ery,** *s.* die Brauerei, das Brauhaus.

briar [ˈbraɪə], *see* **brier.**

brib-e [braɪb], 1. *s.* das Geschenk (zur Bestechung), die Bestechung; *offer a p. a -e*, einen bestechen wollen; *take a -e*, sich bestechen lassen. 2. *v.a.* bestechen, durch Bestechung verleiten **-able,** *adj.* bestechlich. **-ery** [-ərɪ], *s.* die Bestechung; *open to -ery*, bestechlich.

bric-à-brac [ˈbrɪkəbræk], *s.* Antiquitäten (*pl.*), Raritäten (*pl.*), Nippsachen (*pl.*).

brick [brɪk], 1. *s.* der Ziegelstein, Backstein; Würfel, (Bau)Klotz; (*coll.*) famoser Kerl; (*coll.*) *drop a* –, eine Taktlosigkeit begehen, einen Schnitzer machen; *fire--*, feuerfester Ziegelstein; *box of wooden -s*, der Holzbaukasten; *swim like a* –, wie eine bleierne Ente schwimmen; *like a ton of -s*, mit Riesenkrach. 2. *adj* Backstein-; *-colour* (*--red*), *s.* das Ziegelrot; *-facing*, die Backsteinverkleidung; – *wall*, die Backsteinmauer; *he can see through a – wall*, er hört das Gras wachsen, er kann alles. 3. *v.a.* mit Backsteinen bauen *or* pflastern; – *up*, zumauern. **-bat,** *s.* der Ziegelbrocken. **--clay,** *s.* die Ziegelerde. **--dust,** *s.* das Ziegelmehl. **--kiln,** *s.* der Ziegelofen, die Ziegelei **-layer,** *s.* der Maurer. **-laying,** *s.* die Maurerei. **--making,** *s.* das Ziegelbrennen. **-work,** *s.* der Backsteinbau; die Maurerarbeit. **-works,** *pl.*, **-yard,** *s.* die Ziegelei.

brid-al [ˈbraɪdl], 1 *adj.* bräutlich; *-al array*, der Brautschmuck; *-al chamber*, das Brautgemach; *-al wreath*, der Brautkranz, Jungfernkranz. 2. *s.* die Hochzeit, das Hochzeitsfest. **-e** [braɪd], *s.* neuvermählte Frau; die Braut am Tag der Trauung; *-e and -egroom*, das junge Paar, die Neuvermählten; *give the -e away*, Brautvater sein. **-egroom,** *s.* der Bräutigam am Hochzeitstag, junger Ehemann, der Neuvermählte. **-esmaid,** *s.* die Brautjungfer.

[1]**bridge** [brɪdʒ], 1. *s.* die Brücke; der Steg (*of string-instruments*); Rücken (*of the nose*); die (Kommando)Brücke (*Naut.*); – *of boats*, die Schiffsbrücke; *cable-suspension--*, die Drahtseilbrücke; *cantilever* –, die Auslegerbrücke; *chain--*, die Kettenbrücke; *draw-*, die Zugbrücke; *floating* or *flying* –, schwimmende Brücke; *foot-*, der Steg; *girder* –, die Fachwerk- *or* Trägerbrücke; *loading* –, die Verladebrücke; – *of the nose* der Nasenrücken; *suspension--*, die Hängebrücke; *swing* –, die Drehbrücke, *temporary* –, die Notbrücke. 2. *v.a.* eine Brücke schlagen (über (*Acc.*)); überbrücken; – *over*, (*fig.*) überbrücken. **-able,** *adj.* überbrückbar. **--building,** *s.* der Brückenbau. **-head,** *s.* der Brückenkopf (*Mil.*).

[2]**bridge,** *s.* das Bridge (*Cards*).

bridle [ˈbraɪdl], 1. *s.* der Zaum Zügel; *give a horse the* –, einem Pferde die Zügel schießen lassen. 2. *v.a.* zäumen, im Zaume halten, zügeln, bändigen; – *one's tongue*, seiner Zunge einen Zügel anlegen. 3. *v.n.*; (– *up*) sich brüsten; beleidigt tun (*at*, über). **--bit,** *s.* das Stangengebiß. **--hand,** *s.* linke Hand. **--path,** *s.* der Reitweg. **--rein,** *s.* der Zügel.

bridoon [brɪˈdʊ:n], *s.* die Trense (*Saddl.*). **--bit,** *s.* das Trensengebiß.

brief [brɪ:f], 1. *adj.* kurz, knapp, bündig, kurz gefaßt; flüchtig; *in* –, mit wenigen Worten, in kurzem; *be* –, sich kurz fassen. 2. *s.* das Breve (*of the Pope*); der Schriftsatz (*of solicitor for barrister*) (*Law*); *hold a* –, eine Sache vor Gericht vertreten; (*coll*) *hold a – for*, sprechen für, eingenommen sein für; (*coll.*) *hold no – for*, nicht viel übrig haben für. 3. *v a.* in Kenntnis setzen; – *a lawyer*, den Fall einem Rechtsanwalt übergeben. **--case,** *s.* die Aktentasche, Aktenmappe. **-ing,** *s.* die Flugbesprechung (*Av.*), der Einsatzbefehl (*Mil.*), die Instruktion (*Law*). **-less,** *adj.* ohne Praxis (*of lawyers*). **-ly,** *adv.* mit wenigen Worten, in kurzem. **-ness,** *s.* die Kürze, Knappheit.

brier [ˈbraɪə], *s.* der Dornstrauch; wilde Rose; das Bruyèreholz; *sweet--*, die Weinrose.

brig [brɪg], *s.* die Brigg.

brigad-e [brɪˈgeɪd], *s.* die Brigade; Abteilung (*Artil.*); *fire--e*, die Feuerwehr; *-e major*, der Brigadeadjutant. **-ier** [-gəˈdɪə], *s.* der Brigadegeneral.

brigand [ˈbrɪgənd], *s.* der (Straßen)Räuber, Brigant. **-age,** *s.* die Straßenräuberei.

brigantine [brɪgənˈtɪ:n], *s.* die Brigantine, der Briggschoner.

bright [braɪt] *adj.* hell, glänzend, leuchtend, klar; heiter, lebhaft; aufgeweckt, gescheit; – *colour*, lebhafte *or* leuchtende Farbe; – *day*, heiterer Tag; (*coll.*) – *and early*, recht früh; – *eyes*, strahlende Augen; – *prospects*, glänzende Aussichten; *-ly shining*, hellglänzend. **-en** [ˈbraɪtn], 1. *v.a.* glänzend machen, erhellen, erleuchten; (*fig.*) aufhellen; aufheitern; abklären, auffrischen, beleben (*Dye*); *-en up*, polieren, glänzen, glätten; *-en a p. up*, einen aufheitern. 2. *v.n.* (*-en up*) hell werden, sich aufklären, sich aufhellen; *the sky is -ening up*, der Himmel klärt sich auf. **--eyed,** *adj.* helläugig. **--hued,** *adj.* von leuchtender Farbe. **-ness** [ˈbraɪtnɪs], *s.* der Glanz, die Klarheit, Helligkeit; Heiterkeit, Lebhaftigkeit; Helle, Glätte (*as a polish, etc.*).

brill [brɪl], *s.* der Meerbutt (*Icht.*).

brillian-ce, -cy [ˈbrɪljəns(ɪ)], *s.* der Glanz, die Klarheit, Pracht; der Scharfsinn; das Feuer (*of gems*). **-t** [-nt], 1. *adj.* glänzend, leuchtend, strahlend; prächtig; hochbegabt (*a p.*), genial (*an idea*); *-t exploit*, glänzende Tat; *-t gloss*, der Hochglanz; *-t talker*, blendender Redner. 2. *s.* der Brillant; die Brillant(schrift) (*Typ.*).

brim [brɪm], 1. *s.* der Rand; die Krempe (*of a hat*); *fill to the* –, bis zum Rande füllen. 2. *v.n.* bis an den Rand voll sein; – *over*, übervoll sein, überlaufen; (*fig.*) übersprudeln (*with*, von); *-ming eyes*, tränende Augen. **-ful,** *adj.* bis zum Rande voll, übervoll (*of*, an). **-med** [-d], *adj.*; *broad--med hat*, breitkrempiger Hut. **-mer,** *s.* volles Glas; (*coll.*) steifer Strohhut.

brimstone [ˈbrɪmstən], *s.* (*archaic*) der Schwefel; – *butterfly*, der Zitronenfalter.

brindle(d) [ˈbrɪndl(d)], *adj.* gestreift, getigert; scheckig.

brin-e [braɪn], *s.* das Salzwasser, die Salzbrühe, Salzlauge, Sole, Lake. **-e-bath,** *s.* das Solbad. **-e-gauge,** *s.* die Salzwaage. **-y,** 1. *s.* (*coll.*) das Meer. 2. *adj.* salzig.

bring [brɪŋ], *ir.v.a.* bringen; herbringen, mitbringen, tragen, führen; – *about*, zuwege bringen, verursachen, hervorrufen, bewerkstelligen; umdrehen (*Naut.*); – *an action against a p.*, einen gerichtlich belangen, einen unter Anklage stellen; – *away*, wegbringen, wegschaffen; – *back*, zurückbringen; – *it back to mind*, sich dessen entsinnen; – *down*, herunterbringen *or* –holen; zurückverfolgen (*information*); abschießen, niederholen (*an aircraft*); – *down the house*, stürmischen Beifall hervorrufen; – *down prices*, die Preise herabsetzen; – *s.o. down*, einen demütigen; *his illness has brought him down greatly*, seine Krankheit hat ihn sehr geschwächt *or* heruntergebracht; – *down upon s.o.*, einem zufügen; – *down upon o.s.*, sich zuziehen; – *forth*, hervorbringen, ans Licht bringen, mit sich bringen; gebären (*children*), werfen (*animals*); – *forward*, vorwärtsbringen, vorbringen; anführen, zitieren; vortragen, übertragen (*C.L.*); – *home to a p.*, einem nahebringen, einem eindringlich vorstellen, einem zu Gemüte führen; (*sl.*) – *home the bacon*, Erfolg haben; – *in*, hereinbringen, hineinbringen, einführen; einbringen (*a bill*); Gewinn abwerfen, Geld eintragen *or* einbringen; – *in guilty*, für schuldig erklären *or* erkennen; – *in not guilty*, freisprechen; – *into notice*, bekanntmachen; – *into play*, in Gang bringen; – *into the world*, erzeugen, zur Welt bringen; – *off*, fortbringen (*Acc.*); (*coll.*) zustande bringen, fertigbringen, schaffen; – *on*, heranbringen, herbeiführen, verursachen, veranlassen; – *out*, herausbringen, in die Gesellschaft einführen (*a young lady*); aufdecken, an den Tag bringen; zu Gehör bringen, erweisen, hervorheben, herausstellen; herausgeben, veröffentlichen, verlegen (*a book*); auf den Markt bringen (*wares*); – *over*, herüberbringen, herüberziehen; – *a p. over to one's own way of thinking*, einen zu seiner eigenen Denkweise überreden *or* bekehren *or* für (*Acc.*) . . . gewinnen; – *round*, wiederherstellen, wieder zu Bewußtsein bringen; bekehren, umstimmen, überreden; vorfahren (*as a car*); *I will – it round tomorrow*, ich bringe es morgen herüber; – *through*, durchbringen; wiederherstellen; – *to*, beidrehen (*Naut.*); – *a ship to*, ein Schiff beilegen; – *to account*, in Rechnung stellen; – *to bear*, anwenden, anbringen; *be brought to bed* (*of a son*), (von einem Sohne) entbunden werden; – *to book*, zur Rechenschaft ziehen; – *to a close*, zum Abschluß bringen; *I cannot – myself to do it*, ich kann es nicht über mich *or* übers Herz bringen *or* ich bringe mich nicht dahin es zu tun; – *to a head*, zur Entscheidung bringen; – *to heel*, zur Strecke bringen; – *a p. to* (*himself*), einen wieder zu sich bringen; – *to an issue*, zum Austrag bringen; – *s.o. to justice*, einen gerichtlich belangen; – *to light*, ans Licht bringen, aufdecken; – *s.th. to life*, einer S. Leben verleihen; – *to* (*one's*) *mind*, (sich) erinnern an (*Acc.*); – *s.th. to his notice*, ihm etwas bekannt machen; – *to pass*, zustande bringen; – *a p. to his senses*, einen zur Vernunft bringen; – *to subjection*, unterwerfen; – *together*, zusammenbringen, versöhnen; – *under*, bezwingen, überwältigen, unterwerfen; – *things under a heading*, Sachen in einer Gruppe einschließen; – *up*, hinaufbringen, heraufbringen, heranschaffen; vorbringen, anführen, zur Sprache bringen; erziehen, aufziehen (*a child*); ausbrechen, herausbrechen (*food*); aufhalten, zum Stehen, Halten *or* Stillstand bringen (*s.th. moving*); vor Anker legen (*Naut*); – *up the rear*, den Nachtrab bilden, den Rückzug decken (*Mil.*); (*fig.*) der letzte sein; – *up to date*, auf den gegenwärtigen Stand bringen; – *upon o.s.*, sich (*Dat.*) zuziehen.

brink [brɪŋk], *s.* der Rand, das Ufer; *on the – of*, kurz *or* dicht vor, nahe (*Dat.*); *on the – of doing*, im Begriff sein zu tun; *hover on the –*, unschlüssig sein.

briny [ˈbrɑɪnɪ], *see* **brine.**

briquet(te) [ˈbrɪkət, brɪˈkɛt], *s.* das Brikett, die Preßkohle.

brisk [brɪsk], 1. *adj.* lebhaft, frisch, munter, flink; moussierend (*as beer*); – *sale* or *trade*, flotter Absatz. 2. *v.n.*; (*coll.*) – *up*, munter werden. 3. *v.a.* beleben, anfeuern, aufmuntern. **–ness,** die Lebhaftigkeit.

brisket [ˈbrɪskɪt], *s.* das Bruststück (*of meat*).

bristl–e [ˈbrɪsl], 1. *s.* die Borste (*also Bot.*). 2. *v.n.* sich sträuben; –*e* (*up*), auffahren; –*e with*, strotzen von. **–ed** [–d], *adj.*, **–y,** *adj.* borstig, stachelig.

brittle [ˈbrɪtl], *adj.* spröde, brüchig, bröckelig, zerbrechlich. **–ness,** *s.* die Sprödigkeit, Zerbrechlichkeit.

broach [broutʃ], 1. *s.* der Bratspieß (*Cul.*); die Turmspitze (*Arch.*); Ahle, der Pfriem (*Mech.*); Dorn (eines Schlosses). 2. *v.a.* anzapfen, anbohren (*a cask, etc.*); (aus)bohren (*a hole*); das Gespräch bringen auf (*Acc.*), aufs Tapet bringen (*a subject*); – *to*, querschlagen (*Naut*).

broad [brɔ:d], 1. *adj.* breit, weit, ausgedehnt; offen, klar, hell (*as daylight, etc.*); deutlich ausgesprochen (*as a hint*); frei, derb, grob, zu weitgehend; umfassend, umfangreich; *in – daylight*, am hellen *or* lichten Tag; – *hint*, der Wink mit dem Zaunpfahl; – *joke*, derber Spaß; *it's as – as it's long*, es läuft auf eins hinaus, es kommt auf eins heraus; *in – outlines*, in großen *or* groben Umrissen. – *Scots*, im schottischen Dialekt; *in the –est possible sense*, im allerweitesten Sinn; – *stare*, dreistes Angaffen, frecher Blick; – *views*, aufgeklärte, weite, liberale *or* tolerante Gesichtspunkte. 2. *adv.* völlig. **––arrow,** *s.* breitköpfiger Pfeil. **––axe,** *s.* die Streitaxt; das Breitbeil. **––bean,** *s.* die Saubohne. **––brimmed,** *adj.* breitkrempig, breitrandig (*as a hat*). **––built,** *adj.* breitgebaut; breitschult(e)rig, untersetzt. **–cast** [ˈbrɔ:dkɑ:st], 1. *v.a.* & *n.* breitwürfig säen, (*fig.*) verbreiten; durch Rundfunk verbreiten, im Radio übertragen, senden, ausstrahlen, im Rundfunk sprechen, singen, *etc.* 2. *s.* die (Rundfunk)-Sendung *or* Übertragung. 3. *adj.* & *adv.* mit der Hand gesät, ausgestreut; weit verbreitet; *sow –cast*, breitwürfig säen; *–cast programme*, das Rundfunkprogramm; *–cast receiver*, der Radioempfänger. **–caster,** *s.* der Sänger, Vortragende, *etc.* am Radio. **–casting,** *s.* der Rundfunk, das Radio. **–casting station,** *s.* der Sender. **–casting studio,** *s.* der Senderaum. **–cloth,** *s.* feines wollenes Tuch. **–en** [ˈbrɔ:dn], 1. *v.a.* breiter machen, verbreitern, erweitern, ausdehnen. 2. *v.n.* breiter werden, sich weiten *or* erweitern. **––gauged,** *adj.* weitspurig (*more than 1,435 mm.*) (*Railw.*). **–ish,** *adj.* etwas breit. **–ly,** *adv.* allgemein; *–ly speaking*, allgemein gesprochen. **––minded,** *adj.* weitherzig, tolerant, großzügig, duldsam. **–ness,** *s.* die Roheit, Grobheit, Schlüpfrigkeit. **–sheet** [ˈbrɔ:dʃɪ:t], *s.* das Flugblatt, Plakat. **––shouldered,** *adj.* breitschult(e)rig. **–side** [–sɑɪd], *s.* die Breitseite (*Naut.*), Abfeuerung aller Geschütze der Breitseite; volle Lage. **–side on,** *adv.*, **–side to,** *prep.* mit der Breitseite zugekehrt. **–sword** [–sɔ:d], *s.* der Säbel, breites Schwert. **–ways, –wise,** *adv.* der Breite nach.

brocade [broˈkeɪd], *s.* der Brokat. **–d** [–ɪd], *adj.* mit Brokatmuster geschmückt.

broccoli [ˈbrɔkəlɪ], *s.* der Spargelkohl, Broccoli.

brochure [brɔˈʃjuə], *s.* die Broschüre, Flugschrift.

brock [brɔk], *s.* der Dachs.

brocket [ˈbrɔkɪt], *s.* der Spießer, zweijähriger Hirsch.

brogue [broug], *s.* derber plumper Schuh; irischer Akzent.

[1]**broil** [brɔɪl], *s.* der Lärm, Streit, Zank, die Zwistigkeit.

[2]**broil,** 1. *v.a.* auf dem Roste braten, rösten. 2. *v.n.* (*fig.*) (in der Sonne) schmoren. **–ing,** *adj.* glühend *or* brennend heiß.

broke [brouk], *see* **break;** (*sl.*) pleite.

broken [ˈbroukən], *see* **break;** *adj.* gebrochen, zerbrochen; unterbrochen, fehlerhaft, unvollkommen; – *English*, gebrochenes Englisch; –*glass*, zerbrochenes Glas; – *ground*, unebenes Gelände; – *health*, zerrüttete Gesundheit; – *heart*, gebrochenes Herz; – *meat*, übriggebliebene Speisen, Speisereste (*pl.*), die Brocken; (*fig.*) – *reed*, schwankendes Rohr; – *sleep*, unterbrochener Schlaf, gestörte Ruhe; – *spirit*, niedergeschlagener Geist; – *stones*, der Steinschlag; – *time*, der Verdienstausfall; die Kurzarbeit; – *week*, unvollständige Arbeitswoche. **––backed** *adj.* krumm, gekrümmt; mit einem Katzenrücken (*Naut.*). **––down,** *adj.* gebrochen, niedergebrochen; heruntergekommen, verbraucht, unbrauchbar, ruiniert. **––hearted,** *adj.* mit gebrochenem Herzen. **––winded,** *adj.* kurzatmig (*Vet.*).

broker [ˈbroukə], *s.* der Makler, Agent, Vermittler,

Unterhändler, Zwischenhändler; Trödler, Pfandleiher; *exchange*--, der Wechselmakler; *stock*--, der Börsenmakler. **-age,** *s.* die Maklergebühr, Courtage, das Maklergeschäft.
brolly ['brɔlɪ], *s.* (*sl.*) *see* **umbrella.**
brom-ate ['broumeɪt], *s.* bromsaures Salz. **-ic,** *adj.* Brom-; *-ic acid,* die Bromsäure. **-ide** [-ɑɪd], *s.* das Bromid; (*Amer. sl.*) Phrasen (*pl.*); der Gemeinplatz; Phrasendrescher; *-ide of potassium,* das Bromkali. **-ine** [-ɪn], *s.* das Brom.
bronch-ia ['brɔŋkjə], *pl.* die Bronchien (*Anat.*). **-ial,** *adj.* Luftröhren-, bronchial; *-ial cold,* der Bronchialkatarrh; *-ial tube,* die Luftröhre. **-itis** [-'kɑɪtɪs], *s.* der Luftröhrenkatarrh. **-ocele** [-kəsɪ:l], *s.* der Kropf.
bronco ['brɔŋkou], *s.* (*coll.*) wildes Pferd. **--buster,** *s.* (*coll.*) der Zureiter.
bronz-e [brɔnz], 1. *s.* die Bronze; Bronzefigur; Bronzefarbe; *-e age,* das Bronzezeitalter (*Archaeol.*). 2. *v.a.* bronzieren; *his -ed countenance,* sein gebräuntes Gesicht.
brooch [broutʃ], *s.* die Brosche, Spange; Vorstecknadel.
brood [bru:d], 1. *s.* die Brut; Hecke; (*fig.*) Sippe, das Geschlecht. 2. *v.n.* brüten; – *on* or *over a matter,* über einer S. brüten; – *over,* schwer lasten auf (*Dat.*). **--hen,** *s.* die Bruthenne. **--mare,** *s.* die Zuchtstute. **-y** *adj.* brütig (*of hens*).
[1]**brook** [bruk], *s.* der Bach. **-let,** *s.* das Bächlein.
[2]**brook,** *v.n.* (*always neg.*) dulden, sich (*Dat.*) gefallen lassen.
broom [bru:m], *s.* der Besen; Geißklee (*Bot.*); (*fig.*) *new* –, der Auskehrer; (*prov.*) *new -s sweep clean,* neue Besen kehren gut. **-stick,** *s.* der Besenstiel.
brose [brouz], *s.* (*Scots*) die Hafergrütze.
broth [brɔθ], *s.* die Fleischbrühe, Kraftbrühe; – *of a boy,* (*Irish*) famoser Kerl.
brothel ['brɔθl], *s.* das Bordell, (*sl.*) der Puff.
brother ['brʌðə], *s.* der Bruder; (*fig.*) Mitmensch, Mitbruder, Amtsbruder, Kollege; – *in arms,* der Waffenbruder, Kriegskamerad; – *german,* der Vollbruder; *--in-law,* der Schwager; – *officer,* der Kamerad; *-s and sisters,* die Geschwister (*pl.*); *-s in affliction,* Leidensbrüder. **-hood,** *s.* die Bruderschaft, Brüderschaft. **-ly,** *adj.* brüderlich.
brougham [bru:(ə)m], *s.* der Brougham, geschlossener Einspänner.
brought [brɔ:t], *see* **bring.**
brow [brɑu], *s.* die (Augen)Braue; Stirn; das Aussehen, die Miene, der Gesichtsausdruck; Vorsprung (*of a cliff, etc.*); *knit one's* –, die Stirn runzeln; *by the sweat of one's* –, im Schweiße seines Angesichts. **--antlers,** *pl.* die Augensprosse. **-beat,** *v.a.* einschüchtern, grob anfahren.
brown [brɑun], 1. *adj.* braun; bräunlich, brünett; – *bread,* das Weizenschrotbrot; – *coal,* die Braunkohle; (*sl.*) *do* –, hineinlegen; – *paper,* das Packpapier; *in a – study,* in tiefes Nachsinnen versunken; – *sugar,* der Sandzucker; – *ware,* das Steingut. 2. *v.a.* bräunen, braun machen; beizen, braten. **-ie** ['brɑunɪ], *s.* das Heinzelmännchen; Jungmädel. **-ish,** *adj.* bräunlich. **-ness,** *s.* die Bräune, braune Farbe.
browse [brɑuz], 1. *s.* junges Laub, junge Triebe (*pl.*); das Viehfutter. 2. *v.a.* abäsen, abweiden. 3. *v.n.* weiden, äsen; (*fig.*) – *in* or *through,* durchblättern (*a book*).
bruis-e [bru:z], 1. *v.a.* quetschen, zermalmen, zerreiben, zerstoßen; wund *or* braun und blau schlagen; *-e malt,* Malz schroten; *-ed malt,* das Malzschrot. 2. *s.* die Quetschung. **-er,** *s.* die Schleifschale (*Opt.*); Presse, Quetsche; (*sl.*) der Boxer, Preiskämpfer; Kraftmeier.
bruit [bru:t], 1. *s.* das Gerücht. 2. *v.a.* verkünden, verbreiten, aussprengen.
brume [bru:m], *s.* der Nebel, Dunst.
brunette [bru:'nɛt], 1. *s.* die Brünette. 2. *adj.* brünett.
brunt [brʌnt], *s.* der Angriff, Anfall, Anprall; *bear the* –, der Wucht ausgesetzt sein.
brush [brʌʃ], 1. *s.* die Bürste, der Pinsel; der Bürstenstrich, das Abbürsten; die Rute, der Schwanz, Bruch (*Hunt.*); das Unterholz; Scharmützel (*Mil.*); die Lunte (*Artil.*); die Kupfer- *or* Drahtbürste; der Stromabnehmer (*of dynamo*); elektrische Entladung, das Strahlenbüschel (*Elec.*); *bath*--, die Frottierbürste; *blacking*--, die Wichsbürste; *clothes*--, die Kleiderbürste; *curry*--, die Kardätsche; *give me a – down,* bürsten Sie mich ab; *hair*--, die Haarbürste; *scratch*--, die Abkratzbürste. 2. *v.a.* bürsten, abbürsten, abwischen; streichen, bestreichen, streifen; – *against,* streifen, anstreifen, leicht berühren; – *away,* – *off,* abbürsten, wegbürsten, wegfegen, wegwischen; (*fig.*) übergehen; – *on one side,* beiseite schieben, (*fig.*) übergehen; – *past a p.,* einen im Vorbeieilen streifen; – *up,* reinigen; (*fig.*) auffrischen, erneuern. 3. *v.n.*; – *by* or *past,* vorbeieilen. **-able,** *adj.* streichfähig. **--off,** *s.* (*sl.*) *get the --off,* eine Abfuhr erleiden. **--proof,** *s.* der Bürstenabzug (*Typ.*). (*coll.*) **--up,** *s.* das Reinigen, Abbürsten. **-wood,** *s.* das Dickicht, Gestrüpp, Unterholz, Reisig.
brusque [brusk], *adj.* barsch, schroff, kurz angebunden. **-ness,** *s.* die Barschheit, Schroffheit.
brut-al ['bru:tl], *adj.* unmenschlich, brutal, roh, tierisch, viehisch. **-ality** [-'tælɪtɪ], *s.* die Unmenschlichkeit, Roheit, Brutalität. **-alize** [-təlɑɪz], 1. *v.a.* unmenschlich *or* roh behandeln *or* machen. 2. *v.n.* unmenschlich *or* viehisch werden. **-e** [bru:t], 1. *s.* unvernünftiges Wesen, das Tier, Vieh; (*fig.*) roher Mensch, das Scheusal. 2. *adj.* tierisch; unvernünftig, gefühllos, sinnlos; seelenlos; *-e force,* rohe Gewalt. **-ish,** *adj.* tierisch, viehisch; (*fig.*) gefühllos, dumm; *-ish pleasures,* fleischliche Lüste. **-ishness,** *s.* die Roheit, Dummheit.
bryony ['brɑɪənɪ], *s.* die Zaunrübe (*Bot.*).
bubbl-e ['bʌbl], 1. *s.* die Blase, Luftblase, Seifenblase; (*fig.*) leerer Schein, der Schaum, Schwindel; *rise in -es,* wallen, sprudeln; *South Sea -e,* der Südseeschwindel; *-e company,* die Schwindelgesellschaft. 2. *v.n.* (auf)wallen, Blasen aufwerfen, schäumen, perlen, sprudeln, brodeln; (*fig.*) *-e over with,* übersprudeln von. **-y,** 1. *adj.* sprudelnd, perlend, voller Blasen. 2. *s.* (*sl.*) der Champagner.
bubo ['bju:bou], *s.* die Leistenbeule (*Med.*). **-nic** [-'bɔnɪk], *adj.*; *-nic plague,* die Beulenpest. **-nocele** [bju:'bounosɪ:l], *s.* der Leistenbruch.
buccaneer [bʌkə'nɪə], 1. *s.* der Seeräuber, Freibeuter. 2. *v.a.* Seeräuberei treiben.
[1]**buck** [bʌk], 1. *s.* der Bock (*also Gymn.*); Rehbock; Ziegenbock; das Männchen (*of rabbits, etc.*); der Stutzer, Geck, Lebemann, Modeheld; (*sl.*) *pass the* –, die Verantwortung schieben auf. 2. *v.a.*; – *off,* abwerfen (*horseman*). 3. *v.n.* bocken (*as a horse*); (*sl.*) bockig sein; (*coll.*) – *up.* 1. *v.n.* sich beeilen, sich zusammenraffen; (*coll.*) – *up!* mach schnell! Kopf hoch! 2. *v.a.* ermutigen, aufmuntern; (*coll.*) *I am -ed!* ich bin höchsterfreut; (*coll.*) *he tried to – me up,* er versuchte mich aufzumuntern. **--bean,** *s.* der Sumpfklee (*Bot.*). **-board,** *s.* einfacher Wagen (*Amer.*). **--hound,** *s.* der Jagdhund. **--jump,** *v.n.* bocken. **--jumper,** *s.* störrisches Pferd. **-ram,** *s.* das Buckram, Steifleinen; (*fig.*) die Steifheit, Geziertheit. (*sl.*) **-shee,** *adj.* unentgeltlich, kostenfrei, umsonst. **-shot,** *s.* die Rehposten (*pl.*), der Grobschrot. **-skin,** *s.* das Wildleder; Rehfell. **-thorn,** *s.* der Kreuzdorn, Wegedorn (*Bot.*). **-wheat,** *s.* der Buchweizen.
[2]**buck,** 1. *s.* die Lauge, Beuche; – *ashes,* ausgelaugte Asche. 2. *v.a.* mit Laugen behandeln, beuchen.
bucket ['bʌkɪt], 1. *s.* der Eimer, Kübel; die Pütze (*Naut.*); der Lanzenschuh (*Mil.*); der Pumpenkolben; (*sl.*) *kick the* –, ins Gras beißen. 2. *v.n.* schlecht reiten *or* rudern. **-ful,** *s.* der Eimervoll; *in -fuls, adv.* eimerweise. **--shop,** *s.* die Winkelbörse. **--wheel,** *s.* das Zellenrad, Schöpfrad.
buckle ['bʌkl], 1. *s.* die Schnalle, Spange, das Koppelschloß. 2. *v.a.* zuschnallen; biegen, krümmen (*a wheel, etc.*); – *on,* anschnallen, umschnallen; – *up,* zuschnallen, aufschnallen. 3. *v.n.* einknicken, sich krümmen, sich (ver)biegen; (*coll.*) – (*down*) *to a th.,* sich eifrig an eine Sache machen, tüchtig daran gehen. **-r,** *s.* kleiner, runder Schild.
bucolic [bju:'kɔlɪk], 1. *adj.* ländlich, bukolisch, Hirten-; *-poetry,* die Hirtendichtung, Schäferdichtung. 2. *s.* (*usually pl.*) das Hirtengedicht.
bud [bʌd], 1. *s.* die Knospe, das Auge (*Bot.*), der Keim (*Zool.*); *in* –, in der Knospe; *in the* –, im

Keim, im Entstehen; *nipped in the* –, im Keime erstickt. 2. *v.n.* Knospen treiben, knospen, keimen, (*fig.*) sich entwickeln (*into*, zu (*Dat.*)); aufblühen; – *off*, entstehen (*from*, aus). 3. *v.a.* pfropfen, okulieren (*Hort.*); –*ding love*, aufkeimende Liebe; –*ding scholar*, angehender Gelehrter.

buddle [ˈbʌdl], 1. *s.* der Erzwaschtrog. 2. *v.a.* (Erz) waschen.

buddy [ˈbʌdɪ], *s.* (*sl.*) (*Amer.*) der Kamerad.

budge [bʌdʒ], 1. *v.n.* (*coll.*) sich rühren, sich regen. 2. *v.a.* (*coll.*) (*usually negative*) von der Stelle bringen.

budget [ˈbʌdʒɪt], 1. *s.* der Haushaltsplan, Voranschlag, Etat, Staatshaushalt, das Budget (*Parl.*); der Vorrat, Inhalt; – *of news*, der Stoß Neuigkeiten; *open the* –, den Haushaltsplan vorlegen. 2. *v.n.*; – *for*, im Budget vorsehen, (*coll.*) rechnen mit.

buff [bʌf], 1. *s.* das Büffelleder, Sämischleder; die Lederfarbe; (*coll.*) bloße Haut; *in* –, nackt. 2. *adj.* ledergelb, lederfarben, isabellfarbig; – *coat*, – *jerkin*, der Lederkoller. 3. *v.a.* mit Leder polieren.

buffalo [ˈbʌfəlou], *s.* der Büffel. **–-grass,** *s.* das Ellengras. **–-hide,** *s.* die Büffelhaut.

buffer [ˈbʌfə], *s.* der Puffer, die Stoßscheibe, das Stoßpolster; (*sl.*) *old* –, alter Tropf. **– state,** der Pufferstaat. **–-stop,** *s.* der Anschlagblock, Prellbock.

[1]**buffet** [ˈbʌfɪt], 1. *s.* der Puff, Stoß, Faustschlag; –*s of fate*, Schicksalsschläge (*pl.*). 2. *v.a.* puffen, mit der Faust schlagen; (*fig.*) ankämpfen gegen. **–ing,** *s.* die Schläge (*pl.*), der Anprall.

[2]**buffet** [ˈbufeɪ], *s.* das Büfett, der Schenktisch.

buffoon [bəˈfuːn], *s.* der Possenreißer, Narr, Hanswurst. **–ery,** *s.* die Possen (*pl.*), das Possenreißen.

bug [bʌg], *s.* die Wanze (*Ent.*); (*Amer.*) das Insekt, der Käfer; (*coll.*) *pl.* Bakterien; (*sl.*) *big* –, großes Tier, der Bonze; (*Amer. sl.*) *be a – on*, verrückt sein nach. **–gy,** *adj.* verwanzt. **–house,** *s.* (*sl.*) das Irrenhaus.

bugbear [ˈbʌgbɛə], *s.* der Popanz, das Schreckgespenst.

bugger [ˈbʌgə], 1. *s.* der Sodomit (*Law*); (*vulg.*) gemeiner Kerl, der Lump. 2. *v.a.* Unzucht treiben mit. **–y,** *s.* die Unzucht.

buggy [ˈbʌgɪ], *s.* zwei– (*Amer.* vier)rädriger Einspänner.

[1]**bugle** [ˈbjuːgl], **–-horn,** *s.* das Jagdhorn (*Mus.*), Signalhorn (*Mil.*). **–-call,** *s.* das Horn– *or* Trompetensignal. **–r,** *s.* der Hornist, Hornbläser.

[2]**bugle,** *s.* die Schmelzperle, (schwarze) Glasperle.

bugloss [ˈbjuːglɔs], *s.* der Natternkopf (*Bot.*).

buhl [buːl], *s.*, **–-work,** eingelegte Arbeit.

build [bɪld], 1. *ir.v.a.* bauen; erbauen, errichten, konstruieren; bilden, gestalten; – *in*, zubauen, verbauen; – *into*, einbauen in; – *up*, verbauen, zubauen, (*fig.*) aufbauen; – *upon*, setzen *or* bauen auf. 2. *ir.v.n.*; – *up to*, entwickeln zu; – *upon*, bauen *or* sich verlassen auf. 3. *s.* der Bau, Schnitt, Stil, die Form, Gestalt, Bauart; der Körperbau, die Figur. **–er,** *s.* der Baumeister, Bauherr, Bauunternehmer; Erbauer. **–ing,** *s.* das Bauen; Bauwesen; Gebäude, Bauwerk, der Bau, (*pl.*) die Nebengebäude; *public –ing*, öffentliches Gebäude. **–ing-contract,** *s.* der Baukontrakt. **–ing-contractor,** *s.* der Bauunternehmer. **–ing-lot,** *see* **–ing-site.** **–ing-lease,** *s.* die Baupacht. **–ing-line,** *s.* die Bauflucht (*Arch.*). **–ing material,** das Baumaterial, der Baustoff. **–ing-site,** *s.* das Baugrundstück, der Bauplatz, die Baustelle. **–ing-society,** *s.* die Bausparkasse, Baugenossenschaft. **–ing-trade,** *s.* das Baugewerbe.

built [bɪlt], *see* **build;** *adj.* gebaut. **–-up,** *adj.* zusammengesetzt; –-*up area*, geschlossene Ortschaft; –-*up gun*, die Ringkanone.

bulb [bʌlb], *s.* die Zwiebel, Knolle, der Knollen (*Bot.*); die Wurzel (*of hair, etc.*); Kugel (*of thermometer*); der Apfel (*of the eye*); (Glas)Kolben; (*electric*) –, die (Glüh)Birne. **–ous** [–əs], *adj.* zwiebelförmig, zwiebelartig, knollig; –*ous root*, die Knollenwurzel.

bulg–e [bʌldʒ], 1. *v.n.* hervorragen, hervorstehen, vorspringen, sich ausbauchen, sich bauschen, sich aufblähen, anschwellen. 2. *s.* die Anschwellung, Ausbuchtung, Ausbauchung; der Frontvorsprung (*Mil.*); –*e of a cask*, der Bauch eines Fasses. **–y,** *adj.* bauchig, angeschwollen.

bulk [bʌlk], 1. *s.* der Umfang, die Größe, Masse, das Volumen; der Hauptteil, die Hauptmenge, Hauptmasse, größter Teil, die Mehrzahl; die (Schiffs)Ladung (*Naut.*); *break* –, die Ladung zu löschen anfangen (*Naut.*); *in* –, in losen Haufen; unverpackt (*Naut.*); *in* or *by* –, in großen Mengen, im ganzen; *in the* –, in Bausch und Bogen; – *purchase*, der Masseneinkauf. 2. *v.n.* Umfang *or* Bedeutung haben; – *large*, großen Umfang haben, (*fig.*) eine große Rolle spielen. 3. *v.a.* aufhäufen; – *things together*, Sachen zusammennehmen. **–iness,** *s.* die Größe, großer Umfang. **–y** [ˈbʌlkɪ], *adj.* groß, massig, umfangreich, voluminös; unhandlich, sperrig; –*y goods*, das Sperrgut.

bulkhead [ˈbʌlkhɛd], *s.* das Schott (*Naut.*).

[1]**bull** [bul], 1. *s.* der Stier, Bulle; Haussier (*C.L.*); *like a – in a china-shop*, wie ein Elephant im Porzellanladen; *take the – by the horns*, den Stier bei den Hörnern fassen. 2. *v.a.* & *n.* auf Hausse spekulieren; in die Höhe treiben (*prices*) (*C.L.*). **–-baiting,** *s.* die Stierhetze. **–dog** [–dɔg], *s.* die Bulldogge, der Bullenbeißer; (*fig.*) der Starrkopf; (*sl.*) Universitätsdiener. **–doze** [–douz], *v.a.* (*sl.*) einschüchtern. **–dozer,** *s.* der Erdbagger, die Schuttramme; Panzerschaufel. **–fight,** *s.* der Stierkampf. **–finch,** *s.* der Dompfaff, Gimpel (*Orn.*); die Hecke. **–frog,** *s.* der Ochsenfrosch, Brüllfrosch. **–head,** *s.* der Kaulkopf (*Ichth.*). **–-headed,** *adj.* dickköpfig, hartnäckig, dumm. **–-necked,** *adj.* stiernackig. **–ock** [ˈbulək], *s.* der Ochse. **–ring,** *s.* die Stierkampfarena. **–'s-eye,** *s.* die Blendlaterne; das Ochsenauge, Bullauge (*Naut.*); Schießscheibenzentrum, das Schwarze; der Kernschuß; die Konvexlinse (*Opt.*); die Pfefferminzkugel; –*'s-eye glass*, die Butzenscheibe.

[2]**bull,** *s.* päpstliche Bulle.

[3]**bull,** *s.* (*Irish* –) der Unsinn, die Ungereimtheit, der Kalauer.

bullace [ˈbuləs], *s.* die Krieche, Haferschlehe (*Bot.*).

bullet [ˈbulɪt], *s.* das Geschoß, die Kugel; *armour-piercing* –, das Panzergeschoß, Stahlkerngeschoß; *explosive* –, das Sprenggeschoß; *incendiary* –, das Brandkerngeschoß; *spent* –, matte Kugel; *tracer* –, das Leuchtspurgeschoß; (*Prov.*) *every – has its billet*, jede Kugel hat ihre Bestimmung. **–-headed,** *adj.* rundköpfig. **–-hole,** *s.* das Schußloch. **–-proof,** *adj.* kugelsicher, kugelfest, schußsicher; –-*proof glass*, das Panzerglas.

bulletin [ˈbulɪtɪn], *s.* das Bulletin, der Tagesbericht, (kurze) Bekanntmachung.

bullion [ˈbuljən], *s.* der Münzbarren, ungemünztes Edelmetall, die Franse.

bully [ˈbulɪ], 1. *s.* der Raufbold, Renommist; Tyrann (*among schoolboys*); Abschlag (*Hockey*). 2. *v.a.* tyrannisieren, quälen, einschüchtern, schurigeln, kujonieren. 3. *v.n.* (– *off*) abschlagen (*Hockey*). 4. *adj.* (*Amer. sl.*) famos, erstklassig. **–-beef,** *s.* (*coll.*) das Büchsenfleisch.

bulrush [ˈbulrʌʃ], *s.* die Teich– *or* Sumpfbinse (*Bot.*).

bulwark [ˈbulwəːk], *s.* das Bollwerk, die Bastei, Verschanzung (*Fort.*); das Schanzkleid, die Reeling (*of a ship*); (*fig.*) der Schutz, Halt, die Stütze.

bum [bʌm], 1. *s.* (*vulg.*) Hintere(r), *m.*, der Steiß, das Gesäß; (*Amer. sl.*) der Landstreicher, Bummler. 2 *v.n.* (*Amer. sl.*) vagabundieren, sich durchschlagen, herumlungern. **–-bailiff,** *s.* der Büttel, Scherge, Gerichtsdiener. **–-boat,** *s.* das Proviantboot.

bumble-bee [ˈbʌmblˈbɪː], *s.* die Hummel.

bumbledom [ˈbʌmbldəm], *s.* die Wichtigtuerei.

bumf [bʌmf], *s.* (*vulg.*) das Klosettpapier.

bump [bʌmp], 1. *s.* der Schlag, Stoß; die Beule; der Höcker (*Phren.*); (*fig.*) der Sinn, das Organ; *nasty – on his head*, böse Beule am Kopf; – *of locality*, der Ortssinn, Orientierungssinn. 2. *v.a.* stoßen, schlagen (*against*, gegen; *on*, an (*Acc.*)); – *one's head*, mit dem Kopf stoßen, sich (*Dat.*) gegen den Kopf stoßen; (*sl.*) – *off*, töten, umbringen, um die Ecke bringen. 3. *v.n.* (– *into*, – *against*) zusammenstoßen, bumsen. **–y,** *adj.* holperig; böig (*Av.*).

bumper [ˈbʌmpə], *s.* volles Glas; der Humpen;

Prellbock (*Railw.*); Stoßfänger (*Motor.*); volles Haus (*Theat.*) – *crop*, reiche Ernte.
bumpkin [ˈbʌmpkɪn], *s.* der Bauernlümmel, Tölpel.
bumptious [ˈbʌmpʃəs], *adj.* aufgeblasen anmaßend.
bun [bʌn], *s.* das Korinthenbrötchen; der Kauz (*of hair*); *hot cross*--, die Karfreitagssemmel.
bunch [bʌntʃ], 1. *s.* das Bund, Bündel, der Strauß (*of flowers*), Büschel (*of hair, etc.*); das Erznest, der Butzen (*Min.*); (*coll.*) die Gruppe, Gesellschaft; – *of feathers*, der Federbusch; – *of grapes*, die Weintraube; – *of keys*, der Schlüsselbund; – *of radishes*, das Bund Radieschen; *the best of the* –, der (die, das) Beste von allen. 2. *v.n.* (– *together*) sich zusammenschließen; (– *out*) aufschwellen. 3. *v.a.* zusammenbinden. **-y,** *adj.* in Büscheln wachsend, büschelig; buschig; traubenförmig.
buncombe [ˈbʌŋkəm], *s.* (*coll.*) leeres Geschwätz, der Quatsch.
bundle [ˈbʌndl], 1. *s.* das Bund, Bündel, der Pack, das Paket; die Rolle, der Ballen; – *of nerves*, das Nervenbündel. 2. *v.a.*; – *away*, *off* or *out*, eilig fortschicken *or* wegschaffen; – *up*, zusammenrollen, zusammenpacken. 3. *v.n.*; – *off* or *out*, sich packen *or* davonmachen.
bung [bʌŋ], 1. *s.* der Spund, Zapfen. 2. *v.a.* spunden; (*sl.*) werfen, schleudern; – *up*, verspunden, verstopfen; -*ed up*, verschwollen (*eyes*). **--hole,** *s.* das Spundloch.
bungalow [ˈbʌŋgəloʊ], *s.* einstöckiges Sommerhaus.
bungl-e [ˈbʌŋgl], 1. *s.* die Pfuscherei, Stümperei. 2. *v.a.* verpfuschen, verhunzen; -*ed work*, die Pfuscharbeit. 3. *v.n.* stümpern, pfuschen. **-er,** *s.* der Stümper, Pfuscher. **-ing,** *adj.* ungeschickt, stümperhaft.
bunion [ˈbʌnjən], *s.* die Entzündung (an der großen Zehe).
[1]**bunk** [bʌnk], *s.* die Koje. **-er,** *s.* der (Kohlen)-Bunker; Betonunterstand (*Mil.*); die Truhe, Kiste; das Sandloch, Hindernis (*Golf*).
[2]**bunk,** *v.n.*; *do a* –, (*sl.*) ausreißen.
[3]**bunk** (*sl.*), **-um,** (*coll.*) *s. see* **buncombe.**
bunny [ˈbʌnɪ], *s.* (*coll.*) das Kaninchen.
bunt [bʌnt], *s.* der Bauch (*of a sail*); der Weizenbrand (*Bot.*).
[1]**bunting** [ˈbʌntɪŋ], *s.* das Flaggentuch; der Flaggenschmuck, die Flaggen (*pl.*).
[2]**bunting,** *s.* die Ammer (*Orn.*).
buoy [bɔɪ], 1. *s.* die Boje; *bell*--, die Glockenboje; *life*--, die Rettungsboje; *light*--, die Leuchtboje; *whistling* –, die Heulboje. 2. *v.a.* durch Bojen bezeichnen, ausbojen; – *up*, flott *or* schwimmend erhalten, über Wasser halten; (*fig.*) aufrechterhalten, emporheben. **-ancy,** *s.* die Schwimmkraft, das Tragvermögen (*Phys.*); der Auftrieb (*Hydr.*); (*fig.*) die Schwungkraft, Spannkraft, Lebenskraft. **-ancy tank,** der Auftriebstank (*Naut.*). **-ant,** *adj.* schwimmend, schwimmkräftig, tragfähig, leicht; (*fig.*) lebhaft, unbekümmert, in gehobener Stimmung, heiter; steigend (*of prices*) (*C.L.*).
bur [bə:], *s.* die Klette (*Bot.*); *cling like a* –, wie eine Klette haften. **--oak,** *s.* großblättrige Eiche.
burble [ˈbə:bl], *v.n.* murmeln, unverständlich reden.
burbot [ˈbə:bət], *s.* die Aalraupe, Quappe (*Icht.*).
burden [ˈbə:dn], 1. *s.* die Bürde, Last, der Druck, die Belastung; (also *burthen*) Tragkraft, der Tonnengehalt (*of a ship*); (*fig.*) der Hauptgedanke, das Hauptthema, der Kern; das Leitmotiv, der Refrain; *be a* – *to s.o.*, einem zur Last fallen; *beast of* –, das Lasttier; *ship of 2,000 tons* – (or *burthen*), ein Schiff von 2000 Tonnen. 2. *v.a.* belasten, beladen. **-some,** *adj.* drückend, lästig, beschwerlich.
burdock [ˈbə:dɔk], *s.* die Klette (*Bot.*).
bureau [bjʊəˈroʊ], *s.* das Geschäftszimmer, Amt, Kontor, Büro, Bureau, die Amtsstube; Abteilung eines Ministeriums (*Amer.*); verschließbares Schreibpult; die Kommode (*Amer.*); *information*--, die Auskunftsstelle. **-cracy** [-ˈrɔkrəsɪ], *s.* die Bürokratie, Beamtenherrschaft. **-crat,** *s.* der Bürokrat; (*coll.*) Aktenkrämer. **-cratic** [-ˈkrætɪk], *adj.* bürokratisch; (*iron.*) nach Schema F, den Amtsschimmel reitend.
burette [bjuˈrɛt], *s.* die Bürette (*Chem.*).
burgee [bə:ˈdʒɪ:], *s.* dreieckiger Wimpel (*Naut.*).
burgeon [ˈbə:dʒən], 1. *s.* die Knospe, der Sproß, Keim. 2. *v.n.* Knospen treiben, knospen, sprossen, keimen.
burgess [ˈbə:dʒɪs], *s.* der (Wahl)Bürger, Wähler (*Hist.*), Abgeordnete(r), *m.*
burgh [ˈbʌrə], *s.* die Stadt(gemeinde) (*Scots*). **-er** [ˈbə:gə], *s.* (*not only Scots*) der Bürger.
burgl-ar [ˈbə:glə], *s.* der Einbrecher; *cat--ar*, der Fassadenkletterer. **-ar-proof,** *adj.* diebessicher. **-ary** [-rɪ], *s.* der Einbruch, Einbruchsdiebstahl; *insurance against -ary*, die Einbruchsversicherung. **-e** [ˈbə:gl], *v.a.* einbrechen in (*Acc.*).
burgomaster [ˈbə:gomɑ:stə], *s.* der Bürgermeister.
burial [ˈbɛrɪəl], *s.* das Begräbnis, die Beerdigung, Bestattung. **--ground,** *s.* der Begräbnisplatz, Kirchhof, Friedhof, (*poet.*) Gottesacker. **--place,** *s.* die Grabstätte. **-service,** die Trauerfeier, Totenfeier, Totenmesse.
burke [bə:k], *v.a.* heimlich ermorden, ersticken, erwürgen; (*coll.*) vertuschen, unterdrücken; – *inquiry*, Nachforschungen vertuschen.
burl [bə:l], 1. *s.* der Knoten (*in yarn*), (*Amer. also in wood*). 2. *v.a.* noppen (*cloth*). **-ap,** *s.* das Juteleinen, grobe Leinwand.
burlesque [bə:ˈlɛsk], 1. *adj.* burlesk, possenhaft, possierlich, lächerlich. 2. *s.* das Lächerliche, Possenhafte; die Burleske, Posse, Parodie (*Theat.*). 3. *v.a.* lächerlich machen, possenhaft behandeln, travestieren, parodieren.
burly [ˈbə.lɪ], *adj.* stämmig, kräftig; stark, beleibt.
[1]**burn** [bə:n], *s.* der Bach (*Scots*).
[2]**burn,** 1. *ir.v.a.* brennen, in Brand stecken, verbrennen; anbrennen (*meat, etc.*); einbrennen (*a mark, etc.*); bräunen (*of the sun*); – *alive*, lebendig verbrennen; – *one's boats*, alle Brücken hinter sich abbrechen; – *the candle at both ends*, seine Kräfte vergeuden, sich allzusehr ausgeben; – *to death*, verbrennen; – *one's fingers*, sich (*Dat.*) die Finger verbrennen; (*coll.*) *he has money to* –, er hat Geld wie Heu; *the money -s a hole in his pocket*, das Geld juckt *or* brennt ihm in der Tasche; – *down*, abbrennen, niederbrennen; – *out*, ausbrennen, ausräuchern; – *to the ground*, bis auf den Grund niederbrennen; – *up*, aufbrennen. 2. *ir.v.n.* brennen, entbrennen, aufflammen; (*fig.*) glühen, brennen (*with*, vor); *my ears* –, meine Ohren klingen; – *away*, abbrennen; – *into*, sich tief einfressen in (*Acc.*); *it -ed itself into my mind*, es machte auf mich einen unauslöschlichen Eindruck; – *out*, ausbrennen; durchbrennen (*Elec.*); – *up*, aufflammen; gänzlich verbrennen. 3. *s.* das Brandmal, die Brandwunde. **-able,** *adj.* (ver)brennbar. **-ed,** *see* **-t;** -*ed alive*, lebendig verbrannt. **-er,** *s.* der Brenner; *Bunsen -er*, der Bunsenbrenner; *charcoal--er*, der Köhler, Kohlenbrenner. **-ing,** 1. *adj.* brennend (*also fig.*); glühend, leidenschaftlich, feurig; *my ears are -ing*, mir klingen die Ohren; (*B.*) *the -ing bush*, feuriger Busch; -*ing question*, hochwichtige *or* brennende Frage; -*ing shame*, schreiende Ungerechtigkeit, wahre Schmach. 2. *s.* das Brennen, Verbrennen; der Brand; *smell of -ing*, *v.n.* nach Brand riechen; *s.* der Brandgeruch. **-ing-bush,** *s.* der Diptam (*Bot.*). **-ing-glass,** *s.* das Brennglas (*Opt.*). **-ing-test,** *s.* die Verbrennungsprobe. **-t,** *adj.* gebrannt, verbrannt; -*t almonds*, gebrannte Mandeln; -*t bricks*, Backsteine; (*prov.*) *a -t child dreads the fire*, das gebrannte Kind scheut das Feuer; -*t earthenware*, die Terrakotta; -*t gas*, das Abgas, Auspuffgas; -*t sienna*, die Siennaerde; *taste -t*, angebrannt schmecken. **-t-offering, -t-sacrifice,** *s.* das Brandopfer.
burnet [ˈbə:nɪt], *s.* **--saxifrage,** *s.* die Pimpinelle (*Bot.*).
burnish [ˈbə:nɪʃ], 1. *v.a.* glätten, (hoch)polieren, glänzend machen, glanzschleifen, brünieren. 2. *s.* der Hochglanz (*of metals*). **-er,** *s.* der Polierer; Polierstahl, Brünierstahl.
burnous [bə:ˈnu:s], *s.* der Burnus.
[1]**burr** [bə:], *s.* die Klette; *see* **bur.**
[2]**burr,** *s.* das Zäpfchen-r (*as in northern England*); unartikulierte Aussprache (*as in western England*).
[3]**burr,** *s.* der Mühlstein, Schleifstein, Wetzstein; rauhe Kante (*Metall., etc.*).

burrow [ˈbʌroʊ], 1. *s.* der Bau (*rabbits, etc.*). 2. *v.n.* sich eingraben, in eine Erdhöhle verkriechen; (*fig.*) sich vertiefen (*into*, in (*Acc.*)). 3. *v.a.* aufwühlen.
bursar [ˈbəːsə], *s.* der Schatzmeister, Zahlmeister, Kassenwart; Quästor (*Univ.*).; Stipendiat (*in Scottish universities*). **-y,** *s.* das Schatzamt, die Kasse, Quästur; (*Scots*) das Stipendium.
burst [bəːst], 1. *v.n.* bersten, platzen (*with*, vor); aufspringen, zerspringen, explodieren, zerknallen, krepieren (*Artil.*); aufplatzen, zerplatzen (*of a bubble*); – *asunder*, auseinanderspringen; – *forth*, ausbrechen, hervorsprudeln; – *in*, hineinplatzen, hereinplatzen; – *in upon a p.*, auf einen hereinbrechen; – *into blossom*, knospen, aufblühen; – *into flame*, aufflammen; – *into a room*, in ein Zimmer (hinein)platzen; – *into tears*, in Tränen ausbrechen; – *on*, herfallen über; – *open*, aufspringen; – *out*, hervorbrechen, ausbrechen; ausrufen; – *out laughing*, in Lachen *or* Gelächter ausbrechen; – *out with*, herausplatzen mit; – *upon*, stoßen auf; – *with* (usually *be –ing with*), überfließen von. 2. *v.a.* sprengen, zersprengen; *the river –s its banks*, der Fluß durchbricht seine Dämme; *I have – a blood-vessel*, mir ist eine Ader geplatzt; – *one's sides with laughing*, vor Lachen platzen. 3. *s.* das Bersten, Platzen; die Explosion, Detonation, Sprengung; der Stoß (*of gunfire*); der Reifenschaden (*Cycl., Motor.*); (*fig.*) plötzlicher Ausbruch; der Riß, Bruch; – *of applause*, der Beifallssturm; *barrel-–*, der Rohrzerspringer (*Artil.*); – *of fire*, der Feuerstoß (*Gunn.*); *premature –*, der Frühzerspringer (*Artil.*); (*coll.*) – *of speed*, plötzliche Anstrengung, der Spurt. **-ing-charge,** *s.* die Sprengladung.
burthen [ˈbəːðn], *s. see* **burden.**
bury [ˈbɛrɪ], *v.a.* begraben, beerdigen, bestatten; verbergen, eingraben, vergraben; – *alive*, verschütten; – *the hatchet*, die Streitaxt begraben; – *o.s. in one's work*, sich in der Arbeit vergraben, sich in die Arbeit vertiefen. **-ing-ground,** *s.* der Kirchhof, die Begräbnisstätte.
bus [bʌs], 1. *s.* (*pl.* –es) (*coll. for* **omnibus**) der Omnibus, Verkehrskraftwagen; *motor-–*, der Autobus; (*sl.*) die Kiste (*Motor. or Av.*); (*sl.*) *miss the –*, die Gelegenheit verpassen. 2. *v.n.* (*coll.*) mit dem Omnibus fahren. **--bar,** *s.* die Sammelschiene (*Elec.*). **– conductor,** der Autobusschaffner. **– driver,** der Autobusfahrer. **-man,** das Dienstpersonal einer Autobusgesellschaft; *–man's holiday*, die Berufsarbeit in den Ferien. **– stop,** die Autobushaltestelle.
busby [ˈbʌzbɪ], *s.* der Kalpak, die Bärenmütze.
bush [bʊʃ], *s.* der Busch, Strauch; (*pl.*) das Gebüsch; der (Laub)Kranz (*of a tavern*); der Büschel (*of hair*); die Lagerschale, Büchse (*Mach.*); Hülse (*of a pulley, etc.*); *beat about the –*, wie die Katze um den heißen Brei herumgehen; *good wine needs no –*, gute Ware braucht keine Empfehlung. **--fighting,** der Buschkrieg. **-ing,** *s.* die Lagerschale; *–ing insulator*, der Durchführungsisolator (*Elec.*). **-man,** *s.* der Buschmann (*S. Africa & Australia*). **-ranger,** *s.* der Buschklepper, Strauchdieb. **--whacker,** *s.* der Guerillakämpfer (*Amer.*). **-y,** *adj.* buschig; *–y hair*, dichte Haare.
bushel [ˈbʊʃl], *s.* der (englische) Scheffel; *hide one's light under a –*, sein Licht unter den Scheffel stellen.
busily [ˈbɪzɪlɪ], *adv. see* **busy.**
business [ˈbɪznɪs], *s.* das Geschäft, die Beschäftigung, Arbeit, Aufgabe, Pflicht, Obliegenheit; kaufmännischer Beruf, das Geschäftsleben, der Handel, das Gewerbe; *that's my –*, das ist meine Sache; *on –*, geschäftlich, in geschäftlichen Angelegenheiten; *no – done*, ohne Umsatz; *bad –*, schlimme Sache; (*a*) (with *of*) *line* or *branch of –*, die Geschäftsbranche, der Geschäftszweig; (*coll.*) *that is not in my line of –*, das liegt außer meinem Bereich; *man of –*, der Geschäftsmann; *good* (*stroke of*) *–*, gutes Geschäft; (*b*) (*with verbs*) *attend to one's own –*, see *mind one's own –*; (*coll.*) *come to –*, zur Sache kommen; *do –*, Geschäfte machen; *go about one's –*, seine eignen Angelegenheiten verrichten; *go into –*, Kaufmann werden; *have no – there*, dort nichts zu suchen haben; *have no – to do*, kein Recht haben zu tun; *make it one's – to do*, es sich angelegen sein lassen zu tun; *make a – of (doing) a th.*, viel Aufhebens machen über; *mean –*, Ernst machen *or* es ernst meinen; *mind one's own –*, sich um seine eigenen Angelegenheiten kümmern; *that's none of his –*, das geht ihn nichts an; *open a –*, ein Geschäft eröffnen; *retire from –*, sich geschäftlich zur Ruhe setzen; *send a p. about his –*, einen kurz abfertigen, einem die Tür weisen; *set up in –*, ein Geschäft gründen; (*coll.*) *settle s.o.'s – for him*, einen gehörig zurechtsetzen; *transact –*, geschäftliche Verbindungen haben. **--capital,** das Betriebskapital. **– career,** kaufmännische Laufbahn. **--connexions,** Geschäftsverbindungen (*pl.*). **--hours,** *pl.* die Geschäftszeit, Geschäftsstunden (*pl.*). **--like,** *adj.* geschäftsmäßig; sachlich, praktisch. **--manager,** *s.* der Geschäftsführer. **--outlook,** die Geschäftslage, Konjunktur. **--transactions,** *pl.* die Geschäfte.
busk [bʌsk], *s.* die Planchette, Korsettstange .
buskin [ˈbʌskɪn], *s.* der Halbstiefel; Kothurn; (*fig.*) – *style*, tragischer Stil.
buss [bʌs], 1. *s.* (*archaic*) der Kuß, (*dial.*) das Busserl. 2. *v.a.* (*archaic*) küssen.
[1]**bust** [bʌst], *s.* die Büste, weiblicher Busen; die Großaufnahme, Nahaufnahme (*Films*). **--bodice, --improver, --support,** *s.* der Büstenhalter.
[2]**bust,** *s.*; (*vulg. for* burst) *go –*, kaputtgehen, bankrott machen; *go on the –*, eine Bierreise machen, auf den Bummel gehen. **--up,** *s.* (*sl.*) der Krach, Streit.
bustard [ˈbʌstəd], *s.* die Großtrappe, Trappgans (*Orn.*).
[1]**bustl-e** [ˈbʌsl], 1. *v.n.* sich rühren, geschäftig sein, hetzen; *–e about*, geschäftig sein, umherlaufen, umherhantieren. 2. *s.* der Lärm, Tumult, das Getöse, Geräusch, Gewühl, Aufsehen, die Geschäftigkeit, Aufregung.
[2]**bustle,** *s.* die Turnüre, der Bausch (*of dress*).
busy [ˈbɪzɪ], 1. *adj.* beschäftigt; geschäftig, emsig, fleißig, eifrig; – *bee*, emsige Biene; *he is – at work*, er ist fleißig an *or* bei der Arbeit; *be – with a th.*, mit einer S. beschäftigt sein; – *day*, arbeitsreicher Tag; *he is – reading*, er liest eifrig. 2. *v.a.* beschäftigen; – *o.s.*, beschäftigt sein *or* sich beschäftigen (*with*, mit; *about*, in). 3. *s.* (*sl.*) der Detektiv. **-body,** *s.* der Gschaftlhuber. **-ness,** *s.* die Geschäftigkeit, das Beschäftigtsein.
but [bʌt, bət], 1. *conj.* (*a*) aber, allein, sondern; dessen ungeachtet, indessen, nichtsdestoweniger, dennoch, jedoch; *not only . . . – also . . .*, nicht nur . . ., sondern auch . . .; (*b*) (*after neg. or interr. & before inf.*) außer, als; *nothing remains – to thank him*, nichts bleibt als *or* außer ihm zu danken; *one cannot – hope*, man kann nicht umhin zu hoffen, man kann nur hoffen; (*c*) (*introd. subord. clause after neg. or interr.*) ohne daß, daß nicht, ob nicht; *she is not so old – she may learn*, sie ist nicht zu alt um nicht zu lernen; *who knows – he may be ill?* wer weiß ob er nicht vielleicht krank ist? *not – that I have warned him*, nicht als ob ich ihn nicht gewarnt hätte; *there is no doubt – (that) she will come*, es besteht kein Zweifel daß sie kommen wird; – *that*, wenn nicht, wo nicht; *I do not deny – that he . . .*, ich zweifle nicht daß er . . .; *I could do it – that I am afraid*, ich könnte es tun, wenn ich nicht fürchtete; – *then*, aber andererseits; – *yet*, aber doch, dennoch. 2. *prep.* außer; *the last – one*, der vorletzte; *the last line – one*, die vorletzte Zeile; *the last – two*, der drittletzte; *all – he* or *him*, alle außer ihm, alle bis auf ihn, nur er nicht; – *for him*, wenn er nicht gewesen wäre, ohne ihn; – *for me he would have been lost*, ohne mich wäre er tot; *nothing –*, nichts als. 3. *adv.* nur, bloß; gerade erst; *all –*, fast, beinahe, nahezu; *all – impossible*, nahezu unmöglich; *she all – told him*, fast sagte sie es ihm; – *a child*, bloß ein Kind; *anything – clever*, alles andere als klug, nichts weniger als klug; – *last week*, eben erst vorige Woche. 4. (*as rel.* = that . . . not, *after neg. main clause*) *there is nothing here* – (– *that* (*literary*), – *what* (*coll.*)) *is needed*, hier ist nichts das nicht notwendig ist. 5. *s.* das Aber; – *me no –s!* keine Widerrede! komme mir nicht mit deinen Einwendungen!

butcher ['bʊtʃə], 1. *s.* der Fleischer, Metzger, Schlächter; (*fig.*) Mörder, blutgieriger Mensch; *–'s meat*, das Schlächterfleisch; *–'s shop*, der Fleischerladen. 2. *v.a.* schlachten, abschlachten, hinschlachten, niedermetzeln. **--bird,** *s.* der Würger (*Orn.*). **-y,** *s.* das Schlachthaus, die Schlächterei; das Fleischerhandwerk; (*fig.*) die Metzelei, das Gemetzel, die Niedermetzelung, Bluttat, das Blutbad.

butler ['bʌtlə], *s.* der Kellermeister; oberster Diener.

¹butt [bʌt], *s.* das Faß, Stückfaß, die Butte.

²butt, 1. *s.* der Kopfstoß; der Kolben (*of rifle*), dickes Ende (*of tools*), unterer Stamm (*of a tree*), der Stummel (*of a cigar*); der Plattfisch (*generic name of numerous varieties*); (*pl.*) der Scheibenstand (*Gunn.*); (*fig.*) das Ziel, die Zielscheibe; *he is the – of the company*, er dient der ganzen Gesellschaft als Zielscheibe *or* Gegenstand des Spottes; *– and –*, der Anstoß (*Carp., etc.*). 2. *v.n.* mit dem Kopfe stoßen; in einer Linie zusammenstoßen (*Carp.*); (*coll.*) *– in*, sich (unbefugt) einmischen. **--bolt,** *s.* der Stoßbolzen (*Shipb.*). **--end,** *s.* der (Gewehr)Kolben; (*coll.*) das (dicke) Ende. **--hinge,** *s.* das Fischband. **--plate,** *s.* die Kolbenkappe (*of rifle*). **--swivel,** *s.* der Klammerfuß (*of rifle*).

butter ['bʌtə], 1. *s.* die Butter; *bread and –*, das Butterbrot; *she looks as if – would not melt in her mouth*, sie sieht aus, als ob sie kein Wässerchen trüben könnte. 2. *v.a.* mit Butter bestreichen; (*coll.*) (*– up*) schmeicheln (*Dat.*); *know on which side one's bread is –ed*, seinen Vorteil kennen, wissen wo Barthel den Most holt. **--bean,** *s.* die Wachsbohne. **-cup,** *s.* die Butterblume, der Hahnenfuß (*Bot.*). **--dish,** die Butterdose. (*coll.*) **--fingered,** *adj.* ungeschickt im Gebrauch der Hände *or* beim Fangen. (*coll.*) **--fingers,** *s.* einer der nicht fangen kann. **-fly** ['bʌtəflaɪ], *s.* der Schmetterling. **-fly-nut,** *s.* die Flügelmutter. **-fly-valve,** *s.* die Drosselklappe. **-milk,** *s.* die Buttermilch. **--pat,** die Butterscheibe. **--print,** *s.* die Butterform. **-scotch,** *s.* die Butterkaramelle(n). **-y** ['bʌtərɪ], 1. *adj.* butterig, butterartig. 2. *s.* die Speisekammer; Kantine. **-y-hatch,** *s.* die (Halbtür für die) Speiseausgabe.

buttock ['bʌtək] 1. *s.* die Hinterbacke; das Hinterteil; (*usually pl.*) Gesäß.

button ['bʌtn], 1. *s.* der Knopf; Knauf (*of a sword, etc.*); das Korn (*Metall.*); die Knospe (*Bot.*); der Hoden (*Zool.*); *boy in –s*, der Page in Livree; *not care a – for*, sich nicht das geringste machen aus; *covered –*, überzogener Knopf; *press the –*, auf den Knopf drücken; *push-–*, der Druckknopf; *it's not worth a –*, es ist keinen Deut *or* Pfifferling wert. 2. *v.a.* (*– up*) zuknöpfen; *–ed-up*, *adj.* (*coll.*) zugeknöpft, zurückhaltend. **-hole,** 1. *s.* das Knopfloch; die Knopflochblume. 2. *v.a.* anhalten, abhalten, zurückhalten (*a p.*). **-hole stitch,** *s.* der Langettenstich. **--hook,** *s.* der Stiefelknöpfer. **-s** (*coll.*) der Page, Hoteldiener.

buttress ['bʌtrɪs], 1. *s.* der Strebepfeiler; (*fig.*) die Stütze; *flying-–*, der Schwibbogen, Strebebogen. 2. *v.a.* stützen, unterstützen.

butyri-c [bju:'tɪrɪk], *adj.* butterig; *–c acid*, die Buttersäure. **-ne** ['bju:tɪrɪn], *s.* das Butterfett.

buxom ['bʌksəm], *adj.* gesundheitstrotzend, drall, stramm; mollig (*of women only*).

buy [baɪ], 1. *ir.v.a.* kaufen, einkaufen; teuer zahlen, erkaufen (*experience, etc.*): *– a pig in a poke*, die Katze im Sack kaufen; *– and sell*, Handel treiben; *– s.th. for s.o.*, einem etwas kaufen; *– s.th. of* or *from a p.*, etwas von einem kaufen, einem etwas abkaufen; *– a ticket*, eine Karte lösen; *– forward*, auf Spekulation kaufen (*C.L.*); *– in*, einkaufen, sich eindecken mit; zurückkaufen (*at auctions*); *– off*, loskaufen (*a p. from an obligation*), abfinden (*a p.'s interest in a th.*); (*coll.*) durch Versprechungen abbringen *or* abhalten; erkaufen (*a th.*); *– out*, auskaufen, loskaufen (*a p.*), ablösen (*a p. from an obligation*); durch Ankauf um das Eigentum bringen; *– over*, durch Bestechung gewinnen, bestechen (*a p.*); *– up*, aufkaufen. 2. *s.* (*coll.*) der Kauf. **-er,** *s.* der Käufer, Einkäufer, Abnehmer; *–er of a bill*, der Wechselnehmer (*C.L.*); *–ers over*, mehr Geld als Brief (*stock exchange*). **-ing,** *s.* das Kaufen. **-ing power,** *s.* die Kaufkraft.

buzz [bʌz], 1. *v.n.* brummen, summen; dröhnen, schwirren; *– about*, herumschwirren; (*sl.*) *– off*, abhauen, verduften. 2. *s.* das Summen, Brummen, (*fig.*) Gesumme; Geflüster, Gerede. **-er,** *s.* der Summer (*Phone*). **-er-key,** *s.* der Summerknopf. **-er-set,** *s.* der Summerzusatz.

buzzard ['bʌzəd], *s.* der Bussard, Mäusebussard (*Orn.*).

by [baɪ], 1. *prep.* (*a*) (*place*) neben, an, bei, nahebei; (*b*) (*time*) bei, gegen, um, während, bis zu; (*c*) (*direction*) durch, über, auf, an . . . vorüber; (*d*) (*relation*) nach, gemäß, um; (*e*) (*cause*) von, durch, bei, mit, vermöge, vermittelst, (*C.L.*) per; *– the advice of*, auf den Rat von; *– air*, mit dem Flugzeug; *– appearances*, nach dem Anschein; *represented – attorney*, durch einen Anwalt vertreten; *– his bedside*, an seinem Bette; *– birth*, von Geburt; *– blood*, der Abstammung nach; *– boat*, per Schiff; *– the by(e)*, nebenbei (bemerkt), beiläufig, übrigens; *– chance*, durch Zufall, zufällig; *– day*, bei Tage; *day – day*, (tag)täglich, jeden Tag; *– degrees*, allmählich, stufenweise; *– your desire*, auf Ihren Wunsch *or* Ihr Verlangen; *– dint of*, kraft, vermöge; *– the dozen*, dutzendweise; *– experience*, aus Erfahrung; *– far*, bei weitem; *five feet – four feet*, fünf Fuß zu vier Fuß; *– force*, mit Gewalt; *– heart*, auswendig; *– the hour*, stundenweise; *– hundreds*, zu Hunderten; *– the hundredweight*, zentnerweise; *– itself*, (an und) für sich, allein; *– land*, zu Lande; *– the laws of nature*, nach dem Naturgesetz; *– leaps and bounds*, sprunghaft, in raschem Tempo; *– letter*, brieflich; *little – little*, allmählich, nach und nach; *– his looks*, an seinen Blicken; *man – man*, Mann für Mann; *I have no money – me*, ich habe kein Geld bei mir; *– all means*, auf alle Fälle, auf jeden Fall, freilich, gewiß; durchaus, unbedingt; *– no means*, keineswegs; *– means of*, mittels, vermittels; *– mistake*, aus Versehen, versehentlich, *– so much more*, um so mehr; *– name*, mit Namen, dem Namen nach; *he goes – the name of . . .*, er führt den Namen . . .; *– nature*, von Natur; *– next week*, bis spätestens nächste Woche; *– now*, jetzt schon, mittlerweile; *one – one*, einzeln, einer nach dem andern; *– o.s.*, für sich, allein; selbständig, aus eigner Kraft; *– order of*, auf Verordnung (*Gen.*); *– permission of*, mit Erlaubnis (*Gen.*); *point – point*, Punkt für Punkt; *– post*, mit der Post; *– the pound*, pfundweise; *– profession*, von Beruf; *– rail*, mit der Eisenbahn; *– reason of*, wegen; *– right*, von Rechts wegen; *the house – the river*, das Haus am Flusse; *– the nearest road*, auf dem kürzesten Wege; *– sea*, zu Wasser, zur See; *side – side*, Seite an Seite; *– stealth*, verstohlen, heimlich; *fall – the sword*, durch das Schwert umkommen; *– this time*, (jetzt) schon, unterdessen, inzwischen, mittlerweile; *– this time tomorrow*, morgen um diese Zeit; *– trade*, von Beruf; *– which train?* mit welchem Zuge? *be back – Tuesday*, bis Dienstag zurück sein; *travel – Paris*, über Paris fahren; *– turns*, der Reihe nach, wechselweise, abwechselnd, einer nach dem andern; *two – two*, *– twos*, zwei und zwei, zu zweien; *seize – the waist*, um die Hüfte nehmen; *– my watch*, nach meiner Uhr; *– the way*, übrigens, nebenbei bemerkt, beiläufig, *– way of example*, beispielsweise; *– way of trial*, versuchsweise; *– word of mouth*, mündlich; *word – word*, Wort für Wort; *younger – 6 years*, um 6 Jahre jünger. 2. *adv.* nahe dabei; beiseite; vorbei; *– and –*, nächstens, bald, über kurz oder lang, gelegentlich; *close –*, dicht *or* nahe dabei; *go –*, vorbeigehen, vorbeikommen; *hard –*, see *close –*; *– and large*, im großen und ganzen; *lay –*, aufsparen; beiseitelegen, beiseitestellen; *pass –*, vorbeigehen; (*fig.*) *pass a p. –*, einen übergehen; *the passers-–*, die Vorübergehenden; *put –*, see *lay –*; *stand –*, dabei sein, untätig dabeistehen; bereit stehen (*Mil., Naut.*); *those standing –*, die Umstehenden. 3. *prefix* (*also written* **bye**), Neben–, Seiten–, Bei–. **--election,** *s.* die Ersatzwahl, Nachwahl. **-gone,** 1. *adj.* vergangen, veraltet. 2. *s.* (*pl.*) das Vergangene; *let –gones be –gones*, laß die Vergangenheit ruhen *or* begraben sein, (*sl.*) Schwamm darüber! **--lane,** *s.* die Seiten- *or* Nebengasse. **--law,** *s.* das Ortsstatut, städtische *or* örtliche Verordnung; die Satzung. **--pass,** 1. *s.* die Entlastungsstraße, Umgehungsstraße; Ausweichstelle; der Kleinsteller (*gas*). 2. *v.a.* umgehen, umfahren. **--play,** *s.* die Nebenhandlung; das Gebärdespiel. **--product,** *s.* das Nebenprodukt, Abfallprodukt. **--road,** *s.*, **--way,** *s.* der Nebenweg. **-stander,** *s.* der Zuschauer; (*pl.*) die Umstehenden. **-word,** *s.* das Sprichwort; warnendes Beispiel; die Zielscheibe des Spottes.

bye [baɪ], *s.* das Freilos (*Tenn., etc.*); ein Punkt, der ohne das Zutun des Schlägers gerechnet wird, wenn der Ball von den Angreifern nicht schnell genug eingebracht wird (*Crick.*); etwas Nebensächliches; *see* **by the bye.** **--bye,** 1. *s.* (*nursery talk*) das Bett, der Schlaf. 2. *int. see* **good-bye.**

byre [baɪə], *s.* der Kuhstall.

C

C, c [siː], *s.* das C, c; C (*Mus.*); – *flat*, das Ces; – *sharp*, das Cis; – *major*, C-Dur; – *minor*, C-Moll. *See the Index of Abbreviations.*

cab [kæb], 1. *s.* die Droschke, der Fiaker; Führerstand (*Railw.*). **-by,** *s.* (*coll.*), **-man** [–mən], *s.* der Droschkenkutscher. **--rank,** *s.* der Droschkenstand.

cabal [kəˈbæl], 1. *s.* die Kabale, Ränke (*pl.*); die Ränkeschmiederei. 2. *v.n.* Ränke schmieden. **-ler,** *s.* der Ränkeschmied.

cabaret [ˈkæbəreɪ], *s.* das Kabarett, die Kleinkunstbühne, das Überbrettl.

cabbage [ˈkæbɪdʒ], *s.* der Kohl; Kohlkopf. **--butterfly,** *s.* der Kohlweißling. **--lettuce,** *s.* der Kopfsalat. **--rose,** *s.* die Zentifolie. **--tree,** *s.* die Kohlpalme.

cabbal-a [ˈkæbələ], *s.* die Kabbala. **-ism** [–ɪzm], *s.* die Geheimlehre der Kabbalisten. **-ist,** *s.* der Kabbalist. **-istic(al),** *adj.* kabbalistisch.

cabin [ˈkæbɪn], *s.* die Hütte; Kajüte (*Naut.*), Kabine (*Av.*). **--boy,** *s.* der Schiffsjunge. **-ed,** *p.p.* (*poet.*) eingesperrt. **- roof,** *s.* die Haube.

cabinet [ˈkæbɪnɪt], *s.* das Zimmerchen, Kabinett; der Schrank; das Ministerium (*Pol.*); Gehäuse (*Rad., etc.*); (*archaic*) wertvolle Sammlung; *medicine* –, der Medizinschrank. **--council,** *s.* der Ministerrat. **--maker,** *s.* der Kunsttischler. **--making,** *s.* die Kunsttischlerei. **--meeting,** *s.* Ministerrat. **- minister,** *s.* der Staatsminister. **--size,** *s.* das Kabinettformat.

cable [ˈkeɪbl], 1. *s.* das Kabel, Tau, Kabeltau, die Trosse, Stahltrosse, das Seil, Drahtseil; die Depesche; *a –'s length*, eine Kabellänge (= *200 yds.*) (*Naut.*); *anchor* –, das Ankertau; *armoured* –, das Panzerkabel, Armierungskabel; *buried* –, das Erdkabel; *conducting* –, das Zuleitungskabel; *ground* –, see *buried* –; *lead-covered* –, das Bleikabel, Bleimantelkabel; *marine* –, das Seekabel; *overhead* –, das Luftkabel; *power* –, das Kraftkabel; *rubber-insulated* –, das Gummikabel. 2. *v.a.* kabeln (*Tele.*). **-gram,** *s.* die Kabeldepesche. **--moulding,** *s.* die Seilverzierung (*Arch.*). **--railway,** *s.* die Seilbahn, Schwebebahn.

caboodle [kəˈbuːdl], *s.* (*sl.*) der Kram, Schmarren.

caboose [kəˈbuːs], *s.* die Kombüse, Schiffsküche (*Naut.*).

cabriole [ˈkæbrɪoul], *s.* das Stuhlbein in Pfotenform.

cabriolet [kæbrɪoˈleɪ], *s.* das Kabriolett, zweirädriger Einspänner.

ca'canny [kɑːˈkænɪ], *s.* die Produktionseinschränkung, passiver Widerstand.

cacao [kəˈkeɪou], *s.* die Kakaobohne. **--tree,** *s.* der Kakaobaum.

cachalot [ˈkæʃəlɔt], *s.* der Pottwal.

cache [kæʃ], 1. *s.* der Aufbewahrungsort, das Versteck, geheimes Lager. 2. *v.n.* versteckt aufbewahren, verbergen.

cachectic [kəˈkɛktɪk], *adj.* kränklich.

cachet [ˈkɑʃeɪ], *s.* die Arzneikapsel (*Med.*).

cachexy [kæˈkɛksɪ], *s.* ungesunder Zustand, der Körperverfall, die Kachexie (*Med.*).

cachinnation [kækɪˈneɪʃən], *s.* lautes Gelächter.

cackle [ˈkækl], 1. *v.n.* gackern, schnattern; (*fig.*) schwatzen, plappern. 2. *s.* das Gegacker, Geschnatter; (*fig.*) Geschwätz, Geplapper. **-r,** *s.* gackernde Henne, schnatternde Gans; der Schwätzer.

cacophon-ous [kəˈkɔfənəs], *adj.* mißlautend, übelklingend. **-y** [–i], *s.* der Mißklang.

cactus [ˈkæktəs], *s.* der Kaktus.

cad [kæd], *s.* gemeiner Kerl. **-dish,** *adj.* gemein, schuftig.

cadaver [kəˈdɑːvə], *s.* der Leichnam (*Med.*). **-ous** [kəˈdævərəs], *adj.* leichenhaft, leichenblaß, totenblaß.

caddie [ˈkædɪ], *s.* der Golfjunge, Träger.

caddish [ˈkædɪʃ], *see* **cad.**

caddy [ˈkædɪ], *s.* die Teebüchse.

cadence [ˈkeɪdəns], *s.* der Takt, Rhythmus; Tonfall, Ton, die Kadenz (*Mus.*).

cadet [kəˈdɛt], *s.* jüngster Sohn *or* Bruder; der Kadett, Offiziersanwärter, Fahnenjunker (*Mil.*). **-ship,** *s.* die Kadettenstelle.

cadge [kædʒ], 1. *v.n.* (*coll.*) schmarotzen, betteln. 2. *v.a.* (*coll.*) durch betteln erhalten. **-r,** *s.* der Schmarotzer.

cadmium [ˈkædmɪəm], *s.* das Kadmium.

cadre [ˈkɑːdrə], *s.* der Kader (*Mil.*).

caduc-ity [kəˈdjuːsɪtɪ], *s.* die Hinfälligkeit, Vergänglichkeit, das Abfallen (*Bot., Zool.*); Verfallensein (*Law*). **-ous** [kəˈdjuːkəs], *adj.* hinfällig, vergänglich, schnell abfallend, ausfallend, eingehend *or* verwelkend (*Bot., Zool.*).

caecum [ˈsɪːkəm], *s.* der Blinddarm (*Anat.*).

Caesarian [sɪˈzɛːrɪən] **(operation),** *s.* der Kaiserschnitt (*Med.*).

caesura [sɪːˈzjuərə], *s.* der Verseinschnitt, die Zäsur.

café [ˈkæfe], *s.* das Café, Kaffeehaus, alkoholfreies Restaurant (*in England*); der Kaffee; – *au lait*, der Milchkaffee, Kaffee verkehrt.

cafeteria [kæfəˈtɪərɪə], *s.* das Selbstbedienungsrestaurant.

caffeine [ˈkæfɪaɪn], *s.* das Koffein.

cage [keɪdʒ], 1. *s.* der Käfig, das Bauer (*for birds*); Gehege (*for animals*); der Förderkorb, Fahrkorb (*mines*); (*fig.*) das Gefängnis. 2. *v.a.* in einen Käfig tun; einsperren. **-ling,** *s.* der Vogel im Käfig, Zimmervogel. **-y,** *adj.* (*sl.*) schlau, argwöhnisch.

caïque [kɑːˈɪːk], *s.* der Kaik, türkische Barke.

cairn [kɛən], *s.* der Steinhügel, Grabhügel, Steinhaufen. **-gorm** [–ˈgɔːm], *s.* der Rauchtopas.

caisson [ˈkeɪsən], *s.* der Senkkasten, Schwimmkasten; Munitionswagen (*Mil.*).

caitiff [ˈkeɪtɪf], 1. *s.* (*Poet.*) Elende(r), *m.*, der Schurke, Lump. 2. *adj.* elend, schuftig.

cajole [kəˈdʒoul], *v.a.* schmeicheln (*Dat.*), beschwatzen, verführen (*Acc.*) (*into*, zu). **-ry** [–ərɪ], *s.* die Schmeichelei, Lobhudelei, Liebedienerei.

cake [keɪk], 1. *s.* der Kuchen; *–s and ale*, das Wohlleben, die Freudigkeit; *not all –s and ale*, nicht eitel Freude; – *of chocolate*, die Tafel Schokolade; *go like hot –s*, wie warme Semmeln *or* reißend abgehen; *you can't have your – and eat it*, du kannst nicht alles haben; entweder oder!; – *of soap*, das Stück Seife; (*coll.*) *take the* –, den Preis davontragen, alles überbieten. 2. *v.n.* zusammenbacken; *–d with*, dick beschmiert mit. **--walk,** *s.* der Negertanz; (*coll.*) die Spielerei, das Kinderspiel.

calabash [ˈkæləbæʃ], *s.* die Kalabasse, der Flaschenkürbis.

calaboose [kæləˈbuːs], *s.* (*Amer. sl.*) das Gefängnis, der Kerker.

calamanco [kæləˈmæŋkou], *s.* der Kalmank.

calamine [ˈkæləmɪn], *s.* der Galmei, das Zinkerz (*Min.*).

calamint [ˈkæləmɪnt], *s.* die Bergminze (*Bot.*).

calamit-ous [kəˈlæmɪtəs], *adj.* unheilvoll, unglücklich. **-y** [kəˈlæmɪtɪ], *s.* das Elend, Unglück, Unheil.
calamus [ˈkæləməs], *s.* das Schilfrohr, die Rohrflöte, der Kalmus.
calash [kəˈlæʃ], *s.* die Kalesche.
calcareous [kælˈkɛərɪəs], *adj.* kalkig, kalkreich, kalkhaltig; kalkartig, Kalk–; – *earth*, die Kalkerde; – *spar*, der Kalkspat. **-ness**, *s.* die Kalkartigkeit, Kalkhaftigkeit.
calceolaria [kælsɪəˈlɛərɪə] *s.* die Pantoffelblume, Kalzeolarie (*Bot.*).
calci-fy [ˈkælsɪfɑɪ], 1. *v.a.* verkalken. 2. *v.n.* sich verhärten. **-nation** [kælsɪˈneɪʃən], *s.* die Verkalkung, das Kalzinieren, Brennen (*of lime*). **-ne** [ˈkælsɪn], *v.a.* & *n.* verkalken; brennen, einäschern, ausglühen. **-um** [ˈkælsɪəm], *s.* das Kalzium; *-um oxide*, gebrannter Kalk, der Ätzkalk.
calcul-able [ˈkælkjʊləbl], *adj.* berechenbar; verläßlich (*person*). **-ate** [ˈkælkjʊleɪt], 1. *v.a.* berechnen, abschätzen, kalkulieren; bestimmen, einrichten (*for*, für); glauben, vermuten (*Amer.*, *coll.*). 2. *v.n.* rechnen, sich verlassen (*on*, auf). **-ated**, *adj.* wohl überlegt, beabsichtigt; *be -ated for*, dafür *or* dazu geeignet *or* darauf berechnet sein. **-ating-machine**, *s.* die Rechenmaschine. **-ation** [–ˈleɪʃən], *s.* die Berechnung, Veranschlagung, Schätzung, der Kostenanschlag; die Rechnung; *be out in one's -ation*, sich verrechnet haben; *at the lowest -ation*, bei niedrigster Berechnung. **-us** [ˈkælkjʊləs], *s.* der Blasenstein, Nierenstein (*Med.*); die Rechnung; *differential -us*, die Differentialrechnung; *integral -us*, die Integralrechnung.
caldron [ˈkɔːldrən], *s. see* **cauldron.**
calefaction [kælɪˈfækʃən], *s.* die Erwärmung.
calendar [ˈkælɪndə], 1. *s.* der Kalender; die Liste, Rolle (*Law*); – *month*, der Kalendermonat. 2. *v.a.* registrieren, eintragen, einschreiben.
calender [ˈkælɪndə], 1. *s.* der Kalander, die Zylinderglättmaschine, Tuchpresse, das Glättwerk; (*pl.*) die Satiniermaschine (*Pap.*); *glazing -s*, die Glanzpresse. 2. *v.a.* kalandern, glätten, walzen, satinieren.
calends [ˈkælɪndz], *pl.* die Kalenden; *at the Greek* –, niemals.
[1]**calf** [kɑːf], *s.* (*pl.* calves) das Kalb; Junge (*of deer*); *with* or *in* –, trächtig (*of cows*); *bound in* –, im Ledereinband *or* Franzband; – *binding*, der Franzband, Kalbledereinband; *moon*--, der Dummkopf, Tölpel; *calves-foot jelly*, die Kalbspfotensülze. **--love,** *s.* erste *or* die Jugendliebe. **-skin,** das Kalbsfell, Kalbleder.
[2]**calf,** *s.* (*pl.* calves) die Wade (*of the leg*).
calibrate [ˈkælɪbreɪt], *v.a.* & *n.* eichen, kalibrieren.
calibre [ˈkælɪbə], **caliber** [kəˈlɪːbə], *s.* das Kaliber, die Rohrweite, Seelenweite, innerer Durchmesser; (*fig.*) die Beschaffenheit, Qualität, Eigenschaft, Befähigung, der Wert.
calico [ˈkælɪkoʊ], *s.* der Kattun, Zitz.
calipers [ˈkælɪpəz], *pl. see* **callipers.**
caliph [ˈkeɪlɪf], *s.* der Kalif. **-ate** [–ət], *s.* das Kalifat.
calix [ˈkælɪks], *s.* (*pl.* calices [–ɪsɪːz]) der Kelch (*Bot.*).
calk [kɔːk], *v.a.* scharf beschlagen (*a horse*); durchpausen; *see* **caulk.** **-in,** *s.* der (Huf)Stollen.
call [kɔːl], 1. *v.a.* rufen, anrufen, herbeirufen; wecken (*from sleep*); einberufen, zusammenrufen (*a meeting*); heißen, nennen, benennen, bezeichnen, kommen lassen, zitieren; *what do you – that?* wie nennen Sie das? was *or* wie heißt das? – *a p.'s attention to s.th.*, einen auf eine S. aufmerksam machen; (*sl.*) – *it a day*, damit Schluß machen; – *a halt*, Halt machen, Einhalt gebieten (*Dat.*); – *a meeting*, eine Versammlung einberufen; – *a p. names*, einen beschimpfen; – *one's trump* (or *hand*), Trumpf ansagen, (sein Spiel) ansagen (*Cards*); *not a moment to – one's own*, keinen Augenblick für sich; – *the roll*, Appell abhalten (*Mil.*); – *a spade a spade*, das Kind beim rechten Namen nennen; – *aside*, beiseiterufen *or* –nehmen; – *away*, abrufen, wegrufen; – *back*, zurückrufen; – *down*, herunterrufen, herabrufen (*blessings*, *curses*, *etc.*) (*on*, auf); – *for*, abholen (*a p.*); anfordern; – *forth*, hervorrufen; aufrufen, aufbieten; – *in*, hereinrufen; zuziehen (*for advice*); einziehen, einfordern (*money*, *etc.*), kündigen; – *in question*, in Frage stellen, bezweifeln; – *into being*, ins Leben rufen; – *into play*, in Tätigkeit setzen; – *off* abrufen; absagen, rückgängig machen, (*coll.*) abblasen (*a strike*, *etc.*); – *out*, ausrufen, laut rufen; herausfordern; einberufen, aufrufen, aufbieten, ausheben, einsetzen (*troops*); – *over*, verlesen (*names*); (*coll.*) – *a p. over the coals*, einem gehörig den Kopf waschen; – *to account*, zur Rechenschaft ziehen; – *to the bar*, als Advokat zulassen, zum Advokaten ernennen; – *to mind*, (sich) ins Gedächtnis zurückrufen, (sich) erinnern (an (*Acc.*)); – *to order*, zur Ordnung rufen; – *together*, zusammenrufen, einberufen; – *up*, (her)aufrufen, erwecken; anrufen (*Phone*); einziehen, ausheben (*troops*); hervorrufen, wachrufen, vergegenwärtigen (*ideas*, *memories*, *etc.*); beschwören, zitieren (*spirits*). 2. *v.n.* rufen, schreien (*for*, nach); ausrufen; einen Besuch machen, vorsprechen; anlegen (*of a ship*); – *again*, wiederkommen, sich wieder melden; – *at*, vorsprechen bei; – *at a port*, einen Hafen anlaufen (*Naut.*); – *for*, rufen nach (*help*, *etc.*); herausrufen (*Theat.*); fordern, verlangen, bestellen; abholen (*a p. or a th.*); erfordern, erheischen; *an article much -ed for*, vielbegehrter Artikel; *un-ed-for remark*, unberufene *or* unangebrachte Bemerkung; *to be -ed for*, postlagernd (*on letters*); – *in*, einen kurzen Besuch machen, kurz vorsprechen (*on a p.*, bei einem); – *on*, besuchen (*a p.*), auffordern (*a p. to do*); (*B.*) – *on the name of the Lord*, den Namen des Herrn anrufen; *I – on you for aid*, ich ersuche Sie um Unterstützung; – *out*, aufschreien; – *to*, zurufen (*Dat.*); – *upon*, sich wenden an (*Acc.*); see also – *on*; *be* or *feel -ed upon*, sich berufen, gedrungen *or* genötigt fühlen. 3. *s.* der Ruf, Schrei; Anruf, das Gespräch (*Phone*); der Hervorruf (*Theat.*); die Einberufung, Aushebung (*of troops*); (innere) Berufung, der Beruf; die Forderung, der Anspruch; die Nachfrage (*for*, nach); die Aufforderung, Inanspruchnahme (*upon* (*Gen.*)); kurzer Besuch, das Anlaufen (*Naut.*); Signal, die Signalpfeife (*Naut.*); der Lockruf; die Lockpfeife; (*fig.*) die Anziehung(skraft); das Prämiengeschäft (*stock exchange*); *at* –, bereit, des Rufs gewärtig; (*C.L.*) auf tägliche Kündigung, auf Abruf; *bugle* –, das Trompetensignal; – *to arms* or *the colours*, die Einberufung; – *before the curtain*, der Hervorruf (*Theat.*); (*C.L.*) *first* –, erste Notierung; *have the first – on something*, das Vorrecht auf etwas (*Acc.*) haben; – *for help*, der Hilferuf; – *for trumps*, das Trumpf bedienen (*Cards*); (*coll.*) *give me a* –, ruf' mich an; *make a – on a p.*, einen Besuch machen bei einem; eine Anforderung richten an einen; *no – to blush*, keine Veranlassung zu erröten; – *of duty*, der Pflichtbefehl; *obey the – of nature*, seine Notdurft verrichten; *port of* –, der Anlaufhafen; *telephone* –, der Telephonanruf; *urgent* –, dringendes Gespräch (*Phone*); *within* –, in Rufweite, innerhalb Hörweite, gleich zu erreichen. **--bird,** *s.* der Lockvogel. **--box,** *s.* die Fernsprechzelle, öffentlicher Fernsprecher. **--boy,** *s.* der Hoteljunge; Theaterbursche. **-er,** *s.* der Rufer; Besucher; Sprecher (*Phone*); *many -ers*, viel Besuch. **-ing,** *s.* der Beruf, das Geschäft; die Berufung (*Eccl.*); *-ing of the plaintiff*, das Vorrufen des abwesenden Klägers. **-ing-card,** *s.* die Visitenkarte (*Amer.*). **-ing-hour,** *s.* die Sprechstunde. **-ing-out,** *s.* die Einziehung, Einberufung (*Mil.*). **--loan,** *s.* das Darlehen auf tägliche Kündigung. **--money,** *s.* tägliches Geld. **--note,** *s.* der Lockruf (*of birds*). **--office,** *s.* das Fernsprechamt. **--sign, --signal,** *s.* das Rufzeichen. **--up,** *s.* der Stellungsbefehl, Einberufungsbefehl.
calligraph-er [kəˈlɪgrəfə], *s.* der Schreibkünstler, Kalligraph. **-y,** *s.* die Schönschreibekunst.
callipers [ˈkælɪpəz], *pl.* der Taster, Zirkel; *internal* –, der Innen– *or* Lochzirkel; *external* –, der Tast- *or* Greifzirkel.
callisthenic [kælɪsˈθɛnɪk], *adj.* Leibesübungen betreffend, turnerisch. **-s,** *pl.* die Frauengymnastik.
callosity [kæˈlɔsɪtɪ], *s.* die Schwiele, Hautverhärtung.

callous ['kæləs], *adj.* schwielig, verhärtet, harthäutig; (*fig.*) gefühllos, unempfindlich, abgestumpft, dickhäutig. **–ness,** *s.* (*fig.*) die Härte, Gefühllosigkeit, Unempfindlichkeit.
callow ['kælou], *adj.* ungefiedert, kahl; (*fig.*) unerfahren, unreif.
callus ['kæləs], *s.* die Schwiele, Verhärtung (*Med.*), verhärtete Stelle (*Bot.*).
calm [kɑ:m], 1. *adj.* ruhig, still; gelassen, friedlich; – *day,* windstiller Tag; *fall* –, windstill werden (*Naut.*). 2. *s.* die Stille, Ruhe; (*fig.*) der Friede; die Windstille, Flaute (*Naut., etc.*); *dead* –, völlige Flaute; *after a storm comes a* –, auf Regen folgt Sonnenschein. 3. *v.a.* stillen, beruhigen, besänftigen. 4. *v.n.*; – *down,* sich beruhigen, ruhig werden, sich legen. **–ness,** *s.* die Stille, Ruhe; Gemütsruhe.
calomel ['kæloməl], *s.* das Kalomel, Quecksilberchlorür.
calor–escence [kælə'rɛsəns], *s.* der Wechsel von Wärmestrahlen in Lichtstrahlen (*Phys.*). **–ic** [kə'lɔrɪk], *s.* die Wärme; *–ic engine,* die Heißluftmaschine; *–ic unit,* die Wärmeeinheit. **–ie,** *s.* die Wärmeeinheit. **–ific,** *adj.* Wärme erzeugend, erhitzend; *–ific power,* die Heizkraft; *–ific rays,* die Wärmestrahlen; *–ific value,* der Wärmewert. **–imeter** [kælə'rɪmətə], *s.* der Wärmemesser.
calotte [kæ'lɔt], *s.* die Priesterkappe.
caltrop ['kæltrɔp], *s.* die Fußangel; die Sterndistel (*Bot.*).
calumn–iate [kə'lʌmnɪeɪt], *v.a.* verleumden. **–iation** [–nɪ'eɪʃən], *s.* die Verleumdung. **–iator,** *s.* der Verleumder, Ehrabschneider. **–iatory** [–nɪətərɪ], **–ious** [–nɪəs], *adj.* verleumderisch. **–y** ['kæləmnɪ], *s.* die Verleumdung.
calve [kɑ:v], *v.n.* kalben, ein Kalb werfen; Stücke abstoßen (*of icebergs*).
calx [kælks], *s.* der Metallkalk, das Oxyd.
calyx ['keɪlɪks], *s.* der Kelch (*Bot.*).
cam [kæm], *s.* der Daumen, Nocken, die Knagge (*Mach.*). **– -gear,** *s.* die Nockensteuerung. **–shaft,** *s.* die Nockenwelle, Daumenwelle, Steuerwelle.
camber ['kæmbə], 1. *v.a.* wölben, biegen, krümmen. 2. *s.* die Wölbung, Biegung, Krümmung (*of a road, etc.*); der Radsturz (*of a wheel*). **–ed,** *adj.* gekrümmt, geschweift.
cambist ['kæmbɪst], *s.* der Wechsler, Wechselmakler (*C.L.*).
cambric ['keɪmbrɪk], *s.* der Battist, Kambrik.
came [keɪm], *see* **come.**
camel ['kæməl], *s.* das Kamel (*also Naut.*). **– -backed,** *adj.* buckelig. **– -driver, –eer,** *s.* der Kameltreiber. **– -hair,** das Kamelhaar.
camellia [kə'mɪ:ljə], *s.* die Kamelie (*Bot.*).
camelopard ['kæmɪlopɑ:d], *s.* (*archaic*) die Giraffe.
cameo ['kæmɪou], *s.* die Kamee.
camera ['kæmərə], *s.* die Kamera, (photographischer) Apparat (*Phot.*); die Kammer; das Gewölbe (*Arch.*); *in* –, unter Ausschluß der Öffentlichkeit. **– -gun,** *s.* das Lichtbildmaschinengewehr. **– -man,** *s.* der Kameramann, (*coll.*) Kurbler. **– -obscura,** *s.* die Dunkelkammer.
cami–knickers [kæmɪ'nɪkəz], *pl.* die Hemdhose. **–sole** ['kæmɪsoul], *s.* das Kamisol, Damenhemd.
camlet ['kæmlɪt], *s.* der Kamelott.
camomile ['kæməmaɪl], *s.* die Kamille. **– -tea,** *s.* der Kamillentee.
camouflage ['kæmuflɑ:ʒ], 1. *s.* die Tarnung, Maskierung, Deckung, Schutzfärbung, Scheinstellung, Verschleierung, der Blendanstrich; (*fig.*) die Irreführung. 2. *v.a.* tarnen, maskieren, verdecken, verschleiern.
camp [kæmp], 1. *s.* das Lager, Feldlager; (*fig.*) die Anhänger einer Richtung; *pitch* –, das Lager aufschlagen; *strike* or *break* –, das Lager abbrechen. 2. *v.n.* sich lagern, das Lager aufschlagen; – *out,* im Freien lagern, zelten, kampieren. **– -bed,** *s.* das Feldbett. **– -chair,** *s.* der Feldstuhl. **– -fever,** *s.* der Typhus. **– -fire,** *s.* das Lagerfeuer. **– -follower,** *s.* der Schlachtenbummler. **–ing,** *s.* das Lagern im Freien, Zelten. **–ing-place,** *s.,* **–(ing)-site,** *s.* der Lagerplatz. **– -meeting,** *s.* der Feldgottesdienst (*Amer.*). **– -stool,** *s.* der Feldstuhl, Klappstuhl.
campaign [kæm'peɪn], 1. *s.* der Feldzug; (*fig.*) der Kampf; *electoral* –, der Wahlkampf. 2. *v.n.* einen Feldzug mitmachen; (*fig.*) Propaganda machen; *–ing life,* das Soldatenleben. **–er,** *s.* alter Soldat, der Veteran, (*sl.*) Zwölfender; (*fig.*) Kämpfer.
campanile [kæmpə'nɪ:lɪ], *s.* der Glockenturm (*Arch.*).
campanula [kæm'pænjulə], *s.* die Glockenblume.
campeachy-wood [kæm'pɪ:tʃɪwud], *s.* das Kampescheholz, Blauholz.
camphor ['kæmfə], *s.* der Kampfer. **–ated** [–reɪtɪd], *adj.* mit Kampfer gesättigt; *–ated spirit(s),* der Kampferspiritus. **–ic** [–'fɔrɪk], *adj.* kampferhaltig; *–ic acid,* die Kampfersäure.
campion ['kæmpjən], *s.* die Lichtnelke, Feuernelke (*Bot.*).
campus ['kæmpəs], *s.* die Schulanlagen (*pl.*), das Schulgelände (*Amer.*).
camwood ['kæmwud], *s.* das Kam(bal)holz, Rotholz.
[1]**can** [kæn, kən], *ir.v.aux.* kann (*sing.*), können (*pl.*); vermag (*sing.*), vermögen (*pl.*), bin (*etc.*) fähig. **–not** (*coll.* **–'t** [kɑ:nt]), kann *or* können nicht; *I –not but wish,* ich kann nicht umhin zu wünschen; *it –not be denied,* es läßt sich nicht leugnen.
[2]**can,** 1. *s.* die Büchse, Dose; Kanne; *– -spinning frame,* die Kapselspinnmaschine (*Spin.*). 2. *v.a.* in Büchsen einmachen; (*sl.*) – *it!* halt's Maul! **– -buoy,** *s.* die Tonnenboje. **–ned,** *adj.* eingemacht, Büchsen–; (*coll.*) mechanisch hergestellt; (*sl.*) betrunken; *–ned goods,* Konserven; *–ned meat,* das Büchsenfleisch; *–ned music,* die Schallplattenmusik, Musik im Radio. **–nery,** *s.* die Konservenfabrik. **–ning,** *adj.* Konserven–; *–ning industry,* die Konservenindustrie.
canal [kə'næl], *s.* der Kanal, die Wasserstraße; die Röhre, der Gang (*Anat.*). **– -barge, – -boat,** *s.* das Kanalboot, der Schleppkahn. **–ization** [kænəlaɪ'zeɪʃən], *s.* der Kanalbau, die Kanalisation. **–ize,** *v.a.* kanalisieren. **– -lock,** *s.* die Kanalschleuse. **– -navigation,** *s.* die Kanalschiffahrt.
canard [kɑ'nɑ:, kə'nɑ:rd], *s.* die Zeitungslüge, falsches Gerücht, die Ente.
canary [kə'nɛərɪ], *s.* (*archaic* – -bird) der Kanarienvogel. **– -coloured,** *adj.* kanariengelb.
canaster [kə'næstə], *s.*; (– *tobacco*), der Knaster.
cancel ['kænsəl], 1. *v.a.* streichen, ausstreichen, durchstreichen, stornieren, entwerten, ungültig machen; aufheben, absagen, abbestellen, annullieren, widerrufen (*an order*); heben (*figures*) (*Math.*); – *a booking,* eine Karte abbestellen; – *a debt,* eine Schuld tilgen; – *an order,* etwas abbestellen, einen Auftrag stornieren; einen Befehl aufheben; – *a performance,* eine Vorstellung absagen; *until –led,* bis auf Widerruf; – *a will,* ein Testament für nichtig erklären. 2. *v.n.*; – *out,* sich aufheben (*Math.*); (*fig.*) sich gegenseitig widerlegen. **–late** [–ɪt], **–lated,** *adj.* gegittert, netzförmig (*Anat.*). **–lation** [–'leɪʃən], *s.* die Streichung, Durchstreichung, Abschaffung, Aufhebung, Annullierung, der Widerruf, die Entwertung (*of postage-stamps*). **–ling-stamp,** *s.* der Entwertungsstempel (*for stamps*).
cancer ['kænsə], *s.* der Krebs (*also Astr.*); die Krebskrankheit (*Med.*). **–ous** [–rəs], *adj.* krebsartig.
candelabr–um [kændɪ'lɑ:brəm], *s.* (*pl.* –a) (*usually pl. with sing. constr.*) der Kandelaber, Armleuchter.
candescent [kæn'dɛsənt], *adj.* (weiß)glühend.
candid ['kændɪd], *adj.* aufrichtig, ehrlich, redlich, offen. **–ness,** *s. see* **candour.**
candidat–e ['kændɪdeɪt], *s.* der Bewerber, Kandidat (*for,* um). **–ure,** *s.* die Kandidatur, Bewerbung.
candied ['kændɪd], *adj.* überzuckert, kandiert; **– -peel,** das Zitronat.
candle ['kændl], *s.* die Kerze, das Licht; Kerzenlicht; *the game is not worth the* –, die Sache ist der Mühe nicht wert; *burn the* – *at both ends,* seine Gesundheit untergraben; *he couldn't hold a* – *to him,* er konnte ihm das Wasser nicht reichen, konnte mit ihm keinen Vergleich aushalten. **–berry-tree,** *s.* der Kerzennußbaum. **– -end,** *s.* der Lichtstumpf. **– -extinguisher,** *s.* das Lichthütchen. **– -holder,** *s. see* **–stick.** **– -light,** *s.* das Kerzenlicht. **– -power,** *s.* die Normalkerze.

–stick, *s.* der Leuchter. **––wick,** *s.* der Kerzendocht.
candlemas ['kændlməs], *s.* (die) Lichtmeß.
candour ['kændə], *s.* die Offenheit, Redlichkeit, Aufrichtigkeit.
candy ['kændɪ], 1. *s.* (*Amer.*) das Zuckerwerk, Süßigkeiten, Bonbons (*pl.*); *sugar* –, der Kandiszucker. 2. *v.a.* in Zucker einmachen; kristallisieren (*of sugar*). 3. *v.n.* kandieren, kristallisieren. **––store,** *s.* das Bonbongeschäft (*Amer.*).
candytuft ['kændɪtʌft], *s.* die Schleifenblume (*Bot.*).
cane [keɪn], 1. *s.* das Rohr, Schilfrohr; der Rohrstock; (Spazier)Stock; (*sugar*––) das Zuckerrohr. 2. *v.a.* (durch)prügeln. **––brake,** *s.* das Röhricht. **––chair,** *s.* (*––bottomed chair*) der Rohrstuhl. **–ing** ['keɪnɪŋ], *s.* die Tracht Prügel. **––plaiting,** *s.* das Rohrgeflecht. **––sugar,** *s.* der Rohrzucker. **––trash,** *s.* die Bagasse, Zuckerrohrrückstände (*pl.*). **––worker,** *s.* der Rohrflechter.
cani–cular [kə'nɪkjʊlə], *adj.*; *–cular days*, die Hundstage. **–ne** ['keɪnaɪn], *adj.* Hunde–, Hunds–; *–ne madness*, die Tollwut, Hundswut; *–ne teeth*, die Eckzähne, Augenzähne; *–ne varieties*, Hundespielarten.
canister ['kænɪstə], *s.* die Blechbüchse. **––shot,** *s.* die Kartätsche.
canker ['kæŋkə], 1. der Krebs (*Med.*), Rost, Brand, Fraß (*Bot.*); (*fig.*) der Krebsschaden, das Krebsübel, der Wurm. 2. *v.a.* anfressen, zerfressen, vergiften, anstecken. 3. *v.n.* angefressen *or* angesteckt werden, verderben. **–ed,** *adj.* angefressen, zerfressen, verdorben; mürrisch, verdrießlich. **–ous** [–rəs], *adj.* krebsartig, zerstörend, (an)fressend. **––worm,** *s.* schädliche Raupe; (*fig.*) nagender Wurm.
canned, *see* ²**can.**
cannel-coal ['kænlkoʊl], *s.* die Kannelkohle.
cannery ['kænərɪ], *see* ²**can.**
cannibal ['kænɪbl], *s.* der Menschenfresser, Kannibale. **–ism** [–ɪzm] *s.* der Kannibalismus, die Menschenfresserei. **–ize,** *v.a.* (*coll.*) ausschlachten.
cannon ['kænən] 1. *s.* die Kanone, das Geschütz; die Geschütze (*collect.*); Karambolage (*Bill.*). 2. *v.n.* karambolieren (*Bill.*); (*fig.*) – *into*, rennen (gegen). **–ade,** 1. *s.* die Kanonade. 2. *v.a.* beschießen, bombardieren. **––ball,** *s.* die Kanonenkugel. **––bit,** das Mundstück des Stangengebisses. **––bone,** *s.* der Mittelfußknochen, das Sprungbein (*of horse*). **– fodder,** (*fig.*) das Kanonenfutter. **––foundry,** *s.* die Stückgießerei. **––pinion,** *s.* der Zapfen des Minutenzeigers (*Horol.*). **––shot,** *s.* der Kanonenschuß, die Kanonenkugeln (*pl.*); die Schußweite.
cannot ['kænət], *see* ¹**can.**
canny ['kænɪ], *adj.* klug, schlau; vorsichtig, umsichtig.
canoe [kə'nu:], 1. *s.* das Kanu, Kanoe, Paddelboot. 2. *v.n.* paddeln, in einem Kanu fahren. **–ing,** *s.* der Kanusport, das Paddeln.
¹**canon** ['kænən], *s.* kirchliche Vorschrift, der Kanon (*Eccl.*); die Vorschrift, Richtschnur, das Gesetz (*Law*); die kanonischen Schriften der Bibel; die echten Schriften; der Kanon (*Mus.*); die Formel (*Math., Pharm.*); Kanonschrift (*Typ.*); – *law*, das Kirchenrecht; *the sacred* –, die kanonischen Bücher, der Meßkanon. **–ical** [kə'nənɪkl], *adj.* kanonisch, vorschriftsmäßig; *–ical books*, die kanonischen Bücher; *–ical hours*, vorgeschriebene Gebetsstunden; *–ical punishment*, die Kirchenstrafe. **–icals,** *pl.* das Ornat, der Talar, kirchliche Amtstracht. **–icity** [–'nɪsɪtɪ], *s.* die Kirchengemäßheit, das Kanonische, die Echtheit. **–ist,** *s.* der Kirchenrechtslehrer. **–ization,** *s.* die Heiligsprechung. **–ize,** *v.a.* heiligsprechen.
²**canon,** *s.* der Domherr, Stiftsherr, Kanonikus; *regular* –, regulierter Domherr; *secular* –, weltlicher Domherr. **–ess,** *s.* die Stiftsdame. **–ical,** *adj.* domherrlich. **–ry,** *s.* die Stiftspfründe, das Kanonikat.
canoodle [kə'nu:dl], *v.n.* (*sl.*) liebkosen, flirten.
canopy ['kænəpɪ], 1. *s.* der Baldachin, Betthimmel, Thronhimmel, Traghimmel, die Decke, Hülle; (*fig.*) der Himmel, das Firmament; – *of a pulpit*, der Schalldeckel; – *of heaven*, das Himmelszelt. 2. *v.a.* (mit einem Baldachin) bedecken, überdachen.
can't [kɑ:nt], *see* ¹**can.**
¹**cant** [kænt], 1. *s.* die Schrägung, Biegung, Verkantung, geneigte Lage *or* Fläche. 2. *v.a.* (– *over*) auf die Seite legen, kanten, (um)kippen. 3. *v.n.* sich auf die Seite legen. **––hook,** *s.* der Kanthaken (*Naut.*). **––timbers,** *pl.* schräge Spanten.
²**cant,** 1. *s.* die Scheinheiligkeit, Heuchelei; Zunftsprache, Berufssprache, der Jargon; – *phrase*, stehende Redensart, nichtssagendes Schlagwort. 2. *v.n.* scheinheilig reden; sich scheinheilig benehmen; *–ing fellow*, der Scheinheilige, Heuchler, Frömmler.
cantaloup ['kæntəlu:p], *s.* die Beulenmelone.
cantankerous [kæn'tæŋkərəs], *adj.* (*coll.*) mürrisch, streitsüchtig, rechthaberisch.
cantata [kæn'tɑ:tə], *s.* die Kantate.
canteen [kæn'tɪ:n], *s.* die Feldflasche; das Kochgeschirr; die Kantine, der Speiseraum (*in factories, etc.*).
canter ['kæntə], 1. *s.* kurzer Galopp, der Kanter; (*coll.*) *win in a* –, mühelos gewinnen. 2. *v.n.* kantern, im leichten Galopp reiten.
cantharides [kæn'θærɪdɪ:z], *pl.* spanische Fliegen.
canticle ['kæntɪkl], *s.* der Gesang; Lobgesang; *pl.* das hohe Lied Salomonis.
cantilever ['kæntɪlɪ:və], 1. *s.* der Ausleger, vorspringender Träger. 2. *adj.* freitragend.
cantle ['kæntl], *s.* die Hinterzwiesel (*of saddle*).
canto ['kæntoʊ], *s.* (*pl.* –s) der Gesang (*of a long poem*).
canton ['kæntən], 1. *s.* der Bezirk, Kanton (*Switzerland*); das Eckschildchen, Quartier (*Her.*). 2. [*also* kæn'tu:n], *v.a.* unterbringen, einquartieren. **–al,** *adj.* kantonal, Bezirks–. **–ment** [kæn'tu·nmənt], *s.* die Kantonierung, Einquartierung; die (Orts)-Unterkunft, das Quartier.
cantor ['kæntə], *s.* der Kantor, Vorsänger.
canvas ['kænvəs], *s.* das Segeltuch, der Drillich, Kanevas; die Malerleinwand (*Paint.*); Wagenplane, Persenning; Segel (*pl.*) (*Naut.*); (*fig.*) das Zelt; (*fig.*) Gemälde; *under* –, in Zelten; unter Segeln (*Naut.*). **– bucket,** *s.* der Wassersack, die Pütze.
canvass ['kænvəs], 1. *s.* die Stimmenwerbung. 2. *v.a.* prüfen, genau untersuchen, erörtern; werben um (*votes*); bearbeiten (*constituency*); keilen (*Univ. sl.*). 3. *v.n.* Stimmen werben für, sich bewerben um. **–er,** *s.* der Stimmenwerber, Kundenwerber, Abonnentensammler. **–ing,** *s.* die Erörterung, Untersuchung.
canyon ['kænjən], *s.* tiefe Bergschlucht.
caoutchouc ['kɑutʃu:k], *s.* der Kautschuk, Gummi.
cap [kæp], 1 *s.* die Kappe, Mütze, Haube; das Zündhütchen; der Deckel; Aufsatz; das Eselshaupt (*Naut.*); – *and bells*, die Schellenkappe, Narrenkappe; *get one's* –, die Klub– *or* Mannschaftsmütze bekommen, ausgezeichnet werden (*Sport*); – *and gown*, Barett und Talar, akademische Tracht; *forage*––, die Feldmütze (*Mil.*); *that is a feather in his* –, darauf kann er stolz sein; (*prov.*) *if the – fits wear it*, wen's juckt der kratze sich; – *in hand*, demütig; – *of maintenance*, die Schirmhaube; *put on one's thinking*––, die Gedanken zusammennehmen; *she sets her – at him*, (*coll.*) sie sucht ihn zu gewinnen, sie angelt nach ihm; *toe*––, die Schuhspitze. 2. *v.a.* bedecken, mit einem Deckel versehen; krönen, oben liegen auf; (*fig.*) übertreffen, ausstechen; – *a joke*, einen Witz überbieten; – *verses*, Verse um die Wette hersagen. **–ful,** *s.*; *–ful of wind*, leichter *or* vorübergehender Wind. **––paper,** *s.* das Packpapier. **––stone,** *s.* der Schlußstein.
capab–ility [keɪpə'bɪlɪtɪ], *s.* die Fähigkeit, Tauglichkeit, das Vermögen. **–le** ['keɪpəbl], *adj.* fähig, imstande (*of*, zu); tauglich (*of*, zu), empfänglich (*of*, für).
capacious [kə'peɪʃəs], *adj.* weit, umfassend, geräumig, aufnahmefähig. **–ness,** *s.* die Geräumigkeit, Weite.
capacitate [kə'pæsɪteɪt], *v.a.* fähig machen, befähigen; rechtlich befugt machen (*Law*).
capacity [kə'pæsɪtɪ], *s.* der Inhalt, Gehalt, Umfang; die Geräumigkeit, der Raum, die Aufnahmefähigkeit; der Tonnengehalt (*of a ship*); die Kapazität

(*Elec.*); der Gesamthubraum (*of an engine*); (*fig.*) die Fassungskraft; Befähigung, Leistungsfähigkeit, Tüchtigkeit, Fähigkeit; der Charakter, die Eigenschaft; *in his – as*, in seiner Eigenschaft als; *measure of –*, das Hohlmaß; *official –*, dienstliche Eigenschaft; *productive –*, die Leistungsfähigkeit; *filled* or *full to –*, gedrängt *or* gesteckt voll; *working to –*, mit voller Leistungsfähigkeit arbeiten.

cap-à-pie [kæpəˈpɪ:], *adv.* von Kopf (bis) zu Fuß.

caparison [kəˈpærɪsn], *s.* die Schabracke, Pferdedecke; (*fig.*) Ausstaffierung, Ausstattung, Ausrüstung.

[1]**cape** [keɪp], *s.* der Mantelkragen; Kragenmantel, Umhang, das Cape.

[2]**cape,** *s.* das Vorgebirge, Kap.

[1]**caper** [ˈkeɪpə], 1. *s.* der Bocksprung, Luftsprung; *cut –s*, Kapriolen *or* Dummheiten machen. 2. *v.n.* Freudensprünge machen, hüpfen.

[2]**caper,** *s.* der Kapernstrauch, (*usually pl.*) die Kaper. **–-sauce,** *s.* die Kapernsoße.

capercailye [kæpəˈkeɪljɪ], **capercailzie** [–ˈkeɪlzɪ], *s.* der Auerhahn (*Orn.*).

capful [ˈkæpful], *see* **cap.**

capillar–ity [kæpɪˈlærɪtɪ], *s.* die Haarröhrchenwirkung, Kapillarität. **–y** [kəˈpɪlərɪ], 1. *adj.* haarförmig, haarfaserig, haarfein, kapillar; *–y attraction*, die Haarröhrchenanziehung; *–y pyrites*, der Haarkies. *–y repulsion*, die Haarröhrchenabstoßung. 2. *s.* das Kapillargefäß (*Anat.*).

[1]**capital** [ˈkæpɪtəl], 1. *adj.* Todes–, todeswürdig, kapital (*of crimes, etc.*); hauptsächlich, vorzüglich, Haupt–; vortrefflich, vorzüglich, herrlich, glänzend, famos (*also as int.*); *– city*, die Hauptstadt; *– crime*, das Kapitalverbrechen; *– joke*, herrlicher Spaß; *– letter*, großer Anfangsbuchstabe (*Typ.*); *– levy*, die Vermögensabgabe; *– punishment*, die Todesstrafe; *– ship*, das Kriegsschiff; *– stock*, die Stammaktien (*pl.*). 2. *s.* die Hauptstadt; großer Anfangsbuchstabe; das Kapital (*C.L.*); das Unternehmertum; *floating –*, das Betriebskapital; *fixed –*, festes Kapital; *invested –*, das Anlagekapital; *invest* or *sink – in*, Geld in etwas anlegen; *make – out of*, Kapital schlagen aus, Nutzen *or* Vorteil ziehen aus; *unproductive –*, totes Kapital. **–ism** [–lɪzm], *s* der Kapitalismus. **–ist** [–lɪst], *s.* der Kapitalist. **–ize** [–lɑɪz], *v.a.* kapitalisieren, in Kapital umsetzen; mit großen Anfangsbuchstaben schreiben.

[2]**capital** [ˈkæpɪtl], *s.* das Kapitäl, der Säulenknauf (*Arch.*).

capitation [kæpɪˈteɪʃən], *s.* die Kopfzählung, Kopfsteuer. **–-fee,** *s.* das Kopfgeld.

capitol [ˈkæpɪtl], *s.* das Kapitol (*Rome*); das Kongreßgebäude (*Amer.*).

capitular [kəˈpɪtjulə], **–y** [–ərɪ], 1. *adj.* Stifts–; Köpfchen– (*Anat., Bot.*). 2. *s.* der Stiftsherr, Mitglied eines Domkapitels; das Kapitulare (*Hist.*).

capitulat–e [kəˈpɪtjuleɪt], *v.n.* kapitulieren (*to*, vor), sich unterwerfen *or* ergeben (*to* (*Dat.*)), die Waffen strecken. **–ion** [–ˈleɪʃən], *s.* die Übergabe, Kapitulation, Waffenstreckung.

capon [ˈkeɪpən], *s.* der Kapaun. **–ize,** *v.a.* kastrieren.

capot [kəˈpɔt], *s.* der Matsch (im Pikett).

capote [kəˈpout], *s.* die Kapuze, der Kapuzenmantel.

capric–e [kəˈprɪ:s], *s.* die Laune, Grille. **–ious** [kəˈprɪʃəs], *adj.* launisch, unberechenbar, mutwillig, unbeständig. **–iousness,** *s.* die Launenhaftigkeit.

capricorn [ˈkæprɪkɔ:n], *s.* der Steinbock (*Astr.*).

capriole [ˈkæprɪoul], *s.* die Kapriole, der Bocksprung.

capsicum [ˈkæpsɪkəm], *s.* spanischer Pfeffer.

capsize [kæpˈsɑɪz], 1. *v.a.* zum Kentern bringen, umwerfen. 2. *v.n.* kentern, umschlagen, umkippen.

capstan [ˈkæpstən], *s.* die Ankerwinde, das Gangspill (*Naut.*); die Erdwinde (*Mach.*). **–-bar,** *s.* die Gangspillspate.

capsul–ar [ˈkæpsjulə], *adj.* kapselförmig; *–ar ligament*, das Kapselband (*Anat.*). **–e** [ˈkæpsju:l], *s.* die Kapsel; Abdampfschale, der Schmelztiegel (*Chem.*); *primer –e*, die Zündpille.

captain [ˈkæptɪn], *s.* der Kapitän (*Naut.*); Hauptmann (*Mil.*); Rittmeister (*Cavalry*); Mannschaftsführer (*Sport*); Primus (*of a school*); *– of industry*, Großindustrielle(r), *m.*, der Industrieführer. **–cy,** *s.* der Rang eines Hauptmanns, *etc.* **–ship,** *s.* die Führerrolle, Führung.

caption [ˈkæpʃən], *s.* die Überschrift, Unterschrift, der Bildtext; die Einleitungsformel (*Law*); Verhaftung, Wegnahme (*Law*).

captious [ˈkæpʃəs], *adj.* zänkisch, tadelsüchtig; verfänglich, heikel; spitzfindig; *– critic*, der Besserwisser, Nörgler, Meckerer, Kritikaster. **–ness,** *s.* die Tadelsucht; Verfänglichkeit, Spitzfindigkeit.

captivat–e [ˈkæptɪveɪt], *v.a.* fesseln, einnehmen; bestricken, bezaubern. **–ing,** *adj.* bezaubernd, einnehmend.

captiv–e [ˈkæptɪv], 1. *adj.* gefangen; *–e balloon*, der Fesselballon; *take –e*, gefangennehmen. 2. *s.* Gefangene(r), *m.* **–ity** [–ˈtɪvɪtɪ], *s.* die Gefangenschaft, Knechtschaft.

captor [ˈkæptə], *s.* der Fänger, Erbeuter; Kaper (*Naut.*).

capture [ˈkæptʃə], 1. *s.* das Fangen, die Gefangennahme, Einnahme, Eroberung, das Erbeuten; die Prise, Aufbringung, das Kapern (*Naut.*); der Fang, Raub, die Beute; *right of –*, das Prisenrecht. 2. *v.a.* fangen, abfangen; einnehmen, gefangennehmen (*Mil.*); erbeuten (*stores*), ausheben (*a position*), kapern, aufbringen (*a ship*); *be –d*, in Gefangenschaft geraten.

capuchin [kæpuˈʃɪ:n], *s.* die Kapuze; der Kapuziner (*monk*). **–-monkey,** *s.* der Rollschwanzaffe. **–-pigeon,** *s.* die Haubentaube.

car [kɑ:], *s.* der Wagen, Karren; die Gondel (*of a balloon*); der Eisenbahnwagen, Personenwagen, Waggon (*Amer.*); *dining- –*, der Speisewagen; (*motor-*) *–*, das Auto, der Kraftwagen, Wagen; *sleeping- –*, der Schlafwagen; (*tram*) *–*, der Straßenbahnwagen; *triumphal –*, der Triumphwagen. **–-driver,** *s.* der Kraftfahrer. **–-load,** *s.* die Wagenladung. **–-park,** *s.* der Parkplatz.

carabineer [kærəbɪˈnɪ:ə], *s.* der Karabinier.

caracol(e) [ˈkærəkoul], 1. *s.* halbe Wendung, die Schwenkung (*of a horse*). 2. *v.n.* im Zickzack reiten (*a horse*).

carafe [kəˈrɑ:f], *s.* die Wasserflasche, Karaffe.

caramel [ˈkærəmɛl], *s.* das Karamel; gebrannter Zucker; die Karamelle.

carapace [ˈkærəpeɪs], *s.* der Rückenschild.

carat [ˈkærət], 1. *s.* das Karat; der Goldfeingehalt. 2. *adj.* karätig.

caravan [ˈkærəvæn], *s.* die Karawane; der Wohnwagen, Reisewagen; Menageriewagen. **–serai, –sary** [–ˈvænsərɑɪ], *s.* die Karawanserei.

caraway [ˈkærəweɪ], *s.* der Kümmel. **–-seed,** *s.* der Kümmelsamen, (*pl.*) der Kümmel.

carbide [ˈkɑ:bɑɪd], *s.* das Karbid.

carbine [ˈkɑ:bɑɪn], *s.* der Karabiner.

carbohydrate [kɑ:bouˈhɑɪdreɪt], *s.* der Kohlenwasserstoff, das Kohlehydrat.

carbolic [kɑ:ˈbɔlɪk], *adj.* karbolsauer. *– acid*, die Karbolsäure, das Phenolöl (*Chem.*); *– soap*, die Karbolseife.

carbon [ˈkɑ:bən], *s.* der Kohlenstoff; Kohlestift (*Elec.*); die Ölkohle (*in cylinder*); *– dioxide*, das Kohlendioxyd; *– monoxide*, das Kohlenoxyd. **–aceous** [kɑ:bəˈneɪʃəs], *adj.* kohlenhaltig, kohlenreich (*Geol.*), kohlenstoffhaltig (*Chem.*), Kohlen–. **–ate** [ˈkɑ:bəneɪt], 1. *v.a.* mit Kohlensäure sättigen (*Chem.*); karbonisieren (*Manuf.*). 2. [–nɪt], *s.* das Karbonat, kohlensaures Salz; *–ate of soda*, kohlensaures Natron. **– copy,** der Durchschlag. **–-filament lamp,** die Kohlenfadenlampe. **–ic** [kɑ:ˈbɔnɪk], *adj.* kohlensauer, kohlig, Kohlen–; *–ic acid*, die Kohlensäure; *–ic acid gas*, das Kohlensäuregas; *–ic oxide*, das Kohlenoxyd. **–iferous** [kɑ:bəˈnɪfərəs] *adj.* Kohle enthaltend; *–iferous limestone*, der Kohlenkalk; *–iferous Period*, die Steinkohlenzeit, das Karbon. **–ization** [–ˈzeɪʃən], *s.* die Verkohlung, Verkokung; Inkohlung (*Geol.*); *–ization plant*, die Kokerei. **–ize** [ˈkɑ:bənɑɪz], *v.a.* verkohlen, verkoken; *partially –ize*, ankohlen. **–-light,** *s.* das Bogenlicht. **–-paper,** *s.* das Kohlepapier, Durchschlagpapier.

carboy [ˈkɑ:bɔɪ], *s.* die Korbflasche, der Ballon (*Chem.*).

carbuncle ['kɑ:bʌŋkl], *s.* der Karfunkel (*Min.*); Karbunkel, Furunkel (*Med.*).
carbur-ation ['kɑ:bjureɪʃən], *s.* die Vergasung. **-et** ['kɑ:bjurɛt], *v.a.* vergasen. **-etted,** *adj.* mit Kohlenstoff verbunden; *-etted hydrogen,* das Kohlenwasserstoffgas. **-etter, -ettor,** *s.* der Vergaser (*Motor.*).
carcass, carcase ['kɑ:kəs], *s.* der Kadaver, die Tierleiche; (*contempt.*) der Leichnam, Körper; (*fig.*) das Gerippe, Skelett, der Rumpf.
carcinoma [kɑ:sɪ'noumə], *s.* der Krebs (*Med.*).
[1]**card** [kɑ:d], *s.* die Karte, Postkarte, Spielkarte, Visitenkarte; Mitteilung, Geschäftsanzeige; das Programm (*horse-racing*); *see* **-board;** *compass* –, die Windrose; *identification* –, die Ausweiskarte; *have a – up one's sleeve,* einen Plan in Reserve haben; *lay one's -s on the table,* mit offenen Karten spielen; *leave a – on a p.,* bei einem seine Karte abgeben; *on the -s,* durchaus möglich, gut denkbar; *pack of -s,* das Spiel Karten; (*coll.*) *queer* –, seltsamer Kauz; *ration* –, die Lebensmittelkarte, der Bezugsschein; *show one's -s,* die Karten aufdecken; *throw up one's -s,* das Spiel aufgeben; *trump* –, der Trumpf, das Trumpfblatt; – *to view,* die Erlaubniskarte zur Besichtigung; *visiting* –, die Visitenkarte. **-board,** *s.* der Pappdeckel, die Pappe, der Karton; *-board box,* die Pappschachtel. **--case,** *s.* die (Visiten)Kartentasche. **--catalogue, --index,** *s.* die Kartei, Kartothek. **--party,** *s.* die Spielgesellschaft. **--room,** *s.* das Spielzimmer. **-sharper,** *s.* der Falschspieler, Bauernfänger. **--table,** *s.* der Spieltisch. **--trick,** *s.* das Kartenkunststück. **--vote,** *s.* die Stimmenabgabe nach (Mitglieds)Karten.
[2]**card,** 1. *s.* die Karde, Kardätsche, Kratze, Krempel. 2. *v.a.* kardätschen, krempeln. **-er,** *s.* der Krempler, Wollkämmer. **-ing,** *adj.* Krempel-, Kratz-; *-ing machine,* die Kratzmachine.
cardan ['kɑ:dən], **-ic** [kɑ:'dænɪk], *adj.*; **--joint,** *s.* das Kardangelenk. **--shaft,** *s.* die Kardanwelle. *-ic suspension,* kardanische Aufhängung.
cardia-c ['kɑ:dɪæk], *adj.* Herz-; herzstärkend(es Mittel); den Magenmund betreffend. **-lgy** ['kɑ:dɪældʒɪ], *s.* das Sodbrennen (*Med.*).
cardigan ['kɑ:dɪgən], *s.* die Wollweste.
cardinal ['kɑ:dɪnəl], 1. *adj.* vornehmlich, vornehmst, hauptsächlich, Haupt-, Kardinal-; hochrot, scharlachfarben; – *numbers,* die Grundzahlen; (*fig.*) – *point,* der Haupt -*or* Angelpunkt; – *points,* die Kardinalpunkte (*of the compass*); – *virtues,* die Kardinaltugenden. 2 *s.* der Kardinal (*Eccl.*); Kardinal(vogel) (*Orn.*). **-ate** [-əlɪt] *s.* die Kardinalswürde.
cardio- ['kɑ:dɪou], *prefix* Herz-.
cardoon [kɑ:'du:n], *s.* die Kardonenartischocke (*Bot.*).
care [kɛə], 1. *s.* die Sorge, Besorgnis (*for,* um); Fürsorge; Aufmerksamkeit, Vorsicht; der Kummer; die Sorgfalt, Mühe, der Fleiß; die Pflege, Aufsicht, Obhut, der Gegenstand der Sorge *or* Pflege; – *of,* per Adresse, bei; *cast aside all* –, sich jeder Sorge entschlagen; *entrust to the – of s.o.,* jemandes Obhut anvertrauen; *free from* –, sorgenfrei; *have a –! take –!* Vorsicht! Achtung! *in* or *under his* –, in seiner Obhut; *he was under the – of Dr. F.,* er war in der Behandlung des Herrn Doktor F.; *take* –, sich in acht nehmen, acht geben (*of,* auf), sorgen (*of,* für); *take – to do,* nicht vergessen zu tun, trachten zu tun; *take – not to offend him,* sich hüten ihn zu beleidigen; *take – of a p.,* einen pflegen, sich annehmen (*Gen.*); *he is well taken – of,* er ist in guter Obhut, ist gut aufgehoben, ist gut versorgt; *take – of o.s.,* sich schonen; – *will kill a cat,* Kummer macht vor der Zeit alt. 2. *v.n.* sorgen (*for,* für), sich kümmern (*for,* um); sich sorgen (*about,* über *or* um), besorgt sein (*about,* um), sich Sorgen machen (*about,* über); sich etwas daraus machen; *what do I –!* was frage ich danach! was kümmert's mich, was geht's mich an? (*sl.*) *I don't – a damn, I couldn't – less,* ich mache mir nicht das geringste daraus, das ist mir total schnuppe; *nobody -s about it,* danach kräht kein Hahn; *for all I* –, meinetwegen, wenn es nach mir ginge; *I don't – if I do,* ich habe nichts dagegen, es ist mir gleich, meinetwegen; – *for a p.,* einen gern haben, einen schätzen; *-for nobody,* sich um niemanden kümmern; – *for nothing,* nach nichts fragen, sich um nichts kümmern. **-free,** *adj.* sorgenlos. **-ful,** *adj.* besorgt (*for,* für), bedacht, behutsam, sorgsam, achtsam (*of,* auf), vorsichtig; sorgfältig, genau (*inquiry, etc.*); sparsam; *be -ful!* nimm dich in acht! Vorsicht! *be -ful to do,* nicht vergessen zu tun; *be -ful not to do,* sich hüten zu tun. **-fulness,** *s.* die Sorgsamkeit, Behutsamkeit, Achtsamkeit, Sorgfalt; Aufmerksamkeit, Vorsicht; Gründlichkeit, Genauigkeit. **-less,** *adj.* sorglos, unbekümmert (*of,* um); unüberlegt, unbedachtsam, unachtsam, unvorsichtig; nachlässig; *-less about one's appearance,* um sein Aussehen unbekümmert sein. **-lessness,** *s.* die Sorglosigkeit; Unachtsamkeit; Fahrlässigkeit, Nachlässigkeit. **-taker,** *s.* der Hausmeister, Hausverwalter; Wärter, Wächter; Verwalter; *-taker government,* die Übergangsregierung. **--worn,** *adj.* sorgenvoll, abgehärmt.
careen [kə'rɪ:n], 1. *v.a.* kielholen, umlegen (*a ship*). 2. *v.n.* sich auf die Seite legen, krängen (*Naut.*). **-age,** *s.* das Kielgeld; der Kielholplatz.
career [kə'rɪə], 1. *s.* schneller Lauf; die Laufbahn, Karriere; der Flug (*of a hawk*); *enter upon a* –, eine Laufbahn einschlagen; *in full* –, in vollem Laufe. 2. *v.n.* eilen, jagen, rasen. **-ist** [-rɪst], *s.* der Karrieremacher, Postenjäger.
carefree ['kɛəfrɪ:], *see* **care.**
careful ['kɛəful], *see* **care.**
careless ['kɛəlɪs], *see* **care.**
caress [kə'rɛs], 1. *s.* die Liebkosung. 2. *v.a.* liebkosen, herzen, umarmen; streicheln.
caret ['kærət], *s.* das Einschaltungszeichen, Auslassungszeichen (ᵛ).
cargo ['kɑ:gou], *s.* die Fracht, Schiffsladung. **--vessel,** *s.* das Frachtschiff.
caricatur-e [kærɪkə'tjuə], 1. *s.* das Zerrbild, die Karikatur. 2. *v.a.* karikieren; lächerlich machen. **-ist,** *s.* der Karikaturenzeichner.
cari-es ['kɛərɪɪ:z], *s.* der Knochenfraß; die Zahnfäule. **-ous** [-ɪəs], *adj.* angefressen, verfault.
carillon [kə'rɪljən], *s.* das Glockenspiel.
carking [kɑ:kɪŋ], *adj.* kummervoll; – *care,* nagende Sorge.
carl-(e) [kɑ:l], *s.* der Kerl (*Scots*). **-ine,** *s.* altes Weib (*Scots*).
carline ['kɑ:lɪn], *s.,* – *thistle,* die Eberwurz (*Bot.*).
carminative ['kɑ:mɪnətɪv], 1. *adj.* Blähungen beseitigend. 2. *s.* das Mittel gegen Blähungen.
carmine ['kɑ:maɪn], 1. *s.* der Karmin, das Karminrot. 2. *adj.* karminrot.
carnage ['kɑ:nɪdʒ], *s.* das Gemetzel, Blutbad.
carnal ['kɑ:nəl], *adj.* fleischlich, sinnlich; geschlechtlich; weltlich; *have – intercourse with,* geschlechtlichen Umgang haben mit; – *knowledge,* geschlechtlicher Umgang (*of,* mit (*Law*)). **-ity** [-'nælɪtɪ], *s.* die Fleischeslust, Sinnlichkeit.
carnation [kɑ:'neɪʃən], *s.* die Fleischfarbe; Nelke (*Bot.*).
carnelian [kɑ:'nɪ:ljən], *s.* der Karneol.
carnival ['kɑ:nɪvəl], *s.* der Karneval, Fasching; das Kostümfest.
carnivor-e ['kɑ:nɪvɔ:], *s.* das Raubtier, der Fleischfresser. **-ous** [-'nɪvərəs], *adj.* fleischfressend.
carob ['kærəb], *s.,* **--bean,** das Johannisbrot. **--tree,** *s.* der Johannisbrotbaum.
carol ['kærəl], 1. *s.* der Lobgesang, das Lied; *Christmas* –, das Weihnachtslied. 2. *v.n.* singen, jubilieren (*of birds*).
carotid [kə'rɔtɪd], *s.* die Halsschlagader.
carous-al [kə'rauzəl], *s.* das Trinkgelage. **-e** [kə'rauz], 1. *s. see* **-al.** 2. *v.n.* zechen, trinken.
[1]**carp** [kɑ:p], *s.* der Karpfen (*Ichth.*).
[2]**carp,** *v.n.* kritteln, nörgeln (*at,* über *or* an); *-ing criticism,* kleinliche Kritik.
carpal ['kɑ:pəl], *adj.* Handwurzel- (*Anat.*).
carpel ['kɑ:pəl], *s.* das Fruchtblatt (*Bot.*).
carpent-er ['kɑ:pɪntə], 1. *s.* der Zimmermann, Tischler. 2. *v.n.* zimmern. **-er-bee,** die Holzbiene. **-er's bench,** die Hobelbank. **-er's rule,** der Zollstock. **-ry** [-trɪ], *s.* die Tischlerei, das Zimmerhandwerk, die Zimmermannsarbeit.
carpet ['kɑ:pɪt], 1. *s.* der Teppich; *bedside* –, der

Bettvorleger; *stair*--, der Treppenläufer; *on the* –, aufs *or* auf dem Tapet, zur Erörterung; (*coll.*) vor einem Verweis (stehen). 2. *v.a.* mit Teppichen belegen. **--bag,** *s.* der Reisesack. **--bagger,** *s.* (*Amer.*) der Wahlagitator. **--beater,** *s.* der Teppichklopfer. **-ing,** *s.* der Teppichstoff. **--knight,** *s.* der Salonheld. **--rod,** *s.* die Läuferstange. **--slippers,** *pl.* die Hausschuhe (*pl.*). **--sweeper,** *s.* die Teppichkehrmaschine.

carpolite [ˈkɑ:polɑɪt], *pl.* die Fruchtversteinerung (*Geol.*).

carpus [ˈkɑ:pəs], *s.* die Handwurzel.

carrageen [kærəˈgɪ:n], *s.* irländisches Moos (*Bot.*).

carriage [ˈkærɪdʒ], *s.* der Wagen, das Fuhrwerk; der Waggon, Personenwagen (*Railw.*); das Tragen, Fahren, die Beförderung, Verfrachtung, der Transport; das Rollgeld, Fuhrgeld, Frachtgeld, die Transportspesen, Frachtspesen (*pl.*), der Fuhrlohn; die Haltung, das Betragen, Benehmen; die Ausführung, Durchführung, Annahme eines Antrags; der Wagen, das Gestell (*Mach.*), der Schlitten (*of typewriter*), der Karren (*of printing press*), das Fahrgestell (*of aircraft*), die Lafette (*of a gun*); *one-horse* –, der Einspänner; – *and pair*, der Zweispänner; – *by sea*, der Seetransport; *by* –, per Achse. **--body,** die Karosserie. **--builder,** *s.* der Wagenbauer. **--building,** *s.* der Wagenbau. **--door,** *s.* der Kutschenschlag. **--drive,** die Auffahrt. **--entrance,** die Einfahrt. **– forward,** unter Nachnahme, unfrankiert. **--frame,** das Wagengestell. **--free,** *adj.* portofrei, frachtfrei. **--horse,** *s.* das Wagenpferd. **--paid,** *see* **--free.** **--road, --way,** *s.* der Fahrweg.

carrie–d [ˈkærɪd], *see* **carry.** **–r** [ˈkærɪə], *s.* der Fuhrmann; Überbringer, Bote, Träger, Spediteur, Beförderer; Mitnehmer, das Zwischenrad (*Mach.*); der Gepäckträger (*Cycl.*); Bazillenträger (*Med.*); *aircraft* –*r*, das Flugzeugmutterschiff; *common* –*r*, der Lohnfuhrmann; –*r and forwarding-agent*, der Spediteur; *troop* –*r*, das Truppenfahrzeug. **–r-based,** *adj.* Träger–, Bord–, Decklande– (*aircraft*). **–r-pigeon,** *s.* die Brieftaube. **–r-wave,** *s.* die Trägerwelle (*Rad.*).

carrion [ˈkærɪən], *s.* das Aas; (*fig.*) der Unrat. **--crow,** *s.* die Aaskrähe.

carronade [kærəˈneɪd], *s.* die Schiffshaubitze.

carrot [ˈkærət], *s.* die Karotte, Mohrrübe, Möhre, gelbe Rübe; (*vulg.*) –*s*, der Rotkopf. **–y,** *adj.* rötlich, rot (*of hair*).

carr–y [ˈkærɪ], 1. *v.a.* tragen, führen, bringen, befördern, schaffen; mitnehmen, mitführen (*on one's person*); verbreiten, weitertragen (*disease*); übertragen (*figures in adding*); erobern, einnehmen, stürmen (*a position*) (*Mil.*); fahren (*sail*) (*Naut.*); durchbringen (*a motion*); –*y all before one*, alles mit sich wegreißen; –*y arms*, Waffen tragen; –*y the audience with one*, die Zuhörer mit sich fortreißen; –*y coals to Newcastle*, Eulen nach Athen tragen; –*y conviction*, überzeugen, überzeugend wirken; –*y the day*, den Sieg davontragen, siegen; –*y interest*, Zinsen tragen *or* einbringen; –*y it with a high hand*, gebieterisch auftreten; *the motion was –ied*, der Antrag ging durch; –*y a th. too far*, es zu weit treiben; –*y o.s. with courage*, sich tapfer halten *or* benehmen; –*y one's point*, seinen Zweck *or* sein Ziel erreichen, seinen Willen *or* Standpunkt durchsetzen; –*y too much sail*, mit zu vielen Segeln fahren; –*ied unanimously*, einstimmig angenommen; –*y weight*, von Bedeutung sein, Einfluß haben, ins Gewicht fallen; –*y away*, wegtragen, fortschaffen; fortreißen (*also fig.*); *a mast was –ied away*, ein Mast wurde abgebrochen *or* weggerissen; *passion –ied him away*, Leidenschaft verleitete *or* verführte ihn; *be –ied away with* . . ., von . . . fortgerissen *or* hingerissen werden *or* begeistert sein; –*y forward*, vortragen, übertragen (*C.L.*); fortführen, fortsetzen; *amount –ied forward*, der Übertrag; –*y into, effect*, ausführen, durchsetzen; –*y off*, wegführen, abführen, wegtragen, wegnehmen, wegraffen; erringen; –*y off the prize*, den Preis gewinnen; –*y it off well*, es erfolgreich durchführen, mit Erfolg auftreten, sich darüber hinwegsetzen; –*y on*, anführen, betreiben; fortsetzen; (weiter) führen (*a business*); –*y on a conversation*, ein Gespräch führen; –*y out*, durchsetzen, vollstrecken, ausführen; –*y over*, hinüberführen; see –*y forward* (*C.L.*); –*y to a new account*, auf neue Rechnung vortragen (*C.L.*); –*y through*, durchsetzen, durchführen (*a task*); durchbringen, durchhelfen (*Dat.*) (*a p.*); –*y with it*, (*fig.*) mit sich bringen, in sich schließen, nach sich ziehen. 2. *v.n.* tragen, vernehmbar sein (*of sound*), reichen, schießen (*as a gun*); *fetch and –y*, apportieren (*of dogs*); (*coll.*) geschäftig hin- und herlaufen; –*y on*, (*coll.*) sich aufregen, außer sich sein, stark ins Zeug gehen, eine Szene machen; (*coll.*) weiter machen, weiterarbeiten; (*sl.*) sich abgeben, anbändeln, verkehren, ein Verhältnis haben (*with*, mit); *he gave me money to –y on with*, er half mir mit Geld aus. 3. *s.* die Flugstrecke, Reichweite. **–y-on,** *s.* (*sl.*) unliebsame Szene. **–ying,** 1. *s.* das Fuhrwesen, der Transport (*C.L.*); –*ying agent*, der Spediteur; –*ying capacity*, die Ladefähigkeit, das Fassungsvermögen; –*ying roller*, die Laufrolle (*Mach.*); –*ying trade*, das Speditionsgeschäft; –*ying traffic*, der Güterverkehr (*Railw.*). **–yings-on,** *pl.* (*coll.*) auffallendes Benehmen, dumme Streiche.

cart [kɑ:t], 1. *s.* der Karren, Frachtwagen, die Karre; das Fuhrwerk, die Fuhre; *dog*--, zweirädriger Einspänner; *hand*--, der Handkarren; *in the* –, (*sl.*) in der Tinte *or* Klemme, in übler Lage; *put the – before the horse*, das Pferd beim Schwanze aufzäumen, eine Sache verkehrt anpacken. 2. *v.a.* mit einem Karren befördern; – *about*, (*sl.*) mit sich herumschleppen; – *away*, wegschaffen, abkarren, fortschaffen. **–age,** *s.* das Fahren, Karren; der Fuhrlohn, die Transportkosten, das Rollgeld. **–er,** *s.* der Fuhrmann, Kärrner. **--horse,** *s.* das Zugpferd. **--load,** *s.* die Fuhre, Wagenladung, das Fuder; (*coll.*) große Menge; *come down on s.o. like a --load of bricks*, einen tüchtig abkanzeln. **--rut,** *s.* die Radspur. **--wheel,** *s.* das Wagenrad; Radschlagen (*Gymn.*); *turn --wheels*, radschlagen. **–wright,** *s.* der Stellmacher, Wagenbauer.

carte [kɑ:t], *s.* die Quart (*Fenc.*). **--blanche,** *s.* unbeschränkte Vollmacht.

cartel [ˈkɑ:tel], *s.* das Kartell (*C.L.*); der Auslieferungsvertrag (*Pol.*); schriftliche Herausforderung.

cartilag–e [ˈkɑ:tɪlɪdʒ], *s.* der Knorpel. **–inous** [–ˈlædʒɪnəs], *adj.* knorpelig, knorpelartig.

cartography [kɑ:ˈtɔgrəfɪ], *s.* das Kartenzeichnen.

carton [ˈkɑ:tən], *s.* die Pappschachtel, der Karton.

cartoon [kɑ:ˈtu:n], *s.* die Karikatur; der Trickzeichnungsfilm; Entwurf, die Zeichnung, Musterzeichnung. **–ist,** *s.* der Karikaturenzeichner.

cartouche [kɑ:ˈtu:ʃ], *s.* die Kartusche, Randverzierung, der Zierrahmen, die Umrahmung (*Arch.*).

cartridge [ˈkɑ:trɪdʒ], *s.* die Patrone; Spule (*Phot.*); *ball*--, scharfe Patrone; *blank* –, die Platzpatrone; *dummy* –, die Exerzierpatrone. **--base,** der Hülsenboden. **--belt,** *s.* der Patronengurt. **--case,** *s.* die Patronenhülle, Kartuschhülse. **--paper,** *s.* das Zeichenpapier.

caruncle [ˈkærəŋkl], *s.* der Fleischauswuchs; Fruchthüllenauswuchs (*Bot.*).

carv–e [kɑ:v], 1. *v.a.* schneiden, zerschneiden; zerlegen, tranchieren (*a joint, etc.*); schnitzen, ausschneiden, meißeln (*Carp., Sculp., Engr.*); (*fig.*) gestalten, bahnen (*career, etc.*). 2. *v.n.* vorschneiden (*at table*), schnitzen, meißeln; –*ed work*, das Schnitzwerk (*Arch.*), die Schnitzarbeit. **–er,** *s.* der Vorschneider; Holzschnitzer, Bildhauer; das Vorlegemesser; (*pl.*) das Tranchierbesteck. **–ing,** *s.* das Vorschneiden, Tranchieren; Schnitzen, Meißeln; Schnitzwerk; die Bildhauerarbeit. **–ing-knife,** *s.* das Vorlegemesser.

carvel-built [ˈkɑ:vəlˈbɪlt], *adj.* kraweelgebaut (*Naut.*); --*boat*, das Kraweelboot.

cascade [kæsˈkeɪd], 1. *s.* der Wasserfall; – *of sparks*. der Feuerregen. 2. *v.n.* wellig herabfallen.

ˡ**case** [keɪs], 1. *s.* der Kasten, die Kiste, das Futteral, Gehäuse, Etui, der Behälter, das Fach; die Scheide, Hülse, der Überzug (*of a pillow, etc.*); die Bekleidung, der Mantel (*Mach.*); Rahmen (*Min.*) (*a*) (*with nouns or adjectives*) *brief*--, die (Akten-) Mappe; *cigarette* –, das Zigarettenetui; *dispatch* –, die Aktenmappe; *dressing-–*, das Reisenecessaire; *letter-–*, der Schriftkasten (*Typ.*); *lower* (*upper*) –, untere (obere) Hälfte des Schriftkastens; kleine (große) Buchstaben; *map* –, die Kartenschutzhülle; *music-–*, die Notentasche; *packing-–*, die Packkiste; *show–*, der Glaskasten, die Vitrine; *suit–*, die Reisetasche; *violin* –, der Geigenkasten; *watch* –, das Uhrgehäuse, *writing-–*, das Schreibetui, die Schreibmappe, (*b*) (*with prepositions*) – *of bottles*, der Flaschenkeller; – *of instruments*, das Besteck (*Med.*); – *of mathematical instruments*, das Reißzeug; – *of whisky*, die Kiste Whisky. 2. *v.a.* mit einem Überzug *or* Futteral versehen, verschalen, umhüllen, einhüllen. **--harden,** *v.a.* hartgießen, verstählen (*Metall.*), (*fig.*) abhärten. **--hardened,** *adj.* hartgegossen, stahlhart (*Metall.*); (*fig.*) abgehärtet, abgebrüht, unempfindlich; *see* **casing.** **--shot,** *s.* die Kartätsche (*Mil.*).

²**case,** *s.* der Fall, Umstand, die Frage; Rechtssache, der Rechtsfall, Prozeß (*Law*); Vorfall, Zustand, die Lage; der Krankheitsfall (*Med.*); Kasus (*Gram.*); (*coll.*) rechtlicher Grund, wichtige Gründe (*pl.*), der Anlaß, Belang; (*a*) (*with adjectives and prepositions*) *good – for complaint*, guter Anlaß zum Klagen; *there is no – for complaining*, es ist kein Anlaß zu klagen; – *in point*, der Fall, der als Beispiel zitiert wird; *leading* –, der Präzedenzfall; *it is a – of*, es handelt sich um; – *of conscience*, die Gewissensfrage; (*b*) (*with verbs*) *have a strong* or *good* –, ungefähr recht haben; *make out a – for*, (etwas) beweisen *or* zu verteidigen wissen; *take the – of*, nehmen Sie den Fall (von *or* des); *the – is this* es hat (damit) folgende Bewandtnis; *as the – may be*, je nachdem; *as the – stands*, wie die Sache (nun einmal) liegt, wie die Sachen stehen; *state one's* –, seinen Standpunkt vertreten; (*c*) (*after* in) *in* –, im Falle daß, falls; *in – of*, für den Fall, im Falle (*Gen.*); *in – of need*, im Notfall; *in the – of*, betreffs; *in any* –, jedenfalls, auf jeden Fall; *in no* –, keinesfalls, in keinem Falle, auf keinen Fall; *in that* –, wenn das so ist. **--law** auf Präzedenzien beruhendes Recht (*Law*)

casein(e) [ˈkeɪsiːn], *s.* das Kasein, der Käsestoff.

casemate [ˈkeɪsmeɪt], *s.* die Kasematte (*Fort.*).

casement [ˈkeɪsmənt], *s* der Fensterflügel, Flügelrahmen; – *window*, das Flügelfenster

caseous [ˈkeɪsɪəs], *adj* käsig, käseartig.

cash [kæʃ], 1. *s.* das Geld; bares Geld, das Bargeld, die Barzahlung; Kasse; (*coll.*) das Moos; – *and carry*, nur gegen Barzahlung und eigenen Transport; – *down*, bar, gegen Barzahlung; *for* –, gegen Barzahlung, gegen Kasse; *in* –, bar, per Kassa; (*coll.*) *be in* –, bei Kasse *or* Gelde sein; *£15 in* –, 15 Pfund bar, in barer Münze *or* in barem Geld; *net – in advance*, netto Kasse im voraus; – *in bank*, das Bankguthaben; – *in hand*, der Kassenbestand; *loose* –, das Kleingeld, Münzgeld; – *on delivery* (*C.O.D.*), unter Nachnahme; *be out of* –, nicht bei Gelde *or* Kasse sein; *ready* –, sofortige Kasse; *be short of* –, knapp (an Geld) sein; *turn into* –, zu Geld machen. 2. *v.a.* zu Geld machen; einwechseln, einkassieren, einlösen (*cheque, etc.*); (*sl.*) – *in on*, sich zunutze machen, ausnützen. **--account,** *s.* das Kassakonto. **--advance,** *s.* der Barvorschuß. **--book,** *s.* das Kassenbuch, Kassabuch. **--box,** *s.* der Geldkasten, die Schatulle. **--payment,** die Barzahlung. **--price,** *s.* der Preis bei Barzahlung. **– purchases,** die Bareinkäufe. **--register,** *s.* die Kontrollkasse.

cashew [ˈkæʃuː], *s.* der Nierenbaum. **--nuts,** *pl.* Elefantenläuse.

¹**cashier** [kæˈʃɪːə], *s.* der Kassierer (*C.L.*).

²**cashier,** *v.a.* entlassen, kassieren (*Mil.*). **-ing, -ment,** *s.* die Entlassung, Kassierung, Kassation.

cashmere [kæʃˈmɪə], 1. *s.* der Kaschmir. 2. *attrib.* Kaschmir-.

casing [ˈkeɪsɪŋ], *s.* der Überzug, die Hülle, Umhüllung, Verschalung, Verkleidung, Bekleidung; der Mantel, das Gehäuse.

casino [kəˈsiːnoʊ], *s.* das Gesellschaftshaus; das Tanzlokal, Spiellokal.

cask [kɑːsk], 1. *s.* das Faß, die Tonne. 2. *v.a.* auf Fässer ziehen. **-et,** *s.* das Kästchen; der Sarg (*Amer.*).

casque [kæsk], *s* (*archaic*) der Helm.

cassation [kæˈseɪʃən], *s.* die Kassation, Aufhebung (*Law*).

casserole [ˈkæsəroʊl], *s.* die Schmorpfanne.

cassia [ˈkæsɪə], *s* die Kassie.

cassock [ˈkæsək], *s.* der Meßrock, Chorrock; die Soutane (*R.C*).

cassowary [ˈkæsəwərɪ] *s.* der Kasuar (*Orn.*).

cast [kɑːst], 1. *ir.v.a.* & *n.* werfen, hinwerfen, abwerfen, auswerfen, wegwerfen; verlieren (*horns, teeth, etc.*); gießen, formen (*iron*); werfen, gebären (*young*); berechnen, ausrechnen (*accounts*); verteilen (*parts*) (*Theat.*), besetzen (*a play*) (*Theat.*); – *anchor*, den Anker (aus)werfen; – *a balance*, den Saldo ziehen; – *blame on a p.*, einem die Schuld zuschieben *or* geben (*for*, an (*Dat*)); – *the defendant*, den Beklagten zu Kosten verurteilen; *the die is* –, der Würfel ist gefallen; – *one's eyes upon s. th.*, seine Blicke auf eine S. richten; – *a horoscope*, ein Horoskop stellen; – *the lead*, loten; – *lots for*, um (eine S.) losen; – *the parts of a play*, die Rollen eines Stückes verteilen; *the play is well* –, das Stück ist gut besetzt; – *the skin*, sich häuten; – *a spell on s.o.*, einen behexen; – *teeth*, die Zähne verlieren; – *s.th. in a p.'s teeth*, einem etwas vorwerfen; – *one's vote*, seine Stimme abgeben, – *about*, umherwerfen; – *aside*, beiseitelegen, verwerfen; – *away*, verwerfen, wegwerfen; *be – away*, verschlagen *or* schiffbrüchig werden · – *away care*, die Sorgen verbannen; – *behind* zurückwerfen; – *a look behind*, zurückblicken; – *down*, niederwerfen; deprimieren, niederschlagen; senken (*the eyes*); *be – down*, niedergeschlagen *or* bedrückt sein; – *in one's lot with*, sein Schicksal teilen mit, gemeinsame S. machen mit; – *into prison*, ins Gefängnis werfen; – *off*, abwerfen, ablegen, abschütteln; verstoßen (*son, etc.*); abfieren (*Naut.*); – *off stitches*, Maschen abnehmen; – *on stitches*, (die ersten) Maschen aufnehmen; – *out*, (hin)auswerfen, vertreiben; – *up*, in die Höhe werfen; aufschlagen (*the eyes*); berechnen, zusammenrechnen, ausrechnen (*accounts*) 2. *v.n.* die Angel auswerfen; – *about*, umhersuchen, sich umsehen (*for*, nach); umherlavieren (*Naut*); sinnen (*for*, nach). 3. *s.* der Wurf; das Werfen, Auswerfen (*of nets*); die Wurfweite; Gußform; der Guß, Abguß, Abdruck; die Rollenverteilung, Rollenbesetzung (*Theat.*); der Schein, Stich, Farbton, die Nüance, Färbung, Schattierung, der Schimmer; die Art, Manier, der Typ; Angelhaken mit Köder; die Berechnung; *it has a green* –, es spielt ins Grüne; *have a – in one's eye*, schielen; *plaster* –, der Gipsabdruck; Gipsverband (*Med.*); *rough-–*, der Rohputz; *take a* –, prägen, abdrucken. **– iron,** 1. *s.* das Gußeisen, der Grauguß. 2. *adj.* gußeisern; (*fig.*) starr, unbeugsam, fest. **--off,** *adj.* abgelegt; *--off clothes*, abgelegte Kleider. **– steel,** der Gußstahl; (*see* **-ing**).

castanets [kæstəˈnɛts], *pl.* die Kastagnetten.

castaway [ˈkɑːstəweɪ], 1. *adj.* weggeworfen, unnütz, wertlos; schiffbrüchig (*Naut.*). 2. *s.* Schiffbrüchige(r), *m.*; Verworfene(r), *m.*

caste [kɑːst], *s.* die Kaste, gesellschaftliche Stellung; *lose* –, auf gesellschaftliche niedere Stufe herabsinken; – *feeling*, der Kastengeist.

castell-an [ˈkæstələn], *s.* der Kastellan, Burgvogt. **-ated** [-leɪtɪd], *adj.* mit Zinnen *or* Türmen versehen, burgartig.

caster [ˈkɑːstə], *s.* der Werfer; Berechner (*of accounts*); Gießer (*Metall.*); die Möbelrolle, Laufrolle (*see* ²**castor**).

castigat-e [ˈkæstɪgeɪt], *v.a.* züchtigen. **-ion,** *s.* die Züchtigung.

casting [ˈkɑːstɪŋ], 1. *adj.* den Ausschlag gebend, entscheidend; – *vote*, ausschlaggebende *or* entscheidende Stimme. 2. *s.* das Gießen; der Guß, Abguß, Gießstück, Gußteil, (*pl.*) Gießwaren; – *in chills*, der Schalenguß, Kokillenguß; *open sand* –, der Herdguß. **--box,** *s.* der Gießkasten (*Found.*). **--mould,** *s.* die Gießform. **--net,** *s.* das Wurfnetz.

castle [ˈkɑːsl], 1. *s.* die Burg, das Schloß; der Turm (*Chess*); –*s in the air*, Luftschlösser 2. *v.n.* rochieren (*Chess.*). **--builder,** *s.* der Projektemacher.

[1]**castor** ['kɑːstə], *s.* (*obs.*) der Biber; Biberhut; das Bibergeil (*Pharm.*).
[2]**castor** (*also* **caster**), *s.* die Streubüchse; Laufrolle, Möbelrolle. **--sugar,** *s.* der Streuzucker, Puderzucker.
castor-oil ['kɑːstərɔɪl], *s.* das Rizinusöl.
castrat-e [kæs'treɪt], *v.a.* kastrieren, verschneiden, entmannen; verstümmeln. **-ion** [-'treɪʃən], *s.* die Kastration, Entmannung, Verstümmelung; das Ausmerzen (*of passages in a book*).
casual ['kæʒuəl], 1. *adj.* zufällig, gelegentlich, beiläufig; unbestimmt, gleichgültig, nachlässig, inkonsequent; – *acquaintance*, flüchtige Bekanntschaft; – *labourer*, der Gelegenheitsarbeiter; – *ward*, das Asyl für Obdachlose. 2. *s.* Obdachlose(r), *m.*; der Gelegenheitsarbeiter.
casualty ['kæʒuəltɪ], *s.* der Unglücksfall; Todesfall; *pl.* die Verluste (*in battle*); – *list*, – *returns*, die Verlustliste, Liste der Toten und Verwundeten; – *ward*, die Unfallstation.
casuist ['kæʒuɪst], *s.* der Kasuist **-ic(al)** [-'ɪstɪk(l)], *adj.* kasuistisch, spitzfindig. **-ry,** *s.* die Kasuistik; Spitzfindigkeit.
cat [kæt], 1. *s.* die Katze, der Kater; die Katt, der Kattanker (*Naut.*); *tom--*, der Kater; *wild--*, die Wildkatze; *domestic* –, die Hauskatze; *Manx* –, schwanzlose Katze; *neuter* –, verschnittener Kater; *when the cat's away the mice will play*, wenn die Katze nicht zu Hause ist, spielen die Mäuse auf dem Tisch; (*sl.*) *not a – in hell's chance*, nicht die geringste Aussicht; *by night all -s are grey*, alle Kühe (*or* Katzen) sind in der Nacht schwarz (*or* grau); *see how* (or *which way*) *the – jumps*, sehen wie der Hase läuft; *lead a --and-dog life*, wie Hund und Katze leben; *let the – out of the bag*, ein Geheimnis ausplaudern; *a – may look at a king*, sieht doch die Katz' den Kaiser an; *it was raining -s and dogs*, es regnete Bindfaden. 2. *v.a.*; – *the anchor*, den Anker katten. **--block,** *s.* der Kattblock (*Naut.*). **-boat,** *s.* kleines Segelboot. **--burglar,** *s.* der Fassadenkletterer. **--call,** 1. *s.* das Zischen, Auspfeifen. 2. *v.a.* & *n.* zischen, auspfeifen. **-fall,** *s.* der Kattläufer (*Naut.*). **-fish,** *see* **catfish. -gut,** *see* **catgut. --head,** *s.* der Kranbalken, Ankerkran. **--ice,** *s.* unsicheres Eis. **-kin,** *see* **catkin. --o'-nine-tails,** *s.* die neunschwänzige Katze. **-'s-cradle,** *s.* das Abnehmespiel, Schnurspiel. **-'s-eye,** *s.* das Katzenauge (*Min.*), der Rückstrahler (*traffic sign*). **-('s)-lick,** *s.* flüchtiges Waschen. **-'s-paw,** *s.* die Brise, Kühlte (*Naut.*); (*fig.*) ein Werkzeug in den Händen anderer, Gefoppte(r), *m.*; *make a -'s-paw of a p.*, sich (*Dat.*) von einem die Kastanien aus dem Feuer holen lassen. **-ty,** *adj.* (*coll.*) boshaft, gehässig. **-walk,** *s.* der Laufgang, Steg. **--whisker,** *s.* der Kontaktdraht (*Rad.*).
cataclysm ['kætəklɪzm], *s.* die Überschwemmung, Sintflut; verheerende Umwälzung, völliger Umsturz. **-al,** *adj.* umwälzend, umstürzend.
catacomb ['kætəkuːm], *s.* die Katakombe.
catafalque ['kætəfælk], *s.* der Katafalk, das Leichengerüst.
catalectic [kætə'lɛktɪk], *adj.* katalektisch; unvollständig (*Metr.*).
catalep-sy ['kætəlɛpsɪ], *s.* der Starrkrampf (*Med.*). **-tic** [-'lɛptɪk], *adj.* starrsüchtig, kataleptisch.
catalogue ['kætələg], 1. *s.* das Verzeichnis, der Katalog. 2. *v a.* in ein Verzeichnis aufnehmen, einen Katalog aufstellen.
cataly-se ['kætəlɑɪz], *v. a.* katalysieren, eine Katalyse bewirken in. **-sis** [kə'tælɪsɪs], *s.* die Katalyse. **-st** ['kætəlɪst], *s.* der Katalysator (*Chem.*).
catamaran [kætəmə'ræn], *s.* das Floß; zänkisches Weib.
catamenia [kætə'miːnɪə], *s.* der Monatsfluß (*Med.*).
cataplasm ['kætəplæzm], *s.* der Breiumschlag.
catapult ['kætəpʌlt], 1. *s.* die Wurfmaschine, der Katapult; die Schleuder, Zwille. 2. *v.a.* (ab)-schleudern, mit der Zwille schießen.
cataract ['kætərækt], *s.* der Katarakt, Wasserfall; Wolkenbruch; grauer Star (*of the eye*); *couch the* –, den Star stechen.
catarrh [kə'tɑː], *s.* der Katarrh, Schnupfen. **-al** [-rəl], *adj.* katarrhalisch, Schnupfen-.
catastroph-e [kə'tæstrəfɪ], *s.* die Katastrophe (*drama*); der Schicksalsschlag, das Verhängnis, Unheil, großes Unglück. **-ic** [kætəs'trɔfɪk], *adj.* verhängnisvoll katastrophal.
catch [kætʃ], 1. *ir.v.a.* fangen, einfangen, auffangen; fassen, ergreifen, packen, haschen, erwischen; einholen (*a p.*), erreichen (*a train, etc.*), ertappen (*a p. doing s.th.*); klemmen, hängen bleiben mit (*one's fingers, foot, etc.*); sich (*Dat.*) zuziehen, ergriffen *or* angesteckt werden von (*a disease*); vernehmen, verstehen; (*a*) (*with nouns*) – *his attention*, seine Aufmerksamkeit auf sich lenken; – *the ball*, den Ball auffangen; (*coll.*) – *a p. a blow*, einem eins versetzen; – *one's breath*, den Atem anhalten; – *cold*, sich erkälten; – *a crab*, mit dem Ruder im Wasser stecken bleiben; (*coll*) – *one's death* (*of cold*), sich schrecklich erkälten; – *a p.'s eye*, einem ins Auge fallen (*of things*), jemandes Blick auffangen (*of persons*); – *the Speaker's eye*, das Wort erhalten (*Parl.*); – *fire*, Feuer fangen, in Brand geraten; – *a glimpse of*, erblicken; – *hold of*, fassen, ergreifen, anpacken, habhaft werden (*Gen.*); – *a p. napping*, einen bei einer Unaufmerksamkeit ertappen; – *the scent*, wittern (*Hunt.*); – *sight of*, erblicken; – *a Tartar*, übel ankommen, an den Unrechten kommen; – *a train*, einen Zug erreichen; *not – a train*, einen Zug versäumen *or* verpassen; *without -ing a word*, ohne ein Wort zu verstehen *or* festzuhalten; (*b*) (*with pronouns*) (*coll.*) – *it*, was abkriegen; (*coll.*) – *me* (*doing that*), das fällt mir nicht ein! ich werde mich davor hüten! da kannst du lange warten! (*c*) (*with prepositions*) – *a p. at s.th.*, einen bei einer S. ertappen; – *s.o. in the act*, – *a p. on one foot*, einen überrumpeln *or* bei der Tat ertappen; (*d*) (*with adverbs*) – *out*, durch Auffangen (des Balles) erledigen (*the batsman*) (*Crick.*); ertappen, überraschen (*in*, bei); – *up*, auffangen; einholen; – *up on*, herankommen an, überholen. 2. *ir.v.n.* halten, fassen, greifen, ineinandergreifen; einschnappen (*as a lock*); Feuer fangen; – *at*, haschen *or* greifen nach; *caught in the rain*, vom Regen überrascht; – *on*, hängenbleiben (*as a dress on a nail*); (*coll.*) einschlagen, Erfolg haben, Anklang finden bei; (*sl.*) – *on to*, erfassen, begreifen. 3. *s.* das Fangen; Gefangene, der Fang, die Beute, der Gewinn, Griff; Rundgesang (*Mus.*); Sperrhaken, Schließhaken, die Klinke, der Schnäpper (*of locks*); die Falle, Täuschung, der Kniff; (*fig.*) Haken, die Schwierigkeit; das Stocken, Steckenbleiben (*in speaking*); *there is a – in it*, die Sache hat einen Haken; *good* –, guter Fang *or* Fänger (*Crick.*); (*coll.*) *she was a great* –, sie war eine glänzende Partie. **--as--can,** *s.* das Freistilringen. **-ing,** *adj.* ansteckend (*Med.*); gefällig, fesselnd; verfänglich. **-ment,** *s.* die Sammelanlage, Wasserstauung; *-ment basin*, das Staubecken, der Stausee. **--penny,** 1. *s.* der Schund, Flitterkram; Lockartikel. 2. *adj.* marktschreierisch. **--phrase, -word,** *s.* das Stichwort, der Kustos (*Typ.*); das Schlagwort. **-pole, -poll,** *s.* der Büttel, Häscher. **-y,** *adj.* schwierig, verfänglich, heikel; einschmeichelnd, gefällig, packend.
catech-esis [kætə'kiːsɪs], *s.* die Katechese. **-etical** [kætɪ'kɛtɪkl], *adj.* katechetisch. **-ism,** *s.* der Katechismus. **-ist,** *s.* der Katechet. **-ize** ['kætɪkɑɪz], *v.a.* katechisieren; (*fig.*) ausfragen. **-umen** [kætə'kjuːmən], *s.* der Konfirmand; (*fig.*) Neuling, Anfänger.
catechu ['kætɪtʃuː], *s.* das Katechu (*Dye.*).
categor-ical [kætɪ'gɔrɪkl], *adj.* kategorisch; bestimmt, unbedingt. **-y** ['kætɪgərɪ], *s.* die Kategorie; Klasse.
catenar-ian [kætɪ'nɛərɪən], *adj.* kettenartig, Ketten-. **-y** [kə'tɪːnərɪ], 1. *adj. see* **-ian.** 2. *s.* die Kettenlinie.
cater ['keɪtə], *v.n.* Lebensmittel anschaffen *or* einkaufen (*for*, für); (*fig*) sorgen (*for*, für), sich bemühen (*for*, um); – *for*, versorgen, beistellen. **-er** [-rə], *s.* der Lebensmittellieferant, Versorger. **-ing** [-rɪŋ], *s.* die Lebensmittelversorgung; das Verpflegungswesen. **-ing trade,** das Lebensmittelgewerbe.
caterpillar ['kætəpɪlə], *s.* die Raupe. **--tractor** (Reg. trade name), *s.* der Raupenschlepper.

caterwaul ['kætəwɔ:l], *v.n.* schreien, miauen. **-ing,** *s.* die Katzenmusik.
catfish ['kætfɪʃ], *s.* der Seewolf, Katzenwels.
catgut ['kætgʌt], *s.* die Darmsaite, der Katzendarm.
cathar-sis [kæ'θɑ:sɪs], *s.* die Abführung, Reinigung; (*fig.*) die Katharsis (*Theat.*). **-tic** [kə'θɑ:tɪk], 1. *adj.* reinigend, abführend. 2. *s.* das Abführmittel (*Med.*).
cathedra [kə'θɪ:drə], *s.* der Bischofsstuhl; *ex* –, authoritativ, maßgebend.
cathedral [kə'θɪ:drəl], *s.* der Dom, die Kathedrale.
catherine-wheel ['kæθərɪn'wɪ:l], *s.* das Feuerrad (*Firew.*); die Fensterrose, das Radfenster (*Arch.*).
catheter ['kæθətə], *s.* der Katheter (*Surg.*).
cathode ['kæθoʊd], *s.* die Kathode (*Elec.*); – *rays*, die Kathodenstrahlen; –*-ray tube*, die Kathodenröhre.
catholic ['kæθəlɪk], 1. *adj.* katholisch; allumfassend, allgemein, vorurteilslos. 2. *s.* (*Roman* –) der Katholik. **-ism** [kə'θɔlɪsɪzm], *s.* der Katholizismus. **-ity** [kæθə'lɪsɪtɪ], *s.* die Allgemeinheit, Universalität; Vorurteilslosigkeit. **-ize** [kə'θɔlɪsɑɪz], *v.a.* katholisch machen.
catkin ['kætkɪn], *s.* das Kätzchen (*Bot.*).
catling ['kætlɪŋ], *s.* das Zergliederungsmesser (*Surg.*); (*obs.*) die Darmsaite.
catoptric [kæ'tɔptrɪk], *adj.* katoptrisch. **-s,** *pl.* die Katoptrik.
cattle ['kætl], (*s. form, usually pl. constr.*) das Vieh; Hornvieh, Rindvieh; *horned* –, das Hornvieh; *breeding* –, das Zuchtvieh; *6 head of* –, 6 Stück Vieh. **--breeder,** *s.* der Viehzüchter. **--breeding,** *s.* die Viehzucht. **--dealer,** *s.* der Viehhändler. **--drover,** *s.* der Viehtreiber. **--feeder,** *s.* der Futterschütter, Fütterungsapparat. **--lifter,** *s.* der Viehdieb. **--plague,** *s.* die Rinderpest. **--ranch,** *s.* (*Amer.*) die Viehfarm. **--range,** *s.,* **--run,** *s.* die Viehweide, Viehtrift. **--shed,** *s.* der Viehstall. **--show,** *s.* die Viehausstellung, Tierschau. **--stall,** *s.* der Viehständer. **--truck,** *s.* der Viehwagen.
catty ['kætɪ], *see* **cat.**
caucus ['kɔ:kəs], 1. *s.* die Parteiclique; politische Intriguen (*pl.*); (*Amer*) der Parteiausschuß bei Wahlvorbereitungen; *funds*, die Gelder für Parteizwecke. 2. *v.a.* durch den Parteiausschuß beeinflussen.
cauda-l ['kɔ:dəl], *adj.* Schwanz–. **-te,** *adj.* geschwänzt.
caudle ['kɔ:dl], *s.* die Krankensuppe, der Stärkungstrank.
caught [kɔ:t], *see* **catch.**
caul [kɔ:l], *s* die Eihaut (*Anat.*); das Haarnetz.
cauldron ['kɔ:ldrən], *s.* großer Kessel.
cauliflower ['kɔlɪflɑʊə], *s.* der Blumenkohl.
cauline ['kɔ:lɑɪn], *adj.* Stengel–.
caulk [kɔ:k], *v.a.* (ab)dichten, kalfatern (*Naut.*). **-er,** *s.* der Kalfaterer. **-ing,** *s.* das Abdichten, die Abdichtung, Verstemmung, das Kalfatern.
caus-al ['kɔ:zəl], *adj.* ursächlich, kausal. **-ality,** *s.* die Kausalität, kausaler Zusammenhang. **-ation** [–'zeɪʃən], *s.* die Verursachung, Ursächlichkeit; *law of –ation*, das Kausalgesetz. **-ative** [–zətɪv], 1 *adj* verursachend, bewirkend, begründend; kausativ (*Gram.*). 2. *s.* Kausativum (*Gram.*).
cause [kɔ:z], 1. *s.* die Ursache, der Anlaß, Grund; gute *or* gerechte Sache; der Rechtsfall, Prozeß (*Law*); *first* –, der Urgrund, Gott; – *list*, die Terminliste (*Law*); (*a*) (*with verbs*) *give – for*, Anlaß geben zu; *make common – with*, gemeinsame Sache machen mit; *plead a* –, eine Rechtssache führen; *show* –, seine Gründe angeben; (*b*) (*with prepositions*) *for the* –, für die gute Sache *or* unsre Sache; *die in a good* –, für eine gute Sache sterben; *not without some* –, nicht ohne Grund. 2. *v a.* verursachen, veranlassen, Anlaß geben, bewirken; – *s.o. grief*, einem Kummer machen *or* verursachen; *he –d me to be invited*, er ließ mich einladen; *he –d me to be late*, er verursachte daß ich spät ankam. **-less,** *adj.* grundlos, unbegründet, ohne Ursache. **-lessness,** *s.* die Grundlosigkeit. **-r,** *s.* der Urheber.
causeway ['kɔ·zweɪ], *s.* der Fußweg, Damm.
caustic ['kɔ:stɪk], 1. *adj.* ätzend, beizend, brennend, anfressend; (*fig.*) scharf, beißend, satirisch, sarkastisch, kaustisch; – *bath*, das Laugenbad; – *curve*, die Brennlinie; – *potash*, das Ätzkali; – *soda*, das Natriumhydrat, Natriumhydroxyd, Natron; – *wit*, beißender Witz. 2. *s.* das Ätzmittel, die Alkalilauge, Beize. **-ity** [–'tɪsɪtɪ], *s.* die Ätzwirkung; (*fig.*) die Schärfe, der Sarkasmus.
cauter-ization [kɔ:tərɑɪ'zeɪʃən], *s.* das Ausbrennen, die Ätzung, Beizung. **-ize** ['kɔ:tərɑɪz], *v.a.* ausbrennen, einbrennen, abbeizen, wegätzen, wegbeizen. **-y** [–rɪ], *s.* das Brenneisen, Brennmittel, Ätzmittel; das Brennen, die Ätzung.
cautio-n ['kɔ:ʃən], 1. *s.* die Vorsicht, Umsicht, Behutsamkeit; Warnung, Verwarnung; (*sl.*) etwas Bemerkenswertes; (*sl.*) *he is a –n*, er ist eine Nummer für sich; *by way of –n*, als Warnung; *be let off with a –n*, mit einer Verwarnung davonkommen; *ride with –n!* vorsichtig fahren! 2. *v.a.* warnen (*against a th.*, vor (*Dat.*)); verwarnen; *I –ned him against leaving*, ich warnte ihn fortzugehen. **-nary,** *adj.* warnend. **-n-money,** *s.* die Bürgschaftssumme, Kaution. **-us,** *adj.* vorsichtig, behutsam. **-usness,** *s.* die Vorsicht, Behutsamkeit.
cavalcade [kævl'keɪd], *s.* der Reiteraufzug.
cavalier [kævə'lɪə], 1. *s.* der Reiter; Ritter; Kavalier, Liebhaber; Kavalier, Royalist (*Hist*); *–s and Roundheads*, Royalisten und Puritaner. 2. *adj.* anmaßend, hochmütig, rücksichtslos, verächtlich.
cavalry ['kævlrɪ], *s.* die Reiterei, Kavallerie; – *sergeant*, der Wachtmeister; *troop of* –, die Reiterschwadron. **-man,** der Reiter, Kavallerist. **--sword,** der Schleppsäbel, Reitersäbel (*Mil.*).
[1]**cave** [keɪv], 1. *s.* die Höhle, Grube; Parteispaltung, Absonderung (*Pol.*); Sezession; die Abtrünnigen, Sezessionisten (*pl.*) (*Pol.*); (*Amer*) der Erdrutsch. 2. *v.a.* eindrücken, aushöhlen. 3. *v.n.* sich abspalten (*Pol.*); – *in*, einstürzen; (*sl.*) nachgeben, klein beigeben, zusammenklappen. **--dweller,** *s.* der Höhlenbewohner. **-man,** *s.* der Höhlenbewohner; (*sl.*) der Naturmensch, stürmischer Liebhaber.
[2]**cave** *interj.* (*school sl.*) aufpassen! *keep* –, aufpassen.
caveat ['keɪvɪæt], *s.* der Einspruch, die Einwendung (*Law*); Patentanmeldung (*Amer.*); Warnung, der Vorbehalt; *enter a* –, Einspruch einlegen.
cavern ['kævən], *s.* die Höhle. **-ous** [–əs], *adj.* voll Höhlen, höhlenreich; (*fig*) hohl (*cheeks*), tief (*darkness*).
caviar(e) ['kævɪɑ:], *s.* der Kaviar. – *to the general*, Kaviar für das Volk.
cavil ['kævɪl], 1. *v.n.* kritteln, nörgeln (*at* or *about*, an *or* über). 2. *s.* die Spitzfindigkeit, spitzfindiger Einwand; *without* –, ohne Krittelei. **-ler** *s.* der Nörgler, Krittler. **-ling,** 1. *adj.* spitzfindig. 2. *s.* die Krittelei, Nörgelei
cavity ['kævɪtɪ], *s.* die Höhlung, Vertiefung, Mulde; (Körper)Höhle (*Anat.*).
cavort [kə'vɔ:t], *v.n.* sich bäumen, umherspringen.
cavy ['keɪvɪ], *s.* das Meerschweinchen (*Zool.*).
caw [kɔ:], 1. *v.n.* krächzen. 2. *int.* krah!
cay [keɪ], *s.* die Sandbank.
cayenne-pepper ['keɪɛn'pɛpə], *s.* spanischer Pfeffer.
cayman ['keɪmən], *s.* der Kaiman (*Zool.*).
cease [sɪ:s], 1 *v.n.* aufhören, anhalten (mit); ablassen (von). 2. *v.a.* einstellen, aufhören mit; – *fire*, das Feuer einstellen; – *work*, die Arbeit einstellen. **-less,** *adj.* unaufhörlich, unablässig.
cecity ['sɪ:sɪtɪ], *s.* (*fig*) die Blindheit.
cedar ['sɪ:də], *s.* die Zeder (*Bot.*). **-wood,** *s.* das Zedernholz.
cede [sɪ:d], *v.a.* abtreten (*as territory*), überlassen (*to a p.*), zugeben, nachgeben.
cedilla [sɪ'dɪlə], *s.* die Cedille (ç).
ceil [sɪ:l], *v.a.* eine Decke verschalen, täfeln *or* bewerfen. **-ing** [–ɪŋ], *s.* die (Zimmer)Decke; Wegerung, Innenbeplankung (*Naut.*); Gipfelhöhe, Steighöhe (*Av.*); untere Wolkengrenze (*Meteor.*).
celandine ['sɛləndɑɪn], *s.* (*greater* –) das Schellkraut; (*lesser* –) die Feigwurz.
celeb-rant ['sɛlɪbrənt], *s.* der Zelebrant (*Eccl.*). **-rate** ['sɛləbreɪt], *v.a.* & *n.* feiern, festlich begehen; verherrlichen, preisen; abhalten, zelebrieren (*Eccl.*). **-rated,** *adj.* berühmt, gefeiert. **-ration** [–'breɪʃən], *s.* die Feier, das Fest; die Verherr-

lichung; der Preis, das Lob; *-ration of the Lord's supper*, die Abendmahlsfeier. **-rity** [sɪˈlɛbrɪtɪ], *s.* die Berühmtheit, der Ruhm; berühmte Persönlichkeit.
celerity [sɪˈlɛrɪtɪ], *s* die Geschwindigkeit, Schnelligkeit.
celery [ˈsɛlərɪ], *s.* der & die Sellerie (*Bot.*); *stick* of –, rohgegessener Selleriestengel.
celestial [sɪˈlɛstjəl], 1. *adj.* himmlisch, Himmels–. 2. *s.* Selige(r), *m.*; *– body*, der Himmelskörper; *the – empire*, China; *– harmony*, die Sphärenharmonie.
celiba-cy [ˈsɛlɪbəsɪ], *s.* die Ehelosigkeit; lediger Stand; der & das Zölibat (*of clergy*). **-te** [–bɪt], 1. *s.* der Junggeselle, Unverheiratete(r), *m.* 2. *adj.* unverheiratet, ledig.
cell [sɛl], *s.* die Zelle (*of monk, prisoner, etc.*) (*also Bot., Biol., Zool.*); tätige politische Arbeitsgruppe; das Element (*Elec.*); *– formation*, die Zellbildung, Zellenbildung. *– wall*, die Zellwand; (*see* **cellular**).
cellar [ˈsɛlə], 1. *s.* der Keller; *salt-–*, das Salzfäßchen; *keep a good –*, einen guten Weinkeller halten. 2. *v.a.* einkellern. **-age**, *s.* das Kellergeschoß, die Kellerräume (*pl.*), die Kellerei; Kellermiete. **-er** [–rə], *s.* der Kellermeister. **-et** [–rɛt], *s.* der Flaschenschrank, Flaschenständer.
cellist [ˈtʃɛlɪst], *etc.*, *see* **violoncellist**, *etc.*
cellophane [ˈsɛləfeɪn], *s.* das Zellophanpapier.
cellul-ar [ˈsɛljʊlə], *adj.* zellig, zellenartig, zellhaltig, aus Zellen bestehend; *-ar fibre*, die Zellfaser; *-ar substance*, die Zellmasse; *-ar tissue*, das Zellgewebe; *-ar vest*, die Netzjacke. **-e** [ˈsɛljuːl], *s.* kleine Zelle. **-oid** [ˈsɛljʊlɔɪd], *s.* das Zelluloid, Zellhorn. **-ose** [ˈsɛljʊlous], 1. *adj.* zellig, Zellen–. 2. *s.* der Zellstoff, Zellfaserstoff, Holzstoff, die Zellulose.
Celt [kɛlt], *s.* der Kelte; *see the Index of Names.*
cement [sɪˈmɛnt], 1. *s.* der & das Zement, der Mörtel; Kitt; *mastic –*, der Steinkitt; *Portland –*, der Portlandzement; Steinmörtel. 2. *v.a.* zementieren, (an)kitten, zusammenkitten, verkitten; (*fig.*) verbinden, befestigen, schmieden, vereinigen. **-ation** (*of steel*), die Zementstahlbereitung; *steel of -ation*, der Zementstahl. **-ing-furnace**, *s.* der Zementierofen (*Metall.*).
cemetery [ˈsɛmɪtrɪ], *s.* der Friedhof.
cenotaph [ˈsɛnotæf], *s.* das Ehrengrabmal, Ehrendenkmal.
censer [ˈsɛnsə], *s.* das Weihrauchfaß.
censor [ˈsɛnsə], 1. *s.* der Zensor; Sittenrichter (*of*, über). 2. *v.a.* zensieren. **-ial** [–ˈsɔːrɪəl], *adj.* zensorisch, Zensor–, Zensur–. **-ious** [–ˈsɔːrɪəs], *adj.* streng, kritisch (*towards, of*, gegen), tadelnd, tadelsüchtig, krittelig. **-iousness**, *s.* die Tadelsucht, Krittelei. **-ship**, *s.* das Zensoramt, die Zensur.
censur-able [ˈsɛnʃərəbl], *adj.* tadelhaft, tadelnswert. **-e** [ˈsɛnʃə], 1. *s.* der Tadel, die Kritik (*of*, an); der Verweis, die Rüge; *vote of -e*, das Tadelsvotum. 2. *v.a.* tadeln, rügen, verurteilen.
census [ˈsɛnsəs], *s.* die Volkszählung, der Zensus; *take a –*, eine Volkszählung vornehmen. **--paper**, *s.* die Haushaltungsliste.
cent [sɛnt], *s.*; *per –*, Prozent, aufs Hundert; *at 5 per –*, zu 5 Prozent, zu fünf vom Hundert; *a loan at 5 per –*, eine fünfprozentige Anleihe.
centaur [ˈsɛntɔː], *s.* der Zentaur (*Myth.*). **-y**, *s.* das Tausendgüldenkraut, die Flockenblume (*Bot.*).
centen-arian [sɛntɪˈnɛərɪən], 1. *s.* der *or* die Hundertjährige. 2. *adj.* hundertjährig. **-ary** [–ˈtiːnərɪ], 1. *adj.* hundertjährig. 2. *s.* der Zeitraum von hundert Jahren; die Hundertjahrfeier. **-nial** [sɛnˈtɛnjəl], 1. *adj.* hundertjährig. 2. *s.* die Hundertjahrfeier.
center [ˈsɛntə], *s.* (*Amer.*) *see* **centre.**
centesimal [sɛnˈtɛsɪməl], *adj.* hundertteilig; Zentesimal–.
centi-grade [ˈsɛntɪgreɪd], *adj.* hundertgradig, hundertteilig; *-grade scale*, die Zentesimaleinteilung; *-grade thermometer*, das Celsiusthermometer; *20 degrees -grade*, 20 Grad Celsius. **-gramme** [–græm], *s.* das Zentigramm. **-metre** [–miːtə], *s.* das Zentimeter. **-pede**, *s.* der Tausendfuß (*Zool.*).
centner [ˈsɛntnər], *s.* der Zentner (*50 kilogrammes*).
cento [ˈsɛntou], *s.* das Flickwerk.
central [ˈsɛntrəl], *adj.* zentral, den Mittelpunkt bildend, Zentral–, Mittel–, Haupt–; *be –*, im Mittelpunkt sein; *– heating*, die Zentralheizung; *– office*, die Zentrale; *– point*, der Mittelpunkt; *– powers*, die Mittelmächte; *– railway-station*, der Hauptbahnhof. **-ity** [–ˈtrælɪtɪ], *s.* die Zentralität, zentrale Lage. **-ization** [–lɑɪˈzeɪʃən], *s.* die Zentralisation. **-ize** [–lɑɪz], *v.a.* zentralisieren.
centre [ˈsɛntə], 1. *s.* der Mittelpunkt, die Mitte, das Zentrum; *– of an arch*, der Lehrbogen; *– of attraction*, der Anziehungspunkt; *communication –*, die Nachrichtenstelle; *dead –*, der Totpunkt (*Mech.*); *– of gravity*, der Schwerpunkt; *– of impact*, mittlerer Auftreff– *or* Aufschlagpunkt (*Artil.*); *– of interest*, das Hauptinteresse; *– of motion*, der Drehpunkt; *– of resistance*, der Anklammerungspunkt (*Mil.*); *– of rotation*, der Drehpunkt; *storm-–*, das Sturmzentrum, (*fig.*) der Unruheherd; *training –*, das Ausbildungslager. 2. *v.a.* konzentrieren, zentrieren; in den Mittelpunkt stellen; auf den Mittelpunkt zuspielen (*Footb.*). 3. *v.n.* sich konzentrieren, beruhen (*on*, auf (*Dat.*)). **--bit**, *s.* der Zentrumsbohrer. **--board**, *s.* das (Kiel)Schwert (*Naut.*); *--board vessel*, das Schwertboot. **--forward**, *s.* der Mittelstürmer (*Footb.*). **--half**, *s.* der Mittelläufer (*Footb.*). **--piece**, *s.* der Tafelaufsatz. **– section**, das Mittelstück, der Mittelteil.
centrifug-al [sɛnˈtrɪfjʊgəl], *adj.* zentrifugal; *-al force*, die Schwungkraft, Fliehkraft, Zentrifugalkraft; *-al machine*, die Zentrifuge, Schleudermaschine; *-al pump*, die Kreiselpumpe. **-e** [ˈsɛntrɪfjudʒ], 1. *s.* der Schleuder. 2. *v.a.* abschleudern, ausschleudern, abschwingen.
centripetal [sɛnˈtrɪpɪtl], *adj.* zentripetal; *– force*, die Zentripetalkraft.
centupl-e [ˈsɛntʊpl], 1. *adj.* hundertfach, hundertfältig. 2. *v.a.* verhundertfachen. **-icate**, *v.a.* verhundertfältigen.
centurion [sɛnˈtjuərɪən], *s.* der Zenturio.
centur-y [ˈsɛntʃərɪ], *s.* das Jahrhundert; der Satz von Hundert; das volle Hundert (*Crick.*); *-ies old*, jahrhundertealt; *for -ies*, jahrhundertelang.
cephal-ic [sɛˈfælɪk], *adj.* Kopf–, Schädel–. **-opod** [ˈsɛfələpɔd], *s.* der Kopffüßler (*Zool.*).
ceramic [sɛˈræmɪk], *adj.* keramisch; *– art*, **-s**, *pl.* die Keramik, Töpferkunst.
cer-ate [ˈsɪərɪt], *s.* die Wachssalbe. **-ated** [–reɪtɪd], *adj.* mit Wachs überzogen. **-e** [sɪə], *s.* die Wachshaut (*Orn.*). **-cloth**, *s.* das Wachstuch, Leichentuch. **-ments**, *pl.* die Leichentücher.
cereal [ˈsɪərɪəl], 1. *adj.* Getreide–. 2. *s.* die Frühstücksmehlspeise; *pl.* das Getreide, Getreidearten (*pl.*).
cereb-ellum [sɛrɪˈbɛləm], *s.* das Kleinhirn. **-ral** [ˈsɛrɪbrəl], *adj.* Gehirn–. **-ration**, *s.* die Gehirntätigkeit. **-ro-spinal meningitis**, die Genickstarre (*Med.*). **-rum** [ˈsɛrɪbrəm], *s.* das Großhirn.
ceremon-ial [sɛrɪˈmounjəl], 1. *adj.* zeremoniell, feierlich; förmlich. 2. *s.* das Zeremoniell. **-ious** [–jəs], *adj.* zeremoniös, steif, förmlich; *you are too -ious*, Sie machen zu viele Umstände; *take a -ious leave*, sich umständlich verabschieden. **-iousness**, *s.* das Feierliche, Umständliche. **-y** [ˈsɛrɪmənɪ], *s.* die Zeremonie; Feier, Feierlichkeit, feierliche Handlung; die Förmlichkeit; *no -y please!* bitte, keine Umstände! *stand on -y*, förmlich sein; *the master of -ies*, der Zeremonienmeister, Conferencier.
ceriph [ˈsɛrɪf], *s. see* **serif.**
cerise [səˈrɪːz], *adj.* kirschrot.
cerium [ˈsɪːrɪəm], *s.* das Cer, Zer (*Chem.*).
certain [ˈsəːtn], *adj.* (*a*) *pred.* sicher, gewiß, überzeugt; (*b*) *attrib.* gewiß, bestimmt, festgesetzt; unzweifelhaft; unfehlbar, zuverlässig; *be – of a th.*, einer S. gewiß sein, von einer S. überzeugt sein; *feel –*, überzeugt sein; *– of your friends*, einige Ihrer Freunde *or* unter Ihren Freunden; *a – George Miller*, ein gewisser G. M.; *make – of a th.*, sich (*Dat.*) etwas sichern, sich (*Acc.*) einer S. vergewissern; *to my – knowledge*, wie ich gewiß weiß; *a – reluctance*, eine gewisse Abneigung; *come for –*, sicher kommen; *under – circumstances*, unter bestimmten Umständen; *a – cure*, zuverlässiges Heilmittel; *have a – doubt*, einigen Zweifel

haben. **-ly,** *adv.* gewiß, zweifellos, sicher(lich), allerdings, ja. **-ty,** *s.* die Gewißheit, Überzeugung; Bestimmtheit, Sicherheit, Zuverlässigkeit; *for a -ty*, mit Bestimmtheit, ganz bestimmt *or* gewiß; (*coll.*) *a dead -ty*, eine unumstößliche Gewißheit.

certes [sə:ts], *adv.* (*archaic*) fürwahr.

certif-iable ['sə:tɪfɑɪəbl], *adj.* zu bestätigen(d); anmeldepflichtig (*of lunatics*); (*coll.*) wahnsinnig. **-icate** [sə'tɪfɪkɪt], 1. *s.* das Zeugnis, die Bescheinigung, der Schein; *-icate of baptism*, der Taufschein; *-icate of birth*, die Geburtsurkunde; *-icate of character*, das Leumundszeugnis; *-icate of health*, der Gesundheitspaß, das Gesundheitsattest; *-icate of merit*, schriftliche Belobigung; *-icate of posting*, die Postquittung, der Postempfangsschein. 2. [sə'tɪfɪkeɪt], *v.a.* ein Zeugnis ausstellen (*Dat.*), bescheinigen. **-icated,** *adj.* staatlich anerkannt *or* beglaubigt; *-icated teacher*, geprüfter Lehrer. **-ication** [-'keɪʃən], *s.* die Bescheinigung, Beglaubigung; das Zeugnis. **-y** ['sə:tɪfɑɪ], *v.a.* bescheinigen, beglaubigen, bezeugen, bestätigen; versichern; für geisteskrank erklären; *-ied teacher*, geprüfter Lehrer; *this is to -y . . .*, hiermit wird bestätigt *or* bezeugt . . .

certitude ['sə:tɪtju:d], *s.* die Überzeugung, innere Gewißheit.

cerulean [sɪ'ru:ljən], *adj* himmelblau.

cerumen [sə'ru:mən], *s.* das Ohrenschmalz.

ceruse ['sɪəru:s], *s.* das Bleiweiß.

cervical ['sə:vɪkl], *adj.* Nacken-, Hals-.

cervine ['sə:vɑɪn], *adj.* Hirsch-.

cess [sɛs], 1. *s.* (*Irish*) die Steuer; (*sl.*) *bad - to you!* hol' dich der Teufel! 2. *v.a.* besteuern.

cessation [sɛ'seɪʃən], *s.* das Aufhören, der Stillstand, die Beendigung; *without -*, unaufhörlich; *- of hostilities*, die Einstellung der Feindseligkeiten.

cession ['sɛʃən], *s.* der Verzicht (*of*, auf), die Abtretung (*to*, an), Überlassung, Übertragung. **-ary** [-ərɪ], *s.* der Zessionär (*Law*).

cess-pit ['sɛspɪt], **--pool** ['sɛspu:l], *s.* die Senkgrube, Abtrittsgrube, der Pfuhl (*also fig.*).

cestoid ['sɛstɔɪd], *s.* der Bandwurm (*Med.*).

cetace-an [sɪ'teɪʃɪən], 1. *s.* der Wal(fisch). 2. *adj.*, **-ous,** *adj.* walfischartig, Wal-.

chafe [tʃeɪf], 1. *v.a.* warm reiben; wund reiben, (ab)scheuern, (ab)schleifen, abnutzen; (*fig.*) erzürnen, reizen; schamfilen (*Naut.*). 2. *v.n.* sich reiben; (*fig.*) sich entrüsten, sich härmen; toben, wüten.

chafer ['tʃeɪfə], *s.* der (Mai)Käfer.

chaff [tʃɑ:f], 1. *s.* die Spreu; der & das Häcksel, das Kaff; (*coll.*) die Neckerei, das Aufziehen. 2. *v.a.* (*coll.*) aufziehen, necken. **--cutter,** *s.* die Häckselbank, der Häckselschneider.

chaffer ['tʃæfə], *v.n.* handeln, schachern; *- away*, verhandeln, verschachern. **-er** [-rə], *s.* der Händler, Schacherer.

chaffinch ['tʃæfɪntʃ], *s.* der Buchfink (*Orn.*).

chafing-dish ['tʃeɪfɪŋdɪʃ], *s.* die Wärmpfanne.

chagrin [ʃæ'grɪ:n], 1. *s.* der Ärger, Verdruß. 2. *v.a.* ärgern, kränken; *feel -ed at*, sich ärgern über.

chain [tʃeɪn], 1. *s.* die Kette; Meßkette, ein Längenmaß (*about 20 m.*) (*Surv.*); die Folge, Reihe; *pl.* die Püttinge (*Naut.*); *pl.* die Fesseln; *put s.o. in -s*, einen in Ketten legen; *Albert -*, kurze, im Knopfloch getragenen Uhrkette; *curb -*, die Kinnkette (*harness*); *drag -*, die Hemmkette; *- of hills, mountain--*, die Hügelkette, Gebirgskette, Bergkette, der Höhenzug; *link in a -*, das Kettenglied; *surveyor's -*, die Meßkette. 2. *v.a.* (*- up*) anketten, an die Kette legen; (*fig.*) fesseln. **--bridge,** *s.* die Ketten-Hängebrücke. **--cable,** *s.* die Ankerkette. **--drive,** *s.* der Kettentrieb. **--mail,** *s.* der Kettenpanzer. **--pump,** *s.* die Kettenpumpe; das Paternosterwerk (*Hydr.*). **--reaction,** *s.* die Kettenwirkung (*Phys.*). **--shot,** *s.* die Kettenkugel. **--smoker,** *s.* der Kettenraucher. **--stitch,** *s.* der Kettenstich. **--store,** die Zweigverkaufsstelle; *--stores, pl.* das Warenhaus mit vielen Filialen. **--wale,** *s.* die Rüste. **--wheel,** *s.* das Kettenrad.

chair [tʃɛə], 1. *s.* der Stuhl, Sessel; die Bürgermeisterwürde; der Lehrstuhl (*Univ.*); Schienenstuhl (*Railw.*); Vorsitz, Vorsitzende(r), *m.*; *- ! - !*, zur Ordnung! *easy--*, der Lehnstuhl; *folding -*, der Klappstuhl; *sedan -*, der Tragsessel, die Sänfte; *upholstered -*, der Polsterstuhl; (*with verbs*) *address the -*, den Vorsitzenden anreden; *be in the -*, den Vorsitz führen; *hold the - for German*, den Lehrstuhl für Deutsch innehaben; *take a -*, sich setzen; *take the -*, den Vorsitz übernehmen. 2. *v.a.* auf die Schultern nehmen (*a p.*); *- a meeting*, den Vorsitz einer Versammlung übernehmen. **- attendant,** *s.* der Stuhlvermieter. **--back,** *s.* die Stuhllehne. **--bottom,** *s.* der Sitz des Stuhles. **-man,** *s.* Vorsitzende(r), *m.* **-manship,** *s.* der Vorsitz.

chaise [ʃeɪz], *s.* die Chaise, Kalesche.

chalcedony [kæl'sɛdənɪ], *s.* der Chalzedon (*Min.*).

chalcographer [kæl'kɔgrəfə], *s.* der Kupferstecher.

chaldron ['tʃɔ:ldrən], *s.* ein Kohlenmaß (= *36 bushels, about 1200 litres*).

chalet [ʃæ'le], *s.* die Sennhütte; das Sommerhäuschen.

chalice ['tʃælɪs], *s.* der Meßkelch, der Abendmahlsbecher; der Kelch (*Bot.*).

chalk [tʃɔ:k], 1. *s.* die Kreide; der Kreidestift; *coloured -*, der Buntstift; *- formation*, das Kreidegebirge; (*sl.*) *not by a long -*, bei weitem nicht, lange nicht; *red -*, der Rotstift, Rötel; *they are as unlike as - and cheese*, sie gleichen einander wie Tag und Nacht. 2. *v.a.* mit Kreide zeichnen *or* schreiben; *- out*, vorzeichnen, entwerfen; *- up*, ankreiden, anschreiben; (*coll.*) auf Rechnung setzen. **--cutter,** *s.* der Kreidegräber. **--mark,** der Kreidestrich. **--pit,** *s.* die Kreidegrube. **--stone,** *s.* der Gichtknoten (*Med.*). **-y,** *adj.* kreidig, kreideartig, kreideweiß; *-y clay*, der Mergel.

challenge ['tʃælɪndʒ], 1. *s.* die Herausforderung (*to*, zu *or* für), Aufforderung (*to*, an); das Anrufen (*of a sentry*); die Einwendung; Ablehnung (*of jurymen, etc.*); das Anschlagen (*Hunt.*). 2. *v.a.* herausfordern; anrufen (*Mil.*); beanspruchen; ablehnen (*Law*); Einwendungen machen gegen, in Frage stellen, bestreiten; auffordern. **- cup,** der Pokal.

chalybeate [kə'lɪbɪɪt], *adj.* stahlhaltig; *- spring*, die Stahlquelle.

chamade [ʃə'mɑ:d], *s.* die Schamade, der Rückzug (*Mil.*).

chamber ['tʃeɪmbə], *s.* (*Poet.*) die Kammer, das Zimmer, Gemach; die Kammer, das Haus (*Parl.*); die Kammer (*C.L.*); das Kammergericht, Gerichtszimmer (*Law*); der Laderaum, das Ladeloch (*Gun.*); der Hohlraum, die Höhlung (*Anat.*); (*coll.*) *see* **--pot**; *pl.* die Junggesellenwohnung; die Geschäftsräume (*of a barrister*); *ammunition -*, die Munitionskammer; *- of commerce*, die Handelskammer; *combustion -*, der Verbrennungsraum (*Motor.*); *compression -*, der Verdichtungsraum (*Motor.*); *second* or *upper -*, das Oberhaus (*Parl.*). **--concert,** *s.* das Kammermusikkonzert. **--counsel,** *s.* der Rechtskonsulent. **-ed,** *adj.* mit Kammern versehen; *six--ed revolver*, sechsschüssiger Revolver. **-lain** [-lɪn], *s.* der Kämmerer, Kammerherr; *the Lord -lain of the Household*, der Oberhofmeister; *the Lord Great -lain*, der Großkämmerer. **--maid,** *s.* das Zimmermädchen, Stubenmädchen. **--music,** *s.* die Kammermusik. **--pot,** *s.* das Nachtgeschirr, der Nachttopf. **--practice,** *s.* die Privatpraxis eines Anwalts.

chameleon [kə'mɪ:ljən], *s.* das Chamäleon (*Zool.*); (*fig.*) die Wetterfahne. **--like,** *adj.* (*fig.*) wetterwendisch, unbeständig.

chamfer ['tʃæmfə], 1. *v.n.* auskehlen (*Arch.*); abschrägen, abkanten. 2. *s.* die Auskehlung, Hohlrinne (*Arch.*); Schrägkante, Abschrägung (*Carp.*).

chamois ['ʃæmwɑ:, 'ʃæmɪ], *s.* die Gemse (*Zool.*); (*- leather*) das Sämischleder.

champ [tʃæmp], 1. *v.a. & n.* geräuschvoll kauen; (*fig.*) mit den Zähnen knirschen; *- the bit*, auf die Stange beißen. 2. *s.* (*sl.*) *see* **champion** (*fig.*).

champagne [ʃæm'peɪn], *s.* der Champagner, Schaumwein.

champaign [tʃæm'peɪn], *s.* die Ebene, offenes Feld.

champion ['tʃæmpjən], 1. *s.* der Kämpfer, Held, (*archaic*) Kämpe; (*fig.*) der Verfechter; Meister, Sieger; *- boxer*, der Meisterschaftskämpfer, Boxmeister; – *turnip*, preisgekrönte Rübe; – *of the truth*, der Wahrheitsverfechter. 2. *v.a.* eintreten für, verfechten, verteidigen. 3. *adj.* (*coll.*) erstklassig. **-ship**, *s.* die Verteidigung, Verfechtung, das Eintreten (*of*, für); die Meisterschaft (*Sport*).

chance [tʃɑ:ns], 1. *s.* der Zufall; das Schicksal, Geschick, Los; Glück; die Gelegenheit, Chance, Aussicht (*of*, auf), Möglichkeit, Wahrscheinlichkeit; (*coll.*) *not a dog's* or *an earthly* –, nicht die geringste Aussicht; *the -s are that*, es ist mit Wahrscheinlichkeit anzunehmen, daß; *game of* –, ein Glücksspiel; (*a*) (*with adjectives*) *an even* –, eine ebensogute Chance wie gar keine; *happy* –, das Glück; (*coll.*) *look to the main* –, auf den eigenen Vorteil sehen; *mere* –, reiner Zufall; (*coll.*) *on the off-*–, aufs Geratewohl, mit geringer Aussicht; (*b*)(*with verbs*) *give him a* – *!* versuche es mit ihm doch noch einmal!; *leave it to* –, es darauf ankommen lassen, es dem Zufall überlassen; *stand a good* –, gute Aussichten *or* Aussicht haben; *take a* –, es darauf ankommen lassen, sein Glück versuchen; *not take any -s*, auf Nummer Sicher gehen; *take -s*, die Gefahr auf sich nehmen; (*c*) (*with prepositions*) *by* –, zufällig, durch Zufall, von ungefähr; *on the* –, für den Fall. 2. *v.a.* (*coll.*) wagen, auf gut Glück versuchen. 3. *v.n.* sich zufällig ereignen, sich fügen, sich treffen; *I -d to see him*, ich sah ihn zufällig, es traf sich gerade, daß ich ihn sah; *if my letter should* – *to get lost*, falls mein Brief verloren gehen sollte; – *upon s.th.*, auf eine S. zufällig stoßen. 4. *adj.* zufällig; – *comer*, unerwartet Kommende(r), *m.*; – *customer*, zufälliger Kunde.

chancel [ˈtʃɑ:nsəl], *s.* der Altarplatz, Chor.

chancell-ery [ˈtʃɑ:nsələrɪ], *s.* die Kanzlei, das Kanzleramt. **-or** [ˈtʃɑ:nsələ], *s.* der Kanzler (*also Univ.*); *Vice-*-*or*, stellvertretender Kanzler; der Rektor (*Univ.*, *in England it is a life appointment*); -*or of the Exchequer*, der Schatzkanzler, Finanzminister; *Lord High -or*, der Großkanzler (*highest legal authority in England*). **-orship**, *s.* die Kanzlerwürde.

chancery [ˈtʃɑ:nsərɪ], *s.* das Kanzleigericht (*Law*); (*coll.*) *be in* –, sich mit dem Kopf unter dem Arm des Gegners befinden (*Sport*); (*fig.*) in der Klemme sein; *bill in* –, die Rechtsklage bei dem Kanzleigericht; *ward in* –, das unter Aufsicht des Kanzleigerichts gehaltene Mündel.

chancr-e [ˈʃæŋkə], *s.* der Schanker. **-ous**, *adj.* schankerig.

chancy [ˈtʃɑ:nsɪ], *adj.* (*coll.*) gewagt, ungewiß, riskant, unsicher.

chandelier [ʃændɪˈlɪə *s.* der Armleuchter, Kronleuchter.

chandler [ˈtʃɑ:ndlə], *s.* der Lichtzieher; Krämer; *corn-*–, der Kornhändler; *ship-*–, der Schiffslieferant. **-y** [-rɪ], *s.* der Krämerladen, (*coll.*) Krämerwaren (*pl.*).

change [tʃeɪndʒ], 1. *v.a.* wechseln, auswechseln; ändern, abändern, verändern, umändern, umgestalten, verwandeln (*from*, von; *to*, zu; *into*, in); umwechseln, umtauschen (*money*), einwechseln (*a cheque*) (*for*, gegen); ablösen (*a sentry*); trocken legen (*a baby*); – *one's clothes*, sich umziehen, die Kleider wechseln; – *colour*, blaß werden; – *one's condition*, heiraten; sich verändern; – *gear*, einen anderen Gang einschalten, Geschwindigkeiten umschalten (*Motor.*); – *the guard*, die Wache *or* Posten (*pl.*) ablösen; – *hands*, in andere Hände übergehen, den Besitzer wechseln; – *one's lodgings*, umziehen; – *one's mind*, sich anders besinnen; – *step*, den Tritt wechseln; – *trains*, *etc.*, umsteigen. 2. *v.n.* sich (ver)ändern, anders werden, umschlagen; umsteigen (*for*, nach) (*trains*, *etc.*); *all* – *!*, alle umsteigen!; (*coll.*) sich umkleiden; *the moon -s*, es ist Mondwechsel; – *for the better*, sich (ver)bessern, sich zum Besseren wenden; – *for the worse*, sich verschlimmern, sich zum Schlechteren wenden; – *into*, übergehen *or* sich verwandeln in (*Acc.*); – *into evening dress*, einen Frack anziehen. 3. *s.* die Änderung, Veränderung; der Wechsel, Umschwung; die Abänderung, Abweichung, der Wandel die Wandlung; Abwechslung; der Tausch, Austausch; die Ablösung (*of sentries*); (*also small* –) das Kleingeld, Wechselgeld; (*coll.*) die Börse; (*a*) (*with nouns*) – *of air*, die Luftveränderung; – *of carriage*, der Wagenwechsel (*Railw.*); – *of clothes*, die Wäsche *or* der Anzug zum Wechseln; – *of life*. die Wechseljahre (*pl.*); – *of the moon*, der Mondwechsel; – *of name*, die Namensänderung; – *of position*, der Stellungswechsel; – *of the tide*, der Gezeitenwechsel, Wechsel von Ebbe und Flut; – *of voice*, der Stimmwechsel, – *in the* or *of weather*, der Witterungsumschlag; (*b*) (*with verbs*) *have you got* – *for a pound?* können Sie mir ein Pfund wechseln? *give me* – *for a pound*, geben Sie mir auf ein Pfund heraus; (*coll.*) *get no* – *out of s.o.*, aus einem nichts herausbekommen; *I have no* – *about me*, ich habe kein Kleingeld bei mir; *ring the -s*, alle Melodien eines Glockenspiels ertönen lassen; (*fig.*) *ring the -s with a th.*, dasselbe unter stets verschiedener Aufmachung vorbringen, alle Möglichkeiten ausprobieren, das Thema dauernd wechseln; (*c*) (*with prepositions*) *for a* –, zur Abwechslung; – *for the better*, die (Ver)Besserung; – *for the worse*, die Verschlimmerung. **-ability**, *s.* die Veränderlichkeit, Unbeständigkeit, der Wankelmut. **-able**, *adj.* veränderlich, unbeständig, wandelbar, ungleich, wankelmütig. **-ableness**, *s. see* **-ability**. **-ful**, *adj.* (*rare*) wechselvoll, unbeständig, veränderlich. **--gear**, *s.* das Wechselgetriebe. **-less**, *adj.* unveränderlich, beständig. **-lessness**, *s.* die Unveränderlichkeit, Beständigkeit. **-ling**, *s.* der Wechselbalg, untergeschobenes Kind. **--over**, *s.* die Umschaltung (*Mech.*); der Übergang, die Umstellung; Wandlung, Umwälzung, der Wechsel (*from*, von; *to*, auf); --*over switch*, *s.* der Umschalter, Polwender.

[1]**channel** [ˈtʃænl], 1. *s.* der Kanal; das Flußbett; Fahrwasser; die Kille, Rinne, Gosse; Auskehlung, Hohlkehle (*Arch.*); das Frequenzband (*Rad.*), (*fig.*) der Weg; – *of communication*, der Nachrichtenweg; *through diplomatic -s*, auf diplomatischem Wege; *official* –, der Dienstweg, Instanzenweg; *cross-- services*, der Schiffsverkehr über den Ärmelkanal; '*the usual -s*', Vereinbarung zwischen Regierung und Opposition (*Parl.*). 2. *v.a.* furchen, auskehlen; – *out*, rinnenförmig aushöhlen.

[2]**channel**, *s.* (*usually pl.*) die Rüsten (*pl.*) (*Naut.*).

chant [tʃɑ:nt], 1. *s.* der Gesang, die Weise, Kirchenmelodie; liturgischer Kirchengesang; (*fig.*) der Sing-Sang, eintöniges Lied. 2. *v.a.* besingen, preisen, intonieren; (*also v.n.*) singen. **-er**, *s.* der Sänger; Vorsänger (*in a choir*), Kantor; die Diskantpfeife (*of bagpipes*). **-ry**, *s.* die Messenstiftung; gestiftete kleine Kapelle.

chanterelle [tʃæntəˈrɛl], *s.* der Pfifferling.

chanticleer [ˈtʃɑ:ntɪklɪə], *s.* der Hahn.

chao-s [ˈkeɪɔs], *s.* das Chaos; (*fig.*) Durcheinander, die Verwirrung, der Wirrwarr. **-tic**, *adj.* chaotisch, wüst, verworren, wirr.

[1]**chap** [tʃæp], 1. *s.* (*usually pl.*) der Spalt, Sprung, Riß; die (Haut)Schrunde. 2. *v.a.* & *n.* aufspringen, spalten; Risse verursachen *or* bekommen; *-ped hands*, aufgesprungene Hände.

[2]**chap**, *s.* die Kinnbacke, Kinnlade (*of animals*); (*usually pl.*) das Maul, der Kinnbacken. **--fallen**; *adj.* (*fig.*) entmutigt, mutlos, niedergeschlagen.

[3]**chap**, *s.* (*coll.*) der Bursche, Kerl; (*sl.*) *old* –, alter Junge.

chapbook [ˈtʃæpbʊk], *s.* das Volksbuch, die Flugschrift.

chapel [ˈtʃæpəl], *s.* die Kapelle, Betkapelle; das Gotteshaus (*of dissenters*); die Druckerei (*Print.*); *church versus* –, Staatskirche gegen Sekten; – *of ease*, die Filialkirche; *attend* – *regularly*, regelmäßig dem Gottesdienst beiwohnen.

chaperon [ˈʃæpəroʊn], 1. *s.* die Anstandsdame, Begleiterin. 2. *v.a.* als Anstandsdame begleiten, chaperonieren, bemuttern.

chapiter [ˈtʃæpɪtə], *s.* das Kapitäl (*Arch.*).

chaplain [ˈtʃæplɪn], *s.* der Kaplan; Pfarrer, Geistliche(r), *m.*; Hausprediger; *army* –, Feldgeistliche(r), *m.* **-cy** [-sɪ], *s.* die Kaplanstelle.

chaplet [ˈtʃæplɪt], *s.* der Kranz; Rosenkranz (*Eccl.*).

chapman [ˈtʃæpmən], *s.* (*archaic*) der Hausierer, Höker.

chapped [tʃæpt], *adj. see* [1]**chap.**
chapter [ˈtʃæptə], *s.* das Kapitel (*also fig. & Eccl.*), der Abschnitt; (*coll.*) – *of accidents*, die Reihe von Unglückfällen; *and so on to the end of the* –, und so weiter bis ans Ende; *give – and verse for a statement*, eine Behauptung eingehend begründen, genaue Angaben für eine Behauptung geben. **--house,** *s.* das Kapitelhaus.
chaptrel [ˈtʃæptrəl], *s.* der Knauf, Kämpfer (*Arch.*).
char [tʃɑː], 1. *v.a. & n.* scheuern; *go out -ring*, als Scheuerfrau arbeiten. 2. *s.* (*coll.*), **-woman,** *s.* die Putzfrau, Scheuerfrau, Arbeitsfrau.
[2]**char,** *v.a. & n.* verkohlen.
[3]**char,** *s.* die Rotforelle, der Seibling (*Ichth.*).
char-à-banc [ˈʃærəbæŋ], *s.* der Ausflugswagen.
character [ˈkærɪktə], *s.* das Zeichen, Schriftzeichen, der Buchstabe, die Schrift, Ziffer; der Charakter, die Persönlichkeit; Charakterstärke; das Zeugnis; (guter) Ruf; die Art, Eigenschaft, Eigenart, Wesensart, Beschaffenheit, Natur; das Gepräge, Merkmal, der Stempel, das Kennzeichen; der Rang, Stand, die Stellung; Rolle (*Theat.*), Figur, Gestalt (*of a novel*); (*coll.*) das Original, der Sonderling; *a bad* –, ehrloser Mensch; *generic* –, das Gattungsmerkmal (*Biol.*); *she has not a good* –, sie steht in keinem guten Rufe; *give a p. a good* –, einem ein gutes Zeugnis ausstellen; *in* –, der Rolle gemäß; *out of all* –, völlig unpassend; *act out of* –, aus der Rolle fallen; *public* –, bekannte Persönlichkeit; *set the – of a th.*, einer S. das Gepräge geben; *specific* –, das Artmerkmal (*Biol.*); *a strange* –, eigenartiger Mensch; *take away a p.'s* –, einem den guten Ruf nehmen. **-istic,** 1. *adj.* charakteristisch, bezeichnend (*of*, für); *this is -istic of the man*, es charakterisiert *or* kennzeichnet den Mann *or* ist bezeichnend für den Mann; *-istic difference*, der Hauptunterschied; *-istic quality*, das Erkennungszeichen. 2. *s.* das Merkmal, Kennzeichen, charakteristische Eigenschaft, bezeichnender Zug, die Eigentümlichkeit, Besonderheit; Kennziffer (*of a logarithm*). **-ization** [-raɪˈzeɪʃən], *s.* die Kennzeichnung, Charakterisierung; Charakteristik; Charakterzeichnung. **-ize** [-raɪz], *v.a.* charakterisieren, kennzeichnen, charakteristisch sein für; eingehend schildern. **-less,** *adj.* charakterlos.
charade [ʃəˈrɑːd], *s.* das Silbenrätsel, die Scharade.
charcoal [ˈtʃɑːkoʊl], *s.* die Holzkohle, Meilerkohle; *animal* or *bone* –, tierische Kohle. **--burner,** *s.* der Köhler, Kohlenbrenner. **--burning,** *s.* die Köhlerei, Kohlenbrennerei, Holzverkohlung. **--pencil,** *s.* die Reißkohle (*Art.*); der Kohle(n)stift (*Elec.*). **--pile,** der Kohlenmeiler.
charge [tʃɑːdʒ], 1. *s.* die Ladung (*also Gun., Min. & Elec.*) Last, Belastung; Füllung, Beschickung (*Metall.*); Verwahrung, Obhut, Aufsicht, Verantwortung; das Mündel, der Schützling, Pflegebefohlene(r), *m.*; Anvertraute(s), *n.*; die Kosten (*pl.*), die Forderung, der Preis, die Gebühr; Ermahnung, der Hirtenbrief (*Eccl.*); die Rechtsbelehrung (*of a judge to the jury*); der Befehl, Auftrag; das Zeichen zum Angriff, der Angriff, Ansturm (*Mil.*); die Beschuldigung, Anschuldigung, Anklage, der Klagepunkt (*Law*); (*a*) (*with nouns*) *after deduction of all -s*, nach Abzug aller Lasten; *the pastor's* –, die Pfarrkinder, der Pfarrbezirk; *the heads of the* –, die Klagepunkte; (*b*) (*with adjectives*) *blasting* –, die Sprengladung, Bohrladung; *booster* –, die Eingangszündung; *electrical* –, elektrische Ladung; *free of* –, kostenlos, umsonst, unentgeltlich; *multiple* –, gestreckte Ladung; *no – for admission!* Eintritt frei! *-s pending*, schwebende Anklagen; *priming* –, die Zündladung; *weak* –, der Ausbläser (*Artill.*); (*c*) (*with verbs*) *be in – of*, in Obhut haben (*a p.*), leiten, mit der Führung beauftragt werden (*an undertaking*); *bring a – against a p.*, einen anklagen, eine Anklage gegen einen vorbringen; *give in* –, in Gewahrsam übergeben, der Polizei ausliefern (*a p.*), zur Verwahrung geben (*a th.*); *lay s.th. to a p.'s* –, einem etwas zur Last legen; *put s.o. in – of*, einen mit der Führung beauftragen; *sound the* –, das Signal zum Angriff geben; *take – of*, übernehmen, sorgen für; *take a p. in* –, einen in Haft nehmen. 2. *v.a.* beladen, belasten (*also fig.*); beschweren; beschicken (*Metall.*), bestellen, besetzen (*Dye.*), sättigen (*a solution*) (*Chem.*); laden (*Gun., Elec.*); füllen (*glasses*); anklagen, beschuldigen, bezichtigen (*with* (*Gen.*)) (*Law*); zur Last legen (*einem etwas*); beauftragen (*Acc.*), befehlen (*Dat.*); anvertrauen, ans Herz legen, einschärfen (*a p. with a th.*, einem etwas); ermahnen; anrechnen, in Rechnung stellen, anschreiben, zur Last schreiben (*C.L.*); anfallen, anstürmen, angreifen, anrennen, rammen, sich stürzen gegen, anrempeln (*Sport.*); – *the jury*, den Geschworenen Richtlinien geben; *-d at 5s.*, zu 5 Schilling berechnet; *how much do you – for it?* wieviel verlangen, fordern *or* rechnen Sie dafür? – *s.th. to a p.'s account*, einem etwas in Rechnung stellen, jemandes Konto mit etwas belasten; – *a p. with theft*, einen eines Diebstahls beschuldigen *or* anklagen. 3. *v.n.* einen Angriff machen, anstürmen, angreifen. **-able,** *adj.*; *be -able on a p.*, einem zuzuschreiben *or* zuzurechnen sein; *a duty is -able on wine*, Wein ist mit einer Abgabe zu versteuern; *be -able to a p.*, einem zur Last fallen; *this mistake is -able to you*, Sie sind für diesen Fehler verantwortlich; *be -able with s.th.*, mit etwas zu belasten sein, schuld sein an etwas. **-s,** *pl.* die Kosten, Gebühren; Unkosten, Spesen (*C.L.*); (*see* **charging**).
chargé-d'affaires [ˈʃɑːʒeɪdæˈfɛə], *s.* der Geschäftsträger.
charger [ˈtʃɑːdʒə], *s.* das Offizierspferd, Chargenpferd, Schlachtroß; (*archaic*) große flache Schüssel.
charging [ˈtʃɑːdʒɪŋ], *s.* das Laden, die Ladung (*Elec.*); Beschickung (*Metall.*), – *voltage*, die Ladespannung.
chariness [[ˈtʃɛəːrɪnɪs], *s.* die Behutsamkeit, Bedenklichkeit; Sparsamkeit.
charion [ˈtʃɑːrɪən], *s.* die Haut, Schalenhaut.
chariot [ˈtʃærɪət], *s.* der Streitwagen; Triumphwagen. **-eer** [-ˈtɪə], *s.* der Wagenlenker. **--race,** *s.* das Wagenrennen.
charit-able [ˈtʃærɪtəbl], *adj.* wohltätig, mild; gütig, nachsichtig; *-able interpretation*, nachsichtige *or* günstige Auselegung; *-able institution*, milde Stiftung; *-able organization*, der Wohltätigkeitsverein; *for -able purposes*, für mildtätige Zwecke. **-ableness,** *s.* die Mildtätigkeit, Wohltätigkeit; Milde, Nachsicht. **-ies** [ˈtʃærɪtɪz], *pl.* milde Stiftung, wohltätige Einrichtungen (*pl.*). **-y** [ˈtʃærɪtɪ], *s.* die Nächstenliebe, christliche Bruderliebe, die Mildtätigkeit, Freigebigkeit, Güte, Nachsicht; Wohltat, das Almosen, milde Gabe; (*Prov.*) *-y begins at home*, jeder ist sich selbst der Nächste; *as cold as -y*, bitter wie das Brot der Barmherzigkeit; *for -y's sake*, um Gotteslohn; *sister of -y*, barmherzige Schwester. **-y-school,** *s.* die Armenschule, Freischule.
charivari [ʃɑːrɪˈvɑːrɪ], *s.* die Katzenmusik.
charlatan [ˈʃɑːlətən], *s.* der Quacksalber, Kurpfuscher, Charlatan. **-ism,** *s.* das Quacksalbertum, die Kurpfuscherei, **-ry,** *s.* die Marktschreierei, Prahlerei.
charlock [ˈtʃɑːlək], *s.* der Ackersenf (*Bot.*).
charm [tʃɑːm], 1. *s.* das Zauberwort, die Zauberformel; (*fig.*) der Zauber, Reiz, Liebreiz; das Uhrgehänge, Amulet; *break the* –, den Zauber *or* Bann brechen. 2. *v.a.* bezaubern, (*fig.*) entzücken, reizen, fesseln; – *away*, wegzaubern; (*coll.*) *I shall be -ed*, ich werde mich außerordentlich freuen; *-ed with*, bezaubert von, entzückt von; *have* or *bear a -ed life*, fest *or* gefeit sein. **-er,** *s.* der Zauberer, die Zauberin (*also fig.*). *snake--er*, der Schlangenbändiger. **-ing,** *adj.* entzückend, bezaubernd, reizend.
charnel-house [ˈtʃɑːnlhaʊs], *s.* das Leichenhaus, Beinhaus, der Karner.
chart [tʃɑːt], 1. *s.* die Seekarte; Tabelle, Kurve. 2. *v.a.* auf einem Diagramm verzeichnen. **--house,** *s.* das Kartenhaus (*Naut.*).
charter [ˈtʃɑːtə], 1. *s.* die Stiftungsurkunde, Verleihungsurkunde, Verfassungsurkunde; der Gnadenbrief, Freibrief, das Privileg, Patent; die Verfrachtung (*Naut.*); – *of incorporation*, der Schutzbrief, das Patent; *royal* –, königlicher Freibrief. 2. *v.a.* privilegieren; chartern, verfrachten, heuern (*a ship*); mieten (*a vehicle*). **-ed,** *adj.* privilegiert verbrieft; *-ed accountant*, der Wirtschaftsprüfer,

beeidigter Bücherrevisor; *–ed company*, privilegierte *or* gesetzlich geschützte Gesellschaft; *–ed rights*, Privilegien, verbriefte Rechte. **– -party,** *s.* die Chartepartie, der Verfrachtungsvertrag.

charwoman ['tʃɑ:wumən], *s. see* [1]**char.**

chary ['tʃɛərɪ], *adj.* sparsam (*of*, mit); behutsam, vorsichtig, sorgfältig; *– of doing*, abgeneigt zu tun.

[1]**chase** [tʃeɪs], 1. *s.* die Jagd; (*fig.*) Verfolgung; gehetztes Wild; das Gehege, Jagdrevier; *wild-goose –*, vergebliche Bemühung, fruchtloses Unternehmen; *I sent him on a wild-goose –*, ich schickte ihn von Pontius zu Pilatus; *follow the –*, die Jagd verfolgen; *give –*, Jagd machen (*to*, auf (*Acc.*)), nachjagen, nachstellen (*to* (*Dat.*)), verfolgen (*Acc.*); *in – of*, verfolgend. 2. *v.a.* jagen, Jagd machen auf (*Acc.*), nachsetzen (*Dat.*), verfolgen (*Acc.*), hetzen (*Acc.*); *– away*, verjagen, vertreiben, verscheuchen **– -gun,** *s.* das Jagdstück, Buggeschütz (*Naut.*). **–r,** *s.* der Jäger, Verfolger; das Geleitschiff, der U-Bootjäger (*Naut.*); das Jagdflugzeug (*Av.*); (*sl.*) der Nachschluck (Schnaps auf Kaffee, Bier auf Schnaps, *etc.*); *stern-–r*, das Heckgeschütz (*Naut.*).

[2]**chase,** 1. *s.* der Formrahmen (*Typ.*). 2. *v.a.* treiben, ziseliren, ausmeißeln; *–d work*, getriebene Arbeit. **–r,** *s.* der Ziseleur (*Engr.*).

[3]**chase,** das Längsfeld (*Gun.*); die Rinne, Furche.

chasm [kæzm], *s.* der Abgrund, (*fig.*) die Kluft, der Spalt.

chassis ['ʃæsɪ:], *s.* das Fahrgestell, Untergestell (*Motor.*), Montagegestell (*Rad.*).

chaste [tʃeɪst], *adj.* keusch, züchtig, rein, (*fig.*) edel, einfach, ungeziert (*as language*). **–ness,** *s.* die Einfachheit (*of style*); Keuschheit (*see* **chastity**).

chasten ['tʃeɪsn], *v.a.* züchtigen, strafen; mäßigen, läutern, reinigen.

chastise [tʃæs'tɑɪz], *v.a.* züchtigen, strafen. **–ment** ['tʃæstɪzmənt], *s.* die Züchtigung, Strafe.

chastity ['tʃæstɪtɪ], *s.* die Keuschheit, Reinheit; (*fig.*) Einfachheit.

chasuble ['tʃæzjubl], *s.* das Meßgewand.

chat [tʃæt], 1. *v.n.* plaudern, schwatzen. *s.* die Plauderei, das Geplauder; der Schmätzer (*Orn.*); (*coll.*) *back-–*, *s.* die Unverschämtheit, Frechheit; (*see* **chatty**).

chattel ['tʃætl], *s.* (*usually pl.*) bewegliche Habe, bewegliches Vermögen, der Besitz; *goods and –s*, Hab und Gut.

chatter ['tʃætə], 1. *v.n.* plaudern, schwatzen, plappern; zwitschern (*of birds*); plätschern (*of brooks*); klappern (*of teeth*); rattern (*as machinery*); *his teeth are –ing*, er klappert mit den Zähnen. 2. *s.* das Geplauder, Geplapper, Geschwätz; Gezwitscher (*of birds*). **–er,** *s.* der Schwätzer, die Plaudertasche, das Plappermaul; der Seidenschwanz (*Orn.*). **–ing,** *see* – 2; *–ing of the teeth*, das Zähneklappern.

chatty ['tʃætɪ], *adj.* geschwätzig, schwatzhaft; plaudernd, unterhaltsam.

chauffeur [ʃou'fə:, (*coll.*) 'ʃoufə], *m.* der (Kraft)-Fahrer, Kraftwagenführer.

chauvinism ['ʃouvɪnɪzm], *s.* der Chauvinismus, Hurrapatriotismus.

cheap [tʃɪ:p], *adj.* billig, preiswert, wohlfeil; gering, gemein, minderwertig, kitschig; (*coll.*) *dirt –*, spottbillig; (*coll.*) *on the –*, auf billigste Art; *– trip*, der Ausflug mit Fahrpreisermäßigung; (*coll.*) *feel –*, sich würdelos vorkommen, sich beschimpft fühlen; *get off –ly*, mit einem blauen Auge *or* leichten Kaufs davonkommen; *hold* (*a th.*) *–*, geringschätzen, verachten; *make o.s. –*, sich wegwerfen. **–en,** *v.a.* den Preis herabsetzen, billiger machen; (*archaic*) handeln, feilschen (um); *–en o.s.*, see *make o.s. –*. **– -jack,** 1. *s.* der Marktschreier, wahrer Jakob. 2. *adj.* minderwertig, Schund–. **–ness,** *s.* die Billigkeit, Wohlfeilheit.

cheat [tʃɪ:t], 1. s. der Betrug; Betrüger, Schwindler. 2. *v.a.* betrügen, belügen, schwindeln, (*coll.*) mogeln; *– a p.* (*out*) *of a th.*, einen um eine S. betrügen. **–ing,** *s.* die Betrügerei, der Schwindel.

check [tʃɛk], 1. *s.* das Hindernis, der Halt, Einhalt, die Hemmung, Pause; der Rückschlag, die Schlappe; Kontrollmarke, (*Amer.*) der Gepäckschein; karierter Stoff, kariertes Muster; (*Amer.*) *see* **cheque**; das Schach (*Chess*); die Nachprüfung, Kontrolle; der Verlust der Fährte (*Hunt.*); *– !* Schach dem König! (*Chess*); (*sl.*) *hand in one's –s*, krepieren, ins Gras beißen; *keep a p. in –*, einen im Zaume halten; *keep a – on a th.*, etwas unter Kontrolle halten. 2. *v.a.* Einhalt tun (*Dat.*), aufhalten, hemmen (*Acc.*); kontrollieren, probieren, prüfen, nachprüfen, revidieren; nachrechnen; (*Amer.*) *– one's baggage*, das Gepäck aufgeben; *– an invoice*, eine Faktura auf ihre Richtigkeit nachprüfen; (*coll.*) *– up*, *v.a.* kontrollieren, prüfen, vergleichen, nachrechnen. 3. *v.n.* Schach bieten; (*coll.*) *– in*, sich (zur Arbeit) anmelden; (*coll.*) *– out*, sich (von der Arbeit) abmelden. **– -account,** *s.* die Gegenrechnung, Kontrolle. **– -book,** *s.* das Kontrollbuch (*C.L.*). **–ed,** *adj.* kariert. **–mate,** 1. *s.* das Schachmatt. 2. *v.a.* schachmatt machen; (*fig.*) matt setzen. **– -nut,** *s.* die Gegenmutter (*Mech.*). **– -test,** *s.* der Kontrollversuch. (*sl.*) **– -up,** die Kontrolle, Nachprüfung, Durchsicht. **– -valve,** *s.* das Absperrventil, Rückschlagventil.

checkers ['tʃɛkəz], *s.* das Damespiel (*Amer.*).

cheek [tʃɪ:k], 1. *s.* die Backe, Wange; (*sl.*) Unverschämtheit, Frechheit, Stirn; *pl.* die Seitenstücke (*pl.*), Seitenteile (*pl.*) (*Mech.*); (*coll.*) *none of your –!* sei nicht so frech! *he had the – to tell me*, er hatte die Unverschämtheit, mir zu sagen . . .; *with one's tongue in one's –*, schalkhaft; *– by jowl*, dicht aneinander, in vertraulichem Zusammensein. 2. *v.a.* (*coll.*) *– a p.*, frech sein gegen einen. **– -bone,** *s.* der Backenknochen. **– -piece,** *s.* das Kopfstück (*harness*). **– -rail,** *s.* die Backenschiene (*Railw.*). **–y,** *adj.* frech, dreist, unverschämt; *–y fellow*, der Frechdachs.

cheep [tʃɪ:p], *v.n.* piepen.

cheer [tʃɪə], 1. *s.* das Hurra, der Beifallsruf; die Kost, Bewirtung, Speise, das Essen; die Laune, Stimmung, Ermunterung, der Trost, Frohsinn, die Fröhlichkeit; *three –s for*, ein dreifaches Hoch auf (*Acc.*), dreimal Hurra rufen; *be of good –*, guter Dinge *or* guten Mutes sein; *what –?* was gibt's? wie geht's? 2. *v.a.* mit Beifall begrüßen; aufmuntern, aufheitern, ermuntern, ermutigen, erfreuen; *– on*, anspornen. 3. *v.n.* applaudieren, Beifall spenden, Hoch *or* Hurra rufen; (*coll.*) *– to the echo*, applaudieren daß die Wände wackeln; *– up*, Mut fassen; *– up !* nur Mut! **–ful,** *adj.* heiter, munter, froh, fröhlich; erfreuend, erfreulich, freundlich; *do –fully*, willig tun. **–fulness,** *s.*, **–iness,** *s.* der Frohsinn, die Fröhlichkeit, Heiterkeit. (*coll.*) **–io,** *int.* alles Gute! viel Glück! Heil! Prost! auf Wiedersehen! (*coll.*) **– -leader,** *s.* der Anführer (beim Beifallrufen). **–less,** *adj.* freudlos, trostlos. **–y,** *adj.* heiter, munter, froh.

[1]**cheese** [tʃɪ:z], 1. *s.* der Käse; *cream-–*, der Quarkkäse; *as different as chalk from –*, grundverschieden sein. 2. *v.a.*; (*sl.*) *– it !* sei still! halt's Maul! **– -cake,** *s.* der Quarkkuchen. **– -cloth,** *s.* das Nesseltuch. **– -mite,** *s.* die Käsemilbe. **– -paring,** 1. *s.* die Käserinde; (*fig.*) Knauserigkeit. 2. *adj.* knauserig. **– -straw,** *s.* die Käsestange.

[2]**cheese,** *s.* (*sl.*) das einzig Wahre, das eigentlich Richtige.

cheesy ['tʃɪ:zɪ], *adj.* käsig, (*sl.*) schlecht, schäbig, kläglich.

cheetah ['tʃɪ:tɑ], *s.* der Jagdleopard.

chef [ʃɛf], *s.* der Küchenmeister, Küchenchef.

cheiropter-a [kaɪ'rɔptərə], *pl.* die Fledermäuse, Handflügler. **–ous,** *adj.* fledermausartig.

chemical ['kɛmɪkl], 1. *adj.* chemisch. 2. *s.* chemisches Präparat; *pl.* Chemikalien; *– action*, chemischer Eingriff; *– affinity*, chemische Verwandtschaft; *– conversion*, chemische Umsetzung; *– decomposition*, chemischer Abbau; *–ly pure*, chemisch rein; *– structure*, chemischer Bau; *– warfare*, der Gaskrieg; *– works*, chemische Fabrik.

chemise [ʃə'mɪ:z], *s.* das (Frauen)Hemd, das Leibchen.

chemist ['kɛmɪst], *s.* der Chemiker; Apotheker, Drogist; *analytical –*, der Chemiker; *dispensing –*, der Apotheker; *–'s shop*, die Drogerie, Apotheke; *works –*, der Betriebschemiker. **–ry,** *s.* die Chemie; *analytical –ry*, die Scheidekunst; *applied -ry*, angewandte *or* technische Chemie; *–ry of food*, die

Nahrungsmittelchemie; *–ry of plants*, die Pflanzenchemie; *pure –ry*, die Chemie.

chenille [ʃəˈniːl], *s.* die Chenille.

cheque [tʃɛk], *s.* der Scheck, die Zahlungsanweisung; *give a p. a blank –*, (*fig.*) einem freie Hand lassen; *crossed –*, der Verrechnungsscheck; *– for £10*, der Scheck über 10 Pfund; *– on London*, der Scheck auf London. **– -book,** *s.* das Scheckbuch.

chequer [ˈtʃɛkə], 1. *s.* (*often pl.*) kariertes Zeug; das Schachmuster. 2. *v.a.* scheckig *or* bunt machen, karieren. **–ed,** *adj.* bunt, kariert; (*fig.*) bewegt, veränderlich, wechselvoll.

cherish [ˈtʃɛrɪʃ], *v.a.* pflegen, sorgen für; festhalten (an (*Dat.*)); unterhalten, hegen, hochhalten, schätzen; *– a hope*, eine Hoffnung nähren.

cheroot [ʃəˈruːt], *s.* der Stumpen.

cherry [ˈtʃɛrɪ], 1. *s.* die Kirsche. 2. *adj.* kirschrot. **– -brandy,** *s.* das Kirschwasser, der Kirschlikör. **– -stone,** *s.* der Kirschkern. **– -tree,** *s.* der Kirschbaum. **–wood,** *s.* das Kirschbaumholz.

chersonese [ˈkəːsənɪːz], *s.* die Halbinsel.

chert [tʃəːt], *s.* der Feuerstein, Hornstein, Quarz.

cherub [ˈtʃɛrəb], *s.* (*pl.* –im & –s) der Cherub; (*fig.*) liebliches Kind, das Herzchen. **–ic** [tʃɛˈrʌbɪk], *adj.* engelhaft, cherubinisch. **–im** [ˈtʃɛrubɪm], *pl.* die Cherubim.

chervil [ˈtʃəːvɪl], *s.* der Kerbel (*Bot.*).

chess [tʃɛs], *s.* das Schach; *game of –*, das Schachspiel. **–board,** *s.* das Schachbrett. **–man,** *s.* die Schachfigur, der Stein.

chest [tʃɛst], *s.* die Kiste, der Koffer, die Lade, Truhe, der Kasten, Bottich; die Kasse; die Brust, der Brustkasten (*Anat.*); *– of drawers*, die Kommode; *get* (*s.th.*) *off one's –*, seinem Herzen Luft machen, sich (eine Last) von der Seele wälzen; *have – trouble*, brustkrank sein. **–ed,** *adj. suffix* –brüstig. **– -protector,** *s.* der Brustwärmer. **–y,** *adj.* (*coll.*) es auf der Brust haben; (*sl.*) anmaßend, eingebildet.

chesterfield [ˈtʃɛstəfɪːld], *s.* der Überzieher zum Knöpfen; das Schlafsofa.

chestnut [ˈtʃɛsnʌt], 1. *s.* die Kastanie; (*coll.*) (ur)alte Geschichte, abgedroschener Witz; *horse- –*, die Roßkastanie; *pull the –s out of the fire for s.o.*, für einen die Kastanien aus dem Feuer holen; *sweet* or *Spanish –*, die Edelkastanie. 2. *adj.* kastanienbraune; *– horse*, Braune(r), *m.*, der Fuchs. **– -brown,** *s.* das Kastanienbraun. **– -tree,** *s.* der Kastanienbaum.

cheval-de-frise [ʃəˈvældəˈfrɪːz], *s.* Spanischer Reiter (*Fort.*). **cheval-glass,** *s.* großer Drehspiegel.

chevalier [ʃɛvəˈlɪə], *s.* (*archaic*) der Ritter.

cheviot [ˈtʃɛvɪət], *s.* der Wollstoff; das Bergschaf.

chevron [ˈʃɛvrən], *s.* der Sparren (*Her.*); das Dienstabzeichen, der Winkel, die Unteroffiziertresse (*Mil.*); Zickzackleiste (*Arch.*).

chevrotain [ˈʃɛvroutɛɪn], *s.* das Zwergmoschustier (*Zool.*).

chew [tʃuː], *v.a.* kauen; priemen (*tobacco*); (*sl.*) sinnen (*on*, auf (*Acc.*)); *– the cud*, wiederkäuen; (*sl.*) *– the rag*, viel schwätzen, quasseln, quatschen. **–ing-gum,** *s.* das Kaugummi.

chiaroscuro [kɪɑːrəsˈkuərou], *s.* das Helldunkel; die Licht- und Schattenwirkung (*Paint.*).

chibouque [tʃɪˈbuːk], *s.* türkische Pfeife, der Tschibuk.

chic [ʃɪːk], 1. *adj.* schick, elegant. 2. *s.* der Schick, die Eleganz.

chicane [ʃɪˈkeɪn], *v.a.* übervorteilen, schikanieren. **–ry,** *s.* die Spitzfindigkeit, Schikane, Sophisterei. **– weed,** *s.* der Hühnerdarm (*Bot.*).

chick [tʃɪk], (*coll.*) *see* **–en**; liebes Kind, das Herzchen. **–en** [ˈtʃɪkn], *s.* das Hühnchen, Küken, Kücken; das Huhn, Geflügel (*Cook.*); (*sl.*) *no –en*, nicht mehr jung, kein Kind mehr; *count one's –ens before they are hatched*, die Rechnung ohne den Wirt machen, zu früh triumphieren. **–en-broth,** *s.* die Hühnersuppe. (*sl.*) **–en-feed,** *s.* die Lappalie. **–en-hearted,** (*coll.*) **–en-livered,** *adj.* feige, kleinmütig, zaghaft. **–en-pox,** *s.* die Windpocken (*Med.*). **–en-run,** *s.* der Hühnerhof. **– -pea,** *s.* die Kichererbse (*Bot.*). **–weed,** *s.* der Hühnerbiß, die Vogelmiere (*Bot.*)

chicory [ˈtʃɪkərɪ], *s.* die Zichorie (*Bot.*).

chide [tʃɑɪd], *ir.v.a.* & *n.* (aus)schelten.

chief [tʃɪːf], 1. *adj.* höchst, oberst, vornehmlich, wichtigst, hauptsächlich, Ober–, Haupt–; *– clerk*, erster Kommis; *commander-in- –*, der Oberbefehlshaber, Höchstkommandierende(r), *m.*; *– Justice*, der Oberrichter; *– mourner*, Hauptleidtragende(r), *m.*; *– petty officer*, der Oberfeldwebel (*Naut.*). 2. *s.* das Haupt, Oberhaupt; der Vorsteher, Vorgesetzte(r), *m.*, der Anführer, Chef; Hauptteil; das Schildhaupt (*Her.*), (*see* **–tain**); *in –*, hauptsächlich, im besondern, besonders; *– of staff*, der Generalstabschef (*Mil.*). **–ly,** *adv.* größtenteils, hauptsächlich, meistens. **–tain** [–tən], *s.* der Häuptling.

chiffchaff [ˈtʃɪftʃæf], *s.* der Weidenlaubsänger (*Orn.*).

chiffonier [ʃɪfəˈnɪːə], *s.* kleiner Schrank mit Schubladen.

chignon [ˈʃɪnjɔ̃ː], *s.* der (Haar)Wulst, Kauz.

chilblain [ˈtʃɪlbleɪn], *s.* die Frostbeule.

child [tʃɑɪld], *s.* (*pl.* –ren) das Kind; (*obs.*, *often spelt* –e) der Junker; *from a –*, von Jugend *or* Kindheit auf *or* an; *with –*, schwanger; *– murder*, der Kindermord. **– -bearing,** *s.* die Niederkunft; *be past – -bearing*, keine Kinder mehr haben können. **–bed,** *s.* das Wochenbett; *be in –bed*, in den Wochen liegen *or* sein; *die in –bed*, im Wochenbett sterben; *woman in –bed*, die Wöchnerin. **–birth,** *s.* die Niederkunft. **–hood,** *s.* die Kindheit. **–ish,** *adj.* kindisch. **–ishness,** *s.* die Kindischkeit; Kinderei (*of old people, etc.*). **–less,** *adj.* kinderlos. **–like,** *adj.* kindlich, unschuldig. **–ren,** *pl. see –*; *–ren's allowance*, die Kinderbeihilfe; *–ren's books*, Jugendschriften (*pl.*); *–ren's hour*, der Kinderfunk (*Rad.*). **–'s-play,** *s.* das Kinderspiel, die Kleinigkeit.

chiliad [ˈkɪlɪæd], *s.* das Tausend, Jahrtausend.

chill [tʃɪl], 1. *s.* der Schauer, (Fieber)Frost, das Frösteln; die Erkältung; Kälte, Kühle; Gußform, Schale, Kokille (*Found.*); *catch a –*, sich erkälten; *take the – off*, leicht anwärmen; *water with the – off*, verschlagenes Wasser. 2. *adj.* kühl, kalt, frostig. 3. *v.a.* kalt machen, abkühlen, abschrecken, ablöschen (*Found*); (*fig.*) entmutigen, niederschlagen; *it –s my blood*, mein Blut erstarrt; *–ed meat*, das Kühlfleisch; *–ed shot*, das Hartblei. **– -casting,** der Hartguß, Schalenguß, Kokillenguß (*Found.*). **–iness,** *s.* die Kälte. **–ing,** *adj* (*fig.*) frostig, niederdrückend. **–y,** *adj.* frostig, kalt; (*fig.*) kühl; *feel –y*, frösteln.

chillies [ˈtʃɪlɪz], *pl.* die Schoten des Cayennepfeffers.

[1]**chime** [tʃɑɪm], *s.* die Kimme.

[2]**chime,** 1. *s.* (*often pl.*) das Glockenspiel, Läuten (*of bells*); (*fig.*) der Einklang, Zusammenklang 2. *v a.* läuten, ertönen lassen, anschlagen; *– the hours*, die Stunden schlagen. 3. *v.n.* tönen, klingen; schlagen (*of clocks*); zusammenstimmen, im Einklange tönen; übereinstimmen; (*coll.*) *– in*, gelegentlich bemerken; *– in with*, übereinstimmen mit, beistimmen (*Dat*).

chimer–a [kɑɪˈmɪərə], *s.* die Chimäre (*Myth.*); (*fig.*) das Schreckbild; Hirngespinst. **–ical** [–ˈmɛrɪkl], *adj.* (s)chimärisch, phantastisch.

chimney [ˈtʃɪmnɪ], *s.* der Kamin, Schornstein; Rauchfang; Schlot, die Esse; der Ausbruchskanal (*of a volcano*); Zylinder (*for lamps*); enge Schlucht (*Mount.*); *– on fire*, der Kaminbrand. **– -corner,** *s.* die Kaminecke. **– -piece,** *s.* der Kaminsims. **– -pot,** *s.* die Zugröhre, Kaminkappe; (*coll*) der Zylinderhut, (*coll*) die Angströhre. **– -stack,** *s.* der Schornstein, Schlot. **– -sweep,** *s.* der Schornsteinfeger, Essenkehrer. **– -top,** *s* die Schornsteinkappe; *over the – -tops*, über die Giebel.

chimpanzee [tʃɪmpənˈzɪː], *s.* der Schimpanse (*Zool.*).

chin [tʃɪn], 1 *s.* das Kinn; *up to the –*, bis ans Kinn, bis über die Ohren; (*coll*) *keep your – up!* Kopf hoch! 2. *v.n* (*sl*) schwatzen, quasseln. **– -rest,** *s.* der Kinnhalter (*of a violin*). **– -strap,** *s.* der Sturmriemen. **–wag,** *s.* (*sl.*) der Plauscher.

china [ˈtʃɑɪnə], *s.* das Porzellan. **– bark,** die Chinarinde. **– -clay,** *s.* das Kaolin, die Porzellanerde. **– -shop,** *s.* der Porzellanladen; *like a bull in a – -shop*, wie ein Elefant im Porzellanladen. **–ware,** *s.* das Porzellan.

chinchilla [tʃɪnˈtʃɪlə], *s.* die Hasenmaus (*Zool.*); die & das Chinchilla (*fur*).
chine [tʃaɪn], *s.* der Rückgrat, Kreuz; das Rückenstück, Lendenstück (*Butch.*); der Bergrücken, Felsgrat, Kamm (*of mountains*).
[1]**chink** [tʃɪŋk], *s.* die Ritze, der Riß, Spalt.
[2]**chink,** 1. *s.* der Klang, das Klingen, Klirren, (*sl.*) das Moos, die Pinke. 2. *v.n.* klirren, klingen, klimpern (*as money*); anstoßen (*as glasses*). 3. *v.a.* klingen lassen, klimpern mit.
chintz [tʃɪnts], *s.* der Zitz, Kattun.
chip [tʃɪp], 1. *s.* das Schnittchen, Schnitzel, Stückchen; der Splitter, Span, Bast; *a – of the old block*, ein Ast vom alten Stamm, der leibhafte Vater. 2. *v.a.* in kleine Stücke schneiden, abschaben, abschälen, abhacken, beschneiden, behauen; (*prov.*) *from –ping come –s*, wo man Holz haut, da fallen Späne. 3. *v.n.*; (*sl.*) – *in*, sich hineinmischen, unterbrechen, ins Wort fallen (*Dat.*); mitwirken, mitmachen; – *off*, abbröckeln, abbrechen; abspringen, (sich) blättern. **--hat,** *s.* der Basthut. **-munk,** *s.* (*Amer.*) das Eichhörnchen. **-ped,** *adj.* angeschlagen, angestoßen; *–ped potatoes, see* **–s** (*Cook.*). **-py,** *s.* (*sl.*) das Weibsbild. **-s,** *pl.* Späne, Splitter (*pl.*); (*sl.*) Spielmarken (*pl.*); Pommes frites (*Cook.*).
chiro-graph [ˈkaɪrogræf], *s.* Doppel– *or* Tripelurkunde (*Hist.*). **-mancer** [ˈkaɪromænsə], *s.* der Handwahrsager, Chiromant. **-mancy,** *s.* die Handlesekunst, Chiromantie. **-podist** [–ˈrɔpədɪst], *s.* der Hühneraugenoperateur, Pedikeur. **-pody,** *s.* die Fußpflege. **-practic,** *s.* die Chiropraktik. **-practor,** *s.* der Chiropraktiker.
chirp [tʃə.p], *v.n* zirpen, zwitschern; piepsen. **-ing,** *s.* das Zirpen, Gezirp, Zwitschern, Gezwitscher.
chirrup [ˈtʃɪrəp], *v.n. see* **chirp**; schnalzen.
chisel [ˈtʃɪzəl], 1. *s.* der Meißel; das Stemmeisen; der Beitel; *cold –*, der Kaltschrottmeißel, Hartmeißel; *engraver's –*, der Grabstichel; *sculptor's –*, der Bildhauermeißel. 2. *v.a.* (aus)meißeln, (*sl.*) übervorteilen, betrügen; *finely –led features*, feingeschnittene *or* wohlgeformte Gesichtzüge. **-er,** *s.* (*sl.*) der Nassauer.
chit [tʃɪt], *s.* kleines Geschöpf, junges Ding, das Kind; Zettelchen; der Keim, Schoß (*Bot.*).
chitchat [ˈtʃɪttʃæt], *s.* das Geschwätz, Geplauder, der Schickschnack.
chit(ter)lings [ˈtʃɪt(ə)lɪŋz], *pl.* das Gekröse.
chivalr-ic [ˈʃɪvəlrɪk], *adj*, **-ous,** *adj.* ritterlich. **-y** [ˈʃɪvəlrɪ], *s.* die Ritterschaft; das Rittertum, Ritterwesen; die Ritterlichkeit.
chive [tʃaɪv], *s.* der Schnittlauch (*Bot.*).
chlor-al [ˈklɔːrəl], *s.* das Chloral (*Chem.*). **-ate** [–rɪt], *s.* das Chlorat, chlorsaures Salz; *–ate of lime*, chlorsaurer Kalk. **-ic,** *adj.* Chlor–; *–ic acid*, der Chlorsäure. **-ide,** *s.* das Chlorid, die Chlorverbindung, salzsaure Verbindung; *–ide of lime*, der Chlorkalk. **-inate,** *v.a.* chloren, chlorieren. **-ine,** *s.* das Chlor, Chlorgas. **-oform** [ˈklɔːrofɔːm], 1. *s.* das Chloroform. 2. *v.a.* chloroformieren. **-ometer** [klɔːˈrɔmɪtə], *s.* der Chlormesser. **-ophyll** [ˈklɔːrofɪl], *s.* das Blattgrün, Chlorophyll. **-osis** [–ˈrousɪs], *s.* die Bleichsucht (*Med.*). **-otic** [–ˈrɔtɪk], *adj.* bleichsüchtig. **-ous,** *adj* chlorig.
chock [tʃɔk], 1. *s.* der (Stell)Keil, Bremsklotz, Hemmklotz; die Klampe (*Naut*). 2. *v.a.* festkeilen, festlegen. 3. *adv.* eng, dicht, fest. (*coll.*) **--a-block,** *adv.* dicht gedrängt. (*coll.*) **--full,** *adj.* übervoll, gedrängt voll.
chocolate [ˈtʃɔkəlɪt], 1. *s.* die Schokolade, Praline; Schokoladenfarbe; *bar of –*, der Schokoladenriegel. 2. *adj.* schokoladenfarbig; – *creams*, Pralinen (*pl.*), gefüllte Schokoladen (*pl.*)
choice [tʃɔɪs], 1. *s.* die Wahl; Auswahl; das Beste, die Elite, Auslese; *my –*, das von mir Ausgewählte; *at –*, nach Belieben; *by* or *for –*, vorzugsweise, wenn ich wählen muß; *have no –*, keine (Möglichkeit zur) Wahl haben; keins bevorzugen; *have no – but to come*, nicht anders können als kommen; *Hobson's –*, keine Wahl, dies oder gar nichts; *make a –*, wählen, zu wählen haben, die Wahl haben, eine Auswahl treffen; *take one's –*, nach Belieben wählen; *the – is* or *lies with you*, die Wahl liegt bei dir; *wide* or *good –*, reiche Auswahl. 2. *adj.* auserlesen; vorzüglich, vortrefflich, kostbar; wählerisch; – *fruit*, erlesenes Obst. **-ness,** *s.* die Erlesenheit.
choir [ˈkwaɪə], 1. *s.* der (Sänger)Chor; das Chor, der Altarplatz (*Arch.*). 2. *v.a* & *n.* im Chor singen. **--boy,** *s.* der Chorknabe, Chorsänger.
chok-e [tʃouk], 1. *v.a.* ersticken; erwürgen; (*–e up*) verstopfen, versperren; (*fig.*) unterdrücken, hemmen, hindern, dämpfen, drosseln (*Elec.*); (*sl.*) versaufen (*Motor*); würgen (*bore of gun*); (*–e down*) verschlucken, hinunterwürgen (*food*); (*sl.*) *–e a p. off*, einem den Mund stopfen, einen zum Schweigen bringen. 2. *v.n.* ersticken (an (*Dat.*)); sich stopfen. 3. *s.* die Verengung (*Mech.*), Drosselspule (*Elec.*), Luftdüse, Starterklappe (*Motor.*); Würgebohrung (*Artil.*). **-e-coil,** *s.* die Drosselspule (*Rad.*). **-e-damp,** *s.* der Schwaden, das Grubengas, schlagende Wetter (*Min.*). **-er,** *s.* (*sl.*) steifer Kragen, der Stehkragen.
choler [ˈkɔlə], *s.* die Galle; (*fig.*) der Zorn. **-a** [ˈkɔlərə], *s.* die Cholera. **-ic** [ˈkɔlərɪk], *adj.* cholerisch, gallsüchtig, jähzornig.
choos-e [tʃuːz], 1. *ir.v.a.* wählen, auswählen; (*with inf*) vorziehen, wollen, mögen, belieben; *take which you –e*, nehmen Sie welches Ihnen beliebt; *I do as I –e*, ich tue wie mir beliebt. 2. *ir.v.n.* die Wahl haben, wählen; (*archaic*) *he cannot –e but*, er kann nicht umhin zu . . .; *there is not much to –e between them*, es ist fast kein Unterschied zwischen ihnen, der eine ist genau so gut wie der andere; *pick and –e*, wählerisch sein, behutsam auswählen. **-er,** *s.* Wählende(r), *m.*, der Wähler; *beggars cannot be –ers*, in der Not frißt der Teufel Fliegen. **-y,** *adj.* (*sl.*) wählerisch.
[1]**chop** [tʃɔp], 1. *s.* abgehauenes Stück, die Schnitte; der Hieb, Schlag; das Kotelett (*Butch.*); kurzer Wellenschlag; *pl.* (*vulg.*) das Maul. 2. *v a.* hauen, zerhacken, spalten; – *down*, fällen (*trees*); – *off*, abhauen; – *up*, kleinhacken, kleinmachen. 3. *v.n.* umschlagen (*of the wind*); – *and change*, wechseln, sich andauernd ändern, schwanken, unschlüssig sein. **--house,** *s.* das Speisehaus. **-per,** *s.* das Hackmesser, Hackbeil. **-ping-block,** *s.* der Hackblock, Hackklotz. **-ping and changing,** ständiger Wechsel. **-ping-knife,** *s.* das Hackmesser, Wiegemesser. **-py,** *adj.* unbeständig, unterbrochen, abgebrochen: *–py sea*, kabbelige See. **-s and changes,** Schwankungen (*pl.*). **-stick,** *s.* das Eßstäbchen. **--suey,** chinesisches Gericht.
choral [ˈkɔːrəl], 1. *adj.* Chor–; – *society*, der Gesangverein. 2. *s.* **–e** [koˈrɑːl], der Choral.
chord [kɔːd], *s.* der Ton, Akkord (*Mus.*); die Sehne (*Geom*), Saite; das Band (*Anat.*); *strike a –*, einen Ton anschlagen; *touch the right –*, zu rühren verstehen; *common –*, der Dreiklang; *major –*, der Durakkord; *minor –*, der Mollakkord; *spinal –*, das Rückenmark; *vocal –s*, die Stimmbänder (*pl.*); *wing-–*, die Profilsehne (*Av.*).
chore [tʃɔːə], *s.* (*usually pl.*) (*coll.*) die Hausarbeit, Alltagsarbeit, Hausreinigung.
chorea [kɔˈrɪ.ə], *s.* der Veitstanz (*Med.*).
choreograph [ˈkɔrɪogræf], *s.* der Ballettmeister. **-y** [ˈɔgrəfɪ], *s.* die Tanzkunst; Tanzschrift.
choriamb(us) [ˈkɔːrɪæmb, (kɔːrɪˈæmbəs)], *s.* der Choriambus. (—⏑⏑—) (*Metr.*)
chorion [ˈkɔ.rɪən], *s.* die Zottenhaut (*Anat*).
chorister [ˈkɔrɪstə], *s.* der Chorsänger, Chorist, (*Amer.*) Chorleiter.
choroid [ˈkɔːrɔɪd], *s.* die Aderhaut des Auges.
chortle [ˈtʃɔ·tl], 1. *v.n.* laut *or* vergnügt kichern. 2 *s.* vergnügtes Lachen.
chorus [kɔːrəs], 1. *s.* der Chor (*also Theat.*), Sängerchor; Chorgesang, Refrain; *sing in –*, zusammen *or* im Chor singen. 2. *v.a.* gemeinsam ausrufen *or* äußern. **--girl,** *s.* die Revuetänzerin.
chosen, *see* **choose.**
chough [tʃʌf], *s.* die Alpen– *or* Steinkrähe.
chow [tʃau], *s.* 1. (*sl.*) das Essen; 2. eine Hundeart.
chowder [ˈtʃaudə], *s.* (*Amer.*) die Fischsuppe.
chrism [krɪzm], *s.* das Salböl. **-atory,** *s.* das Salbölgefäß.
chrisom [ˈkrɪzəm], *s.* das Taufkleid.
christen [ˈkrɪsn], *v.a.* taufen; nennen. **-dom** [ˈkrɪsndəm], *s.* die Christenheit, christliche Welt. **-ing** [ˈkrɪsnɪŋ], 1. *s.* die Taufe. 2. *attrib.* Tauf–.

Christian ['krɪstjən], 1. *adj.* christlich; – *era*, christliche Zeitrechnung; – *name*, der Vorname, Taufname; –*Science*, der Szientismus. 2. *s.* der Christ. **–ity** [krɪstɪ'ænɪtɪ], *s.* christlicher Glaube, das Christentum. **–ize** [–aɪz], *v.a.* zum Christentum bekehren.

Christmas ['krɪsməs], *s.* (die) Weihnacht(en); das Christfest, Weihnachtsfest; *Father* –, der Weihnachtsmann. **– -box,** das Weihnachtsgeschenk. **– card,** die Weihnachtskarte, der Weihnachtsglückwunsch. **– carol,** das Weihnachtslied. **– Day,** der Christtag, erster Weihnachtstag. **– Eve,** Heiliger Abend, Weihnachtsabend. **– gift, – present,** *see* **– -box. – pudding,** der Plumpudding. **– rose,** die Christrose, schwarze Nieswurz. **– tree,** der Weihnachtsbaum, Christbaum. **–sy,** *adj.* (*coll.*) weihnachtlich.

chromat–e ['kroumeɪt], *s.* chromsaures Salz, das Chromsalz; –*e of iron*, der Chromeisenstein; –*e of potash*, chromsaures Kali. **–ic** [krou'mætɪk], *adj.* chromatisch, Farben–; –*ic printing*, der Farbendruck; –*ic spectrum*, das Farbenspektrum. **–ics,** *pl.* die Farbenlehre. **–ogene** ['kroumətodʒɪ:n], *adj.* farbenerzeugend (*Chem.*). **–ophore,** *s.* der Farbenträger (*Biol.*).

chrom–e [kroum], 1. *s.* das Chrom; Chromgelb. 2. *v.a.* chromieren, verchromen. **–e steel,** der Chromstahl. **–e-yellow,** *s.* das Chromgelb, Bleichromat. **–ic,** *adj.* chromhaltig, Chrom–; –*ic acid*, die Chromsäure; –*ic salt*, das Chromoxydsalz. **–ium** ['kroumɪəm], 1. *s.* das Chrom. 2. *adj.* Chrom–; –*ium-plated*, verchromt. **–olithograph** [kromo'lɪθəgræf], *s.* (*product*), **–olithography** [–lɪ'θəgrəfɪ], *s.* (*process*) die Chromolithographie, lithographischer Farb(en)druck, der Farbensteindruck **–osome** ['kroumosoum], *s.* das Chromosom, der Farbkörper (*Biol.*). **–otype** ['kroumotaɪp], *s.* (*product*), **–otypy,** *s.* (*process*) der Farbendruck, Buntdruck.

chronic ['krɔnɪk], *adj.* chronisch, andauernd, beständig; schleichend; (*coll.*) schlecht.

chronicle ['krɔnɪkl], 1. *s.* die Chronik; das Jahrbuch; (*coll.*) der Bericht, die Erzählung. 2. *v.a.* aufzeichnen, verzeichnen. **–r,** *s.* der Chronikenschreiber, Chronist. **–s,** *pl.* (*B.*) Bücher der Chronika.

chronogr–am ['krɔnəgræm], *s.* das Chronogramm. **–aph,** *s.* der Chronograph.

chronolog–ical [krɔnə'lɔdʒɪkl], *adj.* chronologisch, zeitlich geordnet; *in –ical order*, in der Zeitfolge, der Zeitfolge nach. **–ist,** *s.* der Chronolog(e), Zeit(rechnungs)forscher. **–y** [krə'nɔlədʒɪ], *s.* die Chronologie, Zeitbestimmung, Zeitrechnung, Zeitfolge, chronologische Anordnung.

chronomet–er [krə'nɔmɪtə], *s.* das Chronometer, der Zeitmesser. **–ry,** *s.* die Chronometrie, Zeitmessung.

chrysalis ['krɪsəlɪs], *s.* die Larve, Puppe (*Ent.*).

chrysanthemum [krɪ'sænθəməm], *s.* die Goldblume, das Chrysanthemum.

chryso–lite ['krɪsolaɪt], *s.* der Chrysolith. **–prase** [–preɪz], *s.* der Chrysopras.

chub [tʃʌb], *s.* der Döbel (*Ichth.*). **–by (–by-faced),** *adj.* pausbackig, pausbäckig, rundwangig; plump.

[1]**chuck** [tʃʌk], 1. *v.n.* glucken, schnalzen. 2. *s.* das Glucken; (*coll.*) Schätzchen.

[2]**chuck,** 1. *v.a.* sanft schlagen (*under the chin*); (*coll.*) werfen, schmeißen; (*sl.*) – *it*, aufgeben, nachlassen, sausen lassen; (*sl.*) – (*up*) *a job*, einen Posten aufgeben; (*coll.*) – *out*, an die Luft setzen, hinauswerfen. 2. *s.* sanfter Schlag *or* Stoß; das Bohrfutter, Aufspannfutter, der Spannkopf, Abdrehnagel (*Mach.*); (*sl.*) die Entlassung; *give s.o. the* –, mit einem brechen.

chuckle ['tʃʌkl], *v.n.* kichern, in sich hineinlachen. **–head,** *s.* der Dummkopf.

chug [tʃʌg], *v.n.* (*coll.*) schuckeln, puckern, knattern.

chum [tʃʌm], 1. *s.* (*coll.*) der Kamerad, Genosse, Busenfreund, Stubengenosse. 2. *v.n.*; (*coll.*) – *up with*, sich eng befreunden mit, dicke Freundschaft schließen mit. **–my,** *adj.* intim; eng befreundet.

chump [tʃʌmp], *s.* dickes Ende, der Klotz; die Fleischkeule (*Butch*); (*coll.*) der Dickkopf, Dummkopf; (*sl.*) *off one's* –, verdreht.

chunk [tʃʌŋk], *s.* (*coll.*) dickes Stück, der Klumpen.

church [tʃə:tʃ], 1 *s.* die Kirche; Geistlichkeit; christliche Gemeinschaft; (*without article*) der Gottesdienst; *at* –, in der Kirche; – *of England*, anglikanische Kirche; *enter the* –, see *go into the* –; *established* –, die Staatskirche; *go to* –, zur Kirche gehen; *go into the* –, Geistlicher werden; – *is over*, die Kirche ist aus. 2. *v.a.* Dankgottesdienst nach einer Geburt abhalten; *be* –*ed*, zum ersten Male wieder in die Kirche gehen (*after childbirth*). **– -burial,** *s.* kirchliches Begräbnis. **– -goer,** *s.* der Kirchgänger. **–ing,** *s.* der Kirchgang einer Wöchnerin. **– -lands,** *pl.* das Kirchengut. **–man,** *s.* der Anhänger der anglikanischen Kirche. **– -mouse,** *s.*; *poor as a* – *-mouse*, arm wie eine Kirchenmaus. **– preferment,** *s.* die Pfründe. **– -rate,** *s.* die Kirchensteuer. **– school,** *s.* von der Staatskirche geleitete Volksschule. **– -service,** *s.* der Gottesdienst. **–warden,** *s.* der Kirchenvorsteher; lange Tonpfeife. **–y,** *adj.* (*coll.*) kirchlich (gesinnt). **–yard,** *s.* der Kirchhof; –*yard cough*, (*coll.*) böser Husten.

churl [tʃə·l], *s.* der Flegel, Fitz, Flaps, Grobian; Bauer; verdrießlicher Mensch, der Knicker. **–ish,** *adj.* bäurisch; grob; karg, geizig, filzig, knauserig; mürrisch.

churn [tʃə:n], 1. *s.* das Butterfaß; die Buttermaschine. 2. *v.a.* aufwühlen, kneten. 3. *v.n.* buttern; aufwallen, schäumen. **–ing,** *s.* das Buttern; Aufwallen, heftige Bewegung. **– -staff,** *s.* der Butterstößel, Butterstempel.

chute [ʃu:t], *s.* die Rutsche, Schüttelrinne, abschüssige Bahn, Flußschnelle; (*Amer.*) Gleitbahn; *abbr. for* **parachute,** *q.v*

chutney ['tʃʌtnɪ], *s.* die Würztunke.

chyle [kaɪl], *s.* der Milchsaft, Speisesaft.

chyme [kaɪm], *s.* der Chymus, Spiesebrei.

ciborium [sɪ'bɔ:rɪəm], *s.* das Hostiengefäß, die Monstranz; der Altarüberhang (*Arch.*).

cicada [sɪ'keɪdə], *s.* die Zikade, Grille, Zirpe.

cicatri–ce ['sɪkətrɪs], *s.* die Narbe. **–zation** [–traɪ'zeɪʃən], *s.* die Vernarbung. **–ze** [–traɪz], *v.a. & n.* vernarben.

cicely ['sɪsəlɪ], *s.* die Myrrhe (*Bot.*).

cicerone [tʃɪtʃə'rounɪ], *s.* (*pl.* –ni [–nɪ:]) der Cicerone, Fremdenführer.

cider ['saɪdə], *s.* der Apfelmost. **– -press,** *s.* die Apfelpresse.

cigar [sɪ'gɑ:], *s.* die Zigarre. **– -box,** *s.* die Zigarrenkiste. **– -case,** *s.* das Zigarrenetui. **– -cutter,** *s.* der Zigarrenabschneider. **–ette** [sɪgə'rɛt]; *s.* die Zigarette; –*ette end*, die Kippe; –*ette lighter*, das Feuerzeug. **– -end,** *s.* der Zigarrenstummel **-holder,** *s.* die Zigarrenspitze.

cilia ['sɪlɪə], *pl.* die (Augen)Wimpern; Flimmerhärchen (*Bot.*, *Zool.*). **–ry,** *adj.* Wimper–; –*ry processes*, Ziliarfortsätze. **–te** ['sɪlɪɪt], *adj.* bewimpert.

cinch [sɪntʃ], *s.* der Sattelgurt (*Harn*); (*sl.*) *a* (*dead*) –, todsichere Sache, die Spielerei, Kleinigkeit.

cinchona [sɪŋ'kounə], *s.* die Chinarinde.

cincture ['sɪŋktʃə], 1. *s.* der Gürtel, Kranz (*Arch.*). 2. *v.a.* umgürten.

cinder ['sɪndə], *s.* ausgeglühte Kohle, die Asche; Schlacke (*Metall.*); *live* –, glühende Kohle; *burnt to a* –, zu Kohle verbrannt, verkohlt. **– path, – track,** *s.* die Aschenbahn. **Cinderella** [–'rɛlə], *s.* Aschenbrödel, *n.*

cine– -camera ['sɪnɪ–], *s.* die Filmkamera. **– -film,** *s.* der Kinofilm. **– -projector,** *s.* der Vorführapparat. **–ma** ['sɪnɪmə], *s.* das Kino, Lichtspieltheater; der Film. **–matograph** [sɪnɪ'mætəgræf], *s.* der Kinematograph. **–matographer,** *s.* der Kameramann. **–matographic** [–'græfɪk], *adj.* kinematographisch.

cineraria [sɪnə'rɛərɪə], *s.* das Aschenkraut (*Bot.*).

cinerary ['sɪnərərɪ], *adj.*; – *urn*, die Totenurne, Aschenurne.

cinnabar ['sɪnəbɑ:], *s.* der Zinnober.

cinnamon ['sɪnəmən], *s* der Zimt, Kaneel.

cinque [sɪŋk], *s.* die Fünf (*Dice, Cards*). **–cento** [tʃɪŋkwə'tʃɛntou], *s.* italienische Kunst des 16.

Jahrhunderts. **-foil** [sɪŋkfɔɪl], *s.* das Fünffingerkraut (*Bot.*); Fünfblatt (*Arch.*).

cipher [ˈsɑɪfə], 1. *s.* die Ziffer, Nummer; Null, das Nichts; Monogramm, der Namenszug, Schriftzug; die Chiffre, Geheimschrift; der Schlüssel; *be a mere* –, eine Null sein. 2. *v.n.* rechnen. 3. *v.a.* ausrechnen; chiffrieren.

circle [ˈsə:kl], 1. *s.* der Kreis; Umkreis, Umfang; Bekanntenkreis; die Periode, der Zyklus; Zirkel (*Log.*); Rang (*Theat.*); Ring, Reif; (*a*) (*with adjectives*) *antarctic* –, südlicher Polarkreis; *arctic* –, nördlicher Polarkreis; *dress* –, erster Rang (*Theat.*); *full* –, (*used as adv.*) rund herum, die Reihe herum; *inner* –, die Ringbahn; *upper* –, zweiter Rang (*Theat.*); *vicious* –, der Zirkelschluß. (*b*) (*with verbs*) *argue in a* –, einen Zirkelschluß machen; *describe a* –, einen Kreis beschreiben; *square the* –, den Kreis quadrieren, (*fig.*) Unmögliches leisten. 2. *v.a.* umgehen; umgeben, umkreisen, einschließen. 3. *v.n.* sich im Kreise bewegen, kreisen. **-t** [–klɪt], *s.* kleiner Ring, das Ringlein, der Reif.

circuit [ˈsə:kɪt], 1. *s.* die Kreisbewegung, Umdrehung; der Kreislauf, Umlauf; Umkreis, Umfang; Umweg, die Runde, der Bogen; Gerichtsbezirk, die Rundreise (*of judges, etc.*) (*Law*); der Stromkreis, die Leitung, Schaltung (*Elec.*); *make a* –, einen Umgang machen; *make a* – *of*, herumgehen um; *go on* –, die Assisen abhalten; *within a* – *of 10 miles*, im Umkreise von 10 Meilen; *cinema* –, der Kinoring; *grid* –, der Gitterkreis (*Rad.*); *rejector* –, der Sperrkreis (*Rad.*); *short* –, der Kurzschluß. 2. *v.a.* bereisen, umkreisen. **--breaker,** *s.* der Stromunterbrecher, Trennschalter, Ausschalter. **- diagram,** *s.* das Schaltbild, die Stromlaufskizze. **-ous** [sə:ˈkju:ɪtəs], *adj.* weitläufig, weitschweifig; *-ous route*, der Umweg.

circular [ˈsə:kjulə], 1. *adj.* kreisförmig, rund, Kreis–; – *letter*, das Rundschreiben, der Laufzettel; – *motion*, die Kreisbewegung; – *numbers*, Zirkularzahlen; – *railway*, die Ringbahn; – *saw*, die Kreissäge; – *section*, kreisrunder Querschnitt (*Geom.*); – *style*, der Rundbogenstil; – *ticket*, das Rundreisebillet; – *tour*, die Rundfahrt, Rundreise; – *velocity*, die Umdrehungsgeschwindigkeit. 2. *s.* das Rundschreiben, Zirkular; *Court* –, die Hofnachrichten. **-ize,** *v.a.* durch Rundschreiben benachrichtigen.

circulat-e [ˈsə:kjuleɪt], 1. *v.n.* umlaufen, zirkulieren, im Umlauf sein (*C.L.*); sich im Kreise bewegen; (*sl.*) verkehren. 2. *v.a.* in Umlauf setzen, verbreiten (*rumour, etc.*); girieren (*bills*) (*C.L.*). **-ing,** *adj.* umlaufend; im Umlauf, kursierend; *-ing decimal*, periodischer Dezimalbruch; *-ing library*, die Leihbibliothek; *-ing medium*, das Zahlungsmittel, Tauschmittel, Unlaufsmittel. **-ion** [–ˈleɪʃən], *s.* der Kreislauf (*of blood, etc.*), Umlauf (*of money, etc.*); die Verbreitung (*of a report*); Auflage (*of a paper*); das im Umlauf befindliche Geld; *-ion of air*, die Ventilation, der Durchzug; die Bewetterung (*in mines*); *bank of -ion*, die Girobank; *-ion of bills*, der Wechselverkehr; *in -ion*, im Umlauf; *out of -ion*, außer Kurs.

circum-ambient [sə:kəmˈæmbɪənt], *adj.* umgebend, einschließend. **-ambulate,** 1. *v.n.* herumgehen, (*fig.*) auf den Busch klopfen. 2. *v.a.* herumgehen um. **-cise** [ˈsə:kəmsɑɪz], *v.a.* beschneiden. **-cision** [–ˈsɪʒn], *s.* die Beschneidung **-ference** [sə:ˈkʌmfərəns], *s.* der Umkreis, die Peripherie. **-ferential** [–fəˈrɛnʃəl], *adj.* Umkreis–. **-flex** [ˈsə:kəmflɛks], 1. *s.* der Zirkumflex. 2. *adj.* gebogen, gekrümmt. **-gyrate** [sə:kəmˈdʒɑɪreɪt], *v.n.* sich um die Achse drehen; kreisen. **-jacent** [–ˈdʒeɪsənt] *adj.* umliegend, umgebend. **-locution** [–loˈkju:ʃən], *s.* die Umschreibung; der Umschweif, die Weitschweifigkeit. **-locutory** [–ˈlɔkjutərɪ], umschreibend, weitschweifig. **-navigable** [–ˈnævɪgəbl], *adj.* umschiffbar. **-navigate** [–ˈnævɪgeɪt], *v.a.* umschiffen, umfahren, umsegeln. **-navigation** [–ˈgeɪʃən], *s.* die Umschiffung, Umseglung. **-navigator,** *s.* die Umsegler. **-scribe** [ˈsə:kəmskrɑɪb], *v.a.* umschreiben; begrenzen, einschränken; definieren. **-scription** [–ˈskrɪpʃən], *s.* die Umschreibung, Begrenzung, Beschränkung; Umschrift (*on coins, etc.*). **-spect** [ˈsə:kəmspɛkt], *adj.* umsichtig, vorsichtig. **-spection** [–ˈspɛkʃən], *s.* die Umsicht, Vorsicht, Behutsamkeit. **-stance** [ˈsə:kəmstəns], *s.* der Umstand; Fall, die Einzelheit, Tatsache, das Ereignis; *pl.* nähere Umstände, Verhältnisse, die Sachlage, der Sachverhalt, die Lage, das Nähere; *extenuating -stances*, mildernde Umstände, der Strafmilderungsgrund; *easy -stances*, gute Umstände; *straitened -stances*, beschränkte Umstände; *-stances demand it*, die Verhältnisse bringen es so mit sich; *that depends on the -stances*, das hängt von den Umständen ab; *-stances alter cases*, neue Umstände ergeben neue Verhältnisse; *pomp and -stance*, Pomp und Staat; *in these -stances*, unter diesen Umständen; *on* or *under the -stances*, unter den obwaltenden Umständen; *under no -stances*, unter keinen Umständen, auf keinen Fall. **-stanced,** *adj.* in einer Lage befindlich, in eine Lage versetzt; *-stanced as I was*, in meiner Lage; **-stantial** [–ˈstænʃəl], *adj.* umständlich, eingehend; zufällig; *-stantial evidence*, der Indizienbeweis. **-stantiality** [–stæʃɪˈælɪtɪ], *s.* die Umständlichkeit. **-vallation** [–væˈleɪʃən], *s.* die Umwallung. **-vent** [–ˈvɛnt], *v.a.* überlisten, übervorteilen, hintergehen (*a p.*); verhindern, vereiteln, hintertreiben (*a th.*). **-vention,** *s.* die Überlistung, Vereitelung. **-volution** [–voˈlu:ʃən], *s.* die Umdrehung, Umwälzung; Windung, Säulenschnecke (*Arch.*).

circus [ˈsə:kəs], *s.* der Zirkus; die Arena, der Platz; große Wegkreuzung.

cirrhosis [sɪˈrousɪs], *s.* die Zirrhose.

cirrhus [ˈsɪrəs], *s.* die Ranke (*Bot.*); der Rankenfuß (*Zool.*); die Federwolke (*Meteor.*).

cirro-cumulous [ˈsɪrouˈkju:mələs], *s.* die Schäfchenwolke. **cirro-stratus** [–strɑ:təs], *s.* die Schleierwolke.

cirrous, *adj.* rankig, rankenförmig (*Bot., Zool.*).

cisalpine [sɪsˈælpɑɪn], *adj.* zisalpinisch, diesseits der Alpen gelegen.

cissy [ˈsɪsɪ], 1. *s.* (*sl.*) der Weichling. 2. *adj.* (*sl.*) weichlich, weibisch.

cist [sɪst], *s.* das Steingrab; die Kiste, das Kästchen.

cistern [ˈsɪstən], *s.* die Zisterne; der Wasserbehälter, Tank, Bottich, das Reservoir, Bassin.

cistus [ˈsɪstəs], *s.* die Zistrose (*Bot.*).

citable [ˈsɑɪtəbl], *adj.* anführbar, zitierbar.

citadel [ˈsɪtədəl], *s.* die Burg; Zitadelle.

citat-ion [sɪˈteɪʃən], *s.* die Vorladung (*Law*); Anführung, das Zitieren; Zitat; ehrende Erwähnung, die Belobigung. **-ory** [ˈsɪtətərɪ], *adj.* vorladend, Ladungs– (*Law*); *letters -ory*, schriftliche Vorladung.

cite [sɑɪt], *v.a.* vorladen (*Law*); anführen, zitieren.

cither(n) [ˈsɪθə(n)], *s.* (*Poet.*) die Zither, Laute.

citizen [ˈsɪtɪzən], *s.* der Bürger, Staatsbürger; Einwohner, Bewohner; Städter; *fellow–*–, der Mitbürger; – *of the world*, der Weltbürger. **-ship,** *s.* das Bürgerrecht; die Staatsangehörigkeit; Bürgerkunde.

citr-ate [ˈsɪtrɪt], *s.* das Zitrat, zitronensaures Salz. *-ate of iron*, zitronensaures Eisenoxyd. **-ic,** *adj.*; *-ic acid*, die Zitronensäure. **-on,** *s.* die Zitrone.

city [ˈsɪtɪ], 1. *s.* die Stadt, Großstadt; Altstadt, das Geschäftszentrum, die City. 2. *adj.* städtisch, Stadt–; – *article*, der Börsenbericht, Handelsbericht; – *authorities*, die Stadtbehörden; – *editor*, der Schriftleiter des Handelsteils; – *hall*, das Rathaus; – *man*, der Geschäftsmann, Finanzmann; – *news*, Handelsnachrichten; (*sl.*) – *slicker*, der Stadtbewohner; *freedom of the* –, das (Ehren-) Bürgerrecht der Stadt; – *of Berlin*, die Stadt Berlin.

civet(-cat) [ˈsɪvɪtkæt], *s.* die Zibetkatze.

civic [ˈsɪvɪk], *adj.* bürgerlich, Bürger–; städtisch, Stadt–; – *reception*, der Empfang durch die Stadtverwaltung. **-s,** *s.* die Staatsbürgerkunde, Staatswissenschaft.

civil [ˈsɪvɪl], *adj.* bürgerlich, Bürger–, zivil(rechtlich); höflich; gesittet; – *affairs*, die Zivilverwaltung; – *attitude*, anständige Haltung; – *authorities*, Zivilbehörden (*pl.*); – *aviation*, die Zivilluftfahrt; – *engineer*, der Zivilingenieur; – *law*, das Zivilrecht, bürgerliches Recht; – *list*, die Zivilliste; – *marriage*, standesamtliche Trauung; – *rights*, Bürgerrechte (*pl.*); – *servant*, Staatsbeamte(r), *m.*; – *service*, der Staatsdienst, Beamtendienst; – *suit*, die Zivilklage; *keep a – tongue in one's head*, hübsch höflich bleiben; – *war*, der Bürgerkrieg; – *year*, bürgerliches Jahr. **–ian** [sɪ'vɪljən], *s.* der Bürger, Bürgerliche(r), *m.*, der Zivilist, die Zivilperson; der Staatsbeamte in Indien; *–ian population*, die Zivilbevölkerung, Zivilisten (*pl.*). **–ity** [sɪ'vɪlɪtɪ], *s.* die Artigkeit, Höflichkeit, Gefälligkeit. **–ization** [sɪvɪlɑɪ'zeɪʃən], *s.* die Zivilisation, Kultur, Gesittung. **–ize** ['sɪvɪlɑɪz], *v.a.* zivilisieren, gesittet machen, verfeinern; *–ized nations*, die Kulturvölker. **–izer**, *s.* der Zivilisator, Kulturträger; das Bildungsmittel.

civvies ['sɪvɪz], *pl.* (*coll.*) das Zivil.

clachan ['klækən], *s.* (*Scots*) das Dorf.

clack [klæk], 1. *v.n.* klappern, rasseln; (*coll.*) plappern. 2. *s.* das Klappen, Rasseln; die Klapper; Ventilklappe; (*coll.*) das Plappern, Geplapper. **– -valve**, *s.* das Klappenventil.

clad [klæd], *see* **clothe**; bekleidet; (an)gekleidet.

claim [kleɪm], 1. *v.a.* fordern, beanspruchen, Anspruch machen (auf (*Acc.*)); für sich in Anspruch nehmen; behaupten; reklamieren; – *attention*, Aufmerksamkeit verdienen. 2. *s.* der Anspruch, die Beanspruchung, Forderung, das Recht; der Rechtstitel, das Anrecht (*to*, auf); die Reklamation (*insurance*); Mutung, der Grubenanteil (*Min.*); Kux; *– for compensation*, der Ersatzanspruch; *enter a – for*, Anspruch erheben auf; *give up all – to*, Verzicht leisten auf; *have a – on*, Anspruch haben auf; *lay – to s.th.*, etwas in Anspruch nehmen, Anspruch machen auf eine S.; *place a –*, Schadenersatz beanspruchen; *substantiate a –*, den Rechtsanspruch nachweisen; *put in a – for*, see *enter* . . . . **–able**, *adj.* in Anspruch zu nehmen(d), zu beanspruchen(d). **–ant**, *s.* Beanspruchende(r), *m.*, der Anspruchmacher, Bewerber, Anspruchsberechtigte(r), *m.* (*coll.*) **– jumper**, *s.* einer der den Anteil eines anderen wegnimmt.

clairvoyan–ce [klɛər'vɔɪəns], *s.* das Hellsehen. **–t**, 1. *s.* der Hellseher. 2. *adj.* hellsehend.

clam [klæm], *s.* eßbare Muschel.

clamant ['kleɪmənt], *adj.* lärmend, schreiend.

clamber ['klæmbə], 1. *v.n.* (– *up*) klettern, klimmen. 2. *v.a.*; – *up*, erklettern, erklimmen.

clamm–iness ['klæmɪnɪs], *s.* die Klebrigkeit, Zähigkeit. **–y**, *adj.* feuchtkalt; klebrig, zäh.

clam–orous ['klæmərəs], *adj.* laut, lärmend; ungestüm. **–our** ['klæmə], 1. *s.* das Geschrei, der Lärm, Tumult; laute Klage. 2. *v.n.* schreien (*for*, nach (*Dat.*)); *–our against*, Klage erheben gegen.

[1]**clamp** [klæmp], 1. *s.* die Klampe, Klammer, Krampe, Klemmschraube, Zwinge; Schelle, Einschubleiste (*of a door, etc.*). 2. *v.a.* festklemmen, verklammern, befestigen; *screw–-*, die Schraubzwinge (*Carp.*). **–ing-screw**, *s.* die Klemmschraube (*Mech.*).

[2]**clamp**, 1. *s.* der Haufen, die Miete (*of potatoes, etc.*). 2. *v.a.* aufhäufen, einmieten (*potatoes, etc.*).

clan [klæn], *s.* (*Scots*) der Stamm, Clan; (*coll.*) die Sippe, Familie; Sippschaft, Clique; – *spirit*, das Stammesbewußtsein. **–nish**, *adj.* Stammes–, stammesverbunden; (*fig. coll.*) fest zusammenhaltend. **–nishness**, *s.* das Stammesgefühl; (*fig.*) die Zusammengehörigkeit. **–ship**, *s.* die Stammverbindung, Stammesverbundenheit. **–sman**, *s.* der Stammesgenosse, Stammverwandte(r), *m.*, Angehörige(r) eines Clans.

clandestine [klæn'dɛstɪn], *adj.* heimlich, verstohlen; – *trade*, der Schleichhandel. **–ly**, *adv.* insgeheim.

clang [klæŋ], 1. *s.* der Klang, Schall, das Geklirr. 2. *v.a.* schallen *or* klirren lassen. 3. *v.n.* schallen, klirren; erklingen, ertönen, erschallen. **–orous** [–ərəs], *adj.* schallend, tönend, klingend; schrill, gellend. **–our** [–ə], *s.* der Schall, Klang, das Geschmetter.

clank [klæŋk], 1. *s.* das Gerassel, Geklirr, Klirren. 2. *v.a.* rasseln mit, klirren lassen. 3. *v.n.* rasseln, klirren.

clannish ['klænɪʃ], **clanship**, *see* **clan.**

clap [klæp], 1. *v.n.* in die Hände klatschen, Beifall klatschen. 2. *v.a.* beklatschen, applaudieren; Beifall klatschen (*Dat.*); klopfen, schlagen; (*a*) (*with nouns*) – *one's eyes on*, (*coll.*) bemerken, zu sehen bekommen; – *one's hands*, in die Hände klatschen, Beifall klatschen; – *one's hat on one's head*, den Hut auf den Kopf stülpen; – *a pistol to a p.'s breast*, einem eine Pistole auf die Brust setzen; – *spurs to a horse*, einem Pferde die Sporen geben; (*b*) (*with prepositions*) (*coll.*) – *into prison*, (ohne weiteres) einstecken; – *a p. on the back*, einem auf den Rücken klopfen *or* schlagen; – *to*, zuschlagen, zuwerfen. 3. *s.* der Knall; (*vulg.*) Tripper (*Med.*); das Beifallklatschen; – *of thunder*, der Donnerschlag. **–board**, *s.* die Schindel; Faßhaube. **– -net**, *s.* das Schlagnetz. **–per**, *s.* die Klapper; der Klöppel (*of a bell*); Beifallsklatscher; (*sl.*) die Zunge. **– -trap**, 1. *s.* (*coll.*) die Effekthascherei, der Theaterkniff, Klimbim, das Geschwätz, Blech, die Windbeutelei, Phrasendrescherei. 2. *adj.* effekthaschend, trügerisch, täuschend.

claque [klæk], *s.* die Claque, Claqueure (*pl.*).

clarendon ['klærəndən], *s.* der Fettdruck (*Typ.*).

claret ['klærət], *s.* der Rotwein; das Weinrot; (*sl.*) Blut; – *cup*, die Rotweinbowle; *mulled –*, der Glühwein.

clarif–ication [klærɪfɪ'keɪʃən], *s.* die (Ab)Klärung, Aufhellung, Läuterung. **–ier** ['klærɪfɑɪə], *s.* das Klärmittel; die Klärpfanne, Läuterpfanne. **–y** ['klærɪfɑɪ], *v.a.* (ab)klären, läutern (*fluids*); abschleifen, ausseimen (*sugar*); reinigen (*air*); (*fig.*) aufklären, klarmachen.

clarion ['klærɪən], 1. *s.* (*poet.*) die Zinke, Trompete; das Trompetengeschmetter. 2. *adj.* (*Poet.*) laut, schmetternd.

clari(o)net [klærɪ(ə)'net], *s.* die Klarinette.

clarity ['klærɪtɪ], *s.* die Klarheit, Reinheit.

clary ['klɛərɪ], *s.* das Schlarlachkraut (*Bot.*).

clash [klæʃ], 1. *v.n.* klirren, rasseln, schmettern; zusammenstoßen, kollidieren; widersprechen, in Widerspruch stehen, einander widerstreiten, unvereinbar sein, verstoßen gegen, zuwiderlaufen; nicht harmonieren, sich nicht vertragen, nicht zusammenpassen (*of colours, etc.*). 2. *v.a.* klirren lassen, aneinanderstoßen, zusammenschlagen. 3. *s.* der Stoß, Zusammenprall, das Geklirr, Gerassel, Geschmetter, Getöse; (*fig.*) der Widerstreit, Widerspruch; – *of arms*, bewaffneter Zusammenstoß; – *of opinions*, die Meinungsverschiedenheit.

clasp [klɑ:sp], 1. *v.a.* zuhaken, einhaken, anhaken. festschnallen; ergreifen, umklammern, umarmen, umfangen, umranken (*as tendrils*); umfassen (*the knees, etc.*); – *hands*, sich die Hände reichen; – *one's hands* (*together*), die Hände falten; – *in one's arms*, umarmen; – *to one's bosom*, ans Herz drücken. 2. *s.* der Haken, die Klammer; Schnalle (*of a belt*); (Ordens)Spange (*Mil.*); Umarmung, der Händedruck; die Schließe (*of a book*); das Schließeisen, der Riegelhaken (*of a lock*). **– -knife**, *s.* das Klappmesser. **– -nail**, *s.* der Schindelnagel, Hakennagel.

class [klɑ:s], 1. *s.* die Klasse, Gruppe, Gattung, Form, Sorte; Schulklasse; der Rang, Stand, die Gesellschaftsklasse; der Jahrgang (*of recruits*); *be in the same – with*, gleichwertig sein mit; *first-–*, erster Klasse; erstklassig, hervorragend; *first-– compartment*, das Abteil erster Klasse; *first-– performance*, hervorragende Leistung; *low –*, nicht vornehm; *middle –(es)*, der Mittelstand. 2. *v.a.* in Klassen ordnen, klassifizieren; – *with*, gleichstellen mit. **– -conscious**, *adj.* klassenbewußt. **– -hatred**, *s.* der Klassenhaß. **– -list**, *s.* die Prüfungsliste. **– -mate**, *s.* der Schüler vom selben Jahrgang, der Klassenkamerad. **– -war**, *s.* der Klassenkampf. **–y**, *adj.* (*coll.*) fein, vornehm, erstklassig.

classic ['klæsɪk], 1. *adj.*, **–al**, *adj.* klassisch, vollendet, mustergültig; erstklassig, ausgezeichnet; griechisch-römisch; *–al education*, humanistische Bildung; – *races*, die berühmten Pferderennen; *–al style*, klassischer Stil; *–al scholar*, der Altphilologe. 2. *s.* klassischer Schriftsteller, der Klassiker; griechisch-römischer Schriftsteller. **–ism** ['klæsɪsɪzm], *s.* der Klassizismus; die Klassik (*in German lit.*); klassische Bildung. **–ist**, *s.* klassischer Philologe. **–s**, *pl.* klassische Philologie; klassische (griechisch-römische) Literatur; die Klassiker, die klassischen Schriftsteller; klassische Werke der Literatur.

classif–iable ['klæsɪfɑɪəbl], *adj.* einteilbar, einzuordnen(d). **–ication** [klæsɪfɪˈkeɪʃən], *s.* die Klassifizierung, Einteilung (in Klassen), Anordnung. **–icatory,** *adj.* klassenbildend. **–y** [ˈklæsɪfaɪ], *v.a.* (in Klassen) einteilen, einordnen, gruppieren, klassifizieren.

clatter [ˈklætə], 1. *v.n.* klappern, klirren, rasseln; – *about*, umhertrappeln, umhertrampeln. 2. *v.a.* klirren *or* klappern lassen. 3. *s.* das Gerassel, Geklirr, Geklapper, Getrappel; Geplapper.

clause [klɔ:z], *s.* der Satzteil, das Satzglied; der Vorbehalt, die Klausel (*Law*); *principal* –, der Hauptsatz; *subordinate* –, der Nebensatz.

claustral [ˈklɔ:strəl], *adj.* klösterlich.

claustrophobia [klɔ:strəˈfoubɪə], *s.* die Angst vor geschlossenen Räumen.

clavicle [ˈklævɪkl], *s.* das Schlüsselbein (*Anat.*).

claw [klɔ:], 1. *s.* die Klaue, Kralle, der Fang; die Schere (*of crabs, etc.*); Klaue, der Haken (*Techn.*); – *of a hammer*, die Hammerklaue, gespaltene Finne; (*coll.*) *get one's –s into a p.*, einen zu fassen kriegen. 2. *v.a.* kratzen, zerkratzen; – *off*, vom Ufer abhalten (*Naut.*). **–ed,** *adj.* mit Klauen. **– -hammer,** *s.* der Splitthammer (*Carp.*). **– setting,** *s.* die Ajourfassung (*of a ring*).

clay [kleɪ], *s.* der Ton, Lehm, (*fig.*) die Erde, Staub und Asche; irdische Hülle (*Eccl.*); *china-–*, weißer Ton; *fire-–*, die Schamotte, feuerfester Ton; *potter's* –, der Töpferton; *red-–*, der Bolus. **–ey** [–ɪ:], *adj.* tonig, lehmig, lehmhaltig, Ton–, Lehm–. **– hut,** die Lehmhütte. **– -marl,** *s.* der Tonmergel. **– -pigeon,** *s.* die Tontaube. **– pipe,** die Tonpfeife. **– -pit,** *s.* die Lehmgrube.

claymore [ˈkleɪmɔ:], *s.* (*Scots Hist.*) schottisches Breitschwert.

clean [klɪ:n], 1. *adj* rein; reinlich, sauber, stubenrein (*as animals*); einwandfrei (*as food*); fehlerfrei, schuldlos; leer, unbeschrieben (*paper*); geschickt, tadellos, gut ausgeführt (*as actions*); – *bill of health*, reiner Gesundheitspaß; (*sl.*) *come* –, mit der Sprache herausrücken; *make a – breast of it*, alles frei heraussagen, reinen Wein einschenken; *make a – sweep of*, aufräumen mit, reinen Tisch machen mit. 2. *adv.* (*coll.*) gänzlich, völlig, ganz und gar, absolut, direkt; *cut it – off*, es glatt abschneiden; – *gone*, spurlos verschwunden; *leap – over*, direkt 'rüber springen. 3. *v.a.* reinigen, säubern, reinmachen, putzen; waschen, abschwemmen; – *a gun*, ein Gewehr putzen; – *out*, reinigen, reinmachen; aufräumen, leeren; (*sl*) schröpfen (*a p.*); – *up*, gründlich reinigen, in Ordnung bringen, (*sl.*) einheimsen. **– -cut,** *adj.* scharf abgeschnitten, klar. **–ers,** *pl.* die Reinigungsanstalt; Scheuerfrauen (*pl*). **– -handed,** *adj.* mit reinen Händen; unbestochen, sauber. **–ing,** *s.* die Reinigung; *dry –ing*, chemische Reinigung; *spring-–ing*, großes Reinemachen. **– -limbed,** *adj.* ebenmäßig gebaut. **–liness** [ˈklɛnlɪnɪs], *s.* die Reinheit, Reinlichkeit, Sauberkeit. **–ly** [ˈklɛnlɪ], *adj.* reinlich, säuberlich; nett; geschickt, gewandt. **–ness,** *s.* die Sauberkeit, Reinheit. **– -out,** *s.* (*coll.*) das Reinemachen. **–se** [klɛnz], *v a.* reinigen, befreien; abscheuern, ausputzen (*vessels, etc.*); (ab)beizen (*Metall.*). **–ser,** *s.* das Reinigungsmittel. **– -shaven,** *adj.* glattrasiert **– -up,** *s.* (*coll.*) gründliche Reinigung; die Auswäsche (*Mil.*).

clear [klɪə], 1. *adj* klar, hell, durchsichtig; rein, deutlich, kenntlich, verständlich, übersichtlich; heiter (*of the sky*); scharfsichtig; unbefangen, offen, unbehindert; unschuldig, schuldlos, unbelastet (*of*, mit); ohne Abzug, netto, Rein– (*C.L.*); zuversichtlich, sicher (*Gen*); zweifellos, unleugbar; (*a*) (*with nouns*) *as – as a bell*, glockenrein; – *case*, zweifellose Sache; – *conscience*, reines *or* schuldloses Gewissen; *the – contrary*, genau *or* gerade das Gegenteil; – *day*, heiterer Tag; *four – days*, vier volle Tage; – *head*, klarer Kopf; – *judgment*, scharfsichtiges Urteil; – *profit*, der Reingewinn; – *sky*, heiterer Himmel; – *soup*, klare Kraftbrühe; – *style*, klare Schreibart; – *title*, unbestrittenes Recht; – *voice*, deutliche Stimme; – *water*, offenes Fahrwasser (*Naut.*); reines Wasser; – *weather*, heiteres Wetter; (*b*) (*with verbs*) *all –!* alles klar! fertig! Gefahr vorbei! *be – about*, klar sein über; *be – of debt*, frei von Schuld sein; *the coast is* –, nichts steht im Wege, die Luft ist rein; *it is as – as daylight*, es ist so klar wie die Sonne *or* sonnenklar. 2. *adv.* gänzlich, völlig, ganz under gar; *two weeks* –, zwei volle Wochen; *get – of*, loskommen von; *jump* –, abspringen; *keep – of*, abseits stehen, (*fig.*) sich fernhalten von, meiden; *leap – over*, frei springen über (*Acc.*); *make o.s.* –, sich verständlich machen; *stand* –, abseits stehen. 3. *s.* die Helle; lichte Weite (*Mach., Arch.*); *in the* –, im Lichten; der Klartext. 4. *v.a.* klären, erklären; aufklären; säubern, reinigen; lichten, abholzen, roden (*a wood*); befreien, frei machen, entlasten, reinwaschen (*from guilt*); lösen; aus dem Wege räumen, abräumen, abdecken, aufräumen; ausräumen; bezahlen, ausgleichen, ins Reine bringen, einlösen (*C.L.*); verzollen, klarieren (*at the customs*); hinwegspringen *or* –setzen, überspringen (*an obstacle*); – *accounts*, Rechnungen ausgleichen; – *the coast*, sich von der Küste abhalten (*Naut.*); – *o.s. of a debt*, sich einer Schuld entledigen; – *the decks*, klar machen (*Naut.*); – *a place of the enemy*, einen Ort vom Feinde säubern; – *an estate*, ein Gut entlasten; – *the ground*, ein Stück Land urbar machen; – *a hedge*, über eine Hecke hinüberspringen, eine Hecke nehmen; – *the letter-box*, den Briefkasten leeren; – *the line*, freie Fahrt geben (*Railw.*); – *an obstacle*, ein Hindernis überwinden; – *a port*, aus einem Hafen auslaufen; – *a profit*, einen Reingewinn machen, netto einnehmen, reinverdienen (*by*, an); – *a room*, ein Zimmer (aus– *or* auf)räumen; – *the ship*, die Ladung löschen; – *a ship for action*, ein Schiff klar zum Gefecht *or* gefechtsklar machen; – *the table*, abdecken; – *one's throat*, sich räuspern; – *the way!* Platz da! aus dem Wege! – *away*, wegräumen, abräumen; – *off*, wegbringen, fortschaffen; – *off a debt*, eine Schuld tilgen *or* abbezahlen; – *out*, ausräumen, ausleeren; *his stock was –ed out*, sein Lager wurde ausverkauft; – *up*, aufklären, aufhellen, lösen; aufräumen. 5. *v.n.* sich aufhellen, sich aufklären, sich aufheitern, hell *or* klar werden; klarkommen (*Naut.*); – *away*, abräumen; (*sl.*) – *off*, verduften; (*coll.*) – *out*, sich packen, sich davonmachen, sich aus dem Staube machen; – *up*, see **–. –age,** *s.* die Bodenfreiheit, der Bodenabstand (*of vehicles, etc. from the ground*). **–ance,** *s.* das Reinigen, Aufräumen; die Beseitigung, Abräumung, Räumung; Abrechnung, Verrechnung, Tilgung, volle Bezahlung (*C.L.*); die Lichtweite, der Zwischenraum, Spielraum (*Mech.*); die Lichtung, Abholzung (*of a wood*); Verzollung, Ausklarierung (*at the customs*), der Zollschein. **–ance-sale,** *s.* der (Räumungs-) Ausverkauf. **–ance-space,** *s.* das Toleranzfeld (*Mech*). **– -cut,** *adj.* scharfgeschnitten. **– -eyed,** *adj.* helläugig. **– -headed,** *adj* klardenkend, verständig, scharfsinnig, einsichtig, klar im Kopf. **–ing,** *s.* die Rechtfertigung; Lichtung, Reute, der Kahlschlag, die Ausholzung (*in a wood*); Abrechnung, Verrechnung, der Verrechnungsverkehr, Wertausgleich (*C.L.*); die Klarierung (*customs*). **–ing bank,** *s.* die Girobank. **–ing certificate,** *s.* der Zollabfertigungsschein. **–ing-house,** *s.* die (Londoner) Abrechnungsbörse. **–ing-office,** *s.* die Ausgleichstelle, Verrechnungsstelle. **–ing-station,** *s.* die Verwundetensammelstelle, das Durchgangslager (*Mil.*). **–ly,** *adv.* klar, offenbar. **–ness,** *s.* die Klarheit, Deutlichkeit (*Rad., Phone.*). **– -sighted,** *adj.* scharfsichtig; (*fig.*) scharfsinnig, einsichtig. **– -starch,** *v.a.* stärken, steifen: **– -toned,** *adj.* helltönig.

clear-cole [ˈklɪəkoul], *s.* der Leim(unter)grund.

cleat [klɪ:t], *s.* die Klampe (*Naut.*); Querleiste, das Kreuzholz (*Carp.*); der Keil; Schuhnagel.

cleav–able [ˈklɪ:vəbl], *adj.* spaltbar. **–age** [ˈklɪ:vɪdʒ], *s.* das Spalten; die Spaltung (*also fig.*), Abspaltung, Aufspaltung; (*fig.*) Trennung; Spaltbarkeit (*of crystals*). **–e** [klɪ:v], 1. *ir v.a.* spalten, aufspalten, zerspalten; *–e asunder*, entzweispalten; sich (*Dat.*) bahnen, hauen (*a way*); durchdringen (*the air*). 2. *ir.v.n.* sich spalten, aufspringen, bersten; (*archaic*) kleben, haften, hängenbleiben (*to*, an (*Acc.*)); (*fig.*) anhangen (*to* (*Dat.*)). **–er,** *s.* das Hackmesser. **–ers,** *pl.* das Klebkraut (*Bot.*)

cleek [klɪ:k], *s.* der Golfschläger.

clef [klɛf], *s.* der (Noten)Schlüssel (*Mus.*).

cleft [klɛft], 1. *see* **cleave.** 2. *s.* die Spalte, Ritze, Kluft, der Riß. 3. *adj.*; – *palate*, die Gaumenspalte; *in a – stick*, in der Klemme *or* Patsche.
cleg [klɛg], *s.* (*dial.*) die Pferdefliege, Bremse.
clem [klɛm], 1. *v.n.* (*dial.*) verschmachten. 2. *v.a.* (*dial.*) verschmachten lassen.
clematis [ˈklɛmətɪs], *s.* die Waldrebe (*Bot.*).
clemen–cy [ˈklɛmənsɪ], *s.* die Gnade, Begnadigung, Nachsicht, Milde, Schonung. **–t,** *adj.* gnädig, gütig, nachsichtig; sanft, mild.
clench [klɛntʃ], *v.a.* vernieten (*rivet*); festmachen (*rope*); zusammenpressen; – *one's fist*, die Faust ballen; – *one's teeth*, die Zähne aufeinanderbeißen.
clerestory [ˈklɪəstərɪ], *s.* der Lichtgaden (*Arch.*).
clergy [ˈklə:dʒɪ], *s.* die Geistlichkeit, Geistliche (*pl.*), der Klerus; *benefit of* –, das Vorrecht der Geistlichen vor dem Gericht. **–able,** *adj.* als Geistlicher berechtigt vor dem Gericht nicht zu erscheinen. **–man** [–mən], *s.* Geistliche(r), *m.* der Pfarrer, Pastor.
cleric [ˈklɛrɪk], *s.* Geistliche(r), *m.*, der Pfaffe **–al** [–l], *adj.* geistlich, klerikal; Schreib–; *–al error*, der Schreibfehler; *–al staff*, die Büroangestellten (*pl.*); *–al work*, die Schreibarbeit, Büroarbeit. **–alism,** *s.* der Klerikalismus, das Pfaffentum; die Pfaffenherrschaft; geistlicher Einfluß.
clerk [klɑ:k], *s.* der Schreiber, Schriftführer, Buchhalter; Kontorist, Handlungsgehilfe, kaufmännischer Angestellter, Sekretär, (*Amer.*) Verkäufer; (*archaic*) Geistliche(r), *m.*; Gelehrte(r), *m.*; (*a*) (*with nouns, adjectives, etc.*) *articled* –, junger Jurist der bei einem Rechtsanwalt in die Lehre gegeben ist; *bank-–*, Bankbeamte(r), *m.*, Bankangestellte(r), *m* , *chief* –, see *head* –; *confidential* –, der Geheimsekretär; *correspondence* –, der Korrespondent; *head* –, erster Buchhalter, der Bürovorsteher; *signing* –, der Prokurist; *town-–*, der Stadtsekretär; (*b*) (*with prepositions*) – *of the assizes*, der Gerichtsschreiber; – *of the House of Commons*, der Sekretär des Unterhauses, – *of the weather*, (*hum.*) Petrus, der Wettergott. **–ly,** *adj.* (*archaic*) gelehrt, Schreiber–. **–ship,** *s.* der Buchhalterposten, die Schreiberstelle, das Amt eines Sekretärs.
clever [ˈklɛvə], *adj.* klug, gescheit, begabt, intelligent; geschickt, gewandt; geistreich (*as an answer*); (*coll.*) – –, gerissen, übergescheit. **–ness,** *s.* die Klugheit; Geschicklichkeit, Gewandtheit; Begabung.
clew [klu:] 1. *s.* der Knäuel; *see* **clue**; das Schothorn (*Naut.*). 2 *v.a.* aufgeien (*Naut.*). **– -line,** *s.* das Geitau (*Naut.*).
cliché [ˈklɪ ʃe.], *s.* das Klischee (*Typ.*); (*fig.*) abgedroschene Redensart, der Gemeinplatz.
click [klɪk], 1. *s.* das Ticken, Knacken, Knipsen; Einschnappen; die Sperrklinke, der Sperrhaken; – *of the tongue*, das Schnalzen. 2. *v.n.* ticken, knacken, knipsen, zuschnappen (*as a lock*); (*sl.*) anbandeln; – *one's heels*, die Hacken zusammenschlagen; – *one's tongue*, schnalzen.
client [ˈklaɪənt], *s.* der Klient (*Law*); Kunde. **–age** [–ɪdʒ], *s.*, **–ele** [klaɪənˈtɪ:l, klɪ:ɑ̃:ˈtɛ:l], *s.* die Kundschaft; die Klientel.
cliff [klɪf], *s.* die Klippe, steiler Abhang.
climacteric [klaɪmækˈtɛrɪk], 1. *adj.* entscheidend, kritisch. 2 *s* Wechseljahre (*pl.*), kritisches Alter
climat–e [ˈklaɪmɪt], *s.* das Klima, der Himmelsstrich. **–ic** [–ˈmætɪk], *adj.* klimatisch, Klima–. **–ology** [–əˈtɔlədʒɪ], *s.* die Witterungskunde
climax [ˈklaɪmæks], 1. *s* die Steigerung; höchster Grad, der Gipfel; Höhepunkt. 2. *v.n.* gipfeln, sich steigern. 3. *v.a.* steigern, das Ende herbeiführen.
climb [klaɪm], 1 *v.a.* ersteigen, erklimmen, besteigen, hinaufklettern an, hinaufsteigen auf, umranken (*of plants*). 2. *v.n.* klettern, emporsteigen, steigen (*Av.*); (*fig.*) – *down*, klein beigeben, einen Rückzieher machen, nachgeben. *– -down*, *s.* die Abstandnahme; das Aufgeben, Nachgeben. 3. *s.* der Aufstieg; Steilflug (*Av.*); *rate of* –, die Steigleistung (*Av.*). **–able,** *adj.* ersteigbar **–er,** *s.* der Kletterer, Bergsteiger; die Kletterpflanze, Schlingpflanze; (*fig.*) der Streber. **–ing,** *s.* das Bergsteigen, Klettern. **–ing-irons,** *pl* die Steigeisen (*Mount.*). **–ing-rope,** *s.* das Kletterseil. **–ing turn,** *s.* gezogene Kurve (*Av.*).
clime [klaɪm], *s.* (*poet.*) der Himmelsstrich.
clinch [klɪntʃ], 1. *v.a.* nieten, festmachen; entscheiden, erledigen; – *an argument*, eine Auseinandersetzung entscheiden, zwingende Beweisgründe anführen; *this –ed matters*, das brachte die Sache zum Abschluß, das gab den Ausschlag, damit war die Sache entschieden. 2. *v.n.* sich umklammern (*Boxing*). 3. *s.* die Vernietung; Umklammerung (*Boxing*). **–er,** *s.* (*coll.*) treffender Beweis, das Ausschlaggebende.
cling [klɪŋ], *ir.v.n.* (sich) festhalten, sich klammern, sich heften (*to*, an (*Dat.*)); anhaften, anhangen, treu bleiben (*Dat.*) (*to a p.*); haften, festsetzen (an) (*of things*). **–ing,** *adj.* anhängend, anhänglich; eng anliegend (*as a dress*).
clinic [ˈklɪnɪk], *s.* die Klinik, Poliklinik; klinisches Praktikum. **–al,** *adj.* klinisch; *–al conversion*, die Bekehrung auf dem Sterbebett; *–al thermometer*, das Fieberthermometer. **–ian** [klɪˈnɪʃən], *s.* der Kliniker.
clink [klɪŋk], 1. *s.* das Geklirr; (*sl.*) Gefängnis, der Arrestraum, das Loch, Kittchen. 2. *v.n.* klirren. 3. *v.a.* klirren lassen, klimpern mit; – *glasses*, anstoßen. **–er** [ˈklɪŋkə], *s.* der Klinker, hartgebrannter Ziegelstein (*Build.*); die Schlacke; der Nietnagel (*Mount.*); (*sl.*) das Prachtexemplar. **–er-built,** *adj.* klinkerweise gebaut (*Naut.*). **–er-screen,** *s.* der Schlackensieb. **–ing,** *adj.* (*sl.*) famos.
clinometer [klaɪˈnɔmɪtə], *s.* der Winkel– *or* Neigungsmesser, das Klinometer (*Surv.*).
[1]**clip** [klɪp], 1. *v.a.* beschneiden, stutzen, scheren; kippen (*coin*); (durch)lochen (*tickets*); – *s.o.'s wings*, einem die Flügel beschneiden; – *one's words*, die Silben verschlucken. 2. *s.* die (Schaf)Schur, der Schnitt; (*coll.*) Schlag, (*sl.*) Klaps. **–per,** *s.* der Beschneider; Klipper, Schnellsegler (*Naut.*); (*sl.*) ein Prachtkerl. **–pers,** *pl.* die Schere, Haarschneidemaschine, Schneidzange. **–ping,** *s.* das Abschneiden, Scheren. **–pings,** *pl.* die Abfälle, Zeitungsausschnitte (*pl.*). **–ping-shears,** *pl.* die Pferdeschere, Schafschere.
[2]**clip,** 1. *v.a.* festhalten, befestigen. 2. *s.* die Klammer, Klemme; *paper* –, Büroklammer; *trouser* –, Hosenklammer (*Cycl.*); *cartridge* –, der Patronenrahmen, das Einsteckmagazin; *pipe* –, die Rohrschelle.
cliqu–e [klɪ:k], *s.* die Clique. **–ish, –y,** *adj.* (*coll.*) cliquenhaft.
clitoris [ˈklɪtərɪs], *s.* der Kitzler (*Anat.*).
cloaca [klouˈeɪkə], *s.* die Senkgrube, der Pfuhl; die Kloake (*Anat.*).
cloak [klouk], 1. *s.* der Mantel; (*fig.*) die Decke, der Deckmantel; die Bemäntelung, der Vorwand. 2. *v.a.* einhüllen; (*fig.*) verbergen, bemänteln, vertuschen. **– -room,** *s.* die Garderobe, Toilette; Gepäckaufgabe (*Railw.*).
cloche [klɔʃ], *s.* die Glasglocke (*for plants*).
[1]**clock** [klɔk], 1. *s.* die Uhr; der Fahrpreisanzeiger (*in taxis*); die Federkrone (*of dandelions*); *alarm-–*, die Weckuhr, der Wecker; *musical* –, die Spieluhr; *what o' – is it?* wieviel Uhr ist es? *four o'* –, vier Uhr. 2. *v.n.*; – *in*, den Arbeitsanfang an der Kontrolluhr stempeln; – *out*, das Arbeitsende stempeln. **– -face,** *s.* das Zifferblatt. **– -hand,** *s.* der (Uhr)Zeiger. **–maker,** *s.* der Uhrmacher. **– -movement,** *s.* **–work,** *s* das Uhrwerk; *like –work*, sehr regelmäßig, pünktlich; mechanisch, automatisch. **–wise,** *adv.* rechtsdrehend, rechtslaufend, in Uhrzeigerrichtung, im Uhrzeigersinne; *–wise rotation*, der Rechtslauf; *counter-–wise*, linksdrehend, linkslaufend, der Uhrzeigerrichtung *or* dem Uhrzeigersinne entgegen.
[2]**clock,** *s.* der Zwickel (*in stockings*). **–ed,** *adj.* mit Zwickel.
clod [klɔd], *s.* der Erdklumpen; die Scholle; (*fig.*) der Klotz, Tölpel. **– -crusher,** *s.* der Schollenbrecher; die Ackerwalze. (*coll.*) **–hopper,** *s.* der Bauernlümmel.
clog [klɔg], 1. *v.a.* hindern, hemmen, verstopfen; belasten, beschweren. 2. *v.n.* sich verstopfen. 3. *s.* der Holzklotz; Holzschuh; (*fig.*) die Bürde, Last, das Hindernis; die Verstopfung. **– -dance,** *s.* der Schuhplattler. **–gy,** *adj.* klumpig; hinderlich.

cloist–er ['klɔɪstə], 1 *s.* das Kloster; der Kreuzgang (*Arch.*). 2. *v.a.* ins Kloster stecken. **–ered,** *adj.* mit Kreuzgängen umgeben; (*fig.*) einsam, abgeschieden, zurückgezogen. **–ral,** *adj.* Kloster–; (*fig.*) abgeschlossen, zurückgezogen.

[1]**close** [klous], 1. *adj.* geschlossen (*also Phonet.*), zugeschlossen, eingeschlossen, abgeschlossen, verschlossen, zugemacht; zurückgezogen, dumpf, schwül, drückend (*of air*); verborgen, verschwiegen, zurückhaltend, in sich gekehrt, schweigsam; nahe, dicht, fest, eng; eng anschließend *or* anliegend, gedrängt, knapp, kurz, kompreß (*Typ.*); sparsam, karg, geizig, knickerig, filzig; genau (*resemblance*), getreu (*translation*), gespannt (*attention*); vertraut, innig, intim (*friend*); fast gleich, unentschieden (*contest*); – *argument*, lückenlose(r) Beweis(führung); – *attack*, der Nahangriff; – *box*, der Verschlag (*Naut.*); – *cell*, enge Zelle; – *combat*, der Nahkampf; – *confinement*, strenge Haft; *in* – *conversation*, in eifrigem Gespräche; (*coll.*) – *customer*, verschlossener Mensch; – *fight*, lange unentschiedener Kampf; – *fire*, die Feuerkonzentration (*Mil.*); – *fist*, karge Hand; – *formation*, geschlossene (Marsch– *or* Flug)Ordnung; – *friend*, vertrauter Freund; – *friendship*, innige Freundschaft; – *material*, dichtes Zeug; – *prisoner*, streng bewachter Gefangener; – *proximity*, unmittelbare Nähe; *at* – *quarters*, in nächster Nähe; *come to* – *quarters*, handgemein werden; – *range*, nächste Entfernung, die Kernschußweite; *– –range gun*, das Nahkampfgeschütz; – *scholarship*, bedingtes Stipendium; – *season*, die Schonzeit; (*fig.*) – *shave*, das Entkommen mit knapper Not, knappes Entrinnen; knappes Erreichen; – *study*, gründliches Studium; – *style*, bündiger *or* knapper Stil, (*coll.*) – *thing*, knappes Erreichen, knapper Sieg; – *translation*, genaue Übersetzung; – *weather*, drückendes *or* schwüles Wetter. 2 *adv.* nahe, dicht an, dicht bei; – *by*, dicht dabei *or* daneben; *come* –, nahe herankommen; *cut a th.* –, etwas kurz abschneiden; – *to the ground*, dicht am Boden; *be* – *at hand*, dicht bevorstehen; – *on a hundred*, nahe an 100; *follow – upon a p.*, einem auf den Fersen folgen, dicht hinter einem kommen; *keep* – (*to*), dicht anhalten (bei), dicht anschließen (an); *lie* –, dicht an *or* bei etwas sein; *live* –, knapp *or* sparsam leben; *sail – to the wind*, (dicht, hoch *or* hart) am Winde segeln; (*fig.*) Gefahr laufen, beinahe Anstoß geben; *sit* – (*together*), eng ansitzen; *sit – round the fire*, dicht ums Feuer sitzen; *stick – to a p.*, sich dicht an einen halten. 3. *s.* eingeschlossener Raum; das Gehege; die Umzäunung, Einfriedigung; das Klostergebiet, bischöflicher Machtbezirk, die Domfreiheit, der Domplatz, Hofraum; (*Scots*) Hauseingang. **– –cropped,** *adj.* kurz geschoren **– –fisted,** *adj.* geizig, karg, filzig, knauserig. **– –fitting,** *adj.* eng anschließend *or* anliegend. **– –grained,** *adj.* dichtfaserig. **– –hauled,** *adj.* dicht, hoch *or* hart am Winde (*Naut*). **–ly,** *adv.* fest, dicht; scharf, streng, genau; *–ly allied*, eng verbunden; *attend –ly*, scharf aufpassen; *–ly contested*, hart umstritten. **–ness,** die Verschlossenheit, Verschwiegenheit, Zurückhaltung; Dichtheit, Dichtigkeit, Festigkeit (*of cloth, etc.*); Dumpfheit, Schwüle (*of air*); Kargheit, Knauserigkeit, der Geiz; die Nähe (*as relationship*); Genauigkeit, Treue (*of a translation*); Schärfe (*as confinement*). **– –stool,** *s.* der Nachtstuhl. **– –tongued,** *adj.* verschwiegen, vor sichtig im Gespräch. **– –up,** 1 *s.* die Großaufnahme (*Films*). 2. *adj.*, *-up view*, die Nahansicht.

[2]**close** [klouz], 1 *v.a.* schließen, zuschließen, einschließen, abschließen, verschließen, zumachen, zutun; beschließen, beenden, endigen; (*a*) (*with nouns*) – *an account*, eine Rechnung abschließen; – *accounts with*, abrechnen mit; – *an affair*, einer Sache ein Ende machen, eine S. beendigen; – *a bargain*, ein Geschäft abmachen, einen Kauf abschließen; – *the books*, die Bücher schließen (*C.L.*); – *the current*, den Stromkreis schließen; – *the door on a p.*, die Tür hinter einem zumachen, (*fig.*) einen verstoßen; – *the door on a th.* (*fig.*) den Weg zu etwas abschneiden; – *one's eyes to a th.*, die Augen vor etwas verschließen, etwas absichtlich übersehen; – *one's mind to a th.*, sich einer S. verschließen; – *the ranks*, die Reihen schließen (*Mil.*); – *a sentence*, einen Satz beenden *or* schließen; – *the wind*, an den Wind kommen (*Naut.*); (*b*) (*with adverbs*) – *down*, schließen, einstellen, stillegen; zusperren; – *in*, einschließen; – *off*, abschließen; – *up*, (ver)schließen, zumachen; verbinden (*Typ.*). 2. *v.n.* (sich) schließen, geschlossen werden; sich zusammenschließen (um); zueilen (*of wounds*); aneinandergeraten, sich nähern; aufhören, endigen, abschließen; – *about a p.*, einen umschließen *or* umgeben; – *down*, schließen, stillgelegt werden; – *in*, herankommen, hereinbrechen; umkreisen, umzingeln, auf den Leib rücken (*upon* (*Dat.*)); – *up*, aufschließen, aufrücken, zusammenrücken; sich füllen, sich schließen; – *upon or – with the enemy*, mit dem Feinde handgemein werden, den Feind überfallen; – *with the land*, sich dem Lande nähern (*Naut.*); – *with an offer*, ein Angebot annehmen; *–ed circuit current*, der Ruhestrom (*Elec.*); *–ed shop*, der Gewerkschaftszwang. 3. *s.* der Schluß, Abschluß, das Ende; *bring to a* –, schließen, beendigen; *draw to a* –, sich dem Ende nähern; *at the – of the year*, am Jahresende; (*see* **closing, closure**). **–er,** *s.* der Beschließer, Schließer; Schlußstein (*Arch.*).

closet ['klɔzɪt], 1. *s.* das Kabinett, kleines Zimmer; (*Amer.*) der Wandschrank; (*water*) –, der Abort, Abtritt, das Klosett; – *play*, das Lesedrama. 2. *v.a.*; *be –ed with a p.*, mit einem eine vertrauliche Unterredung haben.

closing ['klouzɪŋ], 1 *adj.*; – *time*, die Polizeistunde (*for taverns, etc.*); der Geschäftsschluß, Feierabend; – *word*, das Schlußwort. 2. *s.* das Schließen; der Schluß, Abschluß, Verschluß (*Tech.*).

closure ['klouʒə], *s.* das Verschließen; der Verschluß, Schluß (der Debatte (*Pol.*)); *apply the* –, den Antrag auf Schluß der Debatte stellen.

clot [klɔt], 1. *s.* der Klumpen, das Klümpchen; Gerinnsel. 2. *v.n.* dick *or* klumpig werden, gerinnen, verdicken, koagulieren, Klümpchen bilden. **-ted** [–tɪd], *adj.* klumpig, geronnen; *–ted cream*, verdickter Rahm.

cloth [klɔθ], *s.* das Tuch, Gewebe, Zeug, der Stoff; die Leinwand (*Bookb.*); (*fig*) geistliche Amtstracht, die Geistlichkeit; *American* –, das Wachstuch; *bolting*– –, das Beuteltuch, *cut one's – according to one's measure*, sich nach der Decke strecken; *lay the* –, den Tisch decken, *remove the* –, abdecken; *saddle*– –, die Satteldecke; *sail*– –, das Segeltuch; *twilled* –, das Köperzeug. **– –beam,** *s.* der Weberbaum. **– binding,** der Leinenband. **– board,** der Leinwanddeckel. **– –merchant,** *s.* der Tuchhändler. **– –printing,** *s.* der Zeugdruck. **– –weaver,** *s* der Tuchweber. **– –worker,** *s.* der Tucharbeiter, Tuchwirker. **– –yard,** *s.* die Tuchelle.

clothe [klouð], *reg. & irreg v.a.* kleiden, ankleiden, bekleiden; anziehen (*a child, etc.*), (*fig*) kleiden, einhüllen (*thoughts, etc*).

clothes [klouðz], *pl.* die Kleider (*pl.*) die Kleidung; Wäsche; (*a*) (*with adjectives, etc.*) *baby* –, die Säuglingswäsche, Windeln; *bed*– –, die Bettwäsche, das Bettzeug; *cast-off* –, alte *or* abgetragene Kleider; *in plain* –, in Zivil; *plain– – officer*, der Geheimpolizist, Spitzel; (*archaic*) *small* –, die Beinkleider; *soiled* –, schmutzige Wäsche; *under*–, die Leibwäsche, Unterwäsche; (*b*) (*with verbs*) *change one's* –, sich umziehen; *put on one's* –, sich ankleiden *or* anziehen; *take off one's* –, sich ausziehen *or* entkleiden. **– –airer,** *s.* der Wäschetrockner. **– –bag,** *s* der Wäschebeutel. **– –basket,** *s.* der Wäschekorb. **– –brush,** *s.* die Kleiderbürste. **– –hanger,** *s.* der Kleiderbügel. **– –horse,** *s.* das Wäschegestell, der Trockenständer. **– –line,** *s.* die Wäscheleine. **– –man,** *s.*; *old– – -man*, der Kleidertrödler, Lumpensammler. **– –peg,** *s.*, **– –pin,** *s.* die Wäscheklammer.

clothier ['klouðɪə], *s.* der Kleiderhändler, Tuchhändler.

clothing ['klouðɪŋ], *s.* die Kleidung, der Anzug; die Bekleidung; *article of* –, das Kleidungsstück; – *allowance*, der Bekleidungszuschuß (*Mil.*); – *coupon*, der Kleiderbezugschein; *under*– –, die Leib– *or* Unterwäsche.

cloud [klaud], 1. *s.* die Wolke; (*fig.*) Haufe, Schar,

Menge; trüber Fleck, der Schatten, die Verdüsterung, Dunkelheit; – *of dust*, die Staubwolke; – *of tobacco smoke*, der Tabaksqualm; *be in the –s*, träumen, in Gedanken vertieft sein; *under a –*, in Ungnade, in Verruf; *cast a – upon* or *over*, trüben; *live in a –*, in höheren Regionen leben *or* schweben. 2. *v.a.* bewölken, trüben, verdunkeln, überschatten; ädern, flammen; moirieren (*materials*). 3. *v.n.* (– *over*) sich bewölken, sich trüben, trübe werden. **–burst,** *s.* der Wolkenbruch. **––capped,** *adj.* von Wolken umgeben, wolkenbedeckt. **––covered,** *adj.* wolkenumhüllt (*as mountains*), bewölkt, wolkenbedeckt (*as sky*). **––Cuckoo-Land,** *s.* das Wolkenkuckucksheim. **––drift,** *s.* der Wolkenzug. **–ed,** *adj.* umwölkt, getrübt; moiriert. **––formation,** *s.* die Wolkenbildung. **–iness,** *s.* die Umwölkung, Trübung, Wolkigkeit, Bewölkung, Unklarheit, Dunkelheit, das Trübe, Dunkle. **–ing,** *s.* die Trübung (*of stones*); Äderung (*in stuffs*). **––layer,** *s.* die Wolkenschicht. **–less,** *adj.* wolkenlos, unbewölkt, klar, hell. **–let,** *s.* das Wölkchen. **––wrapt,** *adj.* in Wolken gehüllt. **–y,** *adj.* wolkig, bewölkt, trübe, getrübt, düster; geädert, moiriert (*of materials*); (*fig.*) finster, traurig; dunkel, unverständlich, verschwommen, unklar.

clout [klaʊt], 1. *s.* (*archaic & dial.*) der Lappen, Wisch; (*archaic*) Fleck, das Flicken (*on shoes, etc.*); die Achsscheibe (*of wheels*); der Mittelpunkt der Schießscheibe; (*coll.*) Schlag; – *on the head*, die Kopfnuß; – *on the ear*, die Ohrfeige. **––nail,** *s.* der Schuhnagel, Blattnagel. 2. *v.a.* (*archaic & dial.*) flicken; beschlagen; (*coll.*) schlagen, ohrfeigen.

[1]**clove** [kloʊv], (*archaic*) *see* **cleave.** **––hitch,** *s.* der Mastwurf (*Naut.*). **–n,** *adj.* gespalten; *–n hoof*, der Spaltfuß, (*fig.*) Teufel; *show the –n hoof*, sein wahres Gesicht zeigen. **–n-hoofed,** *adj.* spaltfüßig, (*fig.*) teuflisch.

[2]**clove,** *s.* die Gewürznelke; (*Poet.*) das Nägelein; *oil of –s*, das Nelkenöl. **––pink,** *s.* die Gartennelke.

[3]**clove,** *s.* die Brutzwiebel, Nebenzwiebel (*Bot.*).

clover [ˈkloʊvə], *s.* der Klee; *be in –*, es gut haben, üppig leben.

clown [klaʊn], *s.* der Grobian, Tölpel; Hanswurst, Clown (*Theat.*). **–ish,** *adj.* bäuerisch, grob, tölpelhaft, närrisch. **–ishness,** *s.* die Grobheit, Plumpheit, Ungeschliffenheit.

cloy [klɔɪ], *v.a.* übersättigen, überladen; (*fig.*) anwidern.

club [klʌb], 1. *s.* die Keule, der Knüppel, Knüttel; Ballstock, Schläger (*Sport*); das Treff, Kreuz, die Eichel (*Cards*); geschlossene Gesellschaft, der Klub, Verein; das Kasino; *Indian –s*, Keulen (*pl*); *Queen of –s*, die Treffdame. 2. *v.a.* mit einer Keule schlagen; – *a musket*, mit dem Kolben dreinschlagen. 3. *v.n.* (*coll.*) (– *together*) sich zusammentun, zusammenschießen, gemeinschaftlich beisteuern; (*coll.*) – *up*, zusammenlegen (*money*). **–foot,** *s.* der Klumpfuß. **–footed,** *adj.* klumpfüßig. **––haul,** *v n.* mit dem Leeanker wenden (*Naut.*). **–house,** *s* das Klublokal, Klubhaus, Kasino. **––law,** *s.* das Faustrecht. **––moss,** *s.* das Kolbenmoos, der Bärlapp (*Bot.*). **–room,** *s.* das Gesellschaftszimmer. **––shaped,** *adj.* keulenförmig.

cluck [klʌk], *v.n.* glucken.

clue [klʊː], *s.* der Faden (*of a tale*); (*fig*) Fingerzeig, Anhaltspunkt, Schlüssel, das Losungswort (*to*, zu, für). **–less,** *adj.* ohne Anhaltspunkt.

clump [klʌmp], 1. *s.* der Klotz, Klumpen; die Gruppe; Doppelsohle; – *of trees*, die Baumgruppe, das Gehölz. 2. *v.a.* mit Doppelsohlen versehen. 3. *v.n.* (*coll.*) schwer auftreten, schwerfällig gehen, trampen, trapsen.

clums-iness [ˈklʌmzɪnɪs], *s.* die Plumpheit, Unbeholfenheit. **–y** [ˈklʌmzɪ], *adj.* plump, schwerfällig, unbeholfen, ungeschickt.

clung [klʌŋ], *see* **cling.**

cluster [ˈklʌstə], 1. *s.* die Traube, der Büschel; Haufen, die Gruppe; der Schwarm; – *of trees*, die Baumgruppe. 2 *v.n.* in Büscheln *or* Trauben wachsen; sich sammeln *or* zusammenscharen; schwärmen (*of bees*); *–ed column*, der Bündelpfeiler (*Arch.*).

[1]**clutch** [klʌtʃ], 1. *s.* der Griff; das Greifen; die Klaue, Kralle; (*fig.*) Macht; Kupplung (*Mach.*); *cone––*, die Kegelkupplung; *disk––*, die Lamellenkupplung; *keep out of his –es*, sich vor seiner Macht hüten; *plate––*, die Scheibenkupplung. 2. *v.a.* greifen, fassen, packen, ergreifen; kuppeln (*Mach.*). **––pedal,** *s.* der Kupplungs(fuß)hebel.

[2]**clutch,** *s.* die Brut.

clutter [ˈklʌtə], 1. *s.* der Wirrwarr, die Unordnung. 2. *v.a.* durcheinanderwerfen, verwirren; *–ed up with*, überhäuft *or* vollgestopft mit.

clype-ate [ˈklɪpɪeɪt], *adj.*, **–iform,** *adj.* schildförmig (*Bot.*)

clyster [ˈklɪstə], *s.* das Klistier (*Med.*). **––pipe,** *s.* die Klistierspritze.

coach [koʊtʃ], 1. *s.* die Kutsche; der Eisenbahnwagen; Privatlehrer; Einpauker (*Univ.*), Trainer (*Sport*); – *and four*, vierspännige Kutsche; *hackney––*, die Mietkutsche; *mail––*, die Postkutsche; *motor––*, der Autobus; *stage––*, die Eilkutsche; *slow–*, (*fig.*) langsamer Mensch, der Trödelfritz. 2. *v.a.* kutschieren, in einer Kutsche fahren; einpauken, trainieren (*for*, zu) (*Sport*). **––box,** *s.* der Kutscherbock. **––builder,** *s.* der Wagenbauer. **––house,** *s.* die Wagenremise. **–ing,** 1. *adj.*; *the old –ing days*, als man noch Kutsche fuhr. 2. *s.* der Privatunterricht; das Training (*Sport*); *–ing fee* das Stundengeld. **–man,** *s.* der Kutscher. **–work,** *s.* die Karosserie. **––wrench,** *s.* der Engländer.

coacti-on [koʊˈækʃən], *s.* das Zusammenwirken. **–ve** [–ˈæktɪv], *adj.* zusammenwirkend, mitwirkend.

coadjutor [koʊˈædʒʊtə], *s.* der Gehilfe, Koadjutor (*Eccl.*).

coagul-ant [koʊˈægulənt], *s.* der Gerinnstoff, das Koagulierungsmittel. **–ate** [–leɪt], 1. *v.n.* gerinnen, erstarren, festwerden, verdicken, koagulieren. 2. *v.a.* gerinnen lassen. **–ation** [–ˈleɪʃən], *s.* das Gerinnen; die Koagulierung, Erstarrung; das Geronnene. **–um** [–ləm], *s.* das Gerinnsel, die Koagulatmasse.

coal [koʊl], 1. *s.* die Kohle, Steinkohle; *bituminous –*, die Fettkohle, bituminöse Kohle; (*coll.*) *call* or *haul a p. over the –s*, einem den Text lesen, einen zur Rechenschaft ziehen; *carry –s to Newcastle*, Eulen nach Athen tragen; *hard –*, der Anthrazit, die Glanzkohle; *heap –s of fire on a p.'s head*, feurige Kohlen auf jemandes Haupt sammeln *or* häufen; *live –*, glühende Kohle; *rich –*, die Fettkohle; *vegetable –*, die Braunkohle. 2. *v.n.* Kohlen einnehmen, bunkern (*Naut.*). 3. *v.a.* bekohlen (*a ship, etc.*). **––black,** *adj.* kohlschwarz. **––box,** *s.* der Kohlenkasten (*Railw.*). **––bunker,** *s.* der Kohlenraum (*Naut.*). **––cellar,** *s.* der Kohlenkeller. **––dust,** *s.* der Kohlengrus. **–field,** *s.* das Kohlengebiet *or* –revier. **– fire,** das Kohlenfeuer. **––formation,** *s.* die Steinkohlenformation (*Geol.*). **––gas,** *s.* das Kohlengas, Leuchtgas, Steinkohlenleuchtgas. **––heaver,** *s.* der Kohlenträger. **––hole,** *s.* der Kohlenraum. **–ing,** *s.* das Kohleneinnehmen; *–ing station*, *s.* die Kohlenstation. **––measures,** *pl.* das Kohlengebirge (*Geol.*). **––merchant,** *s.* der Kohlenhändler. **––mine,** *s.* das Kohlenbergwerk. **–mouse,** *s.* die Tannenmeise (*Orn.*). **––mining,** der Kohlenabbau. **––oil,** *s.* (*Amer*) das Kerosin. **––owner,** *s.* der Bergwerkbesitzer. **––pit,** *s.* die Kohlengrube. **––scuttle,** *s.* der Kohlenkasten, Kohleneimer. **––seam,** *s.* das Kohlenflöz. **––tar,** *s* der (Stein)-Kohlenteer, Teer; *––tar dye*, der Teerfarbstoff; *––tar soap*, die Kohlenseife. **––wharf,** *s.* der Kohlenabladeplatz.

coal-esce [koʊəˈlɛs], *v.n.* sich verbinden, sich verschmelzen, zusammenwachsen; (*fig.*) sich vereinigen. **–escence,** *s.* das Zusammenfließen; die Vereinigung, Verschmelzung. **–ition,** *s.* die Verbindung, Vereinigung, das Bündnis; die Koalition (*Pol.*).

coaming [ˈkoʊmɪŋ], der Süll der Luken (*Naut.*).

coarse [kɔːs], *adj.* grob, rauh, grobkörnig; (*fig.*) roh, plump, gemein, gewöhnlich, ungebildet, unanständig; – *bread*, das Schrotbrot; – *language*, anstößige Redensarten; – *manners*, ungeschliffene Manieren; – *meal*, das Schrotmehl. **––grained,**

adj. grobkörnig; grobfaserig. **–n,** 1. *v.a.* vergröbern, grob machen. 2. *v.n.* grob werden. **–ness,** *s.* die Derbheit, Grobheit, Gemeinheit; Rauheit.

coast [koʊst], 1. *s.* die Küste; der Strand, das Gestade; (*Amer.*) die Rodelbahn; (*fig.*) *the – is clear*, die Luft ist rein; *foul –*, gefährliche Küste (*Naut.*). 2. *v.n.* an der Küste hinfahren (*Naut.*); (*Amer.*) rodeln; (*– along*), mit Freilauf entlangfahren *or* hinunterfahren. **–al,** *adj.* Küsten–. **– -battery,** *s.* die Küstenbatterie. **– -defence,** *s.* die Küstenverteidigung. **–er,** *s.* der Küstenfahrer (*Naut.*); das Servierbrett (*for wine*); (*Amer.*) der Schlitten; *–er-hub*, *s.* die Freilaufnabe (*Cycl.*). **–guard,** *s.* die Küstenwache (*Naut.*). **–ing,** *s.* die Küstenschiffahrt, der Küstenhandel; (*Amer.*) das Rodeln; *–ing trade*, *s.* der Küstenhandel; *–ing vessel*, *s.* das Küstenschiff. **–line,** *s.* die Küstenlinie. **–wise,** 1. *adj.* Küsten–. 2. *adv.* an der Küste entlang; *–wise shipping*, die Küstenschiffahrt.

coat [koʊt], 1. *s.* der Rock, die Jacke; der (Damen)-Mantel, das Damenjackett; Fell, der Pelz (*of beasts*); das Gefieder (*of birds*); der Anstrich, Aufstrich, Auftrag, Belag, Bewurf; Überzug, die Schicht, Lage, Haut; (*a*) (with *of*) *– of arms*, das Wappenschild; *– of dust*, die Staubschicht; *– of mail*, der Panzerharnisch; *– of paint*, der Anstrich; *– of plaster*, der Gipsbewurf; (*b*) (*with nouns & adjective*) *dress-–*, der Frack; *first –*, der Grundanstrich; *fur –*, der Pelzmantel; *frock-–*, der Gehrock; *great-–*, der Überrock, Mantel; (*c*) (*with verbs*) *cut one's – according to one's cloth*, sich nach der Decke strecken; *dust a p.'s –*, einen verprügeln; *turn one's –*, den Mantel nach dem Winde hängen, abtrünnig werden; *wear the king's –*, Soldat sein. 2. *v.a.* überziehen; auftragen, aufstreichen, anstreichen, anlegen, belegen, bestreichen, überstreichen. **–ed,** *adj.* bedeckt, überzogen, bekleidet; belegt (*as the tongue*) (*Med.*); (*as suffix*) –röckig; *black-–ed worker*, der Kopfarbeiter; *become –ed*, beschlagen. **–ee** [koʊ'tiː], *s.* kurzes Damenjackett, die Jacke, Weste. **– -hanger,** *s.* der Kleiderbügel. **–ing,** *s.* der Überzug, Belag, Beschlag, die Schicht; Bedeckung; der Rockstoff. **– -stand,** *s.* der Kleiderständer. **– -tail,** *s.* der Rockschoß; *hang on to s.o.'s –-tails*, sich an jemandes Rockschoß klammern.

coax [koʊks], 1. *v.a.* beschwatzen, überreden; *– a p. into (doing) a th.*, einem gut zureden, daß er etwas tut; *he –ed money out of her*, er gewann ihr Geld durch Schmeicheln ab. 2. *v.n.* zureden.

¹**cob** [kɔb], *s.* starkes Reitpferd, das Halbblut; männlicher Schwan; der Maiskolben; der Klumpen. **– -loaf,** *s.* rundes Brot. **– -nut,** *s.* große Haselnuß.

²**cob,** *s.* die Mischung aus Lehm und Stroh (*Build.*).

cobalt ['koʊbɔːlt], *s.* der Kobalt. **– -blue,** *s.* das Kobaltblau, die Smalte. **– -glance,** *see* **–ine. –ic** [ko'bɔːltɪk], *adj.* Kobalt–. **–ine, –ite** [ko'bɔːl-taɪt], *s.* der Kobaltglanz.

¹**cobble** ['kɔbl], *v.a.* flicken (*shoes*); (*fig.*) pfuschen, zusammenflicken; *–d job*, das Flickwerk, gepfuschte Arbeit. **–r** [–ə], *s.* der Schuhflicker, Schuster; (*fig.*) Pfuscher, Stümper; *–r's wax*, das Schusterpech, Schuhmacherpech, Schnittwachs.

²**cobble,** 1. *s.* der Feldstein, Kiesel; das Kopfsteinpflaster; *pl.* Stückkohlen. 2. *v.a.* mit Kopfsteinen pflastern.

co-belligerent ['koʊbə'lɪdʒərənt], *s.* Mitkriegführende(r), *m.*

coble ['kɔbl], *s.* flaches Fischerboot.

cobra ['koʊbrə], *s.* die Brillenschlange.

cobweb ['kɔbwɛb], *s.* das Spinngewebe, Spinnweb, die Spinnwebe, der Spinnenfaden; feiner Faden, feines Gewebe; *blow away the –s from one's brain*, sich einen klaren Kopf schaffen. **–bed** [–d], *adj.*, **–by,** *adj.* von Spinngeweben bedeckt; (*fig.*) fein, zart, leicht.

coca ['koʊkə], *s.* die Koka (*Bot.*). **– -cola** [–koʊlə], *s.* (*Amer.*) das Cola, Cocacola. **–ine** [–'keɪn], *s.* das Kokain.

coccyx ['kɔksɪks], *s.* das Steißbein (*Anat.*).

cochineal ['kɔtʃɪniːl], *s.* die Cochenille.

cochlea ['kɔklɪə], *s.* die Schnecke (*of the ear*) (*Anat.*).

¹**cock** [kɔk], 1. *s.* der Hahn (*of poultry*); das Männchen (*of any bird*); der Hahn (*of gun, etc.*), Absperrhahn; Heuhaufen, Heuschober; (*coll.*) Kerl, Bursche; (*vulg.*) Schwanz (= *penis*); *blow-off –*, der Ablaßhahn; *fighting –*, der Kampfhahn; (*coll.*) *that – won't fight*, damit geht's nicht; *live like fighting –s*, üppig leben; *at full –*, Hahn gespannt; *at half –*, Hahn in Ruh'; (*coll.*) *old –*, alter Junge; *–-sparrow*, das Sperlingsmännchen; *– of the roost* or *walk*, der Hahn im Korbe. 2. *v.a.* (*– up*) in die Höhe richten, aufrichten, aufschichten, zusammenhäufen, schobern (*hay*); (den Hahn) spannen (*of a gun*); *– one's ears*, die Ohren spitzen; *– one's eye at a p.*, einem mit dem Auge winken; *– one's hat*, den Hut schief *or* keck aufsetzen; (*sl.*) *– a snook*, eine lange Nase machen. **– -a-doodle-doo,** *s.* der Kikeriki. **– -a-hoop,** *s.* frohlockend, anmaßend. **– -and-bull story,** das Lügenmärchen, unglaubliche Geschichte. **– -boat,** *s.* kleines Boot, das Beiboot. **– -crow,** *s.* der Hahnenschrei; (*fig.*) Tagesanbruch. **–ed,** *adj.* aufgebogen, gestülpt; *–ed hat*, dreieckiger Hut, der Dreimaster, Dreispitz; (*coll.*) *knock into a –ed hat*, überrumpeln, zu Brei schlagen. **–erel,** *s.* junger Hahn. **– -eyed,** *adj.* (*sl.*) schief, schielend. **– -fight,** *s.* der Hahnenkampf. **– -loft,** *s.* die Dachkammer. **–pit,** *s.* der Platz für Hahnenkämpfe; (*fig.*) Kampfplatz; Lazarettraum auf dem Orlogdeck (*Naut.*); die Plicht (*Naut.*); der Führersitz, Führerraum, die Kanzel (*Av.*). **– -shy,** *s.* die Zielscheibe. (*coll.*) **–sure,** *adj.* siegesgewiß, selbstbewußt. **– -tread,** *s.* der Hahnentritt (*in egg*). **–y,** *adj.* (*sl.*) keck, frech.

cockade [kɔ'keɪd], *s.* die Kokarde.

cockatoo [kɔkə'tuː], *s.* der Kakadu.

cockatrice ['kɔkətraɪs], *s.* der Basilisk.

cockchafer ['kɔktʃeɪfə], *s.* der Maikäfer.

cocker ['kɔkə], *v.a.* verhätscheln.

cockerel ['kɔkərəl], *see* **cock.**

cocket ['kɔkət], *s.* (*archaic*) das Zollsiegel.

cockle ['kɔkl], 1. *s.* die Kornrade (*Bot.*); Herzmuschel (*Mollusc.*); (*coll.*) *warm the –s of one's heart*, höchst erfreulich sein. 2. *v.n.* sich runzeln, sich kräuseln. **– -shell,** *s.* die Muschelschale.

cockney ['kɔknɪ], 1. *s.* das Londoner Stadtkind. 2. *adj.* Londoner. **–ism** [–ɪzm], *s.* der Londoner Ausdruck.

cockroach ['kɔkroʊtʃ], *s.* die Küchenschabe, der Kakerlak.

cockscomb ['kɔkskoʊm], *s.* der Hahnenkamm; gemeiner Hahnenkamm, der Klappertopf (*Bot.*); (*see also* **coxcomb**).

cockspur ['kɔkspəː], *s.* gemeiner Hahnendorn (*Bot.*).

cocktail ['kɔkteɪl], *s.* halbblütiges Pferd mit gestutztem Schwanz; der Kurzflügler (*Ent.*); der Cocktail.

coco ['koʊkoʊ], *s.* (*–nut-tree*) die Kokospalme. **–nut** ['koʊkənʌt], 1. *s.* die Kokosnuß. 2. *attrib.*; *–nut fibre*, der Kokosbast; *–nut oil*, das Kokosfett.

cocoa ['koʊkoʊ], *s.* der Kakao. **–bean,** *s.* die Kakaobohne. **– -butter,** die Kakaobutter.

cocoon [kɔ'kuːn] 1. *s.* der Kokon, das Gespinst, die Puppe (*of silkworm*). 2. *v.n.* einen Kokon bilden, sich einspinnen.

cocotte [koʊ'kɔt], *s.* die Kokotte, Dirne.

¹**cod** [kɔd], *s.* (*also* **–fish,** *s.*) der Kabeljau, Dorsch; *dried –*, der Stockfisch, Klippfisch. **–ling,** *s.* junger Kabeljau. **– -liver-oil,** der Lebertran, Kabeljautran, Fischtran.

²**cod,** *v.a. & n.* (*sl.*) foppen, narren, beschwindeln.

coddle ['kɔdl], *v.a.* verhätscheln, verzärteln, verwöhnen, verweichlichen.

code [koʊd], 1. *s.* das Gesetzbuch, der Kodex; die Geheimschrift, Schlüsselschrift; *civil –*, die Zivilprozeßordnung; *commercial –*, das Handelsgesetzbuch; *criminal –*, see *penal –*; *– of honour*, der Ehrenkodex; *– of laws*, das Gesetzbuch; *penal –*, das Strafgesetzbuch; *– of signals*, das Flaggensignalsystem. 2. *v.a.* chiffrieren, schlüsseln. **– -name,** *s.* der Deckname. **– -telegram,** *s.* das Schlüsseltelegramm.

codex ['koʊdeks], *s.* alte Handschrift, der Kodex.

codger ['kɔdʒə], *s.* (*coll.*) der Sonderling, Kauz.

codicil ['kɔdɪsɪl], *s.* das Kodizill, der Nachtrag, Zusatz (*to a will*).
codif–ication [koudɪfɪ'keɪʃən], *s.* die Kodifizierung. **–y** [–faɪ], *v.a.* kodifizieren.
codling ['kɔdlɪŋ], *see* [1]**cod**; eine Kochapfelsorte.
co-ed [kou'ɛd], *s.* (*sl.*) (*Amer.*) die Schülerin einer Gemeinschaftsschule.
co-editor [kou'ɛdɪtə], *s.* der Mitherausgeber.
coeducation [kouɛdju'keɪʃən], *s* gemeinschaftliche Erziehung von Knaben und Mädchen, die Koedukation.
coefficient [kouə'fɪʃənt], 1. *adj.* mitwirkend. 2. *s.* der Koeffizient, Beiwert, die Verhältniszahl (*Math.*); – *of linear expansion*, linearer Ausdehnungskoeffizient.
coeliac ['sɪ:lɪæk], *adj.* Unterleibs–, Bauch–.
coenobite ['sɛnobaɪt], *s.* der Klostermönch.
coequal [kou'ɪ:kwəl], *adj.* gleich (*Theol.*).
coerc–e [kou'ə:s], *v.a.* zwingen, erzwingen (*obedience*); nötigen. **–ible,** *adj.* erzwingbar. **–ion** [–'ə:ʃən], *s.* der Zwang; die Nötigung, Zwangsgewalt. **–ive,** *adj* zwingend; *–ive measures*, Zwangsmaßnahmen (*pl.*). **–ively,** *adv.* zwangsweise.
coessential [kouə'sɛnʃəl], *adj.* wesensgleich, gleichen Wesens (*Theol.*).
coeternal [kouɪ'tə:nəl], *adj.* gleich ewig
coeval [kou'ɪ:vəl], *adj.* gleichzeitig, gleichaltrig.
coexecut–or [kouɛg'zɛkutə], *s.* der Mitvollstrecker. **–rix,** *s.* die Mitvollstreckerin.
coexist [kouɛg'zɪst], *v.n.* zugleich vorhanden sein (mit), zu gleicher Zeit da sein (wie), zusammenexistieren (mit). **–ence,** *s.* gleichzeitiges Bestehen *or* Dasein, die Koexistenz, das Mitvorhandensein. **–ent,** *adj.* gleichzeitig (vorhanden).
coexten–d [kouɛks'tɛnd], *v.n.* gleichen Umfang *or* gleiche Dauer haben. **–sion** [–'tɛnʃən], *s.* gleiche Dauer, gleicher Umfang. **–sive** [–'tɛnsɪv], *adj.* von gleicher Dauer, von gleichem Umfang.
coffee ['kɔfɪ], *s.* der Kaffee. **– -bean,** *s.* die Kaffeebohne. **– -cup,** *s.* die Kaffeetasse. **– -grinder,** *s.* die Kaffeemühle. **– grounds,** der Kaffeesatz. **– -house,** *s.* das Kaffeehaus, Café. **– -pot,** *s.* die Kaffeekanne. **– -room,** *s.* das Gastzimmer (*in a hotel, etc.*); Kaffeehaus. **– -service,** *s.* das Kaffeegeschirr, Kaffeeservice. **– -stall,** *s.* der Kaffeeausschank. **– substitute,** *s.* der Kaffeeersatz.
coffer ['kɔfə], *s.* der Koffer, Kasten; die Kiste, Truhe; das Deckenfeld, die Kassette (*Arch.*); gedeckter Verbindungsweg (*Fort.*); (*pl.*) die Schatzkammer, Schätze (*pl.*). **– -dam,** *s.* der Fangdamm (*Bridgeb.*).
coffin ['kɔfɪn], 1. *s.* der Sarg; Karren (*Typ.*). 2. *v.a.* einsargen. **– -bone,** *s.* das Hufbein. **– -nail,** *s.* (*sl.*) schlechte Zigarette, der Sargnagel.
[1]**cog** [kɔg], 1. *s.* der Kamm, Zahn, Mitnehmer. 2. *v.a.* zahnen. **– -rail,** *s.* die Zahnschiene. **–wheel,** *s.* das Kammrad, Zahnrad; *–wheel drive*, der Zahnantrieb; *–wheel railway*, die Zahnradbahn.
[2]**cog,** *v.a.* betrügen; – *the dice*, (beim Würfeln) falsch spielen.
cogen–cy ['koudʒənsɪ], *s.* überzeugende *or* zwingende Kraft; die Überzeugungskraft, Triftigkeit. **–t** [–t], *adj.* zwingend, überzeugend, triftig, schlagend.
cogitat–e ['kɔdʒɪteɪt], 1. *v.n.* denken, sinnen; nachdenken (*upon*, über). 2. *v.a.* denken, ausdenken, ersinnen. **–ion** [–'teɪʃən], *s.* das Denken; Nachdenken, die Überlegung. **–ive** [–ṭətɪv], *adj.* denkend, nachdenklich.
cognac ['kounjæk], *s.* der Kognak, Weinbrand.
cognat–e ['kɔgneɪt], 1. *adj.* verwandt; *–e accusative*, inneres Objekt (*Gram.*); *–e words*, verwandte Wörter. 2. *s.* verwandtes Wort; Verwandte(r), *m.* (*Law*). **–ion** [–'neɪʃən], *s.* (sprachliche) Verwandtschaft.
cogni–tion [kɔg'nɪʃən], *s.* die Kenntnis, Kunde, das Wissen, die Wahrnehmung; das Erkennen, Erkennungsvermögen, die Erkenntnis (*Phil.*). **–tive** ['kɔgnɪtɪv], *adj.* Erkenntnis–. **–zable** ['kɔ(g)nɪzəbl], *adj.* erkennbar, wahrnehmbar; Gerichtsbarkeit unterworfen (*Law*). **–zance** ['kɔ(g)nɪzəns], *s.* die Kenntnis, Erkenntnis, Anerkennung; gerichtliche Erkenntnis, die Gerichtsbarkeit, Zuständigkeit (*Law*); das Abzeichen, Kennzeichen (*Her.*); *take –zance of a th.*, Kenntnis von einer S. nehmen. **–zant** ['kɔ(g)nɪzənt], *adj* wissend; zuständig (*Law*); *be –zant of a th.*, über etwas unterrichtet sein, um etwas wissen.
cognomen [kɔg'noumɛn], *s.* der Zuname, Beiname.
cohabit [kou'hæbɪt], *v.n.* zusammenleben; in wilder Ehe leben. **–ation** [–hæbɪ'teɪʃən], *s.* wilde Ehe, das Beisammenwohnen, der Beischlaf, Geschlechtsverkehr.
coheir [kou'ɛə], *s.* der Miterbe. **–ess** [–rɪs], *s.* die Miterbin.
cohe–re [kou'hɪə], *v.n.* zusammenhängen, zusammenhalten. **–rence** [–rəns], **–rency,** *s.* der Zusammenhang, Zusammenhalt, die Kohärenz; Klarheit (*of ideas*). **–rent** [–rənt], *adj.* zusammenhängend, kohärent; klar, verständlich, logisch. **–rer** [–rə], *s.* der Fritter, Kohärer (*Rad.*). **–sion** [–'hɪ:ʒən], *s.* die Kohäsion, der Zusammenhalt; (*fig.*) Zusammenhang. **–sive** [–'hɪ:sɪv], *adj.* fest zusammenhängend, zusammenhaltend, kohäsiv, Binde–. **–siveness,** *s.* der Zusammenhalt, die Bindekraft, Kohäsion.
cohort ['kouhɔ:t], *s.* die Kohorte; (*poet.*) Kriegsschar, Schar.
coif [kɔɪf], *s.* die Kappe, Haube. **–fure** [kwɑ'fjuə], *s.* der Kopfputz; die Haartracht.
coign [kɔɪn], *s.* (*archaic*) die Ecke; der Eckstein; – *of vantage*, vorteilhafte Stellung.
coil [kɔɪl], 1. *s.* die Rolle; Locke, der Wickel (*of hair, etc.*); die Windung, Wicklung, Spule (*Elec.*); *induction* –, die Induktionsspule; *moving* –, die Schwingspule; *tuning* –, die Abstimmspule (*Rad.*). 2. *v.a.* aufwickeln, aufrollen; aufschießen (*rope*), (auf)spulen; spiralförmig winden (*springs, etc.*). 3 *v.n.* sich winden; – *up*, sich zusammenrollen (*as snakes*). **– -spring,** *s.* die Bandfeder.
coin [kɔɪn], 1. *s.* das Geldstück, die Münze; *base* or *counterfeit* –, falsche Münze; *current* –, gangbare Münze; *small* –, die Scheidemünze; *pay a p. back in his own* –, einem in gleicher Münze heimzahlen. 2. *v.a.* Münzen schlagen; prägen, münzen; (*fig.*) *be –ing money*, schwer verdienen, Geld verdienen wie Heu; – *a phrase*, eine Redewendung erfinden. **–age** [–ɪdʒ], *s.* das Münzen, Prägen; gemünztes Geld; das Münzsystem. **–er,** *s.* der Münzer, Falschmünzer.
coincide [kouɪn'saɪd], *v.n.* zusammentreffen, zusammenfallen; (*fig.*) übereinstimmen, sich decken, entsprechen (*with* (*Dat.*)). **–nce** [–'ɪnsɪdəns], *s.* das Zusammentreffen; (*fig.*) die Übereinstimmung; *mere –nce*, bloßer Zufall. **–nt** [–'ɪnsɪdənt], *adj.* zusammentreffend, zusammenfallend, gleichzeitig; übereinstimmend. **–ntal** [–'dɛntəl], *adj.* zufällig.
coir [kɔɪə], *s.* der Kokosbast, die Kokosfaser.
coit–ion [kou'ɪʃən], *s.*, **–us** ['kouɪtəs], *s.* der Beischlaf, Koitus.
coke [kouk], 1. *s.* der Koks, Gaskoks. 2. *v.a.* verkoken.
col [kɔl], *s.* der Gebirgspaß, das Joch; das Tief (*Meteor.*)
colander ['kʌlɪndə], *s.* der Durchschlag, Seiher, die Seihe, das Sieb.
colchicum ['kɔlkɪkəm], *s.* die Herbstzeitlose (*Bot.*).
colcothar ['kɔlkoθɑ:], *s.* das Eisenrot, Glanzrot, der Kolkothar, rotes Eisenoxyd.
cold [kould], 1. *adj.* kalt, frostig; gleichgültig, kühl, teilnahmlos, zurückhaltend, nüchtern, ruhig; (*a*) (*with nouns*) *in – blood*, kalten Blutes; – *chisel*, der Hartmeißel, Kaltschrottmeißel; – *comfort*, schwacher *or* schlechter Trost; – *cream*, die Hautpomade; – *drawing*, das Kaltstrecken (*Metall.*); (*sl.*) – *feet*, die Angst; – *front*, die Kaltluftfront, Einbruchsfront (*Meteor.*); – *look*, kalter *or* unfreundlicher Blick; – *meat*, kalte Küche, kalte Platte; – *reception*, frostiger Empfang; – *scent*, schwache Fährte (*Hunt.*); *give a p. the – shoulder*, einen kühl *or* geringschätzig behandeln; – *snap*, plötzlich eintrendes kaltes Wetter; – *steel*, blanke Waffe; *throw – water on a th.*, etwas herabsetzen; (*b*) (*with verbs*) *I am* –, mich friert; *be as – as charity*, hart wie Stein sein; *be as – as ice*, eiskalt sein; (*coll.*) *that leaves me* –, das läßt mich kalt; *my*

blood runs –, mich gruselt's. 2. *s.* die Kälte; der Frost; die Erkältung (*Med.*); *catch* –, sich erkälten, sich (*Dat.*) einen Schnupfen holen; *have a* –, sich erkältet haben, einen Schnupfen haben; – *in the head*, der Schnupfen; *keep out the* –, die Kälte abhalten *or* vertreiben; *leave s.o. out in the* –, einen kaltstellen *or* ignorieren. **–-blooded,** *adj.* wechselwarm (*Zool.*); (*fig.*) kaltblütig, gefühllos. **–-hearted,** *adj.* kaltherzig, gefühllos. **–ish,** *adj.* ziemlich kalt, kühl. **–ly,** *adv.* gefühllos, kaltblütig. **–ness,** *s.* die Kälte (*also fig.*). **–-short,** *adj.* kaltbrüchig, spröde (*of metals*). **–-shoulder,** *v.a.* ignorieren. **–-storage,** *s.* die Kaltluftaufbewahrung; (*fig.*) *put into –-storage*, auf die lange Bank schieben. **–-store,** *s.* das Kühlhaus, der Kühlraum.

cole [koʊl], *s.* der Kohl. **–-seed,** *s.* der Raps, Rübsen, Rübsamen. **–wort,** *s.* der Grünkohl.

coleopter–a [kɔlɪˈɔptərə], *pl.* die Käfer. **–ous** [–s], *adj.* käferartig.

coli–c [ˈkɔlɪk], *s.* die Kolik, der Darmkatarrh. **–tis,** *s.* der Dickdarmkatarrh.

collaborat–e [kəˈlæbəreɪt], *v.n.* mitarbeiten, zusammenarbeiten. **–ion,** *s.* die Mitarbeit, Mitwirkung, Zusammenarbeit; *in –ion with*, gemeinsam mit. **–or,** *s.* der Mitarbeiter.

collaps–e [kəˈlæps], 1. *s.* das Zusammenfallen, der Zusammenbruch, Einsturz; Verfall *or* das Sinken der Kräfte; der Kollaps (*Med.*); die Vernichtung (*of hopes*); der Sturz, Krach (*C.L.*). 2. *v.n.* zusammenfallen, einfallen, einstürzen; zusammenbrechen, zu Fall kommen, ins Wasser fallen, vereitelt werden. **–ible,** *adj.* zusammenlegbar, zusammenklappbar; *–ible boat*, das Faltboot.

collar [ˈkɔlə], 1. *s.* der Kragen, Rockkragen, Hemdkragen; das Kumt, Kummet (*Harn.*), Halsband (*dogs, etc.*); Kollier (*of pearls, etc.*); die Halskette, Ordenskette (*Her.*); der Ring, Reif(en), Bund (*Mech.*); *clamping* –, die Schelle; *stand-up* –, der Stehkragen; *turn-down* –, der Umlegekragen; (*coll.*) *get hot under the* –, sich aufregen *or* ärgern. 2. *v.a.* beim Kragen fassen *or* packen; (*sl.*) sich aneignen; (Fleisch) zusammenrollen. **–-beam,** *s.* der Querbalken. **–-bone,** *s.* das Schlüsselbein (*Anat.*). **–et,** *s.* kleiner Damenkragen (*of lace, etc.*); die Halsrüstung, Halsberge. **–-stud,** *s.* der Kragenknopf. **–-work,** *s.* harte Arbeit.

collate [kɔˈleɪt], *v.a.* kollationieren, kritisch vergleichen; einsetzen (*to*, in) (*a living*) (*Eccl.*).

collateral [koʊˈlætərəl], 1. *adj.* seitlich, Seiten–; gleichzeitig, begleitend, Neben–; in der Seitenlinie verwandt; – *circumstances*, Nebenumstände; – *descent*, die Abstammung von einer Seitenlinie; – *relations*, Seitenverwandte; – *security*, die Nebensicherheit. 2. *s.* Seitenverwandte(r), *m.*; die Bürgschaft, Nebensicherheit.

collat–ion [kɔˈleɪʃən], *s.* die Textvergleichung; Übertragung, Einsetzung (*to a living*); der Imbiß. **–or** [–ˈleɪtə], *s.* der Textvergleicher; Pfründenverleiher, Patron (*Eccl.*).

colleague [ˈkɔlɪːg], *s.* der Kollege, Amtsgenosse.

collect [kəˈlɛkt], 1. *v.a.* sammeln, zusammenbringen, auflesen; ansammeln, einsammeln, auffangen; einziehen (*taxes*); eintreiben, einkassieren (*money*); (*coll.*) abholen; – *o.s.*, sich zusammennehmen, sammeln *or* fassen. 2. *v.n.* sich ansammeln, sich versammeln, sich anhäufen. 3. *s.* [ˈkɔlɛkt], kurzes Gebet, die Kollekte. **–ed,** *adj.* gesammelt; (*fig.*) gefaßt. **–edness,** *s.* die Fassung. **–ing centre,** die Sammelstelle. **–ing vessel,** das Sammelbecken, Auffanggefäß. **–ion** [–ˈlɛkʃən], *s.* das Sammeln, die Sammlung, Anhäufung; Eintreibung, das Inkasso (*of money*); die Leerung (*of the letter-box*); das Gesammelte, die Ansammlung, Anhäufung; Kollekte (*Eccl.*); *ready for –ion*, zum Abholen bereit. **–ive,** *adj.* gesammelt, gesamt, vereint, gemeinschaftlich; Sammel–, Kollektiv–; *–ive bargaining*, das Verhandeln der Arbeitgeber- und Arbeitnehmerverbände; *–ive noun*, das Kollektivum, Sammelwort; *–ive ownership*, der Gemein(schafts)besitz. **–ively,** *adv.* insgesamt, im ganzen. **–ivism,** *s.* der Kollektivismus. **–ivist,** *adj.* kollektivistisch. **–or,** *s.* der Sammler; Kassierer, Inkassobeamte(r), *m.* (*C.L.*); der Einnehmer; (Strom)Abnehmer, die Sammelscheibe, der Bügel (*Elec.*); *tax-–or*, der Steuereinnehmer; *ticket-–or*, der Schaffner.

colleen [ˈkɔlɪːn], *s.* (*Irish*) das Mädchen.

colleg–e [ˈkɔlɪdʒ], *s.* höhere Schule, die Akademie, Hochschule, Universität; das College (*Oxford & Cambridge*); Kollegium; *–e of cardinals*, das Kardinalkollegium; *commercial –e*, die Handelsschule; *–e dues*, Studiengebühren; *go to –e*, die Universität beziehen; *military –e*, die Kadettenanstalt; *training –e*, die Lehrerbildungsanstalt. **–ian** [kəˈlɪːdʒɪən], *s.* der Student. **–iate** [kəˈlɪːdʒɪɪt], *adj.* studentisch, akademisch, Universitäts–; *–iate church*, die Stiftskirche; *–iate school*, die Stiftsschule, Stiftung.

collide [kəˈlaɪd], *v.n.* zusammenstoßen (*also fig.*), rennen (*with*, gegen); (*fig.*) im Widerspruch stehen (*with*, zu).

collie [ˈkɔlɪ], *s.* schottischer Schäferhund.

collier [ˈkɔlɪə], *s.* der Kohlenarbeiter, Grubenarbeiter; das Kohlenschiff. **–y** [–rɪ], *s.* das Kohlenbergwerk, die Kohlengrube, Zeche.

colligate [ˈkɔlɪgeɪt], *v.a.* vereinigen, verbinden.

collimat–ion [kɔlɪˈmeɪʃən], *s.* die Kollimation (*Opt.*); das Zielen, Richten, Visieren; *line of –ion*, die Absehlinie, optische Achse. **–or** [ˈkɔlɪmeɪtə], *s.* der Kollimator, das Richtglas, die Visiervorrichtung.

collision [kəˈlɪʒən], *s.* der Zusammenstoß; (*fig.*) Widerspruch, Widerstreit, Konflikt; *come into – with*, in Konflikt geraten mit.

collocat–e [ˈkɔlokeɪt], *v.a.* (zusammen)stellen, (an)ordnen. **–ion** [–ˈkeɪʃən], *s.* die Stellung, Ordnung; Zusammenstellung, Anordnung.

collocutor [ˈkɔləkjuːtə], *s.* der Gesprächsteilnehmer.

collodion [kəˈloudɪən], *s.* das Kollodium (*Chem.*).

collogue [kəˈlɔg], *v.n.* (*coll.*) eine vertrauliche Besprechung halten, heimlich bereden.

colloid [ˈkɔlɔɪd], *s.* das Kolloid.

collop [ˈkɔləp], *s.* die Fleischschnitte.

colloqu–ial [kəˈloukwɪəl], *adj.* Umgangs–, Alltags–, familiär. **–ialism** [–ɪzm], *s.* der Ausdruck der Umgangssprache, familiärer Ausdruck. **–y** [ˈkɔləkwɪ], *s.* formelle Besprechung, das Gespräch.

collotype [ˈkɔlətaɪp], *s.* der Lichtdruck.

collusi–on [kəˈluːʒən], *s.* betrügerisches Einverständnis, die Durchstecherei. **–ve,** *adj.* verabredet, abgekartet.

collywobbles [ˈkɔlɪwɔbəlz], *s.* (*coll.*) das Bauchgrimmen.

colocynth [ˈkɔlosɪnθ], *s.* der Koloquinte (*Bot.*).

[1]**colon** [ˈkoulən], *s.* der Doppelpunkt, das Kolon (*Typ.*).

[2]**colon,** *s.* der Grimmdarm, Dickdarm (*Anat.*).

colonel [ˈkəːnl], *s.* der Oberst; *lieutenant-–*, der Oberstleutnant. **–cy,** *s.* die Oberstenstelle; der Oberstenrang.

colon–ial [kəˈlounjəl], 1. *adj.* Kolonial–, kolonial; *–ial Office*, das Kolonialamt; *–ial preference*, die Politik der Vorzugszölle zwischen Mutterland und Kolonien; *–ial Secretary*, der Kolonialminister. 2. *s.* der Bewohner einer Kolonie. **–ist** [ˈkɔlənɪst], *s.* der Ansiedler, Kolonist. **–ization** [kɔlənaɪˈzeɪʃən], *s.* die Kolonisierung, Kolonisation, Besiedelung. **–ize** [ˈkɔlənaɪz], 1. *v.a.* kolonisieren, besiedeln (*territory*), ansiedeln (*people*). 2. *v.n.* eine Kolonie gründen; sich ansiedeln. **–izer,** *s.* der Kolonisator. **–y** [ˈkɔlənɪ], *s.* die Kolonie, Siedlung; Gruppe (*Zool., etc.*).

colonnade [kɔləˈneɪd], *s.* der Säulengang, die Säulenhalle (*Arch.*); Allee (*of trees*).

colony, *see* **colon–y.**

colophon [ˈkɔləfən], *s.* der Kolophon (*Typ.*).

colophony [koˈlɔfənɪ], *s.* das Kolophonium, Geigenharz.

color, *s.* (*Amer.*) *see* **colour.** **–ation** [kʌləˈreɪʃən], *s.* das Färben; die Färbung, Anfärbung; Farbengebung, das Kolorit (*Paint.*). **–atura** [–rəˈtjʊrə], *s.* die Koloratur (*Mus.*). **–ific** [–ˈrɪfɪk], *adj.* färbend, Farben–. **–imeter,** *s.* der Farbenmesser.

coloss–al [kəˈlɔsəl], *adj* riesenhaft, riesig, Riesen–, ungeheuer, kolossal; massig. **–us** [kəˈlɔsəs], *s.* der Koloß, die Riesengestalt.

colour [ˈkʌlə], 1. *s.* die Farbe; Anstrichfarbe; Färbung, das Kolorit; die Gesichtsfarbe, Hautfarbe; Klangfarbe (*Mus.*); der Anstrich, Anschein; Ton, die Stimmung, Schattierung; der Deckmantel, Vorwand. **–s,** *pl.* die Fahne (*Mil.*); die Auszeichnung als Mannschaftsmitglied (*Sport*); (*a*) (*with nouns & adjectives*) *body-–*, die Deckfarbe; *complementary –*, die Gegenfarbe, Ergänzungsfarbe; *composite –s*, Mischfarben (*pl.*); *fast –*, haltbare Farbe; *fugitive –*, unbeständige Farbe; *local –*, die Lokalfärbung; *national –s*, die Nationalfarben; *oil-–*, die Ölfarbe; *primary –s*, die Grundfarben; *priming –*, die Grundierfarbe; *prismatic –s*, die Prismenfarben; *secondary –s*, die Mischfarben; *water-–*, die Wasserfarbe; das Aquarell; (*b*) (*with genitive*) *coat of –*, der Farbenauftrag; *man of –*, Farbige(r), *m.*; *play of –*, das Farbenspiel; *theory of –s*, die Farbenlehre; *trooping* (*of*) *the –*, die Fahnenparade; (*c*) (*with verbs*) *change –*, verfärben, die Farbe wechseln; erröten; erblassen; *get one's –s*, Mitglied der ersten Mannschaft werden (*Sport*); *give* or *lend – to a th.*, einer S. den Anschein der *or* Anstrich von Wahrscheinlichkeit geben; *have a –*, blühend aussehen; *join the –s*, Soldat werden; *nail one's –s to the mast, stick to one's –s*, hartnäckig bei seinem Standpunkt bleiben; *show one's –s*, Farbe bekennen; *serve with the –s*, im Heere dienen; *troop the –*(*s*), die Fahnenparade abnehmen; (*d*) (*with prepositions*) (*coll*) *be* or *feel off –*, unpäßlich sein, nicht auf der Höhe sein, sich nicht wohl fühlen; *come out in one's true –s*, sich in seinem wahren Lichte zeigen; *paint a p. in his true –s*, einem zeigen wie er ist; *under false –s*, unter falscher Flagge; *come off with flying –s*, den Sieg davontragen. 2. *v.a.* färben, kolorieren, anstreichen, bemalen; (*fig*) einen Anstrich geben (*Dat.*), beschönigen, bemänteln, übertreiben, entstellen; (*fig.*) beeinflussen, sich abfärben auf 3. *v.n.* erröten; *she –ed up to the eyes*, sie wurde über und über rot. **–able** [–rəbl], *adj.* plausibel, annehmbar; fingiert, vorgeblich, mutmaßlich. **– bar,** die Rassenschranke. **–-blind,** *adj.* farbenblind. **–-box,** *s.* der Malkasten, Farbenkasten. **–ed** [ˈkʌləd], *adj.* gefärbt, koloriert; bunt, farbig; beschönigt; *–ed crayon*, die Farbkreide; *–ed gentleman*, Farbige(r), *m.*, der Neger; *–ed impression*, der Buntdruck (*Typ.*); *–ed pencil*, der Farbstift, Buntstift; *–ed ray*, farbiger Strahl (*Phys.*). **–-fast,** *adj.* waschecht, lichtecht. **–ful,** *adj.* farbenreich, farbenprächtig, farbenfreudig. **–-grinder,** *s.* der Farbenreiber. **–ing** [–rɪŋ], *s.* das Färben; die Färbung; Gesichtsfarbe; Farbengebung, Farbkunst, das Kolorit (*Paint*); *–ing agent*, das Farbmittel; *–ing body*, der Farbkörper; *–ing matter*, der Farbstoff. **–ist** [–rɪst], *s.* der Meister der Farbengebung. **–less,** *adj.* farblos; (*fig.*) matt, nichtssagend, neutral. **–man,** *s* der Farbenhändler. **–-photography,** *s.* die Farbphotographie. **–-printing,** *s.* der Farb(en)druck. **– sergeant,** der Fahnenunteroffizier (*Mil.*).

colport-age [ˈkɔlpɔ:tɪdʒ], *s.* der Hausierhandel (mit Büchern). **–eur** [–ə:], *s.* der (Bibel)Hausierer.

colt [koult], *s* das Füllen, Fohlen; (*fig.*) der Neuling. **–ish,** *adj.* mutwillig, wild, ausgelassen. **–sfoot,** *s.* der Huflattich (*Bot.*).

columbine [ˈkɔləmbɑɪn], *s.* die Akelei (*Bot.*).

column [ˈkɔləm], *s.* die Säule (*Arch., of smoke, etc.*), der Pfeiler; die Kolonne (*Mil.*); Spalte, Kolumne (*of a page*); Rubrik (*of a ledger*); *advertisement –*, die Anschlagsäule, Litfaßsäule; *– of figures*, die Zahlenkolumne. **–ar** [koˈlʌmnə], *adj.* säulenförmig, Säulen–. **–ist,** *s.* der Zeitungsartikelschreiber.

colure [kəˈljuːə], *s.* der Kolur (*Meteor.*).

colza [ˈkɔlzə], *s.* der Raps.

[1]**coma** [ˈkoumə], *s.* die Schlafsucht (*Med.*); der Dämmerzustand, die Bewußtlosigkeit. **–tose** [–tous], *adj.* schlafsüchtig.

[2]**coma,** *s.* der Haarbüschel, die Federkrone (*Bot.*); der Schweif (*Astr.*).

comb [koum], 1. *s.* der Kamm, Striegel, die Hechel (*Weav*); Honigwabe; der Kamm (*of a cock*). 2. *v.a.* kämmen; striegeln; krempeln (*wool*), hecheln (*flax*); absuchen (*the ground*) (*Mil.*); *– one's hair*, sich kämmen; *– out*, durchkämmen; sieben, ausmustern (*Mil.*). 3. *v.n.* sich brechen, sich überstürzen (*of waves*). **–er,** *s.* der Wollkämmer, Krempler; die Sturzwelle. **–ings,** *pl.* ausgekämmte Haare (*or* Fasern, *etc.*).

combat [ˈkɔmbət], 1. *s.* der Kampf, das Gefecht, der Streit; *close –*, der Nahkampf; *hand-to-hand –*, das Handgemenge, der Nahkampf; *single –*, der Zweikampf. 2. *v.a.* kämpfen gegen, bekämpfen, bestreiten (*opinions, etc.*). **–ant** [–ənt], *s.* der Kämpfer; Verfechter. **–ive,** *adj.* streitsüchtig, kampflustig, kampfbereit. **–iveness,** *s.* die Streitsucht, Kampflust.

combe [kuːm], *s. see* **coomb.**

combin-ation [kɔmbɪˈneɪʃən], *s* die Vereinigung, Verbindung, das Bündnis, Komplott; der Zusammenschluß, die Verknüpfung, Zusammenstellung, Zusammensetzung, Kombination (*Math.*); das Zusammenspiel (*in sports*); das Motorrad mit Beiwagen *pl.* die Hemdhose; *chemical –ation*, chemische Verbindung; *–ation padlock*, das Buchstabenschloß, Kombinationsschloß. **–e** [kəmˈbɑɪn], 1. *v.a.* verbinden, (in sich) vereinigen, zusammensetzen, zusammenfügen, kombinieren. 2. *v.n.* sich verbinden (*Chem.*), sich vereinigen, eine Einheit bilden; einen Bund schließen. 3 [ˈkɔmbɑɪn], *s.* der Verband, Ring, Trust (*C.L.*). *–ed arms*, gemischte Verbände, der Truppenverband (*Mil.*); *–ed transmitter and receiver*, der Senderempfänger (*Rad.*); *–e harvester*, *s.* der Mähdrescher.

combust-ibility [kəmbʌstɪˈbɪlɪtɪ], *s.* die Brennbarkeit, Entzündbarkeit. **–ible** [kəmˈbʌstɪbl], *adj.* (ver)brennbar, entzündbar, feuergefährlich; leicht erregbar; *–ible matter*, der Zündstoff. **–ibles,** *pl.* der Brennstoff. **–ion** [–ˈbʌstʃən], *s.* die Verbrennung, Entzündung; (*internal-*)*–ion engine*, der Verbrennungsmotor; *spontaneous –ion*, die Selbstentzündung; *–ion-chamber*, *s.* der Verbrennungsraum (*Locom., etc.*).

come [kʌm], *ir.v.n.* kommen; gelangen nach, ankommen (bei, an, in (*Dat.*)); herkommen, näherkommen (*Dat.*); gelingen; entstehen, zum Vorschein kommen, sich bilden, werden; (*coll.*) *it –s expensive*, es wird teuer; *– and go*, hin- und hergehen; wechseln (*as colours*); *I have –*, ich bin gekommen; *how –s it to be yours?* wie sind Sie dazu gekommen? (*coll.*) *how –s it that . . .?* wie ist es möglich daß . . . ? (*coll.*) *– a cropper*, zu Fall kommen (*also fig.*); *the malt –s*, das Malz keimt; (*sl.*) *– the fine gentleman*, den vornehmen Herrn spielen; *there is cheese to –*, es kommt noch Käse; *for a year to –*, ein weiteres Jahr, noch ein Jahr; *the life to –*, künftiges Leben; (*coll.*) *a year – Christmas*, Weihnachten in einem Jahr; *first –, first served*, wer zuerst kommt, mahlt zuerst; (*coll.*) *he's as stupid as they –*, er ist so dumm wie nur möglich; (*as interj.*) *–!* bitte! nun!; *– –!* sachte! na nu!; *– now!* ach gar! geh' doch!; **– about,** sich ereignen, zustandekommen, passieren; sich drehen (*of wind*) (*Naut.*). **– across a p.,** einen (an)treffen, auf einen stoßen; *he came across it accidentally*, es ist ihm zufällig untergekommen. **– after,** folgen (*Dat.*), nachkommen, nachfolgen (*Dat.*); zu erhalten suchen **– again,** wiederkommen; zurückkommen. **– along,** entlangkommen; herankommen, mitkommen; *– along!* los! vorwärts! rasch! **– amiss,** ungelegen kommen **– asunder,** in Stücke *or* auseinander gehen **– at,** gelangen zu, erreichen; losgehen auf (*Acc.*). **– away,** fortkommen; abfallen, abgehen, sich loslösen; *– away empty-handed*, mit leeren Händen ausgehen. **– back,** *v.n.* zurückkommen; wieder ins Gedächtnis kommen. **–-back,** *s.* (*coll.*) neues Auftreten; schlagfertige Antwort. **– behind,** nachkommen, hinterherkommen. **– by,** vorüberkommen, vorbeikommen; erlangen; *– by one's death*, sich (*Dat.*) den Tod holen; *how did you – by that?* wo haben Sie das her? wie kommen Sie dazu? **– down,** *v.n.* herabkommen, herunterkommen, heruntergehen (*of prices*), fallen, sinken; einstürzen, zusammenfallen; gedemütigt werden; herunterreichen (*of a dress, etc.*); (*sl.*) *he came down handsomely*, er zeigte sich sehr freigebig *or* nobel, er ließ sich nicht lumpen; *– down a peg*, mildere Saiten aufziehen, etwas kleinlaut werden; *– down before the wind*, mit dem Wind fahren (*Naut.*); *– down in the world*, herunterkommen; *– down upon a p.*, einem Vorwürfe machen, herfallen über einen, einen scharf rügen *or* schelten; – *down on s.o. like a ton of bricks*, einem die heftigsten Vorwürfe machen; (*coll.*) – *down with*, herausrücken mit. **– -down,** *s.* (*coll.*) die Herabsetzung, Blamage, der Reinfall. **– for,** kommen für *or* wegen, abholen. **– forth,** herauskommen, hervorkommen. **– forward,** vorwärtskommen; sich zeigen, auftreten, hervortreten, hervorkommen, sich melden. **– from,** herkommen *or* herrühren von, stammen aus. **– home,** nach Hause kommen; *it came home to him at last*, es leuchtete ihm endlich ein, es wurde ihm endlich nahegebracht. **– in,** hereinkommen, hereintreten; ankommen, einlaufen, anlangen (*trains, etc.*); eingehen (*of orders*); ans Ziel kommen; aufkommen (*as fashions*); – *in!* herein!; – *in for*, sich zuziehen; teilhaben an (*Dat.*); (*coll.*) – *in for a good thrashing*, sich eine Tracht Prügel aufhalsen, eine Tracht Prügel abkriegen; *that –s in handy* or *useful*, das kommt sehr gelegen; (*coll.*) *where do I – in?* was ist mit mir? wo bleibe ich? *where does the joke – in?* wo steckt der Witz? **– into,** eintreten in; – *into demand*, in Nachfrage kommen; – *into force*, in Kraft treten; – *into one's own*, zur Geltung kommen, wieder zu seinem Recht kommen, Erfolg erzielen, auf seine Rechnung kommen; – *into play*, in Tätigkeit treten; – *into property*, ein Vermögen erben; – *into sight*, in Sicht kommen; – *into the world*, auf die Welt kommen. **– loose,** locker werden. **– near,** sich nähern (*Dat.*); ähnlich sein (*Dat.*), Ähnlichkeit haben mit; nahekommen (*Dat.*), beinahe erreichen; *I came near breaking my neck*, ich hätte mir beinahe den Hals gebrochen. **– next,** darauf folgen. **– of,** abstammen von; entstehen aus, werden aus; – *of it what will*, es entstehe daraus was mag; *this –s of smoking*, das kommt davon wenn man raucht. **– off,** sich loslösen, abfallen, abgehen; ablaufen, erfolgen, stattfinden; (*coll.*) glücken, ausfallen; abschneiden (*of p.*); abgesetzt werden (*of plays*); – *off creditably*, mit Ehren ausgehen, hervorgehen *or* davonkommen; – *off duty*, mit dem Dienst fertig sein; – *off a loser*, dabei verlieren, den Kürzeren ziehen; *the lid won't – off*, der Deckel will nicht ab *or* herunter; (*sl.*) – *off it!* hör' damit auf! **– on,** vorrücken, heranrücken, eintreten, hereinbrechen; fortkommen; vorwärtskommen, vorwärtsschreiten, Fortschritte machen; – *on!* komm mit! komm weiter!; *night is coming on*, die Nacht zieht herauf *or* bricht herein; *it will very likely – on to rain*, es wird wohl Regen geben. **– out,** herauskommen, veröffentlicht werden, erscheinen (*newspapers, etc.*); bekannt werden, an den Tag kommen; hervorgehen, sich zeigen; ausfallen, ausgehen (*as hair*); herausgehen (*as stains*); hervortreten (*as details in a picture*); aufgehen (*puzzles, etc.*); auf Bälle gehen, in die Gesellschaft eingeführt werden (*as a debutante*); – *out in spots*, fleckig werden; – *out on strike*, in Streik treten; *he came out top*, er ging als erster hervor; – *out with s. th.*, mit etwas herausplatzen. **– over,** herüberkommen; befallen, überkommen, überlisten, übervorteilen. **– right,** gut ausgehen. **– round,** sich erholen; sich bedenken, sich anders *or* eines Besseren besinnen; wiederkehren; sich bekehren (*to a point of view*); sich drehen (*as the wind*); vorbeikommen, herüberkommen; wieder zum Bewußtsein kommen; lavieren (*Naut.*). **– short of,** nicht erreichen, nicht gleichkommen, nachstehen (*Dat.*). **– through,** durchkommen; sich entledigen (*Dat.*); (*coll.*) Erfolg haben, das Ziel erreichen. **– to** (*with inf.*), dazu kommen (*with inf.*), zu (*noun*) kommen; – *to do*, dazu kommen es zu tun; – *to believe*, zu der Überzeugung kommen; an, auf *or* in eine *or* zu einer S. kommen; gelangen zu, sich nähern (*Dat.*); – *to an end*, aufhören, zu Ende kommen, ein Ende haben; – *to a bad* or (*sl.*) *sticky end*, ein schlimmes Ende nehmen; *he doesn't know what's coming to him*, er weiß nicht was ihm bevorsteht; *how much* or *what does it – to?* wieviel macht es (aus)? – *to be*, schließlich werden; – *to be considered*, schließlich angesehen werden; – *to be in possession of*, in Besitz gelangen; – *to know*, kennenlernen; – *to regret a th.*, es noch bereuen; – *to blows*, handgemein werden; *he will never – to any good*, aus ihm wird nie etwas Rechtes werden; – *to grief* or *harm*, zu Schaden kommen; – *to hand*, zum Vorschein kommen; *your letter has – to hand*, Ihr Schreiben habe ich erhalten; – *to a head*, sich voll entwickeln; *it has – to my knowledge*, mir ist zu Ohren gekommen; – *to light*, an den Tag kommen; – *to little*, wenig Erfolg haben, wenig ausrichten; – *to nothing*, zu Wasser werden, ins Wasser fallen; – *to o.s.* or *one's senses*, wieder zu sich kommen; – *to pass*, sich ereignen, zustande kommen, erfolgen, sich zutragen; – *to a point*, spitz zulaufen; – *to the point*, zu der Sache kommen; – *to rest*, zur Ruhe kommen; – *to the same* (*thing*), auf eins herauskommen *or* hinauslaufen; – *to terms*, sich einigen; (*coll.*) – *it too strong*, es zu arg treiben. **– true,** sich verwirklichen *or* bewahrheiten, zur Wirklichkeit werden. **– under,** fallen *or* stehen unter (*Dat.*); unterstehen, unterliegen (*Dat.*). **– undone,** sich (los)lösen, abfallen. (*sl.*) **– unstuck,** Mißerfolg haben, einen Rückschlag erleiden. **– up,** heraufkommen, aufgeworfen *or* aufgerollt werden, zur Sprache kommen; aufgehen, keimen (*of plants*); – *up against*, stoßen auf; auftreten gegen; – *up for discussion*, zur Diskussion kommen; – *up smiling*, lächelnd überstehen; – *up to*, erreichen, reichen bis zu *or* an; gleichtun, gleichkommen; zutreten auf (*Acc.*), herantreten an (*Acc.*); – *up to expectations*, Erwartungen entsprechen; – *up to the mark*, den Ansprüchen genügen; – *up to the university*, auf die Universität gehen; – *up with*, einholen; gleichkommen (*Dat.*). **– upon,** kommen *or* stoßen auf (*Acc.*); hereinbrechen über, überfallen, überraschen. **– one's way,** einem unterkommen, sich einem bieten; *no work came his way*, er fand keine Arbeit.

comed-ian [kəˈmiːdɪən], *s.* der Komiker (*Theat.*); Komödiant, Lustspieldichter. **–y** [ˈkɔmɪdɪ], *s.* das Lustspiel, die Komödie; *light –y*, der Schwank, die Posse; *musical –y*, das Singspiel, die Operette.

comel-iness [ˈkʌmlɪnɪs], *s.* die Anmut, Grazie, Schönheit. **–y** [ˈkʌmlɪ], *adj.* anmutig; hübsch.

comer [ˈkʌmə], *s.* der *or* die Kommende; *all –s*, all und jeder; *first –*, der *or* die zuerst Kommende, der *or* die erste Beste; *new–*, der Neuankömmling.

comestible [kəˈmɛstɪbl], *adj.* eßbar. **–s,** *pl.* die Eßwaren, Nahrungsmittel (*pl.*).

comet [ˈkɔmɪt], *s.* der Komet.

comfit [ˈkʌmfɪt], *s.* das Konfekt, Zuckerwerk, die Zuckerware.

comfort [ˈkʌmfət], 1. *s.* die Behaglichkeit, Bequemlichkeit, Gemütlichkeit, der Komfort; Trost, die Stärkung, Erquickung (*to*, für); der Tröster; *cold –*, schlechter Trost; *creature –(s)*, leiblicher Genuß; *derive – from*, Trost finden in; *take –*, sich trösten, Mut fassen; *–s for the troops*, Liebesgaben (*pl.*). 2. *v.a.* trösten; erquicken; erfreuen. **–able,** *adj.* bequem, behaglich, gemütlich, komfortabel; trostreich (*words, etc.*); behäbig, wohlhabend (*of a p.*); ausreichend (*income*); *make o.s. –able*, es sich (*Dat.*) bequem machen; *feel more –able*, Erleichterung spüren (*as an invalid*). **–er,** *s.* der Tröster; *Job's –er*, schlechter Tröster. **–ing,** *adj.* tröstlich. **–less,** *adj.* trostlos; unbequem, unbehaglich; untröstlich, unerfreulich.

comfrey [ˈkʌmfrɪ], *s.* die Schwarzwurz (*Bot.*).

comfy [ˈkʌmfɪ], *adj.* (*coll.*) bequem, behaglich.

comic [ˈkɔmɪk], 1. *adj.* komisch, heiter, Lustspiel–; *see also* **–al.** 2. *s.* (*coll.*) der Komiker; – *actor*, der Komiker; – *paper*, das Witzblatt. – *strip*, *s.* der Karikaturstreifen. **–al,** *adj.* lustig, drollig, spaßig, possierlich. **–ality** [–ˈkælɪtɪ], *s.* das Komische, die Komik.

coming [ˈkʌmɪŋ], 1. *see* **come;** – *Sir!* gleich *or* sofort mein Herr! 2. *adj.* künftig, kommend; – *man*, kommender Mann. 3. *s.* das Kommen, die Ankunft; – *of age*, das Mündigwerden. **– -in,** *s.* der Eintritt. **– -on,** *s.* das Heranrücken, Anrücken.

comity [ˈkɔmɪtɪ], *s.* die Höflichkeit, gutes Einvernehmen; – *of nations*, das Konzert der Mächte; (*frequently used wrongly as if* = company).

comma [ˈkɔmə], *s.* der Beistrich, das Komma; *inverted –s*, die Anführungszeichen, Gänsefüßchen.

command [kəˈmɑːnd], 1. *v.a.* befehlen, gebieten (*Dat.*); fordern, beanspruchen; befehligen, kommandieren, führen (*Mil.*); beherrschen, verfügen über, zu Verfügung haben; abnötigen, einflößen; *her beauty –s love and admiration from all*, ihre Schönheit flößt allen Liebe und Bewunderung ein; *– me, madam!* gnädige Frau, verfügen Sie ganz über mich! *– one's passions*, seine Leidenschaften beherrschen; *– a ready sale*, guten Absatz finden; *– a good price*, einen guten Preis einbringen; *– respect*, Achtung gebieten *or* einflößen; *– silence*, Stillschweigen gebieten; *– a fine view*, eine schöne Aussicht besitzen *or* bieten. 2. *v.n.* den Befehl führen, befehlen, gebieten, herrschen, kommandieren. 3. *s.* die Herrschaft, Führung, Verfügung, Gewalt (*of*, über); der Auftrag, das Gebot, der Befehl; das Kommando, der Oberbefehl (*Mil.*); die Beherrschung (*of a language*); *at my –*, zu meiner Verfügung; *by –*, auf Befehl; *chain of –*, die Befehlerteilungsfolge (*Mil.*); *– of language*, die Sprachgewandtheit; *– over o.s.*, die Selbstbeherrschung; *supreme –*, oberste Heeresleitung; *– performance*, die Aufführung auf Allerhöchsten Befehl; *take – of*, das Kommando übernehmen über; *under the – of*, befehligt von; *word of –*, das Kommandowort (*Mil.*). **–ant** [kɔmən'dænt] *s.* der Befehlshaber, Kommandant, Kommandeur. **–eer** [kɔmən'dɪə], *v.a.* zum Dienst pressen, requirieren (*stores*); (*coll.*) sich aneignen, beschlagnahmen. **–er** [kə'mɑ:ndə], *s.* der Gebieter; Befehlshaber, Chef, Kommandant, Kommandeur, Truppenführer; Fregattenkapitän (*Naut.*); *wing –er*, *s.* der Fliegeroberstleutnant (*Av.*), Komtur (*of Order of Knighthood*); *–er-in-chief*, der Oberbefehlshaber, Höchstkommandierende(r), *m.* **–ery** [kə'mɑ:ndərɪ], *s.* die Komturei. **–ing** [–dɪŋ], *adj.* gebietend, kommandierend; herrschend, hervorragend, überragend (*of situation*); (*fig.*) eindrucksvoll, dominierend, imponierend; *–ing officer*, der Kommandeur, Befehlshaber. **–ment** [–mənt], *s.* das Gesetz, die Vorschrift; das Gebot; *the ten –ments*, die zehn Gebote. **–o** [kə'mɑ:ndoʊ], *s.* das Kommando, die Truppeneinheit; der Sabotagetrupp. **–-post**, *s.* der Gefechtsstand, Feuerleitungsstand (*Mil.*).

commemorat–e [kə'mɛməreɪt], *v.a.* gedenken (*Gen.*), (das Andenken) feiern; gedenkend erwähnen, erinnern an. **–ion** [–'reɪʃən], *s.* die Gedächtnisfeier, das Gedenkfest; *in –ion of*, zum Gedächtnis (*Gen.*) *or* Andenken an (*Acc.*). **–ive** [–rətɪv], *adj.* Gedächtnis–.

commence [kə'mɛns], *v.a.* & *n.* anfangen, beginnen; promovieren (*Univ.*). **–ment**, *s.* der Anfang, Beginn; die Promotion (*Univ.*).

commend [kə'mɛnd], 1. *v.a.* loben, belobigen; empfehlen; anvertrauen. 2. *v.r.* sich empfehlen. **–able**, *adj.* lobenswert, empfehlenswert, löblich. **–ation** ['kɔmɛndeɪʃən], *s.* die Empfehlung; das Lob. **–atory** [kə'mɛndətərɪ], *adj.* empfehlend, lobend; *–atory letter*, das Empfehlungsschreiben.

commensal [kə'mɛnsəl], 1. *adj.* an demselben Tische essend; parasitisch, Schmarotzer– (*Biol.*). 2. *s.* der Tischgenosse; Schmarotzer (*Biol.*).

commensura–bility [kəmɛnʃərə'bɪlɪtɪ], *s.* die Kommensurabilität. **–ble** [kə'mɛnʃərəbl], *adj.* mit gleichem Maße meßbar *or* zu messen(d) (*with*, wie), kommensurabel. **–te** [kə'mɛnʃərɪt], *adj.* von gleichem Umfang *or* gleicher Dauer, entsprechend, angemessen (*to* or *with* (*Dat.*)).

comment ['kɔmɛnt], 1. *v.n.* Bemerkungen machen (*upon*, über (*Acc.*)); kritische Anmerkungen machen (*on*, zu). 2. *s.* der Kommentar, die Erklärung, Erläuterung, Stellungnahme (*on*, zu), Bemerkung, Anmerkung (*on*, über). **–ary** ['kɔməntərɪ], *s.* der Kommentar (*on*, zu); *running –ary*, laufender Kommentar; der Hörbericht (*Rad.*). **–ate** ['kɔmɛnteɪt], *v.a. see* **–** 1. **–ator**, *s.* der Ausleger, Erläuterer, Kommentator; Funkberichter(statter) (*Rad.*).

commerc–e ['kɔmə:s], *s.* der Handel, Außenhandel; (*fig.*) Umgang, Verkehr; *Chamber of –e*, die Handelskammer. **–ial** [kə'mə:ʃəl], 1. *adj.* kaufmännisch, kommerziell, Geschäfts–, Handels–; technisch rein (*of chemicals*); *–ial college*, die Handelshochschule; *–ial education*, kaufmännische Bildung; *–ial hotel*, der Gasthof für Geschäftsreisende; *–ial law*, das Handelsrecht. *–ial plane*, das Zivilflugzeug, Verkehrsflugzeug; *–ial school*, die Handelsschule; *–ial traveller*, Handlungsreisende(r), *m.*, Geschäftsreisende(r), *m.*, der Vertreter. 2. *s.* (*coll.*) see *–ial traveller*. **–ialism**, *s.* der Handelsgeist. **–ialize**, *v.a.* in den Handel bringen, marktfähig machen.

comminat–ion [kɔmɪ'neɪʃən], *s.* die Drohung (*Eccl.*). **–ory** ['kɔmɪnətərɪ], *adj.* drohend.

commingle [kə'mɪŋgl], *v.a.* (& *n.* sich) vermischen, (sich) vermengen.

comminut–e ['kɔmɪnju:t], *v.a.* zerkleinern, zerstückeln; *–ed fracture*, der Splitterbruch (*Med.*). **–ion** [kɔmɪn'ju:ʃən], *s.* die Zerkleinerung; (*fig.*) Verkleinerung, Verringerung.

commiserat–e [kə'mɪzəreɪt], *v.a.* (& *n.* –e with) bemitleiden, bedauern. **–ing**, *adj.* mitleidig. **–ion** [–'reɪʃən], *s.* das Mitleid, Erbarmen, Bedauern (*on*, *of*, mit).

commissar [kɔmɪ'sɑ:], *s.* Beauftragte(r), *m.*, der Kommissar. **–iat** [–'sɛərɪət], *s.* das Kommissariat; Verpflegungsamt, die Intendantur, Nahrungsmittelversorgung. **–y** ['kɔmɪsərɪ], *s.* Bevollmächtigte(r), *m.*, der Kommissär; Intendanturbeamte(r), *m.* (*Mil.*); bischöflicher Vertreter (*Eccl.*). **–y-general**, der Oberproviantmeister.

commission [kə'mɪʃən], 1. *s.* der Auftrag, die Bestellung, Instruktion, Vollmacht; Verübung, Begehung (*Law*); Provision (*C.L.*); Stelle, das Amt; Offizierspatent (*Mil.*); der Ausschuß, die Kommission, das Komitee; *royal –*, der Untersuchungsausschuß; (*a*) (*with verbs*) *discharge a –*, einen Auftrag ausführen; *give a – for*, bestellen; *resign one's –*, seinen Abschied nehmen; (*b*) (*with prepositions*) *in –*, in Dienst gestellt (*of ships*), im Betriebe (stehend); *sell on –*, gegen Provision verkaufen; *put out of –*, außer Dienst (*ships*) *or* Betrieb stellen; *sins of –*, die Begehungssünden. 2. *v.a.* beauftragen, bevollmächtigen; bestellen; das Offizierspatent verleihen (*Dat.*); einen Auftrag geben (*Dat.*); abordnen; dienstbereit machen, in Dienst stellen (*a ship*); *–ed officer*, der (durch Patent angestellter) Offizier; *non- –ed officer*, der Unteroffizier. **–-agent**, *s.* der Kommissionär, Agent. **– business**, das Kommissionsgeschäft. **–aire** [kəmɪʃə'nɛə], *s.* der Dienstmann, Portier. **–er** [kə'mɪʃənə], *s.* Beauftragte(r), *m.*, Bevollmächtigte(r), *m.*; das Mitglied eines Regierungsausschusses; *High –er*, der Vertreter eines Dominions in London; *–er for oaths*, beeidigter Notar; *–er of Works*, der Minister für Staatsbauten.

commissure ['kɔmɪʃə], *s.* die Verbindungsstelle, Naht, das Bindeglied; der Nervenstrang (*Anat.*).

commit [kə'mɪt], *v.a.* begehen, verüben, ausüben (*a crime*); übergeben, einliefern (*a p., etc.*); anvertrauen (*a th. to a p.*, einem etwas); binden, verpflichten (*a p.*) (*also v.r.*); *– adultery*, ehebrechen; *– a crime*, ein Verbrechen begehen; *– to memory*, dem Gedächtnis einprägen; *– to paper*, zu Papier bringen; *– to prison*, einsperren; *stand –ted*, verpflichtet *or* gebunden sein; *– suicide*, Selbstmord begehen; *–ted for trial*, dem Gerichte zur Aburteilung eingeliefert. **–ment**, *s.* die Verhaftung, das Übergeben; die Überweisung, Auslieferung; Verpflichtung, Bindung; *undertake a –ment*, eine Verpflichtung eingehen. **–tal**, *s.* das Übergeben, Überweisen; die Begehung, Verübung, Ausübung; Verpflichtung; der Einsatz (*of forces*) (*Mil.*); *non- –tal*, *adj.* unverbindlich.

committee [kə'mɪtɪ], *s.* der Ausschuß, das Komitee, die Kommission; *go into –*, in Sonderausschüssen beraten (*Parl.*); *– of Imperial Defence*, der Reichsausschuß für Verteidigung; *joint –*, zusammengesetzter Ausschuß; *– of management*, der Verwaltungsausschuß; *standing –*, ständiger Ausschuß; *executive –*, geschäftsführender Ausschuß.

commix [kə'mɪks], (*archaic*) *v.a.* (& *n.* sich) vermischen. **–ture**, *s.* die Mischung, das Gemisch.

commode [kə'moʊd], *s.* der Nachtstuhl; die Kommode.

commodious [kə'moʊdɪəs], *adj.* bequem, geräumig. **–ness**, *s.* die Bequemlichkeit, Geräumigkeit.

commodity [kə'mɔdɪtɪ], *s.* die Ware, der Artikel, *pl.* Gebrauchsgüter.
commodore ['kɔmədɔ:], *s.* der Kommodore, Kapitän zur See, Kommandeur eines Geschwaders.
common ['kɔmən], 1. *adj.* gewöhnlich, üblich, alltäglich; allgemein, öffentlich; gemeinschaftlich, gemeinsam; gemein, niedrig, gewöhnlich, ordinär, vulgär; – *carrier*, öffentliches Transportmittel; *make – cause with*, gemeinsame Sache machen mit; – *charges*, gemeine Figuren (*pl.*) (*Her.*); – *chord*, der Dreiklang; *by – consent*, mit allgemeiner Zustimmung; – *divisor*, gemeinsamer Teiler (*Math.*); (*coll.*) – *or garden*, landläufig, gewöhnlich; – *gender*, doppeltes Geschlecht (*Gram.*); *be on – ground with*, von den gleichen Voraussetzungen ausgehen wie, auf den gleichen Grundlagen fußen wie; *have in – with*, gemeinsam haben mit; *the – herd*, gemeines *or* niedriges Volk; – *law*, das Gewohnheitsrecht; – *measure*, see – *divisor*; – *noun*, der Gattungsname; *the – people*, die gewöhnlichen Leute; *Court of – Pleas*, der Zivilgerichtshof; *Book of – Prayer*, anglikanische Liturgie, anglikanisches Gebetbuch; – *rights*, Menschenrechte; – *salt*, das Kochsalz, Siedesalz, Natriumchlorid; – *soldier*, gemeiner Soldat; – *talk*, das Stadtgespräch; – *time*, gerader Takt (*Mus.*); – *usage*, weit verbreiteter Gebrauch; *the – weal*, das Gemeinwesen, Gemeinwohl; – *woman*, ordinäres Weib, die Hure. 2. *s.* der Gemeindeplatz, die Gemeindewiese; das Gemeinsame, Allgemeine; *have in –*, gemeinschaftlich besitzen; *in – with*, gemeinsam mit, in Übereinstimmung mit, genau wie; *out of the –*, außergewöhnlich, über das Gewöhnliche hinaus; *right of –*, das Mitbenutzungsrecht; – *right of pasturage*, das Weiderecht. **-alty** [–'næltɪ], *s.* gemeines Volk, die Gesamtheit, Korporation. **-er** ['kɔmənə], *s.* Nichtadlige(r), *m.*, Bürgerliche(r), *m.*; das Mitglied des englischen Unterhauses (*Parl.*); der Student der für seine Verpflegung bezahlt hat (*Univ.*). **-ly**, *adv.* meistens, allgemein; gemeinschaftlich. **ness** ['kɔmənɪs], *s.* häufiges Vorkommen, die Gewöhnlichkeit; Gemeinheit; Gemeinschaft. **-place** [–pleɪs], 1. *adj.* alltäglich, gewöhnlich; abgedroschen; *–place book*, das Kollektaneenbuch, Sammelheft. 2. *s.* der Gemeinplatz; das Alltägliche, Platte, Gewöhnliche. **--room**, das Lehrerzimmer (*in schools*); das Klubzimmer des Lehrkörpers (*Univ.*). **-s** [–z], *pl.* die Gemeinen, Bürgerlichen, Nichtadligen; die Ration, gemeinschaftliche Kost; *the* (*House of*) *–s*, das Unterhaus; *be kept on short –s*, nicht satt zu essen bekommen, von schmaler Kost leben. **--sense**, gesunder Menschenverstand, schlichte Vernunft. **-wealth** [–wɛlθ], *s.* das Gemeinwesen; der Staat; die Republik; *the –wealth*, die englische Republik (*1649–60*); *Australian –wealth*, Australischer Staatenbund; *the –wealth of learning*, die Gelehrtenrepublik; *British –wealth of Nations*, Britischer Staatenbund.
commotion [kə'mouʃən], *s.* heftige Bewegung, die Verwirrung, Erregung; der Tumult, Aufruhr; *make a –*, Aufsehen erregen.
commun-al ['kɔmjunəl], *adj.* Gemeinde–, Kommunal–; *–al kitchen*, die Volksküche. **-alize**, *v.a.* eingemeinden. **-e** [kə'mju:n], 1. *v.n.* sich unterhalten; das Abendmahl empfangen, kommunizieren (*Eccl*); *–e with o.s.*, in sich gehen. 2. *s.* ['kɔmju:n], die Gemeinde; Kommune.
communic-able [kə'mju:nɪkəbl], *adj.* mitteilbar, erzählbar; übertragbar (*of disease*); mitteilsam. **-ant**, *s.* der Kommunikant, (regelmäßiger) Abendmahlsgast. **-ate** [–keɪt], 1. *v a.* mitteilen, benachrichtigen; übertragen (*to*, auf) (*disease*). 2. *v.n.* kommunizieren, das Abendmahl empfangen (*Eccl.*); in Verbindung stehen, sich in Verbindung setzen; zusammenhängen, verbunden sein (*of rooms*). **-ation** [–'keɪʃən], *s.* die Mitteilung, Bekanntmachung, Nachricht; der Verkehr, die Verbindung; der Durchgang, Verkehrsweg, Verbindungsweg; *pl.* die Nachschublinien (*Mil.*); *–ation centre*, die Nachrichtensammelstelle; *channel of –ation*, der Nachrichtenweg; *–ation cord*, die Notleine, Notbremse (*Railw.*); (*Prov.*) *evil –ations corrupt good manners*, schlechter Umgang verdirbt gute Sitten; *ground –ation*, die Boden-zu-Bord-Verbindung *or* Verständigung (*Av.*); *inter-–ation*, die Bordverbindung, Eigenverständigung (*Av.*); *line of –ations*, die Etappe (*Mil.*); *means of –ation*, die Verkehrsmittel (*pl.*); *–ation by rail*, die Eisenbahnverbindung; *–ation of motion*, die Fortpflanzung der Bewegung; *–ations trench*, *s.* der Verbindungsgraben, Stichgraben (*Mil.*); *two-way –ation*, der Wechselverkehr; *visual –ation*, die Zeichenverbindung. **-ative** [–kətɪv], *adj.* mitteilsam; redselig, gesprächig. **-ativeness**, *s.* die Mitteilsamkeit. **-ator**, *s.* der Mitteiler; die Notleine (*Railw*).
communion [kə'mju:njən], *s.* die Gemeinschaft, Verbindung, der Verkehr; das Heilige Abendmahl; die Kommunion (*R.C.*); *hold – with s.o.*, mit einem Verkehr unterhalten; – *with o.s.*, die Einkehr bei sich; **--bread**, *s.* das Abendmahlsbrot, die Oblate, Hostie. **--cup**, *s.* der Abendmahlskelch. **--rail**, *s.* das Altargitter. **--service**, *s.* die Abendmahlsfeier. **--table**, *s.* der Altar, Tisch des Herrn.
communiqué [kə'mju:nɪkeɪ], *s.* die Meldung, der Bericht, die Verlautbarung, amtliche Mitteilung.
communis-m ['kɔmjunɪzm], *s.* der Kommunismus. **-t** [–nɪst], 1. *s.* der Kommunist. 2. *adj.* kommunistisch.
community [kə'mju:nɪtɪ], *s.* die Gemeinschaft, Gemeinsamkeit; Körperschaft, Gemeinde; der Staat, das Gemeinwesen; die Allgemeinheit, Gesamtheit; – *of goods*, die Gütergemeinschaft; – *of interests*, die Gemeinsamkeit der Interessen; – *singing*, gemeinsames Singen.
commut-ability [kəmju:tə'bɪlɪtɪ], *s.* die Vertauschbarkeit. **-able** [kə'mju:təbl], *adj.* vertauschbar; ablösbar. **-ation** [kɔmju'teɪʃən], *s.* die Veränderung; Umwandlung, Vertauschung; der Tausch, Umtausch; die Herabsetzung (*of a penalty*), Ablösung (*of obligations*); Umschaltung (*Elec.*); *–ation of sentence*, die Strafmilderung, der Strafnachlaß; *–ation-ticket*, die Abonnementskarte, Dauerkarte (*Amer.*). **-ator** ['kɔmjuteɪtə], *s.* der Umschalter, Gleichrichter, Stromwender (*Elec.*). **-e** [kə'mju:t], *v.a.* austauschen, umtauschen, vertauschen, umwandeln, auswechseln, verändern, mildern, ablösen. **-er**, *s* der Abonnementsinhaber (*Amer.*).
compact [kəm'pækt], 1. *adj.* dicht, fest, kompakt; zusammengedrängt, gedrängt, bündig (*style*). 2. *v.a.* zusammendrängen, verbinden; verdichten. 3. ['kɔmpækt], *s.* der Vertrag, Pakt, die Übereinkunft. **-ness**, *s.* die Dichte, Dichtigkeit, Festigkeit; Knappheit, Bündigkeit (*of style*).
[1]**companion** [kəm'pænjən], 1. *s.* der Gesellschafter, Begleiter; Kamerad, Genosse; das Seitenstück, Gegenstück; *–-in-arms*, der Waffenbruder; *boon –*, der Zechkumpan; – *of the Bath* (*C.B.*), der Ritter des Bath-Ordens; *travelling –*, Mitreisende(r), *m.* 2. (*as attrib.*) dazu passend, zugehörig, Gegen–, Seiten–, Begleit–. **-able**, *adj.* gesellig, umgänglich. **-ableness**, *s.* die Geselligkeit, Umgänglichkeit. **-ate** [–nɪt], *adj.*; *–ate marriage*, die Kameradschaftsehe. **-ship**, *s.* die Kameradschaft, Gesellschaft.
[2]**companion**, *s.* (**--hatch**) das Deckfenster, die Kajütskappe. **--ladder**, *s.* **--way**, *s.* die Kajütentreppe, der Niedergang (*Naut.*).
company ['kʌmpənɪ], *s.* die Begleitung, Gesellschaft, das Zusammensein; die Kompagnie (*Mil.*); Handels)Gesellschaft, Genossenschaft (*C.L.*); Zunft, Innung; der Haufen; die Mannschaft, Besatzung (*of a ship*); – *of actors*, die Schauspielertruppe; *chartered –*, gesetzlich genehmigte Gesellschaft; *be fond of –*, gerne Gesellschaft haben, Geselligkeit lieben, *they have –*, sie haben Gäste; *be good –*, ein guter Gesellschafter sein; *in – with*, zusammen *or* in Gesellschaft mit; *be in the – of s.o.*, in jemandes Begleitung sein; *joint-stock –*, die Aktiengesellschaft; *keep a p. –*, einem Gesellschaft leisten; *keep – with*, Umgang haben mit; *keep – with a girl*, mit einem Mädel verkehren *or* ein Verhältnis haben; *limited* (*liability*) –, die Gesellschaft mit beschränkter Haftung; *part – (with a p.)*, sich (von einem) trennen *or* auseinandergehen; *receive –*, Gesellschaft bei sich empfangen; *see no –*, keinen

Umgang haben; *strolling* –, die Wandertruppe; *trading* –, die Handelsgesellschaft; – *of travellers*, die Reisegesellschaft; –*'s water*, das Leitungswasser.

compar–able ['kɔmpərəbl], *adj.* vergleichbar. **–ative** [kəm'pærətɪv], 1. *adj.* vergleichend, bedingt, relativ; steigernd (*Gram.*); –*ative anatomy*, vergleichende Anatomie; –*ative beauty*, relative Schönheit; –*ative value*, der Vergleichswert. 2. *s.* der Komparativ (*Gram.*). **–atively,** *adv. see* **–ative**; (*coll.*) ziemlich, verhältnismäßig. **–e** [kəm'pɛə], 1. *v.a.* vergleichen (*with, to*, mit); gleichstellen, gleichsetzen, auf eine Stufe stellen (*to*, mit); steigern (*Gram.*); *as –ed with* or *to*, im Vergleich mit *or* zu; *not to be –ed with*, nicht zu vergleichen mit; (*coll.*) –*e notes*, Meinungen austauschen. 2. *v.n.* sich vergleichen (lassen), den Vergleich aushalten, wetteifern (*with*, mit). 3. *s.* der Vergleich (*poet.*); *beyond, past* or *without –e*, unvergleichlich. **–ison** [kəm'pærɪsən], *s.* der Vergleich; die Vergleichsmöglichkeit, Ähnlichkeit; Vergleichung, das Gleichnis; die Steigerung (*Gram.*); *bear –ison with*, den Vergleich aushalten mit, sich sehr wohl vergleichen lassen mit; *beyond –ison*, unvergleichlich; *by –ison*, vergleichsweise, zum Vergleich; *in –ison with*, verglichen mit, im Vergleich mit *or* zu; *make* or *draw a –ison*, einen Vergleich anstellen *or* ziehen.

compartment [kəm'pɑ:tmənt], *s.* die Abteilung; das Fach; die Zelle; das Abteil (*Railw.*); *luggage* –, der Gepäckraum; *smoking* –, das Raucherabteil; *water-tight* –, wasserdichte Abteilung.

compass ['kʌmpəs], 1. *s.* der Umfang, Umkreis, die Ausdehnung; der Zeitraum; der Bezirk, Bereich; Schranken (*pl.*); der Umweg, die Abschweifung; (*magnetic* –) die Bussole, der Kompaß; *prismatic* –, die Patentbussole; *repeater* –, der Tochterkompaß; *point of the* –, der Kompaßstrich; *keep within* –, die Schranken einhalten; *reduce in* –, in engeren Rahmen fassen; – *of the voice*, der Stimmumfang; – *variation*, die Abweichung der Magnetnadel. 2. *v.a.* (*archaic*) *see* **encompass**; bewerkstelligen, zustandebringen, zeitigen; erzielen, erreichen, vollenden, durchsetzen (*one's purpose*); anstiften, planen, anzetteln; – *a p.'s death*, einem nach dem Leben trachten. **– -bearing,** *s.* die Peilung. **– -box,** *s.* das Kompaßgehäuse. **– -card,** *s.* die Kompaßscheibe, Windrose. **– direction,** *s.* die Gradzahl. **–es,** *pl.* der Zirkel; *pair of –es*, der Zirkel; *beam- –es*, der Stabzirkel; *bow- –es*, der Nullenzirkel; *measure with –es*, abzirkeln. **– needle,** *s.* die Magnetnadel. **– -saw,** *s.* die Stichsäge, Lochsäge, Laubsäge.

compassion [kəm'pæʃən], *s.* das Mitleid, Erbarmen (*for* or *with*, mit); *have* or *take – on*, Mitleid empfinden mit. **–ate,** 1. *adj.* mitleidig, mitleidsvoll; –*ate allowance*, das Gnadengehalt; –*ate leave*, der Sonderurlaub aus Familiengründen (*Mil.*). 2. *v.a.* bemitleiden (*Acc.*). **–ateness** [–nɪtnɪs], *s. see* **–**.

compatib–ility [kəmpætɪ'bɪlɪtɪ], *s.* die Verträglichkeit, Vereinbarkeit; –*ility of temper*, verträgliches Gemüt. **–le** [kəm'pætɪbl], *adj.* verträglich, vereinbar (*with*, mit); schicklich, angemessen (*with* (*Dat.*)).

compatriot [kəm'pætrɪət], *s.* der Landsmann.

compeer ['kɔmpɪə], *s.* Gleichstehende(r), *m.*; der Genosse; *have no* –, nicht seinesgleichen haben.

compel [kəm'pɛl], *v.a.* zwingen, nötigen (*a p.*); erzwingen, abnötigen (*a th.*). **–ling,** *adj.* unwiderstehlich.

compendi–ous [kəm'pɛndɪəs], *adj.* kurz, kurz gefaßt, gedrängt. **–ousness,** *s.* die Kürze, Gedrängtheit. **–um** [–ɪəm], *s.* das Handbuch, der Grundriß, Leitfaden, Auszug, die Zusammenfassung.

compensat–e ['kɔmpənseɪt], 1. *v.a.* ersetzen; ausgleichen; entschädigen. 2. *v.n.* aufwiegen, kompensieren, Ersatz geben für. **–ing,** *adj.* ausgleichend, Ausgleichs–. **–ion** [–'seɪʃən], *s.* der Ersatz; Schadenersatz, die Vergütung, Entschädigung; Ausgleichung, Kompensation, der Ausgleich; Lohn, das Gehalt (*Amer.*); *make –ion for*, Ersatz leisten für *as –ion* or *by way of –ion* als Ersatz; *disability –ion*, die Entschädigung für Dienstbeschädigung; *workmen's –ion*, die Unfallversicherung. **–ory** [kəm'pɛnsətərɪ], *adj.* ausgleichend, Entschädigungs–; –*ory vowel-lengthening*, die Ersatzdehnung (*Phonet.*).

compete [kəm'pɪ:t], *v.n.* sich mitbewerben (*for*, um); konkurrieren, wetteifern (*for*, um); sich messen (*with*, mit).

competen–ce ['kɔmpɪtəns], *s.*, **–cy,** *s.* die Fähigkeit, Befähigung, Tauglichkeit, Qualifikation; Zuständigkeit, Befugnis (*Law*); das Auskommen. **–t,** ['kɔmpɪtənt], *adj.*, zuständig, kompetent (*Law*); zulänglich, ausreichend, entsprechend, hinreichend, hinlänglich, angemessen, statthaft; (*coll.*) (leistungs)fähig; –*t authority*, zuständige Behörde; –*t person*, fähiger Kopf.

competit–ion [kɔmpɪ'tɪʃən], *s.* der Wettbewerb; die Konkurrenz (*for*, um; *with*, mit); das Preisausschreiben; *enter a –ion*, an einem Wettbewerb teilnehmen; –*ion in armaments*, das Wettrüsten; *unfair –ion*, unlauterer Wettbewerb. **–ive** [–'pɛtɪtɪv], *adj.* auf Wettbewerb eingestellt, Konkurrenz–, wetteifernd; konkurrenzfähig; –*ive examination*, die Konkurrenzprüfung; –*ive price*, konkurrenzfähiger Preis. **–or** [–'pɛtɪtə], *s.* der Mitbewerber, Konkurrent, Kandidat, Teilnehmer (*for*, um; *in*, an).

compil–ation [kɔmpɪ'leɪʃən], *s.* die Zusammenstellung, Zusammenfassung, Sammlung, Kompilation. **–e** [kəm'pɑɪl], *v.a.* zusammentragen, zusammenstellen, kompilieren (*from*, aus (*Dat.*)). **–er,** *s.* der Kompilator.

complacen–ce [kəm'pleɪsəns], *s.*, **–cy,** *s.* die Selbstgefälligkeit, das Wohlgefallen, Behagen; *self-–cy*, die Selbstzufriedenheit. **–t** [–t], *adj.* selbstgefällig, behaglich.

complain [kəm'pleɪn], *v.n.* klagen, sich beklagen, sich beschweren, Klage führen (*of*, über (*Acc.*)); *he –ed to me of him*, er beklagte sich bei mir über ihn. **–ant,** *s.* der Kläger. **–t,** *s.* die Klage (*also* (*Law*); Klageschrift; Beschwerde, Beanstandung; Krankheit, das Übel (*Med.*); *make –ts about*, sich beklagen *or* beschweren über, Klage führen über; *there were –ts that . . .*, Klagen wurden laut daß. . . .

complaisan–ce [kəm'pleɪzəns], *s.* die Gefälligkeit, Willfährigkeit, Nachgiebigkeit; Höflichkeit. **–t** [–t], *adj.* gefällig, willfährig, nachgiebig; höflich.

complement ['kɔmpləmənt], 1. *s.* die Ergänzung, Vervollständigung; volle Anzahl, Gesamtzahl, der Satz; die Vollständigkeit, Vollzähligkeit; das Komplement (*Math.*); *a full* –, voll besetzt. 2. *v.a.* ergänzen, vervollständigen. **–ary** [kɔmplə'mentərɪ], *adj.* ergänzend; *be –ary*, sich ergänzen; –*ary angles*, die Ergänzungswinkel; –*ary colours*, Komplementärfarben.

complet–e [kəm'plɪ:t], 1. *adj.* vollzählig, vollständig; komplett, ganz, völlig; vollendet, vollkommen; –*e with*, zusammen mit; *be –e with*, ausgestattet sein mit. 2. *v.a.* vervollständigen, ergänzen; beenden, abschließen, erledigen, vollenden. **–eness,** *s.* die Vollständigkeit, Vollkommenheit. **–ion** [–'plɪ:ʃən], *s.* die Vollendung, Vervollständigung; Erfüllung, der Abschluß; *bring to –ion*, zum Abschluß bringen; –*ion of the predicate*, die Ergänzung des Prädikates.

complex ['kɔmplɛks], 1. *adj.* zusammengesetzt; komplex (*Math.*); (*fig.*) verwickelt, kompliziert; – *sentence*, das Satzgefüge. 2. *s.* das Ganze, die Gesamtheit, der Inbegriff; Komplex (*Psych.*); *inferiority* –, das Minderwertigkeitsgefühl. **–ity** [kəm'plɛksɪtɪ], *s.* die Verwick(e)lung, Verflechtung, Verflochtenheit, Verzweigtheit.

complexion [kəm'plɛkʃən], *s.* die Hautfarbe, Gesichtsfarbe, der Teint; das Aussehen, der Charakter, die Natur; *put a fresh – on a th.*, einer S. ein neues Aussehen *or* einen neuen Zug verleihen.

complexity, *see* **complex.**

complian–ce [kəm'plɑɪəns], *s.* die Willfährigkeit, Unterwürfigkeit; Einwilligung; *in –ce with your wishes*, Ihren Wünschen gemäß *or* entsprechend. **–t,** *adj.* nachgiebig, fügsam, willfährig.

complica–cy ['kɔmplɪkəsɪ], *s.* die Verwick(e)lung, Vielgestaltigkeit. **–te** [–keɪt], *v.a.* verwickeln; erschweren. **–ted.** *adj.* verwickelt, kompliziert.

-tion [–ˈkeɪʃən], *s.* die Verflechtung, Verwick(e)lung; Komplikation (*Med.*).
complicity [kəmˈplɪsɪtɪ], *s.* die Mitschuld (*in*, an).
compliment [ˈkɔmplɪmənt], 1. *s.* das Kompliment; (*pl.*) Empfehlungen, Grüße; *give her my –s*, grüßen Sie sie von mir, empfehlen Sie mich ihr; *in – to s.o.*, einem zu Ehren; *pay a p. a –*, einem ein Kompliment machen; *send one's –s to s.o.*, sich einem empfehlen. 2. *v.a.* beglückwünschen (*Acc.*), gratulieren (*Dat.*) (*on a th.*, zu einer S.); beehren. 3. *v.n.* Komplimente machen. **-ary** [kɔmplɪˈmɛntərɪ], *adj.* schmeichelhaft; Höflichkeits–, Ehren–; *–ary copy*, das Freiexemplar.
compl-y [kəmˈplaɪ], *v.n.* willfahren (*Dat.*), sich schicken *or* fügen in, einwilligen in (*Acc.*), nachgeben (*Dat.*); *–y with*, sich halten an, sich unterwerfen (*Dat.*), erfüllen.
component [kəmˈpounənt], 1. *adj.* einen Teil ausmachend; *– part*, der Bestandteil. 2. *s.* der Bestandteil, Einzelteil, die Komponente.
comport [kəmˈpɔ:t], *v.r.* sich betragen, sich verhalten, sich benehmen.
compos-e [kəmˈpouz], *v.a.* zusammensetzen, zusammenstellen, bilden, ausmachen; verfassen, dichten (*a poem, etc.*); komponieren, vertonen (*Mus.*); setzen (*Typ.*); stillen, beruhigen (*the mind, etc.*); beilegen, schlichten, ordnen (*a quarrel*); *–e o.s.*, sich beruhigen; sich fassen; *–e o.s. to sleep*, sich zum Schlafe anschicken. **-ed**, *adj.* gefaßt, gesetzt, gelassen, ruhig; zusammengesetzt; *be –ed of*, bestehen aus. **-edness**, *s.* die Gelassenheit, Ruhe. **-er**, *s.* der Verfasser (*of a poem*); Komponist (*Mus.*). **-ing**, 1. *adj.* Beruhigungs–; *–ing draught*, der Schlaftrunk. 2. *s.* das Komponieren; Dichten; Schriftsetzen. **-ing-machine**, *s.* die Setzmaschine. **-ing-room**, *s.* der Setzersaal (*Typ.*). **-ing-stick**, *s.* der Winkelhaken (*Typ.*). **-ite** [ˈkɔmpəzɪt], *adj.* zusammengesetzt, gemischt; Kornblüter–, Kompositen– (*Bot.*). **-ition** [kɔmpəˈzɪʃən], *s.* die Zusammensetzung, der Aufbau, die Synthese, Gestaltung, Anordnung, Einrichtung, Ausarbeitung, Komposition, Verbindung, Mischung; Beschaffenheit, Art, Anlage, Natur; der Aufsatz, schriftliche Arbeit; die Komposition (*Mus.*); das Setzen, der Satz (*Typ.*); die Übereinkunft, der Vergleich, Kompromiß, Akkord (*C.L.*); die Abfindungssumme; *German –ition*, die Übersetzung ins Deutsche. **-itor** [kəmˈpɔzɪtə], *s.* der Schriftsetzer, Setzer.
compost [ˈkɔmpəst], *s.* der Kompost, Mischdünger (*Agr.*).
composure [kəmˈpouʒə], *s.* die Gemütsruhe, Fassung, Gelassenheit.
compote [ˈkɔmpɔt], *s.* Eingemachte(s), *n.*, das Kompott.
compound [ˈkɔmpaund], 1. *adj.* zusammengesetzt; *– engine*, die Verbundmaschine; *– eye*, das Netzauge; *– fracture*, komplizierter Bruch (*Med.*); *– interest*, der Zinseszins; *– number*, zusammengesetzte Zahl; *– pillar*, der Bündelpfeiler; *– word*, *see* – 2. 2. *s.* zusammengesetztes Wort, das Kompositum; die Zusammensetzung, Assoziation, Mischung, Masse, das Gemisch, Präparat; Körper; die Verbindung (*Chem.*); umzäuntes Gelände. 3. [kəmˈpaund], *v.a.* zusammensetzen, (ver)mischen; beilegen (*a quarrel*); erledigen, entrichten (*a sum of money*), tilgen (*a debt*); *– a felony*, ein Verbrechen (infolge erhaltener Entschädigung) nicht verfolgen (*Law*). 4. *v.n.* sich abfinden; sich vergleichen, akkordieren (*for*, über; *with*, mit); *– with one's creditors*, ein Abkommen mit seinen Gläubigern treffen. **-ed**, *adj.* zusammengesetzt.
comprehen-d [kɔmprɪˈhɛnd], *v.a.* enthalten, einschließen, in sich schließen *or* fassen; begreifen, verstehen, erfassen. **-sible**, *adj.* faßlich, begreiflich, verständlich. **-sion** [–prɪˈhɛnʃən], *s.* das Fassungsvermögen; der Umfang; die Einbeziehung, Einschließung; das Verständnis, der Verstand, die Einsicht. **-sive**, *adj.* umfassend, weit. **-siveness**, *s.* die Weite, Ausdehnung, der Umfang; die Reichhaltigkeit.
compress [kəmˈprɛs], 1. *v.a.* zusammenpressen, –drängen *or* –drücken, komprimieren, verdichten, kondensieren; *–ed air*, die Preßluft, Druckluft; *–ed brick*, der Preßziegel; *–ed style*, gedrängter Stil. 2. [ˈkɔmprɛs], *s.* die Kompresse, Kompressionsbinde (*Surg.*). **-ibility** [–prɛsɪˈbɪlɪtɪ], *s.* die Verdichtbarkeit, Zusammendrückbarkeit. **-ible**, *adj.* zusammendrückbar, komprimierbar, preßbar, verdichtbar. **-ion** [–ˈprɛʃən], *s.* das Zusammendrücken, Pressen, der Druck, die Kompression, Verdichtung; (*fig.*) Zusammendrängung; *–ion chamber*, der Kompressionsraum; *–ion ratio*, der Verdichtungsgrad. **-or**, *s.* der Kompressor, Verdichter, Druckluftkessel, die Preßluftmaschine.
comprise [kəmˈpraɪz], *v.a.* in sich fassen, enthalten, einschließen, einbegreifen, umfassen (*within*, in (*Acc.*)); bestehen aus.
compromise [ˈkɔmprəmaɪz], 1. *s.* gütlicher Vergleich; der Kompromiß. 2. *v.n.* einen Vergleich schließen, sich vergleichen, übereinkommen (*on*, über). 3. *v.a.* kompromittieren, bloßstellen; aufs Spiel setzen, gefährden.
comptometer [kəmˈtɔmɪtə], *s.* die Rechenmaschine.
compuls-ion [kəmˈpʌlʃən], *s.* der Zwang; *under* or *upon –ion*, gezwungen, unter Zwang. **-orily**, *adv.* zwangsweise. **-ory** [–ˈpʌlsərɪ], *adj.* Zwangs–, zwangsmäßig, obligatorisch; *–ory education*, allgemeine Schulpflicht; *–ory lecture*, die Pflichtvorlesung; *–ory military service*, allgemeine Wehrpflicht.
compunction [kəmˈpʌŋkʃən], *s.* Gewissensbisse (*pl.*), die Reue, das Bedenken.
comput-able [kəmˈpju:təbl], *adj.* berechenbar, zu berechnen(d). **-ation** [kɔmpju:ˈteɪʃən], *s.* die Berechnung, Schätzung, der Kostenanschlag, Überschlag (*C.L.*). **-e** [kəmˈpju:t], 1. *v.a.* berechnen, schätzen (*at*, auf). 2. *v.n.* rechnen; *–ed tare*, die Durchschnittstara; *–ing centre*, die Auswertstelle. **-er**, *s.* der Rechner; Kalkulator, Auswerter.
comrade [ˈkɔmrəd], *s.* der Kamerad, Genosse, Gefährte. **-ship**, *s.* die Kameradschaft, Kameradschaftlichkeit.
[1]**con** [kɔn], *s.* (*abbr. of* **contra**); *pro and –*, das Für und Wider; *pros and –s*, Gründe für und wider.
[2]**con**, *v.a.* fleißig studieren, wiederholt lesen.
[3]**con**, *v.a.* steuern (*Naut.*). **-ning-tower**, *s.* der Kommandoturm.
conat-ion [koˈneɪʃən], *s.* der Willenstrieb, das Begehren (*Psych.*). **-ive** [ˈkɔnətɪv], *adj.* Willens–, begehrlich.
concatenat-e [kɔnˈkætɪneɪt], *v.a.* verketten. **-ion**, [–ˈneɪʃən], *s.* die Verkettung, Reihe.
concav-e [kɔnˈkeɪv], 1. *adj.* konkav, hohl, hohlgeschliffen, ausgehöhlt, Hohl–; *double –e*, bikonkav; *–e glasses*, Hohlgläser (*Opt.*); *–e lens*, die Zerstreuungs– *or* Konkavlinse; *–e mirror*, der Hohlspiegel. 2. *s.* die Höhlung, konkave Fläche. **-ity** [–ˈkævɪtɪ], *s.* die Höhlung, Wölbung. **-o-concave**, *adj.* bikonkav. **-o-convex**, *adj.* konkavkonvex, hohlerhaben.
conceal [kənˈsɪ:l], *v.a.* verhehlen, verheimlichen, verschweigen, verbergen, verstecken, gegen Sicht decken (*Mil.*) (*from*, vor). **-ed**, *adj.* verborgen; unübersichtlich (*as a turning*). **-ment**, *s.* die Verheimlichung, Verschleierung, Verhehlung, Verschweigung, Verbergung, Geheimhaltung, Verborgenheit, Deckung (*Mil.*); *–ment of birth*, die Geburtsverschweigung; *in –ment*, verborgen; *–ment of material facts and circumstances*, die Verhehlung wesentlicher Tatsachen; *place of –ment*, das Versteck.
concede [kənˈsɪ:d], *v.a.* einräumen, zugeben, zugestehen, gewähren; (*coll.*) *– a point*, einen Punkt einbüßen.
conceit [kənˈsɪ:t], *s.* die Eitelkeit, Eingebildetheit; der Einfall, die Idee, gesuchter Gedankengang, gedankliche Spielerei; *idle –s*, törichte Einfälle; *out of – with*, unzufrieden mit *or* über; *put a p. out of – with*, einem die Lust (zu einer S.) nehmen. **-ed**, *adj.* eingebildet, eitel (*of*, auf (*Acc.*)).
conceiv-able [kənˈsɪ:vəbl], *adj.* (er)denkbar; begreiflich, faßlich; *the best relation –able*, das denkbar beste Verhältnis. **-e** [–ˈsɪ:v], 1. *v.a.* fassen, begreifen, verstehen (*an idea*); sich (*Dat.*) denken, sich (*Dat.*) vorstellen (*of a th.*, (*Acc.*)); meinen, denken, dafür halten; ersinnen, ausdenken; fassen, hegen (*an inclination, etc.*) (*for*, zu); empfangen

schwanger werden von (*a child*). 2. *v.n.* empfangen, schwanger werden (*of women*); trächtig werden (*of beasts*).

concentrat–e [ˈkɔnsəntreɪt], 1. *v.a.* konzentrieren; massieren, zusammenziehen, vereinigen; richten (*attention*); verdichten, verdicken, verstärken, sättigen (*Chem.*). 2. *s.* das Konzentrat. **–ed** *adj.* dick, stark, kurz (*of a solution*); *–ed, charge*, geballte Ladung; *–ed fire*, zusammengefaßtes *or* geballtes Feuer, das Massenfeuer, die Feuerzusammenfassung. **–ion** [kɔnsənˈtreɪʃən], *s.* die Konzentration; gespannte Aufmerksamkeit; die Verdichtung, Verstärkung, Dichte, Stärke, Grädigkeit, Sättigung; Zusammenziehung, Zusammenfassung, Heranführung; Bereitstellung, Schwerpunktbildung (*Mil.*); *–ion of fire*, die Feuerzusammenfassung. **–ion-camp,** das Konzentrationslager. **–ive,** *adj.* konzentrierend.

concent–re [kɔnˈsɛntə], *v.a.* (*& n.*) (sich) in einem Punkte vereinigen *or* zusammenziehen. **–ric** [–ˈsɛntrɪk], *adj.* konzentrisch. **–ricity** [kɔnsɛnˈtrɪsɪtɪ], *s.* die Konzentrizität.

concept [ˈkɔnsɛpt], *s.* der Begriff. **–ion** [kənˈsɛpʃən], die Empfängnis (*of women*); das Erfassen, Begreifen; das Auffassungsvermögen, die Fassungskraft; die Vorstellung, Auffassung, der Begriff; Entwurf, Plan, die Idee, Anlage; Konzipierung, Durchführung; *immaculate –ion*, unbefleckte Empfängnis; *form a –ion of*, sich (*Dat.*) einen Begriff machen von; *this passes all –ion*, das übersteigt alle Begriffe. **–ional, –ive, –ual,** *adj.* begrifflich, Begriffs–.

concern [kənˈsəːn], 1. *v.a.* betreffen, angehen, anbelangen, interessieren, von Wichtigkeit sein für; *be –ed* (*of persons*), besorgt sein (*about s. th.*, über eine S.; *for a p.*, um einen); beschäftigt sein, sich angelegen sein lassen (*in doing*, zu tun), verwickelt sein (*in*, in); beteiligt sein (*in*, an *or* bei), ein Interesse haben (*in*, an); (*of things*), sich beschäftigen, sich befassen (*with*, mit), behandeln, berührt *or* betroffen werden; *that does not – you*, das geht Sie nichts an; *– o.s.*, sich beschäftigen (*with*, mit), sich kümmern (*about*, um); *those –ed*, die Beteiligten (*pl.*); *see* **–ed.** 2. *s.* das Interesse, der Anteil, die Teilnahme; Unruhe, Beunruhigung, Sorge; Angelegenheit, Sache; (*coll.*) das Ding; die Wichtigkeit, der Belang; die Beziehung, das Verhältnis; Geschäft, die Firma; (*a*) (*with adjectives*) *with deep –*, mit großer Teilnahme; *big –*, der Großbetrieb, großes Unternehmen; *flourishing –*, blühendes Unternehmen; *paying –*, rentables Geschäft; *a matter of the utmost –*, eine Sache von äußerster Wichtigkeit *or* von höchstem Belang; (*b*) (*with verbs*) *have no – for*, sich nicht kümmern um; *have a – in*, Interesse haben an; *have no – with*, nichts zu tun haben mit; *that's your own –*, das ist eure Sache; *that's no – of yours*, das geht dich nichts an; *mind one's own –s*, sich um seine eignen Angelegenheiten kümmern. **–ed,** *adj.* verwickelt (*in*, in (*Acc.*)); beteiligt, interessiert (*in*, an (*Dat.*)); besorgt (*about*, über; *for*, um). **–ing,** *prep.* in betreff, betreffs (*Gen.*), betreffend, hinsichtlich, in Bezug auf (*Acc.*); *–ing him*, was ihn betrifft *or* anbelangt; *–ing it*, mit Bezug darauf, diesbezüglich.

concert [kənˈsəːt], 1. *v.a.* verabreden, vereinbaren, abmachen, planen; vereinigen (*forces*). 2. *v.n.* zusammenarbeiten (*with*, mit). 3. [ˈkɔnsət], *s.* das Einverständnis; Konzert (*Mus.*); *European –*, europäisches Konzert; *in – with*, im Einverständnis mit. **–ed** [kənˈsəːtɪd], *adj.* gemeinsam, Zusammen–; mehrstimmig (*Mus.*); *–ed move*, verabredete Maßnahme. **–ina** [kɔnsəˈtiːnə], 1. *s.* die Ziehharmonika (*Mus.*). 2. *v.a.* zusammendrücken. 3. *v.n.* zusammenklappen. **–o** [kənˈtʃɛːtoʊ], *s.* das Konzert. **– –party,** *s.* die (Künstler)-Truppe; buntes Programm. **– –pitch,** *s.* der Kammerton; (*fig.*) *up to – –pitch*, auf der Höhe. **– –room,** *s.* der Konzertsaal.

concessi–on [kənˈsɛʃən], *s.* die Verleihung; zugeteilter Grund und Boden, die Konzession; das Zugeständnis; Entgegenkommen. **–onaire,** *s.* der Konzessions– *or* Monopolinhaber. **–ve** [–ˈsɛsɪv], *adj.* einräumend; *–ve clause*, der Einräumungssatz, Konzessivsatz (*Gram.*).

conch [kɔŋk], *s.* die (Schale der) Seemuschel (*Mollusc.*); Halbkuppel (*Arch.*). **–oid** [–ˈkɔɪd], *s.* die Schneckenlinie, Konchoide (*Math.*). **–ological** [kɔŋkəˈlɔdʒɪkəl], *adj.* Muschel–. **–ology** [–ˈkɔlədʒɪ], *s.* die Muschelkunde.

conchy [ˈkɔnʃɪ], *s.* (*sl.*) der (Kriegs)Dienstverweigerer.

conciliat–e [kənˈsɪlɪeɪt], *v.a* aussöhnen, beschwichtigen; gewinnen. **–ion** [–ˈeɪʃən], *s.* die Versöhnung, Aussöhnung, der Ausgleich; *–ion board*, der Schlichtungsausschuß. **–or,** *s.* der Vermittler, Versöhner. **–ory** [–ətərɪ], *adj.* versöhnlich, vermittelnd, gewinnend.

concise [kənˈsaɪs], *adj.* kurz, gedrängt, knapp, bündig, prägnant. **–ness,** *s.* die Kürze, Knappheit, Gedrängtheit, Bündigkeit.

conclave [ˈkɔnkleɪv], *s.* das Konklave, die geheime Versammlung; *sit in –*, geheime Sitzung halten.

conclu–de [kənˈkluːd], 1. *v.a.* schließen, (be)-endigen, beenden, zu Ende führen, abschließen, beschließen (*business, etc.*); entscheiden, sich entschließen; folgern (*from*, aus). 2. *v.n.* aufhören, endigen, enden, zu Ende gehen, ein Ende nehmen; schließen, folgern (*from*, aus); *to –de*, zum Schluß, schließlich; *to be –ded*, Schluß folgt. **–ding,** *adj.* schließend, Schluß–, End–. **–sion** [–ˈkluːʒən], *s.* der Schluß, Abschluß, das Ende, Ergebnis; die Schlußfolgerung, der Schluß (*Log.*); die Entscheidung; der Entschluß, Beschluß; *bring to a –sion*, zum Abschluß bringen; *come to the –sion*, zu der Überzeugung *or* dem Schluß kommen; *in –sion*, zum Schluß, schließlich; *–sion of peace*, der Friedensschluß; *try –sions with a p.*, es versuchen mit einem, sich mit einem messen. **–sive** [–ˈkluːsɪv], *adj.* entscheidend, endgültig, überzeugend. **–siveness,** *s.* das Entscheidende, Endgültige, Überzeugende.

concoct [kənˈkɔkt], *v.a.* (zusammen)brauen, auskochen, aussieden, ausziehen; (*fig.*) aussinnen, aushecken (*a plot*). **–ion** [–ˈkɔkʃən], *s.* das Brauen, Auskochen; Gebräu, Präparat, die Mischung; (*fig.*) Erfindung, das Ausbrüten (*of a scheme*).

concomitan–ce [kənˈkɔmɪtəns], *s.*, **–cy,** *s.* das Zusammenbestehen; die Koexistenz (*Eccl.*). **–t,** 1. *adj.* mitwirkend; begleitend. 2. *s.* begleitender Umstand. **–tly,** *adv.* in Begleitung.

concord [ˈkɔŋkɔːd], *s.* die Eintracht, Einmütigkeit, der Einklang; die Übereinstimmung (*also Gram.*); der Wohlklang, Zusammenklang, die Harmonie (*Mus.*); der Vertrag (*Law*). **–ance** [kənˈkɔːdəns], *s.* die Einhelligkeit, Übereinstimmung; Konkordanz (*to the Bible, etc.*); *in –ance with*, in Übereinstimmung mit. **–ant,** *adj.* einstimmig, einhellig, übereinstimmend; harmonisch. **–at** [kənˈkɔːdæt], *s.* das Konkordat, Übereinkommen.

concourse [ˈkɔŋkɔːs], *s.* der Auflauf, das Zusammenkommen, Zusammentreffen; die Versammlung, Menge, das Gewühl.

concret–e [ˈkɔnkriːt], 1. *adj.* wirklich, dinglich, greifbar, wesenhaft, gegenständlich, konkret; benannt (*as a number*); dicht, fest, kompakt; Beton–, betoniert (*Build.*); *–e noun*, das Konkretum, Dingwort. 2. *s.* der Beton, der *or* das Zement, der Steinmörtel (*Build.*); das Konkrete, konkretes Ding (*Log.*); *in the –e*, in Wirklichkeit, im konkreten Falle; *reinforced –e*, der Eisenbeton. 3. *v.a.* zu einer festen Masse verbinden, betonieren. 4. *v.n.* eine feste Masse bilden, fest werden, sich zusammenballen; anschießen (*of crystals*). **–eness,** *s.* die Festigkeit, Körperlichkeit; das Konkrete. **–ion** [kənˈkriːʃən], *s.* das Zusammenwachsen; Festwerden; die Zusammenhäufung, Ablagerung, Konkretion (*Geol.*); Absonderung (*Path.*); feste Masse.

concubin–age [kənˈkjuːbɪnɪdʒ], *s.* wilde Ehe, die Kebsehe, das Konkubinat. **–e** [ˈkɔŋkjubaɪn], *s.* das Kebsweib, die Beischläferin, Konkubine.

concupiscen–ce [kənˈkjuːpɪsns], *s.* sinnliche Begierde, die Sinnlichkeit, Fleischeslust. **–t,** *adj.* lüstern, sinnlich.

concur [kənˈkəː], *v.n.* (*of events*) zusammentreffen, zusammenfallen, zusammenwirken; beitragen; (*of persons*) übereinstimmen, sich vereinigen; *I – with your view*, ich stimme Ihrer Meinung bei.

–rence [–ˈkʌrəns], *s.* das Zusammentreffen, Zusammenwirken; die Übereinstimmung, Zustimmung, das Einverständnis; der Schnittpunkt (*Geom.*). **–rent,** *adj.* zusammenwirkend, mitwirkend; übereinstimmend, gleichzeitig, gleichlaufend; in einem Punkte treffend, sich schneidend (*Geom.*); zustimmend (*Law*); *–rently with*, zusammen *or* gleichzeitig mit.
concuss [kənˈkʌs], *v.a.* erschüttern (*with*, durch); durch Drohung zwingen, einschüchtern. **–ion** [–ˈkʌʃən], *s.* die Erschütterung; *–ion of the brain*, die Gehirnerschütterung. **–ion-fuse,** *s.* der Aufschlagzünder (*Artil.*). **–ive,** *adj.* erschütternd.
condemn [kənˈdɛm], *v.a.* verdammen; verurteilen, schuldig sprechen (*of* (*Gen.*)); mißbilligen, tadeln; für unbrauchbar *or* untauglich erklären; *the ship was –ed*, das Schiff wurde für seeuntüchtig erklärt. **–able** [–nəbl], *adj.* verwerflich, verdammenswert; strafbar. **–ation** [–ˈneɪʃən], *s.* die Verurteilung, Verdammung; Verwerfung. **–atory** [–nətərɪ], *adj.* verurteilend, verdammend.
condens–ability [kəndɛnsəˈbɪlɪtɪ], *s.* die Verdichtbarkeit, Kondensierbarkeit. **–ate,** *s.*, das Niederschlagwasser. **–ation** [kəndɛnˈseɪʃən], *s.* die Verdichtung, Kondensation, Zusammendrängung; (*fig.*) Abkürzung, Zusammenfassung; *–ation trail*, der Kondensstreifen (*Av.*). **–e** [kənˈdɛns], 1. *v.a.* verdichten, eindicken, kondensieren; niederschlagen, verflüssigen; zusammendrängen, zusammenfassen, abkürzen; *–ed milk*, die Kondensmilch. 2. *v.n.* sich verdichten; sich verflüssigen. **–er,** *s.* der Kondensator (*Elec.*, *Rad.*); Kondensor (*Opt.*); das Kühlrohr, der Verdichter, Verflüssiger; *fixed –er*, der Blockkondensator (*Rad.*); *variable –er*, der Drehkondensator (*Rad.*).
condescen–d [kəndɪˈsɛnd], *v.n.* sich herablassen (*to*, zu), leutselig sein (*to*, gegen), geruhen, belieben (*to do*). **–ding,** *adj.* herablassend, leutselig. **–sion** [–ˈsɛnʃən], *s.* die Herablassung, Leutseligkeit.
condign [kənˈdaɪn], *adj.* verdient; gehörig, angemessen (*of punishment*).
condiment [ˈkəndɪmənt], *s.* die Würze, Zutat.
condition [kənˈdɪʃən], 1. *s.* die Beschaffenheit, Lage, der Zustand; Familienstand; Rang, Stand, die Stellung; (*pl.*) Umstände, Verhältnisse; die Bedingung, Voraussetzung; *–s of the ground*, Geländeverhältnisse (*pl.*) (*Mil.*); *all sorts and –s of men*, alle Arten von Menschen; *change one's –*, sich verändern, heiraten; *implied –s*, stillschweigende Bedingungen; *in –*, in guter Verfassung, imstande; *make it a – that*, es zur Bedingung machen daß; *in an interesting –*, in anderen Umständen, schwanger; *on – that*, unter der Bedingung daß; *under existing –s*, unter diesen Umständen; *working –s*, Arbeitsbedingungen (*pl.*). 2. *v.a.* & *n.* bedingen, konditionieren; zur Bedingung machen, Bedingungen machen, bestimmen, ausmachen; prüfen (*textiles, etc.*) (*C.L.*); *be –ed by*, abhängen von. **–al,** 1. *adj.* bedingt (*on, upon*, durch), abhängig (von); freibleibend; konditional (*Gram.*); *–al acceptance*, freibleibende Annahme; *–al clause*, der Bedingungssatz. 2. *s.* die Bedingungsform, das Konditional (*Gram.*). **–ality** [–ˈnælɪtɪ], *s.* die Bedingtheit. **–ally,** *adv.* unter der Bedingung. **–ed,** *adj.* bedingt, (*as suffix*) beschaffen.
condol–atory [kənˈdouˈlətərɪ], *adj.* Beileid bezeigend, Beileids–. **–e** [kənˈdoul], *v.n.* sein Beileid bezeigen *or* bezeugen (*with* (*Dat.*)). **–ence** [–ləns], *s.* (*often pl.*) die Beileidsbezeigung, das Beileid; *letter of –ence*, der Beileidsbrief.
condon–ation [kəndouˈneɪʃən], *s.* die Entschuldigung, Verzeihung, stillschweigende Einwilligung. **–e** [kənˈdoun], *v.a.* verzeihen, vergeben, entschuldigen (einem etwas), gutheißen (*a th. in a p.*, etwas bei einem).
condor [ˈkəndɔ:], *s.* der Kondor (*Orn.*).
conduc–e [kənˈdju:s], *v.n.* beitragen, dienen, führen, förderlich sein (*to*, zu); *–e to*, herbeiführen (*Acc.*). **–ive,** *adj.* förderlich, dienlich.
conduct 1. [ˈkəndʌkt], *s.* die Führung, Leitung, Verwaltung (*of affairs*); das Betragen, Benehmen, Verhalten, Gebaren; *disorderly –*, grober Unfug; *good –*, gute Führung (*Mil.*); *– prejudicial to good order and discipline*, Ordnung und Disziplin gefährdendes Verhalten (*Mil.*); *safe –*, sicheres Geleit, der Geleitsbrief; *– unbecoming a gentleman*, ungebührliches Betragen; *– of war*, die Kriegführung. 2. [kənˈdʌkt], *v.a.* leiten, geleiten, führen, zuführen; verwalten; anorden, leiten, führen (*a business*); dirigieren (*an orchestra*); *– away*, ableiten; *– o.s.*, sich benehmen, sich betragen, sich aufführen; *–ed tour*, die Gesellschaftreise. **–ance,** *s.* die Leitfähigkeit, das Leitungsvermögen (*Elec.*). **–ibility** [–ɪˈbɪlɪtɪ], *s.* die Leitungsfähigkeit. **–ing** [–ˈdʌktɪŋ], 1. *adj.* Leit–, Leitungs–; *–ing ray*, der Leitstrahl; *–ing wire*, der Leitungsdraht (*Elec.*). 2. *s.* das Leiten; *capable of –ing*, leitungsfähig. **–ion** [–ˈdʌkʃən], *s.* die Leitung, Übertragung; Führung, Zuführung. **–ive,** *adj.* leitend, Leitungs–. **–ivity** [–ˈtɪvɪtɪ], *s.* das Leitungsvermögen. **–or** [kənˈdʌktə], *s.* der Führer, Begleiter; Verwalter, Leiter (*also Phys.*); Leitungsdraht (*Elec.*); Dirigent (*Mus.*); Schaffner (*on trams, etc.*), (*Amer.*) Zugführer (*Railw.*); *–or's baton*, der Taktstock; *lightning-–or*, der Blitzableiter; *non-–or*, der Nichtleiter (*Elec.*).
conduit [ˈkəndɪt], *s.* die Leitung, Rohrleitung, Wasserleitung, Röhre; der Kanal; Abzug. **–-pipe,** *s.* das Leitungsrohr.
condyle [ˈkəndɪl], *s.* der Gelenkhöcker (*Anat.*).
cone [koun], *s.* der Kegel (*Geom.*); Zapfen (*of firs*); (Berg)Kegel; *– of dispersion*, die Streugarbe (*Gunn.*); *– of rays*, der Strahlenbüschel; *– of shade*, der Schattenkegel *or* –raum.
coney [ˈkounɪ], *s. see* **cony.**
confab [ˈkənfæb], (*coll.*) *for* **–ulate** *or* **–ulation.** **–ulate** [kənˈfæbjuleɪt], *v.n.* vertraulich plaudern *or* schwatzen. **–ulation** [–ˈleɪʃən], *s.* vertrauliches Gespräch, gemütliches Geplauder.
confection [kənˈfɛkʃən], *s.* die Zubereitung, Zusammensetzung, Mischung; das Konfekt, in Zucker Eingemachte(s), *n.*; der Konfektionsartikel (*ladies' wear*); die Latwerge (*Med.*). **–er,** *s.* der Konditor, Zuckerbäcker; *–er's shop*, die Konditorei. **–ery,** *s.* das Zuckerwerk, Konfekt; die Konditorei; das Kompott.
confedera–cy [kənˈfɛdərəsɪ], *s.* das Bündnis, der (Staaten)Bund; die Verschwörung. **–te** [–rɪt], 1. *adj.* Bundes–, verbündet, verbunden; *–te States of America*, die Südstaaten von Amerika. 2. *s.* Verbündete(r), *m.*, der Bundesgenosse; Mitschuldige(r), *m.*, der Helfershelfer; Südstaatler (*Amer. Civil War*). 3. *v.a.* & *n.* (sich) verbünden. **–tion** [–ˈreɪʃən], *s.* das Bündnis, der (Staaten)Bund.
confer [kənˈfə:], 1. *v.a.* erteilen, verleihen, zuteil werden lassen (*upon* (*Dat.*)); *– a favour on a p.*, einem eine Gunst erweisen. 2. *v.n.* unterhandeln, sich besprechen *or* beraten, beratschlagen (*with s.o. about s.th.*, mit einem über eine S.). **–ence** [ˈkənfərəns], *s.* die Verhandlung, Unterredung, Beratung, Besprechung; Konferenz, Tagung; *hold a –ence*, eine Sitzung (ab)halten; *sit in –ence*, tagen. **–rable,** *adj.* verleihbar, übertragbar.
confess [kənˈfɛs], 1. *v.a.* zugestehen, bekennen (*a crime, etc.*); (ein)gestehen, zugeben, beichten (*sins*); (einem) die Beichte abnehmen (*as a priest*) (*Eccl.*). 2. *v.n.* beichten; ein Bekenntnis ablegen; *– to*, sich bekennen zu. **–ed,** *adj.* offenbar, zugestanden; *stand –ed as a liar*, als Lügner dastehen. **–edly** [–ɪdlɪ], *adv.* zugestandenermaßen; offenbar. **–ion** [kənˈfɛʃən], *s.* das Geständnis, Zugeständnis, Bekenntnis; die Beichte (*Eccl.*); *auricular –ion*, die Ohrenbeichte; *dying –ion*, das Bekenntnis auf dem Sterbebett; *–ion of faith*, das Glaubensbekenntnis. **–ional,** 1. *s.* der Beichtstuhl. 2. *adj.* Beicht–, Bekenntnis–, konfessionell. **–or** [–ə], *s.* der Glaubensbekenner, Glaubenszeuge; *father –or*, der Beichtvater; *Edward the –or*, Eduard der Bekenner.
confid–ant [kənfɪˈdænt], *s.* Vertraute(r), *m.*; der Mitwisser. **–ante,** *s.* die Vertraute, Mitwisserin. **–e** [kənˈfaɪd], 1. *v.a.* anvertrauen, vertraulich mitteilen (*s. th. to a p.*, einem etwas). 2. *v.n.* vertrauen, sich verlassen (*in*, auf). **–ence** [ˈkənfɪdəns], *s.* das Vertrauen, Zutrauen, die Zuversicht (*in*, zu *or* auf); vertrauliche Mitteilung; *be in a p.'s –ence*, das Vertrauen jemandes genießen; *have every –ence*, unbedingte Zuversicht haben; *in –ence*, vertraulich; *–ence in a man*, Vertrauen auf einen Mann *or* zu

einem Manne; *–ence man*, see *–ence trickster*; *place* or *repose –ence in a p.*, Vertrauen zu einem fassen *or* auf einen setzen; *take a p. into one's –ence*, einen ins Vertrauen ziehen; *–ence trick*, die Bauernfängerei; *–ence trickster*, der Bauernfänger, Schwindler. **–ent** [–ənt], *adj.* vertrauend, voll Vertrauen; sicher, zuversichtlich; überzeugt, keck, dreist; *be –ent in* or *of*, vertrauen auf; *–ent of success*, des Erfolges sicher *or* gewiß. **–ential** [kɔnfɪˈdɛnʃəl], *adj.* vertraulich, im Vertrauen; geheim; *–ential clerk*, der Prokurist; *speaking –entially*, unter uns gesagt. **–ently**, *adv.* vertrauensvoll.

configuration [kənfɪgjʊəˈreɪʃən], *s.* die Gestaltung, Gestalt, Struktur; Stellung der Planeten, der Planetenstand.

confine [kənˈfaɪn], 1. *v.a.* begrenzen, einschränken (*to*, auf (*Acc.*)); einsperren; *– o.s. to*, sich beschränken auf; *be –d to bed*, bettlägerig sein, das Bett hüten müssen; *be –d to one's room*, ans Zimmer gefesselt sein; *be –d*, niederkommen, in den Wochen liegen; *be –d of a son*, von einem Sohne entbunden werden, einen Sohn bekommen. 2. *s.* (*usually pl.*) die Grenze; *on the –s of death*, am Rande des Grabes. **–d**, *adj.* eng, beengt; gefesselt, eingesperrt; verstopft (*Med.*). **–ment** [kənˈfaɪnmənt], *s.* die Beengtheit; Gefangenschaft, Haft, der Arrest, die Inhafthaltung; Entbindung, Niederkunft, das Wochenbett; die Einschränkung, Beschränkung (auf (*Acc.*)); *–ment to quarters*, der Stubenarrest (*Mil.*); *solitary –ment*, die Einzelhaft.

confirm [kənˈfəːm], *v.a.* bekräftigen (*a resolve*), festigen (*s.o.'s position*); bestärken; bestätigen (*a rumour, etc.*); konfirmieren (*Prot.*), firmeln (*R.C.*). **–ation** [kɔnfəˈmeɪʃən], *s.* die Bestätigung, Bekräftigung; Festigung; Konfirmation (*Prot.*), Firmelung (*R.C.*); *in –ation of this*, zur Bestätigung dieses. **–ative** [–ˈfəːmətɪv], **–atory**, *adj.* bestätigend, bekräftigend. **–ed**, *adj.* fest, gefestigt, eingefleischt, eingewurzelt, unverbesserlich; *–ed bachelor*, eingefleischter Junggeselle; *–ed drunkard*, der Gewohnheitstrinker, chronischer Trinker; *–ed sceptic*, der Erzzweifler, unverbesserlicher Zweifler.

confiscat–e [ˈkɔnfɪskeɪt], 1. *v.a.* einziehen, beschlagnahmen, konfiszieren. 2. *adj* verfallen, beschlagnahmt. **–ion** [–keɪʃən], *s.* die Einziehung, Beschlagnahme, Wegnahme, Konfiszierung. **–ory** [kənˈfɪskətərɪ], *adj.* Einziehungs–, konfiszierend (*powers, etc.*).

conflagration [kɔnfləˈgreɪʃən], *s.* die Feuersbrunst, großer Brand.

conflict 1. [ˈkɔnflɪkt], *s.* der Zusammenstoß, Kampf, Streit, Konflikt; (*fig.*) Widerstreit, Widerspruch; *mental –*, der Seelenkampf. 2. [kənˈflɪkt], *v.n.* zusammenstoßen, kämpfen, streiten, in Widerspruch stehen, kollidieren (mit); wiederstreiten, widersprechen (*with* (*Dat.*)). **–ing** [kənˈflɪktɪŋ], *adj.* widerstreitend, widersprechend, entgegengesetzt.

conflu–ence [ˈkɔnfluəns], *s.* der Zusammenfluß (*of rivers*); der Zustrom, Zulauf (*of people*). **–ent**, 1. *adj.* zusammenfließend, verwachsen (*Anat.*). 2. *s.* der Nebenfluß. **–x** [ˈkɔnflʌks], *s. see* **–ence**.

conform [kənˈfɔːm], 1. *v.a.* anpassen (*to*, an). 2. *v.n.*; *– to*, entsprechen (*Dat.*), sich fügen, sich richten nach, sich schicken in (*Acc.*), sich anpassen (*Dat. or* an eine S.); gehorchen (*Dat.*); sich der Staatskirche unterwerfen. **–able**, *adj.* gleichförmig, übereinstimmend, vereinbar (mit), gemäß; nachgiebig, fügsam (*to s.o.'s will*); *be –able to*, entsprechen (*Dat.*). **–ance**, *s.* die Anpassung (*to*, an), Übereinstimmung (*with*, mit); *in –ance with*, gemäß. **–ation** [–ˈmeɪʃən], *s.* die Gestaltung, Gestalt, Anordnung, Zusammensetzung; Anpassung, Angleichung (*to*, an (*Acc.*)). **–ity** [kənˈfɔːmɪtɪ], *s.* die Gleichförmigkeit, Übereinstimmung, Anpassung, Fügsamkeit (*to*, gegenüber), Konformität (*Eccl.*); *in –ity with*, gemäß (*Dat.*), in Übereinstimmung mit.

confound [kənˈfaʊnd], *v.a.* vermengen; verwechseln; verwirren, bestürzt *or* verwirrt machen; (*B.*) beschämen; vernichten, zugrunde richten, zerstören; *– him!* zum Teufel mit ihm! *– it!* zum Teufel! Donnerwetter! **–ed**, *adj.* (*coll.*) verflucht, verflixt.

confraternity [kɔnfrəˈtəːnɪtɪ], *s.* die Brüderschaft.

confrère [ˈkɔnfrɛə], *s.* der Kollege, Genosse.

confront [kənˈfrʌnt], *v.a.* entgegenhalten (*a p. with a th.*, einem etwas); entgegentreten, mutig begegnen (*Dat.*); *be –ed with*, vor etwas stehen, gegenüberstehen (*Dat.*). **–ation** [–ˈteɪʃən], *s.* die Gegenüberstellung (*Law*).

confus–e [kənˈfjuːz], *v.a.* vermischen; vermengen, verwechseln, verwirren, außer Fassung bringen. **–ed**, *adj.* verwirrt, bestürzt, verlegen (*of persons*); wirr, verworren (*of things*). **–ion** [–ˈfjuːʒən], *s.* die Verwirrung, Unordnung; der Lärm, das Durcheinander, die Verworrenheit; Verwechs(e)lung; Verlegenheit, Bestürzung.

confut–able [kənˈfjuːtəbl], *adj.* widerlegbar. **–ation** [kɔnfjuːˈteɪʃən], *s.* die Widerlegung. **–e** [kənˈfjuːt], *v.a.* widerlegen, zum Schweigen bringen.

congé [ˈkɔ̃ːʒeː], *s.* der Abschied; Urlaub, die Entlassung, Beurlaubung.

congeal [kənˈdʒiːl], 1. *v.n.* frieren, einfrieren, gefrieren, zusammenfrieren, zu Eis werden; dick *or* fest werden, gerinnen; *be –ed*, erstarren. 2. *v.a.* gefrieren *or* gerinnen lassen; erstarren. **–able**, *adj.* gefrierbar. **–ing**, *s.*, **–ment**, *s.* das Gefrieren, die Zusammenfrierung, das Gerinnen, Erstarren.

congelation [kɔndʒɪˈleɪʃən], *s. see* **congealing.**

congen–er [ˈkɔndʒɪnə], *s.* Stammverwandte(r), *m.*, gleichartiges Wesen *or* Ding. **–ial** [kənˈdʒiːnjəl], *adj.* gleichartig, geistesverwandt; zusagend, sympathisch; passend, angemessen, entsprechend (*to* (*Dat.*)). **–iality** [–nɪˈælɪtɪ], *s.* die Gleichartigkeit, Geistesverwandtschaft; Angemessenheit. **–ital** [–ˈdʒɛnɪtəl], *adj.* angeboren. **–itally**, *adv.* von Geburt (an).

conger [ˈkɔŋgə], *s.* (**– eel**) der Seeaal, Meeraal.

congeries [kɔnˈdʒɛriːz], *s.* der Haufen, die Anhäufung, Masse (*of stars*).

congest [kənˈdʒɛst], 1. *v.n.* sich ansammeln. 2. *v.a.* überfüllen, anhäufen. **–ed**, *adj.* überfüllt, übervölkert; mit Blut überfüllt (*Med.*). **–ion** [–ʃən], *s.* die Anhäufung, Ansammlung, der Andrang, die Stauung, (Blut)Überfüllung (*Med.*); *–ion of the brain*, der Blutandrang nach dem Gehirn; *traffic –ion*, die Verkehrsstockung.

conglob–ate [ˈkɔngləbeɪt], 1. *v.a.* zusammenballen. 2. *adj.* (zusammen)geballt. **–ation** [–ˈbeɪʃən], *s.* die Zusammenballung; Anhäufung.

conglomerat–e [kənˈglɔmərɪt], 1. *adj.* zusammengeballt, zusammengeknäuelt, zusammengewürfelt, gemischt; *–e rocks*, das Trümmergestein, Konglomerat. 2. *s.* das Konglomerat (*Geol.*); Gemisch, die Anhäufung. 3. [–reit], *v.a.* (*& n.*) (sich) zusammenballen *or* –knäueln, (sich) verbinden (*into*, zu). **–ion** [–ˈreɪʃən], *s.* die Anhäufung, Zusammenhäufung; (*fig.*) Masse, das Knäuel, Gemisch.

conglutinat–e [kənˈgluːtɪneɪt], 1. *v.a.* zusammenleimen, zusammenkitten. 2. *v.n.* zusammenkleben. **–ion** [–ˈneɪʃən], *s.* das Zusammenleimen; (*fig.*) die Vereinigung.

congratulat–e [kənˈgrætjʊleɪt], *v.a.* beglückwünschen (*Acc.*), Glück wünschen, gratulieren (*Dat.*) (*on*, zu). **–ion** [–ˈleɪʃən], *s.* (*often pl.*) der Glückwunsch, die Beglückwünschung (*on*, zu). **–or**, *s.* der Gratulant. **–ory** [–lətərɪ], *adj.* (be)glückwünschend, Glückwunsch–.

congregat–e [ˈkɔŋgrɪgeɪt], 1. *v.a.* sammeln, zusammenbringen. 2. *v.n.* sich (ver)sammeln, zusammenkommen. **–ion** [–ˈgeɪʃən], *s.* das Sammeln; die Versammlung, Ansammlung; Gemeinde, Kirchengemeinde. **–ional**, *adj.* kirchengemeindlich; independent (*Eccl.*). **–ionalism**, *s.* die Selbstverwaltung der Kirchengemeinde. **–ionalist**, *s.* der Independent.

congress [ˈkɔŋgrɛs], *s.* die Tagung, Versammlung der Kongreß; die amerikanische gesetzgebende Versammlung. **–ional** [kɔŋˈgrɛʃənəl], *adj.* Kongreß–. **––man**, *s.* (*Amer.*) das Mitglied der gesetzgebenden Versammlung.

congru–ence [ˈkɔŋgruəns], *s.*, **–ency**, *s.* die Übereinstimmung; Angemessenheit, Kongruenz (*Math.*). **–ent**, *adj.* gemäß, passend, entsprechend; übereinstimmend; kongruent (*Math.*). **–ity**, [kɔŋˈgruːɪtɪ], *s.* die Übereinstimmung, Folgerichtigkeit, Angemessenheit; Kongruenz (*Math.*). **–ous** [–gruəs], *adj.* übereinstimmend (*to*, *with*, mit), angemessen, gemäß, entsprechend (*Dat.*).

conic [ˈkɔnɪk], **–al** [–kəl], *adj.* kegelförmig, konisch. **–s,** *s.* die Lehre von den Kegelschnitten; – *frustum*, der Kegelstumpf; – *section*, der Kegelschnitt.

conifer [ˈkounɪfə], *s.* der Nadelbaum, die Konifere; *pl.* die Nadelhölzer. **–ous** [kouˈnɪfərəs], *adj.* zapfentragend, Nadel–, Nadelholz–.

conjectur–able [kənˈdʒɛktʃərəbl], *adj.* zu vermuten(d). **–al,** *adj.* mutmaßlich. **–e** [kənˈdʒɛktʃə], 1. *s.* die Mutmaßung, Vermutung; Idee. 2. *v.a.* mutmaßen, vermuten, vorschlagen. 3. *v.n.* Vermutungen anstellen (über (*Acc.*)).

conjoin [kənˈdʒɔɪn], *v.a.* verbinden. **–t,** *adj.* vereint, verbunden, gemeinsam. **–tly,** *adv.* zusammen, gemeinsam.

conjugal [ˈkɔndʒugəl], *adj.* ehelich, Ehe–; – *love*, die Gattenliebe. **–ity,** *s.* der Ehestand.

conjugat–e [ˈkɔndʒugeɪt], 1. *adj.* gepaart, paarig (*Bot.*); zugeordnet (*Phys.*, *Math.*); wurzelverwandt (*Gram.*). 2. *v.a.* beugen, konjugieren (*a verb*). 3. *v.n.* sich paaren (*Biol.*). **–ion** [–ˈgeɪʃən], *s.* die Konjugation (*Gram.*), Vereinigung (*Biol.*).

conjunct [kənˈdʒʌŋkt], *adj.* verbunden, vereint. **–ion** [–dʒʌŋkʃən], *s.* die Vereinigung, Verbindung; das Zusammentreffen (*of events*); die Konjunktion (*Astr.* & *Gram.*); das Bindewort (*Gram.*); *in –ion with*, zusammengenommen mit. **–iva** [kɔndʒʌŋkˈtaɪvə], *s.* die Bindehaut (*of the eye*) (*Anat.*). **–ive** [kənˈdʒʌŋktɪv], *adj.* verbindend, konjunktional, konjunktivisch (*Gram.*); *–ive mood*, die Möglichkeitsform, der Konjunktiv (*Gram.*). **–ure** [–ˈdʒʌŋktʃə], *s.* die Verbindung; das Zusammentreffen (*of events*); die Krise, der Wendepunkt.

conjur–ation [kɔndʒuəˈreɪʃən], *s.* feierliche Anrufung, die Beschwörung; Zauberformel; Zauberei. **–e,** 1 [kənˈdʒuə], *v.a.* inständig bitten, feierlich anflehen. 2. [ˈkʌndʒə] beschwören; behexen, bezaubern; *–e away*, weghexen, bannen; *–e up*, heraufbeschwören, zitieren (*spirits*). 3. [ˈkʌndʒə], *v.n.* hexen, zaubern, Zauberei treiben; *a name to –e with*, ein Name von mächtigen Einfluß. **–er, –or** [ˈkʌndʒərə], *s.* der Zauberer, Hexenmeister; Taschenspieler. **–ing,** 1. *adj.* Zauber–. 2. *s.* die Zauberei, Hexerei; Taschenspielerei. **–ing trick,** *s.* das Zauberkunststück.

conk [kɔŋk], *s.* (*sl.*) die Nase, Schnauze.

conk out, *v.n.* (*sl.*) aussetzen, versagen (*Mach.* & *fig.*).

conker [ˈkɔŋkə], *s.* (*coll.*) die Roßkastanie. **–s,** *s.* (*coll.*) ein Kinderspiel mit Kastanien.

connat–e [ˈkɔneɪt], *adj.* mitgeboren, angeboren (*with* (*Dat.*)); verwachsen (*Bot.*); *–e notions*, angeborene Begriffe. **–ural** [kəˈnætʃərəl] *adj.* gleicher Natur; verwandt; angeboren.

connect [kəˈnɛkt], 1. *v.a.* verbinden, verknüpfen, zusammenfügen; ankuppeln, koppeln (*Mach.*); schalten, einschalten, anschalten (*Elec.*). 2. *v.n.* in Verbindung treten, in Zusammenhang stehen, sich anschließen, Anschluß haben (*of trains*). **–ed,** *adj.* verbündet, verknüpft, verwandt, zusammenhängend; *–ed by marriage*, verschwägert; *be –ed with*, in Verbindung stehen mit, sich berühren mit; *be –ed with a th.*, in einer S. verwickelt sein; *well–ed*, gute Verbindungen haben, einflußreiche Verwandte haben; *think –edly*, logisch *or* in logischem Zusammenhang denken. **–edness,** *s.* die Folgerichtigkeit, logischer Zusammenhang (*of thought*). **–ing,** *adj.* Binde–; *–ing line*, das Anschlußgleis (*Railw.*); *–ing link*, (*fig.*) das Bindeglied; *–ing passage*, der Durchgang; *–ing piece*, das Ansatzstück; *–ing rod*, die Schubstange, Pleuelstange (*Mach.*). **–ion** [kəˈnɛkʃən], *s. see* **connexion. –ive,** *adj.* verbindend; *–ive tissue*, das Bindegewebe. **–or,** *s.* das Verbindungsstück, die Verbindungsschraube *or* –röhre, (Verbindungs)Klemme (*Elec.*); Kupplung (*Railw.*).

connexion [kəˈnɛkʃən], *s.* die Verbindung; der Anschluß, die Schaltung (*Elec.*), verbindender Teil (*Mach.*); der Zusammenhang, die Beziehung; Verwandte(r), *m.* & *f.*, die Verwandtschaft; persönliche Beziehung, (*pl.*) der Kundenkreis, die Kundschaft, Klientel, Beziehungen, Konnexionen; *business –s*, Handelsverbindungen; *no – between them*, kein Zusammenhang zwischen ihnen; *establish a –*, Verbindungen anknüpfen, einen Anschluß herstellen; *be in – with*, in Verbindung stehen mit; *in this –*, in diesem Zusammenhang, in dieser Beziehung *or* Hinsicht; *miss one's –*, seinen Anschluß versäumen; *run in – with*, Anschluß haben an (*Railw.*); *in – with*, anläßlich, betreffs (*Gen.*), in bezug auf (*Acc.*).

conning tower, *s. see* ³**con.**

conniv–ance [kəˈnaɪvəns], *s.* die Nachsicht, wissentliches Gewährenlassen (*at* or *in*, bei), stillschweigende Einwilligung (*at* or *in*, in) *or* Einverständnis (mit), das Übersehen (*in* (*Gen.*)). **–e** [kəˈnaɪv], *v.n.* stillschweigend dulden, gewähren lassen (*at* (*Acc.*)), (einem) durch die Finger sehen, ein Auge zudrücken (*at*, bei). **–ent,** *adj.* gegeneinander gebogen, zusammenlaufend, konvergierend (*Bot.*); *–ent valves*, Darmfalten (*Anat.*).

connoisseur [kɔnəˈsəː], *s.* der (Kunst)Kenner.

connot–ation [kɔnouˈteɪʃən], *s.* die Mitbezeichnung, (Neben)Bedeutung; der Begriffsinhalt (*Log.*). **–ative,** *adj.* mitbedeutend; umfassend (*Log.*). **–e** [kəˈnout], *v.a.* mitbezeichnen, zugleich bedeuten, in sich schließen, mit einbegreifen.

connubial [kəˈnjuːbɪəl], *adj.* ehelich, Ehe–. **–ity** [–ˈælɪtɪ], *s.* der Ehestand; (*pl.*) eheliche Zärtlichkeiten.

conoid [ˈkounɔɪd], *s.* das Konoid (*Geom.*); die Zirbeldrüse (*Anat.*); das Rotationsparaboloid. **–(al)** [kouˈnɔɪdəl], *adj.* kegelförmig.

conquer [ˈkɔŋkə], 1. *v.a.* besiegen, überwinden (*persons*); erobern, unterwerfen (*territory*); bezwingen, bewältigen, erringen. 2. *v.n.* siegen; Eroberungen machen. **–able** [–rəbl], *adj.* besiegbar, überwindlich. **–ing** [–rɪŋ], *adj.* siegend, siegreich, überwältigend. **–or** [–rə], *s.* der Eroberer, Sieger.

conquest [ˈkɔŋkwɛst], *s.* die Eroberung, Unterwerfung, Unterjochung; der Sieg, die Überwindung; erobertes Land, die Beute; (*coll.*) *make a –*, jemandes Zuneigung gewinnen; *the* (*Norman*) –, die normannische Eroberung.

consanguin–eous [kɔnsæŋˈgwɪnɪəs], *adj.* blutsverwandt. **–ity,** *s.* die Blutsverwandtschaft.

conscience [ˈkɔnʃəns], *s.* das Gewissen; *clear –*, reines Gewissen; (*coll.*) *have the – to do a th.*, die Frechheit haben *or* frech genug sein etwas zu tun; *matter of –*, die Gewissenssache, Gewissensfrage; *make it a matter of –*, sich (*Dat.*) ein Gewissen daraus machen; *in all –*, mit gutem Gewissen, wahrhaftig, sicherlich; *out of all –*, unverschämt, über alle Maßen; *upon my –!* auf mein Wort! *steel one's – to a th.*, ein Auge dabei zudrücken, etwas durchgehen lassen. **– -clause,** *s.* die Gewissensklausel. **–less,** *adj.* gewissenlos. **– -money,** *s.* in die öffentliche Kasse gezahltes Geld (um Steuerhinterziehung gutzumachen). **– -proof,** *adj.* unempfindlich gegen Gewissensbisse. **– -smitten, – -stricken,** *adj.* reuig, reuevoll.

conscientious [kɔnʃɪˈɛnʃəs], *adj.* gewissenhaft; Gewissens–; *– objector*, der Kriegsdienstverweigerer. *– scruples*, *pl.* Gewissensskrupel. **–ness,** *s.* die Gewissenhaftigkeit.

conscious [ˈkɔnʃəs], *adj.* bewußt; bei *or* mit (vollem) Bewußtstein; *– of a th.*, einer S. (*Gen.*) bewußt *or* kundig; *be – that*, wohl wissen daß, davon überzeugt sein daß. **–ly,** *adv.* bewußt, wissentlich. **–ness,** *s.* das Bewußtsein, der Bewußtseinszustand; die Kenntnis (von), das Wissen (um); *lose –ness*, das Bewußtsein verlieren.

conscript [ˈkɔnskrɪpt], 1. *adj.* zwangsweise ausgehoben. 2. *s.* Dienstpflichtige(r), *m.*, der (eingezogene) Rekrut (*Mil.*). 3. [kənˈskrɪpt], *v.a.* zwangsweise ausheben *or* einziehen. **–ion** [kənˈskrɪpʃən], *s.* die (Zwangs)Aushebung, Militärdienstpflicht; *universal –ion*, allgemeine Wehrpflicht.

consecrat–e [ˈkɔnsɪkreɪt], 1. *v.a.* weihen, einweihen, einsegnen; (*fig.*) widmen (*to* (*Dat.*)); heiligsprechen (*Eccl.*). 2. *adj.*, **–ed,** *adj.* geweiht, geheiligt. **–ion** [–ˈkreɪʃən], *s.* die Weihe, Weihung, Einweihung, Einsegnung; Widmung.

consecut-ion [kɔnsɪ'kjuːʃən], *s.* die Folge, (logische) Aufeinanderfolge, Wortfolge, Folgerung. **-ive** [kən'sɛkjutɪv], *adj.* aufeinanderfolgend, zusammenhängend; *-ive clause*, der Folgesatz; *-ive narrative*, zusammenhängende Erzählung; *three -ive weeks*, drei Wochen hintereinander. **-ively,** *adv.* nacheinander, fortlaufend. **-iveness,** *s.* logische Aufeinanderfolge, die Folgerichtigkeit.

consensus [kən'sɛnsəs], *s.* die Übereinstimmung; Sympathie (*Med.*); – *of opinion*, allseitige Zustimmung, übereinstimmende Meinung.

consent [kən'sɛnt], 1. *s.* die Einwilligung (*to*, in), Zustimmung, Genehmigung (*to*, zu); *age of* –, das Mündigkeitsalter; *by common* –, *with one* –, einmütig, einstimmig; *mutual* –, gegenseitige Übereinkunft; *silence gives* –, Stillschweigen bedeutet Zustimmung. 2. *v.n.* einwilligen (*to*, in (*Acc.*)), genehmigen (*Acc.*), zustimmen (*to* (*Dat.*)), beistimmen (*Dat.*). **-aneous** [kɔnsɛn'teɪnɪəs], *adj.* übereinstimmend (mit); einmütig.

consequen-ce ['kɔnsɪkwəns], *s.* die Folge, das Ergebnis, die Wirkung; Folgerung, der Schluß, Schlußsatz (*Log.*); die Wichtigkeit, Bedeutung, der Einfluß; (*pl.*) der Steckbrief (*game*); *in -ce*, folglich, infolgedessen; *in -ce of*, infolge (von *or Gen.*), wegen (*Gen.*), zufolge (*follows Dat.*); *in -ce of which*, weswegen; *of -ce*, bedeutend, wichtig (*to*, für); *man of -ce*, einflußreicher *or* angesehener Mann, Mann von Bedeutung; *of little -ce*, von geringer Bedeutung (*to*, für); *of no -ce*, ohne Bedeutung, unbedeutend, unwichtig (*to*, für); *take the -ces*, die Folgen tragen; *with the -ce that*, mit der Wirkung *or* dem Ergebnis daß. **-t,** 1. *adj.* folgend (*on* or *upon*, auf (*Acc.*)); folgerichtig, konsequent (*Log.*); *-t on*, die Folge sein von, infolge von. 2. *s.* die Folge, Wirkung; Folgeerscheinung, Folgerung, der Schluß; das Hinterglied (*of a ratio*) (*Math.*). **-tial** [-'kwɛnʃəl], *adj.* folgernd (*on*, aus); folgerecht, folgerichtig (*Log.*); wichtigtuend, überheblich; *be -tial on*, folgen *or* sich ergeben aus. **-tly** ['kɔnsɪkwəntlɪ], *conj.* folglich, deshalb, infolgedessen.

conserv-able [kən'səːvəbl], *adj.* erhaltbar. **-ancy** [-vənsɪ], *s.* die Kontrollbehörde (*for waters, forests, etc.*), Fischereikontrolle, Forsterhaltung; *Thames -ancy Board*, die Kontrollbehörde für die Themse. **-ation** [kɔnsəː'veɪʃən], *s.* die Erhaltung, Bewahrung; der Schutz; das Haltbarmachen (*of fruit*); *-ation of energy*, die Energieerhaltung (*Phys.*). **-atism** [kən'səːvətɪzm], *s.* der Konservatismus. **-ative** [-vətɪv], 1. *adj.* erhaltend; mäßig, vorsichtig; konservativ (*Pol.*); *be -ative of*, erhalten, vorsichtig umgehen mit; *-ative estimate*, vorsichtige Einschätzung. 2. *s.* Konservative(r), m. **-atoire,** *s.* das Konservatorium (*Mus.*). **-ator** ['kɔnsəːveɪtə], *s.* der Erhalter, Beschützer; Konservator, Aufseher, Aufsichtsbeamte(r), m. **-atory** [kən'səːvətərɪ], *s.* das Treibhaus, Gewächshaus, der Wintergarten (*for plants*); das Konservatorium (*Mus.*). **-e** [kən'səːv], 1. *v.a.* erhalten, schonen, (auf)bewahren, sparen; einmachen (*fruit*). 2. *s.* Eingemachte(s), *n.*, die Konserve.

consider [kən'sɪdə], 1. *v.a.* sorgfältig ansehen, betrachten, ins Auge fassen; überlegen, erwägen, bedenken, nachdenken über, in Betracht ziehen, in Anschlag bringen; Rücksicht nehmen auf, berücksichtigen, beachten; der Meinung sein, finden, achten, halten für, ansehen für; *I – him a clever person*, ich betrachte ihn als *or* halte ihn für einen klugen Mann; *I – he acted wisely*, ich finde daß er klug gehandelt hat; *he may – himself lucky*, er kann sich glücklich nennen; – *the matter and let me know*, erwägt die Sache und laßt mich wissen; – *a th. on its merits*, etwas auf seinen Wert hin betrachten; – *yourself at home*, tun Sie, als wären Sie zuhause; *they wish to be -ed wise*, sie möchten für weise gelten; *all things -ed*, wenn man alles in Betracht zieht; *-ed action*, wohlüberlegte *or* wohlerwogene Tat. 2. *v.n.* bedenken, nachdenken, erwägen, überlegen. **-able,** *adj.* beträchtlich, ansehnlich, bedeutend; (*coll.*) sehr viel, eine Menge von. **-ate** [kən'sɪdərɪt], *adj.* rücksichtsvoll, aufmerksam (gegen); bedächtig, wohlbedacht, überlegt. **-ateness,** *s.* die Rücksichtnahme, Aufmerksamkeit. **-ation** [-'reɪʃən], *s.* die Betrachtung, Überlegung, Erwägung; Bedeutung, Wichtigkeit, das Ansehen; die Rücksicht, Rücksichtnahme, Berücksichtigung (*for* or *of*, auf); das Entgelt, die Entschädigung, Gegenleistung, Vergütung, das Äquivalent; der Beweggrund, Grund; *want of -ation*, die Rücksichtslosigkeit; der Mangel an Valuta (*C.L.*); *for a -ation*, gegen Entgelt, gegen ein Äquivalent; *it is of no -ation*, es kommt darauf nicht an; *in -ation of*, in Anbetracht von, hinsichtlich (*Gen.*); *a p. of some -ation*, eine P. von einiger Bedeutung; *on further -ation*, bei weiterer Überlegung; *out of -ation for*, aus Rücksicht auf; *take into -ation*, in Betracht ziehen; *that is a -ation*, das ist ein Grund, den man berücksichtigen muß; *the matter is under -ation*, die Sache schwebt noch *or* wird erwogen. **-ing** [kən'sɪdərɪŋ], 1. *prep.* betreffend, in Anbetracht (*Gen.*). 2. *adv.* (*coll.*) wenn man alles in Betracht zieht; *that is very well done -ing*, da ist im ganzen recht hübsch gemacht.

consign [kən'saɪn], *v.a.* übergeben, überliefern, übersenden, übermachen (*Dat.*); verschicken, befördern, abschicken, adressieren (*to*, nach); richten an (*Acc.*), bestimmen für; überweisen, hinterlegen (*money*); anvertrauen (*Dat.*); – *to oblivion*, der Vergessenheit überliefern; – *to writing*, schriftlich aufsetzen. **-ation** [kɔnsɪg'neɪʃən], *s.* die Überweisung, Übersendung, Verschickung; Hinterlegung; *to the -ation of*, unter der *or* an die Adresse von. **-ee** [kɔnsaɪ'niː], *s.* der (Waren)Empfänger, Adressat. **-ment,** *s.* die Verschickung, Zustellung, Versendung, Übergabe, Konsignation, Hinterlegung; Sendung, Lieferung; *-ment note*, der Frachtbrief; *-ment of specie*, die Barsendung; *in -ment*, in Konsignation, mit Rücksenderecht (*C.L.*). **-or** [kɔnsaɪ'nɔː], *s.* der Hinterleger; Verfrachter, Versender; Übersender, Überweiser, Konsignant.

consist [kən'sɪst], *v.a.* bestehen, sich zusammensetzen (*of*, aus (*Dat.*)); – *in*, bestehen in, enthalten, ausmachen; – *with*, zusammen bestehen mit, vereinbar sein mit, sich vertragen.

consisten-ce [kən'sɪstəns], *s.* die Festigkeit, Dichtigkeit, Dicke, Konsistenz. **-cy,** *s. see* **-ce;** die Übereinstimmung, Folgerichtigkeit, Konsequenz. **-t** [kən'sɪstənt], *adj.* fest, dicht, starr; übereinstimmend, vereinbar, verträglich (*with*, mit), gemäß (*Dat.*); folgerichtig, konsequent; *make -t with*, in Einklang bringen mit; *he is at least -t*, er ist wenigstens konsequent.

consistor-ial [kɔnsɪs'tɔːrɪəl], *adj.* Konsistorial-. **-y** [kən'sɪstərɪ], *s.* das Konsistorium, die Kardinalsversammlung (*R.C.*).

consol [kən'sɔl], *s.* (*usually pl.*) konsolidierte Annuität, der Konsol (*C.L.*).

consol-able [kən'souləbl], *adj.* tröstbar, zu trösten(d). **-ation** [kɔnsə'leɪʃən], *s.* der Trost, die Tröstung, das Trösten; *-ation prize*, der Trostpreis; *poor -ation*, schlechter Trost. **-atory** [-'sɔlətərɪ], *adj.* tröstend, tröstlich. **-e** [kən'soul], *v.a. & r.* trösten.

console ['kɔnsoul], *s.* der Kragstein, die Konsole (*Arch.*); *mixing* –, der Mischtisch (*of sound engineer*) (*Rad.*). – *model*, *s.* das Stehmodell (*Rad.*). **--table,** *s.* das Pfeilertischchen.

consolidat-e [kən'sɔlɪdeɪt], *v.a.* verdichten; (be)festigen, stärken; vereinigen, zusammenlegen, konsolidieren, fundieren (*C.L.*). **-ed,** *adj.* dicht, fest, kompakt; vereinigt, konsolidiert (*C.L.*); *see* **consol.** **-ion** [-'deɪʃən], *s.* die Verdichtung, Festigung, der Ausbau, die Vereinigung; Konsolidation (*of funds, etc.*).

consols [kən'sɔlz], *see* **consol.**

consommé ['kɔ̃sɔme], *s.* die Kraftbrühe.

consonan-ce ['kɔnsənəns], *s.* der Einklang, die Konsonanz (*Mus.*); (*fig.*) Übereinstimmung. **-t,** 1. *adj.* zusammenklingend, konsonant (*Mus.*); (*fig.*) übereinstimmend, vereinbar; gemäß. 2. *s.* der Mitlaut(er), Konsonant (*Phonet.*); *back -t*, der Gaumenlaut; *dental -t*, der Zahnlaut; *front -t*, der Palatallaut; *lingual -t*, der Zungenlaut; *lip -t*, der Lippenlaut; *stopped -t*, der Verschlußlaut. **-tal,** *adj.* konsonantisch (*Phonet.*). **-t-shift,** *s.* die Lautverschiebung (*Phonet.*).

consort, 1. ['kɔnsɔːt], *s.* der Gemahl, Gatte; die

Gemahlin, Gattin; das Geleitschiff (*Naut.*); *Prince* –, der Prinzgemahl. 2. [kən'sɔ:t], *v.n.* sich gesellen (*with*, zu), verkehren (mit); (*fig.*) passen (zu), übereinstimmen (mit).

conspectus [kən'spɛktəs], *s.* die Übersicht (*of*, über (*Acc.*)), Zusammenfassung.

conspicuous [kən'spɪkjʊəs], *adj.* deutlich, ersichtlich, auffallend, bemerkenswert, hervorragend (*by*, durch; *for*, wegen); *be* –, in die Augen fallen; *be* – *by one's absence*, durch Abwesenheit glänzen; *make o.s.* –, sich auffällig benehmen, auffallen.

conspir–acy [kən'spɪrəsɪ], *s.* die Verschwörung, das Komplott, geheime Abrede; *–acy of silence*, verabredetes Stillschweigen. **–ator** [–rətə], *s.* der Verschwörer. **–e** [kən'spɑɪə], 1. *v.n.* sich verschwören, sich vereinigen *or* verbünden; *all things –e to make him happy*, alles trifft zu seinem Glücke zusammen. 2. *v.a.* planen, anstiften, anzetteln.

constab–le ['kʌnstəbl], *s.* der Schutzmann, Polizist; Konnetabel (*Hist.*); *Chief –le*, der Polizeipräsident; *Lord High –le of England*, der Großkonnetabel von England; *special –le*, der Hilfspolizist. **–ulary** [kən'stæbjʊlərɪ]. 1 *s.* die Schutzmannschaft, Polizei. 2. *adj.* Polizei–.

constan–cy ['kɔnstənsɪ], *s.* die Standhaftigkeit, Treue; Stetigkeit, Beständigkeit, Beharrlichkeit, Dauer, der Bestand, die Unveränderlichkeit. **–t** ['kɔnstənt], 1. *adj.* beständig, stetig, unveränderlich; gleichmäßig, unaufhörlich, fortwährend; standhaft, beharrlich, treu; konstant, gleichbleibend (*Math.*, *Phys.*); *–t current*, konstanter Strom (*Elec.*); *–t friend*, treuer Freund; *–t noise*, unaufhörliches Geräusch; *–t rain*, anhaltender Regen. 2. *s.* die Kennzahl, unveränderliche Größe, die Konstante (*Math.*).

constellation [kɔnstə'leɪʃən], *s.* das Sternbild, die Konstellation.

consternation [kɔnstə'neɪʃən], *s.* die Bestürzung.

constipat–e ['kɔnstɪpeɪt], *v.a.* verstopfen (*Med.*). **–ion**, *s.* die Verstopfung, Hartleibigkeit (*Med.*).

constituen–cy [kən'stɪtjʊənsɪ], *s.* die Wählerschaft; der Wahlbezirk. **–t** [–jʊənt], 1. *adj.* wählend, Wahl–, verfassunggebend; einen Teil ausmachend, Teil–; *–t body*, der Wahlkörper, die Wählerschaft; *–t parts*, die Bestandteile, wesentliche Elemente. 2. *s.* der Wähler (*Pol.*); Bestandteil, die Komponente; der Auftraggeber, Vollmachtgeber.

constitut–e ['kɔnstɪtjʊ:t], *v a.* festsetzen, einrichten, errichten, gründen; bilden, ausmachen, in sich enthalten; ernennen, bestellen, einsetzen (*a p.*), konstituieren (*Parl.*); *–e o.s. as a judge*, sich als Richter einsetzen; *this –es a precedent*, dies gibt einen Präzedenzfall ab; *the –ed authorities*, die verfassungsmäßigen Behörden. **–ion** [kɔnstɪ'tjʊ:ʃən], *s.* das Festsetzen, die Anordnung, Einrichtung, Errichtung, Bildung; Natur, Gemütsart, Beschaffenheit, Körperbeschaffenheit; Zusammensetzung; (Staats)Verfassung; Satzung, Verordnung, das Statut, der Beschluß; *strong –ion*, kräftiger Körperbau; *by –ion*, von Natur. **–ional**, 1. *adj.* körperlich bedingt *or* begründet, von Natur angeboren, temperamentsmäßig; gesetzmäßig, verfassungsmäßig, konstitutionell; *–ional charter*, die Verfassungsurkunde; *–ional disease*, angeborenes Übel; *–ional liberty*, verfassungsmäßige Freiheit. 2. *s.* (*coll*) der Verdauungsspaziergang. **–ionalism,** *s* verfassungsmäßige Regierungsform. **–ionalist,** *s.* *s.* der Anhänger verfassungsmäßiger Regierungsformen. **–ive** [kən'stɪtjʊtɪv], *adj.* richtunggebend, grundlegend, wesentlich.

constrain [kən'streɪn], *v.a.* zwingen, drängen, nötigen; fesseln. **–ed,** *adj.* gezwungen, unfrei, befangen, verlegen, unnatürlich. **–t,** *s.* der Zwang; die Gezwungenheit, Verlegenheit, Befangenheit, Zurückhaltung; Haft; *under –t*, zwangsweise.

constrict [kən'strɪkt], *v.a.* zusammenziehen, zusammenpressen, einengen. **–ion** [–ʃən], *s.* die Zusammenziehung, Zusammenpressung, Beengtheit. **–or,** *s.* der Schließmuskel (*Anat.*); *boa-–or*, die Abgottschlange, Königsschlange.

constringent [kən'strɪndʒənt], *adj.* zusammenziehend.

construct [kən'strʌkt], *v.a.* errichten, aufführen, aufbauen, (er)bauen (*a building*); konstruieren (*Math.*); (*fig.*) bilden, erdenken, ausarbeiten, ersinnen. **–ion** [–kʃən], *s.* das Bauen, Erbauen, Aufführen, die Errichtung, der Ausbau; Bau, das Gebäude, Bauwerk; der Satzbau, das Satzgefüge, die Wortfügung, Konstruktion; Gestaltung, Bauart, der Aufbau, die Anlage, Form; Auslegung, Deutung; *brick –ion*, der Ziegelbau; *put the worst –ion on a th.*, eine Sache im schlechtesten Sinne auffassen *or* auslegen; *cost of –ion*, die Baukosten (*pl.*); *type of –ion*, die Bauart; *under –ion*, im Bau. **–ional,** *adj.* Bau–. **–ive** [kən'strʌktɪv], *adj.* aufbauend, konstruktiv, schöpferisch; Bau–, Konstruktions–, baulich; gefolgert, abgeleitet, de facto (*Law*); *–ive criticism*, positive Kritik. **–or,** *s.* der Erbauer, Konstrukteur.

construe [kən'strʊ:], 1. *v.a.* konstruieren, richtig ordnen (*Gram.*); wörtlich übersetzen; auslegen, deuten. 2. *v.n.* sich konstruieren *or* grammatisch erklären lassen.

consubstant–ial [kɔnsəb'stænʃəl], *adj.* wesensgleich. **–iality,** *s.* die Wesenseinheit (*Eccl.*). **–iate** [–'stænʃɪeɪt], *v.a.* in demselben *or* zu einem Wesen vereinigen. **–iation,** *s.* die Lehre von der Gegenwart des Leibes und des Blutes Christi im heiligen Abendmahl.

consuetud–e ['kɔnswɪtjʊ:dɪ], *s.* der Brauch, die Gewohnheit. **–inary** [–'tjʊ:dɪnərɪ], *adj.* gewohnheitsmäßig, Gewohnheits–.

consul ['kɔnsəl], *s.* der Konsul. *–-general*, *s.* der Generalkonsul. **–ar** [–sjʊlə], konsularisch, Konsulats–, Konsular–. **–ate** [–sjʊlɪt], *s.* das Konsulat (*office and premises*). **–ship,** *s.* die Konsulswürde.

consult [kən'sʌlt], 1. *v.n.* sich beraten, beratschlagen (*with a p. about a th.*, mit einem über eine S.). 2. *v.a.* zu Rate ziehen, um Rat fragen, konsultieren (*a doctor*); nachschlagen in (*a book*); Rücksicht nehmen auf (*Acc.*), berücksichtigen; ins Auge fassen; *– one's own advantage*, seinen eignen Vorteil bedenken; *– one's pillow*, etwas beschlafen; *– one's watch*, nach der Uhr sehen. **–ant,** *s.* der Spezialarzt, fachärztlicher Berater. **–ation** [kɔnsəl'teɪʃən], *s.* die Beratung, Beratschlagung, Konsultation, Konferenz; *after –ation with*, nach Rücksprache mit. **–ative** [kən'sʌltətɪv], *adj.* beratend. **–ing engineer,** technischer Berater. **–ing-room,** *s.* das Sprechzimmer (*of a doctor*).

consum–able [kən'sjʊ:məbl], *adj.* verzehrbar, zerstörbar. **–e** [–'sjʊ:m], 1. *v.a.* verzehren, aufzehren; aufbrauchen, verbrauchen; vergeuden, verschwenden, durchbringen; hinbringen (*time*); vernichten, zerstören; *be –ed with*, erfüllt sein von, sich verzehren vor; *–ing desire*, brennender Wunsch. 2. *v.n.* sich verzehren, sich abnutzen. **–er,** *s.* der Verbraucher, Abnehmer, Konsument (*C.L.*).

consummat–e 1. *v.a.* ['kɔnsəmeɪt], vollziehen, durchführen, vollenden; *–e the marriage*, den Eheakt vollziehen. 2. *adj.* [kən'sʌmɪt], vollendet; *–e fool*, ausgemachter Narr. **–ion** [–'meɪʃən], *s.* die Vollziehung, Vollendung; das Ende, Ziel; *–ion of the marriage*, die Vollziehung des Eheaktes.

consumpti–on [kən'sʌmpʃən], *s.* der Verbrauch, Aufwand (*of*, an); die Auszehrung, Schwindsucht (*Med.*); der Absatz, Konsum, Bedarf (*C.L.*). **–ve** [–'sʌmptɪv], 1. *adj.* verzehrend; schwindsüchtig. 2. *s.* Schwindsüchtige(r), *m.*

contact ['kɔntækt], 1. *s.* die Berührung, Verbindung, der Anschluß; die Fühlung (*fig.* & *Mil.*); der Kontakt (*Elec.*); Bazillenträger (*Med.*); *point of* –, der Berührungspunkt; *be in – with the enemy*, Feindberührung haben; *come in*(*to*) *– with*, in Berührung kommen mit; *establish* –, Fühlung aufnehmen; *make* –, den Kontakt herstellen (*Elec.*); *– with the rear*, rückwärtige Verbindung (*Mil.*); *– with the soil*, (*fig.*) die Erdverbundenheit. 2. *v.a.* berühren, in Berührung kommen mit, Kontakt herstellen, in Verbindung treten mit. **–-box,** *s.* die Anschlußdose. **–-company,** *s.* die Nahtkompagnie (*Mil.*). **–-mine,** *s.* die Flattermine (*Mil.*). **– print,** der Abzug, die Kopie (*Phot.*).

contagio–n [kən'teɪdʒən], *s.* die Ansteckung; der Ansteckungsstoff; ansteckende Krankheit, die Seuche; Verseuchung. **–us,** *adj.* ansteckend; (*fig.*) verderblich, schädlich.

contain [kən'teɪn], *v.a.* enthalten, umfassen; fassen, messen (*measures and weights*); halten, festhalten, hinhalten, abriegeln, fesseln (*Mil.*); – *o.s.*, (an) sich halten, sich mäßigen, sich zügeln; *I could not – myself for laughing*, ich konnte mich des Lachens nicht enthalten. **–er,** *s.* der Behälter, das Gefäß; **–ing action,** hinhaltendes Gefecht (*Mil.*).

contaminat–e [kən'tæmɪneɪt], *v.a.* beflecken, beschmutzen, verunreinigen, besudeln; anstecken, vergiften, verseuchen (*with gas*). **–ion** [–'neɪʃən], *s.* die Verunreinigung, Besudelung, Verseuchung.

contango [kən'tæŋgoʊ], 1. *s.* das Aufgeld, der Report; die Reportprämie (*C.L.*). **– rate,** *s.* der Reportsatz, die Prolongationsgebühr. 2. *v.n.* Reportgeschäfte machen.

contemn [kən'tɛm], *v.a.* verachten, verschmähen, geringschätzen.

contemplat–e ['kɔntəmpleɪt], 1. *v.a.* betrachten, beschauen; vorhaben, beabsichtigen, im Sinne haben, ins Auge fassen; rechnen mit, voraussehen; überlegen, bedenken, erwägen. 2. *v.n.* nachsinnen, nachdenken (über). **–ion** [–'pleɪʃən], *s.* die Betrachtung, Beobachtung; das Sinnen, Nachdenken; die Beschaulichkeit; Absicht, das Vorhaben; *be in –ion*, beabsichtigt *or* geplant werden; *have in –ion*, vorhaben, beabsichtigen. **–ive** ['kɔntəmpleɪtɪv], *adj.* nachdenklich, gedankenvoll, tiefsinnig; beschaulich.

contempor–aneity [kəntɛmpə'reɪnjɪtɪ], *s.* die Gleichzeitigkeit. **–aneous** [–reɪnjəs], *adj.* gleichzeitig (*with*, mit). **–aneousness,** *s. see* **–aneity. –ary** [kən'tɛmpərərɪ], 1. *adj.* zeitgenössisch, gleichzeitig; *be –ary with*, zeitlich zusammenfallen mit. 2. *s.* der Zeitgenosse, Altersgenosse; *our –ary*, unsere Kollegin (*referring to a newspaper, etc.*).

contempt [kən'tɛmpt], *s.* die Verachtung (*for* (*Gen.*)), Geringschätzung (*for*, gegen); Schmähung, Schmach, Schande; Gehorsamsverweigerung, Mißachtung (*Law*); das Nichterscheinen vor Gericht, die Kontumaz; *beneath –*, verächtlich; *bring into –*, verächtlich machen; *– of court*, vorsätzliches Nichterscheinen, die Mißachtung des Gerichts; *hold in –*, mit Verachtung strafen, verachten; *hold a p. up to –*, einen verächtlich machen. **–ible,** *adj.* verächtlich, verachtungswert, unwürdig, gemein; (*coll.*) *Old –ibles*, britisches Heer in Frankreich, 1914. **–ibleness,** *s.* die Verächtlichkeit. **–uous** [–jʊəs], *adj.* verachtend, verachtungsvoll, geringschätzig; *–uous air*, verächtliche Miene; *be –uous of*, verachten; *speak –uously of s.o.*, von einem mit Verachtung reden. **–uousness,** *s.* verächtliches Wesen; die Verachtung.

contend [kən'tɛnd], *v.n.* kämpfen (*for*, für), ringen, wetteifern, sich bewerben (*for*, um); behaupten; *– for mastery*, um den Vorzug streiten. **–ing,** *adj.* streitend; widerstreitend, entgegenstehend.

[1]**content** [kən'tɛnt], 1. *pred. adj.* (leidlich) zufrieden; einverstanden (*Parl.*); bereit, geneigt, willens; *not –*, dagegen (*Parl.*). 2. *v.a.* befriedigen, zufriedenstellen; *– o.s. with*, sich damit begnügen. 3. *s.* die Zufriedenheit; *to one's heart's –*, nach Herzenslust. **–ed,** *adj.* zufrieden, genügsam; *be –ed with*, sich damit zufrieden geben, sich damit begnügen. **–edness,** *s.* die Zufriedenheit, Genügsamkeit. **–ment,** *s.* die Zufriedenheit.

[2]**content** ['kɔntɛnt], *s.* der Gehalt, Inhalt, Rauminhalt, Umfang; das Volumen, Fassungsvermögen; (*pl.*) der Inhalt; *cubic –*, der Kubikinhalt; *solid –*, das Volumen; *table of –s*, das Inhaltsverzeichnis.

contentio–n [kən'tɛnʃən], *s.* der Streit, Wortstreit; die Behauptung, Beweisführung; *bone of –n*, der Zankapfel. **–us** [–ʃəs], *adj.* streitsüchtig, zänkisch; strittig (*point*); streitig (*Law*); *non-–us*, freiwillig (*Law*). **–usness,** *s.* die Streitsucht.

contents ['kɔntɛnts], *see* [2]**content.**

contermin–al [kɔn'tə:mɪnəl], *adj.* grenzend (*to*, an). **–ous,** *adj. see* **–al**; gleichbedeutend, zusammenfallend (*with*, mit); *be –ous*, eine gemeinsame Grenze haben (*with*, mit).

contest ['kɔntɛst], 1. *s.* der Streit, Kampf (*over* or *about*, über); der Wettkampf (*for*, um). 2. *v.n.* streiten (über), wetteifern (um). 3. [kən'tɛst], *v.a.* bestreiten, streitig machen, streiten um, sich bewerben um, anfechten; *– a seat*, kandidieren (*Parl.*). **–able** [kən'tɛstəbl], *adj.* bestreitbar, anfechtbar, strittig. **–ant,** *s.* der Streiter, streitende Partei; der Kandidat, Bewerber. **–ed,** *adj.* streitig, umstritten, bestritten, angefochten.

context ['kɔntɛkst], *s.* der Zusammenhang; Text, Wortlaut. **–ual,** *adj.* vom Zusammenhang abhängig. **–ure** [kən'tɛkstʃe], *s.* das Gewebe, Gefüge, der Bau, die Zusammensetzung, Struktur.

contigu–ity [kɔntɪ'gjʊ:ɪtɪ], *s.* die Berührung, das Angrenzen; die Nähe, Nachbarschaft, Kontiguität (*Psych.*). **–ous** [kən'tɪgjʊəs], *adj.* anstoßend, angrenzend (*to*, an (*Dat.*)), benachbart.

continen–ce ['kɔntɪnəns], *s.* (geschlechtliche) Enthaltsamkeit, die Keuschheit; Mäßigung. **–t,** *adj.* keusch, enthaltsam; mäßig.

continent ['kɔntɪnənt], *s.* das Festland, der Kontinent; *the Dark –*, der dunkle Erdteil. **–al** [kɔntɪ'nɛntəl], 1. *adj.* Kontinental–; *–al travel*, das Auslandsreisen. 2. *s.* der Bewohner des Festlandes, Fremde(r), *m.*

contingen–cy [kən'tɪndʒənsɪ], *s.* die Zufälligkeit, Möglichkeit, der Zufall, möglicher Fall, zufälliges Ereignis. **–cies,** *pl.* Zufälle, unvorhergesehene Ausgaben (*pl.*). **–t,** 1. *adj.* zufällig; ungewiß; möglich, eventuell; nebensächlich, unwesentlich, nicht notwendig wahr (*Philos.*); an gewisse Bedingungen geknüpft; *–t (up)on*, abhängig von, bedingt durch, verbunden mit. 2. *s.* der Beitrag, Anteil, die Beteiligungsquote, das Kontingent (*of soldiers*).

continu–al [kən'tɪnjʊəl], *adj.* ununterbrochen, fortgesetzt, oft wiederholt; (*coll.*) fortwährend, beständig, unablässig, fortdauernd, anhaltend, unaufhörlich. **–ance,** *s.* die Fortdauer, das Fortbestehen, Anhalten; die Dauer, Beständigkeit; das Verweilen, Bleiben; der Aufschub, die Aussetzung, Vertagung (*Law*). **–ant,** *s.* der Dauerlaut (*Phonet.*). **–ation** [–'eɪʃən], *s.* die Fortsetzung, der Fortbestand; die Weiterführung, Fortdauer; Erweiterung, Verlängerung, das Fortsetzungsstück; die Übertragung, Prolongation (*C.L.*); *–ation school*, die Fortbildungsschule. **–ative** [–jʊətɪv], *adj.* fortführend, fortsetzend. **–e** [–'tɪnjʊ], 1. *v.a.* fortsetzen, fortführen, weiterführen; beibehalten, fortfahren mit; erhalten, behalten, beibehalten, belassen; verlängern (*a line, etc.*); aufschieben, vertagen (*Law*). 2. *v.n.* bleiben, verweilen, verharren, beharren in; anhalten, fortfahren, sich fortsetzen, fortdauern; *please –e!* bitte fahren Sie fort! *–e in sin*, in der Sünde beharren; *to be –ed*, Fortsetzung folgt; *he –ed his story*, er setzte seine Erzählung fort; *he –ed to smoke*, er rauchte weiter. **–ed,** *adj.* fortgesetzt, unaufhörlich, stetig; *–ed fraction*, kontinuierlicher Bruch, der Kettenbruch; *–ed proportion*, stetiges Verhältnis. **–ity** [kɔntɪ'njʊɪtɪ], *s.* die Stetigkeit; innerer Zusammenhang; gleichmäßige Fortdauer; die Kontinuität; das Drehbuch (*Films*); (*fig.*) roter Faden. **–ous** [–əs], *adj.* ununterbrochen, andauernd, fortdauernd, anhaltend, (fort)laufend, stetig, kontinuierlich; *–ous current*, der Gleichstrom (*Elec.*); *–ous operation* or *working*, der Dauerbetrieb. **–um,** *s.* ununterbrochene Reihe, zusammenhängende Substanz, das Kontinuum (*Math.*).

contort [kən'tɔ:t], *v.a.* verdrehen, verzerren, verziehen (*one's features*); zusammenziehen, krümmen. **–ion** [–'tɔ:ʃən], *s.* die Krümmung (*also Geol.*); Verzerrung, Verdrehung. **–ionist,** *s.* der Schlangenmensch, Kautschukmensch.

contour ['kɔntʊə], *s.* der Umriß, die Außenlinie, Kontur. **–-line,** *s.* die Höhenlinie, Isohypse (*Surv.*). **–-map,** *s.* die Höhenkurvenkarte.

contra ['kɔntrə], 1. *prep.* (*usually as prefix*) wider, gegen. 2. *s.* die Kreditseite, Gegenseite (*C.L.*); *per –*, als Gegenrechnung *or* Gegenleistung (*C.L.*). **–band** [–bænd], 1. *adj.* verboten, gesetzwidrig, Schmuggel–. 2. *s.* die Konterbande; Bannware, Schmuggelware; der Schleichhandel, Schmuggel. **–-bass** [–beɪs], *s.* die Baßgeige; der Kontrabaß. **–-bassoon** [–bə'sʊ:n], *s.* das Kontrafagott. **–ception** [–'sɛpʃən], *s.* die Empfängnisverhütung, Schwangerschaftsverhinderung. **–ceptive,** 1. *adj.* empfängnisverhütend. 2. *s.* empfängnisverhütendes Mittel. **–-tenor,** *s.* zweiter Tenor (*Mus.*).

[1]**contract** [ˈkɔntrækt], *s.* der Vertrag, Kontrakt; die Vertragsurkunde; Bestellung, der Auftrag, Lieferungsvertrag; Akkord, die Verdingung; *by* –, in Submission, in Akkord; *by private* –, unter der Hand; *marriage* –, der Ehevertrag; *simple* –, der Kontrakt ohne Siegel; *special* –, der Kontrakt unter Siegel; *under* – *to*, kontraktlich verpflichtet (*Dat.*).

[2]**contract** [kənˈtrækt], 1. *v.a.* zusammenziehen; verengen, beschränken; beengen, einengen (*the mind, etc.*); abkürzen, verkürzen, kontrahieren (*Gram.*); sich (*Dat*) zuziehen (*disease, etc.*); sich (*Dat.*) aneignen, annehmen (*habits, etc.*); eingehen (*obligation*), machen, kontrahieren (*debts*), schließen (*marriage, etc.*); – *one's eyebrows* or *forehead*, die Stirn runzeln; – *a word*, ein Wort zusammenziehen *or* verkürzen. 2. *v.n.* sich zusammenziehen, einschrumpfen, zusammenschrumpfen; enger *or* kürzer werden; einen Handel eingehen, ein Geschäft *or* einen Vertrag abschließen; – *for*, sich kontraktlich verpflichten; – *out*, sich durch Abkommen von etwas befreien; – *out of a th.*, sich von einer S. freizeichnen *or* aus einer S. befreien *or* frei machen. **–ed,** *adj* verkürzt, zusammengezogen; engherzig. **–ibility, -ility** [–tɪˈbɪlɪtɪ, –ˈtɪlɪtɪ], *s.* die Zusammenziehbarkeit. **–ible, –ile** [–tɪbl, –tɑɪl], *adj.* zusammenziehbar, verkürzbar. **–ion** [–ʃən], *s.* die Zusammenziehung, Zusammenfassung, Verkürzung, Abkürzung, Verkleinerung (*also Gram.*); das Eingehen (*of a debt, etc.*); die Zuziehung (*of an illness*); die Abschließung (*of an agreement*). **–or,** *s.* Vertragschließende(r), *m.*, der Kontrahent (*C.L.*); Lieferant; Unternehmer (*Build., etc.*); Schließmuskel (*Anat.*); *builder and –or*, der Bauunternehmer. **–ual** [–juəl], *adj.* vertraglich, vertragsgemäß, Vertrags–.

contradict [kɔntrəˈdɪkt], *v.a.* widersprechen (*a p.* (*Dat.*)); widerrufen (*a statement* (*Acc.*)); in Abrede stellen; – *each other*, sich widersprechen. **–ion** [–ˈdɪkʃən], *s.* der Widerspruch, die Widerrede; Unvereinbarkeit; *spirit of –ion*, der Widerspruchsgeist; *in –ion to*, im Widerspruch zu; *–ion in terms*, innerer Widerspruch, der Widerspruch in sich selbst; *without –ion*, ohne Widerrede. **–ious** [–ˈdɪkʃəs], *adj.* streitsüchtig, widerstreitend. **–oriness** [–ˈdɪktərɪnɪs], *s.* die Unverträglichkeit; der Widerspruchsgeist. **–ory** [–ˈdɪktərɪ], 1. *adj.* (sich) widersprechend, (einander) entgegengesetzt; unvereinbar. 2. *s.* (*with def. art. only*) der Gegensatz, Widerspruch.

contradistinction [kɔntrədɪsˈtɪŋkʃən], *s.* die Unterscheidung; *in – to*, im Gegensatze zu.

contralto [kənˈtræltoʊ], *s.* der Alt, die Altistin; Altstimme (*Mus.*).

contraption [kənˈtræpʃən], *s.* (*coll.*) die Vorrichtung, technische Neuheit, der Apparat, technischer Kniff; (*sl.*) das Dingsda; der Kasten, das Ungetüm.

contrapunt–al [kɔntrəˈpʌntl], *adj.* kontrapunktisch (*Mus.*).

contrar–iety [kɔntrəˈrɑɪətɪ], *s.* der Widerspruch, Gegensatz; die Unvereinbarkeit; Widrigkeit. **–iness** [kən trɛːrɪnɪs], *s.* die Widerspenstigkeit (*of persons*); Widerwärtigkeit. **–iwise,** *adv.* (*coll.*) im Gegenteil; umgekehrt. **–y** [ˈkɔntrərɪ], 1. *adj.* entgegengesetzt, widersprechend (*to* (*Dat.*)); Gegen–, konträr (*Log.*); ungünstig, widrig; (*coll.*) [kənˈtrɛːrɪ] widerspenstig, eigensinnig, mürrisch; *in the –y case*, widrigenfalls. 2. *adv.* (*with* to *used as prepos.*) zuwider (*always follows*), entgegen (*sometimes follows*), gegen. 3 (*with def. art. only*) *s.* das Gegenteil (*to*, zu *or* von); *quite the –y*, ganz im Gegenteil; *on the –y*, im Gegenteil, hingegen; *to the –y*, gegenteilig, dagegen.

contrast [kənˈtrɑst], 1. *v.a.* entgegensetzen, gegenüberstellen; kontrastieren, vergleichen. 2. *v.n.* abheben *or* abstechen (*with*, gegen), konstrastieren (*with*, mit). 3. [ˈkɔntrɑst], *s.* der Gegensatz (*to*, zu), Kontrast (*between*, zwischen); *by – with*, im Vergleich mit; *in – to*, im Gegensatz zu.

contrate [ˈkɔntreit], *adj.*; – *wheel*, das Steigrad.

contra–vene [kɔntrəˈviːn], *v.a.* im Widerspruch stehen mit, bestreiten, widersprechen, zuwiderhandeln (*Dat.*); übertreten (*laws*). **–vention** [–ˈvenʃən], *s.* das Zuwiderhandeln (*of*, gegen); die Übertretung (*Gen.*); *in –vention of*, zuwider, entweder (*Dat. following*), im Widerspruch zu.

contretemps [ˈkɔ̃ːtrətɔ̃ː], *s.* unglücklicher *or* widriger Zufall.

contribut–e [kənˈtrɪbjʊːt], 1. *v.a.* beitragen, beisteuern (*also fig.*). 2. *v.n.* mitwirken (*to*, an), beitragen (*to*, zu); *–e to a paper*, für ein Blatt schreiben. **–ion** [kɔntrɪˈbjʊːʃən], *s.* das Beitragen, die Mitwirkung; der Beitrag; die Beisteuer, Kriegssteuer, Zwangsauflage, Brandschatzung (*Mil*); *lay under –ion*, zu einem Beitrage heranziehen; brandschatzen. **–ive** [–ˈtrɪbjʊtɪv], *adj.* beitragend (zu); mitwirkend (bei). **–or** [–ˈtrɪbjʊtə], *s.* Beisteuernde(r), Beitragende(r), *m.*; der Mitarbeiter (*to*, an *or* bei). **–ory** [–ˈtrɪbjʊtərɪ], 1. *adj.* beitragend, beisteuernd (zu), förderlich (*Dat.*), mitwirkend (bei *or* an); beitragspflichtig. 2. *s.* Beitragspflichtige(r), *m.*

contrit–e [ˈkɔntrɑɪt], *adj.* zerknirscht, reuevoll, reuig, reumütig, bußfertig. **–eness,** *s.*, **–ion** [kənˈtrɪʃən], *s.* die Zerknirschung, Reue.

contriv–able [kənˈtrɑɪvəbl], *adj.* erfindbar, erdenkbar; herstellbar. **–ance** [–vəns], *s.* die Erfindung, Bewerkstelligung; Einrichtung, Vorrichtung, der Apparat; Plan; Kniff, Kunstgriff; die Findigkeit; *full of –ances*, erfinderisch, findig. **–e** [kənˈtrɑɪv], 1. *v.a. & n.* erfinden, ersinnen, erdenken; fertigbringen, bewerkstelligen, zuwegebringen, zustandebringen, es so einrichten daß; *he –ed to come*, es gelang ihm zu kommen; *he –ed means for his escape*, er fand Mittel und Wege zu seiner Flucht.

control [kənˈtroʊl], 1. *s.* die Überwachung, Prüfung (*also Mach.*); der Einhalt, die Einschränkung, der Zwang; die Zwangswirtschaft; Leitung, Oberaufsicht, Aufsicht, Kontrolle; Macht, Herrschaft, Gewalt, Beherrschung; der Regler, die Kontrollvorrichtung; (*pl.*) die Steuerung (*of machinery*); Steuerorgane (*pl.*), das Leitwerk (*Av.*); *dual* –, die Doppelsteuerung; *fire* –, die Feuerleitung (*Artill.*); *he gets beyond my* –, er wächst mir über den Kopf; *be in – of a th.*, etwas unter sich haben; *lose* –, die Beherrschung verlieren; *press-button* –, die Druckknopfsteuerung; *radio* –, die Fernlenkung, Funklenkung; *remote* –, die Fernsteuerung; *be under* –, unter Kontrolle stehen; *bring under* –, bewältigen, meistern (*as a fire, etc.*); *volume* –, der Lautstärkenregler (*Rad.*); *without* –, uneingeschränkt, frei, ohne Aufsicht. 2. *v.a.* nachprüfen, revidieren, überwachen, beaufsichtigen; regulieren, kontrollieren, leiten; zurückhalten, einschränken, beschränken, im Zaum halten; lenken, steuern (*Mach.*); unter Zwangswirtschaft stellen (*industry, etc.*); beherrschen; – *o.s.*, sich beherrschen, sich zurückhalten, sich mäßigen. **--board,** *s.* die Bewirtschaftungstelle (*Econ.*), Schalttafel (*Elec., etc.*). **--column,** *s.* der Steuerknüppel (*Av.*). **--grid,** *s.* der Steuergitter (*Rad.*). **--knob,** *s.* der Bedienungsknopf (*Rad., etc.*). **–lable,** *adj.* kontrollierbar, lenkbar; lenksam. **–ler** *s.* der Aufseher, Kontrolleur; Revisor, Rechnungsprüfer, Leiter; Stromregler (*Elec.*); Fahrschalter (*electric Railw.*). **--lever,** *s.* der Schalthebel. **--panel,** *s.* die Bedienanlage (*Elec.*) **--room,** *s.* die Zentrale (*of submarine*), Befehlszentrale (*Mil.*), der Regieraum (*Rad.*). **--surface,** *s.* die Steuerfläche (*Av.*). **--tower,** *s.* der Kommandoturm (*Naut.*), Kontrollturm (*Av.*). **--valve,** *s.* die Steuerröhre (*Rad.*).

controver–sial [kɔntrəˈvəːʃəl], *adj.* strittig, polemisch, Streit–; streitlustig. **–salist,** *s.* der Polemiker. **–sy** [ˈkɔntrəvəːsɪ], *s.* der Streit, die Diskussion, Kontroverse; Streitfrage; *without –sy*. unstreitig, fraglos. **–t** [ˈkɔntrəvəːt], *v.a.* bestreiten, bekämpfen (*opinions*); widersprechen (*a p* (*Dat*)). **–tible** [–ˈvəːtəbl], *adj.* bestreitbar, anfechtbar.

contumac–ious [kɔntjʊˈmeɪʃəs], *adj.* hartnäckig, halsstarrig, widerspenstig; ungehorsam (*Law*). **–iousness,** *s.*, **–y** [ˈkɔntjʊməsɪ], *s.* die Halsstarrigkeit, Widerspenstigkeit; der Ungehorsam; die Kontumaz (*Law*).

contumel–ious [kɔntjʊˈmɪːlɪəs], *adj.* verächtlich, schändlich; frech, unverschämt, schnöde. **–y** [ˈkɔntjʊmɪlɪ], *s.* die Beschimpfung, der Schimpf; Hohn, die Schmach, Verachtung.

contus–e [kənˈtju:z], *v.a.* quetschen. **–ion** [–ʒən], *s.* die Quetschung; Quetschwunde.

conundrum [kəˈnʌndrəm], *s.* das (Scherz)Rätsel.

convalesce [kɔnvəˈlɛs], *v.n.* genesen, gesund werden. **–nce,** *s.* die Genesung, Gesundung, Rekonvaleszenz. **–nt,** 1. *adj.* genesend; *he is –nt,* er ist gut auf dem Wege der Besserung. 2. *s.* Genesende(r), *m.*, der Rekonvaleszent; *–t home,* das Genesungsheim, die Heilanstalt, Pflegeanstalt.

convection [kənˈvɛkʃən], *s.* die Konvektion (*Phys.*). **–al,** *adj.* Konvektions–.

convene [kənˈvi:n], 1. *v.a.* zusammenrufen, (ein)berufen, versammeln; vorladen (*before,* vor (*Acc.*)) (*Law*). 2. *v.n.* zusammenkommen, zusammentreffen, sich versammeln. **–r,** *s.* der Einberufer; (*Scots*) Vorsitzende(r), *m.*

convenien–ce [kənˈvi:njəns], *s.* die Schicklichkeit, Angemessenheit; Bequemlichkeit, Annehmlichkeit; der Vorteil; bequeme Einrichtung; (*coll.*) die Bedürfnisanstalt; *make a –ce of,* ausnutzen; *marriage of –ce,* die Verstandesheirat; *at your earliest –ce,* baldmöglichst, bei erster Gelegenheit; *every –ce,* aller Komfort, jede Bequemlichkeit; *at one's own –ce,* wenn es einem paßt, gelegentlich, nach Belieben; *suit your own –ce,* tun Sie das ganz nach Ihrem Belieben; *whenever it suits your –ce,* zu jeder Zeit die Ihnen paßt; *public –ce,* die Bedürfnisanstalt. **–t** [–njənt], *adj.* schicklich, passend, (zweck)dienlich; günstig, geeignet, bequem gelegen; *it will not be –t for me to see him to-day,* es paßt mir schlecht, ihn heute zu sehen; *–t for the purpose,* dem Zwecke dienlich, zweckdienlich; (*coll.*) *–t for the station,* nahe an *or* bei dem Bahnhof; *with –t speed,* mit möglichster Eile.

convent [ˈkɔnvənt], *s.* das Kloster, Nonnenkloster.

conventical [kənˈvɛntɪkl], *s.* die Versammlung; das Konventikel (*of Nonconformists*).

convention [kənˈvɛnʃən], *s.* die Versammlung, Tagung; der Vertrag, das Übereinkommen, die Übereinkunft, Abmachung; Konvention (*Pol.*); (*often pl.*) das Herkommen, der Brauch; *national –,* der Nationalkonvent. **–al** [–ˈvɛnʃənəl], *adj.* verabredet, vertragsgemäß; üblich, herkömmlich, konventionell, traditionsgemäß; willkürlich festgesetzt; *–al signs,* Kartenzeichen (*pl.*) (*of a map*); *–al treatment,* die Behandlung nach der Schablone (*Paint.*). **–alism** [–ɪzm], *s.* das Haften am Hergebrachten. **–ality** [–ˈnælɪtɪ], *s.* die Herkömmlichkeit, Schablonenhaftigkeit.

conventual [kənˈvɛntjuəl], *adj.* klösterlich, Kloster–.

converg–e [kənˈvə:dʒ], *v.n.* zusammenlaufen, konvergieren, sich zusammenziehen (*on,* auf). **–ence,** *s.*, **–ency,** *s.* die Annäherung, das Zusammenlaufen, die Konvergenz. **–ent,** *adj.*, **–ing,** *adj.* zusammenlaufend, verjüngend, konvergent, konvergierend; *–ing lens,* die Sammellinse; *–ing point,* der Knotenpunkt.

convers–able [kənˈvə:səbl], *adj.* unterhaltend, gesprächig; gesellig, umgänglich, mitteilsam. **–ableness,** *s.* die Gesprächigkeit; Umgänglichkeit. **–ance** [ˈkɔnvəsəns], *s.* die Vertrautheit. **–ant** [ˈkɔnvəsənt], *adj.* bekannt, vertraut (*with,* mit); geübt, bewandert (*with,* in (*Dat.*)), kundig (*Gen.*), erfahren (in (*Dat.*)). **–ation** [kɔnvəˈseɪʃən], *s.* das Gespräch, die Unterredung, Unterhaltung; (*archaic*) der Umgang, Verkehr; *criminal –ation,* der Ehebruch; *enter into –ation with,* ein Gespräch anknüpfen mit; *–ation piece,* das Genrebild; *subject of –ation,* das Gesprächsthema. **–ational,** *adj.* gesprächig, Unterhaltungs–; gesellig. **–ationalist,** *s.* guter Gesellschafter, gewandter Erzähler. **–azione** [–sætsɪˈounɪ], *s.* die Abendgesellschaft; (literarischer) Unterhaltungsabend.

¹**convers–e** [kənˈvə:s], 1. *v.n.* verkehren (*with,* mit); sich unterhalten, sprechen, reden (*with,* mit). 2. [ˈkɔnvə:s] *s.* (*archaic & poet.*) das Gespräch, die Unterhaltung, Unterredung; gesellschaftlicher Verkehr.

²**convers–e** 1. [ˈkɔnvə:s], *adj.* umgekehrt, gegenteilig. 2. *s.* die Umkehrung, der Gegensatz; umgekehrter Satz (*Math., Log.*). **–ion** [kənˈvə:ʃən], *s.* die Umänderung, Verwandlung, Umwandlung, Umsetzung, Umrechnung, Umstellung; Konvertierung, Einlösung (*C.L.*), Umkehrung (*Log.*); Bekehrung (*Theol.*), Meinungsänderung, der Übertritt; widerrechtliche *or* unberechtigte Verwendung (*Law*); *–ion of equations,* die Umkehrung von Gleichungen; *fraudulent –ion,* unrechtmäßige Veräußerung; *–ion of paper into cash,* die Umwandlung eines Papiers in bares Geld; *–ion loan,* die zu konvertierende Anleihe; *–ion table,* die Umrechnungstabelle.

convert [kənˈvə:t], 1. *v.a.* umändern, umwandeln, verwandeln; konvertieren, einlösen, umwechseln, umsetzen, umrechnen, überführen (*C.L.*); umkehren (*Log.*); bekehren (*Theol., etc.*); verwenden, aptieren (*Law*); erhöhen (*Footb.*); zementieren (*iron*); *– a house,* ein Haus in kleine Wohnungen einteilen; *– everything into money,* alles zu Geld machen; *– a th. to one's own use,* etwas für sich verwenden, sich etwas aneigen; *–ed steel,* der Zementstahl. 2. [ˈkɔnvə:t], *s.* Bekehrte(r), *m.*, der Proselyt; *become a – to,* sich bekehren zu; *make a –,* einen Proselyten machen. **–er** [kənˈvə:tə], *s.* der Bekehrer; Umformer (*Elec.*); die Bessemerbirne (*Metall.*); *rotary –er,* der Drehumformer, Einankerumformer (*Elec.*). **–ibility,** *s.* die Umwandelbarkeit, Verwandelbarkeit; Umsetzbarkeit (*C.L.*). **–ible,** *adj.* umwandelbar, verwandelbar; bekehrbar; verwendbar; umsetzbar, umwechselbar, konvertierbar, einlöslich (*C.L.*); *–ible terms,* gleichwertige *or* gleichbedeutende Ausdrücke.

convex [ˈkɔnvɛks], *adj.* konvex, nach außen gewölbt, erhaben. **–ity** [kənˈvɛksɪtɪ], *s.* konvexe Form.

convey [kənˈveɪ], *v.a.* zuführen, überbringen, übergeben, übersenden, übertragen, übermitteln (*s.th. to s.o.,* einem etwas); befördern, transportieren, versenden (*goods, etc.*); mitteilen, vermitteln (*information*); übertragen, abtreten (*to,* an) (*Law*); fördern, fortpflanzen; *– compliments,* Grüße überbringen *or* bestellen; *– an idea,* einen Begriff geben; *– letters,* Briefe befördern; *– one's meaning clearly,* sich klar ausdrücken; *– by water,* verschiffen. **–ance,** *s* das Wegführen, Forttragen, Fortschaffen; die Übergabe, Abtretung (*Law*); Übertragungsurkunde (*Law*); Beförderung, Übersendung, Übermittlung, der Transport, die Spedition (*C.L.*); Überbringung, Vermittlung, Mitteilung; das Fuhrwerk, Transportmittel; *charges for –ance,* Transportkosten; *bill of –ance,* die Speditionsrechnung; *deed of –ance,* die Übertragungsurkunde; *means of –ance,* das Beförderungsmittel, Transportmittel; *mode of –ance,* die Versendungsart; *–ance by land* (*water*), der Landtransport (Wassertransport). **–ancer,** *s.* der Notar für Übertragungsgeschäfte. **–er, –or,** *s.* der Beförderer; die Förderkette, Becherkette, das Transportband, laufendes Band. **–or-belt,** *s.* laufendes Band, das Förderband, Transportband, Fließband.

convict, 1. [kənˈvɪkt], *v.a.* überführen, für schuldig erklären; *– a p. of an error,* einem einen Irrtum nachweisen *or* zum Bewußtsein bringen; *be –ed of murder,* des Mordes überführt werden. 2. *s.* [ˈkɔnvɪkt], der Sträfling, Zuchthäusler; (*archaic*) überführter Missetäter; *– settlement,* die Sträflingskolonie. **–ion** [kənˈvɪkʃən], *s.* die Überführung, Verurteilung; Schuldigerklärung, Schuldigsprechung; Gewißheit, Überzeugung; *the –ion grows on me,* ich komme immer mehr zu der Überzeugung; *previous* or *prior –ion,* die Vorstrafe; *–ion of sin,* das Sündengefühl; *strong –ion,* feste Überzeugung; *carry –ion,* überzeugend klingen; *live up to one's –ions,* den Überzeugungen leben.

convinc–e [kənˈvɪns], *v.a.* überzeugen; *–e s.o. of a th.,* einem etwas zum Bewußtsein bringen. **–ible,** *adj.* überzeugbar. **–ing,** *adj.* überzeugend; *be –ing,* überzeugen; *–ing proof,* schlagender Beweis.

convivial [kənˈvɪvɪəl], *adj.* gesellig; lustig, heiter; festlich; *– evening,* der Festabend. **–ity** [–ˈælɪtɪ], *s.* die Geselligkeit; Fröhlichkeit (bei Tafel).

convocation [kɔnvoˈkeɪʃən], *s.* die Zusammenberufung, Einberufung; Versammlung; Provinzialsynode (*of Church of England*); gesetzgebende Versammlung einer Universität.

convoke [kənˈvouk], *v.a.* zusammenberufen, einberufen.

convolut–e [ˈkɔnvəluːt], *adj.* zusammengerollt *or* –gewickelt, ringelförmig (*Bot.*). **–ed** [–ˈluːtɪd], *adj.* gebogen, gewunden (*Zool.*). **–ion** [–ˈluːʃən], *s.* die Bindung; Zusammenwick(e)lung (*Bot.*).

convolve [kənˈvɔlv], 1. *v.a.* zusammenrollen, zusammenwickeln, aufrollen. 2. *v.n.* sich zusammenrollen.

convolvulus [kənˈvɔlvjuləs], *s.* die Winde (*Bot.*).

convoy, 1. [kənˈvɔɪ], *v.a.* geleiten, begleiten, decken. 2. [ˈkɔnvɔɪ], *s.* die Begleitung, das Geleit (*also Mil.*); der Geleitzug, Konvoi (*Naut.*); *lorry –*, die Lastkraftwagenkolonne.

convuls–e [kənˈvʌls], *v.a.* erschüttern; *be –ed with laughter*, sich vor Lachen biegen *or* krümmen. **–ion** [–ˈvʌlʃən], *s.* (*often pl.*) die Zuckung, der Krampf (*Med.*); (*fig.*) die Erschütterung; *–ions of laughter*, Lachkrämpfe. **–ive,** *adj.* krampfhaft, krampfartig, zuckend; (*fig.*) erschütternd.

cony, coney [ˈkounɪ], *s.* das Kaninchen; Kaninchenfell.

coo [kuː], *v.n.* girren, gurren; *bill and –*, (sich) schnäbeln; (*coll.*) zärtlich tun, liebkosen. **–ing,** *s.* das Girren; *billing and –ing*, (*coll.*) Zärtlichkeiten (*pl.*).

cook [kuk], 1. *s.* der Koch, die Köchin; (*Prov.*) *too many –s spoil the broth*, viele Köche verderben den Brei. 2. *v.a. & n.* kochen, abkochen, backen, zubereiten; (*coll.*) *– accounts*, den (Rechenschafts)-Bericht fälschen, schminken *or* frisieren; (*sl.*) *– a p.'s goose*, einem den Garaus machen; *– up*, aufwärmen; (*sl.*) zusammenbrauen, fälschen. **– -book** (*Amer.*), *see* **–ery book. –er,** *s.* der Kocher; Kochapparat; das Kochgefäß; (*pl.*) das Kochobst; *the apples are good –s*, die Äpfel lassen sich gut kochen. **–ery** [–ərɪ], *s.* das Kochen; die Kochkunst. **–ery book,** das Kochbuch. **–ery talk,** der Küchenfunk (*Rad.*). **– -house,** *s.* die Feldküche (*Mil.*), die Schiffsküche, Kombüse (*Naut.*). **–ie,** *s. see* **–y. –ing,** 1. *s.* das Kochen, die Küche. 2. *adj.* Koch–; *–ing apple*, der Kochapfel; *–ing range*, der Kochherd. **– -shop,** *s.* die Garküche. **–y,** *s.* (*Scots*) das Brötchen, der Kuchen; (*coll.*) die Köchin.

cool [kuːl], 1. *adj.* kühl, frisch; (*fig.*) gleichgültig, leidenschaftslos, teilnahmlos; ruhig, bedächtig, besonnen, gelassen; (*sl.*) unverfroren, frech; *– cheek*, die Frechheit, Stirn; (*coll.*) *– as a cucumber*, frech wie Oskar; (*coll.*) *– customer*, unverfrorener Bursche. 2. *s.* die Kühle, Frische. 3. *v.a.* kühlen; (*fig.*) abkühlen, mäßigen; *– down*, abkühlen, abschrecken, besänftigen; (*coll.*) *– one's heels*, vergeblich warten. 4. *v.n.* sich abkühlen, kühl werden; (*fig.*) erkalten; *– down*, sich legen, sich beruhigen. **–er,** *s.* der Kühler; (*sl.*) das Kittchen. **– -headed,** *adj.* besonnen, kaltblütig. **–ing,** 1. *s.* die Abkühlung; *air- –ing*, die Luftkühlung; *forced water –ing*, die Druckwasserkühlung; *gravity system water –ing*, die Thermosyphonkühlung. 2. *adj.* kühlend, erfrischend. **–ing fin,** die Kühlrippe (*of an engine*). **–ing tower,** der Kondensationsturm. **–ing water,** das Kühlwasser. **–ish,** *adj.* ziemlich kühl. **–ness,** *s.* die Kühle; (*fig.*) Lauheit, Gleichgültigkeit; Kälte, Kaltblütigkeit; (*sl.*) Frechheit.

coolie [ˈkuːlɪ], *s.* der Kuli, chinesischer Lastträger.

coomb [kuːm], *s.* (*dial.*) die Talmulde, Senkung.

coon [kuːn], *s.* der Waschbär. der Neger (*Amer.*, *pej.*)

coop [kuːp], 1. *v.a.*; (*– up*) einsperren, einpferchen. 2. *s.* der Hühnerkorb.

co-op [ˈkouɔp], *s.* (*coll.*) *see* **co-operative society** *and* **store.**

cooper [ˈkuːpə], 1. *s.* der Küfer, Böttcher, Faßbinder. 2. *v.a. & n.* Fässer machen *or* binden. **–age,** *s.* die Küferei, Böttcherei; der Küferlohn.

co-operat–e [kouˈɔpəreɪt], *v.n.* mitwirken, zusammenwirken, zusammenarbeiten, beitragen (*in*, *to*, zu). **–ion** [–ˈreɪʃən], *s.* die Mitwirkung, das Zusammenarbeiten; Zusammenwirken, die Zusammenarbeit; *army –ion plane*, das Arbeitsflugzeug. **–ive** [–ˈɔprətɪv], *adj.* mitwirkend, zusammenarbeitend; genossenschaftlich; *–ive movement*, die Genossenschaftsbewegung; *–ive society*, der Konsumverein, die Genossenschaft; *–ive store*, der Konsumvereinsladen. **–or,** *s.* Mitwirkende(r), *m.*; das Konsumvereinsmitglied.

co-opt [kouˈɔpt], *v.a.* hinzuwählen, kooptieren. **–ation** [–ˈteɪʃən], *s.* die Zuwahl, Kooptierung.

co-ordinat–e 1. [kouˈɔrdɪnɪt], *adj.* beigeordnet, nebengeordnet, koordiniert; gleichgestellt, gleichartig. 2. [–eɪt], *v.a.* beiordnen, gleichordnen, koordinieren, einheitlich leiten; gleichschalten, zusammenfassen. 3. *s.* die Koordinate; *polar –es*, die Polarkoordinaten; *rectangular –es*, kartesische Koordinaten. **–ion** [–ˈneɪʃən], *s.* die Nebenordnung, Beiordnung, Gleichstellung; Gleichschaltung; Zusammenfassung; das Zusammenwirken.

coot [kuːt], *s.* das Wasserhuhn; *as bald as a –*, völlig kahl.

[1]**cop** [kɔp], *s.* der Kamm, Garnwickel, Kötzen, das Knäuel.

[2]**cop,** 1. *v.a.* (*sl.*) erwischen; (*sl.*) *– it*, Prügel bekommen. 2. *s.* (*sl.*) der Polizist.

copaiba [kouˈpaɪbə], *s.* der Kopaivabalsam (*Pharm.*).

copal [ˈkoupəl], *s.* der Kopal.

coparcen–ary [kouˈpɑːsənərɪ] *s.* gemeinsamer Besitz einer Erbschaft; die Miterbschaft (*Law*). **–er,** *s.* der Miterbe (*Law*).

copartner [kouˈpɑːtnə], *s.* der Teilhaber, Teilnehmer, Mitinhaber, Associé (*C.L.*). **–ship,** *s.* die Teilhaberschaft; das Mitbeteiligungssystem; *labour –ship*, die Gewinnbeteiligung.

[1]**cope** [koup], 1. *s.* der Priesterrock, Chorrock; Außenmantel (*Found.*); die Mauerkappe (*Arch.*); (*fig.*) Decke, das Dach, der Mantel. 2. *v.a.* (be)-decken. **– -stone,** *s.* der Kappenstein; (*fig.*) Schlußstein, die Krönung, Krone.

[2]**cope,** *v.n.* sich messen (mit), gewachsen sein (*Dat.*), es aufnehmen (mit); *– with a th.*, etwas bewältigen, mit einer S. fertig werden.

copeck [ˈkoupɛk], *s.* die Kopeke.

coper [ˈkoupə], *s.* der Pferdehändler.

copied [ˈkɔpɪd], *see* **copy.**

copier [ˈkɔpɪə], *s.* der Abschreiber, Plagiator.

co-pilot [kouˈpaɪlət], *s.* zweiter Pilot, der Mitpilot, Beiflieger.

coping [ˈkoupɪŋ], *s.* die Mauerkappe, Mauerkrönung. **– stone,** *see* **cope-stone.**

copious [ˈkoupjəs], *adj.* reich, reichlich; weitläufig, weitschweifig, wortreich; *– tears*, reichliche Tränen. **–ness,** *s.* die Fülle; der Überfluß; die Weitläufigkeit.

copper [ˈkɔpə], 1. *s.* das Kupfer (*Min.*); (*often pl.*) die Kupfermünze, das Kupfergeld, (*pl.*) das Kleingeld; der (Kupfer)Kessel, das (Kupfer)Gefäß; (*sl.*) der Polizist. 2. *adj.* kupfern, Kupfer–. **–as** [ˈkɔpərəs], *s.* der *or* das Vitriol; *blue –as*, Kupfervitriol; *green –as*, Eisenvitriol; *white –as*, Zinkvitriol. **– -beech,** *s.* die Blutbuche (*Bot.*). **– -bottomed,** *adj.* mit Kupferverkleidung (*Shipb.*), (*fig.*) seetüchtig, kerngesund. **– -coloured,** *adj.* kupferrot. **– -engraving,** *s.* die Kupferstechkunst. **– -glance,** *s.* der Kupferglanz (*Min.*). **–head,** *s.* die Mokassinschlange (*Zool.*). **–plate,** 1. *s.* der Kupferstich. 2. *adj.* Kupferstich–, Kupferstech–; *like –plate*, wie gestochen (*of handwriting*); *–plate engraving*, *s.* der Kupferdruck, Kupferstich; die Kupferdruckerei, Kupferstechkunst. **– pyrites,** *pl.* der Kupferkies. **– sheathing,** der Kupferbeschlag (*Shipb.*). **– sheet, sheet- –,** das Kupferblech. **–smith,** *s.* der Kupferschmied. **– sulphate,** das Kupfersulphat, Kupfervitriol. 3. *v.a.* verkupfern, mit Kupfer beschlagen. **–y,** *adj.* kupferig; kupferhaltig; Kupfer–.

coppice [ˈkɔpɪs], *s.* das Unterholz, Dickicht, Gestrüpp, Gebüsch.

copra [ˈkɔprə], *s.* die Kopra.

copse [kɔps], *s. see* **coppice.**

copula [ˈkɔpjulə], *s.* die Kopula (*Gram.*); das Verbindungsglied (*Anat.*). **–te** [ˈkɔpjuleɪt], *v.n.* sich begatten, sich paaren. **–tion** [–ˈleɪʃən], *s.* die Paarung, Begattung; Verbindung. **–tive** [–lətɪv], 1. *adj.* verbindend, Binde–. 2. *s.* das Bindewort (*Gram.*).

copy [ˈkɔpɪ], 1. *s.* die Abschrift, Kopie; das Muster, Modell; die Nachahmung, Nachbildung (*Paint. Sculp.*); das Exemplar, der Abdruck (*of a book*).

die Nummer (*of a newspaper*); (*without art.*) druckfertiges Manuskript (*Typ.*), der Zeitungsstoff, literarisches Material; die Urkunde, das Instrument (*Law*); *carbon* –, der Durchschlag; *clean* or *fair* –, die Reinschrift; *foul* or *rough* –, die Kladde, das Konzept; die Skizze, erster Entwurf; *make* or *take a* –, eine Abschrift nehmen. 2. *v.a.* abschreiben, kopieren; eine Kopie machen; abzeichnen, nachbilden, nachahmen; – *out*, abschreiben, ins Reine schreiben. 3. *v.n.* kopieren, nachahmen; (vom Nachbar) abschreiben (*at school*). **--book,** *s.* das Schreibheft. (*coll.*) **--cat,** *s.* der Nachahmer. **–hold,** *s.* das Zinslehen; Lehngut. **–holder,** *s.* der Erbpächter, Besitzer eines Lehngutes. **–ing,** 1. *s.* das Abschreiben. 2. *adj.* Kopier–. **–ing-clerk,** der Kopist. **–ing-ink,** *s.* die Kopiertinte; *–ing-ink pencil, s. see* **–ing-pencil. –ing-machine,** *s.*, **–ing-press,** *s.* die Kopiermaschine, Kopierpresse. **–ing-paper,** *s.* das Abdruckpapier, Durchschlagpapier, Pauspapier. **–ing-pencil,** *s.* der Tintenstift. **–ist,** *s.* der Abschreiber, Kopist. **–right,** *s.* das Verlagsrecht, Urheberrecht (*in*, über); *the book is –right*, Nachdruck ist verboten, alle Rechte vorbehalten; *–right edition*, urheberrechtliche Ausgabe.

coquet [kə'kɛt], 1. *v.n.* kokettieren, flirten; (*fig.*) liebäugeln. 2. *adj.* kokett. **–ry** ['koukıtrı], *s.* die Gefallsucht, Koketterie. **–te,** *s.* die Kokette, Gefallsüchtige. **–tish** [ko'kɛtıʃ], *adj.* gefallsüchtig, kokett.

coracle ['kɔrəkl], *s.* das Boot aus überzogenem Flechtwerk.

coracoid ['kɔrəkɔıd], *adj.* Raben– (*Anat., Zool.*); – *bone*, das Rabenbein; – *process*, der Rabenschnabelfortsatz.

coral ['kɔrəl], 1. *s.* die Koralle; der Korallenpolyp. 2. *adj.* Korallen–; – *beads*, Korallen; das Korallenhalsband; – *island*, die Koralleninsel; – *reef*, das Korallenriff. **–lin,** *s.* das Korallin (*Chem.*). **–line,** 1. *adj.* korallenartig; korallenrot; Korallen enthaltend. 2. *s.* die Korallenalge. **–ite,** *s.* fossile Koralle. **–loid,** *adj.* korallenähnlich, korallenartig.

corbel ['kɔ:bəl], 1. *s.* der Kragstein, die Konsole, der Balkenträger (*Arch.*). 2. *v.a.* durch Kragsteine stützen. **--table,** *s.* der auf Kragsteinen ruhende Mauervorsprung, Bogenfries (*Arch.*).

corbie ['kɔ:bı], *s.* der Rabe (*Scots*). **--steps,** *pl.* die Giebelstufen (*Arch.*).

cord [kɔ:d], 1. *s.* der Strick, das Seil, die Leine; Schnur (*also Anat.*); der Strang (*also Anat.*); das Band (*Anat.*); die Klafter (*of wood = 128 cu. ft.*); der Kord (*cloth*); (*pl.*) (*coll.*) die Kordhose; *spinal* –, das Rückenmark; *vocal –s*, die Stimmbänder; – *of wood*, eine Klafter Holz. 2. *v.a.* zuschnüren, festbinden; – *wood*, Holz (auf)klaftern. **–age** [–ıdʒ], *s.* das Tauwerk, Seilwerk. **–ed,** *adj.* verschnürt, zugeschnürt; gerippt (*of cloth*).

cordate ['kɔ:deıt], *adj.* herzförmig.

cordelier ['kɔ:də'lı:ə], *s.* der Franziskanermönch.

cordial ['kɔ:dıəl], 1. *adj.* herzlich, aufrichtig; belebend, herzstärkend, magenstärkend. 2. *s.* der Magenlikör, herzstärkendes *or* magenstärkendes Mittel; (*fig.*) das Labsal. **–ity** *s.* die Herzlichkeit, Wärme.

cordite ['kɔ:dαıt], *s.* das Kordit.

cordon ['kɔ:dən], 1. *s.* die Postenkette, Absperrkette, der Kordon (*Mil.*); der Mauerkranz, Mauersims (*Arch.*); der Spalierbaum (*Hort.*); das Ordensband; *form a* –, Spalier bilden. 2. *v.a.*; – *off*, abriegeln, absperren, umzingeln, einschließen. 3. [kɔ:'dɔ̃], *s.* der Kordon, das Ordensband.

cordovan ['kɔ:dəvən], *s.* das Korduan, Korduanleder.

corduroy ['kɔ:djʊrɔı], *s.* der Kord, Kordstoff; (*pl.*) die Kordhose; – *road*, der Knüppeldamm.

cordwain ['kɔ:dweın], *s. see* **cordovan. –er,** *s.*; *–s' company*, die Londoner Schuhmacherinnung.

core [kɔ:], 1. *s.* das Kerngehäuse, der Griebs, Kern (*in fruit*); (*fig.*) der Kern, das Innerste, Herz, Mark, die Ader; Seele (*of wire, cable, etc.*); *the heart's* –, der Herzensgrund; *rotten at* or *to the* –, im Innersten faul; *to the* –, bis ins Innerste, bis auf den Grund. 2. *v.a.* entkernen.

co-regent [kou'rı:dʒənt], *s.* der Mitregent.

co-religionist [kourı'lıdʒənıst], *s.* der Glaubensgenosse.

co-respondent [kourı'spɔndənt], *s.* mitbeklagter Ehebrecher.

corf [kɔ:f], *s.* der Förderkorb (*Min.*).

coriaceous [kɔrı'eıʃəs], *adj.* Leder–, ledern, lederartig, zäh.

cork [kɔ:k], 1. *s.* der Kork (*Bot.*), die Korkrinde; der Pfropfen, Stöpsel, Kork. 2. *v.a.* (zu)korken, verkorken, zustöpseln; (mit gebranntem Kork) schwärzen (*one's face, etc.*). **–age** [–ıdʒ], *s.* das Pfropfengeld, Korkgeld. **–ed** [–t], *adj.* verkorkt, zugestopft; korkig; nach dem Kork schmeckend (*of wine*). **–er,** *s.* (*sl.*) famose *or* prima Sache, blendender Kerl, Unübertreffliche(s), *n.* **–ing,** *adj.* (*sl.*) famos, knorke, großartig, blendend, pfundig, prima. **--jacket,** *s.* die Kork-Schwimmweste, der Rettungsgürtel. **- leg,** die Korkprothese. **--oak,** *s.* die Korkeiche. **–screw,** 1. *s.* der Korkzieher, Pfropfenzieher. 2. *adj.* spiralförmig, schraubenförmig; *–screw curls*, Ringellocken; *–screw staircase*, die Wendeltreppe. 3. *v.a.* (*coll.*) sich spiralförmig bewegen; *–screw one's way through*, sich durchschlängeln. **- sole,** die Korkeinlegesohle.

cormorant ['kɔ:mərənt], *s.* die Scharbe, der Kormoran, Seerabe (*Orn.*); (*fig.*) Vielfraß.

[1]**corn** [kɔ:n], 1. *s.* das Getreide, Korn; der Weizen, Hafer; (*Amer.*) Maisschnaps; (*fig.*) das Körnchen; *Indian* – (*Amer.* –), der Mais; *give a horse a feed of* –, einem Pferde Hafer zu fressen geben. 2. *v.a.* einsalzen, einpökeln; *–ed beef*, das Pökelfleisch, Büchsenfleisch. **--belt,** *s.* der Getreidegürtel (*U.S.A. Middle West*). **--bin,** *s.* die Kornlade. **--bind,** *s.* die Ackerwinde (*Bot.*). **--chandler,** *s.* der Getreidehändler. **--cob,** *s.* der Maiskolben. **--cockle,** *s.* die Kornrade (*Bot.*). **–crake,** *s.* die Wiesenknarre, der Wiesenläufer (*Orn.*). **--exchange,** *s.* die Getreidebörse. **--factor,** *s.* der Kornmakler; Korn(groß)händler. **–field,** *s.* das Getreidefeld. **–flakes,** *s.* die Frühstücksmehlspeise. **–flour,** *s.* das Maismehl. **–flower,** *s.* die Kornblume (*Bot.*). **--land,** *s.* das Getreideland. **--laws,** *pl.* die Getreidezollgesetze. **--loft,** *s.* der Kornboden, Kornspeicher. **--poppy,** *s.* die Klatschrose (*Bot.*). **–y,** *adj.* kornreich (*see also* [2]**corn**).

[2]**corn,** *s.* das Hühnerauge; die Hornhaut (*Anat.*). **--plaster,** *s.* das Hühneraugenpflaster. **–y,** *adj.* hornig; (*sl.*) schlecht, minderwertig.

cornea ['kɔ:nıə], *s.* die Hornhaut (*of the eye*).

cornel ['kɔ:nəl], die Korneliuskirsche, der Hartriegel (*Bot.*).

cornelian [kɔ:'nı:ljən], *s.* der Karneol (*Min.*).

corneous ['kɔ:nıəs], *adj.* hornig.

corner ['kɔ:nə], 1. *s.* die Ecke, der Winkel; die Schwänze, das Aufkaufen, der Spekulantenring (*C.L.*); (*fig.*) die Verlegenheit, Klemme; *at the* – *of the street*, an der Straßenecke; *blind* –, unübersichtliche Biegung *or* Ecke; *cut off a* –, ein Stück (vom Wege) abschneiden; *all the –s of the earth*, alle Gegenden der Erde; (*fig.*) *be in a* –, in der Klemme sitzen, in Verlegenheit sein; *drive s.o. into a* –, einen in die Enge treiben *or* in Verlegenheit bringen; (*coll.*) *hole-and-corner business*, das Winkelgeschäft, (*sl.*) die Quetsche; *on the street*-–, auf der Straßenecke; (*coll.*) *do in a hole-and- – way*, in verborgenen *or* heimlich tun; *we are not round the* – *yet*, wir sind noch nicht über den Berg; *tight* –, schwierige Lage; *take a* –, eine Kurve nehmen (*Motor.*); *turn the* –, um die Ecke biegen; (*fig.*) über den Berg kommen. 2. *v.a.* (*fig.*) in die Enge treiben, in Verlegenheit bringen; aufkaufen, aufschwänzen (*C.L.*); vertrusten; durch Aufkauf *or* Vereinbarung die Preise erhöhen; – *the market*, den Markt aufkaufen; **--cupboard,** der Eckschrank. **–ed,** *adj.* (*as suffix*) –eckig; (*fig.*) in die Enge getrieben, in Verlegenheit, in der Klemme; aufgekauft, aufgeschwänzt (*C.L.*). **- house,** das Eckhaus. **–(-kick),** *s.* freier Eckstoß (*Footb.*). **–piece,** *s.* der Dreikantbeschlag. **–stone,** *s.* der Eckstein (*Arch.*); (*fig.*) Grundstein. **–wise,** *adv.* diagonal, eckig.

cornet ['kɔ:nıt], *s.* das Ventilkornett, die Zinke (*Mus.*); spitze Tüte; (*archaic*) der Fahnenjunker,

Kornett (*Mil.*). **–cy,** *s.* die Kornettstelle (*Mil.*). **– -player,** *s.* der Kornettbläser.
cornice ['kɔːnɪs], *s.* das Karnies, Gesims, der Sims (*Arch.*); die Wächte (*of snow*). **–d,** *adj.* überwächtet.
cornucopia [kɔːnjuˈkoupjə], *s.* das Füllhorn; (*fig.*) die Fülle.
corny ['kɔːnɪ], *see* [1]**corn** *and* [2]**corn.**
corolla [kəˈrɔlə], *s.* die Blumenkrone (*Bot.*).
corollary [kəˈrɔlərɪ], *s.* der Folgesatz (*Log.*, *Math.*), Zusatz; (*fig.*) die Folge(erscheinung), das Ergebnis.
corona [kəˈrounə], *s.* die Krone, der Hof, Lichtkranz (*Astr.*); die Kranzleiste, das Kranzgesims (*Arch.*); die Zahnkrone; der Randblütenkranz (*Bot.*). **–l,** *adj.* Kranz–, Kronen–, Hof–; *–l bone,* das Stirnbein (*Anat.*); *–l suture,* die Kranznaht.
coronach ['kɔrənæk], *s.* die Totenklage (*Scots*).
coronal ['kɔrənl], 1. *adj.* *see* **corona.** 2. *s.* der Blumenkranz; der Reif, das Diadem.
coronation [kɔrəˈneɪʃən], *s.* die Krönung, Krönungsfeier; *– oath,* der Krönungseid.
coroner ['kɔrənə], *s.* amtlicher Leichenbeschauer; *–'s inquest,* amtliche Totenschau.
coronet ['kɔrənət], *s.* kleine Krone, die Adelskrone; Hufkrone (*of horse*). **–ed,** *adj.* mit einer Krone.
[1]**corporal** ['kɔːpərəl], *s.* Obergefreite(r), Hauptgefreite(r), Korporal (*Mil.*); **lance- –,** Gefreite(r).
[2]**corporal,** 1. *adj.* körperlich, leiblich; *– punishment,* körperliche Züchtigung. 2. *s.* das Korporale, Meßtuch (*Eccl.*). **–ity** [kɔːpəˈrælɪtɪ], *s.* die Körperlichkeit, körperliche Existenz.
corporat-e ['kɔːpərɪt], *adj.* körperschaftlich, korporativ, inkorporiert, vereinigt, verbunden; *–e body,* juristische Person, die Körperschaft; *–e effort,* vereinte Bemühung. **–ion** [kɔːpəˈreɪʃən], *s.* die Körperschaft, Korporation, juristische Person; die Stadtbehörde; Gilde, Zunft, Innung, Handelsgesellschaft; (*sl.*) der Schmerbauch; *mayor and –ion,* Bürgermeister und Rat.
corpore-al [kɔːˈpɔːrɪəl], *adj.* körperlich; materiell; *be –ally present,* persönlich zugegen sein. **–ity** [kɔːpəˈrɪːətɪ], *s.* die Körperlichkeit, körperliche Form.
corposant ['kɔːpəznt], *s.* das (St.) Elmsfeuer.
corps [kɔː], *s.* das (Armee)Korps; der Truppenkörper (*Mil.*).
corpse [kɔːps], *s.* die Leiche, der Leichnam.
corpul-ence ['kɔːpjuləns], *s.*, **–ency,** *s.* die Beleibtheit, Leibesfülle, Korpulenz. **–ent** [–lənt], *adj.* beleibt, korpulent.
corpus ['kɔːpəs], *s.* das Korpus, die Sammlung; *– Christi,* der Fronleichnahm; *– delicti,* der Tatbestand (*Law*).
corpusc-le ['kɔːpəsl], *s.* das Körperchen, Teilchen; das Atom; *blood –le,* das Blutkörperchen. **–ular.** [–ˈpʌskjulə], *adj.* atomistisch, Korpuskular–. **–ule,** *s.* *see* **–cle.**
corral [kəˈræl], *s.* die Hürde, der Pferch, das Gehege, die Einzäunung (*for cattle*); Wagenburg.
correct [kəˈrɛkt], 1. *adj.* richtig, fehlerfrei, genau; regelrecht, sinngemäß; tadellos, korrekt (*of behaviour*); in Ordnung (*C.L.*); *be –,* stimmen (*of things*), recht haben (*of persons*); *that is the – thing to do,* das gehört sich nun einmal; *– manners,* gute Sitten, tadelloses Benehmen; *if found –,* nach Rechtbefinden. 2. *v.a.* berichtigen, verbessern, korrigieren, richtigstellen (*a mistake*); tadeln, zurechtweisen, strafen (*a wrongdoing*); abstellen, beheben (*a defect, etc.*); (*fig.*) mildern; *– proofs,* durchkorrigieren, Korrekturen lesen; *stand –ed,* einen Fehler eingestehen. **–ion** [–ˈrɛkʃən], *s.* die Berichtigung, Verbesserung; Korrektur (*Print.*); der Tadel, Verweis; die Bestrafung, Züchtigung; *house of –ion,* die Besserungsanstalt, das Zuchthaus; *subject to –ion,* ohne Gewähr; *under –ion,* wenn ich (mich) nicht irre; *I speak under –ion,* dies ist meine unmaßgebliche Meinung. **–ional,** *adj.* Besserungs–, verbessernd. **–itude,** *s.* die Korrektheit (*behaviour*). **–ive,** 1. *adj.* verbessernd; mildernd (*Med.*). 2. *s.* das Gegenmittel, Korrektiv; Milderungsmittel, die Abhilfe. **–ness,** *s.* die Richtigkeit, Genauigkeit; Korrektheit (*of behaviour*). **–or,** *s.* der Verbesserer, Zurechtweiser; Korrektor (*Print.*); das Milderungsmittel (*Med.*); Besserungsmittel.
correlat-e ['kɔrɪleɪt], 1. *s.* das Korrelat. 2. *v.n.* sich aufeinander beziehen, in Wechselbeziehung stehen. 3. *v.a.* in Wechselbeziehung bringen, aufeinander beziehen. **–ion** [–ˈleɪʃən], *s.* die Wechselbeziehung; gegenseitiges Verhältnis. **–ive** [kəˈrɛlətɪv], *adj.* wechselseitig bedingt, voneinander abhängig, einander entsprechend.
correspond [kɔrɪsˈpɔnd], *v.n.* übereinstimmen (*with,* mit); entsprechen, passen, gemäß sein (*Dat.*); in Briefwechsel stehen. **–ence,** *s.* die Übereinstimmung, Angemessenheit, das Entsprechen; der Briefwechsel, Schriftverkehr, die Korrespondenz; Verbindung (*C.L.*); *keep up a –ence,* einen Briefwechsel unterhalten; *be in –ence with,* in Briefwechsel stehen mit. **–ent,** 1. *adj.* übereinstimmend (mit), entsprechend (*Dat.*). 2. *s.* der Briefschreiber, Korrespondent, Berichterstatter (*press*), Geschäftsfreund (*C.L.*). **–ing,** *adj.* entsprechend, gemäß (*to* (*Dat.*)).
corridor ['kɔrɪdɔː], *s.* der Korridor, Gang, Flur. **– -train,** *s.* der Durchgangszug, D-Zug.
corrie ['kɔrɪ], *s.* (*Scots*) die Bergschlucht.
corrigible ['kɔrɪdʒəbl], *adj.* verbesserlich; lenksam.
corroborat-e [kəˈrɔbəreɪt], *v.a.* bekräftigen, bestätigen, erhärten. **–ion** [–ˈreɪʃən], *s.* die Bekräftigung, Bestätigung, Erhärtung; *in –ion of,* zur Bestätigung von. **–ive** [–rətɪv], *adj.* bekräftigend. **–or,** *s.* der Bestätiger. **–ory,** *adj.* bekräftigend.
corro-de [kəˈroud] 1. *v.a.* auffressen, einfressen, zerfressen, wegätzen, beizen. 2. *v.n.* zerfressen werden, verfallen, sich wegfressen. **–sion** [–ˈrouʒən], *s.* das Zerfressen, Einfressen; die Anfressung, Verrottung, Zerstörung. **–sive** [–ˈrousɪv], 1. *adj.* fressend, anfressend, zerfressend, ätzend, Ätz–; (*fig.*) nagend, quälend; *–sive sublimate,* das Ätzsublimat. 2. *s.* das Ätzmittel, Beizmittel. **–siveness,** *s.* ätzende Schärfe, die Beizkraft.
corrugat-e ['kɔrugeɪt], *v.a.* wellen; runzeln, (zer)furchen. **–ed,** *adj.* gerunzelt, geriffelt, gewellt; *–ed iron,* das Wellblech; *–ed paper,* das Wellpapier, die Wellpappe. **–ion** [–ˈgeɪʃən], *s.* das Runzeln, Furchen.
corrupt [kəˈrʌpt], 1. *v.a.* verderben, verschlechtern; bestechen, erkaufen: verleiten, verführen; verfälschen, entstellen (*text*); verunstalten (*language*). 2. *v.n.* (ver)faulen, verderben. 3. *adj.* faul, schlecht, verdorben; verfälscht, unecht; verderbt (*morals*); ehrlos, unredlich, bestechlich; *– practices,* die Bestechung (*at elections*); *the text is –,* der Text ist verderbt. **–er,** *s.* der Verderber, Bestecher. **–ibility,** *s.* die Verderblichkeit, Bestechlichkeit. **–ible,** *adj.* verderblich; vergänglich; bestechlich. **–ion** [–ˈrʌpʃən], *s.* die Verwesung, Fäulnis, der Verfall; die Verderbtheit, Verderbnis, Verdorbenheit, Verschlechterung, Entartung; Verfälschung, Entstellung (*of a text, etc.*); Bestechung. **–ive,** *adj.* verderblich, ansteckend. **–ness,** *s.* die Verdorbenheit; Bestechlichkeit; Verderbtheit.
corsage [kɔːˈsæːʒ], *s.* das Mieder, die Taille.
corsair ['kɔːsɛə], *s.* der Seeräuber, Korsar; das Seeräuberschiff.
corse [kɔːs], *s.* (*poet.*) *see* **corpse.**
corset ['kɔːsɪt], 1. *s.* das Korsett. 2. *v.n.* ein Korsett tragen, sich schnüren (*usually p.p.*). **–ed,** *adj.* geschnürt.
cors(e)let ['kɔːslɪt], *s.* der Brustharnisch; Brustschild (*Ent.*).
cortège [kɔːˈtɛʒ], *s.* das Gefolge, der Zug; Leichenzug.
cort-ex ['kɔːtɛks], *s.* die Rinde (*Bot.*); *cerebral –,* äußerer Teil des Großhirns (*Anat.*). **–ical, –icate,** *adj.* rindig, rindenartig; berindet.
corundum [kəˈrʌndəm], *s.* der Korund (*Min.*).
coruscat-e ['kɔrəskeɪt], *v.n.* blitzen, funkeln, glänzen. **–ion,** *s.* der Glanz, Blitz, das Schimmern, Funkeln, Blitzen.
corvette [kɔːˈvɛt], *s.* die Korvette (*Naut.*).
corvine ['kɔːvaɪn], *adj.* rabenartig, krähenartig.
corymb ['kɔrɪm], *s.* die Doldentraube (*Bot.*). **–iferous,** *adj.* Doldentrauben tragend.
coryphaeus [kɔrɪˈfɪːəs], *s.* der Chorführer; (*fig.*) Vornehmste(r), *m.*, der Koryphäe, Leiter.

coryza [kəˈrɑɪzə], *s.* der Schnupfen (*Med.*).
cosecant [koʊˈsɛkənt], *s.* die Kosekante.
[1]**cosh** [kɔʃ], 1. *s.* (*sl.*) der Knüppel. 2. *v.a.* prügeln.
[2]**cosh**, *s.* hyperbolischer Kosinus (*Math.*).
cosher [ˈkɔʃə], *v.a.* verhätscheln.
co-signatory [koʊˈsɪgnətərɪ], *s.* der Mitunterzeichner.
cosily [ˈkoʊzɪlɪ], *adv. see* **cosy.**
cosine [ˈkoʊsɑɪn], *s.* der Kosinus.
cosiness [ˈkoʊzɪnɪs], *s.* die Behaglichkeit, Gemütlichkeit, Traulichkeit.
cosmetic [kɔzˈmɛtɪk], 1. *adj.* kosmetisch. 2. *s.* das Schönheitsmittel. **-s,** die Schönheitspflege, Kosmetik.
cosmic(al) [ˈkɔzmɪk(l)], *adj.* kosmisch, Weltall–; (*fig.*) gewaltig.
cosmo-gony [kɔzˈmɔgənɪ], *s.* die Weltentstehungslehre. **-graphic,** *adj.* kosmographisch. **-graphy** [–ˈmɔgrəfɪ], *s.* die Weltbeschreibung. **-logical,** *adj.* kosmologisch. **-logy** [–ˈmɔlədʒɪ], *s.* die Weltkunde, Kosmologie. **-politan** [–məˈpɔlɪtn], 1. *adj.* weltbürgerlich, kosmopolitisch. 2. *s.* der Kosmopolit, Weltbürger. **-politanism**, *s.* der Kosmopolitismus, das Weltbürgertum.
cosmos [ˈkɔzmɔs], *s.* das Weltall, der Kosmos; die Weltordnung.
cosset [ˈkɔsɪt], *v.a.* verhätscheln.
cost [kɔst], 1. *s.* (*only sing.*) der Preis, die Kosten, Auslagen (*pl.*); *– of living*, Unterhaltungskosten (*pl.*); *– of living bonus*, der Teuerungszuschlag; (*fig.*) das Opfer, der Verlust, Schaden, Nachteil; (*only pl.*) die (Gerichts)Gebühren (*Law*); die Spesen; *at any –, at all –s*, auf jeden Fall, unter allen Umständen, um jeden Preis; *at a heavy –*, unter schweren Opfern; *at the – of his life*, auf Kosten seines Lebens; *excess –*, Mehrkosten (*pl.*); *prime –*, der Gestehungspreis, Selbstkostenpreis (*C.L.*); *to my –*, zu meinem Schaden; *with –s*, nebst (Tragung der) (Gerichts)Kosten; *without counting the –*, ohne Rücksicht auf den Aufwand; *it will not repay the –*, es macht sich nicht bezahlt, es lohnt die Kosten nicht. 2. *v.a. & n.* kosten; *– dear*, teuer zu stehen kommen; *it – me £2*, es kostete mich *or* mir zwei Pfund; *it – him his life*, es kostete ihn das Leben; *it will – him much time and trouble*, es wird ihn viel Zeit und Mühe kosten. 3. *v.a.* Preise festsetzen (*C.L.*). **-ing,** *s.* die Kostenberechnung, Preisfestsetzung. **-liness,** *s.* die Kostbarkeit; Kostspieligkeit. **-ly,** *adj.* kostspielig, kostbar, teuer. **--price,** *s.* der Selbstkostenpreis, Einkaufspreis, Einstandspreis; Gestehungskosten (*pl.*).
costa-l [ˈkɔstl], *adj.* Rippen–. **-te** [ˈkɔstɪt], *adj.* gerippt (*Bot., Zool.*).
co-star [koʊˈstɑ:], *v.n.* als Hauptdarsteller mitspielen (*films, etc.*).
coster(-monger) [ˈkɔstə:mʌŋgə], *s.* der Händler, Höker.
costive [ˈkɔstɪv], *adj.* verstopft, hartleibig (*Med.*); (*fig.*) sparsam, zugeknöpft, geizig. **-ness,** *s.* die Verstopfung; Sparsamkeit.
costum-e [ˈkɔstju:m], *s.* das Kostüm, die Tracht; *tailor-made –e*, das Schneiderkostüm. **-ier** [–ˈtju:mɪə], *s.* der Kostümschneider; Theaterschneider.
cosy [ˈkoʊzɪ], 1. *adj.* behaglich, bequem, traulich, gemütlich. 2. *s.* der Kaffeewärmer, Teewärmer, die Teehaube.
cot [kɔt], *s.* das Kinderbett; die Hängematte, Koje (*Naut.*); das Feldbett, die Pritsche; der (Schaf)-Stall, *see* **cote;** (*Poet.*) die Hütte, Kate.
cote [koʊt], *s.* der Stall; *dove-–*, der Taubenschlag; *sheep-–*, der Schafstall.
coterie [ˈkoʊtərɪ], *s.* die Koterie; geschlossene Gesellschaft, die Clique, der Klüngel.
cothurnus [koʊˈθə:nəs], *s.* der Kothurn; (*fig.*) tragischer *or* erhabener Stil.
cotillion [koˈtɪljən], *s.* der Kotillon.
cottage [ˈkɔtɪdʒ], *s.* das Häuschen, die Hütte, Kate, der Kotten; das Bauernhaus; Landhaus, die Sommerwohnung; *– piano*, das Pianino. **-r,** *s.* der Hüttenbewohner, kleiner Bauer, der Häusler, Kossäte.
cott-ar, -er [ˈkɔtə] **(***Scots***), -ier** [ˈkɔtɪə] (*Irish*), *s. see* **cottager.**
cotter, *s.* der Pflock, Schließkeil, Splint, Bolzen, Sicherungsstift (*Mach.*).
cotton [ˈkɔtn], 1. *s.* die Baumwolle, das Baumwollgarn, der (Baumwoll)Zwirn; das Baumwollzeug, der Kattun; (*pl.*) Baumwollstoffe (*pl.*); *reel of –*, die Zwirnrolle. 2. *adj.* baumwollen, Baumwoll–. 3. *v.n.*; (*coll.*) *– on to a p.*, sich eng an einen anschließen; (*coll.*) *– on to a th.*, sich zu einer S. bequemen, sich mit einer S. abfinden *or* zurechtfinden. **--belt,** *s.* (*Amer.*) die Baumwollgegend. **--cake,** *s.* der Baumwollkuchen (*for cattle*). **--gin,** *s.* die Egreniermaschine. **--goods,** *s.* Baumwollwaren (*pl.*). **--grass,** *s.* das Wollgras (*Bot.*). **--grower,** *s.* der Baumwollpflanzer. **--mill,** *s.* die Baumwollspinnerei. **--plant,** *s.* die Baumwollstaude. **--print,** *s.* gedruckter Kattun. **--reel,** *s.* die Zwirnrolle. **--waste,** *s.* der Baumwollabfall. **--wool,** *s.* die (Roh)Baumwolle; Watte. **-y,** *adj.* baumwollartig, (*fig.*) weich.
cotyledon [kɔtɪˈlɪ:dən], *s.* der Samenlappen (*Bot.*); das Nabelkraut (*Bot.*). **-ous,** *adj.* kotyledarisch.
couch [kɑʊtʃ], 1. *s.* das Ruhebett, Liegesofa, die Chaiselongue; (*Poet.*) das Bett, Lager; die Lagerstätte; Schicht, Lage (*of paint, etc.*); Gautschpresse (*Pap.*). 2. *v.a.* (*only passive*) (nieder)legen; (*also active*) einlegen (*lance, etc.*); fassen, (ein)-kleiden (*thoughts, etc.*); stechen (*a cataract*) (*Med.*); gautschen (*paper*); verbergen. 3. *v.n.* sich niederlegen, sich lagern (*of animals*), (*fig.*) kauern, versteckt liegen, sich ducken. **-ed,** *adj.* im Lager (*Hunt.*); mit erhobenem Kopf liegend (*Her.*).
couch-grass [ˈkɑʊtʃgrɑs], *s.* das Queckengras (*Bot.*).
cougar [ˈku:gɑ:], *s.* der Puma, Kuguar (*Zool.*).
cough [kɔf], 1. *s.* der Husten; (*coll.*) *churchyard –*, böser Husten; *catch a –*, (den) Husten bekommen, sich (*Dat.*) den Husten holen. 2. *v.n.* husten. 3. *v.a.*; *– up*, aushusten (*phlegm*); (*sl.*) herausrücken mit, blechen (*money*). **--drop,** *s.*, **--lozenge,** *s.* der Hustenbonbon. **-ing,** *s.* das Husten. **--mixture,** *s.* Hustentropfen (*pl.*).
could [kʊd, kəd], *see* **can.**
coulisse [ku:ˈlɪ:s], *s.* die Kulisse.
couloir [ˈkulwɑ:], *s.* die Bergschlucht.
coulomb [ˈkulɔm], *s.* das Coulomb, die Amperesekunde (*Elec.*).
co(u)lter [ˈkoʊltə], *s.* die Pflugschar, das Pflugeisen.
council [ˈkɑʊnsl], *s.* die (Rats– *or* beratende) Versammlung, der Rat; das Konzil (*Eccl.*); *cabinet –*, der Kabinettsrat; *common-–*, der Gemeinderat; *county –*, der Grafschaftsrat; *order in –*, der Kabinettsbefehl; *privy –*, geheimer Staatsrat; *– of state*, der Staatsrat; *– of war*, der Kriegsrat (*also fig.*). **--chamber,** *s.* die Ratsstube. **-lor** [–ə], *s.* das Ratsmitglied, der Rat(sherr); *privy-–lor*, der Geheimrat. **--school,** *s.* die Volksschule.
counsel [ˈkɑʊnsl], 1. *s.* die Beratung, Beratschlagung; der Ratschlag; (*often without article*) der Rechtsanwalt, Rechtsbeistand (*Law*); *– for the defence*, der Strafverteidiger, Anwalt der Verteidigung; *– for the prosecution*, der Staatsanwalt, Anklagevertreter; *God's –*, Gottes Rat, der Ratschluß Gottes (*Theol.*); *King's* (*Queen's*) *–* der Kronanwalt; *– of perfection*, idealer Rat; eine Unmöglichkeit; *keep one's* (*own*) *–*, schweigen, etwas für sich behalten; *take –*, sich beraten; *take – of one's pillow*, etwas beschlafen; *take – with*, sich Rat holen bei. 2. *v.a.* raten, (einen) Rat geben *or* erteilen (*Dat.*); beraten; empfehlen (*Dat.*); ermahnen. **-lor** *s.* der Ratgeber; (*Amer.*) der Anwalt. **-or,** *s.* (*Amer.*) *see* **-lor.**
[1]**count** [kɑʊnt], *s.* der Graf.
[2]**count,** 1. *v.a.* zählen; rechnen, berechnen, in Rechnung stellen, mitzählen, mitrechnen; halten für; *– o.s. lucky*, sich glücklich schätzen; *– one's chickens before they are hatched*, die Rechnung ohne den Wirt machen; *without –ing the others*, ohne die anderen zu zählen, abgesehen von den anderen, die anderen abgesehen. **– in,** mitzählen, einrechnen. **– out,** auszählen (*also boxing*); die Sitzung aufheben, vertagen (*Parl.*); (*sl.*) nicht berücksichtigen, ausnehmen. **– over,** durchzählen, durchrechnen, nachzählen. 2. *v.n.* rechnen, zählen, ins Gewicht fallen, von Wert sein; *he does*

not –, auf ihn kommt es nicht an; *that does not* –, das ist ohne Belang; *every minute* –*s*, auf jede Minute kommt es an; – *for nothing*, nichts gelten, von keinem Belang sein; – *on*, sich verlassen auf, rechnen auf. 3. *s.* die Rechnung, Zählung, Abzählung; das Auszählen (*Box.*); die Zahl, Anzahl, Endzahl, das Ergebnis; der Klagepunkt, Klagegrund (*Law*); die Berücksichtigung; *keep* –, genau zählen; *lose* –, sich verzählen; *take the* –, ausgezählt werden (*Box.*); *take no* – *of*, nicht berücksichtigen; *see* [1]**counter, counting.**

countenance ['kaʊntɪnəns], 1. *s.* das Gesicht; der Ausdruck, die Miene; Fassung, Gemütsruhe; Unterstützung, Gunst; *change* (*one's*) –, die Farbe wechseln; *his* – *fell*, er machte ein langes Gesicht; *give* or *lend* – *to*, unterstützen, fördern; *keep one's* –, die Fassung *or* ernste Miene bewahren; *keep a p. in* –, einen ermutigen *or* ermuntern *or* unterstützen; *put a p. out of* –, einen verblüffen *or* aus der Fassung bringen. 2. *v.a.* begünstigen, unterstützen, ermutigen (*a p.*); zulassen, dulden, gutheißen, hingehen lassen (*a th.*).

[1]**counter** ['kaʊntə], *s.* die Spielmarke, der Zahlpfennig (*Cards*); Zahltisch, Ladentisch, Kassenschalter, die Theke; das Zahlwerk, der Zähler, Zählapparat (*Mach.*). **--jumper,** *s.* der Ladenschwengel.

[2]**counter,** *s.* die Brustgrube (*of horse*); Gillung, Gilling (*Naut.*).

[3]**counter,** 1. *adv.* in entgegengesetzter Richtung, entgegen, zuwider; *run* –, zuwiderlaufen (*to* (*Dat.*)). 2. *v.a. & n.* einen Gegenschlag führen (gegen); entgegnen; entgegenwirken, widersprechen. 3. *s.* der Gegenschlag, die Parade (*Fenc.*).

[4]**counter-,** *prefix* Gegen-, entgegen-. **-act,** *v.a.* entgegenhandeln, entgegenwirken (*Dat.*); aufwiegen, widerstehen; hintertreiben, vereiteln. **-action,** *s.* die Entgegenwirkung, Gegenwirkung, der Widerstand. **--attack,** *s.* der Gegenangriff, Gegenstoß. **--attraction,** *s.* entgegengesetzte Anziehung(skraft). **-balance,** 1. *s.* das Gegengewicht. 2. *v.a.* das Gegengewicht *or* die Waage halten (*Dat.*), aufwiegen; ausgleichen. **-blast,** *s.* der Gegenstoß, die Gegenerklärung, kräftige Entgegnung. **-check,** *s.* die Gegenwirkung; das Hindernis, der Einhalt. **--claim,** 1. *s.* der Gegenanspruch, die Gegenforderung. 2. *v.a. & n.* als Gegenforderung verlangen. **--clockwise,** *adv.* linksläufig, dem Uhrzeigersinn entgegen. **--current,** *s.* der Gegenstrom. **--espionage,** *s.* der Abwehrdienst, die Spionageabwehr. **--evidence,** *s.* der Gegenbeweis. **-feit,** 1. *v.a.* nachmachen, nachahmen; fälschen, nachdrucken; heucheln, vorgeben; *-feit illness*, sich krank stellen. 2. *adj.* nachgeahmt, nachgemacht; falsch, unecht; verstellt, erheuchelt. 3. *s.* das Nachgemachte, Gefälschte, Verfälschte; falsche Münze, unrechtmäßiger Nachdruck. **-feiter,** *s.* der Nachmacher, Fälscher, Falschmünzer; Heuchler. **-foil,** *s.* der Kontrollabschnitt; die Quittung, der Kupon, Talon, Appoint, Abreißzettel. **-fort,** *s.* der Strebepfeiler (*Arch.*). **--irritant,** *s.* das Gegenreizmittel. **-mand,** 1. *s.* der Gegenbefehl; die Widerrufung, Abbestellung, Annullierung (*Law*). 2. *v.a.* widerrufen, abbestellen, absagen; umstoßen (*an order*). **-march,** 1. *s.* der Rückmarsch. 2. *v.n.* zurückmarschieren. **-mark,** *s.* das Gegenzeichen. **--measure,** *s.* die Gegenmaßnahme. **-mine,** 1. *s.* die Gegenmine; (*fig.*) der Gegenanschlag. 2. *v.a.* gegenminieren; (*fig.*) entgegenarbeiten (*Dat.*); durch Gegenanschlag vereiteln. **--motion,** *s.* der Gegenantrag (*Parl.*). **--movement,** *s.* die Gegenbewegung, der Gegenzug. **--offensive,** *s.* die Gegenoffensive (*Mil.*). **-pane,** *s.* die Steppdecke, Bettdecke. **-part,** *s.* das Duplikat, die Kopie; das Seitenstück, Gegenstück, die Ergänzung. **-point,** *s.* der Kontrapunkt (*Mus.*). **-poise,** 1. *s.* das Gegengewicht, Gleichgewicht. 2. *v.a.* aufwiegen, entgegenwirken; (*fig.*) im Gleichgewicht halten (*Dat.*). **-scarp,** *s.* äußere Grabenböschung, die Gegenböschung (*Fort.*). **--shaft,** *s.* die Vorlegewelle. **-sign** 1. *s.* die Parole, Losung, das Losungswort, Erkennungswort (*Mil.*). 2. *v.a.* gegenzeichnen, mitunterschreiben, bestätigen. **--signature,** *s.* die Gegenzeichnung. **-sink,** 1. *v.a.* ausfräsen (*a hole*), versenken, einlassen (*a screw*). 2. *s.* der Versenkbohrer; die Senkschraube, der Krauskopfbohrer. **-stroke,** *s.* der Gegenstoß, Rückschlag. **--tenor,** *s.* erster Tenor. **-vail,** *v.a. & n.* aufwiegen, ausgleichen, stark genug sein, ausreichen; *-vailing duty*, der Ausgleichszoll.

countess ['kaʊntɪs], *s.* die Gräfin.

count-ing ['kaʊntɪŋ], 1. *s.* das Rechnen, Zählen. 2. *adj.* Rechen-. **-ing-house,** *s.* das Kontor, die Buchhalterei, das Büro.

countrified ['kʌntrɪfaɪd], *adj.* ländlich; bäurisch.

country ['kʌntrɪ], 1. *s.* das Land; die Gegend, der Landstrich, das Gebiet; das Vaterland, Heimatland; Gelände (*Mil.*); die Einwohner (*pl.*), das Volk, die Nation; die Wähler (*pl.*) (*Pol.*); *foreign* –, das Ausland; *appeal to the* –, an das Volk appellieren (*Parl.*); *fly the* –, landesflüchtig werden; *from all over the* –, aus allen Teilen des Landes; *die for one's* –, für das Vaterland sterben; *in the* –, auf dem Lande; *go into the* –, aufs Land gehen; *go down into the* –, in die Provinz gehen; *go up* –, sich ins Innere des Landes begeben; *God's own* –, (*Amer.*) (*coll.*) Vereinigte Staaten; *mother* –, *native* –, das Vaterland, Heimatland, Geburtsland. 2. *adj.* Land-, ländlich. **--bred,** *adj.* auf dem Lande erzogen. **– bumpkin,** der Bauernlümmel. **– cousin,** der Vetter *or* die Base *or* (*hum.*) die Unschuld vom Lande. **--dance,** *s.* der Bauerntanz, volkstümlicher Tanz. **– folk,** das Landvolk. **– gentleman,** der Gutsbesitzer; Landedelmann. **– house,** der Landsitz, das Landhaus, die Villa. **– life,** das Landleben. **-man,** *s.* der Landsmann, Mitbürger; Landmann, Bauer. **--party,** der Landbund (*Pol.*). **-people,** *see* **– folk. --seat,** *s.* der Landsitz. **-side,** *s.* das Land, die Landschaft, der Landstrich. **– squire,** der Landjunker. **– town,** die Landstadt. **--wide,** *adj.* über das ganze Land ausgedehnt. **-woman,** *s.* die Bäuerin, Bauersfrau; Landsmännin.

county ['kaʊntɪ], *s.* die Grafschaft. **– borough, --corporate,** *s.* die Stadt als Grafschaftsbezirk. **– council,** der Grafschaftsrat. **– councillor,** das Mitglied des Grafschaftsrates. **– court,** das Provinzialgericht für Zivilsachen. **--palatine,** *s.* die Pfalzgrafschaft. **--town,** *s.* die Kreisstadt, Hauptstadt einer Grafschaft.

coup [kuː], *s.* der Streich, Putsch; – *d'état* [– deɪ'tæː], der Staatsstreich; – *de grace*, der Gnadenstoß; – *de main*, der Handstreich; – *d'œil*, flüchtiger Blick.

coupé ['kuːpeɪ], *s.* das Coupé, geschlossener Zweisitzer (*Motor.*); das Halbabteil (*Railw.*).

coupl-e ['kʌpl], 1. *s.* das Paar; Ehepaar, Liebespaar, Tanzpaar; die Koppel (*Hunt.*); *a -e of words*, ein paar Worte; *married -e*, das Ehepaar. 2. *v.a.* koppeln (*dogs*); kuppeln, ankuppeln, einkuppeln, zusammenkuppeln; verbinden; ehelich verbinden, paaren. 3. *v.n.* sich paaren; *-ed axle*, die Kuppelachse; *-ed engine*, die Zwillingsmaschine (*Railw.*). **-er** ['kʌplə], *s.* die Koppel(ung) (*Org.*); der Koppler (*Rad.*). **-et,** *s.* das Reimpaar. **-ing,** *s.* die Kupplung (*Mach.*), Kopplung (*Elec., Rad.*), Verbindung, Paarung (*of animals*); *feed-back -ing, reaction -ing*, die Rückkopplung (*Rad.*). **-ing-box,** *s.* die Muffe. **-ing-coil,** *s.* die Kopplungsspule (*Rad.*). **-ing-rod,** *s.* die Kuppelstange (*Locom.*).

coupon ['kuːpɔn], *s.* der Gutschein, Kupon, Kassenzettel, Bon; Abschnitt.

courage ['kʌrɪdʒ], *s.* der Mut, die Tapferkeit; *Dutch* –, angetrunkener Mut; *have the* – *of one's convictions*, Zivilcourage haben; *pluck up* or *take* –, Mut fassen; *screw up one's* –, *take one's* – *in both hands*, seinen Mut zusammennehmen. **-ous** [kə'reɪdʒəs], *adj.* mutig, tapfer, beherzt.

courier ['kurɪə], *s.* der Eilbote, Kurier; Reiseführer.

course [kɔːs], 1. *s.* der Lauf, Gang; Verlauf (*of time*), Weg, die Richtung, der Kurs (*Naut.*); die Handlungsweise, das Verfahren; der Lehrgang, Kursus (*of lectures, etc.*); die Laufbahn, Karriere, der Lebenslauf; die Reihenfolge, Reihe; der Gang, das Gericht (*of food*); die (Renn)Bahn, der (Golf)-Platz; die Schicht, Lage (*Mas., etc.*); der Kurs, die Notierung (*C.L.*); Hasenhetze (*Hunt.*); (*pl.*) der

Monatsfluß (*Med.*); (*a*) (*with nouns*) – *of action*, die Handlungsweise; – *of exchange*, der Kurs, Wechselkurs, die Notierung; – *of instruction*, der Lehrkursus, Lehrgang; – *of law*, der Rechtsgang; – *of lectures*, die Vortragsreihe; *matter of* –, eine Selbstverständlichkeit; – *of treatment*, die Kur (*Med.*); (*b*) (*with adjectives*) *direct* –, gerader *or* direkter Kurs (*Naut.*); *in due* –, zu seiner Zeit, zur rechten Zeit; *in the ordinary* –, normalerweise; *magnetic* –, mißweisender Kurs; (*c*) (*with verbs*) *adopt a certain* –, einen gewissen Weg einschlagen; *alter* –, den Kurs ändern; *clear the* – ! (macht die) Bahn frei! *plot a* –, den Kurs absetzen; *shape one's* – *for*, den Kurs absetzen nach; *stay the* –, bis zum Ende durchhalten; *let it take its* –, es seinen Weg gehen lassen; (*d*) (*with prepositions*) *in* – *of construction*, im Bau (begriffen); *in the* – *of nature*, nach dem natürlichen Lauf der Dinge; *in* – *of time*, im Laufe der Zeit; *in the* – *of a year*, binnen Jahresfrist; (*e*) (*as adverb*) *of* –, natürlich, selbstverständlich. 2. *v.a.* mit Hunden jagen, verfolgen (*usually hares*). 3. *v.n.* rennen, jagen; rinnen, fließen (*of liquids*). **-r,** *s.* der Renner, das Rennpferd.

coursing [ˈkɔ:sɪŋ], *s.* die Hetzjagd, Hetze.

court [kɔ:t], 1. *s.* der Hof; Vorhof, Platz; (fürstlicher) Hof, (fürstliche) Familie; die Hofgesellschaft, Hofleute, Höflinge; das Gericht, der Gerichtshof; die Cour; die Aufwartung; die Hintergasse; – *of appeal*, die Berufungsinstanz; – *of arbitration*, das Schiedsgericht, die Schlichtungskammer; *at* –, bei Hofe; – *of Chancery*, das Kanzleigericht; – *of equity*, das Billigkeitsgericht für Zivilsachen; *hold a* –, eine Cour abhalten; *in* –, vor Gericht; *bring into* –, vor Gericht bringen, (einen) verklagen; – *of inquiry*, das Untersuchungsgericht; *keep* –, Hofstaat halten; – *of King's* (*Queen's*) *Bench*, das Oberhofgericht; *law*-–, der Gerichtshof; das Gericht; – *of Probate*, das Erbschaftsgericht; *pay* (*one's*) – *to s.o.*, einem den Hof *or* seine Aufwartung machen; *put out of* –, von der Verhandlung ausschließen; *out of* –, (*fig.*) nicht zur Sache gehörig, indiskutabel; *the case was settled out of* –, der Streit wurde außergerichtlich *or* auf gütlichem Wege beigelegt; *summary* –, das Standgericht; *tennis*-–, der Tennisspielplatz; *go to* –, zu Gericht gehen, den Gerichtsweg beschreiten. 2. *v.a.* den Hof machen, huldigen (*a p.*, einem); werben *or* freien um (*a p.*); sich bemühen um (*a th.*); –*ing couple*, das Liebespaar; – *disaster*, (das) Unheil herausfordern; – *favour*, sich um Gunst bemühen, zu gefallen suchen; – *sleep*, Schlaf suchen. **--card,** *s.* die Figur, das Bild (*Cards*). **- chaplain,** der Hofprediger. **--circular,** *s.* die Hofnachrichten. **--dress,** *s.* die Hoftracht. **--house,** *s.* das Gerichtsgebäude. **--martial,** 1. *s.* (*pl.* –s-martial) das Kriegsgericht. 2. *v.a.* vor ein Kriegsgericht stellen. **--plaster,** *s.* Englisches Pflaster. **-shoes,** die (Damen)Pumps. **-yard,** *s.* der Hof, Hofraum.

court-eous [ˈkə:tjəs], *adj.* höflich, liebenswürdig, verbindlich. **-eousness,** *s.* die Höflichkeit, Artigkeit. **-esan, -ezan** [kɔ:tɪˈzæn], *s.* die Buhlerin, Kurtisane. **-esy** [ˈkə:təsɪ], *s.* die Höflichkeit, Artigkeit, Verbindlichkeit, Gefälligkeit (*to*, gegen); Gunstbezeigung; *by* –*esy of Mr. E.*, durch freundliches Entgegenkommen des Herrn E.; –*esy title*, der Höflichkeitstitel. **-ier** [ˈkɔ:trə], *s.* der Höfling. **-ly** [ˈkɔ:tlɪ], *adj.* höfisch; höflich. **-ship** [ˈkɔ:tʃɪp], *s.* das Werben, Freien, Courmachen, Hofmachen.

cousin [ˈkʌzn], *s.* der Vetter, Cousin; (*female* –) die Cousine, Base; *first* –, – *german*, leiblicher Vetter, leibliche Base; –*s german*, Geschwisterkinder; *second* –*s*, Vettern zweiten Grades, Kinder der Geschwisterkinder; (*first*) – *once removed*, das Kind meines Vetters, der Vetter meiner Eltern. **-ly,** *adj.* vetterlich. **-ship,** *s.* die Vetterschaft.

couvade [ˈku:vɑ:d], *s.* das Männerkindbett.

[1]**cov-e** [kouv], 1. *s.* die Bucht; Wölbung (*Arch.*); (*fig.*) der Schlupfwinkel. 2. *v.a.* überwölben (*Arch.*). **-ing,** *s.* die Wölbung, gewölbtes Dach; die Seitenwand (*of a chimney*).

[2]**cove,** *s.* (*sl.*) der Kerl, Bursche.

coven [ˈkʌvən], *s.* die Hexenversammlung.

covenant [ˈkʌvənənt], 1. *s.* der Vertrag; Bund (*also Theol.*), das Bündnis; die Vertragsklausel; *ark of the* –, die Bundeslade (*B.*); *land of the* –, Gelobtes Land (*B.*). 2. *v.n.* übereinkommen (*with*, mit; *for*, um); sich verpflichten. 3. *v.a.* gewähren; vereinbaren, festsetzen. **-er,** *s.* der Vertragskontrahent; das Mitglied des Bundes der schottischen Protestanten.

cover [ˈkʌvə], 1. *v.a.* bedecken; decken (*also C.L. & Mil.*); verdecken, zudecken; (*fig.*) verhehlen; überziehen (*with*, mit), einschlagen, einhüllen (*with*, in), umhüllen, umwickeln; schützen, versichern (*from*, vor); zurücklegen (*a distance*); bestreiten, ausgleichen (*costs, etc.*); umfassen, erstrecken *or* sich ausdehnen über; (*coll.*) berichten über; bespringen, decken (*mares, etc.*); (*a*) (*with nouns*) – *one's head*, sich bedecken; – *the front man*, einen als Vordermann nehmen (*Mil.*); – *a p.*, auf einen zielen; *they* –*ed 20 miles*, sie legten 20 Meilen zurück; *the receipts do not* – *the outlay*, die Einnahme deckt die Kosten nicht; – *one's tracks*, die Spuren verdecken *or* (*fig.*) verhüllen; (*b*) (*with adv.*) – *in*, decken, bedachen; – *over*, überdecken; – *up*, verdecken, zudecken, verhüllen, (*fig.*) bemänteln. 2. *s.* die Decke; der Deckel; Schutz, die Deckung (*Mil.*); der Einband, Umschlag, die Hülle (*of a book*); der Bezug, Überzug, Belag, das Futteral, die Haube; der Mantel (*of tyre*); das Obdach; Lager (*Hunt.*), Dickicht; Gedeck, Kuvert (*at table*); die Bürgschaft (*C.L.*); der Deckmantel, Vorwand; *break* –, aus dem Lager hervorbrechen (*Hunt.*); *from* – *to* –, vom Anfang bis zum Ende (*of a book*); *take* –, Deckung suchen; *under* –, unter Deckung, gedeckt (*Mil.*); *under this* –, eingeschlossen, beiliegend (*as letters*); *under* – *of darkness*, unter dem Schutze der Finsternis; *place under* –, verdeckt aufstellen. **-age,** *s.* die Verbreitung (*of newspaper*), die Reichweite (*radio*). **-ed,** *adj.* gedeckt, überzogen (*buttons*); übersponnen (*strings*); besponnen (*wire*); *be* –*ed*, gedeckt sein; Deckung in Händen haben (*C.L.*); –*ed wagon*, der Planwagen; –*ed way*, gedeckter Gang. **-ing,** 1. *pr.p. & adj.* deckend; 2. *s.* der Beschlag, das Futteral, die Hülle; Bekleidung, Beschalung, Beplankung, Bespannung, Verkleidung; der Überzug, Bezug (*for hats*); die Dachdeckung (*of roofs*); –*ing letter*, das Begleitschreiben; –*ing party*, *s.* der Deckungstrupp (*Mil.*). **-let,** *s.* die Bettdecke.

covert [ˈkʌvət], 1. *adj.* (*archaic*) gedeckt, geschützt; heimlich, versteckt, verborgen; *feme* –, verheiratete Frau (*Law*). 2. *s.* der Zufluchtsort, das Obdach; (*fig.*) der Schutz; das Dickicht, Lager (*Hunt.*). **-ure** [ˈkʌvətʃə], *s.* der Schutz, das Obdach; die Decke, Bedeckung; der Stand einer Ehefrau (*Law*).

covet [ˈkʌvɪt], *v.a.* begehren, ersehnen, trachten nach, sich gelüsten lassen nach. **-ous** [–əs], *adj.* begierig (*of*, nach); geizig, habsüchtig; –*ous of*, -gierig (*as suffix*). **-ousness,** *s.* die Begierde; Habsucht, der Geiz.

covey [ˈkʌvɪ], *s.* die Brut, Hecke, das Volk (*of partridges*).

coving [ˈkouvɪŋ], *see* [1]**cove.**

[1]**cow** [kɑu], *s.* die Kuh; das Weibchen (*of whale, elephant, etc.*). **--bane,** *s.* der Wasserschierling (*Bot.*). **-boy,** *s.* der Rinderhirt. **--catcher,** *s.* der Schienenräumer (*Railw.*). **--dung,** *s.* der Kuhmist. **--heel,** *s.* der Kalbsfuß (in Gelee). **--herd,** *s.* der Kuhhirt. **-hide,** 1. *s.* die Kuhhaut; –*hide* (*whip*), *s.* der Ochsenziemer. 2. *v.a.* auspeitschen. **--house,** *s.* der Kuhstall. **--lick,** *s.* (*sl.*) die Spucklocke. **-like,** *adj.* Kuh-. **--man,** *s.* der Kuhknecht. **--parsley,** *s.* der Wiesenkerbel, das Kerbelkraut (*Bot.*). **--parsnip,** *s.* der Bärenklau (*Bot.*). **-pox,** *s.* die Kuhpocken (*pl.*). **--puncher,** *s.* (*sl.*) *see* **-boy.** **--shed,** *s.* der Kuhstall. **-slip,** *s. see* **cowslip.**

[2]**cow,** *v.a.* einschüchtern (*Acc.*), bange machen (*Dat.*).

coward [ˈkɑuəd], *s.* der Feigling, die Memme. **-ice** [–ɪs], **-liness,** *s.* die Feigheit. **-ly,** *adj. & adv.* feige.

cower [ˈkɑuə], *v.n.* kauern; niederhocken, sich ducken.

cowl [kɑul], *s.* die Mönchskappe; Kapuze; Schornsteinkappe (*Build.*); *it is not the* – *that makes the* *monk*, das Kleid macht nicht den Mann. **–ing,** *s.* die Haube, Verkleidung, Schalung.

cowr–ie, –y ['kaʊrɪ], *s.* die Kauri(muschel), Porzellanschnecke (*Mollusc.*); das Muschelgeld.

cowslip ['kaʊslɪp], *s.* die Schlüsselblume, Primel.

cox [kɔks], *s.* (*coll.*) (*abbr.*) *see* **–swain. –comb** ['kɔkskoʊm], *s.* der Geck, Stutzer, Laffe. **–combry,** *s.* die Geckenhaftigkeit, Affektiertheit. **–swain** ['kɔksn], *s.* der Steuermann, Bootsführer.

coy [kɔɪ], *adj.* spröde, blöde, scheu, schüchtern, zurückhaltend; zimperlich. **–ness,** *s.* die Sprödigkeit, Scheu.

coyote [kɔɪ'oʊtɪ], *s.* der Präriewolf, Steppenwolf.

coz [kʌz], (*archaic*) *abbr. of* **cousin.**

cozen ['kʌzn], *v.a.* (*archaic*) betrügen, prellen (*out of*, um).

[1]**crab** [kræb], *s.* die Krabbe; der Krebs (*also Astr.*), Taschenkrebs; die Winde, das Hebezeug; die Laufkatze; *catch a –*, mit dem Ruder im Wasser stecken bleiben. **– –louse,** *s.* die Filzlaus (*Ent.*).

[2]**crab,** *s.* (**– –apple**) der Holzapfel(baum).

[3]**crab,** 1. *s.* (*sl.*) der Sauertopf, Miesmacher, Nörgler, Querkopf. 2. *v.a.* bekritteln; meckern *or* nörgeln an, heruntermachen; beeinträchtigen. **–bed,** *adj.* mürrisch, grämlich, griesgrämig, kratzbürstig; kritzlig, verzwickt, verworren. **–by,** *adj.* (*coll.*) mürrisch, griesgrämig.

crack [kræk], 1. *v.a.* spalten, zerspalten, zersprengen, zerbrechen; aufknacken (*nuts*); knallen lassen (*a whip*); zerstören, vernichten (*credit*); kracken (*oils*) (*Chem.*); (*coll.*) *– a bottle together*, eine Flasche zusammen trinken; (*sl.*) *– a crib*, in ein Haus *etc.* einbrechen; *– an egg*, ein Ei aufschlagen; *– one's fingers*, mit den Fingern knacken; *– a joke*, einen Witz reißen; (*sl.*) *– up*, anpreisen, rühmen, herausstreichen. 2. *v.n.* Sprünge *or* Risse bekommen, zerspringen, aufspringen; bersten, platzen, sich spalten, reißen; krachen, knallen; brechen, umschlagen (*of the voice*); (*coll.*) (also *– up*) zusammenbrechen. 3. *s.* der Krach, Knall; Schlag; Riß, Sprung, Bruch, Schlitz, Spalt, die Spalte; (*sl.*) der Witz; *the – of doom*, der jüngste Tag, das Jüngste Gericht; *– of a whip*, der Peitschenschlag *or* –knall. 4. *adj.* Elite–; *– horse*, hervorragendes Pferd; *– regiment*, feudales Regiment; *– shot*, der Meisterschütze. 5. *int.* klatsch! patsch! **– –brained,** *adj.* verrückt. **–ed,** *adj.* rissig, gesprungen; *be –ed*, einen Sprung haben; (*coll.*) verrückt sein; *his voice was –ed*, seine Stimme schlug um. **–er,** *s.* der Knallbonbon; Knacker; Schwärmer, Frosch (*Firew.*); Keks, Biskuit; *nut –s*, der Nußknacker. **–erjack,** *adj.* (*sl.*) famos. **–ing,** *s.* die Sprungbildung; Kracking (*oil*); *–ing plant*, *s.* die Krakkingsanlage, Destillieranlage, Fraktionierungsanlage. *–ing process*, *s.* der Krackprozeß, das Krackverfahren, die Krackingdestillation. **– –up,** *s.* (*sl.*) der Bruch (*Av.*). **–le** ['krækl], *v.n.* knistern, knattern, prasseln. **–ling,** *s.* das Geknatter, Geknister; knusprige Kruste (*of roast pork*). **–nel,** *s.* die Brezel.

cradle ['kreɪdl], 1. *s.* die Wiege; (*fig.*) das Anfangsstadium, die Kindheit; das Gestell, die Beinschiene (*Surg.*); der Schwingtrog (*for gold washing*); Stapelschlitten (*Shipb.*); Schienenstuhl (*Railw.*); Korb, das Reff (*of a scythe*); Laufbrett (*Typ.*); die Gabel (*Phone*); das Wiegemesser, Gründungseisen (*Engr.*); *rock the –*, wiegen; *from the –*, von Jugend an *or* auf. 2. *v.a.* in die Wiege legen; (ein)wiegen. **– –snatching,** *s.* der Kinderraub (*also fig.*). **– –song,** *s.* das Wiegenlied.

craft [krɑːft], *s.* das Handwerk, Gewerbe; die Zunft; die Kunst, Fertigkeit, Geschicklichkeit, das Geschick; die List, Verschlagenheit, Geriebenheit; (*sing. or pl.*) das Fahrzeug, Schiff. **–iness,** *s.* die List, Schlauheit, Verschlagenheit, Geriebenheit, Verschmitztheit. **–sman** [–smən], *s.* der Handwerker, Künstler. **–smanship,** *s.* die Kunstfertigkeit, das Künstlertum. **–y,** *adj.* schlau, listig, verschlagen, gerieben.

crag [kræg], *s.* die Klippe, Felsenspitze. **–giness,** *s.* die Felsigkeit, Schroffheit. **–gy,** *adj.* schroff, felsig, uneben. **–sman,** *s.* erfahrener Kletterer.

crake [kreɪk], *s. see* **corn-crake.**

cram [kræm], 1. *v.a.* vollstopfen, vollfüllen, anfüllen; mästen, nudeln (*poultry*); überfüttern, überladen (*with food*); hineinstopfen, hineinzwängen (*into*, in (*Acc.*)); (*sl.*) einpauken; *– s.th. down a p.'s throat*, einem etwas mit aller Gewalt aufdrängen, einem etwas recht deutlich machen. 2. *v.n.* (*sl.*) ochsen, büffeln (*for an examination*). **– –full,** *adj.* vollgepfropft. **–mer,** *s.* (*coll.*) der Einpauker. **–ming,** *s.* das Einpauken, die Einpaukerei; *–ming establishment*, (*coll.*) die Presse.

crambo ['kræmboʊ], *s.* das Reimspiel.

cramp [kræmp], 1. *s.* der Krampf (*Med.*); die Krampe, Klammer, Schraubzwinge (*Mach.*); *writer's –*, der Schreibkrampf. 2. *v.a.* krampfen, krampfhaft verziehen (*Med.*); beengen, einengen, einzwängen, einschränken; hindern, hemmen; befestigen, verklammern, einklammern; *– s.o.'s style*, einem die Bäume nicht in den Himmel wachsen lassen. **–ed,** *adj.* steif, verkrampft; beengt, eng; *–ed hand*, steife Hand(schrift). **– –fish,** *s.* der Zitterrochen (*Ichth.*). **– –iron,** *s.* eiserne Klammer, der Anker (*Arch.*); der Enterhaken (*Naut.*). **–ons** (*pl.*), das Steigeisen.

cranage ['kreɪnɪdʒ], *s.* die Krangebühr, das Krangeld.

cranberry ['krænbərɪ], *s.* die Moosbeere, Kronsbeere, Preiselbeere.

crane [kreɪn], 1. *s.* der Kranich (*Orn.*); Kran (*Mach.*); *feeding –*, der Speisewasserkran (*Railw.*); *hoisting –*, der Hebekran; *travelling –*, der Laufkran. 2. *v.a.*; *– one's neck*, den Hals ausrecken. 3. *v.n.* den Hals ausrecken nach; (*fig.*) zaudern, zögern (*at*, bei, vor (*Dat.*)). **– –jib,** *s.* die Kranausladge. **–sbill** ['kreɪnzbɪl], *s.* der Storchschnabel, das Geranium (*Bot.*).

cran–ial ['kreɪnɪəl], *adj.* Hirn–, Schädel–. **–iology** [kreɪnɪ'ɔlədʒɪ], *s.* die Schädellehre. **–ium** ['kreɪnɪəm], *s.* die Hirnschale (*Anat.*); (*coll.*) der Schädel.

crank [kræŋk], 1. *s.* die Kurbel, der Schwengel, Hebel (*Mech.*); die Kröpfung (*of a shaft*); (*coll.*) verschrobener Mensch, komische Kruke; verschrobener Einfall, die Verdrehung, Schnurre; (*coll.*) *he is a –*, er hat einen Sparren. 2. *adj.* in Gefahr umzukippen, rank (*of a ship*); unsicher, baufällig (*of buildings*). 3. *v.a.*; (*– up*) ankurbeln, andrehen, anwerfen (*Motor.*). **–case,** *s.* das Kurbelgehäuse. **– –handle,** *s.* die Andrehkurbel. **–iness** ['kræŋkɪnɪs], *s.* die Grillenhaftigkeit, Wunderlichkeit. **–shaft,** *s.* die Kurbelwelle, gekröpfte Welle. **–y** ['kræŋkɪ], *adj.* exzentrisch, verdreht, verschroben; voreingenommen, launisch (*of persons*); wackelig, baufällig, unsicher (*of things*).

cranny ['krænɪ], *s.* der Riß, die Ritze, Spalte; das Versteck, der Winkel.

crape [kreɪp], *s.* der Flor, Krepp, Trauerflor.

crapulen–ce ['kræpjʊləns], *s.* der Kater; die Sauferei, Völlerei. **–t,** *adj.* der Völlerei ergeben, unmäßig; verkatert.

[1]**crash** [kræʃ], 1. *s.* der Krach; das Krachen, der Absturz, Bruch (*Av.*), Zusammenstoß (*Motor.*); (*fig.*) Zusammenbruch, Krach. 2. *v.n.* krachen, einstürzen, zusammenstürzen, zusammenkrachen; abstürzen, eine Bruchlandung *or* Bruch machen (*Av.*); zusammenstoßen (*Motor.*). 3. *v.a.* zerbrechen, zerschmettern; zum Absturz bringen (*a plane*); (*sl.*) uneingeladen eindringen (*a party*). **– –dive,** *v.n.* schnell tauchen, (*sl.*) eine Ente machen (*submarines*). **– –helmet,** *s.* der Sturzhelm, die Sturzhaube (*Motor.*). **– –landing,** *s.* die Bruchlandung (*Av.*).

[2]**crash,** *s.* grober Drillich (*fabric*).

crasis ['kreɪsɪs], *s.* die Zusammenziehung, Krasis (*Gram.*).

crass [kræs], *adj.* grob, derb, kraß. **–ness,** *s.* die Derbheit, krasse Dummheit.

crate [kreɪt], *s.* großer Korb; die Lattenkiste; der Verschlag. **– –car,** *s.* der Verschlagwagen (*Railw.*).

crater ['kreɪtə], *s.* der Krater, Trichter, das Loch; der Becher (*Astr.*). **–iform** [–rɪfɔːm], *adj.* kraterförmig.

cravat [krə'væt], *s.* (*archaic*) die Halsbinde, Krawatte.

crave [kreɪv], 1. *v.a.* flehen *or* bitten um. 2. *v.n.* sich sehnen, verlangen (*for*, nach).

craven ['kreɪvn], 1. *adj.* feig(herzig), zaghaft. 2. *s.* die Memme, der Feigling.
craving ['kreɪvɪŋ], *s.* heftiges Verlangen, die Sehnsucht (*for*, nach).
craw [krɔ:], *s.* der Kropf (*of fowls*).
crawfish ['krɔ:fɪʃ], *s. see* **crayfish.**
crawl [krɔ:l], 1. *v.n.* kriechen; schleichen; wimmeln (*with*, von), kribbeln; kraulen (*swimming*). 2. *s.* das Kriechen, Schleichen; Kraulschwimmen; *go at a* –, sehr langsam gehen *or* fahren. **–er,** *s.* kriechendes Ungeziefer, der Kriecher; (*coll.*) langsam fahrendes Fahrzeug. **–ers,** *pl.* das Überkleid für Kleinkinder. **–ing,** 1. *adj.* kriechend; *be –ing with vermin*, von Ungeziefer wimmeln. 2. *s.* das Kriechen.
crayfish ['kreɪfɪʃ], *s.* der Flußkrebs, Bachkrebs; die Languste.
crayon ['kreɪən], *s.* der Farbstift, Buntstift, Zeichenstift, Pastellstift; *red* –, der Rotstift; –*drawing*, die Kreidezeichnung, Pastellzeichnung, das Pastell.
craz–e [kreɪz], 1. *s.* die Verrücktheit; fixe Idee, die Manie; (*coll.*) Schrulle, der Fimmel; die Modetorheit; *be all the –e*, überall Mode sein. 2. *v.a.* zerrütten, verrückt *or* toll machen. **–ed,** *adj.* verrückt; –*ed with fear*, wahnsinnig vor Angst. **–iness,** *s.* die Verrücktheit. **–y,** *adj.* hinfällig, gebrechlich, wacklig, baufällig; verrückt, unsinnig begeistert (*with*, vor), versessen (*about*, auf); –*y pavement*, das Mosaikpflaster; *go –y*, aus dem Häuschen geraten.
creak [krɪ:k], 1. *v.n.* knarren. 2. *v.a.* knarren mit. 3. *s.* das Knarren. **–y,** *adj.* knarrend.
cream [krɪ:m], 1. *s.* die Sahne, der Rahm; die Salbe; (*fig.*) das Beste, die Auslese, Blüte, der Kern; Krem, die Kremspeise (*Conf.*); *clotted* –, verdickter Rahm; *cold* –, die Kühlsalbe; *whipped* –, die Schlagsahne; – *of the joke*, eigentlicher Witz, die Pointe; – *of tartar*, gereinigter Weinstein. 2. *v.a.* abrahmen; zu Krem schlagen. 3. *v.n.* Rahm ansetzen; schäumen. **– -cheese,** *s.* der Rahmkäse, Quarkkäse. **– -coloured,** *adj.* blaßgelb, mattgelb, kremfarbig. **–ery,** *s.* die Butterei; das Milchgeschäft, die Molkerei. **– -laid,** *adj.* gelblichweiße Velin– (*of paper*). **– -tart,** *s.* die Sahnetorte. **–y,** *adj.* voller Sahne, sahnig; (*fig.*) sämig, ölig.
crease [krɪ:s], 1. *s.* die Falte, Bügelfalte (*in trousers, etc.*); der Kniff, das Eselsohr (*in a book*); der Torstrich (*in cricket*). 2. *v.a.* falten, kniffen, umbiegen. 3. *v.n.* Falten werfen. **–proof,** *adj.* knitterfrei.
creat–e [krɪ'eɪt], 1. *v.a.* schaffen, erschaffen, hervorbringen; hervorrufen, machen (*an impression, etc.*), verursachen (*a situation, etc.*); ernennen zu, machen zu. 2. *v.n.* (*sl.*) Aufhebens machen (*about*, über). **–ion,** *s.* die Schöpfung (*also artistic product*); das Geschöpf, Erzeugnis; die Modeschöpfung (*clothes*); Erschaffung, Hervorbringung, Erzeugung; Gestaltung (*of a role*) (*Theat.*), Schaffung, Ernennung (*of peers, etc.*). **–ive,** *adj.* schaffend, erschaffend, Schöpfungs–; schöpferisch (*as genius*). **–iveness,** *s.* schöpferische Kraft, die Schaffenskraft, Schöpferkraft, Produktivität. **–or,** *s.* der Schöpfer, Erzeuger, Urheber. **–ure** ['krɪ:tʃə], *s.* das Geschöpf, Wesen; die Kreatur; (*fig.*) das Werkzeug, der Sklave; *dumb –ures*, die Tiere, stumme Kreaturen; *fellow –ure*, der Mitmensch; *living –ure*, lebendes Wesen, das Lebewesen; –*ure comforts*, das Wohlleben, die materiellen Annehmlichkeiten des Daseins.
crèche [kreɪʃ], *s.* die Kleinkinderbewahranstalt.
credence ['krɪ:dəns], *s.* der Glaube; *see also* **– -table;** *give – to a story*, einer Geschichte Glauben schenken. **– -table,** *s.* der Kredenztisch (beim Altar).
credentials [krɪ'dɛnʃəlz], *pl.* das Beglaubigungsschreiben, Empfehlungsschreiben, der Ausweis; die Kreditive (*Dipl.*).
credib–ility [krɛdɪ'bɪlɪtɪ], *s.* die Glaubwürdigkeit. **–le** ['krɛdɪbl], *adj.* glaublich; *be –ly informed*, von zuverlässiger Seite erfahren.
credit ['krɛdɪt], 1. *s.* der Glaube, die Glaubwürdigkeit, Zuverlässigkeit; der Ruf, guter Ruf, das Ansehen, die Ehre; Anerkennung, das Verdienst; das Guthaben; der Kredit, Borg (*C.L.*); die Kreditseite, das Haben (*C.L.*); Abgangszeugnis; *blank* –, der Blankokredit; – *balance*, das Guthaben; *letter of* –, der Kreditbrief; – *note*, der Gutschein, Überweisungsauftrag; *at* or *on a year's* –, auf ein Jahr Ziel; (*a*) (*with verbs*) *it does him* –, es macht ihm Ehre; *he does me* –, mit ihm lege ich Ehre ein; *give* –, Kredit geben (*for*, auf (*Acc.*) *or* in Höhe von); *give – to a story*, einer Geschichte Glauben beimessen *or* schenken; *give a p.* (*the*) –, einem etwas hoch *or* als Verdienst anrechnen, einem etwas zutrauen (*for a th.* (*Acc.*); *for being*, daß er ist); *open a* –, einen Kredit eröffnen; *reflect – on a p.*, einem Ehre machen *or* einbringen; *take* (*the*) – *for a th.*, sich (*Dat.*) etwas zum Verdienst anrechnen; (*b*) (*with prepositions*) *worthy of* –, glaubwürdig; *on* –, auf Borg, auf Kredit; leihweise; *transactions on* –, Zeitgeschäfte; *get* or *take on* –, auf Kredit bekommen *or* nehmen; *to his* –, zu seinen Gunsten *it is to his – that*, es macht ihm Ehre daß; *place, put* or *enter it to my* –, schreiben Sie es mir gut; *with* –, ehrenvoll. 2. *v.a.* Glauben schenken (*Dat.*), glauben (*Dat.*), trauen (*Dat.*); kreditieren, gutschreiben (*to* (*Dat.*)); erkennen (*a p. with a sum*, einen für eine Summe) (*C.L.*); – *a p. with s.th.*, einem etwas beimessen *or* zuschreiben. **–able,** *adj.* ehrenwert, achtbar; rühmlich; *it is very –able to him*, es macht ihm alle Ehre. **–or,** *s.* der Gläubiger (*C.L.*); –*or's side*, die Kreditseite.
credul–ity [krə'dju:lɪtɪ], *s.* die Leichtgläubigkeit. **–ous** ['krɛdjʊləs], *adj.* leichtgläubig. **–ousness,** *s. see* **–ity.**
creed [krɪ:d], *s.* das Glaubensbekenntnis; der Glaube; *the Apostles'* –, Apostolisches Glaubensbekenntnis.
creek [krɪ:k], *s.* die Bucht; der Nebenfluß, kleiner Fluß, das Flüßchen (*Amer.*).
creel [krɪ:l], *s.* der Weidenkorb, Fischkorb; das Gestell, Gatter (*Weav.*).
creep [krɪ:p], 1. *v.n.* kriechen; schleichen, sich ranken (*of plants*); kribbeln (*as flesh*); – *into a p.'s favour*, sich bei einem einschmeicheln; *I felt my flesh* –, es überlief mich eiskalt, mich überlief eine Gänsehaut; *it makes my flesh* –, es macht mich schaudern; – *forward*, anschleichen; – *in*, hineinkriechen; *an error has crept in*, ein Fehler hat sich eingeschlichen; – *up*, langsam steigen (*of prices*); – *up* (*to*), heranschleichen. 2. *s.* der Rutsch (*Geol.*); (*pl.*, *coll.*) *the –s*, die Gänsehaut, das Gruseln, Kribbeln, der Schauder; *it gives me the –s*, es macht mich schaudern. **–er,** *s.* der Kriecher; das Kriechtier; Rankengewächs, die Schlingpflanze; der Baumläufer (*Orn.*); *Virginia –er*, wilder Wein. **–ing barrage,** *s.* die Feuerwalze, das Rollsperrfeuer (*Artill.*). **–y,** *adj.* kriechend; unheimlich, schauerlich, gruselig, Schauer–.
creese [krɪ:s], *s.* der Kris, malaiischer Dolch.
cremat–e [krɪ'meɪt], *v.a.* einäschern; verbrennen. **–ion** [–'meɪʃən], *s.* die Einäscherung; die Leichenverbrennung. **–ory** ['krɛmətərɪ], *s.* (*Amer.*), **–orium** [krɛmə'tɔ:rɪəm], *s.* die Einäscherungshalle, Feuerbestattungsanstalt, das Krematorium.
crenat–e ['krɪ:neɪt], *adj.*, **–ed** [–'neɪtɪd], *adj.* zackig, gekerbt (*Bot.*). **–ion, –ure** [–nətjʊə], *s.* die Kerbung, Auszackung (*Bot.*).
crenel ['krɛnl], **–le** [krə'nɛl], *s.* die Schießscharte. **–late** ['krɛnəleɪt], *v.a.* mit Schießscharten versehen. **–ation,** *s.* die Bastion; Zinnenbildung, Zackenbildung.
creosote ['krɪ:əsout], 1. *s.* das Kreosot. 2. *v.a.* mit Kreosot durchtränken *or* beschmieren.
crêpe [kreɪp], *s.* der Krepp; *see also* **– -rubber. – paper,** das Kreppapier. **– -rubber,** *s.* das Krausgummi, Kreppgummi.
crepitat–e ['krɛpɪteɪt], *v.n.* knistern, knirschen, knacken, knarren, prasseln. **–ion** [–'teɪʃən], *s.* das Knistern, Knarren; die Krepitation (*Med.*).
crept [krɛpt], *see* **creep.**
crepuscular [krɪ'pʌskjulə], *adj.* dämmend, dämmerig, Dämmerungs–; im Zwielicht erscheinend (*Zool.*).
crescendo [krɪ'ʃɛndou], 1. *adv.* an Stärke zunehmend (*Mus.*). 2. *s.* das Crescendo, zunehmende Stärke.
crescent ['krɛsnt], 1. *adj. see* **– -shaped.** 2. *s.* zunehmender *or* abnehmender Mond, der Halbmond; Schellenbaum (*Mus.*); halbmondförmige

Straße; das Hörnchen (*Bak.*). **--shaped,** *adj.* halbmondförmig.
cress [krɛs], *s.* die Kresse (*Bot.*).
cresset [ˈkrɛsɪt], *s.* die Pechpfanne, Kohlenpfanne; Stocklaterne.
crest [krɛst], *s.* der Kamm (*of a cock*); Schopf, die Haube (*on birds, etc.*); Mähne; der Federbusch, Helmbusch (*of a helmet*); Helmschmuck (*Her.*); Helm; Rücken, Höhenrücken, Kamm, Gipfel; die Bekrönung (*Arch.*); *on the – of the wave*, (*fig.*) auf dem Gipfel des Glücks. **–ed,** *adj.* gehaubt; mit Kamm, Schopf *or* Helmschmuck; *–ed lark*, die Haubenlerche (*Orn.*). **–fallen,** *adj.* niedergeschlagen, beschämt.
cretaceous [krɪˈteɪʃəs], *adj.* kreidig, kreideartig; kreidehaltig; *– period*, die Kreide(zeit).
cretin [ˈkrɛtɪn], *s.* der Kretin. **–ism** [–ɪzm], *s.* der Kretinismus.
cretonne [krɛˈtɔn], *s.* die Kretonne, der Zitz.
crev–asse [krɪˈvæs], *s.* die Gletscherspalte; der Durchbruch (*Geol.*). **--ice** [ˈkrɛvɪs], *s.* der Riß, die Spalte.
[1]**crew** [kru:], *s.* die Schar; der Haufe, die Rotte, Bande; Bemannung, Bedienung (*of a gun*), Mannschaft, Besatzung (*of a ship*). **--space,** *s.* die Kabine (*Av.*), das Logis (*Naut.*).
[2]**crew,** *see* **crow.**
crewel [ˈkrʊ:əl], *s.* feine Wolle. **--work,** *s.* die Plattstichstickerei.
crib [krɪb], 1. *s.* die Krippe, Raufe; der Stall, Stand, das Holzgerüst, die Hütte; Kinderbettstelle; (*coll.*) kleiner Diebstahl, das Plagiat, die Eselsbrücke; (*sl.*) *crack a –*, in ein Haus einbrechen. 2. *v.a.* einsperren; (*coll.*) mausen, stibitzen; abschreiben (*at school*). **--biter,** *s.* der Krippensetzer.
cribbage [ˈkrɪbɪdʒ], *s.* die Kribbage.
cribriform [ˈkrɪbrɪfɔ:m], *adj.* siebförmig (*Anat.*).
crick [krɪk], 1. *s.* der Krampf; *– in the back*, der Hexenschuß; *– in the neck*, das Muskelreißen am Hals, steifer Hals. 2. *v.a.*; *– one's neck*, sich den Hals verrenken.
[1]**cricket** [ˈkrɪkɪt], *s.* die Grille, das Heimchen (*Ent.*); *merry as a –*, vergnügt wie ein Lämmerschwänzchen, kreuzfidel.
[2]**cricket,** *s.* das Kricket; (*coll.*) *not –*, nicht ehrlich *or* fair; (*coll.*) *play –*, ehrlich spielen. **--bat,** *s.* das Schlagholz. **–er,** *s.* der Kricketspieler. **--field,** *s.* der Kricketspielplatz. **--match,** *s.* die Kricketpartie. **– pitch,** der Rasen zum Kricketspielen.
cricoid [ˈkraɪkɔɪd], *adj.* ringförmig; *– cartilage*, der Ringknorpel.
crie–d [kraɪd], *see* **cry.** **–r,** *s.* der Schreier, Ausrufer; *town –r*, öffentlicher Ausrufer.
crim–e [kraɪm], 1. *s.* das Verbrechen; Vergehen; (*fig.*) der Frevel, die Übeltat; *capital –e*, das Kapitalverbrechen; *commit a –e*, ein Verbrechen begehen. 2. *v.a.* (*coll.*) beschuldigen (*a p.*) (*Mil.*). **–inal** [ˈkrɪmɪnəl], 1. *adj.* verbrecherisch, strafbar, Kriminal–, Straf– (*Law*); *–inal code*, das Strafgesetzbuch; *–inal conversation*, der Ehebruch; *–inal law*, das Strafrecht. 2. *s.* der Verbrecher. **–inality** [–ˈnælɪtɪ], *s.* die Strafbarkeit; Schuld; Kriminalität. **–inate** [–neɪt], *v.a.* beschuldigen, anklagen. **–ation,** *s.* die Beschuldigung, Anklage. **–inology** [–ˈnɔlədʒɪ], *s.* die Kriminalistik.
[1]**crimp** [krɪmp], 1. *v.a.* fälteln, kräuseln, knittern; *– fish*, Fische schlitzen (*Cook.*). 2. *s.* die Falte. **–er,** *s.* die Kräuselmaschine.
[2]**crimp,** 1 *v.a.* gewaltsam anwerben, pressen (*sailors, etc.*). 2. *s.* der Werber, Matrosenmakler. **–ing-house,** *s.* die Preßspelunke.
crimson [ˈkrɪmzn], 1 *s.* das Karmesin, Hochrot. 2. *adj.* karmesin, hochrot. 3. *v.n.* erröten.
cring–e [krɪndʒ], 1. *v.n.* sich ducken, sich beugen, kriechen (*to*, vor (*Dat.*)). 2. *s.* kriechende Höflichkeit. **–ing,** 1 *adj.* kriechend. 2. *s.* die Kriecherei.
cringle [ˈkrɪŋl], *s.* der Tauring (*on sails*) (*Naut.*).
crinkl–e [ˈkrɪŋkl], 1. *s.* die Falte, Runzel; Windung, Krümmung. 2 *v.a.* faltig machen; kräuseln. 3 *v.n.* Falten werfen, sich falten, sich krümmen, sich winden. **–y,** *adj.* wellig, faltig, gekräuselt.
crinoline [krɪnolɪn], *s* der Reifrock, die Krinoline; der Roßhaarstoff; das Torpedoabwehrnetz (*Nav.*).
cripple [ˈkrɪpl], 1. *s.* der Krüppel. 2. *adj.* lahm. 3. *v.a.* verkrüppeln, zum Krüppel machen; (*fig.*) entkräften, lähmen. **–d,** *adj.* verkrüppelt, lahm, krüppelhaft; (*fig.*) lahmgelegt.
crisis [[ˈkraɪsɪs], *s.* (*pl.* crises [–sɪ:z]) die Krise; der Entscheidungspunkt, Wendepunkt.
crisp [krɪsp], 1. *adj.* kraus, gekräuselt (*of hair*); bröckelig, knusperig, mürbe (*of cakes*); frisch, scharf (*of air*); klar, entschieden, kurz (*of manner*). 2. *v.a.* kräuseln; mürbe *or* knusperig machen; braun rösten (*meat, etc.*). 3. *v.n.* sich kräuseln, knusperig werden. **–ate** [–eɪt], *adj.* gekräuselt. **–ation,** *s.* das Kräuseln, die Gänsehaut. **–ness,** *s.* die Knusperigkeit; Frische. **–s,** *pl.* geröstete Kartoffelscheiben.
criss-cross [ˈkrɪskrɔs], 1. *s.* das Kreuz, Netz (*of lines*), Gewirr. 2. *adj.* gekreuzt, Kreuz–. 3. *adv.* in die Quere, kreuz und quer. 4. *v.a.* durchkreuzen.
criteri–on [kraɪˈtɪ:ərɪən], *s.* (*pl.* –a *or* –ons) das Kennzeichen, Merkmal; Kriterium; die Norm; *he is no – for*, er ist nicht maßgebend für.
critic [ˈkrɪtɪk], *s.* der Kunstrichter; Rezensent Kritiker; Tadler. **–al,** *adj.* kunstverständig, kritisch (*of a th.*, gegen etwas; *of a p.*, einem gegenüber); entscheidend; bedenklich, gefährlich, brenzlig; tadelsüchtig, krittelig; *–al moment*, entscheidender Augenblick; *–al position*, brenzlige Lage; *–al times*, bedenkliche Zeiten. **–ism** [ˈkrɪtɪsɪzm], *s.* die Kritik; Kunstbeurteilung; Rezension, Besprechung; der Tadel; *above –ism*, über jeden Tadel erhaben; *make –ism*, Kritik üben; *open to –ism*, anfechtbar. **–ize** [ˈkrɪtɪsaɪz], *v.a.* kritisieren, beurteilen; besprechen, rezensieren; tadeln, bemäkeln, kritteln.
critique [krɪˈtɪ:k], *s.* die Besprechung, Kritik, Rezension.
croak [kroʊk], *v.n.* krächzen (*as a raven*); quaken, quäken (*of frogs*); (*fig.*) Unglück prophezeien, unken, jammern; (*sl.*) sterben. **–er,** *s.* (*sl.*) der Unglücksprophet, Miesmacher. **–ing,** *s.* das Gequake, Gekrächze. **–y,** *adj.* krächzend (*as voice*).
crochet [ˈkroʊʃɪ], 1. *s.* die Häkelarbeit, Häkelei. 2. *v.a.* & *n.* häkeln. **–ed** [–ʃɪd], *adj.* gehäkelt. **--hook,** *s.* die Häkelnadel. **–ing** [–ʃɪɪŋ], *s.* das Häkeln. **--work,** *s.* die Häkelarbeit.
crock [krɔk], 1. *s.* der Topf; (*sl.*) unbrauchbarer *or* kranker Mensch; der Krüppel; ausgedientes Pferd; der Karren, Klapperkasten (*vehicle*). 2. *v.n.* (*– up*) (*coll.*) versagen, zusammenbrechen. 3. *v.r.* (*coll.*) sich verletzen. **–ed,** *adj.* (*coll.*) verletzt, untauglich. **–ery,** *s.* das Steingut, irdenes Geschirr, die Töpferware.
crocket [ˈkrɔkɪt], *s.* die Kriechblume, Krabbe (*Arch.*).
crocodile [ˈkrɔkədaɪl], *s.* das Krokodil; (*coll.*) die Schlange (*of schoolchildren*); *– tears*, Krokodilstränen.
crocus [ˈkroʊkəs], *s.* der Krokus, Safran (*Bot.*).
croft [krɔft], *s.* kleines Feldstück, kleines Pachtgut. (*Scots*) **–er,** *s.* der Kleinbauer.
cromlech [ˈkrɔmlɛk], *s.* vorgeschichtlicher Steinbau.
crone [kroʊn], *s.* altes Weib.
crony [ˈkroʊnɪ], *s.* alter Bekannter, vertrauter Freund.
crook [krʊk], 1. *s.* der Haken, Krummstab; Bischofsstab, Hirtenstab; Schwindler, Schieber, Hochstapler; (*coll.*) *by hook or by –*, auf Biegen oder Brechen. 2. *v.a.* krümmen, krumm biegen. **–ed** [ˈkrʊkɪd], *adj.* krumm, gekrümmt, gebeugt, verwachsen, schief, verdreht; unehrenhaft, verbrecherisch; *–ed ways*, krumme Wege. **–edness,** *s.* die Krummheit, Krümmung; Verkrümmung; Verderbtheit.
croon [krʊ:n], *v.n.* leise singen, vor sich hin summen. **–er,** *s.* der Jazzsänger.
crop [krɔp], 1. *s.* der Kropf (*of a fowl*); Peitschenstock, die Reitgerte; (*coll.*) Haufe, Menge; der Stutzkopf; (*often pl.*) die Ernte, der Ertrag, Ernteertrag, das Getreide auf dem Halm, eingebrachtes Getreide; *she has an Eton –*, sie trägt Herrenschnitt; *in –*, in Bebauung; *under –*, angebaut. 2. *v.a.* abschneiden, stutzen (*a tail*); abfressen.

abweiden (*grass*); bepflanzen, bebauen, besäen (*land*). 3. *v.n.* grasen, weiden; Ernte tragen; (*coll.*) – *up*, zum Vorschein kommen, auftauchen. **--eared,** *adj.* mit gestutzten Ohren. **–ped** [–t], *adj.* (ab)geschnitten, gestutzt; beschnitten (*of a book*). **–per,** *s.* der Abschneider, Abmäher; die Kropftaube; (*sl.*) der Fall, Sturz; *a good –per*, guter Träger (*plant, etc.*); (*sl.*) *come a –per*, einen schweren Sturz tun, (*fig.*) entgleisen, Mißerfolg haben.

croquet [ˈkroukeɪ], *s.* das Krocket(spiel).

croquette [krɔˈkɛt], *s.* das Bratklöschen (*Cook.*).

crosier [ˈkrouʒjə], *s.* der Bischofsstab, Krummstab.

cross [krɔs], 1. *s.* das Kreuz; Kruzifix; (*fig.*) Leiden, die Trübsal, Not, Widerwärtigkeit; das Kreuzzeichen (*as signature*); der Kreuzstrich (*on a t*); die Kreuzung, Mischung (*of races*); *fiery* –, das Feuerkreuz; *make the sign of the* –, sich bekreuzigen; *on the* –, schräg; *take up one's* –, sein Kreuz auf sich nehmen; *Red – Society*, der Verein vom Roten Kreuz; *Southern* –, das Kreuz des Südens (*Astr.*). 2. *adj.* kreuzweise, quer, schräg, schief; entgegengesetzt, verkehrt; bös, verstimmt, verdrießlich, übelgelaunt, mürrisch; *be at – purposes*, aneinander vorbeireden; (*coll.*) *as – as two sticks*, äußerst verstimmt. 3. *adv.* quer, schief. 4. *v.a.* kreuzen, kreuzweise legen; unterschlagen (*the arms*); überschreiten, überqueren; hinübergehen (über (*Acc.*)); kreuzen, mischen (*races, plants*); durchkreuzen, vereiteln, hindern, entgegentreten; besteigen (*a horse*); *be –ed in*, gehindert werden in; – *a cheque*, einen Scheck kreuzen; *–ed cheque*, der Verrechnungsscheck; – *each other*, sich kreuzen, sich treffen, sich überschneiden; – *the floor*, zur anderen Seite übergehen (*Pol.*); – *a p.'s hand with money*, einem Geld in die Hand legen; *it –ed my mind*, es fuhr mir durch den Kopf *or* fiel mir ein *or* kam mir in den Sinn; – *o.s.*, sich bekreuzigen; – *off* or *out*, ausstreichen, durchstreichen; – *s.o.'s path*, einem in die Quere kommen; – *s.o.'s purpose*, einem einen Strich durch die Rechnung machen; – *the threshold*, die Schwelle überschreiten. 5. *v.n.* sich kreuzen (*as letters*), sich treffen; – *over to*, hinübergehen auf; *–ed in love*, in der Liebe Pech haben. **--action,** *s.* die Widerklage (*Law*). **--bar,** *s.* der Querbalken, Querriegel, die Querstange; Torlatte (*Footb.*) **--beam,** *s.* der Querbalken, Kreuzträger, Dwarsbalken (*Naut.*). **–bench,** die Querbank (*Parl.*). **–bill,** *s* der Kreuzschnabel (*Orn.*). **--bones,** *pl.* gekreuzte Knochen. **–bow,** *s.* die Armbrust. **--breed,** *s.* die Mischrasse, der Mischling. **--channel,** *adj* ; *--channel steamer*, der Kanaldampfer. **--country,** *adj.* überland, querfeldein; *--country flight*, der Überlandflug; *--country race*, der Geländelauf, Waldlauf; *--country vehicle*, geländegängiger Wagen. **--cut,** *s.* der Querweg; Querschlag (*Min.*); *--cut saw*, die Schrotsäge. **--entry,** *s.* der Gegenposten, die Gegeneintragung, Umbuchung (*C.L.*). **--examination,** *s.* das Kreuzverhör (*Law*). **--examine,** *v.a.* ins Kreuzverhör nehmen, einem Kreuzverhör unterziehen. **--eyed,** *adj.* schielend. **--fire,** *s.* das Kreuzfeuer (*Mil.*). **--grained,** *adj.* wider den Strich geschnitten; (*fig.*) störrisch, eigensinnig, widerspenstig, widerhaarig, widerborstig. **--head,** *s.* der Kreuzkopf. **--heading,** *s.* die Auszeichnungszeile. **–ing,** *s.* der Übergang, die Überfahrt; Durchquerung (*of Africa, etc.*); der Straßenübergang; Kreuzweg; die Vierung (*Arch.*); Kreuzung (*of races*) (*also Railw.*); *level –ing*, der Bahnübergang (*Railw.*); *pedestrian –ing*, der Straßenübergang. **–ing-sweeper,** *s.* der Straßenkehrer. **--legged,** *adj.* mit gekreuzten Beinen. **–ly,** *adv* mürrisch, verdrießlich, ärgerlich. **--modulation,** *s.* die Kreuzmodulation (*Rad.*). **--multiplication,** *s.* kreuzweise Multiplikation. **–ness,** *s.* schlechte Laune, die Verdrießlichkeit. (*coll.*) **--patch,** *s.* der Murrkopf. **--piece,** *s.* der Querbalken; das Querholz. **--purposes,** *pl.* das Rätselspiel; *be at --purposes*, sich mißverstehen, einander unabsichtlich entgegenhandeln. **--question,** *s.* *see* **--examine. --reference,** *s.* der Kreuzverweis. **–road,** *s.* die Querstraße; *–roads*, *pl.* der Kreuzweg, die Wegkreuzung, Straßenkreuzung; (*fig.*) *at the –roads*, am Scheidewege. **--section,** *s.* der Querschnitt, Trennschnitt. **--stitch,** *s.* der Kreuzstich. **--talk,** *s.* das Nebensprechen (*Rad.*). **--trees,** *pl.* der Saling (*Naut.*). **--wind,** *s.* der Dwarswind. **–wires,** *pl.* das Fadenkreuz. **–wise,** *adv.* quer, kreuzweise. **–word (puzzle),** *s.* das Kreuzworträtsel.

crotch [krɔtʃ], *s.* die Gabel(ung).

crotchet [ˈkrɔtʃɪt], *s.* die Viertelnote (*Mus.*); Grille, Schrulle. **–y,** *adj.* schrullenhaft.

croton [ˈkroutn], *s.* der Kroton (*Bot.*); – *oil*, das Krotonöl.

crouch [krautʃ], 1. *v.n.* hocken, sich bücken, sich ducken; kauern, sich schmiegen (*to*, vor (*Dat.*)) (*of dogs, etc.*); (*fig.*) sich demütigen, kriechen (vor (*Dat.*)). 2. *s.* die Hockstellung.

croup [kruːp], *s.* der Krupp (*Med*).

croup(e) [kruːp], *s.* das Kreuz, die Kruppe (*of horses*); der Steiß, Bürzel (*of birds*).

croupier [ˈkruːpɪə], *s.* der Bankhalter.

crow [krou], 1. *s.* die Krähe (*Orn.*); das Krähen (*of a cock*); *hooded* –, die Nebelkrähe; *have a – to pluck with a p.*, ein Hühnchen mit einem zu rupfen haben; *be as hoarse as a* –, heiser wie ein Rabe sein; *as the – flies*, schnurgerade, in der Luftlinie; *white* –, eine Seltenheit. 2. *v.n.* krähen; (*coll.*) frohlocken; triumphieren (*over*, über). **–bar,** *s.* das Brecheisen, Stemmeisen. **–foot,** *s.* der Hahnenfuß (*Bot.*). **–'s-feet,** *pl.* Falten unter den Augen, Krähenfüsse. **–'s-nest,** *s.* der Ausguck, das Krähennest (*Naut.*).

crowd [kraud], 1. *s.* das Gedränge; der Haufe, die Menge (*of people*); der Pöbel, gemeines Volk; *–s of people*, Menschenmassen (*pl.*). 2. *v.a.* überfüllen, vollstopfen, (an)füllen; drängen, pressen; bedrängen, zusammendrängen; – (*all*) *sail*, alle Segel beisetzen; – *out*, verdrängen, ausschalten. 3. *v.n.* sich drängen; – *in*(*to*), sich hineindrängen (in (*Acc.*)); hineindringen; – *in upon*, bedrängen, bestürmen. **–ed,** *adj.* gedrängt, übervoll, angefüllt; *–ed to suffocation*, zum Ersticken voll; *–ed with*, angefüllt mit, wimmelnd von.

crown [kraun], 1. *s.* die Krone; der Kranz; (*fig.*) Gipfel, Schlußstein, die Spitze, Krönung, Vollendung; der Scheitel, Wirbel (*of the head*); (*fig.*) Kopf; das Ankerkreuz; die Zahnkrone; Baumkrone; ein Papierformat (15 *in.* × 20 *in.*); (*rare*) eine Silbermünze (5 *shillings*); *half a* –, eine halbe Krone (= 2*s.* 6*d.*); *from the – of the head to the sole of the foot*, von Kopf zu Fuß, vom Scheitel bis zur Sohle. 2. *v.a.* krönen; (*fig.*) bekränzen; schmücken, zieren; Ehre bringen (*Dat.*); die Krone aufsetzen (*Dat.*), vollenden, vervollkommnen; (*sl.*) auf den Kopf schlagen; *to – all*, als Letztes *or* Höchstes; – *a man*, einen Stein zur Dame machen (*Draughts*); – *a tooth*, einen Zahn eine (neue) Krone aufsetzen; *–ed heads*, gekrönte Häupter. **– colony,** die Kronkolonie, Reichskolonie. **--escapement,** *s.* die Spindelhemmung (*Horol.*). **--glass,** *s.* das Kronglas. **–ing,** *adj.* höchst, letzt, oberst. **--jewels,** *pl.* die Reichskleinodien. **--lands,** *pl.* Krongüter, Staatsdomänen. **– octavo,** das Kleinoktav. **--prince,** *s.* der Kronprinz. **--setting,** *s.* die Kastenfassung (*jewels*). **--wheel,** *s.* das Kronrad (*Horol.*).

crucial [ˈkruːʃəl], *adj.* entscheidend, kritisch; kreuzförmig; – *test*, die Feuerprobe.

crucian [ˈkruːʃɪən], *s.* die Karausche (*Icht.*).

crucible [ˈkruːsɪbl], *s.* der Schmelztiegel; (*fig.*) die Feuerprobe. **--steel,** *s.* der Tiegelgußstahl.

crucif–erous [kruˈsɪfərəs], *adj.*; *–erous plant*, der Kreuzblüter (*Bot.*). **–ix** [ˈkruːsɪfɪks], *s.* das Kruzifix. **–ixion** [–ˈfɪkʃən], *s.* die Kreuzigung. **–orm,** *adj.* kreuzförmig. **–y** [–sɪfaɪ], *v.a.* kreuzigen, ans Kreuz schlagen.

crud–e [kruːd], *adj.* roh, unreif, ungekocht; grell (*as colour*); grob, ungehobelt, ungeschliffen; unfertig, unverarbeitet, unverdaut; *the –e facts*, die nackten Tatsachen; *–e iron*, das Roheisen; *–e oil*, natürliches Öl, das Rohöl; *–e sugar*, roher Zucker. **–eness,** *s.*, **–ity,** *s.* die Roheit, Grobheit; Unreifheit, unreifer Gedanke.

cruel [ˈkruːəl], *adj.* grausam; entsetzlich, schrecklich, hart, unbarmherzig, unmenschlich; (*coll.*)

sehr, äußerst, höchst. **–ity,** *s.* die Grausamkeit; Härte; *–ty to animals*, die Tierquälerei; *society for the prevention of –ty to animals*, der Tierschutzverein.
cruet ['kru:ɪt] *s.* das Öl– *or* Essigfläschchen. **– -stand,** *s.* die Menage.
cruis–e [kru:z], 1. *s.* die Seereise; Erholungsreise, Vergnügungsfahrt zur See. 2. *v.n.* kreuzen (*Naut.*). **–er,** *s.* der Kreuzer (*Nav.*); Segler, die Jacht; *armoured –er*, der Panzerkreuzer. **–ing speed,** *s.* die Marschfahrt, Marschgeschwindigkeit; Sparfluggeschwindigkeit (*Av.*).
crumb [krʌm], 1. *s.* die Krume, Brosame; (*fig.*) das Bißchen. 2. *v.a.* (zer)krümeln; panieren (*Cook.*). **– -brush,** *s.* der Tischbesen. **–le** ['krʌmbl], 1. *v.a.* zerkrümeln, zerbröckeln, zerstückeln. 2. *v.n.* krümeln, zerbröckeln; *–le into dust*, in Staub zerfallen. **–ling** [–blɪŋ], *adj.* bröckelig, hinfällig. **–y,** *adj.* bröckelig, krümelig; (*sl.*) verlaust, lausig, schlecht.
crumpet ['krʌmpɪt], *s.* schwachgebackener Teekuchen; (*vulg.*) die Frau, das Mädchen; (*sl.*) *be off one's –*, eine weiche Birne haben.
crumple ['krʌmpl], 1. *v.a.* zerknüllen, zerknittern, ramponieren; *– up*, zusammenknüllen. 2. *v.n.* faltig *or* zerknittert werden; *– up*, einschrumpfen, (*fig.*) zusammenbrechen.
crunch [krʌntʃ], 1. *v.n.* knirschen. 2. *v.a.* zerknirschen, zermalmen.
crupper ['krʌpə], *s.* der Schwanzriemen; die Kruppe, das Kreuz (*of a horse*).
crural ['kruərəl], *adj.* Bein–, Schenkel–.
crusade [kru:'seɪd], 1. *s.* der Kreuzzug. 2. *v.n.* zu Felde ziehen (*against*, gegen). **–r,** *s.* der Kreuzfahrer.
cruse [kru:z], *s.* (*archaic*) der Topf, Krug, das Gefäß.
crush [krʌʃ], 1. *v.a.* (zer)quetschen, zerdrücken, zermalmen, zerkleinern, zerreiben, zerstoßen, zerstampfen, mahlen (*paper pulp, etc.*); (*fig.*) unterdrücken, vernichten, überwältigen, niederschmettern; *– out*; auspressen; ausdrücken. 2. *v.n.* sich drängen *or* drängeln (*into*, in (*Acc.*)); zusammengedrückt werden; zerknittern (*as a dress*). 3. *s.* das Gedränge, die Menschenmenge; (*sl.*) *have a – on*, verknallt *or* vernarrt sein in. **–er,** *s.* der Zerstoßer, die Brechwalze, Quetsche, Zerkleinerungsmaschine. **– -hat,** *s.* der Klapphut. **–ing-machine,** *s. see* **–er.** **– -room,** *s.* das Foyer, die Wandelhalle (*Theat.*).
crust [krʌst], 1. *s.* die Kruste, Rinde; Schale (*Bot., Zool.*); der Schorf, Grind; die Inkrustation (*Geol.*); der Knust, Anschnitt (*of a loaf*); der Teig, Rand (*of a pie*); Niederschlag (*of wine*); trockenes Stück Brot; *– of a boiler*, der Kesselstein; *earth's –*, feste Erdrinde. 2. *v.a.* mit Kruste *or* Rinde überziehen; *–ed snow*, der Harsch. 3. *v.n.* eine Kruste *or* einen Schorf bilden. **–iness,** *s.* die Krustigkeit; (*coll.*) Reizbarkeit. **–y,** *adj.* krustig; (*coll.*) mürrisch, reizbar.
crustace–a [krʌs'teɪʃɪə], *pl.*, **–ans,** *pl.* Krustentiere, Krustazeen, Krebse. **–ous** [–ʃəs], *adj.* krustenartig, Krustentier–.
crusty ['krʌstɪ], *see* **crust.**
crutch [krʌtʃ], *s.* die Krücke; Stütze; *go on –es*, an Krücken gehen. **–ed,** *adj.* auf Krücken gestützt.
crux [krʌks], *s.* das Kreuz (*Her.*); (*fig.*) die Schwierigkeit, harte Nuß.
cry [krɑɪ], 1. *v.n.* schreien, rufen, ausrufen, verkünden; weinen (*for*, vor (*Dat.*); *at*, über (*Acc.*)); heulen, jammern; bellen, anschlagen; *– for a thing*, etwas unter Tränen verlangen; *– for the moon*, nach Unmöglichem verlangen; (*coll.*) *– off*, zurücktreten, absagen *or* sich lossagen; *– out*, laut aufschreien; *– out against*, sich laut beschweren *or* beklagen über (*Acc.*); *– out for*, verlangen nach; *– over spilt milk*, Geschehenes beklagen, unnütz wehklagen; *– to*, zurufen, anrufen. 2. *v.a.* rufen, schreien; öffentlich ausrufen, ausbieten, verkünden (*wares, etc.*); weinen (*bitter tears, etc.*); *– down*, herabsetzen, herabschmälern, in Verruf bringen, verschreien, niederschreien; (*coll.*) *– off*, zurücktreten von, absagen; *– halt*, Einhalt gebieten; *– one's eyes* or *heart out*, sich (*Dat.*) ausweinen; *– up*, rühmen, preisen, in den Himmel heben, in die Höhe treiben. 3. *s.* der Schrei, Ruf; das Geschrei; der Ausruf, Zuruf, die Bitte; das Schlagwort, Losungswort; Weinen, Klagen, Flehen; Gebell, Anschlagen (*of dogs*); *a far –*, eine weite Entfernung; *in full –*, laut bellend, in voller Jagd; (*fig.*) mit großer Begeisterung; *have a good –*, sich ordentlich ausweinen; *the cries of London*, die Ausrufe der Londoner Straßenverkäufer; *the popular –*, die Volksstimme; das Gerücht; *war- -*, der Kriegsruf; *within –*, in Rufweite. **– -baby,** *s.* der Schreihals. **–ing,** *adj.* schreiend; weinend; (*fig.*) himmelschreiend, dringend; *–ing shame*, schreiendes Unrecht.
crypt [krɪpt], *s.* die Gruft, Krypta; Absonderungsdrüse (*Anat.*). **–ic** ['krɪptɪk], *adj.* verborgen, geheim. **–ogam** [–togæm], *s.* (*pl.* –ogamia) die Kryptogame (*Bot.*). **–ogamous,** *adj.* kryptogamisch (*Bot.*). **–ography** [krɪp'tɔgrafɪ], *s.* die Geheimschrift.
crystal ['krɪstl], 1. *s.* der Kristall; das Kristallglas; Uhrglas (*Horol.*). 2. *adj.* kristallen; kristallhell. **– -gazing,** *s.* die Kristallseherei. **–line,** *adj.* kristallen, kristallinisch, kristallisiert; kristallhell, Kristall– (*Min., etc.*); *–line rock*, der Bergkristall. **–lization** [krɪstəlɑɪ'zeɪʃən], *s.* die Kristallisation, Kristallbildung; *water of –lization*, das Konstitutionswasser. **–lize** ['krɪstəlɑɪz], 1. *v.a.* kristallisieren; kandieren (*fruits*). 2. *v.n.* (*– out*) sich (aus)kristallisieren. **–lography** [krɪstə'lɔgrəfɪ], *s.* die Kristallehre. **–loid,** *adj.* kristallähnlich. **– -set,** *s.* der Kristallempfänger (*Rad.*).
ctenoid ['tɪ:nɔɪd], *adj.* Kamm–, kammartig; *– fish*, der Kammschupper.
cub [kʌb], 1. das Junge (*of many wild animals*); ungeschlachter Bengel; (*wolf-*)–, das Mitglied des Jungvolkes, der Pimpf; *unlicked –*, ungeschliffener Bengel, der Tolpatsch. 2. *v.n.* Junge werfen.
cubature ['kju:bətjuə], *s.* die Rauminhaltsberechnung.
cubby-hole ['kʌbɪ'houl], *s.* (*coll.*) das Kämmerchen, kleiner gemütlicher Raum.
cube [kju:b], 1. *s.* der Würfel, Kubus (*Geom.*); *see* **– number.** 2. *v.a.* in die dritte Potenz erheben, kubieren (*Arith.*); Rauminhalt berechnen; *seven –d*, sieben hoch drei (*Arith.*). **– number,** die Kubikzahl, dritte Potenz. **– root,** die Kubikwurzel. **– -sugar,** *s.* der Würfelzucker; *see* **cubic.**
cubeb ['kju:bɛb], *s.* die Kubebe (*Bot.*).
cubi–c ['kju:bɪk], *adj.* kubisch, Kubik–, Raum–; würfelförmig; *–c content*, der Raum– *or* Kubikinhalt; *–c equation*, kubische Gleichung, Gleichung dritten Grades; *–c metre*, das Kubikmeter; *–c number*, die Kubikzahl. **–cal, –form,** *adj.* würfelförmig, Würfel–.
cubicle ['kju:bɪkl], *s.* abgeschlossener Schlafraum.
cubis–m ['kju:bɪzm], *s.* der Kubismus. **–t** ['kju:bɪst], *s.* der Kubist.
cubit ['kju:bɪt], *s.* (*archaic*) die Elle.
cuboid ['kju:bɔɪd], *adj.* würfelförmig; *– bone*, das Würfelbein (*Anat.*).
cuckold ['kʌkəld], 1. *s.* der Hahnrei. 2. *v.a.* zum Hahnrei machen.
cuckoo ['kuku:], 1. *s.* der Kuckuck; (*coll.*) Dummkopf, Einfaltspinsel. **– -clock,** *s.* die Kuckucksuhr. **– -flower,** *s.* das Wiesenschaumkraut (*Bot.*). **– -pint** [–pɪnt], *s.* gefleckter Aron (*Bot.*). **– -spit,** der Kuckucksspeichel, die Schaumzikade. 2. *adj.* (*sl.*) verdreht, verrückt.
cucumber ['kju:kʌmbə], *s.* die Gurke; (*coll.*) *cool as a –*, gelassen, ohne Aufregung.
cucurbit [kju:'kə:bɪt], *s.* der Kürbis. **–aceous,** [–'teɪʃəs], *adj.* Kürbis–.
cud [kʌd], *s.* zurückgebrachtes Futter zum Wiederkäuen; *chew the –*, wiederkäuen, (*fig., coll.*) nachsinnen (*over*, über).
cuddle ['kʌdl], 1. *v.a.* verhätscheln; herzen, liebkosen; (*sl.*) knutschen. 2. *v.n.*; *– up*, sich schmiegen (*to*, an (*Acc.*)); *– up in bed*, sich im Bett warm einpacken *or* zusammenkuscheln. 3. *s.* (*coll.*) die Umarmung, Liebkosung.
cuddy ['kʌdɪ], *s.* die Kajüte (*Naut.*).
cudgel ['kʌdʒəl], 1. *s.* der Knüttel, Knüppel; *take up the –s for a p.*, für einen eintreten *or* Partei nehmen *or* ergreifen. 2. *v.a.* prügeln; *– one's*

brains about a th., sich (*Dat.*) den Kopf über eine S. zerbrechen. **--play,** *s.* das Stockfechten.

[1]**cue** [kjuː], *s.* der Haarzopf; Billardstock, das Queue (*Bill.*).

[2]**cue,** *s.* das Stichwort (*Theat.*); (*fig.*) der Wink, Fingerzeig; *give a p. his –*, einem die Worte in den Mund legen; *take one's – from s.o.*, sich nach einem richten.

[1]**cuff** [kʌf], 1. *s.* der Puff, Knuff. 2. *v.a.* puffen, knuffen, ohrfeigen.

[2]**cuff,** *s.* die Manschette, Stulpe, der Ärmelaufschlag. **--link,** *s.* der Manschettenknopf.

cuirass [kwɪˈræs], *s.* der Brustharnisch, Panzer, Küraß. **–ier** [kwɪrəˈsɪːə], *s.* der Kürassier.

cuisine [ˈkwɪːsɪːn], *s.* die Küche, Kochkunst.

cul-de-sac [kuldəˈsæk], *s.* die Sackgasse.

culinary [ˈkjuːlɪnərɪ], *adj.* Küchen–, Koch–; *– art*, die Kochkunst; *– herbs*, Küchenkräuter.

cull [kʌl], *v.a.* pflücken; aussuchen, auslesen.

cullender [ˈkʌlɪndə], *s. see* **colander.**

cullet [ˈkʌlɪt], *s.* das Bruchglas.

[1]**culm** [kʌlm], *s.* der Halm, Stengel.

[2]**culm,** *s.* der Kohlenstaub, Kohlengrus, die Staubkohle.

culminat–e [ˈkʌlmɪneɪt], *v.n.* den Höhepunkt erreichen (*in*, mit *or* bei), gipfeln (*in*, in), kulminieren (*Astr.*). **–ion** [–ˈneɪʃən], *s.* die Kulmination (*Astr.*); (*fig.*) der Gipfel, Höhepunkt, die Gipfelhöhe, höchster Stand.

culpab–ility [kʌlpəˈbɪlɪtɪ], *s.* die Strafbarkeit, Schuld. **–le** [ˈkʌlpəbl], *adj.* strafbar, sträflich, tadelnswert.

culprit [ˈkʌlprɪt], *s.* der Verbrecher, Angeklagte(r), Beschuldigte(r), *m.*

cult [kʌlt], *s.* der Kult, Kultus, die Huldigung, Mode.

cultiv–able [ˈkʌltɪvəbl], **–atable** [–veɪtəbl], *adj.* anbaufähig. **–ate** [ˈkʌltɪveɪt], *v.a.* bearbeiten, bebauen, kultivieren (*land*); bauen, ziehen, züchten (*crops, etc.*); (*fig.*) bilden, ausbilden, entwickeln, veredeln, verfeinen, gesittet machen; üben, betreiben; pflegen, hegen. **–ated,** *adj.* bebaut, kultiviert; gebildet, zivilisiert. **–ation** [–ˈveɪʃən], *s.* der Anbau, Ackerbau, die Bebauung, Bestellung, Urbarmachung, Kultivierung; Ausbildung, Gesittung, Verfeinerung, Veredelung; Pflege, Übung. **–ator,** *s.* der Bebauer, Landwirt.

cultur–al [ˈkʌltʃərəl], *adj.* kulturell, Kultur–. **–e** [ˈkʌltʃə], 1. *s.* die Kultur (*also fig.*); Bildung, Zivilisation; Pflege, Zucht; *–e medium*, künstlicher Nährboden (*Bacter.*); *physical –e*, die Körperpflege. 2. *v.a.* kultivieren, ausbilden. **–ed,** *adj.* gebildet, kultiviert.

culver [ˈkʌlvə], *s.* die Waldtaube.

culverin [ˈkʌlvərɪn], *s.* (*archaic*) die Feldschlange (*Artill.*).

culvert [ˈkʌlvəːt], *s.* der Abzugskanal, Abflußgraben, Durchlaß.

cumb–er [ˈkʌmbə], *v.a.* beschweren, überladen; hindern, hemmen. **–ersome,** *adj.* beschwerlich, lästig, hinderlich, schwerfällig. **–ersomeness,** *s.* die Beschwerlichkeit, Lästigkeit, Schwerfälligkeit. **–rous** [–brəs], *adj. see* **–ersome.**

cummerbund [ˈkʌməbʌnd], *s.* der Leibgurt.

cum(m)in [ˈkʌmɪn], *s.* der Kreuzkümmel (*Bot.*).

cumulative [ˈkjuːmjulətɪv], *adj.* sich (an)häufend, sich steigernd, kumulativ, Zusatz– (*C.L.*); hinzukommend, verstärkend (*Law*).

cumulus [ˈkjuːmjuləs], *s.* die Haufenwolke, Kumuluswolke.

cune–ate [ˈkjuːnɪeɪt], *adj.* keilförmig, Keil–. **–iform** [ˈkjuːnɪɪfɔːm], 1. *adj. see* **–ate.** 2. *s.* die Keilschrift.

cunning [ˈkʌnɪŋ], 1. *adj.* listig, schlau, verschlagen, verschmitzt; geschickt, kundig. 2. *s.* die List, Arglist, Schlauheit, Verschlagenheit, Verschmitztheit; Geschicklichkeit.

cup [kʌp], 1. *s.* die Tasse, Schale; der Becher, Kelch (*Bot., Eccl.*); Pokal (*trophy*); Trunk; die (kalte) Bowle; *challenge –*, der Wanderpreis, Preispokal; *claret –*, die Rotweinbowle; *drinking –*, der Trinkbecher; *an early morning – of tea*, eine Tasse Tee vor dem Aufstehen; *be fond of the –*, dem Trunk ergeben sein; *his – was full*, der Kelch seines Leides war voll; *in one's –s*, betrunken, im Rausch; *parting –*, der Abschiedstrunk; *– and saucer*, die Tasse und Untertasse; *there's many a slip 'twixt (the) cup and (the) lip*, es ist noch nicht aller Tage Abend. 2. *v.a.* schröpfen (*Surg.*). **--bearer,** *s.* der Mundschenk. **– final,** das Endspiel (*Footb.*). **–ful,** *s.* die Tassevoll, der Bechervoll. **–ping-glass,** *s.* der Schröpfkopf. **--shaped,** *adj.* becherförmig. **--tie,** *s.* das Pokalspiel.

cupboard [ˈkʌbəd], *s*, der Schrank; Speiseschrank. **--love,** eigennützige Liebe.

cupel [ˈkjuːpəl], 1. *s.* die Kapelle, Kupelle, der Versuchstiegel; Test. 2. *v.a.* abtreiben, läutern, kupellieren (*metals*). **–lation** [–ˈleɪʃən], *s.* die Kupellierung, Läuterung, das Abtreiben (*Metall.*); der Treibprozeß.

cupidity [kjuːpɪdɪtɪ], *s.* die Begierde; Habgier.

cupola [ˈkjuːpələ], *s.* die Kuppel, der Dom, das Gewölbe, Kuppeldach; der Kuppelofen (*Metall.*); Panzerturm (*Mil.*).

cupr–eous [ˈkjuːprɪəs], *adj.* kupfern, kupferhaltig. **–ic, –ous,** *adj.* Kupfer–.

cur [kəː], *s.* der Köter; (*fig.*) Schurke, Halunke.

curab–ility [kjuərəˈbɪlɪtɪ], *s.* die Heilbarkeit. **–le** [ˈkjuərəbl], *adj.* heilbar.

cura–cy [ˈkjuərəsɪ], *s.* die Unterpfarre. **–te** [ˈkjuərət], *s.* Hilfsgeistliche(r), *m.*, der Unterpfarrer.

curative [ˈkjuərətɪv], 1. *adj.* heilend, Heil–. 2. *s.* das Heilmittel.

curator [kjuəˈreɪtə], *s.* der Verwalter, Museumsdirektor; (*Scots law*) Vormund. **–ship,** *s.* das Amt eines Kurators.

curb [kəːb], 1. *s.* die Kinnkette, Kandare (*harness*); (*fig.*) der Einhalt, Zaum, Zügel; der Spat, Hasenfuß (*Vet.*); *see* **kerb.** 2. *v.a.* an die Kandare legen; (*fig.*) zügeln, im Zaume halten, bändigen. **--bit,** *s.* die Kinnkettenstange. **--roof,** *s.* das Mansardendach.

curd [kəːd], *s.* geronnene Milch, der Quark; *turn to –s*, gerinnen; *– soap*, die Talgkernseife; *–s and whey*, dicke Milch. **–le** [ˈkəːdl], 1. *v.n.* gerinnen; (*fig.*) erstarren. 2. *v.a.* gerinnen machen, verdicken; *one's blood –les*, es geht einem durch Mark und Bein. **–ling,** *adj.*; *blood--ing*, grauenvoll, entsetzlich.

cur–e [kjuə], 1. *s.* die Kur, Behandlung; das Heilmittel; die Heilung, Genesung; Seelsorge, seelische Fürsorge; Pfarre; *undergo a –e*, eine Kur durchmachen; *past –e*, unheilbar. 2. *v.a.* heilen; einsalzen, einpökeln, räuchern (*meat*); beizen (*tobacco*); vulkanisieren, schwefeln (*rubber*); trocknen (*hay, etc.*). **–e-all,** *s.* (*coll.*) das Universalmittel. **–ing,** *s.* das Heilen; Einmachen, Einpökeln; die Vulkanisierung (*of rubber*); *–ing pickle*, die Lake.

curfew [ˈkəːfjuː], *s.* das Abendläuten; die Abendglocke; das Ausgehverbot, die Polizeistunde, Sperrstunde.

curia [ˈkjuərɪə], *s.* die Kurie.

curio [ˈkjuərɪou], *s.* die Rarität. **–sity** [kjuərɪˈɔsɪtɪ], *s.* die Neugier, Wißbegierde; Seltenheit, Merkwürdigkeit, Rarität; (*coll.*) komischer Kerl; (*old*) *–sity-shop*, *s.* der Antiquitätenladen.

curious [ˈkjuərɪəs], *adj.* neugierig, wißbegierig; sonderbar, merkwürdig, seltsam. **–ness,** *s.* die Merkwürdigkeit, Seltsamkeit.

curl [kəːl], 1. *s.* die (Haar)Locke; Kräuselung, Wallung; *– of the lip*, das Kräuseln der Lippe; *– of smoke*, die Rauchwindung. 2. *v.a.* kräuseln, locken, ringeln, frisieren (*the hair*). 3. *v.n.* sich kräuseln, sich locken, sich wellen, wogen (*as waves*); sich schlängeln (*as a serpent*); *– down*, in Locken niederfallen. **–ed,** *adj.* gekräuselt, lockig, gelockt, gewellt. **–iness,** *s.* die Lockigkeit, Krausheit. **–ing,** 1. *adj.* kräuselnd. 2. *s.* das Kräuseln; Eisschießen (*Sport*). **–ing-irons, –ing-tongs,** *pl.* das Brenneisen, Kräuseleisen, Onduliereisen. **--paper,** *s.* der Haarwickel. **–y,** *adj.* lockig, gekräuselt. **–y-haired, –y-headed,** *adj.* lockenköpfig.

curlew [ˈkəːljuː], *s.* der Brachvogel.

curmudgeon [kəːˈmʌdʒən], *s.* der Geizhals, Knicker, Filz.

currant [ˈkʌrənt], *s.* die Johannisbeere; Korinthe.

curren–cy [ˈkʌrənsɪ], *s.* der Umlauf, die Zirkulation, Lauffrist (*of a bill*); der Kurs, die Währung, Valuta, das Umlaufmittel, Zahlungsmittel; (*fig.*) die Geltung, allgemeine Annahme; *depreciation of –cy*, der Währungsverfall, die Geldentwertung; *give –cy to a th.*, etwas in Umlauf bringen. **–cy-note,** *s.* die Schatzanweisung. **–t** ['kʌrənt], 1. *adj.* laufend, jetzig, gegenwärtig, augenblicklich (*of time*); kursierend, kurant, gangbar, gültig (*of money*); (*fig.*) anerkannt, allgemein angenommen, umlaufend, verbreitet, zirkulierend (*as a report*); (*archaic*) fließend; *at the – exchange*, zum Tageskurs; *– hand(writing)*, die Kurrentschrift; *– opinion*, gegenwärtige *or* verbreitete Meinung; *pass –*, für gültig *or* voll angenommen werden, gang und gäbe sein; *for – payment*, gegen bar; *– price*, der Tagespreis; *– rate*, der Tageswert; *– year*, laufendes Jahr. 2. *s.* der Strom; die Strömung (*sea or river*); der Lauf, Gang (*of events, etc.*); *– of air*, der Luftzug; *alternating –*, der Wechselstrom (*Elec.*); *continuous* or *direct –*, der Gleichstrom; *down –*, der Abwind (*Meteor.*); *electric –*, der Strom; *induction –*, der Erregerstrom (*Elec.*); *– of modern opinion*, moderne Geistesrichtung; *primary –*, der Erststrom, Primärstrom; *secondary –*, der Sekundärstrom; *three-phase –*, der Drehstrom; *up –*, der Aufwind (*Meteor.*).

curricle ['kʌrɪkl], *s.* zweirädriger Zweispänner.

curriculum [kə'rɪkjuləm], *s.* der Lehrplan. **– vitae,** der Lebenslauf.

currier ['kʌrɪə], *s.* der Lederzurichter, Gerber.

currish ['kə:rɪʃ], *adj.* bissig; mürrisch.

[1]**curry** ['kʌrɪ], *v.a.* zurichten, bereiten (*leather*); striegeln, abreiben (*a horse*); *– favour with a p.*, sich bei einem einschmeicheln, jemandes Gunst zu gewinnen suchen; (*vulg.*) *– a p.'s hide*, einem das Fell gerben, einen durchprügeln. **––comb,** *s.* der Striegel.

[2]**curry,** 1. *s.* indisches Ragoutpulver; gewürztes Reisragout. 2. *v.a.* mit Würzen bereiten **––powder,** *s.* indisches Ragoutpulver.

curs–e [kə:s], 1. *v.a.* verfluchen, verwünschen, verdammen; fluchen auf (*a p.*); *–e him !* zum Teufel mit ihm! 2. *v.n.* fluchen. 3. *s.* der Fluch, die Verwünschung; der Bann, die Verdammnis (*Eccl.*); das Unglück, Elend. **–ed** ['kə:sɪd], *adj.* verflucht; (*coll.*) verflixt; *be –ed with*, gequält *or* bestraft sein mit. **–edness** [–sɪdnɪs], *s.* das Verfluchtsein, die Verfluchtheit.

cursive ['kə:sɪv], *adj.* fließend; kursiv (*as handwriting*).

cursor ['kə:sə], *s.* der Schieber (*Mech., Math.*).

cursor–iness ['kə:sərɪnɪs], *s.* die Flüchtigkeit, Oberflächlichkeit. **–y** ['kə:sərɪ], *adj.* flüchtig, oberflächlich, eilfertig.

curt [kə:t], *adj.* kurz, kurzgefaßt, knapp; kurz angebunden (*with*, mit); barsch (*with*, gegen). **–ness,** *s.* die Kürze, Knappheit; Barschheit.

curtail [kə:'teɪl], *v.a.* abkürzen, verkürzen, kürzen, beschneiden; (*fig.*) beschränken, schmälern, herabsetzen, beeinträchtigen; *be –ed of a th.*, um etwas beraubt werden. **–ment,** *s.* die Abkürzung, Verkürzung, Abschneidung, Schmälerung, Kürzung, Beschränkung.

curtain ['kə:tn], 1. *s.* der Vorhang, die Gardine; der Zwischenfall, die Kurtine (*Fort.*); (*fig.*) Hülle, der Schleier; *fire-proof –*, eiserner Vorhang (*Theat.*); (*a*) (*with verbs*) *draw the –s*, die Gardinen zuziehen *or* vorziehen; (*fig.*) *draw the – over a th.*, etwas zudecken *or* begraben; (*fig.*) *lift the –*, den Schleier lüften; *the – rises*, der Vorhang geht hoch; (*b*) (*with prepositions*) *behind the –*, hinter den Kulissen; *under the – of night*, unter dem Schleier der Nacht. 2. *v.a.* mit Vorhängen umhängen *or* versehen; *– off*, durch Vorhänge abschließen. **––fall,** *s.* das Niedergehen des Vorhangs. **––fire,** *s.* das Sperrfeuer (*Artil.*). **––lecture,** *s.* die Gardinenpredigt. **––pole,** *s.* die Vorhangstange. **––raiser,** *s.* einaktiges Vorspiel, der Eröffnungseinakter. **––rod,** *s.* die Gardinenstange.

curtilage ['kə:tɪlɪdʒ], *s.* die Umfriedung.

curts(e)y ['kə:tsɪ], 1. *s.* der Knicks. 2. *v.n.* (*drop a –*) knicksen, einen Knicks machen (*to*, vor).

curvature ['kə:vətʃə], *s.* die Krümmung, Biegung; *– of the spine*, die Rückgratsverkrümmung.

curve [kə:v], 1. *s.* die Krümmung, Biegung, Kurve (*Railw., Math.*); krumme Linie; der Bogen; *sharp –*, die Steilkurve, Kniebiegung. 2. *v.a.* krümmen, biegen; *–d*, bogenförmig, geschweift, gewölbt, Bogen–; gekrümmt. 3. *v.n.* sich biegen, sich krümmen.

curvet [kə:'vɛt *or* 'kə:vət], 1. *s.* die Kurbette (*of a horse*). 2. *v.a.* kurbettieren.

curvilinear [kə:vɪ'lɪnɪə], *adj.* krummlinig.

cushat ['kʌʃət], *s.* die Ringeltaube.

cushion ['kuʃən], 1. *s.* das Kissen, Polster; die Bande (*Bill.*); das Polsterkapitell (*Arch.*); *– tire*, der Vollgummireifen (*Cycl.*). 2. *v.a.* mit Kissen versehen; polstern, abfedern (*Mach.*); *– a ball*, einen Ball dublieren (*Bill.*); *–ed seat*, die Polsterbank.

cushy ['kuʃɪ], *adj.* (*sl.*) kinderleicht, angenehm, bequem.

cusp [kʌsp], *s.* die Spitze, der Scheitelpunkt (*Arch., Anat.*); das Horn (*of the moon*); *– of an arch*, die Nase eines Bogens. **–idal, –idate(d),** *adj.* gespitzt, zugespitzt, Spitz–.

cuspidor ['kʌspɪdə:], *s.* der Spucknapf.

cuss [kʌs], 1. *s.* (*sl.*) Fluch, die Verwünschung; der Bursche, Kerl; *not care a tinker's –*, sich nicht das geringste daraus machen. 2. *v.n.* (*sl.*) fluchen. **–ed** [–ɪd], *adj.* (*sl.*) verflucht, verwünscht. **–edness** [–ɪdnɪs], *s.* (*coll.*) die Widerhaarigkeit, Widerborstigkeit.

custard ['kʌstəd], *s.* die Vanillesoße. **––apple,** *s.* die Frucht des Flaschenbaums. **––powder,** *s.* das Soßenpulver, Puddingpulver.

custod–ial [kʌs'toudɪəl], 1. *adj.* vormundschaftlich. 2. *s.* das Gefäß für Heiligtümer. **–ian** [kʌs'toudɪən], *s.* der Hüter, Wächter, Kustos. **–y** ['kʌstədɪ], *s.* die Haft, der Gewahrsam; die Aufsicht, Obhut, Bewachung, Verwahrung; der Schutz; *–y of a child*, die Obhut eines Kindes; *hand over to the –y of a p.*, einem in Verwahrung geben; *protective –y*, die Schutzhaft; *take into –y*, in Haft nehmen, verhaften.

custom ['kʌstəm], *s.* die Gewohnheit, der Brauch, Gebrauch; die Sitte, das Herkommen; das Gewohnheitsrecht (*Law*); die Kundschaft (*C.L.*). **–able,** *adj.* zollpflichtig. **–ary** [–ərɪ], *adj.* gebräuchlich, üblich, gewöhnlich; herkömmlich, Gewohnheits–. **–er** [–ə], *s.* der Kunde, Abnehmer, Käufer; (*coll.*) Kerl, Bursche; (*coll.*) *queer –er*, seltsamer Kerl; *regular –er* (*of a restaurant, etc.*), der Stammgast; (*coll.*) *rough –er*, roher Kunde. **–ers,** *pl.* die Kundschaft. **–s** ['kʌstəmz], *pl.* der Zoll, die Steuer; Zollbehörde; *–s clearance*, die Zollabfertigung; *–s declaration* or *entry*, die Zollangabe; *–s examination*, die Zollrevision; *–s-house*, *s.* das Zollamt. *–s-house officer*, Zollbeamte(r), *m.*; *–s-union*, *s.* der Zollverein, die Zollunion.

custos ['kʌstəs], *s.* der Aufseher; *– rotulorum*, der Archivar.

cut [kʌt], 1. *ir.v.a.* schneiden, zerschneiden, abschneiden, zurechtschneiden, zuschneiden, beschneiden, scheren, stutzen; aufschneiden (*bread, a book, etc.*); vorschneiden (*meat*); aushauen, schnitzen (*stone, wood*); schleifen (*gems*), mähen (*corn, etc.*), bohren (*a tunnel*), stechen (*a ditch*), kreuzen, durchschneiden (*a line*); (*fig.*) kürzen; (*a*) (*with nouns*) (*sl.*) *– the cackle*, das Schwatzen sein lassen; *– capers*, Luftsprünge machen; *– the cards*, die Karten abheben; (*Prov.*) *– one's coat according to one's cloth*, sich nach der Decke strecken; (*coll.*) *– a dash*, großtun; *– a figure*, eine Rolle spielen; *– one's finger*, sich in den Finger schneiden; *have one's hair –*, sich die Haare schneiden lassen; (*sl.*) *– no ice*, keinen Eindruck machen (*with*, auf), nicht imponieren (*with* (*Dat.*)); ohne Belang sein; (*fig.*) *– the knot*, den Knoten durchhauen; (*coll.*) *– a lecture*, ein Kolleg schwänzen; *– the line*, die Linie durchschneiden; *the lines – each other*, die Linien schneiden sich; *– one's losses*, die Verluste abschreiben *or* abbuchen; *– a p.* (*dead*), einen ignorieren *or* schneiden *or* nicht sehen wollen; *– the price*, den Preis herabsetzen; *– steps*, Stufen schlagen (*Mount.*); *– one's teeth*, zahnen, Zähne bekommen; (*fig.*) *– one's own throat*, sich ins eigene Fleisch schneiden; den Ast absägen, auf dem man sitzt; *– one's way*, sich (*Dat.*) einen Weg bahnen;

(*fig.*) sich durchschlagen; (*b*) (*with adverbs*) – **away,** abschneiden, abhauen. – **down,** niederhauen, fällen; (ab)mähen (*crops*); (*fig.*) herabsetzen (*prices*), beschneiden (*costs*); verkürzen, vermindern, verringern, zusammenstreichen (*manuscript*). (*coll.*) – *s.th. fine,* etwas auf den letzten Moment ankommen lassen, etwas allzu knapp bemessen, etwas genau berechnen. – *in pieces,* zerhauen; – *in two,* entzweischneiden, durchschneiden. – **loose,** lösen *or* trennen; – *o.s. loose from,* sich lossagen von. – **off,** abschneiden, abhauen; abstellen (*supply*); trennen, unterbrechen (*Elec.*); ausschließen; – *off an entail,* die Beschränkung der Erbfolge aufheben; – *s.o. off with a shilling,* einen im Testament auf einen Pfennig herabsetzen, einen bis auf den letzten Pfennig enterben; – *off hopes,* Hoffnungen vernichten; – *off one's nose to spite one's face,* sich (*Dat.*) die Rache allzu viel kosten lassen; – *off the enemy's retreat,* dem Feinde den Rückzug abschneiden; (*sl.*) *be* – *off,* sterben. – **out,** ausschneiden, zuschneiden (*dresses, etc.*); ausschalten, weglassen, auslassen, fallen lassen (*a p. or th.*); (*coll.*) – *it out!* unterlassen Sie es! *he is* – *out for it,* er ist dafür wie geschaffen; *he has his work* – *out,* er hat genügend zu tun; – *s.o. out with a p.,* einen bei einem verdrängen. – **short,** kurz unterbrechen; *he* – *me short,* er fiel mir ins Wort; *to* – *a long story short,* um es kurz zu machen. – *to pieces* or *bits,* in Stücke hauen, zerstückeln; – *to the quick,* (bis) ins Mark treffen, aufs tiefste verwunden; – *s.o. to the heart,* einem ins Herz schneiden, einen auf bitterste kränken. – **up,** aufschneiden, zerschneiden, zerlegen; (*coll.*) einer vernichtenden Kritik unterziehen, heruntermachen, vernichten; (*coll.*) *he was* – *up about it,* er wurde darüber sehr betrübt *or* mitgenommen. 2. *ir.v.n.* schneiden, hauen; sich schneiden lassen; *it* –*s both ways,* es ist ein zweischneidiges Schwert; – *and come again,* greif tüchtig zu! (*sl.*) – *and run,* sich aus dem Staube machen; *badly* – *about,* übel hergerichtet. – **across,** abschneiden, einen kürzeren Weg einschlagen. – **back,** zurückgreifen auf vorangegangenes (*Films*). – *for deal,* zum Geben abheben (*Cards*). – **in,** plötzlich eingreifen, unterbrechen, sich einmischen; sich (nach Überholen) wieder einreihen (*Motor.*). – **loose,** sich befreien. – **out,** scharf ausbiegen zum Überholen (*Motor.*); aussetzen (*an engine*); *I have my work* – *out,* ich habe genug Arbeit vor mir; – *out for,* bestimmt für, geboren zu, das Zeug haben zu. – *up rough,* (*sl.*) auffällig *or* grob werden; (*coll.*) *be* – *up about,* außer sich *or* aufgeregt sein. 3. *s.* der Schnitt, Hieb, Stich, die Schnittwunde; der Peitschenhieb; Kupferstich, Holzschnitt; Durchschnitt, Abschnitt; (Zu)Schnitt, die Form, Fasson (*of clothes*); der Durchstich, Einschnitt, Graben, die Rinne; Gehaltskürzung, Herabschneidung, Beschneidung, der Abzug, Abstrich (*in pay*); Anschnitt, Aufschnitt, die Schnitte, das Stück(chen) (*of meat, etc.*); die Streichung, Kürzung (*in a play, etc.*); (*fig.*) das Schneiden, Nichtsehenwollen; – *and thrust,* das Hieb- und Stoßfechten; *–-and-thrust weapon,* die Hieb- und Stoßwaffe; (*coll.*) *he is a* – *above me,* er steht eine Stufe über mir; (*coll.*) *that's a* – *above me,* das ist mir zu hoch; (*sl.*) – *of a p.'s jib,* sein Aussehen; *short–-,* der Richtweg, nächster Weg; *whose* – *is it?* wer hebt ab? (*Cards*). 4. *adj.* geschnitten, beschnitten; geschnitzt, geschliffen (*glass*). **–-away,** der Ausschnitt. **–away,** Herrenrock mit abgerundeten Vorderschößen. **–-back,** *s.* die Wiederholung (*Film*). – **and dry** *or* **dried,** abgemacht, (fix und) fertig; schablonenhaft. – **horse,** *s* der Wallach. **–-out,** *s.* der Ausschnitt; Umschalter, Ausschalter, Kurzschließer, Unterbrecher, die Sicherung (*Elec.*). **–-price,** *s.* der Schleuderpreis. **–purse,** *s.* der Beutelschneider, Taschendieb. **–ter,** *s.* Schneidende(r), *m.,* der Zuschneider (*Tail.*); Schnittermeister (*Film*); das Schneidewerkzeug, die Schneidemaschine; Ausstechform (*Conf.*); der Kutter, das Beiboot (*Naut.*); *hair–-ter,* der Haarschneider, Friseur; *wire–-ter,* die Drahtzange, Drahtschere, Kneifzange. **–-throat,** 1. *s.* der Halsabschneider. 2. *adj.* mörderisch; *–-throat competition,* die Konkurrenz auf Leben und Tod. **–ting,** 1. *adj.* scharf, schneidend, beißend; *–ting edge,* die Schneide; *–ting remark,* beißende Bemerkung; *–ting tool,* das Schneidewerkzeug; *–ting torch,* der Schneidebrenner; *–ting wind,* schneidender Wind. 2. *s.* das Schneiden; der Abschnitt, Ausschnitt, Einschnitt; Durchstich (*Railw., etc.*); Ableger, Steckling, Setzling (*Bot.*); (*pl.*) die Schnitzel, Späne, Abfälle; *newspaper –ting,* der Zeitungsausschnitt. **–ting-line,** *s.* die Schnittlinie (*Typ.*). **–ting-out,** *s.* das Zuschneiden (*Tail.*). **–ting-(out) board,** *s* der Zuschneidetisch (*Tail.*). **–water** *s.* das Galion (*Naut.*).

cutaneous [kjuːˈteɪnɪəs], *adj.* Haut–.

cute [kjuːt], *adj.* (*coll.*) klug, scharf, aufgeweckt, schlau; (*Amer. sl.*) niedlich, süß, nett, reizend. **–y,** *s.* (*Amer. sl.*) fesches Mädel.

cuticle [ˈkjuːtɪkl], *s.* die Oberhaut, Epidermis (*Anat., Bot.*).

cutlass [ˈkʌtləs], *s.* kurzer Säbel.

cutler [ˈkʌtlə], *s.* der Messerschmied. **–y** [–rɪ] *s.* das Messerschmiedhandwerk; das Eßbesteck, die Messerwaren.

cutlet [ˈkʌtlɪt], *s.* das Rippchen, Kotelett.

cuttle–-bone [ˈkʌtlboun], *s.* die Schulpe. **–-fish,** der Blackfisch, gemeine Sepie.

cwm [kuːm], *s.* (*dial.*) *see* **coomb.**

cyan–ate [ˈsɑɪənəɪt], *s.* zyansaures Salz. **–ic** [sɑɪˈænɪk], *adj.* Zyan–; *–ic acid,* die Zyansäure. **–ide** [ˈsɑɪənɑɪd], *s.* das Zyanid, blausaure Verbindung; *–ide of potassium,* das Zyankalium. **–ogen** [sɑɪˈænodʒɪn], *s.* das Zyan.

cyclamen [ˈsɪkləmən], *s.* das Alpenveilchen (*Bot.*).

cycl–e [ˈsɑɪkl], 1. *s.* die Periode, der Zyklus, Kreislauf, Umlauf, Kreis, Ring; die Folge, Reihe, der Turnus; (*coll.*) das Fahrrad: *combustion –e,* der Verbrennungsvorgang (*Motor.*); *compression –e,* der Verdichtungstakt (*Motor.*); *exhaust –e,* der Auspufftakt (*Motor.*); *–e of the moon* (*sun*), der Mond–(Sonnen)Zyklus; (*coll.*) *motor–-e,* das Motorrad; *recurring in –es,* periodisch wiederkehrend; *–e track,* *s.* der Radfahrweg 2. *v.n.* radfahren, radeln. **–ic,** *adj.* zyklisch, kreisförmig. **–ing,** *s.* das Radfahren, der Radfahrsport; *–ing club,* der Radfahrverein **–ist,** *s* der Radfahrer. **–oid,** *s.* die Zykloide, Radlinie (*Geom.*). **–oidal,** *adj.* radlinig. **–ometer** [–ˈlɔmɪtə], *s.* der Wegmesser. **–otron,** *s.* das Zyklotron.

cyclone [ˈsɑɪkloun], *s.* der Wirbelsturm; das Tiefdruckgebiet (*Meteor.*).

cyclop–aedia, –edia [sɑɪkloˈpɪːdɪə], *s.* das Konversationslexikon. **–aedic, –edic,** *adj* umfassend, universal. **–ean** [–ˈpɪːən], **–ian** [–ˈkloupɪən], *adj.* zyklopisch; (*fig.*) riesig, ungeheuer. **–s** [ˈsɑɪklɔps], *s.* der Zyklop.

cyclostyle [ˈsɑɪkləstɑɪl], 1. *s.* der Vervielfältigungsapparat. 2. *v.a.* vervielfältigen.

cygnet [ˈsɪgnɪt], *s.* junger Schwan.

cylind–er [ˈsɪlɪndə], *s.* der Zylinder, die Walze, Druckwalze (*Typ.*); Trommel (*Spin, etc.*); *gas –er,* die Gasflasche. **–er-escapement,** *s.* die Zylinderhemmung (*Horol.*). **–er-jacket,** *s* der Zylindermantel (*Locom., etc.*). **–er printing,** der Walzendruck. **–rical** [sɪˈlɪndrɪkl], *adj.* zylindrisch, zylinderförmig, walzenförmig.

cymbal [ˈsɪmbəl], *s* die Zimbel, das Becken (*Mus.*).

cyme [sɑɪm], *s* zymöser Blütenstand (*Bot.*).

cynic [ˈsɪnɪk], *s.* der Zyniker Spötter. **–al,** *adj.* zynisch, spöttisch, höhnisch, schamlos **–ism,** *s.* der Zynismus, Hohn.

cynosure [ˈsɑɪnoʃuə], *s.* kleiner Bär (*Astr.*); (*fig.*) der Leitstern; Anziehungspunkt.

cypher [ˈsɑɪfə], *s.* *see* **cipher.**

cypress [ˈsɑɪprəs], *s.* die Zypresse.

cyst [sɪst], *s.* die Blase, Zelle, Kapselhülle (*Bot., Anat.*); Zyste, Sackgeschwulst (*Path.*). **–ic,** *adj.* Blasen–. **–itis,** *s.* die Blasenentzündung.

cytology [sɑɪˈtɔlədʒɪ], *s.* die Zellenlehre.

czar [zɑː], *s.,* **–ewitch,** *s.,* **–ina,** *s.* *see* **tsar,** *etc.*

D

D, d, *s.* das D, d (*also Mus.*); *– flat*, Des, *n.*; *– sharp*, Dis, *n.*; *for abbreviations see Index at end.*

dab [dæb], 1. *v.a.* leicht schlagen, (*coll.*) antippen; betupfen, abtupfen; klischieren. 2. *s.* der Klaps, sanfter Schlag; das Tupfen; Klümpchen, der Klecks, die Schlampe; der Butt, die Scholle (*Ichth.*); (*coll.*) *be a – at a th.*, sich auf eine S. verstehen. **–ber,** *s.* der Tupfballen, die Filzwalze.

dabble [ˈdæbl], 1. *v.a.* benetzen, bespritzen. 2. *v.n.* plätschern, plantschen; sich aus Liebhaberei abgeben *or* befassen (*in*, mit); pfuschen (*in*, in), sich als Dilettant *or* sich dilettantisch beschäftigen (*in*, mit). **–r,** *s.* der Stümper, Pfuscher, Dilettant.

dabchick [ˈdæbtʃɪk], *s.* der Steißfuß, Zwergtaucher (*Orn.*).

dace [deɪs], *s.* der Weißfisch (*Ichth.*).

dacoit [dəˈkɔɪt], *s.* der ostindischer Bandit.

dactyl [ˈdæktɪl], *s.* der Daktylus. **–ic** [–ˈtɪlɪk], *adj.* daktylisch. **–ogram,** *s.* der Fingerabdruck. **–ology** [–ˈɔlədʒɪ], *s.* die Fingersprache.

dad [dæd], **–a, –dy,** *s.* (*coll.*) Papa, Väterchen, Vati. **–dy-long-legs,** *s.* langbeinige Spinne, die Bachmücke, der Kanker (*Ent.*).

dado [ˈdeɪdoʊ], *s.* untere Wandbekleidung, Wandbemalung *or* Wandtäfelung; der Sockel, Postamentwürfel (*Arch.*).

daemon [ˈdɪːmən], *s. see* **demon.**

daffodil [ˈdæfədɪl], *s.* gelbe Narzisse, der Märzbecher.

daft [dɑːft], *adj.* (*sl.*) albern, einfältig, verdreht, verrückt.

dagger [ˈdægə], *s.* der Dolch; das Kreuzzeichen (*Typ.*); *look –s at a p.*, einen mit Blicken durchbohren; *be at –s drawn*, einander verfeindet sein.

dago [ˈdeɪgoʊ], *s.* (*pej.*) Italiener (*m.*).

dahlia [ˈdeɪljə], *s.* die Georgine (*Bot.*).

daily [ˈdeɪlɪ], *adj.* & *adv.* täglich; ständig, tagtäglich, alltäglich, üblich; *– (help)*, das Tagmädchen; *– (paper)*, die Tageszeitung; (*pl.*) *dailies*, die Tagespresse.

daint-iness [ˈdeɪntɪnɪs], *s.* die Niedlichkeit, Zierlichkeit, Zartheit; wählerisches Wesen, die Verwöhntheit; Leckerhaftigkeit, Schmackhaftigkeit. **–y** [ˈdeɪntɪ], 1. *adj.* niedlich, zierlich (*of person*); lecker, wohlschmeckend, schmackhaft, delikat (*of food*); leckerhaft, wählerisch, verwöhnt, geziert (*of persons*). 2. *s.* der Leckerbissen, die Leckerei; (*pl.* –ies) das Naschwerk.

dairy [ˈdeərɪ], *s.* der Milchraum (*of a farm*); die Milchwirtschaft, das Milchgeschäft; die Molkerei. **– -farm,** *s.* die Meierei, Milchwirtschaft. **– -maid,** *s.* das Milchmädchen. **– -man,** *s.* der Milchhändler, Milchmann. **– produce,** *s.* Molkereiprodukte (*pl.*).

dais [ˈdeɪɪs], *s.* erhöhter Sitz, das Podium.

daisy [ˈdeɪzɪ], 1. *s*, das Gänseblümchen, Maßliebchen (*Bot.*); *push up the daisies*, (*sl.*) tot sein. 2. *adj.* (*sl.*) großartig, reizend. **– -cutter,** *s.* (*sl.*) das Pferd mit schleppendem Gang; (*sl.*) sehr flach geschleudeter Ball (*Crick.*).

dale [deɪl], *s.* das Tal. **–sman** [–zmən], *s.* der Talbewohner.

dall-iance [ˈdælɪəns], *s.* die Tändelei, Liebelei; Verzögerung, der Aufschub. **–y** [ˈdælɪ], *v.n.* tändeln, liebeln, spielen; liebäugeln; Zeit vergeuden.

Daltonism [ˈdɔːltənɪzm], *s.* die Farbenblindheit.

¹dam [dæm], 1. *s.* der Deich, Damm, das Wehr; die Talsperre; *beaver –*, das Biberwehr; *coffer –*, der Fangdamm, Kastendamm. 2. *v.a.* (*– up*) eindeichen, dämmen, abdämmen, eindämmen, stauen; (*fig.*) beschränken, hemmen.

²dam, *s.* die Mutter (*of animals*); *the devil's –*, des Teufels Großmutter.

damag-e [ˈdæmɪdʒ], 1. *s.* der Schaden (*often pl.* Schäden) (*to*, an), die Beschädigung (*to* (*Dat.*)), der Nachteil; *–e by sea*, die Havarie; *do a p. –e*, einem Schaden zufügen; (*sl.*) *what's the –e?* was kostet es? 2. *v.a.* beschädigen (*a th.*), schädigen (*a p.*), Schaden anrichten (*a th.* (*Dat.*)), Schaden zufügen (*a p.* (*Dat.*)); verderben; lahmschießen, krankschießen (*by gunfire*). **–eable,** *adj.* leicht zu beschädigen(d), zerbrechlich. **–ed,** *adj.* beschädigt, schadhaft. **–es,** *pl.* der Schadenersatz; *assess –es*, Schadenersatzansprüche festsetzen; *claim –es*, Schadenersatzansprüche stellen: *pay –es*, Schadenersatz leisten; *recover –es*, entschädigt werden, Schadenersatz erhalten. **–ing,** *adj.* schädlich, nachteilig (*to*, für).

damascene [dæməˈsɪːn], 1. *v.a.* damaszieren. 2. *adj.* damasziert.

damask [ˈdæməsk], 1. *s.* der Damast; *linen –*, das Damastleinen; *silk –*, die Damastseide. 2. *adj.* damasten, rosenrot; *– carpet*, der Damastteppich; *– steel*, Damaszener Stahl. 3. *v.a.* damaszieren (*steel*); damastartig weben; (*fig.*) verzieren. **– -rose,** *s.* die Damaszenerrose.

dame [deɪm], *s.* (*Poet.*) die Dame; weiblicher Ordenstitel; (*sl.*) die Frau, das Mädchen. **–(s')-school** [ˈdeɪm(z)skʊːl], (*archaic*) *s.* die Elementarschule.

damn [dæm], 1. *v.a.* verdammen, verurteilen, verschreien, verwerfen, tadeln, in Verruf bringen; auspfeifen, auszischen (*a play*); *– it!* verdammt! verwünscht! *– you!* hol' dich der Teufel! *know – all*, (*sl.*) garnichts wissen; *a – sight too much*, (*sl.*) verflixt viel; *the –ed*, die Verdammten; (*I'll be*) *–ed if*, ich will verflucht sein wenn. 2. *s.*; (*coll.*) *I don't care a* (*twopenny*) *–*, ich schere mich den Teufel darum, ich mache mir absolut nichts daraus. **–able** [–nəbl], *adj.* verdammenswert, verdammlich, verdammt, verflucht, abscheulich. **–ation** [–ˈneɪʃən], 1. *s.* die Verdammnis, Verdammung. 2. *int.* verwünscht! verflucht! **–atory** [–nətərɪ], *adj.* verdammend, Verdammungs–. **–ing,** *adj.* verdammend, belastend, erdrückend.

damp [dæmp], 1. *adj.* feucht; *– rot*, nasse Fäulnis. 2. *s.* die Feuchtigkeit; *fire– –*, schlagende Wetter (*pl.*), das Grubengas, der Schwaden. 3. *v.a.*, **–en,** *v.a.* befeuchten, benetzen; *– (down)*, auslöschen, (ab)dämpfen; (*fig.*) niederschlagen; *– a p.'s spirits*, einem die Stimmung trüben; *–ed wave*, gedämpfte Welle. 4. *v.n.* feucht werden; *– off*, abfaulen (*of plants*). **– -course,** *s.* die Schutzschicht (*Build.*). **–er,** *s.* der Schieber, die Ofenklappe; der Zugregler (*of stoves, etc.*); Dämpfer (*Mus., fig.*); *be a –er to, cast a –er on*, dämpfen, entmutigen, lähmend wirken. **–ing,** *s.* die Dämpfung (*Phys., Elec.*). **–ish,** *adj.* etwas feucht, dumpfig. **–ness,** *s.* die Feuchtigkeit. **– -proof,** *adj.* beständig gegen Feuchtigkeit, vor Nässe schützend, gegen Feuchtigkeit geschützt. **–s,** *pl. see* **fire- –.**

damsel [ˈdæmzəl], *s.* (*Poet.*) junges Mädchen, das Fräulein, die Jungfrau.

damson [ˈdæmzən], *s.* die Damaszenerpflaume.

danc-e [dɑːns], 1. *v.a.* tanzen; *–e up and down*, wiegen, schaukeln (*baby*); *–e attendance upon* or *on a p.*, bei einem antichambrieren, einem den Hof machen. 2. *v.n.* tanzen; hüpfen (*for joy*). 3. *s.* der Tanz; die Tanzmusik; die Tanzgesellschaft, der Ball; *–e of death*, der Totentanz; *lead the –e*, den Reigen eröffnen; (*coll.*) *lead a p. a –e*, einem viele Mühe bereiten, einen von Pontius zu Pilatus schicken; *St. Vitus's –e*, der Veitstanz. **–e-hall,** *s.* das Tanzlokal. **–e-music,** *s.* die Tanzmusik. **–er,** *s.* der Tänzer. **–ing,** *s.* das Tanzen. **–ing-girl,** *s.* die Tänzerin. **–ing-lesson,** *s.* die Tanzstunde. **–ing-master,** *s.* der Tanzlehrer. **–ing-school,** *s.* die Tanzschule.

dandelion [ˈdændɪlɑɪən], *s.* der Löwenzahn (*Bot.*).

dander [ˈdændə], *s.* (*coll.*) der Zorn, Ärger; *get a p.'s – up*, einen in Wut *or* Harnisch bringen.

dandified [ˈdændɪfɑɪd], *adj.* stutzerhaft, ausgeputzt; *see* **dandy.**

dandle [ˈdændl], *v.a.* auf dem Schoße, auf den Knien *or* in den Armen schaukeln (*a child*).

dandruff [ˈdændrʌf], *s.* der (Kopf)Schorf, Kopfschuppen (*pl.*).

dandy [ˈdændɪ], 1. *s.* der Stutzer, Geck, Modenarr; die Schaluppe mit Treibmast (*Naut.*). 2. *adj.* (*sl.*) großartig, erstklassig (*Amer.*). **–ish,** *adj.* geckenhaft, stutzerhaft. **–ism,** *s.* stutzerhaftes Wesen. **– -roll,** *s.* die Draht(sieb)walze (*Pap.*).

danger ['deɪndʒə], *s.* die Gefahr (*to*, für), Not; *be in – of falling*, Gefahr laufen zu fallen; *in case of –*, im Falle der Not; *go in – of one's life*, in Lebensgefahr schweben. **– area**, das Alarmgebiet, Warngebiet; Sperrgebiet. **–ous** [–rəs], *adj.* gefährlich, gefahrvoll (*to*, für). **– point**, der Gefahrenpunkt. **– signal**, das Notsignal. **– zone**, bestrichener Raum (*Mil.*).
dangle [dæŋgl], 1. *v.n.* (herab)hängen, baumeln, schlenkern mit; *– after girls*, den Mädchen nachlaufen. 2. *v.a.* baumeln lassen, schlenkern.
dank [dæŋk], *adj.* dunstig, dumpfig, feucht, naßkalt.
dapper ['dæpə], *adj.* niedlich, nett; schmuck, flink.
dapple [dæpl], 1. *v.a.* sprenkeln, tüpfeln, scheckig machen. **–d**, *adj.* bunt, scheckig. **--gray**, 1. *adj.* apfelgrau. 2. *s.* (*horse*) der Apfelschimmel.
darbies ['dɑ:bɪz], *pl.* (*sl.*) Handschellen (*pl.*).
dar–e [dɛə], 1. *v.n.* wagen, sich erkühnen, sich erdreisten, sich getrauen, sich unterstehen; *he –e not do it, he does not –e to do it*, er wagt es nicht zu tun; *if I may –e to say so*, wenn ich so sagen darf; *I –e say*, ich gebe zu, ich glaube wohl; *I –e not tell him*, ich getraue mich *or* mir nicht, es ihm zu sagen; *how –e you?* wie können Sie sich unterstehen? 2. *v.a.* herausfordern; trotzen (*Dat.*), Trotz bieten (*Dat.*), unternehmen, riskieren. **–e-devil**, 1. *s.* der Teufelskerl, Wagehals. 2. *adj.* wag(e)halsig, tollkühn. **–ing**, 1. *adj.* kühn, tapfer, wagemutig, verwegen; dreist, unverschämt, anmaßend. 2. *s.* die (Toll)Kühnheit, der Wagemut; die Verwegenheit, Dreistigkeit.
dark [dɑ:k], 1. *adj.* dunkel, finster; schwarz, schwärzlich (*in colour*); brünett (*hair*); geheimnisvoll, verborgen, unklar, unaufgeklärt; trostlos, düster, trübe; blind; böse, verbrecherisch, schwarz (*deed*); *the – ages*, frühes Mittelalter; *--browed, adj.* streng, ernst, finster; *--eyed, adj.* dunkeläugig; (*coll.*) *he is a – horse*, er hat es dick hinter den Ohren; *keep s.th. –*, etwas geheim halten; *– lantern*, die Blendlaterne; *look on the – side*, schwarzsehen; *– slide*, die Kassette (*Phot.*). 2. *s.* das Dunkel, die Dunkelheit; (*pl.*) die Schatten (*Paint.*); *after –*, nach Eintritt der Dunkelheit; *a leap in the –*, ein Sprung ins Ungewisse; (*fig.*) *leave a p. in the –*, einen in Ungewißheit lassen. **–en**, 1. *v.a.* verdunkeln, verfinstern, abblenden; nachdunkeln, abdunkeln (*colours*); (*fig.*) verdüstern, trüben, schwärzen; *I shall never –en his doors again*, ich werde seine Schwelle nie wieder betreten. 2. *v.n.* dunkel werden, dunkeln. **–ish**, *adj.* schwärzlich (*of colour*); etwas dunkel, trübe; dämmerig. **–ling**, 1. *adv.* im Dunkeln. 2. *adj.* dunkel; (*fig.*) düster. **–ness**, *s.* die Finsternis, Dunkelheit; (*fig.*) Unwissenheit, Undeutlichkeit, Verborgenheit; *powers of –ness*, die Mächte der Finsternis. **--room**, *s.* die Dunkelkammer (*Phot.*). **–some**, *adj.* (*Poet.*) finster, dunkel, trübe. **–y** *s.* (*pej.*) Schwarze(r), *m.* der Neger.
darling ['dɑ:lɪŋ], 1. *adj.* teuer, lieb; Herzens–, Lieblings–. 2. *s.* der Liebling, Schatz, das Herzblatt; *– of fortune*, das Glückskind.
darn [dɑ:n], 1. *v.a.* stopfen, ausbessern. 2. *s.* das Gestopfte, gestopftes Loch. **–er**, *s.* die Stopfnadel; das Stopfei, die Stopfkugel. **–ing**, *s.* das Stopfen; *–ing needle*, die Stopfnadel; *–ing wool*, das Stopfgarn.
darnel ['dɑ:nəl], *s.* der Lolch (*Bot.*).
dart [dɑ:t], 1. *s.* der Wurfspieß, Speer; Pfeil; abgenähte Falte, der Abnäher (*in skirts*); plötzliche Bewegung, der Sturz, Sprung; (*pl.*) das Pfeilwurfspiel; *make a – for*, losstürzen auf. 2. *v.a.* schleudern, werfen; schießen; *– a glance at a p.*, einem einen Blick zuwerfen. 3. *v.n.* fliegen, schießen, sich plötzlich bewegen; sich stürzen, losstürmen (*at, on*, auf (*Acc.*)), herfallen (über (*Acc.*)); *– forth*, hervorschießen, hervorbrechen (*from*, aus). **–er**, *s.* der Schlangenhalsvogel (*Orn.*); Spritzfisch (*Icht.*). **–s-board**, *s.* das Zielbrett fürs Pfeilwurfspiel.
dash [dæʃ], 1. *v.a.* schlagen, stoßen, schmeißen, schleudern, werfen (*an*, auf (*Acc.*), gegen); zerschlagen, zerschmettern; übergießen, bespritzen, ausschütten (*water*); (*fig.*) zerstören, vernichten, vereiteln vermischen, vermengen; *– a p.'s hopes*, seine Hoffnungen zunichte machen; *– a p.'s spirits*, einen niederschlagen *or* entmutigen; *– it!* verwünscht! 2. *v.n.* stoßen, schlagen; (sich) stürzen. **– about**, umherjagen. **– against**, schlagen, stoßen, rennen (an *or* gegen eine S.); scheitern (an (*Dat.*)). **– away**, davonstürzen, wegeilen. **– by** *a p.*, an einem vorbeieilen. **– into**, hineinstürzen in, einbrechen in (*Acc.*). **– off**, hinwegeilen, dahinsprengen; (*coll.*) *– off a th.*, etwas flüchtig entwerfen, aufs Papier werfen, in aller Eile schreiben. **– out** *a p.'s brains*, einem den Schädel einschlagen. **– over**, überlaufen; *the water –ed over the ship's side*, das Wasser stürzte über die Seiten des Schiffes. **– through**, sich stürzen durch (*the room, etc.*); *– the pen through a line*, eine Zeile durchstreichen *or* ausstreichen. 3. *s.* das Schlagen, Stoßen, Fallen; der Aufschlag, Angriff, Anlauf, Vorstoß; die Kühnheit, der Schneid, Elan, Glanz, die Eleganz; der Federstrich, Gedankenstrich; Strich (*Mus., Tele.*); die Beimischung, der Schuß, Zuschuß, Anflug; *coffee –*, Kaffee verkehrt; (*coll.*) *cut a –*, eine Rolle spielen, von sich reden machen; *a – of eccentricity*, ein Anflug von Überspanntheit; *make a – for*, losgehen auf; *at one –*, mit einem Schlage *or* Zuge, auf einmal. **--board**, *s.* das Armaturenbrett, Schaltbrett, Instrumentenbrett. **–er**, *s.* der Butterstößel. **–ing**, *adj.* schneidig, forsch, ungestüm, feurig, stürmisch (*attack*); klatschend, platschend, rauschend; (*coll.*) elegant glänzend, fesch, patent.
dastard ['dæstəd], *s.* der Feigling, die Memme. **–liness**, *s.* die Feigheit. **–ly**, *adj.* feig; heimtückisch.
data ['deɪtə], *pl.* Werte, Daten, Angaben, Unterlagen, Grundlagen; *see* **datum.**
[1]**date** [deɪt], 1. *s.* das Datum, die Zeitangabe; der Monatstag, die Jahreszahl; Zeit, Epoche, der Zeitpunkt, Termin, die Frist, Verfall(s)zeit eines Wechsels (*C.L.*); *two months after –*, zwei Monate nach dato von heute (*C.L.*); *at an early –*, in nicht zu langer Zeit; *fix a –*, eine Zeit festsetzen, eine Frist bestimmen; (*sl.*) *have a – with s.o.*, ein Stelldichein *or* eine Verabredung mit einem haben; (*sl.*) *make a –*, sich verabreden; *of this –*, vom heutigen Datum; *of recent –*, modern, neu; *out of –*, veraltet; *at a long –*, auf lange Sicht (*C.L.*); (*down*) *to –*, bis auf den heutigen Tag; *up to –*, zeitgemäß, modern, auf die *or* der Höhe der Zeit. 2. *v.a.* datieren; rechnen; herleiten; Zeit ansetzen *or* festsetzen für; (*coll.*) *we've got him –ed*, wir kennen unsere Pappenheimer. 3. *v.n.* das Datum tragen, datiert sein; *– back*, zurückreichen *or* zurückgehen (*to*, auf *or* bis); sich herleiten (*from*, von), zurückgehen (*from*, auf (*Acc.*)). **–less**, *adj.* ohne Datum, undatiert; zeitlos. **--line**, *s.* die Datumsgrenze. **--stamp**, *s.* der Poststempel, Datumstempel.
[2]**date**, *s.* die Dattel. **--palm**, *s.* die Dattelpalme.
dative ['deɪtɪv], 1. *s.* (*– case*) der Wemfall, Dativ. 2. *adv.* dativisch, Dativ–; verfügbar, gerichtlich bestellt, vergebbar (*Law*).
datum ['deɪtəm], *s.* gegebene Tatsache *or* Größe (*Math.*); die Grundlage; *– line*, die Grundlinie; *– point*, der Bezugspunkt.
daub [dɔ:b], 1. *v.a.* verputzen, bewerfen, beschmieren, überziehen; schmieren, klecksen, sudeln. 2. *v.n.* schmieren, klecksen (*Paint.*). 3. *s.* der Klecks; die Kleckserei, Schmiererei, Sudelei, das Geschmier (*Paint.*); der Lehm. **–er**, *s.* der Schmierer, Farbenkleckser.
daughter ['dɔ:tə], *s.* die Tochter. **–ly**, *adj.* töchterlich. **--in-law**, *s.* die Schwiegertochter.
daunt [dɔ:nt], *v.a.* entmutigen, einschüchtern, schrecken. **–less**, *adj.* furchtlos, unerschrocken.
davenport ['dævnpɔ:t], *s.* der Schreibtisch, Sekretär.
davit ['dævɪt], *s.* (*usually pl.*) der Davit, Bootskran (*Naut.*).
davy ['deɪvɪ], *s.* (*coll.*) der Eid; (*coll.*) *on my –!* auf mein Wort. *--Jones's locker*, *s.* (*coll.*) das Grab in Meerestiefe.
daw [dɔ:], *s.* die Dohle (*Orn.*).
dawdle ['dɔ:dl], 1. *v.n.* bummeln, trödeln; *– one's time away*, die Zeit vertrödeln *or* totschlagen. 2. *s.*,

–r, *s.* der Müßiggänger, Bummler, Trödler, Tagedieb, die Schlafmütze.

dawn [dɔːn], 1. *s.* die (Morgen)Dämmerung, das Morgengrauen, der Tagesanbruch; (*fig.*) Beginn, das Erwachen. 2. *v.n.* dämmern, tagen; *when day –ed*, als der Tag anbrach; *it –ed upon me*, es kam mir zum Bewußtsein, es ging mir ein Licht auf. **–ing,** 1. *s.* (*poet*) *see* – 1. 2. *adj.* dämmernd, beginnend, erwachend.

day [deɪ], *s.* der Tag; das Tageslicht; (*often pl.*) die Lebenszeit, Zeit; der Termin, festgesetzter Tag; **1.** (*with nouns & adjectives*) *all the –*, den ganzen Tag; *every –*, alle Tage; *every second –*, alle zwei Tage, einen Tag um den andern; *end one's –s*, sterben; *fall on evil –s*, ins Unglück geraten; *–s of grace*, Verzugstage (*Law*), Respekttage (*C.L.*); *have had one's –*, überlebt sein; *every dog has his –*, alles hat seine Zeit; *intercalary –*, der Schalttag; *one –*, eines Tages, einst; *one of these –s*, in diesen Tagen, nächstens; *the other –*, neulich; *order of the –*, die Tagesordnung; *some –*, eines Tages, der(mal)einst (*future time*); *some – or other*, irgendeinmal; *student –s*, die Studentenzeit; *what's the time of –?* wie spät ist es?; (*coll.*) *know the time of –*, sich auskennen, genau Bescheid wissen; *win the –*, den Sieg davontragen. **2.** (*without prepositions*) *– and – about*, jeden zweiten Tag; (*coll.*) *call it a –!* mach Schluß! *have a fine – of it*, sich einen vergnügten Tag machen; *thirty if a –*, mindestens 30 Jahre alt; *this many a –*, jetzt schon lange Zeit; *this – month*, heute in *or* über vier Wochen; *this – week*, heute über acht Tage; *this – last week*, heute vor acht Tagen; *these –s*, heutzutage; *a – off*, ein freier Tag; *twice a –*, zweimal am Tage. **3.** (*with prepositions*) *the – after*, tags darauf; *the – after tomorrow*, übermorgen; *– after –, – by –*, Tag für Tag, täglich; *the – before*, tags vorher; *the – before yesterday*, vorgestern; *by –*, bei Tage; *by the –*, tagesweise; *for ever and a –*, für immer und ewig; *from this – forth* or *forward*, von heute an; *from – to –*, von Tag zu Tag; *from one – to another*, von einem Tag zum andern; *in all my born –s*, mein Lebtag; *in his –*, (zu) seiner Zeit, in seinen Tagen; *in those –s*, damals; *– in – out*, tagaus tagein; *in these –s*, heutzutage; *in (the) –s of old*, vormals, in alten Zeiten; *in –s to come*, in zukünftigen Zeiten; *late in the –*, reichlich spät; (*coll.*) *all in the –'s work*, es gehört alles mit dazu; *– to –*, ununterbrochen, dauernd; *– to – money*, tägliches Geld (*C.L.*); *to a –*, (genau) auf den Tag; *to this –*, bis auf den heutigen Tag. **––boarder,** *s.* der Halbpensionär. **–book,** *s.* das Tagebuch, Journal (*C.L.*). **––boy,** *s.* der Tagschüler. **–break,** *s.* der Tagesanbruch. **––dream,** *s.* wacher Traum, die Träumerei; (*pl.*) Phantasiegebilde, Luftschlösser. **––fly,** *s.* die Eintagsfliege. **––labourer,** *s.* der Tag(e)löhner. **–light,** *s.* das Tageslicht, Sonnenlicht; der Zwischenraum; *–light printing paper*, das Lichtpauspapier (*Phot.*); *–light saving*, die Sommerzeit, vorverlegte Stundenzählung; *in broad –light*, am hellen lichten Tage; *as clear as –light*, sonnenklar; (*fig.*) *he begins to see –light*, ihm geht ein Licht auf. **––nursery,** *s.* der Kleinkindergarten. **––out,** *s.* freier Tag, der Ausgang. **––scholar,** *s. see* **––boy.** **––school,** *s.* die Tagesschule, das Externat. **––shift,** *s.* die Tagschicht. **–'s-journey,** *s.* die Tagereise. **–'s run,** *s.* das Etmal (*Naut.*). **––star,** *s.* der Morgenstern. **–'s-work,** *s.* das Tagewerk; (*coll.*) *it's all in the –'s work*, das gehört mit dazu, das muß man mit in Kauf nehmen. **–time,** *s.* der Tag, die Tageszeit; *in the –time*, bei Tage.

daze [deɪz], 1. *v.a.* blenden; betäuben, verwirren. 2. *s.* die Betäubung, Verwirrung, Bestürzung.

dazzl-e [ˈdæzl], *v.a.* blenden. **–e-painting,** *s.* die Tarnung (*Mil.*). **–ing,** *adj.* blendend, grell.

deacon [ˈdiːkən], *s.* der Diakon. **–ess,** *s.* die Diakonisse. **–ry,** *s.* das Diakonat.

dead [dɛd], 1. *adj.* tot, gestorben (*of persons*); leblos, kraftlos, wirkungslos; empfindungslos (*of things*); unempfindlich (*to*, für); leer, öde (*of a district*); abgestorben, dürr (*as plants*); still, flau (*C.L.*); glanzlos, matt, trüb, stumpf, unbelebt (*of colours*); dumpf (*of sound*); verloschen (*as a fire*); tief (*of sleep*); *– as a door-nail*, mausetot; *– angle*, toter Winkel; *– ball*, der Ball außer Spiel; *– bargain*, der Spottpreis, spottbillige Ware; *– body*, der Leichnam; *– calm*, völlige Windstille, die Flaute; *– centre*, toter Punkt; *– certainty*, völlige Gewißheit; *– colouring*, die Grundierung (*Paint.*); *– gold*, mattes Gold; *– ground*, unter totem Winkel liegendes Gelände (*Mil.*); *– heat*, totes *or* unentschiedenes Rennen; *– level*, einförmige Ebene; (*fig.*) die Eintönigkeit, Wirkungslosigkeit; *– load*, die Eigenbelastung, das Eigengewicht; *– loss*, der Totalverlust; *be a – man*, ein Kind des Todes sein; *– men*, (*sl.*) leere Flaschen; *as – as mutton*, mausetot; *– point*, toter Punkt (*Mach.*); *– reckoning*, die Gissung, gegißtes Besteck, der Koppelkurs; *position by – reckoning*, gegißter *or* gekoppelter Standort; *– Sea*, Totes Meer; (*fig.*) *– Sea apples* or *fruit*, Sodomsäpfel (*pl.*); täuschender Reiz, die Täuschung; *– season*, geschäftslose Zeit; *– secret*, tiefes Geheimnis; *– set*, das Stehen (*of a dog*) (*Hunt.*), (*fig.*) entschlossener Angriff; *shoot a p. –*, einen totschießen; *– shot*, der Meisterschütze; *– silence*, die Totenstille; *– steam*, der Abdampf, Abgangsdampf; *– stock*, totes Inventar; unverkaufbare Waren (*pl.*); *come to a – stop*, plötzlich anhalten; *strike –*, erschlagen; *– water*, der Sog, das Kielwasser; *– weight*, das Eigengewicht; (*fig.*) schwere, drückende Last. *– wood*, *s.* das Reisig, (*fig.*) wertloser Plunder. 2. *adv.* völlig, absolut; *be – against*, stark voreingenommen sein gegen; (*coll.*) *– beat*, gänzlich erschöpft, kaputt; (*coll.*) *cut s.o. –*, einen schneiden, einen wie Luft behandeln; *– drunk*, völlig betrunken; *– slow*, langsame Fahrt (*Naut.*); (*fig.*) ganz langsam; *stop –*, plötzlich stehenbleiben; *– sure*, todsicher; *– tired*, todmüde. 3. *s.* die Totenstille; *in the – of the night*, mitten in der Nacht; *in the – of winter*, im tiefsten Winter; *the –*, die Toten (*pl.*); *risen from the –*, von den Toten (*or* vom Tode) auferstanden. **––alive,** *adj.*, **––and-alive,** *adj.* halbtot, langweilig. **––beat,** *s.* (*sl.*) der Schmarotzer (*Amer.*). **–en,** *v.a.* (ab)schwächen, dämpfen, abstumpfen (*sounds, feelings, etc.*); abmatten, mattieren (*gold, etc.*). **––end,** *s.* die Sackgasse. **––eye,** *s.* die Jungfer (*Naut.*). **–head,** *s.* (*sl.*) der Freikarteninhaber; blinder Passagier; der Nassauer. **––letter,** *s.* ungültig gewordenes Gesetz; unbestellbarer Brief; toter Buchstabe; *––letter office*, das Amt für unbestellbare Briefe. **–light,** *s.* der Lukendeckel, die Blende vor dem Kajütenfenster (*Naut.*). **–line,** *s.* der Redaktionsschluß, Drucktermin, Stichtag; (*fig.*) äußerste Grenze, äußerster Termin. **–liness,** *s.* die Tödlichkeit, das Tödliche. **–lock,** *s.* das Riegelschloß; (*fig.*) der Stillstand, völlige Stockung; *come to a –lock*, steckenbleiben, ergebnislos verlaufen, auf ein totes Geleise kommen, an einen toten Punkt gelangen. **–ly** [ˈdɛdlɪ], *adj.* tödlich, todbringend, äußerst schädlich, giftig; unversöhnlich; (*coll.*) äußerst, außerordentlich; *–ly enemy*, der Todfeind; *–ly pale*, totenblaß; *–ly sin*, die Todsünde; *–ly tired*, äußerst müde, todmüde. **–ly-nightshade,** *s.* die Tollkirsche (*Bot.*). **––march,** *s.* der Trauermarsch. **–ness** [ˈdɛdnɪs], *s.* die Erstarrung, Leblosigkeit; Mattheit, Flauheit (*of trade*); Empfindungslosigkeit, Abgestumpftheit. **––nettle,** *s.* die Taubnessel (*Bot.*).

deaf [dɛf], *adj.* taub, schwerhörig; *as – as a post*, stocktaub; *– and dumb*, taubstumm; *turn a – ear to*, taub sein gegen; *– in one ear*, auf einem Ohre taub; *fall on – ears*, kein Gehör finden; *– to*, taub *or* unempfindlich gegen. **–en** [dɛfn], *v.a.* taub machen; betäuben. **––mute,** 1. *adj.* taubstumm. 2. *s.* Taubstumme(r), *m.* **–ness,** *s.* die Taubheit (*to* gegen).

¹deal [diːl], 1. *ir.v.a.* (*usually* – out) aus- *or* zuteilen; geben (*cards*); *– a p. a blow*, einem eins versetzen. 2. *ir.v.n.* handeln, Handel treiben (*in*, in *or* mit); geben (*cards*); *– in foodstuffs*, Lebensmittel führen; *– in politics*, sich mit Politik abgeben; *– with a th.*, etwas behandeln, sich mit etwas befassen, von etwas handeln; *– with a p.*, mit einem verfahren *or* verkehren, bei einem kaufen, mit einem Geschäfte machen *or* zu tun haben; einen behandeln; *I will – with it at once*, ich nehme es sofort in Angriff; *– with difficulties*, mit Schwierigkeiten kämpfen; –

fairly with, anständig behandeln; *it was –t with out of hand*, es wurde kurz abgefertigt, man machte kurzen Prozeß damit. 3. *s.* die Anzahl, Menge, Masse (*only with attrib. adj.*); das (Karten)Geben (*cards*); der Handel; das Geschäft (*C.L.*); die Abmachung, das Abkommen; (*sl.*) *a* – (*of*), viel, weit; (*coll.*) *do a – with*, einen Abschluß machen mit; *a fair* –, anständige Behandlung; *a good* –, ziemlich viel, beträchtlich; *a great* –, sehr viel; *make a great – of a p.*, viel Wesens von einem machen; *think a great – of a p.*, einen hochschätzen, große Stücke auf einen halten; *it's a – !* es gilt! abgemacht! *it's my* –, ich muß geben; *the New* –, (Roosevelts) neue Wirtschaftspolitik; (*sl.*) *raw* –, unfaire Behandlung. **–er,** *s.* der Händler, Krämer; Kartengeber; *double-–er*, der Schieber. **–ing,** *s.* das Austeilen; (*generally pl.*) das Verfahren, die Handlungsweise, Behandlung; der Umgang, Verkehr; das Geschäft, der Handel (*C.L.*); *have –ings with*, mit einem zu tun haben; *there's no –ing with him*, es ist mit ihm nicht auszukommen.

²deal, 1. *s.* die Diele, Bohle, das Brett (*of pine wood*); das Tannenholz, Kiefernholz. 2. *adj.* Kiefern–, Tannen–.

dealt [dɛlt], *see* **¹deal.**

dean [di:n], *s.* der Dechant, Dekan (*also Univ.*); Vorsteher eines Domkapitels. **–ery,** *s.* die Dekanei, Dechantenwürde, Dekanswürde; das Amtshaus eines Dechanten.

dear [dɪə], 1. *adj. & adv.* teuer, kostbar, kostspielig; lieb, teuer, wert, wertvoll; (*coll.*) *there's a – child!* sei lieb! sei artig! *it cost him* –, es kam ihm teuer zu stehen; – *Doctor*, sehr geehrter Herr Doktor! *for – life*, als wenn es ums Leben ginge; – *Madam*, gnädige Frau! *near and* –, nahestehend (*to* (*Dat.*)); *pay – for*, teuer bezahlen; – *Sir*, sehr geehrter Herr! 2. *s.* der Liebling, Schatz; *my* –, meine Liebe *or* Teure; *Lizzie is a* –, Lieschen ist ein gutes Kind *or* ein Engel; *the poor* –, der *or* die Ärmste; *there's a – !* sei doch so nett! 3. *interj.*; *oh – !, – me !, – –!*, du liebe Zeit! ach je! **–ie,** *s.* (*coll.*) das Liebchen, die Liebste. **–ly,** *adv. see* –; *–ly beloved*, innig geliebt, heißgeliebt; *–ly bought*, teuer erkauft. **–ness,** *s.* die Kostspieligkeit; teurer Preis, hoher Wert; *her –ness to me*, ihr Wert für mich, meine Liebe für sie.

dearth [də:θ], *s.* der Mangel, die Teu(e)rung.

death [dɛθ], *s.* der Tod, das Sterben; der Todesfall (*pl. –s*, Todesfälle); *in at the* –, (*fig.*) den Schluß mitmachen *or* miterleben; *bleed to* –, sich verbluten; (*coll.*) *catch one's* –, sich (*Dat.*) den Tod holen; *certificate of* –, der Totenschein; *die the – of a hero*, den Heldentod sterben; *do a p. to* –, einen töten; *be at –'s door*, an der Schwelle des Todes sein, in den letzten Zügen liegen; *hour of* –, die Todesstunde; (*coll.*) *it will be the – of me*, es wird mein Tod sein; *at the point of* –, see *at –'s door*; *put to* –, hinrichten; *send a p. to his* –, einen dem Tod entgegenschicken; *sick to – of a th.*, einer S. überdrüssig; *as sure as* –, totsicher, bombensicher; *tired to* –, todmüde. **–-agony,** *s.* der Todeskampf. **–-bed,** *s.* das Sterbebett, Totenbett. **–-blow,** *s.* der Todesstreich; (*fig.*) Todesstoß. **–-dealing,** *adj.* tötend, tödlich. **–-duty,** die Nachlaßsteuer, Erbschaftssteuer. **–-knell,** *s.* die Sterbeglocke, das Totengeläut; (*fig.*) *sound the –-knell*, das letzte Stündlein läuten, den Rest geben. **–less,** *adj.* unsterblich. **–lessness,** *s.* die Unsterblichkeit. **–-like, –ly,** *adj.* totenähnlich, Toten–, Todes–; *–ly pale*, totenblaß. **–-mask,** *s.* die Totenmaske. **–-penalty,** *s.* die Todesstrafe. **–-rate,** *s.* die Sterblichkeitsziffer. **–-rattle,** *s.* das Todesröcheln. **–-ray,** *s.* der Todesstrahl. **–-roll,** *s.* die Verlustliste, Gefallenenliste, Totenliste, Zahl der Todesopfer. **–-sentence,** *s.* das Todesurteil. **–'s-head,** *s.* der Totenkopf (*also Ent.*). **–-throes,** *pl.* der Todeskampf. **–-trap,** *s.* lebensgefährlicher Platz *or* Raum or Bau. **–-warrant,** *s.* der Hinrichtungsbefehl; das Todesurteil (*also fig.*). **–-watch,** *s.* der Klopfkäfer, die Totenuhr (*Ent.*).

débâcle [dɪˈbɑ:kl], *s.* der Zusammenbruch, Untergang; die Mure, der Eisgang, Bodenfluß, Murgang (*Geol.*).

debar [dɪˈbɑ:], *v.a.* ausschließen (*from*, von), hindern (*from doing*, zu tun); *he is –red the liberty . . .*, ihm ist die Freiheit . . . versagt; – *o.s. of a pleasure*, sich (*Dat.*) ein Vergnügen versagen.

debase [dɪˈbeɪs], *v.a.* verschlechtern, verderben; denaturieren (*Chem.*), fälschen (*coin*). **–ment,** *s.* die Verschlechterung, Verringerung, Verfälschung; Erniedrigung, Entwürdigung.

debat-able [dɪˈbeɪtəbl], *adj.* anfechtbar, strittig, fraglich; *–able claims*, bestreitbare Ansprüche; *–able ground*, umstrittenes Gebiet. **–e** [dɪˈbeɪt], 1. *s.* der Wortstreit, die Debatte, Verhandlung (*Parl.*). 2. *v.a.* debattieren, disputieren, erörtern. 3. *v.n.* debattieren; *–e with o.s.*, bei sich überlegen. **–er,** *s.* der Disputant, Debattierende(r), *m.* **–ing-club, –ing-society,** *s.* der Debattierklub.

debauch [dɪˈbɔ:tʃ], 1. *v.a.* verführen, verleiten; (moralisch) verderben. 2. *s.* die Schwelgerei, Ausschweifung. **–ed,** *adj.* verderbt, ausschweifend, liederlich, unzüchtig. **–ee** [dɛbɔ:ˈtʃi:], *s.* der Wüstling, Schwelger. **–er,** *s.* der Verführer. **–ery,** *s.* die Schwelgerei, Ausschweifung, Liederlichkeit.

debenture [dɪˈbɛntʃə], *s.* der Schuldschein, die Schuldverschreibung, Obligation; der Rückzollschein (*customs*); – *bonds*, festverzinsliche Schuldverschreibungen. **–d,** *adj.* Rückzoll–.

debilit-ate [dɪˈbɪlɪteɪt], *v.a.* schwächen, entkräften. **–ation** [–ˈteɪʃən], *s.* die Schwächung. **–y** [dɪˈbɪlɪtɪ], *s.* die Schwäche (*in health*).

debit [ˈdɛbɪt], 1. *s.* das Soll, Debet; der Schuldposten; die Kontobelastung; Debetseite (*of a ledger*); *to the – of a p.'s account*, zu jemandes Lasten; *place a sum to a p.'s* –, jemandes Konto mit einer Summe belasten; – *and credit*, Soll und Haben; – *side*, die Debetseite, das Debetkonto; – *slip*, der Belastungszettel. 2. *v.a.* belasten, debitieren (*with*, mit), zur Last schreiben (*to a p.*, einem).

debonair [dɛboˈnɛə], *adj.* artig, anmutig, höflich, freundlich, heiter, gutmütig, gutherzig.

debouch [dɪˈbu:ʃ], *v.n.* hervorbrechen, herauskommen, debouchieren (*Mil.*); sich ergießen, einmünden (*into*, in) (*of a river*). **–ment,** *s.* das Hervorbrechen (*Mil.*); die Mündung.

débris [ˈdɛbri:], *s.* Überbleibsel, Bruchstücke (*pl.*); Trümmer (*pl.*) (*Geol.*).

debt [dɛt], *s.* die Schuld (*also fig.*); Verpflichtung, Pflicht; (*a*) (*with nouns*) – *of gratitude*, die Dankesschuld; – *of honour*, die Ehrenschuld; *pay the – of* or *one's – to nature*, sterben; (*b*) (*with adjectives*) *active –s*, Außenstände (*pl.*); *–s active and passive*, Aktiva und Passiva; *bad –s*, schlechte Außenstände (*pl.*); *floating* –, schwebende Schuld *or* Forderung; *national* –, die Staatsschuld; *outstanding –s*, see *active –s*; (*c*) (*with verbs*) *be in* –, verschuldet sein; *be in a p.'s* –, einem schuldig *or* verpflichtet sein; *contract* or *incur –s*, see *run up –s*; *honour a* –, eine Schuld begleichen; *place a p. in one's* –, sich (*Dat.*) einen verpflichten; *run into* –, in Schulden geraten; *run up –s*, Schulden machen. **–or,** *s.* der Schuldner, Debitor; *–or side*, die Debetseite.

debunk [di:ˈbʌŋk], *v.a.* (*sl.*) niedriger hängen, entlarven, des Nimbus berauben.

début [ˈdeby:], *s.* erstes Auftreten, das Debüt. **–ant,** *s.* der Debütant. **–ante** [deby:ˈtɑ:nt], *s.* die Debütantin.

decade [ˈdɛkəd], *s.* das Jahrzehnt; die Zehnergruppe.

decaden-ce [ˈdɛkədəns], *s.* der Verfall, Zerfall, die Abnahme; Dekadenz. **–t,** *adj.* verfallend, im Verfall begriffen, angekränkelt; dekadent.

deca-gon [ˈdɛkəgən], *s.* das Zehneck. **–gram(me),** *s.* das Dekagramm. **–hedron** [dɛkəˈhi:drən], *s.* der Zehnflächner, Dekaeder. **–litre,** *s.* der Dekaliter. **–logue,** [ˈdɛkəlɔg], *s.* die zehn Gebote (*pl.*), der Dekalog. **–metre,** *s.* der *or* das Dekameter. **–pod,** *s.* der Zehnfüßer. **–syllabic,** *adj.* zehnsilbig. **–thlon,** *s.* der Zehnkampf (*of the Greeks*).

decalcify [di:ˈkælsɪfaɪ], *v.a.* entkalken.

decamp [dɪˈkæmp], *v.n.* Lager abbrechen *or* verlassen; (*coll.*) sich aus dem Staube machen, sich davonmachen, ausreißen, türmen. **–ment,** *s.* der Aufbruch, das Abmarschieren aus dem Lager.

decant [dɪˈkænt], *v.a.* umfüllen, abfüllen, abgießen, abklären, abziehen, dekantieren. **–ation,** *s.* das

Abgießen, Umfüllen. **–er,** *s.* die Karaffe (*for wine*).

decapitat–e [dɪˈkæpɪteɪt], *v.a.* enthaupten, köpfen. **–ion,** *s.* die Enthauptung.

decapod [ˈdɛkəpɔd], *see under* **deca–.**

decarbonize [dɪːˈkɑ.bənɑɪz], *v.a.* entkohlen, von Kohlenstoff befreien.

decasyllabic [dɛkəsɪˈlæbɪk], *see under* **deca–.**

decathlon [dəˈkæθlən], *see under* **deca–.**

decay [dɪˈkeɪ], 1. *v.n.* verfallen, zerfallen, verderben, in Verfall geraten; verwesen, (ver)modern, verfaulen, schlecht werden (*of teeth*); (*fig.*) abnehmen, sinken 2. *s.* die Verwesung, Fäule, Fäulnis, Zersetzung; das Schlechtwerden (*of teeth*); der Verfall, die Abnahme; das Verblühen; *fall into* –, in Verfall geraten. **–ed** [–d], *adj.* faul, morsch, angefault, verfault; verfallen, verblüht, heruntergekommen; schlecht, hohl (*of teeth*).

decease [dɪˈsɪːs], 1. *s.* das Hinscheiden, Ableben, der Tod. 2. *v.n.* sterben, verscheiden. **–d** [–t], 1. *s.* Verstorbene(r), *m.*, Tote(r), *m.*, Hingeschiedene(r), *m.* 2 *adj.* verstorben.

decei–t [dɪˈsɪːt], *s.* die Täuschung, Falschheit, List, Tücke, der Betrug, Trug; die Betrügerei, Ränke (*pl.*). **–tful,** *adj.* trügerisch, (hinter)listig, falsch. **–tfulness,** *s.* die Falschheit; Hinterlist, Arglist; Ränke (*pl.*), das Trügerische. **–vable** [dɪˈsɪː-vəbl], *adj.* leicht zu betrügen(d). **–ve** [–ˈsɪːv], *v.a.* täuschen, betrügen, hintergehen; *be –ved*, sich täuschen lassen, sich irren (*in*, in (*Dat.*)); *–ve o.s.*, sich täuschen.

decelerat–e [dɪːˈsɛləreɪt], 1. *v.a.* verlangsamen, die Geschwindigkeit vermindern. 2. *v n.* sich verlangsamen, die Geschwindigkeit verringern, langsamer fahren. **–ion,** *s.* die Geschwindigkeitsverminderung.

dec–ember [dɪˈsɛmbə], *s.* der Dezember. **–emvir** [dɪˈsɛmvə], *s.* der Dezemvir. **–emvirate** [–rɪt], *s.* das Dezemvirat. **–ennary** [dɪˈsɛnərɪ], *s. see* **–ennium. –ennial** [dɪˈsɛnjəl], *adj.* zehnjährig. **–ennially,** *adv.* alle zehn Jahre. **–ennium** [dɪˈsɛnɪəm], *s.* das Jahrzehnt.

decen–cy [ˈdɪːsnsɪ], *s.* die Schlicklichkeit, der Anstand; die Sittsamkeit, Wohlanständigkeit; *for –cy's sake*, anstandshalber; *the –cies, pl.* Anstandsformen (*pl.*). **–t** [ˈdɪːsnt], *adj.* schicklich, anständig, sittsam, züchtig, dezent; bescheiden; (*coll.*) ziemlich gut, ganz nett; *–t behaviour*, anständiges Betragen.

decentraliz–ation [dɪːsɛntrəlɑɪˈzeɪʃən], *s.* die Dezentralisation. **–e** [dɪːˈsɛntrəlɑɪz], *v.a.* dezentralisieren.

decepti–on [dɪˈsɛpʃən], *s.* der Betrug, die Betrügerei; Täuschung. **–ve** [–tɪv], *adj.* trügerisch, täuschend. **–veness,** *s.* die Täuschung.

decide [dɪˈsɑɪd], 1. *v.a.* entscheiden, bestimmen, beschließen; zum Entschluß bringen (*a p.*). 2. *v.n.* (sich) entscheiden *or* entschließen, zu der Meinung *or* Überzeugung kommen; die Entscheidung treffen; den Ausschlag geben; – *on* or *upon a th.*, sich für etwas entschließen; – *to do* or *on doing*, sich entscheiden zu tun; – *against doing*, sich entscheiden nicht zu tun. **–d,** *adj.* entschieden, bestimmt (*as attitudes*), entschlossen (*as persons*); gewiß, unzweifelhaft, deutlich. **–dly,** *adv.* fraglos, sicher, bestimmt, ausgesprochen. **–r,** *s.* der Entscheidungskampf, das Entscheidungsrennen (*Sport*).

deciduous [dɪˈsɪdjʊəs], *adj.* jedes Jahr abfallend, Laub–.

deci–gram(me) [ˈdɛsɪgræm], *s.* das Dezigramm, Zehntelgramm. **–litre,** *s.* das Deziliter. **–metre,** *s.* das Dezimeter.

decimal [ˈdɛsɪməl], 1. *adj.* dezimal; – *fraction*, der Dezimalbruch; – *place*, die Dezimalstelle; – *point*, das Komma; – *system*, das Dezimalsystem. 2. *s.* der Dezimalbruch; *recurring* –, unendliche Dezimalzahl. **–ly,** *adv.* nach dem Dezimalsystem.

decimat–e [ˈdɛsɪmeɪt], *v.a.* den Zehnten hinrichten (von), (*fig.*) dezimieren; vernichten. **–ed,** *adj.* dezimiert; verheert. **–ion** [–ˈmeɪʃən], *s.* die Dezimierung.

decipher [dɪˈsɑɪfə], *v.a.* entziffern, dechiffrieren; (*fig.*) enträtseln. **–able,** *adj.* entzifferbar.

decis–ion [dɪˈsɪʒən], *s.* die Entscheidung (*also Law*); der Entschluß, Beschluß, Entscheid, Bescheid, Anspruch, das Urteil; die Entschlossenheit, Festigkeit (*of character*); *come to a –ion*, zu einem Entschluß kommen (über (*Acc.*)); *a man of –ion*, entschlossener Mann; *–ion of character*, die Charakterstärke. **–ive** [–ˈsɑɪsɪv], *adj.* entscheidend, maßgebend; bestimmend, ausschlaggebend; entschieden; bestimmt, klar; entschlossen (*of persons*); *–ive battle*, der Entscheidungskampf. **–ively,** *adv.* in entscheidender Weise. **–iveness,** *s.* die Entschiedenheit, Endgültigkeit.

deck [dɛk], 1. *v.a.* bekleiden (*also* – out); (aus)schmücken, zieren; mit einem Deck versehen (*Naut.*). 2. *s.* das Deck, Verdeck (*Naut.*); das Spiel, Pack (*of cards*); *below* –, unter Deck; *clear the –s*, das Schiff klar zum Gefecht machen (*also fig.*); *half-*–, das Halbdeck; *lower* –, das Unterdeck; *main* –, das Hauptdeck; *on* –, auf Deck; *go on* –, an Deck gehen; *all hands on* –, alle Mann an Deck; *'tween –s*, das Zwischendeck. **–-chair,** *s.* der Liegestuhl. **– games,** Bordspiele. **–-hand,** *s.* der Matrose (*on fishing boats, etc.*). **–-quoits,** *pl.* das Ringdornspiel. **–-tennis,** *s.* das Ringtennis.

deckle [ˈdɛkl], *adj.*; – *edge*, der Büttenrand.

declaim [dɪˈkleɪm], 1. *v.a.* hersagen, vortragen, deklamieren. 2. *v.n.* deklamieren; – *against* eifern *or* losziehen gegen.

declamat–ion [dɛkləˈmeɪʃən], *s.* die Deklamation, das Deklamieren, schwungvolle Rede. **–ory** [dɪˈklæmətərɪ], *adj.* deklamatorisch; schwülstig, pathetisch.

declar–able [dɪˈklɛːərəbl], *adj.* zollpflichtig, steuerpflichtig. **–ation** [dɛkləˈreɪʃən], *s.* die Erklärung, Aussage, das Manifest; die Deklaration (*customs*); Klageschrift (*Law*). **–ative** [–ˈklærətɪv], *adj.* Erklärungs– *be –ative of*, ausdrücken, aussagen. **–atory** [dɪˈklærətərɪ], *adj.* erläuternd, erklärend; *be –atory of*, erläutern. **–e** [dɪˈklɛə], 1. *v a.* erklären, verkündigen, bekanntmachen, kundtun, aussagen, behaupten; angeben, verzollen (*at the custom-house*); ansagen (*Cards*); *nothing to –e*, nichts zu verzollen (*customs*); *–e o.s.*, sich erklären, seine Meinung kundtun. 2. *v.n.* sich erklären, sich entscheiden (*for*, für; *against*, gegen); vor dem Abschluß des Ganges vom Spiele zurücktreten (*Crick.*); *I –e!* wahrhaftig! so etwas! ich muß sagen! (*coll.*) *–e off*, absagen, aufheben, widerrufen. **–ed,** *adj.* offen.

declension [dɪˈklɛnʃən], *s.* die Abweichung, Neigung; der Verfall; die Beugung, Abwandlung, Deklination (*Gram.*).

declina–ble [dɪˈklɑɪnəbl], *adj.* deklinierbar (*Gram.*) **–ation** [dɛklɪˈneɪʃən], *s.* die Neigung, Abschüssigkeit; Abweichung, Deklination (*Phys.*, *Astr.*); *compass –ion*, die Mißweisung; *local –ion*, die Ortsmißweisung; *magnetic –ion*, die Nadelabweichung. **–tor** [ˈdɛklɪneɪtə], *s.* der Abweichungsmesser (*Phys.*). **–tory** [dɪˈklɑɪnətərɪ], *adj.* abweichend.

decline [dɪˈklɑɪn], 1. *v.a.* neigen; beugen, deklinieren (*Gram.*); ablehnen, abweisen, ausschlagen, verweigern, nicht annehmen; *he –d the honour*, er verbat sich die Ehre. 2. *v.n.* herabneigen, sich niederbeugen; abweichen, abfallen, sich senken; vermindern, verfallen, abnehmen; sich neigen, zu Ende gehen; sich verschlimmern (*of health*); ablehnen, absagen, abweisen, sich weigern; fallen, sinken (*as prices*); *his strength –s*, er kommt von Kräften. 3. *s.* die Abnahme, Verminderung; der Niedergang, Verfall; das Sinken, der Sturz (*of prices*); die Auszehrung (*Med.*); *be on the* –, im Niedergang begriffen sein, zu Ende *or* auf die Neige gehen; heruntergehen, sinken, fallen (*of prices*); *go into a* –, siechen, dahinwelken; – *of life*, der Lebensabend, vorgerücktes Alter.

decliv–itous [dɪˈklɪvɪtəs], **–ous** [dɪˈklɑɪvəs], *adj.* abschüssig, steil. **–ity** [dɪˈklɪvɪtɪ], *s.* der Abhang; die Abschüssigkeit.

declutch [dɪˈklʌtʃ], *v.a.* auskuppeln (*Motor.*).

decoct [dɪˈkɔkt], *v.a.* abkochen; absieden, ausziehen. **–ion** [–ˈkɔkʃən], *s.* das Abkochen; der Absud, die Ausziehung, der Auszug.

decode [dɪːˈkoʊd], *v.a.* entziffern, dechiffrieren.

décolleté [deˈkɔləte], *adj.* dekolletiert (*a lady*), ausgeschnitten (*a dress*).

decolor–ant [dɪːˈkʌlərənt], 1. *adj.* bleichend. 2. *s.* das Bleichmittel. **–ize** [dɪːˈkʌlərɑɪz], *v.a.* entfärben, bleichen.

decompos–able [dɪ.kəmˈpoʊzəbl], *adj.* scheidbar, zersetzbar, zerlegbar. **–e** [dɪːkəmˈpoʊz], 1. *v.a.* zersetzen; zerlegen, scheiden, trennen (*Phys.*). 2. *v.n.* verwesen, sich zersetzen, sich auflösen, zerfallen. **–ed,** *adj.* faul, morsch. **–ition** [dɪːkɔmpəˈzɪʃən], *s.* die Zersetzung, der Zerfall, die Auflösung, Fäule, Fäulnis, Zerlegung, Trennung, Scheidung.

decontaminate [dɪːkənˈtæmɪneɪt], *v.a.* entgiften entgasen (*Mil.*).

decontrol [dɪːkənˈtroʊl], 1 *v.a.* die Zwangswirtschaft aufheben *or* abbauen; freigeben (*goods*). 2. *s.* der Abbau der Zwangswirtschaft; die Freigabe.

decorat–e [ˈdɛkəreɪt], *v.a.* schmücken, zieren; auszeichnen (*a p.*); *–ed style*, englische Gotik (*Arch.*). **–ion** [–ˈreɪʃən], *s.* die Verzierung, Ausschmückung, der Schmuck, Zierrat; die Auszeichnung, das Ehrenzeichen, der Orden; (*pl.*) die Dekoration(en) (*in a theatre, etc.*). **–ive** [–rətɪv], *adj.* zierend, schmückend, dekorativ, Dekorations–, Schmuck–, Zier–. **–or** [–ə], *s.* der Dekorateur, Dekorationsmaler, Anstreicher und Tapezierer.

decor–ous [ˈdɛkərəs], *adj.* geziemend, schicklich; anständig, gebührlich. **–um** [dɪˈkɔːrəm], *s.* der Anstand, die Schicklichkeit.

decorticat–e [dɪˈkɔːtɪkeɪt], *v.a.* abrinden, abschälen. **–ion** [–ˈkeɪʃən], *s.* die Abrindung, Abschälung.

decoy [dɪˈkɔɪ], 1. *v.a.* locken, ködern; (*fig*) verleiten, (ver)locken. 2. *s.* die Entenfalle; Lockspeise, der Köder. **– –bird,** *s.* der Lockvogel.

decrease [dɪːˈkrɪːs], 1. *v.n.* abnehmen, sich vermindern, schwinden. 2. *v.a.* verringern, vermindern. 3. [ˈdɪːkrɪːs], *s.* die Abnahme, Verminderung.

decree [dɪˈkrɪː], 1. *s.* die Verordnung, Verfügung, Vorschrift, der Erlaß, Bescheid, das Dekret; der Entscheid, das Urteil (*Law*); der Ratschluß (*of God*); *– of fate*, die Schicksalsbestimmung; *– nisi*, provisorisches Scheidungsurteil. 2. *v.a.* anordnen, verordnen, verfügen, bestimmen.

decrement [ˈdɛkrəmənt], *s.* die Verminderung, Abnahme.

decrepit [dɪˈkrɛpɪt], *adj.* altersschwach, abgelebt; (*fig.*) verfallen, klapprig. **–ude** [ˈdɪkrɛpɪtjuːd], *s.* die Altersschwäche, Hinfälligkeit, Gebrechlichkeit.

decrepitat–e [dɪˈkrɛpɪteɪt], 1. *v.n.* zerknistern, verpuffen. 2. *v.a.* dekrepitieren lassen (*Chem.*). **–ion** [–ˈteɪʃən], *s.* die Verknisterung, Dekrepitation.

decrescen–do [deɪkrɛˈʃɛndoʊ], *adj.* & *adv* abnehmend (*Mus.*). **–t** [dɪˈkrɛsənt], *adj.* abnehmend (*moon, etc.*).

decret–al [dɪˈkrɪːtəl], 1. *adj.* Dekretal–. 2. *s* das Dekretale, (*pl.*) die Dekretalien (*or* Dekretalen). **–ive, –ory** [ˈdɛkrətərɪ], *adj.* dekretorisch, entscheidend.

decry [dɪˈkrɑɪ], *v.a.* verschreien, verrufen, in Verruf bringen; heruntermachen, herabsetzen.

decubitus [dɪˈkjuːbɪtəs], *s.* das Wundliegen (*Med.*).

decumben–ce [dɪˈkʌmbəns], **–cy,** *s.* das Liegen, Lagern. **–t** [–t], *adj.* liegend (*Bot.*); anliegend (*Zool.*).

decuple [ˈdɛkjupl], 1. *adj.* zehnfach. 2. *s.* das Zehnfache. 3. *v.a.* verzehnfachen.

decussate [dɪˈkʌsɪt], 1. *adj.* sich kreuzend, gekreuzt, kreuzförmig, gegenständig (*Bot.*). 2. [dɪˈkʌseɪt], *v.a.* (& *n.*) (sich) kreuzen.

dedicat–e [ˈdɛdɪkeɪt], *v.a.* weihen, einweihen; widmen (*time or a book*), zueignen (*a book*). **–ion** [–ˈkeɪʃən], *s.* die Weihung; Widmung, Zueignung (*to*, an) (*of a book, etc.*); Zueignungsschrift; das Widmen (*to* (*Dat.*)), die Hingabe (*to*, an). **–or,** *s.* der Widmer, Zueigner. **–ory** [–kətərɪ], *adj.* Widmungs–, Zueignungs–.

deduc–e [dɪˈdjuːs], *v.a.* schließen, folgern (*from*, aus); verfolgen, ableiten, herleiten (*from*, von). **–ible,** *adj.* herzuleiten(d), zu schließen(d).

deduct [dɪˈdʌkt], *v.a.* abziehen, abrechnen; *after –ing . . .*, nach Abzug (von) . . .; *–ing expenses*, abzüglich der Kosten. **–ible,** *adj.* abziehbar. **–ion** [–ˈdʌkʃən], *s.* das Abziehen; der Abzug; Rabatt, Nachlaß (*C.L.*); die Ableitung, Herleitung, (Schluß)Folgerung, der (Erkenntnis)Schluß (*Log.*). **–ive,** *adj.* herleitend, folgernd, deduktiv.

deed [dɪːd], *s.* die Tat, Handlung; Ausführung; Heldentat, Großtat; Urkunde, das Instrument (*Law*); *– of gift*, die Schenkungsurkunde; *in* (*very*) *–*, in Wahrheit, in der Tat; *take the will for the –*, den guten Willen für die Tat nehmen. 2. *v.a.* urkundlich übertragen (*to a p.*, auf einen). **– –box,** *s* die Kassette. **– –poll,** *s.* einseitige Rechtsgeschäftsurkunde.

deem [dɪːm], *v.a.* & *n.* halten für, betrachten, erachten, glauben, denken; *– highly of*, hochschätzen. **–ster,** *s.* der Richter (*Isle of Man*).

deep [dɪːp], 1. *adj.* tief, tiefliegend, niedrig gelegen; (*fig.*) unergründlich, dunkel (*also of colours*); geheim, verborgen; listig, verschlagen; scharfsinnig; gründlich (*of persons*); durchdringend, eindringlich, mächtig, stark (*of influence*); innig empfunden, inbrünstig (*of feelings*); tieftönend (*of sounds*); versunken, vertieft (*in*, in (*Acc.*)); *drawn up two –*, in zwei Gliedern aufgestellt; (*a*) (*with nouns*) *– border*, breiter Rand; *– designs*, versteckte Absichten, geheime Pläne; *– disappointment*, schwere Enttäuschung; *– in debt*, tief verschuldet; (*coll.*) *go off the – end*, die Fassung verlieren; *– fellow*, schlauer Kopf *or* Fuchs; *– grief*, schwerer Kummer; *– influence*, mächtiger Einfluß; *– mourning*, tiefe Trauer; *– into the night*, bis tief in die Nacht; *– sea*, hohe See, die Tiefsee; *– sense of gratitude*, aufrichtiges Dankgefühl; *– silence*, vollkommenes Schweigen; *in – or – in thought*, in Gedanken vertieft; *be in – water*, den Boden unter den Füßen verlieren; (*b*) (*with adverbs*) *drink –*, reichlich trinken; *still waters run –*, stille Wasser sind tief. 2. *s.* (*Poet.*) die Tiefe; See, das Meer. **– –breathing,** *s.* die Atemübung. **–en,** 1. *v.a.* tiefer machen, vertiefen, abteufen (*Min.*); abdunkeln, verdunkeln (*colours*); steigern, verstärken, vergrößern; tiefer stimmen (*tones*). 2. *v.n.* tiefer werden, sich vertiefen; dunkler *or* stärker werden. **– –felt,** *adj.* teifempfunden. **– –laid,** *adj.*; *– –laid schemes*, schlau angelegte Pläne. **–ly,** *adv.*; *–ly affected*, tief ergriffen; *–ly echeloned*, gestaffelt (*Mil.*); *–ly hurt*, schwer gekränkt; *–ly indebted*, zu großem Dank verpflichtet; *–(ly) in love*, sehr verliebt; *–ly offend*, großen Anstoß geben; *–ly read*, sehr belesen. **– –mouthed,** *adj.* von tiefer Stimme (*of dogs*); tieftönend. **–ness,** *s.* die Tiefe. **– –rooted,** *adj.* tiefwurzelnd, (*fig.*) tiefverwurzelt. **– –seated,** tiefsitzend, festsitzend. **– –set,** *adj.* tiefliegend (*as eyes*). **– –throated, – –toned,** *adj.* tieftönend.

deer [dɪə], *s.* (*pl.* –) das Wild, Rotwild, Hochwild; Reh; *fallow –*, der Damhirsch, das Damwild; *red –*, der Edelhirsch, Rothirsch. **– –forest,** *s.* das Hochwildgehege. **– –hound,** *s.* der Jagdhund. **– –hunt,** *s.* die Hochwildjagd. **– –lick,** *s.* die Salzlecke. **– –park,** *s.* der Wildpark. **–skin,** *s.* das Hirschleder, Rehleder. **– –stalker,** *s.* der Pirscher; die Jagdmütze. **– –stalking,** *s.* die Pirsch. **– –stealer,** *s.* der Wilddieb.

deface [dɪˈfeɪs], *v.a.* entstellen, verunstalten; unleserlich machen, verderben. **–ment,** *s.* die Entstellung.

de facto [dɪːˈfæktoʊ], *adv.* tatsächlich (*Law*).

defalcat–e [ˈdɪːfəlkeɪt], *v.n.* eine Veruntreuung machen. **–ion** [dɪːfəlˈkeɪʃən], *s.* die Veruntreuung, Unterschlagung; unterschlagenes Geld.

defam–ation [dɛfəˈmeɪʃən], *s.* die Verleumdung, Schmähung. **–atory** [dɪˈfæmətərɪ], *adj.* verleumderisch; *be –atory of*, verleumden; *–atory libel*, die Schmähschrift. **–e** [dɪˈfeɪm], *v.a.* verleumden, verunglimpfen. **–er,** *s.* der Verleumder, Lästerer.

default [dɪˈfɔːlt], 1. *s.* die Unterlassung, Vernachlässigung, Nichterfüllung, Säumnis, Versäumnis; Zahlungseinstellung; (*archaic*) der Fehler, Mangel; das Nichterscheinen (*Law*); der Verzug; *be in –*, im Verzug sein; *in – of*, in Ermang(e)lung von, mangels; *in – whereof*, widrigenfalls; *let go by –*, unausgenützt vorübergehen lassen, unterlassen; *make –*, nicht erscheinen; nicht nachkommen (*Dat.*), nicht bezahlen; *judgment by –*, das Säumnisurteil. 2. *v.n.* ausbleiben, vor Gericht nicht erscheinen; in Verzug sein, Zahlung einstellen; einer Verpflichtung nicht nachkommen; – *on a debt*, einer Schuld nicht nachkommen. 3. *v.a.* wegen Nichterscheinens verurteilen. **–er,** *s.* säumiger Zahler; Nichterscheinende(r), *m.*, der Insolvent (*C.L.*), Deliquent (*Mil*).

defeas-ance [dɪˈfɪːzəns], *s.* die Ungültigkeitserklärung, Aufhebung, Annullierung; Nichtigkeitsklausel (*Law*). **–ible,** *adj.* anfechtbar.

defeat [dɪˈfɪːt], 1. *s.* die Niederlage; das Zurückschlagen, die Niederschlagung (*of an attack*); Vernichtung, Ungültigkeitserklärung, Vereitelung, *inflict a* –, eine Niederlage beibringen (*on* (*Dat.*)); *suffer* –, eine Niederlage erleiden, geschlagen werden. 2. *v.a.* besiegen, schlagen, überwinden (*an army*), niederschlagen (*an onslaught*); zu Fall bringen (*a motion*); vereiteln, zunichte machen (*hopes, etc.*); anfechten, aufheben (*Law*). **–ism,** *s.* die Flaumacherei. **–ist,** *s.* der Miesmacher.

defecat-e [ˈdɪːfəkeɪt], 1. *v.a.* (ab)klären, reinigen, scheiden, läutern. 2. *v n.* ausleeren, den Darm leeren, Stuhlgang haben. **–ion,** *s.* der Stuhlgang, die Ausleerung.

defect [dɪˈfɛkt], *s.* der Fehler; Defekt, das Gebrechen; die Unvollkommenheit; der Mangel (*of*, an). **–ion** [–ˈfɛkʃən], *s.* der Abfall, die Abtrünnigkeit; Pflichtvergessenheit, der Treubruch. **–ive,** *adj.* mangelhaft, unvollkommen, lückenhaft, unvollständig (*also Gram.*), defekt, schadhaft (*C.L.*); gebrechlich; defektiv (*Gram.*); *be –ive in*, mangeln an (*Dat.*); *mentally –ive*, schwachsinnig. **–iveness,** *s.* die Mangelhaftigkeit, Fehlerhaftigkeit.

defen-ce [dɪˈfɛns], *s.* die Verteidigung (*also Law*); Rechtfertigung (*Law*); der Schutz, die Abwehr; (*pl.*) Befestigungsanlagen, Verteidigungswerke, Abwehrstellungen; *anti-aircraft –ce*, die Fliegerabwehr, der Luftschutz; *coast –ce*, die Küstenverteidigung, *counsel for the –ce*, der Verteidiger; *conduct one's own –ce*, sich selbst verteidigen; *come to the –ce of s.o.*, einen verteidigen; *home –ce*, die Landesverteidigung, der Heimatschutz; *in one's own –ce*, zu seiner Rechtfertigung; *in self-–ce*, in Selbstverteidigung, in Notwehr; *witness for the –ce*, der Entlastungszeuge. **–celess,** *adj.* schutzlos, wehrlos; unbefestigt; hilflos, schwach. **–celessness,** *s.* Schutzlosigkeit. **–d** [dɪˈfɛnd], *v.a.* verteidigen; sichern (*against*, gegen); schützen, bewahren (*from*, vor); rechtfertigen, wahren, aufrechterhalten (*rights, etc.*) **–dant,** *s.* Angeklagte(r), *m.*, Beklagte(r), *m.* (*Law*). **–der,** *s.* der Verteidiger, Beschützer. **–se,** *s.* (*Amer.*) *see* **–ce. –sible,** *adj.* zu verteidigen(d), zu rechtfertigen(d), haltbar, verfechtbar. **–sive,** 1. *adj.* verteidigend, schützend, Abwehr–, Schutz–, Verteidigungs–; *–sive arms*, Schutzwaffen; *–sive position*, die Abwehrstellung; *–sive war*, der Defensivkrieg. 2. *s.* die Defensive, Abwehr, Verteidigung; *act, be*, or *stand on the –sive*, sich defensiv verhalten, sich verteidigen.

defer [dɪˈfəː], 1 *v.a.* aufschieben, verschieben, hinausschieben, zurückstellen (*also v.n.*) (*as military service*); *–red annuity*, erst nach gewisser Frist fällige Rente; *–red payment*, die Ratenzahlung, Abzahlung. 2 *v.n.* zögern, warten; anheimstellen, nachgeben (*to a p.*, einem), sich beugen (vor). **–ence** [ˈdɛfərəns], *s.* die Achtung, Ehrerbietung; Nachgiebigkeit, Unterwerfung (*to*, unter), Rücksichtnahme (*to*, auf (*Acc.*)); *in –ence to*, aus Rücksicht gegen, mit Rücksicht auf (*Acc.*); *out of –ence to*, aus Rücksicht gegen *or* auf (*Acc*); *show –ence to a p.*, einem Achtung zollen, *with all* (*due*) *–ence to*, bei aller Hochachtung vor. **–ential** [dɛfəˈrɛnʃəl], *adj* ehrerbietig. **–ment,** *s.* der Aufschub; die Zurückstellung (*of military service*).

defian-ce [dɪˈfaɪəns], *s* die Herausforderung; der Trotz, Hohn; *bid –ce to*, Trotz bieten, Hohn sprechen (*Dat.*); *in –ce of*, trotz, ungeachtet (*Gen.*), zuwider (*with preceding Dat.*); *in –ce of a p.*, einem zum Trotze; *set at –ce*, see *bid –ce to*. **–t** [–t], *adj.* trotzig, keck, herausfordernd.

deficien-cy [dɪˈfɪʃənsɪ], *s.* der Mangel, die Unzulänglichkeit, Lücke, Unvollständigkeit, Mangelhaftigkeit; der Ausfall, das Defizit, Manko, der Fehlbetrag; *make good a –cy*, das Fehlende ergänzen; *–cy disease*, die Avitaminose (*Med.*). **–t** [dɪˈfɪʃənt], *adj.* mangelhaft, unzulänglich; unzureichend, ungenügend (*in*, an (*Dat.*)); *be –t in*, einer S. (*Gen.*) ermangeln; *mentally –t*, schwachsinnig.

deficit [ˈdɛfɪsɪt], *s.* der Fehlbetrag, Ausfall, das Defizit.

defilade [dɛfɪˈleɪd], 1 *v.a.* gegen Feuer sicherstellen (*Fort*). 2. *s.* die Deckung, gedeckte Stellung (*Mil.*).

[1]**defile** [dɪˈfaɪl], 1 *v.n.* vorbeimarschieren, defilieren (*Mil.*). 2. *s.* der Engpaß, gedeckter Hang, Hohlweg (*Mil.*); *force a* –, an *or* um Engen fechten.

[2]**defile,** *v a.* verunreinigen, besudeln, beschmutzen; (*fig.*) verderben, entehren, schänden, entweihen. **–ment,** *s.* die Verunreinigung, Befleckung, (*fig.*) Schändung.

defin-able [dɪˈfaɪnəbl], *adj.* bestimmbar, erklärbar, definierbar. **–e** [dɪˈfaɪn], *v.a.* begrenzen, abgrenzen, umgrenzen, genau bezeichnen, kennzeichnen, bestimmen; erklären, definieren (*ideas, etc*). **–ite** [ˈdefɪnɪt], *adj.* begrenzt, festgesetzt, bestimmt (*also Gram.*); definitiv, ausdrücklich, deutlich. **–iteness,** *s.* die Bestimmtheit. **–ition** [dɛfɪˈnɪʃən], *s.* die Begriffsbestimmung, Erklärung, Definition; Genauigkeit, Deutlichkeit; Präzision (*Opt.*). **–itive** [dɪˈfɪnɪtɪv], *adj.* bestimmt, entschieden, ausdrücklich; abschließend, endgültig, definitiv.

deflagrate [ˈdɪːfləgreɪt], 1. *v.n.* aufflackern, in Brand geraten. 2. *v a.* abbrennen, verbrennen.

deflat-e [dɪˈfleɪt], 1. *v.a.* die Luft ablassen aus, entleeren; (*fig*) herabsetzen, herunterbringen (*prices*). 2. *v.n.* den Zahlungsmittelumlauf einschränken (*C L.*). **–ion** [–ˈfleɪʃən], *s.* die Entleerung; Deflation (*C L*).

deflect [dɪˈflɛkt], 1. *v.a.* ablenken, abbiegen. 2. *v.n.* abweichen. **–ion,** *s. see* **deflexion**

deflexion [dɪˈflɛkʃən], *s.* die Abweichung, Ablenkung, Abbiegung, der Ausschlag (*Magnet.*); die Beugung (*Opt.*); die Seitenrichtung, der Seitenwinkel (*Artil.*); *lateral* –, die Seitenverschiebung; – *correction*, die Seitenänderung.

deflorat-e [ˈdɪˑfloˑreɪt], *adj.* abgeblüht, verblüht. **–ion,** *s.* die Entjungferung.

deflower [dɪːˈflaʊə], *v.a.* entjungfern; (*fig.*) entehren, schänden.

defoliat-e [dɪːˈfoʊlɪeɪt], *v.a* entblättern. **–ion,** *s.* die Entblätterung, der Blätterfall.

deforest [dɪˑˈfɔrɪst], *v.a.* abholzen, entwalden. **–ation** [dɪːfɔrɪsˈteɪʃən], *s.* die Abforstung, Abholzung.

deform [dɪˈfɔːm], *v.a.* entstellen, verunstalten, verzerren, deformieren. **–ation** [–ˈmeɪʃən], *s.* die Entstellung, Verunstaltung; Formveränderung; Mißbildung. **–ed,** *adj.* entstellt, verunstaltet, mißgestaltet. **–ity,** *s.* die Mißgestaltung, Mißgestalt, Häßlichkeit.

defraud [dɪˈfrɔːd], *v.a.* betrügen (*of*, um); *with intent to* –, in betrügerischer Absicht; – *the revenue*, Steuern hinterziehen. **–ation,** *s.* die Unterschlagung.

defray [dɪˈfreɪ], *v.a.* bezahlen, bestreiten, tragen (*expenses*).

deft [dɛft], *adj.* geschickt, gewandt, flink. **–ness,** *s.* die Gewandtheit, Geschicklichkeit, Flinkheit.

defunct [dɪˈfʌŋkt], 1. *adj.* verstorben. 2. *s.* Verstorbene(r), *m.*

defy [dɪˈfaɪ], *v.a.* herausfordern; Trotz bieten, trotzen, Hohn sprechen (*Dat.*); – *all description*, jeder Beschreibung spotten.

degauss [dɪːˈgaʊs], *v.a.* entmagnetisieren (*mines, etc.*) (*Mil.*).

degenera-cy [dɪˈdʒɛnərəsɪ], *s.* die Entartung, Verderbtheit, Verkommenheit. **–te** [–reɪt], 1. *v.n.* entarten, ausarten; (*fig.*) abgehen, herabsinken. 2. *adj.* [–rɪt], entartet, verderbt, verkommen. 3. *s.* verkommener Mensch. **–tion** [–ˈreɪʃən], *s.* die Entartung; der Abbau (*Chem.*), die Degeneration (*Rad*).

deglutition [dɪːgluˈtɪʃən], *s.* das Schlucken, Verschlucken, Schlingen.

degrad-ation [dɛgrəˈdeɪʃən], *s.* die Absetzung,

Entsetzung; Degradation, Degradierung (*Mil.*); Verringerung, Verminderung; Erniedrigung, Entwürdigung; Verderbtheit, Entartung (*Biol.*), Verwitterung (*Geol.*). **–e** [dɪˈgreɪd], 1. *v.a.* absetzen, entsetzen; heruntersetzen, verkleinern, vermindern, verringern; entwürdigen, entehren, degradieren, erniedrigen; abnutzen, abtragen (*Geol.*); auf ein Jahr zurückstellen (*Univ.*). 2. *v.n.* entarten, herunterkommen. **–ing,** *adj.* entehrend, entwürdigend.

degree [dɪˈgrɪː], *s.* die Stufe, der Grad; Rang, Stand; die Klasse, Ordnung; akademische Würde, akademischer Grad (*Univ.*); das Intervall, die Tonstufe (*Mus.*); (*fig.*) das Maß; (*a*) (*with nouns & adjectives*) *–s of comparison*, die Steigerungsgrade (*Gram.*); *honours –*, akademischer Grad höherer Ordnung; *three –s of frost*, 3 Grad unter Null; *– of latitude*, der Breitengrad; *– of longitude*, der Längengrad; *– of relationship*, der Verwandtschaftsgrad; *men of high –*, Männer von hohem Stande; *ordinary* or *pass –*, akademischer Grad ohne Spezialisierung; (*sl.*) *third –*, Polizeizwangsmaßnahmen um ein Geständnis zu bekommen; (*b*) (*with verbs*) *confer an honorary – on a p.*, einem die Würde eines Ehrendoktors verleihen; *he obtained the doctor's –*, er errang die Doktorwürde; *take one's –*, promovieren, eine akademische Würde erlangen; (*c*) (*with prepositions*) *by –s*, allmählich, nach und nach, stufenweise; *by slow –s*, ganz allmählich; *in no small –*, in nicht geringem Grade; *in no –*, keineswegs; *in some –*, einigermaßen; *to a high –*, (or coll. *to a –*), in hohem Grade *or* Maße, hochgradig, äußerst; *to a certain –*, bis zu einem gewissen Grade, gewissermaßen, ziemlich.

dehiscence [dɪːˈhɪsəns], *s.* das Aufspringen (*of seed pods*) (*Bot.*).

dehortatory [dɪˈhɔːtətərɪ], *adj.* abratend, abmahnend.

dehumanize [dɪːˈhjuːmənaɪz], *v.a.* entseelen, entmenschlichen.

dehydrat–e [ˈdɪːhaɪdreɪt], *v.a.* entwässern; *–ed egg*, das Trockenei. **–ion,** *s.* die Entwässerung, Wasserentziehung.

de-ice [ˈdɪːˈaɪs], *v.a.* enteisen (*Av.*).

deif–ication [dɪːɪfɪˈkeɪʃən], *s.* die Vergötterung. **–orm** [ˈdɪːɪfɔːm], *adj.* gottähnlich, göttlich, von göttlicher Gestalt. **–y** [ˈdɪːɪfaɪ], *v.a.* vergöttlichen; (*fig.*) vergöttern.

deign [deɪn], 1. *v.n.* geruhen, belieben; sich herablassen, sich erniedrigen. 2. *v.a.* gewähren, gestatten, würdigen.

deis–m [ˈdɪːɪzm], *s.* der Deismus. **–t,** *s.* der Deist. **–tic(al)** [–ˈɪstɪk(l)], *adj.* deistisch.

deity [ˈdɪːɪtɪ], *s.* die Gottheit; der Gott.

deject–ed [dɪˈdʒɛktɪd], *adj.* niedergeschlagen, betrübt. **–edness,** *s.* die Niedergeschlagenheit. **–ion** [–ˈdʒɛkʃən], *s.* die Niedergeschlagenheit, der Trübsinn; Stuhlgang, die Ausleerung (*Med.*).

dekko [ˈdɛkoʊ], *s.* (*sl.*) der Blick, Einblick.

delaine [dəˈleɪn], *s.* bunter Damenkleidstoff.

delat–e [dɪˈleɪt], *v.a.* anklagen, anzeigen, denunzieren (*Scots*). **–ion** [ˈleɪʃən], die Anklage, Denunziation.

delay [dɪˈleɪ], 1. *v.a.* verzögern, aufschieben, verschieben, hinhalten, hindern, hemmen, aufhalten; *– payment*, mit der Zahlung säumen. 2. *v.n.* zögern, zaudern, sich in die Länge ziehen, sich aufhalten. 3. *s.* die Verzögerung; der Aufschub, Verzug; *without –*, unverzüglich; *– of payment*, die Stundung (*C.L.*); *–ed action*, die Verzögerung; Zeitzündung (*bombs, etc.*). **–er,** *s.* der Zögerer, Zauderer; *–ing action*, hinhaltendes Gefecht (*Mil.*).

dele [ˈdɪːlɪː], 1. *imperat.* zu tilgen! tilge! 2. *s.* das Deleatur, Tilgungszeichen (*Typ.*).

delecta–ble [dɪˈlɛktəbl], *adj.* erfreulich, ergötzlich, köstlich. **–tion** [diːlɛkˈteɪʃən], *s.* die Ergötzung, das Vergnügen.

delega–cy [ˈdɛləgəsɪ], *s.* die Abordnung, der Ausschuß. **–te** [ˈdɛlɪgeɪt], 1. *v.a.* übertragen, überweisen, anvertrauen (*a th. to a p.*, einem etwas); bevollmächtigen, abordnen (*a p.*); *–te authority to s.o.*, einem Vollmacht erteilen. 2. *s.* [–gət], Abgeordnete(r), *m.*; Bevollmächtigte(r), *m.*, Delegierte(r), *m.*; (*pl.*) die Abordnung, Delegation, der Ausschuß. **–tion,** *s.* die Überweisung (*of a debt, etc.*); Bevollmächtigung; Absendung, Abordnung, Delegation; der Ausschuß, die Abgeordneten (*pl.*).

delet–e [dɪˈlɪːt], *v.a.* (aus)streichen, ausmerzen, auslöschen, ausradieren. **–ion** [–ˈlɪːʃən], *s.* die Streichung, Ausmerzung.

deleterious [dɛlɪˈtɪərɪəs], *adj.* schädlich, verderblich, ungünstig, giftig.

delf(t) [dɛlf(t)], 1. *s.* Delfter Porzellan. 2. *adj.* (*Scots*) Steingut–, irden.

deliberat–e [dɪˈlɪbəreɪt], 1. *v.a.* (*only with clause as complement*) überlegen, erwägen. 2. *v.n.* sich beraten, sich bedenken, beratschlagen, nachdenken (*on* or *upon*, über (*Acc.*)). 3. [–rət], *adj.* vorsätzlich, absichtlich; langsam, bedächtig, vorsichtig, umsichtig, besonnen; überlegt, wohlerwogen. **–eness,** *s.* die Bedachtsamkeit, Bedächtigkeit, Vorsichtigkeit. **–ion** [–ˈreɪʃən], *s.* die Überlegung, Beratung; Vorsicht, Behutsamkeit. **–ive** [–ətɪv], *adj.* überlegend; beratend.

delica–cy [ˈdɛlɪkəsɪ], *s.* die Köstlichkeit, Schmackhaftigkeit; der Leckerbissen, die Delikatesse (*foodstuffs*); Feinheit, Genauigkeit, Zartheit, Zierlichkeit, Niedlichkeit; Empfindlichkeit, Zärtlichkeit, Weichlichkeit, zarte Gesundheit (*of health*); die Nachsicht, Feinfühligkeit, der Takt, das Zartgefühl (*of feelings*); *negotiations of the utmost –cy*, Verhandlungen heikelster *or* kitzligster Natur. **–te** [ˈdɛlɪkɪt], *adj.* schmackhaft, köstlich (*of food*); wählerisch, lecker(haft) (*of persons*); zart, sanft, leicht, dünn, fein (*of materials*); feinfühlig, taktvoll, zartfühlend; zierlich, niedlich, elegant; kränklich, schwächlich, schwach; heikel, kitzlig, bedenklich; empfindlich. **–tessen,** *s.* (*Amer.*) die Feinkost; das Feinkostgeschäft.

delicious [dɪˈlɪʃəs], *adj.* köstlich, wohlschmeckend; lieblich, herrlich. **–ness,** *s.* die Köstlichkeit.

delict [dɪˈlɪkt], *s.* das Vergehen, der Delikt.

delight [dɪˈlaɪt], 1. *s.* die Lust, das Vergnügen, Ergötzen; die Freude, Wonne; *take – in a th.*, an einer S. Vergnügen finden. 2. *v.a.* ergötzen, erfreuen, entzücken. 3. *v.n.* sich (er)freuen, sich ergötzen (*in*, an (*Dat.*)); entzückt sein (über); *– in flowers*, große Freude an Blumen haben; *– in mischief*, schadenfroh sein. **–ed,** *adj.* erfreut, entzückt; *be –ed*, entzückt sein, sich freuen (*with* or *at*, über (*Acc.*)); *I am –ed to accept*, ich nehme mit (dem größten) Vergnügen an. **–ful,** *adj.* entzückend, reizend, köstlich. **–fulness,** *s.* die Ergötzlichkeit.

delimit [dɪːˈlɪmɪt], *v.a.* abgrenzen. **–ation,** *s.* die Abgrenzung.

delineat–e [dɪˈlɪnɪeɪt], *v.a.* entwerfen, skizzieren, zeichnen; abgrenzen; schildern, beschreiben, darstellen. **–ion** [–ˈeɪʃən], *s.* der Entwurf, die Skizze; Schilderung.

delinquen–cy [dɪˈlɪŋkwənsɪ], *s.* die Pflichtvergessenheit; das Vergehen, Verbrechen, die Missetat. **–t,** 1. *adj.* pflichtvergessen; verbrecherisch. 2. *s.* der Verbrecher, Missetäter, Gestrauchelte(r), *m.*

deliquesce [dɛlɪˈkwɛs], *v.n.* zergehen, zerschmelzen, zerfließen (*Chem.*). **–nce,** *s.* die Zerfließbarkeit; das Zerschmelzen. **–nt,** *adj.* zerfließend, zerfließlich, zerschmelzend.

deliri–ous [dɪˈlɪːrɪəs], *adj.* irre redend, phantasierend, im Fieberwahn; (*fig.*) rasend, wahnsinnig; *be –ous*, phantasieren, irre reden. **–um** [dɪˈlɪːrɪəm], *s.* das Phantasieren, Irrereden, der Fieberwahn; (*fig.*) Wahnsinn, die Raserei, Verzückung; *–um tremens*, der Säuferwahnsinn.

deliver [dɪˈlɪvə], *v.a.* (*persons*) befreien (*from*, von or aus), retten, erlösen; entbinden (*a woman of a child*); (*things*) übergeben, überreichen, überlassen, einhändigen (*to a p.*, einem); liefern (*to*, an), abliefern, ausliefern, übergeben, überbringen, aushändigen, ausrichten (*to a p.*, einem); zustellen, austragen (*letters*); *to be –ed at B.*, Erfüllungsort B.; *– a blow*, einen Schlag verabreichen *or* versetzen, losschlagen; *to be –ed in eight days*, mit achttägiger Lieferungsfrist, in acht Tagen lieferbar; *she was –ed of a boy*, sie wurde von einem Knaben entbunden; *– a lecture*, einen Vortrag halten; –

one's opinion, sein Urteil abgeben; – *o.s. of a secret*, ein Geheimnis von sich geben; – *up*, aufgeben, abtreten (*a th.*), überantworten (*a p. to justice*); – *o.s. up*, sich ergeben, sich stellen; – *a warning*, eine Warnung aussprechen *or* loslassen. **–able** [–rəbl], *adj.* zu liefern(d). **–ance** [–rəns], *s.* die Befreiung, Erlösung, Rettung. **–er** [–rə], *s.* der Befreier; Erretter, Erlöser. **–y** [–rı], *s.* die Entbindung, Niederkunft (*Med.*); Übergabe, Lieferung, Ablieferung, Abgabe (*to*, an (*Acc.*)); Zustellung, Austragung (*of letters*); der Vortrag (*of a speech*); das Geben, der Wurf (*of a ball*); *bill of –y*, der Lieferungsschein; *cash on –y*, Betrag bei Lieferung *or* unter Nachnahme; *special –y*, die Lieferung durch Eilbote. **–y-pipe**, *s.* das Ablaufrohr, Ausflußrohr. **–y-note**, der Frachtbrief. **–y-van**, *s.* der Lieferwagen.

dell [dɛl], *s.* enges Tal.

delouse [dı:ˈlaʊz], *v.a.* entlausen.

delphinium [dɛlˈfınıəm], *s.* der Rittersporn (*Bot.*).

delt–a [dɛltə], *s.* das Delta; *–a-connection*, die Dreieckschaltung (*Elec.*). **–oid**, 1. *adj.* deltaförmig (*Anat.*). 2. *s.* der Deltamuskel.

delude [dıˈl(j)u:d], *v.a.* betrügen, täuschen, irreführen; – *a p. into*, einen verleiten zu; – *o.s.*, sich Illusionen hingeben.

deluge [ˈdɛlju:dʒ], 1. *s.* die Überschwemmung; (*B.*) *the* –, die Sintflut; (*fig.*) die Menge, Flut. 2. *v.a.* überfluten, überschütten.

delus–ion [dıˈl(j)u:ʒən], *s.* die Täuschung, Selbsttäuschung, Verblendung; der Irrtum, Wahn; *be* or *labour under the –ion*, in dem Wahn leben. **–ive** [dıˈl(j)u:sıv], *adj.* trügerisch, täuschend. **–iveness**, *s.* das Trügerische, die Trüglichkeit.

delve [dɛlv], *v.n. & a.* graben; (*fig.*) sich eingraben (*into*, in), ergründen.

demagnetize [dı:ˈmægnıtaız], *v.a.* entmagnetisieren.

demagog–ic(al) [dɛməˈgɔdʒık(l)], *adj.* demagogisch. **–ue** [ˈdɛməgɔg], *s.* der Demagog. **–y**, *s.* die Demagogie.

demand [dıˈmɑ:nd], 1. *v.a.* verlangen, fordern, ersuchen, begehren (*of* or *from*, von); erfordern, beanspruchen, anfordern; fragen nach. 2. *s.* das Verlangen, Begehren, Ersuchen, Fordern; die Forderung (*C.L.*), Inanspruchnahme (*on* (*Gen.*)); der Bedarf, die Nachfrage (*for*, nach); der Rechtsanspruch (*upon*, an) (*Law*); die Anforderung, Aufforderung; *supply and* –, Angebot und Nachfrage; *in* –, begehrt, gesucht; *on* –, auf Verlangen, auf Sicht; *bill payable on* –, der Sichtwechsel; *make great –s on*, große Anforderungen stellen an. **–-note**, *s.* die Zahlungsaufforderung.

demarcat–e [ˈdı:mɑ:keıt], *v.a.* abgrenzen (*from*, von *or* gegen). **–ion** [–ˈkeıʃən], *s.* die Abgrenzung; *line of –ion*, die Grenzlinie, Scheidelinie.

demean [dıˈmı:n], 1. *v.r.* sich benehmen *or* betragen. 2. *v.a. & r.* (sich) erniedrigen *or* herabwürdigen. **–our** [–ə], *s.* das Benehmen, Betragen.

demented [dıˈmɛntıd], *adj.* wahnsinnig.

démenti [deıˈmɛntı], *s.* die Richtigstellung, das Dementi.

demerit [dı:ˈmɛrıt], *s.* das Verschulden, der Mangel, Fehler; die Unwürdigkeit.

demesne [dıˈmı:n], *s.* das Erbgut, freies Grundeigentum, die Domäne; der Eigenbesitz; (*fig.*) das Gebiet; *royal* –, das Kronland.

demi– [ˈdɛmı], *prefix* halb, Halb–. **–god**, *s.* der Halbgott. **–john**, *s.* die Korbflasche, der Glasballon. **–-monde**, *s.* die Halbwelt.

demilitarize [dı:ˈmılıtəraız], *v.a.* entmilitarisieren.

demis–able [dıˈmaızəbl], *adj* verpachtbar, übertragbar (*Law*). **–e** [dıˈmaız], 1. *s.* das Ableben, der Tod; die Besitzübertragung, Verpachtung. 2. *v.a.* übertragen, vermachen.

demisemiquaver [ˈdɛmısɛmıˈkweıvə], *s.* die Zweiunddreißigstelnote (*Mus.*).

demission [dıˈmıʃən], *s.* das Niederlegen, die Zurückziehung, Abdankung, der Rücktritt.

demobiliz–ation [dı:moubılaıˈzeıʃən], *s.* die Demobilisierung, Demobilmachung, Abrüstung. **–e** [–laız], *v.a.* auflösen (*an army*), entlassen (*troops*), außer Dienst stellen (*a ship*).

democra–cy [dıˈmɔkrəsı], *s.* die Demokratie **–t** [ˈdɛmokræt], *s.* der Demokrat. **–tic** [dɛməˈkrætık], *adj.* demokratisch.

demoli–sh [dıˈmɔlıʃ], *v.a.* niederreißen, abreißen; (*fig.*) vernichten, zerstören. **–tion** [dɛməˈlıʃən], *s.* das Niederreißen, die Zerstörung, Vernichtung; *–tion charge*, geballte Ladung; *–tion party*, das Sprengkommando.

demon [ˈdı:mən], *s.* böser Geist, der Teufel, Dämon; (*coll.*) Teufelskerl; *a – for work*, unersättlicher Arbeiter.

demonetize [dı:ˈmɔnıtaız], *v.a.* außer Kurs setzen, entwerten.

demon–iac [dıˈmounıæk], 1. *adj.* dämonisch, teuflisch, besessen. 2. *s.* Besessene(r), *m.* **–iacal** [dı:məˈnaıəkl], *adj. see* **–iac**, 1. **–ic**, *adj.* dämonisch, übermenschlich. **–ism** [ˈdı:mənızm], *s.* der Dämonenglaube. **–ology** [dı:məˈnɔlədʒı], *s.* die Dämonenlehre.

demonstra–ble [dıˈmɔnstrəbl], *adj.* sichtbar (*to*, für), beweisbar, erweislich, nachweislich. **–te** [ˈdɛmənstreıt], 1. *v.a.* anschaulich machen, dartun, zeigen, vorweisen, erweisen, beweisen. 2. *v.n.* eine Kundgebung veranstalten, demonstrieren (*Pol.*). **–tion** [–ˈstreıʃən], *s.* anschauliche Darstellung, die Vorführung; Kundgebung, Äußerung, Demonstration; der Beweis, die Beweisführung, Darlegung (*Log.*); der Scheinangriff (*Mil.*). **–tive** [dıˈmɔnstrətıv], *adj.* beweiskräftig; überzeugend, schlagend, bündig; ausdrucksvoll, auffällig, überschwenglich; *be –tive of*, deutlich zeigen, beweisen; *–tive pronoun*, hinweisendes Fürwort (*Gram.*). **–tiveness**, *s.* die Überschwenglichkeit. **–tor** [ˈdɛmənstreıtə], *s.* der Beweisführer, Erklärer; Prosektor (*Anat.*); Demonstrant, Teilnehmer an einer Demonstration.

demoraliz–ation [dımɔrəlaıˈzeıʃən], *s.* die Sittenverderbnis. **–e** [dıˈmɔrəlaız], *v.a.* entsittlichen, moralisch verderben; (*fig.*) entmutigen, entkräften, zermürben. **–ing**, *adj.* verderblich, zermürbend.

demot–e [dı:ˈmout], *v.a.* (*coll.*) degradieren (*Mil.*). **–ion**, *s.* die Degradation, Degradierung (*Mil.*).

demur [dıˈmə:], 1. *v.n.* Einwendungen machen, Anstand nehmen, Bedenken äußern, Schwierigkeiten machen, sich wehren (*to*, gegen); – *to*, abwehren, beanstanden. 2. *s.* der Zweifel, Skrupel; die Einwendung, Bedenklichkeit; *without* –, ohne Einwendung; *make – to*, bezweifeln. **–rer**, *s.* der Einwand, Rechtseinwand.

demure [dıˈmjʊə], *adj.* ernsthaft, gesetzt; zimperlich, spröde. **–ness**, *s.* die Gesetztheit; Sprödigkeit.

demurrage [dıˈmʌrıdʒ], *s.* das Überliegegeld; die Überliegezeit (*Naut.*); *be on* –, die Liegezeit überschreiten.

demurrer [dıˈmə:rə], *see* **demur.**

demy [dıˈmaı], *s.* englisches Papierformat ($17\frac{1}{2}$ *in.* $\times 22\frac{1}{2}$ *in.*). **–ship** [-ʃıp], *s.* ein Universitätsstipendium (*in Oxford*).

den [dɛn], *s.* das Lager, der Bau (*of animals*); (*fig.*) die Höhle, Grube; (*coll.*) Bude; (*B.*) – *of thieves*, die Mördergrube; *robbers'* –, die Räuberhöhle, das Räubernest.

denationalize [dı:ˈnæʃənəlaız], *v.a.* entnationalisieren, des Nationalcharakters berauben; ausbürgern.

denaturalize [dı:ˈnætʃərəlaız], *v.a.* (etwas) seiner Natur berauben; (einen) des Heimatrechts berauben.

denature [dıˈneıtʃə], *adj.* denaturieren (*Chem.*).

dendr–iform [ˈdɛndrıfɔ:m], *adj.* baumförmig. **–ite** [ˈdɛndraıt], *s.* der Dendrit. **–oid**, *adj.* baumähnlich. **–olite**, *s.* die Baumversteinerung. **–ology** [–ˈdrɔlədʒı], *s.* die Baumkunde.

deni–able [dıˈnaıəbl], *adj.* verneinbar, zu verneinen(d), abzuleugnen(d). **–al** [dıˈnaıəl], *s.* die Verneinung, Leugnung; Verweigerung, abschlägige Antwort, Absage; *official –al*, das Dementi; *self-–al*, die Selbstverleugnung.

denigrat–e [ˈdɛnıgreıt], *v.a.* anschwärzen, verunglimpfen, verleumden. **–ion**, *s.* die Anschwärzung.

denim [ˈdɛnım], *s.* grober Drillich.

denizen [ˈdɛnızn], 1. *s.* der Bewohner; eingebürgerter Ausländer. 2. *v.a.* bevölkern.

denominat–e [dɪˈnɔmɪneɪt], *v.a.* (be)nennen. **–ion** [dɪnɔmɪˈneɪʃən], *s.* die Benennung, Bezeichnung, Klasse, (benannte) Einheit (*Math.*); der Nennwert (*currency*); das Bekenntnis, die Sekte, Konfession (*Eccl.*). **–ional,** *adj.* konfessionell, Sekten–; *–ional school,* konfessionelle Schule. **–ive** [dɪˈnɔmɪnətɪv], *adj.* benennend. **–or** [–neɪtə], *s.* der Nenner (*Arith.*); *the common –or,* der Generalnenner.

denot–ation [dɪnoˈteɪʃən], *s.* die Bezeichnung; Bedeutung, der Begriffsumfang (*Log.*). **–ative** [dɪˈnoʊtətɪv], *adj.* bezeichnend, andeutend. **–e** [dɪˈnoʊt], *v.a.* bezeichnen, kennzeichnen, andeuten, bedeuten.

dénouement [deˈnuːmɑ̃ː], *s.* die Lösung, der Ausgang; die Entscheidung.

denounce [dɪˈnaʊns], *v.a.* anzeigen, angeben, androhen, brandmarken, öffentlich anklagen *or* rügen; *– a treaty,* einen Vertag kündigen. **–ment,** *s.* die Anzeige, öffentliche Anklage.

dens–e [dɛns], *adj.* dicht (*as a crowd*); dick (*as a fog*); (*coll.*) beschränkt, dumm, schwerfällig; gut belichtet (*Phot.*); *–e smoke,* der Qualm. **–eness,** *s.* die Dichtigkeit; Schwerfälligkeit, Beschränktheit. **–ity,** *s.* die Dichte, Dichtigkeit, Dichtheit, Festigkeit, Grädigkeit, Undurchsichtigkeit; *field –ity,* die Feldstärke (*Elec.*).

dent [dɛnt], 1. *s.* der Einschnitt, die Kerbe; Beule. 2. *v.a.* auszacken, kerben; einbeulen.

dent–al [dɛntl], 1. *adj.* Zahn–; zahnärztlich; *–al hospital,* die Zahnklinik; *–al sounds,* die Zahnlaute; *–al surgeon,* der Zahnarzt; *–al surgery,* die Zahnheilkunde. 2. *s.* der Zahnlaut, Dental(laut). **–ate(d)** [ˈdɛnteɪt, –teɪtɪd], *adj.* gezähnt (*Bot.*). **–ation** [–ˈteɪʃən], *s.* die Kerbung, Bezahnung (*Bot.*). **–icle** [–tɪkl], *s.* das Zähnchen. **–iculate(d)** [–ˈtɪkjuleɪt(ɪd)], *adj.* gezahnt, gezähnelt, ausgezackt. **–iculation,** *s.* die Auszackung. **–iform,** *adj.* zahnförmig. **–ifrice** [ˈdɛntɪfrɪs], *s.* das Zahnpulver, die Zahnpasta *or* –paste; das Zahnputzmittel. **–il** [ˈdɛntɪl], *s.* der Zahnschnitt, die Zahnverzierung. **–ine** [ˈdɛntɪːn], *s.* das Zahnbein, Dentin. **–ist** [ˈdɛntɪst], *s.* der Zahnarzt. **–istry,** *s.* die Zahnheilkunde. **–ition** [–ˈtɪʃən], *s.* das Zahnen (*of children*); die Zahnordnung. **–ure** [ˈdɛntjʊə], *s.* künstliches Gebiß.

denud–ation [dɪːnjuːˈdeɪʃən], *s.* die Entblößung; Abtragung (*Geol.*). **–e** [dɪˈnjuːd], *v.a.* entblößen, bloßlegen; (*fig.*) berauben.

denunciat–e [dɪˈnʌnsɪeɪt], *v.a. see* **denounce. –ion** [–ˈeɪʃən], *s.* drohende Anzeige, die Anklage. **–or,** *s.* der Angeber, Denunziant. **–ory** [–sɪətərɪ], *adj.* anklagend, angeberisch.

deny [dɪˈnaɪ], *v.a.* verneinen, in Abrede stellen, leugnen, ableugnen, dementieren; verweigern, abschlagen; verleugnen, nicht anerkennen; *– on oath,* abschwören; *– o.s. a pleasure,* sich (*Dat.*) ein Vergnügen versagen, sich ein Vergnügen nicht gönnen; *there's no –ing it, it cannot be denied,* es läßt sich nicht *or* es ist nicht zu leugnen; *– o.s.,* sich verleugnen lassen (*to,* vor); *I have been denied this pleasure,* dies Vergnügen ist mir versagt worden; *he will not be denied,* er läßt sich nicht abweisen.

deodand [ˈdɪːoudænd], *s.* dem Staat verfallenes Gut.

deodor–ant [dɪːˈoʊdərənt], *s.* das Desinfektionsmittel. **–ize** [dɪːˈoʊdəraɪz], *v.a.* von Gerüchen befreien. **–izer,** *s. see* **–ant.**

deoxid–ation [dɪːɔksɪˈdeɪʃən], *s.* die Sauerstoffentziehung. **–ize,** *v.a.* vom Sauerstoff befreien.

depart [dɪˈpɑːt], 1. *v.n.* abreisen; abfahren, abgehen (*as trains, etc.*) (*for,* nach); abweichen (*from,* von); *– from a plan,* einen Plan ändern *or* aufgeben; *– from one's word,* sein Wort nicht halten. 2. *v.a.*; *– this life,* dahinscheiden. **–ed,** 1. *adj.* vergangen; verstorben; (*as adv.*) dahin. 2. *s.* der Verstorbene (*usually pl.*).

department [dɪˈpɑːtmənt], *s.* die Abteilung; Branche, der Geschäftskreis, die Dienststelle; der Zweig; der (Verwaltungs)Bezirk, das Departement; das Ministerium (*usually Amer.*); *– of State,* Auswärtiges Amt (*Amer.*); *– of war,* das Kriegsministerium (*Amer.*). **–al** [dɪːpɑːtˈmɛntl], *adj.* Abteilungs–, Bezirks–; *–al chief,* der Abteilungsvorsteher. **– store,** das Warenhaus.

departure [dɪˈpɑːtʃə], *s.* das Weggehen, der Weggang; die Abreise, Abfahrt, der Abgang; die Abweichung, Abwendung, das Aufgeben; das Abstehen, Ablassen, die Abstandnahme; *a new –,* neuer Weg *or* Anfang, etwas ganz Neues; *a – from the usual practice,* eine Abweichung von dem gewöhnlichen Vorgang; *take one's –,* fortgehen, sich verabschieden. **– -platform,** der Abfahrtsbahnsteig. **– -station,** *s.* die Versandstation, Aufgabestation (*Railw., Tele.*).

depend [dɪˈpɛnd], *v.n.* (*poet.*) herab– *or* herunterhängen; abhängen, abhängig sein (*on,* von); darauf ankommen; bedingt sein (*on,* durch); sich verlassen, sich stützen, angewiesen sein (*on* or *upon,* auf (*Acc.*)); (*usually* be –ing) in der Schwebe sein, schweben (*Law*); *– on it,* verlassen Sie sich darauf; *that –s,* das kommt darauf an, je nachdem; *that –s upon circumstances,* das hängt von den Umständen ab. **–able,** *adj.* zuverlässig, verläßlich. **–ant,** *s.* Unterstützungsberechtigte(r), Angehörige(r), Abhängige(r), *m.*; der Diener, Vasall, Anhänger. **–ence,** *s.* die Abhängigkeit (*on* or *upon,* von); das Bedingtsein, die Verkettung; das Vertrauen, der Verlaß (*on,* auf (*Acc.*)); die Schwebe (*Law*). **–ency,** *s.* die Abhängigkeit (*on* or *upon,* auf); schutzherrliches Gebiet, die Kolonie. **–ent,** 1. *adj.* abhängig, abhängend (*on,* von); bedingt (*on,* durch); angewiesen (*on,* auf); unterworfen, unselbständig (*on* (*Dat.*)). 2. *s. usually* **–ant.**

depict [dɪˈpɪkt], *v.a.* (ab)malen; schildern, beschreiben, darstellen, zeichnen. **–ion,** *s.* das Zeichnen; die Zeichnung, Schilderung, Darstellung.

depilat–e [ˈdɛpɪleɪt], *v.a.* enthaaren. **–ory** [dɪˈpɪlətərɪ], 1. *adj.* enthaarend. 2. *s.* das Enthaarungsmittel, Haarlockerungsmittel, die Haarbeize.

deplane [dɪːˈpleɪn], *v.n.* aus dem Flugzeug steigen.

deplenish [dɪːˈplɛnɪʃ], *v.a.* entleeren.

deplet–e [dɪˈplɪːt], *v.a.* entleeren; (*fig.*) erschöpfen. **–ion** [–ˈplɪːʃən], *s.* die (Blut)Entleerung (*Med.*); (*fig.*) die Erschöpfung. **–ive, –ory** [–ərɪ], *adj.* entleerend.

deplor–able [dɪˈplɔːrəbl], *adj.* bedauerlich, beklagenswert, bejammernswert, kläglich, erbärmlich. **–e** [dɪˈplɔːə], *v.a.* bedauern, beweinen, beklagen, betrauern; mißbilligen.

deploy [dɪˈplɔɪ], *v.a.* (*& n.* sich) aufmarschieren (lassen), entfalten, entwickeln; (*v.n. only*) ausschwärmen (*Mil.*). **–ment,** *s.* die Entfaltung, Entwicklung, der Aufmarsch, das Ausschwärmen (*Mil.*); *–ment area,* das Aufmarschgebiet.

depolariz–ation [dɪːpoulərɑɪˈzeɪʃən], *s.* die Depolarisierung. **–e** [dɪːˈpoulərɑɪz], *v.a.* depolarisieren.

depone [dɪˈpoun], *v.a.* eidlich aussagen (*Scots*). **–nt,** 1. *adj.*; *–nt verb,* das Deponens (*Gram.*). 2. *s.* vereidigter Zeuge.

depopulat–e [dɪːˈpɔpjuleɪt], *v.a.* (*& n.* sich) entvölkern. **–ion** [–ˈleɪʃən], *s.* die Entvölkerung, Aussiedlung.

deport [dɪˈpɔːt], *v.a.* verbannen, deportieren; fortschaffen; ausweisen, abschieben (*aliens*); *– o.s.,* sich benehmen, sich betragen, sich verhalten. **–ation** [dɪːpɔːˈteɪʃən], *s.* die Verbannung, Landesverweisung; Ausweisung, Abschiebung (*of aliens*). **–ee,** *s.* Deportierte(r), *m.* **–ment** [dɪˈpɔːtmənt], *s.* das Benehmen, Betragen; Verhalten, die Haltung (*of things*).

depos–able [dɪˈpouzəbl], *adj.* absetzbar. **–e** [dɪˈpouz], *v.a.* absetzen, entsetzen; entthronen (*a king, etc.*); eidlich bezeugen *or* aussagen.

deposit [dɪˈpɔzɪt], 1. *s.* die Lagerstätte (*Geol.*); das Ablagerungsprodukt, der Niederschlag, Satz, Absatz, Bodensatz; die Abscheidung, Ausscheidung, der Belag; das Depot, die Ablagerung (*of goods*); Einlage, Hinterlegung, Anzahlung, Kaution, das Angeld, Depositum, Unterpfand; *– account,* das Depositenkonto; *– in a bank,* das Bankdepositum; *– in a boiler,* der Kesselstein; *make a –,* eine Anzahlung leisten; *place on –,* deponieren. 2. *v.a.* legen (*eggs*); absetzen, ablagern (*Chem.*); anschwemmen (*land*); einlegen, anzahlen, einzahlen, hinterlegen, deponieren (*money*). 3. *v.n.* anlagern, sich absetzen, absitzen, sich ablagern, niederschlagen. **–ary** [–ərɪ], *s.* der Verwahrer, Depositar. **–ion** [dɛpoˈzɪʃən, diːp–], *s.* (eidliche) Zeugenaussage; die Bekundung; Einzahlung (*of money*); Absetzung, Entsetzung (*from an office, etc.*); Entthronung; Anschwemmung (*of mud, etc.*); Ablagerung, Anlagerung, der Niederschlag; die Kreuzabnahme (*of Christ*). **–or** [dɪˈpɔzɪtə], *s.* der Deponent, Einzahler, Hinterleger; *–or's book*, das Einlagebuch. **–ory** [–rɪ], *s.* der Aufbewahrungsort, die Niederlage; (*fig.*) Fundgrube.

depot [ˈdɛpoʊ], *s.* die Niederlage, Ablage, Lagerstelle, das Lagerhaus; der Bahnhof (*Amer.*); das Lager, Depot, der Park (*Mil.*); – *ship*, das Mutterschiff.

deprav–ation [dɛprəˈveɪʃən], *s.* die Verschlechterung; Entartung, das Schlechtwerden; die Entsittlichung, Verderbtheit, Verkommenheit. **–e** [dɪˈpreɪv], *v.a.* moralisch verderben. **–ed,** *adj.* moralisch entartet, verdorben. **–ity** [dɪˈprævɪtɪ], *s.* die Verderbtheit, Verworfenheit.

deprecat–e [ˈdɛprɪkeɪt], *v.a.* mißbilligen, tadeln, rügen; von sich weisen, abzuwenden suchen. **–ing,** *adj.* abweisend. **–ion** [–ˈkeɪʃən], *s.* die Mißbilligung, der Tadel; die Abbitte. **–ory** [–kətərɪ], *adj.* ablehnend, mißbilligend; abbittend; *–ory letter*, das Bittschreiben.

depreciat–e [dɪˈpriːʃɪeɪt], 1. *v.a.* herabsetzen (*prices*); vermindern (*value*), entwerten; (*fig.*) geringschätzen, herabwürdigen. 2. *v.n.* im Preise fallen, im Werte sinken. **–ion** [–ˈeɪʃən], *s.* die Verringerung, Herabsetzung (*in value, etc.*); Entwertung (*of currency*); (*fig.*) Geringschätzung, abfällige Kritik; die Abschreibung (*for wear and tear*). **–ory** [–ʃɪətərɪ], *adj.* herabsetzend; geringschätzig.

depredat–ion [dɛprɪˈdeɪʃən], *s.* die Verwüstung, Verheerung, Plünderung, der Raub; der Raubbau. **–or** [ˈdɛprədeɪtə], *s.* der Plünderer, Verwüster. **–ory** [ˈdɛprədeɪtərɪ], *adj.* verheerend.

depress [dɪˈprɛs], *v.a.* niederdrücken, herunterdrücken; hemmen, einschränken, abflauen lassen (*trade, etc.*); herabsetzen, herabdrücken (*prices*); niederschlagen, bedrücken (*one's spirits*); mäßigen, senken (*voice*). **–ant,** 1. *adj.* niederdrückend, beruhigend. 2. *s.* das Beruhigungsmittel (*Med.*). **–ed** [–t], *adj.* niedergedrückt, gesenkt; niedergeschlagen, gedrückt; flau (*C.L.*). **–ing,** *adj.* niederdrückend. **–ion** [–ˈprɛʃən], *s.* die Niederdrückung, Senkung, Erniedrigung; Vertiefung (*on surface*); gedrückte Stimmung, die Niedergeschlagenheit, Gedrücktheit (*of spirits*); (Körper-)Schwäche, Entkräftung (*Med.*); Flauheit (*of trade, etc.*); Depression, der Tiefstand (*of a star*); das Fallen, Sinken (*of a barometer*); Tief (*Meteor.*); *–ion line*, die Muldenlinie. **–or,** *s.* der Niederziehmuskel (*Anat.*).

depriv–ation [dɛprɪˈveɪʃən], *s.* die Beraubung; Entsetzung, Absetzung (*Eccl.*); der Verlust, die Entehrung. **–e** [dɪˈpraɪv], *v.a.* (*a p. of a th.*), einen einer S. (*Gen.*)) berauben, (einem etwas) rauben, nehmen, entziehen; fernhalten, ausschließen (*of*, von); entsetzen (*of* (*Gen.*)), absetzen; *this –es us of the pleasure*, dies beraubt uns des Vergnügens *or* raubt uns das Vergnügen; *I must –e myself of that pleasure*, ich muß mir dies Vergnügen versagen.

depth [dɛpθ], *s.* die Tiefe (*also fig.*); Fülle, der Tiefdruck (*of colour*); die Unverständlichkeit, Dunkelheit (*of meaning*); Teufe (*Min.*); (*usually* –s, *pl.*) der Abgrund, das Meer; Innerste; – *of column*, die Marschlänge (*Mil.*); – *of focus*, die Tiefenschärfe (*Phot.*); – *of misery*, der Abgrund des Elends; *in the – of night*, in tiefster Nacht; *in the – of winter*, mitten im Winter; *get out of one's –*, den (sichern) Grund unter den Füßen verlieren; *be out of one's –*, (*fig.*) den Boden unter den Füßen verlieren, ratlos davor stehen. **– -charge,** *s.* die Unterwasserbombe. **– -gauge,** *s.* der Tiefenmesser. **– -sounder,** *s.* das Tiefseelot, Echolot.

depurat–e [ˈdɛpjʊreɪt], *v.a.* reinigen, läutern. **–ion** [–ˈreɪʃən], *s.* die Reinigung, Läuterung. **–ive** [dɪˈpjʊərətɪv], *adj.* reinigend.

deput–ation [dɛpjʊˈteɪʃən], *s.* die Abordnung, Deputation, die Abgesandten (*pl.*). **–e** [dɪˈpjuːt], *v.a.* abordnen, zum Stellvertreter bestellen, bevollmächtigen, mit Vollmacht absenden; übertragen (*to* (*Dat.*)) (*task*). **–ize,** *v.n.* vertreten (*for a p.*, einen), einspringen (für einen). **–y** [ˈdɛpjʊtɪ], *s.* Abgeordnete(r), *m.*, Abgesandte(r), *m.*, der Stellvertreter (*Law*); Bevollmächtigte(r), *m.*, der Geschäftsträger (*C.L.*); *by –y*, durch Stellvertretung; *chamber of –ies*, das Abgeordnetenhaus. **– -chairman,** *s.* stellvertretende(r) Vorsitzende(r) *m.*, der Vizepräsident.

deracinate [dɪˈræsɪneɪt], *v.a.* entwurzeln, ausrotten.

derail [dɪˈreɪl], 1. *v.a.* zum Entgleisen bringen. 2. *v.n.* entgleisen. **–ment,** *s.* die Entgleisung (*Railw.*).

derange [dɪˈreɪndʒ], *v.a.* in Unordnung bringen, verwirren, stören; zerrütten (*the mind*). **–d,** *adj.* verrückt, geistesgestört; verdorben (*as stomach*). **–ment,** *s.* die Unordnung, Verwirrung, Störung; die Geistesstörung, Geisteszerrüttung.

derate [dɪˈreɪt], *v.a.* von städtischer Steuer befreien.

derelict [ˈdɛrɪlɪkt], 1. *adj.* verlassen, herrenlos. 2. *s.* herrenloses Gut; das Wrack. **–ion** [–ˈlɪkʃən], *s.* das Aufgeben, Verlassen, Verlassensein; die Vernachlässigung, Versäumnis; das Zurücktreten (*of the sea*); trocken gelegtes Land; *–ion of duty*, die Pflichtverletzung, Pflichtvergessenheit.

de-restrict [diːrɪˈstrɪkt], *v.a.* Einschränkungen *or* die Bewirtschaftung lockern.

deri–de [dɪˈraɪd], *v.a.* verlachen, verhöhnen, verspotten, verächtlich behandeln. **–der,** *s.* der Spötter, Verspotter, Verhöhner. **–sion** [dɪˈrɪʒən], *s.* der Hohn, Spott; das Gespött, die Zielscheibe des Spottes. **–sive** [–ˈraɪsɪv], *adj.* spöttisch, höhnisch. **–sory,** *adj. see* **–sive**; lächerlich, winzig.

deriv–able [dɪˈraɪvəbl], *adj.* ableitbar, herleitbar (*from*, von), erreichbar (*from*, aus); *be –able from*, sich herleiten von. **–ate** [ˈdɛrɪveɪt], *s.* die Abgeleitete (*Math.*). **–ation** [dɛrɪˈveɪʃən], *s.* die Ableitung, Herleitung; Herkunft, Abstammung, der Ursprung. **–ative** [dəˈrɪvətɪv], 1. *adj.* abgeleitet, hergeleitet. 2. *s.* abgeleitetes Wort, das Derivat(um) (*Gram.*); der Differenzialkoeffizient (*Math.*); der Abkömmling, das Derivat (*Chem.*); abgeleitete Sache. **–e** [dɪˈraɪv], *v.a.* ableiten, herleiten (*from*, von); gewinnen, bekommen, erhalten (*from*, von), verdanken (*from a p.*, einem); *be –ed from*, sich ableiten, herleiten, herstammen *or* herrühren von; *–e pleasure from*, Freude haben an; *–e profit from*, Nutzen ziehen aus *or* haben von.

derm–a [ˈdəːmə], *s.* die Haut (*Anat.*). **–al,** *adj.* Haut–. **–atitis** [–ˈtaɪtɪs], *s.* die Hautentzündung. **–atoid** [ˈdəːmətɔɪd], *adj.* hautähnlich. **–atology** [–əˈtɔlədʒɪ], *s.* die Hautlehre. **–ic,** *adj.* Haut–. **–oid,** *adj. see* **–atoid.**

derogat–e [ˈdɛrogeɪt], *v.n.* & *a.* vermindern, beeinträchtigen, schmälern (*from* (*Acc.*)); Abbruch tun, schaden (*Dat.*); *–e from o.s.*, sich erniedrigen, seiner (*Gen.*) unwürdig handeln, sich etwas vergeben; *–e from rules*, von den Regeln abgehen (*Law*). **–ion** [–ˈgeɪʃən], *s.* die Herabsetzung, Entwürdigung; Beeinträchtigung, Schmälerung, der Abbruch (*from* (*Gen.*)). **–ory** [dəˈrɔgətərɪ], *adj.* schmälernd, beeinträchtigend; nachteilig, schadend (*Dat. or* für (*Acc.*)); herabsetzend, abfällig (*as a remark*); *be –ory to*, schaden (*Dat.*), beeinträchtigen (*Acc.*); *–ory to o.s.*, seiner unwürdig.

derrick [ˈdɛrɪk], *s.* der Ladebaum (*Naut.*); beweglicher Ausleger, der Dreh- und Wippkran; Bohrturm (*over oil-well*).

dervish [ˈdəːvɪʃ], *s.* der Derwisch.

descant [dɪsˈkænt], 1. *v.n.* Diskant *or* Sopran singen (*Mus.*); (*fig.*) sich weitläufig auslassen, breit reden, sich verbreiten (*on* or *upon*, über). 2. *s.* der Diskant, Sopran; die Variation eines Liedes; polyphone Musik.

descend [dɪˈsɛnd], 1. *v.n.* hinab–, hinunter–, herab– *or* heruntersteigen, –fallen, –fließen *or* –kommen; niedersteigen, niedergehen, niederkommen; absteigen, aussteigen; fallen, abfallen, sinken; landen, niedergehen (*Av.*); tiefer werden, fallen (*Mus.*); – *from* (usually: *be –ed from*), abstammen von; – *on*, herfallen über, stürzen auf, einfallen in; einbrechen *or* hereinbrechen über; – *on a p.*, einen überfallen; – *to a p.*, einem anheimfallen, auf einen übergehen, sich auf einen vererben; – *to a th.*, sich zu etwas herablassen *or* erniedrigen, sich auf etwas einlassen; – *upon*, see – *on*; *–ing node*, absteigender Knoten (*Astr.*); *–ing series*, fallende Reihe (*Math.*). 2. *v.a.* herunter- *or* hinuntergehen or –steigen. **–ant**, *s.* der Abkömmling, Nachkomme.

descent [dɪˈsɛnt], *s.* das Hinab– *or* Herabsteigen, der Abstieg; Abhang, Abfall, die Neigung, Senkung, das Fallen, Gefälle (*Surv.*, *Build.*); die Einfahrt (*into a mine*); Abstammung, Herkunft, Geburt; (feindlicher) Einfall (*on*, in (*Acc.*)), die Landung (auf, in (*Dat.*)); der Angriff (*on*, auf (*Acc.*)); der Heimfall, die Übertragung, Vererbung (*of property, etc.*); der Fall, die Erniedrigung; – *from the cross*, die Kreuzabnahme; – *into Hell*, die Höllenfahrt; *make a –*, landen, Landung machen (*Av.*); *parachute –*, der Fallschirmabsprung; *rate of –*, die Sinkgeschwindigkeit (*Av.*).

describ–able [dɪsˈkraɪbəbl], *adj.* beschreibbar. **–e** [dɪsˈkraɪb], *v.a.* beschreiben, schildern, darstellen; bezeichnen (*as*, als); *–e a circle*, einen Kreis zeichnen *or* beschreiben; *–e o.s. as an actor*, sich als Schauspieler ausgeben.

descripti–on [dɪsˈkrɪpʃən], *s.* die Beschreibung, Schilderung, Darstellung; Art, Sorte, Gattung; *beggar –on*, jeder Beschreibung spotten; *past all –on*, unbeschreiblich. **–ve** [–tɪv], *adj.* beschreibend, schildernd, darstellend; vielsagend; *be –ve of*, beschreiben, bezeichnen; *–ve power*, die Darstellungsgabe.

descry [dɪsˈkraɪ], *v.a.* gewahren, wahrnehmen, erspähen.

desecrat–e [ˈdɛsɪkreɪt], *v.a.* entweihen, entheiligen, profanieren. **–ion** [–ˈkreɪʃən], *s.* die Entweihung, Entheiligung.

[1]**desert** [ˈdɛzət], 1. *adj.* wüst, öde, verlassen. 2. *s.* die Wüste, Einöde.

[2]**desert** [dɪˈzəːt], 1. *v.a.* verlassen; im Stiche lassen (*a friend*); abtrünnig *or* untreu werden (*a party, etc.*). 2. *v.n.* fahnenflüchtig werden, überlaufen, desertieren (*Mil.*). **–er** [dɪˈzəːtə], *s.* Fahnenflüchtige(r), *m.*, der Deserteur; der Überläufer (*Mil.*). **–ion** [–ˈzəːʃən], *s.* das Verlassen (*of a place, etc.*); der Abfall (*from a party*); das Imstichlassen (*of a friend*); böswilliges Verlassen (*Law*); die Fahnenflucht, Desertion (*Mil.*).

[3]**desert** [dɪˈzəːt], *s.* (*often* **–s**) das Verdienst, die Verdienstlichkeit, verdienter Lohn, wohlverdiente Strafe; *you have got your –s*, Sie haben die verdiente Strafe bekommen.

deserv–e [dɪˈzəːv], 1. *v.a.* verdienen, verdient haben; Anspruch haben auf, würdig sein (*Gen.*); *he –es* (*is –ing of*) *esteem*, er verdient Achtung. 2. *v.n.* sich verdient machen; *he has –ed well of his country*, er hat sich um sein Vaterland wohlverdient gemacht; *–e well of a p.*, sich (*Dat.*) einen zum Dank verpflichten. **–edly** [–ɪdlɪ], *adv.* verdientermaßen, mit Recht, nach Verdienst. **–ing,** *adj.* wert, würdig, verdienstvoll; *be –ing of*, verdienen; *the –ing poor*, die verschämten Armen (*pl.*).

desicca–nt, *s.* das Trocknungsmittel. **–te** [ˈdɛsɪkeɪt], 1. *v.a.* (aus)trocknen. 2. *v.n.* trocken werden. **–tion** [–ˈkeɪʃən], *s.* das Trocknen, die Austrocknung. **–tive** [–kətɪv], *adj.* austrocknend. **–tor,** *s.* der Trockenapparat, Exsikkator.

desiderat–e [dɪˈzɪdəreɪt], *v.a.* bedürfen (*Gen.*), vermissen, ersehnen. **–ive** [–rətɪv], 1. *adj.* ein Verlangen anzeigend (*also Gram.*). 2. *s.* das Desiderativum (*Gram.*). **–um** [–ˈreɪtəm], *s.* (*pl.* **–a**] das Gewünschte, Erwünschte, Erfordernis, Bedürfnis.

design [dɪˈzaɪn], 1. *v.a.* aufzeichnen, entwerfen, skizzieren; (*fig.*) ersinnen, ausdenken, planen, beabsichtigen, vorhaben, sich (*Dat.*) vornehmen; *his father –ed him for the bar*, sein Vater bestimmte ihn zum Rechtsanwalt. 2. *s.* das Vorhaben, die Absicht; der Plan, Anschlag, Endzweck; das Projekt, die Anordnung, Anlage, Einteilung, Ausführung, Konstruktion, der Bau; die Zeichnung; der Entwurf, Abriß; das Muster Dessin (*of fabrics*); *by accident or by –*, durch Zufall oder beabsichtigt; *have –s on* or *against*, etwas im Schilde führen gegen; *registered –*, das Gebrauchsmuster. **–ate** [ˈdɛzɪgneɪt], 1. *v.a.* bezeichnen, kennzeichnen; betiteln, benennen; ernennen, aussersehen, bestimmen (*for*, zu). 2. *adj.* (*follows noun*) ernannt, ausersehen, designiert. **–ation** [–ˈneɪʃən], *s.* die Bezeichnung, Benennung (*of*, für); Bestimmung, Ernennung (*to*, zu). **–edly,** *adv.* absichtlich, vorsätzlich. **–er** [dɪˈzaɪnə], *s.* der (Muster)Zeichner; Erfinder, Konstrukteur; (*fig.*) Projektenmacher; Ränkeschmied, Intrigant. **–ing,** *adj.* ränkevoll.

desilverize [dɪːˈsɪlvəraɪz], *v.a.* entsilbern.

desirab–ility [dɪzaɪərəˈbɪlɪtɪ], *s.* die Erwünschtheit, das Wünschenswerte. **–le,** *adj.* wünschenswert; erwünscht, angenehm; *it is –le, that*, es wird erwünscht daß; *–le residence*, angenehme Wohnung.

desir–e [dɪˈzaɪə], 1. *v.a.* wünschen, verlangen, begehren; bitten, ersuchen; *as –ed*, wie gewünscht; *if –ed*, auf Wunsch; *leave much* (*nothing*) *to be –ed*, viel (nichts) zu wünschen übriglassen. 2. *s.* das Verlangen, Begehren (*for*, nach); der Wunsch, die Bitte; Begierde, Lust, Sehnsucht; *in accordance with one's –e*, wie gewünscht, wunschgemäß. **–ous** [–rəs], *pred. adj.* begierig, verlangend (*of*, nach); *be –ous of doing*, danach verlangen zu tun; *be –ous to do*, gern tun mögen.

desist [dɪˈsɪst], *v.n.* abstehen, ablassen, Abstand nehmen (*from*, von), sich enthalten (*from* (*Dat.*)). **–ance,** *s.* das Abstehen, Ablassen.

desize [dɪːˈsaɪz], *v.a.* entleimen, entschlichten.

desk [dɛsk], *s.* das Pult; der Schreibtisch; *reading–*–, das Lesepult; *writing–*–, der Schreibtisch.

desolat–e [ˈdɛsolɪt], 1. *adj.* einsam, verlassen; wüst, öde; betrübt, trostlos, niedergeschlagen, traurig (*of persons*). 2. [–leɪt], *v.a.* verwüsten, verheeren; betrübt *or* traurig machen. **–eness,** *s.* das Elend, die Vereinsamung, der Gram. **–ion** [–ˈleɪʃən], *s.* die Verödung, Verwüstung; Einöde; das Elend, der Gram, die Trostlosigkeit.

despair [dɪsˈpɛə], 1. *s.* die Hoffnungslosigkeit, Verzweiflung (*at*, über); *drive to –*, zur Verzweiflung bringen; *he is the – of his teachers*, er gibt seinen Lehrern Grund zur Verzweiflung. 2. *v.n.* verzweifeln, ohne Hoffnung sein, die Hoffnung aufgeben; – *of*, verzweifeln an (*Dat.*); *his life is –ed of*, er stirbt gewiß. **–ing** [–rɪŋ], *adj.* verzweifelnd, verzweiflungsvoll, hoffnungslos.

despatch [dɪsˈpætʃ], *see* **dispatch.**

despera–do [dɛspəˈreɪdoʊ], *s.* der Wagehals, Tollkopf, Heißsporn; Schwerverbrecher, Bandit. **–te** [ˈdɛspərɪt], *adj.* hoffnungslos, verzweifelt; verwegen, tollkühn; (*coll.*) arg, schlecht; ungeheuer, toll; *rendered –te*, zur Verzweiflung gebracht; *–te remedy*, äußerstes Mittel. **–tion** [–ˈreɪʃən], *s.* die Verzweiflung, Hoffnungslosigkeit; Raserei, Wut; *drive to –tion*, rasend machen, zur Verzweiflung bringen.

despicable [ˈdɛspɪkəbl], *adj.* verächtlich; jämmerlich.

despise [dɪsˈpaɪz], *v.a.* verachten, geringschätzen; verschmähen.

despite [dɪsˈpaɪt], 1. *s.* die Verachtung, Beschimpfung; der Trotz, die Widersetzlichkeit; das Übelwollen, der Haß, die Tücke, Bosheit; *in – of you*, dir zum Trotze; *in one's own –*, sich selbst zum Trotze, wider seinen Willen. 2. *prep.* (or *in – of*) trotz (*Dat. or Gen.*), ungeachtet (*Dat.*). **–ful,** *adj.* (*archaic*) boshaft, tückisch.

despo–il [dɪsˈpɔɪl], *v.a.* plündern, berauben. **–liation** [dɪspoʊlɪˈeɪʃən], *s.* die Plünderung, Beraubung.

despond [dɪsˈpɔnd], *v.n.* verzagen, verzweifeln (*of*, an (*Dat.*)). **–ence, –ency,** *s.* die Verzweiflung, Verzagtheit, Mutlosigkeit. **–ent, –ing,** *adj.* verzweifelnd, verzagend, verzagt, mutlos, kleinmütig.

despot [ˈdɛspɔt], *s.* der Gewaltherrscher, Despot; Tyrann. **–ic** [dɛsˈpɔtɪk], *adj.* despotisch, herrisch, gebieterisch, unumschränkt. **–ism** [ˈdɛspətɪzm], *s.* die Gewaltherrschaft, der Despotismus.

desquamat–e [ˈdɛskwəmeɪt], *v.a.* (*& n.*) (sich) abschuppen. **–ion** [dɛskwəˈmeɪʃən], *s.* das Abschuppen (*Med.*), Abblättern (*Geol.*).

dessert [dɪ'zəːt], *s.* der Nachtisch, das Dessert, die Süßspeise. **--spoon,** *s.* der Dessertlöffel.
destination [dɛstɪ'neɪʃən], *s.* die Bestimmung, das Ziel; der Bestimmungsort, das Reiseziel; die Adresse (*of a letter*).
destine ['dɛstɪn], *v.a.* bestimmen; ausersehen (*for*, für); *–d to do*, tun sollen.
destiny ['dɛstɪnɪ], *s.* das Schicksal, Geschick, Verhängnis; die Notwendigkeit, Schicksalsgewalt.
destitut–e ['dɛstɪtjuːt], *adj.* bar, ermangelnd (*of* (*Gen.*)), entblößt (*of*, von); hilflos, mittellos, verarmt, notleidend. **–ion** [–'tjuːʃən], *s.* das Fehlen, der Mangel (*of*, an (*Dat.*)); bittere Not, die Armut.
destroy [dɪs'trɔɪ], *v.a.* zerstören, vernichten, verheeren; niederreißen, zerschlagen, demolieren; töten; aufreiben (*enemy forces*), ausrotten, vertilgen, unschädlich machen; zersetzen, auflösen (*Chem.*); – *one's health*, seine Gesundheit zerrütten; – *s.o.'s hopes*, jemandes Hoffnungen zunichte machen. **–able,** *adj.* zerstörbar. **–er,** *s.* der Zerstörer (*also Naut.*). **–ing,** *adj.* vernichtend, verheerend; *–ing angel*, der Würgengel.
destruct–ibility [dɪstrʌktə'bɪlɪtɪ], *s.* die Zerstörbarkeit. **–ible** [dɪs'trʌktɪbl], *adj.* zerstörbar. **–ion** [dɪs'trʌkʃən], *s.* die Zerstörung, Vernichtung, Zertrümmerung, Verwüstung, Verheerung, das Zugrunderichten; die Tötung, (*fig.*) das Verderben, der Zerfall, Untergang; *work one's own –ion*, seinen eignen Untergang herbeiführen. **–ive** [–tɪv], *adj.* zerstörend, vernichtend; verderblich, schädlich; zersetzend; *be –ive of*, untergraben, zerstören; *–ive criticism*, negative *or* verneinende Kritik. **–iveness,** *s.* zerstörende Gewalt, die Verderblichkeit, Zerstörungswut. **–or,** *s.* die Verbrennungsanlage.
desuetude ['dɛswɪtjuːd], *s.* das Aufhören eines Gebrauchs; die Ungebräuchlichkeit; *fall into –*, außer Gebrauch kommen; *lost by –*, infolge Nichtgeltendmachung verloren.
desulphur–ate [dɪː'sʌlfjuəreɪt], *v.a.*, **–ize** [–raɪz], *v.a.* entschwefeln.
desultor–iness ['dɛsəltərɪnɪs], *s.* die Flüchtigkeit, Planlosigkeit, Oberflächlichkeit; Flatterhaftigkeit, der Unbestand. **–y** ['dɛsəltərɪ], *adj.* unzusammenhängend, planlos, unmethodisch; oberflächlich, flüchtig; flatterhaft, unbeständig; *–y remark*, beiläufige Bemerkung.
detach [dɪ'tætʃ], *v.a.* losmachen, loslösen, ablösen, trennen, abtrennen, abnehmen, absondern; detachieren, abkommandieren (*Mil.*). **–able,** *adj.* abnehmbar, abtrennbar, lösbar, trennbar; – *able magazine*, das Ansteckmagazin. **–ed** [–t], *adj.* getrennt, abgesondert, einzeln (*as events*); freistehend, alleinstehend (*as houses*); abgestellt, abgegeben, zur besonderen Verwendung (*Mil.*); objektiv, unparteiisch, unvoreingenommen; gleichgültig (*as attitudes*). **–ment,** *s.* die Absonderung, Trennung, das Losmachen; die Abteilung, der Trupp (*Mil.*); die Objektivität (*of mind*).
detail [dɪ'teɪl], 1. *v.a.* ausführlich beschreiben, umständlich erzählen; einteilen, abkommandieren (*Mil.*). 2. ['dɪːteɪl], *s.* die Einzelheit; Abteilung (*Mil.*); der Tagesbefehl (*Mil.*); die Detailarbeit, Detailbehandlung; (*pl.*) die Nebenumstände, Einzelheiten, Besonderheiten, nähere Angaben, das Nähere; *in –*, umständlich, ausführlich; *go into* or *come down to –*(*s*), auf Einzelheiten eingehen, ausführlich *or* eingehend erörtern, ins einzelne gehen; *down to the smallest –*, bis ins einzelne. **–ed,** *adj.* eingehend, ausführlich, umständlich.
detain [dɪ'teɪn], *v.a.* aufhalten, abhalten, hindern, warten lassen; nachsitzen lassen (*at school*); zurückhalten, vorenthalten; in Haft behalten, festhalten (*in prison*). **–er,** *s.* die Haft, (widerrechtliche) Vorenthaltung (*Law*); *writ of –er*, der Haftverlängerungsbefehl.
detect [dɪ'tɛkt], *v.a.* entdecken, aufdecken, ertappen; nachweisen, ermitteln, ausfindig machen. **–able** [–əbl], *adj.* entdeckbar. **–ion** [–'tɛkʃən], *s.* die Entdeckung, Ermittlung, der Nachweis. **–ive,** *s.* der Geheimpolizist, Kriminalbeamte(r), *m.*, der Detektiv; *–ive force*, die Geheimpolizei; *–ive story*, die Detektivgeschichte. **–or** [–tə], *s.* der Detektor, Gleichrichter (*Rad.*); Anzeiger.
detent [dɪ'tɛnt], *s.* der Sperrkegel, Sperrhaken (*Horol.*).
détente [de'tɑːnt], *s.* die Entspannung (*Pol.*).
detention [dɪ'tɛnʃən], *s.* die Zurückhaltung, Vorenthaltung; Abhaltung, Beschlagnahme; Haft, Gefangenhaltung (*Law*); der Arrest (*Mil.*); das Nachsitzen (*at school*); – *camp*, das Internierungslager; – *colony*, die Strafkolonie; *preventive –*, die Schutzhaft, Sicherungsverwahrung; *unlawful –*, die Freiheitsberaubung.
deter [dɪ'təː], *v.a.* abschrecken; abhalten, verhindern. **–ment,** *s.* das Abschrecken; Hindernis; Abschreckmittel.
detergent [dɪ'təːdʒənt], 1. *adj.* reinigend. 2. *s.* das Reinigungsmittel.
deteriorat–e [dɪ'tɪərɪəreɪt], 1. *v.a.* verschlechtern, verschlimmern, beeinträchtigen, verderben, herabsetzen. 2. *v.n.* sich verschlimmern *or* verschlechtern, verderben; entarten, verfallen. **–ion** [–'reɪʃən], *s.* die Verschlimmerung, Verschlechterung, Entartung, der Zerfall, Verderb.
determent, *see* **deter.**
determin–able [dɪ'təːmɪnəbl], *adj.* bestimmbar, festsetzbar, entscheidbar. **–ant,** 1. *adj.* bestimmend. 2. *s.* das Bestimmende; die Determinante (*Math.*). **–ate** [dɪ'təːmɪnɪt], *adj.* bestimmt, entschieden, entschlossen, fest(gesetzt); endgültig. **–ateness,** *s.* die Bestimmtheit; Entschlossenheit. **–ation** [dɪtəːmɪ'neɪʃən], *s.* die Entschlossenheit, Entschiedenheit, Bestimmtheit; Festsetzung, Festlegung, Entscheidung, Bestimmung; der Beschluß, Entschluß, Vorsatz; Schluß, das Ende, die Lösung, der Ablauf (*Law*); das Streben, die Richtung, Neigung, Tendenz, der Drang; *man of –ation*, entschlossener Mann. **–ative** [dɪ'təːmɪnɪtɪv], 1. *adj.* bestimmend; einschränkend (*of words, etc.*); entscheidend. 2. *s.* das Charakteristische, Bestimmende; Determinativum (*Gram.*). **–e** [dɪ'təːmɪn], 1. *v.a.* beendigen, entscheiden, abmachen, aufheben; zur Entscheidung bringen, schlichten; bestimmen, festsetzen, feststellen, ausfindig machen, aufklären, aufdecken; veranlassen; *–e s.o. in favour of a p.*, einen für jemand günstig stimmen. 2. *v.n.* beschließen, zu einem Schluß kommen, einen Entschluß fassen; *I am –ed to do it*, ich will es unbedingt tun; *be –ed by*, bestimmt *or* getragen werden von; *–ed on doing*, beschließen zu tun. **–ed,** *adj.* entschlossen, entschieden, bestimmt.
deterrent [dɪ'tɛrənt], 1. *s.* das Abschreckungsmittel (*to*, für). 2. *adj.* abschreckend.
detersive [dɪ'təːsɪv], *s.* & *adj. see* **detergent.**
detest [dɪ'tɛst], *v.a.* verabscheuen. **–able,** *adj.* verabscheuungswürdig, abscheulich. **–ableness,** *s.* die Abscheulichkeit. **–ation** [–'teɪʃən], *s.* die Verabscheuung, der Abscheu (*of* or *for*, gegen *or* vor); *hold in –ation*, verabscheuen.
dethrone [dɪ'θroʊn], *v.a.* entthronen (*also fig.*). **–ment,** *s.* die Entthronung.
detonat–e ['dɪːtoʊneɪt], 1. *v.n.* (ab)knallen, detonieren, explodieren, verpuffen, zerplatzen, losknallen. 2. *v.a.* explodieren *or* verpuffen lassen. *–ing composition*, der Knallsatz, Zündsatz. **–ion** [–'neɪʃən], *s.* der Knall, die Detonation, Explosion, Zündung. **–or,** *s.* der Knallkörper, das Knallsignal (*Railw.*); der Zünder, die Zündkapsel, Sprengkapsel, Zündpatrone.
detour [deɪ'tuə], *s.* der Umweg, Abstecher, die Umgehung, Umleitung.
detract [dɪ'trækt], *v.a.* & *n.* abziehen, wegnehmen, entziehen (*from* (*Dat.*)); – *from a th.*, einer S. Eintrag *or* Abbruch tun, eine S. beeinträchtigen, heruntersetzen, herabsetzen, vermindern *or* schmälern; – *from a p.'s reputation*, einen herabsetzen *or* verunglimpfen. **–ion** [–'trækʃən], *s.* die Herabsetzung, Beeinträchtigung (*from* (*Dat.*)); Verleumdung. **–ive,** *adj.* verleumderisch; *be –ive from*, herabsetzen. **–or,** *s.* der Verleumder; Abziehmuskel (*Anat.*).
detrain [dɪː'treɪn], 1. *v.a.* ausladen, absetzen (*persons*) (*Mil.*). 2. *v.n.* aussteigen. **–ment,** *s.* die Ausladung (*of troops*) (*Mil.*).
detriment ['dɛtrɪmənt], *s.* der Nachteil, Schaden, Abbruch; *to the – of*, zum Schaden (*Gen.*); *with-*

out – to, ohne Schaden für. **–al** [–ˈmɛntl], *adj.* schädlich, nachteilig, ungünstig (*to*, für); *be –al to*, schaden.

detrit–al [dɪˈtrɑɪtəl], *adj.* Steinschutt– (*Geol.*). **–ed** [–tɪd], *adj.* abgenutzt. **–ion** [dɪˈtrɪʃən], *s.* das Abnutzen, Abreiben. **–us** [dɪˈtrɑɪtəs], *s.* das Geröll(e), der Gesteinschutt (*Geol.*).

[1]**deuce** [djuːs], *s.* die Zwei, das Daus (*Cards, Dice*); der Einstand (*Tenn.*); *– ace*, der Wurf Eins und Zwei.

[2]**deuce,** *s.* der Teufel; (*sl.*) *what the – do you mean?* was zum Teufel wollen Sie damit sagen? **–d,** *adj.* (*sl.*) verflucht, verteufelt.

deuteronomy [djuːtəˈrɔnəmɪ], *s.* das fünfte Buch Mose.

devalue [dɪːˈvæljuː], *v.a.* abwerten, entwerten.

devastat–e [ˈdɛvəsteɪt], *v.a.* verwüsten, verheeren. **–ion** [–ˈteɪʃən], *s.* die Verwüstung, Verheerung. **–or,** *s.* der Verwüster.

develop [dɪˈvɛləp], 1. *v.a.* entwickeln (*also Phot.*); entfalten, enthüllen, hervorbringen, erschließen; bekommen, sich zuziehen (*as an ailment*); (*fig.*) herausarbeiten, ausbauen. 2. *v.n.* sich entfalten *or* entwickeln, entstehen; *slow to –*, entwicklungsträge. **–er,** *s.* der Entwickler (*Phot.*). **–ment,** *s.* die Entwickelung, Entwicklung (*Phot.*); Entfaltung, Bildung, der Verlauf, das Wachstum. **–mental,** *adj.* Entwicklungs–, Wachstums–.

deviat–e [ˈdɪːvɪeɪt], *v.n.* abweichen, abkommen, abgehen (*from*, von). **–ion** [–ˈeɪʃən], *s.* die Abweichung, Ablenkung der Nadel (*Magnet.*); *angle of –ion*, der Ablenkungswinkel; *–ion of a balance*, der Ausschlag einer Waage.

device [dɪˈvɑɪs], *s.* die Erfindung; Vorrichtung, das Gerät, Mittel, die Anlage, der Apparat; Plan, Einfall; Anschlag, Kunstgriff; das Sinnbild, der Wappenspruch, Wahlspruch, die Devise (*Her.*); *be left to one's own –s*, sich selbst überlassen werden.

devil [dɛvl], 1. *s.* der Teufel; Laufbursche (*Typ.*); Hilfsanwalt (*Law*); Handlanger; stark gewürztes Gericht (*Cook.*); der (Reiß)Wolf (*Weav.*); *the – !* alle Teufel! zum Henker! (*sl.*) *the – a bit*, nicht das geringste; (*sl.*) *the – a one*, gar keine(r)(s); (*sl.*) *how the –?* wie zum Teufel? *the –'s in it*, das muß mit dem Teufel zugehen; *like the –*, wie verrückt *or* wild; *that's the – of it*, da liegt der Hund begraben; *she–*, das Teufelsweib; *it's the (very) –*, es ist eine tolle Sache; (*a*) (*with nouns*) *the –'s advocate*, der Widerpart; *– of a fellow*, der Teufelskerl, verteufelter Kerl; *printer's –*, der Laufbursche einer Druckerei; (*sl.*) *the – of a time*, eine verdammt aufregende *or* schlechte Zeit; (*b*) (*with verbs*) *cast out the –*, den Teufel austreiben; *needs must when the – drives*, in der Not frißt der Teufel Fliegen; *give the – his due*, einem das Seine einräumen; *go to the –*, zugrunde gehen; *go to the – !* geh' zum Teufel!; *there's the – to pay*, der Teufel ist los; *play the – with*, arg mitspielen (*Dat.*); *– take him !* hol' ihn der Teufel! *talk of the – and he is sure to appear*, wenn man den Teufel an die Wand malt, ist er schon da; (*c*) (*with preposition*) *between the – and the deep sea*, zwischen Scylla und Charybdis. 2. *v.a.* stark gepfeffert rösten; wolfen, krempeln (*Weav.*). **––fish,** *s.* der Seeteufel (*Ichth.*). **–ish,** 1. *adj.* teuflisch, verdammt. 2. *adv.* (*coll.*) kolossal. **–ishness,** *s.* das Teuflische, die Teufelei. **––may-care,** *adj.* sorglos, unbekümmert; burschikos, verwegen. **–ment,** *s.* die Schelmerei, der Ulk, Unfug, Possen (*pl.*); die Tollkühnheit, der Mutwillen. **–ry,** *s.* die Teufelei, teuflische Kunst; die Grausamkeit, Schlechtigkeit. **––worship,** *s.* der Teufelsdienst.

devious [ˈdɪːvɪəs], *adj.* abweichend; abgelegen; gewunden; abwegig, irrig; *– paths*, Abwege; *– step*, der Fehltritt. **–ness,** *s.* die Abweichung, Verirrung.

devis–able [dɪˈvɑɪzəbl], *adj.* erdenkbar, erdenklich; vererbbar (*Law*). **–e** [dɪˈvɑɪz], 1. *v.n.* ersinnen, erdenken, ausdenken, erfinden; (*coll.*) drechseln; hinterlassen, letztwillig vermachen (*Law*). 2. *s.* das Vermachen; das Vermächtnis, Testament (*Law*). **–ee,** *s.* der Legatar, Testamentserbe (*Law*). **–er,** *s.* der Erfinder. **–or** [–ɔː], *s.* der Erblasser.

devitalize [dɪːˈvɑɪtəlɑɪz], *v.a.* der Lebenskraft berauben, entkräften.

devitrif–ication [dɪːvɪtrɪfɪˈkeɪʃən], *s.* die Entglasung. **–y,** [dɪːˈvɪtrɪfɑɪ], *v.a.* entglasen.

devoid [dɪˈvɔɪd], *adj.*; *– of*, ohne (*Acc.*), bar (*Gen.*), frei von, leer an (*Dat.*), –los; *– of fear*, furchtlos; *– of all feelings*, aller Gefühle bar, ohne jedes Gefühl; *– of understanding*, ohne Verständnis, verständnislos.

devoir [ˈdɛvwɑː], *s.* (*archaic*) die Höflichkeitsbezeigung; *pay one's –s*, seine Aufwartung machen (*to* (*Dat.*)).

devol–ution [dɪːvəˈluːʃən], *s.* der Verlauf, Ablauf, das Abrollen (*of time*); der Übergang, das Übergehen (*of a privilege*) (*on*, auf); die Übertragung, der Heimfall (an (*Acc.*)) (*Law*); die Abwälzung (*of responsibility*); Entartung (*Biol.*). **–ve** [dɪˈvɔlv], 1. *v.a.* abwälzen; übertragen (*on*, auf). 2. *v.n.* anheimfallen, zufallen (*to* or *on* (*Dat.*)), übergehen (auf); *the crown –ves on his eldest son*, die Krone fällt an seinen ältesten Sohn; *it –ves upon me to tell him*, es liegt mir ob, es ihm sagen.

devot–e [dɪˈvout], *v.a.* widmen, weihen (*to* (*Dat.*)); hingeben, zuwenden (*time, etc.*) (*to* (*Dat.*)); *–e o.s.*, sich widmen, sich ergeben (*to* (*Dat.*)). **–ed,** 1. *pred. adj.* ergeben; übergeben (*Dat.*). 2. *attr. adj.* treu, hingebungsvoll, zärtlich; dem Untergang geweiht. **–edness,** *s.* die Ergebenheit. **–ee,** *s.* der Verehrer, Verfechter; Betbruder, Frömmler. **–ion** [–ˈvouʃən], *s.* die Widmung, Weihung, Weihe; Hingebung, Aufopferung (*to*, für); Frömmigkeit, Andacht; Zuneigung; innige Liebe (*to* or *for*, zu); die Hingabe (*to*, an), Ergebenheit, Treue (*to*, gegen); der Eifer (*to*, für); (*pl.*) die Andacht, das Gebet, Andachtsübungen (*pl.*); *–ion to duty*, der Eifer in der Erfüllung der Pflicht; *be at one's –ions*, seine Andacht verrichten. **–ional,** *adj.* andächtig, fromm; *–ional book*, das Erbauungsbuch; *–ional frame of mind*, fromme Gemütsart.

devour [dɪˈvɑuə], *v.a.* verschlingen, verzehren, fressen; (*fig.*) vernichten, zerstören, wegraffen; *– a book*, ein Buch (förmlich) verschlingen. **–ing,** *adj.* verschlingend, brennend.

devout [dɪˈvɑut], *adj.* andächtig, fromm; innig, inbrünstig. **–ness,** *s.* die Frömmigkeit, Andächtigkeit, Innigkeit.

dew [djuː], *s.* der Tau; *the – is falling*, es taut. **–berry,** *s.* die Ackerbeere. **–drop,** *s.* der Tautropfen. **–iness,** *s.* die Feuchtigkeit. **––point,** *s.* der Taupunkt. **–y,** *adj.* betaut, tauig, taufeucht.

dewlap [ˈdjuːlæp], *s.* die Wamme, der Triel.

dext–er [ˈdɛkstə], *adj.* recht, recht(s)seitig (*Her.*) (*left of the observer*). **–erity** [–ˈtɛrɪtɪ], *s.* die Gewandtheit, Geschicklichkeit; Flinkheit; Rechtshändigkeit. **–erous,** *adj.* flink; gewandt, geschickt; rechtshändig. **–ral,** *adj.* rechtshändig. **–rality,** *s.* die Rechtshändigkeit. **–rin** [ˈdɛkstrɪn], *s.* das Dextrin; Stärkegummi, Röstgummi. **–ro,** *prefix* rechts–; *–ro-acid*, *s.* die Rechtssäure. **–ro-rotatory,** *adj.* rechtsdrehend. **–rose** [–strous], *s.* der Traubenzucker, die Dextrose. **–rous** [ˈdɛkstrəs], *adj. see* **–erous.**

di– [dɑɪ], *prefix* zwei, doppelt (*Chem.*).

diabet–es [dɑɪəˈbɪːtɪːz], *s.* die Zuckerkrankheit. **–ic,** 1. *adj.* zuckerkrank. 2. *s.* der Diabetiker, Zuckerkranke(r), *m.*

diab–lerie [dɪˈɑːblərɪ], *s.* die Teufelei, Hexerei. **–olic(al)** [dɑɪəˈbɔlɪk(l)], *adj.* teuflisch, böse, boshaft.

di-acid [dɑɪˈæsɪd], *adj.* zweisäurig.

diaconal [dɑɪˈækənəl], *adj.* Diakons–, Diakonats–; treffend.

diacoustics [dɑɪəˈkustɪks], *s.* die Schallbrechungslehre.

diacritic [dɑɪəˈkrɪtɪk], 1. *adj.* diakritisch, unterscheidend. 2. *s.* diakritisches Zeichen.

diadem [ˈdɑɪədɛm], *s.* das Diadem; (*fig.*) die Hoheit, Herrschaft.

diaeresis [dɑɪˈɪːərəsɪs], *s.* die Diärese, Diäresis; das Trema.

diagnos–e [dɑɪəgˈnouz], *v.n.* & *a.* diagnostizieren, (die Krankheit) bestimmen. **–is** [–ˈnousɪs], *s.* die Diagnose; *make a –is*, eine Diagnose stellen. **–tic** [–ˈnɔstɪk], *adj.* diagnostisch. **–tician,** *s.* der Diagnostiker. **–tics,** *pl.* die Diagnostik.

diagonal [dɑɪˈægənəl], 1. *adj.* diagonal, schräg, querlaufend. 2. *s.* die Diagonale, der Schrägschnitt.

diagra-m [ˈdaɪəgræm], *s.* erläuternde Figur, graphische Darstellung, das Diagramm, Schaubild, Schema; *circuit -m*, das Schaltschema, Schaltbild (*Rad.*); *floral -m*, der Blütengrundriß (*Bot.*). **-mmatic** [-grəˈmætɪk], *adj.* schematisch. **-ph,** *s.* der Diagraph.

dial [ˈdaɪəl], 1. *s.* das Zifferblatt (*clock, etc.*); der Wähler, die Wählerscheibe (*Phone.*), Ziffernscheibe, Nummernscheibe; (*sl.*) das Gesicht; *sun--*, die Sonnenuhr. 2. *v.a.* wählen (*Phone.*). **-ling tone,** *s.* das Amtszeichen (*Phone*). **--plate,** *s.* die Skalenscheibe, Strichplatte. **--telephone,** *s.* der Selbstanschlußfernsprecher.

dialect [ˈdaɪəlɛkt], *s.* die Mundart, der Dialekt; *study of -s*, die Mundartenforschung. **-al** [-ˈlɛktəl], *adj.* mundartlich; dialektisch. **-ic,** *s.* die Dialektik (*Philos.*). **-ic(al),** *adj.* dialektisch, logisch; spitzfindig. **-ician** [-ˈtɪʃən], *s.* der Dialektiker, Logiker. **-ics,** *pl.* die Dialektik.

dialogue [ˈdaɪəlɔg], *s.* das Zwiegespräch, der Dialog.

diamet-er [daɪˈæmɪtə], *s.* der Durchmesser; *inner -er* (*of a cylinder*), lichte Weite, die Zylinderbohrung; *in -er*, im Durchmesser. **-rical** [daɪəˈmɛtrɪkl], *adj.* diametrisch, mitten durch; *-rically opposed*, diametral, genau entgegengesetzt.

diamond [ˈdaɪəmənd], *s.* der Diamant, (*Poet.*) Demant; Rhombus, die Raute (*Geom.*); das Karo, Schellen (*pl.*) (*Cards*); die Diamant(schrift) (*Typ.*); *black -*, dunkler Diamant; (*coll.*) Steinkohle; *facetted -*, der Rautenbrillant; *glazier's -*, der Glaserdiamant; *nine of -s*, die Karoneun (*Cards*); *queen of -s*, die Karodame (*Cards*); *rough -*, ungeschliffener Diamant; (*fig.*) Mensch mit rauhem Äußeren aber gutem Kern; *- cut -*, List gegen List; (*coll.*) Wurst wider Wurst. **--cutter,** *s.* der Diamantschleifer. **--mine,** *s.* die Diamantgrube. **--setter,** *s.* der Diamantenfasser. **--shaped,** *adj.* rautenförmig.

diandrian [daɪˈændrɪən], *adj.* zweimännig, diandrisch (*Bot.*).

diapason [daɪəˈpeɪsn], *s.* die Oktave (*Mus.*); Mensur (*of organs*); (*Poet.*) der Einklang, harmonisches Ganze; der Stimmumfang; *open -*, das Prinzipale (*organ*).

diaper [ˈdaɪəpə], 1. *s.* rautenförmig gemusterte Leinwand, rautenförmiges Muster (*Arch.*); die Windel (*of a baby*). 2. *v.a.* rautenförmig mustern.

diaphanous [daɪˈæfənəs], *adj.* durchsichtig, durchscheinend, transparent; diaphan.

diaphoretic [daɪəfəˈrɛtɪk], 1. *adj.* schweißtreibend. 2. *s.* schweißtreibendes Mittel.

diaphragm [ˈdaɪəfræm], *s.* das Zwerchfell (*Anat.*); die Scheidewand; Blende (*Phot.*); Membran, das Schallblech (*Phone.*).

diapositive [daɪəˈpɔzɪtɪv], *s.* das Diapositiv; durchsichtiges Bild.

diarist [ˈdaɪərɪst], *s.* der Tagebuchschreiber.

diarrhoea [daɪəˈrɪə] ,*s.* der Durchfall, die Diarrhöe, Ruhr; (*vulg.*) der Dünnpfiff, Dünnschiß.

diary [ˈdaɪərɪ], *s.* das Tagebuch; der (Taschen)-Kalender; *keep a -*, ein Tagebuch führen.

diastole [daɪˈæstəlɪ], *s.* die Diastole (*Med.*); Dehnung (*Metr.*); (*fig.*) *systole and -*, das Auf und Ab.

diatherm-acy [daɪəˈθə:məsɪ], *s.* die Wärmedurchlässigkeit. **-ic,** *adj.* Wärme durchlassend, diatherman.

diathesis [daɪˈæθɪsɪs], *s.* die Krankheitsanlage, Körperbeschaffenheit.

diatom [ˈdaɪətəm], *s.* die Kieselalge, Diatomee (*Bot.*).

diatonic [daɪəˈtɔnɪk], *adj.* diatonisch (*Mus.*).

diatribe [ˈdaɪətraɪb], *s.* die Stichelei, Schmähung; Schmähschrift; kritischer Ausfall, der Protest.

dibbl-e [dɪbl], 1. *s.* der Pflanzstock, Dibbelstock, Steckholz (*Hort.*). 2. *v.a.* mit dem Pflanzstock säen. **-er,** *s.* (also *-ing-machine*) die Dibbelmaschine.

dice [daɪs], 1. *pl.* (*see* ²**die**) die Würfel (*pl.*). 2. *v.n.* würfeln, knobeln. **--box,** *s.* der Würfelbecher, Knobelbecher.

dicephalous [daɪˈsɛfələs], *adj.* zweiköpfig.

dickens [ˈdɪkɪnz], *s.* (*coll.*) der Teufel; (*coll.*) *what the -?* was zum Teufel?

dicker [ˈdɪkə], 1. *s.* zehn Stück (*especially hides*). 2. *v.n.* (*sl.*) schachern.

¹**dick(e)y** [ˈdɪkɪ], *s.* der Bedientensitz (*of a coach*); Rücksitz (*Motor.*); die Hemdbrust, das Vorhemd, der Schurz, das Lätzchen; (*coll.*) der Esel.

²**dicky,** *adj.* (*sl.*) kränklich, ungesund, unwohl, unpäßlich; (*fig.*) unsicher, wackelig, brüchig, kümmerlich, erbärmlich. **--bird,** *s.* (*coll.*) der Piepmatz.

dicotyledon [daɪkɔtɪˈlɪ:dən], *s.* der Blattkeimer, zweikeimblättrige Pflanze. **-ous** [-əs], *adj.* zwei Samenlappen habend.

dictaphone [ˈdɪktəfoun], *s.* das Diktaphon, der Diktierapparat.

dictat-e [dɪkˈteɪt], 1. *v.a.* vorschreiben, befehlen, gebieten, auferlegen; diktieren, vorsagen; (*fig.*) einflößen, eingeben; *he will not be -ed to*, er läßt sich (*Dat.*) nichts vorschreiben *or* keine Vorschriften machen. 2. *v.n.* befehlen, Befehle geben. 3. [ˈdɪkteɪt], *s.* die Vorschrift, der Befehl; das Gebot, die Mahnung, Eingebung; *-es of conscience*, die Mahnung des Gewissens; *-es of reason*, das Gebot der Vernunft. **-ion** [-ˈteɪʃən], *s.* das Diktieren; Diktatschreiben, Diktat; Geheiß, die Vorschrift; *write from -ion*, nach Diktat schreiben. **-or** [-ˈteɪtə], *s.* der Diktator; Gewalthaber. **-orial** [-təˈtɔ:rɪəl], *adj.* diktatorisch; unumschränkt, gebieterisch, befehlshaberisch. **-orship,** *s.* die Diktatur; unumschränkte Macht, die Gewaltherrschaft.

diction [ˈdɪkʃən], *s.* die Ausdrucksweise, der Stil; die Sprache.

dictionary [ˈdɪkʃənərɪ], *s.* das Wörterbuch; (*fig.*) *walking -*, lebendiges *or* wandelndes Lexikon.

dictum [ˈdɪktəm], *s.* (*pl.* dicta) der Spruch, Ausspruch; geflügeltes Wort, die Redensart.

did [dɪd], *see* **do.**

didactic [dɪˈdæktɪk], *adj.* lehrhaft, didaktisch; belehrend (*of persons*); *- poem*, das Lehrgedicht.

diddle [dɪdl], *v.a.* (*sl.*) beschwindeln, betrügen, prellen (*out of*, um).

¹**die** [daɪ], *v.n.* sterben (*of*, an (*Dat.*); *from*, vor); krepieren (*of animals & sl.*); absterben, eingehen (*as a plant*); untergehen, vergehen, dahinschwinden; (*a*) (*absolute*) *never say -!* Kopf hoch! verzweifle nie! *- an early death*, einen frühen Tod sterben; *- a natural death*, eines natürlichen Todes sterben; *- a rich man*, als reicher Mann sterben; (*b*) (*with nouns and adverbs*) *- away*, sich legen (*as the wind*), sich verlieren, verhallen, ersterben (*as sounds*); *- down*, schwinden, allmählich vergehen; verhallen (*of sound*); erlöschen (*of fire*); *- game*, bis zum letzten Augenblick standhalten; (*coll.*) *- hard*, nicht leicht sterben, (*fig.*) sich lange halten, ein zähes Leben haben; *- off*, absterben, dahinsterben, eingehen; *- out*, aussterben; (*c*) (*with prepositions*) *- by the sword*, durch das Schwert umkommen; *though I were to - for it*, sollte es mir den Kopf kosten; (*coll.*) *I am dying for a letter*, ich schmachte nach einem Brief; *- for love*, vor Liebe sterben; *- in the last ditch*, bis zum letzten Blutstropfen kämpfen; *- in harness*, in den Sielen sterben; *- of hunger*, Hungers *or* vor Hunger sterben; *- of an illness*, an einer Krankheit sterben; (*coll.*) *I am dying to see him*, ich möchte ihn rasend gern sehen; (*coll.*) *- with one's boots on*, eines gewaltsamen Todes sterben; *- with laughing*, sich totlachen, vor Lachen sterben (wollen); *- with shame*, vor Scham vergehen. **--hard,** *s.* hartnäckiger Kämpfer, Unentwegte(r), *m.*; *pl.* Reaktionäre (*pl.*), die Alte Garde (*Pol.*).

²**die,** *s.* (*a*) (*pl.* dice) der Würfel; *the - is cast*, der Würfel ist gefallen; *the dice are loaded against him*, er zieht den kürzeren; *cast of the -* or *dice*, (*fig.*) das Spiel des Zufalls; *straight as a -*, kerzengerade; *risk all on the throw of a -* or *dice*, alles dem Zufall überlassen; (*b*) (*pl.* dies) der (Münz)Stempel, die Gußform, der Prägestock, die Matrize, der Stanzer; Postamentwürfel (*Arch.*). **--block,** *s.* das Gesenk. **--cast,** *s.* der Schalenguß. **--head,** *s.* der Schneidkopf. **--sinker,** *s.* der Stempelschneider. **--stock,** *s.* die Kluppe.

dielectric [daɪəˈlɛktrik], *s.* das Dielektrikum (*Elec.*).

¹**diet** [ˈdaɪət], 1. *s.* die Diät (*Med.*); Ernährung, Nahrung, Kost, Speise; *be on -*, Diät halten; *low -*, magere Kost; *put s.o. on a -*, einen auf Diät setzen.

2. *v.a.* Diät vorschreiben (*Dat.*), auf Diät setzen. 3. *v.n.* (nach) Diät leben, Diät halten. **-ary** [-ərɪ], 1. *adj.* diätetisch. 2. *s.* die Diät; Ration. **-etic** [daɪɪ'tetɪk], *adj.* diätetisch, Diät-. **-etics,** *pl.* die Diätetik.

²diet, *s.* der Landtag, Bundestag, Reichstag; die Tagung, Versammlung.

differ ['dɪfə], *v.n.* sich unterscheiden, verschieden sein, abweichen (*from*, von); andrer Meinung sein (*from*, als); nicht übereinstimmen (*from*, mit); *agree to* –, sich auf verschiedene Standpunkte einigen; *I beg to* –, ich bin leider anderer Meinung. **-ence,** *s.* der Unterschied, die Verschiedenheit, Abweichung; Uneinigkeit, der Zwiespalt, Streit; Streitpunkt; die Differenz (*C.L. & Math.*); Unterscheidung, unterscheidendes Merkmal; *-ence in price*, der Preisunterschied; *that makes a -ence*, das ändert die Sache, es ist von Bedeutung; *that makes all the* or *a great -ence*, das macht einen himmelweiten Unterschied, das gibt der Sache ein ganz anderes Gesicht, es ist wesentlich; *that makes no -ence*, das macht nichts aus; *make up the -ence*, das Fehlende ersetzen; *-ence of opinion*, die Meinungsverschiedenheit; *settle a -ence*, einen Streit beilegen *or* schlichten; *split the -ence*, sich in die Differenz teilen. **-ent** ['dɪfərənt], *adj.* verschieden, verschiedenartig, abweichend (*from*, von), andere(r)(s) (*from*, als), ungleich; *as -ent as chalk from cheese*, so verschieden wie Tag und Nacht; *in a -ent way*, anders. **-ently,** *adv.* anders, unterschiedlich. **-ential** [dɪfə'rɛnʃəl], 1. *adj.* unterscheidend, Unterscheidungs-, differential; *-ential calculus*, die Differentialrechnung; *-ential gear*, das Differentialgetriebe; *-ential tariff*, der Staffeltarif (*C.L.*). 2. *s.* die Differentiale (*Math.*); das Differential(getriebe), Ausgleichsgetriebe (*Motor.*). **-entiate** [dɪfə'rɛnʃɪeɪt], 1. *v.a.* einen Unterschied erkennen, unterscheiden, sondern, differenzieren (*Math.*); *be -entiated, see* **-entiate** 2. 2. *v.n.* sich unterscheiden, sich verschieden entwickeln, sich differenzieren, sich entfernen (*from*, von). **-entiation** [-ʃɪ'eɪʃən], *s.* die Unterscheidung; das Differenzieren (*Math., Biol.*); verschiedenartige Entwicklung (*Biol.*).

difficult ['dɪfɪkəlt], *adj.* schwer, schwierig; beschwerlich, mühsam; unwegsam (*as ground*); schwer zu behandeln (*of persons*); – *of access*, schwer zugänglich. **-y** [-tɪ], *s.* die Schwierigkeit; Mühe, Unverständlichkeit; (*usually pl.*) schwierige Lage, die Verlegenheit; *come up against* or *experience a -y*, auf Widerstand stoßen; *find -y in doing a th.*, es schwierig finden etwas zu tun; *in -ies*, in Verlegenheit; *throw -ies in a p.'s way*, einem Schwierigkeiten bereiten *or* in den Weg legen; *with -y*, mit Mühe.

diffiden-ce ['dɪfɪdəns], *s.* der Mangel an Selbstvertrauen (*in*, zu), die Schüchternheit. **-t,** *adj.* mißtrauisch (*of*, gegen), schüchtern; *be -t in doing*, sich scheuen zu tun.

diffract [dɪ'frækt], *v.a.* brechen, beugen. **-ion** [-'frækʃən], *s.* die Ablenkung, Brechung, Beugung, Diffraktion.

diffus-e 1. [dɪ'fjuːs], *adj.* weitverbreitet, zerstreut; diffus; weitschweifig, weitläufig, wortreich. 2. [dɪ'fjuːz], *v.a.* ausschütten, ausgießen; zerstreuen, ausbreiten, verbreiten. 3. *v.n.* sich verbreiten, sich ergießen, sich vermischen, zerfließen. **-ed** [dɪ'fjuːzd], *adj.* verbreitet; zerstreut. **-eness** [-snɪs], *s.* weite Verbreitung; die Zerstreuung; Weitläufigkeit, Weitschweifigkeit. **-ibility** [-zə'bɪlɪtɪ], *s.* das Diffusionsvermögen. **-ible** [-zəbl], *adj.* verbreitbar, ergießbar, diffusionsfähig. **-ion** [-fjuːʒən], *s.* die Verbreitung; Ausstreuung; Diffusion (*Chem.*). **-ive** [-sɪv], *adj.* sich weit verbreitend; ausgebreitet; weitschweifig, weitläufig. **-iveness,** *s.* die Ausdehnung, Verbreitung; Weitschweifigkeit.

dig [dɪg], 1. *ir.v.a.* graben, umgraben, ausgraben; (*sl.*) schippen; (*coll.*) stoßen, puffen (*spurs, etc.*); – *the ground*, den Boden umgraben; – *a pit for s.o.*, einem eine Grube graben *or* eine Falle stellen; – *potatoes*, Kartoffeln ausgraben; – *a p. in the ribs*, einen in die Rippen stoßen; – *down*, untergraben; – *in*, eingraben; – *o.s. in*, sich verschanzen; – *out*, ausgraben; – *up*, umgraben (*ground*), ausgraben (*potatoes, etc.*); (*coll.*) entdecken, ans Tageslicht bringen (*as new facts*). 2. *ir.v.n.* graben (*for*, nach); (*sl.*) wohnen, Quartier nehmen; – *in*, sich eingraben (*Mil.*); – *into*, eindringen in; – *through*, sich graben *or* dringen durch. 3. *s.* (*coll.*) der Stoß, Puff; Hieb (*at*, auf), böswillige Bemerkung (*at*, gegen); – *in the ribs*, der Rippenstoß; *see* **digger, digging,** and **digs.**

digest [dɪ'dʒɛst], 1. *v.a.* verdauen (*food*); ausziehen, digerieren (*Chem.*); ordnen, einteilen, in ein System bringen; überdenken, durchdenken, verarbeiten (*of the mind*); erdulden, ertragen, hinunterschlucken, verwinden; – *one's anger*, seinen Ärger verbeißen. 2. *v.n.* verdauen; sich auflösen, digerieren (*Chem.*). 3. ['daɪdʒɛst], *s.* die Gesetzessammlung (*Law*); Digesten *or* Pandekten (*pl.*); die Sammlung, der Auszug, Abriß. **-er,** *s.* das Verdauungsmittel; der Digestor, Autoklav, Papinsche Topf (*Phys.*); Dämpfer, Kocher, Kochkessel, Dampfkochtopf (*Cook.*). **-ibility** [-ə'bɪlɪtɪ], *s.* die Verdaulichkeit. **-ible** [-əbl], *adj.* verdaulich. **-ion** [-ʃən], *s.* die Verdauung; Digestion (*Chem.*). **-ive** [-ɪv], 1. *adj.* die Verdauung befördernd, bekömmlich; *-ive biscuits*, leichtverdauliche Keks; *-ive organs*, Verdauungsorgane. 2. *s.* das Verdauungsmittel.

dig-ger ['dɪgə], *s.* der Gräber, Schipper; (*sl.*) Australier; *grave--ger*, der Totengräber. **-ging,** *s.* das Graben, die Erdarbeit, Tiefbauarbeit. **-gings,** *pl.* die Goldmine, Goldfelder (*pl.*); (*coll.*) Bude, Wohnung, das Quartier.

digit ['dɪdʒɪt], *s.* die Fingerbreite, der Finger, die Zehe (*Zool.*); einstellige Zahl (*Arith.*); das Zwölftel des Mond- *or* Sonnendurchmessers. **-al,** 1. *adj.* Finger-; *-al pressure*, der Fingerdruck (*Med.*). 2. *s.* die Taste (*Mus.*). **-alis,** *s.* der Fingerhut (*Bot.*). **-ate** [-eɪt], *adj.* gefingert (*Zool.*), fingerförmig (*Bot.*). **-igrade,** 1. *adj.* auf Zehen gehend. 2. *s.* der Zehengänger (*Zool.*).

digni-fied ['dɪgnɪfaɪd], *adj.* würdevoll, würdig, erhaben **-fy** [-faɪ], *v.a.* auszeichnen, verherrlichen, ehren, zieren; *-fy with the name of . . .*, hochtrabend bezeichnen als . . . **-tary** ['dɪgnɪtərɪ], *s.* der Würdenträger; Prälat. **-ty** ['dɪgnɪtɪ], *s.* die Würde; Ehrenstelle, der Rang, hoher Stand; die Erhabenheit, der Adel; *beneath my -ty*, unter meiner Würde; *stand on one's -ty*, auf Würde halten.

digraph ['daɪgræf], *s.* der Digraph (*Phonet.*).

digress [daɪ'grɛs], *v.n.* abschweifen. **-ion,** *s.* die Abschweifung. **-ive,** *adj.* abschweifend, abwegig.

digs [digz], *s.* (*sl.*) *see* **diggings** (*coll.*).

dihedral [daɪ'hɪːdrəl], *s.* die V-Stellung, V-Form (*Av.*).

dike [daɪk], 1. *s.* der Deich, Damm; Graben, Kanal; die Gesteinsader, der Eruptivgang (*Geol.*). 2. *v.a.* eindeichen, eindämmen. **--reeve,** *s.* der Deichaufseher. **--rocks,** *pl.* Ganggesteine (*pl.*) (*Geol.*).

dilapidat-e [dɪ'læpɪdeɪt], 1. *v.a.* zerstören, verfallen lassen, in Verfall geraten lassen. 2. *v.n.* verfallen. **-ed,** *adj.* verfallen, baufällig, schäbig. **-ion** [-'deɪʃən], *s.* die Zerstörung, Baufälligkeit, der Verfall; das Verfallenlassen.

dilat-ability [daɪlətə'bɪlɪtɪ], *s.* die Streckbarkeit, (Aus)Dehnbarkeit (*Phys.*). **-able** [daɪ'leɪtəbl], *adj.* (aus)dehnbar. **-ation** [daɪlə'teɪʃən], *s.* die Ausdehnung, Erweiterung. **-e** [daɪ'leɪt], 1. *v.a.* ausdehnen, erweitern. 2. *v.n.* sich ausdehnen, sich erweitern; (*fig.*) sich verbreiten, sich auslassen (*on* or *upon*, über). **-ion** [-'leɪʃən], *s. see* **-ation.** **-or,** *s.* der Dilatator (*Anat.*).

dilator-iness ['dɪlətərɪnɪs], *s.* die Saumseligkeit, das Zögern, Zaudern. **-y** ['dɪlətərɪ], *adj.* aufschiebend, hinauszögernd, hinhaltend, zögernd, zaudernd, saumselig; langsam, schleppend; *-y pleas*, dilatorische Einreden (*Law*).

dilemma [dɪ'lɛmə], *s.* das Dilemma (*Log.*); (*fig.*) die Verlegenheit, (*coll.*) Klemme; *in a* – or *on the horns of a* –, in einer Zwickmühle, in Verlegenheit, in der Klemme.

dilettant-e [dɪlɪ'tæntɪ], 1. *s.* (*pl.* -i) der Dilettant, Nichtfachmann, Kunstliebhaber. 2. *adj.* dilettantisch. **-ism** [-tɪzm], *s.* der Dilettantismus.

diligen-ce [ˈdɪlɪdʒəns], *s.* der Fleiß, Eifer, die Emsigkeit; Sorgfalt; (*archaic*) Postkutsche. **-t,** *adj.* fleißig, emsig; sorgfältig.
dill [dɪl], *s.* der Dill (*Bot.*).
dilly-dally [ˈdɪlɪˈdælɪ], *v.n.* (*coll.*) die Zeit vertrödeln.
dilu-ent [ˈdɪljuənt], 1. *adj.* verdünnend. 2. *s.* das Streckmittel, Verdünnungsmittel, Verschnittmittel. **-te** [dɪˈljuːt], 1. *v.a.* verdünnen, strecken, verschneiden, verwässern; (*fig.*) abschwächen; *-te labour*, ungelernte Arbeiter einstellen. 2. *adj.* [ˈdaɪljuːt], **-ted,** *adj.* verdünnt, verwässert, geschwächt. **-tion** [-ˈljuːʃən], *s.* die Verdünnung, Verwässerung.
diluvi-al [dɪˈluːvɪəl], *adj.* sintflutlich; diluvial (*Geol.*). **-an,** *adj.* Sintflut-. **-um** [daɪˈluːvɪəm], *s.* das Diluvium (*Geol.*).
dim [dɪm], 1. *adj.* trübe, düster, dunkel; blaß, matt (*of colours*); undeutlich, schwach (*of sound*); (*fig.*) unklar; (*coll.*) dumm, einfältig. 2. *v.a.* verdunkeln, abmatten, trüben; abblenden (*dazzling light*). **-ness,** *s.* die Mattheit, Dunkelheit; Undeutlichkeit.
dime [daɪm], *s.* das Zehncentstück (*Amer.*).
dimension [dɪˈmɛnʃən], *s.* die Ausdehnung, Erstreckung, das Maß; die Abmessung; der Umfang, das Ausmaß, die Dimension (*Math.*); *of great -s*, sehr groß, umfangreich.
dimeter [ˈdɪmɪtə], *s.* der Dimeter (*Metr.*).
dimin-ish [dɪˈmɪnɪʃ], 1. *v.a.* vermindern, verringern; verkleinern; verjüngen (*Arch.*); (*fig.*) abschwächen, herabsetzen, beeinträchtigen; *-ished interval*, vermindertes Intervall (*Mus.*). 2. *v.n.* abnehmen, sich vermindern (*in*, an). **-uendo** [dɪmɪnjuˈɛndoʊ], 1. *adv.* (an Tonstärke) abnehmend. 2. *s.* das Diminuendo (*Mus.*). **-ution** [-ˈnjuːʃən], *s.* die Verkleinerung, Verminderung, Verringerung, Abnahme; Verjüngung (*Arch.*); Verkürzung der Notenwerte (*Mus.*); das Diminuendo (*Mus.*). **-utive** [dɪˈmɪnjutɪv], 1. *adj.* klein, winzig, verkleinernd (*Gram.*). 2. *s.* das Diminutiv (*Gram.*). **-utiveness,** *s.* die Kleinheit, Winzigkeit.
dimissory [dɪˈmɪsərɪ], *adj.* entlassend; *letter -*, das Entlassungsschreiben.
dimity [ˈdɪmɪtɪ], *s.* geköperter Barchent.
dimness [ˈdɪmnɪs], *see* **dim.**
dimorph-ic, -ous [daɪˈmɔːfɪk, -fəs], *adj.* dimorph, zweigestaltig.
dimple [dɪmpl], 1. *s.* das Grübchen. 2. *v.n.* Grübchen bekommen. 3. *v.a.* Grübchen machen; kräuseln (*as the surface of water*). **-d,** *adj.* mit Grübchen versehen; *-d face*, das Gesicht mit Grübchen.
din [dɪn], 1. *s.* das Getöse, der Lärm; das Geklirr (*clashing*); Gerassel (*rattling*). 2. *v.a.* durch Lärm betäuben; *- into a p.'s ears*, einem in die Ohren schreien, einem dauernd vorpredigen.
din-e [daɪn], 1. *v.n.* essen, speisen; *-e off* (or *on*) *roast pork*, Schweinebraten (zu Mittag) essen; *-e out*, außer dem Hause essen, zu Tisch geladen sein; *-e with s.o.*, bei einem essen; *-e with Duke Humphrey*, nichts zu essen bekommen, das (Mittag)Essen überschlagen. 2. *v.a.* speisen, bei sich zu Gast haben; *a room capable of -ing 300 people*, ein Saal, in dem 300 Personen essen können. **-er,** *s.* der Tischgast; Speisewagen (*Railw.*). **-er-out,** *s.* einer, der (oft) außer dem Hause speist. **-ing-car** [ˈdaɪnɪŋkɑː], *s.* der Speisewagen. **-ing-room,** *s.* das Speisezimmer, der Speisesaal. **-ing-table,** *s.* der Eßtisch.
ding [dɪŋ], *v.a.*; *- s.th. into a p.('s ears)*, *see* **din 2.** **--dong,** 1. *int.* bim bam bum! 2. *s.* der Klingklang; *--dong battle*, hin und her wogender Kampf.
dinghy [ˈdɪŋgɪ], *s.* das Beiboot, die Jolle, kleines Boot; der Kutter (*in the navy*); *rubber -*, das Schlauchboot, der Floßsack.
dinginess [ˈdɪndʒɪnɪs], *s.* dunkle Farbe, das Dunkelbraune; die Schmutzfarbe, schmutziges Äußere.
dingle [dɪŋgl], *s.* die Waldschlucht, waldiges Tal.
dingo [ˈdɪŋgoʊ], *s.* wilder Hund (*of Australia*).
dingy [ˈdɪndʒɪ], *adj.* dunkelfarbig, schmutzigbraun; schmutzig; schäbig.
dinky [ˈdɪŋkɪ], *adj.* (*coll.*) klein, nett.
dinner [ˈdɪnə], *s.* die Hauptmahlzeit, das Mittagessen, Mittagsmahl; Abendessen; Festessen, Diner; (*a*) (*with adjectives*) *early -*, das Mittagessen; *late -*, das Abendessen; *public -*, das Zweckessen; *- is ready*, das Essen steht auf dem Tisch; (*b*) (*with verb*) *ask s.o. to -*, einen zum Essen bitten; *what did you have for -?*, was haben Sie zu Mittag bekommen?; *serve (up) -*, das Essen auftragen; *stay for -*, zum Essen bleiben; (*c*) (*with prepositions*) *after -*, nach dem Essen, nach Tisch. **--bell,** *s.* die Tischglocke, das Glockenzeichen zum Essen. **--hour,** *s.* die Mittagspause. **--jacket,** *s.* der Smoking. **--party,** *s.* die Tischgesellschaft, Abendgesellschaft, das Diner. **--service,** *s.* das Tafelgeschirr, Tafelservice. **--table,** *s.* der Speisetisch. **--time,** *s.* die Essenszeit, Tischzeit. **--wagon,** *s.* der Servierwagen.
dint [dɪnt], 1. *s.* (*archaic*) der Schlag; die Kraft (*only in*) *by - of*, kraft, vermöge, mittels, vermittelst (*Gen.*); der Eindruck, die Druckspur, Vertiefung, Strieme, Beule; *see* **dent.** 2. *v.a.* eindrücken, einbeulen, kerben, furchen.
dioces-an [daɪˈɔsɪsən], 1. *adj.* Diözesan-. 2. *s.* der Diözesanbischof. **-e** [ˈdaɪəsɪs], *s.* der Sprengel, die Diözese.
diode [ˈdaɪoʊd], *s.* die Zweielektrodenröhre (*Rad.*).
diopt-er [daɪˈɔptə], *s.* die Dioptrie. **-ric** [-trɪk], 1. *adj.* dioptrisch. 2. *s.* *see* **-er.** **-rics,** *pl.* die Dioptrik, Lichtbrechungslehre.
dioxide [daɪˈɔksaɪd], *s.* das Dioxyd.
dip [dɪp], 1. *v.a.* (ein)tauchen, eintunken (*in, into*, in (*Acc.*)); anfeuchten (*a hide*); waschen (*sheep*); färben, blauen; senken, herablassen, dippen (*flag*) (*Naut.*); abblenden (*headlights*); ziehen (*candles*); schöpfen (*from* or *out*, aus). 2. *v.n.* (unter)tauchen; eintauchen; sinken (*below*, unter); sich neigen; einen Blick werfen, sich flüchtig einlassen (*into*, in); *- into a book*, ein Buch flüchtig durchblättern; *- deeply into one's purse*, tief in die Tasche greifen. 3. *s.* das Tauchen, Eintauchen; die Neigung, Senkung, der Abhang; kurzes Bad (*Dye.*); das Einfallen (*Min.*); die Höhlung, Vertiefung; Inklination der Magnetnadel; gezogenes Licht; *- in the sea*, das (kurze) Bad (im Meer); *- of the horizon*, die Kimmtiefe, Depression. **--stick,** *s.* der Ölmeßstab.
diphtheri-a [dɪfˈθɪːərɪə], *s.* die Diphtherie, Diphtheritis. **-c,** *adj.*, **-tic** [dɪfθəˈrɪtɪk], *adj.* diphtheritisch.
diphthong [ˈdɪfθɔŋ], *s.* der Doppelvokal, Diphthong. **-al** [-ˈθɔŋgl], *adj.* diphthongisch. **-ization** [-aɪˈzeɪʃən], *s.* die Diphthongierung.
diploma [dɪˈploʊmə], *s.* das Diplom, die Urkunde.
diploma-cy [dɪˈploʊməsɪ], *s.* die Diplomatie; diplomatischer Takt. **-t** [ˈdɪplomæt], *s.*, **-tist** [dɪˈploʊmətɪst], *s.* der Diplomat. **-tic** [-ˈmætɪk], *adj.* diplomatisch; taktvoll; urkundlich. **-tics,** *pl.* Urkundenlehre.
dipper [ˈdɪpə], *s.* der Taucher (*Orn.*); die Schöpfkelle; (*coll.*) der Wiedertäufer (*Rel.*).
dippy [ˈdɪpɪ], *adj.* (*sl.*) verdreht, verrückt.
dipsomania [dɪpsoˈmeɪnɪə], *s.* die Trunksucht. **-c** [-ˈmeɪnɪæk], *s.* Trunksüchtige(r), *m.*
dipter-a [ˈdɪptərə], *pl.* Zweiflügler. **-al,** *adj.*, **-ous,** *adj.* zweiflügelig.
diptych [ˈdɪptɪk], *s.* das Diptychon.
dire [ˈdaɪə], *adj.*, **-ful,** *adj.* schrecklich, gräßlich, grauenhaft, fürchterlich, schauderhaft. **-fulness,** *s.* die Schrecklichkeit, Gräßlichkeit.
direct [dɪˈrɛkt], 1. *adj.* gerade, direkt; unmittelbar; rechtläufig (*Astr.*); offen, klar, deutlich; *- action*, direkte Aktion (*Pol.*); *- current*, der Gleichstrom; *- hit*, der Volltreffer (*Artil.*); *in the - line*, in gerader Linie; *in - opposition to*, genau das Gegenteil von; *- route*, gerader Weg; *- speech*, direkte Rede; *- taxes*, direkte Steuern; *- train*, durchgehender Zug. 2. *v.a.* richten, zielen (*to* or *towards*, auf *or* nach), hinweisen, (ver)weisen (*to*, an); den Weg zeigen (*to*, nach); anordnen, verfügen, bestimmen, befehlen, beauftragen; disponieren, anweisen, leiten, beaufsichtigen; adressieren (*a letter*) (*to*, an (*Acc.*)); *as -ed*, nach Vorschrift *or* Angabe; laut Verfügung. 3. *v.n.* anordnen, befehlen. **-ion** [dɪˈrɛkʃən], *s.* die Rich-

tung; das Richten, Adressieren (*of letters*); die Leitung, Führung, Direktion, das Direktorium; die Anschrift, Adresse (*on letters*); (*usually pl.*) Weisung, Anweisung, Anordnung, Vorschrift, Bestimmung, Verfügung, der Hinweis; *according to –ions*, vorschriftsmäßig; *by –ion of*, auf Anordnung von; *from all –ions*, von allen Seiten; *from that –ion*, aus jener Richtung; *–ions for use*, die Gebrauchsanweisung, Anwendungsvorschrift; *in the –ion of*, in der Richtung nach *or* auf; *in all –ions*, nach allen Richtungen; *in many –ions*, in vieler *or* mancherlei Hinsicht; *–ion of motion*, die Bewegungsrichtung, Bahnrichtung; *–ion of turn*, der Drehsinn; *sense of –ion*, der Richtungssinn, Orientierungssinn, das Ortsgedächtnis; *under the –ion of*, unter der Leitung von. **–ional,** *adj.* Richt–, Richtungs–; *–ional aerial*, die Richtantenne (*Rad.*). **–ion-finder,** *s.* das Peilgerät; die Peilfunkeinrichtung; der Sucher (*Phot.*). **–ion-finding,** *s.* die Standortsbestimmung, Peilung, Ortung. **–ion-line,** *s*, die Normzeile (*Print.*). **–ive,** 1. *s.* die Weisung, Direktive. 2. *adj.* anweisend, richtunggebend, maßgebend. **–ly** [dɪˈrɛktlɪ], 1. *adv.* gerade; direkt, unmittelbar; sofort, gleich, augenblicklich, unverzüglich, bald; *–ly opposed*, gerade *or* genau entgegengesetzt. 2. *conj.* (*coll.*) sobald (als), sowie. **–ness,** *s.* gerade Richtung; die Geradheit, Unmittelbarkeit, Offenheit, Unumwundenheit. **–or** [dɪˈrɛktə], *s.* der Direktor, Leiter, Vorsteher, Chef, Dirigent; Regisseur (*films*); das Richtgerät (*Mech.*); *board of –ors*, der Aufsichtsrat, das Direktorium. **–orate** [–rɪt], *s.* das Direktorat; Direktorium. **–orial** [–ˈtɔːrɪəl], *adj.* leitend; Direktorial–. **–orship,** *s.* das Direktoramt, die Direktor(en)stelle. **–ory** [dɪˈrɛktərɪ], *s.* das Adreßbuch, Fernsprechbuch; das Direktorium (*in France*); die Anweisung, der Leitfaden (*Eccl.*). **–ress** [dɪˈrɛktrɪs], *s.* die Vorsteherin, Leiterin. **–rix** [–trɪks], *s. see* **–ress;** die Leitlinie (*Geom.*).

dirge [ˈdəːdʒ], *s.* der Trauergesang, Grabgesang, das Klagelied, Trauerlied, die Klage.

dirigible [ˈdɪrɪdʒəbl], 1. *adj.* lenkbar. 2. *s.* der Lenkballon, das Luftschiff.

dirk [dəːk], *s.* der Dolch.

dirt [dəːt], *s.* der Schmutz, Dreck, Kot; *as cheap as –*, spottbillig; *have to eat –*, sich demütigen müssen; *spot of –*, der Schmutzfleck; *throw – at a p.*, einen mit Schmutz bewerfen, einen in den Schmutz ziehen; *treat s.o. like –*, einen wie seinen Schuhputzer behandeln. (*coll.*) **– -cheap,** *adj.* spottbillig. **–iness,** *s.* der Schmutz; die Schmutzigkeit; (*fig.*) Gemeinheit, Niederträchtigkeit. **– track,** die Aschenbahn. **–y** [ˈdəːtɪ], 1. *adj.* schmutzig, kotig, dreckig; (*fig.*) gemein, niederträchtig; (*sl.*) *do the –y on s.o.*, einen gemein behandeln; *–y brown*, schmutzigbraun; *–y hands*, Schmutzhände (*pl.*); (*coll.*) *–y look*, scheeler Blick; *–y trick*, die Gemeinheit; *–y weather*, schlechtes Wetter; *–y work*, niedrige Arbeit; (*fig.*) unsauberes Geschäft, verdecktes *or* doppeltes Spiel, die Schurkerei; *–y wound*, septische Wunde. 2. *v.a.* beschmutzen, besudeln. 3. *v.n.* schmutzig werden.

disab–ility [dɪsəˈbɪlɪtɪ], *s.* das Unvermögen, die Unfähigkeit, (*often pl.*) Unzulänglichkeit; Rechtsunfähigkeit (*Law*); Körperbehinderung; *partial –ility*, beschränkte Dienstunfähigkeit (*Mil.*); *permanent –ility*, dauernde Dienstunfähigkeit (*Mil.*); *–ility pension*, die Invalidenrente. **–le** [dɪsˈəɪbl], *v.a.* untauglich *or* unbrauchbar machen, außer Stand setzen; kampfunfähig machen, außer Gefecht setzen (*Mil.*); körperlich behindern, lähmen, verkrüppeln, entkräften; rechtsunfähig machen (*Law*). **–led,** *adj.* körperlich behindert, schwerverletzt; kampfunfähig, dienstunfähig, kriegsversehrt, kriegsbeschädigt (*Mil., Naut.*); *permanently –led*, dauernd untauglich; *–led soldier*, Kriegsbeschädigte(r), *m.* **–lement,** *s.* die Unfähigkeit, Kampfunfähigkeit.

disabuse [dɪsəˈbjuːz], *v.a.* aus dem Irrtum befreien, eines Besseren belehren; *– one's mind of s.th.*, sich (*Dat.*) etwas aus dem Kopfe schlagen.

disaccord [dɪsəˈkɔːd], 1. *v.n.* nicht übereinstimmen. 2. *s.* der Widerspruch, das Mißverhältnis, die Nichtübereinstimmung.

disaccustom [dɪsəˈkʌstəm], *v.a.* abgewöhnen (*a p. to a th.*, einem etwas), entwöhnen (einen einer S.).

disadvantage [dɪsədˈvɑːntɪdʒ], *s.* der Nachteil; Schaden, Verlust; ungünstige Lage; *be at* or *labour under a –*, im Nachteil sein; *be at* or *labour under the – of being . . .*, den Nachteil haben . . . zu sein; *put o.s. at a – with a p.*, sich einem gegenüber in den Nachteil setzen; *sell to –*, mit Verlust verkaufen; *take a p. at a –*, jemandes ungünstige Lage ausnutzen. **–ous** [–ˈteɪdʒəs], *adj.* nachteilig, schädlich, abträglich, ungünstig.

disaffect–ed [dɪsəˈfəktɪd], *adj.* unzufrieden, abgeneigt. **–ion** [–ˈfɛkʃən], *s.* die Unzufriedenheit, Abgeneigtheit; Unzuverlässigkeit, der Treubruch; die Unruhe, Abfallsbewegung; *–ion towards the government*, die Unzufriedenheit mit der Regierung.

disaffirm [dɪsəˈfəːm], *v.a.* aufheben (*Law*).

disafforest [dɪsəˈfɔrɪst], *v.a.* abholzen (*a wood*), des Forstrechts berauben.

disagree [dɪsəˈgrɪː], *v.n.* nicht übereinstimmen, in Widerspruch stehen (*with*, mit); nicht zustimmen (*with* (*Dat.*)); uneins *or* uneinig sein, verschiedener Meinung sein (*on*, über); widersprechen (*with* (*Dat.*)); nicht zuträglich sein, schlecht bekommen (*with* (*Dat.*)) (*as food*). **–able** [–ˈgrɪəbl], *adj.* unangenehm; unliebenswürdig, ungnädig, widerwärtig, verdrießlich. **–ableness,** *s.* die Unannehmlichkeit, Widerwärtigkeit. **–ment** [–ˈgrɪːmənt], *s.* die Verschiedenheit, der Widerspruch; die Mißhelligkeit; *–ment in opinion*, die Meinungsverschiedenheit; *in –ment from*, zum Unterschied von, abweichen von.

disallow [dɪsəˈlɑʊ], *v.a.* nicht zugeben, nicht gestatten, nicht einräumen; nicht gelten lassen, nicht anerkennen; verwerfen, zurückweisen.

disappear [dɪsəˈpɪə], *v.n.* verschwinden; (*coll.*) verlorengehen; *– from circulation*, außer Umlauf kommen (*C.L.*). **–ance** [–rəns], *s.* das Verschwinden.

disappoint [dɪsəˈpɔɪnt], *v.a.* enttäuschen; vereiteln, täuschen (*hopes*); *be –ed*, enttäuscht sein (*at* or *with a th.*, über etwas; *in a p.*, in einem); *be –ed of*, gebracht werden um, nicht erhalten; *it is –ing*, es entspricht nicht den Erwartungen. **–ment,** *s.* die Enttäuschung; Vereitelung, der Fehlschlag, Mißerfolg; *meet with a –ment*, enttäuscht werden.

disapprobat–ion [dɪsæproˈbeɪʃən], *s.* die Mißbilligung. **–ive, –ory** [dɪsˈæprobeɪtərɪ], *adj.* mißbilligend.

disapprov–al [dɪsəˈpruːvəl], *s.* die Mißbilligung, das Mißfallen (*of*, über). **–e** [–ˈpruːv], 1. *v.a.* mißbilligen (*a th.*), tadeln (*a p.*), verwerfen. 2. *v.n.*; *–e of, see* **–e** 1.; *be –ed of*, Mißfallen erregen.

disarm [dɪsˈɑːm], 1. *v.a.* entwaffnen; (*fig.*) unschädlich machen, besänftigen; abrüsten (*Mil.*). 2. *v.n.* abrüsten (*Mil.*). **–ament,** *s.* die Entwaffnung; Abrüstung (*Mil.*).

disarrange [dɪsəˈreɪndʒ], *v.a.* in Unordnung bringen, verwirren. **–ment,** *s.* die Unordnung, Verwirrung.

disarray [dɪsəˈreɪ], 1. *s.* die Unordnung, Verwirrung. 2. *v.a.* verwirren, in Verwirrung bringen; (*poet.*) entkleiden; entwaffnen (*a knight*).

disassemble [dɪsəˈsɛmbl], *v.a.* demontieren, auseinandernehmen.

disast–er [dɪˈzɑːstə], *s.* das Unglück, der Unfall, die Katastrophe, das Mißgeschick; *bring –er*, Unheil bringen. **–rous** [–trəs], *adj.* unglücklich, unheilvoll, unselig, schrecklich, verheerend.

disavow [dɪsəˈvɑʊ], *v.a.* (ab)leugnen, nicht anerkennen, in Abrede stellen, abrücken von. **–al,** *s.* die Nichtanerkennung, Verwerfung; das Ableugnen, Dementi.

disband [dɪsˈbænd], 1. *v.a.* auflösen, entlassen (*troops, etc.*); verabschieden (*an individual*). 2. *v.n.* sich auflösen, auseinandergehen.

disbelie–f [dɪsbɪˈlɪːf], *s.* der Unglaube, Zweifel (*in*, an). **–ve** [–ˈlɪːv], *v.a.* nicht glauben (*a th.* (*Acc.*); *a p.* (*Dat.*)); bezweifeln (*a th.*). **–ver,** *s.* der Zweifler, Ungläubige(r), *m.*

disburden [dɪsˈbəːdən], *v.a.* befreien, entlasten; *– one's heart* or *mind* or *feelings*, sein Herz ausschütten.

disburse [dɪsˈbəːs], *v.a.* auszahlen, ausgeben, auslegen. **–ment,** *s.* die Ausgabe, Auslage, Auszahlung.

disc [dɪsk], *s. see* **disk.**

discard [dɪsˈkɑːd], 1. *v.a.* ablegen, aufgeben (*as old clothes*); abwerfen (*cards*); entlassen, verabschieden (*men*). 2. *v.n.* Karten abwerfen. 3. *s.* das Abwerfen; abgeworfene Karte.

discern [dɪˈsəːn], 1. *v.a.* wahrnehmen, erkennen, bemerken; (heraus)finden, dahinterkommen, auf den Grund kommen (*Dat.*); (*archaic*) unterscheiden. 2. *v.n.* (*archaic*) unterscheiden. **–ible,** *adj.* erkennbar, sichtbar, merklich. **–ing,** *adj.* scharfsinnig, verständig. **–ment,** *s.* die Einsicht, Urteilskraft, der Scharfsinn.

discharg–e [dɪsˈtʃɑːdʒ], 1. *v.a.* abladen, ausladen, löschen (*a cargo*), absetzen, ausschiffen (*passengers*), entladen (*Elec.*); abgeben, abschießen, abfeuern (*a gun*); bezahlen, entrichten (*debts, etc.*); quittieren, einlösen (*a bill*); befriedigen (*one's creditors*); aus dem Dienst entlassen (*servants*); verabschieden, abdanken, ausmustern (*soldiers*); ablohnen (*sailors*); entlassen, freilassen (*a prisoner*); freisprechen, entlasten (*the accused*); erfüllen (*duty*); auslassen (*anger*) (*on*, an (*Dat.*)); ausfließen *or* auslaufen lassen, abführen, ablassen (*liquids*); tilgen, aufheben (*Law*); *–e a bond*, einen Schuldschein einlösen; *–e the debt of nature*, der Natur ihren Tribut bezahlen; *the ulcer –es matter*, das Geschwür eitert; *–e one's office*, das Amt versehen *or* verrichten; *–e smoke*, Rauch aussenden *or* auswerfen. 2. *v.r.* sich ergießen, münden (*into*, in). 3. *v.n.* eitern; ausströmen; sich entladen (*of a gun*). 4. *s.* das Abfeuern, der Abschuß (*of fire-arms*); die Entladung (*Elec.*); der Abfluß, Ausfluß, das Ausströmen (*of water, etc.*); die Eiterung, der Eiterausfluß, Auswurf (*Med.*); die Bezahlung, Entrichtung, Quittung, Begleichung (*C.L., etc.*); (Dienst)Entlassung, Verabschiedung (*Mil., servants, etc.*); Entlassung, Freisprechung, Freilassung (*Law*); Verrichtung, Erfüllung (*of a duty*); Ausladung, Löschung (*of cargo*) (*Naut.*); *–e of a bankrupt*, die Aufhebung des Konkursverfahrens; *get one's –e*, seinen Abschied bekommen; *–e in full*, vollständige Quittung; *port of –e*, der Löschplatz (*Naut.*); *–e with ignominy*, schimpflicher Abschied (*Mil.*). **–e-pipe,** *s.* das Abflußrohr, Ausflußrohr. **–er,** *s.* der Entlader (*Elec.*). **–ing-arch,** *s.* der Entlastungsbogen (*Arch.*). **–ing-rod,** *s.* der Entlader.

disciple [dɪˈsaɪpl], *s.* der Schüler, Jünger; Anhänger. **–ship,** *s.* die Jüngerschaft, Anhängerschaft.

disciplin–able [ˈdɪsɪplɪnəbl], *adj.* gelehrig, folgsam. **–arian** [dɪsɪplɪˈnɛərɪən], *s.* der Zuchtmeister. **–ary** [ˈdɪsɪplɪnərɪ], *adj.* disziplinarisch, erzieherisch, Zucht–; *–ary punishment*, *s.* die Disziplinarstrafe. **–e** [ˈdɪsɪplɪn], 1. *s.* die Zucht, Manneszucht, Schulzucht, Kirchenzucht, Disziplin; moralische Erziehung; das Wissensgebiet, Unterrichtsfach; die Züchtigung, Strafe, Bestrafung; *maintain –e*, Disziplin halten; *military –e*, soldatische Zucht, die Manneszucht. 2. *v.a.* erziehen, schulen, bilden; zur Zucht anhalten; züchtigen, (be)strafen.

disclaim [dɪsˈkleɪm], *v.a.* nicht anerkennen, in Abrede stellen, (ver)leugnen; entsagen (*Dat.*), Verzicht leisten auf (*Acc.*), nicht beanspruchen (*Acc.*). **–er,** *s.* die Verzichtleistung (*Law*); Ableugnung; der Widerruf, das Dementi.

disclos–e [dɪsˈklouz], *v.a.* aufdecken, ans Licht bringen; offenbaren, enthüllen. **–ure** [–ʒə], *s.* die Enthüllung, Erschließung, Offenbarung, Verbreitung; Mitteilung.

discol–oration [dɪskʌləˈreɪʃən], *s.* die Entfärbung, Verfärbung, der Farbverlust; Fleck. **–our** [dɪsˈkʌlə], 1. *v.a.* die Farbe ändern von; (*fig.*) entstellen. 2. *v.n.* sich verfärben, verschießen. **–oured,** *adj.* mißfarbig, verschossen.

discomfit [dɪsˈkʌmfɪt], *v.a.* schlagen, besiegen; entmutigen, verwirren, aus der Fassung bringen. **–ure** [–ʃə], *s.* die Niederlage; Verwirrung.

discomfort [dɪsˈkʌmfət], 1. *s.* das Unbehagen, körperliche Beschwerde. 2. *v.a.* beunruhigen.

discompos–e [dɪskəmˈpouz], *v.a.* in Unordnung bringen, verwirren; aufregen, ärgern, beunruhigen, aus der Fassung bringen. **–ure** [–ʒə], *s.* die Unruhe, Aufregung, Verwirrung.

disconcert [dɪskənˈsəːt], *v.a.* vereiteln, zunichte machen; beunruhigen; verwirren, aus der Fassung bringen.

disconnect [dɪskəˈnɛkt], *v.a.* trennen; abstellen, abschalten, ausschalten (*Elec.*); entkuppeln, ausklinken, freimachen (*Mach.*). **–ed,** *adj.* losgelöst; unzusammenhängend, zusammenhangslos.

disconsolate [dɪsˈkɔnsəlɪt], *adj.* trostlos, untröstlich. **–ness,** *s.* die Trostlosigkeit.

discontent [dɪskənˈtɛnt], 1. *s.* die Unzufriedenheit, das Mißvergnügen. 2. *pred. adj. see* **–ed.** 3. *v.a.* unzufrieden machen. **–ed,** *attr. & pred. adj.* unzufrieden (*with*, mit), mißvergnügt (*with*, über (*Acc.*)); mißmutig. **–edness,** *s.*, **–ment,** *s.* die Unzufriedenheit.

discontinu–ance [dɪskənˈtɪnjuəns], *s.* die Unterbrechung; Einstellung, das Aufhören, die Beendigung; *–ance of a suit*, die Absetzung einer Klage (*Law*). **–ation,** *s.* die Unterbrechung. **–e,** 1. *v.a.* unterbrechen, aussetzen; einstellen, aufgeben, unterlassen; *–e a newspaper*, die Zeitung abbestellen. 2. *v.n.* aufhören, nachlassen. **–ity** [dɪskɔntɪnˈjuɪtɪ], *s.* der Mangel an Zusammenhang. **–ous** [dɪskənˈtɪnjuəs], *adj.* unterbrochen, unzusammenhängend, diskontinuierlich (*Math., Phys.*).

discord [ˈdɪskɔːd], *s.* die Zwietracht, Uneinigkeit, Mißhelligkeit; Dissonanz, der Mißklang, Mißton (*Mus.*); *be at – with*, in Widerspruch stehen mit. **–ance** [dɪsˈkɔːdəns], **–ancy,** *s.* der Mißklang; Widerspruch; die Mißhelligkeit. **–ant,** *adj.* uneinig, nicht übereinstimmend, widersprechend mißtönend; nicht zusammenstimmend (*Mus.*).

discount 1. [ˈdɪskaunt], *s.* der Rabatt, Diskont, das Disagio, der Zinsabzug; *allow a –*, Rabatt gewähren; *be at a –*, unter Pari stehen; (*fig.*) in Mißkredit stehen, unbeliebt *or* nicht geschätzt sein; *sell at a –*, unter Verlust verkaufen. 2. [–ˈkaunt] *v.a.* diskontieren (*a bill*); (*fig.*) nur halbwegs glauben, mit Vorsicht hinnehmen; beeinträchtigen, verringern; nicht mitzählen *or* mitrechnen. **–able** [dɪsˈkauntəbl], *adj.* diskontierbar. **–-broker,** der Wechselmakler, Diskontmakler. **–ing business,** das Diskontogeschäft.

discountenance [dɪsˈkauntɪnəns], *v.a.* offen mißbilligen, nicht unterstützen. **–d,** *adj.* entmutigt, verwirrt.

discourage [dɪsˈkʌrɪdʒ], *v.a.* entmutigen; abschrecken (*from doing*, zu tun); abraten von; mißbilligen, verhindern. **–ment,** *s.* die Entmutigung; Enttäuschung; Verhinderung, das Hindernis; das Abschreckungsmittel.

discourse [dɪsˈkɔːs], 1. *s.* das Gespräch; die Rede, der Vortrag; die Predigt; (*archaic*) Abhandlung. 2. *v.n.* einen Vortrag halten, reden, sprechen, predigen; sich unterhalten (*on*, über).

discourt–eous [dɪsˈkɔːtjəs, dɪsˈkəːtjəs], *adj.* unhöflich, unartig. **–esy** [dɪsˈkəːtɪsɪ], *s.* die Unhöflichkeit.

discover [dɪsˈkʌvə], *v.a.* entdecken, ausfindig machen, auskundschaften; ermitteln, feststellen; einsehen, gewahr werden; (*archaic*) aufdecken, enthüllen; *– check*, maskiertes Schach bieten (*Chess*); *– o.s. to a p.*, einem alles gestehen, sich einem entdecken. **–able** [–rəbl], *adj.* entdeckbar; sichtbar. **–er** [–rə], *s.* der Entdecker. **–y** [dɪsˈkʌvərɪ], *s.* die Entdeckung, Auffindung; Enthüllung, zwangsweise Mitteilung (*Law*); das Entdeckte, der Fund.

discredit [dɪsˈkrɛdɪt], 1. *s.* schlechter Ruf; der Mißkredit, die Unehre, Schande; der Zweifel, das Mißtrauen; *bring a p. into –*, *bring – on a p.*, einen in Mißkredit bringen; *throw – on a th.*, etwas zweifelhaft erscheinen lassen; *to the – of their family*, zur Schande ihrer Familie. 2. *v.a.* nicht glauben, bezweifeln; in übeln *or* schlechten Ruf bringen (*a p.*) (*with*, bei). **–able,** *adj.* entehrend, schimpflich.

discreet [dɪsˈkriːt], *adj.* verständig, umsichtig, vorsichtig, besonnen; taktvoll, verschwiegen.

discrepan–cy [dɪsˈkrɛpənsɪ], *s.* die Verschiedenheit

(*of views*); der Widerspruch, Zwiespalt. **–t,** *adj.* verschieden; widerstreitend.

discrete [ˈdɪskrɪ:t], *adj.* getrennt; unstetig, diskontinuierlich, diskret (*Math.*); disjunktiv (*Log.*).

discretion [dɪsˈkrɛʃən], *s.* die Klugheit, Umsicht, Vorsicht, Besonnenheit; Verschwiegenheit, Diskretion, der Takt, das Feingefühl; das Ermessen, Belieben, Gutdünken; die Freiheit, Vollmacht, Machtbefugnis; *age* or *years of –*, gesetztes Alter, mündiges Alter; *at –*, nach Belieben; *at your –*, von Ihrem Gutdünken abhängig; *– is the better part of valour*, das bessere Teil der Tapferkeit ist Vorsicht; *surrender at –*, sich bedingungslos *or* auf Gnade und Ungnade ergeben; *use one's –*, nach Gutdünken handeln; *act with –*, mit Einsicht *or* taktvoll handeln; *be within one's – to do*, einem freistehen zu tun. **–ary** [–ərɪ], *adj.* willkürlich, unumschränkt, beliebig; *–ary powers*, unumschränkte Vollmacht.

discretive [dɪsˈkrɪ:tɪv], *adj.* trennend, disjunktiv (*Log.*, *Gram.*).

discriminat–e [dɪsˈkrɪmɪneɪt], 1. *v.a.* unterscheiden, abheben, absondern. 2. *v.n.* unterscheiden; *–e against*, nachteilig behandeln, benachteiligen, herabsetzen; *–e between*, unterschiedlich behandeln; *–e in favour of*, begünstigen. **–ing,** *adj.* unterscheidend, charakteristisch; scharf(sinnig); urteilsfähig, umsichtig; *–ing duties*, Differenzialzölle. **–ion** [–ˈneɪʃən], . die Unterscheidung, unterschiedliche Behandlung, die Begünstigung (*in favour of*), Benachteiligung, Zurücksetzung (*against*); der Unterschied; Scharfsinn, das Unterscheidungsvermögen, die Urteilskraft. **–ive** [–nətɪv], **–ory,** *adj.* unterscheidend, charakteristisch; einen Unterschied beobachtend *or* machend; *–ory law*, das Ausnahmegesetz.

discursive [dɪsˈkə·sɪv], *adj.* abschweifend, unzusammenhängend; logisch fortschreitend, diskursiv (*Phil.*): *the – faculty*, logische Denkkraft.

discus [ˈdɪskəs], *s.* die Wurfscheibe, der Diskus; die Scheibe (*Astr.*, *Bot.*). **– –throw,** *s.* der Diskuswurf. **– –throwing,** *s.* (*throwing the –*) das Diskuswerfen.

discuss [dɪsˈkʌs], *v.a.* reden über, diskutieren, erörtern, besprechen, verhandeln; untersuchen, behandeln. **–ion** [–ˈkʌʃən], *s.* die Diskussion, Erörterung, Besprechung, Aussprache; *enter into* or *upon a –ion about s.th.*, etwas zum Gegenstand einer Erörterung machen; *matter for –ion*, das Diskussionsthema; *under –ion*, zur Erörterung stehend.

disdain [dɪsˈdeɪn], 1. *s.* die Verachtung, Geringschätzung, Verschmähung; *hold in –*, geringschätzen. 2. *v.a.* verachten, verschmähen. **–ful,** *adj.* verächtlich, geringschätzig; hochmütig; höhnisch.

disease [dɪˈzɪ:z], *s.* die Krankheit, das Leiden. **–d,** *adj.* krank, leidend; erkrankt.

disembark [dɪsɪmˈbɑ:k], 1. *v.a.* ausschiffen, landen. 2. *v.n.* an Land gehen, landen, aussteigen. **–ation** [–ɛmbɑ:ˈkeɪʃən], *s.* die Landung, Ausschiffung.

disembarrass [dɪsɪmˈbærəs], *v.a.* aus der Verlegenheit ziehen, befreien, loslösen; *– o.s. of*, sich befreien, loslösen *or* freimachen von.

disembod–iment [dɪsəmˈbɔdɪmənt], *s.* die Entkörperlichung; Auflösung (*of troops*). **–y,** *v.a.* entkörperlichen; entlassen, auflösen (*Mil.*).

disembogue [dɪsɪmˈboug], 1. *v.a.* ausgießen, entladen. 2. *v.n.* sich ergießen, münden, sich entladen.

disembowel [dɪsɪmˈbauəl], *v.a.* ausweiden; den Bauch aufschlitzen (*Dat.*).

disenchant [dɪsɪnˈtʃɑ:nt], *v.a.* entzaubern, ernüchtern; befreien (*of*, von) (*illusions, etc.*), enttäuschen. **–ment,** *s* die Entzauberung, Enttäuschung, Ernüchterung.

disencumber [dɪsɪnˈkʌmbə], *v.a.* entlasten, befreien (*of*, von).

disendow [dɪsɪnˈdau], *v.a.* die Pfründe *or* das Einkommen entziehen (*Dat.*). **–ment,** *s.* die Entziehung der Pfründen.

disenfranchise [dɪsənˈfræntʃaɪz], *v.a.* das Wahlrecht entziehen (*Dat.*).

disengage [dɪsɪnˈgeɪdʒ], 1. *v.a.* befreien, freimachen, loslösen, losmachen (*from*, von); entwickeln, auslösen, abscheiden (*Chem.*, *Phys.*); ausrücken (*gear*); loskuppeln, entkuppeln (*Railw.*). 2. *v.n.* sich freimachen; sich absetzen, loskommen (*Mil.*). **–d,** *adj.* frei, unbeschäftigt, zu sprechen. **–ment,** *s.* das Losmachen, die Befreiung; das Ausrücken.

disentangle [dɪsɪnˈtæŋgl], *v.a.* entwirren, auseinanderwickeln (*knots, etc.*); (*fig.*) befreien. **–ment,** *s.* die Entwirrung, Befreiung.

disenthral(l) [dɪsɪnˈθrɔ:l], *v.a.* (von Knechtschaft) befreien.

disestablish [dɪsɪsˈtæblɪʃ], *v.a.* aufheben, abschaffen (*organization*); *– the church*, die Kirche entstaatlichen. **–ment,** *s.* die Entstaatlichung.

disfavour [dɪsˈfeɪvə], 1. *s.* die Ungnade, Ungunst, Mißgunst, das Mißfallen; *fall into –*, in Ungnade fallen; *in – with*, in Ungnade bei; *in his –*, zu seinen Ungunsten. 2. *v.a.* mißbilligen, ungnädig behandeln.

disfigur–ation [dɪsfɪgjuˈreɪʃən], *s.* die Entstellung, Verunstaltung. **–e** [dɪsˈfɪgə], *v a.* entstellen, verunstalten. **–ement,** *s see* **–ation.**

disfranchise [dɪsˈfræntʃaɪz], *v.a.* entrechten, das Wahlrecht nehmen (*Dat.*); die Vorrechte *or* Freiheiten entziehen (*a town*, einer Stadt). **–ment,** *s.* die Entrechtung, Entziehung des Wahlrechts *or* der Vorrechte.

disgorge [dɪsˈgɔ:dʒ], 1. *v.a.* auswerfen, ausstoßen, ausspeien; (*fig.*) wieder herausgeben (*booty, etc.*). 2. *v.n.* sich entladen.

disgrace [dɪsˈgreɪs], 1. *s.* die Ungnade; der Schimpf, die Schande, Unehre (*to*, für); *in –*, in Ungnade; *fall into – with*, in Ungnade fallen bei; *bring – on s.o.*, einem Schande bereiten; *he is a – to his family*, er ist eine Schande *or* ein Schandfleck für seine Familie. 2. *v.a.* in Ungnade stürzen; entehren, schänden; *– o.s.*, sich blamieren; *be –d*, in Ungnade fallen. **–ful,** *adj.* schimpflich, schmählich, schmachvoll, entehrend, schändlich; *be –ful*, zur Schande gereichen.

disgruntled [dɪsˈgrʌntld], *adj.* verstimmt, mürrisch, unzufrieden (*at*, über).

disguise [dɪsˈgaɪz], 1. *v.a.* verkleiden, vermummen, maskieren; (*fig.*) verstellen, verhüllen, bemänteln; *– one's feelings*, seine Gefühle verbergen; *– the truth from a p.*, einem die Wahrheit verhehlen. 2. *s.* die Verkleidung, Vermummung; Maske; Verstellung, der Schein; Vorwand; *in –*, maskiert; *blessing in –*, das Glück im Unglück; *under the – of*, unter dem Vorwand (*Gen.*).

disgust [dɪsˈgʌst], 1. *s.* der Ekel, Widerwille (*at*, über *or* vor); die Abneigung (*at*, gegen). 2. *v.a.* anekeln; *it –s me to do it*, es ekelt mich es zu tun; *be –ed with s.o.*, sehr ärgerlich über einen sein, sich sehr über einen ärgern, Ekel über einen *or* vor einem empfinden; *– a p. with s.th.*, einem etwas zuwider machen; *he has become –ed with life*, das Leben ist ihm zum Ekel geworden. **–ing,** *adj.* ekelhaft, widerlich, zuwider, abscheulich, schauderhaft. **–ingly,** *adv.* (*also coll.*) entsetzlich.

dish [dɪʃ], 1. *s.* die Schüssel, Platte; das Gericht, die Speise; *side- –*, das Zwischengericht. 2. *v.a.* anrichten, auftragen; (*sl.*) vereiteln (*a th.*); (*sl.*) hintergehen, betrügen, überlisten, hereinfallen lassen, abtun, erledigen (*a p.*); (*sl.*) *– up*, auftischen (*a story, etc.*). **– –cloth,** *s.* das Abwaschtuch. **– –cover,** *s.* der Schüsseldeckel, die Schüsselstürze. **– –water,** *s.* das Spülwasser, Abwaschwasser.

dishabille [dɪsəˈbɪ:l], *s.* das Morgenkleid, Hauskleid.

disharmony [dɪsˈhɑ:mənɪ], *s.* der Mißklang, die Mißhelligkeit.

dishearten [dɪsˈhɑ:tn], *v.a.* entmutigen, niedergeschlagen *or* verzagt machen.

dishevel [dɪˈʃɛvl], *v.a.* zerzausen, in Unordnung bringen; *–led hair*, aufgelöstes, zerzaustes, unordentliches *or* wirres Haar.

dishon–est [dɪsˈɔnɪst], *adj.* unehrlich, unredlich. **–esty,** *s.* die Unredlichkeit, Unehrlichkeit. **–our** [–ˈɔnə], 1. *s.* die Schmach, Schande, der Schimpf. 2. *v.a.* entehren, schänden; verächtlich behandeln; nicht honorieren (*a cheque*) (*C.L.*); *–our one's word*, sein Wort nicht einlösen; *return a bill –oured*, einen Wechsel mit Protest zurückschicken. **–ourable** [–ˈɔnərəbl], *adj.* ehrlos; entehrend, schimpflich, schändlich, gemein. **–ourableness,** *s.* die Ehrlosigkeit, Unehrenhaftigkeit, Schändlichkeit.

disillusion [dɪsɪˈlju:ʒən], 1. *s.* die Enttäuschung, Ernüchterung (*with*, über). 2. *v.a.* ernüchtern, von Illusionen befreien. **–ment,** *s. see* – 1. **–ize,** *v.a. see* – 2.

disinclin–ation [dɪsɪnklɪˈneɪʃən], *s.* die Abneigung (*for* or *to*, gegen). **–e** [dɪsɪnˈklaɪn], *v.a.* abgeneigt machen (*from*, gegen). **–ed,** *adj.* abgeneigt.

disinfect [dɪsɪnˈfɛkt], *v.a.* desinfizieren. **–ant,** 1. *s.* das Desinfektionsmittel. 2. *adj.* desinfizierend, keimtötend. **–ion** [–ˈfɛkʃən], *s.* die Desinfektion.

disingenuous [dɪsɪnˈdʒenjuəs], *adj.* unaufrichtig, unredlich, hinterlistig. **–ness,** *s.* die Unredlichkeit, Unaufrichtigkeit.

disinherit [dɪsɪnˈhɛrɪt], *v.a.* enterben. **–ance,** *s.* die Enterbung.

disintegrat–e [dɪsˈɪntəgreɪt], 1. *v.a.* auflösen, aufschließen, aufspalten, trennen, zersetzen, zerteilen, zerfasern, zerkleinern, mahlen. 2. *v.n.* zerfallen, sich auflösen, abbauen (*Chem.*), verfallen, verwittern. **–ion** [–ˈgreɪʃən], *s.* die Auflösung, Trennung, Verwitterung, der Zerfall, die Zersetzung, Zertrümmerung, Zerstörung, Zerstückelung. **–or,** *s.* die Stampfmaschine, der Desintegrator.

disinter [dɪsɪnˈtə:], *v.a.* (wieder) ausgraben; (*fig.*) ans Licht bringen. **–ment,** *s.* die Ausgrabung.

disinterest [dɪsˈɪntrɪst], *v.r.* uninteressiert sein (*from*, an); gleichgültig gegenüber stehen (*from* (*Dat.*)). **–ed** [–ɪd], *adj.* uneigennützig, selbstlos, unparteiisch, unbefangen. **–edness,** *s.* die Uneigennützigkeit, Selbstlosigkeit; Unparteilichkeit.

disinterment [dɪsɪnˈtə:mənt], *see* **disinter.**

disjoin [dɪsˈdʒɔɪn], *v.a.* trennen.

disjoint [dɪsˈdʒɔɪnt], *v.a.* verrenken, ausrenken; zerlegen, zerstückeln; trennen, auseinandernehmen, aus den Fugen bringen. **–ed** [–ɪd], *adj.* abgerissen, zusammenhanglos, unzusammenhängend. **–edness,** *s.* der Mangel an Zusammenhang.

disjunct–ion [dɪsˈdʒʌŋkʃən], *s.* die Trennung, Absonderung. **–ive,** *adj.* trennend; disjunktiv (*Gram.*).

disk [dɪsk], *s.* die Scheibe, Platte, der Teller; (*coll.*) die Schallplatte, Gramophonplatte. **––clutch,** *s.* die Lamellenkupplung (*Motor.*). (*sl.*) **––jockey,** *s.* der Betreuer einer Schallplattensendung; (*Rad.*). **––valve,** *s.* das Tellerventil.

dislike [dɪsˈlaɪk], 1. *s.* die Abneigung; das Mißfallen, der Widerwille; *take a – to a th.*, eine Abneigung gegen eine S. fassen. 2. *v.a.* nicht gern haben, nicht mögen, nicht lieben, nicht leiden mögen *or* können, mißbilligen.

dislocat–e [ˈdɪslokeɪt], *v.a.* verrenken, ausrenken (*Med.*); (*fig.*) in Verwirrung bringen; *–e one's shoulder*, sich (*Dat.*) die Schulter verrenken. **–ion** [–ˈkeɪʃən], *s.* die Verrenkung (*Med.*); Verrückung, Verschiebung (*Geol.*); (*fig.*) Verwirrung.

dislodge [dɪsˈlɔdʒ], *v.a.* verjagen, vertreiben, verdrängen, entfernen.

disloyal [dɪsˈlɔɪəl], *adj.* treulos, untreu, ungetreu, verräterisch. **–ty,** *s.* die Untreue.

dismal [ˈdɪzməl], *adj.* trüb(e), düster; traurig, elend; schrecklich, grausig. **–ness,** *s.* die Traurigkeit, Trübheit, Schrecklichkeit.

dismantle [dɪsˈmæntl], *v.a.* abmontieren, abbauen, zerlegen, auseinandernehmen, niederreißen, abbrechen, schleifen (*Build.*); abtakeln (*a ship*); (*archaic*) entblößen, entkleiden.

dismast [dɪsˈmɑ:st], *v.a.* entmasten.

dismay [dɪsˈmeɪ], 1. *s.* der Schreck(en), die Bestürzung. 2. *v.a.* in Schrecken setzen, erschrecken; bange machen; *be –ed*, bange *or* verzagt sein.

dismember [dɪsˈmɛmbə], *v.a.* zergliedern; zerstückeln. **–ment,** *s.* die Zergliederung, Zerstückelung.

dismiss [dɪsˈmɪs], 1. *v.a.* fortschicken, verabschieden; entlassen (*from office*); wegtreten lassen (*a parade*) (*Mil.*); (*fig.*) aufgeben, ablehnen, hinweggehen über, fallen lassen, abweisen (*Law*); *he was –ed the service*, er wurde aus dem Dienst entlassen; *I –ed him without ceremony*, ich fertigte ihn ohne Umstände ab; *– a th. from one's mind*, sich (*Dat.*) eine S. aus dem Sinn *or* Kopf schlagen. 2. *v.n.* wegtreten, abtreten (*Mil.*). **–al,** *s.* die Entlassung, der Abschied, die Verabschiedung; Abweisung (*Law*).

dismount [dɪsˈmaʊnt], 1. *v.n.* absteigen; absitzen (*Mil.*); *– !* abgesessen! (*Mil.*). 2. *v.a.* absteigen von (*a horse*); vom Pferde werfen, aus dem Sattel heben (*a rider*); demontieren, von der Lafette nehmen (*a gun*); auseinandernehmen (*Mach.*).

disob–edience [dɪsoˈbɪ:djəns], *s.* der Ungehorsam, die Gehorsamsverweigerung. **–edient,** *adj.* ungehorsam (*to*, gegen). **–ey** [dɪsoˈbeɪ], *v.a.* nicht gehorchen (*Dat.*), ungehorsam sein gegen (*Acc.*) (*persons*); verletzen, übertreten, nicht befolgen, mißachten (*commands*); *I will not be –ed*, ich dulde keinen Ungehorsam.

disoblig–e [dɪsoˈblaɪdʒ], *v.a.* ungefällig sein gegen, kränken, verletzen. **–ing,** *adj.* ungefällig, unhöflich, unartig, unfreundlich. **–ingness,** *s.* die Ungefälligkeit.

disorder [dɪsˈɔ:də], 1. *s.* die Unordnung, Verwirrung; der Aufruhr, die Ruhestörung; die Unpäßlichkeit, das Übel, die Krankheit; *mental –*, die Geistesgestörtheit. 2. *v.a.* in Unordnung bringen, stören, verwirren; zerrütten (*body or mind*); *my stomach is –ed*, ich habe mir den Magen verdorben. **–liness,** *s.* die Unordnung, Verwirrung. **–ly,** *adj.* unordentlich, verwirrt, aufrührerisch, liederlich; *–ly behaviour*, liederliches Benehmen; *–ly house*, das Bordell.

disorgan–ization [dɪsɔ:gənaɪˈzeɪʃən], *s.* die Auflösung, Zerrüttung; Unordnung, Verwirrung. **–ize** [dɪsˈɔ:gənaɪz], *v.a.* auflösen, zerrütten, stören, in Unordnung *or* Verwirrung bringen.

disown [dɪsˈoun], *v.a.* nicht (als sein eigen) anerkennen; verstoßen; verleugnen, ableugnen.

disparag–e [dɪsˈpærɪdʒ], *v.a.* herabsetzen, in Verruf bringen, geringschätzen, verunglimpfen; verringern, schmälern, verkleinern. **–ement,** *s.* die Herabsetzung, Schmälerung, der Verruf; *no –ement ! without –ement to you !* ohne Ihnen nahetreten zu wollen! **–ing,** *adj.* geringschätzend, geringschätzig.

dispar–ate [ˈdɪspərət], *adj.* ungleichartig, unvereinbar, disparat. **–ates,** *pl.* Unvereinbarkeiten, unvergleichbare Dinge. **–ity** [dɪsˈpærɪtɪ], *s.* die Ungleichheit, Verschiedenheit.

[1]**dispart** [dɪsˈpɑ:t], 1. *v.a.* kalibrieren. 2. *s.* der Visierwinkel. **––sight,** *s.* das Richtkorn (*Artil.*).

[2]**dispart,** 1. *v.a.* trennen, spalten. 2. *v.n.* sich trennen.

dispassionate [dɪsˈpæʃənɪt], *adj.* leidenschaftslos; ruhig, gelassen; unbefangen, unparteiisch.

dispatch [dɪsˈpætʃ], 1. *v.a.* befördern, absenden, versenden, abgehen lassen; schnell erledigen, abmachen, abfertigen; beseitigen, abtun, töten; (*coll.*) rasch aufessen, verzehren. 2. *s.* schnelle Abfertigung, die Ausführung, Erledigung; Absendung, der Versand; die Eile; Beseitigung; Botschaft, Depesche; *advice of –*, die Versandanzeige; *bearer of –es*, der Eilbote, Depeschenträger, Kurier; *mentioned in –es*, in Depeschen erwähnt (*Mil.*); *with –*, eiligst. **––boat,** *s.* das Depeschenboot, Aviso. **––case,** *s.* die Aktentasche *or* –mappe. **––goods,** *pl.* das Eilgut. **––rider,** *s.* der Meldereiter; der Meldefahrer (*Mil.*).

dispel [dɪsˈpɛl], *v.a.* zerstreuen; (*fig.*) verbannen, vertreiben (*doubt, care, etc.*).

dispens–able [dɪsˈpɛnsəbl], *adj.* erläßlich, entbehrlich, unwesentlich. **–ary** [–ərɪ], *s.* die Armenapotheke; Poliklinik. **–ation** [–ˈseɪʃən], *s.* die Austeilung, Verteilung, der Dispens, die Dispensation, Erlassung (*Eccl.*); Fügung, Ordnung, Einrichtung; *divine –ation*, göttliche Fügung. **–e** [dɪsˈpɛns], 1. *v.a.* austeilen, verteilen, spenden, walten lassen; nach Rezept anfertigen, verabreichen; *–e drugs*, Arzneien verabreichen; *–e justice*, Recht sprechen. 2. *v.n.* Dispensation erteilen; Arzneien verabreichen; *–e with*, erlassen; entbehren, verzichten auf (*Acc.*), fertig werden ohne; *it cannot be –ed with*, es darf nicht unterbleiben; *we can –e with your company*, wir können Ihre Gesellschaft entbehren; *–e with formalities*, von Förmlichkeiten Abstand nehmen. **–er,** *s.* der

Handhaber (*of justice*), Arzneibesteller. **–ing-chemist,** *s.* der Apotheker.

dispers–al [dɪs'pəːsəl], *s.* die Zerstreuung, Verteilung, Verbreitung. **–e** [dɪs'pəːs], 1. *v.a.* zerstreuen, zersprengen, verteilen, verbreiten, ausbreiten, auseinandertreiben. 2. *v.n.* streuen, sich zerstreuen; auseinandergehen, auseinanderziehen, auseinanderlaufen. **–ion** [–'pəːʃən], *s.* die (Farben)-Zerstreuung, Streuung; Verbreitung, Ausbreitung.

dispirit [dɪs'pɪrɪt], *v.a.* entmutigen, niederdrücken. **–ed,** *adj.* mutlos, niedergeschlagen.

displace [dɪs'pleɪs], *v.a.* verlegen, versetzen, verdrängen, verrücken; entlassen, entheben, absetzen; *–d person*, verschleppte Person (*Pol.*). **–ment,** *s.* die Verschiebung, Verdrängung, Versetzung; Absetzung; der Hubraum (*of cylinder*) (*Motor.*); die Wasserverdrängung, das Deplacement (*of ships*); *–ment tonnage*, die Wasserverdrängung.

display [dɪs'pleɪ], 1. *v.a.* entfalten, ausbreiten, offenbaren; ausstellen, zur Schau stellen; *– one's courage*, seinen Mut zeigen; *– one's common sense*, seinen Mutterwitz erkennen lassen. 2. *s.* die Entfaltung, Schaustellung; der Aufwand, Pomp, Prunk; die Auslage (*in windows*); Aufmachung (*Typ.*); *make a great –*, großen Aufwand machen; *make a great – of*, auffällig zur Schau tragen, prunken mit; *grand – of fireworks*, großes Feuerwerk.

displeas–e [dɪs'pliːz], *v.a.* mißfallen (*Dat.*), kränken; *–e the eye*, das Auge beleidigen. **–ed,** *adj.* mißvergnügt; ungehalten (*at*, or *with*, über (*Acc.*)); unzufrieden (mit). **–ing,** *adj.* unangenehm, mißfällig, anstößig. **–ure** [dɪs'plɛʒə], *s.* das Mißfallen, der Unwille, Verdruß (*at* or *over*, über); *incur a p.'s –ure*, sich jemandes Mißfallen zuziehen.

disport [dɪs'pɔːt], *v.n.* & *r.* sich belustigen, sich ergötzen, sich vergnügen.

dispos–able [dɪs'pouzəbl], *adj.* verfügbar, disponibel. **–al** [–zəl], *s.* die Anordnung, Verwendung; Beseitigung, Erledigung; der Verkauf, die Übergabe; Verfügung, Disposition, Willkür, Macht (*of*, über); *be at s.o.'s –al*, einem zur Verfügung stehen; *place at s.o.'s –al*, einem zur Verfügung stellen. **–e** [dɪs'pouz], 1. *v.a.* (an)ordnen, verteilen, einrichten, einteilen, aufstellen, einreihen, zurechtlegen (*things*); geneigt machen, bewegen, stimmen, leiten, lenken (*persons*). 2. *v.n.* ordnen, lenken, verfügen; *man proposes God –es*, der Mensch denkt, Gott lenkt; *–e of*, verfügen, gebieten (über (*Acc.*)), verwenden, anwenden; verkaufen, veräußern, an den Mann bringen (*goods*); erledigen, abfertigen, beseitigen, abtun, abschaffen, wegschaffen, wegschicken, loswerden, unschädlich machen; *–e of a matter*, eine S. abfertigen, sich einer S. entledigen; *–e of a th. by will*, eine S. testamentarisch vermachen; *–e of in marriage*, durch Heirat versorgen, verheiraten; *–e of a p. quietly*, einen heimlich um die Ecke bringen; *–e of once and for all*, ein für allemal aus der Welt schaffen. **–ed,** *adj.* geneigt, gewillt, gesonnen, bereit; *–ed to mirth*, zur Fröhlichkeit aufgelegt; *ill-–ed*, übel gelaunt, mürrisch, schlechter Laune; *ill-–ed towards*, übelgesinnt (*Dat.*); *well-–ed towards*, freundlich geneigt *or* gesinnt (*Dat.*). **–ition** [dɪspə'zɪʃən], *s.* die Anordnung, Aufstellung, Verteilung, Einteilung, Einrichtung; Gliederung, Anlage, der Plan; die Verfügung, Bestimmung, Disposition, Verleihung; Neigung, Gesinnung, Stimmung, der Hang, die Gemütsart, Sinnesart, Charakteranlage; (*pl.*) Vorkehrungen, Vorbereitungen.

dispossess [dɪspə'zɛs], *v.a.* enteignen, (aus dem Besitze) vertreiben; (*fig.*) berauben (*of* (*Gen.*)); befreien (*of*, von). **–ion,** *s.* die Entsetzung, Enteignung, Beraubung.

dispraise [dɪs'preɪz], 1. *v.a.* tadeln, herabsetzen. 2. *s.* der Tadel, die Geringschätzung, Herabsetzung.

disproof [dɪs'pruːf], *s.* die Widerlegung.

disproportion [dɪsprə'pɔːʃən], *s.* das Mißverhältnis. **–ate** [–nɪt], *adj.* in keinem Verhältnis stehend (*to*, zu); unverhältnismäßig, übertrieben.

disprove [dɪs'pruːv], *v.a.* widerlegen.

disput–able ['dɪspjutəbl], *adj.* bestreitbar, strittig. **–ant** [–ənt], *s.* der Streiter, Gegner, Disputant. **–ation** [dɪspjuː'teɪʃən], *s.* der Wortstreit, die Disputation. **–atious, –ative,** *adj.* streitsüchtig. **–e** [dɪs'pjuːt], 1. *s.* der Streit, die Debatte, Kontroverse; *beyond –e*, unstreitig, fraglos; *in –e*, streitig, strittig, umstritten. 2. *v.a.* bestreiten, in Zweifel ziehen, bezweifeln; abstreiten, widerstreben, widerstehen; erörtern, diskutieren; *–e every inch of ground*, jeden Zollbreit Landes streitig machen. 3. *v.n.* (sich) streiten, zanken (*about*, um); disputieren, debattieren; *–e about nothing*, um des Kaisers Bart streiten.

disqualif–ication [dɪskwɔlɪfɪ'keɪʃən], *s.* das Unfähigmachen; die Unfähigkeit, Untauglichkeit; der Nachteil; die Untauglichkeitserklärung, Ausschließung, der Ausschluß (*Sport.*). **–y** [dɪs'kwɔlɪfaɪ], *v.a.* unfähig *or* untauglich machen (*for*, zu); ausschließen (*Sport*).

disquiet [dɪs'kwaɪət], 1. *v.a.* beunruhigen, stören. 2. *s.* die Unruhe, Rastlosigkeit, Gärung; Sorge, Angst. **–ing,** *adj.* beunruhigend. **–ude** [–tjuːd], *s.* *see –*, 2.

disquisition [dɪskwɪ'zɪʃən], *s.* eingehende Rede, die Abhandlung (*on*, über).

disrate [dɪs'reɪt], *v.a.* (her)absetzen, degradieren.

disregard [dɪsrɪ'gɑːd], 1. *s.* die Mißachtung (*of* or *for*, vor *or* gegenüber); Geringschätzung, Vernachlässigung (*of* or *for*, für *or* gegenüber). 2. *v.a.* mißachten, nicht achten auf, nicht beachten, vernachlässigen, außer Acht lassen. **–ful,** *adj.* unachtsam; *be –ful of*, mißachten, vernachlässigen.

disrelish [dɪs'rɛlɪʃ], 1. *s.* der Widerwille, die Abneigung (*for*, gegen). 2. *v.a.* keinen Geschmack finden an (*Dat.*), Abneigung empfinden vor.

disrepair [dɪsrɪ'pɛə], *s.* die Baufälligkeit, der Verfall; *be in a state of –*, baufällig sein; *fall into –*, in Verfall geraten.

disreput–able [dɪs'rɛpjutəbl], *adj.* verrufen, von schlechtem Ruf; gemein, schimpflich. **–e** [dɪsrɪ'pjuːt], *s.* übler Ruf, der Verruf; die Unehre, Schande; *bring into –e*, in Verruf bringen.

disrespect [dɪsrɪ'spɛkt], 1. *s.* die Nichtachtung, Mißachtung; Geringschätzung (*to*, gegenüber); die Unhöflichkeit, Unehrerbietigkeit (*to*, gegen). 2. *v.a.* nichtachten, geringschätzen. **–ful,** *adj.* unehrerbietig; unhöflich (*to*, gegen). **–fulness,** *s.* die Unehrerbietigkeit, Unhöflichkeit.

disrobe [dɪs'roub], 1. *v.a.* entkleiden; (*fig.*) befreien. 2. *v.r.* sich entkleiden.

disroot [dɪs'ruːt], *v.a.* entwurzeln.

disrupt [dɪs'rʌpt], *v.a.* spalten, (auseinander)-sprengen; (*fig.*) trennen, zerreißen, auseinanderreißen. **–ion,** *s.* das Auseinanderreißen, die Zerreißung, Zersetzung, Spaltung; der Bruch, Riß; die Zerrissenheit. **–ive,** *adj.* spaltend, auflösend.

dissatisf–action [dɪsætɪs'fækʃən], *s.* die Unzufriedenheit (*at*, *over* or *with*, über *or* mit). **–actory** [dɪsætɪs'fæktərɪ], *adj.* unbefriedigend. **–ied** [dɪ'sætɪsfaɪd], *adj.* unzufrieden, mißvergnügt, verdrießlich, unbefriedigt. **–y** [dɪ'sætɪsfaɪ], *v.a.* nicht befriedigen; unzufrieden machen; mißfallen (*Dat.*).

dissect [dɪ'sɛkt], *v.a.* zerlegen; zergliedern (*also fig.*); sezieren (*Anat.*); (*fig.*) analysieren. **–ing-knife,** *s.* das Seziermesser. **–ing-room,** *s.* der Sezierraum. **–ion** [–'sɛkʃən], *s.* die Zerlegung; Sektion, das Sezieren (*Anat.*); (*fig.*) die Zergliederung.

dissei–se, –ze [dɪs'siːz], *v.a.* widerrechtlich enteignen (*Law*). **–sin, –zin,** *s.* widerrechtliche Besitzergreifung.

dissemble [dɪ'sɛmbl], 1. *v.a.* verbergen, verhehlen, nicht merken lassen, ignorieren. 2. *v.n.* heucheln, sich verstellen. **–r,** *s.* der Heuchler, Verhehler.

disseminat–e [dɪ'sɛmɪneɪt], *v.a.* ausstreuen (*seed*); (*fig.*) verbreiten, zerstreuen, aussprengen. **–ion** [–'neɪʃən], *s.* die Ausstreuung, Verbreitung. **–or,** *s.* der Ausbreiter, Verbreiter.

dissension [dɪ'sɛnʃən], *s.* die Zwietracht; Uneinigkeit; der Streit, Zwist; *sow –*, Zwietracht stiften.

dissent [dɪ'sɛnt], 1. *s.* abweichende Meinung, die Meinungsverschiedenheit; Abweichung von der Staatskirche, der Dissent (*Eccl.*). 2. *v.n.* nicht übereinstimmen (*from*, mit), anderer Meinung sein (*from*, als); (von der Staatskirche) abweichen. **–er,** *s.* der Dissident; Dissenter, Sektierer, Nonkonformist (*Eccl.*); (*Amer.*) *see* **–ient,** 2. **–ient** [–ˈsɛnʃənt], 1. *adj.* andersdenkend, abweichend, nicht übereinstimmend; *without a –ient vote*, einstimmig. 2. *s.* Andersdenkende(r), *m.*, abweichende Stimme.

dissertation [dɪsəːˈteɪʃən], *s.* gelehrte Abhandlung; die Dissertation (*on*, über); *doctoral* –, die Doktorarbeit.

disservice [dɪsˈsəːvɪs], *s.* der Nachteil; schlechter Dienst; *do s.o. a* –, einem einen schlechten Dienst erweisen.

dissever [dɪˈsɛvə], *v.a.* trennen, absondern; (zer)-teilen. **–ance, –ment,** *s.* die Trennung, Absonderung.

dissiden–ce [ˈdɪsɪdəns], *s.* die Uneinigkeit, Meinungsverschiedenheit. **–t,** 1. *adj.* nicht übereinstimmend, andersdenkend, abweichend. 2. *s.* der Dissident, Andersdenkende(r), *m.*

dissimil–ar [dɪˈsɪmɪlə], *adj.* unähnlich, ungleich-(artig); verschieden (*to* or *from*, von). **–arity** [–ˈlærɪtɪ], *s.* die Ungleichheit, Unähnlichkeit, Verschiedenartigkeit. **–itude,** *s.* die Verschiedenartigkeit, Unähnlichkeit.

dissimulat–e [dɪˈsɪmjʊleɪt], 1. *v.a.* verhehlen, verdecken (*one's feelings*). 2. *v.n.* sich verstellen, heucheln. **–ion** [–ˈleɪʃən], *s.* die Verstellung, Heuchelei.

dissipat–e [ˈdɪsɪpeɪt], 1. *v.a.* zerstreuen, zerteilen; (*fig.*) vertreiben, verscheuchen, verbannen (*care*); vergeuden, verschwenden (*resources*). 2. *v.n.* sich zerstreuen, sich auflösen, verschwinden. **–ed,** *adj.* ausschweifend, liederlich. **–ion** [–ˈpeɪʃən], *s.* die Zerstreuung (*also fig.*); Auflösung, Verflüchtigung, Vertreibung; Verschwendung (*of resources*); der Zeitvertreib, die Ausschweifung, Liederlichkeit, ausschweifendes Leben.

dissoci–able [dɪˈsoʊʃjəbl], *adj.* trennbar. **–ate** [dɪˈsoʊʃɪeɪt], 1. *v.a.* trennen, loslösen, absondern; *–ate o.s. from*, abrücken von, sich lossagen von, nichts zu tun haben mit. 2. *v.n.* sich spalten, aufspalten, zerfallen. **–ation** [–ˈeɪʃən], *s.* die Trennung, Absonderung; Auflösung, Zersetzung, der Zerfall (*Chem.*); die Dissoziation, das Doppelbewußtsein (*Psych.*).

dissolub–ility [dɪsəljʊˈbɪlɪtɪ], *s.* die Auflösbarkeit, Trennbarkeit. **–le** [dɪˈsəljʊbl], *adj.* (auf)lösbar, trennbar.

dissolut–e [ˈdɪsəljuːt], *adj.* ausschweifend, liederlich. **–eness,** die Liederlichkeit, Ausschweifung. **–ion** [dɪsəˈljuːʃən], *s.* die Auflösung (*also fig.*), Zersetzung; Zerstörung, Aufhebung; der Tod; die Trennung; *–ion of an assembly*, die Auflösung einer Versammlung; *–ion of the body*, die Zersetzung *or* der Zerfall des Körpers; *–ion of marriage*, die Auflösung *or* Trennung einer Ehe; *–ion of parliament*, die Auflösung des Parlaments.

dissolv–able [dɪˈzəlvəbl], *adj.* auflösbar, auflöslich, löslich. **–e** [dɪˈzəlv], 1. *v.a.* auflösen (*also fig.*), schmelzen; (*fig.*) trennen, umstoßen, aufheben; *–e a marriage*, eine Ehe lösen; *–e a partnership*, eine Handelsgesellschaft auflösen; *–e one picture in another*, ein Bild in das andere überblenden *or* abblenden *or* übergehen lassen (*Films*). 2. *v.n.* sich auflösen, zerrinnen, zergehen, (zusammen)schmelzen; (*fig.*) vergehen, verschwinden, hinschwinden, auseinandergehen (*as parliament*), in einander übergehen *or* überblenden (*as pictures*); sich zerteilen (*Med.*); *–e into tears*, sich in Tränen auflösen. **–ent,** 1. *adj.* auflösend, zersetzend. 2. *s.* auflösendes Mittel.

dissonan–ce [ˈdɪsonəns], *s.* der Mißklang, die Dissonanz; Uneinigkeit, Mißhelligkeit. **–t,** *adj.* mißtönend, unharmonisch; (*fig.*) unvereinbar, abweichend.

dissua–de [dɪˈsweɪd], *v.a.* abraten (*Dat.*), abbringen. **–sion** [–ˈsweɪʒən], *s.* das Abraten, Abbringen. **–sive,** *adj.* abratend.

dissylabic [dɪsɪˈlæbɪk], *adj. see* **disyllabic.**

distaff [ˈdɪstɑːf], *s.* der Spinnrocken, die Kunkel; – *side*, weibliche Linie, weibliches Geschlecht.

distal [ˈdɪstəl], *adj.* der Körpermitte entfernt (*Anat.*), vorder, an der Peripherie.

distance [ˈdɪstəns], 1. *s.* der Abstand, die Entfernung; Ferne, Weite; Strecke (*Sport*); der Hintergrund (*Paint.*); (*fig.*) die Distanz, Zurückhaltung, Reserve; (*a*) (*with adjectives*) *corrected* or *true* –, tatsächlicher Abstand (*Naut.*); *within driving* –, zu Wagen erreichbar; *within easy* –, bequem zu erreichen; *within striking* –, in Wirkungsabstand; *focal* –, die Brennweite (*Opt.*); *a good* – *off*, ziemlich weit entfernt; *long-– flight*, der Langstreckenflug; *long-– train*, der Fernzug; *stopping* –, die Bremsstrecke (*Motor.*); *visual* –, die Sehweite; (*b*) (*with verbs*) *cover a* –, eine Strecke zurücklegen; *the* – *covered*, die Flug–, Lauf– *or* Marschstrecke; *keep one's* –, zurückhaltend sein, Distanz halten; (*c*) (*with prepositions*) *at a* –, von weitem, von ferne, weit entfernt; *at an equal* –, gleich weit; *action at a* –, die Fernwirkung; *keep at a* –, vom Leibe halten, fernhalten (*a p.*); *at this* - *of time*, bei diesem Zeitabstand; *from a* –, aus einiger Entfernung; *in the* –, in der Ferne; *in the middle* –, in der Mitte (*Paint.*). 2. *v.a.* sich distanzieren, hinter sich lassen (*also fig.*); (*fig.*) übertreffen, überflügeln, überholen. **––post,** *s.* der Distanzpfahl. **––signal,** *s.* das Vorsignal.

distant [ˈdɪstənt], *adj.* fern, weit entfernt; zurückhaltend, kühl; – *allusion*, leichte Anspielung; – *prospect*, (*fig.*) entfernte *or* schwache Hoffnung; – *relation*, weitläufiger Verwandter; – *resemblance*, entfernte Ähnlichkeit; – *signal*, das Vorsignal.

distaste [dɪsˈteɪst], *s.* die Abneigung, der Widerwille (*for*, gegen), der Abscheu (*for*, vor). **–ful,** *adj.* zuwider (*Dat.*), ekelhaft, widerlich; verdrießlich, widerwärtig. **–fulness,** *s.* die Widerwärtigkeit.

[1]**distemper** [dɪsˈtɛmpə], *s.* die Krankheit, Unpäßlichkeit, Verstimmung; Staupe (*of dogs*); politische Unruhe. **–ed,** *adj.* krank, unpäßlich; geistig gestört, zerrüttet.

[2]**distemper,** 1. *s.* die Temperafarbe, Wasserfarbe, Leimfarbe; – *painting*, die Temperamalerei. 2. *v.a.* mit Wasserfarben streichen; in Tempera-manier malen.

disten–d [dɪsˈtɛnd], 1. *v.a.* ausdehnen, aufblasen. 2. *v.n.* sich ausdehnen, ausschwellen, weit ausstrecken. **–sible, –sile,** *adj.* (aus)dehnbar. **–sion** [–ˈtɛnʃən], *s.* das Strecken, Dehnen, Spreizen; die Ausdehnung; Weite.

distich [ˈdɪstɪk], *s.* das Distichon, der Doppelvers. **–ous,** *adj.* in zwei Reihen geordnet (*Bot.*).

distil [dɪsˈtɪl], 1. *v.a.* herabtropfen *or* herabträufeln lassen; destillieren (*Chem.*); brennen (*spirits*); (*fig.*) das Beste abziehen aus; *–led perfumes*, ätherische Öle; *–led water*, destilliertes Wasser. 2. *v.n.* tröpfeln, triefen, traufen, herabtropfen, rinnen, rieseln; destillieren. **–late,** *s.* das Destillat. **–lation** [–ˈleɪʃən], *s.* das Destillieren, die Destillation; das Destillat, der Auszug; *–lation of spirits*, die Branntweinbrennerei. **–ler,** *s.* der Destillateur, Branntweinbrenner. **–lery,** *s.* die Branntweinbrennerei.

distinct [dɪsˈtɪŋkt], *adj.* abgesondert, getrennt, einzeln; unterschieden, verschieden; klar, deutlich, ausgesprochen, ausgeprägt, bestimmt, eindeutig, entschieden. **–ion** [–ʃən], *s.* die Unterscheidung; der Unterschied, die Eigenart, unterscheidendes Merkmal; die Auszeichnung, Würde, Vornehmheit. **–ive** [–tɪv], *adj.* unterscheidend, charakteristisch, spezifisch, ausgeprägt, deutlich, kennzeichnend, eigentümlich, besonder, apart; *be –ive of*, kennzeichnen. **–iveness.** *s.* die Deutlichkeit; Eigentümlichkeit, das Unterscheidende. **–ness,** *s.* die Deutlichkeit, Klarheit, Bestimmtheit.

distinguish [dɪsˈtɪŋgwɪʃ], 1. *v.a.* unterscheiden (*from*, von); kennzeichnen, charakterisieren; bemerken, erkennen; auszeichnen; – *o.s.*, sich auszeichnen; *be –ed by*, sich unterscheiden durch; sich auszeichnen durch. 2. *v.n.* unterscheiden; einen Unterschied machen. **–able,** *adj.* unterscheidbar, kenntlich, bemerkbar. **–ed,** *adj.* hervorragend, ausgezeichnet, vorzüglich, berühmt, vornehm; *–ed by*, kenntlich (*by*, an), bemerkenswert (*by*, durch; *for*, wegen); *–ed service cross*, das Verdienstkreuz (*for common soldiers*); *–ed service order*, der Verdienstorden (*for officers*) (*Mil.*). **–ing,** *adj.* unterscheidend; eigentümlich, bezeichnend, charakteristisch.

distort [dɪsˈtɔ:t], 1. *v.a.* verzerren, verdrehen, verbiegen, verrenken; verziehen; (*fig.*) entstellen. 2. *v.n.* sich werfen, sich ziehen. **–ion** [–ˈtɔ:ʃən], *s.* die Verdrehung, Verbiegung, Verrenkung; Verzerrung, Entstellung; Verzeichnung (*Opt.*).

distract [dɪsˈtrækt], *v.a.* abziehen, ablenken (*the attention*); beunruhigen, stören; von Sinnen bringen, verwirren, quälen, zerrütten. **–ed,** *adj.* zerstreut, von Sinnen, wahnsinnig, verrückt; *be –ed with pain,* verrückt *or* außer sich vor Schmerz sein. **–ion** [–ˈtrækʃən], *s.* die Zerstreutheit (*of mind*); Zerstreuung, Ablenkung; Verwirrung, der Wahnsinn, die Raserei; *to –ion,* bis zur Raserei.

distrain [dɪsˈtreɪn], *v.n.* mit Beschlag belegen (*on a th.,* etwas); pfänden (*on a p.,* einen; *for,* wegen); sich schadlos halten (*on a p.,* an einem). **–able,** *adj.* mit Beschlag belegbar, pfändbar. **–ee,** *s.* Gepfändete(r), *m.* **–er, –or,** *s.* der Pfänder. **–t,** *s.* die Beschlagnahme, Zwangsvollstreckung.

distraught [dɪsˈtrɔ:t], *adj.* erregt, wahnsinnig; zerrüttet (*with,* von).

distress [dɪsˈtrɛs], 1. *s.* die Not, das Elend; die Notlage, der Notstand; Trübsal, Kummer, die Bedrängnis (*of mind*); Qual, Pein; Erschöpfung; der Schmerz (*of body*); die Beschlagnahme, Pfändung, Zwangsvollstreckung; *– at sea,* die Seenot; *be in great – for money,* in großer Geldnot sein; *levy a – on,* pfänden, mit Beschlag belegen; *signal of –,* das Notsignal; *warrant of –,* der Vollstreckungsbefehl (*Law*). 2. *v.a.* quälen, plagen, betrüben, unglücklich machen, peinigen; *see* **distrain. –ed,** *adj.* in Not, notleidend, bedrängt; unglücklich, bekümmert, betrübt, geängstigt; *–ed area,* das Notstandsgebiet. **–ful,** *adj.* unglücklich, kummervoll, qualvoll, unselig, jämmerlich. **–ing,** *adj.* schmerzlich, peinlich.

distribut–able [dɪsˈtrɪbjutəbl], *adj.* verteilbar. **–e** [dɪsˈtrɪbju:t], *v.a.* verteilen, austeilen, verbreiten (*among,* unter (*Acc.*); *to,* an (*Acc.*)); einteilen, anorden; zuteilen, spenden (*alms, etc.*); ablegen (*Typ.*). **–ion** [–ˈbju:ʃən], *s.* die Verteilung, Verbreitung, Ausbreitung, Austeilung; der Absatz, Vertrieb (*of goods*); die Einteilung (*into classes*), Zuteilung; Anwendung auf alle in einer Klasse (*Log.*); das Ablegen (*Typ.*); *–ion of alms,* die Almosenspende, Verteilung milder Gaben. **–ive,** 1. *adj.* austeilend, verteilend; zuteilend, erteilend, einteilend (*Log.*); ausgleichend (*justice*); distributiv (*Gram.*). 2. *s.* das Distributivum (*Gram.*). **–or,** *s.* der Zündverteiler; *–or arm,* *s.* der Verteilerfinger.

district [ˈdɪstrɪkt], *s.* der Bezirk, Kreis, Gau, Verwaltungsbereich; das Gebiet, die Gegend, der Landstrich. **––attorney,** *s.* (*Amer.*) der Staatsanwalt. **––court,** *s.* das Bezirksgericht. **––nurse,** *s.* die Armenkrankenschwester, Diakonisse, Diakonieschwester. **––rate,** *s.* die Kreissteuer, Kommunalsteuer. **––visitor,** der Pfarrkreisgehilfe.

distrust [dɪsˈtrʌst], 1. *v.a.* mißtrauen (*Dat.*). 2. *s.* das Mißtrauen (*of,* gegen); *hold s.o. in –,* mißtrauisch gegen einen sein. **–ful,** *adj.* mißtrauisch (*of,* gegen); *–ful of o.s.,* gehemmt, voll Hemmungen, ohne Selbstvertrauen. **–fulness,** *s.* das Mißtrauen.

disturb [dɪsˈtə:b], *v.a.* in Unordnung bringen; stören; beunruhigen, verwirren, aufregen; aufrühren; *– a train of thought,* einen Gedankengang unterbrechen; *don't – yourself!* lassen Sie sich nicht stören! **–ance,** *s.* die Störung, Beunruhigung; Unruhe, Aufregung, Verwirrung, der Aufruhr, Tumult; die Behinderung, Belästigung, Beeinträchtigung (*Law*); *–ance of the peace,* die Friedensstörung. **–ing,** *adj.* beunruhigend (*to,* für).

disuni–on [dɪsˈju:njən], *s.* die Trennung, Spaltung; (*fig.*) Uneinigkeit, Entzweiung. **–te** [dɪsju:ˈnaɪt], 1. *v.a.* entzweien, trennen. 2. *v.n.* sich trennen. **–ty** [dɪsˈju:nɪtɪ], *s.* die Uneinigkeit.

disuse, 1. [dɪsˈju:s], *s.* der Nichtgebrauch; das Aufhören eines Brauches; *fall into –,* ungebräuchlich werden. 2. [dɪsˈju:z], *v.a.* nicht mehr gebrauchen. **–d,** aufgegeben, außer Gebrauch, veraltet.

disyllab–ic [dɪsɪˈlæbɪk], *adj.* zweisilbig. **–le** [dɪˈsɪləbl], *s.* zweisilbiges Wort.

ditch [dɪtʃ], 1. *s.* der Graben, die Gosse; *anti-tank –,* die Tankfalle, Tankgrube; *drainage –,* der Entwässerungsgraben, Dräniergraben, Abzugsgraben; *foundation –,* die Schachtgrube; *dig a –,* einen Graben ziehen; *to the last –,* (*fig.*) bis zum Äußersten. 2. *v.n.* einen Graben ziehen *or* ausbessern. 3. *v.a.* mit einem Graben umgeben; (*sl.*) notwassern (*an aircraft*). **–er,** *s.* der Grabenbauer. **––water,** *s.* abgestandenes Wasser; *as dull as ––water,* langweilig, fade.

dither [ˈdɪðə], 1. *v.n.* zittern; *– about,* unschlüssig sein, sich verdattern. 2. *s.* das Zittern, der Tatterich; (*coll.*) *all of a –,* tatterig, verdattert.

dithyramb [ˈdɪθɪræm(b)], *s.* der Dithyrambus. **–ic** [–ˈræmbɪk], 1. *adj.* dithyrambisch, schwungvoll. 2. *s.* der Dithyrambus.

dittany [ˈdɪtənɪ], *s.* der Diptam (*Bot.*).

ditto [ˈdɪtoʊ], *adv.* desgleichen, dito.

ditty [ˈdɪtɪ], *s.* das Liedchen; *popular –,* der Gassenhauer.

ditty––bag [ˈdɪtɪbæg], *s.* der Nähbeutel (*Naut.*). **––box,** *s.* der Utensilienkasten (*Naut.*).

diuretic [daɪjuˈrɛtɪk], 1. *adj.* harntreibend. 2. *s.* harntreibendes Mittel.

diurnal [daɪˈə:nəl], *adj.* Tag–, Tages–, täglich.

divagat–e [ˈdaɪvəgeɪt], *v.n.* schweifen, abschweifen, herumschweifen. **–ion** [daɪvəˈgeɪʃən], *s.* die Abweichung, Abwendung, Abkehr; Abschweifung.

divalent [ˈdaɪˈveɪlənt], *adj.* zweiwertig (*Chem.*).

divan [dɪˈvæn], *s.* der Diwan; (*rare*) das Rauchzimmer.

divaricat–e [daɪˈværɪkeɪt], *v.n.* abzweigen, sich trennen, sich gabeln, sich spalten. **–ion** [–ˈkeɪʃən], *s.* die Gabelung; (*fig.*) Abweichung, Mißhelligkeit.

div–e [daɪv], 1. *v.n.* tauchen, untertauchen; einen Kopfsprung machen; einen Sturzflug machen, sturzfliegen (*Av.*); *–e into,* untertauchen in, plötzlich verschwinden in; (*fig.*) tief eindringen in (*Acc.*), sich versenken in (*Acc.*); *–e into one's pocket,* in die Tasche greifen. 2. *s.* das Tauchen; der Kopfsprung; Sturzflug (*Av.*); (*sl.*) verrufenes Lokal, die Spelunke; *make a –e for,* stürzen auf; *nose –e,* der Sturzflug; *power –e,* der Sturzflug (*Av.*); *–e-bomber,* das Sturzkampfflugzeug; *–e-bombing attack,* der Sturzangriff; *make a –e at,* einen Griff tun nach, langen nach. **–er,** *s.* der Taucher (*also Orn.*). **–ing-bell,** *s.* dieTaucherglocke. **–ing-suit,** *s.* der Taucheranzug.

diverg–e [daɪˈvə:dʒ], *v.n.* auseinandergehen (*also fig.*), divergieren; abweichen. **–ence, –ency,** *s.* das Auseinanderlaufen, die Abweichung; Streuung (*Artil.*); Divergenz (*Geom.*). **–ent, –ing,** *adj.* divergierend, auseinanderlaufend, abweichend.

divers [ˈdaɪvəz], *adj.* etliche, verschiedene, mehrere, mancherlei. **–e** [daɪˈvə:s], *adj.* verschieden, ungleich; mannigfaltig. **–ification** [daɪvə:sɪfɪˈkeɪʃən], *s.* die Veränderung; Mannigfaltigkeit. **–ified** [daɪˈvə:sɪfaɪd], *adj.* abwechslungsreich, mannigfaltig. **–ify** [–faɪ], *v.a.* verschieden machen; Mannigfaltigkeit *or* Abwechslung bringen in (*Acc.*). **–ion** [daɪˈvə:ʃən], *s.* die Abwendung, Ableitung, Ablenkung; Umleitung (*of traffic*); der Nebenangriff, die Diversion, das Ablenkungsmanöver (*Mil.*); die Zerstreuung, der Zeitvertreib. **–ity** [daɪˈvə:sɪtɪ], *s.* die Verschiedenheit, Ungleichheit; Mannigfaltigkeit, Abwechslung.

divert [daɪˈvə:t], *v.a.* abwenden, ablenken, ableiten; belustigen, ergötzen, zerstreuen; *– a p. from his purpose,* einen von seinem Vorhaben abbringen; *– attention from . . . to . . .,* die Aufmerksamkeit von . . . zu *or* auf . . . lenken; *– traffic,* Verkehr umleiten.

divest [daɪˈvɛst], *v.a.* entkleiden (*of* (*Gen.*)); (*fig.*) berauben, entblößen (*of* (*Gen.*)); *– o.s. of a th.,* etwas ablegen; (*fig.*) einer S. entsagen, auf eine S. verzichten; *– o.s. of a right,* sich eines Rechtes begeben. **–iture, –ment,** *s.* die Entkleidung, (*fig.*) Beraubung.

divid–e [dɪˈvaɪd], 1. *v.a.* teilen, einteilen; verteilen; absondern, trennen, scheiden; spalten, abteilen; durchschneiden, zerteilen; entzweien, uneinig machen; dividieren (*by,* durch); aufgehen in; *–e 12 by 3,* dividiere 12 durch 3; *3 –es 12,* 3 geht in 12 auf; *he –ed the loaf with his comrade,* er teilte sich in das Brot mit dem Kamerad; *the book is –ed into two parts,* das Buch zerfällt in zwei Teile. 2. *v.n.* sich teilen; sich trennen, sich spalten; sich entzweien; sich auflösen (*into,* in); abstimmen

(*Parl.*). 3. *s.* die Wasserscheide; (*fig.*) Scheidelinie. **-end** [ˈdɪvɪdɛnd], *s.* der Gewinnanteil, die Dividende (*C.L.*); der Dividend, die Teilungszahl (*Arith.*). **-end-warrant,** *s.* der Zinsschein. **-ers** [dɪˈvaɪdəz], *pl.* der Handzirkel, Stechzirkel. **-ing,** *adj.* teilend; *-ing line*, die Trennungslinie, Scheidelinie.

divin-ation [dɪvɪˈneɪʃən], *s.* die Weissagung, Wahrsagung; Ahnung. **-e,** 1. *v.n.* weissagen, wahrsagen, vorhersagen. 2. *v.a.* ahnen; mutmaßen, erraten. **-er,** *s.* der Wahrsager, Weissager, Errater; *water-er*, der Rutengänger. **-ing-rod,** *s.* die Wünschelrute.

divin-e [dɪˈvaɪn], 1. *adj.* göttlich; (*fig.*, *coll.*) herrlich, köstlich, himmlisch; *-e grace*, göttliche Gnade; *-e right of kings*, das Königtum von Gottes Gnaden; *king by -e right*, König von Gottes Gnaden; *-e service*, *-e worship*, der Gottesdienst; *-ely inspired*, gottbegeistert. 2. *s.* Geistliche(r), *m.*, der Theologe. **-ity** [dɪˈvɪnɪtɪ], *s.* die Gottheit; Göttlichkeit; Gottesgelehrsamkeit, Theologie; *professor of -ity*, Professor der Theologie.

divis-ibility [dɪvɪzəˈbɪlɪtɪ], *s.* die Teilbarkeit. **-ible** [dɪˈvɪzəbl], *adj.* teilbar. **-ion** [dɪˈvɪʒən], *s.* die Teilung, Trennung, Einteilung, Verteilung; Abteilung, der Abschnitt, die Stufe, Klasse; Grenze, Grenzlinie; Division (*Mil.*); Spaltung, Zwietracht, Uneinigkeit; Division (*Arith.*); der (Wahl)Bezirk, (Wahl)Kreis; namentliche Abstimmung, die Stimmenzählung (*Parl.*); *cause a -ion between friends*, Freunde entzweien; *go into -ion*, zur Abstimmung schreiten (*Parl.*); *-ion of labour*, die Arbeitseinteilung; *-ion of shares*, die Stückelung; *-ion sum*, die Divisionsaufgabe (*Arith.*); *upon a -ion*, nach Abstimmung (*Parl.*). **-ional** [-əl], *adj.* Teilungs-, Abteilungs-, Divisions-; *-ional commander*, der Divisionskommandeur. **-or,** [dɪˈvaɪzə], *s.* der Teiler, Divisor (*Arith.*).

divorce [dɪˈvɔːs], 1. *s.* die Ehescheidung; (*fig.*) Scheidung, Trennung; *--court*, der Gerichtshof für Ehesachen; *obtain a -*, sich scheiden lassen (*from*, von). 2. *v.a.* scheiden; (*fig.*) verstoßen; trennen; *be -d from*, geschieden sein von; *he -d his wife*, er ließ sich von seiner Frau scheiden. **-e** [dɪvɔːˈsiː], *s.* der (die) Geschiedene.

divot [ˈdɪvət], (*Scots*) das Rasenstück, die Sode.

divulge [daɪˈvʌldʒ], *v.a.* bekanntmachen, bekanntgeben, enthüllen, entdecken, ausschwatzen, ausplaudern, verbreiten. **-ment, -nce,** *s.* die Enthüllung, Verbreitung.

dixie [ˈdɪksɪ], *s.* der Feldkessel.

dizz-iness [ˈdɪzɪnɪs], *s.* der Schwindel; Schwindelanfall, die Benommenheit. **-y** [ˈdɪzɪ], 1. *adj.* schwind(e)lig, benommen; verwirrt, unbesonnen; schwindelerregend, schwindelnd (*height, etc.*). 2. *v.a.* schwindlig machen; verwirren.

¹**do** [duː, də *acc. to emphasis*], 1. *ir.v.a.* tun, machen, verrichten (*to*, an); bewirken, tätigen, ausführen, vollenden, vollbringen, zustandebringen, verfertigen, verrichten, ausüben, ausrichten; bereiten, kochen; gewähren, erweisen, erzeigen, zufügen, verursachen; widerfahren lassen; **(a)** (*with impersonal object, with or without personal object, which may also be indirect with* to) – *battle*, kämpfen; – *better*, sich verbessern, Besseres leisten; – *one's best*, sein möglichstes tun (*to come*, um zu kommen); – *a p.'s bidding*, jemandes Befehl ausführen; – *one's bit*, sein Scherflein beitragen; – *business*, Geschäfte machen; – *a p. credit*, einem Ehre machen; – *a favour*, ein Entgegenkommen erweisen, einen Gefallen tun, Gutes tun; – *a p. good*, einem gut tun *or* bekommen; *it does one's heart good*, es tut dem Herzen wohl; *it -es no good*, es nützt *or* hilft nicht, es richtet nichts aus; – *one's hair*, sich (*Dat.*) die Haare richten *or* kämmen; – *a p. harm*, einem schaden; – *a p. the honour*, einem die Ehre erweisen; – *a p. an ill turn*, einem einen bösen Streich spielen; – *a p. an injustice*, einem Unrecht tun; – *justice to*, Gerechtigkeit widerfahren lassen (*a p.* (*Dat.*)); (*coll.*) tüchtig zusprechen (*a meal* (*Dat.*)); gerecht werden (*a th.* (*Dat.*)); – *justice to o.s.*, seine Fähigkeiten voll entfalten; (*sl.*) – *London*, London besichtigen; (*Scots*) – *the messages*, Wege besorgen, Einkäufe machen; – *8 miles an hour*, 8 Meilen in einer Stunde zurücklegen; – *much* (*to help*), viel ausrichten; (*sl.*) – *the polite*, den Höflichen spielen; – *a mean thing*, gemein handeln; – *right*, recht tun; (*coll.*) – *a room*, ein Zimmer aufräumen *or* ordnen; – *sums*, Rechnungen machen, Aufgaben lösen; (*coll.*) – *the talking*, das Wort führen; (*sl.*) – *time*, absitzen; – *a p. a good turn*, einem einen Dienst erweisen; *if you want a thing done well*, – *it yourself*, selbst ist der Mann! – *wrong*, unrecht tun; **(b)** *with personal object*) (*coll.*) bewirten, bedienen; (*sl.*) betrügen, beschwindeln, prellen, bringen (*out of*, um), anführen; – *o.s. well*, sich gütlich tun; (*sl.*) – *s.o. in the eye*, einen hinters Licht führen; – *a p. to death*, einen töten; **(c)** (*with adverbs*) – *away with*, wegschaffen, beseitigen; – *away with o.s.*, Selbstmord begehen; (*sl.*) – *a p. down*, einen übers Ohr hauen; (*sl.*) – *in*, um die Ecke bringen, töten; – *a p. out of his money*, einen um sein Geld bringen; – *out a room*, ein Zimmer ausräumen *or* ausfegen; (*coll.*) – *over*, überstreichen, überziehen; – *over again*, wieder tun, noch einmal machen, wiederholen; – *up*, zusammenlegen, zurechtmachen, einpacken (*parcel*), zuknöpfen (*coat*), (*coll.*) herrichten, reparieren; (*coll.*) *done up*, müde, abgespannt, erledigt. **2.** *ir.v.n.* tun, handeln, vorgehen, sich betätigen; fertigwerden, zustandekommen, fortkommen, vorankommen; sich befinden, ergehen; dem Zwecke dienen *or* entsprechen, genügen, angehen, passen; *that will –*, das genügt, so ist es recht; *that won't –*, das geht nicht (an), das reicht nicht (aus); *it will – to-morrow*, es hat Zeit bis morgen; *it will – for the present*, es ist für den Augenblick gut genug; *it did perfectly*, es paßte vortrefflich, es ging vorzüglich; *will ordinary paper – ?* ist gewöhnliches Papier gut genug? *how do you – ?* Guten Tag! Wie gehts? *he does well to come*, er tut gut daran, zu kommen; – *as I –*, mach's (so) wie ich; (*Prov.*) *one must – at Rome as the Romans –*, mit den Wölfen muß man heulen; – *badly*, schlechte Geschäfte machen, schlecht daran sein; – *well*, seine Sache gut machen, gut vorwärtskommen, Erfolg haben, gut abschneiden; *he is -ing well*, es geht ihm gut; – *by a p.*, an einem handeln; – *as you would be done by*, was du nicht willst das man dir tu', das füg' auch keinem andern zu; – *for*, passen für, sich eignen für, bestimmt sein für, zusagen (*Dat.*), richtig *or* ausreichend sein für, ausreichen; (*coll.*) verderben, erledigen, abtun, töten, zugrunde richten; (*sl.*) betrügen um; (*coll.*) den Haushalt führen, als Reinemachefrau arbeiten; *he is done for!* mit ihm ist's aus! (*coll.*) er ist geliefert! – *with*, sich begnügen mit, auskommen mit, fertig werden mit, brauchen können; *I could – with a drink*, ich könnte einen Schluck vertragen; *have to – with*, zu tun *or* schaffen haben mit; *what has that to – with me?* was geht das mich an? *what am I to – with it?* was soll ich damit anfangen? *I could – with the money*, ich könnte das Geld gut gebrauchen; *I did not know what to – with myself*, ich wußte nicht was ich anfangen *or* wie ich die Zeit hinbringen *or* (*coll.*) totschlagen sollte; *be done with a th.*, mit etwas fertig sein; *I have done with him*, ich will mit ihm nichts mehr zu schaffen haben, ich bin mit ihm fertig; – *without*, entbehren, auskommen ohne, fertig werden ohne. **3.** *ir. v.aux. & absolute* (*a*) (*interrogative*) – *you learn English?* lernen Sie Englisch? *you learn English, don't you?* Sie lernen Englisch, nicht wahr? (*b*) (*negative*) *I – not know him*, ich kenne ihn nicht; *did you not see him?* sahen Sie ihn nicht? (*c*) (*concessive*) *only once did he come*, nur einmal kam er; (*d*) (*emphatic*) – *make haste!* beeile dich doch! *I did see him*, ich sah ihn tatsächlich *or* auch wirklich; *send it, –!* schicke es doch! (*e*) (*absolute*) *he sings better than he did*, er singt besser als vorher; *he sings better than I –*, er singt besser als ich; *you like the German language? I –!* gefällt Ihnen die deutsche Sprache? ja! *you could surely see him? I did!* Sie konnten ihn doch sicherlich sehen? Gewiß! *or* Jawohl! **4.** *special idiomatic forms*; – *or die*, kämpfen oder untergehen; *it was – or die with him*, es ging bei ihm um Leben oder Tod; *have done!* genug! mach Schluß! hör' auf! *have you done talking?* sind Sie mit Reden

fertig? *it can't be done*, es kann nicht geschehen, es geht nicht; *what is to be done?* was ist zu tun?; *it isn't done*, es schickt sich nicht; *this done . . .*, nachdem dies geschehen war; *well done!* Bravo! *no sooner said than done*, gesagt, getan. **5.** *s.* (*sl.*) der Schwindel; der Schmaus; große Angelegenheit. **-able,** *adj.* (*coll.*) ausführbar, tunlich. **-er,** *s.* der Täter; *evil--er*, der Übeltäter. **-ing,** (*coll.*) *nothing -ing*, nichts zu machen, nichts los; *none of my -ing*, mit mir nichts zu tun; (*coll.*) *up and -ing*, an der Arbeit, tätig. (*coll.*) **-ings,** *pl.* Geschichten (*pl.*), das Treiben; (*sl.*) Sachen (*pl.*). **--nothing,** *s.* der Faulenzer, Taugenichts.

[2]do [doʊ], *s.* das C (*Mus.*).

docil-e ['doʊsɑɪl], *adj.* gelehrig, gefügig, fügsam. **-ity** [-'sɪlɪtɪ], *s.* die Gelehrigkeit, Fügsamkeit.

[1]dock [dɔk], *s.* der Ampfer (*Bot.*).

[2]dock, **1.** *s.* das Dock (*Naut.*); der Kai, die Ladebühne, Verladerampe (*Railw.*); (*pl.*) die Hafenanlagen (*pl.*); *dry--*, *graving--*, das Trockendock; *floating--*, das Schwimmdock; *wet--*, das Hafenbecken, der Dockhafen. **2.** *v.a.* & *n.* eindocken. **-age,** *s.*, **--dues,** *pl.* die Dockgebühren. **-er,** *s.* der Hafenarbeiter, Dockarbeiter. **--gate,** *s.* das Schleusentor. **-yard,** *s.* die (Schiffs)Werft.

[3]dock, **1.** *v.a.* stutzen; (*fig.*) kürzen, beschneiden (*wages, etc.*); abschneiden (*supply*). **2.** *s.* der Stummel, Stumpf, Stutzschwanz; die Schwanzrübe (*Vet.*).

[4]dock, *s.* die Anklagebank; *be in the -*, auf der Anklagebank sitzen; (*sl.*) das Lazarett; *be in -*, im Lazarett liegen (*Mil.*).

docket ['dɔkɪt], **1.** *s.* kurze Inhaltsangabe, das Inhaltsverzeichnis, der Inhaltsvermerk; amtliche Beglaubigung (*C.L.*); die Bescheinigung eines Patentes; der Adreßzettel, Lieferschein, das Etikett; der Terminkalender (*Law*). **2.** *v.a.* (Akten, *etc.*) mit Inhaltsvermerk versehen; (Waren, *etc.*) mit Adreßzetteln, Aufschrift *or* Etikett versehen.

doctor ['dɔktə], **1.** *s.* der Doktor (*Univ.*); Kirchenvater (*Theol.*); Arzt, Doktor; das Abstreichmesser (*for calico*); der Papiermaschinenschaber (*Pap.*); *lady -*, die Ärztin; *- of laws* (*of medicine*), Doktor der Rechte (der Medizin); *take one's -('s degree)* promovieren; *-'s stuff*, die Arznei; *- and Mrs. S.*, Herr und Frau Dr. S.; *dear -*, Sehr geehrter Herr Doktor! **2.** *v.a.* ärztlich behandeln, kurieren; (*fig.*) ausbessern (*a th.*); vermischen, verfälschen (*wine, etc.*); fälschen, zurechtmachen, zustutzen. **3.** *v.n.* als Arzt praktizieren. **-al,** *adj.* Doktor- (*Univ.*). **-and,** *s.* der Doktorand (*Univ.*). **-ate** [-rɪt], *s.* die Doktorwürde, das Doktorat (*Univ.*).

doctrin-aire [dɔktrɪ'nɛə], **1.** *s.* der Prinzipienreiter. **2.** *adj.* doktrinär, schulmeisterlich; *-aire socialism*, der Kathedersozialismus. **-al** [dɔk'traɪnəl], *adj.* Lehr-, dogmatisch, lehrmäßig; *-al theology*, die Dogmatik. **-e** ['dɔktrɪn], *s.* die Lehre; Doktrin, Lehrmeinung, der Grundsatz.

document ['dɔkjumənt], **1.** *s.* die Urkunde, das Dokument, Aktenstück. **--file,** *s.* der Aktenhefter. **2.** *v.a.* beurkunden, urkundlich belegen. **-ary** [-'mɛntərɪ], *adj.* urkundlich, dokumentarisch; *-ary evidence*, das Beweisstück; *-ary film*, der Bildbericht, Lehrfilm, Kulturfilm. **-ation,** *s.* die Urkundenbenutzung, Quellenbenutzung, Heranziehung von Dokumenten.

[1]dodder ['dɔdə], *s.* die Klebe, Seide, der Teufelszwirn (*Bot.*).

[2]dodder, *v.n.* (*coll.*) schwanken, wackeln. **--grass,** *s.* das Zittergras (*Bot.*). **-ing, -y,** *adj.* schwankend, zitternd, quasselnd.

dodeca-gon [doʊ'dɛkəgən], *s.* das Zwölfeck. **-hedral** [-'hɪ:drəl], *adj.* zwölfflächig. **-hedron** [-'hɪ:drən], *s.* das Zwölfflach, der Zwölfflächner, Dodekaeder.

dodge [dɔdʒ], **1.** *v.a.* ausweichen; aus dem Wege gehen; sich entziehen (*Dat.*), vermeiden, entschlüpfen (*Dat.*); zum besten haben, aufziehen; (*coll.*) *- the issue*, den Folgen aus dem Wege gehen. **2.** *v.n.* plötzlich beiseitespringen; ausweichen, sich drücken, Ausflüchte *or* Winkelzüge machen. **3.** *s.* der Seitensprung; Schlich, Kniff, Kunstgriff; die Ausflucht; (*coll.*) das Hilfsmittel, die Handhabe. **-r,** *s.* der Schwindler, hinterhältiger Mensch; der Wetterunterstand (*Naut.*); *artful -r*, der Schlaufuchs.

dodo ['doudoʊ], *s.* die Dronte (*Orn.*).

doe [doʊ], *s.* das Reh, die Hindin; das Weibchen (*of rabbits, etc.*).

doer ['du:ə], *see* **do.**

does [dʌz], *see* **do.**

doff [dɔf], *v.a.* (*poet.*) abnehmen (*hat*), ablegen, ausziehen (*clothes*).

dog [dɔg], **1.** *s.* der Hund; das Männchen (*of fox, etc.*); (*coll.*) der Kerl, Bursche; die Klaue, Klammer; der Mitnehmerstift, Sperrklinkenzahn; das Gestell, der Bock, Kaminbock, Greifhaken; Förderwagen, die Lore (*Min.*); der Hundsstern (*Astr.*); (*a*) (*with adjectives*) *gay* or *jolly -*, lustiger Bursche; (*coll.*) *hot -*, das Brötchen mit Knackwurst; *hunting -*, der Jagdhund; (*coll.*) *lucky -*, der Glückspilz; *old -*, schlauer alter Fuchs; *sly -*, geriebener Bursche; (*coll.*) *spotted -*, der Kloß mit Korinthen; (*b*) (*with genitives*) *not a -'s chance*, nicht die geringste Aussicht; *die a -'s death*, in Elend umkommen; *lead a -'s life*, ein Hundeleben führen; *lead s.o. a -'s life*, einem ein Hundeleben bereiten; (*c*) (*with verbs*) *every - has his day*, jeder hat einmal seine guten Tage; *give a - a bad name*, einen verleumden; *give a - a bad name and hang him*, einen ein für alle Male abtun; *help a lame - over a stile*, einem in der Not helfen; *let slip the -s of war*, die Kriegsfurie entfesseln; *it is hard to teach an old - new tricks*, was Hänschen nicht lernt, lernt Hans nimmermehr; (*d*) (*with prepositions*) *- in a manger*, neidischer Mensch, der Neidhammel; *go to the -s*, vor die Hunde gehen; zugrunde gehen; *throw to the -s*, wegwerfen, opfern, verprassen, an den Haken hängen. **2.** *v.a.* auf dem Fuße folgen (*Dat.*), nachspüren, (*fig.*) unablässig verfolgen; *- s.o.'s steps*, einem auf Schritt und Tritt folgen. **-bane,** *s.* der Hundskohl (*Bot.*). **-berry,** *s.* die Hundsbeere (*Bot.*). **--biscuit,** *s.* der Hundekuchen. **--box,** *s.* das Hundeabteil (*Railw.*). **-cart,** *s.* zweirädriger Einspänner. **--collar,** *d.* das Halsband; (*coll.*) steifer Kragen eines Geistlichen. **--days,** *pl.* die Hundstage. **--ear,** **1.** *s.* das Eselsohr. **2.** *v.a.* durch Eselsohren entstellen (*a book*). **--eared,** *adj.* mit Eselsohren. **--fancier,** *s.* der Hundezüchter, Hundeliebhaber. (*coll.*) **--fight,** *s.* der Einzelkampf (*Av.*); erbitterter Kampf, das Handgemenge. **-fish,** *s.* der Hundshai. **-ged,** *see* **dogged.** **--grass,** *s.* die Hundsquecke (*Bot.*). **--house,** *s.* (*Amer.*) *see* **--kennel;** (*sl.*) *in the --house*, in Ungnade. **--kennel,** *s.* die Hundehütte. **--Latin,** *s.* das Küchenlatein. **--licence,** *s.* die Hundesteuer. **--racing,** *s.* das Hundewettrennen. **-rose,** *s.* wilde Rose (*Bot.*). **-'s-ear,** *see* **--ear.** **--show,** *s.* die Hundeausstellung. **-'s lead,** die Hundeleine. **--sleep,** *s.* leiser Schlaf. **-'s life,** *s.* das Hundeleben. **-'s mercury,** *s.* das Bingelkraut (*Bot.*). **--star,** *s.* der Hundsstern (*Astr.*). (*coll.*) **--tired,** *adj.* hundsmüde, todmüde. **--tooth,** *s.* das Zahnornament (*Arch.*). **--violet,** *s.* geruchloses Veilchen (*Bot.*). **--watch,** *s.* die Hundswache (*Naut.*). **--whip,** *s.* die Hundepeitsche. **-wood,** *s.* der Hartriegel (*Bot.*).

doge [doudʒ], *s.* der Doge (*of Venice*).

dogged ['dɔgɪd], *adj.* verbissen, störrisch; hartnäckig, zäh, unverdrossen; (*coll.*) *- does it*, die Hartnäckigkeit siegt. **-ness,** *s.* die Zähigkeit, Hartnäckigkeit.

dogger ['dɔgə], *s.* eine Art Fischerboot.

doggerel ['dɔgərəl], **1.** *adj.* Knüttel-. **2.** *s.* der Knüttelvers.

doggo ['dɔgou] *adv.*; (*sl.*) *lie -*, sich versteckt halten. **-ne** ['dɔgən], *adj.* (*sl.*) verflucht, verflixt, hundsmäßig.

dogma ['dɔgmə], *s.* der Lehrsatz, Glaubenssatz, das Dogma. **-tic** [-'mætɪk], *adj.* dogmatisch; ausdrücklich, gebieterisch; anmaßend. **-tics,** *pl.* die Dogmatik. **-tism** [-mətɪzm], *s.* der Dogmatismus; die Entschiedenheit. **-tist,** *s.* der Dogmatiker. **-tize,** *v.a.* & *n.* mit Bestimmtheit behaupten, sich dogmatisch äußern (*on*, über), dogmatisieren.

doily ['dɔɪlɪ], *s.* das Deckchen, die Tellerunterlage.

doing ['du:ɪŋ], *see* **do.**

doit [dɔɪt], *s.* der Deut, Heller; (*fig.*) Pfifferling.

doldrums ['dɔldrəmz], *pl.* die Windstillen; Gegend der Windstillen; (*fig.*) die Niedergeschlagenheit, der Trübsinn; *be in the* –, verdrießlich sein, sich langweilen.

[1]**dole** [doʊl], 1. *s.* milde Gabe, das Almosen; die Arbeitslosenunterstützung; *be on the* –, stempeln gehen. 2. *v.a.* (– *out*) (*coll.*) verteilen, austeilen.

[2]**dole,** *s.* (*poet.*) der Kummer, das Leid; die Klage. **–ful,** *adj.* traurig. **–fulness,** *s.* die Traurigkeit, der Kummer; *see also* **dolorous.**

dolichocephalic [dɔlɪkoʊsɛ'fælɪk], *adj.* langköpfig.

doll [dɔl], 1. *s.* die Puppe; *–'s-house*, das Puppenhaus. 2. *v.a.* & *n.*; (*coll.*) – *up*, (sich) herausputzen.

dollar ['dɔlə], *s.* (*Amer.*) der Dollar; (*Engl. sl.*) fünf Schillinge.

dollop ['dɔləp], *s.* (*sl.*) der Klumpen, Happen.

dolly ['dɔlɪ], *s.* das Püppchen; der Rührstock (*for washing*); Stampfer, Stößel, Rührer (*Metall.*); der Kamerawagen, Montagewagen (*Films*). **– -dye,** *s.* die Haushaltfarbe. **– -shot,** *s.* die Fernaufnahme (*Films*). **– -tub,** *s.* das Waschfaß, Schlämmfaß.

dolman ['dɔlmən], *s.* der Dolman, die Husarenjacke.

dolmen ['dɔlmən], *s.* das Hünengrab, Steingrabmal.

dolomite ['dɔləmɑɪt], *s.* der Dolomit, Bitterspat.

dolorous ['dɔlərəs], *adj.* (*Poet.*) traurig, schmerzlich.

dolour ['doʊlə], *s.* (*Poet.*) die Pein, Qual, der Schmerz.

dolphin ['dɔlfɪn], *s.* der Delphin (*Ichth.*); die Dalbe, Ankerboje (*Naut.*).

dolt [doʊlt], *s.* der Tölpel, Einfaltspinsel. **–ish,** *adj.* tölpelhaft. **–ishness,** *s.* die Tölpelhaftigkeit.

domain [do'meɪn], *s.* das Erbgut, Herrengut, Grundeigentum; Staatsgut, die Domäne; (*fig.*) das Gebiet, der Bereich, die Sphäre; Herrschaft.

dome [doʊm], *s.* die Kuppel, der Dom, das Gewölbe, die Wölbung (*Arch.*). **–d,** *adj.* gewölbt. **– -shaped,** *adj.* kuppelförmig.

domesday-book ['du:mzdeɪ'bʊk], *s.* das Reichsgrundbuch (*Engl. hist.*).

domestic [do'mɛstɪk], 1. *adj.* Haushalts–, Haus–, Familien–, häuslich; inländisch, Innen–, Binnen–, einheimisch, Landes–; – *affairs*, häusliche Angelegenheiten; die Innenpolitik; – *animal*, das Haustier; – *appliances*, Haushaltungsgeräte; – *cattle*, das Nutzvieh; – *consumption*, inländischer Verbrauch; – *drama*, bürgerliches Drama; – *duties*, häusliche Pflichten; – *policy*, die Innenpolitik; – *remedy*, die Hausarznei; – *servant*, Hausangestellte(r), *m.* & *f.*, der Dienstbote; – *service*, die Dienstbotentätigkeit; – *trade*, der Binnenhandel; – *washing*, die Hauswäsche. 2. *s.* der Dienstbote. **–ate** [do'mɛstɪkeɪt], *v.a.* ans häusliche Leben gewöhnen; zivilisieren (*savages*); zähmen (*beasts*); *become –ated*, häuslich *or* heimisch *or* zahm werden. **–ation** [–'keɪʃən], *s.* die Eingewöhnung, Zähmung (*also Zool.*); Kultivierung (*Bot.*); häusliches Leben, die Häuslichkeit.

domicil–e ['dɔmɪsɪl], 1. *s.* die Wohnung; der Wohnort, Wohnsitz, das Domizil; der Zahlungsort, die Zahlstelle (*C.L.*), der Gerichtsstand (*Law*). 2. *v.a.* wohnhaft *or* ansässig machen, ansiedeln; domizilieren, auf bestimmten Ort ausstellen (*C.L.*). **–ed,** *adj.* wohnhaft, ansässig, beheimatet; domiziliert (*C.L.*). **–iary** [–'sɪljərɪ], *adj.* Haus–, Wohnungs–; *–iary visit*, die Haussuchung.

domin–ance ['dɔmɪnəns], *s.* das Vorherrschen, die Herrschaft. **–ant** ['dɔmɪnənt], 1. *adj.* herrschend; beherrschend, vorherrschend; weithin sichtbar, emporragend; *–ant chord*, der Dominantakkord; *–ant sex*, herrschendes Geschlecht. 2. *s.* die Dominante (*Mus.*). **–ate** ['dɔmɪneɪt], 1. *v.a.* beherrschen, emporragen über. 2. *v.n.* vorherrschen, beherrschen, herrschen (*over*, über (*Dat.*)). **–ation** [–'neɪʃən], *s.* die Herrschaft. **–eer,** [dɔmɪ'nɪə], *v.n.* den Herrn spielen; despotisch herrschen; *–eer over*, tyrannisieren, knechten. **–eering,** *adj.* herrisch, gebieterisch, tyrannisch; anmaßend.

dominic–al [do'mɪnɪkl], *adj.* des Herrn, Christi; sonntäglich; *–al day*, der Sonntag; *–al letter*, der Sonntagsbuchstabe; *–al prayer*, das Vaterunser; *–al year*, das Jahr des Herrn. **–an** [do'mɪnɪkən], *s.* (*–an friar*) der Dominikaner.

dominie ['dɔmɪnɪ], *s.* (*Scots*) der Schulmeister.

dominion [do'mɪnjən], *s.* die Oberherrschaft; Herrschaft, Gewalt, das Besitzrecht; Herrschaftsgebiet, Gebiet; der Staat im Britischen Staatenbund; selbständige Kolonie; – *of Canada*, das Dominion Kanada; – *status*, das Selbstverwaltungsrecht einer Kolonie.

domino ['dɔmɪnoʊ], *s.* (*pl.* –es) der Domino; Dominostein; Maskenball; (*pl.*) das Dominospiel; *play –es*, Domino spielen.

[1]**don** [dɔn], *s.* der Don (*Spanish title*); Graduierte(r), *m.*, akademische Respektsperson (*Univ.*).

[2]**don,** *v.a.* (*poet.*) anziehen (*clothes*), aufsetzen (*a hat*).

donat–e [doʊ'neɪt], *v.a.* schenken, verleihen. **–ion** [–'neɪʃən], *s.* die Schenkung, Gabe. **–ive** ['doʊnətɪv], 1. *adj.* durch Schenkung übertragend. 2. *s.* offizielle Gabe *or* Schenkung; ohne Präsentation übertragene Pfründe (*Eccl.*).

done [dʌn] 1. *see* [1]**do.** 2. *adj.* fertig, vorbei; gekocht, durchbraten, gar; (*coll.*) erschöpft, kaputt (also – *up*); (*sl.*) betrogen, beschwindelt (also – *brown*); *well-–*, gut gekocht, durchgebraten; – *to a turn*, ausgezeichnet gekocht *or* gebraten; *that's not* –, das schickt sich nicht; (*coll.*) – *for*, verloren, aus, geliefert.

donee [doʊ'nɪ:], *s.* Beschenkte(r), *m.* (*Law*).

donjon ['dɔndʒən], *s.* der Schloßturm, das Burgverlies, der Bergfried.

donkey ['dɔŋkɪ], *s.* der Esel; (*fig.*) Dummkopf; (*sl.*) *for –'s years*, seit anno Tobak. **– -engine,** *s.* die Hilfsmaschine.

donnish ['dɔnɪʃ], *adj.* gravitätisch, steif, *see* [1]**don.**

donor ['doʊnə], *s.* der Geber, Stifter, Schenker, Wohltäter; *blood-–*, der Blutspender.

don't [doʊnt], = do not, *see* [1]**do.** 1. *int.* laß das! nicht doch! bitte nicht! 2. *s.* das Verbot; *dos and –s*, Weisungen und Verbote.

doodah ['du:dɑ:], *s.*; (*sl.*) *all of a* –, aus dem Häuschen.

doom [du:m], 1. *v.a.* verurteilen, verdammen (*to*, zu); bestimmen. 2. *s.* das Urteil (*Law* & *archaic*); Schicksal, böses Geschick; der Untergang, das Verderben; *crack* or *day of* –, Jüngstes Gericht. **–ed,** *adj.* gerichtet, verurteilt, verloren, dem Untergang geweiht. **–sday** [–zdeɪ], *s.* Jüngstes Gericht; (*coll.*) *till –sday*, sehr lange, ewig, immerfort. **–sday-book,** *s. see* **domesday-book.**

door [dɔ:] *s.* die Tür; (*fig.*) der Eingang; *back* –, die Hintertür; *double –s*, die Doppeltür; *front* –, *street-–*, die Haustür; *folding* –, die Flügeltür; *sliding* –, die Schiebetür; (*a*) (*with adjectives*) *the first* – *from the corner*, das erste Haus von der Ecke; *next* –, nebenan, im Nebenhaus *or* nächsten Hause; *next* – *to*, (*fig.*) beinahe, fast, nahezu, nicht weit von; *next* – *but one*, zwei Häuser weiter, übernächstes Haus; (*b*) (*with verbs*) *close* or *shut the* – *against s.o.*, einem die Tür verschließen; *close the* – *on a p.*, die Tür hinter einem zumachen; *close the* – *on one's finger*, sich (*Dat.*) den Finger in der Tür klemmen; *bang, close* or *slam the* – *on a th.*, (*fig.*) etwas unmöglich machen, einer S. den Weg abschneiden; *he shall never darken my* – *again*, er soll mir nie wieder über die Schwelle; *lay a th. at a p.'s* –, einem etwas zur Last legen; *open the* – *to s.o.*, einem öffnen, einen hereinlassen; *open the* – *to* or *for a th.*, etwas möglich machen; *show a p. the* –, einem die Tür weisen; *throw the* – *open to s.th.*, (*fig.*) die Tür offnen für etwas; (*c*) (*with prepositions*) *at the* –, vor der Tür; *at death's* –, am Rande des Grabes; *from* – *to* –, von Haus zu Haus; *in-–work*, die Hausarbeit, Stubenarbeit; *out of –s*, außer *or* aus dem Hause; im Freien; *out-– work*, die Arbeit außer dem Hause; *packed to the –s*, voll besetzt, gedrängt voll; *within –s*, im Hause. **– -bell,** *s.* die Türklingel. **– -case,** *s.*, **– -frame,** *s.* der Türrahmen. **– -handle,** *s. see* **– -knob.** **– -keeper,** *s.* der Pförtner, Portier. **– -knob,** *s.* der Türknopf, Türgriff. **–man,** *s. see* **– -keeper.** **–mat,** *s.* der Fußabtreter, die Fußmatte. **– -money,** *s.* das Eintrittsgeld. **– -nail,** *s.* der Türnagel; *dead as a – -nail*, mausetot. **– -plate,** *s.* das Türschild, Namenschild. **–post,** *s.* der Türpfosten. **– -scraper,** *s.* der Fußabstreicher. **–step,** *s.* die Stufe vor der Haustür. **–way,** *s.* der Torweg; Türeingang.

dope [doʊp], 1. *s.* der Lack, Firnis (*Av.*); (*sl.*) das Gift, Rauschgift, Opium, Narkotikum; (*sl.*) die Nachricht, Informationen (*pl.*), das Neueste; – *fiend*, Opiumsüchtige(r), *m.* 2. *v.a.* lackieren, firnissen (*Av.*); (*sl.*) dopen (*Racing*); *–ed petrol*, das Bleibenzin. **–y,** *adj.* (*sl.*) benebelt, benommen.

dor [dɔ:], *s.* der Roßkäfer; Maikäfer.

dorman–cy [ˈdɔ:mənsɪ], *s.* der Schlafzustand, die Ruhe. **–t** [–t], *adj.* schlafend, ruhend; ungebraucht, unbenutzt, untätig, tot (*C.L., Law*); *lion –t*, schlafender Löwe (*Her.*); *–t capital*, totes Kapital (*C.L.*); *–t partner*, stiller Teilhaber; *–t passions*, schlummernde Leidenschaften; *–t title*, ungebrauchter Titel.

dormer [ˈdɔ:mə], *s.*, **––window,** *s.* das Dachfenster, Bodenfenster.

dormitory [ˈdɔ:mɪtərɪ], *s.* der Schlafsaal. **– suburb,** *s.* das Wohnviertel der großstädtischen Büroangestellten.

dormouse [ˈdɔ:maʊs], *s.* die Haselmaus.

dorsal [ˈdɔ:səl], *adj.* dorsal (*Phonet.*).

[1]dory [ˈdɔ:rɪ], *s.* (also *John –*) der Heringskönig.

[2]dory, *s.* kleines Fischerboot.

dos–age [ˈdoʊsɪdʒ], *s.* die Dosierung. **–e** [doʊs], 1. *s.* die Dosis, das Quantum, die Portion. 2. *v.a.* dosieren, eine Dosis verschreiben; Arznei eingeben; fälschen, pan(t)schen, vermischen (*wine*).

doss [dɔs], 1. *s.* (*sl.*) das Bett; der Schlag. 2. *v.n.* (*sl.*) schlafen. **––house,** *s.* billiges Logierhaus, die Herberge.

dossier [ˈdɔsjə], *s.* das Aktenbündel, Aktenheft.

[1]dot [dɔt], 1. *s.* der Punkt, Tüpfel (*on i's*); Knirps; *– and dash*, didd und da (*Tele.*). 2. *v.a.* tüpfeln (*also Bot.*); punktieren; sprenkeln; verstreuen, verbreiten (also *– about*); (*sl.*) *– s.o. one*, einem eins versetzen; (*coll.*) *– and carry one*, hinken, hinkend gehen; *– the i's and cross the t's*, peinlich genau sein. **–ted,** *adj.* punktiert; *–ted with*, besetzt *or* besät mit. **–ting-needle,** *s.* die Punktiernadel.

[2]dot, *s. see* **dowry.**

dot–age [ˈdoʊtɪdʒ], *s.* das Kindischwerden, die Altersschwäche; *he is in his –age*, er ist wieder zum Kind geworden. **–ard** [ˈdoʊtəd], kindischer Greis. **–e** [doʊt], *v.n.* kindisch sein, faseln; *–e on*, schwärmen für, vernarrt sein in (*Acc.*), zärtlich lieben. **–ing,** *adj.* faselnd, kindisch; verliebt, vernarrt (*on*, in (*Acc.*)).

dotted [ˈdɔtɪd], *see* **[1]dot.**

dott(e)rel [ˈdɔtərəl], *s.* der Regenpfeifer (*Orn.*).

dottle [dɔtl], *s.* der Tabaksrest (*in a pipe*).

dotty [ˈdɔtɪ], *adj.* (*sl.*) verdreht, verrückt; *– on*, vernarrt in.

double [dʌbl], 1. *adj.* doppelt, Doppel–, zwiefach, gepaart; zweideutig; falsch, unaufrichtig, scheinheilig; verdoppelt, verstärkt, vermehrt, vergrößert; *– ale*, das Starkbier; *– the amount*, doppelter *or* zweifacher Betrag; *– chin*, das Doppelkinn; *– first*, Universitätsgrad mit Auszeichnung in zwei Fächern; *– Dutch*, das Kauderwelsch; *– eagle*, der Doppeladler (*Her.*); das Zwanzigdollarstück (*Amer.*); *– flowers*, gefüllte Blumen; *– game*, falsches Spiel; *– line*, das Doppelgleis (*Railw.*); die Doppelleitung (*Tele.*); *– stress*, ebener Nachdruck (*Philol.*); *– track*, das Doppelgleis (*Railw.*); *– usance*, doppelte Wechselfrist (*C.L.*). 2. *adv.* paarweise, zu zweit *or* zweien, doppelt. 3. *s.* das Doppelte, Zweifache; das Seitwärtsspringen; der Kreuzsprung, Seitensprung; die Windung; der Hakenschlag (*of a hare*); das Ebenbild, der Doppelgänger (*of persons*); das Duplikat, Seitenstück (*of things*); der Sturmschritt (*Mil.*); (*pl.*) das Doppelspiel, Doppel (*Tenn.*); *at the –*, im Sturmschritt. 4. *v.a.* (ver)doppeln, doppelt zusammenlegen, (um)falten, umschlagen, umbrechen (*paper, etc.*); ballen (*the fist*); umschiffen, umsegeln, umfahren (*a cape*); *– parts*, zwei Rollen spielen (*Theat.*); *– !* marsch, marsch! *– down*, einschlagen, umfalten (*a leaf in a book*); *– in*, nach innen falten; *– up*, zusammenkrümmen; (*usually pass.*) *–d up with*, sich krümmen vor; *– and twist*, zwirnen (*thread*). 5. *v.n.* sich verdoppeln; einen Haken– *or* Kreuzsprung machen (*of hares*); im Sturmschritt marschieren; *– back*, plötzlich kehrtmachen; (*coll.*) etwas vergelten *or* heimzahlen (*on* (*Dat.*)), *– up*, sich krümmen *or* biegen. **––acting,** *adj.* doppelt wirkend. **––barrel,** *s.* der Doppellauf. **––barrelled,** *adj.* doppelläufig; (*fig.*) zweischneidig; *––barrelled gun*, die Doppelflinte; (*coll.*) *––barrelled name*, der Doppelname. **––bass,** *s.* der Kontrabaß. **––bed,** *s.* das Doppelbett, Ehebett. **––bedded,** *adj.*; *––bedded room*, see **––room.** **––breasted,** *adj.* zweireihig (*coat*). **––chin,** *s.* das Doppelkinn. (*sl.*) **––cross,** *v.a.* betrügen, verraten. **––dealer,** *s.* der Achselträger; Betrüger. **––dealing,** *s.* die Falschheit, Doppelzüngigkeit, der Betrug. **––decker,** *s.* der Doppeldecker (*Av.*). **––dyed,** *adj.* (*fig.*) eingefleischt, Erz–. **––edged,** *adj.* zweischneidend (*also fig.*). **––entry,** *s.* doppelte Buchführung (*C.L.*). **––faced,** *adj.* doppelzüngig, heuchlerisch. **––lock,** *v.a.* doppelt schließen. **––march,** *s.* der Sturmschritt, Laufschritt (*Mil.*). **––meaning,** *s.* der Doppelsinn. **–ness,** *s.* das Doppelte, Zweifache; (*fig.*) die Zweideutigkeit; (*fig.*) Falschheit, Arglist. **––quick,** *adj.* schnellstens, sehr rasch. **––room,** *s.* das Schlafzimmer mit Doppelbett. **––stop,** *v.n.* in Doppelgriffen spielen (*Mus.*). **––tooth,** *s.* der Backzahn.

doublet [ˈdʌblɪt], *s.* das (*or* der) Wams (*Hist.*); die Doppelform, Dublette (*Philol.*); der Pasch (*Dice*).

doubly [ˈdʌblɪ], *adv.* doppelt, zweifach.

doubt [daʊt], 1. *v.n.* zweifeln (*about*, an (*Dat.*); *whether* or *if*, ob; (*negat.*) *but* (*that*), daß); zweifelhaft *or* im Zweifel (über (*Acc.*)) sein; zögern; *I – not but he will cone*, ich zweifle nicht, daß er kommt. 2. *v.a.* bezweifeln, in Zweifel ziehen; mißtrauen (*a p.*, einem); *I – his ability*, ich zweifle ob er die Fähigkeit besitzt; *I – it*, ich bezweifle es; *I – his coming*, ich zweifle, daß er kommt. 3. *s.* der Zweifel (*of* or *about*, an (*Dat.*)), die Ungewißheit, Unsicherheit; das Bedenken, die Besorgnis (*about*, über); *beyond –, no –, without –*, ohne Zweifel, zweifelsohne, unzweifelhaft; *I have no – of it*, ich habe keinen Zweifel daran; *I have no – that*, ich bezweifle nicht daß; *there is no – but* (*that*) *he will come*, es ist *or* besteht kein Zweifel, daß er kommt; *give a p. the benefit of the –*, einen mangels Beweises freisprechen, im Zweifelsfalle die günstige Auslegung für einen annehmen; *clear up* or *dispel all –s*, alle Zweifel heben *or* zerstreuen; *I have my –s about it*, ich habe meine Bedenken darüber; *leave s.o. in no – about*, einen nicht in Zweifel lassen über; *make no –*, keine Zweifel hegen. **–ful,** *adj.* zweifelnd, unschlüssig, bedenklich; zweifelhaft, fraglich, ungewiß, unsicher, schwankend; fragwürdig, unklar, verdächtig; *be –ful of a th.*, an einer S. zweifeln; *–ful characters*, finstere Elemente. **–fulness,** *s.* die Zweifelhaftigkeit, Bedenklichkeit; Ungewißheit. **–less,** *adv.* ohne Zweifel, zweifelsohne, zweifellos, unzweifelhaft; wohl, sicherlich, ich gebe zu.

douce [daʊs], *adj.* (*Scots*) gesetzt, gelassen.

douche [du:ʃ], 1. *s.* die Dusche, Brause; der Irrigator (*Med.*); *throw a cold – on a th.*, (*fig.*) etwas dämpfen. 2. *v.a.* duschen.

dough [doʊ], *s.* der Teig; (*sl.*) das Geld, Moneten (*pl.*). (*sl.*) **–boy,** *s.* amerikanischer Infanterist. **––mixer,** *s.* der Kneter. **–nut,** *s.* der Krapfen, (Berliner) Pfannkuchen. **–y,** *adj.* teigig, weich; klitschig.

dought–iness [ˈdaʊtɪnɪs], *s.* (*Poet.*) die Tapferkeit. **–y** [ˈdaʊtɪ], *adj.* tapfer, beherzt, mannhaft, tüchtig.

dour [dʊə], *adj.* (*Scots*) ernst, streng; störrisch, starrköpfig; starr, herb.

douse [daʊs], *v.a.* begießen; löschen (*fire*), auslöschen (*light*); laufen lassen (*sail*) (*Naut.*).

dove [dʌv], *s.* die Taube; der Liebling, das Täubchen. **––colour** *s.* das Taubengrau. **–cot(e),** *s.* der Taubenschlag. **––like,** *adj.* taubenartig. **–'s foot,** *s.* der Storchschnabel (*Bot.*). **–tail,** 1. *s.* der Schwalbenschwanz (*Carp.*). 2. *v.a.* & *n.* durch Schwalbenschwanz verbinden; (*fig.*) fest verbinden, zusammenfügen, eingliedern (*into*, in), genau passen (*into*, zu).

dowager [ˈdaʊədʒə], *s.* die Witwe von Stande; *queen –*, die Königinwitwe, Königinmutter; *– Lady C.*, die verwitwete Lady C.

dowd–iness [ˈdaʊdɪnɪs], *s.* die Schlampigkeit,

–y [ˈdaʊdɪ], 1. *s.* schlampige Frau, die Schlampe. 2. *adj.* unordentlich angezogen; unelegant; schlampig, nachlässig.

dowel [ˈdaʊəl], 1. *s.* der Dübel, Döbel, Diebel, Zapfen, Holzpflock. 2. *v.a.* mit Dübeln befestigen.

dower [ˈdaʊə], 1. *s.* die Mitgift, das Wittum; (*fig.*) die Begabung. 2. *v.a.* mit einer Mitgift ausstatten; (*fig.*) ausstatten. **–less,** *adj.* ohne Mitgift.

dowlas [ˈdaʊləs], *s.* grobe Leinwand, die Sackleinwand.

[1]**down** [daʊn], *s.* die Daune, Flaumfeder (*of birds*); der Flaum (*of plants, the face, etc.*); – *quilt*, die Daunendecke. **–y,** *adj.* flaumig, weich.

[2]**down,** *s.* (*usually pl.*) die Geest, Heide, das Hügelland, grasbewachsener Höhenzug. **–sman,** *s.* der Geestbewohner, Heidebewohner.

[3]**down, 1.** *adv.* (*direction*) herunter, hinunter, herab, hinab, nieder, nach unten; (*position*) unten, nieder, herunter; (*fig.*) heruntergekommen, niedergedrückt, geschwächt; (*a*) (with *be*) (*coll.*) – *and out*, auf den Hund gekommen, völlig heruntergekommen, völlig mittellos, ruiniert, erledigt; – *at heel*, unordentlich, schäbig, zerlumpt, heruntergekommen; *the blinds are* –, das Rouleau ist heruntergelassen; *two points* –, zwei Punkte zurück (*Sport*); *sugar is* –, Zucker ist billiger geworden; *the temperature is six degrees* – or – *by six degrees*, die Temperatur ist um 6 Grad gefallen; *be* – *for tomorrow*, für morgen angesetzt sein; – *in the mouth*, niedergeschlagen, niedergedrückt, mutlos; *the sun is* –, die Sonne ist untergegangen; *be* – *on one's luck*, Pech *or* kein Glück haben; (*coll.*) *be* – *on a p.*, streng sein gegen einen, über einen herfallen; *be* – *with*, darniederliegen an (*an illness*); (*b*) (*with verbs*) *boil* –, einkochen; *come* – *in the world*, sehr herunterkommen; *get* – *!* komm herunter! *go* –, sich legen (*of wind*); in die Ferien gehen (*Univ.*); die Universität verlassen; (*coll.*) *go* – *well*, Anklang finden; *knock* –, überfahren (*Motor., etc.*); (*coll.*) *let a p.* –, einen preisgeben; *run* or *track* –, endlich finden; *send* –, relegieren (*Univ.*), von der Universität verweisen; *thin* –, verdünnen; *go up and* –, auf- und abgehen; *move up and* –, sich auf- und niederbewegen; (*c*) (*absolute*) £1 –, ein Pfund bar auf den Tisch; ein Pfund ärmer; (*coll.*) – *under*, in Australien; *upside* –, das Oberste zuunterst; *turn upside* –, auf den Kopf stellen; – *for second reading*, zur zweiten Lesung angesetzt; – *from London*, von London. **2.** *prep.* herab, herunter, hinab, hinunter; – *in the country*, auf dem Lande; *go* – *the hill*, den Hügel hinabgehen; *all* – *history*, durch die ganze Geschichte hin; *fall* – *a precipice*, in einen Abgrund fallen; – *the river*, stromabwärts; *further* – *the river*, weiter unten am Fluße; *go* – *the river*, den Fluß hinabfahren; – *town*, unten in der Stadt; – (*the*) *wind*, unter *or* mit dem Winde (*Naut.*). **3.** *int.* nieder! hinab! – *with him!* nieder mit ihm! – (*dog*) *!* lege dich hin! kusch dich! kusch! **4.** *s.*; *have a* – *on s.o.*, einem aufsässig sein, einen nicht leiden können; *the ups and* –*s of life*, die Wechselfälle des Lebens. **5.** *v.a.* niederwerfen, bezwingen, ducken (*a p.*); (*sl.*) hinuntergießen, hinunterstürzen (*drink, etc.*); – *tools*, die Arbeit niederlegen *or* einstellen, streiken. **–cast,** *adj.* niedergeschlagen; –*cast* (*shaft*), einziehender Schacht (*Min.*). **–fall,** *s.* der Sturz, Fall; starker Regenfall; (*fig.*) der Verfall, Untergang, Niedergang. **– grade,** *see* **– gradient**; (*fig.*) das Fallen, Sinken. **– gradient,** die Neigung. **––hearted,** *adj.* niedergeschlagen, gedrückt; (*coll.*) *are we* ––*hearted ?* sind wir bange? **–hill,** 1. *adj.* abschüssig. 2. *adv.* bergab, ins *or* zum Tal, abwärts; *he is going* –*hill*, (*fig.*) es geht mit ihm bergab. **––lead,** *s.* die Einleitung, Niederführung (*Rad.*). **––platform,** *s.* der Bahnsteig für Züge aus London. **–pour,** *s.* der Regenguß, Platzregen. **–right,** 1. *adj.* gerade, offen, offenherzig, redlich, unverstellt, ausgesprochen, positiv, völlig; –*right atheism*, völliger Atheismus; –*right fool*, ausgesprochener Narr; –*right madness*, heller Wahnsinn; –*right nonsense*, barer Unsinn. 2. *adv.* geradezu, positiv, gerade heraus; gehörig, gänzlich, durchaus, tüchtig, völlig. **–rightness,** *s.* die Offenheit, Geradheit. **–stairs,** 1. *adv.* treppab, die Treppe hinab *or* hinunter; *he is* –*stairs*, er ist unten. 2. *adj.*; –*stair(s) room*, unteres Zimmer. **–stream,** *adv.* stromabwärts. **––stroke,** *s.* der Schlag nach unten; Grundstrich (*in writing*); Abstrich (*in violin-playing*); –*stroke of a piston*, der Kolbenniedergang. **––train,** *s.* der Zug von London in die Provinz (*Railw.*). **––trodden,** *adj.* (*fig.*) unterdrückt, mit Füßen getreten, niedergeworfen. **–ward,** *adj.* absteigend, abschüssig, sich neigend, sich senkend; *on the* –*ward grade*, auf der schiefen Ebene. **–ward(s),** *adv.* abwärts, hinab, niederwärts, nach unten. **––wind,** *s.* der Abwind (*Meteor.*).

downsman, *s. see* [2]**down.**

downy [ˈdaʊnɪ], *see* [1]**down.**

dowry [ˈdaʊrɪ], *s.* die Mitgift, Aussteuer, Ausstattung.

[1]**dowse** [daʊs], *see* **douse.**

[2]**dows–e** [daʊz], *v.n.* mit der Wünschelrute Wasser suchen. **–er,** *s.* der Rutengänger. **–ing,** *s.* das Rutengehen. **–ing-rod,** *s.* die Wünschelrute.

doxology [dɔkˈsɔlədʒɪ], *s.* liturgischer Lobgesang.

doxy [ˈdɔksɪ], *s.* (*archaic*) die Dirne, Geliebte.

doyen [ˈdɔɪjən], *s.* der Wortführer, Sprecher.

doze [doʊz], *v.n.* schlummern, dösen; – *off*, einduseln, einschlummern; – *over work*, bei der Arbeit einschlafen. 2. *s.* das Schläfchen, der Schlummer.

dozen [ˈdʌzn], *s.* das Dutzend; *by the* –, dutzendweise; *baker's* –, dreizehn; (*coll.*) –*s of*, Mengen von; *round* –, volles Dutzend; *talk nineteen to the* –, das Blaue vom Himmel schwatzen; (*coll.*) *do one's daily* –, tägliche Körperübungen machen.

[1]**drab** [dræb], *adj.* graubraun, gelblich grau, mausgrau, schmutzfarben; (*fig.*) düster, eintönig.

[2]**drab,** *s.* die Schlampe; Dirne.

drabble [ˈdræbl], *v.a.* beschmutzen.

drachm [dræm], *s.* die Drachme, das Quentchen. **–a** [ˈdrækmə], *s.* die Drachme.

draconi–an [dræˈkoʊnɪən], *adj.*, **–c** [–ˈkɔnɪk], *adj.* drakonisch, streng.

draff [dræf], *s.* der Bodensatz, Treber, Trester; das Spülich; (*fig.*) der Auswurf, Unrat.

draft [drɑːft], 1. *s.* die Tratte, der Wechsel (*C.L.*); die Auswahl, Abordnung, Abteilung; das Kriegsaufgebot, die Aushebung, Musterung; der Ersatz, Nachschub (*Mil.*); Entwurf, Abriß, Aufriß, die Skizze, das Konzept; – *agreement*, der Vertragsentwurf; *make a* – *on*, abheben von (*an account*); *make the* – *payable to a p.*, die Tratte auf einen aufstellen; – *at sight on London*, die Sichttratte auf London. 2. *v.a.* entwerfen, zeichnen, skizzieren, abfassen, aufsetzen (*a lease, etc.*); auswählen, abordnen, detachieren (*soldiers*). **–sman,** *see* **draughtsman.**

drag [dræg], 1. *v.a.* schleppen, schleifen, zerren, eggen (*Agr.*); – *the anchor*, vor Anker treiben; – *one's feet*, mit den Füßen schlurren; (*fig.*) – *in*, an den Haaren herbeiziehen; – *into*, hineinziehen in (*a p.*); – *out* (or *on*), hinschleppen, ausdehnen; (*coll.*) – *up*, unsanft erziehen (*a child*). 2. *v.n.* schleifen, schleppen, schlurren, zerren, ziehen; sich hinschleppen, langweilig werden; mit einem Grundnetz suchen (*for*, nach); – *on*, – *out*, sich hinschleppen, in die Länge ziehen. 3. *s.* die Schleife, der Holzschlitten, schwere Egge (*Agr.*); eine Art Vierspänner; (*––net*) das Schleppnetz, Baggernetz; der Dregghaken; Hemmschuh; Widerstand (*Av.*); (*fig.*) das Hindernis, die Hemmung, Belastung; *he is a great* – *on his family*, er fällt seiner Familie sehr zur Last. **––chain,** *s.* die Hemmkette. **––net,** *s.* das Schleppnetz. **––rope,** *s.* das Zugtau, Schlepptau. **––shoe,** *s.* der Hemmschuh.

draggle [ˈdrægl], 1. *v.a.* durch den Schmutz ziehen, beschmutzen. 2. *v.n.* schleppen, schleifen, nachschleifen. **–d,** *adj.* schmutzig, schlampig. (*coll.*) **––tail,** *s.* die Schlampe.

dragoman [ˈdrægomən], *s.* der Dolmetscher.

dragon [ˈdrægən], *s.* der Drache; (*poet.*) Lindwurm, die Schlange; (*B.*) der Teufel; (*fig.*) böses Weib. **–et** [drægəˈnɛt], *s.* der Spinnenfisch (*Ichth.*). **–fly,** *s.* die Wasserjungfrau, Libelle (*Ent.*). **–'s-blood,** *s.* das Drachenblut (*Bot.*). **–'s teeth** *pl.* das Tankhindernis (*Mil.*). **––tree,** *s.* der Drachenbaum.

dragoon [drəˈguːn], 1. *s.* der Dragoner; (*fig.*) Rohling. 2. *v.a.* schinden, unterdrücken; zwingen (*into*, zu).

drain [dreɪn], 1. *v.a.* abtropfen lassen, abfließen lassen, austropfen lassen (*liquids*); (aus)trocknen, entwässern, trockenlegen, dränieren (*ground*); abziehen, ableiten (*pus, etc.*); (aus)leeren, austrinken (*a jug, etc.*); (*fig.*) verzehren; berauben (*Gen.*), entblößen (von); – *off*, ablassen, abfließen lassen, abtropfen lassen, abführen, abziehen, ableiten. 2. *v.n.* ablaufen, abfließen, sickern; – *away*, abfließen, wegfließen, sich verlaufen. 3. *s.* das Ableiten; der Drän, Entwässerungsgraben, Abzugsgraben, Ablaufkanal, die Gosse, Auffangrinne; Kanüle (*Med.*); der Abfluß (*of money*), Ablauf, Ablaß; (*fig.*) die Inanspruchnahme, Belastung, Schwächung; (*pl.*) die Abflußrohranlage, Kanalisation; *that is a – on my purse*, das nimmt meinen Geldbeutel (zu) stark in Anspruch. **-able**, *adj.* entwässerbar. **-age**, *s.* das Ablaufen, Abfließen, die Entwässerung, Trockenlegung, Dränage; Entwässerungsanlage, Kanalisation (*in the house*); *-age system*, die Entwässerungsanlage. *-age tube*, *s.* die Kanüle, Entleerungsröhre (*Med.*). **--cock**, *s.* der Ablaßhahn, Ablaufhahn. **-er**, *s.* der Ableiter, das Tropfbrett. **-ing**, *adj.* abziehend, Abzugs-. **-ing-board**, *s.* das Abtropfbrett. **-ing-rack**, *s.* der Trockenständer (*Phot.*). **--pipe**, *s.* das Abzugsrohr, Abflußrohr. **--trap**, *s.* der Wasserabschluß, Geruchverschluß.

drake [dreɪk], *s.* der Enterich.

dram [dræm], *s.* der Trunk, Schluck (*of spirits*); Schnaps.

drama [ˈdrɑːmə], *s.* das Schauspiel, Drama; die Schauspielkunst, Dramatik. **-tic** [drəˈmætɪk], *adj.* dramatisch, Schauspieler-, Theater-; handlungsreich, spannend; *-tic art*, die Theaterwissenschaft; *-tic school*, die Schauspielerschule. **-tist** [ˈdrɑmətɪst], *s.* der Dramatiker, Schauspieldichter. **-tization**, *s.* die Dramatisierung. **-tize**, *v.a.* dramatisieren. **-turgy** [-təːdʒɪ], *s.* die Dramaturgie, Theaterwissenschaft.

drank [dræŋk], *see* **drink.**

drape [dreɪp], *v.a.* malerisch behängen, drapieren, in Falten legen. **-r** [-ə], *s.* der Tuchhändler, Zeughändler, Schnittwarenhändler; *-rs' company*, die Tuchhändlerinnung. **-ry** [ˈdreɪpərɪ], *s.* der Tuchhandel; das Tuch, Zeug, der Stoff; die Drapierung, der Faltenwurf (*Paint., etc.*).

drastic [ˈdrɑstɪk], *adj.* kräftig, drastisch, gründlich.

drat [dræt], *v.a.*; (*vulg.*) – *it!* zum Henker damit!

draught [drɑːft], *s.* das Ziehen; der Zug (*also drink, of air, of fish*); Tiefgang (*of a ship*); Schluck; Luftzug; die Arznei, Dosis; *see also* **draft**; *drink off at one –*, auf einen Zug austrinken; *there is a –*, es zieht; (*sl.*) *feel the –*, den kürzeren ziehen; *beer on –*, Bier vom Fasse, das Abzugbier. **-s**, *pl.* das Damespiel; Damebrettsteine (*pl.*); *play at -s*, Dame spielen. **--animal**, *s.* das Zugtier. **--board**, *s.* das Damespielbrett. **--hole**, *s.* das Zugloch. **--horse**, *s.* das Zugpferd. **--marks**, *pl.* die Ahmung, Ahming (*Naut.*). **-sman**, *s.* der Damebrettstein; (*also* **draftsman**) der Zeichner, Konstrukteur; (*usually* **draftsman**) der Entwerfer, Konzipist.

draw [drɔː], 1. *ir.v.a.* ziehen, zerren, schleppen, schleifen; anziehen, an *or* zu sich ziehen, fesseln; strecken, dehnen, ausziehen (*Metall.*); (ab)zeichnen, schildern, darstellen; unentschieden spielen; – *applause from s.o.*, einem Beifall entlocken *or* abringen; – *s.o.'s attention to*, jemandes Aufmerksamkeit lenken auf; – *a bead*, zielen (*on*, nach); – *beer*, Bier abziehen *or* abzapfen; – *a bird*, Geflügel ausnehmen; – *blood*, verwunden; – *the bow*, den Bogen spannen; – *the long bow*, aufschneiden, prahlen; – *breath*, Atem holen, Luft schöpfen; – *comparisons*, Vergleiche aufstellen *or* anstellen; – *a conclusion from*, einen Schluß ziehen aus; – *consolation from a th.*, Trost aus etwas schöpfen; – *fresh courage from s.th.*, neuen Mut aus einer S. schöpfen; – *the curtain*, die Gardine aufziehen *or* zuziehen; *at daggers –n*, auf gespanntem Fuße; – *one's finger over*, mit dem Finger fahren über; – *a full house*, das Haus füllen (*Theat.*); – *a game*, ein Spiel unentschieden machen; – *interest*, Zinsen bringen; (*coll.*) – *the line at*, nicht mehr mitmachen, Schluß machen bei; – *a loser*, eine Niete auslosen; – *lots*, losen; – *money from an account*, Geld von einem Konto abheben; – *a parallel*, eine Parallele ziehen; – *one's pen through*, ausstreichen, durchstreichen; (*coll.*) – *a p.*, einen aushorchen *or* auspumpen; – *a good price*, einen guten Preis erhalten; – *profit*, Vorteil ziehen (*from*, von, aus); – *rein*, die Zügel anziehen; – *a sigh*, einen Seufzer ausstoßen; – *stumps*, dem Spiel ein Ende machen (*Crick.*); – *the sword*, das Schwert ziehen *or* zücken; – *tea*, Tee ziehen lassen; – *a tooth*, einen Zahn ziehen; – *one's wages*, seinen Lohn beziehen *or* in Empfang nehmen; – *water*, Wasser holen *or* schöpfen; – *a wood*, einen Wald durchsuchen *or* durchstöbern. – **after**, nach sich ziehen. – **along**, fortziehen. – **aside**, beiseitenehmen *or* -ziehen. – **away**, wegziehen, zurückziehen, ablenken (*attention*). – **back**, zurückziehen. – **down**, herablassen; auf sich ziehen, herabbeschwören (*curse*). – **forth**, herausziehen, entlocken. – **in**, einsaugen, einziehen; zusammenziehen; einschränken; – *in one's horns*, die Hörner einziehen, sich mäßigen. – **into**, hineinziehen (in (*Acc.*)); anlocken, verleiten (zu). – **off**, abziehen, abzapfen, abfüllen (*fluids*); wegziehen, zurückziehen (*troops*); ablenken (*the attention, etc.*). – **on**, anziehen (*boots, etc.*); anlocken; – *a cheque on one's bank*, einen Scheck auf seiner Bank ziehen. – **out**, herausziehen, herausholen; ausziehen, verlängern, ausdehnen; (*fig.*) in die Länge ziehen; – *out troops*, Truppen detachieren *or* aufstellen; – *a p. out about a th.*, einen über eine S. auspumpen. – **up**, aufstellen, aufrichten; (her)aufziehen, in die Höhe ziehen; – *up boats*, Boote ans Land ziehen; – *up a petition*, eine Bittschrift abfassen *or* aufsetzen; – *up in order of battle*, in Schlachtordnung aufstellen; – *o.s. up*, sich recken, emporrichten, aufrichten *or* erheben. 2. *ir.v.n.* ziehen; eine Karte ziehen; das Schwert ziehen; sich begeben, sich bewegen, herankommen (*to*, an), sich nähern (*to* (*Dat.*)); zeichnen (*Draw.*); Tiefgang haben (*Naut.*); unentschieden spielen (*Sport*); *we must let the tea –*, der Tee muß ziehen; – *at long date*, auf lange Zeit ziehen *or* ausstellen (*bills*); – *for the move*, um den Zug losen. – **aside**, zur Seite gehen, ausweichen. – **away from**, hinter sich lassen, sich entfernen von. – **back**, sich zurückziehen, zurückweichen; abfallen. – **in**, sich neigen; kürzer werden (*as the days*); sich einschränken. – **level**, gleichziehen; – *level with*, einholen, herankommen an. – **near** *or* (*Poet.*) **nigh**, sich nähern, näherkommen, naherrücken, heranrücken (*to*, an); *harvest is -ing near*, es geht auf die Ernte zu, die Ernte steht vor der Tür; *the time is -ing near*, die Zeit naht *or* rückt heran. – **off**, sich zurückziehen. – **on**, nahen, anrücken; sich verlassen auf, heranziehen, in Anspruch nehmen (*Acc.*); trassieren auf (*C.L.*); *the night -s on apace*, die Nacht rückt schnell heran; – *on one's savings*, die Ersparnisse angreifen *or* heranziehen. – **out**, länger werden (*as the days*). – **round** *the table*, einen Kreis um den Tisch bilden. – **to** *a close*, zu Ende gehen, sich dem Ende nähern; – *to a head*, den Höhepunkt erreichen; *I felt -n to him*, ich fühlte mich zu ihm hingezogen. – **together**, zusammenziehen. – **up**, vorfahren, (an)halten (*as a carriage*); herankommen (*to*, an). 3. *s.* das Ziehen, der Zug; das Los, Schicksal; die Ziehung, Verlosung; Anziehungskraft; das Zugstück, der Schlager (*Theat.*); unentschiedenes Spiel, das Remis; *the game ended in a –*, das Spiel blieb unentschieden. **-back**, *s.* der Nachteil, die Kehrseite, Schattenseite; das Hindernis, die Beeinträchtigung; der Rückzoll, die Zollrückvergütung. **-bridge**, *s.* die Zugbrücke. **-ee**, *s.* der Akzeptant, Bezogene(r), *m.*, der Trassat (*C.L.*). **-er**, *s.* [ˈdrɔːə] der Aussteller, Trassant (*C.L.*); Zeichner; [drɔː] die Schublade, das Schubfach; *a chest of -ers*, die Kommode. **-ers** [drɔːz], *pl.* die Unterhose (*for men*), der Schlüpfer (*for women*); *a pair of -ers*, eine Unterhose, ein Schlüpfer; *bathing -ers*, die Badehose. **-ing**, *s.* das Ziehen; Zeichnen; die Zeichnung, Skizze; Ziehung (*in a lottery*); *out of -ing*, verzeichnet; *scale--ing*, das

Meßbild; *working –ing*, die Konstruktionszeichnung. **–ing account,** das Girokonto (*C.L.*). **–ing-board,** *s.* das Zeichenbrett, Reißbrett. **–ing-compasses,** *pl.* der Reißzirkel. **–ing-ink,** *s.* die Tusche. **–ing-master,** *s.* der Zeichenlehrer. **–ing-office,** *s.* das Zeichenbüro (*Surv., etc.*). **–ing-paper,** *s.* das Zeichenpapier. **–ing-pen,** *s.* die Reißfeder. **–ing-pin,** *s.* die Reißzwecke, Heftzwecke. **–ing-room,** *s.* das Gesellschaftszimmer, der Salon; *the King holds a –ing-room today*, heute hat der König großen Empfang. **–ings,** *pl.* die Abhebungen, Bezüge (*of money*). **– well,** *s.* der Ziehbrunnen.

drawl [drɔ:l], 1. *v.a. & n.* affektiert sprechen. 2. *s.* affektierte Sprechweise.

drawn [drɔ:n], 1. *see* **draw.** 2. *adj.*; *– battle*, unentschiedene Schlacht; *– butter*, zerlassene Butter; *– expression*, verzerrtes Gesicht; *– sword*, blankes Schwert. *––(thread)work*, die Hohlsaumarbeit.

dray [dreɪ], *s.* der Rollwagen. **–age,** *s.* das Rollgeld. **––cart,** *s. see* **–. – horse,** *s.* der Karrengaul. **–man,** *s.* der Rollkutscher, Rollfuhrmann, Bierkutscher.

dread [drɛd], 1. *s.* große Furcht, die Scheu, der Schrecken; das Grauen (*of*, vor). 2. *adj.* (*poet.*) furchtbar; gefürchtet, erhaben, hehr. 3. *v.a.* fürchten, sich fürchten vor. **–ful,** 1. *adj.* schrecklich, furchtbar; (*coll.*) sehr, entsetzlich. 2. *s.*; *penny-–ful*, billiger Schauerroman. **–nought,** *s.* das Großkampfschiff; wetterfester Stoff; der Mantel aus solchem.

dream [drɪ:m], 1. *s.* der Traum; die Träumerei, der Traumzustand; (*coll.*) *a – of a dress*, ein Wunder von einem Kleid. 2. *ir.v.a.* träumen. 3. *ir.v.n.* träumen; träumerisch sein; *– away*, verträumen (*time, etc.*); *I –ed that*, mir träumte daß; *I never –t of such a thing*, so etwas ist mir nie im Traume eingefallen *or* habe ich mir nie träumen lassen; *without –ing that he might come*, ohne zu ahnen daß er kommen könnte. **–er,** *s.* der Träumer, Phantast. **–iness,** *s.* die Verträumtheit. **–ing,** *adj.* verträumt. **–less,** *adj.* traumlos. **–like,** *adj.* traumartig. **– reader,** *s.* der Traumdeuter. **–t** [drɛmt], *see* **dream. –y** [ˈdrɪ:mɪ], *adj.* träumerisch, verträumt.

drear [drɪə], (*poet.*) *see* **–y. –iness,** *s.* die Öde, Düsterheit. **–y** [ˈdrɪərɪ], *adj.* traurig, öde, düster; langweilig.

¹**dredge** [drɛdʒ], 1. *s.* das Schleppnetz, Grundnetz, die Kurre; der Bagger. 2. *v.a.* ausbaggern (*Hydr.*); dreggen (*Naut.*); mit Schleppnetzen fangen. **–r** [ˈdrɛdʒə], *s.* der Bagger, die Baggermaschine, das Baggerschiff.

²**dredge,** *v.a.* bestreuen, panieren (*with flour, etc.*), streuen (*flour, etc.*) (*Cook.*). **–r,** *s.* die Streubüchse.

dreg [drɛg], *s.* letzter Rest; (*usually pl.*) die Hefe, der Bodensatz; (*fig.*) der Abschaum, Auswurf; *to the –s*, bis auf den Grund *or* zur Neige.

drench [drɛntʃ], 1. *s.* der Trank, die Arznei (*Vet.*). 2. *v.a.* durchnässen; Arznei eingeben (*to animals*) (*Dat.*); *–ed in tears*, in Tränen gebadet; *–ed with rain*, bis auf die Haut durchnässt. **–er,** *s.* (*coll.*) der Regenguß.

dress [drɛs], 1. *v.a.* anziehen, ankleiden; bekleiden, mit Kleidung (*or Theat.* Kostümen) versorgen; schmücken, putzen, dekorieren (*as a window*); beflaggen (*a ship*); bearbeiten, zurechtmachen, behandeln (*wound*); düngen (*Agr.*), anrichten, zubereiten (*food*), anmachen (*salad*), frisieren, kämmen (*hair*), behauen (*stones*), aufbereiten (*ore*), stärken, appretieren, glätten (*cloth*); zurichten, bereiten (*leather*); abhobeln, bestoßen (*Typ.*); hecheln (*flax*); brechen (*hemp*); ordnen, richten (*also Mil.*); *– the ranks*, sich ausrichten; *– a ship*, die Flaggengala setzen; *– the vine*, den Weinstock beschneiden; *– a wound*, eine Wunde verbinden *or* behandeln; *– o.s.*, sich (an)kleiden *or* anziehen; (*coll.*) *– a p. down*, einen abkanzeln *or* anschnauzen; einem eine Strafpredigt halten; *– a p. out with*, einen aufputzen *or* ausschmücken mit; *– a p. up*, einen verkleiden. 2. *v.n.* sich (an)kleiden, sich anziehen; sich richten (*Mil.*); *– !* richt euch! (*Mil.*); *– by the right*, sich nach rechts ausrichten; *– elegantly*, sich geschmackvoll kleiden; *– up*, sich verkleiden. 3. *s.* der Anzug, die Kleidung; das Kleid; *evening –*, der Gesellschaftsanzug; der Frack (*for men*), die Balltoilette (*for women*); *fancy –*, das Maskenkostüm; *full –*, der Galaanzug, Paradeanzug, die Gala; (*fig.*) das Gewand; *morning –*, der Straßenanzug, schwarzer Rock mit gestreifter Hose. **– allowance,** *s.* das Nadelgeld. **– circle,** *s.* erster Rang (*Theat.*). **––clothes,** *pl.* die Gesellschaftskleidung. **––coat,** *s.* der Frack. **–er** [ˈdrɛsə], *s.* die Ankleiderin (*Theat.*); der Bearbeiter (*leather*); Assistenzarzt (*Med.*); die Anrichte, das Büffet; (*also* **kitchen––er**) der Küchenschrank, Geschirrschrank. *window-–er*, *s.* der Schaufensterdekorateur. **–ing** [ˈdrɛsɪŋ], *s.* das Ankleiden; die Bekleidung; das Behandeln (*of a wound*); der Verband, Verbandstoff (*Surg.*); das Zubereiten, Zurichten (*of food*); die Zutat, Füllung; Soße; Appretur (*of cloth*); Düngen (*Agr.*); *field –ing*, der Notverband (*Mil.*). **–ing-bag,** *s.*, **–ing-case,** *s.* das Toilettenkästchen, das Reisenecessaire. (*coll.*) **–ing-down,** *s.* die Strafpredigt. **–ing-gown,** *s.* der Schlafrock. **–ing-jacket,** *s.* der Frisiermantel. **–ing-room,** *s.* das Ankleidezimmer; Umkleidezimmer (*Sport.*). **–ing-station,** *s.* der Verbandplatz (*Mil.*). **–ing-table,** *s.* der Toilettentisch. **–maker,** *s.* die Damenschneiderin. **–making,** *s.* die Damenschneiderei. **– parade,** die Modeschau. **––preserver,** *s.* das Armblatt, Schweißblatt. **––rehearsal,** *s.* die Generalprobe, Hauptprobe. **––shield,** *s. see* **––preserver. ––shirt,** *s.* das Frackhemd. **––suit,** *s.* der Gesellschaftsanzug. **––sword,** *s.* der Galadegen. (*coll.*) **–y** [ˈdrɛsɪ], *adj.* modisch, elegant (*of clothes*); geputzt, stutzerhaft, modesüchtig, auffallend gekleidet (*of persons*).

drew [drʊ:], *see* **draw.**

dribble [ˈdrɪbl], 1. *v.n.* tröpfeln; geifern (*as a child*); dribbeln (*Footb.*). 2. *v.a.* tröpfeln lassen; vor sich (her)treiben (*the ball*) (*Footb.*).

driblet [ˈdrɪblɪt], *s.* (*coll.*) das Bißchen, die Kleinigkeit; *in –s*, in kleinen Mengen.

drie-d [draɪd], 1. *see* **dry.** 2. *adj.* getrocknet, Trocken–, Dörr–. **–r** [ˈdraɪə], der Trockner, Trockenapparat; das Trockenmittel, Sikkativ.

drift [drɪft], 1. *s.* das Treiben; die Strömung; Abtrift, Trift (*Naut.*), Kursabweichung (*Av.*); das Sichtreibenlassen, Gehenlassen, die Untätigkeit; der Trieb, Antrieb, die Neigung, Richtung, der Lauf; Zweck, die Absicht; der Gedankengang; die Wehe, der Haufen (*of sand, etc.*); das Gestöbe, der Guß (*of rain, etc.*); das Geschiebe (*Geol.*), der Stollen, die Strecke (*Min.*); der Lochhammer, Dorn (*Metall.*); *– from the land*, die Landflucht. 2. *v.n.* getrieben werden; treiben; sich häufen (*of snow*), triftig sein (*Naut.*); sich willenlos treiben lassen (*of persons*); sich entwickeln lassen (*of things*), *– apart*, auseinanderkommen (*also fig.*); *– away*, wegziehen, abwandern; *let things –*, den Dingen ihren Lauf lassen. **––anchor,** *s.* der Treibanker. **–er,** *s.* das Treibnetzfischerboot. **––ice,** *s.* das Treibeis. **––net,** *s.* das Treibnetz. **––sand,** *s.* der Flugsand, Triebsand. **––way,** *s.* die Trift (*for cattle*); die Strecke (*Min.*), Abtrift (*Naut.*). **–wood,** *s.* das Treibholz.

¹**drill** [drɪl], 1. *v.a.* bohren, drillen (*holes*); drillen, ausbilden, unterrichten, einexerzieren, eindrillen, abrichten; in Rillen *or* Furchen säen (*seed*), in Rillen besäen (mit) (*land*); *– a th. into a p.*, einem etwas einpauken; *– a tooth*, einen Zahn ausbohren. 2. *v.n.* exerzieren, gedrillt *or* ausgebildet werden. 3. *s.* der Drillbohrer; der Drill, das Drillen, Exerzieren; die Übung, Schulung (*Mil.*); die Furche, Rille (*Agr.*); *Swedish –*, Freiübungen (*pl.*). **––ground,** der Exerzierplatz. **––harrow,** *s.* die Bohregge. **–ing,** 1. *s.* das Bohren; Exerzieren. **––plough,** *s.* die Sämaschine. **––sergeant,** *s.* der Rekrutenunteroffizier.

²**drill,** *s.* der Drell, Drillich, Zwillich, Zwilch.

drink [drɪŋk], 1. *ir.v.a.* trinken; saufen (*of beasts*); leeren, austrinken (*a glass*); *– one's fill*, sich satt trinken; *– o.s. to death*, sich zu Tode trinken; *– o.s. into an illness*, sich (*Dat.*) eine Krankheit antrinken; *– the health of s.o.*, auf jemandes Wohl *or* Gesundheit trinken; *– s.o. under the table*, einen unter den Tisch trinken; *– the waters*, Brunnen trinken (*at a spa*). **– away,** vertrinken, mit Trinken verbringen. **– in,** (*fig*) einziehen, einsaugen, verschlingen, in sich aufnehmen. **– off, – up,** austrinken, ausleeren. 2. *ir.v.n.* trinken; übermäßig trinken, saufen, zechen; – *deep*, einen tiefen Zug tun; – *like a fish*, wie ein Loch trinken; – *to*, (einem) zutrinken, trinken auf (*Acc.*). 3. *s.* das Getränk; der Trunk, Zug, Schluck; geistiges Getränk; *food and –*, Speise und Getränk *or* Trank; *have a –*, einen Trunk zu sich nehmen; *have a – with s.o.*, mit einem eins trinken; *in –*, betrunken; (*coll.*) *on the –*, dem Trunke frönen; *take a –*, see *have a –*; *take to –*, sich dem Trunke ergeben; *a – of water*, ein Trunk Wasser. **–able** [-əbl], *adj.* trinkbar. **–er,** *s.* der Trinker, Zecher; Säufer, Trunkenbold. **–ing** ['drɪŋkɪŋ], *s.* das Trinken; *given to –(ing)*, dem Trunk ergeben. **–ing-bout,** *s.* das Trink- *or* Zechgelage. **–ing-cup,** *s.* der Becher. **–ing-fountain,** *s.* der Trinkbrunnen. **–ing-horn,** *s.* das Trinkhorn. **–ing-song,** *s.* das Trinklied. **–ing water,** das Trinkwasser.

drip [drɪp], 1. *v.n.* tropfen, abtropfen, ablaufen, tröpfeln (*from*, von), triefen (*with*, von). 2. *s.* das Tröpfeln, (*often pl.*) der Nachlauf; *see also* **– -stone. –ping** ['drɪpɪŋ], 1. *adj.* tröpfelnd; triefend, durchnässt; *–ping wet*, triefend naß. 2. *s.* das Herabtropfen, Tröpfeln, Triefen; Bratenfett, Schmalz (*Cook.*). **–ping-pan,** *s.* die Bratpfanne. **– -stone,** *s.* das Traufdach, der Sims (*Arch.*).

drive [draɪv], 1. *ir.v.a.* treiben, forttreiben; einschlagen (*a nail*), vorwärtsschlagen (*a ball*); antreiben, nötigen, zwingen, dahinbringen; jagen, hetzen (*game*); lenken, fahren (*a car, etc.*); führen (*an engine*); bohren (*a tunnel*); – *all before one*, alles überwinden; – *an argument home*, einen Beweis erbringen; *he –s a hard bargain*, es ist nicht gut mit ihm Kirschen essen, er ist eine harte Nuß; – *a car*, ein Auto lenken *or* chauffieren; – *a coach*, kutschieren; – *a p. hard*, einen schinden, einen in die Enge treiben, einen überanstrengen; – *home*, nach Hause fahren; – *a nail home*, einen Nagel ganz einschlagen; – *a th. home to s.o.*, einem etwas zu Gemüte führen, einem etwas einbleuen; – *a hoop*, einen Reifen schlagen; – *s.o. mad*, einen verrückt machen; *it was enough to – one mad*, es war zum Rasendwerden; – *s.o. from pillar to post*, einen von Pontius zu Pilatus schicken; – *a p. out of his mind* or *senses*, einen um den Verstand bringen; – *s.o. to despair* or *distraction*, einen zur Verzweiflung treiben *or* bringen; – *o.s. to do s.th.*, sich nötigen *or* dahinbringen etwas zu tun. **– away,** vertreiben, zerstreuen. **– back,** zurücktreiben. **– in,** eintreiben (*cattle*), einschlagen (*nails*). **– on,** vorwärtstreiben. **– out,** hinaustreiben, forttreiben, vertreiben, verjagen. **– up,** in die Höhe treiben (*prices*). 2. *ir.v.n.* treiben, dahintreiben, getrieben *or* getragen werden; fahren (*in a vehicle*). (*coll.*) **– at,** hinzielen auf, hinauswollen, meinen; *let – at*, losschlagen auf. **– off,** wegfahren. **– on,** weiterfahren, zufahren. **– out,** ausfahren, spazierenfahren. **– to** *leeward*, abtrieben. **– up,** vorfahren (*to*, vor). 3. *s.* die Spazierfahrt, Fahrt, Ausfahrt; der Fahrweg, die Auffahrt; das Hetzen, die Treibjagd (*of game*); die Stoßkraft, Triebkraft, Energie, der Schwung; Vorstoß (*Mil.*); der Antrieb, das Triebwerk (*Mach.*); der Stoß, Schlag (*Sport*); Weitschlag, erster Schlag (*Golf*), der Treibschlag, Triebschlag (*Tenn.*); *go for* or *take a –*, ausfahren; *remote –*, der Fernantrieb (*Mach.*). **–r** ['draɪvə], *s.* der Treiber (*of oxen, etc.*); Fuhrmann, Kutscher; Fahrer, Kraftfahrer, Führer (*Motor.*); das Triebrad (*Railw., etc.*); der Mitnehmer (*on lathes, etc.*); Rammblock (*Build.*); erster Schläger (*Golf*); *slave- –r*, der Sklavenaufseher, (*fig.*) Leuteschinder; *pile- –r*, die Ramme. **–r's cab,** der Führerstand. **–r's mate,** der Beifahrer. **–r's seat,** der Kutschersitz, Führersitz (*Motor.*). **– shaft,** *s.* die Antriebwelle, Treibachse; *see* **driving.**

drivel ['drɪvl], 1. *v.n.* geifern, sabbern (*as infants*); (*fig.*) schwatzen, faseln. 2. *s.* der Geifer; Unsinn, die Faselei, leeres Geschwätz. **–ler,** *s.* der Faselhans, Schwätzer.

driving ['draɪvɪŋ], *adj.* treibend; Treib–, Trieb–; *be within – distance*, zu Wagen leicht erreichbar *or* zu erreichen sein; – *rain*, strömender Regen. **– -anchor,** *s.* der Treibanker. **– -band,** *s.* das Führungsband (*Artil.*). **– -belt,** der Treibriemen. **– -box,** *s.* der Kutsch(er)bock, Kutschersitz. **– -gear,** *s.* das Gebtriebe; Triebwerk. **– -instructor,** *s.* der Fahrlehrer (*Motor.*). **– -licence,** der Führerschein (*Motor.*). **– -mirror,** der Rück(blick)spiegel. **– -power,** *s.* die Betriebskraft. **– -reins,** *s.* die Leitriemen. **– -seat,** *s.* der Führersitz (*Motor.*). **– -shaft,** *s.* die Triebwelle, Triebachse; Kardanwelle (*Motor.*). **– -test,** *s.* die Führerprüfung. **– -wheel,** *s.* das Treibrad (*Locom.*).

drizzl–e ['drɪzl], 1. *s.* der Sprühregen. 2. *v.n.* rieseln, nieseln. **–y,** *adj.* rieselnd.

drogue [droʊg], *s.* der Windsack.

droit [drɔɪt, drwɔ], *s.* das Recht (*Law*).

droll [droʊl], 1. *adj.* drollig, possierlich. 2. *s.* der Possenreißer. **–ery,** *s.* die Posse, Schnurre, der Spaß; die Spaßhaftigkeit, Komik.

dromedary ['drɔmədərɪ], *s.* das Dromedar.

[1]**dron–e** [droʊn], 1. *s.* das Summen; eintöniges Sprechen; der Brummer (*of the bagpipes*). 2. *v.n.* summen, dröhnen; eintönig reden, leiern. 3. *v.a.* herleiern.

[2]**drone,** 1. *s.* die Drohne, (*fig.*) der Faulenzer, Müßiggänger. 2. *v.n.* faulenzen. 3. *v.a.*; – *away*, müßig verbringen.

drool [dru:l], *v.n.* (*sl.*) *see* **drivel.**

droop [dru:p], 1. *v.a.* sinken lassen, hängen lassen. 2. *v.n.* sich senken, dahinsinken, ermatten, schmachten, (ver)welken (*as flowers*); (*fig.*) den Kopf hängen lassen.

drop [drɔp], 1. *s.* der Tropfen, das Tröpfchen; (*coll.*) der Trunk; die Klappe (*Tele.*); der Fall, das Fallen, Herabfallen, Sinken (*of prices, temperatures, etc.*); die Senkung, der Abgrund; die Falltür (*of gallows*); (*– curtain*) der Vorhang (*Theat.*); (*pl.*) (Arznei)Tropfen (*pl.*), Fruchtbonbons, Zuckerplätzchen (*pl.*) (*Conf.*); *add by –s*, einträufeln; *a – too much*, ein Trunk über den Durst; – *in the ocean*, (*fig*). ein Tropfen auf den heißen Stein. 2. *v.a.* tropfen lassen, tröpfeln; senken, niederlassen, niederschlagen (*one's eyes*), absetzen (*passengers*); fallen lassen; werfen, gebären (*the young of beasts*); fällen, zum Fall bringen; – *anchor*, den Anker auswerfen *or* ausbringen; (*coll.*) – *an acquaintance* or *a person*, sich von einem trennen, nichts mehr mit einem zu tun haben; *the bill was –ped*, der Antrag fiel durch; – *a bird on the wing*, einen Vogel im Flug herunterschießen; – *bombs*, Bomben abwerfen; (*coll.*) – *a brick*, einen groben Schnitzer machen; – *a curtsy*, einen Knicks machen; (*fig.*) – *the curtain*, Schluß machen; – *a goal*, ein Tor durch Sprungtritt machen (*Footb.*); – *one's h's*, das *h* nicht aussprechen; – *a hint*, einen Wink fallen lassen *or* von sich geben; – *into bad habits*, in schlechte Gewohnheiten verfallen; (*coll.*) – *into a good th.*, in eine gute Sache einsteigen; (*coll.*) – *it!* laß das! hör' auf damit! – *a letter in the box*, einen Brief in den Briefkasten werfen; – *me a line*, lassen Sie mir ein paar Zeilen zukommen; – *the matter*, die Sache fallen lassen; – *on a th.*, zufällig auf etwas stoßen; – *money on s.th.*, Geld bei etwas verlieren; (*coll.*) – *on a p.*, einen rügen *or* anfahren; – *the pilot*, den Lotsen entlassen; – *a stitch*, eine Masche fallen lassen; – *a tear*, eine Träne vergießen. 3. *v.n.* tröpfeln, triefen; fallen, (herab)fallen, sinken, zurückgehen; sich senken, sich legen (*as wind*); niederfallen, umfallen, hinsinken; aufhören, eingehen; *so quiet that you could hear a pin –*, mäuschenstill; *be ready to –*, zum Umfallen *or* Hinsinken müde sein; – *asleep*, einschlafen; – *astern*, achteraussacken (*Naut.*), zurückbleiben; – *away*, allmählich abfallen; – *behind*, zurückfallen; – *down*, niederfallen; (*coll.*) – *in*, vorsprechen (*at*, bei), unerwartet kommen (zu (*Dat.*)); – *in at his brother's* or *on his brother*, bei seinem Bruder vorbeikommen *or* vorsprechen, seinen Bruder kurz besuchen *or* aufsuchen; einlaufen (*orders, etc.*); – *off*, abtropfen; abfallen; (*coll.*) zurückgehen, sich vermindern, abnehmen; (*coll.*) einschlafen; – *out*, sich zurückziehen, nicht mehr daran teilnehmen; verschwinden, ausfallen, fortfallen. **– -forge,** *s.* die Gesenkschmiede. **– -hammer,** *s.* das Hammerfallwerk. **– -kick,** *s.* der Sprungtritt (*Footb.*).

--out, *s.* der Sprungtritt aus dem Gedränge (*Footb.*). **-ping,** 1. *adj.*; *-ping-bottle, s.* die Tropfflasche (*Med.*); *-ping-fire,* unregelmäßiges Gewehrfeuer (*Mil.*); *-ping zone,* die Landezone (*Av.*). 2. *s.* das Tropfen, Tröpfeln; (*pl.*) der Mist, Dung, Tierexkremente (*pl.*); *constant -ping wears the stone,* stetes Tropfen höhlt den Stein. **--scene,** *s.* der Vorhang (*Theat.*). **--shot,** *s.* kurzer Flugball (*Tenn.*). **--shutter,** *s.* die Fallscheibe (*Phot.*). **--test,** *s.* die Fallprobe.
drops-ical [ˈdrɔpsɪkl], *adj.* wassersüchtig. **-y** [ˈdrɔpsɪ], *s.* die Wassersucht.
dros(h)ky [ˈdrɔskɪ (ˈdrɔʃkɪ)], *s.* die Droschke.
dross [drɔs], *s.* die Schlacke (*Metall.*); der Unrat, Abfall, Auswurf, Wertlose(s), *n.*
drought [drɑʊt], *s.* die Dürre, Trockenheit; (*archaic*) der Durst. **-y,** *adj.* dürr, trocken; durstig.
drove [droʊv], 1. *see* **drive.** 2. *s.* die Viehherde. **-r,** *s.* der Viehtreiber.
drown [drɑʊn], 1. *v.a.* ertränken, ersäufen; überschwemmen; (*fig.*) übertäuben, betäuben; überschlagen, übertönen (*sounds*); ersticken; *be -ed,* ertrinken, ersaufen; *his voice was -ed by the noise,* seine Stimme wurde vom Lärm übertönt, *like a -ed rat,* durch und durch naß; *-ed in tears,* in Tränen gebadet. 2. *v.n.* ertrinken, ersaufen; *she is -ing,* sie ertrinkt. **-ing,** 1. *adj.*; *-ing man,* Ertrinkende(r), *m.* 2. *s.* das Ertrinken.
drows-e [drɑʊz], 1. *v.n.* schlummern, halb schlafen, schläfrig sein. 2. *v.a.* schläfrig machen. **-iness,** *s.* die Schläfrigkeit. **-y** [ˈdrɑʊzɪ], *adj.* schläfrig, schlaftrunken; einschläfernd.
drub [drʌb], *v.a.* schlagen, prügeln; *- s.th. into a p.,* einem etwas einhämmern. **-bing,** *s.* die Tracht Prügel.
drudge [drʌdʒ], 1. *s.* der Knecht, Sklave, Handlanger, das Aschenbrödel, der Packesel. 2. *v.n.* niedrige Arbeit verrichten; (*fig.*) sich abplacken *or* schinden. **-ry** [ˈdrʌdʒərɪ], *s.* schwere Arbeit, die Plackerei.
drug [drʌg], 1. *s.* die Apothekerware, Droge, das Arzneimittel, Rauschgift; *pl.* Chemikalien, Apothekerwaren (*pl.*); *a - on* or *in the market,* unverkäufliche Ware, der Ladenhüter. 2. *v.a.* betäuben; *- wine,* Wein verfälschen. 3. *v.n.* Rauschgift nehmen. **- addict,** Rauschgiftsüchtige(r), *m.* **--store,** *s.* (*Amer.*) die Drogerie. **-gist,** *s.* der Drogist, Apotheker.
drugget [ˈdrʌgɪt], *s.* grober Wollstoff.
Druid [ˈdruːɪd], *s.* der Druide. **-ess,** *s.* die Druidin. **-ic(al)** [druːˈɪdɪk(l)], *adj.* druidisch; Druiden-. **-ism** [-ɪzm], *s.* das Druidentum.
drum [drʌm], 1. *s.* die Trommel (*Mil., Mech.*); (*sl.*) Pauke; Mittelohrhöhle (*Anat.*); Walze, der Zylinder (*Mech.*); das Trommelmagazin (*of machine-gun*); der Korb; die Büchse, der Behälter; (*archaic*) die Abendgesellschaft; (*archaic*) die Säulentrommel, der Kapitälkelch (*Arch.*); *beat the -,* die Trommel rühren, trommeln; *with -s beating,* mit Trommelschlag *or* klingendem Spiel; *roll of -s,* Trommelwirbel (*pl.*). 2. *v.n.* trommeln; (*fig.*) klopfen, pochen; klimpern (*on piano*); burren (*of partridges*). 3. *v.a.*; *- the table,* auf dem Tisch trommeln; *- s.th. into a p's head,* einem etwas eintrauken; *- out of the regiment,* schimpflich aus dem Heere ausstoßen; *- up,* zusammentrommeln; (*coll.*) werben. **--fire,** *s.* das Trommelfeuer (*Mil.*). **-head,** *s.* das Trommelfell (*Anat.*); das Fell der Trommel; *-head court-martial,* das Standgericht (*Mil.*); *-head service, s.* der Feldgottesdienst (*Mil.*). **--major,** *s.* der Tambourmajor. **-mer,** *s.* der Trommler, Trommelschläger, Tambour. **-stick,** *s.* der Trommelstock, Trommelschlegel.
drunk [drʌŋk], 1. *see* **drink.** 2. *pred. adj.* betrunken; (*fig.*) trunken, berauscht (*with,* von); *blind* or *dead -, - as a lord,* sinnlos betrunken; *get -,* sich betrinken. 3. *s.* (*coll.*) der Trunkenbold; Trunkenheitsfall (*Law*). **-ard** [-əd], *s.* der Trinker; Säufer, Trunkenbold, versoffener Kerl. **-en,** *attrib. adj.* betrunken; dem Trunk ergeben, trunksüchtig; *-en man,* Betrunkene(r), *m.*; *-en sleep,* der Schlaf der Trunkenheit, Rausch; *-en song,* das Zechlied. **-enness** [-ənɪs], *s.* die Trunkenheit, der Rausch; die Trunksucht.
drupe [druːp], *s.* die Steinfrucht.
dry [drɑɪ], 1. *adj.* trocken, getrocknet; dürr, regenarm, regenlos; (*coll.*) durstig; herb (*of wines*); (*fig.*) schmucklos, derb, geistlos, teilnahmlos; unter Alkoholverbot, trocken(gelegt); milchlos, gelt (*as a cow*); *- bread,* Brot ohne Butter; *- cough,* trockener Husten; *the cow is -,* die Kuh gibt keine Milch; *- crust,* das Stück trockenes Brot; *as - as dust* höchst langweilig; *with - eyes,* ohne Tränen; ohne Rührung, ungerührt; *- facts,* nüchterne *or* ungeschminkte Tatsachen; *go -,* das Alkoholverbot einführen; *- humour,* trockener *or* sarkastischer Humor; *run -,* trocken werden; *- shampoo,* das Trockenschampoon; *- spell,* die Trockenperiode. 2. *v.a.* trocknen, abtrocknen, austrocknen; dörren (*fruit*); *- one's hands,* sich (*Dat.*) die Hände abtrocknen; *- o.s.,* sich abtrocknen; *- a meadow,* eine Wiese trockenlegen; *- up,* austrocknen; *- (up) the crocks,* das Geschirr abtrocknen. 3. *v.n.* trocknen, trocken werden; *- out,* austrocknen; *- up,* eintrocknen, vertrocknen, verdorren; (*sl.*) das Maul halten, still sein. **- -as-dust,** 1. *adj.* (*fig.*) trocken, langweilig. 2. *s.* trockener Stubengelehrter. **- cell,** das Trockenelement. **- cleaning,** chemische Reinigung, chemische Wäsche, die Trockenreinigung, Trockenwäsche. **--cure,** *v.a.* dörren (*fruit, etc.*), einsalzen (*meat*). **--dock,** 1. *s.* das Trockendock. 2. *v.a.* ins Trockendock bringen. **--eyed,** *adj.* trockenen Auges. **--fly,** *s.* künstliche Fliege (*fishing*). **--goods,** *pl.* Schnittwaren, Kurzwaren (*Amer.*). **-ing,** 1. *adj.* trocknend, Trocken-. 2. *s.* das Trocknen, Dörren. **-ing-ground,** *s.* der Trockenplatz. **-ing-kiln,** *s.* der Trockenofen. **-ing-loft,** *s.* der Trockenboden. **-ing-oil,** *s.* der Ölfirnis. **-ing-room,** *s.* der Trockenraum. **--measure,** *s.* das Trockenmaß. **-ness,** *s.* die Trockenheit; Dürre; Langweiligkeit. **--nurse,** *s.* die Kinderfrau, trockene Amme. **--plate,** *s.* die Trockenplatte (*Phot.*). **--point,** *s.* die Radiernadel, kalte Nadelarbeit (*Engr.*). **--rot,** *s.* die Trockenfäule, Holzfäule, der Hausschwamm; (*fig.*) Verfall, innere Fäulnis. **-salter,** *s.* der Drogenhändler. **--shod,** *adv.* trockenen Fußes.
dryad [ˈdrɑɪəd], *s.* die Dryade, Waldnymphe.
dual [ˈdjuːəl], 1. *s.* der Dual(is) (*Gram.*). 2. *adj.* doppelt, Zwei-. *- alliance,* der Zweibund; *- carriage-way,* doppelte Fahrbahn (*Motor.*); *- control,* die Doppelsteuerung (*Motor., Av.*); *- monarchy,* die Doppelmonarchie; *- number,* die Zweizahl; der Dual(is) (*Gram.*). **--purpose,** *adj.* Mehrzweck-. **-ism** [-ɪzm], *s.* der Dualismus (*Phil., Pol.*). **-ity** [djuːˈælɪtɪ], *s.* die Zweiheit.
dub [dʌb], *v.a.* zum Ritter schlagen; betiteln, (be)nennen, einen Titel *or* (Spitz)Namen zulegen. (*Dat.*); nachsynchronisieren (*film*); einfetten (*leather*). **-in(g),** *s.* das Lederfett, die Schuhschmiere.
dubi-ety [djuˈbɪːɪtɪ], *s.* die Ungewißheit, Zweifelhaftigkeit. **-ous** [ˈdjuːbɪəs], *adj.* zweifelhaft; ungewiß, unsicher, unschlüssig; unbestimmt, zweideutig; *-ous character,* verdächtiger Charakter. **-ness,** *s.* die Unsicherheit, Unbestimmtheit. **-tation** [djuːbɪˈteɪʃən], *s.* das Zweifeln, Zögern. **-tative,** *adj.* zweifelnd, zögernd, unschlüssig.
ducal [ˈdjuːkəl], *adj.* herzoglich, Herzogs-.
ducat [ˈdʌkət], *s.* der Dukaten.
duch-ess [ˈdʌtʃɪs], *s.* die Herzogin. **-y** [ˈdʌtʃɪ], *s.* das Herzogtum.
[1]**duck** [dʌk], *s.* die Ente; (*coll.*) kein Punkt, die Null (*Crick.*); (*coll.*) der Liebling, das Püppchen; *lame -,* der Pechvogel, krankes Huhn; Zahlungsunfähige(r), *m.*; *play at -s and drakes,* Wasserjungfern werfen; *like water off a -'s back,* ohne den geringsten Eindruck zu machen; *make -s and drakes of* or *play -s and drakes with,* verschleudern, zum Fenster hinauswerfen. **-bill,** *s.* das Schnabeltier (*Zool.*). **--boards,** *pl.* der Holzrost, Bretterrost, das Laufbrett. **-ling,** *s.* das Entchen. **-'s egg,** die Null (*Crick.*). **--shooting,** *s.* die Entenjagd. **-weed,** *s.* die Wasserlinse (*Bot.*). **-y,** *adj.* (*coll.*) lieb(lich), niedlich.
[2]**duck,** 1. *s.* das Neigen, Ducken (*of the head*). 2. *v.n.* untertauchen; sich ducken. 3. *v.a.* (unter)-tauchen; *- one's head,* den Kopf ducken. **-ing,** *s.*

das Tauchen; die Taufe (*Naut.*); *get a good –ing*, tüchtig naß werden. **–ing-stool,** *s.* der Tauchschemel.

[3]**duck,** *s.* das Segeltuch; Schiertuch. **–s,** *pl.* die Segeltuchhose.

duckling [ˈdʌklɪŋ], *s. see under* [1]**duck.**

duct [dʌkt], *s.* der Gang, Kanal (*Bot., Zool., Anat.*); die Röhre, Leitung (*Mach.*). **–ile,** *adj.* dehnbar, ziehbar, streckbar; (*fig.*) fügsam, geschmeidig, lenksam, biegsam. **–ility,** *s.* die Dehnbarkeit, Streckbarkeit; Biegsamkeit, Fügsamkeit. **–less,** *adj.* ohne Kanal; *–less glands*, Hormondrüsen (*pl.*) (*Anat.*).

dud [dʌd], 1. *s.* der Blindgänger (*Artil.*); Versager (*fig. & Artil.*); (*fig.*) Fehlschlag, die Niete; (*pl.*) (*sl.*) alte Kleider, Lumpen, Siebensachen. 2. *adj.* (*sl.*) unbrauchbar, wertlos; *– stock*, Ladenhüter (*pl.*).

dude [djuːd], *s.* (*sl.*) der Geck, Gigerl (*Amer.*).

dudgeon [ˈdʌdʒən], *s.* der Groll, Unwille; (*coll.*) *be* or *take in high –*, sehr übelnehmen.

due [djuː], 1. *adj.* gebührend, geziemend, passend, recht, richtig, genau, angemessen; (*only pred. adj.*) schuldig, fällig (*C.L.*); (*a*) (*with nouns*) *after – consideration*, nach reiflicher Überlegung; *in – course*, zur gehörigen *or* richtigen Zeit zu seiner Zeit; *in – form*, in gehöriger Form, gültig; *take – note*, gehörige Notiz nehmen (*C.L.*); *– respect*, schuldige Achtung; *his – reward*, der ihm gebührende Lohn; *in – time*, zur rechten Zeit; (*b*) (with *be*) *be, become* or *fall –*, fällig sein *or* werden; *the train is – (in) at 8 o'clock*, der Zug soll um 8 Uhr ankommen; *it is already –*, es müßte schon da sein; *he is – for retirement*, er ist reif zur Pensionierung; *this is – to carelessness*, dies ist auf Nachlässigkeit zurückzuführen, dies ist eine Folge *or* infolge der Nachlässigkeit; *I am – to see him today*, ich muß *or* soll ihn heute sehen; *it is – to him*, es gebührt ihm, es kommt ihm zu; es ist ihm zuzuschreiben, ihm verdanken wir (es); *honour to whom honour is –*, Ehre wem Ehre gebührt. 2. *adv.* gerade, genau, direkt; *– east*, gerade östlich, genau nach Osten. 3. *s.* die Schuldigkeit, Schuld, das Recht, der Anteil, Lohn; (*pl.*) die Gebühren, Abgaben (*pl.*), der Zoll; Vereinsbeitrag; *give everyone his –*, jedem das Seine geben, jeden gebührend behandeln; *give the devil his –*, selbst dem Teufel Gerechtigkeit widerfahren lassen; *for a full –*, vollständig, vollkommen (*Naut.*).

duel [ˈdjuːəl], 1. *s.* der Zweikampf, das Duell; *student's –*, die Mensur; *fight a –*, sich duellieren, (*Studs. sl.*) auf die Mensur gehen. 2. *v.n.* sich duellieren; (*Studs. sl.*) pauken. **–ling,** *s.* das Duellieren, (*sl.*) Pauken. **–list,** *s.* der Duellant, (*sl.*) Paukant.

duenna [djuːˈɛnə], *s.* die Anstandsdame.

duet [djuːˈɛt], *s.* das Duett; *play a –*, vierhändig spielen.

duffel, duffle [ˈdʌfl], *s.* der Düffel, dickes Wolltuch.

duffer [ˈdʌfə], *s.* (*coll.*) der Dummkopf, Stümper.

[1]**dug** [dʌg], *s.* die Zitze.

[2]**dug,** *see* **dig. – -out,** *s.* der Unterstand, Bunker, Unterschlupf, (*sl.*) der Heldenkeller (*Mil.*); (*– -out canoe*) der Einbaum.

dugong [ˈduːgɔŋ], *s.* die Seekuh (*Zool.*).

duke [djuːk], *s.* der Herzog. **–dom,** *s.* das Herzogtum; die Herzogswürde.

dulc–et [ˈdʌlsɪt], *adj.* wohlklingend, lieblich. **–ify** [ˈdʌlsɪfaɪ], *v.a.* versüßen; (*fig.*) besänftigen. **–imer** [ˈdʌlsɪmə], *s.* das Hackbrett (*Mus.*).

dull [dʌl], 1. *adj.* (*of persons*) dumm, schwer von Begriff(en), stumpfsinnig, unempfindlich, geistlos, schwerfällig, träge; (*of things*) dumpf (*as pain or sound*), stumpf (*as a knife*), trübe (*as weather*), langweilig (*as a book*), getrübt (*as spirits*), schwach (*as the fire*), matt, dunkel (*as colour*), leblos, glanzlos (*as the eyes*); flau, still, stockend (*as trade*); *– as ditch-water*, höchst langweilig. 2. *v.a.* stumpf machen (*a knife*), abstumpfen, mattieren (*a colour*), trüben (*eyes, etc.*), betäuben, mildern (*pain*). **–ard,** *s.* der Dummkopf. **–ish,** *adj.* etwas *or* ziemlich dumm *or* langweilig. **–ness,** *s.* die Stumpfheit; Stumpfsinnigkeit, Dummheit, der Stumpfsinn; die Schwerfälligkeit, Trägheit; Mattheit, Glanzlosigkeit, Trübheit; Dumpfheit; Flauheit.

duly [ˈdjuːlɪ], *adv. see* **due**; pünktlich, rechtzeitig; gehörig, ordnungsgemäß.

dumb [dʌm], *adj.* stumm; (*sl.*) dumm; *deaf and –*, taubstumm; *– brutes, creatures* or *friends*, stumme Tiere; *strike –*, sprachlos machen, zum Schweigen bringen. **– -bell,** *s.* die Hantel (*Gymn.*); (*sl.*) der Dummkopf. **–found** [dʌmˈfaʊnd], *v.a.* sprachlos machen, verblüffen. **–foundedness,** *s.* die Sprachlosigkeit, Verblüfftheit. **–ness,** *s.* die Stummheit. **– -show,** *s.* stummes Spiel, das Gebärdenspiel, die Pantomime. **– -waiter,** *s.* der Drehtisch, stummer Diener; (*Amer.*) der Speiseaufzug.

dummy [ˈdʌmɪ], 1. *s.* stumme Person, der Statist (*Theat.*); (*fig.*) Strohmann (*also Cards*); die Kleiderpuppe; Puppe, Figur; Attrappe, leere Packung; das Lutschgummi, der Schnuller (*for babies*). 2. *adj.* unecht, Schein–, Schwindel–. **– -cartridge,** *s.* die Exerzierpatrone.

dump [dʌmp], 1. *s.* dumpfer Schlag, der Plumps, Bums; Abfallhaufen, Abladeplatz, die Sammelstelle; Halde (*Min.*); das Lager, Depot, der Park (*Mil.*). 2. *v.a.* abladen, anhäufen, ablagern, kippen; heftig hinwerfen; zu Schleuderpreisen absetzen (*surplus goods, etc.*). **– -cart,** *s.* der Kippwagen. **–er,** *s.* der Schmutzkonkurrent. **–ing** [ˈdʌmpɪŋ], *s.* der Schleuderverkauf ans Ausland, das Dumping. **–ing-ground,** *s.* der Abladeplatz, die Schutthalde.

dumpling [ˈdʌmplɪŋ], *s.* der Kloß.

dumps [dʌmps], *pl.* (*coll.*) trübe Stimmung, schlechte Laune; (*coll.*) *in the –s*, niedergeschlagen, trübsinnig, schwermütig, schlechtgelaunt.

dumpy [ˈdʌmpɪ], *adj.* (*coll.*) untersetzt.

[1]**dun** [dʌn], *adj.* schwarzbraun, graubraun; (*Poet.*) dunkel.

[2]**dun,** 1. *s.* drängender Gläubiger; der Mahnbrief, die Mahnung, Forderung. 2. *v.a.* ungestüm mahnen, (*sl.*) treten; belästigen, plagen (*with*, mit); *–ning letter*, der Mahnbrief.

dunce [dʌns], *s.* der Dummkopf.

dunderhead [ˈdʌndəhɛd], *s.* (*coll.*) der Dummkopf. (*coll.*) **–ed,** *adj.* dumm.

dune [djuːn], *s.* die Düne.

dung [dʌŋ], 1. *s.* der Dünger, Dung, Mist. 2. *v.a. & n.* düngen, misten. **– -beetle,** *s.* der Mistkäfer. **– -heap, – -hill,** *s.* der Misthaufen.

dungaree [dʌŋgəˈrɪ], *s.* grobes Kattunzeug. **–s,** *pl.* der Arbeitsanzug, das Überkleid.

dungeon [ˈdʌndʒən], *s.* das Burgverlies, der Kerker.

duo [ˈdjuːoʊ], *s.* (*pl.* –s) das Duett. **–decimal,** *adj.* duodezimal. **–decimo,** *s.* das Duodez(format); (*pl.*) das Buch im Duodezformat. **–denal** [djuːəˈdɪːnəl], *adj.* Duodenal– (*Anat.*). **–denary,** *adj.* deodekadisch. **–denitis,** *s.* die Zwölffingerdarmentzündung (*Med.*). **–denum** [djuːəˈdɪːnəm], *s.* der Zwölffingerdarm (*Anat.*).

dup–ability [djuːpəˈbɪlɪtɪ], *s.* die Leichtgläubigkeit. **–able** [ˈdjuːpəbl], *adj.* leicht anzuführen(d), leichtgläubig. **–e** [djuːp], 1. *s.* Betrogene(r), *m.*; der Gimpel; *be the –e of*, sich anführen lassen von, sich täuschen lassen von. 2. *v.a.* betrügen, täuschen, anführen. **–ery** [–ərɪ], *s.* die Täuschung.

dupl–e [ˈdjuːpl], *adj.*; *–e time*, der Zweivierteltakt (*Mus.*). **–ex** [ˈdjuːplɛks], *adj.* doppelt, zweifach; *–ex burner*, der Doppelbrenner; *–ex telegraphy*, die Duplex-Telegraphie; *–ex turret*, der Zwillingsturm. **–icate** [ˈdjuːplɪkət], 1. *adj.* doppelt. 2. *s.* das Duplikat, die Kopie, Abschrift; das Seitenstück; *in –icate*, in doppelter Ausführung, in zwei Exemplaren. 3. [–keɪt], *v.a.* verdoppeln, vervielfältigen, in Duplikat herstellen. **–ication** [–ˈkeɪʃən], *s.* die Verdoppelung, Vervielfältigung. **–icator,** *s.* der Vervielfältigungsapparat. **–icity** [djuːˈplɪsɪtɪ], *s.* die Zweiheit, Doppelheit; Falschheit, Doppelzüngigkeit.

durab–ility [djuərəˈbɪlɪtɪ], *s.* die Dauerhaftigkeit, Beständigkeit. **–le** [ˈdjuərəbl], *adj.* dauerhaft, beständig, haltbar. **–leness,** *see* **–ility.**

duralumin [djuˈræljəmɪn], *s.* das Dural.

durance [ˈdjuərəns], *s.* (*Poet.*) der Gewahrsam, die Haft; *keep in –*, gefangen halten.

durat–ion [djuəˈreɪʃən], *s.* die Dauer, Fortdauer; (*coll.*) *for the –ion*, bis Kriegsende. **–ive,** 1. *adj.*

dauernd; Dauer– (*Gram.*). 2. *s.* die Dauerform (*Gram.*).
duress [ˈdjʊərɛs], *s.* der Zwang, Druck, die Nötigung (*Law*); Haft, Freiheitsberaubung (*Law*); *under* –, durch Nötigung.
during [ˈdjʊərɪŋ], *prep.* während (*Gen.*); – *the day*, im Laufe des Tages; – *Her Majesty's pleasure*, auf Lebenszeit.
durst [dəːst], (*Poet.*) *see* **dare.**
dusk [dʌsk], 1. *adj.* (*Poet.*) düster, dämmerig, dunkel, finster. 2. s. die Dämmerung; Abenddämmerung, das Zwielicht; *after* –, nach Einbruch der Dämmerung. **–iness**, *s.* dunkle Farbe. **–y**, *adj.* schwärzlich; düster, trüb.
dust [dʌst], 1. *s.* der Staub; Kehricht, Müll, Schutt; (*coll.*) *bite the* –, ins Gras beißen; *fall to* –, zerfallen; *fine as* –, staubfein; *gather* –, staubig werden; *in the* –, gedemütigt; *make, raise* or (*sl.*) *kick up a* –, Staub aufwirbeln, Lärm machen; *lay the* –, den Staub dämpfen; *reduce to* –, zerstäuben; *shake the* – *off one's feet*, voll Entrüstung fortgehen; *throw* – *into a p.'s eyes*, einem Sand in die Augen streuen; (*sl.*) *down with the* –! heraus mit dem Geld! 2. *v.a.* abwischen, ausklopfen, ausbürsten; entstauben, abstäuben; bestäuben, einpudern, bestreuen. **– -bin**, *s.* der Aschenkasten, Müllkasten. **– -cart**, *s.* der Müllwagen. **– -cloth**, *s*, der Überzug (*for furniture*). **– -coat**, der Staubmantel. **– -cover**, *s.* der Schutzumschlag (*on books*). **–er**, *s.* das Staubtuch, der Wischlappen. **–iness**, *s.* die Staubigkeit, staubiger Zustand. **–ing**, *s.* das Abstauben; (*coll.*) die Tracht Prügel. **– -man**, *s.* der Müllfuhrmann. **– -pan**, *s.* die Kehrichtschaufel. **–y**, *adj.* staubig, voll(er) Staub; staubfarben, schmutzig; (*sl.*) *not so* –*y*, nicht so schlimm, nicht zu verachten.
dut–eous [ˈdjuːtjəs], *see* **–iful. –iable** [ˈdjuːtɪəbl], *adj.* zollpflichtig, steuerpflichtig. **–iful** [ˈdjuːtɪfʊl], *adj.* pflichtgetreu, gehorsam; ehrerbietig. **–ifulness**, *s.* die Pflichttreue; Ehrerbietung; der Gehorsam. **–y** [ˈdjuːtɪ], *s.* die Pflicht, Schuldigkeit (*to* or *towards*, gegen *or* gegenüber); die Ehrerbietung; Dienstpflicht, der Dienst, Kriegsdienst; die Gebühr, Abgabe, Steuer, der Zoll; die Nutzleistung (*Mech.*); (*a*) (*with verbs*) *do one's* –*y by s.o.*, seine Schuldigkeit an einem tun; *pay* –*y on goods*, Waren versteuern *or* verzollen; (*b*) (*with nouns*) *ad valorem* –*y*, der Wertzoll; *customs* –*y*, der Einfuhrzoll; *stamp* –*y*, die Stempelgebühr; *transit* –*y*, der Durchgangszoll; (*c*) (*absolute*) *in* –*y bound*, pflichtschuldig, von Rechts wegen, pflichtgemäß; –*y call*, der Pflichtbesuch; –*y off*, unverzollt; –*y paid*, verzollt, versteuert; (*d*) (*with prepositions*) *neglect of* –*y*, die Pflichtverletzung, Pflichtversäumnis; *tour of* –*y*, die Dienstzeit; *off* –*y*, dienstfrei; *be off* –*y*, nicht im Dienst sein; *on* –*y*, diensttuend, im Dienste; *be on* –*y*, Dienst haben; *go on* –*y*, in den Dienst gehen. **–y-free**, *adj.* zollfrei, steuerfrei, abgabefrei. **–y station**, *s.* der Dienstort.
duumvir [djuːˈʌmvə], *s.* der Duumvir. **–ate**, *s.* das Duumvirat.
dwarf [dwɔːf], 1. *s.* der Zwerg. 2. *adj.* Zwerg– (*Bot.*). 3. *v.a.* im Wachstume hindern; (*fig.*) klein(er) erscheinen lassen, in den Schatten stellen. **–ed**, *adj.* verkümmert, verkrüppelt, zusammengeschrumpft. **–ish**, *adj.* zwerghaft, winzig.
dwell [dwɛl], *v.n.* wohnen, bleiben, verweilen, sich aufhalten; – *on*, verweilen *or* sich aufhalten bei; bestehen *or* Nachdruck legen auf; brüten über; – *upon a subject*, einen Gegenstand ausführlich behandeln *or* erörtern; – *upon a syllable*, eine Silbe anhalten *or* dehnen. **–er**, *s.* der Bewohner. **–ing** [ˈdwɛlɪŋ], *s.* die Wohnung, der Wohnsitz, Aufenthalt. **–ing-house**, *s.* das Wohnhaus. **–ing-place**, *s.* der Wohnort.
dwelt [dwɛlt], *see* **dwell.**
dwindle [ˈdwɪndl], *v.n.* abnehmen, schwinden, zergehen; ausarten, verfallen (*into*, in (*Acc.*)); – *away*, dahinschwinden.
dyad [ˈdaɪæd], *s.* das Paar, die Zwei.
dye [daɪ], 1. *v.a.* färben; – *another colour*, umfärben; – *in the grain* or *wool*, in der Wolle färben; (*fig.*) –*d in the wool*, von echtem Schrot und Korn, unverfälscht. **2.** *v.n.* sich färben (lassen). 3. *s.* der Farbstoff, die Farbe; (*fig.*) Färbung; *fast* –, haltbare *or* echte Farbe; *a rogue of the deepest* –, ein Schurke schlimmster Art. **– -house**, *s.* die Färberei. **–ing**, *s.* das Färben; Färbereigewerbe. **–(ing)-vat**, *s.* das Färb(er)faß, die Küpe; Farbflotte. **–r**, *s.* der Färber. **–r's broom**, der Färberginster (*Bot.*). **–r's weed**, der Wau (*Bot.*). **–stuffs**, *pl.* Farbstoffe. **– -works**, *pl.* die Färberei.
dying [ˈdaɪɪŋ], 1. *see* **die.** 2. *adj.* sterbend; (*fig.*) vergehend, schmachtend; verhallend; *be* –, im Sterben liegen; – *bed*, das Sterbebett, Totenbett; *till his* – *day*, bis zu seinem Todestag; *his* – *wish*, sein letzter Wunsch, sein Todeswunsch; – *words*, letzte Worte, Worte auf dem Sterbebett. **3.** *s.* das Sterben; *the* – (*pl.*), die Sterbenden.
dyke [daɪk], *s. see* **dike.**
dynam–ic(al) [daɪˈnæmɪk(l)], *adj.* dynamisch; (*fig.*) wirksam, kräftig. **–ics** [–ˈnæmɪks], *pl.* die Dynamik; (*fig.*) das Kräftespiel. **–ite** [ˈdaɪnəmaɪt], 1. *s.* das Dynamit. 2. *v.a.* durch Dynamit sprengen. **–o** [ˈdaɪnəmoʊ], *s.* die Dynamo(maschine); Lichtmaschine (*Cycl., etc.*). **–ometer** [–ˈmɔmətə], *s.* der Kraftmesser.
dynast [ˈdɪnæst], *s.* der Herrscher. **–ic** [dɪˈnæstɪk], *adj.* dynastisch. **–y** [ˈdɪnəstɪ], *s.* das Herrschergeschlecht *or* –haus, die Dynastie.
dyne [daɪn], *s.* das Zentimetergramm, die Krafteinheit, das Dyn (*Phys.*).
dysenter–ic [dɪsənˈtɛrɪk], *adj.* ruhrartig; ruhrkrank. **–y** [ˈdɪsəntrɪ], *s.* die Ruhr (*Med.*).
dyspep–sia [dɪsˈpɛpsɪə], *s.* die Verdauungsstörung. **–tic**, 1. *adj.* magenschwach, magenkrank; (*fig.*) schwermütig, mürrisch. 2. *s.* der Dyspeptiker.
dyspnœa [ˈdɪspnɪə], *s.* die Atembeschwerde, Atemnot.

E

E, e [iː], *s.* das E, e (*also Mus.*); *E flat*, das Es; *E minor*, E-Moll; *E sharp*, das Eis. *See Index of Abbreviations at end.*
each [iːtʃ], 1. *adj.* (ein) jeder *or* jedes; (eine) jede; – *one*, see –; – *man*, jeder; – *way*, auf Gewinn beziehungsweise Placierung (*betting*). 2. *pron.* jeder, jede, jedes; – *and all*, jeder einzelne; – *and every*, all und jeder; – *other*, einander; *a shilling* –, ein Schilling das Stück.
eager [ˈiːgə], *adj.* eifrig; begierig (*for*, nach), erpicht (*for*, auf). **–ness**, *s.* der Eifer, die Begierde, heftiges Verlangen, die Ungeduld.
eagle [ˈiːgl], *s.* der Adler. **– -eyed**, *adj.* adleräugig, scharfsichtig. **– -owl**, *s.* die Adlereule. **–t**, *s.* junger Adler.
eagre [ˈiːgə], *s.* die Flutwelle.
[1]**ear** [ɪə], *s.* die Ähre. **–ed**, *adj.* mit Ähren.
[2]**ear**, *s.* das Ohr (*Anat.*), Gehör (*Mus.*); der Henkel; das Öhr, die Öse; (*a*) (*with verbs*) *be all* –(*s*), ganz Ohr sein; *not believe one's* –*s*, es nicht für möglich halten, es seinen Ohren nicht trauen; *give* –, aufmerksam zuhören; *give one's* –*s for*, kein Opfer scheuen um; *have a good* –, feines Gehör haben; *have a quick* –, scharfes Gehör haben; *have the* – *of*, jemandes Vertrauen genießen; *lend an* – *to s.o.*, auf einen hören, einem Gehör schenken; *prick up one's* –*s*, die Ohren spitzen; *turn a deaf* – *to*, taub sein gegen; (*b*) (*with prepositions*) *bring s.th. about a p.'s* –*s*, einem etwas auf den Hals bringen; *by* –, nach dem Gehör; *set* (*them*) *by the* –*s*, (sie) gegen einander hetzen; *send s.o. away with a flea in his* –, einem gehörig den Kopf waschen; *just a word in your* –, ein schnelles Wort im Vertrauen; *in at one* – *and out at the other*, zu einem Ohr hinein und zum anderen wieder hinaus; *fall on deaf* –*s*, taube Ohren finden; *over head and* –*s*, ganz und gar, vollkommen, restlos; befangen (*in*, in); *up to the* –*s*, bis über die Ohren; *come* or *get to s.o.'s* –*s*, einem zu Ohren kommen. **– -ache**, *s.* der Ohrenschmerz, das Ohrenreißen. **– -drops**, *pl.* das Ohrgehänge.

--**drum**, *s.* das Trommelfell. -**ed**, *adj.* mit Ohren *or* Henkel (versehen); *lop--ed*, mit Hängeohren; *quick--ed*, von scharfem Gehör. -**mark**, 1. *s.* (*fig.*) das Kennzeichen. 2. *v.a.* (*fig.*) kennzeichnen; bezeichnen; zurückstellen, zurücklegen (*money*); sich (*Dat.*) vorbehalten. -**phone**, *s.* (*usually pl.*) der Kopfhörer. -**piece**, *s.* die Hörmuschel, der Hörer (*Phone.*). --**piercing**, *adj.* ohrenzerreißend. --**ring**, *s.* der Ohrring. -**shot**, *s.* die Hörweite. --**trumpet**, *s.* das Höhrrohr. --**wax**, *s.* das Ohrenschmalz.

earing ['ɪərɪŋ], *s.* der Nockbändsel, das Nockhorn (*Naut.*).

earl [ə:l], *s.* der Graf. -**dom**, *s.* die Grafschaft; die Grafenwürde. --**marshal**, *s.* königlicher Zeremonienmeister.

earl-ier ['ə:lɪə], 1. *adj.* früher. 2. *adv.* früher, vorher. -**iest** ['ə:lɪəst], 1. *adj.* früheste(r)(s); *at your -iest convenience*, so bald wie möglich, umgehend (*C.L.*). 2. *adv.* frühestens, am frühesten; *at the -iest*, frühestens. -**iness** ['ə:lɪnɪs], *s.* die Frühzeitigkeit, Frühe. -**y** ['ə:lɪ], *adj.* & *adv.* früh, (früh)zeitig, beizeiten, zu früh; *-y in the day*, früh am Tage; *as -y as Chaucer*, schon bei Chaucer; *an -y bird* or *riser*, der Frühaufsteher; *-y closing*, früher Ladenschluß; *an -y death*, ein vorzeitiger Tod; *keep -y hours*, früh schlafen gehen; *-y history*, die Frühgeschichte; *-y in the morning*, früh morgens; *in -y life*, in der Jugendzeit; *-y vegetable*, das Frühgemüse; (*Prov.*) *-y to bed and -y to rise makes a man healthy, wealthy, and wise*, Morgenstunde hat Gold im Munde.

earn [ə:n], *v.a.* erwerben, verdienen, einbringen.

[1]**earnest** ['ə:nɪst], 1. *adj.* ernst, ernsthaft, emsig, eifrig, ernstlich, dringend; im Ernst, aufrichtig. 2. *s.* der Ernst; *in -*, ernst, im Ernst; *in dead* or *good -*, in vollem Ernst; *are you in -?* ist das Ihr Ernst? ist es Ihnen ernst damit? -**ness**, *s.* der Ernst, die Ernsthaftigkeit; der Eifer.

[2]**earnest**, *s.* das Angeld, Aufgeld, Draufgeld, Handgeld, die Anzahlung (*of*, auf); (*fig.*) der Vorbote, Vorgeschmack; *as an - of his determination*, als Beweis dafür, daß er entschlossen ist.

earnings ['ə:nɪŋz], *pl.* der Lohn, Verdienst, das Einkommen; der Gewinn, Ertrag, Einnahmen (*pl.*).

earth [ə:θ], 1. *s.* die Erde; der (Erd)Boden, trockenes Land; Bau (*of a fox, etc.*); die Erdung, Erdleitung, der Erdschluß (*Rad.*); (*pl.*) die Erden (*Chem.*); *the -*, die Erde, Welt, der Erdball; (*coll.*) *of the --y*, erdgebunden, erdnahe; *on -*, auf Erden; *what* or *why on -*, was *or* warum in aller Welt; (*coll.*) *come* (*down*) *to -*, wieder nüchtern denken; *fall to the -*, zur Erde *or* auf den Boden fallen; *run to -*, *v.a.* stellen (*a p.*), ausfindig machen (*a th.*). *v.n.* sich verkriechen. 2. *v.a.* erden (*the aerial*), in den Bau treiben (*a fox*); *- up*, häufeln, mit Erde bedecken (*Agr., Hort.*). 3. *v.n.* in den Bau flüchten (*of a fox*). --**born**, *adj.* erdgeboren, staubgeboren, irdisch, sterblich. --**bound**, *adj.* erdgebunden. --**connexion**, *s.* die Erdung, Erdleitung, der Erdschluß (*Rad.*). -**en** ['ə:ðən], *adj.* Erd-, irden; *-en pot*, irdener Topf. -**enware**, *s.* die Töpferware, das Steingut. -**iness**, *s.* die Erdigkeit, das Erdige. --**light**, *s.* der Erdschein. -**liness**, *s.* das Irdische, Körperliche, die Weltlichkeit. -**ly**, *adj.* irdisch, weltlich; (*coll.*) denkbar; *-ly bliss*, das Erdenglück; *no -ly reason*, kein denkbarer Grund, nicht der geringste Grund; (*sl.*) *not an -ly*, gar keine Chance. -**ly-minded**, *adj.* irdisch gesinnt. --**nut**, *s.* die Erdnuß. -**quake**, *s.* das Erdbeben, der Erdstoß. --**shaking**, *adj.* welterschütternd. -**ward(s)**, *adj.* erdwärts. -**work**, *s.* der Erdwall; (*pl.*) das Erdwerk (*Fort.*). -**worm**, *s.* der Regenwurm. -**y**, *adj.* erdig, Erd-; (*fig.*) irdisch; *-y smell*, der Erdgeruch.

earwig ['ɪəwɪg], *s.* der Ohrwurm (*Ent.*).

ease [ɪ:z], 1. *s.* die Bequemlichkeit, Behaglichkeit, Gemächlichkeit, das Behagen; die Ruhe; Erleichterung, Linderung; Ungezwungenheit, Freiheit, Sorglosigkeit; Leichtigkeit; *at -*, bequem, ruhig, zwanglos; *ill at -*, unbehaglich, unruhig; *at one's -*, ungezwungen, ungeniert, wie zu Hause; *be* or *feel at* (*one's*) *-*, sich behaglich *or* wie zu Hause fühlen; *put* or *set s.o. at his -*, einem die Schüchternheit benehmen; *stand at -!* rührt euch! (*Mil.*); *take one's -*, es sich bequem machen; *with -*, mit Leichtigkeit, leicht. 2. *v.a.* erleichtern, lindern, bequem(er) machen, beruhigen; abhelfen (*Dat.*), befreien, entlasten (*of*, von); auslassen (*a seam*), ausschneiden (*an arm-hole*), locker machen, den Spielraum vergrößern (*Mach.*); *- away*, *- off*, abfieren (*rope*); *- the helm*, mit dem Ruder nachgeben, aufkommen; *- the ship*, die Schiffsgeschwindigkeit mäßigen. 3. *v.n.* nachlassen; *- off*, nachlassen; fallen (*C.L.*). -**ment**, *s.* (*archaic*) die Erleichterung; der Vorteil; das Durchgangsrecht; die Grundstückslast, Servitut (*Law*).

easel ['ɪ:zl], *s.* die Staffelei, das Gestell.

easi-ly ['ɪ:zɪlɪ], *adv.* leicht, mühelos, ohne Schwierigkeit; (*coll.*) bei weitem. -**ness** [-nɪs], *s.* die Bequemlichkeit, Behaglichkeit; Leichtigkeit; Ungezwungenheit; Umgänglichkeit.

east [ɪ:st], 1. *s.* der Osten, Ost (*Naut.*); Orient, das Morgenland; *- by south*, Ost zu Süd; *the three kings from the -*, die Weisen aus dem Morgenlande; *the Far -*, der Ferne Osten; *in the -*, im Osten; *the Near -*, der Nahe Osten; (*to the*) *- of*, östlich von, im Osten von. 2. *adj.* Ost-; *the - End of London*, der Ostteil Londons; *- Side*, Newyork östlich von Broadway. 3. *adv.* östlich, ostwärts.

easter ['ɪ:stə], 1. *s.* das Ostern, Osterfest; *at -*, zu Ostern. 2. *attrib.* Oster-; *- egg*, das Osterei; *- greetings*, Ostergrüße.

east-erly ['ɪ:stəlɪ], 1. *adj.* östlich; östlich gelegen. 2. *adv.* ostwärts, nach Osten. -**ern**, *attrib. adj.* östlich, morgenländisch, orientalisch; nach Osten, östlich gelegen; *far--ern questions*, ostasiatische Fragen. -**ernmost**, *adj.* am weitesten östlich. -**ing**, *s.* zurückgelegter östlicher Kurs; östliche Entfernung; die Ostrichtung; Umschlagung nach Osten (*of wind*) (*Naut.*). -**ward**, *adj.*, -**wards**, *adv.* ostwärts gerichtet.

easy ['ɪ:zɪ], 1. *adj.* leicht, mühelos; bequem, behaglich, frei von Schmerzen; unbesorgt, ruhig (*about*, um); ungezwungen, frei, natürlich (*in manners*); locker (*of morals*); willig, bereitwillig, nachgiebig, gefügig; ruhig, flau (*C.L.*); (*a*) (with *be*) *the work is -*, die Arbeit ist leicht (zu bewältigen); *the language is -*, die Sprache ist leicht (zu erlernen); *free and -*, ohne alle Formalitäten; *I am quite - about the future*, um die Zukunft bin ich ganz unbesorgt; *it is - for you to talk*, da haben Sie gut reden; *the stocks are -*, die Aktien sind nicht gesucht (*C.L.*); (*b*) (with *make*) *make o.s. -*, es sich (*Dat.*) bequem machen; *make your mind -!* beruhige dich! sei unbesorgt!; (*c*) (with *nouns*) *- of access*, leicht zugängig; *- of belief*, leichtgläubig; *in - circumstances*, (*sl.*) *on - street*, in guten Verhältnissen; (*sl.*) *- meat*, kein ernst zu nehmender Gegner; *- money*, billiges Geld; *- style* (*of writing*), glatte Schreibweise; *on - terms*, unter günstigen Bedingungen, auf Abzahlung; *woman of - virtue*, die Hure, Dirne, feiles Weib. 2. *adv.* leicht; *- !* langsam! (*Naut.*); *go -*, nachlassen, sich schonen; (*coll.*) *go - !* nimm nicht zuviel! geh' sparsam damit um! *stand - !* rührt euch! *take things -*, es sich (*Dat.*) bequem machen, sich nicht überanstrengen; *take it - !* nur ruhig! --**chair**, *s.* der Lehnstuhl, Liegestuhl, Sessel. --**going**, *adj.* bequem, träge, gemächlich, lässig; gutmütig, behäbig. --**tempered**, *adj.* gutmütig.

[1]**eat** [ɪ:t], 1. *ir.v.a.* essen; fressen (*of beasts*); zerfressen, ätzen; verzehren; verschlingen; (*sl.*) *what's -ing you*, was ist dir über die Leber gelaufen; (*coll.*) *I will - my hat if*, ich lasse mich hängen, wenn; *- away*, abfressen, zerfressen, abätzen; *- one's fill*, sich anessen, sich satt essen; *the horse -s its head off*, das Pferd frißt mehr als es wert ist; *- one's heart out*, sich vor Gram verzehren; *- a p. out of house and home*, einen arm essen, einen zugrunde richten; *- up*, aufessen, verzehren; *be -en up with*, vergehen *or* sich verzehren vor; *- one's words*, seine Worte zurücknehmen *or* widerrufen. 2. *ir.v.n.* essen; *good to -*, gut zum Essen; *- in(to)*, anfressen; sich einfressen *or* eindringen (*in* (*Acc.*)); *- well*, einen guten Appetit haben (*of persons*), gut schmecken (*of things*). -**able**, *adj.* eßbar, genießbar. -**ables**, *pl.* die Eßwaren, Lebensmittel.

–er ['ɪ:tə], *s.* der Esser. **–ing** ['ɪ:tɪŋ], *s.* das Essen. **–ing-apple,** *s.* der Eßapfel. **–ing-house,** *s.* das Speisehaus. **–ings,** *pl.* (*sl.*) Eßwaren (*pl.*).
eau-de-Cologne [oudəkə'loun], *s.* Kölnisches Wasser.
eaves [ɪ:vz], *pl.* die Traufe, Dachrinne. **–drop,** *v.n.* lauschen, horchen. **–dropper,** *s.* der Lauscher, Horcher.
ebb [ɛb], 1. *s.* die Ebbe; (*fig.*) Ebbe, das Zurückfluten; (*fig.*) Abnahme, Neige, der Verfall; – *and flow*, Ebbe und Flut; *at a low* –, sehr schlecht, heruntergekommen; gedrückt (*of prices*), im Tiefstand; traurig stehen *or* liegen. 2. *v.n.* verebben; (*fig.*) zurückgehen, abnehmen, versiegen, sinken; – *and flow*, ebben und fluten, (*fig.*) steigen und fallen. **––tide,** *s.* die Ebbe.
ebon–ite ['ɛbənaɪt], *s.* das Ebonit, Hartgummi. **–ize** ['ɛbənaɪz], *v.a.* schwarz beizen, schwärzen. **–y** ['ɛbənɪ], *s.* das Ebenholz.
ebri–ate ['ɪ:brɪɪt], *adj.* (*archaic*) berauscht. **–ety** [ɪ:'braɪətɪ], *s.* die Trunkenheit.
ebulli–ent [ɪ'bʌljənt], *adj.* aufwallend, sprudelnd, überkochend. **–ence, –ency,** *s. see* **–tion;** die Überschwenglichkeit. **–tion** [ɛbə'lɪʃən], *s.* die Aufwallung, das Aufbrausen, Sieden; (*fig.*) der Ausbruch (*of passion, etc.*).
eccentric [ɪk'sɛntrɪk], 1. *adj.* nicht zentral, nicht rund, exzentrisch (*also fig.*); (*fig.*) wunderlich, überspannt; – *rod*, die Exzenterstange. 2. *s.* der Exzenter (*Mach.*); exzentrischer Mensch, der Sonderling. **–ity** [ɛksən'trɪsɪtɪ], *s.* die Exzentrizität; Wunderlichkeit, Überspanntheit.
Ecclesiast–es [ɪklɪzɪ'æstɪ:z], *s.* Prediger Salomonis (*B.*). **–ic** [ɪklɪ:zɪ'æstɪk], 1. *s.* Geistliche(r), *m.* 2. *adj. see* **–ical.** **–ical,** *adj.* kirchlich, geistlich; *–ical history*, die Kirchengeschichte. **–icism** [–'æstɪsɪzm], *s.* die Kirchlichkeit, das Kirchentum.
ecdysis [ɛk'daɪsɪs], *s.* die Häutung (*of snakes*).
échelon ['ɛʃələn], 1. *s.* die Staffel(ung), Staffelstellung (*Mil.*); *in* –, staffelförmig 2. *v.a.* staffeln, gliedern, staffelweise aufstellen. **–ment,** *s.* die Staffelung.
echi–dna [ɛ'kɪdnə], *s.* der Ameisenigel (*Zool.*). **–nite** ['ɛkɪnaɪt], *s.* fossiler Seeigel. **–noderm,** *s.* der Stachelhäuter (*Zool.*). **–nus** [ɪ'kaɪnəs], *s.* (*pl.* –i [ɪ'kaɪnaɪ]) der Seeigel (*Zool.*); Wulst am dorischen Kapitell (*Arch.*).
echo ['ɛkou], 1. *s.* der Widerhall, das Echo; *cheer s.o. to the* –, einem begeistert zujubeln. 2. *v.a.* widerhallen; (*fig.*) nachsprechen (*Dat.*). 3. *v.n.* widerhallen (*with*, von). **–less,** *adj.* ohne Echo, echolos. **––sounder,** *s.* das Echolot (*Naut.*). **––sounding,** *s.* die Echolotmessung (*Naut.*).
éclair [e'klɛ:ə], *s.* der Cremekuchen.
éclat ['eklɑ:], *s.* die Auszeichnung; allgemeiner Beifall, offenbarer Erfolg, das Aufsehen.
eclectic [ɛk'lɛktɪk], 1. *adj.* eklektisch, auswählend, zusammengestellt. 2. *s.* der Eklektiker. **–ism** [–tɪsɪzm], *s.* der Eklektizismus.
eclip–se [ɪ'klɪps], 1. *s.* die Verfinsterung, Finsternis; *–se of the moon*, die Mondfinsternis; (*fig.*) die Verdunkelung, das Verschwinden; *in –se*, in Verfall, im Sinken, im Abnehmen. 2. *v.a.* verfinstern; (*fig.*) verdunkeln, in den Schatten stellen, überragen. **–tic** [ɪ'klɪptɪk], *s.* die Ekliptik, Sonnenbahn.
eclogue ['ɛklɔg], *s.* das Hirtengedicht, die Ekloge.
econom–ic [ɪ:kə'nɔmɪk], *adj.* ökonomisch, wirtschaftlich, rationell, rentabel; volkswirtschaftlich, nationalökonomisch, Wirtschafts–; *–ic conditions, pl.* die Wirtschaftslage. **–ical,** *adj.* sparsam, haushälterisch (*of*, mit); billig, preiswert; *–ical cruising speed*, die Sparfluggeschwindigkeit (*Av.*). **–ics** [–ks], *pl. used as sing.* die Volkswirtschaft, Nationalökonomie, Volkswirtschaftslehre. **–ist** [ɪ:'kɔnəmɪst], *s.* sparsamer Haushalter, guter Wirtschafter; *political –ist*, der Nationalökonom, Volkswirtschaftler. **–ize** [–aɪz], 1. *v.n.* sparen (*in*, an (*Dat.*); *with*, mit), sparsam umgehen. 2. *v.a.* sparsam wirtschaften *or* umgehen mit, haushälterisch gebrauchen. **–izer,** *s.* der Vorwärmer (*Mach.*). **–y,** *s.* die Wirtschaft, Ökonomie; Wirtschaftlichkeit, Sparsamkeit; der Organismus, innere Verfassung; *pl.* Sparmaßnahmen (*pl.*), Ersparnisse (*pl.*); *planned –y*, die Planwirtschaft; *political –y*, die Volkswirtschaft(slehre), Nationalökonomie; *wartime –y*, die Kriegswirtschaft.
ecsta–sy ['ɛkstəsɪ], *s.* krankhafte Erregung, die Ekstase (*Med.*); das Entzücken, die Entzückung, Begeisterung, Überschwenglichkeit; Verzückung (*Eccl.*); *be in –sies over*, entzückt sein über. **–tic** [ɛks'tætɪk], *adj.* ekstatisch, verzückt (*Med.*); entzückt, begeistert, hingerissen.
ecto–blast, –derm ['ɛktoublæst, –də:m], *s.* äußeres Keimblatt. **–plasm** [–plæzm], *s.* äußere Protoplasmaschicht.
ecumenic(al) [ɪ:kjʊ:'mɛnɪk(l)], *adj. see* **oecumenical.**
eczema ['ɛkzɪmə], *s.* das Ekzem (*Med.*).
edacious [ɛ'deɪʃəs], *adj.* gefräßig, gierig.
eddy ['ɛdɪ], 1. *s.* der Wirbel, Strudel. 2. *v.n.* wirbeln.
edentate [ɪ:'dɛnteɪt], *adj.* zahnlos (*Zool.*).
edge [ɛdʒ], 1. *s.* die Schärfe, Schneide (*of a knife, etc.*); (scharfe) Kante, die Ecke; der Rand, Saum; Schnitt (*of a book*); (*fig.*) die Feinheit, Abgeschliffenheit, der Schliff (*of wit, etc.*); *blunt the*–, abstumpfen; *cutting*-–, die Schneide, Schneidkante; *with gilt –s*, mit Goldschnitt; *give an – to*, verschärfen, verstärken; *the knife has no* –, das Messer schneidet nicht; *the – of the water*, der Rand des Wassers, das Ufer, Gestade; *take the – off*, abstumpfen, (*fig.*) der Wirkung berauben; *be on* –, nervös sein; *put an – on*, schärfen, schleifen; *put s.o. on* –, einen reizen; *put to the – of the sword*, über die Klinge springen lassen (*B.*); *on the* –, am Rande; (*fig.*) im Begriff, kurz vor; *his nerves were on* –, seine Nerven waren gespannt; *set a th.* (*up*) *on* –, etwas hochkantig stellen; *set s.o.'s teeth on* –, einen nervös machen; – *to* –, Kante auf Kante; *leading* –, die Profilvorderkante, Leitkante (*Av.*); *trailing* –, die Profilhinterkante, Schleppkante (*Av.*). 2. *v.a.* schärfen, (ab)schleifen; mit einem Rand versehen, (um)säumen, einfassen, einschließen; abkanten, beschneiden; unbemerkt bringen, rücken *or* drängen (*into*, in; *out of*, aus); – *o.s. into*, sich unbemerkt eindrängen in, sich hineinschmuggeln in. 3. *v.n.* sich seitwärts (heran)bewegen; – *away*, wegschleichen, heimlich abgehen; – *forward*, langsam vorrücken; – *off*, wegrücken, abhalten von (*Naut.*). **–d,** schneidend, scharf; eingefaßt, gesäumt, (*fig.*) durchsetzt; *two-–d*, zweischneidig; *–(d) tool*, schneidendes Werkzeug; *play with –(d) tools*, mit gefährlichen Dingen umgehen. **–less,** *adj.* stumpf. **––rail,** *s.* die Kantenschiene. **––tool,** *s.* das Schneidwerkzeug. **–ways,** *adv.*, **–wise,** *adv.* seitwärts, seitlich, von der Seite; hochkantig; Kante an Kante; *not get a word in –ways* or *–wise*, kein einziges Wort einwerfen können, gar nicht zu Worte kommen.
edg–ing ['ɛdʒɪŋ], *s.* die Einfassung; Litze, der Besatz. **–y,** *adj.* kantig; (*sl.*) reizbar, verdrießlich, kratzbürstig.
edib–ility [ɛdɪ'bɪlɪtɪ], *s.* die Eßbarkeit, Genießbarkeit. **–le** ['ɛdɪbl], *adj.* eßbar, genießbar.
edict ['ɪ:dɪkt], *s.* die Verordnung, das Edikt.
edif–ication [ɛdɪfɪ'keɪʃən], *s.* (*fig.*) die Erbauung. **–ice** ['ɛdɪfɪs], *s.* das Gebäude; (*fig.*) Gefüge. **–y** ['ɛdɪfaɪ], *v.a.* (*fig.*) erbauen; (*fig.*) belehren. **–ying,** *adj.* erbaulich; belehrend.
edit ['ɛdɪt], *v.a.* herausgeben, edieren, redigieren, druckfertig machen. **–ion** [ɪ'dɪʃən], *s.* die Auflage, Ausgabe; *evening –ion*, die Abendausgabe (*of a paper*); *third –ion*, dritte Auflage (*of a book*); *popular –ion*, die Volksausgabe; *–ion de luxe*, die Prachtausgabe. **–or,** *s.* der Herausgeber (*of a book*); Schriftleiter, Redakteur (*of a journal, etc.*). **–orial** [–'tɔ:rɪəl], 1. *adj.* Redaktions–, redaktionell; *–orial staff*, der Redaktionsstab. 2. *s.* der Leitartikel. **–orship,** *s.* die Schriftleitung, Redaktion; das Amt eines Herausgebers.
educa–ble ['ɛdjʊkəbl], *adj.* erziehbar. **–te** ['ɛdjʊkeɪt], *v.a.* erziehen, (aus)bilden, unterrichten; aufziehen, trainieren, dressieren (*animals*). **–tion** [–'keɪʃən], *s.* die Erziehung, Bildung, Ausbildung; das Erziehungswesen, Schulwesen; *liberal –tion*, gelehrte Bildung; *primary* (or *elementary*) *–tion*, das Volksschulwesen; *secondary –tion*, **höheres Schul-**

wesen; *ministry of –tion*, das Unterrichtsministerium. **–tional,** *adj.* erzieherisch, pädagogisch, Unterrichts–, Erziehungs–, Bildungs–; *–tional establishment*, die Erziehungsanstalt; *–tional film*, der Lehrfilm; *–tional journey*, die Studienreise; *–tional value*, der Erziehungswert. **–tionalist,** *s.* der Schulmann, Pädogog. **–tive,** *adj.* Bildungs–, Erziehungs–. **–tor,** *s.* der Erzieher.

educ–e [ɪˈdjʊ:s], *v.a.* hervorziehen, hervorholen, herausholen; ableiten, ziehen (*from*, aus). **–ible,** *adj.* ableitbar. **–t** [ˈɪ:dʌkt], *s.* das Ausgezogene, Edukt; die Ableitung, Folgerung. **–tion** [ɪˈdʌkʃən], *s.* die Hervorziehung, Entwicklung, Ableitung. **–tion-pipe,** *s.* das Abzugsrohr.

edulcorat–e [ɪ:ˈdʌlkəreɪt], *v.a.* auswässern, reinigen. **–ion** [–ˈreɪʃən], *s.* die Reinigung.

eel [ɪ:l], *s.* der Aal; *as slippery as an –*, glatt wie ein Aal. **––fishing,** *s.* der Aalfang. **––pot,** *s.* die Aalreuse. **––pout,** *s.* die Aalraupe. **––spear,** *s.* die Aalgabel.

e'en [ɪ:n], *Poet. abbr. of* **even.**

e'er [ɛə], *Poet. abbr. of* **ever.**

eerie [ˈɪərɪ], *adj.* furchtsam; unheimlich.

efface [ɪˈfeɪs], *v.n.* auswischen, auslöschen, ausstreichen, tilgen, verwischen, austilgen; (*fig.*) in Schatten stellen; *– o.s.*, sich zurückhalten, in den Hintergrund treten. **–able,** *adj.* tilgbar, auslöschbar. **–ment,** *s.* die Auslöschung, Tilgung; Vertilgung.

effect [ɪˈfɛkt], 1. *s.* die Wirkung, Einwirkung, der Einfluß, die Folge, das Ergebnis; die Kraft, Gültigkeit; der Inhalt, Sinn, Nutzen, Zweck, die Absicht; der Eindruck, Effekt; die Leistung (*of a machine*); *cause and –*, Ursache und Wirkung; *carry into –*, ausführen, bewerkstelligen; zur Ausführung bringen, wahrmachen; *for –*, auf Effekt berechnet, um Eindruck zu machen; *give – to a th.*, einer S. Kraft *or* Wirkung verleihen, etwas in Kraft treten lassen, etwas verwirklichen; *have an – on*, wirken auf; *in –*, in der Tat, in Wirklichkeit; *of no –*, wirkungslos, ohne Erfolg; *take –*, in Kraft treten, Wirkung haben; *bring to –*, see *carry into –*; *to that –*, dementsprechend, diesbezüglich; *to this –*, in der Absicht, zu dem Ende; *to the – that*, dem Sinne nach; *to the following –*, folgenden Inhalts; *to good –*, erfolgreich, mit guter Wirkung; *to no –*, see *without –*; *to the same –*, in demselben Sinne, desselben Inhalts; *with telling –*, mit eindeutigem Erfolg; *without –*, vergeblich, umsonst. 2. *v.a.* bewirken, erwirken, verursachen; bewerkstelligen, ausführen; vollziehen, erledigen, besorgen, zuwegebringen, zustandebringen; *– a junction*, sich anschließen (*with* (*Dat.*)); *– an insurance policy*, eine Versicherung abschließen. **–ive,** 1. *adj.* wirkend; wirksam, wirkungsvoll, kräftig, effektvoll, eindrucksvoll; wirklich, tatsächlich; nutzbar (*Mech.*); diensttauglich, kampffähig; *–ive range*, der Wirkungsbereich, Schußbereich (*Artil.*); *–ive work*, die Nutzleistung. 2. *s.* (*usually pl.*) aktiver Soldat; der Effektivbestand, Istbestand (*Mil.*); das Barguthaben (*C.L.*). **–iveness,** *s.* die Wirksamkeit. **–s** [ɪˈfɛkts], *pl.* die Effekten. Aktiva, Vermögenswerte (*pl.*); das Guthaben, der Barbestand (*C.L.*); bewegliche Habe, bewegliches Eigentum. **–ual** [ɪˈfɛktjʊəl], *adj.* wirksam, kräftig, gültig; *be –ual*, wirken, Wirkung haben. **–uate** [ɪˈfɛktjʊeɪt], *v.a.* ausführen, bewerkstelligen, bewirken.

effemin–acy [ɪˈfɛmɪnəsɪ], *s.* die Verweichlichung, Weichlichkeit, unmännliches Benehmen *or* Wesen. **–ate** [ɪˈfɛmɪnɪt], *adj.* weibisch, weichlich, verweichlicht, verzärtelt.

efferent [ˈɛfərənt], *adj.* nach außen führend.

effervesc–e [ɛfəˈvɛs], *v.n.* brausen, wallen, schäumen, gären, moussieren, aufbrausen, aufwallen. **–ence** [–ns], *s.* das Aufbrausen, Schäumen. **–ent,** *adj.*, **–ing,** *adj.* (auf)brausend, moussierend, schäumend, Brause–.

effete [ɪˈfɪ:t], *adj.* abgenutzt; erschöpft, kraftlos, entkräftet.

efficac–ious [ɛfɪˈkeɪʃəs], *adj.* wirksam, kräftig. **–iousness, –y** [ˈɛfɪkəsɪ], *s.* die Wirksamkeit, Kraft, Wirkungskraft.

efficien–cy [ɪˈfɪʃənsɪ], *s.* die Arbeitsleistung, der Nutzeffekt, Wirkungsgrad (*Mach.*); die Leistungsfähigkeit, Wirksamkeit, Tüchtigkeit. **–t** [ɪˈfɪʃənt], *adj.* leistungsfähig, wirkungsfähig, tüchtig, brauchbar, wirksam, bewirkend.

effigy [ˈɛfɪdʒɪ], *s.* das Bild(nis), Abbild; *burn in –*, im Bilde verbrennen.

effloresce [ɛflɔ:ˈrɛs], *v.n.* aufblühen, ausblühen, ausschlagen, ausbrechen (*Bot.*); beschlagen, auswittern; Kristalle ansetzen (*Chem.*). **–nce** [–ns], *s.* die Blüte, das Aufblühen (*Bot.*); die Ausblühung, Auswitterung, der Ausschlag, Beschlag (*Chem.*). **–nt,** *adj.* (auf)blühend (*Bot.*); beschlagend, auswitternd (*Chem.*).

effluen–ce [ˈɛflʊəns], *s.* der Ausfluß, das Ausströmen. **–t,** 1. *adj.* ausströmend. 2. *s.* der Ausfluß, Abfluß, das Abwasser, Sielwasser.

effluvium [ɪˈflʊ:vɪəm], *s.* (*pl.* –a) die Ausdünstung.

efflux [ˈɛflʌks], *s.* das Ausfließen, Ausströmen, der Abfluß, Ausfluß, Auslauf, Austritt, Erguß, das Abwasser; (*fig.*) das Verfließen.

effort [ˈɛfət], *s.* die Anstrengung, Mühe, Bemühung, das Bestreben; (*coll.*) *a fine –*, eine gute Leistung; *make an –*, sich anstrengen; *make every –*, alles aufbieten, alle Kräfte anspannen; *with an –*, mühsam. **–less,** *adj.* ohne Anstrengung, mühelos.

effrontery [əˈfrʌntərɪ], *s.* die Frechheit, Unverschämtheit.

effulge [ɪˈfʌldʒ], *v.n.* strahlen. **–nce** [ɪˈfʌldʒəns], *s.* das (Aus)Strahlen, der Glanz, Schimmer. **–nt,** *adj.* strahlend, glänzend.

effus–e, 1. [ɪˈfjʊ:s], *adj.* ausgebreitet, sich ausbreitend (*Bot.*). 2. [ɪˈfjʊ:z] *v.a.* ausbreiten; ausgießen, hervorquellen lassen, verbreiten. **–ion** [–ˈfjʊ:ʒən], *s.* das Ausgießen, Vergießen; die Ausgießung, Ergießung, der Erguß, Verlust; (*fig.*) der Herzenserguß, die Überschwenglichkeit; *–ion of blood*, der Blutverlust; *–ion of the Holy Spirit*, die Ausgießung des heiligen Geistes. **–ive** [-sɪv], *adj.* (*fig.*) überschwenglich, übertrieben, herzlich; *–ive rock*, das Effusivgestein. **–iveness,** *s.* die Überschwenglichkeit.

eft [ɛft], *s.* der Wassermolch (*Zool.*).

eftsoon(s) [ɛftˈsʊ:n(z)], *adv.* (*archaic*, *Poet.*) bald nachher.

egad [ɪˈgæd], *int.* (*archaic*) wahrhaftig! meiner Treu!

egalitarian [ɪˈgælɪˈtɛ:ərɪən], *s.* der Gleichmacher.

[1]**egg** [ɛg], *s.* das Ei; (*sl.*) die Bombe (*Av.*); *addled –*, das Windei; *have all one's –s in one basket*, alles auf eine Karte setzen; *bad –*, faules Ei; (*fig.*) der Tunichtgut, Nichtsnutz; *hard* (*soft*) *boiled –*, hart (weich) gekochtes Ei; *like the curate's –*, teilweise gut; *fried –s*, Spiegeleier, Setzeier; (*sl.*) *good – !* glänzend; (*sl.*) *be on a good –*, glänzende Aussichten haben; *poached –s*, verlorene Eier; *rotten –s*, faule Eier; *scrambled –*, Rühreier; *as sure as –s are –s*, so sicher wie nur was; (*coll.*) *teach one's grandmother to suck –s*, Unnötiges erörtern; *white of –*, das Eiweiß; *yolk of –*, der Eidotter, das Eigelb. **––beater,** *s. see* **––whisk.** **––cup,** *s.* der Eierbecher. **––flip,** *s.* der Eierpunsch. **––nog,** *s. see* **––flip.** **––plant,** *s.* die Eierpflanze, Aubergine (*Bot.*). **––shaped,** *adj.* eiförmig. **––shell,** *s.* die Eierschale. **––timer,** *s.* die Eieruhr. **––whisk,** *s.* der Eierschlegel, Schlagbesen.

[2]**egg,** *v.a.*; *– on*, (auf)hetzen, anreizen, aufreizen, antreiben.

eglantine [ˈɛgləntaɪn], *s.* die Heckenrose, wilde Rose.

ego [ˈɛgoʊ], *s.* das Ich. **–centric,** *adj.* egozentrisch. **–ism** [–ɪzm], *s.* die Selbstsucht, Eigennützigkeit, der Egoismus. **–ist,** *s.* der Egoist. **–mania,** *s.* die Selbstgefälligkeit. **–tism** [–tɪzm], *s.* die Selbstgefälligkeit, der Eigendünkel; die Selbstüberhebung, Selbstbespiegelung, das Geltungsbedürfnis. **–tist,** *s.* der oft von sich selbst Redende. **–tistic(al)** [–ˈtɪstɪk(l)], *adj.* alles auf sich beziehend, oft von sich redend, selbstgefällig.

egregious [ɪˈgrɪ:dʒəs], *adj.* ungeheuer, ungeheuerlich, entsetzlich, unerhört.

egress [ˈɪ:grɛs], *s.* der Ausgang, Ausweg, Ausfluß (*of water*); Austritt (*Astr.*). **–ion** [–ʃən], *s.* der Ausgang, Austritt.

egret [ˈɛgrɛt], *s. see* **aigrette** (*Orn.*); die Samenkrone (*Bot.*).

eh [eɪ], *int.* nicht wahr? wie? was? nun?
eider–down [ˈaɪdədaʊn], *s.* Eiderdaunen (*pl.*); (*coll.*) (*–down quilt*) die Daunendecke. **––duck,** *s.* die Eidergans.
eidetic [aɪˈdetɪk], *adj.* anschaulich, wesensmäßig, eidetisch.
eight [eɪt], 1. *num. adj.* acht; *––hour day,* der Achtstundentag; *– times,* achtmal. 2. *s.* die Acht; der Achter (*boat*); die Achtermannschaft; *figure of –,* die Acht; (*sl.*) *have one over the –,* einen zu viel haben, betrunken sein. **–een** [eɪˈtiːn], 1. *num. adj.* achtzehn. 2. *s.* die Achtzehn. **–eenth,** 1. *num. adj.* achtzehnt. 2. *s.* das Achtzehntel. **–fold,** *adj.* achtfach. **–h** [eɪtθ], 1. *num. adj.* achte(r)(s). 2. *s.* das Achtel. **–hly,** *adv.* achtens. **–ieth** [ˈeɪtɪɪθ], 1. *adj.* achtzigst. 2. *s.* das Achtzigstel. **–ies** [ˈeɪtɪz], *pl.* die achtziger Jahre. **–y** [ˈeɪtɪ], 1. *num. adj.* achtzig. 2. *s.* die Achtzig.
eisteddfod [aɪˈstɛðfəd], *s.* walisisches Sängerfest.
either [ˈaɪðə], 1. *adj. & pron.* (irgend)eine(r)(s) von beiden; jede(r)(s), beide; *I did not see – of them,* ich sah keinen von beiden, ich sah beide nicht; *– answer is correct,* beide Antworten sind richtig; *– is correct,* beides ist richtig; *in – case,* in beiden Fällen; *– side,* eine der beiden Parteien (*persons*); *on – side,* auf beiden Seiten; *it can be done – way,* es kann auf die eine oder die andere Art gemacht werden. 2. *conj. entweder; – . . . or . . .,* entweder . . . oder; (*after neg.*) weder . . . noch; *I did not see – him or his son,* ich sah weder ihn noch seinen Sohn; *I did not see him nor his son –,* ich sah ihn nicht, und seinen Sohn auch nicht; *I shall not go –,* ich gehe auch nicht; *without gifts – of mind or of character,* sowohl ohne geistige wie charakterliche Begabung.
ejaculat–e [ɪːˈdʒækjuleɪt], *v.a.* ausstoßen, von sich geben. **–ion** [–ˈleɪʃən], *s.* das Ausstoßen; der Ausruf; das Stoßgebet, der Stoßseufzer. **–ory** [–lətərɪ], *adj.* ausstoßend, Ausstoß–; Stoß–, hastig.
eject [ɪːˈdʒɛkt], *v.a.* hinauswerfen, verstoßen, ausstoßen, vertreiben; exmittieren (*Law*); *– from office,* eines Amtes entsetzen. **–ion,** *s.* die Ausstoßung, Auswerfung, Absetzung (*from office*); Vertreibung (*from possession*). **–ment,** *s.* die Vertreibung, Exmittierung (*Law*). **–or,** *s.* der Vertreiber; die Ausstoßvorrichtung, der Ejektor, Ausblaseapparat (*Mach.*); Auswerfer (*of rifle, etc.*).
eke [ɪːk], 1. *v.a.*; *– out,* ergänzen, ausfüllen, verlängern; *– out a miserable existence,* sich kümmerlich durchschlagen. 2. *conj.* (*archaic*) auch.
elaborat–e 1. [ɪˈlæbəreɪt], *v.a.* (sorgsam) ausarbeiten, herausarbeiten. 2. [–rət], *adj.* sorgfältig ausgearbeitet; ausführlich, umständlich; kompliziert, kunstvoll, vollendet. **–ness,** *s.* sorgfältige Ausarbeitung, die Genauigkeit, Ausgefeiltheit. **–ion** [–ˈreɪʃən], *s.* die Ausarbeitung; Vervollkommnung.
élan [eˈlɑ̃ː], *s.* das Feuer, der Schwung, die Begeisterung.
eland [ˈɪːlænd], *s.* die Elenantilope.
elapse [ɪˈlæps], *v.n.* verfließen, verstreichen, vergehen (*of time*).
elastic [ɪˈlæstɪk], 1. *adj.* elastisch, bruchfest, dehnbar, federnd, spannkräftig; biegsam, geschmeidig; *– band,* das Gummi(band); *– conscience,* dehnbares Gewissen; *––sided boots,* Zugstiefel (*pl.*). 2. *s.* das Gummiband, der Gummizug. **–ity** [–ˈtɪsɪtɪ], *s.* die Elastizität, Bruchfestigkeit, Dehnbarkeit, Federkraft, Spannkraft, Springkraft, Schnellkraft.
elat–e [ɪˈleɪt], 1. *v.a.* erheben, ermutigen, stolz machen. 2. *adj. see* **–ed.** **–ed,** *adj.* erhoben, stolz (*at,* über (*Acc.*); *with,* von); freudig, übermütig, in gehobener Stimmung (über). **–er,** *s.* der Schnellkäfer (*Ent.*); Springfaden (*Bot.*). **–ion** [ɪˈleɪʃən], *s.* die Gehobenheit, der Stolz; die Begeisterung; freudige Stimmung.
elbow [ˈɛlboʊ], 1. *s.* der Ellbogen, Ellenbogen; die Krümmung, Biegung, Ecke, das Knie(stück), der Winkel (*Mach.*); *at one's –,* bei einem, nahe, bei der Hand; *out at –s,* zerlumpt, zerrissen, schäbig; *be up to the –s,* eifrig beschäftigt sein; (*sl.*) *lift the –,* unmäßig trinken. 2. *v.a.* mit dem Ellbogen stoßen, drängen, schieben; *– s.o. out,* einen beiseite drängen, einen verdrängen aus; *– one's way through,* sich drängen durch. **––chair,** *s.* der Armstuhl, Lehnstuhl. (*coll.*) **––grease,** *s.* die Kraft, Energie. **––rest,** *s.* die Armstütze. **––room,** *s.* (*fig.*) die Bewegungsfreiheit, der Spielraum.
eld [ɛld], *s.* (*archaic, Poet.*) das Alter, alte Zeit.
[1]**elder** [ˈɛldə], *s.* (schwarzer) Holunder. **–berry,** *s.* die Holunderbeere.
[2]**eld–er,** 1. *attrib. adj.* älter. 2. *s.* (Kirchen)Älteste(r), *m.*; (*usually pl.*) ältere Person; *my –ers,* ältere Leute als ich; *–ers and betters,* Respektspersonen (*pl.*). **–erly,** *adj.* ältlich; *–erly lady,* ältere Dame. **–ership,** *s.* das Ältestenamt (*Eccl.*). **–est** [ˈɛldəst], *attrib. adj.* ältest, erstgeboren.
elect [ɪˈlɛkt], 1. *v.a.* (aus)wählen, (er)wählen (*to,* zu); auserwählen (*Theol.*); sich entschließen, für richtig halten. 2. *adj.* (aus)erwählt, auserlesen (*Theol.*); designiert; *the –,* die Auserwählten; *bishop –,* designierter Bischof; *bride –,* die Verlobte, Braut. **–ion** [ɪˈlɛkʃən], *s.* die Erwählung, Wahl; Gnadenwahl (*Theol.*). **–ioneer** [–ˈnɪə], *v.n.* um Wahlstimmen werben, Wahlagitation treiben. **–ioneering** [–ˈnɪərɪŋ], *s.* die Wahlagitation; Wahlumtriebe (*pl.*). **–ive** [ɪˈlɛktɪv], *adj.* wählend, Wahl–; durch Wahl, gewählt; wahlberechtigt; *–ive affinity,* die Wahlverwandtschaft. **–or** [ɪˈlɛktə], *s.* (stimmberechtigter) Wähler, der Wahlmann; Kurfürst. **–oral** [–tərəl], *adj.* Wahl–, Wähler–; kurfürstlich; *–oral reform,* die Wahlreform; *–oral roll,* die Wählerliste. **–orate** [–tərɪt], *s.* die Kurwürde; der Kurfürstenstand, das Kurfürstentum; die Wählerschaft (*Parl.*). **–ress,** *s.* die Kurfürstin; weiblicher Wähler.
electri–c [ɪˈlɛktrɪk], 1. *adj.* elektrisch; (*fig.*) wie elektrisiert; *–c battery,* elektrische Batterie; *–c blue,* stahlblau; *–c charge,* elektrische Ladung; *–c current,* elektrischer Strom; *–c eel,* der Zitteraal (*Ichth.*); *–c light,* elektrisches Licht; *–c machine,* die Elektrisiermaschine; *–c railway,* elektrische Eisenbahn; *–c ray,* der Zitterroche (*Ichth.*); *–c shock,* elektrischer Schlag. **–cal,** *adj.* Elektrizitäts–, Elektro–; (*fig.*) elektrisiert; *–cal engineer,* der Elektrotechniker; *–cal engineering,* die Elektrotechnik. **–cian** [ɪlɛkˈtrɪʃən], *s.* der Elektriker, Elektrotechniker. **–city** [–sɪtɪ], *s.* die Elektrizität. **–fication** [–fɪˈkeɪʃən], *s.* die Elektrisierung. **–fy** [ɪˈlɛktrɪfaɪ], *v.a.* elektrifizieren, elektrisieren, elektrisch laden; (*fig.*) entflammen, begeistern.
electro––chemistry [ɪlɛktroˈkɛmɪstrɪ], *s.* die Elektrochemie. **–cute** [ɪˈlɛktrəkjuːt], *v.a.* durch elektrischen Strom töten *or* hinrichten. **–cution** [–ˈkjuːʃən], *s.* die Hinrichtung *or* tödlicher Unfall durch Elektrizität. **–de** [ɪˈlɛktroʊd], *s.* die Elektrode. **––dynamics** [ɪlɛktrodaɪˈnæmɪks], *s.* die Elektrodynamik. **–lier** [ɪlɛktrəˈlɪə], *s.* elektrischer Kronleuchter. **–lysis** [ɪlɛkˈtrɔlɪsɪs], *s.* die Elektrolyse (*Chem.*). **–lyte** [ɪˈlɛktrəlaɪt], *s.* der Elektrolyt. **–lytic,** *adj.* elektrolytisch. **––magnet** [ɪlɛktroˈmægnɪt], *s.* der Elektromagnet. **–magnetic,** *adj.* elektromagnetisch. **––magnetism,** *s.* der Elektromagnetismus. **–n** [ɪˈlɛktrən], *s.* das Elektron. **–nic,** *adj.* Elektronen–. **–plate** [ɪˈlɛktrəpleɪt], 1. *v.a.* galvanisch versilbern. 2. *s.* (galvanisch) versilberte Ware. **–scope** [–skoʊp], *s.* das Elektroskop. **–statics,** *s.* die Elektrostatik. **–therapy** [ɪlɛktrəˈθɛrəpɪ], *s.* die Elektrotherapie. **–type** [ɪˈlɛktrətaɪp], *s.* galvanoplastischer Abdruck, die Vervielfältigung; (*also* **–typing**) die Galvanotypie.
electrum [ɪˈlɛktrəm], *s.* die Goldsilberlegierung.
electuary [ɪˈlɛktjʊərɪ], *s.* die Latwerge (*Pharm.*).
eleemosynary [ɛlɪɪːˈmɔsɪnərɪ], *adj.* Almosen–, Wohltätigkeits–.
elegan–ce [ˈɛlɪgəns], *s.* geschmackvolle Erscheinung, die Zierlichkeit, Anmut, Feinheit, Eleganz; (*also* **–cy**) die Vornehmheit, Gewähltheit, Annehmlichkeit. **–t** [ˈɛlɪgənt], *adj.* fein, zierlich, anmutig, gefällig, gewählt, niedlich, elegant, geschmackvoll.
eleg–iac [ɛlɪˈdʒaɪək], 1. *adj.* elegisch; (*fig.*) klagend. 2. *s.* das Distichon. **–iacs,** *pl.* elegische Verse, Distichen (*pl.*). **–ize** [ˈɛlɪdʒaɪz], *v.a.* in Elegien besingen, eine Elegie schreiben auf. **–y** [ˈɛlɪdʒɪ], *s.* die Elegie, das Klagelied, Trauergedicht.
element [ˈɛlɪmənt], *s.* der Urstoff, Grundstoff; (Grund)Bestandteil; das Element; das (Lebens)-Element, gewohnte Umgebung; (*fig.*) das Körnchen, Bißchen; *be in one's –,* in seinem Element sein, sich

wohl fühlen; *be out of one's* –, sich unglücklich *or* unbehaglich fühlen; *an – of truth*, ein Körnchen Wahrheit. **-al** [ɛlɪˈmɛntl], *adj.* elementar, die Elemente betreffend, urkräftig, Ur–; *-al power*, die Naturgewalt; *-al spirits*, Elementargeister (*pl.*). **-ary** [—ˈmentərɪ], *adj.* Elementar–, Anfangs–, Einführungs–, Grund–; einfach, rudimentär; *-ary education*, das Volksschulwesen; *-ary school*, die Grundschule, Volksschule. **-s**, *pl.* die Grundlagen, Grundzüge, Anfangsgründe, Elemente (*pl.*); Naturgewalten, Wetterverhältnisse (*pl.*), das Wetter; Brot und Wein (*Eccl.*).

elenchus [ɪˈlɛŋkəs], *s.* der Gegenbeweis, die Widerlegung.

elephant [ˈɛlɪfənt], *s.* der Elefant; das Papierformat (28 in. × 23 in.); *white* –, kostspieliger *or* lästiger Besitz. **-iasis** [ɛlɪfænˈtaɪəsɪs], *s.* die Elefantiasis. **-ine** [ɛlɪˈfæntaɪn], *adj.* Elefanten–; (*fig.*) elefantenhaft, ungeheuer, plump, schwerfällig, unbeholfen.

elevat-e [ˈɛlɪveɪt], I. *v.a.* aufheben, erhöhen, emporheben; die Höhenrichtung geben (*Dat.*) (*Artil.*); erheben (*a p. to a position*); heben, veredeln (*the mind, etc.*); aufmuntern, beleben, erheitern (*the spirits, etc.*); *-e the voice*, lauter sprechen, die Stimme heben. 2. *v.n.* Erhöhung nehmen (*Artil.*). **-ed**, *adj.* hoch, erhaben, edel; *-ed with*, erhoben von; *-ed railway*, die Hochbahn; *be -ed with wine*, angeheitert *or* weinselig sein. **-ing**, *adj.* erhebend. **-ion** [–ˈveɪʃən], *s.* das Emporheben, Hochheben; die Erhebung, Erhöhung, Anhöhe, Höhe; Erhabenheit, Vornehmheit, Hoheit, Würde; der Aufriß, die Vorderansicht (*Arch., etc.*); Höhe (*Astr.*); der Erhöhungswinkel, Aufsatzwinkel, Visierwinkel, die Höhenrichtung, Richthöhe (*Artil.*); *high -ion fire*, das Steilfeuer (*Artil.*); *-ion of the pole*, die Polhöhe; *sectional -ion*, der Längsschnitt, Querschnitt; *side -ion*, die Seitenansicht. **-or**, *s.* der Hebemuskel (*Anat.*); Wurzelheber (*Dentistry*); Aufzug, das Hebewerk (*Mach.*); (*Amer.*) der Aufzug, Fahrstuhl; (*Amer.*) Getreidespeicher; das Höhensteuer, Höhenruder (*Av.*); *-or cage*, der Förderkorb (*Min.*). **-ory** [–vətərɪ], *adj.* emporhebend, Hebe–.

eleven [ɪˈlɛvn], I. *num. adj.* elf. 2. *s.* die Elf; Elfermannschaft (*Sport*); *half-past* –, halb zwölf. **-th**, I. *num. adj.* elft; *at the -th hour*, in zwölfter Stunde. 2. *s.* das Elftel.

elf [ɛlf], *s.* (*pl.* elves) der Elf, die Elfe, der Kobold; Zwerg. **-in**, I. *adj.* Zwerg–, Elfen–. 2. *s.* der Zwerg, Elf. **-ish**, *adj.* elfisch, schalkhaft, boshaft. **--locks**, *pl.* der Weichselzopf. verfilztes Haar. **--struck**, *adj.* verhext.

elicit [ɪˈlɪsɪt], *v.a.* herausholen, hervorlocken, herausbekommen, entlocken, ans Licht bringen. **-ation** [–ˈteɪʃən], *s.* das Herauslocken, die Auslösung.

elide [ɪˈlaɪd], *v.a.* elidieren (*Gram.*).

eligib-ility [ɛlɪdʒəˈbɪlɪtɪ], *s.* die Wählbarkeit, Qualifiziertheit, Qualifikation. **-le** [ˈɛlɪdʒəbl], *adj.* wählbar, passend, annehmbar, wünschenswert; (*coll.*) heiratsfähig.

eliminat-e [ɪˈlɪmɪneɪt], *v.a.* ausstoßen, ausschließen, entfernen, entziehen, aussondern, ausscheiden, abscheiden; eliminieren (*Math.*). **-ion** [–ˈneɪʃən], *s.* die Ausstoßung, Ausschaltung, Ausscheidung, Aussonderung, Wegschaffung, das Entfernen; die Elimination (*Math.*). **-or**, *s.* der Sperrkreis, Siebkreis (*Rad.*).

elision [ɪˈlɪʒən], *s.* die Ausstoßung eines Vokals, Elision (*Gram.*).

élite [eˈlɪ:t], *s.* die Elite, das Beste; die Kerntruppe (*Mil.*); die Führerschicht (*of society*).

elixir [ɪˈlɪksə], *s.* der Zaubertrank, das Elixier; der Heiltrank; (*fig.*) die Quintessenz, der Kern.

elk [ɛlk], *s.* der Elch, das Elentier.

ell [ɛl], *s.* die Elle; (*Prov.*) *give him an inch and he'll take an* –, gib ihm den kleinen Finger, so nimmt er die ganze Hand.

ellip-se [ɪˈlɪps], *s.* die Ellipse (*Math.*). **-sis** [ɪˈlɪpsɪs], *s.* (*pl.* -ses [–sɪ:z]) die Ellipse (*Gram.*). **-soid** [–sɔɪd] ,*s.* das Ellipsoid (*Math.*). **-tic(al)** [ɪˈlɪptɪk(l)], *adj.* elliptisch, Ellipsen– (*Math.*). **-tical**, *adj.* elliptisch, unvollständig (*Gram.*).

elm [ɛlm], *s.*, **--tree**, *s.* die Ulme, Rüster.

elocution [ɛləˈkjʊ:ʃən], *s.* der Vortrag, die Vortragskunst; – *classes*, Vortragsübungen. **-ary** [–ərɪ], *adj.* Vortrag–, rednerisch. **-ist**, *s.* der Vortragskünstler, Redekünstler.

elongat-e [ˈɪ:lɔŋgeɪt], I. *v.a.* verlängern, ausdehnen. 2. *adj.* zugespitzt, länglich (*Bot.*). **-ed**, *adj.* verlängert. **-ion** [–ˈgeɪʃən], *s.* die Verlängerung, Ausdehnung; Ausweichung (*of pendulum*); der Winkelabstand (*Astr.*).

elope [ɪˈloʊp], *v.n.* durchgehen (*with a lover*), entlaufen (*from* (*Dat.*)); *he -d with her*, er entführte sie. **-ment**, *s.* das Entlaufen.

eloquen-ce [ˈɛlokwəns], *s.* die Beredtheit, Beredsamkeit, der Redefluß. **-t** [–t], *adj.* beredt, beredsam, redegewandt; (*fig.*) ausdrucksvoll, sprechend (*as eyes, etc.*); *be – of*, deutlich zum Ausdruck bringen.

else [ɛls], I. *adv.* sonst, außerdem, weiter; *anyone* –, irgend ein anderer; *anyone – ?* sonst noch jemand? *anything* –, irgend etwas anderes; *anything – ?* sonst noch etwas? *no one* –, sonst niemand, kein anderer, niemand anders; *nothing* –, sonst nichts; *nowhere* –, sonst nirgends; *something* –, etwas anderes; *somewhere* –, sonst irgendwo, (irgend)wo anders, anderswo; *what – ?* was sonst (noch)? was anderes? *where – ?* wo anders? wo sonst? *who – ?* wer sonst? wer anders? wer weiter? 2. *conj.* sonst, wo nicht, wenn nicht. **-where**, *adv.* sonstwo, anderswo, anderwärts, anderswohin.

elucidat-e [ɪˈlʊ:sɪdeɪt], *v.a.* aufhellen, aufklären; erläutern. **-ion** [–ˈdeɪʃən], *s.* die Erläuterung, Erklärung; Klarstellung, Aufklärung, der Aufschluß. **-ory** [–dətərɪ], *adj.* aufklärend, erläuternd, aufhellend.

elu-de [ɪˈljʊ:d], *v.a.* ausweichen, entgehen (*Dat.*); sich entziehen (*Dat.*); umgehen, vermeiden (*Acc.*); sich entziehen (*Dat.*) (*the understanding, etc.*). **-sion** [ɪˈljʊ:ʒən], *s.* die Umgehung, das Entweichen, Ausweichen. **-sive** [–sɪv], *adj.* ausweichend; (*fig.*) täuschend, schwer faßbar. **-sory** [–sərɪ], *adj.* trügerisch; illusorisch.

elutriat-e [ɪˈljʊ:trɪeɪt], *v.a.* abklären, (ab)schlämmen, abschwemmen, abseihen. **-ion**, *s.* die Abklärung, Schlämmung.

elvish [ˈɛlvɪʃ], *adj. see* **elfish.**

elysi-an [ɛˈlɪzɪən], *adj.* elysisch; (*fig.*) wonnig, himmlisch. **-um** [ɛˈlɪzɪəm], *s.* das Paradies, Elysium.

elzevir [ˈɛlzɪvə], *s.* die Elzevirschrift (*Typ.*).

em [ɛm], *s.* die Einheit (*Typ.*).

emaciat-e [ɪˈmeɪʃɪeɪt], *v.a.* abzehren, ausmerzen, abmagern erschöpfen (*soil*). **-ion** [–ˈeɪʃən], *s.* die Abmagerung, Abzehrung, Auszehrung.

emanat-e [ˈɛməneɪt], *v.n.* ausströmen, ausfließen, ausstrahlen (*from*, von, aus); (*fig.*) herrühren, ausgehen (*from*, von). **-ion** [–ˈneɪʃən], *s.* das Ausströmen, die Ausströmung, Ausstrahlung, Ausdünstung, der Ausfluß, die Emanation (*Phys.*); (*fig.*) Offenbarung.

emancipat-e [ɪˈmænsɪpeɪt], *v.a.* freigeben, freilassen, befreien. **-ed**, *adj.* frei. **-ion** [–ˈpeɪʃən], *s.* die Freilassung; Befreiung, Emanzipation, Gleichstellung (*of women*).

emasculat-e, I. [ɪ:ˈmæskjʊlɪt], *adj.* entmannt, kastriert; (*fig.*) unmännlich, weibisch. 2. [–leɪt], *v.a.* entmannen, kastrieren; (*fig.*) schwächen, verweichlichen. **-ion** [–ˈleɪʃən], *s.* die Entmannung; (*fig.*) Verweichlichung, Schwächung; Verstümmelung (*as a book*).

embalm [ɪmˈbɑ:m], *v.a.* salben, einbalsamieren; (*fig.*) sorgsam bewahren, erhalten; (*fig.*) *be -ed in*, fortleben in (*Dat.*). **-ment**, *s.* die Einbalsamierung.

embank [ɪmˈbæŋk], *v.a.* eindeichen, eindämmen. **-ment** [–mənt], *s.* die Eindeichung, Aufdämmung, Eindämmung; der Deich, Bahndamm (*Railw.*); die Uferanlage; *Thames -ment*, der Themsekai.

embargo [ɛmˈbɑ:goʊ], I. *s.* die Beschlagnahme, der Arrest, das Embargo (*on* (*Gen.*)), die Handelssperre, das Verbot (*on*, von); *lay an – on*, Beschlag legen auf, sperren; *under* –, unter Beschlag. 2. *v.a.* sperren; unter Beschlag legen, in Beschlag nehmen.

embark [ɪmˈbɑ:k], I. *v.a.* einschiffen (*persons*), verladen (*goods*). 2. *v.n.* sich einschiffen; (*fig.*) – *in*, sich einlassen in *or* auf (*Acc.*); – *on*, beginnen. **-ation** [–ˈkeɪʃən], *s.* die Einschiffung; Verladung.

embarrass [ɪm'bærəs], *v.a.* verwirren; in Verlegenheit setzen (*a p.*); erschweren, hindern (*movement*); verwickeln. **-ed,** *adj.* verlegen, bestürzt; in Geldverlegenheit; verwickelt; behindert. **-ing,** *adj.* ungelegen, unbequem, befremdlich. **-ment,** *s.* die Verlegenheit, Verwirrung; das Hindernis, die Schwierigkeit, Störung; Geldverlegenheit.
embassy ['ɛmbəsɪ], *s.* die Botschaft, Gesandtschaft.
¹**embattle** [ɪm'bætl], *v.a.* in Schlachtordnung aufstellen.
²**embattle,** *v.a.* mit Zinnen *or* Schießscharten versehen.
embed [ɪm'bɛd], *v.a.* betten, einbetten, einschließen, einmauern, eingraben, verankern; *be -ed in,* lagern in, vergraben in.
embellish [ɪm'bɛlɪʃ], *v.a.* verschöne(r)n, schmücken; (*fig.*) ausschmücken. **-ment,** *s.* die Verschönerung, Verzierung, Ausschmückung.
¹**ember** ['ɛmbə], *s.* (*usually pl.*) glimmende Kohlen (*pl.*), glühende Asche; (*fig.*) Funken (*pl.*).
²**ember-,** (*in compounds*) **--days,** *pl.* der Quatember. **--goose,** *s.* die Imbergans, der Eistaucher (*Orn.*). **--week,** *s.* die Quatemberwoche.
embezzle [ɪm'bɛzl], *v.a.* veruntreuen, unterschlagen. **-ment,** *s.* die Veruntreuung, Unterschlagung. **-r,** *s.* der Veruntreuer.
embitter [ɪm'bɪtə], *v.a.* verbittern; erbittern (*a p.*). **-ment,** *s.* die Verbitterung.
emblazon [ɪm'bleɪzən], *v.a.* mit Wappenbild bemalen, blasonieren; (*fig.*) feiern, verherrlichen, ausposaunen. **-ment,** *s.* das Bemalen mit Wappenbildern; der Wappenschmuck.
emblem ['ɛmbləm], *s.* das Sinnbild, Symbol, Wahrzeichen, Abzeichen, Erkennungszeichen, Emblem. **-atic(al)** [-'mætɪk(l)], *adj.* sinnbildlich; *be -atic of,* versinnbildlichen. **-atize** [ɛm'blɛmətaɪz], *v.a.* sinnbildlich darstellen.
emblement, ['ɛmblmənt] *s.* die Ernte, der Ernteertrag.
embod-iment [ɪm'bɔdɪmənt], *s.* die Verkörperung, Darstellung; das Verkörpern. **-y** [ɪm'bɔdɪ], *v.a.* verkörpern, zum Ausdruck bringen, darstellen, versinnbildlichen; einverleiben, aufnehmen; in sich vereinigen, umfassen, einschließen.
embolden [ɪm'bouldən], *v.a.* kühn machen, ermutigen.
embolism ['ɛmbəlɪzm], *s.* die Embolie (*Path.*).
embonpoint ['ɑ̃:bɔ̃pwɛ̃], *s.* die Beleibtheit, Körperfülle.
embosom [ɪm'bʊzəm], *v.a.* ins Herz schließen, ans Herz drücken; (*fig.*) einhüllen, einschließen.
emboss [ɪm'bɔs], *v.a.* in erhabener Arbeit anfertigen *or* ausarbeiten, mit erhabener Arbeit schmücken; mit dem Hammer treiben, prägen, bossieren; gaufrieren. **-ed** [-t], *adj.* getrieben, narbig, erhaben gearbeitet, gaufriert; *-ed leather,* genarbtes Leder; *-ed printing,* der Blindendruck; *-ed wallpaper,* die Relieftapete. **-ing,** *s.* erhabene Arbeit, die Bossierarbeit. **-ing-press,** *s.* die Prägepresse.
embouchure [ɔmbu'ʃuə], *s.* die Mündung; das Mundstück (*Mus.*).
embowel [ɪm'bauəl], *v.a.* ausweiden.
embower [ɪm'bauə], *v.a.* (wie) in einer Laube einschließen.
embrace [ɪm'breɪs], 1. *v.a.* umarmen, umfassen, umschließen; annehmen (*a religion*), einschlagen (*a career*), ergreifen (*an opportunity*); sich zu eigen machen, in sich aufnehmen, in sich begreifen, einschließen, zusammenfassen. 2. *v.n.* sich umarmen. 3. *s.* die Umarmung.
embranchment [ɪm'brɑntʃmənt], *s.* die Verzweigung, Gabelung.
embrasure [ɪm'breɪʒə], *s.* die Fenstervertiefung, Türvertiefung, Leibung (*Arch.*), Schießscharte, (*Fort.*).
embrocat-e ['ɛmbrokeɪt], *v.a.* einreiben. **-ion** [-'keɪʃən], *s.* das Einreibemittel (*Pharm.*).
embroider [ɪm'brɔɪdə], *v.a.* sticken (*a design*), mit Stickerei schmücken, besticken (*material, etc.*); (*fig.*) ausschmücken. **-y** [-rɪ], *s.* das Sticken, die Stickerei; *do -y,* sticken; *openwork -y,* durchbrochene Stickerei. **-y-cotton,** *s.* das Stickgarn. **-y-frame,** *s.* der Stickrahmen.
embroil [ɪm'brɔɪl], *v.a.* verwickeln, verwirren. **-ment,** *s.* die Verwick(e)lung, Verwirrung.
embryo ['ɛmbrɪou], *s.* der Fruchtkeim, Embryo; (*fig.*) der Keim; *in* –, im Keim, im Werden, im Entstehen. **-nic** [-'ɔnɪk], *adj.* Embryo–; (*fig.*) unentwickelt.
emend [ɪ'mɛnd], *v.a.* verbessern, berichtigen, korrigieren. **-ation** [ɪ:mɛn'deɪʃən], *s.* die Textverbesserung, Berichtigung. **-ator** ['ɪ:mɛndeɪtə], *s.* der Textverbesserer, Berichtiger. **-atory** [ɪ'mɛndətərɪ], *adj.* textverbessernd, Verbesserungs–.
emerald ['ɛmərəld], 1. *s.* der Smaragd; die Smaragdfarbe; ein englischer Druckschriftsgrad (*Typ.*). 2. *adj.* smaragdfarben, smaragdgrün.
emerge [ɪ'mə:dʒ], *v.n.* herauskommen, hervorgehen, hervortreten, zum Vorschein kommen, in Erscheinung treten, auftreten, entstehen, auftauchen, emporkommen; sich erheben (*from,* aus). **-nce,** *s.* das Sichtbarwerden, Hervortreten. **-ncy** [ɪ'mə:dʒənsɪ], *s.* unerwartetes Ereignis, die Notlage, der Notfall, Notstand, Ernstfall; *in case of* or *in an -ncy,* im Notfalle; *-ncy decree,* die Notverordnung; *-ncy exit,* der Notausgang; *-ncy landing,* die Notlandung (*Av.*); *-ncy ration,* eiserne Ration; *state of -ncy,* der Ausnahmezustand, Notstand. **-nt** [ɪ'mə:dʒənt], *adj.* auftauchend, hervorgehend, emporkommend.
emeritus [ɪ:'mɛrɪtəs], *adj.* emeritiert.
emersion [ɪ'mə:ʃən], *s.* das Auftauchen; der Austritt (*Astr.*).
emery ['ɛmərɪ], *s.* der Schmirgel, Korund. **--cloth,** das Schmirgelleinen. **--paper,** *s.* das Schmirgelpapier. **--wheel,** *s.* die Schmirgelscheibe.
emetic [ɪ'mɛtɪk], 1. *adj.* Erbrechen bewirkend. 2. *s.* das Brechmittel.
emigra-nt ['ɛmɪgrənt], 1. *adj.* auswandernd. 2. *s.* der Auswanderer. **-te** [-greɪt], *v.n.* auswandern. **-tion** [-'greɪʃən], *s.* die Auswanderung.
eminen-ce ['ɛmɪnəns], *s.* die Erhöhung, Anhöhe, Höhe; hohe Stellung, hoher Rang, die Auszeichnung, der Ruhm, Vorrang, Vorzug; die Eminenz (*as title*). **-t** [-t], *adj.* hervorragend, erhaben; berühmt, ausgezeichnet (*in, for,* durch). **-tly,** *adv.* in hohem Maße, ganz besonders, ausnehmend.
emiss-ary ['ɛmɪsərɪ], *s.* der Bote, Abgesandte(r), *m.* **-ion** [ɪ'mɪʃən], *s.* das Aussenden, Ausfließen; die Ausströmung, (Aus)Strahlung, der Ausfluß; die Ausgabe, Emission (*of paper money, etc.*). **-ive,** *adj.* ausstrahlend.
emit [ɪ'mɪt], *v.a.* ausstrahlen, ausströmen, aussenden, auswerfen, von sich geben; ausgeben, in Umlauf setzen, emittieren; – *an opinion,* eine Meinung von sich geben.
emmet ['ɛmɪt], *s.* die Ameise.
emollient [ɪ'mɔlɪənt], 1. *adj.* erweichend. 2. *s.* erweichendes Mittel.
emolument [ɪ'mɔljumənt], *s.* (*often pl.*) Nebeneinkünfte, Nebenbezüge (*pl.*).
emoti-on [ɪ'mouʃən], *s.* die Gemütsbewegung, Erregung, Rührung, das Gefühl (*Psych.*). **-onal,** *adj.* gefühlsmäßig, Gefühls–, Gemüts–; leicht erregbar, gerührt; rührend, herzbewegend. **-onalism,** *s.* die Gefühlsseligkeit. **-onality,** *s.* die Erregbarkeit. **-ve,** *adj.* gefühlsmäßig, Gefühls–.
empanel [ɪm'pænl], *v.a.* ernennen, eintragen; zusammenrufen (*a jury*).
empathy ['ɛmpəθɪ], *s.* die Einfühlung (*Psych.*).
empennage ['ɛmpəneɪdʒ], *s.* das Leitwerk (*Av.*).
emperor ['ɛmpərə], *s.* der Kaiser. – *moth,* Kleines Nachtpfauenauge (*Ent.*). *Purple* –, Großer Schillerfalter (*Ent.*).
empha-sis ['ɛmfəsɪs], *s.* die Betonung, der Akzent; Nachdruck, die Emphase; (*fig.*) der Schwerpunkt. **-size** [-saɪz], *v.a.* betonen, nachdrücklich sagen; (*fig.*) hervorheben, unterstreichen. **-tic** [ɪm'fætɪk], *adj.* nachdrücklich, betont, eindringlich, ausdrücklich.
emphysema [ɛmfɪ'sɪ:mə], *s.* das Emphysem (*Path.*).
empire ['ɛmpaɪe], *s.* das Reich, Kaiserreich; die Herrschaft, Gewalt (*over,* über); *British* –, britisches Weltreich. **--***Day,* *s.* der Reichsfeiertag. – *furniture,* das Empiremöbel. – *produce,* Erzeugnisse des britischen Weltreiches. – *trade,* der Handel innerhalb des britischen Weltreiches.

empiric [ɛmˈpɪrɪk], 1. *adj.*, **-al**, *adj.* auf Erfahrung gegründet, erfahrungsmäßig, empirisch. 2. *s.*, **-ist** [-rɪsɪst], *s.* der Empiriker (*Phil.*); Quacksalber. **-ism** [-rɪsɪzm], *s.* Empirismus, die Quacksalberei.

emplacement [ɛmˈpleɪsmənt], *s.* der Geschützstand; die Bettung.

employ [ɪmˈplɔɪ], 1. *v.a.* gebrauchen, benutzen, anwenden, verwenden, einsetzen (*things*); beschäftigen, anstellen (*persons*); – *o.s.*, sich beschäftigen (*with*, mit *or* in); *be -ed*, angestellt sein (*with*, bei); beschäftigt sein (*on*, an *or* mit; *in doing*, zu tun). 2. *s.* die Beschäftigung; *in s.o.'s* –, bei einem angestellt. **-able**, *adj.* anwendbar, brauchbar. **-é** [ɔmˈplɔɪeɪ], *s.*, **-ee** [-iː], *s.* Angestellte(r), *m.*, der Arbeitnehmer. **-er**, *s.* der Arbeitgeber, Auftraggeber, Dienstherr, Prinzipal. **-ment**, *s.* die Beschäftigung, Arbeit, das Geschäft, der Dienst, Beruf, die Stellung; Anwendung, Verwendung, der Einsatz, Gebrauch; *be in -ment*, in Stellung sein; *be thrown out of -ment*, arbeitslos werden. **-ment-exchange**, *s.* der Arbeitsnachweis.

emporium [ɛmˈpɔːrɪəm], *s.* der Stapelplatz, Handelsplatz; das Warenhaus; die Niederlage, das Magazin.

empower [ɪmˈpaʊə], *v.a.* ermächtigen, bevollmächtigen, befähigen; *be -ed to*, befugt sein zu.

empress [ˈɛmprɪs], *s.* die Kaiserin.

emprise [ɛmˈpraɪz], *s.* (*archaic & Poet.*) ritterliches *or* abenteuerliches Unternehmen, das Wagnis.

empt-iness [ˈɛmptɪnɪs], *s.* die Leere, Leerheit; (*fig.*) Nichtigkeit, Hohlheit, Wertlosigkeit. **-y** [ˈɛmptɪ], 1. *adj.* leer (*of*, an (*Dat.*)), ausgeleert; unbesetzt, unbewohnt; (*fig.*) eitel, nichtig, nichtssagend, hohl; (*coll.*) hungrig, nüchtern; *-y room*, leerstehendes Zimmer; *on an -y stomach*, nüchtern; *-y weight*, das Eigengewicht. 2. *v.a.* leeren, entleeren, ausleeren; abfüllen, ablassen (*boiler*). 3. *v.n.* sich leeren, leer werden; sich ergießen, münden (*as a river*). 4. *s.* (*usually pl.*) leere Flasche, leeres Faß; das Leergut, die Emballagen (*C.L.*); abgeschossene Hülse (*Artil.*); das Leermaterial (*Railw.*). **-y-handed**, *adj.* mit leeren Händen. **-y-headed**, *adj.* hohlköpfig.

empyema [ɛmpɪˈiːmə], *s.* das Empyem (*Med.*).

empyrea-l [ɛmpɪˈrɪːəl], *adj. see* **-n**, 1. **-n**, 1. *adj.* empyreisch, himmlisch. 2. *s.* der Feuerhimmel, Lichthimmel.

empyreumatic [ɛmpɪruːˈmætɪk], *adj.* brenzlich.

emu [ˈiːmjuː], *s.* der Emu, australischer Kasuar (*Orn.*).

emul-ate [ˈɛmjuleɪt], *v.a.* wetteifern (mit), nacheifern (*Dat.*). **-ation** [-ˈleɪʃən], *s.* der Wetteifer, die Nacheiferung; *in -ation of a p.*, einem nacheifernd. **-ative**, *adj.*, **-ous** [-ləs], *adj.* wetteifernd (*of*, mit), nacheifernd (*Dat.*), eifersüchtig (auf).

emulsi-fiable [ɪˈmʌlsɪfaɪəbl], *adj.* emulgierbar. **-fication** [-fɪˈkeɪfən], *s.* die Emulsionsbildung. **-fier**, *s.* der Emulgator, das Emulgiermittel. **-fy** [ɪˈmʌlsɪfaɪ], *v.a.* emulgieren, **-on** [-ʃən], *s.* die Emulsion. **-ve**, *adj.* emulsionsbildend.

emunctory [ɪˈmʌŋktərɪ], 1. *s.* das Absonderungsorgan, Ausscheidungsorgan (*Anat.*). 2. *adj.* Ausscheidungs-.

enable [ɪˈneɪbl], *v.a.* befähigen, in den Stand setzen, ermöglichen, ermächtigen; *be -d*, imstande sein.

enact [ɪˈnækt], *v.a.* verordnen, verfügen, beschließen; erlassen (*a law*); Gesetzeskraft verleihen (*Dat.*); spielen, darstellen (*Theat.*); *be -ed*, sich abspielen, vor sich gehen (*of events*). **-ion**, *s.* die Verfügung, Verordnung. **-ive**, *adj.* Verfügungs-. **-ment**, *s.* gesetzliche Verfügung, die Verordnung; Erhebung zum Gesetz.

enamel [ɪˈnæməl], 1. *s.* das Email, die Emaille, Emailfarbe, der Lack, Schmelz; Zahnschmelz; die Schmelze, Glasur. 2. *v.a.* emaillieren, mit Email *or* Schmelz überziehen; glasieren, firnissen, lackieren; überschmelzen, in Email arbeiten *or* malen; (*fig.*) bunt machen, schmücken. **-ler**, *s.* der Emailleur, Schmelzarbeiter. **-ling**, *s.* das Emaillieren, die Lackierung. **--painting**, *s.* die Emailmalerei.

enamour [ɪˈnæmə], *v.a.* verliebt machen; (*usually*) *be -ed*, verliebt sein (*of*, in (*Acc.*)); (*fig.*) sehr gern haben.

encaenia [ɛnˈsiːnɪə], *s.* die Gründungsfeier (*Oxford Univ.*).

encage [ɪnˈkeɪdʒ], *v.a.* einschließen, einsperren.

encamp [ɪnˈkæmp], 1. *v.a.* lagern lassen. 2. *v.n.* sich lagern, ein Lager aufschlagen; *be -ed*, lagern. **-ment**, *s.* das Lagern; Lager, Zeltlager.

encase [ɪnˈkeɪs], *v.a.* in einen Behälter einschließen; umhüllen.

encash [ɪnˈkæʃ], *v.a.* in Geld umsetzen, einkassieren. **-ment**, *s.* die Einkassierung, das Inkasso (*C.L.*).

encaustic [ɛnˈkɔːstɪk], 1. *adj.* enkaustisch, eingebrannt; – *tiles*, glasierte Ziegel. 2. *s.* eingebrannte Wachsmalerei.

enceinte [ɔnˈsænt], 1. *adj.* schwanger. 2. *s.* die Umwallung (*Fort.*).

encephalitis [ɛnsɛfəˈlaɪtɪs], *s.* die Gehirnentzündung.

enchain [ɪnˈtʃaɪn], *v.a.* anketten, verketten; (*fig.*) fesseln, ketten, festhalten.

enchant [ɪnˈtʃɑːnt], *v.a.* bezaubern, behexen; (*fig.*) entzücken (*with*, von; *at*, über); *-ed castle*, das Zauberschloß. **-er**, *s.* der Zauberer. **-ing**, *adj.* bezaubernd, reizend, entzückend. **-ment**, *s.* die Bezauberung, der Zauber. **-ress**, *s.* die Zauberin.

enchas-e [ɪnˈtʃeɪs], *v.a.* ziselieren, erhaben verzieren (*Engr.*); fassen (*gems, etc.*); (*fig.*) schmücken; *-ed work*, getriebene Arbeit. **-ing-hammer**, *s.* der Treibhammer.

encipher [ɪnˈsaɪfə], *v.a.* verschlüsseln, chiffrieren.

encircle [ɪnˈsəːkl], *v.a.* umringen, umzingeln; einkreisen, einkesseln; (*fig.*) umfassen. **-ment**, *s.* die Einkreisung, Einkesselung.

enclave [ɛnˈkleɪv], *s.* die Enklave.

enclitic [ɪnˈklɪtɪk], 1. *adj.* enklitisch. 2. *s.* das Enklitikon.

enclos-e [ɪnˈkloʊz], *v.a.* einzäunen, einfriedigen; einschließen, einfassen, umgeben, umringen; beilegen, beischließen, beifügen (*a letter, etc.*); in sich schließen, enthalten; begrenzen (*Math.*); *the -ed*, die Einlage, Anlage (*C.L.*). **-ure** [-kloʊʒə], *s.* die Umzäunung, Einfriedigung, Koppel, das Gehöft, Gehege (*in a wood*), der Bezirk; die Anlage, Beilage, Einlage (*in a letter*).

encode [ɪnˈkoʊd], *v.a. see* **encipher.**

encomi-ast [ɛnˈkoʊmɪæst], *s.* der Lobredner, Schmeichler. **-astic(al)** [-ˈæstɪk(l)], *adj.* preisend, lobend, lobpreisend. **-um** [ɛnˈkoʊmɪəm], *s.* die Lobrede, Lobpreisung.

encompass [ɪnˈkʌmpəs], *v.a.* umgeben, umringen, umschließen, einschließen.

encore [ˈɔŋkɔː], 1. *int.* noch einmal! da capo! (*Theat., etc.*). 2. *v.a.* um Wiederholung *or* um eine Zugabe bitten. 3. *s.* die Zugabe; Wiederholung, das Dakapo.

encounter [ɪnˈkaʊntə], 1. *s.* die Begegnung, das Zusammentreffen; der Zusammenstoß, das Gefecht, Treffen. 2. *v.a.* begegnen (*Dat.*), treffen (*Acc.*); zusammentreffen *or* zusammenstoßen mit, entgegentreten (*Dat.*); stoßen auf (*Acc.*); – *opposition*, Widerstand finden.

encourag-e [ɪnˈkʌrɪdʒ], *v.a.* ermutigen, ermuntern, aufmuntern; beleben, anregen, antreiben, anreizen; fördern, unterstützen, Vorschub leisten, bestärken. **-ement**, *s.* die Aufmunterung, Ermutigung; (*fig.*) Förderung, Unterstützung, der Antrieb, die Gunst. **-ing**, *adj.* ermutigend, aufmunternd, hoffnungsvoll.

encroach [ɪnˈkroʊtʃ], *v.n.* unberechtigt eindringen, übergreifen, eingreifen (*upon*, in (*Acc.*)); mißbrauchen, sich vergehen an, beeinträchtigen, schmälern; über Gebühr in Anspruch nehmen; – *upon the land*, Land wegreißen (*of the sea*); – *upon a p.'s kindness*, jemandes Güte mißbrauchen. **-ment**, *s.* der Eingriff, Übergriff, die Anmaßung (*on*, in); das Vordringen, Übergreifen (*as the sea*).

encrust [ɪnˈkrʌst], *v.a.* mit (Rinde, *etc.*) überziehen, inkrustieren.

encumb-er [ɪnˈkʌmbə], *v.a.* belasten, beschweren, beladen; (be)hindern; versperren; *-er an estate*, ein Gut mit Schulden belasten. **-rance** [-brəns], *s.* die Belastung, Last; (*fig.*) Beschwerde, das Hindernis; die Schuldenlast, Hypothekenlast (*Law*);

without –rance(s), ohne Kinder, ohne Lasten. **–rancer,** *s.* der Pfandgläubiger.
encyclical [ɛnˈsaɪklɪkl], 1. *adj.* enzyklisch. 2. *s.* päpstliches Rundschreiben; die Enzyklika.
encyclop–aedia [ɛnsaɪkloˈpɪ:dɪə], *s.* die Enzyklopädie, das Konversationslexikon. **–aedic, –edic,** *adj.* enzyklopädisch.
encyst [ɛnˈsɪst], *v.a.*; (*only pass.*) *–ed, adj.* eingekapselt. **–ation, –ment,** *s.* die Einkapselung.
end [ɛnd], **1.** *s.* das Ende, der Schluß; das Ziel; die Absicht, der Zweck, Endzweck; das Aufhören, Zuendegehen; Endchen, Stück, der Rest; **(a)** (*with nouns*) *the –s of the earth*, das äußerste Ende der Welt; *odds and –s*, Reste, Überreste, allerhand Kleinigkeiten; *rope-– of a spar*, das *or* die Nock (*Naut.*); *rope's –*, der Tamp, das Tauende; *shoemaker's –*, der Pechdraht; *the West – of London*, der Westen Londons, westlicher Teil von London; *no – of trouble*, nichts als Unannehmlichkeiten, unendliche Mühe; *the thin – of the wedge*, ein schwacher *or* einmal ein Anfang; **(b)** (*with verbs*) *there's an – of it*, und damit gut *or* basta; *there must be an – of*, es muß ein Ende haben mit; *there's an – to everything*, alles hat mal ein Ende; *be near one's –*, dem Tode nahe sein; *you will be the – of me*, du wirst mich in den Tod bringen; *gain one's –s*, seine Zwecke erreichen; *the – justifies the means*, der Zweck heiligt die Mittel; (*coll.*) *keep one's – up*, durchhalten, nicht nachgeben; *make an – of*, ein Ende machen (*Dat.*); *make both –s meet*, gerade auskommen, sein Auskommen finden, sich nach der Decke strecken; *put an – to*, see *make an – of*; *serve one's –*, seine Interessen *or* seinen eignen Vorteil wahren; **(c)** (*with prepositions*) *at the – of June*, Ende Juni; *be at an –*, zu Ende sein, vorbei sein, aus sein; *be at a loose –*, nichts zu tun haben, untätig *or* müßig sein; ohne feste Bindung; *have at one's fingers' –s*, am Schnürchen haben; *be at the – of one's tether*, ratlos dastehen, am Ende seiner Kraft sein; *be at one's wits' –*, sich (*Dat.*) nicht mehr zu helfen wissen, am Ende seiner Weisheit sein; *for one's own* (*private*) *–s*, für seine persönlichen Zwecke; *in the –*, am Ende, schließlich; auf die Dauer; *it comes to very much the same thing in the –*, es kommt schließlich auf eins hinaus; (*coll.*) *go off the deep –*, sich aufregen, die Fassung verlieren; *on –*, aufrecht, hochkant; (*fig.*) ununterbrochen, hintereinander; *his hair stood on –*, die Haare standen ihm zu Berge; *– on*, mit dem Ende zugewandt (*to* (*Dat.*)); *– to –*, mit den Enden aneinander; *from – to –*, der Länge nach, von einem Ende zum anderen; *to no –*, vergebens; *to this –*, zu diesem Zwecke; *to the – that*, damit; *to what –?* wozu? *bring to an –*, zu Ende führen *or* bringen; *come to an –*, enden, endigen, zu Ende kommen, ein Ende finden; *come to a bad –*, ein schlechtes Ende nehmen; *to the bitter –*, bis aufs äußerste *or* zum äußersten; *without –*, unendlich, unaufhörlich; *world without –*, von Ewigkeit zu Ewigkeit, für immer und immer. **2.** *v.a.* beenden, beendigen, abschließen, zu Ende bringen *or* führen. 3. *v.n.* enden, endigen, aufhören; *– by saying*, schließlich sagen; (*Prov.*) *all's well that –s well*, Ende gut, Alles gut; *– in*, endigen, auslaufen *or* ausgehen in; *– in nothing* or *smoke*, zu Wasser werden, zu nichts führen; *it will – in your doing*, es führt schließlich dazu, daß du tust; *– with*, ein Ende finden mit, aufhören mit; (*coll.*) *– up in*, see *– in*; *see* **ending, endless. -–paper,** *s.* das Vorsatzpapier (*Bookb.*). **-–plate,** *s.* die Endscheibe. **-–rhyme,** *s.* der Endreim; *see* **endways, endwise.**
endanger [ɪnˈdeɪndʒə], *v.a.* gefährden, in Gefahr bringen.
endear [ɪnˈdɪə], *v.a.* lieb *or* wert *or* teuer machen; *– o.s. to* or *with*, sich lieb Kind machen bei. **–ing** [–rɪŋ], *adj.* zärtlich, lockend (*as words*), reizend, gefällig (*of persons*). **–ment,** *s.* die Liebkosung, Zärtlichkeit; Beliebtheit; *terms of –ment*, Kosenamen, Zärtlichkeitsworte (*pl.*).
endeavour [ɪnˈdɛvə], 1. *s.* die Bemühung, das Bestreben. 2. *v.n.* sich bemühen, sich bestreben; versuchen, suchen (*to do*).
endemic [ɛnˈdɛmɪk], 1. *adj.*, **–al,** *adj.* endemisch, örtlich beschränkt. 2. *s.* endemische Krankheit.
endermic [ɛnˈdə:mɪk], *adj.* auf die Haut wirkend.
ending [ˈɛndɪŋ], *s.* das Ende, der Schluß, Abschluß; die Endung (*Gram.*).
endive [ˈɛndɪv], *s.* die Endivie.
endless [ˈɛndlɪs], *adj.* endlos, unendlich, fortdauernd, unaufhörlich, ununterbrochen, ständig, ohne Ende; *– band*, das Transportband, Raupenband, endloses Band; *– chain*, das Paternosterwerk, die Eimerkette; (*fig.*) endlose Kette (*of events, etc.*); *– screw*, die Schnecke, die Schraube ohne Ende. **–ness,** *s.* die Endlosigkeit, Unendlichkeit.
endocard–itis [ɛndoʊkɑ:ˈdaɪtɪs], *s.* die Herzklappenentzündung (*Med.*). **–ium** [ɛndoʊˈkɑ:dɪəm], *s.* die Herzhaut (*Anat.*).
endo–carp [ˈɛndoʊkɑ:p], *s.* das Endokarp, innere Fruchthaut (*Bot.*). **–crine,** *adj.* mit innerer Sekretion (*of glands*). **–gen** [ˈɛndoʊdʒən], *s.* die Monokotyledone (*Bot.*). **–genous,** *adj.* endogen (*Biol.*), im Erdinneren entstanden (*Geol.*). **–plasm,** *s.* innere Plasmaschicht (*Biol.*). *See* **endosperm.**
endorse [ɪnˈdɔ:s], *v.a.* auf der Rückseite überschreiben, vermerken; indossieren, girieren (*a cheque*); überweisen, übertragen (*to* or *over to* (*Dat.*)); beipflichten, gutheißen, bekräftigen, bestätigen (*opinions, etc.*). **–e,** *s.* der Indossat, Girat. **–ment,** *s.* die Aufschrift, Überschrift; das Indossement, Indossament, Giro, die Übertragung (*C.L.*); Bestätigung, Bekräftigung. **–r,** *s.* der Indossant, Girant.
endosperm [ˈɛndouspə:m], *s.* inneres Nährgewebe (*Bot.*).
endow [ɪnˈdɑʊ], *v.a.* schenken, stiften; subventionieren, dotieren; (*fig.*) ausstatten; *–ed with*, begabt mit; *–ed school*, die Stiftungsschule. **–ment,** *s.* die Ausstattung; Stiftung, Dotation; (*usually pl.*) Gabe, Begabung; *–ment insurance*, abgekürzte Lebensversicherung.
endue [ɪnˈdju:], *v.a.* anziehen, anlegen; kleiden; bekleiden; ausstatten, begaben (*with*, mit).
endur–able [ɪnˈdjʊərəbl], *adj.* erträglich, leidlich. **–ance** [ɪnˈdjʊərəns], *s.* die Dauer, Dauerhaftigkeit, Fortdauer; das Ertragen, Aushalten, die Erduldung; Ausdauer, Geduld, Beharrlichkeit; *beyond* or *past –ance*, unausstehlich, unerträglich; *–ance flight*, der Dauerflug; *–ance test*, die Dauerprüfung (*of material*); (*fig.*) Geduldsprobe; *–ance trial*, die Dauerfahrt (*Motor.*). **–e** [ɪnˈdjʊə], 1. *v.a.* aushalten, ertragen, erdulden; erfahren, durchmachen; (*used negat.*) ausstehen, leiden; *not to be –ed*, nicht auszuhalten, unerträglich. 2. *v.n.* Dauer haben, (fort)-dauern. **–ing** [–rɪŋ], *adj.* dauernd, bleibend, fortdauernd, andauernd.
end–ways [ˈɛndweɪz], **–wise,** *adv.* aufrecht, gerade, mit dem Ende zugewandt (*to* (*Dat.*)).
enema [ˈɛnɪmə], *s.* das Klistier, die Klistierspritze.
enemy [ˈɛnɪmɪ], 1. *s.* der Feind, Gegner; Teufel, der böse Feind (*Theol.*); *sworn –*, der Todfeind; *be one's own –*, sich selbst im Wege stehen; (*sl.*) *how goes the –?* wie spät ist es? 2. *adj.* feindlich, Feind-.
energ–etic [ɛnəˈdʒɛtɪk], *adj.* tatkräftig, energisch; tätig, wirksam; kraftvoll, nachdrücklich. **–ize,** *v.a.* mit Energie füllen (*Mach., Elec.*); (*fig.*) anspornen, kräftigen. **–y** [ˈɛnədʒɪ], *s.* die Tatkraft, Energie, Arbeitsfähigkeit, Kraft; der Nachdruck, Kraftaufwand, die Wirksamkeit; *potential –y*, potentielle Energie; *conservation of –y*, die Erhaltung der Kraft.
enervat–e, 1. [ɪˈnə:veɪt], *adj.* kraftlos, entnervt, schlaff. 2. [ˈɛnəveɪt], *v.a.* entkräften, entnerven, kraftlos machen, schwächen. **–ing,** *adj.* entkräftend, schwächend. **–ion** [–ˈveɪʃən], *s.* die Entkräftung, Entnervung, Schwächung; Schwäche.
enfeeble [ɪnˈfɪ:bl], *v.a.* schwächen, entkräften. **–ment,** *s.* die Schwächung, Entkräftung; Schwäche.
enfeoff [ɪnˈfɛf], *v.a.* belehnen; (*fig.*) ausliefern, übergeben. **–ment,** *s.* die Belehnung; der Lehnsbrief.
enfilad–e [ɛnfɪˈleɪd], 1. *s.* das Flankenfeuer, Längsfeuer (*Artil.*). 2. *v.a.* der Länge nach beschießen *or* bestreichen, enfilieren. **–ing,** *adj* Enfilier-, Flanken-, Flankierungs-.
enfold [ɪnˈfould], *v.a.* einhüllen, einschlagen, umfassen, umschließen; falten.

enforce [ɪnˈfɔːs], *v.a.* erzwingen, durchsetzen, durchführen; erzwingen (*upon*, von); aufzwingen, auferlegen, mit Nachdruck einschärfen (*upon* (*Dat.*)); zur Geltung *or* Durchführung bringen; geltend machen (*an argument, etc.*). **-able,** *adj.* erzwingbar, durchsetzbar. **-d,** *adj.* erzwungen, aufgezwungen, notgedrungen. **-ment,** *s.* die Durchsetzung, Durchführung (*of the law*); Erzwingung, Einschärfung.

enfranchise [ɪnˈfræntʃɑɪz], *v.a.* befreien; politisch frei erklären; das Bürgerrecht *or* Wahlrecht erteilen (*Dat.*); *be -d*, das Wahlrecht erhalten. **-ment,** *s.* die Freilassung, Befreiung; Einbürgerung; Verleihung des Bürger- *or* Wahlrechts.

engag-e [ɪnˈgeɪdʒ], 1. *v.a.* verpflichten, binden; auf sich (*Acc.*) ziehen; (*usually pass.*) beschäftigen, in Anspruch nehmen; anstellen, in Dienst nehmen, engagieren, dingen, (*a servant, etc.*); belegen, besetzen (*seats*); mieten (*room, etc.*); bestellen (*tickets*); einrücken, kuppeln, einschalten (*Mech.*); fesseln, verwickeln (in (*Acc.*)), (*in conversation, etc.*); zum Kampf bringen, im Kampf einsetzen (*troops*); angreifen, stellen, handgemein werden mit (*the enemy*); *-e a p. in conversation*, ein Gespräch mit einem anknüpfen, sich mit einem auf ein Gespräch einlassen; *be -ed*, besetzt *or* beschäftigt sein, versagt sein; *be -ed* (*to be married*), verlobt sein; *the number is -ed*, die Nummer ist besetzt (*Phone*); *become* or *get -ed*, sich verloben (*to*, mit). 2. *v.n.* sich verpflichten, sich binden, Gewähr leisten; sich einlassen (*in*, auf (*Acc.*)), sich befassen *or* abgeben *or* beschäftigen (*in*, mit), sich beteiligen (*in*, an), unternehmen (*Acc.*); angreifen, sich schlagen, in Kampf geraten; einklinken, ineinandergreifen (*Mach.*). **-ed,** *adj.* verpflichtet; beschäftigt; besetzt (*Phone, seat, etc.*); verlobt; nicht abkömmlich (*C.L.*); *-ed couple*, das Brautpaar; *-ed signal*, das Besetztzeichen (*Phone*). **-ement,** *s.* die Verpflichtung, Verbindlichkeit (*to s.o.*, einem gegenüber); Verlobung; das Engagement (*of an actor, etc.*); die Beschäftigung, Anstellung; Einladung, Verabredung, Vereinbarung, das Übereinkommen; das Gefecht, die Kampfhandlung, das Treffen; *break off the -ement*, die Verlobung auflösen; *I have an -ement with him*, ich habe eine Verabredung mit ihm; *meet one's -ements*, seinen Verbindlichkeiten *or* Verpflichtungen nachkommen; *be under an -ement to s.o.*, einem vertraglich verpflichtet sein; *-ement book*, das Merkbuch für Verabredungen; *-ement ring*, der Verlobungsring. **-ing,** *adj.* einnehmend, gewinnend, anziehend.

engender [ɪnˈdʒɛndə], *v.a.* (*fig.*) erzeugen, hervorbringen, hervorrufen, verursachen.

engine [ˈɛndʒɪn], 1. *s.* die Maschine; der Motor; die Dampfmaschine; Lokomotive (*Railw.*); (*fig.*) das Werkzeug, Mittel; *internal combustion* –, der Verbrennungsmotor; *fire-*–, die Feuerspritze; *in-line* –, der Reihenmotor; *marine* –, die Schiffsmaschine; *radial* –, der Sternmotor; *traction-*–, die Zugmaschine, der Traktor, Zieher. 2. *v.a.* mit Maschinen *or* Motoren versehen (*Nav.*). **--builder,** *s.* der Maschinenbauer. **--cowling,** *s.* die Motorhaube. **--driver,** *s.* der Lokomotivführer (*Railw.*). **--failure,** *s.* der Motordefekt, Motorausfall. **--fitter,** *s.* der Maschinenschlosser, Monteur. **--house,** *s.* der Lokomotivschuppen, Lokschuppen (*Railw.*); das Maschinenhaus. **--power,** *s.* die Maschinenleistung. **--room,** *s.* der Maschinenraum. **- trouble,** der Maschinenschaden, die Motorpanne.

engineer [ɛndʒɪˈnɪə], 1. *s.* der Ingenieur, Techniker; Maschinenbauer, Maschinist; Pionier (*Mil.*); Lokomotivführer (*Amer.*); *chief* –, der Oberingenieur; *civil* –, der Bauingenieur, Zivilingenieur; *electrical* –, der Elektrotechniker; *marine* –, der Schiffbauingenieur; *mechanical* –, der Maschinenbauer; *mining* –, der Bergwerksingenieur. 2. *v.a.* (er)bauen, errichten, konstruieren; einrichten, anlegen, durchsetzen, (*coll.*) einfädeln, deichseln, herbeiführen, bewerkstelligen. **-ing,** *s.* das Ingenieurwesen, die Maschinenbaukunst; (*coll.*) die Mache, das Getue, Umtriebe (*pl.*); *civil -ing*, die Ziviltechnik; *electrical -ing*, die Elektrotechnik; *marine -ing*, der Schiffbau; (*archaic*) *military -ing*, das Geniewesen; *mechanical -ing*, der Maschinenbau; *-ing drawing*, die Konstruktionszeichnung.

engir-d [ɪnˈgəːd], *v.a.* (*p.p.* -t) umgürten, umschließen, umgeben.

English [ˈɪŋglɪʃ], *see* **Index of Names.**

engraft [ɪnˈgrɑːft], *v.a.* pfropfen (*upon*, auf); (*fig.*) einpflanzen, einprägen (*in* (*Dat.*)).

engrail [ɪnˈgreɪl], *v.a.* (*usually p.p.*) auszacken (*Her.*). **-ment,** *s.* gezahnter Rand (*Her.*).

engrain [ɪnˈgreɪn], *v.a.* in der Wolle färben, tief färben; (*fig.*) (einem etwas) unauslöschlich einprägen, tief einpflanzen. **-ed,** *adj.* in der Wolle gefärbt; (*fig.*) fest verwurzelt, eingefleischt.

engrav-e [ɪnˈgreɪv], *v.a.* gravieren, stechen; einschneiden, eingraben (*upon*, auf (*Acc.*)); (*fig.*) einprägen. **-er,** *s.* der Graveur, Bildstecher; Kupferstecher; *wood-*-*er*, der Holzschneider. **-ing,** *s.* das Gravieren, die Gravierkunst; der Stich, Kupferstich, Holzschnitt; *copperplate-*- *-ing*, der Kupferstich; *wood-*-*ing*, die Holzschneidekunst; der Holzschnitt.

engross [ɪnˈgroʊs], *v.a.* an sich ziehen *or* reißen, ganz für sich in Anspruch nehmen, monopolisieren; ins reine *or* mit großen Buchstaben schreiben; in gesetzlicher Form ausdrücken, mundieren (*Law*); *-ed by*, eingefangen *or* eingenommen von; *-ed in* or *with*, tief versunken vertieft *or* in (*Acc.*). **-er,** *s.* der Urkundenabschreiber. **-ing,** *adj.* fesselnd, spannend; *-ing hand*, die Kanzleischrift. **-ment,** *s.* der Aufkauf; die Urkunde; Abschrift in großen Buchstaben, Mundierung; völliges Aufgehen, die Inanspruchnahme.

engulf [ɪnˈgʌlf], *v.a.* verschlingen, in einen Abgrund stürzen.

enhance [ɪnˈhɑːns], *v.a.* erhöhen; vergrößern; steigern, übertreiben. **-ment,** *s.* die Erhöhung; Vergrößerung.

enharmonic [ɛnhɑːˈmɔnɪk], *adj.* enharmonisch.

enigma [ɪˈnɪgmə], *s.* das Rätsel. **-tic(al)** [ɛnɪgˈmætɪk(l)], *adj.* rätselhaft; dunkel.

enjambment [ɪnˈdʒæmmənt], *s.* das Enjambement, die Versbrechung.

enjoin [ɪnˈdʒɔɪn], *v.a.* auferlegen, einschärfen (*on a p.*, einem); bestimmen; befehlen (*a p.*, einem).

enjoy [ɪnˈdʒɔɪ], *v.a.* genießen (*Acc.*), sich erfreuen (*Gen.*), sich erfreuen an (*Dat.*), Gefallen finden an (*Dat.*), Freude *or* Vergnügen haben an (*Dat.*); besitzen (*as good health, etc.*); *I – the coffee*, der Kaffee schmeckt mir; *– o.s.*, sich gut unterhalten, sich amüsieren. **-able,** *adj.* genießbar (*of food*); genußreich, erfreulich. **-ment,** *s.* der Genuß, die Freude, das Vergnügen.

enkindle [ɪnˈkɪndl], *v.a.* (*fig.*) entzünden, entflammen.

enlace [ɪnˈleɪs], *v.a.* umschlingen, umgeben, verschlingen, verflechten, verstricken.

enlarge [ɪnˈlɑːdʒ], 1. *v.a.* erweitern, ausdehnen, vergrößern (*also Phot.*); *– one's mind*, seinen Gesichtskreis erweitern; *-d and revised edition*, vermehrte und verbesserte Auflage. 2. *v.n.* sich vergrößern lassen (*Phot.*); sich erweitern, sich ausdehnen; sich weitläufig auslassen, sich verbreiten (*on* or *upon*, über (*Acc.*)). **-ment,** *s.* die Vergrößerung (*also Phot.*), Ausdehnung; Erweiterung (*of the heart, etc.*); Verbreitung (*upon*, über (*Acc.*)). **-r,** *s.* der Vergrößerungsapparat (*Phot.*).

enlighten [ɪnˈlɑɪtn], *v.a.* erleuchten, erhellen; aufklären, belehren, unterrichten (*a person*). **-ed,** *adj.* erleuchtet, aufgeklärt, vorurteilsfrei. **-ment,** *s.* die Aufklärung.

enlist [ɪnˈlɪst], 1. *v.a.* anwerben, einstellen (*soldiers*); eintragen, einschreiben; gewinnen, in Anspruch nehmen; *– s.o.'s sympathy*, Stimmung bei einem machen; *-ed man*, (*Amer.*) der Soldat. 2. *v.n.* sich anwerben lassen, Soldat werden, sich zum Militär melden. **-ment,** *s.* die Anwerbung, Einstellung; Gewinnung; *age at -ment*, das Eintrittsalter; *date of -ment*, der Einstellungstermin.

enliven [ɪnˈlɑɪvn], *v.a.* beleben, beseelen, anfeuern, ermuntern, erheitern.

en masse [ɑ̃ˈmæs], *adv.* als Ganzes.

enmesh [ɪnˈmɛʃ], *v.a.* verstricken, umgarnen.

enmity [ˈɛnmɪtɪ], *s.* die Feindschaft; Feindseligkeit; *at – with*, in Feindschaft mit, verfeindet; *bear no* –, nicht nachtragen.

ennoble [ɪ'noʊbl], *v.a.* adeln, in den Adelsstand erheben; (*fig.*) veredeln. **–ment,** *s.* die Erhebung in den Adelsstand; (*fig.*) Veredelung.
ennui [ɔn'wɪ:], *s.* die Langeweile.
enorm–ity [ɪ'nɔ:mɪtɪ], *s.* die Ungeheuerlichkeit, Abscheulichkeit, der Greuel, Frevel. **–ous** –məs], *adj.* ungeheuer, gewaltig, riesig; (*coll.*) kolossal, enorm. **–ousness,** *s.* ungeheure Größe.
enough [ɪ'nʌf], 1. *adv.* genug; genügend, hinlänglich; *curiously* –, eigentümlicherweise; *like* –, sehr wahrscheinlich; *are you man – to do it?* bist du Manns genug es zu tun?; *natural* –, ganz natürlich; *safe* –, durchaus sicher; – *and to spare*, übergenug; *sure – there he was*, freilich *or* gewiß *or* und richtig, da war er; *true* –, nur zu wahr; *well* –, recht gut, gar sehr, ganz leidlich. 2. *adj.* genug, ausreichend; *I have had – of it*, ich habe genug davon, ich habe es satt; *we have time* – or – *time*, wir haben Zeit genug *or* genug Zeit *or* ausreichende Zeit; *it* (or *that*) *is – for me*, es (*or* das) genügt mir. 3. *s.* die Genüge; *have – to do to get finished*, seine Mühe haben, fertig zu werden; (*Prov.*) – *is as good as a feast*, allzuviel ist ungesund.
enounce [ɪ'nɑuns], *v.a.* verkünden; aussprechen, äußern.
en passant [ɑ̃'pæsɑ̃], *adv.* nebenbei, im Vorbeigehen.
enquire [ɪn'kwɑɪə], *see* **inquire.**
enrage [ɪn'reɪdʒ], *v.a.* wütend machen. **–d,** *adj.* wütend, rasend (*at*, über (*Acc.*)).
enrapture [ɪn'ræptʃə], *v.a.* entzücken.
enrich [ɪn'rɪtʃ], *v.a.* bereichern, anreichern, fruchtbar machen, (aus)schmücken, ausstatten. **–ment,** *s.* die Bereicherung; Verzierung, Ausschmückung.
enrol [ɪn'roʊl], *v.a.* einschreiben, eintragen; anwerben (*Mil.*); als Mitglied aufnehmen (*in a society*); aufzeichnen, protokollieren; – *for lectures*, Vorlesungen belegen (*Univ.*); – *o.s.*, sich einschreiben lassen *or* als Mitglied eintragen lassen. **–ment** [ɪn'roʊlmənt], *s.* die Eintragung, Einschreibung; Einreihung; Aufnahme, Beitrittserklärung (*in society*); Anwerbung (*Mil.*).
ensconce [ɪn'skɔns], *v.a.* verstecken, verbergen; (*usually v.r.*) sich bequem niederlassen.
ensemble [ɑ̃'sɑ:mbl], *s.* das Ganze; das Ensemble(spiel) (*Theat., Mus.*); die Gesamtwirkung.
enshrine [ɪn'ʃrɑɪn], *v.a.* in einen Schrein einschließen, als Heiligtum verwahren. **–ment,** *s.* die Einschließung.
enshroud [ɪn'ʃrɑʊd], *v.a.* (ver)hüllen.
ensign ['ɛns(ɑ)ɪn], *s.* die Schiffsflagge (*Nav.*); Fahne; das Abzeichen, Kennzeichen; (*archaic*) der Fahnenjunker, Fähnrich (*Mil.*). **–cy,** *s.* (*archaic*) die Fähnrichsstelle.
ensilage ['ɛnsɪlɪdʒ], *s.* das Gärfutter, Grünfutter, Süßpreßfutter.
enslave [ɪn'sleɪv], *v.a.* zum Sklaven machen, unterjochen, knechten; (*fig.*) fesseln, binden (*to*, an). **–ment,** *s.* die Unterjochung, Knechtung; Knechtschaft.
ensnare [ɪn'snɛə], *v.a.* fangen, verstricken, bestricken, verführen (*also fig.*).
ensu–e [ɪn'sjʊ:], *v.n.* folgen, erfolgen, sich ergeben (*from*, aus). **–ing,** *adj.* folgend, darauffolgend, bevorstehend.
ensure [ɪn'ʃʊə], *v.a.* sichern, sicherstellen (*against* or *from*, gegen); versichern, garantieren, Gewähr leisten für.
enswathe [ɪn'sweɪð], *v.a.* einhüllen.
entablature [ɪn'tæblətjə], *s.* das Säulengebälk (*Arch.*).
entail [ɪn'teɪl], 1. *s.* unveräußerliches Erbgut, das Erblehen, Fideikommiß (*Law*); *cut off the* –, die Erbfolge aufheben; *in strict* –, als unveränderliches Erblehen. 2. *v.a.* als unveräußerliches Gut vererben, als Fideikommiß vererben (*on*, auf (*Acc.*)); aufbürden, auferlegen (*on* (*Dat.*)); (*fig.*) mit sich bringen, nach sich ziehen, zur Folge haben. **–ment,** *s.* die Übertragung als Fideikommiß.
entangle [ɪn'tæŋgl], *v.a.* verwickeln, verstricken, verwirren; *be –d in*, verstrickt sein in (*Dat.*), sich verwickeln in (*Acc.*); *become –d with*, sich kompromittieren mit. **–ment,** *s.* die Verwick(e)lung, Verwirrung; (*coll.*) Liebschaft; der Verhau (*Mil.*).

entente [ɑ̃'tɑ̃:t], *s.* das Bündnis.
enter ['ɛntə], **1.** *v.a.* einziehen; betreten, hineintreten in, sich begeben in; (*fig.*) eintreten in (*Acc.*), beitreten (*Dat.*), Mitglied werden von (*a society*); einschreiben, eintragen, melden; – *an action against s.o.*, einen verklagen, eine Klage gegen einen einleiten (*Law*); – *the army*, Soldat werden; – *s.th. to the credit of s.o.*, einem etwas gutschreiben; – *s.th. to the debit of s.o.*, einem etwas in Rechnung stellen; – *goods at the custom-house*, Waren deklarieren; – *a harbour*, in einen Hafen einlaufen; – *one's head*, einem in den Sinn kommen (*of thoughts*); – *a horse* (*for a race*), ein Pferd (für ein Rennen) anmelden; – *a hospital*, ein Krankenhaus aufsuchen; – *judgement*, ein Urteil fällen; – *the lists*, in die Schranken treten; *it never –ed my head* or *mind*, es ist mir nie in den Sinn gekommen, mir kam niemals der Gedanke; – *one's name*, sich einschreiben; *have one's name –ed*, sich einschreiben lassen; – *a profession*, einen Beruf ergreifen; – *a protest*, Verwahrung einlegen, Einspruch erheben (*with*, bei; *against*, gegen); *he has –ed my service*, er ist in meine Dienste eingetreten; *the river –s the sea*, der Fluß ergießt sich ins Meer; – *the university*, die Hochschule beziehen; – *the war*, in den Krieg eintreten; – *one's fiftieth year*, das fünfzigste Jahr antreten. **2.** *v.n.* eintreten; sich anmelden (*Sport*); auftreten (*Theat.*); – *into*, (*fig.*) sich hineindenken in; teilnehmen an, sich beteiligen an; sich annehmen (*Dat.*); einen Bestandteil bilden von; eintreten (in (*Acc.*)); – *into an agreement*, einen Vergleich eingehen; – *into correspondence with*, in Korrespondenz treten mit; – *into details*, sich auf Einzelheiten einlassen; – *into a p.'s feelings*, jemandes Gefühle würdigen, mit jemandes Gefühlen sympathisieren; – *into the joke*, auf den Scherz eingehen; – *into partnership with*, sich assoziieren mit, sich geschäftlich verbinden mit; *that does not – into my plan*, das gehört nicht in meinen Plan, (*coll.*) das paßt mir nicht in den Kram; – *into the spirit of an author*, in den Geist eines Schriftstellers eindringen; – *into the spirit of it*, mit bei der Sache sein; – *into a treaty*, einen Vertrag abschließen; – *on* or *upon*, sich einlassen in *or* auf (*Acc.*), eintreten in (*Acc.*); vornehmen beginnen, anschneiden, antreten (*an office*); – *up*, regelrecht buchen. **–ing,** 1. *adj.* Eingangs–, Eintritts–. 2. *s.* der Eintritt, Antritt, Eingang; das Einziehen, Einreihen (*Weav.*). **–ing-ladder,** *s.* die Fallreepstreppe (*Naut.*). **–ing-port,** *s.* die Fallreepsluke.
enter–ic [ɛn'tɛrɪk], *adj.* Darm–; *–ic fever*, der Unterleibstyphus. **–itis** [ɛntə'rɑɪtɪs], *s.* der Darmkatarrh. **–ocele** ['ɛntərosɪ:l], *s.* der Darmbruch.
enterpris–e ['ɛntəprɑɪz], *s.* die Unternehmung, das Wag(e)stück; das Unternehmen, die Spekulation (*C.L.*); der Unternehmungsgeist, die Unternehmungslust; *private –e*, freie Wirtschaft. **–ing,** *adj.* unternehmend, unternehmungslustig; wagemutig, kühn.
entertain [ɛntə'teɪn], 1. *v.a.* unterhalten, aufrechterhalten; gastlich bewirten, gastfreundlich aufnehmen; halten, hegen (*an opinion, resentment*); unterhalten, ergötzen; – *doubts*, Zweifel hegen; – *an idea*, sich mit einem Gedanken tragen; – *an offer*, einem Angebot nähertreten; *he did not – the proposal for a moment*, er ging auf den Vorschlag gar nicht ein, er zog den Vorschlag überhaupt nicht in Erwägung; *he –ed them to dinner*, er lud sie zum Mittagessen ein; – *thoughts of revenge*, Rachegedanken Raum geben. 2. *v.n.* Gäste haben, Gäste bei sich sehen. **–er,** *s.* der Unterhaltungskünstler. **–ing,** *adj.* unterhaltend, ergötzlich. **–ment,** *s.* die Bewirtung, Gastfreundschaft; Unterhaltung, Belustigung, Ablenkung, der Zeitvertreib; die Lustbarkeit; Aufführung, das Schauspiel; *afford –ment*, amüsieren, belustigen; *for their –ment*, zu ihrer Belustigung; *give an –ment*, eine Aufführung veranstalten; *place of –ment*, die Vergnügungsstätte. **–ment-tax,** *s.* die Lustbarkeitssteuer.
enthral, –l [ɪn'θrɔ:l], *v.a.* (*archaic*) unterjochen; (*fig.*) fesseln, einnehmen, bezaubern. **–ment,** *s.* die Unterjochung; (*fig.*) Fesselung.
enthrone [ɪn'θroʊn], *v.a.* auf den Thron setzen;

einsetzen (*Eccl.*); *be –d*, thronen. **–ment,** *s.* die Thronerhebung; Einsetzung (*Eccl.*).

enthus–e [ɪn'θjuːz], *v.n.* (*coll.*) schwärmen, sich begeistern (*about* or *over*, über). **–iasm** [ɪn'θjuːzɪæzm], *s.* die Begeisterung, der Enthusiasmus; die Schwärmerei. **–iast** [–æst], *s.* der Schwärmer, Enthusiast. **–iastic** [–'æstɪk], *adj.* enthusiastisch, begeistert (*about*, über; *for*, für); schwärmerisch.

entic–e [ɪn'taɪs], *v.a.* (an)locken, verlocken, verführen, verleiten; anziehen, reizen. **–ement,** *s.* die Lockung, Anreizung; Verleitung, Verführung; der Reiz. **–ing,** *adj.* verlockend, verführerisch, reizend.

entire [ɪn'taɪə], 1. *adj.* ganz, völlig, vollständig; unversehrt, unbeschadet, ungeschmälert, vollzählig; unvermischt, ungeteilt, uneingeschränkt, echt; nicht kastriert (*of horses*). 2. *s.* das Ganze, die Vollständigkeit. **–ly,** *adv.* völlig, durchaus, lediglich. **–ness,** *s.* die Ganzheit, Vollständigkeit. **–ty** [ɪn'taɪətɪ], *s.* die Ganzheit; Gesamtheit, das Ganze; *in its -ty*, als Ganzes, in seiner Gesamtheit, in seinem ganzen Umfang.

entitle [ɪn'taɪtl], *v.a.* betiteln; *– to*, berechtigen zu, ein Recht geben auf (*Acc.*); *be –d to*, berechtigt sein zu, Anspruch haben auf (*Acc.*).

entity ['ɛntɪtɪ], *s.* die Wesenheit, das Wesen, Dasein.

entomb [ɪn'tuːm], *v.a.* begraben, beerdigen; (*fig.*) vergraben, einschließen. **–ment,** *s.* das Begräbnis, die Beerdigung.

entomo–logical [ɛntəmə'lɔdʒɪkl], *adj.* entomologisch, Insekten–. **–logist** [–'mɔlədʒɪst], *s.* Insektenkundige(r), *m.*, der Entomolog. **–logy** [–'mɔlədʒɪ], *s.* die Insektenkunde, Entomologie. **–philous** [–'mɔfɪləs], *adj.* insektenblütig (*Bot.*).

entophyte ['ɛntəfaɪt], *s.* die Schmarotzerpflanze (*Bot.*).

entourage [ɑ̃tuː'rɑːʒ], *s.* die Umgebung, Begleitung.

entozo–on [ɛntə'zouən], *s.* (*pl.* –a) der Eingeweidewurm.

entr'acte [ɔn'trækt], *s.* der Zwischenakt, das Zwischenspiel (*Theat.*).

entrails ['ɛntreɪlz], *pl.* Eingeweide (*pl.*); (*fig.*) das Innere.

entrain [ɪn'treɪn], 1. *v.a.* verladen (*troops*) (*Mil.*). 2. *v.n.* in den Zug einsteigen, verladen werden.

entrammel [ɪn'træməl], *v.a.* (*fig.*) verwickeln; hemmen.

[1]**entrance** ['ɛntrəns], *s.* der Eintritt, Einzug, die Einfahrt, das Eintreten; der Eingang, Torweg; der Einlaß, Zutritt; das Auftreten (*of an actor*); der Antritt; *at the –*, am Eingang; *give – to*, den Eintritt gestatten (*Dat.*); *no –*, Eintritt verboten; *– upon an office*, der Antritt eines Amtes, Amtsantritt. **––examination,** *s.* die Aufnahmeprüfung. **––fee,** *s.* die Eintrittsgebühr, Einschreibegebühr. **––form,** *s.* das Anmeldeformular. **––hall,** *s.* der Hausflur, die Eingangshalle, Vorhalle. **––money,** *s.* das Eintrittsgeld.

[2]**entrance** [ɪn'trɑːns], *v.a.* entzücken, hinreißen, überwaltigen, in Verzückung versetzen. **–ment,** *s.* die Verzückung.

entrant ['ɛntrənt], *s.* Eintretende(r), *m.*; der Teilnehmer, Bewerber (*Sport*).

entrap [ɪn'træp], *v.a.* fangen; (*fig.*) bestricken, verstricken. **–ment,** *s.* die Verleitung (*Law*).

entreat [ɪn'trɪːt], *v.a.* ersuchen, anflehen, ernstlich bitten (*for*, um) (*person*); erbitten (*of*, von) (*things*). **–ing,** *adj.* flehentlich. **–y,** *s.* dringende Bitte, das Gesuch.

entrée ['ɑ̃ːtreɪ], *s.* der Eintritt, Zutritt (*of*, zu); das Zwischengericht (*Cook.*).

entremets ['ɔntrəmeɪ], *s.* (*pl.* –) das Zwischengericht.

entrench [ɪn'trɛnʃ], *v.a.* mit Graben versehen, befestigen, verschanzen (*Mil.*); *– o.s.*, sich eingraben *or* verschanzen; (*fig.*) sich festsetzen. **–ment,** *s.* die Verschanzung; Feldschanze, der Schützengraben.

entrepôt ['ɑ̃ːtrəpou], *s.* die Niederlage, Warenlage.

entrepreneur [ɑ̃trəprə'nəː], *s.* der Unternehmer.

entresol ['ɑ̃ːtrəsoul], *s.* das Zwischengeschoß.

entropy ['ɛntrəpɪ], *s.* das Wärmegewicht.

entrust [ɪn'trʌst], *v.a.* anvertrauen (*a th.* or *a p. to s.o.*, einem etwas *or* einen), betrauen (*a p. with a th.*, einen mit etwas).

entry ['ɛntrɪ], *s.* das Eintreten; der Einzug, Eintritt, Eingang; Antritt, die Besitzergreifung (*into* or *upon* (*Gen.*)) (*Law*); Eintragung, Buchung, der Eintrag, Posten (*C.L.*); die Einfuhr (*of goods*); Zollangabe, Zolldeklaration (*at the custom-house*); Nennung, Meldung (*for games*); der Bewerber (*Sport*); *pl.* die Nennungsliste, Teilnehmerliste (*Sport*); *make one's –*, seinen Einzug halten; *cross-–*, die Gegenbuchung; *book-keeping by double –*, doppelte Buchführung; *make an – of a th.*, etwas buchen *or* eintragen; *no –!* gesperrt! *unlawful –*, der Hausfriedensbruch (*Law*).

entwine [ɪn'twaɪn], *v.a.* umwinden, umschlingen, umflechten; *– o.s. round*, sich winden um, verflechten.

enucleat–e [ɪː'njuːklɪeɪt], *v.a.* klarlegen, aufklären, erläutern; herausnehmen (*a tumour*) (*Med.*). **–ion** [–'eɪʃən], *s.* die Klarlegung; Bloßlegung.

enumerat–e [ɪ'njuːməreɪt], *v.a.* aufzählen, verzeichnen, spezifizieren. **–ion** [–'reɪʃən], *s.* die Aufzählung; Liste, das Verzeichnis.

enunciat–e [ɪ'nʌnsɪeɪt], *v.a.* verkünden, aussagen; ausdrücken, behaupten; formulieren, aufstellen (*a proposition*); aussprechen. **–ion** [–'eɪʃən], *s.* die Aussprache, Ausdrucksweise, Vortragsart, der Ausdruck; die Kundgebung, Erklärung, der Ausspruch; die Formulierung, Aufstellung (*of a proposition*). **–ive** [–sɪətɪv], *adj.* erklärend, ausdrückend, Ausdrucks–.

envelop [ɪn'vɛləp], *v.a.* einwickeln, verhüllen, einschlagen, einhüllen, umhüllen; umfassen, umzingeln, einkreisen, einkesseln (*Mil.*). **–ment** [–mənt], *s.* die Einwicklung, Einhüllung, Umhüllung, Hülle; Umfassung, Umzingelung (*Mil.*).

envelope ['ɛnvəloup], *s.* die Decke; der (Brief)-Umschlag, das Kuvert; der Vorwall (*Fort.*); die Hülle, Haut (*Av.*); der Kelch (*Bot.*).

envenom [ɪn'vɛnəm], *v.a.* vergiften (*also fig.*); (*fig.*) verbittern, erbittert machen.

envi–able ['ɛnvɪəbl], *adj.* beneidenswert, zu beneiden(d). **–er** ['ɛnvɪə], *s.* der Neider. **–ous** ['ɛnvɪəs], *adj.* neidisch (*of*, auf *or* über (*Acc.*); *because of*, um).

environ [ɪn'vaɪərən], *v.a.* umgeben, umringen; umzingeln. **–ment,** *s.* die Umgebung; Umwelt. **–mental,** *adj.* Umgebungs–. **–s,** *pl.* die Umgegend, Umgebung; *London and its –s*, London und (seine) Umgebung.

envisage [ɪn'vɪzɪdʒ], *v.a.* ins Auge fassen *or* schauen, im Geiste betrachten, in Betracht ziehen; sich vorstellen; intuitiv wahrnehmen (*Philos.*).

envoy ['ɛnvɔɪ], *s.* Gesandte(r), *m.*, der Bote.

envy ['ɛnvɪ], 1. *s.* der Neid (*of a p.*, auf einen; *of* or *at a th.*, über etwas); die Mißgunst (*of*, gegen); der Gegenstand des Neides; *be eaten up with –*, vor Neid vergehen; *be green with –*, grün *or* blaß vor Neid werden. 2. *v.a.* beneiden; *I – (him) his success*, ich beneide ihn um seinen Erfolg; *better envied than pitied*, besser beneidet als bemitleidet.

enwrap [ɪn'ræp], *v.a.* einwickeln, umhüllen.

enzyme ['ɛnzaɪm], *s.* das Enzym, Ferment.

eo–cene ['ɪːosɪːn], *s.* das Eozän (*Geol.*). **–lith** ['ɪːolɪθ], *s.* das Steinwerkzeug. **–lithic** [ɪːə'lɪθɪk], *adj.* frühsteinzeitlich. **–zoic** [ɪːo'zouɪk], *adj.* eozorisch (*Geol.*).

eon ['ɪːən], *see* **aeon.**

epact ['ɪːpækt], *s.* die Epakte (*Astr.*).

epaulement [ɪ'pɔːlmənt], *s.* die Schulterwehr, Brustwehr (*Fort.*).

epaulet(te) ['ɛpɔːlɛt], *s.* die Epaulette, das Epaulett, Schulterstück, Achselstück.

epergne [ɪ'pəːn], *s.* der Tafelaufsatz.

epexegesis [ɪpɛksə'dʒɪːsɪs], *s.* die Hinzufügung, Zutat.

ephemer–a [ɪ'fɛmərə], *s.* die Eintagsfliege; (*fig.*) vorübergehende Erscheinung. **–al,** *adj.* eintägig; kurzlebig, vergänglich, schnell vorübergehend, flüchtig. **–id,** *s.* die Eintagsfliege (*Ent.*). **–is,** *s.* (*pl.* –ides [ɛ'fɛmərɪdɪːz]) astronomischer Almanach. **–on,** *s.* (*pl.* –a) *see* **–a.**

epiblast ['ɛpɪblæst], *s.* äußeres Keimblatt (*Biol.*).

epic ['ɛpɪk], 1. *adj.* episch; (*fig.*) heldenhaft,

Helden–. 2. *s.* das Heldengedicht, Epos. **–al,** *adj.* episch, erzählend.
epicene [ˈɛpɪsɪːn], *adj.* beiderlei Geschlechts (*Gram.*).
epicur–e [ˈɛpɪkjʊə], *s.* der Feinschmecker, Geneißer; Genußmensch; **–ean** [–ˈrɪːən], 1. *adj.* epikureisch; schwelgerisch, genußsüchtig. 2. *s.* der Epikureer; Lebemann, genußsüchtiger Mensch. **–eanism** [–ˈrɪːənɪzm], *s.* die Lehre des Epikur, der Epikureismus; (*fig.*) die Genußsucht. **–ism** [–rɪzm], *s.* die Genußsucht.
epicycl–e [ˈɛpɪsaɪkl], *s.* der Epizykel, Nebenkreis. **–oid** [–ˈsaɪklɔɪd], *s.* die Epizykloide, Radlinie (*Geom.*).
epidemic [ɛpɪˈdɛmɪk], 1. *adj.* seuchenartig, epidemisch; (*fig.*) grassierend. 2. *s.* epidemische Krankheit, die Seuche, Epidemie.
epidermis [ɛpɪˈdəːmɪs], *s.* die Oberhaut, Epidermis.
epidiascope [ɛpɪˈdaɪəskoʊp], *s.* das Epidiaskop.
epigastrium [ɛpɪˈgæstrɪəm], *s.* obere Bauchgegend (*Anat.*).
epiglottis [ɛpɪˈglɔtɪs], *s.* der Kehldeckel.
epigram [ˈɛpɪgræm], *s.* das Sinngedicht, Epigramm. **–matic** [–grəˈmætɪk], *adj.* epigrammatisch; schlagkräftig, kurz und treffend. **–matist** [–ˈgræmətɪst], *s.* der Epigrammatiker.
epigraph [ˈɛpɪgrɑːf], *s.* die Inschrift, Aufschrift; der Denkspruch, das Motto.
epilep–sy [ˈɛpɪlɛpsɪ], *s.* die Fallsucht, Epilepsie. **–tic** [–ˈlɛptɪk], 1. *adj.* fallsüchtig, epileptisch. 2. *s.* der Epileptiker.
epilogue [ˈɛpɪlɔg], *s.* das Nachwort, Schlußwort, der Epilog.
epiphany [ɪˈpɪfənɪ], *s.* das Dreikönigsfest, Epiphaniasfest, Epiphanienfest.
epiphyte [ˈɛpɪfaɪt], *s.* der Scheinschmarotzer (*Bot.*).
episcop–acy [ɪˈpɪskəpəsɪ], *s.* bischöfliche Verfassung; die gesamten Bischöfe (*pl.*). **–al** [–əl], *adj.* bischöflich, Bischofs–. *–al Church*, die Episkopalkirche, (*Scots*) anglikanische Kirche in Schottland. **–alian** [–ˈpeɪlɪən], 1. *adj.* Episkopal–. 2. *s.* das Mitglied der Episkopalkirche, (*Scots*) der Anglikaner. **–ate** [–pɪt], *s.* das Episkopat, die Bischofswürde; das Bistum; die gesamten Bischöfe.
episod–e [ˈɛpɪsoʊd], *s.* die Neben– *or* Zwischenhandlung; Episode. **–ic(al)** [–ˈsɔdɪk(l)], *adj.* eingeschaltet, nebensächlich, episodisch, gelegentlich auftretend.
epistemology [ɪpɪstəˈmɔlədʒɪ], *s.* die Erkenntnislehre (*Phil.*).
epist–le [ɪˈpɪsl], *s.* das Sendschreiben, der Brief; die Epistel; (*coll.*) weitschweifiger Brief; *the –le to the Romans*, der Römerbrief. **–olary** [–tələrɪ], *adj.* brieflich; Brief–.
epistyle [ˈɛpɪstaɪl], *s.* der Architrav (*Arch.*).
epitaph [ˈɛpɪtɑːf], *s.* die Grabschrift, das Totengedicht.
epithalamium [ɛpɪθəˈleɪmɪəm], *s.* das Hochzeitsgedicht.
epithelium [ɛpɪˈθɪːlɪəm], *s.* die Epithelzelle (*Biol.*).
epithet [ˈɛpɪθɛt], *s.* das Beiwort, Attribut, Epitheton; die Benennung, Bezeichnung, der Beiname.
epitom–e [ɪˈpɪtəmɪ], *s.* der Auszug, Abriß, die Inhaltsangabe. **–ize** [–maɪz], *v.a.* einen Auszug machen aus *or* von, kurz darstellen; abkürzen.
epizoo–n [ɛpɪˈzoʊən], *s.* der Hautschmarotzer. **–tic,** *adj.* epidemisch (*of cattle*).
epoch [ˈɪːpɔk], *s.* die Epoche, der Zeitabschnitt; Wendepunkt; *mark an – in history*, einen Markstein in der Geschichte bedeuten. **–al,** *adj.* epochemachend, Epochen–. **–-making,** *adj.* bahnbrechend, epochemachend.
epode [ˈɛpoʊd], *s.* die Epode.
eponym [ˈɛpɒnɪm], *s.* der Stammvater. **–ous** [ɪˈpɔnɪməs], *adj.* namengebend.
epopee [ˈɛpopɪː], *s.* episches Gedicht, epische Dichtung.
epos [ˈɛpəs], *s.* episches Gedicht.
equab–ility [ɛkwəˈbɪlɪtɪ], *s.* die Gleichmäßigkeit, Gleichförmigkeit; der Gleichmut. **–le** [ˈɛkwəbl], *adj.*, **–ly,** *adv.* gleichförmig, gleichmäßig, gleich(bleibend); gleichmütig, ruhig, gelassen.
equal [ˈɪːkwəl], 1. *adj.* gleich (*to* (*Dat.*)), gleichförmig, gleichwertig (*in*, an), gleichmäßig; *be – to.* gleichen (*Dat.*); *be – to a th.*, einer S. gleichkommen, einer S. gewachsen sein; *be – to doing*, imstande *or* fähig sein zu tun; *with – ease*, mit derselben Leichtigkeit; *– to the demand*, der Nachfrage angemessen (*C.L.*). 2. *s.* der Gleiche; *be the – of s.o.*, einem ebenbürtig sein; *he has not his –*, *has no –* or *is without –*, er hat nicht seinesgleichen; *his –s in age*, seine Altersgenossen. **–s,** *pl.* gleiche Dinge; *between –s*, unter Gleichstehenden. 3. *v.a.* gleichen (*in*, an), gleich sein, gleichkommen (*Dat.*). **–ity** [ɪˈkwɔlɪtɪ], *s.* die Gleichheit, Gleichförmigkeit; *be on –ity with*, auf gleicher Stufe stehen mit; *political –ity*, politische Gleichberechtigung; *sign of –ity*, das Gleichheitszeichen (*Math.*). **–ization** [ɪːkwəlaɪˈzeɪʃən], *s.* die Gleichmachung, Gleichstellung. **–ize** [ˈɪːkwəlaɪz], *v.a.* gleichmachen, gleichstellen, ausgleichen. **–izer,** *s.* der Stabilisator (*Av.*), Ausgleicher. **–ly** [ˈɪːkwəlɪ], *adv.* in gleicher Weise, in gleichem Maße, ebenso; *–ly good*, ebensogut; *–ly with*, ebenso wie.
equanimity [ɪːkwəˈnɪmɪtɪ], *s.* der Gleichmut.
equat–e [ɪˈkweɪt], *v.a.* gleichsetzen, gleichstellen (*Math.*); auf gleicher Stufe stellen. **–ion** [–ʃən], *s.* die Gleichung (*Math.*), Ausgleichung, der Ausgleich; *simple –ion*, die Gleichung ersten Grades. **–or** [ɪˈkweɪtə], *s.* der Äquator. **–orial** [ɛkwəˈtɔːrɪəl], *adj.* äquatorial.
equerry [ˈɛkwərɪ], *s.* der Stallmeister.
equestrian [ɪˈkwestrɪən], 1. *adj.* Reit–, Reiter–; *– statue*, das Reiterstandbild. 2. *s.* der Reiter; Kunstreiter. **–ism,** *s.* die Reitkunst.
equi–angular [ɪːkwɪˈæŋgjʊlə], *adj.* gleichwink(e)lig. **–distant,** *adj.* gleich weit entfernt. **–lateral,** *adj.* gleichseitig.
equilibr–ate [ɪːkwɪˈlaɪbreɪt], 1. *v.a.* im Gleichgewicht halten, ins Gleichgewicht bringen. 2. *v.n.* im Gleichgewicht sein. **–ist** [ɪˈkwɪlɪbrɪst], *s.* der Akrobat, Seiltänzer. **–ium** [–ˈlɪbrɪəm], *s.* das Gleichgewicht; *be in* (*a state of*) *–ium*, sich (*Dat.*) das Gleichgewicht halten.
equine [ˈɛkwaɪn], *adj.* pferdeartig, Pferde–.
equino–ctial [ɪːkwɪˈnɔkʃəl], 1. *adj.* äquinoktial; *–ctial gales*, Äquinoktialstürme. 2. *s.* die Äquinoktiallinie, der Himmelsäquator. **–x** [ˈɪːkwɪnɔks], *s.* die Tag- und Nachtgleiche, das Äquinoktium; *vernal –x*, das Frühlingsäquinoktium.
equip [ɪˈkwɪp], *v.a.* ausrüsten (*also Mil.*, *Naut.*), ausstatten, ausstaffieren; *well –ped*, mit allem Nötigen (*or fig.* geistigem Rüstzeug) reichlich versehen. **–age** [ˈɛkwɪpɪdʒ], *s.* die Equipage, der Wagen mit Pferden; die Ausrüstung (*Mil.*); Begleitung, das Gefolge. **–ment,** *s.* die Einrichtung, Ausstattung, Anlage; Ausrüstung (*Mil.*); das Gerät, die Gerätschaft; (*fig.*) geistiges Rüstzeug.
equipoise [ˈɛkwɪpɔɪz], *s.* (*fig.*) das Gleichgewicht; Gegengewicht.
equipollent [ɪːkwɪˈpɔlənt], *adj.* gleichwertig, gleichstark, gleichbedeutend.
equitabl–e [ˈɛkwɪtəbl], *adj.* billig, gerecht, unparteiisch; billigkeitsgerichtlich (*Law*). **–eness,** *s.* die Billigkeit, Unparteilichkeit.
equitation [ɛkwɪˈteɪʃən], *s.* das Reiten; die Reitkunst.
equity [ˈɛkwɪtɪ], *s.* die Billigkeit, Gerechtigkeit, Unparteilichkeit; das Billigkeitsrecht (*Law*); *Court of –*, das Billigkeitsgericht.
equivalen–ce [ɪˈkwɪvələns], *s.* die Gleichwertigkeit. **–t,** 1. *adj.* gleichwertig, gleichbedeutend, äquivalent (*to*, mit); *be –t to*, gleichen Wert haben mit, ebensoviel gelten wie; so viel heißen wie. 2. *s.* der Gegenwert, gleicher Wert, gleicher Betrag (*in*, in); volle Entsprechung, das Seitenstück, Gegenstück (*of*, zu); das Äquivalent (*of*, für) (*Chem.*, *Mech.*).
equivoc–al [ɪˈkwɪvəkəl], *adj.* doppelsinnig, zweideutig, unbestimmt, ungewiß, zweifelhaft (*of things*), fragwürdig, verdächtig (*of persons*). **–alness,** *s.* die Zweideutigkeit. **–ate,** *v.a.* zweideutig *or* doppelzüngig reden; Ausflüchte gebrauchen. **–ation,** *s.* die Zweideutigkeit; Ausflucht. **–ator,** *s.* der Wortverdreher, Doppelzüngler.
era [ˈɪərə], *s.* die Ära, Zeitrechnung, (neuer) Zeitabschnitt, das Zeitalter.
eradica–ble [ɪˈrædɪkəbl], *adj.* ausrottbar; *not –ble,*

nicht auszurotten. **–te** [–keɪt], *v.a.* entwurzeln, ausrotten (*usually fig.*). **–ation** [–ˈkeɪʃən], *s.* die Entwurzelung, Ausrottung.
eras–able [ɪˈreɪzəbl], *adj.* vertilgbar, verlöschbar. **–e** [ɪˈreɪz], *v.a.* auskratzen, ausstreichen, ausradieren; (*fig.*) auslöschen, vertilgen (*from*, aus *or* von). **–er** [–ə], *s.* das Radiermesser; Radiergummi. **–ure** [ɪˈreɪʒə], *s.* das Auskratzen, Ausradieren; die Rasur, ausradierte Stelle.
ere [ɛə], 1. *conj.* (*Poet.*) ehe, bevor. 2. *prep.* vor; – *long*, demnächst, bald; – *now*, schon früher, bis jetzt, bereits, zuvor, vordem; – *this*, schon vorher.
erect [ɪˈrɛkt], 1. *adj.* aufrecht, aufgerichtet, gerade; *with head* –, mit erhobenem Kopf; *spring* –, in die Höhe springen; kerzenspringen (*Gymn.*); *stand* –, gerade stehen. 2. *v.a.* aufrichten; bauen, errichten; aufstellen, aufführen. **–ile** [–tɑɪl], *adj.* hochstehend; anschwellbar, erektil (*Anat.*). **–ion** [ɪˈrɛkʃən], *s.* das Aufrichten, Errichten; die Errichtung, der Aufbau, die Aufführung; der Bau, das Gebäude; die Erektion (*Med.*). **–ness**, *s.* die Gradheit, aufrechte Haltung. **–or**, *s.* der Erbauer, Errichter; Aufrichtmuskel (*Anat.*). **–ing-shop**, *s.* die Montagewerkstatt.
eremite [ˈɛrɪmɑɪt], *s.* der Einsiedler, Eremit.
ergo [ˈəːgoʊ], *adv.* also, folglich.
ergot [ˈəːgət], *s.* das Mutterkorn, der Brand (*Agr.*); der Extrakt aus Mutterkorn (*Pharm.*). **–ism** [–tɪzm], *s.* die Kornstaupe, Kriebelkrankheit.
ermine [ˈəːmɪn], *s.* der Hermelin; der Hermelinpelz; (*fig.*) das Richteramt, die Richterwürde, Richtertracht.
erne [əːn], *s.* der Seeadler, Fischgeier (*Orn.*).
ero–de [ɪˈroʊd], *v.a.* zerfressen, wegfressen. **–sion** [ɪˈroʊʒən], *s.* die Zerfressung (*by acids, etc.*), Auswaschung (*by water*); der Krebs (*Med.*); die Ausbrennung (*of a gun-barrel*).
erotic [ɪˈrɔtɪk], 1. *adj.* erotisch, Liebes–. 2. *s.* erotisches Gedicht. **–ism** [–tɪsɪzm], *s.* die Erotik.
err [əː], *v.n.* sich irren; unrichtig sein, fehlgehen (*of statements*); (*fig.*) abweichen, abirren (*from*, von); (*archaic*) sündigen, auf Abwege geraten.
errand [ˈɛrənd], *s.* der Auftrag, die Botschaft; der Gang, Botengang; *go on an* –, einen Gang tun; *go* or *run –s*, Wege besorgen; *fool's* –, unnützer Gang. **–-boy**, *s.* der Laufbursche.
errant [ˈɛrənt], *adj.* fahrend, wandernd, umherziehend; (*fig.*) abweichend (*from*, von); *knight-–*, fahrender Ritter. **–ry**, *s.* das Umherschweifen; die Irrfahrt (*of a knight*); *knight-–ry*, fahrendes Rittertum.
errata [ɪˈreɪtə], *pl.* das Druckfehlerverzeichnis.
erratic [ɪˈrætɪk], *adj.* wandernd (*Med.*); erratisch (*Geol.*); unregelmäßig, regellos, ungleichmäßig, sprunghaft, wandelbar, launenhaft, unberechenbar.
erroneous [ɪˈroʊnɪəs], *adj.* irrig, irrtümlich, falsch, unrichtig. **–ness**, *s.* der Irrtum, die Irrigkeit.
error [ˈɛrə], *s.* der Irrtum, Fehler, das Vergehen, Versehen, die Übertretung, der Fehltritt; die Abweichung (*of the compass*); der Formfehler (*Law*); *–s excepted*, Irrtümer vorbehalten (*C.L.*); *be in* –, sich irren; *in* –, im Irrtum; – *of judgment*, die Täuschung, irrige Ansicht; *margin of* –, die Fehlergrenze; *writ of* –, der Revisionsbefehl.
erst [əːst], *adv.* (*archaic*) ehedem, einst, vormals. **–while**, 1. *adj.* vormalig, früher, 2. *adv.* *see* **erst.**
eructa–te [ɪˈrʌkteɪt], *v.n.* aufstoßen, rülpsen. **–ion** [–ˈteɪʃən], *s.* das Aufstoßen, Rülpsen.
erudit–e [ˈɛruːdɑɪt], *adj.* gelehrt, belesen. **–ion** [–ˈdɪʃən], *s.* die Gelehrsamkeit, Belesenheit.
erupt [ɪˈrʌpt], *v.n.* ausbrechen (*of volcano*); durchbrechen (*of teeth*); ausschlagen (*of pimples, etc.*). **–ion** [ɪˈrʌpʃən], *s.* der Ausbruch, Durchbruch; der Hautausschlag (*Med.*). **–ive**, *adj.* ausbrechend, hervorbrechend; (*fig.*) losbrechend, gewaltsam; eruptiv (*Geol.*); ausschlagartig, mit Ausschlag begleitet (*Med.*).
eryngo [ɛˈrɪŋgoʊ], *s.* die (Meerstrands) Mannstreu (*Bot.*).
erysipelas [ɛrɪˈsɪpɪləs], *s.* die Rose, Wundrose, der Rotlauf (Med.).
escalade [ɛskəˈleɪd], *s.* die Eskalade, Mauerersteigung; *by* –, mit Sturmleitern. 2. *v.a.* mit Sturmleitern ersteigen, erstürmen.
escalator [ˈɛskəleɪtə], *s.* die Rolltreppe.
escallop [əskˈæləp], *s.* die Jakobsmuschel.
escapade [ɛskəˈpeɪd], *s.* toller Streich, der Jugendstreich.
escap–e [ɪsˈkeɪp], 1. *v.a.* entkommen aus, entrinnen aus; entgehen, entschlüpfen, entwischen (*Dat.*); entfliehen; umgehen; *the meaning –es me*, der Sinn leuchtet mir nicht ein; *the name –ed me*, mir entfiel der Name; *the word –ed me*, das Wort entfuhr mir; *it –ed my notice*, ich übersah es; *it –ed my memory*, es ist mir entfallen; *–e being laughed at*, der Gefahr entgehen, verlacht zu werden. 2. *v.n.* entkommen, entrinnen, entwischen, entschlüpfen (mit dem Leben) davonkommen, ungestraft entkommen; ausströmen, entweichen (*as gas*). 3. *s.* das Entrinnen, Entkommen, die Flucht; das Ausströmen, Entweichen, der Abgang, die Abgabe (*of gas*); *fire-–e*, die Rettungsleiter; *have a narrow –e*, mit knapper Not entkommen; *make* (*good*) *one's –e*, glücklich entrinnen, sich aus dem Staube machen. **–e-apparatus**, *s.* der Tauchretter (*submarines*). **–e-hatch**, *s.* die Notluke (*tanks*). **–ement**, *s.* die Hemmung (*Horol.*). **–e-pipe**, *s.* das Abflußrohr, Abzugsrohr. **–er**, *s.* der Ausreißer, Flüchtling. **–e-valve**, *s.* das Auslaßventil. **–e-wheel**, *s.* das Hemmungsrad (*Horol.*).
escarp [ɪsˈkɑːp], 1. *v.a.* böschen, mit einer Böschung versehen. 2. *s.* innere Grabenböschung, vordere Grabenwand (*Fort.*). **–ment**, *s.* die Böschung, mit Böschung versehene Befestigungsanlage.
eschalot [ɛʃəˈlɔt], *s. see* **shallot.**
eschatology [ɛskəˈtɔlədʒɪ], *s.* die Lehre von den letzten Dingen (*Theol.*).
escheat [ɪsˈtʃiːt], 1. *s.* der Heimfall (*Law*); heimgefallenes Gut. 2. *v.n.* anheimfallen. 3. *v.a.* beschlagnahmen.
eschew [ɪsˈtʃuː], *v.a.* (ver)meiden, unterlassen, scheuen.
escort [ˈɛskɔːt], 1. *s.* die Begleitung; das Geleit, der Schutz, die Begleitmannschaft, Bedeckung, Eskorte (*Mil.*). 2. *v.a.* begleiten; geleiten, decken, eskortieren.
escritoire [ɛskrɪˈtwɑː], *s.* das Schreibpult.
esculent [ˈɛskjʊlənt], 1. *adj.* eßbar, genießbar. 2. *s.* das Nahrungsmittel.
escutcheon [ɪsˈkʌtʃən], *s.* das Wappenschild; Wappen; Namenschild; Schloßblech; *a blot on a p.'s* –, ein Flecken *or* Makel auf jemandes Ruf *or* Namen.
esoteric [ɛsoˈtɛrɪk], *adj.* esoterisch, nur für Eingeweihte bestimmt, vertraulich, geheim.
espalier [ɪsˈpæljə], *s.* das Spalier; der Spalierbaum.
esparto [ɛsˈpɑːtoʊ], *s.* das Alfagras.
especial [ɪsˈpɛʃəl], *adj.* besonder, hauptsächlich, Haupt–, hervorragend, vorzüglich. **–ly**, *adv.* besonders, hauptsächlich, in hohem Maße.
espial [ɪsˈpɑɪəl], *s.* das Spähen, Erspähen, Kundschaften, Spionieren.
espionage [ɛspɪəˈnɑːʒ], *s.* das Spionieren, die Spionage.
esplanade [ɛspləˈneɪd], *s.* die Promenade, freier Platz; die Esplanade (*Fort.*).
espous–al [ɪsˈpɑʊzəl], *s.* das Eintreten, die Parteinahme (*of*, für), der Anschluß (*of*, an), die Verteidigung (*of* (*Gen.*)); (*usually pl.*) die Eheschließung, Vermählung. **–e** [ɪsˈpɑʊz], *v.a.* heiraten (*of the man*); verheiraten (*to*, an (*Acc.*)) (*the girl*); (*fig.*) sich annehmen (*Gen.*), eintreten für, Partei ergreifen für.
esprit [ɛsˈpriː], *s.* der Geist, Witz; – *de corps*, der Korpsgeist, das Zusammengehörigkeitsgefühl.
espy [ɪsˈpɑɪ], *v.a.* erspähen, erblicken, entdecken.
esquire [ɪsˈkwɑɪə], *s.* (*archaic*) der Landedelmann; (*as title following name*) Hochwohlgeboren.
essay 1. [əˈseɪ], *v.a.* versuchen, probieren. 2. [ˈɛseɪ], *s.* der Versuch (*at*, mit); der Aufsatz, die Abhandlung, schriftliche Arbeit, der Essay; *prize* –, die Preisarbeit. **–ist** [ˈɛseɪɪst], *s.* der Verfasser von Essays, Essayist.
essence [ˈɛsəns], *s.* (innerstes) Wesen, der Geist; die Substanz, der Kern, wesentlicher Teil, wesentliche Eigenschaft, das Wesentliche; das Extrakt, der Auszug, die Essenz.

essential [ɪ'sɛnʃəl], 1. *adj.* wesentlich, erforderlich; unentbehrlich, wichtig, durchaus notwendig; ätherisch (*Chem.*); – *oils*, ätherische *or* flüchtige Öle. 2. *s.* (*often pl.*) das Wesentliche, die Hauptsache, wesentlicher Umstand. **–ity,** *s.*, **–ness,** *s.* das Wesentliche.

establish [ɪs'tæblɪʃ], *v.a.* festsetzen; aufstellen, einrichten, einführen, durchsetzen; bilden, gründen, errichten; nachweisen, feststellen, festlegen, außer Frage stellen, bestätigen, begründen, beweisen, darstellen; unterbringen, versorgen (*one's children, etc.*); – *the church*, die Kirche verstaatlichen; *–ed church*, die Staatskirche; – *a connexion*, eine Verbindung herstellen; *–ed facts*, feststehende Tatsachen; *–ed laws*, bestehende Gesetze; – *o.s.*, sich niederlassen, sich etablieren; – *order*, Ordnung schaffen; – *a record*, einen Rekord aufstellen. **–ment,** *s.* die Gründung, Errichtung, Einrichtung, Schaffung, Niederlassung; Festsetzung, Einsetzung; Feststellung, Bestätigung; Versorgung; der Haushalt; die Anstalt, das Institut; Etablissement, Geschäft, die Firma (*C.L.*); der Bestand, die Mannschaft, das Personal; die Sollstärke (*Mil.*); *Church –ment*, staatskirchliche Verfassung; *keep up a large –ment*, ein großes Haus führen; *military –ment*, stehendes Heer, die Kriegsmacht; *naval –ment*, die Flotte; *peace –ment*, der Friedensstand; *separate –ment*, getrennter Haushalt; *war –ment*, die Kriegsstärke.

estate [ɪs'teɪt], *s.* das Besitztum, Vermögen, die Erbschaftsmasse, der Nachlaß; die Konkursmasse (*of a bankrupt*); das Gut, die Güter, der Landsitz, das Grundstück, die Besitzung, das Anwesen; Besitzrecht, die Nutznießung an Besitztum (*Law*); (*archaic*) der Rang, Stand, die Klasse; (*B.*) der Zustand; *fourth* –, (*coll.*) die Presse; *freehold*-*–s*, die Freisassenrechte; *owner of large –s*, der Großgrundbesitzer; *man's* –, das Mannesalter; *come to man's* –, mannbar werden; *personal* –, bewegliche Habe, das Mobiliar(vermögen) (*Law*); *real* –, unbewegliche Habe, der Grundbesitz, das Immobiliarvermögen, Immobilien, Liegenschaften (*pl.*) (*Law*); *–s of the realm*, die Reichsstände; *the three –s of the realm*, die drei Stände des Reiches (= die hohe Geistlichkeit, der Adel, die Gemeinen); *residuary* –, der Nachlaß eines Verstorbenen nach Abzug der Legate; *third* –, dritter Stand. **–-agent,** *s.* der Grundstückmakler. **–-duty,** *s.* die Nachlaßsteuer.

esteem [ɪs'tɪ:m], 1. *v.a.* hochschätzen, achten; erachten als *or* für, halten für. 2. *s.* die Wertschätzung; Achtung (*for*, vor); *be in great – with*, in großem Ansehen stehen bei; *hold in* –, achten.

ester ['ɛstə], *s.* der Ester (*Chem.*).

estima–ble ['ɛstɪməbl], *adj.* schätzenswert, achtungswert. **–te,** 1. ['ɛstɪmeɪt], *v.a.* schätzen, würdigen, beurteilen, bewerten; abschätzen, berechnen, veranschlagen (*at*, auf (*Acc.*)). 2. [–mɪt], *s.* die Schätzung, der Überschlag, Voranschlag, Kostenanschlag; die Abschätzung, Beurteilung; *pl.* veranschlagter Etat (*Parl.*); *form an –te of*, beurteilen, abschätzen; *rough –te*, ungefährer Überschlag. **–tion** [–'meɪʃən], *s.* die Schätzung, Abschätzung, Veranschlagung, Berechnung; Ansicht, Meinung, das Gutachten; die Achtung; *hold in –tion*, hochschätzen; *in my –tion*, nach meiner Ansicht.

estop [ɪ'stɔp], *v.a.* abhalten, hemmen, hindern (*Law*).

estrade [ɛs'trɑ:d], *s.* erhöhter Platz, die Estrade (*Build.*).

estrange [ɪs'treɪndʒ], *v.a.* entfremden, abwendig machen (*from a p.*, einem), abwenden, abhalten (*from*, von). **–ment,** *s.* die Entfremdung.

estreat [ɪs'trɪ:t], *v.a.* vollstrecken, zahlen lassen (*a fine or bail*) (*Law*).

estuary ['ɛstjuərɪ], *s.* der Meeresarm; weite Flußmündung.

et cetera [ɪt'sɛtrə], und so weiter.

etch [ɛtʃ], *v.a.* ätzen, radieren, beizen. **–ing,** *s.* das Ätzen; die Radierung. **–ing-needle,** *s.* die Radiernadel.

etern–al [ɪ'tə:nəl], 1. *adj.* ewig; immerwährend; unveränderlich; (*coll.*) unaufhörlich, beständig; *–al triangle*, dreieckiges Verhältnis. 2. *s.* das Ewige; Gott; *pl.* ewige Dinge. **–alize,** *v.a.* verewigen. **–ity** [ɪ'tə:nɪtɪ], *s.* die Ewigkeit. **–ize** [ɪ'tə:naɪz], *v.a.* verewigen; unsterblich machen.

ether, ['ɪ:θə], *s.* der Äther (*Phys.*, *Chem.*; *also fig.*); *acetic* –, der Essigäther; – *waves*, Ätherwellen. **–eal** [ɪ'θɪərɪəl], *adj.* ätherisch (*also fig.*); (*fig.*) himmlisch, zart, vergeistigt. **–ealize,** *v.a.* ätherisch machen, verflüchtigen; (*fig.*) vergeistigen, verklären. **–ize** ['ɪ:θəraɪz], *v.a.* mit Äther betäuben.

ethic ['ɛθɪk], 1. *s. see* **–s.** 2. *adj. see* **–al.** **–al,** *adj.* sittlich, moralisch, ethisch. **–s,** *pl.* (*sing. constr.*) die Sittenlehre, Ethik, Moral.

ethmoid ['ɛθmɔɪd], *adj.* zellig; – *bone*, das Siebbein.

ethn–ic(al) ['ɛθnɪk(l)], *adj.* ethnisch, volkisch, völkisch; heidnisch. **–ographer** [ɛθ'nɔgrəfə], *s.* der Ethnograph. **–ographic(al)** [–nə'græfɪk(l)], *adj.* ethnographisch. **–ography** [ɛθ'nɔgrəfɪ], *s.* die Völkerbeschreibung. **–ological** [ɛθnə'lɔdʒɪkl], *adj.* völkerkundlich, ethnologisch. **–ologist** [–'nɔlədʒɪst], *s.* der Ethnolog. **–ology** [ɛθ'nɔlədʒɪ], *s.* die Völkerkunde.

ethos ['ɪ:θɔs], *s.* sittlicher Gehalt, das Ethos.

ethyl ['ɛθɪl], *s.* das Äthyl; – *alcohol*, der Äthylalkohol (*Chem.*). **–ene,** *s.* das Äthylen, Kohlenwasserstoffgas.

etiolat–e ['ɪ:tɪoleɪt], *v.a.* (durch Ausschließen des Lichts) bleichen. **–ion** [–'leɪʃən], *s.* das Entfärben Bleichwerden; (*fig.*) Siechtum.

etiquette [ɛtɪ'kɛt], *s.* gesellschaftliche Umgangsformen (*pl.*), die Etikette, das Hofzeremoniell.

etui [ɛ'twɪ:], *s.* der Behälter, das Etui, Futteral.

etymolog–ical [ɛtɪmə'lɔdʒɪkl], *adj.* etymologisch. **–ist** [–'mɔlədʒɪst], *s.* der Etymolog. **–y** [ɛtɪ'mɔlədʒɪ], *s.* die Wortableitung, Etymologie.

etymon ['ɛtɪmɔn], *s.* das Stammwort, Grundwort.

eucalyptus [ju:kə'lɪptəs], *s.* der Eukalyptus.

eucharist ['ju:kərɪst], *s.* heiliges Abendmahl. **–ic** [–'rɪstɪk], *adj.* Abendmahls–.

euchre ['ju:kə], 1. *s.* ein Kartenspiel. 2. *v.a.* (*sl.*) übertreffen, überlisten, schlagen.

eudiometer [ju:dɪ'ɔmətə], *s.* der Eudiometer, Sauerstoffmesser.

eugenic [ju:'dʒɛnɪk], *adj.* rassenhygienisch. **–s,** *pl.* (*sing. constr.*) die Rassenhygiene, Rassenpflege, Eugenik.

eulog–ist ['ju:lədʒɪst], *s.* der Lobredner. **–istic(al)** [–'dʒɪstɪk(l)], *adj.* lobpreisend, lobend. **–ium** [ju:'loudʒɪəm], *s. see* **–y.** **–ize** ['ju:lədʒaɪz], *v.a.* loben, preisen. **–y** ['ju:lədʒɪ], *s.* die Lobrede, Lobpreisung, das Lob.

eunuch ['ju:nək], *s.* Verschnittene(r), *m.*, Entmannte(r), *m.*, der Eunuch.

euonymus [juə'naɪməs], *s.* der Spindelbaum (*Bot.*).

eupep–sia [ju:'pɛpsɪə], *s.*, **–sy,** *s.* gute Verdauung. **–tic,** *adj.* leicht verdaulich; mit guter Verdauung.

euphemis–m ['ju:fɪmɪzm], *s.* beschönigender Ausdruck, sprachliche Verhüllung, der Euphemismus. **–tic(al)** [–'mɪstɪk(l)], *adj.* mildernd, beschönigend, euphemistisch.

euphon–ious [ju:'founɪəs], *adj.* wohlklingend. **–ium** [–nɪəm], *s.* das Baritonhorn (*Mus.*). **–y** ['ju:fənɪ], *s.* der Wohlklang.

euphorbia [ju'fɔ:bɪə], *s.* die Wolfsmilch (*Bot.*).

euphuis–m ['ju:fjuɪzm], *s.* der Euphuismus, gezierte Ausdrucksweise, der Schwulst. **–t,** *s.* gezierter Redner *or* Schriftsteller. **–tic** [–'ɪstɪk], *adj.* geziert, gespreizt.

eurhythmics [ju'rɪðmɪks], *pl.* (*sing. constr.*) rhythmische Gymnastik.

euthanasia [ju:θə'neɪzɪə], *s.* leichter *or* sanfter Tod; die Sterbehilfe.

evacu–ant [ɪ'vækjuənt], 1. *adj.* abführend. 2. *s.* das Abführmittel. **–ate** [ɪ'vækjueɪt], *v.a.* (ent)leeren, ausleeren; evakuieren, abführen (*Med.*); räumen, fortschaffen, abschieben, abtransportieren (*troops*); *–ate the air*, die Luft absaugen. **–ation** [–'eɪʃən], *s.* die Entleerung; das Auspumpen (*of air*); die Ausleerung, der Stuhlgang (*Med.*); die Aussiedlung, Verschickung, der Abtransport, Abschub (*of population*); die Evakuierung, Räumung (*of territory*). **–ee** [–'ɪ:], *s.* Evakuierte(r), Umgesiedelte(r), Verschickte(r), *m.* & *f.*

evade [ɪ'veɪd], *v.a.* ausweichen, sich entziehen, entwischen, entrinnen (*Dat.*); umgehen (*Acc.*).

evaluat-e [ɪ'væljʊeɪt], *v.a.* abschätzen, berechnen. **-ion** [-'eɪʃən], *s.* die Abschätzung, Berechnung, Wertbestimmung.
evanesce [ɛvə'nɛs], *v.n.* (ver)schwinden, vergehen. **-nce** [-ns], *s.* das (Dahin)Schwinden. **-nt,** *adj.* (ver)schwindend; unendlich klein (*Math.*).
evangel [ɪ'vændʒəl], *s.* das Evangelium. **-ic(al)** [ɪ:væn'dʒɛlɪk(l)], *adj.* evangelisch; Evangelien-. **-ical,** *s.* evangelischer Protestant. **-icalism,** *s.* die Lehre der evangelischen Kirche. **-ism,** *s.* die Verkündung des Evangeliums. **-ist** [-dʒəlɪst], *s.* der Evangelist, Wanderprediger. **-ize** [ɪ'vændʒəlaɪz], *v.a.* das Evangelium predigen, bekehren.
evapora-ble [ɪ'væpərəbl], *adj.* verdunstbar, verdampfbar. **-te** [ɪ'væpəreɪt], 1. *v.n.* verdunsten, verdampfen, verfliegen, verflüchtigen; (*fig.*) verschwinden. 2. *v.a.* abdampfen, eindampfen, aufdünsten, verdünsten, einkochen, verdampfen lassen, verdunsten lassen. **-tion** [-'reɪʃən], *s.* die Abdampfung, Abdünstung, Ausdünstung, Verdünstung; das Verdampfen, die Verflüchtigung (*Chem.*); *-ted milk*, die Kondensmilch. **-tive** [-rətɪv], *ad.* Ausdünstungs-, Verdampfungs-. **-tor,** *s.*, **-ting-vessel,** *s.* die Abdampfschale, das Abdampfgefäß.
evasi-on [ɪ'veɪʒən], *s.* das Ausweichen, die Umgehung; Ausflucht, Ausrede. **-ve** [-sɪv], *adj.* ausweichend; *-ve action*, das Ausweichmanöver. **-veness,** *s.* ausweichendes Benehmen.
eve [ɪ:v], *s.* (*poet.*) der Abend; Vorabend; *Christmas* -, der Weihnachtsabend, Heiligabend, Heiliger Abend; *New Year's* -, der Silvester; *on the - of*, am Vorabend (*Gen.*); (*fig.*) nahe an (*Dat.*), unmittelbar vor.
[1]**even** ['ɪ:vən], *s.* (*poet.*) der Abend. **-song,** *s.* das Abendgebet, der Abendgottesdienst. **-tide,** *s.* die Abendzeit; *-tide home*, das Altersheim.
[2]**even,** [ɪ:vn] 1. *adj.* eben, gerade, waagerecht, horizontal, flach, glatt; gleichmäßig, regelmäßig, gleichförmig, gleich, identisch; gelassen, gleichmütig, ausgeglichen, ruhig; unparteiisch; (*coll.*) quitt; *of - date*, gleichen Datums (*C.L.*); *on an - keel*, im Gleichgewicht (*Naut.*); *- number*, gerade Zahl; *on - terms*, in gutem Einvernehmen; *be - with s.o.*, mit einem quitt sein, mit einem abrechnen; *get - with s.o.*, mit einem abrechnen *or* ins reine kommen; *make a th. - with the ground*, etwas dem Boden gleichmachen. 2. *adv.* selbst, sogar, gar; *- as*, gerade als; genau wie; *- if*, see *- though*; *- more*, noch (weit) mehr; *- now*, selbst jetzt; eben jetzt; *not* -, nicht einmal; *or* -, oder auch nur; *- so*, immerhin, jedoch, wenn schon; *- though*, wenn auch, selbst wenn. 3. *v.a.* (ein)ebnen, gleichmachen, glätten; (*fig.*) gleichstellen; *- up*, ausgleichen. **--handed,** *adj.* unparteiisch. **--handedness,** *s.* die Unparteilichkeit. **-ness,** *s.* die Ebenheit, Glätte; Geradheit, Gleichheit; Gleichmäßigkeit, Gleichförmigkeit; Unparteilichkeit; *-ness of temper*, die Seelenruhe, der Gleichmut. **--tempered,** *adj.* gleichmütig, gelassen.
evening ['ɪ:vnɪŋ], 1. *s.* der Abend; geselliger Abend; *in the* -, am Abend, abends; *in the -s*, in den Abendstunden, abends; *on the - of*, am Abend des; *on Sunday -s*, an Sonntagabenden; *one* -, eines Abends; *this* -, heute abend; *yesterday* -, gestern abend. 2. *adj.* Abend-; abendlich; *- dress*, der Gesellschaftsanzug (*for men*); das Abendkleid, die Balltoilette (*for women*); *- party*, die Abendgesellschaft; *- service*, der Abendgottesdienst; *--star*, der Abendstern; *--wrap*, der Abendumhang.
evenness, *see* [1]**even.**
evensong, *see* [2]**even.**
event [ɪ'vɛnt], *s.* das Ereignis, der Vorfall, die Begebenheit, das Vorkommnis; der Ausgang, das Ergebnis; die (Programm)Nummer (*of sports*); *at all -s*, auf alle Fälle; *athletic -s*, sportliche Veranstaltung; *field -s*, Sprung- und Wurfwettkämpfe (*pl.*); *in any* -, sowieso; *in the - of his arrival*, im Falle seiner Ankunft; *in the - of his arriving*, im Falle daß er ankommt; *in the - of his arrival* or *arriving*, falls er ankommen sollte; *table of -s*, das Festprogramm; *track -s*, Laufwettkämpfe (*pl.*). **-ful,** *adj.* ereignisreich, ereignisvoll.
eventide, *see* [1]**even.**
eventu-al [ɪ'vɛntjʊəl], *adj.* schließlich, endlich. **-ality** [-'ælɪtɪ], *s.* die Möglichkeit. **-ally,** *adv.* am Ende, schließlich. **-ate** [ɪ'vɛntjʊeɪt], *v.n.* auslaufen, ausfallen, endigen; stattfinden, sich ereignen.
ever ['ɛvə], *adv.* immer, stets, unaufhörlich; je, jemals; überhaupt, nur; *- after(wards)*, seit der Zeit, von der Zeit an, seitdem; *- and anon*, dann und wann, immer wieder; *as good as* -, so gute wie nur je; *as soon as - I can*, sobald ich nur irgend kann; (*coll.*) *did you - ?* hast du überhaupt so etwas gehört (*or* gesehen)? so etwas!; *for - (and -* or *and a day)*, auf ewig, für immer, in alle Ewigkeit; *Scotland for* -, es lebe Schottland! Schottland hoch! *he is for - making mischief*, er stiftet stets Unheil an; *- increasing*, immer (mehr) wachsend; *more than* -, mehr denn je; (*coll.*) *be - so pleased*, sich wirklich sehr freuen; (*coll.*) *- so much*, wirklich sehr; *- since*, see *- after*; *scarcely* -, fast nie; *were he - so rich*, wäre er noch so reich; (*coll.*) *- so long*, sehr lange; (*coll.*) *not . . . for - so much*, nicht um alles in der Welt; (*coll.*) *- so many*, sehr viele, unzählige; *what* (*where, who, etc.*) *- can it be ?* was (wo, wer, *etc.*) kann es nur sein? *yours* -, immer der Ihrige (*in letters*). **-green** ['ɛvəgrɪ:n], 1. *s.* das Immergrün. 2. *adj.* immergrün. **-lasting,** 1. *adj.* ewig; dauerhaft, unverwüstlich (*cloth*); (*coll.*) unaufhörlich. 2. *s.* die Ewigkeit; *-lasting flower*, die Strohblume, Immortelle. **-more,** *adj.* immerfort, immerzu, ewig; stets; *for -more*, für immer; *now and -more*, auf immer und ewig.
ever-sion [ɪ'və:ʃən], *s.* das Auswärtskehren, Umkehren (*of eyelids*). **-t** [ɪ'və:t], *v.a.* nach außen kehren, umkehren.
every ['ɛvrɪ], *attr. adj.* jeder, jede, jedes; alle; *all* or *each and* -, all und jeder; *- bit as good*, ganz genau so gut; *- day*, alle Tage, täglich (*see* **-day**); *- now and then*, von Zeit zu Zeit, dann und wann; *- once in a while*, hie und da, manchmal; *- one*, jeder einzelne (*see* **-one**); *- one of them*, ein jeder von ihnen; *- other* or *second day* or *- two days*, jeden zweiten Tag, alle zwei Tage, einen Tag um den andern; *- third* or *- three days*, jeden dritten Tag; *- ten days*, alle zehn Tage; *from - side*, von allen Seiten; *- so often*, hin und wieder, regelmäßig; *my - thought*, jeder meiner *or* alle meine Gedanken; *- whit as good*, see *- bit as good.* **-body,** *s.* jeder(mann), ein jeder. **-day,** *adj.* täglich, alltäglich, tagtäglich, Alltags-. **-one,** *s.* *see* **-body.** **-thing,** *s.* alles; (*coll.*) etwas Wichtiges, die Hauptsache; *-thing that*, alles was. **-where,** *adv.* überall, allenthalben.
evict [ɪ'vɪkt], *v.a.* aus dem Besitze vertreiben (*Law*). **-ion** [-'vɪkʃən], *s.* gerichtliche Vertreibung *or* Entsetzung (*Law*).
evidence ['ɛvɪdəns], 1. *s.* der Beweis; das Zeugnis, beeidigte Aussage; das Beweisstück, Beweismittel, Beweismaterial; (*fig.*) die Spur, das (An)Zeichen; *be - of*, beweisen, bezeugen; *- of character*, das Leumundszeugnis; *circumstantial* -, der Indizienbeweis; *documentary* -, urkundlicher Beweis; *external* -, äußere Beweise; *furnish - of*, bezeugen, Zeugnis ablegen für, beweisen; *be in* -, sichtbar sein, zutage treten, auffallen; *be much in* -, stark vertreten sein; *admit in* -, als Beweis zulassen; *call a p. in* -, einen als Zeugen anrufen; *give* -, Beweise erbringen, Zeugenaussage machen, Zeugnis ablegen; *piece of* -, das Beweisstück, der Beleg; *prima facie* -, die Rechtsvermutung, vollgültiger Beweis; *rules of* -, Bestimmungen für die Beweiserhebung; *turn king's* or *queen's* -, Kronzeuge werden, gegen seine Mitschuldigen aussagen. 2. *v.a.* augenscheinlich machen, zeigen, beweisen.
evident ['ɛvɪdənt], *adj.* augenscheinlich, einleuchtend; offenbar, klar, deutlich, offensichtlich.
evil ['ɪ:vl], 1. *adj.* übel, böse, schlimm; schlecht, boshaft, gottlos; *- communications*, schlechte Gesellschaft; *fall on - days*, ins Unglück geraten; *- eye*, böser Blick; *look with an - eye upon a p.*, einen scheel ansehen; *the - One*, der böse Feind. 2. *s.* das Übel, Böse; Unglück; *do* -, Böses tun, sündigen; *full of* -, voll Arges (*B.*); *for good and* -, auf Gedeih und Verderb; *King's* -, Skrofeln (*pl.*), die Skrofulose; *powers of* -, die Mächte der Fin-

sternis; *shun* –, die Sünde meiden; *speak – of*, schlecht sprechen von. **– -disposed,** *adj*, boshaft, übelgesinnt. **– -doer,** *s*. der Übeltäter. **– -minded,** *adj*. bösartig, boshaft. **– -speaking,** 1. *s*. die Verleumdung, üble Nachrede. 2. *adj*. verleumderisch.

evince [ɪ'vɪns], *v.a*. beweisen, bekunden, erweisen, zeigen, dartun.

eviscerat–e [ɪ'vɪsəreɪt], *v.a*. ausweiden; (*fig.*) bedeutungslos machen. **–ion** [–'reɪʃən], *s*. die Ausweidung.

evocat–ion [ɛvo'keɪʃən], *s*. die Hervorrufung; (Geister)Beschwörung. **–ive** [ɪ'vɔkətɪv], *adj*. im Geiste hervorrufend; *be –ive of*, erinnern an.

evoke [ɪ'voʊk], *v.a*. hervorrufen; beschwören (*spirits*).

evol–ute ['ɪ:vəljʊ:t], *s*. die Evolute (*Math.*). **–ution** [ɪ:və'lʊ:ʃən], *s*. die Entwick(e)lung, Bildung, Entfaltung, das Wurzelausziehen (*Math.*); die Evolution (*Biol.*); Reihe, Abfolge; Schwenkung, taktische Bewegung (*Mil.*); (*often pl.*) Bewegung, Umdrehung. **–ary** [–ərɪ], *adj*. Entwicklungs–, Evolutions– (*Biol.*), Schwenkungs– (*Mil.*). **–ve** [ɪ'vɔlv], 1. *v.a*. entwickeln, entfalten, enthüllen; ausscheiden, von sich geben (*Chem.*). 2. *v.n*. entstehen (*from*, aus); sich entwickeln, sich entfalten; *be –ved*, auftreten, entstehen.

ewe [jʊ:], *s*. das Mutterschaf; – *lamb*, das Schaflamm.

ewer ['jʊə], *s*. die Wasserkanne, der Wasserkrug.

ex [ɛks], **1.** *prep*. 1. aus; – *mine*, ab Bergwerk; – *ship*, aus dem Schiffe; – *works*, ab Werk (*C.L.*). – *cathedra*, *adv*. von maßgebender Seite. – *officio*, *adv*. von Amts wegen; 2. ohne, exklusive; – *dividend*, ohne Dividende (*C.L.*). **2.** *prefix* ehemalig, früher; –*-queen*, ehemalige Königin. –*-post-facto*, *adj*. hintennach; –*-post-facto law*, rückwirkendes Gesetz. **– -service-man,** *s*. der Kriegsteilnehmer.

exacerbat–e [ɛk'sæsəbeɪt], *v.a*. verschlimmern (*a th.*); erbittern (*a p.*). **–ion** [–'beɪʃən], *s*. die Erbitterung, Verschärfung; Verschlimmerung (*Med.*).

exact [ɪg'zækt], 1. *adj*. genau, richtig, exakt; sorgfältig, pünktlich, gewissenhaft. 2. *v.a*. eintreiben (*payment*); erpressen (*money*); fordern, erfordern, verlangen, erzwingen, erheischen. **–ing,** *adj*. anspruchsvoll; *he was very –ing*, er stellte hohe Anforderungen, er war sehr genau. **–ion** [–'zækʃən], *s*. die Beitreibung, Eintreibung (*of money, debts, etc.*); unrechtmäßige Forderung; hohe Anforderung; der Tribut, erpreßte Abgabe. **–itude,** *s*. die Genauigkeit, Exaktheit. **–ly,** *adv*. genau, richtig; –*ly!* ganz recht *or* richtig! –*ly the man for the post*, gerade der Richtige für diesen Posten; *not –ly*, nicht eben *or* gerade. **–ness,** *s*. die Genauigkeit, Richtigkeit, Pünktlichkeit, Sorgfalt, Regelmäßigkeit. **–or,** *s*. der Eintreiber; Erpresser; Forderer.

exaggerat–e [ɪg'zædʒəreɪt], *v.a*. übertreiben; hervorheben, verstärken, verschlimmern, zu stark betonen. 2. *v.n*. übertreiben. **–ed,** *adj*. übertrieben. **–ion** [–'reɪʃən], *s*. die Übertreibung.

exalt [ɪg'zɔ:lt], *v.a*. erheben; erhöhen, veredeln; preisen; – *to the skies*, in den Himmel heben. **–ation** [ɛgzɔ:l'teɪʃən], *s*. die Erhebung, Erhöhung; (*fig.*) Begeisterung, Verzückung, Erregung, gehobene Stimmung; höchster Stand (*Astrol.*). **–ed** [ɪg'zɔ:ltɪd], *adj*. erhaben, hoch; (*fig.*) begeistert exaltiert; gehoben (*as style*).

examination [ɪgzæmɪ'neɪʃən], *s*. die Prüfung, das Examen; die Untersuchung, Besichtigung, Durchsicht; (Zoll)Revision; das Verhör, die Vernehmung (*Law*); *competitive* –, die Konkurrenzprüfung; *cross*-–, das Kreuzverhör; *entrance* –, die Aufnahmeprüfung; *fail* (*in*) *an* –, in einer Prüfung durchfallen; *go in for an* –, see *sit an* –; *make an – of*, besichtigen; *medical* –, ärztliche Untersuchung; *pass an* –, eine Prüfung bestehen; (*sl.*) *plough an* –, see *fail an* –; *post-mortem* –, die Leichenöffnung; *get through an* –, see *pass an* –; *sit for* or *take an* –, sich prüfen lassen, sich einer Prüfung unterziehen; *be under* –, erwogen werden; unter Verhör stehen (*Law*); (*up*)*on* –, bei näherer Prüfung. **– -paper,** *s*. die Liste der Fragen bei einer schriftlichen Prüfung.

examin–e [ɪg'zæmɪn], *v.a*. untersuchen, prüfen, revidieren, besichtigen; ausfragen, vernehmen, verhören (*Law*); probieren, einer Prüfung unterwerfen; –*e accounts*, Rechnungen prüfen; *be –ed by a doctor*, sich von einem Arzt untersuchen lassen. **–ee** [–'nɪ:], *s*. der Prüfling, Kandidat. **–er** [–ə], *s*. der Prüfer, Prüfende(r), *m*., Untersuchende(r), *m*., der Examinator; Vernehmer (*Law*).

example [ɪg'zɑ:mpl], *s*. das Beispiel, Vorbild; Muster, Exemplar, die Probe; warnendes Beispiel, die Warnung; *by way of* or (*as*) *for* –, zum Beispiel; *hold up as an – to s.o.*, einem als Beispiel hinstellen; *let this be an – to you*, sei dir dies eine Warnung; *an – of*, das Beispiel für; *make an – of a p.*, ein Exempel an einem statuieren, einen exemplarisch bestrafen; *set an* –, ein Beispiel geben; *set a good* –, mit gutem Beispiele vorangehen, ein gutes Beispiel geben; *set a bad* –, ein schlechtes Beispiel geben; *take – by*, sich (*Dat.*) ein Beispiel nehmen an (*Dat.*).

exasperat–e [ɪg'zæspəreɪt], *v.a*. aufreizen, aufbringen, ärgern, erbittern; verschlimmern (*Med.*). **–ion** [–'reɪʃən], *s*. die Erbitterung, der Ärger, die Entrüstung.

excavat–e ['ɛkskəveɪt], *v.a*. ausgraben, aushöhlen. **–ion** [–'veɪʃən], *s*. die Aushöhlung; Ausgrabung, Ausschachtung, Baugrube, Höhle. **–or** [–ə], *s*. der Trockenbagger, die Ausgrabungsmaschine.

exceed [ɪk'sɪ:d], 1. *v.a*. überschreiten, übertreffen, übersteigen, hinausgehen über (*Acc.*). 2. *v.n*. zu weit gehen, das Maß überschreiten; sich auszeichnen. **–ing,** *adj*. übermäßig, äußerst, außerordentlich; mehr als, übersteigend. **–ingly,** *adv*. überaus, außerordentlich, äußerst, höchst.

excel [ɪk'sɛl], 1. *v.n*. & *r*. sich hervortun, sich auszeichnen, hervorragen. 2. *v.a*. übertreffen. **–lence** ['ɛksələns], *s*. die Vortrefflichkeit, Vorzüglichkeit; Güte, ausgezeichnete Leistung, der Vorzug. **–lency** ['ɛksələnsɪ], *s*. die Exzellenz (*in titles*). **–lent** ['ɛksələnt], *adj*. (vor)trefflich, vorzüglich. **–sior,** *adj*. Prima– (*C.L.*).

except [ɪk'sɛpt], 1. *v.a*. ausnehmen, ausschließen (*from*, von *or* aus), vorbehalten. 2. *conj*. außer daß, es sei denn daß, ausgenommen daß; –*for*, abgesehen von, außer in bezug auf, bis auf. 3. *prep*.; **–ing,** *prep*. außer, mit Ausnahme von, ausgenommen. **–ion,** *s*. die Ausnahme (*to* or *from*, von); Einwendung, der Einwand, Vorbehalt (*to*, gegen); Einwurf, die Einrede, Beanstandung, Ausschließung; *beyond –ion*, unanfechtbar; *admit of no –ion*, keine Ausnahme zulassen; *by way of –ion*, ausnahmsweise; *make an –ion of s.o.*, bei *or* mit einem eine Ausnahme machen, einen als Ausnahme betrachten; *the –ion proves the rule*, die Ausnahme bestätigt die Regel; *he is no –ion to the rule*, er bildet keine Ausnahme; *take –ion to*, Einwände *or* Vorstellungen erheben *or* Einwendungen machen gegen, Anstoß nehmen an, sich stoßen an, übelnehmen; *without –ion*, ausnahmslos; *with the –ion of*, mit Ausnahme von, ausgenommen; *with this –ion*, ausgenommen davon. **–ionable,** *adj*. anfechtbar; tadelnswert, anstößig. **–ional,** *adj*. außergewöhnlich, Ausnahme–. **–ionally,** *adv*. ausnahmsweise, außerordentlich.

excerpt, 1. [ɛk'sə:pt], *v.a*. ausziehen, exzerpieren. 2. ['ɛksə:pt], *s*. der Auszug, das Exzerpt; der Sonderdruck, Separatdruck (*Print.*).

excess [ɪk'sɛs], *s*. das Übermaß (*of*, an (*Dat.*)); Mehr, der Mehrbetrag, Überschuß (*Math.*); die Unmäßigkeit, Ausschweifung; *pl*. Exzesse, Ausschreitungen; *in – of*, mehr als; *be in – of*, überschreiten, übersteigen, hinausgehen über, überwiegen; *in* –, im Übermaß; *carry to* –, übertreiben; *drink to* –, im Übermaß *or* übermäßig trinken; – *fare*, der Zuschlag; – *freight*, die Überfracht; – *luggage*, das Übergewicht; – *postage*, das Strafporto; – *profits duty*, die Kriegsgewinnsteuer. **–ive** *adj*. übermäßig, übertrieben. **–iveness,** *s*. die Übermäßigkeit.

exchange [ɪks'tʃeɪndʒ], 1. *v.a*. (aus–, ein–, um–, ver)tauschen, (um)wechseln (*money*) (*for*, gegen); ersetzen (*for*, durch); – *books, compliments, greetings, ideas*, Komplimente, Grüße, Gedanken austauschen; – *prisoners*, Gefangene austauschen; – *shots*, Schüsse wechseln. 2. *s*. der Tausch, Austausch, das Wechseln, Umwechseln, die Umwechslung, der Umsatz, Wechselverkehr; Tauschhandel (*C.L.*); Wechsel (*Boxing, duelling, etc.*); (Wechsel)-Kurs (*of currency*); die Börse, Vermittlungsstelle; das (Fernsprech)Amt (*Phone*); *bill of* –, der Wechsel; *foreign* –, die Valuta, Devisen (*pl.*); *give in* –, einwechseln; *in – for*, als Entgelt für, gegen; *lose by the* –, schlecht wegkommen; *make an* –, tauschen; – *of money*, der Geldwechsel; *on* –, an *or* auf der Börse; *take in part* –, in Zahlung nehmen; *par of* –, das Wechselpari; – *of prisoners*, der Gefangenenaustausch; *under the quoted* –, unter dem Kurse; *rate of* –, der Wechselkurs; – *of shots*, der Kugelwechsel; *stock*- –, die Effektenbörse, Aktienbörse; *telephone*- –, das Amt, die Zentrale; – *of views*, der Meinungsaustausch, Gedankenaustausch. **–ability** [–ə'bɪlɪtɪ], *s.* die (Aus)Tauschbarkeit. **–able,** *adj.* austauschbar, auswechselbar (*for*, gegen); *–able value*, der Tauschwert. **– –advice,** *s.* der Börsenbericht. **– –broker,** *s.* der Wechselmakler, Börsenmakler, Kursmakler. **– –regulations,** *pl.* Devisenverordnungen.

exchequer [ɪks'tʃɛkə], *s.* das Schatzamt, die Staatskasse; der Fiskus, das Finanzministerium; die Kasse, Börse, der Geldvorrat (*of private firms*); *Chancellor of the* –, der Schatzkanzler, Finanzminister; *Court of* –, das Finanzgericht. **– –bill,** *s.* kurzfristiger verzinslicher Schatzwechsel. **– –bond,** *s.* die Schatzanweisung.

excis–able [ɛk'saɪzəbl], *adj.* steuerbar. **–e** [ɛk'saɪz], 1. *s.* die Verbrauchssteuer, Verbrauchsabgabe, Akzise; Finanzabteilung für indirekte Steuern; *–e duties*, Steuerabgaben (*pl.*). 2. *v.a.* besteuern. **–eman,** *s.* **–e-officer,** *s.* der Steuereinnehmer, Akziseeinnehmer.

excis–e, *v.a.* herausschneiden; (*fig.*) ausschneiden (*from*, aus). **–ion** [ɛk'sɪʒən], *s.* die Ausschneidung (*Surg.*); (*fig.*) Ausrottung, Ausschließung.

excit–ability [ɪksaɪtə'bɪlɪtɪ], *s.* die Erregbarkeit, Reizbarkeit, Nervosität. **–able** [ɪk'saɪtəbl], *adj.* erregbar, reizbar, nervös. **–ableness,** *s. see* **–ability. –ant** ['ɛksɪtənt], *s.* das Reizmittel. **–ation** [ɛksɪ'teɪʃən], *s.* die Reizung, Erregung, Anregung. **–e** [ɪk'saɪt], *v.a.* erregen, reizen, affizieren (*Med.*); aufreizen (*Pol.*); anreizen, erregen, aufregen; hervorrufen, wachrufen; *–e o.s., get –ed*, sich aufregen. **–ement,** *s.* die Erregung, Aufregung; Aufgeregtheit. **–er,** *s.* der Anreger, Erreger; das Reizmittel (*Med.*); die Erregerdynamomaschine (*Elec.*). **–ing,** *adj.* aufregend, erregend; spannend.

exclaim [ɪks'kleɪm], 1. *v.n.* ausrufen, schreien; – *against*, eifern gegen. 2. *v.a.* ausrufen.

exclamat–ion [ɛksklə'meɪʃən], *s.* der Ausruf; *pl.* das Geschrei; *–ion mark*, das Ausrufungszeichen. **–ory** [ɪks'klæmətərɪ], *adj.* ausrufend; *–ory words*, Ausrufeworte.

exclu–de [ɪks'klu:d], *v.a.* ausschließen, ausscheiden, ausstoßen. **–sion** [ɪks'klu:ʒən], *s.* die Ausschließung, Ausschaltung, der Ausschluß (*from*, von); die Präklusion (*Law*); *to the –sion of*, unter Ausschluß von. **–sive** [–sɪv], *adj.* ausschließend; ausschließlich, alleinig, Allein–; vornehm, wählerisch, exklusiv; *–sive of*, abgesehen von; *be –sive of*, ausschließen; *–sive of other charges*, andere Kosten ungerechnet; *–sive report*, der Sonderbericht; *–sive sale*, der Alleinverkauf. **–siveness,** *s.* die Ausschließlichkeit; Exklusivität.

excogitat–e [ɛks'kɒdʒɪteɪt], *v.a.* ausdenken, ersinnen. **–ion** ['teɪʃən], *s.* das Ersinnen, Ausdenken; die Erfindung.

excommunicat–e [ɛkskə'mju:nɪkeɪt], *v.a.* in den Bann tun, exkommunizieren. **–ion** [–'keɪʃən], *s.* der Kirchenbann, die Exkommunikation.

excoriat–e [ɛks'kɔ:rɪeɪt], *v.a.* die Haut abschälen (*Dat.*); wund reiben, abschürfen (*skin*). **–ion** [–'eɪʃən], *s.* das Abschälen, Abschürfen; die Wundreibung.

excrement ['ɛkskrɪmənt], *s.* das Exkrement, der Auswurf, Kot (*Physiol.*). **–al** [–'mɛntl], *adj.* Kot–, kotartig.

excrescen–ce [ɪks'krɛsns], *s.* der Auswuchs, Vorsprung. **–t,** *adj.* auswachsend; überflüssig, überschüssig.

excret–a [ɪks'krɪ:tə], *s. see* **excrement. –e** [ɪks'krɪ:t], *v.a.* ausscheiden, absondern. **–ion** [–'krɪ:ʃən], *s.* die Ausscheidung, Absonderung; der Auswurf. **–ive,** *adj.*, **–ory** [–ərɪ], *adj.* ausscheidend, absondernd, abführend, Ausscheidungs–.

excruciat–e [ɪks'kru:ʃɪeɪt], *v.a.* martern, quälen, foltern. **–ing,** *adj.* peinigend, qualvoll; (*coll.*) peinlich. **–ion** [–'eɪʃən], *s.* das Martern; die Qual.

exculpat–e ['ɛkskʌlpeɪt], *v.a.* entschuldigen, rechtfertigen, freisprechen, reinwaschen (*from*, von). **–ion** [–'peɪʃən], *s.* die Entschuldigung; Rechtfertigung. **–ory** [–'kʌlpətərɪ], *adj.* rechtfertigend, Rechtfertigungs–.

excurs–ion [ɪks'kə:ʃən], *s.* der Ausflug, die Partie; der Abstecher, Streifzug; die Ausweichung (*Astr.*); (*fig.*) Abschweifung. **–ionist,** *s.* der Ausflügler. **–ion-ticket,** *s.* die Ausflüglerfahrkarte. **–ion-train,** *s.* der Sonderzug. **–ive** [ɛks'kə:sɪv], *adj.* unzusammenhängend, ziellos; abschweifend. **–us** [ɛks'kə:səs], *s.* die Abschweifung; der Exkurs.

excus–able [ɪks'kju:zəbl], *adj.* entschuldbar, verzeihlich. **–al,** *s.* die Befreiung (*from taxes*). **–e** 1. [ɪks'kju:z], *v.a.* entschuldigen (*Acc.*); verzeihen (*Dat.*), Nachsicht haben mit (*persons*); entschuldigen, übersehen, als Entschuldigung dienen für, eine Entschuldigung finden für, rechtfertigen (*things*); entheben (*from* (*Gen.*)); befreien (*from*, von); *–e me!* verzeihen Sie! Verzeihung! entschuldigen Sie! bitte! *may I be –ed?* bitte mich zu entschuldigen; *I must be –ed from speaking*, ich muß leider ablehnen zu sprechen; *–e o.s.*, sich entschuldigen, sich rechtfertigen; *he was –ed attendance*, ihm wurde das Erscheinen erlassen; *that does not –e his rudeness*, das dient nicht als Entschuldigung für seine Grobheit. 2. [ɪks'kju:s] *s.* die Entschuldigung, Rechtfertigung; der Milderungsgrund; die Ausrede, Ausflucht, der Vorwand; die Bitte um Verzeihung; *make –es*, Ausflüchte machen; *make one's –es to s.o.*, sich bei einem entschuldigen; *there is no –e for it*, es läßt sich nicht entschuldigen.

exeat ['ɛksɪæt], *s.* der Urlaub.

execra–ble ['ɛksɪkrəbl], *adj.* scheußlich, abscheulich. **–te** ['ɛksəkreɪt], 1. *v.a.* verfluchen; verabscheuen. 2. *v.n.* fluchen. **–tion** [–'kreɪʃən], *s.* die Verwünschung, der Fluch; Abscheu; *hold in –tion*, verabscheuen.

execut–ant [ɛk'sɛkjutənt], *s.* Vortragende(r), Ausübende(r), *m.* & *f.* (*Mus.*). **–e** ['ɛksɪkju:t], *v.a.* ausführen, vollstrecken, vollführen, vollziehen, verrichten; vortragen, spielen (*Theat., Mus.*); ausfertigen, rechtsgültig machen (*Law*); ausüben (*an office*); hinrichten (*a p.*). **–er** [ɛk'sɛkjutə], *s.* der Vollzieher, Vollstrecker. **–ion** [ɛksɪ'kju:ʃən], *s.* die Ausführung, Vollstreckung, Vollziehung, Verrichtung, Ausfertigung (*of a deed*); der Vortrag, das Spiel, die Technik (*Mus.*); (schädliche) Wirkung; die Verheerung; Hinrichtung (*of a criminal*); Zwangsvollstreckung, Pfändung, Exekution (*for debt*); *carry* or *put into –ion*, ausführen; *do –ion*, Wirkung haben, wirken; *do great –ion upon the enemy*, dem Feinde großen Schaden anrichten or zufügen; *take out an –ion against a p.*, einen auspfänden lassen; *take goods in –ion*, Güter exekutieren; *writ of –ion*, der Vollstreckungsbefehl (*Law*). **–ioner,** *s.* der Henker. **–ive** [ɪg'zɛkjutɪv], 1. *adj.* vollziehend, ausübend, Exekutiv–; *–ive committee*, geschäftsführender Ausschuß; *–ive council*, der Ministerrat (*Amer.*); *–ive power*, vollziehende Gewalt. 2. *s.* ausübende Gewalt, die Vollziehungsgewalt, Exekutive (*Pol.*); geschäftsführender Beamter, der Hauptleiter (*C.L.*). **–or** [ɪg'zɛkjutə], *s.* der Testamentsvollstrecker. **–orial,** *adj.* Vollstreckungs–. **–orship,** *s.* das Amt eines Testamentsvollstreckers. **–ory** [–tərɪ], *adj.* ausübend, vollziehend, Ausführungs–, Ausübungs–, Vollziehungs–. **–rix,** *s.* die Testamentsvollstreckerin.

exege–sis [ɛksɪ'dʒɪ:sɪs], *s.* die Bibelauslegung, Bibelerklärung, Exegese. **–te** ['ɛksɪdʒɪ:t], *s.* der Bibelerklärer, Exeget. **–tic(al)** [–'dʒɛtɪk(l)], *adj.* exegetisch, auslegend, erklärend. **–tics,** *pl.* die Exegetik.

exemplar [ɪg'zɛmplə], *s.* das Muster, Vorbild, (typisches) Beispiel, das Musterbeispiel. **–iness**

[-rɪnɪs], *s.* die Musterhaftigkeit. **-y** [-rɪ], *adj.* musterhaft, mustergültig, Muster-, vorbildlich; abschreckend, exemplarisch (*of punishment*).

exemplif-ication [ɪgzɛmplɪfɪ'keɪʃən], *s.* die Beispielgebung, Erläuterung durch Beispiele; das Beispiel, Muster; beglaubigte Abschrift (*Law*). **-y** [ɪg'zɛmplɪfaɪ], *v.a.* durch Beispiele belegen *or* erläutern; als Beispiel *or* Beleg dienen für, illustrieren; eine rechtsgültige Abschrift nehmen (von) (*Law*).

exempt [ɪg'zɛmpt], 1. *v.a.* befreien, freimachen, freistellen, ausnehmen (*from*, von); entheben (*from* (*Dat.*)), verschonen (*from*, mit); zurückstellen (*Mil.*). 2. *pred. adj.*; **-ed,** *adj.* befreit, verschont, frei (*from*, von), zurückgestellt (*Mil.*). 3. *s.* Bevorrechtigte(r), *m.*, Privilegierte(r), *m.*, Befreite(r), *m.* **-ion** [-'zɛmpʃən], *s.* die Befreiung, Zurückstellung (*Mil.*), das Freisein; die Sonderstellung, Ausnahmestellung; *-ion from taxation*, die Steuerfreiheit.

exequatur [ɛksə'kweɪtə], *s.* obrigkeitliche Bestätigung (*of a foreign consular representative*).

exequies ['ɛksɪkwɪz], *pl.* das Leichenbegängnis, die Totenfeier.

exercis-able ['ɛksəsaɪzəbl], *adj.* ausführbar, anwendbar, anzuwenden. **-e** [-saɪz], 1. *v.a.* üben, anwenden, gebrauchen (*the body or mind*); ausüben, geltend machen (*power, influence*); verwalten (*an office*); ausbilden, drillen, einexerzieren, üben (*a p.*) (*in*, in); in Bewegung halten, beschäftigen, beunruhigen; bewegen, in Übung halten (*a horse*); - *authority*, die Herrschaft besitzen; *-e one's mind*, sich geistig beschäftigen; *-e patience*, Geduld üben. 2. *v.n.* exerzieren (*Mil.*), trainieren (*Sport*), sich (*Dat.*) Bewegung machen. 3. *s.* die Übung, Anwendung, der Gebrauch; die Ausübung (*of an art, etc.*); das Exerzieren; die (Schul)Aufgabe; (*often pl.*) regelmäßige Übung, körperliche Bewegung; *in the -e of his duty*, in Ausübung seiner Pflicht; *physical -e(s)*, die Leibesübung; *religious -e(s)*, die Andachtsübung, der Gottesdienst; *take -e*, sich (*Dat.*) Bewegung (im Freien) machen; *written -e*, schriftliche Aufgabe *or* Arbeit.

exert [ɪg'zəːt], *v.a.* anwenden, ausüben; - *o.s.*, sich anstrengen, sich bemühen; - *one's influence*, seinen Einfluß geltend machen. **-ion** [-'zəːʃən], *s.* die Anwendung, Ausübung; Anstrengung, Anspannung, Bemühung.

exeunt ['ɛksɪʌnt], (sie gehen) ab (*Theat.*).

exfoliat-e [ɛks'foulɪeɪt], *v.n.* sich abblättern (*Surg., Min.*). **-ion** [-'eɪʃən], *s.* die Abblätterung.

exhal-ation [ɛksə'leɪʃən], *s.* die Ausdünstung, Ausatmung; der Nebel, Dunst. **-e** [ɛks'heɪl], *v.a.* ausdünsten; aushauchen, von sich geben; *be -ed*, ausdunsten.

exhaust [ɪg'zɔːst], 1. *v.a.* erschöpfen, ermüden; erschöpfend behandeln; aufbrauchen, ausziehen, ausschöpfen, auspumpen, entleeren (*vessel*); - *the air in . . ., . . .* luftleer pumpen. 2. *s.* der Auspuff (*Motor.*), das Abgas, der Abdampf. **-ed,** *adj.* erschöpft, ermattet; verbraucht, abgebaut (*of a mine*); *be -ed*, versiegen; vergriffen sein (*of a book*). **--gas,** das Abgas. **-ible,** *adj.* erschöpflich. **-ing,** *adj.* anstrengend, ermüdend, mühselig. **-ion** [-tʃən], *s.* die Erschöpfung; Ausziehung; das Ausströmen, Auspumpen; der Verbrauch, Konsum; die Exhaustion, Ausschöpfung (*Math.*). **-ive,** *adj.* erschöpfend; vollständig. **-less,** *adj.* unerschöpflich. **--pipe,** *s.* das Auspuffrohr. **--steam,** *s.* der Abdampf. **--valve,** *s.* die Auspuffklappe, das Auslaßventil.

exhibit [ɪg'zɪbɪt], 1. *v.a.* sehen lassen, zeigen; ausstellen; aufweisen, darlegen, an den Tag legen, entfalten, vorbringen, anbringen, vorlegen (*a charge, etc.*) (*Law*). 2. *s.* das Beweisstück, der Beleg, die Anlage; Ausstellung; schriftliche Eingabe (*Law*); der Ausstellungsgegenstand. **-ion** [ɛksɪ'bɪʃən], *s.* die Ausstellung, Auslage; Darlegung, Bekundung, Äußerung; (kleines) Stipendium (*Univ.*); *be on public -ion*, öffentlich ausgestellt sein; *international -ion*, die Weltausstellung; *make an -ion of o.s.*, eine lächerliche Figur machen, sich lächerlich *or* zum Gespött machen. **-ioner,** *s.* der Stipendiat. **-or,** *s.* der Aussteller.

exhilarat-e [ɪg'zɪləreɪt], *v.a.* erheitern, aufheitern. **-ed,** *adj.* heiter, lebhaft. **-ing,** *adj.* erheiternd. **-ion** [-reɪʃən], *s.* die Erheiterung; Heiterkeit.

exhort [ɪg'zɔːt], *v.a.* ermahnen, ermuntern, zureden (*Dat.*) (*to*, zu); dringend raten *or* empfehlen (*Dat.*). **-ation** [ɛgzɔː'teɪʃən], *s.* die Ermahnung. **-atory** [-tətərɪ], *adj.* ermahnend.

exhum-ation [ɛkshjuː'meɪʃən], *s.* die Wiederausgrabung (*of corpses*). **-e** [ɛks'hjuːm], *v.a.* ausgraben; (*fig.*) an Tageslicht bringen.

exig-ence ['ɛksɪdʒəns], **-ency,** *s.* das Erfordernis, großes Bedürfnis; der Notfall, dringender Fall, dringende Not, schwierige Lage. **-ent,** *adj.* dringend, dringlich; anspruchsvoll.

exigu-ity [ɛksɪ'gjuɪtɪ], *s.* die Kleinheit, Winzigkeit, Spärlichkeit, Geringfügigkeit, Unerheblichkeit, Unzulänglichkeit. **-ous** [ɛg'zɪgjuəs], *adj.* klein, winzig, dürftig, unbedeutend, geringfügig.

exile ['ɛksaɪl], 1. *s.* die Verbannung, das Exil; die Abgeschiedenheit; Verbannte(r), *m.*, Vertriebene(r), *m.* 2. *v.a.* verbannen, verweisen (*from*, aus).

exist [ɪg'zɪst], *v.n.* existieren, vorhanden sein, sich finden; leben, dauern, bestehen; vegetieren. **-ence,** *s.* das Dasein, Vorhandensein, die Existenz; das Leben, Fortbestehen, die Dauer; *be in -ence*, existieren, vorhanden sein; *call s.th. into -ence*, etwas ins Leben rufen; *struggle for -ence*, der Daseinskampf. **-ent,** *adj.* vorhanden, bestehend, existierend. **-ential** [-'tɛnʃəl], *adj.* Existenz-, Existenzial- (*Philos.*). **-entialism,** *s.* die Existenzphilosophie, Existenzialphilosophie. **-ing,** *adj.* bestehend.

exit ['ɛksɪt], 1. *v.n.* abgehen, abtreten; (geht) ab (*Theat.*). 2. *s.* der Abgang, das Abtreten; (*fig.*) der Tod; Ausgang, Austritt; *make one's -*, abtreten; (*fig.*) verscheiden.

ex-libris [ɛks'lɪːbrɪs], *s.* das Bucheignerzeichen, Exlibris.

exodus ['ɛksədəs], *s.* der Auszug, die Auswanderung; (*B.*) das zweite Buch Mosis.

ex officio [ɛks o'fɪʃɪou], *see* **ex** 1.

exogen ['ɛksodʒɛn], *s.* die Dikotyledone (*Bot.*). **-ous** [ɛk'sodʒənəs], *adj.* von außen wirkend (*Geol.*), exogen (*Bot.*).

exonerat-e [ɪg'zonəreɪt], *v.a.* entlasten, freisprechen, befreien (*from a charge*), entbinden (*from a duty*). **-ion** [-'reɪʃən], *s.* die Entlastung, Befreiung. **-ive** [-rətɪv], *adj.* entlastend.

exophthalmus [ɛksof'θælməs], *s.* der Augapfelvorfall (*Med.*).

exorbitan-ce [ɪg'zɔːbɪtəns], *s.*, **-cy,** *s.* das Übermaß, die Maßlosigkeit. **-t,** *adj.* übermäßig, übertrieben, maßlos, ungeheuer, anormal.

exorc-ism ['ɛksɔːsɪzm], *s.* die Geisterbeschwörung; Teufelsbannung. **-ist,** *s.* der Geisterbeschwörer. **-ize** [-saɪz], *v.a.* beschwören, bannen, austreiben (*spirits*); befreien, reinigen (*a place*).

exordium [ɛk'sɔːdɪəm], *s.* die Einleitung, der Anfang (*of a speech, etc.*).

exoteric(al) [ɛksou'tɛrɪk], *adj.* öffentlich, populär, gemeinverständlich; exoterisch (*Philos.*).

exotic [ɛk'sotɪk], 1. *adj.* ausländisch, fremdartig, exotisch. 2. *s.* ausländisches Gewächs; das Fremdwort.

expan-d [ɪks'pænd], 1. *v.a.* ausspannen, ausbreiten, ausdehnen; erweitern; *-ding bullet*, das Expansionsgeschoß. 2. *v.n.* sich ausbreiten, sich ausdehnen, sich erweitern; freundlich entgegenkommen (*Dat.*); *his heart -ds with joy*, sein Herz schwillt vor Freude. **-se** [-'pæns], *s.* die Ausdehnung, Weite; weiter Raum, weite Fläche; *the -se of heaven*, die Himmelswölbung. **-sibility,** *s.* die Ausdehnbarkeit. **-sible,** *adj.* (aus)dehnbar. **-sion** [-'pænʃən], *s.* die Ausdehnung, Dehnung, Ausbreitung, Erweiterung; Expansion; der Umfang, Raum. **-sive** [-sɪv], *adj.* ausdehnend; ausdehnungsfähig; (*fig.*) gefühlvoll, überschwenglich, mitteilsam; ausgedehnt, weit, breit, umfassend; *-sive force*, die Ausdehnungskraft. **-siveness,** *s.* die Ausdehnungsfähigkeit; (*fig.*) Freundlichkeit, Offenheit, Mitteilsamkeit.

expatiat-e [ɛks'peɪʃɪeɪt], *v.n.* (*archaic*) sich ungehemmt bewegen; (*fig.*) weitläufig sprechen, sich verbreiten *or* auslassen (*on*, über (*Acc.*)). **-ion**

[–ˈeɪʃən], *s.* weitläufige Erörterung. **–ory** [–ʃɪətərɪ], *adj.* weitläufig, langatmig.

expatriat–e [ɛksˈpætrɪeɪt], *v.a.* (aus dem Vaterlande) verbannen; *–e o.s.*, sein Vaterland verlassen, auswandern. **–ion** [–ˈeɪʃən], *s.* die Verbannung aus dem Vaterlande, Aberkennung der Staatsangehörigkeit; Auswanderung.

expect [ɪksˈpɛkt], *v.a.* erwarten; entgegensehen (*Dat.*); rechnen *or* zählen auf (*Acc.*); (*coll.*) vermuten, denken, glauben; *that is what is –ed of you*, das erwartet man von dir; (*coll.*) *I – so*, ich glaube schon. **–ancy,** *s.* die Erwartung, Aussicht; der Anspruch, die Anwartschaft (auf, (*Acc.*)) (*Law*). **–ant,** I. *adj.* erwartend, erwartungsvoll; *fee –ant*, die zu erwartende Gebühr (*Law*); *heir –ant*, der Anwärter auf ein Erbe, Thronanwärter; *–ant method*, abwartende Methode (*Med.*); *–ant mother*, werdende Mutter. 2. *s.* der Anwärter (auf (*Acc.*)). **–ation** [–ˈteɪʃən], *s.* die Erwartung, das Erwarten; die Hoffnung, Aussicht; (*often pl.*) der Gegenstand der Erwartung; *beyond –ation*, über Erwarten; *in the –ation of a th.*, einer S. entgegensehend; *in the –ation that*, in der Erwartung daß; *fall short of –ations*, die Erwartungen enttäuschen, den Erwartungen nicht entsprechen. *–ation of life*, mutmaßliche Lebensdauer; *contrary to –ation(s)*, wider Erwarten. **–ing,** *adj.*; (*coll.*) *be –ing*, in anderen Umständen sein.

expector–ant [ɛksˈpɛktərənt], *s.* schleimlösendes Mittel (*Med.*). **–ate** [ɛksˈpɛktəreɪt], I. *v.a.* auswerfen, aushusten, ausspeien. 2. *v.n.* spucken; Blut husten. **–ation** [–ˈreɪʃən], *s.* das Auswerfen, Ausspeien; der Schleimauswurf.

expedien–ce [ɪksˈpɪ:dɪəns], *s.* die Zweckdienlichkeit. **–cy,** *s.* die Angemessenheit, Schicklichkeit, Tunlichkeit, Ratsamkeit, Zweckmäßigkeit, Nützlichkeit. **–t** [–dɪənt], I. *adj.* schicklich, angebracht, angemessen, ratsam, passend; nützlich, zweckdienlich, vorteilhaft. 2. *s.* das Hilfsmittel, Behelfsmittel, der Notbehelf, Ausweg, die Ausflucht; *hit on an –t*, einen Ausweg finden.

expedit–e [ˈɛkspɪdɑɪt], *v.a.* beschleunigen, fördern; (ab)senden, befördern, expedieren. **–ion** [ɛkspɪˈdɪʃən], *s.* die Eile, Geschwindigkeit; der Feldzug; die (Forschungs)Reise, Expedition. **–ionary** [–ərɪ], *adj.* Expeditions–. **–ious** [–əs], *adj.* schnell, geschwind, eilig, emsig.

expel [ɪksˈpɛl], *v.a.* ausstoßen, austreiben, ausweisen, verbannen, ausschließen, vertreiben, wegtreiben, verdrängen, verweisen, relegieren (*Univ.*) (*from*, von, aus).

expend [ɪksˈpɛnd], *v.a.* ausgeben (*money*); verwenden, aufwenden (*labour*) (*on*, auf (*Acc.*)); verbrauchen. **–able,** *adj.* verbrauchbar, verzehrbar, Verbrauchs–. **–iture** [–dɪtʃə], *s.* die Ausgabe, Auslage, Verausgabung (*on*, für); Geldausgabe; Aufwendung, der Aufwand, Verbrauch (*of*, an) (*of time, etc.*).

expens–e [ɪksˈpɛns], *s.* die Ausgabe, Auslage, der Aufwand, Verbrauch; *pl.* die Kosten, Unkosten, Spesen (*C.L.*); *at an* or *the –e of*, unter Verlust von, mit einem Aufwand von; *at my –e*, auf meine Kosten; *at great –e*, teuer erkauft; *bear the –e*, die Kosten tragen; *cover –es*, die Auslagen decken; *current –es*, laufende Ausgaben (*pl.*); *cut down –es*, sich einschränken; *go to the –e of*, sich (*Dat.*) der Ausgaben unterziehen; *go to great –e*, sich (*Dat.*) große Kosten machen, es sich viel kosten lassen; *incidental –es*, unvorhergesehene Ausgaben, Nebenausgaben (*pl.*); *out-of-pocket –es*, die Erstattung der Unkosten; *put a p. to great –e*, einen in große Kosten stürzen, einem große Kosten verursachen; *not spare any –e*, keine Kosten scheuen; *travelling –es*, Reiskosten (*pl.*); *working –es*, Betriebsunkosten (*pl.*). **–ive** [sɪv], *adj.* kostspielig, teuer; *come –ive*, teuer (zu stehen) kommen. **–iveness,** *s.* die Kostspieligkeit.

experience [ɪksˈpɪərɪəns], I. *s.* die Erfahrung, das Erlebnis; die Praxis, in der Praxis erworbene Kenntnisse (*pl.*); *know by* or *from –*, aus Erfahrung wissen; *– in*, Erfahrung in; *– of*, Erfahrung an; *man of –*, erfahrener Mann; *– table*, die Sterblichkeitstabelle. 2. *v.a.* erfahren, erleben; aus Erfahrung wissen; erleiden, durchmachen; *– a difficulty*, auf eine Schwierigkeit stoßen. **–d,** *adj.* erfahren, bewandert (*in*, in); *–d in business*, geschäftskundig.

experiment [ɪksˈpɛrɪmənt], I. *s.* der Versuch, das Experiment, die Probe (*on*, an). 2. *v.n.* Versuche anstellen, experimentieren (*on*, an; *with*, mit); versuchen, erproben (*with a th.*, etwas). **–al** [–ˈmɛntl], *adj.* experimentell, Experimental–; erfahrungsgemäß, auf Erfahrung gegründet, Erfahrungs–, Erlebnis–; Versuchs–, versuchend; *–al chemistry*, die Experimentalchemie; *–al model*, der Versuchsmodell. **–alist** [–ˈmɛntəlɪst], *s.*, **–er,** *s.* der Experimentierer. **–alize** [–ˈmɛntəlɑɪz], *v.n.* Versuche anstellen, experimentieren. **–ally,** *adv.* durch Experiment. **–ation,** *s.* das Experimentieren.

expert [ˈɛkspə:t], I. *adj.* erfahren, kundig; geschickt, gewandt, fachmännisch (*work*); *– swimmer*, ausgezeichneter Schwimmer. 2. *s.* Sachverständige(r), *m.*, der Gutachter; Fachmann, Kenner; *be an – at s.th.*, sich auf eine S. verstehen. **–ness,** *s.* die Geschicklichkeit, Gewandtheit.

expia–ble [ˈɛkspɪəbl], *adj.* sühnbar. **–te** [ˈɛkspɪeɪt], *v.a.* (ab)büßen, sühnen, wiedergutmachen. **–tion** [–eɪʃən], *s.* die Sühne, (Ab)Buße, Tilgung. **–tory** [–ətərɪ], *adj.* sühnend, Sühn–, Buß–.

expir–ation [ɛkspɪˈreɪʃən], *s.* die Ausatmung; der Ablauf, Verlauf; (*fig.*) das Ende, der Tod; *at the time of –ation*, zur Verfallzeit (*C.L.*); *on the –ation of*, nach Ablauf von. **–atory** [ɪksˈpɑɪrətərɪ], *adj.* ausatmend, Ausatmungs–, Atem–. **–e** [ɪksˈpɑɪə], *v.n.* aushauchen, ausatmen; sterben, verscheiden; zu Ende gehen, ablaufen (*as time*), erlöschen (*as a title*); verfallen, fällig *or* ungültig werden (*as a contract*). **–ing,** *adj.* sterbend, Todes–. **–y,** *s.* das Ende, der Ablauf.

explain [ɪksˈpleɪn], I. *v.a.* erklären, erläutern, verständlich *or* klar machen; auseinandersetzen; rechtfertigen, begründen; *– away*, wegerklären, beseitigen. 2. *v.n.* eine Erklärung geben, sich erklären. **–able,** *adj.* erklärlich, erklärbar. **–er,** *s.* der Erklärer.

explanat–ion [ɛkspləˈneɪʃən], *s.* die Erklärung (*of*, für), Erläuterung (*of*, zu), Auslegung (*of* (*Gen.*)); (*archaic*) Verständigung; (*archaic*) *come to an –ation with*, sich verständigen mit; *in –ation of*, als Erklärung für, zur Erklärung von, um zu erklären; *make some –ation*, sich erklären, eine Erklärung abgeben. **–ory** [ɪksˈplænətərɪ], *adj.* erklärend, erläuternd.

expletive [ɛksˈplɪ:tɪv], I. *adj.* ausfüllend, Ausfüll–. 2. *s.* das Füllwort, Flickwort; der Lückenbüßer, das Füllsel; der Fluch, die Verwünschung.

explic–able [ˈɛksplɪkəbl], *adj.* erklärlich, erklärbar. **–ation** [–ˈkeɪʃən], *s.* die Erläuterung, Erklärung. **–ative, –atory** [–tərɪ], *adj.* erklärend, erläuternd. **–it** [ɛksˈplɪsɪt], *adj.* ausdrücklich, deutlich, klar (*of statements*); bestimmt; offen, rückhaltlos (*of persons*). **–itness,** *s.* die Deutlichkeit, Bestimmtheit.

explode [ɪksˈploʊd], I. *v.a.* explodieren lassen, detonieren, sprengen; (*fig.*) verwerfen, beseitigen; (*fig.*) *be –d*, überlebt *or* veraltet sein, keine Geltung mehr haben. 2. *v.n.* zerknallen, zersprengen, in die Luft fliegen, explodieren, platzen, bersten, krepieren (*of a shell*).

exploit, I. [ˈɛksplɔɪt], *s.* die Großtat, Heldentat. 2. [ɪksˈplɔɪt], *v.a.* ausnutzen, auswerten (*a th.*); ausbeuten (*a p.*). **–able** [ɪksˈplɔɪtəbl], *adj.* ausnutzbar. **–ation** [–ˈteɪʃən], *s.* die Ausnützung, Ausbeutung.

explor–ation [ɛksplɔ:ˈreɪʃən], *s.* die Erforschung, Untersuchung. **–ative** [ɪksˈplɔ:rətɪv], **–atory** [ɪksˈplɔ:rətrɪ], *adj.* erforschend, untersuchend, Forschungs–, Untersuchungs–; informatorisch. **–e** [ɪksˈplɔ:], *v.a.* erforschen, ausforschen, untersuchen, sondieren. **–er** [–rə], *s.* der (Er)Forscher, Forschungsreisende(r), *m.*

explos–ion [ɪksˈploʊʒən], *s.* der Knall, die Explosion, das Bersten, Platzen, Sprengen; die Sprengung; (*fig.*) der Ausbruch. **–ive** [–ˈploʊsɪv], I. *adj.* explosiv, Spreng–, Explosions–; *–ive bullet*, das Sprenggeschoß; *–ive force* or *power*, die Sprengkraft, Sprengwirkung, Brisanz; *–ive gas*, das Knallgas. 2. *s.* der Sprengstoff, das Sprengmittel; der

Verschlußlaut (*Phonet.*); *high –ive*, der Brisanzsprengstoff. **–iveness,** *s.* die Explosionsfähigkeit.

exponent [ɛks'pounənt], *s.* der Repräsentant; Exponent (*Math.*); Erklärer, Ausleger; – *of a view*, der Vertreter einer Ansicht. **–ial** [–po'nɛnʃəl], 1. *adj.* Exponential– (*Math.*). 2. *s.* die Exponentialgröße.

export, 1. [ɛks'pɔ:t], *v.a.* ausführen, versenden, exportieren. 2. ['ɛkspɔ:t], *s.* die Ausfuhr, der Export; Ausfuhrartikel; *pl.* die Gesamtausfuhr. **–able,** *adj.* ausführbar, Ausfuhr–, exportierbar. **–ation** [–'teɪʃən], *s.* die Ausfuhr, das Exportieren. **– -duty,** *s.* der Ausfuhrzoll. **–er,** *s.* der Exporteur, Ausfuhrhändler. **– -trade,** *s.* der Ausfuhrhandel.

expos–e [ɪks'pouz], *v.a.* aussetzen (*a child, etc.*); preisgeben, ausstellen, auslegen; belichten (*Phot.*); aufdecken, entlarven, enthüllen, an den Tag legen, darlegen; bloßstellen, bloßlegen, entblößen; *be –ed*, freistehen, freiliegen; *be –ed to*, ausgesetzt sein (*Dat.*); *–e o.s.*, sich (*Dat.*) eine Blöße geben; *–e o.s. to ridicule*, sich lächerlich machen; *–e for sale*, zum Verkauf auslegen, feilhalten. **–é,** *s.* die Darlegung; Entlarvung, Enthüllung. **–ed,** *adj.* frei, offen, freistehend, freiliegend; entblößt, ungeschützt; ausgesetzt, preisgegeben (*to* (*Dat.*)); *–ed position*, gefährdete *or* exponierte Lage (*Mil.*). **–ition** [ɛkspə'zɪʃən], *s.* die Erklärung, Auslegung (*of* (*Gen.*)); Ausführung(en), *f.* (*pl.*), Darlegung(en), *f.* (*pl.*); der Kommentar (*of*, über); die Ausstellung, Aussetzung, Preisgabe. **–itor** [ɛks'pɔzɪtə], *s.* der Ausleger, Erklärer, Deuter. **–itory** [–tərɪ], *adj.* erklärend, erläuternd.

expostulat–e [ɪks'pɔstjʊleɪt], *v.n.* ernste Vorhaltungen machen (*with a p.*, einem; *about*, über), zurechtweisen, zur Rede stellen (*with a p.*, einen; *about*, über), protestieren. **–ion** [–'leɪʃən], *s.* die Vorhaltung, der Protest, die Klage. **–ive, –ory** [–lətrɪ], *adj.* Vorhaltungen machend, mahnend; *–ory letter*, eine Beschwerdeschrift.

exposure [ɪks'pouʒə], *s.* die Ausstellung, das Feilhalten (*of goods for sale*); Ausgesetztsein, die Aussetzung, Preisgabe; Enthüllung, Entlarvung, Aufdeckung, Bloßstellung; (ungeschützte) Lage; die Belichtung, Belichtungszeit (*Phot.*); *southern* –, die Südlage; *death from* –, der Tod durch Erfrieren; *time* –, die Zeitaufnahme (*Phot.*).

expound [ɪks'paund], *v.a.* auslegen, erläutern, erklären. **–er,** *s.* der Erklärer, Ausleger.

express [ɪks'prɛs], 1. *v.a.* ausdrücken, auspressen; (*fig.*) äußern, ausdrücken, zum Ausdruck bringen, aussprechen (*opinions*); bezeigen, zu erkennen geben, an den Tag legen (*feelings, etc.*); darstellen, vorstellen, bezeichnen, bedeuten, bekunden (*motives, intentions, etc.*); – *o.s.*, sich äußern, sich ausdrücken; sich zeigen, sich erklären, sich offenbaren. 2. *adj.* ausdrücklich, deutlich; eigen, besonder, expreß; Eil–, Schnell–; – *delivery*, die Eilbeförderung, Eilzustellung; – *letter*, der Eilbrief; – *train*, der Schnellzug, D-Zug. 3. *adv.* eigens, expreß; durch Eilboten; *by* –, per Eilgut (*C.L.*). 4. *s.* der Eilbote; das Eilgut; der Schnellzug, Eilzug. **–ible,** *adj.* ausdrückbar. **–ion** [ɪks'prɛʃən], *s.* der Ausdruck, die Redensart; die Äußerung, Erklärung; Ausdrucksweise; Formel (*Math.*); das Auspressen, Ausdrücken (*of juice*); *beyond –ion*, über alle Beschreibung, unaussprechlich; *give –ion to*, Ausdruck verleihen (*Dat.*); *odd –ion*, seltsamer (Gesichts)Ausdruck. **–ionism,** *s.* der Expressionismus. **–ionless,** *adj.* ausdruckslos. **–ive** [–sɪv], *adj.* ausdrückend, bezeichnend, ausdrucksvoll, nachdrücklich, kräftig; *be –ive of*, ausdrücken. **–iveness,** *s.* das Ausdrucksvolle, die Ausdruckskraft; Ausdrücklichkeit, der Nachdruck. **–ly,** *adv.* ausdrücklich, besonders; eigens.

expropriat–e [ɛks'prouprɪeɪt], *v.a.* enteignen, des Eigentums berauben. **–ion** [-'eɪʃən], *s.* die Enteignung, Eigentumsberaubung.

expulsi–on [ɪks'pʌlʃən], *s.* die Austreibung, Vertreibung, Ausweisung, Ausstoßung (*from*, aus), Abschiebung, Entfernung (*from*, von). **–ve** [–'pʌlsɪv], *adj.* vertreibend, austreibend.

expunge [ɛks'pʌndʒ], *v.a.* ausstreichen, auslöschen; (aus)tilgen.

expurgat–e ['ɛkspə:geɪt], *v.a.* reinigen, säubern (*a book*)(*from*, von). **–ion** [–'geɪʃən], *s.* die Reinigung, Streichung, Ausscheidung. **–ory** [ɪks'pə:gətərɪ], *adj.* reinigend, säubernd.

exquisite ['ɛkskwɪzɪt], 1. *adj.* vortrefflich, vorzüglich, ausgezeichnet, ausgesucht; höchst empfindlich, äußerst fein; ungemein, hochgradig. 2. *s.* (*archaic*) der Stutzer, Geck. **–ness,** *s.* die Vorzüglichkeit, Vortrefflichkeit; Schärfe, Feinheit (*of judgement, etc.*); Heftigkeit, Stärke (*of pain*).

ex-serviceman [ɛks'sə:vɪsmən], *s.* ehemaliger Frontsoldat.

extant [ɛks'tænt], *adj.* existierend, (noch) vorhanden.

extempor–aneous [ɛkstɛmpə'reɪnjəs], *adj.*, **–ary** [ɪks'tɛmpərərɪ], *adj.*, **–e** [ɪks'tɛmpərɪ], *adj.* & *adv.* aus dem Stegreif, unvorbereitet. **–ize** [ɪks·tɛmpəraɪz], *v.a.* & *n.* aus dem Stegreife reden *or* spielen *or* dichten, extemporieren, improvisieren. **–izer,** *s.* der Stegreifredner, –spieler, –dichter, Improvisator.

extend [ɪks'tɛnd], 1. *v.a.* ausdehnen, verlängern, erstrecken, erweitern, fortsetzen, vergrößern; ausstrecken, ausbreiten; (*fig.*) gewähren, erweisen, erzeigen (*to* (*Dat.*)) (*a welcome, etc.*); voll ausschreiben (*abbreviations*), in gewöhnliche Schrift umsetzen (*shorthand*); – *one's hand to s.o.*, einem seine Hand reichen; – *help to s.o.*, einem Hilfe angedeihen lassen; – *a line*, eine Linie ziehen; *–ed order* (*Mil.*) or *formation* (*Av.*), ausgeschwärmte Schützenlinie (*Mil.*), geöffnete Flugordnung (*Av.*). 2. *v.n.* sich erstrecken, reichen, sich ausdehnen (*from*, von; *to*, bis); hinausgehen (*beyond*, über).

extens–ibility [ɪkstɛnsɪ'bɪlɪtɪ], *s.* die Dehnbarkeit. **–ible** [ɪks'tɛnsɪbl], *adj.* dehnbar, streckbar. **–ion** [–'tɛnʃən], *s.* die Ausdehnung; Streckung, Verlängerung, Erweiterung, Vergrößerung; der Umfang; Nebenanschluß (*Phone.*), Anbau (*to a building*); *–ion of leave*, die Urlaubsverlängerung, der Nachurlaub (*Mil.*); *–ion rod*, das Aufsteckrohr; *–ion of the term of payment*, die Verlängerung *or* Hinausschiebung des Zahlungstermins; *university –ion*, die Volkshochschule. **–ive** [–'tɛnsɪv], *adj.* weit erstreckend, ausgedehnt; umfassend, geräumig. **–iveness,** *s.* die Ausdehnung, Weite, Größe, der Umfang. **–or** [ɪks'tɛnsə], *s.* der Streckmuskel, Strecker (*Anat.*).

extent [ɪks'tɛnt], *s.* die Ausdehnung, Weite, Strecke, Größe, Länge, Höhe; der Raum, Umfang; Grad, das Maß; *in* –, an Umfang; *to the* – *of*, bis zum Betrage *or* zur Höhe von; *to a certain* –, gewissermaßen, bis zu einem gewissen Grade; *to the full* –, völlig, bis zum vollen Umfang; *to a great* –, im hohen Grade, großenteils; *to some* –, einigermaßen.

extenuat–e [ɛks'tɛnjʊeɪt], *v.a.* mildern, schwächen; beschönigen, bemänteln; *–ing circumstances*, mildernde Umstände. **–ion** [–'eɪʃən], *s.* die Milderung, Abschwächung, Beschönigung; *in –ion of*, um zu mildern, zur Milderung (*Gen.*).

exterior [ɛks'tɪ:ərɪə], 1. *adj.* äußerlich, äußere(r)(s); – *angle*, der Außenwinkel; – *to*, außerhalb (*Gen.*), abseits von. 2. *s.* das Äußere (*of things*), äußeres Ansehen (*of persons*), die Außenaufnahme (*films*); (*fig.*) Außenseite.

exterminat–e [ɛks'tə:mɪneɪt], *v.a.* ausrotten, vertilgen. **–ion** [–'neɪʃen], *s.* die Vertilgung, Ausrottung.

external [ɛks'tə:nl], 1. *adj.* außen befindlich; äußere(r)(s), äußerlich, Außen– (*Math.*); sichtbar, wahrnehmbar, körperlich; auswärtig; – *to*, außerhalb (*Gen.*); *the* – *world*, die Außenwelt, Erscheinungswelt. 2. *s.* (*usually pl.*) das Äußere; Äußerlichkeiten, Nebensächlichkeiten (*pl.*). **–ize,** *v.a.* veräußerlichen, verkörper(liche)n.

exterritorial [ɛkstɛrɪ'tɔ:rɪəl], *see* **extra-territorial.**

extinct [ɪks'tɪŋkt], *adj.* erloschen, ausgestorben; abgeschafft, aufgehoben; – *race*, untergegangene Rasse; – *species*, ausgestorbene Gattung (*of animals*); – *volcano*, ausgebrannter Vulkan. **–ion** [–'tɪŋkʃən], *s.* das Auslöschen, Aussterben, der Untergang; die (Aus)Löschung, Tilgung (*of debts*); Vernichtung.

extinguish [ɪks'tɪŋgwɪʃ], *v.a.* (aus)löschen, erlöschen, ersticken, vernichten, töten, zerstören, abschaffen, aufheben, tilgen (*debt*); (*fig.*) in den Schatten stellen, zum Schweigen bringen. **–er,** *s.* das

Löschhütchen, Lichthütchen; *fire--er*, der Feuerlöschapparat. **–ment,** *s.* die Aufhebung (*Law*); *see aslo* **extinction.**
extirpat–e [ˈɛkstəːpeɪt], *v.a.* ausrotten; ausschneiden, entfernen (*Surg.*). **–ion,** *s.* die Ausrottung; Ausschneidung (*Surg.*).
extol [[ɪksˈtɔl], *v.a.* erheben, preisen, loben; – *s.o. to the skies*, einen in den Himmel heben.
extort [ɪksˈtɔːt], *v.a.* erpressen, abnötigen; – *a th. from a p.*, einem etwas gewaltsam abzwingen, etwas von einem erzwingen. **–ion** [–ˈtɔːʃən], *s.* die Erpressung, der Wucher. **–ionate** [–ˈtɔːʃənɪt], *adj.* erpresserisch, wucherisch; *–ionate price*, der Wucherpreis. **–ioner,** *s.* der Erpresser, Wucherer.
extra [ˈekstrə], 1. *adj.* besonder, zusätzlich, nachträglich; außergewöhnlich, außerordentlich; Neben–, Sonder–, Extra–; – *charges*, die Nebenspesen, Nebenkosten; – *freight*, die Extrafracht; – *pay*, die Zulage; – *work*, die Strafarbeit (*school*). 2. *adv.* besonders, extra. 3. *s.* das Außergewöhnliche, das was über das Übliche hinausgeht; die Extraausgabe, Sondernummer (*newspaper*); *pl.* der Zuschlag, nachträgliche Ausgaben, Sondergebühren, Extrakosten. **--judicial,** *adj.* außergerichtlich. **--mural,** *adj.* Volkshochschul–. **--territorial,** *adj.* exterritorial (*of diplomats, etc.*). **--time,** *s.* die Verlängerungszeit (*Sport*).
extract, 1. [ɪksˈtrækt], *v.a.* ausziehen, herausziehen (*a tooth, etc.*); einen Auszug machen, ziehen (*extracts, etc.*); ausscheiden, auslaugen, extrahieren (*from*, aus) (*Chem.*); absondern, gewinnen (*from* (*Dat.*)); (*fig.*) herausholen (*from*, aus), abringen, entlocken (*from a p.*, einem), herleiten, ableiten (*from*, von); – *the root of a number*, aus einer Zahl die Wurzel ziehen (*Math.*). 2. [ˈekstrækt], *s.* der Extrakt, Absud (*Chem., etc.*); Auszug, Ausschnitt, das Zitat (*from a book*). **–ion** [ɪksˈtrækʃən], *s.* das (Her)Ausziehen; die Ausziehung, Entziehung, Ausscheidung, Gewinnung, Extraktion, das Auslaugen (*Chem., etc.*); die Ausmahlung (*of flour*); das Ziehen (*Math.*); die Abkunft, Abstammung, Herkunft. **–or** [ɪksˈtræktə], *s.* der Auszieher (*also Artil.*), Entlader (*Artil.*); die Zange (*Surg.*); die Maschine *or* das Werkzeug zum Ausziehen *or* Ausscheiden *or* zur Gewinnung, *e.g. honey--or*, die Honigschleuder.
extradit–able [ɛkstrəˈdɑɪtəbl], *adj.* auslieferbar, auszuliefern(d). **–e** [ˈɛkstrədɑɪt], *v.a.* ausliefern. **–ion** [–ˈdɪʃən], *s.* die Auslieferung.
extrados [ɛksˈtreɪdɔs], *s.* der Bogenrücken (*Arch.*).
extraneous [ɛksˈtreɪnjəs], *adj.* nicht gehörig, von außen (kommend); fremd, fremdartig; unwesentlich; – *to*, nicht gehörig zu.
extraordinar–iness [ɛkˈstrɔːdɪnərɪnɪs], *s.* die Merkwürdigkeit, Ungewöhnlichkeit. **–y,** *adj.* außerordentlich, außergewöhnlich, ungewöhnlich; merkwürdig, seltsam; *ambassador –y*, der Sonderbotschafter; *–y charges*, Extrakosten.
extravagan–ce [ɪksˈtrævəgəns], *s.*, **–cy,** *s.* die Verschwendung; Überspanntheit, Übertriebenheit, das Übermaß, die Extravaganz; Ausschweifung, Zügellosigkeit. **–t** [–ənt], *adj.* verschwenderisch; übertrieben, übermäßig; überspannt, zügellos, ausschweifend. **–za** [ɛkstrævəˈgænzə], *s.* fantastisches Werk, die Burleske, Posse.
extravasat–e [ɛksˈtrævəseɪt], 1. *v.a.* austreten lassen; *–ed blood*, ausgetretenes Blut. 2. *v.n.* ausfließen, heraustreten. **–ion** [–ˈseɪʃən], *s.* der (Blut)Erguß, Austritt (*of blood*).
extrem–e [ɪksˈtrɪːm], 1. *adj.* äußerst, weitest, letzt; (*fig.*) außerordentlich, höchst, übertrieben; *–e case*, der Fall der Not; *–e danger*, höchste Gefahr; *to an –e degree*, im höchsten Grade; *–e measure*, äußerstes Mittel; *–e necessity*, dringendste Not; *–e old age*, sehr hohes Alter; *–e unction*, Letzte Ölung; *–e views*, radikale Ansichten. 2. *s.* das Äußerste, äußerstes Ende, äußerste Grenze, höchster Grad, das Extrem; die Übertreibung, das Übermaß; *at the other –e*, am entgegengesetzten Ende; *in the –e*, übermäßig; *–es of a proportion*, die äußeren Glieder einer Proportion; *carry s.th. to –es*, etwas zu weit treiben; *fly* or *go to the other –e*, ins andre Extrem verfallen; *go to –es*, zum Äußersten schreiten. **–ist,** *s.* Radikale(r), *m.* (*Pol.*). **–ity** [ɪksˈtrɛmɪtɪ], *s.* das Äußerste, äußerstes Ende, äußerste Grenze; die Spitze, der Rand; (*often pl.*) äußerste Verlegenheit *or* Not; (*often pl.*) äußerste Maßnahme; *pl.* Extremitäten, Hände und Füße; *to the last –ity*, bis zum Äußersten; *carry to –ities*, übertreiben, zu weit treiben, auf die Spitze treiben; *proceed to –ities*, zum Äußersten schreiten, die äußersten Maßnahmen ergreifen; *be reduced to –ities*, in äußerster Not sein.
extricat–e [ˈɛkstrɪkeɪt], *v.a.* freimachen, befreien, herausziehen, herauswickeln (*from*, aus, von); entwickeln (*heat, etc.*). **–ion** [–ˈkeɪʃən], *s.* die Befreiung, das Freimachen.
extrinsic [ɛksˈtrɪnsɪk], *adj.* äußere(r)(s), äußerlich, von außen.
extrover–sion [ɛkstroˈvəːʃən], *s.* die Einstellung auf die Außenwelt (*Psych.*). **–t** [ˈɛkstrəvəːt], *s.* Extrovertierte(r), *m.* (*Psych.*).
extru–de [ɛksˈtrʊːd], *v.a.* herauspressen, austreiben, verdrängen. **–sion,** *s.* das Auspressen, die Verdrängung.
exubera–nce [ɪgˈzjʊːbərəns], **–ncy,** *s.* der Überfluß, das Übermaß, die Fülle, Üppigkeit, Überschwenglichkeit; der (Rede)Schwall. **–nt** [–ənt], *adj.* (über)reichlich; üppig, wuchernd, überschwenglich; *–nt spirits*, sprudelnde Laune. **–te** [–eɪt], *v.n.* strotzen (*with*, von).
exud–ation [ɛgsjʊːˈdeɪʃən], *s.* die Ausschwitzung, Auswitterung, Ausblühung, der Ausschlag. **–e** [ɪgˈzjʊːd], *v.a.* & *n.* ausschwitzen, auswittern, ausblühen, ausschlagen; (*fig.*) von sich geben, hervorkommen.
exult [ɪgˈzʌlt], *v.n.* frohlocken (*at*, *over*, über (*Acc.*)), triumphieren (*over*, über). **–ant,** *adj.* frohlockend, jauchzend, triumphierend. **–ation** [ɛgzʌlˈteɪʃən], *s.* das Frohlocken, der Jubel.
eye [ɑɪ], **1.** *s.* das Auge (*also Bot.* & *fig.*), (*fig.*) der Blick; das Öhr, die Öse (*of needle, etc.*); Kausch(e) (*on a sail*) (*Naut.*); Knospe (*of plant*); der Nabel (*of seeds*); **(a)** (*with adjectives*) (*coll.*) *all my* –, Unsinn, Unfug; *evil* –, böser Blick; (*coll.*) *give a p. the glad* –, mit einem kokettieren; *if you had half an* –, wenn du nicht ganz blind wärest; *be born with one's –s open*, Haare auf den Zähnen haben; *be in the public* –, in der Öffentlichkeit bekannt sein; (*coll.*) *keep one's –s skinned* or *peeled*, scharf aufpassen, sich nichts entgehen lassen; **(b)** (*with verbs*) *be all –s*, seine Augen überall haben; (*sl.*) *his –s are bigger than his belly*, seine Augen sind größer als der Magen; *catch the* –, ins Auge fallen, auffallen; *catch a p.'s* –, jemandes Blick treffen, jemandes Aufmerksamkeit fesseln; *catch the Speaker's* –, das Wort erhalten (*Parl.*); (*coll.*) *clap –s on*, zu Gesicht bekommen; *cry one's –s out*, sich ausweinen; *give an – to*, ein Auge haben auf; *have an – for*, Sinn *or* ein (offenes) Auge haben für; *have one's –s about one*, die Augen überall haben; *have an – to*, achten auf, ein Auge haben auf; *keep a strict* or *an – on*, ein wachsames Auge haben auf; *make* (*sheep's*) *–s at*, verliebte Blicke zuwerfen (*Dat.*); *more in it than meets the* –, mehr dahinterstecken als es den Anschein hat; (*coll.*) *mind your – !* paß auf! *open a p.'s –s*, einem die Augen öffnen; *set –s upon*, zu Gesicht bekommen; *shut one's –s to*, die Augen verschließen gegen; *strike the* –, in die Augen springen; **(c)** (*with nouns*) *apple of the* –, der Augapfel; *catch* or *see it with the corner of one's* –, einen flüchtigen Blick von etwas erhaschen; *–s front!* Augen geradeaus! *in the twinkling of an* –, im Nu; *mind's* –, geistiges Auge; *–s like saucers*, Glotzaugen (*pl.*); **(d)** (*with prepositions*) *an – for an* –, Auge um Auge; (*coll.*) *sight for sore –s*, der Lichtblick; *have in one's* –, im Auge haben; *in the –(s) of the law*, vom Standpunkt des Gesetzes; *in my –s*, in meinen Augen, nach meinem Urteil; (*sl.*) *do s.o. in the* –, einen beschwindeln; *find favour in his –s*, vor ihm Gnade finden; *be wise in one's own –s*, sich klug dünken; *in(to) the wind's* –, gegen den Wind; *up to the –s in work*, bis über die Ohren in der Arbeit; *see – to – with a p.*, mit einem völlig übereinstimmen; *with an – to*, mit Rücksicht auf (*Acc.*), . . . im Auge haben; *with the naked* –, mit bloßem Auge; *with one's –s shut*, mit geschlossenen Augen. **2.** *v.a.* ansehen, betrachten, mustern, beobachten, ins

Auge fassen, beäugeln; *– from head to foot, up and down* or *from top to toe*, von oben bis unten mustern. **–ball,** *s.* der Augapfel. **– -bright,** *s.* der Augentrost (*Bot.*). **–brow,** *s.* die Augenbraue. **–d,** *adj. suffix* –äugig. **–glass,** *s.* das Augenglas, Monokel, Lorgnon; (*usually pl.*) die Brille, Augengläser, der Kneifer, Zwicker, Klemmer; das Augenglas; Okular. **– -hole,** *s.* das Guckloch. **–lash,** *s.* die Augenwimper. **–let,** *s.* die Öse, das Loch, Äuglein. **–lid,** *s.* das Augenlid. **– -lotion,** *s.* das Augenwasser. (*coll.*) **– -opener,** *s.* die Überraschung, schlagender Beweis; *it was an – -opener to me*, es belehrte mich eines Besseren, es öffnete mir die Augen. **– -piece,** *s.* das Okular (*Opt.*), Augenfenster (*of gas-mask*). **– -shade,** *s.* der Augenschirm. **–sight,** *s.* die Sehkraft; das Augenlicht. **–sore,** *s.* unschöne Stelle, häßlicher Zug, störender Anblick, der Ekel, Dorn im Auge. **–tooth,** *s.* der Augenzahn, Eckzahn. **–wash,** *s.* das Augenwasser, (*sl.*) der Schwindel, die Augenwischerei; Spiegelfechterei, der Bluff, das Täuschungsmanöver. **– -witness,** 1. *s.* der Augenzeuge. 2. *v.a.* als Augenzeuge beobachten.

eyot [ˈeɪət], *s.* der Werder, das Inselchen.

eyre [ɛə], *s.* die Rundreise der Richter; *justices in –*, das Land bereisende Richter.

eyrie [ˈɛərɪ], *s. see* **aerie.**

F

F, f [ɛf], *s.* das F, f (*also Mus.*); *F flat*, das Fes; *F major*, F-Dur; *F minor*, F-Moll; *F sharp*, das Fis. *See Index of Abbreviations.*

fa [fɑː], *s.* das F (*Mus.*).

fabian [ˈfeɪbɪən], *adj.* zögernd; fabianisch; *– Society*, sozialistischer Verein.

fable [ˈfeɪbl], 1. *s.* die Fabel; das Märchen, erdichtete Geschichte; die Mythe, Legende; Erdichtung, Lüge; *it is a mere –*, es ist völlig aus der Luft gegriffen. 2. *v.a.* erdichten, fabeln, zusammenlügen. **–d,** *adj.* in Fabeln gepriesen, legendenhaft, erdichtet.

fabric [ˈfæbrɪk], *s.* das Gebäude, der Bau; (*fig.*) das Gefüge, System, die Struktur; das Zeug, Gewebe, der Stoff; die Bespannung (*Av.*). **–ate** [ˈfæbrɪkeɪt], *v.a.* verfertigen, anfertigen, herstellen, fabrizieren; (*fig.*) erfinden, erdichten, schmieden. **–ation** [–ˈkeɪʃən], *s.* die Herstellung, Fabrikation; (*fig.*) Erdichtung, Erfindung, Lüge. **–ator,** *s.* der Verfertiger; Erfinder, Erdichter.

fabul–ist [ˈfæbjulɪst], *s.* der Fabeldichter; Erdichter von Lügen. **–ous** [–ləs], *adj.* legendenhaft, mythisch, Fabel–; (*fig.*) fabelhaft, unglaublich, ungeheuer.

façade [fəˈsɑːd], *s.* die Vorderseite, Fassade (*Build.*).

face [feɪs], **1.** *s.* das Gesicht, Antlitz, der (Gesichts)-Ausdruck, die Miene; (*coll.*) die Fratze, Grimasse; Fläche, Oberfläche, Schlagfläche; Vorderseite, Fassade, Außenseite, Front; Bildseite (*of a coin*), das Zifferblatt (*of a clock*), rechte Seite (*of cloth*); (*coll., fig.*) die Stirn, Unverschämtheit, Dreistigkeit; **(a)** (*with verbs*) *have the – to . . .*, die Stirn haben zu . . .; *make* or *pull a –*, Fratzen *or* ein Gesicht schneiden; *make* or *pull a long –*, ein langes Gesicht machen; *put a bold – on the matter*, sich (*Dat.*) etwas nicht sehr zu Herzen nehmen; *put a good* or *the best – on the matter*, gute Miene zum bösen Spiel machen; (*coll.*) *put on one's –*, sich pudern und schminken; *save one's –*, den (An)Schein wahren; seinen Ruf schützen; *set one's – against*, entschieden mißbilligen, sich sträuben, widersetzen, wenden *or* stemmen gegen; *show one's –*, sich sehen lassen; **(b)** (*with prepositions*) *take at – value*, für bare Münze nehmen; *before one's –*, vor jemandes Augen; *in – of*, gegenüber, direkt vor; *in the – of*, im Hinblick auf, angesichts; trotz; *fly in the – of a p.*, einem Trotz bieten, Hohn sprechen *or* zu Leibe gehen, sich offen widersetzen; *look a p. in the –*, einem ins Gesicht sehen; *shut the door in a p.'s –*, einem die Tür vor der Nase zuschlagen; *ruin stared them in the –*, der Untergang starrte ihnen entgegen; *on the – of it*, auf den ersten Blick, augenscheinlich; *to my –*, mir ins Gesicht; *– to –*, Angesicht zu Angesicht, Auge in Auge; *– to – with*, gegenüber (*Dat.*), angesichts (*Gen.*); **(c)** (*with adjectives*) *full- –*, die Vorderansicht; *half- –*, das Profil; *wry –*, schiefes Gesicht. **2.** *v.a.* ins Gesicht sehen (*Dat.*), gegenüberliegen *or* -stehen (*Dat.*); stehen vor, liegen vor (*Naut.*), (hinaus)gehen nach *or* auf (*Acc.*); entgegentreten, die Stirn bieten; bedecken, belegen, bekleiden, verblenden, verkleiden (*a wall*), einfassen, verbrämen, besetzen (*a dress, etc.*); *– death*, dem Tode ins Angesicht sehen; *– the engine*, vorwärts *or* mit dem Gesicht nach vorn fahren; *– facts*, sich mit den Tatsachen abfinden; *this window –s the garden*, dieses Fenster geht auf den Garten; *– a jacket*, Aufschläge auf einen Rock setzen; (*sl.*) *– the music*, seinen Mann stehen; *– (the) south*, nach Süden liegen; *the problem that –s us*, die Aufgabe *or* Frage, die uns hier entgegentritt; (*coll.*) *– it out*, fest durchhalten, es überwinden. 3. *v.n.*; *– about*, sich umwenden, kehrtmachen; *right about –!* rechtsum kehrt! (*Amer. Mil.*); *right –!* rechts um! (*Amer. Mil.*); *– up to a th.*, etwas entgegentreten *or* meistern. **–d,** *adj.*; *–d with cement*, mit Mörtel verkleidet *or* belegt; *–d card*, aufgedeckte Karte; *full- -ed*, mit rundem, vollem Gesicht; *two- -d*, doppelzüngig. **– -ache,** *s.* der Gesichtsschmerz, das Zahnweh. **– -card,** *s.* die Figur, das Bild (*Cards*). **– -cloth,** *s.* der Waschlappen. **– -guard,** *s.* die Schutzmaske. **– -lifting,** *s.* die Gesichtsschönheitspflege. (*coll.*) **–r,** *s.* ein Schlag ins Gesicht, plötzliche Schwierigkeit. **– -saving,** *adj.* den Anschein wahrend. **– -value,** *s.* der Nennwert; *see* **facing.**

facet [ˈfæsɪt], *s.* die Facette, Rautenfläche, geschliffene Fläche.

facetious [fəˈsiːʃəs], *adj.* witzig, drollig, spaßhaft, scherzhaft. **–ness,** *s.* die Drolligkeit, Scherzhaftigkeit.

facial [ˈfeɪʃəl], *adj.* Gesichts–, im Gesicht; *– angle*, der Gesichtswinkel.

facil–e [ˈfæsaɪl], *adj.* leicht (zu tun); gefällig, gefügig, umgänglich, nachgiebig; leicht, gewandt. **–itate** [fəˈsɪlɪteɪt], *v.a.* erleichtern, fördern. **–itation** [–ˈteɪʃən], *s.* die Erleichterung, Förderung. **–ity** [fəˈsɪlɪtɪ], *s.* die Leichtigkeit, Gewandtheit; Nachgiebigkeit; (*usually pl.*) Erleichterung, günstige Gelegenheit, Möglichkeit.

facing [ˈfeɪsɪŋ], 1. *pr.p.* zugekehrt (*Dat.*); *used as prep.* gegenüber. 2. *s.* der Überzug, die Schicht, Verkleidung, Verblendung (*Build.*); (*usually pl.*) der Aufschlag, Besatz (*Tail.*); die Wendung, Schwenkung; *– brick*, der Verblendstein.

facsimile [fækˈsɪmɪlɪ], *s.* das Faksimile, die Kopie, Nachbildung.

fact [fækt], *s.* die Tatsache; Tat, Handlung; (*without art. or pl.*) Wirklichkeit, Tatumstände (*pl.*); der Sachverhalt, Tatbestand (*Law*); *hard –s*, nackte Tatsachen. *matter of –*, 1. *s.* feststehende Tatsache. 2. *adj.* nüchtern, praktisch; *as a matter of –*, tatsächlich; *the – (of the matter) is that . . .*, die Sache ist die daß . . ., offen gesagt; *–s are –s*, Tatsache bleibt Tatsache; *in (point of) –*, wirklich, tatsächlich, in der Tat, eigentlich, vielmehr; *see* **factual.**

factio–n [ˈfækʃən], *s.* die Partei, Faktion; Parteiung, der Parteigeist, die Parteisucht; Zwietracht, Uneinigkeit. **–nist,** *s.* der Parteigänger. **–us** [ˈfækʃəs], *adj.* parteieifrig, Partei–; aufrührerisch. **–usness,** *s.* der Parteigeist, die Parteisucht.

factitious [fækˈtɪʃəs], *adj.* (nach)gemacht, künstlich, unecht, äußerlich.

factitive [ˈfæktɪtɪv], *adj.* faktitiv (*Gram.*).

factor [ˈfæktə], *s.* der Faktor (*also Math. & fig.*); Agent, Kommissionär, Vertreter (*C.L.*); Verwalter (*of an estate*) (*Scots*); (*fig.*) (mitwirkender) Umstand, das Moment; die Erbanlage (*Biol.*); *determining –*, bestimmender Faktor; *safety –*, der Sicherheitskoeffizient. **–age,** *s.* die Kommissionsgebühr. **–ial,** *s.* das Produkt einer arithmetischen Reihe (*Math.*).

factory ['fæktərɪ], *s.* die Fabrik(anlage), das Fabrikgebäude; (*archaic*) die Faktorei, Handelsniederlassung. **--hand,** *s.* der Fabrikarbeiter. **--inspector,** *s.* Gewerbeaufsichtsbeamte(r), *m.* **--system,** *s.* das Fabrikwesen.

factotum [fæk'toutəm], *s.* das Faktotum, der Allerweltskünstler; (*fig.*) die Stütze, rechte Hand.

factual ['fæktjuəl], *adj.* Tatsachen–, tatsächlich.

facult–ative ['fækəltətɪv], *adj.* wahlfrei, beliebig, fakultativ. **–y** ['fækəltɪ], *s.* die Fähigkeit, geistige *or* seelische Kraft, das Vermögen, die Anlage, Gabe, das Talent; die Gewandtheit, Geschicklichkeit; Ermächtigung, Erlaubnis, Befugnis, Dispensation (*R.C.*, *Law*); Fakultät, Fakultätsmitglieder (*pl.*) (*Univ.*); der Lehrkörper (*Amer.*).

fad [fæd], *s.* die Grille, Schrulle, Marotte, Liebhaberei, das Steckenpferd; fixe Idee, die Modetorheit. **–dist,** *s.* der Grillenfänger, Fex, einer der ein Steckenpferd hat. **–dy** [–dɪ], *adj.* grillenhaft, launisch, schrullig.

fad–e [feɪd], 1. *v.n.* (ver)welken; abbleichen, abblassen, abfärben, verblassen, sich entfärben, verschießen; schwinden, vergehen; *–e away*, vergehen, abklingen; *–e out*, dahinschwinden, dunkel werden; verklingen (*Rad.*). 2. *v.a.*; *–e in*, einblenden, aufkommen lassen; *–e out*, abblenden, abklingen lassen (*Films*). **–ed,** *adj.* verschossen, welk. **–eless,** *adj.* lichtecht, unverwelklich. **–ing,** 1. *adj.* vergänglich, lichtunecht (*of colours*). 2. *s.* die Verfärbung; der Schwund, Schwundaffekt, die Schwunderscheinung, Fading (*Rad.*).

faeces ['fɪ:sɪ:z], *pl.* der Kot, Dreck, Auswurf, die Exkremente, Fäkalien.

fag [fæg], 1. *v.n.* sich abmühen *or* abschinden *or* abplagen *or* abplacken, ochsen, büffeln; *– for s.o.*, jemandes Fuchs sein (*in schools*). 2. *v.a.* & *r.* (sich) ermüden. 3. *s.* die Plackerei; (*school sl.*) der Fuchs; (*sl.*) die Zigarette. **–ged,** *adj.* (*–ged out*) erschöpft, ermüdet, ermattet, völlig fertig. **–ging,** 1. *s.* die Plackerei; der Dienst als Fuchs. 2. *attrib.*; *–ging system*, die Einrichtung auf der Schule wonach die Primaner Füchse haben. **--end,** *s.* der Zigarettenstummel, die Kippe; die Salleiste (*of cloth*); aufgedrehtes Tauende (*Naut.*); (*coll.*) letzter Rest, das Ende.

fa(g)got ['fægət], *s.* das Reisigbündel, die Faschine; das Paket (*of steel rods*); gehackter Leberbraten.

faience [faɪ'ɑ̃:s], *s.* die Fayence.

fail [feɪl], **1.** *v.n.* fehlen, mangeln; fehlschlagen, fehlgehen, scheitern, verfehlen, mißlingen; zahlungsunfähig werden, Bankrott machen, fallieren (*C.L.*); durchfallen (*in an examination*); zu Ende gehen, vergehen, schwinden, aufhören, versagen, stocken, aussterben, schwach werden, nachlassen, ermatten; versiegen (*as a well*); nicht aufgehen (*as seed*); *the attempt –ed*, der Versuch schlug fehl; *he –ed in his duty*, er vernachlässigte seine Pflicht; *it –ed in its effect*, es hatte nicht die beabsichtigte Wirkung; *if everything else –s*, wenn alle Stricke reißen; *his strength –s*, seine Kräfte lassen nach; *it never –s*, es verfehlt nie; *they never – to be there*, sie sind immer anwesend; *the plan –ed owing to the weather*, der Plan scheiterte an dem Wetter; *he –ed to see*, es war ihm unmöglich einzusehen; *he cannot – to see*, er muß (unfehlbar) einsehen, er kann nicht umhin einzusehen; *they will not – to win*, sie werden unfehlbar *or* sicher gewinnen; *his voice –ed*, seine Stimme versagte. **2.** *v.a.* im Stich lassen, verlassen; enttäuschen; durchfallen lassen (*in an examination*); *– an examination*, in einer Prüfung durchfallen; *my courage –s me*, mich verläßt der Mut; *he will never – you*, er enttäuscht dich nie, er läßt dich nie im Stich; *words – me*, es fehlen mir Worte. **3.** *s.*; only in *without –*, unfehlbar, unbedingt, ganz bestimmt *or* gewiß. **–ing,** 1. *adj.* schwindend, versagend. 2. *prep.* in Ermangelung (*Gen.*), ohne; *–ing this*, andernfalls, wenn nicht; *–ing which*, widrigenfalls. 3. *s.* der Mangel, Fehler, die Schwäche. **–ure,** *s.* das Fehlen, Ausbleiben (*of*, an); das Versäumnis, die Unterlassung; Ermangelung; Abnahme, der Verfall, Zusammenbruch; das Fehlschlagen, Mißlingen, der Mißerfolg, Fehlschlag; Versager, fehlgeschlagene Sache; untauglicher *or* mißglückter Mensch, der Taugenichts, verkrachte Existenz; die Zahlungseinstellung, der Bankrott (*C.L.*); *crop –ure*, die Mißernte; *be doomed to –ure*, keine Aussicht auf Erfolg haben; *–ure to obey*, die Gehorsamsverweigerung; *–ure to pay*, das Zahlungsversäumnis.

fain [feɪn], 1. *pred. adj.* (*archaic*) froh, geneigt; genötigt. 2. *adv.* gern; only in *I would – do it*, ich möchte es gern tun.

faint [feɪnt], 1. *adj.* ohnmächtig; kraftlos, schwach, leise (*sounds*); matt, blaß (*colour*); (*Prov.*) *– heart never won fair lady*, wer nicht wagt, der gewinnt nicht; *– hope*, leise *or* geringe Hoffnung; *– idea*, leise Ahnung; *– recollection*, undeutliche *or* schwache Erinnerung. 2. *v.n.* ohnmächtig werden, in Ohnmacht fallen (*with*, vor (*Dat.*)); (*Poet.*) schwach werden; (*archaic*) verzagen. 3. *s.* die Ohnmacht, der Ohnmachtsanfall. **–ness,** *s.* die Schwäche, Mattigkeit, das Ohnmachtsgefühl; (*fig.*) die Schwachheit; *–ness of heart*, die Verzagtheit. **--hearted,** *adj.* mutlos, kleinmütig, zaghaft. **--heartedness,** *s.* der Kleinmut, die Verzagtheit.

[1]**fair** [fɛə], **1.** *adj.* schön, hübsch; hell(farbig), blond; heiter, klar, hell, rein, deutlich, sauber, leserlich; offen, frei; günstig, gut, glücklich; unbescholten, ehrlich, redlich, gerecht, anständig, billig, unparteiisch, fair; reichlich, beträchtlich, befriedigend, leidlich, erträglich, ziemlich gut; freundlich, gefällig, angenehm, artig; *– catch*, der Freifang; *have a – chance*, freie Bahn haben; *– copy*, die Reinschrift; *– dealing*, die Redlichkeit; *– game*, jagdbares Wild; *be a – judge*, ziemlich gutes Urteil haben; *by – means*, auf ehrliche Weise, anständig, auf gutem Wege; *– play*, ehrliches Spiel *or* Vorgehen; (*coll.*) *pretty –*, ganz leidlich; *– promises*, schöne Versprechungen; *the – sex*, das schöne Geschlecht; *– trial*, unparteiische Untersuchung; *give a p. – warning*, einen zeitig warnen; *be in a – way*, gute Aussichten haben; *– words*, gefällige Worte. **2.** *adv.* gut, schön; unmittelbar, direkt; ehrlich, gerecht, billig; *bid –*, sich gut anlassen, zu Hoffnungen berechtigen; *promise –*, viel versprechen; *the wind sits –*, der Wind ist günstig; *speak a p. –*, einem gute Worte geben; *– and square*, offen und ehrlich, gerecht; genau. **3.** *s.* die Schöne; *the –*, das schöne Geschlecht. **--haired,** *adj.* mit blondem Haar. **–ly,** *adv.* erträglich, leidlich, ziemlich, mäßig; billig, unparteiisch, gerecht; richtig, passend; vollkommen, gänzlich, wirklich, ganz und gar. **--minded,** *adj.* billig, ehrlich. **–ness,** *s.* die Schönheit; Blondheit; Ehrlichkeit, Redlichkeit, Billigkeit, Unparteilichkeit; *in –ness to a p.*, um einem Gerechtigkeit widerfahren zu lassen, um einem gerecht zu sein. **--spoken,** *adj.* höflich, gefällig, artig. **–way,** *s.* das Fahrwasser, die Fahrrinne (*Naut.*); gepflegte Bahn (*Golf*). **--weather friend,** ein Freund im Glück, unzuverlässiger Freund.

[2]**fair,** *s.* die Messe, der Jahrmarkt; die Ausstellung.

fairly, fairness, *see* [1]**fair.**

fairing, *s.* die Verkleidung, Verschalung (*Av.*).

fairy ['fɛərɪ], 1. *adj.* feenhaft, zauberisch, Feen–, Zauber–. 2. *s.* der Elf, die Fee. **--dance,** *s.* der Feenreigen. **–land,** *s.* das Elfenreich, Feenland; (*fig.*) Märchenland, Zauberland. **–like,** *adj.* feenhaft. **--ring,** *s.* der Feenring, Hexenring (*Bot.*). **--tale,** *s.* das Märchen.

faith [feɪθ], *s.* das Vertrauen (*in*, auf (*Acc.*)); der Glaube (*in*, an (*Acc.*)); das Glaubenbekenntnis; die Treue, Redlichkeit; das Versprechen, die Zusage; (*archaic*) *–! i' –!* meiner Treu! *in* (*all*) *good –*, in gutem Glauben, in guter Absicht, auf Treu' und Glauben; *break* (*one's*) *–*, sein Versprechen brechen; *keep* (*one's*) *–*, Wort halten; *pledge* or *plight one's –*, sein Wort *or* Versprechen geben; *pin one's – on* or *put one's – in*, Vertrauen setzen in (*Acc.*). **--cure,** *s. see* **--healing. –ful,** 1. *adj.* treu (*to* (*Dat.*)), wahrhaft, ehrlich, zuverlässig, glaubwürdig; gewissenhaft, wahr, getreu; gläubig, rechtgläubig. 2. *pl.*; *the –ful*, die Gläubigen. **–fully,** *adv.* treu, ergeben; genau, getreu; *carry out –fully*, genau *or* gewissenhaft ausführen; *yours –fully*, Ihr ergebener (*in letters*). **–fulness,** *s.*

die Treue, Ehrlichkeit; Pflichttreue; Genauigkeit. **--healing,** *s.* das Gesundbeten. **-less,** *adj.* treulos, untreu, trügerisch; ungläubig. **-lessness,** *s.* die Treulosigkeit (*towards*, gegen), der Unglaube.

fake [feɪk], 1. *v.a.* (*sl.*) nachmachen; zurechtmachen, aufputzen (*report*); fälschen. 2. *s.* (*sl.*) der Betrug, Schwindel; Kniff, die Fälschung, Attrappe.

fakir [fɑːˈkɪə], *s.* der Fakir.

falchion [ˈfɔːltʃən], *s.* der Pallasch.

falcon [ˈfɔːlkən], *s.* der Falke; (*archaic*) leichtes Geschütz. **-er,** *s.* der Falkner, Falkenier. **-ry** [-rɪ], *s.* die Falknerei, Falkenbeize.

fall [fɔːl], 1. *ir.v.n.* fallen, niederfallen, herunterfallen; umfallen, zu Boden fallen *or* stürzen; erliegen, zusammenfallen, zusammenbrechen, gestürzt *or* getötet werden (nieder)stürzen; einfallen, einstürzen, sinken, sich senken; abfallen (*as leaves*), niedergehen (*as a curtain*); sich legen, abnehmen (*of wind*); heruntergehen, abnehmen (*of prices*); eintreffen, geschehen, eintreten, hereinbrechen (*of time and events*); geboren werden (*of lambs*); *his face fell*, er machte ein langes Gesicht; *see* **fallen, falling.** – *among*, geraten unter; – *asleep*, einschlafen; – *astern*, hinten– *or* zurückbleiben; – *away*, abfallen (*from*, von); abtrünnig werden (*Dat.*); abnehmen, abmagern; – *a-weeping*, zu weinen anfangen; – *back*, abtreten, zurücktreten, zurückfallen, zurückgehen, sich zurückziehen, zurückweichen; – *back upon*, zurückgreifen *or* zurückkommen auf, einen Rückhalt haben (an (*Dat.*)); seine Zuflucht nehmen zu; – *behind*, zurückbleiben (hinter); – *between two stools*, sich zwischen zwei Stühle setzen; – *calm*, windstill werden; – *down*, niederfallen, auf die Knie sinken; einfallen, einstürzen (*as buildings*); (*sl.*) versagen, Pech haben, zu Schaden kommen (*on*, mit); – *due*, fällig werden; (*sl.*) – *for*, sich einnehmen lassen, gefesselt werden von, reinfallen auf (*Acc.*); – *foul of*, in Konflikt geraten mit, zusammenstoßen mit; – *from*, abfallen (von); *an exclamation of displeasure fell from him*, ihm entfuhr ein Ausruf des Mißfallens; – *from favour*, in Ungnade fallen; – *from grace*, in Sünde fallen; – *ill*, krank werden; – *in*, einfallen, einstürzen (*as houses*); fällig werden, zu Ende gehen; ablaufen (*as lease*); antreten (*Mil.*); – *in love*, sich verlieben (*with*, in); – *in value*, an Wert verlieren; – *in with*, eingehen auf, übereinstimmen mit, einverstanden sein mit, beipflichten (*Dat.*), entsprechen (*Dat.*), passen zu; treffen, stoßen auf; – *into a category*, zu einer Gruppe gehören; – *into conversation*, eine Unterhaltung beginnen; – *into disuse*, außer Gebrauch kommen; – *into four divisions*, in vier Teile zerfallen; – *into error*, in Irrtum verfallen; – *into a habit*, eine Gewohnheit annehmen; – *into line*, antreten, sich einreihen (*Mil.*); (*fig.*) – *into line with*, sich anpassen mit, übereinstimmen mit, sich fügen (*Dat.*), einig gehen *or* sein; – *into oblivion*, in Vergessenheit geraten; – *into place* or *their places*, ohne Schwierigkeit zurechtkommen; – *into a rage*, in Wut geraten; *the river –s into the sea*, der Fluß ergießt sich ins Meer; – *off*, herabfallen, herunterfallen; abfallen, sich zurückziehen (*from*, von); abgehen, abweichen (*Naut.*); (*fig.*) nachlassen, abnehmen, abflauen, sich vermindern; – *on*, herabfallen auf (*Acc.*), stoßen auf, verfallen auf, treffen; überfallen, angreifen, herfallen über (*Acc.*); – *on evil days*, ins Unglück *or* in Not geraten; (*fig.*) – *on one's feet*, auf die Füße fallen; – *on s.o.'s neck*, einem um den Hals fallen; – *on a Sunday*, auf einen Sonntag fallen; – *on one's sword*, sich ins Schwert stürzen; – *out*, ausfallen, vorfallen, sich zutragen, sich ereignen; wegtreten, austreten (*Mil.*); – *out of*, herausfallen aus; – *out of cultivation*, nicht mehr bebaut werden; – *out of use*, außer Gebrauch kommen; – *out with*, zanken mit, sich überwerfen *or* veruneinigen mit; – *out of one's hands*, den Händen entfallen; – *over*, umfallen, umkippen; *her hair –s over her shoulders*, ihre Haare hängen über die Schultern; – *a prey to*, zur Beute fallen (*Dat.*); – *short*, mangeln, knapp werden (*of*, an); nicht zureichen; – *short of*, zurückbleiben hinter, nicht erreichen, nicht entsprechen; – *short of the mark*, das Ziel nicht treffen; (*coll.*) – *through*, ins Wasser fallen, durchfallen, mißlingen; – *to* (*a p.* or *one's lot*), fallen *or* kommen an (*Acc.*), zufallen (*Dat.*), zuteil werden (*Dat.*); (*a th.*) beginnen, anfangen, sich machen an (*Acc.*), sich widmen (*Dat.*); (*coll.*) zulangen (*food*); – *to be considered*, betrachtet werden müssen; (*fig.*) – *to the ground*, scheitern, fehlschlagen, unter den Tisch *or* ins Wasser fallen; – *to one's lot*, einem beschieden sein; *it –s to me to do it*, es liegt mir ob es zu tun; – *to pieces*, zerfallen, in Stücke fallen; (*fig.*) – *under*, gerechnet werden unter, gehören (*Dat.*); – *under censure*, sich dem Tadel aussetzen; – *upon*, see – *on*; – *a victim to* or *of*, zum Opfer fallen (*Dat.*), überwältigt werden von; (*fig.*) – *within*, gerechnet werden in. 2. *s.* der Fall, Sturz; das Fallen, Abfallen (*of leaves*), Niedergehen (*of a curtain*), Sinken (*of prices*); (*fig.*) der Untergang, Niedergang, Abstieg, Verfall, Sturz, Zusammenbruch, die Vernichtung, Niederlage, Einnahme (*of a fortress*); die Senkung, Neigung, der Abhang, das Gefälle (*of a river*); die Geburt, der Wurf (*of animals*); die Kadenz (*Mus.*); (*often pl.*) der Wasserfall; der Herbst (*Amer.*); das Fall (*pl.* Fallen) (*rope of hoisting tackle, also Naut.*); der Niederwurf (*wrestling*); (– *of man*) der Sündenfall; *be on the –*, im Fallen begriffen (*C.L.*); *break s.o.'s –*, einen im Fallen auffangen; – *in prices*, das Fallen der Preise; *sudden – in prices*, der Preissturz; – *of rain*, der Regenfall; *ride for a –*, waghalsig reiten; (*fig.*) auf die schiefe Ebene geraten; *speculate on the –*, auf Baisse spekulieren (*C.L.*); *have* or *sustain a –*, zu Falle kommen, fallen, stürzen.

fallac-ious [fəˈleɪʃəs], *adj.* trügerisch, trüglich, täuschend, irreführend; verfänglich. **-iousness,** *s.* die Trüglichkeit, Verfänglichkeit. **-y** [ˈfæləsɪ], *s.* der Irrtum, Trugschluß (*Log.*); die Trüglichkeit; *fall into a –y*, in einen Irrtum verfallen.

fallen [ˈfɔːlən], *see* **fall;** *adj.*; – *angel*, gestürzter Engel; – *arch*, der Senkfuß; – *woman*, gefallene Frau; *the –*, (*pl.*) die Gefallenen, die Kriegsopfer.

fallib-ility [fælɪˈbɪlɪtɪ], *s.* die Fehlbarkeit. **-le** [ˈfælɪbl], *adj.* fehlbar.

falling [ˈfɔːlɪŋ], *see* **fall;** *s.* das Fallen. **--away,** *s.*, **--off** ,*s.* der Rückgang, die Abnahme. **--out,** *s.* die Mißhelligkeit, Veruneinigung, der Zank. **--sickness,** *s.* die Fallsucht. **--star,** *s.* die Sternschnuppe.

Fallopian [fæˈloupjən], *adj.* fallopisch; – *tubes*, die Muttertrompeten *or* –tuben (*Anat.*).

fallow [ˈfælou], 1. *adj.* fahl, falb, fahlgelb; brach, unbebaut (*Agr.*); – *deer*, das Damwild. 2. *s.* das Brachfeld, die Brache. 3. *v.a.* aufbrechen (*land*). **-ness,** *s.* das Brachliegen.

false [fɔːls], *adj.* falsch, unrichtig, irrig, unwahr; trügerisch, verräterisch, treulos (*to*, gegen) untreu (*to* (*Dat.*)); unecht, gefälscht, nachgemacht, vorgetäuscht, Schein–; – *alarm*, blinder Alarm; – *bottom*, der Doppelboden; – *imprisonment*, ungesetzliche Verhaftung; – *keel*, der Loskiel; – *key*, der Nachschlüssel; *play a p. –*, falsches Spiel mit einem treiben; – *pretence*, irrige Behauptung; *under – pretences*, unter Vorspiegelung falscher Tatsachen; – *start*, der Fehlstart; – *step*, der Fehltritt; – *verdict*, das Fehlurteil. **--hearted,** *adj.* treulos, falsch. **-hood,** *s.* die Lüge, Unwahrheit; Falschheit; *tell a –hood*, eine Unwahrheit sagen. **-ness,** *s.* die Falschheit, Unredlichkeit, Unaufrichtigkeit; Treulosigkeit, der Verrat.

falsetto [fɔːlˈsɛtou], *s.* die Fistel(stimme), das Falsett (*Mus.*).

falsi-fication [fɔːlsɪfɪˈkeɪʃən], *s.* die (Ver)Fälschung. **-fier** [ˈfɔːlsɪfaɪə], *s.* der Fälscher. **-fy** [ˈfɔːlsɪfaɪ], *v.a.* fälschen (*coin*); verfälschen (*writings, etc.*); als falsch erweisen, enttäuschen, vereiteln (*hopes, etc.*). **-ty** [ˈfɔːlsɪtɪ], *s.* die Unrichtigkeit, Falschheit, der Irrtum.

falter [ˈfɔːltə], 1. *v.n.* stottern, stammeln (*in speaking*); stolpern, straucheln, wanken, schwanken (*in walking*); zaudern, stocken. 2. *v.a.* stammeln(d äußern).

fame [feɪm], *s.* der Ruhm, die Berühmtheit, (guter) Ruf; (*archaic*) das Gerücht; *ill-* –, übler Ruf. **-d,** *adj.* berühmt, bekannt (*for*, wegen); *ill-–d*, berüchtigt.

familiar [fəˈmɪljə], 1. *adj.* vertraut, intim; wohlbekannt, wohlvertraut (*with*, mit); gebräuchlich, alltäglich, gewöhnlich; geläufig (*to* (*Dat.*)); (zu) frei, ungezwungen, familiär; – *quotation*, geflügeltes Wort; – *spirit*, der Schutzgeist; – *style*, ungezwungene Schreibart; *be on – terms with*, auf vertrautem Fuße stehen mit. 2. *s.* Vertraute(r), *m.*; der Hausgeist. **–ity** [–ɪˈærɪtɪ], *s.* die Bekanntschaft, Vertrautheit, Vertraulichkeit; Ungezwungenheit, Leutseligkeit; (*Prov.*) *–ity breeds contempt*, allzugroße Vertraulichkeit erzeugt Verachtung. **–ization,** *s.* die Gewöhnung (*with*, an). **–ize** [fəˈmɪljəraɪz], *v.a.* gewöhnen (*with*, an), vertraut machen (*with*, mit).

family [ˈfæmɪlɪ], 1. *s.* die Familie; der Stamm, das Geschlecht, Vorfahren (*pl.*); die Gattung (*of plants and animals*), Gruppe (*Chem., etc.*); *father of a –*, der Familienvater; *of good –*, aus guter Familie *or* gutem Geschlecht, von vornehmer Herkunft; *have a large –*, viele Kinder haben; *old –*, altes Geschlecht; (*coll.*) *in the – way*, in anderen Umständen, guter Hoffnung, schwanger. 2. *attrib.* zur Familie gehörig; – *allowance*, die Familienzulage, Kinderzulage; – *Bible*, die Familienbibel; – *doctor*, der Hausarzt; – *likeness*, die Familienähnlichkeit; – *man*, häuslicher Mensch; – *prayers*, die Hausandacht; – *tree*, der Stammbaum.

famine [ˈfæmɪn], *s.* die Hungersnot; (*fig.*) der Mangel; *water –*, der Wassermangel.

famish [ˈfæmɪʃ], 1. *v.a.* aushungern lassen, verschmachten lassen, darben lassen. 2. *v.n.* hungern, verhungern, darben; (*coll.*) *be –ed*, großen Hunger haben.

famous [ˈfeɪməs], *adj.* berühmt (*for*, wegen); (*coll.*) ausgezeichnet, famos. **–ly,** *adv.* (*coll.*) famos, glänzend.

[1]**fan** [fæn], 1. *s.* der Fächer; die Wanne, Schwinge (*for corn, etc.*); der Ventilator (*Mach.*); die Windfahne (*of windmill*); der (Schrauben)Flügel (*Naut.*); *electric –*, der Lüfter. 2. *v.a.* fächeln, wedeln; schwingen, worfeln (*corn*); (*fig.*) anfachen, entfachen (*into*, zu); entflammen; – *the flame*, Öl ins Feuer gießen. 3. *v.n.*; – *out*, ausschwärmen. **––blade,** *s.* der Windflügel. **–light,** *s.* das Fächerfenster, die Lünette. **––palm,** *s.* die Fächerpalme (*Bot.*). **––shaped,** *adj.* fächerförmig. **–tail,** *s.* (*–tail pigeon*) die Pfautaube. **––tracery,** *s.*, **––vaulting,** *s.* das Fächergewölbe (*Arch.*). **–wheel,** *s.* das Windrad.

[2]**fan,** *s.* (*sl.*) leidenschaftlicher Liebhaber, begeisterter Anhänger (*Sport, etc.*); *film-–*, der Kinofex. **––mail,** Briefe aus dem Anhängerkreis.

fanatic [fəˈnætɪk], 1. *s.* der Fanatiker, Eiferer, Schwärmer. 2. *adj.*, **–al,** *adj.* fanatisch, schwärmerisch. **–ism** [–tɪsɪzm], *s.* der Fanatismus, (religiöse) Schwärmerei. **–ize** [–tɪsaɪz], *v.a.* fanatisch machen.

fanc–ier [ˈfænsɪə], *s.* der Liebhaber, Kenner, Züchter. **–iful** [ˈfænsɪfʊl], *adj.* phantastisch, schwärmerisch; wunderlich, grillenhaft, launisch; eingebildet, unwirklich. **–ifulness,** *s.* die Grillenhaftigkeit, Schwärmerei, Phantasterei. **–y** [ˈfænsɪ], 1. *s.* die Phantasie, Einbildungskraft; Einbildung, das Phantasiegebilde, Wahngebilde, irrige Vorstellung *or* Idee, die Grille, Laune, der Einfall; persönlicher Geschmack, die Neigung (*for*, zu), Vorliebe (*for*, für); (*sl.*) *the –y*, die Sportwelt; (*Poet.*) *tell me where is –y bred?* sagt, woher stammt Liebeslust?; *catch* or *take* or *tickle s.o.'s –y*, einem gefallen, bei einem Anklang finden; *take a –y to*, eine Neigung fassen zu, Gefallen finden an. 2. *v.a.* sich (*Dat.*) einbilden *or* vorstellen *or* denken, meinen, denken, wähnen, halten für; gern haben, eingenommen sein für; (*coll.*) *–y o.s.*, sich wichtig vorkommen; (*just* or *only*) *–y!* denken Sie sich nur! 3. *attrib.* Mode–, Luxus–, Galanterie–; Phantasie–, übertrieben; bunt, vielfarbig, gemustert. **–y cakes,** feines Gebäck, Torten (*pl.*). **–y dress,** das Maskenkostüm; *–y-dress ball*, *s.* der Maskenball, das Kostümfest. **–y-free,** *adj.* liebefrei. **–y goods,** Galanteriewaren, Modewaren (*pl.*). **–y handkerchief,** buntes *or* farbiges Taschentuch. (*coll.*) **–y-man,** *s.* Geliebte(r), *m.*; (*sl.*) der Zuhälter. **–y paper,** das Buntpapier, Fantasiepapier. **–y price,** *s.* übertrieben hoher Preis. **–y-stocks,** *pl.* Spekulationspapiere (*pl.*). **–y-work,** *s.* feine Handarbeit.

fandango [fænˈdæŋgoʊ], *s.* spanischer Tanz.

fane [feɪn], *s.* (*Poet.*) der Tempel.

fanfar–e [ˈfænfɛə], *s.* der Tusch, die Fanfare. **–onade** [fænfærəˈneɪd], *s.* die Prahlerei, Großsprecherei, Großtuerei.

[1]**fang** [fæŋ], *s.* der Fang, Hauer, Hauzahn; Giftzahn (*of snakes*); (*fig.*) die Klaue; Zahnwurzel; der Stift, Zapfen. **–ed,** *adj.* mit (Gift)Zähnen bewaffnet; (*as suffix*) –zähnig.

[2]**fang,** *v.a.* mit Wasser auffüllen, in Tätigkeit setzen (*pump*).

fantas–ia [fænˈteɪzɪə, fæntəˈzɪə], *s.* die Phantasie (*Mus.*). **–tic** [fænˈtæstɪk], *adj.* phantastisch, wunderlich, grotesk, seltsam, eingebildet. **–ticality, –ticalness,** *s.* das Phantastische, Groteske; die Seltsamkeit, Wunderlichkeit. **–y** [ˈfæntəsɪ], *s.* die Phantasie, Einbildung, Einbildungskraft; das Traumgebilde, Hirngespinst.

far [fɑː], **1.** *adj.* fern, entfernt; – *East*, Ferner Osten; *in the – corner*, in der gegenüberliegenden Ecke; *on the – side*, auf der anderen Seite. **2.** *adv.* fern, weit, entfernt, weit entfernt; zum großen Teil, bei weitem, sehr viel; *as – as*, so weit wie, so viel wie, bis (an *or* nach); *as – as that goes*, was das betrifft; *so –*, so weit, bis jetzt; *in as – as*, insofern als; *not so – as I am aware*, nicht daß ich wüßte; *thus –*, so weit, bis dahin; (*a*) (*with verbs*) *carry* (*a th.*) *too –*, (eine S.) zu weit treiben; *he will go –*, er hat eine Zukunft vor sich; *this went – to convince us*, dies trug wesentlich dazu bei, uns zu überzeugen, dies überzeugte uns geradezu; *not – to seek*, nicht weit zu suchen; (*b*) (with *and*) – *and away*, bei weitem, weitaus; – *and near*, nahe und fern; – *and wide*, weit und breit, allenthalben; (*c*) (*with adverbs and prepositions*) – *away*, weit weg, weit entfernt; – *back*, weit zurück; – *better*, viel besser; – *the best*, weitaus *or* bei weitem das beste; *few and – between*, selten, nicht häufig; *by –*, bei weitem; – *be it from me*, es sei fern von mir, es liegt mir fern; – *from being offended*, weit (davon) entfernt, beleidigt zu sein; – *from finished*, weit entfernt vollendet zu sein; (*coll.*) – *from it*, bei weitem nicht, keineswegs; – *from rich*, keineswegs reich; – *into*, tief in . . . hinein; – *into the night*, bis spät in die Nacht; – *off*, weit weg; – *out*, weit draußen; – *up*, hoch oben. **––away** *adj.* entfernt (*place*), vergangen (*time*); (*fig.*) träumerisch. **––famed,** *adj.* weitbekannt, weitberühmt. **––fetched,** *adj.* weit hergeholt, übertrieben, gesucht, an *or* bei den Haaren herbeigezogen. **––flung,** *adj.* weit ausgedehnt. **––gone,** *adj.* weit vorgerückt, (*coll.*) stark benebelt. **–ness,** *s.* die Entfernung. **––reaching,** *adj.* weitreichend, weittragend. (*fig.*) **––seeing,** *adj.* weitsehend. **––sighted,** *adj.* weitsichtig (*also fig.*); *see* **––seeing. ––sightedness,** *s.* die Weitsichtigkeit; (*fig.*) der Scharfsinn.

farc–e [fɑːs], 1. *v.a.* füllen, farcieren. 2. *s.* der Schwank, die Posse (*Theat., also fig.*); *complete –e*, ausgesprochene Komödie. **–ical,** *adj.* possenhaft, absurd.

fardel [ˈfɑːdəl], *s.* (*archaic*) das Bündel; (*fig.*) die Bürde, Last.

fare [fɛə], 1. *v.n.* ausfallen, ergehen (*Dat.*), daran sein; essen; (*archaic*) fahren, reisen; *go farther and – worse*, aus dem Regen in die Traufe kommen; – *well* (or *ill*), gut (*or* schlecht) abschneiden; (*Poet.*) – *thee well*, laß es dir gut gehen. 2. *s.* das Fahrgeld, der Fahrpreis; Fahrgast, Passagier; die Beköstigung, Speise, Kost; *bill of –*, die Speisekarte; *excess –*, der Zuschlag; *poor –*, schmale Kost, schlechte Verpflegung; – *stage*, die Teilstrecke, Tarifgrenze; *what is the – ?* was kostet die Fahrt *or* Fahrkarte? **–well** [fɛəˈwɛl], 1. *int.* lebe wohl! leben Sie wohl! 2. *attrib.* Abschieds–. 3. *s.* das Lebewohl, der Abschied; *bid a p. –well* or *–well to a p.*, einem Lebewohl sagen, von einem Abschied nehmen; *make one's –wells*, sich verabschieden.

farina [fəˈraɪnə], *s.* das Stärkemehl, Kartoffelmehl. **–ceous** [færɪˈneɪʃəs], *adj.* mehlig; stärkehaltig, mehlhaltig; *–ceous food*, Mehlspeisen (*pl.*).

farm [fɑːm], 1. *s.* das Bauerngut, der Bauernhof; das Gehöft, der Pachthof, die Farm (*in the colonies*);

dairy-–, die Meierei; *home –*, selbstbewirtschaftetes Gut; *poultry –*, die Hühnerfarm. 2. *v.a.* bebauen, bewirtschaften, beackern; – *out*, verpachten (*land*); gegen Bezahlung ausgeben (*children*); – *the revenue*, die Staatseinkünfte pachten. 3. *v.n.* Landwirtschaft betreiben. **–-bailiff**, *s.* der Gutsverwalter, Inspektor. **–er**, *s.* der Bauer, Landwirt, Pächter; (Steuer)Pächter (*of revenues, etc.*). **–-hand**, *s.* der Landarbeiter. **–house**, *s.* das Gutshaus. **–ing**, 1. *attrib.* landwirtschaftlich, Acker–; *–ing implements*, Ackergeräte (*pl.*). 2. *s.* die Landwirtschaft, der Ackerbau. **–-labourer**, *s.* der Landarbeiter. **–land**, *s.* das Gutsland, die Ackerfläche. **–-servant**, *s.* der Bauernknecht, die Bauernmagd. **–stead**, *s.* der Bauernhof, das Gehöft. **–yard**, *s.* der (Bauern)Hof, Gutshof, das Gehöft.

farness ['fɑːnɪs], *see* **far**.

faro ['fɛəroʊ], *s.* das Pharo(spiel).

farouche [fə'ruːʃ], *adj.* (menschen)scheu.

farrago [fə'reɪgoʊ], *s.* das Gemisch, der Mischmasch.

farrier ['færɪə], *s.* der Hufschmied; Fahnenschmied (*Mil.*); (*archaic*) der Roßarzt. **–y** [–rɪ], *s.* das Hufschmiedehandwerk.

farrow ['færoʊ], 1. *s.* der Wurf (*of pigs*); *in* or *with* –, trächtig (*of sows*). 2. *v.a.* & *n.* ferkeln, (Ferkel) werfen.

fart [fɑːt], 1. *s.* (*vulg.*) der Furz. 2. *v.n.* (*vulg.*) furzen.

farthe-r ['fɑːðə], *adj.* & *adv. see* **far**; ferner, weiter; entfernter. **–st**, *adj.* & *adv.* fernst, weitest, entferntest.

farthing ['fɑːðɪŋ], *s.* der Heller.

farthingale ['fɑːðɪŋgeɪl], *s.* (*archaic*) der Reifrock.

fasces ['fæsɪːz], *pl.* das Liktorenbündel.

fascia ['fæʃɪə], *s.* das Band, Bandgesims, der Streifen, Gurtsims (*Arch.*); Ring, Gürtel (*Astr.*); die Faszie, Gewebeschicht, Muskelbinde (*Anat.*). **–ted** [–ɪeɪtɪd], *adj.* zusammengewachsen (*Bot.*). **–tion**, *s.* das Verwachsensein (*Bot.*).

fascic-le ['fæsɪkl], *s.* das Bündel, das *or* der Büschel (*Bot.*); die Lieferung, der Teil (*of a book*). **–ular** [fə'sɪkjʊlə], **–ulate**, *adj.* büschelförmig.

fascinat-e ['fæsɪneɪt], *v.a.* bezaubern, bestricken, faszinieren. **–ion** [–'neɪʃən], *s.* die Bezauberung, Bestrickung; der Zauber, Reiz.

fascine [fæ'siːn], *s.* die Faschine, das Geflecht, Strauchbüschel.

fascis-m ['fæʃɪzm], *s.* der Faschismus. **–t**, 1. *s.* der Faschist. 2. *adj.* faschistisch.

fash [fæʃ], (*Scots*) 1. *v.a.* quälen, plagen, ärgern; – *o.s.*, sich ärgern *or* aufregen (*about*, über). 2. *s.* der Ärger, die Plage.

fashion ['fæʃən], 1. *s.* (herrschende) Mode, die Sitte, Art (und Weise), Manier, der Gebrauch; feine Lebensart, gute Manieren (*pl.*); die Gestalt, Form; der Schnitt, die Fasson; *at the height of* –, nach der neuesten Mode; *after the – of*, nach (der) Art von; (*coll.*) *after* or *in a* –, einigermaßen, oberflächlich, nachlässig, halb und halb; *in* (*the*) –, modisch (*of clothes, etc.*), modern (*of persons*); *come into* –, Mode werden; *out of* –, außer Mode, veraltet, unmodern; *people of* –, die Modewelt; *rank and* –, die vornehme Welt; *set the* –, den Ton angeben, in Mode bringen. 2. *v.a.* bilden, gestalten, formen, machen, verfertigen, anfertigen. **–able**, *adj.* modisch, Mode–, modern, fein, elegant; *it is –able*, es ist Mode; *–able party*, feine Gesellschaft; *–able resort*, eleganter Kurort; *–able woman*, modisch gekleidete Dame; *dress –ably*, sich nach der Mode kleiden. **–ableness**, *s.* das Beliebtsein, Modesein; das Modische, Moderne, die Eleganz. **–er**, *s.* der Gestalter. **–ing**, *s.* die Formgebung. **–-monger**, *s.* der Modeheld, Stutzer. **–-parade**, *s.* die Modeschau. **–-plate**, *s.* das Modebild, die Modezeichnung.

[1]**fast** [fɑːst], *adj.* (*pred. only*) fest, befestigt, unbeweglich; (*attrib.* & *pred.*) haltbar, dauerhaft, beständig; schnell, geschwind; vorgehend (*of a watch*); (*coll.*) flott, leichtlebig, locker, ausschweifend; (*a*) (*with nouns*) – *colour*, echte Farbe; – *friend*, standhafter Freund; – *girl*, lockeres *or* leichtlebiges Mädchen; *lead a – life*, ein unmoralisches *or* ausschweifendes Leben führen; – *train*, der Schnellzug, Eilzug; (*b*) (*with verbs*) *be – asleep*, fest schlafen; *my watch is* –, meine Uhr geht vor; *hold* –, festhalten; *make* –, zumachen, verschließen (*as a door*); festmachen, befestigen (*Naut.*); *play – and loose*, Schindluder treiben, leichtsinnig umgehen; *it is raining* –, es regnet stark *or* tüchtig; *stick* –, feststecken, (*fig.*) nicht weiterkommen. **–ness**, *s.* die Festigkeit, Beständigkeit, Echtheit; fester Platz, die Festung, das Bollwerk; die Schnelligkeit.

[2]**fast**, 1. *v.n.* fasten. 2. *s.*, **–ing**, *s.* das Fasten; *break one's* –, frühstücken. **–-day**, *s.* der Fasttag.

fasten ['fɑːsn], 1. *v.a.* festmachen, befestigen, anbinden (*to*, an (*Dat.*)); verschließen, fest zumachen; verbinden, zusammenfügen; – *down*, fest zumachen; – *off*, mit Knoten abschließen (*Sewing*); – *a crime on s.o.*, einen eines Verbrechens beschuldigen; – *a nickname on s.o.*, einen mit einem Spitznamen belegen. 2. *v.n.* schließen (*of door*); sich festhalten; – *upon*, sich heften an, sich stützen auf; sich halten *or* klammern an. – *upon a pretext*, etwas zum Vorwand nehmen; *he –ed his eyes upon her*, er heftete *or* richtete seinen Blick auf sie. **–er** [–nə], *s.* der Befestiger, Verschluß, Hefter, Druckknopf. **–ing** [–nɪŋ], *s.* das Befestigungsmittel, die Verschlußvorrichtung, das Band, der Riegel, das Schloß, die Zurrung (*Naut.*).

fastidious [fæs'tɪdɪəs], *adj.* wählerisch, anspruchsvoll; eigen (*in eating*); schwer zu befriedigen. **–ness**, *s.* wählerisches Wesen; die Mäkelei.

fastness, *s. see* [1]**fast**.

fat [fæt], 1. *adj.* fett; fettig, ölig; dick, korpulent (*of persons*); fruchtbar (*as soil*); bituminös (*of coal*); (*fig.*) einträglich; *grow* –, fett werden; (*coll.*) *a – lot*, (*ironic*) herzlich wenig. 2. *s.* das Fett (*also Chem.* & *fig.*), Schmalz; *live on the – of the land*, üppig leben, aus dem vollen schöpfen; *the – was in the fire*, der Teufel war los. (*coll.*) **–head**, *s.* der Dummkopf. (*coll.*) **–headed**, *adj.* dumm, dickköpfig. **–ling**, *s.* junges Masttier. **–ness**, *s.* die Dicke, Beleibtheit (*of persons*), Fettheit, Fettigkeit. **–ted**, *adj.* only in *kill the –ted calf for s.o.*, einen mit Freuden aufnehmen. *See* **fatten**, *etc.*

fatal ['feɪtl], *adj.* verhängnisvoll, unheilvoll, schicksalsschwer; verderblich, tödlich, lebensgefährlich; – *accident*, tödlicher Unfall; – *stroke*, der Todesstreich; *the – Sisters*, die Parzen (*pl.*). **–ism**, *s.* der Fatalismus, Schicksalsglaube. **–ist**, *s.* der Fatalist. **–istic**, *adj.* fatalistisch; schicksalsmäßig. **–ity** [fə'tælɪtɪ], *s.* der Todesfall, tödlicher Unfall; das Verhängnis, Schicksal; die Verderblichkeit, das Verhängnisvolle.

fata morgana ['fɑːtə mɔː'gɑːnə], *s.* die Luftspiegelung.

fate [feɪt], *s.* das Schicksal, Geschick, Los; Verhängnis, Verderben, der Untergang; *go to one's* –, seinem Schicksal entgegengehen; *seal s.o.'s* –, jemandes Geschick besiegeln *or* entscheiden; *the –s*, die Parzen, Schicksalsgöttinnen (*pl.*). **–-line**, *s.* die Schicksalslinie (*on the hand*). **–tragedy**, die Schicksalstragödie. **–d**, *adj.* vom Schicksal verhängt *or* bestimmt; dem Verderben geweiht, dem Schicksal verfallen. **–ful**, *adj.* verhängnisvoll, schicksalsschwer, schicksalhaft.

father ['fɑːðə], 1. *s.* der Vater; Pater (*R.C.*); *your* –, Ihr (Herr) Vater; *adoptive* –, der Pflegevater, Stiefvater; – *Christmas*, der Weihnachtsmann; *city –s*, die Stadtältesten; – *confessor*, der Beichtvater; *the early –s*, die Kirchenväter; *from – to son*, von Geschlecht zu Geschlecht; *the Holy* –, der Papst; *like – like son*, der Apfel fällt nicht weit vom Stamme; (*Prov.*) *the child is – to the man*, aus Kindern werden Leute; *be gathered to one's –s*, zu seinen Vätern versammelt werden; (*Prov.*) *the wish is – to the thought*, der Wunsch ist der Vater des Gedankens. 2. *v.a.* zeugen, Vater werden von; erzeugen, ins Leben rufen, hervorrufen; väterlich betreuen, verantwortlich sein für; – *a cause*, sich (*Acc.*) einer Sache annehmen; sich (*Acc.*) als Urheber einer S. *or* zu etwas bekennen; – *a child upon a p.*, einen als Vater angeben, einem ein Kind zuschreiben; – *s.th. upon a p.*, einem etwas zuschieben *or* in die Schuhe schieben. **–hood**, *s.*

die Vaterschaft. **--in-law,** *s.* der Schwiegervater. **-land,** *s.* das Vaterland. **-less,** *adj.* vaterlos. **-liness,** *s.* die Väterlichkeit. **-ly,** *adj.* väterlich.

fathom ['fæðəm], 1. *s.* die Klafter, der Faden. 2. *v.a.* loten, sondieren, (*usually fig.*) abmessen, ergründen, erforschen, erfassen, eindringen in (*Acc.*). **-able,** *adj.* meßbar; ergründlich. **-less,** *adj.* unergründlich, bodenlos. **--line,** *s.* die Lotleine, Senkleine. **--wood,** *s.* das Klafterholz.

fatigu-e [fə'tɪ:g], 1. *s.* die Ermüdung, Ermattung, Erschöpfung; schwere Arbeit, die Strapaze; Zermürbeerscheinung (*of materials*); der Arbeitsdienst (*Mil.*); *resistance to -e*, der Zermürbewiderstand. 2. *v.a.* ermüden. **-e-dress,** *s.* die Arbeitskleidung, der Drillichanzug (*Mil.*). **-e-party,** *s.* das Arbeitskommando (*Mil.*). **-e-test,** *s.* der Zermürbversuch. **-ing,** *adj.* ermüdend, mühsam.

fatling ['fætlɪŋ], *see* **fat.**

fatt-en ['fætn], 1. *v.a.* mästen. 2. *v.n.* fett werden, sich mästen (*on*, von), (*fig.*) sich bereichern. **-ening,** *s.* das Mästen. **-iness,** *s.* die Fettheit, Fettigkeit. **-ish,** *adj.* etwas *or* ziemlich dick *or* fett. **-y** 1. *adj.* fettig, fetthaltig, fettartig; *-y acid*, die Fettsäure; *-y degeneration*, die Verfettung; *-y heart*, die Herzverfettung. 2. *s.* (*coll.*) das Dickchen.

fatu-ity [fə'tjʊɪtɪ], *s.* die Albernheit, Dummheit, Einfältigkeit. **-ous** ['fætjʊəs], *adj.* albern, einfältig, dumm.

fauc-al ['fɔ:kəl], *adj.* Kehl-, Rachen-. **-es** ['fɔ:sɪ:z], *pl.* der Rachen, Schlund. **-et** ['fɔ:sɪt], *s.* der Hahn, Zapfen.

faugh [fɔ:], *int.* pfui!

fault [fɔ:lt], *s.* der Mangel; Fehler, Fehltritt, das Versehen, Vergehen, die Schuld; verlorene Spur (*Hunt.*), fehlerhafte Isolierung (*Elec.*); die Verwerfung (*Geol.*), falsch gegebener Ball (*Tenn.*); die Störung, der Defekt (*Mech.*); *it is my* -, ich habe die Schuld, es ist meine Schuld; *be at* -, im Unrecht sein, zu tadeln sein; auf falscher Fährte sein; in Verlegenheit sein; *find* -, tadeln, mißbilligen, kritteln, nörgeln; *find - with*, etwas auszusetzen finden *or* haben an (*Dat.*); *to a* -, bis zum Übermaß; *generous to a* -, allzu freigebig. **--finder,** *s.* der Tadler, Krittler, Nörgler. **-iness,** *s.* die Fehlerhaftigkeit. **-less,** *adj.* fehlerfrei; untadelig, tadellos. **-lessness,** *s.* die Fehlerlosigkeit, Tadellosigkeit. **-sman,** *s.* der Störungssucher (*Tele., Phone.*). **-y,** *adj.* fehlerhaft, mangelhaft, unvollkommen.

faun [fɔ:n], *s.* der Faun.

fauna ['fɔ:nə], *s.* die Tierwelt, Fauna; zoologische Abhandlung.

fauteuil [fo'tɔɪ], *s.* der Lehnsessel; Sperrsitz (*Theat.*).

faux-pas ['foʊ'pɑ], *s.* der Fehltritt, Mißgriff, die Taktlosigkeit, der Schnitzer, Verstoß.

favour ['feɪvə], **1.** *s.* die Gunst, Gnade, Gewogenheit, das Wohlwollen; der Gefallen, die Gefälligkeit, Gunstbezeigung; Genehmigung, Erlaubnis; der Schutz, die Unterstützung, Hilfe, Begünstigung, Bevorzugung, der Vorteil; die (Band-)Schleife, Rosette; *do me the - to . . .*, tun Sie mir den Gefallen und . . .; (*a*) (*with prepositions*) *by - of*, mit gütiger Genehmigung von, begünstigt durch; *by -* or *under the - of*, begünstigt durch; *be in - of a p.* or *a th.*, für einen *or* etwas sein; *be* (*high*) *in a p.'s -* or *be in - with a p.*, bei einem (sehr) gut angeschrieben sein, in jemandes (besonderer) Gunst stehen; *it turned in his* -, es wendete sich zu seinen Gunsten; *balance in your* -, Saldo zu Ihren Gunsten; *under - of night*, unter dem Schutze *or* mit Hilfe der Nacht; *look with - on s.o.*, einen mit Wohlwollen betrachten; (*b*) (*with verbs*) *ask s.o. a -* or *ask a - of s.o.*, einen um einen Gefallen bitten, von einem eine Gefälligkeit erbitten; *bestow one's -s on s.o.* (*of a woman*), einem ihre Liebe *or* Neigung schenken; *curry - with s.o.*, einem schmeicheln, sich bei einem einschmeicheln; *find - in the eyes of* or *with s.o.*, bei einem Gnade *or* Gunst finden; *grant a* -, eine Gunst gewähren; *your - of the 20th inst. received*, Ihr geehrtes Schreiben vom 20. d. Mts. erhalten (*C.L.*); *request the - of s.o.'s company*, sich beehren einen einzuladen; *the - of an early answer is requested*, um gefällige baldige Antwort wird gebeten (*C.L.*). **2.** *v.a.* begünstigen, vorziehen, bevorzugen, geneigt sein (*Dat.*) (*things*); beehren, die Ehre geben (*Dat.*) (*persons*); unterstützen, bestätigen, bekräftigen, hinweisen auf; (*coll.*) gleichen, ähnlich sehen; *the child -s his father*, das Kind ähnelt seinem Vater; *- a p.*, einem günstig gesinnt sein; *- doing*, geneigt sein zu tun; *- me with an answer*, antworten Sie mir gefälligst; *- us with a song*, geben Sie uns ein Lied zum besten. **-able** ['feɪvərəbl], *adj.* vorteilhaft, günstig, passend, gelegen; gefällig; gewogen (*to a p.*, einem); vielversprechend, dienlich, förderlich (*to* (*Dat.*)); zustimmend (*answer*). **-ed** ['feɪvəd], *adj.* begünstigt; *-ed by*, überreicht von (*C.L.*); *the -ed few*, die wenigen Begünstigten; *ill--ed*, häßlich; *well--ed*, wohlgestaltet, hübsch; *most--ed-nation clause*, die Meistbegünstigungsklausel. **-ite** ['feɪvərɪt], 1. *s.* der Günstling (*at court*); Liebling, der (*or* die) Liebste; mutmaßlicher Sieger, der Favorit (*horse racing*). 2. *attrib.* Lieblings-. **-itism** [-tɪzm], *s.* die Günstlingswirtschaft (*at courts*); Bevorzugung, Begünstigung.

[1]**fawn** [fɔ:n], 1. *s.* das Rehkalb, Damkitz; die Rehfarbe, das Bisterbraun. 2. *v.a.* (Rehe) werfen *or* setzen. 3. *adj.* rehfarbig, bisterbraun.

[2]**fawn,** *v.n.* schwänzeln, schweifwedeln (*of dogs*); (*fig.*) sich anschmeicheln (*on* or *upon*, bei), kriechen (vor). **-er,** *s.* der Schmeichler, Kriecher. **-ing,** *adj.* sich anschmeichelnd, schmeichlerisch, kriechend, kriecherisch.

fay [feɪ], *s.* die Fee, Elfe.

fealty ['fɪ:əltɪ], *s.* die Lehnstreue (*Law*); (*fig.*) Treue (*to*, zu), Anhänglichkeit (*to*, an).

fear [fɪə], 1. *s.* die Furcht (*of*, vor), Angst, Sorge, Befürchtung, Besorgnis (*for*, um); die Ehrfurcht, Scheu (*of*, vor); *pl.* die Befürchtungen, die Furcht; *- of death*, die Todesangst; *- of one's life*, die Todesangst; *- of the Lord*, die Furcht Gottes, Ehrfurcht vor dem Herrn; *go* or *stand in - of*, sich fürchten vor (*Dat.*); *for - of*, aus Furcht vor, da . . . zu befürchten ist, um . . . zu verhüten; (*coll.*) *no - !* auf keinen Fall! beileibe nicht! *there is no - of that*, das ist nicht zu befürchten. 2. *v.a.* scheuen, fürchten, befürchten (*things*), Angst haben vor, sich fürchten vor (*persons*); *I - his revenge*, ich fürchte mich vor seiner Rache; *there is nothing to* -, da ist nichts zu befürchten. 3. *v.n.* sich fürchten, Furcht haben; besorgt sein (*for*, um) *never - !* seien Sie unbesorgt! **-ful,** *adj.* furchtsam, sich fürchtend, bange (*of*, vor); furchtbar, fürchterlich, schrecklich; ehrfürchtig. **-fulness,** *s.* die Furchtbarkeit, Fürchterlichkeit, Schrecklichkeit; Furchtsamkeit, Ängstlichkeit. **-less,** *adj.* furchtlos, unerschrocken. **-lessness,** *s.* die Furchtlosigkeit. **-some,** *adj.* schrecklich, furchtbar.

feasib-ility [fɪ:zə'bɪlɪtɪ], *s.* die Durchführbarkeit, Möglichkeit. **-le** ['fɪ:zəbl], *adj.*, **-ly,** *adv.* ausführbar, durchführbar, möglich, angänglich, tunlich; wahrscheinlich.

feast [fɪ:st], 1. *s.* das Fest, der Festtag; das Festmahl, Gastmahl, der Schmaus; (*fig.*) der (Hoch-)Genuß. 2. *v.a.* festlich bewirten; (*fig.*) ergötzen; *- one's eyes on*, seine Augen weiden an. 3. *v.n.* schmausen (*on*, von), sich gütlich tun; (*fig.*) sich ergötzen, sich weiden (*on*, an (*Dat.*)).

feat [fɪ:t], *s.* die Heldentat, Großtat; das Kunststück, die Kraftleistung; *- of arms*, die Waffentat.

feather ['fɛðə], 1. *s.* die Feder; *birds of a - flock together*, gleich und gleich gesellt sich gern; *fine -s make fine birds*, Kleider machen Leute; *fur and* -, Wild und Federwild; *a - in his cap*, die Auszeichnung, Ehre worauf man sich etwas einbilden kann; *light as a* -, federleicht; *show the white* -, sich feige zeigen, sich drücken; *in full* or *high* -, in gehobener Stimmung. 2. *v.a.* befiedern; mit Federn bedecken *or* schmücken; *- a bird*, einen Vogel anschießen; *- one's nest*, sein Schäfchen ins Trockne bringen; *- the oars*, die Riemen flach *or* platt werfen, abscheren. **--bed,** *s.* das Federbett. **--brained,** *adj.* unbesonnen. **--duster,** der Federwisch. **-ed** [-d], *adj.* befiedert, gefiedert; *-ed game*, das Federwild; *the -ed tribe*, die Vogelwelt. **--edge,** *s.* zugespitzte Kante. **--grass,** *s.* das Federgras. **-ing** [-rɪŋ], *s.* das Gefieder; Federn (*rowing*); in Segelstellung (*propeller*). **-ings,** *pl.*

Spitzen der Maßwerkverzierung (*Arch.*). **--stitch,** *s.* der Grätenstich, Hexenstich. **-weight,** *s.* das Federgewicht (*Boxing*). **-y,** *adj.* federartig, federleicht, federweich; gefiedert.

feature ['fi:tʃə], 1. *s.* der Gesichtszug, die Eigenschaft, der Grundzug, Hauptzug, das Kennzeichen, Merkmal, Charakteristische, Gepräge; der Zeitungsartikel; *pl.* die Züge, die Gesichtsbildung; *make a – of doing,* sich besonders hervortun *or* sich angelegen sein lassen zu tun; *– film,* der Spielfilm; *– programme,* die Hörfolge (*Rad.*); *redeeming –,* der Lichtblick; *topographical –s,* die Bodengestaltung. 2. *v.a.* kennzeichnen, bezeichnend sein für, charakterisieren; zur Schau stellen, großartig aufziehen; in der Hauptrolle darstellen (*Films*); *film featuring Greta Garbo,* der Film mit G. G. in der Hauptrolle. **-less,** *adj.* ohne bestimmte Züge, formlos. **-d,** *suffix* mit . . . Gesichtszügen.

febri-fuge ['fɛbrɪfju:dʒ], 1. *s.* das Fiebermittel. 2. *adj.* fiebervertreibend. **-le** ['fi:braɪl], *adj.* fieberhaft, fiebernd, Fieber–.

February ['fɛbruərɪ], *s.* der Februar.

feckless ['fɛklɪs], *adj.* hilflos, unfähig, wirkungslos, wertlos.

feculen-ce ['fɛkjʊləns], *s.* das Trübe, Schlammige; die Hefe, der Bodensatz. **-t,** *adj.* hefig, trübe, schlammig, schmutzig.

fecund ['fi:kənd], *adj.* fruchtbar, schöpferisch. **-ate** ['fi:kəndeɪt], *v.a.* befruchten. **-ation** [–'deɪʃən], *s.* die Befruchtung. **-ity** [fɪ'kʌndɪtɪ], *s.* die Fruchtbarkeit, befruchtende Kraft.

fed [fɛd], *see* **feed.**

federa-cy ['fɛdərəsɪ], *s.* der Staatenbund. **-l,** 1. *adj.* föderativ, Bundes–; föderalistisch (*Amer. Civil War*). 2. *s. see* **-list;** *-l government,* die Bundesregierung; *-l states,* Bundesstaaten. **-lism,** *s.* der Föderalismus. **-list,** *s.* der Föderalist (*Amer.*). **-lize,** *v.a.* verbünden. **-te,** 1. ['fɛdərət], *adj.* verbündet, Bundes–. 2. ['fɛdəreɪt], *v.a.* zu einem Staatenbund vereingen, verbünden. 3. *v.n.* sich verbünden. **-tion** [–'reɪʃən], *s.* der Staatenbund; (Zentral)Verband, die Vereinigung, das Bündnis. **-tive** [–rətɪ)], *adj.* föderativ, bundesmäßig.

fee [fi:], 1. *s.* die Gebühr, Aufnahmegebühr, das Eintrittsgeld; Honorar; die Vergütung, Belohnung; das Trinkgeld; Lehen, Lehngut, Erbgut (*Law*); *pl.* das Schulgeld. **--farm,** *s.* das Erbzinsgut; *retaining –,* vorläufiges Honorar; *– simple,* das Eigengut, Allodialgut; *hold in – (simple),* als volles Eigen besitzen; *estate in – tail,* begrenztes Lehen, das Gut mit Erbbeschränkung. 2. *v.a.* bezahlen, belohnen, honorieren; (*coll.*) ein Trinkgeld geben (*Dat.*), schmieren.

feeble ['fi:bl], *adj.* schwach, kraftlos, (*fig.*) unentschlossen; *– joke,* billiger Witz. **--minded,** *adj.* schwachsinnig. **--mindedness,** *s.* der Schwachsinn. **-ness,** *s.* die Schwäche.

feed [fi:d], 1. *ir.v.a.* füttern (*cattle*); nähren (*on* or *with,* mit); zu essen geben (*Dat.*); ernähren (*on,* von); versorgen mit; unterhalten (*a fire*); zuführen, beschicken (*Mach.*); weiden (*God's flock*); (*coll.*) *– the fishes,* seekrank werden; ertrinken; *– hope,* Hoffnung nähren *or* Nahrung geben; *– o.s.,* sich selbst nähren; *– the eyes on s.th.,* das Auge weiden an einer S.; *– up,* mästen; (*sl.*) *fed up with a th.,* es gründlich satt haben, von etwas überdrüssig *or* gelangweilt. 2. *ir.v.n.* essen; fressen, weiden (*beasts*); leben, sich nähren (*upon,* von); (*fig.*) *– out of a p.'s hand,* aus jemandes Hand fressen, gefügig sein. 3. *s.* das Füttern; Futter; die Weide; Nahrung; Zuführung, Zufuhr, der Zufluß (*of material*); Vorschub (*of a lathe, etc.*); *– of oats,* die Metze Hafer. **-back,** *s.* die Rückkopplung, Rückwirkung (*Rad.*). **--bag,** *s.* der Futtersack. **--cock,** *s.* der Speisehahn, Einfüllhahn. **-er** ['fi:də], *s.* der Esser, Fresser; Fütterer; (Er)-Nährer; Nebenfluß, Zufuhrkanal, Zuflußgraben, Bewässerungsgraben (*Hydr.*); die Speisevorrichtung, der Zuführer (*Mach.*); die Speiseleitung (*Elec.*); der Kinderlatz (*for infants*). **-er-line,** *s.* die Zubringerlinie, Zufuhrbahn, Verbindungslinie. **-ing** ['fi:dɪŋ], *s.* die Nahrung; Fütterung (*of cattle*); (*dial.*) Weide; *forcible -ing,* die Zwangsernährung. **-ing-bottle,** *s.* die Saugflasche. **-ing stuff,** *s.* das Futter. **--pipe,** *s.* die Speiseröhre, das Zufuhrrohr, Zuflußrohr, Zuführungsrohr. **--pump,** *s.* die Speisepumpe. **--tank,** *s.* der Speisewasserbehälter, Zuflußbehälter. **--water,** *s.* das Speisewasser.

feel [fi:l], **1.** *ir.v.a.* fühlen, befühlen, betasten; merken, wahrnehmen, empfinden; spüren, erfahren; halten für; *– the draught,* den Zug merken; (*fig.*) unannehmliche Folgen zu spüren bekommen; *the ship –s the helm,* das Schiff folgt dem Ruder; *– one's legs,* festen Boden unter den Füßen gewinnen *or* haben; *– a p.'s pulse,* einem den Puls betasten; (*fig.*) *– one's way,* vorsichtig vorgehen, sich einfühlen in; *I felt it deeply,* es schmerzte mich tief, ich empfand es sehr schmerzlich; *– it one's duty,* es für seine Pflicht halten; *– this to be important,* glauben daß dies wichtig sei. **2.** *ir.v.n.* fühlen (*for,* nach), durch Fühlen feststellen; sich fühlen, das Gefühl haben von, sich bewußt werden; tief empfinden, Mitleid haben, sich zu Herzen nehmen; den Eindruck geben, sich anfühlen; (*a*) (*with adjectives, etc.*) *I – better,* es geht mir besser; *– certain that,* ein gewisses Gefühl haben daß; *– cold,* frieren; *how do you – ?* wie befinden Sie sich; *– hurt at,* sich beleidigt fühlen über; *– inclined,* sich geneigt fühlen, geneigt *or* aufgelegt sein; *I – queer,* mir ist sonderbar zumute; *– quite o.s. again,* sich ganz wiederhergestellt fühlen; *it –s soft,* es fühlt sich weich an; *I – strongly,* ich bin der entschiedenen Ansicht; es geht mit sehr nahe, es liegt mir sehr viel daran; *– sure of,* überzeugt sein von; *– warm,* sich warm fühlen; (*b*) (*with prepositions*) *– for,* fühlen, greifen *or* tasten nach; Fühlung nehmen mit (*Mil.*); *we – for them,* wir fühlen mit ihnen, sie dauern uns, sie tun uns leid; *I – with him in his bereavement,* ich fühle mit ihm in seinem Verlust mit; (*coll.*) *I do not – up to much,* ich bin nicht ganz auf der Höhe; *I do not – up to work* or *like work,* ich habe keine Lust zur Arbeit; (*c*) (*with verbs*) *I – as if I shall stifle,* es ist mir als wenn ich ersticke; *I – like doing s.th.,* ich habe Lust etwas zu tun; *it made itself felt,* es machte sich fühlbar. **3.** *s.* das Fühlen; Gefühl, die Empfindung; *the – of the cloth,* der Griff des Stoffes; *a homely –,* anheimelndes Gefühl; *rough to the –,* dem Anfühlen nach rauh. **-er,** *s.* der Fühler (*Ent. & fig.*) das Fühlhorn (*Ent.*); (*fig.*) der Versuchsballon; *throw out a -er,* sondieren, einen Fühler ausstrecken. **-ing,** 1. *adj.* fühlend, mitfühlend, gefühlvoll. 2. *s.* das Fühlen; das Gefühl, der Gefühlssinn; die Rührung, Empfindung, Stimmung, Ansicht; Aufregung; *good -ing,* das Feingefühl, Entgegenkommen; *ill -ing,* der Unwille, Verdruß; *man of -ing,* Mann von Gefühl; *hurt a p.'s -ings,* einen kränken *or* verletzen, einem weh tun; *-ing(s) ran high,* die Erregung ging hoch, die Gemüter waren sehr erregt.

feet [fi:t], *see* **foot.**

feign [feɪn], *v.a.* erdichten; sich stellen, heucheln, vorgeben; *– sickness,* sich krank stellen. **-ed,** *adj.* falsch, verstellt, vorgeblich, fingiert, Schein–. **-er,** *s.* der Heuchler. **-ing,** *s.* die Heuchelei.

feint [feɪnt], *s.* Finte (*Fenc. & fig.*); der Scheinangriff (*Mil.*), die Verstellung; *make a – of writing,* sich stellen als ob man schreiben wollte.

feldspar ['fɛldspɑ:], *see* **felspar.**

felicit-ate [fɪ'lɪsɪteɪt], *v.a.* beglückwünschen (*upon,* zu); (*archaic*) beglücken. **-ation** [–'teɪʃən], *s.* die Beglückwünschung, der Glückwunsch. **-ous** [fə'lɪsɪtəs], *adj.* glücklich; gut gewählt, treffend (*expressions*). **-y** [–tɪ], *s.* das Glück, die Glückseligkeit; treffender Ausdruck, glücklicher Griff; die Sicherheit (*in doing*).

feline ['fi:laɪn], *adj.* katzenartig, Katzen–.

[1]**fell** [fɛl], v.a. fällen (*trees*); niederstrecken, hinstrecken (*men*); kappen, (ein)säumen, umnähen (*Sew.-mach.*). **-ing,** *s.* der Hieb, Einschlag (*Forestry*).

[2]**fell,** *adj.* (*Poet.*) grausam, grimmig.

[3]**fell,** *s.* (*dial.*) der Hügel, das Moorland, Hügelland.

[4]**fell,** *s.* das Fell, die (Tier)Haut.

[5]**fell,** *see* **fall.**

fellah ['fɛlə], *s.* (*pl.* -een [–'hɪ:n]) der Fellache.

feller ['fɛlə], *s.* (*vulg.*) der Bursche.

felloe ['fɛlou], *s.* die (Rad)Felge.
fellow ['fɛlou], *s.* Gefährte(r), *m.*, der Genosse, Kamerad; Mitmensch, Zeitgenosse; das Mitglied einer Körperschaft (*Univ.*, *etc.*); (*coll.*) der Kerl, Bursch(e), Mensch; das Gegenstück, das andere eines Paares; *two shoes that are not –s*, zwei unzusammengehörige Schuhe; *where is the – of this glove?* wo ist der andere Handschuh? *be –s*, zusammengehören; *this man has not his –*, dieser Mann hat nicht seinesgleichen; *this – of a barber*, dieser Kerl von Barbier; *cunning –*, schlauer Bursche; *my dear –*, lieber Freund; *my good –*, lieber Mann; *fine* or *good –*, guter *or* netter Kerl, famoser Mensch; (*coll.*) *let a – alone!* laß mich in Frieden! *odd –*, komischer Kauz; *old –*, alter Junge, altes Haus; *poor –*, armer Kerl. **–-being,** *s.* der Mitmensch. **–-citizen,** *s.* der Mitbürger. **–-countryman,** *s.* der Landsmann. **–-creature,** *s.* der Mitmensch. **–-feeling,** *s.* das Mitgefühl. **–-member,** *s.* der Parteigenosse. **–-men,** *pl.* die Mitmenschen. **–-passenger,** *s.* der Reisegefährte, Mitreisende(r), *m.* **–-prisoner,** *s.* Mitgefangene(r), *m.* **–ship,** *s.* die Gemeinschaft, Kameradschaft, gegenseitige Verbundenheit; Brüderschaft, Körperschaft, Mitgliedschaft; das Universitätsstipendium; *good –ship*, die Geselligkeit, Kameradschaft; **–-soldier,** *s.* der Mitkämpfer, Waffenbruder, Kamerad. **–-student,** *s.* der Kommilitone. **–-sufferer,** *s.* der Leidensgefährte. **–-traveller,** *s.* der Reisegefährte; (*coll.*) Sympathisierende(r), *m.*
felly ['fɛlɪ:], *see* **felloe.**
felo-de-se ['fɛloudɪ'sɪ:], *s.* der Selbstmörder; Selbstmord.
felon ['fɛlən], 1. *s.* der Verbrecher, Missetäter. 2. *adj.* (*Poet.*) grausam, böse. **–ious** [fɪ'lounɪəs], *adj.* verbrecherisch (*Law*); (*Poet.*) böse, mit böser Absicht. **–y,** *s.* schweres Verbrechen.
felsp–ar ['fɛlspɑ:], *s.* der Feldspat. **–athic,** *adj.* Feldspat–.
[1]**felt** [fɛlt], *see* **feel;** *– want*, dringendes Erfordernis.
[2]**felt,** 1. *s.* der Filz; *carpet –*, die Teppichunterlage; *– hat*, der Filzhut; *roofing –*, die Dachpappe. 2. *v.a.* (ver)filzen; *–ed cloth*, das Filztuch.
female ['fɪ:meɪl], 1. *adj.* weiblich; *– child*, das Mädchen; *– companion*, die Begleiterin; *– dog*, die Hündin; *– friend*, die Freundin; *– labour*, die Frauenarbeit; *– screw*, die Schraubenmutter; *– servant*, die Magd, das Dienstmädchen; *– student*, die Studentin. 2. *s.* das Weib, die Frau, das Mädchen; Weibchen (*of beasts, etc.*).
feme [fɛm], *s.* die Frau (*Law*); *– covert*, verheiratete Frau (*Law*), Ehefrau; *– sole*, unverheiratete Frau (*Law*).
femin–ine ['fɛmɪnɪn], 1. *adj.* weiblich (*also Gram.*); zart, sanft; weibisch, unmännlich (*of men*). 2. *s.* weibliches Geschlecht (*Gram.*). **–inity** [–'nɪnɪtɪ], *s.* die Weiblichkeit. **–ism** ['fɛmɪnɪzm], *s.* das Frauenrechtlertum. **–ist** [–nɪst], *s.* der Frauenrechtler.
fem–oral ['fɛmərəl], *adj.* Oberschenkel– (*Anat.*). **–ur** ['fɪ:mə:], *s.* (*pl.* –s, femora) der (Ober)Schenkel, das Oberschenkelbein.
fen [fɛn], *s.* der Sumpf, das Moor, Marschland; *pl.* Niederungen (*pl.*). **–-berry,** *s.* die Moosbeere. **–-fire,** *s.* das Irrlicht. **–land,** *s.* das Marschland. **–ny,** *adj.* moorig, sumpfig. **–-shooting,** *s.* die Jagd auf Moorvögel.
fenc–e [fɛns], 1. *s.* die Einfriedigung, Umzäunung, Einzäunung, der Zaun, das Gehege, die Hürde; das Hindernis (*Racing*); Fechten, die Fechtkunst; (*sl.*) der Hehler; *sit on the –e*, das Ergebnis abwarten, unentschlossen sein. 2. *v.a.* einhegen, einzäunen; verteidigen, schützen, sichern. *–e about*, umgeben; *–e in*, einzäunen, umzäunen; *–e off*, abwehren, abhalten, absperren. 3. *v.n.* fechten; (*fig.*) abwehren, parieren, ausweichen; Spiegelfechterei treiben; Diebesgut hehlen. **–eless,** *adj.* offen, uneingezäunt. **–e-month,** *s.* die Schonzeit. **–er** ['fɛnsə], *s.* der Fechter. **–ible** ['fɛnsɪbl], *adj.* (*Scots*) verteidigungsfähig. **–ibles,** *pl.* (*archaic*) die Miliz, Landwehr. **–ing,** *s.* das Fechten, die Fechtkunst; Einfriedung, Einzäunung, Einhegung; Zäune (*pl.*). **–ing club,** der Fechtverein. **–ing-foil,** *s.* das Florett. **–ing-gloves,** *pl.* die Fechthandschuhe. **–ing-master,** *s.* der Fechtmeister. **–ing-school,** *s.* die Fechtschule.
fend [fɛnd], 1. *v.a.* (*– off*) abwehren, abhalten (*from*, von); abscheren (*Naut.*). 2. *v.n.*; *– for*, sorgen für. **–er** ['fɛndə], *s.* der Kaminvorsetzer; die Schutzvorrichtung, der Schutz, Puffer; Fender (*Naut.*); das Schutzholz, Schutzbrett, Schutzblech; der Stoßfänger (*Motor.*); Kotflügel (*Amer.*, *Motor.*).
fenestra–l [fɪ'nɛstrəl], *adj.* Fenster–. **–te,** *adj.* mit kleinen Löchern (*Bot. & Zool.*). **–tion** [fɛnəs'treɪʃən], *s.* die Fensteranlage (*Arch.*).
Fenian ['fɪ:nɪən], 1. *adj.* fenisch. 2. *s.* der Fenier. **–ism** [–ɪzm], *s.* die Politik der Fenier.
fennel ['fɛnl], *s.* der Fenchel (*Bot.*). **–-flower,** *s.* der Schwarzkümmel, Gretchen im Busch (*Bot.*).
fenny ['fɛnɪ], *see* **fen.**
feoff [fɛf], *see* **fief. –ee** [fɛf'ɪ:], *s.* Belehnte(r), *m.* (*Law*). **–er, –or,** *m.* der Lehnsherr (*Law*). **–ment,** *s.* die Belehnung (*Law*).
feral ['fɪ:rəl], *adj.* unkultiviert, wild, roh.
feretory ['fɛrətərɪ], *s.* der Reliquienschrein (*R.C.*).
ferial ['fɪ:ərɪəl], *adj.* Alltags–, Wochentags– (*Eccl.*).
ferment, 1. ['fə:mənt], *s.* die Gärung; das Gärmittel (*also fig.*), der Gärungsstoff; (*fig.*) Aufruhr; *in a –*, gärend. 2. [fə:'mɛnt] *v.a.* gären lassen, in Gärung bringen; (*fig.*) erregen. 3. *v.n.* gären, in Gärung sein, aufbrausen. **–able,** *adj.* gärungsfähig, gärfähig. **-ation** [–'teɪʃən], *s.* die Gärung, der Gärprozeß, das Aufbrausen. **–ing,** 1. *adj.* gärend; *–ing vat*, der Gärbottich. 2. *s.* das Gären.
fern [fə:n], *s.* der Farn, das Farnkraut. **–ery** [–ərɪ], *s.* die Farnkrautpflanzung. **–y,** *adj.* mit Farn(kraut) überwachsen; farnartig.
feroc–ious [fə'rouʃəs], *adj.* wild, grausam; bissig (*as a dog*); *–ious animals*, Raubtiere. **–ity** [fə'rɔsɪtɪ], *s.* die Wildheit, Grausamkeit.
ferreous ['fɛrɪəs], *adj.* eisenhaltig.
ferret ['fɛrɪt], 1. *s.* das Frettchen. 2. *v.a.*; *– out*, aus dem Versteck heraustreiben; (*fig.*) ausforschen, ausspüren, aufstöbern, auskundschaften. 3. *v.n.* mit Frettchen jagen; *– about*, herumsuchen (*for*, nach).
ferr–ic ['fɛrɪk], *adj.* Ferri– (*Chem.*); *–ic compound*, die Eisenoxydverbindung; *–ic oxide*, das Eisenoxyd. **–iferous** [fɛ'rɪfərəs], *adj.* eisenhaltig. **–o–,** *adj. prefix* Ferro–; *–o-concrete*, der Eisenbeton. **–ous** ['fɛrəs], *adj.* Ferro– (*Chem.*); *–ous oxide*, (schwefelsaures) Eisenoxydul. **–uginous** [fɛ'ru:dʒɪnəs], *adj. see* **–iferous;** rostbraun.
ferrule ['fɛrul], *s.* die Zwinge (*on a stick*); der Metallring.
ferry ['fɛrɪ], 1. *s.* die Fähre, das Fährboot; die Fährgerechtigkeit (*Law*); *train-–*, das Trajekt, die Eisenbahnfähre. 2. *v.a. & n.* (hin)übersetzen; überführen (*Av.*). **–-boat,** *s.* das Fährboot. **– command,** *s.* das Überführungskommando, Abholkommando (*Av.*). **–man** [–mən], *s.* der Fährmann.
fertil–e ['fə:tɑɪl], *adj.* fruchtbar, reich (*in*, an (*Dat.*)) (*also fig.*). **–ity** [fə:'tɪlɪtɪ], *s.* die Fruchtbarkeit, der Reichtum (*also fig.*). **–ization** [fə:tɪlɑɪ'zeɪʃən], *s.* die Befruchtung, Fruchtbarmachung. **–ize** ['fə:tɪlɑɪz], *v.a.* befruchten, fruchtbar machen. **–izer,** *s.* das Düngemittel, der Kunstdünger.
ferule ['fɛru:l], 1. *s.* der Stock, die Rute, das Lineal. 2. *v.a.* mit dem Stock züchtigen, mit der Rute schlagen.
ferven–cy ['fə:vənsɪ], *s.* die Glut, Hitze; Inbrunst, der Eifer. **–t** [–nt], *adj.* heiß, glühend, brennend, inbrünstig, heftig, eifrig; *–t prayer*, inniges Gebet; *–t zeal*, glühender Eifer; *–t in spirit*, eifrigen Geistes.
ferv–id ['fə:vɪd], *adj.* (*Poet.*) heiß, brennend, glühend; feurig, hitzig; eifrig. **–our** ['fə:və], *s.* die Hitze; Glut, Leidenschaft, Inbrunst, der Eifer; *–our of love*, die Liebesglut.
fescue ['fɛskju:], *s.* (also *– grass*) der Wiesenschwingel, das Schwingelgras (*Bot.*).
fesse [fɛs], *s.* der (Quer)Balken (*Her.*).
festal ['fɛstl], *adj.* (*Poet.*) festlich, Fest–.
fester ['fɛstə], 1. *v.n.* schwären, eitern; verwesen, verfaulen; (*fig.*) nagen, um sich greifen. 2. *v.a.* zum Schwären *or* Eitern bringen. 3. *s.* das Geschwür, eiternde Wunde.

festiv–al ['fɛstɪvl], *s.* der Festtag, das Fest, die Feier; *–al play*, das Festspiel. **–e** ['fɛstɪv], *adj.* festlich, fröhlich, heiter. **–ity** [fɛs'tɪvɪtɪ], *s.* das Fest, die Festlichkeit; Fröhlichkeit.

festoon [fɛs'tu:n], 1. *s.* die Girlande; das Blumengewinde; Fruchtgehänge, Laubgehänge (*Arch.*). 2. *v.a.* mit Girlanden behängen.

fetch [fɛtʃ], 1. *v.a.* holen, abholen; hervorholen (*from*, aus); einbringen, eintragen; fließen lassen (*tears, blood*); (*coll.*) – *s.o. a blow*, einem einen Schlag versetzen; – *a high price*, einen hohen Preis einbringen *or* erzielen; – *down*, herunterholen, niederschießen; – *out*, herausholen(*from*, aus); zum Vorschein bringen, hervorrufen; – *up*, heraufholen; einholen (*distance*); ausspeien(*food*). 2. *v.n.* Kurs nehmen (*Naut.*); – *and carry*, niedrige Dienste verrichten; apportieren (*as dogs*); – *up*, zum Stehen kommen. 3. *s.* (*coll.*) der Kniff, Kunstgriff, die Finte. **–ed,** *adj.*; *far-–ed*, weit hergeholt. **–ing,** *adj.* (*coll.*) einnehmend, reizend, fesselnd, bezaubernd.

fète [feɪt], 1. *s.* das Fest, die Festlichkeit. 2. *v.a.* feiern.

fetid ['fɛtɪd], *adj.* stinkend.

fetish ['fɛtɪʃ], *s.* der Fetisch. **–ism,** *s.* der Fetischdienst.

fetlock ['fɛtlɔk], *s.* die Köte, das Kötengelenk, Fesselgelenk.

fetter ['fɛtə], 1. *v.a.* fesseln. 2. *s.* die Fessel. **–less,** *adj.* ohne Fesseln.

fettle ['fɛtl], *s.*; (*coll.*) *in good* or *fine* –, in guter Verfassung *or* Form.

fetus ['fi:təs], *s. see* **foetus.**

feu [fju:], (*Scots*) 1. *s.* das Lehen. 2. *v.a.* zum Lehen geben (*land*). **–-duty,** *s.* (*Scots*) der Bodenzins.

[1]**feud** [fju:d], *s.* das Lehen, Lehnsgut (*Law*). **–al,** *adj.* feudal, Lehns–; *–al system*, das Lehnswesen, Feudalsystem. **–alism** [–əlɪzm], *s.* das Lehnswesen, Feudalsystem. **–ality** [–'dælɪtɪ], *s.* die Lehnbarkeit, Lehnsverfassung. **–alize,** *v.a.* lehnbar machen. **–atory,** 1. *s.* der Lehnsmann, Vasall. 2. *adj.* lehnspflichtig, Lehns–, feudal.

[2]**feud,** *s.* die Fehde.

feuilleton ['føɪtõ], *s.* das Feuilleton, der Unterhaltungsteil (*of newspaper*).

fever ['fi:və], *s.* das Fieber; (*fig.*) die Erregung, Aufregung. **–ed** ['fi:vəd], *adj.* fiebrig, fiebernd; (*fig.*) fieberhaft, erregt, aufgeregt. **–ish** [–rɪʃ], *adj.* fiebrig, fieberkrank (*Med.*); (*fig.*) fieberhaft, heiß, glühend, aufgeregt; *be –ish*, Fieber haben. **–ishness,** *s.* das Fieber; die Fieberhaftigkeit.

few [fju:], *s. & adj.* wenig, wenige; *a –, some –*, einige (wenige), ein paar; – *and far between*, sehr selten; *every – days*, alle paar Tage; (*coll.*) *a good –*, eine beträchtliche Anzahl von, ziemlich viel; *the chosen –*, die wenigen Auserwählten; *a select –*, einige Auserwählte; *only a –*, nur wenige. **–er,** *adj.* weniger. **–ness,** *s.* geringe Anzahl.

fez [fɛz], *s.* der Fes.

fiancé [fɪ'ɑ̃:seɪ], *s.* Verlobte(r), *m.*, der Bräutigam. **–e,** *s.* die Braut, Verlobte.

fiasco [fɪ'æskoʊ], *s.* der Mißerfolg, das Fiasko; die Blamage.

fiat ['faɪæt], *s.* der Befehl, Machtspruch; die Erlaubnis (*Law*).

fib [fɪb], 1. *s.* (*coll.*) die Lüge, Flunkerei; *tell a –*, flunkern. 2. *v.n.* lügen, flunkern. **–ber,** *s.* der Flunkerer.

fibr–e ['faɪbə], *s.* die Faser, Fiber; (*fig.*) der Charakter, die Struktur; *animal –e*, der Faserstoff. *–e board*, *s.* die Hartpappe. **–eless,** *adj.* faserlos. **–il,** *s.* das Fäserchen, die Wurzelfaser. **–ilation,** *s.* die Faserbildung. **–oid,** *adj.* Faser–, Bindegewebs–. **–in** ['faɪbrɪn], *s.* der Faserstoff, das Fibrin. **–ous** ['faɪbrəs], *adj.* faserig, faserartig, fibrinös; *–ous membrane*, die Faserhaut.

fibula ['fɪbjʊlə], *s.* (*pl.* –e [–lɪ:], –s) das Wadenbein; die Fibel, Spange.

fickle ['fɪkl], *adj.* wankelmütig, unbeständig, launisch, wandelbar. **–ness,** *s.* der Wankelmut, die Unbeständigkeit.

fictile ['fɪktaɪl], *adj.* Ton–, tönern, irden; – *art*, die Töpferkunst; – *ware*, das Steingut.

fict–ion ['fɪkʃən], *s.* die Erdichtung, Erfindung Fiktion (*Law*); Prosadichtung, Romane (*pl.*); *work of –*, der Roman. **–ional,** *adj.* erdichtet; Roman–. **–itious** [fɪk'tɪʃəs], *adj.* fingiert, fiktiv (*Law*); unecht, nachgemacht; erdichtet, erfunden, angenommen (*as a name*); *–itious bill*, der Reitwechsel (*C.L.*); *–itious purchase*, der Scheinkauf. **–itiousness,** *s.* das Erdichtete, die Unechtheit.

fid [fɪd], *s.* das Schloßholz (*Naut.*).

fiddle ['fɪdl], 1. *s.* die Fiedel, Geige, Violine; *play first* (*second*) –, erste (zweite) Geige spielen; (*fig.*) die Haupt– (Neben)rolle spielen; *with a face as long as a –*, ein langes *or* trauriges Gesicht machen; *fit as a –*, in bester Verfassung sein. 2. *v.n.* geigen; (*coll.*) tändeln, spielen (*with*, mit); geschäftig sein, sich zu tun machen (*with*, mit); (*sl.*) beschwindeln, betrügen; – *about*, nichts vernünftiges tun, herumtändeln. 3. *v.a.* auf der Geige spielen, fiedeln (*a tune*); – *away*, vertändeln (*time*). **–-bow,** *s.* der Fiedelbogen. (*coll.*) **–de-dee!** Unsinn! Quatsch! (*coll.*) **–-faddle,** *s.* die Lappalie, der Unsinn. **–stick,** *s.* der Geigenbogen. (*coll.*) **–sticks!** Unsinn! Quatsch! dummes Zeug! **–-string,** *s.* die Geigensaite.

fiddling, *adj.* (*coll.*) unnütz, trivial, läppisch.

fidelity [faɪ'dɛlɪtɪ], *s.* die Treue (*to*, zu *or* gegenüber); (*fig.*) die Genauigkeit, das Festhalten (*to*, an), die Übereinstimmung (*to*, mit) (*as a translation, etc.*).

fidget ['fɪdʒɪt], 1. *v.n.* unruhig sein, zappeln. 2. *v.a.* nervös machen. 3. *s.* der Zappelphilipp, unruhige Person; (*usually pl.*) nervöse Unruhe; (*coll.*) *have the –s*, nicht ruhig sein können, herumzappeln, (*sl.*) kein Sitzfleisch haben. **–iness,** *s.* die Unruhe, Aufgeregtheit. **–y,** *adj.* unruhig, nervös, zappelig.

fiduciary [fɪ'dju:ʃɪərɪ], 1. *adj.* Treuhänder–; anvertraut, Vertrauens–; ungedeckt (*C.L.*); – *currency*, das Kreditgeld; – *issue*, ungedeckte Notenausgabe. 2. *s.* der Treuhänder, Vertrauensmann.

fie [faɪ], *int.* pfui! – *upon you!* pfui über dich! schäme dich!

fief [fi:f], *s.* das Leh(e)n, Lehngut.

field [fi:ld], 1. *s.* das Feld (*also Her.*); der Grund, die Fläche; das Gebiet, der Bereich; die Teilnehmer an einem Spiel *or* Rennen (*Sport*); (*fig.*) die Gesamtheit der Wettbewerber; (*a*) (*with nouns*) – *of application*, das Verwendungsgebiet; – *of fire*, das Schußfeld (*Artil.*); – *of ice*, das Eisfeld; – *of traverse*, der Schwenkungsbereich (*Artil.*); – *of vision* or *view*, das Gesichtsfeld, Blickfeld; (*fig.*) der Gesichtskreis; (*b*) (*with verbs*) *hold the –*, das Feld behaupten; *keep the –*, den Kampf fortsetzen; *take the –*, ins Feld rücken (*Mil.*), den Spielplatz betreten (*Sport*); (*c*) (*with prepositions*) *back a horse against the –*, auf ein Pferd gegen alle andern Renner setzen; *in the –*, im Felde, im Kampfe (*Mil.*); als Angreifer (*Crick.*); (*fig.*) im Wettbewerb; *bring into the –*, ins Gefecht bringen. 2. *v.n.* als Angreifer *or* Fänger spielen (*Crick.*). 3. *v.a.* auffangen und zurückwerfen (*the ball*) (*Crick.*). **–-ambulance,** *s.* der Sanitätskrankenwagen. **–-allowance,** *s.* die Kriegszulage. **–-artillery,** *s.* die Feldartillerie. **–-battery,** *s.* die Feldbatterie (*Artil.*). **–-cornet,** *s.* der Stadtrichter (*in S. Africa*). **–-day,** *s.* die Felddienstübung; (*fig.*) ereignisvoller Tag. **–-dressing,** *s.* der Notverband. **–dressing-station,** *s.* der Truppenverbandplatz (*Mil.*). **–er,** *s.* der Angreifer, Fänger, Spieler der nichtschlagenden Mannschaft (*Crick.*). **–-events,** *pl.* Sprung- und Wurfwettspiele. **–fare,** *s.* der Krammetsvogel. **–-glass(es),** *s.* der Feldstecher, Krimstecher, das Feldglas. **–-gun,** *s. see* **–-piece.** **–-hospital,** *s.* das Feldlazarett. **–ing,** *adj.* nichtschlagend (*Crick.*). **–-kitchen,** *s.* die Feldküche. **–-marshal,** *s.* der Feldmarschall. **–-mouse,** *s.* die Feldmaus. **–-officer,** *s.* der Stabsoffizier. **–-piece,** *s.* das Feldgeschütz. **–sman,** *s. see* **–er.** **–-sports,** *pl.* der Sport im Freien. **–strength,** *s.* die Feldstärke (*Elec.*). **–-training,** *s.* die Geländeausbildung (*Mil.*). **–-unit,** *s.* die Truppeneinheit. **–-work,** *s.* die Feldschanze.

fiend [fi:nd], *s.* böser Feind, der Teufel; (*fig.*) Unhold, die Furie; (*coll.*) Besessene(r), *m.*, der Fex, Narr. **–ish,** *adj.* teuflisch, unmenschlich; (*coll.*) verflucht, verflixt. **–ishness,** *s.* teuflische Bosheit, die Unmenschlichkeit.

fierce [fɪəs], *adj.* wild, grimmig, wütend, grausam;

heftig, hitzig, ungestüm; grell (*of light*). **–ness,** *s.* die Wildheit, Wut, Grimmigkeit, Grausamkeit; das Ungestüm, die Heftigkeit.

fier–iness ['faɪərɪnɪs], *s.* die Hitze, das Feuer. **–y** ['faɪərɪ], *adj.* Feuer–, glühend, brennend; feurig, hitzig, heftig, leidenschaftlich, unbändig (*as a horse*); *–y red*, feuerrot; *–y temper*, der Jähzorn.

fife [faɪf], 1. *s.* die Querpfeife (*Mus.*). 2. *v.n.* auf der Querpfeife blasen, pfeifen. **–r,** *s.* der Pfeifer.

fifteen [fɪf'tɪ:n], 1. *num. adj.* fünfzehn. 2. *s.* die Fünfzehn; der Fünfzehner; die Rugbymannschaft. **–th,** 1. *num. adj.* fünfzehnt. 2. *s.* der, die, das Fünfzehnte; das Fünfzehntel.

fifth [fɪfθ], 1. *num. adj.* fünft. 2. *s.* der, die, das Fünfte; das Fünftel; die Quinte (*Mus.*). **–ly** ['fɪfθlɪ], *adv.* fünftens.

fiftie–s ['fɪftɪz], *pl.* die fünfziger Jahre; *by –s*, zu Fünfzigen. **–th,** 1. *num. adj.* fünfzigst. 2. *s.* der, die, das Fünfzigste; das Fünfzigstel.

fifty ['fɪftɪ], 1. *num. adj.* fünfzig; *––one*, einundfünfzig. 2. *s.* die Fünfzig. (*coll.*) **––fifty,** 1. *adj.* fünfzigprozentig. 2. *adv.* halbpart, (*coll.*) halb und halb, zu gleichen Teilen. **–fold,** *adj.* fünfzigfach.

[1]**fig** [fɪg], 1. *s.* (*coll.*) der Putz, die Ausrüstung; (only in) *in full –*, in vollem Wichs. 2. *v.a.*; *– out*, herausputzen.

[2]**fig,** *s.* die Feige; der Feigenbaum; (*fig.*) etwas Wertloses; *a – for*, zum Teufel mit . . ., was frage ich nach . . .? *I don't care a – for it*, ich mache mir nichts daraus. **––leaf,** *s.* das Feigenblatt. **–wort,** *s.* die Feigwurz.

fight [faɪt], **1.** *ir. v.n.* kämpfen, fechten, sich schlagen; *– against a th.*, sich einer S. widersetzen; *– back*, sich zur Wehr setzen, widerstehen, abwehren; *– for a th.*, etwas verfechten; *– shy of*, meiden, nicht angehen wollen, aus dem Wege gehen (*Dat.*); *– to the last ditch*, bis zum Letzten kämpfen. **2.** *ir. v.a.* kämpfen (mit *or* gegen); bekämpfen, sich schlagen mit; verfechten, verteidigen (*a question*); im Kampf führen (*troops, ships*); *– a battle*, eine Schlacht kämpfen; *– a duel*, sich duellieren; *– a good –*, sich wacker schlagen; *– a fire*, gegen ein Feuer kämpfen; *– a p.*, mit einem kämpfen *or* boxen, sich mit einem schlagen; *– it out*, es ausfechten; *– one's way*, sich durchschlagen. **3.** *s.* das Gefecht, der Kampf, das Treffen; der Streit, Konflikt; die Schlägerei; der Boxkampf; die Kampflust; *be full of –*, see *show –*; *hand-to-hand –*, das Handgemenge; *there is no – left in him*, er ist kampfmüde *or* abgekämpft; *there is – in him yet*, er ist noch kampffähig, er ist noch nicht geschlagen; *make a – of it*, sich kräftig zur Wehr setzen; *running –*, das Rückzugsgefecht; *put up a good –*, sich wacker schlagen; *show –*, kampfbereit *or* kampflustig sein, nicht nachgeben; *stand-up –*, regelrechter Kampf. **–er,** *s.* der Kämpfer, Streiter, Krieger, Fechter; Jäger, Jagdflieger (*Av.*); *–er aircraft*, der Jagdflieger, Jäger; *–er escort*, der Jagdschutz; *–er pilot*, der Jagdflieger; *–er squadron*, die Jagdstaffel. **–ing,** 1. *adj.* Kampf–; *–ing chance*, die Aussicht auf Erfolg beim Einsatz aller Kräfte; *–ing cock*, der Kampfhahn; *–ing efficiency*, der Gefechtswert (*Mil.*); *–ing equipment*, die Feldausrüstung; *–ing force*, die Kampftruppe; *–ing top*, der Kommandoturm, Gefechtsmars (*Naut.*). 2. *s.* das Gefecht, der Kampf; *way of –ing*, die Kampfesart.

figment ['fɪgmənt], *s.* die Erdichtung.

figurant ['fɪgjʊərənt], *s.* der Ballettänzer; Statist, stumme Person (*Theat.*). **–e** [fɪgʊ:'rɑ:nt], die Ballettänzerin, Statistin.

figurat–e ['fɪgjʊərət], *adj.* verziert. **–ation** [–'reɪʃən] *s.* die Gestaltung, bildliche Darstellung; die Figuration (*Mus.*). **–ive** [–rətɪv], *adj.* figürlich; bildlich, sinnbildlich, übertragen; bilderreich. **–iveness,** *s.* bildliche Darstellung; der Bilderreichtum; das Bildliche, die Sinnbildlichkeit.

figure ['fɪgə], **1.** *s.* die Gestalt, Form, Figur (*also Geom., Math., Mus.*); der Charakter, die Person, Persönlichkeit (*in a play, etc.*); äußere Erscheinung, das Äußere; die Abbildung, Darstellung; Zeichnung, das Diagramm, Muster, Bild; die Zahl, Ziffer, Nummer (*Arith.*); Summe (*of money*); Phrase (*Mus.*), (Tanz)Figur, Tour (*dancing*); Redefigur (*Rhet.*); Statue; Kostümzeichnung (*Theat.*); (*a*) (*with adjectives & nouns*) *– of fun*, komische Figur, groteske Person; *be good at –s*, ein guter Rechner sein, tüchtig im Rechnen sein; *at a high –*, teuer; *lay –*, die Gliederpuppe; *at a low –*, billig; *Roman –s*, römische Zahlen; *solid –*, der Körper (*Geom.*); *– of speech*, die Redefigur, Redewendung; (*b*) (*with verbs*) *cut a poor –*, eine armselige Rolle spielen; *keep one's –*, nicht dick werden, eine gute Figur behalten; *make a – (in the world)*, eine glänzende Rolle spielen; *reach three –s*, 100 Punkte gewinnen; *run into three –s*, in die Hunderte gehen. **2.** *v.a.* (ab)bilden, gestalten, formen; (symbolisch) darstellen; mustern, blümen (*stuffs*); figurieren (*Mus.*); mit Zahlen bezeichnen, mit Figuren versehen (*C.L.*); *– to o.s.*, sich (*Dat.*) denken, sich *or* im Geist vorstellen; *– out*, ausrechnen, berechnen; ausfindig machen, ausknobeln. **3.** *v.n.* eine Rolle spielen, sich zeigen, auftreten, erscheinen (*as*, als); (*coll.*) denken; (*coll.*) *– on*, beabsichtigen, im Auge haben; *– out at*, veranschlagt werden auf. **–d** ['fɪgəd], *adj.* figuriert, gemustert, geblümt (*Weav.*); geschmückt, verziert (*Mus.*); *–d bass*, bezifferter Baß (*Mus.*). **–head,** *s.* die Galionsfigur, der Bugschmuck (*Naut.*); (*fig.*) das Aushängeschild, die Representationsfigur, Puppe. **–-skating,** *s.* das (Eis)Kunstlaufen, Figurenlaufen.

filament ['fɪləmənt], *s.* die (Haar)Faser; der Faden; der Glühfaden (*of a lamp*); Heizfaden, die Kathode (*Rad.*); der Staubfaden (*Bot.*); *– battery*, die Heizbatterie (*Rad.*); *– voltage*, die Heizspannung (*Rad.*). **–ous** [–'mɛntəs], *adj.* faserig, fadenartig.

filbert ['fɪlbət], *s.* die Haselnuß; der Hasel(nuß)-strauch.

filch [fɪltʃ], *v.a.* (*coll.*) mausen, klauen, stibitzen.

[1]**fil–e** [faɪl], 1. *s.* der Aufreihfaden, Aufreihdraht; das Aktenbündel, Aktenheft, die Sammelmappe, der Stoß (*of papers*); Briefakten (*pl.*); der (Brief)-Ordner; die Reihe, Rotte (*Mil.*); *blank –e*, halbe or blinde Rotte; *in –e*, einer hinter dem anderen, im Gänsemarsch (*Mil.*); *in double –e*, zu zweien hintereinander (*Mil.*); *in the –e, on (the) –e*, aufgereiht, unter den Akten; *rank and –e*, Mannschaften (*pl.*) (*Mil.*); die große Masse; *single –e*, die Reihe zu einem Glied, der Gänsemarsch. 2. *v.a.* aufreihen, gliedern, ordnen, heften, einregistrieren; *–e away letters*, Briefe ablegen; *–e a bill*, eine Klage vorlegen; *–e a petition*, ein Gesuch einreichen. 3. *v.n.* defilieren, in Reihe vorbeiziehen; *–e in (out)*, in Reih und Glied eintreten (austreten). **–e copy,** die Aktenkopie. **–e-leader,** *s.* der Rottenführer, Vordermann. **–ing,** *s.* das Aufreihen, die Registrierung; *–ing cabinet*, der Aktenkasten, Zettelkasten, die Kartothek, Kartei.

[2]**fil–e,** 1. *s.* die Feile; *smooth –e*, die Schlichtfeile. 2. *v.a.* feilen; (*fig.*) zurechtfeilen, feilen an, glätten (*style, etc.*). **–e-cutter,** *s.* der Feilenhauer. **–ings,** *pl.* der Feilstaub, das Feilicht, Feilspäne (*pl.*).

filial ['fɪljəl], *adj.* kindlich, Kindes–.

filiation [fɪlɪ'eɪʃən], *s.* die Kindschaft; Abstammung, Abhängigkeit, Abzweigung; das Verwandtschaftsverhältnis, Abhängigkeitsverhältnis (*of languages, etc.*).

filibeg ['fɪlɪbɛg], *s. see* **kilt.**

filibuster ['fɪlɪbʌstə], 1. *s.* der Freibeuter, Filibustier; (*Amer.*) Obstruktionspolitiker; die Obstruktion (*of a debate*). 2. *v.n.* freibeutern; (*Amer.*) Obstruktion treiben, die Debatte lahmlegen.

filigree ['fɪlɪgrɪ:], *s.* das Filigran, die Filigranarbeit.

filing ['faɪlɪŋ], *see* [1]**file.** **–s,** *see* [2]**file.**

fill [fɪl], 1. *v.a.* (an)füllen, einfüllen; (voll)stopfen; ausfüllen; innehaben, besetzen, bekleiden (*a post*); sättigen, befriedigen; vollbrassen (*Naut.*); plombieren (*Dentistry*); spachteln, überfärben (*paintwork*); (*coll.*) *– the bill*, allen Anforderungen *or* Ansprüchen genügen, der geeignete Mann sein; *– a p.'s glass*, einem einschenken; *courage –ed their hearts*, Mut erfüllte ihre Herzen; *– a p.'s place*, jemandes Stelle einnehmen, einen ersetzen; *– a tooth*, einen Zahn füllen *or* plombieren; *– in*, eintragen, einsetzen, hineinschreiben; ergänzen; ausfüllen (*a form*); *– in the time*, die Zeit ausfüllen *or* totschlagen; *– out*, ausfüllen; ausdehnen; vollfüllen; *– up*, nachfüllen, vollfüllen, auffüllen; ausfüllen (*a form*). 2. *v.n.* sich füllen, voll werden (*with*, von); – *out*, schwellen (*as sails*); sich ausdehnen, dicker werden; – *up*, sich anfüllen. 3. *s.* die Fülle, Genüge; *have one's – of*, genug haben von, überdrüssig sein von; *drink* (*eat*) (*gaze*) *one's* –, sich satt trinken (essen) (sehen) (*of*, an (*Dat.*)). **–er,** *s.* der Füller, Auffüller; Trichter, Füllapparat; Spachtel; Füllkörper, das Streckmittel.

fillet ['fılıt], 1. *s.* die Kopfbinde, das Haarband, Stirnband, enger Streifen; das Filet, der Lendenbraten, das Lendenstück (*Butch.*); die Roulade (*Cook.*); Leiste, das Band, der Reif (*Arch.*); Goldstreif, Goldzierrat (*Bookb.*). 2. *v.a.* mit einer Kopfbinde schmücken; mit Reifen *or* Leisten zieren (*Arch.*); mit Goldstreifen verzieren (*Bookb.*); von Gräten befreien (*fish*), zu Roulade herrichten (*meat*).

filling ['fılıŋ], *see* **fill**; 1. *adj.* sättigend; – *station*, die Tankstelle (*Motor.*). 2. *s.* die Füllung, Füllmasse, Einlage, das Füllsel; die Farce (*Cook.*); Plombe (*Dentistry*); der Einschlag (*Weav.*); (*fig.*) die Ergänzung, Zutat.

fillip ['fılıp], 1. *s.* der Schneller, Nasenstüber, das Schnippchen; (*coll.*) der Fips; (*fig.*) die Anregung, der Ansporn, Anreiz (*to*, für). 2. *v.n.* (mit dem Finger) schnellen. 3. *v.a.* einen Nasenstüber geben (*Dat.*); (*fig.*) antreiben, anstrengen (*one's memory*).

filly ['fılı], *s.* das Stutenfüllen; (*vulg.*) ausgelassenes Mädchen.

film [fılm], 1. *s.* das Häutchen, die Membran(e); Lage, Schicht, der Überzug, Anstrich, Belag (*on teeth*); die Trübung (*of eyes*); der Dunst, Schleier; (Roll)Film (*Phot.*), (Ton)Film (*Cinema*); *full-length* –, der Hauptfilm; *silent* –, stummer Film; *talking* –, der Tonfilm; *colour* –, der Farbfilm; *the –s*, das Kino, Lichtspiele (*pl.*). 2. *v.n.* sich mit einem Häutchen überziehen; sich zum Filmen eignen (*Cinema*). 3. *v.a.* (ver)filmen. **– actor,** der Filmschauspieler. **– -fan,** *s.* der Kinofex, Kinonarr. **– -pack,** *s.* die Filmpackung (*Phot.*). **– star,** der Filmstar, die Filmdiva. **– -strip,** *s.* der Bildstreifen. **–y,** *adj.* dünn, häutig; trübe, verschleiert.

filose [faı'lous], *adj.* fadenförmig (*Zool.*).

filoselle [fılou'sɛl], *s.* das Filosellegarn.

filt–er ['fıltə], 1. *s.* das (& der) Filter, das Seihtuch, Sieb, der Sieber, Filtrierapparat; die Siebkette (*Rad.*); *band-pass –er*, das Bandfilter (*Rad.*); *high-pass –er*, der Hochpaß, die Kondensatorkette (*Rad.*); *low-pass –er*, der Tiefpaß, die Spulenkette (*Rad.*). 2. *v.a.* durchseihen, aussieben, filtern, filtrieren, abklären. 3. *v.n.* kolieren, passieren; durchsickern, durchlaufen; (*fig.*) *–er in*, sich einfädeln; (*fig.*) *–er through*, allmählich hervorkommen *or* bekanntwerden. **–er-bed,** *s.* die Kläranlage, das Rieselfeld. **–er-circuit,** *s.* der Sperrkreis (*Rad.*). **–er-paper,** *s.* das Filtrierpapier. **–er-tip,** *s.* das Filtermundstück (*on cigarettes*). **–rate** ['fıltreıt], 1. *s.* das Filtrat, filtrierte Flüssigkiet. 2. *v.a.* durchseihen, filtern, filtrieren, abläutern. **–ration** [–'treıʃən], *s.* das Filtrieren; die Filtrierung.

filth [fılθ], *s.* der Schmutz, Dreck, Kot. **–iness,** *s.* die Unreinlichkeit, Unflätigkeit, Gemeinheit, der Schmutz. **–y,** *adj.* schmutzig; unflätig, zotig (*as conversation*).

fimbriate ['fımbrıeıt], *adj.* mit behaartem Rand, befranst (*Bot., Zool.*).

fin [fın], *s.* die Flosse, Finne; Seitenflosse, Kielflosse (*Av.*); (*sl.*) die Pfote. **–less,** *adj.* ohne Flossen. **–ned,** *adj.* mit Flossen. **–ny,** *adj.* Flossen–, Fisch–.

final ['faınəl], 1. *adj.* letzt, endlich, schließlich, End–, Schluß–; auslautend (*Phonet.*); entscheidend, endgültig, definitiv, rechtskräftig (*Law*); – *aim*, das Endziel; – *cause*, der Endzweck; – *clause*, der Absichtsatz (*Gram.*); – *consonant*, der Endkonsonant; – *result*, das Endergebnis. 2. *s.* die Endrunde, das Endspiel (*Sport*); (*often pl.*) die Schlußprüfung (*Univ.*); *get into the* –, sich in die Schlußrunde spielen (*Sport*). **–e** [fı'nɑ:lı], *s.* das Finale, der Schlußsatz (*Mus.*). **–ist** ['faınəlıst], *s.* der Teilnehmer an der Schlußrunde. **–ity** [faı'nælıtı], *s.* die Endgültigkeit; Zweckbestimmtheit. **–ly** ['faınəlı], *adv.* zuletzt, zum Schluß, endlich, schließlich, letztlich, endgültig; im Auslaut (*Gram.*).

financ–e [fı'næns], 1. *s.* die Finanz, das Finanzwesen; die Finanzwissenschaft, *pl.* Finanzen, (Staats)Einkünfte; (*coll.*) *his –es are low*, er ist nicht bei Kasse. 2. *v.a.* finanzieren, finanziell unterstützen. **–ial** [–'nænʃəl], *adj.* finanziell, Finanz–; *–ial position*, die Finanzlage, Vermögensverhältnisse (*pl.*); *–ial year*, das Rechnungsjahr. **–ier** [–'nænsıə], *s.* der Finanzmann; Kapitalist.

finch [fıntʃ], *s.* der Fink.

find [faınd], **1.** *ir.v.a.* finden; (heraus)finden, herausbekommen, feststellen, erfahren; (an)treffen, (auf)finden, ermitteln, entdecken, gewahr werden; befinden, erklären, erkennen (*Law*); sich verschaffen, für sich auftreiben, aufbringen, beschaffen; versehen, versorgen, ausstatten (*in*, mit); liefern, stellen, bestreiten (*Acc.*); suchen, holen; **(a)** (*with nouns and pronouns*) *all found*, freie Station, volle Unterkunft und Verpflegung; – *a* (*true*) *bill*, die Anklagepunkte für gültig erklären; – *me a car!* suchen *or* holen Sie mir ein Auto! *I will make the dress but you must – the material*, ich mache Ihnen das Kleid, Sie müssen aber den Stoff selbst liefern *or* anschaffen; – *expression*, sich ausdrücken (*of things*); – *fault with a p.*, an einem etwas auszusetzen haben; – *favour with*, Gunst gewinnen bei; (*coll.*) – *one's feet*, Selbstvertrauen gewinnen; sich einarbeiten; sich hineinfinden *or* zurechtfinden; *be found guilty*, für schuldig befunden werden; – *it in one's heart*, es über sich *or* übers Herz bringen; *make a p. – his legs* (*his tongue*), einem Beine machen (die Zunge lösen); – *the money for*, das Geld besorgen für; – *s.o. in pocket-money*, einen mit Taschengeld versorgen; – *pleasure in*, Freude an (einer S.) haben; – *time*, die Zeit aufbringen, sich die Zeit verschaffen; – *one's way*, sich (zurecht)finden (*to*, nach); **(b)** (*reflexive use*) – *o.s.*, sich befinden; seine Kräfte erkennen; *he must – himself in boots*, er muß selbst seine Stiefel stellen; *I found myself surrounded by*, ich sah mich umgeben von; *I found myself in a strange house*, ich befand mich in einem fremden Hause; **(c)** (*with adverbs*) – *out*, erfahren, finden, herausbekommen, entdecken, ergründen (*a th. to be*, daß etwas ist); – *out the secret*, das Geheimnis enträtseln; – *a p. out*, einen erwischen *or* ertappen; *he has been found out*, man ist ihm daraufgekommen; *be found out in a lie*, auf einer Lüge *or* beim Lügen ertappt werden. **2.** *ir.v.n.*; – *for a p.*, zu jemandes Gunsten entscheiden (*Law*). **3.** *s.* der Fund. **–er,** *s.* der Finder, Entdecker; Sucher (*Phot.*); das Suchglas (*Opt.*). **–ing,** *s.* die Entdeckung, das Finden, der Fund; Spruch, das Urteil, die Erkenntnis; (*often pl.*) das Ermittlungsergebnis, der Befund die Feststellung; *the –ing of the jury*, der Wahrspruch *or* Beschluß der Geschworenen.

[1]**fine** [faın], **1.** *adj.* schön, fein, edel, gut; (*coll.*) ausgezeichnet, glänzend, vortrefflich, großartig; dünn (*as hair, etc.*); scharf, spitz (*as an edge or point*); rein (*of metals*), verfeinert, gebildet (*as taste*); zart, zierlich, elegant, hübsch, schmuck (*in appearance*); subtil, diffizil (*as work*); *the – arts*, die schönen Künste; – *bill*, guter Wechsel (*C.L.*); (*coll.*) *one* (*of these*) – *day*(*s*), eines schönen Tages; *these are – doings*, das sind mir schöne Geschichten; – *dust*, feiner Staub; (*Prov.*) – *feathers make – birds*, Kleider machen Leute; *you are a – fellow*, du bist mir ein netter Kerl! – *gentleman*, vornehmer Herr; – *scholar*, großer Gelehrter; *they had – sport*, sie hatten großen Spaß; *a – time*, eine herrliche *or* glänzende Zeit; – *weather*, schönes Wetter; (*Prov.*) – *words butter no parsnips*, schöne Worte machen den Kohl nicht fett; (*coll.*) *that's –!* das ist herrlich! *that is all very –, but . . .*, das ist alles recht gut und schön, aber . . . **2.** *v.a.* (also – *down*) abklären (*wine*), abläutern (*beer*), abtreiben (*metal*). **3.** *adv.* (*coll.*) sehr gut; *cut* or *run it* –, mit der Zeit in die Enge kommen. **4.** *s.* schönes Wetter (only in) *in rain or* –, bei Regen oder Sonnenschein. **– -draw,** *v.a.* fein stopfen, fein zusammennähen; fein ausziehen (*wire*). **– -drawn,** *adj.* sehr dünn, fein ausgesponnen; (*fig.*) subtil. **– -fingered,** *adj.* geschickt. **–ness,** *s.* die Feinheit; Zartheit (*of feelings, etc.*); Reinheit, der Feingehalt (*Metall.*); die Schärfe, Dünnheit, Schönheit, Eleganz, Zier-

lichkeit. **-ry** [–ərɪ], *s.* der Putz, Staat; Frischherd, Frischofen (*Metall.*). **--spoken,** *adj.* schönredend. **--spun,** *adj.* feingesponnen, dünn; (*fig.*) subtil. **-sse** [fɪˈnɛs], 1. *s.* die Feinheit, Finesse; Spitzfindigkeit, Schlauheit, List; das Schneiden, der Impasse (*Whist*). 2. *v.n.* Kunstgriffe anwenden. 3. *v.a.* schneiden, impassieren (*Whist*).

[2]**fine,** 1. *s.* die Geldstrafe, Geldbuße; Abstandsumme (*Law*); *in* –, endlich, schließlich, kurz. 2. *v.a.* zu einer Geldstrafe verurteilen.

finger [ˈfɪŋgə], 1. *s.* der Finger; Zeiger (*of clock, etc.*); *have a – in the pie* (or *many pies*), die Hand (überall) im Spiele haben; *count on the –s of one hand*, an den Fingern abzählen; *his –s are all thumbs*, er ist sehr ungeschickt; *slip through one's –s*, einem entschlüpfen *or* entwischen; *not stir a* –, keinen Finger rühren; *twist a p. round one's little* –, einen um den Finger wickeln. 2. *v.a.* betasten, befühlen, leicht berühren, in die Finger nehmen; den Fingersatz angeben (*Mus.*); mit den Fingern spielen. **--board,** *s.* das Griffbrett (*of the violin*); die Klaviatur (*of a piano*). **--bowl,** *s.* die Spülschale. **-ed** [–d], *adj.* –fing(e)rig; fingerförmig (*Bot.*); *light--ed*, langfingerig, diebisch. **--grass,** *s.* die Fingerhirse, Bluthirse (*Bot.*). **-ing** [–rɪŋ], *s.* die Fingerspur; leichte Berührung, das Betasten; der Fingersatz, die Fingertechnik (*Mus.*). **--language,** *s.* die Fingersprache. **-marks,** *pl.* Berührungsstellen (*pl.*). **-nail,** *s.* der Fingernagel. **--plate,** *s.* der Türschoner (*on doors*). **--post,** *s.* der Wegweiser. **-print,** *s.* der Fingerabdruck. **--stall,** *s.* der Fingerling, Däumling. **--tip,** *s.* die Fingerspitze; *have at one's --tips* (or *--ends*), am Schnürchen haben, im kleinen Finger haben, auswendig können, ganz genau kennen.

finic-al [ˈfɪnɪkl], *adj.* geziert; übertrieben genau, peinlich, knifflig. **-alness,** *s.* die Geziertheit; Peinlichkeit. **-king,** (*coll.*) *adj. see* **-al.**

fining [ˈfaɪnɪŋ], *s.* das Klären, Reinigen; (*usually pl.*) das Reinigungs- *or* Läuterungsmittel.

finis [ˈfaɪnɪs], *s.* das Ende.

finish [ˈfɪnɪʃ], 1. *v.a.* (be)enden, beendigen, vollenden, erledigen; verbrauchen, aufbrauchen; aufessen, auftrinken; aufhören; vervollkommnen, ausarbeiten; fertigmachen, fertigstellen (*goods*); zubereiten, zurichten, appretieren (*cloth*); *– a letter*, einen Brief fertig schreiben; (*coll.*) *– a p.*, einen töten, einem den Rest geben; *– off*, fertigmachen, abtun, vervollständigen, erledigen; (*coll.*) den Rest geben, zugrunde richten; *– up*, aufessen, auftrinken. 2. *v.n.* aufhören, zum Ende kommen, enden; ans Ziel kommen (*Sport*); *– up by doing*, zum Schluß tun, damit schließen daß man tut; *– with*, abschließen mit; *have –ed with*, fertig sein mit. 3. *s.* das Ende, der Schluß, Abschluß; die Entscheidung, der Endkampf (*race, etc.*); die Vollendung, letzte Hand, letzter Schliff, die Ausarbeitung, Ausführung; Appretur (*on cloth*); *be in at the* –, mit in den Endkampf kommen; *fight to the* –, bis zur Entscheidung kämpfen. **-ed,** *adj.* fertig, beendigt, vollendet, vollkommen. **-er,** *s.* der Fertigsteller, Vollender; Appretierer; (*coll.*) vernichtender Schlag. **-ing,** 1. *adj.* abschließend, vollendend; *–ing coat*, der Überzugslack; *–ing governess* (or *school*), die Erzieherin (*or* Schule) die den letzten Schliff geben soll; *put the –ing hand* or *stroke* or *give the –ing touch to a th.*, die letzte Hand an eine S. legen; *–ing stroke*, der Gnadenstoß; *–ing post*, das Ziel (*Sport*). 2. *s.* das Fertigstellen, Beenden, Vollenden; die Verzierung.

finite [ˈfaɪnaɪt], *adj.* endlich, begrenzt; *– verb*, das Verbum finitum. **-ness,** *s.* die Endlichkeit, Begrenztheit.

fin-less, -ned, -ny, *see* **fin.**

fiord, fjord [fjɔːd], *s.* der Fjord, die Förde.

fir [fəː], *s.* die Tanne, Fichte, der Tannenbaum; das Fichtenholz; *Scotch* –, die Kiefer, Föhre; *silver* –, die Weißtanne, Edeltanne, Silbertanne; *spruce-–*, die Rottanne, Gemeine Fichte. **--cone,** *s.* der Kienapfel, Tannenzapfen. **--wood,** *s.* der Nadelwald.

fire [ˈfaɪə], **1.** *s.* das Feuer (*also Mil., of jewels & fig.*); der Brand, die Feuersbrunst; (*fig.*) Flamme, Hitze, Glut, das Fieber, die Begeisterung, Leidenschaft; der Glanz; (*a*) (*with adjectives*) *St. Anthony's* –, der Rotlauf, die Rose (*Med.*); *St. Elmo's* –, das St. Elmsfeuer (*Naut.*); *blind* –, Feuer ohne Zielbeobachtung; *concentrated* –, die Feuerzusammenfassung, das Massenfeuer, Punktschießen (*Mil.*); *wild* –, das Lauffeuer; *withering* –, vernichtendes Feuer; (*b*) (*with verbs*) *catch* –, Feuer fangen; *hang* –, zu spät losgehen (*Gunn.*); (*fig.*) sich verzögern, ohne Wirkung bleiben; *make up the* –, das Feuer schüren; (*fig.*) *miss* –, versagen; *open* –, das Feuer eröffnen, Feuer geben (*Mil.*); *put on the* –, aufs Feuer setzen; *set – to*, in Brand stecken, anstecken, anzünden; *take* –; see *catch* –; (*fig.*) in Wut geraten (*at*, über (*Acc.*)); (*c*) (*with prepositions*) *between two –s*, zwischen zwei Feuern; *sit by the* –, am Ofen sitzen; *be on* –, in Brand stehen, brennen; (*fig.*) in Feuer und Flamme stehen, erregt werden; *like a house on* –, wie der Wind, wie toll; *set on* –, in Brand stecken; (*Prov.*) *set the Thames on* –, Außergewöhnliches leisten; *sit over the* –, in den Ofen kriechen; *over a slow* –, bei langsamem Feuer (*Cook.*); *go through – and water*, durchs Feuer gehen (*for*, für); (*fig.*) *add fuel to the fire*, Öl ins Feuer gießen; *under* –, im Feuer, unter Beschuß (*Mil.*); (*fig.*) angegriffen; *no smoke without* –, ohne nichts kommt nichts. **2.** *v.a.* in Brand stecken, anzünden, entzünden; abfeuern (*a gun*); brennen (*bricks*); (*fig.*) rot machen, entflammen; heizen (*engine, etc.*); *– a broadside*, eine Salve abgeben (*Naut.*); (*sl.*) *– a p.*, einen entlassen; *– off*, abfeuern, losschießen (*gun*). **3.** *v.n.* Feuer fangen, anbrennen; Feuer geben, feuern, schießen (*at, on*, auf (*Acc.*)); *– away*, losschießen, (*coll.*) anfangen; *– up at*, in Feuer und Flammen *or* Hitze *or* Wut geraten *or* auffahren über (*Acc.*). **--alarm,** *s.* der Feuerlärm; Feuermelder. **-arms,** *pl.* Schußwaffen. **-ball,** *s.* die Feuerkugel; Brandkugel (*Mil.*). **--balloon,** *s.* der Feuerballon. **--bar,** *s.* der Roststab. **--box,** *s.* die Feuerbüchse, der Feuerraum (*Locom., etc.*). **-brand,** *s.* brennendes Stück Holz; (*fig.*) der Unruhestifter. **-brick,** *s.* feuerfester Ziegel, der Schamottenstein. **--brigade,** *s.* die Feuerwehr. **--bucket,** *s.* der Feuereimer. **-clay,** *s.* die Schamotte, feuerfester Ton. **--control,** *s.* die Feuerleitung; Feuerleitstelle (*Artil.*). **--cracker,** *s.* der Schwärmer (*Firew.*). **--curtain,** *s.* der Sicherheitsvorhang, eiserner Vorhang (*Theat.*). **-damp,** *s.* das Grubengas; schlagende Wetter (*pl.*). **--dog,** *s.* der Feuerbock. **--drill,** *s.* die Feueralarmübung. **--eater,** *s.* der Feuerfresser; (*fig.*) Renommist, Hitzkopf, Raufbold. **--engine,** *s.* die Feuerspritze. **--escape,** *s.* die Rettungsleiter, Nottreppe. **--extinguisher,** *s.* der Feuerlöscher, chemischer Löschapparat. **--fighter,** *s.* der Feuerwehrmann. **-fly,** *s.* der Leuchtkäfer. **-grate,** *s.* der Feuerrost. **--guard,** *s.* das Kamingitter. **--hose,** *s.* die Schlauchleitung. **--hydrant,** *s.* der Hydrant, Feuerhahn. **--insurance,** *s.* die Feuerversicherung. **--irons,** *pl.* das Kamingerät. **--lighter,** *s.* der Feuerzünder. **-lit,** *adj.* durch Feuer beleuchtet (*as a room*). **-lock,** *s.* das Luntenschloß (*on the gun*); die Muskete. **-man,** *s.* der Heizer (*Locom., etc.*); der Feuerwehrmann; (*pl.* –men) die Löschmannschaft, die Feuerwehr. **--office,** *s.* die Feuerversicherungsanstalt. **--order,** *s.* die Zielansprache (*Mil.*). **-place,** *s.* offener Kamin; der Herd. **--plug,** *s. see* **--hydrant.** **-proof,** 1. *adj.* feuerfest, feuerbeständig, flammsicher; *– proof bulkhead*, das Brandspant, Brandschott. 2. *v.a.* flammsicher machen. **--power,** *s.* die Feuerkraft (*Mil.*). **– raising,** *s.* die Brandstiftung. **--screen,** *s.* der Ofenschirm. **--ship,** *s.* der Brander (*Naut.*). **--shovel,** *s.* die Kohlenschaufel. **-side,** 1. *s.* der Herd, Kamin; (*fig.*) häusliches Leben, der Familienkreis. 2. *adj.* häuslich; *–side chat*, trauliche Plauderei; *–side tale*, eine Geschichte für die ganze Familie. **--station,** *s.* die Feuerwehrwache. **--step,** *s.* der Schützenauftritt. **-stone,** *s.* der Feuerstein. **--tongs,** *pl.* die Feuerzange. **--watcher,** *s.* die Brandwache. (*coll.*) **--water,** *s.* das Feuerwasser, der Branntwein. **-wood,** *s.* das Brennholz. **-work,** *s.* (*usually pl.*) das Feuerwerk; *–work(s) display*, die Feuerwerkveranstaltung. **--worship,** *s.* die Feueranbetung.

firing [ˈfaɪərɪŋ], *s.* das Feuer, Feuern, Schießen (*Mil.*); die Heizung; Feuerung, der Brennstoff; das Brennen (*of bricks, etc.*); *cease* –, Feuer einstellen. – **data,** *s.* Schußwerte, Schießgrundlagen (*pl.*). – **lever,** *s.* der Abfeuerungshebel (*Artil.*). –**-line,** *s.* die Kampffront. –**-party,** *s.*, –**-squad,** *s.* das Exekutionskommando, Hinrichtungskommando; Peloton; die Abteilung für die Ehrensalve (*Mil.*).

firkin [ˈfəːkɪn], *s.* das Viertelfaß; Fäßchen (*of butter*).

firm [fəːm], 1. *adj.* fest, hart; (*fig.*) standhaft, treu; entschlossen, bestimmt (*decree*); – *friends*, enge Freunde; *hold* – *to*, aufrechterhalten; *stand* –, entschlossen dastehen. 2. *s.* die (Handels)Firma, das Geschäft, Unternehmen (*C.L.*). –**ness,** *s.* die Festigkeit; Entschlossenheit, Standhaftigkeit.

firmament [ˈfəːməmənt], *s.* das Himmelsgewölbe, Sternenzelt, Firmament.

firman [ˈfəːmæn], *s.* der Ferman, landesherrlicher Befehl.

first [fəːst], 1. *adj.* erst; – *lieutenant*, der Oberleutnant; – *Lord of the Admiralty*, der Marineminister; – *mate*, der Obersteuermann; – *member of a series*, das Anfangsglied; – *quality*, prima Qualität; – *refusal*, das Vorkaufsrecht; – *Sea Lord*, der Chef des Flottenstabs; *in the* – *place*, zuerst, erstens, an erster Stelle; *at* – *sight*, beim ersten (An)Blick; – *stage*, die Vorstufe; – *thing*, als erstes, an erster Stelle; (*coll.*) in aller Früh; 2. *adv.* zuerst, an erster Stelle, vor anderen; zum ersten Male, erstens, fürs erste, zuvörderst; eher, lieber; *at* –, zuerst, anfangs; im Anfang; – *of all*, vor allen Dingen, in allererster Linie; zuallererst; – *come* – *served*, wer zuerst kommt, mahlt zuerst; – *and foremost*, in erster Linie, zuallererst; *go* –, vorangehen; *head* –, mit dem Kopf voran; kopfüber; – *and last*, alles in allem, in ganzen; – *last and all the time*, ein für alle Mal. 3. *s.* der, die, das Erste; erste Klasse (*Railw.*); (*coll.*) erste Stufe in einer Prüfung (*Univ.*); *pl.* Waren bester Qualität; *from the* –, von vornherein, von Anfang an; – *of exchange*, der Primawechsel; *travel* –, erster Klasse fahren (*Railw.*). –**-aid,** *s.* erste Hilfe, die Nothilfe; –*-aid outfit*, *s.* das Sanitätspäckchen; –*-aid post*, *s.* die Verbandstelle, Sanitätswache. –**-born,** 1. *adj.* erstgeboren. 2. *s.* Erstgeborene(r), *m.* –**-class,** 1. *adj.* erstklassig. 2. *adv.* erster Klasse, (*coll.*) famos, prima. 3. *s.* erste Klasse, höchste Stufe. –**-comer,** *s.* Erstbeste(r), *m.*, erste(r), x-beliebige(r), *m.* –**-cost,** *s.* der Einkaufspreis (*C.L.*). –**-cousin,** *s.* das Geschwisterkind. –**-foot,** *v.a.* (*Scots*) ersten Besuch am Neujahrstag machen (*a p.*, bei einem). –**form,** *s.* die Sexta (*at school*). –**-fruits,** *pl.* Erstlinge; (*fig.*) Erstlingserfolge (*pl.*). –**-hand,** *adj.* unmittelbar; –*-hand account*, der Tatsachenbericht; *at* –*-hand*, aus erster Hand *or* Quelle, unmittelbar; –*-hand bills*, eigene Wechsel (*C.L.*). –**ling,** *s.* der Erstling. –**ly,** *adv.* erstlich, erstens, zum Ersten, zuerst. –**-night,** *s.* die Erstaufführung (*Theat.*). –**-nighter,** *s.* der Besucher einer Erstaufführung. –**-offender,** *s.* Nichtbestrafte(r), *m.* –**-rate,** *adj.* ersten Ranges, erstklassig, ausgezeichnet, vorzüglich, (*coll.*) glänzend, tadellos, vortrefflich, famos, prima.

firth [fəːθ], *s.* (*Scots*) der Meeresarm; die Mündung, Förde.

fiscal [ˈfɪskəl], 1. *adj.* fiskalisch; – *reform*, die Finanzreform; – *year*, das Finanzjahr. 2. *s.* der Fiskal, Fiskusbeamte(r), *m.*

[1]**fish** [fɪʃ], **1.** *s.* der Fisch; (*collect.*) Fische (*pl.*); *drink like a* –, wie ein Bürstenbinder trinken; *feed the* –*es*, seekrank werden; ertrinken; *there are as good* – *in the sea as ever came out of it*, es gibt keinen der nicht zu ersetzen wäre; *freshwater* –, der Süßwasserfisch, Flußfisch; *have other* – *to fry*, andere Dinge zu tun haben; *a pretty kettle of* –, eine schöne Bescherung; *loose* –, lockerer Vogel; *all is* – *that comes to the net*, man muß alles mitnehmen; *queer* –, wunderlicher Kauz; *salt* –, eingesalzener Fisch; *salt-water* –, der Seefisch; *take to s.th. like a* – *to the water*, in seinem Element sein; *be like a* – *out of water*, sich verlassen vorkommen; *neither* – *nor flesh* (*nor good red herring*), weder Fisch noch Fleisch, vollkommen undefinierbar. **2.** *v.a.* fischen, holen, ziehen (*out of*, aus) fangen; abfischen, absuchen (*a river*) (*for*, nach); (*fig.*) – *out*, herausholen (*facts, etc.*); – *up* auffischen, retten. **3.** *v.n.* fischen, angeln; haschen (*for*, nach); – *for compliments*, nach Komplimenten haschen; – *for pike*, nach Hechten angeln *or* fischen; – *in troubled waters*, im Trüben fischen. –**-basket,** *s.* der Fischkorb. –**-bone,** *s.* die Gräte. –**-bowl,** *s.* das Goldfischglas. –**-carver,** *s.* das Fischmesser. –**er** [–ə], *s.* der Fischer; der Zobel, das Zobelwiesel (*Zool.*). –**erman,** *s.* der Fischer, Angler. –**ery** [–ərɪ], *s.* der Fischfang; die Fischerei; das Fischereigebiet. –**-glue,** *s.* der Fischleim. –**-hook,** *s.* der Angelhaken. (*coll.*) –**iness,** *s.* die Zweifelhaftigkeit, Mißlichkeit. –**ing,** *s.* das Fischen, die Fischerei, der Fischfang; *go* –*ing*, auf den Fischfang ausgehen. –**ing-boat,** *s.* das Fischerboot. –**ing-boots,** *pl.* Wasserstiefel. –**ing-fly,** *s.* künstliche Fliege. –**ing-gear,** *s. see* –**ing-tackle.** –**ing-ground,** *s.* der Fischereigrund. –**ing-line,** *s.* die Angelschnur. –**ing-rod,** *s.* die Angelrute. –**ing-smack,** der Fischkutter. –**ing-tackle,** *s.* das Angelgerät, Fischereigerät. –**ing-village,** *s.* das Fischerdorf. –**-knife,** *s.* das Fischmesser. –**-like,** *adj.* fischartig, fischähnlich. –**monger,** *s.* der Fischhändler. –**-oil,** *s.* der Fischtran. –**-pond,** *s.* der Fischteich. –**-slice,** *s.* die Fischkelle. –**-sound,** *s.* die Fischblase. –**wife,** *s.* die Fischverkäuferin, das Fischweib. –**y,** *adj.* fischartig, Fisch–; fischreich; (*coll.*) verdächtig, zweifelhaft, mißlich, anrüchig, faul, nicht geheuer, nicht in Ordnung.

[2]**fish,** 1. *s.* die Lasche (*Railw.*). 2. *v.a.* verbinden, verlaschen; – *the anchor*, den Anker festmachen (*Naut.*). –**-bolt,** *s.* der Laschenbolzen. –**-joint,** *s.* die Schienenstoßverbindung. –**-plate,** *s. see* [2]–.

fiss–ile [ˈfɪsɪl], *adj.* spaltbar. –**ion** [ˈfɪʃən], *s.* die Spaltung; *nuclear* –*ion*, die Kernspaltung. –**ure** [ˈfɪʃə], 1. *s.* der Spalt, Riß, Einriß, Sprung, die Ritze. 2. *v.a. & n.* (sich) spalten.

fist [fɪst], 1. *s.* die Faust; (*sl.*) Klaue; *make money hand over* –, schweres Geld verdienen; *shake one's* – *at s.o.*, einen mit der Faust bedrohen. 2. *v.a.* handhaben (*a sail*) (*Naut.*); – *off*, mit der Faust abwehren. –**ed,** *adj.* (*fig.*) *close-*–*ed* or *tight-*–*ed*, knauserig, geizig. –**icuffs,** *pl.* Faustschläge, der Faustkampf.

fistul–a [ˈfɪstjulə], *s.* die Fistel (*Med.*); Rohrflöte (*of an organ*). –**ar,** *adj.* röhrenförmig. –**ous,** *adj. see* –**ar**; fistelartig.

[1]**fit** [fɪt], **1.** *adj.* passend, geeignet, angemessen, geziemend; (*coll.*) gesund, in (guter) Form (*Sport*); (*only pred.*) tauglich, schicklich; tüchtig, fähig; (*a*) (*absolute*) *it is not* –, es ziemt sich nicht; *more than is* –, über Gebühr, übermäßig; (*coll.*) *as* – *as a fiddle*, in bester Verfassung, gut zu Wege, kerngesund, (*sl.*) sauwohl; *keep* –, sich gesund erhalten, in Form bleiben; *see* or *think* –, für gut, richtig, *or* geeignet halten; (*b*) (*with prepositions*) *be* – *for*, taugen zu, reif sein für; geeignet *or* bereit sein zu; – *for habitation*, bewohnbar; – *for service*, dienstfähig, diensttauglich; (*coll.*) – *to drop*, zum Umsinken erschöpft; (*coll.*) *he laughed* – *to burst*, er lachte daß er beinahe platzte. **2.** *s.* genaues Passen, der Sitz (*of clothes*), die Passung (*Mach.*); *it is a bad* –, es paßt schlecht; *be an excellent* –, wie angegossen sitzen; *be a tight* –, eng *or* knapp passen. **3.** *v.a.* aufstellen, anbringen, montieren, einfügen, einordnen; anstehen (*Dat.*), passen (*Dat, or* für, auf *or* zu), angemessen sein für; passend machen, befähigen (*for*, zu); anpassen, anprobieren (*clothes*); *this coat doesn't* – *me*, dieser Rock paßt *or* sitzt mir nicht; – *s.o. to a T*, einem wie angegossen passen; – *s.o. for*, einen zubereiten *in*, auf; – *in*, einfügen; – *on*, anprobieren; – *out*, ausrüsten, ausstatten; – *together*, *v.n.* zusammenpassen; *v.a.* montieren; – *up*, einrichten, zurechtmachen; ausrüsten, ausstatten; montieren; – *with*, versehen *or* versorgen mit. **4.** *v.n.* sich schicken, tauglich sein; sitzen, passen; *the dress* –*s nicely*, das Kleid paßt *or* sitzt ausgezeichnet; *it* –*s* (*in with*) *my plans*, es trifft sich gut, es paßt mir in den Kram; – *in to*, sich einpassen in *or* an; – *in with*, passen zu; – *into*, sich

(hinein)passen in. **–ment,** *s.* (*usually pl.*) die Einrichtung, der Einrichtungsgegenstand. **–ness,** *s.* die Angemessenheit, Schicklichkeit; Brauchbarkeit, Eignung, Tauglichkeit; Gesundheit, Dienstfähigkeit (*Mil.*); *certificate of –ness*, das Gesundheitsattest; (*Scots*) die Zulassung zum Studium (*Univ.*). **–ted,** *adj.* ausgestattet, ausgerüstet; montiert. **–ter,** *s.* der Zuschneider, Anpasser; Schlosser, Klempner, Monteur; Installateur. **–ting,** 1. *adj.* schicklich, passend; geeignet, angebracht. 2. *s.* die Anprobe (*Tail.*); Anpassung, Aufstellung, Montage, Paßarbeit; *pl.* das Zubehör, die Armatur; Einrichtung, Ausstattung; Zubehörteile, Ausrüstungsgegenstände, Beschläge (*Smith.*); *–ting shop*, die Montagehalle; *–ting yard*, die Bauwerft (*Naut.*).

[2]**fit,** *s.* der Anfall, Ausbruch; die Anwandlung, (*coll.*) Stimmung, Laune; *apoplectic –*, der Schlaganfall; *– of coughing*, der Hustenanfall; *drunken –*, der Rausch; *epileptic –*, epileptischer Anfall; *fainting –*, der Ohnmachtsanfall; *– of hysterics*, hysterischer Anfall; *– of jealousy*, die Anwandlung von Eifersucht; *– of laughter*, der Lachkrampf; (*coll.*) *in –s* (*of laughter*), hilflos vor Lachen; *– of rage*, der Wutanfall; *by –s and starts*, stoßweise, rückweise; dann und wann, von Zeit zu Zeit; *if the – takes me*, wenn mich die Laune anwandelt. **–ful,** *adj.* abwechselnd, unterbrochen, ungleichmäßig, veränderlich, unbeständig, launenhaft, launisch. **–fulness,** *s.* die Unbeständigkeit, Ungleichmäßigkeit, Launenhaftigkeit.

[3]**fit, fytte** [fɪt], *s.* der Abschnitt eines altgermanischen epischen Gedichtes.

five [faɪv], **1.** *num. adj.* fünf; *–-barred gate*, der Schlagbaum mit fünf Barren; *–-figure tables, pl.* fünfstellige Tafeln; *–-finger exercises, pl.* Fingerübungen (*Mus.*); *– times*, fünfmal. 2. *s.* die Fünf; der Fünfer. **–fold,** *adj.* fünffach. (*sl.*) **–r,** *s.* die Fünfpfundnote. **–s,** *pl.* eine Art Wandball. **–s-court,** *s.* die Wandballanlage.

fix [fɪks], **1.** *v.a.* befestigen, festmachen (*to*, an), anheften, einpflanzen, einspannen (*into a frame, etc.*) (*on*, auf; *in*, in); ansetzen, anordnen, festlegen, festsetzen, bestimmen, anberaumen (*a meeting, time, etc.*); fixieren (*Phot. & fig. with one's eyes*); verhärten, fest machen, feste Form geben (*Dat.*), erstarren lassen (*Chem.*); (*coll.*) in Ordnung bringen, richten; *– the attention*, die Aufmerksamkeit fesseln; *– the attention* (*eyes*) *upon a th.*, die Aufmerksamkeit (Augen) auf eine S. richten *or* heften; *– bayonets!* Seitengewehr pflanzt auf! (*Mil.*); *– s.th. in one's memory*, sich etwas einprägen; (*coll.*) *– a quarrel*, einen Streit beilegen; *– on*, sich entschließen für, wählen, festsetzen (*a date, etc.*); (*coll.*) *– up*, anordnen, festsetzen; in Ordnung bringen, herrichten, organisieren, arrangieren; (*sl.*) unterbringen. **2.** *v.n.* (*coll.*) sich niederlassen; sich entscheiden. **3.** *s.* (*coll.*) die Verlegenheit, Klemme. **–ate,** *v.a.* die Augen richten auf; fest machen. **–ation,** *s.* die Fixierung, Festlegung, Festsetzung, Bestimmung; der Komplex (*Psych.*). **–ative** ['fɪksətɪv], *s.* das Fixativ, Fixiermittel. **–ed** [fɪkst], *adj.* fest, festliegend, ständig, fix, nicht flüchtig, feuerbeständig (*Chem.*); bestimmt, ausgemacht; starr (*of eyes*); *–ed acid*, gebundene Säure (*Chem.*); *–ed idea*, fixe Idee; *with –ed ideas*, mit bestimmten Ansichten; *–ed income*, ständiges Einkommen; *–ed prices*, feste *or* stehende Preise; *–ed sight*, *s.* das Standvisier; *–ed star*, der Fixstern; *–ed sum*, bestimmte Summe; *–ed undercarriage*, starres Fahrwerk (*Av.*); (*coll.*) *be well –ed*, gut gestellt sein. **–edly** ['fɪksɪdlɪ], *adv.* fest; unverwandt; standhaft. **–edness** ['fɪksɪdnɪs], *s.* die Festigkeit; (*fig.*) Standhaftigkeit, Beharrlichkeit. **–er,** *s.* das Fixiermittel (*Phot.*). **–ing** ['fɪksɪŋ], *s.* das Aufstellen, Festmachen, Befestigen (*Mech., etc.*); die Fixierung (*Chem. & Phot.*); *pl.* das Zubehör, die Einrichtungen, Garnierung. **–ing-bath,** *s.* das Fixierbad. **–ing-solution,** *s.* die Fixierlösung. **–ity** ['fɪksɪtɪ], *s.* die Festigkeit, Beständigkeit, Stabilität; *–ity of purpose*, die Zielstrebigkeit; *–ity of tenure*, die Ständigkeit des Lehens, festes Lehen. **–ture** ['fɪkstʃə], *s.* feste Verabredung; feste Anlage, das Zubehör, Inventarstück (*Law*); kurzes Darlehen (*stock exchange*); *pl.* feste Einrichtungsgegenstände, Pertinenzstücke; festgesetzte Veranstaltung; (*coll.*) *be a –ture*, ein altes Inventarstück sein; *lighting-–ture*, der Beleuchtungskörper.

fizz [fɪz], 1. *v.n.* zischen, aufwallen, sprudeln. 2. *s.* das Zischen, Sprudeln; (*coll.*) der Champagner. **–le,** 1. *v.n.* zischen, brausen, sprühen; summen; (*Amer. sl.*) mißglücken, durchfallen; *–le out*, verpuffen, abflauen, im Sand verlaufen. 2. *s.* (*sl.*) der Mißerfolg, die Pleite. **–y,** *adj.* (*coll.*) sprudelnd.

flabbergast ['flæbəgɑ:st], *v.a.* (*coll.*) verblüffen; (*coll.*) *be –ed*, platt sein.

flabb–iness ['flæbɪnɪs], *s.* die Schlaffheit. **–y** ['flæbɪ], *adj.* schlaff, weich; matt, welk, lappig; (*fig.*) kraftlos, gehaltlos.

flaccid ['flæksɪd], *adj.* welk, weich, schlaff, schlapp, schlotterig, kraftlos. **–ity** [–'sɪdɪtɪ], *s.* die Schlaffheit, Welkheit.

[1]**flag** [flæg], 1. *s.* die Fahne, Flagge (*Naut.*) *black –*, die Seeräuberflagge; *break out* or *unfurl a –*, die (aufgerollte) Fahne entfalten; *dip the –*, die Flagge niederholen und wieder hissen; *hoist a –*, eine Flagge setzen; *hoist one's –*, den Befehl übernehmen (*of an admiral*); *keep the – flying*, die Fahne hochhalten; *strike* or *lower the –*, die Flagge streichen *or* niederholen; *strike one's –*, den Befehl aufgeben (*of an admiral*); *run up a –*, see *hoist a –*; *– of truce*, die Parlamentärfahne 2. *v.a.* (mit Flaggen) signalisieren, winken; beflaggen; *– a train*, einen Zug anhalten; *– the course*, die Rennbahn ausflaggen. **– -day,** *s.* der Opfertag, die Straßensammlung. **– -lieutenant,** *s.* der Flaggleutnant. **–man,** *s.* der Winker (*Naut.*), Signalgeber. **– -officer,** *s.* der Flaggoffizier, Admiral. **– -ship,** *s.* das Flaggschiff, Admiralsschiff. **– -staff,** *s.* die Fahnenstange, der Flaggenstock. (*sl.*) **– -wagging,** *s.* das Winken.

[2]**flag,** *v.n.* ermatten, erschlaffen, nachlassen, erlahmen (*of interest*); mutlos werden, (*sl.*) schlappmachen. **–ging,** *adj.* schlapp, schlaff, sinkend.

[3]**flag,** 1. *s.*; **–stone,** *s.* die Fliese, Steinplatte. 2. *v.a.* mit Fliesen belegen *or* pflastern; *–ged pavement*, das Fliesenpflaster.

[4]**flag,** *s.* die Schwertlilie, Ilge (*Bot.*); *sweet –*, der Kalmus (*Bot.*).

flagell–ant [flə'dʒɛlənt], 1. *s.* der Geißler, Flagellant. 2. *adj.* geißelnd. **–ate** ['flædʒəleɪt], 1. *v.a.* geißeln. 2. *s.* der Flagellat, das Geißeltierchen (*Zool.*). 3. *adj.* Schößlings– (*Bot.*). **–ation** [–'leɪʃən], *s.* die Geißelung.

flageolet [flædʒo'lɛt], *s.* das Flageolett.

flagitious [flə'dʒɪʃəs], *adj.* abscheulich, schändlich, lasterhaft. **–ness,** *s.* die Abscheulichkeit, Verruchtheit, Schändlichkeit.

flagon ['flægən], *s.* der Bocksbeutel, runde Tafelflasche.

flagran–cy ['fleɪgrənsɪ], *s.* offenkundige Schamlosigkeit, die Schändlichkeit, Abscheulichkeit. **–t** ['fleɪgrənt], *adj.* abscheulich, entsetzlich; offenkundig, schreiend, schamlos, empörend.

flail [fleɪl], *s.* der Dreschflegel.

flair [flɛə], *s.* der Spürsinn, die Witterung, feine Nase (*for*, für); (*fig.*) natürliche Begabung, feiner Instinkt.

flak–e [fleɪk], 1. *s.* die Flocke (*of snow, etc.*); Schicht, Lage; Schuppe, Platte, das Blatt; *oat-–es, pl.* Haferflocken. 2. *v.a.* zu Flocken ballen; ausflocken, abschuppen, abblättern; mit Flocken bedecken, sprenkeln. 3. *v.n.* zu Flocken werden, sich flocken, sich schuppen; *–e off*, abblättern, sich abschuppen, abschälen. **–e-white,** *s.* das Wismutweiß, Bleiweiß. **–iness,** *s.* das Flockige; Schuppige. **–y,** *adj.* flockig, blattförmig, schuppig; blätterig (*as piecrust*); geschichtet, in Schichten.

flambeau ['flæmbou], *s.* die Fackel, der Leuchter.

flamboyan–ce [flæm'bɔɪəns], *s.* überladener Schmuck. **–t** [–t], *adj.* flammend, wellenförmig (*Arch.*); (*fig.*) überladen, auffallend; *–t style*, der Flammenstil (*Arch.*).

flam–e [fleɪm], 1. *s.* die Flamme; das Feuer; die Hitze, Glut, Heftigkeit, Leidenschaft; (*sl.*) Geliebte(r), *m. & f.*, der Schatz; (*sl.*) *old –e*, alte Flamme; *burst into –e(s)*, in Flammen ausbrechen. 2. *v.n.* flammen, lodern; leuchten (*with*, von); *–e up*, aufflammen; erröten; (*fig.*) auffahren, **in Zorn**

geraten. **-e-coloured,** *adj.* feuerfarben. **-e-thrower,** *s.* der Flammenwerfer. **-ing,** *adj.* flammend, lodernd; feurig; (*fig.*) hitzig, glühend, heiß, glänzend, hell.
flamingo [flə'mɪŋgoʊ], *s.* der Flamingo.
flan [flæn], *s.* die (Obst)Torte.
flange [flændʒ], 1. *s.* der Flansch, Flantsch; das Seitenstück, der Gurt, Kragen; der Radkranz, Spurkranz (*of a wheel*). 2. *v.a.* flanschen. **--rail,** *s.* die Randschiene (*Railw.*).
flank [flæŋk], 1. *s.* die Flanke, Weiche (*of animals*); (*fig.*) Seite, der Flügel; *exposed* –, offener Flügel (*Mil.*); *take the enemy in the* –, dem Feinde in die Flanken fallen; *turn the* –, die Flanke aufrollen (*Mil.*); – *attack*, der Flankenangriff; – *guard*, die Seitendeckung. 2. *v.a.* flankieren, umgehen, seitlich herumgehen um, seitlich stehen von; die Flanke decken; die Flanke bedrohen, (einen) in der Flanke angreifen, (einem) in die Flanke fallen. **-er,** *s.* das Flankenwerk; *pl.* Flankierer (*pl.*), Plänkler (*pl.*). **-ing,** *adj.*; *-ing fire*, das Flankenfeuer; *-ing march*, seitlicher Abmarsch; *-ing movement*, das Flankierungsmanöver.
flannel ['flænl], **1.** *s.* der Flanell; (*coll.*) der Waschlappen; (*sl.*) blauer Dunst; *pl.* die Flanellhose, der Flanellanzug, weiße Sportkleidung (*for tennis, cricket, etc.*). **2.** *v.n.* (*sl*) schummeln. **-ette,** *s.* die Flanellimitation.
flap [flæp], 1. *s.* die Krempe (*of a hat*); Klappe (*of a table*); Lasche (*of a shoe*), Patte (*of a pocket*); das Flattern; der Klaps; (Flügel)Schlag; – *amputation*, die Lappenamputation (*Surg.*); *wing* –, die Bremsklappe (*Av.*). 2. *v.a.* schlagen mit (*wings, etc.*), klappen mit. 3. *v.n.* lose herabhängen, sich hin- und herbewegen, baumeln, flappen, killen (*as sails*) (*Naut.*). (*sl.*) **-doodle,** *s.* der Unsinn, Quatsch, Mumpitz. **--eared,** *adj.* schlappohrig. (*coll.*) **-jack,** *s.* der Pfannkuchen. **-per,** *s.* die Klapper, der Klöppel, Schlegel; die Flosse; (*sl.*) der Backfisch, Fratz. (*sl.*) **-per-bracket,** *s.* der Soziussitz (*of motor-cycle*).
flar-e [flɛə], 1. *v.n.* flackern, flammen, lodern; sich bauschen (*as a dress*); überhängen (*as ship's bows*); *-e out*, in Zorn ausbrechen; *-e up*, aufflackern, aufflammen; (*fig.*) aufbrausen, losbrechen, in Hitze geraten. 2. *s.* flackerndes Licht, plötzliches Aufleuchten, das Aufflackern; Lichtsignal, Blendfeuer, die Leuchtkugel, Leuchtbombe (*Av.*); (*coll.*) das Gepränge, die Protzigkeit, Prahlerei. **-ing,** *adj.* aufflackernd; blendend, grell, auffallend. **-e-path,** *s.* die Hindernisbeleuchtung (*Mil.*). (*fig.*) **-e-up,** *s.* das Aufbrausen, der Ausbruch; Skandal.
flash [flæʃ], 1. *s.* plötzliches Aufleuchten *or* Aufflammen, lodernde Flamme, der Blitz; das Mündungsfeuer (*Artil.*); (*fig.*) Aufblitzen, Auflodern; plötzlicher Ausbruch; (*coll.*) kurze Zeit, der Augenblick; – *of hope*, der Hoffnungsstrahl; – *of lightning*, der Blitz(strahl); – *of wit*, witziger Einfall; (*fig.*) – *in the pan*, das Strohfeuer, mißlungener Versuch. 2. *adj.* (*sl.*) prunkend, flimmernd, auffällig, aufgedonnert; falsch, unecht (*as jewels*); – *language*, die Gaunersprache. 3. *v.n.* auflodern, aufblitzen, blitzartig aufleuchten; glänzen, glitzern; (*fig.*) ausbrechen, hervorbrechen; sich plötzlich bewegen, springen, flitzen; *lightnings* –, Blitze zucken; *the thought -ed across my mind*, der Gedanke fuhr mir blitzartig durch den Kopf. 4. *v.a.* auflodern *or* glänzen lassen, durchzucken; blitzschnell verbreiten (*news*); – *a light*, ein Licht aufblitzen lassen; – *a light in s.o.'s face*, durch ein Licht jemandes Gesicht blenden; *his eyes -ed fire*, seine Augen sprühten Feuer. **-iness,** *s.* (*sl.*) äußerer Glanz, auffallender Prunk. **-ing light,** *s.* das Blitzfeuer, Blinkfeuer (*Naut.*). **-lamp,** *s.* die Taschenlampe. **-light,** *s.* das Blitzlicht (*Phot.*); die Taschenlampe. **--point,** *s.* der Flammpunkt. **– spotter,** *s.* der Richtkreisdiopter (*Artil.*). **– spotting,** *s.* das Lichtmeßverfahren (*Artil.*). **-y,** *adj.* (*coll.*) auffallend, aufdringlich.
flask [flɑ:sk], *s.* die Flasche, Feldflasche; der (Glas)-Kolben (*Chem.*).
flat [flæt], **1.** *adj.* platt, flach; eben, glatt; schal, matt, trüb, abgestanden; geschmacklos, plump, fade; seicht, oberflächlich; ausdrücklich, unbedingt, entschieden, klar, rund herausgesprochen; vermindert, tief, erniedrigt (*Mus.*); stimmhaft (*Gram.*); flau, leblos (*C.L.*); (*coll.*) *that's* –, das ist klar, das ist mein letztes Wort; – *beer*, schales Bier; – *car*, der Plattformwagen (*Railw.*); – *denial*, glatte Ableugnung; – *foot*, der Plattfuß; – *price*, der Einheitspreis; – *refusal*, glatte Absage, unbedingte Verweigerung; – *seam*, flache Naht; (*sl.*) *be in a* – *spin*, nicht aus noch ein wissen; – *trajectory*, die Rasanz (*Artil.*); – *tyre*, die Reifenpanne. **2.** *adv.* platt, ausgestreckt; glatt, direkt, rundweg; *fall* –, lang hinfallen; (*coll.*) mißglücken, keinen Anklang finden, durchfallen; *fall as* – *as a pancake*, ein glatter Versager sein, mit Pauken und Trompeten durchfallen; *knock s.o.* –, einen zu Boden strecken; (*fig.*) einen platt machen; *lay* –, platt machen; *lie* –, platt liegen; *sing* –, zu tief singen; *tell s.o.* –, einem rundweg heraussagen. **3.** *s.* die Fläche, Ebene, (*usually pl.*) die Untiefe, das Watt, die Sandbank (*Naut.*); das Flachland, die Niederung; das B (♭ (*Mus.*)); die Mietwohnung, Etagenwohnung; (*Scots*) das Stockwerk, die Etage; ebene Oberfläche (*of a solid body*); flache Seite (*of a sword*); (*sl.*) der Einfaltspinsel; *on the* –, auf ebenem Boden; *sharps and -s*, Kreuze und B's (*Mus.*). **--bottomed,** *adj.* Steh–; *--bottomed boat*, der Prahm. **--fish,** *s.* der Plattfisch. (*sl.*) **-foot,** *s.* der Polizist (*N.B.* – *foot*). **--footed,** *adj.* plattfüßig. **--iron,** *s.* das Plätteisen, Bügeleisen. **-let,** *s.* die Kleinwohnung. **-ly,** *adv.* glatt; geradezu, rundweg. **-ness,** *s.* die Flachheit, Plattheit; Entschiedenheit; Eintönigkeit; Flauheit (*C.L.*). **--nosed,** *adj.* stumpfnasig. **--race, --racing,** *s.* das Flachrennen. **--rate,** *s.* die Pauschalgebühr, der Einheitssatz. **--roofed,** *adj.* mit flachem Dache. **-ten** ['flætn], 1. *v.a.* platt *or* flach machen, ebnen, abflachen, breitschlagen, strecken; abstumpfen (*colours*), erniedrigen (*Mus.*); strecken (*Metall.*); glatt drücken *or* streichen. 2. *v.n.* platt *or* flach werden; – *out*, abfangen, ausschweben (*Av.*). **-tening,** *s.* die Verflachung, Abplattung; Streckung (*Metall.*); flache *or* ebene Stelle. **-ter,** *s.* der Planierer (*Mech.*). **-ting,** *s.* das Platthämmern. **-wise,** *adv.* der Länge nach.
flatter ['flætə], *v.a.* schmeicheln, Komplimente machen (*Dat.*); zu günstig darstellen (*as portraits*); – *s.o.'s hopes*, mit unbegründeten Hoffnungen erfüllen; – *o.s. that*, sich einbilden daß, sich in dem Gedanken gefallen daß; – *o.s. on*, sich beglückwünschen zu; – *s.o.'s vanity*, jemandes Eitelkeit befriedigen. **-ing** [–rɪŋ], *adj.* schmeichelhaft, schmeichlerisch, schmeichelnd; geschmeichelt (*as portraits*). **-y** [–rɪ], *s.* die Schmeichelei.
flatulen-ce ['flætjʊləns], *s.*, **-cy,** *s.* die Blähung; Blähsucht (*Med.*); (*fig.*) Aufgeblasenheit, Nichtigkeit. **-t,** *adj.* blähend, blähsüchtig; (*fig.*) aufgeblasen, aufgebläht, schwülstig, nichtig.
flatus ['fleɪtəs], *s.* die Blähung.
flaunt [flɔ:nt], 1. *v.a.* paradieren *or* prunken mit, zur Schau tragen, prunkhaft zeigen. 2. *v.n.* prangen, prunken, stolzieren, paradieren.
flautist ['flɔ:tɪst], *s.* der Flötenspieler, Flötist.
flavour ['fleɪvə], 1. *s.* der Geschmack; Wohlgeruch, Duft, das Aroma; die Blume (*of wine*); (*fig.*) Würze. 2. *v.a.* Geschmack *or* Duft geben, schmackhaft machen, würzen. **-ed** [–d], *adj.* schmackhaft, würzig; wohlriechend; *full--ed*, schwer, stark (*as cigars*), mit starker Blume (*as wine*), stark gewürzt (*as food*). **-less,** *adj.* geschmacklos, schal, fade.
flaw [flɔ:], *s.* der Fehler, fehlerhafte Stelle; der Sprung, Riß, Bruch; die Blase, Wolke, der Flacken (*in cast metal, gems, etc.*); Formfehler (*Law*). **-less,** *adj.* fleckenlos; fehlerfrei; (*fig.*) tadellos.
flax [flæks], *s.* der Flachs, Lein. **--comb,** *s.* die Flachshechel. **--dresser,** *s.* der Flachsbereiter. **-en,** *adj.* Flachs–, flachsen, flächse(r)n, flachsartig; flachsfarben, flachsgelb. **-en-haired,** *adj.* flachshaarig; *-en-haired child*, kleiner Flachskopf. **--seed,** *s.* der Leinsamen. **-y,** *adj.* Flachs–, flachsfarben.
flay [fleɪ], *v.a.* schinden (*Acc.*), die Haut abziehen (*Dat.*); (*fig.*) heruntermachen, scharf kritisieren.
flea [flɪ:], *s.* der Floh; *with a* – *in one's ear*, entmutigt, niedergeschlagen; *send a p. away with a* –

in his ear, einem gehörig den Kopf waschen. (*sl.*) **--bag**, *s.* der Schlafsack. **–bane**, *s.* das Flohkraut (*Bot.*). **–bite**, *s.* der Flohstich; (*coll.*) geringfügige Verletzung; die Kleinigkeit, Bagatelle. **--bitten**, *adj.* von Flöhen gebissen *or* zerstochen.

fleam [flɪ:m], *s.* die Fliete, Lanzette (*Vet.*).

fleck [flɛk], 1. *v.a.* sprenkeln. 2. *s.* kleiner Fleck. **–less**, *adj.* fleckenlos.

fled [flɛd], *see* **flee.**

fledg–e [flɛdʒ], 1. *v.a.* befiedern, mit Federn bedecken. 2. *v.n.* flügge werden . **–ed**, *adj.* flügge, befiedert; *fully-–ed*, flügge, (*fig.*) erwachsen, fertig. **–(e)ling**, *s.* junger Vogel; (*fig.*) unerfahrener Mensch.

flee [flɪ:], *v.a.* & *n.* fliehen, flüchten; sich fernhalten von; – *one's country*, sein Vaterland verlassen.

fleec–e [flɪ:s], 1. *s.* das Vlies. 2. *v.a.* scheren; (*fig.*) rupfen, berauben, plündern (*of* (*Gen.*)). **–y**, *adj.* wollig; flockig; weich; *–y clouds*, Schäfchen(wolken) (*pl.*).

fleer [flɪə], 1. *v.n.* höhnisch lachen, spotten (*at*, über (*Acc.*)). 2. *s.* der Spott, das Hohnlachen.

fleet [flɪ:t], 1. *adj.* (*Poet.*) schnell, flink, flüchtig; – *of foot* or *–-footed*, schnellfüßig. 2. *v.n.* (*rare*) dahineilen, dahinfliehen, flüchtig sein. 3. *s.* die Flotte; Kriegsflotte; *admiral of the* –, der Großadmiral; – *air arm*, die Marineluftwaffe; – *of cars*, das Heer von Fahrzeugen. **–ing**, *adj.* flüchtig, vergänglich; *–ing target*, das Augenblicksziel (*Mil.*). **–ness**, *s.* die Schnelligkeit, Flüchtigkeit.

flesh [flɛʃ], 1. *s.* das Fleisch; *become one* –, ein Leib und eine Seele werden; *it makes my – creep*, mich überläuft eine Gänsehaut; *in the* –, lebendig; *in* –, dick, wohlbeleibt; (*B.*) *be made* –, Mensch werden; *proud* –, wildes Fleisch; *run to* –, eine Neigung zum Dickwerden haben; *put on* –, dick werden. 2. *v.a.* Fleisch kosten lassen (*hounds*); (*fig.*) kampfmutig machen; abrichten, einweihen, gewöhnen an; vom Fleisch befreien, ausfleischen, abschaben (*skins*); – *one's sword*, das Schwert üben. **--brush**, *s.* die Frottierbürste. **--colour**, *s.* die Fleischfarbe. **--coloured**, *adj.* fleischfarben. **– diet**, die Fleischkost. **–er**, *s.* (*Scots*) der Fleischer. **--hook**, *s.* der Fleischhaken. **–iness**, *s.* die Fleischigkeit, Beleibtheit. **–ings**, *pl.* fleischfarbener (*or* –es) Trikot. **–less**, *adj.* fleischlos, mager. **–liness**, *s.* die Fleischlichkeit, Sinnlichkeit. **–ly**, *adj.* fleischlich, sinnlich; irdisch; (*archaic*) körperlich, weltlich, diesseitig, sterblich. **--pots**, *pl.* Fleischtöpfe. **--wound**, *s.* die Fleischwunde. **–y**, *adj.* fleischig, fleischartig.

fleur-de-lis [flə:də'lɪ:], *s.* die Lilie (*Her.*); Schwertlilie (*Bot.*).

flew [flʊ:], *see* **fly.**

flews [flʊ:z], *pl.* Lefzen (*of hounds*) (*pl.*).

flex [flɛks], 1. *s.* die Litze, der Litzendraht, die Kontaktschnur, (Leitungs)Schnur (*Elec.*). 2. *v.a.* biegen, beugen (*Anat.*). **–ibility**, *s.* die Biegsamkeit, Geschmeidigkeit (*also fig.*). **–ible**, *adj.*, **–ibly**, *adv.* biegsam, geschmeidig; unstarr, bewegungsfrei (*Mach.*); (*fig.*) lenksam, fügsam, anpassungsfähig, nachgiebig; *–ible axle*, die Lenkachse; *–ible defence*, elastische Verteidigung; *–ible mind*, fügsames Gemüt. **–ile** ['flɛksaɪl], *adj.* biegsam, geschmeidig, lenksam. **–ion** ['flɛkʃən], *s.* die Biegung, Beugung; Flexion (*Gram.*). **–ional**, *adj.* Flexions–, flektierend (*Gram.*). **–or**, *s.* der Beugemuskel, Beuger (*Anat.*). **–ure** ['flɛkʃə], *s.* das Biegen, Umbiegen; die Biegung, Beugung, Krümmung; Flexur (*Geol.*).

flibbertigibbet [flɪbətɪ'dʒɪbɪt], *s.* der Kobold; Schwätzer, leichtsinniger *or* unbeständiger Mensch.

flick [flɪk], 1. *s.* leichter, schwungvoller Schlag *or* Hieb. *pl.* (*sl.*) die Flimmerkiste. 2. *v.a.* leicht schlagen *or* berühren, schnellen; – *off*, abklopfen. **–er** [–ə], 1. *v.n.* flackern, flimmern; flattern. 2. *s.* das Flackern, Flimmern; Flattern, Zucken; flackerndes Licht; (*fig.*) der Funken (*of hope, etc.*).

flier ['flaɪə], *s. see* **flyer.**

flight [flaɪt], *s.* die Flucht, das Entrinnen; das Fliegen, der Flug; die Luftfahrt, Fliegerei; der Schwarm, die Schar; der Regen, Hagel (*of missiles*); die Flugstrecke (*Artil.*, *Av.*); Kette, der Verband (*Av.*); (*cross-*)*Atlantic* –, der Ozeanflug; – *of fancy*, der Flug, Schwung *or* Ausbruch der Phantasie; *in the first* –, in der vordersten Reihe, in der Vorhut, an der Spitze; *make* or *take a* –, fliegen (*Av.*); – *of pigeons*, der Flug von Tauben; *put to* –, in die Flucht schlagen; – *of stairs* or *steps*, die Treppenflucht; *take to* –, die Flucht ergreifen, fliehen; – *of time*, der Flug der Zeit. **--commander**, der Kettenführer. **--deck**, das (Ab)Flugdeck (*Naut.*). **–iness**, *s.* die Flüchtigkeit, Fahrigkeit, Flatterhaftigkeit. **--lieutenant**, der Fliegerhauptmann. **--mechanic**, der Bordmonteur, Bordwart, Bordmechaniker (*Av.*). **–y**, *adj.* flüchtig, fahrig, flatterhaft, leichtsinnig, zerstreut.

flim-flam ['flɪmflæm], *s.* (*sl.*) der Unsinn, Unfug, Mumpitz, Schwindel.

flims–iness ['flɪmzɪnɪs], *s.* die Dünnheit, Lockerheit; (*fig.*) Geringfügigkeit, Nichtigkeit. **–y** ['flɪmzɪ], 1. *adj.* locker, lose, dünn; (*fig.*) schwach, dürftig, nichtig. 2. *s.* dünnes Kopierpapier; (*sl.*) die Banknote; *pl.* (*sl.*) das Damenunterzeug.

flinch [flɪntʃ], *v.n.* (zurück)weichen, zurückschrecken (*from*, vor), abstehen (*from*, von); wanken; zurückschaudern; zucken.

fling [flɪŋ], 1. *ir.v.a.* werfen, schleudern; – *away*, wegwerfen, verschleudern; fahren lassen (*a chance, etc.*); – *back*, hitzig erwidern; – *down*, niederwerfen; – *s.th. in a p.'s teeth*, einem etwas vorwerfen *or* ins Gesicht schleudern; – *o.s. into*, (*fig.*) sich stürzen in; – *off*, abwerfen; – *o.s. on s.o.*, sich einem anvertrauen; – *open*, aufreißen (*a door*); – *out*, hinauswerfen; ungestüm ausstrecken (*one's arms*); – *to*, zuwerfen (*a door*); – *up*, in die Höhe werfen, emporwerfen; hinten ausschlagen (*as a horse*); unbändig werden (*of a p.*). 2. *s.* der Wurf ; das Ausschlagen (*of a horse*); (*fig.*) toller Ausbruch; der Hieb, die Stichelei; schottischer Tanz; *have a – at*, werfen nach; (*coll.*) versuchen; *let him have his* –, laß ihn austoben, laß ihn sich die Hörner abstoßen.

flint [flɪnt], *s.* der Kiesel, Feuerstein; (*coll.*) *skin a* –, geizig sein; – *and steel*, das Feuerzeug; *heart of* –, ein Herz wie Stein. **--glass**, *s.* das Kieselglas, Flintglas. **--hard**, *adj.* kieselhart. **–lock**, *s.* das Steinschloß. **–y**, *adj.* kieselartig, kieselhaltig; (*fig.*) hart.

flip [flɪp], 1. *v.a.* leicht schlagen, klapsen, schnellen. 2. *s.* leichter Schlaf, der Klaps, Ruck; (*sl.*) kurze Fahrt, kurzer Flug; *egg-–*, der Eierpunsch.

flippan–cy ['flɪpənsɪ], *s.* die Leichtfertigkeit (im Reden), der Leichtsinn; die Frivolität, Keckheit, schnippisches *or* vorlautes Wesen. **–t** ['flɪpənt], *adj.* vorlaut, schnippisch, leichtfertig, leichtsinnig, frivol, keck. **–tly**, *adv.* leichthin, obenhin.

flipper ['flɪpə], *s.* (*coll.*) der Ruderschwanz, die Flosse; (*sl.*) Hand.

flirt [flə:t], 1. *v.n.* flirten, kokettieren; liebeln; (*fig.*) liebäugeln, spielen. 2. *v.a.* spielen mit, schnellen. 3. *s.* die Kokette; der Courschneider, Schäker. **–ation** [–'teɪʃən], *s.* der Flirt, die Liebelei. **–atious**, *adj.* kokett, flirtend.

flit [flɪt], *v.n.* huschen, flitzen, hin- und herflattern; (*Scots*) umziehen, ausziehen; – *away*, wegflattern; – *by* or *past*, vorbeiflattern, vorbeihuschen.

flitch [flɪtʃ], *s.*; – *of bacon*, geräucherte Speckseite.

flivver ['flɪvə], *s.* (*sl.*) billiges Auto, die Kiste.

float [floʊt], 1. *s.* das Schwimmende; Floss; der Kork(schwimmer) (*angling*); die (Rad)Schaufel (*of a paddle wheel*); das Flott (*of a fishing-net*); die Schwimmblase (*of fishes*); das Reibebrett (*of masons*); Schwimmgestell, der Schwimmer (*of carburettor, etc., also Av.*); der Viehkarren, Förderkarren; (*usually pl.*) das Rampenlicht (*Theat.*). 2. *v.n.* obenauf schwimmen, flott sein (*Naut.*); schweben, (dahin)treiben; gleiten, sich leicht bewegen; in Umlauf sein (*C.L.*). 3. *v.a.* bewässern, überschwemmen, überfluten; tragen, befördern; in Gang bringen, verbreiten, in Umlauf setzen (*rumour*); flott machen (*a ship, etc.*); gründen (*a company*); auflegen, ausgeben (*a loan*). **–able**, *adj.* schwimmfähig, flößbar. **–age** [–tɪdʒ], *s.* die Schwimmfähigkeit, Schwimmkraft; das Schwimmen; Schwimmende(s), *n.* **–ation**, *s.* das Schwimmen, Schweben; die Gründung (*of a company*);

das Auflegen (*of a loan*). **-er,** *s.* Schwimmende(r)(s), *f.*, *m. or n.*; der Gründer (*of a company*); anerkanntes Papier (*stock exchange*). **--gauge,** *s.* der Schwimmer. **-ing,** *adj.* schwimmend, treibend, Schwimm-, Treib-; zirkulierend, im Umlauf (*C.L.*); schwankend, unsicher, beweglich; *-ing anchor*, der Treibanker; *-ing assets*, Aktiven (*pl.*) (*C.L.*); *-ing base*, der Flugstützpunkt (*Av.*); *-ing battery*, schwimmende Batterie; *-ing bridge*, die Floßbrücke; *-ing capital*, das Umlaufskapital, Betriebskapital; *-ing debt*, schwebende Schuld; *-ing dock*, das Schwimmdock; *-ing ice*, das Treibeis; *-ing kidney*, die Wanderniere; *-ing light*, das Leuchtschiff; *-ing mine*, die Treibmine; *-ing population*, schwankende Bevölkerung. **--plane,** *s.* der Seeflugzeug, Schwimmerflugzeug.

flocc-ose [flɔˈkoʊs], *adj.* wollig, flockig (*Bot.*). **-ulate** *v.a.* ausflocken. **-ulent,** *adj.* flockig.

[1]**flock** [flɔk], *s.* die Flocke (*of wool*); *pl.* der Wollabfall (*for cushions, etc.*). **--mattress,** *s.* die Wollmatratze. **--paper,** *s.* die Samttapete, Flocktapete.

[2]**flock,** I. *s.* die Herde (*of sheep*); der Flug (*of birds*); die Gemeinde (*Eccl.*); (*fig.*) der Haufen, die Menge, Schar. 2. *v.n.* sich scharen, zusammenströmen; – *out of the room*, aus dem Zimmer herausströmen; – *to a p.*, einem zuströmen; – *to a meeting*, in Scharen *or* Massen zu einer Versammlung kommen; – *together*, sich zusammenscharen.

floe [floʊ], *s.* die Eisscholle, schwimmendes Eisfeld; *pl.* das Treibeis.

flog [flɔg], *v.a.* (aus)peitschen, prügeln, züchtigen; – *a horse on*, ein Pferd antreiben; – *a dead horse*, offene Türen einrennen. **-ging,** *s.* das Peitschen; die Prügelstrafe, körperliche Züchtigung; *get a -ging*, (durch)geprügelt werden.

flood [flʌd], I. *s.* die Flut, Überschwemmung (*also fig.*), das Hochwasser; (*fig.*) der Erguß, die Fülle, Menge; (*Poet.*) der Strom; (*B.*) die Sintflut; *the tide is at the* –, das Wasser steigt; – *of tears*, die Tränenflut, der Tränenstrom; – *of words*, der Wortschwall. 2. *v.a. & n.* überfluten, überschwemmen, mit Wasser füllen, unter Wasser setzen; fließen, strömen; steigen (*as the tide*); – *in upon*, überfluten, sich ergießen über; – *the tanks*, fluten (*submarines*). **--bound,** *adj.* ringsum von Wasser eingeschlossen. **– disaster,** die Hochwasserkatastrophe. **--gate,** *s.* die Schleuse, das Schleusentor. **-ing,** *s.* das Überschwemmen, Überfluten; die Überflutung; das Fluten (*submarine tanks, etc.*); die Gebärmutterblutung (*Med.*). **-light,** I. *s.* (*usually pl.*) das Bühnenlicht, der Scheinwerfer; (*fig.*) das Schlaglicht. 2. *v.a.* mit Scheinwerfern beleuchten. **-lighting,** *s.* die Scheinwerferbeleuchtung. **-lit,** *adj.* von Scheinwerfern beleuchtet. **--mark,** *s.* das Hochwasserstandszeichen. **--tide,** *s.* die Flut.

floor [flɔː], I. *s.* der Fußboden, die Diele; das Geschoß, Stockwerk (*Build.*); der Grund (*of the sea*), die Tenne (*of a barn*); Sohle (*of a trench, etc.*); (*fig.*) der Sitzungssaal (*Parl.*); *ground--* (Amer. *first* –), das Erdgeschoß, Parterre; *on the first* – (Amer. *second* –), im ersten Stock; – *of the House*, der Sitzungssaal (*Parl.*); *inlaid* –, das Parkett; *have* (*take*) *the* –, das Wort haben (ergreifen) (*Parl.*); *take the* –, tanzen; (*sl.*) *wipe the* – *with a p.*, einen gehörig zurichten *or* vollkommen erledigen. 2. *v.a.* mit Fußboden versehen (*a room*); (*coll.*) zu Boden strecken (*a p.*); (*fig.*) verblüffen, auf den Sand setzen. **--cloth,** *s.* der Wischlappen, Scheuerlappen. **-ing,** *s.* die Dielung, der Fußboden; der Fußbodenbelag. **--lamp,** *s.* (*Amer.*) die Stehlampe. **--polish,** *s.* das Bohnerwachs. **--stain,** *s.* die Bodenbeize. **--timbers,** *pl.* Kielplanken (*Shipb.*). **--walker,** *s.* (*Amer.*) der Empfangschef in großen Warenhäusern. **--wax,** *see* **--polish.**

flop [flɔp], I. *v.n.* (*coll.*) schwerfällig niederfallen, hinplumpsen; lose herunterhängen; (*sl.*) scheitern, zusammenbrechen, durchfallen. 2. *s.* (*sl.*) der Mißerfolg, Versager, Durchfall; die Niete (*of persons*). 3. *int.* plumps! **-py,** *adj.* (*coll.*) schlapp, schlappig, schlotterig.

flor-a [flɔːrə], *s.* die Blumenwelt, Flora. **-al,** *adj.* Blüten-, Blumen-. **-et** [ˈflɔːrɛt], *s.* das Blümchen (*Bot.*). **-iculture** [ˈflɔːrɪkʌltʃə], *s.* die Blumenzucht. **-id** [ˈflɔrɪd], *adj.* auffallend, grell, schreiend; rot, gerötet; überladen, gesucht, dekorativ (*Arch.*), figural (*Mus.*), blumenreich (*as language*); (*archaic*) blühend, blütenreich. **-idity, -idness,** *s.* die Röte; Grellheit; Überladenheit, Blumenpracht, blumenreicher Stil.

florin [ˈflɔːrɪn], *s.* der Gulden (*Holland*), das Zweischillingstück (*England*).

florist [ˈflɔːrɪst], *s.* der Blumenhändler; Blumenzüchter.

floss [flɔs], *s.* die Rohseide, der Seidenflaum, ungezwirnte Seidenfäden (*pl.*). **--silk,** *s.* die Wattseide, Florettseide. **-y,** *adj.* seidenweich, seidenähnlich.

flotation [floˈteɪʃən], *s. see* **floatation.**

flotilla [floˈtɪlə], *s.* die Flotille.

flotsam [ˈflɔtsəm], *s.* das Treibgut, treibendes Wrackgut, die Seetrift.

[1]**flounce** [flaʊns], *v.n.* hastig bewegen; – *in*, angebraust kommen; – *out of the room*, trotzig *or* ungehalten aus dem Zimmer stürzen.

[2]**flounce,** I. *s.* die Falbel, Krause, loser Besatz, der Volant. 2. *v.a.* mit Falbeln *or* Volants besetzen.

[1]**flounder** [ˈflaʊndə], *v.n.* sich abarbeiten *or* wühlen, zappeln, vorwärtswaten; (*fig.*) stolpern, taumeln, umhertappen; stocken (*in speaking*).

[2]**flounder,** *s.* die Flunder (*Ichth.*).

flour [ˈflaʊə], I. *s.* das Mehl; *coarse* –, das Schrot. 2. *v.a.* mit Mehl bestreuen. **--bag,** *s.* der Mehlbeutel. **--mill,** *s.* die Mahlmühle. **-y,** *adj.* mehlig.

flourish [ˈflʌrɪʃ], I. *v.n.* blühen, gedeihen; leben, wirken, tätig sein; Schnörkel machen (*in writing*), sich blumenreich *or* geziert ausdrücken; schmettern (*of trumpets*); (*fig.*) prahlen. 2. *v.a.* schwingen (*a sword*); schwenken (*a flag*). 3. *s.* der Schnörkel, die Floskel; das Schwingen (*of a sword*), Schwenken (*of a flag*), Vorspiel (*Mus.*); *in full* –, in voller Blüte; – *of trumpets*, die Trompetenfanfare, der Tusch; *do with a* –, prahlend tun; *write one's name with a* –, seinen Namen zierlich verschnörkeln. **-ing,** *adj.* blühend, gedeihend.

flout [flaʊt], I. *v.a.* verhöhnen, verächtlich machen. 2. *v.n.* spotten (*at*, über (*Acc.*)); – *at fortune*, dem Glücke Hohn sprechen.

flow [floʊ], I. *v.n.* sich ergießen, strömen, fluten; lose herabhängen, wallen (*as garments, etc.*); – *from*, fließen aus, entfließen, entströmen (*Dat.*); (*fig.*) herrühren von, sich ergeben aus, entstehen *or* entspringen aus; – *off*, *v.n.* abfließen; – *out*, *v.n.* ausströmen. 2. *s.* der Fluß, Lauf, die Strömung, Flut; der Zufluß, Zustrom; Strom, Schwall, Erguß (*of words*); das Wogen, Wallen (*of dress*); der Überfluß, die Ergießung. **-ing** *adj.* fließend, strömend; wehend, wallend, flatternd; *-ing cup*, überschäumender Becher; *-ing language*, fließende Worte (*pl.*).

flower [ˈflaʊə], I. *s.* die Blume; Blüte (*also fig.*); (*fig.*) das Beste, Feinste, die Auslese, Zierde, der Schmuck; Gipfel, Kern; die Vignette, Leiste (*Typ.*); *artificial -s*, künstliche Blumen; *the* – *of chivalry*, die Zierde der Ritterschaft; *cut -s*, Schnittblumen; *in* –, in Blüte; *no -s by request*, Blumenspenden dankend verbeten; *say it with -s!* laßt Blumen sprechen! *-s of rhetoric*, die Redeblüten (*pl.*); *-s of sulphur*, Schwefelblumen (*pl.*); sublimierter Schwefel; *the* – *of the troops*, die Besten *or* Auslese der Truppen. 2. *v.n.* blühen (*also fig.*), in höchster Blüte stehen. 3. *v.a.* mit Blumenmuster schmücken, blümen. **-age** [-rɪdʒ], *s.* der Blütenreichtum, Blumenflor. **--bed,** *s.* das Blumenbeet. **--de-luce,** *s.* (*Amer.*) *see* **fleur-de-lis.** **-ed,** *adj.* geblümt, blumig. **-iness,** *s.* der Blütenreichtum; (*fig.*) blumenreicher Schmuck (*of speech*). **-ing,** I. *adj.* blühend, blütentragend. 2. *s.* die Blüte, das Aufblühen; *-ing time*, die Blütezeit. **--leaf,** *s.* das Blütenblatt. **--pot,** *s.* der Blumentopf. **--show,** *s.* die Blumenausstellung. **--stalk,** *s.* der Blütenstiel. **--vase,** *s.* das Blumengefäß, die Blumenvase. **-y,** *adj.* blütenreich, blumig; (*fig.*) blumenreich, geziert; geblümt (*pattern*).

flowing [ˈfloʊɪŋ], *see* **flow.**

flown [floʊn], *see* **fly.**
flu [flʊ:], *s.* (*coll.*) *see* **influenza.**
fluctuat–e [ˈflʌktjʊeɪt], *v.n.* schwanken, steigen und fallen (*as prices*); schweben (*Phonet.*). **–ing,** *adj.* schwankend, schwebend (*accent*). **–ion** [–ˈeɪʃən], *s.* das Schwanken, Wogen, die Schwankung (*C.L., Elec., etc.*).
¹**flue** [flʊ:], *s.* der Rauchfang, Feuerzug; das Flammrohr, Heizrohr, Wärmerohr; der Orgelpfeifenspalt. **–-gas,** *s.* das Abgas, Abzugsgas.
²**flue,** *s.* der Flaum, die Staubflocke.
³**flue,** *s.* das Schleppnetz.
fluen–cy [ˈflʊ:ənsɪ], *s.* der Fluß (*of speech*); die Geläufigkeit, Sprachfertigkeit. **–t** [ˈflʊ:ənt], *adj.* fließend; geläufig.
fluff [flʌf], 1. *s.* leichte Staubflocke, Federflocke, wollige Masse, der Flaum. 2. *v.a.* zu Flaum machen; (*coll.*) verpfuschen; – *up* or *out*, aufplustern. **–y,** *adj.* flaumig, flockig; mit Flaum bedeckt.
fluid [ˈflʊ:ɪd], 1. *s.* die Flüssigkeit; das Fluidum (*Elec.*); der Saft, die Sekretion. 2. *adj.* flüssig, dünnflüssig; (*fig.*) fließend, in Bewegung, im Fluß. **–ity** [–ˈɪdɪtɪ], *s.* die Flüssigkeit, Leichtflüssigkeit; flüssiger Zustand.
¹**fluke** [flʊ:k], *s.* die Flunder (*Ichth.*).
²**fluke,** *s.* der Ankerarm, Ankerflügel; *pl.* Schwanzflossen (*of a whale*).
³**fluk–e,** *s.* (*coll.*) glücklicher Zufall, der Dusel; Fuchs (*Bill.*); *by a –e*, durch Zufall. **–y,** *adj.* unsicher, Zufalls–.
flume [flʊ:m], *s.* künstlicher Wasserlauf.
flummery [ˈflʌmərɪ], *s.* der Flammeri (*Cul.*); (*fig., coll.*) leere Komplimente (*pl.*), leeres Geschwätz.
flummox [ˈflʌməks], *v.a.* (*sl.*) verblüffen.
flung [flʌŋ], *see* **fling.**
flunk [flʌŋk], 1. *v.n.* (*Amer.*) versagen, durchfallen, kneifen. 2. *v.a.* (*Amer.*) durchfallen lassen.
flunkey [ˈflʌŋkɪ], *s.* Livreebediente(r), *m.*, der Lakei; die Bedientenseele, der Speichellecker. **–dom** [–dəm], *s.* Livreebedienten (*pl.*). **–ism,** *s.* der Knechtssinn, das Kriechertum, die Speichelleckerei.
fluor [ˈflʊ:ɔ:], *s.* das Fluor, der Flußspat. **–ate of,** fluorwasserstoffsauer. **–esce,** *v.n.* schillern, fluoreszieren. **–escence** [–ˈrɛsns], *s.* die Fluoreszenz. **–escent,** *adj.* schillernd, fluoreszierend, zweifarbig. **–ic,** *adj.* Fluor–; *–ic acid*, die Fluorwasserstoffsäure. **–ide,** *s.* das Fluorsalz, die Fluorverbindung; *–ide of*, *s.* Fluor–. **–ine,** *s.* das Fluor. **–ite,** *s.* der Flußspat, Bergfluß, das Fluorkalzium. **–spar,** *s. see* **–ite.**
flurry [ˈflʌrɪ], 1. *s.* die Verwirrung, ängstliche Eile; nervöse Aufregung; das Gestöber; der Windstoß; die Haut, Blume, der Schaum (*Chem.*); – *of arrows*, der Pfeilregen; – *of birds*, der Vogelschwarm; – *of snow*, das Schneegestöber; *in a –*, aufgeregt, verwirrt. 2. *v.a.* aufregen, verwirren, nervös machen, beunruhigen.
flush [flʌʃ], 1. *v.n.* erröten, sich erhitzen; sich ergießen, ins Gesicht steigen (*blood*); sprießen (*Bot.*). 2. *v.a.* erröten machen, erhitzen, erregen, erheben, stolz machen; aufscheuchen, aufjagen (*birds*); überschwemmen; ausspülen, durchspülen, ausschwemmen, abschwenken; eben *or* glatt machen, ausstreichen (*joints*); *–ed with anger*, mit Zornröte übergossen; *–ed with joy*, freudetrunken; – *the sewers*, die Kanäle ausspülen; *–ed with victory*, siegestrunken; *–ed with wine*, vom Wein erhitzt. 3. *s.* das Erröten, die Röte, Glut; Aufwallung (*of joy*); Flut (*of passion*); Fülle, der Glanz, die Blüte, Kraft, der Überfluß; die Flöte (*Cards*); das Wachstum; Ausspülen, Strömen; der Wasserzufluß. 4. *adj.* frisch, blühend, kräftig, üppig, (über)voll, gedeihlich; eben, glatt, in gleicher Ebene (*Carp.*); (*coll.*) *be –*, Geld haben, bei Kasse sein; *fit – together*, *v.a.* planeben zusammenfügen; *v.n.* planeben zusammengefügt sein; – *with the surface*, mit der Oberfläche planeben *or* flach sein; – *deck*, das Glattdeck (*Naut.*); – *rivet*, versenkte Niete.
fluster [ˈflʌstə], 1. *s.* die Verwirrung, Aufregung; *all in a –*, ganz verwirrt. 2. *v.a.* verwirren, aufregen.
flut–e [flʊ:t], 1. *s.* die Flöte (*Mus.*); Rinne, Riefe, Rille, Hohlkehle (*Arch.*); Rüsche, Kräusel (*Dressm., etc.*). 2. *v.a.* riefeln, auskehlen, furchen, kannelieren; kräuseln, fälteln. 3. *v.n.* auf der Flöte spielen, flöten. **–e-player,** *s.* der Flötenspieler, Flötist. **–e-stop,** *s.* das Flötenregister. **–ing,** *s.* die Riefelung, Kannelierung (*Arch.*); das Kräuseln, Rüschen (*Dressm.*).
flutter [ˈflʌtə], 1. *v.n.* flattern, wehen (*as flags*); zittern, unregelmässig klopfen (*as the heart*); – *about*, umherflattern, sich hin und her bewegen. 2. *v.a.* beunruhigen, erregen, aufregen; hin und her bewegen; – *the dovecots*, Unruhe stiften, Verwirrung verursachen. 3. *s.* das Geflatter, Flattern flatternde Bewegung; (*fig.*) die Unruhe; Erregung, Verwirrung; (*coll.*) *have a –*, spekulieren, wetten; *be all in a –*, in großer Aufregung sein.
fluvial [ˈflʊ:vɪəl], *adj.* Fluß–.
flux [flʌks], *s.* der Fluß, Ausfluß, die Strömung (*Phys.*); das Ausströmen, der Strom, die Flut; der Umlauf, ständiger Wechsel; das Flußmittel, der Zuschlag (*Metall., Chem.*); *bloody –*, rote Ruhr (*Med.*); *in –*, im Fluß; – *linkage*, die Induktivkupplung (*Elec.*). **–ion** [ˈflʌkʃən], *s.* der Fluß (*Med.*), die Fluxion, das Differential (*Math.*); *method of –ions*, die Differentialrechnung (*Math.*). **–ional,** *adj.* Fluxions–, Differential–.
fly [flɑɪ], **1.** *ir.v.a.* fliegen; entfliehen, vergehen (as *time*); wehen, flattern (*as flags*); eilen, stürzen; fliehen; *as the crow flies*, nach *or* in der Luftlinie; (*fig.*) – *high*, hohe Ziele haben; *let –*, losschießen, abfeuern; (*fig.*) losschlagen; *let – at*, feuern *or* schießen auf (*Acc.*); (*fig.*) anfahren (*Acc.*), (los)wettern auf (*Acc. or* gegen); (*fig.*) *make the sparks –*, energisch zu Werke gehen; – *about*, herumfliegen; – *at*, anfahren, sich stürzen auf (*Acc.*), herfallen über (*Acc.*); – *at higher game*, höher hinauswollen; – *away*, fortfliegen; – *from*, meiden, sich entziehen (*Dat.*); – *in a p.'s face*, einen anfahren *or* herausfordern; – *in pieces*, zerspringen, zerbrechen; – *into a passion*, in Zorn geraten; – *off*, wegfliegen; (*fig.*) – *off at a tangent*, plötzlich abspringen; – *open*, auffliegen; – *out*, herausstürzen; – *out at a p.*, gegen einen ausfallend werden, auf einen losgehen. **2.** *ir.v.a.* fliegen lassen (*hawks*), steigen lassen (*a kite*); führen (*an aeroplane*); fliegen über, überfliegen; fliehen aus (*the country*); fliehen vor (*danger*); *he flew the Atlantic*, er überflog den Atlantischen Ozean; – *a flag*, eine Fahne hissen *or* führen; (*coll.*) – *a kite*, auf Wechsel borgen (*C.L.*); einen Versuchsballon steigen lassen; – *a sortie*, Einsatz fliegen (*Av.*). **3.** *s.* die Fliege; künstliche Fliege (*angling*), die Angelfliege; der Einspänner, die Droschke; der Flug; das Fliehen; die Unruhe (*Horol.*); der (Hosen)Schlitz; Ausleger (*Typ.*); *pl.* Soffitten (*pl.*) (*Theat.*); *break flies on a wheel*, wegen kleiner Zwecke große Mittel aufbieten; *go for a –*, fliegen, einen Flug machen; *a – in the ointment*, ein Haar in der Suppe; (*sl.*) *there are no –s on him*, auf ihn lasse ich nichts kommen; *he is on the –*, er flieht *or* flüchtet. **4.** *adj.* (*coll.*) schlau, gerissen, pfiffig. **–bane,** *s.* das Leimkraut (*Bot.*). **–blow,** *s.* Fliegeneier (*pl.*), der Fliegenschmutz. **–blown,** *adj.* von Fliegen beschmutzt, (*fig.*) besudelt. **–-by-night,** *s.* (*coll.*) der Nachtschwärmer. **–catcher,** *s.* der Fliegenschnäpper, Fliegenfänger (*Orn.*). **–er,** *s.* Fliegende(r), *m.*; Fliehende(r), *m.* der Flüchtling; Flieger (*Av.*); schnellaufendes Tier, schnellfahrendes Fahrzeug; das Schwungrad; der Spindelflügel (*Spin.*); die Freitreppe. **–-fishing,** *s.* das Angeln mit künstlichen Fliegen. **–ing** [ˈflɑɪɪŋ], 1. *pr.p. & adj.* fliegend; flüchtig, eilig. **2.** *s.* das Fliegen; die Fliegerei, das Flugwesen. **–ing-accident,** *s.* der Flugunfall. **–ing-altitude,** *s.* die Flughöhe. **–ing-boat,** *s.* das Flugboot. **–ing-bomb,** die Raketenbombe, führerloses Flugzeug. **–ing-buttress,** *s.* der Strebebogen, Strebepfeiler. **with –ing colours,** (*fig.*) mit Ehren, glänzend. **–ing column,** fliegende Kolonne (*Mil.*). **–ing-corps,** *s.* das Fliegerkorps. **–ing-fish,** *s.* fliegender Fisch. **–ing-field,** *s.* der Flugplatz. **–ing-fox,** *s.* fliegender Hund (*Zool.*). **–ing-instructor,** *s.* der Fluglehrer. **–ing-jib,** *s.* der Außenklüver, Buten-

klüver. **-ing jump,** *s.* der Sprung mit Anlauf. **-ing-machine,** *s.* (*archaic*) das Flugzeug. **-ing-officer,** *s.* der Oberleutnant der Luftwaffe. **-ing-speed,** *s.* die Fluggeschwindigkeit. **-ing-squad,** *s.* das Überfallkommando. **-ing-squirrel,** *s.* das Flughörnchen. **-ing visit,** *s.* flüchtiger Besuch, der Abstecher, die Stippvisite. **-ing-wing,** *s.* das Nurflügelflugzeug. **-leaf,** *s.* das Vorsatzblatt (*Typ.*). **--over,** *s.*; *--over junction*, kreuzungsfreier Übergang, die Überführung. **--paper,** *s.* das Fliegenpapier. **--past,** *s.* die Luftparade. **--press,** *s.* das Stoßwerk. **-sheet,** *s.* das Flugblatt. **--swatter,** *s.* der Fliegenwedel. **--weight,** *s.* das Fliegengewicht; der Fliegengewichtler (*Boxing*). **-wheel,** *s.* das Schwungrad (*Mach.*).

foal [foʊl], 1. *s.* das Fohlen, Füllen; *with* or *in* –, trächtig. 2. *v.a.* & *n.* fohlen, (ein Füllen) werfen. **--foot,** *s.* der Huflattich (*Bot.*).

foam [foʊm], 1. *s.* der Schaum; – *extinguisher*, das Schaumlöschgerät. 2. *v.n.* schäumen; (*fig.*) wüten, vor Wut schäumen (*at*, über); *he –ed at the mouth*, sein Mund schäumte. **-ing,** *adj.*, **-y,** *adj.* schäumend.

[1]**fob** [fɔb], *s.* (*archaic*) die Uhrtasche (in der Hose).

[2]**fob,** *v.a.* foppen, zum besten haben, betrügen, prellen; – *s.th. off on s.o.*, – *s.o. off with a th.*, einen mit etwas abfertigen *or* abspeisen, einem etwas aufhalsen *or* aufhängen.

focal [ˈfoʊkəl], *adj.* im Brennpunkt stehend; – *distance*, die Brennweite; *--plane shutter*, der Schlitzverschluß.

fo'c'sle [ˈfoʊksl], *s.* (*abbr. of* **forecastle**) die Back (*Naut.*).

focus [ˈfoʊkəs], 1. *s.* (*pl.* foci, –ses) der Brennpunkt (*also fig.*); scharfe Einstellung; *in* –, scharf eingestellt; *bring into* –, scharf einstellen; *out of* –, nicht scharf eingestellt. 2. *v.a.* (richtig *or* scharf) einstellen; im Brennpunkt vereinigen. **-ing,** *s.* die (Scharf)Einstellung (*Opt.*). **-ing-screen,** *s.* die Mattscheibe (*Phot.*).

fodder [ˈfɔdə], 1. *s.* die Fütterung; das Trockenfutter, Dürrfutter; *cannon--*, das Kanonenfutter. 2. *v.a.* füttern.

foe [foʊ], *s.* der Feind, Gegner (*to* (*Gen.*)). **-man** [–mən], *s.* (*Poet.*) der Feind.

foet-al [ˈfɪːtəl], *adj.* fötal, Fötus. **-us** [ˈfɪːtəs], *s.* die Leibesfrucht, der Fötus.

fog [fɔg], 1. *s.* der Nebel; (*fig.*) die Umnebelung, Verwirrung, Unsicherheit; der Dunst, Schleier, Grauschleier (*Phot.*); (*fig.*) *in a* –, in Verwirrung, in Verlegenheit. 2. *v.a.* (*fig.*) umnebeln, verwirren, in Verlegenheit setzen. **--bank,** *s.* die Nebelschicht. **-bound,** *adj.* in Nebel eingehüllt; von Nebel zurückgehalten (*of ships*). **-giness,** *s.* die Nebligkeit. **-gy,** *adj.* neblig, dunstig, mistig (*Naut.*); (*fig.*) umnebelt, wirr, unklar, unsicher; *not the –giest notion*, keine blasse Ahnung. **-horn,** *s.* das Nebelhorn. **--signal,** *s.* das Nebelsignal (*Railw.*).

fogey, fogy [ˈfoʊgɪ], *s.*; (*coll.*) usually *old* –, altmodischer Mensch, alter Knopf, der Philister.

foible [ˈfɔɪbl], *s.* die schwache Seite.

[1]**foil** [fɔɪl], *s.* die Folie, das Metallblättchen; Glanzblättchen (*for gems*); (*fig.*) die Unterlage. Einfassung; der (Spiegel)Belag (*for mirrors*); das Blaumetall; die Blattverzierung, das Laubwerk (*Arch.*); (*fig.*) *be a* – *for* or *act as* – *to*, (einem) zur Folie dienen; *metal* –, das Blattmetall; *tin* –, der Blattzinn.

[2]**foil,** 1. *v.a.* vereiteln, zunichte machen (*efforts, plans, etc.*); verwischen (*the scent*) (*Hunt.*). 2. *s.* das Florett, Rapier; die Fährte, Spur (*Hunt.*).

foist [fɔɪst], *v.a.* unterschieben, heimlich einschieben; – *s.th. on a p.*, einem etwas aufhalsen *or* aufhängen, einen mit etwas anschmieren.

[1]**fold** [foʊld], 1. *s.* die Falte (*in cloth, etc., also Geol.*); der Falz (*Bookb.*); Kniff, Bruch (*in paper, etc.*). 2. *suffix* –fach, –fältig. 3. *v.a.* falten; falzen, umbiegen, kniffen (*paper*); übereinanderlegen, kreuzen (*the arms, etc.*); *with –ed arms*, mit untergeschlagenen *or* verschränkten Armen; – *down a leaf*, ein Blatt einschlagen *or* umkniffen; – *in*, einhüllen; – *in one's arms*, umarmen, in die Arme schließen; – *up*, zusammenlegen. 4. *v.n.* (sich) schließen; sich zusammenlegen lassen (*as doors*), zusammenklappen. **-er,** *s.* der Falzer (*Bookb.*), der Papierfalter, das Falzbein; die Mappe, der Hefter; das Heft, die Broschüre, der Prospekt; *pl.* der Kneifer, Zwicker. **-ing,** *adj.* zusammenlegbar, Klapp–. **-ing-bed,** *s.* das Feldbett, Klappbett. **-ing-boat,** *s.* das Faltboot. **-ing-chair,** *s.* der Klappstuhl. **-ing-door,** *s.* die Flügeltür. **-ing-hat,** *s.* der Klapphut. **-ing-head,** *s.* zusammenklappbares Verdeck (*Naut.*). **-ing-screen,** *s.* spanische Wand. **-ing-seat,** *s.* der Klappsitz. **-ing-stick,** *s.* das Falzbein. **-ing-table,** *s.* der Klapptisch.

[2]**fold,** 1. *s.* die (Schaf)Hürde, der Pferch; die Herde, Gemeinde (*Eccl.*). 2. *v.a.* einpferchen (*sheep, etc.*).

folderol [ˈfɔldərɔl], *s.* der Tand.

folia-ceous [foʊlɪˈeɪʃəs], *adj.* blätterig; Blätter–. **-ge** [ˈfoʊljɪdʒ], *s.* das Laub(werk); das Blattwerk (*Art*). **-te,** 1. [ˈfoʊlɪət], *adj.* blätterig, blattförmig, blattartig; blattreich, Blatt–. 2. [–ɪeɪt] *v.n.* Blätter treiben (*Bot.*); sich in Blättchen spalten (*Geol.*). 3. *v.a.* mit Folie belegen; mit Blattverzierung schmücken (*Arch.*); schiefern (*Geol.*); nach Blättern zählen (*a book*). **-tion** [–lɪˈeɪʃən], *s.* die Blattentwicklung, der Blätterwuchs, die Blattstellung, Belaubung (*Bot.*); das Blattwerk, die Blattverzierung (*Arch.*); das Belegen mit Folie (*of a mirror, etc.*); das Schlagen zu Blättern (*Metall.*); die Lagerung in Schichten (*Geol.*); Blattzählung (*of a book*).

folio [ˈfoʊljoʊ], *s.* das Folio (*also book-keeping*); (Folio)Blatt; Folioformat (*Typ.*); die Seitenzahl (*C.L.*); – *volume*, der Foliant.

folk [foʊk], *s.* (*pl. constr.*) die Leute, (*archaic*) das Volk; *pl.* Leute, (*coll.*) Angehörige. **--dance,** *s.* der Volkstanz. **-lore,** *s.* die Volkskunde. **-lorist,** *s.* der Volkskundler. **-song,** *s.* das Volkslied. **--tale,** *s.* die Volkssage. **-weave,** *s.* handgewebte Stoffe (*pl.*).

follicle [ˈfɔlɪkl], *s.* der Follikel, das Drüsengrübchen.

follow [ˈfɔloʊ], **1.** *v.a.* folgen, nachgehen, nachhängen (*Dat.*) (*a p., also fig.*); verfolgen (*Acc.*) (*a way, etc.*); folgen auf (*Acc.*), nachfolgen (*Dat.*); begleiten; sich anschließen an, dienen (*Dat.*), gehorchen (*Dat.*), befolgen, beobachten (*Acc.*), sich halten an (*Acc.*), sich bekennen zu, anerkennen; folgen aus, die Folge sein von, im Gefolge sein von; treiben, ausüben (*business*); (*coll.*) verstehen, begreifen; *he –s me*, er folgt mir; (*fig.*) *he cannot – me*, er kann mich nicht verstehen; – *his advice*, seinem Rat folgen; – *his example*, seinem Beispiel folgen; – *the fashion*, die Mode mitmachen; – *the hounds*, jagen; – *one's nose*, der Nase nachgehen; – *one's pleasure*, seinem Vergnügen nachgehen; – *the plough*, Landmann sein; – *the sea*, Seemann sein; – *suit*, Farbe bedienen (*Cards*); (*fig.*) sich anschließen (*Dat.*), dem Beispiel folgen; – *out*, befolgen, durchführen, weiterverfolgen; – *up*, *v.a.* & *n.* (eifrig) verfolgen; ausnutzen (*an advantage*); nachlaufen (*Dat.*) (*Bill.*); – *up one th. with another*, auf eine S. eine andere folgen lassen. **2.** *v.n.* folgen, nachfolgen; sich später ereignen; sich ergeben (*from*, aus); *as –s*, wie folgt, folgendermaßen; – *in a p.'s (foot)steps*, einem auf dem Fuße folgen; – *on*, später folgen; sofort wiederauftreten (*Crick.*); – *through*, durchziehen, durchschwingen (*the stroke*) (*Sport*); – *up*, nachstoßen, nachdrängen (*Mil.*). **-er,** *s.* Folgende(r), *m.*, der Verfolger; Nachfolger; Anhänger, Schüler, Jünger; Begleiter, Diener; Zubringer (*Mech.*); *pl.* das Gefolge, der Anhang. **-ing,** 1. *prep.* zufolge; als Folge (*Gen.*), im Anschluß an (*Acc.*). 2. *adj.* folgend, kommend; *on the –ing day*, am Tage darauf; *–ing wind*, der Rückenwind, achterlicher Wind. 3. *s.* Folgende(s), *n.*; der Anhang, das Gefolge, die Anhängerschaft, Gefolgschaft, Anhänger (*pl.*). **--on,** *s.* sofortiges Wiederauftreten (*Crick.*). **--through,** *s.* das Durchziehen, Durchschwingen (*Sport*). **--up,** 1. *adj.*; *--up letter*, zweiter Brief, der die Angelegenheit verfolgt. 2. *s.* weitere Verfolgung, die Nachuntersuchung.

folly [ˈfɔlɪ], *s.* die Torheit, Narrheit, der Unsinn;

piece of –, törichtes Unternehmen, die Torheit, dummer Streich.
foment [fou'mɛnt], *v.a.* warm baden, bähen; (*fig.*) erregen, schüren, fördern, pflegen, anfachen, anstiften. **-ation** [-'teɪʃən], *s.* die Bähung, das Bähen; Dampfbad, Bähmittel, heißer Umschlag; die Anreizung, Schürung. **-er,** *s.* der Unterstützer, Anstifter, Schürer.
fond [fɔnd], *adj.* liebevoll, zärtlich; vernarrt, übertrieben zärtlich; albern, närrisch; – *father*, übertrieben zärtlicher Vater; *be – of*, gern haben, lieben; – *of swimming*, gern schwimmen. **-le** ['fɔndl], 1. *v.a.* liebkosen, streicheln, herzen. 2. *v.n.* kosen, tändeln, spielen. **-ly,** *adv.* in unkritischer Zuversicht; *he -ly imagined*, er bildete sich in seiner Unwissenheit ein. **-ness,** *s.* die Liebe, Zärtlichkeit; Vorliebe (*for*, für), der Hang (*for*, zu).
font [fɔnt], *s.* der Taufstein, das Taufbecken.
fontanel(le) [fɔntə'nɛl], *s.* die Fontanelle (*Anat.*).
food [fu:d], *s.* das Essen, die Speise, Nahrung; das Nahrungsmittel, Lebensmittel (*pl.*), die Verpflegung, Beköstigung; das Futter (*of beasts*); – *and drink*, Essen und Trinken, Speise und Trank; – *for meditation*, der Stoff zum Nachdenken. **--card,** *s.* die Lebensmittelkarte. **--controller,** *s.* der Ernährungsminister. **--hoarder,** *s.* der Hamsterer. **--office,** *s.* das Ernährungsamt. **--shortage,** *s.* die Lebensmittelknappheit. **-stuffs,** *pl.* Nahrungsmittel, Nährmittel, Nährstoffe (*pl.*). **--supply,** *s.* die Verpflegung, Lebensmittelzufuhr; der Lebensmittelvorrat. **--value,** *s.* der Nährwert.
[1]**fool** [fu:l], 1. *s.* der Narr, Tor; (*coll.*) Dummkopf, Gimpel; Hanswurst, Possenreißer; (*a*) (*with verbs*) *he's no* –, er läßt sich nicht hinters Licht führen; *there's no – like an old* –, Alter schützt vor Torheit nicht; *he is a – to . . .*, er ist nichts *or* ein Waisenknabe im Vergleich zu . . .; *make a – of o.s.*, sich blamieren, sich (*Dat.*) eine Blöße geben, sich lächerlich machen; *make a – of a p.*, einen zum Narren halten; *make an April – of a p.*, einen in den April schicken; *play the* –, Possen treiben; (*b*) (*with nouns*) *all -s' day*, der erste April; *-'s errand*, vergebliches Bemühen, vergeblicher Gang; *-'s paradise*, das Schlaraffenland; *live in a -'s paradise*, sich goldene Berge versprechen, gedankenlos dahinleben, in einem verhängnisvollen Irrtum befangen sein; *-'s parsley*, der Gartenschierling (*Bot.*). 2. *v.a.* zum Narren haben, äffen, hänseln; täuschen, betören; prellen, betrügen (*a p. out of s.th.*, einen um etwas); – *away*, unnütz vergeuden, vertrödeln *or* vertändeln. 3. *v.n.* Possen treiben; spielen, tändeln (*with*, mit); – *about*, Possen treiben, Unsinn machen; sich herumtreiben, herumlungern. **-ery,** *s.* die Torheit, Narrheit. **-hardiness,** *s.* die Tollkühnheit. **-hardy,** *adj.* tollkühn. **-ing,** *s.* Faxen (*pl.*); *stop your -ing!* mach keinen Unsinn! **-ish,** *adj.* närrisch, töricht, albern, dumm, unklug; lächerlich, läppisch. **-ishness,** *s.* die Torheit, Narrheit; Albernheit. **-proof,** *adj.* kinderleicht, einfach zu handhaben; betriebssicher (*Mach.*, *etc.*). **-scap** ['fu:lzkæp], *s.* die Narrenkappe; das Kanzleipapier, Aktenpapier; Aktenformat.
[2]**fool,** *s.* die Krem, das Mus (*Cook.*).
foot [fʊt], 1. *s.* der Fuß (*also fig. & measure*); unteres Ende, das Fußende (*of a bed, page, etc.*); der Füßling (*of a stocking*); (*coll.*) das Fußvolk, die Infanterie (*Mil.*); der Versfuß (*Metr.*); (*pl.* -s) der Bodensatz, die Hefe; (*a*) (*with nouns*) *horse and* –, Kavallerie und Infanterie; *--and-mouth disease*, die Maul- und Klauenseuche; (*coll.*) *I know the length of his* –, ich kenne seine Schwächen *or* ihn genau; *the 125th* (*regiment of*) –, das 125. Infanterieregiment; (*b*) (*with verbs*) (*coll.*) *get one's – in*, sich hineindrängen; *have both feet on the ground*, mit beiden Füßen auf der Erde stehen; *have one – in the grave*, mit einem Fuß im Grabe stehen; *put one's – down*, sich widersetzen, Einspruch erheben, energisch auftreten, ein Machtwort sprechen; (*coll.*) *put one's – in it*, schön hereinfallen, sich blamieren, ins Fettnäpfchen treten; *put one's best – foremost*, tüchtig ausschreiten, sich nach Kräften anstrengen; (*fig.*) *put one's – on s.th.*, etwas abstellen, mit etwas ein Ende machen; *run s.o. off his feet*, einen zum Tode hetzen; *set – in* or *on*, betreten; *not stir a – from* or *out of*, sich nicht rühren von . . . weg; (*c*) (*with prepositions*) *at the* –, am Schluß, unten; *at his feet*, ihm zu Füßen; *fall at s.o.'s feet*, einem zu Füßen fallen; *light of* –, leichtfüßig; *sweep s.o. off his feet*, einen fortreißen *or* hinreißen; *on* –, zu Fuß, auf den Beinen, (*fig.*) am Werk, in Tätigkeit; *be on one's feet*, auf den Beinen sein; (*coll.*) *fall on one's feet*, immer Glück haben; *set on* –, in die Wege leiten, in Gang bringen, ins Werk setzen; *get on* or *to one's feet*, sich erheben, aufstehen; *from head to* –, von Kopf zu Fuß; *help s.o. to his feet*, einem auf die Beine helfen; *jump to one's feet*, auf die Füße springen; *under* –, unter dem Fuße, auf dem Boden; (*fig.*) unter die Füße; *tread under* –, mit Füßen treten. 2. *v.a.* Füße anstricken (*socks*); (*coll.*) bezahlen, bestreiten (*a bill*); – *up*, addieren, summieren. 3. *v.n.*; – *it*, tanzen, trippeln, (*archaic*) zu Fuße gehen; – *up to*, sich belaufen auf (*Acc.*). **-age** [-ɪdʒ], *s.* die Gesamtlänge (*films*). **-ball,** *s.* der Fußball; das Fußballspiel. **-baller,** *s.* der Fußballspieler. **-board,** *s.* das Fußbrett; Trittbrett (*Motor.*); Laufbrett, der Tritt (*Railw.*). **-boy,** *s.* der Laufbursche, Page. **-bridge,** *s.* der Steg, Laufsteg. **-ed** [-ɪd], *suffix* -füßig. **-er,** *s.* (*sl.*) *see* **-ball. -fall,** *s.* der Tritt, Schritt. **--fault,** *s.* der Fußfehler (*Tenn.*). **--gear,** *s. see* **-wear. --guards,** *pl.* die Gardeinfanterie, das Garderegiment zu Fuß. **--hills,** *pl.* das Vorgebirge. **-hold,** *s.* die Fußstütze, fester Stand; der Raum zum Stehen; (*fig.*) der Halt, die Stütze; *gain a -hold*, Fuß fassen. **-ing** ['fʊtɪŋ], *s.* der Halt, Stand, die Stellung, fester Fuß; (*fig.*) der Stützpunkt; die Lage, der Zustand; das Verhältnis; Anfußen (*of socks*); *be on a friendly -ing*, auf freundschaftlichem Fuße stehen; *get* or *gain a -ing*, festen Fuß fassen; *lose* or *miss one's -ing*, stolpern, einen Fehltritt machen, ausgleiten; *pay one's -ing*, Einstand bezahlen; *first-ing*, (*Scots*) der Neujahrsbesuch; *on a war -ing*, auf Kriegsstand; *he is not on a -ing with us*, er steht uns nicht gleich; *place* or *put on a -ing with* or *the same -ing as* or *with*, gleichstellen (*Dat.*), auf gleichem Fuße stellen mit. **-lights,** *pl.* die Rampenlichter; *get across the -lights*, auf das Publikum wirken. (*coll.*) **--loose,** frei, unbehindert. **-man,** *s.* der Lakei, Bediente(r), *m.* **-mark,** *s. see* **-print. --muff,** *s.* der Fußwärmer, Fußsack. **-note,** *s.* die Fußnote, Anmerkung. **--pace,** *s.* langsamer Schritt, der Spazierschritt. **-pad,** *s.* der Straßenräuber. **--passenger,** *s.* der Fußgänger. **-path,** *s.* der Fußweg, Fußpfad, Steg. **-plate,** *s.* der Führerstand (*Railw.*). **-plate-man,** *s.* der Lokomotivführer. **--pound,** *s.* das Fußpfund (*Mech.*). **-print,** *s.* die Fußtapfe, (Fuß)Spur. **--race,** *s.* der Wettlauf. **--rest,** *s.* das Fußbänkchen; die Fußruhe (*Cycl.*). **--rot,** *s.* die Fußfäule. **--rule,** *s.* der Zollstock. **--scraper,** *s.* der Fußabtreter. (*sl.*) **--slogger,** *s.* der Fußlatscher. **--soldier,** *s.* der Fußsoldat, Infanterist. **-sore,** *adj.* marschkrank, fußwund. **-stalk,** *s.* der Stengel, Stiel. **-step,** *s.* der (Fuß)Tritt; *follow in one's -steps*, jemandes Beispiel folgen. **--stool,** *s.* der Schemel, die Fußbank. **-wear,** *s.* das Schuhwerk, die Fußbekleidung.
footl-e ['fʊtl], *v.n.* albern *or* kindisch sein. **-ing,** *adj.* albern, blöde; nichtig.
foozle ['fu:zl], *v.a.* (*sl.*) verpfuschen (*Golf*).
fop [fɔp], *s.* der Geck, Stutzer. **-pery,** *s.* der Tand, Flitter; die Geckenhaftigkeit, Ziererei. **-pish,** *adj.* geckenhaft, stutzerhaft.
for [fɔ:, fə], 1. *prep.*; (*a*) (= *in place of, instead of*) für, anstatt; *once – all*, ein für allemal; *will you take this letter for me to the post?* wollen Sie diesen Brief für mich zur Post bringen; (*b*) (= *in support of*) *fight – one's country*, für sein Land kämpfen; *take my word – it*, verlassen Sie sich darauf; *what are you – ?* wofür bist du? (*c*) (= *with the aim of*) *it is – art to express*, es ist Sache *or* die Aufgabe der Kunst auszudrücken; *give up law – the church*, das Rechtsstudium aufgeben um Theolog(e) zu werden; *good* –, gut für *or* zu; *try – a job*, sich um eine Stellung bewerben; *not – the life of me*, beim besten Willen nicht; *write – money*, für Geld schreiben; *all – nothing*, alles umsonst; *be*

good – nothing, nichts taugen; *what –?* warum? weshalb? weswegen? wofür? *he gave orders – the charge to be made*, er gab Befehl anzugreifen; *– hire!* zu vermieten! frei! (*of taxicabs*); *– a holiday*, auf Urlaub; *– sale*, zum Verkauf; *go – a walk*, einen Spaziergang machen, spazieren gehen. (*d*) (*destination*) nach; *leave – the continent*, nach dem Kontinent reisen; *I am off – L.*, ich reise nach L. ab; *it is getting on – midnight*, es geht auf Mitternacht; (*e*) (*striving*) *– God's sake!* um Gottes willen! *now – it!* jetzt ans Werk! nun los! jetzt gilt's! *Oh, – money!* hätte ich nur Geld! *– shame!* pfui! schäme dich! (*f*) (*fitness*) für, zu; *that's the man – me!* das ist mein Mann! *there's a man – you!* das nenne ich einen Kerl! *it is – you to say*, es liegt an dir zu sagen; *there is nothing – it but to go*, weggehen ist der einzige Weg; *it is not – me to . . .*, es ziemt mir nicht *or* geziemt sich nicht für mich zu . . .; (*g*) (*relation*) *tall – his age*, groß für sein Alter; *line – line*, Zeile für *or* um Zeile; *word – word*, Wort für Wort; (*h*) (= *as, as being*) *– certain*, sicherlich, gewiß; *– example*, *– instance*, zum Beispiel; *– the first time*, zum ersten Mal; *count – little*, wenig zählen; *I – one*, ich zum Beispiel, ich meinerseits; *in mistake –*, irrtümlich *or* aus Versehen an Stelle (*Gen.*); *take –*, irrtümlich halten für; *a curse upon thee – a traitor!* fluch dir, Verräter! (*i*) (= *in spite of*) *– all he is so rich*, obgleich er so reich ist; *– all I know*, soviel ich weiß; *– all that*, bei *or* trotz alledem; *nothing happened – all his efforts*, es geschah nichts, trotz *or* ungeachtet aller seiner Anstrengungen; *but – you*, ohne dich; *but – this*, wenn dies nicht wäre, abgesehen von dem; (*j*) (= *as regards, on account of*) *as – me*, meinetwegen, was mich betrifft; *treat – cancer*, auf Krebs behandeln; *– fun*, aus Spaß; *be (in) – it*, einer Bestrafung entgegensehen, keinen anderen Ausweg haben, in der Patsche sitzen; *– joy*, vor Freude; *he could not speak – laughing*, er konnte vor Lachen nicht sprechen; *at a loss –*, verlegen um; *– that matter*, was das betrifft; *– my part*, meinerseits; *– this reason*, aus diesem Grunde; (*k*) (*duration*) *– ages*, schon ewig; *– some days*, einige Tage lang, schon einige Tage; *not – some days*, nicht vor einigen Tagen; *– ever*, für immer, auf ewig *or* immer; *Adenauer – ever!* A. soll leben! *– good*, für *or* auf immer; *– life*, lebenslänglich; *– long*, auf lange Zeit; *– the next 3 weeks*, die *or* in den nächsten 3 Wochen; *– the present*, im Augenblick; *– some time past*, seit längerer Zeit; *– a while*, auf einige Zeit; (*l*) (*with dat. meaning*) *buy – s.o.*, einem kaufen; *earn s.th. – s.o.*, einem etwas einbringen; *hold it – me!* halte es mir! 2. *conj.* denn.

forag–e [ˈfɔrɪdʒ], 1. *s.* das (Pferde)Futter, die Furage; das Furagieren; (*fig.*) *on the –e for*, umherstöbern nach. 2. Futter suchen, furagieren. 3. *v.a.* durch Furagieren ausplündern (*country*); (*fig.*) durchstöbern. **–er,** *s.* der Furier. **–e-cap,** *s.* die Feldmütze. **–ing-party,** *s.* der Furagierzug.

foram–en [foˈreɪmɪn], *s.* (*pl.* –ina [–ˈræmɪnə]) das Loch, die Öffnung (*Zool., Bot., & Anat.*).

forasmuch [fərəzˈmʌtʃ], *adv.* insofern.

foray [ˈfɔreɪ], 1. *s.* räuberischer Einfall, der Raubzug, das Scharmützel. 2. *v.a.* plündern.

forbade [fəˈbæd], *see* **forbid.**

[1]**forbear** [fɔ:ˈbɛə], 1. *ir.v.a.* sich enthalten (*Gen.*), unterlassen (*Acc.*), abstehen von; *I cannot – smiling*, ich kann nicht umhin zu lächeln. 2. *ir.v.n.* sich gedulden; Geduld haben (*with*, mit); unterlassen (*Acc.*), abstehen, ablassen (*from*, von). **–ance,** *s.* die Geduld, Nachsicht; die Unterlassung (*Gen.*), Enthaltung. **–ing** [–rɪŋ], *adj.* geduldig, nachsichtig, langmütig.

[2]**forbear** [ˈfɔ:bɛə], *s.* (*usually pl.*) der Vorfahr, Ahne, Ahnherr.

forbid [fəˈbɪd], *ir.v.a.* verbieten, untersagen (*a p.*, einem; *a th.*, etwas); hindern; *circumstances – it*, die Lage macht es unmöglich; *God –!* Gott behüte *or* bewahre! **–den,** *adj.* verboten; *–den fruit*, unerlaubte Frucht. **–ding,** *adj.* verbietend; abstoßend, abschreckend; *–ding appearance*, bedrohliches Aussehen; *–ding rocks*, gefährliche Klippen.

forbore [fɔ:ˈbɔ:], **forborne,** *see* [1]**forbear.**

[1]**force** [fɔ:s], 1. *s.* die Kraft, Macht, Stärke, Wucht, Gewalt, der Zwang, Druck, Einfluß; die Gültigkeit, bindende Kraft; der Nachdruck, das Gewicht, die Wirkung; Bedeutung, der Gehalt (*of a word, etc.*); die Truppe, Formation, der Verband (*Mil.*); *pl.* Truppen, Streitkräfte; *armed –s*, die Wehrmacht; *by –*, gewaltsam; *by main –*, mit roher Gewalt, mit aller Kraft; *by – of*, vermittels, mit Hilfe von; *centrifugal –*, die Fliehkraft, Schwungkraft; *centripetal –*, die Anziehkraft; *– of circumstances*, die Macht *or* der Zwang der Verhältnisse; *explosive –*, die Brisanz; *field –*, Feldtruppen (*pl.*) (*Mil.*); *– of impact*, die Aufschlagkraft, Einschlagkraft; *in –*, in großer Stärke *or* Zahl; gültig, in Kraft; *in full –*, in voller Kraft; *come into –*, in Kraft treten; *put into –*, in Kraft treten lassen; *land –s*, Landstreitkräfte (*pl.*); *police –*, die Polizei. 2. *v.a.* zwingen, nötigen, treiben; Gewalt antun (*the meaning*); überwältigen, erstürmen, durch Sturm einnehmen (*a city etc.*); aufbrechen, erbrechen, sprengen (*a door, lock, etc.*); aufdrängen, aufnötigen, aufzwingen (*upon* (*Dat.*)); erkünsteln, erzwingen (*smiles*); schänden, notzüchtigen (*a woman*); hochzüchten (*Hort.*); künstlich in die Höhe treiben (*prices, etc.*); zu Tode hetzen (*simile*); zum Trumpfen zwingen (*Cards*); (*fig.*) *– s.th. down s.o.'s throat*, einem etwas aufzwingen; *– a p.'s hand*, einen nötigen; (*fig.*) einen gegen seinen Willen zu etwas antreiben; *– the pace*, das Tempo beschleunigen; *– along*, vorwärtstreiben; *– away*, wegreißen; *– back*, zurücktreiben; *– down*, hinunterdrücken; *be –d down*, notlanden (*Av.*); *– forward*, vorwärtstreiben; *– from*, abbringen, abringen, abpressen; *– on*, antreiben; *– open*, mit Gewalt aufbrechen *or* erbrechen, sprengen; *– out*, heraustreiben; *– out of*, vertreiben aus; *– through*, durchbrechen, durchdrücken, durchquetschen. **–d,** *adj.* gezwungen, erkünstelt, forciert, Zwangs–; *–d labour*, die Zwangsarbeit; *–d landing*, die Notlandung; *–d loan*, die Zwangsanleihe; *–d march*, der Gewaltmarsch, Eilmarsch; *–d smile*, erkünsteltes Lächeln; *–d style*, unnatürlicher Stil. **–ful,** *adj.* kräftig, wirkungsvoll, eindrucksvoll; eindringlich, ungestüm; gehaltvoll (*style*). **–fulness,** *s.* das Ungestüm, die Wucht, der Schwung, Schmiß. **--pump,** *s.* die Druckpumpe, Kompressionspumpe. *See* **forcible, forcing.**

[2]**force,** *v.a. see* **farce 1. –meat,** *s.* gehacktes Füllfleisch, das Füllsel.

forceps [ˈfɔ:sɛps], *s.* die Pinzette, Zange (*Surg.*).

forc–ible [ˈfɔ:sɪbl], *adj.* heftig, gewaltsam, Zwangs–; wirksam, eindringlich, überzeugend, zwingend; *–ible detainer*, gewaltsame Entziehung; *–ible feeding*, zwangsweise Ernährung. **–ing** [ˈfɔ:sɪŋ], *s.* das Zwingen; Treiben (*Hort.*). **–ing-house,** *s.* das Treibhaus.

ford [fɔ:d], 1. *s.* die Furt. 2. *v.a.* durchwaten. **–able,** *adv.* durchwatbar.

fore [fɔ:], 1. *adv.* vorn; *–!* Achtung! (*golf*); *– and aft*, längsschiff, vorn und hinten (*Naut.*); *--and-aft sail*, das Stagsegel; *to the –*, zur Hand, zur Stelle, vorhanden; (*coll.*) am Ruder; *be well to the –*, sehr im Vordergrund stehen; *come to the –*, hervortreten, in den Vordergrund treten, zum Vorschein kommen. 2. *adj.* Vor–, vorder. **–arm** 1. [ˈfɔ:rɑ:m], *s.* der Unterarm. 2. [fɔrˈɑ:m], *v.a.* im voraus bewaffnen. **–bode,** *v.a.* weissagen, voraussagen, vorbedeuten, ankündigen; ahnen. **–boding,** *s.* das Vorzeichen; die Voraussage, Prophezeiung; (böse) Ahnung. **--cabin,** *s.* vordere Kajüte. **–cast,** 1. *s.* die Vorhersage, Voraussage; *weather –cast*, der Wetterbericht, die Wettervorhersage. 2. *v.a.* vorhersehen, voraussagen, im voraus feststellen. **–castle** [ˈfoʊksl], *s.* die Back, das Vorderdeck (*Naut.*); *–castle crew* or *men*, die Backsdivision. **–close,** *v.a.* ausschließen, abweisen, präkludieren (*Law*); *–close a mortgage*, eine Hypothek für verfallen erklären. **–closure** [–ˈkloʊʒə], *s.* die Ausschließung; Verfallserklärung, Präklusion (*Law*). **–court,** *s.* der Vorhof. **--deck,** *s.* das Vorderdeck. **–doom,** *v.a.* vorher bestimmen (*to*, zu, für); im voraus verurteilen. **–fathers,** *pl.* die Vorfahren, Ahnen. **–finger,** *s.* der Zeigefinger. **–foot,** *s.* der Vorderfuß; vorderes Kielende (*of a ship*). **–front,** *s.* die Vorderseite; erste *or* vorderste

Reihe; *–front of the battle*, vorderste Schlachtlinie; (*usually fig.*) *be in the –front*, im Vordergrund stehen. **–go,** *v.a. & n.* vorangehen, vorhergehen (*Dat.*). **–going,** *adj.* vorhergehend, früher erwähnt, obig; (*N.B.* **forgo**). **–gone,** *adj.* von vornherein feststehend, vorherbestimmt, unvermeidlich; *–gone conclusion*, ausgemachte Sache; *–gone opinion*, vorgefaßte Meinung. **–ground,** *s.* der Vordergrund; *in the left –ground*, im Vordergrund links. **–hand,** *s.* die Vorderhand (*of horse*); *–hand stroke*, der Vorhandschlag (*Tenn.*). **–handed** *adj.* mit Vorhand (*Tenn.*). **–head** ['fɔrɪd], *s.* die Stirn. **– –hold,** *s.* der Vorderraum (*Naut.*).

foreign ['fɔrɪn], *adj.* ausländisch, auswärtig; (*fig.*) fremd (*to* (*Dat.*)); nicht gehörig *or* passend (*to*, zu); *– affairs*, die Außenpolitik; *Secretary of State for – Affairs*, der Minister des Äußeren, Außenminister; *– attachment*, die Beschlagnahme fremden Eigentums; *– bill*, der Auslandswechsel; *– body*, der Fremdkörper (*in eye*), Fremdstoff; *– country*, das Ausland; *– exchange*, Devisen (*pl.*); *– language*, die Fremdsprache; *– legion*, die Fremdenlegion; *– Office*, das Ministerium des Äußeren, Außenministerium; Auswärtiges Amt; *– parts*, see *– country*; *– –plea*, der Einspruch gegen den Richter (*Law*); *– policy*, die Außenpolitik; *– to my purpose*, meinem Zwecke fernliegend; *– Secretary*, der Außenminister; *– trade*, der Außenhandel. **–er,** *s.* der Ausländer, Fremde(r), *m.* **–ness,** *s.* die Fremdheit; Fremdartigkeit.

fore– –judge, *v.a.* im voraus *or* voreilig urteilen. **–know** [fɔː'noʊ], *ir.v.a.* vorherwissen, im voraus wissen. **–knowledge,** *s.* das Vorherwissen. **–land,** *s.* das Vorland; Vorgebirge, die Landspitze. **–leg,** *s.* das Vorderbein. **–lock,** *s.* die Stirnlocke; *take time by the –lock*, die Gelegenheit beim Schopfe fassen. **–man,** *s.* der Obmann (*of a jury*); Werkführer, Werkmeister, Vorarbeiter, Polier, Aufseher. **–mast,** *s.* der Fockmast. **–mentioned,** *adj.* vor(her)erwähnt. **–most,** 1. *adj.* vorderst, erst, vornehmst. 2. *adv.* zuerst; voran, an erster Stelle; *first and –most*, zu allererst; *head –most*, mit dem Kopf zuvorderst. **–noon,** *s.* der Vormittag.

forensic [fo'rɛnsɪk], *adj.* gerichtlich, Gerichts–; *– medicine*, gerichtliche Medizin.

fore–ordain [fɔːrɔː'deɪn], *v.a.* vorher bestimmen (*Eccl.*); (*fig.*) vorherbestimmen. **–ordination,** *s.* die Vorherbestimmung (*Eccl.*). **–quarters,** *pl.* die Vorhand (*of a horse*). **– –reach,** *v.a. & n.* überholen, übersegeln (*Naut.*). **–runner,** *s.* der Vorläufer, Vorfahr; (*fig.*) Vorbote, das Vorzeichen. **–sail** ['fɔːsl], *s.* das Focksegel. **–see,** *ir.v.a.* voraussehen, vorhersehen, vorherwissen. **–shadow,** *v.a.* ahnen lassen, vorher andeuten. **–shadowing,** *s.* die Vorahnung. **– –sheet,** *s.* die Fockschot (*Naut.*). **–shore,** *s.* das (Küsten)Vorland, Uferland, der Strand. **–shorten,** *v.a.* in der Verkürzung zeichnen, verkürzen. **–show,** *v.a.* vorher anzeigen, vorbedeuten. **–sight,** *s.* die Voraussicht; Vorsorge, Vorsicht, der Vorbedacht; das (Visier)Korn (*of a gun*). **–skin,** *s.* die Vorhaut (*Anat.*).

forest, 1. *s.* der Wald, Forst, die Waldung. 2. *v.a.* aufforsten, beforsten, mit Wald bedecken. **–er,** *s.* der Förster; Waldarbeiter, Waldbewohner. **– fire,** der Waldbrand. **–ry,** *s.* die Forstkultur, Forstwirtschaft, das Forstwesen.

fore–stall, *v.a.* zuvorkommen (*a p.* (*Dat.*)), vorbeugen (*a th.* (*Dat.*)); vorwegnehmen; vereiteln (*a th.* (*Acc.*)); im voraus aufkaufen (*C.L.*); *–stall the market*, durch Aufkauf den Markt beherrschen. **–stay,** *s.* das Fockstag (*Naut.*). **–taste** ['fɔːteɪst], *s.* der Vorgeschmack. **–tell,** *ir.v.a.* vorhersagen; im voraus anzeigen. **–thought,** *s.* der Vorbedacht, die Vorsorge. **–top,** *s.* der Fockmars, Vormars (*Naut.*). **– –topgallant,** *adj.* Vorbram– (*Naut.*); *– –topgallant mast*, die Vorbramstenge. **– –top-mast,** *s.* die Vormarsstenge.

forever [fɔr'ɛvə], *adv.* auf immer, für immer, ewig.

fore–warn [fɔː'wɔːn], *v.a.* vorher warnen (*of*, vor), vorhersagen. **–woman,** *s.* die Vorsteherin, Aufseherin, Werkführerin. **–word** ['fɔːwəːd], *s.* das Vorwort. **–yard,** *s.* die Fockrahe (*Naut.*).

forfeit ['fɔːfɪt], 1. *v.a.* verwirken, verlieren, einbüßen, verscherzen. 2. *adj.* verwirkt, verfallen. 3. *s.* die Verwirkung; Buße, das Pfand; Reuegeld; *pl.* Pfänderspiel; *pay a –*, ein Pfand geben; *pay the –*, das Reugeld zahlen; *play* (*at*) *–s*, Pfänderspiele machen. **–able,** *adj.* verlierbar, verwirkbar. **–ure** [–fɪtʃə], *s.* die Verwirkung, Einbuße, der Verlust.

forfend [fɔː'fɛnd], *v.a.* verwehren, verhindern, fernhalten, abwehren; *Heaven – !* Gott verhüte!

forgather [fɔːgæðə], *v.n.* zusammenkommen, sich treffen.

forgave [fɔː'geɪv], *see* **forgive.**

forg–e [fɔːdʒ], 1. *v.a.* schmieden; (*fig.*) ausdenken, erfinden, ersinnen, erdichten; fälschen, nachmachen (*a document*); *–e coin*, falschmünzen. 2. *v.n.* mit Wucht dahinfahren; *–e ahead*, immer vorwärtskommen, sich an die Spitze drängen *or* vorarbeiten; die Führung übernehmen. 3. *s.* die Schmiede; der Herd, die Esse, das Schmiedefeuer (*Metall.*); *drop –e*, die Gesenkschmiede. **–eable,** *adj.* schmiedbar. **–er,** *s.* der Schmied; Fälscher; (*fig.*) Erfinder; *–er of coin*, Falschmünzer. **–ery,** *s.* das Fälschen, die Fälschung. **–ing,** *s.* das Schmiedestück.

forget [fə'gɛt], 1. *ir.v.a.* vergessen; unterlassen, vernachlässigen, außer Acht lassen; *– o.s.*, sich vergessen; *never to be forgotten*, unvergeßlich. 2. *ir.v.n.* vergessen; *I –*, ich habe vergessen, ich kann mich nicht (mehr) erinnern, ich weiß nicht mehr; *– about a th.*, eine S. vergessen. **–ful,** *adj.* vergeßlich; *be –ful of*, vergessen. **–fulness,** *s.* die Vergeßlichkeit; Vernachlässigung, Vergessenheit. **– –me-not,** *s.* das Vergißmeinnicht.

forgiv–able [fə'gɪvəbl], *adj.* verzeihlich. **–e** [fə'gɪv], *ir.v.a.* vergeben, verzeihen (*a p.* (*Dat.*)); erlassen (*a debt, etc.*); *his mistake was –en him* or *he was –en his mistake*, sein Fehler wurde ihm verziehen; *not to be –en*, unverzeihlich. **–eness,** *s.* die Vergebung, Verzeihung. **–ing,** *adj.* nachsichtig, versöhnlich, mild. **–ingness,** *s.* die Versöhnlichkeit.

forgo [fɔː'goʊ], *v.a.* verzichten auf (*Acc.*), abstehen von, aufgeben; (*N.B.* **forego**).

forgot [fə'gɔt], **forgotten,** *see* **forget.**

fork [fɔːk], 1. *s.* die Gabel, Forke (*Agr.*); Gabelung, Abzweigung (*of a road, etc.*); *tuning –*, die Stimmgabel (*Mus.*). 2. *v.a.* mit der Gabel aufladen; (*sl.*) *– out money*, Geld herausrücken. 3. *v.n.* sich gabeln, sich spalten; (*sl.*) *– out*, blechen, bluten. **–ed,** *adj.* gabelig, gabelförmig, gespalten.

forlorn [fə'lɔːn], *adj.* verlassen, einsam; hilflos, hoffnungslos, unglücklich, elend; *all –*, mutterseelenallein; *– hope*, der Sturmtrupp, verlorene(r) Posten; (*sl.*) das Himmelfahrtskommando (*Mil.*); (*fig.*) verzweifeltes *or* aussichtsloses Unternehmen.

form [fɔːm], **1.** *s.* die Gestalt, Form, Figur; Ordnung, Anordnung; das Muster, Modell, die Schablone; Erscheinungsform, der Zustand, die Verfassung, Art und Weise, Methode; gesellschaftliche Form, die Förmlichkeit, Zeremonie, Formalität, Äußerlichkeit, Sitte, der Gebrauch; (*usually* **–e**) die Druckform (*Typ.*); Schulbank, der Sitz; die (Schul)Klasse; der Vordruck, das Formular (*C.L., etc.*); (*a*) (*with nouns*) *application –*, das Antragsformular; *matter of –*, die Formsache, leere Förmlichkeit, bloße Äußerlichkeit; *– of prayer*, die Gebetformel; *requisition –*, der Bestellzettel; *– of worship*, vorgeschriebener Gottesdienst; (*b*) (*with adjectives*) *that is bad –*, das schickt sich nicht; *good –*, guter Ton, der Takt; *the second –*, die Quinta; *the sixth –*, die Prima; *mere –*, see *matter of –*; (*c*) (*with prepositions*) *for –'s sake*, der bloßen Form wegen, zum Schein; *in the – of*, in der Erscheinungsform (*Gen.*); *be in –*, in Form *or* guter Verfassung sein (*Sport*); *in due –*, in gehöriger Form, vorschriftsmäßig; (*coll.*) *in good* or *great –*, in bester Verfassung; *out of –*, in schlechter Verfassung (*Sport*); *under the – of*, see *in the – of*. **2.** *v.a.* formen, bilden, gestalten (*into*, zu); ausbilden, heranbilden; hervorbringen, schaffen, entwickeln; (an)ordnen, entwerfen, erdenken, ersinnen (*a plan, etc.*); aufstellen, formieren (*a line of battle*); vereinigen (*into*, in (*Acc.*) *or* zu); ausmachen, dienen als; *– an alliance*, eine Verbindung eingehen, ein Bündnis schließen; *– an estimate*, eine Schätzung machen; – *a habit*, eine Gewohnheit annehmen; – *an idea*, eine Idee fassen; – *an opinion*, sich (*Dat.*) eine Meinung bilden; – *the passive*, das Passiv bilden (*Gram.*). **3.** *v.n.* sich bilden *or* gestalten *or* formen, Gestalt gewinnen; – *up*, antreten (*Mil.*); – *up into line*, sich in einer Linie formieren. **--master,** *s.* der Klassenlehrer. *See* **formless.**

formal ['fɔːməl], *adj.* förmlich, in gehöriger Form, bindend; formell, feierlich, umständlich; steif, streng; gewohnheitsgemäß; äußerlich, scheinbar; formal, wesentlich (*Phil.*). **-ism** [–ɪzm], *s* der Formalismus. **-ist** [–ɪst], *s.* der Formenmensch. **-ity** [–'mælɪtɪ], *s.* die Förmlichkeit, Formsache, Formalität; Steifheit, Umständlichkeit; *without –ities*, ohne Umstände. **-ize,** *v.a.* zur Formsache machen; feste Form geben.

formal-dehyde [fɔː'mældɪhaɪd], *s.*, **-in** ['fɔːməlɪn], *s.* das Formaldehyd, Ameisenaldehyd (*Chem.*).

format ['fɔːmæt], *s.* das Format.

formati-on [fɔː'meɪʃən], *s.* das Bilden, die Formung, Gestaltung; Bildung, Entstehung, der Aufbau, die Gliederung; Formation (*Geol.*, *Mil.*); der Verband, Truppenverband (*Mil.*); die Flugordnung (*Av.*). **-ve** ['fɔːmətɪv], **1.** *adj.* bildend, formend; formbildend (*Gram. & Geol.*); plastisch. **2.** *s.* formbildendes Element (*Gram.*).

form-e [fɔːm], *s.* die (Druck)Form (*Typ.*). **-er** ['fɔːmə], *s.* der Bildner, Gestalter; Spant (*Av.*).

former, *adj.* vorig, früher, vorhergehend, vorherig; ehemalig; ersterwähnt, erste(r)(s), jene(r)(s) (*of two*). **-ly,** *adv.* ehemals, vormals, ehedem, früher.

formic ['fɔːmɪk], *adj.* ameisensauer; – *acid*, die Ameisensäure. **-ary,** *s.* der Ameisenhaufen. **-ation** [–'keɪʃən], *s.* das Ameisenlaufen (*Med.*).

formidable ['fɔːmɪdəbl], *adj.* furchtbar, schrecklich.

formless ['fɔːmlɪs], *adj.* formlos, gestaltlos.

formula ['fɔːmjʊlə], *s.* (*pl.* –e [lɪː], –s), die Formel; das Rezept (*Med.*), die Vorschrift. **-te** [–leɪt], *v.a.* formulieren, darlegen, klarlegen. **-tion** [–'leɪʃən], *s.* die Formulierung.

fornicat-e ['fɔːnɪkeɪt], *v.n.* Unzucht treiben, huren. **-ion** [–'keɪʃən], *s.* die Unzucht, Hurerei. **-or,** *s.* der Hurer, Hurenbock.

forsake [fə'seɪk], *ir.v.a.* aufgeben (*Acc.*); entsagen (*Dat.*), verlassen, im Stich lassen, sitzen lassen. **-n,** *adj.* einsam, verlassen.

forsook [fə'sʊk], *see* **forsake.**

forsooth [fə'suːθ], *adv.* (*iron.*) fürwahr, wahrlich, traun.

forswear [fɔː'swɛə], *ir.v.a.* entsagen; (*archaic*) abschwören, eidlich abieugnen (*a debt, etc.*); – *a p.'s company*, jemandes Umgang meiden; – *o.s.*, einen Meineid leisten.

fort [fɔːt], *s.* das Fort, Festungswerk; die Feste, Schanze; Handelsniederlassung.

forte ['fɔːtɪ], **1.** *adv.* laut (*Mus.*). **2.** *s.* die Stärke, starke Seite, ausgesprochene Fähigkeit.

forth [fɔːθ], *adv.* fort, weiter, von . . . an *or* ab, fortan (*of time*); her, vor, hervor; heraus, hinaus; draußen (*of place*); *from this time* –, von jetzt an, künftighin; *and so* –, und so fort, und so weiter; *back and* –, hin und her; *come* –, hervortreten; *set* –, *v.a.* darlegen, klarlegen; *v.n.* (*archaic*) eine Reise antreten. **-coming,** *adj.* bevorstehend; im Erscheinen begriffen (*of books*); (*fig.*) bereit, entgegenkommend (*of persons*); *be –coming*, erscheinen, eintreten, zum Vorschein kommen, sich zeigen, erfolgen, in die Wege geleitet werden. **-right, 1.** *adj.* gerade, offen. **2.** *adv.* geradeaus. **-with,** adv sogleich, sofort, ohne weiteres.

fortieth ['fɔːtɪɪθ], **1.** *num. adj.* vierzigst. **2.** *s.* der, die, das Vierzigste; das Vierzigstel.

fortif-ication [fɔːtɪfɪ'keɪʃən], *s.* das Stärken, Verstärken; die Befestigung; Befestigungskunst; (*often pl.*) das Befestigungswerk, Festungswerk, die Befestigungsanlage, Festung. **-ied** [–faɪd], *adj. see* **-y. -ier,** *s.* das Stärkungsmittel. **-y** ['fɔːtɪfaɪ], *v.a.* befestigen (*also fig.*); stärken, verstärken, ermutigen; bestärken, bekräftigen, erhärten; *–y o.s. against*, sich wappnen gegen.

fortissimo [fɔːtɪsɪmoʊ], *adv.* sehr laut (*Mus.*).

fortitude ['fɔːtɪtjʊːd], *s.* die Seelenstärke, der Mut.

fortnight ['fɔːtnaɪt], *s.* vierzehn Tage; *this day* –, heute über 14 Tage *or* in 14 Tagen; *a – ago*, heute vor 14 Tagen; *Sunday* –, Sonntag über 14 Tage *or* in 14 Tagen; *this* –, seit 14 Tagen; *a –'s holiday*, ein vierzehntägiger Urlaub. **-ly, 1.** *adj.* vierzehntägig. **2.** *adv.* alle vierzehn Tage. **3.** *s.* die Halbmonatsschrift.

fortress ['fɔːtrɪs], *s.* die Festung.

fortuit-ous [fɔː'tjʊɪtəs], *adj.* zufällig. **-ousness,** *s.* **-y** [fɔː'tjʊɪtɪ], *s.* der Zufall, die Zufälligkeit.

fortun-ate ['fɔːtʃənət], *adj.* glücklich; günstig, glückverheißend. **-ately,** *adv.* glücklicherweise, zum Glück. **-e** ['fɔːtʃʊn, –tjʊn], *s.* das Glück; der Glücksfall, glücklicher Zufall; das Geschick, Schicksal; Vermögen, der Reichtum; die Mitgift; Glücksgöttin (*Myth.*); *turn of –e*, die Schicksalswende, der Glückswechsel; *wheel of –e*, das Glücksrad; (*a*) (*with adjectives*) *bad –e*, see *ill –e*; *good –e*, das Glück; *by good –e*, glücklicherweise, zum Glück; *with good –e*, wenn man Glück hat; *ill –e*, das Unglück; (*b*) (*with verbs*) *be the architect of one's own –e*, seines Glückes Schmied sein; *come into a –e*, ein Vermögen erben; *–e favours the bold*, dem Mutigen lächelt das Glück; *make a –e*, sich (*Dat.*) ein Vermögen erwerben; *make one's –e*, sein Glück machen; *marry a –e*, eine reiche Partie machen; *seek one's –e*, sein Glück suchen; *spend a small –e on*, ein kleines Vermögen geben für; *step into a –e*, see *come into a –e*; *tell –es*, wahrsagen; *have one's –e told*, sich (*Dat.*) wahrsagen lassen; *try one's –e*, sein Schicksal versuchen. **-e-hunter,** *s.* der Mitgiftjäger, Geldfreier. **-eless,** *adj.* vermögenslos. **-e-teller,** *s.* der Wahrsager. **-e-telling,** *s.* das Wahrsagen.

forty ['fɔːtɪ], **1.** *num. adj.* vierzig; (*coll.*) – *winks*, das Schläfchen. **2.** *s.* die Vierzig; *the forties*, die Vierziger.

forum ['fɔːrəm], das Forum; (*fig.*) Tribunal, Gericht.

forward ['fɔːwəd], **1.** *adj.* vorn (befindlich), vorder, vorgerückt, vorwärts gerichtet; bereitwillig, entgegenkommend; voreilig, vorlaut, naseweis; frühreif, frühzeitig; vorgerückt, vorgeschritten; auf Zeit *or* spätere Lieferung (*as contract*) (*C.L.*); – *deal*, das Termingeschäft. **2.** *adv.* vorwärts; weiter, fort; *from this time* –, von jetzt an; *bring* –, vorwärtsbringen; früher beginnen lassen; vorbringen, beibringen (*argument, etc.*); einbringen (*a law, etc.*); vortragen, übertragen (*C.L.*); *brought* or *carried* –, der Übertrag (*C.L.*); *go* –, fortschreiten; (*fig.*) *push o.s.* –, sich hervortun; *look – to*, entgegensehen (*Dat.*). **3.** *v.a.* fördern, beschleunigen; begünstigen; (weiter) befördern, absenden, spedieren; nachschicken (*a letter*); *goods to be –ed*, Speditionsgüter. **4.** *s.* der Stürmer (*Footb.*). **-er,** *s.* der Nachsender; Spediteur. **-ing,** *s.* die Versendung, Spedition. **-ing-agent,** *s.* der Spediteur. **-ing-house,** *s.* das Speditionsgeschäft. **-ing-note,** *s.* der Frachtbrief. **-ness,** *s.* der Eifer; die Frühreife, Frühzeitigkeit; Voreiligkeit, Keckheit, Dreistigkeit. **-s,** *adv. see* – 2; *backwards and –s*, hin und her.

fosse [fɔs], *s.* der Graben; die Höhle, Grube (*Anat.*).

fossil ['fɔsɪl], **1.** *adj.* ausgegraben, fossil, versteinert; (*fig.*) verknöchert, rückständig, veraltet. **2.** *s.* das Fossil, die Versteinerung; (*coll.*) rückständige *or* verknöcherte Person. **-iferous** *adj.* fossilienhaltig. **-ization** [fɔsɪlaɪ'zeɪʃən], *s.* die Versteinerung. **-ize** ['fɔsɪlaɪz], **1.** *v.a.* versteinern. **2.** *v.n.* sich versteinern; (*fig.*) verknöchern.

fossorial [fə'sɔːrɪəl], *adj.* grabend.

foster ['fɔstə], *v.a.* nähren, pflegen, aufziehen; (*fig.*) hegen, begünstigen, befördern, günstig sein (*Dat.*). **--brother,** *s.* der Pflegebruder. **--child,** *s.* das Pflegekind. **-er** [–rə], *s.* der Pflegevater; die Amme. **--father,** *s.* der Pflegevater. **-ling,** *s.* das Pflegekind, der Schützling. **--mother,** *s.* die Pflegemutter; Kükenamme.

fought [fɔːt], *see* **fight.**

foul [faʊl], **1.** *adj.* schmutzig, unrein, verschmutzt; (*fig.*) widerwärtig, widerlich, ekelhaft, garstig, anrüchig, verrucht, unzüchtig, zotig; regelwidrig, ungehörig, unredlich, unehrlich; voll(er) Korrekturen (*Typ.*); unklar (*Naut.*); *fall – of a p.*, bei einem Anstoß erregen, mit einem einen Zusammenstoß haben, über einen herfallen; *run – of*, festfahren auf (*Naut.*); *– air*, die Abluft; *the anchor is –*, der Anker ist unklar; *– bottom*, schlechter (Anker)Grund; bewachsener Boden (*of ship*); *– breath*, übelriechender Atem; *– chimney*, verrußter Schornstein; *– copy*, das Unreine, vielfach korrigiertes Konzept (*Typ.*); *– dealings, pl.* die Betrügerei; *– deed*, die Schandtat; *– fiend*, böser Feind, der Teufel; *– gun-barrel*, verstopftes Rohr; *– language*, gemeine *or* schmutzige Reden (*pl.*), Zoten (*pl.*); *– means*, unredliche Mittel; *– play*, falsches Spiel; (*fig.*) unredliche Machenschaften (*pl.*), die Verräterei; *– proof*, das Unreine (*Typ.*); *– tongue*, böse Zunge, loses Maul; *– water*, trübes *or* verdorbenes Wasser; *– weather*, schlechtes Wetter; *– wind*, widriger Wind. 2. *v.a.* beschmutzen, verschmutzen; (*fig.*) besudeln; anstoßen, anfahren, ansegeln, anrennen (gegen *or* an (*Acc.*)) (*of ships*); verwickeln (*the anchor*); verstopfen, (ver)sperren, hemmen; *– the points*, an der Weiche entgleisen. 3. *v.n.* sich verwickeln (*of anchor*), sich festfahren (*of ship*). 4. *s.* der Zusammenstoß (*Racing*), regelwidriger Stoß *or* Schlag (*Sport*). **–ly,** *adv.* schändlich; unredlich. **– -mouthed,** *adj.* ein loses Maul habend, schmutzige Reden führend. **–ness,** *s.* der Schmutz, die Unreinheit, Trübheit; (*fig.*) Gemeinheit, Unredlichkeit, Falschheit (*of intentions*).

[1]**found** [faʊnd], *see* **find.**

[2]**found,** *v.a.* gründen; stiften; den Grund legen von, errichten, einrichten; stützen, bauen (*on*, auf); *be –ed on*, beruhen auf (*Acc.*); *well- –ed*, gut begründet.

[3]**found,** *v.a.* gießen. **–ing,** *s.* der Guß.

foundation [faʊnˈdeɪʃən], *s.* die Gründung, Grundlegung; der Grund, die Grundlage, Unterlage; Bettung (*of a road, etc.*), das Grundmauerwerk (*of a wall*), Fundament (*of a building*); (*fig.*) der Ursprung, Anbeginn; die Stiftung, das Stift, die Anstalt; das Stipendium; *moral –*, sittliche Unterlage; *pious –*, milde Stiftung; *be on the – of*, ein Stipendiat sein (*Gen.*); *to its very –s*, bis in die Grundfesten. **–er,** *s.* der Stipendiat. **– garment,** *s.* das Korsett, Korselett, die Korsage. **– material,** *s.* das Steifleinen. **– -scholar,** *s.* der Freischüler, Stiftsschüler. **– -school,** *s.* die Stiftsschule. **– -stone,** *s.* der Grundstein.

[1]**founder** [ˈfaʊndə], *s.* der Gründer, Stifter; *–'s day*, der Stiftergedenktag; *–'s shares, pl.* Gründeraktien (*C.L.*).

[2]**founder,** *s.* der Schmelzer, Gießer.

[3]**founder,** *v.n.* sinken, untergehen (*Naut.*); (*fig.*) scheitern, zerschellen, zusammenbrechen; (ein)stürzen, einfallen (*as buildings*); steif werden, lahmen (*of a horse*).

foundling [ˈfaʊndlɪŋ], *s.* der Findling, das Findelkind. **– -hospital,** *s.* das Findelhaus.

foundry [ˈfaʊndrɪ], *s.* die Gießerei, Hütte.

fount [faʊnt], *s.* (*Poet.*) *see* **–ain**; der Satz, die Schrift; der Schriftguß (*Print.*). **–ain** [ˈfaʊntɪn], *s.* die Quelle, der Springbrunnen, das Wasserwerk; (*fig.*) der Ursprung, die Herkunft. **–ain-head,** *s.* (*fig.*) der Urquell, Ursprung, die Quelle. **–ain-pen,** *s.* die Füllfeder.

four [fɔː], 1. *num. adj.* vier. 2. *s.* die Vier; der Vierer, die Viermannschaft (*Rowing*); *on all –s*, auf allen vieren; *be on all –s with*, genau entsprechen (*Dat.*); *carriage and –*, der Vierspänner. **– -barrelled,** *adj.* Vierlings–. **– -cornered,** *adj.* viereckig. **– -edged,** *adj.* vierkantig. **– -engined,** *adj.* viermotorig. (*sl.*) **– -flusher,** *s.* der Schwindler, Mogler. **–fold,** *adj.* vierfach. **– -footed,** *adj.* vierfüßig. **– -handed,** *adj.* vierhändig (*Mus.*). **– -in-hand,** 1. *s.* der Vierspänner, das Viergespann. 2. *adv.*; *drive – -in-hand*, vierspännig fahren. **– -legged,** *adj.* vierbeinig. **– -part,** *adj.* vierstimmig (*Mus.*). **– -poster,** *s.* das Himmelbett. **–score,** *adj.* achtzig. **– -seater,** *s.* der Viersitzer. **–some** [–səm], *s.* der Vierer, das Viererspiel (*Golf*). **–square,** *adj.* viereckig, vierkantig. **– -stroke,** *adj.* Viertakt–. **–teen** [–tiːn], 1. *num. adj.* vierzehn. 2. *s.* die Vierzehn. **–teenth,** 1. *num. adj.* vierzehnt. 2. *s.* der, die, das Vierzehnte; das Vierzehntel. **–th** [ˈfɔːθ], 1. *num. adj.* viert; *–th form*, die Tertia (*school*). 2. *s.* der, die, das Vierte; das Viertel; die Quarte (*Mus.*). **–thly,** *adv.* viertens, zum vierten. **– -wheel,** *adj.*; *– -wheel drive*, der Vierradantrieb. **– -wheeled,** *adj.* vierräd(e)rig. **– -wheeler,** *s.* vierrädriger Wagen, die Droschke.

fowl [faʊl], 1. *s.* das Haushuhn; (*archaic*) der Vogel; *pl.* das Geflügel, Federvieh, die Hühner (*pl.*); *barndoor –*, das Haushuhn. 2. *v.n.* vogelstellen, Vögel fangen *or* schießen. **–er,** *s.* der Vogelfänger, Vogelsteller. **–ing,** *s.* der Vogelfang, die Vogeljagd. **–ing-piece,** *s.* die Vogelflinte. **– -run,** *s.* der Auslauf (für Hühner).

[1]**fox** [fɔks], 1. *s.* der Fuchs; (*fig.*) Schlaukopf; *set the – to keep the geese*, den Bock zum Gärtner machen; (*Prov.*) *with –es one must play the –*, mit den Wölfen muß man heulen. 2. *v.a.* (*sl.*) täuschen, betrügen, hintergehen, überlisten, hereinlegen. **– -brush,** *s.* der Fuchsschwanz. **– -earth,** *s.* der Fuchsbau. **–glove,** *s.* der Fingerhut (*Bot.*). **– -hole,** *s.* das Schlupfloch (*Mil.*), (*fig.*) der Schlupfwinkel. **–hound,** *s.* der Fuchsjagdhund. **–hunt,** *s.* die Fuchsjagd. **– -hunter,** *s.* der Fuchsjäger. **– -hunting,** *s.* die Fuchsjagd. **– -terrier,** *s.* der Foxterrier. **–trot,** *s.* der Foxtrott (*Danc.*). **–y,** *adj.* fuchsartig; schlau, listig; rotbraun.

[2]**fox,** *v.n.* stockfleckig werden. **–ed,** *adj.* stockfleckig.

foyer [ˈfwɑjeɪ, ˈfɔɪeɪ], *s.* die Wandelhalle, der Wandelgang (*Theat.*).

fracas [ˈfrækɑː], *s.* der Lärm, Aufruhr, Spektakel.

fraction [ˈfrækʃən], *s.* das Bruchstück, der Bruchteil; Bruch (*Math.*); *simple –*, gemeiner Bruch; *by a – of an inch*, um ein Haar; *representative –*, der Maßstab (*on maps*). **–al,** *adj.* gebrochen, fraktionär, fraktioniert (*Geol., Chem.*), Bruch–, Teil– (*Math., etc.*); minimal, unbedeutend; *–al distillation*, fraktionierte Destillation. **–ate** [–eɪt], *v.a.* fraktionieren (*Chem.*).

fractious [ˈfrækʃəs], *adj.* ärgerlich, zänkisch, widerspenstig. **–ness,** *s.* die Reizbarkeit, Zanksucht, Widerspenstigkeit.

fracture [ˈfræktʃə], 1. *s.* der Knochenbruch, Bruch, die Fraktur (*Med.*), Bruchfläche, Bruchstelle (*Min., etc.*). 2. *v.a.* (zer)brechen; *– one's leg*, sich (*Dat.*) das Bein brechen; *–d skull*, der Schädelbruch.

fragil–e [ˈfrædʒaɪl], *adj.* zerbrechlich, brüchig; (*fig.*) gebrechlich, hinfällig, schwach, zart. **–ity** [frəˈdʒɪlɪtɪ], *s.* die Zerbrechlichkeit, Brüchigkeit; (*fig.*) Gebrechlichkeit, Hinfälligkeit, Schwachheit, Zartheit.

fragment [ˈfrægmənt], *s.* das Bruchstück, Fragment, der Brocken, Bruchteil. **–al,** *adj.* Trümmer– (*Geol.*). **–ary** [–tərɪ], *adj.* abgebrochen, fragmentarisch, bruchstückartig. **–ation,** *s.* die Splitterwirkung, Zertrümmerung; *–ation bomb*, die Splitterbombe.

fragran–ce [ˈfreɪgrəns], *s.*, **–cy,** *s.* der Wohlgeruch, Duft, das Aroma. **–t** [–t], *adj.* wohlriechend, duftig, aromatisch; *be –t of*, duften von.

[1]**frail** [freɪl], *adj.* schwach, zart, gebrechlich; zerbrechlich, hinfällig; vergänglich; sündhaft. **–ness,** *s.* die Schwäche, Schwachheit, Gebrechlichkeit, Zerbrechlichkeit. **–ty,** *s. see* **–ness**; (moralische) Schwäche, der Fehltritt.

[2]**frail,** *s.* der Binsenkorb.

fraise [freɪz], *s.* das Pfahlwerk (*Fort.*); die Bohrfräse (*Mach.*).

fram–e [freɪm], 1. *v.a.* bilden, formen; einrichten, anpassen (*to* (*Dat.*)); einrahmen, einfassen; (*fig.*) zusammenfügen, zusammensetzen; ausdrücken, aussprechen; entwerfen, erfinden, ersinnen; schmieden; (*sl.*) verleumden, intrigieren gegen, hereinlegen. 2. *v.n.* sich anlassen, sich anschicken. 3. *s.* der Bau, das Gefüge, Gebilde; Gestell, der Bock, das Gerüst (*Mach.*), Spant (*Shipb., Av.*); die Einfassung, Einrahmung; der Rahmen; das Regal, der Chassisrahmen (*Typ.*); der Körperbau, die Form, Figur, Gestalt; *forcing- –e*, der Treibkasten (*Hort.*); *–e of mind*, die Geistesverfassung, Gemütsverfassung, Stimmung; *spectacle –e*, das Brillengestell; *window –e*, der Fensterrahmen. **–e-aerial,** *s.* die Rahmenantenne (*Rad.*). **–er,** *s.* der Bildner; Rahmenmacher; Erfinder. **–e-house,** *s.* das Holzhaus. **–e-saw,** *s.* die Spannsäge. (*sl.*) **–e-up,** *s.* die

Verschwörung; der Schwindel, die Machenschaft, abgekartetes Spiel. **–ework,** *s.* das Gerüst, Gerippe, Fachwerk, Riegelwerk, Gebälk (*Carp.*); Gestell (*Railw.*); (*fig.*) der Rahmen, das System, die Einrichtung; der Bau. **–ing,** *s.* die Einrahmung, Einfassung; die Erfindung, Entwerfung.

franchise ['fræntʃaɪz], *s.* das Vorrecht, Privilegium, die Konzession; das Gerechtsame; Stimmrecht, Wahlrecht, Bürgerrecht.

frangib–ility [frændʒɪ'bɪlɪtɪ], *s.* die Zerbrechlichkeit **–le** ['frændʒɪbl], *adj.* zerbrechlich.

[1]**frank** [fræŋk], *adj.* frei(mütig), offen, aufrichtig, offenherzig. **–ness,** *s.* die Offenheit, Freimütigkeit.

[2]**frank,** 1. *s.* (*archaic*) portofreier Brief; der Frankovermerk. 2. *v.a.* portofrei versenden *or* machen; (von Zahlung) befreien; umsonst befördern. **–ed,** *adj.* postfrei, frankiert.

frankincense [['fræŋkɪnsɛns], *s.* der Weihrauch.

franklin ['fræŋklɪn], *s.* (*archaic*) der Freisasse, kleiner Gutsbesitzer.

frantic ['fræntɪk], 1. *adj.* rasend, toll, wahnsinnig (*with*, von). 2. *adv.* außer sich (*with*, vor).

frap [fræp], *v.a.* sorren (*a rope*) (*Naut.*).

fratern–al [frə'tə:nl], *adj.* brüderlich. **–ity** [frə'tə:nɪtɪ], *s.* die Brüderlichkeit; Brüderschaft; Verbindung, Vereinigung, Gilde. **–ization** [frætə:-naɪ'zeɪʃən]. *s.* die Verbrüderung. **–ize** [–naɪz], *v.n.* sich verbrüdern.

fratricid–al [frætrɪ'saɪdl], *adj.* brudermörderisch; (*fig.*) sich gegenseitig zerstörend. **–e** ['frætrɪsaɪd], *s.* der Brudermord; Brudermörder.

fraud [frɔ:d], *s.* der Betrug, Schwindel (*against*, an (*Dat.*)); (*coll.*) Schwindler, Betrüger. **–ulence,** *s.*, **–ulency,** *s.* der Betrug, die Betrügerei. **–ulent,** *adj.* betrügerisch.

fraught [frɔ:t], *pred. adj.* (*poet.*) beladen; versehen (mit), voll (von); – *with danger*, gefahrvoll; – *with meaning*, bedeutungsvoll, bedeutungsschwer; – *with mischief*, unheilschwanger.

[1]**fray** [freɪ], *s.* die Rauferei, Schlägerei; *eager for the* –, kampflustig.

[2]**fray,** 1. *v.a.* durchreiben, abreiben, abnutzen; ausfransen. 2. *v.n.* sich abnutzen, sich ausfasern.

frazzle ['fræzl], *s.* (*sl.*) die Erschöpfung; *to a* –, bis zur völligen Erschöpfung.

freak [frɪ:k], *s.* die Laune, Grille, drolliger Einfall; -- (*of nature*), das Monstrum, die Mißgeburt. **–ish,** *adj.* grotesk; launenhaft, grillenhaft.

freckle ['frɛkl], 1. *s.* die Sommersprosse; das Fleckchen. 2. *v.a.* sprenkeln, tüpfeln. 3. *v.n.* Sommersprossen bekommen. **–d,** *adj.* mit Sommersprossen bedeckt, sommersprossig.

free [frɪ:], 1. *adj.* frei; ungebunden, unabhängig; uneingeschränkt, ungehemmt; kostenlos, unentgeltlich; erlaubt, zugänglich; ungebunden (*Chem.*); zwanglos, ungezwungen, freiwillig, gutwillig, offenherzig; zügellos, lose, dreist, derb; freigebig; (*a*) (*with nouns*) – *agent*, unabhängige Person; *carriage* –, Fracht bezahlt; – *and unencumbered estate*, unbelastetes *or* hypothekenfreies Erbgut; – *fight*, (*sl.*) *--for-all*, allgemeine Schlägerei; – *gift*, die Gratisprobe (*C.L.*); *have a – hand*, freie Hand haben; – *labour*, unorganisierte Arbeiterschaft; – *library*, die Volksbücherei, öffentliche Lesehalle; – *list*, die Liste der Empfänger von Freikarten *or* Freiexemplaren; – *liver*, der Schlemmer; – *love*, ungebundene Liebe; – *and easy manner*, zwangloses, ungeniertes *or* ungezwungenes Benehmen; – *pass*, die Freikarte; – *passage*, freie Überfahrt; freier Durchgang; – *play*, die Handlungsfreiheit; – *port*, der Freihafen; *post* -, franko; – *quarters*, das Freiquartier; *have the – run* (*of a house*), nach Belieben aus- und eingehen können; – *school*, die Freischule; – *scope*, freie Hand; – *state*, der Freistaat; – *trade*, uneingeschränkter Handel, der Freihandel; – *trader*, der Anhänger des Freihandels; – *translation*, nicht wörtliche Übersetzung; – *travel*, toter Gang (*Mech.*); *of one's own* – *will*, aus freiem Willen; (*b*) (*with verbs*) *he is – to do it*, es steht ihm frei, es zu tun; *make s.o. – of one's house*, einem sein Haus öffnen, einem zu seinem Hause freien Zutritt geben; *make – with a p.*, sich einem gegenüber zu viel herausnehmen, sich (*Dat.*) Freiheiten gegen einen erlauben; *make – with a th.*, mit etwas schalten und walten, etwas wie sein Eigentum behandeln; *set* –, befreien, freilassen, freimachen, entbinden, freigeben; (*c*) (*with prepositions*) – *from care*, sorgenfrei; – *from danger*, unbeschädigt; – *from error*, fehlerfrei; – *from fear*, furchtlos; – *from rules*, von Regeln befreit; – *of charge*, gebührenfrei, spesenfrei, kostenlos; *make a p. – of a city*, einem das Bürgerrecht verleihen; – *of debt*, schuldenfrei; – *of duty*, zollfrei; *be – of the harbour*, aus dem Hafen heraus sein; – *on board*, frei Schiff (*C.L.*); – *on rail*, frei Eisenbahn (*C.L.*); – *with one's money*, freigebig. 2. *v.a.* befreien, freilassen, freimachen, auslösen; – *from*, befreien von; – *from acid*, entsäuern, neutralisieren (*Chem.*). **–board,** *s.* das Freibord, die Tiefladelinie (*Naut.*). **–booter,** *s.* der Freibeuter. **–dman,** *s.* Freigelassene(r), *m.* **–dom,** *see* **freedom. –hand,** *adj.* freihändig; *–hand drawing*, das Freihandzeichnen. **--handed,** *adj.* freigebig. **–hold,** *s.* freier Grundbesitz; (*archaic*) das Freisassengut, Freilehen; *–hold residence*, das Haus auf eigenem Grund und Boden. *–holder*, *s.* der Grundbesitzer; (*archaic*) Freisasse. **--kick,** *s.* der Freistoß (*Footb.*). **–lance,** 1. *s.* freier Schriftsteller; der Freischärler, Söldner; (*fig.*) Unabhängige(r), *m.*, Parteilose(r), *m.* 2. *adj.* selbständig, unabhängig, auf eigene Faust, ohne Parteibindung. **–ly,** *adv.* frei, bereitwillig, ohne Zwang; reichlich, im Überflusse; vertraulich, freimütig; *bleed –ly*, reichlich *or* stark bluten; *drink –ly*, stark trinken. **–man,** *s.* freier Mann; der Ehrenbürger; Bürger; Wahlberechtigte(r), *m.*; der Meister (*of a guild*). **–martin,** *s.* unfruchtbare Kuh. **–mason,** *s.* der Freimaurer. **–masonry,** *s.* die Freimaurerei. **–ness,** *s.* die Freiheit; Offenheit; Freigebigkeit; *–ness of divine grace*, die freie Erteilung der göttlichen Gnade. **--spoken,** *adj.* offen, freimütig. **–stone,** *s.* der Sandstein. **--stone,** *adj.* (*plum, etc.*), die sich vom Steine leicht lösende (Pflaume, *etc.*). **–thinker,** *s.* der Freidenker, Freigeist. **–thinking,** *s.* die Freidenkerei, Freigeisterei. **--wheel,** 1. *s.* der Freilauf. 2. *v.n.* mit Freilauf fahren. **--wheeling,** *s.* der Freilauf. **--will,** 1. *s.* freier Wille, die Willensfreiheit. 2. *adj.* freiwillig.

freedom ['frɪ:dəm], *s.* die Freiheit, Unabhängigkeit, Selbstbestimmung, das Freisein, Befreitsein (*from*, von); Vorrecht, Nutznießungsrecht, freier Zutritt (*of*, zu); die Vertraulichkeit, Freimütigkeit, Ungezwungenheit; *take –s*, sich Freiheiten *or* Vertraulichkeiten herausnehmen (*with*, gegenüber); – *of a city*, das Bürgerrecht; – *of a company*, das Meisterrecht; – *of the seas*, die Freiheit der Meere.

freez–e [frɪ:z], 1. *v.a.* zum Gefrieren bringen (*water*); erfrieren lassen (*living beings*); tief kühlen (*food*); erstarren *or* schaudern machen; sperren, blockieren (*money, etc.*); (*coll.*) *–e s.o. out*, einen hinausekeln (*of*, aus). 2. *v.n.* (ge)frieren, zu Eis werden; einfrieren, zufrieren (*as a pond*), (*fig.*) erstarren; *–e to death*, erfrieren; (*coll.*) *–e on to a th.*, an etwas festhalten. **–er,** *s.* die Gefriermaschine. **–ing,** 1. *adj.* eisig. 2. *s.* das Gefrieren. **–ing-machine,** die Gefriermaschine. **–ing-mixture,** *s.* die Kältemischung. **–ing-point,** *s.* der Gefrierpunkt.

freight [freɪt], 1. *s.* die Fracht, Ladung; das Frachtgeld, der Frachtlohn; das Heuern; Heuergeld (*Naut.*); Speditionsgüter (*pl.*); *bill of* –, der Frachtbrief; – *out* (– *home*), die Hinfracht (Rückfracht). 2. *v.a.* heuern; befrachten, beladen (*a ship*); verfrachten, befördern (*goods*). **–age** [–tɪdʒ], *s.* die Schiffsladung, Fracht, der Transport; das Frachtgeld, die Frachtgebühr. **--car,** *s.* der Güterwagen (*Amer.*). **--carrier,** *s.* das Güterflugzeug. **–er,** *s.* der Verfrachter; Befrachter; Frachtdampfer. **--steamer,** *s.* (*Amer.*) der Frachtdampfer. **--train,** *s.* (*Amer.*) der Güterzug. **--yard,** *s.* (*Amer.*) der Güterbahnhof.

frenz–ied ['frɛnzɪd], *adj.* wahnsinnig, rasend. **–y** ['frɛnzɪ], *s.* der Wahnsinn, die Raserei.

frequen–cy ['frɪ:kwənsɪ], *s.* die Häufigkeit; Frequenz, Schwingungszahl (*Phys.*); *audio –cy*, die Tonfrequenz. *–cy-changer*, *s.* der Umrichter (*Rad.*); *high –cy*, die Hochfrequenz. *–cy selection*, die Grobeinstellung (*Rad.*). **–t** [–t], 1. *adj.* häufig; häufig wiederholt *or* wiederkehrend; *be –t*, häufig vorkommen; *–t visitor*, fleißiger Besucher. 2. *v.a.* [frɪ'kwɛnt], häufig *or* öfters besuchen, frequentieren. **–tative** [[frɪ'kwɛntətɪv], 1. *adj.* frequentativ (*Gram.*). 2. *s.* das Frequentativum (*Gram.*). **–ter** [frɪ'kwɛntə], *s.* fleißiger *or* regelmäßiger Besucher. **–tly,** *adv.* häufig, öfters, oft.

fresco ['frɛskoʊ], 1. *s.* die Freskomalerei, Kalkmalerei; das Freskogemälde, Fresko. 2. *v.a.* in Fresko malen.

fresh [frɛʃ], 1. *adj.* frisch, neu, verschieden, anders; ungesalzen (*as butter*); süß, trinkbar (*as water*); erfrischend, kühl, rein (*as air*); munter, blühend, lebhaft (*as complexion*); (*sl.*) frech, keck, anmaßend, dreist; – *air*, frische Luft; – *arrival*, der Neuankömmling, Neuling; – *water*, das Süßwasser. 2. *s.* das Süßwasser; Oberwasser; die Frühe, Kühle (*of the morning*). **–en,** 1. *v.a.* auffrischen, erfrischen, beleben. 2. *v.n.* frisch werden; *the wind –ens*, der Wind nimmt zu. (*sl.*) **–er,** *s.* der Fuchs (*Univ.*). **–et,** *s.* die Überschwemmung, das Hochwasser, die Flut. **–man,** *see* **–er. –ness,** *s.* die Frische; Neuheit, Unerfahrenheit. **–water,** *adj.* Süßwasser–, Binnenlands–; *–water fish*, der Süßwasserfisch, Flußfisch; *–water tank*, der Trinkwasserbehälter.

[1]**fret** [frɛt], 1. *v.a.* abreiben, aufreiben, verzehren, zerfressen, aushöhlen; kräuseln (*the surface of water, etc.*); (*fig.*) ärgern, reizen, aufregen; – *o.s.*, *see* – 2. 2. *v.n.* sich ärgern, sich Sorgen machen, sich quälen, sich grämen; – *and fume*, sich abärgern (*at*, über (*Acc.*)). 3. *s.* die Aufregung; der Ärger, Verdruß; (*coll.*) *be on the –*, aufgeregt *or* nervös sein. **–ful,** *adj.* ärgerlich, mürrisch, verdrießlich, reizbar. **–fulness,** *s.* der Unmut, die Verdrießlichkeit, Reizbarkeit.

[2]**fret,** 1. *v.a.* mit durchbrochener Arbeit verzieren (*Arch., etc.*). 2. *s.* griechische (Flecht)Verzierung, das Gitterwerk (*Arch.*). **–saw,** *s.* die Laubsäge. **–work,** *s.* die Laubsägearbeit; durchbrochene Arbeit.

[3]**fret,** (*usually pl.*) *s.* der Bund, die Griffleiste (*of a guitar, etc.*).

friab–ility [fraɪə'bɪlɪtɪ], *s.* die Sprödigkeit, Brüchigkeit, Bröckligkeit, Zerreibbarkeit. **–le** ['fraɪəbl], *adj.* mürbe, mulmig, spröde, brüchig, bröcklig, zerreibbar. **–leness,** *s. see* **–ility.**

friar ['fraɪə], *s.* der Mönch, Bettelmönch; *Austin* – der Augustiner; *Black* –, der Dominikaner; *Grey* –, der Franziskaner; *White* –, der Karmeliter; *–'s cowl*, die Mönchskappe (*Bot.*). **–y** [–rɪ], *s.* das (Mönchs)Kloster.

fricassee [frɪkə'sɪː], 1. *s.* das Frikassee. 2. *v.a.* frikassieren; *–d veal*, das Kalbsfrikassee.

fricative ['frɪkətɪv], *s.* der Reibelaut.

friction ['frɪkʃən], *s.* die Reibung (*also fig.*); das Frottieren (*Med.*); (*fig.*) die Schwierigkeit, Spannung, Reiberei. **–al,** *adj.* Reibungs–. **– –clutch,** *s.* die Reibungskupplung. **– –drive,** *s.* der Friktionsantrieb. **– –gear,** *s.* das Reibrädergetriebe. **– –primer,** *s.* der Abreißzünder. **– –wheel,** *s.* das Friktionsrad.

Friday ['fraɪdeɪ], *s.* der Freitag; *Good* –, der Karfreitag.

fried [fraɪd], *see* **fry.**

friend [frɛnd], *s.* der Freund, die Freundin; der Bekannte, Gefährte; Helfer, Förderer; *pl.* die Quäker (*pl.*); *bosom* –, der Busenfreund; – *at court*, einflußreicher Gönner; *a – in need is a – indeed*, in der Not erkennt man seine Freunde; *my honourable* –, mein Parteifreund (*Parl.*); *my learned* –, der Gegenanwalt (*Law*); *make a* –, sich (*Dat.*) einen Freund gewinnen; *make –s with*, sich anfreunden mit, Freundschaft schließen mit; *be –s with*, befreundet sein mit. **–less,** *adj.* freundlos. **–lessness,** *s.* die Freundlosigkeit. **–liness,** *s.* die Freundlichkeit, freundschaftliche Gesinnung, das Wohlwollen. **–ly,** *adj.* freundlich, freundschaftlich; freundschaftlich gesinnt, befreundet, günstig; *–ly match*, das Freundschaftsspiel; *–ly nation, –ly power*, befreundete Macht; *–ly society*, die Unterstützungskasse; *be on –ly terms with* . . ., auf freundschaftlichem Fuße stehen mit . . .; *–ly turn*, der Freundschaftsdienst. **–ship,** *s.* die Freundschaft; freundschaftliche Gesinnung.

frieze [frɪːz], *s.* der Fries (*Arch. & Weav.*).

frigate ['frɪgət], *s.* die Fregatte. **– –bird,** *s.* der Fregattvogel.

fright [fraɪt], 1. *s.* der Schrecken, Schreck, die Furcht, Angst, das Entsetzen; (*fig.*) die Fratze, Scheuche, das Schreckbild, Scheusal; (*coll.*) *get a* –, in Schrecken geraten; (*coll.*) *look a perfect* –, einfach verboten aussehen; *take* –, see *get a* –; scheu werden (*of horses*). 2. *v.a.* (*archaic & Poet.*); **–en,** *v.a.* erschrecken, in Furcht versetzen; *–en away*, verscheuchen; *–en a p. into doing*, einen durch Schreck dahin bringen zu tun; *–en a p. out of doing*, einen durch Schreck abbringen zu tun; *–en a p. out of his wits*, einen bis zum äußersten ängstigen; *–en s.o. to death*, einen in Todesangst versetzen. **–ful,** *adj.* schrecklich, gräßlich, fürchterlich, entsetzlich. **–fully,** *adv.* schrecklich; (*coll.*) äußerst, höchst. **–fulness,** *s.* die Schrecklichkeit; der Greuel, Greultaten (*pl.*).

frigid ['frɪdʒɪd], *adj.* kalt, frostig, eisig; gefühllos; kühl, abstoßend (*manner*); – *zones*, kalte Zonen. **–ity** [–'dʒɪdɪtɪ], *s.* die Kälte, Frostigkeit.

frill [frɪl], 1. *s.* die Halskrause, Handkrause, Rüsche; (Papier)Krause; *pl.* (*fig.*) der Tand, Schmuck. 2. *v.a.* kräuseln; mit einer Krause schmücken. 3. *v.n.* sich falten, sich kräuseln (*Phot.*). **–ing,** *s.* das Kräuseln; Krausen (*pl.*), der Stoff zu Rüschen. **–y,** *adj.* gekräuselt. **–ies,** *pl.* (*coll.*) feine Damenunterwäsche.

fringe [frɪndʒ], 1. *s.* die Franse, der Besatz; Rand, Saum, die Einfassung; (*fig.*) Grenze, äußerer Rand; (*coll.*) (*also pl.*) die Ponyfrisur. 2. *v.a.* mit Fransen besetzen, befransen; (*fig.*) umsäumen, einsäumen.

frippery ['frɪpərɪ], 1. *s.* der Flitterkram, Plunder, Tand. 2. *adj.* wertlos, nichtig, geringfügig.

frisk [frɪsk], 1. *v.n.* hüpfen und springen, umherhüpfen. 2. *v.a.* (*sl.*) durchsuchen. 3. *s.* das Hüpfen und Springen, der Freudensprung. **–iness,** *s.* die Munterkeit, Lebendigkeit. **–y,** *adj.* munter, lustig, lebhaft, ausgelassen.

frit [frɪt], 1. *s.* die Glasschmelzmasse, Fritte. 2. *v.a.* fritten (*glass*).

fritillary [frɪ'tɪlərɪ], *s.* die Schachbrettblume (*Bot.*); der Argusfalter (*Ent.*).

fritter ['frɪtə], 1. *s.* (*often pl.*) gebackener Eierteig (*Cook.*); *apple –s*, Apfelscheiben in Eierteig gebacken. 2. *v.a.* zerschneiden; zerstückeln; – *away*, verzetteln, vertrödeln, vergeuden.

frivol ['frɪvəl]; (*coll.*) – *away*, *v.a.* vertändeln. **–ity** [frɪ'vɔlɪtɪ], *s.* die Leichtfertigkeit, Frivolität; Wertlosigkeit, Nichtigkeit. **–ous** ['frɪvələs], *adj.* nichtig, wertlos, geringfügig unbedeutend (*of things*); leichtfertig, leichtsinnig, frivol (*of persons*).

frizz [frɪz], 1. *v.a.* kräuseln (*hair*). 2. *v.n.* sich kräuseln. 3. *s.* gekräuseltes Haar. **–le** ['frɪzl], 1. *v.n.* zischen. 2. *v.a.* rösten. **–ly,** *adj.*, **–y,** *adj.* kraus, gekräuselt.

fro [froʊ], *adv.*; (only in) *to and* –, hin und her, auf und ab.

frock [frɔk], 1. das (Damen)Kleid; Kinderröckchen; die Kutte (*of monks*); der Kittel. **– –coat,** *s.* der Gehrock. 2. *v.a.* in einen Rock kleiden; (*fig.*) mit einem Amt bekleiden (*a priest, etc.*).

frog [frɔg], *s.* der Frosch; Schnurbesatz, die Quaste (*Mil.*); der Degenhalter (*on belt*); das Kreuzungsstück, Herzstück (*of railway line*); die Gabel, der Strahl (*of hoof*); (*coll.*) *have a – in one's throat*, heiser sein; *leap-–*, das Bockspringen; *tree-–*, der Laubfrosch. **– –bit,** *s.* der Froschbiß (*Bot.*). **– –eater,** *s. see* **–gy** 2. **–ged** [–d], *adj.* mit Schnüren besetzt. **–gy,** 1. *adj.* froschartig, froschreich. 2. *s.* (*sl.*) der Froschesser, Franzose. **–hopper,** *s.* die Schaumzirpe (*Ent.*). **– –spawn,** *s.* der Froschlaich.

frolic ['frɔlɪk], 1. *s.* lustiger Streich, der Spaß, die Posse; Lustbarkeit, Ausgelassenhit. 2. *v.n.* Possen treiben, scherzen, spaßen, tollen, ausgelassen sein. **–some** [–səm], *adj.* lustig, fröhlich, vergnügt, ausgelassen. **–someness,** *s.* die Lustigkeit. Ausgelassenheit.

from [frɔm], *prep.* von; . . . her, von . . . weg, von . . . herab; von . . . an, seit; aus, aus . . . heraus; wegen, infolge von; nach, gemäß, in betreff; *apart* –, abgesehen von; – *the beginning*, vom Anfang an; – *a child*, von Kindheit an; – *day to day*, täglich; *defend* –, schützen vor; *descend* –, abstammen von;

– *my own experience*, aus eigener Erfahrung; *be far – thinking*, weit davon entfernt sein zu denken, einem fern liegen zu denken; – *first to last*, von A bis Z; *hide s.th. – s.o.*, etwas verbergen vor einem, einem etwas verbergen; *to judge – his appearance*, seinem Aussehen nach; *keep s.o. – doing s.th.*, einen abhalten *or* hindern etwas zu tun; – *life*, nach dem Leben; *live – hand to mouth*, von der Hand in den Mund leben; – *my point of view*, meiner Meinung nach; *come – school*, aus der Schule kommen; *suffer* –, leiden an (*Dat.*); *take s.th. – s.o.*, einem etwas wegnehmen; – *time to time*, von Zeit zu Zeit; – *what you have told me*, nach dem, was Sie mir gesagt haben; *where are you –?* wo stammen Sie her? – *above*, von oben herab; – *afar*, von weither, aus der Ferne; – *amidst*, mitten aus; – *among*, aus . . . heraus; – *before*, aus der Zeit vor; – *behind*, von hinten; – *below* or *beneath*, von unten; – *between*, zwischen . . . hervor; – *beyond*, von jenseits; – *on high*, aus der Höhe, von oben; – *out*, aus, aus . . . heraus; – *over*, von jenseits . . . her; – *under*, unter (*Dat.*) . . . hervor; – *within*, von innen; – *without*, von außen.

frond [frɔnd], *s.* der Wedel (*of fern*). **–age,** *s.* das Blattwerk. **–escence** [frɔnˈdɛsns], *s.* die Zeit der Blattbildung (*Bot.*). **–escent,** *adj.* blattbildend (*Bot.*). **–iferous** [–ˈdɪfərəs], *adj.* blättertragend, wedeltragend. **–ose** [–ˈdoʊs], *adj.* wedeltragend, dicht belaubt.

front [frʌnt], 1. *s.* die Vorderseite (*also Arch.*); vorderer Teil; die Frontpromenade (*at the seaside*); (*poet.*) die Stirn; (*fig.*) Kühnheit, Frechheit; falsches Haar; der Einsatz (*of a shirt, etc.*); die Front (*Mil.*); *show a bold* –, mit kecker Stirn auftreten; *at the* –, an der Front (*Mil.*); *cold* –, die Einbruchsfront, Kaltluftfront (*Meteor.*); *in* –, davor, an die *or* der Spitze; *in – of*, vor, gegenüber; *to the* –, nach vorne, voraus, voran; (*fig.*) *come to the* –, in den Vordergrund treten, sich auszeichnen; *warm* –, die Aufgleitfront, Warmluftfront (*Meteor.*). 2. *attrib.* Vorder–; – *bench*, die Ministerbank (*Parl.*); – *box*, die Vorderloge; – *door*, die Haustür; – *elevation*, die Vorderansicht (*Arch.*); – *garden*, der Vorgarten; – *line*, die Kampffront (*Mil.*); – *room*, das Vorderzimmer; – *row*, die Vorderreihe, erste Reihe; – *view*, die Vorderansicht; – *vowel*, der Vorderzungenlaut (*Phonet.*); – *wheel*, das Vorderrad. 3. *v.a.* gegenüberstehen *or* gegenüberliegen (*Dat.*); entgegentreten (*Dat.*); Trotz bieten (*Dat.*) (*a person*). 4. *v.n.* mit der Front liegen (*on to*, nach); *eyes –!* Augen geradeaus! (*Mil.*). **–age,** *s.* die Vorderfront (*Arch.*); die Frontbreite, Frontausdehnung (*Mil.*); *–age line*, die Baufluchtlinie (*Build.*). **–al,** 1. *adj.* Vorder–, Front–; Stirn– (*Anat.*); *–al attack*, der Frontalangriff. 2. *s.* die Fassade (*Arch.*); die Altardecke (*Eccl.*). **–ier** [ˈfrʌntɪə], *s.* die Grenze. **–iersman,** *s.* der Grenzbewohner. **–ispiece** [ˈfrʌntɪspɪːs], *s.* die Vorderseite; das Titelbild, Titelkupfer (*Typ.*). **–let** [ˈfrʌntlɪt], *s.* das Stirnband; die Stirn (*of animals*).

frost [frɔst], 1. *s.* der Frost; (*sl.*) Mißerfolg; *2 degrees of* –, zwei Grad Kälte; *ground* –, der Reif; *hoar* –, der Rauhreif. 2. *v.a.* mit Reif überziehen (*as a window*); mit Staubzucker bestreuen (*Cook.*); mattieren (*glass*). **–bite,** *s.* das Erfrieren, der Frostschaden. **–bitten,** *adj.* vom Frost beschädigt, erfroren. **–ed,** *adj.* bereift; mit Staubzucker bestreut; *–ed cake*, der Kuchen mit Zuckerguß; *–ed glass*, das Milchglas, Mattglas. **–iness,** *s.* der Frost, eisige Kälte (*also fig.*). **–ing,** *s.* die Zuckerglasur. **–y,** *adj.* eisig, eiskalt, frostig (*also fig.*); eisgrau, ergraut.

froth [frɔθ], 1. *s.* der Schaum, Abschaum, die Blume (*of beer*); (*fig.*) Nichtigkeit, Seichtigkeit. 2. *v.a.* zu Schaum schlagen. 3. *v.n.* schäumen, Schaum schlagen (*also fig.*). **–iness,** *s.* das Schäumen; Schäumige; (*fig.*) die Nichtigkeit, Leerheit, Hohlheit, Seichtigkeit, Schaumschlägerei. **–y,** *adj.* schaumartig, schäumig, moussierend; leer, nichtig, phrasenhaft (*of utterance*).

froward [ˈfroʊəd], *adj.* (*archaic*) widerspenstig, eigensinnig, trotzig. **–ness,** *s.* der Eigensinn, Trotz, die Widerspenstigkeit.

frown [fraʊn], 1. *s.* das Stirnrunzeln; finsterer Blick. 2. *v a.* durch finsteren Blick ausdrücken *or* einschüchtern; – *a p. into silence*, einen durch finstere Blicke zum Schweigen bringen. 3. *v.n.* die Stirn runzeln, finster dreinsehen, finster *or* scheel ansehen (*at*, *upon* (*Acc.*)) (*a person*). **–ing,** *adj.* finster, mürrisch.

frow–st [fraʊst], *s.* muffige *or* stickige Luft, der Muff, Mief. **–stiness, –ziness** [ˈfraʊzɪnɪs], *s.* die Muffigkeit, Ranzigkeit; Schmutzigkeit, Unordentlichkeit. **–sty, –zy** [ˈfraʊzɪ], *adj.* muffig, moderig, ranzig; schlumpig, schlampig, schmutzig, unordentlich.

froze [froʊz], *see* **freeze.** **–n** [–n], *adj.* gefroren; (*fig.*) nicht verwertbar (*C.L.*); *–n over* or *up*, zugefroren; *–n to death*, erfroren; *–n capital*, eingefrorenes Kapital; *–n meat*, das Gefrierfleisch; *–n ocean*, das Eismeer.

fruct–iferous [frʌkˈtɪfərəs], *adj.* fruchttragend. **–ification** [frʌtɪfɪˈkeɪʃən], *s.* die Befruchtung, Fruchtbildung. **–ify** [ˈfrʌktɪfaɪ], 1. *v.a.* befruchten (*also fig.*). 2. *v.n.* Früchte tragen. **–ose,** *s.* der Fruchtzucker.

frugal [ˈfruːgəl], *adj.* genügsam, sparsam; mäßig, frugal. **–ity** [–ˈgælɪtɪ], *s.* die Mäßigkeit, Sparsamkeit.

frugivorous [fruːˈdʒɪvərəs], *adj.* von Früchten lebend, fruchtfressend (*Zool.*).

fruit [fruːt], *s.* die Frucht (*also fig.*); Früchte (*pl.*), das Obst; (*fig. usually pl.*) die Folge, das Ergebnis, der Ertrag, Gewinn, Nutzen; *bear* –, Frucht bringen, Früchte tragen; (*fig.*) Nutzen gewähren; *dried* –, das Backobst, Dörrobst; *–s of the earth*, die Früchte der Erde; *the – of all my endeavours*, das Ergebnis aller meiner Bemühungen; *first –-s*, die Erstlinge; *fresh* –, rohes Obst; *stewed* –, das Kompott; *stone-–*, das Kernobst; *wall-–*, das Spalierobst. **–age** [–tɪdʒ], *s.* das Tragen (*of fruit trees*). **–arian** [–ˈtɛərɪən], *s.* der Rohköstler. **–-bearing,** *adj.* fruchttragend. **–-drop,** *s.* das Fruchtbonbon. **–erer** [–ərə], *s.* der Obsthändler. **–ful,** *adj.* fruchtbar; (*fig.*) ergiebig, ergebnisreich, reich (*of* or *in*, an (*Dat.*)). **–fulness,** *s.* die Fruchtbarkeit (*also fig.*). **–ion** [fruˈɪʃən], *s.* der Genuß, Vollgenuß; ersehnter Erfolg. **–less,** [ˈfruːtlɪs] *adj.* unfruchtbar; (*fig.*) fruchtlos, vergeblich, unnütz. **–lessness,** *s.* (*fig.*) die Fruchtlosigkeit. **–-salad,** *s.* der Obstsalat. **–-tree,** *s.* der Obstbaum. **–y** [ˈfruːtɪ], *adj.* fruchtartig; würzig (*of wine*, *also fig.*); (*fig.*) saftig.

frument–aceous [fruːmənˈteɪʃəs], *adj.* weizenartig, getreideartig. **–y** [ˈfruːməntɪ], *s.* süßer Weizenbrei.

frump [frʌmp], *s.* (*coll.*) altmodisch gekleidetes Frauenzimmer; *old* –, alte Schachtel. **–ish,** *adj.* altmodisch gekleidet.

frustrat-e [frʌsˈtreɪt], *v.a.* vereiteln, verhindern; durchkreuzen, zuschanden machen; *–e a p.'s hopes*, einen in seinen Erwartungen täuschen. **–ion** [–ˈtreɪʃən], *s.* die Vereitelung; Enttäuschung.

frustum [ˈfrʌstəm], *s.* der Stumpf (*Geom.*).

[1]**fry** [fraɪ], 1. *v.a.* in der Pfanne braten; *fried eggs*, Spiegeleier, Setzeier; *fried potatoes*, Bratkartoffeln. 2. *s.* Gebratene(s), *n.*; das Gekröse, Kaldauen (*pl.*). **–ing-pan,** *s.* die Bratpfanne; *out of the –ing-pan into the fire*, aus dem Regen in die Traufe.

[2]**fry,** *s.* die Fischbrut, der Fischrogen, junge Fische; (*fig.*) die Brut, Menge, der Haufe(n), Schwarm; *small* –, (*coll.*) kleine Kinder; (*sl.*) unbedeutende Leute.

fuchsia [ˈfjuːʃə], *s.* die Fuchsie (*Bot.*).

fuddle [ˈfʌdl], 1. *v.a.* berauschen. 2. *v.n.* sich betrinken. **–d,** *adj.* (*coll.*) angeheitert, angesäuselt.

fudge [fʌdʒ], 1. *s.* die Aufschneiderei; Täuschung, der Schwindel, das Blech, Flausen (*pl.*); weiches Zuckerwerk. 2. *int.* dummes Zeug! Unsinn! 3. *v.a.* & *n.* pfuschen, schwindeln; zurechtpfuschen.

fuel [ˈfjuːəl], 1. *s.* die Feuerung, das Heizmaterial, der Brennstoff; Kraftstoff, Treibstoff, Betriebsstoff; (*sl.*) Sprit (*Motor., etc.*); – *gas*, das Heizgas; – *gauge*, die Benzinuhr, Benzinlehre, der Kraftstoffmesser; – *level*, der Treibstoffstand; – *oil*, das Brennöl, Heizöl. 2. *v.n.* Brennstoff einnehmen, tanken.

fug [fʌg], *s.* (*sl.*) stickige Luft, muffiger Geruch. **–gy,** *adj.* muffig, stickig.

fug–acious [fjuːˈgeɪʃəs], *adj.* flüchtig, vergänglich. **–acity,** *s.* die Flüchtigkeit, Vergänglichkeit. **–itive** [ˈfjuːdʒətɪv], 1. *adj.* fliehend; flüchtig, unbeständig, vergänglich, kurzlebig, vorübergehend; *–itive colour*, lichtempfindliche Farbe; *–itive to light*, unecht gegen Licht. 2. *s.* der Flüchtling; Ausreißer.

fugal [ˈfjuːgəl], *adj.* Fugen– (*Mus.*).

fugleman [ˈfjuːglmən], *s.* der Flügelmann (*Mil.*); (*fig.*) (Wort)Führer, Sprecher; rechte Hand, der Sekundant.

fugue [fjuːg], *s.* die Fuge (*Mus.*).

fulcrum [ˈfʌlkrəm], *s.* der Stützpunkt, Drehpunkt, Gelenkpunkt, Ruhepunkt (*Mech.*); das Stützorgan (*Bot.*).

fulfil [fʊlˈfɪl], *v.a.* erfüllen, vollziehen, vollbringen; – *o.s.*, sich voll entwickeln. **–ment,** *s.* die Erfüllung, Vollziehung, Vollführung.

fulg–ency [ˈfʌldʒənsɪ], *s.* (*Poet.*) der Glanz. **–ent,** *adj.* glänzend. **–urant,** *adj.* funkelnd, glänzend. **–urate,** *v.n.* glänzen, blitzen.

fuliginous [fjuːˈlɪdʒɪnəs], *adj.* rußig, verußt, Ruß–.

¹full [fʊl], **1.** *adj.* voll (*of*, von); (also – *up*) (voll) besetzt, (*as a room*); gesättigt, (*vulg.*) satt (*of stomach*); plump, dick (*shape*); sättigend (*as a meal*); ganz, vollständig, unverkürzt, völlig, vollkommen, unumschränkt; rein, echt, leiblich (*of relationship*); stark, tief, kräftig (*of light, colour, etc.*); ausführlich, weitläufig, reichlich, genügend, reif; – *age*, die Volljährigkeit, Mündigkeit; *of* – *age*, volljährig, mündig; – *amount*, ganzer Betrag; – *chorus*, voller Chor; – *citizen*, der Vollbürger; – *consent*, volle Zustimmung; – *costs*, sämtliche Kosten; *in* – *cry*, laut bellend, (*fig.*) mit großer Begeisterung; *in* – *daylight*, am hellichten Tage; – *description*, ausführliche Beschreibung; (*at*) – *gallop*, in gestrecktem Galopp; *have one's hands* –, (*fig.*) vollauf zu tun haben; – *hour*, ganze *or* geschlagene Stunde; – *intent*, feste Absicht; – *length*, in ganzer Länge (*N.B.* **––length**); (*fig.*) *at* – *length*, ausführlich; – *moon*, der Vollmond; – *of o.s.*, von sich eingenommen sein; – *pay*, voller Arbeitslohn; – *powers*, unumschränkte Vollmacht; *under* – *sail*, mit vollen Segeln (*also fig.*); alles bei (*Naut.*); (*at*) – *speed*, spornstreichs, im Galopp; mit höchster Geschwindigkeit; – *statement*, ausführlicher Bericht; – *steam ahead*, Volldampf voraus; – *stop*, der Punkt (*Gram.*); *come to a* – *stop*, plötzlich stillstehen, ins Stocken geraten; *be in* – *swing*, in vollem Gange sein; – *throttle*, das Vollgas; *in* – *view* (*of*), gerade gegenüber (*Dat.*). **2.** *adv.* genau, gerade, direkt; recht, sehr, gar; *see compounds*; *look a p.* – *in the face*, einem gerade ins Gesicht sehen; (*poet.*) – *many a*, gar manche; (*poet.*) – *nigh*, fast; – *well*, gar sehr. **3.** *s.* die Fülle, Vollheit, Genüge; (*fig.*) das Ganze, höchstes Maß, der Höhepunkt; *at the* –, auf dem Höhepunkt; – *of the moon*, der Vollmond; *in* –, vollständig, ungekürzt; per Saldo (*C.L.*); *pay in* –, voll bezahlen; *acquittance in* –, die Generalquittung; *to the* –, reichlich. **––back,** *s.* der Verteidiger (*Footb.*); Schlußspieler (*Rugby footb.*). **––blooded,** *adj.* echtblütig (*fig.*) kräftig. **––blown,** *adj.* in voller Blüte, voll aufgeblüht; (*fig.*) voll entwickelt, entfaltet. **––bodied,** *adj.* beleibt; schwer (*as wine*). **––bottomed,** *adj.* breit; *––bottomed wig*, die Allongeperücke. **––dress,** *s.* der Gesellschaftsanzug, Paradeanzug, die Gala (*Mil.*); *––dress rehearsal*, die Generalprobe. **––faced,** *adj.* mit rundem Gesicht, pausbackig; fett (*Typ.*); direkt zugewandt. **––fledged,** *adj.* flügge; (*fig.*) voll entwickelt, selbständig. **––grown,** *adj.* ausgewachsen, voll erwachsen. **––length,** *adj.* in Lebensgröße (N.B. – *length*). **––mouthed,** *adj.* starktönend. **–ness,** *s.* die Fülle, Vollheit, der Reichtum; die Vollständigkeit; Dicke, Weite, Plumpheit; *–ness of the heart*, die Fülle des Herzens; *in the –ness of time*, da die Zeit erfüllt war, zur rechten Zeit. **––orbed,** *adj.* ganz rund; *––orbed moon*, der Vollmond. **––page,** *adj.* ganzseitig. **––rigged,** *adj.* vollgetakelt. **––size,** *adj.* lebensgroß, in Lebensgröße. **––tracked,** *adj.* Gleisketten (*vehicle*). **–y,** *adv.* voll, völlig, gänzlich; ausführlich; *–y twenty seconds*, volle zwanzig Sekunden.

²full, *v.a.* walken. **–er,** *s.* der Walker. **–er's-earth,** *s.* die Walk(er)erde, Bleicherde, Füllerde. **–er's-weed,** *s.* die Weberkarde. **–ing-mill,** *s.* die Walkmühle.

fulmar [ˈfʊlmə], *s.* der Eissturmvogel (*Orn.*).

fulmin–ate [ˈfʌlmɪneɪt], 1. *v.n.* donnern, krachen, (ab)knallen, verpuffen, explodieren; (*fig.*) losdonnern, wettern. 2. *v.a.* zur Explosion bringen; (*fig.*) schleudern (*censures*). 3. *s.* das Knallpulver; knallsaures Salz (*Chem.*); *–ate of mercury*, das Knallquecksilber. **–ating,** *adj.* Knall–, knallend; *–ating powder*, das Knallpulver. **–ation** [–ˈneɪʃən], *s.* das Donnern, der Knall; das Explodieren; (*fig.*) der Bannstrahl, Fluch. **–atory** [–nətərɪ], *adj.* donnernd, Droh–. **–ic** [fʌlˈmɪnɪk], *adj.* knallsauer; *–ic acid*, die Knallsäure.

fulsome [ˈfʊlsəm], *adj.* widerlich, ekelhaft; übermäßig. **–ness,** *s.* die Widerlichkeit, Ekelhaftigkeit.

fumbl–e [ˈfʌmbl], 1. *v.n.* umherfühlen, umhertappen; *–e for*, tappen nach; *–e with*, fummeln an. 2. *v.a.* ungeschickt behandeln (*a ball, etc.*). **–ing,** *adj.* tappend; täppisch, linkisch.

fume [fjuːm], 1. *s.* der Dunst, Dampf, Rauch; (*fig.*) die Aufwallung, Aufregung; *be in a* –, aufgebracht sein. 2. *v.a.* (aus)räuchern. 3. *v.n.* dampfen, rauchen, dunsten; (*fig.*) toben, wüten, aufgebracht sein, aufgeregt sein.

fumigat–e [ˈfjuːmɪgeɪt], *v.a.* anräuchern, durchräuchern; entlausen. **–ing,** *adj.* Räucher–, rauchend. **–ion** [–ˈgeɪʃən], *s.* die (Aus)Räucherung.

fumitory [ˈfjuːmɪtərɪ], *s.* der Erdrauch, Lerchensporn (*Bot.*).

fun [fʌn], *s.* Scherz, Spaß; *it is* –, es macht Spaß; *it is great* –, es ist ein Hauptspaß; (*coll.*) *he is great* –, er ist sehr amüsant; *for* –, zum *or* aus Spaß, im Scherz; *for the* – *of the thing*, des Spaßes wegen; *have good* –, sich ausgezeichnet amüsieren; *in* –, see *for* –; *make* – *of* or *poke* – *at a p.*, einen zum besten haben; *see* **funny.**

function [ˈfʌŋkʃən], 1. *s.* die Funktion (*also Math.*); Tätigkeit, das Wirken; die Aufgabe, Obliegenheit; Amtstätigkeit, Amtsverrichtung, Amtshandlung; das Amt, amtliche Pflicht, der Dienst, Beruf; die Veranstaltung, Feier, Zeremonie; *natural* –, die Notdurft; *official* –, die Repräsentation. 2. *v.n.* fungieren, tätig sein, wirksam sein, funktionieren. **–al,** *adj.* formell, repräsentativ; amtlich, dienstlich; funktionell, Funktions–. **–alism,** *s.* die Zweckmäßigkeit. **–ary** [–ərɪ], *s.* Beamte(r), *m.*, der Amtswalter.

fund [fʌnd], 1. *s.* der Fonds, das Kapital (*C.L.*); der Vorrat, Schatz, die Fülle (*of*, an); *pl.* das Grundkapital; Gelder (*pl.*), Geldmittel (*pl.*); fundierte Staatspapiere *or* Staatsschulden, öffentlicher Fonds; (*coll.*) *in –s*, bei Kasse; *sinking-–*, der Schuldentilgungsfonds; *trust* –, der Treuhandfonds. 2. *v.a.* in Staatspapieren anlegen (*money*); fundieren (*floating debt*). **––holder,** *s.* der Inhaber von Staatspapieren.

fundament [ˈfʌndəmənt], *s.* das Gesäß; der After. **–al** [–l], *adj.* grundlegend, als Grundlage dienend (*to*, für); Grund–, grundsätzlich, wesentlich; *–al science*, die Hauptwissenschaft; *–al tone*, der Grundton; *–al truths*, Grundwahrheiten. **–alism,** *s.* der Buchstabenglaube. **–ally,** *adv.* im Grunde, im wesentlichen. **–als,** *pl.* Grundlagen; Grundwahrheiten, Hauptsachen.

funer–al [ˈfjuːnərəl], 1. *s.* die Beerdigung, Bestattung, das Begräbnis, Leichenbegängnis; feierliche Beisetzung, der Leichenzug; (*coll.*) *that's your* (*own*) *–al*, das ist dein eigener Schaden. 2. *adj.* Begräbnis–, Grab–, Leichen–, Trauer–; *–al march*, der Trauermarsch; *–al oration*, die Leichenpredigt; *–al pile*, der Scheiterhaufen; *–al procession*, der Leichenzug; *–al service*, der Trauergottesdienst; *–al urn*, die Totenurne. **–eal** [–ˈnɪərɪəl], *adj.* begräbnismäßig, Trauer–, Leichen–; traurig, düster, klagend.

fungible [ˈfʌndʒɪbl], *adj.* vertretbar, ersetzbar (*Law*).

fung–i [ˈfʌndʒaɪ], *pl. see* **fungus. –icide,** *s.* das Schädlingsbekämpfungsmittel. **–oid** [ˈfʌŋgɔɪd],

adj., **-ous** [ˈfʌŋgəs], *adj.* pilzähnlich, pilzartig, schwammig; *-oid spores*, der Mehltau. **-us** [ˈfʌŋgəs], *s.* (*pl.* -i [ˈfʌndʒaɪ], -uses) der Pilz, Schwamm; Schimmelpilz, Schmarotzerpilz; krankhafte Geschwulst (*Path.*).
funicular [fjuːˈnɪkjulə], *adj.* Seil-, Band-, Strang-; *- railway* die (Draht)Seilbahn.
funk [fʌŋk], 1. *v.n.* (*sl.*) in Angst geraten. 2. *v.a.* (*sl.*) Angst haben vor, sich fürchten vor, sich drücken von. 3. *s.* (*sl.*) der Bammel, große Angst; Feigling, Angsthase; *blue -*, (*sl.*) die Mordsangst, Heidenangst; *be in a* (*blue*) -, (*sl.*) einen Bammel, Dampf *or* (*vulg.*) Schiß haben (*of* or *about*, vor). **--hole,** *s.* (*sl.*) der Heldenkeller, Schlupfwinkel, das Schlupfloch, der Unterstand. **-y,** *adj.* feige, bange.
funnel [ˈfʌnl], *s.* der Trichter; die Schornsteinröhre, der Rauchfang; Schornstein (*of a ship, etc.*); Luftschacht (*Min.*). **--shaped,** *adj.* trichterförmig.
funny [ˈfʌnɪ], *adj.* komisch; drollig, spaßhaft, ulkig; (*coll.*) *feel -*, sich unbehaglich fühlen; (*coll.*) *I came over -*, es wurde mir elend; (*coll.*) *- business*, unheimliche Sache. **--bone,** *s.* der Musikantenknochen.
fur [fəː], 1. *s.* der Pelz, das Fell; der Pelzmantel; *pl.* das Pelzwerk, Rauchwaren (*pl.*); der Belag (*on the tongue*); Kesselstein (*of a boiler*). 2. *v.a.* mit Pelz füttern *or* besetzen. 3. *v.n.* sich mit Belag *or* Kesselstein überziehen. **-red,** *adj.* mit Pelz besetzt; belegt (*of the tongue*). **-ring,** *s.* der Kesselsteinbelag, die Kesselsteinansetzung. **-ry,** *adj.* pelzartig.
furbelow [ˈfəːbɪlou], 1. *s.* die Falbel; (*fig.*) der Staat, Putz. 2. *v.a.* mit Falbeln besetzen.
furbish [ˈfəːbɪʃ], *v.a.* polieren, blank putzen; *- up*, aufputzen, herrichten.
furcat-e [ˈfəːkeɪt], *adj.* gabelförmig, gegabelt. **-ion,** *s.* die Gabelung.
furious [ˈfjuərɪəs], *adj.* wütend, rasend; (*fig.*) wild, ungestüm. **-ness,** *s.* die Wut, Raserei.
furl [fəːl], *v.a.* zusammenrollen, festmachen, beschlagen (*sails*), aufrollen (*a flag*). *-ing line*, *s.* der Beschlagzeising (*Naut.*).
furlong [ˈfəːlɔŋ], *s.* die Achtelmeile (= 201 Meter).
furlough [ˈfəːlou], 1. *s.* der Urlaub; *on -*, auf Urlaub. 2. *v.a.* beurlauben.
furnace [ˈfəːnɪs], *s.* der Ofen, Brennofen, Schmelzofen; Heizraum; *blast -*, der Hochofen.
furnish [ˈfəːnɪʃ], *v.a.* versehen, versorgen (*with*, mit); möblieren, ausstatten, ausrüsten (*rooms, houses, etc.*); verschaffen, gewähren, darbieten, liefern; *-ed rooms*, möblierte Zimmer. **-er,** *s.* der Lieferant; Möblierer. **-ing,** *s.* die Einrichtung, Ausstattung. **-ings,** *pl.* das Mobiliar; der Schmuck.
furniture [ˈfəːnɪtʃə], *s.* (*no pl.*) die Möbel (*pl.*), das Mobiliar, Hausgerät, der Hausrat; die Ausrüstung, das Schiffsgerät, die Betakelung (*Naut.*); das Geschirr (*of a horse*); Zubehör (*Mach.*). **--polish,** *s.* die Möbelpolitur. **--remover,** *s.* der Möbelspediteur. **--van,** *s.* der Möbelwagen.
furore [fjuəˈrɔːrə], *s.* das Furore, Aufsehen.
furred [fəːd], *see* **fur.**
furrier [ˈfʌrɪə], *s.* der Kürschner; Pelzhändler.
furrow [ˈfʌrou], 1. *s.* die Furche, Rille, Rinne (*Agr., also fig.*); Nut, Nute (*Carp., etc.*); Runzel. 2. *v.a.* (durch)furchen, auskehlen, aushöhlen.
furry [ˈfəːrɪ], *see* **fur.**
furth-er [ˈfəːðə], 1. *adj.* weiter, ferner, entfernter; *-er from*, weiter entfernt von; *till -er notice*, bis auf weiteres; *-er particulars*, Nähere(s), *n.*; *the -er side*, jenseits. 2. *adv.* weiter, ferner, mehr, weiterhin, überdies; *nothing -er?* weiter nichts? sonst noch was? 3. *v.a.* fördern, unterstützen. **-erance** [-rəns], *s.* die Förderung, Unterstützung; *in -erance of*, um . . . zu fördern, zur Förderung von. **-ermore,** *adv.* ferner, überdies, außerdem. **-ermost,** *adj.* weitest, fernst. **-est,** 1. *adj.* weitest, fernst. 2. *adv.* am weitesten.
furtive [ˈfəːtɪv], *adj.* verstohlen, heimlich, unbemerkt (*of actions*); heimlich tuend, hinterlistig, hinterhältig (*of persons*). **-ness,** *s.* die Verstohlenheit.
furuncle [ˈfjuərʌŋkl], *s.* der Furunkel.
fury [ˈfjuərɪ], *s.* die Raserei, Wut; Heftigkeit, das Ungestüm; (*usually pl.*) die Furie, Rachegeister (*pl.*) (*Myth.*).
furze [fəːz], *s.* der Stechginster (*Bot.*).
fuse [fjuːz], 1. *v.a.* schmelzen, flüssig machen. 2. *v.n.* verschmelzen, zerfließen, zusammenfließen, zusammenschmelzen, zusammenschmelzen; durchbrennen (*Elec.*). 3. *v.a.* mit einem Zünder versehen (*Artil.*). 4. *s.* der Zünder, (*archaic*) die Lunte; Sicherung, der Schmelzeinsatz; *the - has blown.* die Sicherung ist durchgebrannt.
fusee [fjuːˈziː], *s.* die Schnecke (*Horol.*); das Windfeuerzeug, Streichholz.
fuselage [ˈfjuːzɪlɪdʒ], *s.* der Rumpf (*Av.*).
fusib-ility [fjuːzɪˈbɪlɪtɪ], *s.* die Schmelzbarkeit. **-le,** *adj.* schmelzbar.
fusi-lier [fjuːzɪˈlɪːə], *s.* der Füsilier. **-lade** [fjuːzɪˈleɪd], 1. *v.a.* beschießen (*a place*), erschießen, füselieren (*a person*). 2. *s.* das Gewehrfeuer, die Salve; (*fig.*) der Hagel (*of stones, etc.*).
fus-ing [ˈfjuːzɪŋ], *s.* das Schmelzen; *-ing point*, der Schmelzpunkt. **-ion** [ˈfjuːʒən], *s.* das Schmelzen; der Zusammenfluß; (*fig.*) Zusammenschluß, die Verschmelzung; Fusion (*C.L.*).
fuss [fʌs], 1. *s.* der Lärm, das Getue, Wesen, Aufheben; *make a - about*, viel Aufhebens machen um. 2. *v.n.* sich aufregen, viel Aufhebens machen (*about* or *over*, über). **-iness,** *s.* die Geschäftigkeit, übertriebene Umständlichkeit. (*sl.*) **--pot,** *s.* der Umstandsmeier. **-y,** *adj.* übertrieben umständlich, geschäftig.
fustian [ˈfʌstɪən], 1. *s.* der Barchent; (*fig.*) Schwulst, Bombast. 2. *adj.* barchent; (*fig.*) schwülstig, hochtrabend.
fustigat-e [ˈfʌstɪgeɪt], *v.a.* prügeln. **-ion,** *s.* die Prügelstrafe.
fust-iness [ˈfʌstɪnɪs], *s.* muffiger Geruch, der Modergeruch. **-y** [ˈfʌstɪ], *adj.* muffig, moderig; (*fig.*) veraltet, verstaubt.
futil-e [ˈfjuːtaɪl], *adj.* nichtig, unnütz; zwecklos, wirkungslos, wertlos; unzulänglich. **-ity** [-ˈtɪlɪtɪ], *s.* die Nichtigkeit, Leerheit, Oberflächlichkeit, Unzulänglichkeit, Zwecklosigkeit, Nutzlosigkeit.
futtock [ˈfʌtək], *s.* der Auflanger, Sitzer; *pl.* die Püttings(wanten) (*Naut.*).
futur-e [ˈfjuːtʃə], 1. *adj.* künftig, zukünftig, Zukunfts-; Termin- (*C.L.*); *-e tense*, das Futurum (*Gram.*). 2. *s.* die Zukunft; das Futurum (*Gram.*); *pl.* Termingeschäfte, Terminwaren (*pl.*) (*C.L.*); *in the -e*, in Zukunft; *for the -e*, künftig. **-ism** [-rɪzm], *s.* der Futurismus (*Art*). **-ity** [-ˈtjuərɪtɪ], *s.* die Zukunft, das Zukünftige; *pl.* zukünftige Ergebnisse.
fuze [fjuːz], *s.* der Zünder (*see* **fuse**).
fuzz [fʌz], 1. *v.n.* sich zerfasern *or* auflösen. 2. *s.* flaumiges Haar, die Fussel; der Flaum (*on fruit*). **-y,** *adj.* flaumig, flockig; kraus, struppig, zottig (*hair*); unbestimmt, verwischt.
fylfot [ˈfɪlfət], *s.* das Hakenkreuz.

G

G, g [dʒiː], *s.* das G, g (*also Mus.*); *G clef*, der Violinschlüssel; *G flat*, das Ges; *G sharp*, das Gis. (*See Index of Abbreviations.*)
gab [gæb], *s.* das Geschwätz, Geplauder; (*vulg.*) *stop your -!* halt deinen Schnabel! *gift of the -*, ein tüchtiges Mundwerk. **-ble,** 1. *v.n.* schnattern (*as geese*); schwatzen, in den Bart reden. 2. *s.* das Geschnatter; Geschwätz.
gab-ardine, -erdine [ˈgæbədɪːn], *s.* der Kittel; Kaftan (*of Jews*); Gabardine [*pron.* -ˈdɪːn], Garbardinemantel.
gabion [ˈgeɪbɪən], *s.* der Schanzkorb. **-ade** [geɪbɪəˈneɪd], *s.* die Schanzkorbbefestigung.

gable ['geɪbl], *s.* der Giebel. **–d,** *adj.* gegiebelt, Giebel–. **--end,** *s.* die Giebelwand. **--window,** *s.* das Giebelfenster.
gaby ['geɪbɪ], *s.* der Trottel, Tropf.
[1]**gad** [gæd], *int.*; (*archaic*) *by –!* meiner Treu!
[2]**gad,** 1. *v.n.*; – *about,* umherstreifen, sich umhertreiben. 2. *s.*; *be on the –,* see – *about.* **--about,** *s.* der Bummler, Pflastertreter. **–fly,** *s.* die Viehbremse, Biesfliege; (*fig.*) lästiger Kerl.
gadget ['gædʒɪt], *s.* technische Vorrichtung; kleines Zubehör.
gaff [gæf], *s.* der Fischhaken (*for salmon*); die Gaffel (*Naut.*); (*sl.*) der Unfug; (*sl.*) *blow the –,* alles verplaudern *or* verraten.
gaffer ['gæfə], *s.* (*coll.*) Alte(r), *m.*, das Väterchen; der Gevatter; Aufseher, Vorarbeiter.
gag [gæg], 1. *v.a.* knebeln; mundtot machen (*Pol.*); (*fig.*) verstopfen. 2. *v.n.* improvisieren, extemporieren (*Theat.*). 3. *s.* der Knebel; die Knebelung; der Debattenschluß (*Parl.*); extemporierte Einschaltung, die Improvisation (*Theat.*); (*coll.*) alter Witz, der Ulk; Schwindel.
gaga ['gægæ], *adj.* (*sl.*) verrückt, albern.
[1]**gage** [geɪdʒ], 1. *s.* das Pfand, Unterpfand, die Bürgschaft; *throw down the –,* (einem) den Fehdehandschuh hinwerfen. 2. *v.a.* verpfänden.
[2]**gage,** (*Amer.*); *see* **gauge**; die Windseite, Luvseite (*Naut.*); *have the weather – of,* windwärts liegen von (*Naut.*); (*fig.*) Vorteil gewinnen über.
gaggle ['gægl], 1. *v.n.* schnattern, gackern. 2. *s.*; – (*of geese*), die (Gänse)Herde.
gai–ety ['geɪətɪ], *s.* die Heiterkeit, Lustigkeit, Fröhlichkeit, der Frohsinn; Putz; die Festlichkeit, Lustbarkeit. **–ly,** *see* **gay.**
gain [geɪn], 1. *s.* der Gewinn, Profit, Vorteil, Nutzen, die Ausbeute; das Verstärkungsmaß (*Rad.*), die Steigerung, Zunahme. 2. *v.a.* gewinnen; bekommen, erhalten, erwerben, erlangen, erreichen; – *the day,* den Sieg erringen *or* davontragen, obsiegen; – *the ear of,* Gehör finden bei; – *one's ends,* seinen Zweck erreichen; – *by force,* erzwingen; – *ground,* Boden gewinnen, um sich greifen, sich durchsetzen; – *the upper hand,* den Sieg davontragen; – *over,* für sich gewinnen (*a person*); – *possession,* Besitz ergreifen. 3. *v.n.* gewinnen (*in,* an); Vorteil haben, Einfluß *or* Boden gewinnen; vorgehen (*of clocks*); – *on,* einholen, überholen (*Acc.*), näherkommen (*Dat.*) (*in a race*); übergreifen auf, sich ausbreiten über; den Vorteil abgewinnen (*Dat.*). **–er,** *s.* der Gewinner; *be the –er by,* gewinnen durch. **–ful,** *adj.* einträglich.
gainsay [geɪn'seɪ], *v.a.* widersprechen (*a person*) (*Dat.*); bestreiten; leugnen (*things*).
gait [geɪt], *s.* die Gangart, Haltung.
gaiter ['geɪtə], *s.* die Gamasche.
gal [gæl] *s.* (*coll.*) see **girl.**
gala ['geɪlə], *s.* die Festlichkeit, Gala.
galact–ic [gə'læktɪk], *adj.* Milchstraßen– (*Astr.*). **–ometer** [gælək'tɔmɪtə], *s.* die Milchwaage, der Milchmesser.
galantine ['gæləntɪ:n], *s.* kalte Platte.
galanty show [gə'læntɪ ʃou], *s.* das Schattenspiel.
galaxy ['gæləksɪ], *s.* die Milchstraße; (*fig.*) glänzende Versammlung.
galbanum ['gælbənəm], *s,* das Galbanharz.
[1]**gale** [geɪl], *s.* frischer *or* heftiger Wind, steife Brise; *it is blowing a –,* es geht ein heftiger Wind; *moderate –,* harter Wind; *fresh –,* stürmischer Wind; *strong –,* der Sturmwind; *whole –,* schwerer Sturm.
[2]**gale,** *s.* periodische Renten–, Zins– *or* Steuerzahlung.
galena [gə'lɪ:nə], *s.* der Bleiglanz, Galenit.
galilee ['gælɪlɪ:], *s.* die (Dom)Vorhalle (*Arch.*).
[1]**gall** [gɔ:l], *s.* die Galle; (*fig.*) Bitterkeit, Bosheit, Erbitterung. **--bladder,** *s.* die Gallenblase. **--duct,** *s.* der Gallengang. **--stone,** *s.* der Gallenstein.
[2]**gall,** *s.* (*--nut*) der Gallapfel. **--fly,** *s.* die Gallwespe.
[3]**gall,** 1. *s.* das Wundreiben; wunde Stelle, (*coll.*) der Wolf. 2. *v.a.* wundreiben; (*fig.*) quälen, peinigen, ärgern, reizen. **–ing,** *adj.* ärgerlich; *it is –ing,* es wurmt einen, es ist ärgerlich.
gallant ['gælənt], 1. *adj.* tapfer, brav, ritterlich, höflich, artig; schön, prächtig, stattlich; aufmerksam gegen Damen, galant, Liebes–. 2. *s.* der Galan, Kurmacher. **–ry,** *s.* die Tapferkeit; der Edelmut; die Galanterie, Artigkeit (*to women*), Buhlerei.
galleon ['gælɪən], *s.* die Galeone, Gallione.
gallery ['gælərɪ], *s.* die Galerie (*also Theat.*), Säulenhalle (*Arch.*); Empore (*of a church*); gedeckter *or* bedeckter Gang, der Minengang (*Fort.*), Stollen (*Min.*); *picture–,* die Gemäldegalerie; *play to the –,* nach Effekt haschen.
galley ['gælɪ], *s.* die Galeere; offenes Ruderboot (*Naut.*); die Schiffsküche, Kombüse (*Naut.*); das Setzschiff (*Typ.*). **--proof,** *s.* der Bürstenabzug, Fahnenkorrekturen (*pl.*) (*Typ.*). **--slave,** *s.* der Galeerensklave, Galeerensträfling.
gallic ['gælɪk], *adj.*; – *acid,* die Gallussäure.
Gallic, *adj.* gallisch. **–an,** *adj.* gallikanisch. **–ism** ['gælɪsɪzm], *s.* der Gallizismus. **–ize,** *v.a.* französeln.
gallimaufry [gælɪ'mɔ:frɪ], *s.* (*fig.*) der Mischmasch.
gallinaceous [gælɪ'neɪʃəs], *adj.* hühnerartig.
galling ['gɔ:lɪŋ], *see* [3]**gall.**
galliot ['gælɪət], *s.* kleine Galeere.
gallipot ['gælɪpɔt], *s.* der Apothekertopf, Salbentopf.
gallivant ['gælɪvænt], *v.n.* sich herumtreiben, umherflanieren.
gallon ['gælən], *s.* die Gallone (= 4·54 Liter; *Amer.* = 3·78 Liter).
galloon [gə'lu:n], *s.* die Tresse, Borte, Litze.
gallop ['gæləp], 1. *s.* der Galopp; *full –,* gestreckter Galopp; (*fig.*) größte Eile; *at a –,* im Galopp. 2. *v.n.* galoppieren; lossprengen (*at,* auf (*Acc.*)); (*fig.*) eilen. 3. *v.a.* galoppieren lassen (*a horse*); *–ing consumption,* galoppierende Schwindsucht. **–ade** [gælə'peɪd], *s.* die Galoppade (*dance*).
gallows ['gælouz], *pl.* (*usually sing. constr.*) der Galgen. **--bird,** *s.* der Galgenvogel, Galgenstrick. **--tree,** *s.* der Galgen.
galoot [gə'lu:t], *s.* (*sl.*) der Kerl.
galop ['gæləp], *s.* der Galopp (*Danc.*).
galore [gə'lɔ:], *adv.* (*coll.*) in Hülle und Fülle, in Menge, mehr als genug.
galosh [gə'lɔʃ], *s.* (*usually pl.*) der Überschuh, Gummischuh, die Galosche.
galvan–ic [gæl'vænɪk], *adj.* galvanisch. **–ism** ['gælvənɪzm], *s.* der Galvanismus. **–ize** ['gælvənaɪz], *v.a.* galvanisieren, verzinken; (*fig.*) beleben, wecken (*to,* zu); *–ized iron,* verzinktes Eisen(blech). **–ometer** [gælvə'nɔmətə], *s.* der Galvanometer.
gambit ['gæmbɪt], *s.* das Gambit (*Chess*); (*fig.*) erster Schritt.
gambl–e ['gæmbl], 1. *v.n.* um Geld *or* um hohen Einsatz *or* Hasard spielen, spekulieren; (*coll.*) *you can –e on it,* darauf können Sie Gift nehmen; *–e with,* aufs Spiel setzen. 2. *v.a.*; *–e away,* verspielen. 3. *s.* das Glücksspiel; Wagnis. **–er,** *s.* der Spieler. **–ing,** *s.* das Spielen (um Geld). **–ing-den,** *s.* die Spielhölle.
gamboge [gæm'bu:dʒ], *s.* das Gummigutt.
gambol ['gæmbəl], 1. *s.* der Luftsprung, Freudensprung. 2. *v.n.* Luftsprünge machen, freudig hüpfen.
game [geɪm], 1. *s.* das Spiel, die Partie; der Scherz, Spaß, die Belustigung; der Plan, Schlich, geheime Absicht; jagdbare Tiere, das Wild; *big –,* das Großwild; – *of chance,* das Glücksspiel, Hasardspiel; – *of skill,* das Spiel das gelernt sein will; *give the – away,* den Plan verraten; *give* or *throw up the –,* das Spiel aufgeben; *losing –,* das Spiel bei dem man verlieren muß; *on one's –,* in Form; *beat s.o. at his own –,* einen mit seinen eignen Waffen schlagen; (*coll.*) *the – is up,* das Spiel ist aus, alles ist verloren; *the – is not worth the candle,* die Sache lohnt die Mühe nicht; *what's his (little) – ?* was führt er im Schilde?; *make – of a p.,* einen zum besten haben; *play the –,* nach den Regeln spielen, mit ehrlichen Mitteln kämpfen; *play a good –,* gut spielen. 2. *v.n.* spielen. 3. *adj.* (*coll.*) mutig, unerschrocken, entschlossen; bereit; *die –,* tapfer sterben; *he is – for anything,* er ist zu allem bereit *or* für alles zu haben. **--bag,** *s.* die Jagdtasche. **--cock,** *s.* der Kampfhahn. **–keeper,** *s.* der

Förster; Wildhüter. **--laws,** *pl.* Wildschutzgesetze (*pl.*). **--licence,** *s.* der Jagdschein. **-ness,** *s.* die Entschlossenheit, der Mut. **--preserve,** *s.* der Wildpark. **-'s master,** der Sportlehrer. **-ster** ['geɪmstə], *s.* der (die) Spieler(in). **--tenant,** *s.* der Jagdpächter. **-y,** *adj.* angegangen, mit Wildgeschmack (*of food*).

gamete [gæ'mɪ:t], *s.* geschlechtliche Fortpflanzungszelle (*Biol.*).

gaming ['geɪmɪŋ], *s.* das Spielen. **--table,** *s.* der Spieltisch.

gammer ['gæmə], *s.* (*archaic*) das Mütterchen, die Gevatterin.

[1]**gammon** ['gæmən], 1. *s.* doppelter Gewinn (*at backgammon*); der Betrug, Schwindel, die Täuschung; der Unsinn. 2. *v.a.* zweimal schlagen (*at backgammon*); betrügen, anführen.

[2]**gammon,** 1. *s.* geräucherter Schinken. 2. *v.a.* räuchern und einsalzen (*ham*).

gamp [gæmp], *s.* (*coll.*) (alter) Regenschirm.

gamut ['gæmət], *s.* die Tonleiter (*Mus.*); (*fig.*) die Skala, der Bereich, Umfang.

gamy ['geɪmɪ], *see* **gamey.**

gander ['gændə], *s.* der Gänserich.

gang [gæŋ], *s.* die Bande, Rotte, Sippschaft; Abteilung, der Trupp (*of workmen*); Satz (*of tools*). **-er,** *s.* der Werkführer. **--plank,** *s.* die (Lauf)-Planke, der Landungssteg (*Naut.*); *see* **gangster, gangway.**

gangli-on ['gæŋglɪən], *s.* (*pl.* -ons, -a) der Nervenknoten (*Anat.*), das Überbein (*Med.*).

gangren-e ['gæŋgrɪ:n], 1. *s.* der Brand (*Med.*), (*fig.*) die Fäulnis. 2. *v.a.* brandig machen. 3. *v.n.* brandig werden. **-ous** [-grənəs], *adj.* brandig.

gangster ['gæŋstə], *s.* bewaffneter Verbrecher.

gangway ['gæŋweɪ], *s.* der (Durch)Gang; das Fallreep, die Fallreepspforte; der Laufgang, Gangbord, die Laufplanke (*Naut.*); der Quergang (*Parl.*); *members below the* –, die Wilden (*Parl.*).

gannet ['gænɪt], *s.* der Tölpel; Weißer Seerabe (*Orn.*).

gantry ['gæntrɪ], *s.* das Faßlager, der Stützblock (*for barrels*); die Kranbahn (*for cranes*); *signal* –, die Signalbrücke (*Railw.*).

gaol ['dʒeɪl], 1. *s.* das Gefängnis, der Kerker. 2. *v.a.* einkerkern. **--bird,** *s.* der Gewohnheitsverbrecher. **--break,** *s.* der Ausbruch aus dem Gefängnis. **-er,** *s.* der Gefangenenaufseher, Kerkermeister; *see* **jail.**

gap [gæp], *s.* die Öffnung, Lücke, Spalte, Kluft, der Riß, die Scharte; Bresche, Gasse (*Mil.*); Schlucht (*Geog.*); *spark*-–, die Funkstrecke; *stop a* –, ein Loch zustopfen; (*fig.*) eine Lücke ausfüllen.

gap-e [geɪp], *v.n.* gähnen; gaffen, starren, glotzen; sich spalten, sich öffnen, klaffen; *-e at*, angaffen, anstarren; *stand -ing*, Maulaffen feil halten. **-ing,** 1. *adj.* weit offen, klaffend. 2. *s.* das Gähnen; Gaffen.

garage ['gærɑ:ʒ], 1. *s.* die Garage. 2. *v.a.* einstellen, unterbringen (*car*).

garb [gɑ:b], *s.* die Tracht, Kleidung, das Gewand.

garbage ['gɑ:bɪdʒ], *s.* der (Küchen)Abfall; (*fig.*) Auswurf; Dreck. **--can,** (*Amer.*) der Kehrichtkasten.

garble ['gɑ:bl], *v.a.* verstümmeln, entstellen; zustutzen, verdrehen, frisieren; (*archaic*) auslesen.

garboard ['gɑ:bɔ:d], *s.* (also – *strake*) der Kielgang (*Naut.*).

garden ['gɑ:dn], 1. *s.* der Garten; *pl.* Gartenanlagen (*pl.*); (*coll.*) *lead s.o. up the – path*, einen zum Narren halten, einen aufs Glatteis führen; *market* –, die (Handels)Gärtnerei; *nursery* –, die Baumschule; *hanging* –, hängender Garten. 2. *v.n.* sich mit Gartenbau beschäftigen; im Garten arbeiten. **– city,** die Gartenstadt. **-er,** *s.* der Gärtner. **-ing** ['gɑ:dnɪŋ], *s.* der Gartenbau, die Gartenarbeit. **--mould,** *s.* die Gartenerde. **--party,** *s.* das Gartenfest. **--roller,** *s.* die Gartenwalze. **--shears,** *pl.* die Heckenschere. **--stuff,** das Gartengemüse, Gartengewächse (*pl.*).

gardenia [gɑ:'dɪ:nɪə], *s.* die Gardenie (*Bot.*).

gargantuan [gɑ'gæntjuən], *adj.* reisig, ungeheuer.

gargle ['gɑ:gl], 1. *s.* das Gurgelwasser. 2. *v.n.* (den Hals) ausspülen, gurgeln.

gargoyle ['gɑ:gɔɪl], *s.* der Wasserspeier (*Arch.*).

garish ['gɛərɪʃ], *adj.* grell, blendend; prunkend, auffallend.

garland ['gɑ:lənd], 1. *s.* der (Blumen)Kranz; das Blumengewinde, Laubgewinde, die Girlande (*also Arch.*); (*fig.*) der Siegespreis, Ehrenpreis; die Blumenlese. 2. *v.a.* bekränzen.

garlic ['gɑ:lɪk], *s.* der Knoblauch.

garment [gɑ:mənt], *s.* das Kleidungsstück, Kleid, Gewand; (*fig.*) die Decke, Hülle.

garner ['gɑ:nə], 1. *s.* der Kornboden, Kornspeicher, die Getreidekammer. 2. *v.a.* aufspeichern.

garnet ['gɑ:nɪt], *s.* der Granat.

garnish ['gɑ:nɪʃ], *v.a.* (*Poet.*) zieren, schmücken, besetzen; garnieren (*Cook.*); vorladen, zitieren (*Law*). **-ing,** *s.* der Schmuck, Zierrat; die Garnierung (*Cook.*). **-ment,** *s.* der Zierrat, Schmuck; die Beschlagnahme (*Law*). **- order,** der Beschlagnahmungsbefehl (*Law*).

garniture ['gɑ:nɪtʃə], *s.* der Schmuck, die Garnitur; das, der *or* die Zubehör.

garret ['gærət], *s.* die Dachstube, Bodenkammer.

garrison ['gærɪsn], 1. *s.* die Garnison, Besatzung; der Standort; *in* –, in Garnison. 2. *v.a.* belegen, besetzen, mit einer Besatzung versehen (*a town*); in Garnison legen (*troops*).

garrotte [gə'rɔt], 1. *s.* die Garrotte; Erdrosselung. 2. *v.a.* garottieren, erdrosseln.

garrul-ity [gə'ru:lɪtɪ], *s.* die Schwatzhaftigkeit, Geschwätzigkeit. **-ous** ['gærʊləs], *adj.* schwatzhaft, geschwätzig, redselig.

garter ['gɑ:tə], 1. *s.* das Strumpfband, der Sockenhalter; *order of the* –, der Hosenbandorden; *knight of the* –, der Ritter des Hosenbandordens. 2. *v.a.* mit dem Strumpfband binden; mit dem Hosenbandorden ehren.

garth [gɑ:θ], *s.* der Hofgarten, Klostergarten.

gas [gæs], 1. *s.* das Gas; Leuchtgas; (*sl.*) Benzin (*Amer.*); der Kampfstoff (*Mil.*); *mustard* –, das Yperit (*Mil.*); *poison* –, das Giftgas, Kampfgas; (*coll.*) *step on the* –, Gas geben (*Motor.*). 2. *v.a.* mit Gas vergiften, vergasen, begasen (*Mil.*). 3. *v.n.* (*sl.*) schwatzen. **--bag,** *s.* die Gaszelle (*of airships*); (*coll.*) der Schwätzer, Windbeutel. **--bracket,** *s.* der Gasarm. **--burner,** *s.* der Gasbrenner. **--chamber,** *s.* die Gaskammer. **--cylinder,** *s.* die Gasflasche. **--detector,** *s.* der Gasanzeiger. **--engine,** *s.* der Gasmotor. **-eous** ['geɪsɪəs, -zɪəs], *adj.* gasförmig, gasartig. **--fire,** *s.* die Gasheizung. **-fitter,** *s.* der Gasinstallateur. **--fittings,** *pl.* die Gasarmaturen (*pl.*). **--gangrene,** *s.* der Gasbrand. **-ify,** *v.a.* in Gas verwandeln, vergasen. **-light,** das Gaslicht, die Gasbeleuchtung; *-light paper*, das Gaslichtpapier (*Phot.*). **--main,** *s.* die Gashauptleitung. **--mantle,** *s.* der Glühstrumpf. **-mask,** *s.* die Gasmaske. **-meter,** *s.* der Gasmesser, die Gasuhr. **-oline,** *s.* der Gasäther, das Gasolin; (*Amer.*) Benzin. **-ometer,** *s.* der Gasbehälter, Gasometer. **--pipe,** *s.* das Gasrohr. **--ring,** *s.* der Gaskocher, Gasbrenner. **-sed,** *adj.* gaskrank, gasvergiftet, vergast. **--shell,** *s.* die Gasgranate. **--stove,** *s.* der Gasofen, Gasherd. **--supply,** *s.* die Gasversorgung. **-sy,** *adj.* gasig; (*sl.*) geschwätzig. **--tar,** *s.* der Steinkohlenteer. **-works,** *pl.* die Gasanstalt, Gasfabrik, das Gaswerk.

gasconade [gæskə'neɪd], 1. *v.n.* prahlen, aufschneiden. 2. *s.* die Prahlerei, Aufschneiderei.

gaseous, *see* **gas.**

gash [gæʃ], 1. *v.a.* tief ins Fleisch schneiden (*Dat.*), aufschlitzen. 2. *s.* klaffende Wunde, die Schnittwunde; der Schmiß, die Schmarre; Spalte.

gasify ['gæsɪfaɪ], *see* **gas.**

gasket ['gæskɪt], *s.* die Dichtung, der Verdichtungsring (*Mach.*); der *or* das Seising, Zeising (*Naut.*).

gasoline ['gæsəlɪ:n], *see* **gas.**

gasometer [gæ'sɔmətə], *see* **gas.**

gasp [gɑ:sp], 1. *s.* das Keuchen, schweres Atmen; *be at one's* or *the last* –, in den letzten Zügen liegen. 2. *v.a.*; – *out*, ausatmen, aushauchen (*one's life*), seufzend äußern (*words, etc.*). 3. *v.n.* schwer atmen, keuchen, schnaufen; – *for breath*, nach Luft schnappen. (*sl.*) **-er,** *s.* billige Zigarette.

gassed [gæst], *see* **gas.**

gastr-ic ['gæstrɪk], *adj.* gastrisch, Magen-; *-ic juice*, der Magensaft. **-itis** [gæs'trɑɪtɪs], *s.* die Magenentzündung. **-onomer** [gæs'trɔnəmə], *s.* der Feinschmecker. **-onomic**, *adj.* feinschmeckerisch. **-onomist** [-mɪst], *see* **-onomer.** **-onomy** [gæ'strɔnəmɪ], *s.* die Kochkunst; Feinschmeckerei.

gat [gæt], *s.* (*sl.*) der Revolver.

gate [geɪt], 1. *s.* das Tor, die Pforte; das Schleusentor; die Sperre, Schranke (*Railw.*); (*fig.*) der Zugang, Weg; die Besucherzahl (*Sport.*); eingenommenes Eintrittsgeld. 2. *v.a.* (*sl.*) den Ausgang verbieten (*Dat.*) (*Univ.*); *he was -d*, ihm wurde verboten, das College zu verlassen. (*coll.*) **--crasher,** *s.* der Eindringling, ungebetener Gast. **-house,** *s.* das Torhaus, das Pförtnerhaus. **--keeper,** *s.* der Pförtner; Schrankenwärter, Bahnwärter (*Railw.*). **--legged table,** der Klapptisch. **-man,** *see* **--keeper.** **--money,** *s.* eingenommenes Eintrittsgeld. **-post,** *s.* der Torpfosten; (*coll.*) *between you and me and the -post*, unter vier Augen. **-way,** *s.* der Torweg, die Einfahrt; (*fig.*) der Zugang, das Tor.

gather ['gæðə], 1. *v.a.* sammeln, ansammeln, aufsammeln, einsammeln, versammeln; ernten, pflücken, lesen, zusammenhäufen, zusammenbringen; schließen, folgern (*from*, aus); gewinnen, erwerben, einziehen (*information, etc.*); zusammenziehen, in Falten legen, falten, kräuseln, aufreihen (*Semp.*); – *breath*, zu Atem kommen; *be -ed to one's fathers*, mit seinen Vorfahren vereint werden; – *in*, einbringen, einsammeln; – *strength*, zu Kräften kommen; – *together*, versammeln; – *oneself together*, sich zusammennehmen; – *up*, aufsammeln, zusammennehmen, auflesen; – *way*, in Fahrt kommen (*Naut.*) (*also fig.*). 2. *v.n.* sich sammeln, sich versammeln; sich häufen, sich vergrößern; sich zusammenziehen; schließen, folgern (*from*, aus); – *to a head*, eitern, reifen (*Med.*); (*fig.*) zur Reife kommen. 3. *s.* die Falte. **-ing,** *s.* das Sammeln; die Versammlung; das Kräuseln (*Semp.*); Eitern, Geschwür (*Med.*); die Lage (*Bookb.*).

gatling ['gætlɪŋ], *attrib.*; – *gun*, das Revolvergeschütz.

gauche [gouʃ], *adj.* linkisch, taktlos.

gaud [gɔ:d], *s.* der Putz, Schmuck, Tand, Flitter. **-iness,** *s.* geschmackloser Putz, prunkhafte Aufmachung. **-y,** *adj.* prunkhaft, aufgeputzt, geziert; bunt, grell.

gaug-e [geɪdʒ], 1. *v.a.* abmessen; abeichen, eichen; (*fig.*) abschätzen, beurteilen (*by*, nach). 2. *s.* das Maß, Eichmaß; die Spur, Spurweite (*Railw.*); der Messer, das Meßgerät, die Lehre; (*fig.*) der Maßstab; *see* **gage**; *broad -e*, die Breitspur; *narrow -e*, die Schmalspur; *oil -e*, der Ölstandzeiger; *pressure -e*, das Manometer, der Druckmesser, die Drucklehre; *rain -e*, der Niederschlagsmesser; *standard -e*, die Normalspur, Regelspur; *wind -e*, das Windmeßgerät, der Windstärkenmesser. **-er,** *s.* der Eichmeister. **-ing-rod,** *s.* das Eichmaß, der Eichstab.

gault [gɔ:lt], *s.* der Flammenmergel, Gault (*Geol.*).

gaunt [gɔ:nt], *adj.* mager, hager, dürr.

[1]**gauntlet** ['gɔ:ntlɪt], *s.* der Handschuh, Stulpenhandschuh, Panzerhandschuh, Fechthandschuh, Reithandschuh; (*fig.*) Fehdehandschuh; *throw down the* –, zum Kampf herausfordern; *take up the* –, die Herausforderung annehmen.

[2]**gauntlet,** *s.*; *run the* –, Spießruten laufen.

gauntry, *see* **gantry.**

gauz-e [gɔ:z], *s.* die Gaze, der Flor; Schleier; *wire -e*, das Drahtgeflecht. **-y,** *adj.* gazeartig, florartig.

gave [geɪv], *see* **give.**

gavel ['gævəl], *s.* der Hammer (*of an auctioneer*).

gavotte [gə'vɔt], *s.* die Gavotte.

gawk [gɔ:k], *s.* der Tölpel; Einfaltspinsel. **-y,** *adj.* tölpelhaft, linkisch, schlaksig.

gawp [gɔ:p], *v.n.* (*sl.*) gaffen, glotzen.

gay [geɪ], *adj.* heiter, lustig, fröhlich; bunt, glänzend, strahlend (*as colours*); sehr geputzt; lebenslustig, flott; auschweifend, liederlich. **-ness,** *s.* die Buntheit, Lebhaftigkeit; *see* **gaiety.**

gaze [geɪz], 1. *v.n.* starren, starr blicken (*on*, auf (*Acc.*)); – *at*, anstarren. 2. *s.* fester *or* starrer Blick; das Anstarren.

gazebo [gæ'zɪ:bou], *s.* der Aussichtsturm (*Fort.*).

gazelle [gə'zɛl], *s.* die Gazelle (*Zool.*).

gazette [gə'zɛt], 1. *s.* das Amtsblatt, der Staatsanzeiger, die Zeitung. 2. *v.a.* amtlich bekanntgeben; *he has been -d captain*, seine Ernennung zum Hauptmann ist im Staatsanzeiger veröffentlicht. **-er** [gæzə'tɪ:ə], *s.* geographisches Lexikon.

gear [gɪ:ə], 1. *s.* das (Pferde)Geschirr; Gerät, Zeug, das *or* die Zubehör; das Gut (*Naut.*); die Übersetzung (*Cycl.*), der Gang (*Motor.*); das Getriebe, Zahnrad, Triebwerk; *bevel* –, das Kegelrad; *change* –, Geschwindigkeiten umschalten; *change into bottom* –, die erste Geschwindigkeit einschalten; *differential* –, das Ausgleichsgetriebe; *high-speed* –, das Schnellganggetriebe, Schonganggetriebe; *high* –, große Übersetzung (*Cycl.*); *in* –, in Gang; *low* –, erster Gang (*Motor.*), kleine Übersetzung (*Cycl.*); (*coll.*) *out of* –, in Unordnung, gestört; *put in* –, einschalten; *spur* –, das Stirnrad; (*fig.*) *throw out of* –, in Unordnung bringen, stören; *top* –, die Höchstgeschwindigkeit; *transmission* –, das Übersetzungsgetriebe. 2. *v.a.* mit Getriebe versehen; – *down*, untersetzen; – *up*, übersetzen. 3. *v.n.* ineinandergreifen; – *with*, zusammenarbeiten mit. **-box,** *s.* der Getriebekasten. **--case,** *s.* der Kettenschützer (*Cycl.*). **--change,** *s.* die Gangschaltung. **-ing,** *s.* die Verzahnung, das Triebwerk, Getriebe (*Mach.*); die Übersetzung (*Cycl.*). **--lever,** *s.*, **--shift,** *s.* die Gangschaltung, der Schalthebel. **-wheel,** *s.* das Zahnrad, Getrieberad.

gee [dʒɪ:], *int.* (*coll.*) mein Gott! nanu! **gee-gee,** *s.* das Pferd (*nursery talk*); – *ho*, – *up*, hott!, hottehü!

geese [gɪ:s], *pl. see* **goose.**

geezer ['gɪ:zə], *s.* (*sl.*) alter Tropf.

gelatin-e ['dʒɛlətɪ:n], *s.* (tierische) Gallerte, das Gallert. **-ize** [dʒə'lætənɑiz], 1. *v.a.* zu Gallert machen. 2. *v.n.* zu Gallert werden. **-ous** [-'lætənəs], *adj.* gallertartig.

geld [gɛld], *reg. & ir.v.a.* verschneiden, kastrieren. **-ing,** *s.* das Beschneiden; der Wallach.

gelid ['dʒɛlɪd], *adj.* eiskalt.

gem [dʒɛm], 1. *s.* der Edelstein; die Gemme; Knospe, das Auge (*Bot.*); (*fig.*) Prachtstück, Glanzstück, die Perle. 2. *v.a.* mit Edelsteinen besetzen.

gemin-ate 1. ['dʒɛmɪneɪt], *v.a.* verdoppeln (*also Gram.*). 2. [-nɪt], *adj.* gepaart, verdoppelt. **-ation** [-'neɪʃən], *s.* die Verdoppelung, Gemination. **-i** ['dʒɛmɪnɑɪ], *pl.* die Zwillinge, Kastor und Pollux (*Astr.*).

gemm-a ['dʒɛmə], *s.* die (Blatt)Knospe (*Bot.*); Gemme, Spore, das Keimkorn (*Zool.*). **-ate** [-eɪt], *adj.* knospig, Knospen- (*Bot.*); Gemmen- (*Zool.*). **-ation** [-'meɪʃən], *s.* die Knospenbildung (*Bot.*); Fortpflanzung durch Gemmen (*Zool.*). **-iferous** [dʒɛ'mɪfərəs], *adj.*, **-iparous** [-'mɪpərəs], *adj.* knospentragend, knospentreibend (*Bot.*), sich durch Gemmen fortpflanzend (*Zool.*).

gendarme ['ʒɔndɑ:m], *s.* der Landjäger, Gendarm.

gender ['dʒɛndə], *s.* das Geschlecht, Genus (*Gram.*).

gene [dʒɪ:n], *s.* das Gen (*Biol.*).

genealog-ical [dʒɪ:nɪə'lɔdʒɪkl], *adj.* genealogisch; *-ical tree*, der Stammbaum. **-ist** [-'ælədʒɪst], *s.* der Genealog. **-ize** [dʒɪ:nɪ'ælədʒɑɪz], *v.n.* die Abstammung erforschen. **-y** [dʒɪ:nɪ'ælədʒɪ], *s.* die Familienforschung, Genealogie; der Stammbaum.

general ['dʒɛnərəl], 1. *adj.* allgemein, allgemein gebräuchlich, üblich, gewöhnlich, verbreitet, durchgängig; allumfassend, uneingeschränkt, unbegrenzt; unbestimmt, vag, unspezifisch; Haupt-, General-; – *approbation*, ungeteilter Beifall; – *cargo*, gemischte Ladung; – *committee*, der Gesamtvorstand; – *dealer*, der Krämer; – *education*, unspezialisierte Erziehung; – *elections*, allgemeine Wahlen (*pl.*); – *Headquarters*, Großes Hauptquartier; – *hospital*, allgemeines Krankenhaus; *in* –, im allgemeinen; *have a* – *invitation*, ein für allemal eingeladen sein; – *manager*, der Generaldirektor; – *order*, der Tagesbefehl; – *Post Office*, das Hauptpostamt; – *practitioner*, praktischer Arzt.

– *purpose, adj.* Mehrzweck–; – *readers*, das große Lesepublikum; *as a – rule*, meistens, in den meisten Fällen; – *servant*, das Mädchen für alles; – *Staff*, der Generalstab; —*Staff officer*, der Generalstäbler; – *strike*, der Generalstreik; *in – terms*, ganz im allgemeinen. 2. *s.* das Allgemeine, das große Ganze; das Volk, Publikum, die Allgemeinheit; der General (*Mil.*), (*fig.*) Feldherr; (*coll.*) das Mädchen für alles; *Lieutenant-* –, der Generalleutnant. **–issimo** [dʒɛnərə'lɪsɪmoʊ], *s.* der Oberbefehlshaber, oberster Heerführer. **–ity** [dʒɛnə'rælɪtɪ], *s.* (*sing. with pl. constr.*) die Allgemeinheit; Mehrzahl, größter Teil; *pl.* allgemeine Äußerungen. **–ization** [–rəlaɪ'zeɪʃən], *s.* die Verallgemeinerung. **–ize** [–laɪz], 1. *v.a.* verallgemeinern, das Allgemeine betonen. 2. *v.n.* allgemeine Schlüsse ziehen (*from*, aus). **–ly**, *adv.* im ganzen, im allgemeinen, überhaupt; meistens, gewöhnlich, in den meisten Fällen; *–ly speaking*, im allgemeinen, im Grunde genommen. **–ship**, *s.* der Generalsrang, die Feldherrnwürde; Feldherrnkunst, Kriegführung; (*fig.*) geschickte Leitung.

generat–e ['dʒɛnəreɪt], *v.a.* zeugen (*Biol.*); hervorbringen, erzeugen, entwickeln (*Chem., Mach., etc.*); (*fig.*) bewirken, verursachen. **–ing-plant**, *s.* die Stromerzeugungsanlage. **–ing-station**, *s.* das Elektrizitätskraftwerk. **–ion** [–reɪʃən], *s.* die Zeugung, Fortpflanzung (*Biol.*); Erzeugung, Hervorbringung, Bildung; Generation, das Geschlecht; Menschenalter, Zeitalter; *people of one's –ion*, die Altersgenossen. **–ive** [–rətɪv], *adj.* zeugend, fruchtbar; *–ive power*, die Zeugungskraft. **–or** [–ə], *s.* der Erzeuger; Grundton (*Mus.*); Stromerzeuger, die Dynamomaschine (*Elec.*); *–or gas*, das Verbrauchergas.

generic [dʒɪ'nɛrɪk], *adj.* generisch; – *name*, der Gattungsname.

gener–osity [dʒɛnə'rɒsɪtɪ], *s.* der Edelmut, die Großmut; Freigebigkeit, Großzügigkeit. **–ous** ['dʒɛnərəs], *adj.* großmütig, edelmütig; freigebig; reichlich, ausgiebig, üppig; voll, stark (*as wine*).

genesis ['dʒɛnɪsɪs], *s.* die Entstehung, Genese, Genesis, das Werden; die Schöpfungsgeschichte; (*B.*) erstes Buch Mosis.

genet ['dʒɛnɪt], *s.* die Ginsterkatze, Genette (*Zool.*).

genetic [dʒɪ'nɛtɪk], *adj.* genetisch, Entstehungs–. **–s**, *pl.* (*sing. constr.*) die Entstehungslehre, Erblehre.

genial ['dʒɪ:njəl], *adj.* belebend, aufheiternd, anregend; freundlich, herzlich, heiter, munter, lustig; warm, mild (*climate*); (*archaic*) fruchtbar; Genie–. **–ity** [dʒɪ:nɪ'ælɪtɪ], *s.* die Freundlichkeit, Herzlichkeit, Wärme; Heiterkeit, Milde (*of climate*).

genital ['dʒɛnɪtl], *adj.* Zeugungs–, Geschlechts–. **–s**, *pl.* die Geschlechtsteile, Genitalien.

genitive ['dʒɛnɪtɪv], *s.* der Wesfall, Genetiv.

genius ['dʒɪ:njəs], *s.* (*pl.* –es) das Genie, genialer Mensch; (*no pl.*) die Anlage, Gabe, Begabung, besondere Fähigkeit, das Genie, geniale Kraft, schöpferische Kraft, das Geniale; die Eigentümlichkeit, das Charakteristische; (pl. *genii*) der Genius, Schutzgeist, Dämon; *good* –, der Schutzgeist; *evil* –, böser Genius; *man of* –, das Genie; *his – does not lie in that direction*, dazu hat er keine Anlage; – *of a period*, der Zeitgeist.

genre [ʒɑ̃:r], *s.* das Genre, die Art und Weise; der Stil. **—painting**, *s.* die Genremalerei.

gent [dʒɛnt], *s.* (*coll.*) feiner Herr. **–eel** [dʒɛn'tɪ:l], *adj.* fein, elegant, vornehm, vornehmtuend.

gentian ['dʒɛnʃən], *s.* der Enzian (*Bot.*).

gentile ['dʒɛntaɪl], 1. *s.* der Heide, die Heidin; der Nichtjude. 2. *adj.* heidnisch; nichtjüdisch.

gentility [dʒɛn'tɪlɪtɪ], *s.* die Vornehmheit, feine Lebensart.

gentle ['dʒɛntl], *adj.* sanft, mild, zart, lind, leicht, weich; gelinde (*as a breeze*); fromm (*as beasts*); mäßig, ruhig, sanft dahinfließend (*as rivers*); *of – birth* or *blood*, von vornehmer Abkunft; – *reader*, geneigter Leser; – *sex*, zartes Geschlecht; – *slope*, leichter Abhang. **–folk(s)**, *pl.* vornehme Leute. **–man**, *s.* der Herr, Ehrenmann, vornehmer Mann, der Mann von Stand, gesellschaftsfähiger Mann; *–man-at-arms*, das Mitglied der königlichen Leibwache; *country –man*, der Landedelmann; *fine –man*, feiner Herr; *–man of private means*, der Rentner; *too much of a –man to* (*do, etc.*), zu sehr Ehrenmann als daß . . .; *he is no –man*, er hat keine Lebensart; *–man of the bedchamber*, königlicher Kammerjunker; *–man's agreement*, stillschweigendes Übereinkommen, der Freundschaftsvertrag; *–man's –man*, der Diener, *–men!* meine Herren! **–man-driver**, *s.* der Herrenfahrer (*Motor.*). **–man-farmer**, *s.* der Gutsbesitzer und Landwirt. **–manlike**, **–manly**, *adj.* vornehm; fein, anständig, ehrenhaft; wohlgesittet, gebildet. **–man-rider**, *s.* der Herrenreiter. **–ness**, *s.* die Milde, Güte, Zartheit, Sanftheit, Sanftmut. **–woman**, *s.* vornehme, gebildete Dame.

gentry ['dʒɛntrɪ], *s.* niederer Adel, der Landadel, besitzende Stände (*pl.*); (*sl.*) Leute (*pl.*).

genufle–ct ['dʒɛnjʊflɛkt], *v.n.* die Knie beugen. **–ction, –xion** [–'flɛkʃən], *s.* die Kniebeugung.

genuine ['dʒɛnjʊɪn], *adj.* echt, wahr, lauter, unverfälscht. **–ness**, *s.* die Echtheit, Wahrheit.

gen–us ['dʒɪ:nəs], *s* (*pl.* –era ['dʒɛnərə]) die Gattung, das Geschlecht (*Biol.*); (*fig.*) die Art, Sorte.

geo–centric [dʒɪ:o'sɛntrɪk], *adj.* geozentrisch. **–de** ['dʒɪ:oʊd], *s.* die Druse, der Adlerstein (*Min.*). **–desy** [dʒɪ'ɒdɪsɪ], *s.* die Geodäsie, Feldmessung, Feldmeßkunst. **–detic** [dʒɪə'dɛtɪk], *adj.* geodätisch. **–gnosy** [dʒɪ'ɒgnəsɪ], *s.* die Erdschichtenkunde, Geologie. **–grapher** [dʒɪ'ɒgrəfə], *s.* der Geograph. **–graphic(al)** [dʒɪə'græfɪk(l)], *adj.* geographisch. **–graphy** [dʒɪ'ɒgrəfɪ], *s.* die Erdkunde, Geographie, Erdbeschreibung. **–logic(al)**, [dʒɪə'lɒdʒɪk(l)], *adj.* geologisch. **–logist** [–'ɒlədʒɪst], *s.* der Geolog. **–logize** [–'ɒlədʒɑɪz], 1. *v.n.* geologische Studien machen. 2. *v.a.* geologisch untersuchen. **–logy** [dʒɪ'ɒlədʒɪ], *s.* die Geologie. **–mancer** ['dʒɪ:omænsə], *s.* der Wahrsager aus Sandfiguren. **–mancy** [–mænsɪ], *s.* die Geomantie; Wahrsagung aus Sandfiguren. **–meter** [–'ɒmɪtə], *s.* der Mathematiker; die Spannerraupe (*Ent.*). **–metric(al)** [–ə'mɛtrɪk(l)], *adj.* geometrisch. **–metry** [–'ɒmɪtrɪ], *s.* die Geometrie, Raumlehre; *plane –metry*, die Geometrie der Ebene, Planimetrie; *solid –metry*, die Stereometrie; *–metry set*, das Reißzeug. **–physics** [dʒɪə'fɪzɪks], *s.* (*sing. constr.*) die Geophysik.

georgette ['dʒɔ:dʒɛt], *s.* der Seidenkrepp.

geranium [dʒɪ'reɪnjəm], *s.* der Storchschnabel, das Geranium (*Bot.*).

gerfalcon ['dʒə:fɔ:kən], *s.* der Gierfalke (*Orn.*).

germ [dʒə:m], *s.* der Keim, die Bazille (*Bot., Zool., Path.; also fig.*); – *carrier*, der Bazillenträger.

german ['dʒə:mən], *adj.* (*following*) leiblich.

German, *adj. & s. see Index of Names.*

germane ['dʒə:meɪn], *pred. adj.* gehörig, passend (*to*, zu), angemessen (*to* (*Dat.*)).

germi–cidal ['dʒə:mɪsɑɪdl], *adj.* keimtötend. **–cide** ['dʒə:mɪsɑɪd], *s.* keimtötendes Mittel. **–nal** ['dʒə:mɪnəl], *adj.* Keim–, Anfangs–, Ur–, unentwickelt. **–nant**, *adj.* keimend, sprossend. **–nate** [–neɪt], *v.n.* keimen, sprossen, sich entwickeln. **–nation** [–'neɪʃən], *s.* das Keimen, Sprossen.

gerrymander ['gɛrɪmændə], *v.a.* durch unlautere Mittel beeinflussen (*an election*) (*Amer.*); (*coll.*) beschönigen.

gerund ['dʒɛrənd], *s.* das Gerundium (*Gram.*). **–ial** [dʒə'rʌndjəl], *adj.* Gerundial–. **–ive** [dʒə'rʌndɪv], *s.* das Gerundiv(um) (*Gram.*).

gestation [dʒɛs'teɪʃən], *s.* die Trächtigkeit (*of beasts*); Schwangerschaft (*of women*).

gesticulat–e [dʒɛs'tɪkjʊleɪt], *v.n.* sich lebhaft gebärden, gestikulieren. **–ion** [–'leɪʃən], *s.* das Gebärdenspiel. **–ive**, *adj.* Gebärden–. **–ory** [–lətərɪ], *adj.* gestikulierend.

gesture ['dʒɛstʃə], 1. *s.* die Gebärde; das Gebärdenspiel; (*fig.*) die Geste. 2. *v.n. see* **gesticulate.**

get [gɛt], **1.** *ir. v.a.* erhalten, bekommen, empfangen, (*coll.*) kriegen; sich (*Dat.*) verschaffen, beschaffen, erwerben, verdienen, gewinnen, erlangen; besorgen, sich (*Dat.*) kaufen; (*a*) (*with p.p.*) lassen, veranlassen; – *one's hair cut*, sich (*Dat.*) die Haare schneiden lassen; – *s.th. done*, etwas machen lassen, etwas fertigbringen; – *you gone!* pack dich! mach dich fort! *I got my suit mended*, ich ließ meinen Anzug ausbessern; (*b*) (*with inf.*) dahinbringen, bewegen, überreden (*a person*); (*c*) (*with* *nouns*) – *the better of a p.*, einen überwinden *or* besiegen; die Oberhand gewinnen (über einen); – *me the book*, verschaff' *or* besorge mir das Buch; – *a glimpse of s.th.*, etwas nur flüchtig zu sehen bekommen; (*sl.*) – *one's goat*, einen reizen *or* ärgern; (*sl.*) – *a big hand*, lauten Beifall erhalten; – *hold of s.th.*, etwas zu fassen kriegen, zu etwas kommen, etwas erwischen; – *a hold on*, beherrschen, unter seinen Einfluß bekommen; – *it into one's head*, sich (*Dat.*) etwas in den Kopf setzen; – *possession of a th.*, sich einer S. bemächtigen, Besitz von etwas ergreifen; (*coll.*) – *the sack*, entlassen werden, den Laufpaß erhalten; – *a sight of*, zu Gesicht bekommen; – *the start of a p.*, einem den Vorsprung abgewinnen; (*fig.*) – *wind of*, erfahren über, Wind bekommen von; (*sl.*) – *the wind up*, Angst *or* Dampf bekommen; – *the worst of the bargain*, den kürzeren ziehen; – *a woman with child*, eine Frau schwängern; (*d*) (*with adv. extension*) bringen, schaffen, befördern, holen; – *away*, wegbringen, fortschaffen; *there is no –ting away from that*, man kann nicht davon loskommen; – *back*, zurückerhalten, wiederbekommen; – *by heart*, auswendig lernen; – *clear*, klarmachen; – *down*, hinunterbringen, hinunterholen; herunterschlucken; – *in*, hineinbringen, zur Aufnahme bringen; einschieben, hineintun; einziehen (*money due*); einbringen (*crops*); (*coll.*) – *one's hand in*, sich üben; – *off*, ausziehen, ablegen (*clothes*); aussteigen aus (*vehicle*); losmachen, loskriegen, wegschaffen, entfernen; lernen (*a task*); Lossprechung bewirken; – *on*, anziehen (*clothes*); besteigen (*a horse, cycle, etc.*); – *out*, herausbringen, herausziehen, herauslocken; – *over*, hinüberbringen; überwinden, hinter sich haben, ein Ende machen (*Dat.*); – *through*, durchbringen, bewältigen (*work*); – *together*, zusammenbringen, zusammenstellen; – *under control*, zähmen, bändigen; – *up*, aufwecken; zustandebringen, veranstalten, ins Werk setzen; ausstatten, einrichten; aufbessern, herausputzen; einstudieren, einpauken; (*sl.*) – *up s.o.'s back*, einen erzürnen; – *up steam*, Dampf aufmachen (*Locom.*); (*fig.*) in Schwung *or* vollen Gang kommen; (*e*) (*idiomatic or slang usage*) *I've got you*, ich habe dich erfaßt, ertappt *or* gefangen; (*sl.*) *they got him*, sie brachten ihn um; *you – me wrong*, du verstehst mich falsch; *he got it at last*, endlich verstand er es; *you'll – it hot*, du wirst dein Fett bekommen; *I'll – you for it*, ich werde dich schon packen *or* fassen; *it –s me*, es geht über meine Begriffe; (*f*) (*periphrastic*) (*coll.*) *have got*, haben, besitzen; *I've got s.th. for you*, ich habe etwas für dich; *have you got this book?* hast du dieses Buch? **2.** *ir.v.n.* gelangen, geraten, kommen, ankommen, anlangen; sich begeben, geben; (*a*) (*with inf.*) dahinkommen; – *to be*, werden; – *to hear*, zu hören bekommen; – *to know*, erfahren (*a th.*), kennenlernen (*a person*); (*b*) (*with adj. or p.p.*) werden; – *better*, sich erholen; – *clear*, frei werden, entwischen; – *dressed*, sich anziehen; – *drunk*, sich betrinken; – *married*, sich verheiraten; – *ready*, sich fertig machen; – *rid of*, loswerden; – *used to*, sich gewöhnen an (*Acc.*); (*c*) (*with pres. part.*) beginnen; – *talking*, zu plaudern anfangen; (*d*) (*with prepositions or adverbs*) – *about*, herumkommen, sich bewegen (können), wieder aufstehen dürfen (*after illness*); umgehen, bekannt werden (*of rumours*); – *abroad*, bekannt werden, unter die Leute kommen; (*coll.*) – *across*, wirken, Erfolg haben, Eindruck machen; – *ahead*, – *along*, weiterkommen, vorwärtskommen; – *along with*, auskommen mit; (*coll.*) – *along with you!* red' doch keinen Unsinn! – *at*, kommen an (*Acc.*), erreichen; (*coll.*) erfahren, herausbekommen (*facts*); (*coll.*) bestechen, herumkriegen, beikommen (*Dat.*) (*a person*); – *away*, wegkommen, davonkommen; – *away with*, Erfolg haben (mit, bei); (*coll.*) den Vogel abschießen; – *away with you!* mach daß du fortkommst; – *back*, zurückkommen; (*sl.*) – *back at a p.*, sich an einem rächen; – *behind*, zurückbleiben; – *by*, durchkommen; – *down*, hinunterkommen; absteigen; (*coll.*) – *down to*, sich heranmachen an; (*sl.*) – *down to business* or *brass tacks*, zur Sache kommen; – *forward*, see – *ahead*; – *home*, nach Hause (an)kommen; – *in*, eintreten, hineinkommen; geraten in (*debt, etc.*); – *into a habit*, eine Gewohnheit annehmen; – *near*, nahekommen (*Dat.*); – *off*, absteigen (*from*, von); davonkommen, freigesprochen werden; starten, loskommen (*as aircraft*); sich entziehen (*Dat.*) (*obligations, etc.*); – *off cheaply*, mit einem blauen Auge davonkommen; (*coll.*) – *off with a p.*, sich mit einem anbändeln; – *on*, Fortschritte machen, vorwärtskommen; – *on!* nur weiter! – *on one's feet*, aufstehen; *be –ting on for*, zugehen auf; – *on in life*, älter werden; – *on in the world*, weiterkommen, vorwärtskommen, es zu etwas bringen; – *on with a p.*, mit einem auskommen, sich mit einem vertragen; – *out*, ausgehen (dürfen), herauskommen; aussteigen; – *out of bed on the wrong side*, mit dem linken Fuß zuerst aufstehen; – *out of one's depth*, den Boden unter den Füßen verlieren (*also fig.*); – *out of doing*, umgehen zu tun; – *over*, hinüberkommen, hinwegkommen über (*Acc.*), überwinden (*difficulties*); sich erholen von (*a loss, an illness*); – *round a p.*, einen für sich gewinnen, einem um den Bart gehen; – *through*, durchkommen (*in an examination*), eine Prüfung bestehen; verbunden werden, Anschluß bekommen (*Tele.*); – *to*, erreichen; – *together*, zusammenkommen, sich versammeln, (*coll.*) sich einigen; – *under way*, in Fahrt kommen; – *up*, aufstehen, sich erheben; (empor)steigen; *the wind is –ting up*, der Wind erhebt sich. (*coll.*) **–-at-able**, *adj.* erreichbar (*of things*), zugänglich (*of persons*). **–-away**, *s.* das Entkommen; *make one's –-away*, auf und davon gehen, sich aus dem Staube machen. (*coll.*) **–-up**, *s.* der Anzug, Putz, Staat, die Ausstaffierung, Aufmachung (*of a book, etc.*); Ausstattung, Inszenierung (*of a drama*).

gewgaw ['gjuːgɔː], *s.* der Tand, die Nichtigkeit; das Spielzeug.

geyser ['gɪːzə], *s.* der Geiser; der Badeofen; Warmwasserapparat.

ghast-liness ['gɑːstlɪnɪs], *s.* gräßliches Aussehen; die Totenblässe. **–ly**, *adj.* & *adv.* geisterhaft, totenbleich; gräßlich grausig, schauderhaft; (*coll.*) entsetzlich, furchtbar, haarsträubend.

gherkin ['gəːkɪn], *s.* die Pfeffergurke, Essiggurke.

ghetto ['gɛtoʊ], *s.* das Getto, Judenviertel.

ghost [goʊst], *s.* der Geist, das Gespenst; (*fig.*) die Spur, der Anflug, Schatten; *give up the –*, den Geist aufgeben; *Holy –*, Heiliger Geist; *lay a –*, einen Geist bannen; *not a* or *the – of a chance*, nicht die geringste Aussicht. **–like**, *adj.*, **–ly**, *adj.* geisterhaft. **–-story**, *s.* die Gespenstergeschichte, Geistergeschichte.

ghoul [guːl], *s.* leichenverzehrender Dämon, der Ghul.

giant ['dʒɑɪənt], **1.** *s.* der Riese. **2.** *adj.* riesenhaft, riesig. **–ess**, *s.* die Riesin. **–-like**, *adj.* riesig, ungeheuer.

gibber ['dʒɪbə], *v.n.* kauderwelsch sprechen. **–ish** ['gɪbərɪʃ], *s.* das Geschnatter, Kauderwelsch.

gibbet ['dʒɪbɪt], **1.** *s.* der Galgen; der Kranbalken (*of a crane*). **2.** *v.a.* (auf)hängen.

gibb-osity [gɪ'bɔsɪtɪ], *s.* die Wölbung; der Buckel, Höcker. **–ous** ['gɪbəs], *adj.* gewölbt; buckelig; *the –ous moon*, der Mond zwischen Vollmond und Halbmond.

gib-e [dʒɑɪb], **1.** *s.* der Spott, die Stichelei. **2.** *v.n.* spotten (*at*, über). **3.** *v.a.* verspotten, höhnen. **–ing**, *adj.* spöttisch, höhnisch.

giblets ['dʒɪblɪts], *pl.* das Gänseklein.

gidd-iness ['gɪdɪnɪs], *s.* der Schwindel; die Unbesonnenheit, der Leichtsinn; die Unbeständigkeit. **–y**, *pred. adj.* schwind(e)lig, taumelnd (*with*, vor *or* von), benommen; *attrib. adj.* (*of persons*) unbeständig; unbesonnen, leichtsinnig; *attrib. adj.* schwindelnd, schwindelerregend (*height, etc.*); (*coll.*) albern, absurd.

gift [gɪft], **1.** *s.* die Gabe, das Geschenk; das Geben, die Schenkung; das Verleihungsrecht, Patronatsrecht; die Gabe, Begabung, das Talent; *the living is in his –*, er hat die Pfründe zu verleihen *or* zu vergeben; *deed of –*, die Schenkungsurkunde; *make a – of*, schenken; (*coll.*) – *of the gab*, ein tüchtiges Mundwerk; – *of tongues*, die Sprachbegabung; (*B.*) das Zungenreden; (*coll. it's a –*, es ist ge-

schenkt; *I wouldn't take it as a –*, ich möchte es nicht geschenkt bekommen. 2. *v.a.* beschenken. **–ed,** *adj.* begabt. **--horse,** *s.*; *look a --horse in the mouth*, einem geschenkten Gaul ins Maul sehen.
gig [gɪg], *s.* zweirädriger, offener Einspänner; das Kommandantenboot, leichtes Ruderboot (*Naut.*); die Rauhmaschine.
gigantic [dʒɑɪ'gæntɪk], *adj.* riesenhaft, gigantisch; ungeheuer.
giggle ['gɪgl], 1. *v.n.* kichern. 2. *s.* das Gekicher.
gigolo ['dʒɪgəloʊ], *s.* der Eintänzer.
[1]**gild** [gɪld], *ir.v.a.* vergolden; zieren, schmücken, übertünchen, verschönern; – *the pill*, die Pille versüßen. **–ed,** *adj.* vergoldet. **–ing,** *s.* die Vergoldung, (*fig.*) Verschönerung.
[2]**gild,** *see* **guild.**
[1]**gill** [gɪl], *s* (*usually pl.*) die Kieme (*Ichth.*); der Kehllappen (*Orn.*); die Lamelle (*of mushrooms*); (*coll.*) das Fleisch unter dem Kinn.
[2]**gill** [gɪl], *s.* (*dial.*) die Bergschlucht.
[3]**gill** [dʒɪl], *s.* die Viertelpinte (= 0·14 litre).
gillie ['gɪlɪ], *s.* der Jagdbegleiter, Bursche, Diener (*Scots*).
gillyflower ['dʒɪlɪflɑʊə], *s.* der Goldlack; die Levkoje; Gartennelke (*Bot.*).
gilt [gɪlt], *see* [1]**gild.** 1. *adj.* vergoldet; – *edges*, der Goldschnitt (*Bookb.*). 2. *s.* die Vergoldung; *take the – off the gingerbread*, einer S. des Glanzes berauben. **--edged,** *adj.* mit Goldschnitt (*Bookb.*); (*coll.*) prima, erstklassig; *--edged securities*, mündelsichere Papiere (*C.L.*).
gimbals ['dʒɪmbəlz], *pl.* Kardanische Aufhängung (*Naut.*).
gimcrack ['dʒɪmkræk], (*coll.*) 1. *adj.* wertlos, nichtig. 2. *s.* der Kram, Flitter, Tand.
gimlet ['gɪmlɪt], *s.* der Handbohrer; – *eye*, scharfspähendes Auge, (*coll.*) das Luchsauge.
gimp [gɪmp], *s.* die Gimpe, Borte, Besatzschnur.
[1]**gin** [dʒɪn], *s.* der Wachholderschnaps, Genever. **--palace,** *s.* großaufgemachte Branntweinschenke, feudales Lokal.
[2]**gin,** 1. *s.* das Hebezeug, die Winde (*Mach.*); Fördermaschine (*Min.*); *cotton-–*, die Egreniermaschine. 2. *v.a.* egrenieren, entkörnen (*cotton*).
[3]**gin,** 1. *s.* der Fallstrick, die Schlinge, Falle. 2. *v.a.* mit einer Schlinge fangen, verstricken.
ginger ['dʒɪndʒə], 1. *s.* der Ingwer; das Gelblichbraun; (*sl.*) der Rotkopf; (*fig.*) (*sl.*) der Mut, Schneid. 2. *v.a.*; (*coll.*) – *up*, anfeuern, aufpulvern, aufrütteln, auffrischen. **--ale, --beer,** *s.* das Ingwerbier. **–bread,** *s.* der Pfefferkuchen, Honigkuchen. **–ly,** *adv.* behutsam, sachte; zimperlich. **--nut,** *s.*, **--snap,** *s.* das Ingwerkeks. **–y,** *adj.* Ingwer–; scharf gewürzt; rötlich.
gingham ['gɪŋəm], *s.* der Gingang.
gingivitis [dʒɪndʒɪ'vɑɪtɪs], *s.* die Zahnfleischentzündung.
gipsy ['dʒɪpsɪ], 1. *s.* der Zigeuner; die Zigeunersprache, das Rotwelsch. 2. *adj.* zigeunerhaft, Zigeuner–. **--moth,** der Schwammspinner (*Orn.*). **--rose,** *s.* Wilde Skabiose (*Bot.*). **--winch,** *s.* kleine Winde (*Naut.*).
giraffe [dzɪ'rɑ:f], *s.* die Giraffe (*Zool.*).
girandole ['dʒɪrəndoʊl], *s.* der Armleuchter; die Feuergarbe, das Feuerrad (*Firew.*).
[1]**gird** [gə:d], *reg. & ir.v.a.* (*Poet.*) gürten (*dress, etc.*); umgürten (*a person*); (*fig.*) umgeben, umschließen; – *o.s. for the fray*, sich zur Schlacht bereit machen *or* gürten (*also fig.*); – *up one's loins*, sich rüsten *or* vorbereiten; – *on*, umgürten, umlegen, anlegen (*sword, etc.*).
[2]**gird,** 1. *v.n.* (*archaic*) sticheln, spotten, schmähen (*at*, über, (*Acc.*)). 2. *s.* der Spott, die Stichelei.
girder ['gə:də], *s.* der Träger, Tragbalken, Balken; Tragbaum, die Stütze (*Build.*); der Holm (*Av.*); Brückenträger (*of bridges*).
girdle [gə:dl], 1. *s.* der Gürtel, Gurt; (*fig.*) Ring, Umfang; die Einfassung (*of a gem*). 2. *v.a.* umgürten, umgeben; ringeln (*trees*).
girl [gə:l], *s.* das Mädchen; (*coll.*) Mädel; Dienstmädchen; (*coll.*) die Liebste, der Schatz; – *guide*, die Pfadfinderin; *shop* –, das Ladenmädchen. **–hood,** *s.* die Mädchenjahre (*pl.*), die Mädchenzeit. **–ish,** *adj.* mädchenhaft. **–ishness,** *s.* das Mädchenhafte.
girt [gə:t], *see* [1]**gird.**
girth [gə:θ], 1. *s.* der (Sattel)Gurt; (*fig.*) Umfang; *in* –, an Umfang. 2. *v.a.* gürten (*a horse*), (also – *up*) aufschnallen, festschnallen (*a saddle*).
gist [dʒɪst], *s.* der Hauptpunkt, Kern, das Wesentliche; (*coll.*) des Pudels Kern.
give [gɪv], **1.** *ir.v.a.* geben (*a p. a th.* or *a th. to a p.*, einem etwas); übergeben, übermitteln, überlassen, hergeben, hingeben, überbringen, abgeben; bieten, anbieten, darbieten; schenken, verleihen, erteilen, zuschreiben, zuerteilen; gewähren, angedeihen lassen, gestatten, zugeben, erlauben; verursachen, bewirken, hervorrufen; mitteilen, übertragen, weitergeben; von sich geben, äußern (*a groan, etc.*); vortragen, zum besten geben (*a song, etc.*); (*a*) (*with nouns*) – *attention to*, Acht geben auf (*Acc.*); – *battle*, eine Schlacht liefern (*to* (*Dat.*)), es zu einer Schlacht kommen lassen (*to a p.*, mit einem); – *birth to*, gebären, zur Welt bringen, (*fig.*) hervorbringen, Veranlassung geben zu; – *chase to*, Jagd machen auf (*Acc.*); – *credit to a report*, einem Bericht Glauben schenken *or* beimessen; – *a cry*, aufschreien; – *a decision*, den Fall entscheiden; – *a p. his due*, einem das Seinige zukommen lassen; – *ear to*, Gehör schenken (*Dat.*), horchen auf (*Acc.*); – *effect to*, in Kraft treten lassen, einer S. Kraft verleihen; – *ground*, zurückweichen, nachgeben, sich zurückziehen; – *a hand*, mithelfen, mitanpacken; – *heed to*, Beachtung schenken, beachten; (*sl.*) – *it to a p.*, einen durchprügeln; einem gehörig die Meinung sagen; – *judgment*, ein Urteil abgeben, sprechen *or* fällen; – *a knock*, anklopfen; – *a laugh*, auflachen; – *lectures on*, Vorlesungen halten über (*Acc.*); – *the lie to s.o.*, einen einer Lüge überführen; – *a p. a lift*, einen ein Stück mitnehmen, einen mitfahren lassen (*Motor.*); – *a p. a look*, einem einen Blick zuwerfen, einen anblicken; – *one's love to a p.*, einen herzlich grüßen lassen; – *one's mind to*, sich verlegen auf (*Acc.*), sich widmen (*Dat.*); – *one's name*, seinen Namen nennen; – *notice*, kündigen; – *offence*, kränken, beleidigen, Anstoß geben, Ärgernis erregen; – *pain*, weh tun; – *a p. a piece of one's mind*, einem unverblümt die Meinung sagen; – *place*, Platz machen (*to* (*Da* .)); ersetzt werden (*to*, von); – *a play*, ein Stück aufführen; – *pleasure*, Freude machen; – *s.o. one's kindest regards*, einen von sich schön grüßen lassen; – *rise to*, veranlassen, verursachen, hervorrufen, herbeiführen, bewirken, Anlaß geben zu; – *a song*, ein Lied zum besten geben; – *a start*, zusammenfahren; – *tongue*, bellen, anschlagen (*of hounds*), Ausdruck geben; – *a toast*, einen Toast ausbringen; – *trouble*, Mühe machen; – *vent to*, freien Lauf lassen (*Dat.*); – *voice to*, Ausdruck verleihen (*Dat.*), äußern; – *way*, nachgeben, nachlassen, weichen (*of persons*), zusammenbrechen, einstürzen (*of things*); – *one's word*, sein Wort verpfänden; (*b*) (*with prepositions & adverbs*) – *away*, weggeben, verteilen (*prizes*); verschenken, hergeben, (*coll.*) verraten, bloßstellen; – *away the bride*, Brautführer sein; – *o.s. away*, sich verraten, sich (*Dat.*) eine Blöße geben; (*coll.*) – *the show away*, das Geheimnis verraten; – *back*, zurückgeben; – *forth*, von sich geben, aussprechen, veröffentlichen; – *in*, einreichen, einliefern (*a petition, etc.*); – *in one's name*, sich einschreiben lassen; – *a th. into s.o.'s charge*, einem etwas anvertrauen; – *off*, abgeben, ausströmen, ausstrahlen, von sich geben; – *out*, verteilen, austeilen; bekanntmachen, bekanntgeben, ankündigen, aussprengen; see – *off*; – *o.s. out to be*, sich ausgeben für; – *over*, aufgeben, ablassen von, abtreten (*rights*); übergeben, überlassen (*to* (*Dat.*)); – *o.s. over to*, sich hingeben, sich ergeben (*Dat.*); – *up*, aufgeben, preisgeben; übergeben, abgeben; verzichten auf, abstehen von; – *o.s. up*, sich freiwillig stellen, sich ergeben, sich ausliefern; – *o.s. up for lost*, sich für verloren halten; – *o.s. up to a th.*, sich einer S. hingeben, ergeben *or* widmen. **2.** *ir.v.n.* geben; nachgeben, weichen, schlapp werden; federn, elastisch sein, sich anpassen (*to*, an); führen (*as roads, doors, etc.*) (*into*, in; *on to*, auf); (hinaus)gehen (*as windows*) (*on to*, auf); *a matter of – and take*, eine Hand wäscht die andere (*see below*); – *in*, nachgeben, weichen, klein beigeben; – *in to*, einwilligen in

(*Acc.*), annehmen (*Acc.*); beitreten (*Dat.*); – *out*, erschöpft *or* verbraucht sein, ausgehen, versiegen, versagen, zu Ende gehen, zur Neige gehen, alle werden (*of things*); nachlassen, zusammenbrechen (*of persons*); (*coll.*) – *over*, – *up*, aufhören, sich geben. **3.** *s.* das Nachgeben, die Elastizität. **--and-take,** *s.* der Ausgleich; (Gedanken–) *or* (Meinungs)-Austausch. **–n,** *attrib. adj.* bestimmt, festgesetzt, bekannt, gegeben (*also Math.*); *pred. adj.* ergeben, geneigt, veranlagt; *I am –n to understand*, man hat mir zu verstehen gegeben. **–r,** *s.* der Geber; *–r of a bill*, der Befehlsaussteller, Trassant.

gizzard [ˈgɪzəd], *s.* der Muskelmagen (*Orn.*); (*coll.*) *stick in one's –*, einem zuwider sein.

glabrous [ˈgleɪbrəs], *adj.* kahl, glatt, unbehaart.

glac-ial [ˈgleɪʃɪəl, ˈglæsɪəl], *adj.* eisig, Gletscher–; *–ial epoch*, die Eiszeit. **–iated** [–ʃɪeɪtɪd, –sɪeɪtɪd], *adj.* vereist, vergletschert. **–ier** [ˈglæsɪə], *s.* der Gletscher.

glacis [ˈgleɪsɪs], *s.* flache Abdachung (*Geol.*); das Glacis (*Fort.*).

glad [glæd], *pred. adj.* froh, erfreut (*of, at*, über (*Acc.*)); *attrib. adj.* heiter, fröhlich, vergnügt; freudig, erfreulich, angenehm; *be – of heart*, frohen Herzens sein; *I am –of it*, ich freue mich darüber, das freut mich; *I am – to see*, zu meiner Freude sehe ich; *I am – to say*, zu meiner Freude kann ich sagen; (*sl.*) *give a p. the – eye*, einem einen verliebten Blick zuwerfen; (*sl.*) *give a p. the – hand*, einen freundlich begrüßen; (*sl.*) – *rags*, Sonntagskleider (*pl.*). **–den,** *v.a.* erfreuen. **–ly,** *adv.* gern, mit Freuden. **–ness,** *s.* die Freude, Fröhlichkeit. **–some,** *adj.* (*Poet., archaic*) freudig, fröhlich; erfreulich.

glade [gleɪd], *s.* die Lichtung, Schneise.

gladiator [ˈglædɪeɪtə], *s.* der Gladiator. **–ial** [–əˈtɔːrɪəl], *adj.* gladiatorisch; *–ial fights*, Gladiatorenkämpfe.

gladiol-us [ˈglædɪouləs], *s.* (pl. –uses, –i [–laɪ]) die Gladiole, Schwertlilie (*Bot.*).

glad-ly [ˈglædlɪ], **–ness, –some,** *see* **glad.**

glair [glɛə], **1.** *s.* das Eiweiß. **2.** *v.a.* mit Eiweiß bestreichen.

glaive [gleɪv], *s.* (*Poet.*) breites Schwert.

glamo-rous [ˈglæmərəs], *adj.* bezaubernd, zauberisch. **–ur** [ˈglæmə], *s.* der Zauber, das Blendwerk; bezaubernde Schönheit, bezaubernder Glanz. **–ur-girl,** die Reklameschönheit.

glance [glɑːns], **1.** *s.* flüchtiger Blick; der Blitz, Schimmer, Schein, Lichtstrahl; das Abprallen; *at a –*, *at (the) first –*, auf den ersten Blick; *cast a – at*, einen Blick werfen in; *take a – at*, flüchtig betrachten. **2.** *v.n.* flüchtig blicken (*at*, auf); strahlen, glänzen, aufblitzen; – *aside*, anstreifen, abprallen, abschwenken, abgleiten; – *at*, Blicke werfen auf (*Acc.*), flüchtig anblicken; anspielen auf (*Acc.*), streifen, kurz berühren; – *off*, see – *aside*; – *over*, flüchtig überblicken.

gland [glænd], *s.* die Drüse (*Anat., Bot.*); Stopfbuchse (*Mach.*).

glander-ed [ˈglændəːd], *adj.* rotzig, rotzkrank (*of horses*). **–s,** *pl.* (*sing. constr.*) der Rotz, die Rotzkrankheit (*of horses*).

glandular [ˈglændjʊlə], *adj.* drüsig, Drüsen–.

glans [glænz], *s.* die Eichel (*Anat.*).

glar-e [glɛə], **1.** *s.* blendendes Licht, blendender Glanz; wilder durchbohrender Blick. **2.** *v.n.* strahlen, glänzen, blenden; starren; *–e at* or *upon a p.*, einen anstarren. **–ing,** *adj.* blendend, grell brennend; schreiend, auffallend, grell (*as colours*); unverhüllt, offenkundig; *–ing sun*, pralle Sonne.

glass [glɑːs], **1.** *s.* das Glas; Trinkglas, Wasserglas; Glasgefäß; Gewächshäuser (*pl.*); der Spiegel; das Stundenglas; das & der Barometer; *pl.* die Brille, die Gläser (*pl.*); das Fernglas, Opernglas; *pair of –es*, die Brille; – *after –*, ein Glas nach dem andern; *broken –*, Glasscherben (*pl.*); *cut –*, geschliffenes Glas; *looking-–*, der Spiegel; *magnifying-–*, das Vergrößerungsglas; *pane of –*, die Fensterscheibe; *plate-–*, das Spiegelglas; *sheet –*, das Tafelglas; *spun –*, die Glaswolle, das Glasgespinst; *stained –*, buntes Glas; *a – too much*, ein Trunk über den Durst; *a – of wine*, ein Glas Wein. **2.** *adj.* gläsern, Glas–. **– bead,** *s.* das Glaskügelchen. **--blower,** *s.* der Glasbläser. **– case,** *s.* der Schaukasten, Glaskasten. **– cover,** die Glasglocke (*for cheese*). **--cutter,** *s.* der Glasschleifer, Glasschneider (*also tool*). **– eye,** *s.* das Glasauge. **--foundry,** *see* **–works. –ful,** *s.* das Glasvoll. **--house,** *s.* das Treibhaus, Gewächshaus (*Hort.*); (*sl.*) Militärgefängnis. **–iness,** *s.* das Glasige, die Glätte. **–paper,** *s.* das Glaspapier. **--ware,** *s.* Glaswaren (*pl.*). **–works,** *pl.* die Glashütte. **–y,** *adj.* gläsern; glasig, starr (*as eye*); glatt (*as water*).

Glauber's salt [ˈglɔːbəzˈsɔːlt], *s.* das Natriumsulphat, schwefelsaures Natrium.

glauc-oma [glɔːˈkoumə], *s.* grüner Star, das Glaukom. **–ous,** *adj.* bläulich grün.

glaz-e [gleɪz], **1.** *v.a.* verglasen, mit Glasscheiben versehen; glasieren (*a cake, etc.*); lasieren (*Paint.*); glätten, satinieren (*paper, etc.*). **2.** *v.n.* gläsern *or* glasig werden; leblos erscheinen. **3.** *s.* der Glanz, die Glasur; Schmelze, Lasur (*Paint.*); Glätte, Satinage (*Paperm.*). **–ed,** *adj.* Glas–, Glanz–; glasig, verglast (*as eyes*). **–er,** *s.* der Glasierer; Feinschleifer (*Cutlery*). **–ier** [ˈgleɪzjə, ˈgleɪʒə], *s.* der Glaser; *–ier's diamond*, der Glaserdiamant; *–ier's putty*, der Glaserkitt. **–ing,** *s.* das Glasieren, die Verglasung; Lasierung (*Paint.*), Glasur (*on china, etc.*), Satinage (*paper*).

gleam [glɪːm], **1.** *s.* der Lichtstrahl, Schein, Schimmer, Glanz; – *of hope*, der Hoffnungsstrahl, der Schimmer von Hoffnung. **2.** *v.n.* glänzen, scheinen, schimmern; leuchten, strahlen.

glean [glɪːn], **1.** *v.a.* nachlesen; auflesen; (*fig.*) sammeln, zusammenbringen, schöpfen (*information, etc.*); – *from*, erfahren von, schließen aus. **2.** *v.n.* Ähren lesen. **–er,** *s.* der Ährenleser; (*fig.*) Sammler. **–ing,** *s.* (*usually pl.*) die Nachlese.

glebe [glɪːb], **1.** *s.* (*Poet.*) die Scholle, der Boden; – *land*, der Pfarracker, das Pfarrland.

glede [glɪːd], *s.* die Gabelweihe (*Orn.*).

glee [glɪː], *s.* die Freude, Fröhlichkeit, Heiterkeit; das Tafellied, der Rundgesang, Wechselgesang; *malicious* or *wicked –*, die Schadenfreude. **--club,** der Gesangverein. **–ful,** *adj.* fröhlich, vergnügt, lustig. **–man** [–mən], *s.* (*archaic*) der Sänger, Spielmann, Barde.

glen [glɛn], *s.* enges Tal, die Bergschlucht. **–garry,** *s.* schottische Mütze.

glib [glɪb], *adj.* glatt, zungenfertig; – *tongue*, geläufige Zunge. **–ness,** *s.* die Zungenfertigkeit. **--tongued,** *adj.* glattzüngig.

glid-e [glaɪd], **1.** *v.n.* gleiten, sanft dahinfließen *or* dahingleiten; im Gleitflug niedergehen (*Av.*). **2.** *s.* das Gleiten, der Gleitflug (*Av.*); Gleitlaut (*Phonet.*). **–er,** *s.* das Segelflugzeug; Segelflieger. **–ing,** *s.* das Segelfliegen, der Segelflug; *–ing ratio*, die Gleitzahl (*Av.*).

glimmer [ˈglɪmə], **1.** *v.n.* flimmern, glimme(r)n; schimmern, flackern. **2.** *s.* der Schein, Schimmer, Glimmer (*Geol.*); *not a – of an idea*, nicht die geringste Idee, kein Schimmer.

glimpse [glɪmps], **1.** *s.* flüchtiger Blick, Anblick *or* Einblick; der Schimmer, Lichtblick; *afford a – of*, einen Einblick gewähren in; *catch* or *get a – of*, nur flüchtig zu sehen bekommen, einen kurzen Blick tun in. **2.** *v.a.* flüchtig blicken (*at*, auf) *or* sehen, plötzlich erblicken.

glint [glɪnt], **1.** *v.n.* glänzen, schimmern, glitzern. **2.** *s.* der Schimmer, Lichtschein, Lichtstrahl.

glissade [glɪˈsɑːd], **1.** *s.* die Abfahrt (*Mount.*); der Schleifschritt (*Danc.*). **2.** *v.n.* abrutschen, abfahren (*Mount.*).

gliste-n [ˈglɪsn], *v.n.*, **–r** [ˈglɪstə], *v.n.* glänzen, glitzern, schimmern.

glitter [ˈglɪtə], **1.** *v.n.* glitzern, glänzen, funkeln, schimmern, flimmern, gleißen. **2.** *s.* das Funkeln, der Glanz, Schimmer. **–ing** [–rɪŋ], *adj.* glänzend, glitzernd.

gloaming [ˈgloumɪŋ], *s.* die Dämmerung.

gloat [glout], *v.n.* (– *on* or *upon*) anglotzen, anstieren, gierig anblicken (*Acc.*); – *over*, sich weiden an (*Dat.*), sich hämisch freuen über. **–ing,** **1.** *s.* die Schadenfreude, hämische Lust. **2.** *adj.* schadenfroh, hämisch.

glob-al [ˈgloubəl], *adj.* weltumfassend, Welt–, Gesamt–. **–ate** [ˈgloubeɪt], *adj.* kugelförmig. **–e**

[gloub], 1. *s.* die Kugel; Erdkugel, der Erdball, die Erde; der Globus (*Geog.*); die Lampenglocke; *habitable –e*, bewohnbarer Erdkreis. 2. *v.a. & n.* zusammenballen. **–e-flower,** *s.* die Trollblume, Kugelranunkel (*Bot.*). (*coll.*) **–e-trotter,** *s.* der Weltbummler. **–ose** [glo'bous], *adj. see* **–ular.** **–osity** [–'bɔsıtı], *s.* die Kugelgestalt, Kugelform. **–ular** ['glɔbjulə], *adj.* kugelförmig, rundlich. **–ule** ['glɔbju:l], *s.*, **–ulet** ['glɔbjəlıt], *s.* das Kügelchen.

glomerat–e ['glɔmərət], *adj.* knäuelförmig, zusammengeballt. **–ion** [–'reıʃən], *s.* die Zusammenballung.

gloom [glu:m], 1. *s.* das Dunkel, die Dunkelheit, Düsterkeit, Düsternis; (*fig.*) Schwermut, der Trübsinn. 2. *v.n.* trüb *or* düster aussehen; schwermütig *or* mürrisch blicken. 3. *v.a.* verdunkeln, verdüstern. **–iness,** *s.* die Düsterheit, Düsterkeit, Düsternis; Schwermut. **–y,** *adj.* dunkel, düster (*also fig.*); (*fig.*) schwermütig, trübsinnig; hoffnungslos; verdrießlich.

glor–ification [glɔ:rıfı'keıʃən], *s.* die Verherrlichung, Lobpreisung. **–ify** ['glɔ:rıfaı], *v.a.* verherrlichen; preisen, lobpreisen; verklären, erhellen. **–iole** ['glɔ:rıoul], *s.* der Heiligenschein, die Strahlenkrone. **–ious** ['glɔ:rıəs], *adj.* glorreich, ruhmreich, ruhmvoll; herrlich, prächtig. **–y** ['glɔ:rı], 1. *s.* der Ruhm, die Ehre; Herrlichkeit, Pracht, der Glanz, Glanzpunkt; die Verklärung; Glorie, Strahlenkrone, der Heiligenschein; (*fig.*) Nimbus. 2. *v.n.* sich freuen, frohlocken (*in*, über (*Acc.*)); stolz sein (*in*, auf (*Acc.*)); seinen Stolz suchen (*in*, in); sich rühmen. (*sl.*) **–y-hole,** *s.* die Rumpelkammer.

[1]**gloss** [glɔs], 1. *s.* die Glosse, Erklärung, erklärende Anmerkung, Randbemerkung. 2. *v.a. & n.* erklären, auslegen, Bemerkungen machen; *– over*, wegdeuten, hinweggehen über. **–ary** ['glɔsərı], *s.* das Glossar; Spezialwörterbuch. **–ographer** [glɔs'ɔgrəfə], *s.* der Glossenschreiber, Kommentator.

[2]**gloss,** 1. *s.* der Glanz, Preßglanz; (*fig.*) Anstrich, äußerer Schein. 2. *v.a.* glänzend machen, glänzen, satinieren, polieren; (*fig.*) *– over*, beschönigen, bemänteln, vertuschen. **–iness,** *s.* der Glanz, die Glätte, Politur. **–y,** *adj.* glänzend, glatt, poliert.

glott–al ['glɔtl], **–ic,** *adj.* Stimmritzen–; *–al stop*, der Knacklaut (*Phonet.*). **–is** ['glɔtıs], *s.* die Stimmritze.

glove [glʌv], *s.* der Handschuh; *a pair of –s*, ein Paar Handschuhe; *fit like a –*, passen wie angegossen; *be hand in – with s.o.*, mit einem (in böser Absicht) zusammenarbeiten; (*fig.*) *take the –s off*, derb werden, unsanft anpacken; *take up the –*, die Herausforderung annehmen; *throw down the –*, den Fehdehandschuh hinwerfen, herausfordern. **–r,** *s.* der Handschuhmacher. **– -stretcher,** *s.* der Handschuhweiter.

glow [glou], 1. *s.* die Glut, das Glühen, der Schein, Glanz, die Helle, Röte; Wärme, das Wohlbehagen; *all in a –*, glühend. 2. *v.n.* glühen, durchglühen; strahlen, glänzen (*as colours*); erröten, rot werden (*with*, vor). **–ing,** *adj.* glühend; heiß, warm; strahlend, glänzend; begeisternd. **– -worm,** *s.* der Leuchtkäfer, das Glühwürmchen.

glower ['glauə], 1. *s.* finsterer Blick. 2. *v.n.* finster aussehen; *– at*, anstieren.

gloze [glouz], 1. *v.a.*; *– over*, beschönigen, vertuschen. 2. *v.n.* schmeicheln, kriechen.

glucose ['glu:kous], *s.* die Glukose, Glykose, der Traubenzucker.

glue [glu:], 1. *s.* der (Tischler)Leim. 2. *v.a.* leimen (*Carp.*); kleben; (*fig.*) heften (*to*, auf *or* an). **– -pot,** *s.* der Leimtiegel. **–y** ['glu:ı], *adj.* klebrig, leimig.

glum [glʌm], *adj.* mißmutig, verdrossen, verdrießlich, mürrisch, sauer, finster.

glum–aceous [glu:'meıʃəs], *adj.* spelzblütig. **–al,** spelzig. **–e** [glu:m], *s.* die Spelze (*Bot.*).

glut [glʌt], 1. *v.a.* übersättigen, überladen, überfüllen; (*fig.*) sättigen, befriedigen; *– the market*, den Markt überschwemmen. 2. *s.* die Überfülle, der Überfluß; die Übersättigung, Überfüllung.

glut–en ['glu:tən], *s.* der Kleber, die Gallerte, das Gluten. **–inous** [–əs], *adj.* leimig, klebrig.

glutton ['glʌtn], *s.* der Fresser, Schlemmer; Vielfraß (*Zool.*); (*fig.*) Schwelger, Unersättliche(r), *m.* Gierige(r), *m.* **–ous** [–əs], *adj.* gefräßig, gierig (*also fig.*) (*of* or *for*, nach). **–y** [–ı], *s.* die Gefräßigkeit, Völlerei, Schlemmerei.

glycerine ['glısərın], *s.* das Glyzerin.

glyp–h [glıf], *s.* die Rille, Furche (*Arch.*); Glypte, Steinfigur. **–tic** ['glıptık], *adj.* Steinschneide–. **–tograph,** *s.* die Gemme, geschnittener Stein. **–tography** [glıp'tɔgrəfı], *s.* die Glyptik, Gemmenkunde.

gnarl [nɑ:l], *s.* der Knorren. **–ed** [nɑ:ld], *adj.* knorrig.

gnash [næʃ], *v.a.* knirschen; *– one's teeth*, mit den Zähnen knirschen.

gnat [næt], *s.* die Mücke; Schnake. **– -bite,** *s.* der Mückenstich.

gnaw [nɔ:], *v.a. & n.* nagen an, zernagen; zerfressen; (*fig.*) zermürben.

gneiss [nɑıs], *s.* der Gneis (*Geol.*).

[1]**gnom–e** [noum], *s.* der Erdgeist, Gnom. **–ish,** *adj.* gnomenhaft.

[2]**gnom–e,** *s.* der Sinnspruch, Denkspruch. **–ic** ['noumık], *adj.* gnomisch. *–ic poetry*, die Spruchdichtung.

gnomon ['noumən], *s.* der Sonnen(uhr)zeiger; Gnomon (*Math.*).

gnos–is ['nousıs], *s.* tiefe religiöse Erkenntnis. **–tic** ['nɔstık], 1. *adj.* gnostisch. 2. *s.* der Gnostiker. **–ticism** ['nɔstısızm], *s.* der Gnostizismus.

gnu [nu:], *s.* das Gnu (*Zool.*).

go [gou], **1.** *ir.v.n.* gehen, laufen, fahren, reisen; verkehren (*of vehicles*), arbeiten, funktionieren (*of engines*); fortgehen, losgehen, abgehen, dahingehen, sich begeben, sich bewegen, sich rühren; vergehen, verfließen (*of time*), in Umlauf sein (*as rumours*), lauten (*of documents*); werden, sich entwickeln, verlaufen, sich gestalten (*of events*); ausgehen, ausfallen, Erfolg haben, gelingen; sich erstrecken, reichen; gelten, gültig sein, angenommen werden; *be –ing to*, im Begriff sein zu; *see* **–ing;** *a week to –*, noch eine Woche übrig, eine weitere Woche; (*coll.*) *– all out*, große Anstrengungen machen; *as far as that –es*, an und für sich, was das anlangt; *let –*, fahren lassen, loslassen; *they let it – at that*, sie haben es dabei bewenden lassen; *as the story –es*, wie man sich erzählt; *as things –*, unter den Umständen; *as times –*, wie die Zeiten nun einmal sind; *how –es the time*, wie spät ist es? *who –es there?* wer da? *here –es!* nun los! *there he –es again!* da fängt er schon wieder an! *–ing, –ing, –ne!* zum ersten, zum zweiten, zum dritten! (a) (*with nouns*) *– bail for*, bürgen für, Bürgschaft leisten für; *– halves with*, teilen mit, sich in die Hälfte teilen; *let – hang*, links liegenlassen, unerledigt liegen bleiben, stehen und liegen lassen; (*coll.*) *– the pace*, schnell gehen; (*fig.*) ein flottes Leben führen; *– shares*, teilen; *– a long way*, weit *or* lange reichen; *– a long way towards*, wesentlich beitragen zu; (b) (*with adjectives*) (*coll.*) *– bad*, verderben; *– blind*, erblinden; (*sl.*) *– broke*, Bankrott machen; (*sl.*) *– bust*, ruiniert sein; *be –ing cheap*, billig zu haben sein; *– easy*, es sich (*Dat.*) bequem machen, sich nicht überanstrengen; *– easy with*, sparsam umgehen mit; *– far towards*, see *– a long way towards*; *– hard*, schlimm *or* übel ergehen (*with* (*Dat.*)); *– hungry*, hungern; *– mad*, verrückt werden; *– short of*, entbehren; *– sick*, sich krank melden; *– steady*, sich vorsichtig verhalten, vorsichtig gehen; (*coll.*) *be –ing strong*, noch auf den Beinen sein; *– unheeded*, unbeachtet bleiben; *– unpunished*, davonkommen; (*sl.*) *– west*, zunichte werden, in die Binsen gehen, flötengehen; *– wrong*, fehlgehen, sich irren, schief gehen; auf Abwege geraten, sich verirren; (c) (*with adverbs & prepositions*) *– aboard*, an Bord gehen, sich einschiffen; *– about*, wenden (*Naut.*); umhergehen; vorhaben, gehen an (*Acc.*), heranmachen an (*Acc.*), sich befassen mit, in Angriff nehmen; *you – the wrong way about it*, Sie fangen das verkehrt an; *– about one's work*, an seine Arbeit gehen; *– abroad*, ins Ausland gehen *or* reisen; *– after*, nachgehen, nachlaufen (*Dat.*); zu erlangen suchen; *– against*, ziehen gegen *or* wider (*an enemy*); zuwiderhandeln (*Dat.*), widerstreben (*Dat.*); –

against the grain, (einem) gegen den Strich gehen; *it –es against his wishes*, es läuft seinen Wünschen zuwider; – *ahead*, vorwärtsgehen; – *ahead!* vorwärts! weiter! – *along*, fortgehen, dahingehen, entlang gehen; – *along with*, begleiten; – *amiss*, schiefgehen; – *astray*, sich verirren; verloren gehen; – *at*, losgehen auf (*Acc.*), angreifen, in Angriff nehmen; – *away*, weggehen, abreisen; – *back*, zurückgehen; – *back on one's promise*, sein Versprechen zurücknehmen *or* nicht einlösen; – *back to*, zurückgehen auf, zurückgreifen auf; – *before*, vorhergehen; vorgehen; – *behind*, folgen (*Dat.*), hinterhergehen; untersuchen, auf den Grund gehen (*Dat.*); – *behind s.o.'s back*, einen hintergehen; – *by*, vorbeigehen, vorübergehen; verfließen, vergehen, verstreichen; sich richten nach, bestimmt werden durch; – *by air*, fliegen, mit dem Flugzeug fahren; – *by the instructions*, sich an die Weisungen halten; – *by the name of . . .*, den Namen . . . führen, unter dem Namen . . . bekannt sein; – *contrary to*, gehen *or* handeln gegen; – *down*, hinuntergehen, herabgehen, sich legen (*as wind*); unterliegen, fallen; (*coll.*) Wirkung haben, Glauben, Anklang, *or* Annahme finden (*with*, bei); (*coll.*) die Universität verlassen, sich exmatrikulieren lassen; – *down in history*, in die Geschichte eingehen; – *down in the world*, herunterkommen; *his name will – down to posterity*, sein Name wird auf die Nachwelt kommen; (*coll.*) *that won't – down with me*, das wird bei mir nicht verfangen, so etwas lasse ich mir nicht gefallen; – *far*, weit gehen; weit reichen; viel gelten (*with*, bei); es weit bringen; – *for*, gehen nach, holen; gehalten werden für, gelten für *or* als; losgehen auf, sich losstürzen auf; – *for a drive*, ausfahren, spazieren fahren; – *for an excursion*, einen Ausflug machen; – *for nothing*, nichts fruchten, wirkungslos *or* vergeblich sein, nichts gelten; – *forth*, hervorgehen; – *forward*, vorwärts gehen, vorrücken; fortschreiten; – *from*, weggehen, verlassen; nicht halten (*one's word*); – *in*, hineingehen; – *in for*, sich eifrig befassen mit, sich legen auf (*Acc.*), sich widmen (*Dat.*); – *in for an examination*, ein Examen machen; – *into*, gehen in (*Acc.*), eintreten in; eingehen auf, teilnehmen an, sich beschäftigen mit; geraten *or* verfallen in (*Acc.*); prüfen, überprüfen; – *into committee*, sich als Kommission konstituieren; – *into court*, klagen; – *into holes*, Löcher bekommen; – *into a matter*, auf eine Sache eingehen, etwas untersuchen; – *into mourning*, trauern, Trauerkleider anlegen; – *into partnership*, sich mit einem geschäftlich verbinden *or* assoziieren; – *off*, weggehen (*as people*), abgehen (*as trains, etc.*); Absatz finden (*as goods*); sich ergehen, vonstatten gehen; losgehen, explodieren (*as a gun*); sich verschlechtern, schlecht werden (*as food*); einschlafen; – *off without a hitch*, reibungslos vonstatten gehen, tadellos klappen; – *on*, vorwärts gehen, fortfahren, vor sich gehen, weitergehen, fortdauern, weiterbestehen; losfahren (*at*, auf (*Acc.*)); (*coll.*) schelten, reden; sich anziehen lassen (*as clothes*); sich benehmen; *be –ing on for*, sich nähern (*Dat.*), gehen auf (*Acc.*); – *on an errand*, einen Gang tun; – *on an expedition*, eine Expedition unternehmen; (*coll.*) – *on the dole*, Arbeitslosenunterstützung beziehen; – *on horseback*, reiten; – *on the parish*, der Gemeinde zur Last fallen; – *on one's way*, sich auf den Weg machen; see – *upon*; – *out*, ausgehen, erlöschen; *my heart –es out to him*, ich fühle mich zu ihm hingezogen; – *out on strike*, streiken; – *out to service*, in Stellung gehen; – *out of business*, das Geschäft aufgeben; – *out of fashion*, aus der Mode kommen; – *out of print*, vergriffen sein; (*fig.*) – *out of one's way*, sich bemühen (*to*, um), sich einsetzen (*to*, für), keine Mühe scheuen; – *over*, gehen über (*Acc.*), übergehen, übertreten (*to*, zu); durchgehen, durchsehen, durchlesen (*a paper*); untersuchen, prüfen (*an account, etc.*); (*sl.*) Erfolg haben, wirken; – *round*, ausreichen (*of food*); – *through*, durchgehen, Annahme finden; erörtern; bestehen, aushalten, mitmachen, durchmachen; – *through with*, durchsetzen, durchführen, zu Ende führen; – *to*, gehen zu; *the property –es to his brother*, das Besitztum fällt an seinen Bruder; – *to the country*, sich an das Volk wenden, das Parlament auflösen, Neuwahlen ausschreiben (*Parl.*); – *to the dogs*, auf den Hund kommen; – *to expense*, sich in Unkosten stürzen; – *to law*, einen Prozeß anfangen, prozessieren; *16 ounces – to a pound*, 16 Unzen gehen auf das Pfund; – *to sea*, Seemann werden; in See stechen; – *to a lot of trouble*, sich viel Mühe geben; – *to war*, Krieg anfangen, Krieg führen; – *to waste*, verkommen, verlottern; – *to work*, an die Arbeit *or* ans Werk gehen; – *to wrack and ruin*, zugrunde gehen; – *together*, zusammengehen; zusammenpassen; – *under*, untergehen, unterliegen, zugrunde gehen; – *under the name of*, unter dem Namen gehen; – *up*, hinaufgehen, aufsteigen; *prices are –ing up*, die Preise steigen; – *up the line*, an die Front geschickt werden; – *up to town*, nach der Hauptstadt reisen; (*coll.*) – *up* (*to the University*), die Universität beziehen; – *upon*, see – *on*; sich gründen *or* stützen auf (*Acc.*), handeln *or* sich richten nach; *nothing to – upon*, keine Unterlagen *or* Vorlagen haben; – *with*, begleiten; es halten mit; passen zu, zusammenpassen mit; *things – well* (*ill*) *with him*, es geht ihm gut (schlecht), es steht gut (schlecht) mit ihm; – *without*, sich behelfen ohne, entbehren; *that –es without saying*, das versteht sich von selbst, das ist selbstverständlich; (**d**) (*with gerund*) – *begging*, betteln gehen (*of a p.*), (*coll.*) um nichts zu haben sein (*of a th.*); – *limping from the room*, hinkend aus dem Zimmer gehen; – *motoring*, eine Autofahrt machen; (**e**) (*–ing with inf.*) *be –ing to do*, im Begriff sein zu tun, tun werden, wollen *or* müssen; *what is –ing to be done?* was wird man tun müssen? was will man tun? **2.** *v.a.* (*coll.*) – *one better than*, überbieten, übertreffen; (*sl.*) – *the whole hog*, die Sache gründlich erledigen, reine Sache machen; (*coll.*) – *it!* nur los! immer zu!; (*coll.*) – *it strong*, entschlossen auftreten. **3.** *s.* (*coll.*) das Gehen, der Gang; Versuch; die Mode; der Schneid, Schwung; Schluck; die Abmachung; (*sl.*) Prüfung; *Great –*, die Hauptprüfung; *Little –*, das Vorexamen, die Aufnahmeprüfung (*Univ.*); *have a – at*, einen Versuch machen mit, probieren (*Acc.*); *be all* or *quite the –*, Furore machen, Mode sein; *it's a –!* abgemacht!; *on the –*, in Bewegung; *it's no –!* es ist nichts zu machen, das geht nicht, es ist zwecklos. **–-ahead,** *adj.* fortschrittlich, modern; unternehmend, aufstrebend, strebsam, energisch, tätig. **–-between,** *s.* der Vermittler, Mittelsmann. **–-by,** *s.* (*sl.*); *give a p. the –-by*, einen ignorieren *or* schneiden. **–-cart,** *s.*, der Gängelwagen. **–er,** *s.* der Geher, Gänger, Läufer. **–-getter,** *s.* (*sl.*) der Draufgänger. **–ing, 1.** *adj.* gehend; im Gange, im Schwange, gutgehend; *be –ing*, (*before an inf.*) im Begriff sein, gedenken, gerade wollen; *he thought he was –ing to die*, er glaubte, er stürbe; *we are –ing to have company tomorrow*, morgen werden wir Gesellschaft haben; *I was just –ing to tell you*, ich wollte dir eben sagen; *–ing concern*, gutgehendes *or* blühendes Geschäft; *the greatest scoundrel –ing*, der größte Schurke, den es gibt. **2.** *s.* das Gehen; der Weggang, die Abfahrt, Abreise; Bodenbeschaffenheit; *–ing back*, das Zurück(gehen); *there is no –ing back*, ein Zurück(weichen) ist unmöglich, das Los ist gefallen; *the –ing was rough*, es war ein beschwerlicher Weg; *while the –ing was good*, bei gutem Wind, solange es Zeit war. **–ings-on,** *pl.* das Verfahren, Benehmen, Treiben, Techtelmechtel.

goad [goud], 1. *s.* der Stachelstock, Treibstock; (*fig.*) der Sporn, Antrieb. 2. *v.a.* (*fig.*) anstacheln, anregen; (an)treiben.

goal [goul], *s.* das Ziel, der Bestimmungsort; das Tor, der Torschuß (*Footb.*); (*fig.*) Zweck, Endzweck, Zielpunkt; (*archaic*) das Mal, Grenzmal; *get* or *score a –*, ein Tor machen. **–-keeper,** *s.* der Torwart, Tormann (*Footb.*). **–-post,** *s.* der Torpfosten (*Footb.*).

goat [gout], *s.* die Ziege, Geiß; der Steinbock (*Astr.*); (*coll.*) Narr, Tölpel; *he-–*, der Ziegenbock; (*sl.*) *get a p.'s –*, einen ärgern; (*coll.*) *play the giddy –*, sich leichtfertig benehmen. **–ee,** *s.* der Ziegenbart, Spitzbart. **–-herd,** *s.* der Ziegenhirt. **–ish,** *adj.* bockig; (*fig.*) geil. **–-moth,** *s.* der Weidenbohrer (*Ent.*). **–'s beard,** *s.* der Ziegenbart, Geißbart,

Bocksbart (*Bot.*). **–skin,** *s.* das Ziegenfell. **–sucker,** *s.* der Ziegenmelker (*Orn.*).

gob [gɔb], *s.* (*vulg.*) der Speichel, Schleimauswurf; taubes Gestein (*Min.*); (*sl.*) (*Amer.*) die Blaujacke. **–bet** [ˈgɔbɪt], *s.* das Stück Fleisch, der Bissen.

gobble [ˈgɔbl], 1. *v.a.* (– *up*) gierig verschlingen. 2. *v.n.* kollern (*as a turkey*). **–r,** *s.* der Vielfraß; Truthahn.

goblet [ˈgɔblɪt], *s.* der Kelch, Becher, Pokal.

goblin [ˈgɔblɪn], *s.* der Kobold. Elf.

goby [ˈgoubɪ], *s.* die Grundel (*Ichth.*).

god [gɔd], *s.* der Gott; die Gottheit; der Götze, (*fig.*) Abgott; *by* –*!* bei Gott! *for* –*'s sake,* um Gottes willen; – *forbid!* Gott behüte!; *good* –*!* großer Gott!; – *grant,* gebe Gott; – *knows,* weiß Gott; *thank* –*!* Gott sei Dank! – *willing,* so Gott will; *would to* –, wollte Gott. **–child,** *s.* das Patenkind. **–daughter,** *s.* die Pate. **–dess,** *s.* die Göttin. **–father,** *s.* der Taufzeuge, Pate, Gevatter; *stand –father to,* Gevatter stehen bei. **––fearing,** *adj.* gottesfürchtig. **––forsaken,** *adj.* gottverlassen, elend, erbärmlich. **––given,** *adj.* von Gott gesandt. **–head,** *s.* die Gottheit. **–less,** *adj.* gottlos. **–like,** *adj.* göttlich, gottähnlich. **–liness,** *s.* die Frömmigkeit, Gottseligkeit. **–ly,** *adj.* fromm, gottesfürchtig. **–mother,** *s.* die Taufzeugin, Patin, Gevatterin. **–parent,** *s.* der Taufpate, die Taufpatin. **–s,** *s.* (*sing. constr.*) (*sl.*) der Olymp (*Theat.*). **–send,** *s.* der Glücksfall, unverhoffter Fund, wahrer Segen. **–son,** *s.* der Pate; Täufling. **––speed,** *s.* der Scheidegruß, das Lebewohl; *bid a p. ––speed,* einem glückliche Reise wünschen.

godwit [ˈgɔdwɪt], *s.* die Uferschnepfe (*Orn.*).

goffer [ˈgɔfə], 1. *v.a.* kräuseln, kniffen, plissieren, gaufrieren. 2. *s.* die Falte, der Plissee.

goggle [ˈgɔgl], *v.n.* stieren, glotzen. **––eyed,** *adj.* glotzäugig. **–s,** *pl.* die Schutzbrille; (*sl.*) Brille.

goitr–e [ˈgɔɪtə], *s.* der Kropf. **–ous,** *adj.* kropfartig.

gold [gould], 1. *s.* das Gold; die Goldmünze; (*fig.*) das Geld, der Reichtum; (*Prov.*) *all is not – that glitters,* es ist nicht alles Gold, was glänzt; *as good as* –, kreuzbrav, sehr artig; *with a heart of* –, (gut)-herzig; *worth one's weight in* –, unbezahlbar, unschätzbar. 2. *adj.* golden, Gold–. **––beater,** *s.* der Goldschläger. **––beater's-skin,** *s.* die Goldschlägerhaut. **– brick,** *s.* (*sl.*) der Schwindel, Schein (*Amer.*); *sell s.o. a – brick,* einen anschmieren. **–crest,** *s.* das Goldhähnchen (*Orn.*). **––digger,** *s.* der Goldgräber. **––dust,** *s.* der Goldstaub. **–en,** *adj.* golden; goldgelb; *–en age,* goldenes Zeitalter; *–en eagle,* der Steinadler (*Orn.*); *–en mean,* goldener Mittelweg; *–en opinions,* hohe Anerkennung; *–en opportunity,* günstige Gelegenheit; *–en oriole,* der Pirol (*Orn.*); *–en pheasant, s.* der Goldfasan (*Orn.*); *–en-rod, s.* die Goldrute (*Bot.*); *–en wedding,* goldene Hochzeit. **–finch,** *s.* der Stieglitz, Distelfink. **–fish,** *s.* der Goldfisch. **––hammer,** *s.* die Goldammer (*Orn.*). **–ilocks,** *s.* Goldgelber Hahnenfuß (*Bot.*); (*coll.*) das Goldköpfchen. **– lace,** die Goldtresse. **––leaf,** *s.* die Goldfolie, das Blattgold. **––mine,** *s.* die Goldgrube (*also fig.*). **––rush,** *s.* der Massenandrang von Goldschürfern. **––size,** *s.* der Goldgrund. **–smith,** *s.* der Goldschmied. **– standard,** *s.* die Goldwährung.

golf [gɔlf], *s.* das Golfspiel. **– club,** der Golfschläger; Golfklub. **–er,** *s.* der Golfspieler. **––links,** *pl.* (*sing. constr.*) der Golfplatz.

golliwog [ˈgɔlɪwɔg], *s.* groteske Puppe, die Negerpuppe.

gondol–a [ˈgɔndələ], *s.* die Gondel (*also Av.*), venetianisches Ruderboot. **–ier** [–ˈlɪə], *s.* der Gondelführer, Gondolier.

gone [gɔn], *see* **go.** 1. *p.p. he has* –, er ist gegangen; *he is* –, er ist fort, weg, abgereist *or* verschwunden; *all his money is* –, sein ganzes Geld ist aufgebraucht *or* (*coll.*) futsch; *years ––by,* vergangene *or* verflossene Jahre; *ten years had* –, zehn Jahre waren vergangen *or* verstrichen; *be* –*! get you* –*!* packt euch! *I must be* –, ich muß fort. 2. *adj.* tot; verloren; (*sl.*) *he is a – coon,* es ist aus mit ihm; *dead and* –, tot und dahin; – *is* –, hin ist hin; (*sl.*) *be – on,* versessen sein auf. **–r,** *s.* (*sl.*) der Mann des Todes.

gonfalon [ˈgɔnfələn], *s.* das Banner.

gong [gɔŋ], 1. *s.* der Gong. 2. *v.a.* durch Gongsignal stoppen.

goniomet–er [gounɪˈɔmɪtə], *s.* der Winkelmesser, **–ry,** *s.* die Winkelmeßkunst.

gono-coccus [ˈgɔnəkɔkəs], *s.* (*pl.* –cocci) der Gonokokkus. **–rrhea** [gɔnəˈrɪə], *s.* der Tripper, die Gonorrhöe.

good [gud], (comp. *better,* sup. *best*) **1.** *adj.* gut; artig, brav (*as children*); gütig, freundlich; echt, gangbar (*as coins*); gültig, annehmbar, triftig (*Law*); sicher, zuverlässig, kreditfähig, zahlungsfähig (*C.L.*); tugendhaft, fromm; günstig, vorteilhaft; genügend, ausreichend, passend, schicklich; angenehm, zuträglich; tüchtig, geschickt (*of persons*) (*at,* in), gründlich, reichlich, gehörig; nützlich, wertvoll, heilsam, tauglich, brauchbar; frisch (*as food*); (*a*) (*with nouns*) – *old age,* hohes Alter; *on – authority,* aus guter Quelle; – *breeding,* die Wohlerzogenheit, feine Lebensart; *be – company,* ein guter Gesellschafter sein; – *day!* guten Tag! *a – deal,* ziemlich viel; – *debts,* sichere Schulden; *in – earnest,* in vollem Ernste; – *Friday,* der Karfreitag; – *God!* see – *Lord!* – *gracious!* du meine Güte! ach du liebe Zeit! *a – half,* reichlich die Hälfte; – *health,* das Wohlbefinden; *a – hour,* eine ganze *or* volle Stunde; – *humour,* gute Laune; – *looks,* die Schönheit; – *Lord!* du großer Gott! – *luck,* das Glück; *a – many,* ziemlich viele; *I have a – mind,* ich hätte wohl Lust; – *news,* erfreuliche Nachricht; – *night!* gute Nacht!; – *sense,* gesunder Menschenverstand; *have a – press,* gute Aufnahme in der Presse finden; *have a – time,* sich amüsieren; *in – time,* zur rechten Zeit; bei Zeiten; – *turn,* die Gefälligkeit; *a – while,* eine gute Weile; – *word,* freundliches Wort; (*b*) (*with verbs*) *be so – as* or *be – enough to do,* sei so gütig *or* gut zu tun; *hold* –, noch gelten (für), sich bewähren; *make* –, *v.a.* ersetzen, vergüten (*a loss*), halten, erfüllen (*a promise*), erweisen (*a claim*), rechtfertigen, wahrmachen, durchsetzen; *v.n.* (*coll.*) Erfolg haben, sich bewähren; *stand* –, see *hold* –; *stand – for,* haften *or* bürgen für; *think* –, für gut halten; (*c*) (*with prepositions*) – *at,* geschickt in (*Dat.*); – *for,* gut gegen (*disease, etc.*) *or* für; fähig sein für, geneigt sein zu, gewachsen sein (*Dat.*); gültig für; (*coll.*) – *for you!* recht von dir! – *for nothing,* nichts wert; *what is it – for?* wozu wird es gebraucht? was soll das helfen? wofür ist es gut? (*d*) (*comparisons*) *as – as,* (eben)so gut wie; *be as – as,* auf dasselbe hinauslaufen; *enough is as – as a feast,* allzuviel ist ungesund; *as – as finished,* so gut wie fertig; *as – as gold,* kreuzbrav; *be as – as one's word,* sein Wort halten; *he gives as – as he takes,* er bleibt nichts schuldig. **2.** *adv.* gut, tüchtig; (*coll.*) – *and ready,* – *and proper,* gehörig, tüchtig; (*coll.*) – *and ready,* ganz *or* durchaus fertig. **3.** *s.* das Gute, Wohl, Beste; *the* – (*pl.*) die Gerechten, Frommen; (*plural forms*) Güter, Waren, bewegliche Habe; *dry––s,* Kurzwaren, Schnittwaren; *soft –s,* Tuchwaren, (Baum)Wollwaren; *–s and chattels,* Hab und Gut; (*sl.*) *be the –s,* der *or* das Richtige sein; (*sl.*) *deliver the –s,* den Erwartungen entsprechen; (*a*) (*with verbs*) *be not much* –, nicht viel taugen; *it's no* –, es ist wertlos *or* zwecklos, es nützt nichts; *what's the – of it?* was nützt es? was kommt dabei heraus? welchen Zweck hat es? *what's the – of complaining?* was für einen Sinn hat es zu klagen; *do* –, Gutes tun; *I can do no – here,* ich kann hier nichts nützen; *I cannot do any – with it,* ich kann damit nichts anfangen; *it does me – to see you,* es macht mir Freude, Sie zu sehen; *much – may it do you!* wohl bekomm' es Ihnen! *what – will it do you?* was wird es Ihnen helfen? (*b*) (*with prepositions*) *for* –, für *or* auf immer, endgültig; *for – and all,* ein für allemal; *a power for* –, eine Kraft zum Guten; *for the – of,* zum Besten von; *to the* –, obendrein; zu Gunsten; *5 marks to the* –, DM. 5 gut haben; *be all to the* –, zum Guten ausschlagen. **––bye,** *s.* das Lebewohl; *––bye!* leb(e) wohl! auf Wiedersehen! adieu! *wish ––bye,* (einem) Lebewohl sagen. **––class,** *adj.* erstklassig. **––fellowship,** *s.* gute Kameradschaft. **––for-nothing,** 1. *s.* der Taugenichts, Nichtsnutz. 2. *adj.* nichtsnutzig, unbrauchbar. **––humoured,** *adj.* aufgeräumt, gutmütig. **–ish,** *adj.* (*coll.*) leidlich, ziemlich, beträchtlich. **–liness,** *s.* die Anmut. **– -looking,** *adj.* gut aussehend, schön. **–ly,** *adj.* schön, anmutig, stattlich; beträchtlich, tüchtig. **–man,** *s.* (*archaic*) der Hausherr, Ehemann. **– -natured,** *adj.* gutmütig, gefällig. **–ness,** *s.* die Güte; Frömmigkeit, Tugend; Gütigkeit, Freundlichkeit; das Gute, die Vortrefflichkeit; *–ness gracious!* du lieber Himmel! *in the name of –ness,* um Himmels willen; *–ness knows!* weiß der Himmel! *for –ness' sake!* um Gotteswillen! *my –ness!* ach je! *thank –ness!* Gott sei Dank! *I wish to –ness,* wollte Gott. **–s,** *see above.* **–s-train,** *s.* der Güterzug. **–s-traffic,** *s.* der Güterverkehr. **– -tempered,** *adj.* gut gelaunt; gutartig, gutmütig. **–wife,** *s.* (*archaic*) die Hausfrau. **– will,** das Wohlwollen, guter Wille, die Zuneigung, Bereitwilligkeit; der Kundschaftswert, Kundenkreis, guter Ruf (*C.L.*). **–y** ['gʊdɪ], 1. *adj.* (*–y-–y*) frömmelnd, zimperlich. 2. *s.* die Gevatterin, das Mütterchen; (*usually pl.*) (*coll.*) das Zuckerwerk, der *or* das Bonbon.

goof [gu:f], *s.* (*sl.*) der Tropf. **–y,** *adj.* (*sl.*) blöd, albern.

goop [gu:p], *s.* (*sl.*) *see* **goof.**

goosander [gu:'sændə], *s.* der Sägetaucher (*Orn.*).

goose [gu:s], *s.* (pl. *geese*) die Gans; (*fig.*) der Narr, Dummkopf; *Mother –,* Frau Holle; *all his geese are swans,* er übertreibt; *cook s.o.'s –,* einen endgültig erledigen; *kill the – that lays the golden eggs,* die Gans schlachten, die goldene Eier legt; *not say boo to a –,* den Mund nicht auftun können; *roast –,* der Gänsebraten; *wild-– chase,* unsinnige Verfolgung, zweckloses Unternehmen. **–berry** ['gʊzbərɪ], *s.* die Stachelbeere; (*coll.*) *play –berry,* die Anstandsdame spielen. **–berry-fool,** *s.* der Stachelbeerkrem. **– -flesh,** *s.* die Gänsehaut (*fig.*). **– -foot,** *s.* der Gänsefuß (*Bot.*). **–gog** ['gʊzgɔg], *s.* (*sl.*) *see* **–berry.** **– -grass,** *s.* das Klebkraut, Gänsekraut (*Bot.*). **– -quill,** *s.* der Gänsekiel, die Gänsefeder. **– -pimples,** *pl. see* **– -flesh.** **– -step,** *s.* der Parademarsch, Stechschritt (*Mil.*). **–y** ['gu:sɪ] *s.* (*coll.*) (dummes) Gänschen.

Gordian ['gɔ:dɪən], *adj.*; *cut the – knot,* den gordischen Knoten zerhauen.

¹gore [gɔ:], 1. *s.* der Zwickel, Keil, das Keilstück, die Gehre, dreieckiges Stück. 2. *v.a.* mit Zwickel versehen, keilförmig zuschneiden.

²gore, *s.* geronnenes Blut, *see* **gory.**

³gore, *v.a.* durchbohren, aufspießen (*with horns*).

gorge [gɔ:dʒ], 1. *s.* die Gurgel, Kehle, der Schlund; die (Berg)Schlucht, der Hohlweg; die Hohlkehle, Rille (*Arch.*); (Festungs)Kehle, (*Fort.*); *my – rises at,* es wird mir übel bei. 2. *v.a.* gierig verschlingen; vollpfropfen; *– o.s.,* sich vollfressen. 3. *v.n.* fressen, sich vollstopfen.

gorgeous ['gɔ:dʒəs], *adj.* prächtig, glänzend, prachtvoll, blendend. **–ness,** *s.* die Pracht, der Glanz, Prunk.

gorget ['gɔ:dʒɪt], *s.* der Ringkragen (*Mil.*), Halsschmuck, das Halstuch, Brusttuch; (*archaic*) die Halsberge.

Gorgon ['gɔ:gən], *s.* die Gorgo, Meduse (*Myth.*); (*fig.*) schreckliche Frau.

gorilla [gə'rɪlə], *s.* der Gorilla.

gormand-ize ['gɔ:məndaɪz], *v.n.* fressen, prassen, schlemmen. **–izing,** *s.* die Schlemmerei.

gorse [gɔ:s], *s.* der Stechginster (*Bot.*).

gory ['gɔ:rɪ], *adj.* blutig, blutbefleckt.

goshawk ['gɔshɔ:k], *s.* der Hühnerhabicht (*Orn.*).

gosling ['gɔzlɪŋ], *s.* das Gänschen.

gospel ['gɔspəl], *s.* das Evangelium (*also fig.*); (*fig.*) die Lehre; *take for* or *as –,* für bare Münze nehmen; *– truth,* buchstäbliche Wahrheit. **–ler,** *s.* der Wanderprediger; (*coll.*) *hot-–ler,* religiöser Eiferer.

gossamer ['gɔsəmə], *s.* Sommerfäden, *pl.*; (*coll.*) der Altweibersommer, das Mariengarn; dünne Gaze.

gossip ['gɔsɪp], 1. *s.* die Klatschbase; der Klatsch, das Geschwätz; die Plauderei (*in newspapers*). 2. *v.n.* schwatzen, klatschen. **–y,** *adj.* geschwätzig, schwatzend, klatschsüchtig.

gossoon [gɔ'su:n], *s.* der Bursche, Diener (*Irish*).

got [gɔt], *see* **get.**

gouge [gaʊdʒ], 1. *s.* das Hohleisen, der Hohlmeißel, Hohlbeitel. 2. *v.a.* (*– out*) ausmeißeln, aushöhlen; herausdrücken (*eyes*).

gourd [gʊəd], *s.* der (Flaschen)Kürbiß;die Kürbisflasche.

gour-mand ['gʊəmənd], 1. *adj.* gefräßig. 2. *s.* der Feinschmecker, Vielfraß. **–met** ['gʊəmeɪ], *s.* der Feinschmecker, Weinkenner.

gout [gaʊt], *s.* die Gicht, das Podagra. **–iness,** *s.* die Anlage zur Gicht. **–y,** *adj.* gichtisch (veranlagt).

govern ['gʌvən], 1. *v.a.* regieren (*also Gram.*), beherrschen, verwalten, lenken, leiten, bestimmen; als Präzedenzfall dienen für (*Law*). 2. *v.n.* regieren, herrschen. **–able,** *adj.* lenkbar, leitbar, lenksam, folgsam. **–ance,** *s.* (*usually fig.*) die Herrschaft, Beherrschung, Kontrolle (*of,* über). **–ess,** *s.* die Erzieherin. **–ing,** *adj.* herrschend, leitend, Vorstands–; *–ing body,* die Leitung, Direktion, der Vorstand, Verwaltungsrat; *–ing principle,* das Leitprinzip. **–ment** [–mənt], *s.* die Regierung (*also Pol.*), Führung, Leitung, Kontrolle, Verwaltung; Beherrschung, Herrschaft (*of,* über (*Acc.*)); Regierungsform; das Ministerium, Kabinett; der Regierungsbezirk; die Rektion (*Gram.*); *local –ment,* die Lokalverwaltung; *military –ment,* die Militärverwaltung; das Gouvernement; *petticoat –ment,* das Weiberregiment; *self-–ment,* die Selbstverwaltung; *–ment control,* die Bewirtschaftung; *–ment grant,* die Staatsunterstützung; *–ment loan,* die Staatsanleihe; *–ment office,* die Verwaltungskanzlei, Staatsstelle; *–ment official,* Staatsbeamte(r), *m.*; *–ment property,* das Landeseigentum; *–ment securities,* die Staatspapiere. **–mental,** *adj.* Regierungs–, Staats–. **–or** ['gʌvənə], *s.* der Herrscher, Regent; Statthalter, Gouverneur (*of a province, etc.*); Verwalter; (Festungs)Kommandant (*Mil.*); Direktor, Leiter, Präsident (*C.L.*); (*sl.*) Vater, Alte(r), *m.*, alter Herr; Prinzipal; Regler, Regulator (*Mach.*); *pl.* das Kuratorium (*of a school*). **–orship,** *s.* die Statthalterschaft.

gowan ['gaʊən], *s.* (*Scots*) das Gänseblümchen (*Bot.*).

gowk [gaʊk], *s.* der Kuckuck (*Orn.*); (*fig.*) Tölpel, Einfaltspinsel.

gown [gaʊn], *s.* das (Damen)Kleid; Amtsgewand, der Talar (*Law & Univ.*); *town and –,* Stadt und Universität, Philister und Akademiker. **–sman,** *s.* der Student.

grab [græb], 1. *v.a.* ergreifen, packen, an sich reißen, (*coll.*) grapsen, grapschen. 2. *v.n.* haschen, greifen, grapsen (*at,* nach). 3. *s.* plötzlicher Griff, der Graps; Greifer, die Klaue, Kranschaufel (*Mech.*); (*coll. fig.*) der Eigennutz; *make a – at,* grapsen nach. **–ber,** *s.* der Geizhals, Habsüchtige(r), *m.*; *land –ber,* der Schnapper, Landgierige(r), *m.*

grace [greɪs], 1. *s.* die Gunst, Gnade, das Wohlwollen; göttliche Gnade, die Barmherzigkeit; Anmut, der Reiz, Liebreiz, Anstand, die Zierde, Grazie; Nachsicht, Gunstbezeigung, Bewilligung, Begünstigung, der Beschluß; die Frist, Gnadenfrist, Wartezeit; das Tischgebet; *your –,* Euer Gnaden; (*a*) (*with nouns*) *act of –,* der Gnadenakt; *days of –,* Respekttage (*C.L.*); *a day's –,* Gnadenfrist von einem Tage, ein Tag Aufschub; *by the – of God,* von Gottes Gnaden; *by – of the Senate,* durch Senatsbeschluß; *by way of –,* auf dem Gnadenwege; *the year of –,* das Jahr des Heils; (*b*) (*with verbs*) *have the – to do,* den Anstand haben zu tun; *the – has been rejected,* der Senat hat den Entwurf abgelehnt; *say –,* das Tischgebet sprechen; (*c*) (*with adjectives*) *with a bad* or *ill –,* unwillig, widerwillig; *with a good –,* gern, willig, mit Anstand; *do s.th. with a good –,* gute Miene zum bösen Spiel machen. 2. *v.a.* schmücken, zieren; (be)ehren, auszeichnen. **–ful,** *adj.* anmutig, hold, reizend, graziös; geziemend, angebracht. **–fulness,** *s.* die Anmut, Grazie, Zierlichkeit. **–less,** *adj.* gottlos, verworfen, verdorben; unverschämt, schamlos. **– -note,** *s.* die Verzierung (*Mus.*). **–s,** *pl.* die Grazien (*Myth.*); *airs and –s,* die Vornehmtuerei; *I am not in his good –s,* ich bin nicht gut bei ihm angeschrieben; *get into a p.'s good –s,* jemandes Gunst erlangen.

gracious ['greɪʃəs], *adj.* gütig, freundlich, wohlwollend; anmutig, reizvoll; herablassend, gnädig (*of rulers*); barmherzig (*of God*); *– me! good(ness)–!*

du meine Güte! lieber Himmel! **–ness,** *s.* die Gnade, Huld, Freundlichkeit, Güte; die Anmut.
gradat–e [grəˈdeɪt], 1. *v.a.* abstufen, abtönen, gegeneinander absetzen. 2. *v.n.* sich abstufen, stufenweise übergehen. **–ion** [–ˈdeɪʃən], *s.* der Stufengang, die Stufenfolge; Abstufung (*Paint.*); der Ablaut (*Gram.*).
grad–e [greɪd], 1. *s.* der Grad, Rang; die Stufe; Neigung (*Railw.*); Qualität, Güte (*C.L.*); (*Amer.*) Schulklasse; *–e crossing,* (*Amer.*) der Bahnübergang; (*coll.*) *he is on the down-–e,* mit ihm geht's bergab. 2. *v.a.* abstufen; einteilen, ordnen, sortieren; *–e up,* aufkreuzen, veredeln (*cattle*). **–ient** [ˈgreɪdjənt], *s.* die Steigung; Neigung; das Gefälle. **–ing,** *s.* die Einstufung, Eingliederung.
gradua–l [ˈgrædjuəl], *adj.* stufenweise fortschreitend; allmählich. **–lly,** *adv.* allmählich, nach und nach. **–te** [–eɪt], 1. *v.a.* in Grade einteilen, mit einer Skala versehen, eichen, einteilen, graduieren; abstufen, staffeln (*taxes*); gradieren, titrieren (*Chem.*); schattieren (*Paint.*). 2. *v.n.* sich abstufen, allmählich übergehen; promovieren (*Univ.*). 3. *s.* [–ət], Graduierte(r), *m.* **–tion** [–ˈeɪʃən], *s.* der Stufengang; die Abstufung, Staffelung; Gradierung (*Chem.*); Gradeinteilung, Teilstricheinteilung (*Phys.*); Promovierung, Promotion (*Univ.*).
¹**graft** [grɑːft], 1. *v.a.* pfropfen (*on,* auf (*Acc.*)); übertragen (*Med.*); (*fig.*) einimpfen, einpflanzen, verpflanzen. 2. *s.* das Pfropfreis.
²**graft,** 1. *s.* (*coll.*) die Schieberei, Bestechung, Korruption; unehrlicher Gewinn, das Bestechungsgeld, Schmiergeld. 2. *v.n.* (*sl.*) schieben.
grail [greɪl], *s.* der Gral; *Knight of the Holy –,* der Gralsritter; *legend of the Holy –,* die Gralssage.
grain [greɪn], 1. *s.* das Korn, Getreide; Samenkorn, Körnchen (*of sand, salt, etc.*); der Gran (*Pharm.*); (*fig.*) die Spur, winziges Quantum; die Struktur, Faser, das Gefüge, Gewebe; die Maserung, Ader, der Strich; *dyed in the –,* in der Wolle gefärbt; (*fig.*) *against the –,* wider den Strich, widerwillig. 2. *v.a.* körnen, granulieren; masern, ädern, marmorieren (*wood*); krispeln, narben (*leather*).
gram [græm], *s.* das Gramm.
gramarye [ˈgræmərɪ], *s.* (*archaic*) die Zauberkunst.
gramercy [ˈgræməsɪ], *int.* (*archaic*) vielen Dank!
gramin–aceous [græmɪˈneɪʃəs], **–eous** [græˈmɪnɪəs], *adj.* grasartig. **–ivorous** [græmɪˈnɪvərəs], *adj.* grasfressend.
gramma–logue [ˈgræmələg], *s.* das Sigel, Kürzel, Kürzungszeichen (*shorthand*). **–r** [ˈgræmə], *s.* die Grammatik; *that is good* (*bad*) *–r,* das ist grammatisch richtig (falsch). **–rian** [grəˈmɛərɪən], *s.* der Grammatiker. **–r-school,** *s.* die Lateinschule, das Gymnasium. **–tical** [grəˈmætɪkl], *adj.* grammatisch, grammatikalisch.
gramme [græm], *see* **gram.**
gramophone [ˈgræməfoun], *s.* das Gram(m)ophon; *– pick-up,* der Tonabnehmer; Gra(m)mophonanschluß; *– record,* die Schallplatte, Gram(m)ophonplatte.
grampus [ˈgræmpəs], *s.* der Butzkopf, Schwertwal; *blow like a –,* wie eine Maschine schnaufen.
granary [ˈgrænərɪ], *s.* der Kornspeicher, die Kornkammer.
grand [grænd], 1. *adj.* groß; vornehm, erhaben, würdevoll, stattlich, prächtig, (*coll.*) großartig, imposant, glänzend, herrlich; wichtig, mächtig, gewaltig; Haupt–, Hoch–, Groß–; *– Fleet,* die Hochseeflotte; *– opera,* große Oper; *– piano,* der Flügel. 2. *s.* see *– piano*; (*sl.*) (*Amer.*) tausend Dollar; *baby –,* der Salonflügel; *concert –,* der Konzertflügel. **–ad,** *s. see* **–-dad. –am,** *s.* (*archaic*) die Großmutter, altes Mütterchen. **–child,** *s.* der (die) Enkel(in), das Enkelkind. **–-dad,** *s.* (*coll.*) der Großvater. **–-daughter,** *s.* die Enkelin. **–-ducal,** *adj.* großherzoglich. **–-duchess,** *s.* die Großherzogin. **–-duchy,** *s.* das Großherzogtum. **–-duke,** *s.* der Großherzog; *Russian –-duke,* russischer Großfürst. **–ee** [grænˈdiː], *s.* der Grande, Magnat (*in Spain*). **–eur** [ˈgrændjə], *s.* die Größe, Hoheit, Herrlichkeit; (*fig.*) Vornehmheit, Erhabenheit. **–father,** *s.* der Großvater. *–father clock,* *s.* große Standuhr. **–-jury,** *s.* großes Geschworenengericht. **–iloquence** [grænˈdɪləkwəns], *s.* die Redeschwulst, Prahlerei. **–iloquent** [–t], *adj.* hochtrabend, schwülstig; großsprecherisch. **–iose** [ˈgrændɪous], *adj.* großartig, grandios, hochtrabend, pompös, prunkvoll. **–ma, –mamma,** *s.* (*coll.*) *see* **–mother. –-Master,** *s.* der Großmeister, Hochmeister (*also Freem.*). **–mother,** *s.* die Großmutter; (*vulg.*) *go teach your –mother to suck eggs,* lehre du mich nur die Welt kennen. **–ness** [ˈgrændnɪs], *s. see* **–eur. –-nephew,** *s.* der Großneffe. **–-niece,** *s.* die Großnichte. **–pa,** *s.* (*coll.*) *see* **–father. –parent,** *s.* der Großvater, die Großmutter; *pl.* die Großeltern. **–sire,** *s.* (*archaic*) der Großvater; Ahnherr (*of animals*). **–son,** *s.* der Enkel. **–-stand,** *s.* die Haupttribüne.
grange [greɪndʒ], *s.* der Meierhof.
graniferous [græˈnɪfərəs], *adj.* körnertragend.
granit–e [ˈgrænɪt], 1. *s.* der Granit. 2. *adj.* granitartig, Granit–. **–ic** [–ˈnɪtɪk], *adj. see* **–e 2.**
grann–ie [ˈgrænɪ], **–y,** *s.* (*coll.*) das Großmütterchen; *–y knot,* falscher Knoten.
grant [grɑːnt], 1. *v.a.* bewilligen, gewähren, gestatten, zusprechen, vergönnen; zugeben, zugestehen, einräumen; übertragen, überweisen, verleihen; *Heaven – that,* gebe der Himmel daß; *– a p.'s life,* einem das Leben schenken; *– a request,* eine Bitte erfüllen, einem Ansuchen Folge leisten; *take for –ed,* als erwiesen *or* selbstverständlich annehmen, voraussetzen; *–ed that,* angenommen *or* gesetzt daß; *–ing this to be true,* angenommen, dies wäre wahr. 2. *s.* die Bewilligung, Gewährung, Erteilung, Verleihung (*to,* an); Übertragung (*to,* auf) (*Law*); übertragene *or* bewilligte Sache; *government –,* der Staatszuschuß; *–-in-aid,* die Notunterstützung, Beihilfe. **–ee** [grɑːnˈtiː], *s.* Begünstigte(r), *m.*, Privilegierte(r), *m.*, der Konzessionär (*Law*). **–or,** *s.* der Verleiher, Zedent (*Law*).
granul–ar [ˈgrænjulə], *adj.* körnig, gekörnt, granuliert; *–ar ore,* das Graupenerz. **–ate** [ˈgrænjuleɪt], *v.a.* körnen, granulieren. **–ated,** *adj.* körnig, granuliert. **–ation** [–ˈleɪʃən], *s.* das Körnen, Granulieren; die Kornbildung, Kristallbildung, Granulation (*Med.*). **–e** [ˈgrænjuːl], *s.* das Körnchen. **–ous** [–juləs], *see* **–ar.**
grape [greɪp], *s.* die Weinbeere, (Wein)Traube; *bunch of –s,* die Weintraube, (*pl.*) die Mauke (*Vet.*). **–-fruit** [ˈgreɪpfruːt], *s.* die Pampelmuse. **–shot,** *s.* die Kartätsche. **–-stone,** *s.* der Weinbeerkern. **–-sugar,** *s.* der Traubenzucker. **–-vine,** *s.* der Weinstock.
graph [grɑːf], *s.* graphische Darstellung, das Kurvenblatt, Schaubild, Diagramm. **–ic(al)** [ˈgræfɪk(l)], *adj.* graphisch, zeichnerisch; anschaulich, lebhaft, getreu.
graphit–e [ˈgræfaɪt], *s.* der Graphit, das Reißblei, die Temperkohle. **–ic** [–ˈfɪtɪk], *adj.* graphitisch.
graphology [græˈfələdʒɪ], *s.* die Handschriftendeutung, Graphologie.
grap–nel [ˈgræpnəl], *s.* der Dregganker, die Dragge, Dregge; der Enterhaken. **–ple** [ˈgræpl], 1. *v.a.* verankern, mit Enterhaken fassen, entern. 2. *v.n.* sich raufen, miteinander ringen, handgemein werden; (*fig.*) *–ple with a th.,* etwas anpacken *or* ernstlich in Angriff nehmen. 3. *s.* der Enterhaken; das Greifzeug, der Greifer. **–pling-hook, –pling-iron,** *s.* der Enterhaken.
grasp [grɑːsp], 1. *v.a.* packen, fassen, ergreifen; (*fig.*) verstehen, begreifen, (er)fassen; *– the nettle,* die Schwierigkeit anpacken. 2. *v.n.*; *– at,* ergreifen; (*fig.*) streben *or* trachten nach; *– at a straw,* sich an die letzte Hoffnung klammern. 3. *s.* der Griff; (*fig.*) der Bereich, die Gewalt; Fassungskraft, das Verständnis; *have a – of a th.,* etwas beherrschen; *no – of,* kein Verständnis für; *in s.o.'s –,* in jemandes Gewalt; *within the – of,* im Bereiche von. **–ing,** *adj.* habgierig, geizig.
grass [grɑːs], 1. *s.* das Gras, der Rasen; die Weide, Wiese; *at –,* auf der Weide; *go to –,* zur Weide gehen; *put* or *turn out to –,* auf die Weide treiben; *not let the – grow under one's feet,* unverzüglich ans Werk gehen, nicht lange zögern. 2. *v.a.* mit Gras bedecken; auf Rasen bleichen (*flax*); abschießen (*a bird*). **–iness,** *s.* der Grasreichtum. **–y,** *adj.* grasig, grasartig; grasreich; (gras)grün. **–-cloth,** *s.*

das Grasleinen, Nesselstuch. **--cutter, --mower,** *s.* die Grasschneidemaschine. **--grown,** *adj.* mit Gras bewachsen. **--green,** *adj.* grasgrün. **-hopper,** *s.* die Heuschrecke, der Grashüpfer. **-land,** *s.* die Wiese, Weide. **- plot,** der Rasenplatz. **--snake,** *s.* die Ringelnatter. **--widow,** *s.* die Strohwitwe. **--widower,** *s.* der Strohwitwer.

¹**grate** [greɪt], *s.* der Rost, Herd, Kamin; das (Kamin)Gitter. **-d,** *adj.* vergittert.

²**grat-e,** 1. *v.a.* abschaben, (zer)reiben; (*fig.*) beleidigen, ärgern, verletzen; *-e the teeth*, mit den Zähnen knirschen. 2. *v.n.* knarren, knirschen, kreischen, rasseln; (*fig.*) zuwider sein ((*up*)*on* (*Dat.*)); *-e upon the ear*, das Ohr beleidigen; *-e upon the nerves*, auf die Nerven gehen. **-er** ['greɪtə], *s.* das Reibeisen. **-ing,** *adj.* knirschend, schrill, grell, mißtönend.

grateful ['greɪtful], *adj.* dankbar, erkenntlich (*to* (*Dat.*)); angenehm, zusagend, wohltuend (*of things*). **-ness,** *s.* die Dankbarkeit; Annehmlichkeit.

graticule ['grætɪkjuːl], *s.* der Strich, das Fadenkreuz.

gratif-ication [grætɪfɪ'keɪʃən], *s.* die Befriedigung, Genugtuung (*at*, über); Freude, das Vergnügen, der Genuß; das Geschenk, Trinkgeld, die Gratifikation. **-y** ['grætɪfaɪ], *v.a.* befriedigen, zufriedenstellen, belohnen; willfahren, gefällig sein (*Dat.*); erfreuen; *be -ied at*, sich freuen über. **-ying,** *adj.* erfreulich.

grating ['greɪtɪŋ], *s.* das Gitter, Gitterwerk, der Rost, die Vergitterung; Gräting (*Naut.*).

gratis ['greɪtɪs], *adv.* unentgeltlich, umsonst.

gratitude ['grætɪtjuːd], *s.* die Dankbarkeit, Erkenntlichkeit; *in - for*, aus Dankbarkeit für; *a debt of -*, eine Dankesschuld; *owe a p. a debt of -*, einem zu (großem) Dank verpflichtet sein.

gratuit-ous [grə'tjuːɪtəs], *adj.* unentgeltlich, freiwillig, unverlangt, ohne Gegenleistung; unberechtigt, unverdient; grundlos, haltlos, mutwillig. **-y** [grə'tjuːɪtɪ], *s.* die Belohnung, Erkenntlichkeit; das Trinkgeld, kleines Geldgeschenk, die Gratifikation.

gravamen [grə'veɪmən], *s.* das Belastende, der Beschwerdepunkt.

¹**grave** [greɪv], *adj.* ernsthaft, gewichtig; gesetzt, feierlich; ernst, wichtig, schwerwiegend; schlicht, prunklos, dunkel(farben) (*as dress*); tief (*as sound*); *- accent*, der Gravis (*Phonet.*).

²**grave,** *s.* das Grab, der Grabhügel; *have one foot in the -*, mit einem Fuß im Grabe stehen; *turn in one's -*, sich im Grabe umdrehen. **--clothes,** *pl.* Sterbekleider. **--digger,** *s.* der Totengräber. **--stone,** *s.* der Grabstein. **--yard,** *s.* der Friedhof.

³**grave,** *reg. & ir.v.a. & n.* (*Poet.*) eingraben, stechen, schnitzen. **-r,** *s.* der Grabstichel.

⁴**grav-e,** *v.a.* kalfatern (*Naut.*). **-ing-dock,** *s.* das Trockendock.

gravel ['grævəl], 1. *s.* der Kies, grober Sand; der Grieß (*Med.*). 2. *v.a.* mit Kies bedecken; (*fig.*) verwirren. **-ly,** *adj.* kiesig. **--pit,** *s.* die Kiesgrube. **--stone,** *s.* der Kieselstein.

graven ['greɪvən], *adj. see* ³**grave;** *- image*, das Götzenbild.

graves [greɪvz], *see* ²**greaves.**

gravid ['grævɪd], *adj.* schwanger. **-ity,** *s.* die Schwangerschaft.

gravimet-er [græ'vɪmɪtə], *s.* der Dichtigkeitsmesser, Schweremesser. **-ric,** *adj.* Gewichts-, gewichtsanalytisch.

gravit-ate ['grævɪteɪt], *v.n.* gravitieren, (hin)neigen (*to*(*wards*), nach), hingezogen werden (*to*, zu). **-ation** [-'teɪʃən], *s.* die Schwerkraft; (*fig.*) Neigung, der Hang. **-y** ['grævɪtɪ], *s.* das Gewicht (*Phys.*); die Schwerkraft; Schwere; Wichtigkeit, der Ernst, die Ernsthaftigkeit; Feierlichkeit, Würde; Tiefe (*of sound*); *centre of -y*, der Schwerpunkt; *force of -y*, die Schwerkraft; *law of -y*, das Gesetz der Schwere; *specific -y*, spezifisches Gewicht.

gravy ['greɪvɪ], *s.* das Bratenfett, der Fleischsaft, die Tunke, Soße. **--boat,** *s.* die Saucière.

gray, *see* **grey.**

grayling ['greɪlɪŋ], *s.* die Äsche (*Ichth.*).

¹**graz-e** [greɪz], 1. *v.a.* abgrasen, abweiden; grasen lassen. 2. *v.n.* grasen, weiden. **-ier,** *s.* der Viehzüchter, Viehmäster. **-ing,** *s.* das Weiden; die Weide, Trift. **-ing-land,** *s.* das Weideland, Grasland.

²**graz-e,** 1. *v.a.* streifen, leicht berühren; abschürfen. 2. *s.* der Querschläger, Streifschuß; die Schramme. **-ing shot,** der Streifschuß.

greas-e, 1. *s.* [griːs] das Fett; die Schmiere; der Schweiß (*of wool*); die Mauke (*Vet.*); *in -e*, in Feist (*of deer*); *in the -e*, ungereinigt (*of wool*). 2. *v.a.* [griːz] einfetten; anfetten, einölen, einschmieren, beschmieren; *-e a cake-tin*, eine Form zum Backen ausstreichen; *-e a p.'s palm*, einen schmieren, einem Schmiergeld bezahlen; *like -ed lightning*, wie ein geölter Blitz. **-e-box,** *s.* die Schmierbüchse. **-e-paint,** *s.* die Schminke. **-e-proof,** *adj.* fettdicht; *-e-proof paper*, das Butterbrotpapier. **-er** [griːzə], *s.* die Schmiervorrichtung, der Schmiernippel. **-e-spot,** *s.* der Fettfleck, Schmierfleck. **-iness** [griːzɪnɪs], *s.* die Schmierigkeit, Fettigkeit. **-y** [griːzɪ], *adj.* schmierig, fettig; fetthaltig, fettartig, ölartig; glitschig, schlüpfrig (*of the ground*); *-y pole*, eingefetteter Kletterbaum.

great [greɪt], 1. *adj.* groß, bedeutend, wichtig, ungeheuer, mächtig; vornehm, berühmt, bewunderungswürdig, wunderbar, prächtig, stattlich, erhaben, ehrwürdig, imponierend; hochherzig, großmütig; (*often attrib.*) (*coll.*) hervorragend, glänzend, großartig, famos; (*coll.*) *she is - on the piano*, sie spielt glänzend Klavier; *- age*, hohes Alter; *- attraction*, die Hauptzugnummer; *- Bear*, Großer Bär (*Astron.*); (*coll.*) *- big*, ungeheuer groß; *- Britain*, Großbritannien; *- dane*, die Dogge; *a - deal*, sehr viel; *in - favour with*, in hoher Gunst bei; *- friend*, intimer Freund; (*sl.*) *- go*, das Schlußexamen (*Univ.*); *- hall*, der Hauptsaal; *a - many*, sehr viele; *it is no - matter*, es macht nicht viel aus; *- poet*, großer Dichter; *the - powers*, die Großmächte; *- Scott!* Großer Gott! *- toe*, große Zehe; *the - War*, erster Weltkrieg; *a - while*, eine lange Zeit, recht lange; *- with young*, trächtig. 2. *pl.* die Großen, Vornehmen; *pl.* das Schlußexamen (*Univ.*). **-coat,** *s.* der Wintermantel. **--grandchild,** *s.* das Urenkelkind. **--grandfather,** *s.* der Urgroßvater. **--great-grandfather,** *s.* der Ururgroßvater. **--hearted,** *adj.* hochherzig. **-ly,** *adv.* in hohen Maße *or* Grade, beträchtlich, sehr, höchst. **-ness,** *s.* die Größe; Bedeutung, Stärke, Gewalt; Erhabenheit, Herrlichkeit.

¹**greaves** [griːvz], *pl.* die Beinschienen.

²**greaves,** *pl.* die (Talg)Grieben, Fettgrieben.

grebe [griːb], *s.* der Steißfuß, Lappentaucher (*Orn.*).

greed [griːd], *s.* die Gier, Habgier. **-iness** [-ɪnɪs], *s.* die Gierigkeit, Gefräßigkeit; *see also* **-.** **-y,** *adj.* gierig, begierig (*of*, nach *or* auf); habgierig; gefräßig.

green [griːn], 1. *adj.* grün; (*fig.*) frisch; unreif (*as fruit*); (*coll.*) unerfahren; *- in one's memory*, noch in frischem Andenken; *- old age*, frisches *or* blühendes Greisenalter; *- with envy*, gelb vor Neid. 2. *s.* das Grün, grüne Farbe; der Grasplatz, Anger, Rasen; das Grün (*Golf*); die Frische, Jugend(kraft); das Laub; *pl.* frisches Gemüse. **-back,** *s.* (*sl.*) die Banknote, das Papiergeld (*Amer.*). **- cheese,** der Kräuterkäse. **-ery,** *s.* das Laub(werk), Grün. **-finch,** *s.* der Grünfink (*Orn.*). **-fly,** *s.* die Blattlaus (*Ent.*). **--fodder,** *s.* das Grünfutter, Futterpflanzen (*pl.*). **-gage,** *s.* die Reineclaude (*Bot.*). **-grocer,** *s.* der Obst- und Gemüsehändler. **-grocery,** *s.* (*often pl.*) Obst- und Gemüsewaren, der Grünkram. **-horn,** *s.* der Grünschnabel, unerfahrener Junge, der Einfaltspinsel. **-house,** *s.* das Gewächshaus, Treibhaus. **-ish,** *adj.* grünlich. **-ness,** *s.* das Grün(e); (*fig.*) die Frische; Unreife; (*sl.*) Unerfahrenheit. **-room,** *s.* das Künstlerzimmer (*Theat.*). **-shank,** *s.* der Grünschenkel (*Orn.*). **--sickness,** *s.* die Bleichsucht. **-stick,** *adj.* Grünholz- (*fracture*) (*Med.*). **-stuff,** *s.* Gemüsewaren (*pl.*), der Grünkram. **-sward,** *s.* der Rasen. **-wood,** *s.* belaubter Wald.

¹**greet** [griːt], *v.n.* weinen, klagen (*Scots*).

²**greet,** *v.a.* (be)grüßen; grüßend empfangen. **-ing** ['griːtɪŋ], *s.* die Begrüßung; der Gruß; *-ings telegram*, das Glückwunschtelegramm.

gregarious [grɪˈgɛərɪəs], *adj.* in Herden *or* Scharen lebend, Herden–; gesellig. **–ness,** *s.* das Zusammenleben in Herden; die Geselligkeit.
grenad–e [grəˈneɪd], *s.* die (Hand)Granate. **–ier,** *s.* der Grenadier.
grenadine [ˈgrɛnədɪ:n], *s.* die Grenadine (*Weav.*) gespickte Fleischschnitte (*Cook.*).
gresorial, *adj.* Stelz–, Schreit– (*Orn.*).
grew [grʊ:], *see* **grow.**
grey [greɪ], 1. *adj.* grau; altersgrau; trübe; – *friar,* der Franziskanermönch, Kapuziner; – *horse,* der Grauschimmel; (*coll.*) *the – mare is the better horse,* die Frau führt das Regiment *or* hat die Hosen an; (*coll.*) – *matter,* graue Substanz, der Verstand. 2. *s.* das Grau, graue Farbe; der Grauschimmel (*horse*). 3. *v.n.* grau werden, grauen. **–beard,** *s.* der Graubart. **– -haired,** *adj.* grauhaarig. **– -headed,** *adj.* grauköpfig. **–hen,** *s.* das Birkhuhn; *see* **black-cock.** **–hound,** *s.* das Windspiel, der Windhund; *–hound-racing,* *s.* das Hunderennen. **–ish,** *adj.* fahlgrau, gräulich. **–lag (goose),** *s.* die Wildgans. **–ness,** *s.* graue Farbe, das Graue. **–wacke,** *s.* die Grauwacke (*Geol.*).
grid [grɪd], *s.* das Gitter (*also Rad.*); Netz; die Überlandzentrale (*Elec.*); (*Amer.*) das Spielfeld (*Footb.*); *control –,* das Steuergitter (*Rad.*); *screen –,* das Schirmgitter (*Rad.*). **–dle** [ˈgrɪdl], *s.* (*dial.*) das Kuchenblech. **– -iron,** *s.* der Bratrost; die Kielbank, der Balkenrost. (*Naut.*); (*coll., Amer.*) das Spielfeld (*Footb.*). **– -leak,** *s.* der Gitterwiderstand (*Rad.*).
grief [grɪ:f], *s.* der Kummer, Schmerz, Gram; *come to –,* zu Schaden kommen, Schaden nehmen *or* erleiden (*of persons*); zu Fall kommen, versagen (*of things*).
griev–ance [grɪ:vəns], *s.* die Beschwerde, der Verdruß, Groll; Grund zur Klage, Mißstand, Übelstand; *nurse a –ance against,* einen Groll hegen gegen; *redress a –ance,* einem Übelstand abhelfen. **–e** [grɪ:v], 1. *v.a.* kränken, betrüben; wehtun (*Dat.*). 2. *v.n.* sich grämen *or* härmen. **–ous,** *adj.* schmerzlich, kränkend, bedrückend, unangenehm, bitter; (*archaic*) arg, schwer, schrecklich. **–ousness,** *s.* das Drückende, Schmerzliche, der Druck.
[1]**griffin** [ˈgrɪfɪn], *s.* der Greif (*Her., Myth.*).
[2]**griffin,** *s.* der Neuling, Anfänger.
griffon [ˈgrɪfən], *s.* der Affenpinscher; *see also* [1]**griffin.** **– -vulture,** *s.* der Gänsegeier.
grig [grɪg], *s.* (*dial.*) die Grille, das Heimchen; der Sandaal.
grill [grɪl], 1. *v.a.* auf dem Roste braten, rösten; (*fig.*) quälen, plagen; (*sl.*) ins Verhör nehmen. 2. *v.n.* braten, schmoren. 3. *s.* der Bratrost; Rostbraten, geröstetes Fleisch. **–age** [ˈgrɪlədʒ], *s.* das Gitterwerk, Pfahlrost (*Arch.*). **–e,** *s.* das Türgitter. **–ing,** *s.* (*sl.*) scharfes Verhör. **–(-room),** *s.* das Speiselokal, der Grillroom.
grilse [grɪls], *s.* junger Lachs.
grim [grɪm], *adj.* grimmig; finster, schrecklich, scheußlich, gräßlich, abstoßend, abschreckend; – *humour,* der Galgenhumor. **–ness,** *s.* die Grimmigkeit, abstoßendes Benehmen.
grimace [grɪˈmeɪs], 1. *s.* die Grimasse, Fratze. 2. *v.n.* Gesichter schneiden.
grimalkin [grɪˈmælkɪn], *s.* die Katze.
grim–e [graɪm], 1. *s.* der Schmutz, Dreck, Ruß. 2. *v.a.* besudeln, beschmutzen. **–iness,** *s.* die Schmutzigkeit, der Schmutz. **–y** [ˈgraɪmɪ], *adj.* schmutzig, rußig, schmierig.
grin [grɪn], 1. *v.n.* grinsen, lächeln, feixen; – *and bear it,* gute Miene zum bösen Spiel machen. 2. *s.* das Grinsen.
grind [graɪnd], 1. *ir.v.a.* abreiben, verreiben, zerreiben, zerkleinern, zermalmen; mahlen, kollern, schroten; schleifen, wetzen; (*fig.*) quälen, schinden; *have an axe to –,* eigennützige Zwecke verfolgen; – *a barrel-organ,* eine Drehorgel leiern; – *colours,* Farben reiben; – *the face of the poor,* die Armen bedrücken, ausnützen *or* ausbeuten; – *to powder,* zermalmen; – *roughly,* schroten; – *one's teeth,* mit den Zähnen knirschen; – *down,* feinmahlen (*corn, etc.*), abwetzen (*knife, etc.*); (*fig.*) unterdrücken; – *out,* mühsam *or* schwerfällig hervorbringen (*music, etc.*). 2. *ir.v.n.* sich mahlen lassen; knirschend reiben (*on,* an; *against,* gegen); (*sl.*) ochsen, büffeln, schuften, sich plagen, sich schinden, sich abmühen (*at,* an). 3. *s.* die Plackerei, Schinderei; (*sl.*) das Ochsen, Büffeln. **–er,** *s.* der Schleifer; Backzahn; (*sl.*) Einpauker. **–ing,** 1. *s.* das Mahlen, Schleifen, der Schliff. 2. *adj.* mühsam, bedrückend, quälend. **–ing-mill,** *s.* die Schleifmühle, Reibmühle; der Mahlgang, das Mahlwalzwerk. **–stone,** *s.* der Mühlstein, Wetzstein, Schleifstein; (*coll.*) *keep one's nose to the –stone,* ochsen, schuften *or* büffeln müssen.
grip [grɪp], 1. *s.* der Griff, Handgriff; das Anpacken, Greifen; der Händedruck; (*fig.*) die Herrschaft, Gewalt (*on* or *of,* über); (*coll.*) *see* **–sack;** *at –s,* handgemein, im Kampf; *in the – of,* in den Klauen von; *have a – on,* in der Gewalt haben; Verständnis haben für; *lose one's – on,* den Halt *or* die Gewalt verlieren über; *come to –s,* handgemein werden mit, anpacken, zupacken, angehen, sich zu fassen kriegen; sich auseinandersetzen mit; *tyre –,* die Griffigkeit der Reifen (*Motor.*). 2. *v.a.* ergreifen, (an)fassen, (an)packen; festhalten, in der Gewalt haben; in Spannung halten. 3. *v.n.* greifen, packen; fassen, halten (*as an anchor*). **–ping,** *adj.* ergreifend, packend. **–sack,** *s.* die Handtasche, Reisetasche (*Amer.*).
grip–e [graɪp], 1. *v.a. see* **grip** 2; zusammenpressen; drücken, zwicken; Bauchgrimmen verursachen (*Dat.*) (*Med.*); zurren, seefest machen (*boats*); *be –ed,* Bauchschmerzen haben. 2. *v.n.* zugreifen; die Kolik haben (*Med.*); luvgierig sein (*Naut.*); (*sl.*) meckern. 3. *s. see* **grip** 1; *pl.* die Kolik, das Bauchgrimmen (*Med.*). **–ing,** 1. *adj.* drückend, nagend (*as pain*), luvgierig (*Naut.*). 2. *s. see* **–e,** 3. (*pl.*).
griskin [ˈgrɪskɪn], *s.* der Schweinsrücken (*Cook.*).
grisly [ˈgrɪzlɪ], *adj.* schrecklich, eklig, entsetzlich, grausig, gräßlich.
grist [grɪst], *s.* das Mahlgut, Mahlkorn; *that's – to his mill,* das ist Wasser auf seine Mühle; *bring – to the mill,* Vorteil *or* Nutzen bringen.
gristl–e [ˈgrɪsl], *s.* der Knorpel; (*fig.*) *in the –e,* unentwickelt, im Entstehen. **–y,** *adj.* knorpelig.
grit [grɪt], 1. *s.* der Kies, Grieß, grober Sand; der Grus, Sandstein (*Min.*); (*coll.*) die Charakterfestigkeit, Entschlossenheit, der Mut; *pl.* die Grütze; das Schrot, grobes Hafermehl. 2. *v.n.* knirschen. 3. *v.a.*; – *one's teeth,* mit den Zähnen knirschen. **–tiness,** *s.* sandige *or* kiesige Beschaffenheit. **–ty,** *adj.* kiesig, sandig.
grizzl–e [ˈgrɪzl], 1. *s.* das Grau, graue Farbe. 2. *v.n.* (*coll.*) nörgeln, quengeln, murren. **–ed,** *adj.* grau(haarig), ergraut. **–y,** 1. *adj.* grau, gräulich 2. *s.* **–y (bear)** grauer Bär.
groan [groʊn], 1. *v.n.* stöhnen, ächzen (*of persons*), knarren, knacken (*as furniture*). 2. *v.a.* unter Stöhnen hervorbringen. 3. *s.* das Stöhnen, Seufzen, Ächzen; Murren.
groat [groʊt], *s.* (*archaic*) der Heller, Groschen (= *4 pence*).
groats [groʊts], *pl.* die Hafergrütze.
grocer [ˈgroʊsə], *s.* der Kolonialwarenhändler, Krämer; *–'s shop,* das Kolonialwarengeschäft. **–y,** *s.* der Kolonialwarenladen; Kolonialwarenhandel; (*often pl.*) Kolonialwaren (*pl.*).
grog [grɔg], 1. *s.* der Grog; (*sl.*) – *blossom,* rote Nase, die Kupfernase. 2. *v.n.* Grog trinken. **–gy,** *adj.* betrunken; steif, abgejagt (*as horses*); (*coll.*) schwankend, anfällig, kränklich (*of persons*); (*coll.*) wackelig, locker (*of things*).
groin [grɔɪn], 1. *s.* die Leiste, Leistengegend (*Anat.*); der Grat, die Rippe (*Arch.*). 2. *v.a.* mit Rippen *or* Gurten versehen (*Arch.*); *–ed ceiling,* gerippte Decke; *–ed vault,* das Kreuzgewölbe.
groom [grʊ:m], 1. *s.* der Stallknecht, Pferdeknecht, Reitknecht; (*coll.*) Bräutigam (bei der Trauung); (*archaic*) Diener; – *in waiting,* diensttuender Kammerjunker; – *of the chamber,* königlicher Kammerdiener. 2. *v.a.* warten, pflegen, striegeln, besorgen (*horses*); (*coll., fig.*) vorbereiten. *well-–ed, adj.* elegant gekleidet, gut gepflegt. **–sman** [–zmən], *s.* der Beistand des Bräutigams (*at the wedding*).

groov-e [gru:v], 1. *s.* die Nut, Nute, Rinne, Furche, Hohlkehle, Auskehlung, Rille, Riese; *pl.* Züge (*of a gun*); (*fig.*) die Gewohnheit, Schablone, gewohntes Geleise; *run in a -e*, immer in demselben Geleise bleiben. 2. *v.a.* auskehlen, einkehlen, aushöhlen, furchen, falzen, nuten, riffeln. **-ed,** *adj.* ausgekehlt, gerillt. **-ing-plane,** *s.* der Nuthobel, Spundhobel.

grope [group], 1. *v.a.* tasten nach; *- one's way*, seinen Weg tastend suchen, im Dunkeln tappen. 2. *v.n.* tasten, tappen, tastend suchen (*for*, nach); *- about*, herumtappen.

grosbeak ['grousbɪ:k], *s.* der Haken- *or* Karmingimpel.

gross [grous], 1. *adj.* sehr dick, fett, feist (*figure*); grob, roh, unfein (*manners*); schwerfällig, stumpf (*mind*); ungeheuerlich, schreiend (*error, etc.*); Brutto-, Roh- (*C.L.*); (*fig.*) grob; *- amount*, die Gesamtsumme, der Bruttobetrag; *- earnings*, Bruttoeinnahmen, der Rohertrag; *- misrepresentation*, grobe Entstellung; *- tonnage*, der Bruttotonnengehalt; *- weight*, das Bruttogewicht. 2. *s.* das Gros, 12 Dutzend; *in the -*, im ganzen, in Bausch und Bogen. **-ly,** *adv.* in hohem Grade, sehr, höchst. **-ness,** *s.* die Grobheit, Unfeinheit, Roheit, Gemeinheit.

grotesque [grou'tɛsk], *adj.* grotesk, wunderlich, phantastisch. **-ness,** *s.* das Groteske.

grotto ['grɔtou], *s.* die Felsenhöhle, Grotte.

grouch [grautʃ], (*Amer. sl.*) *v.n. see* **²grouse.**

¹ground [graund], 1. *s.* der Grund, Boden; Meeresgrund, Meeresboden; das Gelände, Gebiet, die Strecke, Fläche; der Grundbesitz, das Grundstück, Grund und Boden (*without art.*); der Spielplatz (*Sport*), Untergrund, Fond, die Unterlage, Grundfarbe, Grundierung (*Paint.*); (*often pl.*) die Grundlage, Basis, Ursache, Veranlassung, der Beweggrund (*of* or *for*, zu); die Stellung, der Standort; die Erde, der Erdschluß (*Rad., Elec.*); *pl.* (Garten)Anlagen; der (Boden)Satz; die Anfangsgründe; *fishing -*, das Fischereigebiet; *football -*, der Fußballspielplatz; *rising -*, die Steigung, Anhöhe, hügeliges Gelände; (*a*) (*with verbs*) *break new -*, neues Feld umbrechen, (*fig.*) neues Gebiet erschließen; *cover much -*, sich weithin erstrecken, eine Weite Strecke zurücklegen; *cover old -*, ein altes Gebiet behandeln; *cut the - from under a p.'s feet*, einen in die Enge treiben; *gain -*, vorwärtskommen, (an) Boden gewinnen, um sich greifen; *gain - upon a p.*, einem Boden abgewinnen; *hold one's -*, sich *or* die Stellung behaupten; *lose -*, weichen, (an) Boden verlieren; *lose the - from under one's feet*, den Boden unter den Füßen verlieren; *maintain* or *stand one's -*, see *hold one's -*; *take -*, stranden (*Naut.*); *till the -*, Land bestellen; (*b*) (*with prepositions*) *below* (*the*) *-*, unter der Erde; *in its own -s*, auf eignem Grund und Boden; *on German -*, auf deutschem Grund und Boden, auf deutschem Gebiet; *on the - that*, aus dem Grunde daß; *on the - of*, wegen; *on political -s*, aus politischen Gründen *or* Rücksichten; *go over the -*, etwas besprechen, überlegen *or* (*coll.*) durchackern; *go over old - again*, Bekanntes wiederholen; *to the -*, zu Boden, zur Erde; (*coll.*) *down to the -*, von Grund aus, gründlich, in jeder Hinsicht; (*fig.*) *fall to the -*, mißglücken, fehlschlagen, scheitern; *strike to the -*, zu Boden schlagen. 2. *v.a.* auf den Boden stellen *or* setzen; hinlegen, niederlegen; stranden lassen (*Naut.*); vorfärben, grundieren, unterlegen (*Paint.*); erden (*Elec.*); (*fig.*) gründen, begründen (*on* or *in*, auf (*Acc.*)); in den Anfangsgründen unterrichten; abstellen (*aircraft*); *be well -ed*, gute Vorkenntnisse haben; *be -ed in*, gegründet sein auf, wurzeln in. 3. *v.n.* stranden, auflaufen (*Naut.*). **-age,** *s.* Hafengebühren (*pl.*), das Ankergeld. **--angling,** *s.* das Grundangeln. **- attack,** *s.* der Tiefangriff (*Av.*). **--bait,** *s.* der Grundköder. **--bass,** *s.* der Grundbaß. **--cherry,** *s.* die Zwergkirsche. **- clearance,** *s.* die Bodenfreiheit (*of vehicles*). **--coat,** *s.* der Grundanstrich. **--colour,** die Grundfarbe. **- communication,** *s.* der Boden-zu-Bord Verkehr (*Av.*). **--connexion,** *s.* die Erdung, der Erdschluß (*Elec.*). **- crew,** *see* **--staff** (*Av.*). **--floor,** *s.* das Erdgeschoß, Parterre; *on the --floor*, im Erdgeschoß. **--frost,** *s.* der Frost im Boden. **--game,** *s.* nicht fliegendes Wild. **--ice,** *s.* das Grundeis. **-ing,** *s.* die Grundierung (*Paint.*); der Anfangsunterricht; das Stranden (*Naut.*). **--ivy,** *s.* der Gundermann (*Bot.*). **--landlord,** *s.* der Grundeigentümer. **-less,** *adj.* grundlos, unbegründet. **-ling,** *s.* der Gründling (*Ichth.*); *pl.* (*Poet.*) der große Haufe. **- mechanic,** *s.* der Wart (*Av.*). **--nut,** *s.* die Erdnuß. **- panel,** *s.* das Fliegertuch (*Av.*). **--plan,** *s.* der Grundriß. **--plate,** *s.* die Grundplatte, Schwelle (*Build.*) **--rent,** *s.* der Bodenzins. **-sel,** *s.* das Kreuzkraut (*Bot.*); die Grundschwelle (*Arch.*). **-sman,** *s.* der Spielplatzwärter. **--staff,** *s.* das Bodenpersonal (*Av.*). **--story,** *s. see* **--floor.** **--swell,** *s.* die Grundsee, Dünung. **- troops,** *pl.* Erdtruppen (*pl.*). **--water,** *s.* das Grundwasser. **-work,** *s.* der Grund, die Grundlage, Unterlage, das Fundament.

²ground, *see* **grind;** *- glass*, undurchsichtiges Glas; die Mattscheibe (*Phot.*).

group [gru:p], 1. *s.* die Gruppe, Anzahl; der Trupp, das Geschwader (*Av.*). 2. *v.a.* gruppieren, zusammenstellen, anordnen. **--captain,** *s.* der Oberst der Luftwaffe. **-ing,** *s.* die Gruppierung, Anordnung.

¹grouse [graus], *s.* das Moorhuhn; *black -*, das Birkhuhn; *red -*, schottisches Schneehuhn.

²grouse, 1. *v.n.* (*coll.*) murren, grollen, nörgeln, meckern. 2. *s.*; (*coll.*) *have a - against*, einen Groll haben gegen.

¹grout [graut], 1. *s.* das Schrot; dünner Mörtel. 2. *v.a.* mit Mörtel überziehen, ausfüllen, verstopfen (*cracks*). **-ing,** *s.* der Füllstoff.

²grout, 1. *v.a.* aufwühlen (*of pigs*). 2. *v.n.* in der Erde wühlen.

grove [grouv], *s.* das Gehölz; (*Poet.*) der Hain.

grovel ['grɔvl], *v.n.* am Boden kriechen; (*fig.*) kriechen. **-ler,** *s.* der Kriecher. **-ling,** 1. *adj.* kriechend; niedrig, unwürdig. 2. *s.* die Kriecherei.

grow [grou], 1. *ir.v.n.* wachsen, zunehmen (*in*, an); *- angry*, böse werden; *- to be*, werden; *- better*, sich bessern; *- fond of*, lieb gewinnen; *- less*, sich vermindern; *- light*, sich aufklären *or* aufhellen; *- obsolete*, veralten; *- old*, altern, alt werden; *- poor*, verarmen; *- worse*, sich verschlimmern; *- in favour*, an Gunst zunehmen; *- into a habit*, zur Gewohnheit werden; *it -s on me*, es wird mir immer lieber *or* vertrauter, ich gewinne es lieb; es wird mir zur zweiten Natur, es gewöhnt sich mir an; *the conviction grew on him*, er kam mehr und mehr zu der Überzeugung; *- out*, auswachsen, keimen (*as potatoes*); *- out of*, herauswachsen aus; (*fig.*) entwachsen (*Dat.*); die Folge sein (von), sich ergeben (aus), erwachsen *or* entstehen aus; *- out of one's clothes*, aus den Kleidern wachsen; *- out of use*, außer Gebrauch kommen; *- together*, verwachsen, zusammenwachsen; *- up*, aufwachsen; heranwachsen; *- upon*, see *- on.* 2. *ir.v.a.* (an)bauen, züchten, ziehen (*Agr.*); *- a beard*, sich (*Dat.*) einen Bart wachsen lassen. **-er,** *s.* wachsende Pflanze; der Pflanzer, Züchter, Produzent (*Agr.*). **-ing,** 1. *adj.* wachsend, zunehmend; *-ing weather*, fruchtbares Wetter; *-ing pains*, Wachtumschmerzen (*pl.*). 2. *s.* das Wachsen; Züchten; der Wuchs.

growl [graul], 1. *s.* das Knurren, Brummen; Rollen (*of thunder*). 2. *v.n.* knurren, brummen, rollen (*as thunder*); *- at a p.*, einen anknurren *or* anbrummen. **-er,** *s.* knurriger Hund; (*fig.*) der Brummbär.

grown [groun], *see* **grow;** *adj.* erwachsen; *- man*, Erwachesene(r), *m.*; *full--*, ausgewachsen; *- over with*, überwachsen mit. **--up,** 1. *adj.* erwachsen. 2. *s.* Erwachsene(r), *m. & f.*

growth [grouθ], *s.* der Wuchs, das Wachstum, die Bildung, Entwicklung; der Zuwachs, die Zunahme, Vergrößerung; Züchtung, Kultivierung, Erzeugung; das Gewächs (*also Path.*).

groyne [grɔɪn], *s.* die Buhne, der Wellenbrecher.

grub [grʌb], 1. *v.n.* (*coll.*) graben, wühlen; (*vulg.*) essen, futtern. 2. *v.a.*; *- up*, ausgraben, ausroden, ausjäten. 3. *s.* die Larve, Made, Raupe; (*coll.*) schmutzige *or* schlampige Person; (*vulg.*) das Essen, Futter, Fressalien (*pl.*). **-by,** *adj.* (*coll.*) schmutzig, schmierig.

grudg-e [grʌdʒ], 1. *v.a.* mißgönnen, neiden (*a p. a*

th. or *a th. to a p.*, einem etwas), beneiden (*a p. a th.* or *a th. to a p.*, einen um etwas); ungern geben; nicht leiden, erlauben *or* gewähren daß man tut; *not –e doing*, nicht ungern tun; *–e no pains*, sich keine Mühe verdrießen lassen; *–e the time*, sich die Zeit nicht gönnen. 2. *s.* der Groll, Haß, die Mißgunst, der Widerwille; *bear a p. a –e* or *have a –e against a p.*, einen Groll gegen einen hegen. **–er,** *s.* der Neider, Unzufriedene(r), *m.* **–ing,** *adj.* neidisch; ungern gegeben. **–ingly,** *adv.* widerwillig, ungern.
gruel ['gru:əl], *s.* der Haferschleim; (*coll.*) *get one's –*, sein Teil *or* Fett bekommen. **–ling,** *adj.* (*coll.*) anstrengend, strapaziös.
gruesome ['gru:səm], *adj.* schauerlich, grausig, grauenhaft.
gruff [grʌf], *adj.* mürrisch; barsch, schroff, bärbeißig; rauh (*voice*). **–ness,** *s.* die Grobheit, Schroffheit, Barschheit.
grumble ['grʌmbl], 1. *v.n.* murren, brummen, nörgeln (*at*, über (*Acc.*)); rollen, grollen (*as thunder*). 2. *s.* das Murren, Brummen. **–r,** *s.* der Nörgler, (*coll.*) Brummbär.
grum–e [gru:m], *s.* der Blutklumpen. **–ous** [–məs], *adj.* klumpig, geronnen (*of blood*).
grummet ['grʌmɪt], *s.* der Tauring (*Naut.*).
grumpy ['grʌmpɪ], *adj.* (*coll.*) mürrisch, verdrießlich, mißlaunisch.
grunt [grʌnt], 1. *v.n.* grunzen. 2. *s.* das Grunzen. **–er,** *s.* der Grunzer; das Schwein, Ferkel.
gruyère [grʊ'jɛ:ə], *s.* der Schweizerkäse.
gryphon ['grɪfən], *see* [1]**griffin.**
guan–a ['gwɑ:nə], *s.* der Leguan (*Zool.*). **–o** ['gwɑ:noʊ], *s.* der Guano, Vogeldünger.
guarant–ee [gærən'tɪ:], 1. *s.* die Bürgschaft, Gewähr, Sicherheit (*of*, für); die Sicherheitssumme, Pfandsumme; sichergestellter Gläubiger. 2. *v.a.* gewährleisten für, bürgen für, sich verbürgen für, garantieren, Garantie leisten für; sichern, schützen (*against*, gegen); sicherstellen, verbürgen, sich dafür verbürgen (*that*, daß; *to*, zu). **–or** [–'tɔ:], *s.* der Bürge, Gewährsmann, Garant. **–y** ['gærəntɪ], *s.* die Bürgschaft, Sicherheit, Gewährleistung; (*fig.*) Gewähr, Garantie.
guard [gɑ:d], 1. *v.a.* (be)schützen, bewachen, (be)hüten, bewahren, beschirmen, wahren (*from* or *against*, vor (*Dat.*)); achten auf, beaufsichtigen. 2. *v.n.* auf der Hut sein; *– against*, sich hüten *or* in Acht nehmen vor (*Dat.*); verhüten, vorbeugen (*Dat.*). 3. *s.* die Wacht, Bewachung, Hut, Bedekkung; Wache, Aufsicht; der Wächter, die Wachmannschaft (*Mil.*); der Schaffner (*Railw.*); Bahnwärter (*Amer.*); die Auslage, Deckung, Parade (*Fenc.*); Schutzvorrichtung (*Mach.*); das Stichblatt (*of a sword*); *pl.* die Garde, das Gardekorps; *advanced –*, die Vorhut; *body–*, die Leibwache; *fire-–*, das Kamingitter; *frontier –*, die Grenzwache (*troops*), der Grenzwächter (*sentry*); *home –*, die Bürgerwehr; *– of honour*, die Ehrengarde, Ehrenwache; *keep –*, Wache halten; *life –*, die Schwimmwache, Rettungsmannschaft; *mount –*, Wache stehen; *off one's –*, unachtsam, unbedacht; *come off –*, von der Wache kommen; *throw a p. off his –*, einen überraschen; *on –*, auf Wache; *be* or *stand on one's –*, auf seiner Hut sein; *go on –*, die Wache beziehen; auf Wache ziehen; *post –s*, Posten ausstellen; *put a p. on his –*, einen warnen, einem einen Wink geben; *rear-–*, die Nachhut; *watch-–*, die Sicherheitskette. **–-duty,** der Wachdienst. **–ed,** *adj.* vorsichtig, behutsam, zurückhaltend. **–edness,** *s.* die Vorsicht, Behutsamkeit. **–-house,** *s.* die Wache, das Wachtlokal (*Mil.*). **–ian** ['gɑ:dɪən], 1. *s.* der Wächter, Hüter; Vormund (*of*, über) (*Law*); *–ian of the poor*, der Armenpfleger; *board of –ians*, das Armenamt. 2. *adj.* schützend, Schutz–. **–ian-angel,** *s.* der Schutzengel. **–ianship,** *s.* die Obhut, der Schutz; die Vormundschaft. **–-rail,** *s.* das Schutzgeländer; die Leitschiene (*Railw.*). **–-room,** *s.* die Wachtstube. **–-ship,** *s.* das Wachtschiff. **–sman,** *s.* der Gardist; Gardeoffizier.
gubernatorial [gjubənə'tɔ:rɪəl], *adj.* (*Amer.*) Gouverneur–, Statthalter–.
[1]**gudgeon** ['gʌdʒən], *s.* der Gründling; (*fig.*) Einfaltspinsel.
[2]**gudgeon,** *s.* der Zapfen, Bolzen; die Ruderöse; *– pin*, der Kolbenbolzen.
guelder-rose ['gɛldəroʊz], *s.* der Wasserahorn, Schneeball (*Bot.*).
guerdon [['gə:dən], 1. *s.* (*Poet.*) der Lohn, die Belohnung. 2. *v.a.* (*Poet.*) belohnen.
guerilla [gə'rɪlə], *s.* (*– war*) der Kleinkrieg, Guerillakrieg, Partisanenkrieg; der Freischärler, Guerillakrieger, Partisan.
guess [gɛs], 1. *v.a.* & *n.* raten, erraten, mutmaßen, abschätzen (*at*, auf), vermuten; (*sl.*) glauben, denken, annehmen, meinen (*Amer.*) 2. *s.* die Mutmaßung, Vermutung; *by –*, vermutungsweise, aufs Geratewohl; *make a –*, erraten; *make a – at*, (ab)schätzen. **–-rope,** *see* **guest-rope.** **–work,** *s.* die Mutmaßung, Vermutungen (*pl.*); *by –work*, aufs Geratewohl.
guest [gɛst], *s.* der Gast (*at*, bei); Parasit (*Bot.* & *Zool.*); *paying –*, der Pensionär; *– of honour*, der Ehrengast. **–-room,** *s.* das Fremdenzimmer. **–-rope,** *s.* zweite Vertäuleine (*Naut.*).
guffaw [gʌ'fɔ:], 1. *s.* schallendes Gelächter. 2. *v.n.* laut lachen *or* brüllen.
guid-able ['gaɪdəbl], *adj.* lenksam, lenkbar. **–ance,** *s.* die Führung, Leitung, Orientierung, Belehrung. **–e** [gaɪd], 1. *s.* der Führer, Leiter, Reisebegleiter; (*fig.*) Leitfaden, Wegweiser; Anhalt, Anhaltspunkt; die Führung, Leitvorrichtung (*Mach*); das Lehrbuch, der Reiseführer; *girl-–e*, der Mädchenpfadfinder. 2. *v.a.* führen, geleiten, lenken; (*fig.*) leiten, belehren. **–e-book,** *s.* das Reisehandbuch, der Reiseführer. **–ed,** *adj.* gelenkt, gesteuert; *–ed missile*, ferngesteuertes Geschoß. **–e-post,** *s.* der Wegweiser. **–e-rail,** *s.* die Führungsschiene, Laufschiene, Leitschiene, Anlegeschiene. **–e-rope,** *s.* das Leitseil; das Schlepptau (*Av.*). **–ing,** *adj.*; *–ing star*, der Leitstern.
guidon ['gaɪdən], *s.* die Standarte (*of cavalry*).
guild [gɪld], *s.* die Gilde, Zunft, Innung. **–-hall,** *s.* das Gildehaus. **–hall,** *s.* das Londoner Rathaus. **– socialism,** der Gewerkschaftssozialismus.
guile [gaɪl], *s.* die (Arg)List, der Betrug. **–ful,** *adj.* (arg)listig, verräterisch, betrügerisch. **–less,** *adj.* arglos, ohne Falsch. **–lessness,** *s.* die Arglosigkeit.
guillemot ['gɪlɪmɔt], *s.* die Lumme (*Orn.*).
guillotine [gɪlə'tɪ:n], 1. *s.* das Fallbeil, die Guillotine; Beschneidemaschine (*paper*); die Befristung der Abstimmung (*Parl.*). 2. *v.a.* mit dem Fallbeil hinrichten.
guilt [gɪlt], *s.* die Schuld; Strafbarkeit. **–iness,** *s.* die Schuld, das Schuldbewußtsein. **–less,** *adj.* schuldlos, unschuldig; (*fig.*) *–less of*, nicht wissen, unberührt von, ohne. **–y,** *adj.* schuldig, strafbar, schuldbeladen, verbrecherisch; schuldbewußt; *–y conscience*, böses Gewissen; *find –y*, für schuldig erklären (*on a charge*, einer Anklage); *plead –y*, sich schuldig bekennen (*to doing*, getan zu haben).
guinea ['gɪnɪ], *s.* die Guinee (= 21 Schilling). **–-fowl,** *s.* das Perlhuhn. **–-pig,** *s.* das Meerschweinchen; (*coll.*) Versuchskaninchen.
guise [gaɪz], *s.* (*archaic*) äußere Erscheinung, die Gestalt; Maske, der Vorwand. **–r,** *s.* Vermummte(r), *m.*
guitar [gɪ'tɑ:], *s.* die Gitarre, Zupfgeige.
gulch [gʌltʃ], *s.* tiefe Schlucht (*Amer.*).
gules [gju:lz], *s.* das Rot (*Her.*).
gulf [gʌlf], 1. *s.* der Meerbusen, Golf; Abgrund, Schlund; Strudel; *– Stream*, der Golfstrom. 2. *v.a.* (wie in einem Abgrund) verschlingen.
[1]**gull** [gʌl], *s.* die Möwe.
[2]**gull,** 1. *s.* der Einfaltspinsel, Tölpel, Tollpatsch, Tropf, Tor, Narr. 2. *v.a.* übers Ohr hauen, übertölpeln, verleiten (*into*, zu).
gullet ['gʌlɪt], *s.* die Gurgel, Speiseröhre (*Anat.*), der Schlund.
gullib-ility [gʌlɪ'bɪlɪtɪ], *s.* die Leichtgläubigkeit. **–le** ['gʌlɪbl], *adj.* leichtgläubig, einfältig.
gully ['gʌlɪ], *s.* der Sinkkasten, die Abflußrinne, der Abzugskanal; die Schlucht, das Gießbachbett. **–-hole,** *s.* der Schlammfang, das Abflußloch.
gulp [gʌlp], 1. *v.a.* (*– down*) gierig hinunterschlucken; (*fig.*) gierig verschlingen. 2. *v.n.* mit Schwierigkeit schlucken, würgen. 3. *s.* der Schluck; das Schlucken; *at one –*, mit einem *or* auf einen Zug.

[1]**gum** [gʌm], 1. *s.* das Gummi; der Klebstoff; Gummifluß, das (Pflanzen)Harz, der Pflanzenschleim; (*coll.*) das Kaugummi (*Amer.*); *pl.* (*sl.*) Gummischuhe (*pl.*) (*Amer.*); *chewing-–*, das Kaugummi. 2. *v.a.* kleben, ankleben, gummieren; *– down*, aufkleben, zukleben. **–-arabic,** *s.* das Gummiarabikum. **–-elastic,** *s.* der & das Kautschuk; das Gummielastikum. **–-juniper,** *s.* der Sandarak (*Bot.*). **–my,** *adj.* gummiartig, klebrig. **–-resin,** *s.* das Gummiharz. **–shoe,** *s.* (*sl.*) der Spitzel, Spion (*Amer.*). **–-tree,** *s.* der Gummibaum (*Bot.*); (*sl.*) *up a –-tree*, in der Klemme.

[2]**gum,** *s.* (*usually pl.*) das Zahnfleisch. **–boil,** *s.* das Zahngeschwür.

gumption [ˈgʌmpʃən], *s.* (*coll.*) der Mutterwitz, die Schlagfertigkeit.

gun [gʌn], 1. *s.* die Feuerwaffe, Schußwaffe, das Gewehr; Geschütz, die Kanone; der Schütze, Jagdgast; *anti-aircraft –*, die Flugzeugabwehrkanone, Flakkanone; (*coll.*) *big –*, hohes Tier, große Kanone; *blow great –s*, heulen, toben (*of the wind*) (*Naut.*); *machine-–*, das Maschinengewehr; (*vulg.*) *son of a –*, der Kerl; (*fig.*) *stick to one's –s*, nicht weichen, fest bleiben. 2. *v.n.* (*sl.*) auf der Jagd sein (*for*, nach). **–-barrel,** *s.* der Gewehrlauf; das Geschützrohr. **–boat,** *s.* das Kanonenboot. **–-carriage,** *s.* die Lafette. **–cotton,** *s.* die Schießbaumwolle, Kollodiumwolle, Nitrozellulose. **– crew,** *s.* die Geschützbedienung. **–-deck,** *s.* das Batteriedeck. **– emplacement,** *s.* die Geschützbettung. **–fire,** *s.* das Artilleriefeuer. **–-flashes,** *pl.* das Mündungsfeuer. **–-layer,** *s.* der Richtkanonier. **–-licence,** *s.* der Waffenschein. **–man** [–mən], *s.* bewaffneter Räuber (*Amer.*). **–-metal,** *s.* das Kanonenmetall, der Geschützguß. **–nage,** *s.* die Bestückung (*Naut.*). **–ner,** *s.* der Kanonier, Artillerist, Schütze (*Av.*), Feuerwerker. **–nery,** *s.* das Geschützwesen, die Artillerie(wissenschaft). **– pit,** *s.* der Geschützbunker. **–-port,** *s.* die Stückpforte (*Naut.*). **–powder,** *s.* das Schießpulver; *–powder plot*, die Pulververschwörung. **–-room,** *s.* die Kadettenmesse (*Naut.*). **–-running,** *s.* der Waffenschmuggel. **–shot,** *s.* der Kanonenschuß; die Schußweite; *within –shot*, in Schußweite; *–shot wound*, die Schußwunde. **–-shy,** *adj.* flintenscheu (*of dogs*). **–-sight,** *s.* das Visier. **–smith,** *s.* der Büchsenmacher. **–-stock,** *s.* der Gewehrschaft, Gewehrkolben. **–-turret,** *s.* der Geschützturm, die Kanzel (*Av.*). **–wale** [ˈgʌnl], *s.* der Schandeckel; das Strombord, Dollbord (*on row-boats*).

gurgl-e [ˈgəːgl], 1. *v.n.* murmelnd rieseln; glucksen. 2. *s.*, **–ing,** *s.* das Gemurmel, Gurgeln.

gurn-ard [ˈgəːnəd], **–et** [ˈgəːnɪt], *s.* grauer Knurrhahn (*Orn.*).

gush [gʌʃ], 1. *v.n.* hervorströmen, hervorquellen, sich ergießen, strömen, gießen (*from*, aus), entströmen (*from* (*Dat.*)); (*coll.*) schwärmen, sich überschwenglich ausdrücken. 2. *s.* der Guß, Strom; (*fig.*) Erguß; (*coll.*) die Schwärmerei, Überschwenglichkeit. **–y,** *adj.* (*coll.*) überschwenglich, überspannt.

gusset [ˈgʌsɪt], 1. *s.* der Zwickel (*Semp.*), das Winkelstück (*Mach.*). 2. *v.a.* mit einem Zwickel versehen.

gust [gʌst], *s.* der Windstoß, die Bö. **–y,** *adj.* stürmisch, böig.

gust-ation [gʌsˈteɪʃən], *s.* der Geschmack, das Geschmacksvermögen. **–atory,** *adj.* Geschmacks–. **–o** [ˈgʌstoʊ], *s.* (*coll.*) besondere Neigung; der Schwung, Eifer.

gusty [ˈgʌstɪ], *see* **gust.**

gut [gʌt], 1. *s.* der Darm; *pl.* das Eingeweide, Därme (*pl.*), das Gedärm; (*coll.*) das Innere, wesentlicher Inhalt; *pl.* (*sl.*) der Mut, die Unerschrockenheit, Widerstandskraft; Kraft und Saft. 2. *v.a.* ausweiden, ausnehmen; (*fig.*) ausleeren; *the house was –ted* (*by fire*), das Haus war völlig ausgebrannt.

gutta-percha [gʌtəˈpəːtʃə], *s.* die Guttapercha.

gutter [ˈgʌtə], 1. *s.* der Rinnstein, die Rinne, Gosse, Auffangrinne; Dachrinne, Traufrinne, das Ablaufrohr, der Ausguß (*Build.*); die Rille, Hohlkehle; *he picked him up in the –*, er las ihn von der Straße auf. 2. *v.a.* furchen, rillen, aushöhlen. 3. *v.n.* rinnen, triefen; (ab)laufen, tropfen (*as a candle*). **–-press,** *s.* die Schmutzpresse. **–-snipe,** *s.* der Gassenjunge.

guttural [ˈgʌtərəl], 1. *adj.* Kehl–. 2. *s.* der Kehllaut.

gutty [ˈgʌtɪ], *s.* der Golfball (aus Guttapercha).

[1]**guy** [gɑɪ], 1. *s.* der Backstag, das Geitau (*Naut.*); Spannseil, Haltetau. 2. *v.a.* befestigen, verankern. **–-rope,** *s.* die Zeltschnur; das Haltetau (*Av.*).

[2]**guy,** 1. die Vogelscheuche, der Popanz; (*sl.*) der Kerl, Bursche (*Amer.*). 2. *v.a.* lächerlich machen, verulken, foppen.

guzzle [ˈgʌzl], *v.n.* & *a.* unmäßig trinken, saufen; gierig essen, fressen. **–r,** *s.* der Fresser.

gybe [dʒɑɪb], 1. *v.a.* umlegen, halsen (*Naut.*). 2. *v.n.* sich umlegen.

gym [dʒɪm], *s.* (*coll.*) die Turnhalle; *see* **–nasium. –khana** [dʒɪmˈkɑːnə], *s.* das Sportfest, die Sportveranstaltung. **–nasium** [–ˈneɪzjəm], *s.* (*pl.* –nasiums, –nasia [–ˈneɪzjə]) die Turnhalle, der Turnplatz. **–nast** [ˈdzɪmnæst], *s.* der Turner. **–nastic** [–ˈnæstɪk], *adj.* gymnastisch, turnerisch, Turn–. **–nastics,** *pl.* die Leibesübungen, das Turnen, die Turnkunst, Gymnastik (*also fig.*). **–nosophist** [–ˈnɔsəfɪst], *s.* indischer Asket. **–nosperm,** *s.* nacktsamige Pflanze, der Nacktsamer. **–nospermous** [–noˈspəːməs], *adj.* nacktsamig. **–-shoes,** *pl.* Turnschuhe (*pl.*).

gynaecolog-ical [gɑɪnɪkəˈlɔdʒɪkl], *adj.* gynäkologisch. **–ist** [–ˈkɔlədʒɪst], *s.* der Frauenarzt, Gynäkolog(e). **–y** [–ˈkɔlədʒɪ], *s.* die Frauenheilkunde, Gynäkologie.

gynocracy [gɑɪˈnɔkrəsɪ], *s.* die Weiberherrschaft.

gyp [dʒɪp], *s.* (*sl.*) der (Studenten)Diener (*Univ.*).

gyps-eous [ˈdʒɪpsɪəs], **–ous,** *adj.* gipsartig. **–um** [ˈdʒɪpsəm], *s.* der Gips, Leichtspat, das Kalziumsulfat, schwefelsaurer Kalk.

gypsy [ˈdʒɪpsɪ], *s. see* **gipsy.**

gyr-ate [dʒɑɪˈreɪt], *v.n.* kreisen, wirbeln, sich drehen. **–ation** [–ˈreɪʃən], *s.* die Kreisbewegung, Drehung. **–atory** [ˈdʒɑɪrətərɪ], *adj.* sich drehend, Dreh–, Kreis–.

gyro [ˈdʒɑɪro], *s.* der Kreisel. **–-compass** [–kʌmpəs], *s.* der Kreiselkompass. **–mancy** [–mænsɪ], *s.* die Kreiswahrsagerei. **–plane,** *s.* der Tragschrauber, Hubschrauber, das Drehflügelflugzeug, Windmühlenflugzeug (*Av.*). **–scope** [–rəskoʊp], *s.* der Kreisel, die Kreiselvorrichtung, das Gyroskop. **–scopic,** *adj.* Kreisel–; *–scopic stabilizer*, *s.* der Schiffskreisel.

gyves [dʒɑɪvz], *pl.* (Fuß)Fesseln.

H

H, h [eɪtʃ], *s.* das H, h. *See Index of Abbreviations.*

ha [hɑː], *int.* ha!

habeas corpus [ˈhæbɪəsˈkɔːpəs], *s.*; *writ of – –*, der Vorführungsbefehl (*Law.*).

haberdasher [ˈhæbədæʃə], *s.* der Kurzwarenhändler. **–y** [–rɪ], *s.* die Kurzwaren (*pl.*).

habergeon [ˈhæbədʒən], *s.* das Panzerhemd.

habiliment [həˈbɪlɪmənt], *s.* das Kleidungsstück; *pl.* die Kleidung.

habit [ˈhæbɪt], 1. *s.* die Gewohnheit; Beschaffenheit, Verfassung; Wachstumart, Wachstumserscheinung (*Bot.*, *Zool.*); (*archaic*) die Kleidung; *break o.s. of a –*, sich (*Dat.*) etwas abgewöhnen; *from –*, aus Gewohnheit, gewohnheitsmäßig; *be in the – of*, gewöhnt sein zu, pflegen zu; *fall* or *get into the – of*, sich (*Dat.*) etwas angewöhnen; *fall into bad –s*, schlechte Gewohnheiten annehmen, in schlechte Gewohnheiten verfallen; *– of mind*, die Sinnesart, Geistesverfassung; *get out of the – of*, etwas nicht mehr gewöhnt sein; *riding-–*, der Reitanzug. 2. *v.a.* kleiden. **–able** [ˈhæbɪtəbl], *adj.* bewohnbar. **–ableness,** *s.* die Bewohnbarkeit.

-ant, *s.* der Einwohner; der Kanadier französischer Abstammung. **-at** [ˈhæbɪtæt], *s.* der Fundort, die Heimat (*of animals or plants*). **-ation** [-ˈteɪʃən], *s.* das Wohnen; der Wohnsitz, die Wohnung. **-ual** [həˈbɪtjʊəl], *adj.* gewohnt, gewöhnlich, gewohnheitsmäßig, Gewohnheits-. **-uate** [-jʊeɪt], *v.a.* gewöhnen (*to*, an). **-uation,** *s.* die Gewöhnung (*to*, an). **-ude** [ˈhæbɪtjʊ:d], *s.* die Gewohnheit, Veranlagung. **-ué** [həˈbitjueɪ], *s.* ständiger Besucher.

hachure [ˈhæʃʊə], *s.* (*usually pl.*) die Schraffe, Schraffierung, Schraffur (*on maps*).

[1]**hack** [hæk], 1. *v.a.* (zer)hacken; einkerben; mit dem Fuße stoßen (*Footb.*). 2. *v.n.* kurz husten; – *at*, einhauen. 3. *s.* die Kerbe, der Einschnitt; Hieb; Fußtritt (*Footb.*). **-ing,** *adj.*; *-ing cough*, trockener Husten. **--saw,** *s.* die Metallsäge.

[2]**hack,** 1. *s.* gewöhnliches Reitpferd, das Mietpferd; (*fig.*) der Lohnschreiber, literarischer Tagelöhner. 2. *adj.* Miet(s)-, Lohn-, gemietet; – *writer*, der Lohnschreiber; – *lawyer*, der Winkeladvokat; – *saying*, abgedroschene Redensart. 3. *v.a.* abnutzen. 4. *v.n.* ein Reitpferd mieten; im gewöhnlichen Gang reiten.

hackle [ˈhækl], 1. *v.a.* hecheln. 2. *s.* die Hechel; lange Nackenfedern des Hahns; (*fig.*) *with his – up*, kampflustig.

hackney [ˈhæknɪ], 1. *s.* gewöhnliches Reitpferd, das Mietpferd, der Gaul. 2. *adj.* Lohn-, Miet(s)-; – *carriage*, die Mietskutsche, der Fiaker. 3. *v.a.* abnutzen. **-ed,** *adj.* abgenutzt, abgegriffen, abgedroschen.

had [hæd], *see* **have.**

haddock [ˈhædək], *s.* der Schellfisch.

haem-al [ˈhɪ:məl], *adj.* Blut-. **-atin** [-ətɪn], *s.* das Hämatin. **-atite** [ˈhɛmətaɪt], *s.* der Roteisenstein. **-oglobin** [hɪ:məˈgloʊbɪn], *s.* roter Blutfarbstoff, das Hämoglobin. **-philia** [-ˈfɪlɪə], *s.* die Bluterkrankheit, Hämophilie. **-orrhage** [ˈhɛmərɪdʒ], *s.* die Blutung, der Blutsturz. **-orrhoids** [ˈhɛmərɔɪds], *pl.* Hämorrhoiden.

haft [hæft], 1. *s.* das Heft, der Griff, Stiel. 2. *v.a.* mit einem Heft versehen.

hag [hæg], *s.* häßliches altes Weib, das Scheusal. **--ridden,** *adj.* vom Alpdrücken gequält.

haggard [ˈhægəd], 1. *adj.* hager, abgehärmt; verstört; wild, ungezähmt (*falcon*). 2. *s.* ungezähmter Falke.

haggis [ˈhægɪs], *s.* (*Scots*) der Fleischpudding.

haggl-e [ˈhægl], *v.n.* feilschen, knickern, handeln, markten (*about* or *over*, um); (*coll.*) streiten. **-ing,** *s.* das Feilschen.

hagio-grapha [hægɪˈɔgrəfə], *pl.* Hagiographen (*pl.*). **-grapher** [-ˈɔgrəfə], *s.* der Verfasser von Heiligenlegenden. **-graphy,** *s.* die Lebensbeschreibung der Heiligen. **-logy** [-ˈɔlədʒɪ], *s.* die Literatur über Heiligenlegenden.

hah [hɑ:], *int.*; *see* **ha.** **-a** [ˈhɑ:hɑ:], 1. *int. see* **ha ha.** 2. *s.* unsichtbarer Gartengrenzgraben.

[1]**hail** [heɪl], 1. *s.* der Hagel (*also fig.*). 2. *v.n.* hageln. 3. *v.a.*; – *down*, niederhageln lassen (*upon*, auf). **-stone,** *s.* das Hagelkorn, die Schloße. **-storm,** *s.* das Hagelwetter.

[2]**hail,** 1. *v.a.* anrufen, ansprechen; grüßen, begrüßen, zujubeln. 2. *v.n.*; – *from*, kommen von *or* aus, (her)stammen von *or* aus, abstammen von. 3. *s.* der Zuruf; Gruß; *within* –, in Hörweite *or* Rufweite. 4. *int.* (*Poet.*) Heil! Glück zu! **--fellow-well-met,** (*as pred. adj.*) intim, vertraulich.

hair [hɛə], 1. *s.* das (einzelne) Haar; die Haare; *a -'s breadth, see* **-breadth;** *false* –, falsche Haare; *a fine head of* –, schöner Haarwuchs; *to a* –, auf ein Haar, ganz genau; (*sl.*) *keep one's – on*, ruhig *or* gefaßt bleiben; (*vulg.*) *get s.o. by the short -s*, einen vollkommen in der Gewalt haben; *let down one's* –, das Haar auflösen; (*fig.*) sich ungeniert benehmen; *put up one's* –, das Haar aufstecken; *split -s*, Haarspalterei treiben; *tear one's* –, sich die Haare ausraufen; *not touch* or *harm a – of s.o.'s head*, einem kein Haar krümmen; *without turning a* –, ohne mit der Wimper zu zucken, ganz gelassen. **-breadth,** 1. *s.* die Haaresbreite; *within a -breadth*, um ein Haar, ums Haar; *-breadth escape*, das Entkommen mit genauer Not. **--brush,** *s.* die Haarbürste (*for hair*). **– brush,** der Haarpinsel (*of hair*). **--clippers,** *pl.* die Haarschneidemaschine. **-cut,** *s.* der Haarschnitt. **--dresser,** *s.* der Friseur, Haarschneider. **--dressing,** *s.* das Haarschneiden, Frisieren. **--dryer,** *s.* der Föhn. **--dye,** *s.* das Haarfärbemittel. **-ed,** *adj.* behaart; (*in compounds*) -haarig. **--grass,** *s.* die Schmiele (*Bot.*). **-iness,** *s.* die Behaartheit. **-less,** *adj.* unbehaart, ohne Haare, kahl. **--line,** *s.* der Haarstrich, Faden. **--mattress,** *s.* die Roßhaarmatratze. **--net,** *s.* das Haarnetz. **--oil,** *s.* das Haaröl. **-pin,** *s.* die Haarnadel; *-pin bend*, scharfe Kurve *or* Biegung. **--raising,** *adj.* haarsträubend, aufregend. **– restorer,** das Haarwuchsmittel. **--shirt,** *s.* härenes Hemd. **--sieve,** *s.* das Haarsieb. **--slide,** *s.* die Haarspange. **--splitting,** 1. *adj.* haarspaltend. 2. *s.* die Haarspalterei, Wortklauberei. **--spring,** *s.* feine Feder (*Horol.*). **--trigger,** *s.* der Stecher, das Stechschloß (*of a gun*). **--wash,** *s.* das Haarwasser. **-y,** *adj.* haarig, behaart.

hake [heɪk], *s.* der Hechtdorsch, Seehecht (*Ichth.*).

halation [hæˈleɪʃən], *s.* der Lichthof, heller Fleck (*Phot.*); *no* –, lichthoffrei.

halberd [ˈhælbəd], *s.* die Hellebarde. **-ier** [-ˈdɪ:ə], *s.* der Hellebardier.

halcyon [ˈhælsɪən], 1. *s.* der Eisvogel, Königsfischer (*Myth.*). 2. *adj.* friedlich, ruhig.

[1]**hale** [heɪl], *adj.* frisch und gesund; – *and hearty*, rüstig.

[2]**hale,** *v.a.* (*archaic*) ziehen, schleppen.

half [hɑ:f], 1. *s.* (*pl.* halves [hɑ:vz]) die Hälfte; das (Universitäts)Semester; die Seite, Partei (*Law*); *a litre and a* –, anderthalb Liter; (*coll.*) *his better* –, seine Ehehälfte, seine Frau; *centre* –, der Mittelläufer (*Footb.*); *left* –, linker Läufer (*Footb.*); *not good enough by* –, lange nicht gut genug; *do by halves*, nur halb tun; *too clever by* –, überklug; *in* – or *halves*, entzwei; *go halves with s.o.*, mit einem teilen, mit einem halbpart machen. 2. *adj.* halb; – *as long again*, anderthalbmal so lang; – *the amount*, halb soviel, die Hälfte; *be – the battle*, uns dem Ziele nahebringen; – *a crown* or *a – crown*, eine halbe Krone; (*coll.*) *six of one and – a dozen of another*, dasselbe in grün; – *an hour* or *a – hour*, eine halbe Stunde; *have – a mind*, beinahe Lust haben; – *a pound*, ein halbes Pfund; *at – the price*, zum halben Preise; *a – truth*, nur die halbe Wahrheit. 3. *adv.* zur Hälfte, halbwegs, nahezu, beinahe, fast, ziemlich; (*sl.*) *not* –, durchaus, bei weitem; (*sl.*) *not – bad*, gar nicht übel; (*sl.*) *I don't – like him*, ich bin ihm herzlich zugetan; (*sl.*) *he didn't – carry on*, er schimpfte entsetzlich; (*sl.*) *are you coming? not –!* kommst du mit? Und wie!; – *past twelve*, halb eins. **--and-half,** 1. *s.* (*sl.*) eine Mischung von hellem und dunklem Bier. 2. *adj.* zu gleichen Teilen. **--back,** *s.* der Läufer (*Footb.*). **--baked,** *adj.* ungar; (*fig.*) unerfahren, unreif, unverdaut; einfältig. **--binding,** *s.* der Halbfranzeinband, Halbledereinband. **--blood,** *s.* das Halbblut. **--blooded,** *adj.* halbbürtig, Halbblut-. **--bound,** *adj.* in Halbfranz gebunden. **--breed,** *s.* der Mischling. **--brother,** *s.* der Stiefbruder. **--calf,** *s. see* **--binding. --caste,** 1. *adj.* halbbürtig. 2. *s.* der Mischling. **--cloth,** *s.* & *adj.* Halbleinen. **at --cock,** halb gespannt; (*fig.*) in Bereitschaft. **--crown,** *s.* das halbe Kronenstück. **--deck,** *s.* das Halbdeck. **--hearted,** *adj.* lau, gleichgültig, zaghaft. **--holiday,** *s.* freier Nachmittag. **--hourly,** *adv.* halbstündlich, jede halbe Stunde. **--length,** 1. *s.* halbe Länge. 2. *adj.*; *--length portrait*, das Brustbild. **--mast,** *s.* der Halbmast; *at --mast*, halbstocks, halbmast. **--measure,** *s.* die Halbheit, Unvollkommenheit, der Kompromiß. **--moon,** *s.* der Halbmond. **--mourning,** *s.* die Halbtrauer. **--pay,** *s.* halber Sold, das Ruhegehalt; *on --pay*, außer Dienst, zur Disposition (*Mil.*). **-penny** [ˈheɪpənɪ], 1. *s.* halber Penny *three -pence*, anderthalb Penny. 2. *adj.* einen halben Penny wert. **-pennyworth** [ˈheɪpənɪwə:θ] *s.* der Wert eines halben Penny; für einen halben Penny. **--price,** *s.* halber Preis; *at --price*, zum halben Preise. (*coll.*) **--seas-over,** *pred. adj.* beschwipst, bezecht. **--sister,** *s.* die Stiefschwester. **--sovereign,** *s.* das Zehnschillingstück. **--time**, *s.* die Halbzeit (*Footb.*). **--tone**, *s.* der Halbton (*Mus.*); die Autotypie (*etching*). **--tracked**, *adj.* Halbketten–, Zwitter– (*vehicle*). **--volley**, *s.* der Halbflugschlag. **--way**, 1. *adv.* halbwegs, auf halbem Wege. 2. *adj.* auf halbem Wege gelegen; (*fig.*) *--way house*, die Zwischenstation, das Mittelding. **--witted**, *adj.* närrisch, albern, nicht recht gescheit. **--yearly**, *adv.* halbjährlich.

halibut [ˈhælɪbət], *s.* der Heilbutt (*Ichth.*).

halide [ˈhælaɪd], *s.* das Halogen (*Chem.*).

halitosis [hælɪˈtoʊsɪs], *s.* der Mundgeruch (*Med.*).

hall [hɔ:l], 1. *s.* die Halle, der Saal; (Haus)Flur, Vorraum, Vorsaal, die Diele; der Landsitz, das Herrenhaus; der Speisesaal (*in colleges*); das Innungshaus, Logenhaus, Stammhaus, der Sitz; *servants'* –, die Bedientenstube; *town* –, das Rathaus; *I shall not go to – tonight*, ich werde heute abend nicht im Speisesaal (des College) essen. **--mark**, 1. *s.* der Feingehaltsstempel; (*fig.*) Stempel, das Kennzeichen. 2. *v.a.* stempeln, kennzeichnen. **--stand**, *s.* der Schirmständer.

hallelujah [hælɪˈlu:jə], *s.* & *int.* (das) Halleluja.

halliard [ˈhɔ:ljəd], *s. see* **halyard.**

hallo [hɛˈloʊ], 1. *int.* hallo! 2. *s.* der Halloruf. 3. *v.n.* (hallo) rufen.

halloo [həˈlu:], 1 *v.n.* (hallo) rufen; nach den Hunden rufen (*Hunt.*), (*fig.*) schreien; *not – before one is out of the wood*, den Tag nicht vor dem Abend loben, nicht zu früh triumphieren. 2. *int.* hallo! (*Hunt.*). 3. *s.* das Hallo (*Hunt.*).

hallow [ˈhæloʊ], *v.a.* heiligen, weihen. **–e'en** [–ɪ:n], *s.* der Abend vor Allerheiligen (31. Okt.). **–mas**, *s.* (das) Allerheiligen(fest) (1. Nov.).

hallucination [həlu:sɪˈneɪʃən], *s.* die Sinnestäuschung, Halluzination, Wahnvorstellung.

halo [ˈheɪloʊ], *s.* der Hof (*Astr.*); Lichthof (*Phot.*); Glorienschein, Heiligenschein (*Paint.*).

halo–gen [ˈhælədʒən], *s.* das Halogen, der Salzbildner (*Chem.*). **–genation**, *s.* die Halogenierung, Salzbildung. **–genous**, *adj.* salzbildend. **–id** [ˈhælɔɪd], *adj.* Halogen–.

[1]**halt** [hɔ:lt], 1 *v.n.* anhalten, haltmachen. 2. *v.a.* zum Halten bringen, haltmachen lassen. 3. *s.* die Rast, Marschpause; Haltestelle (*Railw.*); *make a* –, haltmachen; *come to a* –, zum Stehen *or* Stillstand kommen, stille stehen, halten.

[2]**halt**, 1. *adj.* (*poet.*) lahm, hinkend. 2. *v.n.* (*archaic*) hinken, lahmen; schwanken, zögern. **–ing**, *adj.* hinkend, schleppend, zögernd, unsicher.

halter [ˈhɔ:ltə], 1. *s.* die, der *or* das Halfter; (*fig.*) der Strick. 2. *v.a.* (an)halftern (*a horse*); erhängen (*a p.*). **– rope**, der Halfterriemen.

halve [hɑ:v], *v.a.* halbieren (*also Golf*), zur Hälfte teilen, um die Hälfte verringern. **–s**, *see* **half.**

halyard [ˈhɔ:ljəd], *s.* das Fall (*Naut.*).

ham [hæm], 1. *s.* der Schinken; Schenkel (*Anat.*); (*coll.*) (*radio*) –, der Radio-Amateur. 2. *adj.* (*coll.*) *– actor*, der Schmierenschauspieler.

hamadryad [hæməˈdraɪæd], *s.* die Waldnymphe.

hame [heɪm], *s.* (*usually pl.*) das Kum(me)t.

hamlet [ˈhæmlɪt], *s.* der Weiler, das Dörfchen, der Flecken.

hammer [ˈhæmə], 1. *s.* der Hammer; *sledge* –, der Vorschlaghammer; (*coll.*) *– and tongs*, mit aller Kraft; *bring to the* –, versteigern lassen; *come under the* –, unter den Hammer kommen, versteigert werden. 2. *v.a.* hämmern, mit dem Hammer schlagen, bearbeiten (*metal*) (*into*, zu); *– in*, einschlagen (*a nail*); (*fig.*) einhämmern, einprägen; *– s.th. into a p.*, einem etwas einhämmern, einbleuen *or* eintrichtern; *– out*, schlagen, schmieden (*metal*); (*fig.*) herausarbeiten, ersinnen; erhellen, klären; *be –ed*, für zahlungsunfähig erklärt werden (*C.L.*). 3. *v.n.* hämmern; *– at s.th.*, anhaltend an einer S. arbeiten. **--beam**, *s.* der Stichbalken (*Build.*). **--blow**, *s.* der Hammerschlag. **--cloth**, *s.* die Kutschsitzdecke. **--head**, *s.* der Hammerhai (*Ichth.*).

hammock [ˈhæmək], *s.* die Hängematte.

[1]**hamper** [ˈhæmpə], *s.* der Packkorb, Eßkorb, Frühstückskorb.

[2]**hamper**, *v.a.* verstricken, verwickeln (*in*, in (*Acc.*)); (*fig.*) hindern, hemmen.

hamshackle [ˈhæmʃækl], *v.a.* fesseln.

hamster [ˈhæmstə], *s.* der Hamster (*Zool.*).

hamstring [ˈhæmstrɪŋ], 1. *s.* die Kniefl echse. 2. *v.a.* die Kniefl echsen zerschneiden (*Dat.*); (*fig.*) lähmen.

hand [hænd], **1.** *s.* die Hand; der Vorderfuß (*of animals*); die Handschrift, Unterschrift; der Zeiger (*Horol.*); die Handbreite (= 4 Zoll); (*usually pl.*) der Arbeiter; Mann, Matrose; das Blatt, Karten (*pl.*) (*cards*); der Büschel, das Bündel (*fruit, etc.*); *all –s on deck!* alle Mann an Deck! *the ship was lost with all –s*, das Schiff ging mit Mann und Maus unter; **(a)** (with *of*) *note of* –, der Handwechsel, Handschuldschein; *by show of –s*, durch Aufheben der Hände; *sleight of* –, der Kunstgriff; *in the turn of a* –, im Handumdrehen; **(b)** (*with adjectives*) (*sl.*) *give s.o. the big* –, einem Beifall klatschen; *keep a firm – over*, streng im Zaume *or* fest in den Zügeln halten; *at first* –, aus erster Hand; *be a good – at a th.*, in einer S. geschickt sein, sich auf etwas verstehen, für etwas Geschicklichkeit *or* Veranlagung haben, sich bei etwas geschickt anstellen; *with a heavy* –, bedrückend, mit großer Strenge; *lend a helping* –, eine hilfreiche Hand leisten; *with a high – or high-–ed*, rücksichtslos, willkürlich, anmaßend, hochfahrend, hochmütig; *an iron* –, eiserne Zucht; *left-–ed compliment*, zweifelhaftes Kompliment; *be an old – at*, ein alter Praktikus sein, gründlich bewandert sein in; *open-–ed*, freigebig; *with one's own* –, mit eigner Hand, *buy second-–*, antiquarisch *or* aus zweiter Hand kaufen; *be short-–ed*, Mangel an Arbeitskräften haben; *the upper* –, die Oberhand; *a wretched* –, ein schlechtes Blatt, schlechte Karten (*Cards*); **(c)** (*with verbs*) *ask the – of Miss E.*, um Fräulein E. anhalten, sich um Fräulein E's Hand bewerben; *be – and* or *in glove with*, sehr befreundet sein mit; *bear a* –, anfassen, mithelfen, Hilfe leisten; *change –s*, in andere Hände kommen *or* übergehen, den Besitzer wechseln; *get one's – in*, sich gewöhnen an, sich einarbeiten in; *give one's – to*, einem die Hand reichen; *give one's – upon a th.*, (einem) die Hand darauf geben; *have a – in*, die Hand im Spiele haben bei, beteiligt sein bei; *have one's –s full*, alle Hände voll zu tun haben, vollauf beschäftigt sein; *hold one's* –, sich zurückhalten, Abstand nehmen; *hold o.s. in* –, sich beherrschen; (*fig.*) *join –s*, sich verbünden, *keep one's – in*, in Übung bleiben; *keep a tight – on*, im Zaume halten; *lay one's –(s) on s.th.*, einer S. habhaft werden; *lay –s on*, ergreifen, anpacken, erhalten; Hand legen an; *lend a* –, helfen, mit anfassen, mit Hand anlegen; *put one's – to*, in Angriff nehmen; *shake –s*, sich (*Dat.*) die Hände geben; *show one's* –, die Karten aufdecken (*also fig.*); *throw in one's* –, sein Blatt wegwerfen (*Cards*), (*fig.*) etwas aufgeben, sich von etwas zurückziehen; *throw up one's –s*, eine verzweifelte Gebärde machen; *try one's – at a th.*, sich bei etwas versuchen; *wash one's –s of a p.*, nichts mit einem zu tun haben wollen; *wash one's –s of a th.*, sich (wegen einer Sache) die Hände in Unschuld waschen; eine Sache gehen lassen, wie sie geht; *win –s down*, spielend leicht gewinnen; **(d)** (*with prepositions*) *at* –, zur Hand, bei der Hand, nah(e); *near at* –, nah(e), nahebei; *at our –s*, seitens *or* von Seiten unser, von uns; *by* –, mit der Hand; durch Boten; *bring up by* –, mit der Flasche nähren (*a child*); *by the – of*, vermittelst, durch; *shake a p. by the* –, einem die Hand geben *or* reichen; *take by the* –, bei der Hand nehmen; *from – to* –, von Hand zu Hand; *from – to mouth*, aus der Hand in den Mund; *in* –, in der Hand, unter Kontrolle; *be well in* –, im Gange sein; *cash in* –, bares Geld; *have s.th. in* –, eine S. unter den Händen haben; *– in* –, Hand in Hand; (*fig.*) *go – in – with*, Schritt halten mit; *the matter in* –, vorliegende Sache; *put in* –, in Ausführung *or* Arbeit nehmen; *take in* –, unternehmen, übernehmen; *fall into s.o.'s –s*, einem in die Hände fallen; *off-–*, auf der Stelle, aus dem Stegreif *or* Handgelenk; *off-–(ed)*, von oben herab, wegwerfend, kurz angebunden; *take off s.o.'s –s*, einem abnehmen; *on* –, vorrätig, auf Lager, verfügbar; (*fig.*) bevorstehend; *on all –s, on every* –, auf *or* von allen Seiten, überall; *on either* –, zu beiden Seiten; *be on a p.'s –s*, einem zur Last fallen; *have s.o. on one's –s*, einen am *or* auf dem Halse haben; *on the one –*, auf der einen Seite, einerseits; *on the other –*, auf der anderen Seite, anderseits; *out of –*, im Handumdrehen, kurzerhand, auf der Stelle; unbändig, außer Zucht; *– over – or – over fist*, in schneller Folge, rasch nacheinander; *to –*, zur Hand, bereit; *your letter to –*, Ihren Brief erhalten (*C.L.*); *come to –*, einlaufen, eintreffen, einlangen, zum Vorschein kommen; *– to –*, Mann gegen Mann; *– to – fighting*, der Nahkampf; *under one's –*, eigenhändig unterschrieben; (e) (*commands*) *–s off!* Hände weg! laß die Hände davon! *–s up!* Hände hoch! **2.** *v.a.* reichen, (über)geben; (*sl.*) *one must – it to him*, man muß ihm Anerkennung zollen, man muß es ihm lassen; *– about*, herumgeben; *– down*, herunterlangen, herunterreichen; hinterlassen, vererben; *– down to posterity*, der Nachwelt überliefern; *– in*, einreichen, abgeben (*a th.*), hineinhelfen in (*Dat.*) (*a. p.*); *– off*, mit der Hand abwehren (*Rugby footb.*); *– on*, weitergeben, weiterreichen; *– out*, ausgeben, austeilen (*a th.*) (*to*, an); heraushelfen (*Dat.*) (*a p.*); *– over*, überlassen, abgeben (*to* (*Dat.*)), abtreten (*to*, an); *– round*, herumreichen; *– up*, hinaufreichen, hinauflangen. **–bag,** *s.* die Handtasche. **–ball,** *s.* der Handball. **–bell,** *s.* die Tischglocke, Schelle. **–bill,** *s.* gedruckter Zettel, das Flugblatt, der Reklamezettel. **–book,** *s.* das Handbuch. **–breadth,** *s.* die Handbreite. **– -cart,** die Handkarre. **–cuff,** 1. *s.* die Handschelle, Handfessel. 2. *v.a.* Handschellen anlegen (*Dat.*), fesseln (*Acc.*). **–ed,** (*in compounds*) –händig. **–ful,** *s.* die Handvoll; (*coll.*) *he is a –ful*, er ist ein ungezogenes Kind, er macht mir viel zu schaffen. **– -gallop,** *s.* kurzer Galopp. **– -grenade,** *s.* die Handgranate. **– -hold,** *s.* der Halt, Handgriff. **–icap,** *see* **handicap. –icraft** ['hændıkrɑːft], *s.* das Handwerk, Gewerbe, Kunsthandwerk. **–icraftsman,** *s.* der Handwerker. **–ily** ['hændılı], *adv.* *see* **handy. –iness,** *s.* die Gewandtheit; Handlichkeit, Bequemlichkeit, Zweckmäßigkeit. **–iwork** ['hændıwəːk], *s.* die Handarbeit; das Werk, die Arbeit, Schöpfung. **–kerchief** ['hæŋkətʃıf], *s.* das Taschentuch. **– -made,** *adj.* mit der Hand gemacht; *– -made paper*, das Büttenpapier. **–maid(en),** *s.* (*B.*) die Dienerin, Magd; (*fig.*) der Gehilfe, Handlanger; (*sl.*) **– -me-downs,** *pl.* gebrauchte Kleidungsstücke, alte Erbstücke. **– -rail,** *s.* das Geländer. **–saw,** *s.* die Handsäge. **–set,** *s.* der Hörer (*Tele.*). **– -shake,** *s.* der Händedruck. **–spike,** *s.* die Brechstange; Handspake, der Hebebaum (*Naut. & Artil.*). **–stand,** *s.* der Handstand (*Gymn.*). **–wheel,** *s.* das Kurbelrad. **–writing,** *s.* die Handschrift. **–y,** *see* **handy.**

handicap ['hændıkæp], 1. *s.* die Vorgabe; (*fig.*) Belastung, Erschwerung, Benachteiligung, Schwierigkeit, das Hindernis; das Vorgaberennen, Ausgleichsrennen, Handikap; der Ausgleichswettbewerb, das Vorgabespiel. 2. *v.a.* extra belasten (*a horse*); (*fig.*) hemmen, hindern, beeinträchtigen, in Nachteil setzen, benachteiligen. **–ped** [–t], *adj.* benachteiligt, gehindert.

handl–e ['hændl], 1. *v.a.* anfassen, befühlen, handhaben, hantieren mit; lenken, leiten; behandeln, sich befassen mit; handeln mit *or* in (*C.L.*). 2. *s.* der Griff, Stiel; die Kurbel (*on a spindle*); der Henkel (*of a vessel*); Schwengel (*of a pump*); (*fig.*) die Handhabe, der Vorwand; *crank –e*, der Kurbelgriff; *door –e*, der Türgriff, Türdrücker, die Türklinke; (*coll.*) *a –e to one's name*, ein Titel vor dem Namen. **–e-bar,** *s.* die Lenkstange (*Cycl.*). **–ing,** *s.* die Handhabung, Führung.

handsel ['hændsəl], 1. *s.* das Neujahrsgeschenk; Handgeld; der Vorgeschmack. 2. *v.a.* zum ersten Mal gebrauchen *or* versuchen, dem Gebrauch einweihen; Handgeld geben.

handsome ['hænsəm], *adj.* hübsch, schön, stattlich; großzügig, freigebig, edelmütig; ansehnlich, beträchtlich; (*Prov.*) *– is that – does*, edel ist wer edel handelt. **–ness,** *s.* die Schönheit, Stattlichkeit.

handy ['hændı], *adj.* zur Hand, leicht erreichbar; bequem, handlich; gewandt, geschickt (*of persons*); *come in –*, gelegen kommen. **–man,** *s.* Mann für alles.

hang [hæŋ], 1. *ir.v.a.* (auf)hängen; einhängen (*doors*); behängen (*a room with pictures*); hängen lassen (*one's head, etc.*). 2. *reg. v.a.* erhängen (*a person*); *– fire*, versagen; (*fig.*) verzögern; *well hung*, gut abgehangen (*Hunt.*); *I'll be –ed if*, ich will mich hängen lassen, wenn; *– it!* zum Teufel *or* Henker!; *– out*, (her)aushängen; *– out the washing*, die Wäsche aufhängen; *– up*, aufhängen; (*fig.*) aufschieben, verschieben, ruhen lassen; den Hörer auflegen (*Tele.*). 3. *reg.v.n.* gehängt werden; 4. *ir.v.n.* hangen, (*now usually*) hängen; baumeln; schweben; *– by a thread*, an einem Faden hängen; (*coll.*) *let it go –*, der Teufel soll es holen, überlaß es sich selbst; *– in the balance*, in der Schwebe *or* unentschieden sein; (*a*) (*with prepositions*) *– about*, herumhängen um; herumlungern in (*a place*); sich hängen an (*a p.*); *– on*, sich hängen *or* anklammern an, hangen an; abhängen von, beruhen auf; *time is –ing on my hands*, die Zeit ist mir lang; *– over*, sich beugen *or* neigen über, hangen *or* schweben über; (*b*) (*with adverbs*) *– about*, faulenzen, umherlungern; *– back*, zögern, sich sträuben *or* zurückhalten; *– down*, herab– *or* herunterhängen; *– on*, festhalten, sich klammern (*to*, an); (*coll.*) ausharren; *– out*, heraushangen; (*sl.*) wohnen; *– over*, überhangen; *– together*, zusammenhalten (*of persons*), zusammenhängen (*of things*). 5. *s.* der Hang, Abhang; die Neigung; der Sitz, Fall (*of clothes, etc.*); (*coll.*) die Bedeutung, der Sinn; (*coll.*) *get the – of a th.*, etwas herausbekommen, hinter etwas kommen; (*sl.*) *not a –*, nicht die Bohne. **– -dog,** 1. *s.* der Galgenvogel, Galgenstrick. 2. *adj.*; *– -dog look*, die Galgenmiene. **–er,** *s.* der Aufhänger, Haken, Henkel; Kleiderbügel; Hirschfänger; *strap- –er*, *s.* stehender Fahrgast. **–er-on,** *s.* (*coll.*) der Anhänger, Mitläufer, Schmarotzer. **–ing,** 1. *s.* das Hängen, Aufhängen; Gehängtwerden. 2. *adj.* Hänge–, hängend; *a –ing matter*, etwas das einen an den Galgen bringen kann. **–ings,** *pl.* die Wandbekleidung, Tapeten (*pl.*). **–man,** *s.* der Henker. **– -out,** *s.* (*sl.*) der Stammplatz. (*sl.*) **–over,** *s.* der Kater, Katzenjammer.

hangar ['hæŋə], *s.* die Flugzeughalle (*Av.*); der Schuppen.

hank [hæŋk], *s.* der *or* das Knäuel, der Wickel, das Bund, die Docke; der Legel (*Naut.*).

hanker ['hæŋkə], *v.n.* verlangen, sich sehnen (*after*, nach), begehren. **–ing** [–rıŋ], *s.* das Verlangen (*after*, nach).

hanky ['hæŋkı], *s.* (*coll.*) *see* **handkerchief. – -panky** [–'pæŋkı], *s.* (*coll.*) der Hokuspokus, Schwindel.

hansel ['hænzl], *see* **handsel.**

hansom ['hænsəm], *s.* zweirädrige Droschke.

hap [hæp], (*archaic*) 1. *v.n.* sich ereignen. 2. *s.* (*archaic*) der Zufall. **–hazard,** 1. der Zufall, das Geratewohl. 2. *adj.* zufällig, wahllos. **–less,** *adj.* unglücklich. **–ly,** *adv.* (*archaic*) vielleicht, ungefähr.

ha'porth ['heıpəθ], *see* **halfpennyworth.**

happen ['hæpən], *v.n.* sich ereignen, sich zutragen, geschehen, zustande kommen; (*coll.*) passieren; *I –ed to read*, ich las zufällig; *as it –s*, wie es sich trifft; *– upon*, durch Zufall treffen, stoßen auf (*Acc.*); *– to him*, ihm zustoßen *or* (*coll.*) passieren. **–ing,** *s.* das Ereignis.

happ–ily ['hæpılı], *adv.* glücklicherweise. **–iness,** *s.* das Glück; die Gewandtheit, Geschicklichkeit, Gefälligkeit, glückliche Wahl. **–y** ['hæpı], *adj.* glücklich; beglückt, günstig, vorteilhaft, erfreulich; treffend, passend, geschickt; *be –y in his friendship*, froh über seine Freundschaft; *I am –y to know*, ich freue mich zu wissen; *–y dispatch*, legaler Selbstmord; *in a –y hour*, zu glücklicher Stunde; *–y retort*, treffende Entgegnung; *many –y returns of the day*, viel Glück zum Geburtstag; *–y thought*, guter Gedanke. **–y-go-lucky,** *adj.* unbekümmert, sorglos.

harangue [hə'ræŋ], 1. *v.a.* eindringlich sprechen zu. 2. *v.n.* eine Ansprache halten. 3. *s.* die Ansprache, Anrede, feierliche Rede.

harass ['hærəs], *v.a.* dauernd belästigen, aufreiben, quälen, plagen, beunruhigen, stören (*also Mil.*); *–ing fire*, das Störfeuer (*Mil.*).

harbinger [ˈhɑ:bɪndʒə], 1. *s.* der Vorbote, Vorläufer. 2. *v.a.* ankündigen.

harbour [ˈhɑ:bə], 1. *s.* der Hafen; (*fig.*) Unterschlupf. 2. *v.a.* beherbergen; schützen, Schutz gewähren (*Dat.*); (*fig.*) hegen (*feelings, etc.*); – *a criminal*, einen Verbrecher verbergen. 3. *v.n.* im Hafen ankern *or* anlegen. **–age** [–rɪdʒ], *s.* die Unterkunft, Herberge, Zuflucht; das Unterkommen im Hafen. **– -dues,** *pl.* Hafengebühren. **– -master,** *s.* der Hafenmeister.

hard [hɑ:d], **1.** *adj.* hart, fest; schwierig, schwer (zu verstehen, tun, *etc.*); mühsam, anstrengend, ermüdend; streng, drückend, schlimm, ungünstig, unbillig, ungerecht, unangenehm, unfreundlich, hartherzig, gefühllos, unbarmherzig, unbeugsam, grausam; karg, geizig; heftig, kräftig; tüchtig, fleißig; herb, sauer, rauh (*as liquor*); kalkhaltig (*of water*); (*a*) (*with nouns*) *drive a – bargain*, aufs äußerste feilschen; – *case*, schwieriger *or* (besonders) harter Fall; eine Härte (*Law*); – *cash*, see – *money*; *a – death*, ein schwerer Tod; – *drinker*, heftiger Trinker, der Säufer; *the – facts*, die unumstößlichen Tatsachen; *no – feelings!* nichts für ungut!; – *labour*, die Zwangsarbeit; (*coll.*) – *lines*, großes Pech, ein hartes Los; (*coll.*) – *luck*, das Unglück; – *money*, das Hartgeld, die Münze; – *pan*, (*Amer.*) fester Untergrund; – *and fast rule*, strenger Brauch, bindende Regel, starre Richtlinie; – *soap*, die Kernseife; – *tack*, der Schiffszwieback (*Naut.*); – *times*, schlimme Zeiten; *for – wear*, unverwüstlich; strapazierfähig (*C.L.*); – *work*, schwere Arbeit; – *worker*, fleißiger Arbeiter; (*b*) (*with verbs*) *be – upon a p.*, hart gegen einen sein; – *to deal with*, schwer auszukommen *or* umzugehen mit; – *to digest*, schwerverdaulich; *he is – to please*, er ist schwer zu befriedigen; – *of hearing*, schwerhörig. **2.** *adv.* heftig, stark, mächtig, wuchtig; fleißig, tüchtig; mit Mühe, schwer, sauer; nahe, dicht; (*a*) (*with verbs*) *be – on s.o.*, einem hart zusetzen, streng mit einem sein; *bear – upon*, drücken; *die –*, ein zähes Leben haben; *drink –*, übermäßig trinken; *go – with*, schlecht ergehen (*Dat.*), schlimm werden für, schwer ankommen (*Dat.*); *look – at*, fest ansehen; *press – for*, ernstlich dringen auf (*Acc.*); – *pressed*, hart *or* schwer bedrängt, in großer Bedrängnis; *be – put to it*, es sich sauer werden lassen; *rain –*, heftig *or* stark regnen; *try –*, sein Äußerstes tun; *work –*, tüchtig, fleißig *or* schwer arbeiten; (*b*) (*with prepositions*) – *at work*, fleißig bei *or* an der Arbeit; – *by*, nahe *or* dicht dabei; – *on his heels*, ihm hart *or* dicht auf den Fersen. **3.** *s.* das Ufer, die Landestelle; (*coll.*) die Zuchthausstrafe; *pl.* Nöte, Mühsale (*pl.*); *pl.* das Werg (*Tech.*). **– -beset,** *adj.* hart bedrängt. **– -bitten,** *adj.* hartnäckig, verbissen. **– -boiled,** *adj.* hartgesotten, hartgekocht; (*sl.*) (kalt)berechnend, nüchtern, abgehärtet, unsentimental, realistisch, geschäftsmäßig. **– -earned,** *adj.* sauer erworben. **–en,** *see* **harden. – -featured,** *adj.* mit harten Gesichtszügen. **– -fisted,** *adj.* geizig, knauserig. **– -headed,** *adj.* nüchtern, praktisch, realistisch. **– -hearted,** *adj.* hartherzig, grausam. **–ihood, –ly,** *see* **hardihood, hardly. – -mouthed,** *adj.* hartmäulig. **–ness,** *see* **hardness. – -set,** *adj.* unbeugsam, hart, streng; starr. **–ship,** *see* **hardship. – -up,** *pred. adj.* in Not, mittellos, nicht bei Kasse; *– -up for*, in Verlegenheit *or* schlimm dran um. **–ware, –wood,** *see* **hardware, hardwood. – -working,** *adj.* fleißig. **–y,** *see* **hardy.**

harden [ˈhɑ:dən], 1. *v.a.* härten, hart machen; stählen, abhärten (*against*, gegen); gewöhnen (*to*, an (*Acc.*)); stärken, verhärten, bestärken (*in sin, etc.*); gefühllos machen. 2. *v.n.* hart werden, sich verhärten *or* verfestigen, erstarren; (*fig.*) unempfindlich werden; steigen, anziehen, fest werden (*of prices*) (*C.L.*). **–er,** *s.* der Härter (*Metall.*). **–ing,** 1. *s.* das Härten. 2. *adj.* Härte– (*Metall.*).

hardi–hood [ˈhɑ:dɪhʊd], *s.* die Kühnheit, Unerschrockenheit; Dreistigkeit. **–ness,** *s.* körperliche Kraft, die Körperkraft, Rüstigkeit.

hardly [ˈhɑ:dlɪ], *adv.* kaum, schwerlich, fast nicht, eben gerade; mit Mühe, mühsam, schwer; hart, streng; – *ever*, fast nie.

hardness [ˈhɑ:dnɪs], *s.* die Härte, Festigkeit; Schwierigkeit, Mühsamkeit, Strenge, Not, der Druck; die Grausamkeit, Hartherzigkeit; der Geiz; – *of heart*, die Hartherzigkeit.

hardship [ˈhɑ:dʃɪp], *s.* die Mühe, Mühsal, Not, Bedrängnis; das Ungemach, die Unbequemlichkeit, Härte, Bedrückung; das Unrecht; *relieve –*, Härten mildern.

hardware [ˈhɑ:dwɛə], *s.* Eisenwaren, Metallkurzwaren (*pl.*).

hardwood [ˈhɑ:dwʊd], *s.* das Hartholz.

hardy [ˈhɑ:dɪ], *adj.* kräftig, abgehärtet; unempfindlich gegen Kälte (*Hort.*); kühn, verwegen; – *annual*, Pflanze, die im Freien überwintern kann; (*fig.*) periodisch wiederkehrende Sache.

hare [hɛə], *s.* der Hase; – *and hounds*, die Schnitzeljagd; *run with the – and hunt with the hounds*, es mit beiden Parteien halten. **– -bell,** *s.* die Glockenblume (*Bot.*). **–brained,** *adj.* unbesonnen, gedankenlos, unstet, zerfahren. **– -lip,** *s.* die Hasenscharte. **–'s-foot,** *s.* der Ackerklee (*Bot.*).

harem [ˈhɛərɛm], *s.* der Harem.

haricot [ˈhærɪkət], 1. *s.* das Hammelragout (*Cul.*); – *bean*, welsche Bohne.

hark [hɑ:k], 1. *v.n.* horchen; – *back*, nach der Fährte zurückgehen (*of hounds*); (*fig.*) zurückkommen, zurückgehen, zurückgreifen (*to*, auf). 2. *int.* horch! hör zu!

harlequin [ˈhɑ:lɪkwɪn], *s.* der Hanswurst, Harlekin. **–ade** [–ˈneɪd], *s.* das Possenspiel.

harlot [ˈhɑ:lət], *s.* die Dirne, Hure. **–ry,** *s.* die Hurerei.

harm [hɑ:m], 1. *s.* der Schaden, das Leid, Unrecht; Übel, Böses, *n.*; *do no –*, nicht(s) schaden; *do a p. –*, einem schaden; *mean no –*, nichts Böses im Sinne haben; *keep out of –'s way*, die Gefahr meiden, sich vorsehen. 2. *v.a.* schädigen, verletzen; schaden (*Dat.*), Leid zufügen (*Dat.*); *not – a hair of his head*, ihm kein Haar krümmen. **–ful,** *adj.* nachteilig, schädlich (*to*, für (*or Dat.*)). **–fulness,** *s.* die Schädlichkeit. **–less,** *adj.* harmlos, unschädlich; schuldlos, arglos. **–lessness,** *s.* die Harmlosigkeit, Unschädlichkeit.

harmon–ic [hɑ:ˈmɔnɪk], 1. *adj.* harmonisch (*Mus.*, *Math.*); übereinstimmend, zusammenstimmend; *–ic proportion*, harmonische Reihe. 2. *s.* die Oberschwingung. **–ica,** *s.* die (Mund)Harmonika. **–ics,** *pl.* (*sing. const.*) die Harmonielehre (*Mus.*). **–ious** [–ˈmoʊnjəs], *adj.* harmonisch, wohlklingend; (*fig.*) zusammenstimmend; einträchtig. **–iousness,** *s.* der Wohlklang; die Eintracht. **–ist** [ˈhɑ:mənɪst], *s.* der Harmonielehrer; Harmoniker (*Rel.*). **–ium** [–ˈmoʊnjəm], *s.* das Harmonium. **–ize,** 1. *v.n.* harmonieren; übereinstimmen. 2. *v.a.* harmonisch machen, in Einklang bringen. **–y** [ˈhɑ:mənɪ], *s.* die Harmonie, der Wohlklang; das Ebenmaß (*Arch.*); (*fig.*) der Einklang, die Eintracht.

harness [ˈhɑ:nɪs], 1. *s.* das Geschirr; (*archaic*) der Harnisch, die Rüstung; (*fig.*) *be in –*, mitten in der Arbeit stehen; (*fig.*) *die in –*, in den Sielen sterben; *parachute –*, das Gurtwerk. 2. *v.a.* anschirren, anspannen (*to*, an (*Acc.*)); einspannen (*to*, in (*Acc.*)); (*fig.*) nutzbar machen (*natural forces*). **– -maker,** *s.* der Sattler.

harp [hɑ:p], 1. *s.* die Harfe (*Mus.*); *Jew's- –*, die Maultrommel. 2. *v.n.* Harfe spielen, harfen; – *on a subject*, dasselbe Thema immer wieder berühren *or* betonen, auf einer S. herumreiten; *be always –ing on the same string*, immer dieselbe Leier anstimmen, eine S. wiederholt aufs Tapet bringen. **–er,** *s.*, **–ist,** *s.* der Harfner.

harpoon [hɑ:ˈpu:n], 1. *s.* die Harpune. 2. *v.a.* harpunieren.

harpsichord [ˈhɑ:psɪkɔ:d], *s.* der Kielflügel, das Cembalo (*Mus.*).

harpy [ˈhɑ:pɪ], *s.* die Harpyie; (*fig.*) raubgierige Person.

harquebus [ˈhɑ:kwɪbəs], *s. see* **arquebus.**

harridan [ˈhærɪdən], *s.* alte Vettel.

harrier [ˈhærɪə], *s.* der Hasenhund (*Hunt.*), die *or* der Weihe (*Orn.*). **–s,** *pl.* Geländeläufer (*pl.*).

harrow [ˈhæroʊ], 1. *s.* die Egge. 2. *v.a.* eggen; (*fig.*) quälen, martern. **–ing,** *adj.* herzzerreißend, qualvoll, schrecklich.

harry [ˈhærɪ], 1. *v.a.* verheeren, verwüsten, plün-

dern (*a land*); ausnehmen, berauben (*a nest*); verfolgen, quälen (*a person*).
harsh [hɑ:ʃ], *adj.* rauh, hart (*touch*); herb, sauer (*taste*); grell (*sound, colour*); (*fig.*) streng, barsch, unsanft, grausam. **-ness,** *s.* die Rauheit, Herbheit; (*fig.*) Härte.
hart [hɑ:t], *s.* der Hirsch; – *of ten*, der Zehnender. **-'s-tongue,** *s.* die Hirschzunge (*Bot.*).
hartebeest [ˈhɑ:təbɪ:st], *s.* der Kama (*Zool.*).
hartshorn [ˈhɑ:tshɔ:n], *s.* das Hirschhorn (*Chem.*).
harum-scarum [ˈhɛərəmˈskɛərəm], 1. *adj.* hastig, wild, unbändig; fahrig, gedankenlos, leichtsinnig. 2. *s.* fahrige Person; der Wildfang.
harvest [ˈhɑ:vɪst], 1. *s.* die Ernte; Erntezeit; (*fig.*) der Gewinn, Ertrag. 2. *v.a.* ernten, (Ernte) einbringen *or* einholen. **--bug,** *s.* die Grasmilbe. **-er,** *s.* der Schnitter; die Mähmaschine mit Selbstbinder; *see also* **--bug.** **--festival,** *s. see* **--thanksgiving.** **--home,** *s.* das Erntefest. **--mite,** *s. see* **--bug.** **--moon,** *s.* der Vollmond im Herbste. **--mouse,** *s.* die Zwergmaus. **--thanksgiving,** das Erntedankfest. **--tick,** *s. see* **--bug.**
has [hæz], *3rd sing. pres. indic. of* **have,** *q.v.* **--been,** *s.* (*coll.*) Überholte(r), *m.*; Ausgespielte(r), *m.*; Vergangene(s), *n.*
hash [hæʃ], 1. *s.* das Haschee, Gehacktes, *n.*, Faschiertes, *n.*; (*fig.*) der Mischmasch, Wiederaufgewärmtes, *n.*; (*sl.*) *make a – of*, verpfuschen; (*sl.*) *settle s.o.'s –*, einen abtun. 2. *v.a.* zerhacken; – *up an old story*, eine alte Geschichte aufwärmen.
hashish [ˈhæʃɪʃ], *s.* das Haschisch.
haslet [ˈhæslɪt], *s.* das (Schweins)Geschlinge.
hasp [hɑ:sp], 1. *s.* die Haspe, Spange; Haspel, der Haken; die Docke (*of yarn*). 2. *v.a.* mit einer Haspe verschließen, zuhaken.
hassock [ˈhæsək], *s.* das Kniekissen, Betkissen.
hast [hæst], (*archaic*) *2nd sing. pres. indic. of* **have.**
hastate [ˈhæsteɪt], *adj.* spießförmig (*Bot.*).
hast-e [heɪst], 1. *s.* die Hast, Eile; Hastigkeit, Übereilung; *make –e*, eilen, sich beeilen; *in –e*, in Eile, eilig; (*Prov.*) *more –e less speed*, eile mit Weile. 2. *v.n.* eilen, sich beeilen. **-en,** 1. *v.a.* beschleunigen, antreiben. 2. *v.n.* eilen, sich beeilen. **-iness,** *s.* die Hastigkeit, Eilfertigkeit, Übereilung; Hitze, Ungeduld. **-y,** *adj.* hastig, eilig; eilfertig, voreilig, übereilt, überstürzt; hitzig, jähzornig. **-y-pudding,** *s.* der Mehlpudding.
hat [hæt], *s.* der Hut; *cardinal's –*, die Kardinalswürde; – *in hand*, mit dem Hut in der Hand, respektvoll; *beat into a cocked –*, in Stücke schlagen; (*coll.*) *my – !* was Sie sagen!; *raise one's –*, den Hut abnehmen; *send round the –*, Geld (ein)sammeln; (*coll.*) *talk through one's –*, übertreiben, aufschneiden, kohlen; *top –*, der Zylinder; *touch one's – to a p.*, einen grüßen; (*coll.*) *under one's –*, geheim. **--block,** *s.* die Hutform. **--box,** *s.* die Hutschachtel. **-less,** *adj.* ohne Hut, barhäuptig. **--pin,** *s.* die Hutnadel. **--stand,** *s.* der Hutständer. **-ter,** *s.* der Hutmacher. **--trick,** *s.* drei Erfolge hintereinander (*Crick. & fig.*).
[1]**hatch** [hætʃ], 1. *v.a.* ausbrüten (*eggs*); (*fig.*) aushecken, ersinnen; – *out*, ausbrüten. 2. *v.n.* ausgebrütet werden; (*fig.*) sich entwickeln. 3. *s.* die Brut, Hecke. **-ery,** *s.* die Brutanstalt.
[2]**hatch,** *s.* die Halbtür; Luke, Lukentür, der Lukendeckel (*Naut.*); Einstieg (*of tank, etc.*); das Servierfenster; *under –es*, unter Deck; in Arrest (*Naut.*). **-way,** *s.* die Luke, Lukenöffnung.
[3]**hatch,** *v.a.* schraffieren; (mit Linien) schattieren. **-ing,** *s.* die Schraffierung.
hatchet [ˈhætʃɪt] *s.* das Beil; *bury the –*, das Kriegsbeil begraben. **--face,** *s.* scharfgeschnittenes Gesicht.
hatchment [ˈhætʃmənt], *s.* das Wappenschild (*Her.*).
hat-e [heɪt], 1. *s.* der Haß (*towards*, gegen, auf (*Acc.*)). 2. *v.a.* hassen, verabscheuen; (*coll.*) nicht mögen. **-eful,** *adj.* verhaßt; hassenswert, gehässig. **-efulness,** *s.* die Gehässigkeit. **-red,** *s.* der Haß, Abscheu, die Abneigung.
haught-iness [ˈhɔ:tɪnɪs], *s.* der Hochmut, Stolz. **-y** [ˈhɔ:tɪ], *adj.* hochmütig, stolz, überheblich.
haul [hɔ:l], 1. *s.* kräftiger Zug; der Fischzug; (*fig.*) Fang, Gewinn, die Beute; (*sl.*) *make a –*, Beute machen; *short –*, kurzer Transportweg. 2. *v.a.* kräftig ziehen, zerren, schleppen; anziehen, (an)holen (*rope*) (*Naut.*); befördern, transportieren; – *down*, niederholen, streichen (*flag*); – *in*, einholen (*Naut.*); – *off*, verholen (*Naut.*); – *a p. over the coals*, einen abkanzeln, einem eine Standpauke halten; – *up*, aufholen (*Naut.*), aufwinden; (*fig.*) abkanzeln. 3. *v.n.*; – (*to*) *the wind*, an den Wind gehen; – *round*, umspringen (*of wind*). **-age** [ˈhɔ:lɪdʒ], *s.* der Transport, die Spedition (*C.L.*); Förderung (*Min.*); Transportkosten; *-age contractor*, der Fuhrwerksunternehmer. **-er,** *s.* **-ier** [ˈhɔ:ljə], *s.* der Schlepper (*Min.*), Spediteur.
haulm [hɔ:m], *s.* der Halm, Stengel.
haunch [hɔ:ntʃ], *s.* die Hüfte (*Anat.*), der Schenkel (*of a horse*); die Keule (*of venison*).
haunt [hɔ:nt], 1. *v.a.* häufig besuchen, heimsuchen, plagen, verfolgen; umgehen in (*as a ghost*); *the place is –ed*, hier spukt es; – *a spot*, sich oft an einem Ort herumschleichen; *–ed by memories*, durch Erinnerungen geplagt. 2. *s.* häufig besuchter Ort, der Aufenthalt; das Lager (*of animals*), der Schlupfwinkel (*of robbers, etc.*). **-ed,** *adj.* verwunschen, gespenstig.
hautboy [ˈoʊbɔɪ], *s.* die Hoboe (*Mus.*).
have [hæv, həv], **1.** *ir.v.a.* haben, besitzen; erhalten, bekommen; hören, erfahren haben; **(a)** (*with nouns*) – *advice*, (den Arzt, *etc.*) zu Rate ziehen; – *a baby*, ein Kind bekommen *or* zur Welt bringen; – *the care of*, Sorge tragen für *or* acht geben auf; – *a care!* vorgesehen! passen Sie auf!; – *a cigarette*, eine Zigarette rauchen; – *a cup of tea!* nehmen Sie eine Tasse Tee! – *food*, essen, Essen einnehmen, Speise zu sich nehmen; – *the 'flu*, an Grippe leiden; – *by heart*, auswendig können; (*coll.*) – *a down on s.o.*, Groll gegen einen hegen; – *the kindness to do!* sei so gut zu tun!; – *a look at a th.*, sich etwas ansehen; – *a lot to do*, viel zu tun haben; – *a mind*, Lust haben; – *no French*, Französisch nicht können *or* verstehen; (*sl.*) – *a p.*, einen betrügen *or* beschwindeln *or* anschmieren; *we shall – rain*, wir werden Regen bekommen; – *one's say*, seine Meinung ausdrücken; *let a p. – a th.*, einem etwas zukommen lassen; *tickets may be had of the conductor*, Fahrscheine sind beim Schaffner zu haben; – *a good time*, eine schöne Zeit genießen *or* erleben; – *a try*, einen Versuch machen, etwas probieren; – *a walk*, einen Spaziergang machen; *you – my word for it*, ich gebe Ihnen mein Wort darauf; **(b)** (*with pronouns*) *there I had him!* da hatte ich ihn *or* konnte ich ihn fassen! *you – it!* Sie haben es getroffen! – *it from s.o.*, von einem erfahren haben; – *it your own way!* meinetwegen, wie du willst! (*coll.*) *let a p. – it*, es einem gehörig geben *or* sagen; *he will – it that*, er behauptet daß; *as good luck would – it*, glücklicherweise; *rumour has it*, es geht ein Gerücht um, man munkelt; (*sl.*) *he's had it*, er darf nichts mehr erwarten; er ist erledigt; **(c)** (*with adverbs*) – *back*, zurückbekommen, sich zurückgeben lassen; – *s.o. in for dinner*, einen zum Abendessen einladen; (*coll.*) – *it in for s.o.*, Groll gegen einen hegen; – *off*, ausgezogen haben (*as a coat*), abgenommen haben (*as a hat*); – *on*, anhaben (*coat, etc.*), aufhaben (*hat, etc.*), tragen; (*coll.*) – – *s.o. on*, einen zum besten haben; (*coll.*) – *it out with s.o.*, sich mit einem auseinandersetzen; (*coll.*) – *s.o. up*, einen vor Gericht ziehen *or* bringen; *I had just as well go*, es wäre ebenso gut, daß ich ginge, ich täte ebenso gut zu gehen; *I had better*, es wäre besser, daß; *I had best*, das beste wäre wohl, daß *or* wenn; – *rather*, lieber haben, vorziehen; **(d)** (*with past participles*) – *one's hair cut*, sich (*Dat.*) die Haare schneiden lassen; *I will not – it discussed*, ich dulde nicht daß es besprochen wird; – *done!* laß das! hör auf! *he had three horses shot under him*, ihm wurden drei Pferde unter dem Leibe erschossen; **(e)** (*with infinitives*) *he has to go*, er muß gehen; *you – but to speak the truth*, Sie brauchen nur die Wahrheit zu sagen; *it has to be done*, es muß getan werden; *I would – you know* or *to know it*, ich möchte daß Sie wissen, nehmen Sie zur Kenntnis; *what would you – me do?* was soll ich tun? **(f)** (*with prepositions*) – *about one*, bei sich

(*Dat.*) haben; – *at*, angreifen, fassen; – *at you!* sieh dich vor! nimm dich in Acht! *he has your happiness at heart*, dein Glück liegt ihm am Herzen, er läßt sich dein Glück angelegen sein; – *in keeping*, in Verwahr(ung) haben, verwahren, aufbewahren; – *nothing on a p.*, einem weit unterlegen sein. **2.** *ir.v.aux.* haben (*with trans. verbs*), sein (*with intrans. verbs*); *he has come*, er ist gekommen; *you – done it, –n't you?* Sie haben es getan, nicht wahr? (*coll.*) *I – got*, ich habe *or* besitze. **3.** *s.* (*usually pl.*) *the –s and the – -nots*, die Besitzenden und die Habenichtse.

haven ['heɪvn], *s.* (*usually fig.*) der Hafen; die Freistätte, der Zufluchtsort.

haversack ['hævəsæk], *s.* der Brotbeutel.

having ['hævɪŋ], *see* **have**; *s.* das Eigentum, die Habe, der Besitz.

havoc ['hævək], *s.* die Verwüstung, Verheerung, Metzelei; *cause* –, Verheerung anrichten; *make – of* or *play – with* or *among*, verwüsten, zerstören.

[1]**haw** [hɔ:], *s.* die Frucht des Hagedorns, Hagebutte; Nickhaut (*of animals*). **–finch,** *s.* der Kernbeißer (*Orn.*).

[2]**haw,** *v.n.* only in *hum and* –, zögernd sprechen, sich räuspern. **– -haw,** *v.n.* laut lachen.

[1]**hawk** [hɔ:k], 1. *s.* der Falke, Habicht; (*fig.*) Gauner; *sparrow- –*, der Sperber. 2. *v.n.* mit Falken beizen *or* jagen. **–er,** *s.* der Falkenjäger. **– -eyed,** *adj.* scharfsichtig, falkenäugig. **–ing,** *s.* die Falkenbeize. **– -moth,** *s.* der Schwärmer. **– -nosed,** *adj.* mit einer Habichtsnase. **–'s-beard,** *s.* der Pippau (*Bot.*). **–'s-bill,** *s.* die Meeresschildkröte. **–weed,** *s.* das Habichtskraut, der Pippau (*Bot.*).

[2]**hawk,** *v.a.* verhökern, feilbieten.

[3]**hawk,** *v.n.* sich räuspern; – *up*, aushusten.

hawse [hɔ:z], *s.* (*– -hole*) die Klüse (*Naut.*). **– -pipe,** *s.* das Rohr des Klüslochs. **–r,** *s.* die Trosse, das Kabeltau.

hawthorn ['hɔ:θɔ:n], *s.* der Weißdorn, Rotdorn, Hagedorn (*Bot.*).

hay [heɪ], 1. *s.* das Heu; *make* –, Heu machen; (*sl.*) *hit the* –, pennen; (*Prov.*) *make – while the sun shines*, das Eisen schmeiden, solange es heiß ist. 2. *v.n.* Heu machen. **– -box,** *s.* die Kochkiste. **–cock,** *s.* der Heuhaufen. **– -fever,** *s.* das Heufieber, der Heuschnupfen. **– -harvest,** *s.* die Heuernte. **– -loft,** *s.* der Heuboden. **–maker,** *s.* der Heumacher. **–making,** *s.* das Heumachen. **– -mow,** *s. see* **–cock.** **–rick,** *s.*, **–stack,** *s.* der Heuschober. **– -seed,** *s.* der Grassame; (*Amer. sl.*) der Bauerntölpel; (*sl.*) **–wire** in *go –wire*, durcheinander geraten, kaputt gehen, nicht in Ordnung sein.

hazard ['hæzəd], 1. *s.* die Gefahr, das Wagnis, Risiko; der Zufall, das Ungefähr; Glückspiel, eine Art Würfelspiel; das Hindernis (*Golf*); *at all –s*, auf alle Fälle; *at the – of one's life*, auf die Gefahr, sein Leben zu verlieren; *at whatever* –, auf jede Gefahr hin; *losing* –, der Verläufer (*Bill.*); *winning* –, der Treffer (*Bill.*). 2. *v.a.* dem Zufall aussetzen, aufs Spiel setzen, wagen. **–ous** [–əs], *adj.* gewagt, gefährlich.

[1]**haze** [heɪz], *s*, leichter Nebel, der Dunst; (*fig.*) die Unklarheit.

[2]**haze,** *v.a.* durch schwere Arbeit bestrafen; (*Amer. sl.*) schinden.

hazel ['heɪzl], 1. *s.* der Hasel(nuß)strauch. 2. *adj.* nußbraun. **– -nut,** *s.* die Haselnuß.

haz–iness ['heɪzɪnɪs], *s.* die Nebligkeit, Dunstigkeit; (*fig.*) Unbestimmtheit, Unklarheit. **–y** ['heɪzɪ], *adj.* dunstig, diesig, neblig; (*fig.*) unklar, undeutlich, unbestimmt, verschwommen.

he [hɪ:], 1. *pers. pron.* er; der, derjenige; – *who*, derjenige, wer; 2. *s.* männliches Tier, das Männchen. **– -goat,** *s.* der Ziegenbock. **– -man,** *s.* der Kraftmensch.

head [hɛd], **1.** *s.* der Kopf; das Haupt (*high style*); Kopfbild; die Spitze, führende Stellung, die Front, oberes Ende; der Bug, das Vorderteil (*of a ship*); die Landspitze, das Vorgebirge (*of land*); die Quelle (*of river*); das Kopfende (*of a bed*); einzelne Person, das Stück (*of cattle*); (*no pl.*) die Anzahl, Menge; der Führer, Anführer, Vorsteher, Direktor, Leiter, Chef; das Oberhaupt, der Häuptling; Höhepunkt, die Krisis, Höhe; der Hauptpunkt, Hauptabschnitt Hauptteil, die Abteilung, Rubrik, Überschrift, der Titelkopf; Rechnungsposten; Schaum (*on liquor*); die Druckhöhe, Fallhöhe, Stauung (*of water*); Spannung, der Druck (*of steam*) (= *pressure per unit area*); Kopfball (*Footb.*); (*fig.*) Kopf, Verstand, Geist; **(a)** (*with nouns*) 40 – *of cattle*, 40 Stück Vieh; *–s of the charges*, die Klagepunkte; – *of the church*, das Oberhaupt der Kirche; *–s of departments*, Abteilungsleiter; *–s of a discourse*, die Hauptpunkte einer Abhandlung; – *of hair*, der Haarwuchs; – *of the stairs*, oberster Teil einer Treppe; – *of the table*, oberes Ende des Tisches, oben am Tische; *–s or tails?* Kopf oder Schrift; **(b)** (*with adjectives*) *civic –s*, die Stadtältesten; *crowned –s*, gekrönte Häupter; (*Prov.*) *you cannot put old –s on young shoulders*, Jugend hat keine Tugend; (*coll.*) *swelled* –, der Größenwahn; **(c)** (*with verbs*) *gather* –, überhandnehmen, zu Kräften kommen; *give a p. his* –, einem freien Lauf lassen; *give a horse his* –, einem Pferde die Zügel schießen lassen; (*coll.*) *have a* –, Schädelbrummen *or* einen Brummschädel haben; *keep one's* –, die Fassung bewahren, nicht den Kopf verlieren; *lose one's* –, sich vergessen, den Kopf verlieren; *not make – or tail of a th.*, daraus nicht klug werden können; *they put their –s together*, sie beraten sich *or* beratschlagen; *puzzle one's – over a th.*, sich (*Dat.*) den Kopf darüber zerbrechen; *my – spins* or *swims*, es schwindelt mir; *take the* –, die Führung übernehmen; (*coll.*) *talk one's – off*, losschwatzen; *turn one's* –, sich umdrehen; *turn a p.'s* –, einem den Kopf verdrehen; **(d)** (*with prepositions*) *at the* –, an der Spitze (*of*, von); *by the* –, vorlastig (*Naut.*); *by – and shoulders*, durchaus, beträchtlich; mit Gewalt, gewaltsam; *win by a* –, um Kopflänge gewinnen; *by a short* –, um eine Nasenlänge; *from – to foot*, von Kopf zu Fuß; *it runs in my* –, es geht mir im Kopfe herum; *get into one's* –, sich (*Dat.*) einprägen; *put s.th. into s.o.'s* –, einem etwas in den Kopf setzen; *take s.th. into one's* –, sich (*Dat.*) etwas in den Kopf setzen; (*coll.*) *off one's* –, verrückt; *on this* –, über diesen Punkt, hierüber; *have s.th. on one's* –, für etwas verantwortlich sein, etwas auf dem Gewissen haben; *he could do it on his* –, er könnte es ohne Schwierigkeit tun; *knock s.th. on the* –, etwas vereiteln *or* zugrunde richten; *stand on one's* –, auf dem Kopfe stehen; *get a th. out of one's* –, sich (*Dat.*) etwas aus dem Sinne schlagen; *over his* –, über dem Kopf (*of roof*); über seinem Haupte (*impending evil*); *be promoted over a p.'s* –, einen (bei einer Beförderung) überspringen; *over a p.'s* –, über jemandes Kopf hinweg; – *over ears*, bis über die Ohren; völlig, gänzlich; – *over heels*, Hals über Kopf; *per* –, pro Kopf *or* Mann; *bring to a* –, zur Entscheidung bringen; *come to a* –, eitern, reif werden; (*fig.*) zur Entscheidung kommen, sich zuspitzen; *go to one's* –, einem zu Kopfe *or* in den Kopf steigen (*as a cold*); **(e)** (*with adverbs*) – *first* or *foremost*, kopfüber. **2.** *v.a.* (an)führen, befehligen (*an army, etc.*); an der Spitze stehen (*Gen.*); vorangehen, vorausgehen (*Dat.*); mit einem Kopfe *or* einer Überschrift versehen; entgegenarbeiten, entgegentreten, sich entgegenstellen (*Dat.*); mit dem Kopfe stoßen (*Footb.*); – *off*, ablenken, umlenken, abdrängen. **3.** *v.n.* Richtung nehmen (*for*, nach), sich wenden (*for*, an), zugehen, losgehen, lossteuern (*for*, auf), einen Kurs haben (*Naut.*); entspringen (*of a river*) (*Amer.*); *how does she –?* welchen Kurs steuert das Schiff? **4.** *adj.* Ober–, Haupt–, Spitzen– (*see compounds below*). **–ache,** *s.* Kopfschmerzen (*pl.*), das Kopfweh. **–band,** *s.* die Kopfbinde. **– -board,** *s.* das Kopfbrett (*of bed*). **– clerk,** *s.* erster Buchhalter *or* Kommis; der Geschäftsführer. **– -dress,** *s.* der Kopfputz. **–ed,** *adj. suffix* –köpfig; *cool- –ed*, kaltblütig; *hot- –ed*, hitzköpfig, ungestüm; *long- –ed*, schlau. **–er,** *s.* das Kopfstück, der Binderstein (*Arch.*); Kopfdreher, Kopfstaucher, das Sammelrohr (*Tech.*); der Kopfsprung (*Sport*); *take a –er*, einen Kopfsprung machen. **–fast,** *s.* das Anhaltetau am Bug (*Naut.*). **– -gear,** *s.* die Kopfbedeckung. **– -hunter,** *s.* der Kopfjäger. **-iness,** *s.* das Berauschende (*of wine*);

(*fig.*) Ungestüm, die Unbesonnenheit, Halsstarrigkeit. **-ing,** *s.* der Titelkopf, die Rubrik, Überschrift (*Typ.*); das Kopfstück (*Tech.*); das Stoßen mit dem Kopfe (*Sport*). **-land** [-lənd], *s.* das Vorgebirge, die Landspitze, Landzunge; ungepflügtes Land. **-less,** *adj.* ohne Kopf, kopflos (*also fig.*); ohne Oberhaupt, führerlos. **-light,** *s.* der Scheinwerfer (*Motor.*), das Mastlicht (*Naut.*). **-line,** *s.* die Schlagzeile, Kopfzeile (*Typ.*). **-long,** 1. *adj.* jäh, ungestüm; (*fig.*) unbesonnen. 2. *adv.* kopfüber, mit dem Kopfe nach vorn; (*fig.*) Hals über Kopf, unbedachtsam. **-man** [-mən], *s.* der Häuptling, Führer; Vorarbeiter, Vorsteher. **-most,** *adj.* vorderst. **-master,** *s.* der Direktor, Rektor (*of school*). **-mastership,** *s.* die Direktorstelle. **-mistress,** *s.* die Direktorin. **--money,** *s.* das Kopfgeld. **--on,** *adj.* direkt gegeneinander *or* aufeinander; *--on collision*, der Zusammenstoß, Aufeinanderstoß. **-phone,** *s.* der Kopfhörer. **--piece,** *s.* der Helm; die Titelvignette (*Typ.*); (*coll.*) der Verstand, Kopf. **- porter,** *s.* erster Portier. **-quarters,** *pl.* (*sing. constr.*) das Hauptquartier (*Mil.*); die Hauptgeschäftsstelle, der Hauptsitz, die Zentrale (*C.L.*); (*fig.*) das Zentrum, die Hauptquelle; *at -quarters*, im Hauptquartier. **--resistance,** *s.* der Stirnwiderstand (*Av.*). **--rest,** *s.* die Kopflehne. **-room,** *s.* obere Höhe (*Arch.*). **--sail,** *s.* das Fockmastsegel. **--sea,** *s.* die Gegensee. **-ship,** *s.* höchste *or* führende Stelle; oberste Leitung. **-sman,** *s.* der Scharfrichter, Henker; Schlepper (*Min.*). **-spring,** *s.* der Hauptquell (*usually fig.*). **--stall,** *s.* das Kopfstück (*of a bridle*). **-stock,** *s.* der Spindelstock (*Tech.*). **-stone,** *s.* der Grabstein. **--stone,** *s.* der Eckstein (*Arch.*). **-strong,** *adj.* starrköpfig, halsstarrig, eigenwillig, eigensinnig. **--voice,** *s.* die Kopfstimme. **-waiter,** *s.* der Oberkellner. **-water,** *s.* (*usually pl.*) der Oberlauf, die Zuflußgewässer (*of river*). **-way,** *s.* das Vorwärtskommen (*Naut.*); (*fig.*) der Fortschritt, Fortschritte (*pl.*); *see also* **-room;** *make -way*, vorwärtskommen, Fortschritte machen. **--wind,** *s.* der Gegenwind. **--work,** *s.* die Kopfarbeit. **-y,** *adj.* berauschend (*of liquor*); ungestüm, übereilt.

heal [hɪ:l], *v.a. & n* heilen; (*fig.*) versöhnen; *- up*, zuheilen. **-er,** *s.* der Heiler; (*fig.*) das Heilmittel. **-ing,** 1. *adj.* heilsam, Heil-; (*fig.*) versöhnend. 2. *s.* die Heilung.

health [hɛlθ], 1. *s.* die Gesundheit; das Heil, Wohl; der Toast; *Ministry of -*, das Gesundheitsministerium; *bad* or *poor -*, die Kränklichkeit; *good -*, das Wohlbefinden; *public -*, öffentliche Gesundheitspflege; *in the best of -*, bei bester Gesundheit; *drink s.o.'s -*, auf jemandes Gesundheit trinken; *here is to the - of . . . . ,* . . . soll leben! es lebe . . .! *your good -!* auf Ihr Wohl! **-ful,** *adj.* heilsam, gesund. **-fulness,** *s.* die Gesundheit. **--giving,** *adj.* gesundheitsfördernd. **-iness,** *s.* die Gesundheit. **- insurance,** die Krankenversicherung. **-y,** *adj.* gesund; gesundheitsfördernd, heilsam.

heap [hɪ:p], 1. *s.* der Haufe(n); (*coll.*) -(*s*), die Menge (*of people, etc.*); (*coll.*) *struck all of a -*, ganz verblüfft; *in -s*, haufenweise; (*coll.*) *-s of time*, viel Zeit; (*coll.*) *-s of times*, viele Male, oftmals; (*coll.*) *-s worse*, viel schlimmer. 2. *v.a.* häufen, beladen, bedecken; (*fig.*) überhäufen (*with*, mit); *- coals of fire on a p.'s head*, feurige Kohlen auf jemandes Haupt sammeln; *-ed spoonful*, gehäufter Löffelvoll; *- up*, aufhäufen, aufstapeln.

hear [hɪə], 1. *ir.v.a.* hören (*a th.*); anhören (*Acc.*), zuhören (*Dat.*) (*a p.*); verhören, vernehmen (*a witness*), verhandeln (*a case*) (*Law*); abhören, überhören (*lessons, etc.*); *make o.s. -d* [hə:d], sich hörbar machen; *- mass*, an der Messe teilnehmen; *- out*, ausreden lassen. 2. *ir.v.n.* hören, zuhören; Nachricht bekommen, erfahren (*of* or *about*, von *or* über); *let me - how . . .*, laß mich wissen, wie . . .; *let me - from you*, laß von dir hören; *I will not - of it*, ich will nichts davon wissen *or* hören; *- say* or *tell*, sagen hören; *- ! - !* hört! hört! (*Parl.*). **-er,** *s.* der Hörer, Zuhörer. **-ing,** *s.* das Hören; Gehör; die Audienz; das Verhör, die Verhandlung (*Law*); *gain a -ing*, sich Gehör verschaffen; *give a p. a -ing*, einen anhören; *hard of -ing*, schwerhörig; *in my -ing*, in meiner Gegenwart; *out of -ing*, außer Hörweite; *within -ing*, in Hörweite. **-say,** *s.* das Hörensagen, Gerede; *by -say*, von Hörensagen; *--say evidence*, Zeugnis vom Hörensagen.

hearken [ˈhɑ:kən], *v.n.* hören, horchen, lauschen (*to*, auf).

hearse [hə:s], *s.* der Leichenwagen, die Bahre. **--cloth,** *s.* das Leichentuch, Bahrtuch.

heart [hɑ:t], *s.* das Herz (*also fig.*); (*fig.*) die Seele, das Inner(st)e, Wesentliche, der Kern; Mut, die Energie; das Mitgefühl; Gemüt; der Schatz, das Herzchen; Herz, die Herzkarte (*cards*). **-s,** *pl.* die Herzfarbe (*cards*); **(a)** (*with nouns*) *- of iron*, fester Mut, die Unerschrockenheit; *- of oak*, das Eichenkernholz; (*fig.*) *-s of oak*, englische Matrosen; *change of -*, der Gesinnungswechsel; *king of -s*, der Herzkönig (*cards*); *ten of -s*, die Herzzehn (*cards*); **(b)** (*with verbs*) *bless my -!* ach du lieber Himmel! *break s.o.'s -*, einem das Herz brechen; *eat one's - out*, sich etwas sehr zu Herzen nehmen; *my - fails me*, see *lose -*; *my - goes out to him*, ich fühle mit ihm; *have one's - in one's mouth*, das Herz klopft einem bis zum Halse; *have no -*, kein Mitgefühl haben; *lose -*, den Mut verlieren; *lose one's - to*, sein Herz verlieren an; *open one's - to a p.*, einem sein Herz ausschütten; *set one's - on a th.*, einen Lieblingswunsch haben, sein Herz hängen an; *take -*, Mut fassen, sich (*Dat.*) ein Herz fassen; *warm the cockles of one's -*, herzerwärmend sein; *wear one's - upon one's sleeve*, seine Gefühle zur Schau tragen; *it wrings my -*, es schmerzt mich tief; **(c)** (*with prepositions*) *after his own -*, nach seinem Wunsch; *at -*, im Herzen; im Innern; *have at -*, auf dem Herzen haben, vom Herzen wünschen; *by -*, auswendig; *from one's -*, vom Herzen, frei von der Leber weg; *in one's - (of -s)*, im Grunde seines Herzens; *I could not find it in my -*, ich konnte es nicht übers Herz bringen; *in good -*, in gutem Zustande, fruchtbar (*of land*); *in the - of*, inmitten, mitten in; *in the very - of*, im Innersten von; *out of -*, mutlos; *get to the - of a matter*, bis ins Innerste einer Angelegenheit dringen; *it goes to my -*, es geht mir zu Herzen; *take to -*, sich (*Dat.*) zu Herzen nehmen; *to one's -'s content*, nach Herzenslust; *- to -*, offen, ehrlich; *with all my -*, herzlich gern, von ganzem Herzen, mit Leib und Seele; *with a heavy -*, schweren *or* blutenden Herzens; *with one's - in one's mouth*, zum Tode erschrocken, in atemloser Spannung. **--ache,** *s.* der Kummer, Gram. **--attack,** *s.* der Herzschlag. **--beat,** *s.* der Herzschlag (*Physiol.*). **--break,** *s.* das Herzeleid. **--breaking,** *adj.* herzzerbrechend, niederdrückend. **--broken,** *adj.* gebrochenen Herzens. **-burn,** *s.* das Sodbrennen. **--burning,** *s.* (*often pl.*) der Groll, Neid. **- disease,** *s.* die Herzkrankheit. **-ed,** *adj. suff.* -herzig. **-en** [ˈhɑ:tn], *v.a.* aufmuntern, ermutigen, anfeuern. **-ening,** *adj.* herzerquickend. **--failure,** *s.* der Herzschlag. **-felt,** *adj.* tiefempfunden, herzlich, innig, aufrichtig. **-ily,** *adv.* herzlich, innig, aufrichtig, von Herzen; tüchtig, kräftig, sehr. **-iness,** *s.* die Herzlichkeit, Offenheit, Aufrichtigkeit; Herzhaftigkeit, Stärke (*of appetite*); Wärme (*of feelings*). **-less,** *adj.* herzlos, gefühllos, grausam. **-lessness,** *s.* die Herzlosigkeit. **--rending,** *adj.* herzzerreißend. **-'s-blood,** *s.* das Herzblut (*also fig.*). **--searchings,** *pl.* Nöte (*pl.*), die Beklemmung. **-sease, -'s-ease,** *s.* das Stiefmütterchen (*Bot.*). **--shaped,** *adj.* herzförmig. **--sick,** *adj.*, **--sore,** *adj.* (*fig.*) tief betrübt, schwermütig. **-some,** *adj.* (*Scots*) erfrischend, ermunternd, erheiternd, belebend. **--strings,** *pl.* (*fig.*) das Herz, Innerste(s), *n.* **-wood,** *s.* das Kernholz. **-y,** 1. *adj.* herzlich, innig, aufrichtig, warm; gesund, frisch, munter; kräftig, kernig; herzhaft, tüchtig, stark (*of appetite*). 2. *s.*; (*coll.*) lustiger Bursche, der Naturbursche.

hearth [hɑ:θ], *s.* der Herd; Schmiedeherd, das Schmiedefeuer; (*fig.*) Heim. **--rug,** *s.* der Kaminvorleger. **--stone,** *s.* die Herdplatte, der Herd; weicher Scheuerstein.

heat [hɪ:t], 1. *s.* die Hitze (*also fig.*); Wärme (*Phys.*); (*fig.*) Erhitzung, Heftigkeit, Leidenschaft, das

Feuer, Ungestüm; die Erregung, der Zorn, Eifer; die Brunst, Brunft, Brunftzeit, Läufigkeit (*of animals*); der Vorlauf, einzelnes Rennen, einzelner Lauf *or* Gang (*Sport*); *dead* –, unentschiedenes *or* totes Rennen; *final* –, letzte Ausscheidungsrunde; *latent* –, gebundene Wärme; *red* –, die Glühhitze; *degree of* –, der Wärmegrad. 2. *v.a.* heiß machen; heizen (*stove, etc.*); erhitzen (*also fig.*). 3. *v.n.* heiß werden. **– engine,** *s.* die Wärmekraftmaschine. **–er,** *s.* der Heizkörper, die Heizanlage, Heizvorrichtung; der Bolzen (eines Plätteisens); Heizdraht, die Heizspule (*Rad.*). **–ing,** *s.* die Heizung; *–ing element*, elektrischer Heizkörper; *–ing surface*, die Heizfläche; *–ing technology*, die Wärmetechnik. **– -proof, – -resisting,** *adj.* hitzebeständig. **– -spot,** *s.* das Hitzbläschen. **– -stroke,** *s.* der Sonnenstich, Hitzschlag. **– -wave,** *s*, die Hitzewelle.

heath [hɪ:θ], *s.* die Heide, das Heideland; Heidekraut (*Bot.*). **– -cock,** *s.* der Birkhahn (*Orn.*).

heathen [ˈhɪ:ðən], 1. *s.* der Heide. 2. *adj.* heidnisch. **–dom** [–dəm], *s.* das Heidentum. **–ish,** *adj.* (*fig.*) heidnisch, roh, wild, ungesittet. **–ism,** *s.* das Heidentum; (*fig.*) die Barbarei.

heather [ˈhɛðə], *s.* die Heide, das Heidekraut, die Erika (*Bot.*). **– -bell,** *s.* die Glockenheide, Sumpfheide (*Bot.*).

heave [hɪ:v], 1. *v.a.* aufheben, emporheben; hochziehen, hochheben, hieven, aufwinden (*Naut.*); werfen, schleudern (*Naut. & coll.*); – *the anchor*, den Anker lichten (*or navy only*) hieven; – *the lead*, das Lot werfen; – *the log*, loggen; – *a sigh*, einen Seufzer ausstoßen; – (*a ship*) *down*, kielholen; – *overboard*, über Bord werfen. 2. *v.n.* sich heben (und senken), (an)schwellen, wogen, sich empordrängen; Brechreiz haben, sich übergeben wollen; getrieben werden, treiben (*as ships*) (*Naut.*); – *away!* – *ho!* zieh! hiev! (*Naut.*); *her breast –ed*, ihr Busen wogte; – *in sight*, in Sicht kommen, sichtbar werden (*Naut.*); – *to*, beidrehen, beilegen, stoppen (*Naut.*). 3. *s.* das Heben, Aufheben; Schwellen, Wogen (*of the breast*); die Verwerfung, Verschiebung (*Geol.*); der Hub. **–r** [ˈhɪ:və], *s.* der Hebebaum, Ablader. **–s,** *pl.* das Keuchen (*Vet.*).

heaven [ˈhɛvn], *s.* (*no art. or pl.*) der Himmel, das Himmelreich; (*fig.*) die Vorsehung, Gott, *m.*; die Seligkeit, himmliches Glück; (*with art. & usually pl.*) der Himmel, das Himmelszelt, Himmelsgewölbe, Firmament; (*fig.*) Klima, die Zone; *the –s*, die himmlischen Mächte; *good –s!* (du) lieber Himmel! *in* –, im Himmel; *thank –s!* Gott sei Dank!; – *forbid!* Gott behüte!; *go to* –, in den Himmel kommen *or* eingehen; *move – and earth*, Himmel und Erde in Bewegung setzen. **– -born,** *adj.* vom Himmel stammend, himmlisch. **–liness,** *s.* das Himmlische. **–ly,** *adj.* Himmels–, himmlisch (*also fig.*); (*fig.*) göttlich; erhaben; (*coll.*) köstlich. **– -sent,** *adj.* vom Himmel gesandt. **–ward,** 1. *adj.* gen Himmel gerichtet. 2. *adv.* **–wards,** *adv.* gen Himmel, himmelwärts.

heav–iness [ˈhɛvɪnɪs], *s.* die Schwere, das Gewicht, der Druck; die Schwerfälligkeit, Schläfrigkeit; Schwermut, Bedrückung. **–y** [ˈhɛvɪ], 1. *adj.* schwer; beladen; massig, schwergebaut; schwerbewaffnet; heftig, gewaltig, stark (*as storm, etc.*); schwerfällig, unbeholfen, träge, schläfrig, benommen, matt; niedergeschlagen, betrübt, trübe, finster; schwer verdaulich (*as food*); klitschig, pappig (*as dough*); unwegsam, aufgeweicht (*as ground*); fett, feucht (*as soil*); ergiebig, reich (*as crops*); schwierig, mühsam, ermüdend (*as work*); kräftig, satt (*as colour*); (*fig.*) *–y book*, langweiliges Buch; *–y cavalry*, schwere Reiterei; *–y cloud*, dicke Wolke; *–y expenses*, drückende Kosten; *–y eyes*, müde Augen; *–y face*, plumpes Gesicht; *–y father*, gestrenger Vater; *–y fire*, das Dauerfeuer (*Mil.*); *–y frost*, strenger Frost; *have a –y hand*, plump sein; *–y industry*, die Schwerindustrie; *–y news*, traurige Nachricht(en); *–y oil*, das Dicköl; *–y swell*, die Bullendünung; *–y type*, der Fettdruck. 2. *adv.* (*in compounds*) schwer–. 3. *s.* (*usually pl.*) schwere Kavallerie, schwere Artillerie (*Mil.*); der Schwergewichtler (*Boxing*); Schwerindustrieaktien (*pl.*) (*C.L.*). **–y-armed,** *adj.* schwerbewaffnet. **– -handed,** *adj.* plump, ungeschickt; (ge)streng. **– -hearted,** *adj.* betrübt, bekümmert. **–y-laden,** *adj.* schwerbeladen. **–weight,** *s.* das Schwergewicht (*über 175 Pfund*) (*Boxing*); der Schwergewichtler. **– -worker,** *s.* der Schwerarbeiter.

hebdomadal [hɛbˈdəmədl], *adj.* wöchentlich, Wochen–; – *council*, höchste akademische Behörde (*Oxford*).

hebet–ate [ˈhɛbɪteɪt], *v.a.* abstumpfen. **–ude** [–tjʊ:d], *s.* (geistige) Stumpfheit, die Abstumpfung.

hecatomb [ˈhɛkətʊ:m], *s.* die Hekatombe.

heckle [ˈhɛkl], *v.a.* durchhecheln (*flax, etc.*); störende Fragen stellen (*Pol.*). **–r,** *s.* störender Fragesteller, der Zwischenrufer (*Pol.*).

hectare [ˈhɛktɛə], *s.* das Hektar.

hectic [ˈhɛktɪk], 1. *adj.* hektisch, auszehrend, schwindsüchtig (*Path.*); fieberrot; (*coll.*) erregt, aufregend. 2. *s.* die Auszehrung, Schwindsucht; Fieberröte.

hecto–gram(me) [ˈhɛktəgræm], *s.* das Hektogramm. **–graph,** 1. *s.* der Hektograph. 2. *v.a. & n.* vervielfältigen, hektographieren. **–litre,** *s.* das Hektoliter.

hector [ˈhɛktə], 1. *s.* der Prahler, Aufschneider, Eisenfresser, Raufbold. 2. *v.a.* bedrohen, einschüchtern, tyrannisieren. 3. *v.n.* prahlen, aufschneiden, renommieren, großtun.

heddle [ˈhɛdl], *s.* (*usually pl.*) die Litze, Helfe. **– -hook,** *s.* die Einziehnadel.

hedge [hɛdʒ], 1. *s.* die Hecke, der Zaun; die Gegendeckung (*C.L.*). 2. *v.a.* einzäunen, einfriedigen, einhegen; umzäunen, umgeben; (*fig.*) einengen, versperren; (durch Gegendeckung) sichern (*C.L.*); – *in*, einzäunen, einschließen, einhegen, umzingeln; – *off*, abzäunen, absperren. 3. *v.n.* Hecken anlegen; sich sichern, sich decken; (*coll.*) sich nicht festlegen, ausweichen, sich winden. **–hog,** 1. *s.* der Igel; (*sl.*) die Igelstellung (*Mil.*). 2. *v.n.* (*sl.*) sich einigeln (*Mil.*). **– -hop,** *v.n.* (*sl.*) tief fliegen (*Av.*). **–row,** *s.* die Baumhecke. **– -school,** *s.* die Winkelschule. **– -sparrow,** *s.* der Waldsperling; die Braunelle, das Graukehlchen (*Orn.*).

hedoni–c [hɪ:ˈdənɪk], *adj.* hedonisch, Lust–. **–sm** [ˈhɪ:dənɪzm], *s.* der Hedonismus. **–st** [ˈhɪ:dənɪst], *s.* der Hedoniker.

heed [hɪ:d], 1. *v.a.* beachten, achtgeben auf (*Acc.*). 2. *v.n.* achten, achtgeben. 3. *s.* die Aufmerksamkeit; *give* or *pay* –, achtgeben (*to*, auf (*Acc.*)); *take* – *of*, sich in acht nehmen vor, beachten. **–ful,** *adj.* achtsam, aufmerksam; behutsam, vorsichtig. **–fulness,** *s.* die Achtsamkeit, Vorsicht. **–less,** *adj.* achtlos, unachtsam, unbedacht, sorglos, unbesonnen, gedankenlos. **–lessness,** *s.* die Unachtsamkeit, Sorglosigkeit.

hee-haw [ˈhɪ:hɔ:], 1. *v.n.* iahen. 2. *s.* das Iah.

¹heel [hɪ:l], 1. *s.* die Ferse, Hacke; der Absatz (*on shoe, etc.*); Fuß, das Ende (*of mast, etc.*); (*sl.*) der Schurke, verräterischer Schuft; *Achilles'* –, die Achillesferse; *at s.o.'s –s*, einem auf den Fersen, dicht hinter einem; *close at* –, dicht hinterher; *down at* –, mit schiefen Absätzen; (*fig.*) zerlumpt, schäbig; *lay by the –s*, erwischen; *on s.o.'s –s*, see *at s.o.'s –s*; *out at –s*, mit zerrissenen (Strumpf)Fersen *or* Strümpfen; *show a clean pair of –s*, *take to one's –s*, ausreißen, Fersengeld geben; *to –!* bei Fuß! (*to a dog*); *bring to* –, zur Strecke bringen, gefügig machen, unterkriegen; *tread on s.o.'s –s*, einem auf die Hacken treten; *turn on one's* –, sich kurz umdrehen. 2. *v.a.* mit Absätzen *or* Hacken versehen (*shoes*), Fersen anstricken (*socks*); – *out*, hinausfersen (*Footb.*). **– -ball,** *s.* das Schusterwachs, Polierwachs. **– -piece,** *s.* der Absatzfleck, das Absatzstück. **– -tap,** *s.* (*coll.*) die Neige, letzter Rest; *no – -taps!* ausgetrunken!

²heel, 1. *v.n.* (– *over*) sich auf die Seite legen *or* neigen, überliegen, krängen, kentern (*Naut.*). 2. *s.* die Krängung.

heft [hɛft], 1. *s.* das Gewicht, der Umfang, das Ausmaß (*Amer.*). 2. *v.a.* heben, hochheben, emporheben; anheben, abwiegen, das Gewicht schätzen (*Amer.*). **–y,** *adj.* (*coll.*) kräftig, muskulös, stramm; (*sl.*) groß, mächtig.

hegemony [hɪˈgɛmənɪ], *s.* die Hegemonie, Oberherrschaft; Vormachtstellung, Führung.

hegira [ˈhɛdʒɪrə], *s.* die Hedschra.
heifer [ˈhɛfə], *s.* die Färse, junge Kuh.
heigh [heɪ], *int.* he! hei! **--ho,** *int.* heisa! heißa!
height [hɑɪt], *s.* die Höhe, Größe; Anhöhe, der Hügel; höchster Punkt, der Höhepunkt, Gipfel; *at the – of*, auf dem Höhepunkt von; *in –*, hoch; *in the – of fashion*, nach der neuesten Mode; *twice the – of*, doppelt so hoch wie; *– of the barometer*, der Barometerstand; *– of folly*, der Gipfel der Torheit; *– to paper*, die Norm der Schrifthöhe (*Typ.*); *what is your – ?* wie groß sind Sie? **–en,** *v.a.* erhöhen, (er)heben; vergrößern, verstärken, vermehren; steigern. **--finder,** *s.* der Höhenmesser.
heinous [ˈheɪnəs], *adj.* abscheulich, verrucht, verhaßt, hassenswert. **–ness,** *s.* die Abscheulichkeit.
heir [ɛə], *s.* der Erbe (*to* (*Gen.*)); *– apparent*, rechtmäßiger *or* gesetzmäßiger Erbe (eines noch Lebenden); *--at-law*, rechtmäßiger *or* gesetzmäßiger Erbe (eines Toten); *– general*, der Universalerbe; *– presumptive*, mutmaßlicher (Thron)Erbe; *– to the throne*, der Thronerbe, Thronfolger; *be – to a th.*, etwas erben. **–dom,** *s.* die Erbschaft, das Erbe. **–ess** [–rəs], *s.* (reiche) Erbin. **–less,** *adj.* ohne Erben, unbeerbt. **–loom,** *s.* das Erbstück. **–ship,** *s.* die Erbschaft.
held [hɛld], *see* **hold.**
helia–cal [ˈhɪːlɪəkl, hɪːˈlɑɪəkl], *adj.* heliakalisch, Sonnen–. **–nthus** [hɪːlɪˈænθəs], *s.* die Sonnenblume (*Bot.*).
helic–al [ˈhɛlɪkl], *adj.* schneckenförmig, schraubenförmig, Schrauben–. **–opter** [hɛlɪˈkɔptə], *s.* der Hubschrauber, das Drehflügelflugzeug (*Av.*).
helio-centric [hɪːlɪoˈsɛntrɪk], *adj.* heliozentrisch. **–chromy,** *s.* die Farbenphotographie. **–graph,** 1. *s.* der Heliograph, Spiegeltelegraph. 2. *v.a.* heliographieren. **–graphic,** *adj.* heliographisch. **–graphy** [–ˈɔgrəfɪ], *s.* die Heliographie, Spiegeltelegraphie. **–gravure,** *s.* die Heligravüre, Photogravüre. **–trope** [ˈhɛljətroʊp], 1. *s.* das Heliotrop, der Chalzedon (*Min.*); die Sonnenblume (*Bot.*); Malvenfarbe. 2. *adj.* malvenfarbig. **–type,** *s.* der Lichtdruck.
helium [ˈhɪːlɪəm], *s.* das Helium.
heli–x [ˈhɪːlɪks], *s.* (*pl.* –ces [ˈhɛlɪsɪːz], –xes) die Schneckenlinie, Spirallinie; Schnecke (*Arch.*); Ohrleiste, Knorpelleiste (*of ear*) (*Anat.*).
hell [hɛl], *s.* die Hölle, Unterwelt; *–!, oh, –!*, zum Teufel!; *to – with . . .*, zum Teufel mit . . .; *what the – . . .?* was zum Teufel . . .?; *gambling –*, die Spielhölle; (*vulg.*) *– of a row*, höllischer Lärm, der Höllenspektakel; (*vulg.*) *like –*, höllisch, riesig, sehr (groß); *give s.o. –*, einem die Hölle heiß machen; *go to –*, zur Hölle fahren; (*fig.*) zum Teufel gehen, sich zum Teufel scheren; *all –'s let loose*, der Teufel ist los; (*sl.*) *raise –*, Krach *or* Krawall machen. **--bent,** *adj.* (*Amer.*) erpicht (*on* or *after*, auf), rücksichtslos. **--broth,** *s.* der Hexentrank. **–cat,** *s.* die Hexe, böses Weib. **–fire,** *s.* das Höllenfeuer. (*coll.*) **--for-leather,** *adv.* in rasendem Tempo, wie der Teufel. **--hound,** *s.* der Höllenhund, abscheulicher Mensch. **–ish** [ˈhɛlɪʃ], *adj.* höllisch, teuflisch, abscheulich. **–ishness,** *s.* das Höllische, Abscheuliche.
hellebore [ˈhɛlɪbɔː], *s.* der Nieswurz (*Bot.*).
hello [hɛˈloʊ], *int.* hallo!
[1]**helm** [hɛlm], *s.* (*Poet. & archaic*) *see* **helmet.**
[2]**helm,** *s.* das Steuer, Steuerrad, Ruder (*Naut. & fig.*); *at the –*, am Ruder; *put the – hard over*, das Ruder in Hartlage legen; *starboard the –!* Steuerbord das Ruder! **–sman,** *s.* der Steuermann, Steurer, Rudergänger.
helmet [ˈhɛlmɪt], *s.* der Helm; Kelch (*Bot.*); *crash –*, der Sturzhelm (*Motor.*); *spiked –*, die Pickelhaube; *steel –*, der Stahlhelm. **–ed,** *adj.* behelmt.
helminth [ˈhɛlmɪnθ], *s.* der Eingeweidewurm.
helot [ˈhɛlət], *s.* der Helote, Sklave. **–ry,** *s.* das Helotentum, die Sklaverei.
help [hɛlp], **1.** *v.a.* helfen, beistehen, Hilfe leisten (*a p.* (*Dat.*); *to do* or (*coll.*) *do* or *in doing*, zu tun; *in* or *with a th.*, bei einer S.); fördern, unterstützen, beitragen zu (*a th.*); (with *can*) abhelfen (*Dat.*), ändern, sich ersparen, unterlassen, hindern, bessern; bedienen, servieren (*at table*); *can I – you?* kann ich Ihnen behilflich sein? *how could he – it?* was konnte er dafür? wie hätte er es vermeiden können? *I cannot – it*, ich kann nichts dafür, ich kann es nicht ändern; *I cannot – laughing* or *but laugh*, ich kann nicht umhin zu lachen, ich muß doch lachen; *I cannot – myself*, ich kann mir nicht helfen, ich kann nicht anders; *I cannot – my looks*, ich kann nichts für mein Aussehen; *it can't be –ed*, dem ist nun nicht abzuhelfen, es läßt sich nicht ändern; *you cannot – being jealous*, man kommt nicht um die Eifersucht herum; *don't be any slower than you can –*, arbeite nicht langsamer als nötig ist; *so – me God!* so wahr mir Gott helfe! *– yourself*, bitte bedienen Sie sich, langen Sie zu; *– down*, hinunterhelfen (*Dat.*); *– forward*, weiterhelfen (*Dat.*), fördern; *– in*, hineinhelfen (*Dat.*); *– a p. off with his coat*, einem den Mantel ablegen helfen; *– on*, see *– forward*; *– out*, aushelfen (*Dat.*); *– a p. out of a difficulty*, einem aus einer Schwierigkeit heraushelfen; *– a p. over a difficulty*, einem über eine Schwierigkeit hinweghelfen; *– through*, durchhelfen (*Dat.*); *– to*, verhelfen (*Dat.*) zu; *she –ed me to the salt*, sie reichte mir das Salz; *may I – you to some bread*, darf ich Ihnen etwas Brot geben; *– o.s. to s.th.*, sich mit etwas bedienen; (*coll.*) sich etwas zunutze machen; *– up*, hinaufhelfen (*Dat.*). **2.** *v.n.* helfen, dienen (*to*, zu). **3.** *s.* die Hilfe, Unterstützung, der Beistand; die Abhilfe, Hilfeleistung; das Hilfsmittel; (*coll.*) die Aushilfe, das Dienstmädchen; *by the – of*, mit Hilfe von; *daily –*, das Tagmädchen; *holiday –*, die Ferienaushilfe; *lady –*, die Stütze der Hausfrau; *mother's –*, das Kinderfräulein; *there is no – for it*, es läßt sich nicht ändern. **–er,** *s.* der Helfer, Hilfeleistende(r), *m. & f.*, der Beistand; Gehilfe, die Gehilfin. **–ful,** *adj.* hilfreich; behilflich, nützlich (*to* (*Dat.*)). **–fulness,** *s.* die Dienstlichkeit, Nützlichkeit (*of things*), die Hilfsbereitschaft (*of persons*). **–ing,** *s.* die Hilfeleistung; Portion (*at table*); *take another –ing!* langen Sie noch zu! **–less,** *adj.* hilflos; (*coll.*) *–lessly drunk*, bis zur Hilflosigkeit *or* über alle Maßen betrunken. **–lessness,** *s.* die Hilflosigkeit. **–mate,** *s.*, **–meet,** *s.* der Helfer, Gehilfe, die Gehilfin, Gattin.
helter-skelter [ˈhɛltəˈskɛltə], 1. *adv.* holterdiepolter, durcheinander, Hals über Kopf, ungestüm. 2. *s.* die Rutschbahn.
helve [hɛlv], 1. *s.* der Stiel, Griff; *throw the – after the hatchet*, die Flinte ins Korn werfen. 2. *v.a.* mit einem Griff versehen (*an axe, etc.*).
[1]**hem** [hɛm], 1. *s.* der Saum. 2. *v.a.* säumen, einfassen; *– in*, einschließen, umgeben, umzingeln. **–stitch,** 1. *s.* der Hohlsaum. 2. *v.a.* mit einem Hohlsaum einfassen.
[2]**hem,** 1. *s.* das Räuspern. 2. *v.n.* sich räuspern; *– and haw*, in der Rede stocken, (*fig.*) unschlüssig sein. 3. *int.* hm!
hematite [ˈhɛmətaɪt], *etc. see* **haematite,** *etc.*
hemi–cycle [ˈhɛmɪsɑɪkl], *s.* der Halbkreis. **–demisemiquaver,** *s.* die Vierundsechzigstelnote. **–plegia,** *s.* einseitige Lähmung (*Path.*). **–ptera** [hɛˈmɪptərə], *pl.* Hemipteren, Wanzen (*Ent.*). **–sphere,** *s.* die Halbkugel, Hemisphäre; Großhirnhälfte (*Anat.*). **–spherical,** *adj.* halbkug(e)lig. **–stich** [–stɪk], *s.* der Halbvers.
hemlock [ˈhɛmlɔk], *s.* der Schierling (*Bot.*); (*fig.*) Schierlingstrank. **--fir,** *s.*, **--spruce,** *s.* die Hemlocktanne, Schierlingstanne.
hemorrhage [ˈhɛmərɪdʒ], *etc. see* **haemorrhage,** *etc.*
hemp [hɛmp], 1. *s.* der Hanf (*Bot.*), die Hanffaser; (*fig.*) der Strick zum Hängen. 2. *adj.*, **–en,** *adj.* hanfen, Hanf–.
hen [hɛn], 1. *s.* die Henne (*fowl*); das Weibchen (*of all birds*); *pea- –*, die Pfauhenne. **–bane,** *s.* das Bilsenkraut; (*fig.*) Gift. **--coop,** *s.* der Hühnerstall. **--harrier,** *s.* die Kornweihe (*Orn.*). **--house,** *s.* *see* **--coop.** (*sl.*) **--party,** *s.* der Kaffeeklatsch, die Frauengesellschaft. (*coll.*) **–peck,** *v.a.* unter dem Pantoffel haben. (*coll.*) **–pecked,** *adj.* unter dem Pantoffel stehend; *–pecked husband*, der Pantoffelheld. **--roost,** *s.* die Hühnerstange; der Hühnerstall. **–'s egg,** das Hühnerei.
hence [hɛns], 1. *adv.* (*of place*) (*archaic*) (*from –*) von hier entfernt, von hinnen, hinweg, fort; (*of*

time) von jetzt an; *six months* –, heute in sechs Monaten; (*consequence*) hieraus, daraus, daher, deshalb, deswegen, folglich. 2. *int*. fort! hinweg! **–forth,** *adv*., **–forward,** *adv*. von nun an, von jetzt ab, künftig, fernerhin, fortan.

henchman [ˈhɛntʃmən], *s*. (*archaic*) der Knappe, Page; (*fig*.) treuer Diener *or* Anhänger; feiler Parteigänger, der Mietling.

hendeca–gon [hɛnˈdɛkəgən], *s*. das Elfeck. **–syllabic,** 1. *adj*. elfsilbig. 2. *s*. elfsilbiger Vers.

hendiadys [hɛnˈdaɪədɪs], *s*. das Hendiadys, Hendiadyoin.

henna [ˈhɛnə], *s*. das (Haar)Färbemittel; der Hennastrauch.

hepat–ic [hɪˈpætɪk], *adj*., **–o–,** *adj*. *pref*. Leber–.

hepta–gon [ˈhɛptəgən], *s*. das Siebeneck. **–gonal** [–ˈtægənəl], *adj*. siebeneckig. **–hedron** [–ˈhɪːdrən], *s*. das Siebenflach. **–rchy** [ˈhɛptɑːkɪ], *s*. die Heptarchie. **–teuch** [–tjuːk], *s*. der Heptateuch.

her [həː], 1. *pers. pron*. (*Acc*.) sie; (*Dat*.) ihr; *he gave – the book*, er gab ihr das Buch; *to* or *for* –, ihr; (*of ships*) ihn, es (*Dat*. ihm); (*of the moon*) (*poet*.) ihn (*Dat*. ihm); (*coll*.) *it's* –, sie ist es. 2. *poss. adj*., ihr, *etc*. (sein, *etc*. *if the noun referred to is masc. or neut*.). **–s, –self,** *see* **hers, herself.**

herald [ˈhɛrəld], 1. *s*. der Herold; (*fig*.) Vorläufer, Vorbote; *College of –s*, das Heroldsamt. 2. *v.a*. feierlich verkünden, ankündigen; – *in*, einführen. **–ic** [həˈrældɪk], *adj*. heraldisch. **–ry,** *s*. die Wappenkunde, Heraldik; (*collect*.) das Wappen, der Wappenschild.

herb [həːb], *s*. das Kraut, Gewächs, die Pflanze; das Gewürzkraut (*Cul*.). **–aceous** [–ˈbeɪʃəs], *adj*. krautartig, Kraut–. **–age** [–bɪdʒ], *s*. Kräuter (*pl*.), das Blätterwerk, Gras; die Weide, Trift; das Weiderecht (*Law*). **–al,** 1. *s*. das Pflanzenbuch, Kräuterbuch. 2. *adj*. Kräuter–. **–alist,** *s*. der Kräuterkenner; Kräutersammler, Kräuterhändler. **–arium** [–ˈbɛərɪəm], *s*. das Herbarium, die Pflanzensammlung. **– –bennet,** *s*. die Nelkenwurz (*Bot*.). **–ivorous** [–ˈbɪvərəs], *adj*. pflanzenfressend. **–orize** [–əraɪz], *v.n*. Pflanzen sammeln, botanisieren. **– –robert,** *s*. das Robertskraut (*Bot*.). **– –tea,** *s*. der Kräutertee.

herculean [həːˈkjulɪən], *adj*. (*fig*.) sehr schwierig, mühevoll (*as a task*); *see also Index of Names*.

herd [həːd], 1. *s*. die Herde; der Haufe; – *of deer*, das Rudel Hochwild; *the common* –, die große Masse; – *instinct*, der Herdentrieb. 2. *v.a*. (eine Herde) hüten; zusammentreiben. 3. *v.n*. in Herden gehen; – *together*, zusammenhausen (*of men*). **–sman** [–zmən], *s*. der Hirt.

here [hɪə], *adv*. hier, an diesem Orte *or* (*fig*.) dieser Stelle; (*fig*.) in diesem Falle; her, hierher (*with verbs of motion*); *be* –, anwesend *or* da sein; *belong* –, hierher gehören; – *below*, hienieden; – *goes!* jetzt geht's los! – *and there*, hier und da; hin und wieder; *that's neither – nor there*, das gehört nicht zur Sache; *it was Lady B*. –, *Lady B. there*, es hieß Lady B. hinten und vorn; – *there and everywhere*, überall; (*vulg*.) *this – chap*, dieser Kerl; *–'s to you!* auf dein Wohl; – *to-day and gone tomorrow*, flüchtig und vergänglich. **–about(s)** [–rəbaut(s)], *adv*. hier herum. **–after** [hɪəˈrɑːftə], 1. *adv*. hernach, künftighin, in Zukunft; im künftigen Leben. 2. *s*. die Zukunft, das künftige Leben. **–by,** *adv*. hierdurch. **–in** [–rɪn], *adv*. hierin. **–inafter,** *adv*. hiernach, nachstehend, hier unten. **–of** [–ˈrɔv], *adv*. hiervon. **–on** [–ˈrɔn], *adv*. hierauf, hierüber. **–to,** *adv*. hierzu. **–tofore,** *adv*. vormals, vordem, ehemals, bis jetzt. **–upon** [–rəˈpɔn], *adv*. hierauf, darauf. **–with,** *adv*. hiermit; beifolgend.

heredit–able [həˈrɛdɪtəbl], *adj*. vererbbar, erblich. **–ament** [hɛrɪˈdɪtəmənt], *s*. das Erbgut (*Law*). **–ary** [hɪˈrɛdɪtərɪ], *adj*. erblich, Erb–, vererbt; ererbt (*of diseases*); althergebracht. **–y** [hɪˈrɛdɪtɪ], *s*. die Erblichkeit, Vererbung.

here–siarch [ˈhɛrəsɪɑːk], *s*. der Erzketzer. **–sy** [ˈhɛrəsɪ], *s*. die Ketzerei, Irrlehre. **–tic** [ˈhɛrətɪk], *s*. der Ketzer. **–tical** [hɪˈrɛtɪkl], *adj*. ketzerisch.

heriot [ˈhɛrɪət], *s*. (*archaic*) der Hauptfall (*Law*).

herit–able [ˈhɛrɪtəbl], *adj*. erbfähig; erblich, sich vererbend. **–age** [ˈhɛrɪtɪdʒ], *s*. die Erbschaft, das Erbe, Erbgut. **–or,** *s*. der Erbe (*Law*).

hermaphrodit–e [həˈmæfrədaɪt], *s*. der Zwitter; die Zwitterpflanze (*Bot*.). **–ism** [–tɪzm], *s*. die Zwitterbildung, der Zwitterzustand.

hermeneutic [həːmɪˈnjuːtɪk], *adj*. erklärend, auslegend. **–s,** *pl*. (*sing. constr*.) die Hermeneutik.

hermetic [həːˈmɛtɪk], *adj*. luftdicht, hermetisch; *–ally sealed*, luftdicht verschlossen.

hermit [ˈhəːmɪt], *s*. der Einsiedler, Eremit. **–age** [–tɪdʒ], *s*. die Einsiedelei, Klause. **– –crab,** *s*. der Einsiedlerkrebs.

hernia [ˈhəːnjə], *s*. der Bruch. **–l,** *adj*. Bruch–.

hero [ˈhɪərou], *s*. der Held; die Hauptgestalt (*in drama, etc*.); – *worship*, der Heroenkultus, die Heldenverehrung. **–ic** [hɪˈrouɪk], *adj*. heldenhaft, heldenmütig; *–ic age*, das Heldenzeitalter; *–ic couplet*, heroisches Reimpaar (*Metr*.); *–ic metre*, epischer Vers; *–ic poem*, das Heldengedicht; *–ic saga*, die Heldensage; *–ic verse*, epische Dichtung. **–ics,** *pl*. Überschwenglichkeiten, Schwärmereien; *go off into –ics*, schwärmen. **–ine** [ˈhɛrouɪn], *s*. die Heldin. **–ism** [ˈhɛrouɪzm], *s*. der Heldenmut, Heldengeist.

heroin [ˈhɛroɪn], *s*. das Heroin.

heron [ˈhɛrən], *s*. der (Fisch)Reiher (*Orn*.). **–ry,** *s*. der Reiherstand.

herpe–s [ˈhəːpɪːz], *s*. die Flechte (*Med*.). **–tic** [–ˈpɛtɪk], *adj*. flechtenartig, Flechten– (*Med*.). **–tology** [həːpəˈtɔlədʒɪ], *s*. die Reptilienkunde (*Zool*.); Flechtenkunde (*Med*.).

herring [ˈhɛrɪŋ], *s*. der Hering; *grilled* –, der Brathering; *kippered* –, der Räucherhering; *pickled* –, der Matjeshering; Rollmops; *red* –, der Bückling, Bücking; (*fig*.) das Ablenkungsmanöver. **– –bone,** 1. *s*. die Heringsgräte; das Grätenmuster; der Grätenstich (*Sew*.); die Zickzackordnung (*Arch*.); der Grätenschritt (*skiing*). 2. *v.a*. mit Grätenstich nähen. **– –gull,** *s*. die Silbermöwe. (*coll*.) **– –pond,** *s*. Atlantischer Ozean.

hers [həːz], *poss. pron*. ihr; der, die *or* das ihre *or* ihrige; *a friend of* –, eine ihrer Freundinnen, eine Freundin von ihr. **–elf** [həːˈsɛlf], *pron*. 1 (*emphatic*) selbst, sie selbst; (*coll*.) *she is not –elf*, sie ist nicht auf der Höhe, sie ist nicht ganz normal *or* ganz bei sich; *by –elf*, von selbst, allein; 2. (*refl*.) sich (*Acc. & Dat*.).

hesita–nce [ˈhɛzɪtəns], **–ncy** [–tənsɪ], *s*. die Unschlüssigkeit, das Zögern. **–nt,** *adj*. zögernd, unschlüssig. **–te** [ˈhɛzɪteɪt], *v.n*. zögern, zaudern, unschlüssig sein, Bedenken tragen, zweifelhaft sein. **–tion** [–ˈteɪʃən], *s*. das Zögern, Zaudern, die Unschlüssigkeit, das Bedenken; *without any –tion*, sogleich, ohne jedes Bedenken; *have no –tion*, kein Bedenken tragen (*in doing*, zu tun). **–tive,** *adj*. *see* **–nt.**

hetero–clite [ˈhɛtərəklaɪt], 1. *s*. unregelmäßiges Wort. 2. *adj*. unregelmäßig, anormal (*Gram*.). **–dox** [ˈhɛtərədɔks], *adj*. irrgläubig, heterodox, abweichend. **–doxy,** *s*. der Irrglaube, abweichende Meinung. **–dyne** [–daɪn], *adj*. Überlagerungs– (*Rad*.). **–geneity** [–dʒɪˈnɪːɪtɪ], *s*. die Ungleichartigkeit, Ungleichförmigkeit, Verschiedenartigkeit. **–geneous** [–ˈdʒɪːnjəs], *adj*. ungleich, verschiedenartig, grundverschieden, fremdartig, heterogen. **–nomy,** *s*. ungleichartige Gliederung (*Biol*.).

hetman [ˈhɛtmən], *s*. der Kosakenführer, ukrainischer Befehlshaber.

heuristic [hjuəˈrɪstɪk], *adj*. heuristisch, wegweisend, richtunggebend; erfinderisch.

hew [hjuː], *v.a*. hauen, hacken; behauen (*masonry*); – *one's way*, sich einen Weg bahnen; – *down*, niederhauen, fällen; – *in pieces*, zerhauen, in Stücke hauen; – *off*, abhauen; – *out*, aushauen. **–er,** *s*. der Holzhauer, Steinhauer; Häuer (*Mining*).

hexa–chord [ˈhɛksəkɔːd], *s*. der & das Hexachord, große Sexte (*Mus*.). **–gon** [–gən], *s*. das Sechseck. **–gonal** [–ˈsægənəl], *adj*. sechseckig. **–hedral,** *adj*. sechsflächig. **–hedron,** *s*. das Hexaeder. **–meter** [hɛkˈsæmɪtə], *s*. der Hexameter, Sechsfüßler (*Metr*.). **–pod,** *s*. der Sechsfüßler (*Zool*.).

hey [heɪ], *int*. he! hei!; – *presto!* sieh mal! und da haben Sie's! **– –day** [ˈheɪdeɪ], *s*. (*fig*.) der Höhepunkt, die Blüte(zeit), Vollkraft, Hochflut, der Sturm (*of passion*).

hi [haɪ], *int*. he! heda!

hiatus [haɪˈeɪtəs], *s.* die Lücke, Kluft, der Spalt; Hiatus (*Gram.*).

hibernat-e [ˈhaɪbəːneɪt], *v.n.* (den) Winterschlaf halten, überwintern; (*fig.*) untätig sein. **–ion** [–ˈneɪʃən], *s.* der Winterschlaf, die Überwinterung.

hibiscus [hɪˈbɪskəs], *s.* der Eibisch (*Bot.*).

hicc-ough, –up [ˈhɪkʌp], 1. *s.* der Schlucken, Schluckauf. 2. *v.n.* den Schlucken haben.

hickory [ˈhɪkərɪ], *s.* das Hickoryholz.

hid [hɪd], *see* **hide. –den,** *adj.* heimlich, versteckt.

[1]**hid-e** [haɪd], 1. *ir.v.a.* verbergen, verstecken (*from,* vor); (*fig.*) verheimlichen (*from* (*Dat.*)). 2. *ir.v.n.* sich verbergen *or* verstecken. **–e-and-seek** (*Amer. –e-and-go-seek, –e-and-coop*) das Versteckspiel; *play at –e-and-seek,* Verstecken spielen. (*coll.*) **–e-out,** *s.* das Versteck, der Schlupfwinkel. **–ing,** *s.* das Verbergen; *be in –ing,* sich im Verborgenen halten. **–ing-place,** *s.* das Versteck, der Schlupfwinkel.

[2]**hide,** *s.* (*archaic*) die Hufe (= *60 to 100 acres*) (*Agr.*).

[3]**hid-e,** 1. *s.* die (Tier)Haut, das Fell; (*fig.*) *thick –e,* dickes Fell. 2. *v.a.* (*coll.*) prügeln. **–ebound,** *adj.* mit eng anschließender Haut *or* Rinde; (*usually fig.*) steif, eng(herzig); *be –ebound by tradition,* im Bann der Überlieferung stecken. (*coll.*) **–ing,** *s.* die Tracht Prügel; *good –ing,* tüchtige Tracht Prügel.

hideous [ˈhɪdɪəs], *adj.* entsetzlich, furchtbar, gräßlich, scheußlich. **–ness,** *s.* die Scheußlichkeit.

hie [haɪ], *v.n.* & *r.* (*Poet.*) eilen.

hier-arch [ˈhaɪərɑːk], *s.* das Oberhaupt, der Priester; Oberpriester. **–archic(al)** [–ˈrɑːkɪk(l)], *adj.* hierarchisch, Priester–, priesterlich. **–archy,** *s.* die Priesterherrschaft; Kirchenverfassung; (*fig.*) Rangordnung; Beamtenhierarchie. **–atic(al)** [–ˈrætɪk(l)], *adj.* priesterlich, Priester–. **–ocracy,** *s.* die Priesterherrschaft. **–oglyph** [–roglɪf], die Hieroglyphe, symbolisches Schriftzeichen; (*fig.*) unleserliches Gekritzel. **–oglyphic** [–oˈglɪfɪk], *adj.* hieroglyphisch; geheimnisvoll, rätselhaft; unleserlich. **–oglyphics,** *pl.* die Hieroglyphen, ägyptische Bilderschrift. **–omancy,** *s.* die Weissagung aus Opfern, Hieromantie. **–ophant,** *s.* der Oberpriester.

higgle [ˈhɪgl], *v.n.* feilschen, handlen, knickern, schachern. **–dy-piggledy,** 1. *adv.* kunterbunt, drunter und drüber, durcheinander, planlos. 2. *s.* das Durcheinander, die Verwirrung.

high [haɪ], 1. *adj.* hoch; hochstehend, erhaben, vornehm; angesehen, bedeutend, wichtig; groß, stark, kräftig, heftig; hochgradig, erstklassig, hochentwickelt, vorgeschritten; stolz, anmaßend, hochtrabend, übertrieben, extrem; abgehangen, angegangen, pikant (*as meat*), teuer (*of price*); laut, stark, lärmend, schrill (*voice, tone*); **(a)** (*with nouns*) *– antiquity,* fernes Altertum, *– birth,* hohe Abstammung; *– colour,* lebhafte *or* blühende Farbe; *– commendation,* großes Lob; *– Commissioner, s.* der Gesandte (der Dominien) in London; *– Court, s.* oberster Gerichtshof; *– dive,* das Turmspringen; *– explosive,* der Sprengstoff; *– farming,* intensive Bewirtschaftung; *in – feather,* in gehobener Stimmung; *– feeding,* reiche *or* üppige Kost; *– German,* Hochdeutsch; *with a – hand,* hochmütig, hochfahrend, rücksichtslos; (*coll.*) *get on one's – horse,* sich aufs hohe Roß setzen; (*coll.*) *– jinks,* ausgelassene Fröhlichkeit; *– jump,* der Hochsprung; *– life,* die vornehme Welt; *– lights,* lichte Stellen; (*fig.*) Glanzpunkte, Lichtpunkte; *– Mass,* das Hochamt; *– sea,* hochgehende See; *– seas, pl.* offenes Meer, hohe See; *– spirits,* gehobene Stimmung, fröhliche, muntere *or* lustige Laune; *– standing,* guter Ruf; *– table,* der Speisetisch der Graduierten (*Univ.*); *– tea,* der Tee mit Fleischspeisen; *– tension,* die Hochspannung; *– time,* höchste Zeit; (*coll.*) *a – old time,* see *– jinks*; *– Tory,* weit rechtsstehend; *– treason,* der Hochverrat; *– voltage,* die Hochspannung; *– wind,* starker Wind; *– words,* heftige Worte; *have – words with,* sich zanken mit; **(b)** (*with prepositions*) *on –,* in die Höhe, hinauf; in der Höhe, oben; *from on –,* von oben, aus der Höhe; **(c)** (*with adjectives*) *– and dry,* gestrandet; (*fig.*) auf dem Trockenen; *– and mighty,* hochmütig, hochfahrend. **2.** *adv.* hoch, in die Höhe; stark, mächtig, heftig, in hohem Grade; *pay –,* teuer zahlen; *play –,* mit hohem Einsatz spielen; *run –,* hochgehen (*of waves*); heftig werden (*of feelings*); *search – and low,* überall *or* an allen Ecken und Enden suchen; *stand –,* in gutem Rufe stehen. **– -altar,** *s.* der Hochaltar. **– -altitude flying,** der Höhenflug. **– -angle fire,** das Steilfeuer. **– -angle gun,** das Steilfeuergeschütz. **– -backed,** *adj.* mit hoher Lehne (*chair*). (*sl.*) **–ball,** *s.* das Getränk aus Spirituosen. **– -born,** *adj.* hochgeboren. **– -bred,** *adj.* vornehm, von hoher Geburt. (*coll.*) **–brow,** 1. *adj.* (bewußt) intellektuell. 2. *s.* der Intellektuelle. **– -Church,** 1. *s.* (anglikanische) Hochkirche. 2. *adj.* hochkirchlich, hochanglikanisch. **– -Churchman,** *s.* der Hochkirchler. **– -class,** *adj.* hochwertig, erstklassig. **– -day,** *s.* der Festtag, Freudentag. **–er,** *comp. adj.* höher; obere, Ober–; höher entwickelt, diffenzierter; *–er certificate,* das Abiturienzeugnis. **–est,** *sup. adj.* höchst, oberst; *at its –est,* auf dem Höhepunkt; *–est bidder,* Meistbietende(r) *m.* **– -explosive,** *adj.* Brisanz–, Spreng–. (*sl.*) **–falutin(g),** *adj.* bombastisch, hochtrabend. (*coll.*) **– -flier,** *s.* der Schwärmer, Draufgänger. **– -flown,** *adj.* überspannt, hochtrabend, überschwenglich, schwülstig. (*fig.*) **– -flying,** *adj.* ehrgeizig, hochfliegend. **– -frequency,** *s.* die Hochfrequenz. **– -grade,** *adj.* hochgradig, hochwertig, Qualitäts–; Vergütungs– (*steel*). **– -handed,** *adj.* anmaßend, willkürlich, gewaltsam. **– -heeled,** *adj.* mit hohen Absätzen. **–land,** 1. *s.* das Hochland; *the* (*Scottish*) *–lands,* schottisches Hochland. 2. *adj.* hochländisch; schottisch. **–lander,** *s.* der Hochländer, Bergschotte. **–ly,** *adv.* hoch, höchst, in hohem Grade; *–ly coloured,* sehr bunt, lebhaft; (*fig.*) übertrieben; *–ly flavoured,* stark gewürzt, pikant; *–ly placed,* hochgestellt; *–ly strung,* überempfindlich, nervös, überspannt; *speak –ly of,* lobend sprechen von; *think –ly of,* viel halten von. **– -minded,** *adj.* hochherzig, großherzig. **– -mindedness,** *s.* die Großherzigkeit. **–ness,** *s.* die Höhe; Hoheit; pikanter Geschmack, der Stich (*of food*); *His Royal –ness,* Seine Königliche Hoheit. **– -pass filter,** die Kondensatorkette (*Rad.*). **– -pitched,** *adj.* steil (*of roof*); in hoher Tonlage (*of sound*). **– -pressure,** 1. *s.* der Hochdruck. 2. *adj.* (*fig. coll.*) konzentriert, energisch. **– -priced,** *adj.* teuer, kostspielig (*goods*); hochstehend (*shares, etc.*). **– -priest,** *s.* Hoher Priester, der Hohepriester. **– -principled,** *adj.* von hohen Grundsätzen. **–road,** *s.* die Landstraße; Hauptverkehrsstraße; *be on the –road to success,* auf dem besten Wege sein, sein Glück zu machen. **– -school,** *s.* höhere (*usually* Mädchen– *or* Töchter)Schule; (*Amer.*) höhere Schule. **– -souled,** *adj.* hochherzig. **– -sounding,** *adj.* hochtönend, hochtrabend. **– -speed,** *adj.* Schnell– (*as railway*); Schnellauf– (*as steel*); schnell laufend, von großer Geschwindigkeit. **– -spirited,** *adj.* munter, lebhaft; feurig (*as horse*). **– -stepping,** *adj.* hochtrabend (*horse; also fig.*). **– -stepper,** *s.* hochtrabendes Pferd; (*sl.*) anmaßendes Frauenzimmer. **– -tension battery,** *s.* die Anodenbatterie (*Rad.*). **– -tide,** *s. see* **– -water. – -toned,** *adj.* erhaben. **– -water,** *s.* das Hochwasser, die Fluthöhe; *– -water mark,* der Hochwasserstand; (*fig.*) der Höchststand. **–way,** *s.* die Landstraße, Hauptstraße, Chaussee, Heerstraße; (*fig.*) die Straße, direkter Weg; *–way robbery,* der Straßenraub. **–wayman** [–weɪmən], *s.* der Straßenräuber.

hight [haɪt], (*archaic* & *Poet.*) *p.p.* genannt.

hik-e [haɪk], *v.n.* wandern. **–er,** *s.* der (Fuß)-Wanderer. **–ing,** *s.* das Wandern.

hilar-ious [hɪˈlɛərɪəs], *adj.* vergnügt, heiter, ausgelassen. **–ity** [hɪˈlærɪtɪ], *s.* die Heiterkeit.

hill [hɪl], *s.* der Hügel; Berg, die Anhöhe, Steigung; *ant–,* der Ameisenhaufen; *up – and down dale,* über Berg und Tal; *as old as the –s,* uralt. **– -climb,** *s.* die Bergfahrt (*Motor.*). **–iness** *s.* die Hügeligkeit. **–ock,** [–ək], *s.* kleiner Hügel. **–y,** *adj.* hügelig. **–side,** *s.* der Bergabhang. **–top,** *s.* die Bergspitze.

hilt [hɪlt], *s.* der Griff, das Heft, (Degen)Gefäß; *up to the –,* bis ans Heft; (*fig.*) ganz und gar.

him [hɪm], *pers. pron.* (*Acc.*) ihn; (*Dat.*) ihm; *to* or *for –,* ihm; (*coll.*) *that's –,* er ist es. **–self**

[hɪmˈsɛlf], *pron.* 1. (*emphatic*) er, ihn *or* ihm selbst; 2. (*refl.*) sich; *by –self*, allein, für sich; *he is not –self*, er ist nicht wohl, er ist nicht bei sich; *of –self*, von selbst; *he came to –self*, er kam zu sich; *he talks to –self*, er redet vor sich hin; *he thinks to –self*, er denkt bei sich; *he thinks –self clever*, er hält sich für klug.

[1]**hind** [haɪnd], *s.* die Hindin, Hirschkuh.

[2]**hind,** *s.* (*Scots*) der Knecht, Bauer, Tagelöhner.

[3]**hind,** *adj.* hinter, Hinter–; *– leg*, das Hinterbein; *– quarter*, das Hinterviertel; *– quarters*, die Hinterhand (*of a horse*); das Hinterteil, Hinterviertel (*pl.*); (*coll.*) das Gesäß. **–er,** *comp. adj. see* **–.** **–most,** *adj.* hinterst, letzt.

hind–er [ˈhɪndə], *v.a.* hindern (*in*, in *or* bei; *from doing*, zu tun): aufhalten, stören (*a p.*); verhindern, hemmen (*a th.*). **–rance,** *s.* das Hindernis (*to*, für), die Hinderung; der Nachteil.

hinge [hɪndʒ], 1. *s.* die Angel (*of a door, etc.*); das Scharnier (*of a box, etc.*); das Gelenk(band); (*fig.*) der Angelpunkt, Wendepunkt; die Hauptsache; *off the –s*, aus den Angeln *or* Fugen; (*fig.*) aus dem Häuschen, in Unordnung. 2. *v.a.* mit Angeln *or* Scharnieren versehen, einhängen. 3. *v.n.* (*fig.*) sich drehen (*on*, um); ankommen (*on*, auf (*Acc.*)); abhängen (*on*, von). **–d,** *adj.* (auf– *or* zusammen)-klappbar. **––pin,** *s.* der Drehzapfen.

hinny [ˈhɪnɪ], *s.* der Maulesel.

hint [hɪnt], 1. *v.a. & n.* andeuten, einen Wink geben; *– at a th.*, auf eine S. anspielen. 2. *s.* der Wink, Fingerzeig; die Andeutung (*of*, von; *as to*, über), Anspielung (*at*, auf), Spur; *broad –*, der Wink mit dem Zaunpfahl; *drop* or *give s.o. a –*, einem einen Wink geben; *take a –*, einen Wink verstehen, es sich (*Dat.*) gesagt sein lassen; *throw out a –*, zu verstehen geben, merken lassen.

hinterland [ˈhɪntəlænd], *s.* das Hinterland.

[1]**hip** [hɪp], *s.* die Hüfte, Lende (*Anat.*), der Walm (*Build.*); (*coll.*) *have s.o. on the –*, einen in der Gewalt haben; (*B.*) *smite – and thigh*, unbarmherzig vernichten, völlig besiegen. **––bath,** *s.* das Sitzbad. **––bone,** *s.* das Hüftbein. **––joint,** *s.* das Hüftgelenk. **––rafter,** *s.* der Gratsparren. **––roof,** *s.* das Walmdach. **––shot,** *adj.* (lenden)lahm.

[2]**hip,** *s.* die Hagebutte (*Bot.*).

[3]**hip,** *v.a.* niederdrücken, trübsinnig machen. (*coll.*) **–ped, –pish,** *adj.* trübsinnig, schwermütig.

hippo–campus [hɪpoˈkæmpəs], *s.* das Seepferdchen (*Ichth.*). **–drome** [–droum], *s.* die Rennbahn, Reitbahn. **–griff, –gryph** [–grɪf], *s.* das Flügelroß, Musenroß. **–phagy** [hɪˈpɔfədʒɪ], *s.* das Essen von Pferdefleisch. **–potamus** [hɪpəˈpɔtəməs] *s.* das Nilpferd, Flußpferd.

hircine [ˈhəːsaɪn], *adj.* bockig, Bocks–; (*fig.*) übelriechend, stinkend.

hire [ˈhaɪə], 1. *v.a.* mieten (*th. or p.*), dingen, in Dienst nehmen, anstellen (*a p.*), heuern (*sailors*); *– out*, vermieten; *– o.s.* (*out*), sich verdingen (*as*, als; *to*, bei); *–ed man*, Angestellte(r), *m.* 2. *s.* die Miete, der Mietspreis, (Arbeits)Lohn; das Mieten; *on –*, zu vermieten; *have* or *take on –*, mieten. **–ling,** 1. *s.* der Mietling. 2. *adj.* feil, käuflich. **––purchase,** *s.* der Abzahlungskauf, die Abzahlung, Teilzahlung, Ratenzahlung. **––purchase-system,** *s.* das Abzahlungssystem.

hirsute [ˈhəːsjuːt], *adj.* haarig, behaart, struppig, zottig; (*fig.*) rauh.

his [hɪz], 1. *poss. pron.* sein(e), seines; der, die *or* das seine *or* seinige; *a book of –*, eins seiner Bücher, *or* eins von seinen Büchern; *it is –*, es gehört ihm. 2. *poss. adj.* sein(e); *he has hurt – finger*, er hat sich (*Dat.*) den Finger verletzt.

hispid [ˈhɪspɪd], *adj.* borstig (*Bot. & Zool.*).

hiss [hɪs], 1. *v.n.* zischen. 2. *v.a.* auszischen, auspfeifen (*Theat.*). 3. *s.* das Zischen, Gezisch, der Zischlaut (*Phonet.*).

hist [hɪst], *int.* (*archaic*) st! still!

histo–logy [hɪsˈtɔlədʒɪ], *s.* die Gewebenlehre (*Med.*). **–lysis,** *s.* der Gewebszerfall.

histor–ian [hɪsˈtɔːrɪən], *s.* der Geschichtschreiber. **–ic** [–ˈtɔrɪk], *adj.* historisch, von geschichtlicher Bedeutung. **–ical,** *adj.* geschichtlich, Geschichts–, zur Geschichte gehörig. **–icity** [hɪstoˈrɪsɪtɪ], *s.* die Geschichtlichkeit. **–iographer** [hɪstɔːrɪˈɔgrəfə], *s.* amtlicher Geschichtschreiber. **–iography** [–ˈɔgrəfɪ], *s.* (amtliche) Geschichtschreibung. **–y** [ˈhɪstrɪ], *s.* die Geschichte, Chronik, Darstellung (des Geschehens), der Werdegang, die Entwicklung; (*without art.*) die Geschichte, Geschichtswissenschaft; (*coll.*) die Vergangenheit; *ancient –y*, die Geschichte des Altertums; (*coll.*) alte Geschichte, abgetane Sache; (*coll.*) *have a –y*, eine Vergangenheit haben; *make –y*, Geschichte machen; *universal –y*, die Weltgeschichte. **–y-book,** *s.* das Geschichtsbuch. **–y-piece,** *s.* historisches Gemälde.

histrionic [hɪstrɪˈɔnɪk], *adj.* schauspielerisch, theatralisch. **–s,** *pl.* die Schauspielkunst; das Schauspielern, die Schauspielerei.

hit [hɪt], 1. *ir.v.a.* schlagen, stoßen; treffen (*the mark, etc.*); (*coll.*) *– it* (*on the head*), (den Nagel auf den Kopf) treffen; *– a p. back*, einen wieder schlagen; *– s.o. a blow*, einem einen Schlag versetzen; *be hard –*, schwer getroffen sein *or* werden (*by*, durch); (*coll.*) *– off*, richtig, überzeugend *or* treffend darstellen *or* schildern; (*coll.*) *– it off*, gut auskommen, übereinstimmen *or* sich vertragen (*with*, mit). 2. *ir.v.n.* schlagen, treffen; *– against*, stoßen gegen; *– on* or *upon*, zufällig treffen *or* finden; kommen, verfallen *or* stoßen auf; *– out*, um sich schlagen; *– or miss*, aufs Geratewohl, auf gut Glück. 3. *s.* der Schlag, Stoß; Hieb, Stich; glücklicher Zufall, der Glücksfall, Treffer, Erfolg, Schlager (*Theat.*); treffende Bemerkung, glücklicher Einfall, gute Idee; *– below the belt*, der Tiefschlag (*Boxing*); (*fig.*) unehrenhaftes Benehmen; *direct –*, der Volltreffer; *stage-–*, der Bühnenschlager. **––and-run raid,** der Einbruchsangriff, Stippangriff (*Av.*). **––song,** der Schlager, das Schlagerlied.

hitch [hɪtʃ], 1. *s.* der Ruck, Zug; Stich, Knoten (*in a rope*) (*Naut.*); (*fig.*) Haken, das Hindernis, die Stockung, Störung, toter Punkt; *there is a – in the business*, das Ding hat einen Haken; *without a –*, reibungslos, ohne die geringste Störung. 2. *v.a.* rücken; festmachen, anspannen; *– up*, hochziehen, hinaufziehen. 3. *v.n.* hinken, humpeln; hängenbleiben, sich festhaken. **––hike,** *v.n.* per Anhalter reisen.

hither [ˈhɪðə], 1. *adv.* hierher; *– and thither*, hin und her, auf und ab. 2. *adj.* diesseitig. **–to,** *adv.* bisher, bis jetzt. **–ward,** *adv. see* **hither.**

hive [haɪv], 1. *s.* der Bienenkorb, Bienenstock; (*fig.*) Sammelpunkt, Brennpunkt; *– of bees*, der Bienenschwarm. 2. *v.a.* (Bienen) in den Stock tun. 3. *v.n.* zusammenwohnen, hausen (*with*, mit). **––bee,** *s.* die Honigbiene.

hives [haɪvz], *pl.* der Ausschlag; Hautausschlag; die Bräune.

ho [hou], *int.* ho! holla! *– there!* holla! wer da?

hoar [hɔː], *adj.* (*Poet.*) weiß; weißgrau; grau bereift; (*fig.*) ehrwürdig. **––frost,** *s.* der (Rauh)Reif. **–iness,** *s.* das Weißgrau, die Grauheit. **–y,** *adj.* weiß, grau, grauhaarig, (*fig.*) ehrwürdig.

hoard [hɔːd], 1. *s.* der Vorrat, Schatz. 2. *v.a. & n.* anhäufen, aufhäufen, sammeln; hamstern, sparen; *– up*, aufhäufen, sparen, zurücklegen. **–ing,** *s.* das Anhäufen, Schätzesammeln, Hamstern.

hoarding [ˈhɔːdɪŋ], *s.* der Bauzaun, Bretterzaun; die Reklamefläche, Litfaßsäule.

hoarse [hɔːs], *adj.* heiser, rauh; krächzend. **–ness,** *s.* die Heiserkeit.

hoary [ˈhɔːrɪ], *see* **hoar.**

hoax [houks], 1. *s.* die Täuschung, der Betrug, Schwindel; die Fopperei, der Schabernack; die (Zeitungs)Ente. 2. *v.a.* zum besten haben, foppen, anführen.

hob [hɔb], *s.* die Kaminseite, der Kaminabsatz; die Nabe (*of wheel*); der Pflock (*as target*).

hobble [ˈhɔbl], 1. *v.n.* humpeln; hinken. 2. *v.a.* fesseln (*a horse*). 3. *s.* das Hinken, Humpeln; die Verlegenheit, Patsche. **––skirt,** *s.* enger Rock.

hobbledehoy [ˈhɔbəldɪˈhɔɪ], *s.* der Taps, Schlaks, linkischer Bursche.

hobby [ˈhɔbɪ], *s.* (*fig.*) das Steckenpferd, die Liebhaberei. **––horse,** *s.* das Steckenpferd, Schaukelpferd.

hobgoblin [ˈhɔbgəblɪn], *s.* der Kobold.

hobnail ['hɔbneɪl], *s.* der Schuhnagel, Hufnagel. **–ed,** *adj.* mit groben Nägeln beschlagen.
hobnob ['hɔbnɔb], *v.n.* (*coll.*) zusammen kneipen; vertraulich plaudern, intim sein, verkehren.
hobo ['houbou], *s.* (*Amer. sl.*) der Landstreicher.
[1]**hock** [hɔk], 1. *s.* das Sprunggelenk, die Hachse, Hechse (*Vet.*). 2. *v.a.* Kniefiechsen zerschneiden (*Dat.*).
[2]**hock,** *s.* der Rheinwein.
[3]**hock,** 1. *s.* (*sl.*) das Pfand; Gefängnis; *in –*, verpfändet (*of things*), im Gefängnis (*of persons*). 2. *v.a.* (*sl.*) verpfänden, versetzen.
hockey ['hɔkɪ], *s.* das Hockey(spiel).
hocus ['houkəs], *v.a.* betrügen; betäuben, berauschen (*a p.*); fälschen, mischen (*wine, etc.*). **–pocus** [–'poukəs], *s.* der Hokuspokus, Schwindel, die Gaukelei.
hod [hɔd], *s.* der Mörteltrog, das Steinbrett. **–man,** *s.* der Mörtelträger; Handlanger.
hodge-podge ['hɔdʒpɔdʒ], *s. see* **hotchpotch.**
hodiernal [hɔdɪ'ə:nəl], *adj.* heutig, gegenwärtig.
hodometer [hɔ'dɔmɪtə], *s.* der Schrittzähler, Wegmesser.
hoe [hou], 1. *s.* die Hacke. 2. *v.a.* hacken, aufbrechen, lockern (*ground*), jäten (*weeds*).
hog [hɔg], 1. *s.* das Schwein, der Keiler; die Rührschaufel (*Dye.*); der Scheuerbesen (*Naut.*); (*fig.*) die Sau, der Lümmel, gemeiner Kerl; (*sl.*) *go the whole –*, die Sache gründlich machen, reine Sache machen, reinen Tisch machen, aufs Ganze gehen. 2. *v.a.* stutzen (*mane*), (*sl.*) an sich reißen, erraffen, wegschnappen, unter den Nägeln reißen; *– down, v.a.* fieren (*Naut.*). **–get,** *s.* einjähriges Schaf. **–gish,** *adj.* schweinisch, saugrob, säuisch, gemein, gefräßig. **–gishness,** *s.* die Schweinerei, Gefräßigkeit. **– -mane,** *s.* gestutzte Mähne. **–'s-back,** *s.* runder Bergrücken. **–shead** ['hɔgzhɛd], *s.* das Oxhoft (*etwa 240 Liter*); großes Faß. (*coll.*) **– -tie,** *v.a.* fesseln, binden. **–wash,** *s.* das Spülwasser; (*vulg.*) der Saufraß; das Gewäsch.
hogmanay ['hɔgməneɪ], *s.* (*Scots*) Silvester.
hoi(c)k [hɔɪk], *v.a.* ruckweise hochziehen (*Av.*).
hoist [hɔɪst], 1. *v.a.* in die Höhe ziehen *or* winden; hochziehen; heißen, hissen (*flags, etc.*) (*Naut.*); *– out a boat*, ein Boot aussetzen; *– with one's own petard*, in seiner eigenen Falle gefangen. 2. *s.* der Aufzug, Kran, die Winde, der Flaschenzug; die Tiefe (*of a flag*). **–ing-engine,** *s.* der Aufzug, die Hebevorrichtung; Fördermaschine (*Min.*).
hoity-toity ['hɔɪtɪ'tɔɪtɪ], 1. *adj.* mutwillig, auslassen; (*coll.*) leicht verletzt, reizbar. 2. *int.* potztausend!
hokey-pokey ['houkɪ'poukɪ], *s.* (*coll.*) der Eiskrem.
hokum ['houkəm], *s.* (*coll.*) der Schwindel, die Übertreibung, der Unsinn, leeres Geschwätz; kitschige Aufmachung (*Theat.*).
hold [hould], **1.** *ir.v.a.* halten, festhalten; gefangenhalten (*a p.*); behalten (*a position*) (*also Mil.*); enthalten, fassen; anhalten, aufhalten, zurückhalten; glauben, behaupten, der Meinung sein, halten für, ansehen, entscheiden; innehaben, besitzen, einnehmen, bekleiden (*a post*); **(a)** (*with nouns*) – *the audience*, die Zuhörer in Spannung halten; – *one's breath*, den Atem anhalten; – *a brief for*, eintreten für; (*coll.*) – *a candle to s.o.*, sich mit einem messen, mit einem einen Vergleich aushalten; – *a conversation*, eine Unterredung führen; – *counsel*, sich beraten; – *the floor*, see – *the stage*; – *one's ground*, see – *one's own*; (*sl.*) – *your horses!* keine Übereilung! sachte!; – *the line*, am Apparat bleiben (*Phone*); – *a meeting*, eine Versammlung abhalten; – *an office*, ein Amt bekleiden, eine Stelle innehaben; – *an opinion*, eine Meinung haben, einer Meinung sein; – *one's own*, sich behaupten, standhalten; – *a party*, ein Fest feiern; – *one's peace*, stillschweigen, sich ruhig verhalten; – *shares*, Aktien besitzen; – *the stage*, im Mittelpunkt stehen; – *sway*, herrschen, vorherrschen; – *one's tongue*, see – *one's peace*; (*coll.*) – *your tongue!* halt's Maul! – *a view*, eine Ansicht vertreten, eine Meinung hegen; – *water*, wasserdicht sein; (*fig.*) stichhalten, stichhaltig sein; **(b)** (*with adjectives or adverbs*) – *o.s. aloof*, sich abseits halten; – *back*, zurückhalten; verschweigen (*the truth*); – *cheap*, gering achten; – *dear*, lieben, wertschätzen; – *down*, niederhalten, unterdrücken; (*coll.*) innehalten, sich halten in (*a job*); – *excused*, für entschuldigt betrachten; – *forth*, bieten, in Aussicht stellen (*hopes*); – *in*, anhalten, im Zügel halten; – *o.s. in*, sich beherrschen; – *off*, abhalten, abwehren; – *out*, aushalten (*against*, gegen); ausstrecken, herhalten, bieten (*hands, etc.*); machen (*offer*); gewähren (*hope*); geben (*promise*); – *out prospects of*, in Aussicht stellen; – *over*, verschieben, aufschieben; – *tight!* Achtung! fest anhalten! – *up*, in die Höhe halten, aufheben; aufrecht halten, stützen; (*fig.*) zeigen, hinstellen; (*coll.*) überfallen; (*coll.*) aufhalten, hindern; – *up to derision*, dem Spott aussetzen; – *up as an example*, als Beispiel hinstellen; – *up one's head*, den Kopf hochhalten; **(c)** (*with prepositions*) – *in check*, in Schach halten; – *s.o. in esteem*, einen achten; – *in suspense*, im Zweifel lassen; – *of no* or *little account*, geringschätzen; – *a p. to his promise*, einen beim Wort halten; – *to ransom*, gegen Lösegeld festhalten. **2.** *ir.v.n.* halten, festhalten; gelten, sich bewähren; erachten, der Meinung sein; andauern, sich halten, standhalten; – *back*, sich zurückhalten (*from doing*, zu tun); – *forth*, Reden halten, predigen, sich ergehen (*on*, über); – *good*, gelten (*of*, von); gültig *or* in Kraft bleiben, sich bestätigen *or* bewähren; (*sl.*) – *hard!* halt! wart mal! – *off*, sich zurückhalten *or* fernhalten (*from doing*, zu tun); zurückgehalten werden, ausbleiben; – *on*, (sich) festhalten; (*fig.*) durchhalten, aushalten; (*coll.*) am Apparat bleiben (*Phone*); (*sl.*) langsam! warte! einen Augenblick! – *out*, sich halten, standhalten, aushalten, andauern, standhaft bleiben, sich behaupten; (*coll.*) zureichen; (*coll.*) zurückhalten; (*coll.*) – *out for*, sich einsetzen für; – *to one's position*, auf dem Platze ausharren; – *together*, zusammenhalten, nicht brechen; – *true*, see – *good*; – *up*, stehenbleiben; sich aufrecht halten; – *with*, übereinstimmen mit, billigen (*views*); es aushalten bei (*persons*). **3.** *s.* der Halt, Griff; die Macht, Gewalt; der Einfluß (*on*, auf; *over*, über); Eindruck (*on*, auf); Schiffsraum, Frachtraum, Laderaum (*Naut.*); (*archaic*) die Haft, der Gewahrsam; (*archaic*) befestigter Platz; das Lager (*of a beast*); *after-–*, hinterer Teil des Laderaums (*in ships*); *catch, lay* or *seize – of*, ergreifen, erfassen, anfassen (*persons*); *get – of*, erwischen, kommen zu; *get a – on s.o.*, einen unter seinen Einfluß bekommen; *have a firm – of* or *on s.th.*, etwas beherrschen *or* meistern; *keep – of*, festhalten; *let go one's –*, loslassen, fahren lassen; *miss one's –*, fehlgreifen; *take – of*, ergreifen, anfassen (*things*); *take a strong – on*, beeindrucken, Eindruck machen auf. **– -all,** *s.* der Behälter, das Necessaire. **– -back,** *s.* das Hindernis. **–er,** *s.* der Haltende; Inhaber, Besitzer, Pächter, Lehnsmann; Halter, Griff (*of pen, etc.*); Behälter; *cigarette –er*, die Zigarettenspitze. **– -fast,** *s.* der Haken, die Klammer, Zwinge. **–ing,** 1. *adj.*; *–ing attack*, der Fesselungsangriff (*Mil.*); *–ing capacity*, das Fassungsvermögen; *–ing company*, die Dachgesellschaft, der Trust (*C.L.*). 2. *s.* das Halten, Abhalten, die Abhaltung; das Pachtgut, der Grundbesitz, das Guthaben; *pl.* der Bestand, Besitz, die Beteiligung, der Anteil (*C.L.*). (*coll.*) **– -over,** *s.* der Rest, das Übrigbleibende. **– -up,** *s.* räuberischer Überfall; die Störung, Stockung, der Stillstand; *traffic – -up*, die Verkehrsstockung.
hole [houl], 1. *s.* das Loch, die Öffnung; Höhle, der Bau (*of animals*); (*sl.*) die Klemme, Patsche, Verlegenheit; *full of –s*, durchlöchert; (*coll.*) *pick –s in*, bekritteln, zerpflücken. 2. *v.a.* aushöhlen, durchbohren, durchlöchern; ins Loch spielen (*ball*) (*Golf*). 3. *v.n.* in die Höhle gehen (*of animals*); ins Loch spielen (*Golf*). **– -and-corner,** *adj.* heimlich, versteckt, zweifelhaft, anrüchig; hinterlistig. **– -board,** *s.* das Lesebrett (*Weav.*). **– -gauge,** *s.* die Lochlehre (*Mach.*).
holiday ['hɔlɪdeɪ], *s.* der Feiertag; freier Tag; *pl.* Ferien (*pl.*), der Urlaub; *half –*, freier Nachmittag; *on –*, in den Ferien; *go on –* or *on one's –s*, in die Ferien gehen; *we have a – today*, wir haben heute frei; *– course*, der Ferienkurs. **– -maker,** *s.* der Sommerfrischler, Ferienreisende(r), *m.*
holiness ['houlɪnəs], *s.* die Heiligkeit (*also title*).
holla ['hɔlə], 1. *s.* der Halloruf. 2. *v.n.* hallo rufen. 3. *v.a.* laut (aus)rufen, zurufen.

holland [ˈhɔlənd], *s.* ungebleichte Leinwand. **–s,** *s.* der Wacholderschnaps.
holl–er [ˈhɔlə], (*sl.*) (*v. only*), **–o, –oa, –ow** (*n. & v.*), *see* **holla.**
hollow [ˈhɔlou], 1. *adj.* hohl, Hohl–; tiefliegend (*eyes*), eingefallen (*cheeks*); dumpf (*sound*); (*fig.*) hohl, leer, nichtssagend, wertlos, gehaltlos; unaufrichtig, falsch (*words, promises*). 2. *adv.*; (*coll.*) *beat* –, völlig *or* gänzlich besiegen, glatt aus dem Felde schlagen. 3. *s.* die Senkung, Vertiefung, Aushöhlung; das Loch, die Höhle, Schlucht, Mulde, das Tal, der Hohlweg; die Nut, Rinne, Hohlkehle; – *of the hand,* die hohle Hand; (*fig.*) *have in the – of one's hand,* völlig in seiner Gewalt haben; – *of the knee,* die Kniekehle. 4. *v.a.* (– *out*) hohl machen, aushöhlen; auskehlen. **–-cheeked,** *adj.* hohlwangig. **–-eyed,** *adj.* hohläugig. **–-ground,** *adj.* hohlgeschliffen. **–ness,** *s.* die Hohlheit, Dumpfheit (*of sound*); (*fig.*) Leerheit. **–-ware,** *s.* Hohlwaren (*pl.*), das Kochgeschirr.
holly [ˈhɔlɪ], *s.* die Stechpalme (*Bot.*).
hollyhock [ˈhɔlɪhɔk], *s.* die Stockrose, Herbstrose, Rosenmalve (*Bot.*).
holm [houm], *s.* der Werder, flaches Uferland.
holm-oak [ˈhoumouk], *s.* die Steecheiche (*Bot.*).
holo-caust [ˈhɔləkɔːst], *s.* das Brandopfer; (*fig.*) große Zerstörung, der Massenmord. **–graph** [–græf], *s.* eigenhändig geschriebene Urkunde.
holster [ˈhoulstə], *s.* die (Pistolen)Halfter.
holt [hoult], *s.* (*Poet.*) das Gehölz, der Hain.
holus-bolus [ˈhouləsˈbouləs], *adv.* im ganzen, alles auf einmal.
holy [ˈhoulɪ], *adj.* heilig. *–-day, s.* kirchlicher Festtag; – *Father,* der Papst; – *Ghost,* Heiliger Geist; – *of Holies,* das Allerheiligste; – *Land,* das Heilige Land; – *Office,* die Inquisition; – *orders, pl.* geistlicher Stand; *take – orders,* Geistlicher werden; – *Spirit,* see – *Ghost*; – *Thursday,* der Himmelfahrtstag; (*usually*) Gründonnerstag; – *water,* das Weihwasser; – *Week,* die Karwoche, Passionswoche; – *Writ,* die Heilige Schrift.
holystone [ˈhoulɪstoun], 1. *s.* der Scheuerstein. 2. *v.a.* scheuern, schrubben (*Naut.*).
homage [ˈhɔmɪdʒ], *s.* die Huldigung, Treuhuldigung; *do, pay* or *render* –, huldigen (*to* (*Dat.*)).
home [houm], **1.** *s.* die Heimat; der Wohnort, Heimatsort; das Haus, Heim, die Wohnung; (*fig.*) Familie, der Familienkreis, Hausstand; das Heim, Asyl, die Anstalt, Pflegestätte (*for sick, aged, etc.*); das Ziel, Mal (*in games*); *at* –, zu Hause; in der Heimat; der Empfangstag; (*fig.*) in seinem Element, ungezwungen; *be at* –, Empfangstag haben; (*fig.*) *be at – in,* vertraut sein mit, bewandert sein in; *make o.s. at* –, tun als ob man zu Hause ist, es sich (*Dat.*) gemütlich machen; *at – to no one,* für niemand zu sprechen; *away from* –, nicht zu Hause, abwesend, verreist; – *for girls,* das Mädchenheim; – *is* – or *there is no place like* –, eigner Herd ist Goldes wert. **2.** *adj.* heimisch, häuslich; inländisch, einheimisch, Inlands–, Innen–; (*fig.*) derb, treffend; – *affairs,* die Innenpolitik; – *circle,* der Familienkreis; – *cinema,* das Heimkino; – *comforts,* häusliche Gemütlichkeit; – *consumption,* einheimischer Verbrauch; – *defence,* – *guard,* die Bürgerwehr; – *farm,* die Hauptfarm; – *gymnastics,* die Zimmergymnastik; – *journey,* die Rückreise, Rückfahrt, Heimkehr; – *market,* der Inlandsmarkt; – *Office,* das Ministerium des Innern; – *port,* der Heimathafen, Einsatzhafen; – *rule,* die Selbstregierung; – *Secretary,* der Innenminister, Minister des Innern; – *stretch,* die Strecke vor dem Ziel; – *trade,* der Binnenhandel; – *town,* die Heimatstadt; – *truth,* ungeschminkte Wahrheit, die Binsenwahrheit. **3.** *adv.* heim, nach Hause; daheim, zu Hause; (*fig.*) am Ziel; nachdrücklich; *be – soon,* bald zu Hause sein; *bring s.th. – to a p.,* einem etwas klarmachen *or* zu Gemüte führen; (*fig.*) *come – to a p.,* einen treffen *or* nahe berühren, einem nahegehen *or* klarwerden; *drive a nail* –, einen Nagel fest einschlagen; *drive a th. – to a p.,* einem etwas nachdrücklich *or* gründlich einprägen; *go* –, nach Hause gehen, (*fig.*) seine Wirkung tun; *the thrust has gone* –, der Hieb hat gesessen; *press – an attack,* einen Angriff wirkungsvoll vortragen; *press – one's point,* seinen Standpunkt durchsetzen; *push the bolt* –, den Riegel vorschieben; *return* –, die Rückkehr nach Hause; *strike* –, den rechten Fleck treffen; *welcome –!* willkommen zu Hause! (*sl.*) *write – about,* prahlen über. **4.** *v.n.* sich einpeilen (*on to,* auf) (*Av.*). **–-baked,** *adj.* hausbacken. **–-brewed,** *adj.* selbstgebraut. **–-coming,** *s.* die Heimkehr. **–-felt,** *adj.* tiefempfunden. **–land,** *s.* die Heimat, das Heimatland, Mutterland. **–less,** *adj.* heimatlos. **–like,** *adj.* behaglich, anheimelnd. **–liness,** *s.* die Häuslichkeit, Gemütlichkeit; Einfachheit, Schlichtheit; (*coll.*) Unschönheit. **–ly,** *adj.* heimisch, behaglich, gemütlich, anheimelnd, einfach, schlicht; (*coll.*) reizlos, unschön, unansehnlich, nicht hübsch; *–ly cooking,* die Hausmannskost. **–-made,** *adj.* zu Hause gemacht; inländisch. **–sick,** *adj.* an Heimweh leidend; *he is –sick,* er hat Heimweh. **–sickness,** *s.* das Heimweh. **–-signal,** *s.* das Hauptsignal (*Railw.*). **–spun,** 1. *adj.* zu Hause gesponnen; (*fig.*) einfach, schlicht. 2. *s.* grober Wollstoff. **–stead,** *s.* das Gehöft; Eigenheim mit Garten; die Heimstätte (*Poet.*). **–-thrust,** *s.* sitzender Hieb, der Treffer. **–ward(s)** [–wəd(z)], *adv.* heimwärts, nach Hause; Rück–. **–ward-bound,** *adj.* auf der Rückreise begriffen (*Naut.*). **–work,** *s.* die Heimarbeit, Hausarbeit.
homici–dal [hɔmɪˈsaɪdl], *adj.* mörderisch. **–de** [ˈhɔmɪsaɪd], *s.* der Totschlag, Mord; Totschläger.
homil–etic [hɔmɪˈlɛtɪk], *adj.* homiletisch. **–etics,** *pl.* die Kanzelberedsamkeit, Homiletik.
homily [ˈhɔmɪlɪ], *s.* die Homilie, Predigt; (*fig.*) Moralpredigt.
homing [ˈhoumɪŋ], 1. *adj.* heimkehrend; – *instinct,* der Heimatsinn; – *loft,* der Heimatschlag; – *pigeon,* die Brieftaube. 2. *s.* das Heimkehren, die Heimkehr (*of pigeons*).
hominy [ˈhɔmɪnɪ], *s.* das Maismehl; der Maisbrei.
homoeopath [ˈhoumɪopæθ], *s.* der Homöopath. **–ic** [–ˈpæθɪk], *adj.* homöopathisch.
homo–geneity [hɔmədʒɪːˈnɪətɪ], *s.* die Gleichartigkeit, Gleichförmigkeit, Einheitlichkeit. **–geneous** [–ˈdʒɪːnjəs], *adj.* gleichartig, gleichförmig, einheitlich, homogen (*Phys.*). **–genesis,** *s.* die Homogenese (*Biol.*). **–genize,** *v.a.* homogenisieren. **–logous** [həˈmɔləgəs], *adj.* homolog, gleichnamig, gleichlautend. **–logue,** *s.* das Homolog. **–logy** [həˈmɔlədʒɪ], *s.* die Übereinstimmung, Ähnlichkeit. **–nym** [ˈhɔmonɪm], *s.* das Homonym, gleichlautendes Wort. **–nymous** [həˈmɔnɪməs], *adj.* homonym, gleichlautend. **–ptera** [həˈmɔptərə], *pl.* Gleichflügler (*Ent.*). **–sexual,** *adj.* homosexuell, gleichgeschlechtlich.
homunculus [houˈmʌŋkjuləs], *s.* der Homunkulus; das Menschlein, der Zwerg.
hone [houn], 1. *s.* der Schleifstein, Wetzstein. 2. *v.a.* abziehen, schärfen (*razors*).
honest [ˈɔnɪst], *adj.* redlich, ehrlich, rechtschaffen, aufrichtig; ehrbar, anständig, sittsam, tugendhaft; echt; *earn* or *turn an – penny,* sich ehrlich durchschlagen; *make an – woman of her,* ihr die Ehre wiedergeben. (*coll.*) **–-to-God, –-to-goodness,** *adj.* echt, wirklich, bieder. **–y** [ˈɔnɪstɪ], *s.* die Ehrlichkeit, Redlichkeit, Aufrichtigkeit, Rechtschaffenheit; Mondviole (*Bot.*); (*Prov.*) *–y is the best policy,* ehrlich währt am längsten.
honey [ˈhʌnɪ], *s.* der Honig; (*fig.*) die Süßigkeit; (*coll.*) der Schatz, Liebling. **–-bag,** *s.* der Honigmagen. **–-bear,** *s.* der Wickelbär. **–-buzzard,** *s.* der Wespenbussard. **–comb,** 1. *s.* die (Honig)-Wabe. 2. *v.a.* wabenartig durchlöchern. **–combed,** *adj.* zellig; löcherig. **–dew,** *s.* der Honigtau; süßlicher Tabak. **–ed,** *adj.* honigsüß (*also fig.*). **–moon,** 1. *s.* Flitterwochen (*pl.*), die Hochzeitsreise. 2. *v.n.* die Flitterwochen verbringen. **–suckle,** *s.* das Geißblatt (*Bot.*).
honied [ˈhʌnɪd], *see* **honeyed.**
honk [hɔŋk], 1. *s.* der Schrei der wilden Gans. 2. *v.a.* schreien (*of geese*); hupen (*Motor.*).
honorar–ium [ɔnəˈrɛərɪəm], *s.* (*pl.* –ia *or* –iums) das Honorar. **–y** [ˈɔnərərɪ], *adj.* ehrend, ehrenvoll, Ehren–; ehrenamtlich; *–y degree,* der Ehrengrad (*Univ.*); *–y member,* das Ehrenmitglied; *–y post,* das Ehrenamt; *–y secretary,* ehrenamtlicher Schriftführer.

honour [ˈɔnə], 1. *s.* die Ehre, Würde, hoher Rang, die Ehrenstelle; der Ruhm, hohe Achtung, die Ehrerbietung, Ehrung, Auszeichnung, guter Ruf *or* Namen; das Ehrgefühl; (Euer *or* Ew.) Ehrwürden *or* Gnaden (*in titles*). **–s,** *pl.* Ehrenbezeigungen, Ehrenverleihungen; das Studium *or* die Prüfung höherer Ordnung (*Univ.*); Honneurs (*pl.*) (*Cards*); *–s are easy*, die Honneurs (*or fig.*) Vorteile sind gleich verteilt; (*a*) (*with nouns*) *affair of –*, die Ehrensache; *code of –*, der Ehrenkodex; *court of –*, das Ehrengericht; *maid of –*, die Ehrendame, Hofdame; *sense of –*, das Ehrgefühl; *word of –*, das Ehrenwort; (*b*) (*with verbs*) *do – to a p.*, einen ehren, einem Ehre erweisen; *do the –s*, die Honneurs machen; *have the – to inform*, die Ehre haben *or* sich beehren mitzuteilen; *an – to his profession*, eine Zierde seines Berufs; *there is – among thieves*, eine Krähe hackt der andern die Augen nicht aus; *– to whom – is due*, Ehre dem Ehre gebührt; (*c*) (*with prepositions*) *in his –*, ihm zu Ehren; *bound in –*, durch Ehrenpflicht gebunden; *on my –!* auf mein Ehrenwort! auf Ehre! *put s.o. on his –*; einen an der Ehre packen; *to his –*, see *in his –*; *be upon one's – to do*, moralisch verpflichtet sein zu tun; *with –*, glorreich, ehrenvoll. 2. *v.a.* ehren (*Acc.*), Ehre erweisen (*Dat.*); beehren (*with*, mit), verherrlichen; honorieren, akzeptieren, einlösen (*a cheque, etc.*) (*C.L.*). **–able** [–rəbl], *adj.* ehrenvoll (*to*, für), rühmlich; ehrenhaft, ehrlich, redlich; ehrenwert (*in titles*); *the –able gentleman, my –able friend*, der Herr Vorredner (*Parl.*); *–able discharge*, ehrenvoller Abschied (*Mil.*); *Right –able*, Hochwohlgeboren (*title*).

hooch [hu:tʃ], *s.* (*sl.*) der Schnaps.

hood [hud], 1. *s.* die Haube, Schutzhaube (*also Motor.*); Kapuze, Kappe; das Verdeck, die Plane (*Motor.*); der Überwurf über Talar (*Univ.*). 2. *v.a.* mit einer Kappe, Haube, *etc.* bedecken. **–ed,** *adj.* mit einer Kappe, (*fig.*) verhüllt; *–ed crow*, die Nebelkrähe (*Orn.*). **–wink,** *v.a.* die Augen verbinden (*Dat.*); (*usually fig.*) täuschen, blenden.

hoodlum [ˈhu:dləm], *s.* (*coll.*) der Strolch, Rowdy, Knote.

hoodoo [ˈhu:du:], *s.* (*coll.*) der Unheilbringer; die Zauberei, das Mißgeschick.

hoof [hu:f], 1. *s.* (*pl.* hooves) der Huf, die Klaue, Schale (*of deer*); (*sl.*) der Fuß; *on the –*, lebend (*of animals*). 2. *v.a.* (*sl.*); *– it*, zu Fuß gehen; (*sl.*) *– out*, hinausschmeißen. **–ed,** [–t], *adj.* behuft; *–ed animal*, das Huftier.

hook [huk], 1. *s.* der Haken, die Klammer; der Widerhaken; (Noten)Schwanz (*Mus.*); Seitenschlag (*Box.*); *clothes –*, der Kleiderhaken; *crotchet –*, die Häkelnadel; *fish –*, der Angelhaken; *grappling –*, der Staken; *picture –*, der Bilderhaken; *reaping –*, die Sichel; *–s and eyes*, Haken und Ösen; *by – or by crook*, auf irgendwelche Weise, gleichgültig wie, so oder so; (*sl.*) *on one's own –*, auf eigene Faust; (*sl.*) *go off the –s*, verrückt werden, überschnappen; (*sl.*) *sling* or *take one's –*, sich aus dem Staube machen, durchbrennen. 2. *v.a.* zuhaken (*dress, etc.*), einhaken, festhaken; angeln, fangen (*fish, also fig.*); (*sl.*) klauen, mausen, stibitzen; von der Außenseite schlagen (*ball*) (*Golf*); mit gekrümmtem Arm in die Seite schlagen (*Boxing*); (*sl.*) *– it*, abhauen, auskratzen. 3. *v.n.* (*– on*) sich einhaken *or* festhaken; (*sl.*) *– up*, heiraten. **–ed,** *adj.* krumm, hakenförmig; *–ed nose*, *see* **––nose. ––nose,** *s.* die Hakennase. (*coll.*) **––up,** *s.* der Anschluß, die Ringsendung (*Rad.*); (*fig.*) das Übereinkommen. **–er, s.** kleines Fischerboot, der Huker (*Naut.*).

hookah [ˈhukə], *s.* orientalische Wasserpfeife.

hooligan [ˈhu:lɪgən], *s.* der Straßenlümmel, Radaubruder, Rowdy. **–ism** [–ɪzm], *s.* das Rowdytum.

[1]**hoop** [hu:p], 1. *s.* der Reifen, Ring, das Band; der Reif (*of dress*); *iron –, –iron*, das Bandeisen. 2. *v.a.* binden, mit Reifen belegen (*a cask*). **–ed,** *adj.* gereift; *–ed petticoat*, der Reifrock. **–er,** *s.* der Böttcher, Küfer, Faßbinder.

[2]**hoop,** *see* **whoop.**

hoopoe, hoopoo [ˈhu:pu:], *s.* der Wiedehopf (*Orn.*).

hoot [hu:t], 1. *v.n.* schreien, heulen; tuten, hupen (*Motor.*); *– at*, auspfeifen, auszischen (*a person, etc.*), verspotten (*an idea, etc.*). 2. *s.* das Geschrei, Geheul; Tuten (*Motor.*); (*sl.*) *not care two –s*, sich (*Dat.*) nicht die Bohne daraus machen. **–er,** *s.* die Hupe (*Motor.*); Sirene, Dampfpfeife.

[1]**hop** [hɔp], 1. *s.* (*often pl.*) der Hopfen, Hopfenzapfen. 2. *v.a.* hopfen (*beer*). 3. *v.n.* Hopfen ernten *or* pflücken. **––back,** *s.* der Läuterbottich (*Brew*). **––garden,** *s.* der Hopfengarten. **––grower,** *s.* der Hopfenbauer. **––kiln,** *s.* die Hopfendarre. **–per,** *s.* der Hopfenpflücker. **––pole,** *s.* die Hopfenstange. **––yard,** *s. see* **––garden.**

[2]**hop,** 1. *s.* das Hupfen, der Sprung; (*coll.*) kurze Strecke, die Etappe; (*sl.*) der Tanz, Tanzabend; *– step and jump*, der Dreisprung; (*sl.*) *catch on the –*, erwischen, ertappen; (*sl.*) *keep s.o. on the –*, einem keine (Rast und) Ruh(e) lassen. 2. *v.n.* hüpfen, springen; (*sl.*) tanzen; (*sl.*) *– it*, (*coll.*) *– off*, verschwinden, verduften, sich aus dem Staube machen. 3. *v.a.* springen über. **––o'-my-thumb,** *s.* der Zwerg, Knirps, Däumling. **–per,** *s.* hüpfendes Insekt, die Käsemade; der Fülltrichter, Füllrumpf (*Tech.*). **–scotch,** *s.* Himmel und Hölle, das Hickeln (*game*).

hope [houp], 1. *s.* die Hoffnung, Zuversicht, das Vertrauen (*of*, auf (*Acc.*)); die Wahrscheinlichkeit; *there is no – for him*, für ihn gibt es keine Hoffnung mehr, es ist aus mit ihm; *in the – of*, in der Hoffnung auf; *set one's –s on*, seine Hoffnung setzen auf; *in the – that*, es ist Hoffnung vorhanden daß; *hold out –s to s.o.*, einem Hoffnungen machen; *forlorn –*, see **forlorn**; *past –*, hoffnungslos. 2. *v.a.* & *n.* hoffen (*for*, auf (*Acc.*)); *v.a.* (*Poet.*) erhoffen; *– against –*, hoffen wo nichts (mehr) zu hoffen ist, wenig *or* geringe Hoffnung darauf setzen; *I – not*, das will ich nicht hoffen; *I – so*, das hoffe ich, hoffentlich. **–ful,** 1. *adj.* hoffnungsvoll, zuversichtlich; vielversprechend; *be –ful of*, Hoffnung setzen auf. 2. *s.* (*young –ful*) (*iron.*) vielversprechender Jüngling. **–fulness,** *s.* die Hoffnungsfreudigkeit. **–less,** *adj.* hoffnungslos, aussichtslos, verzweifelt; unverbesserlich. **–lessness,** *s.* die Hoffnungslosigkeit.

horary [ˈhɔ:rərɪ], *adj.* Stunden–, stündlich.

horde [hɔ:d], *s.* die Horde.

horizon [həˈraɪzn], *s.* der Horizont, Gesichtskreis (*also fig.*); die Kimm (*Naut.*); *artificial –*, der Kreiselhorizont; *rational –*, astronomischer Horizont; *sensible –*, scheinbarer Horizont. **–tal** [hɔrɪˈzɔntl], 1. *adj.* waagerecht, horizontal, Horizont–; liegend (*Mach.*); *–tal bar*, das Reck (*Gymn.*); *–tal line*, die Längslinie; *–tal projection*, der Grundriß. 2. *s.* die Waagerechte.

hormone [ˈhɔ:moun], *s.* das Hormon, der Wirkstoff.

horn [hɔ:n], *s.* das Horn (*of beasts, also substance* & *Mus.*); die Hornsubstanz; (*usually pl.*) das Geweih; Fühlhorn (*Ent.*); die Hupe (*Motor.*); der (Schall)-Trichter (*of gramophone, etc.*); das Trinkhorn; (*fig.*) der Flügel, Arm, Vorsprung; (*fig.*) *draw in one's –s*, gelindere Saiten aufziehen; *be on the –s of a dilemma*, sich in einer Zwickmühle *or* verzwickten Lage befinden; *French –*, das Orchesterblashorn; *– of plenty*, das Füllhorn. **–beam,** *s.* die Weißbuche, Hainbuche (*Bot.*). **–bill,** *s.* der Nashornvogel (*Orn.*). **–blende** [ˈhɔ:nblend], *s.* die Hornblende. **–ed** [hɔ:nd], *adj.* gehörnt, Horn–; *–ed cattle*, das Hornvieh; *–ed mine*, die Bleikappenmine. **–et** [ˈhɔ:nɪt], *s.* die Hornisse; *bring a –et's nest about one's ears*, in ein Wespennest stechen. **–less** [ˈhɔ:nlɪs], *adj.* hornlos. **–pipe** [ˈhɔ:npaɪp], *s.* die Hornpfeife; schneller Einzeltanz, der Seemannstanz (*Naut.*). **––rimmed,** *adj.* Horn– (*of spectacles*). **–y** [ˈhɔ:nɪ], *adj.* hornig, hörnern, Horn–, hornartig.

horo–loge [ˈhɔ:rəlɔdʒ], *s.* die Uhr. **–scope** [ˈhɔrəskoup], *s.* das Horoskop; *cast a –scope*, das Horoskop stellen.

horrible [ˈhɔrɪbl], *adj.* entsetzlich, schrecklich, fürchterlich, abscheulich, scheußlich, grausig. **–ness,** *s.* die Entsetzlichkeit, Schrecklichkeit.

horrid [ˈhɔrɪd], *adj.* schrecklich, greulig, eklig, häßlich. **–ness,** *s.* die Schrecklichkeit, Häßlichkeit.

horrif–ic [hɔˈrɪfɪk], *adj.* schreckenerregend,

entsetzlich. **–y** [ˈhɔrɪfaɪ], *v.a.* erschrecken, entsetzen, empören.

horror [ˈhɔrə], *s.* das Entsetzen, Grausen, der Abscheu, Schauder (*of*, vor); Schrecken, Greuel; *–s of war*, die Kriegsgreuel; (*coll.*) *the –s*, das Grauen; *strike a p. with –*, einem Grauen einflößen. **– -stricken, – -struck,** *adj.* von Grausen *or* Grauen erfaßt.

hors d'œuvre [ɔːˈdəːvr], *s.* die Vorspeise.

horse [hɔːs], 1. *s.* das Pferd, Roß, der Gaul, Hengst; (*collect.*) die Reiterei, Kavallerie; das Gestell, der Bock, Ständer; *clothes –*, der Kleiderständer; (*coll.*) *a dark –*, unbeschriebenes Blatt; *flog a dead –*, offene Türen einrennen; *not look a gift – in the mouth*, einem geschenkten Gaul nicht ins Maul sehen; *get on one's high –*, sich aufs hohe Roß setzen; *lead –*, das Handpferd; *light –*, leichte Kavallerie; *pack –*, das Saumpferd; *saddle –*, das Reitpferd; *towel –*, der Handtuchständer; *vaulting –*, das Pferd (*Gymn.*); *wild –s will not . . .*, nicht vier Pferde werden . . ., keine Kraft der Welt wird . . .; *back the wrong –*, auf die falsche Karte setzen; *give a – its head*, einem Pferde die Zügel schießen lassen; (*sl.*) *hold your –s!* nicht so rasch! *work like a –*, tüchtig *or* mächtig arbeiten; *as strong as a –*, stark wie ein Gaul; *put the cart before the –*, das Pferd beim Schwanze aufzäumen, eine S. verkehrt anfangen, angehen *or* anpacken; *straight from the –'s mouth*, aus bester Quelle; *master of the –*, der Stallmeister; *to –!* zu Pferde! aufgesessen! aufsitzen! *sound to –*, zum Aufsitzen blasen; *take –*, reiten, sich zu Pferde setzen, aufsitzen. 2. *v.a.* mit Pferd(en) versehen; bespannen (*vehicle*); auf dem Rücken tragen; belegen, beschälen (*a mare*). **– -artillery,** *s.* reitende Artillerie. **–back,** *s.*; *on –back*, zu Pferde, beritten; *be* or *go on –back*, reiten. **– -bean,** *s.* die Saubohne. **– -block,** *s.* der Aufsteigeblock. **– -box,** *s.* der Pferde(transport)-wagen. **– -breaker,** *s.* der Bereiter, Zureiter. **– -breeding,** *s.* die Pferdezucht. **– -brush,** *s.* die Kardätsche. **– -chestnut,** *s.* die Roßkastanie (*Bot.*). **– -cloth,** *s.* die Pferdedecke. **– -collar,** *s.* das Kumt, Kummet. **– -coper,** *s.*, **– -dealer,** *s.* der Pferdehändler. (*coll.*) **– -doctor,** *s.* der Roßarzt. **– -drawn,** *adj.* bespannt, Bespannungs–, Fahr–; *– -drawn traffic*, Pferdefuhrwerke (*pl.*). **– -droppings,** *pl.* der Pferdemist, Pferdepillen (*pl.*). **– -flesh,** *s.* das Pferdefleisch; (*collect.*, *sl.*) Pferde (*pl.*). **– -fly,** *s.* die Pferdebremse (*Ent.*). **– -guards,** *pl.* englisches Gardekavallerieregiment. **–hair,** *s.* das Roßhaar, Schweifhaar. **– -laugh,** *s.* wieherndes Gelächter. **– -leech,** *s.* der Pferdeegel (*Zool.*). **–man,** *s.* der Reiter. **–manship,** *s.* die Reitkunst. **– -play,** *s.* derber Scherz, die Rauferei. **– -pond,** *s.* die Pferdeschwemme. **– -power,** *s.* die Pferdestärke, Pferdekraft (*Tech.*). **– -race,** *s.*, **– -racing,** *s.* das Pferderennen. **– -radish,** *s.* der Meerettich (*Bot.*). (*coll.*) **– sense,** gesunder Menschenverstand. **–shoe,** *s.* das Hufeisen. **– -show,** *s.* die Pferdeschau. **–tail,** *s.* der Pferdeschwanz; Schachtelhalm (*Bot.*). **–whip,** 1. *s.* die Reitgerte. 2. *v.a.* mit der Reitgerte schlagen. **–woman,** *s.* die Reiterin.

hors–iness [ˈhɔːsɪnɪs], *s.* der Stallgeruch; die Pferdeliebhaberei. **–y** [ˈhɔːsɪ], *adj.* pferdeliebend, Rennsport liebend; jockeymäßig, stallknechtmäßig; nach dem Stall riechend.

hortat–ive [ˈhɔrtətɪv], **–ory** [–tətərɪ], *adj.* ermahnend, Ermahnungs–.

horticultur–al [hɔːtɪˈkʌltʃərəl], *adj.* Gartenbau–. **–e** [ˈhɔːtɪkʌltʃə], *s.* der Gartenbau, die Gartenkunst. **–ist** [–rɪst], *s.* der Garten(bau)künstler.

hosanna [houˈzænə], *s.* das Hosianna.

hose [houz], 1. *s.* (*collect.*) (*pl. constr.*) (lange) Strümpfe (*pl.*); (*archaic*) das Beinkleid, die Strumpfhose; (pl. *–s*) der Schlauch; *garden –*, der Gartenschlauch. 2. *v.a.* mit einem Schlauch bespritzen. **–pipe,** *s.* die Schlauchleitung.

hosier [ˈhouʒjə], *s.* der Strumpfwarenhändler. **–y** [–rɪ], *s.* die Strumpfwaren, Wirkwaren, Strickwaren, Trikotwaren (*pl.*).

hospice [ˈhɔspɪs], *s.* die Herberge, das Hospiz.

hospitable [ˈhɔspɪtəbl], *adj.* gastlich, gastfreundlich (*to*, gegen), gastfrei (*as a house*).

hospital [ˈhɔspɪtəl], *s.* das Krankenhaus, Hospital, Spital, die Klinik, das Lazarett; (*archaic*) wohltätige Stiftung; *she is in –*, sie liegt im Krankenhaus; *walk the –s*, klinische Ausbildung durchmachen; *– fever*, der Flecktyphus; *– nurse*, die (Kranken)-Schwester, Krankenpflegerin; *– orderly*, der Sanitäter (*Mil.*); *– ship*, das Lazarettschiff; *– Sunday*, der Sonntag für Krankenhauskollekte; *– train*, der Lazarettzug. **–(l)er,** *s.* der Johanniterritter, Barmherziger Bruder.

hospitality [hɔspɪˈtælɪtɪ], *s.* die Gastfreiheit, Gastfreundschaft, Gastlichkeit.

[1]**host** [houst], *s.* der Wirt, Gastwirt; Gastgeber, Hausherr; die Wirtspflanze (*Biol.*, *Bot.*); *reckon without one's –*, die Rechnung ohne den Wirt machen.

[2]**host,** *s.* (*poet.*) das Heer, die Schar; (*coll.*) große Menge, die Unmenge, Unzahl; *Lord of –s*, der Herr der (himmlischen) Heerscharen; *– of questions*, eine Unmenge Fragen; *he is a – in himself*, er kann soviel wie hundert andere.

[3]**host,** *s.* die Hostie (*R.C.*).

hostage [ˈhɔstɪdʒ], *s.* der *or* die Geisel; (*fig.*) das Pfand; *give –s to fortune*, sich Gefahren aussetzen.

hostel [ˈhɔstəl], *s.* die Herberge; *students' –*, das Studentenheim. **–ry,** *s.* (*archaic*) das Gasthaus.

hostess [ˈhoustɪs], *s.* die Wirtin, Gastgeberin.

hostil–e [ˈhɔstaɪl], *adj.* feindlich; feindselig (*to*, gegen); abgeneigt, abhold (*to* (*Dat.*)). **–ity,** [hɔsˈtɪlɪtɪ], *s.* die Feindschaft, Feindseligkeit (*to*, gegen); (*fig.*) der Gegensatz. **–ities,** *pl.* Feindseligkeiten (*pl.*), der Krieg.

hostler [ˈɔslə], *s. see* **ostler.**

hot [hɔt], *adj.* heiß; (*fig.*) hitzig, feurig, eifrig (*of persons*); (*fig.*) heftig, erbittert (*of things*); (*coll.*) geil, lüstern (*of persons*); (*coll.*) verfänglich, schlüpfrig, gestohlen, geschmuggelt (*of things*); beißend, scharf, gewürzt (*of spices*); (*a*) (*with nouns*) *– air*, die Heißluft; (*sl.*) leeres Geschwätz, blauer Dunst; *– bills*, kürzlich emittierte Papiere (*C.L.*); *go like – cakes*, wie warme Semmeln abgehen; *– fight*, heißes *or* heftiges Gefecht; *– scent*, starke Spur (*Hunt.*); *– shot*, glänzender Schuß; (*sl.*) *– stuff*, großartige Sache; forscher Kerl (*also of a girl*); *– water*, das Heißwasser; (*coll.*) *get into – water*, sich in die Patsche setzen, in eine Klemme kommen; *there is – work there*, da geht es heiß her; *– jazz*, die Jazzmusik, Swingmusik; (*b*) (*with verbs*) *get –* (*under the collar*), sich ereifern, erregt werden (*about* or *over*, über); *it got too – for him*, ihm wurde der Boden unter den Füßen zu heiß; (*coll.*) *give it s.o. –*, einen tüchtig verdreschen; (*coll.*) *make it – for s.o.*, einem den Boden zu heiß machen. **–bed,** *s.* das Mistbeet; (*fig.*) die Brutstätte. **–blooded,** *adj.* heißblütig, leidenschaftlich, hitzig. **– -foot,** *adv.* schnellen Schrittes, eiligst. **–head,** *s.* der Hitzkopf. **– -headed,** *adj.* hitzköpfig, ungestüm, unbesonnen. **–house,** *s.* das Treibhaus, (*fig.*) die Brutstätte. **–ly,** *adv.* heiß; hitzig, erregt. **–ness,** *s.* die Hitze; Hitzigkeit, Schärfe (*of spices*). **– -plate,** *s.* die Heißplatte. **– -pot,** *s.* das Eintopfgericht. **– -press,** 1. *s.* die Heißpresse. 2. *v.a.* heiß pressen *or* plätten, dekatieren. **–spur,** *s.* (*archaic*) der Heißsporn, Hitzkopf. **– -short,** *adj.* rotbrüchig (*Metall.*). **– -tempered,** *adj.* heftig, hitzig. **– -water,** *adj.*; *– -water bottle*, die Wärmflasche.

hotchpotch [ˈhɔtʃpɔtʃ], *s.* der Mischmasch; die Gemüsesuppe (*Cook.*).

hotel [houˈtɛl], *s.* das Hotel, der Gasthof, die Gaststätte; *– register*, das Fremdenbuch.

hough [hɔk], *s. see* [1]**hock.**

hound [haund], 1. *s.* der Jagdhund, Spürhund, Hetzhund; Rüde; *follow the –s*, *ride to –s*, an der Parforcejagd teilnehmen. 2. *v.a.* (*usually fig.*) jagen; hetzen (*on*, auf (*Acc.*)). **–s.** *pl.* Backen am Mast (*Naut.*).

hour [auə], *s.* die Stunde; *the –s*, die Horen (*Myth.*), das Stundengebet, Offizium (*R.C.*); (*a*) (*time*) *– after –*, stundenlang; *by the –*, stundenlang, stundenweise; *for –s*, stundenlang; *half an –*, eine halbe Stunde; *a quarter of an –*, eine Viertelstunde; *three-quarters of an –*, dreiviertel Stunde(n); *the question of the –*, die Frage des gegenwärtigen Augenblicks; (*b*) (*with adjectives*) *keep early –s*, früh zu Bett gehen; *at the eleventh* –, in letzter Stunde, im letzten Augenblick; – *flown*, die Flugstunde; *keep late* –*s*, nachts lange aufbleiben; *the last* –, die Todesstunde; *keep regular* –*s*, ein ordentliches Leben führen; *the small* –*s* (*of the night*), frühe Morgenstunden, die Stunden nach Mitternacht; *till the small* –*s*, bis nach Mitternacht; *working* –*s*, Dienststunden (*pl.*), die Arbeitszeit. **--glass,** *s.* das Stundenglas, die Sanduhr. **--hand,** *s.* der Stundenzeiger. **–ly,** *adj.* & *adv.* stündlich; –*ly wage*, der Stundenlohn.

houri ['hʊərɪ], *s.* die Huri.

house [haʊs], **1.** *s.* das Haus (*also Astrol.*); die Wohnung; der Haushalt; (*fig.*) das Geschlecht, die Fürstenfamilie; das Geschäftshaus, Handelshaus, die Firma (*C.L.*); das Parlament, Abgeordnetenhaus, die Kammer (*Parl.*); das College (*Univ.*), Pensionshaus (*school*); (*coll.*) Publikum, Zuhörer (*pl.*), Zuschauer (*pl.*) (*Theat.*); (*a*) (*with nouns*) – *of call*, die Herberge; – *of cards*, das Kartenhaus (*also fig.*); – *of Commons*, das Unterhaus; – *of correction*, die Besserungsanstalt; – *of God*, das Gotteshaus; – *and home*, Haus und Hof; *neither* – *nor home*, weder Dach noch Fach; – *of ill fame*, das Bordell; – *of Lords*, das Oberhaus; – *of mourning*, das Trauerhaus; – *of revenge*, das Rettungshaus, die Besserungsanstalt; – *of Representatives*, das Repräsentantenhaus (*Amer.*); (*b*) (*with verbs, adjectives, & prepositions*) *bring down the* –, stürmischen Beifall finden, das Publikum hinreißen; *constitute a* –, eine beschlußfähige Anzahl Mitglieder aufweisen (*Parl.*); *enter the* –, Mitglied des Parlaments werden; *keep* –, haushalten, den Haushalt führen (*for s.o.*, einem); *keep the* –, das Haus hüten; *keep open* –, offene Tafel halten; (*Prov.*) *my* – *is my castle*, mein Haus ist meine Burg; (*coll.*) *like a* – *on fire*, glänzend; –*-to-– fighting*, der Häuserkampf; –*-to-– search*, die Haussuchung. **2.** *v.a.* [houz], unterbringen, beherbergen; unter Dach (und Fach) *or* in Sicherheit bringen; befestigen (*Naut.*); aufnehmen, empfangen (*as buildings*). **3.** *v.n.* hausen, wohnen. **--agent,** *s.* der Hausmakler, Häusermakler. **--boat,** *s.* das Wohnboot, Hausboot. **--breaker,** *s.* der Einbrecher. **--breaking,** *s.* der Einbruch. **--flag,** *s.* die Reedereiflagge. **--fly,** *s.* die Stubenfliege. **–ful,** *s.* das Hausvoll. **–hold,** 1. *s.* der Haushalt, die Familie; *Royal* –*hold*, die Hofhaltung. 2. *adj.* häuslich, Haus–, Familien–; –*hold bread*, gewöhnliches Brot; –*hold expenses*, Haushaltungskosten. –*hold gods*, die Hausgötter, Penaten; –*hold jam*, billige Marmelade; –*hold linen*, das Weißzeug; –*hold medicine*, die Hausarznei; –*hold soap*, die Haushaltseife; –*hold troops*, Gardetruppen; –*hold washing*, die Hauswäsche; –*hold words*, Alltagsworte, geflügelte Worte. **–holder,** *s.* der Haushaltvorstand, Hausherr, Hausvater. **–keeper,** *s.* die Haushälterin, Wirtschafterin, Hausfrau. **–keeping,** 1. *adj.* Haushaltungs–; –*keeping money*, das Haushaltsgeld, Wirtschaftsgeld. 2. *s.* das Haushalten, Wirtschaften. **--leek,** *s.* die Hauswurz, Dachwurz (*Bot.*). **–maid,** *s.* das Hausmädchen, Stubenmädchen; –*maid's knee*, die Kniescheibenentzündung. **--master,** *s.* der Leiter eines Pensionshauses (*school*). **--painter,** *s.* der Anstreicher. **--party,** *s.* der Logierbesuch im Landhaus. **--physician,** *s.* der Anstaltsarzt der medizinischen Abteilung. **--porter,** *s.* der Hausmann, Pförtner. **--rent,** *s.* die Hausmiete, der Hauszins. **--room,** *s.*; *give* –*-room to*, ins Haus nehmen, Platz *or* Raum machen für. **--surgeon,** *s.* der Anstaltsarzt der Chirurgie. **–top,** *s.*; *proclaim from the* –*tops*, öffentlich verkündigen. **--trained,** *adj.* stubenrein. **--warming,** *s.* die Einzugsfeier. **–wife** ['haʊswaɪf], *s.* die Hausfrau, Wirtschafterin; ['hʌzɪf] der Nähbeutel, das Nähzeug. **–wifely,** *adj.* hausfraulich.

housing ['haʊzɪŋ], 1. *pr.p.* & *adj. see* **house** 2; – *estate*, die Siedlung; – *problem*, die Wohnungsfrage; – *shortage*, die Wohnungsnot. 2. *s.* die Wohnung, Wohngelegenheit, Unterkunft, Unterbringung, Behausung, Wohnbeschaffung; Lagerung, das Lagern; Lagergeld, die Lagermiete (*C.L.*); die Hüsung (*Naut.*); das Gerüst, Gehäuse (*Tech.*); die Schabracke, Satteldecke.

hove [houv], *see* **heave;** *the ship was* or *lay* – *to*, das Schiff wurde beigedreht *or* beigelegt.

hovel ['hɔvəl], *s.* der Schuppen, elende Hütte.

hoveller ['hɔvələ], *s.* der Berger (*of wrecks*).

hover ['hɔvə], *v.n.* (in der Luft) schweben; (*fig.*) schwanken, zögern; – *about* or *round*, schweben; (*fig.*) sich herumtreiben.

how [haʊ], *adv.* wie, auf welche Weise, in welcher Art; – *do you do?* guten Tag; – *are you?* wie geht es Ihnen? – *is your mother today?* wie steht es heute mit Ihrer Mutter? – *is* or *comes it that?* (*Amer. coll.* – *come?*), wie kommt es, daß; *it depends on* –, es hängt davon ab, wie; *do it* – *you can*, mach es so gut du kannst; (*sl.*) *all you know* –, so gut du kannst; – *like him!* das sieht ihm ähnlich! (*coll.*) – *now?* wie geht's? – *many*, wieviel, wie viele; – *much is it?* wieviel (*or coll.* was) kostet es? wieviel macht es? *know* – *to do*, tun können, wissen wie es zu machen ist; *he does not know* – *to say it*, er weiß nicht, wie er es sagen soll. **–beit,** 1. *adv.* (*archaic*) nichtsdestoweniger, wie dem auch sei. 2. *conj.*; (*B.*) –*beit* (*that*), wenngleich. **--d'ye-do,** *s.* (*coll.*) die Patsche, verflixte Lage, schöne Bescherung. **–ever,** 1. *adv.* wie auch immer; *all mistakes* –*ever small*, alle noch so kleinen Fehler; –*ever it may be*, wie dem auch sei; –*ever he may try*, und wenn er es auch noch so sehr versucht *or* soviel er es auch versuchen mag. 2. *conj.* doch, jedoch, dennoch, gleichwohl. **–soever,** *adv.* wie . . . auch immer.

howdah ['haʊdə], *s.* der Sitz auf Elefanten.

howitzer ['haʊɪtsə], *s.* die Haubitze.

howl [haʊl], 1. *v.n.* heulen, brüllen, schreien; laut klagen; (*coll.*) weinen; pfeifen, summen (*Rad.*); – (*s.o.*) *down*, (einen) niederschreien. 2. *s.* das Geheul; Pfeifen (*Rad.*). **–er,** *s.* (*coll.*) grober Schnitzer; *schoolboys'* –*ers*, Schülerweisheiten. **–ing,** *adj.* heulend; (*sl.*) entsetzlich, fürchterlich, gewaltig.

[1]**hoy** [hɔɪ], *s.* das Lichterschiff (*Naut.*).

[2]**hoy,** *int.* holla! hallo! he!; ahoi! (*Naut.*).

hoyden ['hɔɪdən], *s.* ausgelassenes Mädchen.

hub [hʌb], *s.* die Nabe (*of a wheel*); (*fig.*) der Angelpunkt, Mittelpunkt.

hubbub ['hʌbʌb], *s.* der Lärm, das Getöse; der Wirrwarr.

hubby ['hʌbɪ], *s.* (*coll.*) *see* **husband.**

huckaback ['hʌkəbæk], *s.* der Drell.

huckle ['hʌkl], *s.* die Hüfte. **–berry** ['hʌklbərɪ], *s.* amerikanische Heidelbeere (*Bot.*). **--bone,** *s.* der Hüftknochen; Fußknöchel, das Sprungbein.

huckster ['hʌkstə], 1. *s.* der Höker, Krämer. 2. *v.n.* hökern, schachern.

huddle ['hʌdl], 1. *v.n.* sich (zusammen)drängen; – *together*, sich zusammenkauern; – *up*, sich schmiegen (*to*, an). 2. *v.a.* unordentlich durcheinanderwerfen. 3. *s.* (*coll.*) *go into a* –, die Köpfe zusammenstecken.

[1]**hue** [hjʊ:], *s.* die Farbe, Färbung, der (Farb)Ton, das Kolorit. **–d,** *adj.* gefärbt.

[2]**hue,** *s.* (only in) – *and cry*, das Zetergeschrei; (*fig.*) die Hetze; *raise a* – *and cry*, Zeter und Mordio *or* Zetergeschrei erheben (*about*, gegen), mit lautem Geschrei verfolgen (*after a p.*, (*Acc.*)); einen Steckbrief erlassen (*after a p.*, hinter einem).

huff [hʌf], 1. *s.* (*coll.*) der Ärger, die Mißstimmung; *be in a* –, gekränkt sein, sich beleidigt fühlen. 2. *v.a.* anfahren; scharf anfassen, beleidigen; blasen, pusten (*Draughts*). 3. *v.n.* sich beleidigt fühlen. **–iness,** *s. see* **–ishness. –ish,** *adj.* übelnehmerisch, beleidigt; anmaßend, aufgeblasen. **–ishness,** *s.* das Übelnehmen; die Anmaßung, Aufgeblasenheit. **–y,** *adj. see* **–ish.**

hug [hʌg], 1. *v.a.* umarmen, liebkosen; festhalten an; – *o.s.*, sich schmeicheln; – *the wind* (*coast*), dicht an den Wind (die Küste) halten. 2. *s.* die Umarmung; der Griff (*in wrestling*).

huge [hjʊ:dʒ], *adj.* sehr groß, riesig, ungeheuer. **–ly,** *adv.* gewaltig. **–ness,** *s.* ungeheure Größe.

hugger-mugger ['hʌgəmʌgə], *adv.* unordentlich; insgeheim, verstohlen.

hulk [hʌlk], *s.* der Rumpf, der *or* die Hulk *or* Holk (*Naut.*); der Klumpen, Klotz, schwerfällige Masse; schwerfälliger Mensch. **–ing,** *adj.* schwerfällig, ungeschlacht, plump (*of persons*).

hull [hʌl], 1. *s.* die Hülse, Schale (*Bot.*); der Rumpf (*Naut.*, *Av.*); – *down*, weit entfernt, gerade sichtbar (*Naut.*); in Rampenstellung (*of tanks*) (*Mil.*). 2. *v.a.* schälen, enthülsen; den Schiffsrumpf treffen *or* durchschießen.
hullabaloo [hʌləbəˈlʊː], *s.* (*coll.*) der Lärm, Tumult, das Geschrei, der Klamauk.
hullo [hʌˈloʊ], *int.* hallo!
hum [hʌm], 1. *v.n.* summen, brummen; murmeln; – *and haw*, in der Rede stocken, verlegen stottern; – *and haw about a th.*, mit der Sprache nicht herausrücken, nicht anbeißen wollen; (*sl.*) *make things* –, die S. in Schwung bringen, etwas kräftig anfassen. 2. *v.a.* summen (*a tune*). 3. *s.* das Summen, Brummen, Dröhnen, Gebrumme, Gesumme (*of insects, etc.*); Gemurmel (*of conversation*); *mains* –, der Netzbrumm (*Rad.*); – *eliminator*, das Netzfilter (*Rad.*). 4. *int.* hm!
human [ˈhjʊːmən], 1. *adj.* menschlich, Menschen–; – *nature*, die Menschheit; menschliche Natur, die Menschlichkeit; –*ly possible*, menschenmöglich; –*ly speaking*, nach menschlichem Ermessen. 2. *s.* (*coll.*) der Mensch. **–e** [hjʊːˈmeɪn], *adj.* menschenfreundlich, wohlwollend, human; humanistisch; –*e learning*, humanistische Bildung; –*e society*, die Lebensrettungsgesellschaft. **–ism** [ˈhjʊːmənɪzm], *s.* der Humanismus; die Menschlichkeit. **–ist** [–nɪst], *s.* der Humanist. **–istic** [–ˈnɪstɪk], *adj.* humanistisch. **–itarian** [hjʊːmænɪˈtɛərɪən], 1. *s.* der Menschenfreund. 2. *adj.* menschenfreundlich, menschenbeglückend. **–ities** [–ˈmænɪtɪz], *pl.* klassische Philologie; *modern –ities*, neuere Sprachen und Literatur. **–ity** [–ˈmænɪtɪ], *s.* menschliche Natur, die Menschheit, das Menschengeschlecht, Menschen (*pl.*); die Menschlichkeit, Menschenliebe, menschliches Gefühl; lateinische Philologie (*Scots*). **–ization** [–mənaɪˈzeɪʃən], *s.* die Vermenschlichung. **–ize** [ˈhjʊːmənɑɪz], *v.a.* vermenschlichen; gesittet machen, (sich *or* einen) als Menschen vorstellen. **–kind,** *s.* das Menschengeschlecht.
humble [ˈhʌmbl], 1. *adj.* bescheiden, demütig, anspruchslos; niedrig, gering, ärmlich, dürftig; *eat* – *pie*, Abbitte tun, zu Kreuze kriechen, sich erniedrigen; *my* – *self*, meine Wenigkeit; *your* – *servant*, Ihr ergebener. 2. *v.a.* erniedrigen, demütigen. **––bee,** *s.* die Hummel (*Ent.*). **–ness,** *s.* die Niedrigkeit (*of birth, etc.*); Demut.
humbug [ˈhʌmbʌg], 1. *s.* (*coll.*) der Schwindel, Betrug, Humbug, die Täuschung; der Unsinn, Quatsch, Mumpitz; Schwindler, Aufschneider, Schaumschläger. 2. *v.a.* beschwindeln, zum besten haben, foppen; – *s.o. out of s.th.*, einen um etwas bringen *or* betrügen.
humdrum [ˈhʌmdrʌm], *adj.* alltäglich, langweilig, eintönig, fade.
humer–al [ˈhjʊːmərəl], *adj.* Schulter– (*Anat.*). **–us** [ˈhjʊːmərəs], *s.* das Oberarmbein.
humid [ˈhjʊːmɪd], *adj.* feucht, naß. **–ify,** *v.a.* anfeuchten, befeuchten, benetzen. **–ity** [–ˈmɪdɪtɪ], *s.* die Feuchtigkeit, der Feuchtigkeitsgehalt.
humil–iate [hjʊːˈmɪlɪeɪt], *v.a.* erniedrigen, demütigen. **–iating,** *adj.* demütigend, kränkend. **–iation** [–ˈeɪʃən], *s.* die Demütigung, Erniedrigung. **–ity** [–ˈmɪlɪtɪ], *s.* die Demut, Bescheidenheit.
humming [ˈhʌmɪŋ], 1. *adj.* summend, brummend, Brumm–; (*coll.*) lebhaft, kräftig, gewaltig. 2. *s.* das Summen, Brummen. **––bird,** *s.* der Kolibri. **––top,** *s.* der Brummkreisel.
hummock [ˈhʌmək], *s.* kleiner Hügel.
humoral [ˈhjʊːmərəl], *adj.* humoral, Humoral– (*Anat.*).
humor–esque [hjʊːməˈrɛsk], *s.* die Humoreske. **–ist** [ˈhjʊːmərɪst], *s.* der Humorist; (*coll.*) der Spaßvogel. **–ous** [ˈhjʊːmərəs], *adj.* humorvoll, humoristisch; launig, spaßhaft, komisch. **–ousness,** *s.* die Spaßhaftigkeit, der Humor.
humour [ˈhjʊːmə], 1. *s.* das Temperament, die Gemütsart; Stimmung, Laune, Grille; der Humor, Scherz, Spaß; (*archaic*) der (Körper)Saft, die Flüssigkeit; *in the – for*, aufgelegt zu; *in a good* (*bad*) –, gut (schlecht) aufgelegt *or* gelaunt, bei guter (schlechter) Laune; *out of* –, verstimmt, schlecht aufgelegt, mißgelaunt. 2. willfahren (*Dat.*), gewähren lassen (*Acc.*), den Willen tun (*Dat.*). **–less,** *adj.* humorlos. **–some,** *adj.* launisch.
hump [hʌmp], 1. *s.* der Höcker, Buckel; (*coll.*) üble Laune, der Ärger; (*coll.*) *have the* –, verdrießlich sein, üble Laune haben; (*coll.*) *give s.o. the* –, einem üble Laune bereiten. 2. *v.a.* krümmen, buckelig machen; (*coll.*) auf den Rücken nehmen, auf dem Rücken tragen. **–back,** *s.* der Buck(e)lige. **–backed,** *adj.* buck(e)lig, höckerig (*of persons*). **–ed,** *adj.* buckelig (*of things*). **–y,** *adj. see* **–ed;** holperig (*road*), (*coll.*) *see* **–backed.**
humph [hʌmf], *int.* hm!
humpty-dumpty [ˈhʌm(p)tɪˈdʌm(p)tɪ], *s,* kleine dicke Person, (*coll.*) der Stöpsel.
humus [ˈhjʊːməs], *s.* der Humus.
hunch [hʌntʃ], 1. *s. see* **hump;** (*sl.*) das Vorgefühl, die Ahnung, der Animus. 2. *v.a.* krümmen; –*ed up*, hockend, kauernd. **–back,** *etc.*, *see* **humpback,** *etc.*
hundred [ˈhʌndrəd], 1. *num. adj.* hundert; *a* – *people*, hundert Leute; *several* – *men*, mehrere hundert Mann. 2. *s.* das Hundert; der Bezirk, die Hundertschaft (*Hist.*); *by the* –, hundertweise, zu Hunderten; *several* –, mehrere hundert; –*s and* –*s*, Hundert und aber Hunderte; *a* – *per cent*, hundertprozentig; –*s and thousands*, Zuckerkügelchen (*Conf.*). **–fold,** *adj.* hundertfältig, hundertfach. **–th,** 1. *num. adj.* hundertst. 2. *s.* der, die, das Hundertste (*ordinal*), das Hundertstel (*fraction*). **–weight,** *s.* (englischer) Zentner (*Engl. 112 lb.*; *Amer. 100 lb.*); *metrical –weight*, deutscher Zentner.
hung [hʌŋ], *see* **hang;** – *beef*, das Rauchfleisch.
hung–er [ˈhʌŋgə], 1. *s.* der Hunger; (*fig.*) das Verlangen (*for* or *after*, nach); (*Prov.*) –*er is the best sauce*, Hunger ist der beste Koch. 2. *v.n.* hungern; –*er after*, verlangen, sich sehnen *or* dürsten nach. **–er-strike,** *s.* der Hungerstreik. **–ry,** *adj.* hungrig; (*fig.*) verlangend, begierig, dürstend (*for*, nach); unfruchtbar, unergiebig (*as soil*); *be –ry*, Hunger haben; *go –ry*, hungern, verhungern; –*ry Forties*, die Hungerjahre 1840–50.
hunk [hʌŋk], *s.* (*coll.*) dickes Stück.
hunt [hʌnt], 1. *v.a.* jagen, hetzen; nachsetzen (*Dat.*), verfolgen (*a p.*), absuchen (*territory, also fig.*); zur Jagd gebrauchen (*dogs, etc. for hunting*); – *down*, zu Tode hetzen; (*fig.*) zu fassen suchen; – *out* or *up*, ausspüren, aufstöbern. 2. *v.n.* jagen, Jagd machen (*for* or *after*, auf (*Acc.*)); (*fig.*) forschen (*for*, nach), (*coll.*) suchen; oszillieren (*Tech.*). 3. *s.* die Jagd, Hetzjagd (*for foxes, etc.*); das Jagen, die Verfolgung; das Suchen; die Jagdgesellschaft; das Jagdrevier; *the – is up*, die Jagd hat begonnen; *on the – for*, auf der Jagd nach. **–er,** *s.* der Jäger; das Jagdpferd; der Jagdhund; die Doppelkapseluhr (*Horol.*). **–ing,** *s.* das Jagen, die Jägerei; (*poet.*) das Weidwerk. **–ing-box,** *s.* der Jagdsitz, das Jagdhäuschen. **–ing-crop,** *s.* die Jagdpeitsche. **–ing-ground,** *s.* das Jagdrevier. **–ing-horn,** *s.* das Jagdhorn, Jägerhorn. **–ing-lodge,** *s. see* **–ing-box. –ress,** *s.* die Jägerin. **–sman,** *s.* der Jäger, Weidmann. **––the-slipper,** *s.* die Pantoffeljagd.
hurdle [ˈhəːdl], 1. *s.* die Hürde, das Hindernis aus Reisig; die Faschine, der Schanzkorb (*Fort.*). 2. *v.a.* mit Hürden einschließen. 3. *v.n.* über ein Hindernis springen; ein Hürdenrennen machen. **–r,** *s.* der Hürdenläufer. **––race,** *s.*, **–s,** *pl.* das Hürdenrennen.
hurdy-gurdy [ˈhəːdɪgəːdɪ], *s.* die Drehleier, der Leierkasten.
hurl [həːl], 1. *v.a.* werfen, schleudern; (*fig.*) ausstoßen, kräftig äußern (*at*, gegen); – *defiance at a p.*, einem den Fehdehandschuh hinwerfen. 2. *s.* das Schleudern. **–ing,** *s.* das Schleudern; irisches Hockeyspiel.
hurly-burly [ˈhəːlɪbəːlɪ], *s.* der Tumult, Wirrwarr, das Getümmel.
hurra(h) [hʊˈrɑː], 1. *int.* hurra!; – *for*, es lebe. 2. *s.* der Hurraruf.
hurricane [ˈhʌrɪkən], *s.* der Orkan, Sturm, die Windsbraut. **––deck,** *s.* das Oberdeck, Sturmdeck. **––lamp,** *s.* die Sturmlaterne.
hurr–ied [ˈhʌrɪd], *adj.* eilig, schnell; übereilt, flüchtig. **–y** [ˈhʌrɪ], 1. *v.a.* zur Eile (an)treiben *or* drängen, beschleunigen; eilig verrichten, übereilen,

überstürzen; *–y along*, *–y away*, forteilen, eiligst wegbringen; *–y in* (*to*), hineinbefördern, eilig hineinbringen; *–y on*, (an)treiben, drängen; (*coll.*) *–y* (*a p.*) *up*, (einen) antreiben; *–y* (*a th.*) *up*, (etwas) beschleunigen. 2. *v.n.* eilen, sich beeilen, hasten; *–y away*, davoneilen, forteilen; *–y back*, zurückeilen; *–y in*, eilig hereinkommen; *–y off*, see *–y away*; *–y on*, sich eilig weiterbewegen; *–y on to*, zueilen (*Dat.*); *–y over*, eilig *or* flüchtig hinweggehen über, schnell erledigen; (*coll.*) *–y up*, sich beeilen. 3. *s.* große Eile, die Hast; Übereilung; das Drängen; der Drang, Tumult, die Unruhe; *there is no –y*, es hat keine Eile; *be in a –y*, Eile *or* es eilig haben; *in the –y of business*, im Drange der Geschäfte; (*coll.*) *that won't happen in a –y*, das wird nicht so leicht *or* bald geschehen.

hurst [hə:st], *s.* das Gehölz, der Hain.

hurt [hə:t], 1. *ir.v.a.* verletzen, verwunden; wehe tun (*Dat.*); schaden (*Dat.*), Schaden zufügen (*Dat.*); beschädigen; kränken; *feel –*, sich gekränkt fühlen; *not – a hair of s.o.'s head*, einem kein Haar krümmen; *– s.o.'s feelings*, jemandes Gefühle verletzen; *be – at*, sich verletzt fühlen von *or* wegen. 2. *ir.v.n.* wehe tun, schmerzen; (*coll.*) zu Schaden kommen; (*coll.*) *that won't –*, das tut nichts. 3. *s.* die Verletzung, Verwundung; der Schaden, Nachteil. **–er**, *s.* der Stoßring (*Tech.*). **–ful**, *adj.* schädlich, nachteilig, verderblich (*to*, für). **–fulness**, *s.* die Schädlichkeit.

hurtle [hə:tl], *v.n.* (an)stoßen, (an)prallen; sausen, stürzen, prasseln, rasseln (*against*, auf).

husband [ˈhʌzbənd], 1. *s.* der Ehemann, Mann, Gatte, Gemahl; *ship's –*, der Schiffsagent. 2. *v.a.* haushälterisch *or* sparsam umgehen mit, haushalten mit, sparen. **–less**, *adj.* gattenlos. **–man**, *s.* der Landmann, Landwirt. **–ry** [–drɪ], *s.* der Ackerbau, die Landwirtschaft; *animal –ry*, die Tierzucht.

hush [hʌʃ], 1. *int.* still, pst! 2. *s.* die Stille; (*fig.*) Flaute. 3. *v.a.* zum Schweigen bringen; stillen, zur Ruhe bringen, beruhigen, beschwichtigen; *– up*, verschweigen, vertuschen. 4. *v.n.* still sein *or* werden. **–aby** [ˈhʌʃəbaɪ], *int.* still, still! **–ed** [–t], *adj.* still, lautlos. (*coll.*) **– – –**, *pred. & attrib. adj.* geheimtuerisch, heimlich, Geheim–. **– –money**, *s.* das Schweigegeld.

husk [hʌsk], 1. *s.* die Hülse, Schale, Schote; (*fig.*) äußere Form. 2. *v.a.* enthülsen.

husk–iness [ˈhʌskɪnɪs], *s.* die Rauheit, Heiserkeit. **–y** [ˈhʌskɪ], 1. *adj.* hülsig, schalig; rauh, heiser; (*coll.*) kräftig, stark. 2. *s.* der Eskimo; Eskimohund; die Eskimosprache; (*coll.*) der Kraftmeier.

hussar [hʊˈzɑ:], *s.* der Husar.

hussy [ˈhʌzɪ], *s.* das Weibsbild, die Blage.

hustings [ˈhʌstɪŋgz], *pl.* (*usually sing. constr.*) die Rednerbühne; Wahlbühne (*Hist.*).

hustle [hʌsl], 1. *v.a.* drängen, stoßen; *– s.th. through*, etwas durchsetzen *or* fertigbringen. 2. *v.n.* sich drängen, sich einen Weg bahnen; (*Amer.*) tätig *or* arbeitsam sein, sich rühren, sich tüchtig umtun. *– through s.th.*, etwas rasch erledigen, durch etwas eilen. 3. *s.* der Betrieb, das Gedränge, lebhaftes Treiben, der Hochbetrieb; (*Amer.*) die Betriebsamkeit.

hut [hʌt], 1. *s.* die Hütte; Baracke (*Mil.*); *mountain –*, die Schutzhütte, Alpenhütte. 2. *v.a.* in Baracken unterbringen (*Mil.*). **–ment**, *s.* die Unterbringung in Baracken; Feldhütten (*pl.*), das Barackenlager.

hutch [hʌtʃ], *s.* der Kasten, Trog (*for coal, etc.*); die Hütte, der Stall (*for small animals*).

huzza [hʊˈzɑ:], 1. *int.* heisa! heißa! hussa! juchhe! 2. *s.* das Jauchzen. 3. *v.n.* heisa rufen, jauchzen. 4. *v.a.* zujauchzen (*Dat.*).

hyacinth [ˈhaɪəsɪnθ], *s.* die Hyancinthe.

hyal–ine [ˈhaɪəlɪn], *adj.* glasartig, glasklar, durchsichtig; *–ine quartz*, der Glasquarz. **–ite** [–aɪt], *s.* der Hyalit, Glasopal (*Min.*). **–oid**, *adj. see* **–ine.**

hybrid [ˈhaɪbrɪd], 1. *adj.* hybrid(isch), bastardartig, Bastard–, Misch–, Zwitter–. 2. *s.* der Mischling, Bastard, die Zwitterbildung. **–ism** [–dɪzm], *s.* die Bastardierung, Kreuzung. **–ity**, *s.* die Mischbildung, Zwitterbildung, Hybridenbildung. **–ize**, *v.a.* kreuzen, bastardieren.

hydr–a [ˈhaɪdrə], *s.* die Hydra (*Myth.*); der Süßwasserpolyp (*Zool.*). **–a-headed**, *adj.* vielköpfig, hydraköpfig. **–angea** [haɪˈdreɪndʒjə], *s.* die Hortensie (*Bot.*). **–ant** [ˈhaɪdrənt], *s.* der Hydrant, Feuerhahn. **–ate** [–dreɪt], 1. *s.* das Hydrat (*Chem.*). 2. *v.a.* hydrieren. **–ated**, *adj.* wasserhaltig. **–aulic** [–ˈdrɔ:lɪk], *adj.* hydraulisch; *–aulic cement*, der Wassermörtel, Wasserkitt; *–aulic engine*, die Wasserkraftmaschine; *–aulic power*, die Wasserkraft; *–aulic press*, hydraulische Presse, die Wasserpresse; *–aulic pressure*, der Flüssigkeitsdruck. **–aulics**, *pl.* (*sing. constr.*) die Hydraulik. **–iodic** [haɪdrɪˈɔdɪk], *adj.* jodwasserstoffsauer (*Chem.*); *–iodic acid*, die Jodwasserstoffsäure.

hydro– [ˈhaɪdro] (*in compounds*) Wasser–. **–carbon**, *s.* das Kohlenstoffhydrat, der Kohlenwasserstoff (*Chem.*). **–carbonaceous**, *adj.* kohlenwasserstoffhaltig. **–cephalus** [–ˈsɛfələs], *s.* der Wasserkopf (*Med.*). **–chlorate**, **–chloric** [–ˈklɔrɪk], *adj.* salzsauer (*Chem.*); *–chloric acid*, der Chlorwasserstoff, die Salzsäure. **–chloride**, *s.* das Chlorhydrat. **–cyanic**, *adj.*; *–cyanic acid*, die Blausäure, Zyanwasserstoffsäure. **–dynamic** [–daɪˈnæmɪk], *adj.* hydrodynamisch. **–dynamics**, *pl.* (*sing. constr.*) die Wasserdrucklehre, Hydrodynamik. **–electric**, *adj.* hydroelektrisch; *–electric generating station*, das Wasserkraftwerk. **– –extract**, *v.a.* entwässern, zentrifugieren, abschleudern. **–gen** [ˈhaɪdrədʒən], *s.* der Wasserstoff (*Chem.*); *–gen peroxide*, das Wasserstoffsuperoxid; *–gen sulphide*, der Schwefelwasserstoff. **–genation**, *s.* die Hydrierung; *–genation plant*, die Hydrieranlage. **–genize** [haɪˈdrɔdʒənaɪz], *v.a.* hydrieren, härten (*oil*). **–genous** [–dʒɪnəs], *adj.* wasserstoffhaltig, Wasserstoff–. **–graphic**, *adj.* hydrographisch; *–graphic Department*, nautische Abteilung der Kriegsmarine (*in England*). **–graphy**, *s.* die Gewässerkunde, Hydrographie. **–logy** [haɪˈdrɔlədʒɪ], *s.* die Hydrologie, Wasserkunde. **–lysis** [–ləsɪs], *s.* die Hydrolyse. **–lyze**, *v.a.* aufschließen (*starch*). **–meter** [–ˈdrɔmɪtə], *s.* das *or* der Hydrometer, die Senkwaage, der Dichtigkeitsmesser. **–metric** [–ˈmɛtrɪk], *adj.* hydrometrisch. **–pathic** [–ˈpæθɪk], *adj.* hydropathisch; *–pathic establishment*, die Kaltwasserheilanstalt. **–pathy** [–ˈdrɔpəθɪ], *s.* die Wasserheilkunde, Wasserkur. **–phobia** [–ˈfoubɪə], *s.* die Wasserscheu; die Tollwut (*Med.*). **–phobic** [–ˈfoubɪk], *adj.* wasserscheu. **–phone** [ˈhaɪdrəfoun], *s.* das Unterwasserhorchgerät. **–pic** [–ˈdrɔpɪk], *adj.* wassersüchtig. **–plane**, *s.* das Gleitboot (*Naut.*); Tiefensteuer (*of submarines*). **–quinone** [–ˈkwaɪnoun], *s.* das Hydrochinon (*Phot.*). **–sphere**, *s.* die Hydrosphäre. **–static** [–ˈstætɪk], *adj.* hydrostatisch, Wasser–; *–static balance*, die Wasserwaage; *–static pressure*, der Wasserdruck. **–statics**, *pl.* (*sing. constr.*) die Hydrostatik. **–therapy**, *s.* die Wasserheilkunde. **–xide** [haɪˈdrɔksaɪd], *s.* das Hydroxyd, Hydrat (*Chem.*).

hyena [haɪˈɪ:nə], *s.* die Hyäne (*Zool.*).

hygien–e [ˈhaɪdʒɪ:n], *s.* die Körperpflege, Hygiene. **–ic** [haɪˈdʒɪ:nɪk], *adj.* gesundheitlich, hygienisch; *–ic measures*, Gesundheitsmaßnahmen (*pl.*). **–ics**, *pl.* (*sing. constr.*) die Gesundheitslehre, Gesundheitspflege.

hygro–meter [haɪˈgrɔmɪtə], *s.* der Feuchtigkeitsmesser. **–metric** [haɪgrəˈmɛtrɪk], *adj.* hygrometrisch. **–scope** [ˈhaɪgrəskoup], *s.* der Feuchtigkeitszeiger. **–scopic**, *adj.* Feuchtigkeit anziehend, wasserziehend.

hymen [ˈhaɪmɛn], *s.* das Jungfernhäutchen; (*poet.*) die Ehe; der Hymen, Gott der Ehe (*Myth.*). **–eal** [–ˈnɪ:əl], 1. *adj.* hochzeitlich, Hochzeits–. 1. *s.* das Hochzeitslied. **–opter**, *s.* der Hautflügler (*Ent.*). **–opterous**, *adj.* Hautflügler– (*Ent.*).

hymn [hɪm], 1. *s.* das Kirchenlied, die Hymne. 2. *v.a.* preisen, lobpreisen, lobsingen (*Dat.*). **–al** [–nəl], 1. *adj.* hymnisch. 2. *s.*; **– –book**, *s.* das Gesangbuch. **–ic** [–nɪk], *adj. see* **–al**, 1. **–ody** [–nədɪ], *s.* das Hymnensingen, der Hymnengesang; (*collect.*) Hymnen (*pl.*). **–ology** [–ˈnɔlədʒɪ], *s.* die Hymnologie.

hyoid [ˈhaɪɔɪd], *adj.*; *– bone*, das Zungenbein (*Anat.*).

hyper [ˈhaɪpə *prep.* (*in compounds*) über,

übermäßig. **-aesthesia,** *s.* nervöse Reizbarkeit. **-bola** [haɪˈpəːbələ], *s.* die Hyperbel (*Math.*). **-bole** [–bəlɪ], *s.* die Übertreibung, Hyperbel (*Rhet.*). **-bolic,** *adj.* Hyperbel- (*Math.*). **-bolical** [–ˈbəlɪkl], *adj.* übertreibend, hyperbolisch. **-borean** [–ˈbɔːrɪən], 1. *adj.* hyperboreisch, nördlich. 2. *s.* der Hyperboreer. **-catalectic,** *adj.* überzählig (*Metr.*). **-critical,** *adj.* übertrieben kritisch, allzuscharf kritisierend, allzu kritisch, peinlich genau. **-metropia,** *s.* die Übersichtigkeit. **-sarcosis,** *s.* wildes Fleisch. **-sensitive,** *adj.* äußerst empfindlich. **-trophy** [haɪˈpəːtrəfɪ], *s.* die Hypertrophie, übermäßiges Wachstum.

hyphen [ˈhaɪfən], 1. *s.* der Bindestrich; das Divis (*Typ.*). 2. *v.a.*; **-ate** [–neɪt], *v.a.* mit Bindestrich versehen; *–ated name,* der Doppelname.

hypno-id [ˈhɪpnɔɪd], *adj.* schlafähnlich. **-sis** [hɪpˈnoʊsɪs], *s.* die Hypnose. **-tic** [–ˈnɔtɪk], 1. *adj.* hypnotisch, einschläfernd. 2. *s.* der Hypnotisierte; das Schlafmittel, Einschläferungsmittel. **-tism** [ˈhɪpnətɪzm], *s.* der Hypnotismus. **-tist,** *s.* der Hypnotiseur. **-tize** [ˈhɪpnətaɪz], *v.a.* hypnotisieren; (*fig.*) fesseln, faszinieren.

hypo [ˈhaɪpo], 1. *prep.* (*in compounds*) unter, unterhalb. 2. *s.* (abbr. for *sodium hyposulphite*) unterschwefliges Natron, das Fixiersalz (*Phot.*). **-chlorous,** *adj.* unterchlorig. **-chondria** [–ˈkɔndrɪə], *s.* die Hypochondrie, Schwermut, der Trübsinn. **-chondriac** [–ˈkɔndrɪæk], 1. *adj.* hypochondrisch, schwermütig. 2. *s.* der Hypochonder. **-crisy** [hɪˈpɔkrəsɪ], *s.* die Heuchelei. **-crite** [ˈhɪpəkrɪt], *s.* der Heuchler, Andächtler, Scheinheilige. **-critical** [hɪpəˈkrɪtɪkl], *adj.* heuchlerisch; scheinheilig. **-dermic** [haɪpoˈdəːmɪk], *adj.* unter der Haut liegend; *–dermic injection,* hypodermatische Einspritzung. **-gastrium** [–ˈgæstrɪəm], *s.* der Unterleib (*Anat.*). **-geal** [–ˈdʒɪːəl], **-gean** [–ˈdʒɪːən], **-geous** [–ˈdʒɪːəs], *adj.* unter der Erde lebend. **-stasis** [haɪˈpɔstəsɪs], *s.* die Grundlage, Unterlage, Hypostase (*Log.*); Blutstauung, Blutsenkung (*Med.*). **-statize** [–ˈpɔstətaɪz], *v.a.* vergegenständlichen, hypostasieren (*Log.*). **-sulphate** [haɪpoˈsʌlfeɪt], *s.* unterschwefelsaures Salz. **-sulphite** [–faɪt], *s.* das Schwefelhydroxid, Thiosulfat, unterschwefligsaures Salz. **-tenuse** [haɪˈpɔtənjuːz], *s.* die Hypotenuse (*Math.*). **-thec** [ˈhaɪpəθək], *s.* (*Scots*) die Hypothek. **-thecary** [haɪˈpɔθəkərɪ], *adj.* hypothekarisch, pfandrechtlich. **-thecate** [haɪˈpɔθəkeɪt] *v.a.* verpfänden, verschreiben, hypothekarisieren. **-thesis** [haɪˈpɔθəsɪs], *s.* (*pl.* –theses [–sɪːz]) die Hypothese, Annahme. **-thetical** [haɪpəˈθɛtɪkl], *adj.* hypothetisch, mutmaßlich, angenommen; bedingt.

hypso-meter [hɪpˈsɔmətə], *s.* das Höhenmesser. **-metric(al)** [hɪpsəˈmɛtrɪk(l)], *adj.* Höhen–, hypsometrisch. **-metry** [hɪpˈsɔmətrɪ], *s.* die Höhenmessung.

hyssop [ˈhɪsəp], *s.* der Ysop (*Bot.*).

hysterectomy [hɪstəˈrɛktəmɪ], *s.* die Gebärmutterentfernung (*Surg.*).

hysteresis [hɪstəˈrɪːsɪs], *s.* die Hysterese (*Elec.*).

hysteri-a [hɪsˈtɪːrɪə], *s.* die Hysterie. **-c(al)** [hɪsˈtɛrɪk(l)], *adj.* hysterisch. **-cs,** *pl.* die Hysterie, hysterischer Zustand, hysterischer Anfall; *go into* or *have a fit of –cs,* hysterische Anfälle bekommen.

hystero-cele [ˈhɪstərəsɪːl], *s.* der Gebärmutterbruch. **-tomy** [–ˈrɔtəmɪ], *s.* der Kaiserschnitt (*Med.*).

I

[1]I, i [aɪ], *s.* das I, i. *See Index of Abbreviations at end.*

[2]I, *pers. pron.* ich; *it is –,* ich bin es; *– say!* hören Sie mal!

iamb [ˈaɪæmb], *s.* der Jambus. **-ic** [aɪˈæmbɪk], 1. *adj.* jambisch. 2. *s.* (*usually pl.*) *see* **iamb. -us** [aɪˈæmbəs], *s. see* **iamb.**

ibex [ˈaɪbɛks], *s.* der Steinbock (*Zool.*).

ibidem [ɪˈbaɪdəm], *adv.* ebenda.

ibis [ˈaɪbɪs], *s.* (*pl.* ibes [–ɪːz]) der Ibis (*Orn.*).

ice [aɪs], 1. *s.* das Eis; das (Speise)Eis, Gefrorene(s), *n.* (*Conf.*); *broken –,* Eisstücke (*Cook.*), Eisstollen; *floating –,* das Treibeis; *pack –,* das Packeis; *sheet –,* das Glatteis; *break the –,* das Eis brechen (*also fig.*); (*coll.*) *cut no –,* nichts ausrichten, keine Wirkung haben, keinen Eindruck machen; (*fig.*) *skate on thin –,* sich auf dünnes Eis wagen, ein heikles Thema berühren. 2. *v.a.* mit Eis bedecken, in Eis verwandeln, gefrieren machen; überzuckern (*Conf.*); kühlen (*wine*). 3. *v.n.* (*– up*), beeisen, eineisen, vereisen. **--age,** *s.* die Eiszeit. **--axe,** *s.* der Eispickel (*Mount.*). **-berg,** *s.* (schwimmender) Eisberg. **--boat,** *s.* der Segelschlitten. **--bound,** *adj.* eingefroren, eingeeist. **--box,** *s.* der Eisschrank. **--breaker,** *s.* der Eisbrecher. **--cream,** *s.* das (Speise)Eis, Gefrorene(s), *n.*; *--cream parlour,* die Eisdiele. **--fall,** *s.* der Gletscherabbruch. **--ferns,** *pl.* Eisblumen (*pl.*). **--field,** *s.* das Eisfeld. **--floe,** *s.* die Treibscholle, Eisscholle. **--foot,** *s.* der Eisgürtel. **--hockey,** *s.* das Eishockey. **--pail,** *s.* der Eiskübel, Weinkühler. **--plant,** *s.* das Eiskraut. **--plough,** *s.* der Eispflug. **--rink,** *s.* die Eisbahn.

ichneumon [ɪkˈnjuːmən], *s.* das *or* der Ichneumon. **--fly,** *s.* die Schlupfwespe.

ichor [ˈaɪkɔː], *s.* das Götterblut (*Myth.*); Eiter (*Med.*). **-ous** [ˈaɪkərəs], *adj.* eiterig.

ichthyo-logy [ɪkθɪˈɔlədʒɪ], *s.* die Fischkunde, Zoologie der Fische. **-phagous** [–ˈɔfəgəs], *adj.* fisch(fr)essend. **-saurus** [ɪkθɪəˈsɔːrəs], *s.* der Ichthyosaurier.

ici-cle [ˈaɪsɪkl], *s.* der Eiszapfen. **-ness,** *s.* eisige Kälte, die Eiskälte; (*fig.*) Zurückhaltung. **-ng,** 1. *adj.* Eis–, Kühl–; *–ng sugar,* der Puderzucker, Staubzucker. 2. *s.* die Vereisung (*Av.*); der Zuckerguß, Beguß, die Glasur (*Cook.*).

icon [ˈaɪkɔn], *s.* das Abbild; Christusbild, Heiligenbild. **-oclasm** [aɪˈkɔnəklæzm], *s.* die Bilderstürmerei. **-oclast** [–klæst], *s.* der Bilderstürmer. **-oclastic** [–ˈklæstɪk], *adj.* bilderstürmend, Bilderstürmer–. **-ography** [–ˈnɔgrəfɪ], *s.* die Bildniskunde. **-olatry** [–ˈnɔlətrɪ], *s.* die Bilderverehrung, Bilderanbetung. **-ology** [–ˈnɔlədʒɪ], *s. see* **-ography.**

icosahedron [aɪkɔsəˈhɪːdrən], *s.* der Zwanzigflächer, das Ikosaeder.

ictus [ˈɪktəs], *s.* der Starkton, Iktus, rhythmischer Akzent.

icy [ˈaɪsɪ], *adj.* (*adv.* **icily**) eisig; (*fig.*) kalt, frostig; *– cold,* eiskalt.

idea [aɪˈdɪːə], *s.* die Idee (*also Phil.*), Vorstellung, der Begriff; Anhaltspunkt, Gedanke, Einfall, Plan; die Meinung, Ahnung; *form an – of,* sich (*Dat.*) vorstellen *or* eine Vorstellung machen von; *I cannot form any – of it,* ich kann mir keinen Begriff davon machen; *have an – that,* ich denke *or* meine daß, mir kommt es vor, als ob; *have little* (or *no*) *– of,* wenig (*or* keine) Ahnung haben von; (*coll.*) *that's the –,* darum dreht's sich; *the – is that,* man will damit bezwecken *or* erreichen; (*coll.*) *what's the – ?* was soll das (heißen *or* bedeuten)? (*coll.*) *the very – (of doing),* der bloße Gedanke daran (zu tun). **-tion,** *s.* die Vorstellung, Gedankenbildung.

ideal [aɪˈdɪːəl], 1. *adj.* ideal, vollkommen, vollendet; vorbildlich, (*coll.*) ausgezeichnet; ideell, nicht wirklich, eingebildet; gedanklich, Gedanken–, Ideen–. 2. *s.* das Ideal; die Vollendung; das Vorbild, Wunschbild, Mustergültige(s), *n.* **-ism** [–lɪzm], *s.* der Idealismus. **-ist** [–lɪst], *s.* der Idealist. **-istic** [–ˈlɪstɪk], *adj.* idealistisch. **-ity** [–ˈælɪtɪ], *s.* die Idealität. **-ize** [–laɪz], 1. *v.a.* idealisieren, verklären, veredeln, vergeistigen. 2. *v.n.* Ideale bilden.

ideation [aɪdɪˈeɪʃən], *s. see* **idea.**

idée fixe [ˈɪdeɪˈfɪːks], *s.* fixe Idee.

idem [ˈaɪdɛm], *adj.* derselbe, dasselbe, dieselbe.

identi-cal [aɪˈdɛntɪkl], *adj.* derselbe, dasselbe, dieselbe; übereinstimmend, gleich, gleichbedeutend; *–cal twins,* eineiige Zwillinge. **-calness,** *s.* die Übereinstimmung. **-fiable** [aɪdɛntɪˈfaɪəbl], *adj.* feststellbar, identifizierbar. **-fication** [–fɪˈkeɪʃən], *s.* die Identifizierung, Feststellung, Bestimmung; Legimitation, der Ausweis; *–fication card,* die Kennkarte; *–fication light,* das Kennlicht; *–fication* *mark*, das Kennzeichen; *–fication papers*, die Legitimation, Ausweispapiere (*pl.*); *–fication parade*, die Gegenüberstellung, Konfrontierung. **–fy** [aɪˈdɛntɪfaɪ], *v.a.* identifizieren (*Acc.*); ausweisen, legitimieren (*a p.*); nachweisen, bestimmen (*species*); gleichsetzen (*with* (*Dat.*)); *–fy o.s. with*, sich solidarisch erklären mit. **–ty** [–tɪ], *s.* die Identität, Gleichheit; Individualität; *mistaken –ty*, die Personenverwechslung; *prove one's –ty*, sich ausweisen. **–ty-card**, *s.* der (Personal)Ausweis. **–ty-disk**, *s.* die Erkennungsmarke.

ideo-gram, -graph [ˈɪdɪəgræm, –græf], *s.* das Begriffszeichen. **–logical** [aɪdɪəˈlɔdʒɪkl], *adj.* ideologisch. **–logist** [aɪdɪˈɔlədʒɪst], *s.* unpraktischer Theoretiker, der Schwärmer. **–logy** [–ˈɔlədʒɪ], *s.* die Begriffslehre, Begriffsbildung, Ideologie; Schwärmerei, reine Theorie.

ides [aɪdz], *pl.* die Iden.

idiocy [ˈɪdɪəsɪ], *s.* der Schwachsinn, Blödsinn, die Geistesschwäche.

idiom [ˈɪdɪəm], *s.* die Spracheigentümlichkeit; Mundart, der Dialekt, das Idiom; (*fig.*) die Eigentümlichkeit. **–atic(al)** [–ˈmætɪk(l)]. *adj.* idiomatisch, spracheigentümlich.

idio-pathic [ɪdɪoˈpæθɪk], *adj.* idiopathisch (*Med.*). **–syncrasy** [ɪdɪoˈsɪŋkrəsɪ], *s.* abnorme Wesenseigenheit, die Idiosynkrasie; besondere Empfindlichkeit (gegen); krankhafte Abneigung (gegen).

idiot [ˈɪdɪət], *s.* Schwachsinnige(r), Geistesschwache(r), *m.* & *f.*, der Idiot; (*coll.*) Narr, Dummkopf. **–ic** [ɪdɪˈɔtɪk], *adj.* (*usually fig.*) blödsinnig, idiotisch, einfältig, dumm.

idl-e [aɪdl], 1. *adj.* träge, faul; müßig, untätig (*of persons*); eitel, leer, hohl, wertlos, nichtig, zwecklos, unnütz; stillstehend, leerlaufend, nicht in Betrieb (*Mach.*); *–e capital*, totes *or* unproduktives Kapital; *–e fellow*, der Faulenzer, Faulpelz; *–e hour*, die Mußestunde; *–e motion*, der Leergang (*Mach.*); *–e talk*, leeres Geschwätz *or* Gewäsch; *–e wheel*, das Zwischenrad, Leitrad; *–e words*, unnütze Worte; (*Prov.*) *Satan finds mischief for –e hands to do*, Müßiggang ist aller Laster Anfang; *lie –e*, brach liegen (*of land*). 2. *v.n.* faulenzen; *be –ing*, leerlaufen (*Mech.*). 3. *v.a.*; *–e away one's time*, seine Zeit müßig hinbringen. **–eness**, *s.* die Faulheit, Trägheit; Untätigkeit, der Müßiggang; die Nichtigkeit, Unfruchtbarkeit. **–er**, *s.* der Faulenzer, Müßiggänger; das Leitrad. **–ing**, *s.* der Leerlauf (*Mech.*).

idol [aɪdl], *s.* das Götzenbild, Idol; (*fig.*) der Abgott. **–ater** [aɪˈdɔlətə], *s.* der Götzendiener, (*fig.*) Anbeter, Verehrer. **–atress** [aɪˈdɔlətrɪs], *s.* die Götzendienerin. **–atrous** [–trəs], *adj.* abgöttisch, Götzen–. **–atry** [–trɪ], *s.* der Götzendienst, die Abgötterei; (*fig.*) Vergötterung. **–ization** [–aɪˈzeɪʃn], *s.* die Vergötterung. **–ize** [ˈaɪdəlaɪz], *v.a.* vergöttern, anbeten.

idyll [ˈaɪdɪl], *s.* die Idylle, das Schäfergedicht, Hirtengedicht; (*fig.*) das Idyll. **–ic** [aɪˈdɪlɪk], *adj.* idyllisch (*also fig.*).

if [ɪf], 1. *conj.* wenn, falls, wofern; (*after* ask, know, see, try, doubt, *etc.*) ob; *– he should write*, wenn er schreiben sollte; *fifty – a day*, mindestens fünfzig Jahre alt; *– any*, höchstens *or* wenn überhaupt einer; *as –*, als ob, als wenn; *even –*, selbst wenn, wenn auch *or* überhaupt; *– not*, wo nicht; *– so*, in dem Fall, gegebenenfalls; *– so be that*, gesetzt, es wäre. 2. *s.* das Wenn; *without –s or ands*, ohne Wenn und Aber.

igloo [ˈɪgluː], *s.* die Schneehütte.

ign-eous [ˈɪgnɪəs], *adj.* feurig, glühend; Eruptiv– (*Geol.*). **–is fatuus** [ˈɪgnɪs ˈfætjʊəs], (*pl.* –es fatui [ˈɪgnɪːz ˈfætjʊaɪ]) das Irrlicht, (*fig.*) Blendwerk. **–ite** [ɪgˈnaɪt], 1. *v.a.* anzünden, entzünden, in Brand setzen, anstecken; bis zur Verbrennung erhitzen (*Chem.*). 2. *v.n.* sich entzünden, Feuer fangen. **–ition** [–ˈnɪʃən], *s.* das Anzünden; die Erhitzung (*Chem.*); Zündung (*Motor.*, *etc.*); *pre–ition*, vorzeitige Zündung. **–ition-charge**, *s.* die Zündladung. **–ition-key**, der Zündschlüssel (*Motor.*). **–ition-spark**, *s.* der Zündfunke.

ignoble [ɪgˈnoʊbl], *adj.* unedel, niedrig, gemein. **–ness**, *s.* die Gemeinheit, Niedrigkeit.

ignomin-ious [ɪgnoˈmɪnɪəs], *adj.* schmählich, schimpflich, schändlich, schmachvoll, entehrend. **–iousness**, *s.*, **–y** [ˈɪgnəmɪnɪ], *s.* die Schmach, Schande, der Schimpf.

ignora-mus [ɪgnoˈreɪməs], *s.* Unwissende(r), *m.*, der Ignorant. **–nce** [ˈɪgnərəns], *s.* die Unwissenheit; Unkenntnis. **–nt** [ˈɪgnərənt], *adj.* unwissend, unkundig; ungebildet; *be –nt of*, nicht wissen, nicht kennen, nichts wissen von, unbekannt sein mit; *–nt of the world*, ohne Weltkenntnis.

ignore [ɪgˈnɔː], *v.a.* nicht beachten, unbeachtet lassen, nicht wissen; verwerfen, abweisen (*Law*).

iguan-a [ɪˈgwɑːnə], *s.* gemeiner Leguan (*Zool.*). **–odon**, *s.* eine Art Dinosaurier.

ileum [ˈɪlɪəm], *s.* der Krummdarm (*Anat.*).

ilex [ˈaɪlɛks], *s.* die Stechpalme (*Bot.*).

iliac [ˈɪlɪæk], *adj.* Darmbein– (*Anat.*).

Iliad [ˈɪljəd], *s.* die Ilias, Iliade.

ilk [ɪlk], *adj.* (only in) *of that –*, (*Scots*) desselben Namens, (*coll.*) derselben Art, des–, der–, *or* ihresgleichen.

ill [ɪl], **1.** *adj.* schlimm, schlecht; böse, bösartig, feindlich; übel, ungünstig; (*pred. only*) krank; *– blood*, böses Blut; *– breeding*, die Ungezogenheit; *– effect*, schlimme Auswirkung, üble Wirkung, unangenehme Folge; *– fame*, schlechter Ruf; *– feeling*, die Verstimmung, Abneigung, der Verdruß, Unwille; *with an – grace*, unwillig, widerwillig; *– health*, schlechte Gesundheit; *– humour*, schlechte Laune; *– luck*, das Unglück; *as – luck would have it*, unglücklicherweise; *– management*, die Mißwirtschaft; *– nature*, die Bösartigkeit, Böswilligkeit; *– turn*, schlimmer Streich; *– usage*, schlechte Behandlung; (*Prov.*) *– weeds grow apace*, Unkraut vergeht *or* verdirbt nicht; *– will*, das Übelwollen, die Feindschaft, Abneigung, der Groll; *bear s.o. – will*, einen Groll gegen jemanden haben, auf einen schlecht zu sprechen sein; (*Prov.*) *it's an – wind that blows nobody any good*, etwas Gutes ist an allem. **2.** *adv.* schlecht, böse, übel; nicht gut, ungünstig; schwerlich; *accord – with*, schlecht passen zu; *it becomes him –*, es steht ihm schlecht an; *– afford*, nicht leisten können, nicht auf sich nehmen können; *be away –*, krankheitshalber abwesend sein; *be taken –*, see *fall –*; *he can – bear it*, er kann es schwerlich, kaum *or* nicht gut ertragen; *– at ease*, befangen (*with s.o.*, einem gegenüber), unbehaglich; *fall –*, krank werden; *go – with*, übel ergehen (*Dat.*), schlecht stehen um *or* mit; *speak – of s.o.*, schlecht *or* Schlimmes über einen reden; *take –*, übelnehmen. **3.** *s.* das Übel, Böse(s), *n.*; (*often pl.*) das Unglück, Mißgeschick. **--advised**, *adj.* schlecht beraten, nicht ratsam; unbesonnen. **--affected**, *adj.* übel gesinnt (*to* or *towards*, gegen). **--bred**, *adj.* ungebildet, unerzogen, ungezogen, unhöflich. **--conditioned**, *adj.* schlecht beschaffen, in schlechtem Zustand; bösartig. **--disposed**, *adj.* übelgesinnt, unfreundlich, nicht gewogen (*to* or *towards* (*Dat.*)). **--fated**, *adj.* unglücklich, ungünstig. **--favoured**, *adj.* häßlich, unschön. **--gotten**, *adj.* unrechtmäßig *or* unredlich erworben. **--humoured**, *adj.* schlecht gelaunt. **--judged**, *adj.* unbesonnen, unklug. **--mannered**, *adj.* unmanierlich. **--matched**, *adj.* schlecht zusammenpassend. **--natured**, *adj.* boshaft, bösartig; böswillig. **–ness**, *s.* see **illness**. **--omened**, *adj.* von böser Vorbedeutung, Unglücks–. **--pleased**, *adj.* unzufrieden (mit), unbefriedigt (von). **--starred**, *adj.* unglücklich, von Unglück verfolgt. **--tempered**, *adj.* schlecht gelaunt, verdrießlich, mürrisch. **--timed**, *adj.* unpassend, ungelegen. **--treat**, *v.a.* mißhandeln. **–treatment**, *s.* die Grausamkeit. **--usage**, *s.* die Mißhandlung. **--use**, *v.a.* (*usually p.p.*) *see* **--treat.**

illati-on [ɪˈleɪʃən], *s.* der Schluß, die Folgerung. **–ve** [–tɪv], *adj.* folgernd, schließend.

illegal [ɪˈlɪːgəl], *adj.* ungesetzlich, widerrechtlich, rechtswidrig, unrechtmäßig, illegal. **–ity** [ɪlɪːˈgælɪtɪ], *s.* die Ungesetzlichkeit, Widerrechtlichkeit, Unrechtmäßigkeit, Illegalität.

illegib-ility [ɪlɛdʒɪˈbɪlɪtɪ], *s.* die Unleserlichkeit. **–le** [ɪˈlɛdʒɪbl], *adj.* unleserlich.

illegitima-cy [ɪlɪˈdʒɪtɪməsɪ], *s.* die Unehelichkeit; Unrechtmäßigkeit, Unechtheit, Ungültigkeit. **–te**

[–ˈdʒɪtɪmɪt], *adj.* unehelich, illegitim; unrechtmäßig, widerrechtlich.
illiberal [ɪˈlɪbərəl], *adj.* knauserig, karg; engherzig. **–ity** [–ˈrælɪtɪ], *s.* die Knauserei, Kargheit; Engherzigkeit.
illicit [ɪˈlɪsɪt], *adj.* unerlaubt, verboten, rechtswidrig; unzulässig; – *sale*, der Schwarzkauf; – *trade*, der Schwarzhandel, Schleichhandel; – *work*, die Schwarzarbeit.
illimitable [ɪˈlɪmɪtəbl], *adj.* unbegrenzbar, grenzenlos.
illitera–cy [ɪˈlɪtərəsɪ], *s.* die Ungelehrtheit, Unwissenheit; Unkenntnis des Lesens und Schreibens, das Analphabetentum. **–te** [ɪˈltərɪt], 1. *adj.* ungelehrt, ungebildet, unwissend; des Schreibens und Lesens unkundig. 2. *s.* Ungebildete(r), *m.*, der Analphabet.
illness [ˈɪlnɪs], *s.* Krankheit, Unpäßlichkeit, das Unwohlsein.
illogical [ɪˈlɔdʒɪkl], *adj.* unlogisch; folgewidrig; vernunftwidrig.
illum–e [ɪˈljuːm], *v.a.* erleuchten, aufhellen. **–inate** [–ɪneɪt], *v.a.* beleuchten, erleuchten, erhellen; (*fig.*) aufklären, aufhellen; festlich beleuchten, illuminieren (*streets, etc.*); illustrieren, bunt ausmalen (*a manuscript*); *–inated advertising*, die Lichtreklame; *–inated manuscript*, die Bilderhandschrift. **–inati** [–ɪˈneɪtɑɪ], *pl.* die Illuminaten. **–ination** [–ɪˈneɪʃən], *s.* (festliche) Beleuchtung, die Erleuchtung, Illumination; Ausschmückung, Illustration; der Bilderschmuck; die Lichtstärke (*Phot.*). **–inative,** *adj.* erleuchtend, Schmuck–; aufklärend (*Opt.*). **–ine,** *v.a. see* **–inate.**
illus–ion [ɪˈljuːʒən], *s.* die (Sinnes)Täuschung, Einbildung, Illusion; der Wahn. **–ionist,** *s.* der Zauberkünstler. **–ive** [–sɪv], *adj.* täuschend, trügerisch, illusorisch. **–iveness** [–sɪvnɪs], *s.* die Täuschung, Trüglichkeit. **–ory,** *adj. see* **–ive.**
illustrat–e [ˈɪləstreɪt], *v.a.* erläutern, erklären; veranschaulichen; illustrieren (*a book*). **–ion** [–ˈtreɪʃən], *s.* die Erläuterung, Erklärung, Veranschaulichung; (preceded by *in* or *as*, zu), das Beispiel; die Abbildung, Illustration. **–ive,** *adj.* erklärend, erläuternd; *be –ive of*, veranschaulichen, ins rechte Licht rücken; *–ive material*, das Anschauungsmaterial. **–or** [–tə], *s.* der Illustrator; Erläuterer.
illustrious [ɪˈlʌstrɪəs], *adj.* berühmt; erhaben, erlaucht, ausgezeichnet. **–ness,** *s.* die Berühmtheit; Erlauchtheit.
image [ˈɪmɪdʒ], 1. *s.* das Bild, Bildnis; Abbild, Ebenbild; die Vorstellung, Verkörperung; das Standbild, die Bildsäule; das Götzenbild; bildlicher Ausdruck *graven –*, das Götzenbild; *the very – of his father*, das Ebenbild seines Vaters; – *interference*, das Wellenecho (*Rad.*). 2. *v.a.* abbilden, bildlich *or* anschaulich darstellen; widerspiegeln. **–ry,** *s.* das Bildwerk, Bilder (*pl.*); die Bildersprache, bildliche Sprache *or* Darstellung. **––worship,** *s.* der Bilderdienst.
imagin–able [ɪˈmædʒɪnəbl], *adj.* vorstellbar, denkbar; erdenklich; *the finest weather –able*, das denkbar schönste Wetter. **–ary** [–nərɪ], *adj.* eingebildet, nur in der Vorstellung vorhanden; imaginär (*Math.*); *–ary weakness*, eingebildete Schwäche. **–ation** [–ˈneɪʃən], *s.* die Einbildung, Vorstellung, das Denkvermögen; die Einbildungskraft, Phantasie, der Ideenreichtum; *his suggestions lack –ation*, seine Vorschläge sind ideenarm; *I was at your side in my –ation*, ich stand im Geiste dir zur Seite. **–ative** [–nətɪv], *adj.* erfinderisch; ideenreich; phantasievoll, phantasiereich; *–ative faculty*, die Einbildungskraft. **–e** [ɪˈmædʒɪn], *v.a.* sich (*Dat.*) einbilden *or* vorstellen *or* denken; (*coll.*) glauben, vermuten, annehmen; *just –e!* denken Sie (sich) nur!
imago [ɪˈmɑːgoʊ], *s.* vollkommen ausgewachsenes Insekt.
imbecil–e [ˈɪmbɪsɑɪl], 1. *adj.* schwachsinnig, blödsinnig, geistesschwach; (*coll.*) närrisch. 2. *s.* Schwachsinnige(r), *m. & f.*; (*coll.*) der Narr. **–ity** [–ˈsɪlɪtɪ], *s.* der Schwachsinn; die Geistesschwäche; (*coll.*) Dummheit.
imbib–e [ɪmˈbɑɪb], *v.a.* einsaugen, aufsaugen; (*fig.*) geistig *or* in sich aufnehmen, sich zu eigen machen; (*coll.*) trinken.
imbricate [ˈɪmbrɪkɪt], 1. *adj.* dachziegelartig. 2. *v.a.* dachziegelartig übereinanderlegen. 3. *v.n.* dachziegelartig übereinanderliegen.
imbroglio [ɪmˈbroʊlɪoʊ], *s.* die Verwick(e)lung, Verwirrung, der Wirrwarr; verwickelte Lage (*Pol.*).
imbrue [ɪmˈbruː], *v.a.* benetzen, beflecken (*in* or *with*, mit); eintauchen (*usually fig.*).
imbue [ɪmˈbjuː], *v.a.* durchtränken; tief färben; (*usually fig.*) erfüllen; *–d with*, erfüllt von.
imita–ble [ˈɪmɪtəbl], *adj.* nachahmbar. **–te** [ˈɪmɪteɪt], *v.a.* nachahmen (*an example, etc.* (*Dat.*); (*a p.* (*Acc.*); (*a th. from a p.*, etwas einem); nachmachen, nachbilden, nachschaffen (*a th. from s.o.*, etwas einem); kopieren, imitieren. **–ted,** *adj.* künstlich, unecht. **–tion** [–ˈteɪʃən], 1. *s.* die Nachahmung; Nachgeahmte(s), Nachgemachte(s), *n.*; die Nachbildung, Fälschung, Imitation; *in –tion of*, nach dem Muster *or* Vorbild (*Gen.*), als Nachahmung von. 2. *attrib.* unecht, künstlich, Kunst–; *–tion leather*, das Kunstleder. **–tive** [–tətɪv], *adj.* nachahmend, nachgemacht; *–tive word*, lautnachahmendes Wort. **–tor** [–ə], *s.* der Nachahmer.
immaculate [ɪˈmækjʊlɪt], *adj.* unbefleckt, makellos, rein; (*fig.*) fleckenlos, fehlerfrei; – *conception*, unbefleckte Empfängnis. **–ness,** *s.* die Unbeflecktheit, Reinheit.
immanen–ce [ˈɪmənəns], *s.* das Innewohnen, die Immanenz. **–t** [–t], *adj.* innewohnend, immanent (*Phil.*).
immaterial [ɪməˈtɪərɪəl], *adj.* unkörperlich, stofflos, immateriell; (*fig.*) unwesentlich, unbedeutend, unwichtig, nebensächlich; (*coll.*) *be – to me*, mir einerlei sein. **–ity** [–ˈælɪtɪ], *s.* die Unstofflichkeit, Unkörperlichkeit.
immatur–e [ɪməˈtjʊə], *adj.* unreif, unentwickelt. **–ity** [–rɪtɪ], *s.* die Unreife.
immeasurabl–e [ɪˈmɛʒərəbl], *adj.* unermeßlich. **–eness,** *s.* die Unermeßlichkeit.
immedia–cy [ɪˈmiːdjəsɪ], *s.* die Unmittelbarkeit; Unverzüglichkeit. **–te** [ɪˈmiːdjət], *adj.* unmittelbar; augenblicklich, unverzüglich, sofortig; umliegend, nahe, direkt; *–te circle*, enger Kreis; *–te heir*, nächster Erbe. **–tely,** 1. *adv.* sogleich, sofort, augenblicklich, unverzüglich, auf der Stelle; *–tely after*, unmittelbar darauf. 2. *conj.* sobald (als).
immemorial [ɪmɪˈmɔːrɪəl], *adj.* undenklich, uralt; *from time –*, seit unvordenklichen Zeiten.
immens–e [ɪˈmɛns], *adj.* unermeßlich, ungeheuer. **–ity,** *s.* die Unermeßlichkeit, Unendlichkeit; ungeheure Größe, gewaltige Ausdehnung. **–urability** [ɪmɛnʃərəˈbɪlɪtɪ], *s.* die Unermeßlichkeit. **–urable** [ɪˈmɛnʃərəbl], *adj.* unermeßbar, unermeßlich.
immers–e [ɪˈməːs], *v.a.* untertauchen, eintauchen; versenken (*in*, in (*Acc.*)); (*fig.*) *–ed in*, vertieft *or* versunken in; verwickelt *or* verstrickt in. **–ion** [ɪˈməːʃən], *s.* das Untertauchen, Eintauchen; (*fig.*) die Versenkung, Versunkenheit; das Verschwinden (*Astr.*); die Immersionstaufe (*Eccl.*). **–ion-heater,** *s.* der Tauchsieder (*Elec.*).
immigra–nt [ˈɪmɪgrənt], 1. *s.* der Einwanderer. 2. *adj.* einwandernd. **–te** [–greɪt], *v.n.* einwandern. **–tion** [–ˈgreɪʃən], *s.* die Einwanderung.
imminen–ce [ˈɪmɪnəns], *s.* nahes Bevorstehen; drohende Gefahr. **–t** [ˈɪmɪnənt], *adj.* bevorstehend, drohend.
immiscible [ɪˈmɪsɪbl], *adj.* unvermischbar, unmischbar.
immitigable [ɪˈmɪtɪgəbl], *adj.* nicht zu besänftigen, lindern *or* beruhigen, unstillbar.
immobil–e [ɪˈmoʊbɑɪl], *adj.* unbeweglich, ortsfest. **–ity** [–ˈbɪlɪtɪ], *s.* die Unbeweglichkeit. **–ize** [–bɪlɑɪz], *v.a.* unbeweglich machen, festlegen; aus dem Umlauf ziehen, einziehen (*specie*); immobil machen (*troops*).
immoderat–e [ɪˈmɔdərɪt], *adj.* unmäßig, übermäßig, maßlos. **–ion** [–ˈreɪʃən], *s.* die Unmäßigkeit, das Übermaß.
immodest [ɪˈmɔdɪst], *adj.* unbescheiden, frech, anmaßend; unsittlich, unkeusch, unzüchtig, unanständig. **–y,** *s.* die Unbescheidenheit, Frechheit; Unsittlichkeit, Unzüchtigkeit, Unanständigkeit.

immolat–e [ˈɪmoleɪt], *v.a.* opfern, zum Opfer bringen, als Opfer darbringen (*also fig.*). **–ion** [–ˈleɪʃən], *s.* das Opfer, die Opferung (*also fig.*).
immoral [ɪˈmɔrəl], *adj.* unmoralisch, unsittlich. **–ity** [ɪməˈrælɪtɪ], *s.* die Unsittlichkeit, Sittenlosigkeit.
immort–al [ɪˈmɔːtl], 1. *adj.* unsterblich; ewig, unvergänglich. 2. *s.* Unsterbliche(r), *m.* **–ality** [ɪmɔːˈtælɪtɪ], *s.* die Unsterblichkeit. **–alize** [–təlaɪz], *v.a.* unsterblich machen, verewigen. **–elle** [ɪmɔːˈtɛl], *s.* die Immortelle (*Bot.*).
immovab–ility [ɪmuːvəˈbɪlɪtɪ], *s.* die Unbeweglichkeit, (*fig.*) Unerschütterlichkeit. **–le** [ɪˈmuːvəbl] *adj.* unbeweglich (*also Law*); fest, unerschütterlich; unveränderlich. **–les**, *pl.* Liegenschaften, Immobilien (*pl.*).
immun–e [ɪˈmjuːn], *adj.* geschützt, gefeit, immun (*to, from* or *against*, gegen); *–e reaction*, die Immunreaktion (*Med.*). **–ity** [–ɪtɪ], *s.* die Befreiung, Freiheit, Immunität (*from*, von); Straffreiheit, Steuerfreiheit; Unempfänglichkeit (*from*, gegen) (*Med.*); (*often pl.*) das Privileg. **–ization** [–aɪˈzeɪʃn], *s.* die Immunisierung, Impfung (*against*, gegen). **–ize** [ˈɪmjunaɪz], *v.a.* unempfänglich *or* immun machen, immunisieren (*Med.*) (*against*, gegen).
immure [ɪˈmjuə], *v.a.* einmauern, einbauen, einschließen, einsperren, einkerkern; – *o.s.*, sich abschließen *or* vergraben.
immutab–ility [ɪmjuːtəˈbɪlɪtɪ], *s.* die Unveränderlichkeit, Unwandelbarkeit. **–le** [ɪˈmjuːtəbl], *adj.* unveränderlich, unwandelbar.
[1]**imp** [ɪmp], *s.* das Teufelchen, der Kobold; (*coll.*) Schelm, Schlingel, Knirps; *see* **impish.**
[2]**imp**, *v.a.* (*the wings*) den Flug verbessern; (*fig.*) beschwingen.
impact, 1. [ɪmˈpækt], *v.a.* zusammenpressen, einkeilen. 2. [ˈɪmpækt], *s.* der (Zusammen)Stoß; Aufprall, Aufschlag, Einschlag (*Artil.*); *point of* –, der Auftreffpunkt.
impair [ɪmˈpɛə], *v.a.* beeinträchtigen, verschlimmern, verschlechtern, schädigen; schwächen, schmälern, entkräften, verringern, vermindern. **–ment**, *s.* die Schädigung, Schwächung.
impale [ɪmˈpeɪl], *v.a.* einpfählen, aufspießen; (*fig.*) durchbohren; (zwei Wappen) durch einen senkrechten Pfahl verbinden (*Her.*). **–ment**, *s.* Aufspießung, Durchbohrung; Verbindung zweier Wappen in einem Schild (*Her.*).
impalpable [ɪmˈpælpəbl], *adj.* unfühlbar, sehr fein; (*fig.*) unbemerkbar, unfaßbar.
impanel [ɪmˈpænl], *v.a. see* **empanel.**
impart [ɪmˈpɑːt], *v.a.* geben, verleihen, erteilen, mitteilen (*to* (*Dat.*)).
impartial [ɪmˈpɑːʃəl], *adj.* unparteiisch, unvoreingenommen, unbefangen. **–ity** [ɪmpɑːʃɪˈælɪtɪ], *s.* die Unparteilichkeit, Unbefangenheit.
impassable [ɪmˈpɑːsəbl], *adj.* unwegsam, nicht befahrbar (*as roads*), unüberschreitbar, unübersteigbar (*as an obstacle*).
impasse [ˈɪmpæs], *s.* die Sackgasse; das Stocken, völliger Stillstand.
impassib–ility [ɪmpæsɪˈbɪlɪtɪ], *s.* die Unempfindlichkeit, Gefühllosigkeit. **–le** [ɪmˈpæsɪbl], *adj.* unempfindlich, gefühllos (*to*, gegen); leidensunfähig.
impassioned [ɪmˈpæʃənd], *adj.* leidenschaftlich, feurig.
impassiv–e [ɪmˈpæsɪv], *adj.* unempfindlich, leidenschaftslos, teilnahm(s)los; (*fig.*) unbeweglich. **–eness**, *s.*, **–ity** [ɪmpæˈsɪvɪtɪ], *s.* die Unempfindlichkeit.
impast–e [ɪmˈpeɪst], 1. *v.a.* Farben dick auftragen auf (*Acc.*), impastieren, pastös malen (*Paint.*). **–o** [–oʊ], *s.* dickes Auftragen der Farbe, das Impasto.
impatien–ce [ɪmˈpeɪʃəns], *s.* die Ungeduld; Unduldsamkeit (*of*, gegenüber), Abneigung (*of*, gegen), der Unwille (*at* or *with*, über); *await with –ce*, nicht erwarten können. **–t**, *adj.* ungeduldig (*at, of* or *with*, über); unduldsam; begierig (*for*, nach); *be –t of*, nicht dulden *or* ertragen können.
impawn [ɪmˈpɔːn], *v.a.* verpfänden.
impeach [ɪmˈpiːtʃ], *v.a.* beschuldigen, anklagen (*a p. of a th.*, einen einer S.); des Hochverrats anklagen (*a minister*); angreifen; in Zweifel ziehen, in Frage stellen; tadeln, bemängeln, herabsetzen. **–able**, *adj.* anfechtbar, angreifbar, anklagbar. **–ment**, *s.* (öffentliche) Anklage (wegen Hochverrats); die Beschuldigung, Anfechtung, Herabsetzung.
impeccab–ility [ɪmpɛkəˈbɪlɪtɪ], *s.* die Unfehlbarkeit, Sündlosigkeit. **–le**, *adj.* unfehlbar, sündlos.
impecunio–sity [ɪmpəkjunɪˈɔsɪtɪ], *s.* der Geldmangel, die Armut. **–us** [ɪmpəˈkjunɪəs], *adj.* mittellos, geldlos, arm.
imped–ance [ɪmˈpiːdəns], *s.* der Scheinwiderstand, die Impedanz (*Elec.*). **–e**, *v.a.* (be)hindern (*a p.*); verhindern, erschweren (*a th.*). **–iment** [ɪmˈpɛdɪmənt], *s.* das Hindernis (*to*, für); *–iment in one's speech*, der Sprachfehler. **–imenta**, *pl.* das Gepäck; der Troß (*Mil.*).
impel [ɪmˈpɛl], *v.a.* (an)treiben, drängen, zwingen (*to*, zu). **–lent**, 1. *s.* die Triebkraft. 2. *attr. adj.* Trieb–.
impend [ɪmˈpɛnd], *v.n.* hangen, schweben (*over*, über, (*Dat.*)); (*fig.*) bevorstehen, drohen. **–ing**, *adj.* überhangend; (*fig.*) bevorstehend, drohend.
impenetrab–ility [ɪmpɛnətrəˈbɪlɪtɪ], *s.* die Undurchdringlichkeit; (*fig.*) Unerforschlichkeit. **–le** [ɪmˈpɛnɪtrəbl], *adj.* undurchdringlich, unforschbar (*to*, für); (*fig.*) unerforschlich, unergründlich (*to*, für); unempfänglich (*to*, gegen).
impeniten–ce [ɪmˈpɛnɪtəns], *s.* die Unbußfertigkeit, Verstocktheit. **–t**, *adj.* unbußfertig, verstockt, reuelos.
imperative [ɪmˈpɛrətɪv], 1. *adj.* befehlend, befehlerisch, Befehls–, gebietend; dringend notwendig, zwingend; – *mood*, der Imperativ, die Befehlsform (*Gram.*). 2. *s.* see – *mood.*
imperceptib–ility [ɪmpəsɛptɪˈbɪlɪtɪ], *s.* die Unmerkbarkeit, Unmerklichkeit. **–le** [ɪmpəˈsɛptɪbl], *adj.* unbemerkbar, unwahrnehmbar, unmerklich, unmerkbar, verschwindend klein.
imperfect [ɪmˈpəːfɪkt], *adj.* unvollkommen; unvollendet; mangelhaft, fehlerhaft; – *rhyme*, unreiner Reim (*Metr.*); – *tense*, das Imperfekt(um). **–ion** [ɪmpəˈfɛkʃən], *s.* die Unvollkommenheit; der Mangel, Fehler; (*fig.*) die Schwäche.
imperforate [ɪmˈpəːfəreɪt], *adj.* undurchbohrt; ohne Öffnung (*Surg.*); ungezähnt (*postage-stamps*).
imperial [ɪmˈpɪːrɪəl], 1. *adj.* kaiserlich, Kaiser–, Reichs–; Weltreichs– (*of Gt. Britain*); gebietend; stattlich; – *conference*, britische Weltreichskonferenz; – *diet*, deutscher Reichstag (*Hist.*); – *pint*, gesetzliches (englisches) Flüssigkeitsmaß; – *preference*, Zollvergünstigungen innerhalb des britischen Weltreiches. 2. *s.* Kaiserlicher (Soldat); das Imperial(papier) (22 × 32 *in.*); der Knebelbart, die Fliege; der Gepäckbehälter; das Omnibusdach. **–ism**, *s.* die Kaiserherrschaft; der Imperialismus, die Weltherrschaft, Weltmachtpolitik. **–ist**, *s.* Kaiserliche(r), Kaiserlichgesinnte(r), *m.*, der Imperialist. **–istic** [–ˈlɪstɪk], *adj.* imperialistisch.
imperil [ɪmˈpɛrɪl], *v.a.* gefährden.
imperious [ɪmˈpɪːrɪəs], *adj.* gebieterisch, herrisch, anmaßend; dringend (*as necessity*). **–ness**, *s.* gebieterisches Wesen.
imperishable [ɪmˈpɛrɪʃəbl], *adj.* unvergänglich.
impermanen–ce [ɪmˈpəːmənəns], *s.* die Unbeständigkeit. **–t**, *adj.* unbeständig, vorübergehend.
impermeab–ility [ɪmpəːmɪəˈbɪlɪtɪ], *s.* die Undurchdringlichkeit. **–le** [–ˈpəːmɪəbl] *adj.* undurchdringlich (*to*, für), undurchlässig; wasserdicht.
imperson–al [ɪmˈpəːsənl], *adj.* unpersönlich (*also Gram.*). **–ality** [ɪmpəːsəˈnælɪtɪ], *s.* die Unpersönlichkeit. **–ate**, *v.a.* verkörpern, personifizieren, sich ausgeben als; darstellen (*Theat.*). **–ation** [ɪmpəːsəˈneɪʃn], die Verkörperung, Personifizierung, Darstellung. **–ator** [ɪmˈpəːsəneɪtə], *s.* der Darsteller, Imitator (*Theat.*).
impertinen–ce [ɪmˈpəːtɪnəns], *s.* die Frechheit, Unverschämtheit, Ungebührlichkeit, Ungehörigkeit, Belanglosigkeit. **–t**, *adj.* frech, unverschämt; ungehörig, belanglos, unangebracht.
imperturbab–ility [ɪmpətəːbəˈbɪlɪtɪ], *s.* die Gelassenheit, Unerschütterlichkeit, der Gleichmut. **–le** [–ˈtəːbəbl] *adj.* gelassen, unerschütterlich.
impervious [ɪmpəːvjəs], *adj.* undurchdringlich (*to*, für); (*fig.*) unzulänglich (*to*, für), unwegsam; – *to*

water, wasserdicht. **–ness,** *s.* die Undurchdringlichkeit; Unzulänglichkeit.
impetigo [ɪmpəˈtaɪgoʊ], *s.* die Eiterflechte, der Blasengrind (*Med.*).
impet–uosity [ɪmpɛtjʊˈɔsɪtɪ], *s.* die Heftigkeit, das Ungestüm. **–uous** [ɪmˈpɛtjʊəs], *adj.* ungestüm, heftig. **–us** [ˈɪmpətəs], *s.* die Triebkraft, Stoßkraft, der Impuls; (*fig.*) Antrieb, Anstoß; *give a fresh –us to s.th.*, einer S. neuen Antrieb geben.
impiety [ɪmˈpaɪətɪ], *s.* die Gottlosigkeit; Pietätlosigkeit, der Mangel an Ehrfurcht.
impinge [ɪmˈpɪndʒ], *v.n.* stoßen, zusammenstoßen (*on* or *upon*, auf *or* gegen); fallen (*of light*) (*on* or *upon*, auf); (*fig.*) verstoßen (*on* or *upon*, gegen); übergreifen (*on*, in), einwirken (*on* or *upon*, auf). **–ment,** *s.* das Stoßen, der Stoß, Zusammenstoß; Eingriff (*on*, in), Einfluß, die Einwirkung.
impious [ˈɪmpɪəs], *adj.* gottlos, ruchlos; ehrfurchtslos, pietätlos.
impish [ˈɪmpɪʃ], *adj.* koboldartig; (*fig.*) schelmisch.
implacab–ility [ɪmplækəˈbɪlɪtɪ], *s.* die Unversöhnlichkeit. **–le** [ɪmˈplækəbl], *adj.* unversöhnlich, unerbittlich.
implant [ɪmˈplɑːnt], *v.a.* einpflanzen (*also fig.*); (*fig.*) einimpfen, einprägen (*in* (*Dat.*)).
implement, 1. [ˈɪmpləmənt], *s.* das Gerät, Werkzeug, Zubehöhr; (*Scots*) die Ausführung, Erfüllung (*Law*). 2. [ˈɪmplɪmɛnt], *v.a.* ausführen, erfüllen, vollenden, zur Ausführung bringen, in Wirkung setzen.
implicat–e [ˈɪmplɪkəɪt], *v.a.* verwickeln, hineinziehen (*a p.*) (*in*, in (*Acc.*)); in Verbindung or Zusammenhang bringen (*with*, mit), in sich schließen, mit einbegreifen (*a th.*); *be –ed in*, mit enthalten sein in, verflochten sein mit; beeinflußt *or* betroffen werden durch *or* bei (*Med.*). **–ion** [ɪmplɪˈkəɪʃən], *s.* die Verwick(e)lung; selbstverständliche Folgerung, tieferer Sinn; *by –ion*, stillschweigend, ohne weiteres, mittelbar, als selbstverständliche Folgerung.
implicit [ɪmˈplɪsɪt], *adj.* unbeschränkt, unbedingt, blind; inbegriffen, einbegriffen, stillschweigend. **–ly,** *adv.* unbedingt; stillschweigend, ohne weiteres, implizite. **–ness,** *s.* die Unbeschränktheit, Unbedingtheit; das Mitinbegriffensein.
implied [ɪmˈplaɪd], *adj.* miteinbegriffen, stillschweigend verstanden; *see* **imply.**
implor–e [ɪmˈplɔːɹ] *v.a.* anflehen, flehentlich bitten (*a p.*) (*for*, um); *I –e you*, ich beschwöre dich. **–ing,** *adj.* flehentlich, flehend.
imply [ɪmˈplaɪ], *v.a.* mitenthalten, in sich schließen bedeuten, besagen, zu verstehen geben, durchblicken lassen, andeuten; *that may be implied from*, das ergibt sich aus, das ist zu erschließen aus.
impolite [ɪmpoˈlaɪt], *adj.* unhöflich, grob. **–ness,** *s.* die Unhöflichkeit, Grobheit.
import [ɪmˈpɔːt], 1. *v.a.* einführen, importieren (*C.L.*); bedeuten, besagen, mit sich bringen. 2. *v.imp.* (*rare*) von Wichtigkeit sein für, betreffen, angehen. 3. [ˈɪmpɔːt], *s.* die Einfuhr, Zufuhr, der Import (*C.L.*); (*usually pl.*) Einfuhrartikel (*C.L.*); der Sinn, die Bedeutung, Wichtigkeit, Tragweite; *– duty*, der Einfuhrzoll. **–ation** [ɪmpɔːˈteɪʃən], *s.* die (Waren)Einfuhr; der Einfuhrartikel. **–er** [ɪmˈpɔːtə], *s.* der Importhändler, Importeur.
importan–ce [ɪmˈpɔːtəns], *s.* die Wichtigkeit, Bedeutsamkeit, Bedeutung, der Wert, Belang, Einfluß, das Gewicht; (*coll.*) die Wichtigtuerei; *man of –ce*, der Mann von Bedeutung, einflußreicher Mann. **–t,** *adj.* wichtig, bedeutsam, bedeutend, wesentlich (*to*, für); einflußreich; (*coll.*) wichtigtuerisch.
importun–ate [ɪmˈpɔːtjunɪt], *adj.* lästig, zudringlich, aufdringlich. **–e** [ɪmˈpɔːtjuːn], *v.a.* belästigen, behelligen, dringend bitten. **–ity** [ɪmpɔːˈtjuːnɪtɪ], *s.* die Zudringlichkeit, Aufdringlichkeit.
impos–e [ɪmˈpoʊz], 1. *v.a.* auferlegen, aufbürden; aufdrängen, aufbinden (*on* or *upon* (*Dat.*)); ausschießen (*Typ.*). 2. *v.n.* imponieren (*upon* (*Acc.*)); betrügen, täuschen, hintergehen, anschmieren (*upon* (*Acc.*)); *–e upon his good nature*, seine Gutherzigkeit mißbrauchen. **–ing,** *adj.* imponierend, eindrucksvoll, imposant. **–ition** [ɪmpəˈzɪʃən], *s.* das Auflegen (*of hands*); die Auferlegung, Aufbürdung (*of taxes*); Beilegung, Erteilung (*of a name*); Steuer; Bürde; Strafarbeit (*in schools*); Täuschung, der Betrug; Umbruch (*Typ.*); *an –ition on his good nature*, ein Mißbrauch seiner Gutherzigkeit.
impossib–ility [ɪmpɔsɪˈbɪlɪtɪ], *s.* die Unmöglichkeit. **–le** [ɪmˈpɔsɪbl], *adj.* unmöglich, ausgeschlossen; (*coll.*) unerträglich (*of persons*).
impost [ɪmˈpɔst], *s.* die Abgabe, Steuer; der Auflager, Kämpfer (*Arch.*); (*sl.*) das Gewicht (*horse-racing*).
impost–or [ɪmˈpɔstə], *s.* der Betrüger, Schwindler. **–ure** [ɪmˈpɔstʃə], *s.* der Betrug, Schwindel.
impoten–ce, –cy [ˈɪmpətəns(ɪ)], *s.* das Unvermögen, die Unfähigkeit; Impotenz (*Med.*); (*fig.*) Schwäche, Hilflosigkeit. **–t,** *adj.* unfähig; impotent (*Med.*); (*fig.*) schwach, machtlos.
impound [ɪmˈpaʊnd], *v.a.* einpferchen, einsperren, einschließen; beschlagnahmen, mit Beschlag belegen (*Law*).
impoverish [ɪmˈpɔvərɪʃ], *v.a.* arm machen; aussaugen (*land*); *be –ed*, verarmen. **–ment,** *s.* die Verarmung; Erschöpfung (*of soil*).
impracticab–ility [ɪmpræktɪkəˈbɪlɪtɪ], *s.* die Unausführbarkeit, praktische Unmöglichkeit; die Unlenksamkeit, Hartnäckigkeit; Ungangbarkeit (*of roads*). **–le** [ɪmˈpræktɪkəbl], *adj.* unausführbar, untunlich; unlenksam, hartnäckig; unwegsam, ungangbar (*as roads*).
imprecat–e [ˈɪmprɪkeɪt], *v.a.* herabwünschen (*misfortune*) (*upon*, auf (*Acc.*)); *–e curses on*, verwünschen, verfluchen. **–ion** [ɪmprɪˈkeɪʃən], *s.* das Herbeiwünschen; die Verwünschung, der Fluch. **–ory** [ˈɪmprɪkətərɪ], *adj.* verwünschend, Verwünschungs–.
impregnab–ility [ɪmprɛgnəˈbɪlɪtɪ], *s.* die Unüberwindlichkeit, Unbezwingbarkeit. **–le** [ɪmˈprɛgnɪbl] *adj.* uneinnehmbar, unbezwinglich; (*fig.*) unerschütterlich (*to*, gegenüber).
impregnat–e, 1. [ɪmˈprɛgneɪt], *v.a.* schwängern, schwanger machen; befruchten (*Bot.*); (*usually passive*) sättigen, imprägnieren (*Chem.*); (*fig.*) durchtränken, durchdringen, erfüllen. 2. [ɪmˈprɛgnɪt], *adj.* geschwängert, schwanger, befruchtet; (*fig.*) durchtränkt (*with*, mit); voll (*with*, von). **–ion** [–ˈneɪʃən], *s.* Schwängerung; Befruchtung; Sättigung, Imprägnierung; Durchdringung.
impresario [ɪmprəˈzɑːrɪoʊ], *s.* der Impresario, Theaterunternehmer.
imprescriptible [ɪmprɪˈskrɪptɪbl], *adj.* unverjährbar, unverlierbar, unverletzbar (*rights, etc.*).
impress, 1. [ɪmˈprɛs], *v.a.* eindrücken, aufdrücken, (ein)prägen (*on*, auf); (*fig.*) verleihen (*upon* (*Dat.*)); aufzwingen, einschärfen (*upon a p., etc.* (*Dat.*)); erfüllen, durchdringen (*a p.*) (*with*, von); beeindrucken, Eindruck machen auf (*a p.*); pressen (*seamen*); beschlagnahmen (*goods*); *be favourably –ed by*, einen guten Eindruck erhalten von; *–ed by the idea*, durch den Gedanken beeindruckt; *the urgency was –ed on my mind*, die dringende Eile wurde mir eingeschärft *or* nahegelegt; *–ed with the necessity*, von der Notwendigkeit durchdrungen. **2.** [ˈɪmprɛs] *s.* der Abdruck, Stempel, die Prägung; das Gepräge, Merkmal. **–ible** [ɪmˈprɛsɪbl], *adj. see* **–ionable. –ion** [ɪmˈprɛʃən], *s.* der Eindruck, die Einwirkung, Beeindruckung; der Abdruck, Stempel, das Gepräge, Merkmal; (*coll.*) dunkle Erinnerung; die Auflage (*of a book*); *give the –ion of being*, den Eindruck hinterlassen zu sein; *make a favourable –ion upon a p.*, einen günstigen Eindruck auf einen machen; *new –ion*, der Neudruck, neue Auflage (*Print.*); *be under the –ion that*, es schwebt mir dunkel vor daß. **–ionable** [ɪmˈprɛʃənəbl], *adj.* empfänglich, leicht bestimmbar. **–ionism,** *s.* der Impressionismus (*Paint.*). **–ionist,** *s.* der Impressionist (*Paint.*). **–ionistic** [ɪmprɛʃəˈnɪstɪk], *adj.* impressionistisch. **–ive** [ɪmˈprɛsɪv], *adj.* eindrucksvoll, eindringlich, ergreifend, imponierend. **–iveness,** *s.* Eindrucksvolle(s), Ergreifende(s), *n.* **–ment,** *s.* das Pressen (*Naut.*), die Beschlagnahme.
imprest [ˈɪmprɛst], *s.* der Staatsvorschuß.
imprimatur [ɪmprɪˈmeɪtə], *s.* die Druckbewilligung, Druckerlaubnis.
imprint, 1. [ɪmˈprɪnt], *v.a.* auf)drücken, prägen,

aufpressen (*on* or *auf* (*Acc.*)); (*fig.*) einprägen (*on* or *upon* (*Dat.*)). 2. [ˈɪmprɪnt] *s.* der Abdruck, Stempel; (*fig.*) Eindruck, das Gepräge; der Druckvermerk, die Verlagsangabe, das Impressum (*Print.*).

imprison [ɪmˈprɪzən], *v.a.* einkerkern, einsperren, verhaften; (*fig.*) einschließen. **–ment,** *s.* die Verhaftung, Einkerkerung, Inhaftierung; Haft, Gefangenschaft, Freiheitsstrafe, Gefängnisstrafe, das Gefängnis; *false –ment*, ungesetzliche Haft.

improbab–ility [ɪmprɔbəˈbɪlɪtɪ], *s.* die Unwahrscheinlichkeit. **–le** [ɪmˈprɔbəbl], *adj.* unwahrscheinlich, unglaubwürdig.

improbity [ɪmˈproubɪtɪ], *s.* die Unredlichkeit, Unehrlichkeit.

impromptu [ɪmˈprɔmptjʊ], 1. *adj.* & *adv.* aus dem Stegreif, improvisiert. 2. *s.* das Stegreifgedicht; Impromptu (*Mus.*).

improper [ɪmˈprɔpə], *adj.* ungeeignet, untauglich; unschicklich, ungehörig, unanständig; – *fraction*, unechter Bruch (*Arith.*); *see* **impropriety.**

impropriat–e, 1. [ɪmˈprouprɪeɪt], *v.a.* zueignen, zur Nutznießung übertragen (*Eccl.*). 2. [ɪmˈprouprɪət], *adj.* übertragen (*Eccl.*). **–ion** [–ˈeɪʃən], *s.* das Übertragen; übertragene Pfründe. **–or** [–ə], *s.* weltlicher Pfründenbesitzer.

impropriety [ɪmprəˈpraɪətɪ], *s.* die Untauglichkeit, Unangebrachtheit; Unschicklichkeit, Ungehörigkeit.

improv–able [ɪmˈpruːvəbl], *adj.* verbesserungsfähig, verbesserlich, bildsam; anbaufähig (*as lands*). **–e** [ɪmˈpruːv], 1. *v.a.* verbessern, vervollkommnen, aufbessern, anreichern, veredeln, verfeinern, meliorisieren (*land*); benutzen, ausnutzen, sich (*Dat.*) zunutze machen; *–e the occasion*, gleich eine Predigt halten; *–e the shining hour*, seine Zeit vorteilhaft ausnützen. 2. *v.n.* besser werden, sich verbessern, Fortschritte machen; steigen (*prices*); sich erholen (*health*); sich vervollkommnen; *–e* (*up*)*on*, verbessern, überbieten, übertreffen; *be –ing*, auf dem Wege der Besserung sein; *–e on acquaintance*, bei längerer Bekanntschaft gewinnen. 3. *s.*; (*coll.*) *on the –e*, auf dem Wege der Besserung. **–ement,** *s.* die Verbesserung, Vervollkommnung; Ausnutzung, Nutzanwendung, vorteilhafte Anwendung; die Veredelung, Ausbildung; Besserung (*of health*); das Steigen (*of prices*); der Fortschritt, Gewinn (*on* or *upon*, gegenüber); *pl.* Verbesserungen. **–er,** *s.* der Verbesserer; Volontär (*C.L.*); das Verbesserungsmittel; *see* **improving.**

improviden–ce [ɪmˈprɔvɪdəns], *s.* die Unbedachtsamkeit, Unvorsichtigkeit; Sorglosigkeit, der Leichtsinn. **–t,** *adj.* unvorsichtig, unbedacht; sorglos, leichtsinnig.

improving [ɪmˈpruːvɪŋ], *adj.* förderlich, heilsam, wohltätig.

improvis–ation [ɪmprəvaɪˈzeɪʃən], *s.* die Stegreifdichtung; unvorbereitete Veranstaltung, Improvisation (*also Mus.*). **–ator** [–ˈzeɪtə], *s.* der Improvisator, Stegreifdichter. **–e** [ˈɪmprəvaɪz], *v.a.* & *n.* aus dem Stegreif *or* ohne Vorbereitung tun, reden *or* dichten, improvisieren; im Handumdrehen einrichten; (*coll.*) aus dem Boden stampfen, aus dem Ärmel schütteln. **–ed** [–vaɪzd], *adj.* improvisiert, unvorbereitet, aus dem Stegreif, behilfsmäßig, Behelfs–.

impruden–ce [ɪmˈpruːdəns], *s.* die Unklugheit, Unvorsichtigkeit. **–t** [–t], *adj.* unklug, übereilt.

impuden–ce [ˈɪmpjədəns], *s.* die Unverschämtheit, Frechheit, Unverschämtheiten (*pl.*). **–t** [–t], *adj.* unverschämt, frech, schamlos.

impugn [ɪmˈpjuːn], *v.a.* anfechten, bestreiten; angreifen, antasten. **–able,** *adj.* bestreitbar, anfechtbar. **–ment,** *s.* die Bekämpfung, Widerlegung, der Einwand.

impuls–e [ˈɪmpʌls], *s.* der Stoß, Anstoß, Trieb, Antrieb, Drang, Impuls, die Anregung; Regung, Anwandlung, Eingebung; *on the –e of the moment*, unter dem Drang *or* Impuls des Augenblicks; *on an –e*, auf einen Antrieb hin; *on –e*, impulsiv. **–ion** [–ˈpʌlʃən], *s.* der Stoß, Anstoß, Antrieb (*also fig.*); *under the –ion*, durch den Antrieb. **–ive** [–ˈpʌlsɪv], *adj.* leicht erregbar, leidenschaftlich, impulsiv, triebhaft; (an)treibend, Trieb–. **–iveness,** *s.* die Erregbarkeit, Leidenschaftlichkeit.

impunity [ɪmˈpjuːnɪtɪ], *s.* die Straflosigkeit, Straffreiheit; *with –*, ungestraft.

impur–e [ɪmˈpjuːə], *adj.* unrein, schmutzig; unkeusch, unzüchtig; unsauber (*motives*). **–ity** [–ˈpjuːrɪtɪ], *s.* die Unreinheit, Unreinlichkeit; Unkeuschheit. **–ities,** *pl.* fremde Bestandteile (*pl.*), die Verunreinigung.

imput–able [ɪmˈpjuːtɪbl], *adj.* zuzuschreiben(d), zuzurechnen(d), beizumessen(d) (*to* (*Dat.*)). **–ation** [ɪmpjʊˈteɪʃən], *s.* die Anschuldigung, Beschuldigung, Bezichtigung; *–ation on his character*, der Makel auf seinem Charakter. **–e** [ɪmˈpjuːt], *v.a.* zurechnen, zuschreiben, beimessen, zur Last legen (*to* (*Dat.*)). **–ed** [–ɪd], *adj.* unterstellt, zugeschrieben.

in [ɪn], **1.** *prep.* in an; auf; bei; aus; nach; unter; gemäß; zu; von; **(a)** – *1870*, im Jahre 1870; – *the affirmative*, bejahend; – *the afternoon*, nachmittags; – *all*, im ganzen; – *answer to*, in Beantwortung (*Gen.*), als Antwort auf (*Acc.*); – *appearance*, dem Anschein nach; – *arms*, unter Waffen; *infant – arms*, ein Kind, das noch nicht gehen kann; – *the army*, beim Heer; – *any case*, auf jeden Fall; – *the circumstances*, unter den Umständen; – *conclusion*, schließlich; – *contempt*, aus Verachtung; – *the country*, auf dem Lande; – *doubt*, im Zweifel; – *dozens*, zu Dutzenden, dutzendweise; – *due course*, zu rechter Zeit *or* seiner Zeit; – *the day*(*time*), bei Tage; – *debt*, verschuldet; – *his defence*, zu seiner Verteidigung; *blind – one eye*, auf einem Auge blind; – *despair*, in Verzweiflung; – *the evening*, am Abend, abends; – *German*, auf deutsch; – *groups*, gruppenweise; – *good health*, in *or* bei guter Gesundheit; - *his honour*, ihm zu Ehren; – *hopes*, in der Hoffnung; *not one – a hundred*, keiner von Hundert; – *a hurry*, eilig; – *January*, im Januar; – *life*, bei Lebzeiten; – *all likelihood*, aller Wahrscheinlichkeit nach; – *this manner*, auf diese Weise, in dieser Weise; *a woman – a million*, eine Frau wie man sie unter einer Million nicht findet; – *the morning*, am Morgen, morgens; – *number*, an Zahl; – *obedience to*, aus Gehorsam gegen; – *my opinion*, meines Erachtens, nach meiner Meinung, meiner Meinung nach; – *order to do*, um zu tun; – *particular*, im besonderen; *a shilling – the pound*, ein Schilling aufs Pfund; – *praise of*, zum Lobe von; – *the press*, im Druck, unter der Presse; – *print*, im Druck, gedruckt; – *all probability*, höchstwahrscheinlich, – *the rain*, in *or* bei Regen; – *the reign*, unter der Regierung (*of* (*Gen.*)); – *reply to*, als Antwort auf; – *respect of . . .*, was . . . anbelangt *or* betrifft; – *search of*, auf der Suche nach; – *short*, kurz; – *size*, an Größe; – *the sky*, am Himmel; – *his sleep*, während er schlief, im Schlaf; – *stock*, vorrätig; – *the street*, auf der Straße; *equal – strength*, an Stärke gleich; – (*the*) *summer*, im Sommer; – *time*, zur rechten Zeit, rechtzeitig; – *truth*, wahrhaftig; – *turn*, der Reihe nach; – *no way*, auf keine Weise, keineswegs, durchaus nicht; *dressed – white*, weißgekleidet; – *bad weather* bei schlechtem Wetter; – *a week*, in acht Tagen; – *a word*, mit einem Wort, in aller Kürze, kurz; – *writing*, schriftlich; **(b)** (*with pers. prons.*) *be –* or *have a hand – it*, dabei beteiligt sein, es mitmachen; (*coll*) *he's not – it*, er zählt nicht mit; *he has not got it – him*, er hat nicht das Zeug dazu; *there's money – it*, es ist dabei Geld zu verdienen; *there is nothing – it*, es ist nichts daran, es hat keinen Wert, es springt nichts dabei heraus, es lohnt sich nicht; es ist kein großer Unterschied; es ist ganz einfach; *there's something – it*, es steckt etwas dahinter; **(c)** (*with verbs, etc.*) *abound –*, Überfluß haben an; *believe –*, glauben an; *engage –*, sich beteiligen an, sich beschäftigen mit, sich abgeben mit, sich einlassen in *or* auf; *originate –*, seine Ursache haben in, entstehen, entspringen *or* herstammen aus; *participate –*, beteiligt sein an, teilhaben, teilnehmen *or* sich beteiligen an, gemeinsam haben mit; *persist –*, bestehen auf, fest bleiben bei, beharren bei; hartnäckig fortfahren (*doing*, zu tun); *rejoice –*, sich erfreuen (*Gen.*); *trust –*, vertrauen auf; **(d)** (*with gerunds*) – *crossing the road*, beim Überqueren der Straße; *I have much pleasure – informing you*, es freut mich sehr, Ihnen mitteilen zu können; – *making this contribution*, mit der Leistung dieses

Beitrages; *they pass their time – sleeping*, sie bringen ihre Zeit mit Schlafen hin. **2.** *adv.* (*with verbs of movement*) hinein–, herein–; (*with verbs*) ein–; drinnen, innen; – *between*, zwischendurch; *be* –, zu Hause sein; angekommen sein (*of trains*); am Schlagen sein (*Crick.*); an der Regierung *or* am Ruder sein (*Pol.*); *be* – *for*, zu erwarten or befürchten haben; (*coll.*) *be* – *for it*, schön in der Patsche sitzen; *be* – *for an examination*, sich für eine Prüfung gemeldet haben; *breed* –, sich durch Inzucht fortpflanzen; *come* –! herein! *he came* –, er kam herein; *go* –, hineingehen, eintreten; (*coll.*) *go* – *for a th.*, sich mit einer S. beschäftigen; *keep* –, nachsitzen lassen (*in school*); *keep* – *with s.o.*, auf gutem Fuße mit einem sein; *keep one's hand* –, in Übung bleiben; *rub* –, einreiben; *year* – *year out*, jahraus, jahrein; (*Prov.*) – *for a penny*, – *for a pound*, wer A sagt muß auch B sagen. **3.** *s.*; *the* –*s*, die Regierungspartei (*Pol.*); (*coll.*) *the* –*s and outs*, alles was drum und dran ist, die Winkel und Ecken, alle Einzelheiten; Windungen.

inability [ɪnəˈbɪlɪtɪ], *s.* die Unfähigkeit, das Unvermögen; *see* **unable.**

inaccessib–ility [ɪnəksɛsəˈbɪlɪtɪ], *s.* die Unzugänglichkeit (*to*, für), Unnahbarkeit. **–le** [ˈsɛsɪbl], *adj.* unerreichbar, unzugänglich, unnahbar (*to*, für).

inaccura–cy [ɪnˈækjərəsɪ], *s.* die Ungenauigkeit; Unrichtigkeit, der Fehler, Irrtum. **–te** [–rət], *adj.* ungenau; unrichtig.

inact–ion [ɪnˈækʃən], *s.* die Untätigkeit. **–ive** [tɪv], *adj.* untätig; träge; passiv, unwirksam; unbelebt; außer Dienst (*Mil.*); flau (*C.L.*). **–ivity** [–ˈtɪvɪtɪ], *s.* die Untätigkeit; Unbelebtheit, Flauheit (*C.L.*).

inadaptab–ility [ɪnədæptəˈbɪlɪtɪ], *s.* die Unanwendbarkeit. **–le** [–ˈdæptɪbl], *adj.* unanwendbar (*to*, für *or* auf).

inadequa–cy [ɪnˈædəkwəsɪ], *s.* die Unzulänglichkeit, Unangemessenheit. **–te** [–dɪkwət], *adj.* unzulänglich, unangemessen, unzureichend. **–teness,** *s. see* **–cy.**

inadmissib–ility [ɪnədmɪsɪˈbɪlɪtɪ], *s.* die Unzulässigkeit. **–le** [–ˈmɪsɪbl], *adj.* unzulässig, unstatthaft.

inadverten–ce, –cy [ɪnədˈvəːtəns(ɪ)], *s.* die Unachtsamkeit, Nachlässigkeit, Fahrlässigkeit; der Irrtum, das Versehen. **–t,** *adj.* unachtsam, nachlässig, fahrlässig; unbeabsichtigt, unabsichtlich. **–tly,** *adv.* aus Versehen, versehentlich.

inadvisable [ɪnədˈvɑɪzəbl], *adj.* unratsam.

inalienab–ility [ɪneɪlɪənəˈbɪlɪtɪ], *s.* die Unveräußerlichkeit. **–le** [ɪnˈeɪlɪənəbl], *adj.* unveräußerlich.

inalterable [ɪnˈɔːltərəbl], *adj.* unveränderlich.

inamorat–a [ɪnæməˈrɑːtə], *s.* die Verliebte; das Liebchen. **–o** [–toʊ], *s.* Verliebte(r), *m.*, der Liebhaber.

inane [ɪnˈeɪn], *adj.* leer, nichtig, fade, geistlos, sinnlos, albern.

inanimate [ɪnˈænɪmət], *adj.* leblos, geistlos, unbeseelt; (*fig.*) unbelebt; flau (*C.L.*).

inanit–ion [ɪnæˈnɪʃən], *s.* die Schwäche, Entkräftung; Leerheit (*Med.*). **–y** [ɪnˈænɪtɪ], *s.* die Leere, Nichtigkeit, Hohlheit, Albernheit.

inapplicab–ility [ɪnəplɪkəˈbɪlɪtɪ], *s.* die Unanwendbarkeit. **–le** [–ˈplɪkəbl], *adj.* unanwendbar (*to*, auf), ungeeignet, unbrauchbar (*to*, für).

inapposite [ɪnˈæpəzɪt], *adj.* unangemessen, unpassend (*to*, für).

inappreciable [ɪnəˈprɪːʃɪəbl], *adj.* unwahrnehmbar, unbemerkbar, unberechenbar; unbedeutend, unwichtig.

inapprehensible [ɪnæprɪˈhɛnsɪbl], *adj.* unbegreiflich, unfaßbar, unfaßlich.

inapproachable [ɪnəˈproʊtʃəbl], *adj.* unnahbar, unzugänglich.

inappropriate [ɪnəˈproʊprɪət], *adj.* ungeeignet, unpassend, unangemessen, ungehörig. **–ness,** *s.* die Unangemessenheit, Ungehörigkeit.

inapt [ɪnˈæpt], *adj.* unpassend, ungeeignet, untauglich, ungeschickt (*at*, bei). **–itude** [–ɪtjuːd], *s.*, **–ness,** *s.* die Ungeeignetheit, Untauglichkeit (*for*, zu); Ungeschicktheit.

inarch [ɪnˈɑːtʃ], *v.a.* absaugen, ablaktieren (*Hort.*).

inarticulate [ɪnɑːˈtɪkjʊlət], *adj.* unartikuliert; undeutlich, unvernehmlich (*of speech*); ungegliedert (*Zool.*). **–ness,** *s.* die Undeutlichkeit, Unvernehmlichkeit.

inartistic [ɪnɑːˈtɪstɪk], *adj.* unkünstlerisch.

inasmuch [ɪnəzˈmʌtʃ], *adv.*; – *as*, da, weil; (in)sofern (als).

inattent–ion [ɪnɔˈtɛnʃən], *s.* die Unaufmerksamkeit, Unachtsamkeit; –*ion to details*, die Gleichgültigkeit gegen Einzelheiten. **–ive** [–tɪv], *adj.* unaufmerksam, unachtsam (*to*, auf (*Acc.*)); nachlässig, achtlos, gleichgültig (*to*, gegen). **–iveness,** *s.* die Unaufmerksamkeit.

inaudib–ility [ɪnɔːdɪˈbɪlɪtɪ], *s.* die Unhörbarkeit. **–le** [ɪnˈɔːdɪbl], *adj.* unhörbar.

inaugur–al [ɪnˈɔːgjərəl], *adj.* Einweihungs–, Antritts–. **–ate** [–jəreɪt], *v.a.* einweihen, feierlich eröffnen, einführen *or* einsetzen; (*fig.*) beginnen, einleiten (*an era, etc.*). **–ation** [–jəˈreɪʃən], *s.* die Einweihung, feierliche Eröffnung, Einführung *or* Einsetzung; Einleitung, das Beginnen. –*ation Day*, die Amtseinsetzung des Präsidenten (*Amer.*). **–ator** [–reɪtə], *s.* der Einführer. **–atory** [–rətərɪ], *adj. see* **–al.**

inauspicious [ɪnɔːˈspɪʃəs], *adj.* ungünstig, unglücklich, unheilvoll, von böser Vorbedeutung. **–ness,** *s.* üble Vorbedeutung.

inboard [ˈɪnbɔːd], 1. *adv.* binnenbords, im Schiff. 2. *attrib. adj.* Innen– (*Naut.*).

inborn [ˈɪnbɔːn], *adj.* angeboren (*in a p.*, einem).

inbreathe [ɪnˈbrɪːð], *v.a.* einhauchen.

inbre–d [ˈɪnbrɛd], *adj.* angeboren, ererbt. **–ed** [ɪnˈbrɪːd], *v.a.* erzeugen. **–eding,** *s.* die Inzucht.

incalculab–ility [ɪnkælkjʊləˈbɪlɪtɪ], *s.* die Unberechenbarkeit. **–le** [ɪnˈkælkjʊləbl], *adj.* unberechenbar, unermeßlich, unmeßbar; unzuverlässig (*of persons*).

incandescen–ce [ɪnkənˈdɛsəns], *s.* das Weißglühen, die Weißglut. **–t** [–t], *adj.* weißglühend, glühend, leuchtend, Glüh–; –*t mantle*, der Glühstrumpf.

incantation [ɪnkænˈteɪʃən], *s.* die Beschwörung; Beschwörungsformel, der Zauberspruch.

incapa–bility [ɪnkeɪpəˈbɪlɪtɪ], *s.* die Unfähigkeit, Untüchtigkeit, Untauglichkeit. **–ble** [ɪnˈkeɪpəbl], *adj.* unfähig, untauglich, nicht fähig *or* imstande (*of*, zu); nicht berechtigt (*Law*); *drunk and* –*ble*, hilflos betrunken. **–citate** [ɪnkəˈpæsɪteɪt], *v.a.* unfähig machen (*for*, zu). **–citation** [–ˈteɪʃən], *s.* die Unfähigmachung. **–city** [–ˈpæsɪtɪ], *s.* die Unfähigkeit (*for*, für; *for doing*, zu tun), Untüchtigkeit.

incarcerat–e [ɪnˈkɑːsəreɪt], *v.a.* einkerkern; einklammern, einklemmen (*Med.*). **–ion** [–ˈreɪʃən], *s.* die Einkerkerung.

incarna–dine [ɪnˈkɑːnədɑɪn], *adj.* (*Poet.*) fleischfarben. **–te,** 1. [–nɪt] *adj.* fleischgeworden; (*fig.*) eingefleischt, leibhaftig. 2. [–neɪt] *v.a.* mit Fleisch bekleiden, verkörpern; (*fig.*) verwirklichen; konkrete Form geben (*Dat.*). **–tion** [–ˈneɪʃən], *s.* die Fleischwerdung, Menschwerdung; (*fig.*) Verkörperung.

incautious [ɪnˈkɔːʃəs], *adj.* unvorsichtig, unbedacht. **–ness,** *s.* die Unvorsichtigkeit.

incendiar–ism [ɪnˈsɛndjərɪzm], *s.* die Brandstiftung. **–y** [–rɪ], 1. *adj.* Brand–; (*fig.*) aufrührerisch, aufwieglerisch; –*y bomb*, die Brandbombe; –*y fires*, Brandstiftungen. 2. *s.* der Brandstifter; (*fig.*) Aufruhrstifter, Aufwiegler.

[1]**incense** [ˈɪnsɛns], 1. *s.* der Weihrauch (*also fig.*). 2. *v.a.* beweihräuchern, mit Weihrauch *or* Duft erfüllen, durchduften.

[2]**incense** [ɪnˈsɛns], *v.a.* erzürnen, in Wut bringen (*against*, gegen; *with*, über (*Acc.*)).

incentive [ɪnˈsɛntɪv], 1. *adj.* anreizend, auspornend, antreibend. 2. *s.* der Anreiz, Antrieb, Ansporn (*to*, zu).

incept [ɪnˈsɛpt], 1. *v.n.* anerkannt werden (*Univ.*). 2. *v.a.* einnehmen, aufnehmen (*Biol.*). **–ion** [–ʃən], *s.* die Gründung, Eröffnung, das Beginnen; die Aufnahme, Anerkennung, Qualifikation (*Univ.*). **–ive** [–tɪv], *adj.* beginnend, anfangend, Anfangs–; –*ive proposition*, der Vordersatz; –*ive verb*, das Inchoativ(um).

incertitude [ɪnˈsəːtɪtjuːd], *s.* die Ungewißheit.

incessan–cy [ɪnˈsɛsənsɪ], *s.* die Unablässigkeit. **–t** [–ənt], *adj.* unaufhörlich, unablässig, fortgesetzt.

incest [ˈɪnsɛst], *s.* die Blutschande. **–uous** [ɪnˈsɛstjʊəs], blutschänderisch.

inch [ɪntʃ], 1. *s.* der Zoll (*2·54 cm.*); (*fig.*) die Kleinigkeit, das Bißchen, *pl.* die Statur, der Wuchs; *– by –* Schritt für Schritt, allmählich; *by –es*, allmählich, nach und nach, langsam; *flog a p. within an – of his life*, einen fast zu Tode prügeln; *every –*, jeder Zoll, durch und durch; *not yield an –*, nicht einen Zoll weichen; (*Prov.*) *give him an – and he'll take an ell*, gibt man ihm den kleinen Finger, so nimmt er die ganze Hand; *2 –es of rain*, 2 Zoll Regen; *two-–plank*, zweizölliges Brett. 2. *v.n.*; *– forward*, sich langsam vorwärtsbewegen. **–ed,** *adj.* Zoll–, zöllig.

inchoat–e [ˈɪnkoʊɪt], *adj.* angefangen, Anfangs–, unvollkommen, unfertig. **–ive** [–ˈkoʊɪtɪv], 1. *adj.* inchoativ (*Gram.*), *see also* **–e.** 2. *s.* das Inchoativ(um) (*Gram.*).

inciden–ce [ˈɪnsɪdəns], *s.* das Vorkommen, Aufkommen, Eintreten; die Ausdehnung, Ausbreitung, Verbreitung, der Umfang; Einfall (*Phys.*); *angle of –ce*, der Einfallswinkel; *–ce of taxation*, die Steuerbelastung. **–t** [–t], 1. *adj.* eigen, zugehörig (*to* (*Dat.*)); verknüpft, verbunden (*to*, mit); einfallend (*Phys.*). 2. *s.* der Zwischenfall, Vorfall, Zufall, Umstand, das Ereignis; die Begleiterscheinung, der Nebenumstand. **–tal** [ɪnsɪˈdɛntəl], *adj.* zufällig, gelegentlich, nebensächlich, beiläufig, Neben–; *–tal to*, gehörig zu, verbunden mit; *be –tal to*, gehören zu; *be –tal upon*, folgen auf; *–tal expenses*, Nebenausgaben; *–tal images*, Nachbilder; *–tal music*, die Begleitmusik. **–tally,** *adv.* beiläufig, nebenbei, übrigens. **–tals,** *pl.* Nebenausgaben; Nebenumstände, Begleitumstände.

incinerat–e [ɪnˈsɪnəreɪt], *v.a.* zu Asche verbrennen, einäschern. **–ion** [–ˈreɪʃən], *s.* die Einäscherung. **–or** [ɪnˈsɪnəreɪtə], *s.* der Verbrennungsofen.

incipien–ce, –cy [ɪnˈsɪpɪəns(ɪ)], *s.* der Anfang, das Beginnen, erstes Stadium. **–t** [–t], *adj.* beginnend, anfangend, Anfangs–, im Entstehen begriffen.

incis–e [ɪnˈsaɪz], *v.a.* einschneiden in; schneiden, gravieren (*a stone*); *–ed wound*, die Schnittwunde. **–ion** [ɪnˈsɪʒən], *s.* der Einschnitt, Schnitt. **–ive** [ɪnˈsaɪsɪv], *adj.* einschneidend; (*fig.*) schneidend, scharf, durchdringlich, ausdrucksvoll. **–or** [–zə], *s.* der Schneidezahn (*Anat.*).

incit–ation [ɪnsaɪˈteɪʃən], *s.* die Anreizung, Anregung, der Antrieb. **–e** [ɪnˈsaɪt], *v.a.* anreizen, antreiben, anspornen, anstacheln, aufmuntern (*to*, zu). **–ement,** *s.* die Anreizung, Aufreizung, Anregung (*to*, zu).

incivility [ɪnsɪˈvɪlɪtɪ], *s.* die Unhöflichkeit, Grobheit.

incivism [ˈɪnsɪvɪzm], *s.* die Unbürgerlichkeit.

in-clearing [ɪnˈklɪːərɪŋ], *s.* der Gesamtbetrag der zu zahlenden Schecks (*C.L.*).

inclemen–cy [ɪnˈklɛmənsɪ], *s.* die Rauheit, Unbill, Härte (*of the weather*). **–t** [–t], *adj.* unfreundlich, rauh.

inclin–able [ɪnˈklaɪnəbl], *adj.* geneigt. **–ation** [ɪnklɪˈneɪʃən], *s.* die Neigung, Vorliebe, Anlage, der Hang (*for*, zu); Abhang. **–e** [ɪnˈklaɪn], 1. *v.n.* sich neigen (*also fig.*); geneigt sein (*to* or *towards*, zu), einen Hang, eine Anlage *or* Neigung haben, dazu neigen; *–ing to red*, ins Rötliche spielend. 2. *v.a.* neigen, beugen; bewegen, geneigt machen, verleiten; senken (*one's head*). 3. [ˈɪnklaɪn], *s.* die Neigung, der Abhang. **–ed** [ɪnˈklaɪnd], *adj.* geneigt; schief, abschüssig; *–ed plane*, schiefe Ebene; *be –ed to*, aufgelegt *or* geneigt zu.

inclose [ɪnˈkloʊz], *etc.*, *see* **enclose.**

inclu–de [ɪnˈkluːd], *v.a.* einschließen, einrechnen, einbeziehen, rechnen (*among*, unter); umfassen, enthalten, in sich begreifen; *fares –ded*, einschließlich Fahrgeld, Fahrgeld inbegriffen. **–ding** [–dɪŋ], *prep.* einschließlich, eingeschlossen (*follows noun*). **–sion** [–ʒən], *s.* die Einschließung, Einbeziehung, Zugehörigkeit (*in*, zu), der Einschluß (*Min.*); *with the –sion of*, mit Einschluß von. **–sive** [ɪnˈkluːsɪv], *adj.* einschließend, einschließlich, mitgerechnet, alles einbegriffen; *from Monday to Wednesday –sive*, von Montag bis Mittwoch einschließlich; *be –sive of*, in sich schließen; *–sive terms*, Preise einschließlich Licht und Bedienung.

incogni–to [ɪnˈkɔgnɪtoʊ], 1. *adv.* unter fremdem Namen; unerkannt, inkognito. 2. *s.* das Inkognito. **–zance** [–zəns], *s.* das Nichterkennen, Nichtwissen; die Unerkennbarkeit. **–zant** [–zənt], *adj.* nicht erkennend, unbekannt (*of*, mit).

incoheren–ce, –cy [ɪnkoʊˈhɪːərəns(ɪ)], *s.* die Zusammenhangslosigkeit, Unvereinbarkeit, der Widerspruch, die Inkonsequenz. **–t** [–ənt], *adj.* unzusammenhängend, widerspruchsvoll, inkonsequent.

incombustible [ɪnkəmˈbʌstɪbl], *adj.* unverbrennbar.

incom–e [ˈɪnkʌm], *s.* das Einkommen, die Einkünfte (*pl.*); *big –e*, hohes Einkommen; *earned –e*, das Einkommen durch Arbeit; *unearned –e*, das Einkommen aus Vermögen. **–er** [ˈɪnkʌmə], *s.* Hereinkommende(r), *m.*, der Ankömmling; Eindringling, Nachfolger; neuer Eigentümer (*Law*). **–e-tax** [ˈɪnkʌmˈtæks], *s.* die Einkommensteuer; *–e-tax return*, die (Einkommen)Steuererklärung. **–ing** [ˈɪnkʌmɪŋ], 1. *adj.* ankommend; hereinkommend (*as tide*); neueintretend, nachfolgend (*as tenant*); eingehend, fällig (*as payment*). 2. *s.* der Eintritt; Einkünfte; Eingänge.

incommensura–bility [ɪnkəmɛnsjərəˈbɪlɪtɪ], *s.* die Unmeßbarkeit (*Math.*). **–ble** [–ˈmɛnsjərəbl], *adj.* unmeßbar, untereinander nicht meßbar, unvergleichbar, unvereinbar, inkommensurabel (*Math.*). **–te** [–ˈmɛnsjərɪt], *adj.* unvergleichbar, unvereinbar (*to* or *with*, mit).

incommod–e [ɪnkəˈmoʊd], *v.a.* belästigen (*Acc.*), lästig *or* beschwerlich fallen (*Dat.*). **–ious** [–dɪəs], *adj.* unbequem, lästig, beschwerlich.

incommunica–bility [ɪnkəmjuːnɪkəˈbɪlɪtɪ], *s.* die Unmittelbarkeit. **–ble** [–ˈmjuːnɪkəbl], *adj.* unmitteilbar, unausdrückbar. **–tive** [–ˈmjuːnɪkətɪv], *adj.* nicht mitteilsam, verschlossen, zurückhaltend.

incommutable [[ɪnkəˈmjuːtɪbl], *adj.* unveränderlich, unabänderlich; unvertauschbar.

incomparable [ɪnˈkɔmpərəbl], 1. *attrib. adj.* unvergleichlich. 2. *pred. adj.* nicht zu vergleichen (*to* or *with*, mit). **–ness,** *s.* die Unvergleichlichkeit.

incompatib–ility [ɪnkəmpætɪˈbɪlɪtɪ], *s.* die Unvereinbarkeit, Unverträglichkeit, der Widerspruch. **–le** [–ˈpætɪbl], *adj.*, unvereinbar; unverträglich, nicht zusammenpassend.

incompeten–ce [ɪnˈkɔmpɪtəns], *s.* die Unfähigkeit, Unzulänglichkeit, Untauglichkeit. **–cy** [–sɪ], *s.* die Unzuständigkeit, Inkompetenz (*Law*). **–t** [–t], *adj.* unfähig, untüchtig; unzuständig, unbefugt, inkompetent; untauglich, unzulänglich, unbrauchbar.

incomplete [ˈɪnkəmplɪːt], *adj.* unvollendet, unvollständig, mangelhaft, lückenhaft, unvollkommen. **–ness,** *s.* die Unvollständigkeit, Unvollkommenheit.

incomprehensib–ility [ɪnkəmprɪhɛnsɪˈbɪlɪtɪ], *s.* die Unbegreiflichkeit. **–le** [–ˈhɛnsɪbl], *adj.*, unbegreiflich, unverständlich.

incompressib–ility [ɪnkəmprɛsɪˈbɪlɪtɪ], *s.* die Nichtzusammendrückbarkeit. **–le** [–ˈprɛsɪbl], *adj.* nicht zusammendrückbar.

incomputable [ɪnkəmˈpjuːtəbl], *adj.* unberechenbar, nicht errechenbar.

inconceivab–ility [ɪnkənsɪːvəˈbɪlɪtɪ], *s.* die Unbegreiflichkeit, Unfaßbarkeit. **–le** [–ˈsɪːvəbl], *adj.* unbegreiflich (*to*, für), unfaßbar. **–leness,** *s. see* **–ility.**

inconclusive [ɪnkənˈkluːsɪv], *adj.* nicht überzeugend, ohne Beweiskraft, nicht entscheidend, ergebnislos. **–ness,** *s.* der Mangel an Beweiskraft, die Ergebnislosigkeit.

incongru–ity [ɪnkəŋˈgruɪtɪ], *s.* die Nichtübereinstimmung, das Mißverhältnis, die Ungereimtheit, Widersinnigkeit. **–ous** [ɪnˈkɔŋgruəs], *adj.* nicht übereinstimmend, widerspruchsvoll, unvereinbar; ungereimt, widersinnig; unangemessen, unpassend.

inconsequen–ce [ɪnˈkɔnsɪkwəns], *s.* die Folgewidrigkeit, Inkonsequenz. **–t** [–t], *adj.*, **–tial** [–ˈkwɛnʃəl], *adj.* folgewidrig, inkonsequent, unzusammenhängend.

inconsider–able [ɪnkənˈsɪdərəbl], *adj.* unbedeutend, unbeträchtlich, belanglos. **–ate** [–ərət], *adj.* rücksichtslos (*towards*, gegen), unbesonnen,

unüberlegt, unbedacht(sam). **–ateness,** *s.* die Rücksichtslosigkeit, Unbesonnenheit, Unüberlegtheit.
inconsisten–cy [ɪnkən'sɪstənsɪ], *s.* die Unvereinbarkeit, Folgewidrigkeit, innerer Widerspruch, die Inkonsequenz; (*often pl.*), Ungereimtheit; Veränderlichkeit, Unbeständigkeit, Unstetigkeit. **–t** [–t], *adj.* unvereinbar, nicht übereinstimmend, folgewidrig, widersprechend; ungereimt, widersinnig, inkonsequent; unstet, unbeständig.
inconsolable [ɪnkən'souləbl], *adj.*, untröstlich.
inconspicuous [ɪnkən'spɪkjuəs], *adj.* unauffällig, unmerklich. **–ness,** *s.* die Unauffälligkeit.
inconstan–cy [ɪn'kɔnstənsɪ], *s.* die Unbeständigkeit, Veränderlichkeit, Ungleichheit, der Wankelmut; die Untreue, Treulosigkeit. **–t** [–ənt], *adj.* unbeständig, ungleich, veränderlich, unstet, wandelbar, wankelmütig; untreu, treulos.
incontestable [ɪnkən'tɛstɪbl], *adj.* unstreitig, unbestreitbar, unumstößlich, unwiderleglich, unwidersprechlich.
incontinen–ce [ɪn'kɔntɪnəns], *s.* die Unenthaltsamkeit, Unmäßigkeit; Unkeuschheit; das Nichthaltenkönnen, der Harnfluß (*Med.*). **–t** [–ənt], *adj.* unenthaltsam, unmäßig; unkeusch, ausschweifend; nicht imstande zu halten, unaufhörlich; *be –t of,* nicht halten können. **–ly,** *adv.* (*archaic*), sofort, unverzüglich.
incontrovertible [ɪnkɔntrə'və:tɪbl], *adj.* unbestreitbar, unstreitig, unumstößlich.
inconvenien–ce [ɪnkən'vɪ:nɪəns], 1. *s.* die Unannehmlichkeit, Unbequemlichkeit; Lästigkeit, Schwierigkeit. 2. *v.a.* belästigen (*Acc.*), lästig *or* beschwerlich fallen (*Dat.*). **–t** [–ənt], *adj.* unbequem, lästig, beschwerlich; unpassend, ungelegen (*to*, für).
inconvertib–ility [ɪnkənvə:tɪ'bɪlɪtɪ], *s.* die Unverwandelbarkeit, Nichtumsetzbarkeit, Unkonvertierbarkeit (*C.L.*). **–le** [–'və:tɪbl], *adj.* unverwandelbar, nicht umsetzbar, nicht konvertierbar (*C.L.*).
incorpor–ate [ɪn'kɔ:pərɪt], 1. *adj.* einverleibt, vereinigt, inkorporiert; —*ate body*, die Körperschaft. 2. [–reɪt] *v.a.* verbinden, vereinigen (*with*, mit), einverleiben (*in* or *into* (*Dat.*)), aufnehmen (*into*, in); eingemeinden (*towns*); Körperschaftsrechte verleihen; (*fig.*) enthalten, in sich schließen; *–ated*, inkorporiert, (*after union's name*) eingetragener Verein (E.V.); *be –ated*, als Körperschaft anerkannt werden; *be –ated as a member*, als Mitglied einer Körperschaft aufgenommen werden. 3. *v.n.* sich verbinden *or* vermischen (*with*, mit). **–ation,** *s.* die Einverleibung (*into*, in (*Acc.*)); Vereinigung, innige Verbindung; die Inkorporation, Gründung einer Körperschaft, Eintragung in das Vereinsregister (*C.L.*). **–eal** [ɪnkɔ:'pɔ:rɪəl], *adj.* unkörperlich, nicht stofflich, geistig, immateriell. **–eity** [–pə'rɪ:ɪtɪ], *s.* die Unkörperlichkeit, Immaterialität.
incorrect [ɪnkə'rɛkt], *adj.* unrichtig, fehlerhaft, ungenau, irrig, irrtümlich, falsch; ungehörig, unschicklich (*as behaviour*). **–ness,** *s.* die Unrichtigkeit, Fehlerhaftigkeit, Ungenauigkeit.
incorrigib–ility [ɪnkɔrɪdʒɪ'bɪlɪtɪ], *s.* die Unverbesserlichkeit. **–le** [ɪn'kɔrɪdʒəbl], *adj.* unverbesserlich.
incorruptib–ility [ɪnkərʌptɪ'bɪlɪtɪ], *s.* die Unverderblichkeit, Unverweslichkeit; (*fig.*) Unbestechlichkeit. **–le** [–'rʌptɪbl], *adj.*, unverderblich; (*fig.*) redlich, unbestechlich. **–leness,** *s. see* **–ility.**
increas–e, 1. [ɪn'krɪ:s] *v.n.* wachsen, zunehmen, sich vermehren, stärker *or* größer werden (*in*, an (*Dat.*)); (*fig.*) anwachsen, steigen (*as prices*). 2. *v.a.* vermehren, vergrößern, verstärken, erhöhen, steigern. 3. ['ɪnkrɪ:s], *s.* das Zunehmen, Wachsen, Anwachsen, Steigen, die Zunahme, der Zuwachs, das Wachstum, die Vergrößerung, Vermehrung, Verstärkung, Erhöhung, Steigerung; der Ertrag (*of the soil*); *on the –e*, im Zunehmen *or* Wachsen; *–e in price*, die Preissteigerung; *–e in* or *of trade*, der Zuwachs *or* Aufschwung des Handels; *–e in wages*, die Lohnerhöhung, das Steigen der Löhne. **–ing** [ɪn'krɪ:sɪŋ], *adj.* zunehmend, steigend. **–ingly,** *adv.* immer mehr, mehr und mehr, in zunehmendem Maße.
incredib–ility [ɪnkrɛdɪ'bɪlɪtɪ], *s.* die Unglaublichkeit. **–le** [ɪn'krɛdɪbl], *adj.*, unglaubhaft, unglaublich (*also coll.*).
incredul–ity [ɪnkrɪ'dju:lɪtɪ], *s.* die Ungläubigkeit, der Unglaube. **–ous** [ɪn'krɛdjuləs], *adj.* ungläubig.
increment ['ɪnkrɪmənt], *s.* die Zunahme, der Zuwachs (*in*, an), die Zulage, der Ertrag, Mehrertrag; das Differenzial (*Math.*); – *value*, der Wertzuwachs; *unearned – tax*, die Wertzuwachssteuer.
incriminat–e [ɪn'krɪmɪneɪt], *v.a.* eines Vergehens beschuldigen, belasten. **–ion** [–'neɪʃən], *s.* die Beschuldigung, Belastung.
incrustation [ɪnkrʌs'teɪʃən], *s.* die Bekrustung; Kruste; Inkrustation (*Geol.*), der Belag, die (Wand)Bekleidung (*Build.*); der Kesselstein (*on boilers*); die Krustenbildung, der Niederschlag (*Chem.*).
incubat–e ['ɪŋkjubeɪt], 1. *v.a.* ausbrüten. 2. *v.n.* brüten. **–ion** [–'beɪʃən], *s.* das Brüten; die Inkubation (*Med.*). **–or** ['ɪŋkjəbeɪtə], *s.* der Brutapparat.
incubus ['ɪŋkjəbəs], *s.* der Alp, das Alpdrücken; (*fig.*) bedrückende Last.
inculcat–e ['ɪnkʌlkeɪt], *v.a.* einschärfen, einprägen, einimpfen (*on* or *upon* (*Dat.*)). **–ion** [–'keɪʃən], *s.* die Einschärfung.
inculpat–e ['ɪnkʌlpeɪt], *v.a.* beschuldigen, anklagen (*Law*). **–ion** [–'peɪʃən], *s.* die Beschuldigung, der Vorwurf, Tadel. **–ory** [ɪn'kʌlpətərɪ], *adj.* beschuldigend, Anklage–.
incumben–cy [ɪn'kʌmbənsɪ], *s.* die Pfründe, der Pfründenbesitz; (*fig.*) die Obliegenheit. **–t** [–ənt], 1. *adj.* liegend (*on*, auf) (*also Bot.*); obliegend (*on* or *upon* (*Dat.*)), *it is –t on me*, es ist meine Pflicht, es liegt mir ob. 2. *s.* der Pfründeninhaber, Pfründenbesitzer, Amtsinhaber.
incunabula [ɪnkju'næbjulə], *pl.* Erstlingsdrucke, Inkunabeln (*pl.*).
incur [ɪn'kə:], *v.a.* sich (*Dat.*) zuziehen, auf sich laden (*Acc.*), sich aussetzen (*Dat.*) (*danger, etc.*), verfallen in (*fine, etc.*), machen (*debts*).
incurab–ility [ɪnkju:ərə'bɪlɪtɪ], *s.* die Unheilbarkeit. **–le** [ɪn'kju:ərəbl], 1. *adj.* unheilbar. 2. *s.* Unheilbare(r), *m. or f.*
incurious [ɪn'kju:rɪəs], *adj.* gleichgültig, uninteressiert, nicht neugierig.
incursion [ɪn'kə:ʃən], *s.* feindlicher Einfall, der Vorstoß, Streifzug; das Eindringen.
incurve [ɪn'kə:v], *v.a.* krümmen, biegen, beugen.
incuse [ɪn'kju:z], 1. *adj.* eingeprägt, eingehämmert. 2. *v.a.* prägen. 3. *s.* die Prägung.
indanthrene [ɪn'dænθrɪ:n], *s.* das Indanthren.
indebted [ɪn'dɛtɪd], *adj.* verschuldet, verpflichtet; *be – to s.o. for s.th.*, einem für etwas zum Dank verpflichtet sein, einem etwas zu verdanken haben. **–ness** [–nɪs], *s.* die Verschuldung, Verpflichtung.
indecen–cy [ɪn'dɪ:sənsɪ], *s.* die Unanständigkeit. **–t** [–ənt], *adj.* unanständig, ungebührlich; *–t assault*, die Vergewaltigung; *–t exposure*, unzüchtige Entblößung.
indecipherable [ɪndɪ'saɪfərəbl], *adj.* unentzifferbar, unleserlich.
indecisi–on [ɪndɪ'sɪʒən], *s.* die Unentschlossenheit, Unschlüssigkeit. **–ve** [–'saɪsɪv], *adj.* nicht entscheidend, unentschieden (*as a battle*); unentschlossen, unbestimmt. **–veness,** *s.* die Unentschlossenheit, Unentschiedenheit.
indeclinable [ɪndɪ'klaɪnəbl], *adj.* undeklinierbar (*Gram.*).
indecor–ous [ɪn'dɛkərəs], *adj.* unanständig, unziemlich. **–ousness, –um** [ɪndɪ'kɔ:rəm], *s.* die Unanständigkeit, Unschicklichkeit.
indeed [ɪn'dɪ:d], 1. *adv.* (*emph. & usually following*) in der Tat, wirklich, tatsächlich; *he did – !, – he did !*, gewiß!; (*unemph. & preceding*) freilich, allerdings, zwar, ja; (*archaic*) fürwahr; *thank you very much –*, vielen herzlichen Dank. 2. *int.* wirklich!, so!, ich danke!, was Sie sagen! (*archaic*) fürwahr!
indefatigab–ility [ɪndɪfætɪgə'bɪlɪtɪ], *s.* die Unermüdlichkeit, Unverdrossenheit; **–le** [–'fætɪgəbl], *adj.* unermüdlich, unverdrossen.
indefeasib–ility [ɪndɪfɪ:zɪ'bɪlɪtɪ], *s.* die Unverletzlichkeit (*of a title*), Unveräußerlichkeit (*of property*). **–le** [–'fɪ:zəbl], *adj.* unverletzlich, unwiderruflich, unantastbar; unveräußerlich.

indefectible [ɪndɪˈfɛktɪbl], *adj.* unvergänglich, nicht verfallbar; (*fig.*) unfehlbar.
indefensib–ility [ɪndɪfɛnsɪˈbɪlɪtɪ], *s.* die Unhaltbarkeit. **–le** [–ˈfɛnsɪbl], *adj.* unhaltbar, nicht zu verteidigen(d).
indefin–able [ɪndɪˈfaɪnəbl], *adj.* unbestimmbar, undefinierbar, unerklärlich. **–ite** [ɪnˈdɛfɪnɪt], *adj.* unbestimmt (*also Gram.*), unbegrenzt, unklar, undeutlich, verschwommen. **–iteness,** *s.* die Unbestimmtheit, Unklarheit.
indelib–ility [ɪndɛlɪˈbɪlɪtɪ], *s.* die Unauslöschlichkeit. **–le** [ɪnˈdɛlɪbl], *adj.* unauslöschlich, unauslöschbar; (*fig.*) unvertilgbar, unvergänglich; *–le ink*, die Kopiertinte; *–le pencil*, der Tintenstift.
indelica–cy [ɪnˈdɛlɪkəsɪ], *s.* der Mangel an Zartgefühl, die Taktlosigkeit; Unfeinheit, Unanständigkeit. **–te** [–ət], *adj.* unzart, taktlos; unfein, unanständig.
indemni–fication [ɪndɛmnɪfɪˈkeɪʃən], *s.* die Entschädigung, Schadloshaltung, Sicherstellung. **–fy** [ɪnˈdɛmnɪfaɪ], *v.a.* entschädigen, schadlos halten (*for*, für), sicherstellen (*from* or *against*, gegen). **–ty** [–nɪtɪ], *s.* die Entschädigung, Vergütung, Schadloshaltung, Sicherstellung; Straflosigkeit; Indemnität, der Schadenersatz, das Abstandgeld; *act of –ty*, der Indemnitätsbeschluß.
indemonstrable [ɪnˈdɛmənstrəbl], *adj.* unbeweisbar.
indent [ɪnˈdɛnt], 1. *v.a.* einschneiden (*also Geol.*), einzähnen, (ein)kerben, auszacken; einrücken (*a line*) (*Typ.*); bestellen (*goods*); genaue Abschrift(en) ausfertigen *or* anfertigen (*a document*); (ab)schließen (*a contract*) (*Law*). 2. *v.n.*; *– upon a p. for a th.*, bei einem eine S. bestellen, von einem eine S. verlangen, anfordern *or* einfordern. 3. [ˈɪndɛnt], *s.* der Einschnitt, die Kerbe; der Auftrag, die Warenbestellung, amtliche Anforderung *or* Requisition (*for* (*Gen.*)); die Einrückung (*Typ.*). **–ation** [–ˈteɪʃən], *s.* der Einschnitt, die Auszackung, Bucht (*of coastline*), Vertiefung. **–ed** [ɪnˈdɛntɪd], *adj.* gezahnt, eingekerbt, ausgezackt, zackig, buchtig (*as coastline*); *see also* **–ured. –ion** [ɪnˈdɛnʃən], *s.* die (Zeilen)Einrückung (*Typ.*). **–ure** [ɪnˈdɛntʃə], 1. *s.* die Vertragsurkunde, der Vertrag, Kontrakt, Lehrbrief, amtliches Verzeichnis; *take up one's –ures*, die Lehrzeit beenden, ausgelernt haben. 2. *v.a.* verdingen, in die Lehre geben, kontraktlich binden (*a p.*). **–ured,** *adj.* durch Lehrzeit gebunden, kontraktlich verpflichtet.
independen–ce [ɪndɪˈpɛndəns], *s.* die Unabhängigkeit, Selbständigkeit; hinreichendes Auskommen. **–cy** [–sɪ], *s.* der Independentismus (*Theol.*); unabhängiger Staat. **–t** [–dənt], 1. *adj.* unabhängig, selbständig, unparteiisch; *–t fire*, das Schnellfeuer, Einzelfeuer; *–t income* or *means*, eignes Vermögen; *man of –t means*, der Rentner; *–t suspension*, die Einzelaufhängung (*Motor.*); *act –tly*, eigenmächtig *or* auf eigene Faust handeln; *be –t*, auf eigenen Füßen stehen (*of p.*), für sich bestehen (*of th.*). 2. *s.* der Independent (*Eccl.*), Unabhängige(r), *m.* (*Pol.*).
indescribab–ility [ɪndɪskraɪbəˈbɪlɪtɪ], *s.* die Unbeschreiblichkeit. **–le** [–ˈkraɪbəbl], *adj.* unbeschreiblich.
indestructib–ility [ɪndɪstrʌktɪˈbɪlɪtɪ], *s.* die Unzerstörbarkeit. **–le** [–ˈstrʌktɪbl], *adj.* unzerstörbar.
indetermina–ble [ɪndɪˈtəːmɪnəbl], *adj.* unbestimmbar. **–te** [–nɪt], *adj.* unbestimmt, unbestimmbar, unentschieden. **–teness,** *s.* die Unbestimmtheit. **–tion** [–ˈneɪʃən], *s.* die Unschlüssigkeit.
index [ˈɪndɛks], 1. *s.* (*pl.* –es, indices [ˈɪndɪsɪːz]) der Zeiger, Zeigefinger (*Anat.*); das Inhaltsverzeichnis, Sachverzeichnis, Namensverzeichnis, Register (*of a book*); der Index (*R.C.*); (*fig.*) die Verbotliste; der Exponent, die Hochzahl, Kennziffer (*Math.*); das Unterscheidungszeichen, Handzeichen (*Typ.*); (*fig.*) Zeichen, Anzeichen (*of*, für *or* von), der Hinweis (*to*, auf), Wegweiser, Fingerzeig (*to*, für), Maßstab; *card –*, die Kartei, Kartothek; *cost-of-living-–*, der Lebenshaltungsindex; *– of intelligence*, die Intelligenzmeßzahl; *– of refraction*, der Brechungsexponent. 2. *v.a.* mit einem Inhaltsverzeichnis versehen, registrieren. **––card,** *s.* die Karteikarte. **–er,** *s.* der Anfertiger eines Inhaltsverzeichnisses. **––figure,** *see* **––number. ––finger,** *s.* der Zeigefinger. **–ing,** *s.* das Ordnen, Registrieren. **––number,** *s.* die Meßziffer, Indexziffer, Indexzahl, der Index; polizeiliches Kennzeichen (*Motor.*).
India [ˈɪndɪə], *s. see Index of Names.* **–man,** *s.* der (Ost)Indienfahrer. **–n,** *adj. see Index of Names*; *–n club*, die Keule (*Gym.*); *–n corn*, der Mais; *–n file*, der Gänsemarsch; *–n ink*, chinesische Tusche; *–n summer*, der Nachsommer. **––paper,** *s.* dünnes chinesisches Papier. **––rubber,** *s.* der Kautschuk, das Gummi, der Radiergummi (*Draw.*).
indicat–e [ˈɪndɪkeɪt], *v.a.* anzeigen, bezeichnen, andeuten, hinweisen auf; indizieren, erfordern (*Med.*); *–e that*, darauf hinweisen daß; *be –ed*, angedeutet, angezeigt *or* indiziert sein, erforderlich *or* angebracht sein; *–ed horse-power*, indizierte Pferdekraft. **–ion** [–ˈkeɪʃən], *s.* der Hinweis (*of*, auf), die Angabe, Andeutung, Hindeutung (*of*, über); das Zeichen, Anzeichen, Kennzeichen (*of*, für); das Merkmal; *give –ion of*, zeigen, anzeigen; *there is every –ion*, alles deutet darauf hin. **–ive** [ɪnˈdɪkətɪv], 1. *adj.* hinweisend (*of*, auf), andeutend, anzeigend; indikativisch (*Gram.*); *be –ive of*, anzeigen, (hin)deuten auf. 2. *s.* der Indikativ, die Wirklichkeitsform (*Gram.*). **–or** [ˈɪndɪkeɪtə], *s.* der Anzeiger, Zeiger, Messer, Indikator (*Mech.*), Zeigeapparat (*Tele.*); *–or-board*, der Klappenschrank (*Tele.*). **–ory** [–kətərɪ], *adj.* anzeigend, hinweisend (*of*, auf).
indict [ɪnˈdaɪt], *v.a.* anklagen (*for.* wegen, *or Gen.*) (*Law*). **–able** [–təbl], *adj.* anklagbar (*of a p.*), klagbar (*of an offence*). **–ment** [–mənt], *s.* formelle Anklage, die Anklageerhebung, Anklageschrift.
indifferen–ce [ɪnˈdɪfərəns], *s.* die Gleichgültigkeit, Teilnahm(s)losigkeit (*to*, gegen), Unparteilichkeit; Mittelmäßigkeit; *it is a matter of –ce*, es ist unwichtig *or* belanglos. **–t** [–ənt], *adj.* gleichgültig, teilnahm(s)los, unparteiisch; nebensächlich, unwichtig; leidlich, mittelmäßig, ziemlich schlecht; unempfindlich, indifferent (*Chem.*).
indigen–ce [ˈɪndɪdʒəns], *s.* die (Be)Dürftigkeit, Armut, Not. **–t** [–ənt], *adj.* (be)dürftig, arm.
indigen–e [ˈɪndɪdʒɪːn], *s.* Eingeborene(r), *m.*, einheimisches Tier (*Zool.*), einheimische Pflanze (*Bot.*). **–ous** [ɪnˈdɪdʒənəs], *adj.* eingeboren, einheimisch, bodenständig (*Bot., Zool.*).
indigent, *adj. see* **indigence.**
indigest–ed [ɪndɪˈdʒɛstɪd], *adj.* unverdaut (*also fig.*). **–ibility** [–tɪˈbɪlɪtɪ], *s.* die Unverdaulichkeit. **–ible** [–ˈdʒɛstɪbl], *adj.* unverdaulich (*also fig.*). **–ion** [–ˈdʒɛstʃən], *s.* die Verdauungsstörung, Verdauungsschwäche, Magenverstimmung. **–ive** [–ˈdʒɛstɪv], *adj.* schwer verdaulich.
indign–ant [ɪnˈdɪgnənt], *adj.* entrüstet, empört, aufgebracht, verletzt, ungehalten, unwillig, zornig (*at*, über (*Acc.*)); **–ation** [–ˈneɪʃən], *s.* die Entrüstung, Empörung, der Unwille (*at* or *with*, über (*Acc.*)); *–ation-meeting*, die Protestversammlung. **–ity** [ɪnˈdɪgnɪtɪ], *s.* schimpfliche Behandlung, die Beleidigung, Beschimpfung, Schmach.
indigo [ˈɪndɪgoʊ], *s.* der Indigo. **––blue, –tin,** *s.* das Indigoblau, Indigotin.
indirect [ɪndɪˈrɛkt], *adj.* indirekt, mittelbar; nicht gerade, schief, krumm; *– object*, das Dativobjekt (*Gram.*); *– ray*, reflektierte Welle (*Rad.*); *– speech*, indirekte Rede (*Gram.*); *– taxes*, Verbrauchssteuern, indirekte Steuern. **–ness** [–nɪs], *s.* indirekter Weg, indirekte Weise, die Mittelbarkeit; (*fig.*) Anspielung, Andeutung; Unaufrichtigkeit.
indiscernible [ɪndɪˈsəːnəbl], *adj.* nicht wahrnehmbar, unmerklich.
indiscipline [ɪnˈdɪsɪplɪn], *s.* der Mangel an Zucht.
indiscoverable [ɪndɪsˈkʌvərəbl], *adj.* unentdeckbar, nicht feststellbar.
indiscr–eet [ɪndɪsˈkrɪːt], *adj.* unbedachtsam, unbesonnen, unüberlegt; taktlos, unklug. **–etion** [–ˈkrɛʃən], *s.* die Unbedachtsamkeit, Unbesonnenheit, Unklugheit, Taktlosigkeit, Indiskretion (*Pol., etc.*).
indiscriminat–e [ɪndɪsˈkrɪmɪnət], *adj.* unterschiedslos, ohne Unterschied *or* Rücksicht, wahllos, kritiklos. **–ely,** *adv.* wahllos, ohne Unterschied,

aufs Geratewohl. **–ive** [–nətɪv], *adj.* keinen Unterschied machend, kritiklos, blind. **–ion** [–ˈneɪʃən], *s.* die Unterschiedslosigkeit, Kritiklosigkeit.

indispensab–ility [ɪndɪspɛnsɪˈbɪlɪtɪ], *s.* die Unentbehrlichkeit, Unerläßlichkeit (*to* or *for*, für). **–le** [–ˈpɛnsɪbl], *adj.* unentbehrlich, unerläßlich; unabkömmlich (*Mil.*).

indispos–e [ɪndɪsˈpoʊz], *v.a.* abgeneigt machen (*to*, zu), untauglich machen (*for*, für). **–ed** [–d], *adj.* (*usually pred.*) unpäßlich, unwohl; abgeneigt (*to*, gegen). **–ition** [–pəˈzɪʃən], *s.* die Unpäßlichkeit, das Unwohlsein; die Abneigung, Abgeneigtheit.

indisputab–ility [ɪndɪspjuːtəˈbɪlɪtɪ], *s.* die Unbestreitbarkeit. **–le** [–ˈpjuːtəbl], *adj.* unbestreitbar, unstreitig.

indissolub–ility [ɪndɪsəljuˈbɪlɪtɪ], *s.* die Unauflöslichkeit, (*fig.*) Unzertrennbarkeit, Unzerstörbarkeit. **–le** [–ˈsəljəbl], *adj.* unauflöslich, (*fig.*) unzertrennlich, unzerstörbar.

indistin–ct [ɪndɪsˈtɪnkt], *adj.* unklar, undeutlich, verworren, verschwommen. **–ctness** [–nɪs], *s.* die Undeutlichkeit, Verworrenheit, Unklarheit. **–guishable** [–ˈtɪŋgwɪʃəbl], *adj.* ununterscheidbar, nicht zu unterscheiden(d).

indite [ɪnˈdaɪt], *v.a.* (*archaic*) niederschreiben, abfassen.

individual [ɪndɪˈvɪdjʊəl], 1. *adj.* einzeln, Einzel–, persönlich, individuell; besonder, eigentümlich, charakteristisch; – *credit*, der Personalkredit, – *income*, das Privateinkommen; – *psychology*, die Individualpsychologie. 2. *s.* das Einzelwesen, Individuum, die Einzelperson; (*coll.*) Person, der Mensch; *private* –, der Privatmann, die Privatperson. **–ism** [–ɪzm], *s.* der Individualismus. **–ist** [–ɪst], *s.* der Individualist. **–istic** [–ˈlɪstɪk], *adj.* individualistisch. **–ity** [–ˈælɪtɪ], *s* die Individualität, Persönlichkeit; Eigenart, das Kennzeichen. **–ization** [–ɑɪˈzeɪʃən], *s.* die Individualisierung, Einzelbetrachtung. **–ize** [–ˈvɪdjʊəlɑɪz], *v.a.* individualisieren, einzeln darstellen *or* herausheben, ins Einzelne gehen. **–ly**, *adv.* einzeln genommen, für sich; *–ly and collectively*, einzeln und insgesamt.

indivisib–ility [ɪndɪvɪzɪˈbɪlɪtɪ], *s.* die Unteilbarkeit. **–le** [–ˈvɪzɪbl], *adj.* unteilbar.

indocil–e [ɪnˈdoʊsɑɪl], *adj.* ungelehrig, unbändig, unlenksam. **–ity** [ɪndəˈsɪlɪtɪ], *s.* die Ungelehrigkeit, Unbändigkeit.

indoctrinat–e [ɪnˈdəktrɪneɪt], *v.a.* unterweisen, belehren, schulen (*in*, in), erfüllen, durchdringen (*with*, mit). **–ion** [–ˈneɪʃən], *s.* die Belehrung, Schulung, Unterweisung.

indolen–ce [ˈɪndələns], *s.* die Trägheit, Indolenz; Schmerzlosigkeit (*Med.*). **–t** [–t], *adj.* träge, lässig, indolent; schmerzlos (*as a tumour*).

indomitable [ɪnˈdəmɪtəbl], *adj.* unbezwinglich, unbezähmbar. **–ness** [–nɪs], *s.* die Unbezähmbarkeit.

indoor [ˈɪndɔː], *adj.* Haus–, Zimmer–; *––aerial*, die Zimmerantenne; *––game*, das Zimmerspiel; – *relief*, die Anstaltspflege; – *swimming pool*, das Hallenbad. **–s** [–z], *adv.* im Hause, zu Hause; ins Haus.

indorse, *see* **endorse.**

indubitable [ɪnˈdjuːbɪtəbl], *adj.* zweifellos, unzweifelhaft, gewiß, sicher. **–ness** [–nɪs], *s.* die Zweifellosigkeit, Gewißheit.

induce [ɪnˈdjuːs], *v.a.* herbeiführen, verursachen (*a th.*); bewegen, veranlassen, überreden, dahinbringen, verleiten (*a p.*); induzieren, durch Induktion hervorrufen (*Elec.*), durch Induktion ableiten *or* schließen (*Log.*); *–d current*, der Induktionsstrom (*Elec.*). **–ment** [–mənt], *s.* die Veranlassung, der Anlaß, Beweggrund, Anreiz.

induct [ɪnˈdʌkt], *v.a.* einsetzen, einführen (*Eccl.*); einberufen, einziehen (*Mil.*); (*fig.*) geleiten, führen. **–ance** [–əns], *s.* die Induktivität, Induktanz (*Elec.*). **–ion** [–ʃən], *s.* die Einführung, Einsetzung, Einberufung, Anführung; Induktion (*Phys.*, *Log.*), der Schluß (*Log.*); *–ion coil*, der Induktionsapparat, Funkeninduktor (*Elec.*); *–ion current*, der Induktionsstrom (*Elec.*); *–ion order*, der Gestellungsbefehl (*Mil.*); *–ion pipe*, das Einlaßrohr. **–ive** [–tɪv], *adj.* verleitend, führend (*to*, zu); induktiv (*Log.*); Induktions– (*Elec.*). **–or** [–tə], *s.* der Induktionsapparat, Induktor (*Elec.*).

indulge [ɪnˈdʌldʒ], 1. *v.a.* nachgeben (*Dat.*), nachsichtig sein gegen, willfahren (*Dat.*), gefällig sein (*Dat.*); verwöhnen, verziehen, verzärteln (*a p.*); frönen (*Dat.*) (*a th.*); – *s.o. in a th.*, einem etwas nachsehen; – *one's children*, seine Kinder verwöhnen; – *one's desires*, seinen Wünschen frönen *or* nachhängen, sich seinen Wünschen hingeben; – *o.s.*, sich gehen lassen, sich nicht zurückhalten; – *o.s. in a th.*, sich ergehen in *or* schwelgen in etwas, sich etwas erlauben *or* gestatten. 2. *v.n.* (*coll.*) gern trinken; – *in a th.*, sich (*Dat.*) an etwas gütlich tun, sich (*Dat.*) etwas erlauben, leisten, anschaffen *or* gönnen, einer S. (*Dat.*) frönen, sich einer S. (*Dat.*) hingeben, zu etwas greifen. **–nce** [–əns], *s.* die Nachsicht, Duldung, Schonung (*to*, gegen; *of*, für), Verwöhnung, Verzärtelung (*of children*), Befriedigung (*of appetites*), das Frönen (*in* (*Dat.*)); Wohlleben der Genuß; die Gunst, Gunstbezeigung; der Ablaß (*R.C.*); die Stundung (*C.L.*). **–nt** [–ənt], *adj.* nachsichtig, schonend (*to*, gegen), milde.

indurat–e [ˈɪndjʊəreɪt], 1. *v.a.* hart machen, härten, verhärten, abhärten (*to* or *against*, gegen). 2. *v.n.* hart *or* fest werden. **–ion** [–ˈreɪʃən], *s.* die Härtung, Verhärtung, das Hartwerden; (*fig.*) die Verstocktheit.

industr–ial [ɪnˈdʌstrɪəl], *adj.* gewerblich, gewerbetreibend, Gewerbe–, industriell; *–ial alcohol*, denaturierter Sprit; *–ial art*, das Kunstgewerbe; *–ial exhibition*, die Gewerbeausstellung; *–ial revolution*, industrielle Umwälzung; *–ial school*, die Gewerbeschule; die Besserungsanstalt; *–ial town*, die Fabrikstadt. **–ialism** [–ɪzm], *s.* die Gewerbetätigkeit, der Industrialismus. **–ialist** [–ɪst], *s.* Industrielle(r), *m.* **–ialize** [–ɑɪz], *v.a.* industrialisieren. **–ious** [–ɪəs], *adj.* fleißig, arbeitsam, betriebsam, emsig. **–y** [ˈɪndəstrɪ], *s.* der Fleiß, die Betriebsamkeit; das Gewerbe, (*also pl.*) die Industrie, der Industriezweig, die Branche.

indwell [ˈɪndwɛl], 1. *v.n.* wohnen in. 2. *v.n.* bewohnen (*Acc.*) (*fig.*) innewohnen (*Dat.*). **–er**, *s.* der Bewohner.

inebri–ate [ɪnˈiːbrɪət], 1. *adj.* betrunken, berauscht. 2. *s.* der Trunkenbold. 3. [–brɪeɪt], *v.a.* betrunken machen, (*fig.*) trunken machen, berauschen. **–ated** [–brɪetɪd], *adj. see* **–ate** 1. **–ation** [–brɪˈeɪʃən], *s.*, **–ety** [ɪnɪˈbrɪːətɪ], *s.* die Trunkenheit, der Rausch; die Trunksucht (*Med.*).

inedible [ɪnˈɛdɪbl], *adj.* ungenießbar.

inedited [ɪnˈɛdɪtɪd], *adj.* ohne Änderung herausgegeben.

ineffable [ɪnˈɛfəbl], *adj.* unaussprechlich, unbeschreiblich. **–ness**, *s.* die Unaussprechlichkeit.

ineffaceable [ɪnɪˈfeɪsəbl], *adj.* unauslöschlich, unauslöschbar.

ineffect–ive [ɪnɪˈfɛktɪv], *adj.*, **–ual** [–tjʊəl], *adj.* unwirksam, wirkungslos fruchtlos, erfolglos; untauglich, unfähig. **–iveness**, *s.*, **–ualness**, *s* die Unwirksamkeit, Fruchtlosigkeit; Untauglichkeit.

ineffic–acious [ɪnɛfɪˈkeɪʃəs], *adj.* unwirksam. **–acy** [ɪnˈɛfɪkəsɪ], *s.* die Unwirksamkeit, Fruchtlosigkeit. **–iency** [ɪnɪˈfɪʃənsɪ], *s.* die Unfähigkeit, Wirkungslosigkeit, Erfolglosigkeit; Schlamperei. **–ient** [–ˈfɪʃənt], *adj.* (leistungs)unfähig, untauglich, unwirksam, unfruchtbar, wirkungslos, unzulänglich.

inelastic [ɪnɪˈlæstɪk], *adj.* nicht elastisch, (*fig.*) starr, nicht anpassungsfähig. **–ity** [–ˈstɪsɪtɪ], *s.* die Starrheit, Anpassungsunfähigkeit.

inelegan–ce, –cy [ɪnˈɛlɪgəns(ɪ)], *s.* die Geschmacklosigkeit, Unfeinheit. **–t** [–ənt], *adj.* unelegant, geschmacklos, unfein.

ineligib–ility [ɪnəlɪdʒɪˈbɪlɪtɪ], *s.* die Unwählbarkeit, Untauglichkeit. **–le** [ɪnˈɛlɪdʒəbl], *adj.* unwählbar, (*fig.*) (dienst)untauglich, nicht in Betracht kommend, ungeeignet, unwürdig, unerwünscht.

ineluctable [ɪnɪˈlʌktəbl], *adj.* unvermeidlich, unausweichbar, unentrinnbar.

inept [ɪnˈɛpt], *adj.* albern, abgeschmackt, ungeeignet, unangemessen, ungeschickt. **–itude** [–ɪtjuːd], *s.*, **–ness**, *s.* die Albernheit, Abgeschmacktheit, Ungeeignetheit (*for*, zu), Ungeschicklichkeit.

inequality [ɪnɪˈkwəlɪtɪ], *s.* die Ungleichheit, Verschiedenheit, das Mißverhältnis die Unebenheit.

inequit–able [ɪnɪˈkwɪtəbl], *adj.* ungerecht, unbillig. **–y** [ɪnˈɛkwɪtɪ], *s.* die Ungerechtigkeit, Unbilligkeit.
ineradicable [ɪnɪˈrædɪkəbl], *adj.* unausrottbar.
inert [ɪnˈəːt], *adj.* träge, leblos, inaktiv; indifferent, edel (*of gases*); untätig, unwirksam; (*fig.*) schwerfällig, stumpf. **–ia** [–ˈəːʃə], *s.* die Trägheit, Untätigkeit; das Beharrungsvermögen; Trägheitsmoment (*Phys.*). **–ness,** *s.* die Trägheit, Inaktivität, Passivität.
inescapable [ɪnɪsˈkeɪpəbl], *adj.* unvermeidbar, unvermeidlich.
inessential [ɪnɪˈsɛnʃəl], 1. *adj.* unwesentlich, unbedeutend, unwichtig. 2. *s.* unwesentliche Sache, etwas Unwesentliches.
inestimable [ɪnˈɛstɪməbl], *adj.* unschätzbar.
inevitab–ility [ɪnɛvɪtəˈbɪlɪtɪ], *s.* die Unvermeidlichkeit. **–le** [ɪnˈɛvɪtəbl], *adj.* unvermeidlich, unumgänglich. **–leness,** *s. see* **–ility.**
inexact [ɪnɪgˈzækt], *adj.* ungenau. **–itude** [–ɪtjuːd], *s.*, **–ness,** *s.* die Ungenauigkeit, Unrichtigkeit.
inexcusable [ɪnɪksˈkjuːzəbl], *adj.* unverzeihlich, unentschuldbar, unverantwortlich. **–ness,** *s.* die Unverzeihlichkeit, die Unverantwortlichkeit.
inexhausti–bility [ɪnɪgzɔːstɪˈbɪlɪtɪ], *s.* die Unerschöpflichkeit **–ble** [ɪnɪgˈzɔːstɪbl], *adj.* unerschöpflich, unermüdlich. **–ve,** *adj.* unerschöpflich.
inexorab–ility [ɪnɛksərəˈbɪlɪtɪ], *s.* die Unerbittlichkeit. **–le** [ɪnˈɛksərəbl], *adj.* unerbittlich.
inexpedien–cy [ɪnɪksˈpɪːdɪənsɪ], *s,* die Unzweckmäßigkeit, Untunlichkeit, Undienlichkeit. **–t** [–ənt], *adj.* unangemessen, ungeeignet, unpassend, unzweckmäßig, undienlich, unvorteilhaft, nicht ratsam.
inexpensive [ɪnɪksˈpɛnsɪv], *adj.* nicht kostspielig, wohlfeil, billig. **–ness,** *s.* die Wohlfeilheit, Billigkeit.
inexperience [ɪnɪksˈpɪːərɪəns], *s.* die Unerfahrenheit. **–d** [–t], *adj.* unerfahren; nicht geübt (*of sailors*) (*Naut.*).
inexpert [ɪnɪkˈspəːt], *adj.* ungeübt, unbeholfen. **–ness,** *s.* die Ungeübtheit, Unbeholfenheit.
inexpiable [ɪnˈɛkspɪːəbl], *adj.* unsühnbar, unversöhnlich.
inexplic–able [ɪnɪksˈplɪkəbl], *adj.* unerklärlich, unbegreiflich, unfaßlich. **–it** [–ˈplɪsɪt], *adj.* unklar, undeutlich ausgedrückt.
inexpressi–ble [ɪnɪksˈprɛsɪbl], *adj.* unaussprechlich, unsäglich. **–bles,** *pl.* (*coll. archaic*) Beinkleider. **–ve** [–sɪv], *adj.* ausdruckslos, nichtssagend.
inexpugnable [ɪnɪksˈpjuːnəbl], *adj.* unüberwindlich, unbezwinglich.
inextinguishable [ɪnɪksˈtɪŋgwɪʃəbl], *adj.* unauslöschbar, (*fig.*) unauslöschlich.
inextricable [ɪnɪksˈtrɪkəbl], *adj.* unentwirrbar, hoffnungslos verwirrt.
infallib–ility [ɪnfælɪˈbɪlɪtɪ], *s.* die Unfehlbarkeit. **–le** [ɪnˈfælɪbl], *adj.* unfehlbar, untrüglich, zuverlässig; unvermeidlich.
infam–ous [ˈɪnfəməs], *adj.* verrufen, berüchtigt; niederträchtig, schändlich, ehrlos. **–y** [–mɪ], *s.* die Ehrlosigkeit, Schande, Schändlichkeit, Niedertracht.
infan–cy [ˈɪnfənsɪ], *s.* die Kindheit; Minderjährigkeit, Unmündigkeit (*Law*), (*fig.*) der Anfang, erstes Stadium; *be still in its –cy*, noch in den Kinderschuhen stecken. **–t** [ˈɪnfənt], 1. *s.* kleines Kind, das Kleinkind, der Säugling; Unmündige(r), Minderjährige(r), *m. or f.* (*Law*). 2. *adj.* kindlich, Kinder–, Kleinkind–, Säuglings–; (*fig.*) jung, jugendlich; unmündig, minderjährig (*Law*); *–t baptism*, die Kindertaufe; *–t Jesus*, das Jesuskind; *–t mortality*, die Säuglings– *or* Kindersterblichkeit; *–t-school*, *s.* die Kleinkinderschule, der Kindergarten; *–t welfare*, die Säuglingsfürsorge. **–ta** [ɪnˈfæntɑ], *s.* die Infantin. **–te** [ɪnˈfæntə], *s.* der Infant. **–ticide** [ɪnˈfæntɪsɑɪd], *s.* der Kindesmord; Kindesmörder, die Kindesmörderin. **–tile** [ˈɪnfəntɑɪl], *adj.* kindlich, jugendlich, Kindes–, Jugend–; unentwickelt, Anfangs–; kindisch; *–tile paralysis*, die Kinderlähmung. **–tilism** [ɪnˈfæntɪlɪzm], *s.* der Infantilismus. **–tine** [ˈɪnfəntɑɪn], *adj. see* **–tile.**
infantry [ˈɪnfəntrɪ], 1. *s.* die Infanterie, (*archaic*) das Fußvolk. **–man,** *s.* der Infanterist, (*archaic*) Fußsoldat, (*sl.*) Landser.
infatuat–e [ɪnˈfætjueɪt], *v.a.* betören, verblenden (*with*, durch). **–ed** [–ɪd], *adj.* betört, töricht; verliebt, vernarrt (*with*, in (*Acc.*)). **–ion** [–ˈeɪʃən], *s.* die Betörung, Verblendung, Vernarrtheit (*for*, in (*Acc.*)).
infect [ɪnˈfɛkt], *v.a.* anstecken (*also fig.*), infizieren, verpesten, vergiften (*air, etc.*), (*fig.*) beeinflussen. **–ion** [–ˈfɛkʃən], *s.* die Ansteckung, (*fig.*) Vergiftung, das Gift, der Ansteckungskeim, die Seuche; *catch the –ion*, angesteckt werden. **–ious** [ɪnˈfɛkʃəs], *adj.* ansteckend, infektiös. **–iousness,** *s.* ansteckende Beschaffenheit, Ansteckende(s), *n.*
infelicit–ous [ɪnfɪˈlɪsɪtəs], *adj.* unglücklich; unpassend, unglücklich gewählt. **–y** [–tɪ], *s.* die Unglückseligkeit, das Unglück; die Ungeeignetheit; unglücklich gewählter Ausdruck; *–y of style*, der Stilmangel.
infer [ɪnˈfəː], *v.a.* schließen, folgern, ableiten (*from*, aus), schließen lassen auf. **–able** [ˈɪnfərəbl], *adj.* zu folgern(d), zu schließen(d), ableitbar. **–ence** [ˈɪnfərəns], *s.* der Schluß, die Folgerung (*from*, aus). **–ential** [ɪnfəˈrɛnʃəl], *adj.* zu schließen, zu folgern, folgernd, gefolgert. **–entially,** *adv.* durch Schlußfolgerung.
inferior [ɪnˈfɪːrɪə], 1. *adj.* unter, niedriger, tiefer (stehend); geringer, schwächer (*to*, als); minderwertig, mittelmäßig, unbedeutend, gering (*in quality*); untergeordnet, Unter– (*in rank*); *be – to s.o.*, einem nachstehen, hinter einem zurückstehen (*in*, in *or* an); *be – to none*, keinem etwas nachgeben. 2. *s.* Untere(r), Geringere(r), Untergegebene(r), *m.*; *be s.o.'s – in*, einem nachstehen in. **–ity** [–rɪˈɔrɪtɪ], *s.* die Untergeordnetheit, Unterlegenheit, geringerer Stand, Wert, *etc.*; geringere Zahl; die Niedrigkeit, Minderwertigkeit, Inferiorität; *–ity complex*, der Minderwertigkeitskomplex.
infern–al [ɪnˈfəːnəl], *adj.* Höllen–, höllisch, teuflisch; (*coll.*) verflucht; *–al machine*, die Höllenmaschine; *–al regions*, die Unterwelt, Hölle. **–o** [–noʊ], *s.* die Hölle.
infertil–e [ɪnˈfəːtɑɪl], *adj.* unfruchtbar. **–ity** [–ˈtɪlɪtɪ], *s.* die Unfruchtbarkeit.
infest [ɪnˈfɛst], *v.a.* heimsuchen, verheeren, plagen; (*fig.*) überschwemmen; *–ed with*, überschwemmt von. **–ation** [–ˈteɪʃən], *s.* die Heimsuchung, Plage, Überschwemmung.
infeudation [ɪnfjuːˈdeɪʃən], *s.* die Belehnung, die Zehntverleihung (*of tithes*).
infidel [ˈɪnfɪdəl], 1. *adj.* ungläubig, heidnisch. 2. *s.* Ungläubige(r), *m.*, der Heide, Nichtchrist. **–ity** [–ˈdelɪtɪ], *s.* der Unglaube; die Untreue (*to*, gegen).
infield [ˈɪnfɪːld], *s.* dem Hofe naheliegendes Ackerland, das Baugelände; inneres Spielfeld (*Crick.*), nahestehende Fänger (*Crick.*).
infighting [ˈɪnfɑɪtɪŋ], *s.* der Nahkampf (*Boxing*).
infiltrat–e [ɪnˈfɪltreɪt], 1. *v.a.* eindringen *or* durchdringen lassen, infiltrieren, hineinsickern, durchtränken (*with*, mit); *–ed with*, durchtränkt von. 2. *v.n.* durchsickern, eindringen (*into*, in). **–ion** [–ˈtreɪʃən]; *s.* das Durchsickern, Einsickern, die Infiltration; (*fig.*) die Infiltration, das Eindringen (*Mil., Pol.*).
infinit–e [ˈɪnfɪnɪt], 1. *adj.* unendlich, endlos; zahllos, unzählig, ungeheuer. 2. *s.* das Unendliche. **–ely,** *adv.* unendlich, außerordentlich. **–esimal** [–ˈtɛsɪməl], 1. *adj.* unendlich klein; *–esimal calculus*, die Infinitesimalrechnung. 2. *s.* unendlich kleine Größe. **–ival** [–ˈtɑɪvəl], *adj.* infinitivisch, Infinitiv–. **–ive** [ɪnˈfɪnɪtɪv], 1. *s.*; 2. *adj.*; *–ive (mood)*, die Nennform, der Infinitiv. **–ude** [ɪnˈfɪnɪtjuːd], *s.* die Unendlichkeit, Unbegrenztheit, Unermeßlichkeit, unzählige Menge. **–y** [ɪnˈfɪnɪtɪ], *s. see* **–ude**; unendliche Zahl (*Math.*).
infirm [ɪnˈfəːm], *adj.* kraftlos, schwach, gebrechlich; *– of purpose*, unentschlossen, willensschwach. **–ary** [–ərɪ], *s.* das Krankenhaus, Spital. **–ity** [–ɪtɪ], *s.* die Schwäche, Altersschwäche, Schwachheit, Gebrechlichkeit; das Gebrechen, die Krankheit; *–ity of purpose*, die Charakterschwäche, Unentschlossenheit.
infix [ɪnˈfɪks], 1. *v.a.* befestigen, hineintreiben, (*fig.*) einprägen (*in s.o.'s mind*, einem). 2. *s.* die Einfügung, das Infix (*Gram.*).
inflam–e [ɪnˈfleɪm], 1. *v.a.* **entzünden** (*Med.*); (*fig.*)

entflammen, erregen, erhitzen; *-ed with rage*, wutentbrannt. 2. *v.n.* sich entzünden. **-ability** [ɪnflæmə'bɪlɪtɪ], *s.* die Brennbarkeit, Entzündbarkeit; (*fig.*) Erregbarkeit. **-mable** [ɪn'flæməbl], *adj.* brennbar, feuergefährlich, entzündlich; (*fig.*) leicht erregbar, hitzig; *-mable matter*, der Zündstoff. **-mables,** *pl.* brennbare, feuergefährliche *or* leicht entzündbare Stoffe. **-mation** [ɪnflə'meɪʃən], *s.* die Entzündung; (*fig.*) Aufregung, Erregung. **-matory** [ɪn'flæmətərɪ], *adj.* Entzündungs– (*Med.*); (*fig.*) aufreizend, aufhetzend, aufrührerisch; *-matory speech*, die Hetzrede.

inflat-able [ɪn'fleɪtəbl], *adj.* aufblasbar; *-able boat*, das Schlauchboot. **-e** [ɪn'fleɪt], *v.a.* aufblasen, aufblähen (*also fig.*), aufpumpen (*tyres*), hochtreiben (*prices*); *be -ed with*, sich aufblähen vor; *-ed style*, schwulstiger *or* hochtrabender Stil. **-ion** [–'fleɪʃən], *s.* die Aufblähung; (*fig.*) Aufgeblasenheit; Inflation (*C.L.*). **-ionary** [–'fleɪʃənrɪ], *adj.* Inflations–, inflationistisch, inflatorisch. **-or** [–tə], *s.* die Luftpumpe (*Cycl.*).

inflect [ɪn'flɛkt], *v.a.* beugen, biegen, abwandeln, flektieren (*Gram.*), modulieren (*Mus.*). **-ion (inflexion)** [–'flɛkʃən], *s.* die Biegung, Beugung, Flexion (*Gram.*); Modulation (*of the voice*).

inflexib-ility [ɪnflɛksɪ'bɪlɪtɪ], *s.* die Unbiegsamkeit, (*fig.*) Unbeugsamkeit. **-le** [ɪn'flɛksɪbl], *adj.* unbiegsam, (*fig.*) unbeugsam, unerbittlich, unerschütterlich, unbeweglich, starr.

inflexion, *s. see* **inflection.**

inflict [ɪn'flɪkt], *v.a.* auferlegen, zufügen (*on* or *upon* (*Dat.*)), verhängen (*punishment*) (*on*, über (*Acc.*)), beibringen (*a defeat*) (*on* (*Dat.*)); *– o.s. upon a p.*, sich einem aufbürden *or* aufdrängen. **-ion** [–'flɪkʃən], *s.* die Auferlegung, Verhängung (*of penalty*), Strafverfügung; Zufügung (*of wounds*); die Plage, Heimsuchung.

inflorescence [ɪnflɔ:'rɛsəns], *s.* der Blütenstand (*Bot.*), Blüten (*pl.*); (*fig.*), das Aufblühen, die Blüte.

inflow ['ɪnflou], *s.* der Zufluß, Zulauf.

influen-ce ['ɪnflʊəns], 1. *s.* der Einfluß, die Einwirkung (*on* or *upon*, auf; *with*, bei); *-ce over s.o.*, die Macht über einem. 2. *v.a.* Einfluß ausüben auf (*Acc.*), einwirken auf (*Acc.*), beeinflussen, bestimmen. **-tial** [–'ɛnʃəl], *adj.* einflußreich, von Einfluß (*on*, auf (*Acc.*)).

influenza [ɪnflʊ:'ɛnzə], *s.* die Grippe, Influenza.

influx ['ɪnflʌks], *s.* das Einfließen, Einströmen, (*fig.*) Eindringen; der Zufluß, Zustrom, Andrang, das Einmünden (*of a river*); die Zufuhr, Einfuhr (*C.L.*).

inform [ɪn'fɔ:m], 1. *v.a.* benachrichtigen, in Kenntnis setzen, unterrichten (*of*, von *or* über; *about* or *on*, über); erfüllen, beseelen (*with*, mit); *keep o.s. -ed*, sich auf dem laufenden halten. 2. *v.n.* Anzeige erstatten; *– against a p.*, einen denunzieren *or* anzeigen. **-ant** [–ənt], *s.* der Berichterstatter, Einsender, Gewährsmann; Angeber. **-ation** [–'meɪʃən], *s.* (*no pl.*), die Kenntnis, Nachricht, Auskunft, Auskünfte (*pl.*), Informationen (*pl.*) (*about* or *on*, über); die Belehrung, Unterweisung, Benachrichtigung; (*with pl.*) die Anklage, Anzeige (*Law*); *file an -ation against*, Anzeige erstatten gegen; *for your -ation*, zu Ihrer Kenntnisnahme; *gather -ation upon a subject*, Erkundigungen über eine Sache einziehen; *I have no -ation*, ich bin nicht unterrichtet; *Ministry of -ation*, das Aufklärungsministerium. **-ation-bureau,** *s.*, **-ation-office,** *s.* die Auskunftsstelle, Auskunftei, das Auskunftsbüro. **-ation-service,** der Nachrichtendienst. **-er,** *s.* der Angeber, Denunziant; *common -er*, der Spitzel.

informal [ɪn'fɔ:məl], *adj.* zwanglos, ungezwungen, ohne Förmlichkeit, nicht formell, unzeremoniell; formlos, formwidrig. **-ity** [–'mælɪtɪ], *s.* die Ungezwungenheit, Zwanglosigkeit; Formlosigkeit, Formwidrigkeit, der Formfehler.

infra ['ɪnfrə], *adv.* (weiter) unten; (*coll.*) *– dig*, unwürdig; *–-red*, infrarot, ultrarot.

infract [ɪn'frækt], *v.a.* brechen, verletzen. **-ion** [–'frækʃən], *s.* die Verletzung, Übertretung.

infrangible [ɪn'frændʒɪbl], *adj.* unverletzlich, unzerbrechlich.

infrequen-cy [ɪn'frɪ:kwənsɪ], *s.* die Seltenheit. **-t** [–ənt], *adj.* selten, nicht häufig.

infringe [ɪn'frɪndʒ], 1. *v.a.* übertreten, verletzen (*laws*), verstoßen gegen. 2. *v.n.* übergreifen in *or* auf, beeinträchtigen. **-ment** [–mənt], *s.* der Eingriff, Übergriff (*on*, in (*Acc.*)), die Übertretung, Verletzung (*of* (*Gen.*)), der Verstoß (*of*, gegen).

infuriate [ɪn'fjʊ:rɪeɪt], *v.a.* wütend machen, in Wut versetzen.

infus-e [ɪn'fjʊ:z], 1. *v.a.* begießen, aufgießen (*tea, etc.*); einweichen, ziehen lassen (*Chem., Pharm.*); (*fig.*) einflößen, eingeben (*into* (*Dat.*)), erfüllen (*with*, mit). 2. *v.n.* ziehen (*as tea*). **-er** [–ə], *s.* das Teeei. **-ible** [–ɪbl], *adj.* einflößbar; unschmelzbar (*metals*). **-ion** [–ʒən], *s.* das Eingießen, Ziehenlassen, Einweichen; der Aufguß, die Infusion; (*fig.*) Einflößung; der Zustrom, Zufluß; die Beimischung, der Beigeschmack, Anstrich. **-oria** [ɪnfjʊ'zɔ:rɪə], *pl.* Aufgußtierchen, Infusorien (*pl.*). **-orial** [–'zɔ:rɪəl], *adj.* infusorisch, Infusorien–; *-orial earth*, die Kieselgur. **-orian** [–'zɔ:rɪən], *s.* das Aufgußtierchen, Infusorium.

ingathering ['ɪngæðərɪŋ], *s.* das Einernten, Einsammeln.

ingen-ious [ɪn'dʒɪ:nɪəs], *adj.* geistreich, erfinderisch, klug (*of persons*); sinnreich, klug angelegt, kunstvoll (*of things*). **-ue** ['ɪnʒeny], *s.* schlichtes Mädchen (*Theat.*). **-uity** [ɪndʒɪ'njʊɪtɪ], *s.* der Scharfsinn, die Erfindungsgabe, Findigkeit (*of persons*); das Sinnreiche (*of things*). **-uous** [ɪn'dʒɛnjʊəs], *adj.* aufrichtig, offen, bieder, offenherzig, unbefangen, arglos, schlicht, treuherzig. **-uousness,** *s.* die Offenherzigkeit, Biederkeit, Treuherzigkeit, Unbefangenheit, Schlichtheit.

ingest [ɪn'dʒɛst], *v.a.* einnehmen, verschlingen (*nourishment*).

ingle [ɪŋgl], *s.* der Herd, Kamin, das Kaminfeuer. **– nook,** *s.* die Kaminecke.

inglorious [ɪn'glɔ:rɪəs], *adj.* ruhmlos, unrühmlich; schimpflich, schändlich.

ingoing ['ɪngouɪŋ], 1. *s.* das Eintreten, der Antritt. 2. *adj.* eintretend, antretend.

ingot ['ɪŋgət], *s.* der Barren (*gold, etc.*), Stab, Zain (*steel, etc.*). **--mould,** *s.* die Gießform, Kokille. **--steel,** *s.* der Flußstahl.

ingrain ['ɪngreɪn *as attrib.*, ɪn'greɪn *as pred.*], 1. *adj.* in der Wolle gefärbt. 2. *v.a. see* **engrain. -ed** [–d], *adj.* (*fig.*) tief verwurzelt, eingewurzelt, eingefleischt.

ingrat-e ['ɪngreɪt], (*archaic*) 1. *adj.* undankbar. 2. *s.* Undankbare(r), *m.* **-iate** [ɪn'greɪʃɪeɪt], *v.r.* sich beliebt machen, sich einschmeicheln (*with*, bei); *he -iates himself with his superiors*, er setzt sich in die Gunst seiner Vorgesetzten. **-iating,** *adj.* gewinnend, einnehmend. **-itude** [ɪn'grætɪtjʊ:d], *s.* die Undankbarkeit, der Undank.

ingredient [ɪn'grɪ:dɪənt], *s.* der Bestandteil, die Zutat.

ingress ['ɪngrɛs], *s.* der Eintritt (*into*, in (*Acc.*)) (*also Astr.*), der Zutritt, das Eintrittsrecht (*into*, zu).

ingrow-ing ['ɪngrouɪŋ], *adj.* ins Fleisch gewachsen. **-n** [ɪn'groun], *adj.* eingewachsen.

inguinal ['ɪngwɪnl], *adj.* Leisten–.

ingurgitate [ɪn'gə:gɪteɪt], *v.a.* hinunterschlucken, hinunterschlingen, verschlingen.

inhabit [ɪn'hæbɪt], *v.a.* bewohnen (*Acc.*), wohnen (in (*Dat.*)). **-able** [–əbl], *adj.* bewohnbar. **-ancy** [–ənsɪ], *s.* der Aufenthalt, das Wohnrecht. **-ant** [–ənt], *s.* der Bewohner, Einwohner. **-ation** [–'teɪʃən], *s.* das Bewohnen, die Bewohnung.

inhal-ation [ɪnhə'leɪʃən], *s.* die Einatmung, Inhalation (*Med.*). **-e** [ɪn'heɪl], *v.a.* einatmen, inhalieren (*Med.*). **-er,** *s.* der Einatmer, Inhalationsapparat, Respirator.

inharmonious [ɪnhɑ:'mounɪəs], *adj.* unharmonisch, mißtönend; (*fig.*) uneinig. **-ness,** *s.* der Mangel an Harmonie.

inhere [ɪn'hɪ:ə], *v.n.* anhaften, eigen sein, innewohnen (*in* (*Dat.*)). **-nce, -ncy** [–rəns(ɪ)], *s.* das Anhaften, Innewohnen, Verwurzeltsein, die Inhärenz. **-nt** [–rənt], *adj.* anhaftend, angeboren, eigen, innewohnend (*in* (*Dat.*)).

inherit [ɪn'hɛrɪt], 1. *v.a.* erben. 2. *v.n.* erben. **-able** [–əbl], *adj.* erblich, Erb–, vererbbar (*of things*); erbfähig, erbberechtigt (*of person*). **-ance** [–əns], *s.* die Erbschaft, das Erbteil, Erbe (*also* *fig.*), die Vererbung. **–ed** [–ɪd], *adj.* ererbt. **–or** [–ə], *s.* der Erbe. **–ress** [–rɪs], **–rix** [–rɪks], *s.* die Erbin.

inhibit [ɪn'hɪbɪt], *v.a.* hemmen, hindern (*things*); verbieten, untersagen (*persons*) (*from doing*, zu tun). **–ion** [–'bɪʃən], *s.* die Hemmung (*also Psych.*), das Verbot, der Einhalt (*Law*). **–ory** [ɪn'hɪbɪtərɪ], *adj.* verbietend, hemmend, Hemmungs– (*Psych., etc.*).

inhospita-ble [ɪnhɔs'pɪtəbl], *adj.* ungastfreundlich; (*fig.*) unwirtlich, ungastlich, unfreundlich. **–lity** [–'tælɪtɪ], *s.* die Unwirtlichkeit, Ungastlichkeit.

inhuman [ɪn'hjuːmən], *adj.* unmenschlich, grausam, gefühllos. **–ity** [–'mænɪtɪ], *s.* die Unmenschlichkeit.

inhum-ation [ɪnhjʊ'meɪʃən], *s.* die Beerdigung. **–e** [ɪn'hjuːm], *v.a.* beerdigen, begraben.

inimical [ɪn'ɪmɪkl], *adj.* feindlich, schädlich (*to* (*Dat.*)).

inimitable [ɪn'ɪmɪtəbl], *adj.* unnachahmlich, unvergleichlich, einzigartig. **–ness,** *s.* die Unnachahmlichkeit.

iniquit-ous [ɪn'ɪkwɪtəs], *adj.* unbillig, ungerecht; frevelhaft, boshaft. **–y** [–tɪ], *s.* die Ungerechtigkeit; Schlechtigkeit, der Frevel.

initia-l [ɪn'ɪʃəl], 1. *adj.* anfänglich, ursprünglich, Anfangs–, Ausgangs–; Ansatz–, anlautend (*Phonet.*) 2. *s.* der Anfangsbuchstabe; die Initiale (*Art*); *his –ls*, die Anfangsbuchstaben seines Vor- und Familiennamens. 3. *v.a.* mit den Anfangsbuchstaben unterzeichnen. **–te** [–ʃɪeɪt], 1. *v.a.* anfangen, beginnen, ins Leben rufen, als Erster beantragen (*a thing*); einführen, einweihen (*a person*) (*in*, in (*Acc.*)). 2. *s.* Eingeweihte(r), *m.* der Anfänger. **–ted,** *adj.* (*usually fig.*) eingeweiht. **–tion** [–'eɪʃən], *s.* die Einweihung; Einführung, der Anfang. **–tive** [ɪn'ɪʃɪətɪv], 1. *adj.* einweihend, einleitend. 2. *s.* erster Anstoß *or* Schritt, die Anregung, Initiative; der Unternehmungsgeist; das Initiativrecht (*Parl.*); Recht eigenen Handelns; *take the –tive*, die ersten Schritte tun, die Initiative ergreifen (*in*, in); *on one's own –tive*, aus eigenem Antrieb. **–tor** [ɪn'ɪʃɪeɪtə], *s.* der Beginner, Anreger, Urheber. **–tory** [ɪn'ɪʃɪətərɪ], *adj.* beginnend, einführend, einleitend; einweihend.

inject [ɪn'dʒɛkt], *v.a.* einspritzen (*Med., Mach.*), ausspritzen (*Anat.*), (*fig.*) einimpfen, erfüllen. **–ion** [–ʃən], *s.* die Einspritzung, Ausspritzung; das Eingespritzte. **–or** [–tə], *s.* die Strahlpumpe, Einspritzdüse (*Mach.*).

injudicious [ɪndʒʊ'dɪʃəs], *adj.* unverständig, unklug, unbesonnen, unüberlegt. **–ness,** *s.* die Unverständigkeit.

injunction [ɪn'dʒʌŋkʃən], *s.* die Einschärfung, ausdrücklicher Befehl; gerichtliche Verfügung, gerichtliches Verbot, richterlicher Befehl, das Unterlassungsgebot.

injur-e ['ɪndʒə], *v.a.* beschädigen, verletzen (*things*), (*fig.*) beeinträchtigen, schädigen, schwächen, schaden, unrecht tun (*Dat.*) (*people*); *–e one's head*, sich den Kopf verletzen *or* verwunden; *–ed vanity*, gekränkte Eitelkeit. **–ious** [ɪn'dʒʊːərɪəs], *adj.* schädlich, nachteilig (*to*, für); beleidigend, schmähend, boshaft (*as language*); ungerecht; *be –ious to*, schaden (*Dat.*). **–y** ['ɪndʒərɪ], *s.* die Verletzung, Verwundung (*to* (*Gen.*) *or* an (*Dat.*)); der Schaden (*to*, für), die Beschädigung (*to* (*Gen.*)); (*fig.*) Beleidigung, Kränkung, Schädigung, Ungerechtigkeit, das Unrecht; *that adds insult to –y*, zum Schaden hat man noch den Spott.

injustice [ɪn'dʒʌstɪs], *s.* die Ungerechtigkeit, das Unrecht; *do s.o. an –*, einem unrecht tun.

ink [ɪŋk], 1. *s.* die Tinte; *as black as –*, pechschwarz, kohl(raben)schwarz; *Indian –*, die Tusche; *printer's –*, die Druckerschwärze. 2. *v.a.* mit Tinte schwärzen, beschmieren *or* beklecksen; einfärben (*types*). **--bottle,** *s.* die Tintenflasche. **–er,** *s. see* **–ing-roller.** **–iness,** *s.* die Schwärze. **--eraser,** *s.* der Tintengummi. **–ing-roller,** *s.* die Auftragwalze, Farbwalze. **--pad,** *s.* das Farbkissen, Stempelkissen. **--pencil,** *s.* der Tintenstift. **--pot,** *s.* das Tintenfaß. **–stand,** *s.* das Schreibzeug; *see* **--pot.** **--well,** *s.* eingelassenes Tintenfaß. **–y** ['ɪŋkɪ], *adj.* tintig, tintenschwarz.

inkling ['ɪŋklɪŋ], *s.* die Andeutung, leiser Wink, dunkle Ahnung, leise Idee, (*dial.*) das Gemunkel.

inlaid ['ɪnleɪd], *adj.* eingelegt, Mosaik–; *– floor*, der Parkett(fuß)boden; *– woodwork*, die (*or Austr.* das) Holzmosaik; *– work*, die Einlegearbeit.

inland ['ɪnlənd], 1. *adj.* inländisch, binnenländisch, Binnen–, einheimisch, Landes–, Inlands–; *– bill*, der Inlandswechsel; *– duty*, der Binnenzoll; *– navigation*, die Binnenschiffahrt; *– produce*, Landeserzeugnisse, Landesprodukte (*pl.*); *– revenue*, Steuereinnahmen (*pl.*); *– sea*, der Binnensee; *– trade*, der Binnenhandel. 2. *adv.* landeinwärts, im Inlande. 3. *s.* das Binnenland, Inland. **–er,** *s.* der Binnenländer.

inlay [ɪn'leɪ], 1. *v.a.* einlegen, täfeln, fournieren. 2. *s.* eingelegte Arbeit, das Fournier; die Plombe (*Dent.*). **–ing,** *s.* das Einlegen, die Täfelung, eingelegte Arbeit.

inlet ['ɪnlɛt], *s.* der Einlaß, Eingang, die Einfahrt, der Zugang (*also fig.*); kleine Bucht. **--valve,** *s.* das Einlaßventil.

in-line ['ɪn'laɪn], *attrib. adj.* Reihen– (*of engines*).

inly ['ɪnlɪ], *adv.* (*Poet.*) innerlich, innig, heimlich. **–ing** ['ɪnlaɪɪŋ], *adj.* inner–, Innen–.

inmate ['ɪnmeɪt], *s.* der Insasse, Mitbewohner, Hausgenosse.

inmost ['ɪnmoʊst], *adj.* innerst, geheimst, innigst.

inn [ɪn], *s.* der Gasthof, das Gasthaus, Wirtshaus; *–s of Court*, die (Gebäude der) Rechtsschulen (in London). **–keeper,** *s.* der Gastwirt.

innate [ɪ'neɪt], *adj.* angeboren (*in* (*Dat.*)). **–ly,** *adv.* von Natur. **–ness,** *s.* angeborene Eigenschaft.

inner ['ɪnə], *adj.* inner, inwendig, (*fig.*) geheim, verborgen, innerlich; *– diameter*, lichte Weite; *– man*, die Seele; (*coll.*) der Magen; *– tube*, der Luftschlauch (*Cycl., Motor.*). **–most** [–moʊst], *adj.* innerst, innigst.

innervat-e [ɪ'nəːveɪt], *v.a.* Nervenkraft zuführen (*organs*); (*fig.*) beleben, anregen. **–ion,** *s.* die Innervation, Nervenbelebung.

innings ['ɪnɪŋs], *pl.* die Reihe, das Am-Spiel-Sein, Dransein; Spiel, die Spielzeit (*Crick.*); (*fig.*) *have one's –*, an der Macht sein, am Ruder sein.

innocen-ce ['ɪnəsəns], *s.* die Unschuld (*of*, an), Schuldlosigkeit, Harmlosigkeit, Einfalt. **–t** [–ənt], 1. *adj.* unschuldig, schuldlos (*of*, an); harmlos, unschädlich (*as drugs, etc.*); arglos; (*coll.*) *–t of*, frei von, ohne, (*following noun*) bar. 2. *s.* Unschuldige(r), Arglose(r), *m.*; *massacre of the –ts*, Bethlehemitischer Kindermord, (*sl.*) die Nichterledigung der Tagesordnung am Sessionsende (*Parl.*); *–ts' Day*, das Fest der Unschuldigen Kinder (*Dec. 28*).

innocuous [ɪ'nɔkjʊəs], *adj.* unschädlich, harmlos. **–ness,** *s.* die Unschädlichkeit.

innominate [ɪ'nɔmɪneɪt], *adj.* namenlos, unbenannt; *– bone*, das Becken, Hüftbein (*Anat.*).

innovat-e ['ɪnoveɪt], *v.n.* Neuerungen machen *or* einführen. **–ion** [–'veɪʃən], *s.* die Neuerung. **–or** [–tə], *s.* der Neuerer.

innoxious [ɪ'nɔkʃəs], *adj.* unschädlich.

innuendo ['ɪnjʊɛndoʊ], *s.* (*pl.* –oes) versteckte *or* geheime Andeutung *or* Anspielung, die Unterstellung; Stichelei, Anzüglichkeit; untergelegte Bedeutung eines Ausdrucks (*Law*).

innutritious [ɪnjʊ'trɪʃəs], *adj.* nicht nahrhaft.

inobservance [ɪnəb'zəːvəns], *s.* die Nichtbe(ob)achtung (*of* (*Gen.*)), Unaufmerksamkeit, Unachtsamkeit (*of*, gegen).

inoculat-e [ɪ'nɔkjʊleɪt], *v.a.* impfen (*a.p.*) (*Med.*); einimpfen (*serum*) (*into* (*Dat.*)) (*Med.*); okulieren (*Hort.*); (*fig.*) *–e s.o. with s.th.*, einem etwas einimpfen. **–ion** [–'leɪʃn], *s.* die Einimpfung, Impfung; das Okulieren, die Okulierung.

inodorous [ɪ'noʊdərəs], *adj.* geruchlos.

inoffensive ['ɪnə'fɛnsɪv], *adj.* harmlos, arglos, gutartig, einwandfrei, unschädlich. **–ness,** *s.* die Harmlosigkeit.

inofficious [ɪnə'fɪʃəs], *adj.* gegen natürliche Pflichten, sittenwidrig (*Law*).

inopera-ble [ɪn'ɔpərəbl], *adj.* nicht operierbar (*Surg.*). **–tive,** *adj.* unwirksam, ungültig.

inopportune [ɪ'nɔpətjuːn], *adj.* ungelegen, unangebracht, unzeitgemäß, unzeitig.

inordinate [ɪn'ɔːdɪnɪt], *adj.* regellos, ungeregelt,

unregelmäßig, ungeordnet; unmäßig, übermäßig, zügellos. **-ness,** *s.* die Un(regel)mäßigkeit.
inorganic [ɪnɔːˈgænɪk], *adj.* unorganisch, anorganisch (*Chem.*).
inosculat-e [ɪˈnɔskjuleɪt], **1.** *v.a.* verbinden, einfügen (*into*, in (*Acc.*)). **2.** *v.n.* einmünden, eng verbunden sein, in Verbindung stehen, sich berühren. **-ion** [-ˈleɪʃən], *s.* die Einfügung, Verbindung, Vereinigung.
in-patient [ˈɪnˈpeɪʃənt], *s.* Anstaltskranke(r), *m.*
input [ˈɪnput], *s.* die Eingangsenergie, Leistungsaufnahme, zugeführte Energie *or* Leistung (*Mech. & Rad.*); – *amplifier*, der Vorverstärker (*Rad.*); – *circuit*, der Eingangskreis (*Rad.*); – *impedance*, die Gitterkreisimpedanz (*Rad.*); – *terminals*, *pl.* der Speisepunkt (*Rad.*).
inquest [ˈɪnkwɛst], *s.* gerichtliche Untersuchung; *coroner's* –, die Leichenschau.
inquietude [ɪnˈkwaɪətjuːd], *s.* die Unruhe, Ruhelosigkeit.
inquir-e [ɪnˈkwaɪə], **1.** *v.n.* fragen, sich erkundigen (*about*, über); *-e within*, Näheres im Hause; *-e of so-and-so*, zu erfragen bei N.N.; *-e after*, fragen nach, sich erkundigen nach; *much -ed after*, viel verlangt, sehr gesucht; *-e into a th.*, eine S. untersuchen *or* erforschen. **2.** *v.a.* sich erkundigen nach, fragen nach, erfragen (*Acc.*); *-e the way*, nach dem Wege fragen. **-er** [-rə], *s.* der Frager, Untersucher. **-ing** [-rɪŋ], *adj.* forschend, fragend, neugierig (*as a look*). **-y** [-ɪ], *s.* die Erkundigung, Anfrage, Nachfrage (*also C.L.*) (*for*, nach); Untersuchung, Prüfung (*into* (*Gen.*)); *make -ies*, Erkundigungen einziehen (*about*, über; *of a p.*, bei einem); *on -y*, auf Nachfrage, nach Erkundigung. **-y-office,** *s.* die Auskunftsstelle.
inquisit-ion [ɪnkwɪˈzɪʃən], *s.* gerichtliche Untersuchung; das Ketzergericht, die Inquisition (*R.C.*). **-ive** [ɪnˈkwɪzɪtɪv], *adj.* neugierig (*about*, auf), wißbegierig. **-iveness,** *s.* die Neugier(de), Wißbegierde. **-or** [-tə], *s.* der Untersucher, Untersuchungsrichter (*Law*), Inquisitor (*R.C.*). **-orial** [-ˈtɔːrɪəl], *adj.* forschend, neugierig, Untersuchungs-, Inquisitions-.
inroad [ˈɪnroud], *s.* feindlicher Einfall (*in*, in), der Angriff, Überfall (*on*, auf); (*fig.*) Eingriff (*on*, in (*Acc.*)). Übergriff (*on*, auf); (*pl.*) das Eindringen (*of disease, etc.*), die Inanspruchnahme (*on* (*Gen.*)).
insalubrious [ɪnsəˈluːbrɪəs], *adj.* ungesund.
insane [ɪnˈseɪn], *adj.* geisteskrank, wahnsinnig; (*fig.*) unsinnig, sinnlos.
insanitary [ɪnˈsænɪtərɪ], *adj.* ungesund, gesundheitsschädlich.
insanity [ɪnˈsænɪtɪ], *s.* die Geisteskrankheit, der Irrsinn, Wahnsinn; (*fig.*) die Sinnlosigkeit.
insatia-bility [ɪnseɪʃɪəˈbɪlɪtɪ], *s.* die Unersättlichkeit. **-ble** [-ˈseɪʃɪəbl], **-te** [-ˈseɪʃɪeɪt], *adj.* unersättlich.
inscribe [ɪnˈskraɪb], *v.a.* einschreiben, eintragen (*one's name, etc.*); zueignen, widmen (*a book, etc.*) (*to* (*Dat.*)); beschreiben, einzeichnen (*a figure*) (*Geom.*); (*fig.*) einprägen (*on* (*Dat.*)); *-d stock*, eingeschriebene *or* eingetragene Aktien ohne Besitzerschein (*C.L.*).
inscription [ɪnˈskrɪpʃən], *s.* die Einschreibung, Eintragung, Überschrift, Inschrift, Aufschrift; Einzeichnung (*Geom.*); Zueignung, Widmung; Zeichnung ins Aktienverzeichnis (*C.L.*).
inscrutab-ility [ɪnskruːtəˈbɪlɪtɪ], *s.* die Unerforschlichkeit. **-le** [-ˈskruːtəbl], *adj.* unerforschlich, unergründlich, rätselhaft, unverständlich. **-leness,** *s. see* **-ility.**
insect [ˈɪnsɛkt], *s.* das Kerbtier, Insekt. **-icide** [ɪnˈsɛktɪsaɪd], *s. see* **--powder.** **-ivore** [-ɪvɔː], *s.* der Insektenfresser (*Zool.*). **-ivorous** [-ˈtɪvərəs], *adj.* insektenfressend. **--powder,** *s.* das Insektenpulver, Schädlingsbekämpfungsmittel.
insecur-e [ɪnsɪˈkjuːə], *adj.* unsicher, ungewiß. **-ity** [-ˈkjuərɪtɪ], *s.* die Unsicherheit, Ungewißheit.
insen-sate [ɪnˈsɛnseɪt], *adj.* empfindungslos, gefühllos; unsinnig, unvernünftig. **-sibility** [-sɪˈbɪlɪtɪ], *s.* die Bewußtlosigkeit, Ohnmacht; Gleichgültigkeit, Gefühllosigkeit (*to*, gegen), Unempfindlichkeit (*to*, für); (*fig.*) Stumpfheit, der Stumpfsinn. **-sible** [ɪnˈsɛnsɪbl], *adj.* bewußtlos, ohnmächtig; unempfindlich, gefühllos; gleichgültig (*of* or *to*, gegen), unmerklich, nicht bewußt (*of* (*Gen.*)). **-sitive** [-ˈsɛnsɪtɪv], *adj.* unempfindlich (*to*, gegen), unempfänglich (*to*, für). **-tience** [-ˈsɛnʃɪəns], *s.* die Empfindungslosigkeit. **-tient** [-ˈsɛnʃɪənt], *adj.* empfindungslos.
inseparab-ility [ɪnsɛpərəˈbɪlɪtɪ], *s.* die Untrennbarkeit, Unzertrennlichkeit. **-le** [ɪnˈsɛpərəbl], *adj.* untrennbar (*also Gram.*), unzertrennlich. (*coll.*) **-les,** *pl.* unzertrennliche Freunde. **-leness,** *s. see* **-ility.**
insert [ɪnˈsəːt], **1.** *v.a.* einsetzen, einschalten, einfügen, einlassen, einrücken (lassen); aufgeben, inserieren (*advertisement*). **2.** [ˈɪnsəːt] *s.* die Einlage, Beilage, der Zusatz. **-ion** [ɪnˈsəːʃən], *s.* die Einschaltung, Einfügung, Eintragung, Einsetzung; der Einsatz, Zusatz, Einlaß; die Anzeige, das Inserat; der Einwurf (*of coin*).
inset [ˈɪnsɛt], **1.** *s.* der Einsatz, die Einlage, der Eckeinsatz (*in a picture*), das Nebenbild, die Nebenkarte (*in an atlas*); das Einströmen (*of the tide*). **2.** *v.a.* einsetzen, einlegen. **3.** *adj.* Einsatz-, Neben-; – *story*, die Rahmenerzählung.
inshore [ɪnˈʃɔː], **1.** *adv.* an *or* nahe der Küste; – *from the ship*, zwischen dem Schiff und der Küste. **2.** *adj.* Küsten-.
inside [ˈɪnsaɪd], **1.** *adj.* inner, inwendig, Innen-; – *callipers*, der Lochzirkel; – *diameter*, lichte Weite, lichter Durchmesser; (*coll.*) – *information*, direkte Informationen, die Nachricht aus erster Hand; – *left*, der Linksinnen(stürmer) (*Footb.*). **2.** [ɪnˈsaɪd], *adv.* im Innern, ins Innere, drinnen. **3.** [ɪnˈsaɪd] *prep.* innerhalb; (*coll.*) – *of a week*, in weniger als einer Woche. **4.** [ɪnˈsaɪd] *s.* die Innenseite, innere Seite, das Innere; (*coll.*) der Magen, Leib; Innensitzplätze (*pl.*) (*of tramcar, etc.*); (*coll.*) *the – of a week*, nahezu eine Woche, nicht mehr als eine Woche; – *out*, das Innere nach außen; *turn s.th. – out*, etwas völlig umkrempeln; (*coll.*) *know s.th. – out*, etwas in- und auswendig kennen. **-r,** *s.* (*coll.*) Eingeweihte(r), *m.*
insidious [ɪnˈsɪdɪəs], *adj.* hinterlistig, heimtückisch, trügerisch; – *agitation*, die Wühlarbeit. **-ness,** *s.* die Hinterlist, Heimtücke.
insight [ˈɪnsaɪt], *s.* die Einsicht, der Einblick (*into*, in (*Acc.*)), Scharfblick.
insignia [ɪnˈsɪgnɪə], *pl.* Abzeichen, Insignien (*pl.*).
insignifican-ce, -cy [ɪnsɪgˈnɪfɪkəns(ɪ)], *s.* die Bedeutungslosigkeit, Belanglosigkeit, Unerheblichkeit, Unwichtigkeit, Geringfügigkeit. **-t** [-ənt], *adj.* unbedeutend, unwichtig, unerheblich, belanglos, nichtssagend, bedeutungslos, geringfügig, verächtlich.
insincer-e [ɪnsɪnˈsɪːə], *adj.* unaufrichtig, falsch. **-ity** [ɪnsɪnˈsɛrɪtɪ], *s.* die Unaufrichtigkeit, Falschheit.
insinuat-e [ɪnˈsɪnjueɪt], *v.a.* zu verstehen geben (*to a p.*, einem), merken lassen (*to a p.*, einen), anspielen (*auf*, (*Acc.*)); sanft eindrängen, langsam hineinbringen *or* hineinschmuggeln (*into*, in); *-e o.s. into*, sich einschmeicheln bei, sich einschleichen, einschmuggeln, eindringen *or* winden in. **-ing,** *adj.* einschmeichelnd, einnehmend. **-ion** [-ˈeɪʃən], *s.* die Einflüsterung, feine Anspielung, der Wink; leises Eindringen, das Sich-Einschleichen, die Einschmeichelung.
insipid [ɪnˈsɪpɪd], *adj.* unschmackhaft, geschmacklos; (*fig.*) fad(e), schal, abgeschmackt. **-ity** [-ˈpɪdɪtɪ], *s.* die Unschmackhaftigkeit, Geschmacklosigkeit.
insist [ɪnˈsɪst], *v.n.*; – *on* or *upon*, bestehen auf (*Dat.*), beharren auf (*Dat.*), dringen auf (*Acc.*), ausdrücklich verlangen, Gewicht legen auf (*Acc.*), hervorheben, betonen, geltend machen. **-ence** [-əns], *s.* das Beharren (*on*, bei), Bestehen (*on*, auf (*Dat.*)); der Nachdruck, die Eindringlichkeit. **-ent** [-ənt], *adj.* beharrlich, eindringlich, nachdrücklich.
insobriety [ɪnsoˈbraɪətɪ], *s.* die Unmäßigkeit, Trunkenheit.
insole [ˈɪnsoul], *s.* die Einlegesohle, Brandsohle.
insolen-ce [ˈɪnsələns], *s.* die Unverschämtheit, Frechheit, Ungebührlichkeit, Anmaßung. **-t** [-ənt], *adj.* unverschämt, frech, anmaßend.
insolub-ility [ɪnsɔljuˈbɪlɪtɪ], *s.* die Un(auf)löslichkeit. **-le** [ɪnˈsɔljubl], *adj.* un(auf)löslich; (*fig.*) unlösbar, unerklärbar.

insolven–cy [ɪn'sɔlvənsɪ], *s.* die Zahlungsunfähigkeit, Zahlungsschwierigkeit, der Konkurs, Bankrott. **–t** [–t], 1. *adj.* zahlungsunfähig, bankrott, insolvent; *–t estate*, die Konkursmasse. 2. *s.* zahlungsunfähiger Schuldner.

insomnia [ɪn'sɔmnɪə], *s.* die Schlaflosigkeit.

insomuch ['ɪnsoʊmʌtʃ], *adv.* dermaßen, dergestalt (*that*, daß), insofern (*as*, als).

insoucian–ce [ɪn'su:sɪəns], *s.* die Sorglosigkeit, Gleichgültigkeit. **–t** [–ənt], *adj.* sorglos, unbekümmert.

inspect [ɪn'spɛkt], *v.a.* besichtigen, besehen, nachsehen, untersuchen, prüfen, inspizieren (*things*), beaufsichtigen, mustern (*persons*). **–ion** [–'spɛkʃən], *s.* die Besichtigung, Durchsicht, Untersuchung, Prüfung, Inspizierung, Aufsicht; der Appell (*Mil.*); *for your –ion*, zur Ansicht *or* Durchsicht (*C.L.*). **–ion-lamp,** *s.* die Ableuchtlampe. **–or** [–tə], *s.* der Inspektor, Aufsichtsbeamte, Aufseher; *customs –or*, der Zollaufseher; *police –or*, der Polizeikommissar; *–or of schools*, der Schulinspektor. **–oral** [–tərəl], *adj.* Aufsichts–. **–orate** [–tərɪt], *s.* die Aufsichtsbehörde. **–orship,** *s.* das Inspektoramt; die Aufsicht.

inspir–ation [ɪnspɪ'reɪʃən], *s.* das Einatmen, die Eingebung, Begeisterung; *divine –ation*, göttliche Eingebung *or* Erleuchtung; *at the –ation of*, auf Veranlassung von; *on the –ation of the moment*, durch einen plötzlichen Einfall. **–ational,** *adj.* eingegeben, Begeisterungs–. **–ator** ['ɪnspɪreɪtə], *s.* der Inspirierapparat. **–atory** [–'reɪtərɪ], *adj.* Atmungs–, Einatmungs–, **–e** [ɪn'spɑɪə], *v.a.* einatmen, (*fig.*) einhauchen, einflößen (*in a p.*, einem), auslösen, erwecken (*in a p.*, in einem), begeistern, anfeuern (*a p.*); *–e s.o. with s.th.*, einen mit etwas erfüllen *or* beseelen, einem etwas einflößen; *–ed by the government*, durch die Regierung veranlaßt; *the –ed word*, das von Gott eingegebene *or* inspirierte Wort. **–ing,** *adj.* begeisternd, belebend.

inspirit [ɪn'spɪrɪt], *v.a.* anfeuern, beseelen, ermutigen.

inspissat–e [ɪn'spɪseɪt], *v.a.* verdicken, eindicken, eindampfen, einkochen. **–ed** [–'seɪtɪd], *adj.* undurchdringlich, undurchsichtig. **–ion** [–'seɪʃən], *s.* die Verdickung.

instability [ɪnstə'bɪlɪtɪ], *s.* die Unbeständigkeit, Unsicherheit, Labilität; *see* **unstable.**

install [ɪn'stɔ:l], *v.a.* einsetzen, einführen, einweisen (*in office*); anlegen, einbauen, einrichten, installieren, montieren (*apparatus*). **–ation** [–stə'leɪʃn], *s.* die Bestallung, Einsetzung; Anlage, Einrichtung, Installation. **–ed,** *adj.* bestallt; *duly –ed*, wohlbestallt.

instalment [ɪn'stɔ:lmənt], *s.* die Rate, Abzahlung, Teilzahlung, Ratenzahlung, Abschlagszahlung; Lieferung (*of a book, etc.*), Fortsetzung (*of a serial*); *by –s*, ratenweise, in Raten; in Lieferungen; *first –*, die Anzahlung; *– plan*, die Ratenzahlung.

instan–ce ['ɪnstəns], 1. *s.* dringende *or* inständige Bitte, das Bitten, Ansuchen; (besonderer) Fall, das Beispiel; die Instanz (*Law*); *another –ce*, einen zweiten Fall *or* Beweis; *at the –ce of our friend*, auf Ansuchen *or* Veranlassung unseres Freundes; *for –ce*, zum Beispiel; *in the first –ce*, an erster Stelle, in erster Linie, das erste Mal; *Court of first –ce*, das Gericht erster Instanz; *in this –ce*, in diesem einzelnen Fall; *in the last –ce*, letzten Endes. 2. *v.a.* als Beispiel anführen, zitieren, erwähnen. **–t** [–ənt] 1. *adj.* dringend, sofortig, unmittelbar; (usually abbr. *inst.*) gegenwärtig, laufend, dieses Monats; inständig, anhaltend (*of prayer*); *on the 10th –t*, am zehnten dieses *or* laufenden Monats. 2. *s.* der Augenblick, Zeitpunkt; *in an –t*, sofort, augenblicklich; *the –t he spoke*, sobald (als) er sprach; *this –t*, sofort, in diesem Augenblick; *at that –t*, in dem Augenblick. **–taneous** [–'teɪnɪəs], *adj.* augenblicklich, unverzüglich, sofortig; gleichzeitig (*of two events*); Augenblicks–, Moment–; *his death was –taneous*, er war auf der Stelle tot; *–taneous shutter*, der Momentverschluß (*Phot.*) **–taneously,** *adv.* sofort, sogleich (*coll.*) **–ter** [ɪn'stæntə], *adv.* sogleich, sofort. **–tly,** *adv.* sogleich, augenblicklich.

instead [ɪn'stɛd], *adv.* dafür, statt dessen; *– of*, anstatt, statt; *– of me*, statt meiner, an meiner Statt *or* Stelle; *– of my brother*, anstatt meines Bruders; *– of writing*, statt zu schreiben; *be – of*, eintreten, stehen *or* gelten für.

instep ['ɪnstɛp], *s.* der Spann, Rist; (*coll.*) *be high in the –*, die Nase hoch tragen. **–-raiser,** *s.* die Senkfußeinlage, Plattfußeinlage.

instigat–e ['ɪnstɪgeɪt], *v.a.* anreizen, aufreizen, aufhetzen, antreiben (*with infin.*); anstiften (*with Acc.*). **–ion** [–'geɪʃən], *s.* die Anreizung, Aufhetzung, das Antreiben, Betreiben, der Antrieb; *at or on the –ion*, auf Betreiben (*of*, *Gen.*). **–or** ['ɪnstɪgeɪtə], *s.* der Anreizer, Aufhetzer, Anstifter (*of*, zu *or Gen.*).

instil(l) [ɪn'stɪl], *v.a.* eintröpfeln, einträufeln, (*fig.*) einflößen, beibringen (*into s.o.'s mind*, einem). **–lation** [–'leɪʃən], *s.* **–ment,** *s.* das Eintröpfeln, (*fig.*) Einflößen, die Eingebung.

instinct [ɪn'stɪŋkt], 1. *pred. adj.* erfüllt, angeregt, durchdrungen (*with*, von). 2. ['ɪnstɪŋkt], *s.* der Instinkt (*for*, für), Naturtrieb, die Naturanlage, instinktives Gefühl (*for*, für); *by –*, instinktiv, von Natur, durch Naturanlage; *act on –*, instinktiv, instinktmäßig *or* aus Instinkt handeln; *– of self-preservation*, der Selbsterhaltungstrieb. **–ive** [ɪn'stɪŋktɪv], *adj.* instinktmäßig, triebmäßig, unwillkürlich, instinktiv.

institut–e ['ɪnstɪtju:t], 1. *v.a.* einrichten, errichten, stiften, gründen, ins Werk setzen; einführen, einsetzen (*into*, in (*Acc.*)) (*Eccl.*); anstellen, einleiten (*enquiry, comparison, etc.*). 2. *s.* gelehrte Gesellschaft, der Verein, das Institut, die Anstalt, Einrichtung; das Institutsgebäude; *Justinian's –es*, Justinians Institutionen. **–ion** [–'tju:ʃən], *s.* die Einrichtung, Errichtung, Anordnung, Stiftung, Gründung; Verordnung, Satzung, das Gesetz; die Anstalt, Gesellschaft, das Institut; die Einführung, Einsetzung (*Eccl.*); *benevolent –ion*, milde Stiftung; *educational –ion*, die Erziehungsanstalt. **–ional** [–'tju:ʃənl], *adj.* Institutions–, Anstalts–. **–or** ['ɪnstɪtju:tə], *s.* der Stifter, Gründer, Anordner; einführende(r) Geistliche(r), *m.* (*Eccl.*).

instruct [ɪn'strʌkt], *v.a.* unterrichten, unterweisen, lehren, belehren; informieren, anweisen, beauftragen, anleiten; ausbilden; instruieren (*Law*). **–ion** [–'strʌkʃən], *s.* die Unterweisung, Anweisung, Anleitung, der Unterricht; die Ausbildung, Instruktion (*Mil.*); *course of –ion*, der Lehrgang. **–ions,** *pl.* Vorschriften, Anweisungen, Verhaltungsmaßregeln, Anordnungen, Befehle, Aufträge; Instruktionen (*Law*); *contrary to –ions*, gegen ausdrückliche Weisung; *–ions for use*, die Gebrauchsanweisung. **–ional,** *adj.* erzieherisch, Erziehungs–, Lehr–, Unterrichts–; Übungs– (*Mil.*); *–ional film*, der Lehrfilm. **–ive,** *adj.* belehrend, lehrreich. **–iveness,** *s.* die Belehrung; das Belehrende. **–or,** *s.* der Lehrer, Erzieher; (*Amer.*) Dozent; *flying –or*, der Fluglehrer. **–ress,** *s.* die Lehrerin, Erzieherin.

instrument ['ɪnstrumənt], 1. *s.* das Werkzeug (*also fig.*), Gerät, die Vorrichtung, das Instrument (*also Mus.*); die Urkunde, das Dokument (*Law*); (*fig.*) das Mittel; der Handlanger; *–-board*, die Schalttafel (*Motor.*), das Armaturenbrett (*Mach. Elec.*); *chosen –*, auserwähltes Rüstzeug; *musical –*, das Musikinstrument. 2. *v.a.* instrumentieren. **–al** [–'mɛntəl], *adj.* als Mittel *or* Werkzeug dienend (*to* (*Dat.*)), behilflich; Instrumental– (*Mus.*); durch Werkzeuge, Apparate *or* Instrumente verursacht (*Mach.*); (*archaic*) dienlich, förderlich; *–al error*, der Fehler des Apparats; *–al music*, die Instrumentalmusik; *be –al in*, beitragen zu, mitwirken bei, veranlassen, bewirken, es durchsetzen; *he was –al in finding a house for us*, er setzte es durch, daß eine Wohnung für uns gefunden wurde; das Finden einer Wohnung für uns haben wir *or* ist ihm zu verdanken. **–alist** ['–mɛntəlɪst], *s.* der Instrumentspieler (*Mus.*). **–ality** [–'tælɪtɪ], *s.* die Mitwirkung, Vermittlung, das Mittel; *by the –ality of*, durch Vermittlung von. **–ation** [–'teɪʃən], *s.* die Instrumentierung (*Mus.*).

insubordinat–e [ɪnsjə'bɔ:dɪnɪt], *adj.* widersetzlich, unbotmäßig. **–ion** [–'neɪʃən], *s.* die Widersetzlichkeit, Unbotmäßigkeit, der Ungehorsam, die

Gehorsamsverweigerung, Auflehnung, Insubordination.

insubstantial [ɪnsəb'stænʃəl], *adj.* unkörperlich, unwirklich, nicht stofflich. **–ity** [–ʃɪ'ælɪtɪ], *s.* die Unkörperlichkeit, Nicht-Stofflichkeit.

insufferabl–e [ɪn'sʌfərəbl], *adj.* unerträglich, unausstehlich, unleidlich.

insufficien–cy [ɪnsə'fɪʃənsɪ], *s.* die Unzulänglichkeit, Unfähigkeit, Untauglichkeit. **–t** [–ənt], *adj.* unzulänglich, unzureichend, ungenügend, unfähig, untauglich.

insufflation [ɪnsə'fleɪʃən], *s.* das Anhauchen (*R.C.*), Einblasen (*Med.*).

insular ['ɪnsjələ], *adj.* insular, Insel–; (*fig.*) abgeschlossen, beschränkt. **–ity** [–'lærɪtɪ], *s.* insulare Lage; (*fig.*) die Beschränktheit.

insulat–e ['ɪnsjəleɪt], *v.a.* isolieren (*also Elec.*), absondern. **–ing,** *adj.* isolierend, Isolier–; *–ing tape,* das Isolierband. **–ion** [–'leɪʃən], *s.* die Isolierung (*also Elec.*), Absonderung; der Isolierschutz, die Isolation. **–or** ['ɪnsjəleɪtə], *s.* der Isolator, Nichtleiter.

insulin ['ɪnsjəlɪn], *s.* das Insulin.

insult, 1. ['ɪnsʌlt], *s.* die Beleidigung (*to,* für), Beschimpfung (*to* (*Gen.*)). 2. [ɪn'sʌlt], *v.a.* beleidigen, beschimpfen. **–ing,** *adj.* beschimpfend, Schmäh–; *–ing language,* Schimpfworte.

insuperab–ility [ɪnsjʊpərə'bɪlɪtɪ], *s.* die Unüberwindlichkeit. **–le** [ɪn'sjuːpərəbl], *adj.* unüberwindlich; unübersteigbar (*as a barrier*).

insupportable [ɪnsə'pɔːtəbl], *adj.* unerträglich, unausstehlich.

insur–able [ɪn'ʃʊərəbl], *adj.* versicherungsfähig, versicherbar. **–ance** [–rəns], *s.* die Versicherung, Assekuranz; *accident –ance,* die Unfallversicherung; *all-in––ance,* die Gesamtversicherung; *fire –ance,* die Feuerversicherung; *life –ance,* die Lebensversicherung; *marine –ance,* die Seeversicherung; *unemployment –ance,* die Arbeitslosenversicherung. **–ance agent,** *s.* der Versicherungsagent. **–ance broker,** *s.* der Assekuranzmakler. **–ance company,** die Versicherungsgesellschaft. **–ance policy,** *s.* der Versicherungsschein, die Police. **–e** [ɪn'ʃʊə], *v.a.* versichern; (*fig.*) sichern, verbürgen, sicherstellen; *–ed party,* Versicherte(r), *m.* **–ee** [–rɪː], *s.* Versicherte(r), *m.* **–er** [–rə], *s.* der Versicherer. **–ers,** *pl.* die Versicherungsgesellschaft.

insurgent [ɪn'səːdʒənt], 1. *adj.* aufständisch, aufrührerisch. 2. *s.* Aufständische(r), *m.,* der Aufrührer, Rebell.

insurmountable [ɪnsəː'mɑuntəbl], *adj.* unübersteigbar, (*fig.*) unüberwindlich.

insurrection [ɪnsə'rɛkʃən], *s.* der Aufstand, Aufruhr, die Empörung. **–ary** [–ʃənrɪ], *adj.* aufrührerisch, aufständisch.

insusceptib–ility [ɪnsəsɛptɪ'bɪlɪtɪ], *s.* die Unempfänglichkeit, Unzugänglichkeit (*to,* für). **–le** [–'sɛptɪbl], *adj.* unempfänglich, unzugänglich (*to* or *of,* für), unfähig (*of* (*Gen.*)); *–le of pity,* mitleidslos.

intact [ɪn'tækt], *adj.* unberührt, unversehrt, unverletzt.

intaglio [ɪn'tɑːlɪoʊ], *s.* das Intaglio, die Gemme, geschnittener Stein.

intake ['ɪnteɪk], *s.* das Einnehmen, die Einnahme; Einlaßöffnung, das Ansaugrohr (*Motor.*).

intangib–ility [ɪntændʒɪ'bɪlɪtɪ], *s.* die Unberührbarkeit, Unantastbarkeit, Nichtgreifbarkeit. **–le** [ɪn'tændʒɪbl], *adj.* unberührbar, unbetastbar, unfühlbar; (*fig.*) unantastbar, unfaßbar.

integ–er ['ɪntɪdʒə], *s.* das Ganze, ganze Zahl (*Arith.*). **–ral** ['ɪntɪgrəl]. 1. *adj.* ganz, vollständig, Integral– (*Arith.*), (*fig.*) wesentlich; *–ral calculus,* die Integralrechnung; *–ral parts,* wesentliche Bestandteile. 2. *s.* das Integral (*Math.*), Ganze. **–rant** ['ɪntɪgrənt], *adj.* integrierend; wesentlich, notwendig, unerläßlich. **–rate** ['ɪntɪgreɪt], *v.a.* ergänzen, vervollständigen, zusammenfassen (*into,* in), integrieren (*Math.*). **–ration** [–'greɪʃən], *s.* die Ergänzung, Vervollständigung; Integrierung, Berechnung des Integrals (*Math.*). **–rity** [ɪn'tɛgrɪtɪ], *s.* die Ganzheit, Vollständigkeit; Unversehrtheit, Lauterkeit, Echtheit; Rechtschaffenheit, Unbescholtenheit, Redlichkeit.

integument [ɪn'tɛgjʊmənt], *s.* die Decke, Hülle, Deckhaut (*Anat.*).

intellect ['ɪntəlɛkt], *s.* der Verstand, Intellekt, die Urteilskraft, Denkfähigkeit; (*coll.*) kluger Kopf, *pl.* die Intelligenz. **–ion** [–'lɛkʃən], *s.* das Verstehen, der Begriff. **–ual** [–'lɛktjʊəl], 1. *adj.* verstandesmäßig, gedanklich, geistig, Verstandes–, Geistes–; verständig, vernünftig, klug, intellektuell; *–ual powers,* die Geisteskräfte (*pl.*), geistige Kraft. 2. *s.* Intellektuelle(r), *m.,* Gebildete(r), *m.,* der Kopfarbeiter. **–ualism,** *s.* der Intellektualismus. **–uality** [–tjʊ'ælɪtɪ], *s.* die Verstandeskraft, Intelligenz.

intelligen–ce [ɪn'tɛlɪdʒəns], *s.* (*no pl.*) der Verstand, die Intelligenz, Denkfähigkeit, Auffassungsgabe, Klugheit, Einsicht, das Verständnis; die Nachricht, Mitteilung, Kunde, Auskunft; Spionage; (*with pl.*) verständiges *or* vernünftiges Wesen. **–ce-department,** *s.* das Nachrichtenamt, geheimer Nachrichtendienst, der Geheimdienst, die Spionageabteilung (*Mil.*). **–ce-office,** *s.* (*Amer.*) das Auskunftsbüro. **–cer,** *s.* der Kundschafter, Geheimagent, Spion. **–ce-service,** *s.* der Nachrichtendienst (*Mil.*). **–t** [–ənt], *adj.* mit Verstand begabt, denkfähig, verständig, vernünftig, verständnisvoll, intelligent, klug, scharfsinnig, aufgeweckt. **–sia** [–'dʒɛntsɪə], *s.* gebildete (Ober)-Schicht, die Intelligenz.

intelligib–ility [ɪntɛlɪdʒɪ'bɪlɪtɪ], *s.* die Verständlichkeit. **–le** [ɪn'tɛlɪdʒɪbl], *adj.* verständlich, klar (*to,* für).

intempera–nce [ɪn'tɛmpərəns], *s.* die Unmäßigkeit; Trunksucht. **–te** [rət], *adj.* unmäßig, maßlos, zügellos, ungestüm, leidenschaftlich; trunksüchtig.

intend [ɪn'tɛnd], *v.a.* beabsichtigen, vorhaben, im Sinne haben, wollen; meinen, sagen wollen (*by,* mit), bestimmen (*for,* für *or* zu); *as –ed,* wie beabsichtigt; *–ed as,* gemeint als; *the picture is –ed to be me,* das Bild soll ich sein *or* soll mich darstellen. **–ed** [–ɪd], 1. *adj.* geplant, beabsichtigt, absichtlich; (*coll.*) künftig; *–ed husband,* der Bräutigam. 2. *s.* (*coll.*) Zukünftige(r), *m. or f.,* der Bräutigam, die Braut. **–ing,** *adj.* angehend; *–ing purchaser,* der Reflektant.

intendan–cy [ɪn'tɛndənsɪ], *s.* die Oberaufsicht, Intendantur. **–t** [–ənt], *s.* der Vorsteher, Verwalter, Intendant.

intens–e [ɪn'tɛns], *adj.* stark, heftig, intensiv, eindringlich; sehnlichst (*as desires*), tief (*as colour*), (an)gespannt, angestrengt (*as effort*); (*coll.*) empfindsam, überspannt. **–ness,** *s.* die Stärke, Heftigkeit, Anstrengung, Anspannung. **–ification** [–ɪfɪ'keɪʃən], *s.* die Verstärkung (*also Phot.*). **–ifier** [ɪn'tɛnsɪfɑɪə], *s.* der Verstärker (*Phot.*). **–ify** [ɪn'tɛnsɪfɑɪ], 1. *v.a.* verstärken (*also Phot.*), verschärfen, steigern. 2. *v.n.* sich steigern *or* verstärken. **–ity** [–sɪtɪ], *s.* die Heftigkeit, Stärke, Fülle, Tiefe, Größe, hoher Grad; der Stärkegrad, die Intensität (*Phys.*), Stromstärke (*Elec.*); *–ity of light,* Lichtstärke; *–ity of sound,* Tonstärke. **–ive** [ɪn'tɛnsɪv], *adj.* stark, intensiv; angespannt, angestrengt, unablässig; verstärkend, Verstärkungs–, (*Gram.*).

intent [ɪn'tɛnt], 1. *adj.* gespannt, gerichtet, eifrig bedacht, erpicht, versessen (*on,* auf), eifrig beschäftigt (*on,* mit). 2. *s.* die Absicht, das Vorhaben; *proof of –,* der Beweis der Vorsätzlichkeit (*Law*); *to all –s and purposes,* durchaus, in jeder Hinsicht, im Grunde, in Wirklichkeit, praktisch genommen; *to do with –,* absichtlich tun; *with – to do,* in der Absicht zu tun; *with evil –,* in böser Absicht. **–ion** [–'tɛnʃən], *s.* die Absicht, der Vorsatz, das Vorhaben, der Zweck, das Ziel; die Bedeutung, der Sinn; *it is his –ion,* er hat die Absicht. (*coll.*) **–ions,** *pl.* Heiratsabsichten (*pl.*). **–ional** [–'tɛnʃənl], *adj.* absichtlich, vorsätzlich, mit Fleiß. **–ioned** [–'tɛnʃənd], *adj. suff.* –gesinnt. **–ness,** *s.* gespannte Aufmerksamkeit, der Eifer; *–ness of purpose,* die Zielstrebigkeit.

inter [ɪn'təː], *v.a.* beerdigen, begraben; *see* **interment.**

inter- ['ɪntə], *pref.* zwischen, unter, Zwischen–; einander, gegenseitig; *see compounds below.*

interact ['ɪntəækt], 1. *s.* das Zwischenspiel, der

Zwischenakt. 2. [ɪntəˈækt] *v.n.* aufeinander (ein)-wirken, einander *or* sich gegenseitig beeinflussen. **-ion** [-ˈækʃən], *s.* die Wechselwirkung. **-ive** [-ˈæktɪv], *adj.* wechselwirkend.

interbreed [ɪntəˈbrɪ:d], 1. *v.a.* durch Kreuzung züchten. 2. *v.n.* sich kreuzen.

intercala-ry [ɪntəˈkælərɪ], *adj.* eingeschaltet, eingeschoben; *-ry day*, der Schalttag. **-te** [ɪnˈtə:-kəleɪt], *v.a.* einschalten, einschieben. **-tion** [-kəˈleɪʃən], *s.* die Einschaltung.

intercede [ɪntəˈsɪ:d], *v.a.* sich verwenden, sich ins Mittel legen, Fürsprache einlegen (*with*, bei; *for*, für). **-r,** *s.* der Fürsprecher.

intercept, 1. [ɪntəˈsɛpt], *v.a.* abfangen (*also Av.*), auffangen; abhören, ablauschen; unterschlagen (*letters*); (*coll.*) aufchnappen; hemmen, hindern, aufhalten, unterbrechen, abschneiden (*also Av.*); einschließen (*Math.*). 2. [ˈɪntəsɛpt], *s.* der Abschnitt, die Kreuzung (*Math.*). **-ion** [-ˈsɛpʃən], *s.* das Auffangen, Aufhalten, Abfangen; die Unterbrechung, Hemmung; *-ion flight*, der Sperrflug (*Av.*). **-or** [-ˈsɛptə], *s.* der Auffänger, Abfänger; das Jagdflugzeug, der Jäger (*Av.*); *-or service*, *s.* der Horchdienst, Abhördienst (*Rad.*, *Tele.*).

intercess-ion [ɪntəˈsɛʃən], *s.* die Fürbitte, Fürsprache, Verwendung, Vermittlung; *make -ion*, sich verwenden, Fürsprache einlegen (*to*, bei; *for*, für); *service of -ion*, der Fürbittegottesdienst. **-or** [-ˈsɛsə], *s.* der Fürsprecher, Vermittler. **-ory** [-ˈsɛsərɪ], *adj.* fürsprechend, Fürsprech–, vermittelnd.

interchange [ɪntəˈtʃeɪndʒ], 1. *v.a.* gegenseitig *or* untereinander austauschen *or* auswechseln, vertauschen, verwechseln, abwechseln lassen. 2. *v.n.* (ab)wechseln. 3. *s.* der Umtausch, Austausch, die Abwechslung; – *of ideas*, der Gedankenaustausch. **-ability** [-əˈbɪlɪtɪ], *s.* die Auswechselbarkeit, Vertauschbarkeit. **-able** [-ˈtʃeɪndʒəbl], *adj.* auswechselbar, austauschbar, umschaltbar.

intercollegiate [ˈɪntəkəˈlɪ:dʒɪɪt], *adj.* zwischen den Colleges.

intercolonial [ˈɪntəkəˈlounɪəl], *adj.* interkolonial.

intercommun-icate [ɪntəkəˈmjunɪkeɪt], *v.n.* miteinander in Verbindung stehen, untereinander verkehren. **-ication** [-ˈkeɪʃən], *s.* die Verbindung miteinander, gegenseitiger Verkehr, gegenseitige Verständigung; die Eigenverständigung, der Bordverkehr (*Av.*).

interconnect [ɪntəkəˈnɛkt], 1. *v.a.* untereinander verbinden. 2. *v.n.* untereinander verbunden sein *or* werden, sich untereinander verbinden. **-ion** [-ˈnɛkʃən], *s.* gegenseitige Verbindung.

intercostal [ɪntəˈkɔstəl], *adj.* zwischen den Rippen liegend (*Anat.*).

intercourse [ˈɪntəkɔ:s], *s.* der Verkehr, Umgang (*between*, zwischen; *with*, mit); geschlechtlicher Verkehr; *commercial* –, der Geschäftsverkehr; *sexual* –, geschlechtlicher Verkehr.

intercross [ɪntəˈkrɔs], 1. *v.n.* sich *or* einander kreuzen (*as lines*). 2. *v.a.* einander kreuzen lassen.

intercurrent [ɪntəˈkʌrənt], *adj.* dazwischenlaufend, dazwischenkommend, dazukommend, hinzutretend (*Med.*).

interdepend [ɪntədɪˈpɛnd], *v.n.* voneinander abhängen. **-ence,** *s.* **-ency** [-ˈpɛndəns(ɪ)], *s.* gegenseitige Abhängigkeit. **-ent** [-ənt], *adj.* gegenseitig *or* voneinander abhängig; (*fig.*) eng zusammenhängend, ineinandergreifend.

interdict, 1. [ɪntəˈdɪkt], *v.a.* untersagen, verbieten (*to a p.*, einem); sperren, aussperren; mit dem Interdikt belegen (*R.C.*); – *a p.*, einem verbieten (*from doing*, zu tun). 2. [ˈɪntədɪkt], *s.* das Verbot, Interdikt (*R.C.*). **-ion** [-ˈdɪkʃən], *s.* das Verbot, der Kirchenbann. **-ory** [-ˈdɪktərɪ], *adj.* Verbots–, verbietend.

interdigita-l [ɪntəˈdɪdʒɪtəl], *adj.* zwischen den Fingern *or* Zehen liegend. **-te** [-teɪt], *v.n.* ineinandergreifen.

interest [ˈɪntərɛst], **1.** *v.a.* interessieren (*in*, für); angehen, betreffen; Interesse *or* Teilnahme erwecken *or* gewinnen *or* erregen (*in*, an); anziehen, reizen, fesseln, einnehmen, beteiligen (*in*, an), gewinnen (*in*, für) (*also C.L.*); – *o.s. in*, Anteil nehmen an, sich interessieren für. **2.** *s.* das Interesse, die Teilnahme (*in*, für); Beteiligung, der Anteil (*in*, an); das Anrecht (*in*, auf); der Vorteil, Nutzen, Gewinn, Einfluß, die Macht (*with*, bei), die Wichtigkeit, Bedeutung (*to*, für); (*no pl.*) der Zins, die Zinsen (*pl.*) (*C.L.*); **(a)** (*with nouns, adj., etc.*); *arrears of* –, Zinsrückstände (*pl.*); *compound* –, Zinseszinsen (*pl.*); *payment of* –, die Zinszahlung; *self-*–, der Eigennutz; *simple* –, Kapitalzinsen (*pl.*); **(b)** (*with verbs*) *bear* –, sich verzinsen *bearing no* –, unverzinslich; *have an* – *in*, beteiligt sein an *or* bei; *have no* – *for s.o.*, einen nicht interessieren; *lose* – *in*, das Interesse verlieren an; *pay the* – *on the capital*, das Kapital verzinsen; *show much* – *in*, großen Anteil zeigen an; *take an* (*a great* or *great*) – *in*, sich (sehr) interessieren für; **(c)** (*with prepositions*) *ex* –, ohne Zinsen (*C.L.*); *be in* or *to a p.'s* –, in jemandes Interesse liegen, zu jemandes Vorteil sein; *be of small* –, von geringer Bedeutung sein; *lend on* or *at* –, Geld auf Zinsen ausleihen; *with* –, mit Zinsen; (*coll.*) in verstärktem Maße. **-ed,** *adj.* beteiligt, interessiert, eigennützig; *the -ed parties*, die Beteiligten. **-edly,** *adv.* mit Interesse, in interessanter Weise. **-edness,** *s.* der Eigennutz. **-ing,** *adj.* interessant, fesselnd, anziehend, unterhaltend; (*coll.*) *in an -ing condition*, in anderen Umständen.

interfere [ɪntəˈfɪ:ə], *v.n.* sich einmischen *or* einmengen (*in*, in (*Acc.*)), dazwischentreten, sich ins Mittel legen, einschreiten, eingreifen; – *with*, stören, hindern, unterbrechen, beeinträchtigen, in Konflikt geraten mit, dazwischenkommen, zusammenstoßen mit; störend beeinflussen, störend einwirken auf, störend wirken, interferieren, sich kreuzen, aufeinanderschlagen (*as waves*), sich streichen (*Vet.*). **-nce** [-rəns], *s.* das Dazwischentreten, die Einmischung (*in*, in), der Eingriff (*with*, in), die Beeinträchtigung, Interferenz, Störung (*Phys.*); das Störgeräusch (*Rad.*); *elimination of -nce*, die Entstörung (*Rad.*).

interflow [ɪntəˈflou], *s.* das Ineinanderfließen.

interfus-e [ɪntəˈfju:z], *v.a.* (miteinander) vermischen, durchdringen. **-ion** [-ʒən], *s.* die Vermischung, Durchdringung.

interglacial [ɪntəˈglæsɪəl], *adj.* interglazial (*Geol.*).

interim [ˈɪntərɪm], 1. *s.* die Zwischenzeit, das Interim; einstweilige Regelung (*Hist.*); *in the* –, unterdessen, einstweilig, einstweilen, mittlerweile, vorläufig, in der Zwischenzeit. 2. *adj.* einstweilig, vorläufig, Interims–, Zwischen–; – *dividend*, die Abschlagsdividende; – *injunction*, einstweilige Verfügung; – *report*, vorläufiger Bericht.

interior [ɪnˈtɪ:rɪə], 1. *adj.* inner, Innen–, innerlich, inwendig; binnenländisch, Binnen–. 2. *s.* das Innere; Binnenland; die Innenaufnahme (*Phot.*), (*Amer.*) *Department of the* –, das Ministerium des Inneren, Innenministerium. **-ly,** *adv.* innen, im Innern.

interject [ɪntəˈdʒɛkt], *v.a.* einwerfen, dazwischenwerfen (*a remark*), (*fig.*) einschalten, hinzufügen (*a parenthesis*). **-ion** [-ˈdʒɛkʃən], *s.* der Ausruf, die Interjektion (*Gram.*). **-ional,** *adj.* **-ory** [-tərɪ], *adj.* dazwischengeworfen.

interlac-e [ɪntəˈleɪs], 1. *v.a.* verflechten, verschlingen, durchflechten. 2. *v.n.* sich verflechten *or* kreuzen; *-ing arches*, Kreuzbogen (*pl.*).

interlard [ɪntəˈlɑ:d], *v.a.* (*fig.*) spicken, durchsetzen (*with*, mit).

interleave [ɪntəˈlɪ:v], *v.a.* durchschießen (*a book*). **-d,** *adj.* durchschossen.

interline [ɪntəˈlaɪn], *v.a.* zwischen die Zeilen schreiben, einfügen (*a word*). **-ar** [-ˈlɪnɪə], *adj.* zwischenzeilig, Interlinear–. **-ation,** *s.* das Dazwischenschreiben, Zwischengeschriebenes, *n.*, eingefügtes Wort.

interlink [ɪntəˈlɪŋk], *v.a.* verketten.

interlock [ɪntəˈlɔk], 1. *v.n.* ineinandergreifen, ineinanderhaken. 2. *v.a.* zusammenschließen, einschachteln, verschränken.

interlocut-ion [ɪntəloˈkjuʃən], *s.* die Unterredung, das (Zwie)Gespräch. **-or** [-ˈkjutə], *s.* der Mitredende im Zwiegespräch; *my -or*, derjenige mit dem ich spreche. **-ory** [-ˈlɔkətərɪ], *adj.* in Gesprächsform, Gesprächs–; *-ory decree*, die Zwischenentscheidung (*Law*); *-ory question*, die Zwischenfrage.

interlope [ɪntə'loup], *v.n.* sich eindrängen *or* dazwischendrängen; (*archaic*) den Markt aufkaufen, verbotenen Handel treiben (*C.L.*). **–r,** *s.* der Eindringling; (*archaic*) Schleichhändler (*C.L.*).
interlude ['ɪntəljuːd], *s.* das Zwischenspiel, Intermezzo (*Mus.*), die Pause (*Theat.*).
intermarr–iage [ɪntə'mærɪdʒ], *s.* die Wechselheirat. **–y** [–'mærɪ], *v.n.* untereinander heiraten.
intermaxillary [ɪntəmæk'sɪlərɪ], *adj.*; – *bone*, der Zwischenkieferknochen.
intermedia–ry [ɪntə'mɪːdjərɪ], 1. *adj.* dazwischen befindlich, vermittelnd. 2. *s.* der Vermittler, Zwischenhändler (*C.L.*). **–te** [–'mɪːdɪət], 1. *adj.* dazwischen liegend, Mittel–, Zwischen–; *be –te between*, liegen in der Mitte zwischen; *–te examination*, erste Universitätsprüfung (*England*); *–te school*, die Mittelschule (*Amer.*); *–te stage*, das Zwischenstadium; *–te station*, die Zwischenstation; *–te trade*, der Zwischenhandel. 2. *s.* der Vermittler; das Zwischenspiel; (see also *–te examination*). **–tor,** *s.* der Vermittler.
interment [ɪn'təːmənt], *s.* die Beerdigung, Bestattung, Beisetzung.
intermezzo [ɪntə'mɛdzou], *s.* das Intermezzo, Zwischenspiel.
interminable [ɪn'təːmɪnəbl], *adj.* endlos, unendlich, grenzenlos; langwierig. **–ness,** *s.* die Endlosigkeit, Grenzenlosigkeit.
intermingle [ɪntə'mɪŋgl], 1. *v.a.* vermischen, untermischen, durchsetzen. 2. *v.n.* sich vermischen.
intermission [ɪntə'mɪʃən], *s.* das Aussetzen, die Unterbrechung, Aussetzung, Pause; *without* –, unaufhörlich, unausgesetzt, ohne Unterlaß, unablässig.
intermit [ɪntə'mɪt], 1. *v.a.* aussetzen, unterbrechen. 2. *v.n.* nachlassen, aussetzen. **–tence** [–əns], *s.* das Versagen, Aussetzen. **–tent** [–ənt], *adj.* aussetzend, absatzweise, diskontinuierlich, unterbrochen, abwechselnd; *be –tent*, aussetzen; *–tent fever*, das Wechselfieber; *–tent light*, das Blinkfeuer. **–tently,** **–tingly,** *adv.* in Absätzen, abwechselnd.
intermix [ɪntə'mɪks], 1. *v.a.* vermischen, untermischen. 2. *v.n.* sich mischen. **–ture** [–tʃə], *s.* die Mischung, das Gemisch; die Beimischung, der Zusatz.
intern, 1. [ɪn'təːn], *v.a.* internieren. 2. ['ɪntəːn], *s.* der Hilfsarzt im Krankenhaus. **–ee** [–'nɪː], *s.* Internierte(r), *m.* **–ment,** *s.* die Internierung; *–ment camp*, das Internierungslager.
internal [ɪn'təːnəl], *adj.* inner, innerlich; einheimisch, inländisch, Innen–, Binnen–; intern; *–-combustion engine*, der Verbrennungs– *or* Explosionsmotor; – *diameter*, lichte Weite; – *evidence*, innerer Beweis; – *injury*, innere Verletzung; – *pressure*, der Innendruck; – *revenue*, Staatseinkünfte (*pl.*).
international [ɪntə'næʃənəl], 1. *adj.* international, zwischenstaatlich; – *exhibition*, die Weltausstellung; – *language*, die Weltsprache; – *law*, das Völkerrecht; – *relations*, zwischenstaatliche Beziehungen. 2. *s.* die Internationale (*Pol.*), internationaler Spieler (*Sport.*). **–ism,** *s.* der Internationalismus. **–ity** [–'nælɪtɪ], *s.* überstaatlicher Charakter. **–ize,** *v.a.* internationalisieren, unter internationale Kontrolle stellen. **–ly,** *adv.* unter den Nationen, in internationaler Hinsicht, auf internationalem Wege.
internecine [ɪntə'nɪːsaɪn], *adj.* sich gegenseitig zerstörend, Vernichtungs–, mörderisch.
interpellat–e [ɪntə'pɛleɪt], *v.a.* interpellieren. **–ion** [–'leɪʃən], *s.* die Interpellation (*Parl.*).
interpenetrat–e [ɪntə'pɛnɪtreɪt], 1. *v.n.* sich gegenseitig durchdringen. 2. *v.a.* durchsetzen, durchdringen. **–ion** [–'treɪʃən], *s.* gegenseitige Durchdringung.
interplay ['ɪntəpleɪ], *s.* die Wechselwirkung, gegenseitige Beeinflussung, wechselseitiges Spiel, das Ineinandergreifen (*of forces*).
interpolat–e [ɪn'təːpoleɪt], *v.a.* einschalten, unterschieben, einschieben, dazwischenschalten, interpolieren (*also Math.*). **–ion** [–'leɪʃən], *s.* die Interpolation, Interpolierung (*also Math.*), Einschiebung, Einschaltung; das Einschiebsel, die Textfälschung.
interpos–e [ɪntə'pouz], 1. *v.a.* dazwischenstellen, dazwischenlegen, dazwischensetzen, dazwischenschalten, einwerfen, einflechten (*a remark, etc.*), vorbringen, einlegen (*veto*). 2. *v.n.* sich ins Mittel legen, vermitteln (*between*, zwischen), dazwischentreten, dazwischenkommen, (sich) unterbrechen (*in speaking*). **–ition** [–pə'zɪʃən], *s.* das Dazwischentreten, Eingreifen; die Zwischenstellung, Vermittlung.
interpret [ɪn'təːprɪt], *v.a.* auslegen, erklären; verdolmetschen, übersetzen; deuten (*dreams, etc.*), darstellen, wiedergeben (*a rôle*). **–ation** [–'teɪʃən], *s.* die Auslegung, Auswertung, Erklärung, Deutung; Darstellung, Wiedergabe. **–ative** [ɪn'təːprətɪv], *adj.* erklärend, auslegend. **–er** [–prətə], *s.* der Dolmetscher; Ausleger, Darsteller.
interregnum [ɪntə'rɛgnəm], *s.* die Zwischenregierung, (*fig.*) Unterbrechung.
interrelat–ed [ɪntərɪ'leɪtɪd], *adj.* untereinander zusammenhängend. **–ion** [–'leɪʃən], *s.* gegenseitige Beziehung, die Wechselbeziehung.
interrogat–e [ɪn'tɛrəgeɪt], 1. *v.a.* befragen, ausfragen; vernehmen, verhören (*Law*). 2. *v.n.* Fragen stellen. **–ion** [–'geɪʃən], *s.* das Befragen, die Befragung, Vernehmung, Frage; das Verhör (*Law*); *–ion-mark*, *mark* or *note of –ion*, das Fragezeichen; *–ion officer*, der Vernehmungsoffizier (*Mil.*). **–ive** [ɪntə'rɔgətɪv], 1. *adj.* fragend, Frage–. 2. *s.* das Fragewort. **–or** [ɪn'tɛrəgeɪtə], *s.* der Frager, Fragesteller. **–ory** [ɪntə'rɔgətərɪ], 1. *adj.* fragend, Frage–. 2. *s.* die Fragestellung, gerichtliches Verhör (*Law*).
interrupt [ɪntə'rʌpt], *v.a.* unterbrechen, aufhalten, verhindern, stören; – *a p.*, einem in die Rede fallen; *don't let me – you*, lassen Sie sich durch mich nicht stören. **–ed,** *adj.* unterbrochen, verhindert, gestört. **–edly,** *adv.* mit Unterbrechungen. **–er,** *s.* der Unterbrecher (*also Tech.*), Störer, die Fliehbacke (*of a fuze*); *–er gear*, die Steuerung (*Mach.*). **–ion** [–'rʌpʃen], *s.* die Unterbrechung, Stockung, Störung; *without –ion*, ohne Unterbrechung, ununterbrochen.
intersect [ɪntə'sɛkt], 1. *v.a.* (durch)schneiden. 2. *v.n.* sich schneiden *or* kreuzen. **–ion** [–'sɛkʃən], *s.* die Durchschneidung, der Schnittpunkt, die Schnittlinie (*Geom.*), Kreuzung (*Railw. etc.*), Straßenkreuzung.
interspace [ɪntə'speɪs], 1. *s.* der Zwischenraum. 2. *v.a.* einen Zwischenraum lassen zwischen.
intersperse ['ɪntəspəːs], *v.a.* einstreuen, einmischen (*among*, zwischen (*Acc.*)), vermischen, untermengen, durchsetzen (*with*, mit).
interstate ['ɪntəsteɪt], *adj.* zwischenstaatlich (*Amer.*).
intersti–ce [ɪn'təːstɪs], *s.* der Zwischenraum, die Spalte, Lücke. **–tial** [ɪntə'stɪʃəl], *adj.* in den Zwischenräumen.
intertwine [ɪntə'twaɪn], 1. *v.a.* verflechten, verschlingen. 2. *v.n.* sich verflechten *or* verschlingen.
interval ['ɪntəvəl], *s.* der Abstand (*also fig.*), Zwischenraum (*in space*); die Zwischenzeit, Pause (*in time*); das Intervall, der Tonabstand (*Mus.*); *at –s*, dann und wann, hier und da; *at frequent –s*, in häufigen Zwischenräumen; *lucid –s*, lichte Augenblicke. **– signal,** das (Sende)Pausenzeichen (*Rad.*).
interven–e [ɪntə'vɪːn], *v.n.* dazwischenkommen, dazwischentreten, hinzukommen, liegen zwischen; sich erstrecken; eintreten, vorfallen, sich einmischen (*in*, in), sich verwenden (*on behalf of*, für), sich ins Mittel legen, vermitteln (*between*, zwischen), eingreifen, intervenieren (*C.L. & Law*). **–tion** [–'vɛnʃən], *s.* das Dazwischentreten, Dazwischenkommen; die Einmischung, Vermittlung, das Eingreifen, die Intervention (*C.L., Law*).
interview ['ɪntəvjuː], 1. *s.* die Zusammenkunft, Unterredung; Besprechung (zu Pressezwecken), das Interview. 2. *v.a.* (als Berichterstatter) befragen, interviewen, ein Interview haben mit. **–er** [–ə], *s.* befragender Berichterstatter, der Interviewer.
interweave [ɪntə'wɪːv], *ir.v.a.* durchweben, durchwirken, durchflechten, verflechten, verweben; *interwoven with*, verwachsen mit.
intesta–cy [ɪn'tɛstəsɪ], *s.* das Fehlen eines Testa-

ments. **–te** [–teɪt], 1. *adj.* ohne Testament, testamentlos. 2. *s.* Verstorbene(r) ohne Testament.
intestin–al [ɪntɛs'tɑɪnl], *adj.* Eingeweide–, Darm–. **–e** [ɪn'tɛstɪn], 1. *adj.* inner, einheimisch; *–e war*, der Bürgerkrieg. 2. *s.* (*usually pl.*) Eingeweide, Därme (*pl.*), das Gedärm(e); *large –e*, der Dickdarm; *small –e*, der Dünndarm.
intima–cy ['ɪntɪməsɪ], *s.* die Vertraulichkeit, Vertrautheit, Innigkeit, vertrauter Umgang; (unerlaubter) geschlechtlicher Umgang. **–te** [–ət], 1. *adj.* innig, vertraut, intim, vertraulich. 2. *s.* Vertraute(r), *m. or f.*
intimat–e ['ɪntɪmeɪt], *v.a.* andeuten, zu verstehen geben, nahe legen, bekannt machen, mitteilen, ankündigen. **–ion** [–'meɪʃn], *s.* die Andeutung, der Wink, Fingerzeig, die Ankündigung, Anzeige.
intimidat–e [ɪn'tɪmɪdeɪt], *v.a.* einschüchtern, bange machen, abschrecken. **–ion** [–'deɪʃən], *s.* die Einschüchterung. **–ory** [–dətrɪ], *adj.* einschüchternd.
into ['ɪntʊ], *prep.* in (*Acc.*), in . . . hinein; *bribe – secrecy*, durch Bestechung zum Schweigen bringen; *cheat – accepting*, durch List zur Annahme bewegen; *come – property*, zu Vermögen kommen; *convert – money*, zu Geld machen; *dip –*, flüchtig durchlesen, überfliegen (*a book*); *4 divides – 12 three times*, 4 geht in 12 dreimal; *get – a habit*, eine Gewohnheit annehmen; *grow –*, werden zu; *be led – error*, zum Irrtum verleitet werden; *look –*, prüfen, untersuchen; *make – jam*, zu Marmelade verarbeiten; *put – execution*, ausführen; *put – shape*, in Form bringen; *put – writing*, schriftlich niederlegen; *turn – money*, zu Geld machen; *turn – ridicule*, lächerlich machen.
intolera–ble [ɪn'tɔlərəbl], *adj.* unerträglich, unausstehlich. **–bleness**, *s.* die Unerträglichkeit. **–nce** [–əns], *s.* die Unduldsamkeit (*of*, gegen). **–nt** [–ənt], *adj.* unduldsam, unnachsichtig (*of*, gegen), intolerant; *be –nt of*, nicht gelten lassen.
inton–ation [ɪnto'neɪʃən], *s.* das Anstimmen, die Tongebung, der Tonansatz (*Mus.*), die Intonation (*in church*), der Tonfall, Betonung (*Phonet.*). **–e** [ɪn'toʊn], *v.a.* anstimmen, intonieren.
intoxica–nt [ɪn'tɔksɪkənt], 1. *s.* berauschendes Getränk. 2. *adj.* berauschend. **–te** [–keɪt], *v.a.* berauschen. **–ted**, *adj.* berauscht (*also fig.*), betrunken, (*fig.*) trunken (*by* or *with*, von); *be –ted with*, sich berauschen an. **–tion** [–'keɪʃən], *s.* die Berauschung, Trunkenheit (*also fig.*), der Rausch (*also fig.*).
intractab–ility [ɪntræktə'bɪlɪtɪ], *s.* die Unlenksamkeit, Störrigkeit, Halsstarrigkeit, Starrsinnigkeit. **–le** [ɪn'træktəbl], *adj.* unlenksam, widerspenstig, eigensinnig, störrig, halsstarrig, unbändig; schwer zu bearbeiten *or* handhaben (*of materials*). **–leness**, *s. see* **–ility**.
intrados [ɪn'treɪdɔs], *s.* innere Wölbung (*Arch.*).
intramural [ɪntrə'mjʊ:rəl], *adj.* innerhalb der Mauern (einer Stadt, Universität, Anstalt) vorkommend; inner (*Anat.*).
intransigen–ce [ɪn'trænzɪdʒəns], *s.* die Unnachgiebigkeit. **–t** [–ənt], 1. *adj.* unversöhnlich, unnachgiebig. 2. *s.* starrer Parteimann, der Starrkopf (*Pol.*).
intransitive [ɪn'trænsɪtɪv], 1. *adj.* intransitiv. 2. *s.* (*– verb*) das Intransitivum.
intravenous [ɪntrə'veɪnəs], *adj.* intravenös (*Med.*).
intrepid [ɪn'trɛpɪd], *adj.* unerschrocken, unverzagt, furchtlos. **–ity** [ɪntrə'pɪdɪtɪ], *s.* die Unerschrockenheit, Furchtlosigkeit.
intrica–cy ['ɪntrɪkəsɪ], *s.* die Verwick(e)lung, Schwierigkeit, Feinheit, (*coll.*) Kniffligkeit. **–te** [–ət], *adj.* verwickelt, verworren, verschlungen, verzweigt; schwierig, knifflig.
intrigu–e [ɪn'trɪ:g], 1. *s.* das Ränkespiel, die Intrige; der Liebeshandel, die Liebschaft; Verwicklung, Knotenschürzung (*of a drama*); *pl.* Machenschaften, Schliche, Umtriebe, Ränke (*pl.*). 2. *v.n.* Ränke schmieden, intrigieren. 3. *v.a.* (*coll.*) Neugier erregen, fesseln. **–er**, *s.* der Ränkeschmied, Intrigant. **–ing**, *adj.* ränkevoll, arglistig; (*coll.*) fesselnd, interessant.
intrinsic [ɪn'trɪnsɪk], *adj.* innerlich, (*fig.*) wahr, wirklich, wesentlich, eigentlich.

introduc–e [ɪntrə'djʊ:s], *v.a.* einführen (*also Med.*); bekannt machen (*to*, mit), vorstellen (*to* (*Dat.*)) (*people*); einschieben, einbringen (*a bill*); aufbringen (*fashions, etc.*); einleiten, eröffnen (*a book, sentence, etc.*); zur Sprache bringen, vorbringen (a topic); einlassen (*Med., etc.*). **–tion** [–'dʌkʃən], *s.* die Einführung (*also Med.*); Vorstellung, das Bekanntmachen; die Einleitung, Vorrede (*of a book*); die Anleitung, der Leitfaden (*to a subject*); *letter of –tion*, das Empfehlungsschreiben. **–tory** [–'dʌktərɪ], *adj.* einleitend, Einleitungs–; *–tory remarks*, Vorbemerkungen (*pl.*).
introit ['ɪntrɔɪt], *s.* der Introitus, Eingang der Messe.
intromi–ssion [ɪntro'mɪʃən], *s.* die Einführung, Zulassung; unbefugte Einmischung (*Scots law*). **–t** [–'mɪt], *v.n.* einführen, einfügen; sich unbefugterweise einmischen (*in*, in) (*Scots law*).
introspecti–on [ɪntro'spɛkʃən], *s.* die Selbstbeobachtung, Innenschau. **–ve** [–tɪv], *adj.* beschaulich, nach innen gekehrt *or* schauend.
introver–sion [ɪntro'və:ʃən], *s.* das Nachinnengerichtetsein (*also fig.*). **–sive** [–sɪv], *adj.* nach innen gerichtet. **–t**, 1. [–'və:t], *v.a.* nach innen richten (*thoughts, etc.*); einwärts kehren. 2. ['ɪntrovə:t], *s.* der auf das Innenleben gestellte Mensch.
intru–de [ɪn'trʊ:d], 1. *v.n.* sich eindrängen (*into*, in (*Acc.*)); sich aufdrängen (*upon* (*Dat.*)), stören (*Acc.*) lästig fallen (*Dat.*). 2. *v.a.* hineindrängen, einzwängen (*into*, in), aufzwingen, aufdrängen (*upon* (*Dat.*)). **–der** [–ə], *s.* der Eindringling, der Störenfried, Aufdringliche(r), *m.*; der Einbruchsflieger (*Av.*). **–sion** [ɪn'trʊ:ʒən], *s.* das Eindrängen, Eindringen (*into*, in), Aufdrängen (*upon* (*Dat.*)), die Zudringlichkeit; Besitzentziehung, Besitzstörung (*Law*); Intrusion (*Geol.*). **–sive** [ɪn'trʊ:sɪv], *adj.* aufdringlich, zudringlich, lästig (*of persons*), eingedrungen (*of things*), intrusiv (*Geol.*). **–siveness**, *s.* die Zudringlichkeit.
intubation [ɪntjʊ'beɪʃən], *s.* das Einführen einer Röhre (*Med.*).
intuiti–on [ɪntjʊ'ɪʃən], *s.* innere Schau, das Erfassen des Wesentlichen, unmittelbare Erkenntnis, die Intuition. **–ve** [ɪn'tjʊ:ɪtɪv], *adj.* unmittelbar erfaßt, anschaulich, intuitiv; *–ve faculty*, das Anschauungsvermögen.
intumescen–ce [ɪntjʊ'mɛsəns], *s.* die Geschwulst, Anschwellung. **–t** [–ənt], *adj.* geschwulstig, anschwellend.
inundat–e ['ɪnʌndeɪt], *v.a.* überschwemmen (*also fig.*). **–ion** [–'deɪʃən], *s.* die Überschwemmung, Überflutung, das Unterwassersetzen.
inure [ɪn'jʊ:ə], *v.a.* gewöhnen (*to*, an (*Acc.*)); (*fig.*) abhärten (*to*, gegen). **–ment**, *s.* die Gewöhnung.
inutility [ɪnjʊ:'tɪlɪtɪ], *s.* die Nutzlosigkeit.
invade [ɪn'veɪd], *v.a.* einfallen in, eindringen in, angreifen, anfallen, überfallen; (*fig.*) überlaufen, befallen, antasten (*rights*). **–r**, *s.* der Angreifer, Eindringling; *see* **invasion.**
invalid [ɪn'vælɪd], 1. *adj.* rechtsungültig, null und nichtig (*Law*), hinfällig; (*attrib. only*) ['ɪnvəlɪd] krank, kränklich, gebrechlich, Kranken–. 2. ['ɪnvəlɪd] *s.* Kränkliche(r), *m. or f.*, Kranke(r), *m. or f.*; Dienstunfähige(r), *m.*, der Invalide (*Mil., Naut.*); *be a confirmed –*, unheilbar krank sein, dauernd kränklich sein; *– diet*, die Krankenkost. 3. ['ɪnvəlɪd] *v.a.* (*usually pass.*) auf die Invalidenliste setzen, als Invalide entlassen, dienstuntauglich sprechen; *be –ed out of the army*, als Invalide entlassen werden. **–ate** [ɪn'vælɪdeɪt], *v.a.* entkräften, ungültig machen, umstoßen (*Law*). **–ation** [–'deɪʃən], *s.* die Entkräftung, das Ungültigmachen (*Law*). **–ism** ['ɪnvəlɪdɪzm], *s.* dauernde Kränklichkeit, unheilbarer kranker Zustand. **–ity** [ɪnvæ'lɪdɪtɪ], *s.* die Ungültigkeit, Invalidität, Nichtigkeit, Hinfälligkeit (*Law*).
invaluable [ɪn'væljʊəbl], *adj.* unschätzbar. **–ness**, *s.* die Unschätzbarkeit.
invariab–ility [ɪnvɛərɪə'bɪlɪtɪ], *s.* die Unveränderlichkeit, Beständigkeit. **–le** [ɪn'vɛərɪəbl], 1. *adj.* unveränderlich, beständig, unverändert, konstant (*Math.*). 2. *s.* die Konstante, unveränderliche Größe (*Math.*).
invasi–on [ɪn'veɪʒən], *s.* das Eindringen, der Einfall

(*of*, in), Überfall, Angriff, die Invasion; (*fig.*) Eingriff, Anfall. **–ve** [ɪn'veɪsɪv], *adj.* angreifend, eingreifend, anfallend, Angriffs–.

invective [ɪn'vɛktɪv], 1. *s.* die Schmähung, Beschimpfung; *pl.* Schimpfreden. 2. *adj.* schmähend, schimpfend, Schmäh–.

inveigh [ɪn'veɪ], *v.n.*; – *against*, herziehen über (*Acc.*), losziehen gegen, schimpfen *or* schelten auf (*Acc.*).

inveigle [ɪn'vɪ:gl], *v.a.* verlocken, verleiten, verführen (*into*, zu), locken (*into*, in). **–ment,** *s.* die Verlockung, Verführung, Verleitung.

invent [ɪn'vɛnt], *v.a.* erfinden, erdenken, ersinnen, erdichten. **–ion** [ɪn'vɛnʃən], *s.* das Erfinden, Erdichten; die Erfindung, Entdeckung, Erdichtung; Erfindungsgabe, Erfindungskraft, Phantasie. *–ion of the Cross*, die Kreuzerfindung, Kreuzauffindung (*R.C.*). **–ive** [–tɪv], *adj.* erfinderisch, erfindungsreich (*of*, in (*Dat.*)), schöpferisch, phantasievoll, originell. **–iveness,** . die Erfindungsgabe. **–or** [–tə], *s.* der Erfinder.

inventory ['ɪnvəntrɪ], 1. *s.* das Inventar, (Bestands)-Verzeichnis; die Inventur, Bestandaufnahme; der (Lager)Bestand; *draw up* or *take an – of*, see – 2. 2. *v.a.* inventarisieren.

inver–se [ɪn'və:s], 1. *adj.* umgekehrt, entgegengesetzt; *–se proportion*, umgekehrtes Verhältnis, *in the –se ratio*, umgekehrt. 2. *s.* die Umkehrung. **–sion** [ɪn'və:ʃən], *s.* die Umkehrung (*Math.*, *Mus.*, *Log.*), Inversion (*Gram.*). **–t,** 1. [ɪn'və:t], *v.a.* umkehren, umwenden, umstellen (*Gram.*), versetzen, umkehren (*Mus.*), invertieren (*Chem.*, *etc.*). 2. ['ɪnvə:t], *s.* umgekehrter Bogen (*Arch.*); homosexuell Veranlagte(r), *m.* (*Psych.*); *–t sugar*, der Invertzucker. **–ted** [ɪn'və:tɪd], *adj.* umgekehrt, umgestellt; invertiert, pervers (*Psych.*); *–ted arch*, umgekehrter Bogen (*Arch.*); *–ted commas*, Anführungszeichen, Gänsefüßchen (*pl.*); *–ted flight*, der Rückenflug (*Av.*); *–ted interval*, umgekehrtes Intervall (*Mus.*).

invertebrate [ɪn'və:tɪbreɪt], 1. *adj.* wirbellos; (*fig.*) ohne Rückgrat, haltlos. 2. *s.* wirbelloses Tier.

invest [ɪn'vɛst], *v.a.* bekleiden, bedecken (*with*, mit), (*fig.*) belehnen, ausstatten (*with*, mit), einsetzen (*in*, in (*Acc.*)); anlegen, investieren, (*coll.*) hineinstecken (*money*); einschließen, belagern, zernieren, blockieren, abschließen (*Mil.*).

investigat–e [ɪn'vɛstɪgeɪt], *v.a.* erforschen, ergründen, untersuchen (*Acc.*); nachforschen (*Dat.*). **–ion** [–'geɪʃən], *s.* die Erforschung, Untersuchung. **–or** [–geɪtə], *s.* der Forscher, Untersucher.

invest–iture [ɪn'vɛstɪtjʊə], *s.* die Investitur, Einsetzung, Belehnung; (*fig.*) Ausstattung. **–ment** [–mənt], 1. *s.* die Belagerung, Einschließung (*Mil.*); das Anlegen (*of money*); die Geldanlage; die Investitur, Bekleidung; *make an –ment*, Geld anlegen. **–or** [–ə], *s.* einer, der Geld anlegt.

invetera–cy [ɪn'vɛtərəsɪ], *s.* das Eingewurzeltsein; die Hartnäckigkeit (*of disease*). **–te** [–ət], *adj.* eingewurzelt; hartnäckig (*as disease*); eingefleischt, Erz– (*of persons*).

invidious [ɪn'vɪdɪəs], *adj.* gehässig, neiderregend, verhaßt. **–ness,** *s.* die Gehässigkeit.

invigilat–e [ɪn'vɪdʒɪleɪt], *v.n.* die Aufsicht führen. **–ion** [–'leɪʃən], *s.* die Aufsichtführung.

invigorat–e [ɪn'vɪgəreɪt], *v.a.* kräftigen, stärken; (*fig.*) beleben. **–ing,** *adj.* belebend. **–ion** [–'reɪʃən], *s.* die Kräftigung, Stärkung, Belebung.

invincib–ility [ɪnvɪnsɪ'bɪlɪtɪ], *s.* die Unbezwinglichkeit, Unbesiegbarkeit, Unüberwindlichkeit. **–le** [ɪn'vɪnsɪbl], *adj.* unüberwindlich, unbezwinglich, unbesiegbar.

inviola–bility [ɪnvaɪələ'bɪlɪtɪ], *s.* die Unverletzlichkeit, Unverbrüchlichkeit (*of an oath*, *etc.*). **–ble** [ɪn'vaɪələbl], *adj.* unverletzlich, unverbrüchlich, heilig. **–te** [ɪn'vaɪələt], *adj.* unverletzt, unversehrt, unentweiht.

invisib–ility [ɪnvɪzɪ'bɪlɪtɪ], *s.* die Unsichtbarkeit. **–le** [ɪn'vɪzɪbl], *adj.* unsichtbar (*to*, für); *–le ink*, die Geheimtinte; *–le mending*, die Kunststopferei.

invit–ation [ɪnvɪ'teɪʃən], *s.* die Einladung (*to a* p., an einen; *to a meal*, zum Essen); Aufforderung. **–e** [ɪn'vaɪt], *v.a.* einladen; auffordern (*to do*, zu tun), anlocken, ermutigen zu, herausfordern (*criticism*); *–e s.o. in one's house*, einen in sein Haus einladen; *–e s.o. to tea*, einen zum Tee einladen; *–e questions*, um Fragen bitten, Fragen erbitten, zu Fragen anregen. **–ing,** *pr.p.* & *adj.* einladend, verlockend, anziehend.

invocat–ion [ɪnvə'keɪʃən], *s.* das Anrufen; die Anrufung; das Bittgebet. **–ory** [ɪn'vɔkətərɪ], *adj.* anrufend, Bitt–; *see* **invoke.**

invoice ['ɪnvɔɪs], 1. *s.* die Faktura, (Waren)Rechnung, Begleitrechnung; *as per* –, laut Faktura (*C.L.*). 2. *v.a.* fakturieren, in Rechnung stellen; *as –d*, laut Faktura.

invoke [ɪn'voʊk], *v.a.* anrufen, anflehen, appellieren an, beschwören (*spirits*), erflehen (*help*, *etc.*); *see* **invocation.**

involucre [ɪnvə'lju:kə], *s.* die Hülle (*Bot.*).

involuntar–iness [ɪn'vɔləntərɪnɪs], *s.* die Unfreiwilligkeit, Unwillkürlichkeit. **–y** [–tərɪ], *adv.* unfreiwillig, unwillkürlich, unabsichtlich.

involut–e ['ɪnvəlju:t], 1. *adj.* eingerollt (*Bot.*), (*fig.*) verwickelt. 2. *s.* die Evolvente (*Geom.*). **–ion** [–'ju:ʃən], *s.* die Verwirrung, Verwick(e)lung; Involution, Potenzierung, Erhebung in eine Potenz (*Math.*); Einrollung, Einschrumpfung, Rückbildung (*Bot.*, *etc.*).

involve [ɪn'vɔlv], *v.a.* verwickeln in, hineinziehen in (*a p.*) (*in difficulties*, *etc.*); verwirren, verwickelt machen (*a th.*); notwendig machen, zur Folge haben, nach sich ziehen, mit sich bringen, in sich schließen, umfassen, enthalten; (*archaic*) einhüllen, einwickeln; – *o.s. in*, sich verwickeln in. **–d,** *adj.* verworren, verwickelt; einbegriffen; *get* (*o.s.*) *–d in*, sich verwickeln in; *be –d*, in Frage kommen, auf dem Spiele stehen; *–d in debt*, verschuldet.

invulnerab–ility [ɪnvʌlnərə'bɪlɪtɪ], *s.* die Unverwundbarkeit; Unanfechtbarkeit. **–le** [ɪn'vʌlnərəbl], *adj.* unverwundbar; (*fig.*) unangreifbar, unanfechtbar.

inward ['ɪnwəd], 1. *adj.* inner, innerlich, inwendig; (*fig.*) geistig, seelisch. 2. *adv.* einwärts, nach innen, im Inneren, ins Innere. 3. *s.* (*fig.*) das Innere. **–ly,** *adv.* innerlich, im Innern; nach innen, für sich. **–ness,** *s.* innere Natur, die Innerlichkeit. **–s** [–z], 1. *adv.*, *see* – 2. 2. *s.* (*coll.*) der Leib, Eingeweide (*pl.*).

inweave [ɪn'wɪ:v], *v.a.* einweben (*into*, in (*Acc.*)), (*fig.*) einflechten, verflechten.

inwrought ['ɪnrɔ:t], *adj.* hineingearbeitet, verwoben (*in*(*to*), in), verarbeitet, verflochten; geschmückt (*with*, mit).

iod–ic [aɪ'ɔdɪk], *adj.* Jod–, jodsauer. **–ide** ['aɪədaɪd], 1. *s.* das Jodid, die Jodverbindung. 2. *adj.* Jod–. **–ine** ['aɪədɪn], *s.* das Jod; *tincture of –ine*, die Jodtinktur. **–ism** [–dɪzm], *s.* die Jodvergiftung. **–ize** [–daɪz], *v.a.* mit Jod behandeln (*Phot.*). **–oform** [aɪ'oʊdəfɔ:m], *s.* das Jodoform.

iolite ['aɪəlaɪt], *s.* der Iolith (*Geol.*).

ion ['aɪən], *s.* das Ion. **–ization** [–aɪ'zeɪʃən], *s.* die Ionisierung. **–ize** ['aɪənaɪz], 1. *v.a.* ionisieren. 2. *v.n.* sich in Ionen spalten. **–osphere** [aɪ'ɔnəsfɪ:ə], *s.* die Ionosphäre.

iota [aɪ'oʊtə], *s.* das Iota, Jota; (*fig.*) Tüpfelchen.

ipecacuanha [ɪpə'kækjʊænə], *s.* die Brechwurzel, Kopfbeere (*Bot.*).

irascib–ility [ɪræsɪ'bɪlɪtɪ], *s.* die Reizbarkeit, der Jähzorn. **–le** [ɪ'ræsɪbl], *adj.* reizbar, jähzornig.

ir–ate [aɪ'reɪt], *adj.* erzürnt, zornig. **–e** ['aɪə], *s.* (*Poet.*) der Zorn, die Wut. **–eful** ['aɪəfəl], *adj.* (*Poet.*) zornig, wütend.

iridescen–ce [ɪrɪ'dɛsəns], *s.* das Schillern. **–t** [–ənt], *adj.* (farben) schillernd, irisierend.

iridium [ɪ'rɪdɪəm], *s.* das Iridium.

iris ['aɪrɪs], *s.* der Regenbogen, die Regenbogenhaut (*Anat.*); die Schwertlilie (*Bot.*); – *diaphragm*, die Irisblende (*Phot.*).

irk [ə:k], *v.a.* (*usually imp.*) ärgern, verdrießen; (*Poet.*) ermüden. **–some** [–səm], *adj.* lästig, verdrießlich, beschwerlich. **–someness,** *s.* die Lästigkeit, Verdrießlichkeit, Beschwerlichkeit.

iron ['aɪən], **1.** *s.* das Eisen; Bügeleisen, Plätteisen; der Golfschläger; eisernes Werkzeug; *cast* –, das Gußeisen, der Grauguß; *corrugated* –, das Wellblech; *pig* –, das Roheisen; *rod of* –, (*fig.*) eiserne

Stange; *pl.* Fesseln, die (Bein)Schienen (*Orthopaedy*); *in –s*, in Ketten; *have too many –s in the fire*, sich mit vielerlei zugleich befassen, zuviel auf seinen Schultern haben; *put into –s*, in Fesseln schlagen *or* legen; *sheet –*, das Blecheisen, Eisenblech; *soldering –*, der Lotkolben; *strike while the – is hot*, das Eisen schmieden solange es heiß ist, zuschlagen solange das Eisen heiß ist; *will of –*, eiserne Wille; *wrought –*, das Schmiedeeisen, Schweißeisen. **2.** *adj.* eisern, Eisen–; (*fig.*) unbeugsam, fest (*as will*); *the – age*, die Eisenzeit; *– cross*, Eisernes Kreuz; (*archaic*) *– horse*, das Stahlroß (*Cycl.*), das Dampfroß (*Railw.*); *– ration*, eiserne Ration. **3.** *v.a.* bügeln, plätten; (*fig.*) *– out* ausgleichen, beseitigen (*difficulties, etc.*). **––bound,** *adj.* eisenbeschlagen; felsig (*as a coast*). **––casting,** *s.* der Eisenguß. **–clad,** 1. *adj.* gepanzert; (*fig.*) äußerst streng. 2. *s.* das Panzerschiff. **––fisted,** *adj.* geizig, geldgierig. **––founder,** *s.* der Eisengießer. **––foundry,** *s.* die Eisengießerei. **––grey,** *adj.* eisengrau. **––handed,** *adj.* unerbittlich, streng, grausam. **––hearted,** *adj.* hartherzig. **–ing,** *s.* das Plätten, Bügeln; die Wäsche zum Bügeln, ungeplättete Wäsche. **–ing-board,** *s.* das Plättbrett, Bügelbrett. **–master,** *s.* der Eisenhüttenbesitzer. **–monger,** *s.* der Eisenhändler. **–mongery,** *s.* Eisenwaren (*pl.*); die Eisenhandlung. **––mould,** *s.* der Rostfleck. **––ore,** *s.* das Eisenerz. **––pyrites,** *s.* der Schwefelkies. **–sides,** *pl.* Cromwells Reiterei. **––smelting,** *s.* die Eisenverhüttung. **–smith,** *s.* der Eisenschmied. **–stone,** *s.* der Eisenstein. **–ware,** *s.* die Eisenwaren (*pl.*). **–work,** *s.* die Eisenkonstruktion. **–works,** *pl.* (*sing. constr.*) die Eisenhütte, das Eisenwerk.

iron–ic(al) [ɑɪə'rɔnɪk(l)], *adj.* spöttelnd, spöttisch, ironisch. **–y** ['ɑɪərənɪ], *s.* die Ironie.

irradia–nce, –ncy [ɪ'reɪdɪəns(ɪ)], *s.* das Ausstrahlen, der Strahlenglanz. **–te** [–ɪeɪt], *v.a.* bestrahlen, erhellen, erleuchten, (*fig.*) aufklären, Licht werfen auf; strahlend machen, aufheitern; verbreiten, ausstrahlen. **–tion** [–ɪ'eɪʃən], *s.* das Strahlen, die Bestrahlung (*Med.*), Irradiation (*Opt.*); (*fig.*) Aufklärung, Erleuchtung.

irrational [ɪ'ræʃənəl], 1. *adj.* unvernünftig, vernunftwidrig; irrational (*Math., Philos.*). 2. *s.* irrationale Größe (*Math.*). **–ity** [–'nælɪtɪ], *s.* die Unvernunft, Vernunftwidrigkeit; Irrationalität (*Philos.*).

irreclaimable [ɪrɪ'kleɪməbl], *adj.* unwiderruflich, unwiederbringlich; unverbesserlich, nicht kulturfähig (*of land*).

irrecognizable [ɪrɛkəgnɑɪzəbl], *adj.* nicht erkennbar, nicht wiederzuerkennen(d).

irreconcilab–ility [ɪrɛkənsɑɪlə'bɪlɪtɪ], *s.* die Unversöhnlichkeit, Unvereinbarkeit (*to*, mit). **–le** [–'sɑɪləbl], *adj.* unversöhnlich, unvereinbar (*to* or *with*, mit).

irrecoverable [ɪrɪ'kʌvərəbl], *adj.* unwiederbringlich (verloren), unersetzlich, nicht wiedergutzumachen(d). **–ness,** *s.* die Unersetzlichkeit, Unwiederbringlichkeit.

irredeemabl–e [ɪrɪ'dɪ:məbl], *adj.* nicht rückkaufbar *or* wiederkaufbar, nicht einlösbar (*as paper currency*), nicht tilgbar (*as loans*); (*fig.*) unwiederbringlich, hoffnungslos.

irredentis–m [ɪrɪ'dɛntɪzm], *s.* der Irredentismus (*Pol.*). **–t** [–tɪst], *s.* Irredentist.

irreducible [ɪrɪ'djuːsɪbl], *adj.* nicht reduzierbar, nicht zu vermindern(d); nicht verwandelbar, unveränderbar; unüberwindlich; *the – minimum*, das Allergeringste, Äußerste, Unentbehrliche, Mindestmaß (*of*, an).

irrefragab–ility [ɪrɪfrædʒə'bɪlɪtɪ], *s.* die Unwiderleglichkeit, Unumstößlichkeit. **–le** [–'frædʒəbl], *adj.* unwiderleglich, unumstößlich.

irrefrangible [ɪrɪ'frændʒɪbl], *adj.* unverletzbar, unverletzlich (*Law*); unbrechbar (*Opt.*).

irrefutab–ility [ɪrɪfju:tə'bɪlɪtɪ], *s.* die Unwiderlegbarkeit. **–le** [–'fju:tɪbl], *adj.* unwiderleglich, unwiderlegbar.

irregular [ɪ'rɛgjʊlə], *adj.* unregelmäßig (*also Gram.*), regellos, regelwidrig; ungeregelt; uneben, ungleichförmig (*as a surface*), unordentlich, zügellos, liederlich (*of conduct*), irregulär (*Mil.*). **–ity** [–'lærɪtɪ], *s.* die Unregelmäßigkeit (*also Gram.*), Ungleichmäßigkeit, Unebenheit; Regellosigkeit, Regelwidrigkeit, Unordnung; Unordentlichkeit, Ausschweifung, Abweichung von der Norm; der Fehler, Verstoß. **–s** [ɪ'rɛgjʊləz], *pl.* irreguläre Truppen, Freischärler.

irrelevan–ce, –cy [ɪ'rɛləvəns(ɪ)], *s.* die Belanglosigkeit, Unerheblichkeit, Unanwendbarkeit. **–t** [–ənt], *adj.* nicht zur Sache gehörig, ohne Beziehung (*to*, zu); belanglos, ohne Belang, unerheblich (*to*, für); unanwendbar (*to*, auf).

irreligio–n [ɪrɪ'lɪdʒən], *s.* die Irreligiosität, der Unglaube, die Gottlosigkeit, Gottvergessenheit. **–us** [–əs], *adj.* irreligiös, ungläubig, gottlos, gottvergessen.

irremediable [ɪrɪ'mɪ:dɪəbl], *adj.* unheilbar; (*fig.*) unabänderlich, unersetzlich.

irremissible [ɪrɪ'mɪsɪbl], *adj.* unverzeihlich, unerläßlich, verbindlich.

irremovable [ɪrɪ'mu:vəbl], *adj.* nicht entfernbar *or* abnehmbar, unbeweglich; unabsetzbar (*from office, etc.*).

irreparable [ɪ'rɛpərəbl], *adj.* unersetzlich, nicht wieder gutzumachen(d).

irreplaceable [ɪrɪ'pleɪsəbl], *adj.* unersetzbar, unersetzlich.

irrepressible [ɪrɪ'prɛsɪbl], *adj.* nicht zu unterdrücken(d), unbezähmbar.

irreproachable [ɪrɪ'proutʃəbl], *adj. adv.* untadelhaft, tadellos, einwandfrei, unbescholten.

irresistib–ility [ɪrɪzɪstɪ'bɪlɪtɪ], *s.* die Unwiderstehlichkeit. **–le** [ɪrɪ'zɪstɪbl], *adj.* unwiderstehlich, unaufhaltsam.

irresolut–e [ɪ'rɛzəlju:t], *adj.* unschlüssig, unentschlossen, schwankend, zögernd. **–eness, –ion** [–'lju:ʃən], *s.* die Unentschlossenheit, Unschlüssigkeit.

irresolvable [ɪrɪ'zɔlvəbl], *adj.* unauflösbar, unlösbar, unlöslich.

irrespective [ɪrɪ'spɛktɪv], *adj.*; *– of*, ohne Rücksicht auf (*Acc.*), abgesehen von, unabhängig von.

irresponsib–ility [ɪrɪspɔnsɪ'bɪlɪtɪ], *s.* die Unverantwortlichkeit. **–le** [–'pɔnsɪbl], *adj.* unverantwortlich (*deed*), verantwortungslos, nicht verantwortlich für (*person*), unzurechnungsfähig (*Law*).

irresponsive [ɪrɪ'spɔnsɪv], *adj.* teilnahm(s)los, verständnislos (*to*, gegenüber), unempfindlich (*to*, für); *be – to*, nicht reagieren auf.

irretentive [ɪrɪ'tɛntɪv], *adj.* unfähig zu behalten, schwach (*of memory*).

irretrievable [ɪrɪ'trɪ:vəbl], *adj.* unwiederbringlich, unersetzlich, nicht wieder gutzumachen(d).

irreveren–ce [ɪ'rɛvərəns], *s.* die Unehrerbietigkeit, Respektlosigkeit. **–t,** *adj.* unehrerbietig, geringschätzig, respektlos.

irreversib–ility [ɪrɪvə:sɪ'bɪlɪtɪ], *s.* die Unabänderlichkeit. **–le** [–'və:sɪbl], *adj.* unwiderruflich, unabänderlich; nicht umkehrbar (*Mach.*).

irrevocab–ility [ɪrɛvəkə'bɪlɪtɪ], *s.* die Unwiderruflichkeit. **–le** [ɪ'rɛvəkəbl], unwiderruflich, unumstößlich, unabänderlich.

irriga–ble ['ɪrɪgəbl], *adj.* bewässerungsfähig (*as land*). **–te** ['ɪrɪgeɪt], *v.a.* bewässern, berieseln, mit Wasser versorgen (*land*); (aus)spülen (*Med.*). **–tion** [–'geɪʃən], *s.* die Bewässerung, Berieselung.

irrita–bility [ɪrɪtə'bɪlɪtɪ], *s.* die Reizbarkeit. **–ble** ['ɪrɪtəbl], *adj.* reizbar. **–ncy** ['ɪrɪtənsɪ], *s.* (*Scots law*) die Verwirkung, Nichtigmachung; das Ärgernis. **–nt** ['ɪrɪtənt], 1. *adj.* (auf)reizend, erregend, aufregend; verwirkend (*Scots law*). 2. *s.* das Reizmittel, der Reizstoff. **–te** ['ɪrɪteɪt], *v.a.* reizen (*also Med.*), ärgern, erzürnen, aufbringen (*at*, über); entzünden (*Med.*). **–ting** [–tɪŋ], *adj.* ärgerlich, störend, aufreizend, schmerzlich. **–tion** [–'teɪʃən], *s.* die Reizung, Entrüstung, Erbitterung, der Ärger (*at* or *over*, über); der Reiz, Entzündung (*Med.*).

irrupti–on [ɪ'rʌpʃən], *s.* das Hereinbrechen, der Einbruch, Einfall. **–ve** [–tɪv], *adj.* (her)einbrechend.

is [ɪz], (*3rd pers. sing. pres. indic. of* to be, *q.v.*), ist, wird; *it – I*, ich bin es; *it – not for me*, es geziemt mir nicht (*to*, zu), *there – no man who*, es gibt keinen Menschen, der . . .; *that – to say*, das heißt: *how – it that?* woher kommt es, daß? *how – she?* wie geht es ihr? wie befindet sie sich?

ischiatic [ɪʃɪ'ætɪk], *adj.* Hüft–, Sitzbein– (*Anat.*).
isinglass ['ɑɪzɪŋglɑ:s], *s.* der Fischleim, die Hausenblase.
isl–and ['ɑɪlənd], *s.* die Insel; Verkehrsinsel. **–ander** [–ə], *s.* der Inselbewohner. **–e** [ɑɪl], *s.* (*Poet.*) das Eiland, die Insel. **–et** ['ɑɪlɪt], *s.* das Inselchen.
ism [ɪzm], *s.* (*usually pl.*) (*coll.*) die Theorie.
iso–bar ['ɑɪsobɑ:], *s.* die Isobare. **–meric** [–'mɛrɪk], *adj.* isomer, gleichteilig (*Chem.*). **–sceles** [ɑɪ-'sɔsəlɪ:z], *adj.* gleichschenklig (*Geom.*). **–therm** [–θə:m], *s.* die Isotherme. **–thermal** [–'θə:məl], *adj.* isothermisch. **–tope** [–toʊp], *s.* das Isotop.
isolat–e ['ɑɪsəleɪt], *v.a.* absondern (*from*, von), isolieren (*Elec.*, *Med.*); (*fig.*) abschließen, abdichten; rein darstellen (*Chem.*). **–ion** [–'leɪʃən], *s.* die Absonderung, Isolierung; *–ion hospital*, das Krankenhaus für ansteckende Krankheiten. **–ionist,** *s.* der Anhänger der Isolationspolitik.
issu–able ['ɪʃʊəbl], *adj.* auszugeben(d), emittierbar. **–ance** [–əns], *s.* (*Amer.*) die Ausgabe, Verteilung. **–e** ['ɪʃʊ], **1.** *s.* das Herauskommen, Herausgehen, Herausfließen, Herausströmen; der Ausfluß, Abgang (*blood*); Ausweg; Ausgang, das Ergebnis, Resultat, die Folge; der Erlaß, das Erlassen, Herausgeben, die Verkündigung; Ausgabe, Ausstellung, Ausstattung; Verabfolgung, Emission (*C.L.*), Nummer (*of a periodical*); die Nachkommenschaft, Leibeserben (*pl.*); der Streitpunkt, Angelpunkt, Sachverhalt, Streitfrage; Meinungsverschiedenheit. (*a*) (*with nouns or adjectives*), *bank of –e*, die Notenbank; *–e in fact*, die Tatsachenfrage; *–es in kind*, die Naturlieferung; *live –e*, aktuelle Frage; *–e in law*, die Rechtsfrage; *side –e*, nebensächlicher Punkt. (*b*) (*with verbs*) *force an –e*, eine Entscheidung erzwingen; *join –e with*, bestreiten, nicht übereinstimmen mit, abweichen von, gegenteiliger Ansicht sein; *raise the whole –e*, den ganzen Sachverhalt anschneiden. (*c*) (*with prepositions*) *at –e*, strittig, streitig, im Widerspruch, uneinig; *be at –e*, verschieden denken; *point at –e*, strittiger Punkt, der Streitpunkt; *–e at stake*, das zur Rede stehende Problem; *in the –e*, schließlich; *die without –e*, ohne Leibeserben sterben. **2.** *v.a.* erlassen, erteilen, ergehen lassen, ausgeben; emittieren, ausstellen (*bills, etc.*), auflegen (*loans*), liefern (*goods*), herausgeben (*books, etc.*); *–e a p. with*, einen beliefern, ausstatten *or* versehen mit. **3.** *v.n.* herauskommen, herausgehen, herausfließen, herausströmen, hervorbrechen; ausgehen, herkommen, herrühren, entspringen (*from*, von *or* aus); enden, endigen, auslaufen, übergehen (*in*, in (*Dat.*)), zu einem Ergebnis kommen. **–e-department,** *s.* die Abteilung für Notenausgabe. **–eless,** *adj.* ohne Nachkommen. **–er,** *s.* der Aussteller, Ausgeber.
isthmus ['ɪsθməs], *s.* die Landenge, der Isthmus.
it [ɪt], **1.** *pron.* er, es, sie (*Nom.*); ihn, es, sie (*Acc.*); ihm, ihr (*Dat.*); sich (*refl. after prep.*); (*coll.*) unübertrefflich, ideal. (*a*) (*as Nom.*) *from what has been said – follows* or *– is clear*, aus dem Gesagten folgt *or* wird klar; *– is not your fault*, Ihre Schuld ist es nicht; *– is I*, ich bin es; *how is – with . . . ?* wie steht's mit . . .? (*b*) (*as Acc.*) *confound – !* zum Teufel!; *you must fight –*, du mußt kämpfen; (*coll.*) *foot –*, zu Fuß gehen, tanzen; (*sl.*) *go – !* nur zu! (*coll.*) *king –*, den König spielen; (*coll.*) *lord –*, den Herrn spielen; *remember –*, sich daran erinnern; *walk –*, zu Fuß gehen; (*coll.*) *I take – that . . .*, ich nehme an, daß. (*c*) (*with prepositions*) *at –*, daran, darüber, dazu; *by –*, dadurch; *for –*, dafür, deswegen; *there's nothing for – but*, es bleibt nichts übrig als; *there's no remedy for –*, da ist kein Mittel dagegen; *from –*, davon; *in –*, darin; (*coll.*) *not be in – with*, es nicht aufnehmen können mit; *of –*, davon, darüber; (*coll.*) *have a fine time of –*, sich köstlich amüsieren; *to –*, dazu, daran; *with –*, damit; *power carries responsibility with –*, die Macht bringt Verantwortung mit sich; (*emphatic*) *– is on that account*, deshalb, aus diesem Grunde. **2.** *s.* (*sl.*) höchste Vollendung, letztes Wort, das Ideal, der Gipfel; *she has '–'*, sie hat ein gewisses Etwas.
italic [ɑɪ'tælɪk], *adj.* kursiv (*Print.*). **–ize** [–ɪsɑɪz], *v.a.* in Kursivschrift drucken. **–s,** *pl.* der Kursivdruck.
itch [ɪtʃ], **1.** *s.* das Jucken, die Krätze (*Med.*); (*coll.*) das Verlangen, Gelüst(e); *– of desire*, der Sinnenkitzel. **2.** *v.n.* jucken; verlangen, gelüsten (*for*, nach); *I –*, es juckt mich; *my fingers – to do it*, es juckt mir in den Fingern es zu tun. **–ing,** *s.* das Jucken; heftiges Verlangen, das Gelüst(e). **–y,** *adj.* juckend, krätzig.
item ['ɑɪtəm], **1.** *adv.* desgleichen, ferner. **2.** *s.* die Einzelheit, einzelner Gegenstand *or* Punkt; der Posten, die Buchung (*C.L.*); die Zeitungsnotiz. **3.** *v.a.* notieren, anmerken. **–ize** [–ɑɪz], *v.a.* angeben, aufführen, verzeichnen, spezifizieren, detaillieren.
itera–nce, –ncy ['ɪtərəns(ɪ)], *s.* die Wiederholung. **–te** [–eɪt], *v.a.* wiederholen. **–tion** [–'reɪʃən], *s.* die Wiederholung. **–tive** ['ɪtərətɪv], *adj.* sich wiederholend, iterativ (*Gram.*).
itinera–cy, –ncy ['ɪtɪnərə(n)sɪ], *s.* das Umherreisen, Umherziehen. **–nt** [–ənt], **1.** *adj.* (herum)-reisend, umherziehend, Wander–. *–nt judge*, herumziehender Richter; *–nt preacher*, der Wanderprediger; *–nt scholar*, fahrender Schüler. **–ry** [–ərərɪ], **1.** *s.* die Reiseroute; Reisebeschreibung, das Reisebuch, der Reiseführer. **2.** *adj.* Reise–. **–te** [–əreɪt], *v.n.* (umher)reisen.
its [ɪts], *poss. pron.* sein, ihr; dessen, deren.
itself [ɪt'sɛlf], *pron.* (*emph.*) es (*etc.*) selbst, selbst; (*refl.*) sich; *by –*, für sich allein, besonders; *in –*, an sich; *of –*, von selbst.
ivied ['ɑɪvɪd], *adj.* mit Efeu bedeckt *or* umrankt.
ivory ['ɑɪvərɪ], **1.** *s.* das Elfenbein; Elfenbeinweiß. **2.** *adj.* elfenbeinern, Elfenbein–; (*sl.*) *the ivories*, Zähne; Würfel; Klaviertasten (*pl.*); *vegetable –*, Steinnuß.
ivy ['ɑɪvɪ], *s.* der Efeu (*Bot.*).
izard ['ɪzəd], *s.* spanische Gemse (*Zool.*).

J

J [dʒeɪ], *s.* das J, j. *See Index of Abbreviations.*
jab [dʒæb], **1.** *s.* (*coll.*) der Stoß, Stich; linker Gerader (*Boxing*). **2.** *v.a.* (*coll.*) stoßen, stechen.
jabber ['dʒæbə], **1.** *v.a.* & *n.* (*coll.*) schnattern, plappern, schwatzen. **2.** *s.* (*coll.*) das Geschnatter, Geplapper.
jabot ['ʒæboʊ], *s.* das Jabot, die Brustkrause.
jack [dʒæk], **1.** *s. see Index of Names*; der Bube (*Cards*); die Winde, Hebevorrichtung, der Wagenheber (*Motor*); Bratenwender; die Klinke (*Tele.*); der Sägebock; Stiefelknecht; die Zielkugel (*bowls, etc.*); Gösch, Bugflagge (*Naut.*); junger Hecht (*Ichth.*); (*Amer.*) der Esel; (*archaic*) das Männchen (*of small animals*); *– in office*, wichtigtuender Beamter; *– of all trades*, Hans Dampf in allen Gassen; *lifting –*, der Wagenheber; *every man –*, jede Menschenseele; *Union –*, englische Nationalflagge. **2.** *v.a.* (*– up*) (in die Höhe) heben, aufwinden, hochwinden (*Motor.*). **–anapes** [–əneɪps], *s.* der Naseweis, Schlingel, Schelm, Geck, Affenschwanz. **–ass** [–æs], *s.* männlicher Esel; (*fig.*) der Esel, Dummkopf; *laughing –ass*, der Riesenkönigsfischer (*Orn.*). **– -boots,** *s.* Kanonenstiefel, Wasserstiefel, hohe Stiefel (*pl.*). **–daw,** *s.* die Dohle (*Orn.*). **– -in-the-box,** *s.* das Schachtelmännchen. **– -knife,** *s.* großes Klappmesser. **– -leg,** *adj.* (*Amer.*) Winkel– (*as lawyer*). **– -plane,** *s.* der Schropphobel, Schrubhobel. **– -snipe,** *s.* die Sumpfschnepfe (*Orn.*). **– -staff,** *s.* der Göschstock. **– -tar,** *s.* der Matrose, die Teerjacke. **– -towel,** *s.* das Rollhandtuch.
jackal ['dʒækəl], *s.* der Schakal; (*fig.*) Handlanger, Helfershelfer.
jacket ['dʒækɪt], **1.** *s.* die Jacke, Joppe, das Wams; der Schutzumschlag (*of a book*); Mantel, Doppelmantel, das Mantelrohr, die Umhüllung, Muffe (*Tech.*); die Hülle, Schale; *potatoes in their –s*, Pellkartoffeln (*pl.*); (*fig.*) *dust a p.'s –*, einen durch-

prügeln; *water* –, der Kühl(wasser)mantel. 2. *v.a.* auskleiden; *–ed gun*, die Mantelkanone.
Jacob's ladder [ˈdʒeɪkəbzˈlædə], die Himmelsleiter (*Bot.*); Jakobsleiter, Strickleiter (*Naut.*). **–ean** [dʒækəˈbɪ:ən], *adj.* der Zeit Jakobs I.; Dunkeleiche– (*colour*).
jactitation [dʒæktɪˈteɪʃən], *s.* das Herumwerfen *or* Durchschütteln des Körpers (*Path.*); die Zuckung, Ruhelosigkeit; – *of marriage*, die Unterschiebung eines Ehestandes (*Law*).
¹**jade** [dʒeɪd], 1. *s.* die (Schind)Mähre, (*coll.*) Kracke; (*sl.*) das Weibsbild, der Wildfang. 2. *v.a.* abschinden, (*fig.*) abhetzen, ermüden. **–d,** *adj.* abgemattet.
²**jade** [dʒeɪd], *s.* der Nierenstein, Beilstein; das Jadegrün.
jag [dʒæg], 1. *s.* (*coll.*) die Zacke, Kerbe, der Zacken, Stich. 2. *v.a.* kerben, (aus)zacken, stechen. **–ged** [ˈdʒægɪd], *adj.* zackig.
jaguar [ˈdʒægjʊə], *s.* der Jaguar.
jail [dʒeɪl] *see* **gaol.**
jalap [ˈdʒæləp], *s.* die Jalap(p)enwurzel, Purgierwinde.
¹**jam** [dʒæm], *s.* die Marmelade; (*sl.*) *have all the* –, die Rosinen aus dem Kuchen haben. **–my,** *adj.* (*sl.*) spielend leicht.
²**jam** [dʒæm], 1. *v.a.* einzwängen, festklemmen, einklemmen, einkeilen, verstopfen, versperren; blockieren, stören, Verbindung abschneiden (*Rad.*). 2. *v.n.* sich festklemmen, festsitzen, stocken, nicht funktionieren; eine Ladehemmung haben (*of a gun*); (*coll.*) – *on the brakes*, mit voller Kraft bremsen. 3. *s.* das Quetschen, Einzwängen; die Stockung, Stauung, das Gedränge; die Hemmung, Ladehemmung (*of a gun*), die Störung (*Rad.*); (*sl.*) Klemme, Patsche. **–ming,** *s.* das Stören, die Störung (*Rad.*); *–ming station*, der Störsender.
jamb [dʒæm], *s.* der (Tür)Pfosten.
jamboree [ˈdʒæmbərɪ], *s.* das Pfadfindertreffen; die Lustbarkeit.
jamming [ˈdʒæmɪŋ], *s. see* ²**jam.**
jammy [ˈdʒæmɪ], *adj. see* ¹**jam.**
jangl–e [ˈdʒæŋgl], 1. *v.n.* mißtönen, rasseln, kreischen. 2. *v.a.* unharmonisch klingen lassen. 3. *s.* der Mißklang. **–ing,** 1. *adj.* mißtönend, schrill. 2. *s. see* **–e** 3.
janitor [ˈdʒænɪtə], *s.* der Pförtner.
janizary, janissary [ˈdʒænɪzərɪ], *s.* der Janitschar.
jankers [ˈdʒænkəz], *pl.* (*sing. constr.*) (*sl.*) der Lagerarrest (*Mil.*).
January [ˈdʒænjuərɪ], *s.* der Januar.
Japan [dʒəˈpæn], 1. *s. see Index of Names*; japanischer Lack; lackierte Arbeit. 2. *v.a.* schwarz lackieren. **–ning,** *s.* das Lackieren.
jape [dʒeɪp], 1. *s.* der Spott. 2. *v.n.* spotten (*at*, über).
¹**jar** [dʒɑ:], 1. *v.n.* knarren, kreischen, schnarren, rasseln; (sich) zanken, widerstreiten (*Dat.*), in schreiendem Gegensatz stehen (*with*, zu); – *on one's nerves*, einem auf die Nerven gehen; – *upon the ear*, das Ohr beleidigen *or* unangenehm berühren. 2. *v.a.* erschüttern, rütteln. 3. *s.* das Knarren, Schwirren; der Mißton; Streit, die Mißhelligkeit; der Stoß, Schlag, Schock.
²**jar** [dʒɑ:], *s.* der Krug, Topf, Kolben; *Leyden* –, Leydener Flasche. **–ful,** *s.* der Krugvoll.
³**jar** [dʒɑ:], *s.*; *on the* –, angelehnt, halb offen (*of doors*).
jargon [ˈdʒɑ:gən], *s.* das Kauderwelsch; die Berufssprache, Zunftsprache, Standessprache, der Jargon.
jargonelle [dʒɑ:gəˈnɛl], *s.* die Frühbirne.
jasmine [ˈdʒæzmɪn], *s.* der Jasmin (*Bot.*).
jasper [ˈdʒæspə], *s.* der Jaspis (*Geol.*).
jaundice [ˈdʒɔ:ndɪs], *s.* die Gelbsucht (*Med.*); (*fig.*) der Neid. **–d** [–t], *adj.* gelbsüchtig; (*fig.*) scheel(süchtig), neidisch, voreingenommen.
jaunt [dʒɔ:nt], 1. *v.n.* umherstreifen. 2. *s.* der Ausflug, die Wanderung, Spritzfahrt, der Spaziergang. **–iness,** *s.* die Munterkeit, Leichtigkeit im Auftreten, Lebhaftigkeit, Frische. **–y,** *adj.* munter, leicht, lebhaft, flott, schmuck, elegant. **–ing-car,** *s.* zweirädriger Wagen (*Irish*).
javelin [ˈdʒævlɪn], *s.* der Wurfspieß, Speer; *throwing the* –, das Speerwerfen (*Sport.*).
jaw [dʒɔ:], 1. *s.* der Kiefer, Kinnbacken, das Maul (*also coll.*), (*sl.*) die Fresse; (*coll.*) das Reden, Getratsche, der Tratsch; *pl.* der Rachen, Schlund; die Backen, Klauen (*Tech.*); *–s of death* (*hell*), der Todesrachen (Höllenschlund); (*sl.*) *hold one's* –, den Mund halten. 2. *v.a.* (*coll.*) ausschimpfen, anschnauzen, abkanzeln (*a p.*). 3. *v.n.* schwatzen. **– -bone,** *s.* der Kinnbacken. **– -breaker,** *s.* zungenbrecherisches Wort. **– -coupling,** *s.* die Klauenkupplung. **–ing,** *s.* (*coll.*) die Standpauke.
jay [dʒeɪ], *s.* der (Eichel)Häher (*Orn.*); (*fig.*) Schwätzer; (*coll.*) Träumer; (*sl.*) Tölpel. **– -walker,** *s.* unvorsichtiger *or* achtloser Fußgänger.
jazz [dʒæz], *s.* der Jazz, die Jazzmusik. **– -band,** die Jazzkapelle.
jealous [ˈdʒɛləs], *adj.* eifersüchtig, neidisch (*of*, auf (*Acc.*)), argwöhnisch, mißtrauisch (*of*, gegen), eifrig bedacht (*of*, auf), besorgt (*of* or *over*, um). **–ly,** *adv.* eifrig, sorgfältig. **–y** [–ɪ], *s.* die Eifersucht (*of* or *towards*, auf), der Neid (*at* or *over*, über), Argwohn, die Besorgnis; *petty –ies*, Eifersüchteleien.
jean [dʒɪ:n], *s.* der Baumwollköper. **–s,** *pl.* (*Amer.*) die Hose.
jeep [dʒɪ:p], *s.* der Geländewagen (*Mil.*).
¹**jeer** [dʒɪ:ə], 1. *v.a.* verhöhnen. 2. *v.n.* höhnen, spotten (*at*, über (*Acc.*)). 3. *s.* der Spott, die Spötterei. **–ing,** 1. *adj.* höhnisch, spöttisch. 2. *s.* die Spötterei.
²**jeer** [dʒɪ:ə], (*usually pl.*) das Fall der Unterrahe (*Naut.*).
Jehu [ˈdʒɪ:hju], *s.* (*hum.*) der Kutscher.
jejune [dʒɪˈdʒʊ:n], *adj.* unfruchtbar, mager (*of land*), (*fig.*) geistlos, nüchtern, trocken, fade. **–ness,** *s.* (*fig.*) die Nüchternheit, Trockenheit.
jell–ied [ˈdʒɛlɪd], *adj.* in Gelee. **–ify** [–ɪfaɪ], *v.n. see* **–y,** 2. **–y** [ˈdʒɛlɪ], 1. *s.* die Sülze, die Gallerte, das Gelee, Gallert. 2. *v.n.* gelieren, Gelee bilden, gerinnen, verkleistern. **–y-fish,** *s.* die Qualle. **–y-like,** *adj.* gallertartig.
jemmy [ˈdʒɛmɪ], *s.* das Brecheisen.
jennet [ˈdʒɛnɪt], *s.* kleines spanisches Pferd.
jenny [ˈdʒɛnɪ], *s.* das Weibchen (*of small animals*); die Jennyspinnmaschine, der Jennywebstuhl; der Laufkran. **– -ass,** *s.* die Eselin. **– -wren,** *s.* der Zaunkönig.
jeopard–ize [ˈdʒɛpədaɪz], *v.a.* gefährden, aufs Spiel setzen, in Frage stellen. **–y** [–ɪ], *s.* die Gefahr, Gefährdung; *double –y*, zwiefache Straffälligkeit (*Law*); *former –y*, früheres Strafverfahren in gleicher Sache (*Law*).
jerboa [ˈdʒə:boʊə], *s.* die Springmaus.
jeremiad [dʒɛrəˈmaɪæd], *s.* das Klagelied, die Jeremiade.
¹**jerk** [dʒə:k], 1. *s.* plötzlicher Stoß, der Ruck, Krampf, die Zuckung, der Schwung, Satz; *with a* –, plötzlich, mit einem Ruck; *by –s*, stoßweise, ruckweise; (*sl.*) *put a – in it*, tüchtig herangehen; (*coll.*) *physical –s*, Leibesübungen (*pl.*). 2. *v.a.* ruckweise ziehen, stoßen, schleudern, schnellen. 3. *v.n.* zusammenzucken, auffahren. **–y,** *adj.* sprunghaft, krampfartig.
²**jerk** [dʒə:k], *v.a.* in Streifen schneiden und an der Sonne trocknen (*beef*). **–y,** *s.* (*Amer.*) das Pökelfleisch.
jerkin [ˈdʒə:kɪn], *s.* (*archaic*) das Wams; *leather* –, das Koller.
jerry [ˈdʒɛrɪ], *s.* (*sl.*) das Nachtgeschirr; (*sl.*) der Deutsche. **– -builder,** *s.* der Bauspekulant. **– -building,** *s.* unsolide Bauart. **– -built,** *adj.* unsolid gebaut; *– - built house*, die Bruchbude. **–can,** *s.* (*sl.*) der Benzinbehälter (*Mil.*).
jersey [ˈdʒə:zɪ], *s.* die Strickjacke.
jess [dʒɛs], *s.* (*usually pl.*) der Wurfriemen um den Fuß des Falken.
jessamine [ˈdʒɛsəmɪn], *s. see* **jasmine.**
jest [dʒɛst], 1. *s.* der Scherz, Spaß; die Zielscheibe des Scherzes; *in* –, im Scherz *or* Spaß; *make a* –, scherzen (*of*, über). 2. *v.n.* scherzen, spaßen. **–er,** *s.* der Spaßmacher, Possenreißer; *king's –er*, der Hofnarr. **–ing,** *s.* das Scherzen, Spaßen; *no –ing matter*, keine Sache zum Spaßen. **–ingly,** *adv.* scherzweise.

[1]**jet** [dʒɛt], *s.* der Gagat, Jett, die Pechkohle. **--black,** *adj.* pechschwarz, kohlschwarz, (kohl)-rabenschwarz.

[2]**jet** [dʒɛt], 1. *v.n.* ausspritzen, ausströmen, hervorsprudeln. 2. *v.a.* auswerfen, ausspeien. 3. *s.* der Strahl, Strom; die Stichflamme; Röhre, Düse, das Strahlrohr; – *engine*, der Düsenmotor (*Av.*); *--fighter*, der Düsenjäger (*Av.*); *--propelled*, mit Düsenantrieb; *--propulsion*, der Düsenantrieb, Strahlantrieb, Rückstoßvortrieb; – *of water*, der Wasserstrahl.

jet–sam ['dʒɛtsəm], *s.* über Bord geworfene Schiffsladung (*Naut.*); (*fig.*) unnützes Zeug; *flotsam and -sam*, treibendes Wrack- und Strandgut; (*fig.*) die niederen Elemente des Lebens. **-tison** ['dʒɛtɪsən], 1. *s.* das Überbordwerfen der Güter. 2. *v.a.* über Bord werfen (*cargo*); im Notwurf abwerfen (*bombs*); (*fig.*) abwerfen, wegschlagen.

jetty ['dʒɛtɪ], *s.* der Hafendamm, die Mole, der Landungssteg, Pier, die Landungsbrücke, Anlegebrücke.

jewel ['dʒʊːəl], 1. *s.* das Juwel, der Edelstein; Stein (*Horol.*); (*fig.*) das Kleinod. 2. *v.a.* mit Juwelen schmücken. **-ler** [–ə], *s.* der Juwelier. **-lery, -ry** [–rɪ], *s.* der Schmuck, das Geschmeide; (*collect.*) Juwelen, Schmucksachen (*pl.*).

[1]**jib** [dʒɪb], *s.* der Klüver (*Naut.*); (*sl.*) *the cut of his* –, sein Aussehen, seine äußere Erscheinung. **--boom,** *s.* der Klüverbaum.

[2]**jib** [dʒɪb], *s.* der Ausleger, Kranbalken, Kranbaum (*of crane*).

[3]**jib** [dʒɪb], *v.n.* scheuen (*also fig.*), bocken, störrisch sein (*at*, vor) (*of horses*); (*fig.*) stehenbleiben, innehalten (*at*, vor), sich widersetzen (*at*, gegen). **-ber,** *s.* bockiges Pferd.

jib-door ['dʒɪbdɔː], *s.* die Tapetentür.

jibe [dʒaɪb], *see* **gibe.**

jiff, -y ['dʒɪf(ɪ)], *s.* (*coll.*) der Augenblick; (*coll.*) *in a –*(*y*), im Nu.

jig [dʒɪg], 1. *s.* die Gigue (*Mus.*); das Montagegestell (*Mach.*). 2. *v.n.* eine Gigue tanzen; umherhüpfen; scheiden (*ore*). **-ger** [–ə], 1. *s.* der Hüpfer, Tänzer; die Siebvorrichtung, Setzmaschine (*Min.*); die Handtalje (*Naut.*); das Hecksegel (*Naut.*). 2. *v.a.* (*only pass.*) (*coll.*); *I'm -gered*, hol' mich der Teufel. **-ger-mast,** *s.* der Besanmast. **-gery-pokery,** *s.* (*coll.*) der Schwindel, Schliche (*pl.*). **-saw** [–sɔː], *s.* (*Amer.*) die Schweifsäge; *--saw puzzle*, das Puzzle(Spiel), Zusammensetzspiel.

jiggle [dʒɪgl], *v.a.* rütteln, wackeln.

jilt [dʒɪlt], 1. *s.* die Kokette. 2. *v.a.* sitzen lassen (*one's lover*).

Jim Crow ['dʒɪm'kroʊ], *s.* (*Amer.*) (*fig.*) der Neger; *--car*, das Negerabteil.

Jiminy ['dʒɪmɪnɪ], *inter.* (*archaic*) *by –!* bei Gott!

jim-jams ['dʒɪmdʒæmz], *pl.* (*sl.*) das Delerium, Gruseln.

jimp [dʒɪmp], *adj.* (*Scots*) schlank, zierlich, spärlich.

jingle [dʒɪŋgl], 1. *v.n.* klingeln, klimpern, klirren. 2. *v.a.* klingeln lassen. 3. *s.* das Geklingel; Reimgeklingel, Wortgeklingel.

jingo ['dʒɪŋgoʊ], 1. *s.* der Hurrapatriot, Säbelraßler, Chauvinist. 2. *int.*; *by –*, alle Wetter! **-ism,** *s.* der Hurrapatriotismus, Chauvinismus.

jinks [dʒɪŋks] *pl.*; *high –*, übermütige Laune, ausgelassene Lustigkeit.

jinx [dʒɪŋks], *s.* (*Amer. sl.*) der Unglücksrabe.

jitter-bug ['dʒɪtəbʌg], *s.* der Swingtanz. **-s** ['dʒɪtəz], *pl.* (*sl.*) die Angst. **-y,** *adj.* (*sl.*) ängstlich, nervös.

jiu-jitsu, *see* **ju-jitsu.**

jive [dʒaɪv], *s.* die Swingmusik.

[1]**job** [dʒɔb], **1.** *s.* ein Stück Arbeit, die Lohnarbeit, Akkordarbeit; (*coll.*) die Beschäftigung, Stellung, der Beruf; die Verrichtung, Sache, das Geschäft, der Auftrag; das Profitgeschäft, der Kuhhandel, die Schiebung; Akzidenzarbeit, Akzidenz (*Print.*); (*coll.*) *that was a –!* das war ein schweres Stück Arbeit!; *know one's –*, seine Sache verstehen; *what a –!* das ist ja rein zum Verzweifeln! (*a*) (*with adjectives*) *a bad –*, eine schlimme Sache; *make a good – of it*, es ordentlich machen, eine ordentliche Arbeit leisten; (*coll.*) *it is a good –*, es ist ein wahres Glück; *a good – of work*, eine gute Arbeit; (*coll.*) *and a good – too*, und recht so; *odd -s*, Gelegenheitsarbeiten (*pl.*); (*coll.*) *put-up –*, abgekartete Sache; (*coll.*) *soft –*, angenehme Arbeit. (*b*) (*with prepositions*) *by the –*, in Akkord; (*coll.*) *on the –*, tätig; *out of a –*, arbeitslos, erwerbslos. **2.** *v.n.* in Akkord arbeiten; Makler sein, wuchern, schachern, spekulieren. **3.** *v.a.* (– *out*), vermieten, ausmieten (*horses*), in Akkord vergeben (*work*), durch Schiebung befördern (*a p.*). **-ber,** *s.* der Effektenhändler, Zwischenhändler, Börsenspekulant, Schieber, Akkordarbeiter. **-bery,** *s.* die Schiebung, Korruption, der Vertrauensmißbrauch, Amtsmißbrauch. **-bing,** *s.* die Akkordarbeit; das Maklergeschäft, die Börsenspekulation, Schiebung; *-bing cobbler*, der Flickschuster; *-bing printer*, der Akzidenzdrucker; *-bing work*, die Akkordarbeit. **--horse,** *s.* das Mietpferd. **- lot,** der Gelegenheitsankauf. **--master,** *s.* der Pferdevermieter, der Mietwagenbesitzer. **--printer,** see *-bing printer*. **- work,** *s.* see *-bing work*.

[2]**job** [dʒɔb], 1. *v.a.* & *n.* stechen, stoßen (*at*, **nach**). 2. *s.* der Stoß, Stich, Schlag.

jobation [dʒoʊ'beɪʃən], *s.* die Strafpredigt, Standpauke.

jockey ['dʒɔkɪ], 1. *s.* der Jockei. 2. *v.a.* betrügen, prellen (*out of*, um); verleiten, hineintreiben (*into*, zu).

joc–ose [dʒə'koʊs], *adj.* spaßhaft, scherzhaft, heiter, lustig, drollig. **-oseness,** *s.* die Scherzhaftigkeit, Spaßhaftigkeit, Lustigkeit. **-ular** ['dʒɔkjʊlə], *adj.* scherzhaft, spaßhaft, scherzend, spaßig. **-ularity,** *s.* die Heiterkeit, der Humor. **-und** ['dʒoʊkənd], *adj.* fröhlich, munter, lustig. **-undity** [–'kʌndɪtɪ], *s.* die Lustigkeit, Fröhlichkeit.

jodhpurs ['dʒoʊdpʊːəz], *pl.* die Reithose.

jog [dʒɔg], 1. *v.a.* rütteln, schütteln, (an)stoßen; – *his memory*, seinem Gedächtnis nachhelfen. 2. *v.n.*; – *along* or *on*, dahinschlendern, dahintrotten, weitertraben, (*fig.*) gemütlich fortfahren, fortwursteln. 3. *s.* der Stoß, das Stoßen (*of a carriage*). **--trot,** 1. *s.* leichter Trott *or* Trab, (*fig.*) der Schlendrian. 2. *attrib.* behaglich schlendernd.

joggle [dʒɔgl], 1. *v.a.* leicht schütteln *or* rütteln; federn und nuten, fest einfügen *or* zusammenfügen (*Carp.*). 2. *v.n.* sich schütteln. 3. *s.* die Verbindung auf Nut und Feder (*Carp.*).

johnny ['dʒɔnɪ], *s.* (*coll.*) der Kerl, Bursche.

join [dʒɔɪn], **1.** *v.a.* verbinden (*also Geom.*), vereinigen, zusammenfügen (*to*, mit), sich vereinigen *or* verbinden mit, stoßen zu; sich zugesellen zu, beitreten (*Dat.*), sich anschließen (*Dat.*); angrenzen an (*territory*), münden in (*Acc.*) (*tributary*); – *the army*, ins Heer eintreten, Soldat werden; – *battle*, den Kampf beginnen, handgemein werden; – *company with*, sich anschließen (*Dat.*); – *hands with*, die Hand *or* Hände reichen, sich vereinigen mit (*in*, zu); – *in marriage*, ehelich verbinden, verheiraten, vermählen (*with*, mit); – *issue with*, nicht übereinstimmen mit; – *the majority*, sich der Mehrheit anschließen; – *one's regiment*, zu seinem Regiment stoßen; – *a ship*, ein Schiff einholen, sich einschiffen *or* an Bord begeben. **2.** *v.n.* sich verbinden, sich vereinigen, anstoßen, sich berühren, aneinander grenzen; – *in*, teilhaben *or* teilnehmen an, sich beteiligen an (*Dat.*); einstimmen in (*Dat.*), mitmachen (*Acc.*); – *in his praise*, in seinem Lob einstimmen; – *in an undertaking*, sich einer Unternehmung anschließen, gemeinsam unternehmen; – *up*, Soldat werden, sich zum Heeresdienst melden, einrücken; *I – with you in thinking*, ich stimme mit Ihnen überein, ich teile Ihre Ansicht. **3.** 1. *s.* die Verbindungsstelle, Fuge; der Berührungspunkt. **-der** [–də], *s.* die Vereinigung (*Law*). **-er** [–ə], *s.* der Tischler, Schreiner; *-'s bench*, die Hobelbank. **-ery** [–ərɪ], *s.* das Tischlerhandwerk, die Tischlerarbeit. **-t** [–t], *s.* die Verbindung, Fuge, der Verband (*Carp.*), das Gelenk (*Anat.*, *Mech.*), Scharnier (*Mech.*); der Knoten, Blattansatz (*Bot.*); das Fleischstück, der Braten, die Keule (*Butch.*); der Riß, die Querspalte (*Geol.*); (*sl.*) das Lokal, die Kneipe, Spelunke; *ball and socket -t*, das Kugelgelenk; *cold -t*, kalter Braten; *dowel -t*, der Holzdübel; *halved -t*, das Blatt (*Carp.*); *mitre*

–t, die Gehrung (*Carp.*); *out of –t*, verrenkt, (*fig.*) aus den Fugen; *put out of –t*, aus den Fugen bringen; *put one's arm out of –t*, sich (*Dat.*) den Arm verrenken; *put a p.'s nose out of –t*, einen aus der Fassung bringen; *riveted –t*, die Nietung; *universal –t*, kardanisches Gelenk. 2. *v.a.* zusammenfügen; zerlegen, zergliedern. 3. *attrib. adj.* vereint, verbunden, gemeinschaftlich, gemeinsam, Mit–; *–t and several*, solidarisch; *–t action*, gemeinsames Vorgehen; *–t authorship*, gemeinsame Verfasserschaft; *during their –t lives*, solange sie beide (*or* alle) am Leben sind. **–t-account,** *s.* gemeinschaftliche Rechnung, gemeinschaftliches Konto. **–t-Board,** *s.* vereinigter (Prüfungs)Ausschuß (*Univ.*). **–ted** [–tɪd], *adj.* gegliedert, knotig (*Bot.*); zergliedert; *–ted doll*, die Gliederpuppe. **–ter,** *s.* der Schlichthobel, Glatthobel (*Carp.*), das Fugeisen (*Build.*). **–tly,** *adv.* alle zusammen, gemeinschaftlich; *–tly and severally*, samt und sonders. **–t-ownership,** *s.* das Miteigentum. **–t-plaintiff,** *s.* der Mitkläger. **–t-proprietor,** *s.* der Miteigentümer. **–t-stock,** *s.* das Aktienkapital; *–t-stock company*, die Aktiengesellschaft. **–t-tenancy,** *s.* der Mitbesitz. **–t-tenant,** *s.* der Mitpächter. **–ture** [–tʃə], 1. *s.* das Leibgedinge, Wittum. 2. *v.a.* ein Wittum aussetzen (*Dat.*).

joist [dʒɔɪst], 1. *s.* der Querbalken, Streckenbalken, die Schwelle. 2. *v.a.* mit Querbalken belegen.

jok–e [dʒoʊk], 1. *s.* der Scherz, Spaß, Witz; *in –e*, im Scherz; *it's all a –e*, es ist alles nur Spaß; *crack a –e*, einen Witz reißen; *play a (practical) –e upon s.o.*, einem einen Streich spielen; *see* or *take a –e*, einen Spaß verstehen. 2. *v.a.* necken, hänseln (*a p.*) (*about*, über *or* wegen). 3. *v.n.* scherzen, spaßen. **–er,** *s.* der Witzbold, Spaßvogel; Joker (*Cards*). **–ing,** 1. *adj.* scherzhaft. 2. *s.* das Spaßen, Scherzen; *–ing apart!* Scherz beiseite!

joll–ification [dʒɔlɪfɪˈkeɪʃən], *s.* die Lustbarkeit, (*coll.*) das Gelage. **–iness** [ˈdʒɔlɪnɪs], *s.*, **–ity** [ˈdʒɔlɪtɪ], *s.* die Lustigkeit, Munterkeit, Fröhlichkeit. **–y** [ˈdʒɔlɪ], 1. *adj.* lustig, munter, fidel, (*coll.*) angeheitert, (*sl.*) famos; *–y Roger*, die Piratenfahne. 2. *adv.* (*sl.*) sehr, riesig, außerordentlich; *–y good*, famos; *–y well*, ausgezeichnet; *he will –y well have to*, er muß es, ob er will oder nicht; er muß wohl oder übel. 3. *s.* (*sl.*) der Matrose. 4. *v.a.* (*coll.*) aufmuntern, schmeicheln (*Dat.*).

jolly-boat [ˈdʒɔlɪboʊt], *s.* die Jolle, das Beiboot, der Kutter (*Navy only*).

jolt [dʒoʊlt], 1. *v.a. & n.* stoßen, rütteln. 2. *s.* der Stoß. **–ing,** 1. *adj.* stoßend, rüttelnd, holperig. 2. *s.* das Gerüttel.

jonquil [ˈdʒɔŋkwɪl], *s.* die Jonquille, Binsennarzisse (*Bot.*).

jorum [ˈdʒɔːrəm], *s.* großes Trinkgefäß, die Bowle.

joss [dʒɔs], *s.* chinesischer Götze. **–-house,** *s.* chinesischer Tempel. **–-stick,** *s.* der Räucherstock.

josser [ˈdʒɔsə], *s.* (*sl.*) der Bursche, Tölpel.

jostle [ˈdʒɔsl], *v.a. & n.* stoßen, anrennen, anrempeln, verdrängen.

jot [dʒɔt], 1. *s.* das Jota, Pünktchen, (*fig.*) Bißchen; *not a –*, nicht das geringste. 2. *v.a.* (*– down*) notieren, flüchtig hinwerfen, kurz vermerken. **–ter,** *s.* das Schreibheft, die Kladde. **–ting,** *s.* die Notiz, der Vermerk.

Joule [dʒuːl], *s.* die Einheit der elektrischen Energie.

journal [ˈdʒəːnəl], *s.* das Tagebuch, Journal; die Zeitschrift, Zeitung, das Tageblatt; Logbuch (*Naut.*), der (Well)Zapfen (*Mach.*). (*coll.*) **–ese** [–iːz], *s.* der Zeitungsstil. **–ism** [–ɪzm], *s.* das Zeitungswesen, Zeitschriftenwesen, die Schriftstellerei. **–ist** [–ɪst], *s.* der Zeitungsschreiber, Journalist. **–istic** [–ˈlɪstɪk], *adj.* journalistisch

journey [ˈdʒəːnɪ], 1. *s.* die Reise; *the double –*, die Hin- und Rückreise; *day's –*, die Tagereise; *ten-mile –*, die Reise von 10 Meilen; *return –*, die Rückreise. 2. *v.n.* reisen, wandern. **–man,** *s.* der Geselle; *–man-baker*, der Bäckergeselle.

joust [dʒuːst], 1. *s.* das Turnier. 2. *v.n.* turnieren.

jovial [ˈdʒoʊvɪəl], *adj.* lustig, heiter, aufgeräumt, jovial. **–ity** [–ˈælɪtɪ], *s.* die Lustigkeit, Heiterkeit, der Frohsinn, die Jovialität.

jowl [dʒaʊl], *s.* die Backe, Wange; das Kopfstück (*Cook.*); *cheek by –*, dicht bei einander, Seite an Seite.

joy [dʒɔɪ], 1. *s.* die Freude (*at*, über, *in* or *of*, an), Fröhlichkeit, das Vergnügen, Entzücken; *tears of –*, Freudentränen; *it gives me great –*, es macht mir große Freude; *leap for –*, vor Freude hüpfen; *wish s.o. – of*, einem Glück wünschen *or* gratulieren zu. 2. *v.n.* (*Poet.*) sich freuen, entzückt sein. **–ful** [–fəl], *adj.* froh, freudig; erfreulich. **–fulness,** *s.* die Fröhlichkeit, Freude. **–less** [–lɪs], *adj.* freudlos; unerfreulich. **–lessness,** *s.* die Freudlosigkeit. **–ous** [–əs], *adj. see* **–ful.** **–ousness,** *s. see* **–fulness.** **–-ride,** *s.* die Lustfahrt; Schwarzfahrt. **–-stick,** *s.* der (Steuer)Knüppel (*Av.*).

jubil–ant [ˈdʒuːbɪlənt], *adj.* jubelnd, frohlockend. **–ate,** 1. [–eɪt] *v.n.* jubeln, frohlocken. 2. [dʒuːbɪˈlɑːtɪ], *s.* der 3. Sonntag nach Ostern; der 100. Psalm, Jubilate. **–ation** [–ˈleɪʃən], *s.* das Jubeln, Frohlocken, der Jubel. **–ee** [–lɪː], *s.* 50-jähriges Jubiläum; das Jubeljahr, Ablaßjahr (*R.C.*), die Jubelfeier, das Jubelfest, der Jubel; *silver –ee*, 25-jähriges Jubiläum; *diamond –ee*, 60-jähriges Jubiläum.

Judai–c(al) [dʒuːˈdeɪɪk(l)], *adj.* jüdisch. **–sm** [ˈdʒuːdeɪɪzm], *s.* das Judentum, jüdische Religion. **–ze** [–deɪɑɪz], *v.a.* verjuden.

judge [dʒʌdʒ], 1. *s.* der Richter (*also B. and fig.*) (*of*, über), Schiedsrichter (*Sport*), Kenner, Sachverständige(r), *m.* (*of*, in); *book of –s*, das Buch der Richter (*B.*); *be a – of*, sich verstehen auf (*Acc.*); *I am no – of these things*, darüber habe ich kein Urteil; *as God is my –!* so wahr mir Gott helfe! *sober as a –*, vollkommen nüchtern. 2. *v.n.* urteilen (*by* or *from*, nach; *of*, über). 3. *v.a.* richten, Recht sprechen über, entscheiden, beurteilen (*by*, nach); urteilen über, schließen (*from*, aus), halten für, betrachten als; *– Advocate*, der Kriegsgerichtsrat; *– Advocate General*, der Chef des Heeresjustizwesens. **–ment (judgment)** [–mənt], *s.* das Urteil, der Urteilsspruch, gerichtliche Entscheidung; die Urteilskraft, Einsicht, der Verstand, Scharfsinn; die Beurteilung, Meinung, Ansicht; das Strafgericht, göttliches Gericht; *day of –ment* or *the last –ment*, Jüngstes Gericht; *–ment by default*, das Versäumungsurteil; *error of –ment*, das Fehlurteil; *give –ment*, entscheiden, ein Urteil sprechen; *in my –ment*, meines Erachtens, nach meiner Ansicht; *pass* or *pronounce –ment on*, ein Urteil fällen über, urteilen über; *sit in –ment*, zu Gericht sitzen (*upon*, über); *man of –ment*, scharfsinniger *or* einsichtsvoller Mann. **–ment-day,** *s.* Jüngster Tag. **–ment-seat,** *s.* der Richterstuhl. **–ship,** *s.* das Richteramt.

judic–ature [ˈdʒuːdɪkətʃə], *s.* der Gerichtshof, die Richter (*pl.*); die Justizgewalt, Rechtspflege, Rechtsprechung, das Gerichtswesen, Richteramt; *the Supreme Court of –ature*, das Oberlandesgericht. **–ial** [–ˈdɪʃəl], *adj.* gerichtlich, richterlich, Gerichts–, Richter–, (*fig.*) kritisch; *–ial error*, der Rechtsirrtum; *–ial murder*, der Justizmord. *–ial procedure*, das Gerichtsverfahren; *–ial proceedings*, Gerichtsverhandlungen; *–ial system*, das Gerichtswesen. **–iary** [–ˈdɪʃərɪ], 1. *s.* das Rechtswesen, Gerichtswesen, die Rechtsprechung, Justizgewalt. 2. *adj.* richterlich, gerichtlich. **–ious** [–ˈdɪʃəs], *adj.* verständig, vernünftig, klug, einsichtsvoll, wohl überlegt, sinnvoll, zweckentsprechend. **–iousness,** *s.* die Klugheit, Einsicht.

jug [dʒʌg], 1. *s.* der Krug, die Kanne; (*sl.*) das Loch, Kittchen. 2. *v.a.* schmoren, dämpfen (*Cook.*); (*sl*). ins Loch stecken; *–ged hare*, der Hasenpfeffer (*Cook.*). **–ful,** *s.* der Krugvoll.

juggernaut [ˈdʒʌgənɔːt], *s.* der Moloch, Götze, Schreckgespenst, unwiderstehliche Gewalt, unwiderstehlicher Gedanke.

juggins [ˈdʒʌgɪnz], *s.* (*sl.*) der Dummkopf, Tröttel.

juggle [dʒʌgl], 1. *v.n.* gaukeln, Kunststücke machen, jonglieren; betrügen, täuschen, unehrlich verfahren; *– with words*, durch Worte täuschen. 2. *v.a.* betrügen (*out of*, um). 3. *s.* die Gaukelei, das Kunststück; der Betrug. **–r** [–lə], *s.* der Jongleur, Taschenspieler, Zauberkünstler, Gaukler, Betrüger. **–ry** [–lərɪ], *s.* die Gaukelei, Taschenspielerei.

jugula–r [ˈdʒʌgjʊlə], *adj.* Kehl–, Gurgel–; *–r vein,* die Drosselader. **–te** [–eɪt], *v.a.* erdrosseln, (*fig.*) unterdrücken, hemmen.

juic–e [dʒʊ:s], *s.* der Saft (*also fig.*); (*fig.*) die Kraft, der Inhalt, das Wesen; (*sl.*) der Treibstoff, Sprit (*Motor*); (*sl.*) der Strom (*Elect.*); (*sl.*) *stew in one's own –e,* im eigenen Fette schmoren. **–iness,** *s.* die Saftigkeit. **–y,** *adj.* saftig; (*sl.*) erstklassig, würzig.

ju-jitsu [dʒʊ:ˈdʒɪtsʊ], *s.* das Jiu-Jitsu.

ju-ju [ˈdʒʊ:dʒʊ:], *s.* das Tabu, der Fetisch, Zauber.

jujube [ˈdʒʊ:dʒʊ:b], *s.* die Brustbeere (*Bot.*).

julep [ˈdʒʊ:lɪp], *s.* der Julep, Julap, Kühlgetränk.

July [dʒʊ:ˈlaɪ], *s.* der Juli.

jumble [dʒʌmbl], 1. *v.a.* zusammenwerfen, wahllos durcheinanderwerfen, vermengen. 2. *v.n.* durcheinanderkommen, in Unordnung kommen *or* geraten. 3. *s.* das Durcheinander, der Wirrwarr, Mischmasch; (*coll.*) Ramschwaren (*pl.*), der Ramsch, altes Zeug. **– -sale,** *s.* der Ramschverkauf.

jump [dʒʌmp], **1.** *v.n.* springen, hüpfen; steigen, emporschnellen (*in price*), in die Höhe fahren, auffahren. (*a*) (*with prepositions*) – *at the chance,* die Gelegenheit ergreifen, mit beiden Händen zupacken; – *at an idea,* einen Gedanken schnell aufgreifen; – *at conclusions,* see – *to conclusions*; – *at an offer,* ein Angebot freudig annehmen; (*sl.*) – *down a p.'s throat,* auf einen wie ein Wilder losgehen; – *for joy,* vor Freude hüpfen; – *on,* stürzen auf, (*sl.*) anhauen, ausputzen, einem auf die Bude rücken *or* aufs Dach steigen *or* übers Maul fahren; – *on to,* aufspringen auf; – *out of one's skin,* aus der Haut fahren; – *over,* hinüberspringen über; – *to conclusions,* voreilige Schlußfolgerungen ziehen, übereilte Schlüsse ziehen, vorschnell folgern; (*coll.*) – *to it,* rasch 'rangehen. (*b*) (*with adverbs*) – *about,* herumspringen; – *clear of,* wegspringen von; – *down,* abspringen, herunterspringen; – *in,* einspringen; – *off,* abspringen; – *up,* aufspringen; – *up against,* hinaufspringen an. **2.** *v.a.* hinwegspringen über (*Acc.*), überspringen; auslassen; schwenken (*potatoes*); – *a claim,* von Land, auf das ein anderer Anspruch hat, Besitz ergreifen; – *the rails,* entgleisen. **3.** *s.* der Sprung (*also fig.*), Satz, das Auffahren; *pl.* (*coll.*) nervöse Zuckungen; *give a –,* emporschnellen (*of things*), auffahren (*of persons*); – *in price,* die Preissteigerung; *make* or *take a –,* einen Sprung tun, einen Satz machen; *take the –,* das Hindernis nehmen. **–er,** *s.* der Springer; Steinbohrer (*quarrying*); Schaltdraht (*Elec.*); die Käsemade (*Ent.*); der Schlüpfer. **–ing-board,** *s.* das Sprungbrett. **–ing Jack,** *s.* der Hampelmann. **–ing-off point,** der Absprungpunkt; Abflugpunkt (*Av.*). **–ing-off position,** die Ausgangsstellung. **–ing-pole,** *s.* der Sprungstab. **–y,** *adj.* nervös, unruhig.

junct–ion [ˈdʒʌŋkʃən], *s.* die Verbindung, Berührung (*Geom.*), der Knotenpunkt (*Railw.*). **–ion-box,** *s.* die Abzweigdose (*Elec.*). **–ion-line,** *s.* die Verbindungsbahn (*Railw.*). **–ure** [–tʃə], *s.* das Zusammentreffen (*of events*), die Lage der Dinge, kritischer Augenblick, (*archaic*) die Verbindung, das Gelenk; *at this –ure,* an dieser Stelle, zu diesem Zeitpunkt.

June [dʒʊ:n], *s.* der Juni.

jungle [ˈdʒʌngl], *s.* der, das (*or Austr.* die) Dschungel, das Sumpfdickicht.

junior [ˈdʒʊ:nɪə], 1. *adj.* jünger (*to,* als); untergeordnet, tieferstehend; – *class,* – *year,* dritter Jahrgang (*Amer. Univ.*); – *clerk,* zweiter Buchhalter; – *department* (*of a school*), – *school,* die Unterstufe (*Eng.*); – *forms,* Klassen bis zur Tertia; – *partner,* jüngerer Teilhaber. 2. *s.* der (die) Jüngere; der Student des dritten Jahrgangs (*Amer. Univ.*); *he is my – by some years,* er ist einige Jahre jünger als ich. **–ity** [–ˈɔrɪtɪ], *s.* geringeres Alter.

juniper [ˈdʒʊ:nɪpə], *s.* der Wacholder (*Bot.*).

[1]**junk** [dʒʌŋk], *s.*; (*Chinese –*), die Dschonke, Dschunke.

[2]**junk** [dʒʌŋk], *s.* altes Tauwerk (*Naut.*); das Altmaterial, Altwaren (*pl.*), der Trödel, wertloser Plunder; (*sl.*) der Schund, Abfälle (*pl.*), zähes Pökelfleisch (*Naut.*). **– -dealer,** der Altwarenhändler, Trödler. **– -heap,** der Abfallplatz; der Autofriedhof. **– -shop,** *s.* der Trödelladen, Ramschladen.

junket [ˈdʒʌŋkɪt], 1. *s.* dicke Milch; die Festlichkeit, Feier, das Fest. 2. *v.n.* schmausen, ein Fest feiern. **–ing,** *s.* das Lustigsein.

junt–a [ˈdʒʌntə], *s.* die Ratsversammlung, (spanische) Junta. **–o** [–oʊ], *s.* die Clique, geheime Verbindung.

Jurassic [dʒʊəˈræsɪk], *adj.* Jura– (*Geol.*).

juridical [dʒʊˈrɪdɪkl], *adj.* Rechts–, gerichtlich, Gerichts–.

juris–diction [dʒʊrɪsˈdɪkʃən], *s.* die Rechtsprechung, Gerichtsbarkeit; der Gerichtsbezirk; *have –diction over,* zuständig sein für. **–prudence** [–ˈprʊ:dəns], *s.* die Rechtswissenschaft. **–prudential** [–ˈdɛnʃəl], *adj.* rechtswissenschaftlich. **–t** [ˈdʒʊərɪst], *s.* Rechtsgelehrte(r), *m.*, (*Amer.*) der Jurist.

jur-or [ˈdʒʊərə] *s.* Geschworene(r), *m.*, Vereidigte(r), *m.*; der Preisrichter (*of competitions*). **–y** [–rɪ], *s.* die Geschworenen (*pl.*), die Geschworenenbank; das Schwurgericht, Geschworenengericht, die Jury (*Law*); die Preisrichter (*pl.*), das Preisrichterkollegium, Preisgericht (*in competitions*); *grand –y,* die Anklagejury; *petty –y,* die Urteilsjury; *trial by –y,* die Schwurgerichtsverhandlung. **–y-box,** *s.* die Geschworenenbank. **–yman,** *s.*, Geschworene(r), *m.*

jury-mast [ˈdʒʊərɪˈmɑ:st], *s.* der Notmast.

just [dʒʌst], 1. *adj.* gerecht, billig, unparteiisch (*to, gegen*); redlich, rechtschaffen; genau, richtig, gehörig, passend, recht, wahr; rein (*Mus.*); berechtigt, (wohl)begründet, (wohl)verdient, rechtmäßig; *my – right,* mein volles Recht. 2. *adv.* gerade, genau, nicht mehr als; fast, beinahe, eben; eben gerade, soeben, gerade noch, mit knapper Not, (*coll.*) wirklich, geradezu; – *as,* ebenso wie, gerade als, eben als; – *as large,* ebenso groß; – *as well,* ebenso gut; *but –,* eben erst; – *enough,* eben genug; – *a moment!* einen Augenblick, bitte! halt! wart' einmal! nur nicht so eilig! – *now,* soeben gerade, jetzt, jetzt gerade; *that's – right,* das ist gerade recht, das paßt gerade; *that's – it!* das ist es eben; – *let me see!* laß 'mal sehen, zeig einmal her! – *so!* ganz recht! jawohl!; – *tell me,* sage mir (ein)mal *or* doch; – *then,* gerade in dem Moment; – *there,* genau dort; *see* **justly, justness.**

justic–e [ˈdʒʌstɪs], *s.* die Gerechtigkeit, Billigkeit, Richtigkeit; das Recht, Justizwesen; das Gericht; der Richter. (*a*) (*with nouns*) *High Court of –e,* das Reichsgericht; *Lord Chief –e,* der Lord Oberrichter; *–e of the peace,* der Friedensrichter, Laienrichter. (*b*) (*with verbs*) *administer –e,* Recht sprechen; *do –e to him* or *do him –e,* ihm Gerechtigkeit widerfahren lassen; *do o.s. –e,* sich nichts abgeben lassen; *do –e to a dish,* einer Speise tüchtig zusprechen; *see –e done to a p.*, einem Recht verschaffen. (*c*) (*with prepositions*) *in –e,* von Rechts wegen; *in –e to him,* um ihm gerecht zu werden; *bring to –e,* vor den Richter bringen, gerichtlich belangen; *with –e,* mit Recht, gerecht, billig. **–eship,** *s.* das Richteramt. **–iable** [–ˈtɪʃɪəbl], *pred. adj.* der Gerichtsbarkeit unterworfen. **–iary** [–ˈtɪʃɪərɪ], 1. *s.* der Gerichtshalter, Rechtsprecher; *High Court of –iary,* oberstes Kriminalgericht (*Scots*). 2. *adj.* gerichtlich.

justif–iability [dʒʌstɪfaɪəˈbɪlɪtɪ], *s.* die Entschuldbarkeit. **–iable** [ˈdʒʌstɪfaɪəbl], *adj.* zu rechtfertigen(d), berechtigt, rechtmäßig. **–ication** [–fɪˈkeɪʃən], *s.* die Rechtfertigung, Berechtigung; Ausschließung, Justierung (*Typ.*); *in –ication of,* zur Rechtfertigung von. **–icatory** [ˈdʒʌstɪfɪkətərɪ], *adj.* rechtfertigend, Rechtfertigungs–. **–ier** [–faɪə], *s.* der Rechtfertiger; Justierer (*Typ.*). **–y** [–faɪ], *v.a.* rechtfertigen (*to* or *before,* vor (*Dat.*)); freisprechen, lossprechen (*Theol.*); ausschließen, justieren (*Typ.*); *be –ied in doing,* berechtigt sein zu tun; *the end –ies the means,* der Zweck heiligt die Mittel.

just–ly [ˈdʒʌstlɪ], *adv.* mit Recht, richtig, verdientermaßen; *see* **just** 1. **–ness,** *s.* die Gerechtigkeit, Billigkeit; Richtigkeit, Genauigkeit.

jut [dʒʌt], 1. *v.n.* (– *out*) hervorstehen, hervorragen, hinausragen, vorspringen, ausbauchen. 2. *s.* der Vorsprung. **– -window,** *s.* das Erkenfenster.

jute [dʒʊ:t], *s.* die Jute (*Bot.*).

juven–escence [dʒʊ:vəˈnɛsəns], *s.* die **Verjüngung,**

Jugendlichkeit; *well of –escence*, der Jungbrunnen. **–escent** [–ənt], *adj.* sich verjüngend; unentwickelt, unreif. **–ile** [ˈdʒuːvənaɪl], 1. *adj.* jung, jugendlich, Jugend–; *–ile court*, das Jugendgericht; *–ile wear*, Kleidung für Jugendliche. 2. *s.* der Jugendliche. **–ility** [–ˈnɪlɪtɪ], *s.* das Jungsein, die Jugendlichkeit; jugendliche Unreife; jugendlicher Leichtsinn. **–ilities,** *pl.* Kindereien (*pl.*).
juxtapos–e [dʒʌstəˈpouz], *v.a.* nebeneinanderstellen. **–ition** [–pəˈzɪʃən], *s.* die Nebeneinanderstellung.

K

K, k [keɪ], *s.* das K, k. *See Index of Abbreviations.*
Kaffir [ˈkæfə], *s. see Index of Names.*
kale, kail [keɪl], *s.* der Winterkohl, Krauskohl. **––yard,** *s.* (*Scots*) der Gemüsegarten, Küchengarten; *– -yard school*, (*Scots*) schottische Heimatdichtung.
kaleidoscop–e [kəˈlaɪdəskoup], *s.* das Kaleidoskop. **–ic** [–ˈskɔpɪk], *adj.* kaleidoskopisch, (*fig.*) bunt durcheinandergewürfelt.
kali [ˈkeɪlɪ], *s.* das Salzkraut (*Bot.*).
kangaroo [kæŋgəˈruː], *s.* das Känguruh.
kaolin [ˈkeɪəlɪn], *s.* das Kaolin, die Porzellanerde.
kapok [ˈkæpɔk], *s.* das Haar des Kapokbaumes, die Pflanzenfaser.
karma [ˈkɑːmə], *s.* das Schicksal.
kayak [ˈkaɪæk], *s.* der *or* das Kaiak, das Paddelboot.
kedge [kɛdʒ], 1. *s.* (*––anchor*) der Warpanker. 2. *v.a.* warpen, verholen (*a ship*).
kedgeree [ˈkɛdʒərɪː], *s.* ein Gericht aus Reis, Fisch und Eiern.
keel [kɪːl], 1. *s.* der Kiel (*Naut.*); (*Poet.*) das Schiff; *on an even –*, gleich schwer beladen; (*fig.*) ruhig, eben, glatt. 2. *v.n.*; *– over*, umschlagen, umkippen, kieloben liegen, kentern. 3. *v.a.*; *– over*, kieloben legen, umlegen. **–age** [–ɪdʒ], *s.* das Kielgeld. **–ed** [–d], *adj.* kielförmig (*Bot.*). **–haul** [–hɔːl], *v.a.* kielholen, (*fig.*) abkanzeln. **–son,** *s.* das Kielschwein.
[1]**keen** [kɪːn], *adj.* scharf (*as an edge, also fig.*), spitz (*as a point*); (*fig.*) eifrig, erpicht (*on*, auf), interessiert (*on*, für *or* an), begierig (*on*, nach) (*of persons*); durchdringend (*as a glance*), beißend (*as wit, frost, etc.*), schneidend, streng (*as cold*), stark, groß (*as appetite, delight, etc.*), heftig (*as pain, sorrow, etc.*), lebhaft, eingehend (*as interest, desire, attention, etc.*), fein (*as senses*), heiß (*as a contest, etc.*), bitter (*as disappointment*); *– competition*, lebhafter *or* starker Wettbewerb; *– edge*, scharfe Schneide; *as – as mustard*, wild versessen *or* toll (auf (*Acc.*)); *be – on swimming*, ein eifriger Schwimmer sein, gern schwimmen; *– perception of*, feines Gefühl für; *– to go out*, Lust haben auszugehen; *I am not very –*, ich habe wenig Lust. **––edged,** *adj.* scharf geschliffen, mit scharfer Schneide. **––eyed,** *adj.* scharfsichtig. **–ness,** *s.* die Schärfe, Heftigkeit, Strenge, Bitterkeit, der Eifer, Scharfsinn; *–ness of sight*, die Scharfsichtigkeit. **––witted,** *adj.* scharfsinnig.
[2]**keen** [kɪːn], 1. *s.* irische Totenklage. 2. *v.n.* (weh)klagen (um).
keep [kɪːp], **1.** *ir.v.a.* halten, (in Besitz) behalten, aufbewahren; behaupten (*the field*); bewachen, beschützen, bewahren (*from*, vor), abhalten, zurückhalten (*from*, von), hindern (*from*, an (*Dat.*)) (*a p.*); vorenthalten, verheimlichen (*s.th. from s.o.*, einem etwas); erhalten, unterhalten, ernähren (*a p.*); beobachten befolgen (*laws, etc.*); feiern, abhalten (*a festival*); verfolgen, einhalten, innehalten (*a course*); hüten (*one's bed, etc.*); führen (*goods in stock, ledger, etc.*), auf Lager haben. **(a)** (*with nouns*) *– s.o. company*, einem Gesellschaft leisten; *– company with s.o.*, mit einem verkehren, mit einem Beziehungen unterhalten; *– your distance!* bleib mir vom Leibe!; *– an eye on*, im Auge behalten; *– faith with s.o.*, einem die Treue halten; *– one's feet*, sich auf den Füßen halten; *– one's ground*, standhalten; *– guard*, Wache stehen *or* halten; *– a guard over one's tongue*, seine Zunge im Zaume halten; *– one's hand in*, bei Übung bleiben; *– one's head*, besonnen *or* ruhig bleiben; *– late hours*, spät zu Bett gehen, spät aufbleiben; *– house*, die Wirtschaft *or* Haushalt führen; (*coll.*) *– a stiff upper lip*, sich nicht unterkriegen lassen; *– pace with*, Schritt halten mit, mitgehen *or* mitkommen mit; *– the peace*, den Frieden aufrecht erhalten, Ruhe halten; (*coll.*) *– the pot boiling*, durchhalten; *– s.o. prisoner*, einen gefangenhalten; *– a tight rein over a p.*, einen streng halten; *– one's room*, das Zimmer hüten; *– one's seat*, sitzen bleiben; *– a shop*, einen Laden besitzen; *– silence*, Stillschweigen beobachten, still sein; *– one's temper*, sich beherrschen; *– time*, richtig gehen (*of watches*), Takt halten (*Mus.*); *– watch*, Wache stehen, aufpassen, achtgeben (*on* or *over*, auf (*Acc.*)); *– one's word*, sein Wort halten. **(b)** (*with adjectives*) *– a p. advised*, see *– s.o. informed*; *– a th. dark*, etwas verschweigen; *– dry!* vor Nässe zu schützen!; *– s.th. going*, etwas in Gang halten; *– s.o. going*, einen über Wasser halten *or* aufrechthalten; *– s.o. informed*, einen auf dem laufenden halten; *– s.th. secret*, etwas verschweigen, etwas geheimhalten; *– a p. waiting*, einen warten lassen. **(c)** (*with adverbs*) *– apart*, getrennt halten; *– away*, fernhalten; *– back*, zurückhalten; geheimhalten, vorenthalten (*from* (*Dat.*)); *– down*, (nieder)drücken, niederhalten, niedrig halten (*prices*), beschränken (*to*, auf); *– in*, kurz halten, zurückhalten, im Zaume halten, bändigen; anhalten (*one's breath*); nachsitzen lassen (*pupil*); nicht ausgehen lassen (*a fire*); *– off*, abhalten, abwehren; *– on*, anbehalten (*clothes*), aufbehalten (*hat*), behalten, beibehalten (*a servant*), (*sl.*) *– one's hair on*, den Kopf oben behalten; *– out*, nicht hereinlassen, ausschließen, fernhalten; *– under*, niederhalten, im Zaume halten, nicht aufkommen lassen; *– up*, in die Höhe halten, aufrecht(er)halten, behaupten, auf der Höhe halten (*as prices*), (*coll.*) bleiben bei, weiter machen mit, unterhalten (*correspondence, etc.*), stehen lassen (*type*), nicht zu Bett gehen lassen, aufbehalten (*from bed*); *– up appearances*, den Schein wahren; (*coll.*) *– your chin up!* immer feste auf die Weste!; (*coll.*) *– one's end up*, sich behaupten, durchhalten; *– it up*, nicht nachlassen, es immer weitermachen; *– it up!* immer zu!; *– up to the mark*, auf der Höhe halten. **(d)** (*with prepositions*) *– at it*, an etwas festhalten; *– at a distance*, von sich fernhalten; *– s.o. at work*, einen dauernd beschäftigen, einen zur Arbeit anhalten; *– from coming*, verhindern zu kommen; *– from danger*, vor Gefahr schützen; *– s.th. from s.o.*, einem etwas verschweigen, verheimlichen *or* vorenthalten; *– in one's own hands*, selbst verwalten; *– in mind*, im Gedächtnis behalten, daran denken; *– s.o. in money*, einen mit Geld versorgen; *– in repair*, in gutem Zustande erhalten; *– in suspense*, in Ungewißheit halten *or* lassen; *– in view*, im Auge behalten; *– o.s. on £2 a week*, sich von 2 Pfund in der Woche ernähren; *– s.th. out of sight*, etwas verborgen halten; *– o.s. to o.s.*, für sich bleiben; *– s.o. to his promise*, einen zu seinem Wort halten; *– a th. to o.s.*, etwas für sich behalten; (*coll.*) *– a th. under one's hat*, etwas hinter den Spiegel stecken. **2.** *ir.v.n.* sich halten (*of things*); sich aufhalten, sich verhalten, bleiben, nicht aufhören (*doing*, zu tun); *– doing*, fortwährend *or* wiederholt tun; (*coll.*) *how are you –ing?* wie geht's (Ihnen)?; (*coll.*) *the matter will –*, die S. eilt nicht *or* hat Zeit. **(a)** (*with adverbs*) *– abreast with the times*, mit der *or* seiner Zeit fortschreiten *or* Schritt halten; *– aloof*, sich entfernt halten; *– aloof from s.o.*, mit einem nichts zu tun haben wollen; *– away*, sich fernhalten (*from*, von), fernbleiben (*from* (*Dat.*)); *– clear of*, sich fernhalten *or* freihalten von, sich (*Dat.*) vom Leibe halten, aus dem Wege gehen; *– close*, sich zurückziehen; *– dark about a th.*, mit etwas hinterm Berge halten; *– down*, sich geduckt halten; *– in*, sich versteckt halten; *– in with a p.*,

bei einem in Gunst bleiben; – *off*, sich fernhalten, fernbleiben, davonbleiben, sich enthalten (*Gen.*); – *off!* bleib mir vom Leibe! – *on*, fortfahren (mit *or* auf), bleiben (bei); *it kept on raining*, es regnete (immer) weiter *or* fortwährend; – *out*, draußen bleiben; – *quiet*, sich ruhig verhalten; dicht halten; – *up*, sich aufrecht erhalten, Schritt halten; – *up one's spirits*, den Mut nicht sinken lassen; *prices are –ing up*, die Preise behaupten sich; – *up with*, Schritt halten mit, (*fig.*) es gleichtun (*Dat.*). **(b)** (*with prepositions*) – *at*, festhalten an, beharren bei, ununterbrochen arbeiten an (*things*), belästigen (*a p.*); – *from*, sich enthalten (*Gen.*), (*neg. only*), nicht umhin können (*doing*, zu tun); – *in touch with*, Fühlung behalten mit, in Verbindung *or* Berührung bleiben mit; – *off the grass!* das Gras nicht betreten!; – *out of danger*, der Gefahr fernbleiben; – *out of debt*, sich schuldenfrei erhalten; – *out of mischief*, keine bösen Streiche machen; – *out of sight*, sich nicht sehen *or* blicken lassen, außer Sicht bleiben, sich verbergen; – *to*, (sich) halten an, festhalten an, bleiben bei, befolgen; – *to the left!* links fahren! halten Sie sich links!; (*coll.*) – *to o.s.*, für sich bleiben; – *to one's word*, sein Wort halten. **3.** *s.* der Unterhalt, die Kost, Verpflegung (*of persons*), Weide, das Futter (*of cattle*); der Hauptturm, Bergfried, das Burgverlies (*Austr.* Burgverließ); *earn one's –*, gerade soviel verdienen, um sich zu erhalten; (*coll.*) *for –s*, auf *or* für immer, ewig und drei Tage. **–er,** *s.* der Inhaber, Besitzer (*of a hotel, etc.*); Hüter, Wächter, Aufseher, Wärter, Gefängniswärter; Verwahrer, Bewahrer (*as title*); Schutzring, Anker (*of a magnet*); *–er of the great seal*, der Großsiegelbewahrer; *–er of manuscripts*, der Direktor der Handschriftenabteilung; *–er of the privy purse*, der Intendant der königlichen Zivilliste; (*in comps.*) *bee-–er*, der Imker; *box-–er*, der Logenschließer (*Theat.*); *door-–er*, der Pförtner; *game-–er*, der Förster; *gate-–er*, der Torwärter, Pförtner; Bahnwärter (*Railw.*); *inn–er*, der Wirt, Gastwirt; *shop–er*, der Ladenbesitzer, Krämer; *time-–er*, der Zeitmesser, der *or* das Chronometer (*Horol.*); der Zeitmesser (*Sport*); Aufseher; *wicket-–er*, der Torwart, Torhüter (*Crick.*). **–ing,** 1. *adj.* sich haltend; *–ing apples*, Daueräpfel (*pl.*). 2. *s.* die Verwahrung, Aufsicht, Pflege, Obhut, der Gewahrsam; Unterhalt, die Nahrung; Übereinstimmung, der Einklang; *be in (out of) –ing with*, (nicht) übereinstimmen mit, (nicht) stimmen *or* passen zu, (nicht) in Einklang stehen zu; *in safe –ing*, in Verwahrung, in Gewahrsam; *entrust to s.o.'s –ing*, jemandes Obhut anvertrauen. **–sake,** *s.* das Andenken; *as a –sake*, zum Andenken.

kef [kɛf], *s.* der (Haschisch)Rausch, die Verträumtheit.

keg [kɛg], *s.* das Fäßchen.

kelp [kɛlp], *s.* der Seetang, Kelp, die Seetangasche.

kelpie [ˈkɛlpɪ], *s.* (*Scots*) der Wassergeist.

kelson [ˈkɛlsən], *s. see* **keelson.**

ken [kɛn], 1. *s.* der Gesichtskreis, die Sehweite (*also fig.*); *beyond* or *out of one's –*, außerhalb des Gesichtskreises; *within one's –*, innerhalb des Gesichtskreises. 2. *v.a.* (*Scots*) wissen, kennen.

[1]**kennel** [kɛnl], 1. *s.* die Hundehütte, der Hundestall; (*sl.*) das Loch. **–s,** *pl.* der Hundezwinger, die Stallung (*for pack of hounds*); die Meute, Koppel (*hounds*). 2. *v.n.* in einem Loche liegen *or* hausen. 3. *v.a.* in einem Hundestalle unterbringen.

[2]**kennel** [kɛnl], *s.* die Gosse, Rinne, der Rinnstein.

kentledge [ˈkɛntlɪdʒ], *s.* das Ballasteisen (*Naut.*).

kept [kɛpt], 1. *see* **keep.** 2. *adj.*; – *woman*, die Maitresse.

kerb [kə:b], *s.* die Bordkante, Straßenkante; – *market*, inoffizielle *or* schwarze Börse. **--stone,** *s.* der Randstein, Bordstein, Prellstein.

kerchief [ˈkə:tʃɪf], *s.* das Kopftuch, Halstuch.

kerf [kə:f], *s.* die Kerbe, Schnittbreite (*of a saw*).

kermes [ˈkə:mɪz], *s.* der Kermes; *pl.* die Kermeskörner.

kermis [ˈkə:mɪs], *s.* die Kirmes, Kirchweih.

kernel [ˈkə:nl], *s.* der Kern (*of nuts, etc. also fig.*), das Korn (*of oats, etc.*); (*fig.*), das Wesen, Innerste(s), *n.*

kerosene [ˈkɛrəsɪ:n], *s.* das Kerosin, Leuchtöl, Brennöl.

kersey [ˈkə:zɪ], *s.* grobes Wollzeug.

kestrel [ˈkɛstrəl], *s.* der Turmfalke (*Orn.*).

ketch [kɛtʃ], *s.* die Ketsch, kleines zweimastiges Küstenschiff.

ketchup [ˈkɛtʃəp], *s.* kalte pikante Sauce aus Tomaten, Pilzen, u.s.w.

kettle [kɛtl], *s.* der Kessel, Kochtopf, Wassertopf; *a pretty – of fish!* eine schöne Bescherung. **--drum,** *s.* die Kesselpauke. **--drummer,** *s.* der Paukenschläger. **--holder,** *s.* der Anfasser.

key [kɪ:], 1. *s.* der Schlüssel (*also fig.*), die Lösung; Übersetzung; Unterlage; Zeichenerklärung; der Ton, die Tonart (*Mus.*); (*fig.*) der Einklang, die Übereinstimmung; der Keil, Vorsteckbolzen (*Mach.*); Schraubenschlüssel; die Taste (*piano, etc.*), Klappe (*flute, etc.*), der Schalter (*Elec., Tele.*). *in – with*, in Einklang mit; *power of the –s*, die Schlüsselgewalt (*R.C.*); *all in the same –*, alle in derselben Tonart; *turn the –*, abschließen; *speak in a high –*, in hohem Tone sprechen; *keep under lock and –*, unter Schloß und Riegel halten. 2. *v.a.* befestigen; (– *in* or *on*) festkeilen; (*coll.*) – *up* anfeuern. **–board,** *s.* die Tastatur (*typewriter, etc.*), Klaviatur (*piano*). **--bugle,** *s.* das Klapphorn. **–ed** [–d], *adj.* mit Tasten *or* Klappen; *–ed instrument*, das Tasteninstrument; *six-–ed flute*, die Flöte mit sechs Klappen. **–hole,** *s.* das Schlüsselloch. **--industry,** *s.* die Schlüsselindustrie. **–less,** *adj.* ohne Schlüssel; *–less watch*, die Remontoiruhr. **– man,** *s.* unentbehrliche Arbeitskraft. **–note,** *s.* der Grundton (*also fig.*), die Grundstimmung, der Hauptgedanke, die Lösung. **– position,** die Schlüsselstellung. **--ring,** *s.* der Schlüsselring. **–stone,** *s.* der Schlußstein; (*fig.*) Grundpfeiler, die Stütze, Grundlage, der Grundsatz, die Grundlage, das A und O. **--way,** *s.* die (Keil)Nut. **--word,** *s.* das Schlüsselwort, die Losung.

khaki [ˈkɑ:kɪ], 1. *adj.* staubfarbig, graugelb. 2. *s.* das Khaki.

[1]**khan** [kɑ:n], *s.* der Tatarenfürst.

[2]**khan** [kɑ:n], *s.* die Karawanserei.

Khedive [kɪˈdɪ:v], *s.* der Khedive.

kibe [kaɪb], *s.* eiternde Frostbeule.

kibosh [ˈkaɪbɔʃ], *s.* (*sl.*) der Mumpitz, das Blech, höherer Blödsinn; (*sl.*) *put the – on*, erledigen (*Acc.*), ein Ende machen (*Dat.*).

kick [kɪk], **1.** *v.a.* mit dem Fuße stoßen *or* treten, einen Fußtritt geben (*Dat.*), kicken (*Footb.*); (*sl.*) – *the bucket*, ins Gras beißen; – *s.o. downstairs*, einen die Treppe hinunterwerfen; – *one's heels*, ungeduldig *or* müßig warten (müssen); (*coll.*) – *s.o. out*, einen hinausschmeißen; – *up one's heels*, ausschlagen, sich hemmungslos benehmen; (*coll.*) – *up a dust*, viel Staub aufwirbeln; (*coll.*) – *up a row*, Radau schlagen, Spektakel machen. **2.** *v.n.* mit den Füßen stoßen, hinten ausschlagen (*of animals*), stoßen (*fire-arms*), hochfliegen (*of balls*), (*fig.*) sich auflehnen *or* streben (*at* or *against*, gegen); – *against the pricks*, wider den Stachel löcken; – *off*, den ersten Stoß machen, das Spiel beginnen; – *over the traces*, über die Stränge schlagen, über die Schnur hauen. **3.** *s.* der Fußtritt, Stoß; Rückstoß (*of a gun*), (*coll.*) Schwung, Stoßkraft, die Energie, Wirkung (*of a drink*), der Schuß (*Footb.*); das Neueste; (*sl.*) ein Halbschillingstück; *free –*, der Freistoß (*Footb.*); *goal –*, der Torstoß (*Footb.*); *penalty –*, der Elfmeter (*Footb.*); (*sl.*) *get the –*, entlassen werden; (*sl.*) *get a – out of a th.*, viel Spaß daran haben; *get more –s than halfpence*, wenig Dank ernten. **–er,** *s.* der Fußballspieler; Schläger (*horse*); (*coll.*) Nörgler, Quengler. **--off,** *s.* der Anstoß (*Footb.*). **--starter,** *s.* der Trittanlasser (*Motor.*).

kickshaw [ˈkɪkʃɔ:], *s.* der Tand, die Kleinigkeit, Spielerei; Nippsache, Schleckerei, Näscherei.

kid [kɪd], 1. *s.* das Zicklein; Ziegenleder; (*sl.*) Gör; (*sl.*) der Schwindel, Bluff. 2. *v.n.* zickeln. 3. *v.a.* (*coll.*) täuschen, verleiten, hereinlegen, zum Narren haben, anführen, bluffen, nasführen; – *s.o. that it is*, einem etwas weismachen; *you're –ding (me)*, sie scherzen. 4. *adj.* ziegenledern; – *brother* (*sl.*), junger Bruder; – *gloves*, Glacéhandschuhe. **–ding,** *s.* der Schwindel, Bluff. **–dy,** *s.* (*coll.*) das Gör.

kidnap ['kɪdnæp], *v.a.* entführen, rauben, stehlen (*child, etc.*), pressen, kapern (*Mil.*). **-per,** *s.* der Kinderdieb, Menschenräuber, Seelenverkäufer. **-ping,** *s.* der Kinderraub, Menschenraub.
kidney ['kɪdnɪ], *s.* die Niere; (*fig.*) (*coll.*) Art, Sorte, der Schlag. **--bean,** *s.* die Schminkbohne, französische Bohne. **--shaped,** *adj.* nierenförmig.
kilderkin ['kɪldəkɪn], *s.* das Fäßchen (= 18 Gallonen *or* 82 l.).
kill [kɪl], 1. *v.a.* töten, erschlagen, umbringen; schlachten (*cattle*); zerstören, vernichten, unterdrücken, zur Fall bringen (*a bill*) (*Parl.*); dämpfen, übertönen (*sound*); unwirksam machen, ausgleichen (*colours*); totmachen (*a play, etc.*); streichen (*an entry*); – *the ball*, den Ball töten (*Tenn.*); – *two birds with one stone*, zwei Fliegen mit einer Klappe schlagen; (*coll.*) *dressed up* (*fit*) *to* –, geschmacklos aufgeputzt, aufgedonnert; – *time*, die Zeit totschlagen; – *with kindness*, aus Güte schaden (*Dat.*); – *off*, abschlachten (*cattle*); ausrotten, vertilgen, beseitigen; (*coll.*) abmurksen. 2. *s.* die Tötung (*also Tenn.*), (Jagd)Beute. **-er,** *s.* der Totschläger. **-ing,** 1. *adj.* mörderisch; (*coll.*) unwiderstehlich, zum Kaputtlachen. 2. *s.* das Töten. **--joy,** *s.* der Störenfried, Spielverderber. **--or-cure,** *attrib. adj.* drastisch (*remedy*).
kiln [kɪln], *s.* der Brennofen, Röstofen, die Darre; *lime--*, der Kalkofen. **--dry,** *v.a.* darren, dörren.
kilo-gram(me) ['kɪləgræm], *s.* das Kilo(gramm). **-litre,** *s.* das Kiloliter. **-metre,** *s.* das (*or coll. & Swiss* der) Kilometer. **-watt,** *s.* das Kilowatt.
kilt [kɪlt], 1. *s.* das Schottenröckchen. 2. *v.a.* in Falten legen (*Semp.*); aufschürzen. **-ed** [–ɪd], *adj.* Schottenrock *or* Faltenrock tragend; senkrecht gefaltet *or* gefältelt.
kimono [kɪ'mounou], *s.* japanischer Schlafrock.
kin [kɪn], *s.* die (Bluts)Verwandtschaft; Verwandte(r), *m. or f.*, Verwandten (*pl.*); die Familie, das Geschlecht; *next of* –, nächste(r) Verwandte(r), die nächsten Verwandten, *see* **kindred, kinsfolk, kinship, kinsman,** *etc.*
kind [kaɪnd], **1.** *adj.* gut, gütig, freundlich, liebenswürdig (*to*, gegen), gefällig; *be – enough to* or *be so as to* . . ., seien Sie so freundlich *or* gut *or* haben Sie die Güte zu . . .; – *regards*, freundliche Grüße (*to*, an (*Acc.*)); *send one's – regards to a p.*, einen freundlich grüßen lassen. **2.** *s.* die Art, Gattung, das Geschlecht; die Beschaffenheit, Sorte, Art und Weise; Waren (*pl.*), Naturprodukte (*pl.*). **(a)** (*with nouns and pronouns*) *all of a* –, alle von derselben Art (*with*, wie); *all -s of people, people of all -s*, alle Arten Menschen, allerlei Menschen, Menschen jeder Art; *every – of* . . ., see *all -s of* . . .; *nothing of the* –, nichts dergleichen; bewahre! mit nichten!; *something of the* –, etwas derartiges; *this – of person*, diese Art (von) Mensch; (*coll.*) *these – of people*, diese Art Leute; *this – of thing*, derartiges; *just the – of thing I wanted*, gerade dies wünschte ich; *a person of this* –, ein Mensch dieser Art; (*sl.*) – *of*, sozusagen, gleichsam; (*sl.*) *I – of promised*, ich versprach halb und halb; (*coll.*) *a queer – of fellow*, ein etwas merkwürdiger Mensch; *what – of person is he?* was für ein Mensch ist er?, welche Art (von) Mensch ist er? **(b)** (*with prepositions*) *in* –, in Waren, in Natura; *different in* –, in der Sorte verschieden; *taxes paid in* –, Naturalabgaben; *repay in* –, mit gleicher Münze bezahlen. **--hearted,** *adj.* gutherzig, gütig. **-liness,** *s.* die Güte, Freundlichkeit. **-ly,** 1. *adj.* gütig, freundlich, lebenswürdig, wohlwollend, wohltätig; gutartig, günstig (*of climate, etc.*). 2. *adv.* freundlich, liebenswürdig; *-ly give it to me*, bitte geben Sie es mir; *take it -ly of a p.*, einem Dank wissen, einem verbunden sein; *take -ly to a p.*, einen gern haben; *take -ly to a th.*, etwas liebgewinnen; *thank you -ly*, besten Dank! **-ness,** *s.* die Güte, Freundlichkeit; Gefälligkeit, Wohltat.
kindl-e [kɪndl], 1. *v.a.* anzünden, entzünden (*also fig.*), (*fig.*) entflammen, anfeuern, erregen. 2. *v.n.* sich entzünden, Feuer fangen; (*fig.*) entbrennen. **-er,** *s.* (*fig.*) der Aufwiegler. **-ing,** *s.* Anbrennholz.
kind-ly, -ness, *see* **kind.**
kindred ['kɪndrɪd], 1. *s.* die Verwandtschaft, (*pl. constr.*) Verwandten (*pl.*). 2. *adj.* (bluts)verwandt, (*fig.*) verwandt, gleichartig, gleichgesinnt.
kinema ['kɪnəmə], *s. see* **cinema.**
kinetic [kɪ'nɛtɪk], *adj.* kinetisch, bewegend. **-s,** *pl.* (*sing. constr.*) die Kinetik.
king [kɪŋ], 1. *s.* der König (*also Cards & Chess*); die Dame (*Draughts*). 2. *v.a.* zum König machen. 3. *v.n.*; – *it*, den König spielen. **--craft,** *s.* die Regierungskunst, das Herrschertalent. **--cup,** *s.* der Hahnenfuß (*Bot.*). **-dom,** *s.* das Königreich; Reich (*Bot., Zool.*); *animal -dom*, das Tierreich; *vegetable -dom*, das Pflanzenreich; *the -dom of God* or *Heaven*, das Reich Gottes, Himmelreich; (*B.*) *thy -dom come*, dein Reich komme; (*coll.*) *-dom-come*, das Jenseits. **-fisher,** *s.* der Eisvogel (*Orn.*). **-like,** *adj.* königlich. **-liness,** *s.* das Königliche. **-ly,** *adj.* königlich, majestätisch. **--of-arms,** der Wappenkönig. **--pin,** *s.* der Achsschenkelbolzen, Achszapfen (*Motor.*); (*fig.*) Hauptvertreter, die Hauptstütze. **--post,** *s.* die Dachspitze (*Arch.*). **-s,** *pl.* (*B.*) Bücher der Könige. **-'s bench,** das Oberhofgericht. **-'s counsel,** der Kronanwalt. **-'s English,** das reine Englisch. **-'s evidence,** der Hauptzeuge; *turn -'s evidence*, Kronzeuge werden. **-'s evil,** die Skrofeln (*pl.*). **-'s highway,** die (öffentliche) Landstraße. **-'s speech,** die Thronrede. **-ship,** *s.* die Königswürde, das Königtum.
kink [kɪŋk], 1. *s.* die Kink, Schleife (*in rope*), der Knick (*in wire*); (*fig. coll.*) (– *on the brain*), die Grille, der Klaps, Vogel, Sparren. 2. *v.n.* Schleifen bilden. 3. *v.a.* verknoten, knicken.
kinkajou ['kɪŋkədʒuː], *s.* der Wickelbär (*Zool.*).
kino ['kɪːnou], *s.* das Kinoharz, Kinogummi.
kin-sfolk ['kɪnzfouk], *pl.* Verwandten (*pl.*), die Verwandtschaft. **-ship,** *s.* die Verwandtschaft (*to*, mit). **-sman,** *s.* Verwandte(r), *m.* **-swoman,** *s.* die Verwandte.
kiosk ['kɪːɔsk], *s.* der Kiosk; *telephone* –, die Fernsprechzelle.
kip [kɪp], *v.n.* (also – *down*) (*sl.*) pennen.
kipper ['kɪpə], 1. *s.* der Räucherhering, Bückling; der Lachs während und nach der Laichzeit. 2. *v.a.* einsalzen und räuchern.
kirk [kəːɹk], *s.* (*Scots*) die Kirche.
kirtle [kəːtl], *s.* (*archaic*) das Wams, der Frauenrock. **-d,** *adj.* mit einem Frauenrock bekleidet.
kiss [kɪs], 1. *v.a.* küssen; leicht berühren (*Bill.*); (*sl.*) – *the dust*, ins Gras beißen; – *a p. good-bye*, einen zum Abschied küssen, einem einen Abschiedskuß geben; – *s.o.'s hand*, einem die Hand küssen, einem einen Handkuß geben; – *one's hand to a p.*, einem eine Kußhand zuwerfen; – *and make* (*it*) *up*, sich wieder vertragen; – *the rod*, sich ergeben, sich fügen. 2. *s.* der Kuß; *throw s.o. a* –, einem eine Kußhand zuwerfen. **-ing-crust,** *s.* der Anstoß am Brote. **--proof,** *adj.* kußecht.
kit [kɪt], *s.* der Eimer, Zuber; das Fäschen, Tönnchen; die Werkzeugtasche, der Werkzeugkasten; das Handwerkszeug, Arbeitsgerät; die Ausrüstung, das Gepäck (*Mil. & fig.*). **--bag,** *s.* der Seesack.
kitcat ['kɪtkæt], *adj.*; – *portrait*, das Brustbild.
kitchen ['kɪtʃɪn], *s.* die Küche. **--car,** *s.* der Küchenwagen (*Railw.*). **-er,** *s.* der (Patent)-Kochherd; Küchenmeister (*in monasteries*). **-ette,** *s.* die Kochnische, Kleinküche. **--garden,** *s.* der Gemüsegarten, Küchengarten. **--maid,** *s.* die Küchenmagd. **--midden,** *s.* der Küchenabfallhaufen. **--range,** *s.* der Kochherd.
kite [kaɪt], *s.* der Gabelweih(e), (Roter) Milan (*Orn.*); der (Papier)Drache; (*sl.*) Schwindler, Gauner; (*sl.*) der Kellerwechsel, Reitwechsel (*C.L.*); *fly a* –, einen Drachen steigen lassen; (*sl.*) Wechselreiterei treiben (*C.L.*); (*sl.*) (*fig.*) einen Versuchsballon loslassen. **--balloon,** *s.* der Fesselballon. **--flying,** *s.* (*sl.*) die Wechselreiterei (*C.L.*); (*fig.*) das Sondieren.
kith [kɪθ], *s.*; (only in) – *and kin*, Verwandte und Bekannte.
kitten ['kɪtən], 1. *s.* das Kätzchen. 2. *v.n.* Junge werfen (*of cats*). **-ish,** *adj.* kätzchenhaft, (*fig.*) spielerisch.
kittiwake ['kɪtɪweɪk], *s.* die Dreizehenmöwe (*Orn.*).
kittl-e [kɪtl], *adj.* (*coll.*) kitzlig, heikel, schwer zu

behandeln(d) (*of things*), unberechenbar (*of persons*); *–e cattle*, unsicher.
kitty ['kɪtɪ], *s. see* **kitten**; die Kasse (*Cards, etc.*), (*coll.*) gemeinsamer Fonds.
kiwi ['kɪ:wɪ], *s.* der Kiwi, Schnepfenstrauß.
kleptomania [klɛpto'meɪnɪə], *s.* die Kleptomanie, der Stehltrieb, die Stehlsucht; **–c** [–ɪæk], *s.* der Kleptomane.
knack [næk], *s.* (*coll.*) die Fertigkeit, Geschicklichkeit, das Geschick (*at* or *of*, in *or* mit); der Kunstgriff, Kniff; *have the – of a th.*, den Kniff einer S. heraushaben, etwas weghaben.
knacker ['nækə], *s.* der Abdecker, Pferdeschlächter. **–y,** *s.* die Abdeckerei.
knag [næg], *s.* der Knorren, Knoten, Knast, Pflock. **–gy,** *adj.* knorrig, knotig.
knap [næp], *s.* der Gipfel, die Spitze.
knapsack ['næpsæk], *s.* der Tornister, Rucksack, Ranzen.
knapweed ['næpwɪ:d], *s.* die Hockenblume (*Bot.*).
knar [nɑ:], *s. see* **knag.**
knav–e [neɪv], *s.* der Bube (*Cards*); Schuft, Schurke, Spitzbube. **–ery,** *s.* die Schurkerei, Büberei, der Schelmenstreich. **–ish,** *adj.* spitzbübisch, schurkisch; *–ish trick*, der Bubenstreich. **–ishness,** *s.* die Schurkerei.
knead [nɪ:d], *v.a.* kneten, massieren, formen, bilden (*into*, zu). **–ing-trough,** *s.* der Backtrog.
knee [nɪ:], *s.* das Knie (*Anat.*); die Fußwurzel (*Vet.*); das Kniestück, die Kröpfung (*Mach.*); *bow the – to*, das Knie beugen vor; *bring s.o. to his –s*, einen in *or* auf die Knie zwingen; *housemaid's –*, entzündetes Knie; *on one's –s*, kniend; *go on one's –s*, auf die Knie fallen, niederknien (*to*, vor); *on the –s of the gods*, im Schoße der Götter. **––bending** *s.*, **–s bend,** *s.* die Kniebeuge. **––boots,** *pl.* Schaftstiefel, Kanonenstiefel, Kniestiefel (*pl.*). **––breeches,** *pl.* Kniehosen. **–cap,** *s.* die Kniescheibe (*Anat.*); das Knieleder (*Saddl.*). **–d,** *suff.*; *knock––d*, X-beinig; *weak––d*, (*fig.*) schwach, nachgiebig. **––deep,** *adj.* knietief. **––joint,** *s.* das Kniegelenk. **––pan,** *s.* die Kniescheibe. **––timber,** *s.* das Krummholz, Knieholz. **–l** [nɪ:l], *ir.v.n.* (*–l down*) knien, niederknien (*to*, vor). **–ler,** *s.* das Kniekissen.
knell [nɛl], 1. *s.* die Totenglocke, das Grabgeläute. 2. *v.n.* (*archaic*) läuten. 3. *v.a.* (durch Läuten) verkünden.
knelt [nɛlt], *see* **kneel.**
knew [nju:], *see* **know.**
knicker–bockers ['nɪkəbɔkəz], *pl.* Kniehosen; *a pair of –bockers*, eine Kniehose; (*archaic*) *see* **–s.** **–s** ['nɪkəz], *pl.* der (Damen)Schlüpfer, die Schlupfhose; *a pair of –s*, eine Schlupfhose.
knick-knack ['nɪknæk], *s.* der Tand, die Nippsache, Kleinigkeit; *pl.* der Trödelkram.
knife [nɑɪf], 1. *s.* das Messer; *– and fork*, das Besteck; (*coll.*) *have one's – in* or *get one's – into s.o.*, einen verfolgen, einem übelwollen, (*coll.*) einen gefressen haben; *war to the –*, der Krieg bis aufs Messer. 2. *v.a.* erstechen, erdolchen. **––board,** *s.* das Messerputzbrett. **––box,** *s.* der Besteckkasten. **––edge,** *s.* die Messerschneide; (*fig.*) die Schneide, haarscharfer Rand. **––grinder,** *s.* (hausierender) Scherenschleifer. **––rest,** *s.* das Messerbänkchen.
knight [nɑɪt], 1. *s.* der Ritter; unterste Adelsstufe (*England*); der Springer (*Chess*); (*fig.*) Begleiter, Kämpe. **––at-arms,** bewaffneter Ritter. **– of the road,** der Straßenräuber; Handlungsreisende(r). 2. *v.a.* zum Ritter schlagen. **–age,** *s.* (*collect.*) die Ritterschaft, Liste der Ritter. **––errant,** *s.* fahrender Ritter. **––errantry,** *s.* fahrendes Rittertum. **–hood,** *s.* der Ritterstand, die Ritterwürde; (*collect.*) Ritter (*pl.*), die Ritterschaft; (*fig.*) Ritterlichkeit, das Rittertum. **––hospitaller,** *s.* der Johanniter(ritter), Maltheser(ritter). **–liness,** *s.* die Ritterlichkeit. **–ly,** *adj.* ritterlich; Ritter–. **–'s cross,** *s.* brennende Liebe (*Bot.*). **––service,** *s.* der Ritterdienst.
knit [nɪt], 1. *ir.v.a.* stricken; verbinden, zusammenfügen (*Med.*); (*fig.*) vereinigen, (ver)knüpfen; *– up*, zusammenfügen; abschließen (*argument*); *– the brows*, die Brauen zusammenziehen, die Stirn **runzeln.** 2. *ir.v.n.* stricken; (*fig.*) (*– together*) sich verbinden; *well-–*, wohlgebaut. **–ted,** *adj.* Strick–; *–ted goods*, Strickwaren, Wirkwaren (*pl.*). **–ter,** *s.* der Stricker. **–ting,** *s.* das Stricken; Strickzeug; die Strickarbeit. **–ting-machine,** *s.* die Strickmaschine. **–ting-needle,** *s.* die Stricknadel. **–ting-wool,** *s.* das Strickgarn. **–wear,** *s.* die Strickwaren (*pl.*).
knob [nɔb], *s.* der Knopf, Knauf, Griff; Knorren, Auswuchs; (*coll.*) das Stückchen (*of sugar, etc.*); (*sl.*) die Birne; (*sl.*) *with –s on*, und wie! **–bed** [–d], *adj.*, **–by,** *adj.* knorrig, knotig. **–kerrie,** *s.* der Knüppel.
knock [nɔk], **1.** *v.n.* klopfen (*also of engines*), stoßen, schlagen, prallen (*against*, gegen). (*a*) (*with prepositions*) *– against*, zusammenstoßen gegen; (*coll.*) zufällig stoßen auf (*a th.*) *or* treffen (*a p.*). (*b*) (*with adverbs*) *– about*, sich umhertreiben, bummeln; *– off*, aufhören, Schluß machen (*with*, mit), Feierabend machen, Arbeit einstellen; *– together*, aneinanderstoßen; *– under*, nachgeben, sich geschlagen geben, zu Kreuze kriechen; *– up against*, zusammenstoßen mit; (*fig.*) zufällig treffen, in den Weg laufen (*Dat.*). **2.** *v.a.* klopfen, stoßen, schlagen; *– the door*, an die Tür klopfen; *– one's head*, mit dem Kopf stoßen (*against*, gegen). **(a)** (*with adverbs*) *– about*, umherstoßen, arg zurichten (*things*), böse mitnehmen, arg zusetzen (*persons*) (*sl.*) *– back*, heruntergießen (*a drink*); *– down*, niederschlagen, niederwerfen, zu Boden strecken, umstoßen, überfahren (*with a vehicle*), einreißen, abbrechen (*buildings, etc.*), (*fig.*) vernichten, zunichte machen; stark drücken (*prices*), zuschlagen, zusprechen (*to a p.*, einem) (*at auctions*); *– in*, einschlagen; *– off*, abbrechen (*also Typ.*), abschlagen, einstellen (*work*), Feierabend machen; (*coll.*) schnell erledigen, aufgeben, aufhören mit; (*coll.*) abziehen (*from price*); (*sl.*) klauen, (*sl.*) absetzen, abstoßen, an den Mann bringen (*sale*); *– out*, herausarbeiten; kampfunfähig machen, schlagen, besiegen, außer Gefecht bringen, zur Strecke bringen (*Boxing & fig.*), (*coll.*) erschöpfen; *– over*, unwerfen; überfahren; *– together*, zusammenbasteln, behelfsmäßig zusammenbauen; *– up*, in die Höhe schlagen; wecken; (*coll.*) erschöpfen; (*coll.*) schnell entwerfen; (*vulg.*) *–ed up*, schwanger. **(b)** (*with prepositions*) *– against*, stoßen gegen; *– into s.o.'s head*, einem einhämmern *or* einprägen; *– into shape*, Form *or* Gestalt geben, gestalten; *– two rooms into one*, zwei Räume zusammenlegen; *– off the price*, von dem Preise abziehen; *– on the head*, niederschlagen (*a p.*), vereiteln (*a th.*); *– the bottom out of*, zunichte machen. **3.** *s.* der Schlag, Stoß; das Anklopfen, Pochen (*at the door*). **––about,** *adj.* lärmend, unstet, ruhelos; strapazierfähig (*of clothes*); *––about act*, die Clownszene; *––about farce*, das Radaustück. **––down,** *adj.* niederschmetternd, überwältigend; *––down price*, äußerster Preis. **–er,** *s.* der Klopfer, Türklopfer; (*sl.*) Miesmacher, Kritikaster; Nörgler; (*sl.*) *up to the –er*, famos. **–er-up,** *s.* der Wecker (*person*). **––kneed,** *adj.* X-beinig, (*fig.*) hinkend, lahm. **––knees,** *pl.* X-Beine (*pl.*). **––out,** 1. *adj.* entscheidend (*as a blow*), Ausscheidungs– (*Sport*). 2. *s.* der Niederschlag, Knockout (*Boxing*); (*fig.*) entscheidender Schlag; (*sl.*) *he's* or *it's a ––out*, er (es) ist unwiderstehlich.
[1]**knoll** [noʊl], *s.* kleiner Hügel, die Kuppe.
[2]**knoll** [noʊl], 1. *s.* (*archaic*) das Geläut(e). 2. *v.a.* (*archaic*) (zu Grabe) läuten.
knop [nɔp], *s.* die Knospe (*Bot.*); der Knopf, Knauf.
knot [nɔt], 1. *s.* der Knoten, Knorren (*on a stem, etc.*); Ast (*in a board*); die Knospe, das Auge (*Bot.*); Stek, Stich, die Schleife, Docke (*of yarn*); Seemeile (*Naut.*); der Knutt, Isländischer Strandläufer (*Orn.*); (*fig.*) die Schwierigkeit, Verwicklung; die Gruppe, der Haufe; das Achselstück, die Epaulette; *granny's –*, falscher Knoten; *true-lovers' –*, der Liebesknoten; *cut the –*, den Knoten durchhauen; *tie a –*, einen Knoten machen. 2. *v.a.* knoten, verknüpfen, (*fig.*) verwickeln, verwirren; *tie o.s. into –s*, sich in Widersprüche verwickeln. 3. *v.n.* Knoten bilden (*also Bot.*). **––grass,** *s.* der Knöterich (*Bot.*). **––hole,** *s.* das Astloch (*in wood*). **–ted,** *adj.* knotig, knorrig (*as wood*); ver-

knotet (*as cord*); (*fig.*) verwickelt, verschlungen. **-ty,** *adj.* knotig, knorrig (*as wood*); (*fig.*) schwierig, verwickelt, verzwickt. **-work,** *s.* die Knüpfarbeit.
knout [naut], 1. *s.* die Knute. 2. *v.a.* die Knute geben (*Dat.*), mit der Knute schlagen.
know [nou] **1.** *ir.v.a.* wissen (*a matter*) (*of*, über *or* von), sich bewußt sein, kennen (*a p. or th.*), erkennen (*for*, als), unterscheiden (*from*, von), erleben, erfahren. (*a*) (*with pronouns, etc.*) *he -s it*, er weiß es; *he -s him*, er kennt ihn; *- him to be*, erkennen ihn als; wissen, daß er ist; *- how to do*, zu tun verstehen; *as well as he -s how*, mit Einsatz seines ganzen Könnens; *- what to do*, wissen was zu tun ist; (*coll.*) *- what's what*, sich auskennen; *before you - where you are*, ehe man sich's versieht, im Handumdrehen; *- which side one's bread is buttered*, seinen Vorteil kennen; *- by heart*, auswendig wissen *or* können; *- by name*, dem Namen nach kennen; *- by sight*, von Ansehen kennen; *- thyself!* erkenne dich selbst! (*b*) (*with nouns*) (*coll.*) *- the ropes*, sich gut auskennen; *- a thing or two*, etwas verstehen (*about*, von); *- the way*, den Weg kennen *or* wissen; *- one's way about*, sich auskennen *or* zurechtfinden (*a place*, in einem Ort). (*c*) (*with verbs*) *come to -*, erfahren; *come to be -n*, bekannt werden; *get to -*, kennenlernen; *let a p. -*, einen wissen lassen, einen verständigen; *make -n*, bekannt machen; *I have never -n him lie*, meines Wissens hat er niemals gelogen. **2.** *ir.v.n.* wissen (*about* or *of*, um *or* von), (*coll.*) im Bilde sein (*about*, über); *- better than to do*, es besser wissen als zu tun, zu vernünftig sein zu tun; *there is no -ing*, man kann nicht wissen; *not that I - of*, nicht, daß ich wüßte, nicht soviel ich weiß; (*coll.*) *I -*, ich weiß es; selbstverständlich; (*coll.*) *you -* or *don't you -*, nicht wahr, nämlich, verstehen Sie. **3.** *s.*; (*coll.*) *be in the -*, im Bilde sein, gut orientiert sein, eingeweiht sein, Bescheid wissen. **-able,** *adj.* (er)kennbar, kenntlich. **--all,** *s.* (*sl.*) der Alleinwisser, Besserwisser. **--how,** *s.* (*sl.*) die Kenntnis, Erfahrung. **-ing,** *adj.* geschickt, schlau, gerieben, durchtrieben, klug, verständig; *-ing look*, verständnisvoller Blick; (*coll.*) *-ing one*, der Schlauberger. **-ingly,** *adv.* wissentlich, absichtlich, vorsätzlich. **-ingness,** *s.* die Schlauheit, Klugheit. **-ledge** ['nɔlɪdʒ], *s.* (*only sing.*) das Wissen, Kenntnisse (*pl.*) (*of* (*Gen.*) *or* in (*with Dat.*)), die Kenntnis (*also Law*), Kunde, Bekanntschaft (*of a p.*, mit einem); *come to one's -ledge*, einem zur Kenntnis kommen; *be common -ledge*, allgemein bekannt sein; *extensive -ledge*, ausgebreitete Kenntnisse (*pl.*); *have -ledge of*, zur Kenntnis nehmen; *have carnal -ledge of*, geschlechtlichen Umgang haben mit; *out of all -ledge*, so daß man es nicht wiedererkennt; *tree of -ledge*, der Baum der Erkenntnis; (*not*) *to my -ledge*, (nicht) soviel ich weiß, meines Wissens; *to the best of my -ledge* (*and belief*), nach bestem Wissen (und Gewissen); *without my -ledge*, ohne mein Wissen. **-ledgeable,** *adj.* kenntnisreich. **-n** [noun], *adj.* bekannt, anerkannt; *well--n*, (wohl)-bekannt (*for*, durch; *as*, als).
knuckle [nʌkl], 1. *s.* der Knöchel, das (Finger)-Gelenk; Kniestück (*of veal*), Eisbein (*of pork*); *near the -*, gerade noch möglich, bis nahe an die Grenzen des Sittlichen; *rap on* or *over the -s*, der Verweis. 2. *v.a.* mit den Knöcheln pressen *or* reiben. 3. *v.n.*; *- down*, sich beugen, nachgeben (*under*, unter), sich unterwerfen (*under* (*Dat.*)); *- down to*, sich eifrig machen an; *- under*, sich beugen, nachgeben (*to*, unter), sich unterwerfen (*to* (*Dat.*)). **--bones,** *s.* das Knöchelspiel. **--duster,** *s.* der Schlagring, Totschläger. **--joint,** *s.* das (Knöchel- *or* Finger)Gelenk (*Anat.*), die Gliederfuge (*Mach.*).
knurl [nə:l], 1. *v.a.* rändeln, kordieren (*Mach.*). 2. *s.* der Knorren, Ast, Knoten.
knut [nʌt], *s.* der Stutzer, Geck, Zierbengel.
kopje ['kɔpɪ], *s.* kleiner Hügel (*S. Africa*).
Koran [ko'ra:n], *s.* der Koran.
kosher ['kouʃə], *adj.* koscher, rein (*Jew.* (*of food*)).
kotow [kɔ'tau], **kowtow** ['kautau]. 1. *s.* chinesische demütige Ehrenbezeigung. 2. *v.n.* eine Ehrenbezeigung machen (*to*, vor); (*fig.*) sich unterwürfig zeigen (*to* (*Dat.*)), kriechen (*to*, vor).
kraal [krɑ:l], *s.* der *or* das Kral, die Umzäunung, das Hottentottendorf.
kudos ['kju:dɔs], *s.* (*sl.*) der Ruf, Ruhm, das Ansehen, die Ehre.
kukri ['kukrɪ], *s.* der Ghurkadolch.
kulak ['ku:læk], *s.* der Großbauer.
kyanize ['kaɪənaɪz], *v.a.* kyanisieren, mit Sublimat tränken.

L

L, l [ɛl], *s.* das L, l. *See Index of Abbreviations.*
[1]**la** [lɑ:], *s.* die sechste Silbe der Solmisation (*Mus.*).
[2]**la** [lɑ:], *int.* sieh! sieh da! -, -! na, na!
laager [lɑ:gə], 1. *s.* das Burenlager, die Wagenburg. 2. *v.a.* & *n.* (sich) lagern.
lab [læb], *s.* (abbr. for *laboratory*) (*coll.*) das Labor.
label [leɪbl], 1. *s.* der Zettel, das Etikett, die Etikette, Aufschrift, Beschriftung; das Kodizill (*Law*); der Tournierkragen (*Her.*); die Kranzleiste (*Arch.*); (*fig.*) Kennzeichnung, Bezeichnung, Signatur, das Merkmal; *tie-on -*, der Anhänger; *stick-on -*, der Anklebezettel. 2. *v.a.* mit Zettel *or* Aufschrift versehen, etikettieren; (*fig.*) beschriften, bezeichnen, abstempeln (*as*, als).
labi-al ['leɪbɪəl], 1. *adj.* Lippen-, labial. 2. *s.* der Lippenlaut, Labial(laut). **-alize,** *v.n.* labialisieren. **-ate** [-ɪət], 1. *adj.* lippenförmig (*Bot.*). 2. *s.* der Lippenblütler. **-o-dental** ['leɪbɪo'dɛntl], 1. *adj.* labiodental (*sound*). 2. *s.* der Lippenzahnlaut, Reibelaut.
labil-e ['leɪbaɪl], *adj.* labil, unsicher. **-ity** [læ'bɪlɪtɪ], *s.* die Labilität.
laboratory [lə'bɔrətərɪ], *s.* das Laboratorium, Labor; die Werkstatt, Werkstätte; *- assistant*, der Laborant.
laborious [lə'bɔ:rɪəs], *adj.* mühselig, mühsam, mühevoll; arbeitsam, fleißig. **-ness,** *s.* die Mühseligkeit, Arbeitsamkeit, Emsigkeit, der Fleiß.
labour ['leɪbə], 1. *s.* die Arbeit; Mühe, Anstrengung, Beschwerde; Wehen (*pl.*), die Entbindung; Arbeiter (*pl.*), die Arbeiterschaft, der Arbeiterstand; *- camp*, *s.* die Arbeitslager; *- exchange*, *s.* das Arbeitsamt, der Arbeitsnachweis; *hard -*, die Zwangsarbeit; 9 *months* (*imprisonment with*) *hard -*, 9 Monate Zuchthaus; *have one's - for one's pains*, sich umsonst abmühen; *be in -*, in den Wehen liegen; *lose one's -*, sich umsonst anstrengen; *manual -*, körperliche Arbeit. 2. *v.n.* arbeiten (*at*, an), sich anstrengen, sich bemühen, sich abmühen, sich (*Dat.*) (alle *or* viel) Mühe geben (*for*, um); sich mühsam bewegen; schlingern, stampfen (*Naut.*); *- under*, zu kämpfen haben mit, zu leiden haben unter, kranken an (*Dat.*); *- under a delusion*, sich im Irrtum befinden. 3. *v.a.* mühsam fertigbringen *or* ausarbeiten; *- the point*, auf den Punkt ausführlich eingehen. **-age,** *s.* der Arbeitslohn, Arbeitsunkosten (*pl.*). **-ed,** *adj.* langsam, mühsam, gezwungen, schwerfällig. **-er,** *s.* (ungelernter) Arbeiter; *agricultural -er*, der Landmann, Landarbeiter; *casual -er*, der Gelegenheitsarbeiter; *day--er*, der Tagelöhner; *heavy manual -er*, der Schwerarbeiter. **-ing,** *adj.* arbeitend; werktätig, handwerksmäßig, Arbeits-, Arbeiter-; *-ing breath*, schwerer Atem; *-ing classes*, die Arbeiterbevölkerung. (*coll.*) **-ite,** *s.* der Anhänger *or* Abgeordnete der Arbeiterpartei. **- party,** die Arbeiterpartei. **--saving,** 1. *adj.* arbeitersparend. 2. *s.* die Arbeitsersparnis. **--service,** der Arbeitsdienst.
labret ['læbrɪt], *s.* der Lippenpflock.
laburnum [lə'bə:nəm], *s.* der Goldregen (*Bot.*).
labyrinth ['læbərɪnθ], *s.* das Labyrinth, der Irrgarten; (*fig.*) das Gewirr. **-ine** [-'rɪnθaɪn], *adj.* labyrinthisch; (*fig.*) verwickelt, wirr, verworren.
[1]**lac** [læk], *s.* der Gummilack. **--varnish,** *s.* der Lackfirnis.
[2]**lac** [læk], *s.* das Hunderttausend (Rupien).

lac-e [leɪs], 1. *s.* (geklöppelte) Spitze, Spitzen (*pl.*); die Tresse, Borte, Schnur; der Schnürsenkel, das Schuhband, der Schuhriemen. 2. *v.a.* (zu)-schnüren, festschnüren, zubinden; mit Spitzen besetzen, verbrämen; (*coll.*) mit Spirituosen versetzen; (*coll.*) durchprügeln; *–e through*, durchziehen (*with braid*). 3. *v.n.* sich schnüren (lassen). **-e-bobbin,** *s.* der Spitzenklöppel. **-e boots,** *pl.* Schnürstiefel (*pl.*). **-ed** [–t], *adj.* geschnürt, Schnür–; *–ed boots, see* **–e boots.** **-ing,** *s.* das Schnurband. **-e-maker,** *s.* der Spitzenklöppler. **-e-paper,** *s.* das Spitzenpapier. **-e-pillow,** *s.* das Klöppelkissen. **-e-work,** *s.* die Klöppelarbeit.

lacerat-e [ˈlæsəreɪt], *v.a.* zerreißen, zerfleischen; *–ed wound*, die Rißwunde. **-ion** [–ˈreɪʃən], *s.* die Zerreißung, Zerfleischung; der Riß, die Fleischwunde, Rißwunde; Verletzung (*also fig.*).

lacert-ian [læˈsəːʃən], *adj.* **-ine** [–sətɪn], *adj.* eidechsenartig, Eidechsen–.

laches [ˈlætʃɪz], *s.* die Vernachlässigung, Versäumnis, der Verzug (*Law*).

lachrym-al [ˈlækrɪməl], *adj.* Tränen–. **-ator** [–meɪtə], *s.* das Tränengas, der Augenreizstoff (*Mil.*). **-atory** [–ˈmeɪtərɪ], 1. *s.* das Tränengefäß. 2. *adj.* tränenerregend. **-ose** [–moʊs], *adj.* tränenreich, weinerlich, rührselig.

lacing, *s. see* **lace.**

lack [læk], 1. *v.a.* ermangeln (*Gen.*), fehlen an (*Dat.*), nicht haben, entbehren (*Acc.*); *he –s perseverance*, es mangelt ihm an Ausdauer; *he –s nothing in perseverance*, er läßt es nicht an Ausdauer fehlen. 2. *v.n.* fehlen, Mangel leiden (*in*, an). 3. *s.* der Mangel; das Fehlen; *for – of*, aus Mangel an; *there was no – of . . .*, es fehlte nicht an. . . . **-ing,** *adj.* fehlend, mangelnd, arm (*in*, an); *be –ing, see* **–** 2; (*coll.*) einfältig *or* blöde sein. **--lustre,** *adj.* glanzlos, matt.

lackadaisical [lækəˈdaɪzɪkl], *adj.* (*coll.*) schmachtend; schlapp, schlaff.

lacker, *s. see* **lacquer.**

lackey [ˈlækɪ], 1. *s.* der Lakai. 2. *v.n.* unterwürfig dienen *or* aufwarten, den Lakai *or* Schranzen machen (*for s.o.*, einem).

laconi-c [ləˈkɒnɪk], *adj.* lakonisch, kurz und treffend, kurz angebunden, wortkarg. **-cism** [–nɪsɪzm], *s.*, **-sm** [ˈlækənɪzm], *s.* treffende Kürze, knappe *or* gedrängte Redeweise, der Lakonismus.

lacquer [ˈlækə], 1. *v.a.* lackieren. 2. *s.* der Lack, Lackfirnis, die Lackarbeit. **--work,** *s.* die Lackarbeit.

lacquey, *s. see* **lackey.**

lacrosse [ləˈkrɒs], *s.* kanadisches Nationalballspiel.

lact-ate [ˈlækteɪt], *s.* das Laktat; *–ate of*, milchsauer. **-ation** [–ˈteɪʃən], *s.* das Säugen, Stillen. **-eal** [–tɪəl], *adj.* milchig, Milch–. **-eals** [–tɪəlz], *pl.* Milchgefäße, Lymphgefäße (*pl.*). **-ic** [–tɪk], *adj.* milchig, Milch–, milchsauer; *–ic fermentation*, die Milchgärung. **-ometer** [–ˈtɒmɪtə], *s.* die Milchwaage. **-ose** [–toʊs], *s.* der Milchzucker.

lacun-a [læˈkjuːnə], *s.* (pl. *–ae*) die Lücke; der Zwischenraum, Hohlraum (*Anat.*, *Bot.*). **-ar** [–nɑː], 1. *s.* die Kassettendecke (*Arch.*). 2. *adj.* lückig.

lad [læd], *s.*, der Junge, Bursche, Jüngling; (*coll.*) lustiger Geselle.

ladder [ˈlædə], *s.* die Leiter; (*fig.*) Stufenleiter; Laufmasche (*in stockings*); *accommodation –*, die Fallreeptreppe (*Naut.*); *rope –*, die Strickleiter; *step –*, die Treppenleiter; *– to fame*, der Weg zur Berühmtheit; *get one's foot on the –*, einen Anfang machen. **--proof,** *adj.* maschenfest. **--rope,** *s.* das Fallreep.

lad-e [leɪd], *v.a.* laden, beladen (*a ship, etc.*), aufladen, verladen (*goods*); ausschöpfen (*water, etc.*); (*fig.*) verteilen. **-en,** *adj.* beladen. **-ing,** *s.* das Laden, Verladen; die Ladung, Fracht.

la-di-da [ˈlɑːdɪˈdɑː], *adj.* (*sl.*) zimperlich, etepetete.

ladle [leɪdl], 1. *s.* der Schöpflöffel, Kochlöffel; die Schaufel (*Tech.*). 2. *v.a.* (*– out*) ausschöpfen, auslöffeln.

lady [ˈleɪdɪ], *s.* die Dame; Edelfrau, Freifrau, Lady; Frau von . . . (*as title*); (*Poet.*) Herrin, Gemahlin; *leading –*, die Hauptdarstellerin, erste Liebhaberin (*Theat.*); *not a* or *no –*, keine feine Dame; *Our* (*Blessed*) *–*, die Mutter Gottes, Unsere Liebe Frau; *Church of Our –*, die Marienkirche, Frauenkirche; *young –*, (gnädiges) Fräulein; (*coll.*) die Freundin, der Schatz, die Verlobte. **--bird,** *s.* die Marienkäfer (*Ent.*). **--chapel,** *s.* die Marienkapelle. **--cow,** *s. see* **--bird.** **--Day,** *s.* Mariä Verkündigung (*25th March*). **– doctor,** die Ärztin. **–friend,** die Freundin. **--fern,** *s.* der Frauenfarn (*Bot.*). **– help,** die Stütze der Hausfrau. **--in-waiting,** *s.* königliche Kammerfrau, die Hofdame. **--killer,** *s.* der Herzenbrecher, Don Juan. **-like,** *adj.* damenhaft. **--love,** *s.* (*hum.*) die Geliebte. **– Mayoress,** *s.* die Gemahlin des Oberbürgermeisters. **–'s glove,** der Fingerhut (*Bot.*). **–'s handbag,** *s.* die Damenhandtasche. **-ship,** *s.* gnädige Frau, gnädiges Fräulein (*as title*). **–'s laces,** das Mariengras (*Bot.*). **–'s maid,** die Kammerzofe. **–'s man (ladies' man),** *s.* der Damenheld, Salonheld. **–'s mantle,** der Marienmantel, Frauenmantel (*Bot.*). **--smock,** *s.* das Wiesenschaumkraut (*Bot.*). **–'s slipper,** *s.* der Frauenschuh (*Bot.*).

laevulose [ˈlɪːvjəloʊs], *s.* der Fruchtzucker.

[1]**lag** [læg], 1. *v.n.* zögern, langsam gehen, zurückbleiben, sich Zeit lassen; *– behind*, zurückbleiben *or* zurückstehen hinter, nachstehen, nachhinken (*Dat.*); nacheilen (*in phase*) (*Elec.*). 2. *s.* die Verzögerung; der Zeitabstand (*Tech.*); die Rücktrift (*Av.*), Nacheilung (*Elec.*). **-gard** [ˈlægəd], 1. *adj.* zögernd, langsam, lässig, saumselig, träge. 2. *s.* der Zauderer, Saumselige(r), *m.*; der Nachzügler, (*coll.*) Schlappschwanz. **-ging,** *adj.* zögernd, zaudernd.

[2]**lag** [læg], 1. *v.a.* (*sl.*) ins Loch stecken. 2. *s.* (*sl.*) der Knastschieber.

[3]**lag,** 1. *s.* die Daube. 2. *v.a.* verkleiden, mit Dauben belegen (*a boiler, etc.*). **-ging,** *s. see* **–,** 1.

lagan [ˈlægən], *s.* versenktes Wrackgut (*Naut.*).

lager [lɑːgə], *s.* das Lagerbier.

lagoon [ləˈguːn], *s.* die Lagune.

laic [ˈleɪɪk], 1. *s.* der Laie. 2. *adj.* weltlich, laienhaft, Laien–. **-al** [–l], *adj. see* **–,** 2. **-ize** [–saɪz], *v.a.* verweltlichen, säkularisieren.

laid [leɪd], *see* **lay;** (*sl.*) *– off*, arbeitslos; *– out*, (geschmackvoll), angelegt (*as a garden*); angelegt, angewandt (*as money*); (*coll.*) *– up*, bettlägerig (*with*, an); aufgehäuft, angesammelt (*as a stock*); abgetakelt (*as a boat*); *– paper*, gestreiftes *or* geripptes Papier.

lain [leɪn], *see* **lie.**

lair [ˈlɛːə], *s.* das Lager (*of animals*).

laird [lɛːɹd], *s.* der Gutsherr (*Scots*).

laissez-faire [ˈleɪseɪˈfɛːə], *s.* das Gehenlassen.

laity [ˈleɪɪtɪ], *s.* (*pl. constr.*) die Laien (*pl.*), der Laienstand.

[1]**lake** [leɪk], *s.* der See; *on the –*, am See; *– district*, das Seengebiet von Cumberland und Westmorland; *--dwellers, pl.* Pfahlbaubewohner (*pl.*); *--dwellings, pl.* Pfahlbauten (*pl.*); *– poets*, Dichter der englischen Seeschule. **--side,** *s.* das Seeufer, die Seelandschaft; *by the --side*, am See.

[2]**lake** [leɪk], *s.* roter Farbstoff.

lakh [læk], *s. see* **lac.**

lam [læm], 1. *v.a.* (*sl.*) verdreschen, vermöbeln. 2. *s.*; (*sl.*) *on the –*, auf der Flucht.

lama [ˈlɑːmə], *s.* buddhistischer Priester. **-sery** [lɑˈmɑːsərɪ], *s.* buddhistisches Kloster.

lamb [læm], 1. *s.* das Lamm; junges Hammelfleisch; *with –*, trächtig (*of sheep*). 2. *v.n.* lammen. **-ing time,** die Lammzeit. **-kin** [–kɪn], *s.* das Lämmchen. **-like,** *adj.* (*fig.*) sanft, lammfromm; **-skin,** *s.* das Lammfell. **–'s lettuce,** *s.* der Feldsalat (*Bot.*). **–'s-wool,** *s.* die Schafwolle, Lammwolle.

lamben-cy [ˈlæmbənsɪ], *s.* das Strahlen, Funkeln, Züngeln. **-t** [–ənt], *adj.* strahlend, züngelnd, funkelnd (*of light, also fig.*).

lame [leɪm], 1. *adj.* lahm, hinkend (*in*, auf); (*fig.*) unbefriedigend, fehlerhaft, mangelhaft; (*coll.*) *– duck*, krankes Huhn, der Pechvogel; Zahlungsunfähige(r), *m.*, fauler Kunde, der Pleitegeier (*C.L.*); *– excuse*, faule Ausrede; *– verse*, hinkender Vers. 2. *v.a.* lähmen, lahm schlagen. **-ness,** *s.* die Lahmheit, Lähmung; (*fig.*) Schwäche.

lamella [læ'mɛlə], *s.* das Plättchen, Blättchen, die Lamelle. **–r** [–lɑ:], **–te(d)** ['læməleɪt(ɪd)], *adj.* blätterig, lamellenartig.
lameness, *s. see* **lame.**
lament [lə'mɛnt], 1. *v.a.* beklagen, bejammern, betrauern, beweinen. 2. *v.n.* (weh)klagen, jammern, trauern (*for* or *over*, um). 3. *s.* die (Weh)Klage, der Jammer; das Klagelied. **–able** ['læməntəbl], *adj.* beklagenswert; kläglich, jammervoll, jämmerlich, elend. **–ation** [–'teɪʃən], *s.* die Wehklage. **–ations,** *pl.* (*B.*) Klagelieder Jeremiä (*pl.*). **–ed** [lə'mɛntɪd], *adj.* betrauert; *the late –ed*, kürzlich Verstorbene(r).
lamina ['læmɪnə], *s.* das Plättchen, die Schuppe; Blattfläche (*Bot.*); dünne Schicht (*Geol.*). **–r** [–ɑ:], **–ry** [–ərɪ], **–te** [–ət], *adj.* in Plättchen, blätterig. **–te** [–eɪt], 1. *v.a.* auswalzen, strecken (*Metals*); lamellieren (*Elec.*); laminieren (*Spin.*). 2. *v.n.* sich blättern. **–ted** [–eɪtɪd], *adj.* in Schichten, blätterig. **–tion** [–'neɪʃən], *s.* das Plättchen; das (Transformator)Blech.
Lammas ['læməs], **–day, –tide,** *s.* Petri Kettenfeier (*1st Aug.*).
lamp [læmp], *s.* die Lampe; Ampel; (*fig.*) Leuchte, das Licht; *street–*, die Straßenlaterne. **– -black,** *s.* der Lampenruß, Gasruß, Kienruß, Oelruß, das Rußschwarz, Lampenschwarz. **– -chimney,** *s.*, **– -glass,** *s.* der (Lampen)Zylinder. **– -holder,** *s.* die (Lampen)Fassung. **–light,** *s.* das Lampenlicht. **– -lighter,** *s.* der Laternenanzünder. **– -oil,** *s.* das Brennöl, Leuchtöl. **– -post,** *s.* der Laternenpfahl. **– -shade,** *s.* der Lampenschirm, die Lampenglocke.
lampoon [læm'pu:n], 1. *s.* die Schmähschrift, Satire. 2. *v.a.* eine Schmähschrift machen auf (*Acc.*), schmähen. **–er,** *s.* der Verfasser einer Schmähschrift.
lamprey ['læmprɪ], *s.* das Neunauge (*Ichth.*).
lanate ['leɪneɪt], *adj.* wollig, Woll–.
lance [lɑ:ns], 1. *s.* die Lanze, der Speer; *free– –*, 1. *s.* der Freischärler; freier Ausüber einer Kunst. 2. *adj.* frei, unabhängig. 2. *v.a.* (mit einer Lanze) durchbohren; (mit einer Lanzette) aufschneiden (*Surg.*). **– -corporal,** *s.* Gefreite(r), *m.* **–olate** –ɪəleɪt], *adj.* lanzettförmig, spitzzulaufend (*Bot.*). **–r** [–ə], *s.* der Ulan. **–rs** [–əz], *pl.* (*sing. constr.*) Lanciers (*pl.*) (*Dance*). **–t** [–ɪt], *s.* die Lanzette. **–t-arch,** *s.* der Spitzbogen. **–t-window,** *s.* das Spitzbogenfenster.
land [lænd], 1. *s.* das Land; der Grund und Boden, Grundbesitz, das Grundstück; (*fig.*) das Reich, Gebiet; *by –*, zu Lande; *– of the leal*, der Himmel (*Scots*); *pl.* das Gelände, Ländereien (*pl.*); Felder (*pl.*) (*of gun barrel*); *– of the living*, das Reich der Lebendigen; *make* (*the*) *–*, Land sichten (*Naut.*); *– of Nod*, der Schlaf; *ploughed –*, bebauter Acker; *see how the – lies*, sehen, wie die Sache steht; sich umsehen, wie die Dinge liegen. 2. *v.a.* landen (*troops, etc.*), ans Land bringen (*fish*), löschen, ausladen (*cargo*), absetzen, niedersetzen (*a passenger*); (*fig. coll.*) versetzen (*a blow*); gewinnen, kriegen; ans Ziel bringen (*Racing*); *– a p. in a difficulty*, einen in eine Klemme bringen *or* verwickeln; (*coll.*) *– o.s. in* or *be –ed in*, geraten in; *be –ed on*, landen auf. 3. *v.n.* landen, aussteigen (*of passengers*), anlegen (*of ships*), ans Ziel kommen (*Racing*); (*fig.*) ankommen, gelangen; *– on one's head*, auf den Kopf fallen; *– on instruments*, eine Blindlandung machen (*Av.*). **– -agent,** *s.* der Güteragent (*C.L.*). **– -bank,** *s.* die Bodenkreditanstalt, Grundkreditbank, Hypothekenbank. **– -breeze,** *s.* der Landwind. **–ed,** *adj.* Land–, Grund–; *–ed gentry*, niederer Landadel; *–ed interest*, das Interesse des Grundbesitzers; *–ed nobility*, der Landadel; *–ed property*, das Grundeigentum, der Landbesitz, Ländereien (*pl.*); *–ed proprietor*, der Grundbesitzer, Grundeigentümer. **–fall,** *s.* die Landsichtung (*Naut.*), Landung (*Av.*). **– fighting,** *s.* der Erdkampf. **– -forces,** *pl.* Erdtruppen (*pl.*), die Landmacht, das Landheer. **– -girl,** *s.* die Erntearbeiterin, Erntehelferin. **– -grabber,** *s.* der Landräuber, Landschnapper. **–grave,** *s.* der Landgraf. **–holder,** *s.* der Gutsbesitzer, Grundeigentümer. **–ing,** *s.* das Landen, die Landung (*of passengers & aircraft*), das Anlegen (*of ships*), Ausladen (*of goods*); der Treppenabsatz (*of stairs*); *see* **–ing place**; *blind –ing*, die Blindlandung (*Av.*); *forced –ing*, die Notlandung (*Av.*); *pancake –ing*, die Durchsacklandung (*Av.*); *rough –ing*, die Bumslandung (*Av.*); *make a safe –ing*, glücklich landen (*Av.*). **–ing-apron,** *s.* das Schleppsegel (*for seaplanes*). **–ing-charges,** *pl.* die Löschgebühr. **–ing-craft,** das Landungsboot. **–ing-deck,** *s.* das Flugdeck. **–ing facilities,** die Landeanlage. **–ing-gear,** das Fahrwerk, Fahrgestell (*Av.*). **–ing-ground,** der Landeplatz (*Av.*). **–ing-light,** das Landelicht (*Av.*). **–ing-net,** *s.* der Hamen, Ketscher. **–ing-party,** das Landungskommando. **–ing-place,** *s.* der Landungsplatz (*Naut.*). **–ing-stage,** *s.* die Landungsbrücke, schwimmende Landungsstelle. **–ing-strip,** die Landebahn, das Rollfeld (*Av.*). **–ing-wheel,** das Laufrad (*Av.*). **– -jobber,** *s.* der Gütermakler. **–lady,** *s.* die Wirtin. **– -league,** *s.* irische Landliga. **– -locked,** *adj.* vom Lande eingeschlossen. **–lord,** *s.* der Gutsherr, Grundbesitzer; Hausbesitzer, Hausherr, Hauswirt; Gastwirt, Wirt. **– -loper,** *s.* der Landstreicher. **– -lubber,** *s.* die Landratte (*Naut.*). **–mark,** *s.* der Grenzstein, die Grenzlinie, (*fig.*) der Markstein, das Wahrzeichen, der Wendepunkt. **–mine,** *s.* die Flattermine (*Mil.*); die Fallschirmbombe (*Av.*). **–owner,** *s.* der Grundbesitzer, Gutsbesitzer. **–owning,** *adj.* grundbesitzend. **–rail,** *s.* der Wiesenläufer (*Orn.*). **– reform,** *s.* die Bodenreform. **– register,** *s.* das Grundbuch. **–scape,** *s.* die Landschaft; *–scape-gardening*, *s.* die Landschaftsgärtnerei; *–scape-painter*, *s.* der Landschaftsmaler. **– -shark,** *s.* (*sl.*) der Halsabschneider (*Naut.*); (*Amer.*) *see* **– -grabber.** **–slide,** *s.* der Erdrutsch (*Geol.*), (*fig.*) Zusammenbruch, Umsturz, Umschwung; politische Umwälzung, überwältigender Sieg (*Pol.*). **–slip,** *s.* der Erdrutsch, Bergsturz. **–sman,** *s.* der Landbewohner. **– -surveyor,** *s.* der Landmesser. **– -tax,** *s.* die Grundsteuer. **–ward** [–wəd], *adj.* landwärts gelegen. **–ward(s)** [–wədz], *adv.* landwärts.
landau ['lændɔ:], *s.* der Landauer; *state –*, die Staatskutsche, Karosse, der Staatswagen. **–let** [–dolɛt], *s.* der Halblandauer.
lane [leɪn], *s.* der Heckenweg, Pfad (*in the country*); die Gasse, das Gäßchen (*in towns*); der Durchhau, die Schneise (*in a wood*); das Spalier (*of persons*); (*fig.*) die Durchfahrt (*in ice*), Sperrlücke (*in minefield*); *air –*, die Flugschneise (*Av.*); *it is a long – that has no turning*, selbst der längste Weg *or* Tag hat einmal ein Ende.
lang syne ['læŋ'zaɪn], (*Scots*) 1. *adv.* lange her, längst, vor langer Zeit. 2. *s.*; *auld –*, längst vergangene Zeit.
language ['læŋgwɪdʒ], *s.* die Sprache; Worte, Reden (*pl.*); die Ausdrucksweise, Diktion; Terminologie, der Stil; *bad –*, Schimpfworte, gemeine Ausdrücke (*pl.*); *strong –*, Kraftausdrücke (*pl.*).
langu–id ['læŋgwɪd], *adj.* schlaff, matt, mutlos, lappig; träge, schleppend; flau (*C.L.*). **–idness,** *s.* die Mattigkeit, Schlaffheit, Flauheit. **–ish** [–wɪʃ], *v.n.* matt *or* schwach *or* schlaff werden, erschlaffen, erlahmen (*as interest*); dahinsiechen, dahinwelken; verschmachten; sich härmen, schmachten (*for*, nach); darniederliegen (*as trade*). **–ishing,** *adj.* schmachtend; lau, flau (*C.L.*). **–or** ['læŋgə], *s.* die Schwäche, Abspannung, Abgespanntheit, Mattigkeit, Schlaffheit, Trägheit, Stumpfheit, Lauheit, Flauheit. **–orous** [–ərəs], *adj.* matt, schlaff; drückend, schwül.
lank [læŋk], *adj.* mager, lang und dünn, schlank, schmächtig; *– hair*, schlichte *or* glatte Haare (*pl.*). **–iness, –ness,** *s.* die Magerkeit, Schlankheit, Schmächtigkeit. **–y,** *adv.* mager, hager, lang und dünn, hoch aufgeschossen.
lanner ['lænə], *s.* das Weibchen des Würgfalken *or* Blaufußfalken. **–et** [–ərɛt], *s.* männlicher Würgfalke *or* Blaufußfalke.
lanoline ['lænəlɪn], *s.* das Lanolin, Schafwollfett.
lansquenet ['lænskənət], *s.* der Landsknecht (*Cards*).
lantern ['læntən], *s.* die Laterne; der Laternenraum (*of lighthouse*); durchbrochenes Türmchen, der Dachaufsatz (*Arch.*); *Chinese –*, der Lampion; *dark –*, die Blendlaterne. **– -jawed,** *adj.* hohlwangig. **– -jaws,** *pl.* eingefallenes *or* hageres

Gesicht. **--lecture,** *s.* der Lichtbildervortrag. **--slide,** *s.* das Lichtbild, Diopositiv, die Lichtbildplatte.
lanyard ['lænjəd], *s.* das Taljereep (*Naut.*); die Schnur, Schleife, Schlinge.
¹lap [læp], *s.* der Schoß; *on the – of the gods,* im Schoß der Götter. **--dog,** *s.* der Schoßhund. **-ful,** *s.* der Schoßvoll.
²lap [læp], 1. *v.a.* umschlagen, wickeln, falten, einwickeln, einschlagen (*in,* in (*Acc.*)); übereinanderlegen (*boards, etc.*); (*fig.*) (ein)hüllen, einschließen, umgeben, betten (*in,* in (*Acc.*)); überrunden (*Racing*). 2. *v.n.* (*– over*) vorstehen, hinübergreifen *or* hineinragen (*into* or *on to,* in *or* auf). 3. der Vorstoß; Falz (*Bookb.*); Wickel (*Spin.*); übergreifende Kante; die Runde, der Lauf (*Racing*). **-ping,** *s.* das Übergreifen. **-(ping)-machine,** *s.* die Wickelmaschine.
³lap, 1. *s.* das Auflecken, Plätschern, Anschlagen. 2. *v.a.* auflecken (*of animals*); plätschern an *or* gegen (*of water*); (*coll.*) *– up,* verschlingen, verzehren. 3. *v.n.* plätschern, lecken.
lapel [lə'pɛl], *s.* der (Rock)Aufschlag.
lapida-ry ['læpɪdərɪ], 1. *adj.* Stein-, Lapidar-; *-ry style,* wuchtiger Stil. 2. *s.* der Steinschneider. **-te** [-deɪt], *v.a.* steinigen. **-tion** [-'deɪʃən], *s.* die Steinigung.
lapis lazuli ['læpɪs'læʒjulaɪ], der Lasurstein.
lappet ['læpɪt], *s.* der Zipfel (*of a coat*); Lappen (*of skin*).
lapse [læps], 1. *s.* das Dahingleiten; der Lauf (*of a stream*); Verlauf, Ablauf, die Zeitspanne (*of time*); das Fallen, Sinken, Verfallen (*into indolence, etc.*); Abgehen, Abweichen, Abfallen (*from grace, etc.*); der Verfall, Heimfall, das Erlöschen (*Law*); der Fehler, Fehltritt, Mißgriff, das Versehen, die Versäumnis, Entgleisung; der (Sünden)Fall (*of Adam*); *after the – of a considerable time,* nachdem eine beträchtliche Zeit verstrichen war. 2. *v.n.* dahingleiten; verstreichen, verfließen, verlaufen (*as time*); fallen, straucheln, einen Fehltritt tun; verfallen, geraten (*into,* in (*Acc.*)); abfallen (*from,* von); verfallen, heimfallen, erlöschen (*Law*).
lapwing ['læpwɪŋ], *s.* der Kiebitz (*Orn.*).
larboard ['lɑ:bɔ:d], *s.* (*archaic*) das Backbord (*Naut.*).
larceny ['lɑ:sənɪ], *s.* der Diebstahl.
larch [lɑ:tʃ], *s.* die Lärche (*Bot.*).
lard [lɑ:d], 1. *s.* das Schweinefett, Schmalz. 2. *v.a.* spicken (*meat; also fig.*). **-aceous** [-'deɪʃəs], *adj.* fettartig, speckartig (*Med.*). **-er** [-ə], *s.* die Speisekammer, der Speiseschrank. **-ing-needle,** *s.* die Spicknadel. **-on** ['lɑ:dən], *s.* **-oon** [-du:n] *s.* der Speckstreifen.
large [lɑ:dʒ], *adj.* groß, reichlich, beträchtlich, bedeutend; weit, geräumig, ausgedehnt, umfassend; dick, stark; *as – as life,* in Lebensgröße; *at –,* auf freiem Fuß; als Ganzes, in der Gesamtheit; *talk at –,* in den Tag hineinreden; *by and –,* im großen (und) ganzen; *on the – side,* etwas zu weit (*of clothes*); *world at –,* gesamte Welt; *treat* (*of a th.*) *at –,* (eine S.) ausführlich besprechen. **--boned,** *adj.* starkknochig. **--hearted,** *adj.* großherzig, wohltätig. **--limbed,** *adj.* starkgliederig. **-ly,** *adv.* reichlich, in großem Umfange, zum großen Teil, großenteils, größtenteils. **--minded,** *adj.* weitherzig, edel gesinnt, großdenkend, tolerant. **--mindedness,** *s.* edle Gesinnung, die Weitherzigkeit, Toleranz. **-ness,** *s.* die Größe, Weite, Ausdehnung, der Umfang; die Großzügigkeit, Freigebigkeit. **--scale,** *adj.* Groß-. **--sized,** *adj.* von großem Format; groß. **-ss(e),** [-'dʒɛs], *s.* die Freigebigkeit; die Gabe, Schenkung.
lariat ['lærɪət], *s.* der *or* das Lasso.
¹lark [lɑ:k], *s.* die Lerche (*Orn.*); *rise with the –,* mit den Hühnern aufstehen.
²lark [lɑ:k], 1. *s.* (*coll.*) der Spaß, Ulk, Jux, Feez; *what a –!* zum Schießen! *have a –,* seinen Spaß haben. 2. *v.n.* (*– about*) tolle Streiche machen.
larkspur ['lɑ:kspə:], *s.* der Rittersporn (*Bot.*).
larrikin ['lærɪkɪn], *s.* (*sl.*) der Raufbold, Lümmel.
larrup ['lærəp], *v.a.* (*sl.*) verdreschen, vermöbeln.
larva ['lɑ:və], *s.* die Larve, Puppe (*Ent.*). **-l** [-əl], *adj.* Larven-, Raupen-.
laryn-geal [læ'rɪndʒəl], *adj.* Kehlkopf-. **-gitis** [-'dʒaɪtɪs], *s.* die Kehlkopfentzündung. **-gophone** [-'rɪŋgəfoun], *s.* das Kehlkopfmikrophon (*Av.*). **-goscope** [-'rɪŋgəskoup], *s.* der Kehlkopfspiegel (*Med.*). **-x** ['lærɪŋks], *s.* der Kehlkopf (*Anat.*).
Lascar ['læskə], *s.* indischer Matrose.
lascivious [læ'sɪvɪəs], *adj.* lüstern, geil, unzüchtig; **-ness,** *s.* die Geilheit, Lüsternheit.
¹lash [læʃ], 1. *s.* der Peitschenhieb; die Prügelstrafe; Peitschenschnur; (*fig.*) die Geißel, Rute. 2. *v.a.* peitschen, schlagen, hauen; peitschen an, schlagen gegen (*of water*); (*fig.*) geißeln, verspotten; treiben (*into,* zu); *– o.s. into a fury,* wütend werden; *the horse -ed its tail,* das Pferd schlug um sich mit dem Schwanz. 3. *v.n.*; *– down,* niederprasseln (*of rain*); *– out,* um sich schlagen, hinten ausschlagen (*as a horse*); (*fig.*) ausbrechen (*into,* in). **-er,** *s.* der Überfall (*of water*); das Wehr. **-ing,** *s.* das Peitschen, Geißeln; die Tracht Prügel. **-ings,** *pl.* (*sl.*) die Fülle (*of,* an), Menge, Massen (*pl.*) (*of,* von).
²lash [læʃ], *v.a.* festmachen, festbinden (*to* or *on,* an), laschen, zurren, (*Naut.*); *– up,* einzurren, sorren (*Naut.*). **-ing,** *s.* die Zurrung, Zeisung, Lasching, Laschung, das Gebinde; Sorrtau, Rödeltau (*Naut.*); *square -ing,* der Bockschnürbund.
lass [læs], *s.* (*Scots & coll.*) das Mädchen; (*Poet.*) die Liebste, der Schatz. **-ie,** *s.* (*Scots*) kleines Mädchen.
lassitude ['læsɪtju:d], *s.* die Müdigkeit, Mattigkeit, Abspannung, Abgespanntheit.
lasso ['læsu:], 1. *s.* der *or* das Lasso. 2. *v.a.* mit dem Lasso fangen.
¹last [lɑ:st], 1. *adj.* letzt; vorig, vergangen; äußerst, höchst; geringst. (*a*) (*with nouns*) *in the – analysis,* letzten Endes; *the – hope,* die einzig übrigbleibende Hoffnung; *of the – importance,* von der äußersten *or* höchsten Wichtigkeit; *the – judgment,* Jüngstes Gericht; *be on one's – legs,* auf dem letzten Loche pfeifen; *to the – man,* bis auf den letzten Mann; *– meal,* die Henkermahlzeit; *– night,* gestern abend; *the – post,* der Zapfenstreich; *– sacrament,* das Sterbesakrament; *the – thing in . . .,* das Neueste in . . .; *for the – time,* zum letzten Male. (*b*) (*with numerals, etc.*) *– but one,* vorletzt; *– but two,* drittletzt; *– of all,* zum Schluß, endlich, zuletzt, nicht zum wenigsten, allerletzt. 2. *s.*; *the –,* der, die *or* das Letzte *or* Hinterste; das Ende; der Tod. (*a*) (*with verbs*) *breathe one's –,* den letzten Atem aushauchen, den Geist aufgeben; *hear* (*see*) *the – of,* nichts mehr hören (sehen) von; *look one's – on,* den letzten Blick werfen auf. (*b*) (*with prepositions*) *at –,* schließlich, zuletzt; *at long –,* zu guter Letzt; *to the –,* bis zum Ende. 3. *adv.* zuletzt, zum letzten Mal, an letzter Stelle; *– not least,* nicht zuletzt, nicht zum wenigsten, zuletzt aber nicht zumindest. **-ly,** *adv.* zuletzt, schließlich, zum Schluß.
²last [lɑ:st], 1. *v.n.* dauern, bleiben, anhalten, bestehen, währen; (sich) halten (*as colour*); (also *– out*) hinreichen, ausreichen; (*with Dat. person*) ausreichen für, hinreichen für, genügen (*Dat.*); *– well,* dauerhaft sein. 2. *v.a.*; *– out,* ebenso lange aushalten wie, länger aushalten als (*a p.*). **-ing,** *adj.* dauernd, dauerhaft, nachhaltig, anhaltend, beständig; echt, haltbar (*as colour*). **-ness,** *s.* die Dauer(haftigkeit).
³last [lɑ:st], *s.* der Leisten; *put on the –,* über den Leisten schlagen; *stick to one's –,* bei seinem Leisten bleiben.
⁴last [lɑ:st], *s.*; *– of herrings,* 12 Faß Heringe; *– of wheat,* etwa 3.000 l. Weizen; *– of wool,* etwa 2.000 kg. Wolle.
latch [lætʃ], 1. *s.* die Klinke, der Drücker; das Sicherheitsschloß, Schnappschloß; *on the –,* (nur) eingeklinkt. 2. *v.a.* einklinken, zuklinken, zuschließen. 3. *v.n.* sich klinken lassen. **--key,** *s.* der Haus(tür)schlüssel, Schnappschloßschlüssel, Drücker.
latchet ['lætʃɪt], *s.* (*B.*) der Schuhriemen.
late [leɪt], 1. *adj.* spät; zu spät, verspätet; vorgerückt; verstorben, selig; früher, ehemalig, einstig, vormalig; jüngst; *be –,* sich verspäten, Verspätung haben; zurück *or* rückständig sein; *be – in developing,* sich spät entwickeln. *my – brother,* mein seliger *or* verstorbener Bruder; *at a – hour,*

zu später Stunde, sehr spät; *keep – hours*, spät nach Hause kommen, spät aufbleiben; *– owner*, früherer Besitzer; *of – years*, seit einigen Jahren, in den letzten Jahren. 2. *adv.* spät; *as – as yesterday*, noch gestern; *– in the day*, spät am Tage, zu später Stunde; (*coll.*) fast zu spät; *of –*, kürzlich, neulich, in letzter Zeit, seit einiger Zeit; *– of London*, früher wohnhaft in London. **–comer,** *s.* der Spätling, Nachzügler. **––fee,** *s.* der Portozuschlag nach Postschluß. **–ly,** *adv.* kürzlich, vor kurzem, jüngst, unlängst. **–ness,** *s.* die Verspätung, spätes Kommen, späte Entwicklung, die Neuheit; *–ness of the hour*, späte *or* vorgerückte Stunde. **–r,** *comp. adj.* später; *–r on*, späterhin. **–st,** *sup. adj.* spätest, letzt, jüngst; *at (the) –st*, spätestens; *the –st*, das Neueste.

lateen sail [læˈtɪ:nˈseɪl], *s.* das Lateinsegel.

laten–cy [ˈleɪtənsɪ], *s.* das Verborgensein, die Latenz. **–t** [–ənt], *adj.* verborgen, versteckt, latent; gebunden (*Chem.*).

lateral [ˈlætərəl], 1. *adj.* seitlich, Seiten–, Neben–, Quer–; *– axis*, die Querachse; *– branch*, die Seitenlinie (*of a family*); *– controls, pl.* die Quersteuerung (*Av.*); *– error*, die Seitensteuerung; *– pressure*, der Seitendruck; *– thrust*, der Querschub. 2. *s.* der Seitenzweig.

latex [ˈleɪtɛks], *s.* die Gummimilch.

lath [lɑ:θ], *s.* die Latte; *pl.* Stakhölzer (*Build.*); *– and plaster*, die Stakenbauart, der Fachwerkbau. 2. *v.a.* belatten, (mit Latten) verschalen, ausstaken. **–ing, ––work,** *s.* das Lattenwerk.

lathe [leɪð], *s.* die Drehbank, Abdrehmaschine (*Mach.*), Lade, der Schlag (*Weav.*). **––hand,** *s.* der Dreher.

lather [ˈlæðə], 1. *s.* der Seifenschaum. 2. *v.a.* einseifen, (*coll.*) verprügeln. 3. *v.n.* schäumen.

latitud–e [ˈlætɪtju:d], *s.* die Breite (*Geog.*); (*fig.*) Weite, Ausdehnung, der Umfang; Spielraum, die Freiheit; *pl.* der Himmelsstrich, Gegenden, Breiten (*pl.*); *allow o.s. great –e*, sich (*Dat.*) große Freiheiten erlauben; *degree of –e*, der Breitengrad. **–inal** [–ˈtju:dɪnəl], *adj.* Breiten– (*Geog.*). **–inarian** [–ˈnɛ:ərɪən], 1. *adj.* uneingeschränkt, weitherzig, freisinnig, freigeisterisch, freidenkerisch, duldsam (*Theol.*). 2. *s.* der Freigeist, Freidenker (*Theol.*). **–inarianism** [–ˈnɛ:ərɪənɪzm], *s.* die Freigeisterei, Freidenkerei, Duldsamkeit.

latrine [ləˈtrɪ:n], *s.* (*often pl.*) der Abort, das Klosett.

latten [ˈlætən], *s.* (*archaic*) das Messing, Messingblech.

latter [ˈlætə], *adj.* (*archaic*) (only in) *the – end*, das Ende, der Schluß; später, neuer, modern, jetzig (only in) *the – days*, neuere Zeiten; der, die *or* das Letztere, letzterer, letztere(s); dieser, diese(s) (*of two*). **––day** [–deɪ], *adj.* modern, der neueren Zeit; *––day Saints*, Mormonen (*pl.*). **– grass,** das Grummet. **–ly** [–lɪ], *adv.* neuerdings; schließlich, am *or* gegen Ende.

lattice [ˈlætɪs], 1. *s.* das Gitter, Gitterwerk, Gatter. 2. *v.a.*; *– (up)*, vergittern. **––bridge,** die Gitterbrücke. **––window,** *s.* das Gitterfenster, Rautenfenster. **––work,** *s.* das Gitterwerk, die Gitterkonstruktion.

laud [lɔ:d], 1. *s.* (*rare*) das Lob, der (Preis)Lobgesang; *pl.* das Morgenoffizium (*R.C.*). 2. *v.a.* (*Poet.*) loben, preisen, rühmen. **–ability** [–əˈbɪlɪtɪ], *s.*, die Löblichkeit. **–able** [–əbl], *adj.* lobenswert, löblich, empfehlenswert. **–ableness,** *s. see* **–ability. –ation** [–ˈdeɪʃən], *s.* das Lob. **–atory** [–ˈdeɪtərɪ], *adj.* lobend, preisend.

laudanum [ˈlɔ:dənəm], *s.* die Opiumtinktur, das Laudanum.

laugh [lɑ:f], 1. *v.n.* lachen (*also fig.*); (*fig.*) strahlen; *– at*, lachen über (*Acc.*) (*p. or th.*), belachen (*a th.*), auslachen (*a p. for*, einen über); (*coll.*) sich nichts machen aus (*a th.*); *– at a p. to his face*, einem ins Gesicht lachen; *– away*, immer nur zulachen; *– in a p.'s face*, einem ins Gesicht lachen; *– in one's sleeve*, sich (*Dat.*) ins Fäustchen lachen; (*coll.*) *he will – on the wrong side of his face*, ihm wird das Lachen vergehen; *– over*, lachen über (*a th.*). 2. *v.a.* *– a bitter –*, bitter lachen; *– s.th. away*, etwas durch Lachen vertreiben; *– a p. down*, einen durch Lachen zum Schweigen bringen, einen gründlich auslachen; *– a th. off*, sich lachend hinwegsetzen über etwas, etwas mit Lachen abtun; *– a p. out of s.th.*, einen von etwas durch Lachen abbringen; *– s.th. out of court*, etwas restlos lächerlich machen; *– to scorn*, verhöhnen. 3. *s.* das Lachen, Gelächter; *broad –*, lautes Gelächter; *burst into a tremendous –*, eine gewaltige Lache aufschlagen; *get the – of one's life*, lachen wie nie im Leben; *have a good – at*, sich recht lustig machen über; *have the – of s.o.*, über einen triumphieren; (*Prov.*) *the – is always against the loser*, wer den Schaden hat, braucht für den Spott nicht zu sorgen; *have the – on one's side*, die Lacher auf seiner Seite haben; *the – was against him*, die Lacher waren auf der anderen Seite; *raise a –*, Lachen erregen; *with a –*, lachend. **–able,** *adj.* lächerlich. **–ing,** *adj.* lachend, (*fig.*) strahlend; *it is no –ing matter*, es ist nicht zum Lachen. **–ing-gas,** *s.* das Lachgas. **–ing jackass,** *s.* der Riesenkönigsfischer (*Orn.*). **–ing-stock,** *s.* der Gegenstand des Gelächters, die Zielscheibe des Spottes. **–ter** [–tə], *s.* das Gelächter; *roars of –ter*, schallendes Gelächter. **–ter-loving,** *adj.* fröhlich, vergnügt.

launch [lɔ:ntʃ], 1. *v.a.* schleudern (*a spear, etc.*), vom Stapel lassen (*a ship; also fig.*), lancieren (*a torpedo*), aussetzen (*a ship's boat*); (*fig.*) in Tätigkeit *or* Gang setzen, loslassen (*threats, etc.*); *– an attack*, angreifen, einen Angriff ansetzen; *– into eternity*, ins Jenseits befördern; *– a p. into* or *on s.th.*, einen in etwas lancieren. 2. *v.n.* (also *– out, – forth*) sich stürzen, sich hineinbegeben; sich verbreiten, ergehen, auschweifen (*into*, in (*Acc.*)), beginnen, unternehmen (*into* (*Acc.*)). 3. *s.* der Stapellauf (*Shipb.*); die Barkasse; (*motor*) –, das Motorboot. **–ing-cradle,** *s.* das Ablaufgerüst. **–ing-tube,** *s.* das Ausstoßrohr. **–ing-ways,** *pl.* die Bettung, Helling (*Naut.*).

laund–er [ˈlɔ:ndə], 1. *v.a.* waschen (*clothes*), Wäsche bereiten. **–ress** [ˈlɔ:ndrɪs], *s.* die Wäscherin, Waschfrau. **–ry** [ˈlɔ:ndrɪ], *s.* die Wäscherei, Waschanstalt; Waschküche; Wäsche.

laureate [ˈlɔrɪɪt], 1. *adj.* mit Lorbeer gekrönt, lorbeerbekränzt. 2. *s.* gekrönter Dichter; der Hofdichter. **–ship,** *s.* die Würde eines Hofdichters.

laurel [ˈlɔrəl], *s.* der Lorbeer (*Bot.*); (*fig.*) (*usually pl.*) die Ehre, Anerkennung; *gain* or *win one's –s*, Lorbeeren ernten; *rest on one's –s*, auf seinen Lorbeeren ausruhen.

lava [ˈlɑ:və], *s.* die Lava (*Geol.*).

lavatory [ˈlævətərɪ], *s.* der Waschraum, die Toilette; *public –*, die Bedürfnisanstalt.

lave [leɪv], 1. *v.a.* (*Poet.*) waschen, baden; bespülen (*as waves*). 2. *v.n.* sich waschen *or* baden.

lavender [ˈlævəndə], *s.* der Lavendel (*Bot.*).

lavish [ˈlævɪʃ], 1. *adj.* freigebig, verschwenderisch (*of* or *in*, mit); reichlich; *be – of one's promises*, mit Versprechungen um sich werfen. 2. *v.a.* verschwenden, vergeuden; *– favours on*, mit Gunstbezeigungen überhäufen. **–ness,** *s.* die Verschwendung.

law [lɔ:], *s.* das Gesetz; (*often pl.*) das Recht, die Rechtswissenschaft, Rechtskunde, Rechtsgelehrsamkeit, Rechte (*pl.*), Jura (*pl.*); juristische Laufbahn, der Juristenberuf; das Gebot, der Befehl, die Vorschrift, Regel; die Gesetzmäßigkeit; der Vorsprung (*Hunt.*). **(a)** (*with nouns*) *– days*, der Fälligkeitstermin; zugestandene Löschtage (*Naut.*); *–s of the game*, Spielregeln (*pl.*); *– of inheritance*, das Erbrecht; *– of the land*, das Landrecht, Gesetz des Landes; *– of nations*, das Völkerrecht; *– of nature*, das Naturgesetz; *– of the pendulum*, das Pendelgesetz; *workmen's compensation –*, das Arbeiterunfallversicherungsgesetz. **(b)** (*with adjectives*) *civil –*, das Zivilrecht, bürgerliches Recht; *common –*, das Gewohnheitsrecht; *criminal –*, das Strafrecht; *divine –*, göttliches Gesetz; *ecclesiastical –*, das Kirchenrecht; *ex post facto –*, rückwirkendes Gesetz; *international –*, das Völkerrecht; *natural –*, das Naturrecht (*Phil.*); Naturgesetz, wissenschaftliches Gesetz (*Science*); *statute –*, gesetzliches Recht. **(c)** (*with verbs*) *be in the –*, Jurist sein; *become –*, zum Gesetze werden; *give a hare good –*, einem Hasen einen Vorsprung gewähren; *go in for –* Jura studieren; *go to –*, den Rechtsweg beschreiten, vor Gericht gehen; *go to – with s.o.*, einen verklagen; *necessity knows no –*, Not kennt kein Gebot; *lay down the –*, selbstherrlich verfahren; *pass into –*, see *become –*; *practise –*, als Rechtsanwalt praktizieren; *read* or *study –*, Jura studieren; *substantive –*, materielles Recht; *sumptuary –*, das Aufwandgesetz; *take the – into one's own hands*, sich (*Dat.*) selbst Recht verschaffen. **(d)** (*with prepositions*) *according to –*, von Rechts wegen; *at –*, gerichtlich; *be at –*, einen Prozeß führen, prozeßieren; *by –*, gesetzlich, von Rechts wegen; *brother-in-–*, der Schwager; *daughter-in-–*, die Schwiegertochter; *father-in-–*, der Schwiegervater; *good in –*, rechtsgültig; *mother-in-–*; die Schwiegermutter; *sister-in-–*, die Schwägerin; *son-in-–*, der Schwiegersohn; *doctor of –(s)*, Doktor der Rechte; *due process of –*, ordentliches Rechtsverfahren; *contrary to –*, rechtswidrig; *under the –*, auf Grund des Gesetzes, nach dem Gesetz; *under Scottish –*, nach schottischem Recht. **–-abiding,** *adj.* friedlich, ordnungsliebend, den Gesetzen folgend, an die Gesetze haltend; *be –-abiding*, die Gesetze befolgen, sich friedlich benehmen; *–-abiding citizens*, friedliche *or* ruhige Bürger. **–-breaker,** *s.* der Gesetzesübertreter. **–-breaking,** *s.* die Gesetzesüberschreitung. **–-charges,** *pl.* Prozeßkosten, Gerichtsgebühren (*pl.*). **–-court,** *s.* der Gerichtshof. **–ful,** *adj.* gesetzlich, gesetzmäßig, rechtsmäßig, gültig, erlaubt; *–ful age*, die Volljährigkeit, *–ful children*, ehelich geborene Kinder. **–fulness,** *s.* die Gesetzlichkeit, Rechtmäßigkeit, Gültigkeit. **–giver,** *s.*, der Gesetzgeber. **–less,** *adj.* gesetzlos, gesetzwidrig, unrechtmäßig; zügellos, ungefügig. **–lessness,** *s.* die Gesetzlosigkeit; Zügellosigkeit. **–-Lords,** *pl.* Mitglieder des Oberhauses in richterlicher Funktion. **– merchant,** *s.* das Handelsrecht. **–-officer,** *s.* der Rechtsberater der Regierung. **–suit,** *s.* der (Zivil)-Prozeß, Rechtshandel, die Klage; *carry on a –suit*, einen Prozeß führen; *see* **lawyer.**

law(ks) [lɔ:(ks)], *int.* (*vulg.*) herrje!

[1]**lawn** [lɔ:n], *s.* der Rasen, Rasenplatz. **–-mower,** *s.* die Rasenmähmaschine. **–-roller,** *s.* die Rasenwalze. **–-tennis,** *s.* das (Lawn)Tennis.

[2]**lawn** [lɔ́:n], *s.* der Batist.

lawyer [ˈlɔ:jə], *s.* der (Rechts)Anwalt, Rechtsbeistand, Sachwalter; Jurist, Rechtsgelehrte(r), *m.*

lax [læks], *adj.* lose, locker, schlaff (*also fig.*); (*fig.*) nicht genau, nicht streng, lässig, nachlässig, lax; offen, weich (*of bowels*). **–ative** [–ətɪv], 1. *adj.* abführend. 2. *s.* das Abführmittel. **–ity** [–ɪtɪ], *s.* (*usually fig.*), **–ness,** *s.* (*usually lit.*) die Lockerheit, Schlaffheit, Ungenauigkeit, Lässigkeit, Laxheit.

[1]**lay** [leɪ], *adj.* weltlich, Laien–; (*fig.*) nicht fachmännisch, laienhaft; *– habit*, weltliche Kleidung; *– preacher*, der Laienprediger. **–man** [–mən], *s.* der Laie (*also fig.*), (*fig.*) Nichtfachmann.

[2]**lay** [leɪ], *s.* (*Poet.*) das Lied.

[3]**lay** [leɪ], *s.* (*coll.*) die Lage; (*sl.*) das Unternehmen, die Beschäftigung, Betätigung; der Schlag (*Naut.*, *Weav.*); die Richtung, der Strick (*of rope*); *– of the land*, die Lage der Dinge.

[4]**lay** [leɪ], *see* **lie.**

[5]**lay** [leɪ], **1.** *ir.v.a.* legen (*also eggs*), setzen, stellen, hinstellen, niederlegen; wetten (*a sum of money*); richten (*a gun*); bannen (*ghosts*); mäßigen, lindern, beruhigen, zerstreuen, unterdrücken; schlagen, belegen (*a rope*). **(a)** (*with adjectives*) *– bare*, bloßlegen, offen darlegen; *– low*, (*fig.*) zu Falle bringen, stürzen, erniedrigen; *– open*, enthüllen; *– o.s. open to*, sich aussetzen (*Dat.*); *– waste*, verwüsten, verheeren. **(b)** (*with nouns*) *– an ambush*, einen Hinterhalt legen; *– the blame (up)on s.o.*, einem die Schuld zuschreiben; *– claim to*, Anspruch erheben *or* machen (auf (*Acc.*)), in Anspruch nehmen (*Acc.*); *– the cloth*, den Tisch decken; *– one's eyes on*, erblicken; *– a fire*, ein Feuer anlegen; *– hands on*, ergreifen, in Besitz nehmen (*a th.*), Hand anlegen an (*a p.*); *– one's heads together*, die Köpfe zusammen stecken; *– hold of*, see *– hands on*; *– plans*, Pläne ersinnen *or* festlegen; *– a plot*, ein Komplott schmieden; *– the scene in London*, den Schauplatz in London legen; *the scene is laid in London*, die Szene spielt in London; *– siege to*, belagern, bestürmen (*also fig.*); *– a snare for s.o.*, einem eine Falle stellen; *– stress on*, Gewicht *or* Nachdruck legen auf, betonen; *– the table*, den Tisch decken; *– a tax (on a th.)*, (etwas) besteuern; (*on a people*), (einem Volke) eine Steuer auferlegen; *– a trap*, eine Falle legen; *– a wager*, eine Wette machen. **(c)** (*with adverbs*) *– aside*, beiseitelegen, zurücklegen (*money*); *– by*, zurücklegen, sparen (*money, etc.*); aufbewahren, aufspeichern; *– s.th. by for a rainy day*, einen Notgroschen zurücklegen; *– down*, hinlegen, niederlegen (*a post*), aufgeben (*hope, etc.*), hinterlegen, bar bezahlen (*money*); einlegen (*wine*); hingeben (*one's life*); aufstellen, vorschreiben, festlegen (*rules*); anführen (*reasons*); entwerfen, anlegen, aufzeichnen (*plans*); bauen (*a road or railway*); auf Stapel legen (*a ship*); *– down the law*, selbstherrlich auftreten; *– o.s. down*, sich niederlegen; *– it down that*, behaupten *or* die Behauptung aufstellen daß, vorschreiben; *– in*, sich (*Dat.*) anlegen, einlegen, einkaufen, anschaffen, sich eindecken mit, aufspeichern; *– off*, abstechen; (*coll.*) entlassen; *– on*, auftragen (*colours*); anlegen (*water, gas, etc.*); auferlegen (*taxes*); (*sl.*) *– it on*, zuschlagen; übertreiben, dick auftragen; *– out*, auslegen, ausbreiten, zur Schau stellen, ausstellen; aufbahren (*a corpse*); auslegen, ausgeben (*money*); anlegen (*a garden, money*); entwerfen, aufreißen, abstecken, trassieren, planieren; (*sl.*) zu Boden strecken; *– o.s. out*, sich bemühen, sich (*Dat.*) Mühe geben, sich einrichten (*for*, auf); *– over*, belegen, bedecken (*with*, mit); *– to*, beidrehen (*Naut.*); *– up*, aufbewahren, sammeln, zurücklegen; abtakeln, auflegen (*a ship*); einstellen (*a vehicle*); brach liegen lassen (*land*); ans Bett fesseln (*usually pass.*); *laid up with*, darniederlegen an. **(d)** (*with prepositions*) *– at s.o.'s door*, einem in die Schuhe schieben; *– before s.o.*, einem vorlegen *or* zur Ansicht geben; *– s.o. by the heels*, einen zur Strecke bringen, erwischen, kaltstellen; *– in ashes*, einäschern (*a town, etc.*); *– to s.o.'s charge*, einem zur Last legen; *– to rest*, zur letzten Ruhe geleiten, bestatten; *– s.o. under an obligation*, einem eine Verpflichtung auferlegen. **2.** *ir.v.n.* legen (*of hens*); wetten; decken (*the table for s.o.*); *– about one*, um sich schlagen, dreinschlagen; (*sl.*) *– into s.o.*, einen verprügeln; (*sl.*) *– off*, aufhören; *– on*, zuschlagen; *– to*, festliegen, stilliegen (*Naut.*); *– up*, krank sein. **– days,** *pl.* Liegetage (*pl.*), die Liegezeit (*Naut.*). **–er** [–ə], 1. *s.* die Schicht, Lage; der Ableger, Setzling, das Senkreis (*Hort.*); die Legerin (*hen*); der Richtkanonier (*Artil.*); *be a good –er*, gut legen, viele Eier legen; *plate –er*, der Schienenleger (*Railw.*). 2. *v.a.* absenken (*Hort.*). 3. *v.n.* niederliegen, sich legen (*of corn*). **–ette** [–ˈɛt], *s.* die Babyausstattung, Babywäsche. **–ing,** *s.* das Legen, Eierlegen; Richten (*Artil.*); Verputzen *or* Bewerfen mit Mörtel (*Mas.*); *–ing of cables*, die Kabelverlegung; *hens past –ing*, Hennen, die nicht mehr legen. **–-out** [–ɑʊt], *s.* das Abstecken, Anlegen; die Linienführung, Trassierung; Anlage, der Plan, die Anordnung, Gruppierung (*of streets, etc.*), Aufmachung (*Print.*).

lay figure, die Gliederpuppe; (*fig.*) der Strohmann.

lazar-et(to) [læzəˈrɛt(oʊ)], *s.* (*–-house*) das Lazarett, Spital; die Isolierstation, Quarantäneanstalt (*Naut.*).

laz-e [leɪz], 1. *v.n.* faulenzen, nichts tun. 2. *v.a.*; *–e away*, verbummeln, vertändeln. **–iness,** *s.* die Faulheit, Trägheit. **–y** [–ɪ], *adj.* faul, träge. (*coll.*) **–y-bones** [–ɪboʊnz], *s.* der Faulpelz. **–y-tongs,** *pl.* die Gelenkzange.

[1]**lea** [lɪ:], *s.* die Aue, Flur, Wiese, das Weideland.

[2]**lea** [lɪ:], *s.* ein Garnmaß (80 bis 300 Meter).

leach [lɪ:tʃ], *v.a.* auslaugen, durchsickern lassen.

[1]**lead** [lɛd], 1. das Blei; Lot, Senkblei (*Naut.*); die (Blei)Mine, der Bleistift; Durchschuß (*Typ.*); *pl.* Bleiplatten (*pl.*), das Bleidach (*Build.*), Durchschußlinien (*pl.*) (*Typ.*), die Bleifassung (*Glazing*); *black –*, der Graphit, Bleistift; *red-–*, der Mennig, die Mennige; der Rotstift; *white-–*, das Bleiweiß; *under –s*, unter Bleiverschluß; *heave the –*, loten (*Naut.*); *swing the –*, (*sl.*) sich drücken. 2. *v.a.* verbleien, mit Blei überziehen; plombieren;

durchschießen (*Typ.*). **-en** [-ən], *adj.* bleiern, Blei-; bleifarbig; schwerfällig, träge; *-en eyes*, glanzlose Augen. **--line**, *s.* die Lotleine. **--pencil**, *s.* der Bleistift. **--poisoning**, *s.* die Bleivergiftung. **--shot**, *s.* Bleikugeln (*pl.*). **-sman**, *s.* der Lotgast.

[2]**lead** [lɪ:d], **1.** *ir.v.a.* führen, leiten; anführen, befehligen; vorangehen; bewegen, veranlassen, bringen (*to*, zu); anspielen, ausspielen (*Cards*); vorspielen, vorsingen (*Mus.*). **(a)** (*with nouns*) – *captive*, in Gefangenschaft führen; – *a dance*, vortanzen; – *s.o. a (fine) dance*, einem viele Scherereien bereiten, einem gehörig zu schaffen machen *or* zu tun geben; – *s.o. a dog's life*, einem ein Hundeleben bereiten; – *evidence*, (*Scots law*) bezeugen; – *the fashion*, die Mode angeben; – *the field*, die Führung haben, an der Spitze reiten (*Racing*); – *a sedentary life*, eine sitzende Lebensweise führen; – *the way*, vorangehen. **(b)** (*with adverbs*) – *astray*, verleiten, verführen, irreführen; – *off*, ableiten, abführen; – *on*, verlocken; ermutigen, aufmuntern; – *out*, hinausführen. **(c)** (*with prepositions*) – *s.o. by the nose*, einen an der Nase herumführen; – *s.o. into thinking* or *to think*, einen bewegen, verleiten *or* dahin bringen zu denken; einen auf den Gedanken bringen. **2.** *ir.v.n.* vorangehen, als Erster *or* Anführer sein, den Weg bahnen; führen, leiten (*to*, zu *or* nach); die Vorhand haben, ausspielen (*Cards*). **(a)** (*with adverbs*) – *off*, vorangehen, anfangen, beginnen, eröffnen; anspielen (*Footb.*, *Cards*, *etc.*); anstoßen (*Bill.*); – *up to*, einleiten; übergehen *or* überleiten zu. **(b)** (*with prepositions*) – *out of*, in Verbindung stehen mit (*as rooms*); (*fig.*) – *to*, ergeben, hervorbringen (*trouble*, *etc.*). **3.** *s.* die Führung, Leitung, das Führen, Vorangehen (*Hunt.*); Anspielen, der Anwurf, die Vorhand (*Cards.*); der Anstoß (*Bill.*); Vorhalt (*aiming*); Vorsprung (*Racing*); (*fig.*) Fingerzeig, das Beispiel; die Leine (*for dogs*); die Leitung, der Leiter (*Elec.*); führende Rolle, die Hauptrolle (*Theat.*); *give a* –, einen Fingerzeig geben, mit gutem Beispiel vorangehen; *have the* –, die Führung haben, (*fig.*) den Ton angeben, tonangebend wirken; ausspielen, die Vorhand haben (*Cards*); den ersten Wurf haben; anwerfen (*Dice*); *take a* –, vorhalten (*aiming*); *take the* –, die Führung übernehmen, vorangehen, an die Spitze kommen; zuvorkommen (*of* (*Dat.*)). **-er**, *s.* der Führer, Anführer, Leiter; Vormann, Verhandlungsleiter (*Parl.*); erster Geiger (*of an orchestra*), der Chorführer (*in a choir*), Leitartikel (*in a newspaper*); das Vorderpferd, Leitpferd, die Sehne; Spitze, höchster Zweig (*of a tree*); *band -er*, der Kapellmeister; *section -er*, der Zugführer (*Mil.*). **-ership**, *s.* die Führerschaft, Leitung; *-ership principle*, das Führerprinzip. **--in**, *s.* der Zuleitungsdraht (*Rad.*). **-ing**, 1. *adj.* führend, leitend; herrschend, Haupt-, erste(r, s), hervorragend; raum, günstig (*as wind*); *-ing article*, der Leitartikel (*in a newspaper*); die Zugware (*C.L.*); *-ing case*, der Präzedenzfall (*Law*); *-ing edge*, die Leitkante, Nasenleiste, Profilvorderkante (*Av.*); *-ing lady*, die Hauptdarstellerin, erste Liebhaberin (*Theat.*); *-ing man*, der Hauptdarsteller, erster Liebhaber (*Theat.*); *-ing men*, *pl.* führende Geister; *-ing note*, große Septime (*Mus.*); *-ing question*, die Suggestivfrage; *-ing rein*, der Leitzügel. *-ing seaman*, der Obermatrose. *-ing strings*, *pl.* das Gängelband, die Führungsleine; *be in -ing strings*, am Gängelband geführt werden, noch in den Kinderschuhen stecken; *have* or *keep in -ing-strings*, am Gängelband führen. 2. *s.* die Leitung, Führung.

leaf [lɪ:f], *s.* (pl. *leaves* [lɪ:vz]) das Blatt (*tree or book*); der Flügel (*door*); die Klappe, Platte, das Einlegebrett (*of table*); der Schaft (*Weav.*); das Blättchen (*of gold*); (*Poet.*) das Blattwerk, Laub; *in* –, belaubt; *come into* –, Blätter entwickeln, anschlagen; *over the* –, *over*–, auf dem nächsten Blatte; *turn over the leaves of a book*, ein Buch durchblättern; *turn over a new* –, (*fig.*) sich bessern, ein neues Leben beginnen; *take a – out of a p.'s book*, einem nachahmen, jemandes Beispiel folgen, sich (*Dat.*) einen zum Muster nehmen. **-age**, *s.* das Laub. **--bud**, *s.* die Blattknospe. **--gilding**, *s.* die Vergoldung mit Blattgold. **--gold**, *s.* das Buchbindergold, Blattgold. **--green**, *adj.* laubgrün. **-iness**, *s.* die Belaubung, Belaubtheit. **-less**, *adj.* blattlos, blätterlos, unbelaubt, entblättert. **-let**, *s.* das Blättchen; Flugblatt, die Broschüre, der Prospekt. **--mould**, *s.* die Blatterde. **--stalk**, *s.* Blattstiel. **--table**, *s.* der Klapptisch. **--tobacco**, *s.* der Blättertabak. **--valve**, *s.* das Klappenventil. **--work**, *s.* das Blattwerk, Laubwerk (*Art*). **-y**, *adj.* belaubt, blattreich, Laub-.

[1]**league** [lɪ:g], *s.* die Seemeile (= 3 englische Meilen = 4·8 km.).

[2]**league** [lɪ:g], 1. *s.* das Bündnis, der Bund, Verband, Verein; die Liga (*also Hist. & Footb.*); – *of Nations*, der Völkerbund. 2. *v.r.* sich verbünden. **-r**, *s.* Verbündete(r), *m.*, der Bundesgenosse.

leak [lɪ:k], 1. *s.* das Leck (*also Elec.*); die Spalte, der Riß; durchsickerndes Wasser; *spring a* –, ein Leck bekommen. – *current*, der Verluststrom (*Elec.*); *grid* –, – *resistance*, der Gitterwiderstand (*Rad.*), 2. *v.n.* lecken, leck *or* undicht sein, ein Leck haben, Wasser durchlassen; – *out*, auslaufen, ausströmen; (*fig.*) durchsickern, bekannt werden (*as news*). **-age** [-ɪdʒ], *s.* das Lecken, Durchsickern, Auslaufen; Leck, undichte Stelle, die Undichtigkeit; Leckage (*C.L.*); der Abgang, Verlust, die Abnahme. **-ing, -y**, *adj.* leck, undicht; (*fig.*) geschwätzig.

leal [lɪ:l], *adj.* (*Scots*) treu; *land o' the* –, der Himmel, das Paradies.

[1]**lean** [lɪ:n], 1. *ir.v.n.* (imperf. & p.p. *-t* [lɛnt] or *-ed* [lɪ:nd]), (sich) lehnen (*against*, an (*Acc.*) *or* gegen), sich stützen (*on*, auf); schief stehen, sich neigen; (*fig.*) hinneigen (*to*(*wards*), zu); (*fig.*) sich verlassen (*on*, auf (*Acc.*)). 2. *ir.v.a.* lehnen, stützen (*against*, gegen; (*up*)*on*, auf (*Acc.*)); (*fig.*) – *one's ear to*, das Ohr neigen nach. 3. *s.* die Neigung; *on the* –, geneigt, schief. **-ing**, 1. *s.* die Neigung (*to*(*wards*), nach). 2. *adj.* sich neigend, schief. **--to**, 1. *s.* der Anbau (*Build.*). 2. *adj.* Anbau-, angebaut.

[2]**lean** [lɪ:n], 1. *adj.* mager, dürr; (*fig.*) unfruchtbar. 2. *s.* das Magere, mageres Fleisch. **-ness** [-nɪs], *s.* die Magerkeit, Dürre.

leant [lɛnt], *see* [1]**lean.**

leap [lɪ:p], 1. *ir.v.n.* (imperf. & p.p. *-t* [lɛpt] or *-ed* [lɪ:pt]) springen, hüpfen; hervorschießen, hochschießen; aufglühen (*as flames*); – *at a th.*, etwas eifrig ergreifen; – *for joy*, vor Freude hüpfen; – *into fame*, plötzlich berühmt werden; – *into flame*, entflammen, aufflammen; – *to a conclusion*, voreilig schließen; – *to the eye*, ins Auge springen. 2. *ir.v.a.* springen lassen (*as a horse*); überspringen, (hinweg)setzen über (*an obstacle*). 3. *s.* der Sprung, Satz; *take a* –, einen Sprung tun, einen Satz machen; – *in the dark*, der Sprung ins Dunkle *or* Ungewisse; *by -s*, sprungweise, sprunghaft; *by -s and bounds*, in großen Sätzen, in gewaltigen Sprüngen. **--frog**, 1. *s.* das Bockspringen; der Bocksprung. 2. *v.n.* bockspringen; sprungweise vorgehen (*Mil.*). **-t**, *see* –. **--year**, *s.* das Schaltjahr.

learn [lə:n], 1. *ir.v.a.* (imperf. & p.p. *-t* [lə:nt] or *-ed* [lə:nd]) lernen; erlernen, erfahren; – *by heart*, auswendig lernen; – *by rote*, mechanisch auswendig lernen; – *German*, Deutsch lernen; – (*how*) *to swim*, schwimmen lernen; – *the truth*, die Wahrheit erfahren. 2. *ir.v.n.* lernen, erfahren, ersehen, hören (*from*, aus; *of*, von); – *by experience*, aus *or* durch Erfahrung lernen; *I -ed from him that . . .*, ich hörte von ihm daß. . . . **-ed** [ɪd], *adj.* gelehrt; erfahren, bewandert (*in*, in (*Dat.*)). **-er**, *s.* Lernende(r), *m.*, der Anfänger, Lehrling (*also Motor.*). **-ing**, *s.* die Gelehrsamkeit; das Lernen, die Erlernung; *a little -ing is a dangerous thing*, Halbbildung ist schlimmer als Unbildung; *the new -ing*, der Humanismus. **-t**, *see* –.

lease [lɪ:s], 1. *s.* die Verpachtung, Vermietung (*to*, an); Pacht, Miete, das Mietverhältnis; der Pachtbrief, Mietvertrag; die Pachtzeit; – *of life*, die Lebensdauer, Lebensfrist; *a new – of life*, neues Leben; *let* (*out*) *on* –, verpachten, vermieten, in Pacht geben; *take a – of*, *take on* –, pachten, mieten. 2. *v.a.* verpachten, vermieten; pachten, mieten. **-hold**, 1. *s.* die Pachtung. 2. *adj.* Pacht-; *-hold*

estate, das Pachtgut; *–hold residence*, die Wohnung auf Zeitpacht. **–holder,** *s.* der Pächter. **– -(and-) lend act,** das Pacht- und Leihgesetz (*Pol.*).
leash [lɪ:ʃ], 1. *s.* die Koppelleine, der Koppelriemen (*for dogs*); die Koppel (*of dogs*), drei Hunde (*Hunt.*); (*fig.*) *hold in* –, im Zügel halten. 2. *v.a.* koppeln.
leasing [lɪ:sɪŋ], *s.* (*B.*) das Lügen, die Lüge.
least [lɪ:st], 1. *sup. adj.* geringst, kleinst, mindest. 2. *adv.* am wenigsten; – *of all*, am allerwenigsten; *last* (*but*) *not* –, nicht zum wenigsten; *not* –, nicht am wenigsten; (*Prov.*) – *said, soonest mended*, Reden ist Silber, Schweigen Gold. 3. *s.* das Geringste, Minderste; *to say the – of it*, gelinde *or* milde gesagt; *the – said the better*, see – *said soonest mended*; *at* (*the*) –, wenigstens, zum mindesten; *not in the* (*very*) –, nicht im geringsten, durchaus nicht, keineswegs.
leather [ˈlɛðə], 1. *s.* das Leder; (*sl.*) die Haut, das Fell; der (Fuß)Ball; *pl.* die Lederhose, Reithose, Ledergamaschen (*pl.*), das Lederzeug; *upper* –, das Oberleder. 2. *adj.* ledern, Leder–. 3. *v.a.* mit Leder überziehen *or* abdichten; (*coll.*) das Fell gerben (*Dat.*), verdreschen (*Acc.*). 4. *v.n.*; – *away*, arbeiten *or* schuften (*at*, an). **–ette** [–ˈɛt], *s.*, **–oid** [–ɔɪd], *s.* die Lederimitation, das Kunstleder. **–n,** *adj.* (*archaic*) ledern, Leder–. **–y,** *adj.* lederartig, zäh.
[1]leave [lɪ:v], *s.* die Erlaubnis; der Abschied; (also – *of absence*) Urlaub. (*a*) (*with nouns*) *man on* –, der Urlauber; *ticket of* –, das Entlassungszeugnis; *ticket-of- -man*, entlassener Sträfling. (*b*) (*with verbs*) *ask – of s.o.*, einen um die Erlaubnis bitten; *I beg – to contradict*, darf ich so frei sein, zu widersprechen; *grant* –, beurlauben; *have* –, Urlaub haben; *take* –, Abschied nehmen, fortgehen, sich empfehlen; *take one's – of*, Abschied nehmen von; *take French* –, sich heimlich drücken; *take – of one's senses*, den Verstand verlieren; *take – to contradict*, sich zu widersprechen erlauben. (*c*) (*with prepositions*) *by your* –, mit Ihrer Erlaubnis, mit Verlaub; *on* –, auf Urlaub; *go on* –, Urlaub nehmen, auf Urlaub gehen, den Urlaub antreten. **– -taking,** *s.* das Abschiednehmen. **– -train,** *s.* der Urlauberzug.
[2]leave [lɪ:v], **1.** *ir.v.a.* hinterlassen (*also a p.*); vermachen (*only a th.*) (*a th. to a p.* or *a p. a th.*, einem etwas); zurücklassen (*a p. or a th.*); liegenlassen, stehenlassen (*only a th.*); lassen, bestehen lassen, belassen; verlassen, im Stich lassen; überlassen, anheimstellen, freistellen (*to a p.* einem); *to be left*, übrigbleiben; *to be left till called for*, postlagernd; – *go*, fahren lassen, loslassen. **(a)** (*with nouns and pronouns*) – *one's card*, seine Visitenkarte abgeben; – *one's hat*, den Hut liegenlassen; *we left the house*, wir verließen das Haus; – *an impression*, einen Eindruck hinterlassen *or* zurücklassen; *that –s much to be desired*, das läßt viel zu wünschen übrig; – *the service*, aus dem Heere ausscheiden; – *one's umbrella*, den Regenschirm stehenlassen; – *a p. word*, einem sagen lassen, einem Bescheid hinterlassen. **(b)** (*with adjectives*) – *me alone*, laß mich in Ruhe *or* ungestört, stören Sie mich nicht; – *a th. alone*, etwas nicht berühren; – *severely alone*, vollkommen ignorieren; *this –s me cold*, das läßt mich kalt; – *one's children comfortably off*, seine Kinder in guten Verhältnissen zurücklassen; – *nothing undone*, nichts unterlassen *or* ungeschehen lassen; – *a p. wondering*, einen im unklaren lassen. **(c)** (*with prepositions*) – *it at that*, es (so) gut sein lassen, es dabei (bewenden) lassen; – *Kiel for Berlin*, von Kiel nach Berlin abreisen; – *London for the country*, von London aufs Land reisen; – *a p. in the lurch*, einen im Stich lassen; – *the church on one's left*, die Kirche links liegen lassen; *I – it to you to . . .*, ich überlasse es Ihnen, zu . . .; *I – that entirely to you* or *your discretion*, das steht in Ihrem Belieben, ich gebe Ihnen völlig freie Hand; – *s.o. to himself*, einen sich selbst überlassen. **(d)** (*with adverbs*) – *behind*, zurücklassen, hinterlassen, liegen *or* stehen lassen; hinter sich (*Dat.*) lassen; – *off*, aufhören mit (*speaking, etc.*); einstellen (*work*); ablegen (*clothes*); aufgeben, unterlassen (*habits*); – *off crying!* laß das Weinen! – *out*, auslassen, weglassen; – *over*, übriglassen; *left over*, bleibt (übrig) (*Arith.*). **2.** *ir.v.n.* abreisen, fortgehen (*for*, nach); austreten, einen Posten aufgeben; – *off*, aufhören; – *on a journey*, eine Reise antreten; *see* **leaving, left.**
leaved [lɪ:vd], *adj. suff.* –blätt(e)rig; –flügelig (*as a door*) *see* **leaf.**
leaven [ˈlɛvn], 1. *s.* der Sauerteig, die Hefe; (*coll.*) Beigeschmack, die Dosis. 2. *v.a.* säuern; (*fig.*) anstecken, durchsetzen, durchdringen, erfüllen.
leaves [lɪ:vz], *pl. see* **leaf.**
leaving [lɪ:vɪŋ], 1. *adj.*; – *certificate*, das Abgangszeugnis. 2. *s.* das Verlassen, Hinterlassen; *see* **[2]leave. –s,** *pl.* Überbleibsel, Reste (*pl.*).
lecher [ˈlɛtʃə], *s.* der Wüstling. **–ous** [–rəs], *adj.* wollüstig, geil. **–y** [–rɪ], *s.* die Unzucht, Wollust, Geilheit.
lectern [ˈlɛktə:n], *s.* das Lesepult; Chorpult (*Eccl.*).
lectionary [ˈlɛkʃənərɪ], *s.* das Kollektenbuch (*Eccl.*).
lectur-e [ˈlɛktʃə], 1. *s.* der Vortrag, die Vorlesung (*on*, über (*Acc.*)); (*coll.*) die Strafpredigt, der Verweis; *attend –es*, Vorlesungen *or* ein Kolleg hören; *cut a –e*, eine Vorlesung schwänzen; *give a –e*, eine Vorlesung halten (*on*, über (*Acc.*)); *read a p. a –e*, einen abkanzeln, einem eine Strafpredigt halten (*on*, über). 2. *v.n.* Vorlesung(en) *or* einen Vortrag halten, lesen (*on*, über (*Acc.*); *to*, vor). 3. *v.a.* (*coll.*) den Text lesen, eine Moralpredigt halten ((*Dat.*); *for*, wegen). **–e notes,** das Kollegheft. **–er** [–rə], *s.* Vortragender *m.*; *university –er*, der Dozent, außerordentlicher Professor. **–eship,** *s.* die Dozentenstelle, außerordentliche Professur.
led [lɛd], *see* **[2]lead**; – *captain*, der Schmarotzer; – *horse*, das Handpferd.
ledge [lɛdʒ], *s.* der *or* das Sims; die Brüstung; vorstehender Rand, vorstehende Kante; das Felsenriff, der Vorsprung, die Platte, Leiste (*Mount.*); das Lager, die Schicht (*Min.*).
ledger [ˈlɛdʒə], *s.* das Hauptbuch (*C.L.*); der Querbalken (*Build.*). **– -line,** *s.* die Hilfslinie (*Mus.*).
lee [lɪ:], *s.* der Schutz; die Lee(seite) (*Naut.*); *under the – of the shore*, im Schutz der Küste. **– -board,** *s.* das Schwert. **–ward,** 1. *adv.* leewärts, unter dem Winde. 2. *adj.* vom Winde geschützt; *drift* or *drive to –ward*, abtreiben; *fall to –ward*, vom Winde abkommen. **–way,** *s.* die Abtrift, der Abtrieb, Leeweg; (*fig.*) Rückschritt, die Rückständigket; *make –way*, stark abtreiben (*Naut.*); *make up the* or *for –way*, Versäumtes nachholen.
[1]leech [lɪ:tʃ], *s.* der Blutegel (*Zool.*); (*fig.*) Blutsauger, Wucherer.
[2]leech [lɪ:tʃ], *s.* das Liek, Leik (*Naut.*).
leek [lɪ:k], *s.* der Lauch, Porree (*Bot.*).
leer [ˈlɪ:ə], 1. *s.* boshafter Seitenblick. 2. *v.n.* boshaft schielen, Seitenblicke werfen (*at*, nach). **–y,** *adj.* schlau, gerieben, gerissen.
lees [lɪ:z], *pl.* die Hefe, der Bodensatz.
leet [lɪ:t], *s.* (*Scots*) die (Kandidaten)Liste.
leeward [ˈlu:əd], *see* **lee.**
[1]left [lɛft], 1. *adj.* link; – *hand*, linke Hand. 2. *s.* die Linke (*also Pol.*), linke Hand *or* Seite, linker Flügel (*Mil.*); Linke(r), *m.* (*Boxing*); *on the* –, links, zur Linken, linkerhand, zu linker Hand; *on my* –, mir zur Linken, zu meiner Linken; *to the* –, nach links; *the first on* or *to the* –, die erste (Straße) links; *keep to the –!* sich links halten! links fahren! links ausweichen! 3. *adv.* links, nach links, zur Linken; – *turn!* linksum! (*Mil.*). **– -hand,** *attrib. adj.* link; *– -hand-drive*, *s.* die Linkssteuerung (*Motor.*). **– -handed,** *adj.* linkshändig; linksgängig (*Mach.*); (*fig.*) linkisch, ungeschickt; fragwürdig, zweifelhaft; boshaft; *– -handed marriage*, die Ehe zur linken Hand, morganatische Ehe; *– -handed person*, der Linkshänder, (*coll.*) Linkser. **– -handedness,** *s.* die Linkshändigkeit. **– -hander,** *s.* Linke(r), *m.* (*Boxing*), (*coll.*) der Linkser. **–ist,** *s.* Linksradikale(r), *m.*
[2]left [lɛft], *see* **[2]leave**; **– -luggage-office,** *s.* die Gepäckaufbewahrung.
leg [lɛg], 1. *s.* das Bein; die Keule (*of mutton, etc.*); der Schenkel (*of compasses, etc.*); Schaft (*of boots*); die Strecke (*of course*) (*Naut.*); links vom Schläger (*Crick.*); *bandy –s*, O-Beine; *wooden* –, der Stelzfuß, die Prothese; *on one's –s*, auf den Beinen; (*coll.*) *be on one's last –s*, auf *or* aus dem letzten Loch

pfeifen; *set a p. on his –s*, einem (wieder) auf die Beine helfen; *give a p. a – up*, einem aufhelfen *or* auf die Beine helfen; (*fig.*) einem helfen; *not have a – to stand (up)on*, keine Stütze *or* keinen Halt haben, keinen Grund zur Entschuldigung haben; nicht die geringste Aussicht haben; *pull a p.'s –*, einen necken, einen zum Narren haben; *put one's best – foremost*, die Beine unter den Arm nehmen; *shake a –*, das Tanzbein schwingen; *shake a –!* hurtig! mach schnell! heraus aus den Federn! *stand on one's own –s*, auf eigenen Füßen stehen. 2. *v.n.*; (*sl.*) *– it*, sich auf die Beine *or* Socken machen. **– -bail,** *s.* (*coll.*) das Fersengeld. **– -break,** *s.* der Ball mit Effekt nach links (*Crick.*). **–ged** [–ɪd], *adj. suff.* –beinig. **–ging,** *see* **legging. – -guard,** *s.* die Beinschiene (*Crick.*). **–gy,** *adj.* (*coll.*) langbeinig. **–less,** *adj.* ohne Beine. **– -of-mutton,** *adj.* Keulen– (*as sleeves*). **– -pull(ing),** *s.* das Necken, Hänseln, Aufziehen.

legacy [ˈlɛgəsɪ], *s.* das Vermächtnis (*also fig.*), die Erbschaft, das Legat; (*fig.*) Ererbte(s), *n.* **– -duty,** *s.* die Erbschaftssteuer. **– -hunter,** *s.* der Erbschleicher.

legal [ˈlɪ:gəl], *adj.* gesetzlich, rechtsgültig, rechtskräftig, Rechts–, juristisch; *– adviser*, der Rechtsbeistand; *– capacity*, die Rechtsfähigkeit; *– decision*, rechtskräftiges Urteil; *– documents*, Aktenstücke; *– heir*, der Rechtsnachfolger; *– proceedings*, das Rechtsverfahren; *take – proceedings*, see *– steps*; *– remedy*, das Rechtsmittel; *take – steps against s.o.*, gegen einen gerichtlich vorgehen; *– tender*, gesetzliches Zahlungsmittel. **–ity** [lɪˈgælɪtɪ], *s.* die Gesetzlichkeit, Rechtsgültigkeit. **–ization** [–ɑɪˈzeɪʃən], *s.* gerichtliche Beglaubigung; gesetzliche Bestätigung *or* Anerkennung. **–ize** [–ɑɪz], *v.a.* rechtskräftig machen; als gesetzlich anerkennen, amtlich beglaubigen *or* bestätigen.

¹**legat–e** [ˈlɛgət], *s.* päpstlicher Gesandter, der Legat. **–ion** [–ˈgeɪʃən], *s.* die Gesandtschaft; das Gesandtschaftsgebäude; die Botschaft, Sendung.

²**legat–e** [lɪˈgeɪt], *v.a.* vermachen (*to* (*Dat.*)). **–ee** [ˈlɛgətɪ], *s.* der Vermächtnisnehmer, Erbe. **–or** [lɪˈgeɪtə], *s.* der Erblasser.

legato [lɛˈgɑ:toʊ], *adv.* gebunden (*Mus.*).

legend [ˈlɛdʒənd], *s.* die Legende, Heiligengeschichte; Sage, Wundergeschichte, das Märchen; die Inschrift, Umschrift (*on coins*); der Text (*to illustrations*). **–ary** [–ərɪ], *adj.* sagenhaft, legendhaft.

legerdemain [ˈlɛdʒədəmeɪn], *s.* die Taschenspielerei, Taschenspielerkunst; das Kunststück.

legging [ˈlɛgɪŋ], *s.* (*usually pl.*) Gamaschen (*pl.*).

legib–ility [lɛdʒɪˈbɪlɪtɪ], *s.* die Leserlichkeit. **–le** [ˈlɛdʒɪbl], *adj.* leserlich, deutlich.

legion [ˈlɪ:dʒən], *s.* die Legion (*Mil.*); große Menge, Schar; *British –*, britischer Frontkämpferverband; *– of Honour*, französische Ehrenlegion; *foreign –*, die Fremdenlegion. **–ary** [–ərɪ], *s.* der Legionssoldat; Fremdenlegionär.

legislat–e [ˈlɛdʒɪsleɪt], *v.n.* Gesetze geben *or* machen. **–ion** [–ˈleɪʃən], *s.* die Gesetzgebung. **–ive** [–lətɪv], *adj.* gesetzgebend. **–or** [–leɪtə], *s.* der Gesetzgeber. **–ure** [–lətʃə], *s.* gesetzgebende Gewalt *or* Versammlung.

legitim–acy [lɪˈdʒɪtɪməsɪ], *s.* die Gesetzmäßigkeit, Rechtmäßigkeit, Legitimität; (*fig.*) Berechtigung, Richtigkeit (*of conclusions, etc.*); eheliche Geburt (*of children*). **–ate** [–ət], 1. *adj.* gesetzmäßig, rechtmäßig (*ruler, etc.*); wohlbegründet, berechtigt, folgerichtig, einwandfrei (*as arguments*); ehelich geboren, legitim (*of child*); *–ate drama*, echtes Drama. 2. *v.a. see* **–ize. –ation** [–ˈmeɪʃən], *s.* die Gültigkeitserklärung; Legitimation, der Ausweis; das Gültigmachen, die Legitimierung, Ehelicherklärung (*of a child*). **–atize** [–ətɑɪz], *see* **–ize. –ist** [–ɪst], *s.* der Legitimist. **–ize** [–ɑɪz], *v.a.* für gesetzlich *or* gültig erklären, legitimieren; für berechtigt erklären, rechtfertigen; für ehelich erklären (*child*).

legum–e [ˈlɛgjʊ:m], *s.* (*often pl.*) die Hülse, Hülsenfrucht. **–inous** [–ˈgjʊ:mɪnəs], *adj.* Hülsen–, hülsentragend.

leisure [ˈlɛʒə], 1. *s.* die Muße, freie Zeit; *at –*, unbeschäftigt, frei; *at your –*, wann es Ihnen beliebt, bei passender Gelegenheit, gelegentlich. 2. *adj.* müßig, Muße–; *– hour*, freie Stunde; *– time*, freie Zeit, die Freizeit. **–d,** *adj.* frei, unbeschäftigt; *–d classes*, wohlhabende Klassen. **–ly,** *adj. & adv.* gemächlich, mit Ruhe, behaglich, gemütlich.

leit-motif [ˈlɑɪtmoʊˈtɪ:f], *s.* das Leitmotiv (*Mus. & fig.*).

leman [ˈlɛmən], *s.* (*archaic*) Geliebte(r), *f.* (*m.*); die Buhle, Buhler(in), *m.* (*f.*).

lemma [ˈlɛmɑ], *s.* (pl. *–ta* [lɛˈmɑ:tə]) der Hilfssatz, Lehnsatz (*Math.*); das Stichwort, die Überschrift.

lemon [ˈlɛmən], *s.* die Zitrone; der Zitronenbaum; die Zitronenfarbe, das Zitronengelb; *salts of –*, das Kleesalz. **–ade** [–ˈneɪd], *s.* die (Zitronen)-Limonade, der Zitronensaft. **– -cheese, – -curd,** *s.* der Zitronenkrem. **– -juice,** *s.* der Zitronensaft. **– -peel,** *s.* die Zitronenschale. **– -sole,** *s.* die Rotzunge (*Ichth.*). **– -squash,** *s.* der Zitronensaft, das Zitronenwasser. **– -squeezer,** *s.* die Zitronenpresse.

lemur [ˈlɪ:mə], *s.* der Maki, Lemur(e) (*Zool.*).

lend [lɛnd], *ir.v.a.* ausleihen, verleihen (*a th. to a p.* or *a p. a th.*, etwas an einen); leihen (*a th. to a p.* or *a p. a th.*, einem etwas); (*fig.*) gewähren, leisten (*aid*), schenken (*an ear*), hergeben (*one's name to*); *– a hand*, mit Hand anlegen, behilflich sein; *– o.s. to*, sich hergeben **zu**; *– itself to*, sich eignen zu *or* für. **– -(and-)lease bill,** das Leih- und Pachtgesetz. **–er,** *s.* der Verleiher. **–ing-library,** *s.* die Leihbibliothek.

length [lɛŋθ], *s.* die Länge (*also Racing*); lange Strecke, die Weite, Entfernung; Dauer, Zeitdauer (*of time*); *at –*, endlich, zuletzt; ausführlich; *at full –*, der Länge nach; *at great –*, sehr ausführlich; *at arm's –*, möglichst weit entfernt; *full –*, in Lebensgröße; *fall full –*, der Länge nach hinfallen; *in –*, lang; *measure one's – on the floor*, see *fall full –*; *overall –*, *– over all*, die Baulänge, Gesamtlänge; *go (to) the – of saying*, so weit gehen, zu sagen; *go to any –*, alles daransetzen, vor nichts zurückschrecken; *go to all –s*, aufs Ganze gehen; *go to desperate –s*, verzweifelt weit gehen; *go to great* or *extreme –s*, bis zum Äußersten gehen. **–en,** 1. *v.a.* verlängern, ausdehnen; dehnen (*syllables*). 2. *v.n.* sich verlängern, sich ausdehnen, länger werden; *–en out*, sich in die Länge ziehen. **–ening,** 1. *s.* die Verlängerung. 2. *attrib. adj.* Verlängerungs–, Ansatz–. **–iness,** *s.* die Länge; Langwierigkeit. **–ways, –wise,** *adv.* der Länge nach **–y,** *adj.* sehr lang; langwierig, weitschweifig; *have a –y talk with s.o.*, sich mit einem länger unterhalten.

lenien–cy [ˈlɪ:nɪənsɪ], *s.* die Milde, Nachsicht. **–t** [–ɪənt], *adj.* mild(e), nachsichtig, schonend, gelind (*to(wards)*, gegen).

lenit–ive [ˈlɛnɪtɪv], 1. *adj.* lindernd. 2. *s.* das Linderungsmittel. **–y** [–tɪ], *s.* die Milde, Nachsicht.

lens [lɛnz], *s.* die Linse, Optik; *concave –*, die Zerstreuungslinse; *convex –*, die Sammellinse.

¹**lent** [lɛnt], *see* **lend.**

²**lent** [lɛnt], *s.* Fasten (*pl.*), die Fastenzeit; *keep –*, fasten; *– lily*, gelbe Narzisse; *– term*, das Frühjahrsquartal (*Univ.*). **–en,** *adj.* Fasten–; *–en far* karge *or* magere Kost.

lenticular [lɛnˈtɪkjʊlə], *adj.* linsenartig, Linsen– (*Opt. & Bot.*).

lentil [ˈlɛntɪl], *s.* die Linse (*Bot.*).

leonine [ˈlɪənɑɪn], *adj.* löwenartig, Löwen–; *– verses*, leoninische Verse.

leopard [ˈlɛpəd], *s.* der Leopard.

leper [ˈlɛpə], *s.* Aussätzige(r), *m.*; *see* **leprosy, leprous.**

lepidopter–a [lɛpɪˈdɔptərə], *pl.* Schmetterlinge. **–ous** [–əs], *adj.* Schmetterlings–.

leporine [ˈlɛpərɑɪn], *adj.* Hasen–.

lepro–sy [ˈlɛprəsɪ], *s.* der Ausatz. **–us** [ˈlɛprəs], *adj.* aussätzig; *see* **leper.**

lese-majesty [lɪ:zˈmædʒɪstɪ], *s.* die Majestätsbeleidigung; der Hochverrat.

lesion [ˈlɪ:ʒən], *s.* die Verletzung (*Med.*); Schädigung (*Law*).

less [lɛs], 1. *adj.* kleiner, geringer; *little – than*, so gut wie, schon fast; *no – a person than*, kein

Geringerer als. 2. *adv.* weniger, geringer, in geringerem Maße; – *and* –, immer weniger; *no* – *than*, ebensogut wie; *much* – or *still* –, noch viel weniger, geschweige denn; *the* – *the better*, je weniger desto besser; *the* – *so as*, um so weniger als. 3. *prep.* abzüglich (*Gen.*); – *purchase tax*, abzüglich der Warenumsatzsteuer. 4. *s.* der, die, das Geringere *or* Kleinere; *I cannot sell it for* –, ich kann es nicht billiger abgeben; *nothing* –, wenigstens soviel, nicht weniger. **–en** [–n], 1. *v.a.* verkleinern, verringern, vermindern; schmälern, herabsetzen; mildern (*pain*). 2. *v.n.* kleiner *or* geringer werden, abnehmen, sich vermindern *or* verringern. **–er** [–ə], *attrib. adj.* kleiner, geringer, unbedeutender; *the* –*er evil* or –*er of two evils*, das kleinere Übel.

lessee [lɛˈsɪː], *s.* der Mieter, Pächter.

lesson [ˈlɛsən], *s.* die Aufgabe, Lektion; (Lehr)-Stunde; Lehre, Vorschrift; (*fig.*) Warnung, der Denkzettel (*to*, für); das Vorlesestück (*Eccl.*); *pl.* der Unterricht; *let this be a* – *to you* or *teach you a* –, lassen Sie sich das zur Warnung dienen; *give s.o. a* –, einem den Text lesen; *give* –*s*, Stunden geben, Unterricht erteilen; *have* or *take* –*s with*, Stunden nehmen *or* Unterricht haben bei; *home* –*s*, Hausaufgaben; *music* –, die Musikstunde.

lessor [ˈlɛsɔː], *s.* der Vermieter, Verpachter.

lest [lɛst], *conj.* (foll. by *should*) damit nicht, daß nicht; aus Furcht daß, (*foll. expressions of fear*) daß; – *you should not understand me*, damit du mich recht verstehst; – *he understands*, damit er nicht versteht; *fear* –, fürchten daß.

[1]**let** [lɛt], **1.** *ir.v.a.* lassen (*Acc.*); zulassen, gestatten, erlauben (*Dat.*); vermieten, verpachten (*a house, etc.*) (*to*, an). **(a)** (*with nouns*) – *blood*, zur Ader lassen; – *rooms*, Zimmer vermieten. **(b)** (*with adjectives*) – *alone*, in Ruhe *or* Frieden lassen (*a p.*), nicht anrühren *or* berühren, sich nicht mischen in (*a th.*), sein lassen; – *alone anyone else*, geschweige denn ein anderer; – *loose*, loslassen. **(c)** (*with verbs*) – *be*, see – *alone*; – *it come to this*, es darauf ankommen lassen; – *o.s. be deceived*, sich täuschen lassen; – *fall*, fallen lassen (*also fig.*); äußern; – *fly*, abschießen, loslassen; – *go*, gehen lassen; in Freiheit setzen; fahren lassen, loslassen; vergeben (*goods*); – *o.s. go*, sich gehen lassen; – *s.o. have s.th.*, einem etwas zukommen lassen; – *me* (*help*), erlauben Sie mir; – *a p. know*, einen wissen lassen, – *pass*, fahren lassen; – *s.th. pass unnoticed*, sich (*Dat.*) etwas mit ansehen; – *things slide*, die Dinge gehen *or* ihren Lauf nehmen lassen; – *an opportunity slip*, die Gelegenheit entgehen lassen. **(d)** (*aux. as imper.*) – *come what may*, möge kommen was will; – *us go*, wir wollen gehen, gehen wir; – *us suppose*, nehmen wir an; – *me see* or *think*, einen Augenblick; – *him try*, so mag er nur versuchen. **(e)** (*with prepositions*) – *a p. into*, einen einweihen in, einen (etwas) wissen lassen; – *a p. off a punishment*, einen von einer Strafe befreien; – *a p. off a promise*, einen von einem Versprechen entbinden; – *p. over a place*, einen über einen Ort gehen lassen; – *a p. out of*, einen herauslassen aus. **(f)** (*with adverbs*) – *down*, herunterlassen; (*fig.*) – *a p. down*, einen enttäuschen *or* im Stich lassen; – *a p. down gently*, einen glimpflich behandeln; – *in*, einlassen, (hin)einlassen, Zutritt gestatten (*Dat.*); (*fig.*) – *p. in for*, einen hineinlegen *or* bringen um; – *o.s. in for*, sich (*Dat.*) aufhalsen, aufbürden *or* einbrocken; – *a p. in on*, einen aufklären über; – *off*, abschießen, losschießen; (*fig.*) loslassen; – *off steam*, Dampf ablassen; (*fig.*) den Gefühlen freien Lauf geben; – *a p. off*, einem die Strafe erlassen, bei einem ein Auge zudrücken; (*coll.*) einen davonkommen lassen; *be* – *off lightly*, leichten Kaufes davonkommen; – *out*, herauslassen; auslassen (*a dress*); ausplaudern (*a secret*); vermieten, verpachten, vergeben (*rooms, etc.*). **2.** *ir.v.n.* vermietet werden, sich vermieten (*at* or *for*, für); *house to* –, Haus zu vermieten; (*sl.*) – *on*, verraten, merken *or* erkennen lassen, vorgeben, tun (*as if*, als ob); (*sl.*) – *up*, nachlassen, aufhören; – *well alone*, die Dinge gehen lassen. (*sl.*) **––down,** *s.* die Enttäuschung. (*sl.*) **––up,** *s.* das Nachlassen, die Pause, der Unterlaß.

[2]**let** [lɛt], 1. *v.a.* (*archaic*) hindern. 2. *s.* das Hindernis; *without* – *or hindrance*, ohne Hinderung; das Let, die Wiederholung des Anschlages (*Tenn.*).

lethal [ˈlɪːθl], *adj.* tödlich, todbringend, Todes–, Toten–; – *chamber*, die Todeskammer.

letharg–ic(al) [lɛˈθɑːdʒɪk(l)], *adj.* schlafsüchtig, lethargisch; (*fig.*) träge, stumpf, teilnahm(s)los. **–y** [ˈlɛθədʒɪ], *s.* die Schlafsucht, Lethargie (*Med.*); (*fig.*) Interesselosigkeit, Teilnahm(s)losigkeit, Stumpfheit.

lethe [ˈlɪːθɪː], *s.* die Lethe; (*fig.*) Vergessenheit.

letter [ˈlɛtə], 1. *s.* der Buchstabe; die Letter, Type, Schrift (*Typ.*); der Brief, das Schreiben, die Zuschrift, Mitteilung (*to*, an); buchstäbliche Bedeutung. **(a)** (*with nouns*) – *of acceptance*, das Akzept; – *of application*, das Bewerbungsschreiben; – *of attorney*, die Vollmacht; – *of credence*, das Beglaubigungsschreiben; – *of credit*, der Kreditbrief; – *of introduction* or *recommendation*, der Empfehlungsbrief, das Empfehlungsschreiben; – *of the law*, Buchstabe des Gesetzes. **(b)** (*with adjectives*) *black* –, die Fraktur, gotische Schrift (*Typ.*); *capital* –, großer Buchstabe; *covering* –, das Begleitschreiben; *dead* –, toter Buchstabe; ungültig gewordene Vorschrift; unbestellbarer Brief; –*s patent*, der Patentbrief, die Patenturkunde; *prepaid* –, frankierter Brief; *red*-– *day*, der Festtag, Glückstag, Freudentag; *registered* –, eingeschriebener Brief; *roman* –*s*, die Antiqua (*Typ.*); *small* –, kleiner Buchstabe. **(c)** (*with prepositions*) *by* –, brieflich, schriftlich; *in* – *and spirit*, dem Buchstaben und Inhalt nach; *to the* –, buchstäblich. 2. *v.a.* mit Buchstaben bezeichnen; beschriften (*drawings*); betiteln, mit Lettern *or* Titel versehen (*Bookb.*). **––balance,** *s.* die Briefwaage. **––book,** *s.* das Briefbuch, der Briefordner. **––box,** *s.* der Briefkasten, Briefeinwurf. **––card,** *s.* der Kartenbrief. **––case,** *s.* die Brieftasche. **–ed,** *adj.* gelehrt, gebildet; betitelt (*Bookb.*). **––file,** *s.* der Briefordner. **––founder,** *s.* der Schriftgießer. **–ing,** *s.* die Bezeichnung mit Buchstaben; Betitelung (*of a book*); Beschriftung (*of drawings*); Aufschrift, der Aufdruck; das Schriftschreiben (*Art*). **––lock,** *s.* das Buchstabenschloß, Vexierschloß. **––perfect,** *adj.* vollständig und genau. **–press,** *s.* der Druck, Text; –*press printing*, der Pressendruck, Buchdruck. **––press,** *s.* die Kopierpresse. **––rack,** *s.* der Briefhalter, Briefständer. **–s,** *pl.* die Literatur; *man of* –*s*, der Literat. **––weight,** *s.* der Briefbeschwerer. **––writer,** *s.* der Briefschreiber, Briefsteller.

lettuce [ˈlɛtɪs], *s.* der Lattich; *garden* –, (Garten)-Salat; *round-headed garden* –, Kopfsalat.

leuco–cyte [ˈljuːkəsɑɪt], *s.* weißes Blutkörperchen. **–ma** [–ˈkoumə], *s.* die Hornhauttrübung. **–rrhœa** [–rɪə], *s.* Leukorrhöe (*Med.*).

levant [ləˈvænt], *v.n.* (*coll.*) durchbrennen, durchgehen.

[1]**levee** [ˈlɛvɪ], 1. *s.* (*Amer.*) der Uferdamm, Schutzdamm eines Flußes. 2. *v.a.* eindämmen (*a river*).

[2]**levee** [ˈlɛvɪ], *s.* das Lever, der Morgenempfang (eines Fürsten).

level [lɛvl], **1.** *s.* ebene, gerade *or* waagerechte Fläche; gleiche Höhe *or* Stufe, dasselbe Niveau, das Niveau, der Grad, Stand, (*fig.*) Höhestand; die Höhenlage; Wasserwaage, Libelle (*Carp, etc.*), das Richtscheit (*Mas.*); die Sohle, der Stollen (*Min.*); *datum* –, die Bezugsebene; *dead* –, gerade Ebene, (*fig.*) Eintönigkeit; *find one's* –, an die richtige Stelle kommen; sich ausgleichen (*Phys.*); *low-–attack*, der Tiefflugangriff (*Av.*); – *of prices*, das Preisniveau, der Durchschnittspreis; *oil* –, der Ölstand; (*coll.*) *on the* –, ehrlich, offen, vertrauenswürdig; *on a* – *with*, in gleicher Höhe mit, (*fig.*) auf gleicher Höhe *or* Stufe mit; *sea* –, – *of the sea*, der Meeresspiegel, die Meereshöhe; *water* –, der Wasserstand. **2.** *v.a.* waagerecht, gerade *or* eben machen, ebnen, planieren, nivellieren (*ground*); dem (Erd)Boden gleichmachen; (*fig.*) aufs gleiche Niveau bringen, ausgleichen, gleichmachen; zielen, richten (*a weapon*) (*at*, auf (*Acc.*) *or* nach; *against*, gegen); richten (*criticism, etc.*) (*against* or *at*, gegen); – *a reproach at a p.*, einem etwas zum Vorwurf machen; – *down*, herabdrücken, herabsetzen (*as wages*), hinunterdrücken, hinabschrauben, nach unten ausgleichen; – *off*, abfangen (*Av.*); – *up*, auf gleiche Höhe bringen; erhöhen (*as wages*), hinaufschrauben, nach oben ausgleichen; – *with* or *to the ground*, dem (Erd)Boden gleichmachen. **3.** *adj.* waagerecht, horizontal; eben, gerade, flach; (*fig.*) gleich, gleichmäßig, ausgeglichen (*of style*); – *crossing*, der Bahnübergang (*Railw.*); *do one's – best*, sein möglichstes tun; – *race*, ausgeglichenes Rennen; – *stress*, gleichstarke *or* schwebende Betonung (*Phonet.*); – *with*, in gleicher Höhe mit, (*fig.*) auf gleicher Höhe *or* Stufe mit; *draw – with*, einholen, in gleiche Linie kommen mit. **--headed,** *adj.* verständig, klarblickend. **-ling mechanism,** *s.* die Horizontierung (*Gunn.*). **-ling-screw,** *s.* die Stellschraube.

lever ['lɪ:və], 1. *s.* der Hebel, Hebebaum (*Tech.*); Anker (*Horol.*); *hand* –, der Griffhebel. 2. *v.a.* mit einem Hebel heben *or* bewegen. **-age,** *s.* die Hebelwirkung, Hebelanwendung; Hebelkraft, (*fig.*) der Einfluß. **--watch,** *s.* die Ankeruhr.

leveret ['lɛvərɪt], *s.* junger Hase.

leviathan [lɪ'vaɪəθən], *s.* der Leviathan; das Seeungeheuer, (*fig.*) Ungetüm.

levigat-e ['lɛvɪgeɪt], *v.a.* zerreiben, zerstoßen, pulverisieren, abschlämmen. **-ion** [-'geɪʃən], *s.* die Zerreibung.

levitat-e ['lɛvɪteɪt], 1. *v.a.* schweben lassen. 2. *v.n.* frei schweben; leicht werden. **-ion** [-'teɪʃən], *s.* das Schweben.

levity ['lɛvɪtɪ], *s.* die Leichtfertigkeit, der Leichtsinn; die Flüchtigkeit; *with* –, leichtfertig.

levulose ['lɪ:vjəlous], *s.* der Obstzucker, Fruchtzucker (*Chem.*).

levy ['lɛvɪ], 1. *v.a.* erheben (*taxes*); ausheben (*troops*); anfangen (*war*); auferlegen (*a fine*) (*upon* (*Dat.*)). 2. *s.* die Erhebung (*of taxes*), der Beitrag; die Aushebung, das Aufgebot (*Mil.*); ausgehobene Truppen (*pl.*), *capital* –, die Kapitalabgabe.

lewd [lju:d], *adj.* liederlich, unzüchtig. **-ness,** *s.* die Unzucht, Liederlichkeit.

lewis ['lu:ɪs], *s.* der (Stein)Wolf.

lexic-al ['lɛksɪkl], *adj.* lexikalisch, **-ographer** [-'kɔgrəfə], *s.* der Wörterbuchverfasser, Lexikograph. **-on** [-kən], *s.* das Wörterbuch, Lexikon.

liab-ility [laɪə'bɪlɪtɪ], *s.* die Verantwortlichkeit; Verbindlichkeit, Haftbarkeit, Haftpflicht (*C.L.*); das Ausgesetztsein, Unterworfensein (*to* (*Dat.*)); der Hang, die Neigung (*to*, zu); *pl.* Schulden, Belastungen, Passiva, geldliche Verpflichtungen (*C.L.*); *accept* or *incur –ility*, Verantwortlichkeit übernehmen, *joint –ility*, die Gesamthaftung; *limited –ility*, beschränkte Haftpflicht; *discharge* or *meet one's –ilities*, seinen Verbindlichkeiten nachkommen; *–ility to military service*, die Wehrpflicht. **-le** ['laɪəbl], *adj.* ausgesetzt, unterworfen (*to* (*Dat.*)); haftbar, haftpflichtig (*C.L.*); verantwortlich; *be –le*, unterworfen sein, unterliegen (*to* (*Dat.*)); zu gewärtigen haben (*to* (*Acc.*)); neigen (*to*, zu); in Gefahr sein; *be –le for*, haften für; *–le to be forgotten*, in Gefahr sein, vergessen zu werden; *difficulties are –le to occur*, Schwierigkeiten ergeben sich leicht; *this price is –le to discount*, von diesem Preis geht ein Rabatt ab; *–le to duty*, zollpflichtig; *be –le to prosecution*, sich strafbar machen, strafrechtliche Verfolgung zu gewärtigen haben.

liaison [lɪ:'eɪzən], *s.* die Liebschaft; Bindung (*Philol.*); Verbindung, Fühlung, Zusammenarbeit (*Mil.*). **--officer,** *s.* der Verbindungsoffizier.

liana [lɪ'ɑ:nə], *s.* die Schlingpflanze, Liane.

liar ['laɪə], *s.* der Lügner.

lias ['laɪəs], *s.* der & die Lias, schwarzer Jura (*Geol.*).

libation [laɪ'beɪʃən], *s.* das Trankopfer.

libel [laɪbl], 1. *s.* die Klageschrift; Schmähschrift (*Law*); (*coll.*) Verleumdung, Verunglimpfung, Beleidigung; (*coll.*) *it is an absolute* –, es ist ein wahrer Hohn (*on*, auf (*Acc.*)); *action for* –, die Verleumdungsklage. 2. *v.a.* eine Klageschrift einreichen (*a p.*, gegen einen) (*Law*); schriftlich und öffentlich schmähen, verleumden, beschimpfen. **-lant** [-ənt], *s.* der Kläger (*Law*). **-lee** [-'lɪ:], *s.* Beklagte(r), *m.* (*Law*). **-ler** [-ə], *s.* der Schmähschriftschreiber; Verleumder. **-lous** [-ləs], *adj.* verleumderisch, Schmäh–.

liberal ['lɪbərəl], 1. *adj.* freigebig (*of*, mit); ansehnlich, beträchtlich, reichlich (bemessen); großzügig, offen, frei(sinnig), weitherzig, aufgeklärt; unbefangen, vorurteilslos (*as views*); offen; liberal (*Pol.*); – *arts*, freie *or* schöne Künste, Geisteswissenschaften (*pl.*); – *education*, die Allgemeinbildung, allgemeine Bildung; – *interpretation*, ungezwungene *or* freie Auslegung; – *profession*, freier Beruf. 2. *s.* Liberale(r), *m.* (*Pol.*). **-ism,** *s.* der Liberalismus (*Pol.*). **-istic** [-'lɪstɪk], *adj.* liberal gesinnt. **-ity** [-'rælɪtɪ], *s.* die Freigebigkeit; Freisinnigkeit, Unbefangenheit, Unparteilichkeit.

liberat-e ['lɪbəraɪt], *v.a.* befreien (*from*, von); freigeben, freilassen (*slaves*); freimachen, entbinden, ausscheiden (*Chem.*); *be –ed*, auftreten (*Chem.*). **-ion** [-'reɪʃən], *s.* die Befreiung (*from*, von), Freilassung (aus). **-or,** *s.* der Befreier.

libertin-age ['lɪbətɪnɪdʒ], *s. see* **-ism. -e** ['lɪbətɪn], 1. *s.* der Wüstling; römischer Freigelassener, *m.* (*Hist.*); der Freidenker. 2. *adj.* liederlich; freigeistig. **-ism,** *s.* die Liederlichkeit, Auschweifung.

liberty ['lɪbətɪ], *s.* die Freiheit, Ungebundenheit; (*usually pl.*) das Recht, Vorrecht, Privilegium; die Erlaubnis, freie Wahl; der Freibezirk, die (Stadt)-Freiheit; die Ungebührlichkeit, Frechheit; *at* –, frei; *be at* –, freie Hand haben, die Erlaubnis haben, dürfen; *you are at* –, es steht Ihnen frei; *be at – to disclose*, enthüllen dürfen; *set at* –, befreien, freilassen, in Freiheit setzen; – *of conscience*, die Glaubensfreiheit, Gewissensfreiheit; – *of the press*, die Pressefreiheit; *religious* –, die Religionsfreiheit; *take liberties*, sich (*Dat.*) Freiheiten herausnehmen, gestatten *or* erlauben (*with*, gegenüber). **--man,** *s.* der Matrose auf Urlaub.

libid-inous [lɪ'bɪdɪnəs], *adj.* unzüchtig, wollüstig. **-o** ['lɪbɪdou], *s.* der Libido, Geschlechtstrieb, die Lustbegierde (*Psych.*).

libra ['laɪbrə], *s.* die Waage (*Astr.*).

librar-ian [laɪ'brɛ:ərɪən], *s.* der Bibliothekar; *chief –ian*, der Bibliotheksdirektor. **-ianship,** *s.* das Amt eines Bibliothekars. **-y** ['laɪbrərɪ], *s.* die Bibliothek, Bücherei; das Bibliotheksgebäude; die Bücherreihe; *circulating* or *lending –y*, die Leihbibliothek; *free –y*, die Volksbücherei; *reference –y*, die Handbibliothek.

librate ['laɪbreɪt], *v.n.* schwanken, sich im Gleichgewicht halten (*Astr.*).

librett-ist [lɪ'brɛtɪst], *s.* der Librettoschreiber, Textdichter. **-o** [-tou], *s.* das Libretto, Textbuch, der Operntext.

lice [laɪs], *pl. of* **louse.**

licen-ce, -se ['laɪsəns], 1. *s.* die Erlaubnis, Bewilligung, amtliche Genehmigung; die Konzession, Lizenz; der Erlaubnisschein, Schein; die Zügellosigkeit, Ausschweifung; *dog –ce*, die Hundesteuer(marke); *driving –ce*, der Führerschein; *gun-–ce*, der Waffenschein; *poetic –ce*, dichterische Freiheit; *special –ce*, die Sonder-Eheerlaubnis; *take out a –ce*, sich (*Dat.*) eine Konzession beschaffen; *wireless –ce*, die Radiogebühr. 2. *v.a.* (usually *–se*) amtlich genehmigen, bewilligen, konzessionieren (*things*); zulassen, freigeben (*a play*); ermächtigen (*Acc.*); *–sed victualler*, konzessionierter Gastwirt. **-see** [-'sɪ:], *s.* der Konzessionsinhaber, Lizenzinhaber; konzessionierter Gastwirt. **-ser,** *s.* der Aussteller einer Konzession. **-tiate** [laɪ'sɛnʃɪeɪt], *s.* der Lizenziat.

licentious [laɪ'sɛnʃɪəs], *adj.* zügellos, ausschweifend; liederlich. **-ness,** *s.* die Zügellosigkeit Ausschweifung, Liederlichkeit.

lichen [['laɪkən], *s.* die Flechte (*Bot.*, *Med.*).

lich-gate ['lɪtʃgeɪt], *s.* das Friedhofstor.

lick [lɪk], 1. *v.a.* lecken, lecken an, belecken; (*sl.*) verprügeln; besiegen, übertreffen, schlagen; bestreichen (*as waves*); – *s.o.'s boots*, vor einem kriechen; – *the dust*, ins Gras beißen; (*sl.*) *that –s everything*, das ist die Höhe *or* der Gipfel, das übersteigt alles; (*sl.*) *it –s me how . . .*, es geht übr meine Begriffe wie . . .; (*coll.*) **– *into shape*,** zustutzen (*Acc.*), (die richtige) Gestalt *or* Form geben (*Dat.*). 2. *v.n.* züngeln (*of flames*). 3. *s.* das Lecken; (*sl.*) die Eile, der Hetz; *at a tremendous* –, mit rasender Hast; *cat-–, a – and a promise*, die Katzenwäsche; – *of paint*, flüchtiger Anstrich; *salt-–*, die Salzlecke. **-er,** *s.* der Lecker, Öler (*Tech.*). **-erish,** *adj.* naschhaft, lecker; (be)gierig, lüstern (*after* or *for*, nach). **–ing,** *s.* das Lecken; (*sl.*) die Niederlage (*Sport*); (*sl.*) die Tracht Prügel, Schmiere. **–spittle,** *s.* der Speichellecker.

licorice, *s. see* **liquorice.**

lictor ['lɪktə], *s.* der Amtsdiener.

lid [lɪd], *s.* der Deckel; (*sl.*) der Hut; (*eye*)–, das Augenlid; *put the – on a th.*, einer S. die Krone aufsetzen, dem Faß den Boden ausschlagen.

[1]**lie** [lɑɪ], 1. *s.* die Lüge; *tell –s* or *a –*, lügen; *give a p. the –*, einen Lügen strafen, einen als Lügner hinstellen; *give the – to a th.*, etwas als unwahr erweisen; *white –*, die Notlüge. 2. *v.n.* lügen; – *like a book*, lügen wie gedruckt; – *in one's throat*, das Blaue vom Himmel herunterlügen; – *to s.o.*, einen belügen, einem vorlügen.

[2]**lie** [lɑɪ], **1.** *s.* die Lage; – *of the land*, die Lage der Dinge; das Lager (*of animals*). **2.** *ir.v.n.* liegen, ruhen; liegenbleiben; gelegen sein, sich befinden (*of places*); sich lagern, gelagert sein; existieren, bestehen; sich legen, stützen *or* lehnen (*on*, auf (*Acc.*), *against*, an (*Acc.*)); führen, gerichtet sein (*as roads*); anhängig *or* zulässig sein (*appeal, etc.*) (*Law*); (*Prov.*) *let sleeping dogs –*, die S. auf sich beruhen lassen. **(a)** (*with adverbs*) – *about*, umherliegen; – *by*, unbenutzt liegen, brachliegen; (*sl.*) – *doggo*, sich verborgen halten, ruhig liegen; – *down*, sich niederlegen; *take it lying down*, es sich (*Dat.*) gefallen lassen, ohne weiteres hinnehmen; – *hard* or *heavy on*, schwer lasten auf; – *idle*, stillstehen; – *in*, in die Wochen kommen; – *low*, sich verborgen halten, sich nicht verraten, sich abwartend verhalten; – *off*, vom Lande abhalten (*Naut.*); – *open*, ausgesetzt sein, unterliegen (*to* (*Dat.*)); – *over*, aufgeschoben werden, liegenbleiben; – *to*, beilegen (*Naut.*); – *up*, das Bett hüten. **(b)** (*with prepositions*) – *at anchor*, vor Anker liegen; *this –s at his door*, das ist ihm zuzuschreiben, das wird ihm zur Last gelegt; – *at death's door*, am Rande des Grabes liegen; – *at full length*, ausgestreckt daliegen; – *at the mercy of a p.*, jemandes Willkür preisgegeben sein; – *at the root of a matter*, einer Sache zugrunde liegen; – *in*, liegen *or* bestehen in; *her talents do not – in that direction* or – *that way*, dazu hat sie keine Anlagen; *as far as in me –s*, soweit es in meinen Kräften steht; – *in state*, auf dem Paradebett liegen; – *in wait for a p.*, einem auflauern; – *on the bed one has made*, wie man sich bettet so liegt (*or* schläft) man; – *on hand*, (unverkauft) liegen bleiben; – *on a p.*, einem obliegen (*Law*); – *under*, unterliegen (*Dat.*); – *under an imputation*, angeschuldigt *or* beschuldigt sein (*of* (*Gen.*)); – *under the necessity*, genötigt sein; – *under sentence of death*, zum Tode verurteilt worden sein; – *under* (*the*) *suspicion*, unter (dem) Verdacht stehen (*of* (*Gen.*); *of doing*, getan zu haben); – *with*, liegen *or* schlafen bei; beiwohnen (*a woman*); *it –s with him*, es liegt *or* steht bei ihm, es ist an ihm. **--abed,** *s.* der Langschläfer.

lief [lɪ:f], *adv.* (*archaic*) gern; *I had as – go as stay*, ich ginge ebenso gern wie ich bliebe; *I had as – die as go*, ich würde lieber sterben als gehen.

liege [lɪ:dʒ], 1. *adj.* lehnspflichtig, Lehns–; – *lord*, der Lehnsherr. 2. *s.* der Lehnsmann, Vasall; Lehnsherr.

lien [lɪ:ən], *s.* das Zurückbehaltungsrecht, Pfandrecht (*on*, auf).

lieu [lju:], *s.* (only in) *in – of*, anstatt.

lieutenan–cy [lɛf'tɛnənsɪ, *Navy & Amer.* lʊ:'tɛnənsɪ], *s.* der Leutnantsrang; die Statthalterschaft. **–t** [–ənt], *s.* der Oberleutnant (*Mil.*), Kapitänleutnant (*Navy*); Statthalter, Stellvertreter; *first –t*, der Oberleutnant; *lord –t*, der Vertreter des Königs; *second –t*, der Leutnant. **--colonel,** *s.* der Oberstleutnant. **--commander,** *s.* der Korvettenkapitän. **--general,** *s.* der Generalleutnant. **--governor,** *s.* der Unterstatthalter.

life [lɑɪf], *s.* das Leben; belebende Kraft, die Lebenskraft, Seele, Lebendigkeit, Lebhaftigkeit; der Lebenswandel, menschliches Leben, das Menschenleben; die Lebenszeit, Lebensdauer; der Lebenslauf, die Lebensbeschreibung; die auf Lebenszeit versicherte Person (*insurance*). **(a)** (*with nouns*) – *and death struggle*, der Kampf auf Leben und Tod; *a matter of – and death*, eine Sache auf Leben und Tod *or* von höchster Wichtigkeit; *expectation of –*, mutmaßliche Lebensdauer; *–and soul of the party*, die Seele *or* treibende Kraft der Gesellschaft. **(b)** (*with adjectives*) *have a charmed –*, kugelfest *or* unverwundbar sein; – *to come*, zukünftiges Leben, das Leben nach dem Tode; *early –*, die Jugend; *in early –*, in jungen Jahren; – *everlasting*, ewiges Leben; *high –*, das Leben der vornehmen Klassen; *as large as –*, lebensgroß, in Lebensgröße; *low –*, das Leben der niederen Klassen; *still –*, das Stilleben (*Art*). **(c)** (*with verbs*) *give – to*, beleben; *lay down one's – for*, sein Leben hingeben für; *lead a good –*, einen guten Lebenswandel führen; *they lost their lives*, sie verloren ihr Leben, sie kamen ums Leben; *put – into*, see *give – to*; *many lives were saved*, viele Menschen wurden gerettet *or* kamen mit dem Leben davon; *see –*, das Leben genießen *or* kennenlernen; *seek a p.'s –*, einem nach dem Leben trachten; *take a p.'s* (*or one's own*) –, einem (*or* sich) das Leben nehmen; *take one's – in one's hands*, sein Leben riskieren. **(d)** (*with prepositions*) *for –*, lebenslänglich, auf Lebenszeit; *not for the – of me*, nicht um alles in der Welt, um keinen Preis, absolut nicht, beim besten Willen nicht; *run for one's –* or *for dear –*, aus Leibeskräften *or* ums (liebe) Leben davonlaufen; *drawn from –*, nach dem Leben *or* der Natur gezeichnet; *in danger of one's –*, in Todesgefahr; *go in danger of one's –*, in ständiger Lebensgefahr schweben; *come to –*, belebt werden; *come to – again*, wieder aufleben; *to the –*, nach dem Leben, naturgetreu; *upon* (or *'pon*) *my –*, so wahr ich lebe; *enter upon –*, in die Welt eintreten; *with – and limb*, mit heiler Haut. **--annuity,** *s.* die Leibrente. **--assurance,** *s.* die Lebensversicherung. **--belt,** *s.* der Rettungsring. **--blood,** *s.* (*fig.*) das Herzblut. **--boat,** *s.* das Rettungsboot. **--giving,** *adj.* belebend, lebenspendend. **--guard,** *s.* die Leibwache. **--guards,** *pl.* die Garde, das Gardekorps. **--guardsman,** *s.* der Gardist. **--insurance,** *s. see* **--assurance.** **– interest,** *s.* lebenslänglicher Nießbrauch. **--jacket,** *s.* der Rettungsgürtel, die Schwimmweste. **–less,** *adj.* leblos, tot; unbelebt, (*fig.*) unwirksam; kraftlos, schlaff. **–lessness,** *s.* die Leblosigkeit, Kraftlosigkeit. **–like,** *adj.* lebenswahr, naturgetreu. **--line,** *s.* die Rettungsleine; Signalleine (*of diver*); (*fig.*) lebenswichtige Verbindung. **–long,** *adj.* lebenslänglich. **--membership,** *s.* lebenslängliche Mitgliedschaft. **--office,** *s.* die Lebensversicherungsanstalt. **--preserver,** *s.* der Rettungsgürtel, die Schwimmweste; der Bleistock, Totschläger. (*sl.*) **–r,** *s.* lebenslänglicher Zuchthäusler. **--sentence,** *s.* das Urteil auf lebenslänglichen Kerker. **--size, --sized,** *adj.* lebensgroß, in Lebensgröße. **--strings,** *pl.* der Lebensfaden. **--subscription,** *s.* einmaliger Beitrag auf Lebenszeit. **--table,** *s.* die Sterblichkeitstabelle. **–time,** *s.* die Lebenszeit, das Lebensalter. **--work,** *s.* das Lebenswerk.

lift [lɪft], 1. *v.a.* (auf)heben, emporheben, erheben, hochheben; aufschlagen; ernten (*potatoes, etc.*); (*sl.*) klemmen, klauen, mausen; – *down*, herunterholen; – *up one's eyes*, die Augen erheben; *have one's face –ed*, sich die Runzeln entfernen lassen; *not – a finger*, keinen Finger rühren; – *one's hand against*, sich auflehnen gegen, die Hand erheben gegen; – *up one's voice*, die Stimme erheben. 2. *v.n.* sich heben; aufsteigen, sich zerstreuen (*as mist*). 3. *s.* das (Auf)Heben; der Hub, die Hubhöhe (*of a valve, etc.*); der Fahrstuhl, Aufzug; Auftrieb (*Av.*); Hebebaum (*Mach.*); (*Naut.*); (*coll.*) der Beistand; *give s.o. a –*, einen mitfahren lassen; (*fig.*) einem helfen. **–er,** *s.* die Knagge, der Nocken (*Tech.*); *shop-–er*, der Ladendieb; *weight-–er*, der Gewichtheber. **–ing,** *s.* das Heben. **–ing-force,** *s.* die Hebekraft; Hubkraft, der (die) Auftrieb(kraft) (*Av.*). **–ing-jack,** *s.* die Wagenwinde, der Wagenheber. **--up,** *adj.* Klapp–.

ligament ['lɪgəmənt], *s.* das Band, die Sehne, Flechse.

ligat–e [lɑɪ'geɪt], *v.a.* verbinden; unterbinden (*artery*). **–ion** [–'geɪʃən], *s.* das Verbinden, Unterbinden. **–ure** ['lɪgətʃə], *s.* das Band, die Binde, der

Verband; die Unterbindung (*of artery*); Ligatur (*Typ.*), Bindung (*Mus.*).

light [laɪt], **1.** *s.* das Licht; die Beleuchtung, Lampe, Kerze; das Feuer, Leuchtfeuer, der Leuchtturm; das Sonnenlicht, Tageslicht, der Tag, die Helligkeit; Fensteröffnung; (*fig.*) die Einsicht, Erkenntnis, Aufklärung, Erleuchtung; Leuchte (*person*); *pl.* hellere Teile eines Bildes; (*fig.*) Eingebungen, geistige Fähigkeiten (*pl.*). (*a*) (*with verbs*) *give a p. a –*, einem Feuer *or* ein Streichholz geben; *put a – to*, anzünden; *see the –*, das Licht der Welt erblicken; zum ersten Male aufgeführt werden (*of plays*); (*coll.*) überzeugt *or* aufgeklärt werden; *throw* or *shed – (up)on*, Licht werfen auf. (*b*) (*with prepositions*) *according to his –s*, nach bester Einsicht; *by the – of*, beim Schein von; *in a good –*, gut beleuchtet; *in the – of*, unter Heranziehung von, im Hinblick auf, angesichts (*Gen.*); *put a th. in its true –*, etwas in seiner richtigen Beleuchtung stellen; *stand in one's own –*, sich (*Dat.*) selbst im Lichte stehen; *get out of the –*, aus dem Lichte gehen; *bring to –*, ans Licht *or* an den Tag bringen; *come to –*, ans Licht *or* an den Tag kommen. (*c*) (*with nouns & adjectives*) *flashing –*, das Blitzfeuer, Blinkfeuer, Drehfeuer; *harbour –*, das Hafenfeuer; *masthead –*, das Topplicht; *navigation –*, das Feuer; *pierhead –*, das Molenfeuer; *revolving –*, das Drehfeuer; *side––s*, Positionslichter, Seitenlichter. **2.** *adj.* licht, hell; (*fig.*) leuchtend, strahlend; blond; *– blue*, hellblau. **3.** *ir.v.a.* (imperf. & p.p. *lit* or *–ed*) anzünden (*a fire or lamp*); beleuchten, erleuchten (*a thing*); *– a cigar*, sich (*Dat.*) eine Zigarre anzünden; *– a p.*, einem leuchten; *– up*, hell beleuchten, (*fig.*) erleuchten, aufhellen, aufheitern. **4.** *ir.v.n.* (also *– up*) hell werden, leuchten; (*fig.*) aufleuchten (*as the face*); (*coll.*) sich eine Pfeife (usw.) anzünden. **––ball**, *s.* die Leuchtkugel. **–en**, *see* **lighten**. **–er**, *see* **[1]lighter**. **––fitting**, *s.* der Beleuchtungskörper. **–house**, *s.* der Leuchtturm. **–ing**, *see* **lightning**. **–ness**, *s.* die Helligkeit. **–ning**, *see* **lightning**. **–ship**, *s.* das Feuerschiff, Leuchtschiff. **––treatment**, *s.* das Lichtheilverfahren (*Med.*). **–wood**, *s.* das Kienholz.

[2]light [laɪt], I. *adj. & adv.* leicht, nicht schwer, unschwer; flott, flink, behende (*as movements*); leichtfertig, sorglos, oberflächlich (*character, etc.*); locker (*of bread, soil, etc.*); dünn (*of cloth, clothing, etc.*); leicht verdaulich (*of food*); schwach (*of sleep*); unbeladen, leer (*of ships, etc.*); leicht zu tun, tragen *or* ertragen; *make – of*, sich nichts machen aus, auf die leichte Schulter nehmen; *– car*, das Kleinauto; *– heart*, freies *or* sorgloses Herz; *– infantry*, leichtbewaffnete Infanterie; *– literature*, die Unterhaltungsliteratur; *no – matter*, keine Kleinigkeit, geringfügige Sache; *– metal*, das Leichtmetall; *– music*, die Unterhaltungsmusik; *– of foot*, schnellfüßig, leichtfüßig; *– punishment*, milde Strafe; *– railway*, die Kleinbahn; *– weight*, das Mindergewicht, Untergewicht. 2. *v.n.* (*archaic*) absteigen (*from*, von); *– on*, fallen auf (*Acc.*), sich niederlassen auf; (*fig.*) stoßen *or* geraten auf, zufällig treffen. **––armed**, *adj.* leicht bewaffnet. **–en**, I. *v.a.* leichter machen; leichtern, lichten, löschen (*Naut.*); (*fig.*) erleichtern, aufheitern. 2. *v.n.* leichter werden. **–er**, *comp. adj.* leichter; *see also* **[2]light**. **–er-than-air**, *adj.* leichter als Luft, mit natürlichem Auftrieb. **––fingered**, *adj.* langfingerig, diebisch; geschickt. **––footed**, *adj.* leichtfüßig, schnellfüßig. **––handed**, *adj.* leicht belastet, mit leeren Händen. **––headed**, *adj.* wirr im Kopf, schwindlig, benommen; (*fig.*) unbesonnen, leichtfertig. **––headedness**, *s.* die Benommenheit; Unbesonnenheit. **––hearted**, *adj.* leichten Herzens, leichtbeschwingt, wohlgemut, fröhlich. **––heartedness**, *s.* der Frohsinn. **––heavyweight**, *s.* das Leichtschwergewicht (*less than 175 lb.*) (*Boxing*). **––horse**, *s.* leichte Reiterei. **–ly**, *adv.* leicht; oberflächlich, obenhin; gedankenlos, unbesonnen, leichtfertig, flüchtig; (*Prov.*) *–ly come, –ly go*, wie gewonnen, so zerronnen; *take –ly*, auf die leichte Achsel nehmen; *think –ly of*, leicht nehmen, geringschätzen; *treat –ly*, als unerheblich behandeln. **––minded**, *adj.* leichtsinnig. **–ness**, *s.* die Leichtigkeit; Leichtfertigkeit, der Leichtsinn; die Flinkheit (*of movement*); Leichtverdaulichkeit (*of food*); Milde (*of punishment, etc.*); *see also* **[1]light**. **––o'-love**, *s.* (*archaic*) die Trulle. **–some**, *adj.* leicht, behende; fröhlich. wohlgemut. **––weight**, I. *s.* das Leichtgewicht (*less than 135 lb.*) (*Boxing*). 2. *attrib. adj.* Leicht–.

lighten ['laɪtən], I. *v.n.* blitzen; *it –s*, es blitzt *or* leuchtet; hell werden, sich aufhellen. 2. *v.a.* aufhellen (*colour*); *see also* **[2]light**.

[1]lighter ['laɪtə], *s.* der Anzünder; das (Taschen)-Feuerzeug.

[2]lighter ['laɪtə], *s.* der Leichter, Lichter, das Lichterschiff. **–age**, *s.* die Kahnfracht, Lichterkosten (*pl.*), die Löschgebühr. **–man**, *s.* der Lichterschiffer, Löscher.

lighting ['laɪtɪŋ], *s.* die Beleuchtung; *– effect*, die Lichtwirkung. **––up**, *s.* die Erleuchtung; *––up time*, die Zeit eintretender Dunkelheit.

lightning ['laɪtnɪŋ], I. *s.* der Blitz; *forked –*, der Zickzackblitz; *like –*, *quick as –*, wie der Blitz, blitzartig, blitzschnell; *like greased –*, wie geschmiert; *struck by –*, vom Blitz erschlagen; *summer –*, das Wetterleuchten. 2. *adj.* blitzschnell; *with – speed*, mit Blitzesschnelle. **––conductor**, *s.*, **––rod**, *s.* der Blitzableiter.

lights [laɪts], *pl.* die Lunge (*as animal food*).

lightsome ['laɪtsəm], *see* **[2]light**.

lign–eous ['lɪgnɪəs], *adj.* hölzern; holzig, Holz–. **–ify** [–nɪfaɪ], *v.a.* (*& n.*) (sich) in Holz verwandeln, verholzen. **–ine** [–nɪn], *s.* die Holzfaser, der Holzstoff. **–ite** [–naɪt], *s.* die Braunkohle. **–um-vitae** [–nəm'vaɪtɪ], *s.* das Guajakholz.

ligul–a ['lɪgjʊlə], *s.*, **–e** [–jʊ:l], *s.* das Blatthäutchen (*Bot.*). **–ate**, *adj.* strahlblütig, Rand–.

likable ['laɪkəbl], *see under* **[2]like**.

[1]like [laɪk], **1.** *adj.* gleich, ähnlich; wie. (*a*) (*attrib.*) *of – extent*, von gleicher Ausdehnung, ebenso groß; *in – manner*, in gleicher *or* dergleichen Weise, auf gleiche Weise, ebenso; (*Prov.*) *– father, – son*, der Apfel fällt nicht weit vom Stamm; (*Prov.*) *– master, – man*, wie der Herr, so der Knecht; *– sum*, ähnliche Summe. (*b*) (*pred.*) *as – as two peas*, ähnlich wie ein Ei dem andern; *it is – hearing one's own voice*, man hört gleichsam seine eigene Stimme; *I feel – coming*, ich habe Lust *or* ich möchte kommen; *look –*, so aussehen wie; *nothing* or *not anything – as good as*, lange nicht *or* nicht annähernd *or* nicht bei weitem so gut wie; *there is nothing –*, es geht nichts über; (*coll.*) *something –*, etwa; (*sl.*) *that is something –*, das läßt sich hören; *what is he – ?* wie ist er? wie sieht er aus? (*c*) (*with foll. object*) *that is just – him*, das sieht ihm ähnlich; *they are – each other*, sie sind einander ähnlich; *die – a hero*, wie ein Held sterben; *he is – that*, er ist nun einmal so. (*d*) (*archaic, with inf. expressed or understood*) *he is – to die*, er wird wahrscheinlich sterben; *'tis – enough!* es ist wohl glaublich. **2.** *adv.* *– all prophets he is . . .*, er ist, gleich allen Propheten . . .; *she cannot cook – my mother*, sie kann nicht kochen wie meine Mutter; *don't talk – that*, red' nicht so; *a man – that*, so ein Mann; *a thing – that*, so etwas; (*coll.*) *hurry – anything*, *– mad* or *– the dickens*, eilen wie besessen; (*sl.*) *rant – the devil*, lärmen wie verteufelt; (*coll.*) *as – as not*, höchst wahrscheinlich. **3.** *s.* der, die, das Gleiche; *his –*, seinesgleichen; *their –*, ihresgleichen; *the – of it*, so etwas; *the – of these people*, dergleichen wie diese Leute; (*coll.*) *the –s of him*, seinesgleichen, Leute wie er; (*coll.*) *the –s of me*, unsereiner, meine Wenigkeit; *and the* (*or coll.*) *such –*, und dergleichen; *– attracts –*, gleich und gleich gesellt sich gern. **––minded**, *adj.* gleichgesinnt; *be ––minded with*, derselben Meinung sein wie, übereinstimmen mit. **––mindedness**, *s.* die Gesinnungsgleichheit. **–wise**, *adv.* ebenso, gleichfalls, auch, desgleichen. *See* **liken, likeness**.

[2]like [laɪk], I. *v.a.* gern haben *or* sehen, mögen, leiden, lieben; *– well*, gern mögen; *– better*, lieber mögen; *– best*, am liebsten mögen; *how do you – it?* wie findest du es? wie gefällt es dir? *– pancakes*, Pfannkuchen gern essen; *do you – skating?* laufen Sie gern Schlittschuh? *do you – my hat?* gefällt Ihnen mein Hut? *I do not – to interrupt*, ich unterbreche nur ungern; *I do not – it mentioned*, ich habe nicht gern daß es erwähnt wird; *I – that*, (*ironic*) das ist aber die Höhe; – *well* (*better*), gern (lieber) mögen; *I – her*, ich mag sie gern (leiden), *I should – to know*, ich möchte gern wissen; *I should – you to come*, ich hätte gern *or* möchte daß Sie kommen; *make o.s. –d*, sich beliebt machen (*with*, bei). 2. *v.n.* belieben, wollen, Lust haben; (*just*) *as you –*, wie es Ihnen beliebt, wie Sie wollen, ganz nach Belieben; *as you – it*, wie es euch gefällt. 3. *s.*; *–s and dislikes*, Neigungen und Abneigungen. **–able,** *adj.* liebenswürdig, angenehm; *see* **liking.**

likel–ihood [ˈlaɪklɪhud], *s.* die Wahrscheinlichkeit; *in all –ihood*, aller Wahrscheinlichkeit *or* allem Anschein nach; *there is every –ihood of*, es ist sehr wahrscheinlich daß; *there is little –ihood of*, es ist kaum wahrscheinlich daß. **–y,** 1. *adj.* wahrscheinlich; scheinbar passend *or* geeignet; (*coll.*) vielversprechend; *it is –y he will come* or *he is –y to come*, er kommt wahrscheinlich, es ist wahrscheinlich daß er kommt; *most –y candidate*, der scheinbar geeignetste Bewerber; *he is the most –y to win*, er hat die größte Aussicht zu gewinnen. 2. *adv.* (usually *most* or *very –y*) *he is most –y to win*, er wird höchstwahrscheinlich gewinnen; *not –y*, schwerlich, kaum; *as –y as not*, sehr wahrscheinlich.

liken [ˈlaɪkən], *v.a.* vergleichen (*to*, mit).

likeness [ˈlaɪknɪs], *s.* die Ähnlichkeit, Gleichheit; das Bild, Portrait; *have one's – taken*, sich malen *or* photographieren lassen; *in the – of*, in Gestalt (*Gen.*).

likewise, *see under* [1]**like.**

liking [ˈlaɪkɪŋ], *s.* das Gefallen (*for*, an); die Neigung, Zuneigung, der Geschmack (*for*, für); *take a – to*, Gefallen finden an (*Dat.*), liebgewinnen; *is it to your – ?* ist es nach Ihrem Geschmack? sagt es Ihnen zu? *have a – for*, Gefallen haben an.

lilac [ˈlaɪlək] 1. *s.* (spanischer) Flieder (*Bot.*); das Lila, die Lilafarbe. 2. *adj.* lilafarben, Lila–.

liliaceous [lɪlɪˈeɪʃəs], *adj.* Lilien–, lilienartig.

lilt [lɪlt], 1. *s.* fröhliches Lied; rhythmischer Schwung. 2. *v.a.* fröhlich singen, trällern; *–ing gait*, wiegender Gang.

lily [ˈlɪlɪ], *s.* die Lilie; – *of the valley*, das Maiglöckchen. **– -livered,** *adj.* bangbüxig, benaut, memmenhaft, weibisch. **– -white,** *adj.* lilienweiß.

[1]**limb** [lɪm], *s.* das Glied; der Ast (*of a tree*); *artificial –*, die Prothese, das Ersatzglied; (*sl.*) – *of the law*, der Rechtsverdreher; *tear – from –*, in Stücke zerreißen. **–ed,** *adj. suffix* –gliedrig. **–s,** *pl.* Gliedmaßen (*pl.*).

[2]**limb** [lɪm], *s.* der Rand (*Astr.*, *Bot.*).

[1]**limber** [ˈlɪmbə], *adj.* biegsam, geschmeidig.

[2]**limber** [ˈlɪmbə], 1. *s.* die Protze (*of gun-carriage*). 2. *v.a.* (– *up*) aufprotzen. **–s,** *pl.* der Wasserlauf, Wasserlauflöcher (*pl.*) (*of keelson*) (*Naut.*).

limbo [ˈlɪmbou], *s.* die Vorhölle; (*fig.*) Rumpelkammer; Vergessenheit; (*sl.*) das Kittchen.

[1]**lime** [laɪm], 1. *s.* der Kalk (*Chem.*, *Min.*, *etc.*); Vogelleim; *quick –*, ungelöschter Kalk; *slaked –*, gelöschter Kalk. 2. *v.a.* mit Kalk düngen (*Agr.*); mit Vogelleim bestreichen. **– -burner,** *s.* der Kalkbrenner. **– -kiln,** *s.* der Kalkofen. **–light,** *s.* das Kalklicht; der Scheinwerfer (*Theat.*); (*fig.*) das Licht der Öffentlichkeit; *in the –light*, unter Scheinwerferlicht; (*fig.*) im Brennpunkt *or* Mittelpunkt des Interesses; *bring into the –light*, *throw the –light on*, (*fig.*) in helles Licht rücken; *disappear from the –light*, (*fig.*) aus dem Interesse verschwinden. **– -twig,** *s.* die Leimrute. **–stone,** *s.* der Kalkstein. **– -wash,** *s.* die (Kalk)Tünche. **– -water,** *s.* das Kalkwasser; *see* **limy.**

[2]**lime** [laɪm], *s.* die Linde; der Lindenbaum.

[3]**lime** [laɪm], *s.* die Limone; Limette. **– -juice,** *s.* der Limonensaft.

limen [ˈlaɪmən], *s.* die Reizschwelle, Empfindungsgrenze (*Psych.*).

limerick [ˈlɪmərɪk], *s.* fünfzeiliger Schüttelreimvers.

limey [ˈlaɪmɪ], *s.* (*Amer. sl.*) der Engländer.

limit [ˈlɪmɪt], 1. *s.* die Grenze, Schranke, Beschränkung; der Endpunkt, das Ziel; der Grenzwert (*Math.*); zulässiger Spielraum (*Mech.*); äußerster Preis, der Mindestbetrag; Höchstpreis; die Gültigkeitsdauer (*C.L.*); *there is a – to everything*, alles hat seine Grenzen; *set –s to a th.*, einer S. Grenzen setzen; (*coll.*) *that's the* (*absolute*) *– !* da hört doch alles auf! das ist wirklich die Höhe *or* der Gipfel *or* unerhört! (*coll.*) *he is the – !* er ist ohnegleichen *or* einfach unmöglich! *off –s* (*Amer.*), Zutritt verboten; *within –s*, in Grenzen, maßvoll; *without –*, ohne Grenze *or* Schranken. 2. *v.a.* begrenzen, beschränken, einschränken (*to*, auf). **–ation** [–ˈteɪʃən], *s.* die Beschränkung, Begrenzung, Einschränkung; Verjährung (*Law*); (*fig.*) Grenze; *know one's –ations*, seine Grenzen kennen. **–ative** [–ətɪv], *adj.* beschränkend, einschränkend. **–ed** [–ɪd], *adj.* beschränkt (*to*, auf (*Acc.*)); *–ed liability*, beschränkte Haftung; *–ed* (*liability*) *company*, die Gesellschaft mit beschränkter Haftung; *–ed monarchy*, konstitutionelle Monarchie; *–ed* (*train*) (*Amer.*), der Luxus-Schnellzug. **–less,** *adj.* grenzenlos, schrankenlos.

limn [lɪm], *v.a.* (*Poet.*) malen, zeichnen, darstellen. **–er,** *s.* der Portraitmaler.

limn–etic [lɪmˈnɛtɪk], *adj.* Süßwasser–. **–ology** [–ˈnɔlədʒɪ], *s.* die Seenkunde.

limonite [ˈlaɪmənaɪt], *s.* das Limonit, der Brauneisenstein.

limousine [lɪmuˈziːn], *s.* die Limousine.

[1]**limp** [lɪmp], 1. *v.n.* hinken (*also fig.*); humpeln (*with*, infolge). 2. *s.* das Hinken; *walk with a –*, hinken, lahmen.

[2]**limp** [lɪmp], *adj.* weich, welk, schlaff, biegsam; (*fig.*) schlapp, kraftlos.

limpet [lɪmpɪt], *s.* die Napfschnecke (*Zool.*); *– mine*, die Haftmine (*Naut.*).

limpid [lɪmpɪd], *adj.* hell, klar, durchsichtig (*also fig.*). **–ity** [–ˈpɪdɪtɪ], *s.*, **–ness,** *s.* die Klarheit, Durchsichtigkeit.

limy [ˈlaɪmɪ], *adj.* leimig, kalkhaltig, kalkig.

linage [ˈlaɪnɪdʒ], *s.* die Zeilenzahl (*of a page*); das Zeilenhonorar.

linch-pin [ˈlɪntʃpɪn], *s.* die Lünse, der Achsnagel.

linden [ˈlɪndən], *s.* (*Poet.*) die Linde.

[1]**line** [laɪn], *v.a.* füttern, auskleiden, belegen; auspolstern, füllen; – *one's pocket*, Geld machen. **–r,** *s.* das Futter, Futterrohr, die Fugeinlage (*Tech.*); das Einlegerohr, der Einstecklauf (*Artil.*); *see* **lining.**

[2]**line** [laɪn], **1.** *s.* die Linie; der Strich, die Falte, Furche; Reihe; Zeile (*Print.*); der Vers (*Pros.*); der Zug, die Kontur; Leine, Schnur, das Seil, Kabel, der Draht (*esp. Naut.*); die Geschlechtslinie, das Haus, die Familie, der Stamm, das Geschlecht; die Front, vorderste Stellung (*Mil.*); die Leitung (*Elec.*); der Nummernanschluß (*Tele.*); das Tätigkeitsfeld, Geschäft, Gewerbe, Fach, der (Geschäfts)Zweig, die Branche; der Posten, die Partie (*C.L.*); (*fig.*) (*often pl.*) richtunggebendes Verhalten *or* Verfahren, die Art und Weise, Methode; Grundlage, Richtschnur, Regel, Richtlinien (*pl.*); das Muster, richtunggebende Linie, Richtung; Route, Verkehrslinie, Eisenbahnlinie, Strecke; das Geleise, Gleis, die Schiene, der Schienenstrang (*Railw.*); die Bildzeile (*Television*); (*coll.*) das Briefchen; die Wäscheleine; *the –*, der Äquator (*Naut.*); die Linientruppen (*pl.*) (*Mil.*). **–s,** *pl.* (*apart from normal pl. of meanings given*) (*fig.*) das Los, Geschick; die Strafarbeit (*at school*); der Riß, Entwurf, Plan; die Umrißlinie (*of ship, etc.*); *–s of action*, taktische Möglichkeiten; *along these –s*, nach diesen Grundsätzen; *–s of communication*, die Etappe, rückwärtige Verbindungen; (*coll.*) *hard –s*, hartes Los, das Pech; *hard and fast –s*, strenge Grenzlinien; *isobaric –s*, die Isobaren; *marriage –s*, der Trauschein; *on the –s of*, nach dem Muster von; *on broad –s*, auf breiter Grundlage; *on these –s*, auf diese Weise, in diesem Sinne; *work on the wrong –s*, nach einer falschen Methode *or* falschen Richtlinien arbeiten; *study one's –s*, seine Rolle studieren (*Theat.*). **(a)** (*with nouns and* of) – *of argument*, die Beweisführung; – *of battle*, die Schlachtlinie; – *of bearing*, die Peillinie; – *of business*, der Geschäftszweig, die Branche; – *of conduct*, das Verhalten, die Lebensführung; – *of defence*, die Verteidigungslinie; – *of demarcation*, die Trennungslinie; – *of direction*, die Richtungslinie; die Baufluchtlinie) (*Surv.*); – *of elevation*, verlängerte Seelenlänge, die Seelenachsenlinie.

(*Artil.*); – *of fire*, die Schußlinie, Schußrichtung; – *of hills*, die Reihe *or* Kette von Hügeln; – *of march*, die Marschroute; – *of policy*, politische Richtung; – *of resistance*, die Widerstandslinie; *take the – of least resistance*, den Weg des geringsten Widerstandes einschlagen; – *of sight*, die Visierlinie, Schußlinie. **(b)** (*with nouns and adjectives*) – *abreast*, die Dwarslinie (*Naut.*); – *ahead* or *astern*, die Kiellinie (*Naut.*); *building* –, die Bauflucht; das Baufach; *clothes* –, die Wäscheleine; *date* –, die Datumsgrenze; *double* –, zweigleisige Bahnlinie; *down* –, die Strecke von London; *emergency* –, die Notleitung (*Elec.*); *the – is engaged*, die Leitung ist besetzt; *fishing* –, die Angelleine, Angelschnur; *ground* –, die Erdleitung (*Elec.*); *a cheap – in gents' hosiery*, eine preiswerte Partie Herrenstrümpfe; *main* –, die Hauptlinie; *male* –, der Mannesstamm; *overhead* –, die Freileitung (*Elec.*); *railway* –, die Bahnlinie, der Schienenstrang; *rhumb* –, die Loxodrome; *ship of the* –, das Linienschiff; *tram*-–, die Straßenbahnlinie, das Straßenbahngeleise; *up* –, die Strecke nach London. **(c)** (*with verbs*) *passengers must not cross the – !* das Überschreiten der Geleise ist verboten! *draw the* –, haltmachen, Einhalt tun, die Grenze ziehen (*at*, bei); (*coll.*) *drop s.o. a* –, einem ein paar Zeilen schreiben; *form* –, sich einreihen; (*coll.*) *get a – on*, Aufklärung erhalten über; *hold the* –, am Apparat bleiben; *take the – that*, die Ansicht *or* den Standpunkt vertreten daß; *take one's own* –, eigene Wege gehen; *take a strong* –, energisch vorgehen; *toe the* –, in einer Linie antreten; (*usually fig.*) sich einfügen *or* unterwerfen (lernen); sich gleichschalten. **(d)** (*with prepositions*) *all along the* –, auf der ganzen Linie; *read between the –s*, zwischen den Zeilen lesen; *fall in – with*, sich decken mit; *keep in* –, in Reih und Glied bleiben; (*fig.*) bei der Stange bleiben; *that is not in my* –, das erzeuge ich nicht (*C.L.*); (*fig.*) das liegt mir nicht, das schlägt nicht in mein Fach; *in the – of*, nach Art von; *in – with*, in Übereinstimmung mit; *be in – with*, übereinstimmen mit; *bring into* –, ins Einvernehmen *or* in Einklang bringen (*with*, mit); *come* or *fall into – with*, übereinstimmen *or* sich anpassen mit; *come off the* –, entgleisen (*Railw.*); – *upon* –, Zeile auf Zeile. **2.** *v.a.* lini(i)eren, zeichnen; furchen; besetzen, Spalier bilden (in *or* auf (*Dat.*)) (*streets, etc.*); – *in*, einzeichnen; – *off*, abgrenzen; – *out*, entwerfen, skizzieren; – *through*, durchstreichen. **3.** *v.n.*; – *up*, sich in einer Linie aufstellen; Schlange stehen; (*fig.*) sich zusammenschließen. **–-assembly,** *s.* die Fließarbeit. **–-drawing,** *s.* die Linienzeichnung. **–-frequency,** *s.* die Zellenfrequenz (*Television*). **–man,** *s.* der Leitungsmann. **–sman,** *s.* der Streckenwärter (*Railw.*), Linienrichter (*Sport*).

linea–ge [ˈlɪnɪɪdʒ], *s.* das Geschlecht, die Familie, der Stamm; die Abstammung, Abkunft. **–l** [–ɪəl], *adj.* in direkter Linie abstammend; aus Linien bestehend, Längen–; *–l descendant*, direkter *or* geradliniger Nachkomme. **–ment** [–ɪəmənt], *s.* (*usually pl.*) der Gesichtszug. **–r** [–ɪə], *adj.* Linien–, Linear–, linear, geradlinig, linienförmig (*Bot.*); *–r equations*, lineare Gleichungen; *–r expansion*, die Längenausdehnung; *–r measure*, das Längenmaß; *–r numbers*, Linearzahlen; *–r perspective*, die Linearperspektive. **–tion** [–ɪˈeɪʃən], *s.* Striche, Linien (*pl.*), die Linienführung.

linen [ˈlɪnɪn], 1. *s.* die Leinwand (*product*); das Leinen (*raw material*); (*coll.*) die Wäsche, Unterwäsche, das Weißzeug; *dirty* –, schmutzige Wäsche (*also fig.*); *wash one's dirty – in public*, seine schmutzige Wäsche vor aller Welt ausbreiten; *change of* –, Wäsche zum Wechseln; *change one's* –, reine Wäsche anziehen. 2. *adj.* leinen, aus Leinwand. **–-basket,** *s.* der Wäschekorb. **–-draper,** *s.* der Leinwandhändler; Weißwarenhändler. **–-goods,** *pl.* Leinenwaren (*pl.*). **–-press,** *s.* der Wäscheschrank. **– paper,** *s.* das Leinenpapier. **– thread,** *s.* der Leinenzwirn.

liner [ˈlaɪnə], *s.* der Passagierdampfer, Überseedampfer, Fahrgastdampfer; *air*-–, das Verkehrsflugzeug.

linesman [ˈlaɪnzmən], *see* [2]**line.**

[1]**ling** [lɪŋ], *s.* der Leng, Langfisch (*Ichth.*).

[2]**ling** [lɪŋ], *s.* das Heidekraut, gemeine Binsenheide (*Bot.*).

linger [ˈlɪŋgə], *v.n.* zögern, sich hinziehen, zurück bleiben; noch fortleben; – *on*, fortdauern, weilen verweilen, sich lange aufhalten; schmachten, dahinsiechen (*of invalids*). **–ing,** *adj.* langwierig (*as diseases*); langsam; schleichend; verhallend, nachklingend (*sound*), nachhaltend, nachwirkend (*taste, etc.*); *the impression still –s in my mind*, ich kann mich des Eindrucks nicht erwehren.

lingerie [ˈlɛ̃:ʒərɪ], *s.* die Damenunterwäsche.

ling–o [ˈlɪŋgoʊ], *s.* (*coll.*) das Kauderwelsch. **–ual** [–wəl], 1. *adj.* Zungen–. 2. *s.* der Zungenlaut. **–uist** [–wɪst], *s.* der Sprachkenner, Sprachkundige(r), *m.*; Sprachforscher, Linguist; *I am not a good –uist*, ich bin nicht sprachgewandt. **–uistic** [–ˈwɪstɪk], *adj.* sprachwissenschaftlich, Sprach–. **–uistics,** *pl.* (*sing. constr.*) die Sprachwissenschaft, Sprachforschung.

liniment [ˈlɪnəmənt], *s.* die Salbe, das Einreibemittel.

lining [ˈlaɪnɪŋ], *s.* das Futter, die (Aus)Fütterung; Bekleidung, der Besatz, Beschlag; die Verkleidung, Verblendung, Ausmauerung; *brake* –, der Bremsbelag; (*Prov.*) *every cloud has a silver* –, selbst der schlechteste Tag hat ein Ende.

[1]**link** [lɪŋk], 1. *s.* das Glied (*also fig.*), Kettenglied; Getriebeglied, Gelenk, die Kulisse (*Mach.*); (*fig.*) das Band, Bindeglied, die Verbindung; *connecting* –, das Bindeglied; *cuff* –, der Manschettenknopf; – *motion*, die Kulissensteuerung (*Engin.*). 2. *v.a.* verketten, (*fig.*) (also – *up*) verbinden; – *arms*, sich einhaken; *–ed atoms*, gebundene Atome. 3. *v.n.* (also – *up*) sich verbinden. **–age,** *s.* die Verkettung, Verknüpfung, das Gliederwerk. **–-pin,** *s.* der Kettenbolzen.

[2]**link** [lɪŋk], *s.* (*archaic*) die Pechfackel. **–man,** *s.* der Fackelträger.

links [lɪŋks], *pl.* grasbewachsene Küstendünen (*pl.*); (*usually sing. constr.*) der Golf(spiel)platz.

linn [lɪn], *s.* (*Scots*) der Wasserfall; Teich.

linnet [ˈlɪnɪt], *s.* der Hänfling (*Orn.*).

lino [ˈlaɪnoʊ], *s.* (*abbr. for* **–leum**) das Linoleum. **–-cut,** *s.* der Linoleumschnitt. **–leum** [lɪˈnoʊlɪəm], *s.* das Linoleum. **–type** [–taɪp], *s.* die Zeilensetz- und Gießmaschine (*Typ.*).

linseed [ˈlɪnsɪ:d], *s.* der Leinsamen. **–-cake,** *s.* der Leinkuchen, Ölkuchen. **–-oil,** *s.* das Leinöl.

linsey-woolsey [ˈlɪnzɪˈwʊlzɪ], *s.* das Wolle-und-Baumwolle-Mischzeug, Halbwollzeug.

lint [lɪnt], *s.* die Charpie, Zupfleinwand (*Surg.*).

lintel [ˈlɪntl], *s.* der Fenstersturz, die Oberschwelle (*Arch.*).

lion [ˈlaɪən], *s.* der Löwe (*also fig.*); (*fig.*) Held; *literary* –, der Modeschriftsteller; *make a – of s.o.*, einen zum Helden des Tages machen; *–'s share*, der Löwenanteil; *–s of a place*, die Sehenswürdigkeiten (eines Ortes). **–ess,** *s.* die Löwin. **–ize** [–aɪz], *v.a.* die Sehenswürdigkeiten besichtigen; *–ize a p.*, einen zum Helden des Tages machen. **–-hearted,** *adj.* löwenherzig, unverzagt. **–-hunter,** *s.* (*fig.*) der Zelebritätenjäger. **–-like,** *adj.* löwenartig. **–-tamer,** *s.* der Löwenbändiger.

lip [lɪp], 1. *s.* die Lippe (*also Bot.*); der Rand, die Tülle (*of a vessel*), der Saum (*of a hole*); (*sl.*) die Unverschämtheit, Frechheit; *bite one's* –, sich auf die Lippen beißen; *hang on s.o.'s –s*, an jemandes Mund hängen; *from his own –s*, aus seinem eigenen Mund; *keep a stiff upper* –, unverzagt bleiben. 2. *v.a.* mit den Lippen berühren. **–ped,** *adj.* lippig; lippenförmig (*Bot.*). **–-read,** *v.n.* von den Lippen ablesen. **–-reading,** *s.* das Ablesen von den Lippen. **–-salve,** *s.* die Lippensalbe. **–-service,** *s.* der Lippendienst, die Augendienerei. **–stick,** *s.* der Lippenstift.

liqu–ate [lɪkˈweɪt], *v.a.* schmelzen, verflüssigen, abseigern (*Metall.*). **–ation** [–ˈweɪʃən], *s.* das Schmelzen; die Seigerung. **–efaction** [–wɪˈfækʃən], *s.* die Verflüssigung, Schmelzung; Verdichtung (*of gas*); das Geschmolzensein. **–efiable** [ˈlɪkwɪfaɪbl], *adj.* schmelzbar. **–efy** [ˈlɪkwɪfaɪ], 1. *v.a.* schmelzen, flüssig machen, auflösen; verdichten (*gas*). 2. *v.n.* flüssig werden. **–escent** [–ˈkwɛsənt], *adj.* auflösend, sich verflüssigend. **–eur** [–ˈkə:], *s.* der Likör.

-id ['lɪkwɪd], 1. *adj.* flüssig (*also C.L.*), fließend; sanft, angenehm (*Mus.*); rein, hell, klar (*as sounds*); liquid, sofort fällig (*as debts*), sofort realisierbar (*of securities*) (*C.L.*); (*fig.*) unbeständig, schwankend. 2. *s.* die Flüssigkeit; *pl.* Liquida (*pl.*) (*Phonet.*); *-id air*, flüssige Luft; *-id measure*, das Flüssigkeitsmaß; *-id sounds*, Liquida (*pl.*) (*Phonet.*). **-idate** [-wɪdeɪt], *v.a.* bezahlen, abtragen, liquidieren (*also fig.*), saldieren (*debts*); abwickeln, auflösen (*a business, etc.*) (*C.L.*); (*fig.*) beseitigen, hinrichten. **-idation** [-'deɪʃən], *s.* die Tilgung, Liquidation (*of debts*), Auflösung, Abwicklung (*of a business*); (*fig.*) Beseitigung; *go into -idation*, sich auflösen; *-idation proceedings*, das Konkursverfahren. **-idator** [-deɪtə], *s.* der Liquidator. **-idity** [-'wɪdɪtɪ], *s.* die Flüssigkeit, flüssiger Zustand. **-or** ['lɪkə], 1. *s.* die Flüssigkeit, Lauge, Flotte (*Dye.*); geistiges Getränk; *be in -or* or *the worse for -or*, betrunken sein. 2. *v.a.* einweichen. **-orice** ['lɪkərɪs], *s.* das Süßholz, die Lakritze.

lisle [lɑɪl], *s.* der Baumwollfaden.

lisp [lɪsp], 1. *v.a.* & *n.* lispeln, mit der Zunge anstoßen. 2. *s.* das Lispeln. **-ing**, 1. *adj.* lispelnd. 2. *s.* das Gelispel.

lissom(e) ['lɪsəm], *adj.* geschmeidig, biegsam; beweglich, flink. **-ness**, *s.* die Geschmeidigkeit, Flinkheit.

[1]**list** [lɪst], 1. *s.* die Liste, das Verzeichnis; *- of contents*, das Inhaltsverzeichnis; *draw up a -*, *make a - of*, eine Liste aufstellen von; *crew -*, die Musterrolle (*Naut.*); *price -*, die Preisliste; *- of subscribers*, die Zeichnungsliste, Subskriptionsliste. 2. *v.a.* in eine Liste eintragen, einschreiben, verzeichnen, registrieren, aufzählen.

[2]**list** [lɪst], 1. *s.* die Gewebeleiste, Webkante, das Salband; der Rand, Saum. **-s**, *pl.* Schranken (*pl.*); *enter the -s*, in die Schranken treten. 2. *v.a.* mit Salleisten beschlagen (*a door*).

[3]**list** [lɪst], 1. *s.* die Schlagseite (*Naut.*). 2. *v.n.* Schlagseite haben.

[4]**list** [lɪst], *imp. v.a.* (*archaic*) wünschen, belieben, gefallen.

[5]**list** [lɪst], *v.n.* (*archaic*) horchen, hören **auf**; *see* **listen.**

listen ['lɪsən], *v.n.* horchen, lauschen, hören (*to*, auf (*Acc.*)), zuhören, Gehör schenken (*to* (*Dat.*)), anhören (*to* (*Acc.*)); *- for*, aufpassen auf, horchend erwarten; *- in*, Rundfunk *or* Radio hören; *- in on a conversation*, eine Unterredung mithören; *- in to a play*, ein Stück im Radio anhören; *- to reason*, Vernunft annehmen. **-er**, *s.* der Zuhörer, Horcher, Lauscher; Rundfunkhörer; (*Prov.*) *-ers never hear good of themselves*, ein Horcher an der Wand, hört seine eigne Schand'. **-ing(-in)**, *s.* das Rundfunkhören. **-ing-post**, *s.* der (Ab)Horchposten.

listless ['lɪstlɪs], *adj.* gleichgültig, teilnahm(s)los; träge, flau. **-ness**, *s.* die Gleichgültigkeit, Trägheit.

lists [lɪsts], *see* [2]**list.**

lit [lɪt], *see* [1]**light**; (*sl.*) *- up*, besoffen, illuminiert.

litany ['lɪtənɪ], *s.* die Litanei (*also fig.*).

litera-cy ['lɪtərəsɪ], *s.* das Buchwissen, gelehrte Bildung. **-l** [-əl], *adj.* buchstäblich, wortgetreu, wörtlich; prosaisch, nüchtern, pedantisch; förmlich, eigentlich; *-l sense*, eigentliche Bedeutung; *-l truth*, nüchterne *or* ungeschminkte Wahrheit. **-lness**, *s.* die Buchstäblichkeit, wörtliche Auslegung; übertriebene Genauigkeit. **-ry** [-rɪ], *adj.* schriftstellerisch, literarisch, Literar-; *-ry activity*, schriftstellerische Tätigkeit; *-ry historian*, der Literarhistoriker; *-ry history*, die Literaturgeschichte; *-ry language*, die Schriftsprache; *-ry man*, der Schriftsteller, Literat; *-ry property*, geistiges Eigentum; *-ry career*, schriftstellerische Laufbahn. **-te** [-rət], 1. *adj.* gelehrt, gebildet. 2. *s.* Gelehrte(r), *m.*, Gebildete(r), *m.* **-ti** [-'rɑːtɪ], *pl.* Literaten, Gelehrte (*pl.*). **-ture** [-rətʃə], *s.* das Schrifttum, die Literatur; *history of -ture*, die Literaturgeschichte; *light -ture*, die Unterhaltungsliteratur.

litharge ['lɪθɑ·dʒ], *s.* die Bleiglätte, Bleiasche.

lithe [lɑɪð], *adj.* geschmeidig, biegsam; schlank, graziös. **-ness**, *s.* die Geschmeidigkeit. **-some** [-səm], *adj. see* **lithe.** **-someness**, *s. see* **-ness.**

lithium ['lɪθɪəm], *s.* das Lithium (*Chem.*).

litho-chromatic [lɪθokrə'mætɪk], *adj.* Buntdruck-, Farbendruck-. **-graph** ['lɪθogræf], 1. *s.* der Steindruck. 2. *v.a.* & *n.* lithographieren. **-grapher** [lɪ'θɔgrəfə], *s.* der Lithograph. **-graphic** [lɪθo'græfɪk], *adj.* im Steindruck, lithographisch; *-graphic paper*, das Lithographierpapier, Steindruckpapier; *-graphic print*, der Steindruck. **-graphy** [lɪ'θɔgrəfɪ], *s.* die Lithographie, Steindruckerkunst. **-logy** [lɪ'θɔlədʒɪ], *s.* die Gesteinskunde.

litig-ant ['lɪtɪgənt], 1. *adj.* prozessierend. 2. *s.* Prozessierende(r), *m.*, prozessierende Partei (*Law*). **-ate** [-eɪt], 1. *v.n.* prozessieren. 2. *v.a.* prozessieren *or* streiten um. **-ation** [-'geɪʃən], *s.* der Rechtsstreit, Prozeß, die Prozeßführung. **-ious** [lɪ'tɪdʒɪəs], *adj.* prozeßsüchtig, streitsüchtig; *-ious person*, der Querulant. **-iousness**, *s.* die Streitsucht, Prozeßsucht.

litmus ['lɪtməs], *s.* das Lackmus; *- paper*, das Lackmuspapier, Reagenzpapier; *- solution*, die Lackmustinktur; *showing acid reaction to -*, lackmussauer.

litotes [lɑɪ'toutɪz], *s.* die Litotes (*Rhet.*).

litre ['liːtə], (Amer. *liter*) *s.* das & der Liter.

[1]**litter** ['lɪtə], 1. *s.* die Sänfte; Tragbahre; Streu (*for animals*); zerstreute *or* herumliegende Dinge (*pl.*) Reste (*pl.*), der Abfall; die Unordnung; *in a -*, in Unordnung. 2. *v.a.* (*- down*) Streu aufschütten für (*animals*); unordentlich bestreuen, in Unordnung bringen (*a place*); *lie -ed about*, verstreut umherliegen.

[2]**litter** ['lɪtə], 1. *s.* der Wurf, die Brut, Hecke (*of animals*); *a - of pigs*, ein Wurf Ferkel; *at a -*, auf einen Wurf. 2. *v.a.* (& *n.*, Junge) werfen.

little [lɪtl], 1. *adj.* klein, gering; unbeträchtlich, unbedeutend, geringfügig; kurz (*of time, distance, etc.*); wenig; *a -*, etwas, ein wenig; *but -*, nur wenig; *so this is your - game*, also darauf willst du hinaus; (*coll.*) *- Mary*, der Magen; *- Masters*, die Kleinmeister (*German engravers*); *- minds*, kleine Geister; *no - trouble*, viel *or* nicht wenig Mühe; *- or no*, wenig oder kein; *- one*, ein Kleines, das Wurm; *the - ones*, die Kleinen *or* Kinder; *his - ways*, seine Eigenheiten *or* Eigentümlichkeiten. 2. *adv.* wenig, nur wenig; überhaupt nicht; *be it ever so -*, sei es auch noch so wenig; *he - knows*, er weiß gar nicht; *- does he know that . . .*, nur wenig weiß er daß . . .; *in - less than a year*, in nicht viel weniger als einem Jahr. 3. *s.* Weniges, die Kleinigkeit; *a -*, ein wenig, ein bißchen, eine Kleinigkeit; *not a -*, ziemlich viel; *after a -*, nach kurzer Zeit; *- by -*, *by - and -*, allmählich, nach und nach; *for a -*, für kurze Zeit. **--Englander**, *s.* der Gegner der imperialistischen Politik Englands; (*sl.*) **--go**, die Cambridger Aufnahmeprüfung (*Univ.*). **-ness**, *s.* die Kleinheit; Geringfügigkeit; Kleinlichkeit, Niedrigkeit.

littoral ['lɪtərəl], 1. *adj.* Küsten-, Ufer-. 2. *s.* das Uferland.

liturg-ical [lɪ'tɔːdʒɪkl], *adj.* liturgisch. **-y** ['lɪtɔːdʒɪ], *s.* die Liturgie.

[1]**live** [lɪv], **1.** *v.n.* leben; (*fig.*) Leben haben; wohnen, sich aufhalten (*at*, in (*Dat.*)); fortleben, fortdauern; sich nähren (*on*, von) (*on things*), abhängig sein (*on*, von) (*on a person*); sich ernähren, seine Existenz erhalten (*by*, durch, von *or* vermittels); *the boats could not - in the heavy sea*, bei solchem Seegang konnten sich die Schiffe nicht halten; *- a bachelor*, als Junggeselle leben; *- and learn*, man lernt nie aus, man muß immer noch zulernen; *- by writing*, sich durch Schriftstellerei ernähren; *- by one's wits*, mit Schlauheit durchs Leben kommen; *- in clover*, in der Wolle sitzen, leben wie Gott in Frankreich; *- in luxury*, ein üppiges Leben führen; *- on bread*, von Brot leben; *- on one's income*, in den Grenzen seines Einkommens leben; *- on nothing*, von der Luft leben; *they - on bad terms*, sie vertragen sich schlecht; *- out*, auswärts leben (*as servants*); *- through a crisis*, eine Krise erleben *or* durchleben; *- to o.s.*, für sich leben; *- to see*, erleben; *- to a great age*, ein hohes Alter erreichen; *you will - to regret it*, du wirst es noch bereuen; *- up to one's principles*, seinen Grundsätzen entsprechend leben; *- with*, leben (zusammen mit),

wohnen bei; – *with a woman*, mit einer Frau in wilder Ehe leben. **2.** *v.a.* verleben, (ein Leben) führen; (im Leben) verwirklichen *or* ausdrücken; – *a good life*, ein tadelloses Leben führen; – *down*, durch die Lebensweise widerlegen *or* überwinden *or* in Vergessenheit bringen (*bad reputation, etc.*); –*-and-let-*–, leben und lebenlassen. **–d,** *adj. suff.* –lebig. **–long** [–lɔŋ], *adj.* (*Poet.*) (only in) *the –long day*, den ganzen Tag hindurch, den lieben langen Tag. **–r,** *s.* (only in) *fast –r*, der Lebemann; *good –r*, der Schlemmer; *loose –r*, liederlicher Mensch.

²**live** [laɪv], *attrib. adj.* lebend, lebendig; (*fig.*) lebhaft, voll Leben, tätig, energisch; scharf (*as bombs*); geladen, stromführend (*Elec.*); ungebraucht (*as matches*); glühend (*as embers*). **– bait,** lebender Köder. **– issue,** aktuelle Frage. **–n,** *see* **liven.** **–-oak,** *s.* immergrüne, amerikanische Eiche. **– steam,** der Frischdampf. **–stock,** *s.* lebendes Inventar (*Agr.*). **–-weight,** *s.* das Lebendgewicht. **– wire,** *s.* elektrischer Draht, (*coll.*) rühriger Mensch.

livel–ihood [ˈlaɪvlɪhʊd], *s.* der (Lebens)Unterhalt, das Auskommen; *make a* or *one's –ihood, earn one's –ihood*, sein Brot verdienen. **–iness** [–lɪnɪs], *s.* die Lebhaftigkeit, Lebendigkeit. **–y** [–lɪ], *adj.* lebendig; lebenswahr, eindrucksvoll (*description, etc.*); lebhaft, kräftig (*feelings, colours*); stark, fest, eifrig (*as faith, hope*); aufregend (*time, etc.*).

liven [laɪvən], (*coll.*) (usually – *up*), **1.** *v.n.* aufleben, lebendig werden, sich beleben. **2.** *v.a.* lebendig machen, beleben.

¹**liver,** *see* ¹**live.**

²**liver** [ˈlɪvə], *s.* die Leber. **–-coloured,** *adj.* rötlich braun, leberfarbig. **–-complaint,** *s.* die Leberkrankheit. **–ed,** *adj. suff.* –leberig. **–-fluke,** *s.* der Leberegel. **–ish,** *adj.* (*coll.*) leberleidend; mürrisch, griesgrämig. **–-rot,** *s.* die Leberegelseuche. **–wort,** *s.* das Leberblümchen.

livery [ˈlɪvərɪ], *s.* die Livree, Dienstkleidung; Amtstracht (*of guild, etc.*); (*Poet.*) das Gewand; die Übergabe, Übertragung (*Law*); (*archaic*) Versorgung mit Kleidung und Nahrung; Futterlieferung; *liveried*, in Livree; *at* –, in Futter (*of horses*); *sue for* –, die Übergabe eines Besitzes ersuchen. **– companies,** *pl.* wahlfähige Zünfte. **–man,** *s.* das Zunftmitglied; der Mietstallbesitzer. **–-servant,** *s.* der Diener in Livree. **–-stable,** *s.* die Mietstallung.

livid [ˈlɪvɪd], *adj.* bleifarbig, blaugrau; fahl, bleich (*with*, vor). **–ness,** *s.* die Fahlheit, Bleichheit.

living [ˈlɪvɪŋ], **1.** *adj.* lebend, lebendig; brennend, glühend; zeitgenössisch; gewachsen (*as rock*); *the* – (*pl.*), die Lebenden, Lebendigen; *in the land of the* –, im Reiche der Lebendigen; – *death*, trostloses Leben; *no man* –, kein Sterblicher; – *memory*, das Menschengedenken; *while* –, bei Lebzeiten. **2.** *s.* das Leben; der (Lebens)Unterhalt, das Auskommen; die Pfründe (*Eccl.*); Lebensweise, der Lebensstil; *good* or *high* –, das Wohlleben, üppige Lebensweise; *earn one's* –, *work for one's* –, seinen Lebensunterhalt *or* sein Brot verdienen; *make a* –, sich ernähren *or* sein Auskommen haben (*out of*, von); *standard of* –, der Lebensstandard. **–-room,** *s.* das Wohnzimmer. **– wage,** *s.* das Existenzminimum.

lixiviat–e [lɪkˈsɪvɪeɪt], *v.a.* auslaugen. **–ion** [–ˈeɪʃən] *s.* die Auslaugung.

lizard [ˈlɪzəd], *s.* die Eidechse (*Zool.*).

lizzie [ˈlɪzɪ], *s.* (*sl.*) die Karre, Kiste.

llama [ˈlɑːmə], *s.* das Lama (*Zool.*).

lo [loʊ], *int.* (*archaic*) siehe! – *and behold*, und siehe da!

loach [loʊtʃ], *s.* die Schmerle (*Ichth.*).

load [loʊd], **1.** *s.* die Last, Ladung, Fracht; (*fig.*) Bürde; (*cart-*)– Fuhre, Wagenladung, das Fuder (*of hay*); die Belastung, Arbeitsleistung, Tragkraft, Tragfähigkeit (*Mech. & Elec.*). *–s, pl.* (*coll.*) die Menge, Haufen (*pl.*); *axle* –, der Achsdruck; *breaking* –, die Bruchfestigkeit; – *capacity*, die Tragfähigkeit; – *on ground*, der Bodendruck; *pay* –, zahlende Nutzlast; *peak* –, die Belastungsspitze; *permissible* –, die Höchstbelastung; *safe* –, zulässige Belastung; *useful* –, die Nutzlast; *a – is taken off my mind*, mir ist ein Stein *or* eine Last vom Herzen genommen. **2.** *v.a.* laden (*also guns*), beladen, belasten; aufladen (*goods*); überladen, beschweren; (*fig.*) überhäufen; – *dice*, Würfel fälschen *or* beschweren; – *the dice*, (*fig.*) etwas zu seinen Gunsten auslegen. **3.** *v.n.* (– *up*) laden, Ladung einnehmen (*for*, nach); stark kaufen (*C.L.*). **–ed** [–ɪd], *adj.*; *–ed cane*, der Bleistock, Totschläger; *–ed dice*, falsche Würfel; *–ed wine*, gefälschter *or* verschnittener Wein. **–er,** *s.* der Verlader; Auflader; Lader (*of gun*); *breech –er*, der Hinterlader. **–ing,** **1.** *adj.*; *–ing berth*, die Ladestelle (*Naut.*); *–ing limit*, die Belastungsgrenze; *–ing ramp*, die Verladerampe; *–ing tray*, die Ladeschale, der Ladetisch (*Artil.*). **2.** *s.* das Laden; die Ladung, Fracht; Beschwerung. **–-gauge,** *s.* die Ladelehre, der Profilrahmen (*Railw.*). **–-water-line,** *s.* die Ladewasserlinie (*Naut.*). **–star,** *s. see* **lodestar.** **–stone,** *s.* der Magneteisenstein; (*fig.*) Magnet.

¹**loaf** [loʊf], *s.* (pl. *loaves* [loʊvz]) der Laib (Brot), das Brot; (*sl.*) die Bohne, Birne, Rübe, der Dez; – *of sugar*, der Zuckerhut; – *sugar*, der Hutzucker; *half a – is better than no bread*, etwas ist besser als gar nichts; (*sl.*) *use your* – ! sei gescheit! nimm dich zusammen!

²**loaf** [loʊf], **1.** *v.n.* umherlungern, bummeln. **2.** *v.a.*; – *away*, vertrödeln (*time*). **–er,** *s.* der Müßiggänger, Bummler, Drückeberger.

loam [loʊm], *s.* der Lehm, Ton. **–y,** *adj.* lehmig, lehmhaltig.

loan [loʊn], **1.** *s.* die Anleihe (*on*, auf), das Darlehen (*to*, an *or* für), die Leihgabe (*for exhibition*); das (Ver)Leihen, die Darlehnung, Entlehnung; *government* –, die Staatsanleihe; *public* –, öffentliche Anleihe; *have the – of*, borgen, leihen, geliehen haben *or* bekommen; *as a* –, *on* –, leihweise, geliehen; als Anleihe (*C.L.*); *take up a* –, eine Anleihe aufnehmen (*C.L.*). **2.** *v.a.* leihen (*to* (*Dat.*)). **–able,** *adj.* verleihbar. **–-society,** *s.* die Darlehnskasse. **–-word,** *s.* das Lehnwort.

loath [loʊθ], *adj.* abgeneigt, unwillig, nicht willens (*to do*, zu tun; *for s.o. to do*, daß jemand tut); *I am – to do it*, ich tue es ungern; *nothing* –, durchaus nicht abgeneigt. **–ness,** *s.* die Abgeneigtheit, der Unwille.

loath–e [loʊð], *v.a.* mit Ekel ansehen, Ekel empfinden vor; verabscheuen, (*coll.*) nicht gern tun *or* haben. **–ing** [–ɪŋ], *s.* der Widerwille, Ekel, Abscheu (*at*, über *or* vor). **–ingly,** *adv.* mit Ekel *or* Widerwillen. **–some** [–səm], *adj.* ekelhaft, widerlich, abscheulich, ekelerregend, verhaßt. **–someness,** *s.* die Ekelhaftigkeit.

loaves [loʊvz], *pl. of* ¹**loaf.**

lob [lɔb], **1.** *s.* der Hoch(flug)ball, Lob (*Tenn.*), Wurf von unten (*Crick.*). **2.** *v.a. & n.* hoch zurückschlagen (*Tenn.*), von unten werfen (*Crick.*).

lobate [ˈloʊbeɪt], *see* **lobed** (*Bot.*).

lobby [ˈlɔbɪ], **1.** *s.* die Vorhalle, der Vorplatz, Vorraum, Vorsaal, das Vorzimmer, Foyer, der Wandelgang, Korridor, die Wandelhalle; *division* –, der Abstimmungssaal (*Parl.*). **2.** *v.a.* bearbeiten, beeinflussen (*a delegate, etc.*). **3.** *v.n.* sich außerhalb des Verhandlungssaals beraten; im geheimen arbeiten, intrigieren, antichambrieren. **–ist** [–ɪst], *s.* bezahlter Agent, der die Abgeordneten zu beeinflussen sucht (*Amer.*).

lobe [loʊb], *s.* der Lappen; – *of the ear*, das Ohrläppchen. **–d,** *adj.* lappig, gelappt (*Bot., etc.*); *see* **lobular, lobule.**

lobelia [loʊˈbɪːlɪə], *s.* die Lobelie.

lobster [ˈlɔbstə], *s.* der Hummer; *red as a* –, puterrot.

lobul–ar [ˈlɔbjʊlə], *adj.* lappenförmig, Lobulär– (*Med.*). **–e** [–juːl], *s.* das Läppchen.

lobworm [ˈlɔbwəːm], *s.* der Köderwurm.

local [ˈloʊkl], **1.** *adj.* örtlich, Orts–, Stadt–, lokal, Lokal–; – *authority*, die Ortsbehörde, Stadtbehörde; – *branch*, die Ortsgruppe, der Ortsverband, örtliche Zweigstelle *or* Niederlassung; – *call*, das Ortsgespräch; – *colour*, die Lokalfärbung; – *declination*, die Ortsmißweisung (*of compass needle*); – *government*, die Gemeindeverwaltung, Kommunalverwaltung; – *inflammation*, örtliche Entzündung; – *inhabitant*, Ortsansässige(r), *m.*; – *option*, der Ortsentscheid; – *patriotism*, der Lokalpatriotismus; – *time* die Ortszeit; – *traffic*, der

Ortsverkehr, Nahverkehr; – *train*, der Lokalzug. 2. *s.* der Lokalzug; lokale Nachricht; etwas Lokales; *pl.* Ortsbewohner, Ortsansässige (*pl.*). **–e** [loˈkɑːl], *s.* der Schauplatz. **–ism** [–ɪzm], *s.* örtliche (Sprach)-Eigentümlichkeit; (*fig.*) enger Horizont, die Borniertheit. **–ity** [louˈkælɪtɪ], *s.* der Ort, die Örtlichkeit, Ortschaft; Lage; (*coll.*) *bump of –ity*, der Ortssinn, Orientierungssinn. **–ization** [–laɪˈzeɪʃən], *s.* örtliche Bestimmung *or* Beschränkung, die Lokalisierung, Festlegung. **–ize** [–laɪz], *v.a.* (örtlich) beschränken, lokalisieren (*to*, auf (*Acc.*)); (örtlich) bestimmen *or* festlegen.

locat–e [louˈkeɪt], *v.a.* örtlich feststellen, ausfindig machen; die Lage bestimmen, Grenzen abstecken; orten, einpeilen (*Navig.*); (*coll.*) auffinden, ermitteln; *be –ed*, gelegen sein, liegen; wohnhaft sein. **–ion** [–ˈkeɪʃən], *s.* die Lage, Stelle, der Platz, Standort; die Niederlassung, Unterbringung, Anlage, das Anlegen; die Vermietung, Verpachtung (*Law*); Grenzbestimmung, Abmessung (*of land*) (*Amer.*); abgestecktes Stück Land (*Amer.*); der Standort einer Außenaufnahme (*Films*); *on –ion*, auf Außenaufnahme (*Films*).

loch [lɔχ], *s.* (*Scots*) der See; die Bucht.

loci [ˈlousaɪ], *pl. of* **locus.**

[1]**lock** [lɔk], 1. *s.* das Schloß, der Verschluß; die Schleusenkammer (*of canal*); der Griff (*Wrestling*); die Lenkbarkeit (*of a carriage*); (*coll.*) –, *stock, and barrel*, Bausch und Bogen, Stumpf und Stiel; *under – and key*, unter Schloß und Riegel. 2. *v.a.* zuschließen, abschließen (*a door, etc.*); einschließen, verschließen (*a p. or th.*) (*in*, in); (um)schließen, fest (um)fassen (*in one's arms, etc.*); mit Schleusen versehen (*a canal*); verriegeln, sperren; hemmen (*a wheel*); – *in*, einschließen, einsperren; – *out*, aussperren, ausschließen; – *up*, verschließen, einschließen (*a th.*); einsperren (*a p.*); stromaufwärts durchschleusen (*ship*); sperren (*as frost a river*); fest anlegen (*funds*); schließen (*Typ.*). 3. *v.n.* (sich) schließen (lassen); ineinandergreifen (*as gear-wheels*). **–age** [ɪdʒ], *s.* das Schleusengefälle. **–er** [–ə], *s.* verschließbarer Schrank, das Schließfach, Spind; *in Davy Jones's –er*, ertrunken. **–et** [–ɪt], *s.* das Medaillon. **––gates,** *pl.* die Schleusentore. **–jaw,** *s.* der Kinnbackenkrampf. **––keeper,** *s.* der Schleusenwärter. **––nut,** *s.* die Gegenmutter. **––out,** *s.* die Aussperrung. **–smith,** *s.* der Schlosser. **––stitch,** *s.* der Steppstich (*Sew.-mach.*). **––up,** 1. *s.* der Torschluß; feste (Kapitals)-Anlage (*C.L.*); (*coll.*) verschließbare Mietgarage (*Motor.*); (*coll.*) der Karzer. 2. *attrib.* verschließbar.

[2]**lock** [lɔk], *s.* die Locke; Flocke (*of wool*). **–s,** *pl.* Haare (*pl.*).

locomot–ion [loukəˈmouʃən], *s.* die Ortsveränderung, Fortbewegung. **–ive** [–tɪv], 1. *adj.* der Ortsveränderung fähig; fortbewegend; freibeweglich (*as bivalves*); *–ive engine*, die Lokomotive; *–ive power*, die Bewegungskraft. 2. *s.* die Lokomotive. **–or** [–ə], 1. *s.* der Triebwagen. **–or ataxia** [–əəˈtæksɪə], *s.* die Rückenmarksschwindsucht, Rückenmarksdarre.

locum (tenens) [ˈloukəm (ˈtɪːnəns)], *s.* der Stellvertreter.

loc–us [ˈloukəs], *s.* (pl. *–i* [–saɪ]) der Ort, die Stelle; geometrischer Ort (*Math.*).

locust [ˈloukəst], *s.* die Heuschrecke. **––tree,** *s.* die Robinie, falsche Akazie; der Johannisbrotbaum, die Karobe.

locution [loˈkjuːʃən], *s.* der Ausdruck, die Redensart; Sprechweise, Redeweise.

lode [loud], *s.* der Gang, die Ader (*Min.*); der Abzugsgraben. **–star,** *s.* der Polarstern; (*fig.*) Leitstern. **–stone,** *s. see* **loadstone.**

lodg–e [lɔdʒ], 1. *v.a.* beherbergen, aufnehmen, unterbringen (*a p.*); einlagern (*goods*); einzahlen, hinterlegen, deponieren (*money*); (*fig.*) niederlegen, in Verwahrung geben (*with s.o.*, bei einem), anvertrauen (*with* (*Dat.*)); einreichen (*a complaint*), einlegen, erheben (*a protest*), (Klage *or* Beschwerde) führen (*against*, gegen; *with*, bei); hineintreiben, hineinsenden (*in*, in), ans Ziel bringen (*a missile*); *–e information against*, Anzeige erstatten gegen. 2. *v.n.* logieren, zur Miete wohnen; übernachten, einkehren (*with*, bei); steckenbleiben (*as a bullet*). 3. *s.* das Häuschen, Jagdhaus, Forsthaus; Pförtnerhaus, die Portierwohnung; Loge (*Freemasons*). **–er** [–ə], *s.* der Mieter, Kostgänger. **–ing,** *s.* das Wohnen, Logieren; die Wohnung, der Wohnsitz; *night's –ing*, das Logis, Nachtquartier, Obdach, die Unterkunft; *pl.* die (Miets)Wohnung, möbliertes Zimmer. **–ing-allowance,** *s.* das Wohnungsgeld, die Mietentschädigung (*Mil.*). **–ing-house,** *s.* das Logierhaus, die Herberge. **–(e)ment,** *s.* die Hinterlegung, Einzahlung, Deponierung (*of money*); Anhäufung, Ansammlung; Verschanzung, befestigte Stellung (*Mil.*).

loess [ˈlouəs], *s.* der Löß (*Geol.*).

loft [lɔft], 1. *s.* der Boden, Speicher, das Dachgeschoß, die Dachkammer; *organ-–*, der Orgelchor; *pigeon-–*, der Taubenschlag; *hanging –*, der Hängeboden. 2. *v.a.* in die Höhe schlagen (*golf-ball*). **–iness,** *s.* die Höhe; (*fig.*) Erhabenheit, der Hochmut. **–y,** *adj.* hoch, erhaben, hehr, stolz; stattlich.

log [lɔg], 1. *s.* der (Holz)Klotz, unbehauenes Holz, das Scheit; Schiffsjournal, Tagebuch, Log (*Naut.*); *like a –*, wie ein Klotz. 2. *v.a.* loggen, zurücklegen (*distance*) (*Naut.*); ins Logbuch eintragen. **––book,** *s.* das Logbuch, Schiffsjournal; Bordbuch (*Av.*). **––cabin,** *s.*, **––hut,** *s.* das Blockhaus. **–gerhead,** *see* **loggerhead.** (*sl.*) **––roll,** *v.a.* durch Beeinflussung durchbringen. (*sl.*) **––rolling,** *s.* gegenseitige Hilfe, politische Korruption. **–wood,** *see* **logwood.**

logan(-stone) [ˈlougən(stoun)], *s.* der Wagstein.

loganberry [ˈlougənbɛrɪ], *s.* die Kreuzung von Himbeere und Brombeere.

logarithm [ˈlɔgərɪθm], *s.* der Logarithmus. **–ic** [–ˈrɪθmɪk], *adj.* logarithmisch; *–ic tables*, Logarithmentafeln.

loggerhead [ˈlɔgəhɛd], *s.* (*archaic*) der Dummkopf; *be at –s with*, in den Haaren liegen mit.

logi–c [ˈlɔdʒɪk], *s.* die Logik; (*fig.*) überzeugende Kraft. **–cal** [–l], *adj.* logisch, folgerichtig, konsequent. **–cian** [–ˈdʒɪʃən], *s.* der Logiker. **–stic** [–ˈdʒɪstɪk], *adj.* Rechen–. **–stics,** *pl.* (*sing. constr.*) die Rechenkunst; das Verpflegungswesen (*Mil.*).

logo–gram [ˈlɔgəgræm], *s.* das Siegel, die Sigle (*Shorthand*). **–machy** [–ˈgɔməkɪ], *s.* die Wortklauberei.

log-roll, *see* **log.**

logwood [ˈlɔgwud], *s.* das Kampescheholz, Blauholz.

loin [lɔɪn], *s.* (*usually pl.*) die Lende; das Lendenstück (*of meat*). **–s,** *pl.* (*fig.*, *B.*) die Zeugungskraft; *roast –*, der Lendenbraten; – *of veal*, der Kalbsnierenbraten. **––cloth,** das Lendentuch.

loiter [ˈlɔɪtə], 1. *v.n.* bummeln, schlendern, tändeln; – *about*, umherschlendern. 2. *v.a.*; – *away*, vertrödeln. **–er,** *s.* der Müßiggänger, Bummler, Faulenzer. **–ing,** *s.* das Herumstehen, Faulenzen.

loll [lɔl], 1. *v.n.* sich nachlässig lehnen *or* bequem hinstrecken (*upon*, auf (*Acc.*)), sich rekeln *or* fläzen; – *about*, umherlungern; – *back*, sich lang hinstrecken (*in a chair, etc.*); – *out*, heraushängen (*as the tongue*). 2. *v.a.* (– *out*) vorstrecken, herausstrecken (*one's tongue*).

lollipop [ˈlɔlɪpɔp], (*coll.*) *s.* das Zuckerwerk, Naschwerk.

lollop [ˈlɔləp], (*coll.*) *v.n.* schwerfällig gehen, watscheln.

lone [loun], *attrib. adj.* (*Poet.*) einsam; *play a – hand*, für sich *or* auf eigene Faust arbeiten. **–liness,** *s.* die Einsamkeit, Verlassenheit. **–ly,** *adj.*, **–some,** *adj.* einsam, verlassen. **–someness,** *s. see* **–liness.**

[1]**long** [lɔŋ], 1. *adj.* lang (*of space*); lang, langdauernd (*of time*); langsam, langwierig; – *arm*, (*fig.*) weitreichende Macht; auf lange Sicht (*C.L.*); *pull a – face*, ein langes Gesicht machen; – *field*, das Spielfeld hinter dem Schläger (*Crick.*); – *firm*, die Schwindelfirma; *have a – head*, umsichtig *or* schlau sein; – *hundred*, (*archaic*) das Großhundert; – *leg*, der Deckposten (*Crick.*); – *measure*, das Längenmaß; – *memory*, gutes Gedächtnis; – *odds*, schlechte Chance; *it is – odds he . . .*, ich möchte hundert gegen eins wetten daß er . . .; – *primer*, die Korpus(schrift) (*Typ.*); *in the – run*, auf die Dauer, am Ende, zuletzt, schließlich; – *sight*, die Fernsicht;

of – standing, alt, langjährig; – *stop*, der Hintermann (*Crick.*); – *suit*, lange Farbe (*Cards*); *a – time*, lange; – *vacation*, die großen Ferien (*pl.*); *take – views*, von höherer Warte aus betrachten; – *way round*, großer Umweg; *for a – while*, seit langem, lange; – *years of waiting*, langwierige Jahre des Wartens. **2.** *adv.* lange (*of time*); – *ago*, vor langer Zeit; *not – ago*, erst *or* noch vor kurzem; *all day –*, den ganzen Tag; *as – as*, so lange wie; (voraus)-gesetzt daß; *be –*, lange brauchen; *be – (in) coming*, lange Zeit in Anspruch nehmen um zu kommen; *not – before*, kurz *or* nicht lange vorher; *it was not – before*, es dauerte nicht lange bis *or* daß; *how – is it since?* wie lange ist es her? – *since*, see – *ago*; *so – as*, see *as – as*; (*coll.*) *so –!* bis dahin! auf Wiedersehen! **3.** *s.* die Länge; lange Zeit; lange Note (*Mus.*); lange Silbe (*Philol.*); *before –*, (Poet. *ere –*) binnen kurzem, bald; *for –*, lange; *that is the – and the short of it*, das ist das ganze Geheimnis *or* die ganze Geschichte; *the – and the short of it is*, um es kurz zu sagen, kurzum; *take –*, viel Zeit in Anspruch nehmen, lange dauern. **--boat,** *s.* das Beiboot, Großboot. **--bow,** *s.* der Langbogen; (*coll.*) *draw the --bow*, aufschneiden, übertreiben. **– clothes,** *pl.* das Tragkleid(chen). **--continued,** *adj.* lange dauernd. **--dated,** *adj.* langsichtig (*bill*) (*C.L.*). **--delayed,** *adj.* lange verzögert. **--distance,** *adj.* Langstrecken–, Dauer– (*race, runner, etc.*); Fern– (*telephone call, flight, etc.*). **--drawn,** *adj.* sich lange hinziehend. **--eared,** *adj.* langohrig. **–er,** *comp. adj. & adv.* länger, mehr; *no –er*, nicht länger, nicht mehr; *no –er ago than yesterday*, erst gestern; *not any –er*, nicht länger, nicht mehr; *be not much –er for this world*, nicht lange mehr in dieser Welt zu leben haben. **–eron,** *see* **longeron. –est,** 1. *sup. adj.* längste(r, s). 2. *sup. adv.* am längsten; *at the –est*, längstens, spätestens. **–evity,** *see* **longevity. – green,** (*coll.*) das Papiergeld (*Amer.*). **–hand,** *s.* die Kurrentschrift, gewöhnliche Schreibschrift. **--headed,** *adj.* langköpfig; (*fig.*) schlau, gescheit. **--horn,** *s.* langhörniges Vieh. **–ish,** *adj.* etwas lang, länglich. **–itude,** *see* **longitude. – jump,** *s.* der Weitsprung (*Sport*). **--legged** [–lɛgɪd], *adj.* langbeinig. **–lived,** *adj.* lange lebend, langlebig. **--range,** *adj.* weittragend, Fernkampf– (*as gun*). **–shoreman,** *s.* der Hafenarbeiter; Küstenfischer. **--sighted,** *adj.* weitsichtig, fernsichtig; (*fig.*) weitblickend, scharfsinnig; langsichtig (*C.L.*). **--sightedness,** *s.* die Weitsichtigkeit; (*fig.*) der Scharfsinn. **--standing,** *adj.* seit langer Zeit bestehend. **--suffering,** 1. *adj.* langmütig. 2. *s.* die Langmut. **--tongued,** *adj.* geschwätzig. **–ways,** *adv.* der Länge nach. **--winded,** *adj.* langatmig (*also fig.*); (*fig.*) weitschweifig, langweilig. **–wise,** *adv. see* **–ways.**

[2]**long** [lɔŋ], *v.n.* verlangen, sich sehnen (*for*, nach); *I very much – to see you*, ich sehne mich nach dir; *the –ed-for rest*, die ersehnte Ruhe. **–ing,** 1. *adj.* sehnsüchtig, schmachtend. 2. *s.* die Sehnsucht, das Verlangen (*for*, nach).

longe [lɔndʒ], *see* [2]**lunge.**

longeron [ˈlɔndʒərən], *s.* der Rumpflängsholm (*Av.*).

longitud–e [ˈlɔndʒɪtjʊ:d], *s.* (geographische) Länge; *degree of –e*, der Längengrad. **–inal** [–ˈtjʊ:dɪnl], *adj.* Längen–, Längs–; *–inal section*, der Längsschnitt. **–inally,** *adv.* der Länge nach.

loo [lʊ:], 1. *s.* das Lu. 2. *v.a.* beim Luspiel alle Stiche machen.

looby [lʊ:bɪ], *s.* (*coll.*) der Tölpel.

loofah [lʊ:fə], *s.* der Luffaschwamm.

look [lʊk], **1.** *v.n.* (*of persons*) schauen, blicken, sehen (*at* or *on*, auf (*Acc.*) *or* nach); (*of persons & things*) aussehen, scheinen; (*of things*) liegen, sehen, gerichtet sein (*towards*, nach). **(a)** (*with adjective, etc.*) (*coll.*) – *alive*, see – *sharp*; *things – bad*, die Lage sieht schlecht aus; – *before you leap*, erst wägen dann wagen; – *one's best*, vorteilhaft aussehen, sich am besten zeigen; – *blank*, verblüfft *or* verständnislos dreinsehen; – *like*, aussehen wie *or* nach, den Anschein haben; – *much better for*, besser aussehen infolge; – *here!* passen Sie auf! hören Sie mal! – *the other way*, wegblicken (*of persons*), nach der anderen Richtung zeigen (*of things*); – *the part*, danach aussehen; – *and see*, überzeugen Sie sich; – *to see*, nachsehen; (*coll.*) – *sharp* or – *smart*, sich beeilen; (*coll.*) – *you!* sieh, *or* sehen Sie mal! **(b)** (*with adverb*) – *about*, sich umsehen (*for*, nach); – *ahead*, Vorsorge treffen; – *back*, sich umsehen; (*fig.*) zurückblicken (*upon*, auf (*Acc.*)); – *down*, die Augen niederschlagen; (*fig.*) herabsehen, herabblicken (*on*, auf); – *forward to a th.*, etwas (*Dat.*) mit Erwartung entgegensehen, hoffen *or* sich freuen auf etwas; – *in*, vorsprechen (*upon*, bei); – *on*, zuschauen, zusehen (*at*, bei); – *out*, hinaussehen (*through* or *at*, aus); sich vorsehen, aufpassen; einen Ausblick gewähren *or* haben (*on*, auf (*Acc.*) *or* nach); – *out for*, ausschauen *or* sich umsehen nach; sich gefaßt machen auf; – *out!* Achtung! gib acht! – *round*, sich umsehen; – *up*, aufsehen, aufblicken; (*sl.*) sich bessern, einen Aufschwung nehmen (*C.L. & fig.*); anziehen (*of prices*); – *up to s.o.*, einen als Muster ansehen, an *or* zu einem hinaufblicken *or* emporblicken. **(c)** (*with preposition*) – *about one*, um sich sehen; – *after*, nachblicken (*Dat.*); aufpassen *or* achten auf (*Acc.*); sorgen für, sich kümmern um; – *at*, ansehen, betrachten; (*coll.*) *he wouldn't – at it*, er wollte nichts davon wissen; – *for*, suchen *or* sich umsehen nach; erwarten; *be –ed for*, erwartet werden; – *into*, prüfen, nachgehen (*Dat.*), untersuchen; – *on*, ansehen, betrachten; – *on the bright side of things*, das Leben von der heiteren Seite nehmen; – *over*, prüfen, durchsehen, übersehen; verzeihen; – *through*, durchsehen, durchlesen; – *to*, achtgeben *or* sehen auf; – *to a p.*, auf einen rechnen (*for*, wegen); – *to it that*, nimm dich in acht daß; – *upon*, see – *on*. **2.** *v.a.*; – *one's age*, so alt aussehen wie man ist; – *daggers at a p.*, mit den Blicken durchbohren; *he –s a fool*, er sieht wie ein Narr aus; – *s.o. in the face*, einem ins Gesicht sehen; – *one's last at*, zum letzten Male ansehen; (*coll.*) – *a sight*, einen kümmerlichen *or* abstoßenden Anblick darbieten; – *out*, (her)aussuchen; – *over*, mit den Augen prüfen *or* mustern; – *through*, mit den Blicken durchdringen *or* durchbohren; überprüfen, durchlesen, durchblättern; – *up*, aufschlagen, nachschlagen, nachsuchen (*a word, etc.*); (*coll.*) aufsuchen, besuchen (*a p.*). **3.** *s.* der Blick (*at*, auf *or* nach); Anblick; das Aussehen, Ansehen, die Miene; *hang-dog –*, die Galgenmiene; *have a – at*, ansehen, einsehen; (*coll.*) *keep a – out*, aufpassen; (*coll.*) *I don't like the – of it*, die Sache gefällt mir nicht; *wear a – of*, aussehen wie. **–er,** *s.* (*sl.*) einer der gut aussieht, *not much of a –er*, nicht sonderlich aussehen. **–er-on,** *s.* der Zuschauer (*at*, bei). **--in,** *s.* (*sl.*) die Chance. **–ing,** 1. *adj. suff.* aussehend; *good-–ing*, hübsch, schön. 2. *s.* das Blicken. **–ing-glass,** *s.* der Spiegel. **--out,** *s.* der Ausblick, die Ausschau, der Ausguck; *on the --out*, auf der Lauer *or* Ausschau (*for*, nach); (*coll.*) *be on the --out*, aufpassen (*for*, auf); *keep a good --out*, ein wachsames Auge haben, scharf aufpassen (*for*, auf (*Acc.*)); sich wohl vorsehen; (*sl.*) *that's your own --out*, das ist deine Sache *or* Angelegenheit. (*sl.*) die Aussicht; der Wächter, die Wache (*person*). **–s** (*good –s*) *pl.* die Schönheit.

[1]**loom** [lʊ:m], *s.* der Webstuhl, die Webmaschine.

[2]**loom** [lʊ:m], 1. *v.n.* undeutlich sichtbar werden, undeutlich aufragen *or* erscheinen, sich in der Ferne auftun, drohend auftauchen; – *large*, drohend aufragen; (*fig.*) von großer Bedeutung erscheinen. 2. *s.* das Sichtbarwerden, Auftauchen (*Naut.*).

[1]**loon** [lʊ:n], *s.* (*Scots*) der Bengel, Lümmel; Bursche.

[2]**loon** [lʊ:n], *s.* der Eistaucher, Haubentaucher (*Orn.*).

loony [ˈlʊ:nɪ], *adj. & s.* (*coll.*) *see* **lunatic.**

[1]**loop** [lʊ:p], 1. *s.* die Schlinge, Schleife; Öse; Krümmung (*of a river*); der Überschlag, das Looping (*Av.*); *see* **--line.** 2. *v.a.* in Schleifen *or* eine Schleife legen, winden, schlingen; – *the –*, sich überschlagen, einen Schleifenflug *or* ein Looping machen (*Av.*); – *up*, aufnehmen, aufstecken, aufschnüren. 3. *v.n.* eine Schleife bilden, sich winden. **– aerial** *or* **antenna,** die Drehrahmenantenne, Peilantenne (*Rad.*). **–er,** *s.* die Spannerraupe (*Ent.*). **–hole,** 1. *s.* das Guckloch, die Schieß-

scharte (*Fort.*); (*fig.*) das Schlupfloch, die Ausflucht, der Ausweg, die Hintertür. 2. *v.a.* mit Schießscharten versehen. **--line,** *s.* die Schleife (*Railw.*). **--way,** *s.* die Umleitung, der Umweg.

²loop [lu:p], *s.* die Luppe, der Deul (*Metall.*).

loose [lu:s], 1. *v.a.* lösen, befreien, frei machen (*from*, von); losmachen, losbinden, auflösen, aufbinden; loslassen, laufen lassen; – *one's hold* (*on a th.*), (eine S.) loslassen *or* fahren lassen; – *off*, losschießen, abschießen, abfeuern (*a shot, etc.*). 2. *v.n.* die Anker lichten, absegeln. 3. *adj.* los, frei; locker, lose; schlaff, lappig, weit (*as a dress*), lose hängend, fliegend (*as hair*); unverpackt, lose verpackt; zerstreut; (*fig.*) unklar, unbestimmt, unlogisch, ungenau (*of ideas, etc.*); liederlich (*of persons*). (*a*) (*with nouns*) – *bowels*, flüssiger Stuhlgang; – *box*, der Stallabteil (*Railw.*); – *collar*, loser Kragen; – *contact*, der Wackelkontakt (*Elec.*); *at a – end*, ohne feste Beschäftigung; – *fish*, lockerer *or* liederlicher Bursche; – *ice*, offenes Eis; – *money*, das Kleingeld; (*sl.*) *he has a screw* –, bei ihm ist eine Schraube los; – *talk*, gewissenloses Gerede; – *thinking*, unklares *or* wirres Denken; – *tongue*, lose Zunge; – *tooth*, loser *or* lockerer Zahn; – *translation*, freie Übersetzung. (*b*) (*with verbs*) *break* –, sich losreißen; ausbrechen (*from prison*); *come* or *get* –, sich losmachen; losgehen; *hang* –, schlaff hangen; *let* –, loslassen; Luft machen (*Dat.*) (*feelings*); (*coll.*) *play fast and – with*, Schindluder treiben mit. 4. *s.*; (*sl.*) *go on the* –, sumpfen. **--leaf,** *s.* versetzbares Blatt; *--leaf note-book*, das Einlegeheft. **-n,** 1. *v.a.* losmachen, freimachen, losbinden (*a string, etc.*); locker machen (auf)lockern (*earth*); öffnen (*bowels*); lösen (*tongue, cough*). 2. *v.n.* sich lösen *or* lockern, locker werden. **-ness,** *s.* die Lockerheit, Schlaffheit; Unklarheit, Ungenauigkeit; Laxheit, Liederlichkeit; der Durchfall (*Med.*). **-strife,** *s.* der Weiderich, das Pfennigkraut (*Bot.*).

loot [lu:t], 1. *v.n.* plündern. 2. *v.a.* plündern (*town, etc.*), erbeuten (*goods*). 3. *s.* die (Kriegs-)Beute, das Raubgut. **-er,** *s.* der Plünderer. **-ing,** *s.* die Plünderung.

¹lop [lɔp], *v.a.* beschneiden, stutzen (*trees*); – *off*, abhauen, abschneiden. **-pings,** *pl.* abgeschnittene Zweige. **-ping-shears.** *pl.* die Baumschere.

²lop [lɔp], 1. *v.a.* herabhängen lassen. 2. *v.n.* schlaff herunterhängen *or* herabfallen; – *about*, herumlungern. **--eared,** *adj.* mit Hängeohren. **-sided,** *adj.* nach einer Seite hängend, schief; (*fig.*) einseitig.

loquaci-ous [loʊk'weɪʃəs], *adj.* geschwätzig, schwatzhaft. **-ty** [–'wæsɪtɪ], *s.* die Geschwätzigkeit, Schwatzhaftigkeit.

lord [lɔ:d], 1. *s.* der Herr, Gebieter; Feudalherr; Peer, Adlige(r), *m.*; der Lord (*as title*); (*Poet.*) Gemahl, Eheherr; (*coll.*) Magnat; *the* –, Gott der Herr; *the –s*, das Oberhaus; *the –'s Day*, der Tag des Herrn; (*coll.*) *drunk as a* –, voll wie eine Strandkanone; (*coll.*) *good –!* oh Gott! oh je! *the – of Hosts*, der Herr der Heerscharen, Herr Zebaoth; *the House of –s*, das Oberhaus; – *of the manor*, der Grundherr, Lehnsherr; *my* –, gnädiger Herr, Mylord! *our* –, Christus; *the –'s Prayer*, das Vaterunser; *the –'s Supper*, heiliges Abendmahl; *in the year of our* –, im Jahre des Herrn. **– chamberlain,** der Oberkammerherr. **– Chancellor,** der Lordkanzler. **– High Commissioner,** der Oberkommissar. **– Chief Justice,** der Lordoberrichter. **– Lieutenant,** der Vizekönig, Gouverneur; Vertreter der Königin (*of a county*). **– Mayor,** der Oberbürgermeister; – *Mayor's show*, der Festzug des neuerwählten Oberbürgermeisters von London. **– Provost,** der Oberbürgermeister (*Scotland*). **-s spiritual,** geistliche Mitglieder des (englischen) Oberhauses. **-s temporal,** weltliche Mitglieder des (englischen) Oberhauses. 2. *v.a.*; (*coll.*) – *it*, den großen Herrn spielen; – *it over*, dominieren über. **-liness,** *s.* die Hoheit, Würde, der Glanz; die Großmut; der Hochmut. **-ling,** *s.* das Herrchen. **-ly,** *adj.* vornehm, edel, großmütig; stolz, herrisch, gebieterisch, hochmütig. **-s-and-ladies,** *s. see* **cuckoo-pint** (*Bot.*). **-ship,** *s.* die Herrschaft; das Herrschaftsgebiet; *your –ship*, Euer Gnaden.

lore [lɔ:], *s.* die Lehre, Kunde, Überlieferung, überliefertes Wissen.

lorgnette [lɔ:'njɛt], *s.* die Lorgnette, Stielbrille.

loricate ['lɔrɪkeɪt], *adj.* gepanzert, Panzer– (*Zool.*).

lorn [lɔ:n], *adj.* (*archaic*) einsam, verlassen.

lorry ['lɔrɪ], *s.* das Lastauto, der Lastkraftwagen, Frachtwagen (*Motor.*); die Lore, Lori (*Railw.*); der Kipper (*Build., Min.*); *lorried infantry*, motorisierte Infanterie (*Mil.*).

los-e [lu:z], **1.** *ir.v.a.* verlieren; verwirken, einbüßen, kommen um, verlustig gehen (*Gen.*), verlegen; vergeuden, verschwenden (*time, etc.*); zurückbleiben, nachgehen (*as a watch*); loswerden, befreit werden von (*headache, etc.*); verpassen, versäumen (*train, etc.*). (*a*) (*with nouns*) *I lost his answer in the noise*, ich überhörte *or* mir entging seine Antwort bei dem Lärm; *–e colour*, abfärben; *–e ground*, (an) Boden verlieren, (zurück)weichen; (*fig.*) (an) Einfluß verlieren (*with*, bei); *–e one's hair*, das Haar verlieren; *–e heart*, den Mut sinken lassen; *–e one's heart to*, sein Herz verlieren an; *–e height*, absacken (*Av.*); *–e one's hold of*, loslassen, fahren lassen; *–e one's labour*, sich (*Dat.*) unnütze Mühe geben, sich (*Acc.*) umsonst plagen; *–e one's life*, sein *or* das Leben verlieren; *–e an opportunity*, eine Gelegenheit vorbeigehen lassen; *–e (one's) patience*, die Geduld verlieren; *–e sight of*, aus den Augen verlieren; *–e one's temper*, heftig, wütend, *or* hitzig *or* ärgerlich werden, in Zorn geraten; *–e one's voice*, heiser werden; *–e one's way*, sich verirren. (*b*) (*causative*) um den Verlust bringen, bringen um; kosten (*Dat.*). (*c*) (*passive*) *be lost*, verlorengehen, verschwinden; untergehen, den Tod finden; *be lost in*, versunken *or* vertieft sein in; *be lost to*, bar sein *or* nicht mehr empfindlich sein für; *be lost upon*, keinen Eindruck machen auf, erfolglos sein bei, wirkungslos bleiben auf. **2.** *v.r.* den Weg verlieren, sich verirren; sich verlieren (*also fig.*) (*in*, in). **3.** *ir.v.n.* verlieren (*in*, an); Verluste *or* Einbuße erleiden (*by*, durch); geschlagen werden, den kürzeren ziehen; nachgehen (*as a watch*); *–e to a team*, einer Mannschaft unterliegen (*Sport*); *what I –e on the swings I gain on the roundabouts*, ich halte mich schadlos. **-er,** *s.* der Verlierer, Verlierende; *be a –er by*, Schaden *or* Einbuße erleiden durch; *come off a –er*, den kürzeren ziehen. **-ing,** *adj.* verlierend; verlustbringend, unrentabel (*C.L.*); *–ing game*, aussichtsloses Unternehmen; *–ing hazard*, der Verläufer (*Bill.*). **-ings,** *pl.* Verluste (*gambling*). **-t,** *see* **lost.**

loss [lɔs], *s.* der Verlust, Nachteil, Schaden (*to*, für), die Einbuße, der Ausfall, Abgang; *at a* –, mit *or* unter Verlust; *be at a – for*, verlegen *or* in Verlegenheit sein um; *be at a – to . . .*, nicht . . . können; – *of appetite*, die Appetitlosigkeit; – *of blood*, der Blutverlust; *combat –es*, Gefechtsausfälle (*pl.*) (*Mil.*); *dead* –, vollständiger Verlust; – *of memory*, die Amnesie; – *of power*, der Leistungsabfall; – *of time*, der Zeitverlust; – *through shrinkage*, die Zehrung.

lost [lɔst], *adj.* verloren, verlorengegangen, (da)hin; verirrt; vergeudet; *give up as* or *for* –, verloren geben; – *motion*, toter Gang, der Leerlauf (*Mach.*); – *property office*, das Fundbüro; *see* **lose.**

lot [lɔt], 1. *s.* das Los (*also fig.*); (*fig.*) Geschick, Schicksal, die Lage; der Teil, Posten, die Partie (*C.L.*); das Stück Land, die Parzelle (*of land*); (*coll.*) die Menge, Masse; (*coll.*) *bad* –, fauler Kunde; *building* –, der Bauplatz, die Baustelle; *by* –, durch Losen, durch das Los; *cast* or *draw –s*, losen (*for*, um); *fall to one's – to do*, einem zufallen zu tun; *give me the* –, gib sie mir alle; *is that the –?* ist das alles? sind das alle? (*coll.*) *a – of, –s of*, eine Menge *or* Masse, ein Haufen; sehr viel(e); *sell in* or *by small –s*, in kleinen Posten verkaufen (*C.L.*); *throw in one's – with*, das Los teilen mit; (*coll.*) *the whole* –, die ganze Sippschaft. 2. *v.a.* (– *out*) durch Los zuteilen, verlosen; in Parzellen *or* Partien teilen; *see* **lottery.**

loth [loʊθ], *adv. see* **loath.**

lotion ['loʊʃən], *s.* das Waschmittel, Hautwasser; *eye-*–, das Augenwasser.

lottery ['lɔtərɪ], *s.* die Lotterie (*also fig.*), Verlosung, das Glücksspiel. **--ticket,** *s.* das Lotterielos.

lotto [ˈlɔtou], *s.* das Lotto(spiel).
lotus [ˈloutəs], *s.* der Lotos, die Lotusblume; der Lotusklee, Steinklee, Hornklee. **--eater,** *s.* der Lotosesser, Genüßling.
loud [laud], *adj.* laut; lärmend, geräuschvoll; (*fig.*) schreiend, grell, auffallend (*as colours*). **-ness,** *s.* die Lautheit, der Lärm; die Lautstärke (*Rad.*); (*fig.*) das Schreiende, Auffallende. **--speaker,** *s.* der Lautsprecher (*Rad.*).
lough [lɔχ], *s.* (*Irish*) der See, Meerbusen.
lounge [laundʒ], 1. *v.n.* müßiggehen, faulenzen, schlendern, faul herumliegen; – *about*, herumlungern. 2. *v.a.*; – *away*, vertrödeln (*one's time*). 3. *s.* die Diele, Halle, der Gesellschaftsraum, das Foyer; die Chaiselongue. **--chair,** der Klubsessel. **– coat,** der Sakko. (*sl.*) **--lizard,** der Salonlöwe. **-r,** *s.* der Faulenzer, Müßiggänger. **--suit,** *s.* der Straßenanzug.
lour [lauə], *v.n.* drohend *or* finster blicken ((*up*)*on* or *at*, auf (*Acc.*)); (*fig.*) düster werden, sich verfinstern (*of sky*); finster aussehen, drohen (*of events*). **-ing,** *adj.* düster, finster, drohend.
lous–e [laus], *s.* (pl. *lice*) die Laus (*Ent.*). **-iness** [ˈlauzɪnɪs], *s.* die Lausigkeit, verlauster Zustand. **-y** [ˈlauzɪ], *adj.* verlaust; (*fig.*) (*sl.*) lausig.
lout [laut], *s.* der Tölpel, Lümmel. **-ish,** *adj.* tölpelhaft, lümmelhaft, flegelhaft. **-ishness,** *s.* die Tölpelhaftigkeit.
louver, louvre [ˈlu:və], *s.* durchbrochenes Türmchen, Dachfenster (*Arch.*); der Luftschlitz, die Öffnung (*Motor.*).
lov–able [ˈlʌvəbl], *adj.* liebenswürdig, liebenswert. **-ableness,** *s.* die Liebenswürdigkeit. **-age** [–ɪdʒ], *s.* das Liebstöckel (*Bot.*). **-e** [lʌv], 1. *v.a.* lieben; liebhaben, gern haben *or* mögen; Gefallen *or* Vergnügen finden an (*Dat.*); *–e doing* or *to do*, gern tun, mit Vergnügen tun. 2. *v.n.* lieben. 3. *s.* die Liebe; Zuneigung (*of*, *for*, *to*, or *towards*, zu); die Liebschaft; der Schatz, das Liebchen; Amor, der Liebesgott; die Null (*Tenn.*); *my –e*, mein Liebes; *–e all!* beide null! *four* (*to*) *–e*, vier gegen nichts (*Tenn.*); *–e's labour's lost*, die verlorene Liebesmüh. (*a*) (*with nouns*) *–e of one's country*, die Vaterlandsliebe; (*coll.*) *a –e of a dress*, ein allerliebstes Kleid; *–e of glory*, die Ruhmsucht. (*b*) (*with verbs*) *give my –e to your sister*, grüße deine Schwester herzlich von mir; *there is no –e lost between them*, sie haben für einander nichts übrig; *make –e*, den Hof machen (*to* (*Dat.*)); *send one's –e to a p.*, einen herzlich grüßen lassen. (*c*) (*with prepositions*) *for* (*the*) *–e of*, aus Liebe zu; *for the –e of God*, um Gottes willen; *not for –e or money*, nicht für Geld und gute Worte; *play for –e*, um nichts spielen; *be in –e with*, verliebt sein in; *fall in –e with*, sich verlieben in. **-e-affair,** *s.* die Liebschaft, der Liebeshandel. **-e-apple,** *s.* die Tomate. **-e-bird,** *s.* der Sperlingspapagei (*Orn.*). **-e-child,** *s.* das Kind der Liebe, uneheliches Kind. **-e-game,** *s.* das Nullspiel (*Tenn.*). **-e-in-a-mist,** *s.* das Kapuzinerkraut (*Bot.*). **-e-in-idleness,** *s.* das Stiefmütterchen (*Bot.*). **-e-knot,** *s.* der Liebesknoten. **-eless,** *adj.* lieblos. **-e-letter,** *s.* der Liebesbrief. **-e-lies-bleeding,** *s.* roter Fuchsschwanz (*Bot.*). **-eliness,** *s.* die Lieblichkeit, Schönheit, der Reiz. **-e-lock,** *s.* die Schmachtlocke. **-e-lorn,** *adj.* vom Liebchen verlassen; schmachtend. **-ely,** *adj.* lieblich, reizend, (*coll.*) wunderschön. **-e-making,** *s.* das Hofmachen, Kurmachen. **-e-match,** *s.* die Liebesheirat. **-e-potion,** *s.* der Liebestrank. **-er,** *s.* der Liebhaber, Freund, Geliebte(r), *f.* & *m.*; der Verehrer, Anbeter; die Buhle; *pl.* Liebende (*pl.*), ein Liebespaar. **-e-set,** *s.* die Nullpartie (*Tenn.*). **-e-sick,** *adj.* liebeskrank. **-e-song,** *s.* das Liebeslied. **-e-story,** *s.* die Liebesgeschichte. **-e-token,** *s.* das Liebespfand. **-ing,** *adj.* liebend, zärtlich, liebevoll; *–ing care*, liebevolle Fürsorge; *–ing kindness*, die Herzensgüte; *in –ing memory*, in liebendem Gedenken (*of*, an (*Acc.*)); *your –ing mother*, deine dich liebende Mutter. **-ing-cup,** *s.* der Liebesbecher, Freundschaftsbecher.
[1]**low** [lou], 1. *adj.* & *adv.* niedrig; tief, nieder (*of rank*); schwach, leise (*as sound, etc.*); seicht (*as water*); niedergeschlagen, gedrückt (*as the spirits*); mäßig, billig, wohlfeil (*of price*); gemein, niederträchtig, roh (*of persons*); tief ausgeschnitten (*as a dress*); gering, ungünstig, minderwertig (*of opinion, etc.*). (*a*) (*with verbs*) *be –*, niedrig stehen (*C.L.*); *bring a p. –*, einen zu Falle bringen; *feel –*, in gedrückter Stimmung sein, sich krank fühlen; *lay –*, besiegen, stürzen; demütigen; (*sl.*) *lie –*, sich versteckt halten; (*fig.*) nichts unternehmen, abwarten; nichts verraten; (*coll.*) *run –*, zur Neige gehen, knapp werden; *the sands are running –*, die Zeit *or* es geht zu Ende. (*b*) (*with nouns*) *– birth*, niedere Geburt; *– bow*, tiefe Verneigung; *– Church*, puritanische Richtung der anglikanischen Kirche; *– comedy*, das Possenspiel; *the – Countries*, die Niederlande; *– frequency*, die Niederfrequenz; *– gear*, erster Gang (*Motor.*); *– German*, niederdeutsch, plattdeutsch; *– Latin*, das Spätlatein; *–-level attack*, der Tieffliegerangriff; *– life*, das Leben der unteren Stände; *– Mass*, stille Messe; *– neck*, der Ausschnitt; *– opinion*, geringe Meinung; *– pressure*, der Niederdruck; *– spirits*, die Niedergeschlagenheit, gedrückte Stimmung; *– Sunday*, der Sonntag nach Ostern; *– tension*, die Niederspannung (*Elec.*); *– tide*, *– water*, niedrigste Ebbe; *be in – water*, auf dem Trockenen sitzen, nicht bei Kasse sein. 2. *adv.* tief; leise (*of sound*); *– down*, tief unten; *fall –*, tief fallen. **--born,** *adj.* niedrig geboren, aus niederem Stande. **--bred,** *adj.* ungebildet, gemein. **--brow,** 1. *adj.* geistig tiefstehend *or* anspruchslos. 2. *s.* geistig Anspruchsloser, der Spießer. **--church,** *adj.* see *– Church.* (*sl.*) **--down,** *adj.* gemein. *--down trick*, die Gemeinheit. **-er,** 1. *comp. adj.* tiefer; (*only attrib.*) untere(r)(s), niedere(r)(s); Unter–; *–er case*, unterer Schriftkasten; kleine Buchstaben (*Typ.*); *–er classes*, untere *or* niedere Klassen; *–er deck*, das Niederdeck; *–er Empire*, Byzantinisches Kaiserreich; *the –er House*, das Unterhaus; *the –er regions*, die Hölle, Unterwelt; *–er school*, die Unterstufe; *–er sixth*, die Unterprima. 2. *comp. adv.* tiefer; leiser (*of sound*). **-ermost,** 1. *adj.* niedrigst. 2. *adv.* am niedrigsten. **-est,** *sup. adj.* tiefst, unterst; *–est bidder*, Mindestbietende(r), *m.* **-land,** *s.* das Tiefland, Unterland; die Niederung; *pl.* das schottische Tiefland. **-lander,** *s.* der Bewohner des schottischen Tieflandes. **-liness,** *s.* die Demut; Niedrigkeit (*of station*); Armut. **-ly,** 1. *adj.* niedrig, tief, gering; demütig, bescheiden. **--lying,** *adj.* flach. **--minded,** *adj.* niedrig *or* gemein gesinnt. **--necked,** *adj.* tief ausgeschnitten (*dress*). **-ness,** *s.* die Niedrigkeit, Tiefe (*of sound, price, etc.*); *–ness of spirits*, die Niedergeschlagenheit. **--pass filter,** *s.* die Spulenkette, Hochfrequenz-Sperrkette (*Rad.*). **--pitched,** *adj.* flach (*as a roof*); tief(tönend) (*as a sound*). **--pressure,** *adj.* Unterdruck– (*Tech.*), Tiefdruck– (*Meteor.*). **--spirited,** *adj.* gedrückt, niedergeschlagen. **--tension,** *adj.* see *– tension*; *--tension battery*, die Heizbatterie (*Rad.*). **--water mark,** niedrigster Wasserstand; (*fig.*) der Tiefstand, Tiefpunkt. **--wing monoplane,** der Tiefdecker.
[2]**low** [lou], 1. *v.n.* brüllen, muhen. 2. *s.* das Gebrüll, Muhen.
[1]**lower** [ˈlauə], *see* **lour.**
[2]**lower** [ˈlouə], 1. *v.a.* niederlassen, herunterlassen; niederholen, senken, sinken lassen; streichen (*flag*), fieren, zu Wasser bringen *or* setzen (*boats*); niederschlagen (*the eyes*); erniedrigen (*a p., also Mus.*); herabsetzen (*prices*); drücken (*records*); *– one's voice*, leise(r) sprechen. 2. *v.n.* sinken, fallen, abnehmen.
loyal [ˈlɔɪəl], *adj.* treu (*to* (*Dat.*)), loyal; bieder, redlich; *– demonstration*, patriotische Kundgebung; *– toast*, der Trinkspruch auf Herrscher und Herrscherhaus. **-ist,** *s.* Treugesinnte(r), *m.* **-ty,** *s.* die Treue, Loyalität.
lozenge [ˈlɔzɪndʒ], *s.* die Raute, der Rhombus (*Geom., Her.*); die Pastille, Tablette (*Med.*); das Zuckerplätzchen, Bonbon (*Conf.*). **--shaped,** *adj.* rautenförmig.
lubber [ˈlʌbə], *s.* der Lümmel, Flegel, Tölpel; unerfahrener Seemann; (also *land-–*) die Landratte. **-ly,** *adj.* tölpelhaft, plump.
lubric–ant [ˈl(j)u:brɪkənt], *s.* das Schmiermittel. **-ate** [–eɪt], *v.a.* schmieren, ölen (*Mach.*); *–ating*

oil, das Schmieröl. **-ation** [–ˈkeɪʃən], *s.* das Schmieren, Ölen, die Einschmierung, Einölung. **-ator** [–keɪtə], *s.* der Öler, die Schmierbüchse. **-ity** [–ˈbrɪsɪtɪ], *s.* die Schlüpfrigkeit; Unbeständigkeit (*of fortune*); (*fig.*) Lüsternheit, Geilheit.

luce [l(j)uːs], *s.* (ausgewachsener) Hecht.

luc-ency [ˈl(j)uːsənsɪ], *s.* der Glanz. **-ent** [–ənt], *adj.* glänzend, leuchtend, klar. **-id** [–ɪd], *adj.* (*usually fig.*) hell, klar, deutlich; (*archaic & Poet.*) glänzend, leuchtend; *–id intervals*, lichte Augenblicke. **-idity** [–ˈsɪdɪtɪ], *s.* **-idness**, *s.* (*usually fig.*) die Helle; Klarheit, Deutlichkeit. **-ifugous** [–ˈsɪfəgəs], *adj.* lichtscheu.

luck [lʌk], *s.* das Glück, Schicksal, Geschick; der Zufall, die Schicksalsfügung; *bad –*, das Unglück, (*coll.*) Pech; *be down on one's –*, vom Glück verlassen sein, in übler Lage sein; *good –*, das Glück, (*coll.*) Schwein; *by good –*, glücklicherweise; *with good –*, wenn man Glück hat, glücklichenfalls; *good –!* viel Glück! (*coll.*) *hard –*, see *bad –*; *as – would have it*, wie es der Zufall *or* das Schicksal (haben) wollte, glücklicherweise *or* unglücklicherweise; *ill –*, see *bad –*; *be in –*, (*sl.*) Schwein haben; *be out of –*, (*sl.*) Pech haben; *piece of –*, großes Glück; *run of good –*, andauerndes Glück; (*coll.*) *tough –!* see *worse –!*; *try one's –*, sein Glück versuchen; (*coll.*) *worse –!* Pech! leider! **-ily**, *adv.* zum Glück, glücklicherweise. **-iness**, *s.* das Glück. **-less**, *adj.* unglücklich. **-lessness**, *s.* das Unglück. **-y**, *adj.* glücklich; glückbringend, günstig, Glücks–; *be –y*, Glück haben; *–y bag*, *–y dip*, der Glückstopf; *–y dog* or *fellow*, der Glückspilz; *–y hit*, der Glücksfall, Treffer.

lucr-ative [ˈl(j)uːkrətɪv], *adj.* einträglich, gewinnbringend. **-e** [ˈl(j)uːkə], *s.* der Gewinn, Vorteil; die Gewinnsucht, Habsucht; (*sl.*) *filthy –e*, Moneten (*pl.*), das Blech, der Kies, das Moos.

lucubrat-e [ˈl(j)uːkjuːbreɪt], *v.n.* bei Nachtlicht arbeiten. **-ion** [–ˈbreɪʃən], *s.* gelehrte Nachtarbeit; (*usually pl.*) gelehrte Abhandlungen.

ludicrous [ˈl(j)uːdɪkrəs], *adj.* lächerlich; drollig, possierlich. **-ness**, *s.* die Lächerlichkeit; Possierlichkeit.

ludo [ˈl(j)uːdoʊ], *s.* ein Würfelspiel.

lues [ˈluːɪːz], *s.* die Syphilis.

luff [lʌf], 1. *s.* die Luv, Windseite (*Naut.*); Stagkante (*of staysail, etc.*). 2. *v.a.* näher an den Wind bringen (*ship*). 3. *v.n.* (*– up*) anluven.

[1]**lug** [lʌg], *v.a.* (*sl.*) schleppen, zerren; (*fig.*) *– in*, an den Haaren herbeiziehen.

[2]**lug** [lʌg], *s.* der Henkel, das Öhr; der Ansatz, Zapfen, die Zinke, Warze (*Mach.*); (*Scots or vulg.*) das Ohr.

[3]**lug** [lʌg], *s. see* **lug-sail.**

luge [lyːʒ], 1. *s.* der Schlitten. 2. *v.a. & n.* (in einem) Schlitten fahren.

luggage [ˈlʌgɪdʒ], *s.* (*no pl.*) das Gepäck; *free –*, das Freigepäck; *heavy –*, großes Gepäck; *light –*, das Handgepäck; *register the –*, das Gepäck aufgeben. **--carrier**, der Gepäckträger (*Cycl.*). **--grid**, *s.* die Kofferbrücke (*Motor.*). **--office**, *s.* die Gepäckabfertigungsstelle, Gepäckannahme, Gepäckaufgabe, Gepäckausgabe. **--rack**, *s.* das Gepäcknetz (*Railw.*). **--train**, *s.* der Güterzug. **--van**, *s.* der Gepäckwagen.

lug-ger [ˈlʌgə], *s.* der Lugger, Logger (*Naut.*). **--sail**, *s.* das Luggersegel.

lugubrious [l(j)uɡjuːbrɪəs], *adj.* traurig, kummervoll. **-ness**, *s.* die Traurigkeit.

lukewarm [ˈl(j)uːkwɔːm], *adj.* lauwarm; angewärmt, (*fig.*) lau, gleichgültig. **-ness**, *s.* die Lauwärme; (*fig.*) Lauheit.

lull [lʌl], 1. *v.a.* einlullen; (*fig.*) beschwichtigen, beruhigen, überreden (*a p.*) (*into*, zu); *– to sleep*, einschläfern. 2. *v.n.* sich beruhigen, sich legen, nachlassen (*of wind*). 3. *s.* die Ruhepause, Stille (*also fig.*); Windstille, Flaute; (*fig.*) Stockung. **-aby** [ˈlʌləbaɪ], *s.* das Wiegenlied, Schlummerlied.

lumba-go [lʌmˈbeɪgoʊ], *s.* der Hexenschuß. **-r** [ˈlʌmbə], *adj.* Lenden–, lumbal (*Anat.*).

lumber [ˈlʌmbə], 1. *s.* das Gerümpel, der Plunder, Trödelkram; behauenes Bauholz. 2. *v.a.* (*– up*) belasten, vollstopfen (*a room, etc.*). 3. *v.n.* zusammengehäuft umherliegen; poltern, rumpeln; (*– along*) sich schleppen *or* schwerfällig fortbewegen. **-ing**, *adj.* rumpelnd, polternd; schwerfällig, plump, schleppend. **--jack**, *s.*, **-man**, *s.* der Holzfäller. **--mill**, *s.* die Sägemühle. **--room**, *s.* die Rumpelkammer. **--yard**, *s.* der Holzplatz.

lumen [ˈljuːmən], *s.* die Lichteinheit.

lumin-ary [ˈl(j)uːmɪnərɪ], *s.* leuchtender Körper, der Lichtkörper, Himmelskörper; (*fig.*) die Leuchte. **-escence** [–ˈnɛsəns], *s.* die Lichterregung, Lichtausstrahlung. **-escent** [–ˈnɛsənt], *adj.* lichterregend, lichtausstrahlend. **-osity** [–ˈnɒsɪtɪ], *s.* die Helligkeit, der Glanz. **-ous** [ˈl(j)uːmɪnəs], *adj.* leuchtend, strahlend, glänzend, Leucht–; (*fig.*) hell, klar, licht; lichtvoll; *–ous dial*, *s.* das Leuchtzifferblatt; *–ous paint*, die Leuchtfarbe; *–ous ray*, der Lichtstrahl; *–ous screen*, der Leuchtschirm (*Television*).

lump [lʌmp], 1. *s.* der Klumpen, Knollen; die Masse; das Stück; die Luppe, der Deul (*Metall.*); die Beule, Schwellung (*Med.*); (*coll.*) grober *or* plumper Mensch; *a – came in my throat*, mir war die Kehle wie zugeschnürt; *– of gold*, der Goldklumpen; *in the –*, in Bausch und Bogen, im ganzen; *two –s of sugar*, zwei Stücke Zucker; *all of a –*, alles auf einmal; *– sum*, die Pauschalsumme. 2. *v.a.* (*– together*) zusammenwerfen, in einen Topf werfen; zusammenfassen, pauschalieren (*in(to)*, in; *with*, mit; *under*, unter); (*sl.*) *if you don't like it you can – it*, wenn dir's nicht paßt, kannst du's (ja) bleiben lassen *or* mußt du dich damit abfinden. **-er**, *s.* der Hafenarbeiter, Löscharbeiter. **-ish**, *adj.* schwerfällig, unbeholfen, plump, träge, stur. **- sugar**, *s.* der Würfelzucker. **-y**, *adj.* klumpig; unruhig, bewegt (*of sea*).

luna-cy [ˈl(j)uːnəsɪ], *s.* der Irrsinn, Wahnsinn; (*coll.*) große Dummheit. **-r** [–nə], *adj.* Mond–; (*fig.*) blaß, schwach; *–r caustic*, der Höllenstein; *–r month*, der Mondmonat. **-tic** [–nətɪk], 1. *adj.* wahnsinnig, irrsinnig. 2. *s.* Geistesgestörte(r), Wahnsinnige(r), Irre(r), *m.*; *–tic asylum*, die Irrenanstalt. **-tion** [–ˈneɪʃən], *s.* der Mondumlauf.

lunch [lʌntʃ], 1. *s.* der Lunch, das Mittagessen; Gabelfrühstück, der Imbiß. 2. *v.n.* zu Mittag essen. **--counter**, *s.* die Imbißstube. **-eon** [–ən], *s.* formelle Mittagsmahlzeit. **-eon-basket**, *s.* der Speisekorb. **--hour**, *s.* die Mittagspause.

lune [l(j)uːn], *s.* halbmondförmige Figur (*Geom.*). **-tte** [–ˈnɛt], *s.* halbkreisförmiges Fenster, das Halbkreisfeld, Bogenfeld (*Arch.*); die Lünette (*Fort.*).

lung [lʌŋ], *s.* der Lungenflügel (*Anat.*); *pl.* die Lunge; (*fig.*) Grünfläche (*of towns*); *have good –s*, eine kräftige Stimme haben; *inflammation of the –s*, die Lungenentzündung. **-wort**, *s.* das Lungenkraut (*Bot.*).

[1]**lunge** [lʌndʒ], 1. *s.* der Ausfall (*Fenc.*), Stoß, Angriff. 2. *v.n.* ausfallen, einen Ausfall machen (*at*, gegen), losschlagen (*at*, auf (*Acc.*)).

[2]**lunge** [ləndʒ], 1. *s.* die Longe, Laufleine. 2. *v.a.* longieren.

[1]**lupin(e)** [ˈl(j)upɪn], *s.* die Lupine (*Bot.*).

[2]**lupine** [ˈl(j)uːpaɪn], *adj.* wölfisch, Wolfs–.

lupus [ˈl(j)uːpəs], *s.* der Lupus, die Hauttuberkulose.

[1]**lurch** [ləːtʃ], *s.*; (only in) *leave in the –*, im Stiche lassen.

[2]**lurch** [ləːtʃ], 1. *s.* das Überholen, plötzliches Schlingern, Umlegen *or* Rollen (*Naut.*); (*fig.*) der Ruck; das Taumeln. 2. *v.n.* schlingern (*of ship*); taumeln, torkeln (*of persons*).

lurcher [ˈləːtʃə], *s.* der Spürhund.

lure [ljuːə], 1. *s.* der Köder, die Lockspeise (*also fig.*); (*fig.*) der Reiz, Zauber. 2. *v.a.* ködern, anlocken; (*fig.*) anziehen, locken (*into*, in).

lurid [ljuːrɪd], *adj.* helleuchtend, grell (*of colours*); (*fig.*) gespenstisch, unheimlich, grausig; fahlgelb (*Bot.*).

lurk [ləːk], 1. *v.n.* lauern; (*fig.*) sich verstecken, sich versteckt halten, verborgen liegen. 2. *s.*; *on the –*, auf der Lauer. **-ing**, 1. *s.* das Verstecken. 2. *adj.* versteckt, heimlich. **-ing-place**, *s.* das Versteck, der Schlupfwinkel.

luscious [ˈlʌʃəs], *adj.* saftig; lecker, köstlich; übersüß, süßlich. **-ness**, *s.* die Saftigkeit; Süße, Süßigkeit, Süßlichkeit.

lush [lʌʃ], *adj.* saftig, üppig (*of plants*).
lust [lʌst], 1. *s.* sinnliche Begierde, die Wollust; (*fig.*) Gier, Sucht, das Gelüste, leidenschaftliches Verlangen (*after*, *of* or *for*, nach). 2. *v.n.* begehren (*after* (*Acc.*)); verlangen (*after* or *for*, nach); gelüsten, lüsten (*impers.*) (*after* or *for*, nach). **–ful,** *adj.* wollüstig, geil. **–fulness,** *s.* die Lüsternheit, Wollust.
lustiness ['lʌstɪnɪs], *s.* die Rüstigkeit, Stärke, Lebenskraft; *see* **lusty.**
lustra–l ['lʌstrəl], *adj.* Reinigungs–, Weih–. **–te** [–reɪt], *v.a.* reinigen. **–tion** [–'reɪʃən], *s.* die Reinigung; das Reinigungsopfer (*Rel.*).
lustr–e ['lʌstə], *s.* der Glanz (*also Min. & fig.*), Schimmer, Metallglanz; der Kronleuchter; Lüster (*Weav.*). **–eless,** *adj.* glanzlos, matt. **–ine** [–rɪn], **–ing** [–rɪŋ], *s.* seidener Glanzstoff, der Glanztaffet. **–ous** [–rəs], *adj.* glänzend, strahlend (*also fig.*). **–um** [–rəm], *s.* der Zeitraum von 5 Jahren, das Jahrfünft.
lusty ['lʌstɪ], *adj.* rüstig, kräftig; munter, frisch, lebhaft; *see* **lustiness.**
lut–anist ['l(j)ʊ:tənɪst], *s.* der Lautenspieler. **–e** [l(j)ʊ:t], *s.* die Laute (*Mus.*); *rift in the –e*, die Verstimmung. **–ist,** *see* **–anist.** **–estring** [–strɪŋ], *s. see* **lustrine.**
lute [l(j)ʊ:t], 1. *s.* der Kitt; Dichtungsring. 2. *v.a.* verkitten; dichten.
luxat–e [lʌk'seɪt], *v.a.* ausrenken, verrenken. **–ion** [–'seɪʃən], *s.* die Verrenkung.
lux–e [lʌks], *s.*; (only in) *de –e*, Luxus–. **–uriance, –uriancy** [–'jʊ:rɪəns(ɪ)], *s.* die Üppigkeit, der Reichtum (*of*, an). **–uriant** [–'jʊ:rɪənt], *adj.* üppig, wuchernd, fruchtbar, überschwenglich, verschwenderisch; blütenreich, prächtig (*as style*). **–uriate** [–'jʊ:ərɪeɪt], *v.n.* üppig leben; wuchern; sich ergeben, schwelgen (*in*, in (*Dat.*)). **–urious** [–'jʊ:ərɪəs], *adj.* schwelgerisch; üppig, verschwenderisch; reich ausgestattet, prächtig, luxuriös (*of furniture, etc.*). **–uriousness,** *s.* die Üppigkeit, Schwelgerei; der Luxus, das Wohlleben. **–ury** [lʌkʃərɪ], *s.* der Luxus, das Wohlleben, die Üppigkeit; Prachtliebe, Prunksucht, der Aufwand; die Verschwendung; (*often pl.*) der Luxusartikel, das Genußmittel; *live in –ury*, im vollen leben; *in the lap of –ury*, im Schoß des Glückes. **–ury-tax,** *s.* die Luxussteuer.
lyceum [laɪ'sɪəm], *s.* das Lyzeum; die Bildungsanstalt; literarische Gesellschaft; (*Amer.*) die Volkshochschule.
lychnis ['lɪknɪs], *s.* die Lichtnelke (*Bot.*).
lycopodium [laɪkə'poudɪəm], *s.* der Bärlapp; – *powder*, der Bärlappsamen.
lye [laɪ], *s.* die Lauge, das Laugenwasser.
lying ['laɪɪŋ], *see* [1]**lie** & [2]**lie.** 1. *adj.* lügnerisch, lügenhaft. 2. *s.* das Liegen; – *in state*, öffentliche Aufbahrung. **–-in,** 1. *s.* das Wochenbett; *–-in hospital*, die Entbindungsanstalt. **–-to,** das Beiliegen (*Naut.*).
lymph [lɪmpf], *s.* die Lymphe, das Blutwasser (*Anat.*); der Impfstoff (*Med.*); (*Poet.*) das Quellwasser. **–atic** [–'fætɪk], 1. *adj.* lymphatisch, Lymph–; (*fig.*) blutlos, schlapp (*of persons*). 2. *s.* (*usually pl.*) das Lymphgefäß.
lynch [lɪntʃ], *v.a.* lynchen. **–-law,** *s.* die Lynchjustiz, Volksjustiz.
lynx [lɪnks], *s.* der Luchs. **–-eyed,** *adj.* luchsäugig.
lyre ['laɪə], *s.* die Leier, Lyra. **–-bird,** *s.* der Leierschwanz.
lyri–c ['lɪrɪk], 1. *adj.* lyrisch. 2. *s.* lyrisches Gedicht; die Lyrik; der Liedtext (*Mus.*). **–cal** [–əl], *adj.* lyrisch, liedartig. **–cism** [–sɪzm], *s.* lyrischer Charakter, der Gefühlsausdruck. **–st** [–ɪst], *s.* lyrischer Dichter, der Lyriker.
lysol ['laɪsəl], *s.* das Lysol.

M

M, m [ɛm], *s.* das M, m. *See Index of Abbreviations.*
ma [mɑ:], *s.* (*coll.*) *see* **mamma.**
ma'am [mæm], *s. see* **madam.**
Mac, Mc, M' [mək], *prefix* (*Scots*) Sohn des (*in family names*).
macabre [mə'kɑ:br], *adj.* schrecklich, gruselig.
macaco [mə'keɪkou], *s.* der Maki, Lemur (*Zool.*).
macadam [mə'kædəm], 1. *s.* der Schotter. 2. *adj.* beschottert. **–ize** [–ɑɪz], *v.a.* makadamisieren, beschottern.
macaroni [mækə'rounɪ], *s.* Makkaroni (*pl.*); (*fig.*) das Gemisch. **–c** [–'rɔnɪk], *adj.* makkaronisch (*poetry*); *–c poetry*, die Makkaronidichtung.
macaroon [mækə'rʊ:n], *s.* die Makrone.
macaw [mə'kɔ:], *s.* der Makao (*Orn.*); amerikanische Palme (*Bot.*).
[1]**mace** [meɪs], *s.* der Amtsstab, das Zepter; die (Kriegs)Keule. **–-bearer,** *s.* der Zepterträger.
[2]**mace** [meɪs], *s.* die Muskatblüte.
macerat–e ['mæsəreɪt], *v.a.* einweichen; erweichen; entkräften, schwächen, abzehren, abhärmen, kasteien. **–ion** [–'reɪʃən], *s.* die Einweichung; (*fig.*) Ausmergelung; Abhärmung, Kasteiung.
machicolation [mætʃɪko'leɪʃən], *s.* die Pechnasenreihe, der Verteidigungserker (*Arch.*).
machinat–e ['mækɪneɪt], *v.n.* Ränke schmieden. **–ion** [–'neɪʃən], *s.* die Machenschaft, Anstiftung; (*usually pl.*) Machenschaften, Umtriebe, Ränke. **–or,** *s.* der Ränkeschmied.
machin–e [mə'ʃɪ:n] 1. *s.* die Maschine, der Apparat; (*coll.*) das Fahrrad, Flugzeug; die Maschinerie (*of government, etc.*). 2. *v.a.* maschinell bearbeiten. **–e-gun,** 1. *s.* das Maschinengewehr. 2. *v.a.* mit Maschinengewehr beschießen. **–e-made,** *adj.* mit der Maschine gemacht, maschinell hergestellt, Fabrik–, Maschinen–. **–ery** [əri], *s.* die Maschinerie, Apparatur, der Mechanismus, das Triebwerk, Getriebe; Maschinen (*pl.*); *by –ery*, durch Maschinenkraft. **–e-shop,** *s.* die Maschinenfabrik. **–e-tool,** *s.* die Werkzeugmaschine. **–e-works,** *pl.* (*sing. constr.*) die Maschinenfabrik. **–ist,** *s.* der Maschinenbauer; Maschinenarbeiter, Maschinist.
mack [mæk], *s.* (*coll.*) *see* **mackintosh.**
mackerel ['mækərəl], *s.* die Makrele (*Ichth.*). **–-shark,** *s.* der Heringshai. **–-sky,** *s.* mit Schäfchenwolken bedeckter Himmel.
mackintosh ['mækɪntɔʃ], *s.* wasserdichter Mantel, der Regenmantel.
mackle ['mækl], 1. *v.a.* schmitzen, verschmieren, duplizieren (*Print.*); *–d sheets*, der Ausschuß. 2. *s.* der Schmitz, Druckfleck, verwischter Druck.
macrocosm ['mækrəkɔzm], *s.* das Weltall, der Makrokosmos.
macron ['mækrən], *s.* das Längezeichen über Vokalen.
macula [mækjʊlə], *s.* der Fleck; Sonnenfleck (*Astr.*). **–r,** *adj.* gefleckt, Flecken–.
mad [mæd], *adj.* verrückt, wahnsinnig, toll, irre; (*fig.*) närrisch, überspannt; rasend, wütend (*at*, über; *with*, vor); wild, versessen (*after*, *for* or *on*, auf (*Acc.*)); außer sich (*with*, vor); tollwütig (*of dogs*); *drive a p.* –, einen um den Verstand bringen; *go* –, verrückt werden; (*coll*) *as – as a hatter* or *March hare*, völlig verrückt, ganz übergeschnappt; (*coll.*) *like* –, wie toll. **–cap,** 1. *s.* der Tollkopf; Wildfang. 2. *adj.* toll, wild. **–den,** 1. *v.a.* rasend or toll machen. 2. *v.n.* rasend werden. **–-house,** *s.* das Irrenhaus, Tollhaus. **–man,** *s.* Verrückte(r), Wahnsinnige(r), *m.* **–ness,** *s.* der Wahnsinn; die Tollheit, Narrheit; Wut (*at*, über). **–woman,** *s.* Verrückte, Wahnsinnige, *f.*
madam ['mædəm], *s.* gnädige Frau, gnädiges Fräulein.
madder ['mædə], *s.* der Krapp (*Bot.*); Krappfarbstoff, die Färberöte.
made [meɪd], *see* **make**; *adj.* gemacht; gebaut, zusammengesetzt; – *ground*, neu gewonnenes Land; – *man*, gemachter Mann; – *up*, fertig, Kon-

fektions– (*clothes*); zusammengestellt, Fabriks– (*articles*); erfunden, erdacht; geschminkt; – *up of*, bestehend aus.
madrepore [ˈmædrəpɔː], *s.* die Steinkoralle.
madrigal [ˈmædrɪgəl], *s.* das Madrigal.
maelstrom [ˈmeɪlstrəm], *s.* der Wirbel, Strudel.
mafficking [ˈmæfɪkɪŋ], *s.* der Siegestaumel, patriotische Ausgelassenheit, das Johlen.
magazine [mægəˈziːn], *s.* das Magazin (*also of rifle*), Warenlager, die Niederlage; (also *powder*-–) das Pulvermagazin; die Zeitschrift. **–-rifle,** *s.* das Mehrladegewehr.
magdalen [ˈmægdələn], *s.* die Büßerin, reuige Sünderin.
mage [meɪdʒ], *s.* (*archaic*) der Magier.
magenta [məˈdʒɛntə], *s.* das Magentarot, Fuchsin.
maggot [ˈmægət], *s.* die Made, Larve; (*fig.*) Grille. **–y,** *adj.* madig; grillenhaft, wunderlich.
magi [ˈmeɪdʒaɪ], *pl. see* **magus.**
magic [ˈmædʒɪk], 1. *s.* die Magie, Zauberei; (*coll.*) das Wunder. 2. *attrib. adj.* magisch, zauberisch, Zauber–; – *eye*, die Abstimmglimmröhre (*Rad.*); – *lantern*, die Zauberlaterne; Laterna magica; *under a – spell*, verzaubert; – *wand*, der Zauberstab. **–ian** [–ˈdʒɪʃən], *s.* der Zauberer, Magier.
magist–erial [mædʒɪsˈtɪːrɪəl], *adj.* richterlich, obrigkeitlich; (*fig.*) maßgebend; gebieterisch, herrisch, diktatorisch, gewichtig, hochmütig. **–racy** [ˈmædʒɪstrəsɪ], *s.* obrigkeitliches Amt; die Magistratur, Obrigkeit; obrigkeitliche Beamten (*pl.*). **–ral** [ˈmægɪstrəl], *adj.* nicht offiziell (*pharmacy*). **–rate** [ˈmædʒɪstreɪt], *s.* obrigkeitlicher *or* richterlicher Beamter, *m.*; der Friedensrichter, Polizeirichter, ehrenamtlicher Richter (*in England*); der Richter, obrigkeitlicher Beamter.
magnanim–ity [mægnəˈnɪmɪtɪ], *s.* die Großmut. **–ous** [–ˈnænɪməs], *adj.* großmütig.
magnate [ˈmægneɪt], *s.* der Magnat.
magnesi–a [mægˈniːzɪə], *s.* die Magnesia, das Magnesiumoxyd; –*a hydrate*, die Bittererde; –*a limestone*, der Bitterkalk, Dolomit. **–an** [–zɪən], *adj.* magnesisch. **–um** [–zɪəm], *s.* das Magnesium.
magnet [ˈmægnɪt], *s.* der Magnet. **–ic** [–ˈnɛtɪk], *adj.* magnetisch; (*fig.*) anziehend; –*ic compass*, die Bussole; –*ic course*, mißweisender Kurs; –*ic declination, deviation* or *variation*, die Mißweisung; –*ic needle*, die Magnetnadel. **–ics,** *pl.* (*sing. constr.*) die Lehre vom Magnetismus. **–ism** [ˈmægnətɪzm], *s.* der Magnetismus; (*fig.*) die Anziehungskraft. **–ization** [–ˈzeɪʃən]. *s.* die Magnetisierung. **–ize** [–taɪz], *v.a.* magnetisieren; (*fig.*) anziehen, faszinieren, blenden. **–o** [məgˈniːtoʊ], *s.* die Magnetmaschine, magnetelektrische Maschine; der Magnet (*Motor.*). **–o-electric,** *adj.* magnetelektrisch. **–o-generator,** *s.* der Kurbelinduktor. **–ron** [ˈmægnətrən], *s.* die Magnetfeldröhre (*Rad.*).
magnificat [mægˈnɪfɪkət], *s.* der Lobgesang (Mariens). **–ion** [–ˈkeɪʃən], *s.* die Vergrößerung (*Opt.*); (*fig.*) Verherrlichung; *see* **magnify.**
magnificen–ce [mægˈnɪfɪsəns], *s.* die Herrlichkeit, Pracht, der Glanz. **–t** [–ənt], *adj.* herrlich, prachtvoll, prächtig, glänzend; (*coll.*) ausgezeichnet, großartig.
magnif–ier [ˈmægnɪfaɪə], *s.* das Vergrößerungsglas; (*fig.*) der Verherrlicher, Lobpreiser. **–y** [–faɪ], *v.a.* vergrößern (*also fig.*); (*fig.*) übertreiben; (*fig. & archaic*) verherrlichen; –*ying glass*, das Vergrößerungsglas, die Lupe.
magniloquen–ce [mægˈnɪləkwəns], *s.* die Großsprecherei. **–t** [–ənt], *adj.* großsprecherisch, prahlerisch.
magnitude [ˈmægnɪtjuːd], *s.* die Größe, der Umfang, das Ausmaß; die Wichtigkeit, Bedeutung; *star of the first* –, der Stern erster Größe; (*fig.*) *of the first* –, von äußerster Wichtigkeit.
magnolia [mægˈnoʊlɪə], *s.* die Magnolie (*Bot.*).
magnum [ˈmægnəm], *s.* große Flasche (2 *quarts*).
magpie [ˈmægpaɪ], *s.* die Elster (*Orn.*); (*fig.*) der Schwätzer; (*coll.*) zweiter Ring von Außen (*of a target*).
mag–us [ˈmeɪgəs], *s.* (pl. –*i* [–dʒaɪ]) der Magier, Zauberer; persischer Priester; *the three –i*, die drei Weisen aus dem Morgenlande.
mahara–ja [mɑːhəˈrɑːdʒə], *s.* indischer Großfürst. **–nee** [–niː], *s.* die Gemahlin eines indischen Großfürsten.
mahlstick [ˈmɔːlstɪk], *s. see* **maulstick.**
mahogany [məˈhɔgənɪ], *s.* der Mahagonibaum; das Mahagoni(holz); *have one's feet under a p.'s* –, bei einem zu Tisch sein, jemandes Gastfreundschaft genießen.
mahout [məˈhaʊt], *s.* der Elefantentreiber.
maid [meɪd], *s.* junges Mädchen; das Dienstmädchen, die Magd; die Jungfrau; – *of honour*, die Hofdame, Ehrendame; – *of Orleans*, die Jungfrau von Orleans; (*coll.*) *old* –, alte Jungfer; –-*of-all-work*, das Mädchen für alles. **–en,** 1. *s.* das Mädchen, die Jungfrau; (*archaic*) Guillotine. 2. *adj.* jungfräulich, mädchenhaft, Mädchen–, unverheiratet; (*fig.*) neu, frisch; Erstlings–; –*en aunt*, unverheiratete Tante; –*en name*, der Mädchenname; –*en over*, der Spielsatz ohne Läufe (*Crick.*); –*en race*, das Jungfernrennen für Pferde, die noch keinen Preis gewonnen haben; –*en speech*, die Jungfernrede, Erstlingsrede; –*en voyage*, die Jungfernfahrt. **–enhead,** *s.* die Jungfernschaft. **–enhair,** *s.* das Frauenhaar, Venushaar (*Bot.*). **–enhood,** *s.* die Jungfräulichkeit, Jungfernschaft. **–enlike,** *adj.*, **–enly,** *adj.* mädchenhaft. **–servant,** *s.* das Dienstmädchen.
[1]**mail** [meɪl], *s.* der Panzer, die Plattenrüstung; (also *chain*-–) der Kettenpanzer; *coat of* –, das Panzerhemd; (*Poet.*) der Harnisch. **–ed, –-clad,** *adj.* gepanzert (*also fig.*); –*ed fist*, eiserne Faust; (*fig.*) die Waffengewalt.
[2]**mail** [meɪl], 1. *s.* der Briefbeutel; die Post, Postsachen, Postsendungen (*pl.*); *air*-–, die Luftpost; *by* –, per Post; *by return* (*of*) –, postwendend, umgehend; 2. *v.a.* zur Post geben, mit der Post senden. **–able,** *adj.* postversandfähig. **–-bag,** *s.* der Briefbeutel. **–-boat,** *s.* das Paketboot. **–-car,** *s.* der Postwagen (*also Railw.*). **–-coach,** *s.* die Postkutsche. **–-order firm,** *s.* das Postversandgeschäft. **–-steamer,** *s.* der Postdampfer, das Paketboot. **–-train,** *s.* der Postzug. **–-van,** *s. see* **–-car.**
maim [meɪm], *v.a.* verstümmeln, lähmen; zum Krüppel schlagen; verkrüppeln (*also fig.*). **–ed,** *adj.* verstümmelt.
[1]**main** [meɪn], 1. *adj.* hauptsächlich, wichtigst, Haupt–; – *body*, das Hauptkorps, Gros; *have an eye to the – chance*, an seinen eigenen Vorteil denken; *by – force* or *strength*, mit bloßer, aller *or* nackter Gewalt, mit voller Kraft; – *road ahead!* Hauptverkehrsstraße! – *thing*, die Hauptsache. 2. *s.* der Hauptteil, die Hauptsache, der Kern, das Ganze; das Hauptrohr, die Hauptleitung (*water, gas*), das Hauptkabel (*electricity*); die Gewalt, Kraft (only in) *with might and* –, mit aller *or* voller Macht; *in the* –, in der Hauptsache, im ganzen, hauptsächlich, zum größten Teil. **–-boom,** *s.* großer Baum (*Naut.*). **–-brace,** *s.* die Brasse der Großrahe (*Naut.*). **– deck,** das Hauptdeck. **–land,** *s.* das Festland. **– line,** die Hauptstrecke (*Railw.*). **–ly,** *adv.* hauptsächlich, zum größten Teil, vornehmlich. **–mast,** *s.* der Großmast. **–-rail,** *s.* die Reling (*Naut.*). **–s,** *pl.* die Hauptstromleitung, das Stromnetz; *operate on the –s*, sich direkt an die Lichtleitung anschließen lassen; *operating on the –s*, mit Netzanschluß; –*s set*, der Netzanschlußempfänger. **–sail,** *s.* das Großsegel. **–-sheet,** *s.* der Großschot (*Naut.*). **–spring,** *s.* die Uhrfeder (*Horol.*); (*fig.*) die Haupttriebfeder. **–stay,** *s.* das Großstag (*Naut.*); (*fig.*) die Hauptstütze. **–-street,** *s.* die Hautstraße. **–-top,** *s.* der Großmars (*Naut.*). **–-topgallant-mast,** *s.* die Großbramstenge (*Naut.*) **–-topsail,** *s.* das Großmarssegel (*Naut.*). **–-work,** *s.* das Kernwerk (*Fort.*). **–-yard,** *s.* die Großrahe (*Naut.*).
[2]**main** [meɪn], *s.* (*Poet.*) hohe See, das weite Meer.
maintain [meɪnˈteɪn], *v.a.* erhalten; unterhalten, instandhalten, aufrechterhalten (*things*); mit Lebensunterhalt versehen, alimentieren (*a p.*); fortfahren in, weiterführen; behaupten, verfechten, verteidigen (*an opinion*); – *a correspondence*, einen Briefwechsel unterhalten; – *one's ground*, seine

Stellung behaupten, standhalten; (*fig.*) sich behaupten; – *life*, das Leben erhalten; – *one's reputation*, seinen guten Ruf aufrechthalten. **–able,** *adj.* verfechtbar, haltbar, gerechtfertigt, zu rechtfertigen(d). **–er,** *s.* der Versorger, Erhalter; Verfechter.

maintenance ['meɪntənəns], *s.* die Erhaltung, Aufrechterhaltung, Instandhaltung; Ernährung, Beköstigung, der Unterhalt; die Behauptung, Verfechtung, Verteidigung; widerrechtliche Unterstützung (*of a party*) (*Law*); *cost of* –, die Instandhaltungskosten (*pl.*); – *and repair*, die Unterhaltung und Instandsetzung. **– -grant,** *s.* der Unterhaltszuschuß.

maisonnette [meɪzə'nɛt], *s.* kleines Eigenheim.

maize [meɪz], *s.* der Mais.

majest–ic [mə'dʒɛstɪk], *adj.* majestätisch, würdevoll, erhaben. **–y** ['mædʒɪstɪ], *s.* die Majestät, Würde, Erhabenheit, Pracht; königliche Hoheit; die Macht; *His –y*, Seine Majestät.

majolica [mə'jɔlɪkə], *s.* die Majolika.

major ['meɪdʒə], 1. *attrib. adj.* größer; älter (*of two brothers*); – *axis*, die Hauptachse (*Geom.*); *C* –, C-Dur (*Mus.*); – *key*, die Durtonart (*Mus.*); – *offender*, Hauptschuldige(r), *m.*; – *part*, größter Teil (*of* (*Gen.*)); – *premise*, der Obersatz (*Log.*); *the – prophets*, die größeren Propheten; – *repair*, größere Reparatur; *Smith* –, Smith der Ältere; – *third*, große Terz (*Mus.*). 2. *pred. adj.* mündig. 3. *s.* der Major (*Mil.*); Mündige(r), *m.* (*Law*); der Obersatz (*Log.*); das Hauptfach (*Univ.*). **– -domo,** *s.* der Hausmeier (*Hist.*); Haushofmeister. **– -general,** *s.* der Generalmajor. **–ity** [mə'dʒɔrɪtɪ], *s.* die Mehrheit, Mehrzahl; Volljährigkeit, Mündigkeit (*Law*); Majorsstelle, der Majorsrang (*Mil.*); *attain one's –ity*, mündig werden; *the –ity of cases*, die Mehrzahl der Fälle; *join the –ity*, sterben; *–ity principle*, das Majoritätsprinzip; *two-thirds –ity*, die Zweidrittelmehrheit; *vast –ity*, überwiegende Mehrzahl; *–ity* (*of*) *vote*(*s*), die Stimmenmehrheit. **–ship,** *s.* die Majorsstelle, der Majorsrang.

majuscule [mə'dʒʌskju:l], *s.* großer (Anfangs)-Buchstabe, die Versalie.

makar ['mækɑ:], *s.* (*Scots*) der Dichter.

make [meɪk], **1.** *ir.v.a.* machen; (er)bauen, verfertigen, anfertigen, fabrizieren, herstellen (*of*, *from* or *out of*, aus); verarbeiten (*into*, zu); schaffen, formen, bilden; gewinnen, zusammenbringen; lassen (*do*, tun), zwingen (*do*, zu tun), nötigen (*act*, zum Handeln) (*a p.*); bewirken, verursachen, herbeiführen, ergeben, sich belaufen auf; zustandebringen; aufsetzen; ernennen zu. **(a)** (*with nouns*) – *amends for*, Ersatz leisten für, ersetzen, wieder gutmachen; – *arrangements*, Verabredungen *or* Vorkehrungen treffen; – *the bed*, das Bett machen; – *a choice*, eine Wahl treffen; – *contact*, den Strom schließen (*Elec.*); – *a decision*, eine Entscheidung fällen; – *a difference*, ankommen auf; – *no doubt*, keinen Zweifel hegen (*of*, über); – *an example of*, ein Beispiel statuieren; – *excuses*, Ausflüchte gebrauchen; – *faces*, Gesichter schneiden; – *a fool of o.s.*, sich blamieren; – *a fortune*, ein Vermögen erwerben; *two and two – four*, zwei und zwei ist vier; – *friends*, sich anfreunden; – *fun of*, sich lustig machen über; – *haste*, sich beeilen; *not – head or tail of*, sich nicht auskennen; – *headway*, vorwärtskommen; – (*heavy*) *inroads on*, (stark) heimsuchen; – *a bad job of*, verpatzen; – *a good job of*, ordentlich machen; – *the land*, Land sichten (*Naut.*); – *a loss*, einen Verlust erleiden; – *love*, den Hof machen (*to* (*Dat.*)); – *mention of*, erwähnen; – *a mess of*, durcheinanderbringen; – *a name for o.s.*, sich einen Namen machen; – *a noise*, ein Geräusch hervorbringen; – *one of*, sich beteiligen bei, teilnehmen an, sich anschließen (*Dat.*) (*a group*); – *peace*, Frieden schließen; – *a point of s.th.*, sich etwas angelegen sein lassen; – *a port*, einen Hafen anlaufen; – *provision*, sorgen (*for*, für); Vorkehrungen treffen (*against*, gegen); *it –s pleasant reading*, es bietet angenehme Lektüre; – (*a*) *reply*, Antwort geben, erwidern; – *room*, Platz machen; – *a rule*, eine Regel aufstellen; – *a sacrifice*, ein Opfer bringen; – *sail*, das Segel setzen; – *shift*, sich behelfen: – *a speech*, eine Rede halten; – *a stay*, sich aufhalten; – *tea*, Tee bereiten; *they – good teachers*, sie geben gute Lehrer ab; – *trouble*, Unheil anstiften *or* anrichten; – *war upon*, Krieg führen mit; – *way*, vorwärtskommen. **(b)** (*with double objects*) – *it one's business*, es sich angelegen sein lassen; *they made him their chief*, sie machten ihn zu ihrem Anführer; *he was made colonel*, er wurde zum Obersten gemacht *or* ernannt; *I – the distance 100 yards*, ich schätze die Entfernung auf 100 Yard; – *o.s. a name*, sich einen Namen machen; *she made him an ideal partner*, sie war ihm eine ideale Partnerin; – *it a rule*, es zur Regel machen; *what do you – the time?* wie spät ist es? *she –s* (*him*) *a good wife*, sie zeigt sich als gute Ehefrau. **(c)** (*with adjectives*) – *things awkward*, Schwierigkeiten in den Weg legen (*for* (*Dat.*)); – *the best of*, tun was man kann mit, nach Kräften ausnützen; – *the best of a bad job*, gute Miene zum bösen Spiel machen; – *fast*, befestigen; – *good*, wieder gutmachen, ersetzen; bestätigen, als berechtigt erweisen, nachweisen, begründen (*a claim*); glücklich bewerkstelligen (*one's escape*); – *good one's position*, seine Stellung ausbauen; – *good a promise*, ein Versprechen erfüllen, einem Versprechen nachkommen; – *good one's word*, Wort halten; – *known*, verkündigen, bekanntgeben, bekannt machen; – *o.s. known*, sich zu erkennen geben; – *light of a th.*, etwas leicht *or* auf die leichte Schulter nehmen, sich (*Dat.*) nichts aus einer S. machen; – *the most of*, möglichst gut ausnützen, ins beste Licht stellen; – *much of*, viel Wesens machen von, große Stücke halten auf; (*coll.*) – *o.s. scarce*, sich aus dem Staube machen; – *sure of*, sich vergewissern. **(d)** (*with verbs*) – *them agree*, sie zur Übereinstimmung bringen; – *believe*, vorgeben, vorschützen; *she made me do this*, sie zwang mich dazu; – *s.th. do*, es genug sein lassen, sich damit behelfen *or* zufrieden geben; *he –s us feel*, er läßt uns fühlen; (*coll.*) – *things hum*, alles in Schwung bringen; – *s.th. last*, etwas einteilen, daß man damit auskommt *or* daß man das Auskommen findet; – *the passage read as follows*, die Stelle wie folgt abfassen, der S. folgenden Wortlaut geben; – *s.o. sit down*, einen zum Sitzen nötigen. **(e)** (*with adverbs*) – *out*, ausstellen, aufstellen, ausfertigen (*list*, *cheque*, *etc.*); verstehen, erkennen, feststellen, herausbekommen, ausfindig machen; entziffern (*handwriting*); klug werden aus, begreifen; beweisen, erweisen, darstellen, (als glaubwürdig) hinstellen, angeben; – *o.s. out to be*, sich stellen; – *over*, übergeben, überantworten, übertragen (*to* (*Dat.*)); – *up*, ersetzen, wieder gutmachen, (*to* (*Dat.*)); einholen, nachholen (*lost ground*); vervollständigen; zusammensetzen, zusammenstellen, zusammenbringen (*a group*); bilden, ausmachen (*a whole*, *etc.*); aufstellen, verfassen, erfinden (*a story*); abschließen, vereinbaren, beilegen (*quarrel*, *etc.*); ausgleichen (*accounts*); zusammennähen, verfertigen (*dresses*, *etc.*); herrichten, ausstaffieren, zurechtmachen, schminken (*one's face*); umbrechen (*type into pages*); – *it up*, sich aussöhnen; – *up a fire*, das Feuer schüren; – *up one's mind*, sich entschließen; – *it up with a p.*, sich mit einem aussöhnen. **2.** *ir.v.n.* gehen, sich begeben; sich stellen *or* anschicken, versuchen; handeln, sich verhalten; – (*so*) *bold*, sich die Freiheit nehmen, sich erdreisten; – *free with a th.*, frei schalten *or* walten mit etwas; – *free with a p.*, sich einem gegenüber zu viel herausnehmen; – *merry*, sich belustigen, fröhlich *or* lustig sein; – *do with*, fertig werden mit, sich behelfen mit; *the tide –s*, die Flut tritt ein. **(a)** (*with prepositions*) – *after s.o.*, einem nachlaufen *or* nachjagen; – *against*, sprechen gegen; – *at*, losgehen auf (*Acc.*); – *for*, lossteuern, zugehen *or* sich begeben nach (*a place*); beitragen zu, fördern, bewirken, herbeiführen; – *of*, machen aus, denken über; *what do you – of it?* was denken Sie darüber? – *nothing of*, sich nichts machen aus, nicht klug werden aus; – *towards*, zugehen auf (*Acc.*). **(b)** (*with adverbs*) – *away*, sich fortmachen *or* davonmachen; – *away with a p.*, einen um die Ecke bringen; – *away a th.*, etwas entfernen *or* beseitigen; durchbringen (*money*); – *off*, fortgehen, sich fortmachen; ausreißen, durchbrennen; (*sl.*) – *out*, fertig werden, vorankommen; – *up*, sich zurechtmachen, sich schminken; – *up for*, ersetzen (*expenses*); wieder gutmachen, wettmachen, ausgleichen (*loss*); *be made up of*, zusammengesetzt sein *or* bestehen aus; (*coll.*) – *up to*, den Hof machen (*Dat.*), um den Bart gehen (*Dat.*); – *up to s.o. for*, einen entschädigen für. **3.** *s.* die Form, Fasson; der Schnitt (*Tail.*); Bau, das Gefüge, die Bauart, Art, Ausführung, Fassung, Type, Marke, Mache; das Erzeugnis, Fabrikat; die Fabrikation, Herstellung; *at* –, geschlossen (*Elec.*); *be on the* –, auf Gewinn zielen. **--believe,** 1. *s.* die Verstellung, der Schein, Vorwand. 2. *adj.* verstellt, angeblich, vorgeblich. **--contact,** *s.* der Schließkontakt (*Elec.*). **-r,** *s.* der Hersteller, Verfertiger, Fabrikant; Schöpfer, Gott; *boiler--r*, *s.* der Kesselschmied; *peace--r*, *s.* der Friedensstifter. **--ready,** *s.* die Zurichtung (*Typ.*). **-shift,** 1. *s.* der Notbehelf. 2. *adj.* behelfsmäßig, Not–, Behelfs–, Aushilfs–. **--up,** *s.* die Ausstaffierung, Kostümierung, Aufmachung, Zusammensetzung, Struktur, Verfassung, Ausstattung, Verpackung; Erfindung; der Umbruch (*Typ.*). **--weight,** *s.* die Zulage, Zugabe; (*fig.*) der Lückenbüßer, das Anhängsel, fünftes Rad am Wagen; der Ersatz, Notbehelf.

making [meɪkɪŋ], *s.* das Machen, die Verfertigung, Herstellung, Fabrikation; *that was the – of him*, das hat sein Glück gemacht; *be in the* –, in Arbeit, im Bau, Entstehen *or* Werden *or* in der Entwicklung begriffen sein; *it is of my own* –, ich habe es selbst gemacht; *he has the –s of . . .*, er hat das Zeug zu . . .; *go to the – of*, ausmachen, zustande bringen.

malachite [ˈmæləkaɪt], *s.* der Malachit.

maladjustment [mæləˈdʒʌstmənt], *s.* das Mißverhältnis, schlechte Anordnung *or* Einstellung.

maladministration [mælədmɪnɪˈstreɪʃən], *s.* schlechte Verwaltung, die Mißwirtschaft.

maladroit [mæləˈdrɔɪt], *adj.* ungeschickt, linkisch, taktlos. **-ness,** *s.* die Ungeschicklichkeit.

malady [ˈmælədɪ], *s.* die Krankheit.

malaise [ˈmæleɪz], *s.* die Unpäßlichkeit.

malapert [ˈmæləpəːt], *adj.* (*archaic*) ungezogen, vorlaut, naseweis.

malaprop-ism [ˈmæləprɔpɪzm], *s.* die Wortentstellung, Wortverdrehung. **-os** [–prəˈpoʊ], *adv.* zur Unzeit, unangebracht, ungelegen.

malar [ˈmeɪlə], *adj.* Backen– (*Anat.*).

malari-a [məˈlɛːərɪə], *s.* die Malaria, das Sumpffieber. **-al** [–ɪəl], **-ous** [–ɪəs], *adj.* Malaria– (*Med.*).

malcontent [ˈmælkəntɛnt], 1. *adj.* mißvergnügt, unzufrieden. 2. *s.* Mißvergnügte(r), *m.*, Ablehnende(r), *m.*, der Rebell.

male [meɪl], 1. *s.* der Mann; das Männchen (*of birds, etc.*). 2. *adj.* männlich; – *issue*, der Mannesstamm; – *nurse*, der Krankenpfleger; – *rhyme*, männlicher *or* stumpfer Reim; – *screw*, die Schraube(nspindel); – *voice*, die Männerstimme.

maledict-tion [mælɪˈdɪkʃən], *s.* die Verwünschung, der Fluch. **-ory** [–ˈdɪktərɪ], *adj.* Verwünschungs–.

malefactor [ˈmælɪfæktə], *s.* der Übeltäter, Missetäter.

maleficent [məˈlɛfɪsənt], *adj.* unheilvoll, schädlich (*to*, für).

malevolen-ce [məˈlɛvələns], *s.* die Böswilligkeit, Schädlichkeit; Bosheit, Mißgunst, böser Wille. **-t** [–ənt], *adj.* böswilling, übelwollend, feindselig, mißgünstig.

malfeasance [mælˈfɪːzəns], *s.* gesetzwidrige Handlung, die Übertretung, Übeltat, Missetat (*Law*).

malformation [mælfəˈmeɪʃən], *s.* die Mißbildung.

malic [ˈmeɪlɪk], *adj.* apfelsauer; – *acid*, die Apfelsäure (*Chem.*).

malic-e [ˈmælɪs], *s.* die Bosheit, Arglist; der Groll; böse Absicht (*Law*); *with -e aforethought* or *prepense*, mit bösem Vorbedacht, vorsätzlich (*Law*); *bear a p. -e*, einem grollen. **-ious** [–ˈlɪʃəs], *adj.* boshaft, arglistig, gehässig, heimtückisch, hämisch; böswillig, vorsätzlich (*Law*). **-iousness.** *s.* die Bosheit, Boshaftigkeit, Tücke.

malign [məˈlaɪn], 1. *adj.* schädlich, unheilvoll; bösartig (*Med.*). 2. *v.a.* verleumden, lästern. **-ancy** [–ˈlɪgnənsɪ], *s.* die Bosheit, Feindseligkeit, Widrigkeit; Bösartigkeit (*Med.*). **-ant** [–ˈlɪgnənt], 1. *adj.* boshaft, feindselig; bösartig (*Med.*). 2. *s.* Übelgesinnte(r), *m.* **-ity,** *s. see* **-ancy.**

malinger [məˈlɪŋgə], *v.n.* Krankheit vortäuschen, simulieren, sich krank stellen, sich drücken. **-er,** *s.* der Simulant, Drückeberger.

mall [mɔːl], *s.* der Schlegel; schattiger Weg.

mallard [ˈmæləd], *s.* die Stockente, wilde Ente, wilder Enterich (*Orn.*).

malleab-ility [mælɪəˈbɪlɪtɪ], *s.* die Dehnbarkeit, Streckbarkeit; (*fig.*) Geschmeidigkeit. **-le** [ˈmælɪəbl], *adj.* dehnbar, streckbar, hämmerbar; (*fig.*) gefügig, geschmeidig; *-le cast iron*, der Temperguß.

malleolar [ˈmælɪoʊlə], *adj.* Knöchel– (*Anat.*).

mallet [ˈmælɪt], *s.* hölzerner Hammer, der Schlegel, Fäustel, Holzhammer, Schläger, das Schlagholz (*Sport*).

mallow [ˈmæloʊ], *s.* die Malve (*Bot.*).

malm [mɑːm], *s.* kalkreicher Lehmboden.

malmsey [ˈmɑːmzɪ], *s.* der Malvasier.

malnutrition [mælnjʊˈtrɪʃən], *s.* schlechte Ernährung, die Unterernährung.

malodorus [mælˈoʊdərəs], *adj.* übelriechend.

malpractice [mælˈpræktɪs], *s.* die Übeltat; verkehrte Behandlung (*Med.*); *pl.* gesetzwidrige Handlungen, Amtsvergehungen (*Law*).

malt [mɔːlt], 1. *s.* das Malz. 2. *v.a.* malzen; *-ed milk*, die Malzmilch. 3. *v.n.* zu Malz werden. **--house,** *s.* die Mälzerei. **-ing,** *s.* das Malzen. **--kiln,** *s.* die Malzdarre. **-ose,** *s.* der Malzzucker, die Maltose. **-ster,** *m.* der Mälzer.

maltreat [mælˈtrɪːt], *v.a.* schlecht behandeln, mißhandeln. **-ment,** *s.* die Mißhandlung.

malversation [mælvəˈseɪʃən], *s.* das Amtsvergehen, der Amtsmißbrauch, Unterschleif, die Veruntreuung.

mama [ˈmɔmə], *s.* die Mama.

mamill-a [mæˈmɪlə], *s.* die Brustwarze. **-ary** [ˈmæmɪlərɪ], *adj.* Brustwarzen–. **-iform** [–ˈmɪlɪfɔːm], *adj.* brustwarzenförmig (*Anat.*).

mamma [məˈmɑː], *see* **mama.**

mamma-l [ˈmæməl], *s.* das Säugetier. **-lian** [məˈmeɪlɪən], *adj.* Säugetier–. **-ry** [ˈmæmərɪ], *adj.* Brust–.

mammon [ˈmæmən], *s.* der Mammon. **-ism** [–ɪzm], (**--worship**), *s.* der Mammonsdienst.

mammoth [ˈmæməθ], 1. *s.* das Mammut. 2. *adj.* ungeheuer, riesenhaft, riesig.

mammy [ˈmɔmɪ], *s.* (*coll.*) *see* **mama**; (*Amer.* [ˈmæmɪ]) farbiges Kindermädchen.

man [mæn], **1.** *s.* (pl. *men* [mɛn]) der Mann; Mensch, die Person, menschliches Wesen; die Menschen (*pl.*), die Menschheit, das Menschengeschlecht; der Lehnsmann (*Hist.*), Diener, Arbeiter; (*in address*) (*coll.*) Menschenskind!; (Dame)Stein, die Figur (*Draughts, etc.*); *pl.* Soldaten, Matrosen, Gemeine (*pl.*) (*Mil.*); *any* –, jemand, man; *a Cambridge* –, einer der in Cambridge studiert (hat); *be the – for s.th.*, der passende Mann für etwas sein; *oil*–, der Ölhändler; *police*–, der Polizist; *no* –, niemand; *be one's own* –, sein eigener Herr sein; *show yourself a* – ! zeige, daß du ein Mann bist! (*a*) (*with following nouns*) *--at-arms*, der Reiter, bewaffneter (und berittener) Soldat; – *of conscience*, gewissenhafter Mensch; – *of genius*, das Genie; – *of honour*, der Ehrenmann; – *of letters*, der Literat, Schriftsteller; – *of many parts*, vielseitiger Mensch; – *of straw*, der Strohmann; – *in the street*, der Mann von der Straße, der gemeine *or* einfache Mann, der Durchschnittmensch; – *in a thousand*, außergewöhnlicher Mensch; – *about town*, der Lebemann; *--of-war*, das Kriegsschiff; – *and wife*, Mann und Frau; – *of many words*, der Schwätzer; – *of the world*, der Weltmann. (*b*) (*with adjectives*) – *alive!* Mensch(enskind)! *best* –, der Beistand des Bräutigams; *my good* – ! mein lieber Herr! *handy*–, der Mann für alles; *little* –, kleiner Kerl, der Knirps; *medical* –, der Arzt, Hausarzt; *her young* –, ihr Freund *or* Schatz. (*c*) (*with prepositions*) *between – and* –, von Mensch zu Mensch; – *for* –, Mann für Mann; *pro* –, pro Mann; *to a* –, bis auf den letzten Mann, geschlossen. **2.** *v.a.* bemannen (*with troops*, *sailors*); besetzen (*trench, etc.*); – *o.s.*, sich ermannen; – *the yards*, die Rahen zum Salut bemannen. **--ape,** *s.* der Menschenaffe. **--child,** *s.* der Knabe. **--cook,** *s.* der Koch. **--eater,** *s.* der Menschenfresser. **–ful,** *adj.* mannhaft, tapfer. **–fulness,** *s.* die Mannhaftigkeit. **--handle,** *v.a.* (nur) durch Menschenkraft bewegen *or* befördern; (*fig.*) gewaltsam anpacken, rauh behandeln, mißhandeln. **--hater,** *s.* der Menschenfeind. **–hole,** *s.* das Mannloch, die Einsteigeöffnung. **–hood,** *s.* menschliche Natur; die Mannhaftigkeit, Mannesehre; das Mannesalter; (*collect.*) Männer (*pl.*); *–hood suffrage*, das Männerwahlrecht. **--hunt,** *s.* die Männerjagd. **–kind** [–ˈkaɪnd], *s.* (*sing. or pl. constr.*) die Menschheit, das Menschengeschlecht; das Männergeschlecht, die Männerwelt; Männer (*pl.*). **–like,** *adj.* männlich; männisch (*of women*). **–liness,** *s.* die Männlichkeit, Mannhaftigkeit. **–ly,** *adj.* männlich, mannhaft; männisch (*of women*). **–nish,** *adj.* männisch, unweiblich (*of women*). **--power,** *s.* die Menschenkraft; das Menschenmaterial (*Mil.*). **--servant,** *s.* der Diener, Bediente(r), *m.* **–slaughter,** *s.* fahrlässige Tötung, der Totschlag (*Law*). **--trap,** *s.* die Fußangel.

manacle [ˈmænəkl], 1. *s.* die Handfessel, Handschelle. 2. *v.a.* Handschellen anlegen (*Dat.*), fesseln (*Acc.*).

manag–e [ˈmænɪdʒ], 1. *v.a.* handhaben (*tool, weapon, etc.*); führen, leiten, verwalten (*a business, etc*); bewirtschaften (*an estate, etc.*); vorstehen, beaufsichtigen (*a house, etc.*); dirigieren, regulieren; zustande bringen, fertigbringen, zuwege bringen, bewerkstelligen, (*coll.*) deichseln, managen (*a th.*); (*coll.*) herumkriegen, gefügig machen (*a person*); *I can –e it*, ich kann es bewältigen; *I can –e him*, ich kann es mit ihm aufnehmen. 2. *v.n.* die Geschäfte *or* den Haushalt führen, wirtschaften; auskommen; gelingen, es einrichten, fertigbringen; *he –ed to get away*, es gelang ihm zu entkommen, er kam eben noch weg; *I cannot –e to come*, ich kann es nicht so einrichten daß ich komme; *-e very well* or *nicely*, gut auskommen, ganz gut fertig werden. **–eable,** *adj.* handlich, leicht zu handhaben; lenksam, fügsam; manövierierbar (*Naut.*). **–eableness,** *s.* die Handlichkeit, Lenksamkeit. **–ement,** *s.* die Handhabung, Behandlung; Verwaltung, Leitung, Führung; Bewirtschaftung; das Direktorium, die Direktion; kluge Handlungsweise; *under new –ement!* Geschäftsübernahme! **–er,** *s.* der Geschäftsführer, Betriebsleiter, Direktor; Verwalter; *general –er*, der Generaldirektor; Prokurist; *good –er*, guter Verwalter *or* Haushalter; *works-–er*, der Betriebsleiter; *pl.* das Kuratorium (*of a school*); *board of –ers*, das Direktorium. **–eress,** *s.* die Geschäftsführerin, Direktorin, Vorsteherin, Leiterin. **–erial** [–ˈdʒɪːrɪəl], *adj.* Leitungs–, Verwaltungs–; *in –erial capacity*, in leitender Stellung. **–ing,** *adj.* geschäftsführend, leitend; bevormundend (*of character*); *–ing director*, der Betriebsdirektor.

manciple [ˈmænsɪpl], *s.* (*archaic*) der Ökonom, Verwalter, Wirtschafter.

mandamus [mænˈdeɪməs], *s.* der Befehl *or* Mandat eines höheren Gerichtes an ein niederes (*Law*).

mandarin [ˈmændərɪn], *s.* der Mandarin.

mandarin(e) [ˈmændərɪn], *s.* die Mandarine (*Bot.*). **--duck,** *s.* die Mandarinenente (*Orn.*). **--orange,** *s.* die Mandarine.

mandat-ary [ˈmændətərɪ], *s.* (Prozeß)Bevollmächtigte(r), *m.*, der Mandatar (*Law*). **–e,** 1. [–ət], *s.* das Mandat, die Vollmacht, der Auftrag (*Law*). 2. [–ˈdeɪt], *v.a.* einem Mandat unterstellen (*territory*). **–ed** [–ˈdeɪtɪd], *adj.* Mandats–. **–or,** *s.* der Auftraggeber, Mandant. **–ory** [ˈmændətərɪ], 1. *adj.* befehlend, Befehls–, Mandatar–. 2. *s.* die Mandatsmacht, der Mandatarstaat; Mandatar (*Law*).

mandible [ˈmændɪbl], *s.* der Kinnbacken, die Kinnlade.

mandolin(e) [ˈmændəlɪn], *s.* die Mandoline.

mandragora [mænˈdrægərə], *s.*, **mandrake** [ˈmændreɪk], *s.* der Alraun (*Bot.*).

mandrel, mandril [ˈmændrɪl], *s.* der Dorn, die Docke, der Drehstift, die Spindel (*of a lathe*).

mandrill [ˈmændrɪl], *s.* der Mandrill (*Zool.*).

mane [meɪn], *s.* die Mähne. **–d,** *adj.* gemähnt, –mähnig. **--comb,** *s.* der Striegel.

manège [mæˈneɪʒ], *s.* die Reitschule; Zureitung, Reitkunst.

manes [ˈmeɪnɪːz], *pl.* Manen (*pl.*).

mangan-ate [ˈmæŋgənət], *s.* mangansaures Salz. **–ese** [–nɪːz], *s.* das Mangan (*Chem.*).

mang–e [meɪndʒ], *s.* die Räude (*Vet.*). **–iness,** *s.* die Räudigkeit. **–y** [–ɪ], *adj.* räudig; (*fig.*) schäbig.

mangel-wurzel [ˈmæŋglˈwəːzl], *s.* die Runkelrübe (*Bot.*).

manger [ˈmeɪndʒə], *s.* die Krippe; *dog in the –*, der Neidhammel.

manginess [ˈmeɪndʒɪnɪs], *see* **mange.**

[1]**mangle** [mæŋgl], 1. *s.* die Mangel, Wäscherolle. 2. *v.a.* mangeln, rollen (*clothes*).

[2]**mangle** [mæŋgl], *v.a.* zerreißen, zerhauen, zerfleischen, zerstückeln; (*fig.*) verstümmeln.

mango [ˈmæŋgou], *s.* der Mangobaum, die Mangopflanze.

mangold [ˈmæŋgould], *s. see* **mangel-wurzel.**

mangrove [ˈmæŋgrouv], *s.* der Mangelbaum, die Mangrovepflanze.

mangy [ˈmeɪndʒɪ], *see* **mange.**

manhood [ˈmænhud], *see under* **man.**

mani–a [ˈmeɪnɪə], *s.* der Wahnsinn, die Raserei; Manie (*for*, für), Sucht (*for*, nach). **–ac** [–nɪæk], 1. *adj.* wahnsinnig, rasend, toll. 2. *s.* Wahnsinnige(r), *m.* **–acal** [məˈnaɪəkl], *adj. see* **–ac** 1. **–c** [ˈmænɪk], *adj.* manisch, besessen.

manicur–e [ˈmænɪkjuə], 1. *s.* die Handpflege, Nagelpflege, Maniküre. 2. *v.a.* maniküren. **–ist** [–kjuərɪst], *s.* der *or* die Maniküre, die Handpflegerin.

manifest [ˈmænɪfɛst], 1. *adj.* offenbar, offenkundig, augenscheinlich, handgreiflich, deutlich; *make –*, offenbaren, kundtun, klarlegen, klarstellen. 2. *v.a.* offenbaren, kundtun, deutlich zeigen, darlegen, manifestieren; *be –ed*, sich zeigen. 3. *v.n.* öffentlich auftreten; erscheinen, sich zeigen (*of ghost*). 4. *s.* das Schiffsladungsverzeichnis, der Frachtbrief (*Naut.*). **–ation** [–ˈteɪʃən], *s.* die Offenbarung, Kundgebung, Äußerung, Darlegung; (Geister)Erscheinung. **–o** [–ˈfɛstou], *s.* öffentliche Bekanntmachung *or* Erklärung, das Manifest.

manifold [ˈmænɪfould], 1. *adj.* mannigfaltig, mannigfach. 2. *v.a.* vervielfältigen. 3. *s.* die Sammelleitung (*Tech.*). **--writer,** *s.* der Vervielfältigungsapparat.

manikin [ˈmænɪkɪn], *s.* das Männlein, der Zwerg.

manil(l)a [məˈnɪlə], *s.* die Manilazigarre; der Manilahanf; – *paper*, das Manilapapier.

maniple [ˈmænɪpl], *s.* die Armbinde des Meßpriesters (*R.C.*).

manipulat–e [məˈnɪpjuleɪt], *v.a.* behandeln, handhaben, hantieren mit; (künstlich) beeinflussen (*the market*) (*C.L.*). **–ion** [–ˈleɪʃən], *s.* (kunstgerechte) Handhabung, Behandlung *or* Bearbeitung; (künstliche) Beeinflussung, der Kunstgriff; Geschäftskniff (*C.L.*). **–ive** [–lətɪv], *adj.* Handhabungs–, Manipulations–. **–or,** *s.* der Bearbeiter, Handhaber. **–ory,** *adj. see* **–ive.**

mankind, *s.*, **manliness,** *s.*, **manly** *adj.*, *see under* **man.**

manna [ˈmænə], *s.* die & das Manna (*B.*).

mannequin [ˈmænɪkɪn], *s.* die Vorführdame; – *parade*, die Modenschau.

manner [ˈmænə], *s.* die Art, Weise, Art und Weise; das Verhalten, die Manier, der Stil (*Paint., etc.*); *pl. see* **–s**; *adverb of –*, das Umstandswort der Art und Weise; *after the – of*, nach Art von; *all – of*, alle Arten von; *no – of means*, gar kein; *by no – of means*, unter gar keinen Umständen; *in a –*, in gewisser Hinsicht, gewissermaßen, gleichsam; *in like –*, *in the same –*, in gleicher Weise, ebenso; *in such a –*, auf solche Weise; *in this –*, in dieser *or* auf diese Weise; *as to the – born*, als ob es (ihm) angeboren wäre. **–ed,** *adj.* gesittet, geartet. **–ism** [–rɪzm], *s.* die Manieriertheit, Geziertheit, Eigenheit im Benehmen. **–less,** *adj.* unmanierlich **–liness,** *s.* die Manierlichkeit. **–ly,** *adj.* gesittet, höflich, manierlich. **-s** [-z], *pl.* Manieren, Umgangsformen, Sitten, Gewohnheiten, Bräuche (*pl.*), die Lebensart; *bad -s*, see *no -s*; *comedy of -s*, die Sittenkomödie; *no -s*, keine Lebensart; *other times other -s*, andere Zeiten andere Sitten.

mannish ['mænɪʃ], *adj. see under* **man.**

manœuvr-able [mə'nuːvrəbl], *adj.* manövrierfähig, wendig. **-e** [-və], 1. *s.* das Manöver; *pl.* große Truppenübung (*Mil.*); (*fig.*) taktische Bewegung, die Schwenkung; der Kunstgriff, Streich, die List. 2. *v.n.* manövrieren; (*fig.*) geschickt zu Werke gehen. 3. *v.a.* manövrieren lassen; (*fig.*) geschickt handhaben; *-e into*, bringen *or* verleiten zu (*a p.*); *-e o.s. into a position*, sich durch Geschick in eine Lage bringen, sich eine Lage verschaffen.

manometer [mæ'nɔmɪtə], *s.* das Manometer, der Dampfdruckmesser.

manor ['mænə], *s.* das Rittergut; *lord of the -*, der Gutsherr, adliger Grundherr. **--house,** *s.* das Herrschaftshaus, herrschaftliches Schloß, der Herrensitz, das Herrenhaus. **-ial** [mə'nɔːrɪəl], *adj.* herrschaftlich, Herrschafts-, Ritterguts-.

mansard ['mænsɑːd], *s.* (also *--roof*) das Mansardendach.

manse [mæns], *s.* (*Scots*) das Pfarrhaus.

mansion ['mænʃən], *s.* (herrschaftliches) Wohnhaus; *pl.* der Häuserblock mit größeren Einzelwohnungen. **--house,** *s.* das Herrenhaus; die Amtswohnung des Londoner Oberbürgermeisters.

manslaughter ['mænslɔːtə], *s. see under* **man.**

mantel [mæntl], *s.*, (also *-piece*, *-shelf*) der Kaminsims, die Kamineinfassung.

mantilla [mæn'tɪlə], *s.* die Mantille, spanischer Schleier *or* Umhang.

mantis ['mæntɪs], *s.* die Gottesanbeterin (*Ent.*).

mantle [mæntl], 1. *s.* ärmelloser Mantel; (*fig.*) der Schleier, die Hülle; (also *gas--*) der Glühstrumpf; der Formmantel (*Found.*). 2. *v.a.* bedecken, verbergen, verhüllen. 3. *v.n.* (*Poet.*) sich überziehen *or* bedecken, erröten (*of the face*).

mant(e)let ['mæntlɪt], *s.* die Schutzwehr, schußsicherer Schild (*Mil.*).

manual ['mænjuəl], 1. *adj.* mit der Hand gemacht *or* arbeitend, Hand-; eigenhändig; *- aid*, tätige Beihilfe; *- alphabet*, die Fingersprache; *- exercise*, die Griffübung (*Mil.*); *- instruction*, der Handfertigkeitsunterricht; *- labour*, see *- work*; *- press*, die Handpresse; *sign -*, eigenhändige Unterschrift; *- work*, die Handarbeit. 2. *s.* das Handbuch, der Leitfaden, die Vorschrift; das Manual (*of an organ*).

manufact-ory [mænju'fæktərɪ], *s.* (*archaic*) die Fabrik. **-ure** [-'fæktʃə], 1. *s.* die Herstellung, Verfertigung, Fabrikation (*also fig.*); Manufaktur, das Fabrikat; *pl.* Manufakturen (*pl.*), Erzeugnisse (*pl.*). 2. *v.a.* herstellen, verfertigen, fabrizieren (*out of*, aus), verarbeiten (*into*, zu); *-ured article*, der Fabriksartikel, die Fabrikware, das Fabrikat; *-ured goods*, Manufakturen (*pl.*). **-urer** [-'fæktʃərə] *s.* der Hersteller, Fabrikant, Fabrikbesitzer (*C.L.*). **-uring** [-'fæktʃərɪŋ], *adj.* Fabrik-, Industrie-; *-uring classes*, gewerbetreibende Klassen (*pl.*); *-uring expenses*, die Gestehungskosten; *-uring town*, die Fabrikstadt, Industriestadt.

manumi-ssion [mænju'mɪʃən], *s.* die Freilassung (*of slaves*). **-t** [-'mɪt], *v.a.* freilassen.

manur-e [mə'njuːə], 1. *v.a.* düngen. 2. *s.* der Dünger, das Düngemittel, der Mist.

manuscript ['mænjuskrɪpt], 1. *s.* die Handschrift, das Manuskript; die Druckvorlage (*Print.*). 2. *adj.* handschriftlich.

many ['mɛnɪ], 1. *adj.* (*before pl.*) viele, (*before sing.*) manche(r, s), manch eine(r, s); *- another*, manch anderer; *as -*, ebenso viel; *as - as 10*, nicht weniger als 10; *- a man*, mancher (Mann); (*Prov.*) *- men, - minds*, viele Köpfe, viele Sinne; *- a one*, manch einer; *in - respects*, in vielfacher Hinsicht; *- a time*, oft; *- is the time*, gar manches Mal; *like so -*, wie so viele; *in so - words*, ausdrücklich; *one too -*, einer zu viel; *be too - for me*, mir überlegen sein; *in - ways*, see *in - respects*. 2. *s.* (*pl. constr.*) die große Masse, der große Haufe; *a good* (*great*) *-*, eine ziemliche (große) Menge, (*as attrib.*) ziemlich (sehr) viele. **--cornered,** *adj.* vieleckig. **--sided,** *adj.* vielseitig (*also fig.*). **--sidedness,** *s.* die Vielseitigkeit.

map [mæp], 1. *s.* die Karte, Landkarte; Sternkarte (*Astr.*); das Meßtischblatt; *- of the world*, die Weltkarte; (*coll.*) *off the -*, abgelegen, gottverlassen; bedeutungslos. 2. *v.a.* kartographisch darstellen, abbilden, zeichnen, aufzeichen; verzeichnen (*on map*); *- out*, genau aufzeichnen, entwerfen, planen, ausarbeiten; aufteilen (*one's time*). **-ping,** *s.* die Kartenaufnahme, das Kartenzeichnen, die Kartographie.

maple [meɪpl], *s.* der Feldahorn. **--sugar,** *s.* der Ahornzucker.

mapping ['mæpɪŋ], *s. see* **map.**

maquis ['mækɪ], *pl.* Maquisarden (*pl.*) (*Pol.*).

mar [mɑː], *v.a.* verderben, beeinträchtigen; stören (*pleasure*); *make or -*, Glück oder Unglück bringen (*Dat.*).

marabou ['mærəbuː], *s.* der Marabu (*Orn.*).

maraschino [mærə'skiːnou], *s.* der Maraschino (*eine Art Kirschlikör*).

marasm-ic [mə'ræzmɪk], *adj.* entkräftet, Schwäche-. **-us** [-məs], *s.* die Entkräftung, (Alters)Schwäche, körperlicher Zerfall.

maraud [mə'rɔːd], *v.n.* plündern, marodieren. **-er** [-ə], *s.* der Plünderer, Mordbrenner, Marodeur.

marble ['mɑːbl], 1. *s.* der Marmor; das Marmorkunstwerk (*Sculp.*); die Murmel, der Schneller, Klicker (*toy*); *play at -s*, Murmel spielen. 2. *adj.* marmorn, Marmor-; (*fig.*) steinhart; marmorweiß. 3. *v.a.* marmorieren. **--paper,** *s.* marmoriertes Papier.

[1]**march** [mɑːtʃ], 1. *v.n.* grenzen (*upon*, an (*Acc.*)), zusammenstoßen (*with*, mit). 2. *s.* die Grenze, Mark; *pl.* das Grenzgebiet.

[2]**march** [mɑːtʃ], 1. *s.* der Marsch (*also Mus.*); Vormarsch (*on*, auf); Tagesmarsch; Marschschritt; (*fig.*) das Vorwärtsschreiten, der Fortschritt, Gang; *dead -*, der Totenmarsch; *line of -*, die Marschlinie; *- past*, der Parademarsch, Vorbeimarsch (*a p.*, an einem); *steal a - on s.o.*, einem zuvorkommen. 2. *v.n.* marschieren, ziehen (*Mil.*); gehen, schreiten; (*fig.*) vorwärtsschreiten; *- past*, (im Paradeschritt) vorbeimarschieren (*a p.*, an einem); *quick -!* Abteilung marsch! 3. *v.a.* marschieren lassen (*troops*); im Marsch zurücklegen (*distance*); *- off*, abführen. **-ing,** *adj.* Marsch-; *-ing order*, die Marschausrüstung; *-ing orders*, der Marschbefehl; *be under -ing orders*, Marschbefehl haben; *-ing song*, das Marschlied.

[3]**March** [mɑːtʃ], *s.* der März; *- hare*, der Märzhase.

marchioness ['mɑːʃənɪs], *s.* die Marquise.

marchpane ['mɑːtʃpeɪn], *s. see* **marzipan.**

mare ['mɛːə], *s.* die Stute. **-'s-nest,** *s.* (*fig.*) trügerische Entdeckung, der Schwindel, die Zeitungsente. **-'s-tail,** *s.* der Tannenwedel (*Bot.*); *pl.* Wolkenstreifen, Schäfchenwolken (*pl.*).

margar-ic [mɑː'gærɪk], *adj.* Margarin- (*Chem.*). **-ine** [-gə'riːn], *s.* die Margarine, Kunstbutter.

[1]**marge** [mɑːdʒ], *s.* (*Poet.*) der Rand.

[2]**marg(e)** [mɑːg, mɑːdʒ], *s.* (*coll.*) *see* **margarine.**

margin ['mɑːdʒɪn], 1. *s.* der Rand; Spielraum; die Grenze; Verdienstspanne, der Gewinn, Nutzen, Überschuß; die Deckung, Hinterlegungssumme; der Vorsprung, Abstand (*Sport*); *in the -*, am Rande; (*fig.*) *leave a -*, Spielraum lassen; *leave no - (of profit)*, keinen Überschuß gewähren, keinen Gewinn abwerfen; *- of profit*, die Gewinnspanne; *- of safety*, der Sicherheitsfaktor; *on the -*, auf dem Rand. 2. *v.a.* mit Rand(bemerkungen) versehen, am Rand vermerken; decken (*C.L.*). **-al,** *adj.* an *or* auf dem Rande, Rand-, Grenz-, nahe an der untersten Grenze; *-al note*, die Randbemerkung; *-al profit*, knapper Gewinn. **-alia,** *pl.* Randbemerkungen (*pl.*).

margrav-e ['mɑːgreɪv], *s.* der Markgraf. **-iate** [-greɪvɪət], *s.* die Markgrafschaft. **-ine** [-grə'viːn], *s.* die Markgräfin.

marguerite [mɑːgə'riːt], *s.* die Marienblume, großes Maßlieb (*Bot.*).

marigold ['mærɪgould], *s.* die Ringelblume, Dotterblume (*Bot.*).

marina-de [mærɪˈneɪd], *s.* die Marinade, Essigbrühe. **-te** [ˈmærɪneɪt], *v.a.* marinieren.

marine [məˈrɪ:n], 1. *adj.* Meer(es)–, See–; – *cable*, das Seekabel; – *insurance*, die Schiffahrtsversicherung; – *station*, der Hafenbahnhof; – *stores*, Schiffsgegenstände (*pl.*). 2. *s.* der Seesoldat; die Marine, das Seewesen, Schiffs- und Flottenwesen; *pl.* Seetruppen, die Marineinfanterie; *tell that to the -s!* das mach' einem andern weis! **-r** [ˈmærɪnə], *s.* der Seemann, Matrose; *-r's compass*, der Schiffskompaß, die Bussole.

mariolatry [mærɪˈɔlətrɪ], *s.* die Marienvergötterung, der Madonnenkult.

marionette [mærɪəˈnɛt], *s.* die Drahtpuppe, Marionette; (*fig.*) Puppe, Figur.

marital [ˈmærɪtəl], *adj.* ehelich, Ehe–; – *rights*, das Gattenrecht.

maritime [ˈmærɪtaɪm], *adj.* am Meere gelegen *or* lebend; Küsten–; Schiffahrts–, Seehandel treibend; – *affairs*, Schiffahrtsangelegenheiten, das Seewesen; – *court*, das Seeamt; – *law*, das Seerecht; – *nations*, seehandeltreibende Nationen; – *powers*, Seemächte.

marjoram [ˈmɑ:dʒərəm], *s.* der Majoran (*Bot.*).

[1]**mark** [mɑ:k], *s.* die Mark (*currency*).

[2]**mark** [mɑ:k], **1.** *s.* das (Kenn)Zeichen, Anzeichen; Gepräge, Merkmal, der Stempel, die Marke; Narbe, das Mal; Ziel; Schriftzeichen, Kreuz (*as signature*); die Startlinie (*Sport*); Zensur, Nummer, Note, das Zeugnis (*at school*). (*a*) (*with nouns*) *laundry* –, das Wäschezeichen; *man of* –, ein Mann von Bedeutung, markante Persönlichkeit; – *of mouth*, das Alterszeichen (*of horses*); *number of -s*, die Punktzahl (*in examinations*); – *of origin*, das Herkunftszeichen; – *of respect*, das Zeichen der Achtung; *trade* –, die Schutzmarke, Handelsmarke. (*b*) (*with verbs*) *hit the* –, treffen; *leave one's* – *upon*, seinen Stempel aufdrücken (*Dat.*), seine Spur hinterlassen auf; *make one's* –, sich (*Dat.*) einen Namen machen, es zu etwas bringen, Eindruck machen; *miss one's* –, fehlschießen, danebenschießen, (*fig.*) sein Ziel verfehlen; *overshoot the* –, (*fig.*) zu weit gehen. (*c*) (*with prepositions*) *quite beside* or *far from the* –, nicht zur S. gehörig, fehlgeschossen; *up to the* –, den Anforderungen genügend, den Erwartungen entsprechend; (*coll.*) auf der Höhe; *wide of the* –, weit vom Ziel, am Ziel vorbei, (*fig.*) irrig, verfehlt; *within the* –, berechtigt (*in doing*, zu tun). (*d*) (*with adjectives*) *distinguishing* –, das Kennzeichen; *easy* –, leichtes Ziel; (*sl.*) leichtgläubiger Mensch; *poor* –, schlechte Note. **2.** *v.a.* (be)zeichnen, kennzeichnen, ein Zeichen sein für; durch Zeichen ausdrücken, hervorheben, auszeichnen, brandmarken, markieren (*also Mil.*); beachten, sich (*Dat.*) merken; anmerken, notieren; bestimmen (*for*, zu); zensieren, korrigieren (*school-work*); – *with a hot iron*, brandmarken; – *an occasion*, zum Anlaß nehmen; – *time*, auf der Stelle treten (*Mil.*); (*fig.*) nicht vom Fleck kommen; – *my words!* nimm das zur Kenntnis! – *down*, im Preis herabsetzen (*goods*); vormerken (*for*, für); bestimmen (*for*, zu) (*a p.*); – *off*, abgrenzen, abstecken, anzeichnen; abstreichen (*on a list*); – *out*, bestimmen, ausersehen (*for*, für); bezeichnen, abgrenzen, abstecken. **3.** *v.n.* achtgeben; – *you!* wohlgemerkt! passen Sie auf! **-ed**, *adj.* gezeichnet, markiert, gekennzeichnet; ausgeprägt, auffallend, deutlich, markant, ausgesprochen, ausdrücklich; bemerklich; verdächtig; gebrandmarkt; *-ed attention*, gespannte Aufmerksamkeit; *-ed cheque*, bestätigter Wechsel; *-ed coin*, abgestempelte Münze; *-ed man*, Gebrandmarkte(r), *m.*; *-ed progress*, merklicher Fortschritt. **-er**, *s.* der Anzeiger (*at target-practice*); Markör (*Bill.*); (also *book-*–) das Lesezeichen. **-ing**, *s.* die Zeichnung, Markierung; Musterung (*of animals, birds, etc.*); Betonung (*Mus.*); das Hoheitsabzeichen (*Mil. & Av.*). **-ing-ink**, *s.* unauslöschliche Zeichentinte. **-ing-iron**, *s.* das Brenneisen. **-sman**, *s.* der (Meister)Schütze. **-smanship**, *s.* die Schießkunst.

market [ˈmɑ:kɪt], 1. *s.* der Markt; Marktplatz; Geldmarkt (*stock exchange*); Absatz; das Absatzgebiet; die Nachfrage (*for*, nach); der Handelsverkehr; Marktpreis, Marktpreise (*pl.*). (*a*) (*with prepositions*) *at* or *in the* –, auf dem *or* am Markt; *from* –, von dem Markt; *to* –, auf den Markt; *be in the* – *for*, Bedarf haben für; *come into the* –, zum Verkauf angeboten werden, auf den Markt kommen; *on the* –, auf dem Markt; *place* or *put on the* –, auf den Markt bringen; *drug on the* –, unverkäufliche Ware, der Ladenhüter. (*b*) (*with verbs*) *find a* – *for*, an den Mann bringen; *meet with a ready* –, schnellen Absatz finden; *open new -s*, neue Handelsbeziehungen anbahnen. 2. *v.n.* einkaufen; auf dem Markt handeln. 3. *v.a.* auf dem Markt verkaufen, auf den Markt bringen, Absatz finden für. **-able**, *adj.* verkäuflich, gangbar. **--day**, *s.* der Markttag. **--garden**, *s.* die Gemüsegärtnerei, Handelsgärtnerei. **--gardener**, *s.* der Handelsgärtner, Gemüsegärtner. **--hall**, *s.* die Markthalle. **-ing**, *s.* das Besuchen des Marktes; *do one's -ing*, seine Einkäufe machen. **--place**, *s.* der Marktplatz. **--price**, *s.* der Marktpreis; Börsenkurs (*C.L.*). **--rigging**, *s.* (*sl.*) die Kurstreiberei. **--town**, *s.* der Marktflecken, die Kreisstadt.

marl [mɑ:l], 1. *s.* der Mergel. 2. *v.a.* mit Mergel düngen, mergeln. **-y**, *adj.* mergelhaltig.

marline [ˈmɑ:lɪn], *s.* die Marlleine. **--spike**, (**marlinspike**), *s.* der Marlspieker.

marly [ˈmɑ:lɪ], *see* **marl.**

marmalade [ˈmɑ:məleɪd], *s.* die Orangenmarmelade.

marmoreal [mɑ:ˈmɔ:rɪəl], *adj.* marmorartig, marmorn, Marmor–.

marmoset [ˈmɑ:məsɛt], *s.* das Seidenäffchen (*Zool.*).

marmot [ˈmɑ:mət], *s.* das Murmeltier, der Hamster (*Zool.*).

[1]**maroon** [məˈru:n], *adj.* kastanienbraun, rotbraun.

[2]**maroon** [məˈru:n], 1. *s.* der Maron(neger), Buschneger; entlaufener Negersklave. 2. *v.a.* (zur Strafe) an einer öden Küste *or* Insel aussetzen. 3. *v.n.* (*Amer.*) herumlungern; an einem einsamen Platz zelten.

[3]**maroon** [məˈru:n] *s.* der Kanonenschlag, das Signalfeuerwerk.

marplot [ˈmɑ:plɔt], *s.* der Störenfried, Spaßverderber.

marque [mɑ:k] *s.* das Kaperschiff; *letter(s) of* –, der Kaperbrief (*Naut.*).

marquee [mɑ:ˈkɪ:], *s.* großes Zelt; das Offizierszelt (*Mil.*).

marquess [ˈmɑ:kwɪs], *s.* *Engl. form of* **marquis.**

marquet(e)ry [ˈmɑ:kɪtrɪ], *s.* Marketerie, Intarsia, eingelegte Tischlerarbeit.

marquis [ˈmɑ:kwɪs], *s.* der Marquis. **-ate** [-ət], *s.* das Marquisat, die Marquiswürde.

marriage [ˈmærɪdʒ], *s.* die Ehe, der Ehestand; die Eheschließung, Heirat, Hochzeit, Trauung (*to*, mit); (*fig.*) enge Verbindung; *ask a p. in* –, um eine (Frau) anhalten; *by* –, angeheiratet; *related by* –, verschwägert; *civil* –, standesamtliche Trauung; *companionate* –, die Kameradschaftsehe; *consummate the* –, den Eheakt vollziehen; *contract* (*a*) –, eine Ehe schließen; – *of convenience*, die Verstandesheirat; *give a p. in* –, eine (Tochter) verheiraten; *take a p. in* –, eine(n) heiraten; *the child of her first* –, das Kind aus erster Ehe; – *by proxy*, die Ferntrauung. **-able**, *adj.* heiratsfähig, mannbar; *-able age*, die Ehemündigkeit. **--articles**, *pl.* der Ehevertrag. **--bed**, *s.* das Ehebett. **--ceremony**, *s.* die Eheschließung, Trauung. **--certificate**, *see* **--lines.** **--contract**, *s.* *see* **--articles.** **--customs**, *pl.* Hochzeitsbräuche. **--licence**, *s.* amtliche Erlaubnis, eine Ehe zu schließen. **--lines**, *pl.* der Trauschein. **--loan**, *s.* das Ehestandsdarlehen. **--market**, *s.* der Heiratsmarkt. **--portion**, *s.* die Mitgift. **--rites**, *pl.* Hochzeitsbräuche. **--settlement**, *s.* *see* **--articles.**

married [ˈmærɪd], *adj.* verheiratet, vermählt; verehelicht (*Law*); ehelich, Ehe–; *newly* –, neuvermählt; – *life*, das Eheleben; – *man*, der Ehemann; – *people*, Eheleute; – *state*, der Ehestand; *see* [1]**marry.**

marrow [ˈmærou], *s.* das Mark (*also fig.*); (*fig.*) der Kern, Innerstes, *n.*, Bestes, *n.*; *to the* –, bis aufs Mark, bis ins Innerste; *vegetable* –, der Eierkürbis. **--bone**, *s.* der Markknochen. **-fat**, *s.* große Erbse (*Bot.*). **-y**, *adj.* markig, kernig.

¹marr-y ['mærɪ], 1. *v.a.* heiraten (*one's partner*), verheiraten, vermählen (*a daughter, etc.*) (*to*, mit); verheiraten, trauen (*as the priest*); (*fig.*) eng verbinden (*to* or *with*, mit); *be –ied to*, verheiratet sein mit; *get –ied to*, sich verheiraten mit. 2. *v.n.* sich verheiraten, heiraten (*into a family*, in eine Familie); *–y beneath one's station*, eine Mißheirat schließen; (*Prov.*) *–y in haste and repent at leisure*, schnell gefreit wird meist bereut; *–y for love*, aus Liebe heiraten.

²marry ['mærɪ], *int.* (*archaic*) wahrlich! fürwahr! traun!

marsh [mɑːʃ], *s.* der Morast, Sumpf, die Marsch, das Marschland. **--fever,** *s.* das Malariafieber. **--gas,** *s.* das Sumpfgas, Grubengas (*Min.*). **-iness,** *s.* die Sumpfigkeit. **-mallow,** *s.* gemeiner Eibisch, die Althee (*Bot.*). **--marigold,** *s.* die Sumpfdotterblume (*Bot.*). **-y,** *adj.* sumpfig; *–y ground*, der Sumpfboden.

marshal ['mɑːʃəl], 1. *s.* der Marschall; Zeremonienmeister; (*Amer.*) Vollstreckungsbeamte(r), *m.*, der Gerichtsvollzieher; *air–*, der General der Luftwaffe; *field–*, der Feldmarschall (*Mil.*). 2. *v.a.* (an)ordnen, einordnen; aufstellen (*troops, etc.*); ordnungsgemäß setzen, ordnen (*ideas, etc.*); feierlich führen (*into*, in); zusammenstellen (*trains*). **-ling-yard,** *s.* der Verschiebebahnhof, das Abstellgeleise (*Railw.*). **-ship,** *s.* das Marschallamt.

marshiness, marshy, *see under* **marsh.**

marsupial [mɑː'sjuːpɪəl], 1. *adj.* Beuteltier–. 2. *s.* das Beuteltier.

mart [mɑːt], *s.* (*Poet.*) der Markt, Marktplatz, Handelsplatz.

martagon ['mɑːtəgən], *s.* der Türkenbund (*Bot.*).

marten ['mɑːtən], *s.* der Marder (*Zool.*).

martial ['mɑːʃəl], *adj.* kriegerisch, soldatisch, militärisch, Kriegs–, Militär–; *– bearing*, soldatische Haltung; *– law*, das Kriegsrecht, Standrecht; *– music*, die Militärmusik.

martin ['mɑːtɪn], *s.* die Mehlschwalbe, Hausschwalbe; Uferschwalbe (*Orn.*).

martinet [mɑːtɪ'nɛt], *s.* strenge(r) Vorgesetzte(r), *m.*, strenger Zuchtmeister.

martingale ['mɑːtɪŋgeɪl], *s.* der Sprungriemen (*Saddl.*); das Stampfstag (*Naut.*).

martinmas ['mɑːtɪnməs], *s.* der Martinstag (*11th November*).

martyr ['mɑːtə], 1. *s.* der Märtyrer, Blutzeuge; Dulder, das Opfer; *be a – to gout*, beständig an Gicht leiden; *make a – of o.s.*, sich opfern; *a – in the cause of* or *a – to science*, ein Opfer der Wissenschaft. 2. *v.a.* zum Märtyrer machen, martern, peinigen; *–ed with*, gequält von. **-dom** [-dəm], *s.* das Märtyrertum, der Märtyrertod; die Marterqualen (*pl.*). **-ize,** *v.a.* quälen, opfern. **-ology** [-'rɔlədʒɪ], *s.* die Geschichte der Märtyrer; das Martyrologium.

marvel [mɑːvl], 1. *s.* das Wunder; *it is a – to me*, es ist für mich eine wunderbare *or* erstaunliche S.; *he is a –*, er ist ein wunderbarer *or or* beispielloser Kerl; *– of Peru*, die falsche Jalape, Wunderblume. 2. *v.n.* sich wundern, staunen (*at*, über). **-lous** [-vələs], *adj.* wunderbar, erstaunlich; unglaublich. **-lousness,** *s.* das Wunderbare.

marzipan [mɑːzɪ'pæn], *s.* das Marzipan.

mascot ['mæskət], *s.* der Talisman; *radiator–*, die Kühlerfigur (*Motor.*).

masculin-e ['mæskjulɪn], 1. *adj.* männlich (*also Gram. & Pros.*), Mannes–; mannhaft, männisch (*of women*); stumpf (*of rhyme*). 2. *s.* das Maskulinum (*Gram.*). **-ity** [-'lɪnɪtɪ], *s.* die Männlichkeit, Mannhaftigkeit.

mash [mæʃ], 1. *s.* das Gemisch, Mus, der Brei; das Mengfutter (*for horses*); die Maische (*Brew.*). 2. *v.a.* zerstoßen, zerquetschen; maischen (*Brew.*); *–ed potatoes*, der Kartoffelbrei, gestampfte Kartoffeln. **-(ing)-tub,** *s.* der Maischbottich.

masher ['mæʃə], *s.* (*sl.*) der Geck, Damenheld.

mashie ['mæʃɪ], *s.* der Golfschläger mit Stahlkopf.

mask [mɑːsk], 1. *s.* die Maske, Larve; (*fig.*) der Vorwand, Deckmantel; Maskierte(r), *m. & f.*, Vermummte(r), *m. & f.*; *death–*, die Totenmaske; *gas–*, die Gasmaske; *throw off the –*, die Maske abwerfen; *under the – of*, unter dem Deckmantel (*Gen.*). 2. *v.a.* maskieren, verkleiden, vermummen; (*fig.*) verbergen, verdecken; tarnen (*Mil.*); *–ed ball*, der Maskenball; *–ed battery*, maskierte *or* verdeckte Batterie. **-er** [-ə], *s.* der Maskenspieler; die Maske, maskierte Person.

masochism ['mæzəkɪzm], *s.* der Masochismus.

mason ['meɪsən], 1. *s.* der Maurer; Freimaurer. 2. *v.a.* mauern. **-ic** [mə'sɔnɪk], *adj.* freimaurerisch, Freimaurer–. **-ry** ['meɪsənrɪ], *s.* die Maurerei, Maurerarbeit, das Maurerhandwerk; Mauerwerk; die Freimaurerei; *bound –ry*, das Quaderwerk.

masque [mɑːsk], *s.* das Maskenspiel (*Theat.*). **-rade** [-ə'reɪd], 1. *s.* der Maskenball, das Maskenfest, die Maskerade; (*fig.*) Verkleidung. 2. *v.n.* (*fig.*) maskiert gehen; sich verstellen *or* ausgeben. **-rader,** *s.* der Versteller, Vortäuscher.

¹mass [mæs], *s.* die Messe (*R.C., Mus.*); *– for the dead*, die Seelenmesse; *attend* or *go to –*, zur Messe gehen; *say –*, die Messe lesen.

²mass [mæs], 1. *s.* die Masse (*also Phys.*); großer Haufe, die Menge; Allgemeinheit (*of people*); größerer Teil, die Mehrzahl (*of things*); *the –es*, die Massen, niederen Klassen (*pl.*); (*coll.*) *be a – of*, bedeckt sein mit, voll sein von; *– of cloud*, die Wolkenmasse; *– of fire*, das Feuermeer; *in the –*, im allgemeinen *or* ganzen. 2. *v.a.* (an)häufen, aufhäufen, sammeln, zusammenziehen; versammeln, konzentrieren. 3. *v.n.* sich ansammeln *or* häufen, Massen bilden; *– action*, die Massenwirkung; *– meeting*, die Massenversammlung; *– production*, die Massenherstellung, Reihenproduktion.

massacre ['mæsəkə], 1. *s.* das Gemetzel, Blutbad, der Massenmord. 2. *v.a.* niedermetzeln.

mass-age ['mæsɑːʒ, mæ'sɑːʒ], 1. *s.* das Massieren, die Massage. 2. *v.a.* massieren. **-eur** [-'səː], *s.* der Masseur. **-euse** [-'səːz], *s.* die Masseuse.

massif ['mæsɪf], *s.* die Bergmasse, der Gebirgsstock.

massive ['mæsɪv], *adj.* massiv, massig, sehr groß, schwer, Massen–; (*fig.*) mächtig, gediegen. **-ness,** *s.* Massive(s), *n.*, Schwere(s), *n.*; die Schwere; Gediegenheit.

¹mast [mɑːst], 1. *s.* der Mast; *aerial –*, der Antennenmast, Antennenturm; *at half–*, auf Halbmast; *mooring –*, der Ankermast. 2. *v.a.* bemasten; *three–ed vessel*, der Dreimaster. **-er,** *s.*; (*as suffix*) *three–er*, der Dreimaster. **-head,** *s.* der Topp, Mastkorb, Mars (*Naut.*); *–head light*, das Topplicht.

²mast [mɑːst], *s.* die Mast, das Mastfutter.

master ['mɑːstə], **1.** *s.* der Meister, Arbeitgeber, Prinzipal; Herr, Eigentümer, Besitzer; Hausherr; Herrscher, Gebieter; Vorsteher, Leiter; Kapitän (*of a merchant-vessel*); Lehrer, Studienrat (*in German schools*); Magister (*Univ.*); Lehrmeister (*of a trade*); junger Herr (*before Christian names*); Virtuose, großer Maler. (*a*) (*with verbs*) *be – of*, beherrschen; *be one's own –*, sein eigner Herr sein; *make o.s. – of*, beherrschen, sich erwerben. (*b*) (*with nouns*) *like – like man*, wie der Herr so der Knecht; *– of Arts*, der Magister der philosophischen Fakultät; *– of ceremonies*, der Conferencier; *– of the horse*, der Oberstallmeister; *– of the lodge*, der Meister vom Stuhl (*Freem.*); *– of the revels*, der Leiter der Hoflustbarkeiten; *– of the rolls*, der Oberarchivar, Direktor des Staatsarchivs. (*c*) (*with adjectives*) *old –*, ein Maler *or* ein Bild der Renaissance; *second* or *senior –*, der Oberstudienrat. **2.** *v.a.* meistern (*an art*), beherrschen (*a language*), bewältigen (*a problem*); Herr werden über, besiegen (*a p.*); bändigen, zähmen. **--at-arms,** *s.* der Polizeioffizier (*in navy*). **--builder,** *s.* der Baumeister. **--clock,** *s.* die Normaluhr, Zentraluhr, Hauptuhr. **--compass,** *s.* der Mutterkompaß. **--copy,** *s.* die Originalkopie (*Films*). **-ful,** *adj.* herrisch, gebieterisch; meisterhaft, großartig. **--hand,** *s.* die Meisterhand. **--key,** *s.* der Hauptschlüssel. **-less,** *adj.* herrenlos. **-liness,** *s.* das Meisterhafte, die Meisterschaft. **-ly,** *adj.* meisterhaft. **--mind,** *s.* führender Geist. **-piece,** *s.* das Meisterstück. **-ship,** *s.* die Herrschaft, Meisterschaft; das Amt *or* die Würde eines Meisters *or* Vorstehers *or* Lehrers. **--stroke,** *s.* der Meisterzug; (*fig.*) das Meisterstück, genialer Streich.

--tailor, *s.* der Schneidermeister. **-y,** *s.* die Herrschaft, Gewalt, Macht (*of* or *over*, über); der Vorrang, die Oberhand, Überlegenheit, Meisterschaft (*in* or *of*, in (*Dat.*)), Beherrschung (*of* (*Gen.*)); *-y of the air*, die Beherrschung der Luft; *gain the -y over*, die Oberhand gewinnen (über (*Acc.*)).
mastic ['mæstɪk], *s.* der Mastix; das Mastixharz; der Kitt.
masticat-e ['mæstɪkeɪt], *v.a.* kauen. **-ion** [-'keɪʃən], *s.* das Kauen. **-or,** *s.* die Knetmaschine. **-ory** [-kətərɪ], *adj.* Kau-.
mastiff ['mæstɪf], *s.* der Bullenbeißer, Mastiff.
mastitis [mæs'tɑɪtɪs], *s.* die Brustdrüsenentzündung.
mastodon ['mæstədən], *s.* urzeitlicher Elefant.
mastoid ['mæstɔɪd], *adj.* brustförmig.
masturbat-e ['mæstə:beɪt], *v.n.* onanieren. **-ion** [-'beɪʃən], *s.* die Onanie.
1**mat** [mæt], 1. *s.* die Matte, Fußdecke, der Läufer; (*sl.*) *be on the -*, in der Tinte sitzen; *table--*, der Strohteller. 2. *v.a.* mit Matten bedecken *or* belegen; ineinanderflechten, verflechten, verfilzen; *-ted hair*, verwirrtes *or* verfilztes Haar. 3. *v.n.* sich verfilzen; *see* **matting.**
2**mat** [mæt], 1. *adj.* matt, mattiert, glanzlos. 2. *v.a.* mattieren, matt schleifen.
matador ['mætədɔ:], *s.* der Matador; Haupttrumpf (*Cards*).
1**match** [mætʃ], *s.* das Zündholz, Streichholz; die Lunte, Zündschnur (*Artil.*). **--box,** *s.* die Zündholzschachtel. **--head,** *s.* die Zündholzmasse. **-lock,** *s.* das Luntengewehr; Luntenschloß (*Gun.*). **-wood,** *s.* Holzsplitter (*pl.*), das Kleinholz; *break into* or *reduce to -wood*, in tausend Splitter zerbrechen, bis auf Kleinholz zersplittern.
2**match** [mætʃ], 1. *s.* der, die, das Gleiche *or* Ebenbürtige; die Heirat, Heiratspartie; der Wettkampf, das Wettspiel, Treffen, die Partie; *be* (*more than*) *a - for*, gewachsen sein (*Dat.*); *boxing -*, der Boxkampf; *exact -*, genaue Bemusterung; *find one's -*, see *meet one's -*; *football -*, das Fußball(wett)-spiel, Fußballtreffen; *good -*, gute Partie; ausgezeichnetes Paar; *his -*, seinesgleichen; *ill-assorted -*, schlecht zusammenpassendes Ehepaar; *meet one's -*, seinen Mann finden. 2. *v.a.* ehelich verbinden, passend verheiraten (*to* or *with*, mit); sich messen mit, es aufnehmen mit, ebenbürtig *or* gewachsen sein (*Dat.*); vergleichen (*with*, mit), in Gegensatz stellen (*against*, gegen); anpassen, zusammenpassen, passend machen, abmustern; passen zu, entsprechen; Passendes *or* Gleiches finden; *be well--ed*, gut zusammenpassen *or* zueinander passen; *this colour is hard to -*, zu dieser Farbe läßt sich schwer etwas Passendes finden; *I know nothing to - it*, ich kenne seinesgleichen nicht. 3. *v.n.* zusammenpassen, übereinstimmen, gleich sein (*with*, mit); sich (*Dat.*) entsprechen; *envelopes to -*, die dazu passenden Umschläge. **--board,** *s.* genutetes Holzbrett. **-less,** *adj.* unvergleichlich, unübertrefflich, ohnegleichen. **-maker,** *s.* der Ehestifter, Ehevermittler.
1**mate** [meɪt], 1. *s.* der Gefährte, Genosse, Kamerad (*among workmen, etc. & coll.*); Gehilfe (*at work*); Gatte, die Gattin; das Männchen, Weibchen (*of birds*); der Maat, Steuermann (*Naut.*); das Glied eines Paares. 2. *v.a.* verheiraten (*with*, mit); paaren (*animals*). 3. *v.n.* sich verheiraten; sich paaren, sich gatten. **-y,** *adj.* (*coll.*) vertraulich, kameradschaftlich.
2**mate** [meɪt], 1. *s.* das Matt (*chess*). 2. *v.a.* matt setzen.
maté ['mæteɪ], *s.* der Matebaum; Mate, Paraguaytee.
material [mə'tɪ:ərɪəl], 1. *s.* das Material, der Stoff, Werkstoff; Bestandteil, Bestandteile (*pl.*), Elemente (*pl.*); *pl.* Materialien; Unterlagen (*for*, zu); *building -s*, Baustoffe (*pl.*); *cleaning -s*, das Putzzeug; *raw -*, der Rohstoff; *raw -s*, Materialien (*pl.*); *writing -s*, das Schreibgerät. 2. *adj.* materiell (*also Log.*); stofflich, körperlich; sachlich, Sach-; (*fig.*) weltlich, irdisch; sinnlich; wichtig, wesentlich (*to*, für); *- goods*, Sachgüter. **-ism** [-ɪzm], *s.* der Materialismus. **-ist** [-ɪst], 1. *s.* der Materialist. 2. *adj.*, **-istic** [-'lɪstɪk], *adj.* materialistisch. **-ity** [-ɪ'ælɪtɪ], *s.* die Materialität, Körperlichkeit; Wesentlichkeit, Wichtigkeit, Erheblichkeit (*Law*). **-ization** [-aɪ'zeɪʃən], *s.* die Materialisierung, Verkörperung. **-ize** [-ɑɪz], 1. *v.a.* verkörpern; materialisieren, stoffliche Form geben (*Dat.*) (*spirit*); verwirklichen, materiell machen. 2. *v.n.* sich verwirklichen, erfüllen *or* realisieren, zum Abschluß *or* zustande kommen; sichtbar werden, Wirklichkeit werden, feste Gestalt annehmen; in körperlicher Form erscheinen (*of spirit*).
materia medica [mə'tɪ:ərɪə'mɛdɪkə], *s.* die Arzneimittellehre; Arzneimittel (*pl.*).
matériel [mæterɪ'ɛl], *s.* Erfordernisse (*pl.*), das Rüstzeug, Material.
matern-al [mə'tə:nəl], *adj.* mütterlich, Mutter-; mütterlicherseits; *-al love*, die Mutterliebe; *-al mortality*, die Muttersterblichkeit; *-al uncle*, der Onkel mütterlicherseits. **-ity** [-nɪtɪ], *s.* die Mutterschaft; *-ity centre*, die Mütterberatungsstelle; *-ity hospital*, die Entbindungsanstalt.
matey ['meɪtɪ], *see* **maté.**
mathematic, -al [mæθə'mætɪk(l)], *adj.* mathematisch; *-al instruments*, das Reißzeug. **-ian** [-mə'tɪʃən], *s.* der Mathematiker. **-s** [-tɪks], *pl.* (*sing. constr.*) die Mathematik; (*pl. constr.*) die Rechenkunst.
matin ['mætɪn], *adj.* (*Poet.*) Morgen-, früh; die Matutin (*R.C.*). **-ée** [-eɪ], *s.* die Nachmittagsvorstellung (*Theat.*). **-s** [-z], *pl.* der Frühgottesdienst (*C. of E.*).
matrass ['mætrəs], *s.* der Distillierkolben.
matri-archy ['meɪtrɪɑ:kɪ], *s.* die Mutterherrschaft, das Mutterrecht. **-cidal** [-sɑɪdl], *adj.* muttermörderisch. **-cide** [-sɑɪd], *s.* der Muttermord; Muttermörder.
matriculat-e [mə'trɪkjuleɪt], 1. *v.a.* immatrikulieren (*Univ.*). 2. *v.n.* sich immatrikulieren lassen. **-ion** [-'leɪʃən], *s.* die Immatrikulation, (also *-ion examination*) Aufnahmeprüfung (*Univ.*), Abitur (*at school*).
matrimon-ial [mætrɪ'mounɪəl], *adj.* ehelich, Ehe-; *-ial agency*, das Ehevermittlungsbüro; *-ially inclined*, heiratslustig. **-y** ['mætrɪmənɪ], *s.* die Ehe, der Ehestand.
matrix ['meɪtrɪks], *s.* die Gebärmutter (*Anat.*), der Mutterboden (*also fig.*); der Gang, die Gangart (*Min.*); Matrize, Hohlform, Gießform, Schablone, das Gesenk (*Tech.*); (*fig.*) der Nährboden.
matron ['meɪtrən], *s.* die Matrone, verheirate Frau; die Vorsteherin (*of a boarding school*); Oberin (*of a hospital*). **-ly,** *adj.* matronenhaft, mütterlich; (*fig.*) gesetzt.
matt [mæt], *adj. see* 2**mat** 1.
matter ['mætə], **1.** *s.* der Stoff, die Materie, Substanz, Masse, der Körper; Inhalt, Gehalt, Gegenstand; die Sache, Angelegenheit; der Eiter (*Med.*); Satz, das Manuskript (*Typ.*). (*a*) (*with pronoun*) *no -*, es macht nichts; *no - which*, was auch immer, einerlei was; *no - how long*, ohne Rücksicht darauf *or* ungeachtet wie lange; *s.th. is the -*, es ist etwas los *or* vorgefallen *or* nicht in Ordnung; *for that -*, was das anbelangt, übrigens, überhaupt; *what - ?* was liegt daran? *what's the - ?* was ist los? was gibt's? was geht vor? *what's the matter with you?* was fehlt dir? wie steht es mit dir? (*coll.*) *that's what the - is*, da liegt der Hund begraben. (*b*) (*with nouns*) *it is a - for congratulation*, es ist zu begrüßen; *a - of consequence*, wichtige Angelegenheit; *a - of course*, die Selbstverständlichkeit, ausgemachte Sache; *a - of fact*, (selbständige) Tatsache; der Tatbestand (*Law*); *as a - of fact*, in der Tat, tatsächlich, wirklich, sogar; *the - in hand*, vorliegende Sache; *it's a - of indifference to me*, es ist mir ganz einerlei *or* völlig gleichgültig; *it is a - of life and death*, es geht um Leben und Tod; *be a - of £7*, auf etwa sieben Pfund kommen; *it is a - for regret*, es ist höchst bedauerlich *or* zu bedauern; *- of taste*, die Geschmackssache; *- of time*, die Frage der Zeit; *a - of 10 years*, etwa zehn Jahre. (*c*) (*with adjectives*) *no laughing -*, keine S. zum Lachen; *printed -*, die Drucksache. (*d*) (*with verbs*) *not mince -s*, kein Blatt vor den Mund nehmen; *as -s stand*, wie die Dinge liegen. **2.** *v.n.* von Bedeutung sein (*to*, für), daran gelegen sein, darauf ankommen (*to a p.*, einem); *it does not -*, es macht *or* tut nichts; *what does it - ?* was macht *or* tut das? *it -s little*, es

ist ziemlich einerlei. **--of-course,** *pred. adj.* selbstverständlich. **--of-fact,** *adj.* tatsächlich; prosaisch, nüchtern. **-s** [-z], *pl.* Dinge, Umstände (*pl.*), die Lage.

matting [ˈmætɪŋ], *s.* der Mattenstoff; das Material zu Matten *or* Läufern.

mattins [ˈmætɪnz], *see* **matins.**

mattock [ˈmætək], *s.* die Hacke, Haue, Queraxt.

mattress [ˈmætrɪs], *s.* die Matratze; *hair* –, die Roßhaarmatratze; *spring* –, die Sprungfedermatratze; – *cover*, der Matratzenschoner.

matur-ate [ˈmætjʊreɪt], *v.a.* eitern (*Med.*); zur Reife kommen (*Psych.*). **-ation** [-ˈreɪʃən], *s.* die Eiterung; das Reifen, die Entwicklung zur Reife. **-ative** [-ˈtjuːərətɪv], *adj.* zum Eitern *or* zur Reife bringend. **-e** [-ˈtjuːə], 1. *adj.* reif, voll entwickelt; (*fig.*) wohldurchdacht, durchgebildet, reiflich (erwogen); fällig (*C.L.*). 2. *v.a.* reifen, zur Reife *or* Vollendung bringen, vollenden, ausreifen lassen. 3. *v.n.* reifen, reif werden, ausreifen; fällig werden, verfallen (*C.L.*). **-ed** [-ˈtjʊ.əd], *adj.* ausgereift (*plan*); abgelagert (*wine*); fällig (*bill*). **-ity** [-ˈtjuːərɪtɪ], *s.* die Reife; Fälligkeit, Verfall(s)zeit (*of a bill*); *at* or *on -ity*, zur Verfall(s)zeit, bei Verfall (*of a bill.*).

matutinal [məˈtjuːtɪnəl], *adj.* morgendlich, früh, Morgen–.

maudlin [ˈmɔːdlɪn], *adj.* weinselig, benebelt; rührselig, gefühlvoll.

maul [mɔːl], 1. *s.* der Schlegel. 2. *v.a.* mißhandeln, durchprügeln; beschädigen, zerzausen; rücksichtslos anfassen, übel zurichten, scharf mitnehmen, herunterreißen (*by criticism*); *badly -ed*, schwer angeschlagen (*as troops*).

maulstick [ˈmɔːlstɪk], *s.* der Malerstock.

maunder [ˈmɔːndə], *v.n.* gedankenlos schlendern, dösen; faseln.

maundy [ˈmɔːndɪ], *s.* die Fußwaschung (*R.C.*). **--money,** die Almosenverteilung am Gründonnerstag. **--Thursday,** *s.* der Gründonnerstag.

mausoleum [ˈmɔːsəlɪəm], *s.* das Mausoleum, Grabmal.

mauve [moʊv], 1. *s.* die Malvenfarbe. 2. *adj.* hellviolett, malvenfarbig, mauve.

maverick [ˈmævərɪk], *s.* (*Amer.*) das Vieh ohne Brandzeichen; Kalb ohne Muttertier; (*fig.*) der Einzelgänger (*esp. Pol.*).

mavis [ˈmævɪs], *s.* (*Poet.*) die Singdrossel.

maw [mɔː], *s.* der (Tier)Magen; (*fig.*) Rachen, Schlund.

mawkish [ˈmɔːkɪʃ], *adj.* rührselig, gefühlsselig; süßlich. **-ness,** *s.* die Gefühlsduselei; Süßlichkeit.

maxilla [mækˈsɪlə], *s.* der Kinnbacken, die Kinnlade. **-ry** [-ərɪ], 1. *adj.* Kinnbacken–. 2. *s.* der Backenknochen.

maxim [ˈmæksɪm], *s.* die Maxime, der Grundsatz

maximum [ˈmæksɪməm], 1. *s.* das Maximum, der Höhepunkt; höchster Grad, Preis *or* Wert, der Höchstbetrag, Höchststand, die Höchstzahl, das Höchstmaß, Höchste. 2. *adj.* höchst, größt, Maximal–; – *load*, die Höchstbeanspruchung; – *price*, der Höchstpreis; – *thermometer*, das Maximalthermometer; – *wages*, der Spitzenlohn.

[1]**May** [meɪ], 1. *s.* der Mai, (*Poet., fig.*) Lenz, die Jugend; die Weißdornblüte (*Bot.*). **--day,** *s.* erster Mai. **--flower,** *s.* die Maiblume; der Primelstrauch (*Amer.*). **--fly,** *s.* die Eintagsfliege (*Ent.*). **-pole,** *s.* der Maibaum.

may [meɪ], *aux. v.* (only pres.; pret. *might*) mag, kann, darf; *pl.* mögen, können, dürfen; *aux. forming subjunctive, you – well ask*, du kannst gut fragen; *be that as it –*, es mag sein wie es will; *he – come today*, er kommt vielleicht heute; *come what –*, komme, was wolle; *– he go?* darf er gehen? *it might happen*, es könnte geschehen; *it might have happened*, es hätte geschehen können; *– it please your Majesty*, Euer Majestät mögen geruhen; *I am afraid he – not return*, ich fürchte, er kehrt nicht zurück; *I was afraid he might not return*, ich fürchtete, daß er nicht zurückkehrte. **-be** [-bɪ], *adv.*, (*archaic*) **-hap** [-hæp], *adv.* vielleicht, möglicherweise.

mayhem [ˈmeɪhəm], *s.* schwere Verletzung (*Law*).

mayonnaise [meɪjəˈneɪz], *s.* die Mayonnaise.

mayor [ˈmɛːə], *s.* der Bürgermeister; *Lord* –, der Oberbürgermeister. **-al** [-ərəl], *adj.* bürgermeisterlich. **-alty,** *s.* das Bürgermeisteramt; die Amtsdauer des Bürgermeisters. **-ess** [-ərɛs], *s.* die Bürgermeisterfrau (*as wife*); Bürgermeisterin (*in her own right*); *Lady -ess*, die Frau Oberbürgermeister.

mazarine [mæzəˈriːn], *adj.* dunkelblau.

maz-e [meɪz], 1. *s.* der Irrgarten, das Labyrinth; (*fig.*) die Verwirrung, Bestürzung; *be in a -e*, bestürzt *or* verwirrt sein. 2. *v.a.* (*esp. p.p.*) verwirren, bestürzt machen. **-y,** *adj.* labyrinthisch, verwickelt; wirr, verwirrt.

mazurka [məˈzəːkə], *s.* die Masurka.

me [miː], 1. *pers. pron.* (*Acc.*) mich; (*Dat.* also *to* –) mir; (*coll nom.*) ich; *dear – !* mein Gott; *not for the life of –*, nicht um alles in der Welt; (*coll.*) *it's –*, ich bin's. 2. *refl. pron.*; *I looked about –*, ich sah mich um; (*Poet.*) *I laid – down*, ich legte mich nieder.

[1]**mead** [miːd], *s.* der Met.

[2]**mead** [miːd], *s.* (*Poet.*) *see* **meadow.**

meadow [ˈmɛdoʊ], *s.* die Wiese, der Anger, die Flur, Matte **--grass,** das Rispengras (*Bot.*). **--lark,** die Feldlerche (*Orn.*). **--saffron,** *s.* die Herbstzeitlose (*Bot.*). **--sweet,** *s.* das Mehlkraut. **-y,** *adj.* Wiesen–, wiesenartig.

meagre [ˈmiːgə], *adj.* ärmlich, dürftig, kärglich (*of ideas, etc.*); unfruchtbar, dürr (*soil, etc.*); mager (*persons*). **-ness,** *s.* die Dürftigkeit, Ärmlichkeit, Armseligkeit; Dürre; Magerkeit.

[1]**meal** [miːl], *s.* das Mahl, die Mahlzeit; *eat* or *have a –*, eine Mahlzeit zu sich nehmen; *make a – of*, verzehren; *take one's -s*, essen, seine Mahlzeiten zu sich nehmen. **--time,** *s.* die Essenszeit.

[2]**meal** [miːl], *s.* (grobes) Mehl, (*Scots*) das Hafermehl. **-ie(s),** *s.* (*pl.*) der Mais (*in S. Africa*). **-iness,** *s.* die Mehligkeit. **-y,** *adj* mehlig; staubbedeckt; blaß. **-y-mouthed,** *adj.* nicht freimütig, zurückhaltend, kleinlaut, sanftredend, zimperlich, frömmelnd.

[1]**mean** [miːn], *adj* gering, unbedeutend; gemein, schäbig, geizig, knauserig, filzig, knickerig; niedrig (*rank, etc.*); ärmlich, armselig, erbärmlich (*as streets*); *no – achievement*, keine geringe Leistung; *no – artist*, ein Künstler von gewisser Bedeutung. **-ness,** *s* die Gemeinheit; Ärmlichkeit; Filzigkeit; Niedrigkeit. **--spirited,** *adj.* niederträchtig.

[2]**mean** [miːn], 1. *adj.* mittlere(r, s), Mittel–; mittelmäßig; durchschnittlich, Durchschnitts– (*Math.*); – *annual temperature*, mittlere Jahreswärme, das Wärmejahresmittel; – *chord*, die Profilsehne (*Av.*); – *sea level*, mittlerer Meeresspiegel, das Normalnull; – *number*, die Durchschnittszahl, der Mittelwert; – *time*, mittlere (Sonnen)Zeit (*Astr.*); – *value*, der Mittelwert 2. *s.* die Mitte, arithmetisches Mittel, die Durchschnittszahl (*Arith.*); *geometrical* –, geometrisches Mittel; *golden* or *happy* –, goldener Mittelweg. **-s,** *pl see* **means. -time, -while,** 1. *adv.* mittlerweile, unterdessen, indessen, inzwischen, einstweilen. 2. *s* die Zwischenzeit.

[3]**mean** [miːn], 1 *ir.v.a.* vorhaben, beabsichtigen, gedenken, im Sinn *or* Auge haben; willens, entschlossen *or* gesonnen sein (*with inf.*); meinen, sagen wollen; bedeuten, zu bedeuten haben (*to*, für); bestimmen (*for*, zu). (*a*) (*with nouns*) – *business*, Ernst machen, es ernst meinen, nicht spaßen; – *no harm*, es nicht böse meinen; – *a p. well* (*ill*), es gut (schlecht) mit einem meinen; *this -s war*, dies bedeutet *or* heißt Krieg. (*b*) (*with pronouns*) *you don't – it*, das kann nicht dein Ernst sein; *he -s it for our good*, er meint es gut mit uns; *say what one -s*, sagen was man im Sinne hat; *without -ing it*, ohne es zu wollen. (*c*) (*with verbs*) *I – to say*, ich will sagen; *I did not – to . .*, es war nicht meine Absicht zu . . .; *what do you – by this?* was meinen Sie damit *or* wollen Sie damit sagen? *what do you – by coming?* was fällt dir ein daß du kommst? 2 *ir.v.n.*; – *well* (*ill*), es gut (schlecht) meinen (*by*, mit); *see* **meaning.**

meander [miːˈændə], 1. *v.n.* sich winden, sich schlängeln; ziellos umherirren, mäandern. 2. *s.* die Windung, der Umweg; das Zierband, Mäanderlinien (*pl.*) (*Arch.*). **-ing** [-ərɪŋ], *adj.* gewunden; umherirrend.

meaning ['mɪ:nɪŋ], 1. *adj.* bedeutsam, bedeutungsvoll; *well-–*, wohlwollend. 2. *s.* die Bedeutung, der Sinn; *with –*, bedeutungsvoll; *what's the – of all this?* was soll dies alles heißen *or* bedeuten? *with the same –*, mit derselben Bedeutung. **–ful,** *adj.* bedeutungsvoll, bedeutsam. **–less,** *adj.* bedeutungslos; ausdruckslos.
meanness ['mɪ:nnɪs], *s. see* ¹**mean.**
means [mɪ:nz], *pl.* (*sing. & pl. constr.*) das (Hilfs)-Mittel, der Weg (*to an end*); (*pl. constr.*) (Geld)-mittel (*pl.*), das Vermögen. (*a*) (*with nouns & verbs*) *– of communication*, Verkehrsmittel (*pl.*); *– of conveyance*, see *– of transport*; *man of* (*independent*) *–*, bemittelter Mann; *– test*, der Bedürftigkeitsnachweis; *be a – of*, Schuld sein an (*Dat.*); *find the –*, Mittel und Wege finden; *– of transport*, Verkehrsmittel, Beförderungsmittel (*pl.*). (*b*) (*with prepositions*) *live beyond one's –*, über seine Verhältnisse leben; *by – of*, mittels, vermittelst; *by all –*, auf jeden Fall, auf alle Fälle, jedenfalls; sicherlich, ganz gewiß; *by fair –*, im guten, in Güte; *by foul –*, im bösen, mit Gewalt; *by no –*, auf keinen Fall, keinesfalls, keineswegs; *by no manner of –*, durchaus nicht, ganz gewiß nicht; *by some – or* (*an*)*other*, auf die eine oder andere Art; *by this* or *these –*, hierdurch, dadurch.
meant [mɛnt], *see* ³**mean.**
measl–ed ['mɪ:zəld], *adj.* finnig (*as pigs*). **–es** [–zəlz], *pl.* (*sing. constr.*) Masern (*pl.*) (*Med.*); Finnen (*pl.*) (*Vet.*); *German –es*, Röteln (*pl.*) (*Med.*). **–y** [–lɪ], *adj.* maserig (*Med.*), finnig (*Vet.*); fleckig; (*sl.*) erbärmlich, elend, wertlos.
measur–able ['mɛʒərəbl], *adj.* meßbar; (*fig.*) absehbar. **–e** ['mɛʒə], 1. *s.* das Maß (*also fig.*); Maßinstrument; die Maßeinheit, das Maßsystem; der Maßstab, das Verhältnis; Versmaß, Metrum (*Pros.*); der Takt (*Mus.*); die Maßregel, Maßnahme. (*a*) (*with adjectives & nouns*) *coercive –es*, Zwangsmaßnahmen (*pl.*); *common –e*, gemeinsamer Teiler (*Arith.*); *–e of capacity*, *cubic –e*, das Raummaß; *dry –e*, das Trockenmaß; *liquid –e*, das Flüssigkeitsmaß; *square –e*, *superficial –e*, das Flächenmaß; *tape –e*, das Meßband, Bandmaß; *temporary –e*, vorübergehende Maßnahme. (*b*) (*with verbs*) *make to –e*, nach Maß machen (*clothes*); *set –es*, Grenzen *or* Maß und Ziel setzen (*to* (*Dat.*)), begrenzen (*to* (*Acc.*)); *take a p.'s –e*, einem Maß nehmen (*for*, zu); (*fig.*) einen abschätzen *or* taxieren; *take legal –es*, den Rechtsweg einschlagen; *take –es*, Maßnahmen treffen, Maßregeln ergreifen (*against*, gegen); *tread a –e*, tanzen, sich im Takt drehen. (*c*) (*with prepositions*) *beyond –e*, über alle Maßen; *in –e as*, in dem Maße wie; *in a –e*, in gewissem Maße; *in* (*a*) *great –e*, in großem Maße, großenteils; *in some –e*, gewissermaßen. 2. *v.a.* messen (*also fig.*), abmessen, ausmessen (*material, etc.*), vermessen (*Surv.*); (*fig.*) abwägen, abschätzen (*by*, an), beurteilen (*by*, nach); *–e one's length*, der Länge nach hinfallen; *–e swords*, die Degen kreuzen; (*fig.*) sich messen (*with*, mit); *–e a p. for*, einem Maß nehmen; *–e the length of s.th.*, eine S. der Länge nach ausmessen; *–e a p. with one's eyes*, einen von oben bis unten messen. 3. *v.n.* messen, einen Umfang haben von; *it –es 2 ft.*, es ist zwei Fuß lang. **–ed** ['mɛʒəd], *adj.* (ab)gemessen (*also fig.*); regelmäßig, gleichmäßig, maßvoll, gemäßigt; *with –ed steps*, gemessenen Schrittes. **–eless,** *adj.* unermeßlich. **–ement** [–mənt], *s.* das Maß; Messen, die Messung; Größe, das Ausmaß. **–ing,** *s.* das Messen, die Messung. **–ing-instrument,** *s.* das Meßinstrument. **–ing-tape,** *s.* see *tape-–e.*
meat [mɪ:t], 1. *s.* das Fleisch; (*archaic*) die Speise; (*fig.*) der Gehalt, Inhalt, die Substanz; *butcher –*, (*Scots*) das Fleisch; *canned* or *tinned –*, das Büchsenfleisch; *frozen –*, das Gefrierfleisch; *mince–*, eine Pastetenfüllung aus gemischtem Trockenobst; *minced –*, Gehackte(s), *n.*, das Hackfleisch; *pickled –*, das Pökelfleisch; *potted –*, eingemachtes Fleisch; *preserved –*, die Fleischkonserve; *roast –*, der Braten; *it is – and drink to me*, es ist für mich ein großer Genuß (*with inf.*); (*Prov.*) *one man's – is another man's poison*, des einen Tod ist des andern Brot. **–-ball,** *s.* das Fleischklößchen. **–-chopper,** *s.* das Hackmesser. **–-jack,** *s.* der Bratenwender. **–less,** *adj.* fleischlos. **–-pie,** *s.* die Fleischpastete. **–-safe,** *s.* der Speiseschrank, Fliegenschrank. **–-tea,** *s.* die Abendmahlzeit mit kalter Platte. **–y,** *adj.* fleischig; (*fig.*) (*sl.*) kernig, markig, gehaltvoll.
meatus [mɪ'eɪtəs], *s.* der Gang, Kanal (*Anat.*).
mechani–c [mə'kænɪk], *s.* der Mechaniker, Maschinist, Monteur; Handwerker; *flight –c*, der Bordwart (*Av.*). **–cal** [–ɪkl], *adj.* Maschinen–, mechanisch; (*fig.*) handwerksmäßig, automatisch; *–cal engineering*, der Maschinenbau; *–cal equivalent of heat*, mechanisches Wärmeäquivalent; *–cal properties*, Fertigkeitseigenschaften (*pl.*). **–calness,** *s.* das Mechanische. **–cian** [mɛkə'nɪʃən], *s.* (*archaic*) der Mechaniker; Maschinenmaat (*Navy*). **–cs,** *s.* (*sing. constr.*) die Mechanik. **–sm** ['mɛkənɪzm], *s.* der Mechanismus, das Triebwerk; die Technik (*Art*); mechanistische Auffassung (*Phil.*). **–st** [–ɪst], *s.* (*archaic*) der Mechaniker; mechanistischer Philosoph (*Phil.*). **–stic** [–'nɪstɪk], *adj.* mechanistisch. **–zation,** *s.* die Mechanisierung, Motorisierung (*Mil.*). **–ze,** *v.a.* mechanisieren, motorisieren (*Mil.*); *–zed unit*, mechanisierter Verband (*Mil.*).
mecon–ic [mɛ'kɔnɪk], *adj.*; *–ic acid*, die Mekonsäure, Mohnsäure (*Chem.*). **–ium** [mɛ'kounɪəm], *s.* das Kindspech (*Med.*).
medal ['mɛdl], *s.* die Denkmünze, Medaille, das Ehrenabzeichen, der Orden. **–lion** [mə'dælɪən], *s.* die Medaille, das Medaillon. **–list** ['mɛdəlɪst], *s.* der Medaillenschneider; Münzenkenner; Inhaber einer Ehrenmedaille.
meddle ['mɛdl], *v.n.* sich (unberufen) befassen *or* abgeben (*with*, mit), sich einlassen (*with*, in (*Acc.*)); sich (ein)mischen (*in*, in (*Acc.*)); *– with things that don't concern one*, sich mit Sachen abgeben, die einen nicht angehen. **–r,** *s.* einer, der sich in fremde Angelegenheiten mischt, Unberufene(r), *m.* **–some** [–səm], *adj.* zudringlich, aufdringlich, vorwitzig, lästig, naseweis. **–someness,** *s.* die Zudringlichkeit, Aufdringlichkeit.
media ['mɪ:dɪə], *s.* stimmhafter Verschlußlaut, die Media (*Phonet.*).
mediaeval [mɛdɪ'ɪ:vəl], *adj. see* **medieval.**
media–l ['mɪ:dɪəl], *adj.* mittlere(r, s); inlautend (*Phonet.*); *–l sound*, der Inlaut (*Phonet.*). **–lly,** *adv.* in der Mitte liegend; im Inlaut (*Phonet.*). **–n** [–ɪən], 1. *adj.* in der Mitte liegend (*usually scientific*), mittlere(r, s) (*statistics*); *–n line*, die Mittellinie (*Geog.*, *Bot.*). 2. *s.* die Mittellinie; der Mittelwert (*statistics*). **–nt** [–ɪənt], *s.* die Mediante (*Mus.*). **–te** [–ɪeɪt], 1. *adj.* mittelbar, indirekt. 2. *v.n.* vermitteln, sich ins Mittel schlagen (*between*, zwischen (*Dat.*)); ein Bindeglied bilden. 3. *v.a.* vermitteln, zustande bringen (*armistice, etc.*). **–tion** [–ɪ'eɪʃən], *s.* die Vermittlung, Fürbitte. **–tize** [–ətaɪz], *v.a.* mediatisieren, der Landeshoheit unterwerfen; einverleiben. **–tor** [–ɪeɪtə], *s.* der Vermittler, Fürbitter; Mittler (*Theol.*). **–torial** [–ɪə'tɔ:rɪəl], *adj.* vermittelnd, fürbittend, Vermittler–, Mittler–; *–torial office of Christ*, das Mittleramt Christi. **–torship,** *s.* das Mittleramt. **–trix** [–'eɪtrɪks], *s.* die Vermittlerin; die Fürbitterin.
medic ['mɛdɪk], *s.* (*sl.*) der Arzt, Mediziner. **–able** [–əbl], *adj.* heilbar. **–al** [–əl], *adj.* ärztlich, medizinisch, Kranken–, Sanitäts–, Heil–; *–al advice*, ärztlicher Rat; *–al attendant*, der Hausarzt; *–al board*, die Sanitätsbehörde; *Royal Army –al Corps*, das Sanitätskorps; *–al jurisprudence*, gerichtliche Medizin; *–al man*, der Arzt, Mediziner; *–al officer*, der Sanitätsoffizier (*Mil.*); *–al officer of health*, der Amtsarzt; *–al orderly*, der Sanitäter (*Mil.*); *–al practitioner*, praktischer Arzt; *–al service*, das Sanitätswesen, der Gesundheitsdienst; die Staatskrankenkasse; *–al student*, der Mediziner, Medizinstudent; *–al superintendent*, der Chefarzt. **–ament** [–'dɪkəmənt], *s.* das Heilmittel, die Arznei. **–ate** [–eɪt], *v.a.* mit Arznei versetzen, vermischen *or* imprägnieren; medizinisch behandlen; *–ated soap*, medizinische Seife. **–ation** [–'keɪʃən], *s.* das Vermischen *or* die Imprägnierung (mit etwas medizinischem); medizinische Behandlung. **–ative,** *adj.*

heilkräftig, heilsam. **–inal** [–ˈdɪsɪnəl], *adj.* medizinisch, heilkräftig, heilsam, Heil–; *–inal herbs*, Arzneikräuter; *–inal properties*, Heilkräfte; *–inal springs*, Heilquellen. **–ine** [ˈmɛdsɪn], *s.* die Arznei, Medizin; Heilkunde, Heilkunst, Medizin; der Zauber; *student of –ine*, der Student der Medizin, Mediziner; *–ine ball*, der Medizinball; *–ine-chest*, der Arzneischrank, die Hausapotheke; *–ine-man*, der Medizinmann. **–o** [–koʊ], *s.* (*coll.*) der Arzt.

medieval [mɛdɪˈɪ:vəl], *adj.* mittelalterlich. **–ism,** *s.* die Mittelalterlichkeit; Vorliebe für das Mittelalter. **–ist,** *s.* der Forscher des Mittelalters.

mediocr–e [ˈmɪ:dɪoʊkə], *adj.* mittelmäßig, zweitklassig. **–ity** [–ˈɔkrɪtɪ], *s.* die Mittelmäßigkeit; unbedeutender Mensch.

meditat–e [ˈmɛdɪteɪt], 1. *v.n.* nachdenken, nachsinnen, grübeln (*on* or *upon*, über (*Acc.*)), überlegen (*Acc.*). 2. *v.a.* im Sinne haben, sinnen auf, beabsichtigen. **–ion** [–ˈteɪʃən], *s.* das Nachdenken, Nachsinnen; die Andacht, fromme Betrachtung. **–ive,** *adj.* nachdenklich, sinnend. **–iveness,** *s.* die Nachdenklichkeit.

medium [ˈmɪ:dɪəm], 1. *adj.* mittlere(r, s), Mittel–, Durchschnitts–; – *paper*, das Medianpapier; – *price*, der Durchschnittspreis; – *size*, mittlere Größe, die Mittelgröße; Durchschnittsgröße; *of – size*, *–-sized*, mittelgroß; – *wave*, mittlere Wellenlänge (*Rad.*). 2. *s.* (pl. *–s & media*) die Mitte, der Mittelweg, Mittelsatz, das Mittelglied, Mittelding; Mittelwerkzeug, die Vermittlung, das Medium (*also spiritualism*); der Träger, das Agens (*Phys.*); Lebenselement, Milieu, die Umgebung, Lebensbedingungen (*pl.*); der Nährboden (*Biol.*); *by* or *through the – of*, durch (die) Vermittlung von. **–istic** [–ˈmɪstɪk], *adj.* Medium– (*spiritualism*).

medlar [ˈmɛdlə], *s.* die Mispel; der Mehlbeerbaum (*Bot.*).

medley [ˈmɛdlɪ], 1. *s.* das Gemisch, der Mischmasch, das Potpourri (*Mus.*). 2. *adj.* gemischt, bunt.

medulla [məˈdʌlə], *s.* das (Rücken)Mark. **–ry** [–rɪ], *adj.* Mark–, markig.

meed [mɪ:d], *s.* (*Poet.*) die Belohnung, der Lohn.

meek [mɪ:k], *adj.* sanft(mütig); demütig, bescheiden; *as – as a lamb*, lammfromm. **–ness,** *s.* die Sanftmut; Demut.

meerschaum [ˈmɪ:əʃəm], *s.* der Meerschaum; (also *–-pipe*), *s.* die Meerschaumpfeife.

[1]**meet** [mɪ:t], **1.** *ir.v.a.* begegnen (*Dat.*); treffen (*Acc.*); stoßen auf (*Acc.*); zusammentreffen mit, münden in; feindlich entgegentreten (*Dat.*); entgegenkommen (*Dat.*) (*views, opinions, etc.*); antworten auf, entgegnen (*Dat.*); widerlegen (*objections, etc.*); entsprechen, nachkommen (*Dat.*), erfüllen (*wishes, obligations, etc.*); honorieren (*bill*); tragen, bestreiten (*expenses*); – *s.o. at the station*, einen vom Bahnhof abholen; *be met*, empfangen werden; *come* (*go*) *to –*, entgegenkommen (entgegengehen) (*Dat.*); – *the case*, tun was nötig ist, dem Zweck entsprechen; – *competition*, dem Wettbewerb entgegentreten; – *all contingencies*, gegen alle unvorhergesehene Fälle gewappnet werden; *in order to – your demands* (*the exigencies of the case*), um Ihrem Verlangen (den Umständen) gerecht zu werden; – *the ear*, zu Gehör kommen, das Ohr treffen; – *a p.'s eye*, einem ins Auge fallen; – *one's match*, seinen Mann finden; – *one's reward*, den Lohn erhalten; – *a p. half-way*, einem auf halbem Wege entgegenkommen (*usually fig.*); *well met!* gut daß wir uns treffen, das trifft sich gut; *pleased to – you*, sehr erfreut, Sie kennen zu lernen *or* Ihre Bekanntschaft zu machen. **2.** *ir.v.n.* sich (*Dat.*) *or* einander begegnen, sich treffen, sich kennenlernen; zusammentreffen, zusammentreten, zusammenkommen, sich versammeln, sich vereinigen; sich berühren; zusammenstoßen (*as enemies*); *make both ends –*, auskommen; – *with*, (*sl.*) – *up with*, zufällig stoßen auf, zufällig treffen; erleiden, erfahren; – *with an accident*, verunglücken, einen Unfall haben; – *with approval*, gebilligt werden; – *with a denial*, bestritten *or* verneint werden (*of a statement*); – *with difficulties*, auf Schwierigkeiten stoßen; – *with a loss*, einen Verlust erleiden; – *with a good reception*, gut aufgenommen werden; – *with a refusal*, abgewiesen werden, eine abschlägige Antwort bekommen. **3.** *s.* das (Zusammen)Treffen; die Jagdzusammenkunft. **–ing** [–ɪŋ], *s.* die Begegnung, Zusammenkunft; Versammlung, Sitzung, Tagung, Konferenz; Versammlungsteilnehmer (*pl.*); das Zusammentreffen (*of two lines*); der Zusammenfluß (*of rivers*); das Treffen (*Sport*); Stelldichein, Rendezvous; *at a –ing*, auf einer Sitzung; *call a –ing for 10 a.m.*, eine Versammlung auf 10 Uhr einberufen. **–ing-house,** *s.* das Bethaus (*of Quakers*). **–ing-place,** *s.* der Versammlungsort. **–ing-point,** *s.* der Treffpunkt, Berührungspunkt. **–ing-room,** *s.* der Sitzungssaal.

[2]**meet** [mɪ:t], *adj.* (*archaic*) passend, geeignet; schicklich.

mega–cephalic [mɛgəsɛˈfælɪk], *adj.* großköpfig. **–cycle** [–saɪkl], das Megahertz (*Rad.*). **–lith** [ˈmɛgəlɪθ], *s.* der Megalith, großer Steinblock. **–lithic** [–ˈlɪθɪk], *adj.* megalithisch. **–lomania** [–ləˈmeɪnɪə], *s.* der Größenwahn. **–phone** [ˈmɛgəfoʊn], *s.* das Megaphon, Sprachrohr, der Schalltrichter. **–therium** [–ˈθɪ:ərɪəm], *s.* das Riesenfaultier.

megass [məˈgæs], *s.* die Bagasse.

megger [ˈmɛgə], *s.* (*coll.*) der Isolationsmesser (*Elec.*).

megilp [məˈgɪlp], *s.* der Leinölfirnis.

megohm [ˈmɛgoʊm], *s.* eine Million Ohm, die Einheit des Widerstandes (*Elec.*).

megrim [ˈmɪ:grɪm], *s.* die Migräne; Grille; *pl.* Schwermut, Melancholie; der Koller (*Vet.*).

meiosis [maɪˈoʊsɪs], *s.* die Litotes.

melanchol–ia [mɛlənˈkoʊlɪə], *s.* die Schwermut, Melancholie. **–iac** [–ɪək], *s. see* **–ic** 2. **–ic** [–ˈkɔlɪk], 1. *adj.* schwermütig, melancholisch. 2. *s.* der Melancholiker. **–y** [ˈmɛlənkəlɪ], 1. *s.* die Melancholie; Schwermut, der Trübsinn. 2. *adj.* schwermütig, trübsinnig, melancholisch; düster, traurig.

mélange [meˈlɑ:nʒ], *s.* die Mischung, das Gemisch.

melan–ism [ˈmɛlənɪzm], *s.* der Melanismus, die Schwarzsucht. **–osis** [–ˈnoʊsɪs], *s.* die Melanose, abnorme Schwärze.

melee [ˈmɛleɪ], *s.* das Handgemenge.

meliorat–e [ˈmɪ:lɪəreɪt], *v.a.* (ver)bessern. **–ion,** *s.* die (Ver)besserung.

melli–ferous [məˈlɪfərəs], *adj.* honigtragend. **–fluence** [–fluəns], *s.* der Honigfluß; die Lieblichkeit. **–fluent** [–fluənt], *adj.* (*archaic*), **–fluous** [–fluəs], *adj.* (*fig.*) honigsüß; lieblich.

mellow [ˈmɛloʊ], 1. *adj.* reif, saftig (*of fruit*); weich, mürbe; sanft (*in tone*); mild (*as wine*); gereift, ausgereift (*as age*); heiter, freundlich; (*sl.*) angeheitert, benebelt. 2. *v.a.* mild *or* weich machen; reif machen, reifen lassen. 3. *v.n.* mild *or* weich *or* mürbe *or* reif werden, reifen; sich mildern, ausreifen. **–ness,** *s.* die Reife, Mürbheit (*of fruit*); Milde, Sanftheit, Weichheit, Gereiftheit.

melod–ic [məˈlɔdɪk], *adj.*, **–ious** [–ˈloʊdɪəs], *adj.* melodisch, wohlklingend. **–iousness,** *s.* der Wohlklang. **–ist** [ˈmɛlədɪst], *s.* der Sänger *or* Komponist von Liedern. **–rama** [ˈmɛlodrɑ:mə], *s.* das Melodrama; Volksstück; (*fig.*) die Sensation. **–ramatic** [–drəˈmætɪk], *adj.* melodramatisch. **–y** [ˈmɛlədɪ], *s.* die Melodie, Singweise; der Wohlklang, Wohllaut; die Weise, das Lied, der Gesang.

melon [ˈmɛlən], *s.* die Melone.

melt [mɛlt], 1. *v.a.* schmelzen, zerlassen, zerfließen lassen (*into*, in); weich machen, rühren (*persons*); – *down*, einschmelzen, zusammenschmelzen. 2. *v.n.* schmelzen, zerschmelzen; sich auflösen, schwinden, zergehen (*clouds, etc.*); aufgehen, übergehen (*into*, in (*Acc.*)); auftauen (*of persons*); – *in the mouth*, auf der Zunge schmelzen; – *into tears*, in Tränen zerfließen; – *away*, zerschmelzen, zergehen, zusammenschmelzen, schwinden. **–ing,** 1. *adj.* schmelzend; rührend, schmachtend, weich, sanft; *–ing point*, der Schmelzpunkt, Fließpunkt; *–ing pot*, der Schmelztiegel; *be in the –ing pot*, in völliger Umgestaltung begriffen sein; *put into the –ing pot*, (*fig.*) gänzlich ummodeln. 2. *s.* das Schmelzen.

member [ˈmɛmbə], 1. *s.* das Glied (*Anat.*, *Math.* & *fig.*); der Teil; das Mitglied; – *of parliament*, Abgeordnete(r), *m.* 2. *attrib. adj.* Glied–. **–ed,** *adj.* gegliedert; (*in comp.*) –gliedrig. **–ship,** *s.* die Mitgliedschaft, Zugehörigkeit; Mitgliederzahl. **–ship-card,** *s.* die Mitgliedskarte.

membran–e [ˈmɛmbreɪn], *s.* das Häutchen, die Membran(e); *–e of a cell*, die Zellwand (*Bot.*); *mucous –e*, die Schleimhaut. **–(e)ous** [ˈmɛmbrənəs, mɛmˈbreɪnəs], *adj.* häutig, Membran–.

memento [məˈmɛntoʊ], *s.* (pl. *–es*) das Erinnerungszeichen, Andenken (*of*, an); – *mori*, die Todesmahnung.

memo [ˈmɛmoʊ], *s.* (*coll.*) die Notiz, der Vermerk (*of*, über); *see* **memorandum.**

memoir [ˈmɛmwɑː], *s.* die Denkschrift, der Bericht; wissenschaftliche Abhandlung; *pl.* Memoiren, (Lebens)Erinnerungen, Aufzeichnungen (*pl.*).

memora–bilia [mɛmərəˈbɪlɪə], *pl.* Denkwürdigkeiten (*pl.*). **–ble** [ˈmɛmərəbl], *adj.* denkwürdig, erinnerungswert. **–bleness,** *s.* die Denkwürdigkeit. **–ndum** [–ˈrændəm], *s.* (pl. *–nda*) der Vermerk, die Notiz (*of*, über); das Memorandum, Merkblatt, die Denkschrift, Eingabe (*Pol.*); die Nota, Rechnung (*C.L.*). **memo(randum)-book,** *s.* das Notizbuch.

memori–al [məˈmɔːrɪəl], 1. *adj.* zum Andenken (dienend), Gedächtnis–, Gedenk–; *–al service*, die Gedenkfeier. 2. *s.* das Denkmal, Ehrenmal; Andenken, die Denkschrift; Bittschrift, Eingabe; Klageschrift (*Law*); *as a* or *in –al of*, zum Andenken an. **–alist,** *s.* der Unterzeichner einer Bittschrift, Bittsteller. **–alize,** *v.a.* eine Bittschrift einreichen (*a p.*, einem); erinnern an (*a th.*). **–ze** [ˈmɛmərɑɪz], *v.a.* auswendig lernen; (*archaic*) zur Erinnerung aufzeichnen.

memory [ˈmɛmərɪ], *s.* das Gedächtnis, Erinnerungsvermögen; Andenken, die Erinnerung (*of*, an); *that has escaped my –*, das ist mir entfallen; *from –*, auswendig, aus dem Gedächtnis; *in the – of man*, seit Menschengedenken; *in – of*, zum Andenken an (*Acc.*); *of blessed –*, seligen Andenkens; *if my – serves me right*, wenn ich mich recht entsinne; *commit to –*, auswendig lernen; *within living –*, noch in Erinnerung vieler Lebenden.

men [mɛn], *see* **man. –folk,** *s.* (*coll.*) Mannsleute (*pl.*), Mannsbilder (*pl.*).

menac–e [ˈmɛnəs], 1. *s.* die Drohung, drohende Gefahr (*to*, für), die Bedrohung (*to* (*Dat.*)). 2. *v.a.* drohen (*Dat.*), bedrohen, gefährden. **–ing,** *adj.* drohend, bedrohlich.

ménage [ˈmɛnɑːʒ], *s.* der Haushalt.

menagerie [məˈnædʒərɪ], *s.* die Menagerie, Tierschau.

mend [mɛnd], 1. *v.a.* reparieren, ausbessern; flicken (*clothes*); (*archaic*) besser machen, (ver)bessern; – *a fire*, das Feuer schüren; – *one's pace*, den Schritt beschleunigen; – *one's ways*, sich bessern. 2. *v.n.* besser werden, sich bessern, genesen; *be –ing*, auf dem Wege der Besserung sein. 3. *s.* die Ausbesserung, ausgebesserte Stelle; *on the –*, see *be –ing*. **–ing,** *s.* das Ausbessern, Flicken, Stopfen; *invisible –ing*, das Kunststopfen; *–ing-wool*, die Stopfwolle.

mendaci–ous [mɛnˈdeɪʃəs], *adj.* lügnerisch, lügenhaft, verlogen. **–ty** [–ˈdæsɪtɪ], *s.* die Lügenhaftigkeit, Verlogenheit.

mendic–ancy [ˈmɛndɪkənsɪ], *s.* die Bettelei. **–ant** [–kənt], 1. *adj.* bettelnd; Bettel–. 2. *s.* der Bettler; Bettelmönch (*R.C.*). **–ity** [–ˈdɪsɪtɪ], *s.* der Bettelstand, das Bettelwesen; die Bettelei; *reduce to –ity*, an den Bettelstab bringen.

mending [ˈmɛndɪŋ], *see* **mend.**

menfolk [ˈmɛnfoʊk], *see* **men.**

menhaden [mɛnˈheɪdn], *s.* der Bunker (*Ichth.*).

menhir [ˈmɛnɪə], *s.* der Druidenstein, Hünenstein.

menial [ˈmiːnɪəl], 1. *adj.* gemein, niedrig, knechtisch; Gesinde–. 2. *s.* der Diener, Knecht; *pl.* das Gesinde.

mening–es [mɪːˈnɪŋgɪːz], *pl.* Hirnhäute (*pl.*) **–itis** [mɛnɪnˈdʒɑɪtəs], *s.* die Hirnhautentzündung. **–ocele** [mɛˈnɪŋoʊsɪːl], *s.* der Hirnhautbruch.

menisc–us [məˈnɪskəs], *s.* (pl. *–i*) konvex-konkave Linse, das Meniskenglas (*Opt.*).

menopause [ˈmɛnopɔːz], *s.* Wechseljahre (*pl.*), das Klimakterium.

mens–es [ˈmɛnsɪːz], *pl.* der Monatsfluß; (*coll.*) die Regel. **–trual** [–strʊəl], *adj.* monatlich; Monats– (*Astr.*); Menstruations–. **–truate** [–strʊeɪt], *v.n.* menstruieren; (*coll.*) die Regel haben. **–truation** [–ˈeɪʃən], *s.* die Menstruation, der Monatsfluß, (*coll.*) die Regel.

mensura–bility [mɛnʃərəˈbɪlɪtɪ], *s.* die Meßbarkeit. **–ble** [–əbl], *adj.* meßbar. **–tion** [–ˈreɪʃən], *s.* das Abmessen, die Messung, Vermessung; Meßkunst.

mental [mɛntl], 1. *adj.* geistig, Geistes–; (*coll.*) geisteskrank; – *arithmetic*, das Kopfrechnen; – *case*, (*coll.*) Geisteskranke(r), *m.*; – *disease* or *disorder*, die Geisteskrankheit, Geistesstörung; – *hospital*, die Nervenklinik, Irrenanstalt; – *patient*, see – *case*; – *power*, die Geisteskraft; – *reservation*, geistiger Vorbehalt (*Theol.* & *fig.*); – *state*, der Geisteszustand. **–ity** [–ˈtælɪtɪ], *s.* die Geistesrichtung, Denkungsart, Denkweise, Mentalität.

menthol [mɛnθl], *s.* das Menthol.

mention [ˈmɛnʃən], 1. *s.* die Erwähnung; *honourable –*, ehrenvolle Erwähnung; *make – of*, erwähnen. 2. *v.a.* erwähnen; *not to –*, geschweige denn; *don't – it!* bitte sehr! gern geschehen! *not worth –ing*, nicht der Rede wert. **–able** [–əbl], *adj.* erwähnenswert.

mentor [ˈmɛntɔː], *s.* treuer Ratgeber, der Berater, Mentor.

menu [ˈmɛnjʊ], *s.* die Speisenfolge, das Menü; die Speisekarte.

mephiti–c [mɛˈfɪtɪk], *adj.* verpestet, giftig; *–c air*, see **–s. –s,** *s.* die Stickluft, faule Ausdünstung.

mercantil–e [ˈməːkəntɑɪl], *adj.* Handels–, handeltreibend, kaufmännisch; *–e classes*, kaufmännische Klassen, der Kaufmannsstand; *–e marine*, die Handelsmarine; *–e system* or *theory*, das Merkantilsystem; *–e town*, die Handelsstadt. **–ism** [–ˈkæntɪlɪzm], *s.* der Merkantilismus, das Merkantilsystem.

mercenar–iness [ˈməːsənərɪnɪs], *s.* die Käuflichkeit, Feilheit. **–y** [–ərɪ], 1. *adj.* feil, käuflich; gewinnsüchtig; *–y marriage*, die Geldheirat; *–y soldiers*, Söldner, gedungene Soldaten, Lohntruppen. 2. *s.* der Söldner.

mercer [ˈməːsə], *s.* der Seidenhändler, Schnittwarenhändler. **–ize** [–rɑɪz], *v.a.* merzerisieren (*cotton*), Seidenglanz geben (*Dat.*). **–y** [–rɪ], *s.* Seidenwaren, Schnittwaren (*pl.*); das Schnittwarengeschäft.

merchan–dise [ˈməːtʃəndɑɪz], *s.* (*no pl.*) Waren, Handelswaren, Güter (*pl.*); *article of –dise*, die Ware. **–t** [–ənt], 1. *s.* der Kaufmann, Großhändler, Handelsherr; Krämer; *the –ts*, die Kaufmannschaft; (*sl.*) Bursche, die Person; (*sl.*) *speed –t*, rücksichtsloser Fahrer. 2. *adj.* Handels–, Kaufmanns–. **–table,** *adj.* gangbar, marktfähig. **–tman,** *s.* das Handelsschiff, Kauffahrteischiff. **–t prince,** *s.* der Großkaufmann, Handelsfürst. **–t service,** *s.* die Handelsschiffahrt. **–t-tailor,** *s.* der Schneidermeister und Tuchhändler.

merci–ful [ˈməːsɪfʊl], *adj.* barmherzig, mitleidvoll; gnädig (*as God*); (*coll.*) erfreulich. **–fully,** *adv.* (*coll.*) erfreulicherweise. **–fulness,** *s.* die Barmherzigkeit, Gnade. **–less,** *adj.* unbarmherzig, erbarmungslos, schonungslos, hartherzig, grausam. **–lessness,** *s.* die Unbarmherzigkeit, Grausamkeit; *see* **mercy.**

mercur–ial [məːˈkjʊərɪəl], 1. *adj.* Quecksilber–, Merkur–, quecksilberhaltig, merkurialisch; (*fig.*) lebhaft, beweglich, unbeständig. **–ialism,** *s.* die Quecksilbergiftung. **–ialize,** *v.a.* mit Quecksilber behandeln. **–ic** [–ˈkjʊrɪk], *adj.* Quecksilber–; *–ic chloride*, das Sublimat. **–ous** [–ˈkjʊrəs], *adj. see* **–ic. –y** [ˈməːkjərɪ], *s.* das Quecksilber (*Chem.*); der Merkur (*Myth.*, *Astr.*); (*fig.*) Bote; *the –y is rising*, das Barometer steigt.

mercy [ˈməːsɪ], *s.* die Barmherzigkeit, das Mitleid, Erbarmen; die Gnade; (*coll.*) Wohltat, der Segen; *at s.o.'s –*, einem auf Gnade und Ungnade ausgeliefert, in jemandes Gewalt; *at the – of s.th.*, einer S. preisgegeben; (*coll.*) *it is a – that . . .*, es ist ein Segen *or* eine wahre Wohltat daß . . .; *Lord have – upon us!* Herr erbarme Dich unser!; *Sister* *of* –, barmherzige Schwester; *throw o.s. on s.o.'s* –, sich einem auf Gnade und Ungnade ergeben; – *on us!* Gott sei uns gnädig! *have – on him*, sich seiner erbarmen; *leave to the tender mercies of*, der Gnade jemandes ausliefern; *show – to him* or *show him* –, see *have – on him*; *small* –, wenig Rücksicht; *be thankful for small mercies*, sich mit wenigem zufrieden geben. **--killing,** *s.* der Gnadentod, die Euthanasie. **--seat,** *s.* der Gnadenstuhl (Gottes).

[1]**mere** ['mɪ:ə], *adj.* bloß, nichts als; allein, rein, lauter; *no – imitator*, kein bloßer *or* nicht nur Nachahmer; *the –st chance*, der reinste Zufall. **–ly,** *adv.* nur, bloß, lediglich.

[2]**mere** ['mɪ:ə], *s.* der Weiher, See.

meretricious [mɛrɪ'trɪʃəs], *adj.* buhlerisch; (*fig.*) verführerisch; unecht, hohl, kitschig.

merganser [mə.'gænsə], *s.* der Mittelsäger, Schopfsäger (*Orn.*).

merge [mə·dʒ], 1. *v.a.* verschmelzen (*in*, mit), aufgehen lassen (*in*, in); aufheben, tilgen (*Law*); *be –d in*, aufgehen in. 2. *v.n.* verschmelzen (*in*, mit), aufgehen (*in*, in (*Dat.*)). **–nce** [–əns], *s.* das Verschmelzen (*into*, mit), Aufgehen (*in*, in). **–r** [–ə], *s.* das Aufgehen (*Law*); die Verschmelzung, Vereinigung, der Zusammenschluß (*C.L., Pol.*).

mericarp ['mɛrɪka:p], *s.* die Teilfrucht (*Bot.*).

meridi–an [mə'rɪdɪən], 1. *s.* der Meridian, die Mittagslinie, der Längenkreis (*Geog.*); (*Poet.*) Mittag; Kulminationspunkt (*of sun or star*); (*fig.*) Höhepunkt, Gipfel. 2. *adj.* Mittags–, mittäglich; (*fig.*) höchst; *–an altitude*, die Mittagshöhe. **–onal,** 1. *adj.* mittäglich, südlich. 2. *s.* der Südländer.

meringue [mə'ræŋ], *s.* das Baiser, Schaumgebäck, die Meringe.

merino [mə'rɪ:noʊ], *s.* das Merinoschaf. **--wool,** *s.* die Merinowolle

merit ['mɛrɪt], 1. *s.* das Verdienst; der Wert, die Vortrefflichkeit, der Vorzug; *pl.* Hauptpunkte (*pl.*) (*Law*); *enquire into the –s of a case*, der Sache auf den Grund gehen; *on the –s of the case*, nach Lage der Dinge; *make a – of a th.*, sich etwas aus einer S. zugute tun; *in order of* –, nach Verdienst *or* Leistung geordnet; *Order of* –, der Verdienstorden; *on its own –s*, nach dem inneren Wert, für sich allein, gesondert. 2. *v.a* verdienen. **–ed,** *adj.* (wohl)verdient. **–orious** [–'tɔ.rɪəs], *adj.* verdienstlich. **–oriousness,** *s* die Verdienstlichkeit.

merle [mə:l], *s* die Amsel (*Orn.*).

merlin ['mə:lɪn], *s.* der Zwergfalke, Merlin (*Orn.*).

merlon ['mə·lən], *s.* die Mauerzacke, Schartenbacke (*Fort.*).

mer–maid ['mə:meɪd], *s.* die Seejungfer, Wassernixe. **–man** [–mən], *s.* der Nix, Wassermann; Triton (*Myth.*)

merr–iment ['mɛrɪmənt], *s.* die Fröhlichkeit, Lustigkeit, Belustigung. **–iness,** *s.* die Heiterkeit, der Frohsinn. **–y,** *adj.* lustig, vergnügt, fröhlich; scherzhaft, ergötzlich, spaßhaft; (*coll.*) angeheitert, beschwipst; *–y Christmas!* fröhliche Weihnachten! *as –y as a cricket*, kreuzfidel; *–y England*, das fröhliche (Alt)England; *make –y*, vergnügt sein, sich belustigen, sich lustig machen (*over*, über (*Acc.*)); *the more the –ier*, je mehr desto besser **–y-andrew,** *s.* der Hanswurst. **–y-go-round,** *s.* das Karussell. **–y-making,** *s.* die Belustigung, Lustbarkeit, das Fest. **–y-thought,** *s.* das Gabelbein, Brustbein (*of poultry*).

mésalliance [meza'lɪ:ɑ:ns], *s.* die Mißheirat.

meseems [mɪ'sɪ:mz], *imp.v.* (*archaic*) es scheint mir.

mesenter–ic [mɛsɛn'tɛrɪk], *adj.* Gekröse–. **–y** ['mɛsəntərɪ], *s.* das Gekröse.

mesh [mɛʃ], 1. *s.* die Masche; *pl.* das Netzwerk; (*fig.*) die Schlingen, Stricke (*pl.*); *in* –, ineinandergreifend, zusammenarbeitend (*of gears*). 2 *v.a.* im Netz fangen; (*fig.*) bestricken, umstricken, verstricken, umgarnen. 3. *v.n.* ineinandergreifen, sich verbinden (*of gears*). **--connexion,** *s.* die Dreieckschaltung (*Elec.*). **–ed,** *adj. suff.*; *e.g close* or *fine –ed*, engmaschig. **--work,** *s.* das Netzwerk, Maschen (*pl.*), das Gespinnst.

mesmeri–c [mɛz'mɛrɪk], *adj.* hypnotisch, heilmagnetisch. **–sm** ['mɛzmərɪzm], *s.* tierischer Magnetismus, der Heilmagnetismus. **–st,** *s.* der Heilmagnetiseur. **–ze,** *v.a.* hypnotisieren; (*fig.*) fesseln, faszinieren.

mesne [mɪ:n], *adj.* dazwischentretend, Mittel–, Zwischen– (*Law*); – *lord*, der Afterlehnsherr; – *process*, der Nebenprozeß.

meso– ['mɛsoʊ], *adj. prefix* (*in compounds*) mittel–. **–lithic** [–'lɪθɪk], *adj.* mesolithisch, mittelsteinzeitlich. **–thorax,** *s.* der Mittelbrustring (*Ent.*). **–zoic** [–'zoʊɪk], *adj.* mesozoisch (*Geol.*).

mess [mɛs], 1. *s.* (*coll.*) die Unordnung, das Durcheinander; der Schmutz, die Schweinerei; die Klemme, Patsche; Messe, das Kasino (*Mil.*); die Back, Backmannschaft (*Naut.*); der Mischmasch, die Speise, das Gericht; *in a* –, in Verwirrung *or* Unordnung (*of things*), in der Patsche (*of persons*); *make a* –, Schmutz machen; *make a – of o.s.*, sich beschmutzen; *make a – of s.th.*, etwas verderben, verpatzen, verpfuschen *or* verhunzen; *officers'* –, das Offizierskasino; (*B.*) – *of pottage*, das Linsengericht; (*fig.*) der Mischmasch, unappetitliches Gericht. 2. *v.n.* gemeinsam essen (*with*, mit); – *together*, in derselben Messe essen; – *about*, sich zu schaffen machen (*with*, mit), herumfummeln, herumpüttieren (*with*, an); herumbummeln. 3. *v.a.* (also – *up*) beschmutzen; in Unordnung bringen, verderben. **--jacket,** *s.* blaue Jacke (*Mil.*). **--mate,** *s.* der Tischgenosse, (*coll.*) Kamerad. **–ing,** *s.* die Verpflegung (*Mil.*). **–y,** *adj.* schmutzig, unsauber. **--tin,** *s.* das Kochgeschirr (*Mil.*).

message ['mɛsɪdʒ], *s.* die Botschaft, Mitteilung (*to*, an (*Acc.*)); *go on* or *take a* –, eine Botschaft ausrichten; *send s.o. a* –, einen benachrichtigen; *wireless* –, die Funkmitteilung, Funkmeldung; – *blank*, die Meldekarte (*Mil.*).

messenger ['mɛsəndʒə), *s.* der Bote, Kurier; das Kabelar (*Naut.*); *special* –, der Eilbote. **--boy,** *s.* der Ausläufer. **--dog,** *s.* der Meldehund.

messuage ['mɛswɪdʒ], *s.* das Wohnhaus mit Grundstück, das Anwesen (*Law*).

messy ['mɛsɪ], *see* **mess.**

mestizo [mɛs'tɪ:zoʊ], *s.* der Mestize.

met [mɛt], *see* **meet.**

meta-bolic [mɛtə'bɔlɪk], *adj.* veränderlich, wandelbar. **–bolism** [mə'tæbəlɪzm], *s.* die Formveränderlichkeit; der Stoffwechsel. **–carpal** [–'ka.pl], *adj.* Mittelhand–. **–carpus** [–'ka.pəs], *s.* die Mittelhand. **–centre** [–'sɛntə], *s.* das Metazentrum (*Shipb.*). **–genesis** [–'dʒɛnɪsɪs], *s.* der Generationswechsel.

metage ['mɪ:tɪdʒ), *s.* das Messen von Kohlen; Meßgeld.

metal ['mɛtl], 1. *s.* das Metall; die Glasmasse (*Glassw.*); der Schotter, die Beschotterung (*for roads*); *pl.* das Geleise, Schienen (*pl.*) (*Railw.*); *white* –, das Weißmetall; Lagermetall; *run off the –s*, entgleisen. 2. *v.a.* beschottern (*roads, etc.*); *–led road*, die Chaussee, Landstraße, Schotterstraße. **–lic** [mə'tælɪk], *adj.* metallisch, Metall–; metallen (*of sound*); *–lic currency*, das Metallgeld. **–liferous** [–'lɪfərəs], *adj.* metallhaltig, metallführend. **–line** [–lɪn], *adj.* metallisch, Metall–. **–ling** [–lɪŋ], *s.* die Beschotterung. **–lize** [–la.ɪz], *v.a.* metallisieren. **–loid** [–lɔɪd], 1. *s.* das Metalloid. 2. *adj.* metallähnlich. **–lurgic(al)** [–'lə.dʒɪk(l)], *adj.* metallurgisch, Hütten–. **–lurgist** [–'tælə:-dʒɪst], *s.* der Metallurge. **–lurgy** [–'tælə.dʒɪ), *s.* die Hüttenkunde, Metallurgie. **--plating,** *s.* die Plattierung.

metamorph–ic [mɛtə'mɔ:fɪk], *adj.* gestaltverändernd. **–ism** [–'mɔ:fɪzm], *s.* die Umwandlung (*Geol.*). **–ose** ['mɔ:foʊz], *v.a.* verwandeln, umgestalten, umbilden. **–osis** [–'foʊsɪs], *s.* die Verwandlung, Umgestaltung, Metamorphose.

metaphor ['mɛtəfə], *s.* bildlicher *or* übertragener Ausdruck, die Metapher. **–ic(al)** [–'fɔrɪk(l)], *adj.* bildlich, übertragen, figürlich, metaphorisch.

metaphrase ['mɛtəfreɪz], *s.* wörtliche Übersetzung *or* Übertragung.

metaphysic–(al) [mɛtə'fɪzɪk(l)], *adj.* metaphysisch, übersinnlich. **–ian** [–'zɪʃən], *s.* der Metaphysiker. **–s,** *s.* die Metaphysik.

meta–stasis [mə'tæstɔsɪs], *s.* die Versetzung des

Krankheitsstoffes (*Med.*); der Stoffwechsel (*Biol.*). **–tarsal** [–ˈtɑːsəl], *adj.* Mittelfuß–. **–tarsus** [–ˈtɑːsəs], *s.* der Mittelfuß.
metathesis [məˈtæθəsɪs], *s.* die Buchstabenversetzung, Metathese.
métayage [ˈmɛtɛjɑːʒ], *s.* die Halbpacht.
¹**mete** [miːt], *v.a.* (*Poet.*) messen; – *out*, zumessen (*punishment*) (*to* (*Dat.*)).
²**mete** [miːt], *s.* die Grenze; *–s and bounds*, Maß und Ziel.
metempsychosis [mɛtəmpsɪˈkoʊsɪs], *s.* die Seelenwanderung.
meteor [ˈmiːtɪə], *s.* das Meteor, die Sternschnuppe; Lufterscheinung (*Phys.*). **–ic** [–tɪˈɔrɪk], *adj.* meteorisch, Meteor–; (*fig.*) meteorartig, plötzlich, flüchtig. **–ite** [–raɪt], *s.* der Meteorstein. **–ological** [–rəˈlɔdʒɪk(l)], *adj.* meteorologisch; *–ological conditions*, Witterungsverhältnisse (*pl.*); *–ological observatory*, die Wetterwarte; *–ological office*, das Amt für Wetterdienst; *–ological report*, der Wetterberichte. **–ologist** [–ˈrɔlədʒɪst], *s.* der Meteorologe. **–ology** [–ˈrɔlədʒɪ], *s.* die Meteorologie, Wetterkunde.
meter [ˈmiːtə], *s.* der Messer, das Meßgerät; der Zähler (*for gas, electricity, etc.*); (*Amer.*) see **metre**; *gas* –, die Gasuhr.
methane [ˈmɛθeɪn], *s.* das Sumpfgas, Methan, der Kohlenwasserstoff.
methinks [mɪˈθɪŋks], *v.imp.* (*archaic*) mich dünkt, mir scheint.
method [ˈmɛθəd], *s.* die Methode; das Verfahren, die Arbeitsweise, Lehrweise; Denkmethode; Unterrichtsmethode; das System, die Ordnung, der Plan. **–ic(al)** [məˈθɔdɪk(l)], *adj.* methodisch, planmäßig, folgerecht. **–ism** [–dɪzm], *s.* der Methodismus (*Eccl.*). **–ist** [–dɪst], *s.* der Methodist (*Eccl.*). **–istic(al)** [–ˈdɪstɪk(l)], *adj.* methodistisch (*Eccl.*). **–ize** [–aɪz], *v.a.* planmäßig ordnen. **–ology** [–ˈdɔlədʒɪ], *s.* die Methodenlehre, Unterrichtsmethodik.
methought, *see* **methinks.**
methyl [ˈmɛθɪl], *s.* das Methyl; – *alcohol*, der Methylalkohol, Holzgeist, das Methanol. **–ate,** *v.a.* mit Methyl mischen, denaturieren; *–ated spirits*, denaturierter Spiritus, der Methylalkohol, Brennspiritus. **–ene,** *s.* das Methylen. **–ic,** *adj.* Methyl–.
meticulous [məˈtɪkjʊləs], *adj.* übergenau, peinlich genau.
métier [ˈmɛtɪeɪ], *s.* das Gewerbe; (*usually fig.*) Gebiet.
metonymy [mɛˈtɔnɪmɪ], *s.* die Begriffsvertauschung, Metonymie.
metope [ˈmɛtoʊp], *s.* das Zwischenfeld, Schmuckfeld (*Arch.*).
metr–e [ˈmiːtə], *s.* das Versmaß, Metrum; der *or* das Meter. **–ic** [ˈmɛtrɪk], *adj.* metrisch; *–ic system*, metrisches System. **–ical** [–ɪkl], *adj.* metrische; Vers– (*Metr.*). **–ics,** *pl.* die Metrik, Verslehre.
metronome [ˈmɛtrənoʊm], *s.* der Taktmesser, Tempogeber (*Mus.*).
metropol–is [mɛˈtrɔpəlɪs], *s.* die Hauptstadt, Metropole. **–itan** [–trəˈpɔlɪtən], 1. *adj.* hauptstädtisch; Metropolitan– (*Eccl.*). 2. *s.* der Großstadtbewohner; Erzbischof, Metropolit (*Greek Church*); älteste Ringbahnstrecke der Londoner Untergrundbahn.
mettle [ˈmɛtl], *s.* der (Grund)Stoff, das Wesen; (*fig.*) die Naturanlage, Naturkraft; Rassigkeit, der Mut, das Feuer; *be on one's* –, alle Kräfte anspannen, sein möglichstes tun; *put a p. on his* –, einen zur Aufbietung aller Kräfte anspornen. **–d,** *adj.*, **–some,** *adj.* feurig, mutig, rassig.
¹**mew** [mjuː], *s.* die Möwe (*Orn.*).
²**mew** [mjuː], 1. *s.* das Miauen. 2. *v.n.* miauen.
³**mew** [mjuː], 1. *s.* der (Mauser)Käfig. 2. *v.n.* (sich) mausern. 3. *v.a.* (*archaic*) abwerfen (*plumage*); (also – *up*), abschließen, einsperren.
mewl [mjuːl], *v.n.* wimmern, quäken.
mews [mjuːz], 1. *pl.* königlicher Marstall. 2. *pl.* (*sing. constr.*) die Stallung, Stallgasse.
mezzanine [ˈmɛzənɪːn], *s.* der Halbstock, das Halbgeschoß, Zwischengeschoß, Mezzanin.
mezzo–soprano [ˈmɛzoʊsəˈprɑːnoʊ], *s.* der Mezzosopran; die Mezzosopransängerin. **–tint,** *s.* der Kupferstich in Schabmanier.
mho [moʊ], *s.* die Einheit der Leistungsfähigkeit (*Elec.*).
mi [miː], *s.* dritter Ton der diatonischen Tonleiter (*Mus.*).
miaow [mɪˈaʊ], *s.* & *v.n. see* ²**mew.**
miasma [maɪˈæzmə], *s.* der Ansteckungsstoff, Krankheitsstoff. **–l,** *adj.*, **–tic,** *adj.* miasmatisch, ansteckend.
mica [ˈmaɪkə], *s.* der Glimmer. **–ceous** [–ˈkeɪʃəs], *adj.* glimmerartig, glimmerhaltig, Glimmer–. **––schist,** *s.*, **––slate,** *s.* der Glimmerschiefer.
mice [maɪs], *see* **mouse.**
Michaelmas [ˈmɪkəlməs], *s.* das Michaelsfest, Michaelis; *at* –, zu Michaelis. **––daisy,** *s.* die Strandaster. **––day,** *s.* der Michaelistag. **––term,** *s.* das Herbstsemester (*Univ.*).
mickle [mɪkl], *adj.* (*Scots*) groß, viel.
micro–be [ˈmaɪkroʊb], *s.* die Mikrobe, Bakterie. **–bial** [–ˈkroʊbɪəl], *adj.* Mikroben–, Bakterien–. **–cephalic** [–səˈfælɪk], **–cephalous** [–ˈsɛfələs], *adj.* kleinköpfig. **–cosm** [–kɔzm], *s.* der Mikrokosmus, die Welt im Kleinen. **–meter** [–ˈkrɔmɪtə], *s.* das Mikrometer. **–n** [ˈmaɪkrən], *s.* das Mikron, Mikromillimetre. **––organism,** *s.* kleinstes Lebewesen. **–phone** [ˈmaɪkrəfoʊn], *s.* das Mikrophon; (*coll.*) das Radio, der Rundfunk. **–scope** [ˈmaɪkrəskoʊp], *s.* das Mikroskop. **–scopic** [–ˈskɔpɪk], *adj.* mikroskopisch; (*fig.*) verschwindend klein, peinlich genau. **–scopical,** *adj.* mikroskopisch. **–scopy** [–ˈkrɔskəpɪ], *s.* die Mikroskopie. **–some** [ˈmaɪkrəsoʊm], *s.* das Körnchen im Protoplasma (*usually pl.*). **–spore** [ˈmaɪkrəspɔː], *s.* die Mikrospore, Kleinspore. **–structure,** *s.* das Kleingefüge. **–wave** [ˈmaɪkrəweɪv], *s.* die Mikrowelle (*Rad.*).
mictur–ate [mɪktjʊreɪt], *v.n.* Harn lassen. **–ition** [–ˈrɪʃən], *s.* der Urindrang, das Harnlassen.
mid [mɪd], 1. *adj.* mitten in, in der Mitte, Mittel–; *in – air*, mitten in der Luft; *in – career*, in vollem Lauf; – *May*, Mitte Mai; *in – ocean*, auf offenem Meer. 2. *prep.* see **amid. –day,** 1. *s.* der Mittag. 2. *adj.* mittäglich; Mittags–; *–day meal*, das Mittagessen. **–land,** 1. *s.* das Mittelland. 2. *adj.* mittelländisch, Binnen–. **–lands,** *pl.* Mittelengland. **–night,** 1. *s.* die Mitternacht; *–night sun*, die Mitternachtssonne; *burn the –night oil*, bei Nachtlicht arbeiten. 2. *adj.* Mitternachts–, mitternächtlich. **––off,** *s.* (**––on,** *s.*) der Spieler zwischen Werfer und Schläger und rechts (links) vom Werfer (*Crick.*). **–rib,** *s.* die Mittelrippe (*Bot.*). **–riff,** *s.* (*coll.*) das Zwerchfell. **–shipman,** *s.* der Seekadett. **–ships,** *adv.* mittschiffs. **–st,** 1. *s.* die Mitte, (only in) *in the –st of*, mitten in, inmitten (*Gen.*); *from their –st*, aus ihrer Mitte, *etc.* 2. *adv.* (*Poet.*) in der Mitte. **–stream,** *s.* die Mitte des Flusses. **–summer,** *s.* der Hochsommer; *–summer day*, der Johannistag, die Sommersonnenwende; *–summer holiday*, Sommerferien (*pl.*); *–summer madness*, heller Wahnsinn. **–way,** 1. *adv.* auf halbem Wege, mitten auf dem Wege. 2. *adj.* (*Poet.*) mittlere(r, s). **–wife,** *s.* die Hebamme. **–wifery,** *s.* die Geburtshilfe.
midden [ˈmɪdən], *s.* der Misthaufen, die Müllgrube; der Kehrichthaufen (*Archaeol.*).
middl–e [mɪdl], 1. *s.* die Mitte, mittlerer Teil; die Taille, Hüftlinie; *in the –e of his speech*, mitten in seiner Rede; *the –e of June*, Mitte Juni. 2. *attrib. adj.* mittlere(r, s), in der Mitte, Mittel–; *–e age*, mittleres Alter; *–e ages*, das Mittelalter; *–e-aged*, in *or* von mittlerem Alter; *–e class*, die Mittelklasse; *–e classes*, der Mittelstand; *–e course*, der Mittelweg; *–e English*, das Mittelenglisch; *–e finger*, der Mittelfinger; *–e rhyme*, der Binnenreim; *–e-sized*, von mittlerer Größe; *–e* (*term*), das Mittelglied (*Log.*); *–e watch*, die Hundewache; *–e weight*, das Mittelgewicht (*Box.*) (*under 160 lb.*); der Mittelgewichtler (*boxer*). **–eman,** *s.* der Zwischenhändler, die Mittelsperson (*C.L.*). **–ing** [–lɪŋ], 1. *adj.* mittelmäßig, leidlich, Durchschnitts–. 2. *adv.* ziemlich, leidlich. 3. *s.* (*usually pl.*) die Mittelsorte, Ware mittlerer Qualität (*C.L.*); *pl.* das Mittelmehl.
middy [ˈmɪdɪ], *s.* (*coll.*) *see* **midshipman,** *under* **mid.**
midge [mɪdʒ], *s.* die Mücke. **–t** [–ɪt], *s.* der Zwerg.

midinette [mɪdɪ'nɛt], *s.* das Ladenmädchen.
midland ['mɪdlənd], *see* **mid.**
midnight ['mɪdnɑɪt], *see* **mid.**
midrib ['mɪdrɪb], *see* **mid.**
midriff ['mɪdrɪf], *see* **mid.**
midship-man ['mɪdʃɪpmən], **-s** ['mɪdʃɪps], *see* **mid.**
midst [mɪdst], *see* **mid.**
midstream ['mɪdstrɪ:m], *see* **mid.**
midsummer ['mɪdsʌmə], *see* **mid.**
midway ['mɪdweɪ], *see* **mid.**
midwife ['mɪdwɑɪf], **-ry** ['mɪdwɪfrɪ], *see* **mid.**
mien [mɪ:n], *s.* (*Poet.*) die Miene, der Gesichtsausdruck.
[1]**might** [mɑɪt], *see* **may.**
[2]**might** [mɑɪt], *s.* die Macht, Gewalt; Kraft, Stärke; *with all one's –*, *with – and main*, mit voller Kraft, mit aller Gewalt, aus Leibeskräften; (*Prov.*) *– is right*, Macht geht vor Recht. **-ily,** *adv.* gewaltig, mächtig, kräftig; (*coll.*) sehr. **-iness,** *s.* die Macht, Gewalt; (*coll.*) Größe. **-y,** 1. *adj.* mächtig, gewaltig, heftig; (*coll.*) groß. 2. *adv.* (*coll.*) (*before adj. or adv.*) sehr, höchst.
mignonette [mɪnjə'nɛt], *s.* die Reseda, Resede (*Bot.*).
migraine ['mɪ:grəɪn], *s.* die Migräne.
migra-nt ['mɑɪgrənt], 1. *s.* der Zugvogel (*Orn.*); das Wandertier (*Zool.*); der Auswanderer. 2. *adj.* Zug-, Wander-. **-te** [-'greɪt], *v.n.* (fort)ziehen, auswandern (*to*, nach). **-tion** [-'greɪʃən], *s.* die Wanderung, das Fortziehen; der Zug, die Auswanderung; *-tion of peoples*, die Völkerwanderung; *right of free -tion*, die Freizügigkeit. **-tory** ['mɑɪgrətərɪ], *adj.* umherziehend, wandernd; nomadisch, Zug-; *-tory animals*, Wandertiere; *-tory birds*, Zugvögel.
mikado [mɪ'kɑ:doʊ], *s.* der Mikado, Kaiser von Japan.
[1]**mike** [mɑɪk], *s.* (*sl.*) *see* **microphone.**
[2]**mike** [mɑɪk], *v.n.* (*sl.*) faulenzen, sich drücken.
milch [mɪltʃ], *adj.* milchgebend, melk. **--cow,** *s.* die Milchkuh (*also fig.*); *look on as a --cow*, als melkende Kuh betrachten.
mild [mɑɪld], *adj.* mild, sanft, mäßig, gelinde, freundlich, angenehm (*weather*, *character*); leicht (*disease*, *cigar*); warm, lind (*weather*). **--cured,** *adj.* leicht gesalzen. **-ness,** *s.* die Milde, Sanftmut; *to put it -ly*, gelinde *or* milde gesagt. **--steel,** *s.* der Flußstahl.
mildew ['mɪldjʊ:], 1. *s.* der Meltau, Schimmel; Brand (*in grain*); Moder, Moderflecke (*pl.*) (*in paper*); Stockflecke (*pl.*) (*in cloth*). 2. *v.n.* (usually pass. *be -ed*) verschimmeln; schimmelig, moderig, brandig *or* stockig werden.
mildness ['mɑɪldnɪs], *see* **mild.**
mile [mɑɪl], *s.* die Meile; *statute –*, englische Meile (= 1609·3 Meter); *nautical* or *geographical –*, die Seemeile (= 1853·2 Meter); *for -s*, meilenweit; *from -s*, meilenweit her; *miss by a –*, meilenweit davon bleiben, hoffnungslos danebentreffen. **-age** [-ɪdʒ], *s.* die Meilenlänge *or* Meilenzahl; das Kilometergeld; *-age recorder*, **-ometer** [-'lɔmɪtə], der Kilometerzähler. **-r** *s.* der Meilenläufer. **--post,** der Meilenzeiger. **-stone,** der Meilenstein, (*fig.*) Markstein.
milfoil ['mɪlfɔɪl], *s.* die Schafgarbe (*Bot.*).
miliar-ia [mɪlɪ'ɛ:rɪə], *s.* Frieseln (*pl.*) (*Med.*). **-y** ['mɪlɪərɪ], *adj.* hirsekornförmig; *-y fever*, *see* **-ia.**
milita-ncy ['mɪlɪtənsɪ], *s.* der Kriegsgeist, Kampfgeist; Kampf, Kriegszustand. **-nt** [-ənt], *adj.* kämpfend, kriegführend, streitend; kriegerisch, kampflustig, streitbar. **-rily** [-tərɪlɪ], *adv.* in militärischer Hinsicht. **-rism** [-tərɪzm], *s.* der Militarismus. **-rist** [-tərɪst], *s.* der Militarist. **-ristic** [-'rɪstɪk], *adj.* militaristisch, kriegerisch. **-ry** [-ərɪ], 1. *adj.* militärisch, Militär-; Kriegs-; *-ry academy*, die Kriegsschule; *-ry age*, militärpflichtiges Alter; *-ry court*, das Militärgericht, Kriegsgericht; *-ry cross*, das Militär(verdienst)kreuz; *-ry dictatorship*, die Militärdiktatur; *-ry district*, der Wehrkreis; *-ry equipment*, die Heeresausrüstung; *-ry forces*, die Wehrmacht; *-ry government*, die Militärregierung, Besatzungsbehörde; *-ry intelligence*, Meldungen über den Feind; *-ry law*, das Militärrecht, die Militärgesetzgebung; *-ry man*, der Offizier; *-ry matters*, das Wehrwesen; *-ry outfitter*, der Militärschneider; *-ry police*, die Militärpolizei, Feldpolizei; *-ry science*, die Wehrwissenschaft; *-ry service*, der Heeresdienst, Militärdienst, Wehrdienst; (*un*)*fit for -ry service*, militär(un)tauglich; *universal compulsory -ry service*, allgemeine Wehrpflicht *or* Dienstpflicht; *-ry song*, das Soldatenlied; *-ry stores*, das Gerät, Kriegsmaterial, die Kriegsbedürfnisse (*pl.*). 2. *s.* das Militär, Soldaten (*pl.*).
militate ['mɪlɪteɪt], *v.n.* sprechen (*against*, gegen), widerstreiten, entgegentreten, entgegenwirken (*against* (*Dat.*)).
militia [mɪ'lɪʃə], *s.* die Miliz, Bürgerwehr. **-man,** *s.* der Milizsoldat.
milk [mɪlk], 1. *s.* die Milch; (*fig.*) *– and water*, 1. *s.* die Weichlichkeit, Seichtheit. 2. *attrib. adj.* weichlich, seicht, zimperlich, verwässert; *skim*(*med*) –, die Magermilch; *full cream* or *rich –*, die Vollmilch; *it's no use crying over spilt –*, geschehene Dinge sind nicht zu ändern; *– of human kindness*, die Menschlichkeit, menschliche Güte. 2. *v.a.* melken; (*sl.*) anzapfen; schröpfen, rupfen; belauschen, abfangen (*Tele.*); *– the ram* or *bull*, einen Mohren weißwaschen wollen. **--bar,** *s.* die Milch(trink)halle. **--can,** *s.* die Milchkanne. **--diet,** die Milchkost. **-er,** *s.* der Melker, die Melkerin; Milchkuh. **--fever,** *s.* das Milchfieber. **--float,** *s.* der Milchwagen. **-iness,** *s.* die Milchartigkeit, Milchähnlichkeit. **--jug,** *s.* der Milchtopf. **-maid,** *s.* das Milchmädchen. **-man,** *s.* der Milchmann, Milchhändler. **--round,** *s.* die Runde des Milchmannes. **--shake,** *s.* Milch mit Sodawasser. **-sop,** *s.* das Muttersöhnchen, der Weichling. **--sugar,** *s.* der Milchzucker. **– of sulphur,** die Schwefelmilch. **--tooth,** *s.* der Milchzahn. **-weed,** *s.* die Wolfsmilch (*Bot.*). **--white,** *adj.* milchweiß. **-wort,** *s.* die Kreuzblume (*Bot.*). **-y,** *adj.* milchig, Milch-; milchweiß; *-y Way*, die Milchstraße.
[1]**mill** [mɪl], 1. *s.* die Mühle; Spinnerei; Fabrik, das Werk; Prägwerk (*Mint.*); *rolling--*, das Walzwerk; (*coll.*) *go through the –*, eine harte Schule *or* viel durchmachen; (*coll.*) *he has been through the –*, er hat schwere Prüfungen hinter sich; (*coll.*) *put s.o. through the –*, einen durch eine harte Schule schicken; *that is grist to his –*, das ist Wasser auf seine Mühle. 2. *v.a.* mahlen (*corn*); prägen (*money*); walzen (*paper*, *metal*); walken (*cloth*); rändeln, rändern (*coins*, *etc.*); fräsen (*wood*, *etc.*); *-ed edge*, die Rändelung. 3. *v.n.* sich schlagen, kämpfen; sich im Kreise bewegen (*as cattle*); (*coll.*) *– around*, zwecklos umherirren. **-board,** *s.* starke Pappe, der Pappdeckel. **--dam,** *s.* das Mühlwehr. **-er,** *s.* der Müller (*also Ent.*). **--hand,** *s.* der Mühlenarbeiter, Spinnereiarbeiter. **--hopper,** *s.* der Mühltrichter, Mühlrumpf. **-ing,** 1. *adj.* Fräs-, *etc.*; *-ing crowd*, drängende, wogende Menschenmenge; *-ing cutter*, der Fräser, die Fräse. 2. *s.* das Mahlen, Walken, Fräsen, Rändeln; *-ing-machine*, die Fräsmaschine; Walke. **--owner,** *s.* der Mühlenbesitzer, Spinnereibesitzer, Fabrikbesitzer. **--pond,** *s.* der Mühlteich. **--race,** *s.* der Mühlgraben. **-stone,** *s.* der Mühlstein. **--stream,** *s.* der Mühlbach. **--wheel,** *s.* das Mühl(en)rad. **-wright,** *s.* der Mühlenbauer.
[2]**mill** [mɪl], *s.* ein Tausendstel (*Amer.* $\frac{1}{10}$th cent).
millen-arian [mɪlə'nɛ:ərɪən], 1. *adj.* tausendjährig; zum tausendjährigen Reiche gehörig (*Theol.*). 2. *s.* der Chiliast. **-arianism,** *s.* der Chiliasmus. **-ary** [-'lɛnərɪ], 1. *adj.* tausendjährig, Jahrtausend-. 2. *s.* die Tausendjahrfeier, Jahrtausendfeier; das Jahrtausend. **-nial** [-'lɛnɪəl], *adj.* tausendjährig. **-nium** [-'lɛnɪəm], *s.* das Jahrtausend, die Jahrtausendfeier, tausendjähriges Reich (*Theol.*); (*fig.*) das Zeitalter des Glücks und Friedens.
mille-pede, *see* **millipede.** **-simal** [mɪ'lɛsɪməl], 1. *adj.* tausendst; tausendfach. 2. *s.* das Tausendstel.
millet ['mɪlɪt], *s.* die Hirse. **--grass,** *s.* das Flattergras, die Waldhirse.
milli-ard ['mɪlɪəd], *s.* die Milliarde. **-bar** [-bɑ:], *s.* das Millibar, die Luftdruckeinheit (0·75 mm.).

-gram, *s.* das Milligramm. **-metre** [–mɪːtə], *s.* der *or* das Millimeter.
milliner [ˈmɪlɪnə], *s.* die Putzmacherin, Modistin. *man-–*, *s.* der Putzmacher. **-y** [–rɪ], *s.* Modewaren, Putzwaren (*pl.*); *-y-business*, das Putzgeschäft, die Modewarenhandlung.
million [ˈmɪlɪən], *s.* die Million; (*after figures*: *pl. also* –) 3 –(*s*), drei Millionen; *the* –, die große Menge, der große Haufe, das Volk; *by the* –, nach Millionen; *be worth* 2 *-s*, zwei Millionen Pfund besitzen. **-aire** [–ˈnɛːə], *s.* der Millionär. **-airess** [–ˈnɛːərɪs], *s.* die Millionärin. **-fold,** *adv.* millionenfach. **-th,** 1. *num. adj.* millionst. 2. *s.* der, die, das Millionste; das Millionstel.
millipede [ˈmɪlɪpɪːd], *s.* der Tausendfuß (*Zool.*).
milt [mɪlt], 1. *s.* die Milz; Milch (*of fish*). 2. *v.n.* den Rogen befruchten. **-er,** *s.* der Milchner.
mim-e [mɑɪm], *s.* der Mimus; Mime, Possenspieler. **-eograph** [ˈmɪmɪoʊgræf], *s.* der Vervielfältigungsapparat. **-esis** [mɪˈmɪːsɪs], *s.* die Nachahmung, Mimikry (*Zool.*, *etc.*). **-etic** [mɑɪˈmɛtɪk], *adj.* mimisch, nachahmend, nachgeahmt, nachgemacht. **-ic** [ˈmɪmɪk], 1. *adj.* nachahmend, mimisch; nachgemacht, nachgeahmt; Schein–. 2. *s.* der Gebärdenspieler, Possenreißer; Nachäffer. 3. *v.a.* nachahmen, nachäffen. **-icry** [ˈmɪmɪkrɪ], *s.* die Nachahmung, Nachäfferei; Mimikry, Angleichung an die Umgebung (*Zool.*).
mimosa [mɪˈmoʊzə], *s.* die Sinnpflanze, Mimose (*Bot.*).
mina-cious [mɪˈneɪʃəs], *adj.*, **-tory** [ˈmɪnətərɪ], *adj.* drohend, bedrohlich.
minaret [ˈmɪnərɛt], *s.* das Minarett.
minatory, *see* **minacious.**
minc-e [mɪns], 1. *v.a.* zerhacken, kleinschneiden, klein hacken (*meat*); (*fig.*) mildern, schwächen; *not -e matters* or *one's words*, nichts beschönigen *or* bemänteln, kein Blatt vor den Mund nehmen; *-e one's steps*, (einher)trippeln; *-e one's words*, geziert, affektiert *or* zimperlich sprechen. 2. *v.n.* zimperlich tun, sich zieren; *-ing steps*, zimperliche Tritte. 3. *s.* (also *-ed meat*) gehacktes Fleisch, Gehackte(s), *n.* **-er,** *s.* die Fleischhackmaschine. **-e-meat,** *s.* eine Pastetenfüllung aus gemischtem Dürrobst; (*coll.*) *make -e-meat of*, zerstückeln; (*fig.*) keinen guten Faden lassen an (*Dat.*), herunterreißen, vernichten (*a p.*). **-e-pie,** *s.* die Pastete mit Füllung aus gemischtem Dürrobst. **-ing,** *adj.* affektiert, geziert. **-ing-machine,** *s. see* **-er.**
mind [mɑɪnd], **1.** *s.* der Geist, Verstand; die Gesinnung, Seele, das Gemüt; die Absicht, das Vorhaben, der Wille; die Meinung, Ansicht, Überzeugung, Neigung, Lust; das Gedächtnis, die Erinnerung, der Sinn; die Beachtung, Aufmerksamkeit. (*a*) (*with nouns*) *the -'s eye*, geistiges Auge; *frame of* –, die Gesinnung, Geistesverfassung; *presence of* –, die Geistesgegenwart; *things of the* –, geistige Dinge; *the workings of the* –, der Gedankenvorgang, die Vorstellungsweise; *many men many -s*, viele Köpfe viele Sinne. (*b*) (*with verbs*) *there can be no two -s about*, es kann keine geteilte Meinung sein über; *cast one's – back*, sich im Geiste zurückversetzen (*to*, in *or* nach); *change one's* –, sich anders besinnen; *enter one's* –, einem in den Sinn kommen; *give one's – to a th.*, sich einer S. befleißigen; *have a* (*no*) –, (nicht) Lust haben, geneigt sein *or* willens sein; *have half a – to go*, beinahe Lust haben zu gehen; *have an open* –, unvoreingenommen *or* unbeeinflußt sein (*on* or *about*, in (*Dat.*)); *know one's own* –, wissen, was man will; *make up one's* –, sich entschließen, sich klar werden, zu dem Schluß *or* der Überzeugung kommen; *read a p.'s* –, jemandes Gedanken lesen; *set one's – on a th.*, seinen Sinn auf eine S. richten; *speak one's* –, seine Meinung sagen, freimütig sein, frei herausreden. (*c*) (*with prepositions*) *in my* –, nach meiner Meinung, meines Erachtens; *in his right* –, ganz bei Verstand; *bear* or *keep in* –, denken *or* sich erinnern an (*Acc.*), bedenken, berücksichtigen (*Acc.*), eingedenk sein (*Gen.*), im Gedächtnis *or* Auge behalten, nicht vergessen; *have it in* –, sich wohl erinnern; *put a p. in* –, einen erinnern (*of*, an); *be in two -s*, mit sich im unklaren, geteilter Meinung *or* unschlüssig sein (*about*, über); *come into one's* –, einem in den Sinn fallen; *have it in – to do*, beabsichtigen zu tun; *of one* –, einmütig; *be of a p.'s* –, einer Meinung mit einem sein, einem beistimmen; *give s.o. a piece of one's* –, einem gründlich die Meinung sagen; *have it off one's* –, nicht mehr an eine S. zu denken brauchen; *have on one's* –, auf dem Herzen haben; *out of his* –, nicht bei Trost, Sinnen *or* Verstand, verrückt; *put out of one's* –, sich (*Dat.*) aus dem Sinn schlagen; *time out of* –, vor undenklichen Zeiten; *to my* –, see *in my* –; *bring back* or *call to* –, ins Gedächtnis zurückrufen, sich erinnern an. **2.** *v.a.* achten *or* merken (auf (*Acc.*)), sorgen für, sehen nach, sich kümmern um, sich beschäftigen *or* befassen mit, beachten; sich in acht nehmen vor, auf der Hut sein vor; (*in neg. or interr. clauses*) sich stoßen an, nicht gern sehen, etwas einzuwenden haben gegen; (*archaic*) sich erinnern, in Erinnerung haben (*a th.*), erinnern (*a p.*); *never – him!* kümmere dich nicht um ihn! *he doesn't – it*, er macht sich (*Dat.*) nichts daraus; *– your own business!* bekümmere dich um deine Sachen!; *– the children*, auf die Kinder aufpassen; *– the door*, auf die Tür achtgeben; *I don't – giving something*, ich habe nichts dagegen etwas beizutragen; *– one's P's and Q's*, vorsichtig sein, sich sehr in acht nehmen daß man sich richtig benimmt; *I don't – saying*, ich möchte wohl behaupten; *do you – my smoking?* stört es Sie wenn ich rauche?; *– the step!* Vorsicht! Stufe! **3.** *v.n.* acht geben, sich darum kümmern, sich viel machen aus; etwas dagegen haben; *– you*, wohlgemerkt; *– you come*, denk daran *or* sieh, daß kommst; *I don't* –, meinetwegen, ich habe nichts dagegen, es macht mir nichts aus; *I don't – if I do*, wenn ich bitten darf; *never – !* laß gut sein! mach dir nichts daraus! es macht nichts aus! es macht *or* tut nichts!; *if you don't* –, wenn Sie nichts dagegen haben; *would you – helping me?* Würden Sie mir bitte helfen? **-ed** [–ɪd], *adj.* geneigt, gewillt, gesonnen, eingedenk (*with inf.*); gesinnt, –mütig. **-er,** *s.* der Wärter, Aufseher. **-ful,** *adj.* eingedenk (*of* (*Gen.*)), achtsam (*of*, auf (*Acc.*)); *be -ful of*, achten auf, eingedenk sein. **-fulness,** *s.* die Achtsamkeit. **-less,** *adj.* achtlos, unachtsam, ohne Rücksicht (*of*, auf (*Acc.*)), uneingedenk (*of* (*Gen.*)), unbekümmert, unbesorgt (*of*, um); dumm, geistlos.
[1]**mine** [mɑɪn], 1. *poss. pron.* der, die, das Meinige; mein, meiner; *a book of* –, eines meiner Bücher, ein Buch von mir; *this boy of* –, mein Sohn hier, dieser mein Sohn; *this house is* –, dieses Haus gehört mir. 2. *poss. adj.* (*archaic*) see **my;** *– host*, der Herr Wirt. 3. *s.* die Mein(ig)en (*pl.*).
[2]**min-e** [mɑɪn], 1. *s.* das Bergwerk, die Grube, Zeche (*Min.*); Mine (*Mil. & Naut.*); (*fig.*) Fundgrube; *pl.* die Montanindustrie, der Bergbau (*C.L.*); *anti-tank -e* die Tankmine; *contact -e*, die Tretmine; *floating -e*, die Treibmine; *-e of information*, die Fundgrube der Belehrung; *spring a -e*, eine Mine springen lassen. 2. *v.a.* gewinnen, abbauen (*ore*); unterminieren, untergraben (*also fig.*); mit Minen belegen, verminen (*a harbour, etc.*). 3. *v.n.* minieren, graben (*for*, nach); vergraben, sich eingraben (*of animals*). **-er,** *s.* der Bergmann, Bergarbeiter, Grubenarbeiter; Mineur (*Mil.*); Minenleger (*Nav.*); *-ers' association*, die Knappschaft; *-er's lamp*, die Grubenlampe. **-ed,** *adj.* vermint (*Mil., Naut.*); *-ed area*, das Minensperrgebiet. **-e-detector,** *s.* das Minensuchgerät. **-e-field,** *s.* das Minenfeld. **-e-layer,** *s.* der Minenleger. **-e-owner,** *s.* der Zechenbesitzer. **-e-sweeper,** *s.* das Minenräumboot, Minensuchboot. **-e-thrower,** *s.* der Minenwerfer. **-ing,** 1. *s.* der Bergbau, Bergwerksbetrieb. 2. *adj.*; *-ing academy*, die Bergakademie; *-ing disaster*, das Grubenunglück, Bergwerksunglück; *-ing industry*, der Bergbau, die Montanindustrie; *-ing share*, der Kux.
mineral [ˈmɪnərəl], 1. *s.* das Mineral; *pl.* das Mineralwasser. 2. *adj.* mineralisch, Mineral–; anorganisch (*Chem.*); *– deposit*, die Lagerstätte; *– kingdom*, das Mineralreich, Steinreich; *– oil*, das Mineralöl; *– spring*, die Mineralquelle, der Gesundbrunnen; *– tar*, der Bergteer; *– waters*, das Mineralwasser. **-ize,** *v.a.* vererzen; versteinern, mit anorganischen Stoffen durchsetzen (*Chem.*).

-ogical [-ˈlɔdʒɪkl], *adj.* mineralogisch. **-ogist** [-ˈrælədʒɪst], *s.* der Mineraloge. **-ogy** [-ˈrælədzɪ], *s.* die Mineralogie.
minever, *s., see* **miniver.**
mingle [ˈmɪŋgl], 1. *v.a.* (ver)mischen, (ver)mengen. 2. *v.n.* sich vermischen *or* vereinigen, sich (ein)mischen (*in*, in); verkehren, sich mischen (*among*, unter).
mingy [ˈmɪndʒɪ], *adj.* (*sl.*) knickerig, knauserig, filzig.
miniatur-e [ˈmɪnɪətjuə], 1. *s.* die Miniatur; das Miniaturbild; *in -e*, im kleinen. 2. *adj.* Klein-, im kleinen; *-e camera*, die Kleinbildkamera, Kleinkamera; *-e rifle shooting*, das Kleinkaliberschießen. **-ist,** *s.* der Miniaturmaler.
minify [ˈmɪnɪfaɪ], *v.a.* verkleinern, verminder; (*fig.*) herabsetzen, geringschätzen.
minikin [ˈmɪnɪkɪn], 1. *adj.* winzig; (*fig.*) geziert, affektiert. 2. *s.* kleine Stecknadel.
minim [ˈmɪnɪm], *s.* halbe Note (*Mus.*); der Tropfen, das Sechzigstel Drachme (*Pharm.*); (*fig.*) etwas Winziges, das Tüttelchen. **-al** [-əl], *adj.* minimal, minderst, kleinst. **-ize** [-aɪz], *v.a.* möglichst klein darstellen, auf ein Mindestmaß verringern; unterschätzen, herabsetzen. **-um** [-əm], *s.* (pl. *-a*) das Minimum, Mindestmaß; *at a -um*, sehr niedrig (*C.L.*); *existence -um*, das Existenzminimum; *-um wage*, der Mindestlohn. **-us** [-əs], *s.* (*school sl.*) Jüngste(r), *m.* (von drei Brüdern).
mining [ˈmaɪnɪŋ], *see* [2]**mine**; *- equipment*, das Gezähe.
minion [ˈmɪnjən], *s.* der Günstling, Liebling; die Kolonel(schrift) (*Typ.*).
minist-er [ˈmɪnɪstə], 1. *s.* Geistliche(r), *m.* (*Rel.*), der (Staats)Minister (*Pol.*); Gesandte(r), *m.*; (*archaic*) der Gehilfe, Diener. 2. *v.n.* dienen, aufwarten; behilflich sein (*to* (*Dat.*)) (*a p.*), beitragen (*to*, zu) (*a th.*); ministrieren; den Gottesdienst abhalten. 3. *v.a.* darreichen, spenden (*the sacrament*). **-erial** [-ˈtɪːərɪəl], *adj.* dienend, Hilfs-; kirchlich, geistlich (*Rel.*); ministeriell, Minister- (*Pol.*); *-erial benches*, Sitze der Regierungspartei; *be -erial to*, dienen (*Dat.*); *-erial to the needs*, die Bedürfnisse befriedigen. **-erialist,** *adj.* dienend, Schutz-. **-rant** [-trənt], 1. *adj.* dienend (*to* (*Dat.*)). 2. *s.* der Meßdiener, Ministrant. **-ration** [-ˈtreɪʃən] *s.* der Dienst (*to* (*Dat.*)), die Hilfe (*to*, für); Darreichung, Verwaltung (*of* (*Gen.*)); *pl.* kirchliche Amtsübungen (*pl.*). **-rative** [-trətɪv], *adj.* dienend. **-ry** [-trɪ], *s.* der Dienst; kirchliches *or* geistiges Amt (*Rel.*); das Ministerium, Kabinett (*Pol.*).
minium [ˈmɪnɪəm], *s.* die Mennige.
miniver [ˈmɪnɪvə], *s.* das Feh, Grauwerk.
mink [mɪŋk], *s.* der Nerz, Nörz; das Nerzfell.
minnow [ˈmɪnou], *s.* die Elritze (*Ichth.*).
minor [ˈmaɪnə], 1. *adj.* kleiner, geringer, weniger, jünger; Neben-, Unter- (*Log.*); unbedeutend, geringfügig, klein; Moll- (*Mus.*); *A-*-, A-dur; *Asia -*, Kleinasien; *- chord*, der Mollakkord; *- clergy*, niedere Geistlichkeit; *of - importance*, von zweitrangiger Bedeutung; *- key*, die Molltonart; *- operation*, leichte Operation; *- planets*, die Planetoiden, Asteroiden; *- point*, die Nebensache; *- premiss*, der Untersatz; *- prophets*, kleine Propheten; *- third*, kleine Terz; *Hobson -*, der jüngere Hobson. 2. *s.* Minderjährige(r), *m.*, Unmündige(r), *m.*; der Untersatz (*Log.*); das Nebenfach (*Univ.*). **-ite,** *s.* der Minorist, Franziskaner. **-ity** [-ˈnɔrɪtɪ], *s.* die Minderjährigkeit, Unmündigkeit (*Law*); Minderheit, Minderzahl, Minorität; *-ities problem*, das Minoritäten-problem (*Pol.*); *-ity report*, der Bericht der Minderheit (eines Ausschusses).
minster [ˈmɪnstə], *s.* das Münster, die Stiftskirche, Kathedrale.
minstrel [ˈmɪnstrəl], *s.* der Sänger, Minnesänger, Spielmann (*Hist.*); Dichter, Barde; *Negro -s*, die Negersänger. **-sy** [-sɪ], *s.* die Spielmannsdichtung, der Minnesang; Sängerchor, Spielleute (*pl.*); (*Poet.*) die Dichtkunst, der Bardengesang.
[1]**mint** [mɪnt], *s.* die Minze (*Bot.*); *- sauce*, saure Minztunke.
[2]**mint** [mɪnt], 1. *s.* die Münze; Münzstätte, Münzanstalt; Quelle, Fundgrube; *a - of money*, großer Haufen Geld. 2. *adj.* unbeschädigt; *- condition*, wie neu, tadellos erhalten. 3. *v.a.* prägen (*also fig.*), münzen, schlagen (*money*). **-age** [-ɪdʒ], *s.* die Prägung (*also fig.*), das Münzen; geprägtes Geld; die Münzgebühr.
minue-nd [ˈmɪnjuɛnd], *s.* der Minuend (*Math.*). **-t** [-juˈɛt], *s.* das Menuett (*Mus.*).
minus [ˈmaɪnəs], 1. *prep.* weniger, minus; (*coll.*) ohne. 2. *adj.* negativ, Minus-; *- quantity*, negative Größe; *- sign*, das Minuszeichen. 3. *s.* das Minus(zeichen).
minuscule [mɪˈnjuskəl], *s.* die Minuskel, kleiner Buchstabe.
[1]**minute** [ˈmɪnɪt], 1. *s.* die Minute; (*fig.*) der Augenblick, kurze Zeit; bestimmter Zeitpunkt; kurzer Entwurf, das Konzept, die Denkschrift; *pl.* das Protokoll; *at the last -*, im letzten Augenblick; *for a -*, eine Minute; *keep the -s*, das Protokoll führen; *make a - of*, zu Protokoll nehmen, notieren, vermerken; *to the -*, auf die Minute. 2. *v.a.* zu Protokoll nehmen, protokollieren, notieren, vermerken. **--book,** *s.* das Protokollbuch. **--gun,** *s.* das Minutengeschütz. **--hand,** *s.* der Minutenzeiger.
[2]**minute** [maɪˈnjuːt], *adj.* sehr klein, winzig; peinlich genau, sorgfältig, minuziös; unbedeutend. **-ly,** *adv.* umständlich, peinlich genau, eingehend, ausführlich. **-ness,** *s.* die Kleinheit, Winzigkeit; Umständlichkeit, Genauigkeit.
minutiae [mɪˈnjuːʃɪə], *pl.* Einzelheiten.
minx [mɪŋks], *s.* (*coll.*) ausgelassenes Mädchen, der Wildfang, die Range.
miocene [ˈmaɪosɪːn], *adj.* miozän, Miozän- (*Geol.*).
mirac-le [ˈmɪrəkl], *s.* das Wunder; die Wundertat; Wunderkraft; *work -les*, Wunder tun; (*coll.*) *next door to a -le*, ans Wunderbare grenzend. **-le-play,** *s.* das Mirakelspiel. **-ulous** [mɪˈrækjuləs], *adj.* wunderbar; übernatürlich. **-ulously,** *adj.* wie durch ein Wunder. **-ulousness,** *s.* das Wunderbare; Übernatürliche.
mirage [mɪˈrɑːʒ], *s.* die Luftspiegelung, Fata Morgana; (*fig.*) Täuschung, das Luftbild.
mir-e [maɪə], 1. *s.* der Schlamm, Kot, Dreck, Sumpf; (*coll.*) *be deep in the -e*, tief in der Tinte, Klemme *or* Patsche sitzen; (*fig.*) *drag through the -e*, verunglimpfen, durch den Dreck ziehen. 2. *v.a.* (*usually pass.*) im Sumpf festhalten; (*fig.*) verwickeln, in Ungelegenheiten stürzen; beschmutzen, besudeln. **-y** [ˈmaɪərɪ], *adj.* schlammig, kotig, dreckig.
mirror [ˈmɪrə], *s.* der Spiegel; (*fig.*) das Vorbild, Muster, Spiegelbild; *hold up the - to*, den Spiegel vorhalten (*Dat.*).
mirth [məːθ], *s.* der Frohsinn, die Freude, Fröhlichkeit, Heiterkeit. **-ful,** *adj.* fröhlich, heiter. **-fulness,** *s.* see **-.** **-less,** *adj.* freudlos.
miry [ˈmaɪərɪ], *see* **mire.**
misadventure [mɪsədˈvɛntʃə], *s.* der Unglücksfall, das Mißgeschick.
misalliance [mɪsəˈlaɪəns], *s.* die Mißheirat.
misanthrop-e [ˈmɪsənθroup], *s.* der Menschenfeind. **-ic(al)** [-ˈθrɔpɪk(l)], *adj.* menschenfeindlich. **-ist** [-ˈænθrəpɪst], *s.* der Menschenhasser. **-y** [-ˈænθrəpɪ], *s.* der Menschenhaß.
misappl-ication [mɪsæplɪˈkeɪʃən], *s.* falsche Anwendung; der Mißbrauch. **-y** [-ˈplaɪ], *v.a.* falsch anwenden; mißbrauchen, zu unerlaubten Zwecken verwenden.
misapprehen-d [mɪsæprɪˈhɛnd], *v.a.* mißverstehen. **-sion** [-ˈhɛnʃən], *s.* das Mißverständnis, falsche Auffassung; *be* or *labour under a -sion*, sich in einem Irrtum befinden; *be under no -sion as to . . .*, sich völlig klar sein über . . . (*Acc.*).
misappropriat-e [mɪsəˈprouprɪeɪt], *v.a.* sich (*Dat.*) widerrechtlich aneignen, unterschlagen. **-ion** [-prɪˈeɪʃən], *s.* widerrechtliche *or* unrechtmäßige Aneignung, Unterschlagung.
misbecom-e [mɪsbɪˈkʌm], *v.a.* sich nicht schicken *or* ziemen (*a p.*, für einen), nicht geziemen, schlecht anstehen (*a p.*, einem). **-ing,** *adj.* unschicklich.
misbegotten [mɪsbɪˈgɔtən], *adj.* unehelich; (*fig.*) ekelhaft, scheußlich; unnatürlich.
misbehav-e [mɪsbɪˈheɪv], *v.n.* & *r.* sich schlecht *or* ungebührlich betragen *or* benehmen. **-iour** [-jə], *s.* ungebührliches *or* schlechtes Betragen, die Ungezogenheit, Unart.

misbelie–f [mɪsbɪˈlɪ:f], *s.* der Irrglaube. **–ver** [–ˈlɪ:və], *s.* Irrgläubige(r), *m.*
miscalculat–e [mɪsˈkælkjəleɪt], 1. *v.a.* falsch (be)rechnen *or* beurteilen. 2. *v.n.* sich verrechnen. **–ion** [–ˈleɪʃən], *s.* falsche (Be)Rechnung; der Rechenfehler, falsches Urteil.
miscall [mɪsˈkɔ:l], *v.a.* falsch benennen; (*dial.*) beschimpfen.
miscarr–iage [mɪsˈkærɪdʒ], *s.* das Mißlingen, Fehlschlagen, Mißglücken; Verlorengehen (*of a letter, etc.*); die Fehlgeburt (*Med.*), der Fehlgriff (*Law*); *–iage of justice*, die Rechtsbeugung, das Fehlurteil. **–y** [–ˈkærɪ], *v.n.* mißlingen, fehlschlagen, mißglücken, scheitern (*of plans*); verlorengehen (*as letters*); fehlgebären (*Med.*).
miscegenation [mɪsɪdʒəˈneɪʃən], *s.* die Rassenmischung.
miscellan–ea [mɪsəˈleɪnɪə], *pl.* vermischte Schriften, Miszellen. **–eous** [–ɪəs], *adj.* gemischt, vermischt; vielseitig, verschiedenartig. **–eousness,** *s.* die Gemischtheit; Mannigfaltigkeit, Vielseitigkeit. **–y** [–ˈsɛlənɪ], *s.* das Gemisch; der Sammelband, die Sammlung.
mischance [mɪsˈtʃɑ:ns], *s.* das Mißgeschick, der Unfall; *by –*, durch einen unglücklichen Zufall.
mischie–f [ˈmɪstʃɪf], *s.* das Unheil, der Schaden, Übelstand, Nachteil; die Zwietracht; der Unfug, Possen (*pl.*); der Schelm, Strick; die Ursache des Unheils, der Schädling; *do –f*, Unheil anrichten; *do s.o.* (*a*) *–f*, einem Schaden zufügen; *get into –f*, Unfug machen; *make –f*, Zwietracht säen; *mean –f*, Böses im Schilde führen; *what the –f . . . !* was in aller Welt . . .! was zum Teufel . . .!; *the –f is that . . .*, das Unglück ist daß . . . . **–f-maker,** *s.* der Störenfried, Unheilstifter. **–vous** [–tʃɪvəs], *adj.* schädlich, nachteilig, verderblich; boshaft, schadenfroh; mutwillig, schelmisch. **–vousness,** *s.* die Schädlichkeit, Nachteiligkeit, Verderblichkeit; Bosheit; Mutwilligkeit.
miscible [ˈmɪsɪbl], *adj.* mischbar.
misconce–ive [mɪskənˈsɪ:v], 1. *v.a.* mißverstehen, falsch auffassen. 2. *v.n.* eine irrige Meinung haben (*of*, von). **–ption** [–ˈsɛpʃən], *s.* das Mißverständnis, falsche Auffassung.
misconduct, 1. [mɪsˈkɔndʌkt], *s.* schlechtes Benehmen *or* Betragen, schlechte Amtsführung *or* Verwaltung; der Fehltritt; unerlaubter geschlechtlicher Verkehr, der Ehebruch. 2. [mɪskənˈdʌkt], *v.a.* schlecht führen *or* verwalten. 3. *v.r.* sich schlecht aufführen, betragen *or* benehmen; Ehebruch *or* einen Fehltritt begehen.
misconstru–ction [mɪskənˈstrʌkʃən], *s.* die Mißdeutung, irrige Auslegung; *put a –ction on a th.*, einer S. eine falsche Auslegung geben. **–e** [–ˈstrʊ:], *v.a.* mißdeuten, falsch auslegen, mißverstehen.
miscount [mɪsˈkaʊnt], 1. *v.a.* falsch (be)rechnen *or* zählen. 2. *v.n.* sich verrechnen. 3. *s.* die Verrechnung, der Rechenfehler, falsche Zählung.
miscreant [ˈmɪskrɪənt], 1. *s.* der Bösewicht, Schurke. 2. *adj.* schurkisch, gemein, ruchlos.
miscue [mɪsˈkjʊ:], 1. *s.* der Kicks, Fehlstoß (*Bill.*). 2. *v.n.* einen Fehlstoß machen.
misdate [mɪsˈdeɪt], 1. *s.* falsches Datum. 2. *v.a.* falsch datieren.
misdeal [mɪsˈdɪ:l], 1. *ir.v.n.* sich vergeben. 2. *v.a.* vergeben (*cards*). 3. *s.* das Vergeben.
misdeed [mɪsˈdɪ:d], *s.* die Missetat, das Vergehen.
misdeem [mɪsˈdɪ:m], *v.a.* (*Poet.*) verkennen, falsch beurteilen.
misdemean [mɪsdɪˈmɪ:n], *v.r.* sich schlecht aufführen. **–ant** [–ənt], *s.* der Missetäter (*Law*). **–our** [–ə], *s.* strafbares Vergehen (*Law*); schlechtes Betragen; die Missetat; das Vergehen.
misdirect [mɪsdɪˈrɛkt], *v.a.* irreleiten, falsch unterrichten (*a p.*); falsch adressieren (*a letter*); (*fig.*) falsch anbringen *or* verwenden, schlecht zielen. **–ion** [–ˈrɛkʃən], *s.* das Irreführen, die Irreleitung, falsche Auskunft, Adresse *or* Verwendung.
misdoing [mɪsˈdʊ:ɪŋ], *s.* die Missetat, Übeltat.
misdoubt [mɪsˈdaʊt], *v.a.* (*archaic*) bezweifeln, zweifeln an (*Dat.*); mißtrauen.
misemploy [mɪsəmˈplɔɪ], *v.a.* schlecht anwenden, mißbrauchen. **–ment,** *s.* schlechte Anwendung, der Mißbrauch.
mise-en-scène [ˈmɪ:zɑnˈsɛ:n], *s.* die Inszenierung (*Theat. & fig.*).
miser [ˈmaɪzə], *s.* der Geizhals, Filz, Knicker. **–liness,** *s.* der Geiz, die Knauserigkeit. **–ly,** *adj.* geizig, filzig.
miser–able [ˈmɪzərəbl], *adj.* elend, armselig, ärmlich, kläglich, jämmerlich, erbärmlich, verächtlich, schlecht; unglücklich, traurig. **–ere** [–ˈrɪ:rə], *s.* das Miserere (*Mus.*), 51. Psalm; die Klage, der Hilferuf. **–icord** [–ˈzɛrɪkɔ:d], *s.* das Trinkrefektorium (*in monasteries*); die Stütze an der unteren Seite eines Klappsitzes (*for support when standing*); der Dolch für den Gnadenstoß. **–y** [–ɪ], *s.* das Elend, die Not; Trübsal, der Jammer.
miserl–iness [ˈmaɪzəlɪnɪs], *s.*, **–y** [–lɪ:], *adj. see* **miser.**
misery [mɪzərɪ], *see under* **miser–y.**
misfeasance [mɪsˈfɪ:zəns], *s.* das Vergehen, die Übertretung; unrichtiges Vorgehen, schuldhaftes Handeln (*Law*).
misfire [mɪsˈfaɪə], 1. *v.n.* versagen (*Artil.*); aussetzen, fehlzünden (*Motor.*). 2. *s.* der Versager (*Artil.*); die Fehlzündung (*Motor.*).
misfit [ˈmɪsfɪt], *s.* nichtpassendes Stück (*clothing, etc.*); (*fig.*) der Schädling.
misfortune [mɪsˈfɔ:tjʊn], *s.* das Unglück, Mißgeschick, der Unglücksfall.
misgiv–e [mɪsˈgɪv], 1. *ir.v.a.* mit Zweifel *or* Befürchtung erfüllen, Böses ahnen lassen (*about*, über); (only in) *my mind* or *heart –es me*, mir ahnt nichts Gutes, ich habe ein banges Vorgefühl *or* das unangenehme Gefühl. 2. *v.n.* (*Scots*) scheitern, fehlgehen. **–ing** [–ˈgɪvɪŋ], *s.* böse Ahnung, die Befürchtung, Besorgnis, der Zweifel; *have –ings*, Bedenken tragen.
misgovern [mɪsˈgʌvən], *v.a.* schlecht regieren. **–ment,** *s.* schlechte Regierung, die Mißregierung.
misguid–ance [mɪsˈgaɪdəns], *s.* die Irreleitung, Verleitung. **–e** [–ˈgaɪd], *v.a.* (*esp. p.p.*) irreführen, verleiten.
mishandle [mɪsˈhændl], *v.a.* mißhandeln; (*fig.*) schlecht handhaben, (*coll.*) verkorksen.
mishap [ˈmɪshæp], *s.* der Unfall, das Unglück.
mishear [mɪsˈhɪ:ə], *v.a.* (*& n.*) (sich) verhören.
mishmash [ˈmɪʃmæʃ], *s.* der Mischmasch.
misinform [mɪsɪnˈfɔ:m], *v.a.* falsch unterrichten *or* berichten. **–ation** [–fəˈmeɪʃən], *s.* falsche Auskunft, falscher Bericht.
misinterpret [mɪsɪnˈtə:prɪt], *v.a.* mißdeuten, falsch deuten *or* auslegen *or* verstehen. **–ation** [–ˈteɪʃən], *s.* die Mißdeutung, falsche Auslegung.
misjudg–e [mɪsˈdʒʌdʒ], *v.a.* falsch beurteilen. **–ment,** *s.* irriges Urteil.
mislay [mɪsˈleɪ], *v.a.* verlegen.
mislead [mɪsˈlɪ:d], *ir.v.a.* irreführen, irreleiten, verführen, verleiten (*into doing*, zu tun); *be misled*, sich verleiten lassen. **–ing,** *adj.* irreführend.
mislike [mɪsˈlaɪk], (*archaic*) *see* **dislike.**
mismanage [mɪsˈmænɪdʒ], *v.a.* schlecht führen *or* verwalten. **–ment,** *s.* schlechte Verwaltung, die Mißwirtschaft.
misnomer [mɪsˈnoumə], *s.* falsche Benennung, unrichtige Bezeichnung; der Namensirrtum (*Law*).
misogam–ist [mɪˈsɔgəmɪst], *s.* der Ehefeind. **–y** [–mɪ], *s.* die Ehescheu.
misogyn–ist [mɪˈsɔdʒɪnɪst], *s.* der Weiberfeind, Misogyn. **–y** [–nɪ], *s.* der Weiberhaß.
misplace [mɪsˈpleɪs], *v.a.* an die falsche Stelle legen *or* setzen; übel anbringen (*confidence*); verlegen. **–d** [–t], *adj.* übel angebracht, unangebracht, unberechtigt. **–ment,** *s.* das Verstellen, Versetzen.
misprint [ˈmɪsprɪnt], 1. *v.a.* verdrucken, falsch drucken. 2. *s.* der Druckfehler.
misprision [mɪsˈprɪʒən], *s.* das Vergehen, die Versäumnis; unterlassene Anzeige (*of a crime*) (*Law*).
misprize [mɪsˈpraɪz], *v.a.* unterschätzen, verkennen, verachten.
mispron–ounce [mɪsprəˈnaʊns], *v.a. & n.* falsch aussprechen. **–unciation** [–nʌnsɪˈeɪʃən], *s.* falsche Aussprache.
misquot–ation [mɪsˈkwouteɪʃən], *s.* falsche Anführung, falsches Zitat. **–e** [–ˈkwout], *v.a.* falsch zitieren *or* anführen.

misread [mɪsˈrɪːd], *v.a.* falsch lesen *or* deuten, mißdeuten.
misrepresent [mɪsˈrɛprɪzɛnt], *v.a.* falsch *or* ungenau darstellen, verdrehen, entstellen. **–ation** [–ˈteɪʃən], *s.* falsche Darstellung *or* Angabe, die Verdrehung.
misrule [mɪsˈrʊːl], *s.* schlechte Regierung, die Mißregierung; Unordnung, der Tumult, Aufruhr.
¹**miss** [mɪs], *s.* (*as title*) Fräulein; gnädiges Fräulein; (*coll.*) der Backfisch, das (Schul)Mädchen.
²**miss** [mɪs], 1. *v.a.* missen, vermissen, entbehren; verfehlen, nicht treffen; nicht bekommen, verlustig gehen (*Gen.*); sich (*Dat.*) entgehen lassen, verpassen; nicht verstehen (*also of a joke*); überhören (*a remark*); (also – *out*) überspringen, auslassen, fortlassen; – *one's aim*, das Ziel verfehlen; – *fire*, versagen (*firearms*), aussetzen (*motor*); (*fig.*) (*coll.*) erfolglos sein, nicht klappen; – *one's footing*, ausgleiten, fehltreten; (*coll.*) – *one's guess*, falsch tippen; (*coll.*) – *the mark*, danebenschießen; *we – him very much*, er fehlt uns sehr, wir vermissen ihn sehr; – *one's opportunity*, die günstige Gelegenheit verpassen, versäumen *or* vorübergehen lassen; – *school*, die Schule versäumen; – *one's step*, see – *one's footing*; – *one's train*, den Zug verpassen *or* versäumen; – *one's way*, den Weg verfehlen. 2. *v.n.* fehl gehen, verfehlen; nicht treffen (*Shooting*). 3. *s.* der Verlust; das Verpassen, Verfehlen; der Fehlschuß, Fehlstoß; (*coll.*) *give a p. a –*, einen übergehen, umgehen *or* meiden; (*coll.*) *give s.th. a –*, etwas vermeiden, von einer S. ablassen; (*Prov.*) *a – is as good as a mile*, verfehlt ist verspielt; *near –*, der Nächsttreffer. *See* **missing.**
missal [ˈmɪsəl], *s.* das Meßbuch (*R.C.*).
missel [ˈmɪsəl], *s.*, **–-thrush,** *s.* die Misteldrossel (*Orn.*).
misshapen [mɪsˈʃeɪpən], *adj.* ungestaltet, mißgestaltet, unförmig.
missile [ˈmɪsaɪl], 1. *s.* das Wurfgeschoß; *guided –*, ferngesteuertes Raketengeschoß. 2. *adj.* Wurf–, Schleuder–.
missing [ˈmɪsɪŋ], *adj.* abwesend, fehlend, nicht zu finden(d); verschollen, vermißt (*Mil.*); *be –*, fehlen (*also with imp. subj.*); vermißt werden; *be reported –*, als vermißt erklärt werden; – *link*, fehlendes Glied, die Zwischenstufe.
mission [ˈmɪʃən], *s.* die Sendung; Gesandtschaft; der Auftrag, die Aufgabe, Botschaft, diplomatische Mission; die Bestimmung, der Lebenszweck, innerer Beruf; die Mission, Aussendung (*Rel.*); das Missionshaus, die Missionsstation; *foreign –*, äußere Mission; *home –*, innere Mission; – *in life*, der Lebenszweck, die Bestimmung; *on a –*, in einer Mission. **–ary** [–ərɪ], 1. *adj.* Missions–. 2. *s.* der Missionar. **–ary-society,** *s.* die Missionsgesellschaft.
missis [ˈmɪsɪs], *s.* (*sl.*) *see* **missus.**
missive [ˈmɪsɪv], *s.* das Sendschreiben.
misspell [mɪsˈspɛl], *v.a.* falsch buchstabieren *or* schreiben. **–ing,** *s.* falsche Buchstabierung.
misspend [mɪsˈspend], *v.a.* schlecht verwenden (*time, etc.*); vertun, vergeuden (*money, etc.*).
misstate [mɪsˈsteɪt], *v.a.* falsch angeben. **–ment,** *s.* falsche Angabe.
miss–us [ˈmɪsəs], *s.* (*sl.*) die Frau, Ehefrau; gnädige Frau. **–y,** *s.* (*coll.*) kleines Fräulein.
mist [mɪst], 1. *s.* der Nebel; (*fig.*) Schleier; *Scotch –*, der Sprühregen, starker Nebel; (*fig.*) *in a –*, ver-verdutzt, verwirrt, in Verlegenheit. 2. *v.a.* umnebeln, umwölken. 3. *v.n.* (*rare*) nebeln, neblig werden. **–iness,** *s.* die Nebligkeit, (*fig.*) Unklarheit. **–y,** *adj.* neb(e)lig; (*fig.*) unklar, verschwommen.
mistak–able [mɪsˈteɪkəbl], *adj.* verkennbar, mißzuverstehen(d). **–e** [mɪsˈteɪk], 1. *ir.v.a.* verwechseln (*things or persons*) (*for*, mit); fälschlich halten (*for*, für); verkennen (*a p.*); mißverstehen (*a p.'s intentions*), falsch verstehen (*a th.*); *–e one's way*, sich verirren. 2. *ir.v.n.* (*usually pass.*) sich irren, sich verrechnen; *be –en*, sich irren (*in*, in), im Irrtum sein (*in*, über). 3. *s.* der Irrtum, Fehler (*of doing*, zu tun); das Versehen, Mißverständnis; *by –e*, irrtümlich, versehentlich, aus Versehen; (*coll.*) *and no –e*, bestimmt, sicher(lich), unzweifelhaft, ohne Zweifel, zweifelsohne; *in –e for*, an Stelle (*Gen.*); *make a –e*, sich irren. **–en,** *adj.* irrig, verfehlt, falsch, mißverstanden, im Irrtum (befangen); *–en ideas*, falsche Ideen; *–en identity*, die Personenverwechslung; *see* **–e** 2.
mister [ˈmɪstə], *s.* (*as title*) (normally written *Mr.*) Herr; – *Speaker*, Herr Vorsitzender (*Parl.*).
mistime [mɪsˈtaɪm], *v.a.* zur Unzeit tun; einen falschen Zeitpunkt wählen für. **–d,** *adj.* unzeitig, unangebracht.
mistletoe [ˈmɪsəltoʊ], *s.* die Mistel (*Bot.*).
mistral [ˈmɪstrəl], *s.* der Südwind vom Mittelmeer.
mistranslat–e [mɪstrænzˈleɪt, mɪstrænsˈleɪt], *v.a.* falsch übersetzen. **–ion** [–ˈleɪʃən], *s.* falsche Übersetzung.
mistress [ˈmɪstrɪs], *s.* die Herrin; Gebieterin; Meisterin, Besitzerin; Hausfrau; Lehrerin; Geliebte, Maitresse; *form-–*, die Klassenlehrerin; – *of the robes*, oberste Kammerfrau; *she remained – of herself*, sie wußte sich zu beherrschen.
mistrial [mɪsˈtraɪəl], *s.* falsch geführte Untersuchung (*Law*).
mistrust [mɪsˈtrʌst], 1. *v.a.* mißtrauen, nicht trauen (*Dat.*). 2. *s.* das Mißtrauen (*of*, gegen), der Argwohn. **–ful** [–fʊl], *adj.* mißtrauisch (*of*, gegen); *be –ful of*, mißtrauen (*Dat.*).
misty [ˈmɪstɪ], *see* **mist.**
misunderstand [mɪsʌndəˈstænd], *ir.v.a.* mißverstehen; sich irren in (*Dat.*). **–ing** [–ɪŋ], *s.* das Mißverständnis; die Mißhelligkeit, Uneinigkeit.
misus–age [mɪsˈjuːzɪdʒ], *s.* die Mißhandlung, verkehrte Anwendung. **–e,** 1. [–ˈjuːz], *v.a.* mißbrauchen, mißhandeln; falsch anwenden. 2. [mɪsˈjuːs], *s.* der Mißbrauch.
¹**mite** [maɪt], *s.* die Milbe, Made (*Zool.*).
²**mite** [maɪt], *s.* der Heller, das Scherflein; Stückchen, Bißchen; (*coll.*) kleines Kind, Ding *or* Wesen, kleines Wurm, das Würmchen (*of a child*).
mitigat–e [ˈmɪtɪgeɪt], *v.a.* mildern, mäßigen (*punishment*); lindern (pain, *grief, etc.*); besänftigen, beruhigen (*anger, etc.*). **–ion** [–ˈgeɪʃən], *s.* die Milderung, Linderung, Besänftigung.
mitosis [maɪˈtoʊsɪs], *s.* die Zellteilung, Mitose (*Biol.*).
mitrailleuse [mɪtrɑˈjəːz], *s.* die Mitrailleuse, Kugelspritze.
¹**mitre** [ˈmaɪtə], 1. *s.* die Bischofsmütze, Mitra, Inful; (*fig.*) Bischofswürde, der Bischofshut. 2. *v.a.* mit der Bischofswürde bekleiden.
²**mitre** [ˈmaɪtə], 1. *s.* die Gehrung, Gehre (*Carp.*). 2. *v.a.* gehren. **–-block,** *s.* die Gehrungslade. **–-gear,** *s.* der Kegeltrieb. **–-wheels,** *pl.* Kegelräder.
mitt [mɪt], *s.* (*sl.*) die Pfote, Tatze, Flosse; der Spitzenhalbhandschuh, Pulswärmer. **–en,** *s.* der Fausthandschuh, Fäustling, Pulswärmer; (*sl.*) *get* (*give*) *the –en*, einen Korb bekommen (geben). **–ens,** *pl.* (*sl.*) Boxhandschuhe (*pl.*).
mittimus [ˈmɪtɪməs], *s.* der Haftbefehl (*Law*); (*coll.*) die Entlassung, der Laufpaß.
mix [mɪks], 1. *v.a.* vermischen, vermengen, anrühren, zusammenmischen, melieren; – *up*, tüchtig mischen, (*coll.*) verwechseln, verwirren; (*coll.*) *be –ed up with*, verwickelt sein in. 2. *v.n.* sich mischen (lassen); (*fig.*) sich vertragen; verkehren, Umgang haben. **–ed** [–t], *adj.* gemischt, vermischt, Misch–; meliert (*of hair, cloth*); (*coll.*) verschiedenartig, bunt, zusammengewürfelt; zweifelhaft; verwirrt; *ready –ed*, anstrichfertig (*of paint*); *–ed bathing*, das Familienbad; *–ed company*, bunte *or* gemischte Gesellschaft; *–ed doubles*, gemischtes Doppelspiel (*Tenn.*); *–ed marriage*, die Mischehe; *–ed pickles*, pikant eingemachtes Gemüse, Mixpickles (*pl.*); *–ed school*, die Gemeinschaftsschule. **–er,** *s.* der Mischer, die Mischmaschine; das Mischgerät (*Rad.*); (*coll.*) *good –er*, geselliger Mensch. **–ture** [–tʃə], *s.* die Mischung, Zusammensetzung; Mixtur (*Pharm.*); (*fig.*) das Gemisch, Gemenge. (*coll.*) **–-up,** *s.* das Durcheinander, die Verwirrung; das Handgemenge, die Schlägerei.
miz(z)en [ˈmɪzən], *s.* der Besan (*Naut.*). **–-mast,** *s.* der Besanmast; Kreuzmast (*on square-riggers*). **–-sail,** *s.* das Besansegel. **–-topsail,** *s.* das Kreuz(mars)segel.

mizzle ['mɪzəl], 1. *v.n.* fein regnen, rieseln, nieseln. 2. *s.* der Staubregen, Sprühregen.
mnemo-nic [nɛ'mɔnɪk], 1. *adj.* Gedächtnis–, mnemotechnisch. 2. *s.* die Gedächtnishilfe. **-nics,** *pl.* (*sing. constr.*), **-techny** [nɛmoʊ'teknɪ], *s.* die Gedächtniskunst, Mnemotechnik.
mo [moʊ], *s.* (*sl.*) der Augenblick, der *or* das Nu.
moan [moʊn], 1. *s.* das Stöhnen. 2. *v.n.* stöhnen, ächzen; (*coll.*) wehklagen, jammern.
moat [moʊt], *s.* der Burggraben, Festungsgraben, Stadtgraben. **-ed,** *adj.* mit einem Wassergraben umgeben.
mob [mɔb], 1. *s.* das Gesindel, der Pöbel, Pöbelhaufen, lärmende Menge, die Menschenmenge. 2. *v.a.* lärmend herfallen über, bedrängen *or* anfallen. **--law,** *s.* das Faustrecht, die Volksjustiz, Lynchjustiz. **-ocracy** [–'ɔkrəsɪ], *s.* (*coll.*) die Herrschaft des Pöbels.
mob-cap ['mɔbkæp]], *s.* die Morgenhaube.
mobil-e ['moʊbaɪl], *adj.* (leicht) beweglich; unstet; mobil, motorisiert (*Mil.*); *-e warfare*, der Bewegungskrieg. **-ity** [–'bɪlɪtɪ], *s.* die Beweglichkeit. **-ization** [moʊbɪlaɪ'zeɪʃən], *s.* die Mobilmachung (*Mil.*); Flüssigmachung (*C.L.*). **-ize** ['moʊbɪlaɪz], 1. *v.a.* mobil machen, mobilisieren (*also C.L.*); flüssig machen (*C.L.*). 2. *v.n.* mobil gemacht werden.
moccasin ['mɔkəsɪn], *s.* der Mokassin, Indianerschuh; die Mokassinschlange, der Kupferkopf (*Zool.*).
mocha ['moʊkə], *s.* der Mokka(kaffee); Mochastein, heller Chalzedon.
mock [mɔk], 1. *v.a.* verspotten, verlachen, verhöhnen; necken, narren, aufziehen; nachahmen, nachäffen; täuschen, vereiteln. 2. *v.n.* spotten, spötteln (*at*, über (*Acc.*)). 3. *s.* der Spott, Hohn; die Verhöhnung; Nachahmung; *make a – of*, spotten über, lächerlich machen. 4. *attrib. adj.* nachgemacht, Schein–; Schwindel–; – *fight*, das Scheingefecht; – *hare*, falscher Hase. *--heroic, adj.* komisch-heroisch; – *king*, der Schattenkönig; – *modesty*, vorgetäuschte Sittsamkeit; – *sun*, die Nebensonne (*Astr.*). **-er,** *s.* der Spötter. **-ery,** *s.* der Spott (*of*, über), die Verhöhnung; das Gespött; der Schein, das Blendwerk, die Gaukelei, das Possenspiel; *make a -ery of*, verhöhnen, zum Gespött machen; *turn a th. into -ery*, mit einer S. Spott *or* sein Gespött treiben. **-ing,** 1. *adj.* spöttisch, höhnisch, Spott–. 2. *s.* das Gespött, der Hohn. **-ing-bird,** *s.* die Spottdrossel.
mod-al [moʊdl], *adj.* die Form *or* Art und Weise betreffend; durch Umstände bedingt; modal (*Gram. & Log.*); *-al verb*, modales Hilfszeitwort (*Gram.*). **-ity** [mo'dælɪtɪ], *s.* die Modalität, Art und Weise des Seins *or* Geschehens. **-e** [moʊd], *s.* die Art und Weise; der Brauch, die Sitte, Mode; Tonart (*Mus.*); der Modus (*Gram.*); die Erscheinungsform, Beschaffenheit; (*coll.*) *be all the -e*, modern *or* ganz Mode sein. **-ish** [–ɪʃ], *adj.* modern, modisch, Mode–. **-iste** [mo'dɪ:st], *s.* die Modistin.
model [mɔdl], 1. *s.* das Modell, Muster; Vorbild, die Type; Vorführdame (*for dresses*); *act as* –, Modell stehen (*to* (*Dat.*)); *after* or *on the – of*, nach dem Vorbild von; *artist's* –, lebendes Modell; – *of truthfulness*, das Muster der Wahrhaftigkeit. 2. *v.a. & n.* modellieren; Form geben (*a th.*, einer S.); formen, bilden, gestalten, modeln (*after* or *on*, nach); – *o.s. on*, sich ein Muster nehmen an. 3. *adj.* vorbildlich, musterhaft, Muster–; – *farm*, die Musterwirtschaft. **-ler,** *s.* der Modellierer. **-ling,** *s.* das Modellieren, die Formgebung, Formung; Modellierkunst.
moderat-e, 1. ['mɔdərət], *adj.* mäßig, gemäßigt, mild; niedrig, billig (*price*), bescheiden (*demand*), mittelmäßig. 2. [–reɪt], *v.a.* mildern, mäßigen, beruhigen, einschränken. 3. *v.n.* abnehmen, nachlassen, sich mäßigen. 4. [–rət], *s.* Gemäßigte(r), *m.* **-eness,** *s.* die Mäßigkeit; Mittelmäßigkeit. **-ion** [–'reɪʃən], *s.* die Mäßigung; Mäßigkeit, das Maß; *pl.* erste Universitätsprüfung (*Oxford*); *in -ion*, mit Maß, mäßig. **-or** [–'reɪtə], *s.* (*Scots*) Vorsitzende(r) der schottischen Kirche, *m.*; der Prüfungskommissar für die Universitätsprüfung (*Oxford*) *or* Universitätsprüfung in Mathematik (*Cambridge*).
modern ['mɔdən], 1. *adj.* modern, neu, jetzig; – *history*, neuere Geschichte; – *languages*, neuere Sprachen; – *side*, die Realabteilung (*of school*); – *times*, die Neuzeit. 2. *pl.* die Neueren (*pl.*). **-ism,** *s.* die Neuerung, moderne Richtung, moderner Ausdruck; der Modernismus (*Theol.*). **-ity** [mo'də:nɪtɪ], *s.* die Moderne; Modernität. **-ization** [mɔdənɪ'zeɪʃən], *s.* die Modernisierung. **-ize** [–'naɪz], *v.a.* modernisieren, erneuern. **-ness,** *s.* die Modernität, Neuzeitlichkeit.
modest ['mɔdɪst], *adj.* bescheiden; maßvoll, mäßig, anspruchslos; anständig, sittsam. **-y** [–dəstɪ], *s.* die Bescheidenheit, Sittsamkeit.
modicum ['mɔdɪkəm], *s.* das Wenige, Bißchen, kleine Menge.
modif-iable ['mɔdɪfaɪəbl], *adj.* abänderlich, änderungsfähig, modifizierbar. **-ication** [–fɪ'keɪʃən], *s.* die Änderung, Abänderung, Veränderung, Umänderung, Modifikation (*to*, an); Einschränkung; Umstellung; der Umlaut (*Gram.*). **-y** [–faɪ], *v.a.* abändern, modifizieren; einschränken, beschränken, mäßigen; umlauten (*Gram.*).
mod-ish, -iste, *see under* **modal.**
modulat-e ['mɔdjuleɪt], 1. *v.a.* regulieren, abmessen, abtönen, abstufen, anpassen. 2. *v.n.* modulieren, übergehen, die Tonart wechseln. **-ed,** *adj.* abgestimmt (*Rad.*). **-ion** [–'leɪʃən], *s.* die (Ton)Abstufung, Abwandlung, Anpassung, Regelung; Abstimmung (*Rad.*), Modulation (*Mus. & Rad.*). **-or** [–leɪtə], *s.* Regulierende(r, s), *m.*, *f. or n.*, der Modulator.
modul-e ['mɔdju:l], *s.* das Verhältnismaß; der Modul, Model (*Arch.*). **-us** [–jələs], *s.* (pl. *-i*) der Modul, konstanter Koeffizient (*Math.*).
mogul ['moʊgʌl], *s.* der Mogul, orientalischer Herrscher.
mohair [mo'hɛ:ə], *s.* das Angoraziegenhaar, der Mohär; Mohärstoff.
moiety ['mɔɪətɪ], *s.* der Teil; die Hälfte.
moil [mɔɪl], *v.n.* sich abplacken *or* abquälen.
moir-e [mwɑ:], *s.* (also *-e antique*) der Mohr, Wasserglanz (*on material*); geflammter *or* gewässerter Stoff, der Moiréstoff, der *or* das Moiré. **-é** [–'reɪ], 1. *s.* der Wasserglanz (*on material*), wolkenartiger Schimmer (*on metal*). 2. *adj.* moiriert, geflammt, gewässert.
moist [mɔɪst], *adj.* feucht; naß; – *sugar*, der Sandzucker; – *steam*, der Naßdampf. **-en** ['mɔɪsn], *v.a.* anfeuchten, befeuchten. **-ness,** *s.*, **-ure** ['mɔɪstʃə], *s.* die Feuchtigkeit, Nässe.
moke [moʊk], *s.* (*sl.*) der Esel.
molar ['moʊlə], 1. *adj.* zermalmend, mahlend; – *tooth*, der Backenzahn. 2. *s.* der Backenzahn.
molasses [mə'læsɪz], *pl.* (*sing. constr.*) die Melasse; der Zuckersyrup.
1**mole** [moʊl], *s.* das Muttermal, der Leberfleck.
2**mole** [moʊl], *s.* der Maulwurf (*Zool.*). **-hill,** *s.* der Maulwurfshaufen; *make a mountain out of a -hill*, aus einer Mücke einen Elefanten machen.
3**mole** [moʊl], *s.* die Mole; der Hafendamm.
4**mole** [moʊl], *s.* das Mondkalb (*Vet.*).
molecul-ar [mə'lɛkjulə], *adj.* molekular, Molekular–. **-e** ['mɔlɪkju:l], *s.* das Molekül, die *or* das Molekel.
molest [mə'lɛst], *v.a.* belästigen; lästig *or* beschwerlich fallen (*Dat.*). **-ation** [moləs'teɪʃən], *s.* die Belästigung.
mollif-ication [mɔlɪfɪ'keɪʃən], *s.* die Besänftigung. **-y** ['mɔlɪfaɪ], *v.a.* besänftigen, beruhigen; mildern; erweichen (*wax, etc.*).
mollusc ['mɔlʌsk], *s.* das Weichtier, die Molluske. **-a** [–'lʌskə], *pl.* Weichtiere (*pl.*). **-oid** [–'lʌskɔɪd], *adj.* molluskenartig. **-ous** [–'lʌskəs], *adj.* Mollusken–; (*fig.*) weich, schwammig, wabbelig.
mollycoddle ['mɔlɪkɔdl], 1. *s.* der Weichling, Schlappschwanz; das Muttersöhnchen. 2. *v.a.* verhätscheln, verzärteln.
moloch ['moʊlək], *s.* der Moloch, (*fig.*) Götze.
molten ['moʊltən], *adj.* geschmolzen, gegossen; flüssig; – *mass*, die Schmelze.
molybd-ate [mə'lɪbdeɪt], *s.* molybdänsaures Salz. **-enum** [–dənəm], *s.* das Molybdän. **-ic** [–dɪk], *adj.* Molybdän–, molybdänsauer.
moment ['moʊmənt], *s.* der Augenblick; die

Wichtigkeit, Tragweite, Bedeutung, der Belang, das Moment (*Phys.*); *at the* –, gerade jetzt *or* damals, augenblicklich; *at the – of writing*, während ich dies schreibe; *at this* –, in diesem Augenblick; *at the last* –, im letzten Augenblick; *the – he had done it*, sobald er es getan hatte; *the* (*very*) – *that*, gerade als; *for the* –, gerade jetzt; *this* (*very*) –, *in a* –, sogleich, sofort, auf der Stelle; *one* –, *half a* –, (wart) einen Augenblick; *it is of no great* –, es ist ohne Belang; – *of a force*, statisches Moment, das Moment einer Kraft; – *of a force about a point*, das Drehungsmoment einer Kraft; – *of inertia*, das Trägheitsmoment; – *of resistance*, das Widerstandsmoment. **–arily** [–ərɪlɪ], *adv.* für einen Augenblick nur. **–ary** [–ərɪ], *adj.* augenblicklich, momentan; flüchtig, vorübergehend, vergänglich. **–ous** [mə'mɛntəs], *adj.* wichtig, gewichtig, bedeutend, folgenschwer. **–ousness,** *s.* die Wichtigkeit, Bedeutung, Tragweite. **–um** [mə'mɛntəm], *s.* das Moment, die Kraftwirkung; Wucht, Schwungkraft, Triebkraft; der Antrieb; Impuls; *gather –um*, an Schwung gewinnen.

monachism ['mɔnəkɪzm], *s.* das Mönch(s)tum, Mönchswesen.

monad ['mɔnæd], *s.* die Monade (*Phil.*); das Urkörperchen, die Einzelzelle, organische Einheit (*Biol.*); einwertiges Element (*Chem.*). **–elphous** [–nə'dɛlfəs], *adj.* monadelphisch (*Bot.*). **–ic** [–'nædɪk], *adj.* monadisch. **–ism** ['mɔnədɪzm], *s.* die Monadenlehre, Monadologie.

monandrous [mo'nændrəs], *adj.* einmännig, mit nur einem Staubgefäß (*Bot.*).

monarch ['mɔnək], *s.* der Monarch, (Allein)-Herrscher. **–al** [mə'nɑ:kl], *adj.*, **–ic(al)** [mə'nɑ:kɪk(l)], *adj.* monarchisch, Monarchie–; monarchistisch, monarchiefreundlich. **–ism** ['mɔnəkɪzm], *s.* der Monarchismus. **–ist** [–kɪst], 1. *s.* der Monarchist. 2. *attrib. adj.* monarchistisch. **–y** [–kɪ], *s.* die Monarchie.

monast–ery ['mɔnəstrɪ], *s.* das (Mönchs)Kloster. **–ic** [mə'næstɪk], *adj.* klösterlich, Mönchs–; (*fig.*) abgeschlossen. **–icism** [–'næstɪsɪzm], *s.* das Mönch(s)tum; Mönchswesen, Klosterwesen.

Monday ['mʌndɪ], *s.* der Montag; *on* –, am Montag; *on –(s)*, montags; *Black* –, (*sl.*) der Schulanfang.

monet–ary ['mʌnɪtrɪ], *adj.* Geld–, Finanz–, Münz–; *–ary standard*, der Münzfuß. **–ize** [–tɑɪz, 'mɔnɪtɑɪz], *v.a.* den Münzfuß festsetzen; in Umlauf setzen (*coin*).

money ['mʌnɪ], *s.* das Geld; *call* –, Geld auf Abruf (*C.L.*); *demand* –, das Tagesgeld (*C.L.*); – *down*, see *ready* –; *make* –, Geld verdienen (*by*, an *or* bei); *make – of*, zu Geld machen; *public* –, öffentliche Gelder; *ready* –, bares Geld; *short of* –, nicht bei Kasse; **––bag,** *s.* der Geldbeutel. **––bags,** *pl.* (*coll.*) das Geld, der Reichtum; steinreicher Mensch. **––box,** *s.* die Sparbüchse. **––changer,** *s.* der Geldwechsler, Geldmakler. **–ed,** *adj.* vermögend, reich; *–ed classes*, besitzende Klassen, Kapitalisten; *–ed interest*, die Finanz(welt). **––grubber,** *s.* der Geizhals. **––lender,** *s.* der Geldverleiher. **––making,** 1. *adj.* gewinnbringend, einträglich. 2. *s.* der Gelderwerb. **––market,** *s.* die Börse. **––matters,** *pl.* Geldangelegenheiten (*pl.*). **––order,** *s.* die Postanweisung. **–'s-worth,** *s.* der Geld(es)wert; *his* (*full*) *–'s-worth*, etwas Vollwertiges für sein Geld. **––transactions,** *pl.* Geldgeschäfte.

monger ['mʌŋgə], *s.* (*usually in compounds*) der Krämer, Händler; *fish–*, der Fischhändler; *news–*, der Neuigkeitskrämer; *scandal––*, die Klatsche, das Lästermaul; *sensation––*, der Sensationsmacher, Sensationsschmied.

mongoose ['mɔŋgu:s], *s.* der Mungo (*Zool.*).

mongrel ['mʌŋgrəl], 1. *s.* der Mischling, die Kreuzung (*animals*), der Bastard (*animals & men*). 2. *adj.* Misch–, Bastard–.

monis–m ['mɔnɪzm], *s.* der Monismus (*Phil.*). **–t** [–ɪst], *s.* der Monist. **–tic** [–'nɪstɪk], *adj.* monistisch.

monit–ion [mo'nɪʃən], *s.* die Mahnung, Warnung; Vorladung (*Law*). **–or** ['mɔnɪtə], *s.* der (Er)-Mahner, Warner; Klassenordner, Lehrgehilfe (*in school*); Überwachungstechniker (*Rad.*); Monitor, Küstenpanzer (*Naut.*); Waran (*Zool.*). **–orial,** [–'tɔ:rɪəl], *adj.* ermahnend, warnend; *–orial system*, das Monitorsystem (*in schools*). **–orship,** *s.* die Stellung des Klassenordners. **–ory** [–trɪ], 1. *adj.* ermahnend, warnend, Ermahnungs–. 2. *s.* das Ermahnungschreiben (*Eccl.*).

monk [mʌŋk], *s.* der Mönch; verschmierte Stelle (*Print.*). **–ery,** *s.* das Mönchswesen, Mönchtum; Klosterleben; Mönche. **–ish,** *adj.* mönchlich, klösterlich. **–'s-hood,** *s.* der Eisenhut (*Bot.*).

monkey ['mʌŋkɪ], 1. *s.* der Affe (*also fig.*); (*sl.*) fünfhundert Pfund *or* Dollar; die Ramme, der Rammbär, Fallblock, Rammklotz (*Techn.*); (*coll.*) *little* –, der Nichtsnutz, kleiner Strolch, kleines Äffchen; (*sl.*) *get one's – up*, in Zorn geraten; (*sl.*) *put s.o.'s – up*, einen reizen *or* aufbringen. 2. *v.n.* Possen treiben, Dummheiten machen (*with*, mit), herumpfuschen (*with*, an); (*coll.*) – *about*, herumfummeln, leichtsinnig umgehen (*with*, mit). 3. *v.a.* nachäffen. (*coll.*) **––business,** *s.* der Unfug. **––engine,** *s.* die Rammaschine. **––gland,** die Verjüngungsdrüse. **––house,** *s.* das Affenhaus. **––jacket,** *s.* die Matrosenjacke. **––puzzle,** *s.* die Araukarie (*Bot.*). **––tricks,** *pl.* Narrenspossen. **––wrench,** *s.* der Engländer, Universalschraubenschlüssel.

monk–ish [mʌŋkɪʃ], *see* **monk.**

mono–basic [mɔnoʊ'beɪsɪk], *adj.* einbasig (*Chem.*). **–carpic** [–'kɑ:pɪk], *adj.* nur einmal fruchtend. **–carpous** [–'kɑ:pəs], *adj.* einfrüchtig. **–chromatic** [–krə'mætɪk], *adj. see* **–chrome** 2. **–chrome** ['mɔnəkroʊm], 1. *s.* einfarbiges Gemälde. 2. *adj.* einfarbig. **–cle** ['mɔnəkl], *s.* das Einglas, Monokel. **–clinal** [–'klɑɪnl], *adj.* mit nur einer Neigungsfläche (*Geol.*). **–clinic** [–'klɪnɪk], *adj.* monoklin, mit drei ungleichwertigen Achsen (*Min.*). **–coque** ['mɔnəkɔk], *s.* der Stromlinienrumpf (*Av.*). **–cotyledon** [–kɔtɪ'lɪ:dən], *s.* einkeimblättrige Pflanze. **–cular** [mə'nɔkjʊlə], *adj,* einäugig; für ein Auge. **–dactylous** [–'dæktɪləs], *adj.* einzehig (*Zool.*). **–dy** ['mɔnədɪ], *s.* die Monodie, der Einzelgesang. **–gamous** [mə'nɔgəməs], *adj.* monogam. **–gamy** [mə'nɔgəmɪ], *s.* die Einehe, Monogamie. **–gram** ['mɔnəgræm], *s.* das Monogramm. **–graph** ['mɔnəgrɑ:f], *s.* die Monographie. **–lith** ['mɔnəlɪθ], *s.* der Monolith, einzeln bearbeiteter Steinblock. **–logue** ['mɔnəlɔg], *s.* der Monolog, das Selbstgespräch. **–mania** [–'meɪnɪə], *s.* fixe Idee, die Zwangsvorstellung, Monomanie. **–maniac** [–'meɪnɪæk], *s.* der Monomane. **–metallism** [–'mɛtəlɪzm], *s.* einheitliche Währung. **–mial** [mə'noʊmɪəl], 1. *s.* einfache Größe (*Math.*). 2. *adj.* monomisch (*Math.*). **–phase** ['mɔnəfeɪz], *adj.* einphasig, Einphasen– (*Elec.*). **–plane** ['mɔnəpleɪn], *s.* der Eindecker (*Av.*); *high-wing –plane*, der Hochdecker; *low-wing –plane*, der Tiefdecker. **–polist** [mə'nɔpəlɪst], *s.* der Monopolist, Alleinhersteller, Alleinhändler. **–polize** [mə'nɔpəlɑɪz], *v.a.* monopolisieren; für sich allein in Anspruch nehmen, allein beherrschen, an sich reißen, mit Beschlag belegen. **–poly** [mə'nɔpəlɪ] *s.* das Alleinverkaufsrecht, Alleinherstellerrecht, Monopol (*of*, auf); (*fig.*) ausschließliches Recht (*of*, auf), die Alleinherrschaft (*of*, über). **–rail** ['mɔnəreɪl], 1. *adj.* einschienig. 2. *s.* die Einschienenbahn. **–syllabic** [mɔnəsɪ'læbɪk], *adj.* einsilbig. **–syllable** [mɔnəsɪləbl], *s.* einsilbiges Wort; *in –syllables*, einsilbig. **–theism** ['mɔnəθɪ:ɪzm], *s.* der Monotheismus. **–theist** ['mɔnəθɪ:ɪst], *s.* der Monotheist. **–theistic** [–'ɪstɪk], *adj.* monotheistisch. **–tone** ['mɔnətoʊn], *s.* eintönige Wiederholung, die Eintönigkeit; (*fig.*) das Einerlei. **–tonous** [–'nɔtənəs], *adj.* eintönig, monoton; (*fig.*) einförmig, langweilig. **–tony** [–'nɔtənɪ], *s.* die Eintönigkeit, Monotonie; (*fig.*). Einförmigkeit. **–type** [–tɑɪp], *s.* die Monotype-(setzmachine). **–xide** [mə'nɔksɑɪd], *s.* das Monoxyd.

monsoon ['mɔnsu:n], *s.* der Monsun; *dry* –, der Wintermonsun; *wet* –, der Sommermonsun.

monster ['mɔnstə], 1. *s.* das Ungeheuer, Scheusal; die Mißbildung, Mißgestalt, Mißgeburt, das Monstrum (*Physiol.*); – *of ugliness*, der Ausbund von Häßlichkeit, wahres Scheusal. 2. *adj.* ungeheuer groß, Riesen–.

monstrance ['mɔnstrəns], *s.* die Monstranz.
monstro-sity [mɔn'strɔsɪtɪ], *s.* die Ungeheuerlichkeit; Mißgestalt, Mißbildung. **-us** ['mɔnstrəs], *adj.* ungeheuer, riesig; mißgestalt(et), unförmig, ungestalt, unnatürlich; ungeheuerlich, fürchterlich, gräßlich, entsetzlich, scheußlich, abscheulich; (*coll.*) haarsträubend, absurd. **-usness,** *s.* die Ungeheuerlichkeit, Entsetzlichkeit, Abscheulichkeit.
montage ['mɔntɑ:ʒ], *s.* die Zusammensetzung, Aufstellung, Montage (*film, etc.*).
month [mʌnθ], *s.* der Monat; *this last* –, seit vier Wochen; *this day* –, heute in einem Monat; *by the* –, (all)monatlich; *for* –*s*, monatelang; *once a* –, einmal im Monat; (*coll.*) – *of Sundays*, unabsehbare Zeit; *give a* –*'s notice*, mit vierwöchentlicher Wirkung kündigen. **-ly,** 1. *adj.* monatlich, Monats–. 2. *adv.* monatlich. 3. *s.* die Monatsschrift. **-lies,** *pl.* (*coll.*) monatliche Regel.
montic(u)le ['mɔntɪk(ju:)l], *s.* die Erhebung, das Hügelchen.
monument ['mɔnjəmənt], *s.* das Denkmal (*also fig.*), Grabmal (*to*, für). **-al** [mɔnju'mɛntl], *adj.* Denkmal–, Grabmal–, Gedenk–; (*fig.*) hervorragend, monumental, kolossal, gewaltig, imposant.
moo [mu:], 1. *v.n.* muhen (*of cows*). 2. *s.* das Muhen. **--cow,** *s.* (*nursery talk*) die Muhkuh.
mooch [mu:tʃ], *v.n.* (*sl.*) (also – *around* or *about*) herumlungern; – *along*, einherlatschen.
[1]**mood** [mu:d], *s.* der Modus (*Gram., Log.*); *subjunctive* –, die Möglichkeitsform, der Konjunktiv; *verb of* –, see *modal verb*.
[2]**mood** [mu:d], *s.* die Gefühlslage, Stimmung, Laune; *in a melancholy* –, niedergeschlagen; *be in the* (*in no*) –, (nicht) aufgelegt sein, (keine) Lust haben (*for*, zu); ***when the* – *is on me***, wenn ich in der Stimmung bin; *man of* –*s*, launischer Mensch. **-iness,** *s.* die Launenhaftigkeit, Verdrießlichkeit, üble Laune. **-y,** *adj.* launisch, launenhaft; schwermütig, verstimmt, mürrisch, verdrießlich.
moon [mu:n], 1. *s.* der Mond; (*fig., Poet.*) Monat; *cry for the* –, Unmögliches verlangen; *full* –, der Vollmond; *face like a full* –, das Vollmondgesicht; *new* –, der Neumond; *once in a blue* –, nur alle Jubeljahre (einmal); *there is a* (*no*) –, der Mond scheint (nicht). 2. *v.n.*; (*coll.*) – *about*, umherschweifen, herumlungern. 3. *v.a.*; (*coll.*) – *away one's time*, die Zeit vertrödeln. **--beam,** *s.* der Mondstrahl. **--calf,** *s.* das Mondkalb; (*fig.*) der Tölpel. **-ed,** *adj. suff.* –mondförmig. **-light,** 1. *adj.* mondhell; (*coll.*) –*light flit*, heimliches Ausziehen bei Nacht. 2. *s.* das Mondlicht, der Mondschein. **-lit,** *adj.* mondhell. **-rise,** *s.* der Mondaufgang. **-shine,** *s.* der Mondschein; (*fig.*) leerer Schein, der Schwindel, Unsinn; (*Amer.*) geschmuggelter Alkohol. (*sl.*) **-shiner,** *s.* (*Amer.*) der Alkoholschmuggler. **-stone,** *s.* der Mondstein, echter Adular. **-struck,** *adj.* mondsüchtig. (*coll.*) **-y,** *adj.* träumerisch, zerstreut.
[1]**moor** ['mu:ə], *s.* das Moor, (*often pl.*) Hochmoor, Heideland, die Bergheide. **-cock,** *s.* das Männchen des Teichhuhns. **-fowl,** *s.*, **-hen,** *s.* das Teichhuhn. **-land,** *s.* das Heideland.
[2]**Moor,** *s. see Index of Names.*
[3]**moor** ['mu:ə], 1. *v.a.* verankern, vertäuen, anlegen (*Naut.*); (*fig.*) festmachen, sichern; *be* –*ed*, *see* – 2. 2. *v.n.* vor Anker gehen *or* liegen, ankern. **-age** [–rɪdʒ], *s.* der Ankerplatz. **-ing** [–rɪŋ], 1. *s.* das Vertäuen, (Ver)Ankern; *pl.* die Vertäuung; der Ankerplatz. 2. *attrib. adj.* Anker–. **-ing-mast,** *s.* der Ankermast (*Av.*). **-ing-post,** *s.* der Vertäuungspfahl. **-ing-rope,** *s.* die Halteleine.
moose [mu:s], *s.* amerikanischer Elch, das Elen(tier) (*Zool.*).
moot [mu:t], 1. *v.a.* erörtern, aufwerfen, anschneiden (*a problem*). 2. *adj.* strittig, umstritten, zweifelhaft, zu erörtern(d). 3. *s.* die Volksgerichtsversammlung (*Hist.*), Erörterung (*Law*); (*fig.*) Tagung, das Lagertreffen.
[1]**mop** [mɔp], 1. *s.* der Scheuerlappen, Wischlappen; Schrubber, Dweil (*Naut.*); (*fig.*) Wust (*of hair*). 2. *v.a.* abwischen, aufwischen; säubern (*Mil.*); (*sl.*) – *up*, aufwischen, abtrocknen; verschlucken; an sich reißen, sich aneignen. **--head,** *s.* der Krauskopf, Strubelkopf. **-ping-up operation,** die Säuberungsaktion (*Mil.*).
[2]**mop** [mɔp], 1. *v.n.*; – *and mow*, Grimassen *or* Gesichter schneiden. 2. *s.*; –*s and mows*, Grimassen.
[3]**mop** [mɔp], *s.* der Jahrmarkt.
mop-e [moʊp], 1. *v.n.* niedergeschlagen, schwermütig *or* teilnahmslos sein, den Kopf hängen lassen, Trübsal blasen. 2. *v.a.* (*only pass.*); *be* –*ed*, entmutigt, niedergeschlagen *or* betrübt sein. 3. *s.* der Kopfhänger, Trübsalbläser; (*coll.*) *the* –*es*, der Trübsinn, heulendes Elend. **-ing, -ish,** *adj.* niedergeschlagen, mutlos; betrübt, trübsinnig, griesgrämig, verdrießlich. **-ishness,** *s.* der Trübsinn, die Mutlosigkeit, Niedergeschlagenheit, Verdrießlichkeit, Griesgrämigkeit.
moppet ['mɔpɪt], *s.* (*coll.*) das Püppchen (*also fig.*), die Krabbe.
moquette [mo'kɛt], *s.* das Mokett, Plüschgewebe.
moraine [mo'reɪn], *s.* die Moräne.
moral ['mɔrəl], 1. *adj.* moralisch, sittlich, tugendhaft, sittenrein, lauter; vernunftgemäß, innerlich, charakterlich, gefestigt; Moral–, Sitten–; – *certainty*, voraussichtliche *or* zuversichtliche Gewißheit; – *character*, gefestigter Charakter, die Charakterfestigkeit; – *courage*, sittliche Entschlossenheit; – *law*, das Sittengesetz; – *philosophy*, die Sittenlehre, Moralphilosophie; – *sense*, das Sittlichkeitsgefühl; – *support*, innerliche Unterstützung; – *victory*, moralischer Sieg. 2. *s.* die Nutzanwendung, Lehre (*of a story, etc.*); sittlicher Standpunkt *or* Grundsatz; *pl.* die Sittlichkeit, Moral, Moralität, Tugend, sittliches Verhalten; *pl.* (*sing. constr.*) die Sittenlehre, Ethik (*Phil.*); *point the* –, die Nutzanwendung ziehen, den sittlichen Standpunkt betonen. **-e** [mo'rɑ:l], *s.* die Moral, (Mannes)Zucht, Haltung (*esp. Mil.*). **-ist** ['mɔrəlɪst], *s.* der Sittenlehrer, Sittenrichter, Sittenprediger; Ethiker. **-ity** [mə'rælɪtɪ], *s.* sittliches Verhalten, sittliche Reinheit, die Tugend, Moral, Sittlichkeit; Sittenlehre, Ethik; Sittenpredigt; Moralität (*Theat.*). **-ize** ['mɔrəlaɪz], 1. *v.n.* moralisieren, sittenpredigen (*about* or *on*, über (*Acc.*)). 2. *v.a.* sittlich veredeln *or* beeinflussen.
morass [mo'ræs], *s.* der Morast, Sumpf; (*fig.*) die Wirrnis.
moratorium [mɔrə'tɔ:rɪəm], *s.* die Stundung, das Moratorium, der (Zahlungs)Aufschub.
morbid ['mɔ:bɪd], *adj.* krankhaft, angekränkelt; – *anatomy*, pathologische Anatomie. **-ity** [–'bɪdɪtɪ], *s.* die Krankhaftigkeit; Krankheitsziffer (*statistics*). **-ness,** *s.* die Krankhaftigkeit.
morbidezza [mɔ:bɪ'dɛtsə], *s.* die Zartheit der Fleischfarben (*Paint.*).
mordan-cy, ['mɔ:dənsɪ], *s.* die Schärfe, das Beißende. **-t** [–ənt], 1. *adj.* beißend, ätzend (*also fig.*); brennend, fressend, zerstörend; (*fig.*) sarkastisch. 2. *s.* die Beize, das Beizmittel.
mordent ['mɔ:dənt], *s.* der Pralltriller (*Mus.*).
more ['mɔ:ə], 1. *comp. adj.* mehr; noch, weitere (*pl.*); – *and* –, immer mehr; *no* – *money*, kein Geld mehr; *not a word* –, kein Wort mehr; – *or less*, mehr oder weniger; –*'s the pity!* leider Gottes!; *some* – *water*, noch etwas Wasser; *some* – *people*, noch einige Leute; *ten* – *miles* or *miles* –, noch *or* weitere zehn Meilen. 2. *adv.* mehr; weiter, wieder(um); (*in forming comp. adj. & adv.*) –er; – *often*, öfter; – *silently*, stiller, ruhiger; – *and* –, immer mehr; – *and* – *stupid*, immer dummer; *the* – *so*, um so mehr (*as*, als; *because*, da); – *or less*, einigermaßen, ungefähr; *once* –, noch einmal; – *so*, in höherem Maße; – *than anxious*, übereifrig, äußerst begierig; (*coll.*) *make* – *of a th. than it is*, eine S. übertreiben *or* aufbauschen; *so much the* –, see *the* – *so*; *not any* or *no* – *than*, ebensowenig wie; *say no* –, nicht(s) mehr sagen; *be no* –, tot sein; *no* – *will I*, ich auch nicht; – *than repay*, überreichlich bezahlen; *and* – *than that*, und was noch mehr ist; *the* – *the merrier*, je mehr desto besser; – *to the purpose*, zweckmäßiger. 3. *s.* das Mehr; *see* – *of*, öfter sehen.
moreen [mo'rɪ:n], *s.* moirierter Wollstoff.
morel [mo'rɛl], *s.* der Nachtschatten (*Bot.*); saure Kirsche, die Morelle (*Bot.*); Morchel (*Bot.*).

moreover [mɔːˈrouvə], *adv.* überdies, außerdem, weiter, ferner, noch dazu, übrigens, auch.
morganatic [mɔːgəˈnætɪk], *adj.* morganatisch.
morgue [mɔːg], *s.* das Leichenhaus, die Leichenhalle.
moribund [ˈmɔrɪbʌnd], *adj.* im Sterben (liegend), sterbend.
morion [ˈmɔrɪən], *s.* die Sturmhaube (*Hist.*).
morn [mɔːn], *s.* (*Poet.*) der Morgen.
morning [ˈmɔːnɪŋ], 1. *s.* der Morgen, Vormittag; *the – after*, am Morgen darauf (*adv.*) *or* nach (*prep.*); (*coll.*) *the – after the night before*, der Katzenjammer, Kater; *in the –*, morgens, des Morgens, am Morgen; (*coll.*) morgen (früh), am nächsten *or* andern Morgen; *early in the –*, frühmorgens; *on Monday –*, am Montagmorgen; *one –*, eines Morgens; *this –*, heute morgen *or* früh; *tomorrow –*, morgen früh; *yesterday –*, gestern morgen *or* früh. 2. *attrib. adj.* Morgen–, Vormittags–, Früh–; *– break*, die Frühpause; *– call*, der Vormittagsbesuch; *––coat*, der Cut, Cutaway; *– cup of tea*, eine Tasse Tee vor dem Aufstehen; *– dress*, der Straßenanzug, schwarzer Rock mit gestreifter Hose; *– paper*, die Morgenzeitung; *– performance*, die Vormittagsvorstellung; *– prayers*, das Morgengebet; *––room*, das Frühstückszimmer; *––sickness*, morgendliche Übelkeit; *––suit*, see *– dress*; *– watch*, die Frühwache (*Naut.*).
morocco [məˈrɔkou], 1. *adj.* Saffian-. 2. *s.* der Saffian, Maroquin, das Saffianleder.
moron [ˈmɔrən], *s.* der Schwachsinnige.
morose [məˈrous], *adj.* mürrisch, grämlich, verdrießlich. **–ness**, *s.* die Grämlichkeit, Verdrießlichkeit.
morphi–a [ˈmɔːfɪə], *s.*, **–ne** [–fɪːn], *s.* das Morphium (*Chem.*). **–nism**, *s.* die Morphiumsucht, der Morphinismus.
morpholog–ical [mɔːfəˈlɔdʒɪkl], *adj.* morphologisch. **–y** [–ˈfɔlədzɪ], *s.* die Morphologie; Formenlehre (*Gram.*).
morris [ˈmɔrɪs], *s.* (*– dance*) kostümierter Volkstanz; *– tube*, der Einstecklauf.
morrow [ˈmɔrou], *s.* (*Poet.*) folgender Tag; *on the – of*, am Tage *or* in der Zeit unmittelbar nach.
[1]**morse** [mɔːs], *s.* (*archaic*) das Walroß.
[2]**morse** [mɔːs], *v.n. & a.* morsen; *– alphabet*, *– code*, das Morse-Alphabet, die Morseschrift.
morsel [mɔːsl], *s.* der Bissen; das Stückchen, Bißchen.
[1]**mort** [mɔːt], *s.* das Hornsignal bei Erlegung des Wildes (*Hunt.*).
[2]**mort** [mɔːt], *s.* (*dial.*) die Menge.
mortal [mɔːtl], 1. *adj.* sterblich, vergänglich; menschlich; todbringend, tödlich, Tod–, Todes–; (*coll.*) gewaltig, ungeheuer, Mords–; *– combat*, der Kampf auf Leben und Tod; (*coll.*) *in all my – days*, mein Leben lang *or* lebelang; *– foe*, der Todfeind; *– fright*, die Todesangst; *– hatred*, tödlicher Haß; *– hour*, die Todesstunde; (*coll.*) *two – hours*, zwei geschlagene Stunden; (*coll.*) *– hurry*, die Mordseile; *– sin*, die Todsünde; *– wound*, tödliche Verletzung, die Todeswunde. 2. *s.* Sterbliche(r), *m.* **–ity** [–ˈtælɪtɪ], *s.* die Sterblichkeit; das Sterben; die Sterblichkeitsziffer.
mortar [ˈmɔːtə], *s.* der Mörser (*Artil.*, *Chem.*); Mörtel, Speis, die Speise (*Build.*). **––board**, *s.* das Mörtelbrett; (*coll.*) viereckige Akademikermütze.
mortgag–e [ˈmɔːgɪdʒ], 1. *s.* gepfändetes Grundstück, die Hypothek, der Pfandbrief, Hypothekenbrief; *–e bond* or *deed*, der Pfandbrief, die Pfandverschreibung; *lend on –e*, auf Hypothek leihen; *raise a –e on*, eine Hypothek aufnehmen. 2. *v.a.* verpfänden (*to*, an); mit Hypothek belasten. **–ee** [–ˈdʒɪː], *s.* der Hypothekengläubiger, Hypothekar. **–er, –or** [–dʒə], *s.* der Hypothekenschuldner.
mortician [mɔːˈtɪʃən], *s.* (*Amer.*) der Leichenbestatter.
mortif–ication [mɔːtɪfɪˈkeɪʃən], *s.* der Brand, die Nekrose (*Path.*); Kasteiung (*of the flesh*); Demütigung, Erniedrigung; der Ärger, Verdruß; die Kränkung. **–y** [ˈmɔːtɪfaɪ], 1. *v.a.* absterben lassen; abtöten, kasteien (*the flesh*); demütigen, kränken; *deeply –ied at*, tief gekränkt über. 2. *v.n.* absterben, brandig werden (*Path.*).
mortise [ˈmɔːtɪs], 1. *s.* das Zapfenloch; die Nut; *– and tenon*, Nut und Zapfen. 2. *v.a.* mit einem Zapfenloch versehen; verzapfen. **––chisel**, *s.* der Lochbeitel. **––lock**, *s.* das Einsteckschloß.
mortmain [ˈmɔːtmeɪn], *s.* tote Hand; unveräußerliches Gut (*Law*); *alienation in –*, die Veräußerung an die tote Hand.
mortuary [ˈmɔːtjuərɪ], 1. *adj.* Toten–, Leichen–; *– chapel*, die Begräbniskapelle. 2. *s.* die Totenhalle, Leichenhalle, Begräbnishalle.
mosaic [moˈzeɪɪk], 1. *adj.* Mosaik–. 2. *s.* das Mosaik.
moschatel [mɔskəˈtɛl], *s.* das Bisamkraut, Moschuskraut (*Bot.*).
moselle [moˈzɛl], *s.* der Moselwein.
mosque [mɔsk], *s.* die Moschee.
mosquito [mɔsˈkɪːtou], *s.* der Moskito. **––bite**, *s.* der Moskitostich. **––curtain**, *s.*, **––net**, *s.* das Moskitonetz.
moss [mɔs], *s.* das Moos (*Bot.*); das (Torf)Moor, der Morast; Torf. **––clad**, *adj.*, **––grown**, *adj.* bemoost, moosbewachsen. **––hag**, *s.* das Moorbruch, der Torfboden. **–iness**, *s.* die Moosbedeckung, der Moosüberzug. **––rose**, *s.* die Moosrose. **––troopers**, *pl.* berittene Straßenräuber (*Hist.*). **–y**, *adj.* moosig, bemoost, Moos–.
most [moust], 1. *sup. adj.* (*before sing. subj.*) meist; größt; (*without art. before pl. subj.*) die meisten, die Mehrzahl von, fast alle; *for the – part*, größtenteils, meistenteils, zum größten Teil; *– men*, die meisten Menschen. 2. *adv.* meist(ens), am meisten; (*before adj. or adv.*) **höchst**, überaus; (*to form sup. of adj. or adv.*) –(e)st; *––favoured nation clause*, die Meistbegünstigungsklausel; *– happy*, überaus glücklich; *– of all*, am meisten; *– probably*, höchstwahrscheinlich. 3. *s.* (*as sing.*) das meiste, Höchste; (*as pl. with pl. constr.*) die meisten; *at* (*the*) *–*, höchstens, allenfalls; *make the – of*, aufs beste *or* möglichst gut ausnutzen, möglichst viel machen aus, ins beste Licht stellen; *– of the rest*, fast alle übrigen. **–ly**, *adv.* meistens, größtenteils, meistenteils, hauptsächlich.
mote [mout], *s.* das (Sonnen)Stäubchen; (*B.*) der Splitter.
motet [mouˈtɛt], *s.* die Motette.
moth [mɔθ], *s.* die (Kleider)Motte; der Nachtfalter, Spinner, die Eule. **––eaten**, *adj.* **–y**, *adj.* von Motten angefressen *or* zerfressen.
[1]**mother** [ˈmʌðə], 1. *s.* die Mutter. 2. *v.a.* bemuttern. *– Carey's chicken*, die Sturmschwalbe (*Orn.*); *– church*, die Mutterkirche; *– country*, das Mutterland, Vaterland. **–craft**, *s.* die Mutterkunde. **– Earth**, die (Mutter) Erde. **––in-law**, die Schwiegermutter. **–hood**, *s.* die Mutterschaft. **–less**, *adj.* mutterlos. **–liness**, *s.* die Mütterlichkeit. **–ly**, *adj.* mütterlich. *– of a family*, die Hausmutter; *– of pearl*, die Perlmutter, das Perlmutt; *a –'s heart*, ein Mutterherz; *–'s help*, das Kinderfräulein, die Stütze; *– ship*, das Mutterschiff; *–s' meeting*, die Sitzung eines Hausfrauenvereins; *every –'s son*, jeder(mann). **– Superior**, die Oberin. **– tongue**, *s.* die Muttersprache. **– wit**, *s.* der Mutterwitz.
[2]**mother** [ˈmʌðə], *s.* (also *– of vinegar*) die Essigmutter; *– batch*, die Grundmischung; *– of salt*, die Salzsohle. **––liquor**, *s.*, **––lye**, *s.*, **––solution**, *s.*, **––water**, *s.* die Mutterlauge. **––substance**, *s.* hefiger Rückstand. **–y**, *adj.* trübe, hefig.
mothy [ˈmɔθɪ], *see* **moth**.
motif [mouˈtɪf], *s.* das Leitmotiv, der Leitgedanke.
motil–e [ˈmoutaɪl], *adj.* bewegungsfähig. **–ity** [–ˈtɪlɪtɪ], *s.* die Bewegungsfähigkeit.
motion [ˈmouʃən], 1. *s.* die Bewegung, der Gang, Bewegungsvorgang (*also Mach.*); Antrieb, die Regung (*also fig.*); der Antrag (*Parl.*, *etc.*); Stuhlgang, Stuhl (*Med.*); *alternating –*, die Hin- und Herbewegung; *bring forward a –*, see *propose a –*; *carry a –*, einen Antrag durchbringen; *the – was carried*, der Antrag ging durch *or* wurde angenommen; *free –*, der Spielraum; *idle –*, der Leerlauf, Leergang; *the – was lost*, der Antrag wurde abgelehnt; *oscillatory –*, schillernde Bewegung; *perpetual –*, beständige Bewegung; *propose a –*, einen Antrag stellen (*for*, auf); *put in –*, see *set in –*;

the – was put to the meeting, der Antrag wurde der Versammlung zur Abstimmung vorgelegt; *second a –*, einen Antrag unterstützen; *set in –*, in Gang bringen; *slow-–*, die Zeitlupe (*film*). 2. *v.a.* anweisen, auffordern, verständigen. 3. *v.n.* winken, ein Zeichen andeuten (*to* (*Dat.*)). **–less,** *adj.* bewegungslos, regungslos, unbeweglich. **–-picture,** *s.* der Film.

motiv-ate [ˈmoutɪveɪt], *v.a.* begründen, motivieren. **–ation** [–ˈveɪʃən], *s.* die Begründung, Motivierung. **–e** [ˈmoutɪv], 1. *s.* das Motiv, der Beweggrund, Antrieb (*for*, zu); das Motiv (*Art*). 2. *adj.* Trieb–, Motiv–, bewegend. 3. *v.a.* (*usually pass.*); *be –ed* (or usually *–ated*) *by*, motiviert, begründet, verursacht, angetrieben *or* herbeigeführt werden durch. **–eless,** *adj.* grundlos. **–ity,** *s.* die Bewegungskraft.

motley [ˈmɔtlɪ], 1. *adj.* buntscheckig, bunt (*also fig.*). 2. *s.* buntes Gemisch.

motor [ˈmoutə], 1. *s.* der Motor, die Kraftmaschine (*Mech.*); das Auto(mobil), der (Kraft)Wagen. 2. *attrib. adj.* bewegend, Bewegungs–, motorisch; Motor–, Auto–, Kraft–. 3. *v.n.* im Auto fahren. 4. *v.a.* im Auto befördern. **–-accident,** *s.* der Autounfall. **–-ambulance,** *s.* der Krankenwagen. **– bicycle, – bike,** *s. see* **– cycle. – boat,** *s.* das Motorboot. **– bus,** *s.* der Autobus. **–-car,** *s.* der Kraftwagen, das Auto(mobil), (*coll.*) der Wagen. **– coach,** *s.* der Verkehrskraftwagen. **– cycle,** *s.* das Motorrad, Kraftrad; Krad (*Mil.*). **– cyclist,** *s.* der Motorradfahrer. **–-driven,** *adj.* mit Motorantrieb. **– engine,** *s.* die Kraftmaschine. **– generator,** *s.* der Generator (*Elec.*). **– horn,** *s.* die Hupe. **–ial** [moˈtɔːrɪəl], *adj.* bewegend, Bewegungs–, motorisch. **–ing,** *s.* das Autofahren; Automobilwesen; der Autosport. **–ist,** *s.* der Kraftfahrer, Autofahrer. **–ize,** *v.a.* motorisieren (*esp. Mil.*). **– launch,** *s.* die Motorbarkasse. **– lorry,** *s.* der Lastkraftwagen, das Lastauto. **–man,** *s.* der Wagenführer (*Elec.*, *Railw.*). **–-mechanic,** *s.* der Autoschlosser. **– noise,** der Motorenlärm. **– oil,** *s.* das Treiböl, Motorenöl. **– plough,** *s.* der Motorpflug. **– pump,** *s.* die Kraftfahrspritze (*fire brigade*). **–-road,** *s.* die Autobahn. **– scooter,** *s.* der Motorroller. **– ship,** *s.* das Motorschiff. **–-show,** *s.* die Autoausstellung. **–-spirit,** *s.* das Benzin. **– torpedo-boat,** *s.* das E-Boot, Schnellboot (*Naut.*). **– tractor,** *s.* der Schlepper, Traktor, Trecker. **– transport,** *s.* der Kraftwagentransport. **– truck,** *s.* der Elektrokarren. **– van,** *s.* der Lieferwagen. **– vehicle,** das Kraftfahrzeug. **– works,** *pl.* die Autofabrik, das Motorenwerk.

mottle [mɔtl], *v.a.* sprenkeln, melieren, masern, marmorieren. **–d,** *adj.* gefleckt, gesprenkelt; meliert.

motto [ˈmɔtou], *s.* der Wahlspruch, das Motto.

moujik [ˈmuːʒɪk], *s.* russischer Bauer.

[1]**mould** [mould], 1. *s.* der Schimmel, Moder; Schimmelpilz; *iron-–*, der Rostfleck, Stockfleck. 2. *v.n.* schimmelig werden, schimmeln. **–iness,** *s.* das Schimmelige, die Moderigkeit. **–y,** *adj.* schimmelig, moderig, stockfleckig; (*fig.*, *coll.*) morsch, schal, schlecht, minderwertig.

[2]**mould** [mould], *s.* die Gartenerde, lockere Erde, der Humusboden. **–er,** *v.n.* zerbröckeln, zerfallen, zu Erde *or* Staub werden; vermodern; *–er away*, wegfaulen; *see also* [1]**mould.**

[3]**mould** [mould], 1. *s.* die Form (*also fig.*), Hohlform, Preßform, Gießform, Gußform; Matrize, Schablone, Kokille; Puddingform (*Cook.*); (*fig.*) das Muster, Vorbild; der Charakter, Bau, die Natur, Beschaffenheit; *bullet –*, die Kugelform; *casting –*, die Gußform; *firing –*, die Brennform. 2. *v.a.* formen (*also fig.*), gießen (*candles*), kneten (*dough*); (*fig.*) bilden, gestalten, schaffen (*on*, nach dem Muster von; *into*, zu). **–-candle,** *s.* gegossenes Licht. **–er,** *s.* der Former, Gießer, (*fig.*) Bildner. **–ing,** *s.* das Formen, Formgeben, Modellieren, die Formung; das Gesims, der Fries, die (Zier)Leiste, Kehlung (*Arch.*). **–ing-board,** *s.* das Formbrett. **–ing-box,** *s.* der Formkasten, Gießkasten, Gußkasten. **–ing-chain,** *s.* die Fräskette. **–ing-machine,** *s.* die Formmaschine (*Found.*); Kehlmaschine (*Join.*). **–ing-press,** *s.* die Prägepresse. **–ing-sand,** *s.* der Formsand. **–ing-wax,** *s.* das Modellierwachs, Bossierwachs. **–-loft,** *s.* der Schnürboden (*Shipb.*).

mouldy [ˈmouldɪ]. *see* [1]**mould.**

moult [moult], 1. *v.n.* (sich) mausern, sich häuten. 2. *v.a.* wechseln, abwerfen, verlieren (*feathers*). **–ing,** *s.* das Mausern; die Mauser(ung); Häutung.

[1]**mound** [maund], *s.* der Erdhügel, Erdwall, Damm; Grabhügel.

[2]**mound** [maund], *s.* der Reichsapfel (*Her.*).

[1]**mount** [maunt], 1. *s.* (*Poet.*) der Berg; (*without art. in geogr. names*) – (usually abbr. *Mt.*) *Etna*, der Ätna; die Lafette (*Artil.*); (*coll.*) das Reitpferd; (*B.*) – *of Olives*, der Ölberg; *Sermon on the –*, die Bergpredigt. 2. *v.a.* besteigen (*mountain, horse, throne, bicycle, etc.*); mit einem Pferd versehen (*a p.*); beritten machen (*troops*); stellen, (hoch)setzen (*a th.*) (*on*, auf); montieren, in Stellung bringen (*a gun*); aufstellen, anbringen, einbauen (*machinery, etc.*); inszenieren (*a play*); *be –ed*, zu Pferde sitzen, reiten; hochsitzen (*on*, auf); bestückt sein (*of a ship*) (*with*, mit); *be –ed with*, führen, haben (*guns*); – *guard*, auf Wache ziehen; – *the trenches*, die Schützengräben beziehen. 3. *v.n.* (empor)steigen; (hin)aufsteigen (*to*, zu); aufsitzen, zu Pferde steigen (*on horseback*); *– !* aufgesessen! (*Mil.*); – *on*, steigen auf (*a th.*), besteigen (*horse*); – *up*, sich vermehren; – *up to*, sich belaufen auf, betragen (*C.L.*). **–ed,** *adj.* beritten (*on horses*); montiert (*Tech.*). **–ing,** *s.* die Aufstellung, Montierung; Lafette (*Artil.*), der Vorbau (*Tech.*).

[2]**mount** [maunt], 1. *s.* die Einfassung (*of stones*), der Rahmen (*of pictures*), der Karton zum Aufkleben (von Bildern). 2. *v.a.* (ein)fassen (*stones*); einrahmen, aufziehen, aufkleben (*pictures*); besetzen, belegen, beschlagen (*with*, mit). **–ed,** *adj.* (ein)gefaßt (*stones*), aufgezogen (*pictures*). **–ing,** *s.* die Einfassung; Einrahmung, das Aufziehen; der Beschlag; *pl.* Beschläge (*pl.*), die Armatur, Garnitur, das Zubehör.

mountain [ˈmauntɪn], *s.* der Berg; *pl.* Berge (*pl.*), das Gebirge; *a range of –s*, ein Gebirge; (*fig.*) die Masse, der Haufen; *–s high*, berg(e)hoch, turmhoch; *make a – of a molehill*, aus einer Mücke einen Elefanten machen. **– air,** *s.* die Höhenluft. **– artillery,** *s.* die Gebirgsartillerie. **– ash,** die Eberesche (*Bot.*). **– chain,** *s.* die Gebirgskette, der Höhenzug. **–eer,** 1. *s.* der Bergsteiger, Hochtourist; Bergbewohner. 2. *v.n.* Berge steigen, Bergpartien machen. **–eering,** 1. *s.* das Bergsteigen. 2. *attrib. adj.* Bergsteig–. **–ous,** *adj.* bergig, gebirgig, Gebirgs–; (*fig.*) berghoch, gewaltig, riesig. **– pasture,** *s.* die Alp, Alpentrift. **– railway,** *s.* die Gebirgsbahn. **– range,** *s. see* **– chain. – ridge,** der Gebirgskamm, das Joch. **– scenery,** *s.* die Gebirgslandschaft. **– sickness,** *s.* die Bergkrankheit. **–side,** *s.* der Bergabhang. **–-top,** *s.* die Bergspitze, der Gipfel.

mountebank [ˈmauntəbæŋk], *s.* der Marktschreier, Quacksalber.

mount-ed [ˈmauntɪd], *adj.*, **–ing** [–ɪŋ], *s. see* [1]**mount** & [2]**mount.**

mourn [mɔːn], 1. *v.a.* trauern um, betrauern (*a p.*), beklagen (*one's lot*). 2. *v.n.* trauern (*for* or *over*, um), Trauer anlegen. **–er,** *s.* Leidtragende(r), *m.* **–ful,** *adj.* trauervoll, traurig, düster, Trauer–; klagend. **–fulness,** *s.* die Traurigkeit, Düsterheit. **–ing,** 1. *adj.* Trauer–. 2. *s.* die Trauer(kleidung); das Trauern; *be in –ing*, Trauer haben; *go into –ing*, Trauer anlegen (*for*, um); *go out of –ing*, Trauer ablegen. **–ing-band,** *s.* der Trauerstreifen. **–ing-border,** *s.* der Trauerrand. **–ing-crape,** *s.* der Trauerflor. **–ing-paper,** *s.* das Briefpapier mit Trauerrand.

mouse [maus], 1. *s.* (pl. *mice*) die Maus; (*sl.*) blaues Auge; *as quiet as a –*, mäuschenstill. 2. *v.n.* mausen, Mäuse fangen. **–-deer,** *s.* das Moschustier (*Zool.*). **–-ear,** *s.* das Mausöhrlein, Habichtskraut (*Bot.*), Hornkraut (*Bot.*). **–-hole,** *s.* das Mauseloch. **–r,** *s.* mäusefressendes Tier, der Mäusefänger. **–-tail,** *s.* der Mäuseschwanz (*Bot.*). **–trap,** *s.* die Mausefalle; *see* **mousy.**

moustache [məˈstɑːʃ], *s.* der Schnurrbart.

mousy [ˈmausɪ], *adj.* mauseartig; mausefarbig, mausgrau; mäuschenstill.

mouth 1. [mauθ], *s.* der Mund; das Maul, der Rachen, die Schnauze (*of beasts*); die Mündung (*of a river, a cannon*); Öffnung (*of a bag, a well, etc.*); der Eingang (*of a cave*); die Gicht, das Loch (*of a furnace*); Mundstück (*of wind-instruments*). (*a*) (*with verbs*) *give* –, anschlagen, bellen, Laut geben (*Hunt.*); *make –s* or *a* –, ein schiefes Gesicht *or* Maul ziehen (*at*, über); *stop a p.'s* –, einem den Mund stopfen. (*b*) (*with prepositions*) (*sl.*) *down in the* –, niedergeschlagen, kopfhängerisch; *be in everybody's* –, in aller Leute Munde sein; *put the words in a p.'s* –, einem die Worte in den Mund legen; *by word of* –, mündlich; *take the words out of a p.'s* –, einem die Worte aus dem Munde nehmen; *with a hard* –, hartmäulig. 2. [mauð] *v.a.* in den Mund nehmen (*food*); affektiert *or* gespreizt (aus)sprechen (*words*). 3. *v.n.* den Mund vollnehmen; salbungsvoll, geschwulstig *or* affektiert reden; Gesichter schneiden. **–ed** [mauðd], *adj. suff.* –mäulig; *see* **foul, open. –ful,** *s.* der Mundvoll, Bissen; (*sl.*) *say a –ful*, eine bedeutende Äußerung machen. **–-lotion,** *s.* das Mundwasser. **–-organ,** *s.* die Mundharmonika. **–piece,** *s.* das Mundstück (*Mus.*, *Saddl.*); der Schalltrichter (*Phone*); (*fig.*) das Sprachrohr, der Wortführer. **–-wash,** *s. see* **–-lotion.**

mov–able ['mu:vəbl], *adj.* beweglich, lose, verstellbar; *–able property, see* **–ables. –ableness,** *s.* die Beweglichkeit. **–ables,** *pl.* bewegliche Habe, Mobilien (*pl.*). **–e** [mu:v], **1.** *v.a.* fortbewegen, fortbringen, fortschaffen, fortschieben, fortrücken (*a th.*); in Bewegung setzen (*a th.*); bewegen, antreiben (*a p.*) (*to*, zu); reizen, rühren, ergreifen (*a p.*) (*at*, über; *by*, durch; *with*, vor); erregen, anregen, aufregen, erwecken (*feelings*); vorschlagen, vorbringen, einbringen (*a resolution*); beantragen (*Parl.*); *–e an amendment*, einen Abänderungsantrag einbringen; *–e on*, vorwärtstreiben (*crowds*); *–e a p. to anger*, einen erzürnen; *–e s.o. to do a th.*, einen bewegen, anregen, angehen *or* antreiben etwas zu tun; *be –ed to pity*, zu Mitleid gerührt sein; *–e to tears*, zu Tränen rühren. **2.** *v.n.* sich bewegen, sich regen, sich rühren; sich fortbewegen, (ab)marschieren, aufbrechen, abziehen, umziehen (*to*, nach); ziehen, einen Zug machen (*Chess, etc.*); (*fig.*) fortschreiten, weitergehen (*as time*), vorgehen, Schritte tun (*in a matter*); *–e about*, umherziehen; *–e away*, fortziehen, sich fortbegeben, sich entfernen, davongehen; *–e for the rejection*, die Ablehnung beantragen; *–e in*, einziehen; *–e in good society*, sich in guter Gesellschaft bewegen; *–e into new rooms*, eine neue Wohnung beziehen; *–e off*, sich davonmachen; *–e on*, weitergehen; *–e out*, ausziehen; *the train –es out of the station*, der Zug fährt aus dem Bahnhof heraus; *–e round*, sich umdrehen; *–e up and down*, auf- und abgehen. **3.** *s.* die Bewegung, das Aufbrechen, der Umzug; Zug (*at Chess, etc*); (*fig.*) Schritt, die Maßregel, Maßnahme; *whose –e is it?* wer hat zu ziehen? wer ist am Ziehen? (*Chess, etc.*); (*sl.*) *get a –e on*, sich rühren *or* beeilen; *make a –e*, eine Maßnahme ergreifen; (*coll.*) die Tafel aufheben; einen Zug machen (*Chess, etc.*); *make the first –e*, den ersten Schritt tun; *on the –e*, in Bewegung, fortschreitend; auf dem Marsche, im Abzug. **–ement,** *s.* die Bewegung (*also Rel., Pol., Mech., Mil.*), Regung, Erregung (*of emotions*); Entwicklung, das Fortschreiten, der Gang, die Handlung (*of events, narrative, etc.*); das Tempo (*Mus.*); der Rhythmus, rhythmische Bewegung (*Pros.*); der Satz (*Mus.*); das Gehwerk (*of a watch*); (*fig.*) der Schwung, Fluß, das Leben, Feuer; die Massenbewegung, Massenbestrebung, Richtung (*Rel., Pol., etc.*); *freedom of –ement*, die Freizügigkeit; *–ement of the bowels*, der Stuhlgang (*Med.*); *watch a p.'s –ements*, einem auflauern. **–er,** *s.* Bewegende(r), *m.*, der Anstifter, Anreger, Urheber; Antragsteller (*Parl., etc.*); die Triebkraft (*also fig.*), bewegende Kraft (*Tech.*); *prime –er*, der Antriebsmotor, Hauptantrieb (*Mech.*); (*fig.*) Anstifter, Urheber. **–ie,** (*Amer.*) *attrib. adj.* Film–, Kino–, Lichtspiel–. **–ies,** *pl.* (*Amer.*) das Kino, die Kinovorstellung, der Film, die Filmvorführung; das Filmwesen. **–ie-star,** *s.* (*Amer.*) der Filmstar. **–ing,** 1. *adj.* beweglich, sich bewegend, treibend, Trieb–; (*fig.*) rührend; *–ing band*, laufendes Band; *–ing coil*, die Drehspule (*Elec.*); *–ing-day*, der Umzugstag; *–ing force*, bewegende Kraft, die Triebkraft; *–ing-iron*, das Weicheisen (*Elec.*); *–ing pictures, see* **movies;** *–ing spirit*, anregender Geist, der Führer; *–ing staircase*, die Rolltreppe. 2. *s.* das Umziehen.

[1]**mow** [mou], *s.* der (Getreide- *or* Heu)Haufen, Schober, Feim, Feimen, die Feime; der Scheunenraum, Boden, die Banse (*in barn*).

[2]**mow** [mou], 1. *reg. & ir.v.a.* mähen (*grass*), abmähen (*field*); – *down*, niedermähen (*usually fig.*). **–er,** *s.* der Mäher, Schnitter; die Mähmaschine. **–ing,** *s.* das Mähen, die Mahd. **–ing-machine,** *s.* die Mähmaschine.

much [mʌtʃ], 1. *adj.* viel; – *ado about nothing*, viel Lärm um nichts. 2. *adv.* sehr, (*before compar.*) viel, (*before superl.*) weit, bei weitem; fast, beinahe, annähernd; – *less* . . ., geschweige denn . . .; – *more likely*, viel wahrscheinlicher; – *the most likely*, bei weitem das Wahrscheinlichste; (*sl.*) *not–*, sicher nicht (*as reply*); – *obliged*, sehr verbunden; – *too* –, viel zu sehr. (*a*) (with *as*) – *as* (*if*), etwa wie *or* etwa als wenn; – *as it was*, ziemlich dasselbe; *as* – *as*, soviel wie; *as* – *as to say*, als wenn man sagen wollte; *as* – *again*, noch einmal soviel. (*b*) (with *so*) (*ever*) *so* – *better*, sehr viel besser; *so* – *the better*, um so besser; *so* – *the better for*, um so viel besser für; *so* – *the best*, bei weitem das beste; *not so* – *as*, nicht einmal; *without so* – *as*, ohne auch nur; *so* – *for his appearance*, soweit sein Äußeres; *so* – *for the present*, genug für diesmal; *so* – *so*, und zwar so sehr. 3. *s.* das Viel (*of*, von); *he is too* – *for me*, ich bin ihm nicht gewachsen; *not come to* –, nichts Bedeutendes ergeben; *make* – *of*, mit besonderer Aufmerksamkeit behandeln; viel Wesens machen aus *or* Rühmens machen von; *think* – *of*, viel halten von; *expect, say, think, etc. as* –, eben *or* gerade das erwarten, sagen, denken, *etc.*; *not* – *of a scholar*, kein großer Gelehrter; *so, this* or *that* – *is certain*, so viel ist gewiß; *too* – *of a good thing*, des Guten zuviel. **–ly,** (*sl.*) *adv.* sehr, äußerst. **–ness,** *s.* (*coll.*) die Größe; – *of a –ness*, praktisch *or* so ziemlich dasselbe.

mucilag–e ['mju:sɪlədʒ], *s.* der Pflanzenschleim; Klebstoff. **–inous** [–'lædʒɪnəs], *adj.* schleimig; klebrig.

muck [mʌk], 1. *s.* der Mist (*also fig.*), Kot, Unrat, Schmutz, Dreck (*also fig.*); (*sl.*) *make a* – *of*, verhunzen, verpfuschen, verpatzen. 2. *v.a.* düngen; (*vulg.*) beschmutzen, verpfuschen. 3. *v.n.*; (*sl.*) – *about*, herumlungern. **–er,** *s.* (*sl.*) der Sturz, Hereinfall; Schuft, Außenseiter; (*sl.*) *come a –er*, stürzen, verunglücken. **–-heap,** *s.* der Misthaufen. **–-rake,** *s.* die Mistgabel, Mistharke. **–-raker,** *s.* der Sensationsmacher, Korruptionsaufdecker. **–-worm,** *s.* der Mistkäfer. **–y,** *adj.* (*coll.*) schmutzig, dreckig.

muc–ous ['mju:kəs], *adj.* schleimig; *–ous membrane*, die Schleimhaut. **–us** ['mju:kəs], *s.* der Schleim.

mud [mʌd], *s.* der Schlamm, Schlick, Schmutz, Dreck; *drag in the* –, in den Schmutz ziehen; *throw* – *at a p.*, einen mit Schmutz bewerfen; *stick in the* –, im Schlamme stecken bleiben (*also fig.*). **–-bath,** *s.* das Moorbad. **–diness,** *s.* die Schlammigkeit, Schmutzigkeit. **–dy,** 1. *adj.* schlammig, trüb; schmutzig; (*fig.*) verschwommen, konfus (*as style*). 2. *v.a.* trüben; beschmutzen. **–-flat,** *s.* der Schlickboden, die Schlickstrecke, *pl.* Watten. **–-floor,** *s.* der Lehmfußboden. **–guard,** *s.* das Schutzblech, der Kotflügel (*Motor.*). **–lark,** *s.* der Schmutzfink. **–-pie,** *s.* der Sandkuchen. **–-slinging,** *s.* (*coll.*) die Herabwürdigung, Verleumdung, das Beschmutzen. **–-wall,** *s.* die Lehmwand.

muddiness, *see* **mud.**

muddle [mʌdl], 1. *v.a.* verwirren, in Verwirrung bringen, durcheinanderwerfen; verpfuschen; konfus machen, benebeln; – *up*, durcheinanderwerfen, durcheinanderbringen. 2. *v.n.*; – *on*, weiterwursteln; – *through*, mit mehr Glück als Verstand durchkommen, sich mit Mühe und Not *or* mit Ach und Krach durchbringen, sich durchwursteln, den

Dingen ihren Lauf lassen. 3. *s.* die Verwirrung, Unordnung, das Durcheinander, der Wirrwarr. **--headed,** *adj.* wirr, verworren; benebelt. **-r,** *s.* der Wirrkopf.

muddy ['mʌdɪ], *see* **mud.**

[1]**muff** [mʌf], 1. *s.* (*sl.*) der Dummkopf, Tropf, Stümper; *make a – of*, see – 2. 2. *v.a.* verpfuschen; fallen lassen, ungeschickt schlagen (*ball*) (*usually in Crick.*).

[2]**muff** [mʌf], *s.* der Muff; die Muffe (*Tech.*). **-etee** [-ə'tɪ:], *s.* der Pulswärmer.

muffin ['mʌfɪn], *s.* flacher, runder Kuchen. **-eer** [–'ɪ:ə], *s.* der Salzstreuer, Zuckerstreuer.

muffle [mʌfl], 1. *v.a.* & *r.* umwickeln, umhüllen, einhüllen; (*fig.*) dämpfen (*drum, etc.*), unterdrücken (*curse*); – *o.s. up*, sich einhüllen *or* verhüllen. 2. *s.* die Muffel (*Tech.*), der Schmelztiegel (*Chem.*); – *furnace*, der Muffelofen. **-d,** *adj.* bewickelt, umhüllt; (*fig.*) dumpf, gedämpft. **-r** [–lə], *s.* wollenes Halstuch, der Schal; Auspufftopf, Schalldämpfer (*Motor.*); Dämpfer (*of a piano*).

mufti ['mʌftɪ], *s.* der Mufti, mohammedanischer Rechtsgelehrter; der Zivilianzug (*Mil.*); *in –*, in Zivil(kleidung).

[1]**mug** [mʌg], *s.* die Kanne; der Krug, Becher.

[2]**mug** [mʌg], 1. *s.* (*sl.*) der Schnabel, das Maul; die Fresse, Fratze; (*sl.*) der Tropf, Tölpel, Stümper. 2. *v.n.* (*sl.*) ochsen, büffeln. 3. *v.a.* einpauken. **-gins,** *s.* (*coll.*) der Tölpel. **-gy,** *adj.* dumpfig, schwül, muffig, feucht. **-wort,** *s.* der Beifuß (*Bot.*). **-wump,** *s.* der Einzelgänger, Unabhängige(r), *m.*, Wilde(r), *m.* (*Amer.*, *Pol.*); (*fig.*) hohes Tier.

mulatto [mju'lætou], 1. *s.* der Mulatte, die Mulattin. 2. *adj.* Mulatten–.

mulberry ['mʌlbərɪ], *s.* die Maulbeere; der Maulbeerbaum.

mulch [mʌltʃ], *s.* die Mistbedeckung, Strohbedeckung.

mulct [mʌlkt], 1. *s.* die Geldstrafe. 2. *v.a.* mit Geldstrafe belegen.

mul–e [mju:l], *s.* das Maultier, der Maulesel; Mischling, Bastard (*Bot.*, *Zool.*); die Mulemaschine, Jennymaschine (*Spin.*); der Schlepper, Traktor, Trekker; (*fig.*) störrischer Mensch. **-eteer** [–ə'tɪ:ə], *s.* der Maultiertreiber. **-e-track,** *s.* der Saumpfad. **-ish,** *adj.* eigensinnig, störrisch. **-ishness,** *s.* die Störrigkeit, der Eigensinn.

muliebrity [mju:lɪ'ɛbrɪtɪ], *s.* die Weiblichkeit, Frauenhaftigkeit.

[1]**mull** [mʌl], *s.* das (*or Austr.* der) Mull.

[2]**mull** [mʌl], 1. *v.a.* verpfuschen. 2. *v.n.*; (*sl.*) – *over*, grübeln über. 3. *s.*; *make a – of it*, etwas verderben.

[3]**mull** [mʌl], *v.a.* aufglühen und würzen (*wine, etc.*). **-ed,** *adj.*; *–ed ale*, das Warmbier; *–ed claret*, der Glühwein.

[4]**mull** [mʌl], *s.* (*Scots*) das Vorgebirge.

mullein ['mʌlɪn], *s.* das Wollkraut (*Bot.*).

muller ['mʌlə], *s.* der Reibstein (*Paint.*).

[1]**mullet** ['mʌlɪt], *s.* die Meerbarbe, Meeräsche (*Ichth.*).

[2]**mullet** ['mʌlɪt], *s.* das Spornrädchen (*Her.*).

mulligatawny [mʌlɪgə'tɔ:nɪ], *s.* dicke gewürzte Suppe.

mulligrubs ['mʌlɪgrʌbz], *s.* (*sl.*) das Bauchgrimmen; üble Laune.

mullion ['mʌlɪən], *s.* der Mittelpfosten (*of a window*). **-ed,** *adj.* mit Mittelpfosten, durch Längspfosten geteilt.

mullock ['mʌlək], *s.* (*dial.*) taubes Gestein (*gold-mining*); der Schutt.

mult–angular [mʌlt'æŋgjulə], *adj.* vielwinklig. **-eity** [–'ɪ:ɪtɪ], *s.* die Vielheit.

multi–coloured [mʌltɪ'kʌləd], *adj.* bunt, vielfarbig. **--engined,** *adj.* mehrmotorig (*Av.*). **-farious** [–'fɛ:rɪəs], *adj.* mannigfaltig. **-fariousness,** *s.* die Mannigfaltigkeit. **-form,** *adj.* vielgestaltig. **-graph,** *s.* der Vervielfältigungsapparat. **-lateral,** *adj.* vielseitig. **-millionaire** [–mɪlɪə'nɛ:ə], *s.* vielfacher Millionär. **-parous** [–'tɪpərəs], *adj.* vielgebärend. **-partite,** *adj.* vielteilig. **-ple** ['mʌltɪpl], 1. *adj.* vielfach, mehrfach, mannigfaltig; multipel (*Math.* & *Med.*); *–ple connexion*, die Vielfachschaltung (*Elec.*); *–ple demand*, der Mehrbedarf; *–ple-lens camera*, *s.* der Reihenbildapparat; *–ple proportions*, multiple Proportionen (*Chem.*); *–ple-purpose*, *attrib. adj.* Mehrzweck–; *–ple shop*, *–ple stores*, das Einheitsgeschäft, der Kettenladen; *–ple telegraphy*, die Mehrfachtelegraphie. 2. *s.* das Vielfache; *least common –ple*, kleinstes gemeinsames Vielfache. **-plex** ['mʌltɪplɛks], *adj.* vielfach, mehrfach, Mehrfach– (*Elec.*, *etc.*). **-pliable** ['mʌltɪplaɪəbl], *adj.* zu vervielfältigen(d). **-plicand** [–plɪ'kænd], *s.* der Multiplikand (*Math.*). **-plication** [–plɪ'keɪʃən], *s.* *s.* die Vervielfältigung, Vermehrung; Multiplikation (*Math.*); *–plication sign*, das Malzeichen, Multiplikationszeichen; *–plication table*, das Einmaleins. **-plicity** [–'plɪsɪtɪ], *s.* die Vielfältigkeit, Vielheit, Menge. **-plier** ['mʌltɪplaɪə], *s.* der Vermehrer, Verstärker; Multiplikator (*Math.*). **-ply** ['mʌltɪplaɪ], 1. *v.a.* vermehren (*also Bot.*, *Zool.*); vervielfachen, vervielfältigen; multiplizieren (*by*, mit) (*Arith.*). 2. *v.n.* sich vermehren. **-plying,** *adj.* Vergrößerungs–, Verstärk–; Multiplikations–, Rechen–. **-tude,** *s.* die Vielheit, große Zahl, die Menge; großer Haufen, niederes Volk, der Pöbel. **-tudinous,** *adj.* zahlreich, mannigfach. **-valent,** *adj.* mehrwertig. **-valve,** 1. *adj.* vielschalig (*Zool.*), mehrröhrig (*Rad.*). 2. *s.* vielschalige Muschel.

multure ['mʌltʃə], *s.* das Mahlgeld.

[1]**mum** [mʌm], 1. *adj.* stumm, ganz still; *–'s the word!* nicht ein Wort! 2. *v.n.* pst! still!

[2]**mum** [mʌm], *s. see* **mummy.**

mumbl–e ['mʌmbl], 1. *v.a.* & *n.* murmeln, mummeln, muffeln. 2. *s.* das Gemurmel, Gemummel.

Mumbo Jumbo ['mʌmbou'dʒʌmbou], *s.* (*coll.*) der Popanz.

mummer ['mʌmə], *s.* der Vermummte, Spieler in einem Mummenschanz; (*sl.*) Komödiant, Possenreißer. **-y** [–rɪ], *s.* der Mummenschanz, die Pantomime, Maskerade, Verstellung.

mumm–ification [mʌmɪfɪ'keɪʃən], *s.* die Einbalsamierung, Mumifizierung, Mumifikation. **-ify** ['mʌmɪfaɪ], 1. *v.a.* mumifizieren. 2. *v.n.* vertrocknen, verdörren (*usually fig.*). **-y** ['mʌmɪ], *s.* die Mumie; (*coll.*) *beat to a –y*, windelweich *or* breiweich schlagen.

mummy ['mʌmɪ], *s.* (*coll.*) die Mutti, Mama.

mump [mʌmp], *v.n.* betteln; schwindeln; greinen. **-ish,** *adj.* verdrießlich, grämlich, übel gelaunt. **-s,** *pl.* (*sing. constr.*) der Ziegenpeter (*Med.*); (*coll.*) *in the –s*, übler Laune.

munch [mʌntʃ], *v.a.* & *n.* hörbar *or* schmatzend kauen.

mundane ['mʌndeɪn], *adj.* weltlich, irdisch, Welt–.

municipal ['mju:nɪsɪpl], *adj.* städtisch; Stadt–, Gemeinde–, Kommunal–. **-ity** [–'pælɪtɪ], *s.* der Stadtbezirk, die Stadt mit Selbstverwaltung; Stadtverwaltung, Stadtobrigkeit. **-ize** [–'nɪsəpəlaɪz], *v.a.* verstadtlichen; die Obrigkeitsgewalt verleihen (*a town*, einer Stadt).

munificen–ce [mju'nɪfɪsəns], *s.* die Freigebigkeit. **-t** [–ənt], *adj.* freigebig, großmütig.

muniment ['mju:nɪmənt], *s.* die Urkunde, Urkundensammlung. **--room,** *s.* das Archiv.

munition [mju'nɪʃən], 1. *s.* (*usually pl.*) die Munition, Rüstung, das Kriegsmaterial, der Kriegsvorrat. 2. *v.a.* mit Munition versehen. **--factory,** *s.* die Rüstungsfabrik. **--worker,** *s.* der Munitionsarbeiter.

mural ['mju:rəl], 1. *adj.* Mauer–, Wand–; – *painting*, das Wandgemälde. 2. *s.* das Wandgemälde.

murder ['mə:də], 1. *s.* der Mord (*of*, an), die Ermordung (*of* (*Gen.*)); (*fig.*) Vernichtung, Verhunzung, das Totschlagen; *commit –*, Mord begehen; (*coll.*) *the –'s out*, nun kommt die Wahrheit heraus. 2. *v.a.* (er)morden; verhunzen, entstellen; radebrechen. **-er** [–ərə], *s.* der Mörder. **-ess** [–ərɛs], *s.* die Mörderin. **-ous** [–ərəs], *adj.* mörderisch; todbringend, tödlich; blutig, blutdürstig; unerträglich.

mure ['mju:ə], *v.a.* (*archaic*) einmauern, einpferchen; einsperren.

murex ['mju:rɛks], *s.* die Stachelschnecke (*Zool.*).

muriat–e ['mju:rɪeɪt], *s.* salzsaures Salz (*Chem.*);

–e of lead, das Bleihornerz; *–e of lime*, der Chlorkalk. **–ic** [–ɪ'ætɪk], *adj.* salzsauer; *–ic acid*, die Salzsäure.
murky ['mə:kɪ], *adj.* dunkel, finster, trüb, düster.
murmur ['mə:mə], 1. *s.* das Murmeln, Rauschen; Gemurmel, Murren (*of discontent*); (Atem)-Geräusch (*Med.*). 2. *v.a.* & *n.* murmeln; rauschen; murren (*against* or *at*, gegen *or* über). **–ous,** *adj.* murmelnd; murrend.
murphy ['mə:fɪ], *s.* (*Irish*) die Kartoffel.
murrain ['mʌrɪn], *s.* die Viehseuche, Maul- und Klauenseuche.
musca–del [mʌskə'dɛl], *s.*, **–dine** ['mʌskədɪn], *s.*, **–t** ['mʌskət], *s.*, **–tel** [–kə'tɛl], *s.* die Muskatellertraube; der Muskatellerwein.
muscavado [mʌskə'vɑ:doʊ], *s.* der Rohzucker, Kassaunzucker.
muscle ['mʌsl], *s.* der & die Muskel; (*fig.*) die Muskelkraft; *pl.* (*coll.*) das Muskelfleisch, Muskeln (*pl.*); *without moving a –*, ohne mit der Wimper zu zucken.
musco–id ['mʌskɔɪd], *adj.* moosartig, Moos–. **–logy** [–'kɔlədʒɪ], *s.* die Mooskunde.
muscula–r ['mʌskjʊlə], *adj.* Muskel–; muskulös; kräftig. **–rity** [–kjə'lærɪtɪ], *s.* die Muskelstärke, Muskelkraft, der Muskelbau. **–ture** ['mʌskjələtʃə], *s.* die Muskulatur.
[1]**muse** [mju:z], *s.* die Muse.
[2]**muse** [mju:z], 1. *s.*; *be in a –*, *see* **–** 2. 2. *v.n.* sinnen, nachdenken, grübeln (*on*, über); *see* **musing.** **–r,** *s.* Sinnende(r), *m.*, der Träumer.
musette [mjʊ:'zɛt], *s.* kleiner Dudelsack.
museum [mjʊ:'zɪ:əm], *s.* das Museum, die Sammlung; das Museumsgebäude, die Gemäldegalerie.
mush [mʌʃ], 1. *s.* das Mus, der Brei; (*Amer.*) Maismehlbrei; (*fig. sl.*) Unsinn; (*sl.*) der Regenschirm. 2. *v.n.* durch den Schnee waten *or* stapfen; mit einem Hundeschlitten fahren (*Amer.*). **–y,** *adj.* weich, breiig; (*fig.*) rührselig, gefühlsduselig.
mushroom ['mʌʃru:m], 1. *s.* der Champignon; eßbarer Pilz; (*fig.*) der Emporkömmling; *shoot up like –s*, wie Pilze aus der Erde schießen. 2. *adj.* (*fig.*) neu, eben aufgetaucht, plötzlich entstanden *or* emporgeschossen, Eintags–. 3. *v.n.* Pilze sammeln; (*fig.*) sich pilzartig breitschlagen (*bullet*).
mushy ['mʌʃɪ], *see* **mush.**
music ['mju:zɪk], *s.* die Musik, Tonkunst; Noten (*pl.*), Musikalien (*pl.*); die Melodie, der Wohlklang, Wohllaut; *have you brought any – ?* haben Sie Noten mitgebracht? *copy –*, Noten abschreiben; (*coll.*) *face the –*, einstehen für das was man getan hat, die Verantwortung auf sich nehmen, die Suppe auslöffeln; der Gefahr ins Gesicht sehen; *Master of the Queen's –*, königlicher Hofkapellmeister; *play from –*, vom Blatt spielen; *set to –*, in Musik setzen, vertonen. **–al** [–əl], *adj.* musikalisch, Musik–; wohlklingend; *–al box*, die Spieldose; *–al chairs*, die Stuhlpolonaise; *–al glasses*, die Glasharmonika; *–al instrument*, das (Musik)Instrument; *–al pitch*, die Tonhöhe; *–al setting*, die Vertonung. **–ality** [–'kælɪtɪ], *s.*, **–alness,** *s.* der Wohlklang. **– –book,** *s.* das Notenheft. **– –hall,** *s.* das Variété(theater); buntes Programm (*Rad.*). **–ian** [mjʊ'zɪʃən], *s.* der Musiker; *she is a good –ian*, sie ist sehr musikalisch; sie spielt *or* singt gut. **– –master,** *s.* der Musiklehrer. **– –paper,** *s.* das Notenpapier. **– –room,** *s.* das Musikzimmer. **– –shop,** *s.* die Musikalienhandlung. **– –stand,** *s.* der Notenständer, das Notenpult. **– –stool,** *s.* der Klavierstuhl.
musing ['mju:zɪŋ], (*see* [2]**muse**) 1. *adj.* nachdenklich, sinnend, träumerisch. 2. *s.* das Grübeln, Nachsinnen; (*often pl.*) die Betrachtung, Träumerei.
musk [mʌsk], *s.* der Moschus, Bisam; die Moschuspflanze (*Bot.*). **– –deer,** *s.* das Moschustier. **– –ox,** *s.* der Moschusochse, Bisamochse. **– –rat,** *s.* die Bisamratte. **– –rose,** *s.* die Moschusrose (*Bot.*). **–y,** *adj.* nach Moschus riechend.
musket ['mʌskɪt], *s.* die Muskete, Flinte. **–eer** [–'tɪ:ə], *s.* der Musketier. **–ry** [–rɪ], *s.* die Schießkunst, der Schießunterricht. **–ry-fire,** *s.* das Handgewehrfeuer. **–ry-instructor,** *s.* der Schießlehrer.
musky ['mʌskɪ], *see* **musk.**
muslin ['mʌzlɪn], *s.* der Musselin.
musquash ['mʌskwɔʃ], *s.* die Bisamratte (*Zool.*); das Bisamfell.
muss [mʌs], 1. *s.* (*Amer.*) das Durcheinander, die Verwirrung, Unordnung. 2. *v.a.* verwirren, in Unordnung bringen.
mussel ['mʌsl], *s.* die Muschel.
[1]**must** [mʌst], *ir.v.aux.* müssen (*only pres.* & *past tenses*); (*with neg.*) dürfen (*only pres. tense*); *I* (*he*) –, ich (er) muß(te); *I* (*he*) *– not*, ich (er) darf nicht; *he – have lost his way*, er muß sich verirrt haben; *he – have heard it*, er hätte es hören müssen.
[2]**must** [mʌst], *s.* der Most.
[3]**must** [mʌst], *s.* der Moder, die Modrigkeit, Muffigkeit. **–iness,** *s.* die Muffigkeit, Dumpfigkeit. **–y,** *adj.* modrig, muffig, dumpf; schimmelig, stockfleckig.
mustachio [mʊs'tɑ:ʃoʊ], *s.* (*archaic*) der Schnurrbart.
mustang ['mʌstæŋ], *s.* der Mustang, halbwildes Präriepferd.
mustard ['mʌstəd], *s.* der Senf (*also Bot.*), Mostrich; (*sl.*) treffliche Sache *or* Person. **– –gas,** *s.* das Gelbkreuz(gas), Yperit. **– –plaster,** *s.* das Senfpflaster. **– –poultice,** *s.* die Senfpackung. **– –seed,** *s.* der Senfsame; (*B.*) *grain of – –seed*, das Senfkorn.
muster ['mʌstə], 1. *s.* die Musterung, Parade, der Appell (*Mil.*); die Versammlung; *pass –*, (*fig.*) geduldet werden, Zustimmung finden, hingehen, gelten (*as*, als). 2. *v.a.* mustern (*Mil.* & *fig.*); aufbringen, zusammenbringen, auftreiben, sammeln; *– troops into service*, Soldaten einstellen; *– troops out of service*, Soldaten entlassen; *– up*, zusammenraffen (*courage, etc.*). 3. *v.n.* sich einfinden, sich sammeln *or* ansammeln. **– –roll,** *s.* die Stammrolle.
must–iness, –y, *see* [3]**must.**
mutab–ility [mjʊtə'bɪlɪtɪ], *s.* die Veränderlichkeit; Wankelmütigkeit. **–le** ['mju:təbl], *adj.* veränderlich; (*fig.*) wankelmütig, unbeständig.
muta–nt ['mju:tənt], *s.* die Variante, der Abweicher (*Bot., Zool.*). **–ted** [–'teɪtɪd], *adj.* umgelautet (*Gram.*). **–tion** [–'teɪʃən], *s.* die Veränderung, der Wechsel; die Umformung (*of energy*); Abänderung, Mutation (*Biol.*); der Umlaut (*Gram.*). **–tive,** *adj.* veränderlich.
mutch [mʌtʃ], *s.* (*Scots*) die Frauenhaube.
mute [mju:t], 1. *adj.* stumm (*also Phonet.*), lautlos, still; *– vowel*, der Verschlußvokal. 2. *s.* Stumme(r), *m.*, der Statist (*Theat.*); (*fig.*) Dämpfer, die Sordine (*Mus.*); der Verschlußlaut. 3. *v.a.* dämpfen (*Mus.*). **–ness,** *s.* die Stummheit, Schweigsamkeit.
mutilat–e ['mju:tɪleɪt], *v.a.* verstümmeln. **–ion** [–'leɪʃən], *s.* die Verstümmelung.
mutin–eer [mju:tɪ'nɪ:ə], *s.* der Meuterer. **–ous** ['mju:tɪnəs], *adj.* meuterisch, rebellisch, aufrührerisch. **–y** ['mju:tɪnɪ], 1. *s.* die Meuterei, Auflehnung, der Aufruhr. 2. *v.n.* meutern, sich empören.
mutt [mʌt], *s.* (*Amer. sl.*) der Tölpel, Dummkopf.
mutter ['mʌtə], 1. *v.a.* murmeln. 2. *v.a.* murmeln; murren (*at*, über; *against*, gegen). **–ing,** *s.* das Gemurmel.
mutton ['mʌtən], *s.* das Hammelfleisch; *leg of –*, die Hammelkeule. **– chop,** das Hammelrippchen; *– chop whiskers*, der Kotelettenbart. **– –suet,** *s.* das Hammelfett, Hammeltalg.
mutual ['mju:tʃʊəl], *adj.* gegenseitig, wechselseitig, beiderseitig; gemeinsam; *by – consent*, durch gegenseitige Übereinkunft; *– effect*, die Wechselwirkung; *our – friend*, unser gemeinsamer Freund; *– insurance* (*company*), die Versicherung(sgesellschaft) auf Gegenseitigkeit; *on – terms*, zu gegenseitigem Vorteil. **–ity** [–'ælɪtɪ], *s.* die Gegenseitigkeit.
muzzle ['mʌzl], 1. *s.* das Maul, die Schnauze; die Mündung, Rohrmündung (*of a gun*); der Maulkorb (*for a dog*). 2. *v.a.* einen Maulkorb anlegen (*Dat.*); (*fig.*) den Mund stopfen (*Dat.*), zum Schweigen bringen, mundtot machen, knebeln (*press, etc.*). **– –loader,** *s.* der Vorderlader. **– –velocity,** *s.* die Anfangsgeschwindigkeit, Mündungsgeschwindigkeit.
muzzy ['mʌzɪ], *adj.* (*sl.*) wirr, verwirrt, duselig.
my [mɑɪ], *poss. adj.* mein(e); *– head is aching*, mir

tut der Kopf weh; (*coll.*) *oh – !* du meine Güte! – *eye!* potztausend.
myalgia [maɪ'ældʒɪə], *s.* der Muskelrheumatismus.
myc–elium [maɪ'sɪ:lɪəm], *s.* das Fadengeflecht der Pilze, Myzel. **–ology** [–'kɔlədʒɪ], *s.* die Pilzkunde.
myelitis [maɪə'laɪtɪs], *s.* die Rückenmarksentzündung.
myocarditis [maɪoka:'daɪtɪs], *s.* die Herzmuskelentzündung.
myology [maɪ'ɔlədʒɪ], *s.* die Muskellehre, Muskelkunde.
myop–e ['maɪoʊp], *s.* Kurzsichtige(r), *m.* **–ia** [–pɪə] *s.* die Kurzsichtigkeit. **–ic** [maɪ'oʊpɪk], *adj.* kurzsichtig. **–y,** *s. see* **–ia.**
myosotis [maɪə'soʊtɪs], *s.* das (Sumpf)Vergißmeinnicht.
myri–ad ['mɪrɪəd], *s.* die Myriade, Unzahl, unzählige Menge. 2. *adj.* zahllos, unzählig. **–apod,** *s.* der Tausenfüß(l)er.
myrmidon ['mə:mɪdən], *s.* der Helfershelfer, Scherge, Häscher; – *of the law,* der Vollstrecker der Gerechtigkeit.
myrrh [mə:], *s.* die Myrrhe (*Bot.*).
myrtle ['mə:təl], *s.* die Myrte (*Bot.*).
myself [maɪ'sɛlf], *pron.* (*emph.*) ich selbst, (*refl.*) mich, mir; *I saw it –,* ich sah es selbst *or* mit eigenen Augen; *I – am doubtful,* persönlich *or* was mich betrifft, bin ich skeptisch; *I have hurt –,* ich habe mich verletzt *or* mir weh getan.
myster–ious [mɪs'tɪ:ərɪəs], *adj.* geheimnisvoll, rätselhaft, mysteriös, schleierhaft. **–iousness,** *s.* das Geheimnisvolle, Rätselhafte, Dunkel. **–y** ['mɪstərɪ], *s.* das Geheimnis, Rätsel (*to,* für); Dunkel; die Geheimlehre, Geheimkunst; das Mysterienspiel, Mysterium. **–y-play,** *s.* das Mysterienspiel; Kriminalstück. **–y-ship,** *s.* die U-bootfalle. **–y-trip,** *s.* die Fahrt ins Blaue.
myst–ic ['mɪstɪk], 1. *adj.* geheimnisvoll, mystisch, rätselhaft, mysteriös, geheim, dunkel; tiefsinnig, symbolisch, sinnbildlich. 2. *s.* der Mystiker. **–ical** [–l], *adj. see* **–ic** 1; (*esp.*) geheimnisvoll, mystisch, übervernünftig. **–icism** [–sɪzm], *s.* die Mystik, der Mystizismus. **–ification** [–fɪ'keɪʃən], *s.* die Täuschung, Irreführung, Fopperei, Mystifikation. **–ified,** *adj.* (*coll.*) verblüfft. **–ify,** *v.a.,* hinters Licht führen, irreführen, täuschen, foppen, mystifizieren, (*esp. pass.*) verblüffen, verwirren.
myth (mɪθ], *s.* der Mythus, die Mythe, Göttersage; (*fig.*) Fabel, Erfindung, Erdichtung. **–ic** (*Poet.*), **–ical** [–ɪk(l)], *adj.* mythisch, sagenhaft; (*fig.*) fiktiv, erfunden, erdichtet. **–ological** [–ə'lɔdʒɪkl], *adj.* mythologisch. **–ologist** [–'θɔlədʒɪst], *s.* der Mythologe. **–ology** [–'θɔlədʒɪ], *s.* die Mythologie. **–opoeic** [–o'pɪ:ɪk], *adj.,* **–opoetic** [–opoʊ'ɛtɪk], *adj.* mythenbildend.

N

N, n [ɛn], *s.* das N, n; *n-th,* 6^n (*six to the n-th*), sechs hoch n (*Math.*); (*coll.*) *to the n-th degree,* im höchsten Grade. *See Index of Abbreviations.*
nab [næb], *v.a.* (*sl.*) erhaschen, erschnappen (*a th.*), erwischen, schnappen (*a p.*)
nabob ['neɪbɔb], *s.* der Nabob, (*fig.*) Krösus.
nacelle [næ'sɛl], *s.* der Flugzeugrumpf (*of aeroplane*); Ballonkorb (*of balloon*); die Gondel (*of airship*).
nacr–e ['neɪkə], *s.* die Perlmutter, das Perlmutt. **–(e)ous** [–kr(ɪ)əs], *adj.* perlmutterartig, Perlmutter–; *–(e)ous lustre,* der Perlenglanz.
nadir ['neɪdə], *s.* der Nadir, Fußpunkt; (*fig.*) tiefster Stand, der Tiefstand, Nullpunkt.
naevus ['nɪ:vəs], *s.* das Muttermal.
[1]**nag** [næg], *s.* kleines Pferd, der Gaul.
[2]**nag** [næg], 1. *v.a.* keifen, nörgeln *or* meckern mit. 2. *v.n.* nörgeln, meckern, quengeln (*at a p.,* mit einem). **–ging,** 1. *s.* die Nörgelei, das Meckern, Quengeln. 2. *adj.* (*coll.* **–gy**) nörgelnd, nörglig.
naiad ['naɪæd], *s.* die Najade, Wassernymphe.
nail [neɪl], 1. *s.* der Nagel (*on fingers, etc., also of metal*); der Spieker (*Naut.*); die Kralle, Klaue; *drive a – into,* einen Nagel einschlagen in; *a – in his coffin,* ein Nagel zu seinem Sarg; (*coll.*) *on the –,* auf der Stelle, unverzüglich; *pay on the –,* bar zahlen; *wire –,* der Drahtstift; *as hard as –s,* stahlhart. 2. *v.a.* nageln; verspiekern (*Naut.*); benageln, mit Nägeln beschlagen (*boots, etc.*); (*fig.*) festnageln; *– a lie,* eine Lüge festnageln; *– down,* zunageln (*a box, etc.*); *– a p. down to,* einen festnageln auf; *– one's eyes on,* die Augen heften auf; *– to the cross,* ans Kreuz schlagen, kreuzigen; *– to the spot,* auf dem Fleck festnageln; *– up,* annageln, zunageln, festnageln, vernageln. **– -brush,** *s.* die Nagelbürste. **–er,** *s.* der Nagelschmied; (*sl.*) Prachtkerl, die Kanone. **– -head,** *s.* der Nagelkopf. **–ing,** *adj.* (*sl.*) famos, großartig. **– -nippers,** *pl.* die Nagelzange. **– -scissors,** *pl.* die Nagelschere. **– varnish,** die Nagelpolitur.
nainsook [neɪn'sʊk], *s.* eine Art Musselin.
naissant ['neɪsənt], *adj.* hervorkommend (*Her.*).
naïve [nɑ:'ɪ:v], **naive** [neɪv], *adj.* unbefangen, naiv, ungekünstelt. **–té** [nɑ:'ɪ:vte], *s.,* **–ty** [nə'ɪ:vtɪ], **naïvety** ['neɪvtɪ], *s.* die Unbefangenheit, Naivität.
naked ['neɪkɪd], *adj.* nackt, bloß, unbedeckt; hilflos, schutzlos, wehrlos; kahl, unbeschützt, offen; unverhüllt; *with the – eye,* mit bloßem *or* unbewaffnetem Auge; *– facts,* nackte Tatsachen; *with – fists,* mit bloßer Faust; *– Lady,* die Herbstzeitlose (*Bot.*); *– sword,* blankes Schwert; *– truth,* nackte, einfache *or* reine Wahrheit; *strip –,* ganz ausziehen. **–ness,** *s.* die Nacktheit, Blöße; (*fig.*) Kahlheit; Offenheit, Klarheit, Einfachheit.
namable ['neɪməbl], *see* **nameable.**
namby-pamby ['næmbɪ'pæmbɪ], *adj.* (*coll.*) sentimental, süßlich, verweichlicht, geziert.
name [neɪm], **1.** *s.* der Name, die Benennung, Bezeichnung, der Titel; guter Name, der Ruhm, Ruf, die Berühmtheit, berühmte Person; die Familie, Linie, das Geschlecht; *Christian –,* der Taufname, Vorname; *family –,* der Familienname. (*a*) (*with verbs*) *call a p. –s,* einen beschimpfen; *give one's –,* seinen Namen nennen; *give a dog a bad – (and hang him),* einen ein für alle Male abtun; *give it a – !* heraus damit! *he has a bad –,* er hat einen schlechten Ruf; *have a – for being,* im Rufe (*with Gen. noun*) stehen, im Rufe stehen (*with adj.*) zu sein, verschrien sein als; *what is your – ?* wie heißen Sie ?; *make a – for o.s., make one's –,* sich (*Dat.*) einen Namen machen; *don't mention –s !* werden Sie nicht persönlich!; *put one's – down for,* sich bewerben um; sich vormerken lassen für (*library book, etc.*); *send in one's –,* sich melden. (*b*) (*with prepositions*) *by –,* mit Namen, namens, dem Namen nach; *call by –,* beim *or* mit Namen rufen; *know by –,* dem Namen nach kennen; *mention by –,* mit Namen nennen; *by the – of,* unter dem Namen; *a man by the – of,* ein Mann namens; *in the –,* im Namen (*of* (*Gen.*)); *in s.o.'s –* or *in the – of s.o.,* auf *or* in jemandes Namen, um jemandes willen; *issue a ticket in the – of John,* eine Karte auf den Namen John ausstellen; *what's in a – ?* was bedeutet schon ein Name?; *in – only,* nur dem Namen nach; *in one's own –,* auf eigene Faust; *not have a penny to one's –,* nicht einen Groschen haben; *reduce to a –,* auf einen bloßen Namen bringen; *under the – of,* see *by the – of.* **2.** *v.a.* nennen (*a p.*), benennen (*a th.*) (*after,* nach); erwähnen (*a th.*); mit Namen nennen, namhaft machen (*a p.*); ernennen (*to* or *for,* zu); festsetzen, bestimmen (*a day*), angeben (*a date*); zur Ordnung rufen, von der Sitzung ausschließen (*a deputy*) (*Parl.*). **–able,** *adj.* (be)nennbar. **– -day,** *s.* der Namenstag; Skrontierungstag (*stock exchange*). **–less,** *adj.* namenlos, anonym; unbekannt, nicht berühmt, unerwähnt; unaussprechlich, unsäglich, unbeschreiblich. **–lessness,** *s.* die Namenlosigkeit. **–ly,** 1. *adv.* nämlich. 2. *adj.* (*Scots*) berühmt (*for,* wegen). **– -part,** *s.* die Titelrolle. **–plate,** *s.* das

Türschild; das Firmenschild (*C.L.*). **–sake,** *s.* der Namensvetter.
nankeen [næŋ'kɪ:n], *s.* der Nanking(stoff); *pl.* Nankinghosen.
nanny ['nænɪ], *s.* das Kindermädchen, die Kinderpflegerin. **--goat,** *s.* die Ziege.
[1]**nap** [næp], 1. *s.* das Schläfchen, (*coll.*) Nickerchen; *take a –*, ein Schläfchen halten. 2. *v.n.* schlummern, einnicken; *catch a p. –ping*, einen überraschen *or* überrumpeln.
[2]**nap** [næp], 1. *s.* die Noppe. 2. *v.a.* noppen. **–less,** *adj.* glatt, kahl; fadenscheinig.
[3]**nap** [næp], *s.* Napoleon (*Cards*); (also – *selection*) die Voraussage, Ausrechnung (*Racing*); *go –*, Stiche für alle Karten ansagen (*Cards*); (*fig.*) alles aufs Spiel setzen (*on*, für).
nape [neɪp], *s.* (usually – *of the neck*) der Nacken, das Genick.
napery ['neɪpərɪ], *s.* (*Scots*) das Tischzeug, Leinenzeug.
naphtha ['næfθə], *s.* das Naphtha, Erdöl, Steinöl. **–lene, –line, –lin** [–lɪn], *s.* das Naphthalin.
napkin ['næpkɪn], *s.* (also *table-–*) das Mundtuch, die Serviette; Windel (*for baby*); (*Amer.*) Monatsbinde (*for women*). **--ring,** *s.* der Serviettenring.
napless ['næplɪs], *see* [2]**nap.**
napoo [nɑ:'pu:], *pred. adj.* (*sl.*) futsch, fertig.
nappy ['næpɪ], (*coll.*) *s.* die Windel.
narcissism ['nɑ:sɪsɪzm], *s.* der Narzissmus, krankhafte Selbstbewunderung, die Verliebtheit in sich selbst (*Psych.*).
narcissus [nɑ:'sɪsəs], *s.* die Narzisse (*Bot.*).
narco–sis [nɑ:'kousɪs], *s.* die Narkose. **–tic** [–'kɔtɪk], 1. *adj.* einschläfernd, narkotisch. 2. *s.* das Betäubungsmittel, Einschläferungsmittel, Rauschgift. **–tism** ['nɑ:kətɪzm], *s.* narkotischer Zustand. **–tize** ['nɑ:kətaɪz], *v.a.* narkotisieren.
nard [nɑ:d], *s.* die Narde (*Bot.*); Nardensalbe.
narghile ['nɑ:gɪlə], *s.* türkische Wasserpfeife.
nark [nɑ:k], 1. *s.* (*sl.*) der Spitzel. 2. *v.a.* & *n.* (*sl.*) ärgern.
narrat–e [nə'reɪt], *v.a.* erzählen. **–ion** [–'reɪʃən], *s.* die Erzählung. **–ive** ['nærətɪv], 1. *adj.* erzählend, Erzählungs–. 2. *s.* die Erzählung, Geschichte; Schilderung, Darstellung, der Bericht. **–or** ['nærətə], *s.* der Erzähler.
narrow ['nærou], 1. *adj.* eng, schmal; eingehend; (*fig.*) beschränkt, eingeschränkt, engherzig, kleinlich, geizig; *in – circumstances*, in dürftigen *or* kümmerlichen Verhältnissen; *bring into a – compass*, kurz zusammenfassen; *have a – escape*, mit genauer *or* knapper Not entkommen; – *finish*, knappe Entscheidung. – *gauge*, 1. *s.* die Schmalspur. 2. *attrib. adj.* schmalspurig; – *majority*, knappe Mehrheit; – *pass*, der Hohlweg; – *seas*, see – 4. *pl.*; *in the –est sense*, im beschränktesten Sinne; (*coll.*) – *squeak* see – *escape*; – *views*, beschränkte Ansichten. 2. *v.a.* verengern, schmäler *or* enger machen; beschränken; einengen, beengen; (Maschen) abnehmen (*knitting*). 3. *v.n.* sich verengern, schmäler *or* enger werden. 4. *s.* der Engpaß; (*usually pl.*) die Meerenge. **–ly,** *adv.* nur eben, mit Mühe. **--minded,** *adj.* engherzig. **--mindedness,** *s.* die Engherzigkeit. **–ness,** *s.* die Enge, Schmalheit; Beschränktheit, Engherzigkeit.
narwhal ['nɑ:wəl], *s.* der Narwal.
nasal ['neɪzl], 1. *adj.* Nasen–, Nasal–; näselnd (*sound*); – *bone*, das Nasenbein; – *twang*, das Näseln. 2. *s.* der Nasallaut. **–ity** [–'zælɪtɪ], *s.* die Nasalität. **–ization** [–zəlɑɪ'zeɪʃən], *s.* die Nasalierung, nasale Aussprache. **–ize** [–əlɑɪz], 1. *v.n.* durch die Nase sprechen, näseln; nasalieren (*Phonet.*). 2. *v.a.* durch die Nase aussprechen. **–ly** [–əlɪ], *adv.* durch die Nase, als Nasallaut.
nascent ['næsənt], *adj.* entstehend, wachsend, werdend; freiwerdend (*Chem.*); – *state*, der Entwicklungszustand.
nastiness ['nɑ:stɪnɪs], *s.* der Schmutz, die Schmutzigkeit; der Unflat, die Unflätigkeit, Schlüpfrigkeit, Ekelhaftigkeit, Widerlichkeit. *See* **nasty.**
nasturtium [nə'stə:ʃəm], *s.* die Kapuzinerkresse.
nasty ['nɑ:stɪ], *adj.* unangenehm, widerlich, eklig, ekelhaft, garstig; schmutzig, schlüpfrig, unflätig, unzüchtig; bedenklich, ernst, schwer (*as accident*); mürrisch, gehässig (*to*, gegen); (*coll.*) – *one*, der Treffer (*of remark*); (*sl.*) – *piece of work*, übler Kunde (*of p.*).
natal ['neɪtl], *adj.* Geburts–; – *day*, der Geburtstag. **–ity** [nə'tælɪtɪ], *s.* die Geburtenziffer.
nata–nt ['neɪtənt], *adj.* schwimmend. **–tion** [nə'teɪʃən], *s.* das Schwimmen. **–torial** [neɪtə-tɔ':rɪəl], **–tory** ['neɪtətərɪ], *adj.* Schwimm–.
nation ['neɪʃən], *s.* die Nation, das Volk; *League of –s*, der Völkerbund; – *state*, der Nationalstaat. *--wide*, *adj.* allgemein; **–al** ['næʃənl], 1. *adj.* national, staatlich, Staats–, National–, Volks–, Landes–, volkstümlich, öffentlich; *–al anthem*, die Nationalhymne; *–al character*, der Volkscharakter; *–al characteristics*, völkische Eigenart; *–al costume*, die Volkstracht, Landestracht; *–al debt*, die Staatsschuld; *–al festival*, das Volksfest; *–al flag*, die Nationalflagge; *–al Gallery*, die Nationalgallerie; *–al insurance*, die Volksversicherung; *–al mourning*, die Volkstrauer; *–al park*, das Naturschutzgebiet; *–al prosperity*, der Volkswohlstand, das Volksvermögen. *–al-Socialism*, *s.* der Nationalsozialismus; *–al team*, die Ländermannschaft; *–al trust*, der Ausschuß für Naturschutzgebiete. 2. *s.* Staatsangehörige(r), *m.*; *pl.* Landsleute. **–alism** [–əlɪzm], *s.* der Nationalismus, das Nationalgefühl. **–alist** [–əlɪst], *s.* der Nationalist. **–ality** [–'nælɪtɪ], *s.* die Staatsangehörigkeit, Nationalität; der Nationalcharakter, nationale Eigenart; der Patriotismus, das Nationalgefühl; die Nation, das Volk; nationale Einheit *or* Unabhängigkeit. **–alization** [–ɑɪ'zeɪʃən], *s.* die Nationalisierung, Sozialisierung, Verstaatlichung. **–alize** [–əlɑɪz], *v.a.* verstaatlichen, nationalisieren, verstaatlichen. **–ally,** *adv.* in nationaler Hinsicht. **–hood,** *s.* nationale Geschlossenheit *or* Einheit.
native ['neɪtɪv], 1. *adj.* gebürtig (*of*, aus), heimisch (*of*, in (*Dat.*)); angeboren (*to* (*Dat.*)), von Natur aus, natürlich, ungekünstelt; gediegen (*as metals*); – *country*, das Vaterland; – *language*, die Muttersprache; – *place*, der Geburtsort; – *rock*, gewachsener Fels; – *town*, die Vaterstadt; – *troops*, einheimische Truppen. 2. *s.* Eingeborene(r), *m.*, das Landeskind; einheimische Pflanze (*Bot.*); einheimisches Tier (*Zool.*); künstlich gezüchtete Auster; *a – of Hanover*, geborener Hannoveraner.
nativity [nə'tɪvɪtɪ], *s.* die Geburt; Geburt Christi (*Eccl.*); Nativität, das Horoskop (*Astrol.*); – *play*, das Christfestspiel, Krippenspiel.
natron ['neɪtrən], *s.* das Natron.
natterjack ['nætədʒæk], *s.* die Kreuzkröte (*Zool.*).
natty ['nætɪ], *adj.* (*coll.*) nett, schmuck, zierlich.
natural ['nætʃərəl], 1. *adj.* natürlich, Natur–; physisch; real; normal, üblich, gewöhnlich; angeboren, eigen, eigentümlich (*to* (*Dat.*)); einfach, ungekünstelt, ungezwungen, naturhaft, naturwüchsig, frei, ehrlich, offen; unehelich, außerehelich (*of children*); ohne Vorzeichen (*Mus.*); – *colour*, die Naturfarbe, Eigenfarbe; *come –*, ganz selbstverständlich sein (*to* (*Dat.*)); *die a – death*, eines natürlichen Todes sterben; – *disposition*, das Naturell, die Charaktereigentümlichkeit; – *forces*, Naturkräfte (*pl.*); – *history*, die Naturgeschichte; – *key*, die C-Dur Tonart; – *law*, das Naturgesetz; – *period*, die Eigenperiode; – *philosopher* (*esp. Scots*), der Naturwissenschaftler, Physiker; – *philosophy*, die Naturphilosophie, Naturwissenschaft, Physik; – *religion*, die Naturreligion; – *science*, die Naturwissenschaft; – *selection*, natürliche Zuchtwahl. 2. *s.* Blödsinnige(r), *m.*, Schwachsinnige(r), *m.*, der Idiot; weiße Taste (*piano*), der Ton ohne Vorzeichen, das Auflösungszeichen (*Mus.*). **–ism** [–ɪzm], *s.* der Naturalismus (*Art, etc.*). **–ist** [–ɪst], 1. *s.* der Naturforscher, Naturaliensammler; Tierhändler; Tierausstopfer; Präparator; Naturalist (*Art, Phil.*). **–istic** [–'lɪstɪk], *adj.* naturalistisch (*Arts, Phil.*). **–ization** [–ɑɪ'zeɪʃən], *s.* die Naturalisierung, Einbürgerung. **–ize** [–ɑɪz], *v.a.* naturalisieren, einbürgern (*a p.*); akklimatisieren, heimisch machen (*Bot., Zool.*); (*fig.*) einführen, verbreiten; *become –ized*, sich naturalisieren lassen. **–ly,** *adv.* natürlich; von Natur; naturgemäß, instinktmäßig, auf natürlichem

Wege; ohne Schwierigkeit, von selbst, natürlicherweise, selbstverständlich. **–ness,** *s.* die Natürlichkeit, Ursprünglichkeit, (*fig.*) Ungezwungenheit, Unmittelbarkeit, Echtheit.
nature [ˈneɪtʃə], *s.* (*without art.*) die Natur (*also fig. & personified as fem.*); (*often with indef. art. or posses.*) das Wesen, die Natur(anlage), Charakteranlage, das Naturell; (*with def. art.*) die Art, Sorte, Form, Beschaffenheit; *all –*, die ganze Natur; *by –*, von Natur; *from –*, nach der Natur (*Art*); *good –*, die Gutherzigkeit, Gutartigkeit; *human –*, menschliche Natur; *in his –*, seiner Natur nach; *in the – of*, in Form von, nach Art von, gleichsam als; *in the – of the case* or *of things*, wie die Umstände nun einmal liegen, nach Lage der Dinge; *beauties of –*, Schönheit der Natur(erscheinungen); *law of –*, das Naturgesetz; *be second – with s.o.*, einem zur zweiten Natur geworden sein; *of this –*, dieser Art; *in a state of –*, im Naturzustand, in natürlichem Zustand, nackt; *pay one's debt to –*, der Natur seinen Tribut zahlen; *return to –*, die Rückkehr zur Natur. **– -cure,** *s.* die Naturheilkunde. **–d,** *adj. suff.* geartet, –artig. **– -lover,** *s.* der Naturliebhaber. **– -myth,** *s.* der Naturmythus. **– -printing,** *s.* der Naturselbstdruck. **– -study,** *s.* der Naturanschauungsunterricht. **– -worship,** *s.* die Naturanbetung.
naught [nɔ:t], *pred. adj. & s.* (*archaic & poet.*) nichts; *bring to –*, zum Scheitern bringen; *set at –*, unbeachtet lassen, sich hinwegsetzen über; *see* **nought.**
naught-iness [ˈnɔ:tɪnɪs], *s.* die Ungezogenheit, Unartigkeit. **–y,** *adj.* unartig, ungezogen.
nause-a [ˈnɔ:sɪə], *s.* der Brechreiz, die Übelkeit, das Erbrechen; die Seekrankheit; (*fig.*) der Ekel. **–ate** [–ɪeɪt], 1. *v.n.* Ekel empfinden (*at*, vor). 2. *v.a.* anekeln, mit Ekel erfüllen (*a p.*); (*rare*) mit Ekel zurückweisen (*food, etc.*); *be –ated*, sich ekeln (*at*, vor). **–ating,** *adj.*, **–ous** [–ɪəs], *adj.* ekelhaft, eklig, widerlich, widrig. **–ousness,** *s.* die Ekelhaftigkeit, Widerlichkeit.
nauti-cal [ˈnɔ:tɪkl], *adj.* nautisch, See–, Schiffs–; *–cal almanac*, nautisches Jahrbuch; *–cal chart*, die Seekarte; *–cal mile*, die Seemeile. **–lus** [–tɪləs], *s.* der Nautilus; das Schiffsboot.
naval [ˈneɪvl], *adj.* See–, Marine–, Flotten–, Schiffs–; *– aerodrome*, der Seeflughafen; *– agreement*, das Flottenabkommen; *– air arm*, die Marineluftwaffe; *– airplane*, das Seeflugzeug; *– architect*, der Schiffsbauingenieur; *– architecture*, die Schiffsbaukunst; *– attaché*, der Marine-Attaché; *– aviation*, das Seeflugwesen; *– base*, der Flottenstützpunkt; *– battle*, die Seeschlacht; *– cadet*, der Seekadett; *– college*, die Seekadettenschule; *– conference*, die Flottenkonferenz; *– construction*, der Flottenbau; *– disarmament*, die Flottenabrüstung; *– dockyard*, die Marinewerft; *– engagement*, see *– battle*; *– estimates*, der Marineetat; *– forces*, Marinestreitkräfte (*pl.*), die Seemacht; *– officer*, der Seeoffizier; *– port*, der Kriegshafen; *– power*, die Seemacht; *– prestige*, die Seegeltung; *– station*, der Kriegshafen; *– warfare*, der Seekrieg.
[1]**nave** [neɪv], *s.* das (Kirchen)Schiff, Hauptschiff, Mittelschiff.
[2]**nave** [neɪv], *s.* die (Rad)Nabe.
navel [neɪvl], *s.* der Nabel; (*fig.*) die Mitte, das Zentrum. **– -string,** *s.* die Nabelschnur.
navicert [ˈnævɪsə:t], *s.* der Warenpaß, Geleitschein.
navicular [nəˈvɪkjʊlə], 1. *adj.* bootförmig, nachenförmig. 2. *s.* das Kahnbein (*Anat.*).
naviga-bility [nævɪgəˈbɪlɪtɪ], *s.* die Schiffbarkeit (*of waterway*), Lenkbarkeit (*of aircraft*), Fahrbarkeit (*of road*). **–ble** [ˈnævɪgəbl], *adj.* schiffbar, fahrbar; *–ble balloon*, lenkbares Luftschiff. **–te** [ˈnævɪgeɪt], 1. *v.a.* befahren (*river, etc.*); durchziehen, durchmessen (*the air*); steuern (*also fig.*); lenken (*ship, aircraft, etc.*). 2. *v.n.* segeln, schiffen, zu Schiff fahren. **–tion** [–ˈgeɪʃən], *s.* die Schiffahrt, der Schiffsverkehr; die Steuermannskunst, Schiffahrtskunde, Navigation; *–tion acts*, Navigationsakte (*pl.*); *aerial –tion*, die Luftfahrtskunst; *celestial –tion*, astronomische Navigation; *–tion laws*, Schiffahrtsgesetze; *–tion light*, die Positionslampe, das Kennlicht; *–tion officer*, der Schiffsoffizier. **–tor** [ˈnævɪgeɪtə], *s.* der Seefahrer; Steuermann; Luftschiffer, Orter, (*coll.*) Franz (*Av.*).
navvy [ˈnævɪ], *s.* der Erdarbeiter, Streckenarbeiter; *steam –*, der Löffelbagger, Schipper.
navy [ˈneɪvɪ], *s.* die (Kriegs)Marine, (Kriegs)-Flotte; *– bill*, die Flottenvorlage, Flottennovelle; *– blue*, *adj.* marineblau; *– list*, die Marinerangordnung.
nawab [nəˈwɔ:b], *s.* indischer Fürst.
nay [neɪ], 1. *adv.* (*archaic*) nein; nein vielmehr; ja sogar. 2. *s.* das Nein, abschlägige Stimme.
naze [neɪz], *s.* die Landspitze, das Vorgebirge.
neap [nɪ:p], 1. *s.* (also *– -tide, s.*) die Nippflut. 2. *v.n.* niedriger werden (*of tides*). 3. *v.a.* (*usually pass.*); *be –ed*, wegen Nippflut nicht durchkommen (*of ships*).
near [nɪ:ə], 1. *attrib. adj.* nahe (gelegen); nahe verwandt; eng befreundet, vertraut; genau, (wortge)treu (*as a translation*); (*esp. comp. & sup.*) kurz, gerade (*as the way*); knapp (*as an escape*); karg, knauserig (*of persons*); link (*of vehicles & animals*); (*coll.*) fast, beinahe; *– beer*, das Dünnbier; *– escape*, knappes Entrinnen; *– future*, nahe Zukunft; *– hit*, der Nächsttreffer; *the – horse*, das Sattelpferd; *– miss*, der Fehltreffer; *– race*, knappes Rennen; *the – side*, die Sattelseite, linke Seite (*of road, horse, vehicle, etc.*); *– silk*, die Halbseide; (*coll.*) *a – thing!* um ein Haar! *–est way*, nächster *or* kürzester Weg; *the – wheeler*, das Stangensattelpferd. 2. *adv.* nahe (bei), nahe bevorstehend (*in time*); *– at hand*, dicht dabei, in der nächsten Nähe, vor der Tür (*of time*); *– by*, naheliegend, (ganz) in der Nähe; (*coll.*) *be* or *come – (doing)*, see *– to*; *draw –*, heranrücken, sich nähern (*to*, an); *Christmas draws –*, es geht auf Weihnachten zu; (*coll.*) *not – so big as*, see **–ly**; *sail – the wind*, hart am Winde segeln; *– to*, nahe (bei); *–er to me*, mir näher; *–est to me*, mir am nächsten; *come* or *go – to (doing)*, fast *or* beinahe (tun); *– upon*, nahe an, fast um (*with expressions of time*). 3. *prep.* nahe an *or* bei, unweit von; *– Christmas*, nahe an Weihnachten; *come – a th.*, einer S. nahekommen; *no –er doing*, nicht näher daran zu tun; *– fulfilment*, der Erfüllung nahe; *lie – one's heart*, einem nahegehen. **–by** [–baɪ], 1. *adj.* nahe gelegen. 2. *adv.* in der Nähe. **–ly** [–lɪ], *adv.* nahe; fast, beinahe, ungefähr; *it –ly concerns me*, es geht mich nahe an; *not –ly*, bei weitem nicht, nicht annähernd; noch lange nicht; *they are –ly related*, sie sind nahe verwandt; *for –ly 12 hours*, fast 12 Stunden lang. **–ness,** *s.* die Nähe (*to*, an *or* bei), nahe Verwandtschaft; die Kargheit, Knauserigkeit; Genauigkeit. **– -sighted,** *adj.* kurzsichtig. **– -sightedness,** *s.* die Kurzsichtigkeit.
[1]**neat** [nɪ:t], *adj.* reinlich; ordentlich, sauber; zierlich, niedlich, nett; rein, unverdünnt (*of liquor*); (*coll.*) geschickt, treffend. **–ness,** *s.* die Nettigkeit, Sauberkeit; Zierlichkeit, Niedlichkeit; (*coll.*) Geschicklichkeit.
[2]**neat** [nɪ:t], *s.* das Rind, der Ochse; (*collect. pl. constr.*) das Rindvieh. **–'s-foot-oil,** *s.* das Klauenfett.
neath [nɪ:θ], *prep.* (*Poet.*) *see* **beneath.**
neb [nɛb], *s.* (*Scots*) der Schnabel, die Schnauze; Spitze.
nebul-a [ˈnɛbjʊlə], *s.* (pl. *–ae*) der Nebelfleck (*Astr.*). **–ar** [–lɑ], *adj.* Nebel(fleck)–, Nebular–. **–osity** [–ˈlɔsɪtɪ], *s.* die Nebligkeit; (*fig.*) Nebelhaftigkeit, Undeutlichkeit. **–ous,** *adj.* wolkig, neblig, Nebel– (*Astr.*); (*fig.*) undeutlich, unbestimmt, nebelhaft.
necessar-ily [ˈnɛsəsərɪlɪ], *adv.* notwendig(erweise), durchaus. **–y** [–ərɪ], 1. *adj.* notwendig, durchaus nötig, unentbehrlich (*to* or *for*, für); unumgänglich, unvermeidlich, zwangsläufig, (not)gezwungen; *it is –y that I should go*, es ist notwendig daß ich gehe; *it is –y to go*, man muß unbedingt gehen; *absolutely –y*, unumgänglich notwendig; *–y evil*, notwendiges Übel; *if –y*, nötigenfalls. 2. *s.* das Bedürfnis, Erforderns, der Bedarfsartikel (*C.L.*); notwendiger Unterhalt (*Law*); *–ies of life*, Lebensbedürfnisse (*pl.*); (*sl.*) *the –y*, das nötige Geld; (*coll.*) *do the –y*, das Notwendige tun.
necessit-arian [nəsɛsɪˈtɛ:ərɪən], 1. *s.* der Determinist. 2. *adj.* deterministisch. **–ate** [–ˈsɛsɪteɪt],

v.a. erfordern, notwendig machen (*a th. being done*, daß etwas geschieht), zwingen (*a p. to do*, einen zu tun). **–ous** [–ˈsɛsɪtəs], *adj.* bedürftig, arm; dürftig, notleidend. **–y** [–ˈsɛsɪtɪ], *s.* die Notwendigkeit (*to do* or *of doing*, zu tun); Unumgänglichkeit, Unvermeidlicheit, der Zwang; dringendes Bedürfnis (*for*, für *or* nach); die Armut, Not; *as a –y*, notwendig(erweise); (*Prov.*) *–y is the mother of invention*, Not macht erfinderisch; (*Prov.*) *–y knows no law*, Not kennt kein Gebot; *no –y for* or *of*, durchaus nicht nötig, daß; *of –y*, notgedrungen, notwendigerweise; *be under the –y of doing*, sich gezwungen sehen zu tun; *make a virtue of –y*, aus der Not eine Tugend machen.

neck [nɛk], *s.* der Hals (*also of a bottle*), Nacken; das Genick; Nackenstück (*of meat*); die Landenge, der Paß (*of land*), der Ausschnitt (*of a dress*); die Verbindungsröhre (*Mach.*); (*sl.*) Schnoddrigkeit; – *of land*, die Landzunge; – *and* –, Kopf an Kopf (*Racing*); *break one's* –, das Genick brechen; *break the – of a th.*, das Schwerste an einer S. überstehen *or* hinter sich bringen *or* haben; *crane one's* –, sich den Hals verrenken *or* ausrecken; – *and crop*, mit Sack und Pack; (*sl.*) *get it in the* –, eins aufs Dach *or* auf den Hut kriegen, einen Wischer *or* sein Fett kriegen; (*sl.*) *give s.o. a pain in the* –, einen anekeln; – *or nothing*, alles oder nichts, auf jede Gefahr hin, blindlings; (*attrib. adj.*) blind, verzweifelt; *save one's* –, seine Haut retten; *take by the* –, beim Kragen fassen; *be up to one's – in work*, bis über die Ohren in der Arbeit stecken; *win by a* –, um eine *or* mit Halslänge gewinnen. **––band,** *s.* der Halsbund. **––bone,** *s.* der Halswirbel. **––cloth,** *s.* (*archaic*) das Halstuch, die Krawatte. **–ed,** *adj. suff.* -halsig, -nackig. **–erchief,** *s.* das Halstuch. **–lace,** *s.*, **–let,** *s.* das Halsband, die Halskette, der Halsschmuck. **––mould,** *s.* der Säulenhals (*Arch.*). **––plate,** *s.* der Ringkragen (*of armour*). **––tie,** *s.* die Halsbinde, Krawatte, der Schlips. **–wear,** *s.* die Krawatten (*pl.*), Kragen (*pl.*).

necro–logy [nəˈkrɔlədʒɪ], *s.* der Nachruf; die Totenliste. **–mancer,** *s.* der Schwarzkünstler, Zauberer, Geisterbeschwörer. **–mancy** [ˈnɛkrəmænsɪ], *s.* die Geisterbeschwörung, Schwarzkunst. **–polis** [nɛˈkrɔpəlɪs], *s.* der Friedhof, Beggräbnisplatz. **–sis** [nɛˈkrousɪs], *s.* die Nekrose, der Brand.

nectar [ˈnɛktə], *s.* der Nektar; Göttertrank (*Myth.*). **–ean** [–ˈtɛərɪən], *adj.*, **–eous** [–tɛːərɪəs], *adj.* Nektar–; (*fig.*) süß, köstlich. **–rine** [ˈnɛktərɪːn], *s.* die Nektarine. **–y** [ˈnɛktərɪ], *s.* die Honigdrüse, das Honiggefäß, Nektarium (*Bot.*).

neddy [ˈnɛdɪ], *s.* (*coll.*) der Esel.

née [neɪ], *adj.* geborene; *Mrs. Smith, – Miller*, Frau Smith, geb. Miller.

need [nɪːd], 1. *s.* die Not; Notwendigkeit, das Bedürfnis; der Mangel (*of*, an), Bedarf; die Notdurft, Armut, Bedrängnis, Bedürftigkeit; *if – arise* or *be*, nötigenfalls, im Notfall; *be no – for . . .*, nicht nötig sein daß . . .; *there is no* –, es ist kein Grund vorhanden (*for*, daß); *have no – for*, keinen Grund haben zu; *have – of* or *be* or *stand in – of*, nötig haben, brauchen, benötigen; *in* –, in Not; *a friend in – is a friend indeed*, Freunde erkennt man in der Not; *in case of* –, im Notfalle. 2. *v.a.* nötig haben, erfordern, brauchen, erheischen; bedürfen (*Gen.*); *that is more than is –ed*, das ist mehr als nötig ist. 3. *v. aux.* müssen, brauchen; *what – I care?* was brauche ich danach zu fragen; *it –ed saying*, es mußte (einmal) gesagt werden. **–ful,** 1. *adj.* notwendig, nötig (*for* or *to*, für). 2. *s.* das Nötige; (*sl.*) das nötige Geld. **–iness,** *s.* die Armut, Dürftigkeit. **–less,** *adj.* unnötig, überflüssig. **–lessness,** *s.* die Unnötigkeit, Überflüssigkeit. **–s** *adv.* (only with *must*) durchaus, notwendigerweise, schlechterdings, ausgerechnet; *–s must when the devil drives*, Not bricht Eisen. **–y,** *adj.* arm, bedürftig, mittellos, notleidend.

needle [nɪːdl], 1. *s.* die Nadel; der Obelisk (*Arch.*); *darning-*–, die Stopfnadel; *pine* –, die Fichtennadel, Tannennadel; *gramophone* –, die Grammophonnadel; *hypodermic* –, die Injektionskanüle; *knitting-*–, die Stricknadel; *sewing-*–, die Nähnadel; – *of a balance*, das Zünglein an der Waage; – *of the compass*, die Magnetnadel; – *of rock*, die Felszinne; *–'s eye*, das Nadelöhr; *as sharp as a* –, haarscharf; (*sl.*) *get the* –, eine Wut kriegen; Lampenfieber bekommen (*Theat.*); *look for a – in a haystack* or *bottle of hay*, sich mit nutzlosem Suchen abmühen. 2. *v.a.* mit der Nadel arbeiten an (*Dat.*); durchstechen; – *one's way through*, sich durchwinden. 3. *v.n.* sich winden. **––bath,** *s.* das Brausenduschenbad. **––case,** *s.* die Nadelbüchse. **––galvanometer,** *s.* das Zeigergalvanometer (*Elec.*). **––gun,** *s.* das Zündnadelgewehr. **––maker,** *s.* der Nadler. **––point,** *s.* die Nadelspitze. **––telegraph,** *s.* der Zeigertelegraph. **––threader,** *s.* der Einfädler (*Sew.-mach.*). **–woman,** *s.* die Näherin. **–work,** *s.* die Handarbeit, Näherei.

need–less, –s, –y, *see* **need.**

ne'er [nɛːə], (*Poet.*) *see* **never.** **––do-well** (*Scots* **––do-weel**), 1. *s.* der Taugenichts. 2. *adj.* nichtsnutzig.

nefarious [nəˈfɛːərɪəs], *adj.* schändlich, ruchlos, böse, frevelhaft, verrucht. **–ness,** *s.* die Ruchlosigkeit, Bosheit.

negat–e [nɪˈgeɪt], *v.a.* verneinen, leugnen; aufheben, negieren. **–ion,** *s.* das Verneinen, die Verneinung, Leugnung, Verwerfung, Aufhebung, Negierung, Negation; Null. **–ive** [ˈnɛgətɪv], 1. *adj.* verneinend, negierend, abschlägig (*as answer*); negativ (*Phot.*, *Elec.*, *Math.*); ergebnislos, unfruchtbar (*as criticism*). 2. *s.* die Verneinung, das Verneinungswort (*Gram.*); verneinende Stimme, der Einspruch, das Veto; Negativ (*Elec.*, *Phot.*); *in the –ive*, verneinend; *answer in the –ive*, verneinen. 3. *v.a.* verneinen; ablehnen, verwerfen; widerlegen, neutralisieren, unwirksam machen.

neglect [nɪˈglɛkt], 1. *s.* die Vernachlässigung, Nachlässigkeit, Geringschätzung, Versäumnis, Unterlassung; Verwahrlosung; – *of duty*, die Pflichtvergessenheit. 2. *v.a.* vernachlässigen; versäumen, verfehlen, unterlassen (*a duty, etc.*); geringschätzig behandeln; außer acht lassen (*precaution*). **–ed,** *adj.* verwahrlost. **–ful,** *adj.* nachlässig, unachtsam (*of*, auf); *be –ful of*, vernachlässigen, außer acht lassen.

neglig–é [ˈnɛglɪʒeɪ], *s.* das Negligé, Hauskleid, Morgenkleid. **–ence** [–dʒəns], *s.* die Nachlässigkeit, Unachtsamkeit; Fahrlässigkeit (*Law*); *contributory –ence*, das Mitverschulden (*Law*); *gross –ence*, grobe Fahrlässigkeit. **–ent** [–dʒənt], *adj.* nachlässig, gleichgültig (*of*, gegen); fahrlässig (*Law*); *be –ent of*, vernachlässigen; *–ent of duty*, pflichtvergessen. **–ible** [–dʒɪbl], *adj.* nicht zu beachten(d), unbedeutend, unwesentlich, nebensächlich, geringfügig.

negotia-bility [nɪˈgouʃɪəbɪlɪtɪ], *s.* die Verkäuflichkeit, Börsenfähigkeit, Handelsfähigkeit (*C.L.*). **–ble** [–əbl], *adj.* übertragbar, verkäuflich, umsetzbar, begebbar, börsenfähig (*C.L.*); (*fig.*) gangbar, befahrbar (*as road*), übersteigbar, überwindbar (*as obstacle*); *–ble instrument*, begebbare Urkunde (*C.L.*); *not –ble*, nur zur Verrechnung (*C.L.*). **–te** [–ʃɪeɪt], 1. *v.a.* zustande bringen, vermitteln, herbeiführen, abschließen (*treaty, loan, etc.*); verhandeln über; begeben (*cheque, etc.*); (*fig.*) setzen über, nehmen, übersteigen, überwinden (*obstacle*). 2. *v.n.* verhandeln *or* unterhandeln (*with*, mit). **–tion** [–ʃɪˈeɪʃən], (*often pl.*) *s.* das Verhandeln, Unterhandeln, die Verhandlung, Unterhandlung; Vermittlung; Begebung (*of a bill*); (*fig.*) Überwindung (*of obstacles*); *–tion for time*, das Zeitgeschäft; *enter into –tions*, in Verhandlungen eintreten. **–tor** [–eɪtə], *s.* der Unterhändler, Vermittler.

Negr–ess [ˈnɪːgrɛs], *s.* (*pej.*) **die Negerin.**

Negr–o [ˈnɪːgrou], 1. *s.* der Neger, die Negerin. 2. *adj.* Neger–; *–o minstrels*, die Negersänger. **–oid** [–rɔɪd], *adj.* negerartig, negroid.

¹negus [ˈnɪːgəs], *s.* der Glühwein.

²negus [ˈnɪːgəs], *s.* der König von Abessinien.

neigh [neɪ], 1. *v.n.* wiehern. 2. *s.* das Wiehern.

neighbour [ˈneɪbə], 1. *s.* der Nachbar; (*B.*) Nächste(r), *m.*, der Mitmensch. 2. *adj.* Nachbar–, benachbart. 3. *v.a.* grenzen an (*Acc.*). **–hood** [–hud], *s.* die Nachbarschaft, Nähe (*also fig.*); Gegend, Umgebung; Nachbarn (*pl.*); *in the –hood of*, in

der Nähe von; (*fig.*) ungefähr. **-ing** [-rɪŋ], *adj.* benachbart, angrenzend; *see* **–** 2. **–liness** [–lɪnɪs], *s.* gutes nachbarliches Verhältnis, die Geselligkeit. **–ly,** *adj.* nachbarlich; gesellig, freundlich.
neither ['naɪðə, 'nɪ:ðə], 1. *adj.* & *pron.* keine(r, s) (von beiden); – *of us*, keiner von uns beiden; – *way* or *of the ways*, keiner von den beiden Wegen; *beer or wine?* – *!* Bier oder Wein? keins von beiden! 2. *adv.* – . . . *nor*, weder . . . noch; *no* or *nor* or *not* . . . –, . . . auch nicht. 3. *conj.* (*after neg. clause*) auch nicht, noch auch; *I cannot come, – can he*, ich kann nicht kommen, er auch nicht.
nelly ['nɛlɪ], *s.* der Riesensturmvogel (*Orn.*).
nemat–ode ['nɛmətoʊd], *s.*, **–oid,** *s.* der Fadenwurm. **–ophore,** *s.* das Nesseltier (*Zool.*).
nemesis ['nɛməsɪs], *s.* (*fig.*) die Vergeltung.
nenuphar ['nɛnjʊfə], *s.* weiße Wasserlilie (*Bot.*).
neolith ['nɪ:əlɪθ], *s.* jungsteinzeitliches Gerät. **–ic** [–'lɪθɪk], *adj.* jungsteinzeitlich; *–ic period*, das Neolithikum.
neolog–ism [nɪ'ɔlədʒɪzm], *s.*, **–y,** *s.* sprachliche Neubildung, die Sprachneuerung, neuer Ausdruck; rationalistische Ansicht (*Theol.*).
neon ['nɪən], *s.* das Neon (*Chem.*).
neo–phyte ['nɪ:əfaɪt], *s.* Neubekehrte(r), Neugetaufte(r), *m.* der Novize; (*fig.*) Neuling, Anfänger. **–plasm** [–plæzm], *s.* die Neubildung, das Gewächs (*Path.*). **–platonism** [nɪo'pleɪtənɪzm], *s.* der Neuplatonismus. **–teric** [nɪə'tɛrɪk], *adj.* modern, neu aufgekommen. **–zoic** [–'zoʊɪk], *adj.* neozoisch (*Geol.*).
nepenthe [nə'pɛnθɪ], *s.* der Zaubertrank.
nephew ['nɛfjʊ], *s.* der Neffe.
nephology [nɛ'fɔlədʒɪ], *s.* die Wolkenkunde.
nephr–ite ['nɛfraɪt], *s.* der Nephrit, Bitterstein. **–itic** [–'frɪtɪk], *adj.* Nieren-. **–itis** [–'fraɪtɪs], *s.* die Nierenentzündung.
nepotism ['nɪ:pətɪzm], *s.* der Nepotismus; die Vetternwirtschaft.
nereid ['nɪərɪd], *s.* die Nereide, Wassernymphe.
nerv–ation [nə:'veɪʃən], *s.* die Äderung, Nervatur (*Bot., Zool.*). **–e** [nə:v], 1. *s.* der Nerv; (*poet.*) die Sehne; (*fig.*) Kraft, Stärke, der Mut; die Rippe, Ader (*Bot.*); Nervenfaser, das Nervenbündel (*Anat.*); (*coll.*) die Unverfrorenheit; *pl.* Nerven (*pl.*); *pl.* (*coll.*) die Nervenschwäche, Nervosität; (*coll.*) *of all the –e!* so eine Unverschämtheit! (*coll.*) *a bundle of –es*, ein Nervenbündel; *fit of –es*, der Nervenschock; *get on s.o.'s –es*, einem auf die Nerven fallen; (*coll.*) *have the –e*, die Unverschämtheit haben; *lose one's –e*, den Mut verlieren; *strain every –e*, die allergrößten Anstrengungen machen. 2. *v.a.* kräftigen, stärken, ermutigen; *–e o.s.*, sich zusammenraffen, Mut fassen. **–e-centre,** *s.* das Nervenzentrum. **–ed,** *adj.* nervig; gerippt, –adrig (*Bot.*). **–eless,** *adj.* kraftlos, schlapp (*also fig.*); ohne Rippen (*Bot.*) *or* Adern (*Ent.*) *or* Nerven. **–e-racking,** *adj.* nervenaufreibend. **–e-strain,** *s.* die Nervenüberanstrengung. **–ine** [–aɪn], 1. *adj.* nervenstärkend. 2. *s.* nervenstärkendes Mittel. **–ous** [–əs], *adj.* nervös, erregbar; befangen, ängstlich; Nerven–; (*rare*) sehnig, markig, nervig, kräftig; gediegen, kraftvoll; *–ous breakdown*, der Nervenzusammenbruch; *–ous system*, das Nervensystem. **–ousness,** *s.* die Nervenschwäche, Nervosität; Ängstlichkeit, Befangenheit; (*rare*) Nervigkeit, Stärke. **–y,** *adj.* (*coll.*) nervös, erregbar; (*sl.*) unverfroren, frech.
nescien–ce ['nɛsɪəns], *s.* das Nichtwissen, die Unwissenheit (*of*, in). **–t** [–ənt], *adj.* unwissend (*of*, in (*Dat.*)).
ness [nɛs], *s.* das Vorgebirge.
nest [nɛst], 1. *s.* das Nest; die Brut, Brutstätte; der Satz, die Serie, Zahl (*of boxes, etc.*); *build* or *make one's* –, nisten; (*fig.*) *feather one's* –, sich bereichern, sein Schäfchen ins Trockene bringen; *rob a* –, ein Nest ausnehmen; *mare's* –, die Zeitungsente. 2. *v.n.* nisten, horsten, sich niederlassen; Nester ausnehmen. 3. *v.a.* (wie im Nest) legen, setzen *or* einpacken; ineinanderlegen, ineinanderpacken. **--egg,** *s.* das Nestei; (*fig.*) der Heckpfennig, Notpfennig, Notgroschen. **–le** [nɛsl], 1. *v.n.* sich einnisten; (an)schmiegen (*against, on,* or *close to,* an); *–le down*, sich behaglich niederlassen. 2. *v.a.* schmiegen, drücken (*one's head, etc.*) (*against*, an). **–ling** ['nɛs(t)lɪŋ], *s.* der Nestling.
[1]**net** [nɛt], 1. *s.* das Netz, Maschenwerk; der Tüll, Musselin; (*fig.*) das Netz(werk); die Falle, Schlinge, der Fallstrick, das Garn. 2. *v.a.* mit Netz fangen (*fish, etc.*); mit einem Netze fischen (*a river*, in einem Flusse); ins Netz schlagen (*the ball*) (*Tenn.*); knüpfen, in Filet arbeiten. 3. *v.n.* Filet arbeiten, Netzarbeit machen. **--ball,** *s.* der Netzball, das Netzballspiel. **--play,** *s.* das Spiel dicht am Netz (*Tenn.*). **–ting,** *s.* das Netzstricken; die Filetarbeit; das Netz(werk), Geflecht; die Netzfischerei; *wire –ting*, das Drahtnetz. *–ting-needle*, die Filetnadel. *–ting stitch*, der Netzstich. **–work,** *s.* die Netzarbeit, Filetarbeit; das Netzwerk. Geflecht; Sendernetz (*Rad.*); Eisenbahnnetz.
[2]**net** [nɛt], 1. *adj.* netto, Rein–; – *amount*, der Reinbetrag; – *price*, der Nettopreis; – *proceeds* or *profit*, der Reingewinn; – *weight*, das Nettogewicht. 2. *v.a.* netto einbringen *or* ergeben.
nether ['nɛðə], *adj.* niedere(r, s), untere(r, s); – *lip*, die Unterlippe; – *regions*, – *world*, die Unterwelt. **–most,** *adj.* niedrigst, unterst.
netting ['nɛtɪŋ], *see* [1]**net.**
nettle ['nɛtl], 1. *s.* die Nessel (*Bot.*); *dead-–*, die Taubnessel; *stinging –*, die Brennessel. 2. *v.a.* mit *or* an Nesseln brennen; (*usually fig.*) ärgern, wurmen; *be –d*, geärgert sein (*at*, über). **--rash,** *s* das Nesselfieber, die Nesselsucht.
neum(e) [nju:m], *s.* die Neume (*Mus.*).
neur–al ['nju:rəl], *adj.* Nerven–. **–algia** [–'rældʒə], *s.* der Nervenschmerz, die Neuralgie. **–algic** [–'rældʒɪk], *adj.* neuralgisch. **–asthenia** [–əs'θɪ:nɪə], *s.* die Nervenschwäche, Neurasthenie. **–asthenic** [–əs'θɪ:nɪk], 1. *adj.* nervenschwach. 2. *s.* der Neurastheniker. **–ation** [–'reɪʃən], *s.* die Aderanordnung (*Bot., Zool.*). **–itis** [–'raɪtɪs], *s.* die Nervenentzündung. **–ologist** [–'rɔlədʒɪst], *s.* der Neurolog. **–ology** [–'rɔlədʒɪ], *s.* die Nervenlehre, Neurologie. **–opath** [–əpæθ], *s.* Nervenleidende(r), Nervenkranke(r), *m.* **–opathic** [–ə'pæθɪk], *adj.* nervenleidend. **-opathist** [–'rɔpəθɪst], *s.* der Nervenarzt. **–opathy** [–əpəθɪ], *s.* das Nervenleiden. **–opter** [–'rɔptə], *s.* der Netzflügler. **–opterous** [–'rɔptərəs], *adj.*; *–opterous fly*, *see* **–opter. –osis** [–'roʊsɪs], *s.* die Neurose, Nervenkrankheit, Nervenstörung. **–otic** [–'rɔtɪk], 1. *adj.* neurotisch, nervenkrank; Nerven–. 2. *s.* Nervenkranke(r), *m.*; das Nervenmittel.
neuter ['nju:tə], 1. *adj.* geschlechtslos (*Bot., Zool.*); sächlich (*of nouns*); intransitiv (*of verbs*); – *cat*, verschnittener Kater. 2. *s.* geschlechtsloses Tier *usw.*; das Neutrum, Intransitivum (*Gram.*).
neutral ['nju:trəl], 1. *adj.* neutral, parteilos, unparteiisch; gleichgültig, unbeteiligt, indifferent, unausgesprochen, unbestimmt, farblos; – *conductor*, der Nulleiter; – *gear*, die Ruhelage; – *line*, die Indifferenzzone (*Magnet.*); – *point*, der Nullpunkt; – *position*, die Nullstellung, Ruhestellung. 2. *s.* Neutrale(r), *m.*, Parteilose(r), *m.*; die Ruhelage (*Motor.*). **–ity** [–'trælɪtɪ], *s.* die Neutralität, Parteilosigkeit; *armed –ity*, bewaffnete Neutralität. **–ization** [–laɪ'zeɪʃən], *s.* die Neutralisierung, Ausgleichung; Neutralitätserklärung (*Mil.*). **–ize** [–laɪz], *v.a.* neutralisieren, unwirksam machen; für neutral erklären (*Mil.*); *–ize each other*, sich gegenseitig aufheben.
névé ['nɛveɪ], *s.* der Firn (*Mount.*).
never ['nɛvə], *adv.* nie, niemals, nimmer; nicht einmal, auf keine Weise, überhaupt *or* durchaus *or* gar nicht; – *fear!* nur nicht bange! (*coll.*) *well, I –!* nein, so was!; – *mind!* macht *or* tut nichts! hat nichts zu sagen! laß gut sein! mach dir nichts draus!; – *to be forgotten*, unvergeßlich; – *say die!* nur nicht ängstlich!; (*coll.*) – *so* . . . *as to*, doch nicht so . . . um zu; – *so*, auch noch so, so sehr auch. **--ceasing,** *adj.* unaufhörlich. **--ending,** *adj.* unaufhörlich, ohne Ende. **--failing,** *adj.* unfehlbar; nie versiegend. **–more** [–mɔ:ə], *adv.* nie wieder, nimmermehr. **–theless** [–ðəlɛs], *conj.* nichtsdestoweniger, dennoch.
new [nju:], 1. *adj.* neu, unbekannt (*to* (*Dat.*)), ungewohnt (*to*, für), nicht vertraut (*to*, mit), frisch, neuerschienen (*book*); neuentdeckt (*facts. etc.*);

unerforscht (*ground*); modern; unerfahren, ungeübt (*to*, in (*Dat.*)); – *bread*, frisch gebackenes Brot; – *brooms sweep clean*, neue Besen kehren gut; – *building*, der Neubau; *turn over a – leaf*, sich bessern, ein neues Leben beginnen; *the – learning*, die Renaissance; – *moon*, der Neumond; – *style*, Gregorianische Zeitrechnung, Neuer Stil; – *Testament*, Neues Testament; – *World*, Neue Welt; – *Year*, Neues Jahr; *after the – Year*, nach Neujahr; – *Year's Day*, der Neujahrstag; – *Year's Eve*, der Silvester; – *Year's greetings*, der Neujahrswunsch; *nothing* –, nichts Neues. **--born,** *adj.* neugeboren, eben geboren. **--comer,** *s.* der Ankömmling, Neuling. **– Deal,** Roosevelt's neue Wirtschaftspolitik. **--fangled,** *adj.* erneuerungssüchtig; neumodisch. **--fledged,** *adj.* flügge geworden, (*fig.*) neugebacken. **--laid,** *adj.* frisch(gelegt); *--laid eggs*, frische Eier. **-ly,** *adv.* jüngst, kürzlich; *-ly married*, neuvermählt. **--mown,** *adj.* frisch gemäht. **-ness,** *s.* das Neue, die Neuheit. **-s,** *see* **news.**

newel ['nju:əl], *s.* die (Treppen)Spindel (*of winding stair*); der Treppenpfosten.

news [nju:z], *pl.* (*sing. constr.*) die Nachricht (*of*, über), Neuigkeit, Neuigkeiten (*pl.*), das Neue; der Nachrichtendienst (*Rad.*); *it is – to me*, es ist mir neu; *in the* –, in allen Zeitungen; *be in the* –, von sich reden machen; *what's the – ?* was gibt's Neues? *a piece of* –, eine Neuigkeit; *no – is good* –, keine Nachricht ist auch eine Nachricht; *we have had* –, wir haben erfahren *or* gehört. **-agent,** *s.* der Zeitungshändler. **--boy,** *s.* der Zeitungsjunge, Zeitungsausträger. **--editor,** *s.* der Nachrichtenredakteur. **--letter,** *s.* das Rundschreiben. **-monger,** *s.* der Neuigkeitskrämer. **-paper,** *s.* die Zeitung; *-paper hoax*, die Zeitungsente; *-paper man*, der Journalist; *-paper report*, der Zeitungsbericht, die Zeitungsnachricht; *-paper reporter*, der Berichterstatter. *-paper-wrapper*, das Kreuzband. **--print,** *s.* das Zeitungspapier. **--reel,** *s.* die Wochenschau (*film*). **--room,** *s.* der Lesesaal. **--vendor,** *s.* der Zeitungsverkäufer.

newt [nju:t], *s.* der Wassermolch (*Zool.*).

next [nɛkst], 1. *adj.* nächst, nächststehend, nächstfolgend; (*a*) (*with nouns, etc.*) – *best*, zweitbeste(r, s); *be the – best th. to*, fast so gut sein wie; *the – day*, am folgenden Tage, am Tage darauf; *in the – few days*, in den nächsten Tagen; – *door*, nebenan; – *door but one*, zwei Häuser weiter; – *door to*, nahe bei; fast, beinahe; *that is – door to felony*, das grenzt an Verbrechen; (*the*) – *moment*, im nächsten Augenblick; – *but one*, übernächst; *week after* –, übernächste Woche; *what – ?* was noch?, und dann ? (*b*) (*with adverbs & prepositions*) – *after*, gleich nach; – *before*, direkt vor; – *to*, nächst, gleich *or* erst nach (*order*), nahe bei (*position*); *most important – to*, – *to in importance*, nächstwichtigst nach; – *to in length*, nächstlängst nach; – *to impossible*, nahezu unmöglich; – *to nothing*, fast (gar) nichts; *for – to nothing*, fast umsonst. *--of-kin*, nächster Verwandte(r), *pl.* die nächsten Verwandten. 2. *prep.* nächst, bei, an; gleich neben (*Dat.*); – *your skin*, auf dem Leibe. 3. *adv.* zunächst, gleich darauf, nächstens, demnächst; an nächster Stelle; das nächste Mal.

nexus ['nɛksəs], *s.* die Verbindung, Verknüpfung, der Zusammenhang.

nib [nɪb], *s.* die (Feder)Spitze; *cocoa -s*, das Kakaopulver.

nibble [nɪbl], 1. *v.a.* knabbern an (*Dat.*), abbeißen, abnagen; anbeißen (*as fish*). 2. *v.n.*; – *at*, nagen, knabbern an (*Dat.*); (*fig.*) bekritteln. 3. *s.* das Anbeißen, Knabbern, Nagen.

nice [naɪs], *adj.* wählerisch (*about*, in); lecker, wohlschmeckend (*of food*); heikel, schwierig, kitzlig, bedenklich; genau, gewissenhaft, peinlich, sorgfältig; fein, scharf, ausgebildet; freundlich, gütig (*to*, zu *or* gegen); (*coll.*) hübsch, nett, artig, niedlich, angenehm; (*coll.*) – *and fat*, schön *or* hübsch dick; – *discernment*, scharfes Beurteilungsvermögen; – *distinction*, genaue Unterscheidung; – *mess!* schöne Bescherung! – *point*, kitzliger *or* heikler Punkt. **– ly,** *adv.* (*coll.*) fein, ausgezeichnet; *beg -ly!* Schön! (*to a dog*); *do -ly*, ausgezeichnet sein *or* passen; *be doing -ly*, besser gehen (*Dat.*); *talk -ly*, gute Worte geben (*to* (*Dat.*)). **-ness,** *s.* die Genauigkeit, Feinheit; Verwöhntheit; Niedlichkeit, Annehmlichkeit. **-ty** ['naɪsɪtɪ], *s.* die Feinheit, Schärfe; peinliche Genauigkeit, Spitzfindigkeit; *pl.* Feinheiten, kleine Unterschiede; *to a -ty*, bis aufs Haar; *not stand upon -ties*, es nicht so genau nehmen, (*coll.*) fünf gerade sein lassen.

niche [nɪtʃ], *s.* die Nische; (*fig.*) passender Ort. **-d,** *adj.* in einer Nische stehend *or* in eine Nische gestellt.

[1]**nick** [nɪk], *s.*; (*coll.*) *Old* –, der Deibel, Kuckuck.

[2]**nick** [nɪk], 1. *s.* der Einschnitt, die Kerbe; hoher Wurf (*of dice*); *in the – of time*, gerade zur rechten Zeit. 2. *v.a.* (ein)kerben; (*sl.*) treffen, erfassen, erwischen, ertappen; stehlen, betrügen um.

nickel [nɪkl], 1. *s.* das (*or Austr.* der) Nickel; (*Amer. coll.*) das Fünfcentstück. 2. *adj.* Nickel–, vernickelt. 3. *v.a.* vernickeln. **-odeon** [–ə'loʊdɪən], *s.* (*Amer. coll.*) der Musikautomat. **--plating,** *s.* die Vernickelung.

nicker ['nɪkə], *v.n.* (*Scots*) wiehern.

nick-nack ['nɪknæk], *s. see* **knick-knack.**

nickname ['nɪkneɪm], 1. *s.* der Spitzname. 2. *v.a.* einen Spitznamen geben (*Dat.*), mit Spitznamen bezeichnen.

nicot-ian [nɪ'koʊʃɪən], *adj.* Tabaks–. **-ine** ['nɪkətɪ:n], *s.* das Nikotin. **-inism** [–tɪnɪzm], die Nikotinvergiftung.

nictitat-e ['nɪktɪteɪt], *s.* (mit den Augenlidern) blinzeln; *-ing membrane*, die Nickhaut, Blinzhaut (*Orn.*).

nid-e [naɪd], *s.* die Brut (*of pheasants*). **-ificate** ['nɪdɪfɪkeɪt], **-ify** ['nɪdɪfaɪ], *v.n.* nisten. **-us** ['naɪdəs], *s.* das Nest (*Zool.*); (*fig.*) der Sitz, die Lagerstätte.

niece [nɪ:s], *s.* die Nichte.

niello [nɪ'ɛloʊ], *s.* der Schwarzschmelz; *work in* –, niellieren.

niff [nɪf], 1. *s.* (*sl.*) das Gestänk. 2. *v.n.* (*sl.*) stinken.

nifty [nɪftɪ], *adj.* (*sl.*) schmuck.

niggard ['nɪgəd], 1. *s.* der Geizhals, Knicker, Knauser, Filz. 2. *adj.* geizig, knauserig, karg, sparsam (*of*, mit). **-liness,** *s.* der Geiz, die Knauserei. **-ly,** *adj. see* – 2.

nigger ['nɪgə], *s.* (*pej.*) der Neger, Schwarze(r), *m.*; *the – in the woodpile*, der wirkliche Grund, der Hase im Pfeffer; *work like a* –, wie ein Pferd arbeiten, schuften.

niggl-e [nɪgl], *v.n.* trödeln, die Zeit vertrödeln, sich in Einzelheiten verlieren. **-ing, -y,** *adj.* kleinlich, überfein; krittelig.

nigh [naɪ], (*Poet.*) 1. *adv.* nahe; (usually *well* –) beinahe, fast; *draw* –, sich nähern (*to* (*Dat.*)). 2. *prep.* nahe bei, neben.

night [naɪt], *s.* die Nacht, der Abend; (*fig.*) die Dunkelheit; (*a*) (*with adjectives, etc.*) *all* – (*long*), die ganze Nacht (hindurch); *first* –, die Erstaufführung, Premiere; *good – !* gute Nacht!, guten Abend!; *have a good* –, gut schlafen; *last* –, gestern abend; in der vergangenen Nacht; – *out*, der Ausgang (*servants*); *have a – out*, abends ausgehen; *tomorrow* –, morgen abend. (*b*) (*with verbs*) *make a – of it*, die ganze Nacht durchmachen, bis in die Morgenstunden feiern *or* zechen; *stay the* –, übernachten (*at*, in). (*c*) (*with prepositions*) – *after* –, jeden Abend, Nacht für Nacht; *at* –, nachts, abends; *late at* –, spät abends; *the – before*, am vorhergehenden Abend; *by* –, *during the* –, *in the* –, bei Nacht, nachts, des Nachts; *at dead of* –, in tiefer Nacht; *on a dark* –, in einer dunklen Nacht; *on the – of Jan. 1st*, am Abend des 1. Jan.; *over* –, über Nacht. **--bell,** *s.* die Nachtglocke. **--bird,** *s.* (*fig.*) der Nachtschwärmer. **--cap,** *s.* die Schlafmütze, (*fig.*) der Schlummertrunk. **--clothes,** *pl.* das Nachtzeug. **--club,** *s.* das Nachtlokal, der Nachtklub. **--dress,** *s.* das Nachthemd, Nachtgewand, der Schlafanzug (*for women*). **-fall,** *s.* das Dunkelwerden, der Einbruch der Nacht. **--gown,** *s. see* **--dress.** **-hawk,** *s.* (*Amer.*) der Nachtfalke. **-ingale,** *s.* die Nachtigall (*Orn.*). **-jar,** *s.* der Ziegenmelker, die Nachtschwalbe (*Orn.*). **--long,** 1. *adj.* eine ganze Nacht dauernd. 2. *adv.* die ganze Nacht hindurch. **-ly,** 1. *adj.* nächtlich,

Nacht–. 2. *adv.* jede Nacht, (all)nächtlich. **–mare,** *s.* das Alpdrücken, böser Traum; (*fig.*) der Alpdruck, das Angstgefühl, Schreckgespenst. **–marish,** *adj.* beängstigend, erschreckend. **– -porter,** *s.* der Nachtportier. **– -school,** *s.* die Abendschule. **–shade,** *s.* der Nachtschatten (*Bot.*). **– -shift,** *s.* die Nachtschicht. **– -shirt,** *s.* das Nachthemd (*for men*). **– -soil,** *s.* der Inhalt der Senkgruben. **– -stool,** *s.* der Nachtstuhl. **– -time,** *s.* die Nachtzeit. **– -watch,** *s.* die Nachtwache. **– -watchman,** *s.* der Nachtwächter. **– -work,** *s.* die Nachtarbeit. **–y,** *s.* (*coll.*) *see* **– -dress.**

nigrescen–ce [naɪ'grɛsəns], *s.* das Schwarzwerden; die Dunkelheit. **–t** [–ənt], *adj.* schwärzlich.

nihili–sm ['naɪɪlɪzm], *s.* der Nihilismus. **–st** [–lɪst], 1. *s.* der Nihilist. 2. *adj.*, **–stic** [–'lɪstɪk], *adj.* nihilistisch.

nil [nɪl], *s.* das Nichts, die Null; – *return*, die Fehlanzeige (*C.L.*).

nimble [nɪmbl], *adj.* flink, behend, hurtig, gewandt. **–ness,** *s.* die Behendigkeit, Gewandtheit.

nimbus ['nɪmbəs], *s.* der Heiligenschein, Nimbus; die Regenwolke.

nimiety [nɪ'maɪɪtɪ], *s.* (*rare*) das Übermaß, die Überfülle.

niminy-piminy ['nɪmɪnɪ'pɪmɪnɪ], *adj.* etepetete, zimperlich, geziert, affektiert.

nincompoop ['nɪnkəmpu:p], *s.* (*coll.*) der Einfaltspinsel, Dussel.

nine [naɪn], 1. *num. adj.* neun; – *days' wonder*, die Sensation, das Ereignis des Tages; – *times out of ten*, im allgemeinen. 2. *s.* die Neun; – *of hearts*, die Herzneun (*Cards*); (*coll.*) *to the –s*, vollkommen, im höchsten Maße; *dressed up to the –s*, aufgedonnert. **–fold,** *adj.* neunfach. **–pin,** *s.* der Kegel. **–pins,** *pl.* (*sing. constr.*) das Kegelspiel; *play at –pins*, Kegel schieben, kegeln; *fall over like –pins*, wie Kegel umpurzeln. **–teen** ['naɪn'tɪ:n], 1. *num. adj.* neunzehn. 2. *s.* die Neunzehn; *talk –teen to the dozen*, das Blaue vom Himmel herunterreden. **–teenth,** 1. *num. adj.* neunzehnte(r, s); *–teenth hole*, die Bar im Klubhaus (*Golf*). 2. *s.* das Neunzehntel. **–ties,** *pl.* die neunziger Jahre. **–tieth,** 1. *num. adj.* neunzigst. 2. *s.* das Neunzigstel. **–ty** ['naɪntɪ], 1. *num. adj.* neunzig. 2. *s.* die Neunzig.

ninny ['nɪnɪ], *s.* (*coll.*) der Einfaltspinsel, Tropf, das Kamel.

ninth [naɪnθ], 1. *num. adj.* neunte(r, s). 2. *s.* das Neuntel; die None (*Mus.*). **–ly,** *adv.* neuntens.

[1]**nip** [nɪp], 1. *v.a.* kneifen, zwicken, klemmen; durch Frost beschädigen *or* zerstören *or* töten; – *in the bud*, im Keime ersticken; – *off*, abzwicken, abkneifen. 2. *v.n.* zwicken; schneiden, beißen (*as wind*); (*sl.*) sich schnell bewegen; (*sl.*) – *in*, hineinschlüpfen, sich hineindrängen. 3. *s.* das Kneifen, Zwicken; der Zwick, Biß, Knick (*of a rope*); der Frostbrand; (*coll.*) (*Amer.*) – *and tuck*, harter Kampf; – *in the air*, frostige Luft; *see* **nipper, nipping, nippy.**

[2]**nip** [nɪp], 1. *s.* das Schlückchen (*of brandy, etc.*). 2. *v.a. & n.* nippen.

nipp–er ['nɪpə], *s.* (*coll.*) der Dreikäsehoch, Kiekindiewelt; der Schneidezahn (*of a horse*); die Kralle, Schere (*of a crab*); die Seising (*Naut.*); *pl.* die Kneifzange, der Kneifer; (*sl.*) Handschellen (*pl.*). **–ing,** *adj.* beißend, schneidend. **–y,** 1. *adj.* (*coll.*) *see* **–ing;** schnell, flink, behende. 2. *s.* (*sl.*) die Kellnerin.

nipple [nɪpl], *s.* die Brustwarze; das Gummihütchen, Saughütchen (*of a baby's bottle*); der Zündkegel, Zündstift (*of a gun*); *oiling –*, der Öler. **– -shield,** *s.* der Warzenschutz. **–wort,** *s.* das Warzenkraut (*Bot.*).

nisi ['naɪsaɪ], *conj.*; *decree –*, vorläufiges Scheidungsurteil (*Law*); – *prius*, die Verhörung von Zivilklagen vor den Geschworenen in der Grafschaft (*Law*); *court of – prius*, das Grafschaftsgericht für Zivilklagen (*Law*).

nit [nɪt], *s.* die Nisse, das Lausei.

nitr–ate ['naɪtreɪt], 1. *s.* das Nitrat, salpetersaures Salz; *silver –ate* or *–ate of silver*, salpetersaures Silber. 2. *v.a.* nitrieren, mit Salpetersäure behandeln. **–e** [–tə], *s.* der Salpeter. **–ic** [–trɪk], *adj.* salpetersauer, Salpeter–; *–ic acid*, die Salpetersäure; *–ic oxide*, das Stick(stoff)oxyd. **–ify** [–trɪfaɪ], *v.a.* in Salpeter verwandeln. **–ite** [–traɪt], *s.* das Nitrit, salpetrigsaures Salz. **–o-cellulose,** *s.* die Schießbaumwolle, das Kollodium, Pyroxylin. **–ogen** [–trədʒən], *s.* der Stickstoff. **–ogenous** [–'trɔdʒənəs], *adj.* stickstoffhaltig. **–o-glycerine,** *s.* das Nitroglyzerin, Sprengöl. **–o-hydrochloric** *or* **–o-muriatic acid,** das Königswasser, Goldscheidewasser, die Salzpetersalzsäure. **–ous** [–trəs], *adj.* salpetrig; *–ous acid*, salpetrige Säure; *–ous gases*, nitrose Gase; *–ous oxide*, das Stick(stoff)oxydul, Lachgas.

nitwit ['nɪtwɪt], *s.* (*coll.*) der Nichtswisser, Nichtskönner, Dummkopf.

[1]**nix** [nɪks], *s.* (*sl.*) nichts, niemand.

[2]**nix** [nɪks], *s.* der Nix, Wassergeist. **–ie,** *s.* die (Wasser)Nixe; (*Amer.*) unbestellbarer Brief.

no [nou], 1. *adj.* kein; *on – account*, (*coll.*) alles andere als, nur nicht; – *ball*, der Fehlball, spielwidriger Wurf (*Crick.*); – *good books*, keine guten Bücher; *that is – concern of yours*, das geht Sie nichts an; – *date*, ohne Jahr (*Print.*); *there is – denying*, es läßt sich nicht leugnen; – *doubt*, ohne Zweifel, zweifelsohne; (*coll.*) – *end of*, sehr groß ungeheuer; – *flowers*, Blumenspenden dankend verbeten; (*coll.*) *it's – go*, das geht nicht; – *gratuities!* Trinkgeldablösung! *there is – knowing*, man kann nicht wissen; – *man*, niemand; – *mean writer*, ein bedeutender Schriftsteller; *by – means*, auf keine Weise, keineswegs; *and – mistake*, sicherlich, ohne Zweifel; – *obligation*, ohne jegliche Verpflichtung (*C.L.*); – *one*, keiner; – *one man*, nicht einer; – *parking*, Parkverbot; – *Popery*, kein Pfaffentum; – *such things*, nichts dergleichen; – *thoroughfare!* Durchgang *or* Durchfahrt gesperrt!; *at – time*, nie; *in – time*, im Handumdrehen, sehr bald, in kürzester Zeit; – *trumps!* ohne Trumpf! *of – use*, nutzlos, ohne Nutzen, zwecklos; – *wonder*, kein Wunder. 2. *adv.* nicht; *whether or –*, auf alle Fälle; – *more*, nichts mehr; nicht mehr, nie wieder; – *more than*, ebensowenig wie; – *more will I*, ich auch nicht; *be – more*, tot sein; – *sooner*, nicht eher. 3. *part.* nein. 4. *s.* das Nein; *the –es*, die Stimmen mit Nein *or* dagegen; *the –es have it*, die Mehrheit ist dagegen. **–body** [–bədɪ], *s.* niemand; *–body else*, sonst niemand *or* keiner, niemand anders; (*with indef. art.*) (*fig.*) unbedeutender Mensch, die Null. **– -confidence,** *s.*; *vote of – -confidence*, das Mißtrauensvotum. **– -load,** *s.* der Leerlauf (*Mach.*). (*coll.*) **–how,** *adv.* durchaus nicht, auf keine Weise; *look –how*, nach nichts aussehen. **– -man's-land,** *s.* das Niemandsland, herrenloses Terrain. **–way(s), –wise,** *adv.* keineswegs; *see* **nowhere.**

nob [nɔb], *s.* (*sl.*) der Dez; (*sl.*) feines Aas. **–by,** *adj.* (*sl.*) noblig, fein mit Ei.

nobble [nɔbl], *v.a.* (*sl.*) auf seine Seite ziehen, bestechen; betrügen; stehlen, mausen.

nobili–ary [no'bɪlɪərɪ], *adj.* Adels–; *–ary particle*, das Adelsprädikat. **–ty** [no'bɪlɪtɪ], *s.* der Adel; die Vornehmheit; hoher Adel, der Adel(sstand), die Adligen (*pl.*); *–ty and gentry*, hoher und niedriger Adel; *–ty of soul*, der Seelenadel.

nobl–e [noubl], 1. *adj.* adlig, Adels–; edel, vornehm, erhaben, eindrucksvoll; großmütig; prächtig; vortrefflich, herrlich; *–e art*, das Boxen; *–e metal*, das Edelmetall. 2. *s.* (hoher) Adlige(r), *m.*, der Edelmann; (Rose)Nobel (*gold coin*) (*Hist.*). **–eman** [–mən], *s.* (hoher) Adlige(r). **–e-minded,** *adj.* edelgesinnt, edeldenkend, hochherzig. **–eness,** *s.* der Adel, die Würde, Vornehmheit, der Edelsinn, Edelmut. **–ewoman,** *s.* die Adlige, Edelfrau.

nobody ['noubədɪ], *see* **no.**

nock [nɔk], 1. *s.* die Kerbe, der Einschnitt (*of arrow*). 2. *v.a.* einkerben.

noctambul–ant [nɔk'tæmbjulənt], *adj.* nachtwandelnd. **–ist,** *s.* der Nachtwandler.

nocturn ['nɔktə:n], *s.* die Nachtmette (*R.C.*). **–al** [–'tə:nəl], *adj.* nächtlich, Nacht–. **–e,** *s.* das Notturno (*Mus.*), Nachtstück (*Paint.*).

nocuous ['nɔkjuəs], *adj.* schädlich, giftig.

nod [nɔd], 1. *v.a.* nicken, durch Nicken andeuten; – *assent*, beistimmend nicken, durch Kopfnicken zustimmen; – *one's head*, mit dem Kopfe nicken. 2. *v.n.* nicken, sich neigen; (*fig.*) unachtsam sein; – *off*, einnicken, einschlafen, einschlummern; – *to s.o.*, einem zunicken, einen grüßen; *–ding acquaintance*, die Grußbekanntschaft, flüchtige *or* oberflächliche Bekanntschaft; *on –ding terms*, auf dem Grußfuße. 3. *s.* das (Kopf)Nicken; der Wink; (*coll.*) *Land of* –, der Schlaf; (*sl.*) *on the* –, auf Borg. **–dle** [ˈnɔdl], *s.* (*coll.*) der Bregen.

nod–al [noʊdl], *adj.* Knoten–; *–al line*, die Schwingungslinie. **–e** [noʊd], *s.* der Knoten (*Bot.*, *Astr.*, *etc.*); Gichtknoten (*Med.*); Schwingungsknoten (*Acoust.*, *Rad.*, *etc.*). **–ose** [noˈdoʊs], *adj.* Knoten–, knotig, knorrig. **–osity** [–ˈdɔsɪtɪ], *s.* knotige Beschaffenheit; der Knoten, die Schwellung. **–ular** [ˈnɔdjʊlə], *adj.* knötchenartig, Knoten–. **–ule** [ˈnɔdjuːl], *s.* das Knötchen (*Bot.*), Klümpchen, der Knollen (*Geol.*). **–us** [ˈnoʊdəs], *s.* (*fig.*) die Schwierigkeit, Verwick(e)lung.

noel [noʊˈɛl], *s.* die Weihnacht.

nog [nɔg], 1. *v.a.* mit Holznägeln befestigen; mit Holz einfassen *or* ausmauern (*Build.*). 2. *s.* der Holznagel, Holzpflock, Holzbolzen, Holzklotz, Holm.

noggin [ˈnɔgɪn], *s.* kleiner (hölzener) Krug; ein Flüssigkeitmaß (= ¼ *pint*).

nohow [ˈnoʊhaʊ], *see* **no.**

noil [nɔɪl], *s.* der Kämmling, kurze Wollfaser.

nois–e [nɔɪz], 1. *s.* der Lärm, das Geräusch, Getöse, Geschrei; Fremdgeräusch (*Rad.*); (*fig.*) *make a –e*, viel Aufhebens machen, Aufsehen erregen, von sich reden machen; *hold one's –e*, mit Lärmen aufhören; (*sl.*) *big –e*, gewichtige Person *or* Persönlichkeit, großes *or* hohes Tier; *–e suppression*, die Entstörung (*Rad.*). 2. *v.a.*; *–e abroad*, als Gerücht verbreiten, aussprengen (*rumour*); *be –ed abroad*, als Gerücht umlaufen, ruchbar werden. **–eless**, *adj.* geräuschlos, still. **–elessness**, *s.* die Geräuschlosigkeit. **–iness**, *s.* das Geräusch, Getöse, der Lärm; *see* **noisy.**

noisome [ˈnɔɪsəm], *adj.* schädlich, ungesund; widerlich. **–ness**, *s.* die Schädlichkeit, Widerlichkeit.

noisy [ˈnɔɪzɪ], *adj.* geräuschvoll, lärmend; (*fig.*) laut, grell, auffallend.

noli-me-tangere [ˈnoʊlaɪmɪːˈtændʒərɪ], *s.* das Springkraut, Rührmichnichtan (*Bot.*).

nolle prosequi [ˈnɔləˈprɔsəkwɪ], die Zurücknahme der Klage, Aufgabe des Prozesses (*by plaintiff*); Einstellung des Verfahrens (*by prosecutor*).

nomad [ˈnɔmæd], 1. *adj.* nomadisch, Nomaden–. 2. *s.* der Nomade. **–ic** [–ˈmædɪk], *adj.*; *see* – 1; (*also fig.*) unstet. **–ism**, *s.* das Nomadentum, Nomadenleben.

no-man's land [ˈnoʊmænzlænd], *s. see under* **no.**

nom-de-guerre [ˈnɔmdəˈgɛːə], *s.* der Deckname.

nom-de-plume [ˈnɔmdəˈpluːm], *s.* der Schriftstellername.

nomenclature [ˈnoʊmənkleɪtʃə], *s.* die Namengebung, Terminologie, das Benennungssystem, Namenverzeichnis, Bezeichnungen (*pl.*); die Fachsprache, Nomenklatur.

nomin–al [ˈnɔmɪnəl], *adj.* nominal, Nominal– (*Gram.*, *etc.*); namentlich, Namen–, Nenn–; nominell, nur dem Namen nach; *–al capital*, das Stammkapital (*C.L.*); *–al fine*, unbedeutende Geldstrafe; *–al list*, die Namenliste; *–al rank*, der Titularrang; *–al rent*, geringe Miete; *–al roll*, see *–al list*; *–al sum*, die Nominalsumme; *–al value*, der Nennwert. **–alism** [–ɪzm], *s.* der Nominalismus (*Phil.*). **–ate** [–eɪt], *v.a.* ernennen zu, einsetzen (*to*, in (*Acc.*)), zur Wahl vorschlagen, als Kandidaten aufstellen. **–ation** [–ˈneɪʃən], *s.* die Ernennung, Berufung (*to*, zu), Einsetzung (*to*, in), Aufstellung für die Wahl, Vorwahl; das Vorschlagsrecht; *be in –ation*, als Kandidat aufgestellt sein (*for*, für); *–ation day*, der Wahlvorschlagstermin. **–ative** [–ətɪv], 1. *adj.* Nominativ–. 2. *s.* der Werfall, Nominativ (*Gram.*). **–ator** [–eɪtə], *s.* der Ernenner. **–ee** [–ɪː], *s.* Vorgeschlagene(r), Ernannte(r), *m.*

non- [nɔn], *pref.* nicht, Nicht–, un– **––acceptance**, *s.* die Annahmeverweigerung, Nichtannahme (*of a bill*). **––adhesive**, *adj.* nicht klebend. **––aggression pact**, *s.* der Nichtangriffspakt. **––appearance**, *s.*, **––attendance**, *s.* das Ausbleiben, Nichterscheinen, Fehlen. **––collegiate**, *adj.* keinem College angehörig. **––combatant**, 1. *s.* der Nichtkämpfer. 2. *adj.* am Kampf nicht beteiligt. **––commissioned**, *adj.* nicht bevollmächtigt, unbestallt; *––commissioned officer*, der Unteroffizier. **––committal**, 1. *adj.* nicht bindend, unverbindlich; zurückhaltend. 2. *s.* freie Hand, die Unverbindlichkeit. **––compliance**, *s.* die Nichterfüllung, Nichtbefolgung; Zuwiderhandlung (*with*, gegen), Weigerung. **– compos (mentis)**, *adj.* unzurechnungsfähig. **––conductor**, *s.* der Nichtleiter (*Phys.*). **–conformist** [nɔnkənˈfɔːmɪst], 1. *s.* der Dissident, Nonkonformist. 2. *attrib. adj.* nonkonformistisch. **–conformity** [nɔnkənˈfɔːmɪtɪ], *s.* mangelnde Übereinstimmung (*with*, mit) *or* Anpassung (*to*, an); der Dissent (*Eccl.*). **––cooperation**, *s.* passiver Widerstand (*Pol.*). **––crystalline**, *adj.* unkristallinisch. **––delivery**, *s.* die Nichtbestellung (*of letters*, *etc.*). **–descript**, *adj.* schwer klassifizierbar *or* beschreibbar, unbestimmt. **––effective**, 1. *adj.* (dienst)untauglich. 2. *s.* Dienstuntaugliche(r), *m.* **––ego**, *s.* das Nicht-Ich. **––essential**, 1. *adj.* unwesentlich. 2. *s.* die Nebensächlichkeit. **––existence**, *s.* das Nicht(da)sein. **––existent**, *adj.* nicht vorhanden, nicht existierend. **––explosive**, *adj.* nicht explosiv. **––feasance**, *s.* die Unterlassung (*Law*). **––freezing**, *adj.* ungefrierbar, kältebeständig, Kälte–. **––fulfilment**, *s.* die Nichterfüllung. **––halation**, *adj.* lichthoffrei (*Phot.*). **––inductive**, *adj.* induktionsfrei. **––inflammable**, *adj.* unbrennbar, unentzündbar, feuersicher. **––intervention**, *s.* die Nichteinmischung (*Pol.*). **––juring**, *adj.* eidverweigernd. **––juror**, *s.* der Eidverweigerer. **–liquet**, *s.* der Urteilsausfall wegen mangelnden Beweises (*Law*). **––member**, *s.* das Nichtmitglied. **––metallic**, *adj.* Nichtmetall–; *––metallic element*, das Metalloid. **––negotiable**, *adj.* nicht übertragbar (*C.L.*). **––observance**, *s.* die Nichtbeobachtung. **–pareil** [nɔnpərˈɛl], 1. *s.* das Unvergleichliche, die Nonpareille(schrift) (*Typ.*). 2. *adj.* unvergleichlich. **––party**, *adj.* nicht parteigebunden, ohne Parteibindung, überparteilich. **––payment**, *s.* die Nichtzahlung. **––performance**, *s.* die Nichterfüllung. **––resident**, 1. *adj.* nicht ansässig, nicht amtierend, abwesend; auswärtig (*member*). 2. *s.* Nichtansässige(r), *m.*, der Passant. **––rigid**, *adj.* unstarr (*of airships*). **–sense** [ˈnɔnsəns], 1. *s.* der Unsinn; *–sense!* dummes Zeug!, Blödsinn!, Quatsch!; *stand no –sense*, nicht mit sich spaßen lassen. 2. *attrib.*; *–sense verse*, burleske Verse (*pl.*). **–sensical** [nɔnˈsɛnsɪkl], *adj.* unsinnig, sinnlos. **––sequitur**, *s.* irrige Folgerung. **––skid**, *adj.* Gleitschutz–. **––smoker**, *s.* der Nichtraucher. **––smoking**, *adj.* Nichtraucher– (*compartment*) (*Railw.*). **––stop**, *adj.* durchgehend (*tram*), Dauer–, ohne Zwischenlandung (*Av.*), ununterbrochen, pausenlos, Ohnehalt–. **–such**, *s.* die Luzerne (*Bot.*), der Nonpareilleapfel (*Bot.*); (*fig.*) das Unvergleichliche, die Person *or* Sache ohnegleichen. **–suit**, 1. *s.* die Zurücknahme, Abweisung *or* Sistierung (*of a case*) (*Law*). 2. *v.a.* nicht stattgeben, sistieren (*a case*) (*Law*). **––transparent**, *adj.* undurchsichtig. **––volatile**, *adj.* nicht flüchtig.

nonage [ˈnɔnɪdʒ], *s.* die Minderjährigkeit, (*fig.*) Unreife.

nonagenarian [nɔnədʒəˈnɛːərɪən], 1. *adj.* neunzigjährig. 2. *s.* Neunzigjährige(r), *m.*

nonce [nɔns], *s.*; (only in) *for the* –, für dies eine Mal, einstweilen, nur für diesen Fall. **––word**, *s.* für einen bestimmten Zweck geprägtes Wort.

nonchalan–ce [ˈnɔnʃələns], *s.* die Nachlässigkeit, Gleichgültigkeit. **–t** [–ənt], *adj.* (nach)lässig, gleichgültig; unbekümmert.

nonconformist, *see under* **non–.**

none [nɔn], 1. *pron.* (*usually pl. constr.*) keine(r, s); – *but the best*, nur das allerbeste; – *but fools*, nur Narren; – *more so than I*, keiner mehr als ich; *she will have – of me*, sie will nichts von mir wissen;

– *of them*, keiner von ihnen; *it's – of the best*, es is keins von den besten, es ist keineswegs gut; – *of that*, nichts dergleichen; *it's – of your business*, es geht Sie nichts an; – *of your tricks!* (unter)laß deine Späße! – *other than*, kein anderer als. 2. *adv*. (*with compar. adj. prec. by def. art.*) in keiner Weise, nicht im geringsten; (*with adv. & adj.*) keineswegs; – *the better for it*, deshalb nicht besser daran; – *the less*, nichtsdestoweniger; – *the wiser*, um nichts klüger, so klug wie zuvor; – *too good* or *well*, nicht gerade gut; – *too soon*, keineswegs zu früh, fast zu spät.

nonentity [nɔ'nentɪtɪ], *s*. das Nichtsein, unbedeutender Mensch, die Null.

nones [nounz], *pl*. Nonen; das Mittagsoffizium (*R.C.*).

nonesuch, *s*. (*rare*) *see under* **non–**.

nonplus [nɔn'plʌs], 1. *v.a.* in Verlegenheit setzen, in die Enge treiben. 2. *s*. die Verlegenheit, Klemme; *at a* –, in Verlegenheit. **–sed**, *adj*. verblüfft, verdutzt.

nonsense, *see under* **non–**.

nonsuit, *see under* **non–**.

[1]**noodle** [nu:dl], *s*. (*coll*.) der Dussel.

[2]**noodle** [nu:dl], *s*. (*usually pl*.) (*Amer*.) die Nudel.

nook [nuk], *s*. der Winkel, die Ecke.

noon [nu:n], 1. *s*. (*also* **–day, –tide**) der Mittag, die Mittagszeit; *at* –, zu Mittag. 2. *attrib. adj*. Mittags–.

noose [nu:s], 1. *s*. die Schleife, Schlinge. 2. *v.a.* schlingen (*a rope*) (*round*, um)); mit einer Schlinge fangen (*an animal*).

nor [nɔ:], *conj*. (*after neg*.) noch; auch nicht; – *I* (*n*)*either*, ich auch nicht; *neither* . . . – . . ., weder . . . noch . . .

norm [nɔ:m], *s*. die Norm, Regel, Richtschnur, das Muster. **–al** [–əl], 1. *adj*. normal, Normal–, regelrecht; senkrecht (*Geom*.); *–al school*, das Lehrerseminar; *–al time*, die Einheitszeit. 2. *s*. das Normale, der Normalstand, Normaltyp, Normalwert; üblicher Zustand; die Senkrechte (*Geom*.). **–alcy** [–əlsɪ], *s*., **–ality** [–'mælɪtɪ], *s*. die Normalität, Regelmäßigkeit, der Normal(zu)stand. **–alization** [–əlɑɪ'zeɪʃən], *s*. die Normalisierung, Normung. **–alize** [–əlɑɪz], *v.a.* normalisieren, normieren, normen, vereinheitlichen, regeln. **–ally**, *adv*. normalerweise.

north [nɔ:θ], 1. *s*. der Norden, (*Poet*.) Nord; die Nordstaaten (*of U.S.A.*); *to the – of*, nördlich von; *magnetic* –, magnetisch Nord; *true* –, geographisch Nord; – *by east*, Nord zu Ost. 2. *adv*. nördlich (*of*, von); *go* –, nach Norden gehen; – *and south*, von Norden nach Süden; in nordsüdlicher Richtung. 3. *adj*. nördlich, Nord–; – *Britain*, Schottland; – *Country*, Nord-England; *––countryman*, der Bewohner von Nordengland; – *Pole*, der Nordpol; – *Sea*, die Nordsee; – *wind*, der Nordwind, (*Poet*.) Nord. **––east** [–'ɪ:st], 1. *s*. der Nordosten; *––east by east*, Nordost zu Ost. 2. *adj*. Nordost–. 3. *adv*. nordöstlich (*of*, von). **––easter** [–'ɪ:stə], *s*. der Nordostwind. **––easterly** [–'ɪstəlɪ], 1. *adv*. nordöstlich. 2. *adj*. nordöstlich, Nordost–. **––eastern** [–'ɪ:stən], *adj*. nordöstlich. **––eastward**, 1. *adv*. nordöstlich. 2. *s*. der Nordosten. **–erly** ['nɔ:ðəlɪ], 1. *adj*. nördlich, nach Norden (*course*), von Norden (*wind*). 2. *adv*. im *or* nach Norden. **–ern** ['nɔ:ðən], *attrib. adj*. nördlich, Nord–; *–ern China*, Nordchina; *–ern lights*, das Nordlicht. **–erner**, *s*. der Nordländer. **–ernmost**, *adj*. nördlichst. **–ing** ['nɔ:θɪŋ], *s*. nördliche Richtung, der Kurs *or* die Entfernung nach Norden. **–ward**, 1. *s*. nördliche Gegend *or* Richtung. 2. *adv*. (also *–wards*) nordwärts; nördlich (*of* or *from*, von). **–man** ['nɔ:θmən], *s*. der Skandinavier, Nordländer. **––west, ––wester, ––westerly, ––western, ––westward,** *for forms see under* **––east**, *etc*.

nose [nouz], 1. *s*. die Nase (*also fig*.); offenes Ende, die Öffnung, Mündung; Schnauze, Spitze; Flugzeugstirn, Rumpfspitze (*Av*.); der Bug (*Naut*.); das Kopfteil (*of a shell*); der Geruch (*of tea, hay, etc*.); (*sl*.) (Polizei)Spitzel; *bite a p.'s – off*, see *snap a p.'s – off*; *cut off one's – to spite one's face*, sich ins eigene Fleisch schneiden; *follow one's* –, immer der Nase nach gehen; *have a good – for*, eine feine Nase (*or coll*. einen guten Riecher) haben für; *hold one's* –, sich die Nase zuhalten; *lead a p. by the* –, einen an der Nase herumführen; *look down one's – at*, ein verdrießliches Gesicht machen über; *pay through the* –, tüchtig zahlen *or* bluten müssen; *pick one's* –, in der Nase bohren; *poke, put* or *thrust one's – into*, seine Nase stecken in; *put s.o.'s – out of joint*, einen ausstechen *or* aus dem Sattel heben; *not see beyond one's* –, die Hand vor Augen nicht sehen können; (*fig*.) beschränkt *or* kurzsichtig sein; *snap a p.'s – off*, einen hart anfahren; *speak through one's* –, durch die Nase sprechen; *under a p.'s* (*very*) –, einem direkt vor der Nase. 2. *v.n.* schnuppern, schnüffeln; – *about*, herumschnüffeln (*after* or *for*, nach); (*coll*.) – *round*, herumspähen. 3. *v.a.* riechen, wittern, spüren; mit der Nase stoßen an *or* gegen; – *out*, ausspüren, aufspüren, erkunden, ausfindig machen. **––bag**, *s*. der Futterbeutel. **––band**, *s*. der Nasenriemen (*Saddl*.) **–d**, *adj. suff*. –nasig. **––dive**, 1. *s*. der Sturzflug (*Av*.). 2. *v.n.* abdrehen, einen Sturzflug machen (*Av*.). **–gay**, *s*. der Blumenstrauß. **––heavy**, *adj*. buglastig (*Naut*.); vorderlastig, kopflastig (*Av*.). **––piece**, *s*. das Objektivende (*of a microscope*); *see* **––band**. **–r**, *s*. der Kopfwind. (*coll*.) **–y**, *adj*. neugierig; *–y Parker*, der Topfgucker, Pottkieker.

nosing ['nouzɪŋ], *s*. hervorstehende Kante (*Build*.).

nosology [nɔ'zɔlədʒɪ], *s*. die Krankheitslehre.

nostalgi–a [nɔ'stældʒɪə], *s*. die Sehnsucht, das Heimweh (*for*, nach). **–c**, *adj*. Heimweh–.

nostril ['nɔstrɪl], *s*. das Nasenloch; die Nüster (*of animals*).

nostrum ['nɔstrəm], *s*. das Geheimmittel, (*fig*.) Heilmittel.

nosy ['nouzɪ], *adj*. stinkig; muffig (*as hay*); aromatisch (*as tea*); *see also* **nosey.**

not [nɔt], *adv*. nicht; – *a*, kein(e); – *a few*, nicht wenige; – *at all*, keineswegs, durchaus nicht; – *at home*, ausgegangen, nicht zu sprechen; *I could – but*, ich konnte nicht umhin (zu); *certainly* –, gewiß nicht, nicht doch; – *if I know it*, nicht wenn es nach mir geht; – *that I know*, nicht als ob *or* nicht daß ich wüßte; *is it – ?* nicht wahr?; – *long ago*, vor kurzer Zeit; – *proven*, unbewiesen (*Scots Law*); *more often than* –, in den meisten Fällen; *I think* –, ich glaube es ist nicht so; – *too good*, es dürfte besser sein; – *yet*, noch nicht.

notab–ility [noutə'bɪlɪtɪ], *s*. die Bedeutung, Merkwürdigkeit, Bemerkenswertes, *n*., wichtige Persönlichkeit. **–le** ['noutəbl], 1. *adj*. bemerkenswert, denkwürdig; ansehnlich, hervorragend; merklich, feststellbar (*Chem*.); *–le housewife*, fleißige Hausfrau. 2. *s*. angesehene Person, die Standesperson.

notar–ial [no'tɛ:ərɪəl], *adj*. notariell, Notariats–; notariell beglaubigt. **–y** ['noutərɪ], *s*. (also *–y public*) der Notar.

notation [no'teɪʃən], *s*. die Bezeichnung (*Arith., Geom., Mus*.); (*rare*) Aufzeichnung; *arithmetical* –, das Zahlensystem; *unit of* –, die Maßeinheit.

notch [nɔtʃ], 1. *s*. die Kerbe, der Einschnitt, Ausschnitt; die Kimme (*on gun*); *take a p. down a* –, einen demütigen. 2. *v.a.* (ein)kerben, einschneiden; falzen, nuten (*Carp*.).

note [nout], 1. *s*. die Anmerkung; (*usually pl*.) Aufzeichnung, Notiz; der Zettel, kurzer Brief; die Rechnung, Nota (*C.L.*); Note, Taste (*Mus*.); der Ton, Klang; Gesang (*of birds*); (*fig*.) die Tonart; das Kennzeichen, Merkmal; die Bedeutung, Wichtigkeit; Beachtung; Banknote; *compare –s about* or *on a th*., über eine S. die Meinungen *or* Ansichten austauschen; – *of exchange*, der Kurszettel; *exchange of –s*, der Notenaustausch (*of diplomats*); – *of exclamation*, das Ausrufungszeichen; – *of hand*, der Schuldschein, Schuldbrief, die Schuldverschreibung; – *of interrogation*, das Fragezeichen; *man of* –, der Mann von Ruf *or* Ansehen; *make* or *take a – of a th*., etwas notieren *or* aufschrieben; *promissory* –, see – *of hand*; *speak without –s*, frei sprechen; *strike the* –, die Tasten anschlagen; (*fig*.) *strike the right* –, den rechten Ton anschlagen; *take – of s.th*., sich (*Dat*.) etwas merken, etwas berücksichtigen; *take –s of* or ***about***, sich (*Dat*.) Notizen machen über; *treasury* –, der Schatzschein; *worthy of* –, beachtenswert. 2. *v.a.*

bemerken, beachten; (also – *down*) aufschreiben, niederschreiben, buchen, notieren; – *a bill*, einen Wechsel protestieren (*C.L.*). **--book,** *s.* das Taschenbuch, Notizbuch. **-d** [-ɪd], *adj.* berühmt, bekannt; berüchtigt (*for*, wegen). **-dly,** *adv.* besonders; deutlich ausgesprochen. **--case,** *s.* die Brieftasche. **--paper,** *s.* das Briefpapier. **-worthy,** *adj.* bemerkenswert, beachtenswert.

nothing [ˈnʌθɪŋ], **1.** *pron.* & *s.* nichts; das Nichts, die Kleinigkeit, unbedeutende S. *or* P.; die Null (*Arith., also fig. of a p.*); *pl.* Nichtigkeiten. (*a*) (*with verbs*) *be* –, ohne Bedeutung sein für (*a p.*), nichts im Vergleich sein (*to*, zu); *be as* –, nichts bedeuten; *there is – in it*, das hat nichts auf sich; *come to* –, mißlingen, zunichte werden; *it will come to* –, daraus wird nichts; (*coll.*) – *doing*, nichts zu machen, es geht nicht; *feel like – on earth*, sich hundeelend fühlen; *make – of*, sich (*Dat.*) nichts machen aus *or* anfangen können mit; *to say – of*, geschweige denn; (*Prov.*) – *venture*, – *have*, frisch gewagt ist halb gewonnen. (*b*) (*with prepositions*) *for* –, umsonst, vergebens; *good for* –, untauglich, zu nichts zu gebrauchen; *not for – that*, nicht umsonst daß; *there is – for it but*, es bleibt nichts übrig als; *to* –, in *or* zu nichts; *next to* –, fast nichts; – *to what* . . ., nichts im Vergleich zu dem *or* was . . .; *come to* –, zunichte *or* zu Wasser werden. (*c*) – *but*, – *except*, nichts als, nichts außer, nur, lediglich; – *else than*, nichts anderes als; – *if not stupid*, überaus dumm; – *important*, nichts Wichtiges; *there is – like*, es geht nichts über; – *much*, nichts Bedeutendes. **2.** *adv.* keineswegs, in keiner Weise, durchaus nicht; – *like finished*, in keiner Weise vollendet, längst nicht fertig; – *like so* . . ., bei weitem nicht so . . .; – *loath*, durchaus nicht abgeneigt; – *short of*, geradezu, wirklich. **-ness,** *s.* das Nichts, Nichtsein; die Nichtigkeit.

notice [ˈnoʊtɪs], **1.** *s.* die Anzeige, Notiz, kurzer Bericht (*in newspaper*), die Nachricht, Meldung; Kündigung (*to leave*), Warnung; Aufmerksamkeit, Kenntnis, Beachtung; –*!* zur Beachtung! Bekanntmachung! (*a*) (*with verbs*) *to avoid* –, um Aufsehen zu vermeiden; *escape* –, unbeachtet bleiben; *give s.o.* –, einem kündigen (*for*, zu); *give a week's* –, eine Woche vorher *or* mit achttägiger Frist kündigen; *give – that*, Nachricht geben von, benachrichtigen; *give – of*, ankündigen, anzeigen, bekanntgeben; *give – of appeal*, Berufung einlegen; *give a p. very short* –, einem wenig Zeit lassen, einen sehr spät benachrichtigen; *have – of*, Kenntnis haben von; – *to quit*, die Kündigung; *he was given – to quit*, ihm wurde gekündigt; *receive* –, Nachricht bekommen; *take* –, aufachten (*as a child*); Notiz nehmen (*of a p.*, von einem), beachten; Kenntnis nehmen (*of a th.*, von etwas), achtgeben auf (*a th.* (*Acc.*)); *take no – of*, nicht beachten, nicht achten auf, ignorieren. (*b*) (*with prepositions*) *at a day's* –, innerhalb eines Tages; *at a moment's* –, zu jeder Zeit, jederzeit, fristlos; *at short* –, sofort; *beneath one's* –, unter jemandes Würde, nicht der Beachtung wert; *come into* –, Aufmerksamkeit erregen; –*s of births, marriages and deaths*, Geburts-, Trauungs- und Todesanzeigen; *worthy of* –, der Beachtung wert, beachtenswert; *till further* –, bis auf weiteres; *bring to s.o.'s* –, zu jemandes Kenntnis bringen; *come under s.o.'s* –, zu jemandes Kenntnis kommen, einem bekannt werden; *until further* –, see *till further* –. **2.** *v.a.* feststellen, wahrnehmen, beobachten; bemerken, erwähnen, anzeigen; besprechen (*a book*); Notiz nehmen von, beachten, anerkennen, mit Aufmerksamkeit behandeln (*a person*). **-able,** *adj.* wahrnehmbar, merklich, bemerkbar, sichtbar; bemerkenswert. **--board,** *s.* schwarzes Brett, die Anschlagtafel.

notif-iable [ˈnoʊtɪfaɪəbl], *adj.* (an)meldepflichtig. **-ication** [-fɪˈkeɪʃən], *s.* die Anzeige, Ankündigung, Bekanntmachung, Meldung. **-y** [ˈnoʊtɪfaɪ], *v.a.* anzeigen, bekanntgeben, melden, kundtun, amtlich mitteilen (*a th. to a p.*, einem etwas), benachrichtigen, in Kenntnis setzen (*a p. of a th.*, einen von *or* über etwas).

notion [ˈnoʊʃən], *s.* der Begriff, die Vorstellung, Anschauung, Ahnung, Idee, (*of*, von); Meinung, Ansicht; das Vorhaben, die Absicht, Neigung, der Gedanke (*of doing*, zu tun); *pl.* (*Amer.*) Kurzwaren, Galanteriewaren; *airy* –*s*, leere Einfälle; *I have a – that* . . ., ich denke mir *or* bilde mir ein, daß . . .; *I had no* (or *not the slightest* or *vaguest*) – *that* . . ., ich hatte keine (*or* nicht die leiseste) Ahnung, daß . . .; *put –s into s.o.'s head*, einem den Kopf vollmachen. **-al,** *adj.* Begriffs–, begrifflich, gedanklich, spekulativ; imaginär, nur gedacht, phantastisch, launenhaft.

notori-ety [notəˈraɪətɪ], *s.* die Offenkundigkeit, das Bekanntsein, Berüchtigtsein; weitbekannte Persönlichkeit; *unenviable* –, nicht beneidenswerte Berühmtheit. **-ous** [noˈtɔːrɪəs], *adj.* allgemein bekannt, allbekannt, offenkundig; berüchtigt, anrüchig, nur zu bekannt (*for*, wegen); (*only attrib.*) notorisch.

notwithstanding [nɔtwɪðˈstændɪŋ], 1. *prep.* ungeachtet (*Gen.*), trotz (*Gen. or Dat.*)– *that* or *that.* –, dessenungeachtet. 2. *conj.*; – *that*, obgleich. 3. *adv.* dennoch, nichtsdestoweniger.

nougat [ˈnʌgɪt], *s.* der Nugat.

nought [nɔːt], *s.* die Null (*Arith.*); (*archaic*) das Nichts; *bring to* –, zerstören, zum Scheitern bringen; *come to* –, fehlschlagen, zunichtewerden; zu Wasser werden; *set at* –, unbeachtet lassen, sich hinwegsetzen über, nicht achten, in den Wind schlagen; *see* **naught.**

noumenon [ˈnaʊmənən], *s.* bloße Idee, reines Gedankending, das Noumenon (*Phil.*).

noun [naʊn], *s.* das Hauptwort, Nennwort, Substantiv; *proper* –, der Eigenname.

nourish [ˈnʌrɪʃ], *v.a.* ernähren (*on*, von); (*fig.*) nähren (*with*, mit), erhalten, unterhalten; pflegen, hegen, stärken (*feelings, etc.*). **-ing,** *adj.* nahrhaft, Nähr–. **-ment,** *s.* die Ernährung; Nahrung (*also fig.*), das Nahrungsmittel.

nous [naʊs], *s.* der Verstand (*Phil.*); (*sl.*) der Mutterwitz, die Grütze.

nova [ˈnoʊvə], *s.* neuer Stern (*Astr.*).

[1]**novel** [ˈnɔvəl], *s.* der Roman; *psychological* –, der Bildungsroman; – *with a purpose*, der Tendenzroman; *short* –, die Novelle. **-ette,** *s.* kitschige Novelle, die Schundlektüre. **-ist,** *s.* der Romanschriftsteller.

[2]**novel** [ˈnɔvəl], *adj.* neu(artig), ungewohnt. **-ty,** *s.* die Neuheit; Neuartigkeit, Neuerung; *the -ty*, das (Aller)Neueste, Ungewohnte. **-ties,** Scherzartikel.

November [noˈvɛmbə], *s.* der November.

novercal [noˈvəːkəl], *adj.* stiefmütterlich.

novice [ˈnɔvɪs], *s.* der Neuling, Anfänger; Novize (*Eccl.*).

novitiate [noˈvɪʃɪət], *s.* die Probezeit, das Noviziat (*Eccl.*), die Lehrzeit, Lehrlingszeit.

now [naʊ], 1. *adv.* nun, gegenwärtig, soeben; dann, darauf(hin), damals, zu jener Zeit; bald; – –*!* sachte, sachte! – *and again*, dann und wann, hin und wieder; ab und zu, gelegentlich, zuweilen; *come –!* nur ruhig! – *if*, wenn nun aber; *just* –, gerade jetzt, soeben; – *at length*, jetzt endlich; (*every*) – *and then*, see – *and again*; – *then*, nun also, wohlan, genug jetzt; – *this – that*, bald dies, bald das; *what is it – ?* was gibt's schon wieder. 2. *conj.*; – (*that*), da nun, nun da, jetzt wo. 3. *s.* das Jetzt; *before* –, schon früher, schon einmal; *by* –, (schon) jetzt, mittlerweile; *from* –, von jetzt an; *up to* –, bis jetzt. **-adays,** *adv.* heutzutage.

noway(s), *see under* **no.**

nowhere [ˈno(h)wɛːə], *adv.* nirgends, nirgendwo, nirgendwohin; (*sl.*) *be* –, weit zurück sein, nicht in Betracht kommen; (*coll.*) – *near*, bei weitem nicht, nicht annähernd.

nowise, *see under* **no.**

noxious [ˈnɔkʃəs], *adj.* schädlich, verderblich. **-ness,** *s.* die Schädlichkeit.

nozzle [nɔzl], *s.* die Düse, Ausgußröhre (*of a hose*); Tülle, Schneppe (*of vessels*); (*sl.*) Schnauze.

nuance [ˈnjuəns], *s.* die Abtönung, Schattierung, Nuance.

nub, -ble [ˈnʌb(l)], *s.* der Klumpen, Auswuchs, das Knötchen.

nubil-e [ˈnjubɪl], *adj.* heiratsfähig, mannbar (*of females*). **-ity** [-ˈbɪlɪtɪ], *s.* die Heiratsfähigkeit.

nucle-ar [ˈnjuːklɪə], *adj.* Kern–; –*ar energy*, die Kernenergie, Atomenergie; –*ar research*, die

Atomkernforschung. **-us** [–klɪəs], *s.* der Kern (*also fig.*); (*fig.*) Mittelpunkt; Samenkern (*Bot.*); Zellkern (*Biol.*).
nud-e [njuːd], 1. *adj.* nackt, bloß; nichtig, ungültig (*Law*). 2. *s.* nackte Figur, der Akt (*Paint.*). **-ist,** *s.* der Anhänger der Nacktkultur. **-ity,** *s.* die Nacktheit, (*fig.*) Blöße, Kahlheit, Dürftigkeit; nackte Figur (*Paint.*).
nudge [nʌdʒ], 1. *s.* leichter (Rippen)Stoß. 2. *v.a.* leise anstoßen, einen Rippenstoß geben (*Dat.*).
nugatory [ˈnjuːgətərɪ], *adj.* wertlos, wirkungslos, unwirksam, nichtig, albern.
nugget [ˈnʌgɪt], *s.* der (Gold)klumpen.
nuisance [ˈnjuːsəns], *s.* Unangenehmes, Lästiges, Anstößiges, *s.*; der Skandal, Unfug, Mißstand, das Ärgernis, die Unannehmlichkeit; Plage, Pest, lästiger Mensch; *abate a –*, einen Mißstand beseitigen; *be a – to s.o.*, einem lästig fallen; *commit no –!* Verunreinigung dieses Ortes verboten! *make a – of o.s.*, sich lästig machen; *public –*, öffentliches Ärgernis, öffentlicher Skandal; *what a –!* wie ärgerlich! wie unangenehm! wie dumm! **--raid,** *s.* der Störflug (*Av.*).
null [nʌl], *pred. adj.* nichtig, ungültig; wertlos, nichtssagend, gehaltlos, leer; *– and void*, null und nichtig. **-ification** [–ɪfɪˈkeɪʃən], *s.* die Aufhebung, Vernichtung, Ungültigmachung, Nichtigkeitserklärung. **-ify** [–ɪfɑɪ], *v.a.* ungültig machen, aufheben, vernichten, für null und nichtig erklären. **-ity** [–ɪtɪ], *s.* die Nichtigkeit, Ungültigkeit.
numb [nʌm], 1. *adj.* erstarrt, starr, empfindungslos (*with*, vor). 2. *v.a.* starr machen, erstarren lassen, betäuben. **-ness** [–nɪs], *s.* die Starrheit, Erstarrung, Betäubung.
number [ˈnʌmbə], **1.** *s.* die Zahl, Ziffer, Nummer; Anzahl, Summe; Menge, Schar (*of persons*); der Numerus (*Gram.*); das Heft, die Lieferung, Nummer (*of a work*); *pl.* 4. Buch Mose, Numeri (*B.*); das Versmaß, der Rhythmus; *back –*, die Zeitung älteren Datums; (*coll.*) der Ladenhüter, Mensch mit veralteten Ansichten; *cardinal –*, die Grundzahl; *even –*, gerade Zahl; *in –*, an Zahl; *in round –s*, in runder Zahl, rund; *published in –s*, in Lieferungen herausgegeben; *in large –s*, in großen Mengen; *odd –*, ungerade Zahl; *a great – of*, sehr viele; *a – of*, mehrere, eine Anzahl (*Gen.*); *the – of times*, die vielen Male; *three times the –*, dreimal so viel; *times out of –*, see *times without –*; *by force of –s*, durch Übermacht; *ordinal –*, die Ordnungszahl; *one of their –*, einer aus ihren Reihen; (*coll.*) *his – is up*, seine Stunde ist gekommen; *– one*, die eigene Person, der eigene Vorteil; (*as attrib. adj.*) erstklassig; *a – nine*, eine Abführpille (*Mil.*); *– 10*, die Wohnung des englischen Premierministers; *plural –*, die Mehrzahl; *singular –*, die Einzahl; *times without –*, unzählige Male. **2.** *v.a.* (zusammen)zählen, numerieren (*houses, etc.*); betrachten, rechnen (*among*, unter *or* zu); betragen, sich belaufen auf (*Acc.*); *– (off)*, abzählen (*Mil. & fig.*); *my hours are –ed*, meine Stunden sind gezählt; *the seats are –ed*, die Plätze sind numeriert. **-less,** *adj.* zahllos, unzählig. **--plate,** *s.* das Nummernschild (*Motor.*)
numbness, *see* **numb.**
numer-able [ˈnjuːmərəbl], *adj.* zählbar. **-al** [–əl] 1. *adj.* Zahl–. 2. *s.* das Zahlzeichen, die Zahl, Ziffer, Nummer; das Zahlwort (*Gram.*). **-ation** [–ˈreɪʃən], *s.* das Zählen, die Zählung, Numerierung, Rechenkunst. **-ative** [–ətɪv], *adj.* Zähl–. **-ator** [–eɪtə], *s.* der Zähler (*of a fraction*). **-ical** [–ˈmɛrɪkl], *adj.* zahlenmäßig, Zahl–, Zahlen–, numerisch. **-ically,** *adv.* zahlenmäßig, an Zahl, in Zahlen. **-ous** [–əs], *adj.* zahlreich; *–ously attended*, stark besucht. **-ousness,** *s.* die Menge, Anzahl, große Zahl.
numismat-ic [njumɪzˈmætɪk], *adj.* numismatisch, Münzen–, Münz–. **-ics,** *pl.* (*sing. constr.*) die Münzkunde. **-ist** [–ˈmɪzmətɪst], *s.* der Münzkenner.
nummulite [ˈnumjəlɑɪt], *s.* der Nummulit, Kalkmünzstein.
numskull [ˈnʌmskʌl], *s.* (*coll.*) der Dummkopf, Tölpel, Tropf.
nun [nʌn], *s.* die Nonne, Klosterfrau, Schwester; Blaumeise (*Orn.*). **--buoy,** *s.* die Spitztonne (*Naut.*). **-nery,** *s.* das Nonnenkloster.
nunci-ature [ˈnʌnʃətjuə], *s.* die Nunziatur (*R.C.*). **-o** [–ʃɪoʊ], *s.* der Nunzius (*R.C.*).
nuncupative [ˈnʌnkjəpeɪtɪv], *adj.* mündlich; *will*, mündliche letztwillige Verfügung (*Law*).
nunnery [ˈnʌnərɪ], *see* **nun.**
nuptial [ˈnʌpʃəl], *adj.* Hochzeits–, Ehe–, Trauungs–*bed*, das Brautbett. **-s** [–z], *pl.* die Hochzeit.
nurs-e [nəːs], 1. *s.* die Krankenschwester, Krankenwärterin; Amme, Kinderwärterin, Kinderfrau, das Kindermädchen; (*fig.*) die Nährmutter; *children's –e*, das Kindermädchen; *male –e*, der Krankenwärter; *Red-Cross –e*, die Rote-Kreuz-Schwester; *trained –e*, die (Kranken)Schwester; *wet-–e*, die Amme; *put (out) to –e*, in Pflege geben. 2. *v.a.* säugen, stillen; die Brust geben (*Dat.*) (*an infant*); pflegen, warten (*the sick, etc.*); durch schonende Behandlung kurieren (*a cold, etc.*); schonen, hätscheln (*an injury, one's voice, etc.*); auf den Schoß nehmen; (*usually pass.*) aufziehen, großziehen; (*fig.*) nähren, hegen, pflegen, fördern (*plants, growth, etc.*); sparsam verwalten, schonend umgeben mit (*resources, etc.*); *–e a cold*, wegen Erkältung das Zimmer hüten; *–e a grievance*, einen Groll hegen; *–e one's leg*, das eine Bein über das andere schlagen. **-e-maid,** *s.* das Kindermädchen. **-ery** [–ərɪ], *s.* die Kinderstube; Pflanzschule, Baumschule (*Hort.*); (*fig.*) die Pflanzstätte, Zuchtstätte. **-ery cannon,** *s.* die Karambolageserie (*Bill.*). **-ery garden,** *s.* die Pflanzschule. **-ery-governess,** *s.* das Kinderfräulein. **-eryman,** *s.* der Kunstgärtner. **-ery-rhyme,** *s.* der Kinderreim, das Kinderlied. **-ery-school,** *s.* der Kindergarten. **-ery stakes,** *s.* das Rennen für Zweijährige (*horse-racing*). **-ing,** *s.* das Stillen, Säugen; (also *sick-–ing*) die Pflege, Krankenpflege; *–ing-bottle*, die Saugflasche; *district –ing*, die Armenkrankenpflege; *–ing home*, die (Privat)Klinik; *–ing mother*, stillende Mutter; die Pflegemutter. **-(e)ling** [–lɪŋ], *s.* der Säugling, Pflegling; Liebling.
nurture [ˈnəːtʃə], 1. *s.* die Nahrung; (*fig.*) Pflege, Erziehung. 2. *v.a.* (er)nähren; (*fig.*) erziehen, aufziehen.
nut [nʌt], 1. *s.* die Nuß; (also *screw-–*) (Schrauben)-Mutter; der Frosch (*on a violin-bow*); (*coll.*) Geck, Zierbengel; (*sl.*) die Birne; *pl.* Nußkohlen; (*sl.*) *be –s* (*on*, versessen sein auf, vernarrt sein in; *crack –s*, Nüsse knacken; *a hard* or *tough – to crack*, eine harte Nuß zu knacken; (*coll.*) *not for –s*, überhaupt nicht; (*sl.*) *go –s*, überschnappen, verrückt werden; (*sl.*) *off one's –*, verrückt. *lock-–*, die Gegenmutter. 2. *v.a.* Nüsse sammeln *or* pflücken. **--brown,** *adj.* nußbraun. **--butter,** *s.* die Nußbutter. **-cracker,** *s.* der Tannenhäher, Nußhäher (*Orn.*); *pl.* der Nußknacker. **--gall,** *s.* der Gallapfel. **-hatch,** *s.* der Kleiber (*Orn.*). **-meg,** *s.* die Muskatnuß. **-shell,** *s.* die Nußschale; *in a –shell*, in knappster Form, in aller Kürze, in wenigen Worten; *lie in a –shell*, sich kurz zusammenfassen lassen. **--tree,** *s.* der Haselnußbaum. **-ty,** *adj.* Nuß–, nußartig; nußreich; (*fig.*) würzig, pikant; (*sl.*) *–ty on*, see *be –s on.*
nutat-e [ˈnjuteɪt], *v.n.* sich neigen (*Bot.*) *or* krümmen. **-ion** [–ˈteɪʃən], *s.* das Schwanken der Erdachse, die Nutation (*Astr.*); die Krümmung(s-bewegung) (*Bot.*).
nutmeg, *see* **nut.**
nutria [ˈnjuːtrɪə], *s.* der Biberrattenpelz.
nutri-ent [ˈnjutrɪənt], 1. *adj.* nährend, nahrhaft, Ernährungs–. 2. *s.* der Nährstoff. **-ment** [–trɪmənt], *s.* die Nahrung, der Nährstoff (*also fig.*). **-tion** [–ˈtrɪʃən], *s.* die Ernährung; Nahrung. **-tious** [–ˈtrɪʃəs], *adj.* nahrhaft, nährend. **-tiousness,** *s.* die Nahrhaftigkeit. **-tive** [–trɪtɪv], 1. *adj.* Ernährungs–; *see also* **-tious.** 2. *s.* der Nährstoff, das Nährmittel. **-tiveness,** *see* **-tiousness.**
nutty [ˈnʌtɪ], *see* **nut.**
nux vomica [nʌksˈvɔmɪkə], *s.* die Brechnuß; der Brechnußbaum (*Bot.*).
nuzzle [nʌzl], 1. *v.a.* mit der Schnauze berühren *or* aufwühlen; liebkosen, hätscheln (*children*). 2. *v.n.* schnüffeln, stöbern, mit der Schnauze wühlen; sich anschmiegen *or* drücken.
nyctalopia [nɪktəˈloupɪə], *s.* die Nachtblindheit.
nylg(h)au [ˈnɪlgɔː], *s.* die Nilgauantilope.

nymph [nɪmf], *s.* die Nymphe; Larve, Puppe (*Ent.*). **-al,** *adj.* Puppen– (*Ent.*). **–ean,** *adj.*, **--like,** *adj.* nymphenhaft.
nymphomania [nɪmfəˈmeɪnɪə], *s.* die Mannstollheit. **–c** [–nɪæk], *s.* mannstolles Weib.
nystagmus [nɪˈstægməs], *s.* das Augenzittern.

O

O, o [oʊ], 1. *s.* das O, o; die Null (*Arith.*); *see Index of Abbreviations.* 2. *int.* (*when followed by another word without intervening punctuation*) ach! o! oh!; *see* **oh.**
O' [oʊ], abbr. of *of*, (*Irish*) der Nachkomme *or* Sohn von.
oaf [oʊf], *s.* der Dummkopf, Einfaltspinsel, Lümmel. **–ish,** *adj.* dumm, einfältig, tölpelhaft.
oak [oʊk], 1. *s.* die Eiche, der Eichbaum, das Eichenholz; Eichenlaub; *pl.* Fohlenrennen zu Epsom (*horse-racing*); *sport one's –*, nicht zu sprechen sein, die Tür verschließen (*Univ.*). 2. *adj.*, (*Poet.*) **–en,** eichen, Eichen–. **--apple,** *s.*, **--gall,** *s.* der Gallapfel. **--tree,** *s.* der Eichbaum.
oakum [ˈoʊkəm], *s.* das Werg; *pick –*, Werg zupfen.
oar [ɔ:], 1. *s.* das Ruder (*also fig.*); der (Boots)-Riemen (*Naut.*); Ruderer; *bank of –s*, die Ruderbank; *pull a good –*, gut rudern; *put one's – in*, seine Hand im Spiele haben, seinen Senf dazu geben; *rest on one's –s*, aufhören zu rudern; (*fig.*) auf seinen Lorbeeren ausruhen; *ship the –s*, die Riemen einlegen *or* klarmachen *or* beinehmen. 2. *v.a.* & *n.* (*Poet.*) rudern. **–ed,** *adj. suff.* mit Rudern, -rudrig. **–sman** [ˈɔ:zmən], *s.* der Ruderer. **–smanship,** *s.* die Ruderkunst. **–swoman,** *s.* die Ruderin.
oasis [oʊˈeɪsɪs], *s.* (pl. *oases*) die Oase.
oast [oʊst], *s.* die Hopfendarre. **--house,** *s.* die (Turm)Hopfendarre.
oat [oʊt], 1. *s.* (*usually pl.*) der Hafer (*Agr.*); *false –*, der Wiesenhafer (*Bot.*); *Quaker –s*, die Haferflocken; *sow one's wild –s*, sich die Hörner ablaufen. 2. *adj.*, (*Poet.*) **–en,** *adj.* Hafer–, Hafermehl–; *–en pipe*, die Hirtenpfeife. **–cake,** *s.* der Haferkuchen. **–meal,** *s.* das Hafermehl, die Hafergrütze.
oatmeal [ˈoʊtmɪ:l], *see* **oat.**
oath [oʊθ], *s.* der Eid, Schwur; Fluch. (*a*) (*with nouns & adjectives*) *– of allegiance*, der Lehnseid, Treueid; *false –*, der Falscheid; *– of loyalty to the colours*, der Fahneneid; *– of office*, *official –*, der Diensteid. (*b*) (*with verbs*) *administer* or *tender an* or *the – to a p.*, einen vereidigen, einem den Eid abnehmen, einem einen Eid zuschieben; *swear* or *take an –*, einen Eid ablegen, schwören (*on* or *to*, auf (*Acc.*)); *take the –*, den Eid leisten; *I will take my – that . . .*, ich beschwöre *or* will darauf schwören, daß . . .; *utter an –*, fluchen. (*c*) (*with prepositions*) *by* (*an*) *–*, eidlich; *in lieu of* (*an*) *–*, an Eides Statt, eidesstattlich; *on* (*one's*) *–*, auf Eid; *be on one's –*, unter Eid stehen, eidlich verpflichtet sein; *put s.o. on his –*, einen schwören lassen; *on my solemn –*, bei meinem Eide; *under an –*, unter Eid, eidlich verpflichtet; *under the – of secrecy*, unter dem Siegel der Verschwiegenheit; *upon –*, see *on –*. **--taking,** *s.* die Eidesleistung (*to*, auf).
obbligato [əblɪˈgɑ:toʊ], 1. *s.* selbständig geführte Stimme (*Mus.*). 2. *adj.* selbständig geführt (*Mus.*).
obdura–cy [ˈəbdjurəsɪ], *s.* die Verstocktheit, Halsstarrigkeit. **–te** [–ət], *adj.* verstockt, halsstarrig.
obedien–ce [oˈbɪ:dɪəns], *s.* der Gehorsam (*to*, gegen); (*fig.*) die Abhängigkeit (*to*, von), Obedienz, Obrigkeitssphäre (*R.C.*); *absolute –ce*, der Kadavergehorsam; *in –ce to*, entsprechend, gemäß, im Verfolg (*Gen.*), unter dem Druck von. **–t** [–ənt], *adj.* gehorsam (*to* (*Dat.*)), folgsam; (*fig.*) abhängig (*to*, von); *your –t servant*, Ihr sehr ergebener.
obeisance [əˈbeɪsəns], *s.* die Verbeugung; Huldigung, Ehrerbietung; *make one's – to*, sich beugen vor; *make, do* or *pay – to a p.*, einem huldigen.
obel–isk [ˈəbəlɪsk], *s.* der Obelisk (*Arch.*); das Kreuz (*Typ.*). **–us** [–ləs], *s.* (pl. *–i*) der Obelus (*Typ.*).
obes–e [oʊˈbɪ:s], *adj.* beleibt, fettleibig, korpulent. **–eness,** *s.*, **–ity** [–ɪtɪ], *s.* die Beleibtheit, Fettleibigkeit, Korpulenz.
obey [oˈbeɪ], 1. *v.a.* & *n.* gehorchen (*Dat.*). 2. *v.a.* Folge leisten (*Dat.*), befolgen.
obfuscat–e [ˈəbfʌskeɪt], *v.a.* verdunkeln, (*fig.*) trüben, verwirren. **–ion** [–ˈkeɪʃən], *s.* die Verdunk(e)lung, (*fig.*) Verwirrung.
obit [ˈəbɪt], *s.* (*archaic*) die Seelenmesse, Todesgedenkfeier. **–uary** [əˈbɪtjərɪ], 1. *s.* die Todesanzeige, der Nachruf. 2. *adj.* Toten–, Todes–; *–uary notice*, die Todesanzeige.
[1]**object** [ˈəbdʒəkt], *s.* der Gegenstand, das Objekt (*also Gram.*); der Zweck, das Ziel; *make it one's –*, es sich darauf angelegen sein lassen; *money* (*is*) *no –*, Geld ist Nebensache *or* spielt keine Rolle; *salary no –*, auf Gehalt wird nicht gesehen; *what is his – ?* was bezweckt er? **--glass,** *s.*, **--lens,** *s.* das Objektiv. **–ify** [əbˈdʒɛktɪfɑɪ], *v.a.* vergegenständlichen, objektivieren. **–ive** [–tɪv], 1. *adj.* objektiv, sachlich, gegenständlich, unpersönlich, vorurteilslos; *–ive case*, der Objektsfall (*Gram.*); *–ive genitive*, objektiver Genetiv; *–ive point*, das (Operations)Ziel (*Mil.*). 2. *s.* das Objektiv (*Phot., etc.*), der Objektsfall (*Gram.*), (End)Ziel, Reiseziel, Operationsziel (*Mil.*). **–iveness,** *s.* **–ivity** [əbdʒɛkˈtɪvɪtɪ], *s.* die Objektivität. **–less,** *adj.* gegenstandlos; ziellos; zwecklos. **--lesson,** *s.* die Anschauungsstunde, der Anschauungsunterricht, (*fig.*) lehrreiches *or* anschauliches Beispiel.
[2]**object** [əbˈdʒɛkt], 1. *v.a.* vorhalten, vorwerfen (*to* or *against* (*Dat.*)); (*fig.*) einwenden, vorbringen (*to*, gegen). 2. *v.n.* Einspruch erheben, protestieren (*to*, gegen); etwas einwenden, etwas dagegen haben (*to my smoking*, wenn ich rauche). **–ion** [–kʃən], *s.* die Einwendung, der Einwand; Widerwille, die Abneigung; *have no –ion*, nichts dagegen haben, nichts einzuwenden haben; *make an –ion*, einen Einwand erheben (*to*, gegen); *raise* or *start –ions*, Einwendungen machen *or* Einwände erheben (*to*, gegen); *right of –ion*, das Einspruchsrecht; *take –ion to*, Einspruch *or* Protest erheben; *no –ion to a married man*, verheiratete Bewerber nicht ausgeschlossen. **–ionable,** *adj.* nicht einwandfrei, anstößig, unangenehm (*to*, für), unzulässig. **–or** [əbˈdʒɛktə], *s.* der Gegner; *conscientious –or*, der Kriegsdienstverweigerer.
objurgat–e [ˈəbdʒə:geɪt], *v.a.* tadeln, schelten. **–ion** [–ˈgeɪʃən], *s.* der Tadel. **–ory** [əbˈdʒə:gətərɪ], *adj.* tadelnd.
[1]**oblate** [oʊbˈleɪt], *adj.* abgeplattet. **–ness,** *s.* die Abplattung.
[2]**oblat–e** [ˈəbleɪt], *s.* der Laienbruder, die Laienschwester (*R.C.*). **–ion** [–leɪʃən], *s.* das Opfer, die Opfergabe. **–ory** [ˈəblətərɪ], *adj.* Opfer–.
obligat–e [ˈəblɪgeɪt], *v.n.* (*usually pass.*) zwingen, nötigen (*Law*). **–ion** [–ˈgeɪʃən], *s.* die Verbindlichkeit, Verpflichtung, Obliegenheit (*to*, gegenüber); Schuldverschreibung, Obligation (*C.L.*); *be* or *lie under an –ion*, verbunden *or* zu Dank verpflichtet sein (*to* (*Dat.*)); *incur an –ion*, eine Verbindlichkeit eingehen; *lay* or *put s.o. under an –ion*, einen verpflichten; *meet one's –ions*, seinen Verpflichtungen nachkommen; *of –ion*, obligatorisch; *without –ion*, unverbindlich, freibleibend. **–ory** [–ˈlɪgətərɪ], *adj.* verbindlich, bindend, verpflichtend, obligatorisch (*on* or *upon*, für).
oblig–e [əˈblaɪdʒ], 1. *v.a.* verpflichten, verbinden; nötigen, zwingen; *be –ed to go*, gehen müssen; *be –ed to a p.*, einem verbunden *or* zu Dank verpflichtet sein; *–e a p.*, einem gefällig sein, dienen *or* einen Gefallen tun; *–e me by asking him*, wollen Sie die Güte haben *or* so freundlich sein, ihn zu fragen? *to –e you*, Ihnen zu Gefallen; *much –ed*, sehr verbunden, danke schön *or* bestens. 2. *v.n.* (*coll.*) zur Unterhaltung beitragen (*with*, mit *or*

durch), etwas zum besten geben; *please –e with an early reply*, um baldige Antwort wird gebeten (*C.L.*); *early reply will –e*, für baldige Antwort bin ich sehr verbunden (*C.L.*). **–ee** [ɔblɪˈdʒɪː], *s.* der Gläubiger (*Law*). **–ing** [–ˈblɑɪdʒɪŋ], *adj.* verbindlich, gefällig, zuvorkommend, dienstfertig. **–ingness,** *s.* die Gefälligkeit, Zuvorkommenheit. **–or** [ˈɔblɪgɔː], *s.* der Schuldner (*Law*).

obliqu–e [oˈblɪːk], *adj.* schief, schräg; (*fig.*) mittelbar, indirekt, versteckt; heimtückisch, unaufrichtig; abhängig (*Gram.*); *–e angle*, schiefer Winkel; *–e case*, abhängiger Fall; *–e fire*, das Schrägfeuer (*Artil.*); *–e glance*, der Seitenblick; *–e speech*, indirekte Rede (*Gram.*). **–eness,** *s.*, **–ity** [–ˈblɪkwɪtɪ], *s.* die Schiefheit, Schrägheit, schiefe Richtung; die Schiefe (*of the ecliptic*); (*fig.*) Unredlichkeit; Unregelmäßigkeit, Verirrung, der Abweg.

obliterat–e [obˈlɪtəreɪt], *v.a.* auslöschen, ausradieren, (ver)tilgen; entwerten (*stamps*); (*fig.*) verwischen, vernichten. **–ion** [–ˈreɪʃən], *s.* die Auslöschung, das Verwischen; (*fig.*) die Vernichtung, Vertilgung.

oblivi–on [oˈblɪvɪən], *s.* die Vergeßlichkeit; Vergessenheit; *act of –on*, der Gnadenerlaß, Straferlaß, die Amnestie; *fall* or *sink into –on*, in Vergessenheit geraten. **–ous** [–ɪəs], *adj.* vergeßlich; *be –ous of*, vergessen; *be –ous to*, blind sein gegen. **–ousness,** *s.* die Vergeßlichkeit.

oblong [ˈɔblɔŋ], 1. *adj.* länglich. 2. *s.* das Rechteck.

obloquy [ˈɔbləkwɪ], *s.* die Schmähung, Verleumdung; Schande, Schmach, schlechter Ruf, der Verruf.

obnoxious [əbˈnɔkʃəs], *adj.* gehässig, anstößig; höchst unangenehm, verhaßt (*to* (*Dat.*)); (*archaic*) unterworfen, ausgesetzt (*to* (*Dat.*)); *I am – to him*, ich bin ihm ein Dorn im Auge. **–ness,** *s.* die Gehässigkeit, Anstößigkeit, Verhaßtheit.

obo–e [ˈoubou], *s.* die Oboe. **–ist** [–bouɪst], *s.* der Oboist.

obscen–e [ɔbˈsɪːn], *adj.* schlüpfrig, zotig, unzüchtig, obszön. **–ity** [–ɪtɪ], *s.* die Schlüpfrigkeit, Unzüchtigkeit; *pl.* Zoten (*pl.*).

obscur–ant [ɔbˈskjuːərənt], *s.* der Obskurant, Dunkelmann, Bildungsfeind. **–antism** [–ræntɪzm], *s.* der Obskurantismus, Bildungshaß, die Verdummung. **–antist** [–ræntɪst], *s. see* **–ant. –ation** [–ˈreɪʃən], *s.* die Verdunkelung (*Astr.*). **–e** [əbˈskjuːə], 1. *adj.* dunkel, finster, düster; (*fig.*) unklar, unverständlich, undeutlich; unberühmt, unbekannt, unbedeutend, unauffällig, unscheinbar; obskur; verborgen, abgelegen. 2. *v.a.* verdunkeln, verfinstern (*also fig.*); (*fig.*) undeutlich *or* unverständlich machen; verbergen, in den Schatten stellen. **–ely,** *adv.* sang- und klanglos, unbekannt. 3. *s.* (*Poet.*) die Dunkelheit. **–ity** [–rɪtɪ], *s.* die Dunkelheit, das Dunkel; (*fig.*) die Undeutlichkeit, Unklarheit, Unverständlichkeit; Verborgenheit, Unbekanntheit; Niedrigkeit (*of birth*).

obsecration [ɔbsɪˈkreɪʃən], *s.* flehentliche Bitte; das Bittgebet, die Bittformel (*Eccl.*).

obsequies [ˈɔbsɪkwɪz], *pl.* das Leichenbegängnis, die Leichenfeier.

obsequious [əbˈsɪːkwɪəs], *adj.* unterwürfig, kriechend, knechtisch. **–ness,** *s.* die Unterwürfigkeit, Kriecherei.

observ–able [əbˈzəːvəbl], *adj.* zu beachten(d), bemerkbar; bemerkenswert. **–ance** [–vəns], *s.* das Einhalten, die Beobachtung, Befolgung, Innehaltung (*of laws, etc.*); Vorschrift, Sitte, herkömmlicher Brauch; religiöse Feier, die Heilighaltung; Ordensregel, Observanz. **–ant** [əbˈzəːvənt], *adj.* beobachtend, befolgend, haltend (*of* (*Acc.*)); aufmerksam, achtsam, wachsam (*of*, auf (*Acc.*)); *be –ant of a th.*, etwas befolgen. **–ation** [ɔbzəˈveɪʃən], *s.* die Beobachtung, Wahrnehmung; Beobachtungsgabe, das Beobachtungsvermögen; die Befolgung, Innehalten; Äußerung, Bemerkung (*on*, über); *fall under a p.'s –ation*, von einem bemerkt werden; *keep under –ation*, bewachen, beobachten; *make an –ation*, eine Bemerkung machen. **–ation-balloon,** *s.* der Fesselballon. **–ation-car,** *s.* der Aussichtswagen (*Railw.*). **–ation-plane,** *s.* das Aufklärungsflugzeug. **–ation-post,** *s.* die Beobachtungsstelle. **–ation-tower,** *s.* der Aussichtsturm. **–ationward,** *s.* die Beobachtungsstation. **–atory** [əbˈzəːvətərɪ], *s.* die Sternwarte, Wetterwarte. **–e** [əbˈzəːv], 1. *v.a.* beobachten, wahrnehmen, feststellen, bemerken, äußern; halten, feiern (*holidays*); befolgen, innehalten, ausüben. 2. *v.n.* Beobachtungen *or* Bemerkungen machen (*on*, or *upon*, über (*Acc.*)), sich äußern. **–er,** *s.* der Beobachter (*also Av.*), Zuschauer, Befolger (*of rules*), Orter (*Av.*). **–er corps,** der Flugmeldedienst.

obsess [əbˈsɛs], *v.a.* quälen, heimsuchen, verfolgen; *–ed with* or *by*, besessen von. **–ion** [–ˈsɛʃən], *s.* fixe Idee, die Besessenheit, der Verfolgungswahn.

obsidian [əbˈsɪdɪən], *s.* der Obsidian, Feuerkiesel (*Min.*).

obsolescen–ce [ɔbsəˈlɛsəns], *s.* das Veralten. **–t** [–ənt], *adj.* veraltend.

obsolete [ˈɔbsəlɪːt], *adj.* veraltet, außer Gebrauch, überholt; abgenutzt, verbraucht; unvollkommen entwickelt, rudimentär (*Biol.*). **–ness,** *s.* das Veraltetsein, die Verbrauchtheit; unvollkommene Entwicklung (*Biol.*).

obstacle [ˈɔbstəkl], *s.* das Hindernis (*to*, für), die Sperre. **–-race,** *s.* das Hindernisrennen.

obstetric–(al) [əbˈstɛtrɪk(l)], *adj.* geburtshilflich, Geburts–, Entbindungs–. **–ian** [–ˈtrɪʃən], *s.* der Geburtshelfer. **–s,** *pl.* (*sing. constr.*) die Geburtshilfe.

obstina–cy [ˈɔbstɪnəsɪ], *s.* die Hartnäckigkeit (*also Med.*), Halsstarrigkeit, Unbeugsamkeit, der Eigensinn. **–te** [–nət], *adj.* hartnäckig (*also Med.*), halsstarrig, starrsinnig, eigensinnig, störrisch.

obstreperous [əbˈstrɛpərəs], *adj.* lärmend, geräuschvoll, überlaut; widerspenstig, eigensinnig, eigenwillig. **–ness,** *s.* das Lärmen; die Widerspenstigkeit.

obstruct [əbˈstrʌkt], 1. *v.a.* versperren (*the way, etc.*); verstopfen; aufhalten, nicht durchlassen, hindern, hemmen, lahmlegen (*traffic*); (*fig.*) verhindern, vereiteln. 2. *v.n.* Obstruktion treiben (*Parl., etc.*). **–ion** [–kʃən], *s.* die Verstopfung (*also Med.*), Versperrung, Hemmung, Behinderung; das Hindernis (*to*, für). **–ionism,** *s.* die Obstruktionspolitik. **–ionist,** *s.* der Obstruktionist. **–ive** [–tɪv], 1. *adj.* hinderlich (*of* or *to*, für); *be –ive of*, (ver)hindern. 2. *s.* das Hindernis; *see also* **–ionist.**

obtain [əbˈteɪn], 1. *v.a.* erlangen, erreichen, bekommen, erhalten, erzielen, sich (*Dat.*) verschaffen *or* besorgen; *– by entreaty*, erbitten; *– by flattery*, (sich (*Dat.*)) erschmeicheln; *– expert opinion*, ein Gutachten einholen; *– the prize*, den Preis gewinnen; *– the victory*, den Sieg davontragen; *– one's wish*, seinen Willen durchsetzen; *further information may be –ed from*, Näheres erfährt man von. 2. *v.n.* bestehen, herrschen, in Gebrauch sein, Geltung haben, anerkannt werden, sich behaupten. **–able,** *adj.* erreichbar, zu erlangen(d), erhältlich. **–ment,** *s.* die Erlangung.

obtru–de [əbˈtruːd], 1. *v.a.* aufdrängen, aufnötigen, aufzwingen (*on* or *upon* (*Dat.*)); *–de o.s.* see *–de* 2. 2. *v.n.* sich aufdrängen (*on* or *upon* (*Dat.*)), zudringlich sein *or* werden. **–der,** *s.* Aufdringliche(r), *m.* **–sion,** [–ʃən], *s.* das Aufdrängen, die Aufnötigung. **–sive** [–sɪv], *adj.* aufdringlich, zudringlich. **–siveness,** *s.* die Aufdringlichkeit.

obturat–e [ˈɔbtjureɪt], *v.a.* verstopfen, abdichten, verschließen. **–ion** [–ˈreɪʃən], *s.* die Abdichtung, Verschließung; Liderung (*Gun.*). **–or,** *s.* die Schließvorrichtung, Abdichtungsvorrichtung; der Schließmuskel (*Anat.*); Liderungsring (*Gun.*).

obtuse [obˈtjuːs], *adj.* stumpf (*Geom.*); (*fig.*) dumpf (*as pain*); dumm; *– angle*, stumpfer Winkel. **–ness,** *s.* die Stumpfheit; Dummheit.

obvers–e [əbˈvəːs], 1. *adj.* dem Betrachter zugewandt, Vorder–; umgekehrt (*Bot.*). 2. *s.* die Vorderseite, Bildseite, der Avers (*of a coin*); das Gegenstück, die andere Seite. **–ely,** *adv.* umgekehrt. **–ion** [–ʃən], *s.* die Umkehrung (*Log.*).

obviat–e [ˈɔbvɪeɪt], *v.a.* vorbeugen (*Dat.*), begegnen (*Dat.*); abwenden; verhindern, verhüten; überflüssig *or* unnötig machen; beseitigen, aus dem Wege räumen (*difficulties*). **–ion** [–ˈeɪʃən], *s.* die Abwendung, Beseitigung.

obvious [ˈɔbvɪəs], *adj.* handgreiflich, augenfällig;

klar, deutlich, offenbar, unverkennbar; *be* –, einleuchten, auf der Hand liegen, in die Augen springen. **–ness,** *s.* die Augenscheinlichkeit, Unverkennbarkeit, Deutlichkeit.
occasion [ə'keɪʃən], 1. *s.* die Veranlassung, der Anlaß, Grund, zufällige Ursache (*of* (*Gen.*); *for*, zu); die Gelegenheit (*for*, für *or* zu); das Bedürfnis, die Notwendigkeit (*for*, zu); das Ereignis, der Vorfall; *as – serves*, wenn sich die Gelegenheit (dar)bietet; *be the – of*, veranlassen; *for the –*, eigens zu diesem Zwecke; *there is no – for*, es ist nicht nötig (*him to do*, daß er tut); *give –*, Anlaß *or* Gelegenheit geben; *have – to do*, tun brauchen; *on –*, bei Gelegenheit, wenn nötig, gelegentlich; *on the – of*, anläßlich *or* gelegentlich (*Gen.*); *on this –*, bei dieser Gelegenheit; *be equal* or *rise to the –*, sich den Umständen gewachsen zeigen. 2. *v.a.* veranlassen, verursachen, bewirken, zeitigen. **–al,** *adj.* zufällig, gelegentlich; *–al poems*, Gelegenheitsgedichte; *–al showers* or *rain*, vereinzelte Regenfälle; *–al furniture*, das Kleinmöbel. **–ally,** *adv.* gelegentlich, bei Gelegenheit, dann und wann.
occident ['ɔksɪdənt], *s.* (*Poet.*) der Westen, Abend; das Abendland. **–al** [–'dɛntl], *adj.* abendländisch, westlich.
occip–ital [ɔk'sɪpɪtəl], *adj.* Hinterkopf–. **–ut** ['ɔksɪpət], *s.* das Hinterhaupt, der Hinterkopf.
occlu–de [ɔ'klu:d], *v.a.* verschließen,a bschließen (*Tech.*), verstopfen, okkludieren; adsorbieren (*Chem.*). **–sion** [–ʃən], *s.* die Schließung, der Verschluß; die Verstopfung, Okklusion; die Adsorption (*Chem.*).
occult [ɔ'kʌlt], 1. *adj.* verborgen, geheim, geheimnisvoll, magisch, Okkult–. 2. *v.a.* bedecken, verfinstern (*Astr.*); *–ing light*, das Blinkfeuer (*Naut.*). 3. *v.n.* verschwinden, bedeckt werden. **–ation** [–'teɪʃən], *s.* die Verfinsterung, Verdeckung, Bedeckung (*Astr.*). **–ism,** *s.* der Okkultismus, die Geheimlehre.
occup–ancy ['ɔkjupənsɪ], *s.* die Besitznahme; Besitzergreifung (*Law*); Inanspruchnahme, das Innehaben, der Besitz. **–ant** [–ənt], *s.* der Besitzer, Inhaber, Insasse (*of a vehicle*), Bewohner (*of a house*); Besitzergreifer. **–ation** [–'peɪʃən], *s.* der Besitz, das Innehaben; die Besitznahme, Besitzergreifung; Besetzung (*Mil.*); der Beruf, das Geschäft, Gewerbe, Handwerk; die Beschäftigung; *army of –ation*, das Besatzungsheer, die Okkupationsarmee; *by –ation*, von Beruf *or* Profession; *–ation troops*, die Besatzung, Besatzungstruppen (*pl.*). **–ational** [–'peɪʃənl], *adj.* beruflich, Berufs–; *–ational disease*, die Berufskranhkeit. **–ier** ['ɔkjupaɪə], *s.* der Bewohner, Inhaber, Besitzer. **–y** ['ɔkjupaɪ], *v.a.* in Besitz nehmen; besetzen (*Mil.*); innehaben, besitzen; einnehmen, ausfüllen (*a space*); bewohnen (*a house*); (*fig.*) bekleiden (*a position, post, etc.*); dauern, in Anspruch nehmen (*time*); beschäftigen (*attention, etc.*); *–y o.s.* or *be –ied*, sich beschäftigen (*with* or *in*, mit).
occur [ə'kə:], *v.n.* vorkommen, sich finden (*in*, bei); sich ereignen, vorfallen, eintreten; zustoßen (*to a p.* (*Dat.*)); einfallen (*an idea, etc.*) (*to a p.* (*Dat.*)). **–rence** [ə'kʌrəns], *s.* das Vorkommen; der Vorfall, Vorgang, das Vorkommnis, Ereignis; *of frequent –rence*, häufig vorkommend.
ocean ['ouʃən], *s.* das (Welt)Meer, der Ozean; (*coll.*) *–s of*, Riesenmengen *or* Unmengen von. **–ic** [ouʃɪ'ænɪk], *adj.* Meeres–, Ozean–, ozeanisch. **––going,** *adj.* Hochsee–. **–ographic(al)** [–ə'græfɪk(l)], *adj.* meereskundlich. **–ography** [–'nɔgrəfɪ], *s.* die Meerskunde.
ocell–ate(d) ['ɔsəleɪt(ɪd)], *adj.* mit Augenflecken *or* Punktaugen versehen (*Bot., Zool., etc.*). **–us** [ou'sɛləs], *s.* das Punktauge, die Ozelle (*Zool.*).
ocelot ['ousələt], *s.* die Pardelkatze (*Zool.*).
ochlocracy [ɔk'lɔkrəsɪ], *s.* die Pöbelherrschaft.
ochre ['oukə], *s.* der Ocker; *red –*, der Roteisenocker; *yellow –*, der gelbe (Eisen)Ocker. **–ous** ['ouk(ə)rəs], *adj.* **(ochrous)** ockerhaltig, Ocker–.
o'clock [ə'klɔk], *see* [1]**clock.**
octa–gon ['ɔktəgən], *s.* das Achteck (*Geom.*). **–gonal** [ɔk'tægənəl], *adj.* achteckig, achtseitig. **–hedral** [–'hɪ:drəl], *adj.* achtflächig, Oktaeder–. **–hedron** [–'hɪ:drən], *s.* das Oktaeder. **–nt** ['ɔktənt], *s.* der Oktant, Achtelkreis. **–ve** [–tɪv], *s.* die Oktave (*Mus.*); achter Tag, achttägige Feier (*Eccl.*). **–vo** [ɔk'teɪvou], 1. *s.* das Oktav(format), Oktavband. 2. *adj.* Oktav–.
octe–nniel [ɔk'tɛnɪəl], *adj.* achtjährig, achtjährlich. **–t(te)** [–'tɛt], *s.* das Oktett (*Mus.*).
octillion [ɔk'tɪlɪən], *s.* die Oktillion, eine Million zur achten Potenz (*N.B. Amer.* ein Tausend zur neunten Potenz).
Octo–ber [ɔk'toubə], *s.* der Oktober. **–de** ['ɔktoud], *s.* die Achtelektrodenröhre (*Rad.*). **–decimo** [ɔktə'dɛsɪmou], *s.* das Oktodez(format). **–genarian** [ɔktədʒə'nɛ:ərɪən], 1. *adj.* achtzigjährig. 2. *s.* Achtzigjährige(r), *m.* **–pod** ['ɔktəpɔd], *s.* der Achtfüßler (*Zool.*). **–pus** ['ɔktəpəs], *s.* der Kopffüßer, Krake, achtfüßiger Tintenfisch; (*fig.*) viel verzweigte Organisation. **–roon** [ɔk'tru:n], *s.* der Mischling von Weißen und Quarteronen. **–syllabic** [ɔktəsɪ'læbɪk], *adj.* achtsilbig. **–syllable** [–'sɪləbl], *s.* das Wort *or* der Vers von acht Silben.
octroi ['ɔktrwɑ], *s.* kommunale Abgate (*Hist.*).
ocul–ar ['ɔkjulə], 1. *adj.* augenscheinlich, Augen–; *–ar demonstration*, sichtbarer Beweis; *–ar inspection*, der Augenschein, die Okularinspektion. 2. *s.* das Okular. **–ist,** *s.* der Augenarzt.
odd [ɔd], *adj.* ungerade (*of numbers*); einzeln, vereinzelt (*of a set*); etwas über, einige (*before numbers*), und einige (*after numbers*); übrig, überzählig; gelegentlich, ungerechnet, nicht eingerechnet *or* berücksichtigt; seltsam, sonderbar, wunderlich; *50 –*, einige 50; *50 lb. –*, etwas über 50 Pfund; *– fellow*, wunderlicher Mensch; *– glove*, einzelner Handschuh; *– jobs*, gelegentliche kleine Arbeiten; (*coll.*) häusliche Reparaturen, *usw.*; *at – moments*, zwischendurch; *still some – money*, noch etwas Geld übrig; *– number*, ungerade Zahl; *the – shillings*, die übrigen Schillinge; *at – times*, dann und wann, gelegentlich; *– trick*, letzter *or* dreizehnter Stich (*Whist*); *3 – volumes*, 3 vereinzelte Bände; *twenty and – men*, zwanzig und einige Mann; *twenty –*, einige Zwanzig; *twenty pounds –*, etwas über zwanzig Pfund; *an – way of doing things*, eine seltsame *or* ungewöhnliche Art und Weise zu handeln. **–ity,** *s.* wunderlicher Kauz, der Sonderling, das Original; die Wunderlichkeit, Seltsamkeit. **–ly,** *adv.* seltsam. **–ments,** *pl.* Reste, Überbleibsel; Ramschwaren (*pl.*). **–ness,** *s.* die Seltsamkeit, Wunderlichkeit. **–s,** *pl.* (*often sing. constr.*) ungleiche Dinge; die Ungleichheit, der Unterschied; Streit, die Uneinigkeit; der Vorteil, das Übergewicht, die Überlegenheit, Übermacht; Vorgabe (*Sport*); ungleiche Wette, die Wahrscheinlichkeit, Chance; *–s and ends*, allerlei Reste *or* Kleinigkeiten, Überreste, Abfälle. (*a*) (with *to be*) *the –s are on his side* or *in his favour* (*against him*), der Vorteil ist *or* die Chancen sind für ihn *or* auf seiner Seite (gegen ihn); *the –s are ten to one*, die Chancen stehen zehn zu eins; *the –s are that*, es ist sehr wahrscheinlich, daß; (*sl.*) *there's not much –s between them*, sie sind einander so ziemlich gleich; (*coll.*) *what's the –s?* was macht es aus? was schadet es? was tut's?. (*b*) (*with verbs*) *give s.o. –s*, einem vorgeben; *lay* (*the*) *–s*, eine ungleiche Wette eingehen (*with*, mit); *it makes no –s*, es macht keinen Unterschied, es macht nichts; *take –s*, sich (*Dat.*) vorgeben lassen, eine Vorgabe erhalten; *take the –s*, eine ungleiche Wette eingehen. (*c*) (*with prepositions*) *against tremendous –s*, gegen große Überzahl, Überlegenheit *or* Übermacht; *at –s*, uneinig uneins; *by long –s*, gegen die Wahrscheinlichkeit **––man-out,** *s.* Abgeschlagene(r), Zurückgewiesene(r), *m.*
ode [oud], *s.* die Ode.
odious ['oudɪəs], *adj.* verhaßt; abscheulich; widerlich, abstoßend, ekelhaft. **–ness,** *s.* die Verhaßtheit; Widerwärtigkeit, Abscheulichkeit; Widerlichkeit.
odium ['oudɪəm], *s.* der Haß; Vorwurf, Tadel, Schimpf, Makel; *bring – upon*, verhaßt *or* unbeliebt machen.
odometer [ou'dɔmətə], *s.* der Kilometerzähler.
odont–algia [ɔdən'tældʒɪə], *s.* der Zahnschmerz. **–ic** [ɔ'dɔntɪk], *adj.* Zahn–. **–ology** [–'tɔlədʒɪ], *s.* die Zahnheilkunde.

odor, *s.* (*Amer.*) *see* **odour. -ant** [-rənt], *adj.*, **-iferous** [–ˈrɪfərəs], *adj.*, **-ous** [-rəs], *adj.* wohlriechend, duftend.
odour [ˈoʊdə], *s.* der Geruch (*also fig.*); Wohlgeruch, Duft; – *of sanctity*, der Geruch der Heiligkeit; *be in bad* –, in schlechtem Rufe stehen. **-less,** *adj.* geruchlos, geruchfrei.
œcology [ɪːˈkɔlədʒɪ], *s.* die Ökologie.
œcumenical [ɪːkjʊˈmɪːnɪkl], *adj.* ökumenisch (*Rel.*).
œdema [ɪːˈdɪːmə], *s.* das Ödem.
o'er, (*poet.*) *abbr. of* **over.**
œsophagus [ɪːˈsɔfəgəs], *s.* die Speiseröhre.
of [ov, əv], *prep.* (*origin*) von, aus; (*cause*) an, nach, vor; (*relation*) von, an, über, betreffs, hinsichtlich; (*material or contents*) aus; (*Gen. object*) vor, zu, bei; (*Gen. particle*) von, unter; (*possess. Gen.*) *the genitive of the article*; in, von, vor. (*a*) (*before nouns*) – *one's own accord*, aus eigenem Antrieb; – *an afternoon*, an einem Nachmittag, eines Nachmittags; – *age*, mündig; *2 years – age*, 2 Jahre alt; – *course*, natürlich, selbstverständlich; – *his doing*, sein Werk; – *an ancient family*, aus alter Familie; – *necessity*, notwendigerweise; *be – the opinion*, der Meinung sein; *be – a party*, zu einer Gesellschaft gehören; – *all people*, vor allen anderen; – *right*, von Rechts wegen, mit Recht; – *all shops*, bei allen Geschäften; – *all things*, vor allen Dingen; – *a serious turn – mind*, sehr ernsthaft; – *no value*, wertlos, ohne Wert; *six feet – water*, 6 Fuß Wasser; – *recent years*, in den letzten Jahren. (*b*) (*before adjectives and adverbs*) – *late*, neulich, kürzlich; – *old*, vor alters (her); (*Poet.*), – *yore*, ehemals, vor alters. (*c*) (*after nouns*) *battle – Waterloo*, die Schlacht bei Waterloo; *city – London*, die Stadt London; *fear – death*, die Furcht vor dem Tode, Todesfurcht; *a friend – mine*, einer meiner Freunde, ein Freund von mir; *glass – wine*, das Glas Wein; *hope* –, die Hoffnung auf; *wish s.o. joy* –, einem Glück wünschen zu; *love – God*, die Liebe zu Gott, Gottesliebe; *man – genius* (*letters*), das Genie (ein Gelehrter); *man – wealth*, wohlhabender Mann; *month – May*, der Monat Mai; *within 3 miles* –, innerhalb 3 Meilen von; *be in need* –, bedürfen (*Gen.*); *one – a thousand*, einer unter tausend; *pair – boots*, das Paar Stiefel; *plenty* –, Überfluß an (*Dat.*); *thing – the past*, etwas Vergangenes *or* Überwundenes; *university – Bonn*, die Universität Bonn, die Bonner Universität; *this world – ours*, diese unsre Welt. (*d*) (*after pronouns & adjectives*) *all – them*, sie alle; *afraid* –, bange vor; *the best – all*, der, die *or* das Beste von *or* unter allen; *blind – an eye*, auf einem Auge blind; *foolish – me*, dumm von mir; *be ignorant* –, nicht wissen, nicht gehört haben (*Acc.*); *kind* –, lieb(enswürdig) von; *none* –, nichts von; *none – that*, nichts dergleichen; *proud* –, stolz auf; *regardless* –, unbekümmert um; *short* –, knapp an; *sick* –, erkrankt an; (*fig.*) überdrüssig (*Gen.*); *south* –, südlich von; *true – every case*, in jedem Falle wahr; *wide – the mark*, weit vom Ziel; (*fig.*) irrig, verkehrt. (*e*) (*after verbs*) *come* –, abstammen von; *complain* –, klagen über; *cure* –, heilen von; *deprive* –, berauben (*Gen.*); *die* –, sterben an (*Dat.*); *made* –, gemacht aus; *remind* –, erinnern an (*Acc.*); *repent* –, bereuen; *smell* –, riechen nach; *suspect* –, in Verdacht haben wegen; *think* –, denken an (*Acc.*); *treat* –, handeln von.
off [ɔf, ɔːf], **1.** *adv.* (*position*) entfernt, von hier (*place*), von jetzt **an** (*time*); (*direction*) fort, weg, davon; (*removal*) abgefallen, abgenommen, ausgezogen (*of clothes*); (*cessation*) abgesperrt, abgeschnitten (*gas, etc.*); (*with verbs denoting separation*) ab–, weg–; (*coll.*) nicht frisch (*as meat*), (*fig.*) nicht wohl; – *and on*, dann und wann, ab und zu; *far* –, weit entfernt, weit weg; *a great way* –, sehr weit von hier; *well* –, wohlhabend, gut daran; – *like a shot*, auf und davon; (*with verbs*) *be* –, weggehen, fortgehen; (*coll.*) nicht mehr zu haben sein (*goods*); *be badly* –, schlecht daran sein (*for*, mit); abgeschaltet *or* abgeschnitten sein; (*coll.*) *the affair* is –, die Sache ist aus; *how is he – for . . .?* wie ist er daran in Beziehung auf . . .? *break* –, abbrechen (*also fig.*); *cool* – , abkühlen; *fall* –, abnehmen; *get* –, davonkommen; (*sl.*) *get – with a p.*, mit einem anbändeln; *pass* –, vergehen; *see s.o.* –, einen zur Abreise begleiten, einen fortbegleiten; *take a day* –, sich einen Tag freimachen; *turn* –, abdrehen, abstellen. **2.** *prep.* (*movement*) fort von, von weg; herunter–; (*position*) von . . . ab; vor, auf der Höhe von (*Naut.*); *fall* –, herunterfallen von; *go – one's head*, den Kopf verlieren; *a yard – me*, ein(en) Meter von mir; *street – Cheapside*, die Seitenstraße *or* Nebenstraße von Cheapside; – *duty*, nicht im Dienst, dienstfrei; – *form*, in schlechter Form, nicht auf der Höhe; *please keep – the grass*, das Betreten des Rasens ist verboten; *never – one's legs*, immer auf den Beinen; – *limits*, (*Amer.*) Zutritt verboten; – *the map*, am Ende der Welt; – *the point*, nicht zur Sache gehörig, belanglos; – *Portsmouth*, auf der Höhe von Portsmouth; *two miles – the road*, zwei Meilen von der Straße ab; – *work*, außer Arbeit. **3.** *adj.* recht (*of vehicles, etc.*); rechts vom Schläger (*Crick.*); – *chance*, schwache *or* entfernte Möglichkeit, geringe Aussicht; – *day*, freier Tag; der Tag wo alles schief geht; – *side*, rechte Seite (*of a horse, etc., also of batsman* (*Crick.*)). **--colour,** 1. *s.* die Fehlfarbe. 2. *adj.* (*fig.*) nicht in Ordnung, unpäßlich. **--hand,** *adj.* aus dem Stegreif; auf der Stelle; ungezwungen; *in an --hand manner*, ganz ungezwungen, so leichthin. **-ing,** *s.* hohe See, der Seeraum; *in the -ing*, auf hoher See; (*fig.*) in einiger Entfernung. **-ish,** *adj.* (*coll.*) zurückhaltend, steif, kühl, reserviert. **--licence,** *s.* der Ausschank über die Straße (*or Austr.* Gasse). **--peak,** *adj.* nicht auf dem Höchststand. **--print,** *s.* der Sonderabdruck, das Separatum. **-scourings,** *pl.* der Kehricht, Abschaum, Auswurf. **-set,** 1. *s.* die Gegenrechnung, der Ausgleich (*C.L.*); der Mauerabsatz, Mauervorsprung (*Build.*); die Ordinate (*Surv.*); die Biegung (*of a pipe*); der Offsetdruck, Gummidruck (*Typ.*); der Absenker, Ableger, Sproß, Sprößling (*Hort.*); (*fig.*) Seitenzweig, Ausläufer, die Abzweigung; *-set bulb*, die Brutzwiebel (*Hort.*); *-set machine*, die Offsetpresse, Gummidruckmaschine (*Print.*). 2. *v.a.* ausgleichen, aufrechnen (*C.L.*); mit Vorsprung versehen (*Build.*); (*fig.*) unschädlich machen, wettmachen. **-shoot,** *s.* der Sprößling, Ableger, Sproß, Ausläufer; die Abzweigung, Seitenlinie, der Seitenzweig. **--shore,** *adj.* vom Lande entfernt; *--shore wind*, der Landwind. **-side,** *s.* die Abseite (*Footb.*). **-spring,** *s.* (*only sing.*) der Abkömmling; die Nachkommenschaft, Nachkommen (*pl.*); (*fig.*) das Ergebnis, die Frucht.
offal [ˈɔfəl], *s.* der Abfall, Fleischabfall, geringe Fischsorte; (*fig.*) der Ausschuß, Schund.
offen-ce [əˈfens], *s.* der Anstoß, das Ärgernis, die Beleidigung, Kränkung; das Vergehen, der Verstoß (*against*, gegen); Angriff, die Offensive; *no -ce!* nichts für ungut! *cause* or *give -ce*, Anstoß *or* Ärgernis erregen; *give -ce to a p.*, einen beleidigen; *take -ce at*, Anstoß nehmen an, sich beleidigt fühlen über, übelnehmen; *weapons of -ce*, Angriffswaffen. **-d** [əˈfɛnd], 1. *v.a.* beleidigen, verletzen (*the eye, ear, etc.*); ärgern, erzürnen, kränken (*a p.*, (*Acc.*)), zu nahe treten (*a p.*, (*Dat.*)); *be -ded*, aufgebracht (*at a th.*, über etwas; *by a th.*, durch etwas, *with a p.*, über einen). 2. *v.n.* sich vergehen, verstoßen, sündigen (*against*, gegen). **-der,** *s.* der Beleidiger, Verbrecher, Missetäter; *be a first -der*, nicht vorbestraft sein. **-se,** *s.* (*Amer.*) *see* **-ce. -sive,** 1. *adj.* widerwärtig, widrig, ekelhaft (*to* (*Dat.*)); beleidigend, anstößig; offensiv, Angriffs–. 2. *s.* die Offensive, der Angriff; *be on the -sive*, in der Offensive sein; *assume* or *take the -sive*, die Offensive ergreifen. **-siveness,** *s.* das Anstößige, Beleidigende; die Widerwärtigkeit, Ekelhaftigkeit.
offer [ˈɔfə], 1. *v.a.* anbieten, darbieten, hinhalten, zur Verfügung stellen; zum Verkauf anbieten, offerieren (*C.L.*); bieten (*a sum*); (also – *up*) darbringen, opfern; – *battle*, sich kampfbereit stellen; – *one's hand*, die Hand reichen (*to a p.*, einem); – *one's hand* (*in marriage*), die Hand (zur Heirat) anbieten (*to a lady*, einer Dame); – *one's reasons*, seine Gründe vorbringen; – *resistance*, Widerstand leisten; – *one's services*, seine Dienste anbieten; – *violence to a p.*, einem Gewalt antun. 2. *v.n.* sich

(dar)bieten, sich zeigen; sich erbieten, Miene machen (*to*, zu). 3. *s.* das Anerbieten, Angebot, die Offerte (*C.L.*); gebotene Summe; – *of marriage*, der Heiratsantrag; *on* –, zum Verkauf angeboten. **–er,** *s.* Darbietende(r), *m.*, der Opferer. **–ing,** *s.* das Anerbieten, Geschenk, der Antrag; das Opfer. **–tory** [–tərɪ], *s.* die Kollekte, das Offertorium (*R.C.*); das Opfer, die (Geld)Sammlung.

offic–e [ˈɔfɪs], *s.* das Amt, öffentliches *or* staatliches Amt, der Dienst, Beruf, Posten; die Dienstleistung, Aufgabe, Funktion; der Gottesdienst, das Offizium (*Eccl.*); das (Amts)Büro, die Amtsstube, das Geschäftszimmer, Kontor; Ministerium, Ministerialgebäude; (*fig.*) der Liebesdienst, die Gefälligkeit; *pl.* Wirtschaftsräume, Küchenräume, Geschäftsräume, Verwaltungsgebäude, Nebengebäude, Stallungen, Wirtschaftsgebäude. (*a*) (*with verbs*) *do s.o. a kind –e*, einem einen guten Dienst erweisen; *hold* or *fill an –e*, ein Amt bekleiden; *perform the last –es to a p.*, einem die letzte Ehre erweisen; *resign –e*, vom Amt zurücktreten; *take –e*, das Amt übernehmen *or* antreten. (*b*) (*with prepositions*) *–e for the dead*, der Totengottesdienst; *be in –e*, ein öffentliches Amt bekleiden; im Ministerium sein (*minister*), an der Regierung sein (*cabinet*); *come into –e* or *enter upon –e*, das Amt antreten, ins Ministerium kommen (*Pol.*); *go to the –e*, ins Büro gehen; *through the good –es of*, durch die gütige Vermittlung von. (*c*) (*with attrib.*) *booking –e*, der Fahrkartenschalter; *divine –e*, katholischer Gottesdienst; *Foreign –e*, das Ministerium des Äußern; *Holy –e*, die Inquisition; *Home –e*, das Ministerium des Innern; *inquiry –e*, das Auskunftsbüro; *life –e*, die Lebensversicherungsgesellschaft; *lost-property –e*, das Fundbüro; *post –e*, das Postamt; *record –e*, das Archiv; *War –e*, das Kriegministerium. **–e appliances,** der Kanzleibedarf. **–e-bearer,** *s.* der Amtsinhaber. **–e-boy,** *s.* der Laufbursche, Bürodiener. **–e clerk,** der Kontorist. **–e-furniture,** *s.* Büromöbel (*pl.*). **–e-hours,** *pl.* Geschäftsstunden, Dienststunden (*pl.*). **–e-hunter,** *s.* der Postenjäger. **–er** [–ə], 1. *s.* Beamte(r), *m.*; der Offizier (*Mil.*); *commanding –er*, der Befehlshaber, Kommandeur; *petty –er*, der Maat (*Naut.*); *police –er*, der Polizist, Schutzmann; *warrant –er*, der Feldwebelleutnant. 2. *v.a.* (*usually pass.*) mit Offizieren versehen. **–ial** [əˈfɪʃəl], 1. *adj.* amtlich, Amts–, Dienst–; offiziell, formell; *through –ial channels*, auf dem Dienstwege; *–ial duties*, Amtspflichten; Amtshandlungen; *–ial reports*, amtliche Berichte; *–ial residence*, die Amtswohnung; *–ial stamp*, die Dienstmarke. 2. *s.* (Staats)Beamte(r), *m.* **–ialdom,** *s.* das Beamtentum; der Amtsschimmel, Bureaukratismus. **–ially,** *adv.* offiziell, formell. **–iant** [əˈfɪʃɪənt], *s.* amtierender Geistlicher. **–iate** [əˈfɪʃɪeɪt], *v.n.* amtieren; fungieren (*as*, als); *–iate at a wedding*, den Traugottesdienst abhalten; *–iating clergyman*, amtierender Geistlicher. **–inal** [əˈfɪsɪnəl], *adj.* offizinell, arzneilich, Arznei–. **–ious** [əˈfɪʃəs], *adj.* zudringlich, aufdringlich, übertrieben dienstfertig; halbamtlich, offiziös (*Pol.*). **–iousness,** *s.* übertriebene Dienstfertigkeit, Zudringlichkeit.

offing, *see under* **off.**

offish, *see under* **off.**

offscourings, *see under* **off.**

offset, *see under* **off.**

offshoot, *see under* **off.**

offspring, *see under* **off.**

oft [ɔft, ɔ:ft], *adv.* (*obs., poet., except in compounds*) *see* **–en.** **–en** [ɔfn, ɔ:fn], *adv.* oft, öfters, oftmals, häufig; *ever so –en*, sehr oft, unzählige Male, immer wieder; *as –en as not, more –en than not*, meistens, des öfteren.

ogee [oʊˈdʒɪ:], *s.* die Kehlleiste, Glockenleiste, der S-Bogen, Karnies (*Arch.*); – *arch*, der Eselsrücken.

ogiv–al [oˈdʒaɪvl], *adj.* Spitzbogen–, Ogival–. **–e** [ˈoʊdʒaɪv, oˈdʒaɪv], *s.* gotischer Spitzbogen; die Gratrippe (*of a vault*).

ogle [oʊgl], 1. *v.a.* liebäugeln, zärtlich anblicken. 2. *v.n.* liebäugeln (*with*, mit). 3. *s.* liebäugelnder Blick . **–r,** *s.* Liebäugelnde(r), *m.*

ogre [ˈoʊgə], *s.* der Oger, Menschenfresser. **–ss,** *s.* die Menschenfresserin, weibliches Ungeheuer.

oh [oʊ], *int.* ach! *see* **o**!

ohm [oʊm], *s.* das Ohm. **–meter,** *s.* das Ohmmeter, der Widerstandsmesser.

oho [oˈhoʊ], *int.* oho!

oil [ɔɪl], 1. *s.* das Öl; (*Amer.*) Petroleum; *pl.* die Ölmalerei; *crude* –, das Rohöl; *essential* or *volatile –s*, flüchtige *or* ätherische Öle; *fatty* or *fixed –s*, fette Öle; (*coll.*) *burn the midnight* –, spät in die Nacht arbeiten; *mineral* –, das Mineralöl; *vegetable* –, das Pflanzenöl; – *of vitriol*, die Schwefelsäure; *paint in –s*, in Öl malen; *pour – on troubled waters*, die Gemüter beruhigen; *pour* or *throw – on the flames*, Öl ins Feuer gießen; *strike* –, Petroleum entdecken; (*fig.*) Glück haben. 2. *v.a.* (ein)ölen, einfetten; schmieren; – *a p.'s palm*, einen schmieren *or* bestechen; *a well –ed tongue*, ein gutes Mundwerk; (*coll.*) – *the wheels*, den Karren schmieren. **–-bearing,** *adj.* ölhaltig. **–-brake,** *s.* die Öldruckbremse. **–-cake,** *s.* der Ölkuchen, Leinkuchen. **–-can,** *s.* der Öler, die Ölkanne. **–cloth,** *s.* das Wachstuch. **–-colour,** *s.* die Ölfarbe. **–-engine,** der Ölmotor. **–er,** *s.* der Öler, die Ölkanne. **–-field,** das Petroleumfeld, Erdölfeld. **– fuel,** die Ölfeuerung, das Treiböl, Heizöl. **–iness,** *s.* die Öligkeit, Fettigkeit; (*fig.*) glattes Wesen, die Schmeichelei. **–man,** *s.* der Ölhändler. **–-painting,** *s.* die Ölmalerei; das Ölgemälde. **–skin,** *s.* das Öltuch, die Ölleinwand; *pl.* das Ölzeug **–stone,** *s.* der Ölstein. **–-tanker,** *s.* das Öltankschiff. **–-well,** *s.* das Ölbohrloch, der Petroleumbrunnen. **–y,** *adj.* ölig, fettig, schmierig; (*fig.*) schmeichlerisch, salbungsvoll.

ointment [ˈɔɪntmənt], *s.* die Salbe; *a fly in the* –, ein Haar in der Suppe.

old [oʊld], *adj.* alt; abgenutzt, verbraucht; altertümlich, früher, veraltet. (*a*) (*with nouns*) – *age*, hohes Alter, das Greisenalter; *–-age pension*, die Altersrente; (*sl.*) – *bean*, altes Haus; – *boy*, früherer Schüler; (*coll.*) – *boy*, – *chap*, alter Freund; – *English*, Altenglisch; – *fellow*, see – *boy*, – *chap*; – *gold*, das Mattgold; – *hand*, alter Praktikus (*at*, in); *as – as the hills*, uralt; – *maid*, alte Jungfer; (*coll.*) *the – man*, der Alte, Chef, Prinzipal, Kapitän; (*coll.*) – *man*, alter Freund; (*sl.*) *my – man*, mein Alter, mein Mann; – *Man's Beard*, das Greisenhaar (*Bot.*); *the – Masters*, die Alten Meister (*Art*); (*coll.*) – *Nick*, der Teufel; – *offender*, vielfach vorbestrafter Verbrecher; – *salt*, erfahrener Seemann; *of – standing*, altehrwürdig, althergebracht; – *style*, Alter Stil (*calender*); (*coll.*) *any – thing*, eine x-beliebige Sache; (*coll.*) *a high – time*, eine glänzende Zeit; *the good – times*, die gute alte Zeit; (*coll.*) *any – way*, auf jede Weise, in x-beliebiger Weise; – *woman*, altes Waschweib (*of men*); (*sl.*) *my – woman*, meine Alte, meine Frau. (*b*) (*with verbs*) *grow* –, altern; *have grown – in vice*, in Laster ergraut sein. (*c*) (*with prepositions*) *of* –, ehedem, vor *or* seit alters; *times of* –, alte Zeiten. **–-clothes-man,** *s.* der Trödler. **–en,** *adj.* (*poet.*) alt. **–er,** *comp. adj.* älter. **–est,** *sup. adj.* ältest. **–-established,** *adj.* alt(hergebracht). **–-fashioned,** *adj.* altmodisch. **–ish,** *adj.* ältlich. **–ness,** *s.* das Alter, Altsein. **–ster,** *s.* (*coll.*) alter Knabe. **–-time,** *adj.* aus alter Zeit. **–-timer,** *s.* alterfahrener Mensch. **–-world,** *adj.* altmodisch, rückständig.

oleaginous [oʊlɪˈædʒɪnəs], *adj.* ölig, ölhaltig, fettig.

oleander [oʊlɪˈændə], *s.* der Oleander (*Bot.*).

oleate [ˈoʊlɪeɪt], 1. *adj.* ölsauer. 2. *s.* ölsaures Salz.

oleograph [ˈoʊlɪogrɑ:f], *s.* der Öldruck.

olfactory [ɔlˈfæktərɪ], *adj.* Geruchs–; – *nerve*, der Geruchsnerv.

oligarch [ˈɔlɪgɑ:k], *s.* der Oligarch. **–ic(al)** [–ˈgɑ:kɪk(l)], *adj.* oligarchisch. **–y,** *s.* die Oligarchie.

oligocene [ˈɔlɪgosɪ:n], *adj.* oligozän (*Geol.*).

olive [ˈɔlɪv], 1. *s.* die Olive; der Ölbaum; die Olivenfarbe. 2. *adj.* olivenfarbig. **–-branch,** *s.* der Ölzweig (*also fig.*). **–-oil,** *s.* das Olivenöl. **–-tree,** *s.* der Ölbaum.

olla podrida [ˈɔləpəˈdrɪ:də], *s.* (*fig.*) der Mischmasch.

olympi–ad [əˈlɪmpɪæd], *s.* die Olympiade. **–an** [–pɪən], **–c** [–pɪk], *adj.* olympisch; *–c games, see* **–ad.**

ombre [ˈɔmbə], *s.* das Lomber(spiel) (*Cards*).
omelet(te) [ˈɔmlɪt], *s.* der Eierkuchen, das Omelett; *you cannot make an – without breaking eggs*, um etwas zu erreichen muß man die Nachteile in Kauf nehmen.
omen [ˈoumən], 1. *s.* das Vorzeichen, Omen, die Vorbedeutung. 2. *v.a.* anzeigen, vorhersagen; *ill–ed*, verhängnisvoll, unheilvoll.
omentum [oˈmɛntəm], *s.* das Darmnetz (*Anat.*).
ominous [ˈɔmɪnəs], *adj.* unheilvoll, verhängnisvoll, von übler Vorbedeutung. **–ness**, *s.* das Ominöse.
omissi–ble [oˈmɪsəbl], *adj.* auslaßbar, auszulassen(d). **–on** [–ˈmɪʃən], *s.* die Auslassung, Weglassung, Unterlassung (*also Theol.*), Versäumnis.
omit [oˈmɪt], *v.a.* auslassen, weglassen, fortlassen (*from*, aus *or* von), unterlassen, versäumen; übergehen.
omnibus [ˈɔmnɪbʌs], 1. *s.* der Omnibus, Autobus; Sammelband, die Sammlung (*Bookb.*). 2. *attrib.* Sammel–, Mantel–.
omnifarious [ɔmnɪˈfɛːərɪəs], *adj.* Allerlei–; – *knowledge*, das Wissen aller Art.
omnipoten–ce [ɔmˈnɪpətəns], *s.* die Allmacht. **–t** [–ənt], *adj.* allmächtig.
omnipresen–ce [ɔmnɪˈprɛsəns], *s.* die Allgegenwart. **–t** [–ənt], *adj.* allgegenwärtig.
omniscien–ce [ɔmˈnɪsɪəns], *s.* die Allwissenheit. **–t** [–ənt], *adj.* allwissend.
omnium [ˈɔmnɪəm], *s.* die Gesamtsumme, der Gesamtwert; die Generalschuldverschreibung (*C.L.*). (*coll.*) **– –gatherum**, *s.* das Sammelsurium, gemischte Gesellschaft.
omnivorous [ɔmˈnɪvərəs], *adj.* alles verschlingend *or* fressend.
omophagous [oˈmɔfəgəs], *adj.* rohes Fleisch fressend.
omoplate [ˈouməpleɪt], *s.* das Schulterblatt.
omphal–ic [ɔmˈfælɪk], *adj.* Nabel–. **–ocele** [–əsɪːl], *s.* der Nabelbruch. **–os** [ˈɔmfələs], *s.* der Schildbuckel; (*fig.*) Mittelpunkt.
on [ɔn], **1.** *prep.* auf, an, zu, bei, in, nach, von über. (*a*) (*before nouns*) *payment – account*, die Akontozahlung; – *account of*, wegen; – *the air*, in Betrieb (*Rad.*); – *analysis*, bei näherer Untersuchung; *with a lady – his arm*, eine Dame am Arme führend; – *my arrival*, gleich nachdem ich ankam, gleich nach meiner Ankunft; – *good authority*, aus guter Quelle; – *an average*, im Durchschnitt; – *board*, an Bord; – *bread and water*, bei Wasser und Brot; – *call*, auf Abruf; – *the coast*, an der Küste; – *the committee*, im Komitee; – *these conditions*, unter diesen Bedingungen; – *further consideration*, bei reiflicher Überlegung; – *the continent*, auf dem Kontinent; – *the contrary*, im Gegenteil; – *demand*, auf Antrag; (*coll.*) – *the dot*, auf die Minute; – *entering*, beim Eintritt *or* Eintreten; – *the eve of*, unmittelbar vor; (*coll.*) – *the fence*, neutral, unentschlossen; – *fire*, in Brand, in Flammen; – *the first of April*, am ersten April; – *or before the first of April*, bis zum ersten April; – *foot*, zu Fuß; – *all fours*, auf allen vieren; – *half-pay*, auf Halbsold; – *hand*, auf Lager; – *the right hand*, zur Rechten; – *hearing the news*, als er (*etc.*) die Nachricht hörte; – *my honour*, bei meiner Ehre; – *horseback*, zu Pferd; – *a journey*, auf einer Reise; – *leave*, auf Urlaub; – *the left*, zur Linken; *loss – loss*, Verlust auf *or* über Verlust, ein Verlust nach dem andern; – *Monday*, am Montag; – *Mondays*, montags; – *the morning of*, am Morgen des; – *an optimistic note*, in zuversichtlicher Weise; – *this occasion*, bei dieser Gelegenheit; – *my part*, meinerseits; – *penalty of death*, bei Todesstrafe; – *the piano*, auf dem Klavier; – *publication*, gleich nach Erscheinen; – *purpose*, mit Absicht; – *receipt*, nach *or* bei Empfang; – *the river*, am Flusse; – *sale*, zum Verkauf; – *shore*, am Ufer, ans Ufer; – *side*, im Spiele (*Footb.*); – *this side*, auf dieser Seite; – *the spot*, auf der Stelle; – *the staff*, im Stabe (*Mil.*); – *an empty stomach*, mit einem leeren Magen; – *a sudden*, plötzlich, auf einmal; – *my theory*, nach meiner Theorie; – *time*, zur festgesetzten Zeit; – *the wall*, an der Wand; – *the whole*, im ganzen. (*b*) (*after nouns*) *the agreement –*, das Abkommen über; *the attack –*, der Angriff auf; *a curse – him!* Fluch über ihn! *an increase – last year*, eine Steigerung gegen letztes Jahr; *a lecture –*, ein Vortrag über; *a joke – me*, ein Scherz auf meine Kosten; *the march –*, der Marsch auf; *have pity – me!* habt Mitleid mit mir! (*c*) (*after adjectives*) *keen –*, erpicht auf (*Acc.*), gern haben; *mad –*, wild *or* versessen auf, außer sich vor. (*d*) (*with verbs*) (*coll.*) *this is – me*, dies geht auf meine Rechnung; *bestow –*, verleihen (*Dat.*); *call –*, besuchen; auffordern; *draw a bill – a p.*, einen Wechsel auf einen ziehen; (*coll.*) *have you a match – you?* haben Sie Streichhölzer bei sich? (*coll.*) *have nothing – a p.*, nichts vor einem voraus haben; einem nichts vorzuhalten haben; *live –*, leben von; *start – a journey*, eine Reise antreten; *think –*, nachdenken über; *throw – the floor*, auf den Boden werfen; *write –*, schreiben über. **2.** *adv.* (*position*) darauf; an, auf; (*direction*) vorwärts, heran, weiter, weiter–, fort–; – *and –*, immer weiter; – *and off*, hin und wieder, ab und zu; *far –*, weit vorgerückt; *later –*, später; *and so –*, und so weiter; *be –*, an, auf, dabei *or* darauf sein, im Gange *or* in Tätigkeit *or* los sein; gespielt *or* gegeben werden (*Theat.*); *the water is –*, das Wasser ist an; *what's – today?* was ist heute los? was wird heute gegeben? (*Theat.*); *I can't get my boots –*, ich kann meine Stiefel nicht anziehen; *have one's coat –*, den Mantel anhaben; *with his hat –*, mit dem Hute auf; *it's getting – for six*, es geht auf sechs Uhr zu; *go –!* weiter! fahren Sie fort! *he went – whistling*, er pfiff weiter; (*sl.*) *be – to a th.*, Kenntnis haben von einer S. **3.** *adj.*; *the – side*, die Seite links vom Schläger (*Crick.*). **4.** *s.* see *– side*. **–coming** [ˈɔnkʌmɪŋ], *adj.* herankommend. **– –licence**, *s.* die Schankkonzession. **– –looker** [ˈɔnlukə], *s.* der Zuschauer. **–rush** [ˈɔnrʌʃ], *s.* der Sturm, Ansturm. **–set** [ˈɔnsɛt], *s.* der Angriff, Anfall; Anfang. **–slaught** [ˈɔnslɔːt], *s.* der Angriff. **–ward** [ˈɔnwəd], 1. *adv.* vorwärts, weiter. 2. *adj.* fortschreitend, vorwärtsschreitend. **–wards** [ˈɔnwədz], *adv. see* **–ward** 1.
onager [ˈɔnəgə], *s.* wilder Esel.
onanism [ˈounənɪzm], *s.* die Onanie, Selbstbefleckung.
once [wʌns], 1. *adv.* einmal; ein einziges Mal; einst, vormals, ehedem; dereinst; – *and again*, einige Male; *at –*, (so)gleich, sofort; zugleich, zu gleicher Zeit, auf einmal; *all at –*, auf einmal, plötzlich; alle gleichzeitig; *for –*, für diesmal, ausnahmsweise; *for – in a way*, einmal zur Abwechslung; – *for all*, ein für allemal; – *in a while*, gelegentlich, zuweilen; (*coll.*) – *in a blue moon*, in hundert Jahren einmal; *more than –*, mehrmals, mehrere Male; – *more*, noch einmal; *this –*, dieses eine Mal; – *upon a time*, einmal; (*Prov.*) – *bit, twice shy*, das gebrannte Kind scheut das Feuer. 2. *conj.* sobald, wenn einmal; – *there, we shall . . .*, sind wir einmal da, so werden wir. . . . (*sl.*) **– –over**, *s.* flüchtiger Überblick.
one [wʌn, wɔn], **1.** *num. adj.* ein; *twenty– –*, einundzwanzig; – *hundred*, hundert; – *thousand*, tausend; – *o'clock*, ein Uhr; *half past –*, halb zwei. **2.** *dem. adj.* eine(r, s), eins; (*emphatic*) einzig; *all –*, ganz gleich, alles eins, einerlei; – *and all*, alle zusammen; – *another*, einander; *at –*, einige; – *by –*, einer nach dem andern; – *day*, eines Tages; – *of these days*, dieser Tage; *I for –*, ich für meinen Teil; *on the – hand*, einerseits; (*coll.*) – *in the eye*, der Wischer, Denkzettel; *all in –*, zusammen, zugleich; *as – man*, einstimmig, einmütig; – *more song*, noch ein Lied; – *thing or another*, dies und jenes; *for – thing*, zunächst einmal; – *time*, einmal; – *of these works*, eins dieser Werke; – *or two*, einige; – *too many*, einer zuviel; – *and the same*, ein und derselbe; – *with another*, eins ins andere gerechnet, im Durchschnitt. **3.** *indef. pron.* (irgend)eine(r), (irgend)ein; jemand, man; – *Mr. Smith*, ein gewisser Herr Schmidt; – *knows*, man weiß; *it drives – mad*, es macht einen verrückt; *–'s impression was*, der Eindruck, den man bekam, war; *lose –'s life*, das Leben verlieren; *it gives – a shock*, es gibt einem einen Stoß; *any– –*, irgend einer, irgend jemand; *every–*, jeder; *many a –*, manch einer; *no –*, keiner, niemand; *such a –*, ein solcher, so einer; *such –s*, solche; – *or other*, einer oder der andere; *the – who*, derjenige der; *the*

–*s who*, diejenigen die; *this* –, dieser; *these –s*, diese; *that* –, jener; *those –s*, jene; *which – ?* welcher? *which –s ?* welche? *like – lost*, wie ein Verlorener; *I am not – to . . .*, ich bin kein Mann, der . . .; *be – of a party*, dabei sein; *your view is the right* –, Ihre Ansicht ist die richtige; *the great –s of the earth*, die Großen der Erde; *my little –s*, meine Kleinen, meine Kinder; *a sly* –, ein Schlauberger; *cry –'s eyes out*, sich (*Dat.*) die Augen ausweinen; *take –'s meals*, das Essen einnehmen. **4.** *s.* der Einer; die Eins (*Arith.*); *a row of –s*, eine Reihe Einsen; (*coll.*) *take care of number* –, für sich selbst sorgen. **--act,** *adj.*; *--act play*, der Einakter. **--edged,** *adj.* einkantig; einschneidig. **--eyed,** *adj.* einäugig. **--handed,** *adj.* einhändig. **--horse,** *adj.* einspännig; (*sl.*) dürftig, zweitrangig. **--legged,** *adj.* einbeinig. **--man,** *adj.*; *--man show*, die Einzelleistung. **-ness,** *s.* die Einheit, Gleichheit, Identität; Einigkeit, Übereinstimmung, Harmonie. **--price shop,** *s.* das Einheitspreisgeschäft. (*sl.*) **-r,** *s.* die Kanone (*at*, in) (*person*); die Prachtleistung; krasse Lüge; der Schlag. **-self,** I. *emph. pron.* selbst. 2. *refl. pron.* sich. **--sided,** *adj.* einseitig, voreingenommen. **--sidedness,** *s.* die Einseitigkeit. **--storied,** *adj.* einstöckig. **--time,** *attrib. adj.* (*rare*) einstig, früher. **--way,** *adj.*; *--way street*, die Einbahnstraße.

onerous ['ɔnərəs], *adj.* lästig, beschwerlich, drükkend (*to*, für). **-ness,** *s.* die Lästigkeit, Beschwerlichkeit, Last.

onion ['ʌnjən], *s.* die Zwiebel.

onlooker, *s. see under* **on.**

only ['ounlɪ], I. *adj.* einzig, alleinig; *one and* –, einzigst. 2. *adv.* nur, bloß, allein; erst; – *after*, erst nachdem; *if* –, wenn nur; – *just*, eben erst *or* gerade, kaum; *not – . . .*, *but . . .*, nicht nur . . ., sondern (auch) . . .; – *yesterday*, erst gestern. 3. *conj.* nur daß, jedoch. **--begotten,** *adj.* (*B.*) eingeboren. **--beloved,** *adj.* einzig geliebt.

onomastic [ɔnə'mæstɪk], *adj.* Namens–. **-on** [–ən], *s.* das Namensverzeichnis.

onomatop–œia [ɔnə'mætəpɪ:ə], *s.* die Tonmalerei, Wortmalerei, Lautmalerei, Lautnachahmung, Onomatopöie. **–œic** [–pɪɪk], **-oetic** [–pou'ɛtɪk], *adj.* lautnachahmend, onomatopoetisch.

onrush, *see under* **on.**

onset, *see under* **on.**

onslaught, *see under* **on.**

onto–genesis [ɔnto'dʒɛnɪsɪs], *s.* die Ontogenese (*Biol.*). **-logy** [ɔn'tələdʒɪ], *s.* die Ontologie (*Phil.*).

onus ['ounəs], *s.* die Last, Verpflichtung, Verantwortung; – *of proof*, die Beweislast.

onward, –s, *see under* **on.**

onyx ['ɔnɪks], *s.* der Onyx.

oodles ['u:dəlz], *pl.* (*sl.*) Unmengen (*pl.*).

oof [u:f], *s.* (*sl.*) das Moos, Blech, der Kies, Knöpfe (*pl.*), Moneten (*pl.*).

oogamous [ou'ɔgəməs], *adj.* oogam (*Biol.*).

oolit–e ['ouəlaɪt], *s.* der Oolith, Rogenstein; Dogger (*Geol.*). **–ic,** *adj.* Oolith–.

oosp–erm ['ouəspə:m], *s.* befruchtetes Ei (*Zool.*). **–ore** [–pɔ:], *s.* befruchtetes Keimkorn (*Bot.*).

ooz–e [u:z], I. *v.n.* (durch)sickern; triefen (*with*, von); (*fig.*) *–e away*, (dahin)schwinden; (*fig.*) *–e out*, durchsickern. 2. *s.* der Schlamm, Matsch, Schlick; das Gerbextrakt, die Lohbrühe (*Tan.*); der Fluß, durchgesickerte Flüssigkeit. **–y,** *adj.* schlammig, schlickerig; (*fig.*) flüssig.

opacity [o'pæsɪtɪ], *s.* die Undurchsichtigkeit; Deckkraft (*of paint*); (*fig.*) Dunkelheit.

opal ['oupəl], *s.* der Opal. **–esce** [–'lɛs], *v.n.* opalisieren, schillern. **–escence** [–'lɛsəns], *s.* das Opalisieren, die Opaleszenz. **–escent** [–'lɛsənt], *adj.* opalisierend, bunt schillernd. **–ine** [–aɪn], I. *adj.* Opal–. 2. *s.* das Opalglas.

opaque [o'peɪk], **I.** *adj.* undurchsichtig, undurchlässig; deckfähig (*as paint*); (*fig.*) unverständlich, unklar, dunkel; – *colour*, die Deckfarbe. 2. *s.*, **–ness,** *s. see* **opacity**; die Dunkelheit, Unklarheit.

open ['oupən], **1.** *adj.* offen, offenstehend, auf; unbedeckt, bloß, offenliegend, frei; zugänglich (*to*, für); offenkundig, offenbar, öffentlich; offenbleibend, unentschieden; offen(herzig), aufrichtig, unbefangen, aufgeschlossen (*to*, für); eisfrei (*as a harbour*); laufend (*as accounts*) (*C.L.*); durchbrochen, durchlöchert; unterworfen, ausgesetzt (*to* (*Dat.*)); *a little* –, klaffend (*as a door*). (*a*) (*with nouns*) – *air*, freie Luft, das Freie; *in the – air*, unter freiem Himmel; *with – arms*, mit offenen Armen; (*fig.*) – *book*, offener Mensch; – *bowels*, der Stuhlgang; *in – court*, öffentlich, vor Gericht; *with – doors*, bei offenen Türen; *with one's eyes* –, mit offenen Augen; – *field*. freies Feld; – *fire-place*, see – *hearth*; – *hand*, freigebige Hand; – *hearth*, offener Herd; – *house*, gastfreies Haus; – *lecture*, öffentliche Vorlesung; – *letter*, offener Brief; – *mind*, unbefangener Sinn, die Aufgeschlossenheit; – *order*, geöffnete *or* aufgelöste Ordnung; – *question*, offene Frage; *in the – sea*, auf hoher See; – *season*, die Jagdzeit; *over – sights*, über Kimme und Korn (*Gun.*); – *spaces*, unbebautes Gelände; – *steam*, direkter Dampf; *in the – street*, auf offener Straße; – *throttle*, das Vollgas; – *verdict*, unentschiedener Urteilsspruch; – *vat*, die Wanne; – *weather*, klares Wetter (*Naut.*); – *winter*, milder Winter; – *work*, durchbrochene Arbeit; – *working*, der Tagbau (*Min.*). (*b*) (*with verbs*) *be – to a p. to do*, einem freistehen zu tun; *break* –, aufbrechen, erbrechen; *keep one's eyes* –, die Augen offenhalten; *lay* –, aufdecken, klarlegen; *lay o.s.* –, sich aussetzen (*to* (*Dat.*)); *throw* –, aufreißen (*a door*); zugängig machen, eröffnen (*to a p.*, einem); ausschreiben (*to competition*). (*c*) (*with prepositions*) *be – to conviction*, mit sich reden lassen, sich überzeugen lassen, Beweisgründen zugänglich sein; – *to criticism*, nicht frei von Schuld; *be – to discussion*, zur Diskussion stehen; *be – to doubt*, Zweifel (*Dat.*) unterliegen; *be – to an offer*, mit sich handeln lassen. **2.** *v.a.* öffnen, aufmachen; aufschlagen (*a book*); entkorken (*a bottle*); enthüllen (*a th. to a p.*, einem etwas), zugänglich machen (*to*, für); anfangen, beginnen, eröffnen (*hostilities, Parliament, an account, a shop*); – *a case*, einen Prozeß eröffnen; – *a correspondence*, einen Briefwechsel anknüpfen; – *the door to a p.*, einem die Tür öffnen (*N.B. to let him in*); – *the door for a p.*, einem die Tür öffnen (*N.B. because he cannot*); – *a p.'s eyes*, einem die Augen öffnen (*to*, für); – *one's eyes*, große Augen machen; – *one's heart*, sein Herz ausschütten *or* aufschließen; (*fig.*) – *one's mouth*, sich verraten; – *negotiations*, Verhandlungen beginnen *or* anknüpfen; – *a suit*, eine Farbe anspielen (*Cards*); (*with adverbs*) – *out*, ausbreiten, entfalten; – *up*, erschließen (*country, etc.*). **3.** *v.n.* sich öffnen *or* auftun, aufgehen; offen sein *or* haben (*as shops*); aufblühen (*as flowers*); beginnen, anfangen; sich erschließen *or* zeigen (*to one's view*); führen, (hinaus)gehen (*as rooms, etc.*) (*into*, in *or* nach; *on* or *on to*, auf; *out of*, aus); – *to a p.*, einem die Tür öffnen; (*with adverbs*) – *out*, sich ausdehnen; offen bekommen (*Naut.*); (*fig.*) sich aussprechen *or* offenbaren, mitteilsam werden; Vollgas geben (*Motor.*); – *up*, sich zeigen *or* auftun; das Feuer eröffnen (*of guns*). **4.** *s.* die freie Luft, das Freie *or* freie Feld *or* offene Meer; *in the* –, im Freien, unter freiem Himmel, auf freier Flur; (*fig.*) *come into the* –, offen reden (*about*, über), kein Hehl machen (*about*, aus). **--air,** *adj.* Freilicht–, Freiluft–, im Freien. **-er,** *s.* der Öffner (*p. or instrument*), Eröffner (*of a debate*). **--eyed,** *adj.* mit offenen Augen (*to*, für), wach, wachsam. **--handed,** *adj.* freigebig. **--hearted,** *adj.* offenherzig, aufrichtig. **--hearth,** *adj.*; *--hearth furnace*, der Siemens-Martin-Ofen; *--hearth process*, das Martinverfahren. **-ing,** I. *adj.* Anfangs–, Eröffnungs–, einleitend; *-ing price*, der Eröffnungskurs, Anfangskurs; *-ing remarks*, die Eingangsworte; *-ing speech*, die Eröffnungsrede. 2. *s.* das Öffnen; die Eröffnung (*of a shop, Parliament, etc.*), Erschließung (*of a country*); Öffnung, Mündung, das Loch, der Riß, Spalt, Durchgang; die Bresche; (*Amer.*) Lichtung (*in a wood*); der Absatzweg, Markt; günstige Aussicht; die Gelegenheit (*for*, für); der Anfang, Beginn, einleitender Teil. **--minded,** *adj.* unbefangen, unvoreingenommen, aufgeschlossen. **--mindedness,** *s.* die Vorurteilslosigkeit, Unvoreingenommenheit, Aufgeschlossenheit. **--mouthed,** *adj.* mit aufgesperrtem Munde;

gaffend. **-ness,** *s.* die Offenheit; Offenherzigkeit, Aufgeschlossenheit. **--work,** see – *work.*

opera [ˈɔpərə], *s.* die Oper; Opernmusik, Opern (*pl.*); – *bouffe* or *comic* –, komische Oper; *grand* –, große Oper. **--cloak,** *s.* der Theatermantel. **--dancer,** *s.* der Ballettänzer. **--glass,** *s.* (*usually pl.*) das Opernglas. **--hat,** *s.* der Klapphut. **--house,** *s.* das Opernhaus, die Oper. **– singer,** der Opernsänger. **-tic** [-ˈrætɪk], *adj.* Opern–; (*fig.*) opernhaft; *-tic singer,* see – *singer.*

opera-ble [ˈɔpərəbl], *adj.* operierbar (*Surg.*). **-te** [-eɪt], 1. *v.n.* (ein)wirken, eine Wirkung haben (*on,* auf (*Acc.*)); tätig *or* wirksam sein, arbeiten, funktionieren; operieren (*on* (*Acc.*), *also Mil.*); spekulieren (*C.L.*); *be -ted on,* operiert werden (*Surg.*). 2. *v.a.* bewirken; in Gang *or* Betrieb bringen; handhaben, regulieren, hantieren, betätigen (*a business, etc.*); bedienen (*signals*). **-ting,** *adj.* Operations– (*Med.*), Betriebs– (*Tech.* & *C.L.*); *-ting costs,* Betriebskosten (*pl.*); *-ting-instructions,* Bedienungsvorschriften (*pl.*); *-ting-room,* der Operationssaal (*Surg.*); *-ting-surgeon,* der Operateur; *-ting-table,* der Operationstisch (*Surg.*); *-ting-theatre,* see *-ting-room*; *-ting voltage,* die Betriebsspannung (*Elec.*). **-tion** [-ˈreɪʃən], *s.* die Operation (*Surg., Mil.* & *Maths.*) (*on a p.* (*Gen.*)); chirurgischer Eingriff; das Wirken, die Wirkung (*on,* auf (*Acc.*)); Tätigkeit, Wirksamkeit; Verrichtung; der Vorgang, das Verfahren. der Betrieb; die Handhabung, Bedienung, Betätigung (*Tech.*); Spekulation (*C.L.*); *-tion for appendicitis,* die Blinddarmoperation; *in -tion,* in Tätigkeit; *come into -tion,* in Kraft treten; *-tion on the leg,* die Operation am Bein; *-tion on my father,* die Operation meines Vaters; *scene of -tions,* der Kriegsschauplatz, das Operationsfeld, Operationsgebiet (*Mil.*); *undergo an -tion,* sich einer Operation unterziehen. **-tional** [-ˈreɪʃənəl], *adj.* Operations– (*Mil.*). **-tive** [ˈɔpərətɪv], 1. *adj.* wirkend, tätig (eingreifend); praktisch, wirksam; Betriebs– (*Tech.*); operativ (*Surg.*); *become -tive,* in Kraft treten, wirksam werden; *make -tive,* in Kraft treten lassen. 2. *s.* der (Fabrik)Arbeiter. **-tor** [-eɪtə], *s.* Wirkende(r), *m.*; operierender Arzt, der Operateur (*Surg., also films*); Kameramann (*films*); Bediener einer Maschine; das Telefonfräulein; der Telegrafist; Unternehmer, Arbeitgeber; Schieber, Spekulant (*C.L.*); *telephone -tor,* das Telefonfräulein; *telegraph -tor,* der Telegrafist; *wireless -tor,* der Funker.

opercul-ar [oˈpəːkjulə], **-ate(d)** [-leɪt(ɪd)], *adj.* Deckel– (*Bot.*), Kiemendeckel– (*Ichth.*) **-um** [-əm], *s.* der Deckel (*Bot.*), Kiemendeckel (*Ichth.*).

operetta [ɔpəˈrɛtə], *s.* die Operette, leichte Oper.

operose [ˈɔpərous], *adj.* mühsam, beschwerlich. **-ness,** *s.* die Mühsamkeit, Beschwerlichkeit.

ophicleide [ˈɔfɪklaɪd], die Ophikleide (*Mus.*).

ophi-dian [oˈfɪdɪən], 1. *s.* die Schlange. 2. *adj.* Schlangen–. **-olater** [-ˈɔlətə], *s.* der Schlangenanbeter. **-olatry** [-ˈɔlətrɪ], der Schlangenkult, die Schlangenanbetung, Schlangenverehrung, Ophiolatrie.

ophit-e [ˈɔfaɪt], *s.* der Ophit (*Geol.*). **-ic** [əˈfɪtɪk], *adj.* Ophit–.

ophthalm-ia [ɔfˈθælmɪə], *s.* die Augenentzündung, Ophthalmie. **-ic** [-mɪk], 1. *adj.* Augen–; augenkrank. 2. *s.* das Augenmittel. **-itis** [ɔfθəlˈmaɪtɪs], *s. see* **-ia.** **-ologist** [-ˈmɔlədʒɪst], *s.* der Augenarzt, Ophthalmologe. **-ology** [-ˈmɔlədʒɪ], *s.* die Augenheilkunde, Ophthalmologie. **-oscope** [ɔfˈθælməskoup], *s.* der Augenspiegel, das Ophthalmoskop.

opi-ate [ˈoupɪeɪt], 1. *adj.* einschläfernd (*also fig.*). 2. das Schlafmittel, Opiat; (*fig.*) Beruhigungsmittel. **-um** [-əm], *s.* das Opium; *-um-eater, s.* der Opiumesser. **-umism** [-əmɪzm], *s.* die Opiumvergiftung.

opine [oˈpaɪn], *v.n.* (*archaic*) meinen, der Meinung sein, dafürhalten (*that,* daß).

opinion [əˈpɪnjən], *s.* die Meinung, Ansicht, Überzeugung (*of* or *about,* über); das Gutachten, Urteil (*of* or *on,* über); *be of the* –, der Meinung *or* Ansicht sein; *get another* –, das Gutachten eines anderen einholen; *have* or *hold an* –, eine Ansicht vertreten *or* hegen; *have a high* – *of,* eine hohe Meinung haben von; (*often neg.*) *have no* (*high*) – *of,* nicht viel halten von; *have the courage of one's -s,* zu seiner Meinung stehen; *in my* –, meiner Meinung nach, nach meiner Meinung, meines Erachtens; *incline to the* –, zu der Ansicht neigen; *remain of the* –, der Ansicht bleiben; *matter of* –, die Ansichtssache; *public* –, öffentliche Meinung. **-ated** [-eɪtɪd], *adj.* von sich eingenommen, eigensinnig, starrsinnig, eigenwillig. **-atedness,** *s.* der Eigensinn, Starrsinn, der Eigenwille, Trotz **-ative** [-eɪtɪv], *adj. see* **-ated.**

opisometer [ɔpɪˈsɔmɪtə], *s.* der Kurvenmesser.

opium, *see under* **opiate.**

opopanax [əˈpɔpənæks], *s.* das Gummiharz, der Opanax, Opopanax.

opossum [əˈpɔsəm], *s.* die Beutelratte, das Opossum (*Zool.*).

oppidan [ˈɔpɪdən], 1. *s.* der Externe, nicht in der Schulanstalt wohnender Stadtschüler (*at Eton*); (*rare*) der Stadtbewohner. 2. *adj.* in der Stadt wohnend, auswärtig.

oppilat-e [ˈɔpɪleɪt], *v.a.* verstopfen (*Med.*). **-ion** [-ˈleɪʃən], die Verstopfung.

opponen-cy [əˈpounənsɪ], *s.* (*rare*) die Gegnerschaft. **-t** [-ənt], 1. *s.* der Gegner (*of* (*Gen.*)), Widersacher; Gegenspieler (*sport*), Konkurrent. 2. *adj.* gegnerisch, entgegengesetzt; (*rare*) gegenüberstehend, entgegengestellt, Gegen–.

opportun-e [ˈɔpətjuːn], *adj.* gelegen, günstig, passend; rechtzeitig. **-ely,** *adv.* zu gelegener Zeit, im passenden Augenblick. **-eness,** *s.* die Rechtzeitigkeit, passende Gelegenheit, günstiger Zeitpunkt. **-ism** [-ɪzm], *s.* der Opportunismus, Anpassungssinn; (*coll.*) die Gesinnungslumperei. **-ist,** 1. *s.* der Opportunist, auf den eigenen Nutzen bedachter Mensch. 2. *adj.* opportunistisch, auf den eigenen Nutzen bedacht. **-ity** [-ˈtjuːnɪtɪ], (günstige) Gelegenheit (*of doing* or *to do,* zu tun); vorteilhafte Lage, günstiger Zeitpunkt; die Möglichkeit, Chance; *pl.* Möglichkeiten (*for,* für *or* zu); *at* or *on the first -ity,* bei der ersten Gelegenheit; *miss the -ity,* die Gelegenheit verpassen; *an -ity presents itself,* eine Gelegenheit bietet sich; *seize* or *take the -ity,* die Gelegenheit ergreifen.

oppos-e [əˈpouz], *v.a.* bekämpfen, entgegentreten, widerstehen (*a th.* or *a p.* (*Dat.*)); im Wegen stehen (*a th.* (*Dat.*)), zuwiderlaufen, hemmen (*a th.*); gegenüberstellen, entgegenstellen (*to* or *with a th.* (*Dat.*)). **-ed,** *adj.* feindlich, abhold, zuwider (*to a p.* (*Dat.*)); entgegengesetzt (*to a th.* (*Dat.*)); *be -ed to a p.,* jemandem feindlich gegenüberstehen; *be -ed to a th.,* einer S. feindlich gegenüberstehen, (*coll.*) dagegen sein. **-ing,** *adj.* entgegengesetzt, zusammenstoßend, konfliktierend; widerstreitend, widersprechend, unvereinbar (*ideas, etc.*), gegnerisch (*forces, etc.*). **-ite** [ˈɔpəzɪt], 1. *adj.* gegenüberstehend, gegenüberliegend; entgegengesetzt; verschieden (*to* or *from,* zu *or* von); gegenständig, opponiert (*Bot.*); *-ite angles,* Scheitelwinkel, *pl.* (*Geom.*); *be -ite to,* gegenüberstehen (*Dat.*) (*also fig.*), gegenüberliegen (*Dat.*); (*fig.*) grundverschieden sein von; *in an* or *the -ite direction,* in entgegengesetzter Richtung; (*coll.*) *-ite number,* der Partner, Mitspieler; Gegenspieler, Widersacher, Gegner; das Seitenstück, Gegenstück, entsprechendes Stück, die Entsprechung, das Pendant; *on the -ite side to,* auf der gegenüberliegenden Seite von. 2. *adv.* gegenüber. 3. *prep.* gegenüber (*Dat.*). 4. *s.* das Gegenteil, der Gegensatz; *just the -ite, the very -ite,* das gerade Gegenteil. **-itifolious** [əpɔzɪtɪˈfoulɪəs], *adj.* gegenblätterig (*Bot.*). **-ition** [ˈɔpəzɪʃən], *s.* der Widerstand (*to,* gegen), Gegensatz (*to,* zu); Widerstreit, Widerspruch (*to* or *with,* mit); das Gegenüberstehen, Gegenüberliegen; die Opposition (*to,* zu) (*Pol., Astr.,* & *fig.*), Konkurrenz (*C.L.*); *act in -ition to his wishes,* seinen Wünschen zuwiderhandeln; *be in -ition,* der Opposition angehören (*Pol.*), in Opposition stehen (*to,* zu) (*Astr.*), (*fig.*) Opposition machen (*to,* gegen); *-ition benches,* die Oppositionsbänke (*Pol.*); *encounter* or *meet with -ition,* auf Widerstand stoßen; *-ition meeting,* die Protestversammlung; *offer -ition to,* Widerstand leisten gegen; *-ition party,* die Oppositionspartei, Opposition. *-ition of the thumb,* die Gegenüberstellung des Daumens;

-itive [əˈpɔzɪtɪv], *adj.* (*rare*) gegensätzlich, entgegengesetzt.

oppress [oˈprɛs], *v.a.* unterdrücken, niederdrücken, niederhalten; bedrücken, beklemmen (*spirits*). **-ion** [–ʃən], *s.* die Unterdrückung, Vergewaltigung; der Druck, die Bedrückung; Beklemmung, Bedrücktheit, trübe Stimmung; die Bedrängnis, das Elend. **-ive,** *adj.* tyrannisch, grausam; niederdrückend, bedrückend; drückend, schwül (*weather*). **-iveness,** *s.* die Schwüle, der Druck. **-or** [–ə], *s.* der Tyrann, Unterdrücker, Bedrücker.

opprobri–ous [əˈproʊbrɪəs], *adj.* schimpflich, schändlich, schmählich, ehrenrührig, Schimpf–, Schmäh–. **-um** [–ɪəm], *s.* der Schimpf, Schmach, die Schande (*to*, für).

oppugn [əˈpju:n], *v.a.* bestreiten, bekämpfen, für falsch erklären.

opsimath [ˈɔpsɪmæθ], *s.* (*rare*) lerneifriger Greis. **-y,** *s.* das Studium im Alter; spät erworbene Kenntnisse.

opsoni–c [ɔpˈsɔnɪk], *adj.* Opsonin–. **-n** [ˈɔpsənɪn], *s.* das Opsonin, der Blutserumstoff.

opt [ɔpt], *v.n.* sich entscheiden, optieren (*for*, für). **-ative** [ɔpˈteɪtɪv], 1. *adj.* Wunsch–; *–ative mood*, 2. *s.* der Optativ, die Wunschform (*Gram.*).

optic [ˈɔptɪk], 1. *adj.* Seh–, Augen–. 2. *s.* (*coll.*) das Auge. **-al,** *adj.* optisch. **-ian** [ɔpˈtɪʃən], *s.* der Optiker. **-s,** *pl.* (*sing. constr.*) die Optik.

optime [ˈɔptɪmɪ], *s.* der Student in der 2. oder 3. Klasse bei der mathematischen Abschlußprüfung (*Cambridge*).

optimis–m [ˈɔptɪmɪzm], *s.* der Optimismus, die Fortschrittsgläubigkeit, Zuversichtlichkeit. **-t,** *s.* der Optimist. **-tic** [–ˈmɪstɪk], *adj.* optimistisch, zuversichtlich, hoffnungsfroh.

optimum [ˈɔptɪməm], 1. *s.* das Beste, der Bestfall, das Höchstmaß. 2. *adj.* bestmöglich, Best–.

option [ˈɔpʃən], *s.* die Wahl, freie Wahl or Entscheidung; das Optionsrecht, befristetes Kaufangebot (*C.L.*), das Prämiengeschäft (*Stock-Exchange*), die Möglichkeit (*Law*), wahlfreies Fach (*Univ.*); *at your –*, nach Wahl; *have no –*, keine Wahl haben, keine andere Möglichkeit haben (*but to do*, als zu tun); *leave it to his –*, es ihm freistellen; *he gave me the – on the house*, er gab mir das Haus an Hand; *have the – on a purchase*, einen Kauf an Hand haben. **-al,** *adj.* freistehend, freigestellt, anheimgestellt; beliebig, wahlfrei, fakultativ, nicht pflichtmäßig.

opulen–ce [ˈɔpjʊləns], *s.* die Fülle, Üppigkeit, der Reichtum, Überfluß (*of*, an); (*coll.*) Wohlstand, Luxus. **-t,** *adj.* üppig, reich; (*coll.*) vermögend, luxuriös; reichlich.

opus [ˈoʊpəs], *s.* das (Ton)Werk, Opus; *magnum –*, das Hauptwerk. **-cule** [oˈpʌskjʊl], *s.* kleine Arbeit, die Studie, das Werkchen, Opusculum.

[1]**or** [ɔ:], das Gold (*Her.*).

[2]**or** [ɔ:, ɔ, ə], *conj.* oder; (*after neg.*) noch; *either . . . – . . .*, entweder . . . oder . . .; *– else*, sonst, wenn nicht; *not fame – riches*, kein *or* nicht Ruhm noch Reichtum; *one – two*, einige; *a tree – two*, einige Bäume.

orach [ˈɔrɪtʃ], *s.* Wilder Spinat, die Melde (*Bot.*).

orac–le [ˈɔrəkəl], *s.* das Orakel, die Weissagung; (*fig.*) (unfehlbare) Autorität; (*coll.*) *work the –le*, hinter den Kulissen arbeiten. **-ular** [oˈrækjʊlə], *adj.* orakelhaft, Orakel–; maßgebend (*of a p.*); (*fig.*) rätselhaft, schwer verständlich, dunkel.

oral [ˈɔ:rəl], *adj.* mündlich; Mund– (*Anat.*).

orange [ˈɔrɪndʒ], 1. *s.* die Apfelsine, Orange; der Orangenbaum; die Orangefarbe. 2. *adj.* Orange–; orangefarbig. **-ade** [ˈɔrɪnˈdʒeɪd], *s.* die Orangeade. **--blossom,** *s.* die Orangeblüte. **--peel,** *s.* die Apfelsinenschale. **--coloured,** *adj.* orangegelb, rötlich gelb. **-ry,** *s.* die Orangerie, das Treibhaus.

orang-outang [ˈoʊræŋˈju:tæŋ], **orang-utan** [–ˈʊ:tæn], *s.* der Orang-Utan (*Zool.*).

orat–e [ɔ:ˈreɪt], *v.n.* (*coll.*) lange Reden halten, predigen (*on*, über). **-ion** [oˈreɪʃən], *s.* (feierliche) Rede; die Rede (*Gram.*). **-or** [ˈɔrətə], *s.* der Redner. **-orical** [ɔrəˈtɔrɪkl], *adj.* (schön)rednerisch, Redner–; rhetorisch, oratorisch, sprachkünstlerisch. **-orio** [ɔrəˈtɔ:rɪoʊ], *s.* das Oratorium (*Mus.*). **-ory** [ˈɔrət(ə)rɪ], *s.* die Beredsamkeit, Redegabe; Redekunst, Rhetorik; (Privat)Kapelle (*R.C.*); (*coll.*) *mere –ory*, bloßes Gerede.

orb [ɔ:b], *s.* die Kugel; der Reichsapfel (*Her.*); (*Poet.*) der Himmelskörper; (*Poet.*) das Auge, der Augapfel. **-icular** [–ˈbɪkjʊlə], *adj.* kugelrund, kreisrund, kreisförmig, ringförmig. **-iculate** [–ˈbɪkjʊleɪt], *adj.* kugelrund, gerundet (*Bot.*). **-it** [ˈɔ:bɪt], *s.* die Augenhöhle (*Anat.*), Planetenbahn (*Astr.*); (*fig.*) Bahn, der Bereich, das Wirkungsgebiet. **-ital,** *adj.* Augenhöhlen–.

orc(a) [ˈɔ:k(ə)], *s.* der Schwertwal, Butzkopf (*Ichth.*).

orchard [ˈɔ:tʃəd], *s.* der Obstgarten.

orchest–ic [ɔ:ˈkɛstɪk], *adj.* Tanz–. **-ics,** *s.* die Tanzkunst, Orchestik. **-ra** [ˈɔ:kəstrə], *s.* das Orchester (*Mus.*, *Theat.*), der Orchesterraum (*Theat.*); *–ra stalls*, das Parkett (*Theat.*). **-ral** [ɔ:ˈkɛstrəl], *adj.* Orchester–. **-rate** [ˈɔ:kəstreɪt], *v.a.* & *n.* orchestrieren, instrumentieren. **-ration** [–ˈtreɪʃən], *s.* die Orchestrierung, Instrumentierung.

orchid [ˈɔ:kɪd], *s.* die Orchidee. **-aceous** [–ˈdeɪʃəs], *adj.* Orchideen–.

orchi–s [ˈɔ:kɪs], *s.* die Hode (*Anat.*), das Knabenkraut (*Bot.*); *see also* **orchid.** **-tis** [ɔ:ˈkaɪtɪs], *s.* die Hodenentzündung.

orcin [ˈɔ:kɪn], *s.* das Orzin (*Chem.*).

ordain [ɔ:ˈdeɪn], *v.a.* fügen, ausersehen, bestimmen (*also fig.*) (*as God*); (*fig.*) festsetzen, anordnen, verordnen; ordinieren (zu) (*Eccl.*).

ordeal [ˈɔ:dɪ:l, ˈɔ:dɪ:əl], *s.* schwere Prüfung, die Heimsuchung; Qual, Pein; (Feuer)Probe, das Gottesurteil, Gottesgericht (*Hist.*).

order [ˈɔ:də], **1.** *v.a.* in Ordnung bringen, ordnen, regulieren, einrichten (*things*); befehlen (*a p.* (*Dat.*); *to do*, zu tun *or* daß er tut), beauftragen (*a p.* (*Acc.*); *to do*, zu tun); beordern, herbestellen, fortschicken (*a p.*) (*to*, nach); verordnen, anordnen (*as a doctor*); bestellen (*goods*) (*C.L.*); *– about*, hin und her schicken, schurigeln, schikanieren; *– in advance*, im voraus bestellen, vorausbestellen; *– arms!* Gewehr ab! (*Mil.*); *be –ed*, Befehl erhalten. **2.** *s.* der Befehl (*also Mil.*), Erlaß, die Verfügung, Vorschrift, Verordnung; Bestellung, Order (*C.L.*); geordneter Zustand, die Ordnung; Reihenfolge, Anordnung; Aufstellung (*Mil.*); Gattung, Art, Klasse, Ordnung (*Nat. Hist.*); Stellung, der Rang, Grad; (Ritter)Orden; das Ordenszeichen; religiöser Orden, die Körperschaft; Uniform, Kleidung (*Mil.*); (Säulen)Ordnung (*Arch.*); *pl.* geistlicher Stand; *–! –!* zur Sache *or* Ordnung! (*Parl.*). **(a)** (*with nouns*) *banker's –*, der Zahlungsauftrag an die Bank; *– of battle*, die Schlachtordnung (*Mil.*); Gefechtsformation (*Nav.*); *– in council*, der Kabinettserlaß ohne Parlamentsgenehmigung; *– of the day*, der Tagesbefehl (*Mil.*), die Tagesordnung (*Parl., etc.*); (*fig.*) *be the – of the day*, an der Tagesordnung sein; *pass to the – of the day*, zur Tagesordnung übergehen; *doctor's –s*, ärztliche Anordnung; *– of firing*, die Zündfolge (*of engines*); *– of the Garter*, der Hosenbandorden; *– of the Purple Heart*, (*Amer.*) das Verwundetenabzeichen; *law and –*, Ruhe und Ordnung; *– of magnitude*, das Größenverhältnis (*Math.*); *– of march*, die Marschfolge; *– of merit*, die Rangordnung; *money –*, *post-office –*, die Postanweisung (für größere Beträge bis £40), Zahlungsanweisung; *– of precedence*, die Rangordnung; *– of succession*, die Reihenfolge, der Ablauf. **(b)** (*with adjectives*) *close –*, geschlossene Ordnung (*Mil.*); *your esteemed –*, Ihr geschätzter Auftrag; *extended –*, offene Ordnung (*Mil.*); *in good –*, in guter Ordnung (*Mil.*); wohlbehalten; *of a high –*, hochgradig; *holy –s*, der geistliche Stand; *the lower –s*, die untere Gesellschaftsschicht; *marching –*, die Marschausrüstung; *marching –s*, der Marschbefehl; (*coll.*) Laufpaß; *open –*, see *extended –*; *postal –*, die Postanweisung (für kleinere Beträge); *sailing –s*, die Reiseinstruktion; *in skirmishing –*, ausgeschwärmt; *standing –s*, feststehende Geschäftsordnung; (*coll.*) *tall –*, arge Zumutung, zuviel verlangt; *warning –*, der Vorbefehl, das Ankündigungskommando. **(c)** (*with verbs*) *cancel an – (for s.th.)*, (etwas) abbestellen, eine Bestellung rückgängig machen; *give –s* or *the* or *an –*, Befehl geben; *keep –*, die Ordnung aufrechterhalten, Ordnung halten; *– to pay*, der Zahlungsbefehl; *place an – for s.th.*, eine S. in Auftrag geben (*with*, bei), etwas bestellen; *take an – for*, einen Auftrag erhalten auf (*Acc.*); *take –s*, Geistlicher werden. **(d)** (*with prepositions*) *at the –*, mit Gewehr bei Fuß (*Mil.*); *by –*, auf Befehl; *by – of*, auf Befehl *or* Verordnung *or* im Auftrage *or* (*C.L.*) auf Order von; *by – of the court*, auf Gerichtsbeschluß; *in –*, in Ordnung; in der richtigen Reihenfolge; zulässig (*Parl., etc.*); (*coll.*) am Platze; *be in –s*, Geistlicher sein; *not in –*, ordnungswidrig, nicht zur Geschäftsordnung; *keep in –*, in Ordnung halten, beaufsichtigen; *put in –*, in Ordnung bringen, ordnen; *take in –*, der Reihe nach nehmen; *in – that*, damit; *in – to . . .*, um zu . . .; *love of –*, die Ordnungsliebe; *citation in –s*, besondere Erwähnung (*Mil.*); *disobedience of –s*, der Ungehorsam; *on –*, bestellt, in Bestellung; *on the –(s) of*, auf Befehl (von); *out of –*, in Unordnung, außer der Reihenfolge; unzulässig (*Parl.*); gestört, angegriffen (*Med.*), defekt (*Tech.*); *per –*, laut Bestellung (*C.L.*); *till further –s*, bis auf weitere Befehle; *to –*, (wie) auf Befehl; auf Bestellung, an Order (*C.L.*); *call to –*, der Ordnungsruf; *he was called to –*, er wurde zur Ordnung gerufen; *make to –*, nach Maß *or* auf Bestellung herstellen *or* anfertigen; *rise to (a point of) –*, zur Geschäftsordnung sprechen, beantragen daß zur Geschäftsordnung gesprochen wird; *be under –s*, Befehl haben. **--book,** *s.* das Bestellungsbuch, Kommissionsbuch (*C.L.*). **--form,** *s.* der Bestellzettel, Bestellschein. **-ing,** *s.* die Anordnung, Einrichtung. **-less,** *adj.* ohne Ordnung. **-liness,** *s.* die Regelmäßigkeit, Ordnung; Ordnungsliebe, Ordentlichkeit. **-ly,** 1. *adj.* regelmäßig, ordnungsgemäß; methodisch, geregelt, wohlgeordnet, ordentlich; ruhig, gesittet, ordnungsliebend (*of persons*); diensttuend, Ordonanz– (*Mil.*); *-ly officer*, der Offizier vom Dienst, Ordonanzoffizier. 2. *s.* die Ordonanz; der (Offiziers)Bursche; *hospital* or *medical -ly*, der Krankenwärter, Lazarettgehilfe (*Mil.*). **-ly-book,** *s.* das Parolebuch. **-ly-room,** *s.* das Geschäftszimmer, die Schreibstube, Dienststube (*Mil.*); *-ly-room sergeant*, der (Bataillons)Schreiber. **--paper,** *s.* das Sitzungsprogramm, Programm der Tagesordnung.

[1]**ordinal** ['ɔ:dınəl], 1. *adj.* Ordnungs–, Ordinal–; *– number*, die Ordnungszahl. 2. *s.* die Ordnungszahl.

[2]**ordin-al** ['ɔ:dınəl], *s.* das Ritual (für die Ordinierung) (*Eccl.*). **-ance** [–əns], *s.* die Verordnung; festgesetzter Brauch, der Ritus (*Eccl.*). **-and** [–ənd], *s.* zu ordinierende(r) Geistliche(r), *m.* **-ation** [–'neıʃən], *s.* die Ordination, Priesterweihe.

ordinary ['ɔ:dınərı], 1. *adj.* gewöhnlich, üblich, gebräuchlich, alltäglich, regelmäßig, normal, Durchschnitts–; festangestellt, ordentlich; *– debts*, Buchschulden (*pl.*); *judge –*, festangestellter Richter; *– seaman*, der Leichtmatrose; *– share*, die Stammaktie. 2. *s.* das Gewöhnliche *or* Übliche; (*archaic*) gemeinsame Tafel, fester Mittagstisch; das Speisehaus; feste Ordnung, herkömmlicher Brauch (*Eccl.*); der (Erz)Bischof; ordentlicher Richter (*Law*); *in –*, festangestellt, Leib–, Hof–; *chaplain in – to the King*, der Hauskaplan *or* Hofkaplan des Königs; *physician in –*, der Leibarzt, Hausarzt; *s.th. out of the –*, etwas Außerordentliches *or* Außergewöhnliches.

ordinate ['ɔ:dıneıt], *s.* die Ordinate (*Geom.*).

ordination, *see* **ordin-ation.**

ordnance ['ɔ:dnəns], *s.* (*only sing.*) schweres Geschütz; *Army – Corps*, das Zeugkorps; *Army – Department*, die Feldzeugmeisterei; *Director-General of the –*, der Generalfeldzeugmeister; *piece of –*, das Geschütz. **--depot,** *s.* das Heeresgerätlager. **--map,** *s.* die Generalstabskarte, das Meßtischblatt. **--survey,** *s.* amtliche Landesvermessung. **--survey map,** *s. see* **--map.**

ordure ['ɔ:djuə], *s.* der Unrat, Kot; (*fig.*) Schmutz.

ore [ɔ:], *s.* das Erz; (*Poet.*) Metall.

organ ['ɔ:gən], *s.* das Organ (*also Anat. & fig.*), Werkzeug (*also fig.*); (menschliche) Stimme; die Orgel (*Mus.*); (*fig.*) der Träger, das Sprachrohr, die Zeitung; *American –*, das Harmonium; *sense –*, das Sinnesorgan; *– of public opinion*, der Träger der öffentlichen Meinung. **--builder,** *s.* der Orgelbauer. **--grinder,** *s.* der Leierkastenmann. **-ic** [–'gænık], *adj.* organisch; (*fig.*) zusammenhängend, organisiert, gesetzmäßig, wesenhaft; *-ic chemistry*, organische Chemie. **-ism** ['ɔ:gənızm], *s.* der Organismus (*also fig.*). **-ist** [–ıst], *s.* der Organist. **-ization** [–ı'zeıʃən], *s.* die Organisierung, Organisation, Einrichtung, Ordnung, Gliederung, Gestaltung, Bildung; der Bau, Organismus, das Gefüge; die Körperschaft. **-izational** [–ı'zeıʃənl], *adj.* organisatorisch. **-ize** ['ɔ:gənaız], 1. *v.a.* organisieren, gliedern, einrichten, veranstalten, arrangieren. 2. *v.n.* sich organisieren. **-izer,** *s.* der Organisator. **--loft,** *s.* das *or* der Orgelchor. **-on** ['ɔ:gənən], *s.* das Werkzeug zur Erkenntnis der Wahrheit (*Phil.*). **--recital,** das Orgelkonzert. **--screen,** *s.* das Orgelpostament. **--stop,** *s.* das Orgelregister.

organdie [ɔ:'gændı], *s.* das Organdin.

organzine ['ɔ:gənzı:n], *s.* das Organsin.

orgasm ['ɔ:gæzm], *s.* höchste Wollust; (*fig.*) höchste Wallung.

org-iastic [ɔ:dʒı'æstık], *adj.* zügellos, schwelgend. **-y** ['ɔ:dʒı], *s.* die Orgie, Schwelgerei, Ausschweifung; das Fest.

oriel ['ɔ:rıəl], *s.* der Erker.

orient ['ɔ:rıənt], 1. *adj.* (*poet.*) aufgehend; glänzend. 2. *s.* das Morgenland, der Orient; (*Poet.*) Osten, Morgen. 3. *v.a.* orientieren, orten, die Lage *or* Richtung bestimmen (*with Gen.*); osten (*a church*); (*fig.*) informieren. **-al** [–'ɛntəl], 1. *adj.* östlich, morgenländisch; *-al scholar*, see **-alist.** 2. *s.* der Orientale. **-alist** [–'ɛntəlıst], *s.* der Orientalist. **-ate** [–eıt], *v.a. see* **–** 3. **-ation** [–'teıʃən], *s.* die Orientierung, Ortung; Richtung, Anlage; Ostung (*of a church*); der Orientierungssinn.

orifice ['ɔrıfıs], *s.* die Mündung, Öffnung.

oriflamme ['ɔrıflæm], *s.* die Fahne; (*fig.*) das Wahrzeichen, Fanal.

origin ['ɔrıdʒın], *s.* der Ursprung, die Quelle; der Anfang; die Entstehung, Herkunft, Provenienz (*C.L.*); *– of a force*, der Angriffspunkt einer Kraft. **-al** [ə'rıdʒınəl], 1. *adj.* ursprünglich, Ur–, original, Original–, originell, neuartig, einzigartig; erfinderisch, schöpferisch; unabhängig; *-al cause*, die Grundursache; *-al inhabitants*, Ureinwohner (*pl.*); *-al position*, die Ausgangsstellung; *-al sin*, die Erbsünde; *-al state*, der Anfangszustand; *-al thinker*, selbständiger, unabhängiger *or* schöpferischer Denker. 2. *s.* das Original (*also of persons*), Urbild, die Urschrift, Urform, der Urtext, Urtypus (*Bot., Zool.*); die Vorlage. **-ality** [ərıdʒı'nælıtı], *s.* die Ursprünglichkeit, Ureigenheit, Eigenart, Echtheit, Originalität, Selbständigkeit. **-ate** [ə'rıdʒıneıt], 1. *v.a.* hervorbringen, ins Leben rufen, verursachen. 2. *v.n.* entstehen (*in*, in *or* (*fig.*) aus; *with*, bei *or* durch (*a p.*)), seinen Ursprung *or* seine Ursache haben (*in*, in), herstammen, entspringen (*in*, aus), ausgehen (*with*, von (*a p.*)), beginnen (*with*, bei (*a p.*)). **-ally** [ə'rıdʒınəlı], *adv.* ursprünglich, anfangs. **-ation** [ə'rıdʒı'neıʃən], *s.* die Hervorbringung, Entstehung; Abstammung, der Ursprung. **-ative** [ə'rıdʒınətıv], *adj.* schöpferisch. **-ator** [ə'rıdʒıneıtə], *s.* der Urheber, Schöpfer, Gründer, Beginner.

oriole ['ɔ:rıoul], *s.* der Pirol, die Golddrossel (*Orn.*) der Stärling (*Amer.*).

orison ['ɔrızən], *s.* (*Poet.*) das Gebet.

orlop ['ɔ:ləp], *s.* das Orlopdeck (*Naut.*).

ormolu ['ɔ:məlu:], *s.* das Malergold, Muschelgold, die Goldbronze.

ornament ['ɔ:nəmənt], 1. *s.* der Schmuck, Putz, die Verzierung, der Zierrat (*Art, Arch.*); (*fig.*) die Zierde, Zier (*of persons*) (*to*, für); *pl.* der Schmuck, Schmucksachen (*pl.*); *by way of –*, zur Verzierung. 2. *v.a.* verzieren, schmücken. **-al** [–'mɛntəl], *adj.* zierend, Zier–, schmückend, dekorativ; *be -al*, zieren, verschönern, zur Zierde gereichen. **-ation** [–'teıʃən], *s.* die Ornamentierung, Verzierung, Ausschmückung.

ornate [ɔ:'neıt], *adj.* geziert, geschmückt (*of style, etc.*).

ornitho-logical [ɔ:nıθə'lɔdʒıkl], *adj.* ornithologisch. **-logist** [–'θɔlədʒıst], *s.* der Ornitholog(e). **-logy** [–'θɔlədʒı], *s.* die Vogelkunde, Ornithologie.

-mancy [-ˈnɪθəmænsɪ], *s.* die Wahrsagung aus dem Flug der Vögel. **-pter** [-ˈθɔptə], *s.* der Schlagflügler (*Av.*). **-rhyncus** [-θoˈrɪŋkəs], *s.* das Schnabeltier (*Zool.*).

oro-graphy [əˈrɔgrəfɪ], *s.* die Gebirgsbeschreibung. **-logy** [əˈrɔlədʒɪ], *s.* die Gebirgskunde, Gebirgslehre.

orotund [ˈɔ:rɔtʌnd], *adj.* klangvoll, volltönend (*of the voice*), bombastisch, schwülstig (*of style*). **-ity** [-ˈtʌndɪtɪ], *s.* der Bombast.

orphan [ˈɔ:fən], 1. *s.* die Waise, das Waisenkind. 2. *adj.* verwaist; – *child*, das Waisenkind. 3. *v.a.* (*usually pass.*); *be -ed*, Waise werden, verwaisen. **-age** [-ɪdʒ], *s.* das Waisenhaus; die Verwaistheit, das Verwaistsein.

orphrey [ˈɔ:frɪ], *s.* die Goldverbrämung (*Eccl.*).

orpiment [ˈɔ:pɪmənt], *s.* das Rauschgelb.

orpine [ˈɔ:pɪn], *s.* die Fetthenne, das Johanniskraut (*Bot.*).

orrery [ˈɔrərɪ], *s.* das Planetarium.

orris [ˈɔrɪs], *s.* die Schwertlilie; – *root*, die Veilchenwurzel.

ortho-chromatic [ɔ:θoʊkrəˈmætɪk], *adj.* orthochromatisch, tonrichtig wiedergebend, farbenempfindlich (*Phot.*). **-clase** [ˈɔ:θoʊkleɪz], *n.* der Orthoklas (*Geol.*). **-dox** [ˈɔ:θədɔks], *adj.* rechtgläubig, strenggläubig, orthodox; (*fig.*) üblich, richtig, landläufig, anerkannt; *-dox Church*, griechisch-katholische Kirche. **-doxy** [-dɔksɪ], *s.* die Rechtgläubigkeit, Strenggläubigkeit, Orthodoxie. **-epist** [ɔ:ˈθoʊəpɪst], *s.* der Aussprachelehrer. **-epy** [-əpɪ], *s.* richtige Aussprache. **-gonal** [ɔ:ˈθɔgənəl], *adj.* rechtwinklig. **-graphic(al)** [ɔ:θoʊˈgræfɪk], *adj.* orthographisch; senkrecht (*Surv.*). **-graphy** [ɔ:ˈθɔgrəfɪ], *s.* die Rechtschreibung. **-paedic** [ɔ:θəˈpɪ:dɪk], *adj.* orthopädisch. **-paedist,** *s.* der Orthopäde. **-paedy** [ˈɔ:θəpɪ:dɪ], *s.* die Orthopädie. **-ptera** [ɔ:ˈθɔptərə], *pl.* Geradflügler (*Ent.*).

ortolan [ˈɔ:tələn], *s.* die Fettammer, der Ortolan (*Orn.*).

orts [ɔ:ts], *pl.* der Abfall, Überreste (*pl.*).

oscill-ate [ˈɔsɪleɪt], 1. *v.n.* schwingen, pendeln, oszillieren; (*fig.*) schwanken. 2. *v.a.* ins Schwingen bringen. **-ating,** *adj.* Schwing-, Schwingungs-, Pendel-; *-ating circuit*, der Schwingungskreis. **-ation** [-ˈleɪʃən], *s.* die Schwingung; (*fig.*) Schwankung, das Schwanken; *axis of -ation*, die Schwingungsachse; *damped -ation*, gedämpfte Welle; *natural -ation*, die Eigenschwingung. **-ator** [-leɪtə], *s.* der Oszillator, Schwinger (*Rad.*). **-atory** [əˈsɪlətərɪ], *adj.* schwingend, Schwingungs-, oszillierend. **-ograph** [əˈsɪləgræf], *s.* der Oszillograph.

oscula-r [ˈɔskjʊlə], *adj.* Kuß-, küssend, sich berührend. **-te** [-leɪt], 1. *v.n.* sich eng berühren (*Geom.*). 2. *v.a.* küssen; *-ting circle*, der Berührungskreis. **-tion** [-ˈleɪʃən], *s.* das Küssen, der Kuß; die Berührung höherer Ordnung (*Geom.*). **-tory** [-lətərɪ], *adj.* Kuß-.

osier [ˈoʊzɪə], *s.* die Korbweide. **--bed,** *s.* die Weidenpflanzung.

osmi-c [ˈɔzmɪk], *adj.* Osmium-. **-um,** *s.* das Osmium (*Chem.*).

osmosis [ɔzˈmoʊsɪs], *s.* die Osmose.

osmund [ˈɔzmənd], *s.* das Rispenfarn (*Bot.*).

osprey [ˈɔsprɪ], *s.* der Fischadler (*Orn.*); Federschmuck, Reiherfederbusch.

oss-eous [ˈɔsɪəs], *adj.* knöchern, Knochen-. **-icle** [-ɪkl], *s.* das Knöchelchen. **-ification** [-fɪˈkeɪʃən], *s.* die Verknöcherung. **-ify** [ˈɔsɪfaɪ], 1. *v.a.* verknöchern (*also fig.*); (*fig.*) härten. 2. *v.n.* verknöchern; (*fig.*) sich erhärten, erstarren. **-uary** [-jʊərɪ], *s.* das Beinhaus, der Karner.

ossifrage [ˈɔsɪfrɪdʒ], *s. see* **osprey.**

osten-sible [ɔsˈtɛnsɪbl], *adj.* vorgeblich, angeblich, anscheinend, scheinbar. **-sive** [-sɪv], *adj.* vorgeblich, anschaulich darstellend. **-sory** [-ˈtɛnsərɪ], *s.* die Monstranz. **-tation** [-ˈteɪʃən], *s.* die Schaustellung; Prahlerei, das Gepränge. **-tatious** [-ˈteɪʃəs], *adj.* prangend, prunkhaft, prahlend. **-tatiousness** [-ˈteɪʃəsnɪs], *s.* die Prahlerei, Großtuerei.

osteo-blast [ˈɔstɪəblæst], *s.* der Knochenbildner. **-logy** [-ˈɔlədʒɪ], *s.* die Knochenlehre, Knochenkunde. **-ma** [-ˈoʊmə], *s.* die Knochengeschwulst, das Osteom. **-malacia** [-məˈleɪʃɪə], *s.* die Knochenerweichung. **-path** [ˈɔstɪəpæθ], *s.* Knochenheilkundige(r), *m.*

ostler [ˈɔslə], *s.* der Stallknecht.

ostrac-ism [ˈɔstrəsɪzm], *s.* das Scherbengericht; (*fig.*) die Verbannung, Ächtung. **-ize** [- aɪz], *v.a.* verbannen, ächten, verfemen.

ostrich [ˈɔstrɪtʃ], *s.* der Strauß. **--egg,** *s.* das Straußenei. **- policy,** *s.* die Vogelstraußpolitik.

other [ˈʌðə], 1. *adj.* andere(r, s) (*than*, als), verschieden (*than*, von), sonstig, übrig, weiter. (*a*) (*with nouns*) *the – day*, vor einigen Tagen, vor einiger Zeit, neulich; *every – day*, einen Tag um den andern, alle zwei Tage, jeden zweiten Tag; *on the – hand*, andererseits, hingegen; *the – morning*, neulich morgens. (*b*) (with *than*) *far – than*, ganz anders als, ganz verschieden von; *not – than*, nicht anders als, nur; *any p. – than yourself*, jeder außer dir. 2. *pron. & s.* der, die *or* das andere; *each –*, einander; *do no –*, nichts anderes tun; *no – than*, kein anderer als; *one after the –*, einer nach dem anderen; *one or – of them*, der eine oder der andere von ihnen; *somebody or –*, irgend jemand; *some day or –*, irgendeinmal; *some way or –*, auf irgendeine Weise. 3. *adv.* anders (*than*, als). **-s** [-z], *pl.* andere; *the four –s*, die vier anderen, die anderen Vier; *some –s*, noch ein paar *or* einige. **-wise** [-waɪz], 1. *adv.* anders, andernfalls, anderweitig, verschieden. 2. *conj.* wenn nicht, sonst; *not -wise than*, nicht anders als, genau so wie; *rather than -wise*, am liebsten, viel lieber; *rather pleased than -wise*, eher zufrieden als nicht; *-wise engaged*, anderes vorhaben, anderweitig beschäftigt. **--worldliness,** *s.* die Jenseitigkeit. **--worldly,** *adj.* jenseitig.

otios-e [oʊʃɪˈoʊs], *adj.* unnütz, überflüssig, zwecklos; (*rare*) müßig. **-ity** [-ˈɔsɪtɪ], *s.* die Zwecklosigkeit; Muße, der Müßiggang.

oto-logy [oˈtɔlədʒɪ], *s.* die Ohrenheilkunde. **-scope,** *s.* der Ohrenspiegel.

otter [ˈɔtə], *s.* die Otter; der Otterpelz; das Minenräumgerät (*Nav.*). **--dog,** *s.*, **--hound,** *s.* der Otterhund.

ottoman [ˈɔtəmən], *s.* der Ottomane, Türke; die Ottomane, das Sofa, der Liegestuhl.

oubliette [u:blɪˈɛt], *s.* das Verlies.

[1]**ought** [ɔ:t], *v.aux.* (*only pres. & imp.*) sollte; *I – to go*, ich sollte (eigentlich) gehen; *it – to be done*, es sollte geschehen; *he – to have gone*, er hätte gehen sollen; *you – to know*, du solltest *or* müßtest wissen; *if she had done as she –*, hätte sie gehandelt wie sie sollte.

[2]**ought** [ɔ:t], *s.* (*coll.*) die Null.

[1]**ounce** [aʊns], *s.* die Unze (= 28½ g; *gold, silver, etc.* = 31 g); *by the –*, nach (dem) Gewicht; *half an –*, ein Lot.

[2]**ounce** [aʊns], *s.* der Irbis (*panthera uncia*); (*archaic*) der Luchs.

our [ˈaʊə], *poss. adj. & pron.* unser(e); – *Father*, das Vaterunser; *in the year of – Lord*, im Jahre des Herrn. **-s** [-z], *poss. pron.* unser(e), der, die *or* das unsrige *or* unsere; *a friend of -s*, ein Freund von uns, einer von unseren Freunden; *in this world of -s*, in dieser unserer Welt; *become -s*, unser werden; *that's -s*, das gehört uns. **-self** [-ˈsɛlf], *emph. pron.*; *we -self*, wir selbst (*editorial language*); Wir Höchstselbst (*of a king*). **-selves** [-ˈsɛlvz], 1. *emph. pron. pl.* wir selbst (*Nom.*), uns selbst (*Dat. & Acc.*); *of -selves*, aus unserm eigenen Antriebe, von selbst. 2. *refl. pron.* (*Acc. & Dat.*) uns.

ousel [u:zl], *s. see* **ouzel.**

oust [aʊst], *v.a.* ausstoßen, vertreiben, entfernen (*from*, aus); entheben, entsetzen (*from office*, des Amtes); berauben (*a p.* (*Dat.*), *of a th.* (*Gen.*)) (*Law*); (*fig.*) ersetzen, verdrängen.

out [aʊt], **1.** *adv.* (*a*) (*movement*) hinaus, hinaus-, heraus, heraus-; (*fig.*) aus, entgegen; (*b*) (*position*) (usually with *to be*) draußen; nicht zu Hause, ausgegangen, nicht daheim, fort, verreist; außer dem Hause, im Freien; auf See (*Naut.*); im Felde (*Mil.*); in Blüte; verrenkt; nicht mehr im Dienst *or* Ministerium *or* Amt *or* am Ruder *or* Spiel; im Irrtum; aus, erloschen; völlig erschöpft, verbraucht, kampfunfähig (*Box.*); aus der Mode, vorbei, vorüber, vergangen, abgelaufen, (bis) **zu** Ende;

hörbar, laut; offen, frei, ohne Zurückhaltung, enthüllt, entdeckt, offenbar; gesellschaftsfähig, ballfähig (*of a girl*). **(a)** (*with nouns*) *evening* –, der Ausgehabend (*of servants*); *the best thing* –, das Beste in der Welt; *voyage* –, die Ausreise, Hinreise; *way* –, der Ausgang, (*fig.*) Ausweg; *some way* –, in einiger Entfernung vom Ufer. **(b)** (*with verbs*) *be* (*quite*) –, auf dem Holzwege sein, sich im Irrtum befinden; *blue is quite* –, blau ist völlig aus der Mode; *the calculation is* –, die Rechnung stimmt nicht; *be – in one's calculations*, sich in der Rechnung irren; *the batsman is* –, der Schläger ist aus dem Spiel; *the book is just* –, das Buch ist eben erschienen; *the fire is* –, das Feuer ist aus; *before many days were* –, ehe viele Tage verstrichen waren; *my hand is* –, ich bin aus der Übung; – *of the business*, aus dem Geschäfte ausgetreten; – *of business*, nicht mehr geschäftstätig; *be £10* –, um £10 ärmer sein, £10 eingebüßt haben; *the secret is* –, das Geheimnis ist entdeckt; *the tide is* –, es ist Ebbe; *his time is* –, seine Lehrzeit ist vorüber; *break* –, ausbrechen; *come* –, herauskommen; (*fig.*) enthüllt werden; in die Gesellschaft eingeführt werden, ballfähig werden (*of a young girl*); *cry* –, laut ausrufen; *find* –, entdecken, ausfindig machen; *go – for a walk*, einen Spaziergang machen; *hear a p.* –, einen ganz anhören; (*coll.*) *have it – with s.o.*, sich mit einem gründlich auseinandersetzen; *hold* –, entgegenhalten; (*fig.*) standhalten; *keep* –, nicht einlassen; sich nicht einmischen; *look* –, hinaussehen, heraussehen; aufpassen; *read* –, vorlesen; laut lesen; *ring* –, laut tönen; *see a p.* –, einen hinausbegleiten; *see a th.* –, etwas bis zu Ende mitmachen; *speak – !* heraus damit! *stretch* –, ausstrecken; *tire* –, ganz ermüden; *turn a p.* –, einem die Tür weisen; *blood will* –, Blut setzt sich durch, Blut bricht sich Bahn; *murder will* –, die Sonne bringt es an den Tag. **(c)** (*with prepositions*) *be – at elbows*, Löcher in den Ärmeln haben, (*fig.*) in schlechten Verhältnissen leben; *be* (*all*) *–for*, auf der Suche *or* verlangend sein nach, bedacht *or* versessen sein auf, hinter her sein, trachten nach, abzielen auf; – *in revolt*, in offener Empörung; – *of*, aus, aus . . . heraus; von außerhalb; außer, nicht in; nicht gemäß, unrichtig; abstammend von, gezüchtet aus; *by X – of Y*, dessen Vater X, dessen Mutter Y ist (*horses, dogs, etc.*); (*of* with nouns) – *of breath*, atemlos, außer Atem; – *of date*, veraltet; – *of doors*, im Freien; – *of fear*, aus Furcht; – *of drawing*, falsch gezeichnet; – *of fashion*, aus der Mode; – *of focus*, unscharf; – *of the frying-pan into the fire*, aus dem Regen in die Traufe; – *of hand*, sofort, unverzüglich, auf der Stelle; außer Zucht, unbeherrscht; *get – of hand*, über die Stränge schlagen; – *of humour*, schlecht gelaunt; – *of joint*, aus den Fugen; – *of love*, aus Liebe; *be – of love with*, nicht mehr leiden mögen; – *of money*, nicht bei Kasse; – *of order*, außer der Reihenfolge, in Unordnung; unzulässig (*Parl., etc.*); gestört (*Med.*); defekt (*Tech.*); – *of play*, aus dem Spiel, tot (*Footb.*); – *of pocket*, nicht bei Kasse; *be – of pocket*, ausgeben, auslegen, daraufzahlen; – *of practice*, außer Übung; – *of print*, vergriffen; – *of all proportion*, in keinem Verhältnis; – *of the question*, unzweifelhaft, fraglos, ohne Frage; *be – of the running*, nicht mehr in Frage kommen; – *of sight*, außer Sicht; (*Prov.*) – *of sight*, – *of mind*, aus den Augen, aus dem Sinn; (*coll.*) *be – of sorts*, unpäßlich *or* nicht recht auf dem Damm sein; – *of temper*, schlecht gelaunt; *nine – of ten*, neun von zehn; – *of town*, verreist; *ten miles – of the town*, zehn Meilen außerhalb der Stadt; – *of training*, außer Übung; – *of tune*, verstimmt (*also fig.*); *play – of tune*, unrein spielen; – *of the way*, abseits, abgelegen; abwegig, ungewöhnlich; *be – of the way*, aus dem Wege sein, nicht auf dem Wege liegen; *get – of the way*, aus dem Weg gehen; *go – of one's way*, sich besondere Mühe geben, keine Mühe scheuen; *keep – of the way*, sich abseits halten; *put – of the way*, aus dem Wege schaffen (*a th.*), um die Ecke bringen (*a p.*); *take a p. – of his way*, einen einen Umweg machen lassen; – *of the wood*, überm Berg; – *of work*, arbeitslos; (*of* with verb) *be – of* . . ., . . . nicht haben, ohne . . . sein, entbehren, nicht vorrätig haben; *cheat – of*, betrügen *or* prellen um; *feel – of it*, sich (wie) verdrängt *or* ausgeschlossen fühlen; *manufacture – of*, herstellen *or* verfertigen aus *or* von; *throw – of the window*, zum Fenster hinaus werfen; *be – to do*, darauf ausgehen zu; – *upon him!* pfui über ihn! **(d)** (*with adverbs*) – *and about*, auf den Beinen; – *and away*, bei weitem; – *and* –, (*pred.*) ganz und gar, durch und durch; (*attrib.*) vollkommen, völlig, ausgesprochen, gründlich; – *there*, da draußen. **2.** *s.* die Auslassung (*Typ.*); (*coll.*) der Ausweg, die Entschuldigung; *pl.* Oppositionsmitglieder (*Parl.*); *the ins and –s*, alle Einzelheiten, Winkelzüge; Windungen (*of a road, etc.*). **3.** *adj.* auswärtig. **–-and-outer,** *s.* (*sl.*) ein Hauptkerl, Mordskerl; (*sl.*) eine famose Sache. **–-of-date,** *adj.* unzeitgemäß, veraltet, altmodisch. **–-of-doors,** *adv.* außer dem Hause, draußen, im Freien; *–-of-doors relief*, die Hauspflege. **–-of-fashion,** *adj.* veraltet, aus der Mode (gekommen). **–-of-pocket,** *adj.*; *–-of-pocket expenses*, Barauslagen (*pl.*). **–-of-the-way,** *adj.* abgelegen, entlegen; ungewöhnlich; seltsam, wunderlich, kurios. **–'balance,** *v.a.* überwiegen, übertreffen. **–'bid,** *ir.v.a.* überbieten. **'–board,** *adj.* Außenbord–. **'–-'brave,** *v.a.* Trotz bieten (*Dat.*); an Glanz *or* Tapferkeit übertreffen. **'–break,** *s.* der Ausbruch. **'–building,** *s.* das Nebengebäude. **'–burst,** *s.* der Ausbruch, das Hervorbrechen. **'–cast,** 1. *adj.* ausgestoßen, verstoßen. 2. *s.* Ausgestoßene(r), *m.*; der Ausschuß (*Tech.*). **–'class,** *v.a.* schlagen, übertreffen. **'–come,** *s.* das Ergebnis, die Folge; *be the –come of*, entspringen aus. **'–crop,** 1. *s.* das Zutageliegen; (*fig.*) Zutagetreten; Zutageliegende(r), *m.* 2. *v.n.* zutagetreten. **'–cry,** *s.* das Geschrei; der Aufschrei, Entrüstungsschrei. **–-'distance,** *v.a.* weit überholen, hinter sich (*Dat.*) zurücklassen; (*fig.*) überflügeln. **–'do,** *ir.v.a.* es zuvortun (*Dat.*), übertreffen. **'–door,** *adj.* im Freien, außer dem Hause; *–door department*, der Ausschank über die Gasse; *–door dress*, der Ausgehanzug; *–door relief*, die Unterstützung der nicht im Armenhause wohnenden Armen; *–door sports*, Spiele im Freien; *–door temperature*, die Außentemperatur; *–door work*, die Arbeit außer dem Hause. **–'doors,** *adv.* draußen, im Freien. **'–er,** *adj.* äußere(r, s), Außen–; *–er man*, äußerer Mensch; *–er wall*, die Umfassungsmauer; *–er world*, die Außenwelt. **'–ermost,** *adj.* äußerst. **–'face,** *v.a.* aus der Fassung bringen; Trotz bieten (*Dat.*). **'–fall,** *s.* der Ausfluß, Abfluß, Ableitungskanal (*Hydr.*). **'–field,** *s.* das Außenfeld (*Crick.*); (*fig.*) unbestimmtes Gebiet. **'–fielder,** *s.* der Spieler in Außenfeld (*Crick.*). **'–fit,** 1. *s.* die Ausrüstung, Ausstattung; (*sl.*) Belegschaft, Mannschaft. 2. *v.a.* ausrüsten, ausstatten. **'–fitter,** *s.* der Ausrüstungslieferant, Inhaber eines Konfektionsgeschäftes, Händler. **–'flank,** *v.a.* überflügeln, umgehen; *–flanking movement*, die Umgehung. **'–flow,** *s.* der Ausfluß. **–go,** 1. [aʊt'goʊ], *v.a.* schneller gehen als (*Nom.*); zuvorkommen (*Dat.*); (*fig.*) übertreffen, übertreffen, überbieten (*Acc.*). 2. ['aʊtgoʊ], *s.* die Ausgabe. **'–going,** 1. *adj.* abgehend (*post*), ausziehend (*tenant*), abtretend (*representative*). 2. *s.* das Ausgehen; *pl.* die Auslagen, Ausgaben. **–'grow,** *ir.v.a.* schneller wachsen als, über den Kopf wachsen (*a p.*), herauswachsen aus, zu groß werden für (*garments*); entwachsen (*Dat.*) (*one's toys, etc.*); verwachsen (*a scar, etc.*); *–grow one's strength*, zu schnell wachsen. **'–growth,** *s.* der Auswuchs; das Ergebnis, Nebenprodukt. **–-'herod,** *v.a.* übertreffen. **'–house,** *s.* das Nebengebäude, der Anbau, Schuppen. **'–ing,** *s.* der Ausflug, die Partie. **–'landish,** *adj.* fremdartig, seltsam; abgelegen; rückständig. **–'last,** *v.a.* überdauern, überleben. **'–law,** 1. *s.* Geächtete(r), *m.*, Vogelfreie(r), *m.* 2. *v.a.* ächten, für vogelfrei erklären. **'–lawry,** *s.* die Acht, Ächtung, Verfemung. **'–lay,** *s.* die Auslage, Ausgabe; Auslagen, Ausgaben (*pl.*) (*on*, für). **'–let,** *s.* der Ausgang, Ausfluß, Abfluß, Ablaß, Auslaß (*also fig.*); Ausguß, Auslauf, Abzug, die Öffnung; das Absatzgebiet, der Absatzmarkt (*C.L.*); (*fig.*) Ausweg; *find an –let for s.th.*, einer S. (*Dat.*) Luft machen *or* Ausdruck geben. **'–line,** 1. *s.* der Umriß, die Umrißlinie, Kontur;

(*fig.*) der Entwurf, Abriß, die Skizze; *pl.* Hauptlinien, Hauptzüge (*pl.*). 2. *v.a.* umreißen, skizzieren, im Umriß darstellen. **'–lined,** *adj.* scharf abgehoben. **–'live,** *v.a.* überleben, überdauern. **'–look,** *s.* die Aussicht; (*fig.*) der Ausblick; Ausguck, die Warte; der Standpunkt, die Auffassung, Anschauungsweise, Weltanschauung, Einstellung. **'–lying,** *adj.* außenliegend, abseitsliegend, abgelegen, entlegen, Außen–, auswärtig. **–ma'nœuvre,** *v.a.* im Manövrieren überlegen sein (*Dat.*); überlisten. **–'march,** *v.a.* schneller marschieren als. **–'match,** *v.a.* übertreffen, überflügeln. **–'mode,** *v.a.* (*usually pass.*) aus der Mode bringen. **'–most,** *adj.* äußerst. **–'number,** *v.a.* an Zahl übertreffen, zahlenmäßig überlegen sein (*Dat.*), die Übermacht haben. **–'pace,** *v.a.* schneller vorwärtskommen als (*also fig.*). **'––patient,** *s.* der ambulant behandelte Patient; *––patient's department*, die Poliklinik, Ambulanz; *––patient treatment*, ambulante Behandlung. **'–post,** *s.* der Vorposten. **'–pouring,** *s.* das Ausströmen, der Erguß (*also fig.*), Ausfluß. **'–put,** *s.* die Produktion, Arbeitsleistung; Ausbeute, der Ertrag, das Rendement; das Förderquantum (*Min.*); *actual –put*, die Nutzleistung; *normal –put*, die Nennleistung; *–put valve*, die Endverstärkerröhre (*Rad.*); *–put voltage*, die Ausgangsspannung (*Rad.*). **'–rage,** 1. *v.a.* schmählich behandeln, mißhandeln; Gewalt antun (*Dat.*), schänden; beleidigen. 2. *s.* die Gewalttätigkeit, Gewalttat, Ausschreitung, der Exzeß; grobes Vergehen (*on, gegen*), grobe Beleidigung *or* Beschimpfung (*on* (*Gen.*)). **–'rageous,** *adj.* wütend, heftig, übermäßig, zügellos; abscheulich, empörend, unerhört, schmählich, schändlich. **–'rageousness,** *s.* das Übermaß, die Zügellosigkeit; Abscheulichkeit. **–'range,** *v.a.* an Schußweite übertreffen. **–'reach,** *v.a.* übertreffen, hinausreichen über, weiter reichen als. **–'ride,** *ir.v.a.* schneller reiten als; trotzen (*Dat.*) (*of ships*). **'–rider,** *s.* der Vorreiter. **'–rigger,** *s.* der Ausleger; Luvbaum (*Naut.*); Holm, Längsträger (*Artil.*); das Auslegerboot. **–'right,** *adv.* gerade heraus, unverblümt; gänzlich, völlig; sogleich, unverwandt, auf der Stelle; *kill –right*, auf der Stelle töten; *laugh –right*, laut auflachen; *sell –right*, fest verkaufen. **–'rival,** *v.a.* übertreffen, überflügeln. **–'run,** *ir.v.a.* schneller laufen als, (im Laufen) übertreffen; (*fig.*) vorauseilen (*Dat.*). **'–runner,** *s.* der Vorläufer, Vorreiter. **'–set,** *s.* der Anfang, Beginn; *from the –set*, von Anfang an. **–'shine,** *ir.v.a.* überstrahlen. **–'side,** 1. *adj.* äußere(r, s), Außen–; außenstehend, von außen kommend; (*fig.*) fremd; äußerst (*as price*); *–side broker*, der Winkelmakler (*C.L.*); *–side diameter*, äußere Weite; *–side edge*, die Außenkante; *–side opinion*, die Ansicht der Draußenstehenden. 2. *adv.* außen; draußen; nach außen, hinaus; (*sl.*) außer, ausgenommen; *–side of*, außerhalb (*Gen.*). 3. *s.* das Äußere, die Außenseite; Oberfläche; das Äußerste; *at the* (*very*) *–side*, (aller)höchstens; *from the –side*, von außen, von der Außenseite; *on the –side of the bus*, außen auf dem Autobus; *–side right*, der Rechtsaußen (*Footb.*). 4. *prep.* außerhalb (*Gen.*), außer, jenseits. **–'sider,** *s.* Nichteingeweihte(r), *m.*, der Nichtfachmann; Außenstehende(r), *m.*, Fernstehende(r); der Außenseiter (*in races*; *also fig.*). **'–size,** *s.* große Weite (*of clothes*). **'–skirts,** *pl.* die Umgebung, das Randgebiet, äußerer Rand, die Peripherie. (*sl.*) **–'smart,** *v.a.* überlisten. **–'spoken,** *adj.* freimütig, offen. **–'spokenness,** *s.* die Offenheit, Freimut. **'–standing,** *adj.* hervorstechend, hervorragend; offenstehend, ausstehend; unausgeglichen; *–standing debts*, Außenstände (*C.L.*); *–standing event*, das Hauptereignis. **–'stay,** *v.a.* länger bleiben als (*Nom.*); *–stay one's welcome*, länger bleiben als dem Wirte lieb ist. **'–stretch,** *v.a.* ausstrecken. **–'strip,** *v.a.* überholen; (*fig.*) übertreffen. **–'vote,** *v.a.* überstimmen. **'–ward,** 1. *adj.* äußere(r, s), Außen–, äußerlich; *–ward passage*, die Hinreise. 2. *adv.* nach auswärts, nach außen; *–ward-bound*, nach auswärts fahrend, auf der Hinreise. **'–wardly,** *adv.* (nach) außen, äußerlich, nach außen hin. **'–wards,** *adv. see* **–ward** 2. **–'weigh,** *v.a.* aufwiegen, überwiegen, übertreffen. **–'wit,** *v.a.* überlisten. **–work,** 1. ['ɑutwə:k], *s.* das Außenwerk, Bollwerk (*Fort.*); 2. [ɑut'wə:k], *v.a.* länger *or* mehr arbeiten als. **–'worn,** *adj.* abgenutzt, verbraucht; abgetragen (*as clothes*); veraltet (*as beliefs*).

ouzel ['u:zl], *s.* die Ringamsel; Wasseramsel (*Orn.*).

oval ['ouvl], 1. *adj.* oval, eirund. 2. *s.* das Oval.

ovar–ian [o'vɛ:əriən], *adj.* Eierstock–. **–y** ['ouvəri], *s.* der Eierstock (*Anat.*); der Fruchtknoten (*Bot.*).

ovate ['ouveit], *adj.* eirund (*Bot.*).

ovation [o'veiʃən], *s.* die Huldigung, Ehrenbezeigung, Ovation.

oven ['ʌvən], *s.* der Backofen; Ofen (*Tech.*). **––bird,** *s.* der Töpfervogel.

over ['ouvə], **1.** *adv.* über, über–, über . . . hin, herüber, hinüber, auf die andere Seite, über . . . hinaus; drüben, auf der anderen Seite, darüber, darüber . . . hin, jenseits; übrig, mehr, zuviel, allzu (*amount*); vorüber, vorbei, aus (*time*); *– and –*, einmal über das andere; *– and – again*, immer wieder; *– again*, noch einmal; *– against*, gegenüber, im Gegensatz zu; *all –*, über und über, überall, allenthalben; *be all – with*, aus, vorbei *or* vorüber sein mit; *all – and done with*, total erledigt; (*coll.*) *come all – goose-pimples*, ein kribbliges Gefühl am ganzen Körper empfinden; *fifty times –*, fünfzigmal hintereinander; *all the world –*, durch die ganze *or* auf der ganzen Welt; *ask a p. –*, einen herüberbitten; *carried –*, der Übertrag (*C.L.*); *deliver –*, ausliefern, zustellen; *fall –*, umfallen; *go – to*, übergehen zu; *have –*, übrig haben; *lean –*, sich überlehnen; *make –*, übertragen, vermachen; *read a th. –*, etwas durchlesen; *run –*, überfließen; *see –*, siehe nächste Seite, siehe umstehend; *talk a th. –*, etwas gründlich besprechen; *turn –*, umdrehen, herumdrehen. **2.** *prep.* (*position*) über; (*movement*) über, über . . . hin; (*fig.*) mehr als; *– and above what*, außer dem, was; *give this the preference – that*, diesem vor jenem den Vorzug geben. (*a*) (*with nouns*) *all – Europe*, durch ganz Europa; *from all – Europe*, aus allen Teilen Europas; *– the fire*, am Kaminfeuer; *– a glass of wine*, bei einem Glase Wein; *– our heads*, über unsere(n) Köpfe(n); (*fig.*) über unsern Verstand *or* Horizont; über unsere Köpfe hinweg; *– one's signature*, über seiner Unterschrift, unter seinem Namen, unterzeichnet von; *– the way*, gegenüber, auf der anderen Seite; *– a year*, mehr als ein Jahr. (*b*) (*with verbs*) *be – s.o.*, über einem stehen; (*coll.*) *get – s.th.*, etwas überwinden *or* überstehen; *lord* (*it*) *–*, herrschen *or* dominieren über; *mourn –*, trauern über, beklagen (*Acc.*); *show us – your house*, führen Sie uns in Ihrem Hause herum; *spread – a series of years*, auf einige Jahre verteilen. **3.** *s.* der Wechsel, Satz von sechs Würfen (*Crick.*). **––a'bundance,** *s.* der Überfluß, die Fülle (*of*, an). **––a'bundant,** *adj.* übermäßig, übertrieben. **–(-)'act,** *v.a.* & *n.* übertreiben, des Guten zuviel tun. **'–all,** 1. *adj.* Gesamt–, einschließlich allem. 2. *s.* (*often pl.*) der Schutzkittel, Arbeitsanzug, das Überkleid; (*only pl.*) Galahosen (*Mil.*). **––'anxious,** *adj.* überängstlich. **–'arch,** *v.a.* überwölben. **'–arm,** *adj.* Hand-über-Hand (*swimming*), über die Schulter (*bowling*). **–'awe,** *v.a.* einschüchtern. **–'balance,** 1. *v.a.* überwiegen; aus dem Gleichgewicht bringen, umkippen, umstoßen. 2. *v.n.* das Gleichgewicht verlieren, umkippen, überkippen. 3. *s.* das Übergewicht. **–'bear,** *ir.v.a.* überwältigen, überwinden; überwiegen; unterdrücken, niederdrücken. **–'bearance,** *s.* die Anmaßung. **–'bearing,** *adj.* herrisch, anmaßend. **–'blow,** *v.n.* zublasen (*Mus.*). **–'blown,** *adj.* verblüht, ausgeblüht. **'–board,** *adv.* über Bord (*also fig.*). **–'brim,** 1. *v.n.* überfließen (*with*, von). 2. *v.a.* fließen über. **–'build,** *ir.v.a.* überbauen, zu sehr (be)bauen. **–'burden,** *v.a.* überladen, überlasten, überbürden. **–'call,** *v.n.* überbieten (*Cards*). **–'cast,** 1. *ir.v.a.* überziehen, bedecken, bewölken, umwölken; umnähen (*Semp.*). 2. *adj.* bedeckt, bewölkt, trüb (*as sky*); überwendlich genäht (*as seam*). **–charge,** 1. [–'tʃɑ:dʒ], *v.a.* überladen, überfüllen; überfordern (*a p.*); überteuern (*a th.*). 2. ['–tʃɑ:dʒ], *s.* der Überdruck, die Überladung; Überforderung, Überteuerung (*C.L.*). **–'cloud,** *v.a.* überwölken; bewölken, trüben. **'–coat,** *s.* der Überrock,

Überzieher. **–ˈcome,** *ir.v.a.* überwinden (*obstacle*), überwältigen, übermannen, besiegen (*a p.*); *–come with rage*, von Wut hingerissen. **– –ˈconfidence,** *s.* allzu großes Selbstvertrauen, der Hang zur Überhebung, die Vermessenheit. **– –ˈconfident,** *adj.* überheblich, vermessen. **– –ˈcredulous,** *adj.* allzu leichtgläubig. **–ˈcrop,** *v.a.* zugrunde wirtschaften (*land*). **–ˈcrowd,** *v.a.* überfüllen. **–ˈcrowding,** *s.* die Überfüllung. **– –deˈvelop,** *v.a.* überentwickeln (*Phot.*). **–ˈdo,** *ir.v.a.* zu weit treiben, übertreiben; zu sehr kochen *or* braten (*meat, etc.*); *–do it*, zu weit gehen; sich überanstrengen. **–ˈdone,** *adj.* übertrieben; übergar (*Cook.*). **–dose,** 1. [ˈ–ˈdoʊs], *s.* zu starke Dosis. 2. [–ˈdoʊs], *v.a.* eine zu starke Dosis geben (*Dat.*). **ˈ–draft,** *s.* die Überziehung (*of an account*); überzogener Betrag. **–ˈdraw,** *ir.v.a.* überspannen, übertreiben; überziehen (*an account*). **– –ˈdress,** *v.a.* (sich) übertrieben putzen *or* schmücken. **–drive,** 1. [ˈ–draɪv], *s.* der Schnellgang (*Motor.*). 2. [–ˈdraɪv], *ir.v.a.* zu weit treiben, übertreiben; abhetzen, überanstrengen. **–ˈdue,** *adj.* verfallen, überfällig; *be –due*, Verspätung haben (*trains, etc.*), vermißt werden, ausgeblieben sein (*ships*). **–ˈeat,** *v.n. & r.* sich überessen. **– –ˈestimate,** 1. [–eɪt] *v.a.* überschätzen, zu hoch bewerten. 2. [–ət], *s.* zu hohe Wertung *or* Schätzung. **– –exˈcite,** *v.a.* überreizen, **– –exˈcitement,** *s.* übergroße Aufregung. **– –exˈert,** *v.a.* überanstrengen. **– –exˈpose,** *v.a.* überbelichten (*Phot.*). **ˈ–fall,** *s.* die Sturzsee; Abfließvorrichtung. **– –faˈtigue,** 1. *s.* die Übermüdung. 2. *v.a.* übermüden, überanstrengen. **ˈ–fault,** *s.* überliegende Falte, die Deckfalte (*Geol.*). **–ˈfeed,** *v.a.* überfüttern. **–flow,** 1. [ˈ–floʊ], *s.* der Überfluß; die Überschwemmung, Überflutung; das Überfließen, Übergehen (*Pros.*); *–flow meeting*, die Parallelversammlung; *–flow pipe*, das Überlaufrohr. 2. [–ˈfloʊ], *v.a.* überfließen, überfluten, überschwemmen (*also fig.*); *–flow the banks*, austreten, über die Ufer treten. 3. *v.n.* überfließen, überlaufen, sich ergießen (*into*, in). **–ˈflowing,** 1. *adj.* überschwänglich, überfließend. 2. *s.* das Überfließen; *full to –flowing*, zum Platzen voll, bis auf den letzten Platz besetzt. **ˈ–fold,** *s.* die Decke (*Geol.*). **–ˈfond,** *adj.* überzärtlich. **–ˈgrow,** *ir.v.a. & n.* überwachsen, überwuchern; bewachsen; hinauswachsen über, zu groß werden für. **–ˈgrown,** *adj.* überwachsen; zu groß, schmächtig. **ˈ–hand,** *adj.* den Handrücken nach oben gekehrt; *see also* **–arm;** *–hand service*, der Hochaufschlag (*Tenn.*). **–hang,** 1. [–ˈhæŋ], *ir.v.a.* überhängen; hervorstehen (über (*Acc.*)). 2. *ir.v.n.* überhängen. 3. [ˈ–hæŋ], *s.* der Vorsprung, Überhang. **–ˈhaul,** 1. *v.a.* einholen, überholen (*Naut.*); überprüfen, reparieren, nachsehen, in Ordnung bringen. 2. *s.* die Überholung, Überprüfung, Untersuchung. **–head,** 1. [–ˈhɛd], *adv.* oben, droben; *–head!* Vorsicht! Dacharbeiter! 2. [ˈ–hɛd], *adj.* oberirdisch, über der Erde befindlich (*as cables, etc.*); *–head cable*, die Freileitung, Oberleitung, das Luftkabel; *–head expenses*, laufende Unkosten; *–head railway*, die Hochbahn. (*coll.*) **–heads** [ˈ–hɛdz], *pl.* laufende Unkosten (*pl.*). **–ˈhear,** *ir.v.a.* zufällig hören; (be)lauschen, horchen. **– –ˈheat,** 1. *v.a.* überheizen. 2. *v.n.* zu heiß werden. **– –ˈheated,** *adj.* überheizt; warmgelaufen (*of an engine*). **– –inˈdulge,** *v.a.* zu nachsichtig behandlen (*a p.*); frönen, huldigen, nachgeben (*a habit*); *– –indulge in*, sich zu sehr ergehen in. **– –inˈdulgence,** *s.* zu große Nachsicht; übermäßiger Genuß. **– –inˈdulgent,** *adj.* zu nachsichtig; *be – –indulgent in*, *see* **– –indulge.** **– –ˈissue,** 1. *s.* die Papiergeldinflation. 2. *v.a.* zu viel ausgeben (*notes, etc.*). **–ˈjoyed,** *adj.* hocherfreut, entzückt (*at*, über). **– –ˈladen,** *adj.* zu stark beladen, überladen. **–land,** 1. [ˈ–lænd], *adj.* Überland–; *–land route*, der Landweg. 2. [–ˈlænd], *adv.* über Land. **–lap,** 1. [–ˈlæp], *v.n.* übereinandergreifen, übereinanderliegen; (*fig.*) sich decken, sich überschneiden. 2. *v.a.* überragen, hinüberragen über, hinausgehen über, übergreifen in *or* auf. 3. [ˈ–læp], *s.* das Übergreifen (*on*, auf); überragender Teil. **–ˈlapping,** *adj.* übereinandergreifend. **–lay,** 1. [–ˈleɪ], *ir.v.a.* überziehen, überlagern, belegen, bedecken (*with*, mit). 2. [ˈ–leɪ] *s.* die Bedeckung, Auflage, Planpause. **–ˈleaf,** *adv.* umstehend, umseitig. **–ˈleap,** *v.a.* überspringen, auslassen; springen über, weit hinausgehen über. **–ˈlie,** *ir.v.a.* liegen auf (*Dat.*), durch Liegen ersticken *or* erdrücken (*a child*). **–load,** 1. [–ˈloʊd], *v.a.* überladen, überlasten. 2. [ˈ–ˈloʊd], *s.* die Überbelastung, Überlastung. **–ˈlong,** *adj.* zu lang. **–ˈlook,** *v.a.* übersehen, nicht beachten, vernachlässigen; verzeihen; ignorieren (*a fault, etc.*); überblicken, hinabblicken auf, Ausblick *or* Aussicht haben auf *or* über; beaufsichtigen, überwachen. **ˈ–lord,** *s.* der Oberlehnsherr. **–ˈlordship,** *s.* die Oberherrschaft. **–ly,** *adv.* (*Amer.*) übermäßig. **ˈ–man,** *s.* der Aufseher, Steiger (*Min.*). **ˈ–mantel,** *s.* der Kaminaufsatz, Kaminsims. **–ˈmaster,** *v.a.* bemeistern, überwältigen. **–ˈmastering,** *adj.* hinreißend. **–ˈmuch,** 1. *adj.* allzuviel. 2. *adv.* allzusehr, übermäßig. **–night,** 1. [–ˈnaɪt], *adv.* über Nacht, während der Nacht. 2. [ˈ–naɪt], *adj.* Nacht–, nächtlich. **–ˈpay,** v.a. zu hoch bezahlen, überreichlich belohnen. **– –parˈticular,** *adj.* zu genau. **– –ˈpeopled,** *adj.* übervölkert. **–perˈsuade,** *v.a.* gegen jemandes Willen überreden. **–ˈpitch,** *v.a.* zu weit werfen; (*fig.*) übertreiben. **–ˈplay,** 1. *v.n.* übertreiben. 2. *v.a.*; *–play one's hand*, zu weit gehen. **ˈ–plus,** *s.* der Mehrbetrag, Überschuß. **– –ˈpopulate,** *v.a.* übervölkern. **–ˈpower,** *v.a.* überwältigen. **– –ˈpressure,** *s.* die Überbürdung. **–print,** 1. [–ˈprɪnt], *v.a.* überdrucken; überkopieren (*Phot.*). 2. [ˈ–prɪnt], *s.* erweiteter Aufdruck (*on stamps*). **– –proˈduce,** *v.a. & n.* im Übermaß herstellen. **– –proˈduction,** *s.* die Überproduktion. **ˈ–proof,** *adj.* über Normalstärke. **–ˈrate,** *v.a.* überschätzen. **–ˈreach,** *v.a.* überlisten, übervorteilen; *–reach o.s.*, zu weit gehen, sich übernehmen, sich zuviel zumuten. **–ˈride,** *ir.v.a.* überreiten; (*fig.*) umstoßen, über den Haufen werfen, sich hinwegsetzen über; unterdrücken (*a p.*); gleiten über, sich legen über. **– –ˈride,** *v.a.* zuschanden reiten (*a horse*). **– –ˈripe,** *adj.* überreif. **–ˈrule,** *v.a.* verwerfen, umstoßen, beiseitesetzen, zurückweisen; anders entscheiden, außer Kraft setzen; überstimmen (*a p.*). **–ˈrun,** *ir.v.a.* überrennen, überschwemmen, sich verbreiten über; hinausgehen über, überschreiten; verwüsten, verheeren (*country*); umbrechen (*Typ.*); (*p.p.*) überwachsen, bedeckt; *be –run with*, wimmeln von. **ˈ–sea,** *adj.* überseeisch, Übersee–, Auslands–. **–ˈseas,** 1. *adv.* über See. 2. *s.* die Übersee. **–ˈsee,** *ir.v.a.* beaufsichtigen, überwachen. **ˈ–seer,** *s.* der Aufseher, Inspektor, Faktor (*Print.*); Polier (*Build.*); Steiger (*of a mine*); Armenpfleger (*of the poor*). **–ˈset,** *v.a.* umwerfen, umstürzen. **ˈ–sew,** *v.a.* überwendlich nähen. **– –ˈsexed,** *adj.* geschlechtlich überreizt. **–ˈshadow,** *v.a.* überschatten, beschatten, schirmen, verdunkeln; (*fig.*) in Schatten stellen. **ˈ–shoe,** *s.* der Überschuh. **–ˈshoot,** *ir.v.a.* hinausschießen über; *–shoot o.s.* or *the mark*, übers Ziel hinausschießen, des Guten zuviel tun, zu weit gehen. **ˈ–shot,** *adj.* oberschlächtig. **ˈ–sight,** *s.* das Versehen; die Aufsicht (*of*, über); *by an –sight*, aus Versehen. **–ˈsleep,** *ir.v.a. & r.* sich *or* die Zeit verschlafen. **ˈ–sleeves,** *pl.* Ärmelschoner. **–ˈspend,** 1. *ir.v.a.* überschreiten (*one's income*). 2. *v.n. & r.* sich verausgaben. **ˈ–spill,** *s.* der Überschuß. **– –ˈstaffed,** *adj.* mit zu großer Belegschaft. **–ˈstate,** *v.a.* zu hoch angeben, zu stark betonen, übertreiben; *–state one's case*, in seinen Behauptungen zu weit gehen. **– –ˈstatement,** *s.* die Übertreibung. **–ˈstay,** *v.a.* überschreiten (*time*); *–stay one's welcome*, länger bleiben als erwünscht ist. **–ˈstep,** *v.a.* überschreiten. **–ˈstock,** *v.a.* überladen, überfüllen. **–ˈstrain,** 1. *v.a.* überanstrengen; *–strain o.s.*, sich verrenken. 2. *s.* die Überanstrengung, Überspannung. **ˈ–ˈstrained,** *adj.* (*fig.*) überspitzt. **–strung,** *adj.* [ˈ–strʌŋ], kreuzseitig (*piano*); (*fig.*) [–ˈstrʌŋ], überanstrengt. **–subˈscribe,** *v.a.* überzeichnen. **– –suppˈly,** *s.* das Überangebot, der Überfluß, zu reiche Zufuhr. **–ˈtake,** *ir.v.a.* überholen (*also Motor.*), einholen, ereilen, erreichen; überfallen, überraschen. **–ˈtask,** *v.a.* übrbeürden, zu stark in Anspruch nehmen.

–'**tax**, *v.a.* zu hoch besteuern; (*fig.*) überbürden, zu sehr in Anspruch nehmen; *–tax one's strength*, sich zuviel anmuten. **–throw**, 1. [–'θroʊ], *ir.v.a.* umwerfen, umstürzen, umstoßen, niederreißen, vernichten; stürzen, besiegen. 2. ['–θroʊ], *s.* der Sturz, Umsturz, Untergang, die Vernichtung, Niederlage (*Mil.*); zu weit zurückgeworfener Ball (*Crick.*). **–time**, 1. ['–taɪm] *s.* die Überzeit, Überstunden (*pl.*); die Mehrarbeit; *work '–time*, Überstunden machen. 2. [–'taɪm], *adv.* über die Zeit hinaus; *work –'time*, nach Arbeitsschluß weiterarbeiten. –'**tire**, *v.a.* übermüden. '**–tone**, *s.* der Oberton (*Mus.*). –'**top**, *v.a.* überragen, übertreffen. –'**tower**, *v.n.* überragen. –'**train**, *v.a.* übertrainieren. –'**trump**, *v.a.* übertrumpfen (*also fig.*). **–turn**, 1. [–'tə:n], *v.a.* umkehren, umwerfen, umstoßen, umstürzen. 2. *v.n.* umschlagen, kentern, sich überschlagen (*Naut.*). 3. ['–tə:n], *s.* der Umsturz. **–valu'ation**, *s.* die Überschätzung, Überwertung. –'**value**, *v.a.* überschätzen, überwerten, zu hoch einschätzen. –'**weening**, *adj.* eingebildet, anmaßend. **–weight**, 1. ['–weɪt] *s.* das Übergewicht. 2. [–'weɪt], *v.a.* überladen, überlasten. –'**whelm**, *v.a.* überhäufen, überschütten, verschütten; begraben; überwältigen, übermannen; überfluten, überschwemmen; bestürmen. –'**whelming**, *adj.* überwältigend. –'**wind**, *v.a.* zu weit aufziehen (*a watch*). –'**work**, 1. *v.a.* überarbeiten, mit Arbeit überladen. 2. *v.n.* sich überarbeiten. 3. *s.* die Überarbeitung, übermäßige Arbeit. **––'wrought**, *p.p.* überarbeitet; (*fig.*) überreizt.

overt [oʊ'və:t], *adj.* offenbar, offensichtlich. *– act*, offenkundige Handlung; *– market*, offener *or* öffentlicher Markt.

overture ['oʊvətʃʊə], *s.* die Ouvertüre (*Mus.*); (*fig.*) Einleitung, das Vorspiel; der Antrag; *pl.* Annäherungen, Vorschläge (*pl.*) (*to*, an); *– of marriage*, der Heiratsantrag.

ov–iduct ['oʊvɪdʌkt], *s.* der Eileiter, die Muttertrompete. **–iform** [–fɔ:m], *adj.* eiförmig. **–iparous** [o'vɪpərəs], *adj.* eierlegend. **–iposit** [oʊvɪ'pɔzɪt], *v.n.* Eier legen (*of insects*). **–ogenesis** [ovoʊ'dʒɛnɪsɪs], *s.* die Eibildung. **–oid** ['oʊvɔɪd], *adj.* eiförmig. **–ular** [–vjʊlə], *adj.* Ei–. **–ulation** [–'leɪʃən], *s.* die Eibildung. **–ule** ['oʊvju:l], *s.* unbefruchtetes Ei (*Zool.*). **–um** ['oʊvəm], *s.* (pl. *–a*) das Ei.

ow–e [oʊ], *v.a.* & *n.* schuldig sein, schulden; verpflichtet sein, verdanken (*a p. a th.* or *a th. to a p.*, einem etwas); *–e a p. a grudge*, einem grollen. **–ing**, *pred. adj.* schuldig; *be –ing*, zu zahlen sein (*to*, an (*Acc.*)), noch offenstehen; *have –ing*, ausstehen haben; *–ing to*, infolge von, vermöge (*Gen.*), dank (*Dat.*); *be –ing to* herrühren von, verursacht sein durch, zu verdanken sein (*Dat.*).

owl [aʊl], *s.* die Eule; der Uhu, Kauz. **–et** [–ɪt], *s.* junge Eule. **–ish** [–ɪʃ], *adj.* eulenhaft; (*fig.*) dumm.

[1]**own** [oʊn], 1. *adj.* (*only after poss. pron. or gen. noun*) eigen; wirklich, richtig; *make one's – clothes*, sich die Kleider selbst machen; *God's – country*, Land von Gottes Gnaden; *with my* (*his, etc.*) *– eyes*, mit eigenen Augen; *be one's – master*, sein eigener Herr sein; *the King's –*, das Leibregiment; *countess in her – right*, geborene Gräfin; *my – self*, ich selbst. 2. *s.*; (*coll.*) *get one's – back*, etwas heimzahlen (*on a p.*, einem); *hold one's –*, standhalten; sich behaupten (*also fig.*); *have for one's –*, sein eigen nennen; *come into one's –*, zu seinem Rechte kommen; *of one's –*, einem zu eigen; *a house of one's –*, sein eigenes Haus; *have a way of one's –*, eine eigene Art haben; *on one's –*, allein; *left on one's –*, sich selbst überlassen; (*coll.*) *on one's –*, aus eigenem Antrieb, von selbst, selbständig, auf eigene Verantwortung *or* Faust.

[2]**own** [oʊn], 1. *v.a.* besitzen; bekennen, gestehen, zugeben, zugestehen, einräumen, anerkennen; *– o.s. defeated*, zugeben daß man geschlagen ist. 2. *v.n.* sich bekennen (*to*, zu); *he –ed to being*, er gestand zu sein; (*coll.*) *– up*, gestehen, beichten; *– up to s.th.*, etwas offen zugeben *or* bekennen. **–ed** [–d], *adj.* gehörig (*by* (*Dat.*)), im Besitze (*by*, von). **–er** [–ə], *s.* der Eigentümer, Besitzer; *at –er's risk*, auf eigene Gefahr. **–er-driver**, *s.* der Selbstfahrer. **–ership**, *s.* das Eigentumsrecht; der Besitz.

ox [ɔks], *s.* (pl. *–en*) der Ochse, das Rind. **––eye**, *s.* das Ochsenauge; *––eye daisy*, großes Maßlieb, die Marienblume (*Bot.*). **––eyed**, *adj.* ochsenäugig. **–lip**, *s.* hohe Schlüsselblume (*Bot.*). **––hide**, *s.* die Ochsenhaut. **–tail**, *s.* der Ochsenschwanz. **––tongue**, *s.* die Ochsenzunge.

oxal–ate ['ɔksəleɪt], *s.* oxalsaures Salz. **–ic** [ɔk'sælɪk], *adj.* oxalsauer; *–ic acid*, die Oxalsäure, Kleesäure, Kleesalzsäure.

oxid–ate ['ɔksɪdeɪt], *see* **–ize** 1. **–ation** [–'deɪʃən], *see* **–ization**. **–e** ['ɔksaɪd], *s.* das Oxyd, die Sauerstoffverbindung; *ferrous –e*, das Eisenoxydul. **–ization** [–daɪ'zeɪʃən], *s.* die Oxydierung, Oxydation, Verbrennung. **–ize** ['ɔksɪdaɪz], 1. *v.a.* oxydieren, mit Sauerstoff verbinden, verbrennen, säuern. 2. *v.n.* rosten.

oxy–acetylene [ɔksɪə'sɛtəlɪn], *adj.* Azetylensauerstoff–; *––acetylene welding*, autogene Schweißung. **–gen** ['ɔksɪdʒən], *s.* der Sauerstoff; *–gen apparatus*, der Sauerstoffapparat; *–gen starvation*, der Sauerstoffmangel. **–genate** [–'sɪdʒəneɪt], **–genize** [–'sɪdʒənaɪz], *v.a.* oxydieren, mit Sauerstoff verbinden *or* behandeln. **–hydrogen** [–'haɪdrədʒən], *adj.* Hydrooxygen–; *–hydrogen blowpipe*, das Knallgasgebläse; *–hydrogen gas*, das Knallgas; *–hydrogen light*, Drummondsches Licht. **–moron** [–'mɔ:rən], *s.* das Oximoron. **–tone** ['ɔksɪtoʊn], *s.* auf der Endsilbe betontes Wort.

oyer ['ɔɪə], *s.* das Verhör; die Untersuchung; *– and terminer*, das Hören und Entscheiden (*Law*).

oyez [oʊ'jɛz], *int.* (*archaic*) hört!

oyster ['ɔɪstə], *s.* die Auster. **––bed**, *s.* die Austernbank. **––catcher**, *s.* der Austernfischer (*Orn.*). **––farm**, *s.* der Austernpark.

ozokerit(e) [o'zɔkeraɪt], *s.* der Ozokerit, das Erdwachs, Bergwachs (*Geol.*).

ozon–e ['oʊzoʊn], *s.* das Ozon. **–ic** [–'zɔnɪk], *adj.* Ozon–, ozonisch, ozonhaltig. **–iferous** [–ɔ'nɪfərəs], *adj.* ozonerzeugend. **–ize** ['oʊzənaɪz], *v.a.* mit Ozon behandeln; in Ozon verwandeln. **–izer**, *s.* der Ozonerzeuger.

P

P, p [pɪ:], *s.* das P, p; *see Index of Abbreviations*. (*coll.*) *mind one's P's and Q's*, sich sehr in acht nehmen.

pa [pɑ:], *s. see* **papa.**

pabulum ['pæbjʊləm], *s.* die Nahrung.

paca ['pækə], *s.* das Paka (*Zool.*).

[1]**pace** [peɪs], 1. *s.* der Schritt (*also as measure*); Gang; die Gangart, der Tritt, Paßgang (*of horse*); das Tempo. (*a*) (*with verbs*) (*coll.*) *go the –*, schnell gehen; (*fig.*) ein flottes Leben führen; *keep –*, Schritt halten (*with*, mit); (*fig.*) mitgehen mit; *make* or *set the –*, Schrittmacher sein; *take a –*, einen Schritt tun *or* machen. (*b*) (*with prepositions*) *at a great –*, sehr schnell, in raschem Tempo; *put a horse through his –s*, ein Pferd alle Gangarten machen lassen; *put a p. through his –s*, einen auf Herz und Nieren prüfen. 2. *v.n.* (einher)schreiten; im Paßgang gehen (*of horse*). 3. *v.a.* abschreiten (*a room, etc.*); im Paßgang gehen lassen (*a horse*); Schrittmacher sein für (*Sport*). **–d** [–t], *adj. suff.*; *slow––d*, langsam schreitend; *thorough––d*, durchtrieben, Erz–. **–r**, *s.* Schreitende(r), *m.*; der Paßgänger; Schrittmacher. **––maker**, *s.* der Schrittmacher.

[2]**pace** ['peɪsɪ], *prep.* (*liter.*) mit Erlaubnis (*Gen.*).

pacha [pɑ:ʃə], *s. see* **pasha.**

pachyderm ['pækɪdə:m], *s.* (pl. *–s* or *–ata*) der Dickhäuter (*Zool.*). **–atous** [–'də:mətəs], *adj.* dickhäutig, Dickhäuter–.

pacif–ic [pəˈsɪfɪk], *adj.* friedlich, friedfertig, Friedens–. **–ication** [pæsɪfɪˈkeɪʃən], *s.* die Besänftigung, Beruhigung; Befriedigung; Frieden(s)-stiftung, der Friedensvertag. **–ier** [ˈpæsɪfɑɪə], *s.* der Friedensstifter. **–ism** [ˈpæsɪfɪzm], *s.* der Pazifismus. **–ist** [–fɪst], 1. *s.* der Pazifist. 2. *adj.* pazifistisch. **–y** [ˈpæsɪfɑɪ], *v.a.* beruhigen, besänftigen; den Frieden bringen (*Dat.*); befriedigen (*a country*).

pack [pæk], 1. *s.* das (*or Austr.* der) Pack, Bündel, Paket; Gepäck; der Rucksack, Tornister; Ballen, Sack (*of flour*) (= *280 lb.*); Haufen, die Menge (*of things*); Bande, Rotte (*of thieves*); Meute, Koppel (*of hounds*); das Rudel (*of wolves & submarines*); Spiel (*of cards*); die Packung (*Med.*); Stürmer (*pl.*) (*Rugby Footb.*); – *of cards*, das Spiel Karten; – *of lies*, ein Paket Lügen; – *of nonsense*, lauter Unsinn; *the whole – of them*, das ganze Lumpenpack. 2. *v.a.* packen, einpacken, zusammenpacken; fest zusammenpacken, zusammenpressen; füllen, vollstopfen; verpacken, fest verbinden; abdichten (*Med.*); lidern (*Mach.*); in Dosen einmachen, konservieren (*fish, fruit, etc.*); beladen, bepacken (*beasts*); (usually – *off*) fortschicken; *–ed house*, volles Haus (*Theat.*); *–ed like sardines*, wie die Heringe (gepreßt). 3. *v.n.* packen, seine Sachen einpacken; sich packen (lassen) (*as goods*); sich zusammenscharen *or* ballen; (*coll.*) *send a p. –ing*, einen fortjagen; (*sl.*) – *up*, aufhören, außer Betrieb geraten. **–age** [–ɪdʒ], *s.* die Packung, das Paket; die Verpackung, Emballage; *pl.* Kolli (*pl.*) (*C.L.*). **--animal,** *s.* das Saumtier. **--artillery,** *s.* die Gebirgsartillerie. **--cloth,** *s.* die Packleinwand. **--drill,** *s.* das Exerzieren mit Gepäck (*Mil.*). **–er,** *s.* der (Ver)Packer; die Packmaschine. **–et** [–ɪt], *s.* das Paket, Päckchen; (also *–et-boat*) das Paketboot, der Postdampfer. **--horse,** *s.* das Packpferd, Saumpferd; (*fig.*) Lasttier. **--ice,** *s.* das Packeis. **–ing,** *s.* das Packen, die Verpackung; Packung, das Packmaterial; die Dichtung, Liderung (*Mach.*); *do one's –ing*, packen. **–ing-bush,** *s.* die Stopfbüchse. **–ing-case,** *s.* die Packkiste. **–ing-needle,** *s.* die Packnadel. **–ing-paper,** *s.* das Packpapier. **–ing-ring,** *s.* der Dichtungsring. **–ing-sheet,** *s.* das Packtuch. **--saddle,** *s.* der Packsattel. **–thread,** *s.* der Bindfaden, Packzwirn. **--train,** *s.* die Tragtierkolonne.

pact [pækt], *s.* der Vertrag, Pakt.

[1]**pad** [pæd], 1. *s.* (*archaic*) der Weg, die Straße; *gentleman* or *knight of the –*, der Straßenräuber. 2. *v.a. & n.* (*sl.*) – *along*, dahintrotten. (*sl.*) – *it*, – *the hoof*, zu Fuß gehen. **--nag,** *s.* der Gaul, Klepper, Paßgänger.

[2]**pad** [pæd], 1. *s.* das Polster, Kissen, die Unterlage; Pfote, der Fußballen (*of dog, etc.*); die Beinschiene (*Crick.*); (also *writing-–*) der (Schreib)Block. 2. *v.a.* (aus)polstern; wattieren; durch leere Worte ausfüllen (*a sentence*); *–ded cell*, die Gummizelle. **–ding,** *s.* das Auspolstern, die Polsterung, Wattierung, Einlage; Watte; (*fig.*) leere Phrasen, die Schwafelei, das Zeilenfüllsel, Geschreibsel.

paddl–e [pædl], 1. *v.n. & v.a.* paddeln (*a boat*); (*fig.*) *–e one's own canoe*, sich auf sich selbst verlassen. 2. *v.n.* pla(n)tschen (*in water*); watscheln. 3. *s.* die Paddel, (kurzes) Ruder; *see* **–e-board;** die Rührstange, das Rührholz, Rührscheit (*Tech.*). **–e-board,** *s.* die Radschaufel. **–e-box,** *s.* der Radkasten. **–e-steamer,** *s.* der Raddampfer. **–e-wheel,** *s.* das Schaufelrad. **–ing,** *s.* das Paddeln, Plantschen. **–ing-pool,** *s.* der Plantschbecken.

[1]**paddock** [ˈpædək], *s.* (*Scots*) der Frosch; (*archaic*) die Kröte.

[2]**paddock** [ˈpædək], *s.* die Pferdekoppel, das Gehege; der Sattelplatz (*Racing*).

[1]**paddy** [ˈpædɪ], *s.* der Reis in Hülsen.

[2]**paddy** [ˈpædɪ], *s.* (*coll.*) der Wutanfall, Wutausbruch.

padlock [ˈpædlək], 1. *s.* das Vorhängeschloß, Vorlegeschloß. 2. *v.a.* mit Vorhängeschloß verschließen.

padre [ˈpɑːdrɪ], *s.* (*coll.*) Militärgeistliche(r), *m.*

paean [ˈpiːən], *s.* das Siegeslied, Triumphlied; – *of praise*, das Loblied, Lobgesang, die Lobrede, Lobeserhebung.

paederasty [ˈpiːdəræstɪ], *s.* die Knabenliebe, Päderastie.

pagan [ˈpeɪgən], 1. *adj.* heidnisch. 2. *s.* der Heide, die Heidin. **–ism,** *s.* das Heidentum.

[1]**page** [peɪdʒ], 1. *s.* die Seite, Buchseite; (*fig.*) das Buch, Blatt, Schriftstück, die Schrift, Episode; *–s of history*, die Tafeln der Geschichte. 2. *v.a.* paginieren. **--proof,** *s.* der Abzug eines Umbruchs.

[2]**page** [peɪdʒ], 1. *s.* der Page, Edelknabe (also *--boy*) junger Diener, der Hoteldiener; Amtsbote (*Amer.*). 2. *v.a.* durch Pagen holen *or* suchen lassen.

pageant [ˈpædʒənt], *s.* historischer Aufzug, das Festspiel, großartiges Schauspiel *or* Schaustück. **–ry,** *s.* das Gepränge, der Prunk; (*fig.*) leerer Schein.

pagina–l [ˈpædʒɪnəl], *adj.* Seiten–. **–te** [–neɪt], *v.a.* paginieren. **–tion** [–ˈneɪʃən], *s.* die Paginierung, Seitenzählung.

paging [ˈpeɪdʒɪŋ], *s. see* **pagination.**

pagoda [pəˈgoudə], *s.* die Pagode. **--tree,** *s.* die Sophora; *shake the --tree*, in Indien sein Glück machen.

paid [peɪd], *see* **pay;** frei! franko! (*on letters, etc.*). **--up,** *adj.*; *--up capital*, eingezahltes Kapital.

pail [peɪl], *s.* der Eimer, Kübel. **–ful,** *s.* der Eimervoll.

paillasse [ˈpæljæs], *s.* der Strohsack.

pain [peɪn], 1. *s.* der Schmerz, die Pein; das Leid, Leiden, der Kummer; *pl.* Geburtswehen (*pl.*); die Mühe; *be at –s to do*, sich bemühen zu tun; *for my* (*his*, etc.) *–s*, als Belohnung; *be in –*, leiden, Schmerzen haben; – *in the head*, Kopfschmerzen (*pl.*); (*sl.*) *give s.o. a – in the neck*, einem auf die Nerven gehen; *spare no –s*, keine Mühe scheuen; *take –s*, sich Mühe geben; (*up*)*on* or *under – of death*, bei Todesstrafe; *upon – of my displeasure*, bei Verlust meines Wohlwollens; *go to great –s to do*, sich sehr bemühen zu tun; *hear with –*, mit Wehmut hören. 2. *v.a.* schmerzlich berühren, quälen, peinigen, weh tun (*Dat.*), schmerzen (*Acc. or Dat.*). **–ed,** *adj.* schmerzvoll; *–ed expression*, der Ausdruck des Schmerzes. **–ful,** *adj.* schmerzlich, schmerzhaft; peinlich, mühsam; *–ful cut*, schmerzhafte Schnittwunde; *–ful effort*, mühsame Anstrengung; *–ful scene*, peinliche Szene. **–fulness,** *s.* die Schmerzlichkeit; Schmerzhaftigkeit, Peinlichkeit. **--killer,** *s.* schmerzstillendes Mittel. **–less,** *adj.* schmerzlos. **–lessness,** *s.* die Schmerzlosigkeit. **–staking,** 1. *adj.* sorgfältig, gewissenhaft, unverdrossen; arbeitsam, fleißig, emsig. 2. *s.* die Arbeitsamkeit, Sorgfalt.

paint [peɪnt], 1. *v.a.* malen, anmalen, anstreichen, bemalen, schminken (*the face*); (*fig.*) ausmalen, schildern; pinseln (*as with iodine*); *– a door*, eine Tür anstreichen; – *one's face*, das Gesicht schminken; – *in*, bemalen; – *out*, übermalen; – *a picture*, ein Bild malen; – *s.o.'s portrait*, einen malen; (*coll.*) – *the town red*, Radau machen. 2. *v.n.* malen, sich schminken; – *from nature*, nach der Natur malen. 3. *s.* die Farbe; der Anstrich (*of a wall, etc.*); die Schminke; *coat of –*, der Anstrich; *fresh as –*, schmuck, frisch und munter; *wet –!* frisch gestrichen! **--box,** *s.* der Malkasten. **--brush,** *s.* der Malpinsel, Anstrichpinsel. **–ed Lady,** *s.* der Distelfalter (*Ent*). **–er,** *s.* der Maler; Dekorationsmaler, Anstreicher; *–er in watercolours*, der Aquarellmaler; *–er in oils*, der Ölmaler. **–er's-colic,** *s.* die Malerkrankheit, Bleikolik. **–ing,** *s.* das Malen, die Malerei; das Gemälde; das Schminken (*of the face*); *–ing on glass*, die Glasmalerei. **--remover,** *s.* das Abbeizmittel.

painter [ˈpeɪntə], *s.* die Fangleine, das Bootstau (*Naut.*); (*coll.*) *cut the –*, seinen eignen Weg gehen, sich (von den andern) loslösen (*esp. Pol.*); *see also under* **paint.**

pair [pɛə], 1. *s.* das Paar; der, das *or* die andere (von einem Paar), das Gegenstück; (Ehe)Paar; *carriage and –*, der Zweispänner; – *of boots*, das Paar Stiefel; *two –s of boots*, zwei Paar Stiefel; – *of drawers*, die Unterhose; – *of horses*, das Gespann Pferde; – *of scissors*, die Schere; *two –s of scissors*, zwei Scheren; – *of spectacles*, die Brille; – *of steps*, die Trittleiter; *two-- back (room)*, das Zimmer nach hinten, zwei Treppen hoch. 2. *v.a.* paaren (*animals*) (also – *off*) in Paaren anordnen. 3. *v.n.* sich paaren (*animals, also fig.*); sich gatten (*animals*); (*fig.*) passen (*with*, zu); – *off*, zu zweien gehen, sich paarweise anschließen; (*coll.*) heiraten (*with*, (*Acc.*)). **–ing** [–rɪŋ], *s.* die Paarung. **--oar,** *s.* der Zweier (*rowing*).

pal [pæl], 1. *s.* (*coll.*) der Kamerad, Genosse, Freund. 2. *v.n.*; – *up*, sich anfreunden, Freund sein (*with*, mit).

palace [ˈpæləs], *s.* der Palast, das Schloß. **--yard,** *s.* der Schloßhof.

paladin [ˈpælədɪn], *s.* der Paladin.

palaeo–grapher [pælɪˈɔgrəfə], *s.* der Paläograph. **–graphy,** *s.* die Handschriftenkunde. Paläographie. **–logy** [–ˈɔlədʒɪ], *s.* die Paläologie, Altertumskunde. **–ntologist** [–ənˈtɔlədʒɪst], *s.* der Paläontolog. **–ntology** [–ənˈtɔlədʒɪ], *s.* die Paläontologie. **–zoic** [–əˈzouɪk], *adj.* paläozoisch.

palanquin [ˈpælənkɪːn], *s.* der Palankin, Tragsessel, die Sänfte.

palat–able [ˈpælətəbl], *adj.* schmackhaft, wohlschmeckend; (*fig.*) angenehm. **–al** [–təl], 1. *adj.* Palatal–, Gaumen–. 2. *s.* der Gaumenlaut, Palatal(laut). **–alize** [–təlɑɪz], *v.a.* palatalisieren (*Phonet.*). **–e** [ˈpælət], *s.* der Gaumen; (*fig.*) Geschmack; *hard –e*, der Vordergaumen; *soft –e*, der Hintergaumen. **–ine** [–tɪn], 1. *adj. see* **–al.** 2. *s.* der Gaumenknochen.

palatial [pəˈleɪʃəl], *adj.* palastartig, prächtig, Palast–.

palaver [pəˈlɑːvə], 1. *s.* die Besprechung, Unterredung, (*coll.*) das Geschwätz, Gewäsch; (*sl.*) die Kiste, der Laden. 2. *v.n.* schwatzen, klatschen. 3. *v.a.* (*coll.*) beschwatzen (*a p.*).

[1]**pale** [peɪl], 1. *adj.* blaß, bleich, schwach, matt (*as light*); hell (*as colour*); – *ale*, helles Bier; – *blue*, blaßblau, hellblau; *as – as a ghost*, kreideblaß; *grow –, see –* 2; abblassen (*as colours*); *turn –*, see – 2. 2. *v.n.* erblassen, erbleichen, bleich *or* blaß werden; (*fig.*) verblassen (*beside*, vor). **--face,** *s.* das Bleichgesicht, Angehörige(r) der weißen Rasse. **--faced,** *adj.* mit bleichem Gesicht. **–ness,** *s.* die Blässe, Farblosigkeit.

[2]**pale** [peɪl], *s.* der Pfahl, die Einpfahlung; Grenze; der Bereich, das Gebiet, (*coll.*) *beyond the –*, unkultiviert, unmanierlich, ungeleckt; *English –*, der englische Bezirk (*in Ireland*); *within the – of the church*, im Schoß der Kirche. *see* **paling.**

paletot [ˈpælətou], *s.* der Überrock, Mantel.

palette [ˈpælət], *s.* die Palette; (*fig.*) Farbenskala. **--knife,** *s.* das Palettmesser, Streichmesser.

palfrey [ˈpɔːlfrɪ], *s.* der Zelter.

palimpsest [ˈpælɪmpsɛst], *s.* das Palimpsest.

palindrome [ˈpælɪndroum], *s.* das Palindrom.

paling [ˈpeɪliŋ], *s.* der Lattenzaun, Pfahlzaun.

palin–genesis [pælɪnˈdʒɛnɪsɪs], *s.* die Wiedergeburt. **–ode** [–noud], *s.* die Palinodie, dichterischer Widerruf.

palisade [pælɪˈseɪd], 1. *s.* das Staket, der Schanzpfahl, die Palisade (*Mil.*); 2. *v.a.* verschanzen, mit einer Palisade umgeben.

[1]**pall** [pɔːl], 1. *s.* das Bahrtuch, Leichentuch; die Deichsel (*Her.*); der (Papst)Mantel, das Pallium (*R.C.*); (*fig.*) der Mantel, die Decke, Wolke. 2. *v.a.* einhüllen. **--bearer,** *s.* der Bahrtuchhalter.

[2]**pall** [pɔːl], 1. *v.n.* jeden Reiz verlieren, schal werden (*on*, für), langweilen. 2. *v.a.* (über)sättigen; anwidern.

palladium [pəˈleɪdɪəm], *s.* das Palladium (*also Chem.*); (*fig.*) der Schutz, Hort.

[1]**pallet** [ˈpælɪt], *s.* das Strohbett, die Pritsche, Matratze.

[2]**pallet** [ˈpælɪt], *s.* das Streichmesser (*Pott.*); der Spindellappen (*Horol.*), die Sperrklappe (*Organ*); *see also* **palette.**

palliasse [ˈpælɪæs], *s. see* **paillasse.**

palliat–e [ˈpælɪeɪt], *v.a.* lindern; (*fig.*) bemänteln, beschönigen. **–ion** [–ˈeɪʃən], *s.* die Linderung; Bemäntelung, Beschönigung; *in –ion of*, als Entschuldigung für. **–ive** [–lɪətɪv], 1. *adj.* lindernd, Linderungs–; (*fig.*) bemäntelnd, beschönigend. 2. *s.* das Linderungsmittel, die Beschönigung.

pall–id [ˈpælɪd], *adj.* bleich, blaß. **–idness,** *s.* **–or** [–ə], *s.* die Blässe.

[1]**palm** [pɑːm], *s.* (also *--tree*), die Palme (*Bot.*); (*fig.*) Palme des Sieges, der Sieg; *bear* or *win the –*, den Sieg erringen; *give the –*, den Preis zuerkennen (*to* (*Dat.*)). **–aceous,** *adj.* Palmen–. **--house,** *s.* das Palmenhaus. **--oil,** *s.* das Palmöl; *see also* **palm**[2]. **--Sunday,** *s.* der Palmsonntag. **–y,** *adj.* (*poet.*) palmenreich; (*coll.*) erfolgreich, blühend, glücklich, glorreich; (*coll.*) *–y days*, die Glanzzeit, Blütezeit.

[2]**palm** [pɑːm], 1. *s.* (also – *of the hand*) die Handfläche, flache Hand; die Handbreite (*as measure*); Schaufel (*of antlers or anchor*); *grease a –*, einen bestechen *or* schmieren. 2. *v.a.* in der hohlen Hand verbergen; – *a th.* (*off*) *on a p.*, einem etwas aufdrehen, *or* aufhängen *or* anhängen; – *o.s. off as*, sich ausgeben als. **–ar,** *adj.* Hand–, Handflächen–. **–ate,** *adj.* handförmig. (*coll.*) **--grease, --oil,** *s.* das Schmiergeld, Bestechungsgeld. **–iped** [ˈpælmɪpɛd], *adj.* schwimmfüßig (*Orn.*). **–ist,** *s.* der Handwahrsager. **–istry,** *s.* die Handwahrsagerei, Chiromantie.

palmitic [pælˈmɪtɪk], *adj.*; – *acid*, die Palmitinsäure.

palp [pælp], *s.* (pl. *–i*) der Fühler, Taster, das Fühlhorn. **–ability** [–əˈbɪlɪtɪ], *s.* die Fühlbarkeit; Handgreiflichkeit. **–able** [–əbl], *adj.* fühlbar, greifbar; (*fig.*) handgreiflich, offenbar, leicht zugänglich. **–ate** [–eɪt], *v.a.* betasten (*Med.*). **–ation** [–ˈpeɪʃən], *s.* die Betastung (*Med.*).

palpebral [ˈpælpəbrəl], *adj.* Augenlid–.

palpitat–e [ˈpælpɪteɪt], *v.n.* heftig klopfen, unregelmäßig schlagen (*as the heart*); beben, zittern (*with*, vor). **–ion** [–ˈteɪʃən], *s.* (*also pl.*) das Herzklopfen (*Med.*).

palpus [ˈpælpəs], *s. see* **palp.**

pals–ied [ˈpɔːlzɪd], *adj.* gelähmt, (*fig.*) zitterig. **–y** [–zɪ], 1. *s.* die Lähmung, der Schlagfluß; (*B.*) *sick of the –y*, Gichtbrüchige(r), *m.* 2. *v.a.* lähmen.

palter [ˈpɔːltə], *v.n.* zweideutig handeln (*with*, an (*Dat.*) *or* gegen), Spiegelfechterei *or* sein Spiel treiben (*with*, mit), feilschen.

paltr–iness [ˈpɔːltrɪnɪs], *s.* die Kleinlichkeit, Armseligkeit, Erbärmlichkeit. **–y** [–trɪ], *adj.* kleinlich, armselig, erbärmlich, wertlos; *–y excuse*, lahme *or* lumpige Entschuldigung.

paludal [pəlˈjuːdəl], *adj.* sumpfig, Sumpf–.

pampas [ˈpæmpəs], *pl.* die Pampas, südamerikanische Grasebenen *or* Steppen. **--grass,** *s.* das Pampasgras.

pamper [ˈpæmpə], *v.a.* reichlich füttern; (*fig.*) verwöhnen, verzärteln, verhätscheln, verpimpeln.

pamphlet [ˈpæmflɪt], *s.* die Flugschrift, Broschüre. **–eer,** *s.* der Flugschriftenschreiber.

[1]**pan** [pæn], 1. *s.* die Pfanne; Zündpfanne (*Gun.*); das Setzschiff (*Print.*); *brain--*, die Hirnschale; (*flush –*) das Spülbecken, Klosettbecken; (*hard--*) fester Untergrund; – *out* 1. *v.a.* im Setzkasten waschen (*gold-bearing gravel*), (*fig.*) ergeben, hervorbringen. 2. *v.n.*; (also – *out well*) (*fig.*) Erfolg haben, einschlagen. **–cake,** 1. *s.* der Pfannkuchen, Eierkuchen; *–cake day*, *s.* die Fastnacht; *flat as a –cake*, flach wie ein Brett; *–cake landing*, *s.* die Durchsacklandung, Bumslandung (*Av.*). 2. *v.n.* durchsacken, absacken, bauchlanden (*Av.*).

[2]**pan** [pæn], *prefix*, All–, Pan–; *--Europe*, das Pan-Europa; *--German*, alldeutsch. **–acea** [–əˈsɪːə], *s.* das Allheilmittel, Universalmittel.

panache [pæˈnæʃ], *s.* der Federbusch, (*fig.*) Prunk.

panada [pəˈnɑːdə], *s.* der Semmelbrei.

pan–chromatic [pænkrəˈmætɪk], *adj.* für alle Farben empfindlich, panchromatisch (*Phot.*). **–cratic** [–ˈkrætɪk], *adj.* athletisch, Pankration–; pankratisch (*Opt.*). **–cratium** [–ˈkreɪʃɪəm], *s.* das Pankration, der Allkampf.

pancrea–s [ˈpæŋkrɪəs], *s.* die Bauchspeicheldrüse. **–tic** [–rɪˈætɪk], *adj.* Bauchspeichel–; *–tic juice*, der Bauchspeichel.

panda [ˈpændə], *s.* der Katzenbär, Panda (*Zool.*).

pandects [ˈpændɛkts], *pl.* Pandekten (*pl.*).

pandemic [pænˈdɛmɪk], *adj.* allgemein verbreitet, pandemisch.

pandemonium [pændəˈmounɪəm], *s.* die Hölle, Lästerstätte, das Pandämonium; (*coll.*) der Höllenlärm.

pander ['pændə], 1. *s.* der Kuppler. 2. *v.a.* verkuppeln. 3. *v.n.* fröhnen, willfahren, Vorschub leisten (*to* (*Dat.*)).
pane [peɪn], *s.* die Fensterscheibe, Scheibe; rechteckiges Feld *or* Fach; die Füllung (*of a door*); Finne (*of a hammer*).
panegyri-c [pænə'dʒɪrɪk]. 1. *s.* die Lobrede, der Lobgesang, die Lobeserhebung (*on*, auf). **-cal,** *adj.* Lob-, Lobes-. **-st** ['pænədʒərɪst], *s.* der Lobredner. **-ze** [-raɪz], *v.a.* & *n.* lobpreisen.
panel ['pænəl], 1. *s.* vertieftes, viereckiges Feld *or* Fach, die Füllung (*of a door*), das Einsatzstück (*of a dress*), die Schalttafel (*Elec.*), getäfelte Wandbekleidung, das Paneel (*Arch.*); (also *ground--*) das Grundtuch, Fliegertuch (*Av.*); die Geschworenenliste (*of a jury*), Geschwornen (*pl.*) (*Law*), das Schiedsgericht, der Ausschuß; die Liste, das Verzeichnis (der Krankenkassenärzte); Angeklagte(r), *m.* (*Scots Law*); *instrument* –, das Armaturenbrett; *on the* –, zur Kassenpraxis zugelassen. 2. *v.a.* täfeln, paneelieren; *-led ceiling*, getäfelte Decke. **--doctor,** *s.* der Kassenarzt. **-ling,** *s.* die Täfelung, das Täfelwerk, Getäfel, die Paneelierung. **--patient,** *s.* der Kassenpatient. **--work,** *s.* das Täfelwerk.
pang [pæŋ], *s.* stechender Schmerz, der Stich; (*fig.*) aufschießende Pein, Qual *or* Angst; *-s of conscience*, Gewissensbisse.
pangolin [pæŋ'goulɪn], *s.* der Pangolin (*Zool.*).
panhandle ['pænhændl], *v.n.* (*Amer. coll.*) betteln.
[1]**panic** ['pænɪk], 1. *adj.* panisch. 2. *s.* die Panik, panischer Schrecken, die Bestürzung. (*coll.*) **-ky,** *adj.* beunruhigend; unruhig (*at*, über). **--monger,** *s.* der Bangemacher. **--stricken,** *adj.* von Schrecken ergriffen.
[2]**panic** ['pænɪk], *s.* die Kolbenhirse (*Bot.*).
panicle ['pænɪkl], *s.* die Rispe (*Bot.*).
panjandrum [pæn'dʒændrəm], *s.* der Wichtigtuer, großes Tier.
pannage ['pænɪdʒ], *s.* die Buchmast, Eichelmast; das Mastgeld.
pannier ['pænɪə], *s.* der Tragkorb; Reifrock; Aufwärter (*in the Inns of Court*).
pannikin ['pænɪkɪn], *s.* das (Trink)Kännchen.
panning ['pænɪŋ], *s.* (*coll.*) die Panoramierung(*film*).
panopl-ied ['pænəplɪd], *adj.* vollständig ausgerüstet, geschmückt. **-y** [-plɪ], *s.* vollständige Rüstung, (*fig.*) der Schmuck.
panoram-a [pænə'ræmə], *s.* das Panorama, die Gesamtansicht; der Rundblick, Überblick (*of*, über). **-ic** [-mɪk], *adj.* Panorama-; (*fig.*) umfassend; *-ic lens*, das Weitwinkelobjektiv (*Phot.*).
pansy ['pænzɪ], *s.* das Stiefmütterchen (*Bot.*); (*sl.*) der Zierbengel, Gigerl.
pant [pænt], *v.n.* schwer atmen, keuchen, schnaufen, schnauben, nach Luft schnappen; (*fig.*) lechzen (*after* or *for*, nach); *– for breath*, nach Luft schnappen. 2. *s.* das Keuchen.
pantaloon ['pæntəlu:n], *s.* der Hanswurst. **-s,** *pl.* das Beinkleid, *see* **pants.**
pantechnicon [pæn'teknɪkən], *s.* der Möbelspeicher; Möbelwagen.
pantheis-m ['pænθiɪzm], *s.* der Pantheismus. **-t** [-ɪst], *s.* der Pantheist. **-tic** [-ɪstɪk], *adj.* pantheistisch.
pantheon ['pænθiən], *s.* die Ruhmeshalle, Gedächtnishalle, das Pantheon.
panther ['pænθə], *s.* der Panther (*Zool.*).
panties ['pæntɪz], *pl.* (*coll.*) der (Damen)Schlüpfer.
pantile ['pæntaɪl], *s.* die Dachpfanne, der Pfannenziegel.
panto-graph ['pæntəgræf], *s.* der Storchschnabel. **-mime** [-maɪm], *s.* das Gebärdenspiel, Mienenspiel; die Pantomime (*Hist.*); Weihnachtsrevue, revueartiges Märchenspiel. **-mimic** [-'mɪmɪk], *adj.* pantomimisch.
pantry ['pæntrɪ], *s.* die Speisekammer, Anrichte; der Anrichteraum (*Naut.*).
pants [pænts], *pl.* die (Herren)Unterhose; *a pair of* –, eine Unterhose; (*Amer.*) das Beinkleid, die Hose.
[1]**pap** [pæp], *s.* die Brustwarze; der Kegel, runde Hügel.
[2]**pap** [pæp], *s.* der Brei, Kinderbrei, Papp. **-py,** *adj.* breiartig, breiig, pappig, pampig.

papa [pə'pɑ:], *s.* der Papa.
papa-cy ['peɪpəsɪ], *s.* das Papsttum; die Papstherrschaft. **-l** [-əl], *adj.* päpstlich; *see* **papist.**
papaver-aceous [pæpəvə'reɪʃəs], *adj.* **-ous** [pə'peɪvərəs], *adj.* mohnartig, Mohn-.
papaw [pə'pɔ:], *s.* der Melonenbaum.
paper ['peɪpə], 1. *s.* (*no pl.*) das Papier; Aktien, Wechsel, Wertpapiere, Effekten (*pl.*), (also *--money*), das Papiergeld; (*with pl.*) das Dokument, Schriftstück, der Zettel; die Zeitung, das Blatt; der Aufsatz, die Abhandlung, (also *wall--*) die Tapete; der Fragebogen (*in examinations*); das Päckchen, der Brief (*of pins, etc.*); *pl.* amtliche Papiere, Legitimationspapiere (*pl.*), die Legitimation, der Ausweis; Briefschaften, Akten (*Law*); Prüfungsarbeiten (*pl.*); *brown* –, das Packpapier; *carbon* –, das Kohlenpapier; *commit to* –, zu Papier bringen; *daily* –, die Tageszeitung, das Tageblatt; *kraft* –, das Packpapier; *– of patterns*, das Musterbuch, die Musterkarte; *on* –, auf dem Papier, schriftlich; *read a* –, einen Vortrag halten (*on*, über); *sand–*, das Sandpapier; *send in one's –s*, den Abschied nehmen; *silver* –, das Silberpapier; *tissue* –, das Seidenpapier; *tracing* –, das Pauspapier; *wall--*, die Tapete; *waste* –, das Altpapier. 2. *adj.* papieren, Papier-; dünn; leicht; *– army*, ein Heer auf dem Papier. 3. *v.a.* tapezieren (*a room*); (*sl.*) durch Freikarten füllen (*Theat.*); *– up*, in Papier verpacken. **--bag,** *s.* die Tüte. **--carriage,** *s.* der (Schreibmaschinen)Wagen. **--chase,** *s.* die Schnitzeljagd. **--clip,** *s.* die Heftklammer, Büroklammer. **- cover,** *s.* die Papierdeckung (*C.L.*). **- credit,** *s.* der Wechselkredit (*C.L.*). **- currency,** *s.* das Papiergeld, der Papier(geld)umlauf. **--cutter,** *s.* die Papierschneidemaschine (*Bookb.*); see **--knife. --fastener,** *s.* see **--clip. --folder,** *s.* das Falzbein. **--hanger,** *s.* der Tapezierer. **--hangings,** *pl.* Tapeten. **--mill,** *s.* die Papierfabrik. **- money,** *s.* das Papiergeld. **- war,** *s.* der Federkrieg, Pressekrieg, die Pressefehde. **--weight,** *s.* der Papierbeschwerer; das Papiergewicht (*Boxing*). **-y,** *adj.* papieren, Papier-; papierartig, papierähnlich, (papier)dünn.
papier-mâché ['pæpjə'mæʃeɪ], *s.* das Papiermache.
papilionaceous [pə'pɪljə'neɪʃəs], *adj.* Schmetterlings-.
papill-a [pə'pɪlə], *s.* die Papille, Warze, das Wärzchen. **-ary** ['pæpɪlərɪ], *adj.* warzig, warzenartig, Papillar-. **-ate** ['pæpɪleɪt], *adj.*, **-ose** [-ous], *adj.* warzig.
papist ['peɪpɪst], *s.* der Papist. **-ic(al)** [pə'pɪstɪk(l)], *adj.* papistisch. **-ry** ['peɪpɪstrɪ], *s.* die Papisterei, der Papismus.
papoose [pə'pu:s], *s.* das Indianerkind.
papp-us ['pæpəs], *s.* (pl. *-i*), die Haarkrone (*Bot.*).
pappy, *see* [2]**pap.**
papul-a ['pæpjulə], *s.* see **-e. -ar** [-lɑ], *adj.* Knötchen-. **-e** [-ju:l], *s.* das Bläschen, Knötchen, die Pustel.
papyr-us [pæ'paɪrəs], *s.* (pl. *-i*), der Papyrus, die Papyrusstaude (*Bot.*); die Papyrusrolle.
par [pɑ:], *s.* die Gleichheit; das Pari, der Nennwert (*C.L.*); die Einheit (*Golf*); *at* –, pari, zu Nennwert; *above* –, über Pari; *below* or *under* –, unter Pari; (*fig.*) *below* –, flau, nicht auf der Höhe (*of health*); *on a – with*, gleich (*Dat.*); *put on a – with*, gleichstellen (*Dat.*); *– of exchange*, die Wechselparität. **--value,** der Nennwert.
para- ['pærə], *prefix.* abnorm, anomal; ähnlich; *--military*, halbmilitärisch.
parab-le ['pærəbl], *s.* die Parabel, das Gleichnis. **-ola** [pə'ræbələ], *s.* die Parabel (*Geom.*). **-olic** [pærə'bɔlɪk], *adj.* gleichnisartig, Gleichnis-, in Gleichnissen; parabolisch, Parabol- (*Geom.*). **oloid** [pə'ræbəlɔɪd], *s.* das Paraboloid.
parachut-e ['pærəʃu:t], 1. *s.* der Fallschirm (*Av.*). *-e cords*, Fangleinen (*pl.*); *-e harness*, der Fallschirmgurt; *-e jump*, der Fallschirmabsprung; *-e mine*, die Luftmine; *-e troops*, Fallschirmtruppen (*pl.*), *see* **paratroops.** 2. *v.n.* mit Fallschirm abspringen. **-ist,** *s.* der Fallschirmspringer; Fallschirmjäger (*Mil.*).
paraclete ['pærəkli:t], *s.* der Früsprecher (*Theol.*).
parade [pə'reɪd], 1. *s.* der Staat, Prunk, das

Gepränge; die Parade, der Appell (*Mil.*); die Promenade, Esplanade; *make a – of*, prunken mit. 2. *v.a.* in Parade aufziehen lassen (*troops*); protzen *or* prunken mit, zur Schau tragen; – *the streets*, die Straßen prunkend durchschreiten. 3. *v.n.* in Parade aufziehen *or* vorbeimarschieren (*Mil.*); (*fig.*) sich breit machen. **--ground,** der Paradeplatz.

paradigm ['pærədɪm], *s.* das Musterbeispiel, Paradigma. **-atic** [-dɪg'mætɪk], *adj.* paradigmatisch.

paradis-aic, -aical [pærədɪ'zeɪɪk(l)], *adj.* paradiesisch. **-e** ['pærədɑɪs], *s.* das Paradies; der Himmel; *in -e*, im Paradiese; *bird of -e*, der Paradiesvogel; *fool's -e*, verhängnisvoller Irrtum.

parados ['pærədəs], *s.* die Rückenwehr, Rückendeckung.

paradox ['pærədəks], *s.* widersprüchliche Behauptung, der Widerspruch, das Paradox(on). **-ical** [-'dəksɪk(l)], *adj.* paradox, widersinnig, widersprüchlich.

paraffin ['pærəfɪn], *s.* das Paraffin; – *oil*, das Paraffinöl, Leuchtpetroleum; – *wax*, das Paraffin.

paragon ['pærəgən], *s.* das Muster, Vorbild; der Musterknabe.

paragraph ['pærəgrɑ:f], *s.* der Absatz, Abschnitt, Paragraph; kurzer Zeitungsartikel; das Paragraphenzeichen (*Typ.*). **-er,** *s.*, **-ist,** *s.* der Kleinartikelschreiber.

parakeet ['pærəkɪ:t], *s.* der (Halsband)Sittich.

paralipomena [pærəlɪ'pɔmɪnə], *pl.* nachgelassene Schriften; Nachträge (*pl.*).

paralla-ctic [pærə'læktɪk], *adj.* parallaktisch. **-x** ['pærəlæks], *s.* die Parallaxe.

parallel ['pærəlɛl], 1. *adj.* gleichlaufend, parallel (*to* or *with*, mit); (*fig.*) entsprechend, ähnlich; – *bars*, der Barren (*Gymn.*); – *connexion*, die Parallelschaltung; – *ruler*, das Parallellineal; *run – to*, parallel laufen mit. 2. *s.* die Parallele (*also fig.*), Parallellinie; der Parallelfall, das Gegenstück; der Parallelkreis, Breitenkreis (*Geog.*); (*fig.*) die Übereinstimmung, Ähnlichkeit; der Vergleich; – *of latitude*, der Breitenkreis (*Geog.*); *draw a – between*, einen Vergleich anstellen *or* eine Parallele ziehen zwischen, mit einander vergleichen; *without* –, einzig, ohnegleichen, ohne Parallele. 3. *v.a.* parallel machen; als gleich *or* ähnlich hinstellen, vergleichen (*with*, mit); gleich sein (*with*, mit), Gleichartiges finden (*to*, für), gleichkommen (*Dat.*); *to be -led*, sich vergleichen lassen mit, entsprechen (*Dat.*). **-ism** [-ɪzm], *s.* der Parallelismus, parallele Richtung (*to*, zu; *with*, mit). **-ogram** [-'lɛləgræm], *s.* das Parallelogram.

paralogism [pə'rælədʒɪzm], *s.* der Trugschluß, Fehlschluß.

paraly-sation [pærəlɑɪ'zeɪʃən], *s.* die Lähmung. **-se** ['pærəlɑɪz], *v.a.* lähmen, paralysieren; (*fig.*) entkräften, (*with*, durch *or* von); unwirksam machen, lahmlegen. **-sis** [pə'rælɪsɪs], *s.* die Lähmung, Paralyse; (*fig.*) Lahmlegung. **-tic** [pærə'lɪtɪk], 1. *adj.* gelähmt, paralytisch. 2. *s.* der Paralytiker, Gelähmte(r), *m.*

parameter [pæ'ræmɪtə], *s.* der Parameter (*Math.*).

paramount ['pærəmɑʊnt], 1. *adj.* oberst, Ober-; höchst, größt, ausschlaggebend; *be* –, über alles gehen, an erster Stelle stehen, ausschlaggebend sein; *be – to*, höher stehen als, wichtiger sein als. 2. *s.* (*lord* –) der Oberlehnsherr. **-ly,** *adv.* vornehmlich, vor allem.

paramour ['pærəmu:ə], *s.* der Buhler, Geliebte(r), *m.*

parapet ['pærəpɛt], *s.* die Brustwehr; das (Schutz)-Geländer; die Brüstung.

paraph ['pærəf], *s.* der Namenszug, Handzug; der Schnörkel (*of signature*).

paraphernalia [pærəfə'neɪlɪə], *pl.* das Paraphernalgut (*Law*); (*coll.*) das Zubehör, Drum und Dran.

paraphras-e ['pærəfreɪz], 1. *s.* die Umschreibung, Paraphrase, freie Wiedergabe. 2. *v.a. & n.* umschreiben, frei wiedergeben. **-tic** [-'fræstɪk], *adj.* umschreibend, paraphrastisch.

paraplegia [pærə'plɪ:dʒɪə], *s.* beiderseitige Lähmung.

parasit-e ['pærəsɑɪt], *s.* der Schmarotzer, Parasit; (*coll.*) Nassauer (*of persons*). **-ic(al)** [-'sɪtɪk(l)], *adj.* schmarotzend, Schmarotzer-, parasitisch. **-ism,** *s.* das Schmarotzertum, Parasitentum.

parasol [pærə'sɔl, 'pærəsɔl], *s.* der Sonnenschirm.

parata-ctic [pærə'tæktɪk], *adj.* nebengeordnet, parataktisch. **-xis** [-'tæksɪs], *s.* die Nebenordnung, Beiordnung.

parathyroid [pærə'θɑɪrɔɪd], *s.* (also – *gland*) die Nebenschilddrüse.

paratroops ['pærətru:ps], *pl.* Fallschirmtruppen (*pl.*) (*Mil.*).

paratyphoid [pærə'tɑɪfɔɪd], *s.* der Paratyphus.

paravane ['pærəveɪn], *s.* das Bugschutzgerät (*against mines*) (*Naut.*).

parboil ['pɑ:bɔɪl], *v.a.* halb kochen, aufkochen lassen, ankochen, abbrühen; (*fig.*) überhitzen.

parbuckle [pɑ:bʌkl], 1. *s.* das Jolltau. 2. *v.a.* mit Jolltau heben (*Naut.*).

parcel [pɑ:sl], 1. *s.* das Paket; die Menge; Parzelle (*of land*); der Posten, die Partie (*C.L.*); (*coll.*) *part and – of*, wesentliches Bestandteil von: *bill of -s*, die Faktura (*C.L.*). 2. *v.a.* (also – *out*) abteilen, austeilen, verteilen; parzellieren (*land*); (also – *up*) umwickeln, einpacken, zusammenpacken (*goods*); schmarten (*Naut.*). 3. *adv.* (*archaic*) teilweise, halb-. **-ling,** *s.* die Einteilung; Schmarting (*Naut.*). **-(s)-office,** *s.* die Gepäckabfertigung(stelle). **– post,** *s.* die Paketpost.

parcen-ary ['pɑ:sənərɪ], *s.* der Mitbesitz (durch Erbschaft) (*Law*). **-er** [-sənə], *s.* der Miterbe.

parch [pɑ:tʃ], 1. *v.a.* dörren, austrocknen; *be -ed with thirst*, vor Durst verschmachten; *-ed corn*, gerösteter Mais; *-ed lips*, trockene Lippen. 2. *v.n.* vertrocknen, eintrocknen; verschmachten. **-edness** [-tnɪs], *s.* die Dürre. **-ing,** *adj.* sengend, brennend.

parchment ['pɑ:tʃmənt], *s.* das Pergament, die (Pergament)Urkunde. **-y,** *adj.* Pergament-, pergamentartig.

pard [pɑ:d], *s.* (*sl.*) der Partner.

pardon ['pɑ:dən], 1. *s.* die Verzeihung, Vergebung; Begnadigung; der Ablaß (*Eccl.*); *I beg your* –, wie bitte! verzeihen Sie! *ask* or *beg s.o.'s* –, einen um Verzeihung bitten; *general* –, die Amnestie; *a thousand -s*, ich bitte tausendmal um Verzeihung. 2. *v.a.* verzeihen, vergeben (*a p.* (*Dat.*)), entschuldigen, begnadigen (*Acc.*); – *me!* verzeihen *or* entschuldigen Sie! **-able,** verzeihlich. **-ableness,** *s.* die Verzeihlichkeit. **-er,** *s.* der Ablaßkrämer (*Hist.*).

pare ['pɛ:ə], *v.a.* (be)schneiden (*nails, etc.*); schälen (*apples, etc.*); – *away* or *off*, abschneiden, abschaben, beschneiden, zurichten. *See* **paring.**

paregoric [pærə'gɔrɪk], 1. *adj.* schmerzstillend. 2. *s.* das Linderungsmittel.

parenchyma [pə'rɛnkɪmə], *s.* das Parenchym (*Anat.*), Zellgewebe (*Bot.*).

parent ['pɛərənt], 1. *s.* der Vater, die Mutter; das Muttertier (*Zool.*), die Mutterpflanze (*Bot.*); (*fig.*) Ursache, Quelle, der Urheber, Ursprung; *pl.* Eltern. 2. *adj.* Mutter-, Ur-, Ursprungs-; – *cell*, die Mutterzelle; – *company*, das Stammhaus; – *form*, die Urform. **-age** [-ɪdʒ], *s.* die Abkunft, Abstammung, Familie, Elternschaft; (*fig.*) Herkunft, Urheberschaft, der Ursprung. **-al** [pə'rɛntl], *adj.* elterlich, väterlich, mütterlich; (*fig.*) ursprünglich; *-al roof*, das Elternhaus. **-hood** [-hud], *s.* die Elternschaft. **-less,** *adj.* elternlos.

parenthe-sis [pə'rɛnθəsɪs], *s.* die Einschaltung, Parenthese; (usually pl. *-ses* [-sɪ:z]) (runde) Klammern (*Typ.*); *by way of -sis*, beiläufig. **-size** [-sɑɪz], *v.a.* einschalten; einklammern (*Typ.*). **-tic(al)** [pærən'θɛtɪk(l)], *adj.* eingeschaltet; eingeklammert (*Typ.*); in Parenthese (*Typ. & fig.*). **-tically,** *adv.* beiläufig, nebenbei.

paresis ['pærəsɪs], *s.* die Parese (*Med.*).

par excellence [pɑ:'ɛksəlɑ:ns], vor allen anderen, im wahren Sinne des Wortes.

parget ['pɑ:dʒɪt], 1. *s.* die Tünche, der Bewurf, (Wand)Putz. 2. *v.a.* tünchen, putzen. **-ing,** *s.* das Tünchen, Putzen, der (Wand)Putz.

parhelion [pɑ:'hɪ:lɪən], *s.* die Nebensonne, das Parhelium (*Astr.*).

pariah [pə'rɑɪə], *s.* der Paria; (*fig.*) Ausgestoßene(r), *m.*

parietal [pə'rɪ:ətl], 1. *adj.* parietal (*Anat.*). 2. *s.* (– *bone*) das Scheitelbein.
paring ['pɛ:rɪŋ], 1. *s.* das Abschneiden, Abschaben; Schnitzel; *pl.* Späne, Abschabsel; Schaben (*of fruit*). 2. *attrib. adj.* Schab–, Schäl–.
parish ['pærɪʃ], 1. *s.* das Kirchspiel, der Pfarrbezirk, Sprengel, die Gemeinde; (*collect.*) die Gemeindemitglieder; *come on the* –, der Gemeinde zur Last fallen; *go on the* –, Armenunterstützung erhalten. 2. *attrib. adj.* Pfarr–, Kirchen–, Gemeinde–; –*church*, die Pfarrkirche; – *clerk*, der Küster; – *council*, der Gemeinderat; – *priest*, der Ortspfarrer; ––*pump politician*, der Kirchturmpolitiker; – *register*, das Kirchenbuch; – *relief*, die Gemeindeunterstützung. **–ioner** [–'rɪʃənə], *s.* das Pfarrkind, Gemeindemitglied.
parisyllabic [pærɪsɪ'læbɪk], *adj.* gleichsilbig.
parity ['pærɪtɪ], *s.* die Gleichheit, Gleichberechtigung; Parität, der Umrechnungskurs, Pariwert (*C.L.*); *at* –, pari, zu Pari (*C.L.*).
park [pɑ:k], 1. *s.* der Park, die Parkanlage, öffentliche Anlage; der Parkplatz (*Motor.*); die Sammelstelle, der Fuhrpark, Geschützpark (*Mil.*). 2. *v.a.* aufstellen, aufbewahren, abstellen; parken (*motor-cars*). 3. *v.n.* parken. **–ing,** *s.* das Parken. **–ing-place,** *s.* (*Amer.* **–ing-lot**) der Parkplatz. **––keeper** *s.* der Parkaufseher. **–y,** *adj.* (*coll.*) frisch, kühl.
parkin ['pɑ:kɪn], *s.* der Honigkuchen.
parlance ['pɑ:ləns], *s.* die Redeweise; *in common* –, wie man sich gewöhnlich ausdrückt.
parley ['pɑ:lɪ], 1. *v.n.* verhandeln, unterhandeln, parlamentieren (*Mil.*). 2. *v.a.* (*sl.*) sprechen (*a language*). 2. *s.* die Unterhandlung, Unterredung; *beat* or *sound a* –, Schamade schlagen.
parliament ['pɑ:ləmənt], *s.* das Parlament; *act of* –, das Reichsgesetz; *enter, get into* or *go into* –, ins Parlament gewählt werden; *in* –, im Parlament; *member of* –, das Parlamentsmitglied, Abgeordnete(r) *m.* **–arian** [–'tɛ:ərɪən], 1. *s.* der Parlamentsanhänger (*Hist.*); Parlamentarier. 2. *adj.* parlamentarisch. **–arianism** [–'tɛ:ərɪənɪzm], *s.* der Parlamentarismus. **–ary** [–'mɛntərɪ], *adj.* Parlaments–, parlamentarisch, (*fig.*) höflich; –*ary language*, höfliche Redensart; –*ary secretary*, der Parlamentssekretär; (*archaic*) –*ary train*, der Bummelzug.
parlour ['pɑ:lə], *s.* das Wohnzimmer, gute Stube, der Salon; das Empfangszimmer, Sprechzimmer; Gästezimmer (*in inns*); *beauty*––, der Schönheitssalon; *ice-cream* –, die Eisdiele. **––car,** *s.* der Luxuswagen, Salonwagen (*Amer.*). **––game,** *s.* das Gesellschaftsspiel. **––maid,** *s.* das Stubenmädchen.
parlous ['pɑ:ləs], *adj.* (*archaic*) gefährlich, schlimm, kritisch.
parochial [pə'roukɪəl], *adj.* Pfarr–, Gemeinde–; (*fig.*) eng(herzig), beschränkt, begrenzt; – *politics*, die Kirchturmpolitik. **–ism,** *s.* die Engherzigkeit, Beschränktheit, das Spießbürgertum, die Kirchturmpolitik.
parod–ist ['pærədɪst], *s.* der Verfasser von Parodien. **–y** [–dɪ], 1. *s.* die Parodie (*of*, auf), Parodierung; (*fig.*) Entstellung, Verzerrung. 2. *v.a.* parodieren.
parole [pæ'roul], 1. *s.* das Ehrenwort; Bewährungsfrist, der Straferlaß; die Parole, Losung, das Losungswort, Erkennungswort, Kennwort (*Mil.*); mündliche Erklärung (*Law*); *by* –, mündlich (*Law*); *on* –, auf Ehrenwort; *release on* –, bedingte Begnadigung. 2. *v.a.* auf Ehrenwort verpflichten.
paronym [[pærənɪm], *s.* stammverwandtes Wort. **–ous** [–'rɔnɪməs], *adj.* stammverwandt.
paroquet ['pærəkɛt], *see* **parokeet.**
parotid [pə'rɔtɪd], *adj.*; – *gland*, die Ohrspeicheldrüse.
paroxysm ['pærəksɪzm], *s.* der (Krampf)Anfall (*also fig.*); – *of laughter*, der Lachanfall. **–al** [–'sɪzməl], *adj.* krampfartig.
paroxytone [pə'rɔksɪtoun], *s.* das Paroxytonon (*Pros.*).
parpen ['pɑ:pən], *s.* der Tragstein, Binder (*Build.*).
parquet [pɑ:'kɛt], *s.* das Parkett (*also Theat.*); der Parkett(fuß)boden. **–ry,** *s.* das Parkett, getäfelter Fußboden.
parr [pɑ:], *s.* junger Lachs.
parricid–al [pærɪ'sɑɪdl], *adj.* vatermörderisch, muttermörderisch. **–e** ['pærɪsɑɪd], *s.* der Vatermörder, Muttermörder, Elternmörder; Landesverräter; Vatermord, Muttermord, Elternmord; Landesverrat.
parrot ['pærət], 1. *s.* der Papagei; (*fig.*) Nachschwätzer; *repeat* ––*fashion*, gedankenlos nachplappern. 2. *v.a.* nachplappern.
parry ['pærɪ], 1. *s.* die Parade (*Fenc.*), Abwehr, der Fangstoß. 2. *v.a.* & *n.* parieren, abwehren.
pars–e [pɑ:z], *v.a.* grammatisch zerlegen, zergliedern *or* analysieren. **–ing,** *s.* die Satzzergliederung.
parsimon–ious [pɑ:sɪ'mounɪəs], *adj.* sparsam, karg (*of*, mit); knauserig, knickerig. **–iousness, –y** ['pɑ:sɪmənɪ], *s.* die Sparsamkeit, Knauserei; Knauserigkeit.
parsley ['pɑ:slɪ], *s.* die Petersilie (*Bot.*).
parsnip ['pɑ:snɪp], *s.* die Pastinake, der Pastinak (*Bot.*).
parson ['pɑ:sən], *s.* (*coll.*) der Pfarrer, Geistliche; Pfaffe; (*coll.*) –'*s nose*, der Bürzel, Steiß von Geflügel. **–age** [–ɪdʒ], *s.* das Pfarrhaus; die Pfarre.
part [pɑ:t], **1.** *s.* der Teil; das Stück, Glied; die Gegend, der Bezirk (*usually pl.*); Anteil, die Beteiligung; Partei, Seite, Sache; Lieferung (*of a book*); Rolle (*Theat.* & *fig.*); Einzelstimme, das Einzelinstrument (*Mus.*); Obliegenheit, Aufgabe, Schuldigkeit, Pflicht, das Amt; *pl.* geistige Gaben, Fähigkeiten *or* Anlagen; see also *privy* –*s*. (*a*) (*with adjectives*) *the better* –, see *the greater* –; *component* –, der Bestandteil; *a great* – *of*, ein großer Teil von; *the greater* –, der größte Teil, das Meiste, die Mehrheit; die längste Zeit; *the most* –, der größte Teil; *privy* –*s*, die Schamteile (*pl.*). (*b*) (*with verbs*) *act a* –, see *play a* –; *be* – *and parcel of*, ein wesentlicher Bestandteil sein von; *be art and* – *in*, Anteil haben an; *do one's* –, seine Schuldigkeit tun; *form a* – *of*, einen Teil bilden von; *have neither* – *nor* or *no* – *or lot in*, nicht das geringste zu tun haben mit; *play a* –, eine Rolle spielen (*also fig.*), (*fig.*) von Bedeutung sein; *play one's* –, seinen Teil dazu beitragen; *take a* –, eine Rolle übernehmen; *take s.o.*'s –, *take* – *with a p.*, jemandes Partei ergreifen; *take* – *in*, teilnehmen an (*Dat.*). (*c*) (*with prepositions*) *for the most* –, meisten(teil)s, größtenteils; *for my* –, was mich (an)betrifft, meinerseits, ich für meinen Teil; *from all* –*s*, von allen Ecken und Enden; *in* –, teilweise, zum Teil; *in* –*s*, in Lieferungen (*as a book*); *in large* –, zum großen Teil; *in foreign* –*s*, im Auslande; *payment in* –, die Teilzahlung, Zahlung auf Abschlag; *take in good* (*bad*) –, gut (übel) aufnehmen; *in these* –*s*, hierzulande, in dieser Gegend; *of* –*s*, talentvoll, begabt, geweckt; vielseitig ausgezeichnet; – *of speech*, der Redeteil, die Wortklasse; *on the* – *of*, von seiten, seitens (*Gen.*); *on my* –, meinerseits. **2.** *attrib. adj.* Teil–; *in* – *exchange*, in Zahlung; – *payment*, die Abschlagszahlung; *in* – *payment*, auf Aufschlag; – *owner*, der Mitbesitzer. **3.** *adv.* teils, teilweise, zum Teil; – . . . – . . ., teils . . . teils . . .; ––*time work*, die Nebenbeschäftigung; ––*time worker*, der Aushilfsarbeiter. **4.** *v.a.* teilen, zerteilen; trennen; zertrennen, auseinandertrennen, auseinanderhalten; abgrenzen (*from*, gegen); scheiden (*Chem.*); scheiteln (*the hair*); – *company*, sich trennen (*with*, von). **5.** *v.n.* sich trennen (*as roads*); auseinandergehen, scheiden; brechen, zerreißen (*Naut.*); –*from*, sich trennen, scheiden *or* Abschied nehmen von (*a p.*); – *with*, aufgeben, abgeben, loswerden, verlieren, verkaufen, sich für immer trennen von (*a th.*); – *friends*, als Freunde auseinandergehen. **–ing,** *see* **parting. –ite,** *see* **partite. –ition,** *see* **partition. –itive,** *see* **partitive. –ly,** *see* **partly. ––music,** *s.* mehrstimmige Musik. **––owner, ––payment,** *see under* **– 2. ––singing,** *s.* mehrstimmiger Gesang. **––song,** *s.* mehrstimmiges Lied. **––time,** *adj. see under* **– 2.**
partake [pɑ:'teɪk], *ir.v.n.* teilnehmen, teilhaben in *or* an (*Dat.*); – *of*, etwas an sich (*Dat.*) haben von; – *of a meal*, eine Mahlzeit einnehmen, genießen *or* zu sich nehmen. **–r,** *s.* der Teilnehmer, Teilhaber (*of*, an (*Dat.*)).
parterre [pɑ:'tɛ:ə], *s.* das Blumenbeet (*Hort.*); Parterre (*Theat.*).

parthenogenesis [pɑ:θəno'dʒɛnɪsɪs], *s.* die Parthenogenese, Jungfernzeugung.

partial ['pɑ:ʃəl], *adj.* partiell, unvollständig, Halb–, Teil–, einseitig, parteiisch, eingenommen (*to*, für); *be – to*, sehr gerne haben, eine besondere Vorliebe haben für; *– acceptance*, bedingte Annahme; *– bond*, der Teilschuldschein; *– eclipse*, partielle Verfinsterung; *– success*, der Halberfolg; *– umbel*, das Doldchen (*Bot.*). **–ity** [–ʃɪ'ælɪtɪ], *s.* die Parteilichkeit; besondere Vorliebe (*to* or *for*, für). **–ly**, *adv.* zum Teil, teilweise.

particip–ant [pɑ:'tɪsɪpənt], *s.* der Teilnehmer (*in*, an). **–ate** [–peɪt], *v.n.* teilhaben, teilnehmen, sich beteiligen, beteiligt sein (*in*, an (*Dat.*)). **–ating**, *adj.* gewinnbeteiligt, gewinnberechtigt (*C.L.*). **–ation** [–'peɪʃən], *s.* die Mitwirkung, Teilnahme (*in*, an (*Dat.*)); Teilhaftigkeit, der Genuß (*of* (*Gen.*)); die (Gewinn)Beteiligung, Teilhabe. **–ator** [–'tɪsɪpeɪtə], *s.* der Teilnehmer (*in*, an (*Dat.*)).

particip–ial [pɑ:tɪ'sɪpɪəl], *adj.* partizipial (*Gram.*). **–le** ['pɑ:tɪsɪpl], *s.* das Partizip(ium).

particle ['pɑ:tɪkl], *s.* das Teilchen, Stückchen; Stoffteilchen, Körperchen; die Partikel (*Gram.*); (*coll.*) *not a – of*, kein bißchen *or* Fünkchen *or* keine Spur von.

parti-coloured [pɑ:tɪ'kʌləd], *adj.* bunt.

particular [pɑ:'tɪkjʊlə], 1. *adj.* einzeln, individuell, besonder; sonderbar, ungewöhnlich; ausführlich, umständlich, peinlich, genau, vorsichtig, wählerisch; *be – about*, es genau nehmen mit, Wert legen auf; *not be too –*, nicht zu genau nehmen, nicht zu wählerisch sein; *be – not to*, vorsichtig sein, daß man nicht; *he is not – to a day*, es kommt ihm auf einen Tag nicht an; *nothing –*, nichts Besonderes. 2. *s.* einzelner *or* besonderer Punkt *or* Umstand, die Einzelheit; *in –*, insbesondere, im besonderen, besonders, vornehmlich; *argue from the general to the –*, vom Allgemeinen auf das Besondere schließen; *on this –*, in diesem Punkt; *see* **–s. –ism** [–rɪzm], *s.* der Partikularismus, die Kleinstaaterei; Sonderbestrebung. **–ity** [–'lærɪtɪ], *s.* die Genauigkeit, Ausführlichkeit, Umständlichkeit; Besonderheit, besondere Bewandtnis. **–ization** [–ləraɪ'zeɪʃən], *s.* die Einzelbehandlung, Detailschilderung. **–ize** [–'tɪkjʊləraɪz], 1. *v.a.* einzeln *or* ausführlich angeben, spezifizieren, umständlich anführen, eingehend darstellen. 2. *v.n.* ins Einzelne gehen. **–ly**, *adv.* besonders, vorzüglich, insbesondere, im besonderen; (*more*) *–ly as*, um so mehr als; *not –ly*, nicht sonderlich. **–s** [–ləz], *pl.* Einzelheiten, nähere Umstände (*pl.*), nähere Auskunft, Näheres, *n.* (*with regard to, about* or *of*, über); *for –s apply within*, Näheres hierbei; *for –s apply to . . .*, Näheres durch . . .; *enter* or *go into –s*, ins Einzelne gehen.

parting ['pɑ:tɪŋ], 1. *attrib. adj.* Scheide–, Abschieds–; *– breath*, letzter Atemzug; *– kiss*, der Abschiedskuß; (*fig.*) *– shot*, letztes boshaftes Wort; *– tool*, der Geißfuß. 2. *s.* das Teilen, die Teilung, Trennung; das Scheiden, der Abschied; die Scheidung (*Chem.*); der Scheitel (*of hair*); das Zerreißen, der Riß (*Naut.*); *– of the ways*, die Wegscheide, Weggabelung; (*fig.*) der Scheideweg; *at –*, beim Weggehen *or* Abschied.

[1]**partisan** [pɑ:tɪ'zæn], *s.* der Anhänger, Parteigänger; Freischärler, Partisan (*Mil.*); *– spirit*, der Parteigeist. **–ship**, *s.* das Parteigängertum, die Parteianhängerschaft, lebhafte Parteinahme; die Parteiwirtschaft, Cliquenwirtschaft.

[2]**partisan** ['pɑ:tɪzən], *s.* die Partisane (*Hist.*).

partite ['pɑ:taɪt], *adj.* geteilt (*Bot.*).

partition [pɑ:'tɪʃən], 1. *s.* die Teilung, Unterteilung, Verteilung, Zerteilung, Aufteilung (*of a country*), Trennung, Absonderung; Abteilung, der Teil, das Fach (*of cupboard, etc.*), die Scheidewand (*also Bot.*); der Verschlag; *– wall*, die Brandmauer, Zwischenmauer. 2. *v.a.* (ver)teilen, aufteilen (*a country*); *– off*, abteilen, abtrennen.

partitive ['pɑ:tɪtɪv], 1. *adj.* Teil–, teilend; partitiv (*Gram.*). 2. *s.* das Partitivum (*Gram.*).

partly ['pɑ:tlɪ], *adv.* teils, zum Teil; *– . . ., – . . .*, teils . . ., teils . . .; *–ly closed*, teilweise geschlossen.

partner ['pɑ:tnə], *s.* der Teilnehmer (*in* or *of*, an), Genosse; Teilhaber, Kompagnon, Associé, Sozius (*C.L.*); Mitspieler, Partner (*Sport, Cards*); Tanzpartner; Gatte, die Gattin; *pl.* Fischungen (*Naut.*); *senior –*, älterer Teilhaber; *sleeping –*, stiller Teilhaber; *be a – in*, Teil haben an (*Dat.*); *be –s*, zusammen spielen. **–ship**, *s.* offene Handelsgesellschaft, die Genossenschaft, Teilhaberschaft (*in*, an); *limited –ship*, die Kommanditgesellschaft; *deed of –ship*, der Gesellschaftsvertrag; *enter into –ship*, sich assoziieren (*with*, mit); *take s.o. into –ship*, einen als Teilhaber aufnehmen.

partridge ['pɑ:trɪdʒ], *s.* das Rebhuhn (*Orn.*).

parturi–ent [pɑ:'tjʊ:ərɪənt], *adj.* gebärend, kreißend, schwanger. **–tion** [–'rɪʃən], *s.* das Gebären.

party ['pɑ:tɪ], 1. *s.* die Partei (*Pol., Law, etc.*), Gruppe; der Kläger *or* Beklagte(r), *m.* (*Law*); der Teilhaber, Interessent, Beteiligte(r), *m.* (*to*, an); (*coll.*) die Person, der Mensch, Kunde, das Individuum; die Gesellschaft; Veranstaltung; das Kommando, die Abteilung (*Mil.*); *be a – to*, beteiligt sein *or* teilnehmen an *or* bei, zu tun haben mit; *give a –*, eine Gesellschaft geben; *the parties concerned*, die Betroffenen *or* Beteiligten (*pl.*); *contracting –*, der Kontrahent; *hunting –*, die Jagdgesellschaft; *offended –*, beleidigter Teil; *make one of the –*, mit dabei sein, sich einer Gesellschaft anschließen; *tea –*, die Teeveranstaltung; *third –*, der Dritte; *go to a –*, eingeladen sein. 2. *attrib. adj.* Partei–. **– boss**, *s.* der Parteibonze. **– line**, *s.* Parteidirektiven (*pl.*) (*Pol.*); *follow the – line*, Parteidisziplin halten. **– -line**, *s.* der Sammelanschluß (*Tele.*). **– man**, *s.* der Parteimann. **– spirit**, *s.* der Parteigeist. **– -wall**, *s.* die Brandmauer, Scheidewand, gemeinsame Mauer.

parvenu ['pɑ:vənjʊ], *s.* der Emporkömmling.

parvis ['pɑ:vɪs], *s.* der Vorhof (*Arch.*).

paschal ['pæskl], *adj.* Passah–, Oster–.

pasha ['pɑ:ʃə, 'pæʃə], *s.* der Pascha.

pasque-flower ['pæsk'flauə], *s.* die Küchenschelle, Osterblume.

pasquinade [pæskwɪ'neɪd], *s.* die Schmähschrift, das Pasquill.

pass [pɑ:s], **1.** *v.n.* sich bewegen, gehen, ziehen, fahren, fließen, *etc.*; vorbeigehen, vorbeiziehen, vorbeifahren, vorbeifließen, *etc.* (*by*, an (*Dat.*)); vergehen, vorübergehen, vorüberfließen, *etc.*; verschwinden, verstreichen, zu Ende gehen (*of time, etc.*), vor sich gehen, geschehen, vorfallen, sich ereignen, abspielen *or* zutragen, passieren; werden (*into*, zu), übergehen (*from*, von; (*in*)*to*, zu); durchgehen, durchkommen, bewilligt werden (*as a bill*); bestehen (*as an examination*); angenommen *or* geduldet werden, hingehen, angehen; in Umgang, bekannt *or* gangbar sein; gehalten werden, gelten (*for* or *as*, für); ausfallen (*Fenc.*); überspringen (*of sparks*) (*Elec.*); passen (*Footb., Cards, etc.*); *let –*, (vorüber)gehen *or* vorbeigehen lassen; *let – unpunished*, unbestraft lassen; *it came to –*, es geschah. (*a*) (*with adverbs*) *– along*, weitergehen; *– away*, fortgehen, weggehen; sterben; dahinschwinden, zu Ende gehen, aufhören, vergehen (*of time*); (*fig.*) *– by*, vorbeigehen, vorübergehen; vergehen, verfließen; *– off*, vorübergehen, vergehen, verschwinden; vor sich gehen, vonstatten gehen, ablaufen, verlaufen; *– on*, vorwärtsgehen, weitergehen, übergehen (*to*, zu); sterben; *– out*, hinausgehen; (*coll.*) ohnmächtig werden; *– over*, übergehen (*into*, in), hinübergehen (*to*, auf). (*b*) (*with prepositions*) *– beyond*, hinausgehen über, überschreiten; *– by*, vorübergehen an; *– by the name* (*of*), unter dem Namen (. . .) bekannt sein; *– over*, hinübergehen über; mit der Hand streichen über; *– through*, gehen *or* reisen durch; dringen durch; (*fig.*) durchmachen, erleben, erfahren; *– to*, übergehen an, fallen an. **2.** *v.a.* vorbei– *or* vorüber(gehen, fahren, ziehen, fließen, *etc.*) an; überschreiten, übersteigen, hinausgehen über, überholen; zubringen, hinbringen, verbringen, vergehen lassen, verleben (*time*); reichen, verabfolgen, befördern, weitergeben, in Umlauf bringen; einbringen, durchbringen (*a bill*) (*Parl.*); anerkennen, gelten lassen, genehmigen, zulassen; vorbeigehen *or* vorbeiziehen lassen, durchgehen lassen, vorbeilassen, durchlassen; Annahme finden bei, gebilligt werden von; bestehen (*examination*); abgefertigt werden von (*customs*). (*a*) (*with nouns*) *– an act*, ein

Gesetz ergehen lassen; – *the ball*, den Ball weitergeben *or* zuspielen (*Footb.*); – *the bounds of moderation*, die Grenzen der Mäßigung überschreiten; – *the butter, please!* bitte reichen Sie mir die Butter! darf ich um die Butter bitten; *he has –ed the chair*, er ist Vorsitzender gewesen; – *a cheque*, einen Scheck einlösen; *that –es my comprehension*, das geht über meine Begriffe; – *criticism on*, Kritik üben an; – *one's eye over*, flüchtig überblicken; – *one's hand over*, die Hand gleiten lassen über, mit der Hand fahren über; *the bill has –ed the house*, der Gesetzentwurf ist vom Parlament angenommen worden; – *judgement on*, ein Urteil fällen über; – *muster*, Zustimmung finden (*with*, bei); gelten (*as*, als); – *one's opinion upon*, seine Meinung äußern über; – *sentence*, das Urteil fällen (*on*, über); – *a string round s.th.*, etwas umschnüren; (*coll.*) – *the time of day*, grüßen; – *a vote of thanks*, im Namen aller Anwesenden den Dank aussprechen; – *water*, Wasser lassen. (*b*) (*with prepositions*) – *for clearance*, zur Einfuhr freigeben (*into*, nach); – *for military service*, für diensttauglich erklären; – *in review*, vorbeimarschieren lassen; (*fig.*) Revue passieren lassen; – *over to justice*, an das Gericht ausliefern; – *through a filter*, durchsieben, abfiltrieren, durch ein Sieb passieren; – *through a lock*, durchschleusen (*a ship*); – *to a p.'s account*, einem in Rechnung stellen *or* bringen; – *to a p.'s credit*, einem gutschreiben (*C.L.*). (*c*) (*with adverbs*) – *away*, verbringen (*time*); – *by*, übergehen; übersehen, unbeachtet lassen; – *in*, einreichen; (*sl.*) – *in one's cheques*, sterben; – *off*, ausgeben (*as* or *for*, als); – *on*, weiterschicken, weitergeben (*to*, an); – *over*, weitergeben (*to*, an); übergehen (*a p.*), auslassen (*a th.*); hingehen lassen (*a misdemeanour*); – *over in silence*, stillschweigend übergehen *or* hingehen lassen; – *round*, herumreichen, herumgehen lassen; (*sl.*) – *up*, vorübergehen lassen, aufgeben, verzichten auf. **3.** *s.* der Paß, Engpaß, das Gebirgsjoch; der Durchgang, Gang, Weg; Kanal, die Durchfahrt (*Naut.*); das Streichen, die Bestreichung (*mesmerism*); der Paß, (Personal)Ausweis, Passierschein; Urlaubschein (*Mil.*); die Freikarte (*Theat.*, *Railw.*); kritischer Zustand, kritische Lage; der Stoß, Ausfall (*Fenc.*); das Zuspielen (*Footb.*); Bestehen, Durchkommen (*in examinations*); gewöhnlicher Grad (*Univ.*); *at a desperate –*, in einer verzweifelten Lage; *bring to –*, vollführen, ausführen, bewirken, fertigbringen, zustandebringen; *come to –*, sich ereignen *or* zutragen, eintreten; *things have come to such a –*, die Dinge haben sich derart zugespitzt. **–able,** *adj.* gangbar, befahrbar, passierbar; gültig, erträglich, leidlich, passabel. **– -book,** *s* das Bankkontobuch. **– -cheque,** der Passierschein. **–er-by,** *see* **passer-by.** **– -examination,** *s.* gewöhnliche Universitätsprüfung. **–ing,** *see* **passing.** **– -key,** *s.* der Hauptschlüssel; Drücker. **–port,** *see* **passport.** **–word,** *see* **password.** *See also* **past.**

passage [ˈpæsɪdʒ], 1. *s.* die Durchfahrt, Durchreise; Seereise, Überfahrt; der Durchzug (*of birds*); das Durchgehen, Durchkommen, Inkrafttreten, die Annahme (*of a bill*); der Übergang, Flur, Gang, Korridor (*Build.*); Weg; die Stelle, der Passus (*in a book*); die Passage, der Lauf (*Mus.*); Verlauf (*of time*); *air –*, der Luftkanal; – *of arms;* der Waffengang; *connecting –*, der Verbindungsgang; – *home*, die Rückfahrt; *book one's –*, die Schiffskarte lösen; *work one's – (out)*, die Überfahrt durch Arbeit an Bord bezahlen. 2. *v.n.* seitwärts reiten; sich seitwärts bewegen (*as a horse*). **– -money,** *s.* das Überfahrtsgeld. **– -way,** *s.* der Korridor, Durchgang.

pass–ant [ˈpæsənt], *adj.* schreitend (*Her.*). **–é** [ˈpɑse], *adj.* vorüber, veraltet. **–ée,** *adj.* verblüht (*of women*).

passement [ˈpæsəmənt], *s.* die Tresse, Borte. **–erie,** *s.* Posamentierwaren (*pl.*).

passenger [ˈpæsəndʒe], *s.* der Fahrgast, Passagier, Reisende(r), *m.*, der Fluggast (*Av.*); (*coll.*) der Drückeberger. **– -pigeon,** *s.* die Wandertaube. **– -traffic,** *s.* der Personenverkehr. **– -train,** *s.* der Personenzug.

passe-partout [ˈpæsəpɑːˈtʊ], *s.* der Papierrahmen; – *frame*, der Wechselrahmen; – *binding* (*reel*), die Klebestreifenrolle.

passer-by [ˈpɑːsəˈbɑɪ], *s.* Vorübergehende(r), *m.*

passerine [ˈpæsərɪn], 1. *adj.* Sperlings–, sperlingartig; Sitzfüßler–. 2. *s.* der Sitzfüßler (*Orn.*).

passib–ility [pæsɪˈbɪlɪtɪ], *s.* die Leidensfähigkeit (*Theol.*). **–le** [–ɪbl], *adj.* leidensfähig (*Theol.*).

passim [ˈpæsɪm], *adv.* hie und da, an verschiedenen Orten.

passing [ˈpɑːsɪŋ], 1. *adj.* vorübergehend, flüchtig, beiläufig. 2. *adv.* (*archaic*) sehr, überaus. 3. *s.* das Durchgehen, Inkrafttreten (*of a bill*); Bestehen (*of examination*); (Ver)Schwinden, Dahinschwinden, Hinscheiden; *in –*, im Vorbeigehen, beiläufig. *no –!* Überholen verboten! **– -bell,** *s.* die Totenglocke. **– -note,** *s.* die Durchgangsnote (*Mus.*).

passion [ˈpæʃən], *s.* die Leidenschaft; Wut, der Zorn, heftiger Ausbruch; heiße Liebe, heftige Neigung, die Vorliebe (*for*, für); Begierde, das Verlangen (*for*, nach); Leiden (*pl.*); die Passion (*of Christ*); *be a – with s.o.*, seine Leidenschaft sein; *have a – for*, eine Vorliebe haben für; – *for gambling*, die Spielwut; *in a –*, in Wut; *fly into a –*, in Wut geraten; *with –*, leidenschaftlich. **–al** [–əl], *s.* das Passionsbuch, die Passional (*Eccl.*). **–ate** [–ɪt], *adj.* leidenschaftlich; heftig, hitzig; jähzornig. **–ateness,** *s.* die Leidenschaftlichkeit; der Jähzorn. **–less,** *adj.* leidenschaftslos. **– -play,** *s.* das Passionsspiel. **– Sunday,** der Sonntag Judica. **– week,** die Karwoche, Stille Woche.

passiv–e [ˈpæsɪv], *adj.* leidend, duldend, widerstandslos, teilnahm(s)los, willensträge, passiv; Leide– (*Gram.*); untätig, nicht zinstragend (*C.L.*); *–e resistance*, passiver Widerstand; *–e verb*, intransitives Zeitwort; *–e voice*, die Leideform, das Passiv. **–eness,** *s.* **–ity** [–ˈsɪvɪtɪ], die Passivität, Teilnahm(s)losigkeit, Geduld, Ergebung.

passover [ˈpɑːsovə], *s.* das Passah, Osterlamm.

passport [ˈpɑːspɔːt], *s.* der (Reise)Paß; (*fig.*), der Geleitbrief, die Empfehlung (*to*, für); der Weg(öffner) (*to*, zu). **– -office,** *s.* die Paßstelle.

password [ˈpɑːswəːd], *s.* das Losungswort, die Losung, Parole.

past [pɑːst], *see* **pass.** 1. *adj.* vergangen, ehemalig, vorig, früher; Vergangenheits– (*Gram.*); (*pred. only*) vorbei, vorüber; *for some time –*, seit einiger Zeit; – *master*, ehemaliger Meister vom Stuhl (*Freem.*); (*fig.*) wahrer *or* unübertreffbarer Meister (*in*, in (*Dat.*); *of* (*Gen.*)); – *participle*, das Mittelwort der Vergangenheit (*Gram.*). 2. *s.* die Vergangenheit, das Vergangene; die Vergangenheitsform (*Gram.*); *in the –*, früher, ehemals; *have a –*, ein Vorleben haben. 3. *prep.* an . . . vorbei, an . . . vorüber, (*fig.*) über . . . hinaus; – *all belief*, unglaublich; *be – his comprehension*, über seine Begriffe gehen; – *cure* or *help*, unheilbar; – *due*, überfällig (*C.L.*); – *hope*, hoffnungslos; – *saving*, rettungslos verloren; – *all shame*, ohne jede Scham; *half – twelve*, halb eins; *a quarter – twelve*, (ein) Viertel nach zwölf, (ein) Viertel eins. 4. *adv.* vorbei, vorüber; *hurry –*, vorbeieilen.

past–e [peɪst], 1. *s.* der Teig (*Cook.*); Klebstoff, Kleister; die Paste (as *fish– –e*, *tooth– –e*, and artificial jewels). 2. *v.a.* kleben, kleistern, bekleben (*with*, mit); (*sl.*) verprügeln; *–e on*, aufkleben; *–e up*, ankleben (*a notice*); zukleben (*a hole*). **–eboard,** 1. *s.* die Pappe, der Karton; (*coll.*) die Visitenkarte, Spielkarte. 2. *attrib. adj.* Papp–, aus Pappe; (*fig.*) unecht, Kitsch–. **–e-pot,** *s.* der Kleistertopf. **–y,** 1. *adj.* teigig, teigartig; (*fig.*) blaß. 2. *s.* die Fleischpastete.

pastel [ˈpæstl], *s.* das Pastell, der Pastellstift; das Pastellbild; Waid, das Waidblau (*Dye.*). **–(l)ist,** *s.* der Pastellmaler.

pastern [ˈpæstən], *s.* die Fessel (*of horse*). **– -joint,** *s.* das Fesselgelenk.

pasteur–ization [pɑːstəraɪˈzeɪʃən], *s.* die Pasteurisierung, Haltbarmachung. **–ize,** *v.a.* pasteurisieren, entkeimen, haltbar machen.

pastiche [pæsˈtɪːʃ], *s.* das Flickwerk, Machwerk.

pastille [ˈpæstɪl], *s.* das Räucherkerzchen; das Plätzchen, die Pastille (*Pharm.*).

pastime [ˈpɑːstaɪm], *s.* der Zeitvertreib, die Belustigung; *as a –*, zum Zeitvertreib.

pastor [ˈpɑːstə], *s.* der Pfarrer, Pastor, Seelsorger, Seelenhirt. **–al** [–rəl], 1. *adj.* Hirten–, Schäfer–, ländlich; seelsorgerisch, Pastoral– (*Eccl.*); *–al duties*, geistliche Pflichten; *–al letter*, der Hirtenbrief; *–al play*, das Schäferspiel; *–al poet*, der Idyllendichter; *–al poetry*, die Hirtendichtung, Schäferdichtung; *–al staff*, der Krummstab (*Eccl.*). 2. *s.* das Hirtengedicht, Idyll; der Hirtenbrief; ländliches Gemälde. **–ale,** das Pastorale (*Mus.*). **–ate,** *s.* das Pfarramt, Pastorat; Pastoren (*pl.*).

pastry [ˈpeɪstrɪ], *s.* der Teig; das Gebäck, Backwerk; Pasteten, Torten (*pl.*); *flaky* –, der Blätterteig; *short* –, der Mürbeteig. **– -board,** *s.* das Teigbrett. **– -cook,** *s.* der Feinbäcker, Konditor.

pastur–age [ˈpɑːstjərɪdʒ], *s.* das Weiden; Grasfutter, Weideland, die Weide. **–e** [–tjə], 1. *s.* die Weide, Wiese, das Weideland, Grasland. 2. *v.a.* weiden (*cattle*), abweiden (*grassland*). 3. *v.n.* weiden. **–e-land,** *s.* das Weideland, Grasland.

pasty, *see* **paste.**

[1]**pat** [pæt], *attrib. adj.* & *adv.* passend, zutreffend, gelegen, zur Hand; *answer* –, schlagfertig antworten; *very* –, eben *or* gerade recht; *have* or *know it off* –, es am Schnürchen haben *or* können; *stand* –, aus der Hand spielen (*Poker*), (*sl.*) am alten festhalten.

[2]**pat** [pæt], 1. *s.* der Klaps, leichter Schlag, der Taps, Tapsen; das Stückchen, Klümpchen (*of butter*). 2. *v.a.* leicht schlagen, klapsen; tätscheln; – (*o.s.*) *on the back*, (sich) klapsen, (*fig.*) beglückwünschen. 3. *v.n.* tapsen. **– -a-cake,** *s.* backe-backe-Kuchen.

patch [pætʃ], 1. *s.* der Lappen, Flicken, Fleck, Flecken; das Pflaster, Schönheitspflaster; die Augenbinde; der Tuchstreifen (*Mil.*), das Stückchen (*of land*); (*coll.*) *not a* or *no* – *on*, sich nicht messen können an, gar nichts gegen; (*coll.*) *strike a bad* –, auf Schwierigkeiten stoßen; *in –es*, stellenweise; *–es of fog*, neblige Stellen. 2. *v.a.* flicken, ausbessern; – *up*, zusammenflicken, zusammenschustern, zusammenstoppeln, zusammenstümpern; (*fig.*) übertünchen, beschönigen; (*coll.*) beilegen (*a quarrel*). **–work,** *s.* das Flickenwerk, (*fig.*) Flickwerk; *–work quilt*, die Flickendecke. **–y,** *adj.* voller Flicken; zusammengestoppelt; fleckig; (*coll.*) ungleichmäßig.

patchouli [pæˈtʃuːlɪ], *s.* das Patschuli (*Bot.*).

patchy, *see* **patch.**

pate [peɪt], *s.* (*coll.*) der Schädel, Kopf. **–d,** *adj. suffix*, –köpfig.

pâté [ˈpæteɪ], *s.* die Pastete.

patella [pæˈtɛlə], *s.* die Kniescheibe (*Anat.*). **–r,** *adj.* Kniescheiben–.

paten [ˈpætən], *s.* der Napf, flache Schüssel, der Hostienteller (*Eccl.*).

paten–cy [ˈpeɪtənsɪ], *s.* die Offenkundigkeit; das Offensein (*Anat.*). **–t** [–ənt], 1. *adj.* offen(kundig), offenbar, zugängig; patentiert, durch Patent geschützt, Patent–, Marken–, (*coll.*) patent, großartig; *as is –t from*, wie erhellt aus; *–t fastener*, der Druckknopf; *–t fuel*, Briketts, Preßkohlen (*pl.*); *–t leather*, das Glanzleder; *–t (leather) boot*, der Lackstiefel; *letters –t*, die Privilegsurkunde, Bestallungsurkunde; der Freibrief, das Patent; *–t medicine*, die Markenarznei. 2. *s.* der Patentbrief, das Patent, Privileg, Privilegium, die Bestallungsurkunde, (*fig.*) der Freibrief; *take out a* **-t** *for*, sich (*Dat.*) (eine S.) patentieren lassen, ein Patent anmelden für; *–t applied for*, Patent angemeldet; *–t of nobility*, der Adelsbrief. 3. *v.a.* patentieren, gesetzlich schützen; patentieren lassen. **–table,** *adj.* patentierbar. **–t-agent,** der Patentanwalt. **–tee** [–ˈtɪ], *s.* der Patentinhaber. **–t-office,** das Patentamt. **–t-roll,** *s.* das Patentregister.

pater [ˈpeɪtə], *s.* (*sl.*) der Vater. **–familias** [–fæˈmɪːlɪəs], *s.* der Hausvater, Familienvater. **–nal** [pəˈtəːnəl], *adj.* väterlich, Vater–; *–nal grandmother*, die Großmutter väterlicherseits. **–nity** [pəˈtəːnɪtɪ], *s.* die Vaterschaft; väterliche Abkunft; (*fig.*) die Herkunft, Urheberschaft, der Ursprung. **–noster** [ˈpeɪtənɔstə], *s.* das Vaterunser; der Rosenkranz; *–noster pump*, die Kettenpumpe.

path [pɑːθ], *s.* der Fußweg; Pfad, Weg (*also fig.*); die Bahn (*of comets, etc.*); *bridle* –, der Reitweg; *tow(ing)* –, der Treidelweg. **–finder,** *s.* der Pfadfinder; Zielbeleuchter (*Av.*); (*fig.*) der Bahnbrecher. **–less,** *adj.* pfadlos, unwegsam. **–way,** *s.* der Pfad, Fußsteig, Fußweg.

pathetic [pəˈθɛtɪk], *adj.* rührend, ergreifend; kläglich, armselig, bemitleidenswert; pathetisch.

patho–genous [pæˈθɔdʒənəs], *adj.* krankheitserregend. **–logical** [pæθəˈlɔdʒɪkl], *adj.* pathologisch, krankhaft. **–logist** [pæˈθɔlədʒɪst], *s.* der Patholog. **–logy** [pæˈθɔlədʒɪ], *s.* die Krankheitslehre, Pathologie.

pathos [ˈpeɪθɔs], *s.* das Pathos, die Gefühlsbewegung, Gefühlserregung, Leidenschaftlichkeit, Ergriffenheit.

pathway, *see* **path.**

patien–ce [ˈpeɪʃəns], *s.* die Geduld; Ausdauer; Beharrlichkeit; Nachsicht, Langmut; Patience, das Geduldspiel (*Cards*); *my –ce is at an end*, jetzt reißt mir die Geduld; *have –ce*, gedulden; *have no –ce with*, nicht leiden können; *the –ce of Job*, die Engelsgeduld; *lose* (*all* or *one's*) *–ce with*, ungehalten werden über; *out of –ce with*, aufgebracht gegen *or* über. **–t** [–ənt], 1. *adj.* geduldig; nachsichtig (*towards*, gegen); langmütig; ausdauernd, beharrlich; *be –t of*, geduldig ertragen; (*fig.*) zulassen. 2. *s.* der Patient, Kranke(r), *m.*

patina [ˈpætɪnə], *s.* der Edelrost, die Patina.

patio [ˈpɑːtɪoʊ], *s.* der Lichthof.

patois [ˈpætwɑ], *s.* die Mundart.

patriarch [ˈpeɪtrɪɑːk], *s.* der Patriarch, Erzvater; (*fig.*) Altmeister, ehrwürdiger Alter. **–al** [–ˈɑːkl], *adj.* patriarchalisch; (*fig.*) ehrwürdig. **–ate** [–trɪɑːkət], *s.* das Patriarchat; *see also* **–y. –y** [–ɑkɪ], *s.* das Vaterrecht, die Vaterherrschaft.

patricia–n [pəˈtrɪʃən], 1. *adj.* patrizisch; Patrizier–; (*fig.*) adlig. 2. *s.* der Patrizier. **–te** (–jət], *s.* das Patriziat.

patrimon–ial [pætrɪˈmoʊnɪəl], *adj.* ererbt, Erb–. **–y** [ˈpætrɪmənɪ], *s.* väterliches Erbgut *or* Erbteil; das Kirchengut, Patrimonium.

patriot [ˈpeɪtrɪət, ˈpætrɪət], *s.* der Patriot, Vaterlandsfreund. **–ic** [–ˈɔtɪk], *adj.* vaterländisch, patriotisch. **–ism,** *s.* die Vaterlandsliebe, der Patriotismus.

patristic [pəˈtrɪstɪk], *adj.* patristisch. **–s,** *pl.* (*sing. constr.*) die Patristik.

patrol [pəˈtroʊl], 1. *s.* der Spähtrupp, die Patrouille, Streife (*Mil., etc.*); Runde, das Patrouillieren. 2. *v.n.* die Runde machen, patrouillieren. 3. *v.a.* durchstreifen; abfliegen (*Av.*); – *the streets*, die Straßen abstreifen.

patron [ˈpeɪtrən], *s.* der Schutzherr, Patron; Beschützer, Gönner, Mäzen; Kirchenpatron (*Eccl.*); Schutzheilige(r), *m.*; der Kunde (*C.L.*). **–age** [ˈpætrənɪdʒ], *s.* die Begünstigung, Protektion, Gönnerschaft, der Schutz; das Mäzenatentum; Patronatsrecht, Besetzungsrecht (*Eccl.*); die Kundschaft (*C.L.*). **–ess** [ˈpeɪtrənɛs], *s.* die Schutzherrin, Patronin; Gönnerin; Schutzheilige (*Eccl.*); Kundin (*C.L.*). **–ize** [ˈpætrənaɪz], *v.a.* in Schutz nehmen, beschützen, begünstigen, unterstützen; gönnerhaft behandeln (*other people*); Kunde sein bei (*C.L.*). **–izer,** *s.* der Beschützer, Gönner. **–izing,** *adj.* gönnerhaft.

patronymic [pætrəˈnɪmɪk], 1. *adj.* patronymisch. 2. *s.* der Geschlechtsname.

patten [ˈpætən], *s.* der Holzschuh; Sockel (*Arch.*).

[1]**patter** [ˈpætə], 1. *v.n.* platschen, prasseln, klatschen (*as rain*); – *along*, trippeln; – *down*, niederplatschen. 2. *s.* das Platschen, Prasseln (*of rain*), Trippeln, Getrappel (*of feet*).

[2]**patter** [ˈpætə], 1. *v.a.* (her)plappern, schnattern; (*sl.*) – *flash*, Gaunersprache sprechen. 2. *s.* die Gaunersprache, der Jargon; das Geplapper. **– -song,** *s.* schnell gesungenes Lied.

pattern [ˈpætən], 1. *s.* das Muster, Vorbild; die Schablone, Gießform; das Schnittmuster (*Tail.*); die Musterprobe (*of cloth*); das Modell, Probestück; Trefferbild (*on target*); *dress* –, der Schnitt; *needlework* –, das Stickmuster; *paper* –, das Schnittmuster; *take* – *by*, sich (*Dat.*) ein Beispiel nehmen an (*Dat.*); *according to* –, *on the* – *of*, nach Muster, nach dem Vorbild von. 2. *attrib.* musterhaft, Muster–; – *pupil*, der Musterschüler. **– -book,** *s.* das Musterbuch. **– -maker,** *s.* der Musterzeichner; Modellmacher.

patty ['pætɪ], *s.* das Pastetchen. **-pan,** *s.* das Pastetenblech.
patulous ['pætjuləs], *adj.* ausgedehnt, ausgebreitet.
paucity ['pɔ:sɪtɪ], *s.* geringe Anzahl *or* Menge, kleine Zahl, der Mangel.
paunch [pɔ:ntʃ], *s.* der Dickbauch, Wanst; Pansen (*Zool.*). **-y,** *adj.* dickbäuchig, beleibt.
pauper ['pɔ:pə], 1. *s.* Arme(r), *m.* Almosenempfänger, unter Armenrecht Klagende(r), *m.* (*Law*). 2. *attrib.*; Armen-. **-ism,** *s.* dauernde Armut, allgemeine Verarmung, die Massenarmut, der Pauperismus. **-ization** [-rɑɪ'zeɪʃən], *s.* die Verarmung. **-ize,** *v.a.* arm machen, in Armut bringen.
pause [pɔ:z], 1. *s.* die Pause, Unterbrechung, das Innehalten, Zögern; der Absatz, Gedankenstrich (*Typ.*); die Fermate (*Mus.*); *give – to s.o.*, einem zu denken geben, einen innehalten lassen; *make a –*, innehalten, pausieren; *without a –*, ohne Unterbrechung. 2. *v.n.* innehalten, anhalten, pausieren; zögern; verweilen (*upon*, bei); *– upon a note*, einen Ton anhalten.
pavage ['peɪvɪdʒ], *s.* das Pflastern, Straßenanlegen, die Pflasterung, Straßenanlage; das Pflastergeld.
pavan ['pævən], *s.* die Pavane.
pav–e [peɪv], *v.a.* pflastern (*also fig.*); *–e the way*, den Weg ebnen, bahnen *or* bereiten (*for* (*Dat.*)). **-ement,** *s.* das Pflaster, Straßenpflaster; der Fußsteig, Bürgersteig, Gehweg, das Trottoir, *crazy* or *tesselated –ement*, das Mosaikpflaster. **-ement-artist,** *s.* der Pflastermaler. **-er,** *s.* der Pflasterer. **-ing,** *s.* das Pflastern, die Pflasterung. **-ing-stone,** *s.* der Pflasterstein.
pavilion [pə'vɪljən], *s.* großes Zelt; das Wappenzelt (*Her.*); der Pavillon, das Gartenhäuschen (*Arch.*).
paving, *see* **pave.**
paviour ['peɪvɪə], *s. see* **paver.**
pavonine ['pævənɑɪn], *adj.* pfauenartig.
paw [pɔ:], 1. *s.* die Pfote, Klaue; (*sl.*) Tatze (= *hand*). 2. *v.n.* scharren, stampfen (*as horse*). 3. *v.a.* (*sl.*) derb *or* ungeschickt anfassen, fummeln an; *– the ground*, auf den Boden stampfen, scharren.
pawky ['pɔ:kɪ], *adj.* (*Scots*) schlau, pfiffig.
pawl [pɔ:l], *s.* der Sperrhaken, die Sperrklinke.
[1]**pawn** [pɔ:n], *s.* der Bauer (*Chess*), (*fig.*) die Schachfigur, Strohmann.
[2]**pawn** [pɔ:n], *s.* das Pfand, die Verpfändung; das Pfandobjekt, Pfandstück; *in –*, verpfändet, versetzt; *give in –*, verpfänden, versetzen. 2. *v.a.* verpfänden (*also fig.*), versetzen. **-broker,** *s.* der Pfandleiher. **-broking,** *s.* das Pfandleihgeschäft. **-ee,** *s.* der Pfandinhaber. **-er,** *s.* der Verpfänder. **--shop,** *s.* das Leihhaus, die Pfandleihe. **--ticket,** *s.* der Pfandschein.
pax [pæks], 1. *s.* die Reliquientafel (*Eccl.*). 2. *int.* (*sl.*) Friede! Waffenstillstand!
[1]**pay** [peɪ], **1.** *ir.v.a.* zahlen (*what one owes*); Geld geben (*for*, für), bezahlen (*a p.*); (*fig.*) belohnen, geben, schenken, erweisen, bezeugen, zollen, abstatten. (*a*) (*with nouns*) *– an account*, eine Rechnung begleichen; *– attention*, Aufmerksamkeit schenken (*to* (*Dat.*)), achtgeben (*to*, auf (*Acc.*)); *– a call on s.o.*, einen Besuch machen bei einem; *– cash* (*down*), bar bezahlen; *– a compliment*, ein Kompliment machen (*to* (*Dat.*)); eine Ehrenbezeigung erweisen (*Mil.*); *– a p. the compliment*, einem die Ehre erweisen (*of doing*, zu tun); *– the costs*, die Kosten tragen; *– one's debts*, seine Schulden bezahlen; *– heed*, see *– attention*; *– homage to s.o.*, einem huldigen; *it –s a p. to do*, es nützt einem *or* es lohnt sich für einen zu tun; *– the piper*, die Zeche bezahlen, die Kosten tragen; die Suppe auslöffeln, der Dumme sein; *– regard to*, beachten; *– one's respects to a p.*, sich einem empfehlen; einem seine Aufwartung machen; *– a sum of money*, einen Betrag entrichten; *– a visit to a p.*, einem einen Besuch abstatten; *– wages*, löhnen, Lohn auszahlen; *– one's way*, seinen Verbindlichkeiten nachkommen; auf eigenen Füßen stehen, ohne Zuschuß auskommen, genug zum Leben verdienen; sich bezahlt machen, auf seine Kosten kommen. (*b*) (*with adverbs*) *– away*, ausgeben, auszahlen (*money*), see *– out*; *– back*, zurückzahlen; *– a p. back in his own coin*, einem mit gleicher Münze heimzahlen, Gleiches mit Gleichem vergelten; *– down*, bar bezahlen; *– in*, einzahlen; *– off*, voll bezahlen, abzahlen, tilgen (*debts*); entlohnen, auszahlen, abmustern (*a crew*); *– out*, auszahlen, auslegen; ausgeben, langsam schießen lassen (*rope, etc.*) (*Naut.*); (*coll.*) *– s.o. out*, einem heimzahlen; *– up*, voll bezahlen; voll einzahlen (*shares*). **2.** *ir.v.n.* zahlen, Zahlung leisten, sich bezahlt machen, sich lohnen *or* rentieren; *it –s hand over fist*, es macht sich glänzend bezahlt; *– through the nose*, tüchtig zahlen *or* bluten müssen, schwer draufzahlen; *– for*, die Kosten tragen *or* aufbringen für; (*fig.*) büßen; *– for the seat*, den Platz bezahlen; *he had to – dearly for it*, es kam ihm teuer zu stehen; *– off*, abfallen, vom Winde abhalten (*Naut.*). **3.** *s.* die Bezahlung; das Gehalt, der (Arbeits)Lohn; Sold, die Löhnung; (*fig.*) Belohnung; *in s.o.'s –*, in jemandes Sold; *on half –*, zur Disposition gestellt (*Mil.*). **-able,** *adj.* zahlbar (*to*, an); fällig, abgelaufen (*as bills*) (*C.L.*); ertragreich, ergiebig, rentabel (*Min.*). **--day,** *s.* der Zahltag; Löhnungstag (*Mil.*). **-ee** [-'ɪ:], *s.* der (Zahlungs)Empfänger, Wechselinhaber, Präsentant (*C.L.*). **--envelope,** *s.* die Lohntüte. **-er** [-ə], *s.* der Zahler; Trassat, Bezogene(r) *m.* (*of a cheque*) (*C.L.*). **-ing,** *adj.* zahlend; lohnend, einträglich, vorteilhaft; *–ing concern*, einträgliches Geschäft; *–ing guest*, der Pensionär; *–ing ore*, das Scheideerz. **--load,** *s.* die Nutzlast (*C.L.*, *Av.*). **-master,** *s.* der Zahlmeister; (*fig.*) Zahler, Unterstützer. **-ment,** *s.* die (Be)Zahlung; Einlösung (*of a cheque*); der Lohn; Sold, die Löhnung (*Mil.*); (*fig.*) Belohnung; *against –ment*, gegen Bezahlung; *–ment by instalments*, die Ratenzahlung; *as –ment for*, see *in –ment of*; *make –ment for*, bezahlen; *–ment in advance*, die Vorauszahlung; *–ment in cash*, die Barzahlung; *–ment in kind*, die Naturalleistung; *in –ment of*, zum Ausgleich von; *–ment on account*, die Abschlagszahlung, Akontozahlung; *on –ment of*, gegen Bezahlung von, nach Eingang von. **--office,** *s.* das Lohnbüro, die Zahlstelle, das Rechnungsamt. **--parade,** *s.* der Löhnungsappell (*Mil.*). **--sheet,** *s.* die Lohnliste, Zahlliste.
[2]**pay** [peɪ], *v.a.* schmieren (*Naut.*).
paynim ['peɪnɪm], *s.* (*Poet. & archaic*) der Heide.
pea [pɪ:], *s.* die Erbse; *green –s*, Schoten (*pl.*); *sweet –*, Spanische Wicke; *as like as two –s*, so ähnlich wie ein Ei dem anderen. **-cock,** *s. see* **peacock.** **--green,** *adj.* erbsgrün. **--jacket,** *s.* die Seemannsjacke. **-nut,** *s. see* **peanut.** **--pod,** *s.* die Erbsenschote. **--shooter,** *s.* das Blasrohr, Pustrohr. **- soup,** die Erbsensuppe (*also fig.*). (*coll.*) **--souper,** *s.* dicker Nebel.
peace [pɪ:s], 1. *s.* der Friede(n); die Ruhe, Friedlichkeit, Eintracht; *breach of the –*, die Ruhestörung; *justice of the –*, der Friedensrichter. (*a*) (*with nouns*) *the King's –*, der Landfrieden, öffentliche Ruhe; *– of mind*, die Seelenruhe, Gemütsruhe. (*b*) (*with verbs*) *break the –*, öffentliche Ruhe stören; *have no –*, keine Ruhe haben; *hold one's –*, schweigen, sich ruhig verhalten; *keep the –*, Ruhe *or* Frieden halten, die Sicherheit wahren; *leave s.o. in –*, einen in Ruhe *or* Frieden lassen; *make –*, Frieden schließen; *make – between*, versöhnen; *make one's – with*, sich aussöhnen mit. (*c*) (*with prepositions*) *at –*, in Frieden(szustand), in Eintracht; *in – and quietness*, in Ruhe und Frieden. 2. *int.* still! ruhig! **-able,** *adj.* friedliebend, friedfertig; ruhig, ungestört, friedlich. **-ful,** *adj.* friedlich, ruhig. **-fulness,** *s.* die Friedlichkeit. **-maker,** *s.* der Friedensstifter. **--offering,** *s.* das Sühnopfer.
[1]**peach** [pɪ:tʃ], *s.* der Pfirsich; (*sl.*) *a – of a . . .*, ein(e) prächtige(r, s) . . . *or* prachtvolle(r, s) . . . *or* pfundige(r, s); *a – of a girl*, ein Pfundsmädel. **--colour,** *s.* die Pfirsichfarbe. **--tree,** *s.* der Pfirsichbaum. (*sl.*) **-y,** *adj.* glänzend, prachtvoll, pfundig.
[2]**peach** [pɪ:tʃ], *v.n.* (*sl.*) angeben; *– on a p.*, einen angeben *or* verraten. **-er,** *s.* der (die) Angeber(in).
pea--chick ['pɪ:tʃɪk], *s.* junger Pfau. **-cock** [-kɔk], *s.* der Pfau (*Orn.*); *–cock butterfly*, das Tagpfauenauge. **-fowl** [-fɑul], *s.* der Pfau, die Pfauhenne. **-hen** [-hɛn], *s.* die Pfauhenne.

[1]**peak** [pɪ:k] 1. *s.* der Gipfel (*also fig.*), die Spitze, (*fig.*) Höhe, der Höhepunkt; Scheitelpunkt (*of a curve*); die Piek (*Naut.*); – *of a mast* (or *spar*), das *or* die (Gaffel)Nock; – (*of a cap*), der (Mützen)-Schirm. 2. *v.a.* senkrecht heben, toppen (*Naut.*). **–ed** [–t], *adj.* spitz, Spitz–. **– -hour,** *s.* die Stunde des Hochbetriebs. **– -load,** *s.* die Spitzenbelastung (*Elec.*). **– -power,** *s.* die Spitzenleistung. **– -season,** *s.* die Hochkonjunktur. **–y,** *adj.* spitz, Spitz–.
[2]**peak** [pɪ:k], *v.n.*; – *and pine*, dahinsiechen, sich abhärmen (*over*, über). (*coll.*) **–y,** *adj.* kränklich, abgehärmt.
peal [pɪ:l], 1. *s.* das Läuten; Geläute; Glockenspiel; (*fig.*) Brausen, Getöse, der Krach; *–s of applause*, der Beifallssturm; *–s of laughter*, schallendes Gelächter. 2. *v.n.* erschallen, schmettern; (*fig.*) donnern, brausen, dröhnen. 3. *v.a.* läuten (*bells*); ertönen *or* erschallen lassen; (*fig.*) laut verkünden.
peanut ['pɪ:nʌt], *s.* die Erdnuß (*Bot.*); – *butter*, die Erdnußbutter; (*sl.*) – *politics*, politisches Intrigenspiel.
pear [pɛ:ə], *s.* die Birne. **– -shaped,** *adj.* birnenförmig. **– -tree,** *s.* der Birnbaum.
pearl [pə:l], 1. *s.* die Perle (*also fig.*); Perl(schrift) (*Typ.*); Pille (*Pharm.*); *cast –s before swine*, Perlen vor die Säue werfen. 2. *attrib.* Perlen–, Perl–, Perlmutter–. 3. *v.n.* perlen, tropfen, Perlen bilden. **– -barley,** *s.* Perlgraupen (*pl.*). **– -button,** *s.* der Perlmutterknopf. **– -diver,** *s.* der Perlfischer. **– -eye,** *s.* das Perlenauge, der Augenstar. **– -fisher,** *s.* der Perlenfischer. **– -fishery,** *s.* die Perlenfischerei. **– -grey,** *adj.* perlgrau. **– -oyster,** *s.* die Perlmuschel. **– -white,** *s.* das Perlweiß. **–y,** *adj.* perlenartig; perlenweiß; perlend; perlenreich; *–y lustre*, der Perlenglanz.
peasant ['pɛzənt], 1. *s.* der Bauer, Landmann, Landarbeiter. 2. *attrib.* bäuerlich, Bauern–; – *boy*, der Bauernjunge; – *proprietor*, bäuerlicher Grundbesitzer; – *woman*, die Bäuerin, Bauersfrau. **–ry,** *s.* Bauern (*pl.*), die Bauernschaft, das Landvolk.
pease [pɪ:z], *pl.* (*coll.*) Erbsen; – *pudding*, der Erbsenbrei.
peat [pɪ:t], *s.* der Torf; das Stück Torf. **– -bog,** *s.* das Torfmoor. **– -cutter** *or* **– -digger,** *s.* der Torfstecher. **– -moss,** *s. see* **– -bog.** **–y,** *adj.* torfartig, Torf–.
pebbl–e ['pɛbl], *s.* der Kiesel(stein); Achat, Bergkristall (*Opt.*); (*pl.*) das Geröll; *he is not the only –e on the beach*, man ist auf ihn allein nicht angewiesen. **–y** [–ɪ], *adj.* kieselig, Kiesel–.
pecca–bility [pɛkə'bɪlɪtɪ], *s.* die Sündhaftigkeit. **–ble** ['pɛkəbl], *adj.* sündig, sündhaft. **–dillo** –'dɪlou], *s.* leichte Sünde. **–ncy** ['pɛkənsɪ], *s.* die Sündhaftigkeit; Faulheit (*Med.*). **–nt** [–ənt], *adj.* sündig, böse; faul (*Med.*).
peccary ['pɛkərɪ], *s.* das Nabelschwein.
[1]**peck** [pɛk], *s.* der Viertelscheffel (= *9 liter*); (*fig.*) die Menge, der Haufen (*of trouble, etc.*).
[2]**peck** [pɛk], 1. *s.* das Picken; (*coll.*) der Kuß. 2. *v.a.* & *n.* picken (*at*, nach) (*as a bird*); hacken, hauen (*with an axe*); – *up*, aufpicken. **–er,** *s.* die Hacke, Picke; (*sl.*) *keep one's – up*, den Mut nicht sinken lassen. (*coll.*) **–ish,** *adj.* hungrig.
pecten ['pɛktən], *s.* der Kamm (*Anat.*); die Kammmuschel (*Zool.*).
pect–ic ['pɛktɪk], *adj.* Pektin–. **–in** [–tɪn], *s.* das Pektin.
pectinate ['pɛktɪnət], *adj.* kammförmig, kammartig, Kamm–.
pectoral ['pɛktərəl], 1. *adj.* Brust–. 2. *s.* das Brustmittel, Hustenmittel; Brustschild (*Her.*); die Brustflosse (*Ichth.*).
peculat–e ['pɛkjuleɪt], *v.a.* unterschlagen, veruntreuen. **–ion** [–'leɪʃən], *s.* die Unterschlagung, Veruntreuung, der Unterschleif. **–or** [–leɪtə], *s.* der Betrüger, Veruntreuer, Kassendieb.
peculiar [pɪ'kju:lɪə], 1. *adj.* eigen(tümlich) (*to* (*Dat.*)), besonder; eigenartig, seltsam; (*coll.*) verdreht. 2. *s.* eigner Besitz, das Sondereigentum, Sondervorrecht. **–ity** [–lɪ'ærɪtɪ], *s.* die Eigenheit, Eigentümlichkeit, Eigenartigkeit, Seltsamkeit. **–ly,** *adv.* besonders, vornehmlich; seltsam.
pecuniary [pɪ'kju:nɪərɪ], *adj.* geldlich, Geld–, pekuniär.
pedagog–ic(al) [pɛdə'gɔdʒɪk(l)], *adj.* erzieherisch, Erziehungs–, pädagogisch. **–ics,** *pl.* (*sing. constr.*) die Pädagogik. **–ue** ['pɛdəgɔg], *s.* der Pädagog, Erzieher, Schulmeister; Pedant, Schulfuchs (*contemptuous*). **–y** [–gɔgɪ, –gɔdʒɪ], *s. see* **–ics.**
pedal ['pɛdəl], 1. *s.* das Pedal (*also Cycl.*), der Fußhebel; die Tretkurbel (*Cycl.*); *loud* –, das Fortepedal (*Mus.*); *soft* –, das Pianopedal (*Mus.*); (*fig.*) *apply the soft* –, einen sanften Ton anschlagen. 2. *v.n.* radfahren, Pedal treten; *back–*–, rücktreten; *back–– brake*, die Rücktrittbremse (*Cycl.*). 3. *v.a.* fahren (*a cycle*); treten. 4. *attrib.* Fuß–, Pedal– (*Zool.*).
pedant ['pɛdənt], *s.* der Pedant, Schulfuchs, Kleinigkeitskrämer. **–ic** [pə'dæntɪk), *adj.* schulmeisterlich, pedantisch, kleinlich. **–ry** [–rɪ], *s.* die Pedanterie, Kleinlichkeit.
pedate ['pɛdət], *adj.* fußförmig (*Zool.*).
peddl–e ['pɛdl], 1. *v.a.* hausieren, hökern mit; (*fig.*) hausieren gehen mit. 2. *v.n.* hausieren, hökern; (*fig.*) sich mit Kleinigkeiten abgeben. **–ing** [–lɪŋ], 1. *adj.* hausierend; (*fig.*) kleinlich, nichtig, geringfügig, unbedeutend; *see* **pedlar.**
pedestal ['pɛdəstəl], *s.* das Postament, Fußgestell, Piedestal; der Ständer; Sockel, Säulenfuß (*Arch.*); (*fig.*) die Grundlage.
pedestrian [pə'dɛstrɪən], 1. *adj.* zu Fuß gehend; Fuß–; (*fig.*) alltäglich, prosaisch, langweilig; – *crossing*, der Übergang für Fußgänger; – *traffic*, der Fußgängerverkehr. 2. *s.* der Fußgänger. **–ism,** *s.* das Fußreisen, Wandern.
pedic–el ['pɛdɪsəl], *s.*, **–le** ['pɛdɪkl], *s.* kleiner Stiel *or* Stengel (*Bot.* & *Zool.*). **–ellate** ['pɛdɪsələt], **–ulate** [pə'dɪkjulət], *adj.* gestielt.
pedicure ['pɛdɪkjuə], *s.* die Fußpflege; der Fußpfleger.
pedigree ['pɛdɪgrɪ], *s.* der Stammbaum; – *horse*, das Zuchtpferd.
pediment ['pɛdɪmənt], *s.* der (Zier)Giebel (*Arch.*).
pedlar ['pɛdlə], *s.* der Hausierer (*of*, mit). **–y** [–rɪ], *s.* das Hausieren; Hausierwaren (*pl.*).
pedometer [[pə'dɔmɪtə], *s.* der Schrittmesser, Schrittzähler.
pedunc–le [pə'dʌŋkl], *s.* der Blumenstiel, Fruchtstiel (*Bot.*). **–ular** [–kjulə], *adj.* Stiel–. **–ulate** [–kjulət], *adj.* gestielt.
pee [pɪ:], *v.n.* (*coll.*) pinkeln.
peek [pɪ:k], 1. *v.n.* (*coll.*) gucken. 2. *s.* flüchtiger Blick. **– -a-boo,** *s.* das Versteckspiel.
[1]**peel** [pɪ:l], 1. *v.a.* schälen; – *off*, abschälen; (*sl.*) ausziehen, abstreifen (*one's clothes*). 2. *v.n.* (also – *off*) sich (ab)schälen, sich abblättern; (*sl.*) sich ausziehen. 3. *s.* die Schale, Rinde. **–ed,** *adj.* (*coll.*) offen (*of eyes*). **–ing,** *s.* (*often pl.*) die Schale.
[2]**peel** [pɪ:l], *s.* der Brotschieber, die Backschaufel.
peeler ['pɪ:lə], *s.* (*archaic*) der Schutzmann.
peelings ['pɪ:lɪŋz], *see* **peel.**
peen [pɪ:n], *s.* die Finne (*of hammer*).
[1]**peep** [pɪ:p], 1. *v.n.* piepen, piepsen. 2. *s.* das Piepen.
[2]**peep** [pɪ:p], 1. *v.n.* gucken, neugierig *or* verstohlen blicken; hervorgucken, sich zeigen, zum Vorschein kommen (*out of*, aus); – *at*, angucken, begucken; – *out*, hervorgucken, sich zeigen, zum Vorschein kommen. 2. *s.* verstohlener Blick; *take a* –, heimlich sehen; – *of day*, der Tagesanbruch. (*sl.*) **–er,** *s.* (*usually pl.*) das Auge. **– -hole,** *s.* das Guckloch, der Sehschlitz, Sehspalt. **–ing Tom,** neugieriger Mensch. **– -show,** *s.* der Guckkasten. **– -sight,** *s.* die Richtvorrichtung.
[1]**peer** [pɪə], *s.* Gleiche(r), *m.*, Ebenbürtige(r), *m.*; der Pair; *be the – of*, den Vergleich aushalten mit; *one's –(s)*, seinesgleichen; *without a* –, unvergleichlich, ohnegleichen. **–age** [–rɪdʒ], *s.* Pairs (*pl.*); die Pairswürde; der (Reichs)Adel; Adelskalender. **–ess,** *s.* die Gemahlin eines Pairs; *–ess in her own right*, Adlige aus eignem Recht, *f.* **–less,** *adj.* unvergleichlich. **–lessness,** *s.* die Unvergleichlichkeit.
[2]**peer** [pɪə], *v.n.* blicken, schauen, gucken, spähen (*into*, in; *for*, nach); erscheinen, sich zeigen; – *at*, angucken, begucken.
peev–e [pɪ:v], *v.a.* (*coll.*) (*usually p.p.*) ärgern. **–ish,** *adj.* verdrießlich, mürrisch, grämlich. **–ishness,** *s.* die Verdrießlichkeit, Grämlichkeit.

peewit ['pɪ:wɪt], *s.* der Kiebitz (*Orn.*).
peg [pɛg], 1. *s.* der (Holz)Pflock, Zapfen, Dübel; Stift (*Shoem.*); Haken (*for hat & coat*); die Klammer (*for washing*); der Wirbel (*of violin, etc.*); (*fig.*) Grad, die Stufe; der Vorwand; (*sl.*) Schluck (Schnaps); *take a p. down a* – (*or two*), einen demütigen; *come down a* – (*or two*), einen Pflock zurückstecken; *be a square – in a round hole*, an der unpassenden Stelle stehen. 2. *v.a.* festpflöcken, anpflöcken, begrenzen, einschränken, einengen; (stabil)halten, stützen, festlegen (*prices*); – *down*, festnageln (*to*, auf (*Acc.*)); – *out*, abstecken (*a claim* (*Min.*)). 3. *v.n.*; – *at*, zielen auf (*Acc.*), werfen nach; – *away*, emsig arbeiten, drauf losarbeiten (*at*, an); (*sl.*) – *out*, krepieren. **--top,** *s.* der Kreisel.
pegamoid ['pɛgəmɔɪd], *s.* das Kunstleder.
peignoir ['peɪnwɑə], *s.* der Frisiermantel.
pejorative [pɪ'dʒɔrətɪv], *adj.* verschlechternd.
pekoe ['pɪ:koʊ], *s.* der Pekoetee.
pelage ['pɛlɪdʒ], *s.* die Hautbedeckung (*Zool.*).
pelag-ian [pɛ'leɪdʒən], **-ic** [-'lædʒɪk], *adj.* Hochsee-, ozeanisch.
pelargonium [pɛlə'goʊnɪəm], *s.* die Pelargonie (*Bot.*).
pelerine ['pɛlərɪ:n], *s.* die Pelerine, der Umhang.
pelf [pɛlf], *s.* (*sl.*) der Mammon, Moneten (*pl.*).
pelican ['pɛlɪkən], *s.* der Pelikan (*Orn.*).
pelisse [pə'lɪ:s], *s.* langer (Damen-, Kinder- *or* Husaren-)Mantel.
pellet ['pɛlɪt], *s.* das Kügelchen; das Schrotkorn, die Schrotkugel; Pille.
pellic-le ['pɛlɪkl], *s.* das Häutchen. **-ular** [pɛ'lɪkjʊlə] *adj.* Häutchen-.
pellitory ['pɛlɪtərɪ], *s.* das Glaskraut; die Bertramkamille (*Bot.*).
pell-mell ['pɛl'mɛl], 1. *adj.* kunterbunt, unordentlich. 2. *adv.* unterschiedslos, durcheinander. 3. *s.* das Durcheinander.
pellucid [pɛ'ljʊ:sɪd], *adj.* durchsichtig, (*fig.*) klar. **-ity** [-'sɪdɪtɪ], **-ness,** *s.* die Durchsichtigkeit, Klarheit.
pelmet ['pɛlmɪt], *s.* die (Vorhangs)Falbel.
[1]**pelt** [pɛlt], *s.* der Pelz, das Fell, rohe Haut. **-ry,** *s.* Pelze, Häute, ungegerbte Felle (*pl.*); Pelzwaren (*pl.*), das Rauchwerk. **-ry-man,** *s.* der Rauchwarenhändler, Kürschner. **--wool,** *s.* die Sterblingswolle.
[2]**pelt** [pɛlt], 1. *v.a.* werfen (*a p.*, nach einem; *with* (*Acc.*)); bewerfen (*with*, mit); (*fig.*) bestürmen, bombardieren. 2. *v.n.* niederprasseln; – *ing rain*, der Platzregen. 3. *s.* das (Be)Werfen; Prasseln; (*fig.*) (*at*) *full* –, in höchster Eile.
pelvi-c ['pɛlvɪk], *adj.* Becken-. **-s,** *s.* das Becken (*Med.*).
pemmican ['pɛmɪkən], *s.* harter Fleischkuchen, das Dauerfleisch.
[1]**pen** [pɛn], 1. *s.* die (Schreib)Feder; (*fig.*) Schreibart, der Stil; die Schriftstellerei; *fountain--*, die Füllfeder; *put* or *set – to paper*, die Feder ansetzen. 2. *v.a.* (nieder)schreiben; verfassen, abfassen. **– and ink,** 1. *s.* das Schreibmaterial. 2. *adj.*; *--and-ink-drawing*, die Federzeichnung. **--case,** *s.* der Federbüchse. **--feather,** *s.* die Schwungfeder. **-holder,** *s.* der Federhalter. **-knife,** *s.* das Taschenmesser. **-manship,** *s.* die Schreibkunst. **--name,** *s.* der Schriftstellername. (*coll.*) **--pusher,** *s.* der Schreiber; Vielschreiber. **-wiper,** *s.* der Tintenwischer.
[2]**pen** [pɛn], 1. *s.* die Hürde, Koppel, das Gehege; der Laufstall, Hühnerstall; die Bunkeranlage (*Naut.*). 2. *v.a.* (also – *in*) einpferchen, einschließen. **-stock** [-stɔk], *s.* die Stauanlage, das Wehr, die Schleuse.
penal ['pɪ:nəl], *adj.* Straf-, strafbar; – *code*, das Strafgesetz(buch); – *colony*, die Strafkolonie; – *law*, das Strafgesetz, Strafrecht; – *reform*, die Reform des Strafrechts; – *servitude*, die Zuchthausstrafe. **-ize,** *v.a.* als strafbar erklären, mit Strafe belegen; bestrafen, belasten, benachteiligen. **-ty,** *s.* die Strafe; (*fig.*) der Nachteil, die Buße; der Strafpunkt (*in competition*); *under -ty of*, bei einer Strafe von; *on -ty of death*, bei Todesstrafe; *under -ty of death*, zur Todesstrafe verurteilt; *-ty area*, der Strafraum (*Footb.*); *-ty kick*, der Strafstoß, Elfmeter (*Footb.*).
penance ['pɛnəns], *s.* die Buße; *do* –, Buße tun.
pence [pɛns], *pl. of* **penny.**
penchant ['pɑ̃ʃɑ̃], *s.* der Hang, die Neigung (*for*, zu), Vorliebe (*for*, für).
pencil ['pɛnsɪl], 1. *s.* der Bleistift, Stift; Strahlenbüschel, das Strahlenbündel (*Opt., etc.*); (*archaic*) der Pinsel (*Paint.*); *in* –, mit Bleistift, in Blei; *indelible* –, der Tintenstift; *lead* –, der Bleistift; *propelling* –, der Drehstift; *red* –, der Rotstift. 2. *v.a.* zeichnen, entwerfen; mit Bleistift schreiben, zeichnen *or* anstreichen. **-led,** *adj.* (mit Bleistift) gezeichnet; büschelig (*Opt.*). **--case,** *s.* der Bleistifthalter. **--shaped,** *adj.* büschelig. **--sharpener,** *s.* der Bleistiftspitzer.
pend-ant, -ent ['pɛndənt], *s.* das Gehänge, Ohrgehänge, Anhängsel; die Hängelampe, der Wimpel (*Naut.*); Hängeschmuck (*Arch.*); (*fig.*) das Seitenstück, Gegenstück, Pendant. **-ent, -ant,** *adj.* (herab)hängend, niederhängend, überhängend, Hänge-; schwebend; unentschieden. **-entive** [pə'dɛntɪv], *s.* das Pendentif (*Arch.*). **-ing,** 1. *adj.* unentschieden, schwebend, anhängig, in der Schwebe. 2. *prep.* während; bis (zu); *-ing further instructions*, bis auf weiteres.
pendul-ate ['pɛndjʊleɪt], *v.n.* pendelartig schwingen, pendeln, baumeln; (*fig.*) schwanken, zögern. **-ine** [-lɪn], *adj.* hängend (*as a nest*) (*Orn.*). **-ous** [-ləs], *adj.* (herab)hängend, hängend; pendelnd, schwebend; *-ous motion*, die Pendelbewegung. **-um** [-əm], *s.* das Pendel; (*fig.*) die Pendelbewegung (*of opinion, etc.*).
penetra-bility [pɛnətrə'bɪlɪtɪ], *s.* die Durchdringbarkeit, Durchdringlichkeit. **-ble** ['pɛnətrəbl], *adj.* durchdringbar, durchdringlich, (*fig.*) erfaßbar. **-lia** [-'treɪlɪə], *pl.* das innere Heiligtum; Geheimnisse (*pl.*). **-te** ['pɛnɪtreɪt], *v.a. & n.* durchdringen, erfüllen (*with*, mit), eindringen in (*Acc.*); vordringen (*to*, bis), durchschlagen; (*fig.*) forschen, ergründen, erfassen, durchschauen. **-ting,** *adj.* durchdringend; (*fig.*) durchdringend, scharfsinnig, eindringlich. **-tion,** *s.* das Durchdringen (*into* (*Gen.*)), Eindringen (*in*, in (*Acc.*)); der Durchbruch, die Durchdringung, der Einbruch (*Mil.*); Scharfsinn, die Einsicht; Durchschlagskraft (*Artil.*). **-tive,** *adj. see* **-ting.**
penguin ['pɛŋgwɪn], *s.* der Pinguin (*Orn.*).
penholder, *see* [1]**pen.**
penicillate ['pɛnɪsɪlɪt], *adj.* pinselförmig, bündelförmig.
peninsula [pə'nɪnsjʊlə], *s.* die Halbinsel. **-r** [-lɑ], *adj.* halbinselförmig; Halbinsel-; *-r War*, der Krieg in Spanien (1808–14).
penis ['pɪ:nɪs], *s.* der Penis.
peniten-ce ['pɛnɪtəns], *s.* die Reue, Buße. **-t** [-ənt], 1. *adj.* reuig, bußfertig. 2. *s.* der Bußfertige, Büßer; das Beichtkind (*R.C.*). **-tial** [-'tɛnʃəl], 1. *adj.* bußfertig, Buß-. 2. *s.* das Bußbuch. **-tiary** [-'tɛnʃərɪ], 1. *adj.* Buß-; Besserungs-. 2. *s.* das Gefängnis, Zuchthaus; die Besserungsanstalt, Korrektionsanstalt; der Bußpriester, Beichtvater (*R.C.*).
penknife, *see* [1]**pen.**
penmanship, *see* [1]**pen.**
pennant ['pɛnənt], *s.* der Wimpel, das Fähnchen (*Naut.*).
penniform ['pɛnɪfɔ:m], *adj.* federförmig, kielförmig.
penniless ['pɛnɪləs], *adj.* ohne (einen Pfennig) Geld, arm, mittelos.
pennon ['pɛnən], *s.* das (Lanzen)Fähnchen (*Mil.*), Fähnlein, die Wimpel.
penny ['pɛnɪ], *s.* (pl. *pennies, pence*) englischer Penny; (*Amer. coll.*) das Eincentstück; das Geld, Kleingeld; (*fig.*) der Heller, die Kleinigkeit; *in for a – in for a pound*, wer A sagt muß auch B sagen; *turn an honest – by*, sich gern einen Groschen verdienen mit; *a pretty* –, eine schöne Summe; *not worth a* –, keinen Heller wert. **--a-liner,** *s.* der Zeilenschinder. (*sl.*) **--dreadful,** *s.* das Schauerblatt; der Schauerroman, Schundroman. **--in-the-slot machine,** der Automat. **-royal,** *s.* die Polei (*Bot.*). **-weight,** *s.* ein Gewichtmaß (= *1·55 g.*). **--wise,** *adj.* sparsam im kleinen; *be --wise and pound-foolish*, am unrechten Ende sparen. **-wort** [-wə:t], *s.* das Nabelkraut (*Bot.*).

-worth [–wə:θ], *s.* der Pfennigwert; *a –worth of sweets*, für einen Penny Bonbons.
penolog-ical [pɪ:nəˈlɔdʒɪkəl], *adj.* strafrechtlich, Strafrechts–, kriminalkundlich. **-y,** *s.* die Strafrechtslehre, Kriminalstrafkunde.
pensile [ˈpɛnsɑɪl], *adj.* Hänge–, hängend, schwebend.
pension [ˈpɛnʃən], 1. *s.* das Ruhegehalt, die Pension, Rente, das Jahrgeld; Kostgeld; die Pension, das Fremdenheim, Pensionat; *old-age –*, die Altersversorgung; *retiring –*, das Ruhegehalt. 2. *v.a.* ein Jahrgeld geben (*Dat.*); *– off*, mit Ruhegehalt entlassen, pensionieren. **-able,** *adj.* pensionsberechtigt (*a p.*), pensionsfähig (*age*). **-ary,** *s.* **-er,** *s.* der Ruhegehaltsempfänger, Pensionär; (*fig.*) Mietling.
pensive [ˈpɛnsɪv], *adj.* nachdenklich, tiefsinnig, ernst, schwermütig. **-ness,** *s.* die Nachdenklichkeit, Tiefsinnigkeit; Schwermut.
penstock, *see* [2]**pen.**
pent [pɛnt], *adj.* (also *– up*) eingepfercht, eingeschlossen, gefangen; (*fig.*) *– up*, verhalten (*as anger, etc.*).
penta-cle [ˈpɛntəkl], *s.* der Drudenfuß. **-d** [ˈpɛntæd], *s.* der Zeitraum von 5 Jahren; die Zahl 5. **-gon** [–gən], *s.* das Fünfeck. **-gonal** [–ˈtægənəl], *adj.* fünfeckig. **-gram** [–græm], *see* **-cle. -grid** [–grɪd], *s.* die Fünfgitterröhre (*Rad.*). **-hedral** [–ˈhɪ:drəl], *adj.* fünfflächig. **-hedron** [–ˈhɪ:drən], *s.* das Fünfflach, Pentaeder. **-meter** [–ˈtæmɪtə], *s.* der *or* das Pentameter (*Metr.*). **-teuch** [–tɔɪk], *s.* der Pentateuch (*B.*). **-thlon** [–θlən], *s.* der Fünfkampf (*Sport.*).
pentecost [ˈpɛntəkɔst], *s.* das Pfingstfest, Pfingsten. **-al** [–ˈkɔstəl], *adj.* Pfingst–, pfingstlich.
penthouse [ˈpɛnthɑʊs], *s.* das Schutzdach, Wetterdach.
pentode [ˈpɛntoʊd], *s.* die Dreigitterröhre, Fünfelektrodenröhre (*Rad.*).
pentstemon [pɛntˈstɪ:mən], *s.* Skrofulariazeen (*pl.*) (*Bot.*).
penult [pɪˈnʌlt], *s.* vorletzte Silbe. **-imate** [–ɪmət], *adj.* vorletzt.
penumbra [pɪˈnʌmbrə], *s.* der Halbschatten. **-l,** *adj.* halbdunkel, Halbschatten–.
penur-ious [pɪˈnjʊ:ərɪəs], *adj.* dürftig, ärmlich; karg, geizig, knauserig, filzig. **-y** [ˈpɛnjʊrɪ], *s.* die Armut; Knappheit, der Mangel (*of*, an (*Dat.*)).
peon [pɪ:ən], *s.* der Bote, Schutzmann; Tagelöhner; Leibeigene(r), *m.* **-age** [–ɪdʒ], die Leibeigenschaft.
peony [ˈpɪ:ənɪ], *s.* die Pfingstrose, Päonie (*Bot.*).
people [pɪ:pl], 1. *s.* (*only sing. normally pl. constr.*) Leute, Menschen (*pl.*); (*after poss. pron.*) gemeines Volk, Untertanen; die Dienerschaft, das Gefolge; die Wählerschaft; Verwandte, Angehörige (*pl.*), die Familie; (*impers.*) man; (*sing. & pl.*) das Volk, die Nation; *he of all –*, er vor allen anderen; *country –*, Landbewohner; *many –*, viele (Leute); *what will – say?* was wird man sagen? *the Scottish –*, die Schotten; *some –*, manche. 2. *v.a.* bevölkern (*with*, mit).
pep [pɛp], 1. *s.* (*sl.*) der Schwung, Schmiß, Elan. 2. *v.a.*; *– up*, anfeuern. (*sl.*) **-py,** *adj.* forsch.
pepper [ˈpɛpə], 1. *s.* der Pfeffer. 2. *v.a.* pfeffern; bestreuen, sprenkeln; (*fig.*) beschießen, bewerfen (*with missiles*), überhäufen (*with questions, etc.*); durchprügeln. 3. *v.n.*; *– away at*, losschießen auf (*Acc.*). **--and-salt,** *adj.* gelblich-grauweiß. **--box,** *s.*, **--caster,** *s.* die Pfefferbüchse. **-corn,** *s.* das Pfefferkorn. **-mint,** *s.* die Pfefferminze (*Bot.*); das Pfefferminz(plätzchen). **-y,** *adj.* pfefferig, gepfeffert; (*fig.*) beißend, scharf; heftig, hitzig (*of p.*).
peppy, *see* **pep.**
pep-sin [ˈpɛpsɪn], *s.* das Pepsin. **-tic** [–tɪk], *adj.* verdauungsfördernd, Verdauungs–. **-tone** [–toʊn], *s.* das Pepton, verdauter Eiweißstoff.
[1]**per** [pə:], *prep.* pro; per, mit, für, durch, laut, gemäß; *as –*, laut, gemäß (*C.L.*); *– annum*, pro Jahr; *– bearer*, durch den Überbringer; *– cent*, Prozent, vom Hundert; *see* **percentage**; *– contra*, die Gegenbuchung (*C.L.*); *– diem*, täglich, pro Tag; *– pound*, das Pfund; *– pro.*, per Prokura, in Vollmacht (*C.L.*); *– rail*, per Eisenbahn; *– se*, für sich, an sich.
[2]**per-** [pə:], *pref.* Per–, Über– (*Chem.*).
peradventure [pɛrædˈvɛntʃə], 1. (*archaic*) *adv.* von ungefähr, vielleicht, *if –*, wenn etwa *or* zufällig. 2. *s.* die Ungewißheit, der Zweifel.
perambulat-e [pəˈræmbjʊleɪt], *v.a.* durchwandern, durchschreiten; bereisen, besichtigen, inspizieren (*boundaries, etc.*). **-ion** [–ˈleɪʃən], *s.* die Durchwanderung, Besichtigung; Inspektionsreise, die Grenzbegehung. **-or** [–ˈræmbjʊleɪtə], *s.* der Kinderwagen.
percale [pə:ˈkeɪl], *s.* der Perkal.
perceive [pəˈsɪ:v], *v.a.* wahrnehmen, (be)merken, gewahr werden; (ver)spüren, verstehen, empfinden.
percentage [pəˈsɛntɪdʒ], *s.* der Prozentsatz, Prozente (*pl.*); die Provision, Tantieme (*C.L.*); der (Prozent)Gehalt.
percept [ˈpə:sɛpt], *s.* wahrgenommener Gegenstand (*Phil.*). **-ibility** [pəsɛptɪˈbɪlɪtɪ] *s.* die Wahrnehmbarkeit. **-ible** [–ˈsɛptɪbl], *adj.* wahrnehmbar, vernehmlich, bemerkbar, merklich, fühlbar. **-ion** [–ˈsɛpʃən], *s.* die Wahrnehmung, das Wahrnehmungsvermögen; intuitive Erkenntnis, die Vorstellung, der Begriff. **-ive** [–ˈsɛptɪv], *adj.* wahrnehmend, Wahrnehmungs–; auffassungsfähig. **-ivity** [–ˈtɪvɪtɪ], *s.* das Wahrnehmungsvermögen, Auffassungsvermögen.
[1]**perch** [pə:tʃ], *s.* der Barsch (*Ichth.*).
[2]**perch** [pə:tʃ], 1. *s.* die (Auf)Sitzstange, Hühnerstange; (*fig.*) (sicherer) Sitz; die Rute (= 5·03 *m.*); der Langbaum (*of a wagon*); (*coll.*) *fall off one's –*, vom Stengel fallen. (*coll.*) *knock a p. off his –*, einen vernichten; (*sl.*) *take one's –*, sich setzen; 2. *v.n.* aufsitzen, sich setzen *or* niederlassen (*on*, auf (*Acc.*)); (*fig.*) hoch sitzen. **-ed,** *adj.* sitzend, hoch gelegen. 3. *v.r.* sich setzen.
perchance [pəˈtʃæns], *adv.* vielleicht, zufällig, von ungefähr.
perchloric, *see* [2]**per.**
percipien-ce [pəˈsɪpɪəns], *s.* das Wahrnehmen. **-t** [–ənt], 1. *adj.* wahrnehmend, *be –t of*, wahrnehmen. 2. *s.* wahrnehmende Person.
percolat-e [ˈpə:kəleɪt], 1. *v.n.* durchsickern (*also fig.*), durchlaufen. 2. *v.a.* durchsickern lassen, durchseihen, filtrieren, kolieren. **-ion** [–ˈleɪʃən], *s.* das Durchsickern, Durchseihen. **-or** [–tə], *s.* der Filtriertrichter; Kaffeefilter.
percuss [pəˈkʌs], *v.a.* beklopfen, perkutieren (*Med.*). **-ion** [–ˈkʌʃən], *s.* die Erschütterung, der Schlag, Stoß; das Beklopfen, die Perkussion (*Med.*); das Schlagzeug (*Mus.*); *–ion cap*, *s.* das Zündhütchen. *–ion fuse*, *s.* der Aufschlagzünder; *–ion instrument*, das Schlaginstrument (*Mus.*). **-ive** [–sɪv], *adj.* schlagend, Schlag–.
perdition [pəˈdɪʃən], *s.* ewige Verdammnis (*Rel.*), das Verderben.
perdu(e) [pəˈdjʊ:] *adj. & adv.* auf der Lauer, im Hinterhalt; im Verborgenen, verborgen.
perdurab-ility [pədjʊ:rəˈbɪlɪtɪ], *s.* die Dauerhaftigkeit. **-le** [–ˈdjʊ:rəbl], *adj.* sehr dauerhaft, lange dauernd.
peregrin-ate [ˈpɛrəgrɪneɪt], *v.n.* wandern, herumreisen. **-ation** [–ˈneɪʃən], *s.* die Wanderschaft, Wanderung. **-(e)** [–grɪ(:)n], *s.* (*–(e) falcon*), der Wanderfalke.
peremptor-iness [pəˈrɛmptərɪnɪs; (*Law*) ˈpɛrəmtrɪnɪs], *s.* die Entschiedenheit, Bestimmtheit; absprechende Art, hartnäckiges Beharren. **-y** [pəˈrɛmptərɪ, (*Law*) ˈpɛrəmtrɪ], *adj.* bestimmt, entschieden, entscheidend, unbedingt, peremptorisch, zwingend; herrisch, gebieterisch, diktatorisch; absprechend.
perennial [pəˈrɛnɪəl], 1. *adj.* das ganze Jahr dauernd; perennierend (*Bot.*); beständig, Dauer–. 2. *s.* perennierende Pflanze.
perfect, 1. [ˈpə:fɪkt], *adj.* vollkommen, vollendet, vollkommen ausgebildet, vollständig; gründlich, fehlerlos, tadellos, makellos; (*coll.*) rein, lauter (*rubbish, etc.*); *– tense*, see – 2. 2. *s.* das Perfektum. 3. [pəˈfɛkt], *v.a.* vollenden; vervollkommnen, ausbilden. *– o.s. in*, sich vervollkommnen in. **-ibility** [–ɪˈbɪlɪtɪ], *s.* die Vervollkommnungsfähigkeit. **-ible** [–ˈfɛktɪbl], *adj.* vervollkommnungsfähig. **-ion** [–ˈfɛkʃən], *s.* die Vollendung, Vervollkomm-

nung; Vollkommenheit; (Vor)Trefflichkeit; *to –ion*, vollkommen, vortrefflich, meisterhaft, in hoher Vollendung; *bring to –ion*, vollenden, vervollkommnen. **–ly,** *adv.* see – 1; ganz, gänzlich, völlig, geradezu.

perfervid [pəˈfəːvɪd], *adj.* glühend, heiß, innig.

perfid–ious [pəːˈfɪdɪəs], *adj.* treulos, verräterisch, heimtückisch, falsch, hinterlistig. **–iousness, –y** [ˈpəːfɪdɪ], *s.* die Treulosigkeit, Tücke, Hinterlist.

perfoliate [pəːˈfoʊlɪeɪt], *adj.* durchwachsen (*Bot.*).

perforat–e [ˈpəːfəreɪt], 1. *v.a.* durchbohren, durchlöchern; lochen, perforieren (*stamps, etc.*). 2. *v.n.* eindringen, sich hineinbohren (*into*, in (*Acc.*)). 3. [–ət], *adj.* durchlöchert. **–ion** [–ˈreɪʃən], *s.* die Durchbohrung, Durchlöcherung; Lochung; Öffnung, das Loch. **–or,** *s.* der Locher.

perforce [pəːˈfɔːs], *adv.* gezwungen, notgedrungen.

perform [pəːˈfɔːm], 1. *v.a.* machen, tun, leisten, bewerkstelligen, verrichten; ausführen, durchführen, vollbringen, vollziehen; erfüllen, nachkommen (*Dat.*) (*obligation*); aufführen, vortragen, spielen (*Mus., Theat.*). 2. *v.n.* auftreten, spielen (*Theat., etc.*), funktionieren. **–able,** *adj.* ausführbar, durchführbar; aufführbar (*Theat., etc.*). **–ance** [–əns], *s.* die Ausführung, Verrichtung, Vollziehung, Vollbringung, Erfüllung; Vorstellung, Aufführung (*of a play, etc.*), (*Theat.*); schauspielerische Leistung, die Darstellung (*of a character*) (*Theat.*); Arbeit, Tat, Leistung, das Spiel; *promises without –ance*, Worte, ohne Taten, Versprechungen ohne Erfüllung. **–er,** *s.* der Vollzieher, Verrichter; Schauspieler; Künstler, Virtuose (*Theat., etc.*). **–ing,** *attrib. adj.* dressiert, abgerichtet (*as dogs, etc.*).

perfume [ˈpəːfjuːm], 1. *s.* der Wohlgeruch, Duft; das Parfüm, Parfum, der Riechstoff. 2. *v.a.* parfümieren, durchduften. **–r** [–ə], *s.* der Parfümeriehändler, Parfümeur. **–ry** [–ərɪ], *s.* die Parfümerie; das Parfümeriegeschäft.

perfunctor–iness [pəˈfʌŋktərɪnɪs], die Nachlässigkeit, Flüchtigkeit, Oberflächlichkeit. **–y** [–tərɪ], *adj.* nachlässig, oberflächlich, flüchtig; mechanisch, gewohnheitsmäßig; *in a –y manner*, obenhin.

perfus–e [pəːfjuːz], *v.a.* begießen, besprengen, durchtränken, durchsetzen. **–ion** [–ʒən], *s.* die Begießung, Durchtränkung.

pergola [ˈpəːgoulə], *s.* offener Laubengang.

perhaps [pəˈhæps], *adv.* vielleicht, möglicherweise.

peri [ˈpɪːərɪ], *s.* die Peri, Fee, Elfe.

peri–anth [ˈpɛrɪænθ], *s.* die Blütenhülle (*Bot.*). **–carditis** [–kɑːˈdɑɪtɪs], *s.* die Herzbeutelentzündung (*Med.*). **–cardium** [–ˈkɑːdɪəm], *s.* der Herzbeutel (*Anat.*). **–carp** [–kɑːp], *s.* die Fruchthülle (*Bot.*). **–gee** [–dʒɪː], *s.* die Erdnähe (*Astr.*). **–helion** [–ˈhɪːlɪən], *s.* die Sonnennähe (*Astr.*).

peril [ˈpɛrɪl], *s.* die Gefahr; *at your –*, auf Ihre Gefahr *or* Verantwortung, auf Ihr Risiko; *in – of one's life*, in Lebensgefahr; *the yellow –*, die gelbe Gefahr. **–ous** [–əs], *adj.* gefährlich.

perimeter [pəˈrɪmɪtə], *s.* der Umkreis (*Geom. & fig.*).

perineum [pɛrɪˈnɪːəm], *s.* der Damm, das Mittelfleisch (*Anat.*).

period [ˈpɪːrɪəd], *s.* die Umlaufszeit, periodischer Zeitraum, die Periode; der Zeitabschnitt, das Zeitalter; die Zeitspanne, Zeit; Pause, der Absatz (*Rhet.*); der Punkt (*Typ.*); die Schwingungsdauer (*Elec., etc.*); (Lehr)Stunde, Unterrichtsstunde (*in school*); (also *monthly –*) die Periode, (*coll.*) Regel; *for a – of*, auf die Dauer von; *dress of the –*, die Kleidung des Tages, zeitgenössische Tracht; *girl of the –*, modernes Mädchen; *– of office*, die Amtsdauer, Amtszeit; *– of transition*, die Übergangszeit. **–s** [–z], *pl.* rhetorische Sprache, das Satzgefüge, Perioden (*pl.*); die Periode, Regel (*of women*). **–ic** [pɪːrɪˈɔdɪk], *adj.* periodisch, rhetorisch, wohlgefügt (*Rhet.*). **–ical** [–ˈɔdɪkl], 1. *adj.* periodisch, regelmäßig wiederkehrend; Zeitschriften–; *–ic motion*, der Kreislauf. 2. *s.* die Zeitschrift. **–icity** [–ɔˈdɪsɪtɪ], *s.* die Periodizität.

peri–osteum [pɛrɪˈɔstɪəm], *s.* die Knochenhaut. **–ostitis** [–ɔsˈtɑɪtɪs], *s.* die Knochenhautentzündung (*Med.*). **–patetic** [–pəˈtɛtɪk], 1. *adj.* peripatetisch, umherziehend, Wander–. 2. *s.* der Peripatetiker. **–pheral** [pəˈrɪfərəl], *adj.* peripherisch, Rand–. **–phery** [pəˈrɪfərɪ], *s.* die Peripherie; (*fig.*) der Rand, die Grenze. **–phrasis** [pəˈrɪfrəsɪs], *s.* (pl. *–es* [–sɪːz]), die Umschreibung. **–phrastic** [pɛrɪˈfræstɪk], *adj.* umschreibend, periphrastisch. **–scope** [ˈpɛrɪskoʊp], *s.* das Periskop, Sehrohr, der Beobachtungsspiegel.

perish [ˈpɛrɪʃ], *v.n.* umkommen, sterben, (*sl.*) krepieren (*with*, vor), untergehen, eingehen, zugrunde gehen (*by*, durch *or* an (*Dat.*)); verdammt sein (*Theol.*). **–able** [–əbl], 1. *adj.* vergänglich; leicht verderblich, nicht haltbar (*as goods, etc.*). 2. *pl.* leicht verderbliche Waren. **–ableness,** *s.* leichte Verderblichkeit (*of goods*); die Vergänglichkeit. **–ed** [–t], *adj.* zugrunde gegangen; verdorben (*as goods*); (*coll.*) *be –ed* (*with cold*), schwach *or* hilflos *or* zitternd vor Kälte sein. (*sl.*) **–er,** *s.* der Hundsfott. (*coll.*) **–ing,** *adj.* grimmig (*as cold*); (*sl.*) verflixt.

peri–stalsis [pɛrɪsˈtælsɪs], *s.* die Peristaltik. **–staltic** [–ˈstæltɪk], *adj.* peristaltisch, wurmförmig (*Physiol.*). **–style** [ˈpɛrɪstɑɪl], *s.* der Säulengang, (*Arch.*). **–toneum** [–ˈtoʊnɪəm], *s.* das Bauchfell (*Anat.*). **–tonitis** [–təˈnɑɪtɪs], *s.* die Bauchfellentzündung (*Med.*). **–wig** [ˈpɛrɪwɪg], *s.* die Perücke. **–winkle** [ˈpɛrɪwɪŋkl], *s.* die Uferschnecke (*Mollusc.*); das Immergrün, Singrün (*Bot.*).

perjur–e [ˈpəːdʒə], *v.r.* eidbrüchig werden, meineidig werden, falsch schwören. **–er** [–ərə], *s.* Meineidige(r), *m.*, der Eidbrecher. **–y** [–ərɪ], *s.* der Meineid.

perk [pəːk], 1. *v.n.* sich brüsten, die Nase hoch tragen; (*coll.*) *– up*, sich wieder erholen. 2. *v.a.* putzen, schmücken; *– o.s.*, sich aufputzen; *– up*, emporrecken; *– up one's ears*, die Ohren spitzen. **–iness** [–ɪnɪs], *s.* die Keckheit; Selbstbewußtheit; Lebhaftigkeit. **–y,** *adj.* keck, unverschämt, übermütig; schmuck, geschniegelt, geputzt.

perks [pəːks], *pl.* (*coll.*) *see* **perquisites.**

perm [pəːm], *s.* (*coll.*) *see* **permanent wave.**

permanen–ce, –cy [ˈpəːmənəns(ɪ)], *s.* die (Fort)Dauer, Ständigkeit, Dauerhaftigkeit (*of colours, etc.*); *have no –cy*, nicht von Dauer sein; (*coll.*) *a –cy*, feste Anstellung, die Stellung von Dauer. **–t** [–ənt], *adj.* (be)ständig, (fort)dauernd, bleibend; ortsfest, bodenständig; nachhaltig, dauerhaft, Dauer–; *–t abode*, fester Wohnsitz; *–t appointment*, die Lebensstellung; *–t committee*, ständiger Ausschuß; *–t wave*, die Dauerwelle (*Hairdressing*); *–t way*, die Gleisanlage, der Oberbau, Bahnkörper (*Railw.*).

permanganate [pəˈmæŋgəneɪt], *s.* das Permanganat; *– of potash*, übermangansaures Kali.

permea–bility [pəːmɪəˈbɪlɪtɪ], *s.* die Durchdringbarkeit, Durchlässigkeit. **–ble** [ˈpəːmɪəbl], *adj.* durchdringbar, durchlässig (*to*, für). **–te** [ˈpəːmɪeɪt], 1. *v.a.* durchdringen. 2. *v.n.* eindringen (*into*, in (*Acc.*)), dringen (*through*, durch) sich verbreiten (*among*, unter). **–tion** [–ˈeɪʃən], *s.* das Durchdringen, Eindringen.

permiss–ible [pəˈmɪsɪbl], *adj.* erlaubt, zulässig, statthaft. **–ion** [–ˈmɪʃən], *s.* die Erlaubnis, Bewilligung, Genehmigung; *ask s.o.'s –ion*, einen um Erlaubnis bitten. **–ive** [–sɪv], *adj.* zulassend, gestattend; gestattet, zugelassen, zulässig.

permit [pəːˈmɪt], 1. *v.a.* erlauben, gestatten (*a th.*, es; *a p.*, ihm); *he was –ted to go*, er durfte gehen, ihm wurde gestattet *or* erlaubt zu gehen, man erlaubte ihm zu gehen; *– o.s. a th.*, sich (*Dat.*) etwas erlauben *or* gönnen; *weather –ting*, bei günstiger Witterung. 2. *v.n.* es erlauben; *if time –s*, wenn es die Zeit erlaubt; *– of*, zulassen. 3. [ˈpəːmɪt] *s.* der Erlaubnisschein, Ausweis, Passierschein, Einreisebewilligung, Ausreisebewilligung, Ausfuhrerlaubnis, der Bezugschein, die Lizenz.

permut–ation [pəːmjuˈteɪʃən], *s.* die Permutation (*Math.*); Umsetzung, Vertauschung; Lautverschiebung (*Gram.*). **–e** [–ˈmjuːt], *v.a.* vertauschen, umsetzen.

pernicious [pəːˈnɪʃəs], *adj.* schädlich, verderblich (*to* (*Dat.*)); bösartig.

pernickety [pəːˈnɪkətɪ], *adj.* (*coll.*) heikel, schwierig

(*of things*); pedantisch, kleinlich, wählerisch (*of persons*).
perorat–e ['pɛrəreɪt], *v.n.* eine Rede schließen; (*fig.*) hochtrabend reden. **–ion** [–'reɪʃən], *s.* der Redeschluß, zusammenfassender Schluß, die Schlußerörterung.
peroxide [pə'rɔksaɪd], *s.* das Superoxyd.
perpend [pə:'pɛnd], *v.a.* & *n.* (*rare*) erwägen, überlegen.
perpendicular [pə:pən'dɪkjulə], 1. *adj.* senkrecht, lotrecht (*to*, auf (*Dat.*)); rechtwink(e)lig (*to*, auf (*Dat.*)); sehr steil, aufrecht; – *style*, englische Spätgotik (*Arch.*). 2. *s.* senkrechte Linie, die Senkrechte, Lotrechte, das Lot, der *or* das Perpendikel; das Senklot, die Senkwaage; *raise* or *let fall a* –, ein Lot errichten (*or* fällen); *out of* (*the*) –, nicht senkrecht *or* lotrecht. **–ity** [–'lærɪtɪ], *s.* senkrechte Richtung.
perpetrat–e ['pə:pɪtreɪt], *v.a.* verüben, begehen (*a crime, etc.*); (*coll.*) ausführen, machen; verbrechen (*a pun, etc.*). **–ion** [–'treɪʃən], *s.* die Verübung, Begehung. **–or** [–treɪtə], *s.* der Begeher, Verüber, Täter, Frevler.
perpetu–al [pə:'pɛtjuəl], *adj.* unaufhörlich, andauernd, fortwährend, ununterbrochen; lebenslänglich, unabsetzbar; ewig, unablösbar, unkündbar (*C.L.*); (*coll.*) häufig, wiederholt, ständig; *–al motion*, das Perpetuum mobile. **–ate** [–tjueɪt], *v.a.* verewigen, fortbestehen lassen, immerwährend fortsetzen. **–ation** [–tju'eɪʃən], *s.* die Verewigung, immerwährende *or* stete Fortdauer, endlose Fortsetzung. **–ity** [pə:pɪ'tjuɪtɪ], *s.* stete Fortdauer, die Unaufhörlichkeit, Ewigkeit; lebenslängliche Rente; *in* or *to –ity*, auf ewig, für immer, in alle Ewigkeit.
perplex [pə:'plɛks], *v.a.* verwirren, verblüffen, bestürzt machen. **–ed** [–t], *adj.* verwirrt, verlegen, bestürzt. **–ing,** *adj.* verwirrend. **–ity,** *s.* die Verwirrung, Bestürzung, Verlegenheit, Verworrenheit, das Durcheinander.
perquisite ['pə:kwɪzɪt], *s.* (*often pl.*) Akzidenzien, Sporteln, Nebeneinkünfte, Nebeneinnahmen, Nebenbezüge (*pl.*), der Nebenverdienst.
perron ['pɛrən], *s.* der Beischlag (*Arch.*).
persecut–e ['pə:sɪkju:t], *v.a.* verfolgen; belästigen, plagen, drangsalen, drangsalieren. **–ion** [–'kju:ʃən], *s.* die Verfolgung; *–ion mania*, der Verfolgungswahn. **–or,** *s.* der Verfolger.
persever–ance [pə:sɪ'vɪərəns], *s.* die Beharrlichkeit, Ausdauer. **–ant** [–ənt], *adj.* beharrlich. **–ate** [pə:'sɛvəreɪt], *v.n.* spontan auftreten (*Psych.*). **–e** [–'vɪ:ə], *v.n.* beharren (*in*, bei), festhalten (*in*, an), standhaft fortfahren *or* weiterarbeiten (*with*, mit). **–ing** [–'vɪərɪŋ], *adj.* beharrlich, standhaft.
persiflage ['pə:sɪflɑ:ʒ], *s.* die Verspottung.
persimmon [pə'sɪmən], *s.* die Dattelpflaume.
persist [pə:'sɪst], *v.a.* beharren *or* bleiben (*in*, bei), bestehen (*in*, auf), hartnäckig fortfahren (*in doing*, zu tun); beharrlich weiterarbeiten (*with*, an); fortdauern, andauern, fortbestehen. **–ence** [–əns], *s.* das Beharren (*in*, bei), hartnäckiges Fortfahren (*in*, in), das Fortdauern, Andauern, wiederholtes Vorkommen. **–ency** [–ənsɪ], *s.* die Ausdauer, Beharrlichkeit; Hartnäckigkeit; *see also* **–ence.** **–ent** [–ənt], *adj.* beharrlich, hartnäckig; dauernd, nachhaltig; anhaltend, (be)ständig.
person ['pə:sən], *s.* die Person, der Mensch, das Wesen, Einzelwesen; der Körper, Äußere(s) *n.*; die Rolle, der Charakter (*Theat.*); *the – who*, derjenige, welcher; *a* –, einer, jemand; *fictitious* –, – *at law*, juristische Person; *in* –, persönlich, selbst; *in one's own* –, in eigener Person; *no* –, niemand; *not a* –, keine Seele; *carry on one's* –, an *or* bei sich tragen; *have respect of –s*, die Person ansehen. **–able,** *adj.* ansehnlich, stattlich. **–age** [–ɪdʒ], *s.* die Person, (hohe) Persönlichkeit, die Figur; der Charakter (*Theat.*). **–al** [–əl], *adj.* persönlich, individuell, eigen, Privat–; anzüglich (*remarks*); beweglich (*Law*); *–al appearance*, körperliches Aussehen; persönliches Auftreten (*Theat.*); *become –al*, anzüglich werden; *–al call*, die Voranmeldung (*Phone*); *–al column*, persönliche Anzeigen (*pl.*); *–al life*, das Privatleben; *–al opinion*, eigene Meinung; *–al pronoun*, persönliches Fürwort, das Personalpronomen; *–al property*, bewegliches Eigentum; *–al tax*, die Personalsteuer. **–ality** [–'nælɪtɪ], *s.* die Persönlichkeit, Individualität; (*normally pl.*) Anzüglichkeit, anzügliche Bemerkung. **–alty,** *s.* bewegliches Eigentum. **–ate** ['pə:səneɪt], 1. *v.a.* darstellen; fälschlich ausgeben als, (fälschlich) vorstellen *or* verkörpern, nachahmen. 2. *v.n.* eine Rolle spielen. **–ation** [–'neɪʃən], *s.* die Darstellung; (fälschliches) Nachahmen *or* Ausgeben. **–ification** [–sɔnɪfɪ'keɪʃən], *s.* die Verkörperung, Personifizierung. **–ify** [–'sɔnɪfaɪ], *v.a.* darstellen, personifizieren; verkörpern, versinnbildlichen. **–nel** [pə:sə'nɛl], *s.* das Personal, die Belegschaft; die Mannschaften (*Mil.*), die Besatzung (*Naut.*); *–nel division*, die Personalabteilung.
perspective [pə:'spɛktɪv], 1. *adj.* perspektivisch, Perspektiv–. 2. *s.* die Perspektive; Fernsicht, Fernschau; perspektivische Ansicht, perspektivisch richtige Darstellung *or* Zeichnung; (*fig.*) die Aussicht, der Ausblick; *in* (*true*) –, perspektivisch richtig, in richtiger Perspektive.
perspicaci–ous [pə:spɪ'keɪʃəs], *adj.* scharfsichtig, weitsichtig, scharfsinnig. **–ty** [–'kæsɪtɪ], *s.* der Scharfblick, Scharfsinn, die Scharfsichtigkeit.
perspicu–ity [pə:spɪ'kjuɪtɪ], *s.* die Deutlichkeit, Klarheit, Verständlichkeit. **–ous** [–'spɪkjuəs], *adj.* klar, deutlich, leicht verständlich.
perspir–ation [pə:spɪ'reɪʃən], *s.* der Schweiß; das Schwitzen, (*fig.*) die Ausdünstung. **–e** [–'paɪe], 1. *v.n.* schwitzen, transpirieren. 2. *v.a.* ausschwitzen, ausdünsten.
persua–de [pə:'sweɪd], *v.a.* überzeugen (*of*, von), überreden, bereden (*to do* or *into doing*, zu tun); *–de o.s.*, sich (*Dat.*) einreden *or* einbilden, *be –ded*, überzeugt sein (*of*, von), sich überreden lassen. **–sion** [–'sweɪʒən], *s*, die Überredung; Überzeugung, fester Glaube; die Sekte, der Glaube (*Rel.*); die Art, Gattung. **–sive** [–'sweɪsɪv], *adj.* überredend, überzeugend. **–siveness,** *s.* überzeugende Kraft; die Überredungsgabe.
pert [pə:t], *adj.* keck, vorlaut, schnippisch, naseweis. **–ness,** *s.* die Keckheit.
pertain [pə:'teɪn], *v.n.* gehören (*to*, zu), angehören, zukommen (*to* (*Dat.*)); betreffen (*to* (*Acc.*)); *–ing to*, betreffend.
pertinaci–ous [pə:tɪ'neɪʃəs], *adj.* beharrlich, standhaft; hartnäckig. **–ousness,** *s.* **–ty** [–'næsɪtɪ], *s.* die Standhaftigkeit, Beharrlichkeit; Hartnäckigkeit.
pertinen–ce ['pə:tɪnəns], **–cy** [–əns(ɪ)], die Angemessenheit, Gemäßheit, Eignung (*to*, für). **–t** [–ənt], *adj.* gehörig (*to*, zu), passend, schicklich (*to*, für), angemessen (*to* (*Dat.*)); treffend, einschlägig; *be –t to*, Bezug haben auf. **–ts,** *pl.* das Zubehör.
perturb [pə:'tə:b], *v.a.* beunruhigen, aufregen, verwirren. **–ation,** *s.* die Störung (*also Astr.*), Beunruhigung.
peruke [pə'ru:k], *s.* die Perücke.
perus–al [pə'ru:zəl], *s.* das Durchlesen, die Durchsicht; *for –al*, zur Einsicht. **–e** [–'ru:z], *v.a.* durchsehen, durchlesen.
perva–de [pə:'veɪd], *v.a.* durchdringen, erfüllen, durchziehen. **–sion** [–'veɪʒən], *s.* die Durchdringung. **–sive** [–'veɪsɪv], *adj.* durchdringend.
perver–se [pə:'və:s], *adj.* verkehrt, Fehl– (*of things*); verstockt, störrisch, widerspenstig; widernatürlich, verderbt, böse, schlecht (*of persons*). **–seness,** *s.* der Eigensinn, die Widerspenstigkeit, Verstocktheit. **–sity** [–'və:sɪtɪ], *s.* die Verkehrtheit, Widernatürlichkeit, Verderbtheit, Perversität; *see also* **–seness.** **–sion** [–'və:ʃən], *s.* die Verkehrung, Verdrehung, Entstellung; Verirrung, Abkehr, Abwendung. **–sive,** *adj.* verderblich (*of*, für); verkehrend, verdrehend. **–t** [–'və:t], 1. *v.a.* verkehren: verdrehen, entstellen (*meaning, etc.*); verführen, verderben (*a p.*). 2. ['pə:və:t], *s.* Abtrünnige(r), *m.* (*Rel.*); (*sexual*) *–t*, perverser Mensch.
pervious ['pə:vɪəs], *adj.* gangbar, offen, zugänglich (*to*, für); durchlässig. **–ness,** *s.* die Durchlässigkeit (*to*, für).
pesky ['pɛskɪ], *adj.* (*sl.*) verteufelt, vertrackt.
pessary ['pɛsərɪ], *s.* das Pessar, der Scheidenring, (Gebär)Mutterhalter; das Okklusivpessar.
pessimis–m ['pɛsɪmɪzm], *s.* der Pessimismus; die Kopfhängerei, Schwarzseherei. **–t** [–mɪst], 1. *s.*

der Pessimist, Schwarzseher. 2. *adj.*; **-tic** [–ˈmɪstɪk], *adj.* pessimistisch.
pest [pɛst], *s.* die Pest, Plage; der Schädling. **--house,** *s.* (*archaic*) das Spital für Pestkranke. **-ology** [–ˈtɔlədʒɪ], *s.* die Schädlingsbekämpfung.
pester [ˈpɛstə], *v.a.* plagen, quälen, belästigen.
pest-iferous [pɛsˈtɪfərəs], *adj.* Pest–, pestartig; (*fig.*) schädlich, verderblich, verpestend. **-ilence** [ˈpɛstɪləns], *s.* die Seuche, Pestilenz, Pest. **-ilent** [ˈpɛstilənt], *adj.* schädlich, giftig, tödlich; (*coll.*) lästig. **-ilential** [–ˈlɛnʃəl], *adj.* Pest–, pestartig; verpestend, ansteckend; (*fig.*) bösartig, schädlich; widerlich, ekelhaft; lästig.
pestle [ˈpɛsl], *s.* die Mörserkeule, der Stößel; das Pistill (*Chem.*).
pestology, *see* **pest.**
[1]**pet** [pɛt], *s.* gezähmtes *or* zahmes Tier, das Lieblingstier, Haustier; (*coll.*) der Liebling, verzogenes Kind, das Schoßkind; (*coll.*) *be a – and* . . ., sei gut *or* sei so lieb *or* nett und. . . . 2. *attrib.* Lieblings–; Schoß–; – *aversion*, höchster *or* größter Greuel; – *dog*, der Schoßhund; – *mistake*, ein Lieblingsfehler; – *name*, der Kosename. 3. *v.a.* hätscheln, verzärteln, liebkosen.
[2]**pet** [pɛt], *s.* schlechte *or* üble Laune, der Verdruß; *in a* –, ärgerlich, schlecht gelaunt; *take* (*the*) – *at*, sich ärgern über, übelnehmen.
petal [ˈpɛtl], *s.* das Blumenblatt. **-(l)ed,** *adj.*, **-ous** [ˈpɛtələs], *adj.* mit Blumenblättern.
petard [pəˈtɑːd], *s.* die Petarde, Sprengbüchse; *be hoist with one's own* –, in die Grube fallen, die man andern gegraben hat.
peter [ˈpɪːtə], *v.n.*; (*coll.*) – *out*, zu Ende gehen, sich totlaufen, zerrinnen, abflauen.
petiol-ar [ˈpɛtɪoulə], *adj.* stielförmig, Stiel–. **-ate** [–leɪt], *adj.* bestielt. **-e** [–tɪoul], *s.* der Blattstiel (*Bot.*).
petition [pəˈtɪʃən], 1. *s.* die Bitte; das Gesuch, die Eingabe, Bittschrift, Petition (*to*, an; *for*, um), Klage, der Antrag (*Law*); – *of Rights*, die Erklärung der konstituellen Rechte (*Hist. 1628*); *file one's* – *in bankruptcy*, den Konkurs anmelden. 2. *v.a.* eine Bittschrift reichen an (*Acc.*), eine Bittschrift einreichen (*Dat.*), bitten, ersuchen, angehen (*for*, um). 3. *v.n.* ersuchen, bitten (*for*, um); – *for divorce*, die Scheidung beantragen. **-er,** *s.* der Bittsteller, Antragsteller; Kläger (*Law, esp. in divorce proceedings*).
petrel [ˈpɛtrəl], (also *storm--* or *stormy* –), der Sturmvogel (*Orn.*); (*fig.*) *stormy* –, der Unruhestifter, unruhiger Geist.
petrif-action [pɛtrɪˈfækʃən], *s.* die Versteinerung; *pl.* Fossilien (*pl.*). **-y** [ˈpɛtrɪfaɪ], 1. *v.a.* versteinern; (*fig.*) starr machen, bestürzen; *-ied with*, starr vor. 2. *v.n.* zu Stein werden.
petrograph [ˈpɛtrogrɑːf], *s.* die Felsinschrift.
petrol [ˈpɛtrəl], *s.* das Benzin, der Kraftstoff, Treibstoff; *--pump*, *--station*, die Tankstelle. **-eum** [pɪˈtroulɪəm], *s.* das Erdöl, Petroleum; *-eum ether*, der Petroläther; *-eum jelly*, die Vaseline.
petrology [pɛˈtrɔlədʒɪ], *s.* die Gesteinskunde.
petrous [ˈpɛtrəs], *adj.* steinhart, steinig, felsig; – *bone*, das Felsenbein (*Anat*).
petticoat [ˈpɛtɪkout], 1. *s.* der (Frauen)Unterrock; (*sl.*) das Frauenzimmer, Weibsbild; (*coll.*) *in -s*, in Kinderröckchen. 2. *attrib.*; – *government*, die Weiberherrschaft; *--hold*, das Kunkellehen (*Law*).
pettifog [ˈpɛtɪfɔg], *v.n.* Schliche *or* Kniffe anwenden (*Law*). **-ger,** *s.* der Winkeladvokat (*Law*); Haarspalter. **-ging,** 1. *adj.* schikanös, rabulistisch; armselig, lumpig. 2. *s.* die Rabulistik, Haarspalterei; Rechtskniffe (*pl.*).
pettiness [ˈpɛtɪnɪs], *s.* die Kleinlichkeit, Geringfügigkeit.
pettish [ˈpɛtɪʃ], *adj.* empfindlich, launisch, verdrießlich. **-ness,** *s.* die Empfindlichkeit, Verdrießlichkeit.
pettitoes [ˈpɛtɪtouz], Schweinsfüße (*pl.*).
petty [ˈpɛtɪ], *adj.* klein, gering(fügig), unbedeutend; kleinlich; – *cash*, geringe Beträge (*pl.*); *--cashbook*, *s.* das Kleinkassenbuch; – *jury*, kleine Jury; – *larceny*, kleiner Diebstahl; – *offence*, das Vergehen; – *officer*, der Maat, Unteroffizier (*Nav.*); – *prince*, der Duodezfürst; – *wares*, Kurzwaren.
petulan-ce [ˈpɛtjʊləns], *s.* die Gereiztheit, Verdrießlichkeit, Ungeduld. **-t** [–ənt], *adj.* ungeduldig, verdrießlich, gereizt, launenhaft, schmollend, mürrisch.
petunia [pɪˈtjʊːnɪə], *s.* die Petunie (*Bot.*).
pew [pjʊː], *s.* der Kirchenstuhl, Kirchensitz; (*sl.*) Stuhl, Sitz; (*sl.*) *take a* –, nehmen Sie Platz, setzen Sie sich. **-age** [–ɪdʒ], *s.* die Kirchenstuhlmiete.
pewit [ˈpɪwɪt], *s. see* **peewit.**
pewter [ˈpjʊːtə], 1. *s.* das Hartzinn, Britanniametall; Zinngerät, Zinngefäß; (*sl.*) der Preispokal. 2. *adj.* zinnern, Zinn–. **-er,** *s.* der Zinngießer.
phaeton [ˈfeɪtn], *s.* der Phaethon, vierrädriger Wagen.
phag-ed(a)ena [fædʒəˈdɪːnə], *s.* fressendes Geschwür. **-ocyte** [ˈfægəsaɪt], *s.* die Phagozyte.
phalan-ge [ˈfælændʒ], *s.* die Phalanx; *pl.* Phalangen (*Anat.*). **-ger,** *s.* der Fingerbeutler, Kletterbeutler *Zool.*). **-x** [ˈfælæŋks], *s.* (pl. *-xes* [–sɪz], *-ges* [fəˈlændʒɪz]), die Phalanx; (*fig.*) Schlachtreihe, geschlossene Reihe; *in -x*, *-xed*, in Reihen aufgestellt, geschlossen.
phall-ic [ˈfælɪk], *adj.* phallisch. **-us** [–əs], *s.* (pl. *-i* [–aɪ]) der Phallus, männliches Glied.
phant-asm [ˈfæntæzm], *s.* das Trugbild, Hirngespinst; Wahngebilde, Gespenstererscheinung. **-asmagoria** [–təzməˈgɔːrɪə], *s.* das Blendwerk, Trugbilder, Gaukelbilder (*pl.*). **-asmagoric** [–təsməˈgɔrɪk], *adj.* trügerisch, gaukelhaft, traumhaft. **-asmal** [–ˈtæzməl], *adj.* geisterhaft, gespensterhaft, eingebildet, unwirklich. **-om** [–təm], 1. *s.* das Gespenst, die Erscheinung, der Geist; das Hirngespinst, Wahngebilde, Trugbild, Phantom, der Schein. 2. *attrib.* Schein–, Gespenster–; *-om circuit*, die Viererleitung (*Elec.*); *-om ship*, das Geisterschiff.
pharis-aic(al) [færɪˈzeɪɪk(l)], *adj.* pharisäisch, scheinheilig. **-aism** [–zeɪɪzm], *s.* die Scheinheiligkeit. **-ee** [–sɪː], *s.* der Pharisäer; (*fig.*) Scheinheiliger.
pharmac-eutical [fɑːməˈsjʊːtɪkl, –ˈkjʊtɪkl], *adj.* pharmazeutisch, arzneikundlich. *-eutical chemist*, der Apotheker. **-eutics** [–ˈsjʊːtɪks, –ˈkjʊːtɪks], *pl.* (*sing. constr.*) die Arzneiwissenschaft, Pharmazeutik. **-ist** [ˈfɑːməsɪst], *s.* der Pharmazeut, Drogist, Apotheker. **-ologist** [–ˈkɔlədʒɪst], *s.* der Pharmakolog. **-ology** [–ˈkɔlədʒɪ], *s.* die Arzneimittellehre. **-opoeia** [–kəˈpɪːə], *s.* amtliches Arzneibuch. **-y** [ˈfɑːməsɪ], *s.* die Apothekerkunst; Drogerie, Apotheke.
pharos [ˈfɛːərəs], *s.* (*archaic*) der Leuchtturm.
pharyn-g(e)al [fæˈrɪndʒ(ɪ)əl], *adj.* Kehlkopf–, Rachenkopf–, Schlundkopf. **-gitis** [færɪnˈdʒaɪtɪs], *s.* der Rachenkatarrh (*Med.*). **-x** [ˈfærɪŋks], *s.* (pl. *-ges* [–ˈrɪndʒɪːz], *-xes* [–ɪŋksɪz]) der Schlund(kopf), die Rachenhöhle.
phase [feɪz], *s.* die Phase (*Astr., Elec.*); (*fig.*) das Stadium, die (Entwicklungs)Stufe.
pheasant [ˈfɛzənt], *s.* der Fasan; – *shooting*, *s.* die Fasanenjagd. **-ry,** *s.* die Fasanerie.
phen-acetin [fəˈnæsɪtɪn], *s.* das Phenazetin. **-ate** [ˈfɪːneɪt], die Phenolverbindung. **-ic** [–ɪk] karbolsauer. **-ol** [–əl], *s.* die Karbolsäure, das Karbol, Phenol, Benzophenol. **-olate** [–əleɪt] **of,** karbolsauer. **-yl** [ˈfɪːnɪl], *s.* das Phenyl. **-ylic acid** [fɪːˈnɪlɪk], die Karbolsäure.
phenomen-al [fəˈnɔmənəl], *adj.* phänomenal, Erscheinungs– (*Phil.*); (*coll.*) außerordentlich, erstaunlich, einzigartig, großartig, fabelhaft. **-alism** [–ɪzm], *s.* der Phänomenalismus (*Phil.*). **-on** [–ənən], *s.* (pl. *-a* [–ənə]) das Phänomen, die Erscheinung, (*fig.*) das Wunder; *infant -on*, das Wunderkind.
phenyl, *see under* **phen-yl.**
phew [fjʊː], *int.* puh!
phial [ˈfaɪəl], *s.* das Fläschchen, die Phiole, Ampulle.
philander [fɪˈlændə], *v.n.* tändeln, schäkern, Liebelei treiben. **-er** [–ərə], *s.* der Courmacher, Hofmacher, Schäkerer, Schürzenjäger, Schwerenöter.
philanthrop-ical [fɪlənˈθrɔpɪkl], *adj.* menschenfreundlich, philanthropisch. **-ist** [fɪˈlænθrəpɪst], *s.* der Menschenfreund, Philanthrop. **-y** [fɪˈlænθrəpɪ], *s.* die Menschenliebe.

philatel–ic [fɪlə'tɛlɪk], *adj.* Briefmarken–. **–ist** [fɪ'lætəlɪst], *s.* der Markensammler. **–y** [fɪ'lætəlɪ], *s.* die Briefmarkenkunde, das Briefmarkensammeln.
philharmonic [fɪlhɑ:'mɔnɪk], *adj.* musikliebend, philharmonisch.
philhellenic ['fɪlhə'lɛnɪk], *adj.* griechenfreundlich.
philippic [fɪ'lɪpɪk], *s.* die Philippika, Standrede, Brandrede, Schmährede.
philippin–a [fɪlə'pɪ:nə], **–e** [–'pɪ:n], *s.* das Vielliebchen.
philistin–e ['fɪlɪstɪn], 1. *s.* der Philister, Spießer, Spießbürger. 2. *adj.* spießig, spießbürgerlich, spießerisch, philisterhaft, philiströs. **–ism,** *s.* das Spieß(bürg)ertum, Philistertum.
philolog–ical [fɪlə'lɔdʒɪkl], *adj.* sprachwissenschaftlich, philologisch. **–ist** [fɪ'lɔlədʒɪst], *s.* der Sprachforscher, Philolog. **–y** [fɪ'lɔlədʒɪ], *s.* die Sprachwissenschaft, Philologie.
philopoena [fɪlə'pɪ:nə], *see* **philippina.**
philosoph–er [fɪ'lɔsəfə], *s.* der Philosoph; *natural –er,* der Naturforscher; *–ers' stone,* der Stein der Weisen. **–ic(al)** [fɪlə'sɔfɪk(l)], *adj.* philosophisch; (*fig.*) einsichtig, weise, beherrscht, mäßig. **–ize** [fɪ'lɔsəfɑɪz], *v.n.* philosophieren. **–y** [fɪ'lɔsəfɪ], *s.* die Philosophie; Weltanschauung, Weisheit; *natural –y,* die Naturwissenschaft.
philtre ['fɪltə], *s.* der Liebestrank, Zaubertrank.
phiz [fɪz], *s.* (*sl.*) die Visage.
phleb–itis [flə'bɑɪtɪs], *s.* die Venenentzündung. **–otomize** [flə'bɔtəmɑɪz], 1. *v.a.* zur Ader lassen, (*a p.*). 2. *v.n.* eine Ader öffnen. **–otomy** [–'bɔtəmɪ] *s.* der Aderlaß.
phlegm [flɛm], *s.* der Schleim (*Med.*); (*fig.*) das Phlegma, die Stumpfheit, geistige Trägheit, der Gleichmut. **–atic** [flɛg'mætɪk], *adj* phlegmatisch, träge, stumpf, gleichmütig, gleichgültig. **–on** ['flɛgmən], *s.* die Phlegmone (*Path.*). **–y** ['flɛmɪ], *adj.* schleimig.
phlogistic [flɔ'dʒɪstɪk], *adj.* entzündlich (*Med.*).
phlox [flɔks], *s.* die Flammenblume.
phoenix ['fɪ:nɪks], *s.* der Phönix (*Myth.*).
phon–e [foʊn], 1. *s.* der Phon (*Phonet.*); (*coll.*) das Telephon, der Fernsprecher; *be on the –e,* Telephonanschluß haben; *be wanted on the –e,* am Telephon verlangt werden. 2. *v.a.* anrufen, telephonieren. 3. *v.n.* telephonieren. **–etic** [fə'nɛtɪk], *adj.* Laut–, phonetisch; *–etic spelling,* die Lautschrift. **–etician** [fonə'tɪʃən], *s.* der Phonetiker. **–etics** [fə'nɛtɪks], *pl.* (*sing. constr.*) die Phonetik. **–ic** ['foʊnɪk], *adj.* Laut–, akustisch, lautlich.
phon(e)y ['foʊnɪ], *adj.* (*sl.*) unecht, falsch, Schein–.
phono–gram ['foʊnəgræm], *s.* das Lautzeichen. **–graph** [–grɑ:f], *s.* der Phonograph, die Sprechmaschine. **–logy** [fo'nɔlədʒɪ], *s.* die Lautlehre.
phos–gene ['fɔzdʒɪ:n], *s.* das Phosgen, Chlorkohlenoxyd. **–phate** ['fɔsfɑɪt], *s.* das Phosphat, phosphorsaures Salz; das Kali (*Agric.*); *–phate of,* phosphorsauer. **–phide** ['fɔsfɑɪd], *s.* die Phosphorverbindung; *–phide of iron,* das Phosphoreisen. **–phite** [–fɑɪt], *s.* phosphorigsaures Salz. **–phor** [–fɔ:], *attrib.* Phosphor–. **–phorate** [–fəreɪt], *v.a.* (*usually p.p.*) phosphorisieren. **–phoresce** [–fə'rɛs], *v.n.* phosphoreszieren, im Dunkeln leuchten. **–phorescence** [–fə'rɛsns], *s.* die Phosphoreszenz; *–phorescence of the sea,* das Meeresleuchten. **–phorescent** [–'rɛsnt], *adj.* phosphoreszierend. **–phoric** [fɔs'fɔrɪk], *adj.* Phosphor–. **–phorous** [–fərəs], *adj.* phosphorig, phosphorigsauer, phosphorhaltig. **–phorus** [–fərəs], *s.* der Phosphor; *–phorus necrosis,* der Knochenbrand. **–phuretted** [–fə'rɛtɪd], *adj.* mit Phosphor verbunden; *– –phuretted hydrogen,* der Phosphorwasserstoff.
photo ['foʊtoʊ], (*coll.*) *see* **–graph. – –electric,** *adj.* photoelektrisch. **– –engraving,** *s.* die Buchdruckätzung, Photogravüre. **– –finish,** *s.* die Entscheidung durch Zielphotographie (*Sport*). **– –flash,** *s.* das Blitzlicht. **–genic** [–dʒɛnɪk], *adj.* bildwirksam, zum Photographieren geeignet. **–grammetry** [–'græmətrɪ], *s.* das Meßbildverfahren. **–graph** ['foʊtoʊgrɑ:f], 1. *s.* das Lichtbild, die Photographie; *take a –graph,* eine Aufnahme machen. 2. *v.a.* photographieren, (*coll.*) knipsen. 3. *v.n.* photographieren, photographiert werden; *–graph well,* gut auf Bildern werden. **–grapher** [fə'tɔgrəfə], *s.* der Photograph. **–graphic** [–'græfɪk] *adj.* photographisch, Bild–; (*fig.*) naturgetreu; *–graphic interpretation,* die Lichtbildauswertung. **–graphy** [fə'tɔgrəfɪ], *s.* die Lichtbildkunst, Photographie. **–gravure** [foʊtoʊgrə'vjʊə], *s.* die Photogravüre, Heliogravüre, der Kupfertiefdruck. **–lithograph** [foʊtoʊ'lɪθəgrɑ:f], *s.* der Photolithograph. **–lithography** [–lɪ'θɔgrəfɪ], *s.* die Photolithographie. **–meter,** *s.* der Belichtungsmesser, Licht(stärke)messer. **–metric** [–'mɛtrɪk], *adj.* photometrisch. **–n** ['foʊtɔn], *s.* das Photon. **–sphere** [–sfɪ:ə], *s.* die Photosphäre (*Astr.*). **–stat** [–stæt], 1. *s.* die Photokopie (*of manuscripts, etc.*). 2. *v.a.* photokopieren. **– –survey,** *s.* die Geländeaufnahme. **– –telegraphy,** *s.* die Bildtelegraphie. **–type** [–tɑɪp], 1. *s.* die Lichtdruckplatte; Lichtpause, Phototypie. 2. *v.a.* durch Lichtdruck vervielfältigen.
phrase [freɪz], 1. *s.* die Phrase (*also Mus.*), Redensart, (Rede)Wendung, der Ausdruck; (kurzer) Satz (*Gram.*), der Tonsatz (*Mus.*). 2. *v.a.* ausdrücken, nennen; phrasieren (*Mus.*). **– –monger,** *s.* der Phrasendrescher. **–ology** [–ɪ'ɔlədʒɪ], *s.* die Redeweise, Ausdrucksweise, Phraseologie.
phrenetic [frə'nɛtɪk], *adj.* irrsinnig, wahnsinnig, rasend, toll.
phrenic ['frɛnɪk], *adj.* Zwerchfell–.
phrenolog–ical [frɛnə'lɔdʒɪkl], *adj.* phrenologisch. **–ist** [frə'nɔlədʒɪst], *s.* der Phrenolog(e). **–y** [frɛ'nɔlədʒɪ], *s.* die Schädelforschung, Phrenologie.
phthis–ical ['(f)θɪsɪkl], *adj.* schwindsüchtig. **–is** [–sɪs], *s.* die Schwindsucht.
phut [fʌt], *adv.*; (*sl.*) *go –,* futsch *or* kaputt gehen.
phylactery [fɪ'læktərɪ], *s.* der Gebetriemen (*of Jews*), (*fig.*) religiöse Selbstgefälligkeit.
phylloxera [fɪlɔk'sɪ:ərə], *s.* die Reblaus (*Ent.*).
physic ['fɪzɪk], 1. *s.* die Arzneikunde, Heilkunst; (*coll.*) die Arznei, das (Heil)Mittel. 2. *v.a.* Arznei geben (*Dat.*), herumdoktern an (*Dat.*), kurieren (*a p.*). **–al** [–əl], *adj.* physisch, physikalisch, naturwissenschaftlich, Natur–; körperlich, leiblich, Körper–; *–al condition,* der Gesundheitszustand; *–al culture,* die Körperpflege; *–al fitness,* körperliche Tüchtigkeit *or* Tauglichkeit; *–al force,* die Körperkraft; bewaffnete Macht (*Pol.*); *–al geography,* physikalische Geographie; *–al impossibility,* absolute Unmöglichkeit; (*coll.*) *–al jerks,* Leibesübungen (*pl.*); *–al science,* die Naturwissenschaft; *–al training,* körperliche Ertüchtigung, Leibesübungen (*pl.*), das Turnen. **–ian** [–'zɪʃən], *s.* der Arzt. **–ist** ['fɪzɪsɪst], *s.* der Physiker. **–s,** *pl.* (*sing. constr.*) die Physik.
physiognom–ist [fɪzɪ'ɔ(g)nəmɪst], *s.* der Mienendeuter, Physiognom. **–y** [–mɪ], *s.* die Physiognomie, Gesichtsbildung; (*coll.*) das Gesicht; die Physiognomik, Mienenkunde.
physiography [fɪzɪ'ɔgrəfɪ], *s.* die Naturbeschreibung.
physiolog–ical [fɪzɪə'lɔdʒɪkl], *adj.* physiologisch. **–ist** [–'ɔlədʒɪst], *s.* der Physiolog. **–y** [–'ɔlədʒɪ], *s.* die Physiologie.
physique [fɪ'zɪ:k], *s.* der Körperbau, die Körperbeschaffenheit.
phyto–graphy [fɑɪ'tɔgrəfɪ], *s.* die Pflanzenbeschreibung. **–phagous** [–'tɔfəgəs], *adj.* pflanzenfressend.
pian–issimo [pɪə'nɪsɪmoʊ], *adv.* sehr leise (*Mus.*). **–ist** ['pɪənɪst], *s.* der Klavierspieler, Pianist. **–o,** 1. [pɪ'ɑ:noʊ], *adv.* leise (*Mus.*). 2. [pɪ'ænoʊ], *s.* das Klavier; *at the –o,* am Klavier; *cottage –o,* das Pianino; *grand –o,* der Flügel; *on the –o,* auf dem Klavier; *upright –o,* see *cottage –o*; *–o duet,* vierhändiges Spiel. *–o-player, s. see* **–ist;** *see* **–ola;** *–o recital,* der Klaviervortrag; *–o score,* der Klavierauszug; *–o stool,* der Klavierstuhl. **–oforte** [pɪ'ænoʊ 'fort(ɪ)], *s. see* **–o** 2. **–ola** [pɪə'noʊlə], *s.* das Pianola.
piastre [pɪ'æstə], *s.* der Peso (*Spanish*), Gersch (*Turkish*).
piazza [pɪ'æzə], *s.* der (Markt)Platz, Hof (*Italian*); Balkon, die Veranda (*Amer.*).
pibroch ['pɪ:brɔχ], *s.* die Kriegsmusik *or* Kampfmusik (auf dem Dudelsack).
pica ['pɑɪkə], *s.* die Cicero(schrift) (*Typ.*).
picador ['pɪkadɔ:], *s.* der Stierfechter zu Pferd.

picar–esque [pɪkəˈrɛsk], *adj.* Abenteuer–, Schelmen–; *–esque novel*, der Schelmenroman. **–oon** [–ruːn], *s.* der Seeräuber, Abenteurer.

piccalilli [pɪkəˈlɪlɪ], *s.* eingepökeltes Gemüse.

piccaninny [pɪkəˈnɪnɪ], *s.* (*pej.*) das Negerkind.

piccolo [ˈpɪkəlou], *s.* die Piccoloflöte.

pick [pɪk], **1.** *v.a.* hacken, aufhauen (*ground*); (auf)picken (*as birds*); pflücken, sammeln (*flowers, etc.*), lesen (*vegetables, corn, etc.*), scheiden (*ore*), rupfen (*poultry*); abnagen (*a bone*); ausfasern, zupfen (*wool, oakum*); (*fig.*) sorgsam aussuchen *or* auswählen; – *a bone with s.o.*, mit einem ein Hühnchen rupfen; – *a. p.'s brains*, jemandes Kenntnisse ausbeuten; – *and choose*, auswählen, wählerisch sein; (*fig.*) – *holes* or *a hole in a p.*, einem etwas am Zeuge flicken, etwas an einem auszusetzen haben; . . . *in a th.*, etwas bekritteln; – *a lock*, ein Schloß erbrechen; – *one's nose*, in der Nase bohren; – *s.o.'s pocket*, einen bestehlen, jemandes Tasche plündern; – *a quarrel*, Streit *or* Händel suchen, anbändeln; – *one's teeth*, sich (*Dat.*) die Zähne (aus)stochern; – *one's way*, sich (*Dat.*) mühsam einen Weg suchen; – *off*, (ab)pflücken; herausschießen; – *out*, sich sorgsam auswählen *or* aussuchen, herausheben, hervorheben (*a pattern*); herausfinden, erkennen, unterscheiden (*meaning*); nach Gehör spielen (*melody*); – *to pieces*, zerpflücken, in Stücke reißen; (*fig.*) herunterreißen, herziehen über; – *up*, aufhacken (*ground*); aufheben, aufnehmen, in die Hand nehmen; auflesen, auftreiben, erwerben, erstehen; mitnehmen (*passengers*); sich aneignen, erlernen, aufschnappen (*a language, etc.*); anleuchten (*by searchlight*); aufnehmen, auffangen (*Rad., etc.*); zufällig kennenlernen (*a p.*) *or* erfahren (*a fact*); abholen (*a p.*); – *up cheap* (or *for a song*), (spott)billig erstehen; – *up courage*, Mut fassen; – *up a living*, sich mühsam durchschlagen *or* durchbringen; – *o.s. up*, sich erheben. **2.** *v.n.* (langsam *or* bissenweise) essen; (*coll.*) mausen, stibitzen; – *at*, picken an; (*sl.*) mäkeln an; – *on*, sich entscheiden für; aufsässig sein (*Dat.*); – *up*, auf Touren kommen (*of motor*); sich erholen. **3.** *s.* die (Spitz)Hacke, Picke; der Spieß (*Print.*); die Auswahl, Auslese, die Besten (*pl.*); – *of the bunch* or *basket*, der, die *or* das Beste von allen. **–axe** [–æks], *s.* die (Spitz)Hacke; Picke, Haue. **–ed** [–t], *adj.* erlesen, ausgesucht; *–ed troops*, Kerntruppen (*pl.*). **–ing,** *s.* das Pflücken, Lesen, Zupfen; *pl.* zweifelhafte Nebeneinkünfte (*pl.*), der Raub, unehrlicher Gewinn; Überreste, Überbleibsel (*pl.*). **–lock,** *s.* der Dietrich; Einbrecher. (*coll.*) **– -me-up,** *s.* die (Magen)Stärkung. **–pocket,** *s.* der Taschendieb. **– -up,** *s.* die Aufnahme; Beschleunigungskraft (*Motor.*); elektrischer Tonabnehmer, die Abtastdose (*gramophone*); (*sl.*) die Flitsche, Nutte, das Flittchen.

pick-a-back, pickaback [ˈpɪkəbæk], *adv.* huckepack.

pickerel [ˈpɪkərəl], *s.* junger Hecht.

picket [ˈpɪkɪt], **1.** *s.* der Holzpfahl, Absteckfahl (*Surv.*); Pflock; Zaun; die Feldwache (*Mil.*); der Streikposten; *anchoring* –, der Ankerpfahl. **2.** *v.a.* einzäunen, einpfählen; an einen Pfahl binden (*an animal*); als (Feld)Wache aufstellen; als Streikposten einsetzen, mit Streikposten besetzen (*a factory*). **3.** *v.n.* auf (Feld)Wache stehen, Streikposten stehen.

pickl–e [ˈpɪkl], **1.** *s.* der Pökel, die (Salz)Lake, Salzbrühe, Beize, das Abbeizmittel (*Metall.*); Eingepökelte(s) *n.*; (*coll.*) die Patsche, Verlegenheit; (*coll.*) der Trotzkopf, Wildfang; (*coll.*) *in –e*, in Bereitschaft; (*coll.*) *be in a –e*, in Verlegenheit sein, in der Patsche sitzen; *mixed –es*, gemischte Essigfrüchte; *have a rod in –e for s.o.*, mit einem ein Hühnchen zu rupfen haben. **2.** *v.a.* einpökeln, einsalzen; (ab)beizen (*metal*). **–ed** [–d], *adj.* Essig–, Salz–, Pökel–; (*sl.*) berotzt. **–ing,** *s.* das Einpökeln.

picnic [ˈpɪknɪk], **1.** *s.* das Picknick, die Mahlzeit im Freien, die Landpartie, (*sl.*) eine Leichtigkeit, wahres Vergnügen; (*sl.*) *no* –, keine leichte S. **2.** *v.n.* ein Picknick abhalten. **–ker,** *s.* der Picknickteilnehmer.

picquet [ˈpɪkɪt], *see* **picket** (*Mil.*).

picric [ˈpɪkrɪk], *adj.* Pikrin–.

picto–graph [ˈpɪktəgrɑːf], *s.* das Bildzeichen, Bildsymbol, Bilddiagramm, die Statistik mit bildlichen Zahlen. **–rial** [pɪkˈtɔːrɪəl], **1.** *adj.* Maler–, malerisch; Bild–, bildlich; illustriert, Bilder– (*edition*); *–rial advertising*, die Bildwerbung. **2.** *s.* illustrierte Zeitung.

picture [ˈpɪktʃə], **1.** *s.* das Gemälde, Bild, Porträt; die Zeichnung, (Bild)Tafel (*in a book*); Aufnahme, Photographie (*Phot.*); der Film (*Films*); (*fig.*) das Ebenbild; die Schilderung, anschauliche Darstellung, Veranschaulichung, Verkörperung; (*coll.*) *the –s*, das Kino, die Kinovorstellung; *be in the* –, sichtbar sein, von Bedeutung sein; *come into the* –, in Erscheinung treten; *be* or *look the – of health*, blühend aussehen, von Gesundheit strotzen; *form a – of*, sich ein Bild machen von; *go to the –s*, ins Kino gehen; *on the –s*, beim Film; *she is a perfect* –, sie ist zum Malen schön; *the dress is a* –, das Kleid ist ein Gedicht. **2.** *v.a.* malen; (*fig.*) schildern; – *to o.s.*, sich vorstellen *or* ausmalen. **– -book,** *s.* das Bilderbuch. **– -card,** *s.* das Bild (*Cards*). **– -frame,** *s.* der Bilderrahmen. **– -gallery,** *s.* die Gemäldegallerie. **– -goer,** *s.* der Kinobesucher. **– -hat,** *s.* breitkrempiger Hut. **– -house,** *s.*, **– -palace,** *s.* das Lichtspieltheater, Kino. **– -postcard,** *s.* die Ansichtskarte. **– -puzzle,** *s.* das Vexierbild, Bilderrätsel. **– -rail,** *s.* die Bilderleiste. **–sque** [–ˈrɛsk], *adj.* malerisch. **–squeness,** *s.* das Malerische, malerische Schönheit. **– -transmission,** die Bildübertragung, der Bildfunk (*Rad.*) **– -writing,** *s.* die Bilderschrift.

piddle [ˈpɪdl], *v.n.* (*vulg.*) pinkeln, schiffen.

pidgin [ˈpɪdʒɪn], *s.* (*sl.*) die Sache; – (*English*), die Verkehrssprache zwischen Engländern und Ostasiaten.

[1]**pie** [pɑɪ], *s.* die (Fleisch)Pastete; (Frucht)Torte; *eat humble* –, Abbitte tun, zu Kreuze kriechen; *have a finger in the* –, die Hand im Spiele haben.

[2]**pie** [pɑɪ], *s. see* **magpie.**

[3]**pie** [pɑɪ], *s.* durcheinandergefallener Satz, Zwiebelfische (*pl.*) (*Typ.*); (*fig.*) *printer's* –, der Wirrwarr, Mischmasch, die Verwirrung, das Durcheinander; (*sl.*) *make – of*, verwirren, durcheinanderbringen.

pie–bald [ˈpɑɪbɔːld], *adj.* bunt, scheckig; *–bald horse*, die Schecke. **–d,** *adj.* buntscheckig; *–d Piper* (*of Hamelin*), der Rattenfänger von Hameln.

piece [piːs], **1.** *s.* das Stück, (Musik)Stück, (Theater)-Stück, Gemälde; (Geld)Stück; Geschütz, die Kanone, Flinte, Pistole; (Schach)Figur, (*sl.*) das Weibsbild, Weibsstück; (*coll.*) das Stück Weg, die Wegstrecke. (*a*) (*with nouns*) – *of advice*, der Ratschlag; – *of bread and butter*, das Butterbrot; – *of folly*, die Torheit; – *of furniture*, das Stück Möbel; – *of impudence*, die Unverschämtheit; *give s.o. a – of one's mind*, einem seine Meinung sagen; – *of music*, Musikstück; – *of news*, die Neuigkeit, Nachricht; – *of poetry*, das Gedicht; – *of wallpaper*, die Rolle Tapete; – *of work*, das Stück Arbeit. (*b*) (*with prepositions*) *by the* –, stückweise, nach dem Stück (*C.L.*); *in –s*, in Stücke zerbrochen, entzwei; *fall in –s*, zerfallen, in Stücke fallen; *tear in –s*, zerreißen; (*all*) *of a* –, aus einem Stück; gleichmäßig, übereinstimmend; eins (*with*, mit); *to –s*, in Stücke, auseinander; *break to –s*, zerbrechen; *fall to –s*, in Stücke gehen; *go to –s*, zusammenbrechen; *pull to –s*, zerpflücken; *take to –s*, zerlegen, auseinandernehmen. **2.** *v.a.* anstücken, ansetzen, einsetzen, zusammensetzen, flicken; – *out*, verlängern, ergänzen; – *together*, zusammensetzen, zusammenstücken; – *up*, ausbessern, ausflicken, wiederherstellen. **– -goods,** *pl.* Schnittwaren, Stückwaren, Manufakturwaren (*pl.*). **–meal,** *adj.* & *adv.* stückweise, Stück für Stück, einzeln. **– -work,** *s.* die Akkordarbeit, Stückarbeit. **– -worker,** *s.* der Akkordarbeiter.

pied [pɑɪd], *see under* **piebald.**

pier [pɪːə], *s.* der (Brücken)Pfeiler; Hafendamm, Kai, die Mole, Anlegestelle, Landebrücke, der Landungsplatz, Ausladeplatz, Löschplatz. **–age** [–ɪdʒ], *s.* das Kaigeld. **– -glass,** *s.* langer Spiegel. **– -head,** *s.* der Molenkopf.

pierc–e [ˈpɪːəs], 1. *v.a.* durchstechen, durchbohren, durchstoßen, durchlöchern; anstechen (*a cask*); (*fig.*) durchdringen, durchschauen, erkennen; eindringen in (*Acc.*); (*fig.*) *–e a p.'s heart*, einem ins Herz schneiden. 2. *v.n.* eindringen (*into*, in (*Acc.*)), dringen, (*through*, durch). **–ing,** *adj.* schneidend, scharf, durchdringend, rührend.
pierr–ette [pɪːəˈrɛt], *s.* die Kabarettspielerin. **–ot** [ˈpɪːərou], *s.* der Kabarettspieler (in Harlekintracht).
piet–ism [ˈpɑɪətɪzm], *s.* der Pietismus. **–ist** [–tɪst], *s.* der Pietist. **–istic** [–ˈtɪstɪk], *adj.* pietistisch. **–y** [ˈpɑɪətɪ], *s.* die Frömmigkeit, Ehrfurcht, Pietät; *filial –y*, kindliche Liebe.
piffle [pɪfl], *s.* (*coll.*) der Quatsch, Unsinn, das Geschwätz.
pig [pɪg], 1. *s.* das Schwein; Ferkel; die Massel, Mulde (*of lead*), der Rohblock, Barren (*Metall.*); *buy a – in a poke*, die Katze im Sack kaufen; *make a – of o.s.*, sich zum Schweine machen, sich wie ein Ferkel benehmen. 2. *v.n.* ferkeln, frischen; (*coll.*) *– it*, zusammengepfercht hausen. **–gery,** *s.* der Schweinestall; (*fig.*) die Schweinerei. **–gish,** *adj.* schweinisch; (*fig.*) gemein, gierig. **–gy,** 1. *s.* (*coll.*) das Schweinchen. 2. *adj. see* **–gish.** **–headed,** *adj.* dickköpfig, störrisch, eigensinnig. **–headedness,** *s.* die Störrigkeit. **– -iron,** *s.* das Roheisen. **– -lead,** *s.* das Muldenblei. **–let,** *s.* das Schweinchen, Ferkel. **–nut,** *s.* die Erdnuß. **–'s bladder,** *s.* die Schweinsblase. **–skin,** *s.* das Schweinsleder; (*sl.*) der Sattel. **–sticking,** *s.* die Wildschweinjagd, das Schweineschlachten. **–sty** [–stɑɪ], *s.* der Schweinestall (*also fig.*). **–tail,** *s.* der Zopf. **–wash,** *s.* das Schweinefutter.
pigeon [ˈpɪdʒən], *s.* die Taube; (*sl.*) der Gimpel; *–'s milk*, das Mückenfett. **– -breasted,** *adj.* mit einer Hühnerbrust. **– -fancier,** *s.* der Taubenzüchter. **– -hole,** 1. *s.* das (Schub)Fach, Ablegefach. 2. *v.a.* in ein Schubfach legen; einordnen, klassifizieren; beiseitelegen, zurücklegen, aufheben, die Erledigung von . . . hinausschieben. **– -house, – -loft,** *s.* der Taubenschlag. (*coll.*) **– -livered,** *adj.* bangbüxig. **– -pie,** *s.* die Taubenpastete.
pig–gery, –gish, –gy, –headed, –let, *see under* **pig.**
pigment [ˈpɪgmənt], 1. *s.* der Farbstoff, die Farbe; das Pigment (*Nat. Hist.*). 2. *v.a.* färben, pigmentieren. **–al** [–ˈmɛntəl], *adj.*, **–ary** [–ərɪ], *adj.* Pigment–. **–ation** [–ˈteɪʃən], *s.* die Färbung. **– -print,** *s.* der Pigmentdruck.
pigmy [ˈpɪgmɪ], *s. see* **pygmy.**
pig–-nut, –sticking, –sty, –tail, –wash, *see under* **pig.**
pi-jaw [ˈpɑɪdʒɔː], 1. *s.* (*sl.*) die Standpauke, Gardinenpredigt. 2. *v.a.* anschnauzen.
¹pike [pɑɪk], *s.* die Pike, der Spieß (*Mil.*); Hecht (*Ichth.*). **–man,** *s.* der Pikenträger; Häuer (*Min.*). **–staff,** *s.* der Pikenschaft; *as plain as a –staff*, sonnenklar.
²pike [pɑɪk], *s. see* **turnpike.** **–man,** *s.* Zolleinnehmer. **–r,** *s.* (*sl.*) vorsichtiger Spieler (*Amer.*).
pikelet [ˈpɑɪklɪt], *s.* runder Teekuchen.
pilaster [pɪˈlæstə], *s.* der Pilaster, Wandpfeiler.
pilch [pɪltʃ], *s.* der Kinderschlüpfer (über die Windeln getragen).
pilchard [ˈpɪltʃəd], *s.* die Sardine (*Ichth.*).
¹pile [pɑɪl], 1. *s.* der Haufen, Stoß, Stapel; Satz, die Partie; der Holzstoß, Meiler; Scheiterhaufen; das Gebäude, hohes Bauwerk; die Säule (*Elec.*); (*coll.*) der Haufen Geld, das Vermögen; *atomic –*, das Pile, die Atomkraftanlage, Atomsäule; *galvanic –*, galvanische Säule; (*sl.*) *make one's –*, sich ein Vermögen machen; (*coll.*) *–s of money*, Geld wie Heu. 2. *v.a.* (also *– up*) aufhäufen, auftürmen, aufstapeln, aufschichten, zusammensetzen (*arms*); (*fig.*) bedecken, überhäufen (*table*) (*with*, mit); (*coll.*) *– it on*, übertreiben; (*coll.*) *– on the agony*, die Erwartung auf höchste spannen. 2. *v.n.* (*sl.*) *– in*, hineindrängen, scharenweise besteigen; *– up*, aufhäufen, auftürmen; (*sl.*) Bruch machen (*Av.*).
²pile [pɑɪl], 1. *s.* der Pfahl, Pfeiler, das Brückenjoch; der Spitzpfahl (*Her.*). 2. *v.a.* mit Pfählen verstärken *or* stützen. **– -driver,** *s.*, die Ramme, der Rammklotz. **– -dwelling,** *s.* der Pfahlbau.
³pile [pɑɪl], 1. *s.* weiches Haar, die Daune (*of animals*); der Flor, die *or* der Felbel (*of velvet*); weiche *or* haarige Seite, das Rauhe, die Noppe (*of cloth*). 2. *attrib.*; *double- –*, doppelflorig; *three- –*, dreifach gewebt.
piles [pɑɪlz], *pl.* Hämorrhoiden (*pl.*).
pilfer [ˈpɪlfə], *v.a.* klauen, mausen, stibitzen. **–age,** *s. see* **–ing.** **–er,** *s.* der Dieb, Langfinger. **–ing,** *s.* kleiner Diebstahl, die Dieberei, Mauserei, das Mausen, Stibitzen.
pilgrim [ˈpɪlgrɪm], *s.* der Pilger, Wallfahrer; *the – Fathers*, die Pilgerväter. **–age** [–ɪdʒ], 1. *s.* die Wallfahrt, Pilgerfahrt (*to*, nach); *place of –age*, der Wallfahrtsort. 2. *v.n.* wallfahren, wallfahrten, wallen.
pill [pɪl], 1. *s.* die Pille, Tablette; (*sl.*) Kugel; (*sl.*) der Ball; *pl.* (*vulg.*) Eier (*pl.*); *gild the –*, der S. die unangenehme Seite nehmen; (*coll.*) *swallow a bitter –*, in den sauern Apfel beißen; (*sl.*) *game of –s*, das Spiel Billard. 2. *v.a.* (*sl.*) durchfallen lassen, ablehnen (*a candidate*). **– -box,** *s.* die Pillenschachtel; der Bunker, Unterstand (*Mil.*).
pillage [ˈpɪlɪdʒ], 1. *s.* die Plünderung, der Raub. 2. *v.a.* & *n.* plündern, rauben, brandschatzen.
pillar [ˈpɪlə], 1. *s.* die Säule, der Pfeiler, Ständer, Träger; (*fig.*) die Stütze; *from – to post*, von Pontius zu Pilatus. 2. *v.a.* mit Pfeilern stützen *or* schmücken. **– -box,** *s.* freistehender Briefkasten. **–ed,** *p.p.* & *adj.* mit Pfeilern gestützt *or* geschmückt; säulenförmig.
pillion [ˈpɪlɪən], *s.* der Damensattel, das Sattelkissen; der Sozius(sitz) (*on motor-cycle*); *ride –*, auf dem Sozius mitfahren. **– -rider,** *s.* der Soziusfahrer.
pilliwinks [ˈpɪlɪwɪŋks], *s.* die Daumschraube(n) (*Hist.*).
pillory [ˈpɪlərɪ], 1. *s.* der Pranger; *in the –*, am Pranger. 2. *v.a.* an den Pranger stellen; (*fig.*) anprangern, lächerlich machen.
pillow [ˈpɪlou], 1. *s.* das Kopfkissen, der Pfühl; das (Zapfen)Lager, die Lagerschale, Pfanne (*Tech.*); *lace –*, das Klöppelkissen. *take counsel of one's –*, eine S. beschlafen. 2. *v.a.* auf ein Kissen legen; mit Kissen stützen; *– up*, hoch betten. **– -case,** *s.* Kissenüberzug, Kissenbezug. **– -fight,** *s.* die Kissenschlacht. **– -lace,** *s.* Klöppelspitzen (*pl.*). **– -slip,** *s. see* **– -case.**
pil–ose [ˈpɑɪlous], **–ous** [–əs], *adj.* haarig; behaart (*Bot.*).
pilot [ˈpɑɪlət], 1. *s.* der Lotse, Pilot (*Naut.*), Flugzeugführer, Pilot (*Av.*); (*fig.*) Führer; *automatic –*, der Selbststeurer, das Selbststeuergerät (*Av.*); *–'s seat*, der Führersitz (*Av.*). 2. *v.a.* lotsen, steuern; führen (*also fig.*), steuern, fliegen (*Av.*). **–age,** *s.* das Lotsen; die Flugkunst; das Lotsengeld; (*fig.*) die Leitung, Führung. **– balloon,** *s.* der Pilotballon. **– -boat,** *s.* das Lotsenboot. **– burner,** *s.* der Sparbrenner. **– -cloth,** *s.* dunkelblauer Fries. **– engine,** *s.* die Leerfahrtlokomotive. **– -flag,** *s.* die Lotsenflagge. **– lamp,** *s.* die Kontrollampe (*Elec.*). **–less,** *adj.* führerlos. **– -officer,** *s.* der Fliegerleutnant.
pilous, *adj. see* **pilose.**
pilule [ˈpɪljuːl], *s.* kleine Pille.
pimento [ˈpɪmɛntou], der Nelkenpfeffer, Piment.
pimp [pɪmp], 1. *s.* der Kuppler. 2. *v.n.* kuppeln.
pimpernel [ˈpɪmpənəl], *s.* die Pimpernelle (*Bot.*).
pimpl–e [ˈpɪmpl], *s.* die Pustel, Finne, der Pickel, das Bläschen. **–ed,** *adj.*, **–y,** *adj.* voll(er) Pusteln, finnig, pickelig.
pin [pɪn], 1. *s.* die Stecknadel, Nadel; Zwecke, Pinne; der Dübel, Stift, Pflock (*of wood*), Bolzen (*of metal*); Wirbel (*Mus.*); Kegel (*at ninepins*); *pl.* (*sl.*) Beine; *crank –*, der Kurbelzapfen; *dowel –*, der Dübel, Diebel; *drawing –*, der Reißnagel, die Zwecke; *firing –*, der Schlagbolzen; *hair –*, die Haarnadel; *hinge –*, der Angeldorn, Scharniernagel; *retaining –*, der Schlüsselbolzen; *rolling –*, das Rollholz; *safety –*, die Sicherheitsnadel; *split –*, der Federsplint; (*coll.*) *I don't care two –s*, es ist mir piepe, wurst *or* schnuppe; *–s and needles*, das Ameisenlaufen; *on –s and needles*, (wie) auf glühenden Kohlen; *not worth a –*, keinen Deut wert. 2. *v.a.* stecken, anheften, durchbohren (*also fig.*); befestigen; packen, festhalten; *– one's faith on* or *to*, sein ganzes Vertrauen setzen auf (*Acc.*), fest bauen auf; *– down*,

festhalten (*to*, an), binden (*enemy forces*); – *a p. down*, einen festlegen *or* festnageln (*to*, auf), zur Verantwortung ziehen; – *up*, aufstecken; aufschürzen. **–cushion,** *s.* das Nadelkissen. **– –feather,** *s.* die Stoppelfeder. **– –head,** *s.* der Stecknadelkopf; (*fig.*) die Kleinigkeit; der Dummkopf. **– –hole,** *s.* das Nadelloch, winziges Loch. **–money,** *s.* das Nadelgeld. **– –point,** 1. *s.* die Nadelspitze; (*fig.*) *– –point bombing*, der Bombenpunktwurf. 2. *v.a.* genau zielen nach. **– –prick,** *s.* der Nadelstich (*also fig.*); die Stichelei, spitzige Bemerkung. (*coll.*) *– –up* (*girl*), fesches Frauenbild.

pinafore ['pɪnəfɔː], *s.* die Schürze, das Lätzchen.

pince-nez ['pɪnsneɪ], *s.* der Kneifer, Klemmer.

pincer– –movement [pɪnsə'muːvmənt], *s.* die Umklammerung (*Mil.*). **–s** ['pɪnsəz], *pl.* die Kneifzange; *pair of –s*, eine Kneifzange; die Krebsschere.

pinch [pɪntʃ], 1. *v.a.* kneifen, zwicken, klemmen, quetschen, drücken; (*sl.*) klauen, klemmen; verhaften, festnehmen; *be –ed*, darben, in Not *or* Verlegenheit sein (*for*, um); (*sl.*) *get –ed*, verhaftet werden; – *off*, abzwicken, abkneifen. 2. *v.n.* drücken; (*fig.*) sich nichts vergönnen, darben, geizen, knausern; *know where the shoe –es*, wissen, wo der Schuh drückt; – *and scrape*, sich alles von Munde absparen. 3. *s.* das Drücken, Kneifen, Zwicken; (*fig.*) der Druck, die Klemme; Prise (*snuff, salt, etc.*); (*coll.*) *at a –*, zur Not, wenn alle Stricke reißen; (*fig.*) *with a – of salt*, mit Vorsicht. **–ed,** *adj.* zusammengedrückt; (*fig.*) abgehärmt, abgemagert, abgezehrt; *–ed with cold*, halb erfroren; *–ed with hunger*, halb verhungert; *–ed circumstances*, beschränkte *or* bedrückte Verhältnisse.

pinchbeck ['pɪntʃbɛk], 1. *s.* der Tombak, das Talmi. 2. *adj.* Tombak–, Talmi–, (*fig.*) minderwertig, unecht, nachgemacht.

[1]**pine** [paɪn], *s.* die Fichte, Kiefer, Föhre, Pinie. **–apple,** *s.* die Ananas. **– –cone,** *s.* der Tannenzapfen. **– –marten,** *s.* der Baummarder. **–ry,** *s.* das Ananashaus; die Fichtenpflanzung (*of pine-trees*). **– –tree,** *s. see* **–**. **– –wood,** *s.* der Fichtenwald; das Fichtenholz.

[2]**pine** [paɪn], *v.n.* sich grämen *or* abhärmen; – *away*, verschmachten, vor Gram vergehen; – *for*, sich sehnen nach, schmachten nach.

pineal ['pɪːnɪəl], *adj.*; – *gland*, die Zirbeldrüse.

pinfold ['pɪnfoʊld], *s.* (*archaic*) die Viehhürde.

ping [pɪŋ], 1. *s.* das Pfeifen (*of bullets*). 2. *v.n.* pfeifen, schwirren. **– –pong,** *s.* das Tischtennis.

pinic ['pɪːnɪk], *adj.*; – *acid*, die Pinsäure.

[1]**pinion** ['pɪnɪən], 1. *s.* die Flügelspitze; (also *– –feather*) die Flugfeder; (*poet.*) die Schwinge, der Flügel. 2. *v.a.* beschneiden (*wings*); (*fig.*) binden, fesseln.

[2]**pinion** ['pɪnɪən], *s.* das Ritzel, Zahnrad (*Tech.*).

[1]**pink** [pɪŋk], 1. *s.* die Federnelke (*Bot.*); das Blaßrot, Rosa; roter Jagdrock (*Hunt.*); (*fig.*) der Gipfel, die Krone, Höhe, höchster Grad; *in the –* (*of condition*), in allerbester Gesundheit; *the – of perfection*, das Muster der Vollkommenheit. 2. *adj.* blaßrot, rosa. **–ish,** *adj.* rötlich.

[2]**pink** [pɪŋk], *s.* die Pinke, das Heckboot (*Naut.*).

[3]**pink** [pɪŋk], *v.a.* ausbohren, durchbohren, kunstvoll ausschneiden (*leather*), auszacken (*an edge*). **–ing-iron,** *s.* das Auszackeisen.

[4]**pink** [pɪŋk], *v.n.* klopfen (*Motor.*).

pinna ['pɪnə], *s.* die Ohrmuschel (*Anat.*); Flosse (*Zool.*); Fieder (*Bot.*).

pinnace ['pɪnəs], *s.* die Pinasse, Barkasse, das Beiboot.

pinnacle ['pɪnəkl], *s.* die Zinne, der Spitzturm (*Arch.*); die Felsspitze; (*fig.*) der Gipfel.

pinn–ate ['pɪnət], *adj.* gefiedert (*Bot.*). **–igrade** [–ɪgreɪd], *s.*, **–iped** [–ɪpɛd], *s.* der Flossenfüßer. **–ule** [–juːl], *s.* kleine Flosse (*Zool.*), das Fiederblättchen (*Bot.*).

pinny ['pɪnɪ], *s.* (*coll.*) *see* **pinafore.**

pint [paɪnt], *s.* die Pinte, der Schoppen (= 0·57 (*Amer.* = 0·47) Liter).

pintail ['pɪnteɪl], *s.* (also – *duck*), die Spießente.

pintle ['pɪntl], *s.* der Bolzen, Protznagel (*Artil.*); Ruderhaken (*Naut.*).

pinto ['pɪntoʊ], *s.* der Scheck, die Schecke (*horse*).

pioneer ['paɪənɪːə], 1. *s.* der Pionier (*Mil.*); (*fig.*) Bahnbrecher, Vorkämpfer, Wegbereiter. 2. *v.n.* den Weg bahnen. 3. *v.a.* bahnen, bereiten, vorangehen mit.

pious ['paɪəs], *adj.* fromm, gottesfürchtig.

[1]**pip** [pɪp], *s.* das Auge (*cards*), der Punkt (*dice*); Stern als Rangabzeichen (*Mil.*).

[2]**pip** [pɪp], *s.* der (Obst)Kern (*of apples, etc.*).

[3]**pip** [pɪp], *s.* der Pips (*in fowls*); (*coll.*) der Ärger, Unmut; (*coll.*) *give s.o. the –*, einen verdrießen *or* zu Tode ärgern; *have the –*, grollen, sich erzürnen. **– –squeak,** *s.* (*sl.*) lächerliche S. *or* Person.

[4]**pip** [pɪp], 1. *v.a.* (*coll.*) besiegen, überlisten; durchfallen lassen. 2. *v.n.* (*coll.*) durchfallen.

pip–e [paɪp], 1. *s.* die Pfeife (*Mus.* & *tobacco*), Tabakspfeife, das Rohr, die Röhre, Leitung (*gas, etc.*); das Pfeifen (*of birds*); die Stimme; die Pipe (= *105 gallons*, = *477 l.*) (*of wine*); *pl.* der Dudelsack; *pl.* (*coll.*) Atmungskanäle (*pl.*); *lay –es*, die Leitung legen; (*coll.*) *put that in your –e and smoke it*, laß dir das gesagt sein. 2. *v.n.* & *a.* auf der Pfeife spielen; pfeifen (*as the wind*), piepen (*of birds*), piepsen, quieken (*of persons*); durch Pfeifensignal zusammenrufen (*the crew*) *or* empfangen (*the admiral*) (*Naut.*); paspelieren, mit Schnurbesatz versehen (*a dress*); mit Rohren versehen (*a house*), leiten (*gas, etc.*), absenken (*Hort.*); (*sl.*) *–e in*, mitreden; (*sl.*) *–e down*, sich beruhigen, es billiger geben; *–e up*, zu spielen beginnen, loslegen, zunehmen (*of wind*). **–e-bowl,** *s.* der Pfeifenkopf. **–e-clay,** *s.* der Pfeifenton; (*fig.*) der Kommiß (*Mil.*). **–e-clip,** *s.* die Rohrschelle. **–e-dream,** *s*, der Wunschtraum. **–eful,** *s.* die Pfeifevoll (*of tobacco*). **–e-line,** *s.* die Rohrleitung, Röhrenleitung, Ölleitung. **–e major,** *s.* der Musikmeister (der Dudelsackspfeiferkapellen). **–er,** *s.* der (Dudelsack)Pfeifer; *pay the –er*, die Kosten tragen, die Zeche bezahlen, der Dumme sein. **–e-rack,** *s.* der Pfeifenständer. **–e-stem,** *s.* der Pfeifenstiel. **–ing,** 1. *adj.* pfeifend, schrill; **–ing hot,** siedend heiß; *the –ing times of yore*, die guten alten Zeiten. 2. *s.* das Pfeifen, Piepen; Röhrenwerk, die Röhrenanlage; der Schnurbesatz, die Kleiderborte, Paspel, Litze (*Tail.*).

pipette [pɪ'pɛt], *s.* die Pipette, der Stechheber.

pipit ['pɪpɪt], *s.* der Pieper (*Orn.*).

pipkin ['pɪpkɪn], *s.* irdenes Töpfchen.

pippin ['pɪpɪn], *s.* der Pippingapfel.

piquan–cy ['pɪkənsɪ], *s.* die Würze, Schärfe, Pikantheit, das Pikante. **–t** [–ənt], *adj.* würzig, scharf, pikant, prickelnd.

pique [pɪːk], 1. *s.* der Groll, Unwille, die Gereiztheit, Pikiertheit. 2. *v.a.* reizen, Unwillen erregen, ärgern; – *o.s. on*, sich (*Dat.*) etwas einbilden **auf**, sich zugute tun auf. **–d,** *adj.* pikiert (*at*, über).

piqué ['pɪːkeɪ], *s.* der Pikee.

piquet ['pɪkɪt], *s.* das Pikett.

pira–cy ['paɪrəsɪ], *s.* die Seeräuberei; (*fig.*) unerlaubter Nachdruck. **–te** [–ət], 1. *s.* der Seeräuber, das Seeräuberschiff; (*fig.*) unrechtmäßiger Nachdrucker; konkurrierender Privatomnibus; unoffizieller Radiosender. 2. *v.a.* ohne Erlaubnis nachdrucken. **–tical** [–'rætɪkl], *adj.* (see)räuberisch; Raub–.

pirouette [pɪrʊ'ɛt], 1. *s.* die Pirouette, Kreisdrehung. 2. *v.n.* pirouettieren.

pisc–ary ['pɪskərɪ], *s.*; *common of –ary*, die Fischereigerechtigkeit, das Fischereirecht. **–atorial** [–'tɔːrɪəl], *adj.*, **–atory** [–tərɪ], *adj.* Fischerei–, Fischer–, Fisch–. **–es** ['pɪseɪs], *pl.* die Fische (*Astr.*). **–iculture** ['pɪsɪkʌltʃə], *s.* die Fischzucht. **–ina** [–sɪːnə, –saɪnə], *s.* das Wasserbecken, der Schwimmteich, Fischbehälter; das Abspülbecken (*Eccl.*). **–ivorous** [pɪs'kɪvərəs], *adj.* fischfressend.

pisé ['pɪːzə], *s.* die Stampfmasse, der Pisee; Piseebau, Stampfbau.

pish [pɪʃ], *int.* pfui!

pisiform ['pɪsɪfɔːm, 'pɪzɪfɔːm], *adj.* Erbsen–.

piss [pɪs], 1. *s.* (*vulg.*) der Harn, die Pisse, Schiffe. 2. *v.n.* (*vulg.*) harnen, pissen, schiffen, seichen.

pistachio [pɪs'teɪʃɪoʊ, –'tæʃoʊ], *s.* die Pistazie (*Bot.*).

pistil ['pɪstɪl], *s.* der Stempel, das Pistill (*Bot.*). **–late,** *adj.* mit Stempel; weiblich (*Bot.*).

pistol ['pɪstəl], 1. *s.* die Pistole. 2. *v.a.* mit der

Pistole (er)schießen. **--shot,** *s.* der Pistolenschuß; *within --shot,* in Pistolenschußweite.
piston [ˈpɪsˈtən], *s.* der Kolben. **--rod,** *s.* die Kolbenstange, Pleuelstange. **--stroke,** *s.* der Kolbenhub.
pit [pɪt], 1. *s.* die Grube, Höhle, der Schacht, Stollen; Abgrund; die Hölle; der Hahnenkampfplatz; die Getreidebörse (*C.L.*); Tankstelle (*Motor-racing*); (Blatt)Narbe; das Parterre (*Theat.*); *– of the stomach,* die Magengrube; *the bottomless –,* der Höllenschlund. 2. *v.a.* vergraben (*potatoes, etc.*); feindlich gegenüberstellen (*against* (*Dat.*)), ausspielen (*against,* gegen); mit Narben zeichnen; *–ted with smallpox,* blatternarbig. 3. *v.n.* sich senken, eine Grube bilden (*Path.*). **–fall,** *s.* die Fallgrube; (*fig.*) Falle, der Irrtum. **--head,** *s.* der Grubenkopf, das Förderhaus, Schachthäuschen, die Schachtmündung, (Schacht)Kaue, der Füllort *--head baths,* die Waschkaue; *--head price,* der Preis frei Grube. **–man,** *s.* der Grubenarbeiter, Bergmann. **--pony,** *s.* das Grubenpferd. **--props,** *pl.* das Grubenholz. **--saw,** die Schrotsäge.
pit-a-pat [ˈpɪtəpæt], 1. *adv.* ticktack (*of the heart*); klippklapp, tripptrapp (*of the feet*). 2. *s.* das Getrippel, Getrappel (*of feet*), Herzklopfen.
[1]**pitch** [pɪtʃ], 1. *s.* das Pech; *as black as –,* pechrabenschwarz. 2. *v.a.* (aus)pichen, teeren (*a ship*). **--blende,** *s.* die Pechblende (*Min.*). **– black, – dark,** *adj.* pechschwarz, stockdunkel. **--pine,** *s.* die Pechtanne, Pechkiefer. **–y,** *adj.* Pech–, pechartig, pechschwarz.
[2]**pitch** [pɪtʃ], 1. *s.* der Wurf; Aufschlag (*of the ball*) (*Crick.*); das Stampfen (*of ship*); der Stand, Standort; die Spielbahn, das Spielfeld (*Crick.*); höchster Punkt, der Grad, die Stufe, Höhe; Tonhöhe, Tonstufe, der Kammerton (*Mus.*); die Pfeilhöhe, Abdachung, Neigung, der Neigungsgrad (*Arch.*), die Steighöhe, Steigung (*of a screw*); Zahnteilung, Kettenteilung, Gradteilung (*Tech.*); *at the highest –,* auf der Höhe; *to the highest –,* aufs äußerste; *queer a p.'s* or *the –,* (einem) einen Strich durch die Rechnung machen. 2. *v.a.* werfen, schleudern; feststecken; aufschlagen (*a tent, etc.*); einschlagen; einstecken; aufstellen, errichten, anlegen; zum Verkauf ausstellen; pflastern (*street*); ordnen, ansetzen, festsetzen; (ab)stimmen (*Mus.*); (*fig.*) abstimmen, (auf)laden (*hay, etc.*); *–ed battle,* regelrechte Schlacht; *high--ed voice,* hohe Stimme. 3. *v.n.* sich lagern, sich niederlassen; aufschlagen (*as a ball*), (nieder)stürzen, hinfallen; stampfen (*Naut.*); abfallen, sich neigen (*as a roof*); *–ed work,* die Steinpackung, das Pachwerk; (*coll.*) *– in,* sich ins Zeug legen, tüchtig einhauen, kräftig ans Werk gehen; (*coll.*) *– into,* herfallen über (*Acc.*); *– (up)on,* sich entscheiden für, verfallen auf. **--and-toss,** *s.*; *play at --and-toss,* Kopf oder Wappen spielen. **–er,** *s.* der Ballwerfer (*Sport*). **–fork,** 1. *s.* die Heugabel, Mistgabel. 2. *v.a.* mit der Heugabel werfen; (*fig.*) gewaltsam drängen, rücksichtslos versetzen, lancieren. **--pipe,** *s.* die Stimmpfeife.
pitcher [ˈpɪtʃə], *s.* der Krug; (*Prov.*) *little –s have long ears,* kleine Pötte haben große Ohren; (*Prov.*) *the – goes often to the well but is broken at last,* der Krug geht so lange zum Brunnen bis er bricht. **–ful,** *s.* der Krugvoll.
pitchy [ˈpɪtʃɪ], *see* [1]**pitch.**
piteous [ˈpɪtɪəs], *adj.* kläglich, erbärmlich; rührend, mitleiderregend, herzzerreißend.
pitfall [ˈpɪtfɔːl], *s. see* **pit.**
pith [pɪθ], *s.* das Mark (*Bot. & fig.*); das Wesentliche, der Kern, die Quintessenz; Kraft, Bedeutung, das Gewicht. **–iness,** *s.* das Markige, die Prägnanz, Kraft. **–y,** *adj.* markig, kernig, kräftig, prägnant.
pithecanthropus [pɪθɪˈkænθrəpəs], *s.* der Javamensch.
piti-able [ˈpɪtɪəbl], *adj.* bejammernswert, jämmerlich, erbärmlich, kläglich. **–ful** [–fʊl], *adj.* mitleidig, mitfühlend; mitleiderregend, rührend; jämmerlich, läppisch. **–fulness,** *s.* die Erbärmlichkeit, Jämmerlichkeit. **–less** [–lɪs], *adj.* mitleidslos, unbarmherzig, gefühllos. **–lessness,** *s.* die Unbarmherzigkeit.
pitman [ˈpɪtmən], *s. see* **pit.**
pittance [ˈpɪtəns], *s.* kleine Portion, kleiner Anteil, armseliges Auskommen, der Hungerlohn.
pituitary [pɪˈtjʊɪtərɪ], *adj.* schleimabsondernd, Schleim–; *– gland,* der Hirnanhang, die Hypophyse.
pit–y [ˈpɪtɪ], 1. *s.* das Mitleid, Erbarmen (*on,* mit); der Grund zum Bedauern; *what a –y!* wie schade! *it's a (great) –y,* es ist (sehr) schade; *it is a thousand –ies,* es ist jammerschade; *the –y of it is,* der einzige Nachteil ist; *for –y's sake,* um Gottes willen; *feel –y for,* Mitleid haben mit; *have* or *take –y on,* Mitleid haben mit. 2. *v.a.* bemitleiden, bedauern; *I –y you,* du tust mir leid. **–ying,** *adj.* mitleidsvoll, mitleidig.
pivot [ˈpɪvət], 1. *s.* der Drehpunkt, (Schwenk)Zapfen; die Angel; der Flügelmann (*Mil.*); (*fig.*) Angelpunkt. 2. *v.n.* sich drehen (*on,* um). 3. *v.a.* drehbar lagern. **–al,** *adj.* Haupt–, Schlüssel, zentral; *–al point,* der Angelpunkt.
pixie, pixy [ˈpɪksɪ], *s.* der Elf, die Fee, das Wichtelmännchen.
pizzle [ˈpɪzl], *s.* die Rute.
placab–ility [plækəˈbɪlɪtɪ], *s.* die Versöhnlichkeit. **–le** [ˈplækəbl], *adj.*, versöhnlich, nachgiebig. **–leness,** *s. see* **–ility.**
placard [ˈplækɑːd], 1. *s.* der Anschlag, das Plakat. 2. *v.a.* anschlagen, durch Anschlag bekanntmachen; mit Plakaten bekleben (*wall*).
placate [pləˈkeɪt], *v.a.* versöhnen, besänftigen.
place [pleɪs], **1.** *s.* der Platz, Ort, die Stätte; Stadt, das Dorf, der Aufenthaltsort, Wohnort, Wohnsitz, Herrensitz (*esp. in the country*); Sitz, die Stelle; der Dienst, das Amt, die Stellung, der Stand, Rang; Raum. (*a*) (*with adjectives*) (*coll.*) *every –,* überall; (*coll.*) *no –,* nirgends; *no – for,* kein Raum für; *sore –,* wunde Stelle. (*b*) (*with nouns*) *decimal –,* die Dezimalstelle; *– for delivery,* der Erfüllungsort; *– in the sun,* der Platz an der Sonne; *– of amusement,* die Vergnügungsstätte: *– of refuge,* der Zufluchtsort; *– of worship,* das Gotteshaus. (*c*) (*with verbs*) *change –s,* den Platz tauschen; *find one's –,* sich zurechtfinden; *give –,* Platz machen (*to* (*Dat.*)); ersetzt werden (*to,* von); (*sl.*) *go –s,* die Sehenswürdigkeiten besuchen, Vergnügungsstätten aufsuchen, herumreisen; *it is not his –,* es ist nicht seines Amtes (*to,* zu); *keep s.o. in his –,* einen in seinen Grenzen halten; *know one's –,* wissen, was sich geziemt *or* wohin man gehört; *put o.s. in s.o.'s –,* sich in jemandes Lage versetzen; *put s.o. in his –,* einen in die Schranken weisen; *take –,* stattfinden, eintreten, erfolgen; *take your –s,* setzen Sie sich; *take a p.'s –,* an jemandes Stelle treten, jemandes Stelle einnehmen, einen ersetzen. (*d*) (*with prepositions*) *at his –,* bei ihm zu Hause; *at this –,* hier; *from – to –,* von Ort zu Ort; *in –,* in richtiger Lage, an der ursprünglichen Stelle; (*fig.*) am Platze, angebracht; *in – of,* anstatt, an Stelle von; *in –s,* an gewissen Stellen, stellenweise; *in their –s,* auf ihren Plätzen (*of persons*); *in another –,* anderswo, an anderer Stelle; im Oberhaus (*Parl.*); *in the first –,* erstens, an erster Stelle; gleich von Anfang an, überhaupt; *in his –,* an seiner Stelle, in seiner Lage; *the right man in the right –,* der rechte Mann an der rechten Stelle; *in some –,* irgendwo; *in the wrong –,* am unrichtigen Orte, an der falschen Stelle; *in two –s,* an zwei Orten *or* Stellen; *of that –,* dort(ig); *of this –,* hiesig(en Ortes); *out of –,* nicht an der rechten Stelle, am unrechten Orte; (*fig.*) nicht am Platze, unangebracht. **2.** *v.a.* stellen, legen, setzen; anlegen (*money*); vergeben, erteilen (*contract*); der ersten, zweiten *or* dritten Platz sichern (*Dat.*) (*Racing*); (ein)ordnen; anstellen, ernennen; unterbringen (*a p.*); aufstellen (*a guard, etc.*); aufsetzen, placieren (*the ball*); *be –d,* sich befinden; unter den drei Ersten sein (*Racing*); *– confidence in,* Vertrauen setzen auf; *– a p.,* einem Stellung, Rang *or* Platz anweisen; *– a th.,* Ort *or* Herkunft einer S. feststellen, etwas identifizieren; *– beyond a doubt,* über allen Zweifel erheben; *– on record,* verzeichnen; *– to s.o.'s account,* auf jemandes Rechnung setzen; *– to a p.'s credit,* einem gutschreiben. **--card,** *s.* die Platzkarte (*at banquets*). **--hunter,** *s.* der Stellenjäger. **--kick,** *s.* der Freistoß (*Footb.*). **–man,** *s.* der Stelleninhaber; Postenjäger. **--name,** *s.* der Ortsname.

placenta [plə'sɛntə], *s.* der Mutterkuchen, die Nachgeburt; die Samenleiste (*Bot.*). **–l,** *adj.* Mutterkuchen–.
placer ['pleɪsə], *s.* erzhaltige Stelle (*Min.*).
placet ['pleɪsɪt], *s.* die Jastimme, Zustimmung; *non-–*, die Neinstimme, Ablehnung.
placid ['plæsɪd], *adj.* sanft, mild, friedlich; ruhig, gelassen. **–ity** [–'sɪdɪtɪ], *s.* die Milde; (Gemüts)-Ruhe, Gelassenheit.
placket ['plækɪt], *s.* der Schlitz (*Dressm.*); die Tasche (*in woman's skirt*).
plagiar–ism ['pleɪdʒɪərɪzm], *s.* das Plagiat, literarischer Diebstahl. **–ist,** *s.* der Plagiator. **–ize,** 1. *v.a.* ausschreiben. 2. *v.a.* plagiieren, abschreiben, ausschreiben.
plagu–e [pleɪg], 1. *s.* die Pest, Seuche; Heimsuchung, Geißel; (*fig.*) Plage, Qual, der Quälgeist (*also of a p.*); *–e on it!* hol's der Teufel! 2. *v.a.* plagen, quälen, peinigen, ärgern. **–e-spot,** *s.* die Pestbeule. **–y,** *adj.* (*coll.*) verwünscht, verflixt.
plaice [pleɪs], *s.* die Scholle (*Ichth.*).
plaid [plæd, pleɪd], 1. *s.* der & das Plaid, das Plaidtuch. 2. *adj.* bunt gewürfelt *or* kariert.
plain [pleɪn], 1. *adj.* & *adv.* einfach, schlicht, schmucklos, ungemustert; einfarbig, nicht farbig; flach, eben, glatt; unansehnlich, unschön, nicht hübsch (*as a face*); klar, deutlich, leicht verständlich offen(kundig); rein, nackt, bar; *as – as can be* or *as a pikestaff*, sonnenklar, so klar wie nur etwas; *make – to s.o.*, einem deutlich zu verstehen geben. (*with nouns*) *– clothes*, der Zivilanzug, das Zivil; *– cooking*, bürgerliche Küche; *– dealing*, offene Handlungsweise; *in – English*, frei *or* gerade heraus, auf gut Deutsch; *– knitting*, die Glattstrickerei; *– postcard*, einfache Postkarte; *– sailing*, (*fig.*) einfache Sache. *– sewing*, das Weißnähen; *– speaking*, offene Meinungsäußerung. *– speech*, offene *or* ehrliche Sprache; *– tea*, Tee und Gebäck; *in – terms*, see *in – English*; *– text*, der Klartext; *– truth*, nackte Wahrheit. 2. *s.* die Ebene, Fläche; *pl.* die Prärie, Steppe. **– -clothes,** *adj.*; *– -clothes officer*, der Geheimpolizist. **–ness,** *s.* die Ebenheit; Einfachheit, Schlichtheit; Häßlichkeit; Klarheit, Deutlichkeit; Offenheit, Redlichkeit. **–sman,** *s.* der Präriebewohner, Steppenbewohner. **– -song,** *s.* gregorianische Kirchenmusik, einstimmiger Choralgesang. **– -spoken,** *adj.* offen, ehrlich, freimütig.
plaint [pleɪnt], *s.* (*Poet.*) die Klage; Klageschrift, Beschwerde (*Law*). **–iff** [–ɪf], *s.* der Kläger (*Law*). **–ive** [–ɪv], *adj.* klagend, traurig, kläglich, Klage–. **–iveness,** *s.* die Kläglichkeit, Traurigkeit.
plait [plæt], 1. *s.* der Zopf, die Flechte (*of hair*); das Geflecht (*of straw*). 2. *v.a.* flechten.
plan [plæn], 1. *s.* der Plan, Entwurf, die Anlage; der Grundriß (*Surv., etc.*); das Verfahren, System, Mittel, der Weg, die Methode, Anordnung; das Projekt, Vorhaben, die Absicht; *according to –*, planmäßig; *make –s*, Pläne schmieden. 2. *v.a.* einen Plan entwerfen zu; ersinnen, planen, beabsichtigen. **–less,** *adj.* planlos, ziellos. **–ner,** *s.* der Plänemacher. **–ning,** *s.* die Planung; *economic –ning*, die Bewirtschaftung, Planwirtschaft.
planchet ['plæntʃɪt], *s.* die (Münz)Platte (*Mint*).
[1]**plane** [pleɪn], 1. *adj.* eben, flach, ebenflächig; Plan–; *– mirror*, der Planspiegel. 2. *s.* die Fläche, Ebene; (*fig.*) Stufe, das Niveau, der Bereich; Förderstrecke (*Min.*); Tragfläche, (*Av.*); (*coll.*) das Flugzeug; der Hobel (*Carp.*); *– of direction*, die Visierebene (*Artil.*); *inclined –*, schiefe Ebene; *– of projection*, die Projektionsebene; *on the same – as*, auf demselben Niveau als; *on the upward –*, ansteigend, im Anstieg; *vertical –*, senkrechte Ebene, Vertikalebene; *– sailing*, das Plansegeln. 3. *v.a.* ebnen, glätten; (ab)hobeln (*Carp.*); bestoßen (*types*). 4. *v.n.* (usually *– down*) gleiten, im Gleitflug heruntergehen (*Av.*). **–r,** *s.* die Hobelmaschine. **– -table,** *s.* der Meßtisch.
[2]**plane** [pleɪn], *s.* (also *– -tree*) die Platane (*Bot.*).
planet ['plænɪt], *s.* der Planet. **–arium** [–'tɛːrɪəm], *s.* das Planetarium. **–ary** [–ərɪ], *adj.* planetarisch, Planeten–; (*fig.*) umherirrend. **–oid** [–ɔɪd], *s.* der Planetoid.
plangen–cy ['plændʒənsɪ], *s.* die Tonstärke, Tonfülle. **–t** [–ənt], *adj.* (laut)tönend, durchdringend.
planimet–er ['plænɪmɪːtə], *s.* der Flächenmesser. **–ry,** *s.* die Planimetrie.
planish [plænɪʃ], *v.a.* glätten, planieren, schlichten, polieren (*Metall.*). **–ing-hammer,** *s.* der Schlichthammer.
plank [plænk], 1. *s.* die Planke, Bohle, Diele, das Brett; (*coll.*) parteipolitischer Grundsatz, der Programmpunkt (*Pol.*); *walk the –*, ertränkt werden. 2. *v.a.* mit Planken *or* Bohlen belegen, dielen, verschalen (*Carp.*); beplanken (*ship*); (*sl.*) *– down*, hinlegen, hinterlegen (*money*); *– bed*, die Pritsche. **–ing,** *s.* die Beplankung (*Naut.*); Verschalung, Bekleidung, der Belag (*Carp.*); Planken (*pl.*),
plankton ['plænktən], *s.* das Plankton.
plan–less, –ner, –ning, *see* **plan.**
plant [plɑːnt], 1. *s.* die Pflanze, das Gewächs (*Bot.*); Wachstum; die Fabrikanlage, Betriebsanlage, Betriebseinrichtung; das Betriebsmaterial, Gerät, die Maschinerie, Gerätschaften (*pl.*), (*sl.*) der Spion; Betrug, Kniff, die Falle. 2. *v.a.* pflanzen, anpflanzen, einpflanzen, setzen, senken; bepflanzen (*ground*); aufpflanzen, aufstellen (*flag, etc.*); (*fig.*) errichten, anlegen, stiften, gründen, einführen; ansiedeln (*colonists*); postieren (*a person*); einprägen, einimpfen (*in*, in (*Acc.*)); (*sl.*) als Spion aufstellen; *– o.s.*, sich hinpflanzen *or* hinstellen; (*sl.*) *– s.th. on s.o.*, einem etwas anschmieren; *– out*, in Abständen pflanzen, umpflanzen. **–ation,** *s.* die Pflanzung, Anpflanzung, Schonung, Ansiedlung, Plantage. **–er,** *s.* der Pflanzer, Siedler, Plantagenbesitzer; die Pflanzmaschine, Sämaschine (*Agr.*). **– -house,** *s.* das Gewächshaus. **– -louse,** *s.* die Blattlaus.
plantain ['plæntɪn], *s.* der Wegerich (*Bot.*); *water-–*, der Froschlöffel (*Bot.*); (also *– -tree*) der Pisang(baum), die Paradiesfeige (*Bot.*).
plant–ar ['plæntə], *adj.* Fußsohlen–. **–igrade,** 1. *adj.* auf den Fußsohlen gehend. 2. *s.* der Sohlengänger (*Zool.*).
plaque [plæk], *s.* die Schmuckplatte, Agraffe, Gedenktafel. **–tte,** *s.* die Plakette.
[1]**plash** [plæʃ], *v.a.* ineinanderflechten, zu einer Hecke flechten (*twigs*).
[2]**plash** [plæʃ], 1. *v.n.* & *a.* plan(t)schen, plätschern (*in*, mit *or* auf (*Dat.*)). 2. *s.* die Pfütze, Lache, der Pfuhl; das Plätschern. **–y,** *adj.* plätschernd, plantschend, patschig, schlammig, matschig.
plasm ['plæzm], *s.* das (Proto)Plasma. **–a** [–mə], *s.* das Blutplasma. **–atic** [–'mætɪk], *adj.* Plasma–. **–ic** [–mɪk], *adj.* (Proto)Plasma–.
plaster ['plɑːstə], 1. *s.* das Pflaster (*Pharm.*); der Mörtel, (Ver)Putz, Stuck, Bewurf, die Tünche; *– cast*, der Gipsabdruck, Gipsverband (*Med.*); *court-–*, englisches Pflaster; *– of Paris*, gebrannter Gips; *sticking–*, das Heftpflaster. 2. *v.a.* ein Pflaster legen auf (*Acc.*); (also *– over*) verputzen, vergipsen, (über)tünchen (*Build.*); (*fig.*) überhäufen (*with*, mit). **–er,** *s.* der Gipsarbeiter, Stuckarbeiter. **–ing,** *s.* die Stuckarbeit, Stukkatur.
plastic ['plæstɪk], *adj.* plastisch, biegsam, formbar, knetbar, gestaltungsfähig, bildungsfähig, bildsam, bildend, formend, gestaltend; deutlich, hervortretend, anschaulich; *– art*, bildende Kunst; *– surgery*, plastische Chirurgie. **–ine,** *s.* die Knetmasse, das Plastilin. **–ity** [–'tɪsɪtɪ], *s.* die Knetbarkeit, Formbarkeit, Bildsamkeit, Gestaltungsfähigkeit, Plastizität. **–s** [–tɪks], *pl.* die Preßmasse, der Kunststoff (*pl.* Kunststoffe), das Kunstharz (*pl.* Kunstharze), der Spritzguß.
plastron ['plæstrən], *s.* die Brustplatte (*armour*), das Schutzpolster (*Fenc.*); der Hemdeinsatz, Brusteinsatz (*Dressm., etc.*).
[1]**plat** [plæt], *s. see* [1]**plot.**
[2]**plat** [plæt], *see* **plait.**
[3]**plat** [plɑ], *s.* das Gericht, die Speise.
plate [pleɪt], 1. *s.* die Platte (*also Phot.*), Scheibe, Metallplatte, Metalltafel, das Metallschild; das Blech; der Deckel, das Blatt, die Lamelle (*Tech.*); Anode (*Rad.*), Elektrode (*Elec.*); Dachplatte, Schwelle (*Arch.*); Druckplatte, Stereotypplatte, der Stich (*Engr.*); die Tafel, Illustration, das Bild (*in a book*); Goldgeschirr, Silbergeschirr, Tafel-

geschirr; der Teller; der Preis, Pokal (*at races*); (*coll.*) künstliches Gebiß; *baffle* –, die Schlingerwand; *book*--, das Exlibris; *dental* –, die Gaumenplatte, Zahnplatte; *door*--, das Namenschild; *electro*--, das Galvano; *name*--, das Namenschild; *soup*--, der Suppenteller; – *of soup*, der Teller Suppe; *steel* –, die Panzerplatte, Stahlplatte; (*coll.*) *have enough on one's* –, genug auf den Schultern haben. 2. *v.a.* plattieren, dublieren, überziehen, panzern (*a ship*); stereotypieren (*Typ.*). **--armour,** *s.* die Plattenpanzerung. **--basket,** *s.* der Besteckkorb. **– circuit,** *s.* der Anodenstromkreis (*Rad.*). **--cover,** *s.* der Schüsseldeckel. **–d** [–ɪd], *adj.* plattiert, dubliert, metallüberzogen, versilbert, vergoldet, verchromt; *electro--d*, galvanisch versilbert. **–ful,** *s.* der Tellervoll. **– glass,** *s.* das Spiegelglas, Scheibenglas. **--holder,** *s.* die Kassette (*Phot.*). **--layer,** *s.* der Schienenleger, Streckenarbeiter (*Railw.*). **--mark,** *s.* der Feingehaltstempel, Geschirrstempel. **--powder,** *s.* das Putzpulver. **--rack,** *s.* das Tellergestell, Tellerbrett. **--warmer,** *s.* der Tellerwärmer, Schüsselwärmer.

plateau [plæ'toʊ], *s.* (pl. *–x* or *–s* [–'toʊz]) die Hochebene, das Plateau.

platen [plætən], *s.* der (Druck)Tiegel, die Druckplatte; (also *--roller*) Walze (*of typewriter*).

platform ['plætfɔːm], *s.* die Plattform, Rampe, Terrasse; der Bahnsteig (*Railw.*); Perron (*of a tramcar*); die Bettung (*Artil.*); (Redner)Bühne, Tribüne, das Podium (*in halls, etc.*); (*fig.*) das Parteiprogramm, politischer Standpunkt (*of a party, etc.*). **--car,** *s.* offener Güterwagen (*Railw.*). **--scale,** *s.* die Brückenwaage. **--stage,** *s.* die Plattformbühne (*Theat.*). **--ticket,** *s.* die Bahnsteigkarte.

plating ['pleɪtɪŋ], *s.* die Plattierung (*Metall.*); (Schiffs)Panzerung, Panzerplatten (*pl.*).

platin–ic [plæ'tɪnɪk], *adj.* Platin–. **–ize** [plætɪnaɪz] *v.a.* mit Platin überziehen. **–otype** [plə'tɪnoʊtaɪp], *s.* der Platindruck. **–um** ['plætɪnəm], *s.* das Platin; *–um blonde*, *s.* helle Blondine.

platitud–e ['plætɪtjʊd], *s.* die Seichtheit, Plattheit, der Gemeinplatz. **–inarian** [–dɪ'nɛːərɪən], *s.* der Schwätzer. **–inize** [–'tjʊːdɪnaɪz], *v.n.* quatschen, seichen. **–inous** [–'tjʊːdɪnəs], *adj.* seicht, nichtssagend.

platonic [plə'tɔnɪk], *adj.* platonisch, seelisch, unsinnlich; (*coll.*) harmlos (*of friendship, etc.*).

platoon [plə'tuːn], *s.* der Zug (*Mil.*); das Aufgebot (*of police*); – *commander*, der Zugführer; – *firing*, – *volleys*, das Pelotonfeuer.

platter ['plætə], *s.* (*archaic & Amer.*) die Schüssel.

platy–pus ['plætɪpʌs], *s.* das Schnabeltier (*Zool.*). **–(r)rhine** [–raɪn], 1. *adj.* breitnasig. 2. *s.* breitnasiger Affe (*Zool.*).

plaudit ['plɔːdɪt], *s.* (*usually pl.*) lauter Beifall, das Beifallklatschen, der Beifallssturm.

plausib–ility [plɔːzɪ'bɪlɪtɪ], *s.* die Wahrscheinlichkeit, Glaubwürdigkeit; gefälliges Äußeres (*of a person*). **–le** ['plɔːzɪbl], *adj.* annehmbar, überzeugend, nicht unwahrscheinlich, einleuchtend (*as reason*); äußerlich gefällig, einnehmend (*of persons*).

play [pleɪ], **1.** *v.n.* spielen (*also Mus., Theat. & fig.*), sich unterhalten *or* belustigen, sich tummeln; musizieren (*Mus.*), agieren, auftreten (*Theat.*); sich leicht bewegen, springen, hüpfen, fliegen, gleiten; freien Spielraum haben, im Gange sein (*Tech.*). (*a*) (*with adverbs*) – *fair*, ehrlich *or* fair spielen (*or fig.*) handeln; – *fast and loose with s.o.*, einen zum Narren *or* besten halten, mit einem ein zweideutiges Spiel treiben; – *up*, tüchtig spielen, sich anstrengen; (*coll.*) – *up to s.o.*, sich einem anpassen *or* anbiedern, einem schöntun. (*b*) (*with prepositions*) – (*at*) *ball*, Ball spielen; – (*at*) *a game*, ein Spiel spielen; (*coll.*) – *at a th.*, etwas nebenbei betreiben, sich nur flüchtig mit einer S. abgeben; – *by ear*, nach dem Gehör spielen; – *for love*, um nichts spielen; – *for time*, trachten um Zeit zu gewinnen; – *from memory*, nach dem Gedächtnis spielen; – *into the hands of a p.*, einem in die Hände spielen; – *on*, bespritzen, spritzen gegen (*with water*), beleuchten (*with light*), schießen auf (*Mil.*); sein Spiel treiben mit; – *on words*, in Wortspielen reden; – *round the idea*, mit dem Gedanken spielen; – *to a p.*, einem vorspielen (*Mus.*); – *to the gallery*, an den Pöbel appellieren; – *upon*, see – *on*; – *with*, spielen mit (*also fig.*), scherzen *or* tändeln mit. **2.** *v.a.* spielen (*a game, piece of music or drama or role*); vorstellen, aufführen (*Theat.*); (aus)spielen (*a card*); spielen lassen (*light*) (*on*, über (*Acc.*); (*water*) (*on*, gegen)); werfen (*light*) (*on*, auf); richten (*a gun, hose or light*) (*on*, auf (*Acc.*)). (*a*) (*with nouns*) – *one's best*, nach besten Kräften spielen; – *billiards*, Billard spielen; – *the devil, the dickens* or *old Harry with*, arg mitspielen (*Dat.*), Schindluder treiben mit; – *second fiddle*, eine Nebenrolle spielen; – *the fool*, sich albern benehmen; – *the game*, ehrlich spielen *or* handeln, sich anständig benehmen; – *a losing game*, ohne Aussicht spielen; – *havoc with*, auf den Kopf stellen, durcheinanderbringen; – *a hose on*, bespritzen; – *a p. false*, gegen einen unehrlich handeln; *his memory –ed him false*, sein Gedächtnis ließ ihn im Stich *or* täuschte ihn; – *a team*, gegen eine Mannschaft spielen; – *a p. a trick*, einem einen Streich spielen; – *tricks*, Streiche *or* Dummheiten machen; – *truant*, die Schule schwänzen. (*b*) (*with adverbs*) – *music at sight*, Musik vom Blatt spielen; – *off*, austragen, zur Entscheidung bringen (*a game*); – *one p. off against another*, einen gegen den andern ausspielen; – *out*, ausspielen, zu Ende spielen; *be –ed out*, erschöpft *or* erledigt sein, ausgespielt haben; (*sl.*) – *a p. up*, einen reizen *or* ärgern. **3.** *s.* das Spiel (*also Tech.*); Schauspiel, (Theater)-Stück, Drama (*Theat.*); Glücksspiel, der Zeitvertreib, Scherz, die Spielerei, Kurzweil; Tätigkeit, der Gang, Spielraum, das Verfahren (*Tech. & fig.*); Farbenspiel; *at* –, beim Spiel; *at the* –, im Theater; *fair* (*foul*) –, (un)ehrliches Spiel, (un)redliches Verfahren; *give free* – *to*, freien Spielraum gewähren (*Dat.*); *in* –, im Spiel (*of ball*); (*said*) *in* –, im Scherz (gesagt); *in full* –, in voller Tätigkeit; *bring into* –, in Gang bringen, spielen lassen; *come into* –, in Gang kommen; *make* – *with*, ausnützen, breittreten, Effekt machen mit; – *of colours*, das Farbenspiel; – *on words*, das Wortspiel. **–able,** *adj.* spielbar, zu spielen(d) (*ball or music*), zum Spielen geeignet (*ground*). **--back,** *s.* die Wiedergabe (*of a recording*). **--bill,** *s.* der Theaterzettel. **--book,** *s.* das Textbuch. **–er,** *s.* der Spieler; Berufsspieler (*Sport*); Schauspieler (*Theat.*); *–er piano*, elektrisches Klavier. **–fellow,** *s.* der Spielgefährte, die Spielgefährtin. **–ful,** *adj.* spielend, spielerisch, scherzhaft, spaßhaft, mutwillig, neckisch, launig. **–fulness,** *s.* der Mutwille, die Scherzhaftigkeit. **–goer,** *s.* der Theaterbesucher. **–ground,** *s.* der Spielplatz; Schulhof (*in school*). **–house,** *s.* das Schauspielhaus; Kino. **–ing,** *s.* das Spielen; *to the –ing of*, unter dem Spiel von. **–ing-cards,** *pl.* Spielkarten. **–ing-field,** *s.* der Sportplatz. **–let,** *s.* kurzes Schauspiel. **–mate,** *s. see* **–fellow.** **--off,** *s.* das Wiederholungsspiel, Entscheidungsspiel. **–thing,** *s.* das Spielzeug, *pl.* Spielsachen (*pl.*). **–time,** *s.* die Spielzeit, Freizeit. **–wright,** *s.* der Schauspieldichter, Bühnenschriftsteller, Dramatiker.

plea [plɪː], *s.* dringende Bitte (*for*, nach), das Gesuch; die Ausrede, Entschuldigung, der Vorwand, Einwand, die Einrede, Einwendung, Verteidigungsrede, der Einspruch (*Law*); der Prozeß, Rechtshandel (*Hist.*); – *of guilty*, das Schuldgeständnis: *make a – against*, Einspruch erheben gegen; *put in a – for*, eifrig befürworten; – *in bar*, peremptorische Einrede; *on the – of*, unter dem Vorwande von.

plead [plɪːd], 1. *v.n.* plädieren, vor Gericht reden, sich verwenden (*for*, für; *with*, bei), bitten, flehen (*for*, um), sprechen (*for*, für; *against*, gegen); – *guilty*, sich schuldig bekennen (*to s.th.* (*Dat.*)). 2. *v.a.* verteidigen, vertreten (*a cause*), vorschützen, sich entschuldigen mit, als Beweis *or* Entschuldigung anführen, geltend machen. **–able,** *adj.* rechtlich zu verteidigen(d), rechtsgültig, triftig. **–er,** *s.* der (Rechts)Anwalt, Verteidiger, Sachwalter. **–ing,** 1. *adj.* bittend, flehend. 2. *s.* das Bitten, Flehen; die Verteidigung, das Plädoyer,

pl. gerichtliche Verhandlungen, Prozeßakten, Aussagen der Prozeßparteien (*pl.*). *special –ing*, einseitige Beweisführung, die Sophisterei.
pleasan–ce ['plɛzəns], (*Poet.*) das Vergnügen, der Genuß. **–t** [–ənt], *adj.* angenehm, erfreulich, freundlich, liebenswürdig; *–t odour*, der Wohlgeruch; *–t taste*, der Wohlgeschmack. **–tness,** *s.* die Annehmlichkeit, Freundlichkeit. **–try** [–əntrɪ], *s.* der Scherz, Spaß, Witz; die Lustigkeit, Heiterkeit.
pleas–e [plɪ:z], 1. *v. imp.* & *n.* gefallen, belieben (*Dat.*); *–e!* bitte sehr! wenn ich bitten darf, gefälligst, mit Verlaub; *he insulted me, if you –e*, er beschimpfte mich, man denke sich; *as you –e*, wie es Ihnen beliebt *or* gefällt, wie Sie wollen; *–e God*, so Gott will. 2. *v.a.* gefallen, zusagen, gefällig sein (*Dat.*); erfreuen, befriedigen, zufriedenstellen; belieben, geruhen (*formal or iron.*); *be –ed with*, befriedigt sein von, Freude finden an; *I am –ed to say*, ich freue mich sagen zu können; *hard to –e*, schwer zufrieden zu stellen *or* zu befriedigen; *–e o.s.*, tun was einem beliebt; *it –ed me*, es gefiel mir; *the king has been –ed to grant*, Seine Majestät hat geruht zu gewähren. **–ed,** *adj.* erfreut (*at*, über), zufrieden (*with*, mit); *as –ed as Punch*, höchst erfreut; *I am only too –ed to help*, ich helfe mit dem größten Vergnügen; *I am very –ed to meet you*, es ist mir eine Freude, Sie kennen zu lernen. **–ing,** *adj.* gefällig, angenehm.
pleasur–able ['plɛʒərəbl], *adj.* angenehm, erfreulich. **–e** ['plɛʒə], *s.* das Vergnügen, der Genuß, die Freude (*in*, an); (*after poss. pron.*) das Belieben, Gutdünken; *at one's –e*, nach Belieben; *it is our –e*, wir geruhen (*of royalty*); *what is your –e?* was steht zu Diensten? *do me the –e*, machen Sie mir das Vergnügen (*of coming*, zu kommen); *during Her Majesty's –e*, auf Lebenszeit (*Law*); *for the –e of it*, aus reinem Vergnügen; *give s.o. –e*, einem Vergnügen bereiten, einen erfreuen; *have the –e of doing*, das Vergnügen haben zu tun; *take –e in*, Vergnügen finden an (*Dat.*); *take one's –e*, sich amüsieren; *with –e*, mit Vergnügen. **–e-boat,** *s.* der Vergnügungsdampfer. **–e-ground,** *s.* der Rasenplatz; *pl.* (Garten)Anlagen (*pl.*). **–e-loving,** *adj.*, **–e-seeking,** *adj.* vergnügungssüchtig. **–e-trip,** *s.* der Ausflug, die Vergnügungsreise.
pleat [plɪ:t], 1. *v.a.* fälteln, plissieren (*Tail.*). 2. *s.* die Falte, das Plissee.
pleb–eian [plɪ:'bɪən], 1. *adj.* plebejisch, gemein, pöbelhaft. 2. *s.* der Plebejer. **–eianism,** *s.* das Plebejertum. **–iscite** ['p'ɛbɪsɪt], *s.* die Volksabstimmung, der Volksentscheid (*Pol.*). **–s** [plɛbz], *s.* die Plebs, der Pöbel.
plectrum ['plɛktrəm], *s.* das Schlagstäbchen, der Schlagring.
pled [plɛd], (*Scots*) *pret.* & *p. p. of* **plead.**
pledge [plɛdʒ], 1. *s.* das Pfand, Unterpfand, die Bürgschaft, Sicherheit; das Versprechen (*to*, gegenüber); das Zutrinken, der Toast; (*fig.*) das Kind; die Bürge, der *or* die Geisel, das Faustpfand (*Hist.*); *as a –*, als Pfand; *in – of*, als Pfand für; *be in –*, verpfändet sein; *hold in –*, als (Unter)Pfand in Händen haben; *put in –*, verpfänden, versetzen; *take the –*, Abstinenzler werden; *take out of –*, aus der Verpfändung lösen; *under the –*, unter dem Pfand (*of* (*Gen.*)). 2. *v.a.* verpfänden (*a th. to a p.*, einem etwas); verpflichten (*a p.*) (*to*, zu); *– one's word*, sein Ehrenwort geben; *– a p.*, einem zutrinken. *– o.s.*, geloben, sich verpflichten. **–able,** *adj.* verpfändbar. **–e** [–ɪ], *s.* der Pfandnehmer, Pfandleiher. **–r** [–ə], *s.* (also *pledgor*) der Pfandgeber, Verpfänder.
pleistocene ['plaɪstəsɪ:n], *s.* das Diluvium, Pleistozän.
plenary ['plɪ:nərɪ], *adj.* völlig, vollständig, Voll–, Plenar–; *– indulgence*, vollkommener Ablaß; *– powers*, die Vollmacht; *– session*, die Plenarsitzung, Vollversammlung.
plenipotentiary [plɛnɪpə'tɛnʃərɪ], 1. *adj.* bevollmächtigt, unbeschränkt, unumschränkt, absolut. 2. *s.* Bevollmächtigte(r), *m.*, der Gesandte mit unbeschränkter Vollmacht.
plenish [plɛnɪʃ], *v.a.* (*Scots*) füllen. **–ing,** *s.* (also pl. *–ings*) das Hausgerät, die Hauseinrichtung, Mobiliar (*pl.*).
plenitude ['plɛnɪtjʊd], *s.* die Vollkommenheit; Fülle; der Reichtum (*of*, an).
plent–eous ['plɛntɪəs], *adj.* (*Poet.*) reich(lich) (*in*, an). **–eousness,** *s.* die Fülle, Reichlichkeit, der Überfluß. **–iful,** *adj.* reichlich, im Überfluß vorhanden. **–ifulness,** *s.* die Fülle (*of*, an). **–y,** 1. *s.* die Fülle, der Überfluß (*of*, an), die Menge; *horn of –y*, das Füllhorn; *in –y*, in *or* im Überfluß; *–y to do*, vollauf zu tun; *–y of money*, eine Menge *or* viel Geld; *–y of time*, viel Zeit; *–y of times*, viele Male. 2. *pred. adj.* reichlich. 3. *adv.* (*coll.*) reichlich.
plenum ['plɪ:nəm], *s.* vollkommen ausgefüllter Raum; die Vollversammlung, das Plenum (*Pol.*).
pleonas–m ['plɪ:ənæzm], *s.* der Pleonasmus; Wortüberfluß, überflüssiger Zusatz. **–tic,** *adj.* überflüssig, pleonastisch.
plethor–a ['plɛθərə, plɪ'θɔ:rə], *s.* die Vollblütigkeit (*Med.*); (*fig.*) Überfülle (*of*, an). **–ic** [plɪ'θɔrɪk], *adj.* vollblütig, vollsaftig; (*fig.*) überreich, überladen.
pleur–a ['plu:rə], *s.* das Brustfell, Rippenfell. **–al** [–rəl], *adj.* Brustfell–. **–isy** [–rɪsɪ], *s.* die Rippenfellentzündung, Brustfellentzündung. **–ocarpous** [–o'ka:pəs], *adj.* seitenfrüchtig (*Bot.*). **–o-pneumonia** [–onju'mounɪə], *s.* die Brustseuche (*Vet.*).
plex–imeter [plɛk'sɪmɪtə], *s.* der Plessimeter. **–or** [–ə], *s.* der Perkussionshammer. **–us** [–əs], *s.* das Geflecht; Nervenbündel; (*fig.*) Netzwerk, Flechtwerk.
plia–bility [plaɪə'bɪlɪtɪ], *s.* die Biegsamkeit, Geschmeidigkeit. **–ble** ['plaɪəbl], *adj.* biegsam, geschmeidig; nachgiebig, fügsam. **–ncy** ['plaɪənsɪ], *s.* die Biegsamkeit. **–nt** ['plaɪənt], *adj. see* **–ble.**
plica [plɪ:kə], *s.* die Hautfalte; der Weichselzopf (*Med.*). **–te** [–ət], 1. *adj.* gefaltet (*Bot.* & *Zool.*). 2. *v.a.* (*usually pass.*) falten. **–tion** [plɪ'keɪʃən], *s.* die Falte, Faltung.
pliers ['plaɪəz], *pl.* die (Draht)Zange; *pair of –*, die Zange.
[1]**plight** [plaɪt], *s.* schlimmer Zustand; traurige Lage, die Zwangslage.
[2]**plight** [plaɪt], 1. *v.a.* verpfänden; *– one's faith* (or archaic) *troth*, Treue schwören (*to* (*Dat.*)); verloben (*to*, mit); *–ed troth*, gelobte Treue. 2. *s.* feierliche Verpflichtung, die Verlobung.
plinth [plɪnθ], *s.* die Säulenplatte, Fußplatte, Plinthe (*Arch.*).
pliocene ['plaɪəsɪ:n], *s.* das Pliozän, jüngste Schicht des Tertiärs.
plod [plɔd], *v.n.* & *a.* mühsam *or* schwerfällig gehen, sich hinschleppen; (*fig.*) sich placken, sich abmühen; (*coll.*) schuften, büffeln, ochsen(*at*, an). **–der** [–ə], *s.* der Büffler. **–ding,** 1. *adj.* schwerfällig, mühsam; arbeitsam, unverdrossen arbeitend. 2. *s.* das Schuften.
plop [plɔp], 1. *v.n.* (& *a.*) plumpsen (lassen). 2. *s.* der Plumps, das Plumpsen. 3. *int.* plumps.
plosive ['plousɪv], 1. *s.* der Verschlußlaut. 2. *adj.* Verschluß– (*Phonet.*).
[1]**plot** [plɔt], *s.* das Stück, der Flecken Land, die Parzelle; *building –*, der Bauplatz.
[2]**plot** [plɔt],— *s.* das Komplott, der Anschlag; die Verschwörung, Intrige; Fabel, Handlung (*of a play, etc.*); *lay a –*, ein Komplott schmieden. 2. *v.a.* anstiften, anzetteln, heimlich planen, es absehen auf, abzielen auf; entwerfen, aufzeichnen, planzeichnen; *– a course*, den Kurs bestimmen, absetzen *or* abstecken. 3. *v.n.* Ränke schmieden, intrigieren, sich verschwören, Anschläge machen, Pläne machen. **–ter,** *s.* der Anstifter, Intrigant, Verschwörer.
plough [plau], 1. *s.* der Pflug; das Ackerland; der Falzhobel, Kehlhobel (*Carp.*); Großer Bär, der Wagen (*Astr.*); (*sl.*) das Durchfallen, der Mißerfolg; *put one's hand on the –*, Hand ans Werk legen. 2. *v.a.* pflügen; (durch)furchen (*the sea*), furchen (*the brow, etc.*); (*sl.*) durchfallen lassen; *be –ed*, durchfallen, (durch)rasseln, versieben; *– in*, unterpflügen; *– up*, aufroden (*crops*), umpflügen (*land*); *– one's way*, sich einen Weg bahnen. 3. *v.n.* sich vorwärtsarbeiten *or* (durch)arbeiten (*through*, durch); (*coll.*) *– through a book*, ein Buch durchackern. **– -boy,** *s.* der Ackerknecht. **–ing,** *s.* das

Pflügen. **--land,** das Ackerland. **-man,** *s.* der Pflüger, Ackersmann. **-share,** *s.* die Pflugschar. **--tail,** *s.* der Pflugsterz.
plover ['plʌvə], *s.* der Regenpfeifer, Kiebitz (*Orn.*).
plow [plɑu], (*Amer.*) *see* **plough.**
ploy [plɔı], *s.* (*dial.*) die Beschäftigung, das Unternehmen, Vorgehen, Verfahren.
pluck [plʌk], 1. *v.a.* (ab)pflücken, abbrechen (*flowers*); rupfen (*birds*); zerren, zupfen; (*coll.*) plündern, berauben (*a p.*); (*sl.*) durchfallen lassen, (*usually pass.*) *be -ed,* durchfallen; *have a crow to - with s.o.,* mit einem ein Hühnchen zu pflücken (*or* rupfen) haben; *- up courage,* Mut fassen. 2. *v.n.* zupfen, zerren, greifen (*at,* nach). 3. *s.* das Pflücken, Zupfen, Zerren, Rupfen; das Geschlinge (*of animal*); (*coll.*) der Mut, Schneid, die Schneidigkeit; (*sl.*) das Durchrasseln, Durchfallen (*in examinations*). **-iness,** *s.* der Mut, die Beherztheit. **-y,** *adj.* mutig, beherzt, schneidig; scharf (*Phot.*).
plug [plʌg], 1. *s.* der Pflock, Stöpsel, Pfropf(en), Zapfen, Spund, Döbel, die Zahnplombe (*Dentistry*); (also *wall--*) der Stecker (*Elec.*); Priem (*of tobacco*); *fire--,* der Feuerhahn, Hydrant; *sparking--,* die Zündkerze (*Motor.*); *wander--,* der Wanderstecker (*Elec.*). 2. *v.a.* (also *- up*) verstopfen, zustopfen, (zu)pfropfen, stöpseln; plombieren (*teeth*); verspunden (*Coop.*); (*sl.*) *- s.o.,* einen anschießen *or* erschießen; *- in,* einstecken, einstöpseln; einschalten (*Elec.*); *--in lamp,* die Ansteckbirne; (*sl.*) *- a th.,* etwas anpreisen, für etwas Reklame machen. 3. *v.n.*; (*sl.*) *- along* or *away,* schuften, ochsen (*at,* an). **--adaptor,** *s.* der Umstecker. **--box, --contact, --socket,** *s.* die Steckdose, der Steckkontakt. (*sl.*) **--ugly,** *s.* der Raufbold, Straßenlümmel, Rowdy (*Amer.*).
plum [plʌm], *s.* die Pflaume; Rosine; (*coll.*) das Beste, auserlesener Teil, begehrenswerte Stelle; (*sl.*) hübsches Stück Geld, £100,000; (*coll.*) *take all the -s,* sich die Rosinen aus dem Kuchen klauben. **-cake,** *s.* der Rosinenkuchen. **-duff,** *s.* der Rosinenpudding. **-my,** *adj.* pflaumenreich, pflaumenartig; (*coll.*) begehrenswert. **- pudding,** *s.* der Plumpudding, Weihnachtspudding. **- tart,** *s.* die Zwetschgentorte. **--tree,** *s.* der Pflaumenbaum.
plumage ['plu:mıdʒ], *s.* das Gefieder.
plumb [plʌm], 1. *s.* das Senkblei, Lotblei, Lot; *out of -,* nicht (mehr) im Lot *or* senkrecht. 2. *adj.* senkrecht, lotrecht; seiger (*Min.*). 3. *adv.* senkrecht; gerade, genau; (*sl.*) schier. 4. *v.a.* sondieren, loten, lotrecht machen, (*fig.*) ergründen. 5. *v.n.* klempnern, Röhre legen. **-ago** [-'beıgoʊ], *s.* das Reißblei, der Graphit; die Bleiwurz (*Bot.*). **-eous** [-bıəs], *adj.* bleiartig; bleifarbig. **-er** ['plʌmə], *s.* der Klempner, Spengler, Installateur, Rohrleger. **-ic** [-bık], *adj.* Blei- (*Chem.*); *-ic acid,* das Bleisuperoxyd. **-iferous** [-'bıfərəs], *adj.* bleihaltig. **-ing** ['plʌmıŋ], *s.* die Klempnerarbeit; Rohrleitung, Röhren (*pl.*). **-ism** [-bızm], *s.* die Bleivergiftung. **--line,** *s.* die Lotleine, Senkschnur. **--rule,** *s.* die Senkwaage, das Lot.
plume [plu:m], 1. *s.* die Feder; Straußenfeder; der Federbusch (*Mil.*); (*fig.*) Streifen (*of smoke, etc.*); *borrowed -s,* fremde Federn. 2. *v.a.* putzen (*feathers*); mit Federn schmücken; *- o.s.,* sich putzen (*of birds*); sich mit fremden Federn schmücken; sich brüsten (*on,* mit). **-less,** *adj.* ungefiedert.
plummet ['plʌmıt], *s.* das Bleigewicht, Senkblei, Senklot, die Senkwaage, Lotleine.
plummy, *see* **plum.**
plumose [plu'moʊs], *adj.* gefiedert, flaumig (*Bot. & Zool.*).
[1]**plump** [plʌmp], 1. *adj.* dick, fett, rundlich, drall. 2. *v a.* (also *- out* or *up*) aufschwemmen, aufschwellen, dick machen, runden. **-er,** *s.* der Bausch. **-ness,** *s.* die Dicke, Rundlichkeit.
[2]**plump** [plʌmp], 1. *v.a.* plumpsen *or* fallen lassen. 2. *v.n.* plump hinfallen, hinplumpsen; *- down,* hinplumpsen; (*coll.*) *- for,* ohne Bedenken stimmen *or* entscheiden für; (*coll.*) *- out with,* herausplatzen mit. 3. *adv.* plumps, rundweg, glattweg. 4. *adj.* glatt, plump. 5. *s.* der Plumps, Platzregen. **-er,** *s.* plumpe Lüge; ungeteilte Wahlstimme (*Pol.*).
plum-ulaceous [plu:mju'leıʃəs], *adj.* daunig, flaumartig. **-ule** ['plu:mju:l], *s.* die Blattanlage (*Bot.*); Flaumfeder, Daunenfeder (*Orn.*). **-y** ['plu:mı], *adj.* federartig, gefiedert, befiedert.
plunder ['plʌndə], 1. *s.* der Raub, Gewinn, die Beute. 2. *v.a.* plündern (*a country, etc.*), rauben (*a th.*), berauben (*a p.*) (*of* (*Gen.*)). **-er** [-ərə], *s.* der Plünderer, Räuber.
plunge [plʌndʒ], 1. *v.a.* (ein)tauchen (*into water, etc.*); stoßen (*a sword, etc.*); stecken (*one's hand*); (*fig.*) stürzen, treiben, versetzen. 2. *v.n.* (unter)-tauchen, sich werfen *or* stürzen (*into,* in (*Acc.*)); springen und ausschlagen (*as a horse*); stampfen (*of a ship*); (*fig.*) sich versenken; (*sl.*) spekulieren, es wagen. 3. *s.* das (Unter)tauchen, Eintauchen; der Sturz; das Ausschlagen (*of a horse*); *take a -,* sich ins Wasser stürzen; *take the -,* den entscheidenden Schritt tun, ein Wagnis auf sich nehmen, es wagen. **-r** [-ə], *s.* der Taucher; (*coll.*) Spekulant; Tauchkolben, Plunger (*Mach.*). **--bath,** *s.* das Tauchbad.
plunk [plʌŋk], 1. *s.* (*Amer.*) der Plumps; (*coll.*) Dollar. 2. *v.a.* hinschmeißen, hinhauen. 3. *v.n.* plump hinfallen, hinplumpsen.
pluperfect ['plu'pə:fıkt], *s.* (also *- tense*) das Plusquamperfektum.
plural ['pluərəl], 1. *s.* die Mehrzahl, der Plural. 2. *adj.* Plural-, pluralisch; *- number, see* **-** 1; *- vote, - voting,* das Mehrstimmenwahlrecht, die Pluralwahl. **-ism** ['pluərəlızm], *s.* der Besitz mehrerer Pfründen (*Eccl.*), der Pluralismus (*Phil.*). **-ist,** *s.* der Inhaber mehrerer Pfründen. **-ity** [plu'rælıtı], *s.* die Mehrheit, Mehrzahl; Vielheit, große Menge; der Besitz mehrerer Pfründen (*Eccl.*); *-ity of gods,* die Vielgötterei; *-ity of votes,* die Mehrstimmenwahl; *-ity of wives,* die Vielweiberei. **-ize** ['pluərəlaız], 1. *v.a.* die Mehrzahl bilden von, in den Plural setzen. 2. *v.n.* mehrere Pfründen innehaben.
plus [plʌs], 1. *prep.* und, plus, dazu, zuzüglich. 2. *adv.* und mehr. 2. *adj.* Mehr-, Extra-, extra; positiv (*Math. & Elec.*). 2. *s.* das Plus, Mehr, der Überschuß; das Pluszeichen (*Print.*). **--fours,** *pl.* die Golfhose, Pumphose; Knickerbocker (*pl.*).
plush [plʌʃ], *s.* der Plüsch. **-y,** *adj.* plüschartig.
plut-archy ['plu:tɑkı], *s.,* **-ocracy** [-'tɔkrəsı], *s.* die Geldherrschaft, Geldsackherrschaft; Geldaristokratie, Geldprotzen (*pl.*). **-ocrat** [-təkræt], *s.* der Kapitalist, Geldprotz. **-ocratic** [-tə'krætık], *adj.* Geld-, auf Geldbesitz aufgebaut, (*coll.*) breitlebig, feudal.
plutoni-an [plu:'toʊnıən], *adj.* plutonisch, Pluto-, (*Anat.*). **-c** [-'tɔnık], *adj.* plutonisch (*Geol.*). **-sm** ['plu:tənızm], *s.* der Plutonismus. **-um** [-'toʊnıəm], *s.* das Plutonium (*Chem.*).
pluvi-al ['plu:vıəl], *adj.* regnerisch, Regen-. **-ometer** [-'ɔmıtə], *s.* der Regenmesser. **-ous** [-vıəs], *adj. see* **-al.**
ply [plɑı], 1. *v.a.* fleißig handhaben, emsig anwenden, hantieren; betrieben (*one's business*); zusetzen (*Dat.*) (*with questions*); *- a p. with a th.,* einen überhäufen *or* reichlich versehen mit etwas, einem etwas wiederholt anbieten *or* aufdrängen, auf einen eindringen mit etwas; *- a p. with drinks,* einen mit Getränken traktieren; *- one's needle,* die Nadel emsig führen. 2. *v.n.* regelmäßig fahren *or* verkehren; *- to windward,* aufkreuzen, lavieren. 3. *s.* die Falte (*of cloth*), Strähne (*of rope*); (*fig.*) der Hang, die Neigung; *three--,* dreifach. **--wood,** *s.* das Sperrholz.
pneum-a ['nju:mə], *s.* die Seele, der Lebenshauch. **-atic** [-'mætık], 1. *adj.* pneumatisch, Luft-; luftenthaltend (*Zool.*); Luftdruck-, Preßluft-; *-atic boat, s.* das Schlauchboot, der Floßsack; *-atic drill, s.* der Preßluftbohrhammer; *-atic post,* die Rohrpost; *-atic tire,* der Luftreifen. 2. *s.* der Luftreifen. **-atics,** *pl.* (*sing. constr.*) die Pneumatik. **-atology** [-'tɔlədʒı], *s.* die Lehre vom, Heiligen Geist (*Theol.*), Dämonenlehre. **-onia** [-'moʊnıə], *s.* die Lungenentzündung. **-onic** [-'mɔnık], *adj.* Lungen-, Lungenentzündungs-.
poach [poʊtʃ], 1. *v.a.* wildern in (*private land*); unbefugt fangen (*protected game*); zertreten, niedertreten, aufwühlen, aufweichen (*ground*); (*coll.*) durch unerlaubte Mittel erreichen (*advantage,*

lead, etc.); ohne Schale kochen (*eggs*); *–ed egg*, verlorenes Ei. 2. *v.n.* wildern, Wilddieberei treiben; matschig sein *or* werden (*of ground*); (*fig.*) *– on*, übergreifen auf; *– on a p.'s preserves*, einem ins Gehege eindringen. **–er,** *s.* der Wilderer, Wilddieb. **–ing,** *s.* das Wildern, die Wilddieberei.

pochard [ˈpoutʃəd, ˈpoukəd], *s.* die Tafelente (*Orn.*).

pochette [pɔˈʃɛt], *s.* das Handtäschchen.

pock [pɔk], *s.* (*usually pl.*) die Pocke, Blatter (*Med.*). **--mark,** *s.* die Blatternarbe. **--marked,** *adj.*, blatternarbig.

pocket [ˈpɔkɪt], 1. *s.* die Tasche (*also Bill.*); der Beutel (*Anat.*), das Erzlager (*Min.*); der Sack (*of hops, wool, etc.*); *air--*, die Fallbö, das Luftloch (*Av.*); *be £1 in –*, £1 gewonnen haben, sich um £1 bereichern (*by*, durch); *have a p. in one's –*, einen in der Gewalt *or* Tasche haben; *be £1 out of –*, £1 auslegen *or* draufzahlen; *put one's hand in one's –*, die Hand in die Tasche stecken; (*fig.*) Geld ausgeben; *– of resistance*, das Widerstandsnest (*Mil.*). 2. *v.a.* in die Tasche stecken; einstecken (*also fig.*); in den Beutel treiben (*Bill.*); (*fig.*) sich aneignen, einheimsen; hinnehmen, auf sich sitzen lassen; *– an affront*, eine Beleidigung auf sich sitzen lassen; *– one's pride*, sich demütigen lassen; *– a shilling*, einen Schilling in die Tasche stecken. **--battleship,** *s.* schnelles Panzerschiff. **--book,** *s.* das Taschenbuch, Notizbuch. **--edition,** *s.* die Taschenausgabe. **–ful,** *s.* die Taschevoll. **– handkerchief,** *s.* das Taschentuch. **--knife,** *s.* das Taschenmesser. **--money,** *s.* das Taschengeld. **--size(d),** *adj.* in Taschenformat. **--torch,** *s.* die Taschenlampe.

pod [pɔd], 1. *s.* die Schote, Hülse, Schale (*Bot.*), der Kokon (*Ent.*). 2. *v.n.* Schoten ansetzen. 3. *v.a.* ausschoten, enthülsen (*peas*). **--net,** *s.* die Aalreuse.

podagra [pəˈdægrə], *s.* das Podagra, die (Fuß)-Gicht.

podgy [ˈpɔdʒɪ], *adj.* (*coll.*) untersetzt, klein und dick.

podium [ˈpoudɪəm], *s.* das Podium, Podest.

poe–m [ˈpouɪm], *s.* das Gedicht. **–sy** [–ɪsɪ], *s.* (*Poet.*) die Poesie, Dichtkunst. **–t** [–ɪt], *s.* der Dichter; *–t laureate*, der Hofdichter, gekrönter Dichter; *minor –t*, der Dichter zweiten Ranges. **–taster** [–ɪˈtæstə], *s.* der Dichterling. **–tess** [–ɪtəs], *s.* die Dichterin. **–tic** [–ˈɛtɪk], *adj.* dichterisch, poetisch; *–tic licence*, dichterische Freiheit. **–tical** [–ˈɛtɪkl], *adj.* Vers–, in Versen; phantasievoll. **–ticize** [–ˈɛtɪsaɪz], *see* **–tize. –tics** [–ˈɛtɪks], *pl.* (*sing. constr.*) Poetik. **–tize** [–ɪtaɪz], 1. *v.n.* dichten. 2. *v.a.* in Verse setzen, in Versen bringen. ausdrücken *or* darstellen, dichterisch verherrlichen, **–try** [–ɪtrɪ], *s.* die Dichtkunst, Poesie, Dichtung, Gedichte, Dichtwerke (*pl.*).

pogrom [ˈpɔgrəm], *s.* das Pogrom, die Judenverfolgung, Judenhetze.

poignan–cy [ˈpɔɪnjənsɪ], *s.* die Schärfe, das Scharfe, Schmerzhafte. **–t** [–ənt], *adj.* scharf, beißend, stechend, brennend, heftig, nagend, schmerzlich.

point [pɔɪnt], **1.** *s.* der Punkt, das Punktzeichen (*Typ.*); Komma (*Math.*); der Fleck, kleiner Raum. (also *– lace*) genähte Spitzen (*pl.*); die Schärfe; Absicht, der (End)Zweck; Zielpunkt, das Ziel; der Zeitpunkt, Augenblick; die (Teil)Frage, Einzelheit, der Abschnitt; besondere Eigenschaft, charakteristischer Zug; die Pointe, springender Punkt, die Hauptfrage, Kernfrage, wesentlicher Punkt, besonderer Wert, der Anziehungspunkt, Nachdruck, Grad, die Stufe; der Spieler rechts vom Schläger (*Crick.*); die Spitze, Landspitze, Landzunge; Radiernadel, Ahle; das Geweihende; die Nähspitze; der Steckkontakt (*Elec.*); (*fig.*) die Schärfe; *pl.* Weichen (*Railw.*). (*a*) (*with nouns*) *– d'appui*, der Stützpunkt, Rückhaltspunkt (*Mil.*); *at the – of the bayonet*, mit blanker Waffe; *– of the compass*, der Kompaßstrich; *– of contact*, der Berührungspunkt; *at the – of death*, im Sterben, dem Tode nahe; *– of honour*, der Ehrenpunkt, die (unbedingte) Satisfaktion (*by a duel, etc.*); *the –s of a horse*, die hervorstechenden Merkmale eines Pferdes; *– of impact*, der Auftreffpunkt; *– of interest*, interessante Frage, die Merkwürdigkeit, Sehenswürdigkeit; *– of intersection*, der Schnittpunkt; *on the – of the nose*, auf der Nasenspitze; *– of order*, die Tagesordnung (*Parl.*); *– of origin*, die Versandstation (*C.L.*); *at the – of the revolver*, mit vorgehaltenem Revolver; *– of time*, der Zeitpunkt, Augenblick; *– of view*, der Standpunkt, Gesichtspunkt; *from this – of view*, von diesem Standpunkt aus. (*b*) (*with adjectives*) *boiling –*, der Siedepunkt; *cardinal –s*, die (vier) Himmelsgegenden; *freezing –*, der Gefrierpunkt; *good –s*, gute Seiten; *small –*, unwichtige Sache; *strong –*, die Stärke (*of character*); *weak –*, schwache Seite, die Blöße (*of character*). (*c*) (*with verbs*) *argue the – with*, sich auseinandersetzen mit; *that's the – !* darauf kommt es an! darum geht es *or* handelt es sich! das ist es ja *or* gerade! *there's no – in doing*, es hat keinen Zweck zu tun; *there's not much – in it*, es hat wenig an sich; *carry* or *gain one's –*, seine Ansicht durchsetzen, seine Absicht *or* sein Ziel erreichen; *give – to a th.*, einer S. Nachdruck verleihen; *give –s to*, vorgeben (*Dat.*); überlegen sein (*Dat.*); *make a – of*, sich angelegen sein lassen, sich zum Prinzip *or* zur Aufgabe machen, Wert legen auf, bestehen (auf (*Dat.*)); *make the – that*, hervorheben *or* die Feststellung machen daß; *prove one's –*, seinen Satz beweisen; *stretch a –*, eine Ausnahme machen, ein Auge zudrücken; *uphold one's –*, recht behalten, fünf gerade sein lassen; *yield a – to*, recht geben (*Dat.*). (*d*) (*with prepositions*) *at all –s*, in jeder Hinsicht, ganz und gar; *at many –s*, an vielen Stellen; *at this –*, in diesem Augenblick; *beside the –*, unangebracht, abwegig; *– by –*, Punkt für Punkt; *wander from the –*, von der Sache abschweifen; *in –*, treffend, passend, angemessen, angebracht, geeignet; *a case in –*, ein zutreffender Fall, ein Beispiel; *cite as a case in –*, als Begründung anführen; *the case in –*, der vorliegende Fall; *in – of . . .*, in Hinsicht auf . . . (*Acc.*); *in – of fact*, tatsächlich; *in many –s*, in vierlerlei Hinsicht; *off the –*, nicht zur Sache (gehörig); unzutreffend; *on the – of going*, im Begriff zu gehen; *victory on –s*, der Punktsieg; *win on –s*, nach Punkten siegen; *to a –*, vollkommen; *up to a –*, bis zu einem gewissen Grade; *to the –*, zur Sache (gehörig), sachgemäß, zutreffend; *come to the –*, zur Sache kommen; *when it came to the –*, als es soweit war; *keep to the –*, bei der Sache bleiben; *to the – of*, bis an die Grenze von; *to bursting –*, zum Bersten. **2.** *v.a.* (an)spitzen; zeigen, aufzeigen; bekräftigen, unterstreichen; ausfüllen (*brick-work*); richten (*at*, auf (*Acc.*)); *– the finger*, mit Fingern zeigen (*at*, auf (*Acc.*)); *– a moral*, eine Lehre ziehen, moralische Betrachtungen anstellen; *– out*, hinweisen auf, klarmachen, aufdecken; *as was –ed out*, wie ausgeführt wurde; *I –ed it out to him*, ich machte ihn darauf aufmerksam. **3.** *v.n.* zeigen, deuten, (hin)-weisen (*at* or *to*, auf (*Acc.*)); (vor)stehen (*of hounds*). **--blank,** *adj.* & *adv.* schnurgerade; (*fig.*) direkt, gerade heraus, rundweg; *--blank range*, die Kernschußweite; *--blank refusal*, glatte Weigerung; *--blank shot*, der Kernschuß. **--duty,** *s.* der Verkehrsdienst; *--duty policeman*, der Verkehrspolizist. **–ed** [–ɪd], *adj.* spitz, zugespitzt, spitzig; (*fig.*) deutlich, zutreffend; beißend, anzüglich; *–ed arch*, der Spitzbogen. **–edness,** *s.* die Spitze, Spitzigkeit; (*fig.*) Schärfe, Deutlichkeit. **–er,** *s.* der Zeiger, Zeigestock, Zeigestab; Vorstehhund, Hühnerhund (*Hunt.*); (*coll.*) Wink. **–ing,** *s.* die Richtung; das Fugenverstreichen (*Mas.*); die Interpunktion. **--lace,** *s.* genähte Spitzen (*pl.*). **–less,** *adj.* stumpf; (*fig.*) gehaltlos, sinnlos, zwecklos. **–sman,** *s.* der Weichensteller. **--to-point race,** das Querfeldeinrennen.

poise [pɔɪz], 1. *s.* das Gleichgewicht, die Schwebe; (Körper)Haltung, (*fig.*) Ausgeglichenheit. 2. *v.a.* im Gleichgewicht erhalten, balancieren; *be –d*, im Gleichgewicht ruhen. 3. *v.n.* schweben.

poison [ˈpɔɪzən], 1. *s.* das Gift; *hate like –*, tödlich hassen. 2. *v.a.* vergiften (*also fig.*); *–ed finger*, infigierter Finger. **–er,** *s.* der Vergifter, Giftmischer. **--fang,** *s.* der Giftzahn. **– gas,** *s.* das Giftgas. **–ing,** *s.* die Vergiftung. **–ous** [–əs], *adj.* giftig, Gift–; (*coll.*) widerlich, ekelhaft; *–ous snake*, die Giftschlange.

[1]**poke** [poʊk], *s.* (*archaic*) die Tasche, der Beutel; (*Scots*) die Tüte; *buy a pig in a* –, eine Katze im Sack kaufen.

[2]**poke** [poʊk], 1. *s.* der Stoß, Puff. 2. *v.a.* stoßen, puffen, schieben; schüren (*the fire*); vorstrecken, vorstecken (*head, etc.*); – *fun at*, sich lustig machen über, aufziehen; – *one's nose into*, die Nase stecken in (*Acc.*). 3. *v.n.* (herum)tappen, tasten; – *about*, herumschnüffeln. **--bonnet,** *s.* der Kiepenhut, die Schute. **–r,** *s.* der Feuerhaken, das Schüreisen; der Pedell (*Studs. sl.*); *as stiff as a –r*, steif wie ein Brett. **–r-work,** *s.* die Brandmalerei.

[1]**poker** [ˈpoʊkə], *s.* das Poker (*Cards*).

[2]**poker** [ˈpoʊkə], *s.* (*rare*) das Schreckgespenst, der Popanz.

poky [ˈpoʊkɪ], *adj.* (*coll.*) eng, dumpf(ig); erbärmlich, kleinlich.

polar [ˈpoʊlə], 1. *adj.* Polar– (*Geog.*); polar (*Phys.*); (*fig.*) genau entgegengesetzt; – *air*, arktische Kaltluft; – *axis*, die Polarachse; – *bear*, der Eisbär; – *circle*, der Polarkreis; – *distance*, der Polabstand; – *sea*, das Eismeer; – *star*, der Polarstern. 2. *s.* die Polare (*Geom.*). **–ity** [–ˈlærɪtɪ], *s.* die Polarität; (*fig.*) Gegensätzlichkeit, Wechselbeziehung. **–ization** [–raɪˈzeɪʃn], *s.* die Polarisation. **–ize,** *v.a.* polarisieren.

polder [ˈpoʊldə], *s.* der Koog.

[1]**pole** [poʊl], *s.* der Pol (*Astr., Geog., Elec.*); (*fig.*) entgegengesetztes Extrem; (*fig.*) *–s apart*, himmelweit verschieden; – *reversal*, die Umpolung (*Elec.*). **--star,** *s.* der Polarstern; (*fig.*) Leitstern.

[2]**pole** [poʊl], 1. *s.* die Stange, der Pfahl, Stab, die Deichsel (*of a cart*); Rute (= 5·03 *m.*), Meßrute (*Surv.*); *under bare –s*, vor Topp und Takel (*Naut.*); (*sl.*) *up the –*, klapsig, plemplem. 2. *v.a.* mit einer Stange treiben, staken (*as a boat*), mit Stangen stützen (*hops, etc.*). **--axe,** *s.* die Streitaxt, das Schlachtbeil; Enterbeil (*Naut.*). **–cat,** *s.* der Iltis (*Zool.*). **--jump, --vault,** *s.* der Stabhochsprung. **--jumping, --vaulting,** das Stabspringen. **--pin,** *s.* der Deichselbolzen.

polemic [pəˈlɛmɪk], 1. *adj.* streitsüchtig, polemisch, Streit–. 2. *s.* der Polemiker; Meinungsstreit; (*usually pl.*) die Fehde, Polemik.

polenta [poʊˈlɛntə], *s.* der Maisbrei.

police [pəˈlɪːs], 1. *s.* die Polizei; (*pl. constr.*) Polizisten. 2. *v.a.* überwachen, in Ordnung halten. **--constable,** *s. see* **–man. --court,** *s.* das Polizeigericht. **--inspector,** *s.* der Polizeikommissar. **–man,** *s.* Polizeibeamte(r), *m.*, der Schutzmann, Polizist. **–(men),** Schutzleute, die Polizei. **--officer,** *s.* Polizeibeamte(r), *m.* **--raid,** *s.* die Razzia. **--station,** *s.* die Polizeiwache. **--trap,** *s.* die Autofalle (*Motor.*).

[1]**policy** [ˈpɔlɪsɪ], *s.* die Politik; Diplomatie, Regierungskunst; politischer Grundsatz, politische Rücksicht, politisches Verfahren; *from motives of –*, aus kluger Rücksicht; *domestic –*, die Innenpolitik; *foreign –*, die Außenpolitik; *honesty is the best –*, ehrlich währt am längsten.

[2]**policy** [ˈpɔlɪsɪ], *s.* die (Versicherungs)Police, der Versicherungsschein (*C.L.*). **--holder,** *s.* der Policeinhaber.

poliomyelitis [pɔlɪomaɪəˈlaɪtɪs], *s.* spinale Kinderlähmung.

polish [ˈpɔlɪʃ], 1. *s.* die Glätte, Politur; das Bohnerwachs, die Schuhcreme, Wichse; (*fig.*) der Glanz, Schliff, die Vollkommenheit. 2. *v.a.* glätten, polieren, wichsen (*leather*), putzen (*shoes*), bohnern (*floors*); abschleifen, (*fig.*) feilen, verfeinern; (*coll.*) – *off*, erledigen, abtun, abmurksen. 3. *v.n.* glatt *or* blank werden, glänzend werden, sich putzen lassen. **–ed** [–t], *adj.* glatt, poliert; (*fig.*) gesittet, höflich; fein, elegant (*as manners*). **–er,** *s.* der Polierer; die Politur, das Glanzmittel; die Polierscheibe. **–ing,** *s.* das Polieren; *–ing brush*, *s.* die Glanzbürste, Polierbürste; *–ing powder*, *s.* das Putzpulver.

polite [pəˈlaɪt], *adj.* höflich, artig (*to*, gegen); fein, verfeinert, gebildet; – *literature*, schöne Literatur; (*coll.*) *do the –*, sich höflich benehmen. **–ness,** *s.* die Höflichkeit, Artigkeit.

politic [ˈpɔlɪtɪk], *adj.* politisch, weltklug, berechnend; *body –*, der Staat, Staatskörper. **–al** [pəˈlɪtɪkl], *adj.* politisch; staatskundig; Staats–; *–al economist*, der Volkswirtschaftler, Nationalökonom; *–al economy*, die Volkswirtschaft, Nationalökonomie; *–al science*, die Staatswissenschaft; *–al system*, das Regierungssystem. **–ian** [pɔlɪˈtɪʃən], *s.* der Staatsmann, Politiker. **–s,** *pl.* (*sing. constr.*) die Politik, Staatskunst; (partei)politische Gesinnung *or* Richtung; (*coll.*) *practical –s*, durchführbar; *talk –s*, politisieren.

polity [ˈpɔlɪtɪ], *s.* politische Ordnung, die Verfassung, Regierungsform, Staatsform; der Staat, das Gemeinwesen.

polka [ˈpɔlkə], *s.* die Polka.

[1]**poll** [poʊl], 1. *s.* die Wahl, Abstimmung, Stimmenzählung; der Wahlort; die Stimmenzahl; (*coll. or archaic*) der (Hinter)Kopf, Schädel; (*archaic*) die Person; *at the –s*, an der Wahlurne; *be at the head of the –*, die meisten Stimmen erhalten haben; *challenge to the –s*, die Ablehnung eines Geschworenen (*Law*); *go to the –*, zur Wahl gehen. 2. *v.a.* kappen, köpfen, stutzen, abschneiden; in die Wahlliste eintragen, erhalten (*votes*). 3. *v.n.* stimmen, die Stimme abgeben. 4. *adj.* ohne Hörner; von einer Partei ausgeführt (*Law*). *deed –*, die Urkunde über einseitiges Rechtsgeschäft. **--book,** *s.* die Wählerliste, Wahlliste. **–ing,** *s.* das Wählen, Abstimmen, die Wahl, Abstimmung. **–ing-booth,** *s. see* **–ing-station. –ing-day,** *s.* der Wahltag. **–ing-district,** *s.* der Wahlbezirk. **–ing-station,** *s.* das Wahllokal. **--tax,** *s.* das Kopfgeld, die Kopfsteuer.

[2]**poll** [pɔl], *s.*; (*sl.*) *the –*, *pl. of* **–man. –degree,** *s.* der gewöhnliche Grad eines B.A. (*in Cambridge*). **–man,** *s.* der Student, der sich auf den gewöhnlichen Grad vorbereitet.

[3]**poll** [pɔl], *s.* (*coll.*) der Papagei.

pollack [ˈpɔlək], *s.* der Pollack (*Ichth.*).

pollard [ˈpɔləd], 1. *s.* gekappter Baum; ungehörntes Tier; der Hirsch, der Hörner abgeworfen hat; die Kleie. 2. *v.a.* kappen (*tree*).

poll–en [ˈpɔlən], *s.* der Pollen, Blütenstaub; *–en grain*, das Blütenstaubkorn. **–inate** [–ɪneɪt], *v.a.* bestäuben. **–ination** [–ɪˈneɪʃən], *s.* die Bestäubung.

polling [ˈpoʊlɪŋ], *see* [1]**poll.**

pollock [ˈpɔlək], *s. see* **pollack.**

pollut–e [pəˈljuːt], *v.a.* beflecken, besudeln; verunreinigen, beschmutzen; (*fig.*) entweihen; verderben. **–ion** [–ljuːʃən], *s.* die Befleckung, Besudelung, Verunreinigung, Entweihung, Pollution (*Physiol.*).

polo [ˈpoʊloʊ], *s.* das Polo(spiel). **--stick,** *s.* der Poloschläger.

polonaise [pɔləˈnaɪz], *s.* die Polonaise.

polony [pəˈloʊnɪ], *s.* eine Wurst aus halbgarem Schweinefleisch.

poltroon [pɔlˈtruːn], *s.* die Memme. **–ery** [–ərɪ], *s.* die Feigheit.

poly– [ˈpɔlɪ], *prefix* viel, Viel–. Poly–. **–ˈandrian, –ˈandrous,** *adj* vielmännig (*Bot.*). **ˈ–andry,** *s.* die Vielmännerei. **–ˈanthus,** *s.* die Tuberose (*Bot.*). **–ˈbasic,** *adj.* mehrbasig. **–ˈcarpous,** *adj.* aus vielen Fruchtblättern. **–chroˈmatic,** *see* **–chrome** 1. **ˈ–chrome,** 1. *adj.* vielfarbig, bunt. 2. *s.* die Vielfärbigkeit; mehrfarbige Plastik. **ˈ–chromy,** *s.* der Vielfarbendruck (*Print.*), vielfarbige Darstellung. **–ˈclinic,** *s.* die Klinik für alle Krankheiten. **–gamist** [pəˈlɪgəmɪst], *s.* der Anhänger der Vielweiberei. **–gamous** [pəˈlɪgəməs], *adj.* polygamisch. **–gamy** [pəˈlɪgəmɪ], *s.* die Vielweiberei, Mehrehe. **ˈ–glot,** 1. *adj.* vielsprachig. 2. *s.* der Polyglotte. **ˈ–gon,** *s.* das Vieleck, Polygon. **–gonal** [pəˈlɪgənəl], *adj.* polygon, vieleckig. **–ˈhedral,** *adj.* vielflächig. **–ˈhedron,** *s.* das Polyeder, Vielflach. **–ˈhistor,** *s.*, **ˈ–math,** *s.* der Polyhistor, vielseitiger Gelehrter. **ˈ–merism,** *s.* die Polymerie. **–ˈmorphic,** *adj.*, **–ˈmorphous,** *adj.* vielgestaltig, polymorph. **–ˈnomial,** 1. *adj.* polynomisch. 2. *s.* das Polynom (*Math.*). **ˈ–p,** *s.* der Polyp, Hydrozoe (*Zool.*). **ˈ–pary,** *s.* der Polypenstock. **ˈ–pe,** *see* **–p. ˈ–phase,** *adj.* mehrphasig, vielphasig; *–phase current*, der Drehstrom (*Elec.*). **–ˈphonic,** *adj.* vielstimmig, polyphon(isch). **ˈ–pite,** *s.* der Einzelpolyp (*Zool.*). **ˈ–pod,** *s.* der Vielfüßer. **–ˈpodium,** *s.* der Tüpfelfarn (*Bot.*). **ˈ–pore, –ˈporus,** *s.* der Löcherpilz (*Bot.*).

'-pous, *adj.* Polypen- (*also Med.*). **'-pus,** *s.* der Polyp (*Med.*). **-sy'llabic,** *adj.* mehrsilbig, vielsilbig. **-'syllable,** *s.* vielsilbiges Wort. **-'technic,** 1. *adj.* polytechnisch. 2. *s.* polytechnische Fachschule. **'-theism,** *s.* die Vielgötterei. **-'valent,** *adj.* mehrwertig (*Chem.*). **-'zoa,** *pl.* die Moostierchengattung.
pomace ['pʌməs], *s.* der (Apfel)Trester.
poma-de [pə'meɪd, pə'mɑ:d], 1. *s.* die Pomade. 2. *v.a.* mit Pomade einreiben. **-tum** [-'meɪtəm], *s. see* **-de** 1.
pom-e [poum], *s.* die Kernfrucht. **-egranate** [pəmɪ'grænɪt], *s.* der Granatapfel; Granatapfelbaum. **-iculture** [poum'ɪkʌltʃə], *s.* die Obstbaumzucht. **-ology** [pə'mɔlədʒɪ], *s.* die Obstbaukunde.
pommel ['pʌml], 1. *s.* der Knauf (*of a sword*); Sattelknopf (*of a saddle*). 2. *v.a.* schlagen; puffen, knuffen.
pomology, *see under* **pom-ology.**
pomp [pɔmp], *s.* der Pomp, Prunk, die Pracht, das Gepränge.
pom-pom ['pɔmpɔm], *s.* die Flugabwehrmaschinenkanone, das Schnellfeuergeschütz.
pompon ['pɔmpɔn], *s.* der Büschel, die Quaste, Troddel.
pomp-osity [pɔm'pɔsɪtɪ], *s.* die Prahlerei, Pomphaftigkeit, der Prunk, Bombast. **-ous** ['pɔmpəs], *adj.* prunkvoll, pomphaft, wichtigtuend, prahlerisch (*of p.*), hochtrabend, bombastisch, schwülstig (*as style*).
ponce [pɔns], *s.* (*sl.*) der Zuhälter.
poncho ['pɔntʃou], *s.* der Regenumhang.
pond [pɔnd], *s.* der Teich, Weiher, Tümpel; *horse--*, die Schwemme. **-age** [-ɪdʒ], *s.* die Wassermenge in einem Teich. **-weed,** *s.* das Laichkraut.
ponder ['pɔndə], 1. *v.a.* erwägen, bedenken, überlegen. 2. *v.n.* nachdenken, nachsinnen, grübeln (*on* or *over*, über (*Acc.*)). **-ability** [-rə'bɪlɪtɪ], *s.* die Wägbarkeit. **-able,** *adj.* wägbar. **-ance,** *s.* die Wichtigkeit, der Ernst, das Gewicht. **-ation,** *s.* das Abwägen, Abwiegen. **-osity** [-'rɔsɪtɪ], *s.* das Gewicht, die Schwere; (*fig.*) Gewichtigkeit, Schwerfälligkeit, Plumpheit. **-ous** ['pɔndərəs], *adj.* schwer, wuchtig, massig; (*fig.*) schwerfällig, plump. **-ousness,** *s. see* **-osity.**
pone [poun], *s.* das Maisbrot (*Amer.*).
pong [pɔŋ], *v.n.* (*sl.*) muffeln.
pongee [pʌn'dʒɪ], *s.* chinesische Seide.
poniard ['pɔnɪəd], 1. *s.* der Dolch. 2. *v.a.* erdolchen.
pontif-f ['pɔntɪf], *s.* der Hohepriester; Papst. **-ical** [-'tɪfɪkl], 1. *adj.* oberpriesterlich; bischöflich; päpstlich. 2. *s.* das Pontifikale; *pl.* bischöfliche Amtstracht, Pontifikalien (*pl.*). **-icate** [-'tɪfɪkət], 1. *s.* das *or* der Pontifikat. **-y** [-tɪfaɪ], *v.n.* sich Unfehlbarkeit anmaßen; mit dreister Selbstverständlichkeit auftreten.
pont--levis ['pɔnt'lɛvɪs], *s.* die Zugbrücke. **-oneer, -onier** [pɔntə'nɪ:ə], *s.* der Brückeningenieur. **-oon** [-'tu:n], *s.* der Ponton, Brückenkahn (*Mil.*); *-oon-bridge*, die Schiff(s)brücke.
pontoon [pɔn'tu:n], *s.* das Vingt-et-un (*Cards*).
pony ['pounɪ], *s.* der & das Pony, das Kleinpferd, Zwergpferd, Pferdchen, kleines Pferd; kleines Bierglas; (*sl.*) £25 Sterling; (*sl.*) die Eselsbrücke. **--engine,** *s.* kleine Rangierlokomotive (*Railw.*).
poodle ['pu:dl], *s.* der Pudel.
pooh [pu:], *int.* pah! ach was! **--pooh,** *v.a.* über die Achsel ansehen, geringschätzig behandeln *or* abtun, die Nase rümpfen über.
¹pool [pu:l], 1. *s.* der Tümpel, Pfuhl, Teich, stehendes Wasser, die Lache. 2. *v.a.* schrämen (*Min.*).
²pool [pu:l], 1. *s.* der (Spiel)Einsatz, die Kasse (*Cards, etc.*); Interessengemeinschaft, der Ring, das Kartell, gemeinsamer Fonds, gemeinsame Kasse (*C.L.*); das Poulespiel (*Bill.*); *football* –, der Fußballtoto. 2. *v.a.* zusammenschließen, vereinigen, zusammenwerfen, gemeinsam einsetzen; verteilen (*profits*).
poop [pu:p], 1. *s.* die Kampanie, (Achter)Hütte, das Heck, Hinterteil (*Naut.*). 2. *v.a.* über das Achterschiff treffen (*of waves*); *be -ed*, eine Sturzsee von hinten bekommen, (*fig.*) gefährlich getroffen sein.
poor ['pu:ə], 1. *adj.* arm (*in*, an (*Dat.*)); dürftig, armselig, gering, unbedeutend, schlecht, schwach, unzureichend, mager, unfruchtbar, dürr (*as soil*); – *consolation*, schlechter Trost; – *crop*, unergiebige Ernte; *a* – *head for . . .*, keinen Kopf *or* wenig Begabung für . . .; – *health*, schwache Gesundheit. *a* – *look-out*, traurige *or* schlechte Aussichten. – *me!* ich Armer! *have a* – *night*, eine unruhige Nacht verbringen; *have a* – *opinion of*, wenig halten *or* eine geringe Meinung haben von; *in my* – *opinion*, meiner unmaßgeblichen Meinung nach; *make but a* – *shift*, sich kümmerlich behelfen; – *visibility*, unsichtiges Wetter. 2. *s. the* – (*pl.*), die Armen; (*B.*) *the* – *in spirit*, die da geistlich arm sind. **--box,** *s.* die Armenbüchse, Almosenbüchse. **--house,** *s.* das Armenhaus. **--law,** *s.* das Armengesetz, Armenrecht. **-ly,** 1. *adv.* schwach, dürftig; *-ly off*, schlimm daran; *think -ly of*, nicht viel halten von. 2. *pred. adj.* unwohl, unpäßlich. **-ness,** *s.* die Armut, der Mangel (*of*, an); die Dürftigkeit, Armseligkeit, Unfruchtbarkeit (*of soil*); Schwäche, Beschränktheit. **--rate,** *s.* die Gemeindearmensteuer. **--relief,** *s.* die Armenfürsorge. **--spirited,** *adj.* verzagt, mutlos, kleinmütig.
pop [pɔp], 1. *s.* der Paff, Knall; (*coll.*) Gespritztes, *n.*; (*coll.*) *ginger--*, das Ingwerbier; (*coll.*) *have a* – *at*, schießen nach; (*sl.*) *in* –, verpfändet. 2. *adv.* plötzlich, mit einem Knall; *go* –, knallen, platzen, losgehen. 3. *int.* paff! klatsch! 4. *v.n.* knallen, losgehen, explodieren; paffen, puffen, schnell gehen *or* kommen, huschen; – *along*, forthuschen; – *in*, hereinplatzen, auf einen Sprung kommen; – *off*, entwischen, forthuschen; (*sl.*) hops gehen; – *out*, einen Sprung hinaus machen; – *up*, plötzlich auftauchen. 5. *v.a.* plötzlich bringen, schieben *or* stecken, rösten (*corn*); knallen lassen, losschießen; (*coll.*) verpfänden; (*coll.*) – *the question*, einen Heiratsantrag machen. **--corn,** *s.* der Röstmais. **--eyed,** *adj.* glotzäugig. **--gun,** die Knallbüchse.
pope [poup], *s.* der Papst. **-dom,** *s.* das Papsttum. **-ry** [-ərɪ], *s.* die Papisterei, das Pfaffentum.
popinjay ['pɔpɪndʒeɪ], *s.* der Geck, Laffe, Fatzke.
popish [poupɪʃ], *adj.* papistisch, Pfaffen-.
poplar ['pɔplə], *s.* die Pappel.
poplin ['pɔplɪn], *s.* die Popeline.
popliteal [pɔp'lɪtɪəl], *adj.* Kniekehl-.
poppet ['pɔpɪt], *s.* der Schlittenständer (*Naut.*); die Docke (*of a lathe*); (*coll.*) das Püppchen, Täubchen. **--head,** *s.* die Docke (*of a lathe*). **--valve,** *s.* das Tellerventil.
popping ['pɔpɪŋ], *s. see* **pop. --crease,** *s.* die Schlagmallinie (*Crick.*).
popple ['pɔpl], 1. *v.n.* Wellen schlagen. 2. *s.* der Wellenschlag, Wellengang.
poppy ['pɔpɪ], *s.* der Mohn; *opium* –, der Schlafmohn. – *Day*, der Waffenstillstandstag, englischer Heldengedenktag (*11th Nov.*). (*sl.*) **-cock,** *s.* der Quatsch, Unsinn.
popul-ace ['pɔpjuləs], *s.* das Volk, der große Haufen, der Pöbel. **-ar** [-lə], *adj.* Volks-, volkstümlich, volksmäßig, volksnah; populär, gemeinverständlich, leichtfaßlich, verbreitet, allgemein, beliebt; *-ar front*, die Volksfront (*Pol.*); *-ar government*, die Volksherrschaft; *at -ar prices*, zu volkstümlichen, mäßigen *or* erschwinglichen Preisen; *-ar song*, der Schlager; *-ar tradition*, volkstümliche Überlieferung. *-ar writer*, vielgelesener Schriftsteller; *make o.s. -ar*, sich beliebt machen (*with*, bei). **-arity** [-'lærɪtɪ], *s.* die Volkstümlichkeit, Beliebtheit, Volksgunst, Popularität (*with*, bei; *among*, unter). **-arize** ['pɔpjuləraɪz], *v.a.* gemeinverständlich *or* volkstümlich *or* populär machen, leichtfaßlich darstellen; in den weitesten Kreisen verbreiten, unter das Volk bringen, popularisieren. **-ate** [-leɪt], *v.a.* bevölkern, besiedeln. **-ation** [-'leɪʃən], *s.* die Bevölkerung; Einwohnerzahl; Zahl. **-ous** [-pjuləs], *adj.* dicht bevölkert, volkreich. **-ousness,** *s.* die Bevölkerungsdichte.
porcelain ['pɔ:slɪn], 1. *s.* das Porzellan. 2. *adj.* Porzellan-; – *clay*, *s.* das Kaolin, die Porzellanerde.
porch [pɔ:tʃ], *s.* die Vorhalle; (*Amer.*) Veranda.
porc-ine ['pɔ:saɪn], *adj.* Schwein(e)-. **-upine** [-kjupaɪn], *s.* das Stachelschwein; die Kammwalze, Hechelmaschine (*Tech.*).

[1]**pore** [ˈpɔːə], *s.* die Pore.
[2]**pore** [ˈpɔːə], *v.n.* (usually – *over*) fleißig *or* eifrig studieren, hocken über.
pork [pɔːk], *s.* das Schweinefleisch. **--butcher,** *s.* der Schweineschlächter. **-er,** *s.* das Mastschwein, Mastferkel. **- pie,** *s.* die Schweinefleischpastete; *--pie hat*, runder Filzhut. **-y,** *adj.* fett, fettig.
pornograph-ic [pɔːnəˈgræfɪk], *adj.* Schmutz–, unzüchtig, zotig. **-y** [–ˈnɔgrəfɪ], *s.* die Pornographie, Schmutzliteratur.
poro-sity [pɔːˈrɔsɪtɪ], *s.* die Durchlässigkeit, Porosität. **-us** [–rəs], *adj.* durchlässig, porös.
porphyr-itic [pɔːfɪˈrɪtɪk], *adj.* Porphyr–. **-y** [ˈpɔːfɪrɪ], *s.* der Porphyr.
porpoise [ˈpɔːpəs], *s.* das Meerschwein, der Tümmler.
porridge [ˈpɔrɪdʒ], *s.* der Haferbrei, Haferschleim, die Hafergrütze.
porrigo [pəˈraɪgoʊ], *s.* der Grind (*Med.*).
porringer [ˈpɔrɪndʒə], *s.* der Suppennapf.
[1]**port** [pɔːt], *s.* der Hafen, Hafenplatz, die Hafenstadt; (*fig.*) Zuflucht; – *of call*, der Anlegehafen, Anlaufhafen; *call at a* –, einen Hafen anlaufen; – *of clearance*, der Abgangshafen; *clear a* –, aus einem Hafen auslaufen; – *of destination*, der Bestimmungshafen, Einlaufhafen; *free* –, der Freihafen; – *of London Authority*, die Londoner Hafenbehörde; – *of registry*, der Heimatshafen; – *charges*, – *dues*, *pl.* die Hafengebühren (*pl.*).
[2]**port** [pɔːt], *s.* das Tor, die Pforte, Ladepforte, Pfortluke, das Schießloch (*Naut.*), die Öffnung, Ventilöffnung, der Abzug (*Tech.*); *exhaust* –, der Auspuffkanal. **--hole,** *s.* die Luke.
[3]**port** [pɔːt], 1. *s.* das Backbord; die Backbordseite; – *beam*, das Backbord querab: – *bow*, das Backbord voraus; – *quarter*, das Backbord achteraus; *on the* – *tack*, mit Backbordhalsen. 2. *v.a.* nach links halten (*the helm*).
[4]**port** [pɔːt], *s.* der Portwein.
[5]**port** [pɔːt], 1. *s.* die (Körper)Haltung, der Anstand, das Benehmen. 2. *v.a.* schräg vorm Körper halten (*arms*). **-able** [–əbl], *adj.* tragbar, transportierbar, fahrbar, Reise–; (*fig.*) handlich, beweglich; *-able chair*, der Rollstuhl; *-able gramophone*, das Koffergrammophon; *-able railway*, die Feldbahn; *-able engine*, die Lokomobile; *-able typewriter*, die Reiseschreibmaschine; *-able wireless set*, der Kofferempfänger. **-age** [–ɪdʒ], 1. *s.* das Tragen, der Transport; das Rollgeld, Frachtgeld, die Zustellungsgebühr, der Botenlohn; die Tragstelle (*between navigable waters*); das Umsetzen (*Canoeing*). 2. *v.a.* umsetzen, transportieren (*a canoe*).
portal [pɔːtl], 1. *s.* das Portal (*Arch.*); der (Haupt)-Eingang, das Haupttor, die Pforte; (*fig.*) der Eingang. 2. *adj.*; – *vein*, die Pfortader.
portamento [pɔːtəˈmɛntoʊ], *s.* das Portament, Hinüberschleifen (*Mus.*).
portcullis [pɔːtˈkʌlɪs], *s.* das Fallgatter.
porte [pɔːt], *s.*; *Sublime* –, Hohe Pforte.
porten-d [pɔːˈtɛnd], *v.a.* vorbedeuten, verkündigen; anzeigen, (hin)deuten auf (*Acc.*). **-t** [ˈpɔː-tɛnt], *s.* die Vorbedeutung, Voraussage; schlimmes Anzeichen, das Wunder. **-tous,** *adj.* unheilvoll, unheilverkündend, verhängnisvoll; (*coll.*) furchtbar, gewaltig.
[1]**porter** [ˈpɔːtə], *s.* der Pförtner, Portier.
[2]**porter** [ˈpɔːtə], *s.* der (Gepäck)Träger (*Railw.*); Dienstmann; Packträger, Lastträger. **-age,** *s.* *see* **portage,** 1. *under* [5]**port.**
[3]**porter** [ˈpɔːtə], *s.* das Porterbier.
portfire [ˈpɔːtfaɪə], *s.* die Zündrute, Lunte (*Hist.*).
portfolio [pɔːtˈfoʊlɪoʊ], *s.* die Aktentasche, (Akten)-Mappe; das (Minister)Portefeuille (*Pol.*); *without* –, ohne Geschäftsbereich (*Pol.*).
portico [ˈpɔːtɪkoʊ], *s.* die Säulenhalle.
portière [pɔːˈtjɛːə], *s.* der Türvorhang.
portion [ˈpɔːʃən], 1. *s.* der Teil, das Quantum, die Menge, Anteil (*of*, an); die Portion (*of food*); das Erbteil, die Aussteuer, Mitgift; *legal* –, der Pflichtteil. 2. *v.a.* einteilen; (also – *off*) aussteuern, ausstatten (*a daughter*) (*with*, mit); – *out*, austeilen (*to*, unter (*Acc.*)). **-less,** *adj.* ohne Aussteuer.
portl-iness [ˈpɔːtlɪnɪs], *s.* die Behäbigkeit; Würde, Stattlichkeit. **-y** [–lɪ], *adj.* wohlbeleibt, behäbig; würdevoll, stattlich.
portmanteau [pɔːtˈmæntoʊ], *s.* (pl. –x) *s.* der Handkoffer; – *word*, das Schachtelwort.
portra-it [ˈpɔːtrɪt], *s.* das Porträt, Bildnis, Bild; (*fig.*) die Beschreibung, Schilderung; *paint a p.'s -it*, einen malen. *take a p.'s -it*, einen photographieren. **-itist** [–ɪst], *s.* der Porträtmaler. **-iture** [–jʊə], *s.* die Porträtmalerei; (*fig.*) Schilderung, Darstellung, das Bild. **-y** [–ˈtreɪ], *v.a.* malen, abbilden, portraitieren; (*fig.*) schildern, darstellen. **-yal** [–ˈtreɪəl], *s.* die Darstellung, Schilderung.
pose [poʊz], 1. *s.* die Pose, Positur, Haltung. 2. *v.a.* aufstellen (*assertion*); aufwerfen (*question*); hinstellen, in Pose stellen; (*fig.*) in Positur stellen. 3. *v.n.* sich (*Dat.*) in Pose *or* Positur stellen; posieren, figurieren, auftreten, sich ausgeben (*as*, als). **-r** [–ə], *s.* der Examinator (*at Eton*); verblüffende Frage, harte Nuß. **-ur** [–ˈzəː], *s.* der Wichtigtuer.
posh [pɔʃ], *adj.* (*sl.*) vornehm, elegant, fein, fesch; erstklassig, tipptopp.
posit [ˈpɔzɪt], *v.a.* voraussetzen, postulieren.
position [pəˈzɪʃən], *s.* die Stellung (*also Mil.*), Lage; Lagerung; der Zustand, Rang, Stand, das Amt, die Behauptung, Bejahung (*Philos.*); die Position (*Astr.*, *Mil.*); (*fig.*) der Standpunkt, die Einstellung; *financial* –, die Vermögensverhältnisse (*pl.*), die Finanzlage; *hold a* –, ein Amt *or* eine Stelle bekleiden; *take up a* –, einen Standpunkt vertreten *or* einnehmen; *be in a* – *to*, in der Lage sein zu; *in my* –, in meiner Lage. **-al,** *adj.* Stellungs–. **--finder,** *s.* das Ortungsgerät. **--finding,** *s.* die Ortsbestimmung, Ortung. **--light,** *s.* das Positionslicht. **- report,** *s.* die Standortmeldung.
positiv-e [ˈpɔzɪtɪv], 1. *adj.* ausdrücklich, bestimmt, fest, feststehend, ausgemacht, sicher, unwiderruflich; selbstsicher, überzeugt, entschieden, rechthaberisch, hartnäckig (*of persons*); positiv (*Math.*, *Gram.*, *etc.*), tatsächlich, wirklich, gegeben (*Philos.*); (*coll.*) durchaus, absolut; *be -e of* or *about*, überzeugt sein von, gewiß behaupten; *-e degree*, der Positiv, die Grundstufe (*Gram.*); *-e electrode*, die Anode (*Elec.*); *-e order*, ausdrücklicher Befehl; *proof -e* or *-e proof*, sicherer *or* unwiderlegbarer Beweis; *-e quantity*, positive Größe; *-e statement*, bejahende Aussage (*Gram.*); *-e theology*, die Dogmatik. 2. *s.* der Positiv, die Grundstufe (*Gram.*); das Positiv (*Phot.*) (*also fig.*). **-eness,** *s.* die Bestimmtheit, Wirklichkeit; (*fig.*) Gewißheit, Hartnäckigkeit. **-ism,** *s.* der Positivismus (*Philos.*).
posse [ˈpɔsɪ], *s.* das Aufgebot, die Schar, der Trupp; – *comitatus*, der Landsturm.
possess [pəˈzɛs], *v.a.* besitzen, im Besitz haben, innehaben (*a th.*); beherrschen, in der Gewalt haben (*a p.*); – *o.s. of a th.*, sich einer Sache bemächtigen; – *one's soul in patience*, sich in Geduld fassen; – *a woman*, eine Frau genießen. **-ed,** *adj.* besessen; *be -ed of*, besitzen, im Besitze sein von; *become -ed of*, in den Besitz kommen (*Gen.*); *be -ed with*, eingenommen *or* erfüllt sein von; *a man -ed*, ein Besessener. **-ion** [–ˈzɛʃn], *s.* der Besitz, das Besitztum, die Besitzung; Besessenheit (*by an idea*); *British -ions*, englische Besitzungen; *have -ion of*, sich im Besitz befinden (*Gen.*); im Besitz sein (*Gen.*); *be in -ion of*, besitzen (*of a p.*); gehören, im Besitz sein von (*of a th.*); *come into the -ion of*, in den Besitz kommen von (*of a p.*), in den Besitz kommen (*of a th.* (*Gen.*)); *take -ion of*, Besitz ergreifen von (*a th.*), sich bemächtigen (*of a p.* (*Gen.*)); *vacant -ion*, sofort zu beziehen (*of houses*). **-ive,** 1. *adj.* besitzanzeigend (*Gram.*); besitzgierig (*of a p.*); *-ive case*, der Genitiv; *-ive instinct*, der Instinkt für Besitz; *-ive pronoun*, besitzanzeigendes Fürwort. 2. *s.* der Genitiv, besitzanzeigendes Fürwort (*Gram.*). **-or,** *s.* der Besitzer, Inhaber. **-ory,** *adj.* Besitz–.
posset [ˈpɔsɪt], *s.* heißes Würzgetränk.
possib-ility [pɔsɪˈbɪlɪtɪ], *s.* die Möglichkeit (*of*, für *or* zu); etwas Mögliches; *pl.* Entwicklungsmöglichkeiten, Fähigkeiten (*pl.*); *by any -ility*, auf irgendeine Weise; *human -ility*, das Menschenmögliche. **-le** [ˈpɔsɪbl], *adj.* möglich, angängig; nur möglich; denkbar, eventuell, etwaig; (*coll.*) leidlich, erträglich; *if -le*, womöglich, wenn (irgend) möglich;

best -le way or *best way -le*, denkbar bester Weg. **-ly,** *adv.* möglicherweise, vielleicht; *if I -ly can*, wenn ich irgend kann; *I cannot -ly come*, ich kann unmöglich kommen; *how can I -ly?* wie kann ich nur; *is it not -ly . . .?* ist es nicht etwa . . .?

possum ['pɔsəm], *s.* die Beutelratte (*Zool.*); (*coll.*) *play* –, sich unschuldig *or* krank stellen, sich drücken; äußerst vorsichtig sein.

¹post [poʊst], 1. *s.* der Pfahl, Pfosten, die Stange; *from pillar to* –, von Pontius zu Pilatus; *rudder*--, der Rudersteven (*Naut.*); *starting*--, die Startlinie; *winning*--, das Ziel; *be beaten at* or *on the* –, kurz vor dem Ziel geschlagen werden; *be left at the* –, nicht starten, zurückbleiben; *as deaf as a* –, stocktaub. 2. *v.a.* (usually – *up*) anschlagen, ankleben; bekanntmachen; *-ed as missing*, für vermißt *or* ausgeblieben erklären; – *a wall with bills*, eine Mauer mit Zetteln bekleben; *see* **poster.**

²post [poʊst], 1. *s.* der Posten (*also Mil.*), die Stelle, das Amt, die Stellung, der Platz, Standort; *at one's* –, auf seinem Posten; *last* –, der Zapfenstreich (bei Begräbnissen); *trading* –, der Handelsplatz, die Handelsniederlassung. 2. *v.a.* aufstellen, postieren (*soldiers, etc.*), ernennen (*to a rank*) (*Mil.*).

³post [poʊst], 1. *s.* die Post, Briefpost; das Postamt; die Postaustragung; Postsachen (*pl.*); der Eilbote, Kurier; die Postkutsche; *by* –, per Post, mit der Post; *by to-day's* –, mit der heutigen Post; *by return of* –, postwendend, umgehend; *general* –, das Plätzewechseln. 2. *adv.* (*archaic*) eilig, in Eile; *ride* –, Kurier reiten; *travel* –, mit der Post reisen. 3. *v.a.* zur Post bringen *or* geben, in den Briefkasten stecken, per Post schicken (*a letter, etc.*); eintragen (*an item*) (*C.L.*); – (*up*) *books*, die Bücher ins reine bringen; (*coll.*) (*usually pass.*) informieren; *keep s.o. -ed*, einen auf dem laufenden halten. 4. *v.n.* mit der Post reisen; (*fig.*) eilig reisen, eilen. **-age** [-ɪdʒ], *s.* das Porto, die Postgebühr; *-age due*, das Strafporto, die Nachgebühr; *-age free*, see **--free;** *-age stamp*, die Briefmarke, das Postwertzeichen. **-al** [-əl], *adj.* Post-; *-al order*, die Postanweisung (unter £40); *-al tuition*, der Briefunterricht; *-al Union*, der Weltpostverein. **--bag,** *s.* der Postbeutel. **'-card,** *s.* die Postkarte; *picture -card*, die Ansichtskarte. **--chaise** [-ʃeɪz], *s.* die Postkutsche. **-e restante,** 1. *adv.* postlagernd. 2. *s.* die Briefaufbewahrungsstelle. **--free,** *adj.* portofrei, franko. **--'haste,** *adv.* in Eile. **-ilion, -illion** [pəs'tɪlɪən], *s.* der Postillon. **'-man,** *s.* der Briefträger, Postbote. **'-mark,** 1. *s.* der Poststempel. 2. *v.a.* abstempeln. **'-master,** *s.* der Postmeister, Postamtsvorsteher; *-master-general*, *s.* der Reichspostminister. **'-mistress,** *s.* die Postmeisterin, Postamtsvorsteherin. **'--office,** *s.* das Postamt; *general --office*, das Hauptpostamt, die Hauptpost; *--office clerk*, Postbeamte(r), *m.*; *--office savings-bank*, die Postsparkasse. **--paid,** *adj.* franko, frankiert.

⁴post- [poʊst], *pref.* Nach-; **--'date,** *v.a.* nachdatieren (*a letter*); später datieren (*a fact*). **--di'luvial,** *adj.* nacheiszeitlich. **--di'luvian,** *adj.* nachsintflutlich. **--'entry,** *s.* nachträglicher Eintrag (*C.L.*) *or* Meldung (*Racing*). **'-fix,** *s.* das Suffix (*Gram.*). **--'glacial,** *adj.* nachglazial. **--'graduate,** 1. *s.* der Forschungsarbeiter nach Abschluß des Studiums. 2. *adj.* vorgeschrittene Forschungs-, Doktoranden-. **– hoc,** nach diesem, also deswegen. **-me'ridian,** *adj.* Nachmittags-, nachmittägig. **-me'ridiem,** *adv.* nachmittags. **– 'mortem,** 1. *adj.* nach dem Tode eintretend. 2. *s.*; *--mortem* (*examination*), die Leichenöffnung. **--'natal,** *adj.* nach der Geburt stattfindend. **--'nuptial,** *adj.* nach der Verheiratung stattfindend. **--'obit,** 1. *adj.* nach dem Tode in Wirkung tretend (*Law*). 2. *s.*; *--obit* (*bond*), nach dem Tode fällig werdende Schuldschein. **-pone,** *see* **postpone. -po'sition,** *s.* die Nachstellung; nachgestellte Präposition (*Gram.*). **-'positive,** *adj.* nachgestellt (*Gram.*). **-'prandial,** *adj.* nach dem Mittagessen stattfindend; *-prandial nap*, das Nachmittagsschläfchen. **'-script,** *s.* die Nachschrift. **--'war,** *adj.* Nachkriegs-.

poster ['poʊstə], *s.* das Plakat, der Anschlag; *bill*--, der Plakatankleber.

poste restante, *see under* **³post.**

poster-ior [pɔs'tɪːərɪə], 1. *adj.* später, hinter, Hinter-; *be -ior to*, später sein als, folgen auf (*Acc.*). 2. *s.* der Hintere, das Hinterteil. **-iority** [-rɪ'ɔrɪtɪ], *s.* das Spätersein, späteres Eintreten. **-ity** [-'tɛrɪtɪ], *s.* die Nachkommenschaft; Nachwelt.

postern ['pɔstən], *s.* (also – *gate*) die Hintertür, Seitentür, Nebentür.

posthumous ['pɔstjuməs], *adj.* nachgeboren, hinterlassen, nachgelassen, postum (*as writings*); nach dem Tode; – *child*, nach dem Tode des Vaters geborenes Kind; – *fame*, der Nachruhm.

postiche [pɔs'tɪːʃ], *s.* der Ersatz, die Imitation.

postil ['pɔstɪl], *s.* die Randbemerkung (*Hist.*).

postilion, *see under* **³post.**

postliminy [poʊst'lɪmɪnɪ], *s.* die Wiederherstellung des früheren Rechtzustandes, Wiedergewinnung der Rechte.

postpone [poʊs'poʊn], *v.a.* aufschieben, verschieben, hinausschieben; nachstellen, zurückstellen, unterordnen (*to* (*Dat.*)). **-ment,** *s.* der Aufschub, die Verschiebung, Zurückstellung.

postul-ant ['pɔstjulənt], *s.* der Bewerber (um Aufnahme in einen religiösen Order) (*Eccl.*).

postul-ate ['pɔstjuleɪt], 1. *s.* das Postulat, die Forderung, Grundvoraussetzung (*Log.*). 2. *v.a.* fordern; (als gegeben) voraussetzen. **-ation** [-'leɪʃən], *s.* das Gesuch, die Forderung; unentbehrliche Annahme.

posture ['pɔstʃə], 1. *s.* körperliche Haltung, die Positur, Stellung; der Zustand, die Lage. 2. *v.n.* sich stellen, posieren, figurieren, auftreten. 3. *v.a.* in eine bestimmte Lage stellen (lassen). **--maker,** *s.* der Akrobat.

posy ['poʊzɪ], *s.* der Blumenstrauß; (*archaic*) Denkspruch.

pot [pɔt], 1. *s.* der Topf, Kessel; Krug, die Kanne (*as measure*); der (Schmalz)Tiegel, (*coll.*) Nachttopf; (*sl.*) großer Wetteinsatz, große Summe (Geldes); der Preispokal; Schuß. *chimney*--, die Kaminkappe; (*coll.*) der Zylinderhut; *glue*--, der Leimtiegel; *ink*--, das Tintenfaß; (*sl.*) *big* –, großes Tier; (*Prov.*) *the – calls the kettle black*, ein Esel schimpft den andern Langohr; (*sl.*) *he has -s of money*, er sitzt im Fett *or* hat Geld wie Heu; *keep the – boiling*, die Sache in Gang halten; (*sl.*) *go to* –, auf den Hund kommen, zugrunde gehen, fehlschlagen; (*sl.*) *take a – at*, schießen auf *or* nach. 2. *v.a.* in einen Topf tun; in Töpfe setzen (*plants*); einmachen (*meat, etc.*); (nieder)schießen; *-ted meat*, Fleischkonserven. 3. *v.n.* schießen (*at*, auf *or* nach). **-able** ['poʊtəbl], *adj.* (*coll.*) trinkbar. **-ash,** *see* **potash. -ation,** *s. see* **potation.** (*vulg.*) **--belly,** *s.* der Dickbauch. **--boiler,** *s.* die Brotarbeit, Lohnarbeit, das Schundwerk, der Wälzer. **--boy,** *s.* der Bierkellner. **--herb,** *s.* das Küchenkraut. **--hole,** *s.* das Schlagloch (*Motor.*); der Gletschertopf, die Gletschermühle, der Strudelkessel (*Geol.*); unterirdische Höhle. **--holing,** *s.* die Höhlenforschung. **--hook,** *s.* der Kesselhaken. **--house,** *s.* das Bierhaus, die Kneipe. **--hunter,** *s.* der Preisjäger. (*coll.*) **– luck,** *s.*; *take – luck*, fürliebnehmen mit dem, was es gerade (zu essen) gibt. **-man,** *see* **--boy. --pourri,** *s. see* **potpourri. --roast,** *s.* der Schmorbraten. **--scrubber,** *s.* der Topfschrubber. **-sherd,** *s. see* **potsherd. --shot,** *s.* der Zufallsschuß. **-tage,** *s. see* **pottage. -ter,** *s. see* **potter. --valiant,** *adj.* vom Trinken mutig.

potas-h ['pɔtæʃ], 1. *s.* die Pottasche, das Kali, die Kaliumverbindung, das Kaliumkarbonat; Kalidünger (*Agr.*); *bicarbonate of -h*, das Kaliumantimonyltartrat; *caustic -h*, das Ätzkali, Kalihydrat, Kaliumhydroxyd; *caustic -h solution*, die Kalilauge. **-sium** [pə'tæsɪəm], *s.* das Kalium; *-sium bicarbonate*, doppelkohlensaures Kalium; *-sium bromide*, das Bromkali (*Phot.*); *-sium carbonate*, das Kaliumkarbonat, kohlensaures Kali, die Pottasche; *-sium permanganate*, übermangansaures Kalium.

potation [pə'teɪʃən], *s.* (*often pl.*) der Trunk, das Zechen.

potato [pə'teɪtoʊ], *s.* (pl. *-es*) die Kartoffel; **--blight, -disease, --rot,** *s.* die Kartoffelkrankheit.

poteen [pəˈtɪ:n], *s.* (heimlich gebrannter) irischer Whisky.

poten-cy [ˈpoʊtənsɪ], *s.* die Macht, Stärke; Wirksamkeit, Kraft; (*fig.*) der Einfluß, Durchschlagskraft, die Gewalt. **-t** [-ənt], *adj.* mächtig, stark, wirksam, einflußreich, durchschlagend, gewaltig, zwingend, überzeugend. **-tate** [-ənteɪt], *s.* der Machthaber, Herrscher. **-tial** [pəˈtɛnʃəl], 1. *adj.* möglich, denkbar, latent, potentiell (*Phys.*); *-tial energy*, latente Kraft, die Energie der Lage (*Phys.*). 2. *s.* die Möglichkeit; Spannung, das Potential (*Elec.*); *-tial difference*, die Potentialdifferenz, der Spannungsabstand. **-tiality** [-ʃɪˈælɪtɪ], *s.* die Möglichkeit, Macht; innere Kraft. **-tiometer,** *s.* das Potentiometer, der Spannungsteiler (*Elec.*).

potheen, *see* **poteen.**

pother [ˈpɔðə], 1. *s.* der Lärm, die Aufregung; Rauch, Dunst. 2. *v.n.* viel Aufhebens machen (*about*, um). 3. *v.a.* verwirren, belästigen.

potion [ˈpoʊʃən], *s.* der (Arznei)Trank.

potpourri [poʊˈpu:rɪ], *s.* wohlriechende Kräuter; das Potpourri (*Mus.*).

potsherd [ˈpɔtʃə:d], *s.* (*archaic*) die Scherbe.

pottage [ˈpɔtɪdʒ], (*archaic*) die Suppe.

[1]**potter** [ˈpɔtə], *s.* der Töpfer; *-'s clay*, der Töpferton; *-'s wheel*, die Töpferscheibe. **-y** [-rɪ], *s.* die Töpferei; Töpferwaren, Tonwaren, Steinwaren (*pl.*) das Steingeschirr.

[2]**potter** [ˈpɔtə], 1. *v.n.* (also – *about*) herumbummeln, herumlungern. 2. *v.a.*; – *away*, vertrödeln, vertandeln (*one's time*).

pottle [ˈpɔtl], *s.* (*archaic*) der Maßkrug (*etwa 2, 3 liter*); das Obstkörbchen.

potty [ˈpɔtɪ], *adj.* (*sl.*) verrückt (*about*, über), vernarrt (*about*, in); unbedeutend.

pouch [paʊtʃ], 1. *s.* die Tasche, der Beutel, die Patronentasche (*Mil.*), der Tabaksbeutel. 2. *v.a.* in die Tasche stecken, einstecken; bauschen. 3. *v.n.* sich bauschen. **-ed** [-t], *adj.* Beutel-.

pouf, -fe [pu:f], *s.* rundes Sitzkissen.

poult-erer [ˈpoʊltərə], *s.* der Geflügelhändler. **-ry** [trɪ], *s.* das Geflügel, Federvieh. **-ry-market,** *s.* der Geflügelmarkt. **-ry-yard,** *s.* der Hühnerhof.

poultice [ˈpoʊltɪs], 1. *s.* heißer Breiumschlag. 2. *v.a.* einen Breiumschlag auflegen (*auf* (*Acc.*)).

[1]**pounce** [paʊns], 1. *s.* (*archaic*) die Klaue, Kralle; das Herabschießen, Losstürzen (*upon*, auf (*Acc.*)). (*coll.*) *be on the* –, sprungbereit sein; *make a* – *upon*, herfallen über. 2. *v.n.* springen, stürzen (*at*, auf); – *upon*, herabschießen auf (*Acc.*); (*fig.*) sich stürzen auf (*Acc.*), herfallen über (*Acc.*).

[2]**pounce** [paʊns], 1. *s.* das Bimssteinpulver. 2. *v.a.* mit Bimsstein abreiben, bimsen; durchpausen. **-d,** *adj.* nach einem Muster durchlöchert.

[1]**pound** [paʊnd], *s.* das Pfund (*weight and money*); – *avoirdupois*, englisches Handelspfund (= *453·6g.*); – *troy*, das Apothekerpfund (= *373·25 g.*); – *sterling*, das Pfund Sterling; *five* – *ten*, 5 Pfund und 10 Schilling; *four -s of sugar*, vier Pfund Zucker; *two shillings a* –, zwei Schilling das Pfund; *two shillings in the* –, zehn Prozent; *pay twenty shillings in the* –, voll bezahlen. **-age** [-ɪdʒ], *s.* die Bezahlung pro Pfund Gewicht, die Provision der Pfund (*C.L.*). **-er** [-ə], *suffix*, der -pfünder.

[2]**pound** [paʊnd], 1. *s.* die Hürde, der Pfandstall. 2. *v.a.* einpferchen, einsperren.

[3]**pound** [paʊnd], 1. *v.a.* zerstoßen, zerstampfen, schlagen, hämmern, hämmern *or* trommeln auf. 2. *v.n.* losschlagen, loshämmern (*at* or *on*, auf); – *along*, stampfen, wuchtig einhergehen; – *away*, drauflosfeuern. **-er,** *s.* der Stößel.

pour [pɔ:], 1. *v.a.* gießen, schütten (*from* or *out of*, aus; *into*, in (*Acc.*); *on*, auf (*Acc.*)); – *oil on the flame*, Öl ins Feuer gießen; – *oil upon troubled waters*, Öl auf die Wogen gießen *or* schütten, die Wogen glätten; – *cold water on a p.*, einem einen Dämpfer aufsetzen; – *forth*, schleudern, aussenden, hervorstoßen. – *off*, abgießen; – *out*, einschenken, eingießen, ausschütten, ausgießen (*one's heart, grief, etc.*). 2. *v.n.* strömen, fließen, gießen, sich ergießen (*from*, aus); – *with rain*, in Strömen gießen; *it never rains but it -s*, ein Unglück kommt selten allein. (*a*) (*with prepositions*) – *down*, herabfließen; – *into*, strömen in (*Acc.*), sich ergießen in (*Acc.*). (*b*) (*with adverbs*). – *down*, niederströmen; – *in*, in Mengen einlaufen; – *in upon*, sich ergießen auf, hereinströmen auf; – *out*, herausströmen; – *over*, überfließen. 3. *s.* der Guß (*Found.*). **-ing** [-rɪŋ], 1. *adj.* strömend (*rain*). 2. *s.* das Strömen, Fließen.

pourboire [pu:əˈbwɑ:], *s.* das Trinkgeld.

pourparler [ˈpu:əpɑ:ˈleɪ], *s.* die Besprechung.

pout [paʊt], 1. *v.n.* schmollen, die Lippen spitzen, vorstehen (*of lips*). 2. *v.a.* aufwerfen, spitzen (*lips*). 3. *s.* das Schmollen. **-er,** *s.*, **-er-pigeon,** *s.* die Kropftaube.

poverty [ˈpɔvətɪ], *s.* die Armut; (*fig.*) Dürftigkeit (*of* (*Gen.*)), der Mangel (*of*, an). **--stricken,** *adj.* verarmt; (*fig.*) armselig.

powder [ˈpaʊdə], 1. *s.* der Staub, das Pulver, der Puder; *grind to* –, pulverisieren; *not worth* – *and shot*, keinen Schuß Pulver wert; *the smell of* –, die Kriegserfahrung. 2. *v.a.* zerreiben, pulverisieren; pudern (*the face*), bestreuen, bepudern (*with*, mit); *-ed milk*, die Trockenmilch; *-ed sugar*, der Puderzucker. **--magazine,** *s.* das Pulvermagazin, (*fig.*) Pulverfaß. **--mill,** *s.* die Pulverfabrik. **--puff,** *s.* die Puderquaste. **--train,** der Pulversatz. **-y** [-rɪ], *adj.* staubig, pulverig, pulverartig; zerreibbar; *-y snow*, der Pulverschnee.

power [ˈpaʊə], *s.* das Vermögen, die Macht, Fähigkeit, Kraft, Energie; Gewalt, Herrschaft; der Einfluß (*over*, über); die Potenz (*Math.*), der Starkstrom (*Elec.*); die Stärke, Vergrößerungskraft (*Opt.*); Vollmacht, Ermächtigung, Befugnis (*Law*); die Leistung (*of a machine*); Sendestärke, Sendeleistung (*Rad.*); (*coll.*) *a* – *of*, eine Masse *or* große Menge von; *balance of* –, das Gleichgewicht der Kräfte (*Pol.*); *the -s that be*, die maßgebenden Stellen. (*a*) (*with nouns*) – *of attorney*, die Vollmacht; *-s of description*, das Talent zur Beschreibung; *-s of the mind*, Geisteskräfte; – *of resistance*, die Widerstandskraft. (*b*) (*with attrib.*) *belligerent -s*, kriegführende Mächte; *brake* –, die Bremsleistung; *discretionary* –, die Vollmacht beliebig zu handeln; *effective* –, die Nutzkraft; *great European -s*, europäische Großmächte; *full -s*, die Vollmacht; *horse--*, die Pferdekraft, Pferdestärke; *mechanical* –, mechanische Kraft; *military* –, die Kriegsmacht; *penetrating* –, die Durchschlagskraft; *plenary -s*, unumschränkte Vollmacht; *rated* –, die Nennleistung; *reasoning* –, die Urteilskraft; *sea* –, die Seemacht; *steam* –, die Dampfkraft; *water* –, die Wasserkraft. (*c*) (*with prepositions*) *in* –, an der Macht, am Ruder; *in his* –, in seiner Gewalt; *do all in one's* –, alles tun, was in seiner Kraft *or* Macht steht; *come into* –, zur Macht gelangen *or* kommen; *out of one's* –, außer seiner Macht; *raise to the fourth* –, in die vierte Potenz erheben (*Math.*). **--cable,** *s.* die Starkstromleitung. **--circuit,** *s.* der Kraftstromkreis. **--current,** *s.* der Starkstrom. **--driven,** *see* **--operated.** **-factor,** *s.* der Leistungsfaktor. **-ful,** *adj.* stark, kräftig, mächtig, einflußreich, leistungsfähig, wirksam. **--house,** *s. see* **--station.** **-less,** *adj.* kraftlos, machtlos, hilflos, unfähig, ohnmächtig. **-lessness,** *s.* die Machtlosigkeit, Ohnmacht. **--load,** *s.* der Kraftstrom. **--loom,** *s.* mechanischer Webstuhl. **--loving,** *adj.* machtliebend. **--operated,** *adj.* kraftgetrieben. **--plant,** *s.* die Kraftanlage. **--politics,** *pl.* die Machtpolitik. **--shovel,** *s.* die Löffelbagger. **--station,** *s.* das Kraftwerk, Elektrizitätswerk. **--supply,** *s.* die Kraftversorgung, Stromversorgung (*Elec.*), der Netzanschluß (*Rad.*). **--unit,** *s.* das Triebwerk. **--valve,** *s.* die Lautsprecherröhre (*Rad.*). **--winch,** *s.* die Kraftwinde.

pow-wow [ˈpaʊwaʊ], 1. *s.* indianischer Medizinmann; die Krankheitsbeschwörung; (*coll.*) Besprechung. 2. *v.n.* (*coll.*) besprechen, debattieren. 3. *v.a.* beschwören (*an illness*).

pox [pɔks], 1. *pl.* (*sing. constr.*) die Pocken; (*coll.*) die Syphilis.

practicab-ility [præktɪkəˈbɪlɪtɪ], *s.* die Durchführbarkeit, Ausführbarkeit, Tunlichkeit. **-le** [ˈpræktɪkəbl], *adj.* ausführbar, möglich, tunlich; wegsam, gangbar, fahrbar (*of roads*); brauchbar.

practical [ˈpræktɪkl], *adj.* tatsächlich, wirklich, faktisch; praktisch *or* in der Praxis tätig, ausübend;

erfahren, für die Praxis geeignet (*of p.*), praktisch, praktisch angewandt, praktisch anwendbar, ausführbar, zweckmäßig, brauchbar, möglich; – *chemistry*, angewandte Chemie; – *joke*, der Jux, handgreiflicher Spaß, grober Scherz; – *joker*, der Spaßvogel; – *man*, der Mann der Praxis; – *politics*, das (politisch) Erreichbare. **–ity** [–ˈkælɪtɪ], *s. see* **–ness. –ly,** *adv.* sachdienlich; praktisch, faktisch, nahezu, so gut wie. **–ness,** *s.* das Praktische, die Tunlichkeit.

practic–e [ˈpræktɪs], *s.* die Praxis (*also Law, Med.*), Verfahrungsweise, Gewohnheit, der Brauch, übliches Verfahren; praktische Tätigkeit, die Ausübung, Kundschaft (*Law, Med.*), die Übung (*Mus., etc., Mil.*); Welsche Praktik (*Arith.*); *pl.* Praktiken, Ränke, Kniffe, Schliche (*pl.*); (*Prov.*) *–e makes perfect*, Übung macht den Meister; *in –e*, in der Praxis, wirklich, tatsächlich; in der Übung; *make a –e of*, es sich (*Dat.*) zur Gewohnheit machen; *put into –e*, in die Praxis umsetzen, praktisch anwenden, ausführen, verwirklichen. **–e-ammunition,** *s.* die Übungsmunition. **–e-ground,** *s.* der Übungsplatz. **–ian** [–ˈtɪʃən], *s.* der Praktiker, praktischer Mensch.

practise [ˈpræktɪs], 1. *v.a.* in die Praxis umsetzen, ausführen, ausüben (*a profession, etc.*); ausbilden, drillen (*a p.*); sich üben in, üben, einüben (*piece of music, etc.*). 2. *v.n.* sich üben, sich einspielen (*esp. Mus.*), ausüben, praktizieren; – *at the bar*, als Rechtsanwalt praktizieren; – *upon*, hintergehen, zu besten haben. **–d,** *adj.* geübt, geschult (*in*, in).

practitioner [prækˈtɪʃənə], *s.* der Praktiker; Rechtsanwalt; *general* or *medical* –, praktischer Arzt.

prae–cipe [ˈprɪːsɪpɪ], *s.* die Aufforderung, der Befehl (*Law*). **–munire** [prɪːmjuːˈnɪːərɪ], *s.* die Vorladung, wegen Überschreitung der Kirchengewalt (*Law*). **–poster** (also *preposter*) [prɪˈpɔstə], *s.* see **prefect. –tor** [ˈprɪːtə], *s.* der Prätor. **–torian** [prɪˈtɔːrɪən], prätorisch.

pragmati–c [prægˈmætɪk], *adj.* pragmatisch (*Phil.*); systematisch, sachlich, sachkundig; (*fig.*) nüchtern, praktisch, geschäftig, aufdringlich, vorwitzig, rechthaberisch; *–c sanction*, die Staatssanktion (*Hist.*). **–cal** [–l], *adj.* pragmatisch, praktisch, nüchtern; eingebildet, von sich eingenommen. **–sm** [ˈprægmətɪzm], *s.* der Pragmatismus. **–ze** [–taɪz], *v.a.* als real darstellen.

prairie [ˈprɛːərɪ], *s.* die Prärie, Steppe, Grasebene. **––dog,** *s.* der Präriehund.

praise [preɪz], 1. *s.* das Lob, die Anerkennung, der Preis; *in – of*, zum Lobe, zu Ehren; *be loud in one's –s*, des Lobes voll sein; *unstinted* –, uneingeschränktes Lob. 2. *v.a.* loben, rühmen; preisen, lobpreisen (*Eccl.*) (*for*, wegen); – *to the sky* or *skies*, in den Himmel erheben. **–worthiness,** *s.* die Preiswürdigkeit, Löblichkeit. **–worthy,** *adj.* lobenswert.

[1]**pram** [præm], *s.* der Prahm (*Naut.*).

[2]**pram** [præm], *s.* (*coll. for*) **perambulator.**

prance [prɑːns], *v.n.* sich bäumen (*as horses*); einherstolzieren, paradieren, sich brüsten.

prandial [ˈprændɪəl], *adj.* auf die Mahlzeit bezüglich.

prank [præŋk], 1. *s.* der Possen, Streich; *play –s on s.o.*, einem einen Streich spielen, einem übel mitspielen. 2. *v.a.*; – *up*, herausputzen, schmücken. 3. *v.n.* prunken.

prase [preɪz], *s.* der Pras, Prasem (*Min.*).

prat–e [preɪt], 1. *v.n.* schwatzen, plappern. 2. *v.a.* ausplappern. 3. *s.* das Geschwätz, Geplapper. **–er** [–ə], *s.* der Schwätzer. **–ing,** 1. *adj.* schwatzhaft, geschwätzig. 2. *s.* das Schwatzen, Geschwätz. **–tle** [ˈprætl], 1. *v.n.* (kindisch) schwatzen, plappern, plaudern. 2. *s.* das Geschwätz, Geplapper. **–tler** [–lə], *s.* der Schwätzer.

prawn [prɔːn], *s.* die Steingarnele (*Ichth.*).

pray [preɪ], 1. *v.n.* beten (*to*, zu; *for*, um); bitten (*for*, um); – *tell me* . . ., bitte, sagen Sie mir . . . . 2. *v.a.* (inständig) bitten, ersuchen (*for*, um) (*a p.*); erbitten, erflehen (*a th.*). **–er** [ˈprɛːə], *s.* das Gebet, die Andacht (*Eccl.*); Bitte; *at –er*, beim Gebet; *offer a –er*, ein Gebet verrichten; *put up a –er*, ein Gebet emporsenden; *say one's –ers*, beten, sein Gebet verrichten; *book of Common –er*, see **–er-book;** *Lord's –er*, das Vaterunser; *morning –ers*, die Morgenandacht. **–erful,** *adj.* andächtig, andachtsvoll; inständig. **–erless,** *adj.* ohne Gebet, gottlos. **–er-book,** *s.* das Gebetbuch, die Agende *or* Liturgie der anglikanischen Kirche.

preach [prɪːtʃ], 1. *v.n.* predigen (*to*, vor); (*fig.*) ermahnen, Moral predigen. 2. *v.a.* predigen; – *a sermon*, eine Predigt halten. **–er** [–ə], *s.* der Prediger. (*coll.*) **–ify,** *v.n.* salbadern. **–ing,** *s.* das Predigen. (*coll.*) **–ment,** *s.* langweilige Predigt, die Salbaderei. (*coll.*) **–y,** *adj.* salbungsvoll, moralisierend.

preamble [prɪːˈæmbl], *s.* die Einleitung; Vorrede (*Law*).

prearrange [prɪːəˈreɪndʒ], *v.a.* vorbereiten, vorher bestimmen. **–ment,** *s.* vorherige Bestimmung.

prebend [ˈprɛbənd], *s.* die Pfründe, Präbende (*Eccl.*). **–al** [–əl], *adj.* Pfründen–, Stifts–, Präbende–. **–ary** [–ərɪ], *s.* der Pfründner, Stiftsherr, Domherr.

precarious [prɪˈkɛːərɪəs], *adj.* widerruflich (*Law*); (*fig.*); unsicher, prekär, bedenklich, gefährlich. **–ness,** *s.* die Ungewißheit, Unsicherheit.

precatory [ˈprɛkətərɪ], *adj.* eine Bitte enthaltend, Bitt–.

precaution [prɪˈkɔːʃən], *s.* die Vorsicht, Vorsichtsmaßregel; *as a –*, der Vorsicht halber; *take –s*, Vorsichtsmaßregeln treffen. **–ary** [–ərɪ], *adj.* vorbeugend, Vorsichts–, Warnungs–; *–ary measures*, Vorsichtsmaßregeln.

preced–e [prɪˈsɪːd], 1. *v.a.* vorangehen, vorausgehen, vorgehen (*Dat.*), den Vortritt haben vor (*of persons*), vorhergehen, vorangehen, vorausgehen, den Vorrang haben von (*of things*); *–e hostilities by a declaration of war*, Feindseligkeiten (*Dat.*) eine Kriegserklärung vorausschicken, Feindseligkeiten (*Acc.*) durch eine Kriegserklärung einleiten *or* einführen. 2. *v.n.* vorangehen, vorausgehen, vorhergehen. **–ence,** *s.*, (*archaic*) **–ency,** *s.* [ˈprɛsɪdəns(ɪ), prɪˈsɪːdəns(ɪ)], das Vorhergehen, die Priorität, der Vortritt, Vorrang; das Dienstalter; *order of –ence*, die Rangordnung; *take –ence*, den Vortritt *or* Vorrang haben (*of* or *over*, vor); *yield –ence to*, den Vorrang einräumen (*Dat.*). **–ent** [ˈprɛsɪdənt, prɪˈsɪːdənt], 1. *adj.* (*archaic*) vorhergehend. 2. *s.* der Präzedenzfall (*Law, also fig.*), das Präzendenzurteil (*Law*); *create* or *set a –ent*, einen Präzedenzfall schaffen *or* abgeben; *without* (*a*) *–ent*, ohne Beispiel, noch nicht dagewesen. **–ing** [prɪˈsɪdɪŋ], 1. *adj.* vorhergehend. 2. *prep.* vor.

precentor [prɪˈsɛntə], *s.* der Vorsänger, Kantor (*Eccl.*).

precept [ˈprɪːsɛpt], *s.* die Vorschrift, Regel, Richtschnur, das Gebot; schriftlicher Befehl (*Law*); die Verordnung, Lehre, Unterweisung. **–ive** [prɪˈsɛptɪv], *adj.* verordnend; didaktisch, belehrend. **–or** [prɪˈsɛptə], *s.* der Lehrer, Erzieher.

precession [prɪˈsɛʃən], *s.* das Vorrücken (der Nachtgleichen) (*Astr.*).

precinct [ˈprɪːsɪnkt], *s.* die Umfriedung, der Domplatz; *pl.* (*fig.*) der Bereich, die Umgebung, Nachbarschaft; Grenzen (*pl.*).

precio–sity [prɛʃɪˈɔsɪtɪ], *s.* die Affektiertheit, Geziertheit. **–us** [ˈprɛʃəs], 1. *adj.* kostbar, edel (*stones, metals, etc.*); (*fig.*) wertvoll, unschätzbar (*to*, für); geziert, preziös; (*coll. iron.*) schön, nett, höchst, recht; (*coll.*) *–us scoundrel*, der Erzschurke; (*coll.*) *–us little*, verflucht wenig; *my –us*, mein Liebling; *–us stone*, der Edelstein. **–usness,** *s.* die Kostbarkeit; Affektiertheit.

precipi–ce [ˈprɛsɪpɪs], *s.* der Abgrund; *on the brink of a –ce*, am Rande des Abgrunds. **–table** [prɪˈsɪpɪtəbl], *adj.* fällbar, abscheidbar, niederschlagbar (*Chem.*). **–tance, –tancy** [prɪˈsɪpɪtəns(ɪ)], *s.* die Eile, Hast, Übereilung, Überstürzung. **–tant** [prɪˈsɪpɪtənt], 1. *s.* das Abscheidungsmittel, Fällmittel, Fällungsmittel (*Chem.*). 2. *adj.* übereilt. **–tate** [–ˈsɪpɪteɪt], 1. *v.a.* jäh hinabstürzen; (*fig.*) jäh versetzen, überstürzen, übereilen, beschleunigen, herbeiführen (*events*); niederschlagen, (aus)fällen (*Chem.*), verflüssigen (*of water vapour* (*Meteor.*)). 2. *v.n.* sich ablagern *or* absetzen, niedergeschlagen werden, ausfallen, ausscheiden. 3. [–pɪtət], *adj.* schleunig, hastig, plötzlich, jählings, unüberlegt, übereilt, überstürzt. 4. *s.* der Niederschlag, das Präzipitat. **–tateness** [–tətnɪs], *s.* die Überstürzung, Übereiltheit. **–tation** [–ˈteɪʃən], *s.* das Herabstürzen, der Sturz; die Hast, Übereilung, Überstürzung; Ablagerung, Abscheidung, (Aus)-Fällung, Präzipitation (*Chem.*); der Niederschlag (*Meteor.*). **–tous** [–təs], *adj.* jäh, steil; übereilt. **–tousness**, *s.* die Steilheit.

précis [ˈpreɪsɪ], *s.* gedrängte Darstellung, die Zusammenfassung, Übersicht, Inhaltsangabe, der Auszug.

precis–e [prɪˈsɑɪs], *adj.* bestimmt, genau, präzis, gewissenhaft; richtig, korrekt, steif, pedantisch, pünktlich, umständlich, peinlich. **–eness**, *s.* die Genauigkeit, ängstliche Gewissenhaftigkeit, Pedanterie, Pünktlichkeit. **–ian** [–ˈsɪʒən], *s.* der Rigorist, Pedant. **–ion** [–ˈsɪʒn], *s.* die Genauigkeit, Exaktheit, Präzision; *–ion instrument*, das Präzisionsinstrument.

preclu–de [prɪˈklu:d], *v.a.* ausschließen (*from*, von); zuvorkommen, vorbeugen (*Dat.*); hindern (*a p.*) (*from*, an). **–sion** [–ˈklu:ʒən], *s.* die Ausschließung, der Ausschluß (*from*, von), die Verhinderung. **–sive** [–ˈklu:sɪv], *adj.* ausschließend.

precoci–ous [prɪˈkoʊʃəs], *adj.* frühreif (*also of p.*), frühzeitig; altklug (*of p.*). **–ousness**, *s.*, **–ty** [–ˈkɔsɪtɪ], *s.* die Frühzeitigkeit, Frühreife.

precognition [prɪ:kəgˈnɪʃən], *s.* die Vorkenntnis; Voruntersuchung (*Scots Law*).

preconce–ive [prɪ:kənˈsɪ:v], *v.a.* sich (*Dat.*) vorher ausdenken *or* vorstellen. **–ived**, *adj.* vorgefaßt (*opinion*). **–ption** [–ˈsɛpʃən], *s.* vorgefaßte Meinung, das Vorurteil.

preconcert [prɪ:kənˈsə:t], *v.a.* vorher verabreden *or* abmachen.

preconize [ˈprɪ:kənɑɪz], *v.a.* öffentlich verkünden *or* (*R.C.*) bestätigen (*appointment*).

precursor [prɪˈkə:sə], *s.* der Vorläufer, Vorgänger, Vorbote. **–y** [–rɪ], *adj.* vorbereitend, einleitend.

preda–cious [prɪˈdeɪʃəs], *adj.* vom Raube lebend, Raub(tier)–. **–tory** [ˈprɛdətərɪ], *adj.* plündernd; räuberisch, Räuber–, Raub–.

predate [ˈprɪ:ˈdeɪt], *v.a.* vordatieren.

predece–ase [prɪ:dɪˈsɪs], *v.a.* früher sterben als, vorher sterben. **–ssor** [ˈprɪ:dɪsɛsə], *s.* der Vorgänger, *pl.* Vorfahren, Ahnen (*pl.*).

predestin–ate, 1. [prɪˈdɛstineɪt], *v.a.* (vorher)-bestimmen, auserwählen, ausersehen, prädestinieren. 2. [–nət], *adj.* auserwählt, prädestiniert. **–ation** [–ˈneɪʃən], *s.* die Vorherbestimmung; Gnadenwahl, Prädestination (*Theol.*). **–e** [prɪˈdɛstɪn], *v.a.* vorherbestimmen, auserwählen, ausersehen.

predetermin–able [prɪ:dɪˈtə:mɪnəbl], *adj.* vorherbestimmbar. **–ate** [–mɪnət], *adj.* vorherbestimmt. **–ation** [–ˈneɪʃən], *s.* die Vorherbestimmung. **–e** [–ˈtə:mɪn], *v.a.* vorherbestimmen, vorher festsetzen.

predial [ˈprɪ:dɪəl], *adj.* Land–, Grund–, Guts–, Prädial– (*Law*).

predica–ble [ˈprɛdɪkəbl], *adj.* aussagbar, belegbar. **–bles** [–blz], *pl.* Prädikabilien, Prädikate, Allgemeinbegriffe (*pl.*) (*Log.*). **–ment** [prɪˈdɪkəmənt], *s.* die Kategorie (*Log.*); (*fig.*) schlimme *or* mißliche Lage. **–te**, 1. [ˈprɛdɪkeɪt], *v.a.* aussagen, behaupten; prädizieren (*Log.*). 2. [–kət], *s.* das Prädikat, die Aussage (*Gram. & Log.*). **–tion** [–ˈkeɪʃən], *s.* die Aussage, Behauptung (*Log.*). **–tive** [prɪˈdɪkətɪv], *adj.* prädikativ (*Gram.*), aussagend, Aussage–.

predict [prɪˈdɪkt], *v.a.* vorhersagen, weissagen, prophezeien. **–able** [–əbl], *adj.* vorhersagbar. **–ion** [–ˈdɪkʃən], *s.* die Vorhersage, Weissagung, Prophezeiung. **–or** [–ˈdɪktə], *s.* der Vorhersager, Prophet; das Zielrechengerät (*Artil.*), Kommandogerät (*Av.*).

predilection [prɪ:dɪˈlɛkʃən], *s.* die Vorliebe, Voreingenommenheit (*for*, für).

predispos–e [prɪ:dɪsˈpoʊz], *v.a.* im voraus geneigt machen (*to*, zu *or* für); empfänglich machen, einnehmen, prädisponieren (*to*, für). **–ition** [–pəˈzɪʃən], *s.* die Geneigtheit, Neigung (*to*, zu), Empfänglichkeit (*Med. & fig.*) (*to*, für).

predomina–nce [prɪˈdɔmɪnəns], *s.* das Vorwiegen, Vorherrschen (*in*, in), Übergewicht. **–nt** [–ənt], *adj.* vorherrschend, vorwiegend, überwiegend, überlegen; *be –nt*, vorherrschen, vorwiegen, überwiegen. **–te** [–eɪt], *v.n.* vorherrschen, vorwiegen, überwiegen, das Übergewicht *or* die Herrschaft haben (*over*, über). **–ting** [–eɪtɪŋ], *adj.* vorherrschend, vorwiegend, überwiegend.

pre––eminen–ce [prɪ:ˈɛmɪnəns], *s.* der Vorrang (*above*, vor), die Überlegenheit (*over*, über), der Vorzug, überlegene Stellung. **–t** [–ənt], *adj.* hervorragend; *be –t*, hervorragen, sich hervortun (*among*, unter).

pre––empt [prɪ:ˈɛmpt], *v.a.* durch Vorkaufsrecht erwerben. **–ion** [–ˈɛmpʃən], *s.* der Vorkauf; das Vorkaufsrecht (*Amer.*). **–ive** [–ˈɛmptɪv], *adj.* Vorkaufs–.

preen [prɪ:n], *v.a.* putzen (*feather*) (*of birds*); – *o.s.*, sich putzen (*of birds*); (*fig.*) sich brüsten (*on*, mit), sich einbilden (*on*, auf).

pre––engage [prɪ:ɪnˈgeɪdʒ], *v.a.* im voraus verpflichten (*a p.*), vorherbestellen (*a th.*). **–ment**, *s.* vorher eingegangene Verbindlichkeit, das vorhergegangene Versprechen, vorherige Verpflichtung *or* Bestellung, die Vorherbestellung.

pre––exist [prɪ:ɪgˈzɪst], *v.n.* vorher vorhanden *or* da sein, früher existieren, präexistieren (*of the soul*). **–ence**, *s.* früheres Vorhandensein *or* Dasein, die Präexistenz. **–ent**, *adj.* früher vorhanden, vorher-existierend.

prefab [ˈprɪ:fæb], *s.* (*coll.*) das Fertighaus. **–ricate** [–ˈfæbrɪkeɪt], *v.a.* vorfabrizieren.

prefa–ce [ˈprɛfəs], 1. *s.* die Vorrede, Einleitung, das Vorwort. 2. *v.a.* einleiten, mit einer Vorrede versehen, einleiten (*by* or *with*, mit). **–tory** [–tərɪ], *adj.* einleitend, Einleitungs–; *–tory note*, die Vorbemerkung, das Vorwort.

prefect [ˈprɪfɛkt], *s.* der Präfekt (*Pol.*), Aufsichtsschüler, Vertrauensschüler; – *of police*, der Polizeipräsident (*of Paris*); – *system*, die Schuldisziplin, wobei die Verantwortung älteren Schülern übergeben wird. **–ure** [–fɛktʃə], *s.* die Präfektur.

prefer [prɪˈfə:], *v.a.* vorbringen, einreichen (*to*, bei) (*complaint*, *request*, *etc.*); erheben, befördern (*to*, zu); vorziehen (*to* (*Dat.*)), bevorzugen; – *to do*, lieber tun; – *it done*, lieber haben *or* sehen, daß es getan wird; *–red stock*, Prioritätsaktien, Vorzugsaktien (*pl.*). **–able** [ˈprɛfərəbl], *adj.* (*usually predic.*) vorzuziehen(d) (*to* (*Dat.*)), wünschenswerter, vorzüglicher (*to*, als). **–ably**, *adv.* lieber, am liebsten *or* besten. **–ence** [ˈprɛfərəns], *s.* der Vorzug, die Bevorzugung, der Vorrang (*to*, vor); die Vorliebe (*for*, für); der Vorzugstarif, Begünstigungstarif; *by –ence*, mit (besonderer) Vorliebe; *do from –ence*, vorziehen zu tun, mit Vorliebe tun, vorzugsweise tun; *give –ence to*, den Vorzug geben (*Dat.*), vorziehen, bevorzugen; *in –ence to*, lieber als; *–ence stock*, die Vorzugsaktien (*pl.*). **–ential** [prɛfəˈrɛnʃəl], *adj.* bevorzugt, bevorrechtet, Vorzugs–; *–ential duty*, der Begünstigungszoll. **–entially**, *adv.* vorzugsweise. **–ment** [prɪˈfə:mənt], *s.* die Beförderung (*to*, zu); das Ehrenamt (*Eccl.*).

prefigur–ation [ˈprɪfɪgəˈreɪʃən], *s.* vorherige Darstellung; das Urbild, Vorbild. **–e** [–ˈfɪgə], *v.a.* vorher darstellen, vorbilden; vorbildlich darstellen.

prefix [ˈprɪ:fɪks], 1. *v.a.* vor(an)setzen (*to* (*Dat.*)), hinzufügen (*to*, zu), vorausgehen lassen. 2. *s.* die Vorsilbe, das Präfix (*Gram.*).

pregnan–cy [ˈprɛgnənsɪ], *s.* die Schwangerschaft (*of women*); Trächtigkeit (*of animals*); (*fig.*) Gedankenfülle, Bedeutungsschwere, der Bedeutungsgehalt, die Schöpferkraft. **–t** [–ənt], *adj.* schwanger (*of women*); trächtig (*of animals*); (*fig.*) bedeutungsvoll, gewichtig, schwerwiegend, bedeutsam, prägnant, gedankenreich, schwer, voll (*with*, von), reich (*with*, an (*Dat.*)).

preheat [ˈprɪ:ˈhɪ:t], *v.a.* vorwärmen, anwärmen.

prehensi–le [prɪˈhɛnsɑɪl], *adj.* Greif–, zum Greifen geeignet. **–lity** [–ˈsɪlɪtɪ], *s.* die Greifkraft. **–on** [–ʃən], *s.* das Greifen, (*fig.*) Erfassen.

prehistor–ic [prɪ:hɪsˈtɔrɪk], *adj.* vorgeschichtlich, urgeschichtlich, prähistorisch. **–y** [prɪ:ˈhɪstərɪ], *s.* die Vorgeschichte, Urgeschichte.

prejudge [prɪ:ˈdʒʌdʒ], *v.a.* im voraus, vorher *or* zu früh urteilen über *or* entscheiden.

prejudic–e [ˈprɛdʒʊdɪs], 1. *s.* das Vorurteil, die Voreingenommenheit; der Schaden, Nachteil, Abbruch. *have a –e against*, ein Vorurteil haben gegen; *to the –e of*, zum Nachteil von; *without –e*, ohne Verbindlichkeit *or* Nachteil, unter Vorbehalt; *without –e to*, unbeschadet (*Dat.*). 2. *v.a.* beeinträchtigen, schädigen; Abbruch tun (*Dat.*), einnehmen, beeinflussen (*against*, gegen; *in favour of*, für); mit einem Vorurteil erfüllen. **–ed** [–t], *adj.* voreingenommen. **–ial** [prɛdʒʊˈdɪʃəl], *adj.* schädlich, nachteilig (*to*, für).
prela–cy [ˈprɛləsɪ], *s.* die Prälatenwürde; (*collect.*) Prälaten (*pl.*). **–te,** *s.* der Prälat. **–tic(al)** [–ˈlætɪk(l)], *adj.* Prälaten–, bischöflich.
prelect [prɪˈlɛkt], *v.n.* Vortrag halten (*on*, über; *to*, vor); lesen (*Univ.*). **–ion** [–kʃən], *s.* die Vorlesung. **–or,** *s.* der Dozent.
preliminary [prɪˈlɪmɪnərɪ], 1. *adj.* vorläufig, einleitend, vorbereitend, Vor–; – *advice*, die Voranzeige; – *estimate*, der Voranschlag; – *examination*, die Aufnahmeprüfung (*Univ.*), das Physikum (*Med.*); – *inquiry*, die Voruntersuchung (*Law*); – *round*, das Vorrundespiel (*Sport*); – *steps*, vorbereitende Schritte. 2. *s.* (*usually pl.*) die Einleitung, Vorbereitung, Vorbereitungen, Vorverhandlungen, erste Schritte, Präliminarien (*pl.*).
prelude 1. [ˈprɛːljuːd], *s.* das Präludium (*Mus.*), Vorspiel, die Enleitung. 2. [ˈprɛːljuːd, prɪˈljuːd], *v.a.* einleiten. 3. *v.n.* präludieren (*Mus.*); als Einleitung dienen (*Dat.*).
prematur–e [ˈprɛmətjʊə], *adj.* frühzeitig, frühreif; vorzeitig, verfrüht, unzeitig; voreilig, vorschnell; *–e birth*, die Frühgeburt; *–e burst*, der Frühsprenger (*Artil.*); *–e ignition*, die Frühzündung (*Motor.*). **–eness,** *s.* **–ity** [–ˈtjuːərɪtɪ], *s.* die Frühreife, Frühzeitigkeit, Vorzeitigkeit; die Voreiligkeit, Übereiltheit.
premeditat–e [prɪˈmɛdɪteɪt], *v.a.* vorher überlegen, bedenken *or* ausdenken. **–ed,** *adj.* vorbedacht, vorsätzlich, mit Vorbedacht. **–ion** [–ˈteɪʃən], *s.* der Vorbedacht.
premier [ˈprɪːmɪə, ˈprɛmɪə], 1. *adj.* erste(–r, –s). 2. *s.* der Premierminister. **–ship,** *s.* das Amt des Premierministers.
première [prəmɪˈɛːə], *s.* die Premiere (*Theat.*).
premis–e [ˈprɛmɪs], 1. *v.a.* vorausschicken; vorher erwähnen. 2. *s.* die Prämisse, der Vordersatz (*Log.*), die Voraussetzung. **–es** [–ɪsɪz], *pl.* das Haus nebst Zugehör; Grundstück; das Obenerwähnte, obenerwähntes Grundstück (*Law*); *on the –es*, im Hause; am Schankort; an Ort und Stelle. **–s** [ˈprɛmɪs], *s.* die Prämisse, der Vordersatz (*Log.*).
premium [ˈprɪːmɪəm], *s.* die Prämie, Belohnung, der Preis; das Agio, Aufgeld, die Extradividende; die Versicherungsprämie (*C.L.*); das Lehrgeld (eines Lehrlings); *be at a –*, über Pari stehen (*C.L.*); (*fig.*) hoch im Kurse stehen, nur für teures Geld zu haben sein, sehr gesucht *or* geschätzt sein; *sell at a –*, mit Gewinn verkaufen.
premonit–ion [prɪːməˈnɪʃən], *s.* die Warnung, Vorahnung, das Vorgefühl. **–ory** [prɪˈmɔnɪtərɪ], *adj.* warnend, anzeigend.
prenatal [prɪːˈneɪtl], *adj.* vorgeburtlich, vor der Geburt eintretend.
prentice [ˈprɛntɪs], *s.* (*archaic*) *see* **apprentice.**
preoccup–ancy [prɪːˈɔkjʊpənsɪ], *s.* (das Recht der) vorherige(n) Besitznahme, die Inanspruchnahme; das Beschäftigtsein (*in*, mit). **–ation** [–ˈpeɪʃən], *s.* das Vorurteil, die Voreingenommenheit; Hauptttätigkeit; Befangenheit, Zerstreutheit; *see also* **–ancy.** **–y** [–ˈɔkjʊpaɪ], *v.a.* vorher *or* vor einem andern in Besitz nehmen, vorwegnehmen, ganz in Anspruch nehmen, ausschließlich beschäftigen; *be –ied*, ganz in Anspruch genommen sein; zerstreut, geistesabwesend *or* in Gedanken sein.
preordain [prɪːɔːˈdeɪn], *v.a.* vorher bestimmen *or* anordnen.
prep [prɛp], *s.* (*sl.*) das Vorbereiten (*of lessons*); die Vorschule, Vorbereitungsschule.
prepaid [prɪˈpeɪd], *adj.* voraus bezahlt, portofrei, frankiert; *see* **prepay.**
prepar–ation [prɛpəˈreɪʃən], *s.* die Vorbereitung, Bereitstellung, Zubereitung (*of food, etc.*), Herstellung, Anfertigung, Aufbereitung (*of ores, etc.*); das Präparat, Arzneimittel; Präparieren, Vorbereiten (*of lessons*). **–ative** [prɪˈpærətɪv], 1. *adj. see* **–atory.** 2. *s.* die Vorbereitung (*for*, auf *or* für), vorbereitender Schritt (*to*, zu). **–atory** [prɪˈpærətərɪ], *adj.* vorbereitend, Vorbereitungs–, Vor–; *–atory department*, die Vorschule; *–atory exercise*, die Vorübung; *–atory school*, die Vorbereitungsschule; *–atory work*, Vorarbeiten (*pl.*); *be –atory to*, vorbereiten; *–atory to his departure*, vor seiner Abreise; *–atory to departing*, bevor (er, *etc.*) abreiste. **–e** [prɪˈpɛːə], 1. *v.a.* vorbereiten (*for*, für, zu *or* auf), geeignet *or* geneigt machen (*for*, zu), gefaßt machen (*for*, auf); ausrüsten, ausbilden (*for*, für), herstellen, (zu)bereiten (*food*); zurichten, zurechtmachen, anrichten, beschicken, bestellen, präparieren (*Tech.*); aufbereiten (*ore, etc.*); *–e for action*, bereitstellen (*troops*); *–e a document*, eine Schrift aufstellen; *–e the ground for*, den Boden bereiten für; *–e one's lessons*, sich für die Schule vorbereiten; *–e o.s. for*, sich rüsten für, sich gefaßt machen auf; *–e the way*, Bahn brechen (*for* (*Dat.*)). 2. *v.n.* sich vorbereiten *or* anschicken, Vorbereitungen treffen; *–e to dismount!* fertig zum Absitzen! **–ed,** *adj.* fertig, bereit, vorbereitet; gefaßt; präpariert (*Tech.*); *be –ed*, bereit *or* gewillt sein. **–edness** [–ˈpɛːrɪdnɪs], *s.* die Bereitschaft, das Vorbereitetsein, Gefaßtsein (*for*, auf).
prepay [prɪːˈpeɪ], *v.a.* vorausbezahlen, im voraus *o* pränumerando bezahlen; frankieren (*a letter*). **–ment,** *s.* die Vorausbezahlung, Frankierung; *see* **prepaid.**
prepense [prɪˈpɛns], *adj.* vorbedacht, vorsätzlich (*Law*); *with* or *of malice –*, in böswilliger Absicht.
prepondera–nce [prɪˈpɔndərəns], *s.* das Übergewicht (*also fig.*); (*fig.*) Schwergewicht, überwiegende Zahl, das Überwiegen. **–nt** [–ənt], *adj.* überwiegend; *be –nt*, überwiegen. **–te** [–eɪt], *v.n.* überwiegen, vorwiegen, vorherrschen; das Übergewicht haben (*over* über), übersteigen.
preposition [prɛpəˈzɪʃən], *s.* die Präposition. **–al,** *adj.* präpositional.
prepositive [prɪˈpɔzɪtɪv], *adj.* vor(an)gesetzt.
prepossess [prɪːpəˈzɛs], *v.a.* (*esp. pass.*) im voraus einnehmen *or* erfüllen (*with*, mit; *in favour of*, für; *against*, gegen); günstig beeindrucken *or* beeinflussen (*a p.*). **–ed** [–ˈzɛst], voreingenommen; eingenommen (*by*, durch). **–ing,** *adj.* einnehmend, anziehend. **–ion** [–ˈzɛʃən], *s.* die Voreingenommenheit, vorgefaßte Meinung, das Vorurteil.
preposterous [prɪˈpɔstərəs], *adj.* verkehrt, unsinnig, widersinnig, widernatürlich, unnatürlich; albern, lächerlich, absurd. **–ness,** *s.* die Widersinnigkeit, Lächerlichkeit.
prepoten–ce, –cy [prɪˈpoutəns(ɪ)], *s.* die Vorherrschaft, stärkere Kraft, die Übermacht; stärkere Vererbungskraft (*Biol.*). **–t** [–ənt], *adj.* vorherrschend; stärker vererbend.
prepuce [ˈprɪpjuːs], *s.* die Vorhaut (*Anat.*).
prerequisite [prɪːˈrɛkwɪzɪt], 1. *s.* die Vorbedingung. 2. *adj.* voraussetzend, notwendig (*to*, für).
prerogative [prəˈrɔgətɪv], 1. *s.* das Vorrecht; Hoheitsrecht, die Prärogative. 2. *adj.* bevorrechtet, Vorzugs–.
presage [ˈprɛsɪdʒ], 1. *s.* die Vorbedeutung, das Anzeichen, Vorzeichen; Vorgefühl, die Ahnung. 2. *v.a.* vorhersagen, voraussagen, prophezeien, weissagen, vorher verkünden; anzeigen, vorbedeuten.
presbyopi–a [prɛzbɪˈoupɪə], *s.* die Weitsichtigkeit. **–c** [–pɪk], *adj.* weitsichtig.
presbyter [ˈprɛzbɪtə], *s.* Kirchenälteste(r), *m*, der Kirchenvorsteher; Priester. **–ian** [–ˈtɪːərɪən], 1. *adj.* presbyterianisch. 2. *s.* der Presbyterianer. **–ianism** [–ˈtɪːərɪənɪzm], *s.* der Presbyterianismus. **–y** [ˈprɛzbɪtərɪ], *s.* das Presbyterium, Presbyterkollegium; das Pfarrhaus (*R.C.*); der Chor (*Arch.*).
prescien–ce [ˈprɛʃɪəns], *s.* das Vorherwissen, die Voraussicht. **–t** [–ənt], *adj.* vorherwissend; *be –t of*, vorherwissen, voraussehen.
prescind [prɪˈsɪnd], 1. *v.a.* absondern, entfernen trennen, loslösen (*from*, von). 2. *v.n.*; – *from*, beiseite lassen.
prescri–be [prɪˈskraɪb], 1. *v.a.* vorschreiben (*a th. to a p.*, einem etwas); verordnen, verschreiben

(*Med.*) (*to* or *for a p.*, einem; *for*, gegen *or* für). 2. *v.n.* verjähren, Verjährungsrecht beanspruchen *or* geltend machen (*for*, für) (*Law*). **–pt** [ˈprɪ:-skrɪpt], *s.* die Vorschrift, Verordnung. **–ption** [prɪˈskrɪpʃən], *s.* die Vorschrift, Verordnung; das Rezept (*Med.*); (also *positive –ption*) die Erwerbung durch ständigen Genuß, Ersitzung (*Law*); *negative –ption*, die Verjährung, Verjährungsfrist (*Law*); (*fig.*) althergebrachter Brauch. **–ptive** [–ˈskrɪptɪv], *adj.* verordnend; durch ständigen Genuß verbrieft, durch Brauch gefestigt, ersessen; *–ptive debt*, die Verjährungsschuld; *–ptive right*, das Gewohnheitsrecht.

presence [ˈprɛzəns], *s.* die Gegenwart, Anwesenheit, das Beisein, Vorhandensein, Auftreten; die Nähe; Gesellschaft; Äußere(s), *n.*, äußere Erscheinung; das Benehmen, die Haltung; stattliche Erscheinung, geisterhaftes Wesen; *the –*, die hohen Herrschaften selbst; *in the – of these dangers*, angesichts dieser Gefahren; *– of mind*, die Geistesgegenwart; *page of the –*, der Leibpage. **– -chamber,** *s.* das Audienzzimmer.

[1]**present** [ˈprɛzənt], **1.** *adj.* (*of time*) gegenwärtig, jetzig, momentan, heutig, laufend, Gegenwarts–; (*of space*) anwesend, vorhanden, zugegen (*at*, bei *or* in), vorliegend; *– !* hier! (*a*) (*with nouns*) *– case*, vorliegender Fall; *– company*, die Anwesenden; *the – day*, die gegenwärtige Zeit; *the – king*, der jetzige König; *of the – month*, vom laufenden Monat; *– participle*, das Mittelwort der Gegenwart, Partizipium präsentis; *– position*, der Abschußpunkt (*Artil.*); *– tense*, die Gegenwart, das Präsens; *– time*, see *– day*; *– value*, der Gegenwartswert; *the – writer*, der Verfasser dieser Zeilen. (*b*) (*with prepositions*) *be – at*, zugegen sein bei, beiwohnen (*Dat.*); *– to my mind*, mir gegenwärtig. **2.** *s.* die Gegenwart, gegenwärtige Zeit; das Präsens (*Gram.*). *at* (*the*) *–*, gegenwärtig, jetzt, im Augenblick; *by the –*, durch Gegenwärtiges (*C.L.*); *by these –s*, durch Gegenwärtiges, hiermit (*Law*); *for the –*, für jetzt, vorläufig, einstweilen. **–ly,** *adv.* kurz darauf, (als)bald, nach kurzer Zeit; (*Scots*) augenblicklich, jetzt.

[2]**present** [prɪˈzɛnt], **1.** *v.a.* (dar)bieten, vorbringen, vorlegen, einreichen; darstellen; präsentieren (*Mil. & C.L.*); vorstellen, vorführen (*to* (*Dat.*)); einführen (*to*, bei); vorschlagen, empfehlen (*to*, für); anlegen, richten (*a weapon*) (*at*, auf (*Acc.*)); überreichen, übergeben, schenken (*a th. to a p.*, einem etwas), beschenken (*a p.*) (*with*, mit); *– one's apologies*, sich entschuldigen; *– an appearance of*, erscheinen als; *– arms*, das Gewehr präsentieren; *– a bill of exchange*, einen Wechsel präsentieren *or* zum Akzept vorlegen; *– one's compliments to a p.*, sich einem empfehlen; *– at Court*, bei Hofe einführen; *that –s difficulties*, das bietet Schwierigkeiten dar; *– o.s.*, sich vorstellen, sich melden (*to*, bei; *for*, zu); sich einfinden, erscheinen; sich bieten (*of a th.*). **2.** *s.*; *at the –*, in Präsentierhaltung (*Mil.*). **–able,** *adj.* vorstellbar (*to*, für), zur Darbietung geeignet, präsentierbar; (*coll.*) annehmbar, ansehnlich, präsentabel. **–ation** [prɛzənˈteɪʃən], *s.* der Vorschlag (*to*, zu) (*Eccl.*), das Vorschlagsrecht, die Einreichung, Überreichung, Eingabe (*of a petition, etc.*); Schenkung, Gabe, Aufführung, Darbietung, Darstellung, Wiedergabe (*Theat. & Arts*); das Vorlegen, Vorzeigen, die Präsentation (*C.L.*); die Lage, Stellung (*Med.*), Vorstellung (*Psych.*); Einführung, formelle Vorstellung (*at court*) (*to*, bei); *–ation copy*, das Freiexemplar, Dedikationsexemplar; *on –ation*, bei Vorzeigung (*C.L.*).

[3]**present** [ˈprɛzənt], *s.* das Geschenk (*to*, an *or* für); *make a p. a – of*, einem ein Geschenk machen mit, einem (etwas) zum Geschenk machen; *make a p. a –*, einem etwas schenken, einem ein Geschenk machen.

presentiment [prɪˈzɛntɪmənt], *s.* die (Vor)Ahnung, das Vorgefühl, die Vorempfindung.

presently [ˈprɛzəntlɪ], *see* [1]**present.**

presentment [prɪˈzɛntmənt], *s.* das Bild, die Schilderung, Darstellung, Darbietung, Aufführung, Vorstellung (*Theat.*); die von der Anklagejury erhobene Anklage (*Law*).

preserv–able [prɪˈzə:vəbl], *adj.* erhaltbar. **–ation** [prɛzəˈveɪʃən], *s.* die (Auf)Bewahrung (*from*, vor); Erhaltung, Rettung; das Einmachen, die Konservierung (*of fruit*); *–ation of the countryside*, der Natur- und Heimatschutz; *in* (*a*) *good* (*state of*) *–ation*, gut erhalten, in gut erhaltenem Zustande. **–ative** [prɪˈzə:vətɪv], 1. *adj.* bewahrend, erhaltend, schützend, Schutz–. 2. *s.* das Schutzmittel, Vorbeugungsmittel (*against* or *from*, gegen), Konservierungsmittel. **–e** [prɪˈzə:v], 1. *v.a.* bewahren, behüten (*from*, vor (*Dat.*)) (*a p.*), erhalten, aufrechthalten (*a th.*), (bei)behalten; aufbewahren, in gutem Zustande erhalten, konservieren, schützen und hegen (*game*), einmachen, einlegen; *Heaven –e me!* der Himmel bewahre mich! *–e one's gravity*, ernst bleiben; *–e silence*, still bleiben, Stillschweigen bewahren. 2. *s.* das Gehege (*Hunt.*); (*also pl.*) Eingemachtes, *n.*, die Konserve, (*fig.*) das Sondergebiet, Sonderinteresse. **–ing,** *adj.* bewahrend. **–ing-jar,** *s.* das Einmachglas.

preside [prɪˈzaɪd], *v.n.* den Vorsitz führen, präsidieren, die Aufsicht führen (*at* or *over*, über (*Acc.*)). **–ncy** [ˈprɛzɪdənsɪ], *s.* der Vorsitz, das Präsidium, die Oberaufsicht, Präsidentschaft, Präsidialperiode (*Pol.*). **–nt** [ˈprɛzɪdənt], *s.* Vorsitzende(r), *m.*, der Präsident (*also Pol.*); Direktor (*C.L.*); *Lord –nt of the Council*, der Vorsitzende des Staatsrates. **–ntial** [–ˈdɛnʃəl], *adj.* Präsidenten–; *–ntial address*, die Ansprache des Vorsitzenden. **–ntship,** *s.* die Präsidentschaft (*Pol.*).

[1]**press** [prɛs], 1. *v.a.* drücken, pressen; bügeln (*clothes*), keltern (*grapes*); (*fig.*) drücken auf, in die Enge treiben, bedrücken, bedrängen, bestürmen; drängen, antreiben, überreden, zwingen, zusetzen (*Dat.*); aufdrängen, aufnötigen, eindringlich empfehlen (*on a p.*, einem); *–ed beef*, das Büchsenfleisch; *– the button*, auf den Knopf drücken; *he –ed my hand*, er drückte mir die Hand; *– a p. for s.th.*, einem etwas abpressen; *be –ed for*, in Verlegenheit sein um; *–ed for time*, keine Zeit *or* es eilig haben; *hard –ed*, bedrängt; *– home an advantage*, einen Vorteil ausnützen. 2. *v.n.* drücken, Druck ausüben, schwer liegen (*upon*, auf), (sich) drängen (*of persons*); drängen, dringlich sein, pressieren (*of time*); *the matter is not –ing*, die Sache hat keine Eile; *– for*, drängen auf, verlangen, dringend bitten um; *– forward*, vorwärtsdrängen; *– on*, vorwärtstreiben, weitereilen. 3. *s.* das Drücken, der Druck; Andrang, das Gedränge (*of people*); das Drängen; der Drang, die Dringlichkeit, Hast; die Presse (*Tech.*), der Schrank (*for linen, etc.*); die Druckerpresse, Druckerei; das Drucken, der Druck (*Typ.*); das Zeitungswesen, die Presse; *have a bad –*, ungünstig beurteilt *or* aufgenommen werden; *pass for –*, das Imprimatur erteilen (*Dat.*); *ready for –*, druckreif; *come from the –*, die Presse verlassen; *get ready for –*, zum Druck fertig machen; *in the –*, unter der Presse, im Druck; *see a th. through the –*, den Druck einer S. überwachen; *go to –*, in Druck gehen; *send to –*, in Druck geben. **– -agency,** *s.* das Nachrichtenbüro. **– -box,** *s.* die Presseloge. **– -button,** *s.* der Druckknopf; *– -button tuning*, die Drucktastenabstimmung (*Rad.*). **– copy,** *s.* der Durchschlag; das Rezensionsexemplar. **– cutting,** der Zeitungsausschnitt. **–er,** *s.* der Presser, Drucker, Quetscher, die Druckwalze. **– -fastener,** *s.* der Druckknopf. **– -gallery,** *s.* die Gallerie für die Presse (*House of Commons*). **– -guide,** *s.* der Zeitungskatalog. **–ing,** 1. *adj.* drückend, pressend; drängend, dringend, dringlich, angelegentlich, eilig; aufdringlich (*of a p.*); *be –ing*, drängen. 2. *s.* das Pressen, Drücken; das Preßstück (*Tech.*). **–ing-iron,** *s.* das Bügeleisen, Plätteisen. **–ing-roller,** *s.* die Druckwalze. **–man,** *s.* der Drucker; Journalist, Pressevertreter. **– -mark,** *s.* die Standortnummer, Signatur. **– photographer,** *s.* der Bildberichter. **– -proof,** *s.* letzte Korrektur. **– -reader,** *s.* der Korrektor. **– -room,** *s.* das Druckerzimmer. **– -stud,** *s.* der Druckknopf. **–ure** [ˈprɛʃə], *s.* das Drücken, der Druck (*also Meteor. & fig.*), die Druckkraft (*Tech.*); (*fig.*) das Drängen, der Drang, die Knappheit, Not, Verlegenheit, Klemme; Bedrückung, der Zwang; *atmospheric –ure*, der Luftdruck; *blood-–ure*, der Blutdruck; *–ure of*

business, der Drang der Geschäfte; *high -ure*, der Hochdruck; *work at high -ure*, mit Hochdruck arbeiten; *low -ure*, der Tiefdruck; *monetary -ure*, der Geldmangel, die Geldnot, Geldknappheit; *put -ure on*, einen Druck *or* Zwang ausüben auf; *-ure of space*, der Raummangel; *under -ure*, unter Druck. **-ure-cabin,** *s.* die Höhenkabine. **-ure-cooker,** *s.* der Schnellkocher. **-ure-gauge,** *s.* der Druckmesser. **-ure-pump,** *s.* die Druckpumpe. **--work,** *s.* die Druck(er)arbeit.

[2]**press** [prɛs], 1. *v.a.* pressen; *– into service*, in Dienst pressen (*also fig.*). 2. *s.* das Aufgreifen, (Matrosen)-Pressen (*Hist.*). **-gang,** *s.* die Aushebungsmannschaft.

prestidigitat-ion [prɛstɪdɪdʒɪ'teɪʃən], *s.* die Taschenspielerkunst. **-or** [-'dɪdʒɪteɪtə], *s.* der Taschenspieler.

prestige [prɛs'tɪ:ʒ, 'prɛstɪdʒ], *s.* das Ansehen, der Nimbus, das Prestige.

prest-issimo [prɛs'tɪsɪmoʊ], *adv.* sehr schnell (*Mus.*). **-o** ['prɛstoʊ], *adv.* schnell, geschwind (*Mus.*); (*coll.*) *hey -o*, im Handumdrehen, wie der Blitz.

presum-able [prɪ'zjʊ:məbl], *adj.* vermutlich, mutmaßlich: wahrscheinlich, voraussichtlich. **-e** [prɪ'zjʊ:m], 1. *v.a.* als gegeben annehmen, vermuten, voraussetzen. 2. *v.n.* sich erkühnen *or* erdreisten, sich (*Dat.*) herausnehmen *or* anmaßen, wagen; *-e (up)on*, sich etwas einbilden auf, pochen auf, voraussetzen. **-ed** [-d], *adj.*, **-edly** [-ɪdlɪ], *adv.* mutmaßlich, vermeintlich; *-ed dead*, verschollen. **-ing,** *adj.* anmaßend, vermessen. **-ption** [prɪ'zʌmpʃən], *s.* die Vermutung, Mutmaßung, Annahme, Wahrscheinlichkeit, die Vermessenheit, Anmaßung, der Dünkel; *the -ption is that*, die Vermutung besteht daß; *on the -ption that*, in der Annahme daß; *-ption of fact*, die Tatsachenvermutung (*Law*). **-ptive** [-'zʌmptɪv], *adj.* mutmaßlich, präsumtiv; *-ptive evidence*, der Indizienbeweis (*Law*); *heir -ptive*, mutmaßlicher Erbe. **-ptuous** [-'zʌmpʃəs], *adj.* anmaßend, vermessen. **-ptuousness,** *s.* die Anmaßung, Vermessenheit.

presuppos-e [prɪ:sə'poʊz], *v.a.* im voraus annehmen, voraussetzen, zur Voraussetzung haben. **-ition** [-sʌpə'zɪʃən], *s.* die Voraussetzung.

preten-ce [prɪ'tɛns], *s.* die Vorspiegelung, der Vorwand, Scheingrund, Schein, die Verstellung, Maske, Finte, der Anspruch (*to*, auf); *abandon the -ce*, die Maske fallen lassen; *under false -ces*, unter Vorspiegelung falscher Tatsachen; *make a -ce of*, vortäuschen; *make no -ce of being*, sich nicht den Anschein geben zu sein; *under the -ce*, unter dem Vorwand. **-d** [-'tɛnd], 1. *v.a.* vorgeben, vortäuschen, vorspiegeln, vorschützen, (er)heucheln, simulieren. 2. *v.n.* sich verstellen, sich ausgeben für, vorgeben; *-d to*, Anspruch machen auf (*Acc.*), sich (*Dat.*) einbilden *or* anmaßen; *-d to sleep*, tun, als ob man schliefe. **-ded** [-'tɛndɪd], *adj.* vorgetäuscht, vorgeblich, angeblich, vermeintlich. **-der** [-'tɛndə], *s.* der Heuchler, Scharlatan, Anspruchmachende(r) *m.* (*to*, auf); *-der to the throne*, der Thronbewerber, Prätendent (*Hist.*). **-sion** [-'tɛnʃən], *s.* der Anspruch (*to*, auf), die Anmaßung, der Dünkel. **-tious** [-'tɛnʃəs], *adj.* anspruchsvoll, anmaßend, prunkhaft. **-tiousness,** *s.* die Anmaßung, Anmaßlichkeit.

preterite ['prɛtərɪt], 1. *adj.* Vergangenheits-. 2. *s.* das Präteritum. **--present,** *s.* das Präteritopräsens.

preter-ition [prɪ:tə'rɪʃən], *s.* die Unterlassung, Übergehung. **-mission** [-'mɪʃən], *s.* die Unterlassung; Übergehung (*Rhet.*). **-mit** [-'mɪt], *v.a.* unterlassen, übergehen. **-natural** [-'nætʃərəl], *adj.* übernatürlich, abnorm, anormal.

pretext ['prɪ:tɛkst], *s.* der Vorwand, die Entschuldigung, Ausflucht, das Vorgeben; *make a – of*, vorschützen, vorgeben; *on* or *under the –*, unter dem Vorwande *or* Schein (*of* (*Gen.*)).

pretonic [prɪ:'tɔnɪk], *adj.* vortonig (*Phonet.*).

prett-ify ['prɪtɪfaɪ], *v.a.* verschönern. **-iness** [-nɪs], *s.* die Niedlichkeit, Nettigkeit, Anmut, Artigkeit; Geziertheit, Gespreiztheit (*of style*). **-y** ['prɪtɪ], 1. *adj.* hübsch, schön, niedlich, nett, anziehend; (*coll.*) fein, prächtig, beträchtlich; *-y face*, das Puppengesicht; *-y mess*, schöne Bescherung; *my -y one*, mein Liebchen; *a -y penny*, ein gutes Stück Geld. 2. *adv.* (*coll.*) ziemlich, leidlich, einigermaßen; *-y considerable*, ziemlich beträchtlich; *-y good*, nicht schlecht; *-y much the same*, ungefähr *or* nahezu dasselbe.

prevail [prɪ'veɪl], *v.n.* die Oberhand gewinnen, den Sieg davontragen (*over*, über), sich durchsetzen, herrschen, vorherrschen, vorwiegen; *– against*, erfolgreich sein; *– over*, die Oberhand bekommen, den Sieg davontragen (über (*Acc.*)); *– (up)on*, bereden, bewegen (*a p.*); *– (up)on o.s.*, es nicht übers Herz bringen. **-ing,** *adj.* herrschend, vorherrschend, allgemein geltend.

prevalen-ce ['prɛvələns], *s.* das Vorherrschen, Herrschen, Überhandnehmen, weite Verbreitung. **-t** [-ənt], *adj.* überwiegend, vorherrschend, weit *or* allgemein verbreitet.

prevaricat-e [prɪ'værɪkeɪt], *v.n.* Ausflüchte machen *or* gebrauchen. **-ion** [-'keɪʃən], *s.* die Umgehung der Wahrheit, Ausflüchte (*pl.*). **-or** [-'værɪkeɪtə], *s.* der Wortverdreher, Wahrheitumgeher.

prevent [prɪ'vɛnt], *v.a.* abhalten, hindern (*from*, an), verhindern, verhüten, zuvorkommen, vorbeugen. **-able,** *adj.* verhütbar, zu verhüten(d). **-ative,** *see* **-tive.** **-ion** [-'vɛnʃən], *s.* die Verhinderung, Verhütung; *society for the -ion of cruelty to animals*, der Tierschutzverein. **-ive,** 1. *adj.* verhütend, Verhütungs-, vorbeugend; *-ive custody*, die Schutzhaft, Sicherheitsverwahrung; *-ive medicine*, die Präventivbehandlung; *-ive service*, der Küstenschutzdienst. 2. *s.* das Vorbeugungsmittel, Präventivmittel, Schutzmittel, Abwehrmittel.

previous ['prɪ:vɪəs], 1. *adj.* vorhergehend, vorangehend (*to* (*Dat.*)), vorläufig; (*coll.*) übereilt, voreilig; *– conviction*, die Vorstrafe; *– examination*, das Vorexamen (*at Cambridge*); *move the – question*, das Übergehen zur Tagesordnung beantragen (*Parl.*). 2. *adv.*; *– to*, vor (*Dat.*). **-ly,** *adv.* vorher. **-ness,** *s.* (*coll.*) die Voreiligkeit.

prevision [prɪ:'vɪʒən], *s.* das Vorhersehen, die Voraussicht, Ahnung.

pre-war [prɪ:'wɔ:], *adj.* Vorkriegs-.

prey [preɪ], 1. *s.* der Raub, die Beute; (*fig.*) das Opfer; *beast of –*, das Raubtier; *bird of –*, der Raubvogel; *be, become* or *fall a (an easy) –*, (leicht) zur Beute *or* zum Opfer fallen (*to* (*Dat.*)). 2. *v.n.*; *– upon*, Beute machen auf, fressen (*of animals*); (*fig.*) berauben, plündern, verwüsten, nagen *or* zehren an; *it -ed on his mind*, es bedrückte ihn, es ging ihm die ganze Zeit im Kopf herum.

price [praɪs], 1. *s.* der Preis (*of*, für), Wert, Gegenwert; *at any –*, um jeden Preis; *long (short) –*, ungünstige (günstige) Wette; *opening –*, der Eröffnungskurs; *set a – on*, einen Preis setzen auf (*Acc.*); *what is the – of?* wieviel kostet? *what – . . . ?* welche Chance . . . ? (*Racing*), (*sl.*) wie denkst du über . . . ? 2. *v.a.* den Preis ansetzen für; (*coll.*) nach dem Preis fragen; *-d catalogue*, der Katalog mit Preisangaben. **--control,** *s.* die Zwangswirtschaft. **--current,** *s. see* **--list.** **--cutting,** *s.* das Unterbieten. **-less,** *adj.* unschätzbar, unbezahlbar, (*coll.*) köstlich. **--limit,** die Preisgrenze. **--list,** *s.* die Preisliste.

prick [prɪk], 1. *v.a.* (durch)stechen, durchlochen, punktieren, prickeln in *or* an *or* auf; (*fig.*) antreiben, anspornen (*a p.*), *– the bubble*, den Schwindel aufdecken; *– one's finger*, sich in den Finger stechen; *his conscience -s him*, das Gewissen schlägt ihm, er verspürt Gewissensbisse; *he was -ed to the heart*, es ging ihm durchs Herz; *– out*, auspflanzen, umpflanzen (*seedlings*); ausstecken, ausprickeln (*a pattern*); *– up one's ears*, die Ohren spitzen. 2. *v.n.* stechen, prickeln; (*archaic*) die Sporen geben, jagen, sprengen; *– up*, sich aufrichten (*of ears*). 3. *s.* der Stich (*of insect, needle, etc.*), der Stachel, Dorn, die Spitze; (*fig.*) stechender Schmerz, der Stichel; *kick against the -s*, wider den Stachel lecken *or* löcken; *– of conscience*, der Gewissensbiß. **-er,** *s.* der Pfriem, die Pfrieme, Ahle; Schießnadel (*Min.*). **--eared,** *adj.* mit gespitzten Ohren. **-et** [-ɪt], *s.* der Bock im 2. Jahr. **-le** [-l], 1. *s.* der Stachel, Dorn. 2. *v.n.* prickeln, stechen. **-ly** [-lɪ], *adj.* stach(e)lig, Stachel-; prickelnd; *-ly heat*, Hitzblattern (*pl.*) (*Med.*); *-ly pear*, die Feigendistel, indische Feige.

pride [praɪd], 1. *s.* der Stolz (*in*, auf), Hochmut, Übermut, die Überhebung; (*fig.*) Pracht, der Glanz, die Blüte, Zierde; der Federschmuck (*of a peacock*); der Trupp, das Rudel, die Schar (*of lions*); (*Prov.*) – *goes before a fall*, Hochmut kommt vor dem Fall; – *of place*, der Ehrenplatz, bevorzugte Stellung; (*fig.*) der Standesdünkel; *give – of place to*, große Bedeutung einräumen (*Dat.*); *take – of place*, den ersten Rang einnehmen; *take a – in*, stolz sein auf (*Acc.*), seinen Stolz *or* Ehrgeiz setzen in. 2. *v.r.* stolz sein (*on*, auf), sich brüsten mit.

priest [prɪ:st], *s.* der Priester, Geistliche(r), *m.* **–craft,** *s.* der Pfaffentrug; die Pfaffenpolitik. **–hood,** *s.* das Priesteramt, die Priesterschaft, Priester (*pl.*). **–liness,** *s.* die Priesterlichkeit. **–ly,** *adj.* priesterlich, Priester–. **––ridden,** *adj.* von Pfaffen beherrscht.

[1]**prig** [prɪg], 1. *s.* selbstgefälliger Pedant, dünkelhafter Tugendheld; der Fant. **–gish,** *adj.* selbstgefällig, dünkelhaft. **–gishness,** *s.* die Eingebildetheit, der Dünkel.

[2]**prig** [prɪg], (*sl.*) 1. *s.* der Dieb. 2. *v.a.* mausen.

prim [prɪm], 1. *adj.* steif, formell, gedrechselt, geziert, affektiert, zimperlich, spröde. 2. *v.a.* affektiert verziehen (*the mouth*). **–ness,** *s.* die Steifheit, Förmlichkeit, Geziertheit.

primacy [ˈpraɪməsɪ], *s.* der & das Primat (*also Eccl.*), der Vorrang, Vorzug, bevorzugte Stellung.

prima donna [ˈprɪ:məˈdɔnə], erste Sängerin, die Primadonna.

prima-facie [ˈpraɪməˈfeɪʃɪeɪ], 1. *adv.* auf den ersten Blick, beim ersten Anschein. 2. *adj.* (scheinbar) glaubhaft; – *evidence*, glaubhafter Beweis.

primage [ˈpraɪmɪdʒ], *s.* das Primgeld, der Frachtzuschlag (*Naut.*); der Wassergehalt (im Dampf).

prima–l [ˈpraɪməl], *adj.* erst, frühest; ursprünglich, wesentlich. **–rily** [–mərəlɪ], *adv.*, **–ry** [–ərɪ], 1. *adj.* erst, frühest, ursprünglich, Ur–, Anfangs–, Elementar–, Grund–; hauptsächlich, Haupt–, primär (*Geol.*); *–ry cell*, das Primärelement; *–ry coil*, die Primärspule; *–ry colours*, Grundfarben (*pl.*); *–ry election*, die Vorwahl (*Amer.*); *–ry feather*, die Schwungfeder; *of –ry importance*, von höchster Wichtigkeit; *–ry instinct*, der Urinstinkt; *–ry instruction*, der Volksschulunterricht; *–ry meaning*, die Hauptbedeutung; *–ry meeting*, die Wahlversammlung (*Amer.*); *–ry school*, die Grundschule, Volksschule, Elementarschule. 2. *s.* der Hauptplanet; see also *–ry election*; *pl.* see *–ry feathers*.

primate [ˈpraɪmət], *s.* der Primas; – *of England*, der Erzbischof von York; – *of all England*, der Erzbischof von Canterbury. **–ship,** *s.* der & das Primat. **–s** [ˈmeɪtɪ:z], *pl.* Primaten (*pl.*) (*Zool.*).

prime [praɪm], 1. *adj.* erst, frühest, ursprünglich, wichtigst, Haupt–; Prima–, erstklassig (*coll. & C.L.*); – *cost*, der Einkaufspreis, Selbstkostenpreis, Gestehungskosten (*pl.*); – *minister*, der Premierminister; – *mover*, bewegende Kraft, die Antriebsmaschine, der Schlepper; – *number*, die Primzahl. – *vertical* (*circle*), erster Vertikal(kreis) (*Astr.*). 2. *s.* höchste Vollkommenheit, die Blüte, Vollkraft, der Kern; die Primzahl (*Arith.*); erste Gebetstunde (*R.C.*); die Prime (*Mus. & Fenc.*); *in his* –, im besten Mannesalter, in der Blüte seiner Jahre. 3. *v.a.* mit Zündpulver versehen *or* laden (*guns*); scharf machen (*bombs*); in Tätigkeit setzen (*pumps*); anschärfen, verschärfen (*Dye.*); grundieren (*Paint.*), (*fig.*) ausstatten, ausrüsten (*a p.*); mit Information versehen, vorbereiten, einweihen, instruieren; (*sl.*) betrunken machen. **–r** [–ə], *s.* die Zündpille, Sprengkapsel, der Zünddraht, die Zündnadel, Zündschraube; der Grundierer (*Paint.*); das Elementarbuch, die Fibel, Einführung; *great –r*, die Tertia (*Typ.*); *long –r*, die Korpus(schrift) (*Typ.*).

primeval [praɪˈmɪ:vəl], *adj.* uranfänglich, uralt, Ur–.

[1]**priming** [ˈpraɪmɪŋ], *s.* die Grundierung (*Paint.*); Zündung, Zündmasse (*Artil.*); – *of the tide*, die Verfrühung *or* das frühere Eintreten der Flut. **––charge,** die Beiladung. **––colour,** *s.* die Grundierfarbe. **––horn,** *s.* das Pulverhorn. **––powder,** *s.* das Zündpulver. **––wire,** *s.* der Zünddraht.

primitive [ˈprɪmɪtɪv], 1. *adj.* erst, frühest, ursprünglich; Grund– (*of colours*), Stamm– (*Gram.*); Ur–, uralt, urzeitlich, altertümlich, altmodisch, einfach, primitiv; – *Church*, die Urkirche; – *races*, Naturvölker, Urvölker (*pl.*); – *verb*, das Stammzeitwort. 2. *s.* das Stammwort; der Frühmeister, Maler der Frührenaissance. **–ness,** *s.* die Ursprünglichkeit; Einfachheit, Primitivität.

primness, *see* **prim.**

primogenit–or [praɪməˈdʒɛnɪtə], *s.* der Ahnherr, frühester Vorfahr. **–ure** [–ˈdʒɛnɪtjə], *s.* die Erstgeburt; das Erstgeburtsrecht (*Law*).

primordial [praɪˈmɔ:dɪəl], *adj.* ursprünglich, uranfänglich, Primordial– (*Biol.*).

primrose [ˈprɪmroʊz], 1. *s.* schaftlose Schlüsselblume (*Bot.*); blaßgelbe Farbe; – *League*, der Primelbund; – *path*, der Weg der Freude *or* des Vergnügens. 3. *adj.* blaßgelb.

primula [ˈprɪmjʊlə], *s.* die Gattung der Primeln (*Bot.*).

prince [prɪns], *s.* der Fürst, Prinz; (*fig.*) Magnat. *––bishop*, der Fürstbischof; – *Bismarck*, Fürst Bismarck; *Black* –, schwarzer Prinz; – *of the blood*, der Prinz von königlichem Geblüt; – *Consort*, der Prinz-Gemahl; – *of darkness*, Satan, der Höllenfürst; *merchant* –, reicher Kaufherr; *a – of poets*, ein Dichterfürst; *poet* –, fürstlicher Dichter; – *Regent*, der Prinzregent; – *of Wales*, englischer Kronprinz. **–like,** *adj.* fürstlich. **–ly,** *adj.* fürstlich, Fürsten–; prinzlich; (*fig.*) stattlich, prächtig. **–ss** [–ɛs, –ˈɛs], 1. *s.* die Fürstin, Prinzessin; *–ss-royal*, älteste Tochter des englischen Königs. 2. *attrib.* Prinzeß– (*of dress*); *see* **principality.**

principal [ˈprɪnsɪpəl], 1. *adj.* erst, führend, hauptsächlich, Haupt–; – *actor*, erster Schauspieler; – *axis*, die Hauptachse; – *boy*, die Heldendarstellerin (*pantomime*); – *clause*, der Hauptsatz; – *creditor*, der Hauptgläubiger; – *parts*, die Stammzeiten (*of verbs*). 2. *s.* die Hauptperson, das Haupt, der Vorsteher, Rektor (*of a college, etc.*); Prinzipal, Chef, Auftraggeber, Selbstkontrahent (*C.L.*), Haupttäter, Hauptschuldige(r) (*Law*), Duellant (*in a duel*), die Hauptfigur (*Theat.*), der Hauptbalken, Hauptsparren (*Build.*); das Kapital (*C.L.*); – *and interest*, Kapital und Zinsen; – *in the first degree*, Hauptschuldige(r), *m.*, der Täter (*Law*); – *in the second degree*, der Helfershelfer (*Law*). **–ly,** *adv.* hauptsächlich, besonders.

principality [prɪnsɪˈpælɪtɪ], *s.* das Fürstentum.

principle [ˈprɪnsɪpl], *s.* der Grundsatz, das Prinzip, der Grundgedanke, Grundbegriff; Ursprung, Urgrund, Urstoff; Grundbestandteil (*Chem.*); *in* –, im Grunde *or* Prinzip; *make* (*it*) *a* –, es sich (*Dat.*) zum Prinzip machen (*of doing*, zu tun); *man of* –, der Mann von hohen Grundsätzen. *on* –, aus Prinzip, grundsätzlich, prinzipiell; *on the* –, nach dem Grundsatz. **–d,** *adj. suffix* (also *high –d*) von (hohen) Grundsätzen.

print [prɪnt], 1. *v.a.* drucken, drucken lassen, in Druck geben (*Typ.*); bedrucken (*cloth, etc.*); abdrucken (*a pattern*); kopieren, abziehen (*Phot.*); aufdrücken (*on*, auf); (*fig.*) einprägen (*on a p.'s mind*, einem); in Druckschrift *or* Blockbuchstaben schreiben; *be –ing*, im Druck sein, gedruckt werden; *have –ed*, in Druck geben. 2. *s.* der Druck (*also Typ.*), Abdruck, Abzug, die Kopie (*Phot.*); das Zeichen, Mal, der Eindruck, die Spur; Druckschrift, Gedruckte(s), *n.*; der Stich, Schnitt (*Engr.*); das Modell, der Stempel, die Druckform; das Druckzeug, bedruckter Kattun; *blue-–*, die Lichtpause; *coloured* –, farbiger Stich; – *dress*, das Kattunkleid; *in* –, gedruckt; im Druck erschienen, veröffentlicht; erhältlich; *appear in* –, im Druck erscheinen; (*coll.*) *in cold* –, schwarz auf weiß; *out of* –, vergriffen. **–ed** [–ɪd], *adj.*; *–ed fabric*, das Druckzeug; *–ed form*, das Druckformular; *–ed matter*, die Drucksache. **–er** [–ə], *s.* der (Buch)Drucker, Druckereibesitzer; *–er's devil*, der Setzerjunge; *–er's error*, der Druckfehler; *–er's ink*, die Druckerschwärze; *–er's mark*, das Druckerzeichen; *–er's pie*, Zwiebelfische (*pl.*). **–ing,** *s.* das Drucken, der Druck; das Abziehen, Kopieren (*Phot.*); die Buchdruckerkunst; der Tuchdruck; die Druckschrift; *–ing-block*, *s.* das Klischee; *–ing-frame*, *s.* der Kopierrahmen (*Phot.*);

–*ing-ink*, *s.* die Druckerschwärze; –*ing-machine*, *s.* die Schnellpresse; –*ing-office*, *s.* die (Buch)Druckerei; –*ing-out paper*, das Kopierpapier; –*ing-paper*, *s.* das Lichtpauspapier (*for blue-prints*); Kopierpapier (*Phot.*); –*ing-press*, *s.* die Druckpresse, Schnellpresse; Druckerei; –*ing-types*, *pl.* die Lettern; –*ing-works*, (*sing. constr.*) see –*ing-office*. **--works,** *pl.* (*sing. constr.*) die Kattunfabrik.

prior ['praɪə], 1. *adj.* früher, eher, älter (*to*, als); vorhergehend (*to* (*Dat.*)); – *claim*, das Vor(zugs)-recht (*to*, auf (*Acc.*)); – *condition*, erste Voraussetzung. 2. *adv.*; – *to*, vor (*Dat.*). 3. *s.* der Prior. **-ate** [–ərət], *s.* das Amt eines Priors. **-ess** [–ərəs], *s.* die Priorin. **-i** [prɪ'ɔːrɪ], *adv.*; *a –i*, von vornherein, aus Vernunftgründen. **-ity** [–'ɔrɪtɪ], *s.* die Priorität, der Vorrang, Vorzug (*over*, vor); das Vor(zugs)recht (*over*, vor); –*ity of birth*, die Erstgeburt; *take –ity over*, den Vorrang haben vor; –*ity share*, die Vorzugsaktie. **-y** [–ərɪ], *s.* die Priorei.

prism [prɪzm], *s.* das Prisma; – *binoculars*, *pl.* das Prismenglas. **-atic** [–'mætɪk], *adj.* primatisch, Prismen–; –*atic colours*, die Regenbogenfarben.

prison ['prɪzən], *s.* das Gefängnis, die Strafanstalt; *in* –, im Gefängnis; *put in* or *send to* –, ins Gefängnis werfen. **--break,** *s.* der Ausbruch aus dem Gefängnis. **--breaking,** *s.* das Ausbrechen aus dem Gefängnis. **-er** [–ə], *s.* Gefangene(r), *m.*, Angeklagte(r), *m.*, der Sträfling (*Law*); –*er at the bar*, Untersuchungsgefangene(r), *m.*; *be a –er to*, gefesselt sein an; *keep s.o. a –er*, einen gefangen halten; *make –er*, *take –er*, gefangennehmen; –*er of war*, Kriegsgefangene(r), *m.* **-er's-base,** *s.* das Barlaufspiel. **--van,** *s.* der Gefangenenwagen.

pristine ['prɪstɪn], *adj.* ursprünglich, vormalig, ehemalig.

prithee ['prɪðɪ], *int.* (*archaic*) bitte!

privacy ['prɪvəsɪ], *s.* die Heimlichkeit, Geheimhaltung, Zurückgezogenheit, Stille; *in* –, geheim.

private ['praɪvɪt], 1. *adj.* heimlich, geheim; vertraulich, zurückgezogen; Privat–, privat, persönlich, nicht öffentlich; nicht beamtet, ohne Beruf; – *account*, das Geheimkonto; – *affairs*, Privatangelegenheiten, persönliche Angelegenheiten; – *arrangement*, gütlicher Vergleich; – *bill*, der Antrag eines Abgeordneten; – *business*, see – *affairs*; – *chapel*, die Hauskapelle; – *company*, geschlossene Gesellschaft; – *and confidential*, vertraulich; *sell by – contract*, unter der Hand verkaufen; – *gentleman*, der Privatmann; – *hand*, die Privathand; – *hotel*, das Fremdenheim; – *house*, das Privathaus; – *information*, vertrauliche Mitteilung; *keep* –, geheim halten; – *means*, das Privatvermögen; – *member*, nicht beamteter Abgeordneter; – *parts*, Geschlechtsteile (*pl.*); – *property*, das Privatvermögen; – *road*, nicht öffentliche Straße; – *school*, die Privatschule; – *secretary*, der Privatsekretär; – *soldier*, Gemeine(r), *m.*; – *theatre*, das Liebhabertheater; – *tutor*, der Hauslehrer; *for – use*, zum eigenen Gebrauch; – *view*, geschlossene Besichtigung (*of exhibition*). 2. *s.* Gemeine(r), *m.* (*Mil.*); (*coll.*) Landser; *in* –, insgeheim, im geheimen *or* Vertrauen, unter vier Augen; *pl.* Geschlechtsteile.

privateer ['praɪvətɪːə], *s.* der Kommandant eines Kaperschiffs; das Kaperschiff. **-ing** [–'tɪːərɪŋ], *s.* die Kaperei.

privat-ion [praɪ'veɪʃən], *s.* die Entziehung, Wegnahme, Entbehrung, Not, der Mangel. **-ive,** 1. *adj.* beraubend, ausschließend; verneinend (*Gram.*). 2. *s.* die Verneinungspartikel (*Gram.*).

privet ['prɪvət], *s.* der Liguster, die Rainweide (*Bot.*). --*hawk* (*moth*), *s.* der Ligusterschwärmer (*Ent.*).

privilege ['prɪvɪlɪdʒ], 1. *s.* das Vorrecht, Sonderrecht, Privileg(ium); *it is my* –, es steht mir frei; *breach of* –, die Übertretung der Machtbefugnis. *Committee of –s*, der Ausschuß zur Regelung von Übergriffen (*Parl.*). 2. *v.a.* (*usually pass.*) bevorzugen, bevorrechten, privilegieren, befreien (*from*, von); *be –d*, die Ehre haben.

privity ['prɪvɪtɪ], *s.* das Mitwissen, Mitwisserschaft, das Eingeweihtsein, rechtliche Beteiligung, das Rechtsverhältnis, gemeinsame Interessenbeziehung (*Law*).

privy ['prɪvɪ], 1. *adj.* mitwissend (*to*, um), eingeweiht (*to*, in), (mit)beteiligt, mitinteressiert (*to*, an) (*Law*); (*archaic*) geheim, heimlich; *be – to s.th.*, mit um eine S. wissen; – *Council*, der Staatsrat, Geheimer Rat; – *Councillor*, der Geheimrat, Mitglied des Staatsrats; – *parts*, Schamteile, Geschlechtsteile; – *purse*, königliche Privatschatulle; – *seal*, das Geheimsiegel; *Lord – Seal*, der Geheimsiegelbewahrer. 2. *s.* der Mitinteressent, Teilhaber (*to*, an) (*Law*); Abtritt, Abort.

[1]**prize** [praɪz], 1. *s.* der Preis, Gewinn, die Belohnung, Prämie, das Los (*lottery*); *first* –, großes Los (*in a lottery*); –*s of a profession*, erstrebenswerte Posten eines Berufes. 2. *v.a.* (hoch)schätzen, würdigen. **--fight,** *s.* der Preisboxkampf. **--fighter,** *s.* der Preisboxer. **--fighting,** *s.* der Preiswettkampf. **--list,** *s.* die Gewinnliste. **-man,** *see* **- winner.** **--money,** *s.* der Geldpreis. **- poem,** preisgekröntes Gedicht. **- winner,** *s.* der Preisträger. **--winning,** *adj.* preisgekrönt.

[2]**prize** [praɪz], 1. *s.* die Prise, Beute (*Naut.*); *make – of*, als Prise kapern. 2. *v.a.* aufbringen, als Prise nehmen. **--court,** *s.* das Prisengericht. **--crew,** *s.* das Prisenkommando. **--money,** *s.* Prisengelder (*pl.*).

[3]**prize** [praɪz], 1. *s.* der Hebel, die Hebekraft. 2. *v.a.*; – *open*, aufbrechen, erbrechen; (*fig.*) erschließen; – *up*, mit einem Hebel heben.

[1]**pro** [proʊ], 1. *prep.* & *prefix* für, an Stelle von, pro, per; vor–, vorwärts–. 2. *s.* die Ja-Stimme, Stimme dafür; *the –s and cons*, das Für und Wider. **--Boer,** 1. *s.* der Burenfreund. 2. *adj.* burenfreundlich. **- forma,** *adj.* nur der Form wegen, Proforma–, Schein–, fingiert. **- rata,** *adv.* verhältnismäßig, anteilmäßig. **--rector,** *s.* der Prorektor. **- tem-(pore),** *adv.* & *adj.* gegenwärtig, vorübergehend.

[2]**pro** [proʊ], *s.* (*coll.*) *see* **professional** (*Sport*).

proa ['proʊə], *s.* malaiisches Segelboot.

probab-iliorism [prɔbə'bɪlɪərɪzm], *s.* der Probabiliorismus (*R.C.*). **-ilism** ['prɔbəbəlɪzm], *s.* der Probabilismus, Wahrscheinlichkeitsstandpunkt (*R.C.*). **-ility** [–'bɪlɪtɪ], *s.* die Wahrscheinlichkeit, wahrscheinliches Ereignis; *in all –ility*, aller Wahrscheinlichkeit nach; *theory of –ility*, die Wahrscheinlichkeitsrechnung (*Math.*). **-le** ['prɔbəbl], *adj.* wahrscheinlich, vermutlich, mutmaßlich; –*ly not*, schwerlich.

probang ['proʊbæŋ], *s.* die Schlundsonde (*Med.*).

probate ['proʊbeɪt], *s.* gerichtliche Bestätigung eines Testaments; beglaubigte Abschrift eines Testaments; – *court*, das Hinterlegungsgericht; – *duty*, die Erbschaftssteuer.

probation [prə'beɪʃən], *s.* die Probe, Prüfung; Probezeit; das Noviziat (*Eccl.*); die Bewährungsfrist, bedingte Freilassung (*Law*); *on* –, auf Probe, widerruflich; unter Zubilligung von Bewährungsfrist (*Law*); *place on* –, unter Aufsicht stellen; – *officer*, der Bewährungshelfer; – *year*, das Probejahr. **-al,** *adj.*, **-ary,** *adj.* Prüfungs–, Probe–. **-er,** *s.* der Novize (*Eccl.*), (Probe)Kandidat; provisorische Krankenschwester; bedingt freigelassener Sträfling; (*fig.*) der Neuling.

probative ['proʊbətɪv], *adj.* beweisend (*of*, für), als Beweis dienend.

probe [proʊb], 1. *s.* die Sonde (*Surg.*), Sondierung, der Stich. 2. *v.a.* sondieren, abtasten; (*fig.*) untersuchen, prüfen. **--scissors,** *pl.* die Wundschere.

probity ['proʊbɪtɪ], *s.* die Rechtschaffenheit, Redlichkeit.

problem ['prɔbləm], *s.* die Aufgabe, das Problem (*also Math.*), Rechenexempel (*Math.*); schwierige Frage, die Schwierigkeit, das Rätsel; *it is a – to me*, es ist mir rätselhaft *or* ein Rätsel; *be brought up against a* –, vor ein Problem gestellt werden; – *drama*, das Problemdrama; *set a* –, eine Aufgabe stellen, ein Problem aufstellen. **-atic(al)** [–'mætɪk(l)], *adj.* problematisch, fraglich, zweifelhaft.

proboscis [prə'bɔskɪs], *s.* der Rüssel (*also hum.* = *nose*), (*vulg.*) der Zinken, Schnorchel (= *nose*).

procedure [prə'sɪːdjə], *s.* das Verfahren, Verhalten, Vorgehen, der Vorgang, die Arbeitsweise, Handlungsweise; *law of* –, das Prozeßrecht (*Law*); *legal* –, gerichtliches Verfahren, das Prozeßverfahren.

proceed [pro'sɪːd], *v.n.* sich begeben; vorwärtsgehen, weitergehen, weiterreisen, (fort)schreiten, weiterschreiten (*to*, nach); vor sich gehen, vonstatten gehen, sich entwickeln (*of actions*); fortfahren (*with*, in *or* mit), im Sprechen fortfahren; übergehen, (an)gelangen (*to*, zu); vorgehen, verfahren, handeln; ausgehen, herkommen, herrühren (*from*, von), entstehen, hervorgehen (*from*, aus); – *against s.o.*, gerichtlich gegen einen vorgehen *or* einschreiten; – *on a journey*, eine Reise fortsetzen; – *to the attack*, zum Angriff schreiten; – *to business*, beginnen, ans Werk gehen; – *to a degree*, einen (höheren Universitäts)Grad erwerben *or* erlangen; – *upon a principle*, einen Grundsatz befolgen; – *with s.th.*, eine S. in Angriff nehmen *or* fortsetzen. **-ing**, *s.* das Verfahren, Vorgehen, die Handlung, Maßnahme; *pl.* das (Prozeß)Verfahren, der Rechtsgang, Prozeß, die Gerichtsverhandlung (*Law*); Verhandlungem, Sitzungsberichte, (Prozeß)-Akten, Protokolle (*pl.*); *-ings at law*, der Rechtsgang; *take* (*legal*) *-ings*, gerichtlich vorgehen (*against*, gegen). **-s** ['prousɪ:dz], *pl.* der Ertrag, Erlös, Gewinn, Einnahmen (*pl.*); *gross -s*, der Bruttobetrag; *net -s*, der Reinertrag, Nettoertrag.

[1]**process** ['prousɛs], 1. *s.* das Fortschreiten, der Fortgang; Vorgang, das Verfahren, die Arbeitsweise; der Verlauf (*of time*); die Vorladung (*Law*); der Prozeß (*Chem.*, *Law*); die Verlängerung, der Fortsatz, vorspringender Teil (*Bot.*, *Zool.*, *Anat.*); photomechanisches Reproduktionsverfahren (*Print.*); – *of decomposition*, der Verwesungsvorgang; *in* –, im Gange; *in the* –, dabei, bei dem Verfahren; *in – of construction*, im Bau befindlich *or* begriffen; *in – of time*, mit der Zeit, im Laufe der Zeit; – *of manufacture*, der Arbeitsprozeß. 2. *v.a.* gerichtlich belangen (*Law*); photomechanisch herstellen *or* reproduzieren (*Typ.*); (chemisch) behandeln, aufbereiten, verarbeiten, fertigstellen (*Phot.*). **--block**, *s.* das Klischee (*Typ.*). **-ing**, *s.* die Aufbereitung, Behandlung, Bearbeitung.

[2]**process** [pro'sɛs], *v.n.* (*coll.*) in einem Zuge gehen. **-ion** [-'sɛʃən], *s.* feierlicher Zug, der Umzug, Aufzug, die Prozession, Reihe; das Ausströmen (*of the Holy Ghost*); *funeral -ion*, der Leichenzug. **-ional**, 1. *adj.* Prozessions– (*also Ent.*). 2. *s.* das Prozessionsbuch; die Prozessionshymne. **-ionary**, *adj.* Prozessions– (*Ent.*).

proclaim [prə'kleɪm], *v.a.* öffentlich ausrufen *or* verkünden, bekanntmachen, ankündigen, proklamieren; erklären als (*a p.*); (*fig.*) kundgeben; in Bann erklären (*a district*); verbieten (*a meeting*).

proclamation [prɔklə'meɪʃən], *s.* die Ausrufung, Verkündigung, Bekanntmachung, der Aufruf, die Proklamation (*to*, an); Erklärung des Bannes *or* der Ausnahmezustand (*in a district*); – *of war*, die Kriegserklärung.

proclitic [pro'klɪtɪk], 1. *adj.* proklitisch. 2. *s.* proklitisches Wort (*Gram.*).

proclivity [prə'klɪvɪtɪ], *s.* die Neigung, der Hang, Trieb, natürliche Anlage (*to*, zu).

proconsul [prou'kɔnsʌl], *s.* der (Provinzial)-Statthalter. **-ar**, *adj.* Statthalter–. **-ate**, *s.* das Amt *or* die Amtsdauer eines Statthalters.

procrastinat-e [pro'kræstɪneɪt], 1. *v.n.* zögern, zaudern. 2. *v.a.* (*rare*) aufschieben, verzögern, auf die lange Bank schieben. **-ion** [-'neɪʃən], *s.* der Aufschub, die Verzögerung, das Zaudern, die Saumseligkeit.

procrea-nt [prou'krɪənt], *adj.* zeugend, hervorbringend. **-te** [-ɪeɪt], *v.a.* zeugen, hervorbringen; (*fig.*) erzeugen. **-tion** [-ɪ'eɪʃən], *s.* die Zeugung, Hervorbringung. **-tive** ['prɔkrɪətɪv], *adj.* zeugungsfähig, zeugend, Zeugungs–; fruchtbar.

proctor ['prɔktə], *s.* der Anwalt (*Law*); Disziplinarbeamte(r), *m.* (*Univ.*); *-'s man*, der Pedell. **-ial** [-'tɔ:rɪəl], *adj.* Proktor–. **-ize** ['prɔktəraɪz], *v.a.* vor den Proktor laden (*Univ.*). **-ship**, *s.* das Proktoramt.

procumbent [pro'kʌmbənt], *adj.* am Boden liegend (*Bot.*).

procurable [prə'kjuːərəbl], *adj.* erlangbar, zu verschaffen(d).

procurat-ion [prɔkjuː'reɪʃn], *s.* die Besorgung, Verschaffung; Prokura, Vollmacht (*C.L.*); Maklergebühr; Kuppelei; *by -ion*, per Prokura (*C.L.*). **-or**, *s.* der Sach(ver)walter, Vertreter, Bevollmächtigte(r), *m.*

procure [prə'kjuːə], 1. *v.a.* beschaffen, verschaffen, besorgen (*a p. a th.* or *a th. for a p.*, einem etwas); erlangen, erwerben, sich (*Dat.*) verschaffen *or* anschaffen; bewerkstelligen, bewirken, herbeiführen. 2. *v.n.* kuppeln, Kuppelei treiben. **-ment**, *s.* die Besorgung, Verschaffung, Beschaffung; Erwerbung, Veranlassung, Vermittlung, Bewerkstelligung. **-r** [-rə], *s.* der Beschaffer; Kuppler, Zuhälter. **-ss** [-rəs], *s.* die Kupplerin.

prod [prɔd], 1. *v.a.* stechen, stoßen. 2. *s.* das Stechen, Anspornen; der Stich, Stoß; Stachelstock, die Ahle.

prodigal ['prɔdɪgəl], 1. *adj.* verschwenderisch (*of*, mit); *be – of*, verschwenderisch umgehen mit; (*B.*) – *son*, verlorener Sohn. 2. *s.* der Verschwender. **-ity** [-'gælɪtɪ], *s.* die Verschwendung; Üppigkeit, Fülle (*of*, an). **-ize** [-lɑɪz], *v.a.* verschwenden.

prodig-ious [prə'dɪdʒɪəs], *adj.* ungeheuer, gewaltig; erstaunlich, wunderbar. **-y** ['prɔdɪdʒɪ], 1. *s.* das Wunder (*of* (*Gen.*)); *infant -y*, das Wunderkind. 2. *attrib.* Wunder–.

produc-e [prə'djuːs], 1. *v.a.* vorlegen, vorbringen, vorzeigen; hervorholen, hervorziehen (*from*, aus); verursachen, bewirken, erzeugen, hervorbringen, hervorrufen; erzielen, eintragen, einbringen (*profit, etc.*); verlängern (*a line*) (*Math.*); verfassen (*poetry, books*); verfertigen, herstellen, produzieren (*manufactures*); bauen, ziehen (*Agr.*); einstudieren, inszenieren (*a play*) (*Theat.*); beibringen (*witness, evidence, etc.*); anführen (*reasons, etc.*); *be -ed*, entstehen. 2. *s.* ['prɔdjuːs] das Erzeugnis, Produkt; der Ertrag, die Ausbeute, Frucht; (*coll.*) Produkte, Erzeugnisse (*pl.*); *-e market*, der Warenmarkt; *net -e*, der Reinertrag. **-er**, *s.* der Verfertiger, Hersteller, Erzeuger, Produzent; Regisseur, Theaterleiter (*Theat.*); Spielleiter (*Rad.*, *etc.*); (Gas)-Generator. **-er-gas**, *s.* das Generatorgas. **-ible**, *adj.* erzeugbar, herstellbar, produzierbar; vorzeigbar, aufweisbar, beizubringen(d).

product ['prɔdəkt], *s.* das Erzeugnis, Produkt (*also Math.*); Werk, Ergebnis, Resultat, die Wirkung, Frucht. **-ion** [prə'dʌkʃən], *s.* die Hervorbringung, Beibringung, Vorzeigung, Erzeugung, Herstellung, Gewinnung, Produktion; das Erzeugnis, Produkt, Fabrikat, Werk, die Schöpfung; Verlängerung (*of a line*); Aufführung, Vorführung, Inszenierung, Regie (*Theat.*), Spielleitung (*Rad.*, *etc.*); *cost of -ion* or *-ion costs*, Gestehungskosten (*pl.*); *-ion figures*, Ausstoßzahlen (*pl.*); *-ion line*, die Montagerampe. **-ive** [prə'dʌktɪv], *adj.* hervorbringend, schaffend, erzeugend, herstellend, produzierend; fruchtbar, ertragreich, ausgiebig, ergiebig; schöpferisch, produktive; *be -ive*, hervorbringen, erzeugen, führen zu; *-ive capacity*, die Leistungsfähigkeit. **-iveness**, *s.*, **-ivity** [prɔdək'tɪvɪtɪ], *s.* die Fruchtbarkeit, Produktivität, Ergiebigkeit, Leistungsfähigkeit, Ertragsfähigkeit, Rentabilität.

proem ['prouɪm], *s.* die Vorrede, Einleitung. **-ial** [-'ɪ:mɪəl], *adj.* einleitend, Einleitungs–.

profan-ation [prɔfə'neɪʃən], *s.* die Entweihung, Entheiligung, Profanierung. **-e** [prə'feɪn], 1. *adj.* profan, weltlich, nicht kirchlich; ungeweiht, unheilig, gottlos, ruchlos; *-e language*, das Fluchen. 2. *v.a.* entweihen, entheiligen, profanieren, mißbrauchen. **-ity** [prə'fænɪtɪ], *s.* die Gottlosigkeit, Ruchlosigkeit; (*often pl.*) die Profanierung, Lästerung, das Fluchen, Flüche (*pl.*).

profess [prə'fɛs], *v.a.* öffentlich erklären, bekennen; sich bekennen zu; behaupten, versichern, angeben, vorgeben, sich anmaßen, sich ausgeben als; ausüben, betreiben (*a profession*). **-ed** [-'fɛst], *adj.* angeblich, vorgeblich; erklärt (*as an enemy*), ausgesprochen; Berufs–. **-edly** [-'fɛsədlɪ], *adv.* erklärtermaßen, nach eigener Angabe; angeblich. **-ion** [-'fɛʃən], *s.* das Bekenntnis (*Rel.*), heiliges Versprechen, das Gelübde; die Erklärung, Versicherung, Beteuerung; (freier *or* gelehrter) Beruf, der Stand; (*coll.*) *the -ion*, die Gesamtheit der Berufsgenossen; *by -ion*, von Beruf; *learned -ions*, gelehrte Berufe; *-ion of arms*, der Soldatenstand; *-ion of friendship*, die Freundschaftsbeteuerung. **-ional** [-'fɛʃənl], 1. *adj.* beruflich, Berufs–, berufsmäßig, Fach–; *-ional attendance*, ärztliche Behandlung (*Med.*); *-ional classes*, höhere Berufsklassen; *–ional duties*, Berufspflichten; *–ional education*, berufliche Ausbildung; *–ional examination*, die Fachprüfung; *–ional player*, der Berufsspieler; *–ional honour*, die Standesehre, berufliches Ethos; *–ional man*, der Geistesarbeiter, Kopfarbeiter; *of a –ional nature*, berufsmäßig; *–ional politician*, der Berufspolitiker. 2. *s.* der Fachmann, Kopfarbeiter; Berufskünstler, Berufssänger, Künstler, Sänger, *etc.* von Fach (*Theat.*, *Arts*, *etc.*), Berufsspieler (*Sport*). **–ionalism** [–ˈfɛʃənəlɪzm], *s.* die Berufsausübung; das Berufsspielertum (*Sport.*). **–or** [–ˈfɛsə], *s.* der (Universitäts)Professor; *assistant –or*, außerordentlicher Professor (*Amer.*); *full –or*, ordentlicher Professor, der Ordinarius. **–orial** [prɔfəˈsɔːrɪəl], *adj.* Professor–; *–orial chair*, der Lehrstuhl. **–oriate** [prɔfəˈsɔːrɪət], s. der Lehrkörper, Professoren (*pl.*). **–orship** [–ˈfɛsəʃɪp], *s.* die Professur.

proffer [ˈprɔfə], 1. *v.a.* anbieten. 2. *s.* das Anerbieten.

proficien–cy [prəˈfɪʃənsɪ], *s.* die Tüchtigkeit, Fertigkeit. **–t** [–ənt], 1. *adj.* tüchtig, geübt, bewandert (*in*, in). 2. *s.* der Meister (*in*, in).

profile [ˈproufiːl], 1. *s.* das Profil, die Seitenansicht, das Seitenbild; senkrechter Durchschnitt (*Arch.*); der Längsschnitt, Querschnitt; (*fig.*) knappe biographische Skizze; *in* –, im Profil. 2. *v.a.* im Profil darstellen, profilieren.

profit [ˈprɔfɪt], 1. *s.* der Vorteil, Nutzen, Gewinn; (*usually pl.*) Profit (*C.L.*); *derive – from*, Nutzen ziehen aus; *leave a* –, einen Gewinn abwerfen (*C.L.*); *– and loss*, Gewinn und Verlust; *make a – on*, einen Gewinn ziehen aus; *sell at a* –, mit Gewinn verkaufen; *to his* –, zu seinem Vorteil. 2. *v.n.* gewinnen, profitieren (*by* or *from*, aus) (*of things*); Nutzen ziehen (*by* or *from*, aus), sich zu Nutzen machen (*by* or *from* (*Acc.*)) (*of persons*); *– by an opportunity*, eine Gelegenheit benutzen. 3. *v.a.* nützen, Nutzen bringen (*a p.*, einem). **–able**, *adj.* nützlich, vorteilhaft (*to*, für); einträglich, rentabel (*C.L.*). **–ableness**, *s.* die Nützlichkeit; Einträglichkeit. **–eer** [prɔfɪˈtɪːə], 1. *s.* der (Kriegs)-Gewinnler, Schieber. 2. *v.n.* schieben, Schiebergeschäfte machen. **–eering** [–ˈtɪːərɪŋ], *s.* die Schiebung, Preistreiberei, Wuchergeschäfte (*pl.*). **–less**, *adj.* nutzlos; nicht einträglich. **– -sharing**, *s.* die Gewinnbeteiligung. **– -taking**, *s.* die Gewinnsicherung (*stock exchange*).

profliga–cy [ˈprɔflɪgəsɪ], *s.* die Verworfenheit, Liederlichkeit; Verschwendung. **–te** [–gət], 1. *adj.* verworfen, liederlich; verschwenderisch. 2. *s.* liederlicher Mensch.

profound [prəˈfaʊnd], *adj.* tief, tiefsitzend, tiefreichend, tiefgründig; gründlich, in die Tiefe gehend; tiefsinnig, inhalt(s)schwer, dunkel; – *ignorance*, krasse Unwissenheit; – *indifference*, vollkommene Gleichgültigkeit; – *interest*, starkes Interesse; – *reverence*, tiefe Verbeugung; – *sleep*, tiefer Schlaf. **–ly**, *adv.* tief, aufrichtig. **–ness**, *s.* *see* **profundity.**

profundity [prəˈfʌndɪtɪ], *s.* die Tiefe, der Abgrund; (*fig.*) die Gründlichkeit, Tiefgründigkeit, Tiefsinnigkeit.

profus–e [prəˈfjuːs], *adj.* überreich, übermäßig, reichlich; verschwenderisch, freigebig (*of* or *in*, mit). **–eness**, *s.* die Übermäßigkeit, der Überfluß, Reichtum; verschwenderische Freigebigkeit. **–ion** [–ˈfjuːʒən], *s.* der Überfluß, Reichtum (*of*, an), die Fülle (*of*, von); Verschwendung, der Luxus; *in –ion*, überreichlich, in Hülle und Fülle, im Überflusse.

prog [prɔg], 1. *s.* (*sl.*) Lebensmittel (*pl.*), die Nahrung, der (Reise)Proviant; Proktor (*Univ. sl.*). 2. *v.a. see* **proctorize** (*Univ. sl.*).

progen–itive [prouˈdʒɛnɪtɪv], *adj.* Zeugungs–, zeugungsfähig. **–itor** [–tə], *s.* der Vorfahr, Ahn. **–itress** [–trɪs], *s.* die Ahne. **–iture** [–tjə], *s.* das Zeugen, die Zeugung; Nachkommenschaft. **–y** [ˈprɔdʒənɪ], *s.* die Nachkommenschaft; Brut, Junge(n) (*pl.*) (*of beasts*); Kinder (*pl.*) (*of man*); (*fig.*) das Produkt, die Frucht.

proggins [ˈprɔgɪnz], *s.* (*sl.*) der Proktor (*Univ.*).

proglottis [prouˈglɔtɪs], *s.* das Glied des Bandwurms.

prognath–ic [prɔgˈnæθɪk], **–ous** [–ˈneɪθəs], *adj.* vorspringend (*of jaws*). **–ism** [ˈprɔgnəθɪzm], *s.* vorspringende Kieferbildung, die Prognathie.

prognos–is [prɔgˈnousɪs], *s.* (pl. *–es* [–ɪːz]) die Prognose (*Med.*). **–tic** [–ˈnɔstɪk], 1. *adj.* voraussagend, vorbedeutend (*of* (*Acc.*)). 2. *s.* das Vorzeichen, die Voraussage, Vorbedeutung (*of* (*Gen.*)). **–ticable** [–ˈnɔstɪkəbl], *adj.* voraussagbar. **–ticate** [–ˈnɔstɪkeɪt], *v.a.* vorhersagen, vorbedeuten; anzeigen, andeuten. **–tication** [–ˈkeɪʃən], *s.* die Voraussage; Weissagung, Vorbedeutung. **–ticator** [–ˈnɔstɪkeɪtə], *s.* der Wahrsager.

program(me) [ˈprougræm], *s.* das Programm; programmäßige Darbietung, die Sendefolge, Hörfolge (*Rad.*); der Theaterzettel (*Theat.*); die Tanzkarte (*Danc.*); der Arbeitsplan; das (Partei)Programm (*Pol.*); *draw up a* – (*of work*), einen Arbeitsplan aufstellen; (*coll.*) *what is the – for to-day?* was haben wir heute vor? **– -music**, *s.* die Programmmusik.

progress [ˈprougrɛs], 1. *s.* das Vorschreiten, Vorrücken, der Fortgang, Fortlauf; Fortschritt, Fortschritte (*pl.*), die Entwicklung (zum Besseren); das Überhandnehmen, Umsichgreifen; festliche Rundreise, offizielle Reise; *in* –, im Gange; *make* –, vorwärtsschreiten; Fortschritte machen, fortschreiten (*in* or *with*, in); *much* –, grosse *or* viele Fortschritte; *report* –, den Stand der Verhandlungen kurz berichten (*Parl.*). 2. [proˈgrɛs], *v.n.* weitergehen, weiterschreiten; (*fig.*) weiterkommen, vorwärtskommen, fortschreiten, seinen Fortgang nehmen; Fortschritte machen, sich weiterentwickeln, sich bessern. **–ion** [–ˈgrɛʃən], *s.* das Fortschreiten (*also Mus.*), Vorrücken, der Verlauf, Fortgang, Fortschritt; die Reihe, Progression (*Math.*). **–ional** [–ˈgrɛʃənl], *adj.* fortschreitend, Fortschritts–. **–ionist** [–ˈgrɛʃənɪst], *s.* der Fortschrittler (*Pol.*). **–ive** [–ˈgrɛsɪv], 1. *adj.* fortschreitend, (nach und nach) aufsteigend *or* zunehmend, progressiv, gestaffelt; fortschrittlich (*Pol.*); *–ive form*, die Dauerform (*of a verb*); *–ive party*, die Fortschrittspartei; *–ive step*, der Schritt vorwärts, Fortschritt. 2. *s.* der Fortschrittler (*Pol.*). **–ively**, *adv.* stufenweise, nach und nach, nacheinander, allmählich.

prohibit [proˈhɪbɪt], *v.a.* verbieten, verhindern (*a th. being done*, daß etwas geschieht); – *a p. from doing*, einem verbieten *or* einen verhindern zu tun; *–ed area*, das Sperrgebiet. **–ion** [–ˈbɪʃən], *s.* das Verbot; Alkoholverbot; *writ of –ion*, der Sistierungsbefehl (*Law*). **–ionist** [–ˈbɪʃənɪst], *s.* der Schutzzöllner; Alkoholgegner, Antialkoholiker. **–ive** [–ˈhɪbɪtɪv], *adj.*, **–ory** [–ˈhɪbɪtərɪ], *adj.* verbietend, verhindernd, Prohibitiv–, Sperr–; *–ive duty*, der Schutzzoll; *–ive price*, unerschwinglicher Preis.

project [prəˈdʒɛkt], 1. *v.a.* (vorwärts)werfen, schleudern; werfen (*an image*); entwerfen, planen, projektieren (*a plan*); – *one's thoughts* or *o.s. into*, sich in Gedanken versetzen in. 2. *v.n.* hervorragen, vorspringen, vorstehen. 3. [ˈprɔdʒəkt], *s.* der Entwurf, Plan, Anschlag, das Projekt, Vorhaben. **–ile** [prəˈdʒɛktaɪl], 1. *adj.* Wurf– (*weapon*); Stoß–, Trieb– (*force*). 2. *s.* das Projektil; Geschoß (*Artil.*). **–ing**, *adj.* vorgelagert, vorstehend, hinausragend. **–ion** [–ˈdʒɛkʃən], *s.* das Werfen, Schleudern, der Wurf; das Vorspringen, Horvorragen, Hervortreten, der Vorsprung, Überhang; die Projektion (*Math.*); das Entwerfen, der Entwurf, Plan, Vorsatz; die Darstellung, das Abbild; Wurfbild, Wandbild; *–ion room*, der Vorführungsraum (*cinema*). **–or** [–ˈdʒɛktə], *s.* der Pläneschmied, Projektemacher; Bildwerfer, Projektionsapparat (*Opt.*, *Films*); Scheinwerfer.

prolaps–e, –us [proˈlæps(əs)], *s.* der Vorfall, Prolaps (*Med.*).

prolate [ˈprouleɪt], *adj.* gestreckt (*Math.*).

prolegomen–al [proulɪˈgɔmɪnəl], **–ary** [–nərɪ], *adj.* einleitend. **–on** [–nən], *s.* (*usually pl.* –a [–nə]) die Vorbemerkung, Einleitung. **–ous** [–nəs], *adj.* einleitend; (*fig.*) langatmig.

prolep–sis [prouˈlɛpsɪs], *s.* vorwegnehmende Antwort, die Vorwegnahme Prolepsis (*Rhet.*). **–tic** [-ˈtɪk], *adj.* vorwegnehmend, vorgreifend.

proletaria–n [proulɪ'tɛ:ərɪən], 1. *adj.* proletarisch, Proletarier–. 2. *s.* der Proletarier. **–t** [–rɪət], *s.* das Proletariat.
prolif–erate [prə'lɪfəreɪt], *v.n.* sich fortpflanzen, wuchern. **–eration** [–'reɪʃən], *s.* die Sprossung, Wucherung, Prolifikation (*Bot.*). **–ic** [–'lɪfɪk], *adj.* fruchtbar (*also fig.*); befruchtend; (*fig.*) reich (*of*, an); produktiv; *be –ic of*, verursachen, hervorbringen.
prolix [pro'lɪks, 'proulɪks], *adj.* weitschweifig, wortreich. **–ity** [–'lɪksɪtɪ], *s.* die Weitschweifigkeit.
prolocutor ['proulәkju:tә, prә'lәkjәtә], *s.* der Wortführer, Vorsitzende(r), *m.* (der Synode) (*Eccl.*).
prolog–ize ['prouləd3aɪz], *see* **–uize.** **–ue** ['proulәg], *s.* der Prolog, die Vorrede, Einleitung, das Vorwort; (*fig.*) Vorspiel, der Auftakt. **–uize** ['proulәgaɪz], *v.n.* einen Prolog machen.
prolong [prә'lәŋ], *v.a.* verlängern, ausdehnen; dehnen (*Phonet.*); prolongieren (*C.L.*). **–ation** [prolәŋ'geɪʃən], *s.* die Verlängerung, Ausdehnung; Prolongierung, Prolongation (*C.L.*). **–ed** [–'lәŋgd], *adj.* anhaltend.
prolusion [pro'lju3әn], *s.* der Versuch, Essay.
promenade [prәmә'nɑ:d, –'neɪd], 1. *s.* der Spaziergang; Spazierweg, Strandweg (*on sea-front*); die Wandelanlage, Anlagen (*pl.*), die Promenade. 2. *v.n.* spazierengehen, auf und ab gehen, promenieren. 3. *v.a.* auf und ab schreiten, umherspazieren in *or* auf (*a place*); spazieren führen, umherführen (*a p.*). **– concert,** *s.* das Promenadenkonzert. **– deck,** *s.* das Promenadendeck.
prominen–ce ['prәmɪnәns], *s.* das Hervorragen, Vorspringen; der Vorsprung, die Protuberanz; (*fig.*) Wichtigkeit, Bedeutung; *bring into –ce*, klar herausstellen, berühmt machen; *come into –ce*, hervortreten, in den Vordergrund treten. **–t** [–әnt], *adj.* hervorragend, vorspringend; (*fig.*) hervorstechend, prominent; in die Augen fallend, führend.
promiscu–ity [prәmɪs'kjuɪtɪ], *s.* die Gemischtheit, Vermischung, das Durcheinander; die Promiskuität, zwangloser geschlechtlicher Verkehr. **–ous** [prә'mɪskjuәs], *adj.* gemischt, vermischt, untermischt; gemeinschaftlich; unterschiedslos; gelegentlich, zufällig. **–ously,** *adv.* durcheinander, unterschiedslos, zufällig.
promis–e ['prәmɪs], 1. *s.* das Versprechen (*to a p.*, einem gegenüber); die Verheißung, Hoffnung (*of*, zu *or* auf), Erwartung (*of*, auf); *breach of –e*, der Bruch des Eheversprechens; *of great –e*, vielversprechend, verheißungsvoll; *keep a –e*, ein Versprechen halten *or* einlösen; *make a –e*, ein Versprechen geben. 2. *v.a.* versprechen, in Aussicht stellen (*a p. a th.* or *a th. to a p.*, einem etwas); Hoffnungen erwecken, hoffen lassen, erwarten lassen, befürchten lassen; (*coll.*) versichern; (*B.*) *–ed land*, gelobtes Land. 3. *v.n.* Erwartungen erwecken; *he –es well*, er läßt sich gut an; *it –es fine*, das Wetter verspricht gut zu werden. 4. *v.r.* in Aussicht nehmen, der festen Hoffnung sein auf. **–ee** [–'sɪ], *s.* der Empfänger einer Promesse, Promissar (*Law*). **–ing,** *adj.* vielversprechend, hoffnungsvoll, verheißungsvoll, günstig; *–ing weather*, günstiges Wetter; *–ing youth*, vielversprechender Jüngling. **–or** ['prәmɪsә], *s.* der Geber einer Promesse (*Law*). **–sory** ['prәmɪsәrɪ], *adj.* vielversprechend; *–sory note*, die Promesse, der Schuldschein, eigner Wechsel, der Solawechsel (*C.L.*).
promontory ['prәmәntәrɪ], *s.* das Vorgebirge; stumpfer Vorsprung (*Anat.*).
promot–e [prә'mout], *v.a.* befördern (*a p.*), erheben zu (*a rank*); fördern, beleben, begünstigen; befürworten; gründen (*a company, etc.*); unterstützen, einbringen (*a law*). **–er,** *s.* der Förderer, Befürworter; Anstifter (*of a plot, etc.*); Gründer (*of a company*). **–ion** [–'mouʃәn], *s.* die Förderung, Begünstigung, Befürwortung; Beförderung (*to*, auf) (*in rank*); Gründung (*C.L.*); (*Amer.*) Reklame, Propaganda, Werbung. **–ional,** *adj.* Propaganda–, Reklame–, Werbe–. **–ive,** *adj.* (be)fördernd; *be –ive of*, fördern.
prompt [prәmpt], 1. *adj.* schnell, rasch, pünktlich, prompt, sofortig, unverzüglich, umgehend (*reply*); bereit, (bereit)willig; *– cash*, die Barzahlung (*C.L.*). 2. *s.* der Zahlungstag, die Zahlungsfrist (*C.L.*). 3. *v.a.* & *n.* soufflieren (*Theat.*), zuflüstern (*Dat.*); einflößen, eingeben; (an)treiben, veranlassen (*to*, zu). **– –book,** *s.* das Souffleurbuch. **– –box,** *s.* der Souffleurkasten. **–er,** *s.* der Souffleur (*Theat.*), Anreger, Antreiber; *–er's box*, see **– –box.** **–ing,** *s.* (*often pl.*) die Eingebung. **–itude** ['prәmptɪtju:d], *s.*, **–ness,** *s.* die Schnelligkeit, Unverzüglichkeit, Pünklichkeit, Promptheit: Bereitwilligkeit. **– –note,** *s.* der Mahnzettel (*C.L.*).
promulgat–e ['prәmәlgeɪt], *v.a.* bekanntmachen, verkündigen, verbreiten. **–ion** [–'geɪʃәn], *s.* die Bekanntmachung, Verkünd(ig)ung, Verbreitung. **–or,** *s.* der Verbreiter.
pron–ate ['prouneɪt], *v.a.* strecken (*a limb*). **–ator** [–'neɪtә], *s.* der Pronator (*Anat.*). **–e** [proun], *adj.* vorwärts geneigt; hingestreckt, auf dem Gesicht *or* Bauch liegend; abschüssig (*as ground*); (*fig.*) *–e to*, geneigt zu. **–eness** ['prounnɪs], *s.* die Neigung, Geneigtheit, der Hang (*to*, zu).
prong [prәŋ], *s.* die Zinke, Zacke, Spitze; Gabel; das Horn (*of animals*). **–ed** [–d], *adj.* zackig, gezinkt, –hörnig. **– –buck, – –horn(ed antelope),** *s.* die Gabelantilope.
prono–minal [pro'noumɪnl], *adj.* pronominal (*Gram.*). **–un** ['prounaun], *s.* das Fürwort, Pronomen.
pronounc–e [prә'nauns], 1. *v.a.* aussprechen (*words*); verkünd(ig)en, verhängen, fällen (*on*, über) (*a verdict*); (bestimmt) erklären (*to be*, für); *–e o.s. in favour of*, sich dafür aussprechen. 2. *v.n.* sich aussprechen *or* erklären (*for*, für; *against*, gegen), sich äußern (*on*, über). **–eable** [–әbl], *adj.* aussprechbar, auszusprechen(d). **–ed** [–t], *adj.*, ausgesprochen, (*fig.*) bestimmt, entschieden, deutlich ausgeprägt. **–ement** [–mәnt], *s.* die Äußerung, Erklärung, Verkünd(ig)ung. **–ing,** *adj.* Aussprache–.
pronto ['prәntou], *adv.* (*sl.*) schnellstens, bald; prompt.
pronunciation [prә'nʌnsɪ'eɪʃәn], *s.* die Aussprache, das Aussprechen.
proof [pru:f], 1. *s.* der Beweis (*of*, für), Nachweis, Erweis; die Probe (*also Arith.*), Prüfung; der (Probe)Abdruck, Abzug, Korrekturbogen, die Korrektur (*Typ.*); das Probebild (*Phot.*); die Beweisaussage, Beweisaufnahme (*Law*); die Normalstärke (*of alcohol*); (*fig.*) Festigkeit, Undurchdringlichkeit; *– before letters*, der Abzug vor Eintragung der Schrift (*Engr.*); *burden of –*, die Beweislast; *first –*, erste Korrektur (*Typ.*); *give – of*, unter Beweis stellen, Beweise abgeben von; *in – of*, zum Beweise von; *of –*, undurchdringlich; *press- –*, letzte Korrektur (*Typ.*); (*Prov.*) *the – of the pudding is in the eating*, in der Praxis allein zeigt sich die Bewährung; *put to* (*the*) *–*, auf die Probe stellen; *under –*, unter Normalstärke. 2. *adj.* undurchdringlich; beständig, echt, fest, hart; erprobt, bewährt; sicher (*against*, vor), stichhaltig, gesichert, gefeit, gewappnet (*against*, gegen); *bomb- –*, bombensicher; *fire- –*, feuerfest; *fool–*, sicher vor der gröbsten unfachmännischen Behandlung; *water- –*, wasserdicht. 3. *v.a.* imprägnieren. **– –mark,** *s.* der Probestempel. **– –reader,** *s.* der Korrekturleser, Korrektor. **– –reading,** *s.* das Korrekturlesen; die Korrektur. **– –sheet,** *s.* der Korrekturbogen. **– –spirit,** der Normalweingeist.
prop [prәp], 1. *s.* die Stütze (*also fig.*), der (Stütz)-Pfahl, die Strebe; (*fig.*) der Pfeiler, Halt. 2. *v.a.* (also *– up*) (unter)stützen; pfählen (*vines, etc.*).
propaedeutic(–al) [prәpә'djuɪtɪk(l)], *adj.* einführend, propädeutisch. **–s** [–tɪks], *pl.* (*sing. constr.*) die Propädeutik.
propagand–a [prәpә'gændә], *s.* die Propaganda, Werbung; *carry on* or *make –a for*, Propaganda treiben für. **–ist** [–'gændɪst], *s.* der Propagandist. **–istic** [–gæn'dɪstɪk], *adj.* propagandistisch. **–ize** [–'gændaɪz], *v.n.* Propaganda treiben, propagieren.
propagat–e ['prәpәgeɪt], *v.a.* fortpflanzen (*also fig.*); erzeugen; verbreiten, ausbreiten (*also Rad.*); Propaganda machen für; *be –ed*, sich fortpflanzen. **–ion** [–'geɪʃәn], *s.* die Fortpflanzung (*also fig.*); Verbreitung, Ausbreitung (*Rad.*). **–or,** *s.* der Fortpflanzer; Verbreiter.

propel [prə'pɛl], *v.a.* vorwärtstreiben, forttreiben. **–lant** [–ənt], *s.* das Treibmittel, vorwärtstreibende Kraft, der Antrieb. **–lent** [–ənt], 1. *adj.* vorwärtstreibend. 2. *s. see* **–lant, –ler** [–ə], *s.* (also *screw-–ler*) der Propeller, die Luftschraube, Schiffsschraube. **–ler-blade,** das Propellerblatt, der Schraubenflügel. **–ling,** *adj.* Trieb–; *–ling charge,* die Treibladung (*Artil.*); *–ling force,* die Triebkraft; *–ling pencil,* der Dreh(blei)stift.

propensity [prə'pɛnsɪtɪ], *s.* die Neigung, der Hang (*to* or *for,* zu).

proper ['prɔpə], *adj.* eigentümlich, eigen (*to* (*Dat.*)); geeignet, passend (*to,* für); geziemend, angebracht, korrekt, schicklich; (*coll.*) anständig; zuständig, maßgebend, richtig, genau; (*following noun*) eigentlich; (*coll.*) gründlich, tüchtig; – *behaviour,* anständiges Benehmen; *do as you think* –, handeln Sie wie Sie es für gut finden *or* geeignet halten; – *fraction,* echter Bruch (*Math.*); *the garden* –, der eigentliche Garten; – *name* or *noun,* der Eigenname; *he is a – scoundrel,* er ist durchaus ein Schuft; *in the – sense of the word,* im richtigen *or* eigentlichen Sinne des Wortes; *that's the – thing to do,* das ist das (einzig) Richtige; *at the – time,* zur richtigen *or* passenden Zeit. **–ly,** *adv.* richtig, genau, eigentlich; anständig; (*coll.*) gehörig, gründlich, tüchtig; *–ly speaking,* streng genommen.

propert–ied ['prɔpətɪd], *adj.* besitzend, begütert. **–y** ['prɔpətɪ], *s.* das Eigentum, Besitztum, der Besitz, das Vermögen; (*also with art.*) der Grundbesitz, die Besitzung, das Landgut; Ländereien, Immobilien (*pl.*); die Eigenschaft (*also Log.*), Eigentümlichkeit, Eigenheit; das Eigentumsrecht (*Law*); *pl.* (Bühnen)Requisiten (*Theat.*); *common –y,* das Gemeingut; *house–y,* der Hausbesitz; *literary –y,* literarisches Eigentum(srecht); *man of –y,* vermögender Mann; *lost –y,* Fundsachen (*pl.*); *lost-–y office,* das Fundbüro; *personal –y,* bewegliche Habe; *public –y,* öffentliches Eigentum. **–y-market,** *s.* der Grundstücksmarkt. **–y-master,** *s.* der Requisitenmeister (*Theat.*). **–y-room,** *s.* die Requisitenkammer (*Theat.*). **–y-tax,** *s.* die Vermögenssteuer.

prophe–cy ['prɔfəsɪ], *s.* die Prophezeiung, Weissagung. **–sy** ['prɔfəsɑɪ], 1. *v.a.* prophezeien, vorhersagen (*a th. for a p.,* einem etwas). 2. *v.n.* weissagen. **–t** [–fɪt], *s.* der Prophet, Wahrsager, Weissager, Seher; *major –t,* großer Prophet; *minor –t,* kleiner Prophet; *a –t is not without honour save in his own country,* ein Prophet gilt nichts in seinem Vaterlande. **–tess** [–fɪtəs], *s.* die Prophetin. **–tic** [prə'fɛtɪk], *adj.* prophetisch; *be –tic of,* prophezeien, vorhersagen.

prophyla–ctic [prɔfɪ'læktɪk], 1. *adj.* vorbeugend, Vorbeugungs–, prophylaktisch. 2. *s.* das Vorbeugungsmittel, Abwehrmittel. **–xis** [–'læksɪs], *s.* die Vorbeugung, Prophilaxe.

propinquity [prə'pɪŋkwɪtɪ], *s.* die Nähe (*in place, time*); enge Verwandtschaft.

propiti–ate [prə'pɪʃɪeɪt], *v.a.* sich (*Dat.*) günstig stimmen *or* geneigt machen; besänftigen; versöhnen. **–ation** [–'eɪʃən], *s.* die Versöhnung, Sühne; das Sühnopfer. **–atory** [–'pɪʃɪətərɪ], *adj.* versöhnend, versöhnlich, besänftigend; Sühne–, Sühn–. **–ous** [–'pɪʃjəs], *adj.* günstig, vorteilhaft (*to,* für); geneigt, gnädig. **–ousness,** *s.* die Gnade, Gunst, Milde.

proponent [prə'pounənt], *s.* der Verfechter.

proportion [prə'pɔ:ʃən], 1. *s.* das Verhältnis, Maß; Ebenmaß, Gleichmaß, die Symmetrie, die Größe, der Umfang; Teil, Anteil; die Proportion, Regeldetri (*Math.*); *pl.* das Ausmaß, Dimensionen (*pl.*); *in* –, verhältnismäßig; *in – to,* im Verhältnis zu; *in – as,* im Verhältnis *or* in dem Maße wie, je nachdem wie; *out of* –, unverhältnismäßig; *out of all – to,* in keinem Verhältnis zu; *sense of* –, der Sinn für richtige Proportion; (*fig.*) der Maßstab für die Wirklichkeit. 2. *v.a.* in ein richtiges Verhältnis bringen (*to,* mit *or* zu); gehörig anpassen (*to,* an); verhältnismäßig austeilen (*to,* an). **–able,** *adj.* entsprechend (*to* (*Dat.*)). **–al,** 1. *adj.* verhältnismäßig, Verhältnis–; *–al numbers,* Proportionalzahlen; *–al representation,* das Verhältniswahlsystem. 2. *s.* die Proportionale (*Math.*). **–ality** [–'nælɪtɪ], *s.* die Proportionalität. **–ate** [–ʃənət], 1. *adj.* angemessen, entsprechend (*to* (*Dat.*)), im Verhältnis (*to,* zu) proportioniert, ausgeglichen. 2. *v.a.* verhältnismäßig ausmessen *or* abmessen *or* bemessen. **–ately,** *adv.* entsprechend. **–ed,** *adj.* angemessen; (*as suffix*) –geformt, –proportioniert.

propos–al [prə'pouzəl], *s.* der Plan, Vorschlag, Antrag; Heiratsantrag. **–e** [prə'pouz], 1. *v.a.* vorschlagen (*a p. or th.*) (*for,* zu *or* als; *a th. to a p.,* einem etwas), beantragen; *–e as candidate,* als Kandidaten aufstellen; *–e marriage,* einen Heiratsantrag machen; *–e a riddle,* ein Rätsel aufgeben; *–e s.th. to o.s.,* sich (*Dat.*) vornehmen; *–e the toast of s.o.,* den Toast auf einen ausbringen; *–e a vote of censure,* ein Mißtrauensvotum stellen *or* beantragen; *–e a vote of thanks,* den Antrag stellen, einem Dank auszusprechen. 2. *v.n.* sich vornehmen, vorhaben, in Aussicht nehmen, beabsichtigen; anhalten (*for,* um), einen (Heirats)Antrag machen (*to* (*Dat.*)); (*Prov.*) *man –es, God disposes,* der Mensch denkt, Gott lenkt. **–er,** *s.* der Antragsteller, Vorschlagende(r), *m.* **–ition** [prɔpə'zɪʃən], *s.* der Antrag, Vorschlag, die Behauptung, der (Lehr)Satz (*Math. and Log.*), (*coll.*) die Aufgabe, der Plan; das Geschäft, Unternehmen. **–itional,** *adj.* Satz–.

propound [prə'pɑund], *v.a.* vorschlagen, vortragen (*to* (*Dat.*)), vorbringen, vorlegen; – *a will,* auf Anerkennung eines Testaments klagen. **–er,** *s.* der Antragsteller, Vorschlagende(r), *m.*

propriet–ary [prə'prɑɪətərɪ], 1. *adj.* einem Eigentümer gehörig; gesetzlich *or* patentlich geschützt; *–ary article,* der Markenartikel; *–ary classes,* besitzende Klassen; *–ary right,* das Eigentumsrecht. 2. *s.* der Eigentümer, Besitzer (*also pl.*); das Eigentumsrecht. **–or** [–tə], *s.* der Eigentümer, Besitzer, Inhaber. **–orship,** *s.* das Eigentumsrecht (*in,* an). **–ress** [–trɪs], **–rix** [–trɪks], *s.* die Eigentümerin, Besitzerin, Inhaberin.

propriet–y [prə'prɑɪətɪ], *s.* der Anstand, die Schicklichkeit, Richtigkeit, Angemessenheit; *the –ies,* Anstandsformen (*pl.*), die Wohlanständigkeit; *–y of conduct,* anständiges Betragen.

props [prɔps], *pl.* (*sl.*) (Bühnen)Requisiten.

propulsi–on [prə'pʌlʃən], *s.* der Antrieb; *jet-–on,* der Strahlvortrieb (*Av.*). **–ve** [–sɪv], 1. *adj.* vorwärts treibend, Trieb–. 2. *s.* die Triebkraft.

propylaeum [prɔpɪ'leɪəm], *s.* der Eingang, das Tor.

prorog–ation [prourə'geɪʃən], *s.* die Vertagung. **–ue** [pro'roug], *v.a.* vertagen.

prosaic(al) [prou'zeɪɪk(l)], *adj.* prosaisch, alltäglich, nüchtern, trocken.

proscenium [prou'sɪ:nɪəm], *s.* das Proszenium, die Vorbühne.

proscri–be [pro'skrɑɪb], *v.a.* ächten, verbannen; verbieten. **–ption** [–'skrɪpʃən], *s.* die Ächtung, Acht; Verbannung, Ausschließung, das Verbot. **–ptive** [–'skrɪptɪv], *adj.* ächtend, Ächtungs–.

prose [prouz], 1. *s.* die Prosa; (*fig.*) Alltäglichkeit, das Prosaische, Alltägliche; (*coll.*) die Übersetzung in die Fremdsprache. 2. *adj.* Prosa–. 3. *v.n.* langweilig erzählen. 4. *v.a.* in Prosa schreiben. **–-writer,** *s.* der Prosaiker, Prosaschriftsteller.

prosector [prou'sɛktə], *s.* der Prosektor (*Anat.*).

prosecut–e ['prɔsɪkju:t], 1. *v.a.* verfolgen (*enquiry*); betreiben (*an activity*); gerichtlich verfolgen, belangen, anklagen (*for,* wegen) (*Law*); einklagen, erwirken (*a right or claim*). 2. *v.n.* die Anklage vertreten (*Law*). **–ion** [–'kju:ʃən], *s.* die Verfolgung, Durchführung; Anklage, das Betreiben, gerichtliche Verfolgung; Anklagevertreter (*pl.*); *witness for the –ion,* der Belastungszeuge; *director of public –ions,* der Staatsanwalt. **–or** ['prɔsɪkju:tə], *s.* der Verfolger; Kläger, Ankläger (*Law*); *public –or,* der Staatsanwalt.

proselyt–e ['prɔsəlɑɪt], *s.* der Überläufer, Übergetretene(r), *m.*, der Proselyt. **–ism** [–lətɪzm], *s.* der Bekehrungseifer, Proselytismus. **–ize** [–lətɑɪz], *v.n.* Anhänger werben, Proselyten machen.

prosiness ['prouzɪnɪs], *s.* die Langweiligkeit, Eintönigkeit, Weitschweifigkeit.

prosody ['prɔsədɪ], *s.* die Lehre von der Silbenmessung, Prosodie.

prospect, 1. ['prɔspɛkt], *s.* die Aussicht (*also fig.*)

(*of*, auf), der Blick (*of*, auf), die Landschaft; Anwartschaft; Schürfstelle, der Schurf, die Erzprobe (*Min.*); (*fig.*) voraussichtlicher Ertrag; voraussichtlicher Kunde, der Reflektant; *there is a* –, es ist Aussicht vorhanden (*of*, auf; *that*, daß); *hold out a* –, in Aussicht stellen (*of a th. to a p.*, einem etwas); *pleasures in* –, Freuden in Aussicht; *have in* –, in Aussicht haben. 2. [prəs'pɛkt], *v.n.* schürfen (*Min.*) (*for*, nach); (*fig.*) Umschau halten, suchen, forschen (*for*, nach); versprechen (*well or ill*). 3. *v.a.* durchforschen, prüfen, untersuchen (*a district*) (*Min.*); (*fig.*) überblicken. **-ive** [–'pɛktɪv], *adj.* vorausblickend, zukünftig, in Aussicht stehend, voraussichtlich; *–ive customer*, angehender Kunde, der Reflektant. **-or** [–'pɛktə], *s.* der Schürfer (*Min.*). **-us** [–'pɛktəs], *s.* die Ankündigung, Werbeschrift, Anzeige, der Prospekt (*of*, von *or* über).

prosper ['prɔspə], 1. *v.a.* begünstigen, segnen; hold sein (*Dat.*). 2. *v.n.* gedeihen, gelingen, glücken, Glück haben. **-ity** [prəs'pɛrɪtɪ], *s.* das Gedeihen, Glück, die Wohlfahrt, der Wohlstand. **-ous** ['prɔspərəs], *adj.* gedeihlich, glücklich, günstig, (*coll.*) wohlhabend, reich.

prostate ['prɔsteɪt], *s.* (also – *gland*) die Vorsteherdrüse, Prostata (*Anat.*).

prosthe-sis ['prɔsθəsɪs], *s.* die Vorsetzung einer Silbe, Prothese (*Gram.*); Prothese (*Surg.*). **-tic** [prɔs'θɛtɪk], *adj.* prothetisch.

prostitut-e ['prɔstɪtju:t], 1. *v.a.* preisgeben, hergeben (*to*, zu); mißbrauchen, schändigen, entehren, erniedrigen; *–e o.s.*, sich fortwerfen. 2. *s.* die (Straßen)Dirne, Prostituierte. **-ion** [–'tju:ʃən], *s.* gewerbsmäßige Unzucht, die Prostitution; (*fig.*) Schändung, Entehrung, Herabwürdigung.

prostrat-e ['prɔstrət], 1. *adj.* hingestreckt; niedergestreckt; erschöpft, entkräftet (*with*, von *or* vor), niedergeworfen, niedergeschlagen, gebrochen (*with*, vor); fußfällig, gedemütigt; niederliegend (*Bot.*); *fall –e before a p.*, einem zu Füßen fallen; *–e with grief*, vor Kummer schwer gebeugt. 2. [prɔs'treɪt] *v.a.* niederwerfen, hinwerfen; zerstören, vernichten; (*usually pass.*) entkräften, erschlaffen (*with*, vor *or* von); *–e o.s.*, niederfallen, einen Fußfall tun, sich demütigen (*before*, vor). **-ion** [–'treɪʃən], *s.* die Niederwerfung; Verbeugung, der Fußfall; die Niedergeschlagenheit, Erschlaffung, Entkräftung.

prostyle ['proustaɪl], *s.* das Säulentor, die Säulenhalle.

prosy ['prouzɪ], *adj.* prosaisch, langweilig, weitschweifig.

protagonist [prou'tægənɪst], *s.* der Vorkämpfer; (*fig.*) die Hauptfigur, Hauptperson (*Theat.*).

protasis ['prɔtəsɪs], *s.* der Vordersatz (*also Rhet.*), voranstehender Bedingungssatz (*Gram.*).

protean ['proutɪən], *adj.* proteusartig, vielgestaltig.

protect [prə'tɛkt], *v.a.* (be)schützen (*from*, vor; *against*, gegen), (be)schirmen; sichern (*Mil.*), durch Schutzzoll schützen (*Pol.*); honorieren (*a bill*). **-ion** [–'tɛkʃən], *s.* der Schutz; die Förderung, Protektion, Deckung, Sicherung (*Mil.*); der Zollschutz (*C.L.*); die Honorierung (*of a bill*); der Schutzbrief; das (Schutz)Mittel; *live under s.o.'s –ion*, von einem ausgehalten werden (*of women*). **-ionism**, *s.* das Schutzzollsystem. **-ionist**, 1. *s.* der Schutzzöllner. 2. *attrib.* Schutzzoll–. **-ive** [–'tɛktɪv], *adj.* schützend, Schutz–; *–ive custody*, die Schutzhaft; *–ive system*, das Schutzzollsystem; *–ive tariff* der Schutzzoll. **-or** [–'tɛktə], *s.* der Beschützer, Gönner, Schutzherr, Schirmherr; Reichsverweser (*Engl. Hist.*) (*fig.*) Schützer, das Schutzmittel, die Schutzvorrichtung. **-orate** [–'tɛktərət], *s.* die Schutzherrschaft, das Protektorat (*Engl. Hist.*); Schutzgebiet. **-orship**, *s.* die Reichsverweserschaft. **-ory** [–'tɛktərɪ], *s.* die Anstalt für verwahrloste Kinder (*R.C.*). **-ress** [–'tɛkrɪs], *s.* die Beschützerin.

protégé ['prɔtəʒeɪ], *s.* der Schützling.

protein ['proutɪn], *s.* das Protein, Eiweißkörper (*Chem.*).

protest, 1. ['proutɛst], *s.* der Einspruch, Protest, die Verwahrung, der (Wechsel)Protest (*C.L.*); *enter, lodge* or *make a* –, Verwahrung einlegen *or* Protest erheben (*with*, bei; *against*, gegen); *in – against*, als Protest gegen; *under* –, unter Protest; *by way of* –, als *or* zum Protest. 2. [prə'tɛst], *v.a.* beteuern; protestieren (*a bill*). 3. *v.n.* Einspruch *or* Protest erheben, Verwahrung einlegen, protestieren; sich verwahren (*against*, gegen). **-ant** ['prɔtəstənt], 1. *adj.* protestantisch. 2. *s.* der Protestant. [prə'tɛstənt] 1. *adj.* protestierend. 2. *s.* Protestierende(r), *m.* **-antism** ['prɔtəstəntɪzm], *s.* der Protestantismus. **-ation** [prɔtəs'teɪʃən], *s.* die Beteuerung, feierliche Versicherung, der Protest, Einspruch, die Verwahrung (*against*, gegen). **-er** [prə'tɛstə], *s.* der Beteuerer, Protestierende(r), *m.* (*C.L.*). **–-meeting**, *s.* die Protestversammlung.

prothalamium [prouθə'leɪmɪəm], *s.* der Hochzeitsgesang.

proto- ['proutou], *prefix* erst, frühest, vor. **-chloride**, *s.* das Chlorür. **-col** ['prɔtəkɔl], 1. *s.* die Niederschrift, das Protokoll. 2. *v.a.* zu Protokoll nehmen, protokolieren. 3. *v.n.* (das) Protokoll führen. **-'genic**, *adj.* zuerst entstanden. **-n** ['proutən], *s.* das Proton (*Chem.*, *Elec.*). **-notary** ['proutə'noutərɪ, prə'tɔnətərɪ], *s.* erster (Gerichts)-Sekretär. **-plasm** ['proutəplæzm], *s.* das Protoplasma. **-plast**, *s.* der Zellkörper, das Protoplast (*Biol.*). **-type** ['proutətaɪp], *s.* das Urbild, Vorbild, Muster(bild). **-xide** [prou'tɔksaɪd], *s.* das Oxydul (*Chem.*). **-zoa** [proutə'zouə], *pl.* Urtierchen, Protozoen. **-zoic**, *adj.* protozoisch (*Geol.*).

protract [prə'trækt], *v.a.* in die Länge ziehen, hinausziehen, hinausschieben, aufschieben, verzögern; nach einem Maßtab entwerfen (*Surv.*). **-ed** [–tɪd], *adj.* lang, in die Länge gezogen, langwierig. **-ile** [–taɪl], *adj.* verlängerungsfähig. **-ion** [–ʃən], *s.* die Verlängerung, Hinausziehung, Hinausschiebung, Verzögerung. **-or** [–tə], *s.* der Gradbogen, Winkelmesser, (Richt)Zirkel, Transporteur, die Schmiege (*Draw.*).

protru-de [prə'tru:d], 1. *v.a.* vorstoßen, vorschieben, hervorstrecken. 2. *v.n.* hervorragen, hervorstehen, hervortreten, heraustreten, vordringen, überhangen (*beyond*, über (*Acc.*)). **-sile** [–'tru:saɪl], *adj.* ausstreckbar, vorstreckbar. **-sion** [–'tru:ʒən], *s.* das Vordringen, Hervorstoßen, Hervorragen, Hervorstehen, Hervortreten; der Vorsprung, vorspringender Teil. **-sive** [–'tru:sɪv], *adj.* vordringend, hervortretend, hervorspringend.

protuberan-ce [prə'tju:bərəns], *s.* der Auswuchs, Höcker, die Beule, Erhöhung. **-t** [–ənt], *adj.* geschwollen (*as a joint*); (her)vorstehend (*as eyes*).

proud [praud], *adj.* stolz (*of*, auf); hochmütig, eingebildet, eitel; prächtig, stattlich, herrlich; (*coll.*) *do o.s.* –, sich (*Dat.*) gütlich tun; *do a p.* –, einen königlich bewirten; – *flesh*, wildes Fleisch (*Med.*).

provable ['pru:vəbl], *adj.* erweislich, beweisbar.

prove [pru:v], 1. *v.a.* prüfen, erproben; beweisen, unter Beweis stellen (*it to be*, daß es ist), erweisen, bestätigen, beglaubigen (*a will*); – *one's identity*, sich ausweisen; – *a th.* (*to be*) *true*, etwas als wahr erweisen *or* nachweisen; – *o.s.* (*to be*) *able*, sich als fähig erweisen. 2. *v.n.* sich erweisen, sich herausstellen, sich bewähren, sich bestätigen; sich ergeben, ausfallen; – (*to be*) *correct*, sich als richtig erweisen *or* herausstellen; –(*false*) *true*, sich (nicht) bestätigen *or* bewähren; *it –d to be false*, es stellte sich heraus, daß es falsch war; *he will – a good soldier*, er wird noch einen guten Soldat abgeben. **-n** [–ən], *adj.* (*Scots*) erwiesen; *not –n*, Schuldbeweis nicht erbracht (*Law*).

provenance ['prɔvənəns], *s.* der Ursprung, die Herkunft.

provender ['prɔvəndə], *s.* das (Trocken)Futter, Viehfutter; (*coll.*) die Nahrung, der Proviant.

proverb ['prɔvə:b], *s.* das Sprichwort; *pl.* die Sprüche Salomonis (*B.*). **-ial** [prə'və:bɪəl], *adj.* sprichwörtlich; *be –ial*, sprichwörtlich, allgemein bekannt *or* berüchtigt sein.

provide [prə'vaɪd], 1. *v.a.* anschaffen, beschaffen, verschaffen, besorgen, beistellen, liefern (*a p. with a th.* or *a th. for a p.*, einem etwas); versehen, versorgen (*with*, mit). 2. *v.n.* Vorsorge treffen, Maßnahmen ergreifen (*for*, für; *against*, gegen); festsetzen, bestimmen, vorsehen (*Law*); – *for a th.*, etwas versehen *or* in Rechnung stellen; Deckung schaffen für etwas (*C.L.*); – *for a p.*, für einen sorgen; *be –ed for*, versorgt sein; – *against a th.*, etwas verhindern *or* unmöglich machen. **–r,** *s.* der Fürsorger, Versorger, Lieferant (*C.L.*); *universal –r*, das Warenhaus. **–d** [–ɪd], 1. *adj.* vorbereitet, gefaßt (*for*, auf); *–d school*, die von der Lokalbehörde unterhaltene Volksschule. 2. *conj.* (also *–d that*) vorausgesetzt daß; unter der Bedingung; es sei denn daß; wofern *or* wenn nur.

providen–ce [ˈprɔvɪdəns], *s.* die Vorsorge, Voraussicht; Sparsamkeit; Vorsehung, Fügung (*Theol.*). **–t** [–ənt], *adj.* voraussehend, fürsorglich, vorsorglich, haushälterisch, sparsam; *–t fund*, die Unterstützungskasse; *–t society*, der Wohlfahrtsverein, Unterstützungsverein. **–tial** [–ˈdɛnʃəl], *adj.* durch Fügung *or* Vorsehung bewirkt, günstig, gnädig, glücklich.

provider, *see* **provide.**

providing [prəˈvaɪdɪŋ], *conj.* (also – *that*), see *provided* (*that*).

provinc–e [ˈprɔvɪns], *s.* die Provinz; der Bezirk, Distrikt; (*fig.*) das Gebiet, Fach, Amt, die Sphäre, der Bereich, Zweig; *pl.* die Provinz; *that is not within my –e*, das schlägt nicht in mein Fach, das ist nicht meines Amtes. **–ial** [prəˈvɪnʃəl], 1. *adj.* Provinzial–, Provinz–, provinziell; kleinstädtisch, ländlich; *–ial town*, die Provinzstadt. 2. *s.* der Provinzler, Provinzbewohner. **–ialism,** *s.* provinzielle Abgeschlossenheit, der Provinzialismus, das Provinzlertum, Spießbürgertum; mundartlicher Ausdruck. **–iality** [–vɪnʃɪˈælɪtɪ], *s.* beschränkter Gesichtskreis, das Spießbürgertum.

provision [proˈvɪʒən], 1. *s.* die Vorkehrung, Anstalt, Fürsorge, Vorsorge (*for*, für; *against*, gegen); Beschaffung, Bereitstellung; Verordnung, Verfügung, Maßregel, Bestimmung, Bedingung; der Vorrat (*of*, an (*Dat.*)), die Vorrichtung, Einrichtung, (*for*, für); Deckung, Rimesse (*C.L.*); *pl.* Lebensmittel (*pl.*), der Proviant, Mundvorrat, die Verpflegung; *make – for* (*against*). Vorkehrungen *or* Anstalten treffen für (gegen), sorgen für (sich schützen gegen). 2. *v.a.* mit Proviant *or* Nahrungsmitteln versehen, verproviantieren. **–al** [–ənl], *adj.* vorläufig, provisorisch, behelfsmäßig, Interims– (*C.L.*); *–al order*, (vorläufige) Verwaltungsverfügung; *–al receipt*, die Interimsquittung; *–al result*, das Zwischenergebnis (*Sport*). **– -dealer,** *s.* **– -merchant,** *s.* der Kolonialwarenhändler.

proviso [prəˈvaɪzoʊ], *s.* der Vorbehalt, die Bedingung, (Bedingungs)Klausel. **–ry** [–zərɪ], *adj.* bedingt, vorbehaltlich, einstweilig, provisorisch.

provocati–on [provəˈkeɪʃən], *s.* der Antrieb, die Aufreizung, Herausforderung; *without –on*, ohne Anlaß. **–ve** [prəˈvɔkətɪv], 1. *adj.* (zum Widerspruch) herausfordernd, aufreizend, anreizend (*of*, zu). 2. *s.* das Reizmittel, der Antrieb, Anreiz (*to*, zu).

provok–e [proˈvoʊk], *v.a.* anreizen, antreiben (*a p.*), herausfordern, erregen (*feelings*), hervorrufen, bewirken, veranlassen, verursachen; erbittern, erzürnen, aufbringen (*against*, gegen). **–ing,** *adj.* herausfordernd, aufreizend, ärgerlich, unausstehlich.

provost [ˈprɔvəst], *s.* der Bürgermeister (*Scots*), der Vorsteher, Leiter (*of college and Eton*); *Lord –*, der Oberbürgermeister (*Scots*). [prəˈvoʊ] *s.* der Profoß (*Mil.*). **– -court,** *s.* das Feldgericht (*Mil.*). **– -marshal,** *s.* der Generalprofoß, Chef der Militärpolizei.

prow [praʊ], *s.* das Vorschiff, der Bug, Schiffsschnabel.

prowess [ˈpraʊɪs], *s.* die Tapferkeit, der Heldenmut.

prowl [praʊl], *v.n.* umherstreifen, umherschleichen; herumlungern. 2. *s.* das Umherstreifen; *on the –*, umherstreifend. **–er,** *s.* der Bummler, Vagabund.

proxim–al [ˈprɔksɪməl], *adj.* körpernah, proximal (*Anat.*). **–ate** [–mət], *adj.* nächst, naheliegend, unmittelbar. **–e** [–meɪ], *adv.* am nächsten; *–e accessit*, zweiter Preisträger. **–ity** [–ˈsɪmɪtɪ], *s.* die Nähe. **–o** [–moʊ], *adj.* nächsten Monats (*C.L.*).

proxy [ˈprɔksɪ], *s.* der Stellvertreter; die Vollmacht, Stellvertretung. *by –*, durch einen Stellvertreter, in Vertretung; *stand – for*, als Stellvertreter fungieren für.

prud–e [pruːd], *s.* die Spröde. **–ery,** *s.* die Prüderie, Ziererei, Sprödigkeit. **–ish,** *adj.* zimperlich, prüde, spröde.

pruden–ce [ˈpruːdəns], *s.* die Klugheit, Vorsicht. **–t** [–ənt], *adj.* umsichtig, vorsichtig, klug, weltklug, politisch. **–tial** [–ˈdɛnʃəl], *adj.* klug, verständig, Klugheits–; *–tial considerations*, Klugheitsrücksichten.

prudery, prudish, *see* **prude.**

pruinose [ˈpruːɪnoʊs], *adj.* bereift, bestäubt (*Bot.*, *Zool.*).

[1]**prun–e** [pruːn], *v.a.* beschneiden (*also fig.*), zurecht stutzen, (*fig.*) säubern, befreien (*of*, von). **–er,** *s. see* **–ing shears.** **–ing,** *s.* das Ausputzen, Beschneiden. **–ing-knife,** *s.* das Gartenmesser, Baummesser. **–ing shears,** *pl.* die Baumschere.

[2]**prun–e** [pruːn], *s.* die Backpflaume. **–ella** [pruˈnɛlə], *s.* der Prunell (*fabric*); die Halsbräune (*Med.*). **–ello** [pruˈnɛloʊ], *s.* die Prünelle.

prurien–ce, –cy [ˈprʊrɪəns(ɪ)], *s.* die Lüsternheit (*for*, nach), der (Sinnen)Kitzel. **–t** [–ənt], *adj.* lüstern, unzüchtig.

prurig–inous [pruˈrɪdʒɪnəs], *adj.* juckend (*Med.*). **–o** [pruˈrɪːgoʊ], *s.* die Juckflechte, Juckkrankheit.

prussi–ate [ˈprʌʃɪət], *s.* das Zyanid, blausaures Salz (*Chem.*); *–ate of potash*, das Zyankalium. **–c** [–sɪk], *adj.* blausauer; *–c acid*, die Blausäure, Zyanwasserstoffsäure.

[1]**pry** [praɪ], *v.n.* spähen, neugierig sein: – *into*, die Nase stecken in (*Acc.*). **–ing,** *adj.* neugierig, naseweis.

[2]**pry** [praɪ], *v.a.* (– *open*) (*coll.*) aufbrechen, erbrechen.

psalm [sɑːm], *s.* der Psalm; *book of –s*, die Psalmen (*B.*). **–ist,** *s.* der Psalmist. **–ody** [–ədi, ˈsælmədɪ], *s.* der Psalmgesang; die Psalmensammlung. **– -book,** *s.* der Psalter.

psalter [ˈsɔːltə], *s.* der Psalter, das Psalmenbuch, Buch der Psalmen. **–ium** [–ˈtɪːrɪəm], der Blättermagen (*Zool.*). **–y** [–erɪ], *s.* der Psalter (*Mus.*).

pseudo– [ˈsjuːdoʊ], *prefix* Schein–, Irr–, Pseudo–, falsch. **–carp,** *s.* die Scheinfrucht. **–morph,** *s.* das Afterkristall, die Pseudomorphose. **–nym,** *s.* der Deckname, falscher Name, das Pseudonym. **–ˈnymity,** *s.* die Verwendung eines Decknamens. **–nymous** [–ˈdɔnɪməs], *adj.* pseudonym, unter einem Decknamen.

pshaw [(p)ʃɔː], *int.* pah!

psittacosis [(p)sɪtəˈkoʊsɪs], *s.* die Papageienkrankheit.

psoas [ˈpsoʊæs], *s.* der Lendenmuskel (*Anat.*).

psor–a [ˈpsɔːrə], *s.* die Krätze (*Med.*). **–iasis** [–rɪˈeɪsɪs], *s.* die Schnuppenflechte (*Med.*).

psyche [ˈsaɪkɪ], *s.* die Seele, der Geist.

psychiatr–ic [saɪkɪˈætrɪk], *adj.* psychiatrisch. **–ist** [səˈkaɪətrɪst], *s.* der Psychiater, Irrenarzt. **–y** [səˈkaɪətrɪ], *s.* die Psychiatrie, Irrenheilkunde.

psychic [ˈsaɪkɪk], 1. *adj.* psychisch, seelisch, spiritistisch, übersinnlich. **–al** [–l], *adj. see* – (*esp. Med.*); *–al research*, der Spiritismus.

psycho-analysis [saɪkoʊəˈnæləsɪs], *s.* die Psychoanalyse. **–analist** [–ˈænəlɪst], *s.* der Psychoanalytiker. **–analyse** [–ˈænəlaɪz], *v.a.* psychoanalytisch behandeln. **–logical** [saɪkəˈlɔdʒɪkl], *adj.* psychologisch; *the –logical moment*, der richtige Augenblick. **–logist** [saɪˈkɔlədʒɪst], *s.* der Psychologe. **–logy** [–ˈkɔlədʒɪ], *s.* die Psychologie. **–path** [ˈsaɪkopæθ], *s.* der Psychopath. **–pathic** [–əˈpæθɪk], *adj.* psychopathisch, geistesgestört. **–sis** [saɪˈkoʊsɪs], *s.* die Psychose, Geistesstörung. **–therapeutic** [saɪkoθɛrəˈpjutɪk], *adj.* psychotherapeutisch. **–therapy** [–ˈθɛrəpɪ], *s.* die Psychotherapie.

ptarmigan [ˈtɑːmɪgən], *s.* das Alpenschneehuhn.

ptero– [(p)tɛroʊ], *prefix* Flug–, Flügel–. **–dactyl** [–əˈdæktɪl], *s.* ausgestorbener Flugeidechse. **–pod** [ˈ(p)tɛrəpɔd], *s.* der Flossenfüsser (*Zool.*). **–saur** [ˈ(p)tɛrəsɔː], *s. see* **–dactyl.**

ptomaine [ˈptoʊmeɪn, təˈmeɪn], *s.* das Ptomain.

pub [pʌb], *s.* (*coll.*) see *public house*; (*sl.*) – *crawl*, die Bierreise.

pub–erty [ˈpjuːbətɪ], *s.* die Mannbarkeit, Geschlechtsreife, Pubertät; *age of –erty*, das Pubertätsalter, Entwicklungsjahre (*pl.*). **–es** [ˈpjuːbeɪs], *s.* das Schamhaar, die Schamgegend (*Anat.*).

–escence [–ˈbɛsəns], *s.* die Geschlechtsreife, Mannbarkeit; Behaarung (*Bot., Zool.*). **–ic** [–ɪk], *adj.* Scham–. **–is** [ɪs], *s.* das Schambein.

public [ˈpʌblɪk], **1.** *adj.* öffentlich, Staats–, national, Volks–; allgemein bekannt, offenkundig; *make –*, öffentlich bekanntmachen; *– address system*, die Lautsprecheranlage; *– appointment*, die Staatsanstellung; *– assistance*, staatliche Wohlfahrt; *– auction*, öffentliche Versteigerung; *– call box*, öffentlicher Fernsprecher; *– convenience*, öffentliche Bedürfnisanstalt; *– conveyance*, öffentliches Verkehrsmittel; *– debt*, die Staatsschuld; *– enemy*, der Staatsfeind; *the – eye*, das Auge der Öffentlichkeit; *be in the – eye*, im Brennpunkt des öffentlichen Lebens stehen; *– figure*, der Mann der Öffentlichkeit; *– funds* Staatsgelder (*pl.*); *– health service*, öffentlicher Gesundheitsdienst; *– highway*, see *– road*; *– holiday*, gesetzlicher Feiertag; *– house*, das Wirtshaus, die Schankwirtschaft, Gaststätte; *– institution*, gemeinnütziges Unternehmen; *– law*, das Staatsrecht; *– lecture*, öffentliche Vorlesung; *– library*, die Volksbibliothek, Volksbücherei; *– money*, see *– funds*; *– notary*, der Notar; *– nuisance*, öffentliches Ärgernis; *– opinion*, öffentliche Meinung; *– property*, das Staatseigentum; *– prosecutor*, der Staatsanwalt; *– relations*, Beziehungen eines (öffentlichen) Betriebes zur Öffentlichkeit, die Werbe- und Reklametätigkeit; *– relations officer*, der Fachmann für Presse, Reklame und Werbung; *– revenue*, Staatseinkünfte (*pl.*); *– road*, der Verkehrsweg; *– school*, exklusive Internatsschule (*Eng.*); die Volksschule (*Scots and Amer.*); *– servant*, Staatsbeamte(r), *m.*; *– service*, der Staatsdienst; *– spirit*, der Gemeinsinn; *–-spirited*, *adj.* gemeinsinnig, gemeinnützig; *– thoroughfare*, see *– road*; *– utility*, öffentliche Einrichtung, öffentlicher Versorgungsbetrieb; *– welfare*, die Fürsorge; *– works*, öffentliche Bauten; *– worship*, öffentlicher Gottesdienst. **2.** *s.* das Publikum, die Leute (*pl.*); (*fig.*) die Welt; (*coll.*) see *– house*; *in –*, in der Öffentlichkeit, vor der Welt, öffentlich. **–an** [–ən], *s.* der Gastwirt, Schankwirt; (*B.*) Zöllner. **–ation** [–ˈkeɪʃən], *s.* öffentliche Bekanntmachung, die Veröffentlichung, Herausgabe (*of a work*); Schrift, Publikation, das (Verlags)-Werk; *new –ation*, die Neuerscheinung; *monthly –ation*, die Monatsschrift. **–ist** [–sɪst], *s.* der Publizist. **–ity** [–ˈlɪsɪtɪ], *s.* die Öffentlichkeit, Offenkundigkeit; Werbung, Reklame, Propaganda; *give –ity to*, (der Öffentlichkeit) bekanntmachen; *no –ity*, strengste Diskretion; *–ity agent*, der Pressechef; *–ity department*, die Propagandaabteilung; *–ity manager*, der Werbeleiter; *–ity office*, das Werbebüro.

publish [ˈpʌblɪʃ], *v.a.* öffentlich bekanntmachen, verkündigen, veröffentlichen, in Umlauf setzen; herausgeben, verlegen (*a book, etc.*); *– the banns*, das Aufgebot (von der Kanzel) verkündigen; *just –ed*, eben erschienen; *not yet –ed*, noch unveröffentlicht; *–ed by Cassell's*, im Cassell-Verlag erschienen. **–er** [–ə], *s.* der Verleger, Verlagsbuchhändler; Verbreiter (*of news*); (*firm of*) *–ers*, der Verlag, die Verlagsanstalt. **–ing**, *adj.* Verlags–; *–ing business*, der Verlagsbuchhandel; *–ing house*, der Verlag, das Verlagshaus, die Verlagsbuchhandlung.

puce [pjuːs], *adj.* braunrot, dunkelbraun.

puck [pʌk], *s.* der Kobold, Hausgeist; die Eishockeyscheibe.

pucker [ˈpʌkə], **1.** *s.* die Falte; Runzel; (*coll.*) Verlegenheit, Erregung (*about*, über). **2.** *v.a.* falten, einhalten (*sewing*); zusammenziehen (*lips*), runzeln (*brow*). **3.** *v.n.* sich falten *or* zusammenziehen *or* kräuseln, Falten werfen.

puddening [ˈpʊdənɪŋ], *s.* der Taukranz, das Bündel von Tauenden (*Naut.*).

pudding [ˈpʊdɪŋ], *s.* der Pudding, die Süßspeise, Mehlspeise; Wurst; *see also* **puddening.** *black –*, die Blutwurst; *white –*, die Leberwurst. **–-faced**, *adj.* mit feistem Gesicht, mit Vollmondsgesicht. **–-head**, *s.* der Dummkopf. **–-stone**, *s.* der Puddingstein.

puddl–e [ˈpʌdl], **1.** *s.* die Pfütze, Lache, der Pfuhl; der Lehmschlag, Lehmestrich (*Build.*). **2.** *v.n.* plan(t)schen, manschen; (*fig.*) herumpfuschen. **3.** *v.a.* trüben (*water*), puddeln (*iron*), mit Estrich ausfüllen *or* anfüllen, bereiten (*clay and sand*); *–ed clay*, der Lehmschlag. **–er**, *s.* der Puddler, Puddelarbeiter (*Metall.*). **–ing**, *s.* das Ausfüllen (*Build.*); Puddeln (*Metall.*); die Estrichfüllung. **–ing-furnace**, *s.* der Puddelofen.

puden–cy [ˈpjʊdənsɪ], *s.* die Bescheidenheit, Schüchternheit. **–da** [–ˈdɛndə], *pl.* Geschlechtsteile, Schamteile (*pl.*). **–t** [–ənt], *adj.* schüchtern, verschämt.

pudgy [ˈpʌdʒɪ], *adj.* dick, untersetzt.

pueril–e [ˈpjuːəraɪl], *adj.* knabenhaft, kindisch. **–ity** [pjʊəˈrɪlɪtɪ], *s.* die Knabenhaftigkeit, Kindhaftigkeit, Kinderei.

puerperal [pjuˈəːpərəl], *adj.* Kindbett–.

puff [pʌf], **1.** *s.* der Hauch, Windstoß, Luftstoß, Zug, Puff; Paff (*of a pipe*); die Puffe, der Bausch, Wulst, (also *powder-–*) die Puderquaste; leichtes Backwerk, der Windbeutel (*Cook.*); marktschreierische Anzeige, die (Schwindel)Reklame; *– of smoke*, die Rauchwolke. **2.** *v.n.* blasen; pusten, schnaufen, schnauben, keuchen; puffen, paffen (*as trains*); (marktschreierisch) Reklame machen (*at an auction*); *– and blow*, schnauben, keuchen; *– at a cigar*, an einer **Zigarre** paffen. **3.** *v.a.* ausblasen, ausstoßen, auspaffen (*smoke*); (also *– out*) aufblasen, aufblähen, aufbauschen (*as cheeks*); *– up*, hochtreiben, in die Höhe treiben (*prices*); marktschreierisch *or* überschwenglich anpreisen (*wares*), über den Klee loben; (*coll.*) *–ed* [–t] or *–ed out*, außer Atem; *–ed sleeve*, der Puffärmel; *–ed up*, geschwollen, aufgeblasen (*with*, vor). **–-adder**, *s.* die Puffotter. **–-ball**, *s.* der Bovist, Bofist. **–-box**, *s.* die Puderdose. **–er**, *s.* der Marktschreier, der Preistreiber, Scheinbieter (*at auctions*), der Zug (*nursery talk*). **–iness**, *s.* die Aufgeblasenheit, Aufgedunsenheit; Schwülstigkeit; Aufbauschung, Schwellung. **–ing**, *s.* die Aufbauschung; Marktschreierei; unsaubere Reklame. **–-pastry**, *s.* der Blätterteig. **–-puff**, *s.* der Puffpuff (*nursery talk*). **–y**, *adj.* aufgeblasen, geschwollen, schwülstig; kurzatmig; böig.

puffin [ˈpʌfɪn], *s.* der Papageitaucher (*Orn.*).

[1]**pug** [pʌg], *s.* (also *–-dog*) der Mops; (*dial.*) Fuchs; (*sl.*) erster Dienstbote. **–-nose**, *s.* die Stupsnase, Stülpnase. **–-nosed**, *adj.* stumpfnasig, stupsnäsig.

[2]**pug** [pʌg], **1.** *s.* der Lehm, Lehmschlag. **2.** *v.a.* bereiten, schlagen, kneten (*clay*); ausfüllen, verdichten, verschmieren (*with clay*). **–ging**, *s.* das Lehmstampfen, die Lehmfüllung.

[3]**pug** [pʌg], *s.* die Fährte, Fußspur.

pugilis–m [ˈpjuːdʒɪlɪzm], *s.* der Faustkampf, das Boxen, die Boxkunst. **–t** [–ɪst], *s.* der Faustkämpfer, Boxer. **–tic** [–ˈlɪstɪk], *adj.* Box–.

pugnaci–ous [pʌgˈneɪʃəs], *adj.* kampflustig, kämpferisch, streitsüchtig. **–ty** [–ˈnæsɪtɪ], *s.* die Kampflust, Streitsucht.

puisne [ˈpjuːnɪ], **1.** *adj.* jünger, Unter– (*Law*). **2.** *s.* der Unterrichter (*Law*).

puissan–ce [ˈpwɪːsəns], *s.* (*Poet.*) die Macht, Stärke, Herrschaft. **–t** [–ənt], *adj.* mächtig, gewaltig.

puke [pjuːk], *v.n.* (*vulg.*) kotzen.

pukka [ˈpʌkə], *adj.* (*sl.*) erstklassig, tadellos, ausgezeichnet, prächtig, prachtvoll, knorke, großartig.

pule [pjuːl], *v.n.* winseln, wimmern.

pull [pʊl], **1.** *s.* das Ziehen; der Zug, Ruck, die Anziehungskraft; der Griff, Schwengel; die Ruderfahrt; mühsamer Anstieg; der Abzug vom Satz (*Typ.*); (*coll.*) der Vorteil, Einfluß, die Protektion, Beziehungen, Konnexionen (*pl.*); *give a – at*, ziehen an; *go for a –*, eine Ruderfahrt machen; *have the – of* or *on* or *over a p.*, den Vorteil vor einem haben; *take a – at the bottle*, einen Zug aus der Flasche tun. **2.** *v.a.* ziehen; zerren, reißen, zupfen, raufen; pflücken (*Scots*); abziehen (*a proof*); (*sl.*) zurückhalten (*a horse*); *– the chestnuts out of the fire* (*for a p.*), (einem) die Kastanien aus dem Feuer holen; *– a face* (or *faces*), ein Gesicht (*or* Fratzen *pl.*) schneiden; *– a long face*, ein langes Gesicht ziehen *or* machen; (*sl.*) *– the job*, das Ding drehen; *– a p.'s leg*, einen zum besten *or* Narren haben; (*sl.*) *– a fast one*, ein unredliches Spiel treiben; *– a* *muscle*, sich eine Muskelzerrung zuziehen; – *a good oar*, gut rudern; – *a pistol on*, anlegen *or* feuern auf; – *a p. by the sleeve*, einen am Ärmel zupfen; – *the strings* (*or wires*), die Fäden in der Hand haben, der Drahtzieher *or* das Gangelband sein; – *the trigger*, das Gewehr abdrücken; (*coll.*) – *one's weight*, sich anstrengen, tüchtig mitarbeiten; – *about*, herumstoßen, unsanft traktieren; – *down*, niederreißen, einreißen (*a house, etc.*); schwächen, entkräften (*a p.'s health*); herunterziehen, herunterlassen (*blinds*); – *in*, hineinziehen, anziehen, anhalten (reins), zügeln (*a horse*); – *off*, abziehen (*also Typ.*), abreißen; abnehmen (*a hat, etc.*) (*to*, vor), ausziehen (*clothes, boots*); wegziehen (*a p. etc.*); (*coll.*) davontragen (*a prize*), Glück haben mit, hereinbringen; – *on*, anziehen (*clothes*); – *out*, ausziehen, herausziehen, hervorziehen; – *round*, wiederherstellen; – *through*, durchziehen, durchführen; – *a p. through*, einem durchhelfen (*a difficulty*), einen durchbringen (*an illness*); – *to pieces*, zerreißen, zerpflücken; (*fig.*) herunterreißen, gründlich abrechnen mit, einer vernichtenden Kritik unterziehen; – *o.s. together*, sich zusammennehmen *or* zusammenreißen, sich aufraffen; – *up*, hochziehen, hissen (*flag, etc.*); ausreißen (*flowers, etc.*); zum Stehen bringen, anhalten, aufhalten; unterbrechen, Einhalt tun, zur Rede stellen. **3.** *v.n.* ziehen, zerren, reißen (*at*, an); rudern; – *at a pipe*, an einer Pfeife einen Zug tun; – *against the bit*, pullen; – *back*, (sich) zurückziehen; – *in*, hineinrudern (*boats*); anhalten (*vehicles*); – *into the station*, in den Bahnhof einfahren; – *off*, sich fortbewegen (*boats*); – *out*, abgehen, abfahren, abdampfen; (*sl.*) abziehen, das Feld räumen, sich zurückziehen; – *out of the station*, aus dem Bahnhof fahren; – *through*, glücklich bestehen, überstehen, durchkommen durch (*an illness*), sich durchschlagen *or* durchwinden; – *together*, zusammenarbeiten, zusammenhalten, am gleichen Strang ziehen; – *up*, halten, anhalten, haltmachen, stehenbleiben, zum Stehen kommen; bremsen (*vehicle*); aufholen, einholen (*Racing*); *–ed figs*, getrocknete Tafelfeigen. **–er,** *s.* der Ruderer; Zieher (*horse*). **–over** [ˈpulouvə], *s.* der Pullover, die Überziehjacke, Strickjacke. **––through** [ˈpulθruː], *s.* der Wischstrick (*for rifles*). **––up** [ˈpulʌp], *s.* die Rast(stätte), der Halteplatz.

pullet [ˈpulɪt], *s.* das Hühnchen.

pulley [ˈpulɪ], *s.* die Rolle, Flasche (*Mech.*), Talje (*Naut.*); *belt-–*, die Riemenscheibe; *a set of –s*, der Flaschenzug, Rollenzug. **––block,** *s.* der Kloben.

pullulat–e [ˈpuljuːleɪt], *v.n.* treiben, keimen, sprossen; (*fig.*) wuchern, aus dem Boden schießen, sich verbreiten, um sich greifen, grassieren. **–ion,** [–juˈleɪʃən], *s.* das Keimen, Sprossen, die Forpflanzung.

pulmon–ary [ˈpulmənərɪ], *adj.* Lungen–. **–ate** [–neɪt], *adj.* Lungen– (*Zool.*). **–ic** [–ˈmɔnɪk], *adj.* *see* **–ary.**

pulp [pʌlp], 1. *s.* breiige Masse, der Brei; das Fruchtfleisch, Pflanzenmark; die (Zahn)Pulpa, das Zahnmark; das Ganzzeug, der Papierbrei, Papierstoff (*Pap.*); die Maische (*sugar*); *beat* or *reduce to* –, zu Brei schlagen; (*fig.*) windelweich schlagen. 2. *v.a.* zu Brei *or* breiig machen; einstampfen (*paper stock*). 3. *v.n.* breiig werden. **–er,** *s.* der Ganzzeugholländer (*Pap.*). **–ify,** *v.a.* zu Brei machen. **–iness,** *s.* die Weichheit. **–y,** *adj.* breiig fleischig, weich.

pulpit [ˈpulpɪt], *s.* die Kanzel; (*collect.*) die Geistlichkeit; *in the* –, auf der Kanzel.

pulsat–e [ˈpʌlseɪt, pʌlˈseɪt], *v.n.* schlagen, pochen, klopfen, puls(ier)en. **–ile** [ˈpʌlsətaɪl], *adj.* pulsierend; Schlag– (*Mus.*). **–ion** [–ˈseɪʃən], *s.* das Schlagen, Klopfen, Pulsieren; der Schlag, Pulsschlag.

[1]**pulse** [pʌls], 1. *s.* der Puls, Pulsschlag; die Schwingung; *feel a p.'s* –, einem den Puls fühlen (*Med.*); (*fig.*) einem auf den Zahn fühlen, bei einem auf den Busch klopfen; (*fig.*) *have one's finger on the* –, an den Puls fühlen (*of* (*Dat.*)). 2. *v.n.* *see* **pulsate.**

[2]**pulse** [pʌls], *s.* die Hülsenfrüchte (*pl.*).

pulveriz–ation [pʌlvəraɪˈzeɪʃən], *s.* die Zerreibung, Zerstäubung, Pulverisierung; **–e** [ˈpʌlvəraɪz], 1. *v.a.* mahlen, zerkleinern, zermalmen, zerstoßen, zerreiben, pulverisieren, levigieren; zerstäuben. 2. *v.n.* zu Staub werden. **–izer,** *s.* der Zerstäuber.

pulverulent [pʌlˈvɛrulənt], *adj.* staubig, Staub–.

pulvinate(d) [ˈpʌlvɑnət, –neɪtɪd], *adj.* kissenförmig, polsterförmig, bauchig.

puma [ˈpjuːmə], *s.* der Puma, Kuguar.

pumice [ˈpʌmɪs], 1. *s.* (also *––stone*) der Bimsstein. 2. *v.a.* (ab)bimsen, mit Bimsstein abreiben.

pummel [ˈpʌml], *v.a.* schlagen, puffen.

[1]**pump** [pʌmp], 1. *s.* die Pumpe. 2. *v.a.* pumpen; (*coll.*) ausforschen, ausfragen, ausholen (*a p.*); – *the bilges*, lenzen (*Naut.*); – *out* or *dry*, auspumpen, leerpumpen; (*vulg.*) – *ship*, pissen; – *up*, aufpumpen (*Cycl.*). 3. *v.n.* pumpen; arbeiten (*of heart*); lenzen (*Naut.*). **––handle,** *s.* der Pumpenschwengel. **–ing-station,** *s.* die Pumpanlage. **––room,** *s.* die Trinkhalle, Kurhalle. **––water,** *s.* das Brunnenwasser.

[2]**pump** [pʌmp], *s.* (*usually pl.*) der Tanzschuh, Turnschuh.

pumpkin [ˈpʌmpkɪn], *s.* der Kürbis.

pun [pʌn], 1. *s.* das Wortspiel (*on*, über *or* mit). 2. *v.n.* mit Worten spielen; ein Wortspiel machen, witzeln (*on*, über *or* mit); *see* **punster.**

[1]**punch** [pʌntʃ], *s.* der Punsch. **––bowl,** *s.* die Punschbowle. **––ladle,** *s.* der Punschlöffel.

[2]**punch** [pʌntʃ], 1. *s.* der Faustschlag, Stoß, Puff, Knuff; (*fig.*) die (Tat)Kraft, Schlagkraft, Energie, das Gewicht, der Nachdruck, Schwung, Schmiß. 2. *v.a.* mit der Faust schlagen, stoßen, puffen, knuffen; (*Amer.*) antreiben (*cattle*). **–(ing)-ball,** *s.* der Übungsball beim Boxen.

[3]**punch** [pʌntʃ], *s.* der Stöpsel, kleine dicke Person; starkes, untersetztes (Zug)Pferd. **–y,** *adj.* (*coll.*) untersetzt.

[4]**punch** [pʌntʃ], 1. *s.* die Punze, der Punzen, Dorn; Locher, Lochstecher, das Locheisen, die Lochzange, der Stempel, die Stanze, Patrize. 2. *v.a.* durchbohren, durchlöchern, auslochen, durchlochen; punzen, punzieren, stanzen, stempeln; lochen, knipsen (*tickets*). **–er,** *s.* der Locher; *cow-–er* (*Amer.*) der Viehhirt. **–ing-machine,** *s.* die Lochmaschine, Stanzmaschine.

puncheon [ˈpʌntʃən], *s.* der Pfriem; (*archaic*) das Faß (*liquid measure* = *330–550 l.*); (*Amer.*) das Querbrett (*Carp.*).

punchinello [pʌntʃɪˈnɛlou], *s.* der Hanswurst.

punctate [ˈpʌŋktət], *adj.* punktiert (*Bot., Zool.*).

punctilio [pʌŋkˈtɪlɪou], *s.* kitzliger *or* heikler Punkt; peinliche Genauigkeit; die Förmlichkeit. **–us** [–ˈtɪlɪəs], *adj.* förmlich, formell, steif; peinlich, genau; spitzfindig. **–usness,** *s.* peinliche Genauigkeit.

punctuat–e [ˈpʌŋktjueɪt], *v.a.* interpunktieren, interpungieren; unterbrechen (*speech*); hervorheben, betonen, unterstreichen. **–ion** [–ˈeɪʃən], *s.* die Zeichensetzung, Interpunktion. **–ion-mark,** *s.* das Satzzeichen, Interpunktionszeichen.

puncture [ˈpʌŋktʃə], 1. *s.* der (Ein)Stich, die Punktur, das Loch, die (Durch)Lochung; Radpanne, Reifenpanne, der Reifenschaden (*Motor., Cycl.*); Durchschlag (*Elec.*); *we had a* –, uns platzte der Reifen. 2. *v.a.* durchstechen; punktieren, anstechen (*Surg.*). 3. *v.n.* platzen (*tyres, etc.*); – *outfit*, das Flickzeug (*Motor.*).

pundit [ˈpʌndɪt], *s.* gelehrter Brahmine; (*coll.*) Fachgelehrte(r), *m.*, die Autorität; der Vielwisser, gelehrtes Haus.

pungen–cy [ˈpʌndʒənsɪ], *s.* das Stechende, Beißende, die Schärfe. **–t** [–ənt], *adj.* beißend, stechend, scharf (*also fig.*).

punish [ˈpʌnɪʃ], *v.a.* (be)strafen (*for*, wegen); (*coll.*) mit den Fäusten bearbeiten (*Boxing*); arg zurichten *or* mitnehmen; stark beanspruchen; (*coll.*) tüchtig zusprechen (*Dat.*) (*food*). **–able,** *adj.* strafbar. **–ment,** *s.* die Strafe, Bestrafung, der Schaden; *as* or *for a –ment*, als *or* zur Strafe; *capital –ment*, die Todesstrafe; *corporal –ment*, körperliche Züchtigung; *bring to –ment*, zur Strafe ziehen; *take –ment*, (viel) einstecken müssen (*Boxing*).

punitive [ˈpjuːnɪtɪv], *adj.* strafend, Straf–.

punk [pʌŋk], 1. *s.* faules Holz, der Zunder, das Zunderholz; (*sl.*) der Unsinn, Quatsch. 2. *adj.* faul (*of timber*); (*sl.*) schäbig, armselig; unwohl.
punkah [pʌŋkə], *s.* der Zimmerfächer, die Fächervorrichtung.
punster [ˈpʌnstə], *s.* der Witzbold, Wortspielmacher; *see* **pun.**
[1]**punt** [pʌnt], 1. *s.* flacher Flußkahn, der Prahm. 2. *v.a.* mit Staken fortbewegen, staken. 3. *v.n.* in einem Flußkahn fahren.
[2]**punt** [pʌnt], 1. *s.* der Fallstoß (*Footb.*). 2. *v.a.* (den fallenden Ball) wuchtig stoßen.
[3]**punt** [pʌnt], *v.n.* (*coll.*) wetten, setzen auf (*Gambling*). **–er,** *s.* Wettende(r) *m.*; der Spekulant.
punty [ˈpʌntɪ], *s.* das Hefteisen (*Glassw.*).
puny [ˈpjuːnɪ], *adj.* winzig, schwächlich, kümmerlich.
pup [pʌp], 1. *s.* (*coll.*) junger Hund; (*sl.*) der Laffe; *in* –, trächtig (*of dogs*); (*sl.*) *sell s.o. a* –, einen übers Ohr hauen, einem etwas auf die Nase binden. 2. *v.n.* Junge werfen.
pupa [ˈpjuːpə], *s.* die Puppe, Larve (*Ent.*). **–l,** *adj.* Puppen–. **–tion** [–ˈpeɪʃən], *s.* die Puppenbildung.
[1]**pupil** [ˈpjuːpɪl], *s.* die Pupille (*Anat.*). **–(l)ary** [–ˈpɪlərɪ], *adj.* Pupillen–.
[2]**pupil** [ˈpjuːpɪl], *s.* der Schüler, Zögling; Minderjährige(r), *m.* der (*Austr. n.*) *and* die Mündel (*Law*). **–age** [–ɪdʒ], *s.* die Minderjährigkeit (*Law*); Schülerjahre, Lehrjahre (*pl.*); (*fig.*) das Anfangsstadium. **–(l)ary** [–ərɪ], *adj.* minderjährig, Mündel–, pupillarisch (*Law*).
puppet [ˈpʌpɪt], *s.* die Drahtpuppe, Marionette; (*fig.*) Puppe, das Werkzeug. **–ry,** *s.* die Puppenspielerei. **– -play,** *s.* das Puppenspiel.
puppy [ˈpʌpɪ], *s.* junger Hund; (*fig.*) der Geck, Laffe. **–hood,** *s.* (*fig.*) Flegeljahre (*pl.*).
purblind [ˈpəːblaɪnd], *adj.* halbblind, schwachsichtig; (*fig.*) kurzsichtig.
purchas–able [ˈpəːtʃəsəbl], *adj.* käuflich. **–e** [ˈpəːtʃəs], 1. *v.a.* kaufen, einkaufen, erstehen, (durch Kauf) erwerben; (*fig.*) erkaufen, erringen (*victory, etc.*); aufwinden, hochwinden (*anchor, etc.*) (*Naut.*); *–e s.th. from a p.*, einem etwas abkaufen. 2. *s.* der Ankauf, Einkauf, die Erwerbung, der Jahresertrag (*Law*); Kauf, das Kaufobjekt; die Hebevorrichtung (*Tech.*); das Takel, Spill, die Talje (*Naut.*); der Halt, Griff; Anhaltspunkt, Angriffspunkt, Stützpunkt; Einfluß, die Macht, *at two years –e*, zum Zweifachen des Jahresertrags; *his life is not worth an hour's –e*, er hat keine Stunde mehr zu leben; *by –e*, käuflich; *make –es*, Einkäufe machen. **–er,** *s.* der Käufer, Abnehmer, Kunde. **–e–price,** *s.* der Einkaufspreis. **–ing,** *adj.* Kauf–; *–ing power*, die Kaufkraft.
purdah [ˈpəːdɑ], *s.* der Schleier.
pure [ˈpjuːə], *adj.* rein (*also fig.*), unvermischt, lauter, echt, gediegen; keusch, unbefleckt, unschuldig; (*fig.*) bloß, pur, nichts als; *– -blood, attrib. adj.*, *– -bred, adj.* reinrassig; *– gold*, das Feingold; *– mathematics*, reine Mathematik; *– nonsense*, reiner *or* purer Unsinn; *– silk*, die Glanzseide. **–ly,** *adv.* rein, bloß, glatt, gänzlich, völlig, ausschließlich, lediglich. **–ness,** *s.* die Reinheit, Unschuld, *see* **purity.**
purée [pyˈre], *s.* der Brei, die Püree.
purfl–e [ˈpəːfl], 1. *s.* gestickter Rand, die Borte (*of dress*). 2. *v.a.* schmücken, verzieren (*Arch.*). **–ing,** *s.* der Randschmuck; Flödel (*of violins, etc.*).
purgat–ion [pəːˈgeɪʃən], *s.* die Reinigung (*Law and Rel.*); das Abführen, die Stuhlentleerung (*Med.*). **–ive** [ˈpəːgətɪv], 1. *adj.* abführend, Abfuhr– (*Med.*), Reinigungs– (*Law*). 2. *s.* das Abführmittel. **–orial** [pəːgəˈtɔrɪəl], *adj.* Fegefeuer. **–ory** [ˈpəːgətərɪ], *s.* das Fegefeuer (*also fig.*).
purge [pəːdʒ], 1. *v.a.* reinigen (*also fig.*), befreien (*of*, from, von); läutern, klären (*liquids*); ein Abführmittel geben (*Dat.*) (*Med.*); *– away*, säubern, entfernen; *– o.s. of*, sich reinwaschen von (*Law*). 2. *v.n.* abführen (*of medicines*). 3. *s.* die Ausleerung; das Abführmittel (*Med.*); (*fig.*) die Reinigung; Säuberung(saktion) (*Pol.*).
purif–ication [pjuːrɪfɪˈkeɪʃən], *s.* die Reinigung, Läuterung; *the –ication*, Mariä Reinigung (*R.C.*). **–icator** [ˈpjuːrɪfɪkeɪtə], *s.* das Purifikatorium, Reinigungstüchlein (*Eccl.*). **–icatory** [ˈpjuːrɪfɪkeɪtərɪ], *adj.* reinigend, Reinigungs–. **–ier** [ˈpjuːrɪfaɪə], *s.* der Reiniger, das Reinigungsmittel, Reinigungsgerät. **–y** [ˈpjuːrɪfaɪ], *v.a.* reinigen, läutern; klären, schlämmen, raffinieren (*Tech.*).
puris–m [ˈpjuːərɪzm], *s.* der Purismus, die Sprachreinigung(ssucht). **–t** [–ɪst], *s.* der Sprachreiniger.
puritan [ˈpjurɪtən], 1. *s.* der Puritaner, Frömmler. 2. *adj.* puritanisch. **–ical** [–ˈtænɪkl], *adj.* puritanisch; sittenstreng, frömmelnd. **–ism** [–ɪzm], *s.* der Puritanismus.
purity [ˈpjuːrɪtɪ], *s.* die Reinheit (*also fig.*), Klarheit, Feinheit, Echtheit, Gediegenheit; Makellosigkeit, Keuschheit, Unschuld.
[1]**purl** [pəːl], 1. *s.* gewundenes Gold– *or* Silberdraht; das Linksstricken, *pl.* gestickte Borte, die Häkelkante, Zäckchen (*pl.*). 2. *v.a.* umsäumen, einfassen. 3. *v.n.* linksstricken. **– -stitch,** *s.* linke Masche.
[2]**purl** [pəːl], 1. *s.* das Rieseln, Murmeln, Rauschen (*of a brook*). 2. *v.n.* rieseln, murmeln, sanft rauschen.
[3]**purl** [pəːl], 1. *v.n.* sich drehen, wirbeln; (*coll.*) umfallen, umkippen. 2. *v.a.* (*sl.*) umwerfen. 3. *s.* (*coll.*) der Fall, Sturz. **–er** [–ə], *s.* (*coll.*) der Sturz, Fall; Schlag, Stoß; *come* or *go a –er*, stürzen, heftig fallen.
purlieu [ˈpəːljuː], *s.* der Bezirk, Bereich; (*usually pl.* [–z], die Umgebung, Umgebungen (*pl.*).
purlin [ˈpəːlɪn], *s.* die Pfette.
purloin [pəːˈlɔɪn], *v.a.* entwenden, stehlen, mausen.
purpl–e [ˈpəːpl], 1. *s.* der Purpur; die Kardinalswürde; (*fig.*) Herrscherwürde, fürstliche Würde; 2. *adj.* purpurrot, purpurfarben, purpurn; *–e Emperor*, der Schillerfalter (*Ent.*); *–e Heart*, das Verwundetenabzeichen (*Amer.*); *–e patches*, Glanzstellen (*pl.*). **–ish,** *adj.* purpurfarbig.
purport, 1. [ˈpəːpɔːt], *s.* der Inhalt, Sinn, die Bedeutung. 2. [pəːˈpɔːt] *v.a.* besagen, bedeuten, zum Inhalt haben; es sich zur Aufgabe machen; *it –s to describe*, es will beschreiben; *it –s to contain*; es enthält scheinbar, es will den Eindruck erwecken als enthielte es.
purpos–e [ˈpəːpəs], 1. *s.* der Vorsatz, Entschluß; Zweck, das Ziel, die Absicht; Sache; der Erfolg, die Wirkung; *for all practical –es*, praktisch genommen; *answer the –e*, zweckentsprechend sein; *be at cross –es*, aneinander vorbeireden, einander unbewußt entgegenhandeln; *for this –e*, in dieser Absicht, zu diesem Zweck; *for what –e?* wozu? *for the –e of doing*, um zu tun; *fitness for –e*, zweckdienliche Eignung; *fixity of –e*, die Zielstrebigkeit; *strength of –e*, die Entschlußkraft, Willensstärke; *weakness of –e*, die Schwachheit im Entschluß; *of set –e*, absichtlich, vorsätzlich (*Law*); *on –e*, absichtlich, vorsätzlich, mit Willen, mit Fleiß; *on –e that*, damit; *on –e to do*, um zu tun, in der Absicht zu tun; *suit one's –e*, einem zweckdienlich sein; *to all intents and –es*, praktisch genommen; *to the –e*, zweckdienlich, zur Sache; *to little –e*, mit geringem *or* ohne rechten Erfolg; *to no –e*, umsonst, vergeblich; *be* (*much*) *to the same –e*, (fast) ebendasselbe sein, auf (ungefähr) dasselbe hinauslaufen, (beinahe) dieselbe Wirkung haben; *to some –e*, mit gutem Erfolg; *novel with a –e*, der Tendenzroman. 2. *v.a.* beabsichtigen, vorhaben, sich (*Dat.*) vornehmen. **–eful,** *adj.* zielbewußt, entschlossen (*character*); zweckvoll, beabsichtigt, planmäßig (*action*). **–eless,** *adj.* zwecklos, ziellos; vergeblich. **–ely,** *adv.* absichtlich, vorsätzlich, mit Fleiß, in der Absicht. **–ive,** *adj.* zweckvoll, zweckdienlich, zweckbetont; entschlossen, zielbewußt, zielstrebig.
purpur–a [ˈpəːpjurə], *s.* der Purpurausschlag (*Med.*); die Gattung der Purpurschnecken (*Zool.*). **–ic** [pəːˈpjuːərɪk], *adj.* Purpur–. (*Chem. and Med.*).
purr [pəː], *v.n.* schnurren; (*fig.*) sich geschmeichelt fühlen.
purse [pəːs], 1. *s.* der Geldbeutel, die Geldtasche, Börse, das Portemonnaie; der Beutel, die Damentasche, (*fig.*) die Geldsumme, der Schatz, Fonds; der Geldpreis, das Geldgeschenk. (*a*) (*with adjectives*) *common* –, gemeinsame Fonds, gemeinschaftliche Kasse; *light* –, der Geldmangel; *long* –, großer Geldbeutel, der Reichtum; *privy* –, königlicher

liche Privatschatulle *public* –, der Staatsschatz. (*b*) (*with verbs*) *make up a* – *for*, Geld sammeln für. 2. *v.a.* (also – *up*) zusammenziehen; – *one's lips*, den Mund spitzen. **--bearer**, *s.* der Großsiegelträger. **--net**, *s.* das Beutelnetz. **--proud**, *adj.* geldstolz, protzig. **--seine**, *s.* der Kä(t)scher, Ke(t)scher. **--strings**, *pl.* Beutelschnüre (*pl.*); (*fig.*) der Geldbeutel; *hold the* --*strings*, über den Geldbeutel verfügen; *keep a tight hand on the* --*strings*, die Hand *or* den Daumen auf dem Beutel halten, den Beutel zuhalten.

purser [ˈpəːsə], *s.* der Zahlmeister, Proviantmeister (*Naut.*).

pursiness [ˈpəːsɪnɪs], *s.* die Kurzatmigkeit, *see* **pursy.**

purslane [ˈpəːslɪn], *s.* der Portulak (*Bot.*).

pursuan-ce [ˈpəːsjuːəns], *s.* die Verfolgung, Ausführung; *in* –*ce*, im Verfolg, zur Fortsetzung (*of*, (*Gen.*) *or* laut (*Dat.*), zufolge *or* gemäß (*Dat. usually precedes*); *in* –*ce of which*, demzufolge. **–t** [–ənt], *adj.*; – *to*, zufolge, gemäß (*Dat. usually precedes*), in Ausführung (*Gen.*).

pursu-e [pəːˈsjuː], 1. *v.a.* verfolgen (*also fig.*), nachsetzen (*Dat.*); (*fig.*) ständig begleiten; einschlagen (*a course*); ausüben, betreiben (*a profession*), nachgehen (*Dat.*) (*a matter, studies, etc.*); weiter fortsetzen, fortfahren in (*Dat.*). 2. *v.n.* fortfahren; Klage erheben (*Scots Law*). **er** [–sjuːə], *s.* der Verfolger; Ankläger, Kläger (*Scots Law*). **–it** [–ˈsjuːt], *s.* die Verfolgung; Jagd (*of*, auf (*Acc.*), (*fig.*) nach); das Streben, Trachten (*of*, nach), die Betreibung (*of* (*Gen.*)), Beschäftigung (*of*, mit), der Beruf; *pl.* Geschäfte, Arbeiten, Studien; *give* –*it*, verfolgen; *in hot* –*it*, hart auf den Fersen (*of* (*Dat.*)); *in* –*it of a p.*, hinter einem her, auf der Jagd nach einem; *in* –*it of a th.*, im Verfolg einer S.; *the* –*it of knowledge*, der Wissendrang. **–it-plane**, *s.* das Jagdflugzeug.

pursuivant [ˈpəːswɪvənt], *s.* der Persevant (*Her.*); (*Poet.*) Verfolger.

pursy [ˈpəːsɪ], *adj.* beleibt, fettleibig, kurzatmig; zusammengezogen, gefaltet (*of cloth*).

purtenance [ˈpəːtənəns], *s.* (*archaic*) das Geschlinge.

purulen-ce, *s.*, **–cy** [ˈpjuːrələns(ɪ)], *s.* das Eitern, die Eiterung; der Eiter. **–t** [–ənt], *adj.* eiternd, eitrig, Eiter–.

purvey [pəːˈveɪ], 1. *v.a.* liefern (*to*, für), versorgen mit. 2. *v.n.*; – *for*, beliefern, versorgen. **–ance** [–ˈveɪəns], *s.* die Beschaffung, Lieferung. **–or** [–ˈveɪə], *s.* der Lieferant, Traiteur; –*or to the King*, königlicher Hoflieferant.

purview [ˈpəːvjuː], *s.* der Wirkungskreis, Gesichtskreis, Spielraum, Bereich, das Blickfeld, Gebiet; der Wirkungsbereich, die Verfügung (*Law*).

pus [pʌs], *s.* der Eiter.

push [puʃ], **1.** *v.a.* stoßen, drücken, rücken, drängen (*also fig.*); treiben, schieben, ausführen, durchführen, durchdrücken, durchsetzen (*a claim*); (*fig.*) (an)treiben, beschleunigen, vorwärtsbringen; betreiben (*a business*), fördern (*sales*), aufdrängen, verkaufen wollen (*goods*). (*a*) (*with nouns*) – *an advantage*, einen Vorteil ausnützen; – *money on s.o.*, einem Geld aufdrängen; – *one's nose into*, seine Nase stecken in; – *s.th. down a p.'s throat*, einem etwas glaubhaft machen wollen; – *s.th. too far*, etwas zu weit treiben; – *one's way*, sich vordrängen *or* durchdrängen; *be* –*ed for*, in Not *or* Verlegenheit sein wegen *or* um; *be* –*ed for money*, in Geldverlegenheit sein; *be* –*ed for time*, keine Zeit haben. (*b*) (*with adverbs*) – *aside*, beiseiteschieben, beseitigen; – *back*, zurückstoßen, zurückdrängen; zurückwerfen, aufrollen (*Mil.*); – *forward*, vorwärtsbringen, beschleunigen; – *o.s. forward*, sich vordrängen; – *off*, abstoßen, losschlagen (*goods*); – *open*, aufstoßen (*door*); – *out*, hinausstoßen, fortjagen (*a p.*); vorschieben, vorstrecken (*one's arm, etc.*); aussenden, hervortreiben (*shoots*); – *through*, durchdrücken, durchsetzen; – *the door to*, die Tür zuschlagen; – *up*, in die Höhe treiben, hochtreiben (*prices*). **2.** *v.n.* stoßen, schieben, drücken, drängen; (*with adverbs*) (*coll.*) – *along*, weggehen, weitergehen; – *forward*, sich vordrängen, vorwärtsdrängen, vorstoßen (*Mil.*); – *off*, abstoßen (*of a boat*); (*coll.*) sich auf den Weg machen; (*sl.*) verduften, (*sl.*) beginnen; – *on*, vordringen, vorwärtsdrängen; – *out*, vorstoßen, vordringen (*to*, nach); in See stechen. **3.** *s.* der Stoß, Schub, Druck; horizontaler Druck (*Arch.*); (*fig.*) der Anstoß, Antrieb; dringender Fall, der Notfall, entscheidender Augenblick; der Vorstoß (*for*, auf) (*Mil*); (*coll.*) die Energie, Strebsamkeit, der Ehrgeiz; Entschluß, das Selbstbewußtsein, die Reklame; *at a* –, im Notfall, wenn es aufs Äußerste kommt; (*sl.*) *get the* –, entlassen werden, fliegen; *give a p. a* –, einem einen Stoß geben; (*sl.*) *give a p. the* –, einen entlassen; *bring to the last* –, auf die Spitze *or* aufs Äußerste treiben. **--ball**, *s.* der Stoßball. (*coll.*) **--bike**, *s.* das Fahrrad. **--button**, *s.* der Druckknopf. **--cart**, *s.* der Schiebkarren, die Schiebkarre. **--chair**, *s.* der Sportkinderwagen. **–er**, *s.* Stoßende(r), Treibende(r), *m.*; der Streber, Draufgänger, Emporkömmling; –*er aeroplane*, das Flugzeug mit Schubschraube. **–ful**, *adj.*, **–ing**, *adj.* energisch, unternehmend, strebsam, rührig; aufdringlich, zudringlich. **--pull amplification**, die Gegentaktverstärkung (*Rad.*). **--rod**, *s.* die Stoßstange, Schubstange.

pusillanim-ity [pjuːsɪləˈnɪmɪtɪ], *s.* der Kleinmut. **–ous** [–ˈlænɪməs], *adj.* kleinmütig, verzagt, feig(e).

puss [pus], *s.* die Katze, Mieze, das Kätzchen; der Hase; – *in boots*, gestiefelter Kater; --*in-the-corner*, *s.* das Kämmerchenvermieten (*game*). **– moth,** *s.* der Gabelschwan (*Ent.*). **–y**, *s.* (also **–y-cat**) *see* –. (*sl.*) **–yfoot**, 1. *s.* der Abstinenzler. 2. *v.n.* (*sl.*) heimlich tun, sich ausschweigen (*on*, über); leise schleichen; Entscheidungen aus dem Wege gehen (*Amer.*). 3. *adj.* saftlos, lappig. **–y footer**, *s.* (*Amer.*) der Schleicher, Leisetreter. **–y footing, adj.** (*Amer.*) leisetreterisch.

pustul-ar [ˈpʌstjulə], *adj.* Pustel–. **–ation** [–ˈleɪʃən] *s.* die Pustelbildung. **–e** [ˈpʌstjuːl], *s.* die Pustel, der Pickel, das Eiterbläschen.

put [put], **1.** *ir.v.a.* (*also imperf. & p.p.*) legen, setzen, stellen, stecken (*on*, auf; *to*, an); (*coll.*) tun, ansetzen; abschätzen (*at*, auf); stellen, vorlegen (*questions*); werfen, schleudern (*a stone, hammer*). **(a)** (*with nouns*) – *his age at* 50, sein Alter auf 50 schätzen; – *the blame on s.o.*, einem die Schuld beimessen *or* zuschieben; – *the cart before the horse*, das Pferd hinter den Wagen spannen; – *the case to him!* lege ihm die Sache vor! – *a construction on s.th.*, einer S. eine Auslegung geben; – *an end to s.th.*, der S. ein Ende machen; – *an end to one's life*, sich (*Dat.*) das Leben nehmen; – *a good face on it*, gute Miene zum bösen Spiel machen; – *one's best foot forward*, sich nach Kräften anstrengen; – *one's hand to the plough*, energisch zugreifen; *that* –*s the lid on it*, das setzt der S. die Krone auf; – *pen to paper*, die Feder ansetzen *or* ergreifen; – *a question to a p.*, einem eine Frage stellen, eine Frage an einen richten; – *the shot* or *weight*, kugelstoßen; – *your signature to it*, unterschreiben *or* zeichnen Sie (es); – *a spoke in a p.'s wheel*, einem einen Knüppel zwischen die Beine werfen; – *a stop to*, see – *an end to*; – *words into a p.'s mouth*, einem Worte in den Mund legen. **(b)** (*with prepositions*) – *it* **across** *s.o.*, einen hintergehen; – *a p.* **at** *his ease*, einen beruhigen; – *a horse at a fence*, ein Pferd über einen Zaun setzen lassen; – **before** *a p.*, einem vorlegen, vor einem ausbreiten; – *o.s.* **in** *s.o.'s care*, sich in seine Obhut begeben; – *s.o. in charge of s.th.*, einem etwas beauftragen, einen mit der Leitung *or* Führung einer S. betrauen; – *o.s. in s.o.'s hands*, sich in seine Hände begeben; – *in commission*, in Dienst stellen; – *in gaol*, ins Gefängnis stecken; – *in mind of*, erinnern an; – *in order*, in Ordnung bringen; – *o.s. in a p.'s place*, sich an seine Stelle *or* in seine Lage versetzen; – *in one's pocket*, in die Tasche stecken *or* tun; – **into** *circulation*, in Umlauf setzen; – *into force*, in Kraft setzen; – *into German*, ins Deutsche übersetzen; – *into s.o.'s head*, einem in den Kopf setzen; – *into practice*, in die Praxis umsetzen, ausführen, verwirklichen; – *into shape*, in Form bringen; – *into words*, in Worte kleiden *or* ausdrücken; – *a p.* **off** *his guard*, seine Aufmerksamkeit ablenken; – **on** *a diet*, auf Diät setzen; – *a p. on his guard*, einen warnen; – *money on a horse*, Geld auf ein Pferd setzen; – *on the last*, über den Leisten schlagen; – *on oath*, vereidigen; – *on the shelf*, an den Nagel hängen; – *on the stage*, auf die Bühne bringen; – *s.o. on to an idea*, einen auf eine Idee bringen; – *s.o. on to a p.*, einen mit einem in Verbindung bringen; – **out** *of action*, außer Betrieb setzen, kampfunfähig machen (*Mil.*); – *out of countenance*, aus der Fassung bringen; – *out of circuit*, ausschalten; – *out of reach*, außer der Reichweite stellen *or* legen; unerreichbar *or* unerschwinglich machen; – *it* **through** *a test*, es einer Prüfung unterziehen; – *s.o. through it*, einen auf Herz und Nieren prüfen; – **to** *account*, in Rechnung stellen; – *to bed*, zu Bett bringen; – *to the blush*, beschämen; – *to death*, hinrichten; – *to expense*, Unkosten machen (*Dat.*); – *to flight*, in die Flucht schlagen; – *to rights*, wieder in Ordnung bringen, zurechtsetzen; – *to sleep*, schmerzlos beseitigen (*animals*); – *to the sword*, über die Klinge springen lassen; – *a th. to good use*, etwas vorteilhaft anwenden; – *it to s.o.*, es seiner Entscheidung *or* ihm anheimstellen *or* anheimgeben; einen fragen *or* bitten; – *to shame*, beschämen; – *to the test*, auf die Probe stellen; – *to a trade*, für ein Gewerbe bestimmen; – *it to the vote*, darüber abstimmen lassen; – *o.s.* **under** *s.o.'s care*, see – *o.s. in s.o.'s care*; – *o.s. in a p.'s place*, sich an seine Stelle *or* in seine Lage versetzen. **(c)** (*with adverbs*) – *it clearly*, es klar ausdrücken; – *it mildly*, es milde *or* gelinde ausdrücken; – *s.th. right*, etwas in Ordnung bringen; (*sl.*) – *a p. wise*, einen aufklären, einem reinen Wein einschenken; **– about,** verbreiten, in Umlauf setzen (*a rumour*); in Aufregung versetzen, beunruhigen; Unannehmlichkeiten bereiten (*Dat.*) (*a p.*); umlegen (*Naut.*); – *o.s. about*, sich beunruhigen (*for*, wegen); *be – about*, in Aufregung sein; **– across,** glücklich durchführen; **– aside,** beiseitelegen, weglegen; **– away,** weglegen, beiseitelegen, wegräumen, wegschaffen, wegtun, auf die Seite legen (*a th.*); fortschicken (*a p.*); ablegen, verbannen (*care*); (*coll.*) einsperren (*a p.*), beseitigen (*animals*); verzehren, verputzen (*food*); **– back,** nachstellen, zurückstellen (*a clock*); wieder hinstellen, verschieben, aufschieben; zurückversetzen (*in schools*); **– by,** zurücklegen, beiseitelegen, aufbewahren (*money, etc.*); ablenken, abwenden, ausweichen (*Dat.*); **– down,** niederlegen, niedersetzen, hinlegen, hinsetzen, hinstellen, aus der Hand legen; niederschreiben, aufschreiben; anrechnen, zuschreiben (*to* (*Dat.*)); abschaffen (*abuses, etc.*), unterdrücken, niederschlagen (*opposition*); absetzen, abfertigen, kurz abweisen; ducken, zum Schweigen bringen (*a p.*); (*coll.*) halten, auslegen, einschätzen (*as*, als), schätzen, festlegen (*at*, auf); – *one's name* or *o.s. down*, den Namen *or* sich eintragen; – *s.o. down for*, einen vormerken für; – *down in writing*, niederschreiben, vormerken, schriftlich niederlegen; – *down to s.o.'s account*, einem in Rechnung stellen; – *it down to ignorance*, es der Unwissenheit zuschreiben, es als Unwissenheit auslegen; **– forth,** hervorbringen, treiben (*buds, etc.*); aufbieten, aufwenden (*strength, etc.*); vorbringen, vortragen, behaupten, ausgeben (*as*, als); **– forward,** vorbringen, unterbreiten, zur Geltung *or* zum Vorschein bringen; – *forward the date*, vordatieren; (*fig.*) – *o.s. forward*, sich hervortun; **– in,** (hin)einsetzen, (hin)einstecken, (hin)einlegen, (hin)einstellen; aufstellen, einstellen, anstellen (*a p.*); einreichen (*application*); einrücken (*advertisement, etc.*), einschalten (*omission*), einschieben, machen (*claim*) (*for*, auf); einspannen (*horses*); einsetzen (*bailiff*); anbringen, vorbringen (*evidence, etc.*), verbringen, aufwenden (*at*, für), widmen (*at* (*Dat.*)) (*time*); leisten, stellen (*bail*); einlaufen (*Naut.*); – *in an appearance*, erscheinen; – *in a claim for a th.*, etwas in Anspruch nehmen, Anspruch auf eine S. machen; eine Forderung auf eine S. einreichen; – *in one's oar*, sich in eine Sache (ein)mischen; – *in a plea*, einen Rechtseinwand erheben; – *in a word*, ein Wort mitsprechen; – *in a word for*, ein Wort einlegen für; **– off,** ausziehen, ablegen, abnehmen (*clothes*); (*fig.*) abstreifen; hindern (*from*, an; *from doing*, zu tun), abbringen (*from doing*, zu tun); vertrösten, hinhalten, abfertigen, abspeisen (*a p.*) (*with*, mit); verschieben, aufschieben, auf die lange Bank schieben (*doing*, zu tun); *that – me off completely*, das brachte mich völlig aus der Fassung; **– on,** anziehen, anlegen (*clothes*); aufsetzen (*spectacles, hat*); ansetzen, annehmen (*countenance*); aufschlagen (*addition*) (*to the price*, auf den Preis); wetten, setzen (*money*) (*on*, auf); anziehen (*brakes*); anstellen (*a p.*) (*to a job*, für eine Aufgabe); einstellen (*a train, men*); andrehen, aufdrehen (*tap*); aufführen, ansetzen (*play*); verstärken, beschleunigen (*speed*); vorstellen, vorrücken (*clock*); vorsetzen (*a meal*); (*coll.*) vorspiegeln, vortäuschen, sich stellen, heucheln, schauspielern; – *the screw on*, die Schraube anziehen, einen Druck ausüben; – *on one's thinking-cap*, sich (*Dat.*) die Sache überlegen; – *on weight*, (an Gewicht) zunehmen; **– out,** hinaussetzen, hinauslegen, ausstellen (*a th.*); hinauswerfen (*a p.*), kampfunfähig machen, ausmachen (*Sport*); ausstrecken (*hand*); herausstrecken (*tongue*); aushängen (*flag*); aussetzen (*a boat*); herausgeben (*a book*); anlegen, ausleihen (*money*); in Pflege geben (*child*); in Submission geben, ausgeben (*work*); löschen (*fire*); auslöschen (*a light*); (*coll.*) verstimmen, verwirren, irremachen, ärgern, aus der Fassung *or* dem Konzept bringen (*a p.*); ausrenken (*limb*); – *o.s. out*, sich bemühen *or* ereifern (*about*, über); – *out a p.'s eyes*, einem die Augen ausstechen; – *out to service*, in Dienst geben; **– over,** mit Erfolg durchsetzen *or* ausführen, zustandebringen, zuwegebringen, fertigbringen; (*coll.*) – *it over*, das Publikum gewinnen, Erfolg sichern; – *it over on s.o.*, einem etwas aufbinden *or* weismachen *or* aufhalsen; – *o.s. over*, sich durchsetzen (*with*, bei); **– through,** ausführen, durchführen, zu Ende führen, abschließen, beendigen (*a task*); verbinden (*a p.*) (*to*, mit), herstellen (*telephone call*); **– together,** zusammensetzen, zusammenstellen; montieren (*Tech.*); – *one's heads together*, die Köpfe zusammenstecken; – *two and two together*, seine Schlüsse ziehen, die S. zurechtkombinieren; **– up,** hochziehen, hochschieben (*window, etc.*); aufstellen; errichten, montieren, installieren (*structure*); aufschlagen (*beds*); aufstecken (*one's hair*); aufspannen (*umbrella*); aufhängen (*picture*); aufstellen (*candidate*); vorbringen (*proposition*); beiseitelegen, weglegen, wegpacken, verpacken, verwahren, aufbewahren (*goods*); heraufsetzen, erhöhen (*prices*); anschlagen (*placard*); verlesen lassen (*the banns*); leisten (*resistance*); aufjagen, aufstöbern (*game*); ausstellen, ausbieten, anbieten (*for sale*), sprechen, emporsenden (*prayer*); (*coll.*) aufnehmen, unterbringen, beherbergen (*a p.*), einstellen, einpferchen (*a horse*); hinterlegen (*money*); antreiben, anstiften, anzetteln, verleiten (*to*, zu) (*a p.*); verständigen (*a p. to a th.*, einen über etwas), eröffnen (*a p. to a th.*, einem etwas), bekanntmachen (*a p. to a th.*, einen mit etwas); (*coll.*) – *s.o.'s back up*, einen ärgern, verstimmen *or* verdrießlich machen; – *up a* (*good*) *fight*, sich (energisch) wehren, (zähen) Widerstand leisten, einen (harten) Kampf liefern; – *up one's sword*, das Schwert einstecken; (*sl.*) – *the wind up a p.*, – *a p.'s wind up*, einen einschüchtern. **2.** *ir.v.n.*; *stay* –, festbleiben, sich nicht rühren; – *about*, wenden (*Naut.*); – *back*, zurückkehren, zurückfahren (*Naut.*); – *forth*, auslaufen, in See gehen (*Naut.*); – *in*, einlaufen (*at a port*); – *in for*, sich bewerben um; – *into a port*, einen Hafen anlaufen, in einen Hafen einlaufen; – *off*, abstoßen, abfahren, auslaufen, in See gehen *or* stechen (*Naut.*); – (*out*) *to sea*, auslaufen, in See stechen *or* gehen; *be* (*hard*) – *to it*, (hart) bedrängt *or* (stark) zugesetzt werden (*Dat.*), (große) Mühe haben; – *up*, auftreten, (*as candidate*); einkehren, absteigen (*at*, in) (*an inn*); sich bewerben (*for*, um); – *up with*, sich abfinden mit, sich zufrieden geben mit, sich (*Dat.*) gefallen lassen, dulden, einstecken (*an insult*); (*coll.*) – *upon a p.*, einem (zu) viel zumuten, einen ausnutzen. **3.** *s.* der Kugelstoß (*Sport*); *see* **putt;** die Rückprämie, der Zeitkauf, das Prämiengeschäft (*C.L.*); – *and call*, *s.* die Stellage; (*C.L.*). (*sl.*) **– -off,** *s.* die Ausrede, Ausflucht. (*coll.*) **– -up,** *adj.* abgekartet. *See* **putting.**

putative [ˈpju:tətɪv], *adj.* vermeintlich, mutmaßlich.

putlock ['pʌtlək], **putlog** ['pʌtləg], *s.* die Rüststange, der Rüstbaum, Rüstbalken (*Arch.*).
putr–efaction [pjuːtrɪ'fækʃən], *s.* die Fäulnis, Verwesung. **–efactive,** *adj.* fäulniswirkend, faulig. **–efy** ['pjuːtrɪfaɪ], *v.n.* in Fäulnis übergehen, faul werden, (ver)faulen, verwesen, modern. **–escence** [–'trɛsəns], *s.* die Fäulnis. **–escent** [–'trɛsənt], *adj.* faulend, angefault. **–id** ['pjuːtrɪd], *adj.* faul, verfault, moderig; (*fig.*) verderbt; (*sl.*) ekelhaft, saumäßig, Sau–. **–idity** [–'trɪdɪtɪ], *s.*, **–idness,** *s.* die Fäulnis, (*fig.*) Verderbtheit.
putt [pʊt], 1. *v.a.* einlochen (*Golf*). 2. *s.* leichter Schlag auf dem Grün. **–er,** *s.* der Einlochschläger (*Golf*). **–ing,** *s.* das Stoßen (*Sport*); das Einlochen (*Golf*); *–ing the shot* or *weight,* das Kugelstoßen. **–ing-green** *s.* das Grün, der Kleingolfplatz.
puttee ['pʊtɪː], *s.* (*often pl.* [–z]) die Wickelgamasche.
putti ['pʊtɪ], *pl.* Putten, Kindergestalten (*pl.*) (*Arts*).
puttock ['pʌtək], *s.* (*dial.*) die Reihe, der Bussard (*Orn.*).
putty ['pʊtɪ], 1. *s.* (also *glazier's* –) der Kitt, Glaserkitt; *jeweller's* –, see **––paste;** *plasterer's* –, der Kalkkitt. 2. *v.a.* (also – *up*) (ver)kitten, zukitten. **––knife,** das Spachtelmesser. **––paste,** *s.* die Zinnasche.
puzzl–e ['pʌzl], 1. *s.* das Rätsel, Problem, schwierige Frage; die Verlegenheit, Verwirrung; das Geduldspiel, Vexierspiel. 2. *v.a.* verwirren, irremachen, in Verlegenheit setzen; zu denken geben (*Dat.*); *be –ed,* in Verlegenheit sein (*for,* um), nicht wissen; *–e out,* enträtseln, austüfteln, herausfinden, herausbekommen; *–e one's head* or *brains,* sich (*Dat.*) den Kopf zerbrechen. 3. *v.n.* sich (*Dat.*) den Kopf zerbrechen (*over,* über). **–e-headed,** *adj.* konfus, wirr. **–e-lock,** *s.* das Kombinationsschloß, Vexierschloß. **–er,** *s.* das Verwirrende, Problematische, schwierige Frage. **–ing,** *adj.* verwirrend, irremachend.
pyaemia [paɪ'ɪːmɪə], *s.* das Wundfieber, Eiterfieber, die Blutvergiftung (*Med.*).
pyelitis [paɪə'laɪtɪs], *s.* die Nierenbeckenentzündung (*Med.*).
pygm–ean [pɪg'mɪːən], *adj.* pygmäisch, Zwerg–, zwerghaft. **–y** ['pɪgmɪ], 1. *s.* der Pygmäe, Zwerg. 2. *attrib. adj.* Zwerg– (*Zool.*); (*fig.*) zwerghaft, winzig, unbedeutend.
pyjamas [pɪ'dʒɑːməz], *pl.* der Schlafanzug, das *or* der Pyjama.
pylon ['paɪlən], *s.* der Turm, freitragender Mast, der Leitungsmast (*Elec.*), die Wendemarke (*Av.*).
pylor–ic [paɪ'lɔrɪk], *adj.* Pförtner–, Pylorus– (*Anat.*). **–us** [paɪ'lɔːrəs], *s.* der Pförtner (*Anat.*).
pyo–genesis [paɪə'dʒɛnɪsɪs], *s.* die Eiterbildung. **–rrhœa** [–'rɪːə], *s.* die Zahnfleischeiterung; der Eiterfluß.
pyramid ['pɪrəmɪd], *s.* die Pyramide (*Arch. & Math.*). **–al** [pɪ'ræmɪdəl], *adj.* pyramidal, pyramidisch, pyramidenförmig.
pyre ['paɪə], *s.* der Scheiterhaufen.
pyre–tic [paɪə'rɛtɪk, pɪ'rɛtɪk], 1. *s.* das Fiebermittel. 2. *adj.* fieberhaft; Fieber–; fiebermildernd. **–xia** [paɪ'rɛksɪə], *s.* der Fieberanfall, Fieberzustand.
pyridine ['paɪərɪdɪn, 'pɪrɪdɪn], *s.* das Pyridin (*Chem.*).
pyriform ['paɪərɪfɔːm], *adj.* birnenförmig (*Anat.*).
pyrites [pɪ'raɪtɪːz], *s.* der Schwefelkies, Pyrit; *iron*-–, der Eisenkies.
pyro ['paɪərou], 1. *s.* (*coll.*) *see* **–gallol** (*Phot.*). 2. *prefix* Feuer–, Brand–, Wärme–, Hitze–. **–gallic** [–'gælɪk], *adj.*; *–gallic acid, see* **–gallol. –gallol** [–'gæləl], *s.* die Pyrogallussäure. **–genous** [–'rɔdʒənəs], *adj.* pyrogen (*Geol.*). **–graphy** [–'rɔgrəfɪ], *s.* die (Holz)Brandmalerei. **–latry** [–'rɔlətrɪ], *s.* die Feueranbetung. **–mania** [–'meɪnɪə], *s.* der Brandstiftungstrieb. **–meter** [–'rɔmɪtə], *s.* der Pyrometer. **–technic** [–'tɛknɪk], *adj.* Feuerwerks–, (*fig.*) glänzend, blendend. **–technics,** *pl.* (*usually pl. constr.*) die Feuerwerkerei, Pyrotechnik, das Feuerwerk; (*fig.*) die Glanzentfaltung. **–technist,** *s.* der Feuerwerker. **–xylin** [–'rɔksəlɪn], *s.* die Schießbaumwolle, Kollodiumwolle.
pyrrhic ['pɪrɪk], *adj.*; – *verse,* der Vers aus zwei Kürzen (*Pros.*); – *victory,* der Pyrrhussieg.
python ['paɪθən], *s.* die Riesenschlange. **–ess,** *s.* die Orakelpriesterin.
pyuria [paɪ'uːrɪə], *s.* das Eiterharnen (*Med.*).
pyx [pɪks], 1. *s.* die Pyxis, Monstranz (*Eccl.*); Büchse; Münzproben (*Mint.*). 2. *v.a.* auf ihr Gewicht prüfen (*coins*).

Q

Q, q [kjuː], *s.* das Q. q. *See Index of Abbreviations.* **––boat,** *s.* die U-bootsfalle, das Kriegsschiff als Handelsschiff getarnt.
qua [kwɑ], *conj.* als, in der Eigenschaft als.
[1]**quack** [kwæk], 1. *v.n.* quaken. 2. *s.* das Quaken, Gequake.
[2]**quack** [kwæk], 1. *v.n.* quacksalbern, herumpfuschen. 2. *s.* der Quacksalber, Kurpfuscher, Schwindler, Schaumschläger, Großspecher. 3. *attrib.*; Quacksalber–, Wunder–, Schwindel–, quacksalberisch. **–ery,** *s.* die Quacksalberei, Kurpfuscherei, der Schwindel; **–salver,** *s. see* – (2).
quad–rable ['kwɔdrəbl], *adj.* quadrierbar. **–ragenarian** [–dʒən'ɛərɪən], 1. *s.* Vierzigjährige(r), *m.* 2. *adj.* vierzigjährig. **–ragesima** [–'dʒɛsɪmə], *s.* erster Fastensonntag. **–ragesimal** [–'dʒɛsɪml], *adj.* Fasten–. **–rangle** ['kwɔdræŋgl], *s.* das Viereck (*Math.*); viereckiger Hof *or* Häuserblock. **–rangular** [–'ræŋgjulə], *adj.* viereckig. **–rant** [–rənt], *s.* der Quadrant, Viertelkreis; *–rant elevation,* der Erhöhungswinkel. **–rat** [–rət], *s.* das Quadrat, großer Ausschluß (*Typ.*). **–rate,** 1. [kwə'dreɪt], *v.n.* übereinstimmen (*with,* mit). 2. [–rət] *adj.* quadratisch, Quadrat– (*Anat.*). 3. *s.* das Quadrat. **–ratic** [kwə'drætɪk], 1. *adj.* quadratisch. 2. *s.* quadratische Gleichung. **–rature** [–rətʃə], *s.* die Quadratur. **–rennial** [kwə'drenɪəl], *adj.* vierjährlich, alle vier Jahre; vierjährig. **–riga** [kwə'draɪgə], *s.* römisches Viergespann. **–rilateral** [–rɪ'lætərəl], 1. *adj.* vierseitig. 2. *s.* vierseitige Figur, das Viereck. **–rille** [kwə'drɪl], *s.* die Quadrille (*Danc.*). **–rillion** [kwə'drɪlɪən], *s.* die Quadrillion (= 10^{24} *Eng.*); Billiarde (= 10^{15} *French, Amer.*). **–rinomial** [–rɪ'noumɪəl], *adj.* viergliedrig. **–ripartite** [kwɔdrɪ'pɑːtaɪt], *adj.* vierteilig (*Bot.*) **–roon** [kwə'druːn] *s.* der Quarteron. **–rumanous,** [kwɔd'ruːmɪnəs] *adj.* vierhändig (*Zool.*). **–ruped** [–rupɛd], 1. *s.* der Vierfüß(l)er. 2. *adj.* vierfüssig. **–ruple** [–rupl], 1. *adj.* vierfach; *–ruple of* or *to,* viermal so groß wie; *–ruple alliance,* die Quadrupelallianz; *–ruple pact,* das Viermächteabkommen; *–ruple rhythm* or *time,* der Viervierteltakt (*Mus.*). 2. *s.* das Vierfache. 3. *v.a. & n.* (sich) vervierfachen. **–ruplet** [–druplɪt], *s.* (*usually pl.*) der Vierling. **–ruplicate,** 1. [kwə'druːplɪkeɪt], *v.a.* viermal *or* vierfach ausfertigen, vervierfachen. 2. [kwə'druːplɪkət], *adj.* in vierfacher Ausfertigung. 3. *s.* vierfache Ausfertigung. **–ruplication** [kwɔdruːplɪ'keɪʃən], *s.* die Vervierfachung.
quaestor ['kwɪːstə], *s.* der Quästor. **–ial** [–'stɔːrɪəl], *adj.* Quästor–. **–ship,** *s.* die Quästur.
quaff [kwɔf], 1. *v.n.* tüchtig trinken, zechen. 2. *v.a.* (also – *off*) hinunterstürzen, in großen Zügen trinken, austrinken, (aus)leeren.
quag [kwæg], *s.*, **–mire,** *s.* der Sumpf, Morast (*also fig.*), Sumpfboden; Moorboden. **–gy,** *adj.* sumpfig.
quagga ['kwægə], *s.* das Quagga (*Zool.*).
[1]**quail** [kweɪl], *s.* die Wachtel (*Orn.*).
[2]**quail** [kweɪl], *v.n.* verzagen, den Mut sinken lassen; zittern, beben, zurückweichen (*before,* vor); *his spirit –ed,* ihm sank der Mut.
quaint [kweɪnt], *adj.* altmodisch, anheimelnd; seltsam, wunderlich, drollig, putzig. **–ness,** *s.* das Altmodische, anheimelnde Schlichtheit; die Seltsamkeit, Wunderlichkeit.

quak–e [kweɪk], 1. *v.n.* zittern, beben (*for* or *with*, vor); *–e in one's shoes*, vor Angst außer sich (*Dat.*) sein. 2. *s.* das (Erd)Beben, die Erschütterung. **–er** [–ə], *s.* der Quäker; *–er oats*, Haferflocken (*pl.*). **–erish,** *adj.* quäkerhaft. **–erism,** *s.* das Quäkertum. **–ing,** *adj.* zittrig, bebend. **–ing-grass,** *s.* das Zittergras.

qualif–ication [kwɔlɪfɪˈkeɪʃən], *s.* die Befähigung, Tauglichkeit, Eignung, Qualifikation (*for*, für), Fähigkeit (*for*, zu); Einschränkung, Modifikation, Vorbedingung, Voraussetzung, das Erfordernis; *my –ications for*, was mich qualifiziert für; *without any –ication*, ohne jede Einschränkung. **–ied,** *adj.* geeignet, befähigt, qualifiziert, bedingt, eingeschränkt; *in a –ied sense*, mit Einschränkung(en). **–y** [ˈkwɔlɪfaɪ], 1. *v.a.* befähigen, qualifizieren (*for*, für); einschränken, mildern, mäßigen, modifizieren; ausweisen, bezeichnen (*as*, als); näher bestimmen (*Gram.*); verdünnen, vermischen, verschneiden (*drinks*). 2. *v.n.* sich qualifizieren *or* ausbilden (*as*, als), die Befähigung besitzen (*as*, als); die nötige Befähigung nachweisen (*as*, als; *for*, für).

qualit–ative [ˈkwɔlɪtətɪv], *adj.* qualitativ. **–y** [–tɪ], *s.* die Beschaffenheit, Gattung, Art, Natur, das Wesen; die Qualität (*also C.L.*), Eigenschaft, charakterische Eigenart, die Klangfarbe (*of sound*); Güte, der Wert, Gehalt (*C.L.*); (*archaic*) Rang, (vornehmer) Stand; *the –y*, die vornehme Welt; *person of –y*, die Standesperson.

qualm [kwɑ:m, kwɔ:m], *s.* die (Anwandlung von) Übelkeit; *pl.* Gewissensbisse, Zweifel (*pl.*). **–ish,** *adj.* unwohl, übel.

quandary [ˈkwɔndərɪ, kwɔnˈdɛ:ərɪ], *s.* die Schwierigkeit, Verlegenheit, verzwickte Lage.

quant [kwɔnt], *s.* die Stake *or* (Boots)Stange mit Tellerkappe.

quant–ic [ˈkwɔntɪk], *s.* homogene Funktion (*Math.*). **–ify** [–ɪfaɪ], *v.a.* quantitativ bestimmen. **–itative** [–tɪteɪtɪv, –ˈtɪtətɪv], *adj.* quantitativ; *–itative analysis*, die Mengenbestimmung. **–ity** [ˈkwɔntɪtɪ], *s.* die Menge, Quantität (*also Mus. and Gram.*), große Menge, Zahl *or* Portion; bestimmte Menge, das Quantum; die Größe (*Math.*); das Silbenmaß, Zeitmaß (*Metr.*); *in –ities*, in großer Menge, in großen Mengen; *unknown –ity*, unbekannte Größe (*also fig.*). **–um** [–əm], *s.* die Menge, Zahl, Größe; der Teil, bestimmter Anteil; das Quantum; Energiequantum, Energieatom (*physics*); *–um theory*, die Quantentheorie.

quarantine [ˈkwɔrəntɪ:n], 1. *s.* die Quarantäne (*of a ship*); Isolierung (*of a person*). 2. *v.a.* unter Quarantäne stellen.

quarrel [ˈkwɔrəl], 1. *s.* der Streit, Zank, Zwist, Hader; *have no – with*, nichts auszusetzen haben an; *pick* or *seek a – with*, Händel suchen mit. 2. *v.n.* streiten, hadern; sich streiten, sich zanken (*with*, mit; *for*, wegen; *about* or *over*, um *or* über); *– with one's bread and butter*, mit seinem Los unzufrieden sein, sich ins eigene Fleisch schneiden; *– with each other*, miteinander streiten; *– with a th.*, sich über etwas beklagen, etwas bemängeln, etwas an einer S. auszusetzen haben. **–some** [–səm], *adj.* zänkisch, streitsüchtig. **–someness,** *s.* die Streitsucht.

quarr–ier [ˈkwɔrɪə], *s.* der Steinbrecher, Steinhauer. **–y** [ˈkwɔrɪ], 1. *s.* der Steinbruch, (*fig.*) die Fundgrube, Quelle. 2. *v.a.* brechen, hauen (*stone*), aushöhlen (*a mountain*); (*fig.*) mühsam erarbeiten, gewinnen (*from*, aus). **–yman,** *s. see* **quarrier.**

[1]**quarry** [ˈkwɔrɪ], *s.* die Jagdbeute, verfolgtes Wild; (*fig.*) (verfolgte) Beute.

[2]**quarry** [ˈkwɔrɪ], *s.* viereckige Fensterscheibe.

[1]**quart** [kwɔ:t], *s.* das Quart(maß) (= 1·14 *l.*; *Amer.* = 0·95 *l.*).

[2]**quart** [kɑ:t], *s.* die Quarte (*Mus.*), Quart (*Fenc.*).

quartan [ˈkwɔ:tən], *adj.* viertägig, Quartan (*fever*).

quarter [ˈkwɔ:tə], **1.** *s.* das Viertel; (*time*) das Vierteljahr, Quartal; die Viertelstunde, das Viertelstundenzeichen, Viertel; (Mond)Viertel; (*space*) die Himmelsrichtung, Himmelsgegend, Windrichtung; Gegend, das Viertel (*of a town*); (*fig.*) die Richtung, Seite; Windvierung (*of a ship*); (*measure*) der Viertelzentner (= 28 *lb.*); englisches Trockenmaß (= 8 *bushels* = 290 *l.*); (*coll.*) das Viertelmeilenrennen (*Sport*); (*Amer.*) der Vierteldollar, das 25-Cent-Stück; das Feld eines Gevierts (*Her.*); die Gnade, der Pardon (*Mil.*); (*fig.*) die Schonung, Nachsicht; *pl.* das Quartier (*Mil.*), (*coll.*) die Wohnung, Unterkunft, das Nachtlager, der Aufenthalt; das Hinterviertel, Hinterteil, die Kruppe (*of an animal*). (*a*) (*with nouns*) *– of a century*, ein Vierteljahrhundert; *– of an hour*, eine Viertelstunde; *– of mutton*, das Viertel Hammel. (*b*) (*with verbs*) *find no –*, keine Schonung finden; *give –*, Pardon geben; *give no –*, nichts schonen; (*coll.*) *it has gone the –*, es hat ein Viertel geschlagen; *strike the –s*, die Viertel schlagen (*of a clock*); *take up one's –s*, Quartier nehmen, sein Quartier aufschlagen (*Mil.*); (*coll.*) *take up one's –s with*, sich einquartieren bei. (*c*) (*with prepositions*) *at* (*a*) *– to three*, (um) Viertel vor drei; *by the –*, quartalsweise; *from all –s*, von allen Seiten; *the wind blows from another –*, der Wind bläst aus einer andern Richtung; *from a good –*, aus zuverlässiger *or* guter Quelle; *from another –*, von anderer Seite; *in this –*, hier, hierzulande, in dieser Gegend; *in the proper –*, bei der zuständigen Stelle; *divide into –s*, in vier Teile schneiden; *on the –*, backstagsweise (*Naut.*); *on the starboard –*, am Steuerbord achteraus (*Naut.*); *confined to –s*, Zimmerarrest haben. (*d*) (*with adjectives*) *close –s*, (nächste) Nähe; *come to close –s*, handgemein werden; *free –s*, das Freiquartier; *not a – as good*, bei weitem nicht so gut; *hind –s*, die Hinterhand (*of horse*), (*coll.*) das Hinterteil, der Hintere; *official –*, amtliche Seite. **2.** *v.a.* in vier Teile teilen, vieren, in vier Felder teilen (*Her.*); vierteilen (*a criminal*); einquartieren (*Mil.*); zwangsweise unterbringen (*upon*, bei); durchstöbern, durchqueren (*ground*) (*Hunt.*); *– o.s. upon a p.*, sich bei einem einquartieren; *be –ed at*, in Quartier liegen in; *be –ed upon*, im Quartier liegen bei. **–age** [–ɪdʒ], *s.* die Vierteljahrszahlung, das Vierteljahrsgehalt. **--bend,** *s.* die Krümme (*plumbing*). **--binding,** *s.* der Band mit engem Lederrücken. **--day,** *s.* der Quartalstag, Mietezahltag. **--deck,** *s.* das Achterdeck (*Naut.*). **–ing,** *s.* das Vierteilen; die Schildteilung (*Her.*); Einquartierung (*Mil.*); das Vierblatt, Sparrenholz (*Build.*). **–ly,** 1. *adv.* vierteljährlich, quartalsweise, Vierteljahres–. 2. *s.* die Vierteljahrsschrift. **–master,** *s.* der Feldzeugmeister, Quartiermeister (*Mil.*), Steuermann(smaat) (*Naut.*); *–master-sergeant*, der Furier (*Mil.*). **–n,** *s.* das Viertel (*as measure*); *–n loaf*, das Vierpfundbrot. **--plate,** *s.* die Plattengröße 9 × 12 cm. (*Phot.*). **--sessions,** *pl.* vierteljährliche Gerichtssitzungen, das Grafschaftsgericht. **–staff,** *s.* langer, dicker Stab (*as weapon*). **--tone,** *s.* das Viertelton-intervall (*Mus.*). **--wind,** *s.* der Backstagswind.

quart–et(te) [kwɔ:ˈtɛt], *s.* das Quartett. **–ile** [ˈkwɔ:taɪl], *s.* der Geviertschein, die Quadratur. **–o** [ˈkwɔ:toʊ], *s.* das Quart(format).

quartz [kwɔ:ts], *s.* der Quartz. **–ite** [–ɑɪt], *s.* der Quarzit, Quarzfels.

quash [kwɔʃ], *v.a.* aufheben, annullieren, zurückweisen, verwerfen; (*fig.*) unterdrücken, zunichte machen.

quasi [ˈkweɪsɑɪ], *prefix* Halb–, halb und halb, Schein–, scheinbar, gewissermaßen, gleichsam, sozusagen Quasi–; *--crime*, *s.* das verbrechenähnliche Delikt.

quassia [ˈkwæsɪə, ˈkwæʃə, ˈkwɔʃə], *s.* die Quassie, der Bitterholzbaum.

quater–centenary [kwætəsənˈtɪ:nərɪ], *s.* die Vierhundertjahrfeier. **–nary** [kwəˈtə:nərɪ], 1. *adj.* aus vier bestehend; Qua(r)tär– (*Geol.*); quaternär (*Chem.*); *–nary number*, die Vierzahl. 2. *s.* die Vierzahl (*Math.*), Quartärperiode (*Geol.*). **–nion** [kwəˈtə:nɪən], *s.* die Vier(zahl); Gruppe von vier; die Quaternione (*Math.*). **–nity,** *s.* die Gruppe von vier.

quatr–ain [ˈkwɔtrən], *s.* vierzeilige Strophe mit abwechselnden Reimen. **–efoil** [ˈkætrəfɔɪl, ˈkætəfɔɪl], *s.* das Vierblatt (*Arch. & Her.*).

quattrocento [kwɔtroˈtʃɛntoʊ], *s.* der Frührenaissancestil (*Art*).

quaver [ˈkweɪvə], 1. *v.n.* zittern; trillern, vibrieren, tremulieren. 2. *v.a.* stammeln, stammelnd äußern, trillernd singen. 3. *s.* der Triller; die Achtelnote (*Mus.*). **-y,** *adj.* zitternd.

quay [kɪ:], *s.* der Kai, die Kaimauer, der Hafendamm, die Uferstraße. **-age** [-ɪdʒ], *s.* das Kaigeld, die Kaigebühr.

quean [kwɪ:n], *s.* (*rare*) freche Dirne, das Weibsbild.

queas-iness [ˈkwɪ:zɪnɪs], *s.* die Übelkeit, der Ekel; übertriebene Empfindlichkeit. **-y** [ˈkwɪ:zɪ], *adj.* unwohl, übel; zum Erbrechen geneigt; überempfindlich (*stomach, conscience*).

queen [kwɪ:n], 1. *s.* die Königin (*also Chess*), Dame (*Cards*), (*fig.*) Herrscherin; – *Anne's bounty*, der Unterstützungsfond für arme Geistliche; – *Anne is dead*, das sind olle Kamellen; *the king and his* –, der König und seine Gemahlin; *the – of Hearts*, die Herzkönigin; – *of the May*, die Maienkönigin. 2. *v.a.* zur Königin machen (*Chess*); – *it*, die Herrin *or* große Dame spielen. **– bee,** *s.* die Bienenkönigin, der Weisel. **– dowager,** *s.* die Königinwitwe. **-hood,** *s.* der Rang *or* die Stellung einer Königin. **-ly,** *adj.* königlich, majestätisch. **– mother,** *s.* die Königinmutter. **--post,** *s.* (doppelte) Hängesäule (*Arch.*). **--regnant,** *s.* regierende Königin. **-'s-metal,** *s.* das Weißmetall, Lagermetall.

queer [kwɪ:ə], 1. *adj.* seltsam, wunderlich, sonderbar, eigentümlich; (*coll.*) unwohl, übel, nicht recht wohl; (*coll.*) *be in* – *Street*, in Geldverlegenheiten *or* Zahlungsschwierigkeiten sein. 2. *v.a.*; – *his pitch*, ihm in die Quere kommen, ihm einen Strich durch die Rechnung machen, seine Pläne durchkreuzen, seine Aussichten verderben. **-ness,** *s.* die Seltsamkeit, Wunderlichkeit.

quell [kwɛl], *v.a.* bezwingen, niederwerfen, überwältigen, dämpfen, unterdrücken, ersticken, beschwichtigen, überwinden.

quench [kwɛntʃ], *v.a.* löschen, stillen (*thirst*), auslöschen (*fire*); ersticken, unterdrücken (*feelings*); abschrecken, abkühlen (*Metall.*); *-ed spark*, der Löschfunke (*Elec.*).

quenelle [kəˈnɛl], *s.* das Fleischklößchen.

querist [ˈkwɪ:ərɪst], *s.* der Fragesteller.

quern [kwə:n], *s.* die Handmühle.

querulous [ˈkwɛrələs], *adj.* unzufrieden, klagend, mürrisch, murrend, nörgelnd, verdrossen; kläglich, jämmerlich (*as a voice*). **-ness,** *s.* stetes Klagen, das Jammern, die Nörgelei.

query [ˈkwɪ:ərɪ], 1. *s.* die Frage; der Zweifel; die Beanstandung; das Fragezeichen. 2. *v.a.* bezweifeln, in Zweifel ziehen, in Frage stellen, beanstanden, mit einem Fragezeichen versehen (*a word, etc.*). 3. *v.n.* fragen, zweifeln (*whether*, ob).

quest [kwɛst], 1. *s.* das Suchen, Forschen, die Suche (*of* or *for*, nach); *in* – *of*, auf der Suche nach. 2. *v.n.* suchen (*of hounds*) (*for* or *after*, nach); – *about*, herumsuchen. 3. *v.a.* (*Poet.*) aufsuchen, aussuchen.

question [ˈkwɛstʃən], **1.** *s.* die Frage, Fragestellung, Untersuchung, Streitfrage, der Streitpunkt, das Problem, die Angelegenheit; der Zweifel; die Anfrage, Interpellation (*Parl.*); *leading* –, die Suggestivfrage (*Law*). (*a*) (*with verbs*) *the – does not arise*, die Frage ist belanglos (*or* nicht zutreffend (*Law*)); *ask -s*, Fragen stellen; *beg the* –, dem wahren Sachverhalt ausweichen; *the – is*, es handelt sich darum, die Frage ist; *that is not the* –, das gehört nicht zur Sache; *there is no – but* or *that*, es ist keine *or* steht außer Frage, daß; *there is no – of*, es kann nicht die Rede sein von; *there can be no – of*, es kann kein Zweifel sein an; *be a – of*, sich darum handeln (*doing*, zu tun); *what is the –?* worum handelt es sich? *make no – of*, nicht bezweifeln; (*coll.*) *pop the* –, einen Heiratsantrag machen (*to* (*Dat.*)); *put a – to a p.*, eine Frage an einen richten, einem eine Frage stellen. (*b*) (*with prepositions*) *beyond* –, ohne Frage, fraglos, unzweifelhaft, außer Zweifel; *in* –, bewußt, betreffend, fraglich, um das es sich handelt; *call in* –, in Zweifel ziehen, bezweifeln; *be out of the* –, außer Frage stehen, nicht in Betracht *or* Frage kommen, ausgeschlossen sein; *open to* –, fraglich; *without* –, see *beyond* –. **2.** *v.a.* fragen, ausfragen, befragen, verhören (*a p.*); in Frage stellen, bezweifeln, in Zweifel ziehen (*facts*); – *a p. about a th.*, einen fragen nach etwas, einem Fragen stellen über etwas. **3.** *v.n.* Fragen stellen. **-able,** *adj.* fraglich, zweifelhaft, ungewiß, strittig; fragwürdig, bedenklich, anfechtbar, verdächtig. **-ableness,** *s.* die Zweifelhaftigkeit, Fragwürdigkeit. **-er,** *s.* der Fragesteller. **-ing,** *s.* das Ausfragen, Verhör. **--mark,** *s.* das Fragezeichen. **-naire** [kɛstɪəˈnɛ:ə], *s.* der Fragebogen, die Liste von Fragen. **--paper,** *s.* Prüfungsaufgaben (*pl.*). **--time,** *s.* die Interpellationszeit (*Parl.*).

queue [kjʊ:], 1. *s.* lange Reihe, die Anstellreihe, Schlange; der Zopf; *take one's place* or *wait in a* –, Schlange stehen, anstehen, sich anstellen. 2. *v.a.* in einen Zopf flechten. 3. *v.n.* (also – *up*), anstehen, Schlange stehen.

quibbl-e [ˈkwɪbl], 1. *s.* die Ausflucht, Spitzfindigkeit, Sophisterei; das Wortspiel. 2. *v.n.* Ausflüchte gebrauchen *or* machen, Worte klauben, Haare spalten; – *about*, tüfteln *or* tifteln über, deuteln an. **-er,** *s.* der Wortklauber, Haarspalter, Sophist. **-ing,** 1. *adj.* spitzfindig. 2. *s.* die Wortklauberei, Haarspalterei, Sophisterei.

quick [kwɪk], 1. *adj.* schnell, geschwind, rasch, eilig; hastig, hitzig; munter, lebhaft, behende, regsam, beweglich, gewandt; unverzüglich, ohne Verzug, bald zahlbar (*C.L.*); scharf, fein (*eye, ear*); lebendig. (*a*) (*with nouns*) – *child*, aufgewecktes Kind; – *ear*, feines Gehör; – *eye*, scharfes Auge; – *fire*, kräftiges Feuer; – *hedge*, lebende Hecke; – *lunch*, eiliges Mittagessen; – *march*, der Schnellschritt (*Mil.*); – *returns*, schneller Umsatz; – *step*, der Schritt im Marschtempo; – *temper*, die Reizbarkeit, der Jähzorn; (*coll.*) *that was – work*, das ist schnell gegangen. (*b*) (*with prepositions*) *be – about a thing*, sich mit etwas beeilen; *be – at repartee*, schlagfertig sein; *be – at understanding*, schnell begreifen; *be – of scent*, eine feine Nase haben; *be – with child*, (hoch)-schwanger sein. 2. *s.* lebendes Fleisch; *the* – (*pl.*), die Lebenden (*B.*); (*fig.*) das Leben, Innerste; *to the* –, bis ins Fleisch; (*fig.*) bis ins Innerste, bis aufs Blut; *cut* or *touch a p. to the* –, einen tief kränken, einem nahegehen. **--change,** *adj.*; *--change actor*, der Verwandlungskünstler. **--eared,** *adj.* feinhörig. **-en,** 1. *v.a.* beleben, beseelen, anfeuern, schärfen, beschleunigen. 2. *v.n.* schneller werden, sich beschleunigen; angefeuert *or* belebt werden, Leben zeigen, lebendig werden, sich regen; Leben fühlen (*in pregnancy*). **--firer,** *s.* das Schnellfeuergeschütz. **--firing,** *adj.* Schnellfeuer–. **-lime,** *s.* gebrannter *or* ungelöschter Kalk. **-ly,** *adv.* schnell, rasch, geschwind, bald, gleich. **--match,** *s.* die Zündschnur. **-ness,** *s.* die Schnelligkeit, Raschheit, Lebhaftigkeit, Beweglichkeit (*of imagination, etc.*), Schärfe, Feinheit (*of senses*), das Fassungsvermögen, die Fassungskraft, der Scharfsinn; *-ness of temper*, die Reizbarkeit, Hitze, Übereiltheit. **-sand,** *s.* der Triebsand, Treibsand, Flugsand, Schwimmsand, Schwemmsand, Schluff. **-set,** *s.* der Setzling, Hagedorn; lebende Hecke. **--sightedness,** *s.* die Scharfsichtigkeit. **-silver,** 1. *s.* das Quecksilber. 2. *v.a.* mit Quecksilber beziehen *or* belegen (*glass*). **--tempered,** *adj.* reizbar, hitzig **--witted,** *adj.* scharfsinning, schlagfertig.

¹quid [kwɪd], *s.* der Priem, das Stück Kautabak.

²quid [kwɪd], *s.* (*sl.*) das Pfund Sterling.

³quid [kwɪd], *s.* (*Latin*) etwas; – *pro quo*, die Gegenleistung, Entschädigung, der Gegenwert, Ersatz, das Entgelt, Äquivalent (*for*, für); Mißverständnis, die Verwechslung.

quiddity [ˈkwɪdɪtɪ], *s.* eigentliches Wesen, die Eigenheit; Spitzfindigkeit.

quidnunc [ˈkwɪdnʌŋk], *s.* naseweise Person, der Neuigkeitskrämer; Kannegießer.

quiesce [kwɪ:ˈɛs], *v.n.* ruhig *or* still werden. **-nce** [-əns], *s.* die Ruhe, Stille; das Stummsein (*Gram.*). **-nt** [-ənt], *adj.* ruhend, ruhig, bewegungslos; still, schweigsam; stumm (*Gram.*).

quiet [ˈkwaɪət], 1. *adj.* ruhig, still; sanft, friedlich, gelassen, behaglich, beschaulich; ungestört, flau (*C.L.*); *be* –, ruhig sein, schweigen; *keep* –, schweigen, Stillschweigen bewahren (*about*, über); ruhig *or* still bleiben, sich ruhig verhalten; *keep a th.* –, etwas für sich behalten; *as – as a mouse*, mäuschenstill; – *horse*, frommes Pferd; – *dress*, schlichtes Kleid; – *colour*, ruhige Farbe. 2. *s.* die Ruhe, Stille, Ungestörtheit; der Friede; innere Ruhe, die Seelenruhe; *on the* –, insgeheim, im geheimen, unter der Hand. 3. *v.a.* (also *–en*) beruhigen, stillen, besänftigen; abstehen lassen (*Chem.*). 4. *v.n.* (usually *–(en) down*), sich beruhigen, ruhiger werden; nachlassen, sich legen. **–ism** [–ɪzm], *s.* der Quietismus (*Theol.*). **–ist,** *s.* der Quietist. **–ly,** *adj.* ruhig, still, geräuschlos; unauffällig. **–ness,** *s.* die Ruhe, Stille, Geräuschlosigkeit, Friedlichkeit. **–ude** [–jʊd], *s.* (innere) Ruhe *or* Stille, die Friedfertigkeit, Gelassenheit, der Gleichmut. **–us** [kwɪ:ˈeɪtəs], *s.* der Tod, das Lebensende; der Rest, die Endquittung; *give the –us to a th.*, einer S. ein Ende machen; *give s.o. his –us*, einem den Rest geben *or* Garaus bereiten.

quiff [kwɪf], *s.* die Stirnlocke.

quill [kwɪl], 1. *s.* der Federkiel; (also – *pen*) die Feder; der Stachel (*of a porcupine*); die (Rohr)-Pfeife, das Rohr; die (Weber)Spule; *drive the* –, schreiben. 2. *v.a.* in Falten legen, falten, fälteln; aufspulen (*thread*). (*coll.*) **––driver,** *s.* der Federfuchser, Schmierer. **––feather,** *s.* der Schwungfeder. **–ing,** *s.* die Rüsche, Krause. **– pen,** *s.* *see* **–.**

quilt [kwɪlt], 1. *s.* die Steppdecke, (gesteppte) Bettdecke. 2. *v.a.* steppen, durchnähen; wattieren, füttern, polstern. **–ing,** *s.* das Steppen, Wattieren, Polstern; die Stepperei, gesteppte Arbeit, das Pikee. **–ing-seam,** *s.* die Steppnaht.

quinary [ˈkwaɪnərɪ], *adj.* aus fünf bestehend, Fünf–.

quince [kwɪns], *s.* die Quitte (*Bot.*).

quin–centenary [kwɪnsənˈtɪ:nərɪ], 1. *adj.* fünfhundertjährig. 2. *s.* die Fünfhundertjahrfeier. **–cuncial** [–ˈkʌnʃəl], *adj.* nach Fünfform geordnet. **–cunx** [ˈkwɪŋkʌŋks], *s.* die Quincunxanordnung; Pflanzung in Fünfform, Kreuzpflanzung (*Hort.*).

quini–ne [kwɪˈnɪ:n], *s.* das Chinin. **–sm** [ˈkwɪ:nɪzm], *s.* die Chininvergiftung, der Chininrausch.

quinqu–agenarian [kwɪŋkwədʒəˈnɛ:ərɪən], 1. *adj.* fünfzigjährig. 2. *s.* Fünfzigjährige(r), *m.*, der Fünfziger. **–agesima** [–ˈdʒɛsɪmə], *s.* der Sonntag Quinquagesimä. **–e** [ˈkwɪŋkwə], *prefix* Fünf–, fünf–. **–ennial** [–ˈkwɛnɪəl], *adj.* fünfjährig, fünfjährlich, alle fünf Jahre wiederkehrend. **–ennium** [–ˈkwɛnɪəm], *s.* das Jahrfünft. **–ereme** [ˈkwɪŋkwərɪ:m], *s.* die Galeere mit fünf Ruderbänken.

quinquina [kwɪŋˈkwaɪnə, kɪŋˈkɪ:nə], *s.* die Chinarinde.

quinsy [ˈkwɪnzɪ], *s.* die Bräune; Mandelentzündung (*Med.*).

quint, *s.* [kwɪnt], die Quinte (*Mus.*); [kɪnt] die Quint(e) (*Cards*). **–al** [–əl], (metrischer) Zentner (= 100 *kg.*). **–an** [–ən], *adj.* fünftägig, Fünftage–, Quintan–. **–e** [kænt], *s.* die Quinte (*Fenc.*).

quintessence [kwɪnˈtɛsəns], *s.* die Quintessenz; (*fig.*) der Kern, Inbegriff; das Beste.

quint–et(te) [kwɪnˈtɛt], *s.* das Quintett (*Mus.*). **–illion** [–ˈtɪlɪən], *s.* die Quintillion (*Eng.* = 10^{30}); Trillion (*French, Amer.* = 10^{18}). **–uple** [ˈkwɪntjʊpl], 1. *adj.* fünffach. 2. *s.* fünffacher Betrag. 3. *v.a.* verfünffachen. 4. *v.n.* sich verfünffachen. **–uplets** [ˈkwɪntjʊplɪts], *pl.* Fünflinge. **–uplicate** [–ˈtjʊ:plɪkət], 1. *adj.* *see* **–uple** 1. 2. *s.* der Satz von fünfen. **–uplication** [–ˈkeɪʃən], *s.* die Verfünffachung.

quip [kwɪp], 1. *s.* treffender Stich *or* Hieb, treffende Bemerkung, witziger Einfall, die Stichelei; Spitzfindigkeit; Wunderlichkeit; *–s and quirks*, Schnurren und Schnaken. 2. *v.n.* scherzen, treffende Bemerkungen machen.

quire [kwaɪə], *s.* das Buch (Papier) (= *24 sheets*); *in –s*, in Lagen (*Bookb.*).

quirk [kwə:k], *s.* plötzliche Wendung, der Einfall, Kniff, Witz, die Witzelei, Spitzfindigkeit, Finte; der Schnörkel; die Hohlkehle (*Arch.*); *see* **quip.**

quisling [ˈkwɪzlɪŋ], *s.* (*coll.*) der Landesverräter.

quit [kwɪt], 1. *v.a.* (imperf. & pp. *–ed* or –) verlassen, sich zurückziehen von, aufgeben, verzichten auf; (*coll.*) aufhören (*doing*, zu tun); (*poet.*) vergelten. 2. *v.r.* (*archaic*) sich entledigen (*of* (*Gen.*)); – *you(rselves) like men*, benehmt euch tapfer; *see* **acquit.** 3. *v.n.* räumen, ausziehen, fortgehen; *notice to* –, die Kündigung; *give notice to* –, kündigen; *have notice to* –, gekündigt werden. 4. *pred. adj.* quitt; los, (los und) ledig (*of*, von); *be* (*well*) – *of a th.*, einer S. (zum Glück) los sein *or* loswerden; (*archaic*) *go* –, frei ausgehen. **––claim,** 1. *s.* der Verzicht, die Verzichtleistung (*Law*). 2. *v.a.* Verzicht leisten auf (*Acc.*), überlassen (*to* (*Dat.*)). **––rent,** *s.* (*archaic*) (geringes) Pachtgeld (anstatt Dienstleistung). **–s,** *pred. adj.* (*coll.*) quitt; *be* or *get –s with a p.*, es einem heimzahlen; *call* or *cry –s*, klein beigeben. **–tance,** *s.* (*poet.*) die Befreiung (*from*, von), Quittung, Vergeltung (*of*, für); *omittance is no –tance*, unterlassene Mahnung heißt keine Quittung *or* Befreiung (von einer Schuld). **–ter,** *s.* (*sl.*) der Drückeberger, Kneifer, Angsthase.

quitch(-grass) [ˈkwɪtʃgrɑ:s], *s.* die Quecke (*Bot.*).

quite [kwaɪt], *adv.* ganz, gänzlich, völlig; (*coll.*) durchaus, wirklich, wahrhaftig; ziemlich; – *a different matter*, eine ganz *or* völlig andere S.; – *a* (*big*) *do*, eine regelrechte Festlichkeit, eine große Sache; – *delighted*, wirklich entzückt; – *so!* ganz recht! das stimmt! allerdings! – *spoilt*, schon gänzlich verdorben; – *the thing*, das Gegebene; große Mode, der letzte Schrei; (*coll.*) *she's – pretty*, sie ist ja recht hübsch; (*coll.*) *I – like her*, ich hab' sie wirklich lieb.

quits, quittance, quitter, *see* **quit.**

[1]**quiver** [ˈkwɪvə], *s.* der Köcher; *have a shaft left in one's –*, nicht hilflos sein, noch eine letzte Zuflucht haben; *a – full of children*, eine kinderreiche Familie.

[2]**quiver** [ˈkwɪvə], 1. *v.n.* zittern, beben (*with*, vor). 2. *v.a.* schlagen mit (*wings*). 3. *s.* das Zittern; Zucken (*of eyelids*); bebende Stimme.

qui vive [kɪ:ˈvɪ:v], *s.*; *on the – –*, auf der Hut *or* dem Quivive.

quixotic [kwɪˈksɔtɪk], *adj.* donquichottisch, schwärmerisch, überspannt, weltfremd. **–ism** [ˈkwɪksətɪzm], **–ry** [ˈkwɪksətrɪ], *s.* die Donquichotterie, Narretei, aussichtsloses Unternehmen; der Donquichotismus, weltfremde Abenteuersucht.

quiz [kwɪz], 1. *s.* (*archaic*) komischer Kauz; der Spottvogel; (*coll.*) die Reihe von mündlich zu beantwortenden Fragen, das Frage(-und Antwort)-spiel (*Rad.*). 2. *v.a.* herausfordernd *or* spöttisch ansehen; sich belustigen über (*a p.*); durch ein Monokel betrachten. **–zical** [–ɪkl], *adj.* komisch, spaßig; lächerlich; spöttisch, höhnisch.

quoad [ˈkwouæd], *prep.* was betrifft; – *hoc*, was dies betrifft.

[1]**quod** [kwɔd], *pron.* was.

[2]**quod** [kwɔd], *s.* (*sl.*) das Loch (i.e. *prison*).

quoin [kwɔɪn], 1. *s.* (vorspringende) Ecke (*Arch.*); der Eckstein (*Build.*); (Form)Keil (*Typ.*); Richtkeil (*Gun.*). 2. *v.a.* mit einem Eckstein schließen (*Build.*); einkeilen (*Typ.*); stützen, festkeilen (*Gun.*).

quoit [kwɔɪt], *s.* der Wurfring, die Wurfscheibe; *pl.* (*sing. constr.*) das Wurfringspiel.

quondam [ˈkwɔndæm], *adj.* früher, ehemalig.

quorum [ˈkwɔ:rəm], *s.* beschlußfähige Anzahl; *be a* –, beschlußfähig sein.

quota [ˈkwoutə], *s.* die Quote, das Kontingent, der (Teil)Beitrag; prozentuale Beteiligung, (verhältnismäßiger) Anteil (*of*, an); *– –goods*, kontingentierte Waren.

quot–able [ˈkwoutəbl], *adj.* anführbar, zitierbar; notierbar (*C.L.*). **–ation** [kwoˈteɪʃən], *s.* das Zitat, zitierte Stelle; die Anführung, das Zitieren; der Kurs, die (Kurs- *or* Preis)Notierung; der Kostenanschlag (*C.L.*); *familiar –ations*, geflügelte Worte. **–ation-marks,** *pl.* Anführungsstriche, Anführzeichen, (*coll.*) Gänsefüßchen (*pl.*). **–ative** [ˈkwoutətɪv], *adj.* Zitierungs–, zitierend. **–e** [kwout], 1. *v.a.* zitieren (*a passage*) (*from*, aus), anführen (*as*, als); heranziehen, Bezug nehmen auf, zitieren, angeben, nennen (*an author*); angeben, veranschlagen, (*coll.*) machen (*price*) (*C.L.*), notieren (*at*, zu *or* mit) (*Stock Exchange*). 2. *v.n.* zitieren (*from*, aus). 3. *s.* (*coll.*) das Zitat; *pl.* (*coll.*) *see* **–ation-marks.**

quoth [kwouθ], *v.n.* (*1st & 3rd sing. pret. only*; *usually precedes subject*) (*archaic*) sagte.

quotidian [kwoˈtɪdɪən], 1. *adj.* täglich, Quotidian–

(*fever*, *etc.*); alltäglich, abgedroschen. 2. *s.* das Quotidianfieber.
quotient ['kwouʃənt], *s.* der Quotient (*Math.*).

R

R, r [ɑ:], das R, r; *the three Rs*, die Grundlagen der elementaren Bildung (Lesen, Schreiben, Rechnen); *the r months*, September bis April (die Saison für Austern). *See Index of Abbreviations at the end.*
rabbet ['ræbət], 1. *s.* der Falz, die Fuge, Nut(e), Verbindungsritze (*Carp.*); der Stoßstahl (*Engin.*). 2. *v.a.* nuten, (aus)falzen; zusammenfugen, einfugen. **--joint,** *s.* überfalzte (*or* Falz)Verbindung, die Nut- und Feder (*or* Spund)Verbindung. **--plane,** *s.* der Falz- *or* Nut- *or* Simshobel.
rabbi ['ræbɑɪ], *s.* der Rabbi, Rabbiner. **-nical** [rə'bɪnɪkl], *adj.* rabbinisch.
rabbit ['ræbɪt], *s.* das Kaninchen; (*sl.*) der Stümper (*at sports*); *Welsh* –, geröstetes Käsebrot. **--hutch,** *s.* der Kaninchenstall. **--punch,** *s.* der Nackenschlag (*Boxing*). **--warren,** *s.* das Kaninchengehege, (*fig.*) der Irrgarten, das Labyrinth.
[1]**rabble** ['ræbl], *s.* lärmender Haufe; der Pöbel(haufen).
[2]**rabble,** 1. *s.* die Rührstange. 2. *v.a.* umrühren (*Metall.*), (*coll.*) verstricken, verwirren.
rabi-d ['ræbɪd], *adj.* wütend, rasend, toll, fanatisch; tollwütig (*Vet.*). **-dness,** *s.* die Wut, Tollheit. **-es** ['reɪbɪ:z], *s.* die Tollwut, Hundswut.
raccoon, *see* **racoon.**
[1]**race** [reɪs], *s.* das Geschlecht, der Stamm, die Familie; Rasse, Art, Gattung, Klasse, der Schlag; die Abkunft, Abstammung; *human* –, das Menschengeschlecht; – *hatred*, der Rassenhaß.
[2]**race,** 1. *s.* der Lauf (*also fig.*), die Strömung, Stromschnelle; das Gerinne, Flußbett; die Nute, Gleitbahn (*Tech.*); der Wettlauf, das Wettrennen; (*fig.*) der Kampf (*for*, um); *pl. the* -*s*, Pferderennen (*pl.*); *ball*--, die Laufrille; *boat*--, der Ruderwettkampf, das Wettrudern; *mill*--, das Mühlgerinne; *his* – *is run*, er hat die längste Zeit gelebt; (*sl.*) *play the* -*s*, beim Pferderennen wetten. 2. *v.n.* um die Wette laufen *or* fahren; rennen, schnell laufen *or* fahren, rasen; durchgehen (*Mach.*); Rennpferde halten. 3. *v.a.* um die Wette laufen mit; rennen *or* laufen lassen (*horses*); einholen; ankommen *or* fertigwerden vor (*a p.*); laufen lassen (*an engine*); – *through*, hetzen durch. **--card,** *s.* das Rennprogramm. **--course,** *s.* die Rennbahn. **-horse,** *s.* das Rennpferd. **--meeting,** *s.* das (Pferde)-Rennen. **-r** [-ə], *s.* das Rennpferd, Rennboot, Rennrad, die Rennmaschine, der Rennwagen; Rennfahrer. **--track,** *s. see* **-course.** *See also* **racing.**
racem-e [rə'sɪ:m], *s.* die (Blüten)Traube; razemöser Blütenstand. **-ic** [-'sɪ:mɪk], *adj.* Trauben- (*Chem.*). **-ose** ['ræsɪmous], *adj.* razemös (*Bot.*).
rachi-s ['rɑ:kɪs], *s.* die Spindel, Hauptachse (*Bot.*); das Rückgrat (*Anat.*). **-tic** [rə'kɑɪtɪk], *adj.* rachitisch. **-tis** [rə'kɑɪtɪs], *s.* Englische Krankheit, die Rachitis.
racial ['reɪʃl], *adj.* rassisch, völkisch, Rassen-. **-ism** [-ɪzm], *s.* das Rassenbewußtsein; die Rassentheorie.
raci-ness ['reɪsɪnɪs], *s.* das Pikante, die Würze; das Rassige, die Urwüchsigkeit. *See* **racy.** **-ng** [-ɪŋ], 1. *attrib. adj.* Renn-; *-ng car*, der Rennwagen; *-ng driver*, der Rennfahrer; *-ng man*, der Freund des Pferderennens. 2. *attrib. & pred. adj.* reißend. 3. *s.* das Wettrennen.
[1]**rack** [ræk], 1. *s.* die Folter(bank); – (*and pinion*) *railway*, die Zahnradbahn; *towel* –, der Handtuchhalter; *on the* –, auf der Folter; (*fig.*) in Folterqualen, in höchster Spannung, in quälender Ungewißheit; *put on the* –, auf die Folter spannen; (*fig.*) in quälende Ungewißheit bringen. 2. *v.a.* recken, strecken; foltern, auf die Folterbank spannen; (*fig.*) quälen, martern; aufs höchste (an)-spannen *or* anstrengen, erschüttern; ausnützen, aussaugen, hochschrauben (*rent*), erschöpfen (*land*); – *one's brains*, sich (*Dat.*) den Kopf zerbrechen. **--railway,** *s.* die Zahnradbahn. **--rent,** 1. *s.* wucherische Miete, die Wucherpacht. 2. *v.a.* wucherische Miete auferlegen (*Dat.*). **--wheel,** *s.* das Zahnrad.
[2]**rack,** 1. *s.* das Gestell, Gerüst, Stativ; der (Hut)-Ständer; das (Gepäck)Netz (*Railw.*); die Zahnstange (*Mach.*); die (Futter)Raufe (*in stables*); *bomb*--, das Bombenmagazin (*Av.*); *draining* –, der Trockenständer (*Phot.*); *hat-and-coat*--, die Kleiderleiste; *rifle*--, der Gewehrmicken (*Mil.*); – *and pinion*, das Zahnstangengetriebe. 2. *v.a.* auf ein Gestell legen (*hay*, *fodder*, *etc.*); (also -*up*) mit Futter versehen, füttern (*animals*).
[3]**rack,** 1. *s.* ziehendes *or* fliegendes Gewölk. 2. *v.n.* dahinziehen, vom Winde getrieben werden (*of clouds*).
[4]**rack,** 1. *s.* der Paß(gang). 2. *v.n.* im Paßgang gehen.
[5]**rack,** *s.*; *go to* – *and ruin*, völlig zugrunde gehen, zerfallen.
[6]**rack,** *v.a.* (also – *off*) abziehen, abfüllen (*wine*).
[7]**rack,** *see* **arrack.**
[1]**racket** ['rækɪt], *s.* der (Tennis)Schläger, das Rakett, (*Amer.*) der Schneeschuh, Schneereifen. **-s,** *pl.* das Racketspiel. **--tail,** *s.* Art Kolibri (*Orn.*).
[2]**racket,** 1. *s.* der Lärm, Spektakel, das Getöse, Geschrei; der Trubel, Taumel; (*coll.*) die Schiebung, Erpressung; (*coll.*) *go on the* –, sumpfen; (*coll.*) *stand the* –, die Verantwortung *or* Folgen tragen, durchhalten. 2. *v.n.* lärmen. **-eer** [-'tɪ:ə] der Schieber, Gangster. **-eering** [-'tɪ:ərɪŋ], *s.* Schiebungen (*pl.*), das Gangstertum. **-y,** *adj.* lärmend, vergnügungssüchtig.
racoon [rə'ku:n], *s.* der Waschbär.
racy ['reɪsɪ], *adj.* rassig, urwüchsig, kräftig, feurig, würzig, gehaltvoll; lebhaft, geistreich, lebendig, sprudelnd; (*coll.*) zotig; – *of the soil*, bodenständig, erdrüchig.
radar ['reɪdɑ:] *s.* das Funkmeßverfahren.
raddle ['rædl], 1. *v.a.* mit Rötel bemalen, rot anstreichen. 2. *s.* der Rötel, Roteisenstein.
radia-l ['reɪdɪəl], *adj.* strahlenförmig, Strahl(en)-, radial, Radial-; Speichen- (*Anat.*); *-l engine*, der Sternmotor; *-l nerve*, der Speichennerv. **-nce,** **-ncy** [-ɪəns(ɪ)], *s.* das Strahlen, der Glanz. **-nt** [-ɪənt], 1. *adj.* strahlend, glänzend, leuchtend (*with*, von *or* vor) (*also fig.*); *-nt energy*, strahlende Energie; *-nt point*, der Strahlungspunkt. 2. *s.* der Strahlungspunkt. **-te** [-ɪeɪt], 1. *v.n.* strahlen, glänzen; ausstrahlen, sich strahlenförmig ausdehnen. 2. *v.a.* ausstrahlen, verbreiten; *-te health*, von Gesundheit strahlen. 3. [-ɪət], *adj.* strahlenförmig; Strahl(en)- (*Bot.*, *etc.*). **-tion** [-ɪ'eɪʃən], *s.* das Strahlen, die Strahlung, Ausstrahlung; *cosmic -tion*, die Höhenstrahlung. **-tor** [-ɪeɪtə], *s.* der Heizkörper; die Heizsonne; der Strahlensender; Kühler (*Motor.*).
radic-al ['rædɪkəl], 1. *adj.* wurzelhaft; Wurzel- (*also Gram.*, *Math.*, *Bot.*); (*fig.*) eingewurzelt, angeboren, ursprünglich, gründlich, wesentlich, fundamental, Ur-; Radikal-, radikal (*Pol.*), Grund- (*Chem.*, *also Bot.*), Stamm- (*Gram.*); *-al cure*, die Radikalkur; *-al difference*, die Grundverschiedenheit; *-al error*, der Grundirrtum; *-al sign*, das Wurzelzeichen. 2. *s.* Radikale(r), *m.* (*Pol.*); der Wurzelbuchstabe, das Wurzelwort, Stammwort (*Gram.*); die Wurzel (*Gram.*, *Math.*); das Radikal (*Chem.*). **-alism** [-əlɪzm], *s.* der Radikalismus. **-ally,** *adv.* gründlich, ursprünglich, durchaus. **-le** [-ɪkl], *s.* das Würzelchen, die Wurzelfaser (*Bot.*).
radio ['reɪdɪou], 1. *s.* das Radio, Funkwesen; der Rundfunk, drahtlose Telegraphie; Röntgenstrahlen (*pl.*); *on the* –, im Rundfunk. 2. *v.a.* funken, drahtlos senden; ein Röntgenbild aufnehmen von (*Phot.*); mit Radium bestrahlen *or* behandeln. **-'active,** *adj.* radioaktiv. **-ac'tivity,** *s.* die Radio-

aktivität. **--amateur,** *s.* der Funkbastler, Funkfreund; Radioamateur. **--beacon,** *s.* die Peilbake, der Peilturm, das Funkfeuer. **--beam,** *s.* die Richtfunkbake, der Funkstrahl. **--bearing,** *s.* die Funkpeilung. **- commentator,** *s.* der Rundfunkberichterstatter. **- communication,** *s.* die Funkverbindung. **--control,** *s.* die Fernlenkung. **-direction-finder,** *s.* der Funkpeiler. **-drama,** *s.* das Hörspiel. **- engineering,** *s.* die (Rund)-Funktechnik. (*coll.*) **- fan,** *s. see* **--amateur. --frequency,** *s.* die Funkfrequenz. **-gram,** *s.* das Funktelegramm; (*coll.*) das Grammophon mit eingebautem Radioapparat. **-graph,** *s.* das Röntgenbild, die Röntgenaufnahme. **-graphy** [-ˈɔgrəfɪ], *s.* die Röntgenphotographie. (*coll.*) **- ham,** *s.* der Radioamateur. **-loˈcation,** *s.* die Funkortung, Funkpeilung. **-logist** [-ˈɔlədʒɪst], *s.* der Radiolog(e), Röntgenolog(e). **-logy** [-ˈɔlədʒɪ], *s.* die Strahlenlehre, Röntgenlehre. **--message,** *s.* der Funkspruch. **-meter** [-ˈɔmɪtə], *s.* die Lichtmühle, der Strahlungsmesser. **- network,** *s.* das Funknetz. **-operator,** *s.* der Funker; Bordfunker (*Av.*). **-photograph,** *s.* der Bildfunk. **- pirate,** *s.* der Schwarzhörer. **- receiver,** *s.* der Radioempfänger. **- reception,** *s.* der Funkempfang. **-scopy** [-ˈɔskəpɪ], *s.* die Röntgendurchleuchtung. **- set,** *s.* das Funkgerät, der Radioapparat. **- station,** *s.* die Funkstation, Funkstelle. **-telegram,** *s.* der Funkspruch, das Funktelegramm. **- telegraphy,** *s.* die Funktelegraphie, der Funk(verkehr). **- telephony,** *s.* die Funktelephonie, das Funkfernsprechen; der Rundfunk. **- therapeutics,** *pl.* (*sing. constr.*), **- therapy,** *s.* die Strahlentherapie, Radiotherapie, Röntgentherapie. **--tracer,** *s.* radioaktiver Spurenfinder. **-traffic,** *s.* der Funkverkehr. **--transmitter,** *s.* der (Funk)Sender. **--wave,** *s.* die Radiowelle.

radish [ˈrædɪʃ], *s.* der Rettig.

radium [ˈreɪdɪəm], *s.* das Radium; – *therapy*, die Radiumbehandlung, Strahlentherapie.

radi-us [ˈreɪdɪəs], *s.* (pl. *-i* [-dɪɪ:]) der Halbmesser, Radius; Strahl (*Bot.*); die Speiche (*Anat.*); (*fig.*) der Umkreis (*of*, von); Wirkungsbereich, die Reichweite; *cruising -us*, der Fahrbereich, Flugbereich; *turning -us*, die Achsenverschränkbarkeit (*of vehicles*).

radi-x [ˈreɪdɪks], *s.* (pl. *-ces* [-dɪsɪ:z, rəˈdɪ:sɪ:z]) die Grundzahl, Wurzel (*Math.*).

raffia [ˈræfɪə], *s.* die Raphia, Nadelpalme (*Bot.*); der (Raffia)Bast. **--work,** *s.* die Bastarbeit.

raffish [ˈræfɪʃ], *adj.* liederlich, pöbelhaft.

[1]**raffle** [ˈræfl], 1. *v.a.* auswürfeln, auslosen. 2. *v.n.* würfeln, losen (*for*, um). 3. *s.* die Lotterie, Verlosung, Auslosung.

[2]**raffle,** *s.* das Gerümpel, der Kram, Schund (*Naut.*).

raft [rɑ:ft], 1. *s.* das Floß; (*Amer.*) zusammengebundes Treibholz. 2. *v.a.* flößen. **-sman** [-smən], *s.* der (Holz)Flößer.

rafter [ˈrɑ:ftə], *s.* der Sparren, Dachbalken; *pl.* das Sparrenwerk.

[1]**rag** [ræg], 1. *s.* der Lumpen, Fetzen; Lappen, das Lumpenleinen; (*sl.*) Schundblatt, Schmierblatt, Hetzblatt; *pl.* zerlumpte Kleidung; –, *tag and bobtail*, Krethi und Plethi; (*sl.*) *chew the* –, quatschen; meckern (*over*, an); *like a red – to a bull*, wie ein rotes Tuch wirken (*to*, auf); *not a* –, keine Spur (*of*, von); *not a – to one's back*, nicht einen Fetzen auf dem Leibe; *in -s*, zerlumpt. **-amuffin** [-əmʌfɪn], *s.* der Straßenbengel, Lumpenkerl, Lump. **--and-bone man,** *s.* der Lumpensammler, Lumpenhändler. **--doll,** *s.* die Stoffpuppe. **--book** *s.* unzerreißbares Bilderbuch. **- fair,** *s.* der Trödelmarkt. **-ged** [-ɪd], *adj.* zerrissen, zerfetzt, zerlumpt, lumpig, schäbig; rauh, zottig, uneben, unregelmäßig, holperig; zackig, ausgezackt; mangelhaft, abgerissen, fehlerhaft unvollkommen (*as rhymes*); *-ged robin*, die Kuckucksblume. **-edness,** die Zerlumptheit; Unregelmäßigkeit. **-man,** *s.*, **-picker,** *s.* der Lumpensammler. **- paper,** holzfreies Papier, das Haderpapier. **-(stone),** *s.* der Kieselsandstein. **--time,** *s.* synkopierte (Neger)-Musik. **-wort,** *s.* das (Jakobs)Kreuzkraut.

[2]**rag,** 1. *s.* (*sl.*) die Neckerei, der Scherz; Radau, Spektakel, Krach; *fancy-dress* –, das Studentenkostümfest. 2. *v.n.* (*sl.*) sich raufen, Radau machen. 3. *v.a.* (*sl.*) übel mitspielen (*Dat.*), einen Schabernack spielen (*Dat.*), seinen Ulk treiben mit, necken.

rag-e [reɪdʒ], 1. *s.* die Wut, Raserei; der Zorn; die Heftigkeit, das Toben (*of the wind, etc.*); die Sucht, Manie, Gier (*for*, nach); Begeisterung, der Taumel, das Entzücken; *be* (*all*) *the -e*, allgemein Mode sein. 2. *v.n.* wüten, rasen (*against*, gegen), in Wut sein (*at*, über); toben (*as wind, sea*); *-ing toothache*, heftige *or* rasende Zahnschmerzen.

raglan [ˈræglən], *s.* der Raglan.

ragout [rəˈgu:], *s.* das Ragout.

raid [reɪd], 1. *s.* der Einfall, Streifzug, Raubzug, Beutezug; die Razzia (*police*); der Angriff, Überfall; *air-*–, der Luftangriff; *bombing* –, der Bombenangriff; *naval* –, der Flottenstreifzug, die Kaperfahrt. 2. *v.a.* einen Einfall machen in, eine Razzia machen auf, überfallen; drücken (*the market*) (*C.L.*); *-ing party*, die Streifabteilung (*Mil.*).

[1]**rail,** [reɪl], *s.* die Ralle (*Orn.*).

[2]**rail,** *v.n.* schimpfen, schmähen; – *at* or *against*, beschimpfen, verspotten, herziehen über. **-er** [-ə], *s.* der Schmäher, Spötter. **-ing,** *s.* die Schmähung, der Spott. **-lery** [-ərɪ], *s.* die Neckerei, der Scherz, Spott.

[3]**rail** [reɪl], 1. *s.* das Querholz, der Riegel; die Reling (*Naut.*); Leiste (*for pictures*); das Gitter, Geländer, die (Eisenbahn)Schiene, das Gleis, Geleise, der Schienenstrang (*Railw.*); *pl.* Eisenbahnaktien (*pl.*); *by* –, mit der Eisenbahn, per Bahn; *guide* –, die Führungsschiene; *live* –, die Stromschiene; *off the -s*, entgleist, (*fig.*) aus dem Gleis; *go* or *run off the -s*, entgleisen. 2. *v.a.* (also – *in*) einfriedigen, mit einem Geländer *or* Gitter umgeben; mit Schienen auslegen (*railway-route*); mit der Bahn befördern; – *off*, durch ein Geländer abtrennen. **-car,** *s.* der Triebwagen. **--chair,** *s.* die Schienenklammer. **--fence,** *s.* der (Holz)Zaun. **-head,** *s.* die Endstation, Kopfstation; der Ausladebahnhof, Verteilerbahnhof (*Mil.*). **-ings,** *s.* das Gelände; die Reling (*Naut.*). **-road,** *s.* (*Amer.*), **-way** *s.* die Eisenbahn; *-way accident*, das Eisenbahnunglück; *-way carriage*, der Eisenbahnwagen; *-way company*, die Eisenbahngesellschaft; *-way guide*, das Kursbuch; *-way junction*, der Eisenbahnknotenpunkt; *-way line*, die Eisenbahnlinie; *-way porter*, der Gepäckträger; *-way station*, der Bahnhof; *-way terminus*, der Endbahnhof; *-way ticket*, die (Eisenbahn)Fahrkarte, der Schein, das Billet; *-way train*, der (Eisenbahn)Zug. **-wayman** [-weɪmən], *s.* der Eisenbahner.

raiment [ˈreɪmənt], *s.* (*Poet.*) die Kleidung.

rain [reɪn], 1. *s.* der Regen; *pl.* Regenfälle, Regengüsse; *the -s*, tropische Regenzeit; – *of blows*, der Hagel von Schlägen; – *of tears*, der Strom von Tränen; *be pouring with* –, in Strömen regnen; (*coll.*) *as right as* –, frisch und munter. 2. *v.n.* regnen (*also fig.*); (*fig.*) hageln, herabfallen, herabprasseln; *it -s in*, es regnet herein *or* durch; – *in torrents*, in Strömen regnen; (*Prov.*) *it never -s but it pours*, ein Unglück kommt selten allein. 3. *v.a.* fallen lassen, herniedersenden; *it -s cats and dogs*, es regnet Bindfaden *or* Strippen *or* in Strömen, es gießt wie mit Mollen; – *kisses*, Küsse schütten; – *stones upon*, Steine schleudern auf; – *tears*, Tränen vergießen. **-bow,** *s.* der Regenbogen. **-coat,** *s.* der Regenmantel. **-drop,** *s.* der Regentropfen. **-fall,** *s.* der Regen(fall); die Regenmenge, der Niederschlag (*Meteor.*). **--gauge,** *s.* der Regenmesser. **-iness** [-ɪnɪs], *s.* das Regenwetter. **-proof** 1. *adj.* regendicht, wasserdicht. 2. *s. see* **-coat. -storm,** *s.* heftiger Regenguß. **--water,** *s.* das Regenwasser. **-y** [-ɪ], *adj.* regnerisch, verregnet, Regen-; *-y day*, der Regentag; (*fig.*) die Zeit der Not, schlimme Tage (*pl.*); *lay by* or *save up for a -y day*, sich (*Dat.*) einen Notpfennig zurücklegen; *-y season*, die Regenzeit.

raise [reɪz], 1. *v.a.* aufrichten, aufrecht stellen, aufheben; emporheben, (in die Höhe) heben; hoch ziehen, hochwinden (*by a crane*); errichten, (er)-bauen, aufstellen, aufführen, (*a structure*); erheben, befördern, (*a p.*) (*to*, zu); aufziehen (*children*), stärken, (ver)mehren, vergrößern; sichten (*land, etc.*) (*Naut.*); in Aufruhr bringen, aufrühren, aufwiegeln (*against* or *upon*, gegen) (*to revolt*); antreiben, anfeuern, anregen; anstiften. (*a*) (*with nouns*) – *an army*, ein Heer aufstellen *or* auf die Beine bringen; – *a blister*, eine Blase ziehen; – *Cain* or *the devil* or *hell*, Krach *or* Skandal machen; – *cattle*, Vieh züchten; – *a claim*, einen Anspruch *or* Einspruch erheben; – *a cry*, ein Geschrei erheben; – *the curtain*, den Vorhang aufziehen; – *difficulties*, Schwierigkeiten machen; – *a dust*, Staub aufwirbeln; – *expectations*, Erwartungen erwecken; – *one's eyes*, die Augen aufheben *or* aufschlagen; – *feelings*, Gefühle erwecken *or* erregen; *not* – *a finger*, keinen Finger krümmen; – *one's glass to a p.*, einem zutrinken; – *one's hat*, den Hut abnehmen *or* lüften; – *one's hat to s.o.*, einen begrüßen; – *hopes*, Hoffnungen erwecken; – *a hornet's nest*, in ein Wespennest greifen *or* stechen; – *a hue and cry*, Lärm schlagen; – *a laugh*, Gelächter hervorrufen; – *a loan*, eine Anleihe aufnehmen; – *money*, Geld aufbringen *or* auftreiben; – *the nap of cloth*, das Tuch aufrauhen; – *objections*, Einwendungen *or* Einwände erheben (*to*, gegen); – *plants*, Pflanze ziehen; – *prices*, Preise steigern; – *a report*, ein Gerücht verbreiten *or* in Umlauf setzen; – *a question*, eine Frage anregen *or* aufwerfen, etwas zur Sprache *or* auf die Tagesordnung bringen, etwas erörtern *or* anhängig machen (*with s.o.*, bei einem); – *salary*, das Gehalt erhöhen (*by*, um; *to*, auf); – *a shout*, aufschreien; – *a siege*, eine Belagerung aufheben; (*coll.*) – *a song*, großen Krach schlagen; – *spirits*, Geister beschwören *or* zitieren; – *steam*, Dampf aufmachen; – *taxes*, Steuern erheben *or* beitreiben; – *troops*, Truppen ausheben; – *vegetables*, Gemüse bauen; – *one's voice*, die Stimme erheben; (*fig.*) *voices were* –*d*, Stimmen wurden laut; (*sl.*) – *the wind*, sich (*Dat.*) das nötige Geld verschaffen. (*b*) (*with prepositions*) – *from the dead*, vom Tode *or* von den Toten erwecken; – *to the throne*, auf den Thron erheben. **2.** *s.* (*coll.*) die Erhöhung, Gehaltszulage. **–d,** *adj.* erhöht; erhaben, getrieben (*Tech.*); *with* or *in a* –*d voice*, mit erhobener Stimme. **–r** [–ə], *s.* der Erbauer, Pflanzer (*Hort.*); Züchter (*of cattle*); Erheber.

raisin [ˈreɪzɪn], *s.* die Rosine.

raison d'être [rɛzɔ̃ˈdɛtr], *s.* die Daseinsberechtigung.

raj [rɑːdʒ], *s.* die Herrschaft. **–ah** [ˈrɑːdʒɑ], *s.* der Radscha.

[1]**rake** [reɪk], 1. *s.* der Rechen, die Harke, Scharre; der Feuerhaken, das Kratzeisen; *as thin as a* –, klapperdürr, spindeldürr, spillerig. 2. *v.a.* harken, rechen (*Hort.*); bestreichen (*Mil.*, *Naut.*); (*fig.*) mit den Augen absuchen; durchstöbern; (*coll.*) – *out*, auskundschaften; – *together* or *up*, zusammenscharren, zusammenharken; (*fig.*) zusammenholen, zusammenkratzen, zusammenraffen; (*coll.*) – *up*, aufrühren (*an old story, etc.*). (*sl.*) **– -off,** der Gewinnprofit.

[2]**rake,** 1. *s.* das Überhangen, die Neigung. 2. *v.n.* überhangen, sich nach hinten neigen. **–ish** [–ɪʃ], *adj.* überhangend, ausfallend; (*fig.*) flott, schnittig.

[3]**rak–e,** *s.* der Wüstling. **–ish,** *adj.* wüst, liederlich, ausschweifend.

[1]**rally** [ˈrælɪ], 1. *v.a.* wieder sammeln, zusammentrommeln, scharen (*Mil.*); aufmustern, anfeuern, in Schwung bringen (*a p.*); zusammenraffen, sammeln (*energy*). 2. *v.n.* sich wieder sammeln; sich sammeln *or* scharen (*round*, um); sich anschließen (*to*, an); (also – *round*) sich erholen (*also fig. of prices, the market, etc.*), wieder zu Kräften kommen. 3. *s.* das Sammeln, die Wiedervereinigung; Zusammenkunft, Tagung, Massenversammlung, Kundgebung, das Treffen; die Erholung (*also C.L.*); der Appell (*Mil.*); schneller Ballwechsel (*Tenn.*). **–ing-point,** *s.* der Sammelplatz, Sammelpunkt.

[2]**rally,** *v.a.* aufziehen, zum besten haben, hänseln, sich lustig machen über (*a p.*).

ram [ræm], 1. *s.* der Widder (*also Astr.*), Schafbock; (also *battering* –), Sturmbock (*Mil.*); (also – *-bow*) der Sporn, Rammbug (*Naut.*); die Ramme, der Rammstoß, Rammbär (*Tech.*). 2. *v.a.* rammen (*also Naut.*), verrammen; ansetzen (*Artil.*); – *down*, fest einrammen, eintreiben; – *s.th. down a p.'s throat*, einem etwas einpauken *or* einbleuen; – *in*, einrammen, hineinstopfen, hineinstecken; – *up*, verrammeln, verstopfen. *See* **rammer, ramrod.**

rambl–e [ˈræmbl], 1. *v.n.* wandern, umherstreifen; ranken (*Bot.*); planlos reden, vom Thema abschweifen, sich im Reden verlieren; drauflos reden, unzusammenhängend reden (*delirium*). 2. *s.* die Wanderung, der Ausflug, Streifzug. **–er** [–ə], *s.* der Wanderer, Umherstreicher; die Kletterrose. **–ing,** 1. *adj.* wandernd, umherziehend umherschweifend; weitschweifig, planlos, unzusammenhängend, abschweifend; langgestreckt, unregelmäßig gebaut (*as buildings*); kletternd, sich rankend, wuchernd (*Bot.*); –*ing club*, der Wanderverein. 2. *s.* das Wandern, Umherstreifen.

ramie [ˈræmɪ], *s.* die Gattung der Nesselgewächse (*Bot.*).

ramif–ication [ræmɪfɪˈkeɪʃən], *s.* die Verzweigung, Verästelung (*also fig.*); *pl.* Zweige (*also fig.*). **–y** [ˈræmɪfaɪ], 1. *v.a.* (*usually pass.*) verzweigen, in Zweige zerteilen, zweigartig anlegen. 2. *v.n.* sich verzweigen (*also fig.*).

rammer [ˈræmə], *s.* der Stampfer, die (Hand)-Ramme; der (Geschoß)Ansetzer, Ladestock (*Artil.*).

ramose [rəˈmoʊs], *adj.* ästig, verzweigt.

[1]**ramp** [ræmp], *s.* (*coll.*) der Schwindel, die Geldschneiderei, das Erpressungsmanöver.

[2]**ramp** [ræmp], 1. *v.n.* sich zum Sprunge erheben, auf den Hinterbeinen stehen (*of animals*); wuchern (*of plants*); toben, rasen, wüten; rampenartig ansteigen *or* absteigen (*Arch.*). 2. *v.a.* mit einer Rampe versehen. 3. *s.* die Rampe, Auffahrt; Abdachung (*Arch.*), Biegung (*in a stair-rail*), Klappe (*of landing barge*). **–age** [ræmˈpeɪdʒ], 1. *v.n.* herumtoben, herumtollen; herumwüten, herumrasen. 2. *s.*; *be on the* –*age*, toben. **–ageous** [–əs], *adj.* tobend, lärmend, ausgelassen. **–ancy** [ˈræmpənsɪ], *s.* das Umsichgreifen, Überhandnehmen, Grassieren, Wuchern. **–ant** [ˈræmpənt], *adj.* überhandnehmend, umsichgreifend, grassierend, üppig wuchernd; zügellos, ausgelassen; aufgerichtet, steigend (*Her.*); *be* –*ant*, um sich greifen, überhandnehmen, grassieren; Unwesen treiben.

rampart [ˈræmpɑːt], 1. *s.* der Wall (*Fort.*); (*fig.*) die Schutzwehr. 2. *v.a.* umwallen.

rampion [ˈræmpɪən], *s.* die Rapunzel (*Bot.*).

ramrod [ˈræmrɔd], *s.* der Ladestock.

ramshackle [ˈræmʃækl], *adj.* baufällig, wackelig.

ramson [ˈræmsən], *s.* der Bärenlauch (*Bot.*).

ran [ræn], 1. *see* **run.** 2. *s.* die Docke Bindfaden, aufgerolltes Tau (*Naut.*); (*coll.*) *also*– –, *s.* erfolgloser Bewerber.

ranch [ræntʃ], *s.* (*Amer.*) die Viehwirtschaft, Viehweide. **–er** [–ə], *s.* der Viehhirte, Farmer.

rancid [ˈrænsɪd], *adj.* ranzig. **–ity** [–ˈsɪdɪtɪ], *s.*, **–ness,** *s.* die Ranzigkeit.

ranco–rous [ˈrænkərəs], *adj.* erbittert, boshaft, giftig. **–ur** [ˈrænkə], *s.* der Groll, Haß, die Erbitterung.

randan [rænˈdæn], *s.* das Boot für drei Ruderer; (*coll.*) der Radau; *on the* –, auf dem Bummel.

randem [ˈrændəm], *s.* der Wagen mit drei Pferden.

random [ˈrændəm], 1. *s.*; *at* –, aufs Geratewohl, auf gut Glück, blindlings, wahllos. 2. *adj.* zufällig, Zufalls–, ziellos, wahllos; – *shot*, der Schuß ins Blaue; – *test*, die Stichprobe.

randy [ˈrændɪ], *adj.* (*Scots*) lärmend, ausgelassen; (*dial.*) bockig, widerspenstig (*of cattle, etc.*); (*vulg.*) geil, wollüstig.

ranee [ˈrɑːnɪ], *s.* indische Fürstin.

rang [ræŋ], *see* **ring.**

range [reɪndʒ], 1. *v.a.* anordnen, in Reihen stellen, aufstellen; durchstreifen, durchwandern (*a place*); – *the coast*, an der Küste entlang fahren; – *o.s. with* or *on the side of*, sich stellen zu *or* auf seiten (*Gen.*); – *a gun on*, ein Geschütz richten auf. 2. *v.n.* streifen, wandern; sich ausdehnen, sich erstrecken, reichen; in einer Reihe *or* Linie stehen, liegen *or* sich bewegen, eine Linie bilden; vorkommen, zu finden sein; sich bewegen, schwanken, variieren (*from* . . . *to* . . ., zwischen . . . und . . .); in gleichem Range stehen (*with*, mit), sich stellen, gehören, zählen, passen (*with*, zu); – *wide*, weit ausholen. 3. *s.* die

Reihe; Kette (*of hills*) (*also fig.*); der Raum, die Fläche, Ausdehnung; (*fig.*) der Umfang, Bereich, Spielraum, Grenzen (*pl.*); die Reichweite, Tragweite, Schußweite, Entfernung, der Schußbereich (*Artil.*); Flugbereich (*Av.*); die Weidefläche; der (Stimm)Umfang (*of a voice*); Herd, Kochherd; (also *firing-–* or *shooting-–*) der Schießplatz. (*a*) (*with nouns*) – *of action*, das Arbeitsfeld, der Spielraum, Aktionsradius; – *of goods*, die Warensammlung, das Sortiment; – *of prices*, die Preislage; *rifle* –, der Schießstand; – *of thought*, der Ideenkreis; – *of vision*, das Gesichtsfeld. (*b*) (*with verbs*) *get the* –, sich einschießen (*Artil.*); *give one's fancy free* –, seiner Einbildungskraft freien Lauf lassen; *have a long* –, weit tragen; *long-– gun*, das Fernkampfgeschütz; *have a wide – of goods*, eine reiche Auswahl von Waren haben; *shorten* –, zurückverlegen (*Gun.*). (*c*) (*with prepositions*) *at close* –, aus naher Entfernung; *at a – of*, in einer Entfernung von; *out of* –, außer Schußbereich. **–-finder,** *s.* der Entfernungsmesser. **–r** [–ə], *s.* der Herumstreifer; Förster, Waldaufseher, Waldwärter; der Jäger, leichter Reiter (*Mil.*).

¹**rank** [ræŋk], 1. *s.* die Reihe, Linie; Klasse; der Rang, Stand, Dienstgrad (*Mil., etc.*); *the –s, pl.* see – *and file*. (*a*) (*with nouns*) *taxi* –, die Taxihaltestelle; – *and file* (*pl. constr.*) Mannschaften, Gemeinen, gemeine *or* einfache Soldaten (*pl.*); (*fig.*) gewöhnliche Mitglieder (*pl.*), die breite Masse. *all –s and classes*, alle Stände und Klassen; – *and fashion*, die vornehme Welt. (*b*) (*with verbs*) *break* –, aus der Reihe treten; *join the –s*, ins Heer eintreten; *keep –s!* in Reihe und Glied bleiben; *take – of*, den Vorrang haben vor; *take – with*, im Rang gehören zu, rangieren mit; *thin the –s*, die Reihen lichten. (*c*) (*with prepositions*) *rise from the –s*, von der Pike auf dienen; *in – and file*, in Reih und Glied; *in the first* –, an erster Stelle; *in the –s*, als einfacher Soldat; *fall into the second* –, zweitrangig werden; *man of* –, der Mann von Stand; *of the first* –, ersten Ranges; *of high* –, hohen Standes; *reduce to the –s*, degradieren. 2. *v.a.* in eine Reihe (auf)stellen, einreihen, ordnen; eine Stellung anweisen (*Dat.*); stellen, rechnen, zählen (*with*, zu), (*Amer.*) rangieren über; den Vortritt haben vor. 3. *v.n.* sich reihen, sich ordnen, sich aufstellen; gerechnet *or* gezählt werden (*with*, zu; *among*, unter); – *above*, rangieren über; – *first among*, im Rang an erster Stelle gehören unter; – *high*, hoch stehen, eine hohe Stellung einnehmen; – *next to* . . ., im Range gleich nach . . . kommen; *high-–ing officer*, hoher Offizier. **–er** [–ə] (*coll.*) der Offizier, der von der Pike auf gedient hat.

²**rank,** *adj.* üppig; fruchtbar, fett (*as soil*); stinkend, ranzig; (*fig.*) kraß, offenkundig; – *nonsense*, reiner *or* blühender Unsinn; – *outsider*, krasser Außenseiter; – *bad taste*, schreiende Geschmacklosigkeit. **–ness** [–ˈnɪs], *s.* üppiger Wuchs, die Üppigkeit; Ranzigkeit (*of smell, etc.*).

rankle [ˈræŋkl], *v.n.* (*Poet.*) eitern, schwären; (*fig.*) um sich *or* weiter fressen, nagen, wühlen.

ransack [ˈrænsæk], *v.a.* durchwühlen, durchstöbern, durchsuchen (*for*, nach); plündern.

ransom [ˈrænsəm], 1. *s.* das Lösegeld; der Loskauf; die Erlösung; (*fig.*) *king's* –, gewaltige Summe; *hold to* –, gegen Lösegeld festhalten. 2. *v.a.* loskaufen, auslösen; (*B.*) erlösen.

rant [rænt], 1. *s.* die Schwulst, der Redeschwall, Wortschwall, leeres Gerede. 2. *v.n.* hochtrabend *or* schwülstig reden; eifern, toben, lärmen. 3. *v.a.* schwülstig *or* theatralisch hersagen. **–er** [–ə], *s.* hochtrabender Schwätzer; der Prahler, Großsprecher, Kulissenreißer (*Theat.*).

ranunculus [rəˈnʌŋkjʊləs], *s.* der Hahnenfuß, die Ranunkel (*Bot.*).

¹**rap** [ræp], 1. *s.* leichter Schlag, der Klaps; das Klopfen (*at*, an); *there is a – at the door*, es klopft; – *on* or *over the knuckles*, (*fig.*) der Verweis; – *on the nose*, der Nasenstüber; (*coll.*) *take the* –, bestraft werden. 2. *v.n.* schlagen, klopfen, pochen (*at*, an; *on*, auf). 3. *v.a.* schlagen (auf); – *a p.'s fingers*, einem auf die Finger klopfen; – *out*, ausstoßen, herausplatzen mit; durch Klopfen mitteilen (*a message*) (*Spiritualism*).

²**rap,** *s.* der Heller, Deut; *I don't care* or *give a* – (*for it*), das ist mir ganz gleich(gültig), einerlei *or* egal. ich gebe keinen Pfifferling dafür.

rapaci-ous [rəˈpeɪʃəs], *adj.* raubgierig, (*fig.*) (hab)-gierig; *–acious bird*, der Raubvogel. **–ousness, –ty** [rəˈpæsɪtɪ], *s.* die Raubgier; (*fig.*) Habgier.

¹**rape** [reɪp], 1. *s.* (*Poet.*) der Raub, die Entführung; Notzucht, Vergewaltigung, Schändung (*Law*); *murder and* –, der Lustmord. 2. *v.a.* (*Poet.*) rauben, entführen; notzüchtigen, vergewaltigen (*Law*).

²**rape,** *s.* der Raps, Rübsen. **–-oil,** *s.* das Rüböl. **–-seed,** *s.* der Rübsamen.

³**rape,** *s.* (*dial.*) der Gau, Bezirk.

⁴**rape,** *s.* (*often pl.*) ausgepreßte Traubenschalen (*pl.*), der Trester, Essigfilter. **–-wine,** *s.* der Tresterwein.

rapid [ˈræpɪd], 1. *adj.* schnell, geschwind, rasch (*as growth*); reißend (*as water*); (*fig.*) plötzlich, jäh; – *fire*, das Schnellfeuer (*Mil.*). 2. *s.* (*usually pl.*) die Stromschnelle. **–ity** [ræˈpɪdɪtɪ], *s.* die Geschwindigkeit, Schnelligkeit.

rapier [ˈreɪpɪə], *s.* das Rapier.

rapine [ˈræpɪn], *s.* (*Poet.*) der Raub, die Plünderung.

rappee [rəˈpiː], *s.* grober Schnupftabak.

rapprochement [ræˈprɔʃəmɑ̃], *s.* die Wiederannäherung (*Pol.*); (*fig.*) Versöhnung.

rapscallion [ræpˈskælɪən], *s.* der Lump(enkerl).

rapt [ræpt], *p.p.* & *adj.* hingerissen, entzückt, außer sich (*Dat.*) (*with*, vor); verloren, versunken (*in*, in); gespannt (*as attention*).

raptorial [ræpˈtɔːrɪəl], 1. *adj.* räuberisch; Raub–. 2. *s.* der Raubvogel.

raptur-e [ˈræptʃə], *s.* das Entzücken, die Begeisterung, Ekstase, der Taumel; *in –es*, begeistert, entzückt, außer sich (*Dat.*) vor Entzücken (*at*, über; *with*, von); *go into –es*, in Verzückung geraten (*over*, über). **–ous** [–rəs], *adj.* leidenschaftlich, stürmisch (*applause, etc.*); verzückt (*expression*).

rara avis [ˈrɛːrəˈeɪvɪs], (*fig.*) seltene Erscheinung.

¹**rar-e** [rɛːə], *adj.* selten, rar, ungewöhnlich, außergewöhnlich; vereinzelt, spärlich; dünn, verdünnt, fein (*Phys., etc.*); (*coll.*) nicht durchgebraten (*of roast*); (vor)trefflich, ausgezeichnet; *–e earths*, seltene Erden; *–e gas*, das Edelgas. **–ebit** [ˈrɛːbɪt], *s. see under* **rabbit. –ee-show** [ˈrɛːrɪʃoʊ], *s.* der Guckkasten, Raritätenkasten, (*fig.*) das Schauspiel. **–efaction** [rɛːərɪˈfækʃən], *s.* die Verdünnung. **–efy** [ˈrɛːərɪfaɪ], 1. *v.a.* verdünnen; (*fig.*) verfeinern. 2. *v.n.* sich verdünnen. **–eness** [ˈrɛːənɪs], *s.* die Dünnheit; Seltenheit; (*fig.*) Vortrefflichkeit, Kostbarkeit. **–ity** [ˈrɛːrɪtɪ], *s. see* **–eness;** seltene *or* kostbare S., die Seltenheit.

rascal [ˈræskəl], 1. *s.* der Schuft, Schurke, Lump, (*coll.*) Spitzbube, Schelm, Halunke. 2. *adj.* nichtswürdig, schuftig. **–dom** [–dəm], *s.* das Lumpenpack. **–ity** [–ˈskælɪtɪ], *s.* die Schurkerei. **–ly,** *adv.* schurkisch, Schurken–, schuftig, erbärmlich.

rase [reɪz], *v.a. see* **raze.**

¹**rash** [ræʃ], *adj.* hastig, übereilt, vorschnell; unbesonnen, tollkühn, waghalsig. **–ness** [–nɪs], *s.* die Hast, Übereilung, Unbesonnenheit.

²**rash,** *s.* der Hautausschlag.

rasher [ˈræʃə], *s.* die Schinkenschnitte, Speckschnitte.

rasorial [reɪˈsɔːrɪəl], *adj.* Hühner–; scharrend (*of fowl*).

rasp [rɑːsp], 1. *s.* die Raspel, Sägefeile, das Reibeisen. 2. *v.a.* abraspeln, abkratzen, abschaben. 3. *v.n.* kratzen, krächzen; (*fig.*) verletzen, beleidigen (*feelings, etc.*). **–atory** [–ətərɪ], *s.* die Knochenfeile (*Surg.*). **–er** [–ə], *s.* das Schabeisen, Kratzeisen. **–ing,** 1. *adj.* kratzend, krächzend. 2. *s.* das Raspeln; *pl.* Raspelspäne.

raspberry [ˈrɑːzbərɪ], *s.* die Himbeere; (*sl.*) der Rüffel, Verweis, Wischer, Ausputzer. **–-cane,** der Himbeerstrauch.

rat [ræt], 1. *s.* die Ratte; (*coll.*) der Überläufer, Abtrünnige(r), *m.*; *–s!* Unsinn! unglaublich! *smell a* –, Lunte *or* den Braten riechen, Unrat wittern; *like a drowned* –, pudelnaß. 2. *v.n.* Ratten fangen; (*coll.*) überlaufen, abtrünnig werden, die Farbe wechseln, abfallen. **–-catcher,** *s.* der Rattenfänger. **–sbane,** *s.* das Rattengift. **–-tail,** *s.* der Rattenschwanz (*Vet.*). **–-tailed,** *adj.* Rattenschwanz–; *--tailed file*, der Rattenschwanz. **--trap,** *s.* die Rattenfalle; das Zackenpedal (*Cycl.*).

ratable ['reɪtəbl], *adj.* (ab)schätzbar, abzuschätzen(d) (*at*, auf (*Acc.*)); steuerbar, steuerpflichtig, zollpflichtig.

ratafia ['ɪætəfɪə], *s.* der Fruchtlikör.

rataplan [rætə'plæn], 1. *s.* der Trommelwirbel. 2. *v.n. & a.* trommeln.

rat-a-tat, *see* **rat-tat.**

ratch [rætʃ], *s.*, **–et** [–ɪt], *s.* gezahnte Sperrstange, der Zahnbogen (*Tech.*); die Auslösung (*Horol.*). **–et-wheel,** *s.* das Sperrad.

[1]**rate** [reɪt], 1. *s.* das Maß, Verhältnis; der Preis, Tarif, Kurs, die Taxe, Rate, der Anteil; der Grad, Rang, die Klasse; (*usually pl.*) Kommunalsteuern, Gemeindesteuern, Gemeindeabgaben (*pl.*); (*coll.*) die Schnelligkeit, Geschwindigkeit. (*a*) (*with nouns*) *birth--*, die Geburtenziffer; *– of climb*, die Steigeschwindigkeit (*Av.*); *– of the day*, der Tageskurs; *– of discount*, der Diskontsatz; *– of exchange*, der Wechselkurs; *– of fire*, die Feuergeschwindigkeit, Schußfolge; *– of insurance*, die Versicherungsprämie; *– of interest*, der Zinsfuß; *mortality –*, die Sterblichkeitsziffer; *– of wages*, der Lohnsatz. (*b*) (*with prepositions*) *at any –*, auf jeden Fall, wenigstens; *at a great –*, sehr schnell; *at the same –*, in demselben Maße; (*coll.*) *at that –*, auf diese Weise, in diesem Falle, unter diesen Umständen; *at this –*, auf diese Art; *at the – of*, zum Preise *or* Kurse von, (*coll.*) mit einer Geschwindigkeit von. (*c*) (*with adjectives*) *first--*, erstklassig (*coll.*) vortrefflich; *second--*, zweitklassig; (*coll.*) *third--*, minderwertig. 2. *v.a.* veranschlagen, bewerten; abschätzen, einschätzen; rechnen (*among* unter *or* zu), betrachten (*as*, als) (*a p.*). 3. *v.n.* angesehen, *or* gerechnet werden, rangieren (*as*, als). **–d,** *adj.* Nenn– (*Tech.*); *be –d as*, in eine Klasse eingereiht werden (*Naut.*); *be highly –d*, hoch besteuert sein; *–d altitude*, die Nennhöhe, Volldruckhöhe (*Av.*). **–payer,** *s.* der Kommunalsteuerzahler. *See* [1]**rating.**

[2]**rate,** 1. *v.a.* ausschelten (*for*, wegen). 2. *v.n.* schelten, schimpfen (*at*, über (*Acc.*)). *see* [2]**rating.**

ratel [reɪtl], *s.* der Honigdachs, Ratel (*Zool.*).

[1]**rath** [ræθ], *s.* vorgeschichtliche Hügelfestung (*Irish*).

[2]**rath** [ræθ], **–e** [reɪð], **–eripe, –ripe,** *adj.* (*poet.*) früh, frühreif.

rather ['rɑ:ðə], *adv.* eher, lieber; vielmehr, eigentlich; (*coll.*) ziemlich, etwas; (*coll. as interj.*) freilich! und ob! *or –*, oder vielmehr; *I would* or *had –*, ich möchte lieber (*with inf.*), mir wäre es lieber (*with* daß); *I – think*, ich glaube fast, ich möchte glauben; *– late*, etwas, ziemlich *or* recht spät; *in – a mess*, in einer ziemlichen Patsche.

ratif–ication [rætɪfɪ'kaɪʃən], *s.* die Bestätigung, Gutheißung, Ratifikation, Ratifizierung. **–y** ['rætɪfaɪ], *v.a.* bestätigen, gutheißen, ratifizieren.

[1]**rating** ['reɪtɪŋ], *s.* die Steuereinschätzung, der (Kommunal)Steuersatz; die Schiffsklasse (*Naut.*); der Dienstgrad (*of a p.*); (*usually pl.*) der Matrose; die Bewertung, Leistung (*Tech.*).

[2]**rating,** *s.* der Verweis, die Rüge.

ratio ['reɪʃɪoʊ], *s.* das Verhältnis; *be in the inverse –*, sich umgekehrt verhalten (*to*, zu).

ratiocinat–e ['ræʃɪoʊsɪneɪt], *v.n.* logisch schließen, folgern. **–ion** [–'neɪʃən], *s.* der Vernunftschluß, die Folgerung. **–ive** [–'oʊsɪnətɪv], *adj.* vernunftmäßig, folgernd.

ration ['ræʃən], *s.* 1. die Ration, Verpflegung; *pl.* Nahrungsmittel (*pl.*); *emergency* or *iron –*, eiserne Ration (*Mil.*). 2. *v.a.* rationeren, in Rationen verteilen *or* zuteilen (*goods*). **--book,** *s.* **--card,** *s.* die Lebensmittelkarte, der Bezugschein. **–ing,** *s.* die Rationierung, Bewirtschaftung; Verpflegung. **--strength,** die Verpflegungsstärke (*Mil.*).

rational ['ræʃənəl], *adj.* vernunftgemäß, rationell, beweisfähig; zweckmäßig, praktisch; vernünftig, verständig, mit Vernunft begabt, rational (*Math.*); *– dress*, die Reformkleidung. **–e** [–neɪlə] *s.* (*rare*) wissenschaftlich begründete Erklärung, rationelle Grundlage. **–ism** [–ɪzm], *s.* der Rationalismus (*Phil.*); rationeller Standpunkt, die Zweckmäßigkeit. **–ist** [–ɪst], 1. *s.* der Rationalist, Verstandesmensch. 2. *adj.* rationalistisch, Verstandes–. **–istic** [–'lɪstɪk], *adj.* rationalistisch, verstandesmäßig, vernunftgemäß. **–ity** [–'nælɪtɪ], *s.* die Vernunftigkeit, Vernunftmäßigkeit, Verstandesmäßigkeit; das Vernunftvermögen. **–ization** [–laɪ'zeɪʃən] *s.* die Rationalisierung, Vereinfachung; vernunftgemäße Erklärung. **–ize** [–laɪz], 1. *v.a.* vernunftmäßig erklären, rationalisieren; vereinfachen (*as an industry*). 2. *v.n.* rationalistisch denken *or* vorgehen.

ratlin(e) ['rætlɪn], **ratling** ['rætlɪŋ], *s.* (*usually pl.*) die Webeleine (*Naut.*).

ratoon [rə'tu:n], 1. *s.* der (Zuckerrohr)Schößling. 2. *v.n.* Schößlinge treiben.

rat(t)an [rə'tæn], *s.* Spanisches Rohr; der Rohrstock.

rat-tat(-tat) [rætə'tæt], *s.* lautes Pochen.

ratten ['rætən], *v.a.* an der Arbeit hindern.

ratter ['rætə], *s.* der Rattenfänger.

rattl–e ['rætl], 1. *v.n.* rasseln, klappern, klirren, knattern, prasseln; röcheln (*of dying p.*); (*coll.*) plappern; (*coll.*) *–e away*, drauflosreden. 2. *v.a.* rattern an (*the door, etc.*); klirren mit (*crockery, etc.*); (*coll.*) *–e off*, herunterleiern (*prayers, etc.*). 3. *s.* das Gerassel, Geklapper; (*coll.*) Geplapper Röcheln; die Klapper; Rassel, Schnarre; der Klappertopf, das Läusekraut (*Bot.*). **–e-brained,** *adj.* lärmend, geschwätzig, windig. (*coll.*) **–ed,** *adj.* verwirrt, außer Fassung, ängstlich. **–e-pate,** *s.* der Windbeutel, Schwätzer. **–er** [–lə], *s.* die Klapperschlange (*Amer.*). **–esnake,** *s.* die Klapperschlange. (*coll.*) **–e-trap,** *s.* der Klapperkasten; *pl.* der Tand. **–ing,** *adj.* (*coll.*) famös, großartig, prächtig, schneidig; *at a –ing pace*, in schneidigem Tempo.

ratty ['rætɪ], *adj.* rattenartig; (*sl.*) ärgerlich.

raucous ['rɔ:kəs], *adj.* heiser, rauh.

ravage ['rævɪdʒ], 1. *s.* die Verwüstung, Verheerung; *pl.* verheerende Wirkung; *–s of time*, der Zahn der Zeit. 2. *v.a.* verwüsten, verheeren, plündern, heimsuchen.

rave [reɪv], *v.n.* rasen, toben; wüten, tosen (*as the sea*); irre reden, phantasieren, faseln, schwärmen; *see* **raving.**

ravel ['rævəl], 1. *v.a.* verwirren, verwickeln; *– out*, auftrennen, entwirren, ausfasern. 2. *v.n.* sich aufdrehen, ausfasern. 3. *s.* die Verwirrung, Verwicklung; loser Faden.

ravelin ['rævlɪn], *s.* das Außenwerk, die Vorschanze (*Fort.*).

[1]**raven** ['rævən], 1. *v.n.* rauben, plündern; gierig sein, dürsten, Heißhunger haben (*for*, nach). 2. *v.a.* gierig essen, verschlingen. **–ing,** *adj.* (*poet.*) raubend, plündernd, wild, gierig. **–ous** [–əs], *adj.* raubgierig; gierig, gefräßig, heißhungrig; *–ous appetite*, der Heißhunger. **–ousness,** *s.* die Raubgier, Gier, Gefräßigkeit, der Heißhunger.

[2]**raven** ['reɪvən], 1. *s.* der Rabe; *black as a –*, (kohl)rabenschwarz. 2. *adj.* rabenschwarz.

ravine [rə'vi:n], *s.* die (Berg)Schlucht, Klamm.

raving ['reɪvɪŋ], 1. *adj.* rasend, faselnd; *– mad*, rasend. 2. *s.* das Rasen, Faseln; *pl.* der Fieberwahn; die Faselei.

ravish ['rævɪʃ], *v.a.* schänden, entehren, entführen (*a woman*); (*fig.*) hinreißen, entzücken, (*archaic*) rauben, entreißen, fortraffen. **–er** [–ə], *s.* der Schänder, Entführer (*of a woman*). **–ing,** *adj.* hinreißend, entzückend. **–ment,** *s.* die Entführung, Schändung; Entzückung, Verzückung.

raw [rɔ:], 1. *adj.* roh, ungekocht; unbearbeitet, unverarbeitet, Roh–; ungesponnen (*cotton*); ungewalkt (*cloth*); ungemischt, unverdünnt (*spirits*); ungegerbt (*hides*); wundgerieben (*of the skin*); (*fig.*) unerfahren, ungeübt, unausgebildet (*as a recruit*); rauh, naßkalt (*as the weather*); (*sl.*) *– deal*, unfaire Behandlung *or* Abfertigung; *– edge*, die Schnittkante (*of cloth*); *– material*, der Rohstoff, Werkstoff; *– meat*, rohes Fleisch. 2. *s.* wunde Stelle; der Rohstoff (*C.L.*); *touch a p. on the –*, einen an seiner wunden Stelle treffen. 3. *v.a.* wundreiben (*Vet.*). **--boned,** *adj.* hager. **–hide,** *s.* die Reitpeitsche. **–ness,** *s.* roher Zustand; die Rauheit; Wundheit; (*fig.*) Unerfahrenheit.

[1]**ray** [reɪ], 1. *s.* der (Licht)Strahl; Strahl (*also Bot. &*

fig.), (*fig.*) Funken, Schimmer, die Spur; *pencil of -s*, der Lichtbüschel; *X--s*, Röntgenstrahlen (*pl.*). 2. *v.n.* (aus)strahlen. 3. *v.a.* bestrahlen. **-ed** [-d], *adj.* strahlenförmig, -strahlig. **--treatment,** *s.* die Bestrahlung, Strahlenbehandlung.

[2]**ray,** *s.* der Roche(n) (*Ichth.*).

rayon [ˈreɪən], *s.* die Kunstseide.

raze [reɪz], *v.a.* zerstören, schleifen; *– to the ground*, dem Boden gleichmachen; (*fig.*) tilgen, ausmerzen.

razee [ræˈziː], *s.* (*obs.*) rasiertes Kriegsschiff.

razor [ˈreɪzə], *s.* das Rasiermesser; *be on a –* or *the –'s edge*, auf des Messers Schneide stehen; *safety-–*, der Rasierapparat; *set a –*, ein Rasiermesser abziehen; *as sharp as a –*, haarscharf. **--back,** 1. *adj.* scharfkantig. 2. *s.* der Finnwal (*Zool.*); *-backed whale, see* **--back,** 2. **--bill,** *s.* der Tordalk (*Orn.*). **--blade,** *s.* die Rasierklinge. **--edge,** *s.* haarscharfe Kante, (*fig.*) äußerster Rand, kritische Lage. **--fish,** *s.* der Schermesserfisch (*Ichth.*). **--shell,** *s.* die Muschel des Schermesserfisches. **--strop** *s.* der Streichriemen.

razzia [ˈræzɪə], *s.* der Raubzug.

razzle(-dazzle) [ˈræzl(ˈdæzl)], *s.* (*sl.*) das Zechgelage; *be* or *go on the –*, auf den Bummel gehen.

[1]**re** [reɪ], *s.* zweiter Ton der Tonleiter (*Mus.*).

[2]**re** [riː], *prep.* in Sachen (*Law*); (*coll.* & *C.L.*) betreffs, bezüglich.

[3]**re-** [riː], *prefix* = wieder, noch einmal.

reabsor-b [riːəbˈzɔːb], *v.a.* wiedereinsaugen, wiederaufnehmen, resorbieren. **-ption** [-ˈzɔːpʃən], *s.* die Wiederaufsaugung, Resorbierung.

reach [riːtʃ], 1. *v.n.* reichen, langen, greifen, die Hand ausstrecken (*for*, nach); sich erstrecken *or* ausdehnen; *as far as the eye can –*, so weit wie das Auge sehen kann. 2. *v.a.* reichen; erreichen, ankommen an *or* in (*a place*); *– a p. a blow*, einem einen Schlag verabreichen; einem eins langen; *– home*, nach Hause gelangen; *– a third edition*, eine dritte Auflage erleben; *– the age of discretion*, ein gesetztes Alter erzielen *or* erreichen; *– no conclusion*, zu keinem Schluß gelangen; *your letter -ed me*, ich erhielt Ihren Brief, Ihr Brief traf bei mir ein *or* kam in meine Hände; *– the bottom*, den Grund finden; *– a p.'s ear*, einem zu Ohren kommen; *– down*, herunterreichen, herunterlangen; *– forth* or *out*, ausstrecken. 3. *s.* das Reichen, Erreichen; die Reichweite, Tragweite, der Bereich, Umfang; (*fig.*) die Fassungskraft, Leistungsfähigkeit; der Lauf, die (Strom)Strecke; *beyond* or *out of his –*, außer *or* über seiner Reichweite; *beyond* or *out of –*, unerreichbar; unerschwinglich (*of*, für); *within –*, erreichbar; *within his –*, innerhalb seiner Reichweite; *within easy – of the town*, von der Stadt leicht zu erreichen; *within the – of all*, allen zugänglich. **-able,** *ad.j* erreichbar. **--me-down,** (*sl.*) 1. *adj.* Konfektions-. 2. *s. usually pl.* die Konfektionskleidung.

react [riːˈækt], *v.n.* beeindruckt *or* erregt werden; reagieren, antworten, eine Gegenwirkung *or* Rückwirkung ausüben, (*fig.*) eingehen (*to*, auf (*Acc.*)); einen Gegenangriff machen (*Mil.*); *– against*, entgegenarbeiten, entgegenwirken (*Dat.*), auftreten gegen; *– (up)on*, einwirken auf, Rückwirkung haben auf, zurückfallen auf; *slow to –*, reaktionsträge (*Chem.*). **-ance,** *s.* die Reaktanz, der Blindwiderstand (*Elec.*). **-ive,** *adj.* rückwirkend, reaktionsempfänglich (*to*, für). **-ion** [-ʃən], *s.* die Gegenwirkung, der Rückschlag (*from* or *against*, gegen); die Reaktion (*to*, auf) (*Chem.*, *Pol.* & *fig.*); Einwirkung (*on*, auf) (*Chem.*); Rückwirkung, Rückkopplung (*Rad.*); der Gegenstoß (*Mil.*); (*fig.*) die Rückkehr, der Rückschlag, Rückschritt, Umschwung, rückläufige Einwirkung, rückwirkender Einfluß; *-ion-coupling*, die Rückkopplung (*Rad.*); *-ion-time*, die Reaktionszeit. **-ionary** [-ʃənərɪ], 1. *adj.* rückwirkend, gegenwirkend; rückschrittlich, reaktionär (*Pol.*). 2. *s.* der Reaktionär. **-or** [-tə], *s.* die Drossel(spule) (*Elec.*); Umwandlungsanlage (*Phys.*).

[1]**read** [riːd], 1. *ir.v.a.* lesen, (an)zeigen (*of meters etc.*); *– the character*, den Charakter durchschauen; *– a dream*, einen Traum deuten; *– law*, Jura studieren; *– a p. a lesson*, einem eine Lektion lesen; *– music*, Noten lesen; *– a paper*, ein Referat halten; *– a riddle*, ein Rätsel lösen; *– aloud*, laut (vor)lesen; *– into*, hineinlesen in; *what do you – into this?* wie legen Sie dies aus?; *– off*, ablesen; *– out*, vorlesen; verlesen (*a proclamation, etc.*); *– over* or *through*, durchlesen; *– to*, vorlesen (*Dat.*); *– to o.s.*, für sich lesen; *– s.o. to sleep*, einen durch Lesen in den Schlaf versetzen; *– up*, sich einarbeiten in, einstudieren. 2. *ir.v.n.* lesen; *it -s as follows*, es lautet wie folgt; *– for an examination*, sich auf eine Prüfung vorbereiten; *– for the press*, Korrekturen lesen; *it -s well*, es liest sich gut. **-able** [-əbl], *adj.* lesbar. **-ableness,** *s.* die Lesbarkeit. *See* **reader** & **reading.**

[2]**read** [rɛd], 1. *adj.* gelesen (*of a book*); belesen (*of a p.*); *well –*, sehr belesen. 2. *imp.* & *pp. see* [1]**read.**

readdress [riːəˈdrɛs], *v.a.* neu adressieren, umadressieren.

reader [riːdə], *s.* der Leser; Vorleser (*also Eccl.*); Buchliebhaber; Korrektor (*Typ.*); das Lesebuch; der Dozent (*Univ.*). **-ship,** *s.* die Dozentenstelle (*Univ.*).

readi-ly [ˈrɛdɪlɪ], *adv.* bereit, bereitwillig, gern; leicht, schnell, sogleich. **-ness,** *s.* die Bereitwilligkeit; Leichtigkeit, Gewandtheit, Schnelligkeit; Bereitschaft; *-ness for war*, die Kriegsbereitschaft; *in -ness to*, bereit zu; *place in -ness*, bereitstellen; *-ness of mind* or *wit*, die Geistesgegenwart; *-ness of speech*, die Redegewandtheit; *see* **ready.**

reading [ˈriːdɪŋ], 1. *adj.* lesend; studierend; *--desk*, das Lesepult; *--glass*, die Lupe, das Vergrößerungsglas; *– man*, der fleißig Studierende; *– matter*, der Lesestoff; *the – public*, das Lesepublikum; *--room*, der Lesesaal. 2. *s.* das Lesen, die Durchsicht; das Vorlesen; der Lesestoff; die Leseprobe (*Theat.*); Lesung (*Parl.*); Lesart, der Wortlaut (*of a MS.*); die Auffassung, Deutung, Erklärung; Ablesung, der Stand (*of a meter, etc.*); die Belesenheit; *make interesting –*, interessant zu lesen sein; *give a – from a work*, aus einem Werk vortragen; *a man of wide –*, ein Mann von umfassender Belesenheit.

readjust [riːəˈdʒʌst], *v.a.* wieder in Ordnung bringen. **-ment,** *s.* die Wiederherstellung.

readm-ission [riːədˈmɪʃən], *s.* die Wiederzulassung. **-it** [-ˈmɪt], *v.a.* wieder zulassen. **-ittance,** *see* **-ission.**

ready [ˈrɛdɪ], 1. *pred. adj.* bereit, fertig (*for*, zu); klar (*Naut.*) (*for*, zu); bereitwillig, geneigt (*to*, zu); im Begriffe (*to*, zu); gefaßt (*for*, auf); *– ? go!* fertig? los! (*Sport*); *be – with*, bereit haben *or* halten; *get* or *make –*, bereiten, fertig machen; sich fertig machen; Vorbereitungen treffen; *– at* or *to hand*, leicht zur Hand; *– for sea*, seeklar; *– for use*, gebrauchsfertig. 2. *pred.* & *attrib. adj.* schnell, sofortig, prompt; gewandt, geschickt (*at* or *in*, in); bequem, leicht, nahe, naheliegend, direkt; *– acceptance*, sofortige Annahme; *– market*, schneller Absatz; *– money*, 1. *s.* bares Geld; *for – money*, gegen bar; 2. *attrib.* Bar-, Kassa-; *– reckoner*, die Rechentabelle; *– wit*, die Geistesgegenwart, Schlagfertigkeit. 3. *s.*; *at the –*, schußfertig (*Mil.*). **--made,** *adj.* (gebrauchs)fertig; *--made clothes*, die Konfektion; *--made shop*, das Konfektionsgeschäft; **--to-wear,** *attrib.* fertig, Fertig- (*clothes*). **--witted,** *adj.* schlagfertig.

reaffirm [riːəˈfəːm], *v.a.* nochmals versichern. **-ation** [rɪæfəˈmeɪʃən] *s.* erneute Beteuerung *or* Versicherung.

reafforest [riːəˈfɔrɪst], *v.a.* aufforsten. **-ation** [-ˈteɪʃən], *s.* die Aufforstung.

reagent [riːˈeɪdʒənt], *s.* das Reagens (*Chem.*).

[1]**real** [ˈriːəl], *s.* spanische Silbermünze.

[2]**real** [ˈriːəl], 1. *adj.* wahr, echt, wirklich, tatsächlich, faktisch, objektiv, real; dinglich, Real-; Effektiv-, unbeweglich, Grund- (*C.L.*, *Law*); *– action*, die Realklage; *– estate*, der Grundbesitz; *– life*, das Leben der Wirklichkeit; *– property*, das Grundeigentum, Immobilien (*pl.*), Liegenschaften (*pl.*); (*sl.*) *the – thing*, das einzig Wahre. 2. *adv.* (*sl.*) sehr, äußerst. 3. *s.* das Reale, die Wirklichkeit (*Phil.*). **-ism** [-ɪzm], *s.* der Realismus (*Phil.*); Wirklichkeitssinn, Tatsachensinn; wirklichkeitstreue Darstellung. **-ist** [-ɪst], *s.* der Realist; Wirklichkeitsmensch, Tatsachenmensch. **-istic** [-ˈlɪstɪk], *adj.*

realistisch, sachlich; wirklichkeitstreu, wirklichkeitsnah, Wirklichkeits–. **–ity** [–'ælɪtɪ], *s.* (*no pl.*) die Wirklichkeit, Tatsächlichkeit, Realität; wahre Natur, das Wesen (*of* (*Gen.*)); die Wirklichskeitstreue ; (*with pl.*) reales Faktum, reale S.; *in –ity*, wirklich, tatsächlich. **–ly** ['rɪ:əlɪ], *adv.* wirklich, tatsächlich, in der Tat.

realgar [rɪ'ælgə], *s.* das Realgar, Schwefelarsenik.

realiz–able ['rɪ:əlaɪzəbl], *adj.* realisierbar, ausführbar, zu verwirklichen(d); zu verwerten(d). **–ation** [–'zeɪʃən], *s.* die Verwirklichung, Ausführung, Realisierung; Vergegenwärtigung, Vorstellung, Ausschauung (*in the mind*); Verwertung, Liquidation, Glattstellung, das Realisieren, Zugeldemachen (*C.L.*). **–e** ['rɪ:əlaɪz], *v.a.* verwirklichen, ausführen, realisieren; sich (*Dat.*) vergegenwärtigen, sich (*Dat.*) vorstellen, klar einsehen *or* erkennen, zur Erkenntnis *or* Bewußtsein kommen; gegenwärtig werden lassen (*to a p.*, einem); zu Geld machen, realisieren, liquidieren (*C.L.*); erzielen, einbringen, erweben (*profit*); *I now –e*, es leuchtet mir jetzt ein.

realm [rɛlm], *s.* das Reich (*also fig.*), Königreich; (*fig.*) das Gebiet, der Bereich.

realt–or ['rɪ:əltə], *s.* der Landmakler. **–y** [–tɪ], *s.* der Grundbesitz, unbewegliches Eigentum.

[1]**ream** [rɪ:m], *s.* das Ries; (*fig.*) *–s and –s of*, große Mengen von.

[2]**ream,** *v.a.* erweitern, ausbohren, ausräumen (*a hole*). **–er,** *s.* die Reibahle, Fräse.

reanimat–e [rɪ:'ænɪmeɪt], *v.a.* wiederbeleben. **–ion** [–'meɪʃən], *s.* die Wiederbelebung, Neubelebung.

reap [rɪ:p], 1. *v.n.* schneiden, mähen, ernten. 2. *v.a.* schneiden, mähen (*corn, etc.*); abernten (*a field*); einernten (*a crop*); (*fig.*) ernten; *– advantage*, Nutzen ziehen (*from*, von *or* aus). **–er** [–ə], *s.* der Schnitter; die Mähmaschine. **–er-binder,** die Mäh- und Bindemaschine. **–ing,** *s.* das Ernten, Schneiden, Mähen. **–ing-hook,** *s.* der Sichel. **–ing-machine,** *s.* die Mähmaschine.

reappear [rɪ:ə'pɪ:ə], *v.n.* wiedererscheinen. **–ance** [–rəns], *s.* das Widererscheinen.

reappl–ication [rɪ:æplɪ'keɪʃən], *s.* wiederholte Anwendung; erneutes Gesuch. **–y** [rɪ:ə'plaɪ], *v.a.* wiederholt beantragen; sich wiederholt bewerben (*for*, um).

reappoint [rɪ:ə'pɔɪnt], *v.a.* wieder anstellen, einsetzen *or* ernennen. **–ment,** *s.* die Wiederanstellung, Wiederernennung.

[1]**rear** [rɪ:ə], 1. *s.* der Hintergrund, hintere Seite, hinterer Teil; der Nachtrab, die Nachhut (*Mil.*); (*coll.*) der Abort, Abtritt; *bring up the –*, die Nachhut bilden (*Mil.*); (*fig.*) zuletzt kommen; *at the – of*, hinter (*Dat.*); *in the –*, im Rücken *or* Hintergrund; *to the –*, nach hinten. 2. *attrib. adj.* hinter, Hinter–, Nach–, rückwärtig. **––admiral,** *s.* der Konteradmiral. **––arch,** *s.* innerer Bogen. **––guard,** *s.* die Nachhut (*Mil.*). **––gunner,** *s.* der Heckschütze (*Av.*). **––lamp, ––light,** *s.* das Schlußlicht (*Motor.*), das Katzenauge (*Cycl.*). **–most,** *adj.* hinterst. **––rank,** *s.* das hintere Glied (*Mil.*). **––sight,** *s.* das Visier. **–ward** [–wəd], 1. *adj.* hinter. 2. *adv.* nach hinten, rückwärts. 3. *s.* der Nachtrab; *in the –ward*, hinter (*Dat.*). **–wards** [–wədz], *adv.* nach hinten, rückwärts. **–wheel,** *s.* das Hinterrad.

[2]**rear,** 1. *v.a.* (er)heben, aufrichten; errichten (*an edifice*); erziehen, großziehen (*children*); ziehen (*plants*), züchten (*animals*). 2. *v.n.* sich aufrichten *or* bäumen (*as horse*); *– up*, emporragen.

rearm [rɪ:'ɑ:m], 1. *v.a.* bewaffen; neu ausrüsten. 2. *v.n.* aufrüsten. **–ament** [–əmənt], *s.* die (Wieder)-Aufrüstung.

rearrange [rɪ:ə'reɪndʒ], *v.a.* neu ordnen, umordnen, umändern. **–ment,** *s.* die Neuordnung, Umordnung; neue Anordnung.

reason ['rɪ:zən], **1.** *s.* die Ursache (*for* (*Gen.*)), der Grund (*for* (*Gen.*) *or* für); die Vernunft, der Verstand, die Einsicht; das Recht, Recht und Billigkeit; *age of –*, die (Zeit der) Aufklärung; *– of state*, die Staatsräson (*Hist.*, *Pol.*). (*a*) (*with verbs*) *all the more – for coming*, ein um so triftigerer Grund, daß man kommt; *there is – for supposing*, es ist Grund zur Vermutung vorhanden; *there is – in all he says*, was er sagt, hat Hand und Fuß; *there is every – to believe*, alles spricht dafür; *have good – to do* or *for doing*, mit gutem Grunde tun; *lose one's –*, den Verstand verlieren; *the – why he came*, der Grund weshalb er kam; *an added – why he should come*, um so mehr Grund weshalb er kommen soll. (*b*) (*with prepositions*) *by – of*, auf Grund von, wegen; *for the – that*, aus dem Grunde weil; *for this very –*, schon aus diesem Grunde; *in* (*all*) *–*, mit gutem Recht; *allow anything in –*, alles in einem vernünftigen Ausmaße bewilligen; *out of all –*, maßlos, unverschämt; *bring to –*, zur Vernunft bringen, zurechtsetzen; *listen to* or *see –*, Vernunft annehmen; *it stands to –*, es versteht sich (von selbst); *with –*, mit Recht *or* Grund; *without rhyme or –*, ohne Sinn und Verstand. **2.** *v.n.* vernunftig denken (*about*, über (*Acc.*)); urteilen, schließen (*from*, aus); *– with s.o.*, einen zu überzeugen suchen, einem Vernunft einreden wollen. **3.** *v.a.* logisch *or* vernunftig erörten *or* anordnen. *–ed*, wohldurchdacht; *–* (*a p.*) *into s.th.*, (einem) durch Zureden zu etwas bringen; *–* (*s.th.*) *out*, (etwas) durchdenken; *– a p. out of a th.*, einem etwas ausreden, einen abbringen von etwas. **–able** [–əbl], *adj.* vernünftig, verständig; gerecht, angemessen, billig, annehmbar (*offer, demand, etc.*); mäßig (*price*); *be –able*, Einsicht haben, maßvoll sein; *–able doubt*, berechtigter Zweifel, gerechtfertigtes Bedenken. **–ableness,** *s.* die Vernünftigkeit, Verständigkeit; Mäßigkeit (*of prices*). **–ably,** *adv.* vernünftigerweise, billigerweise, leidlich, ziemlich. **–ing,** *s.* das Urteilen, Schließen; der Gedankengang, die Beweisführung.

reassemble [rɪ:ə'sɛmbl], 1. *v.a.* wieder zusammenbauen; wieder versammeln. 2. *v.n.* sich wieder versammeln.

reassert [rɪ:ə'sə:t], *v.a.* wieder *or* wiederholt behaupten, wieder geltend machen.

reassess [rɪ:ə'sɛs], *v.a.* nochmals abschätzen. **–ment,** *s.* nochmalige Abschätzung *or* Wertung.

reassume [rɪ:ə'sju:m], *v.a.* wieder einnehmen (*one's place*), wieder annehmen (*a post, shape*), wieder aufnehmen (*activity*).

reassur–ance [rɪ:ə'ʃu:ərəns], *s.* erneute Versicherung *or* Bestätigung; die Beruhigung. **–e** [–'ʃu:ə], *v.a.* wieder beteuern *or* versichern; beruhigen. **–ing** [–'ʃu:ərɪŋ], *adj.* beruhigend.

rebapt–ism [rɪ:'bæptɪzm], *s.* die Wiedertaufe. **–ize** [rɪ:'bæptaɪz], *v.a.* wiedertaufen, umtaufen.

rebate ['rɪ:beɪt], *s.* der Rabatt, Nachlaß, Abzug (*on*, auf) (*C.L.*).

rebel 1. *s.* ['rɛbl], der Aufständige, Aufrührer, Rebell. 2. *attrib. adj.* rebellisch, Rebellen–; *– troops*, die Rebellen, Aufständigen. 3. *v.n.* [rɪ'bɛl], sich empören, sich auflehnen, rebellieren (*against*, gegen). **–lion** [rɪ'bɛlɪən], *s.* der Aufruhr, Aufstand, die Erhebung, Rebellion, Auflehnung. **–lious** [rɪ'bɛlɪəs], *adj.* aufrührerisch, aufständisch, rebellisch; (*fig.*) widerspenstig. **–liousness,** *s.* die Widerspenstigkeit.

rebind [rɪ:'baɪnd], *v.a.* neu binden.

rebirth [rɪ:'bə:θ], *s.* die Wiedergeburt.

rebite [rɪ:'baɪt], *v.a.* nachätzen (*Engr.*).

reborn [rɪ:'bɔ:n], *adj.* neugeboren, wiedergeboren.

rebound [rɪ:'baund], 1. *v.n.* zurückprallen, zurückschnellen, zurückfedern; (*fig.*) zurückschlagen. 2. *s.* der Rückprall, Rückschlag; *take on the –*, beim Aufprallen schlagen (*Footb.*); (*fig.*) den Rückschlag ausnützen.

rebuff [rɪ'bʌf], 1. *s.* die Abweisung, Zurückweisung, Zurücksetzung; der Rückschlag, die Niederlage, Abfuhr; *meet with a –*, kurz abgewiesen werden. 2. *v.a.* abweisen, zurückweisen; eine Abfuhr erteilen (*Dat.*).

rebuild [rɪ:'bɪld], *v.a.* wieder (auf)bauen, wiederherstellen.

rebuke [rɪ'bju:k], 1. *s.* der Tadel, Vorwurf, Verweis. 2. *v.a.* zurechtweisen, ausschelten, tadeln.

rebus ['rɪ:bəs], *s.* der & das Rebus, das Bilderrätsel.

rebut [rɪ'bʌt], *v.a.* zurückweisen, abstoßen; widerlegen. **–tal** [–əl], *s.* die Widerlegung. **–ter** [–ə] *s.* die Quadruplik (*Law*).

recalcitra–nce [rɪ'kælsɪtrəns], *s.* die Widerspenstigkeit. **–nt** [–ənt], (*adj.*) widerspenstig, wider-

haarig (*to*, gegen). **-te** [–eɪt], *v.n.* widerspenstig sein, sich sträuben (*against*, gegen).
recall [rɪːˈkɔːl], 1. *v.a.* zurückrufen, abberufen (*a p.*); widerrufen, zurücknehmen (*a statement*); ins Gedächtnis zurückrufen; wieder lebendig machen, aufrühren *or* wachrufen (*feelings*); kündigen (*money lent, etc.*); – *s.th. to s.o.*, or *to a p.'s mind*, einen erinnern an etwas, einem etwas ins Gedächtnis zurückrufen; – *s.th.* (*to one's mind*), sich (*Dat.*) etwas ins Gedächtnis zurückrufen, sich (*Acc.*) an etwas erinnern; – *having seen*, sich erinnern gesehen zu haben; *until –ed*, bis auf Widerruf. 2. *s.* die Zurückrufung; Abberufung; der Widerruf; das Signal der Heimkehr (*Mil.*); *past –*, unwiderruflich.
recant [rɪˈkænt], *v.a.* & *n.* widerrufen, zurücknehmen; Abbitte tun (für). **–ation** [rɪːkænˈteɪʃən], *s.* der Widerruf, die Widerrufung.
recapitulat–e [rɪːkəˈpɪtjuleɪt], *v.a.* kurz wiederholen *or* zusammenfassen, rekapitulieren. **–ion** [–ˈleɪʃən], *s.* kurze Wiederholung *or* Zusammenfassung, die Rekapitulation. **–ive** [–tɪv], **–ory** [–tərɪ], *adj.* zusammenfassend.
recapture [rɪːˈkæptʃə], 1. *s.* die Wiedernahme; Wiederergreifung, Wiedereinnahme (*of a town*). 2. *v.a.* wieder ergreifen; wieder erlangen.
recast [rɪːˈkɑːst], 1. *v.a.* umgießen (*Metall.*); (*fig.*) umformen, umarbeiten, ummodeln; neu besetzen (*a play*), neu verteilen (*the parts*) (*Theat.*). 2. *s.* der Umguß; die Umarbeitung, Umformung, Umgestaltung; Neubesetzung (*Theat.*).
reced–e [rɪˈsɪːd], *v.n.* zurücktreten (*before*, von), zurückgehen, weichen (*from*, von); (*fig.*) abstehen (*from*, von); verschwinden, entschwinden; an Wert verlieren, im Wert zurückgehen (*C.L.*); *–e into the background*, in den Hintergrund treten; *–ing forehead*, zurückfallende Stirn.
receipt [rɪˈsɪːt], 1. *s.* der Empfang (*a letter*), Eingang (*goods*), die Einnahme (*money*); Quittung, Empfangsbeschreinigung, der Empfang(s)schein, Ablieferungsschein; *–s and expenditures*, Einnahmen und Ausgaben; *give* or *make out a –*, eine Quittung ausstellen; *be in – of*, in Besitz sein von; *against –*, gegen Quittung; *on – of*, bei *or* nach Empfang ((*Gen.*) *or* von). 2. *v.a.* quittieren. **–-book**, *s.* das Quittungsbuch. **–-stamp**, *s.* der Quittungsstempel, die Quittungsmarke.
receiv–able [rɪˈsɪːvəbl], *adj.* annehmbar, zulässig; gesellschaftsfähig; *be –able*, als Zahlungsmittel gelten (*C.L.*); *bills –able*, Rimessen (*pl.*). **–e** [–ˈsɪːv], 1. *v.a.* empfangen (*also Rad.*), erhalten, (*coll.*) bekommen; in Empfang nehmen, entgegennehmen; (*fig.*) annehmen, einnehmen, aufnehmen, als gültig anerkennen; auffangen; standhalten (*Dat.*) (*Mil.*); *–e attention*, Aufmerksamkeit *or* Beachtung finden; *–e a blow*, einen Schlag erdulden *or* erleiden *or* hinnehmen; *–e an impression*, einen Eindruck empfangen; *–e a welcome*, ein Willkommen erleben *or* erfahren; *–e into one's house*, in seinem Hause aufnehmen; *–e the sacrament*, das heilige Abendmahl empfangen; *–e stolen goods*, Diebesgut verbergen *or* an sich nehmen; *–ed with thanks*, dankend erhalten; *–ed tradition*, allgemein anerkannte Überlieferung; *–ed text*, echter Text; *–ed pronunciation*, vorschriftsmäßige Aussprache. 2. *v.n.* Besuch empfangen; Abendmahl empfangen; Empfänger sein. **–er** [–ə], *s.* der Empfänger; Annehmer, Einnehmer; Behälter, Sammelbecker (*Tech.*); das Sammelgefäß, die Vorlage (*Chem.*); der Hörer (*Phone.*); Empfänger, das Empfangsgerät (*Rad.*); der Konkursverwalter (*in bankruptcy*); Hehler (*of stolen goods*). **–ing**, *s.* der Empfang; *–ing hopper*, der Auffangtrichter; *–ing office*, die Annahmestelle. *–ing-order*, die Ernennung eines Konkursverwalters (*Law*); *–ing-set*, das Empfangsgerät (*Rad.*). *–ing-station*, die Empfangsstation (*Rad.*).
recency [ˈrɪːsənsɪ], *s.* die Neuheit, Frische; *see* **recent.**
recension [rɪˈsɛnʃən], *s.* die Revision (*of texts*); revidierte Ausgabe.
recent [ˈrɪːsənt], *adj.* neu, modern, jung, kürzlich geschehen; *of – date*, von neuestem Datum. **–ly**, *adv.* neulich, unlängst, kürzlich, vor kurzem, jüngst; *as –ly as*, erst noch. **–ness**, *s. see* **recency.**
receptacle [rɪˈsɛptəkl], *s.* der Behälter, das Behältnis, Gefäß; der Fruchtboden (*Bot.*).
recepti–ble [rɪˈsɛptɪbl], *adj.* empfänglich, aufnahmefähig (*of*, für). **–on** [–ʃən], *s.* der Empfang (*also Rad.* & *of persons*), die Annahme, Aufnahme (*impressions, etc.*); der Empfangsabend; *meet with a favourable –on*, eine günstige Aufnahme finden. **–onist**, *s.* die Empfangsdame. **–on-room**, *s.* das Empfangszimmer. **–ve**, [–tɪv], *adj.* aufnahmefähig, empfänglich, rezeptiv (*of* or *to*, für); nur aufnehmend. **–vity** [rɪːsɛpˈtɪvɪtɪ], *s.* die Aufnahmefähigkeit, Empfänglichkeit.
recess [rɪˈsɛs], 1. *s.* Ferien (*pl.*) (*Parl.*); die Pause, Unterbrechung; Nische, Vertiefung, abgeschiedener Ort, der Schlupfwinkel; (*fig. often pl.*) Tiefen (*pl.*), geheime Winkel (*pl.*), geheimes Innere, der Schoß. 2. *v.a.* mit Vertiefung(en) versehen; vertiefen, einsenken, zurücksetzen. 3. *v.n.* sich vertagen (*Parl.*). **–ion** [–ˈsɛʃən], *s.* das Zurückgehen, Zurückweichen, Zurücktreten (*from*, von), der Rückgang (*trade, etc.*). **–ional** [–ʃənəl], 1. *adj.* mit dem Zurückgehen verbunden. 2. *s.* der Schlußchoral; *–ional hymn*, der Schlußchoral. **–ive** [–sɪv], *adj.* rezessiv (*Biol.*).
recharge [rɪːˈtʃɑːdʒ], wieder laden (*Gun.*), aufladen (*Elec.*).
recherché [rəˈʃɛːʃe], *adj.* sorgfältig ausgewählt, gesucht.
recidivis–m [rɪˈsɪdɪvɪzm], *s.* die Rückfälligkeit, der Rückfall in die Kriminalität. **–t** [–vɪst], *s.* rückfälliger Verbrecher.
recipe [ˈrɛsɪpɪ], *s.* das Rezept.
recipien–t [rɪˈsɪpɪənt], 1. *s.* der Empfänger; *be the –t of*, empfangen. 2. *adj.* empfänglich, aufnahmefähig. **–cy** [–ənsɪ], *s.* die Aufnahmefähigkeit.
reciproc–al [rɪˈsɪprəkl], 1. *adj.* wechselseitig, gegenseitig; entsprechend; Gegen–; reflexiv (*Gram.*); reziprok (*Math.*); *be –al*, auf Gegenseitigkeit beruhen; *–al action*, die Wechselwirkung; *–al bearing*, die Gegenpeilung. 2. *s.* das Gegenstück; reziproker Wert (*Math.*). **–ate** [–keɪt], 1. *v.n.* abwechselnd wirken; hin- und hergehen (*Mach.*); sich erkenntlich zeigen. 2. *v.a.* erwidern, vergelten, austauschen; *–ating engine*, die Kolbenmaschine. **–ation** [–ˈkeɪʃən], *s.* die Hin- und Herbewegung (*Mech.*); Wechselwirkung, Erwiderung, der Austausch. **–ity** [rɛsɪˈprɔsɪtɪ], *s.* gegenseitige Beziehung; die Gegenseitigkeit, Wechselwirkung, Reziprozität.
recit–al [rɪˈsɑɪtl], *s.* das Vorlesen, Vortragen, Hersagen, Aufzählen; die Erzählung, der Bericht; die Rezitation; der (Solo)Vortrag (*Mus.*); einleitender Teil (*of a deed*); die Darstellung des Sachverhalts (*Law*); *organ-–al*, das Orgelkonzert. **–ation** [rɛsɪˈteɪʃən], *s.* das Aufsagen, Hersagen, Vortragen, Rezitieren; der Vortrag, die Rezitation. **–ative** [rɛsɪtəˈtɪːv], 1. *attrib. adj.* Rezitativ–. 2. *s.* das Rezitativ, der Sprechgesang. **–e** [rɪˈsɑɪt], 1. *v.a.* aussagen, hersagen, vortragen, rezitieren. 2. *v.n.* vortragen, rezitieren, deklamieren. **–er** [–ə], *s.* der Vortragskünstler, Rezitator, Deklamator.
reck [rɛk], *v.n.* (*poet. in interr.* & *neg. only*) sich kümmern (*of*, um); wissen (*of*, von).
reckless [ˈrɛklɪs], *adj.* sorglos, unbesonnen, leichtsinnig, tollkühn; rücksichtslos, unbekümmert (*of*, um); *be – of*, sich nicht kümmern um. **–ness**, *s.* die Unbesonnenheit, Tollkühnheit; Unbekümmertheit, Rücksichtslosigkeit.
reckon [ˈrɛkən], 1. *v.a.* (be)rechnen, zählen, halten für, betrachten, schätzen, beurteilen; (*coll.*) annehmen, der Meinung sein, vermuten, glauben; – *up*, zusammenrechnen, zusammenzählen. 2. *v.n.* (ab)rechnen; – (*up*)*on*, rechnen *or* sich verlassen auf (*Acc.*); – *with a p.*, mit einem abrechnen; – *with a th.*, mit einer S. rechnen; – *without one's host*, die Rechnung ohne den Wirt machen. **–er** [–ə], *s.* der Rechner; die Rechentabelle. **–ing**, *s.* das Rechnen; die Berechnung, Schätzung; Rechnung, Zeche (*hotel, etc.*); die Abrechnung (*also fig.* & *Rel.*); Gissung (*Naut.*); *day of –ing*, der Tag der Abrechnung; *dead –ing*, gegißtes Besteck (*Naut.*); *be out in one's –ing*, sich verrechnen *or* verrechnet haben; *according to my –ing*, meines Erachtens.
reclaim [rɪːˈkleɪm], *v.a.* (*fig.*) zurückbringen,

zurückführen, zurücklenken; bekehren, bessern; trockenlegen, urbar machen (*land*); gewinnen, regenerieren (*from waste products*); zivilisieren, zähmen; beanspruchen; zurückfordern, reklamieren (*a th.*); *past* –, unverbesserlich. **-able,** *adj.* (ver)besserungsfähig; zähmbar; kulturfähig (*as land*).

reclamation [rɛklə'meɪʃən], *s.* das Zurückbringen, die Besserung, Bekehrung, Rückforderung; der Einspruch, die Beschwerbe, Reklamation; die Urbarmachung, (*of land*), Gewinnung, Nutzbarmachung.

reclin-e [rɪ'klɑɪn], 1. *v.a.* lehnen, hinlegen, niederlegen, legen. 2. *v.n.* liegen, ruhen, sich lehnen. **-ing-chair,** *s.* (verstellbarer) Liegestuhl.

recluse [rɪ'klu:s], 1. *adj.* einsam, abgeschieden, zurückgezogen (*from*, von); absiedlerisch. 2. *s.* der Einsiedler.

recoal [rɪ:'koʊl], 1. *v.a.* mit Kohlen versehen (*a ship, etc.*). 2. *v.n.* Kohlen einnehmen.

recoat [rɪ:'koʊt], *v.a.* neu anstreichen.

recogn-ition [rɛkəg'nɪʃən], *s.* die (Wieder)-Erkennung (*of a p. or th.*), Anerkennung (*of a fact*); *in -ition of*, als Anerkennung für; *past* (*all*) *-ition*, nicht wiederzuerkennen; *win -ition*, sich durchsetzen; *-ition signal*, das Kennsignal, die Kennung (*Av.*). **-izable** [-'nɑɪzəbl], *adj.* (wieder)-erkennbar. **-izance** [rɪ'kɔgnɪzəns], *s.* schriftliche Verpflichtung, der Schuldschein; das Anerkenntnis; die Kaution(ssumme) (*Law*); *enter into -izances*, sich gerichtlich verbinden. **-izant,** *adj.*; *be -izant of*, anerkennen. **-ize** ['rɛkəgnɑɪz], *v.a.* anerkennen (*as*, als); (wieder)erkennen (*by*, an); Notiz nehmen von, lobend anerkennen.

recoil [rɪ'kɔɪl], 1. *v.n.* zurückspringen, zurückprallen, zurücklaufen (*Artil.*) zurückfahren, zurückweichen, zurückschrecken, zurückschaudern (*at* or *from*, vor (*Dat.*)) (*of persons*); zurückfallen (*on*, auf (*Acc.*)). 2. *s.* das Zurückspringen, Zurückprallen; der Rückstoß, Rücklauf (*of a gun*); das Zurückschrecken (*from*, vor (*Dat.*)).

recoin [rɪ:'kɔɪn], *v.a.* umprägen. **-age** [-ɪdʒ], *s.* die Umprägung.

recollect [rɛkə'lɛkt], *v.a.* sich erinnern ((*Gen.*) *or* an (*Acc.*)), sich besinnen auf (*Acc.*). **-ion** [-'lɛkʃən], *s.* die Erinnerung; das Gedächtnis; *to the best of my -ion*, soweit ich mich erinnere; *beyond my -ion*, mir nicht mehr in Erinnerung; *within my -ion*, mir wohl in Erinnerung.

recommence [rɪ:kə'mɛns], *v.a.* wieder *or* von neuem anfangen, wieder aufnehmen. **-ment,** *s.* der Wiederbeginn.

recommend [rɛkə'mɛnd], *v.a.* empfehlen, anvertrauen; raten, anempfehlen (*Dat.*); *he was -ed to do*, ihm wurde (an)empfohlen zu tun; *he was -ed to me*, er wurde mir (als geeignet) empfohlen. **-able** [-əbl], *adj.* zu empfehlen(d), empfehlenswert (*to* (*Dat.*)). **-ation** [-'deɪʃən], *s.* die Empfehlung (*to*, an); empfehlende Eigenschaft; das Empfehlungsschreiben, der Befähigungsnachweis; *letter of -ation*, das Empfehlungsschreiben; *on the -ation of*, auf Empfehlung von. **-atory** [-'mɛndətərɪ], *adj.* empfehlend, Empfehlungs-.

recommission [rɪ:kə'mɪʃən], *v.a.* neu beauftragen, wiederanstellen; wieder einstellen (*ship, etc.*).

recommit [rɪ:kə'mɪt], *v.a.* wiederübergeben, anvertrauen (*to* (*Dat.*)); an eine Kommission zurückweisen (*a bill*) (*Parl.*); – *to prison*, wieder ins Gefängnis abführen. **-ment, -tal,** *s.* die Rückverweisung.

recompense ['rɛkəmpens], 1. *v.a.* ersetzen, wiedergutmachen, vergüten; belohnen, entschädigen; vergelten (*Dat.*); – *a p. for his kindness*, einem seine Güte vergelten. 2. *s.* der Ersatz, die Entschädigung, Vergütung; Belohnung.

recompos-e [rɪ:kəm'poʊz], *v.a.* neu anordnen *or* zusammensetzen, umgestalten, umgruppieren; neu setzen (*Typ.*); wieder beruhigen *or* in Ordnung bringen. **-ition** [rɪ:kəmpə'zɪʃən] *s.* die Umgestaltung, Umgruppierung, Umbildung, Umarbeitung; neuer Satz (*Typ.*).

reconcil-able ['rɛkənsɑɪləbl], *adj.* vereinbar, verträglich (*with*, mit). **-e** ['rɛkənsɑɪl], *v.a.* versöhnen, aussöhnen (*to* or *with*, mit); beilegen, schlichten, ausgleichen (*a quarrel*); vereinbaren, in Einklang bringen (*with*, mit); *-e o.s.* or *become -ed to*, sich aussöhnen, abfinden *or* befreunden mit, sich finden in (*Acc.*). **-iation** [-sɪlɪ'eɪʃən], *s.* die Aussöhnung, Versöhnung (*to* or *with*, mit); Ausgleichung, Schlichtung, Beilegung (*of a quarrel*).

recondite ['rɛkəndɑɪt, rɪ'kɔndɑɪt], *adj.* wenig bekannt, geheim, dunkel; geheimnisvoll, unverständlich, abstrus.

recondition [rɪ:kən'dɪʃən], *v.a.* wieder instandsetzen, überholen. **-ing,** *s.* die Instandsetzung.

reconnaissance [rɪ'kɔnɪsəns], *s.* die Aufklärung, Erkundung, Rekognoszierung; Streife (*Mil.*); – *party*, der Spähtrupp; – *plane*, das Aufklärungsflugzeug.

reconnoitre [rɛkə'nɔɪtə], *v.a.* auskundschaften; aufklären, erkunden, rekognoszieren (*Mil.*).

reconqu-er [rɪ:'kɔŋkə], *v.a.* wiedererobern, zurückerobern. **-est** [-kwɛst], *s.* die Wiedereroberung, Zurückeroberung.

reconsider [rɪ:kən'sɪdə], *v.a.* von neuem erwägen, nochmals überlegen *or* in Erwägung ziehen; nachprüfen. **-ation** [-'reɪʃən], *s.* nochmalige Überlegung *or* Erwägung; *on -ation*, bei *or* nach nochmaliger Überlegung.

reconstitu-ent [rɪ:kən'stɪtjuənt], 1. *adj.* neubildend, wiederaufbauend (*Med.*). 2. *s.* wiederaufbauendes Mittel. **-te** [rɪ:'kɔnstɪtju:t], *v.a.* neu aufbauen *or* bilden.

reconstruct [rɪ:kən'strʌkt], *v.a.* wieder aufbauen, umbauen; wiederherstellen. **-ion** [-ʃən], *s.* der Wiederaufbau, die Wiederherstellung, Rekonstruktion, Sanierung, der Umbau. **-ive,** *adj.* wieder aufbauend, Aufbau-.

record 1. *v.a.* [rɪ'kɔ:d], schriftlich aufzeichnen, eintragen, niederschreiben; zur Protokoll nehmen, protokollieren (*Law*); registrieren, niederlegen; bezeigen, bezeugen (*satisfaction, etc.*); ablegen (*a vote*); aufnehmen, festhalten (*gramophone*); *-ed music*, die Schallplattenmusik; *self -ing thermometer*, das Registrierthermometer. 2. *s.* ['rɛkɔ:d], die Urkunde, das Protokoll (*Law*); die Niederschrift, Aufzeichnung, schriftlicher Bericht, das Verzeichnis; *pl.* Akten (*pl.*) das Archiv; die Höchstleistung, der Rekord (*Sport*); die Grammophonplatte, Schallplatte; (*fig.*) der Ruf, die Vergangenheit; *bear – of*, bezeugen; *beat* or *break the –*, den Rekord brechen; *a good –*, ein guter Ruf *or* Leumund; *keep a – of*, Buch führen über; *a matter of –*, verbürgte Tatsache; *off the –*, nicht für die Öffentlichkeit, nicht protokolliert; *on –*, geschichtlich *or* urkundlich nachgewiesen, niedergeschrieben; nachweisbar; *left on –*, geschichtlichen Aufzeichnungen zufolge; *the largest poll on –*, die größte bisher verzeichnete Stimmenabgabe; *place on –*, zu Protokoll geben; *put a th. on –*, eine maßgebende Äußerung über etwas machen; *service –*, das Führungszeugnis (*Mil.*). *set up a –*, einen Rekord aufstellen; *a shady –*, eine dunkle Vergangenheit. **--breaker,** *s.* der Rekordmann. **automatic --changer,** *s.* automatischer Plattenwechsler. **-er** [rɪ'kɔ:də], *s.* der Registrator, Protokollführer; Stadtrichter, Stadtsyndikus; Registrierapparat; die Blockflöte (*Mus.*). **-ing apparatus** [rɪ'kɔ:dɪŋ], *s.* der Aufnahmeapparat. **--office,** *s.* das Staatsarchiv.

[1]**recount** [rɪ'kɑunt], *v.a.* aufzählen; eingehend erzählen *or* berichten.

[2]**recount** [rɪ:'kɑunt], 1. *v.a.* nachzählen. 2. *s.* die Nachzählung.

recoup [rɪ:'ku:p], *v.a.* zurückbehalten, abziehen (*Law*); entschädigen, schadlos halten (*a p.*) (*for*, für); wieder einholen *or* einbringen (*a loss*); – *o.s.* sich schadlos halten (*from*, aus). **-ment,** *s.* die Zurückbehaltung, Einbehaltung; Schadloshaltung, Entschädigung; Wiedereinbringung.

recourse [rɪ'kɔ:s], *s.* die Zuflucht (*to*, zu); der Regreß, Ersatzanspruch, Rückanspruch (*C.L.*); *have – to*, greifen zu, seine Zuflucht nehmen **zu**; *have – to law*, den Rechtsweg beschreiten; *without –*, ohne Regreß (*C.L.*).

[1]**recover** [rɪ'kʌvə], 1. *v.a.* wiedererhalten, wiederbekommen, wiederfinden; wiedergewinnen, zurückgewinnen, wiedererobern, zurückerobern

(*territory, etc.*); betreiben, eintreiben (*money*); nachholen, wieder einholen (*time*); ersetzen, wiedergutmachen (*a loss*); retten, befreien (*a p.*) (*from*, von *or* aus), wieder zum Leben *or* Bewußtsein bringen; – *one's balance*, das Gleichgewicht wiedererlangen; – *consciousness*, wieder zum Bewußtsein kommen; – *damages*, Schadenersatz erhalten; – *one's legs*, wieder auf die Beine kommen; – *one's losses*, seine Verluste ersetzt erhalten; – *o.s.*, zu sich kommen; *be –ed*, wiederhergestellt sein. 2. *v.n.* sich erholen, genesen (*from*, von); entschädigt werden, den Prozeß gewinnen (*Law*); in die Auslage zurückgehen (*Fenc.*). 3. *s.* die Auslagestellung (*Fenc.*). **–able** [–rəbl], *adj.* eintreibbar (*debt*), wieder erlangbar; wiedergutzumachen(d) (*loss*); heilbar, wiederherstellbar (*Med.*). **–y** [–rɪ], *s.* die Wiedererlangung, Wiedergewinnung; Eintreibung (*of debts*), Wiederherstellung, Genesung (*Med.*); Erlangung (*Law*); *–y of damages*, der Schadenersatz; *beyond* or *past –y*, unwiederbringlich *or* unrettbar verloren; unheilbar (*Med.*).

²**recover** [rɪ:ˈkʌvə], *v.a.* neu beziehen (lassen) (*umbrellas, etc.*).

recrean–cy [ˈrɪ:krɪənsɪ], *s.* (*Poet.*) schmähliche Feigheit; die Abtrünnigkeit. **–t** [–ənt], 1. *adj.* (*Poet.*) abtrünnig, feig. 2. *s.* Abtrünnige(r), *m.*; der Feigling, Ruchlose(r).

¹**recreat–e** [ˈrɛkrɪeɪt], 1. *v.a.* erquicken, erfrischen, auffrischen; unterhalten, ergötzen; *–e o.s.*, sich erfrischen, erholen *or* ergötzen. 2. *v.n.* sich erfrischen *or* erholen, sich ergötzen. **–ion** [–ˈeɪʃən], *s.* die Unterhaltung, Belustigung, das Spiel, der Sport; die Erholung, Erfrischung. **–ion-ground,** *s.* der Sportplatz, Spielplatz. **–ive** [–ɪətɪv], *adj.* erquicken, erfrischend, erheiternd, Unterhaltungs–.

²**recreat–e** [rɪ:krɪˈeɪt], *v.a.* neu schaffen. **–ion** [–ˈeɪʃən], *s.* die Neuschaffung.

recrement [ˈrɛkrɪmənt], *s.* das Sekret (*Physiol.*); (*rare*) der Auswurfstoff, Ausschuß.

recriminat–e [rɪˈkrɪmɪneɪt], *v.n.* Gegenbeschuldigungen vorbringen. **–ion** [–ˈneɪʃən], *s.* die Gegenbeschuldigung. **–ive** [–ˈkrɪmɪnətɪv], **–ory** [–krɪmɪˈneɪtərɪ], *adj.* Gegenschuldigungs–.

recross [rɪ:ˈkrɔs], *v.a.* wieder überschreiten, wieder kreuzen.

recrudesce [rɪ:kruːˈdɛs], *v.n.* wieder aufbrechen (*wounds*), wieder ausbrechen. **–nce** [–ˈdɛsəns], *s.* das Wiederaufbrechen (*wound*); Wiederausbrechen, der Wiederausbruch; (*fig.*) das Wiederaufleben. **–nt** [–ˈdɛsənt], *adj.* wiederausbrechend, wiederauflebend.

recruit [rɪˈkruːt], 1. *v.a.* (an)werben, rekrutieren (*soldiers*); ergänzen (*an army, etc.*); anziehen, gewinnen (*followers*); (*fig.*) wiederherstellen, stärken, auffrischen; *be –ed from*, sich zusammensetzen, ergänzen *or* rekrutieren aus. 2. *v.n.* Rekruten anwerben (*Mil.*), (*fig.*) sich erholen. 3. *s.* der Rekrut (*Mil.*); (*fig.*) der Neuling, neues Mitglied, der Nachwuchs. **–al** [–əl], *s.* die Wiederherstellung. **–ing,** *s.* das Werben; *–ing-office*, das Wehrbezirkskommando. *–ing-officer*, der Werbeoffizier.

rectal [ˈrɛktəl], *adj.* Rektal–; – *syringe*, die Klistierspritze.

rectang–le [ˈrɛktæŋgl], *s.* das Rechteck. **–ular** [–ˈtæŋgjʊlə], *adj.* rechtwink(e)lig, rechteckig.

rectif–iable [ˈrɛktɪfɑɪəbl], *adj.* verbesserungsfähig, zu verbessern(d), zu berichtigen(d), rektifizierbar (*Math.*). **–ication** [–ɪˈkeɪʃən], *s.* die Berichtigung, Verbesserung; Rektifikation (*Geom., Chem.*); Gleichrichtung (*Rad.*). **–ier** [–fɑɪə], *s.* der Berichtiger; Rektifizierer, Rektifikator (*Chem.*); Gleichrichter (*Rad.*). **–y** [–fɑɪ], *v.a.* berichtigen, richtigstellen, (ver)bessern, in Ordnung bringen; rektifizieren (*Chem., Geom.*); gleichrichten (*Rad.*).

rectilinear [rɛktɪˈlɪnɪə], *adj.* geradlinig.

rectitude [ˈrɛktɪtjuːd], *s.* charakterliche Geradheit, die Redlichkeit, Rechtschaffenheit.

recto [ˈrɛktoʊ], *s.* rechte Seite, die Vorderseite (*Bookb.*).

rector [ˈrɛktə], *s.* der (Ober)Pfarrer; gewählter Vertreter der Studentenschaft (*Scottish Univ.*); der Direktor (*of Scottish school*). **–ial** [–ˈtɔːrɪəl], *adj.* Pfarr–; *–ial election*, die Abstimmung für den Studentenschaftsvertreter (*Scottish Univ.*). **–y** [–tərɪ], *s.* das Pfarrhaus.

rectum [ˈrɛktəm], *s.* der Mastdarm.

recumben–cy [rɪˈkʌmbənsɪ] *s.* liegende Stellung. **–t** [–ənt], *adj.* liegend, lehnend, ruhend.

recuperat–e [rɪˈkjuːpəreɪt], *v.n.* sich erholen; vorholen (*Gun.*). **–ion** [–ˈreɪʃən], *s.* die Erholung. **–ive** [–pərətɪv], *adj.* kräftigend, stärkend; *–ive power*, die Erholungsfähigkeit. **–or** [–tə], *s.* die Vorholeinrichtung (*Gun.*).

recur [rɪˈkəː], *v.n.* zurückkommen, wiederkehren, sich wiedereinstellen, wieder auftauchen, sich wiederholen; einfallen, wieder ins Gedächtnis kommen; zurückkehren (*to*, zu), zurückkommen (*to*, auf). **–rence** [–ˈkʌrəns], *s.* die Wiederkehr; das Wiederauftreten. **–rent** [–ˈkʌrənt], *adj.* wiederkehrend, zurückkehrend, sich wiederholend; rückläufig; Rekurrens– (*Anat.*); *–rent fever*, das Rückfallfieber. **–ring** [–ˈkəːrɪŋ], *adj.* zurückkehrend; periodisch (*of decimals*).

recurv–ate [rɪˈkəːvət], *adj.* zurückgebeugt (*Bot.*). **–e** [rɪːˈkəːv], 1. *v.a.* zurückbiegen. 2. *v.n.* zurückwenden.

recus–ancy [rɪˈkjuːzənsɪ], *s.* hartnäckige Weigerung, die Widerspenstigkeit. **–ant** [ˈrɛkjuːzənt], 1. *adj.* widerspenstig, dissidierend (*Hist.*). 2. *s.* Verweigere(r), *m.*, der Dissident; Widerspenstige(r), *m.* **–e** [rɪˈkjuːz], *v.a.* ablehnen (*Law*).

red [rɛd], **1.** *adj.* rot; (*coll.*) kommunistisch, anarchistisch; – *Admiral*, der Admiral (*Entom.*); – *book*, das Rotbuch (*Pol.*), der Adelskalender; – *cabbage*, der Rotkohl; – *Cross*, das Rote Kreuz; – *currant*, rote Johannisbeere; – *deal*, das Kiefernholz; – *deer*, der Rothirsch, Edelhirsch; – *ensign*, britische Handelsflagge; – *eyes*, entzündete Augen; – *flag*, rote Fahne, das Warnungssignal; – *grouse*, schottisches Schneehuhn; – *gum*, der Rieseneukalyptus (*Bot.*); – *hat*, der Kardinalshut; – *heat*, die Rotglut; – *herring*, der Bückling; (*fig.*) das Ablenkungsobjekt, Ablenkungsmanöver; *draw a – herring across the path*, Ablenkungsmanöver betreiben; – *Indian*, der Indianer; (*coll.*) – *lane*, die Kehle; – *lead*, die Mennige, das Bleizinnober; – *light*, (*sl.*) das Bordell; (*fig.*) das Warnlicht; *see the – light*, ein Unglück kommen sehen; – *man*, die Rothaut, der Indianer; – *ochre*, die Eisenmennige; – *rag*, rotes Tuch; *be a – rag to him*, auf ihn wie ein rotes Tuch wirken; – *rot*, das Sonnenkraut, der Sonnentau (*Bot.*); – *sanders*, rotes Sandelholz; – *snow*, der Blutschnee; – *spider*, die Spinnmilbe; – *tape*, rotes Aktenband; (*fig.*) Schema; (*also* **– -tapery, – -tapism**), der Bürokratismus, Amtsschimmel, die Beamtenwirtschaft, der Zopf. **2.** *s.* das Rot, rote Farbe; Rote(r), *m.*, der Kommunist, Anarchist, Linksradikale(r), *m.* (*Pol.*); *paint the town –*, Spektakel machen; *see –*, rasend werden. **– -blooded,** *adj.* lebenskräftig; (*coll.*) feurig, kräftig. **–breast,** *s.* das Rotkehlchen. **– -cap,** *s.* (*coll.*) der Feldpolizist (*Mil.*). **–coat,** *s.* der Rotrock, englischer Soldat. **– -Cross Society,** der Verein vom Roten Kreuz. **– -haired,** *adj.* rothaarig. **– -handed,** *adj.* auf frischer Tat. **– -hot,** *adj.* feuerrot, rotglühend; (*sl.*) hitzig, heftig, feurig, wild, blindwütig. *– -hot poker*, die Hyazinthenaloe, Kniphofia (*Bot.*). **– -letter day,** der Heiligentag, Festtag; Freudentag, Glückstag. **–ness,** *s.* die Röte. **– -poll,** *s.* der Rothänfling (*Orn.*). **–shank,** *s.* der Wasserläufer, Rotschenkel (*Orn.*). **– -short,** *adj.* rotbrüchig (*Metall.*). **–skin,** *s.* die Rothaut, der Indianer. **–start,** *s.* das Rotschwänzchen (*Orn.*). **– -tapery, – -tapism,** see – *tape*. **– -water,** *s.* das Blutharnen, die Piroplasmose (*Vet.*); *– -water fever*, das Texasfieber **–wing,** *s.* die Rotdrossel (*Orn.*). **–wood,** *s.* das Rotholz, Kaliforniaholz.

redact [rɪˈdækt], *v.a.* abfassen; herausgeben, redigieren. **–ion** [–ʃən], *s.* die (Ab)Fassung, Redaktion, Revision, Neuarbeitung. **–or** [–tə], *s.* der Herausgeber.

redan [rɪˈdæn], *s.* der Redan, die Flesche.

redbreast, *see under* **red.**

redcoat, *see under* **red.**

redd [rɛd], *v.a.* (*Scots*) (also – *up*) ordnen, in Ordnung bringen, aufräumen, reinigen.

redd–en ['rɛdən], 1. *v.n.* rot werden, sich röten; erröten (*at*, über (*Acc.*); *with*, vor). 2. *v.a.* rot färben, röten. **–ish** [–ɪʃ], *adj.* rötlich. **–le** [–l], *s.* der Rötel, Rotstein.
rede [rɪ:d], 1. *v.a.* & *n.* (*Poet.*) raten (*Dat.*). 2. *s.* (*Poet.*) der Rat; die Entscheidung.
redecorat–e [rɪ:'dɛkəreɪt], *v.a.* neu dekorieren. **–ion** [–'reɪʃən], *s.* die Neudekorierung.
redeem [rɪ'dɪ:m], *v.a.* zurückkaufen, zurückgewinnen, wiedererlangen; loskaufen, freikaufen (*captives, etc.*); einlösen (*a pledge*); ablösen, tilgen, amortisieren (*a loan*); erlösen (*Theol.*); wiedergutmachen, ersetzen, ausgleichen. **–able,** *adj.* zurückkäuflich, wiederkäuflich, amortisierbar, ablösbar, einlösbar (*C.L.*); wiedergutzumachen(d), auslösbar, kündbar (*loan*); erlösbar (*Rel.*). **–er** [–ə], *s.* der Erlöser, Heiland (*Eccl.*). **–ing,** *adj.* versöhnend.
redeliver [rɪ:dɪ'lɪvə], *v.a.* wieder austragen, übermitteln, ausliefern, abliefern; wieder befreien.
redempt–ion [rɪ'dɛmpʃən], *s.* der Rückkauf; die Einlösung, Ablösung; Tilgung, Amortisation (*of a loan*); Rückzahlung (*of capital*); Befreiung, der Loskauf, Freikauf (*of captives, etc.*); die Erlösung (*Theol.*); *past –ion*, unrettbar *or* unwiederbringlich verloren; *–ion value*, der Rückkaufswert. **–ive** [–tɪv], *adj.* Erlösungs– (*Theol.*), erlösend.
redeployment [rɪ:dɪ'plɔɪmənt], *s.* die Neuaufstellung, Neuentfaltung.
redintegrat–e [rɪ'dɪntɪgreɪt], *v.a.* wiederherstellen, erneuern. **–ion** [–'greɪʃən], *s.* die Wiederherstellung, Erneuerung.
redirect [rɪ:dɪ'rɛkt], *v.a.* umadressieren, nachsenden (*of letters*).
rediscover [rɪ:dɪs'kʌvə], *v.a.* neuentdecken, wieder entdecken. **–y,** [–vərɪ], *s.* die Neuentdeckung, Wiederentdeckung.
redistribut–e [rɪ:'dɪstrɪbju:t], *v.a.* wiederverteilen, neuverteilen. **–ion** [–'bju:ʃən], *s.* die Wiederverteilung, Neuverteilung.
redivide [rɪ:dɪ'vaɪd], *v.a.* wieder (ver)teilen.
redness, *see under* **red.**
re-do [rɪ:'du:], *v.a.* noch einmal tun, renovieren.
redolen–ce ['rɛdələns], *s.* der Wohlgeruch. **–t** [–ənt], *adj.* wohlriechend, duftend (*of*, nach); (*fig.*) *be –t of*, atmen, erinnern an, einen Anstrich habend von.
redouble [rɪ:'dʌbl], 1. *v.a.* (*fig.*) verdoppeln; verstärken. 2. *v.n.* sich verdoppeln *or* verstärken; Rekontra gehen (*Cards*).
redoubt [rɪ'daʊt], *s.* die Redoute, Schanze.
redoubtable [rɪ'daʊtəbl], *adj.* gefürchtet, furchtbar.
redound [rɪ'daʊnd], *v.n.* gereichen, beitragen, ausschlagen (*to*, zu); sich ergeben, zuteil werden, zufließen (*to* (*Dat.*); *from*, aus); zurückwirken, zurückfallen ((*up*)*on* auf); *– to s.o.'s advantage*, einem zum Vorteil dienen *or* ausschlagen.
redpoll, *see under* **red.**
redraft [rɪ:'drɑ:ft], 1. *s.* neues Entwurf; der Rückwechsel, die Rücktratte (*C.L.*). 2. *v.a.* neu entwerfen.
redraw [rɪ:'drɔ:], *v.a.* gegentrassieren, zurücktrassieren (*C.L.*); *see* **draw.**
redress [rɪ'drɛs], 1. *s.* die Abhilfe, Abstellung, Behebung; Genugtuung, der Ersatz, Regreß; *legal –*, die Rechtshilfe. 2. *v.a.* wiedergutmachen; wiederherstellen; abhelfen (*Dat.*), beheben, beseitigen; abfangen (*Av.*).
re-dress [rɪ:'drɛs], 1. *v.a.* neu kleiden; neu verbinden (*wound*). 2. *v.n.* sich umkleiden.
redshank, *see under* **red.**
redskin, *see under* **red.**
reduc–e [rɪ'dju:s], 1. *v.a.* vermindern, verkleinern, verringern, verjüngen; schwächen, verdünnen, verschneiden, strecken (*Chem.*), reduzieren (*Math., Chem.*); beschränken, einschränken (*to*, auf), herabsetzen, herabdrücken (*to*, zu), ermäßigen (*prices*); herunterbringen, heruntersetzen, herabwürdigen, degradieren; bezwingen, unterwerfen; zwingen, bringen (*a p.*) (*to*, zu); wiederherstellen; zurückführen (*to*, auf), anpassen (*to*, an), bringen (*to*, auf *or* in), machen (*to*, zu); verwandeln (*to*, in *or* zu); wiedereinrenken (*Surg.*). (*a*) (*with nouns*) *–e one's expenses*, sich einschränken; *–e a fortress*, eine Festung zur Übergabe zwingen; *–e by boiling*, verkochen; *–e by liquation*, ausseigern. (*b*) (with *to*) *–e to absurdity*, ad absurdum führen; *–e to ashes*, einäschern, in Asche verwandeln; *–e to beggary*, an den Bettelstab bringen; *–e to certain classes* or *heads*, nach gewissen Gesichtspunkten anordnen *or* einteilen; *–e fractions to a common denominator*, Brüche gleichnamig machen; *–e to despair*, zur Verzweiflung bringen; *–e a proposition to its simplest form*, einen Satz auf seinen einfachsten Ausdruck zurückführen; *–e whole numbers to fractions*, ganze Zahlen in Brüche verwandeln; *–e to half-pay*, verabscheiden (*Mil.*); *–e to nothing*, vernichten; *–e to obedience*, zum Gehorsam zwingen; *–e to order*, in Ordnung bringen; *–e shillings to pence*, die Schillinge in Pence verwandeln; *–e to powder*, pulvern, zu Pulver reiben; *–e to the ranks*, degradieren (*Mil.*); *–e to a system*, in ein System bringen; *–e to tears*, zu Tränen rühren. **–ed** [–t], *adj.*; *–ed scale*, verjüngter *or* verkleinerter Maßstab; *–ed to a skeleton*, zu einem Skelett abgemagert; *at –ed prices*, zu herabgesetzen *or* ermäßigten Preisen; *–ed circumstances*, bedrängte *or* zerrüttete Verhältnisse. **2.** *v.n.* eine Abmagerungskur machen. **–er** [–ə], *s.* das Verdünnungsmittel, Verschnittmittel; der Abschwächer (*Phot.*); verjüngte Muffe (*Tech.*). **–ible** [–ɪbl], *adj.* zurückführbar, reduzierbar (*to*, auf); verwandelbar (*to*, in); *be –ible*, sich zurückführen *or* verwandeln lassen. **–ing-agent,** *s.* das Reduktionsmittel; Entfettungsmittel (*Med.*). **–ing-scale,** *s.* verjüngtes Maßstab. **–ing-valve,** *s.* das Reduzierventil. **–tion** [rɪ'dʌkʃən], *s.* das Zurückführen, Zurückbringen (*to*, auf); Verwandlung ((*in*)*to*, in); die Reduktion (*Math., Chem.*); Herabsetzung, Reduzierung, Ermäßigung (*of prices*); der Abbau (*in salary*); Abzug, Rabatt; die Verminderung, Verkleinerung, Verringerung; Unterwerfung (*of a town, etc.*); Einrenkung (*Surg.*); Degradierung (*Mil.*); Kürzung (*of a fraction*); Verjüngung (*of a scale*); der Verschnitt (*Chem.*); *make a –tion*, eine Ermäßigung eintreten lassen, Rabatt geben. **–tion-compasses,** *pl.* der Reduktionszirkel. **–tion-gear,** *s.* das Untersetzungsgetriebe.
reduit [rə'dwɪ:], *s.* das Kernwerk (*Fort.*).
redundan–ce, –cy [rɪ'dʌndəns(ɪ)], *s.* die Überfülle, der Überfluß (*of*, an). **–t** [–ənt], *adj.* überflüssig, übermäßig; weitschweifig, überladen.
reduplicat–e [rɪ:'dju:plɪkeɪt], *v.a.* verdoppeln, wiederholen; reduplizieren (*Gram.*). **–ion** [–'keɪʃən], *s.* die Verdoppelung, Wiederholung; Reduplikation (*Gram.*).
redwing, *see under* **red.**
redwood, *see under* **red.**
re-echo [rɪ:'ɛkoʊ], *v.a.* & *n.* wiederhallen (*with*, von).
reed [rɪ:d], *s.* das Rohr (*also of organ*), Schilfrohr, Ried; die Rohrpfeife; das (Rohr)Blatt (*of reed instruments*); die Zunge (*organ*); das Webblatt, der Webekamm, das Riet (*Weav.*); *broken –*, schwankendes Rohr. **– -bunting,** *s.* die Rohrammer (*Orn.*). **–iness,** *s.* die Piepsigkeit (*of voice*). **– -mace,** *s.* das Rohrkolbenschilf (*Bot.*). **– -pipe,** *s.* die Rohrpfeife; die Zungenpfeife (*Org.*). **– -stop,** *s.* das Pfeifenwerk, Rohrwerk, Schnarrwerk (*Org.*). **– -warbler,** *s.* der Teichrohrsänger (*Orn.*). **–y** [–ɪ], *adj.* schilfreich; schrill, piepsig (*as a voice*).
re-edit [rɪ:'ɛdɪt], *v.a.* neu herausgeben.
reedling ['rɪ:dlɪŋ], *s.* die Bartmeise, Schilfmeise (*Orn.*).
re-education [rɪ:ɛdju'keɪʃən], die Umschulung.
[1]**reef** [rɪ:f], *s.* das Riff, die Felsenklippe; goldführende Ader (*Min.*). **–y,** *adj.* riffig.
[2]**reef,** 1. *s.* das Reff (*Naut.*); *take in a –*, einreffen. 2. *v.a.* reffen (*Naut.*); *close –ed*, dicht gerefft. **–er** [–ə], *s.* der Reffer; Seekadett; die Seemannsjacke. **– -knot,** *s.* der Reffknoten, Kreuzknoten.
reek [rɪ:k], 1. *s.* (*Scots*) der Rauch, Dampf, Dunst; Qualm; Geruch, Gestank. 2. *v.n.* dampfen. rauchen, dunsten (*with*, vor); riechen (*of* or *with*, nach). **–y,** *adj.* rauchig, dunstig.
reel [rɪ:l], 1. *s.* die Weise; Winde, (Garn)Haspel, (Garn)Rolle; Farbbandspule (*typewriter*), Schnur-

rolle (*fishing line*), Schlauchrolle (*garden-hose*); Trommel (*hawsers*); Spule (*films*); *news*--, die Wochenschau (*Cinema*). 2. *v.a.*; (also – *up*) (auf)-winden, haspeln, spulen, wickeln; – *off*, abhaspeln, abwinden, abwickeln; (*fig.*) herunterhaspeln, herunterleiern, herunterplappern. 3. *v.n.* taumeln, schwanken; sich drehen, wirbeln; *my head* –*s*, mir schwindelt. 4. *s.* der Taumel, Wirbel; schottischer Volkstanz.

re-elect [rɪːɪˈlɛkt], *v.a.* wiederwählen. **-ion** [-ʃən], *s.* die Wiederwahl.

re-eligible [rɪːˈɛlɪdʒəbl], *adj.* wiederwählbar.

re-embark [rɪːəmˈbɑːk], *v.a.* (& *n.*) (sich) wieder einschiffen. **-ation** [rɪːɛmbɑːˈkeɪʃən], *s.* die Wiedereinschiffung.

re-emerge [rɪːɪˈməːdʒ], *v.n.* wieder auftauchen *or* auftreten. **-nce** [-əns], *s.* das Wiederauftauchen, Wiederauftreten.

re-enact [rɪːəˈnækt], *v.a.* neu verordnen; wieder in Kraft *or* Szene setzen; neu inszenieren (*Theat.*); (*fig.*) wiederholen. **-ment,** *s.* wiederholte Inkraftsetzung, die Wiederholung; Neuinszenierung.

re-engage [rɪːɛnˈgeɪdʒ], 1. *v.a.* wieder anstellen *or* einstellen. 2. *v.n.* wieder in Dienst treten. **-ment,** *s.* die Wiederanstellung, Wiedereinstellung.

re-enlist [rɪːɛnˈlɪst], 1. *v.n.* sich wieder anwerben lassen, weiterdienen, kapitulieren. 2. *v.a.* wieder anwerben. **-ment,** *s.* die Wiederanwerbung.

re-ent-er [rɪːˈɛntə], 1. *v.a.* wieder betreten; neu eintragen (*in a book*), eindrucken (*colour*). 2. *v.n.* von neuem eintreten. **-ering** [-ərɪŋ], 1. *adj. see* **-rant** 1. 2. *s.* das Eindrucken (*Cal. Prin.*). **-rance** [-trəns], erneutes Eintreten *or* Auftreten. **-rant** [-trənt], 1. *adj.* einspringend (*angle*) (*Geom.*). 2. *s.* einspringendes Winkel. **-ry** [-trɪ], *s.* das Wiedereintreten, der Wiedereintritt (*Law*).

re-establish [rɪːɛˈstæblɪʃ], *v.a.* wiederherstellen. **-ment,** *s.* die Wiederherstellung.

¹reeve [rɪːv], *s.* (*archaic*) der Vogt, Schultheiß, Amtmann.

²reeve, *s.* das Weibchen des Kampfläufers (*Orn.*); *see* **¹ruff.**

³reev-e, *v.a.* (ein)scheren (*rope*) (*Naut.*) (*to*, an). **-ing-line,** *s.* das Schertau.

re-examin-ation [rɪːɛgzæmɪˈneɪʃən], *s.* die Nachprüfung; nochmaliges Verhör, nochmalige Vernehmung (*Law*). **-e** [-ˈzæmɪn], *v.a.* nachprüfen, neu prüfen; neu vernehmen *or* verhören (*Law*).

re-exchange [rɪːɛksˈtʃeɪndʒ], *s.* abermaliger Tausch; der Rückwechsel, Rikambio, die Ritratte (*C.L.*).

re-export 1. *v.a.* [rɪːɛksˈpɔːt], wieder ausführen. 2. *s.* [rɪːˈɛkspɔːt] die Wiederausfuhr.

refashion [rɪːˈfæʃən], *v.a.* neu formen, umgestalten, ummodeln.

refect-ion [rɪːˈfɛkʃən], *s.* die Erfrischung, der Imbiß. **-ory** [-tərɪ], *s.* der Speisesaal; das Refektorium (*in convents, etc.*); *-ory table*, langer schmaler Tisch.

refer [rɪˈfəː], 1. *v.a.* aufmerksam machen (*to*, auf), verwiesen (*to*, an); überlassen, übergehen, überweisen, zurückstellen (*to*, an); zuschrieben, zuweisen, zuordnen (*to* (*Dat.*)); beziehen (*to*, auf); – *to drawer*, an den Aussteller zurück (*C.L.*). 2. *v.n.* hinweisen, verweisen, anspielen, sich beziehen, Bezug haben *or* nehmen (*to*, auf); – *to a th.*, etwas erwähnen *or* andeuten; – *to a book*, nachschlagen in *or* (sich) Rat in *or* aus einem Buch, ein Buch heranziehen; – *to a p.*, sich an einen wenden *or* auf einen berufen, einen befragen, es auf einen ankommen lassen; *-red to*, betreffend, bezüglich, fraglich; *-ring to my letter*, bezugnehmend auf meinen Brief. **-able** [-rəbl], *adj.* bezüglich, zu beziehen(d) (*to*, auf); zuzuschreibend(d), zuzurechnen(d) (*to* (*Dat.*)). **-ee** [rɛfəˈrɪː], 1. *s.* der Schiedsrichter (*Sport*), Ringrichter (*Box.*), Referent, Sachverständige(r), *m.* (*Law*); Unparteiische(r), *m.* 2. *v.n.* (& *a.*) als Schiedsrichter fungieren (bei). **-ence** [ˈrɛfərəns], 1. *s.* die Beziehung (*to*, zu), Bezugnahme, der Bezug (*to*, auf); die Verweisung (*to*, an) (*Law*); der Hinweis (*to*, auf), Beleg; die Empfehlung, Referenz (*also p. referred to*), das Nachschlagen (*to*, in); das (einem Ausschuß zugewiesene) Arbeitsgebiet; *cross -ence*, der Kreuzverweis; *for -ence*, zur Informierung; zum Nachschlagen (*books*); *terms of -ence*, Richtlinien; *work of -ence*, das Nachschlagewerk; *have -ence to*, sich beziehen auf (*Acc.*); *make -ence to*, erwähnen, verwiesen auf; *in* or *with -ence to*, in *or* mit Bezug auf (*Acc.*), hinsichtlich (*Gen.*); *without -ence to*, ohne Bezug auf (*Acc.*). 2. *v.a.* mit Verweisen versehen (*book*). **-ence book,** *s.* das Nachschlagebuch. **-ence library,** *s.* die Nachschlagebibliothek, Handbibliothek. **-ence mark,** *s.* das Verweisungszeichen. **-ence number,** *s.* das Aktenzeichen, die Geschäftsnummer. **-ence point,** *s.* der Anhaltspunkt (*maps*). **-endum** [rɛfəˈrɛndəm], *s.* der Volksentscheid (*on*, über). **-ential** [-ˈrɛnʃəl], *adj.* hinweisend, Verweisungs–, Vermerk–.

refill 1. *v.a.* [rɪːˈfɪl], wieder füllen, auffüllen. 2. *v.n.* sich wieder füllen. 3. *s.* [ˈrɪːfɪl], die Neufüllung, Ersatzfüllung; das Ersatzblei (*for pencils*); die Ersatzbatterie (*for electric torch*); Einlage (*for ring-book*).

refin-e [rɪˈfaɪn], 1. *v.a.* reinigen, läutern, klären; vergüten; raffinieren, abläuten (*sugar, etc.*), frischen, abscheiden, abtreiben, abbrennen (*metal*); (*fig.*) bilden, verfeinern, veredeln. 2. *v.n.* sich verfeinen *or* verbessern, klar *or* rein werden; klügeln, grübeln, sich verbreiten ((*up*)*on*, über (*Acc.*)); *-e on a th.*, etwas verbessern *or* verfeinern (wollen). **-ed,** *adj.* geläutert, verfeinert, raffiniert, Fein–; (*fig.*) fein, gebildet, gepflegt, vornehm; *-ed lead*, das Weichblei; *-ed steel*, der Edelstahl; *-ed sugar*, der Feinzucker, die Raffinade. **-ement** [-mənt], *s.* die Reinigung, Läuterung; (*fig.*) Verfeinerung, Bildung, Klügelei, Spitzfindigkeit, Feinheit. **-er** [-ə], *s.* der Raffineur, Frischer (*Metall.*); (Zucker)Sieder; Raffinierapparat, die Frischanlage; Feinmühle (*Papermaking*); (*fig.*) Verfeinerer; Haarspalter, Klügler. **-ery** [-ərɪ], *s.* die Raffinerie, Siederei, der Frischofen. **-ing** [-ɪŋ], *s.* die Läuterung, Scheidung, Raffinierung, das Frischen. **-ing-furnace,** *s.* der Frischofen. **-ing-hearth,** *s.* der Zerrenherd.

refit [rɪːˈfɪt], 1. *v.a.* ausbessern, wieder instandsetzen (*a ship*); neu ausrüsten. 2. *v.n.* ausgebessert *or* überholt werden. 3. *s.* die Wiederinstandsetzung, Ausbesserung.

reflect [rɪˈflɛkt], 1. *v.a.* zurückwerfen, widerspiegeln (*also fig.*), zurückstrahlen, zurückbiegen, reflektieren (*light, etc.*); (*fig.*) wiedergeben; – *credit upon a p.*, einem Ehre machen; – *disgrace on a p.*, einem Schande einbringen; *be -ed*, zurückfallen, sich (wider)spiegeln. 2. *v.n.* nachdenken ((*up*)*on*, über), überlegen; (*fig.*) – (*up*)*on a p.*, auf einen zurückwirken *or* zurückfallen *or* schiefes *or* schlechtes Licht werfen, einen in schiefes *or* schlechtes Licht setzen, einem nicht gerade zu Ehre gereichen; (*fig.*) *be -ed in*, sich spiegeln in, (*fig.*) seinen Niederschlag finden in. **-ing,** *adj.* Reflexions–, Spiegel–. **-ion** [-ʃən], die Zurückwerfung, Zurückstrahlung, Reflexion, das (Wider)Spiegeln, Zurückfallen; Spiegelbild; der Widerschein, Reflex; (*fig.*) die Widerspiegelung; Überlegung, Erwägung, der Gedanke, die Bemerkung; (*fig.*) der Tadel (*on*, an), Vorwurf (*on*, für), die Herabsetzung (*on* (*Gen.*)); *angle of -ion*, der Reflexionswinkel; *on -ion*, bei *or* nach näherer Erwägung; *be a -ion on*, schlechtes Licht werfen auf; *cast -ions upon*, herabsetzen. **-ive** [-tɪv], *adj.* zurückstrahlend, Rückstrahl–; reflektierend, nachdenkend. **-or** [-tə], *s.* der Reflektor, Hohlspiegel; Scheinwerfer; Rückstrahler, das Katzenauge (*Cycl.*).

reflex [ˈrɪːflɛks], 1. *adj.* Reflex–, Rück–, rückwirkend; zurückgebogen (*Bot.*); – *action*, die Reflexbewegung; – *camera*, die Spiegelreflexkamera. 2. *s.* der Widerschein, das Lichtspiel, Spiegelbild, der (Licht)Reflex; (*fig.*) die (Wider)Spiegelung; der Reflex, die Reflexbewegung (*Physiol.*). **-ible** [rɪːˈflɛksɪbl], *adj.* reflektierbar, zurückstrahlbar. **-ion,** (*Phys., etc.*) *see* **reflection. -ive** [rɪːˈflɛksɪv], 1. *adj.* rückbezüglich, reflexiv (*Gram.*). 2. *s.* das Reflexivpronomen, rückbezügliches Zeitwort.

refloat [rɪːˈflout], 1. *v.a.* wieder flott machen. 2. *v.n.* wieder flott werden.

refluen-ce [ˈrɛfluːəns], das Zurückfließen. **-t** [-ənt], *adj.* zurückfließend.

reflux [ˈrɪːflʌks], *s.* das Zurückfließen; der Rückfluß, die Ebbe.
refoot [rɪːˈfʊt], *v.a.* einen Füßling neu anstrichen.
[1]**reform** [rɪˈfɔːm], 1. *v.a.* umgestalten, umformen (*a th.*); bessern, reformieren (*a p.*). 2. *v.n.* sich bessern. 3. *s.* die Reform, Umgestaltung, Neugestaltung, Verbesserung; Besserung; – *movement*, die Reformbewegung. **-ation** [rɛfɔːˈmeɪʃən], *s.* die Umgestaltung, Umformung, Reformierung, Verbesserung; Besserung; *the -ation*, die Reformation (*Eccl.*). **-ative** [-ətɪv], *adj.*, *see* **-atory** 1. **-atory** [-ətərɪ], 1. *adj.* Besserungs–, Reform–, reformatorisch. 2. *s.* die Besserungsanstalt. **-ed** [-d], *adj.* umgestaltet, Reform–, verbessert; gebessert, umgewandelt; reformiert (*Eccl.*). **-er** [-ə], *s.* der Verbesserer, Reformer (*Pol.*); Reformator (*Eccl.*).
[2]**re-form** [rɪːˈfɔːm], 1. *v.a.* neu gestalten, umgestalten; neu formieren *or* gliedern (*Mil.*). 2. *v.n.* sich neu formieren *or* gliedern. **-ation** [–ˈmeɪʃən], *s.* die Neugestaltung, Umgestaltung; Neuformierung.
refract [rɪˈfrækt], *v.a.* brechen; (*fig.*) ablenken. **-ing,** *adj.* lichtbrechend, Brechungs–; *-ing telescope*, der Refraktor. **-ion** [-ʃən], *s.* die (Strahlen)Brechung; *index of -ion*, der Brechungsexponent. **-ive** [-tɪv], *adj.* Brechungs–; Refraktions–. **-or** [-tə], *s.* der Refraktor.
refractor-iness [rɪˈfræktərɪnɪs], *s.* die Widerspenstigkeit; Widerstandskraft (*to*, gegen); Strengflüssigkeit (*Metall.*). **-y** [-tərɪ], *adj.* widerspenstig, widerhaarig; hartnäckig (*as disease*); widerstandsfähig (*to*, gegen), strengflüssig (*Metall.*); feuerfest; *-y clay*, die Schamotte.
[1]**refrain** [rɪˈfreɪn], 1. *v.n.* sich enthalten(*from* (*Gen.*)), Abstand nehmen (*from*, von); – *from doing*, sich zurückhalten zu tun, unterlassen. 2. *v.a.* zurückhalten.
[2]**refrain,** *s.* der Kehrreim, Refrain.
refrangible [rɪˈfrændʒɪbl], *adj.* brechbar.
refresh [rɪˈfrɛʃ], 1. *v.a.* erfrischen; (*fig.*) erquicken, auffrischen. 2. *v.n.* sich erfrischen. **-er,** *s.* die Erfrischung, der Trank; (*fig.*) die Auffrischung, das Extrahonorar (*Law*); *-er course*, der Wiederholungskurs, Übungskurs. **-ing,** *adj.* erfrischend, kühlend; (*fig.*) erquickend, anregend. **-ment,** *s.* die Erfrischung, Erquickung (*to*, für); (*usually pl.*) der Imbiß. **-ment room,** *s.* der Erfrischungsraum, die Restauration, das (Bahnhofs)Restaurant, Büfett. **-ment Sunday,** *s.* (der Sonntag) Lätare.
refrigera-nt [rɪˈfrɪdʒərənt], 1. *adj.* kühlend. 2. *s.* das Kühlmittel. **-te** [-reɪt], *v.a.* (ab)kühlen, gefrieren. **-tion** [–ˈreɪʃən], *s.* die Abkühlung; das Kühlen, die Kälteerzeugung. **-tor** [-reɪtə], *s.* der Kühlschrank, Eisschrank, Kühlraum, Kühlapparat, die Kühlanlage. *-tor car*, der Kühlwagen (*Rail.*). **-tory** [-rətərɪ], 1. *adj.* kühlend, Kühl–. 2. *s.* der Verdampfer (*of a still*).
reft [rɛft], *p.p.*, *adj.* (*Poet.*) beraubt (*of*, *Gen.*).
refuel [rɪːˈfʊːəl], 1. *v.a.* mit Brennstoff nachfüllen, auftanken. 2. *v.n.* Brennstoff einnehmen, tanken.
refug-e [ˈrɛfʊːdʒ], 1. *s.* die Zuflucht, der Schutz (*also fig.*) (*from*, vor); Zufluchtsort, die Schutzstätte; Verkehrsinsel (*in street*); (*fig.*) das Schutzmittel, Hilfsmittel, der Ausweg, die Ausflucht; *house of -e*, das Nachtasyl; *seek* or *take -e*, Schutz *or* (seine) Zuflucht suchen. 2. *v.n.* Zuflucht suchen. 3. *v.a.* (*Poet.*) Zuflucht gewähren (*Dat.*). **-e hut,** die Schutzhütte. **-ee** [–ˈdʒɪː], *s.* der Flüchtling.
refulgen-ce [rɪˈfʌldʒəns], *s.* der Glanz, Schein. **-t** [-ənt], *adj.* glänzend, leuchtend, strahlend.
refund [rɪːˈfʌnd], 1. *v.a.* zurückzahlen, rückvergüten, zurückerstatten, ersetzen (*money*, *etc.*) (*to a p.*, einem); schadlos halten (*a p.*). 2. *v.n.* Geld zurückzahlen. 3. *s.*; **-ment,** *s.* die Rückvergütung, Rückerstattung, Rückzahlung.
refurbish [rɪːˈfəːbɪʃ], *v.a.* aufpolieren.
refurnish [rɪːˈfəːnɪʃ], *v.a.* neu möbilieren *or* ausstatten.
refus-al [rɪˈfjʊːzl], *s.* die (Ver)Weigerung, abschlägige Antwort; die Vorhand, der Vorkauf, das Vorkaufsrecht, freie Wahl (*C.L.*); *in case of -al*, im Weigerungsfalle; *first -al of*, erstes Anrecht auf; *give s.o. the -al of*, einem etwas an Hand geben; *have the -al of*, etwas an Hand haben; *meet with a -al*, eine abschlägige Antwort bekommen, eine Fehlbitte tun; *take no -al*, keine abschlägige Antwort annehmen. **-e** [rɪˈfjʊːz], 1. *v.a.* verweigern (*obedience*, *etc.*), Annahme verweigern; ablehnen, abweisen, zurückweisen; abschlagen (*a request*); ausschlagen (*an offer*); *-e a p.*, einem eine Bitte abschlagen; *-e a suitor*, einen Bewerber ablehnen; *-e a p. a th.*, einem etwas verweigern, abschlagen *or* versagen; *he -ed the money*, er schlug das Geld aus; *he -ed to accept the money*, er weigerte sich, das Geld anzunehmen, er verweigerte die Annahme des Geldes; *the horse -es the obstacle*, das Pferd sträubt sich, das Hindernis zu nehmen. 2. *v.n.* ablehnen, sich weigern; sich sträuben zu springen (*as a horse*); nicht bedienen.
refuse [ˈrɛfjʊːs], *s.* der Abfall, der & das Kehricht, der Müll, (*coll.*) die Schlempe; der Ausschuß, die Ausschußware (*C.L.*); (*fig.*) der Abschaum, Auswurf. **--consumer,** *s.*, **--destructor,** *s.* der Müllverbrennungsofen. **--water,** das Spülwasser, Spülicht.
refut-able [rɪˈfjʊːtəbl], *adj.* widerlegbar. **-al, -ation** [rɛfjʊˈteɪʃən], *s.* die Widerlegung. **-e** [rɪˈfjʊːt], *v.a.* widerlegen.
regain [rɪːˈgeɪn], *v.a.* wiedergewinnen, wiedererhalten, widererreichen (*place*); – *one's feet*, wieder festen Fuß fassen.
regal [ˈrɪːgəl], *adj.* königlich, Königs–; (*fig.*) stattlich. **-ia** [rɪːˈgeɪlɪə], *pl.* Krönungsinsignien (*pl.*); königliche Hoheitsrechte (*pl.*); (*fig.*) Insignien (*pl.*). **-ism** [-ɪzm], *s.* die Oberherrschaft des Königs (*Eccl.*). **-ity** [rɪːˈgælɪtɪ], *s.* die Königswürde, das Königsprivileg; *pl.* Hoheitsrechte, königliche Privilegien (*pl.*).
regale [rɪːˈgeɪl], 1. *v.a.* (festlich) bewirten; (*fig.*) ergötzen, erquicken; – *o.s.*, sich weiden *or* laben (*with*, an). 2. *v.n.* schmausen (*on*, von), sich gütlich tun (*on*, an). 3. *s.* (*rare*) das Festmahl, der Schmaus; (*archaic*) der Leckerbissen.
regard [rɪˈgɑːd], 1. *v.a.* ansehen, betrachten; (be)achten, achtgeben auf, berücksichtigen; (*rare*) schätzen, (hoch)achten; – *as*, ansehen als, halten für; *be -ed as*, gelten für; *as -s me*, was mich (an)betrifft. 2. *s.* der Blick; der Bezug, die Bezugnahme, Hinsicht, Beziehung; Achtung (*for*, vor), Rücksicht (*for*, auf); Beachtung, Aufmerksamkeit; (Hoch)Achtung (*for*, vor); *pl.* Grüße, Empfehlungen (*pl.*); *have no – for* or *to*, keine Rücksicht nehmen auf (*Acc.*), nicht berücksichtigen; *give her my kind -s*, grüße sie herzlich von mir; *hold in high* –, hochachten, hochschätzen; *stand in high* –, hoch angeschrieben sein (*with*, bei); *pay* (*no*) – *to*, (nicht) (be)achten; *in this* –, in dieser Hinsicht; *with kind -s*, mit (den) besten Empfehlungen, mit herzlichsten Grüßen; *with – to*, in Hinsicht *or* Bezug auf (*Acc.*), hinsichtlich, betreffs (*Gen.*); *with due – to*, mit gebührender Rücksicht auf; *without – to*, ohne Rücksicht auf (*Acc.*). **-ant** [-ənt], *adj.* zurückblickend (*Her.*). **-ful** [-fʊl], *adj.* rücksichtsvoll (*of*, gegen); *be -ful of*, (be)achten. **-ing,** *prep.* hinsichtlich, betreffs (*Gen.*). **-less,** 1. *adj.* rücksichtslos (*of*, gegen); unbekümmert, sorglos (*of*, um). 2. *adv.* (*coll.*) ohne Rücksicht auf die Kosten.
regatta [rɪˈgætə], *s.* die Regatta.
regen-cy [ˈrɪːdʒənsɪ], *s.* die Regentschaft, Regentschaftszeit. **-t** [-ənt], 1. *adj.* herrschend, regierend. 2. *s.* der Regent, Reichsverweser. **-ship,** *s.* die Regentschaft.
regenerat-e [rɪːˈdʒɛnəreɪt], 1. *v.a.* wiedererzeugen, neu hervorbringen; wiedergewinnen, erneuern, verjüngen, regenerieren (*Tech.*); *be -ed*, wiedergeboren werden (*Theol.*). 2. *v.n.* sich neu *or* wieder bilden (*Med.*), sich regenerieren (*Tech.*). **-ion** [–ˈreɪʃən], *s.* die Wiedererzeugung, Neubildung; Wiederlebung, Regenerierung (*Tech.*); Rückkopplung (*Rad.*); Wiedergeburt (*Theol.*). **-ive** [-ərətɪv], *adj.* Erneuerungs–, Verjüngungs–; *-ive circuit*, die Rückkopplung (*Rad.*); *-ive furnace*, der Regenerationsofen, Vorwärmer. **-or** [-reɪtə], *s.* der Erneuerer; Regenerationsofen.
regent, *see* **regen-t.**
regicid-al [rɛdʒɪˈsaɪdl], *adj.* Königsmord–. **-e** [ˈrɛdʒɪsaɪd], *s.* der Königsmörder; Königsmord.
régime [reˈʒɪːm], *s.* die Regierungsform; (*fig.*) (althergebrachtes) Verfahren.

regimen [ˈrɛdʒɪmən], *s.* die Lebensordnung, Diät, Kost (*Med.*); Rektion (*Gram.*).
regiment [ˈrɛdʒ(ɪ)mənt], 1. *s.* das Regiment (*Mil.*); (*fig.*) die Schar. 2. *v.a.* in Regimenter einteilen; (*usually fig.*) organisieren, kontrollieren, disziplinieren, reglementieren. **-al** [-ɪˈmɛntl], *adj.* Regiments-. **-als,** *pl.* die (Regiments)Uniform. **-ation** [-ɪmɛnˈteɪʃən], *s.* die Organisierung, Disziplinierung, Kontrolle, Reglementierung.
region [ˈrɪ:dʒən], *s.* das Gebiet, die Gegend, Region, der (Korper)Teil, die Gegend (*of the body*); (*fig.*) der Bereich, Bezirk, die Sphäre. **-al,** *adj.* örtlich, Orts-, lokal, räumlich begrenzt.
register [ˈrɛdʒɪstə], 1. *s.* das Verzeichnis, Register; Grundbuch (*Scots Law*); Schiffsregister, Schiffsverzeichnis (*Naut.*); die Klappe, das Ventil (*of a boiler*); Register (*of an organ*), der Stimmumfang, die Tonlage (*Mus.*); genaue Einstellung (*Tech.*); der Registrierapparat; – *of births*, das Geburtsverzeichnis; *cash*--, die Registrierkasse, Kontrollkasse; – *of electors*, die Wählerliste; *parish* –, das Kirchenbuch; *University* –, die Universitätsmatrikel. 2. *v.a.* eintragen, einschreiben, buchen, registrieren; einschreiben (lassen) (*letters*), gesetzlich schützen (lassen) (*a patent*), aufgeben (*luggage*); verzeichnen (*Mach.*); sich (*Dat.*) einprägen (*in one's memory*), von sich geben, zur Schau tragen; – *o.s.*, sich eintragen. 3. *v.n.* sich eintragen *or* anmelden. **-ed,** *adj.* eingetragen (*company*), eingeschrieben (*letter*), patentiert, gesetzlich geschützt (*C.L.*); *-ed design*, das Gebrauchsmuster; *-ed mark*, die Registermark (*currency*). **-ing** [-t(ə)rɪŋ], *adj.* Registrier-.
registr-ar [ˈrɛdʒɪstrɑ], *s.* der Registrator, Archivar, Standesbeamte(r), *m.* *-ar-general*, *s.* der Leiter des Statistischen Amts; *-ar's office*, das Standesamt, die Registratur. **-ation** [-ˈstreɪʃən], *s.* die Eintragung, Anmeldung, Registrierung, das Einschreiben (*of a letter*); *-ation of luggage*, die Gepäckaufgabe; *-ation fee*, die Einschreibegebühr. *-ation form*, der Meldezettel. **-y** [-trɪ], *s.* die Registrierung; Registratur, das Standesamt; der Arbeitsnachweis, das Stellenvermittlungsbüro (*for servants*); *-y office*, das Standesamt; *married at a -y* (*office*), standesamtlich getraut.
Regius [ˈrɪ:dʒɪəs], *adj.* königlich; – *professor*, der Inhaber einer vom König gestifteten Professur (*Univ.*).
reglet [ˈrɛglɪt], *s.* der Zeilendurchschuß, Reglette (*Typ.*).
regna-l [ˈrɛgnəl], *adj.* Regierungs-; *-l day*, der Regierungsantrittstag. **-nt** [-nənt], *adj.* regierend; (*fig.*) (vor)herrschend.
regorge [rɪ:ˈgɔ:dʒ], 1. *v.a.* (wieder) ausspeien. 2. *v.n.* zurückströmen.
regress 1. *v.n.* [rɪˈgrɛs], zurückkehren (*Astr. & fig.*). 2. *s.* [ˈrɪ:grɛs], das Zurückkommen, Rückschreiten, die Rückkehr, der Rückschritt, Rückgang. **-ion** [rɪˈgrɛʃən], *s.* die Rückkehr; der Rückfall, Rückschlag. **-ive** [rɪˈgrɛsɪv], *adj.* rückläufig, rückgängig, rückwirkend, regressiv.
regret [rɪˈgrɛt], 1. *s.* das Bedauern, die Reue (*at*, über); Trauer, der Schmerz, Kummer (*for*, um); *to my* –, zu meinem Bedauern; *with many -s*, mit dem Ausdruck tief(st)en Bedauerns. 2. *v.a.* bedauern, beklagen, mit Bedauern denken an, zurückwünschen, schmerzlich vermissen; bereuen; *I – I cannot come* or *I – not being able to come*, ich bedauere nicht kommen zu können; *I – to see*, es tut mir leid sehen zu müssen, ich sehe mit Bedauern; *it is to be -ted*, es ist zu beklagen. **-ful,** *adj.* mit Bedauern, bedauernd, bereuend. **-table** [-əbl], *adj.* bedauerlich, bedauernswert, zu bedauern(d).
regroup [rɪ:ˈgru:p], *v.a.* umgruppieren, neu gruppieren.
regulable [ˈrɛgjʊləbl], *adj.* regulierbar.
regular [ˈrɛgjʊlə], 1. *adj.* ordentlich; regelmäßig (*also Gram.*), gleichmäßig, symmetrisch; gewohnheitsmäßig; regelrecht, ordentlich, geordnet, richtig, normal, anerkannt; genau, pünktlich; regulär (*Geom., Mil.*); (*coll.*) wirklich, echt, vollkommen, förmlich; – *clergy*, die Ordensgeistlichkeit; – *customer*, der Stammgast; – *doctor*, der Hausarzt; – *service*, fahrplanmäßiger Verkehr; – *soldier*, aktiver Soldat. 2. *s.* (*usually pl.*) Ordensgeistliche(r), *m.* (*Eccl.*); aktiver Soldat, der Berufsoldat; *pl.* reguläre Truppen. **-ity** [-ˈlærɪtɪ], *s.* die Regelmäßigkeit, Gleichmäßigkeit, Gesetzlichkeit; Richtigkeit, Ordnung. **-ize** [-ləraɪz], *v.a.* regeln, gesetzlich festlegen.
regulat-e [ˈrɛgjʊleɪt], *v.a.* regeln, ordnen, einrichten, bemessen, regulieren, stellen (*clocks, etc.*), anpassen (*to*, an); *-ing screw*, die Stellschraube. **-ion** [-ˈleɪʃən], 1. *s.* die Regulierung, Regelung; Verordnung, Anordnung, Vorschrift; *pl.* Satzungen, Bestimmungen, Statuten; *contrary to -ions*, vorschriftswidrig; *Queen's -ions*, die Dienstvorschrift, Null-acht-fünfzehn. 2. *attrib.* vorschriftsmäßig; Kommiß- (*Mil.*). **-ive** [-lətɪv], *adj.* ordnend, regelnd, regulativ. **-or** [-leɪtə], *s.* der Regler, Ordner, Regulator, die Reguliervorrichtung, Steuerung (*Tech.*); Wanduhr (*Horol.*).
regulus [ˈrɛgjʊləs], *s.* der Regulus, Metallkönig (*Chem.*); das Goldhähnchen (*Orn.*).
regurgitat-e [rɪ:ˈgə:dʒɪteɪt], 1. *v.a.* wiederausstoßen; *be -ed*, wieder hochkommen (*food*). 2. *v.n.* zurückfließen. **-ion** [-ˈteɪʃən], *s.* das Erbrechen.
rehabilitat-e [rɪ:həˈbɪlɪteɪt], *v.a.* wieder einsetzen, rehabilitieren, wieder zu Ehren bringen. **-ion** [-ˈteɪʃən], *s.* die Wiedereinsetzung, Rehabilitierung, Ehrenrettung.
rehash [rɪ:ˈhæʃ], 1. *v.a.* (*fig.*) aufwärmen, wieder aufbringen. 2. *s.* das Wiederaufwärmen (*of old ideas*); aufgewärmter Brei.
rehear [rɪ:ˈhɪ:ə], *v.a.* einmal untersuchen *or* verhandeln (*Law*). **-ing** [-rɪŋ], *s.* erneute Verhandlung.
rehear-sal [rɪˈhə:səl], *s.* das Wiederholen, Hersagen; die Probe (*Mus., Theat.*); *at -al*, bei der Probe, beim Proben; *be in -al*, einstudiert werden (*of a play*); *dress -al*, die Hauptprobe. **-e** [rɪˈhə:s], 1. *v.a.* wiederholen, hersagen. 2. *v.a. & n.* proben (*Theat.*).
rehouse [rɪ:ˈhaʊz], *v.a.* in einer neuen Wohnung unterbringen.
reign [reɪn], 1. *v.n.* regieren, herrschen (*over*, über (*Acc.*)); (*fig.*) (vor)herrschen. 2. *s.* die Herrschaft (*also fig.*), Regierung(szeit); (*fig.*) das Regiment; *in the – of*, unter der Regierung von; – *of Terror*, die Schreckensherrschaft.
reimburse [rɪ:ɪmˈbə:s], *v.a.* zurückerstatten, zurückzahlen (*money*); entschädigen (*a p.*); decken (*C.L.*); – *o.s.*, sich schadlos halten. **-ment,** *s.* die Rückzahlung; Entschädigung; Deckung (*C.L.*).
reimport 1. *v.a.* [rɪ:ɪmˈpɔ:t], wieder einführen. 2. *s.* [rɪ:ˈɪmpɔ:t] die Wiedereinführ; (*usually pl.*) wieder eingeführte Ware.
rein [reɪn], 1. *s.* der Zügel, Zaum (*also fig.*); *assume the -s of government*, die Zügel der Regierung ergreifen; *draw* –, anhalten; *give a horse the* –(*s*), dem Pferd die Zügel geben; (*fig.*) *give* –, die Zügel schießen lassen, freien Lauf lassen (*to* (*Dat.*)); *keep a tight – on*, straff im Zügel halten. 2. *v.a.* (also – *in*) zügeln, im Zaume halten (*also fig.*). **-less,** *adj.* zügellos.
reincarnat-e [rɪ:ɪnˈkɑ:neɪt], 1. *v.a.* wieder fleischliche Gestalt geben. 2. *v.n.* wieder Fleisch werden. **-ion** [-ˈneɪʃən], *s.* die Wiederfleischwerdung.
reindeer [ˈreɪndɪ:ə], *s.* das Renntier.
reinforce [rɪ:ɪnˈfɔ:s], 1. *v.a.* verstärken; (*fig.*) stärken, bekräftigen; *-d concrete*, der Eisenbeton. 2. *s.* die Verstärkung (*Tech.*). **-ment,** *s.* die Stärkung; (*fig.*) Bekräftigung; *pl.* Verstärkungstruppen (*pl.*), die Verstärkung, der Nachschub (*Mil.*).
reinless, *see* **rein.**
reins [reɪnz], *pl.* (*B.*) Nieren (*pl.*).
reinstall [rɪ:ɪnˈstɔ:l], *v.a.* wiedereinsetzen. **-ment,** *s.* die Wiedereinsetzung.
reinstate [rɪ:ɪnˈsteɪt], *v.a.* wiedereinsetzen (*a p.*); wiederherstellen (*a th.*). **-ment,** *s.* die Wiedereinsetzung; Wiederherstellung.
reinsur-ance [rɪ:ɪnˈʃʊ:ərəns], die Rückversicherung. **-e** [-ˈʃʊ:ə], *v.a.* rückversichern.
reinvest [rɪ:ɪnˈvɛst], *v.a.* wiedereinsetzen (*in*, in (*Acc.*)); wieder bekleiden (*with*, mit); wieder anlegen (*money*). **-iture** [-ɪtʃʊ:ə], *s.* die Wiedereinführung, Wiedereinsetzung. **-ment,** *s.* die Wiederanlegung, Wiederanlage (*of money*).

reinvigorate [riːɪnˈvɪgəreɪt], *v.a.* von neuem stärken.
reissue [riːˈɪʃ(j)uː], 1. *v.a.* wieder ausgeben; neu herausgeben (*books*). 2. *s.* die Wiederausgabe; unveränderte Neuausgabe.
reitera-nt [riːˈɪtərənt] *adj.* wiederholend. **-te** [-reɪt], *v.a.* ständig wiederholen. **-tion** [-ˈreɪʃən], *s.* ständige Wiederholung. **-ative** [-rətɪv], *adj.* ständig wiederholend.
reject [rɪˈdʒɛkt], *v.a.* ablehnen, ausschlagen, nicht annehmen; zurückweisen, nicht anerkennen, verwerfen; abweisen (*a p.*); verschmähen (*a suitor*); wieder von sich geben (*of the stomach*). **-ion** [-ʃən], *s.* die Ablehnung, Zurückweisung, Verwerfung, Abweisung; *pl.* Exkremente (*pl.*). **-or circuit**, *s.* der Drosselkreis.
rejoic-e [rɪˈdʒɔɪs], 1. *v.a.* erfreuen; *be -ed*, sich freuen, erfreut sein (*over* or *at*, über (*Acc.*)). 2. *v.n.* sich freuen (*at* or *over*, über); *-e in s.th.*, sich einer S. (*Gen.*) erfreuen. **-ing**, 1. *adj.* freudig, freudevoll; froh. 2. *s.* die Freude (*over*, über); *pl.* Freudenbezeigungen, Festlichkeiten (*pl.*).
[1]**rejoin** [rɪˈdʒɔɪn], *v.n.* erwidern (*usually Law*). **-der** [-də], *s.* die Erwiderung; Duplik (*Law*).
[2]**rejoin** [riːˈdʒɔɪn], *v.a.* wieder zusammenfügen; sich wieder vereinigen mit, wieder zurückkehren zu; wieder treffen (*a p.*).
rejuven-ate [rɪˈdʒuːvəneɪt], *v.a.* (& *n.*), (sich) verjüngen. **-ation** [-ˈneɪʃən], *s.* die Verjüngung. **-esce** [-ˈnɛs], *v.a.* (& *n.*) (sich) verjüngen, (sich) neu beleben (*Biol.*, *etc.*). **-escence** [-ˈnɛsəns], *s.* die Verjüngung, Neubelebung (*Biol.*). **-escent** [-ˈnɛsənt], *adj.* (sich) verjüngend. **-ize** [-naɪz], *v.a.* verjüngen.
rekindle [riːˈkɪndl], 1. *v.a.* wieder entzünden *or* anzünden; (*fig.*) neu beleben. 2. *v.n.* sich wieder entzünden, (*fig.*) wieder aufleben.
relapse [riːˈlæps], 1. *v.n.* zurückfallen, wieder verfallen (*into*, in); rückfällig werden; einen Rückfall bekommen (*Med.*). 2. *s.* der Rückfall (*into*, in), das Zurückfallen.
relat-e [riːˈleɪt], 1. *v.a.* berichten, erzählen (*to* (*Dat.*)); in Beziehung *or* Verbindung bringen, verknüpfen (*with*, mit; *to*, zu), verbinden, Beziehung herstellen zwischen. 2. *v.n.* sich beziehen (*to*, auf (*Acc.*)); in Bezug stehen (*to*, zu); *-ing to*, mit Bezug auf (*Acc.*). **-ed** [-ɪd], *adj.* verwandt; in Beziehung zueinander stehend; *be -ed to*, verwandt sein mit; *-ed by marriage*, verschwägert. **-ion** [-ʃən], *s.* die Erzählung, der Bericht; die Beziehung, der Bezug, Zusammenhang; das Verhältnis (*to*, zu), die Verbindung; Verwandtschaft (*to*, mit); (Bluts)Verwandte(r), *f.* (*m.*); *pl.* Beziehungen (*pl.*) (*with*, mit *or* zu); *in -ion to*, in bezug auf (*Acc.*); in Beziehung zu; *have -ion to*, in Beziehung stehen zu; *have -ion*, rückwirkende Kraft haben (*Law*); *be out of -ion to*, in keiner Beziehung stehen zu. **-ionship**, *s.* die Verwandtschaft (*to*, mit); das Verhältnis, die Verbindung. **-ive** [ˈrɛlətɪv], 1. *adj.* relativ (*also Gram.*); bezüglich (*also Gram.*), sich beziehend (*to*, auf (*Acc.*)); bedingt, verhältnismäßig, proportional, entsprechend (*to* (*Dat.*)); *be -ive to*, sich beziehen auf, in Beziehung stehen zu, entsprechen; bedingt sein durch; *-ive pronoun*, das Relativpronomen; 2. *s.* das Relativpronomen; Verwandte(r), *f.* (*m.*). **-iveness** [ˈrɛlətɪvnɪs], *s.* die Bedingtheit. **-ivism** [ˈrɛlətɪvɪzm], *s.* der Relativismus. **-ivity** [rɛləˈtɪvɪtɪ], *s.* die Relativität; Bedingtheit; *theory of -ivity*, die Relativitätstheorie.
relax [riːˈlæks], 1. *v.a.* entspannen, lockern, schlaff, lose *or* locker machen, öffnen (*bowels*); (*fig.*) schwächen, mildern, mäßigen, vermindern; *- one's efforts*, in seinen Bemühungen nachlassen. 2. *v.n.* sich entspannen *or* lockern, erschlaffen; nachlassen, mäßiger *or* milder werden. **-ation** [-ˈseɪʃən] *s.* die Lockerung, Entspannung, Erschlaffung; Milderung, Erleichterung (*Law*); Zerstreuung, Erholung; *without -ation*, ohne Nachlassen. **-ed** [-t], *adj.* entspannt, schlaff, matt. **-ing**, *adj.* erschlaffend, weich.
[1]**relay** [rɪˈleɪ], 1. *s*, frischer Vorspann, der Pferdewechsel; Ort des Pferdewechsels; Relaiposten, die Ablösung(smannschaft) (*Mil.*); das Relais (*Tele.*); die Übertragung (*Rad.*); *in -s*, im rollenden Einsatz (*Mil.* & *fig.*). 2. *v.a.* ablösen; übertragen (*Rad.*). **--race**, *s.* der Staffellauf, Stafettenlauf.
[2]**relay** [riːˈleɪ], *v.a.* umlegen, neu legen (*a pavement, etc.*).
release [rɪˈliːs], 1. *v.a.* loslassen, losgehen lassen, fallen lassen; entlassen, freilassen, befreien (*from*, aus) (*also fig. from*, von); (*fig.*) erlösen (*from*, von), entheben, entbinden (*from* (*Dat.*)), aufgeben (*a right*), erlassen (*a debt*), übertragen (*land*) (*to* (*Dat.*)), freigeben (*to the public*) (*Theat.*, *Film*, *etc.*); auslösen, ausrücken, ausschalten (*Tech.*). 2. *s.* das Loslassen, Fallenlassen; die Entlassung, Freilassung; Befreiung, Erlösung; Entlastung, Entbindung (*from*, von); Verzichtleistung, der Verzicht (*of*, auf (*Acc.*)), die Rechtsübertragung, die Verzichturkunde (*Law*); Freigabe (*of films, goods, etc.*); Auslösung, Ausklinkung (*Tech.*).
relegat-e [ˈrɛləgeɪt], *v.a.* verweisen (*to*, an), verbannen, relegieren (*a p.*); verurteilen (*to*, nach); übergeben, zuweisen (*to* (*Dat.*)). **-ion** [-ˈgeɪʃən], *s.* die Verbannung, Verweisung, Überweisung.
relent [rɪˈlɛnt], *v.n.* sich erweichen lassen, nachgiebig *or* weich *or* mitleidig werden. **-ing**, *adj.* nachgiebig, mitleidig, mitleidsvoll. **-less**, *adj.* unnachgiebig, unbarmherzig, unnachsichtig, hartnäckig. **-lessness**, *s.* die Unnachgiebigkeit, Unbarmherzigkeit.
re-let [riːlɛt], *v.a.* wieder vermieten *or* verpachten.
relevan-ce, -cy [ˈrɛləvəns(ɪ)], *s.* die Erheblichkeit, Wichtigkeit, Bedeutung (*to*, für); Angemessenheit. **-t** [-vənt], *adj.* erheblich, wichtig (*to*, für), sachdienlich, entsprechend (*to* (*Dat.*)), anwendbar (*to*, auf), gehörig (*to*, zu), einschlägig.
reliab-ility [rɪlaɪəˈbɪlɪtɪ], *s.* die Zuverlässigkeit. **-le** [-ˈlaɪəbl], *adj.* zuverlässig, verläßlich, glaubwürdig.
relian-ce [rɪˈlaɪəns], *s.* das Vertrauen (*on*, auf), die Zuversicht (*in* or (*up*)*on*, in *or* auf), der Verlaß; *have -ce in* or *on*, vertrauen auf, Vertrauen haben zu; *place -ce on*, vertrauen auf, Vertrauen setzen in (*Acc.*). **-t** [-ənt], *adj.* vertrauend (*on*, auf (*Acc.*)); *self--t*, voll Selbstvertrauen.
relic [ˈrɛlɪk], *s.* die Reliquie (*of a saint, etc.*); das Andenken, Gedenkstück; letzter Rest, letzte Spur; *pl.* Überreste (*of a p. or th.*), Überbleibsel (*of a th.*).
relict [ˈrɛlɪkt], *s.* (*rare*) Hinterbliebene, *f.*, die Witwe.
relief [rɪˈliːf], *s.* die Erleichterung, Entlastung, Befreiung (*from*, von); Linderung, der Trost; Erlaß, die Abhilfe (*Law*); die (Armen)Unterstützung; Erholung, angenehme Abwechslung (*to*, für); die Ablösung (*of a sentry*); der Entsatz (*of a town*); erhabene Arbeit, das Relief (*Sculp.*, *etc.*); das Hervortreten, Hervorhebung, plastische Darstellung (*Paint.*); die Höhengestaltung, das Hochbild (*maps*); *throw into -*, hervortreten lassen, hervorheben; *stand out in bold -*, sich scharf abheben, deutlich hervortreten; *to my -*, zu meinem Trost. **- column**, *s.* Hilfstruppen (*pl.*), der Entsatz. **--fund**, *s.* der Unterstützungsfond, Hilfsfond. **--map**, *s.* die Hochbildkarte, Reliefkarte. **--train**, der Vorzug, außerfahrplanmäßiger Zug (*Railw.*). **--work**, *s.* die Notstandsarbeit, das Hilfswerk. **--worker**, *s.* der Ersatzarbeiter, Hilfsarbeiter.
reliev-e [rɪˈliːv], *v.a.* erleichtern, mildern, lindern, abschwächen, abhelfen; helfen (*Dat.*), unterstützen (*the poor*); ablösen (*sentry*), entsetzen (*a town*); entlasten, entbinden (*of*, von (*or Dat.*)), befreien (*of*, von); entheben, berauben (*a p.*) (*of*, (*Gen.*)); hervorheben, abheben (*Paint, etc.*); (*fig.*) angenehm unterbrechen; beruhigen (*one's mind*); *-e one's feelings*, seinen Gefühlen Luft machen; *-e the monotony*, die Eintönigkeit beleben, Abwechslung bringen (*of*, in); *-e nature*, sein Bedürfnis verrichten; *be -ed to hear*, leichter zumute werden, als man erfährt. **-ing**, *adj.* erleichternd; *-ing arch*, der Entlastungsbogen; *-ing officer*, der Armenpfleger. **-o** [-voʊ], *s.* das Relief, erhabene Arbeit.
religio-n [rɪˈlɪdʒən], *s.* die Religion; (*fig.*) fromme Pflicht, heiliger Grundsatz. **-nist** [-ɪst], *s.* reli-

giöser Schwärmer *or* Eiferer. **-sity** [-ɪ'ɔsɪtɪ], *s.* die Religiosität, Frömmelei. **-us** [-dʒəs], *adj.* religiös, fromm, gottesfürchtig; gewissenhaft, streng; *-us house*, das Ordenshaus; *-us orders*, geistliche Orden; *-us service*, der Gottesdienst; *-us silence*, andächtiges Stillschweigen.
relinquish [rɪ'lɪŋkwɪʃ], *v.a.* loslassen; abstehen von, verzichten auf; aufgeben, abtreten (*to*, an), überlassen (*to* (*Dat.*)). **-ment**, *s.* das Überlassen; Aufgeben (*Gen.*), der Verzicht (*auf* (*Acc.*)).
reliquary ['rɛlɪkwərɪ], *s.* das Reliquienkästchen.
relish ['rɛlɪʃ], 1. *s.* der Geschmack; Reiz, Wohlgeschmack; das Wohlbehagen, (Wohl)Gefallen, Genuß (*for*, an (*Dat.*)), die Neigung (*for*, zu); pikante Beigabe, die Würze, der Appetitanreger; (*fig.*) Beigeschmack, Anstrich; *have no* –, nicht schmecken; *have no – for*, keinen Geschmack finden an, keine Neigung haben zu; *eat with* –, es sich (*Dat.*) schmecken lassen. 2. *v.a.* mit Behagen genießen, Geschmack *or* Gefallen finden an (*Dat.*); *do you – your dinner?* schmeckt *or* mundet dir das Mittagessen?
relive [rɪ:'lɪv], *v.a.* wieder erleben *or* durchleben.
reload [rɪ:'loud], *v.a. & n.* wieder laden (*Gun.*), umladen (*Railw., etc.*).
reluctan-ce [rɪ'lʌktəns], *s.* die Abneigung, das Widerstreben, der Widerwille (*to*, gegen); magnetischer Widerstand (*Elec.*); *with -ce*, ungern, widerstrebend. **-t** [-ənt], *adj.* widerwillig, widerstrebend, abgeneigt; *be -t to do*, ungern tun, es widerstrebt (*Dat.*) zu tun. **-tly**, *adv.* ungern, wider Willen.
rely [rɪ'laɪ], *v.n.* sich verlassen, vertrauen, bauen, zählen ((*up*)*on*, auf (*Acc.*)).
remain [rɪ'meɪn], *v.n.* zurückbleiben, übrigbleiben, noch vorhanden *or* übrig(geblieben) sein; bleiben; verbleiben (*in letters*); *he -s himself*, er bleibt derselbe; *– of the opinion*, (bei) der Meinung bleiben; *it -s to be proved*, es bedarf noch des Beweises; *it -s to be seen*, es bleibt abzuwarten; *it -s to be told*, es muß noch berichtet werden; *nothing -s to me but*, nichts bleibt mir übrig als. **-der** [-də], 1. *s.* das Überbleibsel, der Rest, Rückstand (*also Arith.*); Übriggebliebene (*pl.*) (*things*), Überlebende (*pl.*) (*persons*); Restbestände (*C.L.*); die Restauflage (*books*); das Anfallsrecht, die Anwartschaft (*Law*). 2. *v.a.* billig abstoßen (*books*). **-ing,** *adj.* übrig(geblieben); Rest–; *have -ing*, übrig haben; *-ing stock*, der Restbestand; *the -ing*, die Übrigen. **-s** [-z], *pl.* (*also sing. constr.*) Überbleibsel, Überreste, Reste; irdische Überreste; (*fig.*) letzte Reste (*pl.*); *literary -s*, hinterlassene Werke (*pl.*), literarischer Nachlaß.
remake [rɪ:'meɪk], *ir.v.a.* wieder machen, erneuern.
remand [rɪ'mɑ:nd], 1. *v.a.*; (also *– into custody*) in die Untersuchungshaft zurücksenden. 2. *s.* die Zurücksendung in die Untersuchungshaft; *appear on* –, nach der Untersuchung wieder vor Gericht erscheinen; *prisoner on* –, Untersuchungsgefangene(r), *m.*
remark [rɪ'mɑ:k], 1. *s.* die Bemerkung, Äußerung; der Vermerk, die Anmerkung; *excite* –, Aufmerksamkeit erregen; *without* –, ohne Kommentar, stillschweigend. 2. *v.a.* bemerken, vermerken, beobachten, gewahr werden; (*followed by* that) bemerken, äußern. 3. *v.n.* sich äußern, Bemerkungen machen ((*up*)*on*, über); *– on*, erwähnen. **-able,** *adj.* bemerkenswert, einzigartig, auffallend, merkwürdig, außerordentlich, erstaunlich. **-ableness,** *s.* die Merkwürdigkeit.
remarr-iage [rɪ:'mærɪdʒ], *s.* die Wiederverheiratung. **-y** [-'mærɪ], 1. *v.n.* wieder heiraten, sich wieder verheiraten. 2. *v.a.* wieder verheiraten (*to*, mit).
remed-iable [rɪ'mɪ:dɪəbl], *adj.* abstellbar; abzuhelfen(d); heilbar. **-ial** [-dɪəl], *adj.* heilend, heilsam, Heil–, abhelfend, Abhilfs–; *-ial gymnastics*, die Heilgymnastik; *-ial measures*, Abhilfsmaßnahmen (*pl.*). **-iless** ['rɛmɪdɪləs], *adj.* unheilbar, unersetzbar; hilflos, machtlos. **-y** ['rɛmɪdɪ], 1. *s.* das (Heil)Mittel, die Arznei (*for*, gegen); das Hilfsmittel, Gegenmittel; das Rechtsmittel, die Abhilfe (*Law, etc.*). 2. *v.a.* helfen (*Dat.*); (*fig.*) abhelfen (*Dat.*), abstellen.
rememb-er [rɪ'mɛmbə], 1. *v.a.* sich erinnern *or* entsinnen ((*Gen.*) *or* an (*Acc.*)), sich besinnen auf (*Acc.*), sich (*Dat.*) ins Gedächtnis zurückrufen; im Gedächtnis behalten, sich (*Dat.*) vor Augen halten, denken an, gedenken *or* eingedenk sein (*Gen.*); bedenken (*in one's will*); grüßen; *-er me to your sister*, grüße deine Schwester von mir; *-er o.s.*, sich auf sich selbst besinnen; *I -er seeing* or *having seen him*, ich erinnere mich ihn gesehen zu haben; *she wishes to be -ered to you*, sie läßt dich grüßen. 2. *v.n.* sich erinnern, entsinnen, besinnen *or* bedenken. **-rance** [-brəns], *s.* die Erinnerung (*of*, an); das Gedächtnis; Andenken; *pl.* Empfehlungen, Grüße (*pl.*); *call to -rance*, in die Erinnerung rufen; *escape one's -rance*, seinem Gedächtnis entfallen; *give my kind -rances to him*, grüßen Sie ihn bestens von mir, empfehlen Sie mich ihm bestens; *have in -rance*, in der Erinnerung haben; *in -rance of*, zum Andenken an (*Acc.*); *within my -rance*, soweit ich mich erinnere; *-rance service*, der Gedächtnisgottesdienst. **-rancer** [-brənsə], *s.* der Mahner, Erinnerer (*of*, an (*Acc.*)); Schatzkammerbeamte(r), *m.* (*Hist.*).
remind [rɪ'maɪnd], *v.a.* erinnern, mahnen (*of*, an (*Acc.*)); *you – me of him*, du rufst die Erinnerung an ihn in mir wach; *that -s me*, da(bei) fällt mir (etwas) ein. **-er** [-ə], *s.* der Wink, die Mahnung (*of*, an; *to*, an *or* für); *be a -er of*, erinnern an. **-ful,** *adj.* erinnernd, mahnend (*of*, an (*Acc.*)).
reminisce ['rɛmɪnɪs], *v.n.* (*coll.*) Erinnerungen erzählen. **-nce,** [-'nɪsəns], *s.* die Erinnerung; der Anklang (*of*, an (*Acc.*)); *pl.* Erinnerungen, Reminiszenzen (*pl.*). **-nt** [-'nɪsənt], *adj.* erinnernd, Erinnerungs–; *be -nt of*, erinnern an, die Erinnerungen wachrufen an.
[1]**remise** [rɪ'maɪz], 1. *v.a.* zurückerstatten, überlassen (*Law*). 2. *s.* die Zurückerstattung, Überlassung (*Law*).
[2]**remise** [rə'mɪ:z], 1. *s.* der Wagenschuppen; Nachstoß, Nachhieb (*Fenc.*). 2. *v.n.* einen Nachhieb versetzen (*Fenc.*).
remiss [rɪ'mɪs], *adj.* (nach)lässig, säumig, träge. **-ible** [-ɪbl], *adj.* erläßlich, verzeihlich. **-ion** [-'mɪʃən], *s.* die Abnahme, das Nachlassen; die Vergebung (*of sins*); Erlassung (*of debt, penalty*), Ermäßigung (*of fees, taxes*). **-ness** [-'mɪsnɪs], *s.* die (Nach)Lässigkeit.
remit [rɪ'mɪt], 1. *v.a.* übersenden, überweisen (*to* (*Dat.*)) (*money*); vergeben (*sins*), erlassen (*debt, penalty*), nachlassen in, mäßigen; zurückverweisen (*Law*), verweisen (*to*, an), ausliefern (*to* (*Dat.*)). 2. *v.n.* nachlassen, abnehmen; Zahlung leisten, remittieren (*C.L.*). **-tal** [-əl], *s.* die Erlassung; Verweisung (*Law*). **-tance** [-əns], *s.* die Rimesse, Tratte, Geldsendung; Übersendung, Remittierung; *make a -tance*, remittieren. **-tee** [-'tɪ:], *s.* der Empfänger einer Geldsendung. **-tent** [-'mɪtənt], 1. *adj.* nachlassend, remittierend (*Med.*). 2. *s.* remitterendes Fieber. **-ter** [-tə], *s.* der Remittent, Geldsender (*C.L.*); die Wiedereinsetzung (*to*, in) (*Law*), Verweisung (*to*, an).
remnant ['rɛmnənt], *s.* der (Über)Rest, das Überbleibsel; der (Stoff)Rest; (*fig.*) letzter Rest. **--sale,** der Resterausverkauf.
remodel [rɪ:'mɔdəl], *v.a.* umbilden, umformen, umgestalten, ummodeln.
remonetiz-ation [rɪ:mʌnɪtaɪ'zeɪʃən], *s.* die Wiederinkurssetzung. **-e** [rɪ:'mʌnɪtaɪz], *v.a.* wieder in Kurs *or* Umlauf setzen.
remonstra-nce [rɪ'mɔnstrəns], *s.* die Vorstellung, Einwendung, der Einspruch, Protest. **-nt** [-ənt], 1. *adj.* protestierend, remonstrierend. 2. *s.* der Remonstrant (*Hist.*). **-te** ['rɛmənstreɪt], 1. *v.n.* Vorstellungen *or* Einwendungen machen (*on*, über; *with a p.*, einem), remonstrieren, protestieren, einwenden. **-tion** [rɛmən'streɪʃən], *s.* die Einwendung. **-tive** [rɪ'mɔnstrətɪv], *adj.* protestierend, remonstrierend.
remontant [rɪ'mɔntənt], 1. *adj.* wiederholt blühend, remontierend (*Bot.*). 2. *s.* die Remontante, remontierende Pflanze (*Bot.*).
remora ['rɛmərə], *s.* (*rare*) die Stockung, das Hindernis; Schildfisch (*Ichth.*).
remorse [rɪ'mɔ:s], *s.* (*only sing.*) Gewissensbisse

(*pl.*), die Reue, Gewissensnot (*at*, über; *for*, wegen). **–ful,** *adj.* reuevoll, reumütig. **–fulness,** *s.* die Reumütigkeit. **–less,** *adj.* (*fig.*) unbarmherzig, hartherzig, gefühllos, grausam. **–lessness,** *s.* die Gefühllosigkeit, Umbarmherzigkeit.

remote [rɪˈmoʊt], *adj.* entfernt (*also fig.*), entlegen (*from*, von); abgelegen, einsam; (*fig.*) weit entfernt, schwach, vage; – *antiquity*, das graue Altertum; *not the –st idea*, nicht die geringste Ahnung; – *relation*, entfernte(r) Verwandte(r); – *control*, die Fernlenkung, Fernsteuerung. **–ness,** *s.* die Entlegenheit, Entfernung.

remould [rɪːˈmoʊld], *v.a.* umformen, umgestalten.

remount [rɪːmaʊnt], 1. *v.n.* wieder besteigen, aufsteigen *or* ersteigen; zurückkehren (*to*, zu), zurückgehen (*to*, auf), zurückreichen (*to*, (bis) in). 2. *v.a.* wieder besteigen (*a horse*); mit frischen Pferden versehen (*cavalry*); wieder aufstellen (*a machine*). 3. *s.* die Remonte; das Remontepferd (*Mil.*).

remov–ability [rɪmuːvəˈbɪlɪtɪ], *s.* die Entfernbarkeit; Absetzbarkeit (*of officials*). **–able** [rɪˈmuːvəbl], *adj.* entfernbar, abnehmbar; zu beseitigen(d), absetzbar (*as officials*). **–al** [rɪˈmuːvl], *s.* das Wegschaffen, Fortschaffen; (*fig.*) die Beseitigung, Entfernung, Versetzung; Entlassung, Absetzung (*of a p.*) (*from*, aus); der Umzug, das Ausziehen (*from a house, etc.*). **–e** [rɪˈmuːv], 1. *v.a.* (*with things*) wegschaffen, fortschaffen, wegräumen, forträumen, entfernen; beseitigen, beheben (*doubts*); ablegen (*one's clothes*), abnehmen (*one's hat, the receiver, a bandage, etc.*); zurückziehen, zurücknehmen (*one's hand*); tilgen, verwischen (*traces*); (*with persons*) entfernen (lassen), abführen, fortnehmen; beseitigen, töten (lassen); entlassen (*from office*) (*from*, aus); versetzen; *–e from the agenda*, von der Tagesordnung absetzen; *–e the cloth*, (den Tisch) abdecken; *–e furniture*, Möbeltransport ausführen, besorgen *or* unternehmen; *–e mountains*, Berge versetzen; *–e into hospital*, ins Krankenhaus schaffen; *–e with acid*, wegätzen. 2. *v.n.* ausziehen, (um)ziehen, verziehen (*from a house*); sich entfernen *or* wegbegeben (*from*, von), ziehen (*to*, nach); *–e into*, einziehen in, beziehen. 3. *s.* die Versetzung (*in school*); Stufe, Klasse (*in some schools*); Entfernung, der Abstand; Verwandschaftsgrad; *but one –e from*, nur ein Schritt von; *get one's –e*, versetzt werden. **–ed,** *adj.* entfernt; *cousin twice –ed*, der Vetter zweiten Grades. **–er** [–ə], *s.* der Möbeltransporteur, Möbelspediteur; *stain –er*, das Fleckenreinigungsmittel.

remuner–able [rɪˈmjuːnərəbl], *adj.* vergeltbar, vergütbar. **–ate** [–əreɪt], *v.a.* vergelten (*Dat.*), belohnen (*a p.*); vergüten, entschädigen, bezahlt machen (*of things*). **–ation** [–ˈreɪʃən], *s.* die Belohnung, Vergütung, das Honorar, der Lohn. **–ative** [–rətɪv], *adj.* (be)lohnend, einträglich.

renaissance [rəˈneɪsəns], *s.* die Renaissance, (*fig.*) Wiedergeburt, das Wiedererwachen.

renal [ˈrɪːnəl], *adj.* Nieren–.

rename [rɪːˈneɪm], *v.a.* umnennen, anders benennen, umtaufen.

renascen–ce [rɪˈnæsəns], *s.* die Wiedergeburt, Erneuerung, das Wiederaufleben. **–t** [–ənt], *adj.* wieder auflebend, sich erneuend.

rencounter [rɛnˈkaʊntə], *s.* (*rare*) zufälliges Zusammentreffen, der Zusammenstoß; das Treffen.

rend [rɛnd], *ir.v.a.* & *n.* reißen, aufreißen, (also – *asunder*) zerreißen, losreißen; – *in two*, entzweireißen; (*fig.*) durchdringen, erschüttern (*of cries*).

render [ˈrɛndə], 1. *v.a.* zurückgeben, zurückerstatten; übergeben, überreichen (*to* (*Dat.*)), abtreten (*to*, an); (*fig.*) leisten (*help*), erstatten (*to* (*Dat.*)); vergelten (*evil for good, etc.*) (*for*, mit); übersetzen, übertragen, wiedergeben (*also Art*); vortragen (*Mus.*), darstellen (*Art*); angeben (*reasons*); abstatten (*thanks*); zahlen (*tribute*), erweisen (*service*); (*with pred. adj.*) machen; (*with noun*) machen zu; ausschmelzen, auslassen (*fat*); verputzen, bewerfen (*Build.*); – *an account*, Rechenschaft ablegen (*of*, von *or* über); Rechnung (vor)legen (*C.L.*); *for services –ed*, für treue Dienste; *to account –ed*, laut erhaltener Rechnung (*C.L.*); – *possible*, ermöglichen; – *up*, herausgeben. 2. *s.* die Zahlung, Gegenleistung; der Bewurf (*Build.*). **–ing** [–ərɪŋ], *s.* die Rückgabe, Wiedergabe (*also fig.*), Darstellung (*Art*); der Vortrag (*Mus., etc.*); die Übersetzung, Übertragung; der Bewurf (*Build.*); *–ing of accounts*, die Rechnungsablegung, Rechnungsaufstellung; *–ing of thanks*, die Danksagung.

rendezvous [ˈrɔndɪvuː], 1. *s.* (*pl.* – [–z]) das Stelldichein, Rendezvous, die Zusammenkunft; der Treffpunkt, Sammelplatz (*Mil.*). 2. *v.n.* zusammenkommen, sich einstellen *or* versammeln.

rendition [rɛnˈdɪʃən], *s.* (*rare*) die Übergabe, Zurückgabe; Übersetzung, Wiedergabe.

renega–de [ˈrɛnɪgeɪd], 1. *s.* Abtrünnige(r), *m.*, der Renegat, Überläufer. 2. *v.n.* abtrünnig werden. **–tion** [–ˈgeɪʃən], *s.* der Abfall, die Verleugnung.

renew [rɪˈnjuː], *v.a.* erneuern, wieder herstellen, ersetzen, wiederholen; wieder beginnen, neu aufnehmen; verlängern, prolongieren (*C.L.*). **–able,** *adj.* erneuerbar, zu erneuern(d), verlängerbar. **–al,** *s.* die Erneuerung, Prolongation (*C.L.*). **–er,** *s.* der Erneu(e)rer, die Erneuerin.

reniform [ˈrɪːnɪfɔːm], *adj.* nierenförmig.

[1]rennet [ˈrɛnɪt], *s.* das Lab.

[2]rennet, *s.* die Renette (*Bot.*).

renounce [rɪˈnaʊns], 1. *v.a.* (*with things*) entsagen (*Dat.*), verzichten (auf (*Acc.*)); abstehen von, aufgeben, sich lossagen von, ablehnen, zurückweisen; abschwören (*beliefs*); nicht bedienen (*Cards*); (*with persons*) verleugnen. 2. *v.n.* Verzicht leisten; nicht bekennen können (*Cards*). 3. *s.* die Renonce (*Cards*). **–ment,** *s.* die Entsagung, der Verzicht.

renovat–e [ˈrɛnəveɪt], *v.a.* erneuern, wiederherstellen, renovieren. **–ion** [–ˈveɪʃən], *s.* die Erneuerung. **–or** [–veɪtə], *s.* der Erneuerer.

renown [rɪˈnaʊn], *s.* der Ruhm, guter Ruf *or* Name. **–ed,** *adj.* berühmt, namhaft.

[1]rent [rɛnt], *s.* der Riß, die Spalte; *see also* **rend.**

[2]rent, 1. *s.* die (Haus)Miete, Wohnungsmiete (*of house*), Pacht, der Pachtzins, Mietzins (*of land*). 2. *v.a.* mieten, pachten (*from*, von); vermieten, verpachten (*to* (*Dat.*)). 3. *v.n.* vermietet *or* verpachtet werden (*at*, zu). **–al,** 1. *attrib.* Miets–, Pacht–; *–al allowance*, der Wohnungsgeldzuschuß. 2. *s.* die Mietsumme, Pachtsumme; der Mietsatz, Pachtsatz; das Zinsbuch. **– -charge,** *s.* der Erbzins. **– -day,** *s.* der Mietzahlungstag. **– -free,** *adj.* mietfrei, pachtfrei. **– -roll,** *s.* das Zinsbuch.

renunciation [rɪnʌnsɪˈeɪʃən], *s.* der Verzicht (*of*, auf), die Entsagung, Ablehnung; (Selbst)Verläugnung.

reoccup–ation [rɪːɔkjuˈpeɪʃən], *s.* die Wiederbesetzung. **–y** [–ˈɔkjupaɪ], *v.a.* wieder besetzen *or* einnehmen.

reopen [rɪˈoupən], 1. *v.a.* wieder öffnen; (*fig.*) wieder eröffnen, beginnen, aufnehmen *or* in Betrieb setzen. 2. *v.n.* sich wieder öffnen; wieder anfangen.

reorgan–ization [rɪːɔːgənaɪˈzeɪʃən], *s.* die Neugestaltung; Sanierung (*C.L.* & *Pol.*); Umgruppierung (*Mil.*). **–ize** [rɪːˈɔːgənaɪz], *v.a.* neugestalten, umgestalten; sanieren (*C.L.* & *Pol.*); umgruppieren (*Mil.*).

reorientat–e [rɪːˈɔːrɪənteɪt], *v.a.* neu orientieren. **–ion** [–ˈteɪʃən], *s.* die Neuorientierung, Umorientierung.

[1]rep [rɛp], *s.* (*coll.*) verrufener Mensch.

[2]rep(p) [rɛp], **reps** [–s], *s.* der Rips.

repack [rɪːˈpæk], *v.a.* umpacken.

repaint [rɪːˈpeɪnt], *v.a.* neu anstreichen, übermalen.

[1]repair [rɪˈpɛːə], 1. *s.* die Ausbesserung, Reparatur (*to*, an); Instandsetzung, Wiederherstellung; *pl.* Instandsetzungsarbeiten (*pl.*); *in good* or *thorough* –, in gutem Zustande, gut erhalten; *in need of* –, reparaturbedürftig; *out of* –, baufällig; *under* –, in Reparatur. 2. *v.a.* ausbessern, reparieren; (*coll.*) flicken; (*fig.*) wieder herstellen; wiedergutmachen (*a wrong*), ersetzen (*a loss*). **–able** [–rəbl], *adj.* reparierbar, reparaturfähig. **–er** [–rə], *s.* der Ausbesserer; *shoe-–er*, *s.* der Schuster. **– -outfit,** *s.* der Flickkasten, Reparaturkasten (*Cycl.*). **– -shop,** *s.* die Reparaturwerkstatt.

[2]repair, *v.n.*; sich begeben, ziehen (*to*, **nach**).

repaper [rɪːˈpeɪpə] *v.a.* neu tapezieren.

repara–ble [ˈrɛpərəbl], *adj.* (*fig.*) wiedergutzumachen(d), ersetzbar. **–tion** [–ˈreɪʃən], *s.* die Entschädigung, Genugtuung, der Ersatz (*for*, für); *pl.* Reparationen, Reparationszahlungen (*pl.*); *make –tion(s)*, Ersatz *or* Genugtuung leisten.
repartee [rɛpɑːˈtɪː], *s.* schlagfertige Antwort; die Schlagfertigkeit; *quick at –*, schlagfertig.
repartition [rɪːpɑːˈtɪʃən], 1. *s.* die (Wieder)Einteilung *or* Aufteilung, Neuverteilung. 2. *v.a.* neu aufteilen, einteilen *or* verteilen.
repass [rɪːˈpɑːs], 1. *v.n.* zurückgehen, zurückkommen. 2. *v.a.* wieder vorbeigehen *or* vorbeikommen an (*Dat.*).
repast [rɪˈpɑːst], *s.* die Mahlzeit, das Mahl.
repatriat–e [rɪːˈpætrɪeɪt], *v.a.* in die Heimat zurücksenden. **–ion** [–ˈeɪʃən], *s.* die Zurucksendung in die Heimat, Heimkehr ins Vaterland, Heimschaffung.
repay [rɪːˈpeɪ], 1. *v.a.* zurückzahlen; (*fig.*) heimzahlen, vergelten, entschädigen (*a p.*), erwidern (*greeting, etc.*), lohnen (*trouble*), entschädigen für; *it –s reading*, es lohnt sich gelesen zu werden. 2. *v.n.* sich lohnen, der Mühe wert sein; zurückzahlen. **–able,** *adj.* rückzahlbar. **–ment,** *s.* die Rückzahlung; Erwiderung; Vergeltung.
repeal [rɪˈpɪːl], 1. *v.a.* widerrufen, aufheben, abschaffen (*a law*). 2. *s.* die Aufhebung, Abschaffung, der Widerruf. **–able** [–əbl], *adj.* widerruflich.
repeat [rɪˈpɪːt], 1. *v.a.* wiederholen (*to*, gegenüber); weitererzählen, weiterverbreiten (*rumours, etc.*); aufsagen, hersagen, vortragen (*a poem, etc.*); noch einmal tun; *– an order*, nachbestellen (*C.L.*). 2. *v.n.* sich wiederholen; repetieren (*Horol.*); *be –ed*, sich wiederholen, wiederkehren; (*usually neg.*) einen Nachgeschmack haben. 3. *s.* die Wiederholung (*also Mus.*); das Wiederholungszeichen (*Mus.*); (also **– –order**) die Nachbestellung, Neubestellung (*C.L.*). **–ed** [–ɪd], *adj.* wiederholt, mehrmalig. **–er** [–ə], *s.* die Repetieruhr (*Horol.*); periodischer Dezimalbruch (*Arith.*); das Mehrladegewehr; der Verstärker (*Tele.*); *–er compass*, *s.* der Tochterkompaß. **–ing,** *adj.* wiederholend, Wiederholungs–, Repetier–. **– –order,** *s.* die Nachbestellung, Neubestellung. **– –performance,** die Wiederholung (*Theat.*).
repel [rɪˈpɛl], *v.a.* abwehren, zurückschlagen (*attack*), zurücktreiben (*enemy*), zurückstoßen (*also Phys.*), abstoßen (*Phys. & fig.*), zurückdrängen (*feelings*), zurückweisen, abweisen (*persons, also suggestion, etc.*); (*fig.*) anwidern (*a p.*); *– one another*, einander abstoßen (*Phys.*). **–lent,** *adj.* abstoßend (*also fig.*).
[1]**repent** [rɪˈpɛnt], 1. *v.a.* bereuen (*a th.*; *doing*, getan zu haben); (*archaic*) *I – me of*, ich bereue (*Acc.*). 2. *v.n.*; *– of*, Reue empfinden über, bereuen. **–ance,** *s.* die Reue. **–ant,** *adj.* reuig (*of*, über), bußfertig.
[2]**repent** [ˈrɪːpənt], *adj.* kriechend (*Bot., Zool.*).
re-people [rɪːˈpɪːpl], *v.a.* neu bevölkern.
repercussi–on [rɪːpəˈkʌʃən], *s.* der Rückstoß, das Rückprallen; (*fig.*) der Widerhall, die Rückwirkung (*on*, auf). **–ve** [–ˈkʌsɪv], *adj.* widerhallend, rückwirkend.
repert–oire [ˈrɛpətwɑː], *s.* der Spielplan, das Repertoire (*Theat.*). **–ory** [–tərɪ], *s.* das Repertorium; (*fig.*) die Fundgrube (*of*, für *or* von); *see* **–oire.** **–ory theatre,** *s.* das Theater mit stehender Truppe und wechselndem Spielplan.
repet–end [rɛpəˈtɛnd], *s.* die Periode (*of a decimal*). **–ition** [–ˈtɪʃən], *s.* die Wiederholung; das Hersagen, Aufsagen; die Wiederkehr, wiederholtes Vorkommen (*of events, etc.*); die Nachbildung, Kopie (*of a pattern*); Gedächtnisaufgabe (*at school*). **–itive** [rəˈpɛtɪtɪv], *adj.* sich widerholend; *be –itive*, sich wiederholen.
repin–e [rɪˈpɑɪn], *v.n.* klagen, murren, mißvergnügt *or* unzufrieden sein (*at*, über). **–ing,** 1. *adj.* mißvergnügt, unzufrieden, mürrisch. 2. *s.* das Murren, die Unzufriedenheit.
replace [rɪːˈpleɪs], *v.a.* wieder (hin)stellen *or* (hin)legen; wieder zurückgeben *or* zurückerstatten (*things taken*); ersetzen (*with* (*a th.*) or *by* (*a p.*), durch); verdrängen (*a th.*), vertreten (*a p.*), Stelle ausfüllen (*of a th.*), Stelle einnehmen (*of a p. or th.*); wieder einsetzen (*in office*); *– the receiver*, den Hörer wieder auflegen (*Tele.*). **–able** [–əbl], *adj.* ersetzbar (*by*, durch). **–ment,** *s.* die Ersetzung, der Ersatz; die Verdrängung (*Geol.*); der Ersatzmann (*Sport*); *pl.* der Nachschub, Ergänzungsmannschaften (*pl.*) (*Mil.*); *–ment value*, der Ersetzungswert.
replant [rɪːplɑːnt], *v.a.* versetzen, umpflanzen (*plants*), neu bepflanzen (*soil*).
replay [rɪːˈpleɪ], *s.* das Wiederholungsspiel.
replenish [rɪˈplɛnɪʃ], *v.a.* (wieder) füllen, anfüllen (*with*, mit); nachsetzen, auffrischen (*Dye.*). **–ment,** *s.* das Anfüllen, Nachfüllen; die Ergänzung.
replet–e [rɪˈplɪːt], *adj.* voll, angefüllt (*with*, von); satt. **–ion** [–ʃən], *s.* das Gefülltsein, Vollsein; die (Über)Fülle; *full to –ion*, voll bis zum Rande; satt.
replev–in [rɪˈplɛvɪn], *s.* (*archaic*) die Wiedererlangung eines Besitzes gegen Kaution (*Law*). **–y** [–ɪ], *v.a.* wiedererlangen gegen Kaution (*Law*).
replica [ˈrɛplɪkə], *s.* die Kopie, Nachbildung (*Art*): (*fig.*) das Ebenbild. **–te** 1. *adj.* [–ət], zurückgeschlagen, zurückgebogen. 2. *v.a.* [–eɪt], (*rare*) zurückbiegen (*Bot.*). **–tion** [–ˈkeɪʃən], *s.* (*rare*) die Antwort, Erwiderung; Replik (*Law*); Kopie; Nachbildung.
reply [rɪˈplɑɪ], 1. *v.a.* antworten. 2. *v.n.* antworten, erwidern; *– to*, beantworten, erwidern auf (*Acc.*). 3. *s.* die Antwort, Erwiderung, Entgegnung; *in – to*, in Erwiderung auf (*Acc.*), in Beantwortung (*Gen.*); *say in – to*, erwidern auf; *make a –*, erwidern; *– paid*, Rückantwort bezahlt; *– postcard*, die Postkarte mit Rückantwort.
report [rɪˈpɔːt], 1. *s.* der Bericht (*of* or *on*, über); Jahresbericht; das (Schul)Zeugnis, die Zensur; das Gutachten, Referat (*of an expert*); die Meldung, Nachricht; das Gerücht (*about* or *of*, über); der Ruf, Name (*good or bad*), der Knall, Schall (*of a gun, etc.*); *annual –*, der Jahresbericht; *– has it*, es geht das Gerücht; *Law –s*, Berichte über Entscheidungen des Obergerichts; *newspaper –*, der Zeitungsbericht; *official –*, das Protokoll; *– of proceedings*, der Verhandlungsbericht; *– stage*, das Erörterungsstadium einer Vorlage (*Parl.*). 2. *v.a.* berichten *or* Bericht erstatten über (*in the press, etc.*); erzählen, berichten; beschreiben, darstellen; Beschwerde führen über, anzeigen (*a p.*) (*to*, bei; *for*, wegen); *it is –ed*, man sagt; *he is –ed to be*, es wird von ihm berichtet, es sei er soll sein; *he is –ed as saying*, er soll gesagt haben; *– o.s.*, sich melden; *– progress*, über den Fortgang berichten. 3. *v.n.* erzählen; melden (*to authorities*); Bericht erstatten (*to* (*Dat.*); (*up*)*on*, über); sich melden, sich stellen (*Mil.*); *– to the police*, sich bei der Polizei melden, sich der Polizei stellen. **–ed** [–ɪd], *adj.* indirekt (*Gram.*). **–er,** *s.* der Berichterstatter. **–ing,** *s.* die Berichterstattung; Anmeldung.
repose [rɪˈpouz], 1. *s.* die Ruhe, der Schlaf, die Erholung (*from*, von). (*fig.*) Gemütsruhe, innere Ruhe, der Friede, die Stille, Gelassenheit, Untätigkeit; *in –*, ruhend, untätig. 2. *v.n.* schlafen, (sich) ausruhen, ruhen (*also fig.*) (*in*, in *or* auf); (*fig.*) beruhen, gegründet sein (*on*, auf). 3. *v.a.* setzen (*in*, auf) (*confidence, etc.*). **–ful,** *adj.* ruhevoll, ruhig.
repository [rɪˈpɔzɪtərɪ], *s.* das Behältnis, der Behälter; Aufbewahrungsort, Speicher, die Vorratskammer, das Lager, Warenlager, die Niederlage.
repossess [rɪːpəˈzɛs], *v.a.* wiedereinsetzen (*a p.*) (*in*, in); *– o.s.*, sich wieder in Besitz setzen (*of* (*Gen.*)). **–ion** [–ʃən], die Wiedergewinnung.
re-post [rɪːˈpoust], *v.a.* umaddressieren (*a letter*).
repoussé [rəˈpuːseɪ], 1. *adj.* getrieben, gehämmert, erhaben (*metalwork*). 2. *s.* getriebene Arbeit.
repp, *see* [2]**rep.**
reprehen–d [rɛprɪˈhɛnd], *v.a.* tadeln, rügen, verweisen. **–sible** [–ˈhɛnsɪbl], *adj.* tadelswert, verwerflich. **–sion** [–ˈhɛnʃən], *s.* der Tadel, Verweis.
represent [rɛprɪˈzɛnt], *v.a.* darstellen (*also a character, Theat.*), vorstellen, zu Gemüte führen, nahebringen, vorhalten (*to* (*Dat.*)); bildlich darstellen, abbilden (*graphically*), schildern, beschreiben (*in words*), aufführen (*Theat.*); Vertreter sein, Stelle vertreten (*of a p.*); entsprechen (*Dat.*); bedeuten, symbolisch darstellen (*a th.*); *– to o.s.*, sich (*Dat.*) vorstellen; *be –ed*, vertreten sein (*at*,

bei). **–ation** [–ˈteɪʃən], *s.* bildliche Darstellung, das Bild; die Schilderung, Beschreibung; Aufführung (*Theat.*); Darstellung (*of a role*) (*Theat.*); Vorhaltung, Vorstellung; Vertretung (*Parl.*); Stellvertretung; *false –ations*, falsche Angaben, die Vorspiegelung falscher Tatsachen; *make –ations to s.o.*, einen Vorhaltungen machen; *make diplomatic –ations*, auf diplomatischen Wege vorstellig werden (*to*, bei); *system of –ation*, das Repräsantativsystem (*Parl.*). **–ational** [–ˈteɪʃənəl], *adj.* begrifflich, Vorstellungs–. **–ative** [–ˈzɛntətɪv], 1. *adj.* darstellend, verkörpend (*of* (*Acc.*)), bezeichnend, typisch (*of*, für), vertretend, repräsentierend, Repräsentativ– ; vorstellend, Vorstellungs–, Begriffs–; *be –ative of*, darstellen, verkörpern; *–ative government*, die Repräsentativverfassung. 2. *s.* der Stellvertreter, Vertreter, Beauftrage(r), *m.*, der Agent, Repräsentant, Volksvertreter, Verkörperer; *natural –ative*, der Rechtsnachfolger (*Law*); *House of –atives*, das Unterhaus, die Volksvertretung (*Amer.*). **–ativeness**, *s.* repräsentativer Charakter.

repress [rɪˈprɛs], *v.a.* unterdrücken; zurückhalten, hemmen, zügeln; verdrängen (*Psych.*). **–ion** [–ˈprɛʃən], *s.* die Unterdrückung, Zügelung, Hemmung; Verdrängung (*Psych.*). **–ive** [–sɪv], *adj.* unterdrückend, Unterdrückungs–; hemmend, Repressiv–.

reprieve [rɪˈprɪ:v], 1. *s.* die Begnadigung; der (Straf– *or* Vollstreckungs)Aufschub, (*fig.*) die Atempause, Frist. 2. *v.a.* Strafaufschub gewähren (*Dat.*), begnadigen; (*fig.*) Atempause *or* eine kleine Frist gewähren (*Dat.*).

reprimand [ˈrɛprɪmɑ:nd], 1. *s.* ernster Tadel *or* Verweis. 2. *v.a.* einen Verweis erteilen (*Dat.*).

reprint 1. *v.a.* [rɪ:ˈprɪnt], neu *or* wieder (ab)drucken, neu herausgeben. 2. *s.* [ˈrɪ:prɪnt], der Neudruck, neuer Abdruck.

reprisal [rɪˈprɑɪzl], *s.* die Vergeltungsmaßregel, Vergeltungsmaßnahme; *pl.* Repressalien; *make –s*, Vergeltungsmaßregeln ergreifen (*on*, gegen).

reprise [rɪˈprɑɪz], *s.* die Wiederholung (*Mus.*); Wiederaufnahme (*of an attack*); *pl.* jährliche Abzüge (*Law*).

reproach [rɪˈproutʃ], 1. *s.* der Vorwurf; die Schande, Schmach (*to*, für); *bring* or *cast – upon s.o.*, einem Schande einbringen; *heap –es on s.o.*, einen mit Vorwürfen überhäufen; *term of –*, der Ausdruck des Vorwurfs; *be a – to*, Abbruch tun (*Dat.*), schaden; *without –*, ohne Tadel. 2. *v.a.* Vorwürfe machen (*Dat.*), tadeln (*for*, wegen); *– s.o. with a th.*, einem etwas vorwerfen *or* zur Last legen; *– o.s.*, sich (*Dat.*) vorwerfen. **–ful**, *adj.* vorwurfsvoll. **–less**, *adj.* tadellos.

reprobat–e [ˈrɛprəbeɪt], 1. *adj.* verworfen, ruchlos; verdammt (*Theol.*). 2. *s.* Verworfene(r), *m.*, ruchloser Mensch. 3. *v.a.* verdammen, verurteilen, mißbilligen, verwerfen. **–ion** [–ˈbeɪʃən], *s.* die Mißbilligung, Verwerfung; Verdammnis (*Theol.*).

reproduc–e [rɪ:prəˈdjʊ:s], 1. *v.a.* (wieder) hervorbringen (*also fig.*); erzeugen, schaffen (*Biol.*), vervielfältigen, wiederabdrucken, reproduzieren, wiedergeben (*also Mus.*). 2. *v.n.* sich fortpflanzen (*Biol.*); (*fig.*) sich vervielfältigen. **–ible**, *adj.* reproduktionsfähig. **–tion** [–ˈdʌkʃən], *s.* die Wiedergabe, Nachbildung, Vervielfältigung, Reproduktion; Fortpflanzung, Wiedererzeugung (*Biol.*). **–tive** [–ˈdʌktɪv], *adj.* (wieder)hervorbringend; Fortpflanzungs–, Reproduktions–. **–tiveness**, **–tivity** [–ˈtɪvɪtɪ], *s.* die Reproduktionsfähigkeit, Reproduktivität.

[1]**reproof** [rɪˈpru:f], *s.* der Tadel, Verweis, die Rüge.

[2]**re-proof** [rɪ:ˈpru:f], *v.a.* wieder wasserdicht machen (*raincoats*).

reprov–al [rɪˈpru:vl], *s.* der Tadel, die Mißbilligung. **–e** [–ˈpru:v], *v.a.* tadeln, rügen (*a p.*), mißbilligen (*a th.*). **–ing**, *adj.* tadelnd, rügend, mißbilligend.

reps, *see* [2]**rep.**

rept–ant [ˈrɛptənt], *adj.* kriechend (*Bot.*, *Zool.*). **–ile** [–tɑɪl], 1. *s.* das Reptil; (*fig.*) der Kriecher. 2. *adj.* kriechend, Kriech–; (*fig.*) gemein, kriecherisch. **–ilian** [–ˈtɪlɪən], 1. *adj.* Reptilien–, Kriechtier–, reptilienartig. 2. *s.* das Reptil, Kriechtier.

republic [rɪˈpʌblɪk], *s.* die Republik, der Freistaat; *– of letters*, die Gelehrtenwelt. **–an** [–ən], 1. *adj.* republikanisch. 2. *s.* der Republikaner. **–anism** [–ənɪzm], *s.* republikanische Gesinnung *or* Regierungsform.

republi–cation [rɪ:pʌblɪˈkeɪʃən], *s.* die Neuauflage, der Neudruck; die Wiederveröffentlichung. **–sh** [rɪ:ˈpʌblɪʃ], *v.a.* wieder veröffentlichen, neu auflegen.

repudiat–e [rɪˈpju:dɪeɪt], 1. *v.a.* nicht anerkennen (*debts, etc.*), ableugnen, von sich weisen (*thoughts*), verwerfen, zurückweisen (*as unwarranted*), verstoßen (*a wife*). 2. *v.n.* Staatsschuld nicht anerkennen (*Pol.*). **–ion** [–ˈeɪʃən], *s.* die Nichtanerkennung, Verwerfung, Zurückweisung, Verstoßung.

repugn [rɪˈpju:n], 1. *v.a.* (*rare*) abstoßen, anwidern. 2. *v.n.*; *– against*, kämpfen gegen. **–ance, –ancy** [rɪˈpʌgnəns(ɪ)], *s.* die Abneigung, der Widerwille (*against* or *to* (*a th.*) or *for* (*a p.*), gegen); die Unvereinbarkeit, der Widerspruch. **–ant** [rɪˈpʌgnənt], *adj.* im Widerspruch stehend, unvereinbar (*with*, mit), unverträglich (*to*, mit), widerstrebend (*to* (*Dat.*)); widerwillig; widerlich, zuwider (*to a p.*, einem).

repuls–e [rɪˈpʌls], 1. *s.* das Zurücktreiben, Zurückschlagen (*enemy*); die Zurückweisung, abschlägige Antwort; *meet with a –e*, zurückgeschlagen werden (*Mil.*); (*fig.*) abgewiesen werden, eine abschlägige Antwort bekommen. 2. *v.a.* zurückschlagen, zurückwerfen, zurücktreiben (*enemy*); zurückweisen (*also Law*), abweisen (*a p.*). **–ion** [–ʃən], *s.* die Abstoßung (*Phys.*); (*fig.*) Abneigung, der Widerwille. **–ive** [–sɪv], *adj.* abstoßend (*Phys.*, *also fig.*); (*fig.*) widerwärtig, widerlich. **–iveness**, *s.* die Widerlichkeit, Widerwärtigkeit.

repurchase [rɪ:ˈpə:tʃəs], 1. *v.a.* wiederkaufen, zurückkaufen. 2. *s.* der Wiederkauf, Rückkauf.

reput–able [rɪˈpju:təbl], *adj.* angesehen, ehrbar, achtbar. **–ation** [rɛpjʊˈteɪʃən], *s.* der Ruf, guter Name, das Ansehen, der Leumund; *have the –ation of being*, im Rufe stehen zu sein; *have a –ation for*, bekannt sein wegen. **–e** [rɪˈpju:t], 1. *v.a.* (*only pass.*) *be –ed to be*, gehalten werden für, gelten für *or* als. 2. *s.* der Ruf, das Ansehen; *by –e*, dem Rufe nach; *of good –e*, von hohem Rufe; *in high –e*, in hohem Ansehen; *house of ill –e*, das Bordell. **–ed** [–ɪd], *adj.* berühmt; scheinbar, angeblich, vermeintlich. **–edly**, *adv.* dem Rufe *or* Leumund nach, angeblich.

request [rɪˈkwɛst], 1. *s.* das Gesuch, Ansuchen, Ersuchen, die Bitte, der Wunsch; *at the – of*, auf Ersuchen von; *at his –*, auf seine Bitte; *by –*, auf Wunsch; *no flowers by –*, Blumenspenden dankend verbeten; *in –*, gesucht, begehrt; *make a –*, eine Bitte stellen *or* richten (*to*, an); bitten (*for*, um). 2. *v.a.* bitten, ersuchen (*a p.*); erbitten, bitten *or* ersuchen um (*a th.*); *as –ed*, auf Ihre Bitte, wie erbeten, wunschgemäß; *– a favour of a p.*, einen um eine Gefälligkeit ersuchen; *– to be allowed*, um die Erlaubnis bitten.

requiem [ˈrɛkwɪəm], *s.* das Requiem, die Seelenmesse, Totenmesse.

require [rɪˈkwɑɪə], *v.a.* verlangen, fordern (*of a p.*, von einem); erfordern; bedürfen, brauchen, müssen; *it –s*, es erfordert (*Acc.*), es bedarf (*Gen.*); *be –d*, notwendig *or* erforderlich sein; *– a th. to be done*, verlangen daß etwas geschieht; *– a p. to do*, einen befehlen zu tun; *–d angle*, gesuchter Winkel; *–d subject*, das Pflichtfach; *as –d*, nach Bedarf; *if –d*, wenn nötig, auf Wunsch. **–ment**, *s.* die Forderung, Bedingung, Anforderung, das Erfordernis; Bedürfnis; *pl.* der Bedarf; *meet the –ments*, den Anforderungen entsprechen *or* Ansprüchen genügen; *educational –ments*, Bildungsvoraussetzungen (*pl.*).

requisit–e [ˈrɛkwɪzɪt], 1. *adj.* erforderlich, notwendig (*for* or *to*, für). 2. *s.* das Erfordernis, notwendige Bedingung; *pl.* Bedarfsartikel (*pl.*). **–ion** [–ˈzɪʃən], 1. *s.* die Forderung; notwendige Bedingung; die Requirierung, Requisition, Beitreibung (*Mil.*); das Ersuchen, die Aufforderung (*Law*); *put in –ion*, requirieren, in Beschlag nehmen. 2. *v.a.* requirieren, beschlagnehmen; beanspruchen, in Anspruch nehmen, anfordern. **–ioning**, *s.* die Beitreibung (*Mil.*).

requit–al [rɪˈkwɑɪtl], *s.* die Vergeltung; Belohnung. **–e** [rɪˈkwɑɪt], *v.a.* vergelten (*a th.* (*Acc.*); *a p.* (*Dat.*)); belohnen, heimzahlen (*a p.* (*Dat.*)).
re-read [rɪːˈrɪːd], *v.a.* noch einmal (durch)lesen.
reredos [ˈrɪːərədɔs], *s.* der Altaraufsatz, die Rückwand eines Altars.
resale [ˈrɪːseɪl], *s.* der Wiederverkauf.
resci–nd [rɪˈsɪnd], *v.a.* aufheben, umstoßen, für ungültig erklären, rückgängig machen, kündigen. **–ssion** [rɪˈsɪʒən], *s.* die Aufhebung, Umstoßung, Nichtigkeitserklärung.
rescript [ˈrɪːskrɪpt], *s.* amtlicher Bescheid *or* Erlaß, die Verfügung, Verordnung.
rescue [ˈrɛskjuː], 1. *v.a.* (gewaltsam) befreien, retten, freilassen (*a p.*) (*from*, aus *or* von); retten, bewahren (*a th.*) (*from*, vor); – *from oblivion*, der Vergessenheit entreißen. 2. *s.* die Rettung; (gewaltsame) Befreiung. **–r** [–ə], *s.* der Befreier, Retter. **––party**, *s.* die Rettungsmannschaft. **––work**, *s.* Rettungsarbeiten (*pl.*), die Bergung.
research [rɪˈsəːtʃ], 1. *v.a.* genau untersuchen, erforschen. 2. *s.* die Suche, Nachforschung (*for* or *after*, nach); (*often pl.*) wissenschaftliche Untersuchung, die Forschung, Forschungsarbeit (*on*, über); *make –es*, Nachforschungen anstellen (*into*, über). **–er** [–ə], *s.* der Forscher; Erforscher (*into*, über). **––student**, *s.* fortgeschrittener Student. **––work**, *s.* die Forschungsarbeit.
reseat [rɪːˈsɪːt], *v.a.* mit neuen Sitzen versehen (*church, etc.*); mit neuem Sitz versehen (*a chair*); neuen (Hosen)Boden einnähen (*trousers*).
resect [rɪˈsɛkt], *v.a.* herausschneiden (*Surg.*). **–ion** [rɪˈsɛkʃən], *s.* die Resektion (*Surg.*).
reseda [rɪˈsɪːdə], *s.* der Wau, die Reseda (*Bot.*); graugrüne Farbe.
re-seize [rɪːˈsɪːz], *v.a.* wieder in Besitz nehmen.
resell [rɪːˈsɛl], *v.a.* wiederverkaufen.
resembl–ance [rɪˈzɛmbləns], *s* die Ähnlichkeit (*to*, mit); *bear* or *have a –ance*, Ähnlichkeit haben (*with*, mit), ähnlich sehen (*with* (*Dat.*)). **–e** [rɪˈzɛmbl], *v.a.* gleichen, ähneln, ähnlich sehen (*Dat.*).
resent [rɪˈzɛnt], *v.a.* übelnehmen, verübeln. **–ful**, *adj.* grollend (*against*, gegen); (*rare*) empfindlich (*of*, über); *be –ful of*, ärgerlich sein auf. **–ment**, *s.* die Verstimmung, das Befremden, der Verdruß, Ärger, die Empörung, Entrüstung (*at*, über), der Groll (*at*, über; *against*, gegen).
reserv–ation [rɛzəˈveɪʃən], *s.* der Vorbehalt; das Reservat, Reservatsrecht (*Law*); Naturschutzgebiet (*in America*); die Vorbestellung (*of seats*); *mental –ation*, geheimer Vorbehalt; *without –ation*, ohne Vorbehalt, bedingungslos. **–e** [rɪˈzəːv], 1. *v.a.* aufsparen, aufbewahren; zurücklegen, zurückstellen, zurückbehalten, vorbehalten, reservieren (*to* or *for a p.*, einem); belegen *or* reservieren lassen (*a seat*); *–e o.s. for*, seine Kräfte aufsparen für; *–e to o.s.*, sich (*Dat.*) vorbehalten, für sich behalten; *–e the right*, sich (*Dat.*) das Recht vorbehalten; *all rights –ed*, all Rechte vorbehalten. 2. *s.* der (Not)-Vorrat (*of*, an); die Reserve (*also fig.* & *Mil.*); reserviertes Gebiet; der Reservemann, Ersatzmann (*Sport*); Vorbehalt, die Einschränkung; (*fig.*) Zurückhaltung, Verschlossenheit, (Selbst)-Beherrschung, zurückhaltendes Wesen; *pl.* Reserven (*pl.*) (*Mil.*); Rücklagen (*pl.*) (*C.L.*); *in –e*, in Bereitschaft *or* Reserve, im Rückhalt; vorrätig (*C.L.*); *keep in –e*, aufsparen; *place to –e*, dem Reservefonds überweisen (*C.L.*); *with certain –es*, unter gewissen Einschränkungen; *without –e*, ohne Vorbehalt. **–ed** [–d], *adj.* vorbehalten, zurückbehalten, reserviert (*also fig.*), vorgemerkt; Reservats– (*Law*); (*fig.*) zurückhaltend; *–ed seat*, numerierter *or* reservierter Platz; *–e forces*, *pl.* die Reservetruppen (*Mil.*); *–e fund*, *s.* der Reservefonds (*C.L.*); *–e price*, der Einsatzpreis, Vorbehaltspreis (*at auctions*). **–ist**, *s.* der Reservist (*Mil.*).
reservoir [ˈrɛzəvwɑː], *s.* das Behältnis, Bassin, der (Wasser)Behälter; Stausee, das Reservoir; der Wasserturm, Hochbehälter; (*fig.*) das Sammelbecken, der (Reserve)Vorrat (*of*, an). **– condenser**, der Speicherkondensator (*Rad.*).
reset [rɪːˈsɛt], *v.a.* neu einfassen (*gems*); (neu) abziehen (*knives*); wieder setzen (*Typ.*).
resettle [rɪːˈsɛtl], *v.a.* wieder ansiedeln (*population*); neu ordnen; beruhigen. **–ment**, *s.* die Neuansiedlung; Neuordnung.
reshape [rɪːˈʃeɪp], *v.a.* umformen, umgestalten.
reship [rɪːˈʃɪp], *v.a.* wieder verschiffen *or* verladen, umladen. **–ment**, *s.* die Rück(ver)ladung.
reshuffle [rɪːˈʃʌfl], 1. *v.a.* neu mischen (*Cards*); (*fig.*) umgruppieren, umstellen, umbilden (*government, etc.*). 2. *s.* die Umgruppierung, Umstellung.
reside [rɪˈzɑɪd], *v.n.* wohnen, ansässig sein, residieren (*of persons*); zustehen, zukommen (*of rights*) (*in a p.*, einem); (*fig.*) ruhen, liegen (*in*, in; *with*, bei), innewohnen (*in* (*Dat.*)). **–nce** [ˈrɛzɪdəns], *s.* das Wohnen; der Wohnort, Wohnsitz; die Wohnung, das Wohnhaus, die Residenz (*of a prince*); der Aufenthalt; *official –nce*, die Amtswohnung; *take up one's –nce*, seinen Wohnsitz aufschlagen. **–ncy**, *s.* die Residentschaft; Amtswohnung, Residenz. **–nt** [ˈrɛzɪdənt], 1. *adj.* wohnhaft, ansässig; im Hause *or* am Orte wohnend; (*fig.*) innewohnend (*in* (*Dat.*)), vorhanden; *–nt birds*, Standvögel; *–nt surgeon*, der Anstaltsarzt; *–nt tutor*, der Internatslehrer. 2. *s.* der Bewohner, Ansässige(r), *m.*; der Ministerresident, Regierungsvertreter. **–ntial** [–ˈdɛnʃəl], *adj.* Wohn–, Wohnsitz–; *–ntial district*, das Wohnviertel, Villenviertel. **–ntiary** [–ˈdɛnʃərɪ], *adj.* seßhaft, ansässig, wohnhaft, 2. *s.* residenzpflichtiger Geistlicher. **–ntship**, *s.* das Amt *or* die Stellung eines Ministerresidenten.
residu–al [rəˈzɪdjuəl], 1. *adj.* übrig, restlich, übrigbleibend, übriggeblieben, zurückgeblieben, zurückbleibend (*Math.*); *–al analysis*, die Differenzialbrechung (*Chem.*); *–al product*, das Nebenprodukt. 2. *s.* der Rest(betrag), die Differenz. **–ary** [–uərɪ], *adj.* übrig, restlich; *–ary legatee*, der Erbe nach Abzug der Schulden. **–e** [ˈrɛzɪdjuː], *s.* der Rest(betrag), Rückstand; das Residuum (*Chem.*); der Erbnachlaß nach Abzug der Schulden (*Law*). **–um** [–ˈzɪdjuəm], *s.* der Rückstand, das Residuum (*Chem.*); niedrigste Schicht, die Hefe (*of a population*).
[1]**resign** [rɪˈzɑɪn], 1. *v.a.* aufgeben (*also fig.*), abtreten, verzichten auf (*Acc.*); niederlegen (*an office*), überlassen, übergeben (*to* (*Dat.*)); *– o.s.*, sich ergeben (*to*, in); sich versöhnen *or* abfinden (*to*, mit). 2. *v.n.* abdanken; austreten (*from*, aus), zurücktreten (*from*, von), verzichten (*from*, aus). **–ation** [rɛzɪgˈneɪʃən], *s.* der Rücktritt, Abschied; das Abschiedsgesuch; die Entlassung; Niederlegung (*of office*), Verzichtleistung, Entsagung, der Verzicht (*of*, auf), die Ergebung (*to*, in (*Acc.*)); *send in one's –ation*, sein Abschiedsgesuch *or* seine Entlassung einreichen. **–ed** [–d], *adj.* ergeben, resigniert. **–edly** [–ədlɪ], *adv.* mit Ergebung.
[2]**re-sign** [rɪːˈsɑɪn], *v.a.* & *n.* nochmals (unter)-zeichnen.
resilien–ce, –cy [rɪˈzɪlɪəns(ɪ)], *s.* das Zurückspringen, Abprallen; die Springkraft; (*fig.*) Spannkraft, Elastizität, der Schwung; die Federung (*mattress*). **–t** [–ɪənt], *adj.* zurückspringend, abprallend; federnd; (*fig.*) elastisch, geschmeidig.
resin [ˈrɛzɪn], 1. *s.* das Harz; Kolophonium (*for violin-bow*). 2. *v.a.* mit Harz behandeln *or* einreiben. **–aceous** [–ˈneɪʃəs], *adj.* harzhaltig, harzig. **–ate** [–eɪt], *s.* das Harzsäuresalz. **–ify** [–ˈzɪnɪfɑɪ], *v.a.* & *n.* verharzen. **–ous** [–əs], *adj.* harzig, Harz–.
resist [rɪˈzɪst], 1. *v.a.* Widerstand leisten, widerstehen (*Dat.*), sich widersetzen, widerstreben (*Dat.*); *I cannot – doing*, ich kann nicht umhin zu tun. 2. *v.n.* Widerstand leisten. 3. *s.* die Schutzbeize. **–ance**, *s.* der Widerstand (*also Elec.*) (*to*, gegen); die Festigkeit, Widerstandsfähigkeit (*Mech.*), Widerstandskraft; *offer –ance*, Widerstand; leisten (*to* (*Dat.*)); *passive –ance*, passiver Widerstand; *–ance to wear and tear*, die Verschleißfestigkeit; *–ance coil*, die Widerstandsspule (*Elec.*); *–ance movement*, die Widerstandsbewegung. **–ant**, 1. *adj.* widerstehend, widerstrebend, widerstandsfähig, Widerstands–. 2. *s.* Widerstandleistende(r), *m.*; das Schutzmittel. **–ible**, *adj.* zu widerstehen(d). **–ing**, *adj.* widerstehend, widerstrebend (*Dat.*). **–less**, *adj.* unwiderstehlich. **–or**, *s.* der Widerstand (*Elec.*).
resit [rɪːˈsɪt], *v.a.* & *n.* wiederholen (*an examination*).

resole [rɪːˈsoul] *v.a.* neu besohlen.
resolut–e [ˈrɛzəljuːt], *adj.* entschlossen (*for* zu), standhaft, fest. **–eness,** *s.* die Entschlossenheit, Festigkeit, Standhaftigkeit. **–ion** [–ˈjuːʃən], *s.* die Entschlossenheit, Festigkeit, der Mut; die Auflösung (*Phys.*, *Chem.*, *Mus.*); Zerlegung, Zerteilung (*of a tumour, etc.*); Behebung (*of doubt*), Lösung (*of a question*); der Entschluß, Beschluß, die Beschlußfassung, Resolution (*Parl.*); *good –ions*, gute Vorsätze; *come to* or *form a –ion*, zu einem Entschluß kommen; *propose a –ion*, eine Entschließung beantragen (*Parl.*). **–ive** [–juːtɪv], *adj.* zerteilend, auflösend (*Med.*).
resolv–able [rɪˈzɔlvəbl], *adj.* auflösbar (*into*, in). **–e** [rɪˈzɔlv], 1. *v.a.* auflösen (*Chem.*, *Math.*, *Mus.*), zerlegen, umwandeln (*into* in), lösen, (er)klären (*problems*), beheben (*doubt*); zerteilen (*Med.*); entscheiden, bestimmen, beschließen, den Beschluß fassen zu; *the house –es itself into a committee*, das Haus tritt als Ausschuß zusammen. 2. *v.n.* sich auflösen (*into*, in); beschließen (*on* (*Acc.*)); sich entschließen (*upon*, zu). 3. *s.* der Entschluß, Beschluß; die Beschlußfassung (*Amer.*); Entschlossenheit. **–ed** [–d], *adj.* fest entschlossen (*on*, zu). **–ent** [–ənt], 1. *adj.* auflösend (*Chem.*, *Med.*). 2. *s.* das Auflösungsmittel (*Med.*)
resona–nce [ˈrɛzənəns], *s.* die Klangfülle, Resonanz, das Mitschwingen (*Accoust.*); (*fig.*) der Widerhall. **–nt** [–ənt], *adj.* widerhallend (*with*, von), nachklingend, mitschwingend. **–te** [–eɪt], *v.n.* widerhallen, mitschwingen. **–tor** [–eɪtə], *s.* der Resonator.
resor–b [rɪˈzɔːb], *v.a.* (wieder) aufsaugen, resorbieren (*Biol.*). **–ption** [–ˈzɔːpʃən], *s.* die Resorption.
resort [rɪˈzɔːt], 1. *s.* das Zusammenkommen, die Zusammenkunft; der Versammlungsort; (*fig.*) die Zuflucht, letztes (Hilfs)Mittel; *as a* or *in the last –*, als letzte Ausweg, wenn Not am Mann ist; letzten Endes, schließlich; *without – to force*, ohne Gewalt anzuwenden, ohne zu Gewalt zu greifen; *bathing* or *seaside –*, das Seebad, der Badeort; *health –*, der Kurort. 2. *v.n.*; *– to*, sich begeben zu *or* nach, oft besuchen; (*fig.*) seine Zuflucht nehmen zu, Gebrauch machen von, greifen zu.
resound [rɪˈzaund], 1. *v.n.* widerhallen (*with*, von), erschallen, ertönen. 2. *v.a.* widerhallen lassen; *– his praises*, sein Lob laut verkünden.
resource [rɪˈsɔːs], *s.* das Mittel, die Zuflucht; Findigkeit, Wendigkeit, Erfindungskraft, Geistesgegenwart, das Geschick; (*rare*) die Zerstreuung, der Zeitvertrieb; (*usually pl.*) die Hilfsquelle, das Hilfsmittel; Geldmittel (*pl.*); *natural –s*, Bodenschätze (*pl.*); *thrown back on one's own –s*, auf sich selbst gestellt *or* angewiesen; *as a last –*, *see under* **resort.** **–ful,** *adj.* findig, wendig, fähig sich zu helfen, erfinderisch.
respect [rɪˈspɛkt], **1.** *v.a.* berücksichtigen, schonen, Rücksicht nehmen auf; (hoch)achten, schätzen; *– o.s.*, etwas auf sich halten. **2.** *s.* der Bezug, die Beziehung; Hinsicht, der Betracht; die Rücksicht (*to*, auf), (Hoch)Achtung, Verehrung, Ehrerbietung; *pl.* Empfehlungen, Grüße (*pl.*). (*a*) (*with verbs*) *give one's –s to a p.*, einen grüßen lassen; *have* (*a*) *– for*, Ehrfurcht haben vor; *have – to*, sich beziehen auf (*Acc.*); *be held in high –*, hoch geachtet werden; *pay one's –s*, sich empfehlen, seine Aufwartung machen (*to* (*Dat.*)). (*b*) (*with prepositions*) *in all –s*, *in every –*, in jeder Hinsicht; *in – of*, *with – to*, in Bezug auf (*Acc.*), hinsichtlich, betreffs (*Gen.*); was . . . (*Acc.*) anbetrifft; *out of – for*, aus Ehrerbietung vor; *without – of persons*, ohne Ansehen der Person. **–ability** [–əˈbɪlɪtɪ], *s.* der Anstand, die Anständigkeit, Schicklichkeit, Achtbarkeit; das Ansehen; die Konventionalität; Respektspersonen (*pl.*). **–able** [–əbl], *adj.* anständig, schicklich; angesehen, achtbar, ehrbar, konventionell; solid, reell (*C.L.*); (*coll.*) beträchtlich, ansehnlich, leidlich. **–er** [–ə], *s.*; *be no –er of persons*, ohne Ansehen der Person handeln, keinen Unterschied der Person machen. **–ful** [–ful], *adj.* ehrerbietig, höflich; *be –ful of*, achten, respektieren; (*in letters*) *–fully*, ergebenst, hochachtungsvoll. **–fulness,** *s.* die Ehrerbietung, Höflichkeit. **–ing** [–ɪŋ], *prep.* in Bezug auf (*Acc.*), hinsichtlich, betreffs (*Gen.*). **–ive** [–ɪv], *adj.* besonder, betreffend, respektiv; *to their –ive homes*, jeder nach seinem Hause; *the –ive amounts of £5 and £10*, die Beträge von 5 beziehungsweise 10 Pfund. **–ively,** *adv.* beziehungsweise, respektive, oder; nacheinander, der Reihe nach.
respir–ation [rɛspɪˈreɪʃən], *s.* das Atmen, die Atmung (*also of plants*); Respiration, der Atemzug **–ator** [ˈrɛspɪreɪtə], *s.* der Respirator (*also Med.*), das Atemgerät, die Gasmaske (*Mil.*). **–atory** [ˈrɛspɪrətərɪ], *adj.* Atem–, Atmungs–; *–atory organs*, die Atmungsorgane. **–e** [rɪˈspaɪə], 1. *v.n.* atmen, Atem holen; (*fig.*) aufatmen. 2. *v.a.* atmen, einatmen.
respite [ˈrɛspaɪt], 1. *s.* die Stundung; (Stundungs)-Frist, der Aufschub, (*fig.*) die Ruhepause, Erholung. 2. *v.a.* Frist *or* Aufschub gewähren, Urteilsvollstreckung aufschieben (*Dat.*) (*a p.*); aufschieben, verschieben (*a th.*), einstellen, zurückhalten (*payment*); (*fig.*) Erleichterung gewähren (*Dat.*) (*a p.*).
resplenden–ce, –cy [rɪˈsplɛndəns(ɪ)], *s.* der Glanz; (*fig.*) die Pracht. **–t** [–ənt], *adj.* glänzend, strahlend.
respon–d [rɪˈspɔnd], 1. *v.n.* antworten (*also Eccl.*), erwidern (*to* (*Dat.*)); (*fig.*) entgegenkommen (*Dat.*), eingehen *or* reagieren (*to*, auf (*Acc.*)); empfänglich sein (*to*, für); gehorchen (*to* (*Dat.*)) (*Mach.*); haften (*to*, für) (*Amer.*); *–d to a call*, einem Rufe folgen; *–d to a letter*, einen Brief beantworten. 2. *v.a.* Genüge leisten (*Dat.*) (*Law*). 3. *s.* das Responsorium (*Eccl.*), der Wandpfeiler, Strebepfeiler (*Arch.*). **–dence** [–əns], *s.* die Entsprechung, entsprechendes Verhältnis; die Reaktion (*to*, auf). **–dency** [–ənsɪ], *s.* die Entsprechung. **–dent,** 1. *adj.* antwortend (*to* (*Dat.*)); (*fig.*) reagierend (*to*, auf); beklagt (*Law*). 2. *s.* der Verteidiger; Beklagte(r), Angeklagte(r) *m.* (*esp. divorce cases*). **–se** [–ɔns], *s.* die Antwort, Erwiderung; das Responsorium (*Eccl.*); (*fig.*) das Eingehen, die Reaktion (*to*, auf), die Aufnahme, der Widerhall (*to*, für); *pl.* [–sɪz] Responsorien (*pl.*) (*Eccl.*); *in –se to*, als Antwort auf, in Erwiderung auf; *meet with a good –se*, Widerhall finden, Erfolg haben. **–sibility** [–sɪˈbɪlɪtɪ], *s.* die Verantwortlichkeit, Verantwortung, Verpflichtung; Zahlungsfähigkeit (*C.L.*); *on one's own –sibility*, auf eigene Verantwortung. **–sible** [–sɪbl], *adj.* verantwortlich (*to* (*Dat.*); *for*, für) verantwortungsvoll, zuverlässig, vertrauenerweckend; zahlungsfähig (*C.L.*); *be –sible for*, haften für, einstehen für, die Verantwortung tragen für; *make o.s. –sible for*, die Verantwortung übernehmen für; verantwortlich zeichnen für (*C.L.*); *–sible partner*, persönlich haftender Teilnehmer (*C.L.*); *–sible position*, der Vertrauensposten. **–sions** [–ˈspɔnʃənz], *pl.* die Aufnahmeprüfung (*Oxford Univ.*). **–sive** [–sɪv], *adj.* (be)antwortend; (*usually fig.*) entgegenkommend (*to* (*Dat.*); zugänglich, verständnisvoll; empfänglich, empfindlich (*to*, für)). **–siveness,** *s.* das Verständnis, die Empfänglichkeit (*to*, für). **–sory** [–sərɪ], *s.* das Responsorium.
[1]**rest** [rɛst], 1. *s.* die Ruhe; Rast, der Schlaf; das Ausruhen, die Erholung (*from*, von); (*Poet.*) ewige Ruhe, der Tod; der Ruheplatz; die Unterkunft, das Heim (*for sailors, etc.*); der Ruhepunkt, die Pause (*Mus.*). Zäsur (*Metr.*); der Ständer, Halter, Steg, die Stütze, Lehne, Auflage; *at –*, ruhig; *set s.o.'s mind at –*, einen beruhigen; *set a matter at –*, eine S. erledigen; *in –*, eingelegt (*as a lance*); *come to –*, zur Ruhe kommen; *lay to –*, begraben, bestatten; *retire to –*, sich zur Ruhe begeben, schlafen gehen; *take a –*, sich ausruhen; (*coll.*) *give a th. a –*, mit etwas aufhören, etwas auf sich beruhen lassen; *have a good night's –*, sich ausruhen *or* ausschlafen. 2. *v.n.* (*of a p.*) rasten (aus)ruhen; schlafen; zur Ruhe kommen, sich erholen; (*of a th.*) liegen, sich stützen *or* lehnen (*on*, auf (*Acc.*)); stehenbleiben, stillstehen, beruhen, begründet sein, sich verlassen ((*up*)*on*, auf (*Acc.*)); *the matter cannot – here*, so kann die Sache nicht bleiben; *let a matter –*, etwas auf sich beruhen lassen, etwas dabei bewenden lassen; *– up*, sich ausruhen *or* erholen (*Amer.*); *it –s with him*, es bleibt ihm überlassen, es ist *or* liegt bei ihm *or* in seinen Händen, es hängt von ihm ab. 3. *v.a.* ruhen lassen, Ruhe gönnen or gewähren (*Dat.*) (*a p.*), ruhen, legen,

stützen (*on*, auf (*Acc.*)); lehnen (*against*, an (*Acc.*)); (be)gründen (*in*, auf) (*a th.*); – *the case*, die Beweisaufnahme schließen (*Law*); – *o.s.*, sich ausruhen; *God – his soul!* Gott hab' ihn selig! **--cure,** *s.* die Liegekur. **--day,** *s.* der Ruhetag. **-ful,** *adj.* ruhig, friedlich; beruhigend. **--house,** *s.* die Herberge. **-ing,** *attrib. adj.* Ruhe–; *-ing place*, der Ruheplatz. **-less,** *adj.* rastlos, ruhelos; unruhig, unstet; *-less night*, schlaflose Nacht. **-lessness,** *s* die Rastlosigkeit, Ruhelosigkeit; Schlaflosigkeit, Unruhe. **--room,** *s.* das Ausruhzimmer.

[2]**rest,** 1. *s.* der Rest(teil), Überrest; das übrige, die übrigen (*pl.*); der Reservefonds; Saldo; die Bilanzierung (*C.L*); der Gang (*Tenn.*); *and all the – of it*, und was sonst noch; und alles übrige; *the – of us*, wir übrigen; – *of a debt*, der Rückstand einer Schuld; *for the –*, in übrigen, übrigens. 2. *v.n.* bleiben, sein; übrig(geblieben) sein; – *assured*, sich darauf verlassen, versichert sein.

restart [rɪːˈstɑːt], 1. *v.a.* wieder in Gang bringen. 2. *v.n.* wieder beginnen *or* starten.

restate [rɪːˈsteɪt], *v.a.* wiederholt feststellen *or* darlegen, neu formulieren. **-ment,** *s.* die Neuformulierung; wiederholte Darlegung.

restaura-nt [ˈrɛstərənt], *s.* das Restaurant, die Gaststätte. *-nt-car*, *s.* der Speisewagen. **-teur** [ˈrɛstɔræˈtəː], *s.* der Gastwirt.

restful, *see* **rest.**

resting, *see* **rest.**

restitution [rɛstɪtjuʃən], *s.* die Wiederherstellung; Zurückerstattung, Zurückgabe, Wiedererstattung, Wiedergabe, der Ersatz; das Zurückkehren in die vorige Lage (*by elasticity*); *make – for*, Ersatz leisten für; *make – of*, wiederherstellen.

restive [ˈrɛstɪv], *adj.* störrisch, widerspenstig; unruhig, ungeduldig, nervös; bockig (*as horse*). **-ness,** *s.* die Widerspenstigkeit, der Starrsinn, die Unruhe, Nervosität, Bockigkeit (*of horse*).

restock [rɪːˈstɔk], *v.a.* neu versorgen (*with*, mit), wieder auffüllen (*warehouse*).

restor-ation [rɛstəˈreɪʃən], *s.* die Wiederherstellung; Wiedereinsetzung, Rückerstättung, Rückgabe, Restauration (*also Hist.*), Ausbesserung; Restaurierung (*Art, etc.*). **-ative** [rəˈstɔːrətɪv], 1. *adj.* stärkend. 2. *s.* das Stärkungsmittel, Belebungsmittel. **-e** [rɪˈstɔː], *v.a.* wiederherstellen, restaurieren, rekonstruieren, erneuern, ausbessern (*Art, etc.*); wiedereinsetzen (*Pol.*) (*to*, in), zurückbringen (*to*, zu) (*a p.*); zurückerstatten, wiedergeben, zurückgeben (*to* (*Dat.*)); *-e a p. to health*, einen wiederherstellen; *-e a p. to liberty*, einem die Freiheit schenken; *-e to life*, ins Leben zurückrufen; *-e a th. to its place*, etwas an seinen Ort zurückstellen; *-e to the throne*, wieder auf den Thron setzen. **-er** [-rə], *s.* der Wiederhersteller; Restaurator (*Art, etc.*); *hair -er*, das Haarstärkungsmittel.

restrain [rɪˈstreɪn], *v.a.* zurückhalten, abhalten (*from*, von), in Schranken *or* im Schach halten, Einhalt tun (*Dat.*); hindern (*from*, an (*Dat.*); (*from doing*, zu tun)); unterdrücken, bezähmen (*feelings*); beschränken, einschränken (*power*). **-able,** *adj.* zurückzuhalten(d), bezähmbar. **-ed** [-d], *adj.* beherrscht, zurückhaltend, maßvoll; gehemmt, gedämpft. **-t,** *s.* die Zurückhaltung, Beherrschung, Zucht, Enthaltsamkeit; Beschränkung, Einschränkung, Hinderung, Hemmung, der Zwang, Einhalt; die Haft, Freiheitsbeschränkung; *under -t*, in Gewahrsam, unter Aufsicht *or* Beobachtung, (*fig.*) im Zaum; *without -t*, frei, ungezwungen.

restrict [rɪˈstrɪkt], *v.a.* beschränken, einschränken (*to*, auf (*Acc.*)); *be -ed*, sich darauf beschränken müssen; *-ed*, nur für den Dienstgebrauch; *-ed area*, das Sperrgebiet. **-ion** [-ʃən], *s.* die Beschränkung, Einschränkung (*on* (*Gen.*)), Hemmung; der Vorbehalt; *-ion on payment*, die Zahlungsbeschränkung. **-ive** [tɪv], *adj.* beschränkend, einschränkend, Einschränkungs–.

result [rɪˈzʌlt], 1. *a.* das Ergebnis, Resultat (*also Arith.*), die Folge, Wirkung, der Ausfall; *as a –*, die Folge war; *without –*, ergebnislos, ohne Folge *or* Wirkung. 2. *v.n.* sich ergeben, herrühren, folgen (*from*, aus *or* von), seinen Ursprung haben (*from*, in); (hin)auslaufen in; – *in*, zur Folge haben, enden *or* (hin)auslaufen in; zurückfallen (*to*, an) (*Law*). **-ant,** 1. *adj.* sich ergebend, entstehend, resultierend (*from*, aus). 2. *s.* die Resultante, Mittelkraft (*Math., Mech.*), (*fig.*) das Endergebnis.

resumé [rəˈzuːmeɪ], *s.* die Zusammenfassung, kurze Übersicht, das Resümee.

resum-e [rɪˈzjuːm], 1. *v.a.* wieder beginnen, fortführen, wieder aufnehmen (*work, etc.*); wieder einnehmen (*a seat*); wieder übernehmen (*an office, command, etc.*); zusammenfassen, resümieren; *be -ed*, wieder einsetzen, fortgeführt werden. 2. *v.n.* die Arbeit wieder aufnehmen; fortfahren. **-ption** [rɪˈzʌmpʃən], *s.* die Wiederaufnahme, der Wiederbeginn; die Zurücknahme, Wiederübernahme.

resupinat-e [rɪːsjuːpɪnət], *adj.* nach oben gebogen, resupiniert (*Bot.*). **-ion** [-ˈneɪʃən], *s.* umgekehrte Lage (*Bot.*).

resurgen-ce [rɪˈsəːdʒəns], *s.* das Wiederaufleben, der Wiederaufstieg. **-t** [ənt], *adj.* wiederauflebend, sich wiedererhebend.

resurrect [rɛzəˈrɛkt], *v.a.* (*coll.*) ausgraben, wieder einführen, aufleben lassen. **-ion** [-ʃən], *s.* die Auferstehung, das Fest der Auferstehung Christi; (*fig.*) das Wiedererwachen, Wiederaufleben. **-ionism,** *s.* der Leichenraub. **-ionist,** *s.* der Leichenräuber. **-ion man,** *s. see* **-ionist.** **-ion pie,** *s.* (*coll.*) die Restepastete.

resuscitat-e [rɪˈsʌsɪteɪt], *v.a.* wiedererwecken, wiederbeleben, ins Leben zurückrufen; (*fig.*) erneuern. **-ion** [-ˈteɪʃən], *s.* die Wiederbelebung, Wiedererweckung, (*fig.*) Erneuerung. **-ive** [-tətɪv], *adj.* wiedererweckend, wiederbelebend.

ret [rɛt], *v.a.* einweichen, rösten, rötten (*flax*).

retable [rɪˈteɪbl], *s.* der Altaraufsatz.

retail 1. *v.a.* [rɪːˈteɪl], einzeln, im kleinen *or* in Detail verkaufen (*C.L.*); (*fig.*) umständlich erzählen *or* wiederholen, nacherzählen, weitergeben (*news*) (*to* (*Dat.*)). 2. *v.n.* im Detail verkauft werden (*at*, zu). 3. *s.* [ˈrɪːteɪl], der Kleinhandel, Einzelverkauf, das Detailgeschäft; *at* or *by –*, im kleinen *or* Detail, stückweise; – *dealer*, der Kleinhändler; – *price*, der Einzelpreis, Ladenpreis; – *shop*, der Kramladen; – *trade*, der Detailhandel, Kleinhandel, Einzelverkauf. **-er** [rɪːˈteɪlə], *s.* der Kleinhändler, (*fig.*) der Verbreiter, Erzähler (*of news*).

retain [rɪˈteɪn], *v.a.* (*a th.*) behalten, bewahren; beibehalten, festhalten an (*Dat.*); in Gedächtnis behalten; (*a p.*) bei sich behalten; bestallen, sich (*Dat.*) sichern (*a lawyer*); bestellen, belegen (*places, etc.*); festhalten, stützen (*Arch.*); zurückhalten, anstauen (*water*). **-er** [-ə], *s.* der Gefolgsmann, Lehnsmann (*Hist.*); Anwaltsvorschuß (*Law*); der Kugelkäfig (*Mech.*); *pl.* das Gefolge. **-ing,** *adj.*; *-ing dam*, das Stauwehr; *-ing fee*, der Anwaltsvorschuß (*Law*); *-ing wall*, die Stützmauer.

retake [rɪːˈteɪk], 1. *ir.v.a.* wiedernehmen; wieder einnehmen, wieder erobern. 2. *s.* zweite Aufnahme (*Films*).

retaliat-e [rɪˈtælɪeɪt], 1. *v.a.* (wieder) vergelten (*upon*, an; *by*, *mit*); heimzahlen (*upon* (*Dat.*)). 2. *v.n.* Vergeltung üben (*upon*, an (*Dat.*)). Vergeltungsmaßnahmen treffen (*against*, gegen). **-ion** [-ˈeɪʃən], *s.* die Wiedervergeltung; *in -ion for*, als Wiedervergeltung für. **-ory** [-ɪətrɪ], *adj.* (Wieder)Vergeltungs–.

retard [rɪˈtɑːd], 1. *v.a.* aufhalten, hindern (*a p.*); bremsen, hemmen, zurückhalten, verzögern, hinausschieben (*a th.*); *-ed ignition*, die Spätzündung; *-ed motion*, verzögerte Bewegung; *-ed velocity*, verlangsamte Geschwindigkeit. 2. *s.* die Verzögerung. **-ation** [-ˈdeɪʃən], *s.* die Verzögerung, Verlangsamung; der Verzug, Aufschub; Vorhalt (*Mus.*). **-ment,** *s. see* **-ation.**

retch [rɛtʃ], *v.n.* (sich) würgen, sich erbrechen.

retell [rɪːˈtɛl], *v.a.* noch einmal erzählen, wiederholen.

retent-ion [rɪˈtɛnʃən], *s.* das Behalten, Zurückhalten; die Beibehaltung, Erhaltung; Zurückbehaltung; Verhaltung (*Med.*); *-ion of shape*, die Formbeständigkeit. **-ive** [-tɪv], *adj.* behaltend, zurückhaltend; Gedächtnis–; *be -ive of*, behalten, bewahren; *-ive memory*, gutes Gedächtnis. **-iveness,** *s.* die Gedächtniskraft.

reticen–ce [ˈrɛtɪsəns], *s.* die Zurückhaltung, Verschwiegenheit; Verschweigung (*of facts*). **–t** [–ənt], *adj.* zurückhaltend, schweigsam; verschwiegen (*about* or *on*, über).
reti–cle [ˈrɛtɪkl], *s.* das Fadenkreuz (*Opt.*). **–cular** [rəˈtɪkjʊlə], *adj.*, **–culate,** 1. [–ˈtɪkjʊlət], *adj.* netzförmig, netzartig. 2. [–ˈtɪkjʊleɪt], *v.a.* netzförmig verzieren; *v.n.* sich netzförmig ausdehnen. **–culated,** *adj.* netzförmig, Netz–. **–culation** [–ˈleɪʃən], *s.* das Netzwerk (*also fig.*). **–cule** [ˈrɛtɪkjʊ:l], *s.* der Strickbeutel, die (Damen)-Handtasche; *see also* **–cle.** **–culum** [–ˈtɪkjʊləm], *s.* (*pl.* –a [–lə]) der Wiederkäuermagen (*Zool.*), (*fig.*) netzförmiges Gefüge. **–form** [ˈrɛtɪfɔ:m], *adj.* netzförmig. **–na** [ˈrɛtɪnə], *s.* die Netzhaut. **–nal,** *adj.* Netzhaut–. **–nitis** [–ˈnɑɪtɪs], *s.* die Netzhautentzündung.
retinue [ˈrɛtɪnjʊ:], *s.* das Gefolge.
retir–al [rɪˈtɑɪərəl], *s.* (*Scots*) *see* **–ement.** **–e** [rɪˈtɑɪə], 1. *v.a.* zurückziehen (*troops*); einlösen (*a bill*); verabschieden, pensionieren, in den Ruhestand versetzen (*a p.*). 2. *v.n.* sich zurückziehen, zurückweichen; zurücktreten, abtreten (*from*, von), sich entfernen, ausscheiden (*from*, aus), in den Ruhestand treten; zu Bett *or* schlafen gehen; *–e from business*, sich zur Ruhe setzen, zurückziehen; *–e from active service*, seinen Abschied aus dem aktiven Dienst nehmen; *–e into the country*, sich aufs Land zurückziehen. 3. *s.* der Rückzug. **–ed** [–d], *adj.* zurückgezogen, einsam; pensioniert, verabschiedet, im Ruhestand; außer Dienst (*Mil.*); *–ed life*, zurückgezogenes Leben; *–ed list*, die Pensioniertenliste; *place* or *put on the –ed list*, verabschieden, pensionieren, in den Ruhestand versetzen (*Acc.*), den Abschied geben (*Dat.*); *–ed pay*, das Ruhegehalt, die Pension. **–edness** [rɪˈtɑɪədnɪs], *s.* die Zurückgezogenheit. **–ement,** *s.* das Sichzurückziehen, Ausscheiden, der Austritt, Rücktritt (*from*, von); das Privatleben, die Zurückgezogenheit; Pensionierung, der Ruhestand; *go into –ement*, ins Privatleben zurücktreten. **–ing** [–rɪŋ], *adj.* zurückhaltend, bescheiden, unaufdringlich; ausscheidend; *–ing age*, das Pensionierungsalter; *–ing pension*, das Ruhegehalt, die Pension; *–ing-room*, das Privatzimmer.
[1]**retort** [rɪˈtɔ:t], 1. *v.n.* scharf erwidern *or* entgegnen. 2. *v.a.* zurückgeben (*on* (*Dat.*)), zurückwerfen (*on*, auf), begegnen (*Dat.*), erwidern, vergelten (*on*, an). 3. *s.* scharfe *or* treffende Entgegnung *or* Erwiderung, schlagfertige Antwort. **–ion** [–ʃən], *s.* die Erwiderung, Wiedervergeltung, Retorsion (*Law*); Zurückbiegung, das Zurücklegen.
[2]**retort** [rɪˈtɔ:t], *s.* die Retorte, Destillierblase, der Destillationskolben (*Chem.*).
retouch [rɪ:ˈtʌtʃ], 1. *v.a.* überarbeiten, aufarbeiten, retuschieren (*Phot.*). 2. *s.* das Retuschieren, die Retusche, Überarbeitung.
retrace [rɪ:ˈtreɪs], *v.a.* zurückführen (*to*, auf); zurückverfolgen (*the way*); *– one's steps*, denselben Weg zurückgehen, (*fig.*) wiederholen; eine S. rückgängig machen.
retract [rɪˈtrækt], 1. *v.a.* zurückziehen (*the skin*); einziehen (*claws, etc.*); (*fig.*) rückgängig machen, wiederrufen, zurücknehmen. 2. *v.n.* sich zurückziehen, zurücktreten, wiederrufen; *no –ing*, kein Zurück. **–able** [–əbl], *adj.* einziehbar (*Av.*), (*fig.*) zurückziehbar, wiederruflich; *–able undercarriage*, das Einziehfahrwerk (*Av.*). **–ation** [–ˈteɪʃən], *s. see* **–ion.** **–ile** [–tɑɪl], *adj. see* **–able.** **–ion** [ʃən], *s.* die Zurückziehung, Zusammenziehung; Zurücknahme, der Widerruf. **–or** [–ə], *s.* der Retraktionsmuskel (*Anat.*); der Wundrandhalter (*Surg.*).
retrain [rɪ:ˈtreɪn], *v.a. & n.* umschulen.
retranslat–e [rɪ:trɑnsˈleɪt], *v.a.* (zu)rückübersetzen; neu übersetzen. **–ion** [–ˈleɪʃən], *s.* die Rückübersetzung.
retread [rɪ:ˈtrɛd], 1. *v.a.* wieder betreten. 2. *v.a.* mit neuer Lauffläche versehen (*tyres*).
retreat [rɪˈtrɪ:t], 1. *s.* der Rückzug (*also Mil.*); das Rückzugssignal, der Zapfenstreich (*Mil.*); die Zurückgezogenheit; der Zufluchtort, die Zuflucht; *beat* (*sound*) *the –*, den Zapfenstreich schlagen (blasen) (*Mil.*); (*fig.*) *beat a –*, sich zurückziehen *or* aus dem Staube machen. 2. *v.n.* sich zurückziehen, zurückweichen; *–ing forehead*, zurücktretende Stirn.
retrench [rɪˈtrɛntʃ], 1. *v.a.* kürzen, beschneiden, einschränken, abbauen (*expenses*); entfernen, auslassen, weglassen; verschanzen (*Fort.*). 2. *v.n.* sich einschränken. **–ment,** *s.* die Kürzung, Einschränkung; Auslassung; Verschanzung (*Fort.*).
retrial [rɪˈtrɑɪəl], *s.* erneute Untersuchung *or* Verhandlung.
retributi–on [rɛtrɪˈbjʊ:ʃən], *s.* die Vergeltung, Strafe. **–ve** [rəˈtrɪbjʊtɪv], *adj.* vergeltend, Wiedervergeltungs–.
retriev–able [rɪˈtrɪ:vəbl], *adj.* wiederbringlich, wiedergutzumachen(d), ersetzlich. **–e** [rɪˈtrɪ:v], 1. *v.a.* auffinden, apportieren (*of dogs*); wiedergewinnen, wiederbekommen, wiedererlangen; wiedergutmachen, wettmachen (*a loss*); retten, bewahren (*a p.*) (*from*, vor). 2. *v.n.* apportieren. **–er** [–ə], *s.* der Apportierhund, Stöberhund.
retro– [ˈrɪ:troʊ *except where shown*], *prefix* rück–, zurück–, rückwärts–, wieder–. **–ˈact,** *v.n.* (zu)-rückwirken. **–ˈaction,** *s.* die Rückwirkung. **–ˈactive,** *adj.* rückwirkend. **ˈ–cede** [–sɪ:d], 1. *v.n.* zurückgehen; nach innen schlagen (*Med.*). 2. *v.a.* wiederabtreten (*estate, etc.*). **–ˈcedent,** *adj.* zurückgehend; nach innen schlagend (*Med.*). **–ˈcession,** *s.* das Zurückgehen, die Wiederabtretung, Rückgabe (*to*, an) (*Law*). **–ˈcessive,** *adj. see* **–cedent.** **ˈ–choir** [–kwɑɪə], *s.* der Rückchor. **–ˈflected, ˈ–flex(ed)** [–flɛktɪd, –flɛks(t)], *adj.* nach rückwärts gebeugt. **–ˈflexion** [–flɛkʃən], *s.* die Beugung nach rückwärts. **–gradation** [rɛtroʊgrəˈdeɪʃən], *s.* das Zurückgehen; der Rückgang; (scheinbar) rückläufige Bewegung (*Astr.*). **–grade** [ˈrɛtrəgreɪd], 1. *adj.* rückläufig, Rückwärts–; (*fig.*) rückgängig; *–grade step*, der Rückschritt. 2. *v.n.* zurückgehen (*also fig.*), rückwärts gehen. **ˈ–gress,** *v.n.* zurückgehen, rückwärts gehen, verschlechtern, entarten. **–ˈgression** [–grɛʃən], *s.* das Rückwärtsgehen; (*fig.*) der Rückgang, die Verschlechterung. Entartung. **–ˈgressive,** *adj.* rückschreitend, Rück–; (*fig.*) zurückgehend. **–spect** [ˈrɛtrəspɛkt], *s.* der Rückblick, die Rückschau; *in –spect*, rückschauend. **–ˈspection** [–spɛkʃən], *s.* die Rückschau, Rückerinnerung. **–ˈspective** [–spɛktɪv], *adj.* rückblickend, rückschauend, Rück–, rückwirkend (*Law*); *–spective view*, der Rückblick. **–ˈversion** [–və:ʃən], *s.* die Rückwärtslagerung, Rückwärtsbeugung (*of the uterus*). **ˈ–vert** [–və:t], *v.a.* nach rückwärts verlagern. **ˈ–verted** [–və:tɪd], *adj.* rückwärtsverlagert (*of the uterus*).
retroussé [rəˈtru:seɪ], *adj.* nach oben gebogen; *– nose*, die Stülpnase.
re-try [rɪ:ˈtrɑɪ], *v.a.* von neuem verhören (*a p.*) *or* verhandeln (*a case*) (*Law*).
return [rɪˈtə:n], **1.** *v.n.* zurückkehren, zurückkommen; wiederkehren, wiederauftreten, wiederkommen; wieder zurückkommen (*to*, auf (*Acc.*)); zurückfallen (*to*, an (*Acc.*)); antworten, entgegen, erwidern; *– to dust*, wieder zu Staub werden; *– home*, nach Hause zurückkehren *or* zurückgehen. **2.** *v.a.* zurückbringen, zurückgeben, zurücksenden, zurückschicken, zurückbefördern, zurückerstatten, wiedergeben; zurückwerfen (*rays*), zurückschlagen (*a ball*), zurückzahlen (*money*), abstatten (*a visit, thanks*); erwidern (*accusation, greeting*); abgeben (*a vote*), aussprechen (*a verdict*); berichten, angeben, melden (*information*); als Abgeordneten wählen (*to*, in); *– a compliment*, ein Kompliment erwidern; *be –ed guilty*, schuldig erklärt werden; *– good for evil*, Böses mit Gutem vergelten; *– like for like*, Gleiches mit Gleichem vergelten; *– a profit*, Gewinn abwerfen *or* einbringen; *– a visit*, einen Gegenbesuch machen *or* abstatten. **3.** *s.* die Rückkehr; Rückreise, Rückfahrt; Wiederkehr, das Wiederauftreten (*of disease*); der Wechsel, Umlauf (*of the seasons, etc.*); die Wiedergabe, Rückgabe; Rückzahlung, Gegenleistung, Entschädigung, Vergeltung, der Ersatz; die Erwiderung, Antwort; das Zurückschlagen, der Rückschlag (*of a ball*); (*often pl.*) das Wiedereinkommen, der (Kapital)-Umsatz, Gewinn, Ertrag (*C.L.*); (amtlicher) Bericht; der Wahlbericht (*Parl.*); Seitenflügel,

Seitenteil, vorspringende Ecke (*Arch.*); die Krümmung, Biegung (*Tech.*); (*coll.*) die Rückfahrkarte; *pl.* Ergebnisse (*pl.*), der Ertrag; statistische Aufstellungen (*pl.*); das Rückgut (*C.L.*), Remittende (*books, etc.*); der Feinschnitt (*tobacco*). (*a*) (*with nouns*) – *of affection*, die Gegenliebe; *election –s*, die Wahlergebnis; – *of health*, wiederkehrende Gesundheit; *income-tax* –, die Einkommensteuererklärung; *by – of post*, postwendend, mit umgehender Post; *on sale or* –, in Kommission; *sales –s*, Verkaufsergebnisse (*pl.*); – *of a salute*, der Gegengruß; *strength* –, die Stärkemeldung (*Mil.*). (*b*) (*with verbs*) *wish a p. many happy –s* (*of the day*), einem herzliche Glückwünsche zum Geburtstage aussprechen; *yield a good* –, viel einbringen; *yield quick –s*, schnellen Umsatz haben, schnell abgehen. (*c*) (*with prepositions*) *in* –, dafür, dagegen; *in – for*, (als Ersatz) für. **–able**, *adj.* zurückzugeben(d), zurückzustellen(d); umtauschbar (*goods*). **– cargo**, *s.* die Rückfracht. **–ed** [–d], *adj.* zurückgekommen, zurückgekehrt; zurückgesandt; *–ed letter*, unbestellbarer Brief. **–er** [–ə], *s.* Zurückkehrende(r); Rückzahlende(r), *m.* **–ing officer**, *s.* der Wahlkommissar. **– journey**, *s.* die Rückreise. **– line**, *s.* die Rückleitung (*Phone.*). **– match**, *s.* die Revanchepartie. **– movement**, *s.* die Rücklaufbewegung. **– postage**, *s.* das Rückporto. **– service**, *s.* die Gegenleistung. **– ticket**, *s.* die Rückfahrkarte, der Rückfahrschein. **– valve**, *s.* das Rückschlagventil.

reuni–on [rɪːˈjuːnɪən], *s.* die Wiedervereinigung, das Wiedertreffen, Wiedersehen; Treffen. **–te** [rɪːjuˈnɑɪt], *v.a.* (& *n.* sich) wiedervereinigen.

rev [rɛv], 1. *s.* (*coll.*) die Umdrehung. 2. *v.a.* (& *n.*) (*coll.*) (sich) drehen; – *up the engine*, den Motor auf Touren bringen (*Av.*).

revaccinat–e [rɪːˈvæksɪneɪt], *v.a.* wieder impfen. **–ion** [–ˈneɪʃən], *s.* die Wiederimpfung.

reval–orization [rɪːvælərɑɪˈzeɪʃən], *s.* die Aufwertung, Umwertung, Neubewertung. **–orize** [rɪːˈvælərɑɪz], *v.a.* aufwerten, neu bewerten. **–uation** [–juˈeɪʃən], *s. see* **–orization**. **–ue** [–ˈvæljuː], *v.a. see* **–orize**.

[1]**reveal** [rɪˈvɪːl], *v.a.* aufdecken, enthüllen, verraten (*to* (*Dat.*)); offenbaren (*also Theol.*); zeigen. **–able**, *adj.* enthüllbar. **–ing**, *adj.* aufschlußreich.

[2]**reveal**, *s.* innere Bogenfläche, die Leibung, Laibung (*Arch.*).

réveillé [rəˈvælɪ], *s.* die Reveille, das Wecken (*Mil.*).

revel [ˈrɛvəl], 1. *s.* das Gelage; die Lustbarkeit. 2. *v.n.* schmausen; sich weiden *or* ergötzen (*in*, an); schwelgen (*in*, in (*Dat.*)). **–ler**, *s.* der Schwelger (*in*, in); Zecher, (Nacht)Schwärmer. **–ry**, *s.* die Schwelgerei, laute Lustbarkeit.

revelation [rɛvəˈleɪʃən], *s.* die Offenbarung (*to*, für) (*also Theol.*), Entdeckung, Enthüllung; – *of St. John*, die Offenbarung Johannis.

revel–ler, –ry, *see* **revel**.

revenant [ˈrəvənɑ̃], *s.* der Geist, das Gespenst, Wiederaufgestandene(r), *m.*

revenge [rɪˈvɛndʒ], 1. *s.* die Rache, Rachgier; Revanche (*Cards, etc.*); *have one's* –, sich revanchieren; *take* (*one's*) –, sich rächen (*on*, an); *in* –, aus Rache. 2. *v.a.* rächen (*on*, an (*Dat.*)); *be –d* or *– o.s.*, sich rächen (*on*, an). **–ful**, *adj.* rachsüchtig. **–fulness**, *s.* die Rachgier, Rachsucht.

revenue [ˈrɛvənju], *s.* das Einkommen, (Staats)-Einkünfte (*pl.*); *inland* –, Steuereinnahmen (*pl.*); *inland – office*, die Staatssteuerkasse. **– cutter**, *s.* der Zollschiff. **– officer**, *s.* Zollbeamte(r), *m.* **– stamp**, *s.* die Banderole, Steuermarke.

reverbera–nt [rɪˈvəːbərənt], *adj.* (*Poet.*) widerhallend. **–te** [–eɪt], 1. *v.n.* widerhallen, ertönen; zurückstrahlen (*light*); (*fig.*) zurückwirken (*on*, auf), sich verbreiten. 2. *v.a.* zurücksenden; zurückwerfen (*light*). **–tion** [–ˈreɪʃən], *s.* der Widerhall; das Widerhallen; Zurückstrahlen, Zurückwerfen (*of light*). **–tory** [–bərətərɪ], *adj.* zurückwerfend, zurückstrahlend; *–tory furnace*, der Flammofen.

rever–e [rɪˈvɪːə], *v.a.* (ver)ehren. **–ence** [ˈrɛvərəns], 1. *s.* die Verehrung, Ehrerbietung, Ehrfurcht, der Respekt (*for*, vor); die Reverenz, Verbeugung; *your –ence*, Euer Ehrwürden. 2. *v.a.* (ver)ehren. **–end** [–ənd], *adj.* ehrwürdig; *Most* or *Right* or *Very –end*, hochwürdig; Hochwürden (*title*); *–end Sir*, Euer Ehrwürden. **–ent** [–ənt], **–ential** [–ˈrɛnʃəl], *adj.* ehrerbietig, ehrfurchtsvoll.

reverie [ˈrɛvərɪ], *s.* die Träumerei.

rever–s [rəˈvɛːə, (*coll.*) rəˈvɪːə], *usually pl.* der Aufschlag, Revers. **–sal** [rɪˈvəːsəl], *s.* die Umkehrung; das Umschlagen; die Umstoßung; Aufhebung (*Law*); Umsteuerung (*of engines, etc.*); *–sal of fortune*, die Schicksalswende. **–se** [rɪˈvəːs], 1. *v.a.* umdrehen, umkehren; aufheben, umstoßen, umstürzen (*decree*); umsteuern (*engines*); *–se arms*, Gewehre mit dem Kolben nach oben halten; *–se the order*, die Reihenfolge umkehren; *–se the order of things*, die Weltordnung umstürzen. 2. *v.n.* rückwärtsfahren (*Motor.*), linksherum tanzen (*in a waltz*). 3. *s.* die Rückseite, Kehrseite (*of coin, etc.*); linke Seite (*of page*); Umgekehrte(s), *n.*, das Gegenteil; der Rückschlag, Umschlag (*of fortune*), (Glücks)Wechsel, (Schicksals)Schlag, die Niederlage, Schlappe (*Mil.*), der Rückwärtsgang (*Motor.*); *quite the –se*, gerade umgekehrt; *in –se*, im Rücken, von hinten (*Mil.*), rückwärtsfahrend (*Motor.*); *meet with a –se*, eine Schlappe erleiden. 4. *adj.* umgekehrt, Rück–, Kehr–; entgegengesetzt (*to* (*Dat.*)); *–se current*, der Gegenstrom; *–se direction*, entgegengesetzte Richtung; *–se fire*, das Rückenfeuer; *–se gear*, der Rücklauf, Rückwärtsgang (*Motor.*); *–se order*, umgekehrte Reihenfolge; *–se side*, die Rückseite, Kehrseite. **–sibility**, *s.* die Umdrehbarkeit, Umkehrbarkeit; Umstoßbarkeit. **–sible**, *adj.* umdrehbar, umkehrbar; umstoßbar (*Law*); umsteuerbar; wendbar, auf beiden Seiten zu tragen (*as cloth*). **–sing**, *adj.* Umsteuerungs–; *–sing-gear*, *s.* die Umsteuerung(svorrichtung); *–sing-switch*, *s.* der Stromwender. **–sion** [–ʃən], *s.* die Umkehrung (*also Math.*); der Rückfall, Heimfall (*to*, auf (*Acc.*)) (*Law*); Atavismus, Rückschlag, die Rückkehr (*Biol., etc.*); *in –sion*, zu erwarten(d). **–sional** [–ʃənəl], **–sionary** [–ʃənərɪ], *adj.* anwartschaftlich; Anwartschafts– (*Law*); atavistisch (*Biol.*); *–sionary heir*, der Nacherbe; *–sionary interest*, der Erbanspruch; *–sionary property*, die Anwartschaft auf späteren Besitz. **–sioner** [–ʃənə], *s.* der Anwärter (*Law*). **–t** [–t], 1. *v.n.* zurückkehren (*to*, zu), zurückgreifen, zurückkommen (*to*, auf (*Acc.*)) (*in talk*); heimfallen, zurückfallen (*to*, an (*Acc.*)) (*Law*); rückschlagen (*Biol.*); *–t to a type*, in einem Typ zurückfallen. 2. *v.a.* zurückwenden (*the eyes*); umkehren (*a series*). 3. *s.* Wiederbekehrte(r), *m.* (*Eccl.*). **–tible**, *adj.* zurückfallbar (*to*, an).

revet [rəˈvɛt], *v.a.* verkleiden, bekleiden (*wall, etc.*). **–ment, –ting**, *s.* die Verkleidung, Verschalung; Futtermauer.

revictual [rɪːˈvɪtl], *v.a.* (& *n.*) (sich) neu verproviantieren.

review [rɪˈvjuː], 1. *v.a.* nachprüfen, rividieren, einer Revision unterziehen; überblicken, überschauen, zurückblicken auf; durchgehen, durchsehen, besprechen, rezensieren (*a book, etc.*); mustern, inspizieren, Parade abhalten über (*Acc.*) (*Mil.*). 2. *v.n.* rezensieren. 3. *s.* die Durchsicht, Nachprüfung, Revision; der Überblick, Rückblick (*of*, auf *or* über); die Besprechung, Rezension, Kritik (*of a book*); Rundschau, Zeitschrift, Revue; Parade, Truppenschau, Truppenmusterung; *pass in* –, mustern, (*fig.*) Rückschau halten über, überblicken. **–al** [–əl], *s.* die Revision, Nachprüfung. **–er**, *s.* der Rezensent; *–er's copy*, das Rezensionsexemplar.

revile [rɪˈvɑɪl], *v.a.* schmähen, verleumden, verunglimpfen. **–ment**, *s.* die Schmähung.

revis–al [rɪˈvɑɪzl], *s.* die Revision, Nachprüfung. **–ary** [–ərɪ], *adj.* Revisions–. **–e** [rɪˈvɑɪz], 1. *v.a.* durchsehen, revidieren; abändern, verbessern; nachprüfen (*Law*); *–ed Version*, die Revision der Bibel; *–ing barrister*, der Prüfer der Wahllisten. 2. *s.* nochmalige Durchsicht, die Revision; zweite Korrektur (*Typ.*); (also *–e-proof*) der Revisionsbogen (*Typ.*). **–er** [–ə], *s.* der Nachprüfer; Korrektor (*Typ.*). **–ion** [rɪˈvɪʒən], *s.* die Revision (*also Typ.*), nochmalige Durchsicht, revidierte Ausgabe. **–ory** [–ərɪ], *adj.* (Über)Prüfungs–, Überwachungs–.

revisit [rɪːˈvɪzɪt], *v.a.* wieder besuchen.

revitalize [rɪːˈvɑɪtəlɑɪz], *v.a.* neu beleben.

reviv–al [rɪˈvɑɪvl], *s.* das Wiederaufleben, Wiederaufblühen, Wiedererwachen; die Wiederbelebung; Erweckung, Erweckungsbewegung (*Rel.*); Neuherausgabe (*book*); Wiederaufführung, Neuaufnahme (*Theat.*); *–al of learning*, die Renaissance. **–alism** [–əlɪzm], *s.* der Erweckungseifer; die Glaubenserweckung (*Rel.*). **–alist** [–əlɪst], *s.* der Erweckungsprediger. **–e** [rɪˈvɑɪv], 1. *v.a.* wieder zum Bewußtsein bringen; wiederherstellen, erneuern, wieder auffrischen, wieder *or* neu beleben, wieder erwecken (*feelings*), wieder aufleben lassen, wieder ins Leben rufen, wieder einführen (*customs*); wieder zur Sprache bringen (*a subject*); wieder aufführen *or* auf die Bühne bringen (*a play, etc.*); frischen (*Metall.*). 2. *v.n.* wieder zum Bewußtsein kommen, das Bewußtsein wiedergewinnen; wieder aufleben *or* aufblühen *or* auftreten, wieder lebendig werden. **–er** [–ə], *s.* das Erfrischungsmittel, Renovierungsmittel; (*sl.*) der Erfrischungstrunk. **–ification** [rɪːvɪvɪfɪˈkeɪʃən, das Wiederaufleben. **–ify** [rɪˈvɪvɪfɑɪ], *v.a.* wiederbeleben. **–iscent** [rɪːvɪˈvɪsənt], *adj.* wiederauflebend; (*fig.*) wiederbelebend.

revo–cable [ˈrɛvəkəbl], *adj.* widerruflich. **–cation** [–ˈkeɪʃən], *s.* der Widerruf; die Aufhebung (*Law*). **–ke** [rɪˈvoʊk], 1. *v.a.* widerrufen, zurücknehmen; aufheben. 2. *v.n.* nicht bedienen, Farbe nicht bekennen (*Cards*). 3. *s.* das Nichtbekennen, die Renonce (*Cards*).

revol–t [rɪˈvoʊlt], 1. *s.* die Empörung, Auflehnung (*against*, gegen), der Aufruhr, Aufstand; Abfall (*from allegiance*). 2. *v.n.* sich empören (*against*, gegen); sich abwenden, abfallen (*from*, von); (*fig.*) sich sträuben (*against* or *from*, gegen), Widerwille empfinden (*at*, über). 3. *v.a.* empören, abstoßen (*a p.*) (*by*, durch). **–ting,** *adj.* (*fig.*) abstoßend, empörend, ekelhaft. **–ute** [ˈrɛvəl(j)uːt], *adj.* zurückgerollt (*Bot.*). **–ution** [rɛvəˈl(j)uːʃən], *s.* die Umdrehung, Drehung, Tour, der Umlauf, Kreislauf; Umschwung, die Umwälzung; Revolution, (Staats)Umwälzung, der Umsturz (*Pol.*); *–ution counter*, der Tourenzähler. **–utionary** [–ʃənərɪ], 1. *adj.* revolutionär (*also fig.*), umstürzlerisch, Umsturz–, (staats)umwälzend; (*fig.*) epochemachend. 2. *s.* der Revolutionär, Umstürzler. **–utionist,** *s. see* **–utionary** 2. **–utionize** [–ʃənɑɪz], *v.a.* revolutionieren, in Aufruhr bringen; (*fig.*) umwälzen, gänzlich umgestalten. **–ve** [rɪˈvɔlv], 1. *v.n.* sich drehen, rotieren, kreisen (*on* or *round*, um (*Acc.*)); umlaufen, wiederkehren. 2. *v.a.* (um)drehen; (*fig.*) überlegen, erwägen (*in one's mind*). **–ver** [rɪˈvɔlvə], *s.* der Revolver. **–ving** [–vɪŋ], *adj.* sich drehend, drehbar, Dreh–; *–ving bookcase*, drehbarer Bücherständer; *–ving chair*, der Drehstuhl; *–ving light*, das Blinkfeuer (*Naut.*); *–ving pencil*, der Drehbleistift; *–ving shutter*, der Rolladen; *–ving stage*, die Drehbühne.

revue [rɪˈvjuː], *s.* die Revue (*Theat.*).

revulsi–on [rɪˈvʌlʃən], *s.* der Umschwung, Umschlag (*of feeling, etc.*); das Ableiten, die Ableitung (*Med.*). **–ve** [–sɪv], *adj.* ableitend (*Med.*).

reward [rɪˈwɔːd], 1. *s.* die Belohnung, Vergütung; der Finderlohn; (*fig.*) die Vergeltung, der Lohn. 2. *v.a.* belohnen; vergelten (*services, etc.*). **–ing,** *adj.* lohnend.

reword [rɪːˈwəːd], *v.a.* neu formulieren.

rewrite [rɪːˈrɑɪt], *ir.v.a.* neu schreiben, umarbeiten. **––man**[ˈrɪːrɑɪtˈmæn], *s.* der Überarbeiter (*press*).

rexine [ˈrɛksɪːn], *s.* das Kunstleder.

Reynard [ˈreɪnɑːd], *s.* Reineke (Fuchs).

rhapsod–ic(al) [ræpˈsɔdɪk(l)], *adj.* begeistert, überschwenglich, ekstatisch, rhapsodisch. **–ist** [ˈræpsədɪst], *s.* der Rhapsode (*Greek*); begeisterter Sänger. **–ize** [ˈræpsədɑɪz], *v.n.* begeistert *or* überschwenglich reden (*about, on* or *over*, über). **–y** [ˈræpsədɪ], *s.* die Rhapsodie, der Wortschwall; überschwenglicher Vortrag; *go into –ies over*, sich in überschwenglichen Lob ergehen über (*Acc.*).

rhatany [ˈrætənɪ], *s.* der Ratanhiastrauch, die Krameria (*Bot.*), Ratanhiawurzel.

rhea [ˈrɪːə], *s.* der Nandu (*Orn.*).

rheostat [ˈrɪːəstæt], *s.* der Rheostat, Regulierwiderstand, Widerstandsregler (*Elec.*).

rhetor [ˈrɪːtɔː], *s.* der Redner. **–ic** [ˈrɛtərɪk], *s.* die Redekunst, Rhetorik; der Redeschwall. **–ical** [rəˈtɔrɪkl], *adj.* rhetorisch, rednerisch; schönrednerisch, phrasenhaft, schwülstig. **–ician** [rɛtəˈrɪʃn], *s.* der Redekünstler, Schönredner.

rheum [ruːm], *s.* (*archaic*) die Flüssigkeit, der Schleim, Schnupfen. **–atic** [–ˈmætɪk], 1. *adj.* rheumatisch. 2. *pl.* (*coll.*) *see* **–atism.** **–atism** [ˈruːmətɪzm], *s.* der Rheumatismus, das Gliederreißen. **–atoid** [–ətɔɪd], *adj. see* **–atic.** **–y** [ˈruːmɪ], *adj.* (*archaic*) wässerig (*eye, etc.*).

rhinoceros [rɑɪˈnɔsərəs], *s.* das Nashorn, Rhinozeros (*Zool.*).

rhizo–me [ˈrɪːzoʊm], *s.* der Wurzelstock, das Rhizom. **–phagous** [rɪːˈzɔfəgəs], *adj.* wurzelfressend. **–pod** [ˈrɪːzəpɔd], *s.* der Wurzelfüßer *Zool.*).

rhodium [ˈroʊdɪəm], *s.* das Rhodium (*Chem.*); (*also* *––wood*) das Rhodiumholz.

rhododendron [roʊdəˈdɛndrən], *s.* das Rhododendron, die Alpenrose (*Bot.*).

rhomb [rɔm], *s.* die Raute, der Rhombus. **–ic** [–bɪk], *adj.* rautenförmig, rhombisch. **–ohedral** [–bəˈhɪːdrəl], *adj.* rhomboedrisch. **–ohedron** [–bəˈhɪːdrən], *s.* das Rhomboeder. **–oid** [–bɔɪd], 1. *s.* das Rhomboid. 2. *adj.* **–oidal** [–ˈbɔɪdl], *adj.* rautenförmig; rhomboidisch. **–us** [–bəs], *s. see* **–.**

rhubarb [ˈruːbɑːb], *s.* der Rhabarber.

rhumb [rʌm], *s.* der Kompaßstrich. **––line,** *s.* die Kompaßlinie.

rhym–e [rɑɪm], 1. *s.* der Reim; Reimvers; das Reimgedicht, Gedicht; Reimwort (*to*, auf); *without –e or reason, with neither –e nor reason*, ohne Sinn und Verstand; *in –e*, in Reimversen; *nursery –e*, der Kinderreim, das Kinderlied. 2. *v.n.* (sich) reimen; Verse machen. 3. *v.a.* reimen (*with*, auf (*Acc.*)), zusammen reimen, in Reimen abfassen. **–ed** [–d], *adj.* gereimt, Reim–. **–eless,** *adj.* reimlos. **–er, –ester** [–stə], *s.* der Reimschmied, Versemacher, Dichterling. **–ing,** *s.* das Reimen; *–ing-dictionary*, *s.* das Reimwörterbuch.

rhythm [rɪðm], *s.* der Rhythmus, Takt (*Mus.*); das Versmaß (*Metr.*); (*fig.*) der Pulsschlag, das An- und Abschwellen, regelmäßige Wiederkehr. **–ic(al)** [–mɪk(l)], *adj.* rhythmisch, taktmäßig, abgemessen; regelmäßig wiederkehrend, an- und abschwellend.

riant [ˈrɑɪənt], *adj.* heiter, lächelnd.

rib [rɪb], 1. *s.* die Rippe (*Anat.*), (Blatt)Ader (*Bot.*); Schirmstange, der Schirmstab (*of an umbrella*); rippenartiger Streifen (*in cloth*); rippenartige Verstärkung (*Arch.*); die Schiffsrippe, das Inholz, Spant (*Shipb.*); (*coll.*) die Ehehälfte; *– of beef*, das Rindsrippenstück. 2. *v.a.* rippen, riefen, wellen; (*sl.*) aufziehen (*a p.*). **–bed** [–d], *adj.* gerippt; geädert (*Bot.*) **––vault(ing),** *s.* das Rippengewölbe. **–wort,** *s.* Spitzer Wegerich (*Bot.*).

ribald [ˈrɪbəld], 1. *adj.* lüstern, schlüpfrig, zotig, lose, respektlos. 2. *s.* loser *or* respektloser Mensch, der Spötter; Zotenreißer. **–ry,** *s.* die Liederlichkeit, unzüchtige Rede, das Zotenreißen.

riband [ˈrɪbənd], *s.*; *Blue –*, Blaues Band.

ribband [ˈrɪbənd], *s.* die Sente (*Shipb.*); der Rödelbalken (*Bridgeb.*).

ribbon [ˈrɪbən], 1. *s.* das Band, Seidenband, die Borte; das Farbband (*of typewriter*); (*fig.*) Ordensband; der Fetzen; schmaler Streifen; *pl.* (*sl.*) Zügel (*pl.*); (*coll.*) *tear to –s*, in Fetzen zerreißen. 2. *v.a.* bebändern. **––development,** *s.* der Serienbau (entlang der Landstraße). **––fish,** *s.* der Bandfisch.

rice [rɑɪs], *s.* der Reis. **––flour,** *s.* das Reismehl. **––paper,** *s.* das Reispapier. **––pudding,** *s.* der Milchreis.

rich [rɪtʃ], *adj.* reich (*in*, an (*Dat.*)), wohlhabend; fett, fruchtbar (*as soil*); reichhaltig, reichlich, ergiebig; wertvoll, kostbar, prächtig, glänzend; voll, klangvoll (*as voice*); satt, warm (*as colour*); nahrhaft (*as food*); kräftig, gehaltvoll (*as wine*); (*coll.*) köstlich, gelungen (*as a joke*); (*sl.*) unsinnig; *the –* (*pl.*), die Reichen; *– coal*, die Fettkohle. **–es** [–ɪz], *pl.* der Reichtum, Reichtümer (*pl.*). **–ly,** *adv.* reich, prächtig; reichlich, völlig, höchst, durchaus; *–ly deserved*, reichlich verdient. **–ness,** *s.* der Reichtum (*in* or *of*, an), die Pracht, Reichhaltigkeit, Fülle; Fruchbarkeit, Ergiebigkeit; Klangfülle, der Wohlklang (*of a voice*).

rick [rɪk], 1. *s.* der (Heu)Schober. 2. *v.a.* in Schobern aufstellen.
ricket–s [ˈrɪkɪts], *pl.* (*sing. constr.*) Englische Krankheit, die Rachitis. **–y,** *adj.* rachitisch (*Med.*); (*fig.*) wack(e)lig, baufällig; (*coll.*) gebrechlich, hinfällig.
ricochet [ˈrɪkəʃeɪ], 1. *s.* das Abprallen, Aufprallen, das Rikoschet, der Rollschuß, Prellschuß, Abpraller. 2. *v.n.* rikoschettieren, aufprallen, aufschlagend abprallen.
rictus [ˈrɪktəs], *s.* der Schlund.
rid [rɪd], *ir.v.a.* (*also imperf. & p.p.*) befreien, freimachen (*of*, von); – *o.s.*, sich (*Dat.*) entledigen (*of* (*Gen.*)) *or* vom Halse schaffen (*of* (*Acc.*)); *be* – *of*, los sein (*Acc.*); *get* – *of*, loswerden (*Acc.*). **–dance** [–əns], *s.* die Befreiung (*from*, von); *a good –dance to him, he is a good –dance*, ein Glück daß man ihn los wird *or* ihn endlich los ist.
ridden [ˈrɪdən], *see* **ride**; (*fig.* beherrscht, verfolgt, geplagt (*by*, von); *disease-–*, von Krankheit heimgesucht.
¹**riddl–e** [ˈrɪdl], 1. *s.* das Rätsel, Geheimnis. 2. *v.a.* enträtseln, auflösen. 3. *v.n.* in Rätseln sprechen. **–ing,** *adj.* rätselhaft.
²**riddle,** 1. *s.* das (Draht)Sieb; der Rätter (*Min.*). 2. *v.a.* sieben (*also fig.*), rättern (*Min.*); (*fig.*) durchlöchern.
ride [raɪd], **1.** *ir.v.n.* reiten (*on horse*); fahren (*on bicycle, in vehicle*); krumm stehen (*Typ.*); getragen werden, treiben, sich bewegen, dahinziehen; ruhen, schweben (*on*, auf) (*of things, vessels*); zum Reiten geeignet sein (*as ground*); *the rope –s*, das Tau läuft unklar; – *with one's back to the engine*, rückwärts fahren; – *pillion*, auf dem Soziussitz fahren; – *at anchor*, vor Anker liegen; – *at a fence*, ein Pferd auf ein Hindernis lenken; – *at a walking pace*, (im) Schritt reiten; – *behind a p.*, hinter einem herreiten; hinten aufsitzen (*on the same horse*); – *for a fall*, wild darauflos *or* waghalsig reiten; (*fig.*) Unglück heraufbeschwören; *in a perambulator*, im Kinderwagen aus(ge)fahren (werden); – *on a bicycle*, radeln, radfahren; – *out*, hinausreiten; – *over a p.*, einen überfahren; – *roughshod over a p.*, sich über einen hinwegsetzen, einen vergewaltigen, roh *or* rücksichtslos behandeln *or* schurigeln; – *to hounds*, in der Parforcejagd reiten; – *up*, sich hochschieben. **2.** *ir.v.a.* reiten, rittlings sitzen auf (*a horse*), fahren (*a bicycle*); (*fig.*) (*often pass. see* **ridden**) beherrschen, bedrücken, plagen; (*fig.*) ruhen auf, sitzen auf, schwingen auf, schweben auf; – *a bicycle*, radfahren, radeln; – *the country*, über Land reiten, das Land durchreiten; – *a horse at a fence*, ein Pferd auf ein Hindernis lenken; – *the high horse*, sich aufs hohe Roß setzen; – *to death*, zu Tode hetzen (*a theory, etc.*); – *a race*, in einem Rennen reiten *or* fahren; – *full speed*, mit voller Geschwindigkeit fahren; – *the waves*, auf den Wellen reiten; – *down*, niederreiten, überfahren; – *out a gale*, einen Sturm überstehen *or* aushalten. **3.** *s.* der Ritt; die Fahrt (*in a vehicle*); der Reitweg; die Schneise (*in a wood*); *give s.o. a* –, einen reiten *or* fahren lassen; *go for* or *take a* –, ausreiten, ausfahren; (*sl.*) *take s.o. for a* –, einen aufs Glatteis führen; einen umbringen. **–r** [–ə], *s.* der Reiter (*also Tech.*); Fahrer (*on a bicycle*); die Strebe (*Arch.*); der Nachtrag, Zusatz, die Zusatzklausel (*Law*), Zusatzaufgabe (*Math.*), (Wechsel)Allonge (*C.L.*), das Laufgewicht (*Tech.*); *see* **riding.**
rideau [rɪˈdoʊ], *s.* die Geländewelle.
ridge [rɪdʒ], 1. *s.* der Rücken (*also of the nose*); (Berg)Kamm, Grat (*also Arch.*), die Hügelkette, Kammlinie (*Geog.*), der (Furchen)Rain (*Agr.*); (Dach)First (*Build.*); – *of hills*, die Hügelkette; *a* – *of high* (*low*) *pressure*, ein Zwischenhoch (Zwischentief) (*Meteor.*). 2. *v.a.* furchen. **–-pole,** der Dachfirstbalken; horizontale Zeltstange. **–-tile,** *s.* der Firstziegel. **–way,** *s.* der Kammlinienweg.
ridicul–e [ˈrɪdɪkju:l], 1. *s.* das Lächerliche, der Spott; *hold up to –e*, lächerlich machen; *turn to –e*, ins Lächerliche ziehen. 2. *v.a.* verspotten, lächerlich machen, bespötteln. **–ous** [rɪˈdɪkjuləs], *adj.* lächerlich, unsinnig. **–ousness,** *s.* die Lächerlichkeit.
¹**riding** [ˈraɪdɪŋ], *s.* das Reiten; der Reitweg. **–-boots,** *pl.* Reitstiefel. **–-breeches,** *pl.* die Reithose. **–-habit,** *s.* das (Damen)Reitkleid. **Red–-Hood,** *see Index of Names.* **–-lamp,** *s.* das Ankerlicht (*Naut.*). **–-lesson,** *s.* die Reitstunde. **–-whip,** *s.* die Reitgerte, Reitpeitsche.
²**riding,** *s.* der Verwaltungsbezirk (*in Yorkshire*).
rife [raɪf], *pred. adj.* häufig, vorherrschend, weitverbreitet; voll, erfüllt (*with*, von); *be* –, grassieren.
riff-raff [ˈrɪfræf], *s.* das Gesindel, der Pöbel; Auswurf.
¹**rifle** [ˈraɪfl], *v.a.* berauben (*of* (*Gen.*)), (aus)plündern.
²**rifl–e,** 1. *v.a.* riffe(l)n, riefen; ziehen (*gun-barrels*). 2. *s.* das Gewehr, die Büchse; *pl.* Schützen (*pl.*) (*Mil.*). **–e-corps,** das Schützenkorps. **–e-green,** *adj.* jägergrün. **–e-grenade,** *s.* die Gewehrgranate. **–eman,** *s.* der Schütze, Jäger. **–e-pit,** *s.* der Schützengraben, das Schützenloch. **–e-range,** *s.* der Schießstand; die Schußweite. **–e-shot,** *s.* der Gewehrschuß; die Gewehrschußweite; der Schütze. **–ing,** *s.* Züge (*pl.*) (*in gun-barrels*); der Drall; das Riefen, Ziehen.
rift [rɪft], 1. *s.* die Ritze, Spalte, der Riß, Spalt, Schlitz; – *in the lute*, die Verstimmung. 2. *v.a.* spalten.
¹**rig** [rɪg], 1. *s.* Possen (*pl.*), der Streich, Schwindel; *run a* –, einen Streich spielen. 2. *v.a.* necken, frozzeln; betrügerisch handhaben; – *the market*, die Kurse *or* den Markt beeinflussen (*C.L.*).
²**rig,** 1. *s.* die Takelung (*Naut.*); (*coll.*) Kleidung, Ausrüstung, Ausstaffierung. 2. *v.a.* auftakeln (*Naut.*), ausrüsten, montieren (*Av.*); (*coll.*) zur Not errichten *or* aufstellen; *fore-and-aft –ged*, mit Schratsegeln getakelt; *full-–ged ship*, das Vollschiff; *square-–ged*, mit Rahsegeln getakelt; (*coll.*) – *out*, aufputzen, ausstaffieren; (*coll.*) – *up*, zur Not ausstatten *or* einrichten, zusammendrechseln. **–ger** [–ə], *s.* der Takler (*Naut.*), Monteur (*Av.*). **–ging,** *s.* das Takelwerk, die Takelung, Takelage (*Naut.*), Verspannung (*Av.*); *standing –ging*, stehendes Gut; *running –ging*, laufendes Gut. **–ging-loft,** *s.* der Schnürboden (*Theat.*).
right [raɪt], **1.** *adj.* recht (*also of angles*), richtig, wahr, in Ordnung, ordnungsgemäß, angemessen, passend; gesund, wohl; (*coll.*) – *oh!* or – *you are!* jawohl! gern! durchaus! schön! gut! *all* – *!* alles in Ordnung! ganz richtig! recht so! gewiß! gut! schön! abgemacht! – *and proper*, recht und billig. (*a*) (*with nouns*) *at* – *angles*, rechtwink(e)lig; – *ascension circle*, der Stundenkreis; – *hand*, rechte Hand; (*fig.*) der treue Beistand, die Hauptstütze; *at* or *on the* – *hand*, rechts, zur Rechten; – *side*, rechte Seite, die Vorderseite; *the error is on the* – *side*, der Fehler wirkt sich gut aus; *keep on the* – *side of a p.*, mit einem in Güte fertig werden; *on the* – *side of 40*, noch nicht 40 Jahre alt; *the* – *thing*, das Richtige; *the* – *way*, (in der) richtig(en Weise); *go the* – *way to work*, etwas richtig angreifen. (*b*) (*with verbs*) *be* –, recht *or* richtig *or* in Ordnung sein, sich gehören; recht haben; *that's* – *!* recht so! so ist's! jawohl!; (*coll.*) *not quite* – *in the head, not in his* – *mind*, nicht ganz normal, nicht bei Trost *or* Verstand; *it is* – *for you to* . . ., Sie tun recht, wenn Sie . . .; *feel quite all* –, sich wohl befinden; *get it* –, es klarlegen, es in Ordnung bringen; *put* or *set* –, in Ordnung bringen, berichtigen (*a th.*); *set s.o.* –, einen zurechtweisen *or* aufklären. **2.** *adv.* rechts; regelrecht, vollkommen, in hohem Grade, sehr; rechtmäßig; – *and left*, von *or* nach rechts und links *or* allen Seiten; – *ahead*, geradeaus; – *away*, sogleich; *come* –, in Ordnung kommen; *do* –, recht handeln; – *in front*, ganz vorn; *eyes* – *!* Augen rechts! – *Honourable*, Exzellenz (*title*); *put o.s.* – *with s.o.*, sich mit einem gut stellen; – *turn!* rechtsum! *it serves us* –, es geschieht uns recht. **3.** *s.* das Recht; die Billigkeit; rechte Seite *or* Hand, die Rechte (*also Pol.*); begründeter Anspruch (*to*, auf (*Acc.*)); das Anrecht, Vorrecht, Privilegium; Rechte(r), *m.* (*Boxing*); *pl.* wahrer, Sachverhalt; *civil –s*, bürgerliche Ehrenrechte; *all –s reserved!* alle Rechte vorbehalten! *the –s and wrongs of a matter*, die Sache von allen Seiten betrachtet. (*a*) (*with nouns*) *in* – *of his mother*, von seiten seiner Mutter, rechtmäßig für seine Mutter; – *of possession*, das Eigentumsrecht; – *of way*, das Recht einen Weg zu

benutzen; das Vorfahrrecht (*Motor*). (*b*) (*with verbs*) *do a p.* –, einem Gerechtigkeit *or* Billigkeit widerfahren lassen; *have a* –, ein Recht *or* Anrecht haben (*to*, auf (*Acc.*)), Recht haben zu. (*c*) (*with prepositions*) *by* –(*s*), von Rechts wegen, eigentlich; *by – of*, kraft, vermöge (*Gen.*); *be in the* –, recht haben; *in her own* –, durch Geburt, aus eigenem Recht; *of* –, rechtmäßig; *on the* –, rechts (*of*, von), zur Rechten; *stand on one's –s*, auf seinen Rechten bestehen; *to the* –, rechts (*of*, von); *keep to the* –, rechts fahren, rechts halten; *put* or *set to –s*, in Ordnung bringen. **4.** *v.a.* Recht widerfahren lassen *or* verschaffen (*Dat.*); berichtigen, wiedergutmachen; wiederaufrichten; – *o.s.*, sich wieder aufrichten, wieder hochkommen; – *itself*, sich wieder ausgleichen (*as a fault*). **5.** *v.n.* sich (wieder) aufrichten (*Naut.*). **--about turn,** die Kehrtwendung. **--and-left shot,** der Doppeltreffer, die Dublette. **--angle(d),** *adj.* rechtwinklig; *--angle bend*, das Kniestück. **--down,** *adj.* & *adv.* (*coll.*) regelrecht, vollkommen, wahr. **-eous** [-ʃəs], *adv.* gerecht, rechtschaffen. **-eousness,** *s.* die Rechtschaffenheit. **-ful** [-ful], *adj.* rechtmäßig, gerecht. **--hand,** *adj.* zur Rechten stehend; rechtshändig, rechtsseitig; rechtsläufig (*screw*); *--hand man*, rechter Nebenmann, (*fig.*) rechte Hand. **--handed,** *adj.* rechtshändig. **--hander,** *s.* Rechte(r), *m.* (*Boxing*). **--lined,** *adj.* geradlinig. **-ly,** *adv.* mit Recht, richtig; *remember -ly*, sich recht entsinnen. **--minded,** *adj.* rechtschaffen. **--mindedness,** *s.* die Rechtschaffenheit. **-ness,** *s.* die Richtigkeit; Rechtlichkeit; Geradheit (*of a line*).

rigid [ˈrɪdʒɪd], *adj.* steif, starr, unbeugsam (*also fig.*); (*fig.*) streng, hart; – *airship*, das Starrluftschiff. **-ity** [rɪˈdʒɪdɪtɪ], *s.* die Steifheit, Starrheit; (*fig.*) Strenge, Härte.

rigmarole [ˈrɪgmərоul], *s.* leeres Geschwätz, das Gewäsch, die Salbaderei.

rigor [ˈrɪgə, ˈraɪgə], *s.* der Schüttelfrost (*Med.*); – *mortis*, die Totenstarre (*Path.*). **-ism** [ˈrɪgərɪzm], *s.* die Starrheit, übertriebene Strenge. **-ist** [-rɪst], *s.* der Rigorist. **-ous** [-rəs], *adj.* streng, hart, unerbittlich, genau; rauh (*of climate*).

rigour [ˈrɪgə], *s.* die Strenge (*also Law*), Härte, Starrheit, Erstarrung; Genauigkeit, Schärfe; *pl.* Unbilden (*pl.*) (*of climate*).

rile [raɪl], *v.a.* (*coll.*) ärgern, aufbringen.

rill [rɪl], *s.* das Bächlein.

rim [rɪm], 1. *s.* der Rand; Radkranz, die Felge (*of a wheel*). 2. *v.a.* mit einem Rand versehen; befelgen (*a wheel*). **--brake,** *s.* die Felgenbremse. **-less,** *adj.* ohne Rand.

¹rim-e [raɪm], *s.* (*Poet.*) der Reif, Rauhfrost. **-y,** *adj.* bereift.

²rime, *see* **rhyme.**

rim-ose [ˈraɪmous], **-ous** [ˈraɪməs], *adj.* rissig, spaltig.

rind [raɪnd], *s.* die (Baum)Rinde, Borke; Käserinde (*of cheese*); Schale, Hülse (*of fruit*), Kruste, Schwarte.

rinderpest [ˈrɪndəpɛst], *s.* die Rinderpest.

¹ring [rɪŋ], 1. *s.* der Ring (*also Sport., C.L.,* & *fig.*); Reif; die Öse; der Hof (*of the moon*); Kreis (*of persons*); das Kartell, der Verband (*C.L.*); die Ringbahn, Schranke, Arena; Buchmacher (*pl.*), die Boxerwelt, Boxer (*pl.*); *judging* –, der Schiedsrichterplatz; *wedding*-–, der Trauring. 2. *v.a.* einen Ring anlegen (*Dat.*), (be)ringen (*pigeons, etc.*); ringeln (*trees, etc.*); in Ringe schneiden (*apples*); – *in*, umringen, einkreisen (*cattle*). 3. *v.n.* (spiralförmig) ansteigen (*as hawks*), sich im Kreise bewegen. **---roses,** *s.* der Ringelreihen. **--bone,** *s.* das Überbein. **--dove,** *s.* die Ringeltaube. **--fence,** *s.* die Umzäunung. **--finger,** *s.* der Ringfinger, Goldfinger. **-leader,** *s.* der Rädelsführer. **-let,** *s.* das Ringlein; die Haarlocke, Ringellocke. **--master,** *s.* der Zirkusdirektor. **--neck,** *s.* die Ringelmoorente (*Orn.*); *--necked plover*, der Halsbandregenpfeifer (*Orn.*). **--ouzel,** *s.* die Ringdrossel (*Orn.*). **-side,** *s.* der Zuschauerplatz am Ring. **--snake,** *s.* die Ringelnatter. **--tail,** *s.* der Blaufalken (*Orn.*); das Weibchen des Kornweihs (*Orn.*). **-worm,** *s.* die Ringelflechte (*Med.*).

²ring, 1. *s.* der Klang, Schall; das Klingen, Läuten, Klingeln; Anrufen, Rufzeichen (*Tele.*); *answer the* –, die Tür öffnen; – *of bells*, das Glockengeläute, Glockenspiel; *there is a – at the door*, es klingelt *or* läutet; *give me a* –, rufe mich an; *the – of truth*, der echte Klang der Wahrheit. 2. *ir.v.n.* läuten, klingeln; klingen (*as coins*); erklingen, erschallen, widerhallen (*with*, von); *does this bell –?* läutet diese Glocke? – *for the maid*, nach dem Mädchen klingeln; – *for tea*, zum Tee klingeln; – *in s.o.'s ears*, einem in den Ohren klingen; – *out*, erklingen, laut tönen; – *off*, abläuten, den Hörer abhängen (*Phone*); – *true*, echt *or* wahr klingen; *the town –s with his fame*, die Stadt ist erfüllt *or* voll von seinem Ruhm. 3. *ir.v.a.* klingen lassen; läuten; – *the bell*, klingeln; (*sl.*) den Vogel abschießen; – *the changes*, das Geläut erklingen lassen; (*fig.*) immer wiederholen *or* zurückkehren (*on*, zu), immer in neuer Fassung vorbringen (*on* (*Acc.*)); – *the knell of*, zu Grabe läuten; – *s.o.'s praises*, jemandes Lob verkünden; – *down*, niedergehen lassen (*the curtain*); – *in*, einläuten; – *out*, feierlichen Abschied nehmen von; – *up*, hochgehen lassen (*the curtain*); anrufen, anklingeln (*a p.*) (*Phone*). **-er** [-ə], *s.* der Glockenläuter. **-ing,** 1. *adj.* klingend, schallend, widerhallend, laut. 2. *s.* das Klingen; *he has a -ing in his ears*, ihm klingen die Ohren.

rink [rɪŋk], *s.* die Rollschuhbahn; künstliche Eisbahn.

rins-e [rɪns], *v.a.* (also *-e out*), ausspülen, abspülen, ausschwenken, abschwemmen (*clothes*). **-ing,** *s.* das (Aus)Spülen, Abspülen; *pl.* das Spülwasser, Spülicht.

riot [ˈraɪət], 1. *s.* der Aufruhr, (Volks)Auflauf, Tumult; die Schwelgerei, Ausschweifung; (*fig.*) der Überfluß; *run* –, wuchern (*plants*); (*fig.*) sich austoben, schwelgen, schwärmen, ausschweifen. 2. *v.n.* Ausschreitungen begehen, an einem Aufruhr teilnehmen, meutern, sich zusammenrotten; toben, sich austoben, umherschwärmen, ausschweifen, schwelgen. **– act,** *s.* das Aufruhrgesetz (*Hist.*); *read the – act to*, verwarnen. **-er** [-tə], *s.* der Aufrührer, Meuterer; (*fig.*) Schwelger. **-ous** [-təs], *adj.* aufrührerisch; tobend, lärmend; zügellos, ausschweifend, ausgelassen, schwelgerisch. **-ousness,** *s.* das Lärmen; die Ausgelassenheit, Zügellosigkeit, Schwelgerei.

¹rip [rɪp], 1. *v.a.* auftrennen (*a seam, etc.*); (*coll.*) (zer)reißen; – *off*, abreißen; – *open*, aufreißen, aufschlitzen; – *out*, ausreißen; – *up*, (in Stücke) zerreißen. 2. *v.n.* (zer)reißen, platzen, sich spalten, (*coll.*) drauflosstürmen; (*sl.*) *let it – !* laß es laufen. 3. *s.* der Riß. **--cord,** *s.* die (Ab)Reißleine (*Av.*). **--saw,** *s.* die Schrotsäge, Kerbsäge.

²rip, *s.* der Taugenichts; alter Klepper (*horse*).

riparian [raɪˈpɛːərɪən], 1. *adj.* Ufer–. 2. *s.* der Besitzer von einem am Ufer gelegenen Grundstück.

ripe [raɪp], *adj.* reif (*for*, für), bereit, fertig (*for*, zu); (*fig.*) (aus)gereift, entwickelt, ausgewachsen, vollendet; wie geschaffen, geradezu gemacht (*for*, für); *when the time is* –, wenn die rechte Zeit gekommen ist; – *age*, hohes Alter; – *scholar*, vollendeter Gelehrter; – *wine*, ausgereifter Wein. **-n,** 1. *v.n.* reif werden, (heran)reifen, sich entwickeln (*into*, zu). 2. *v.a.* reif machen, zur Reife bringen. **-ness,** *s.* die Reife; das Reifsein.

riposte [rɪˈpoust], 1. *s.* der Nachstoß, Gegenstoß, Nachhieb, die Riposte (*Fenc.*); (*fig.*) rasche Antwort. 2. *v.n.* einen Gegenstoß machen; (*fig.*) schnell erwidern.

ripp-er [ˈrɪpə], *s.* (*sl.*) der Prachtkerl, das Prachtexemplar. **-ing** [-ɪŋ], *adj.* (*sl.*) famos, kolossal, hervorragend.

¹ripple [ˈrɪpl], 1. *v.n.* kleine Wellen schlagen, sich kräuseln; plätschern, murmeln. 2. *v.a.* kräuseln (*water*). 3. *s.* kleine Welle, leises Kräuseln (*of water*); das Rieseln, Murmeln, Geplätscher, Geriesel; – *of laughter*, leises Gelächter.

²ripple, 1. *v.a.* kämmen, riffeln (*flax*). 2. *s.* die Flachsriffel, Raffkamm.

rise [raɪz], **1.** *ir.v.n.* aufstehen, sich erheben; emporsteigen, aufsteigen (*to*, zu); in die Höhe gehen, steigen, anschwellen; anziehen (*of prices*); aufgehen (*as the sun, etc., curtain* & *dough*), hochgehen (*curtain*); stärker werden, sich verstärken, wachsen, zunehmen; entspringen, entstehen (*from*, aus); auftreten, aufkommen, erscheinen, sich zeigen, sichtbar werden, emporragen; vorwärtskommen (*in the world*), befördert werden; an die Oberfläche kommen, anbeißen (*as fish*); die Sitzung aufheben, sich vertagen, aufbrechen (*as an assembly*); sich empören (*against*, gegen); auferstehen (*from the dead*, von den Toten); – *above*, erhoben sein über; *my gorge –s at it*, es ekelt mich an; *his hair –s*, ihm stehen die Haare zu Berge; – *in arms*, zu den Waffen greifen; – *to a bait*, (*coll.*) – *to it*, anbeißen, darauf hereinfallen; – *to one's feet*, aufstehen; – *to one's lips*, einem auf die Lippen kommen; – *to the occasion*, sich der Lage gewachsen zeigen; – *to* (*a point of*) *order*, beantragen daß zur Geschäftsordnung gesprochen wird; – *up in arms*, see – *in arms*; – *upon the view*, sich dem Auge zeigen. **2.** *ir.v.a.* aufsteigen lassen; an die Oberfläche locken (*fish*); aufjagen (*a bird*); in Sicht bekommen (*a ship*); hochverstellen (*camera-front*). **3.** *s.* das Hochkommen, der Aufstieg (*to*, zu); das Emporkommen (*in life*); Steigen (*in price*; *of voice*), Aufgehen, der Aufgang (*of the sun*); das Hochgehen (*of the curtain*); die Steigung, Anhöhe, Höhe, Stufe (*of a step, etc.*); Steigerung, das Wachsen (*in*, an), Anschwellen, der Zuwachs, die Zunahme, Zulage (*of salary*); die Hauße (*C.L.*); der Ursprung, die Entstehung; das Anbeißen (*of fish*); (*coll.*) *get* or *take a – out of s.o.*, einen in die Wolle bringen; *give – to*, hervorrufen, veranlassen, bewirken, herbeiführen, Anlaß geben zu; *have its – in*, *take its – from*, entspringen aus; – *in price*, die Preiserhöhung; – *in prices*, das Steigen der Preise; *be on the –*, steigen; *buy for a –*, auf Hauße spekulieren (*C.L.*). **–n** [ˈrɪzən], *see* **rise**; *the –n Christ*, der Auferstandene; *the –n sun*, die aufgegangene Sonne. **–r** [–ə], *s.* Aufstehende(r), *m.*; die Treppenstufe; *early –r*, der Frühaufsteher; *see* **rising.**

risib–ility [rɪzɪˈbɪlɪtɪ], *s.* das Lachvermögen; die Lachlust. **–le** [ˈrɪzɪbl], *adj.* Lach–, lachlustig; lächerlich.

rising [ˈrɑɪzɪŋ], *see* **rise**; **1.** *adj.* emporkommend, aufstrebend (*a p.*), ansteigend (*ground*); – *generation*, heranwachsendes Geschlecht, der Nachwuchs; – *ground*, die Anhöhe; – *gust*, die Steigbö (*Meteor.*); – *stress*, steigender Akzent, der Auftakt; – *sun*, aufgehende Sonne; – *twelve*, von nahezu zwölf (Jahren). 2. *s.* das Aufstehen; (Auf)Steigen, Emporsteigen, Vorwärtskommen; die Steigerung, Zunahme; das Aufbrechen, der Aufbruch, die Vertagung (*of an assembly*); Empörung, der Aufstand; Aufgang (*of the sun, etc.*); die Auferstehung (*from the dead*); Steigung, Anhöhe (*Geog.*); Anschwellung, Geschwulst (*Med.*); – *of a vault*, die Wölbhöhe, Pfeilhöhe.

risk [rɪsk], 1. *s.* die Gefahr, das Wagnis; Risiko (*C.L.*); *at the –*, auf die Gefahr hin (*of doing*, zu tun); *at the – of his life*, auf eigene Lebensgefahr; *at one's own –*, auf eigene Gefahr; *run* or *take –s* or *a* or *the –*, Gefahr laufen, sich der Gefahr aussetzen (*of doing*, zu tun). 2. *v.a.* wagen, aufs Spiel setzen, riskieren. **–y,** *adj.* gewagt, gefahrvoll; heikel, riskant.

risqué [ˈrɪ:skeɪ], *adj.* heikel, schlüpfrig.

rissole [ˈrɪsoul], *s.* die Frikadelle.

rit–e [rɑɪt], *s.* der Ritus, die Liturgie; anerkannter Brauch; *funeral –es*, die Totenfeier; *nuptial –es*, die Hochzeitsbräuche. **–ual** [ˈrɪtjuəl], 1. *attrib. adj.* rituell, ritual, kirchlich; vorschriftsmäßig; feierlich; 2. *s.* das Ritual; die Gottesdienstordnung. **–ualism** [–ɪzm], *s.* der Ritualismus; Anglokatholizismus (*in England*). **–ualist** [–ɪst], *s.* der Ritualist; Anglokatholik, Hochkirchler. **–ualistic** [–ˈlɪstɪk], *adj.* ritualistisch, hochkirchlich.

rival [ˈrɑɪvl], 1. *s.* der Nebenbuhler, Rival(e) (*to* (*Gen.*)), Mitbewerber, Konkurrent (*for*, um); *without –*, ohnegleichen. 2. *attrib. adj.* wetteifernd, nebenbuhlerisch; Konkurrenz–. 3. *v.a.* wetteifern, konkurrieren *or* rivalisieren mit (*in*, an *or* in); gleichkommen, nacheifern (*Dat.*), es aufnehmen mit. **–ry,** *s.* die Nebenbuhlerschaft; Rivalität; der Wetteifer, Wettbewerb, die Konkurrenz.

riv–e [rɑɪv], 1. *ir.v.a.* (zer)spalten, zerreißen (*also fig.*). 2. *ir.v.n.* sich spalten. **–en** [ˈrɪvən], *pp.* & *adj.*, *see* **–e.**

river [ˈrɪvə], *s.* der Fluß; Strom (*also fig.*); (*fig.*) die Flut (*of tears*); – *Thames*, die Themse; *down the –*, stromab(wärts); *on the –*, am Flusse; *up the –*, stromauf(wärts). **–ain** [–reɪn], 1. *adj. see* **–ine.** 2. *s.* der Flußbewohner. **– –basin,** das Stromgebiet. **– –bed,** *s.* das Flußbett. **– –channel,** *s.* das Fahrwasser. **– –head,** *s.* die Flußquelle. **– –horse,** *s.* das Flußpferd (*Zool.*). **–ine** [–rɑɪn], *adj.* Fluß–, am Fluß gelegen. **–side,** 1. *s.* das Flußufer. 2. *attrib.* am Fluß *or* Wasser (gelegen); Fluß–. **– –traffic,** *s.* der Flußverkehr. **– –trout,** die Bachforelle.

rivet [ˈrɪvɪt], 1. *v.a.* (fest)nieten, vernieten; (*fig.*) befestigen (*to*, an), verankern (*in*, in), heften (*on*, auf) (*eyes*), fesseln (*attention*); festnageln (*an error*). 2. *s.* die Niete, der *or* das Niet. **–ing,** *s.* das Nieten. **–ing-hammer,** *s.* der Niethammer.

rivulet [ˈrɪvjulɪt], *s.* das Flüßchen, Bach.

[1]**roach** [routʃ], *s.* das Rotauge, die Plötze (*Ichth.*); *as sound as a –*, kerngesund.

[2]**roach,** *s.* die Gilling, Gillung (*Naut.*).

road [roud], *s.* die (Land)Straße; der Weg (*also fig.*), die Förderstrecke (*Min.*); (*Amer.*) das Geleise, Eisenbahn(linie) (*Railw.*); *pl.* die Reede (*Naut.*); *by –*, zu Fuß; per Auto; *the main* or *high –*, die Landstraße; *in the –*, auf der Straße; (*coll.*) hinderlich, im Wege; *in the –s*, auf der Reede (*Naut.*); *on the –*, auf dem Wege, unterwegs (*to*, nach); auf der Wanderschaft; (*coll.*) *get out of the –*, aus dem Wege gehen; *royal –*, leichter *or* bequemer *or* sicherer Weg (*to*, zu); – *to success*, der Weg zum Erfolg; *take to the –*, Landstreicher werden; *rule of the –*, die Fahrordnung, Straßenverkehrsordnung. **– –bed** *s.* der Bahnkörper. **– –hog,** *s.* (*coll.*) der Kilometerfresser, rücksichtsloser Fahrer. **– –house,** *s.* die Gaststätte *or* Wirtschaft (an der Landstraße). **– intersection,** *s.* die Wegkreuzung. **– junction,** *s.* der Straßenknotenpunkt. **– –making,** *s.* der Straßenbau. **–man,** *s.* der Straßenarbeiter. **– –map,** *s.* die Autokarte, Straßenkarte. **–mender,** *s.* der Straßenarbeiter. **– –metal,** *s.* die Straßenbeschotterung. **– –sense,** *s.* das Gefühl für Verkehrsordnung. **–side,** 1. *s.* die Straßenseite, Straßengegend; 2. *attrib.*; *–side inn*, das Gasthaus an der Landstraße. **– –sign,** *s.* der Wegzeiger. **–stead,** *s.* die Reede. **–ster,** *s.* das Tourenrad (*Cycl.*), offener Tourenwagen (*Motor.*), das Reisepferd; das Schiff vor Anker auf der Reede (*Naut.*). **– surface,** *s.* die Straßendecke. **– test,** *s.* die Probefahrt (*Motor.*). **–way,** *s.* der Fahrweg, Fahrdamm, die Fahrbahn. **–worthy,** *adj.* (zum Fahren) tauglich (*of vehicle*).

roam [roum], 1. *v.n.* streifen, ziehen, wandern; – *about*, umherstreifen. 2. *v.a.* durchstreifen, durchwandern, durchziehen.

roan [roun], 1. *adj.* rötlichgrau. 2. *s.* der Rotschimmel; weiches Schafleder (*Bookb.*).

roar [rɔ:], 1. *s.* das Gebrüll, Brüllen (*of beasts*); lautes Schreien (*of people*); das Brausen, Heulen, Toben (*of wind, etc.*); Krachen (*of thunder*); der Donner (*of cannon*); das Getöse; – *of laughter*, schallendes Gelächter; *set the company in a –*, die Gesellschaft zu lautem Lachen bringen. 2. *v.n.* brüllen, heulen (*of animals*), laut schreien (*of a p.*) brausen, tosen (*as water*), toben (*as wind*); krachen (*as thunder*), donnern (*of cannon*), dröhnen, sausen (*as machinery*); (also – *with laughter*) laut lachen; keuchen (*of a horse*). 3. *v.a.* (– *out*) (heraus)brüllen; – *down*, niederschreien. **–er** [–rə], *s.* der Brüller, keuchendes Pferd. **–ing** [–rɪŋ], 1. *adj.* brüllend, (*coll.*) ungeheuer, enorm, kolossal, famos; *–ing fire*, loderndes Feuer; *–ing forties*, stürmisches Meergebiet (zwischen 40° und 50° nördlicher Breite); *–ing night*, stürmische Nacht; *–ing trade*, flottes Geschäft. 2. *s.* das Brüllen, Heulen, Brausen, *etc.*; Keuchen (*of horses*).

roast [roust], 1. *v.a.* braten, rösten (*also metal, coffee*), brennen (*metal, coffee*); (*sl.*) aufziehen, necken. 2. *v.n.* gebraten werden. 3. *s.* der Braten; *rule the –*, herrschen, die Herrschaft führen; – *beef*, der Rinderbraten; – *meat*, der Braten; – *pork*, der Schweinebraten. **–er** [–ə], *s.* der (Brat)Rost; das

Spanferkel (*for roasting*); der Kaffeebrenner, Röstofen (*Metall.*). **-ing-jack,** *s.* der Bratenwender.

rob [rɔb], *v.a.* rauben, stehlen (*a th.*), berauben (*a p.*) (*of* (*Gen.*)), plündern, ausrauben (*a place*); – *s.o. of his inheritance*, einen um sein Erbe bringen; (*coll.*) – *Peter to pay Paul*, hier anpumpen um dort zu bezahlen, ein Loch aufreißen um das andere damit zu stopfen. **-ber** [-ə], *s.* der Räuber; Dieb; *highway -ber*, der Straßenräuber, Wegelagerer; *-ber knight*, der Raubritter. **-bery** [-ərɪ], *s.* der Raub (*of* or *from*, an (*Dat.*)), Diebstahl; (*coll.*) die Aubeutung, Erpressung, Geldschneiderei.

rob-e [roub], 1. *s.* der Talar, Umhang; (*archaic*) die Robe, das Damenkleid; (*usually pl.*) die Amtstracht, Amtskleidung; *academic -es*, akademischer Ornat, Barett und Talar; *long -es*, das Einschlagtuch (*of a baby*); *gentlemen of the* (*long*) *-e*, Gerichtsherren, Advokaten, Richter (*pl.*); *master of the -es*, der Oberkämmerer; *state -e*, das Staatskleid. 2. *v.a.* feierlich ankleiden. 3. *v.n.* sich ankleiden *or* schmücken. **-ing-room.** *s.* das Ankleidezimmer.

robin [ˈrɔbɪn], *s.* das Rotkehlchen; die Wanderdrossel (*Amer.*). **--redbreast,** *s.* das Rotkehlchen.

roborant [ˈroubərənt], 1. *adj.* stärkend, roborierend. 2. *s.* das Stärkungsmittel.

robot [ˈroubət], 1. *s.* der Roboter, Maschinenmensch, selbsttätiger Mechanismus. 2. *attrib.* automatisch, selbsttätig, Maschinen–.

robust [rouˈbʌst], *adj.* kräftig, stark, robust; gesund, kernig, rüstig; derb (*humour*). **-ious,** *adj.* (*rare*) lärmend, laut, heftig, ungestüm. **-ness,** *s.* die Kraft, Stärke.

roc [rɔk], *s.* der Vogel Rock (*Myth.*).

rocambole [ˈrɔkəmboul], *s.* die Perlzwiebel, Rockenbolle (*Bot.*).

rochet [ˈrɔtʃɪt], *s.* der Chorrock (*of bishops*).

[1]**rock** [rɔk], *s.* der Felsen; Fels, die Klippe; Felsen (*pl.*), felsiges Gestein; *firm as a –*, felsenfest; *see -s ahead*, die Klippen vor sich (*Dat.*) sehen; *on the -s*, festgefahren (*Naut.*); (*coll.*) in Geldnot, auf dem Trocknen, pleite. **--bed,** *s.* der Felsengrund. (*coll.*) **--bottom,** *adj.* allerniedrigst, äußerst (*price*); *at --bottom*, in Wirklichkeit, im Grunde. **--bound,** *adj.* von Felsen eingeschlossen, felsumgürtet. **--cake,** *s.* hartgebackener Kuchen. **--cork,** *s.* das Bergholz, Bergleder, Bergkork, Holzasbest. **--crystal,** *s.* der Bergkristall. **--drill,** *s.* die Gesteinbohrmaschine. **-ery,** *s.*, **--garden,** *s.* der Steinziergarten. **-iness** [-ɪnɪs], *s.* felsige Beschaffenheit, das Felsige, der Klippenreichtum. **--leather,** *s. see* **--cork.** **--oil,** *s.* das Petroleum, Erdöl, Steinöl. **-plant,** *s.* die Alpenpflanze. **--rose** *s.* die Zistrose (*Bot.*). **--salt,** *s.* das Steinsalz, Viehsalz. **--wood,** *see* **--cork.** **--work,** *s.* das Grottenwerk. **-y,** *adj.* felsig, voller Felsen; (*fig.*) felsenhart.

[2]**rock,** 1. *v.a.* schaukeln, wiegen (*a cradle*), in den Schlaf wiegen (*a child*); rütteln, schütteln (*Min.*), erschüttern, ins Schwanken bringen. 2. *v.n.* (sich) schaukeln, schwanken, wackeln. **-er** [-ə], *s.* gekrümmte Kufe (*of a cradle*); der Schaukelstuhl; Schwingtrog; (*sl.*) *be off one's -er*, einen Klaps, Knacks, Piep, Rappel, Sparren *or* Vogel haben. **-er-arm,** *s.* der Kipphebel. **-ing-chair,** *s.* der Schaukelstuhl. **-ing-horse,** *s.* das Schaukelpferd. **-ing-screen,** *s.* das Schüttelsieb, Schwingsieb. **-ing-stone,** *s.* der Wagstein. **-y,** *adj.* (*coll.*) wacklig, wackelnd, schwankend.

[1]**rocket** [ˈrɔkɪt], 1. *s.* die Rakete. 2. *v.n.* senkrecht auffliegen (*of birds, etc.*). **--plane,** *s.* das Raketenflugzeug. **--propelled,** *adj.* mit Raketenantrieb.

[2]**rocket,** *s.* die Rauke, der Raukenkohl, Senfkohl; die Nachtviole (*Bot.*).

rockiness, *see* [1]**rock.**

rocky, *see* [1]**rock** & [2]**rock.**

rococo [rəˈkoukou], 1. *s.* das Rokoko (*esp. Arch.*). 2. *adj.* Rokoko–; (*fig.*) Schnörkel–.

rod [rɔd], *s.* der Stab, die Rute, Gerte (*Bot.*); Stange (*Mach.*); (Meß)Rute (= *5,028 m.*); das Stäbchen (*in retina*); (*Amer. sl.*) die Pistole; *connecting –*, die Pleuelstange (*Motor*); *divining* or *dowsing –*, die Wünchelrute; *fishing –*, die Angelrute; *Black –*, der Träger des Elfenbeinstabs (*Parl.*); *kiss the –*, sich unter der Rute beugen; *I have a – in pickle for him*, ich habe mit ihm noch ein Hühnchen zu rupfen. **– iron,** *s.* das Stangeneisen.

rode [roud], *see* **ride.**

rodent [ˈroudənt], 1. *s.* das Nagetier. 2. *adj.* nagend, Nage–; fressend (*Path.*).

rodeo [ˈroudɪou], *s.* der Sammelplatz; die Wildwestschau.

rodomontade [ˈrɔdəmənˈteɪd], 1. *s.* die Prahlerei, Aufschneiderei. 2. *v.n.* prahlen, aufschneiden.

[1]**roe** [rou], *s.* (also *hard –*) der (Fisch)Rogen; *soft –*, die Milch. **--stone,** *s.* der Rogenstein.

[2]**roe,** *s.* (also *--deer*) das Reh; Rehwild, die Hirschkuh, Ricke. **-buck,** *s.* der Rehbock.

rogation [rəˈgeɪʃn], *s.* die Bitte (*Eccl.*), *pl.* Bittgänge (*R.C.*). – *Sunday*, der Sonntag Rogate; – *week*, *s.* die Himmelfahrtswoche, Bittwoche.

rogu-e [roug], *s.* der Schurke, Schuft, (*coll.*) Schelm, Schalk; Landstreicher; minderwertige Pflanze (*Hort.*); (also *-e elephant*) bösartiger Elefant; *-es' gallery*, das Verbrecheralbum. **-ery** [-ərɪ], *s.* die Schurkerei; Spitzbüberei, (*coll.*) Schelmerei, Schalkhaftigkeit. **-ish,** *adj.* schurkisch; schelmisch, schalkhaft.

roister [ˈrɔɪstə], *v.a.* lärmen, poltern, toben. **-er** [-rə], *s.* der Polterer. **-ing** [-rɪŋ], *adj.* tobend, lärmend.

rôle, role [roul], *s.* die Rolle (*also fig.*); (*fig.*) Funktion.

roll [roul], 1. *v.a.* rollen (*also one's eyes, r's*), herumrollen, herumdrehen; einwickeln, einhüllen (*in*, in); aufrollen, zusammenrollen; wälzen, strecken (*metals*); (*fig.*) herumwälzen (*in one's mind*); – *a cigarette*, eine Zigarette drehen; – *the lawn*, den Rasen walzen; – *out*, glätten, rollen (*dough*); – *over*, umwerfen; – *up*, aufrollen, einwickeln, hochkrempeln (*sleeves, etc.*). 2. *v.n.* rollen, sich wälzen; sich drehen *or* herumrollen; donnern, brausen, wirbeln; schlingen (*as a ship*), schlenkern (*as a p.*); abrollen, ablaufen (*time, etc.*); dahinrollen, dahinfließen (*water*); wallen, wogen (*sea*); sich ausdehnen (*land*); dröhnen (*Org.*); – *in*, hereinrollen; (*coll.*) hereinkommen, hereinschneien; *be -ing* (*in money*), Geld wie Heu haben, in Geld schwimmen. – *over*, sich herumdrehen. – *up*, sich zusammenrollen; (*sl.*) kommen, auftauchen. 3. *s.* die Rolle (*also Tech.*); Locke (*Spin.*); das Brötchen, Rundstück, die Semmel (*Bak.*); das Verzeichnis, die Namenliste, Urkunde; Schnecke, Volute (*Arch.*); Walze (*Tech.*); das Schlingern (*Naut.*); der Überschlag (*Av.*); Trommelwirbel; das Rollen, Brausen (*thunder, etc.*); Schlenkern, wiegender Gang; *call the –*, die Namen verlesen; *Master of the -s*, der Präsident des Reichsarchivs; – *of Honour*, die Ehrentafel der Gefallenen; *put on the –*, in die Liste eintragen; *strike off the -s*, von der Liste streichen; disqualifizieren (*lawyer, doctor, etc.*). **--call,** *s.* der Appell (*Mil.*), Namensaufruf. **-ed** [-d], *adj.* gerollt, Roll–; gewalzt, Walz– (*Metall.*); *-ed gold*, das Doubleegold; *-ed ham*, der Rollschinken; *-ed metal*, das Walzblech; *-ed r*, das Zungen-r. **-er** [-ə], *s.* die Rolle, Walze, der Zylinder (*Mach.*); die Flutwelle, Sturzwelle, Brandungswelle, Woge; Blaurake (*Orn.*), *pl.* das Walzwerk; *feed*(*ing*) *-er*, die Auftragswalze (*Print.*); *steam* or *road -er*, die Straßenwalze; *-er bandage*, die Rollbinde; *-er bearing*, das Rollenlager; *-er blind*, die Rolle, der Rollvorhang, das Rouleau; *-er-blind shutter*, der Schlitzverschluß (*Phot.*); *-er skate*, der Rollschuh; *-er towel*, endloses Handtuch. **– film,** *s.* der Rollfilm (*Phot.*). **-ing** [-ɪŋ], 1. *s.* das Rollen, Walzen, Strecken; Schlingen (*Naut.*). 2. *adj.* rollend, Roll–, wellig, wellenförmig (*land*); *set the ball -ing*, die Sache in Gang setzen; *-ing capital*, das Betriebskapital; *-ing stone*, (*fig.*) umsteter Mensch; (*Prov.*) *a -ing stone gathers no moss*, ein rollender Stein setzt kein Moos an; *-ing barrage*, die Feuerwalze (*Artil.*). **-ing-mill,** *s.* das Walzwerk. **-ing-pin,** *s.* das Rollholz. **-ing-press,** *s.* das Walzwerk; die Rotationsdruckpresse (*Typ.*). **-ing-stock,** *s.* rollendes Material (*Railw.*). **--moulding,** *s.* die Schneckenleiste (*Arch.*). **--top desk,** *s.* das Rollpult.

rollick [ˈrɔlɪk], *v.n.* herumtollen, ausgelassen *or*

übermütig sein. **–ing,** *adj.* ausgelassen, übermütig, lustig.
roly-poly [roulɪ'poulɪ], (*coll.*) 1. *s.* gerollter Marmeladepudding. 2. *attrib.* rundlich und dick.
roman–ce [ro'mæns], 1. *s.* die Romanze, romantische Erzählung, der Abenteuerroman, Liebesroman; das Romantische; (*fig.*) die Übertreibung, Erdichtung. 2. *v.n.* Erdichtungen erzählen, erdichten, fabeln, aufschneiden. **–cer** [–ə], *s.* der Romanzendichter, Romanschreiber; (*fig.*) Aufschneider. **–tic** [tɪk], 1. *adj.* romantisch (*also Lit.*), phantastisch, schwärmerisch (*of a p.*); malerisch; Romanzen–, Abenteuer–. 2. *s.* der Romantiker. **–ticism** [–tɪ'sɪzm], *s.* das Romantische; die Romantik (*Lit., etc.*). **–ticist** [–tɪ'sɪst], *s. see* **–ic.** **–ticize** [–tɪseɪz], *v.a.* romantisch machen.
Romance. *See Index of Names.*
romp [rɔmp], 1. *s.* die Range, der Wildfang; das Tollen, Balgen. 2. *v.n.* herumtollen, toben, sich herumtummeln *or* balgen; – *home*, leicht gewinnen (*Racing*); – *through*, spielend hindurchkommen. **–ers,** *pl.* der Spielanzug.
rond–eau ['rɔndou], *s.* das Reigenlied, Rondeau (*Metr.*). **–el,** *s.* 14-zeiliges Rondeau. **–o,** *s.* das Rondo (*Mus.*). **–ure,** *s.* (*Poet.*) der Kreis.
Röntgen ['rʌntjən], *attrib.* Röntgen–. **–ogram,** *s.* das Röntgenbild. **–'ography,** *s.* die Röntgenphotographie. **–o'therapy,** *s.* die Röntgenbestrahlung. **--rays,** *pl.* Röntgenstrahlen (*pl.*).
rood [ruːd], *s.* (*archaic*) das Kruzifix; die Rute; der Viertelmorgen (= *etwa 10 a*). **--loft,** *s.* die Empore des Lettners (*Eccl.*). **--screen,** *s.* der Lettner (*Eccl.*).
roof [ruːf], 1. *s.* das Dach; *coach-–*, das Wagendeck; – *of heaven*, das Himmelsgewölbe; – *of the mouth*, harter Gaumen; *under my* –, in meinem Hause. 2. *v.a.* bedachen; (also – *over*), überdachen. **–age** [–ɪdʒ], *s. see* **–ing.** **–er** [–ə], *s.* der Dachdecker. **--garden,** *s.* der Dachgarten. **–ing,** *s.* die Bedachung, das Dachwerk; *–ing felt*, die Dachpappe; *–ing-tile*, der Dachziegel. **–less,** *adj.* ohne Dach; (*fig.*) obdachlos. **--tree,** *s.* der Dachbalken, Firstbalken; (*fig.*) das Dach.
rook [ruk], 1. *s.* die Saatkrähe (*Orn.*); der Turm (*chess*); (*fig.*) Gauner, Betrüger. 2. *v.a.* betrügen. **–ery** [–ərɪ], *s.* die Krähenkolonie; Brutstätte (*of other birds*). **–ie,** *s.* (*sl.*) der Rekrut (*Mil.*); (*fig.*) Neuling, Anfänger.
room [ruːm], 1. *s.* der Raum, Platz; das Zimmer, die Stube; (*fig.*) der Spielraum; Anlaß, die Gelegenheit (*for*, zu); die Anwesenden (*pl.*); *pl.* die Wohnung; *no – for hope*, nichts zu hoffen, keine Hoffnung mehr; *have no – for complaint*, über nichts zu beklagen haben; *make – for*, Platz machen (*a p.*, einem), Raum schaffen für (*a th.*); *in the next* –, im Nebenzimmer; *in the – of*, (*rare*) an Stelle von, statt; *plenty of* –, viel Platz; *no – to swing a cat in*, sehr beengter Raum; *take up much* or *a lot of* –, viel Platz in Anspruch nehmen. 2. *v.n.* wohnen, logieren (*at*, in; *with*, bei); – *together*, zusammenwohnen. **–ed** [–d], *adj. suff.* –zimmerig. **–er,** *m.* (*Amer.*) der Untermieter. **–ful,** *s.* der Raumvoll, das Zimmervoll (*of*, von). **–iness,** *s.* die Geräumigkeit. **–ing-house,** *s.* (*Amer.*) das Logierhaus. **–y,** *adj.* geräumig, weit.
roost [ruːst], 1. *s.* der Schlafsitz (*of birds*); die Sitzstange, Hühnerstange; der Hühnerstall; *at* –, ruhend, schlafend; *cock of the* –, der Hahn im Korb; (*coll.*) *go to* –, zur Ruhe gehen. 2. *v.n.* aufsitzen, (sitzend) schlafen; (*coll.*) hausen. **–er** [–ə], *s.* der Hahn.
[1]**root** [ruːt], 1. *s.* die Wurzel (*also fig., Gram. & Math.*); der Quell, Grund, Ursprung; die Grundlage, das Wesen, der Gehalt, Kern; *be at the – of*, der Grund *or* die Ursache sein von; – *and branch*, mit Stumpf und Stiel, vollständig, ganz und gar, gänzlich; *cube* –, die Kubikwurzel; *go to the – of a th.*, einer S. auf den Grund gehen; *have one's –s in*, seine Grundlage haben in; *square* –, die Quadratwurzel; *take* or *strike* (*deep*) –, (tief) Wurzel schlagen *or* fassen. 2. *v.a.* einwurzeln, tief einpflanzen; (*fig.*) einimpfen; verwurzeln; (*fig.*) fesseln (*to*, an); – *out*, ausrotten. 3. *v.n.* Wurzel schlagen *or* fassen. **– cause,** die Grundursache, eigentliche Ursache. **--crop,** die Rübenernte, Hackfrüchte (*pl.*). **–ed** [–ɪd], *adj.* eingewurzelt, verankert, verwurzelt; *be –ed in*, fest verwachsen sein in, wurzeln in; *–ed to the spot*, wie angewurzelt. **–edness,** *s.* die Verwurzelung, Verankerung. **--grafting,** *s.* die Wurzelhalsveredelung. **– idea,** der Grundgedanke. **–less,** *adj.* ohne Wurzel; (*fig.*) ohne festen Boden. **–let,** *s.* die Wurzelfaser. **--sign,** *s.* das Wurzelzeichen (*Math.*). **--stock,** *s.* der Wurzelstock, das Rhizom. **--treatment,** *s.* die Wurzelbehandlung (*Dentistry*). **–y,** *adj.* wurzelreich; wurzelartig, Wurzel–.
[2]**root,** 1. *v.n.* mit der Schnauze wühlen (*for*, nach); – *about*, herumwühlen. 2. *v.a.* aufwühlen, umwühlen (*earth*); – *out*, (*fig.*) ausgraben, ausfindig machen.
rope [roup], 1. *s.* das Seil, der Strick; das Tau, (Tau)Ende, Reep (*Naut.*); die Strähne, das Bund, Bündel (*onions, etc.*); die Schnur (*pearls*); (*fig.*) Bewegungsfreiheit; *pl.* das Tauwerk (*Naut.*); die (Seil)Einzaunung (*Sport*); *give a p.* –, einen gewähren lassen; (*coll.*) *know the –s*, sich auskennen, den Kniff 'raushaben, den Rummel verstehen; *on the* –, angeseilt (*Mount.*); *on the high –s*, hochfahrend, hochmütig, hochgestimmt. 2. *v.a.* mit einem Seil festbinden, zusammenbinden *or* befestigen; anseilen (*climbers*); (*fig.*) hineinziehen (*into*, in), verlocken (*into*, zu); – *in*, durch ein Seil einschließen (*space*); (*coll.*) einfangen, gewinnen (*a p.*); – *off*, mit einem Seil absperren (*a space*). 3. *v.n.* Fäden bilden *or* ziehen, dick werden (*syrup*); sich anseilen (*Mount.*); – *down*, abseilen (*Mount.*). **--dancer,** *s.* der Seiltänzer. **--end,** *s. see* **–'s-end.** **--ladder,** *s.* die Strickleiter. **--maker,** *s.* der Seiler, Reeper, Reepschläger. **--moulding,** *s.* die Seilleiste (*Arch.*). **--railway,** *s.* die Seilbahn. **–ry,** *s.* die Seilerei. **–'s-end,** 1. *s.* das (Tau)Ende, der Tamp (*Naut.*). 2. *v.a.* mit dem Tauende verprügeln. **--walk,** *s.* die Seilerbahn; Reeperbahn. **--walker,** *s.* der Seiltänzer. **--yard,** *s.* die Seilerbahn, Seilerei. **--yarn,** *s.* das Kabelgarn.
rop–iness ['roupɪnɪs], *s.* die Klebrigkeit, Dickflüssigkeit. **–y,** *adj.* klebrig, dickflüssig, fadenziehend.
rorqual ['rɔːkwəl], *s.* der Finnwal (*Zool.*).
rosace ['rouzeɪs], *s.* das Rosenornament; Rosenfenster (*Arch.*). **–ous** [rou'zeɪʃəs], *adj.* Rosen– (*Bot.*).
rosar–ian [ro'zɛːərɪən], *s.* der Rosenzüchter; Rosenkreuzbruder (*R.C.*). **–ium** [–rɪəm], *s.* der Rosengarten. **–y** [–ərɪ], *s.* der Rosenkranz (*R.C.*); das Rosenbeet (*Hort.*).
[1]**rose** [rouz], *s.* die Rose (*Bot.*); Brause (*of a watering-can*); das Rosenrot, die Rosafarbe, Röte; Rosette (*Arch.*); *the* –, die Rose, der Rotlauf (*Med.*); *on a bed of –s*, auf Rosen gebettet; *milk and –s*, wie Milch und Blut; *under the* –, im Vertrauen. **–ate** [–ɪət], *adj.* rosig (*also fig.*); (*fig.*) strahlend, goldig, optimistisch. **--bud,** *s.* die Rosenknospe. **--bush,** *s.* der Rosenstrauch, Rosenstock. **--coloured,** *adj.* rosenrot, rosafarben; (*fig.*) rosig. **--diamond,** *s.* der Rosenstein, die Rosette. **--gall,** *s.* der Rosenschwamm. **--leaves,** *pl.* Rosenblätter. **–mary** [–mərɪ], *s.* der Rosmarin (*Bot.*). **–ola** [–'ɪːələ], *s.* Röteln (*pl.*) (*Med.*). **--pink,** 1. *s.* das Rosa. 2. *adj.* rosa–. **--rash,** *s.* Röteln (*pl.*). **--red,** *adj.* rosenrot. **--tree,** *s.* der Rosenstrauch, Rosenstock. **–tte** [–'zɛt], *s.* die Rosette (*also Arch.*), das Rosenornament. **--water,** *s.* das Rosenwasser, (*fig.*) die Affektiertheit. **– window,** *s.* die Fensterrose. **–wood,** *s.* das Rosenholz. *See* **rosiness, rosy.**
[2]**rose,** *see* **rise.**
rosin ['rɔzɪn], 1. *s.* das Harz, Terpentinharz, Kolophonium. 2. *v.a.* mit Kolophonium einreiben.
rosiness ['rouzɪnɪs], *s.* die Rosenfarbe; rosiges Aussehen. *See* **rose.**
roster ['roustə], *s.* die Dienstliste (*Mil.*).
rostra–l ['rɔstrəl], *adj.* schnabelförmig. **–te(d)** ['rɔstreɪt(ɪd)], *adj.* Schnabel–, schabelförmig.
rostrum ['rɔstrəm], *s.* die Rednerbühne, Kanzel, das Dirigentenpult; der Schnabel (*Zool. & Bot.*); Schiffsschnabel; schnabelförmiger Vorsprung.
rosy ['rouzɪ], *adj.* rosenrot, rosa; (*fig.*) rosig, blühend, glänzend. **--cheeked,** rosenwangig.

rot [rɔt], 1. *v.n.* (also – *away*) (ver)faulen, verwesen, (ver)modern; (*fig.*) verkommen, verrotten 2. *v.a.* zum Faulen bringen; (*sl.*) verderben; (*coll.*) hänseln, necken. 3. *s.* die Fäulnis, Verwesung, Vermoderung, Fäule; (*sl.*) der Unsinn, Blech, Quatsch; *the* –, die (Leber)Fäule (*in sheep*); (*sl.*) schlechte Spielperiode (*Sport*); (*sl.*) *talk* –, quasseln. 4. *int.* (*sl.*) Blödsinn! Quatsch!

rota [ˈroʊtə], *s.* die Dienstliste, der Lauf, Turnus; das päpstliche Appellationsgericht (*R.C.*). **–ry** [–ərɪ], *adj.* sich drehend, kreisend, rotierend, Rotations–, Dreh–, drehbar (*Mach.*); *–ry beacon*, das Drehfeuer; *–ry club*, der Rotaryclub, Rotarier (*pl.*); *–ry converter*, der Drehumformer (*Elec.*); *–ry current*, der Drehstrom; *–ry drier*, die Trockentrommel; *–ry engine*, der Umlaufmotor; *–ry motion*, die Drehbewegung, Kreisbewegung; *–ry machine*, die Rotationsmaschine, Schnellpresse; *–ry printing*, der Rotationsdruck; *–ry switch*, die Drehschaltung. **–te** [roˈteɪt], 1. *v.n.* sich um eine Achse drehen, umlaufen, rotieren; der Reihe nach abwechseln. 2. *v.a.* drehen; wechseln lassen (*as crops*). 3. [ˈroʊteɪt], *adj.* radförmig (*Bot.*). **–tion** [roˈteɪʃən], *s.* die (Um)Drehung, Rotation, der Kreislauf, Umlauf; (*fig.*) Wechsel, die Abwechslung; *–tion of crops*, der Fruchtwechsel; *direction of –tion*, der Drehsinn; *by* or *in –tion*, der Reihe nach, abwechselnd. **–tory** [ˈroʊtətərɪ], *adj. see* **–ry**; abwechselnd; *–tory storm*, der Wirbelsturm.

rote [roʊt], *s.*; *by* –, durch bloße Übung, rein mechanisch, auswendig.

rotifer [ˈroʊtɪfə], *s.* das Rädertierchen (*Zool.*).

rotor [ˈroʊtə], *s.* der Rotor, Anker (*Elec.*); rotierender Zylinder.

rotten [ˈrɔtən], *adj.* faul (*also fig.*), verfault, vermodert, verfallen; wurmstichig (*as fruit*); morsch (*as soil, also fig.*), mürde, brüchig (*as ice*); (*fig.*) verderbt, bestechlich, korrupt; (*sl.*) schlecht, niederträchtlich, kläglich; – *eggs*, faule Eier; – *to the core*, kernfaul, (*fig.*) grundschlecht, hoffnungslos korrupt; (*coll.*) – *luck*, das Saupech. **–ness,** *s.* die Fäulnis, Fäule; (*fig.*) Verderbtheit, Korruptheit.

rotter [ˈrɔtə], *s.* (*sl.*) verdorbener Mensch, der Lump, Schuft.

rotund [roˈtʌnd], *adj.* rund(lich), abgerundet; geblümt, ölig, ausgewogen (*style*); klangvoll, volltönend (*voice*). **–a** [–ə], *s.* der Rundbau (*Arch.*). **–ate** [–ət], *adj.* (ab)gerundet (*Bot.*). **–ifolius** [–ɪˈfoʊlɪəs], *adj.* rundblättrig (*Bot.*). **–ity** [–ɪtɪ], *s.* die Rundung; Rundheit, Rundlichkeit, Dicke.

roué [ˈruːeɪ], *s.* der Wüstling.

rouge [ruːʒ], 1. *adj.* rot (*Her.*); *––royal* (*marble*), rötlicher Marmor. 2. *s.* (rote) Schminke, (rotes) Polierpulver; – *et noir*, ein Glückspiel (*Cards*). 3. *v.a.* (*& n.*) (sich) rot schminken.

rough [rʌf], **1.** *adj.* rauh (*also fig.*), uneben, holperig; rauhhaarig, zottig, struppig; wild, stürmisch, heftig, ungestüm; barsch, grob, schroff, derb, ungeschliffen, ungehobelt, ungebildet (*as manners*); streng, hart (*with*, gegen); anstrengend (*life*); roh, Roh–; flüchtig, annähernd, ungefähr; herb (*taste*); – *balance*, rohe Bilanz; – *calculation*, der Überschlag; – *copy*, erster Entwurf, die Skizze; – *customer*, grober Gesell; – *diamond*, ungeschliffener Diamant; (*fig.*) das Rauhbein; – *draft*, see – *copy*; – *luck*, das Pech (*on*, für); (*coll.*) *it is* – *on him*, es ist hart für ihm; – *passage*, stürmische Überfahrt; – *and ready*, Notbehelfs–, behelfsmäßig; unfertig, urwüchsig; roh, ungeschliffen, im groben bearbeitet; – *sketch*, die Faustzeichnung, der Abriß, flüchtige Skizze; – *and tumble*, 1. *s.* das Handgemenge; 2. *attrib.* rauh, heftig. **2.** *s.* das Rauhe, Grobe; rauhe Seite; roher *or* unfertiger Zustand; unebener Boden (*Golf*); der Grobian, Lümmel, Rowdy; *in the* –, im groben, noch unfertig, in Bausch und Bogen; *take the* – *with the smooth*, die Dinge nehmen wie sie sind, das Schlechte mit dem Guten in Kauf nehmen. **3.** *v.a.* roh bearbeiten *or* behauen; flüchtig entwerfen; rauh machen, schrubben; rauh schleifen (*Glassw.*); schärfen (*horseshoes*); – *it*, ein hartes Leben führen, sich mühselig durchschlagen; – *in*, im groben skizzieren; – *out*, im groben behauen *or* formen *or* skizzieren, in großen Umrissen entwerfen; – *up*, wider den Strich fahren (*Dat.*). **–age** [–ɪdʒ], *s.* der Abfall; grobe Nahrung. **––cast,** 1. *v.a.* im groben *or* rohen entwerfen; mit Rohputz bedecken (*Build.*). 2. *s.* der Rohputz (*Build.*). 3. *adj.* im rohen entworfen; roh verputzt. **––drill,** *v.a.* vorbohren. **––dry,** *v.a.* bügelfertig machen. **–en,** 1. *v.a.* rauh machen, aufrauhen, anrauhen. 2. *v.n.* rauh werden. **––hew,** *v.a.* im groben formen, schnitzen, behauen *or* bearbeiten. **––hewn,** *adj.* flüchtig *or* im groben bearbeitet, unfertig; (*fig.*) ungeschliffen, ungehobelt. **–ly,** *adv.* roh, grob, unsanft; im groben; ungefähr, annähernd; *–ly speaking*, etwa, annähernd. **––neck,** *s.* (*sl.*) der Rowdy, das Rauhbein. **–ness,** *s.* die Rauheit, Unebenheit, rauhe Stelle; die Rohheit, Grobheit, Schroffheit, Ungeschliffenheit; Härte, Herbheit; Heftigkeit, das Ungestüm, die Stürmischkeit, wilde Bewegung. **––plane,** *v.a.* vorhobeln. **––rider,** *s.* der Bereiter, Zureiter; irregulärer Kavalerist. **–shod,** *adj.* scharf *or* roh beschlagen (*horses*); *ride –shod over a p.*, einen rücksichtslos behandeln; einen mißhandeln; (*fig.*) einen schurigeln *or* zwiebeln.

roul–ade [ruːˈlɑːd], *s.* die Roulade, Passage (*Mus.*). **–ette** [–ˈlɛt], *s.* das Roulett (*gambling*); Rollrädchen (*Engr.*).

round [raʊnd], **1.** *adj.* rund (*also fig.*), rundlich, dick; Rund–; (*fig.*) beträchtlich, ansehnlich, vollständig, gut; glatt, fließend (*style*); voll, abgerundet; offen(herzig), ehrlich, aufrichtig; – *answer*, offen(herzig)e *or* klare Antwort; – *arch*, der Rundbogen; – *cheeks*, dicke Wangen; – *dance*, der Rundtanz; – *dozen*, volles Dutzend; – *game*, das Gesellschaftspiel; – *number*, abgerundete Zahl; – *oath*, kräftiger Fluch; *at a* – *pace*, in schnellem *or* gutem Schritt; *a* – *peg in a square hole*, fehl am Ort; – *robin*, der Sammelbrief mit Unterschriften im Kreise; – *shot*, die Kanonenkugel; – *sum*, runde Summe; – *table conference*, die Konferenz am runden Tisch; – *Table*, die Tafelrunde (*of Arthur*); *in* – *terms*, rundweg; – *tour* or *trip*, die Rundreise, die Hin- und Rückfahrt; – *vowel*, gerundeter Vokal. **2.** *adv.* rundum(her), ringsum(her), rundherum, ringsherum; herum; im Umkreise, in der Runde; *all* –, *see* – 2; (*fig.*) überall, von allen Seiten; auf der ganzen Linie, allgemein, allesamt; *all the year* –, das ganze Jahr (hin)durch; *the country* – (*about*), die Umgegend; *for a mile* –, im Umkreis von einer Meile; – *about*, rund, rings(her)um; ungefähr, etwa; – *about way*, der Umweg; *ask a p.* –, einen zu sich bitten; *bring a p.* –, (*fig.*) einen herumkriegen, überzeugen *or* bekehren; einen wieder zum Bewußtsein bringen; *come* –, vorbeikommen, vorsprechen; wiederkehren, wiederkommen; lavieren (*of a ship*); sich drehen (*of wind*); sich bekehren (*to*, zu); wieder zu Bewußtsein kommen; *go* –, einen Umweg machen; *go* – (*and* –), herumgehen; kreisen; *go* – *to a p.*, bei einem vorsprechen *or* Besuch machen; *hand* –, herumreichen; *look* –, sich umsehen (*at*, nach); *order* –, vorfahren lassen (*a carriage*); *show* –, herumführen; *sleep the clock* –, zwölf volle Stunden schlafen; *turn* –, (sich) herumdrehen; *a long way* –, ein langer Umweg; **3.** *prep.* rings(um), um, um . . . herum; *just* – *the corner*, gerade *or* gleich um die Ecke; – *me*, um mich her; *a tour* – *the world*, eine Weltreise; *get* – *a p.*, einen herumkriegen; *he looked* – *him*, er sah sich (nach allen Seiten) um. **4.** *s.* die Runde; der Umlauf, Kreislauf, Ablauf, Gang, Rundgang; die Ronde, Patrouille (*Mil.*); der Kreis, Ring, die Reihe; Scherbe, Schnitte (*of bread, etc.*); Sprosse (*of a ladder*); das Rund, Rundteil, der Rundbau; der Rundgesang, Kanon (*Mus.*); Schuß, die Ladung. Salve (*Artil.*); – *of applause*, Hurrarufe (*pl.*); – *of ammunition*, die Ladung, der Schuß; *20 –s*, 20 Schuß; – *of beef*, die Rindskeule; *in the* –, in plastischer Gestalt; (*fig.*) vollkommen; *daily* –, täglicher Ablauf; *go* or *make the –s*, die Runde machen, herumgehen (*also fig.*). **5.** *v.a.* runden, rund machen; herumfahren, herumgehen *or* herumsegeln um; fließend gestalten (*style*); *–ed edges*, abgestumpfte Ecken; *–ed figure*, rundliche Gestalt; – *off*, abrunden, (*fig.*) abschließen; – *up*, (zusammen)treiben (*cattle*); zusammenbringen; umstellen.

ausheben. **6.** *v.n.* rund werden, sich runden; (*coll.*) – *on a p.*, einen anfahren; – *to*, beidrehen (*Naut.*). **-about,** 1. *adj.* weitläufig, weitschweifig, umständlich; abwegig; *-about way*, der Umweg. 2. *s.* der Umschweif, Umweg, der Kreisverkehr (*traffic*); das Karussel. **-(-)arm,** *adj.* mit dem Arm in Schulterhöhe (*Boxing, Crick.*). **-el** [-əl], *s.* runde Scheibe, das Medaillon (*Her.*). **-elay** [-əleɪ], *s.* der Rundgesang, Rundtanz. **-er,** *s.* der Lauf (beim Ballspiel dieses Namens); *pl.* eine Art Ballspiel. **–hand,** *s.* die Rundschrift. **-head,** *s.* der Puritaner, Rundkopf, Stutzkopf (*Hist.*). **--headed,** *adj.* rundköpfig (*as nail, also Ethn.*). **--house,** *s.* die Wache, das Gefängnis; der Lokschuppen (*Railw.*). **--iron,** *s.* das Stabeisen, Rundeisen. **-ing** [-ɪŋ], *s.* die Rundung (*also Phonet.*), Abrundung, Labialisierung (*Phonet.*). **-ish,** *adj.* rundlich. **-ly,** *adv.* rundweg, rundheraus, unumwunden, rückhaltlos, gründlich, tüchtig. **-ness,** *s.* die Rundung, Rundheit; Offenheit. **--nose(d),** *adj.* rundnäsig; *--nose pliers*, die Rundzange. **-sman** [-zmən], *s.* der Laufbursche. **– turn,** *s.* einfacher Knoten (*Naut.*). **--up,** *s.* das Zusammentreiben.

[1]roup [ruːp], *s.* die Luftröhrenseuche, Darre (*in poultry*).

[2]roup [rɑup] (*Scots*) 1. *s.* die Auktion. 2. *v.a.* versteigern.

rous-e [rɑuz], 1. *v.a.* (auf)wecken, erwecken (*from*, aus); aufjagen (*game*); (*fig.*) ermuntern, anreizen, aufreizen, aufrütteln; erregen, entflammen, anstacheln, aufpeitschen (*feelings, etc.*); *-e o.s.*, sich aufraffen *or* aufrappeln; *-e a p.'s anger*, einen aufbringen. 2. *v.n.* aufwachen, wach werden. 3. *s.* das Wecken (*Mil.*). **-er,** *s.* der Rührapparat (*Brew.*); (*sl.*) große Überraschung, gewaltige Lüge. **-ing,** *adj.* anregend; (*coll.*) gewaltig, stürmisch; begeistend, zündend; rauschend, brausend.

[1]rout [rɑut], 1. *s.* wilde Flucht; wirrer Haufe, die Rotte; der Auflauf, Aufruhr; große Abendgesellschaft; *put to* –, in die Flucht schlagen, gänzlich vernichten *or* auseinander treiben. 2. *v.a.* in Verwirrung setzen; in die Flucht schlagen.

[2]rout, 1. *v n.* mit der Schnauze aufwühlen (*as swine*); (*fig*) – *about*, herumwühlen, herumstöbern. 2. *v.a.*; (*coll.*) – *out*, aufstöbern, ausfindig machen, hervorholen; – *out of bed*, aus dem Bett herausholen.

route [ruːt], 1. *s.* der Weg, die Strecke, Route; [*also* rɑut] Marschroute, der Marschbefehl (*Mil.*); *en* –, unterwegs. 2. *v.a.* die Route bestimmen für; die Strecke kennzeichnen an (*a ticket*). **--map,** *s.* die Karte mit eingezeichneter Marschroute. **--march,** *s.* der Übungsmarsch.

routin-e [ruːˈtiːn], 1. *s.* gewohnheitsmäßiger Brauch, festes Geleise, übliche Pflicht, alltäglicher Geschäftsgang, alter Schlendrian; handwerksmäßige Gewandtheit, Routine, Schablone. 2. *adj.* üblich, Gewohnheits-, schablonenmäßig; *-e business*, die Geschäftsroutine, geistlose Beschäftigung; *-e order*, der Tagesbefehl. **-ist,** *s.* der Routinier, Schablonenmensch.

[1]rov-e [rouv], 1. *v.n.* umherschweifen, umherziehen, umherstreifen, wandern; streifen, schweifen (*as eyes*); *-ing commission*, der Wanderauftrag. 2. *s.* die Wanderschaft. **-er** [-ə], *s.* der Herumstreicher, Durchstreifer, Wanderer; das Wandertier; der Seeräuber; älterer Pfadfinder; *shoot at -ers*, nach einem gelegentlichen Ziel, aufs Geratewohl *or* (*fig.*) ins Blaue schießen.

[2]rove, 1. *v.a.* vorspinnen, zum Gespinst verarbeiten. 2. *s.* die Strähne, das Vorgespinst. **-r,** *s.* die Vorspinnmaschine.

[1]row [rou], *s.* die Reihe; Sitzreihe (*Theat.*); Straße, Häuserreihe; *in -s*, reihenweise.

[2]row [rou], 1. *v.a. & n.* rudern, pullen (*Naut.*); – *a long stroke*, lang ausholen; – *a steady stroke*, gleichmäßig rudern. 2. *s.* das Rudern, die Ruderfahrt, Ruderpartie. **-ing,** *s.* das Rudern. **-(ing)-boat,** *s.* das Ruderboot; *see* **rowlock.**

[3]row [rɑu], 1 *s.* (*coll.*) der Lärm, Spektakel, heftiger Streit; (*coll.*) *kick up a* –, Krach, Spektakel *or* Skandal machen; *have a – with*, Streit *or* Krach haben mit; (*sl.*) *what's the – ?* was ist los? *get into a* –, eins aufs Dach kriegen. 2. *v.a.* (*coll.*) abkanzeln, übers Maul fahren.

rowan [ˈrouən, ˈrɑuən], *s.* (also *--tree*) (*esp. Scots*) die Eberesche.

rowd-iness [ˈrɑudɪnɪs], *s.* die Pöbelhaftigkeit, Rohheit. **-y** [ˈrɑudɪ], 1. *s.* der Lärmer, Spektakelmacher; Rohling, Raufbold, Rowdy. 2. *adj.* laut, lärmend, pöbelhaft, roh. **-yism** [-dɪɪzm], *s.* rohe Gewalt, das Rowdytum, die Gewalttätigkeit.

rowel [ˈrɑuəl], 1 *s.* das Spornrädchen. 2. *v.a.* anspornen, die Sporen geben (*Dat.*).

rowing, *see* **[2]row.**

rowlock [ˈrʌlək], *s.* die Rudergabel, Dolle.

royal [ˈrɔɪəl], 1. *adj.* königlich, Königs-; (*fig.*) fürstlich, prächtig, herrlich; – *Academy*, Königliche Akademie der Künste; – *antler*, dritte Sprosse eines Hirschgeweihs; – *assent*, königliche Einwilligung; *battle* –, der Hauptkampf; *blood* –, (*fig.*) die königliche Familie; – *blue*, das Königsblau; – *Exchange*, die Londoner Börse; *the – and ancient game*, das Golfspiel; – *Highness*, Königliche Hoheit; – *mast*, die Oberbramstenge, Royalstenge; – *paper*, das Royal(format) (*Print.*); – *prince*, der Prinz von königlichem Geblüt; *Princess* –, des Königs älteste Tochter; – *road*, (*fig.*) bequemer *or* müheloser Weg; – *sail*, das Oberbramsegel; – *Society*, die Königliche Gesellschaft der Naturwissenschaften; – *stag*, der Kapitalhirsch, Zwölfender; – *standard*, die Königsstandarte; – *time*, köstliche *or* herrliche Zeit. 2. *s.* das Royalpapier; das Reuelstengesegel (*Naut.*). **-ism** [-ɪzm], *s.* die Königstreue, der Royalismus. **-ist** [-ɪst], *s.* der Monarchist, Royalist, Königstreue(r), *m.* **-istic** [-ˈlɪstɪk], *adj.* königstreu, royalistisch. **-ty** [-tɪ], *s.* das Königtum; die Königswürde, das Königreich; monarchistische Regierung; das Mitglied der königlichen Familie; (*usually pl.*) königliches Privileg, das Regal, Abgaben an den König; die Patentabgabe, Pacht (*Min.*); das Krongut, die Domäne; die Lizenzgebühr; (Autoren)Tantieme; der Gewinnanteil, Ertragsanteil.

rub [rʌb], 1. *s.* das Reiben, (*fig.*) die Reibung; Hindernis, Schwierigkeit, Unannehmlichkeit; der Hieb, Strich, die Stichelei; *give a th. a* –, etwas ein wenig reiben; (*coll.*) *there's the – !* da ist der Haken *or* liegt der Hase im Pfeffer! 2. *v.a.* reiben (*against* or *on*, an), streifen, schleifen, abreiben; frottieren, (ab)wischen, putzen, wischen, scheuern; abklatschen (*Engr.*), levigieren (*Tech.*); – *one's hands*, sich (*Dat.*) die Hände reiben; – *shoulders*, verkehren, in enge Berührung kommen (*with*, mit); – *s.o.* (*up*) *the wrong way*, einen ärgern *or* reizen, einen vor den Kopf stoßen; – *away*, abreiben; – *down*, abreiben, verreiben; striegeln (*horses*), anreiben (*colours*); – *in*, einreiben (*liniment*); (*coll.*) unter die Nase reiben; – *off*, abreiben, abwischen, abschleifen; – *out*, wegwischen, ausradieren, (*sl.*) umbringen; – *up*, polieren; (*fig.*) auffrischen (*memory*); see – *s.o. the wrong way.* 3. *v.n.* sich reiben (*against* or *on*, an (*Dat.*)); (*coll.*) – *along*, durchhalten, auskommen, sich durchbringen, sich durchschlagen, sich über Wasser halten; – *off*, sich abreiben lassen, abfärben, abschmutzen. **--a-dub** [-ədʌb], *s.* der Trommelwirbel, Bumbum. **--down,** *s.* das Abreiben; *have a --down*, sich abreiben. **-ber** [-ə], 1. *s.* der Reiber, Frotteur, Reibstein, die Reibfläche, das Reibkissen, Reibzeug, Frottiertuch, der Wischlappen; *see* **rubber.** **-bing** [-ɪŋ], *s.* das Reiben, die Reibung; der Abklatsch (*Engr.*); *-bing brush*, die Wischbürste; *-bing-cloth*, *s.* das Frottiertuch.

[1]rubber [ˈrʌbə], *s.* das Gummi, der Kautschuk; der (Radier)Gummi; *pl.* Gummischuhe, Turnschuhe (*pl.*); – *dinghy*, das Schlauchboot. **-ize,** *v.a.* mit Gummi imprägnieren. (*sl.*) **-neck,** *s.* Neugierige(r), Schaulustige(r), *m.* **--plant,** *s.* die Parakautschukpflanze. **– stamp,** *s.* der Gummistempel, (*fig.*) (*coll.*) willenloses Werkzeug. **– solution,** *s.* die Gummilösung. **– truncheon,** *s.* der Gummiknüppel. **– tyre,** *s.* der Gummireifen. **-y,** *adj.* gummiweich, schwammig.

[2]rubber, *s.* der Robber (*Cards*); die Reihe von 5 Spielen.

rubbish [ˈrʌbɪʃ], *s.* der Schutt, Abfall, Müll, Kehricht; Schund, Plunder; die Ausschußware; (*fig.*) der Unsinn, Quatsch. **--heap,** *s.* der Schutthaufen. **-ing, -y,** *adj.* minderwertig, schlecht, Schund-.

rubble [ˈrʌbl], *s.* der Steinschutt, Bauschutt; Schotter, Bruchstein, Rollstein (*Build.*); das Geschiebe, Geröll (*Geol.*). **--stone,** *s.* der Rollstein. **--work,** *s.* das Bruchsteinmauerwerk, Füllwerk.
rube-facient [ru:bɪˈfeɪsɪənt], 1. *adj.* (haut)rötend. 2. *s.* hautrötendes Mittel. **-fy** [ru:bɪfaɪ], *v.a.* röten, rot färben. **-scence** [ru:ˈbɛsəns], *s.* das Rotwerden, Erröten. **-scent** [-ənt], *adj.* errötend.
rubicund [ˈru:bɪkənd], *adj.* rötlich, rot.
rubidium [ru:ˈbɪdɪəm], *s.* das Rubidium (*Chem.*).
rubify, *see* **rubefy.**
rubric [ˈru:brɪk], 1. *s.* roter Titel(Buchstabe); die Rubrik (*Typ.*); liturgische Anweisung (*Eccl.*). 2. *adj.* rot gedruckt. **-ate** [-eɪt], *v.a.* rot bezeichnen; mit Rubriken versehen, rubrizieren.
ruby [ˈru:bɪ], 1. *s.* der Rubin; die Rubinfarbe, das Rot; die Parisienne (*Typ.*). 2. *adj.* (rubin)rot, hochrot.
ruch-e [ru:ʃ], *s.* die Rüsche. **-ing,** *s.* Rüschen (*pl.*), der Rüschenbesatz.
[1]**ruck** [rʌk], 1. *s.* die Runzel, Falte. 2. *v.a.* runzeln, zerknüllen, ramponieren. 3. *v.n.* sich runzeln, knittern, zerknüllen; hochrutschen; – *up,* zerknittern. **-le,** *v.a.* & *n. see* –.
[2]**ruck,** *s.* (großer) Haufe (*also Racing*), der Durchschnitt; *rise out of the* –, sich aus der großen Menge herausheben.
rucksack [ˈrʌksæk], *s.* der Rucksack.
ruction [ˈrʌkʃən], *s.* (*sl.*) (*often pl.*) der Spektakel, Krach.
rudd [rʌd], *s.* das Rotauge, die Rotfeder (*Ichth.*).
rudder [ˈrʌdə], *s.* das Steuerruder; das Seitensteuer, Leitwerk (*Av.*). **-less,** *adj.* ruderlos; (*fig.*) führlos, hilflos.
rudd-iness [ˈrʌdɪnɪs], *s.* die Röte. **-y** [ˈrʌdɪ], *adj.* rot, rötlich; (*sl.*) verflucht.
rude [ru:d], *adj.* ungebildet, grob, unverschämt, unhöflich (*to,* gegen); derb, heftig, wild, ungestüm, gewaltsam, grausam; rauh, streng, unwirtlich (*as climate*); robust, kräftig (*as health*); roh, primitiv, ungesittet, unzivilisiert; uneben, holperig, unfertig, unvollkommen, kunstlos, einfach. **-ness,** *s.* die Unhöflichkeit, Grobheit; Derbheit, Wildheit, das Ungestüm; die Rauheit, Rohheit; Einfalt, Kunstlosigkeit.
rudiment [ˈru:dɪmənt], *s.* der Anfang; Ansatz, erste Spur; *pl.* Grundlagen, Anfangsgründe (*pl.*). **-al** [-ˈmɛntl], **-ary** [-ˈmɛntərɪ], *adj.* rudimentär, Anfangs–, Elementar–.
[1]**rue** [ru:], *v.a.* bereuen, beklagen, verwünschen. **-ful,** *adj.* reuig, traurig, kläglich. **-fulness,** *s.* die Traurigkeit, der Gram, Kummer.
[2]**rue,** *s.* die Raute (*Bot.*).
rufescent [ru:ˈfɛsənt], *adj.* rötlich (*Zool.*).
[1]**ruff** [rʌf], *s.* die Krause; der Kampfläufer, die Kampfschnepfe (*Orn.*); der Federring (*of bird*), Haarring (*of animal*).
[2]**ruff,** 1. *s.* das Stechen, Trumpfen (*Cards*). 2. *v.a.* & *n.* stechen, trumpfen.
[3]**ruff,** *s.* der Kaulbarsch (*Ichth.*).
ruffian [ˈrʌfɪən], *s.* der Raufbold, roher Bursche. **-ism** [-ɪzm], *s.* die Roheit, Brutalität, das Rowdytum. **-ly,** *adj.* brutal, roh, wild, wüst.
ruffle [ˈrʌfl], 1. *s.* die Krause, Handkrause, Halskrause, der Federring (*of birds*); das Kräuseln (*of water*); (*coll.*) die Aufregung. 2. *v.a.* kräuseln, kraus machen, zerknittern, zerzausen; sträuben (*feathers*); (*fig.*) außer Fassung bringen, verwirren, aufregen; – *one's feathers,* sich aufplustern; (*fig.*) sich aufregen. 2. *v.n.* prahlen, aufschneiden, renommieren.
rufous [ˈru:fəs], *adj.* fuchsrot, rötlichbraun.
rug [rʌg], *s.* die (Reise)Decke; kleiner Teppich; der Vorleger; *travelling* –, die Reisedecke. **--work,** *s.* die Wollstickerei.
Rugby [ˈrʌgbɪ], *s.* eine Art Fußballspiel.
rugged [ˈrʌgɪd], *adj.* rauh (*also fig.*), uneben, holperig (*as a way*); zackig, zerklüftet, wild (*as scenery*); gefurcht, runzelig (*as a face*); (*fig.*) schroff, unfreundlich. **-ness,** *s.* die Rauheit, Schroffheit.
rugger [ˈrʌgə], *s.* (*coll.*) *see* **Rugby.**
rugose [ru:ˈgous], *adj.* runzig, gerunzelt.
ruin [ˈru:ɪn], 1. *s.* der Sturz, Verfall, Untergang, Zusammenbruch, die Vernichtung, das Verderben, der Ruin; (*fig.*) die Vereitelung; die Ruine (*castle, etc.*); *pl.* Trümmer (*pl.*); *it will be his* – or *the* – *of him,* es wird sein Untergang sein; *bring to* –, zugrunde richten, ins Verderben stürzen; *go to* –, verfallen. 2. *v.a.* vernichten, zerstören; (*fig.*) vereiteln; zugrunde richten, ruinieren (*a p.*), verführen (*a girl*). **-ation** [-ˈneɪʃən], *s.* die Zerstörung; (*fam.*) das Verderben. **-ed** [-d], *adj.* verfallen, zerfallen (*building, etc.*), ruiniert (*a p.*). **-ous** [-əs], *adj.* verfallen, baufällig; (*fig.*) verderblich, schädlich, gefährlich; (*coll.*) übermäßig, enorm (*as price*). **-ously,** *adv.* (*coll.*) enorm (*dear*). **-ousness,** *s.* die Baufälligkeit; Verderblichkeit, (*coll.*) Abnormität (*of prices*).
rul-e [ru:l], **1.** *s.* die Regel (*also Arith., Eccl., & fig.*); Ordensregel (*Eccl.*), Spielregel (*Sport.*); Vorschrift, Satzung, (Ver)Ordnung, Verfügung; Richtschnur, Norm, Gewohnheit, der Grundsatz, Maßstab; das Lineal, Richtsheit, der Zollstock; die Herrschaft; *as a* –*e,* in der Regel. (*a*) (*with nouns*) *carpenter's* –*e,* die Schmiege; –*e of the road,* die Straßenordnung; –*e of three,* die Regeldetri; –*e of thumb,* die Faustregel, praktisches Erfahrungsverfahren; *by* –*e of thumb,* erfahrungsmäßig, auf praktischem Wege. (*b*) (*with adjectives*) *fixed* –*e,* die Satzung; *folding* –*e,* die Schmiege; *foot* –*e,* der Zollstock; *hard and fast* –*e,* ausnahmsloser Grundsatz; –*e nisi,* vorläufige Entscheidung (*Law*); *parallel* –*e,* das Parallellineal; *standing* –*e,* die Satzung. (*c*) (*with verbs*) *be the* –*e,* die Regel sein; *become the* –*e,* zur Regel *or* allgemein üblich werden; *break a* –*e,* gegen eine Regel verstoßen; *lay down a* –*e,* eine Regel aufstellen; *make it a* –*e,* es sich (*Dat.*) zur Regel machen. **2.** *v.a.* linieren (*paper, etc.*); ziehen (*line*); anorden, verfügen, regeln, entscheiden, zu der Entscheidung kommen; (also –*e over*) beherrschen; –*e the roost,* die Oberhand haben, das Wort führen; –*e out,* ausschließen, ausscheiden, nicht zulassen; –*e s.o. out of order,* einem verbieten zu sprechen (*Parl.*); *be* –*ed by,* sich führen *or* leiten lassen von. **3.** *v.n.* herrschen; vorherrschen; stehen, liegen (*as prices*). **-ed,** *adj.* liniert; –*ed paper,* das Linienpapier. **-er** [-ə], *s.* der Herrscher; das Lineal (*Draw.*). **-ing,** 1. *adj.* herrschend, vorherrschend; bestehend, laufend, Durchschnitts– (*C.L.*). 2. *s.* die Herrschaft; amtliche Entscheidung; das Linieren; *judicial* –*ing,* der Gerichtsentscheid.
[1]**rum** [rʌm], *s.* der Rum. **--running,** *s.* der Alkoholschmuggel.
[2]**rum** [rʌm], *adj.* (*sl.*) wunderlich, seltsam.
rumba [ˈrʌmbə], *s.* der Rumba.
rumbl-e [ˈrʌmbl], 1. *s.* das Rumpeln, Poltern, Rollen, Dröhnen; der Gepäcksitz, Bedientensitz (*of coach*). 2. *v.n.* rumpeln, rasseln, poltern, dröhnen; rollen (*of thunder*); knurren (*of stomach*). 3. *v.a.* (*sl.*) kapieren, klein kriegen, fressen, schalten.
rumbustious [rʌmˈbʌstʃəs], *adj.* (*coll.*) lärmend, ungestüm.
rum-en [ˈru:mən], *s.* der Pansen, erster Magen der Wiederkäuer. **-inant** [-ɪnənt], 1. *adj.* wiederkäuend. 2. *s.* der Wiederkäuer. **-inate** [-ɪneɪt] 1. *v.n.* wiederkäuen; (*fig.*) grübeln, (nach)sinnen (*about* or *upon,* über (*Acc.*)). 2. *v.a.* nachdenken über. **-ination** [-ɪˈneɪʃən], *s.* das Wiederkäuen; (*fig.*) das Nachsinnen, Grübeln. **-inative** [-ɪnətɪv], *adj.* sinnend, nachdenklich.
rummage [ˈrʌmɪdʒ], 1. *v.n.* stöbern, wühlen, kramen; – *about,* herumstöbern. 2. *v.a.* durchsuchen, durchstöbern; – *out,* hervorholen, auskramen. 3. *s.* der Ausschuß, Ramsch, Restwaren (*pl.*); das Durchsuchen, Durchstöbern. **--sale,** *s.* der Ramschverkauf.
rummer [ˈrʌmə], *s.* der Römer, Humpen.
[1]**rummy** [ˈrʌmɪ], *adj.* (*sl.*) *see* [2]**rum.**
[2]**rummy** [ˈrʌmɪ], *s.* das Rommé (*Cards*).
rumour [ˈru:mə], 1. *s.* das Gerücht (*of,* über); – *has it, the* – *is* or *runs,* es geht das Gerücht. 2. *v.a.* (*usually pass.*); *it is* –*ed,* es geht das Gerücht.
rump [rʌmp], 1. *s.* der *or* das Hinterteil; der Steiß; Bürzel (*of fowl*); (*coll.*) das Kreuz; – *Parliament,* das Rumpfparlament. **-steak,** *s.* das Rumpsteak.
rumple [ˈrʌmpl], 1. *v.a.* zerknittern, zerknüllen; zerzausen (*hair*). 2. *s.* die Falte.
rumpus [ˈrʌmpəs], *s.* (*coll.*) der Spektakel, Krawall.
run [rʌn], **1.** *ir.v.n.* (*also imperf.* & *p.p.*) rennen,

laufen; eilen, (los)stürzen; (dahin)fliehen, weglaufen; verkehren (*vehicle*), schwimmen, wandern (*fish*), rollen (*ball*), fahren (*steamers, & rope through a block*), segeln (*sailing ships*), sich drehen (*wheels*), in Betrieb sein, arbeiten, gehen (*engines*); verfließen, hinfließen, vergehen, hingehen (*time*); sich erstrecken, dauern, abgehalten *or* gegeben werden; fließen (*as liquids*), eitern (*as a sore*); zerfließen (*as colours*); schmelzen (*as metals*); auftauen (*as ice, etc.*); in Kraft bleiben, in Umlauf sein, Gültigkeit haben, gelten; herrschen, sich stellen (*as prices*); lauten, den Wortlaut haben (*as text*); sich verbreiten, umlaufen, umgehen (*as rumours*); sich ergießen, triefen, strömen (*with*, von); tropfen (*as a candle*); *the boat -s on Sundays*, der Dampfer verkehrt sonntags; *two days -ning*, zwei Tage nacheinander, zwei aufeinanderfolgende Tage; *the play ran for 100 nights*, das Stück wurde 100 Mal gegeben (*Theat.*); – *riot*, wuchern (*plants*), (*fig.*) sich austoben, einen hemmungslosen Lauf nehmen; *a heavy sea is -ning*, es ist hoher Seegang; *his taste does not – that way*, dafür hat er keinen Sinn; *trains – 6 times a day*, es gehen täglich 6 Züge ab. **(a)** (*with adjectives*) *my blood -s cold*, mich gruselt's; – *dry*, versiegen, vertrocknen; – *foul of*, anfahren, festfahren auf, übersegeln (*Naut.*); (*fig.*) herfallen über; – *high*, hochgehen (*waves*), heftig, erregt *or* lebhaft werden (*feelings*); – *hot*, sich warm laufen (*of engines*); – *low*, auf die Neige gehen, erschöpft *or* knapp werden; – *mad*, toll *or* verrückt, werden; – *short*, zu Ende gehen, ausgehen, knapp werden (*of*, an); – *wild*, ausarten, wild wachsen, ins Kraut schießen (*Hort.*); (*fig.*) wild *or* ohne Aufsicht aufwachsen, verwildern. **(b)** (*with adverbs*) – *about*, umherlaufen; – *aground*, auflaufen, stranden; – *amuck*, wie wild herumlaufen; – *ashore*, see – *aground*; – *away*, davonlaufen, fortlaufen (*from*, von (*or Dat.*)); durchgehen (*as horses*) (*also fig.*); – *away from*, aufgeben; sich entfernen von (*a subject*); – *away with*, entführen; durchgehen mit; aufbrauchen, aufzehren; *don't – away with the idea that*, bilden Sie sich nur nicht ein daß, setzen Sie sich (*Dat.*) nur nicht in den Kopf daß; – *counter to*, zuwiderlaufen (*Dat.*); – *down*, hinablaufen (*tears, etc.*); ablaufen (*clock*); – *for one's life*, ausreißen; – *in*, hineinlaufen; übereinstimmen (*with*, mit); – *off*, davonlaufen; ablaufen (*as water*); – *off with*, durchgehen mit; – *on*, fortlaufen, auflaufen; unablässig schwatzen, fortplaudern; – *out*, hinauslaufen; zu Ende gehen, ablaufen (*time*), zu Ende sein, ausverkauft sein, ausgehen (*stock*); sich erstrecken; – *over*, überlaufen; – *up*, hinauflaufen; einlaufen, eingehen (*cloth*); sich belaufen, zulaufen (*to*, auf (*Acc.*)); schnell wachsen, hochschießen; – *up against*, stoßen auf. **(c)** (*with prepositions*) – *across*, zufällig treffen; – *after*, nachjagen, nachlaufen (*a th.* (*Dat.*)), herlaufen hinter (*a p.*); – *against*, laufen gegen, zusammenstoßen mit; sich (im Laufen) messen mit (*Sport*); – *at*, losstürzen auf (*Acc.*); – *before*, herlaufen vor (*a p.*); – *before the wind*, vor dem Winde segeln; – *for*, laufen nach; wettlaufen um (*a prize*); sich bewerben um (*a position*); (*coll.*) – *for it*, ausreißen; sich eilen; – *in the blood*, im Blute liegen *or* stecken; – *in debt with him*, in seine Schuld fallen; *it -s in his head*, es geht ihm im Kopf herum; – *into*, auffahren auf (*Acc.*); (hinein)rennen *or* (hinein)fahren in (*Acc.*); sich entwickeln zu, anwachsen zu, aufgehen in, sich belaufen auf (*Acc.*); – *into debt*, sich in Schulden stürzen, in Schulden geraten; – *into four editions*, vier Auflagen erleben; – *into money*, ins Geld laufen; *the colours – into one another*, die Farben laufen *or* fließen ineinander; – *into a p.*, einen zufällig treffen, einem in den Hals rennen; – *into a port*, einen Hafen ansegeln; – *off the rails*, entgleisen (*also fig.*); – *on*, see – *upon*; – *out of*, knapp werden mit, nicht mehr vorrätig haben; – *over*, gleiten über; – *over a p.*, einen überfahren; – *through*, laufen durch; durchlaufen; durchlesen, kurz behandeln; durchmachen, erleben; durchbringen (*a fortune*); – *to*, sich belaufen auf, kommen auf; ausreichen für; erreichen, sich entwickeln zu; – *to extremes*, ins Extrem fallen; – *to fat*, Fett ansetzen; – *to seed*, in Samen schießen; – *upon*, zielen *or* sich beziehen auf (*Acc.*); sich beschäftigen mit (*of the mind*), bevorzugen, neigen zu; – *with*, übereinstimmen mit; – *with the hare and hunt with the hounds*, zwei Herren dienen; – *with sweat*, vom Schweiß triefen; – *with tears*, in Tränen schwimmen. **2.** *ir.v.a.* laufen, verfolgen, einschlagen (*a course*); durchlaufen, durchfahren (*a distance*); (wett)rennen *or* laufen lassen; verkehren *or* gehen lassen; in Gang halten (*machine*); führen, leiten, betreiben (*a business*); aufstellen (*candidate*); schmelzen; gießen (*metal*); verfolgen (*game*); bohren, stechen, stoßen (*a weapon*). **(a)** (*with nouns*) – *the blockade*, die Blockade brechen; – *brandy*, Branntwein schmuggeln; – *cattle*, Vieh weiden lassen; – *one's course*, seinen Gang gehen; – *debts*, Schulden machen; – *errands*, Besorgungen machen, Wege besorgen; – *the gauntlet*, Spießruten laufen; – *a race*, um die Wette laufen, wettrennen; – *risks* or *the risk*, sich der Gefahr aussetzen; Gefahr laufen; (*coll.*) – *the show*, die Sache schmeißen; – *the streets*, sich auf der Straße herumtreiben; – *a temperature*, Fieber haben. **(b)** (*with adjectives*) – *a p. close*, einem nahe kommen, einem dicht auf den Fersen sein; (*fig.*) einem ebenbürtig sein; (*coll.*) – *it fine*, es knapp bemessen; – *the tank dry*, den Behälter leeren *or* erschöpfen; – *a p. hard*, einem tüchtig zusetzen, einen in die Enge treiben. **(c)** (*with prepositions*) – *one's head against*, mit dem Kopf rennen gegen; – *a p. for president*, einen zum Präsidenten aufstellen; (*sl.*) – *a p. for a th.*, einen wegen einer S. belangen; – *o.s. into*, sich stürzen in; – *a knife into a p.*, einem ein Messer in den Leib jagen *or* stechen; – *a nail into one's foot*, sich (*Dat.*) einen Nagel in den Fuß treten; – *one's hand over*, mit der Hand fahren über; – *one's fingers through*, mit den Fingern fahren durch; – *one's pen through*, durchstreichen; – *to earth*, zur Strecke bringen; (*fig.*) aufspüren, ausfindig machen. **(d)** (*with adverbs*) – *aground*, auflaufen lassen, auf den Strand setzen; – *down*, niederrennen (*a p.*), totjagen, zu Tode hetzen, zur Strecke bringen (*a stag*); in den Grund bohren (*a ship*); entladen, erschöpfen (*a battery*); (*coll.*) aufstöbern, entdecken (*a th.*); (*coll.*) heruntermachen (*a p.*); *be – down*, herunter *or* abgespannt sein; – *in*, einfahren (*an engine*); (*coll.*) einstecken, einlochen (*a p.*); – *off*, ablaufen lassen (*liquid*), herzählen, herunterrasseln (*speech*), entscheiden (*races*); – *o.s. out*, sich durch Laufen erschöpfen; – *over*, wiederholen; durchsehen, überblicken; – *through*, durchbohren; – *up*, hissen (*a flag*), schnell aufbauen *or* errichten (*houses*); in die Höhe treiben (*prices*); auflaufen *or* anwachsen lassen (*an account*); zusammennähen (*a seam*). **3.** *s.* das Laufen, Rennen, der Lauf, Dauerlauf; Anlauf; Laufschritt; (*fig.*) (Ver)Lauf, Gang, Fortgang, die Richtung; Bahn (*bob-sleigh*); (*Amer.*) der Bach; Zulauf, Zustrom (*of customers*), starke Nachfrage (*on*, nach), der Ansturm (*on a bank*, auf eine Bank); schneller Lauf, die Passage (*Mus.*); Fahrt; Reihe, Folge, Dauer, Zeitdauer; Aufführungsserie (*Theat.*), Arbeitsperiode, Arbeitszeit (*of machines*); Sorte, Qualität (*of goods*) (*C.L.*); freier Zugang, freie Benutzung; der Auslauf (*for fowl, also Av.*); die Trift, der Weidegrund (*for cattle*); Mühlgang (*Mill.*); die Laufmasche (*stockings*); das Abflußrohr, die Laufschiene, Laufplanke (*Tech.*); Piek (*Naut.*); *common* –, durchschnittliche Art; *the common – of mankind*, die Allgemeinheit, Majorität, Menschheit im allgemeinen; *the general – of things*, die meisten Dinge, die Dinge im Durchschnitt; *go for a* –, einen Dauerlauf machen; (*coll.*) eine Spazierfahrt machen; *have a – for one's money*, etwas nicht umsonst bekommen; *have the – of a th.*, freien Zutritt haben zu etwas; *a – on this article*, starke Nachfrage nach diesem Artikel; *have a – of 40 nights*, 40 mal nacheinander gegeben werden (*Theat.*); *trial* –, die Probefahrt; *a – of luck*, fortdauerndes Glück, die Glücksserie; *take a* –, einen Anlauf nehmen; *in the long* –, schließlich, auf die Dauer; – *of office*, die Amtsdauer; *on the* –, auf der Flucht; auf den Beinen, immer tätig; *come down with a* –, heftig herabstürzen. **-about,** *s.* (*coll.*) das Kleinauto. **-away,** 1. *adj.* entlaufen, fortgelaufen, davongelaufen; durchgegangen (*horse*); *-away match*, die Heirat nach vorheriger Entführung. 2. *s.* der Ausreißer; Durchgänger (*horse*). **--in,** *s.* das Laufen über die Seitenlinie (*Footb.*). **-ner** [-ə], *s.* der Renner, Läufer, Rennläufer, Sprinter; Bote, Laufbursche; Melder (*Mil.*); Schmuggler; das Drehreep (*Naut.*); die Laufschiene, Laufrolle, Laufwalze (*Tech.*); Kufe (*sledge*); der Schieber (*of an umbrella*); Ausläufer (*Bot.*); Laufvogel, die Ralle (*Orn.*); schmaler Teppich, der (Tisch)-Läufer, Zimmerläufer; *edge -ner*, der Kollergang (*Mill.*); *scarlet -ner*, die Feuerbohne. **-ner-up,** *s.* zweiter Sieger *or* Preisträger. **-ning** [-ɪŋ], 1. *adj.* fortlaufend, ununterbrochen; eiternd (*sore*); *5 times -ning*, 5 mal hintereinander; *-ning account*, laufende Rechnung; *-ning-board*, das Trittbrett (*Motor.*); *-ning commentary*, laufender Kommentar, der Hörbericht (*on*, über) (*Rad.*); *-ning fight*, das Rückzugsgefecht; *-ning fire*, das Trommelfeuer, Schnellfeuer; *-ning hand*, die Kurrentschrift; *-ning head(line)*, see *-ning title*; *-ning jump*, der Sprung mit Anlauf; *-ning knot*, die Schlinge, Schleife; *-ning speed*, die Umlaufgeschwindigkeit; die Fahrgeschwindigkeit (*Motor.*); *-ning stitch*, der Vorderstich; *-ning stone*, der Mahlstein; *-ning title*, der Kolumnentitel; *-ning water*, das Fließwasser, fließendes Wasser. 2. *s.* das Rennen, Laufen; der Gang (*Mach.*); *be in the -ning*, Aussichten haben; in Betracht kommen; *be out of the -ning*, keine Aussichten haben; nicht in Betracht kommen; *make the -ning*, das Rennen machen, gut abschneiden; *put s.o. out of the -ning*, einen verdrängen *or* außer Konkurrenz setzen. **--off,** *s.* der Entscheidungslauf, das Entscheidungsrennen. **--on,** *adj.* an die nächste Seite übergehend (*Typ.*). *See* **runway.**

runcinate [ˈrʌnsɪnət], *adj.* sägeförmig.

run-e [ruːn], *s.* die Rune. **-ic,** *adj.* runisch, Runen-.

[1]**rung** [rʌŋ], *s.* die Sprosse (*of a ladder*); (*fig.*) Stufe.

[2]**rung,** *see* [2]**ring.**

runic, *see* **rune.**

runnel [ˈrʌnl], *s.* die Rinne, der Kanal.

runner, running, *see* **run.**

runway [ˈrʌnweɪ], *s.* die Startbahn, Rollbahn, Landebahn (*Av.*).

runt [rʌnt], *s.* der Zwergochse; verbuttetes Tier; (*vulg.*) untersetzte Person.

rupee [ruːˈpiː], *s.* die Rupie.

rupture [ˈrʌptʃə], 1. *s.* das Brechen, Platzen, Sprengen; der Bruch (*also Med. & fig.*); (*fig.*) das Abbrechen, der Abbruch. 2. *v.a.* brechen, sprengen, zerreißen (*also Med.*); (*fig.*) abbrechen; *be -d*, einen Bruch bekommen; (*fig.*) trennen. 3. *v.n.* einen Bruch bekommen. **--support,** *s.* das Bruchband.

rural [ˈruːrəl], *adj.* ländlich; Land-; landwirtschaftlich, Ackerbau-; *- dean*, der Dekan eines Landbezirkes; *- District Council*, ländlicher Verwaltungsbezirk; *- poetry*, die Dorfpoesie. **-ize** [-ɑɪz], 1. *v.a.* ländlichen Charakter geben (*Dat.*). 2. *v.n.* aufs Land gehen, ländliches Leben führen.

ruse [ruːz], *s.* die List; der Kniff.

[1]**rush** [rʌʃ], *s.* die Binse; *not worth a -*, keinen Deut *or* Pfifferling wert. **--bearing,** *s.* das Kirchweihfest. **-light,** *s.* das Binsenlicht; (*fig.*) schwacher Schimmer, matter Schein. **--mat,** *s.* die Schilfmatte.

[2]**rush,** 1. *s.* das Stürzen, der Schwung, Ansturm, Anfall, Andrang, das Gedränge; die Massenwanderung; lebhafte Nachfrage (*on* or *for*, nach) (*C.L.*); der Drang, Hochbetrieb (*of business*); Vorstoß (*Footb.*); *make a - for*, sich stürzen nach, sich drängen um; *with a -*, plötzlich; *--hour*, die Hauptgeschäftzeit; *--order*, eiliger Auftrag. 2. *v.n.* (*of a p.*) sich beeilen, sich werfen (*on*, auf), (sich) stürzen (*into*, in); eilen, rasen; (*of things*) herabstürzen, sich wälzen (*water*), stürmen, rauschen, sausen (*as wind*); (*fig.*) fliegen, schießen; *- in*, hineinstürzen, hereinstürzen; *- into print*, voreilig an die Öffentlichkeit treten. 3. *v.a.* schnell drängen *or* treiben; eilig befördern (*to*, nach); rasch erledigen (*work*); hinwegsetzen über (*an obstacle*); erstürmen, im Sturm nehmen (*Mil.*); hetzen, jagen (*a p.*); *- a bill through*, ein Gesetz in Eile durchbringen; *- matters*, die Dinge überstürzen; *be -ed for time*, Eile haben, in großer Eile sein, keine Zeit haben; *- up*, in aller Eile heranbringen *or* herbeibringen (*reinforcements*), in die Höhe treiben (*prices*).

rusk [rʌsk], *s.* der Zwieback.

russet [ˈrʌsɪt], 1. *adj.* rotbraun. 2. *s.* das Rotbraun; der Rötling (*apple*); die Bauernkleidung (*Hist.*).

rust [rʌst], 1. *s.* der Rost (*also Bot. & fig.*); Rostpilz, Brand (*Bot.*). 2. *v.n.* rosten, anrosten, rostig werden; (*fig.*) einrosten, verrosten. 3. *v.a.* rostig machen, oxydieren. **-iness,** *s.* die Rostigkeit; (*fig.*) das Eingerostetsein. **-less, -proof,** *adj.* nichtrostend, rostfrei. **--stained,** *adj.* rostfleckig. **-y,** *adj.* rostig, verrostet; rostfarbig; (*fig.*) eingerostet, vernachlässigt, außer Übung.

rustic [ˈrʌstɪk], 1. *adj.* ländlich, bäuerlich, Land-; einfach, schlicht; bäuerisch, grob; aus Baumästen hergestellt. 2. *s.* der Landmann, Bauer. **-ate** [-eɪt], 1. *v.n.* aufs Land senden; zeitweise ausschließen, relegieren (*Univ.*); mit Bossenwerk verzieren (*Arch.*). **-ation** [-ˈkeɪʃən], *s.* ländliche Zurückgezogenheit; zeitweise Ausschließung, die Relegierung (*Univ.*). **-ity** [-ˈtɪsɪtɪ], *s.* die Ländlichkeit; ländliche Einfachheit, die Plumpheit, bäurisches Wesen. **--work,** *s.* das Bossenwerk, die Rustika (*Arch.*).

rustiness, *see* **rust.**

rustle [ˈrʌsl], 1. *v.n. & a.* rascheln, rauschen, knistern; (*Amer.*) stehlen (*cattle*); (*sl.*) *- o.s.* sich anstrengen, sich beeilen. **-r,** *s.* (*Amer.*) der (Vieh)-Dieb. 2. *s.* das Rascheln.

rust-less, -y, *see* **rust.**

[1]**rut** [rʌt], 1. *s.* die Brunft (*of deer*), Brunst (*other animals*). 2. *v.n.* brunsten, brunften. **-ting,** 1. *s.* der Brunstzustand. 2. *adj.* Brunst-. **-tish,** *adj.* brünftig, brünstig.

[2]**rut,** 1. *s.* das (Wagen)Geleise; die (Rad)Spur, Furche; (*fig.*) altes Geleise; *get out of the -*, sich zu etwas aufschwingen; *stay in the -*, beim alten Schlendrian verbleiben. 2. *v.a.* furchen. **-ted** [-ɪd], *adj.* durchfurcht, ausgefahren.

ruth [ruːθ], *s.* (*archaic*) das Erbarmen, Mitleid. **-less** [-lɪs], *adj.* erbarmungslos, unbarmherzig, grausam. **-lessness,** *s.* die Unbarmherzigkeit.

ruthenium [ruˈθiːnɪəm], *s.* das Ruthenium (*Chem.*).

rye [rɑɪ], *s.* der Roggen. **--grass,** *s.* der Lolch (*Bot.*).

ryot [ˈrɑɪət], *s.* indischer Bauer.

S

S, s [ɛs], das S, s. *See List of Abbreviations.*

's [z], 1. *gen. part.*; *father's*, (des) Vaters; *Lyon's*, die Firma Lyon; *St. Michael's*, die Michaelikirche. 2. (*coll.*) *remainder of word after elision*: (*a*) = *is*; *he's*, *she's*, or *it's here*, er, sie, *or* es ist hier; (*b*) = *has*; *he's*, *she's*, or *it's made*, er, sie, *or* es hat gemacht; (*c*) = *us*; in *let's go*, gehen wir! (*d*) (*archaic*) = *God's* in *'sblood*, mein or großer Gott!

Sabaism [ˈseɪbeɪzm], *s.* die Sternenanbetung.

sabbat-arian [sæbəˈtɛːrɪən], *s.* der Sabbatarier, Sabbatist. **-h** [ˈsæbəθ], *s.* der Sabbat, Ruhetag; *break the -h*, den Sabbat entheiligen; *keep the -h*, den Sabbat heiligen; *witches' -h*, der Hexensabbat. **-h-breaker,** *s.* der Entheiliger des Sabbats, Sabbatschänder. **-h-breaking,** *s.* die Sabbatentheiligung. **-ical** [səˈbætɪkl], *adj.* Sabbat-; *-ical year*, das Sabbatjahr. **-ize** [ˈsæbətɑɪz], *v.a.* als Sabbat feiern.

[1]**sable** [ˈseɪbl], 1. *s.* der Zobel (*Zool.*); Zobelpelz. 2. *attrib. adj.* Zobel-.

[2]**sable,** 1. *s.* das Schwarz (*Her.*); see also *- antelope*; *pl.* (*Poet.*) die Trauerkleidung. 2. *adj.* schwarz, düster (*Her. & Poet.*); *- antelope*, die Rappenantilope; *his - Majesty*, der Höllenfürst, Herrscher der Finsternis.

sabot ['sæbou], *s.* der Holzschuh. **-ed** [-boud], *adj.* mit Holzschuhen.
sabot-age ['sæbətɑ:ʒ], 1. *s.* die Sabotage. 2. *v.a.* sabotieren. 3. *v.n.* Sabotage treiben *or* üben. **-eur** [-tə:], *s.* der Saboteur.
sabre ['seɪbə], 1. *s.* der Säbel; (*fig.*) Kavallerist; *rattle the* –, mit dem Säbel rasseln, mit Angriff drohen. 2. *v.a.* niedersäbeln. **--rattling,** *s.* das Säbelrasseln, Säbelgerassel. **-tache** [-tæʃ], *s.* die Säbeltasche. **--toothed tiger,** der Säbelzahntiger. **-ur** [sæ'brə:], *s.* schneidiger Kavallerieoffizier.
sabu-lous ['sæbjʊləs], *adj.* Sand–, sandig; *-lous matter,* der Harngrieß, Blasengrieß, körnige Ablagerungen in der Harnblase (*Med.*). **-rra** [-'bʌrə], *s.* bösartige Ablagerung im Magen (*Med.*).
sac [sæk], *s.* der Beutel, Sack, sackartige Höhle; krankhafter Hohlraum, die Zyste, Geschwulst. **-cate** [-eɪt], *adj.* sackförmig, taschenförmig (*Bot.*). **-ciform** [-sɪfɔ:m], *adj.* sackförmig, taschenförmig, beutelartig. **-cule** [-ju:l], *s.* das Säckchen, Beutelchen (*Anat.*). **-cular** [-kjʊlə], **-culate(d)** [-kjʊlət, -kjʊleɪtɪd], *adj.* mit Zystenbildung, zystisch, zystös, geschwulstmäßig. **-culation** [-kjʊ'leɪʃən], *s.* die Zystenbildung.
sacchar-ate ['sækəreɪt], *adj.* zuckersauer (*Chem.*). **-ic** [sæ'kærɪk], *adj.* Zucker– (*Chem.*); *-ic acid,* die Zuckersäure. **-iferous** [sækə'rɪfərəs], *adj.* zuckerhaltig. **-ify** ['sækərɪfaɪ], *v.a.* in Zucker verwandeln (*starch*). **-imeter** [-'rɪmɪtə], *s.* das Polarisationssaccharimeter, der Zuckergehaltsmesser (durch Drehung der Schwingungsebene des polarisierten Lichts). **-in(e)** ['sækərɪn], *s.* das Saccharin, der Süßstoff. **-ine** ['sækərɪ:n], *adj.* Zucker–, Süßstoff–. **-oid** ['sækərɔɪd], *adj.* körnig (*Geol.*). **-ometer** [-'rɔmɪtə], *s.* das Aräometer, der Zuckergehaltsmesser (durch Messung des spezifischen Gewichts) (*Brew.*). **-ose** ['sækərous], *s.* der Rohrzucker.
sacciform, saccule, saccular, sacculate(d), sacculation, *see under* **sac.**
sacerdotal [sæsə'doutl], *adj.* priesterlich, Priester–. **-ism** [-təlɪzm], *s.* das Priestertum, die Priesterherrschaft.
sachem ['seɪtʃəm], *s.* der Indianerhäuptling (*Amer.*).
sachet ['sæʃeɪ], *s.* das Parfümtäschchen, der Parfümbeutel.
[1]**sack** [sæk], 1. *s.* der Sack; *a – of corn,* ein Sack Korn, (*coll.*) *get the* –, entlassen werden, den Laufpaß bekommen; (*coll.*) *give a p. the* –, einen den Laufpaß geben, einen fristlos entlassen. 2. *v.a.* einsacken, in Säcke tun; (*coll.*) fristlos entlassen. **-cloth,** *s.* die Sackleinwand, das Sacktuch. **-ful,** *s.* der Sackvoll. **-ing,** *s. see* **-cloth. --race,** *s.* das Sacklaufen.
[2]**sack** [sæk], 1. *s.* die Plünderung; *put to* –, plündern. 2. *v.a.* plündern.
[3]**sack** [sæk], *s.* (*archaic*) spanischer Wein.
sackbut ['sækbʌt], *s.* (*archaic*) die Posaune.
sack-ful, -ing, *see* [1]**sack.**
sacral ['seɪkrəl], *adj.* Kreuzbein– (*Anat.*).
sacrament ['sækrəmənt], *s.* das Sakrament, Heiliges Abendmahl. *last* –, letzte Ölung; *take the* –, das Abendmahl nehmen. **-al** [-'mɛntl], *adj.* sakramentlich, Sakrament(s)–; gnadenbringend, heilig. 2. *s.* (*usually pl.*) heilige Handlung (*R.C.*); *-al wafers,* die Oblaten; *-al wine,* der Abendmahlswein. **-arian** [-mən'tɛ:ərɪən], *s.* der Sakramentarier, Zwinglianer (*Eccl.*).
sacrarium [sæ'krɛ:ərɪəm], *s.* das Allerheiligste, die Altarstätte.
sacred ['seɪkrɪd], *adj.* heilig; kirchlich, Kirchen–; biblisch; (*fig.*) unverletzlich, unverbrüchlich; – *music,* die Kirchenmusik. **-ness,** *s.* die Heiligkeit.
sacrific-e ['sækrɪfaɪs], 1. *s.* das Opfer (*also fig.*), das Opfern; (*fig.*) die Hingabe, Aufgabe; der Verlust (*C.L.*) *fall a -e to,* zum Opfer fallen (*Dat.*); *make a -e of a th.,* etwas opfern *or* aufgeben; *make -es,* Opfer bringen; *sell at a -e,* mit Verlust verkaufen. 2. *v.a.* opfern; (*fig.*) zum Opfer bringen (*to* (*Dat.*)), aufgeben; unter Verlust verkaufen (*C.L.*). *-e o.s. for,* sich (auf)opfern für. 3. *v.n.* opfern. **-ial** [-'fɪʃəl], *adj.* Opfer–.
sacrileg-e ['sækrɪlɪdʒ] *s.* die Entweihung, Schändung, der Kirchenraub. **-ious,** [-'lɪdʒəs], *adj.* kirchenschänderisch, gotteslästerlich, ruchlos, frevelhaft. **-ist** [-'lɪdʒɪst], *s.* der Schänder, Frevler.
sacrist ['seɪkrɪst], *s.* der Mesner (*R.C.*). **-an** ['sækrɪstən], *s.* der Kirchendiener, Küster.
sacrosanct ['sækrəsæŋkt], *adj.* unverletzlich.
sacrum ['seɪkrəm], *s.* das Kreuzbein (*Anat.*).
sad [sæd], *adj.* traurig, niedergeschlagen, betrübt, (*at,* über); betrübend, beklagenswert; klitsch(ig), schliff, sitzengeblieben (*as bread*); satt, dunkel (*as colours*); (*fig.*) arg, kläglich, elend. **-den** [-əd], 1. *v.a.* betrüben, traurig stimmen *or* machen; abtrüben, abdunkeln, nachdunkeln (*colours*). 2. *v.n.* betrübt werden. **-ly,** *adv.* betrübt, beklagenswert; sehr, überaus. **-ness,** *s.* die Traurigkeit, Niedergeschlagenheit; Trauer.
saddle ['sædl], 1. *s.* der Sattel, (Fahrrad)Sitz; die Klampe, das Querholz (*Naut.*); die Senkung (*between hills*); *in the* –, fest im Sattel, an der Macht, im Amt; – *of mutton,* der Hammelrücken, das Hammellendenstück. 2. *v.a.* satteln; (*fig.*) (*often pass.*) belasten; – *s.o. with a th.,* einen etwas aufbürden, aufladen *or* aufhalsen. **-back,** *s.* die Senkung zwischen zwei Bergen; das Dach zwischen zwei Giebeln; das Männchen des Grönlandwals (*Zool.*); die Nebelkrähe (*Orn.*). **-backed,** *adj.* hohlrückig. **--bag,** *s.* die Satteltasche. **--bow,** *s.* der Sattelbogen. **--cloth,** *s.* die Satteldecke, der Woilach. **--horse,** *s.* das Reitpferd. **-r** [-lə], *s.* der Sattler; *-r's wax,* das Sattlerpech. **-ry** [-lərɪ], *s.* die Sattlerei; der Sattelraum; Sattelwaren (*pl.*), das Sattelzeug. **--tree,** *s.* der Sattelbock (*Cycl.*).
sadis-m ['seɪdɪzm], *s.* der Sadismus. **-t** [-ɪst], *s.* der Sadist. **-tic** [sə'dɪstɪk], *adj.* sadistisch.
sadness, *see* **sad.**
safe [seɪf], 1. *adj.* sicher, unversehrt, heil, wohlbehalten, glücklich (*arrival, etc.*); geschützt (*from,* von), in sicherem Gewahrsam, sicher aufgehoben, nicht länger gefährdet *or* gefährlich, außer Gefahr, gefahrlos; Sicherheit bietend (*of things*); zuverlässig, vertrauenswürdig; vorsichtig, bedächtig (*of a p.*); *it is – to say,* man kann getrost *or* ruhig sagen; (*coll.*) *he is – to win,* er wird sicher gewinnen; *as – as houses,* absolut sicher, todsicher; *the bridge is* –, die Brücke hält; *with a – conscience,* mit ruhigem *or* gutem Gewissen; – *custody,* sicherer Gewahrsam; – *driver,* vorsichtiger Fahrer; *be on the – side,* sicher gehen; – *and sound,* gesund und munter; *not* –, gefährlich. 2. *s.* der Geldschrank; (also *meat*-–) Speiseschrank. **--breaker,** *s.* der Geldschrankknacker. **– conduct,** *s.* freies, sicheres *or* bewaffnetes Geleit; der Schutzbegleiter; Geleitsbrief. **– deposit,** *s.* das Bankfach. **-guard** [-gɑ:d], 1. *s.* der Schutz, die Sicherheit, Bürgschaft, Vorsichtsmaßnahme, Sicherheitsklausel (*Law*); der Geleitsbrief. 2. *v.a.* schützen; verwahren, sichern, wahrnehmen, sicherstellen. **– keeping,** *s.* sicherer Gewahrsam. **-ness,** *s.* die Sicherheit, Zuverlässigkeit. **-ty** [-tɪ], *s.* die Sicherheit; *in -ty,* in Sicherheit; *-ty first,* erst an die eigene Sicherheit denken, der Schutz gegen Unfall; *flee for -ty,* sich flüchten; *play for -ty,* vorsichtig spielen; *there is -ty in numbers,* in der Menge geht man unter; *place of -ty,* der Sicherheitsort, Zufluchtsort; *carry to -ty,* in Sicherheit bringen; *jump to -ty,* sich durch einen Sprung in Sicherheit bringen. **-ty-belt,** *s.* der Rettungsgürtel (*Naut.*), Anschnallgurt (*Av.*). **-ty-catch,** *s.* die Sicherung (*of a rifle*). **-ty-curtain,** *s.* eiserner Vorhang. **-ty factor,** *s.* der Sicherheitsfaktor. **-ty-fuse,** *s.* der Sicherheitszünder. **-ty-glass,** *s.* das Schutzglas. **-ty-lamp,** *s.* die Sicherheitslampe. **-ty-lock,** *s.* das Sicherheitsschloß. **-ty-matches,** *pl.* Sicherheitszünder (*pl.*). **-ty-pin,** *s.* die Sicherheitsnadel. **-ty-razor,** *s.* der Rasierapparat. **-ty-valve,** *s.* das Sicherheitsventil, (*fig.*) der Ausweg.
saffian ['sæfɪən], *s.* das Saffianleder.
safflower ['sæflɑʊə], *s.* der Saflor, die Färberdistel, wilder Safran (*Bot.*).
saffron ['sæfrən], 1. *s.* echter Safran (*Bot.*); das Safrangewürz; Safrangelb; 2. *adj.* Safran–, safrangelb.
sag [sæg], 1. *v.n.* sich senken, niederhängen; absacken, sinken, fallen, nachlassen, (*of prices*); – *to leeward,* nach Lee abtreiben (*Naut.*). 2. *s.* das Sacken, die Senkung, Absackung, der Durchgang.

saga [ˈsɑːgə], *s.* die Saga.
sag-acious [səˈgeɪʃəs], *adj.* klug, scharfsinnig. **-acity** [-ˈgæsɪtɪ], *s.* der Scharfsinn, die Klugheit. **-e** [seɪdʒ], 1. *adj.* weise, klug, urteilsfähig. 2. *s.* Weise(r), *m.*
sage [seɪdʒ], *s.* der & die Salbei (*Bot.*).
sagg-ar, -er [ˈsægə], *s.* feuerfestes Gefäß.
Sagittarius [sægɪˈtɛːərɪəs], *s.* der Schütze (*Astr.*).
sago [ˈseɪgoʊ], *s.* der Sago.
Sahib [ˈsɑːhɪb], *s.* Herr (*as title following name*); der Engländer, Europäer (*in India.*).
said [sɛd], *see* **say**; *adj.* vorerwähnt, besagt.
sail [seɪl], 1. *s.* das Segel; (*fig.*) (*no pl.*) das Segelschiff; der Flügel (*of a windmill*); die Segelfahrt; *hoist* –, die Segel hissen; *in full* –, mit vollen Segeln; *make* –, die Segel beisetzen; *set* –, auslaufen, in See gehen; *shorten* –, die Segel einziehen; *strike* –, die Segel streichen; *under* –, unter Segel; *under full* –, alles bei. 2. *v.n.* segeln; absegeln, abreisen, sich einschiffen (*for*, nach); zu Schiff fahren *or* reisen; gleiten, fliegen (*in the air*); (*fig.*) schwimmen, dahinschweben; – *close* or *near to the wind*, nah am Winde *or* hoch an den Wind segeln; (*fig.*) Gefahr laufen sich strafbar zu machen *or* gegen die Moral zu verstoßen; (*fig.*) – *in*, majestätisch hereinkommen; (*coll.*) sich ins Mittel legen; *ready to* –, seeklar. 3. *v.a.* durchsegeln (*the sea*), durchfliegen, durchschweben (*the air*); führen (*a boat*). **--cloth,** *s.* das Segeltuch. **-er,** *s.* der Segler, das Segelschiff. **-ing,** 1. *pr.p.* & *adj.* segelnd, Segel–. 2. *s.* das Segeln, die (Segel)Schiffahrt; Abfahrt (*for*, nach); *pl.* Abfahrtszeiten; *plain -ing*, eine einfache S. **-ing-boat,** *s.* das Segelboot. **-ing orders,** *pl.* der Befehl zum Auslaufen, die Fahrtordnung. **-ing-vessel,** *s.* das Segelschiff. **--loft,** *s.* der Schnürboden. **-maker,** *s.* der Segelmacher. **-or** [-ə], *s.* der Matrose, Seemann; *be a good -or*, seefest sein; nicht leicht seekrank werden; *be a bad -or*, nicht seefest sein, leicht seekrank werden; *-or's knot*, der Schifferknoten; *-or hat*, der Matrosenhut. **-oring,** *s.* das Seemannsleben. **-or-man,** *s.* (*coll.*) der Matrose. **-plane,** *s.* das Segelflugzeug.
sainfoin [ˈseɪnfɔɪn], *s.* die Esparsette, der Schildklee (*Bot.*).
saint [seɪnt], 1. *s.* Heilige(r), *m.*; frommer *or* unschuldiger Mensch; Scheinheilige(r), *m.*, der Frömmler (*satirical*); *patron* –, Schutzheilige(r), *m.*; *-'s day*, der Heiligentag; *All -s' day*, Allerheiligen (*pl.*). 2. [sənt, sɪnt, snt, sn], *adj.* (*before names*) heilig, Sankt; *St. Andrew's Cross*, das Andreaskreuz; *St. Anthony's Fire*, die Rose, das Erysipel (*Med.*); *St. Elmo's Fire*, das Elmsfeuer; (*Court of*) *St. James('s)*, der Großbritannische Hof; *St. John's wort*, das Johanniskraut (*Bot.*); *St. Leger*, das Septemberrennen zu Doncaster; *St. Martin's summer*, der Altweibersommer; *St. Valentine's day*, der Valentinstag; *St. Vitus's dance*, der Veitstanz. 3. *v.a.* heiligsprechen. **-ed,** *adj.* heiliggesprochen; selig; geheiligt, geweiht, heilig. **-like,** *adj. see* **-ly. -liness,** *s.* die Heiligkeit. **-ly,** *adj.* heilig; (*fig.*) fromm.
sake [seɪk], *s.*; *for God's* or *goodness* –, um alles in der Welt, um Gottes willen; *for his* –, um seinetwillen, ihm zuliebe; *for my own* –, um meiner selbst willen; *for the* – *of doing*, in der Absicht zu tun; *for the* – *of a th.*, aus Rücksicht auf eine S., um einer S. willen, wegen einer S., in der Absicht eine S. zu bekommen, im Interesse einer S.; *for the* – *of peace*, um des (lieben) Friedens willen.
saker [ˈseɪkə], *s.* weiblicher Sakerfalk (*Orn.*). **-et** [-rɪt], *s.* männlicher Sakerfalk (*Orn.*).
sal [sæl], *s.* das Salz (*Chem.*); – *ammoniac*, der Salmiak, das Chlorammonium; – *volatile*, das Hirschhornsalz.
salaam [səˈlɑːm], 1. *s.* mohammedanische Begrüßung(sform). 2. *v.n.* nach mohammedanischer Art grüßen.
salable [ˈseɪləbl], *adj.* verkäuflich, gangbar.
salac-ious [səˈleɪʃəs], *adj.* wollüstig, geil, zotig. **-ousness, -ity** [-ˈlæsɪtɪ], *s.* die Wollust, Geilheit.
salad [ˈsæləd], *s.* der Salat, grüner Salat; – *days*, Jugendjahre (*pl.*). **--bowl, --dish,** *s.* die Salatschüssel. **--dressing,** *s.* die Salatsoße. **--oil,** *s.* das Olivenöl.
salamander [ˈsæləmændə], *s.* der Salamander, Molch (*Zool.*); Feuersalamander, Feuergeist; das Schüreisen, die Eisenschaufel (*Cook.*).
salar-ied [ˈsælərɪd], *adj.* besoldet, bezahlt; *-ied employee*, der Gehaltsempfänger. **-y** [-rɪ], 1. *s.* das Gehalt, die Besoldung. 2. *v.a.* besolden.
sale [seɪl], *s.* der Verkauf; Ausverkauf; Abgang; Absatz; die Auktion, Versteigerung; *forced* –, der Zwangsverkauf; *forward* –, der Terminverkauf; *for* –, zum Verkauf, verkäuflich; *put up for* –, feilbieten; versteigern; *bill of* –, die Verkaufsrechnung, der Kaufkontrakt; *on* –, zu verkaufen(d); *on* – *or return*, in Kommission; *by private* –, unter der Hand; *meet with a ready* –, schnellen Absatz finden; – *of work*, der Verkauf zu Wohltätigkeitszwecken. **--price,** *s.* der Verkaufspreis. **--room,** *s.* das Auktionslokal. **-sman** [-zmən], *s.* der (Laden)-Verkäufer; Geschäftsreisende(r), *m.* **-smanship,** *s.* die Verkaufstüchtigkeit, Verkaufsgewandheit. **-sroom** [-zruːm], *s.* der Verkaufsraum. **-swoman** *s.* die (Laden)Verkäuferin.
Salic [ˈsælɪk], *adj.* salisch; – *law*, salisches Gesetz.
salic-in [ˈsælɪsɪn], *s.* das Salizin, Weidenbitter (*Chem.*). **-yl** [-sɪl], *s.* das Salizyl. **-ylic** [-ˈsɪlɪk], *adj.* Salizyl–, salizylsauer.
salient [ˈseɪlɪənt], *adj.* hervorspringend, hervortretend, hervorragend, Haupt–; vorspringend (*Arch.*); springend (*Her.*). 2. *s.* vorspringender Winkel; vorspringende Verteidigungslinie (*Mil.*).
sali-ferous [sæˈlɪfərəs], *adj.* salzhaltig. **-ne** [ˈseɪlaɪn], 1. *adj.* Salz–, salzig, salzhaltig. 2. *s.* die Saline, Salzquelle. **-nity** [sæˈlɪnɪtɪ], *s.* die Salzhaltigkeit, Salzigkeit.
saliva [səˈlaɪvə], *s.* der Speichel. **-ry** [-ərɪ], *adj.* Speichel–. **-te** [ˈsælɪveɪt], 1. *v.a.* durch den Speichelfluß reinigen. 2. *v.n.* Speichel absondern. **-tion** [-ˈveɪʃən], *s.* der Speichelfluß.
[1]**sallow** [ˈsæloʊ], *s.* die Salweide (*Bot.*).
[2]**sallow** [ˈsæloʊ], *adj.* gelblich, fahl, farblos, bleich, bläßlich. **-ness,** *s.* fahle *or* gelbliche Farbe, die Blässe.
sally [ˈsælɪ], 1. *s.* der Ausfall (*Mil.*); (*fig.*) Ausbruch, witziger Einfall. 2. *v.n.* (often – *forth*) aufbrechen, sich aufmachen; – *out*, ausfallen, einen Ausfall machen. **--port,** *s.* das Ausfallstor.
Sally-Lunn [ˈsælɪˈlʌn], *s.* eine Art Teekuchen.
salmagundi [sælməˈgʌndɪ], *s.* das Ragout; (*fig.*) der Mischmasch.
salmon [ˈsæmən], *s.* der Lachs, Salm; (also *--pink* or *--colour*) die Lachsfarbe. **- trout,** *s.* die Lachsforelle.
salon [ˈsælɔn], *s.* der Salon.
saloon [səˈluːn], *s.* der Saal, Gesellschaftssaal; erste Klasse (auf Schiffen); die Kneipe; *dancing* –, das Tanzlokal; *gambling* –, die Spielhölle; – *bar*, vornehmerer Ausschank; – *cabin*, die Kabine erster Klasse (*on ships*); – *deck*, *s.* das Oberdeck, Salondeck. **--car,** *s.* der Salonwagen, Luxuswagen (*Railw.*); die Limousine (*Motor.*).
sals-afy, -ify [ˈsælsəfɪ], *s.* der Bocksbart (*Bot.*).
salt [sɔːlt], 1. *s.* das Salz; (*fig.*) der Saft, die Würze; (*coll.*) der Seemann; *pl.* Riechsalze (*pl.*), das Abführmittel; *above* (*below*) *the* –, oben (unten) am Tisch; *common* –, das Kochsalz; Chlornatrium (*Chem.*); *eat a p.'s* –, jemandes Gast sein; *the* – *of the earth*, die Würze; *Epsom* –, englisches Salz; *in* –, eingesalzen, gepökelt; *grain of* –, das Körnchen Salz; (*coll.*) *with a grain of* –, mit einiger Vorsicht; *old* –, alter Seebär; *smelling -s*, Riechsalze; *table* –, das Tafelsalz; *not worth one's* –, nichts taugen. 2. *adj.* salzig, gesalzen; – *beef*, gepökeltes Rindfleisch; – *butter*, gesalzene Butter; – *meat*, das Pökelfleisch; – *tears*, bittere Tränen; – *water*, das Salzwasser. 3. *v.a.* salzen (also – *down*) einsalzen, einpökeln (*meat, etc.*); (*fig.*) würzen; pfeffern, (*prices*); (*sl.*) frisieren; (*fig.*) – *down* beiseitelegen. **--cellar,** *s.* das Salzfäßchen. **-ed** [-ɪd], *adj.* (*fig.*) abgehärtet, ausgekocht, ausgepicht. **-er,** *s.* der Salzhändler; Salzsieder. **-ern,** *s. see* **-works. -ing,** *s.* das Einpökeln; (*usually pl.*) salzreiches Schwemmland; *-ing-tub*, das Pökelfaß. **-less,** *adj.* ungesalzen, salzlos, ohne Salz; (*fig.*) seicht. **--lick,** *s.* die Salzlecke. **- marsh,** *s.* der Salzwassermorast. **--mine,** *s.*

die Saline, das Salzbergwerk. **-petre,** *see* **saltpetre.** **--pit,** *s.* die Salzgrube. **--spring,** *s.* die Salzquelle, Salzsole. **-works,** *s.* das Salzbergwerk, die Saline. **-y,** *adj.* salzig, (*fig.*) würzig.
salt-ant [ˈsæltənt], *adj.* springend (*Her.*). **-ation** [-ˈteɪʃən], *s.* das Springen, der Sprung. **-atory** [ˈsæltətərɪ], *adj.* springend, Spring–, sprunghaft. **-igrade** [-tɪgreɪd], *s.* die Springspinne (*Zool.*).
saltire [ˈsæltɑɪə], *s.* das Schrägkreuz (*Her.*).
saltpetre [sɔːltˈpiːtə], *s.* der (Kali)Salpeter, das Kaliumnitrat (*Chem.*).
salty [ˈsɔːltɪ], *see* **salt.**
salu-brious [səˈl(j)uːbrɪəs], *adj.* heilsam, gesund, zuträglich, bekömmlich (*climate, etc.*). **-brity** [-brɪtɪ], *s.* die Heilsamkeit, Zuträglichkeit. **-tariness** [-ˈljuːtərɪnɪs], *s. see* **-brity.** **-tary** [-ljutərɪ], *adj.* heilsam, gesund, ersprießlich.
salut-ation [sæljuˈteɪʃən], *s.* der Gruß, die Begrüßung; *in -tation,* zum Gruß, zur Begrüßung. **-atory,** *adj.* grüßend, Begrüßungs–; Eröffnungs- (*Amer.*). **-e** [səˈl(j)uːt], 1. *s.* der Gruß (*also Mil.*), die Begrüßung; (*archaic*) der Kuß; Salut (*of guns*); das Salutieren; *in -e,* zum Gruß; *give a -e,* grüßen; *give the -e,* den Salut leisten; *return a -e,* einen Gruß erwidern, wiedergrüßen; *stand at the -e,* salutieren; *take the -e,* den Salut entgegennehmen (*of* (*Gen.*)), die Parade abnehmen (*of,* über); *-e of twelve guns,* der Salut von 12 Schüssen. 2. *v.a.* grüßen (*also Mil.*), salutieren (*Mil.*), (*fig.*) begrüßen. 3. *v.n.* grüßen, salutieren.
salva-ble [ˈsælvəbl], *adj.* rettbar; einbringbar (*a ship*); errettbar, erlösbar. **-ge** [ˈsælvɪdʒ], 1. *s.* die Bergung, Einbringung (*ship, etc.*); Rettung; (Abfall)Verwertung; das Bergegut, Aufräumungsgut; geworbenes Gut; das Bergegeld. 2. *v.a.* bergen. **-ge-dump,** *s.* die Beutesammelstelle.
salvation [sælˈveɪʃən], *s.* die Erlösung, das Seelenheil (*Eccl.*); (*fig.*) die Rettung, Befreiung; der Retter, das Heil (*of a p.*); *be the – of,* der Retter sein von; *work out one's own –,* (*fig.*) auf eigenen Beinen stehen, auf eigene Faust selig werden. **– Army,** die Heilsarmee. **-ist,** *s.* das Mitglied der Heilsarmee.
[1]**salve** [sælv], *v.a.* retten, bergen (*Naut.*).
[2]**salve** [sælv], 1. *s.* die Salbe, der Balsam; (*fig.*) das Heilmittel, Linderungsmittel. 2. *v.a.* einsalben; (*usually fig.*) heilen, beruhigen, lindern; *– one's conscience,* sein Gewissen beruhigen.
salver [ˈsælvə], *s.* der Präsentierteller.
[1]**salvo** [ˈsælvou], *s.* der Vorbehalt, die Vorbehaltsklausel.
[2]**salvo** [ˈsælvou], *s.* die Salve (*Mil.*).
salvor [ˈsælvə], *s.* der Berger, das Bergungsschiff.
same [seɪm], *adj.*; *the –,* derselbe, dieselbe, dasselbe; *all the –,* dennoch, gleichwohl, nichtsdestoweniger; *it is all the – to me,* es ist mir einerlei *or* ganz gleich; *just the –,* genau dasselbe, genau so; gleichwohl; *no longer the – man,* nicht mehr der alte; *much the –,* (so) ziemlich dasselbe; *one and the –,* ein und derselbe; *think the –,* genau so denken über; *at the – time,* zur gleichen *or* selben Zeit (*as,* wie); (*fig.*) zugleich, ebenfalls; (*coll.*) *the – to you,* gleichfalls; *it comes to the – thing,* es kommt auf dasselbe hinaus; *the very –,* ganz *or* eben derselbe. **-ness,** *s.* die Gleichheit, Identität; Eintönigkeit, Einförmigkeit.
samlet [ˈsæmlɪt], *s.* junger Lachs.
sampan [ˈsæmpæn], *s.* chinesisches Flußboot.
sample [ˈsæmpl], 1. *s.* die Probe (*also fig.*), das Muster (*C.L.*); *according to, as per* or *up to –,* mustergemäß, laut Probe; *– post,* Muster ohne Wert. 2. *v.a.* eine Probe nehmen von, nach Proben beurteilen; (*fig.*) probieren, kosten. **-r** [-lə], *s.* das Stickmuster.
sanat-ive [ˈsænətɪv], *adj.* heilend, heilkräftig, Heil–, heilsam. **-orium** [-ˈtɔːrɪəm], *s.* (pl. *-ia*) die Heilanstalt, das Sanatorium, Erholungsheim. **-ory** [-tərɪ], *adj. see* **-ive.**
sanctif-ication [sæŋktɪfɪˈkeɪʃən], *s.* die Heiligung, Heiligsprechung, Weihe. **-y** [ˈsæŋktɪfɑɪ], *v.a.* heiligen (*also fig.*), weihen; rechtfertigen.
sanctimon-ious [sæŋktɪˈmounɪəs], *adj.* scheinheilig. **-iousness,** *s.*, **-y** [ˈsæŋktɪmənɪ], *s.* die Scheinheiligkeit.
sanction [ˈsæŋkʃən], 1. *s.* die Bestätigung, Genehmigung, das Gutheißen; die Sanktion, Strafmaßnahme, Zwangsmaßnahme (*Law*); *pl.* Sanktionen (*pl.*) (*Pol.*); *give – to,* unterstützen, bekräftigen, dulden; *impose -s,* Sanktionen auferlegen. 2. *v.a.* gutheißen, genehmigen; bekräftigen, sanktionieren.
sanctit-ude [ˈsæŋktɪtjuːd] (*rare*), **-y** [-tɪtɪ], *s.* die Heiligkeit, Unverletzlichkeit; Reinheit.
sanctu-ary [ˈsæŋktjuərɪ], *s.* das Heiligtum, die Hochaltarstätte (*Eccl.*); (*fig.*) heiliger Zufluchtsort, das Asyl, die Freistatt. **-m** [ˈsæŋktəm], *s.* das Heiligtum, Allerheiligste; (*coll.*) das Privatzimmer. **-s** [-təs], *s.* der Meßhymnus (*R.C.*).
sand [sænd], 1. *s.* der Sand; *pl.* das Sandufer, die Sandbank, die Sandwüste; *build on –,* auf Sand bauen; *make ropes of –,* leeres Stroh dreschen; *his -s are running out,* seine Zeit ist bald um, seine Augenblicke sind gezählt. 2. *v.a.* mit Sand bestreuen. **-bag,** 1. *s.* der Sandsack. 2. *v.a.* mit Sandsäcken bedecken *or* ausbauen; (*coll.*) niederschlagen. **-bank,** *s.* die Sandbank. **--blast,** *s.* das Sandstrahlgebläse. (*coll.*) *happy as a* **--boy,** kreuzfidel. **--drift,** *s.* der Flugsand, Treibsand. **-erling,** *s.* kleiner Wasserläufer (*Orn.*). **-glass,** *s.* die Sanduhr. **--grouse,** *s.* das Sandhuhn (*Orn.*). **--hill,** *s.* die Düne. **-hopper,** *s.* der Strandfloh (*Zool.*). **-iness,** *s.* sandige Beschaffenheit. **-man,** *s.* das Sandmännchen. **--martin,** *s.* die Uferschwalbe (*Orn.*). **-paper,** 1. *s.* das Sandpapier. 2. *v.a.* mit Sandpapier abreiben. **– piper,** *s.* der Strandläufer (*Orn.*). **--pit,** *s.* die Sandgrube. **--shoes,** *pl.* die Strandschuhe. **-stone,** *s.* der Sandstein. **-storm,** *s.* der Sandsturm. **-wich,** *see* **sandwich.** **-wort,** *s.* das Sandkraut (*Bot.*). **-y,** *adj.* sandig; sandfarbig; (*coll.*) rotblond (*hair*).
sandal [ˈsændl], *s.* die Sandale. **-ed,** *adj.* in Sandalen. **-wood,** *s.* das Sandelholz.
sandever, sandiver [ˈsændɪvə], *s.* die Glasgalle (*Glassmaking*).
sandiness *see* **sand.**
sandwich [ˈsændwɪtʃ], 1. *s.* belegtes Butterbrot. 2. *v.a.* (also *– in*) (*fig.*) einlegen, einschieben, einklemmen, einpferchen. **--board,** *s.* wandelndes Plakat. **--box,** *s.* die Butterbrotsdose. **--man,** *s.* der Plakatträger. **– spread,** *s.* der Brotaufstrich.
sandy, *see* **sand.**
sane [seɪn], *adj.* geistig, gesund, bei gesundem Verstande; vernünftig; *see* **sanity.**
sang, *see* **sing.**
sang-froid [sæŋˈfrwɑː], *s.* die Kaltblütigkeit, Geistesgegenwart.
sangrail [sænˈgreɪl], *s.* Heiliger Gral.
sangui-fication [sæŋgwɪfɪˈkeɪʃən], *s.* die Blutbildung. **-nary** [ˈsæŋgwɪnərɪ], *adj.* blutig, mörderisch, blutbefleckt; blutdürstig, grausam. **-ne** [ˈsæŋgwɪn], *adj.* (*fig.*) leichtblütig, lebhaft, heiter, optimistisch; zuversichtlich (*of,* auf); blutrot (*Her. & Poet.*); (*archaic*) blutreich, vollblütig, heißblütig (*Med.*); *most -ne expectations,* die kühnsten Erwartungen; *-ne person,* der Sanguiniker, Optimist. **-neous** [-ˈwɪnɪəs], *adj.* Blut–; blutreich, vollblütig; blutrot.
sanhedrin [ˈsænɪdrɪn], *s.* das Synedrium.
sanita-ry [ˈsænɪtərɪ], *adj.* Gesundheits–, sanitär, Sanitäts–; gesund, hygienisch; *-ry arrangements,* sanitäre Einrichtungen; *-ry inspector,* der Beamte der Gesundheitspolizei; *-ry towel,* die (Damen)-Binde. **-tion** [-ˈteɪʃən], *s.* sanitäre Einrichtungen (*pl.*), das Gesundheitswesen.
sanity [ˈsænɪtɪ], *s.* geistige Gesundheit, die Zurechnungsfähigkeit; gesunder Verstand, die Vernunft.
sank [sæŋk], *see* **sink.**
sans [sænz], *prep.* ohne. **-culotte** [-kjuːˈlɔt], *s.* extremer Republikaner (*French Hist.*). **-erif** [sænˈserɪf], *s.* die Schrift ohne Feinstriche.
[1]**sap** [sæp], *s.* der Saft (*Bot.*); (*fig.*) das Mark, Lebensmark, die Kraft. **-less,** *adj.* saftlos, kraftlos, dürr; seicht. **-ling,** *see* **sapling.** **-piness,** *s.* die Saftigkeit. **-py,** *adj.* saftig; (*fig.*) markig, kräftig. **--wood,** *s.* der Splint, das Grünholz.
[2]**sap,** 1. *s.* bedeckter Laufgraben, die Sappe (*Fort.*). 2. *v.n.* sappieren. 3. *v.a.* unterminieren, untergraben; (*fig.*) schwächen, erschöpfen, auszehren (*strength*). **-head,** *s.* der Sappenkopf, die Sackgrube (*Fort.*). **-per,** *s.* der Pioneer (*Mil.*).

[3]**sap,** 1. *s.* (*sl.*) der Büffler; Tölpel. 2. *v.n.* (*sl.*) büffeln, ochsen. **-py,** *adj.* (*sl.*) lappig, schwächlich, dumm.
sapid ['sæpɪd], *adj.* schmackhaft, saftig; interessant. **-ity** [sæ'pɪdɪtɪ], die Schmackhaftigheit.
sapien-ce ['seɪpɪəns], *s.* die Weisheit (*often ironic*), Scheinweisheit. **-t** [-ənt], *adj.* weise (*ironic*), überklug.
sapling ['sæplɪŋ], *s.* junger Baum, der Schößling; (*fig.*) junger Windhund; der Jüngling, grüner Junge.
sapon-aceous [sæpə'neɪʃəs], *adj.* seifig, seifenartig, seifenhaltig, Seifen-. **-ification** [sæpɔnɪfɪ'keɪʃən], *s.* die Seifenbildung, Verseifung. **-ify** [-'pɔnɪfaɪ], *v.a.* (& *n.*) zur Seife machen (werden), verseifen.
sapphic ['sæfɪk], 1. *adj.* sapphisch. 2. *s.* (*usually pl.*) sapphische Verse (*pl.*), sapphische Strophe.
sapphire ['sæfaɪə], 1. *s.* der Saphir; das Saphirblau. 2. *adj.* Saphir-; blau (*Her.*).
sappiness, *see* [1]**sap.**
sappy, *see* [1]**sap,** [3]**sap.**
saraband, *s.* spanischer Tanz.
sarcas-m ['sɑ:kæzm], *s.* bitterer Hohn, beißender Spott, der Sarkasmus. **-tic** [-'kæstɪk], *adj.* sarkastisch, höhnisch, beißend.
sarcenet ['sɑ:sənɪt], *s.* der Seidentaft.
sarco-de ['sɑ:koud], *s.* tierisches Protoplasma. **-ma,** *s.* das Fleischgewächs. **-phagous** [-'kɔfəgəs], *adj.* fleischfressend. **-phagus** [-'kɔfəgəs], *s.* der Sarkophag.
sard [sɑ:d], **-ius** [-ɪəs], *s.* der Sarder.
sardine [sɑ:'dɪ:n], *s.* die Sardine (*Ichth.*); *packed like -s,* eng zusammengedrängt, zusammengepfercht wie Schafe.
sardonic [sɑ:'dɔnɪk], *adj.* sardonisch, höhnisch, hämisch, bitter.
sardonyx ['sɑ:dənɪks], *s.* der Sardonyx.
sark [sɑ:k], *s.* (*Scots*) das Hemd.
sarment-ose ['sɑ:məntous], **-ous** [sɑ:'mɛntəs], *adj.* rankig, rankend (*Bot.*).
sarong [sə'rɔŋ], *s.* der Sarong.
sarsaparilla [sɑ:s(ə)pə'rɪlə], *s.* die Sassaparilla.
sarsen ['sɑ:sən], *s.* (also *--stone*) der Sandsteinfindling (*Geol.*).
sartori-al [sɑ:'tɔ:rɪəl], *adj.* Schneider-, Kleider-. **-us** [-ɪəs], *s.* der Schneidermuskel (*Anat.*).
[1]**sash** [sæʃ], *s.* die Schärpe, Leibbinde.
[2]**sash,** *s.* schiebbarer Fensterrahmen. **--cord,** *s.* der Fenstergurt. **--window,** *s.* das Schiebefenster, Aufziehfenster.
Sassanach ['sæsənæχ], *s.* (*Scots*) der Engländer.
sassafras ['sæsəfræs], *s.* der Sassafras (*Bot.*).
sat, *see* **sit.**
Satan ['seɪtən], *s.* der Teufel, Satan. **-ic(al)** [sə'tænɪk(l)], *adj.* satanisch, Satans-; (*fig.*) teuflisch.
satchel ['sætʃl], *s.* der Ranzen, die Schulmappe, Schultasche.
sate [seɪt], *v.a.* (*usually pass.*) (über)sättigen. **-less,** *adj.* (*Poet.*) unersättlich.
sateen [sæ'tɪ:n], *s.* der Satin, Baumwollatlas, Englisches Leder.
satellite ['sætəl t], *s.* der Trabant, Satellit (*Astr.*); (*fig.*) Anhänger; *- state,* der Satellitenstaat.
sati-ate ['seɪʃɪeɪt], *v.a.* übersättigen, befriedigen, saturieren. **-ation** [- 'eɪʃn], *s.* die (Über)Sättigung. **-ety** [sə'taɪətɪ], *s.* die Sattheit, Übersättigung, der Überdruß, Ekel.
satin ['sætɪn], 1. *s.* der Atlas, Seidensatin. 2. *v.a.* satinieren, glätten (*paper*). 3. *adj.* Atlas-; glatt, glänzend. **-et(te)** [-'nɛt], *s.* der Halbatlas. **-y,** *adj.* glatt, glänzend. **-paper,** *s.* das Atlaspapier. **-wood,** *s.* das Satinholz.
satir-e ['sætaɪə], *s.* die Satire, das Spottgedicht; die Ironie, der Hohn (*on,* auf). **-ic(al)** [sə'tɪrɪk(l)], *adj.* satirisch, spöttisch, höhnisch. **-ist** ['sætɪrɪst], *s.* der Satiriker. **-ize** ['sætɪraɪz], *v.a.* verspotten, bespötteln, geißeln.
satisf-action [sætɪs'fækʃən], *s.* die Befriedigung; Zufriedenheit, Genugtuung (*of doing,* zu tun); Satisfaktion (*duel*); Sühne (*Theol.*); Bezahlung (*of a debt*); *find -action,* Befriedigung finden (*in doing,* zu tun); *give -action,* befriedigen; Satisfaktion geben (*duelling*); sich bewähren; *to the -action of,* zur Zufriedenheit von. **-actoriness** [-'fæktərɪnɪs], *s.* das Befriedigende. **-actory** [-'fæktərɪ], *adj.* befriedigend; beruhigend, zufriedenstellend (*to,* für); sühnend (*Theol*); *be -actory for,* sühnen, (*Theol.*). **-y** ['sætɪsfaɪ], 1. *v.a.* befriedigen; erfüllen (*request*); genügen (*demands*); stillen, sättigen (*hunger*); nachkommen (*Dat.*) (*obligations*); zufriedenstellen, überzeugen (*a p.*), bezahlen (*a debtor*); *be -ied,* satt sein, genug haben; überzeugt sein (*of,* von; *that,* daß); *be -ied with,* sich begnügen *or* zufrieden sein mit; *-y o.s.,* sich überzeugen, sich vergewissen. 2. *v.n.* Genüge leisten, Genugtuung geben (*Dat.*). **-ying** [-faɪɪŋ], *adj.* befriedigend, ausreichend, genügend, hinlänglich; sättigend.
satrap ['sætrəp), *s.* der Satrap, tyrannischer Statthalter. **-y** [-pɪ], *s.* die Satrapie, Statthalterschaft.
satura-ble [sætʃərəbl], *adj.* zu sättigen(d). **-nt** [-ənt], 1. *adj.* sättigend. 2. *s.* neutralisierendes *or* Säuren absorbierendes Mittel. **-te** [-eɪt], *v.a.* durchtränken, durchsetzen; imprägnieren, sättigen (*Chem.*); (*coll.*) *be -ted,* durchnäßt sein *or* werden, pudelnaß sein; (*fig.*) *-te o.s. in,* sich versenken *or* vertiefen in. **-ted** [-eɪtɪd], *adj.* durchnäßt, durchtränkt, gesättigt (*with,* von); satt, kräftig (*colour*). **-tion** [-'reɪʃən], *s.* die Durchnässung, Durchsetzung, Durchwässerung; Sättigung (*Chem.*); *-tion point,* der Sättigungspunkt.
Saturday ['sætədɪ], *s.* der Samstag, Sonnabend.
Saturn ['sætə:n], *see Index of Names*; das Schwarz (*Her.*). **-alia** [-'neɪlɪə], *s.* Saturnalien (*pl.*). **-alian** [-'neɪlɪən], *adj.* saturnalisch. **-ine** ['sætənaɪn], *adj.* saturnisch (*Astr.*); (*fig.*) finster, düster.
satyr ['sætə], *s.* der Satyr, Waldgott; (*fig.*) lüsterner Mensch. **-iasis** [-tɪ'raɪəsɪs], *s.* abnormer Geschlechtstrieb des Mannes. **-ic** [sə'tɪrɪk], *adj.* satyrartig, Satyr-.
sauc-e [sɔ:s], 1. *s.* die Soße, Sauce, Tunke; (*fig.*) Würze; (*coll.*) Frechheit, Unverschämtheit; (*Prov.*) *what's -e for the goose is -e for the gander,* was dem einen recht ist, ist dem andern billig; (*Prov.*) *hunger is the best -e,* Hunger ist der beste Koch. 2. *v.a.* würzen; unverschämt sein zu, frech reden mit. **-e-boat,** *s.* die Sauciere, Soßenschüssel, der Soßennapf. **-epan,** *s.* der Kochtopf, Schmortopf, die Pfanne. **-er** [-ə], *s.* die Untertasse; *-er-eyes, pl.* Glotzaugen. **-iness** [-ɪnɪs], *s.* (*coll.*) die Frechheit, Unverschämtheit, Keckheit. **-y** [-ɪ], *adj.* (*coll.*) unverschämt, frech; keck; naseweis; flott, schmuck.
saunter ['sɔ:ntə], 1. *s.* das Schlendern; gemächlicher Spaziergang. 2. *v.n.* schlendern; bummeln; *- about,* umherschlendern.
saurian ['sɔ:rɪən], 1. *s.* der Saurier. 2. *adj.* Saurier-, Eidechsen-.
sausage ['sɔsɪdʒ], *s.* die (Brat)Wurst. **--balloon,** s. der Fesselballon. **--roll,** *s.* die Wurstpastete.
sauté ['souteɪ], *adj.* geschwenkt (*Cul.*).
savable ['seɪvəbl], *adj.* rettbar, zu erretten(d).
savage ['sævɪdʒ], 1. *adj.* wild; wütend; brutal, roh; grausam; primitiv, barbarisch, unzivilisiert; (*coll.*) ärgerlich. 2. *s.* der Barbar, Wilde(r), *m.* 3. *v.n.* anfallen (*of a horse*). **-ness,** *s.* die Wildheit, Grausamkeit, Rohheit, Wut, Heftigkeit. **-ry** [rɪ], *s.* die Wildheit, Barbarei.
savanna(h) [sə'vænə], *s.* die Savanne, Steppe (*Amer.*).
savant ['sævã:], *s.* Gelehrte(r), *m.*
save [seɪv], 1. *v.a.* retten, befreien (*from,* aus *or* von); erlösen (*Theol.*); bergen (*Naut.*); schützen, bewahren, sichern (*from,* vor); aufbewahren, aufheben, aufsparen, sparsam umgehen mit, schonen; verschonen mit, ersparen (*a p.* (*Dat.*)); *to - appearances,* (um) den Schein (zu) wahren; *- your breath,* schone deine Lunge; *- the expression,* entschuldigen Sie den Ausdruck; *- one's face,* sich vor Demütigung schützen; *God - the Queen!* Gott schütze *or* erhalte die Königin! *- a p.'s life,* einem das Leben retten; *- money,* Geld sparen; *- o.s.,* sich schonen; *- o.s. the trouble,* sich (*Dat.*) die Mühe ersparen; *- the situation,* die Situation retten; *to - time,* um keine Zeit zu verlieren. 2. *v.n.* (also *- up*) sparen. 3. *prep.* & *conj.* außer, ausgenommen; *- and except,* mit alleiniger Ausnahme von; *- for,* abgesehen von; *the last - one,* der Vorletzte; *- only he,* ausgenommen er allein; *- that,*

außer daß. 4. *s.* die Abwehr, Verhinderung eines Tores (*Footb.*). **--all,** *s.* der Lichtsparer, Tropfenfänger. **-r,** *s.* der Retter, Sparer; das Ersparnis (*of*, an); *life -r*, der Lebensretter; *labour -r*, das Arbeitsersparnis; *see* **saving, saviour.**

saveloy ['sævəlɔɪ], *s.* die Zervelatwurst.

saving ['seɪvɪŋ], 1. *adj.* sparsam, haushälterisch (*of*, mit); (*as suffix*) -ersparend; Vorbehalts- (*Law*); - *clause*, der Vorbehalt, die Vorbehaltsklausel; - *grace*, rettender Umstand. 2. *s.* das Sparen, Ersparnis (*of*, an); (*usually pl.*) Ersparnisse (*pl.*), der Vorbehalt (*Law*). 3. *prep.* & *conj.* außer, ausgenommen; - *you*, ausgenommen du, dich ausgenommen, außer dir; - *your presence*, mit Verlaub zu sagen. **-s-bank,** *s.* die Sparkasse.

saviour ['seɪvjə], *s.* der Retter; Erlöser, Heiland (*Theol.*).

savoir-faire ['sævwɑːˈfɛːə], *s.* die Gewandtheit, Takt. **--vivre** [-'viːvr], *s.* die Lebensart.

savour ['seɪvə], 1. *s.* (charakterischer) Geschmack; (*fig.*) der Beigeschmack, Anflug. 2. *v.n.* (*usually fig.*) schmecken, riechen (*of*, nach); einen Anstrich haben von, aussehen wie. 3. *v.a.* würdigen, auskosten, recht genießen. **-iness** [-ərɪnɪs], *s.* die Schmackhaftigkeit; der Wohlgeschmack, Wohlgeruch. **-less,** *adj.* geschmacklos, fad(e). **-y** [-ərɪ], 1. *adj.* schmackhaft, würzig, pikant. 2. *s.* pikantes Vor- oder Nachgericht.

savoy [sə'vɔɪ], *s.* der Wirsingkohl.

[1]**saw** [sɔː], *see* **see.**

[2]**saw,** *s.* der Spruch, das Sprichwort.

[3]**saw,** 1. *s.* die Säge. 2. *v.a.* sägen. 3. *v.n.* sich sägen lassen; - *up*, zerschneiden, zersägen. **-bones,** *s.* (*sl.*) der Chirurg. **-dust,** *s.* das Sägemehl. **--fish,** *s.* der Sägefisch. **-ing-horse, -ing-jack,** *s.* der Sägebock. **-mill,** *s.* die Sägemühle. **--set,** *s.* das Schränkeisen. **-tooth,** *adj.* Kipp- (*Elec.*). **-toothed,** *adj.* zackig. **-yer,** *s.* der (Holz)Säger.

sawney ['sɔːnɪ], *s.* (*coll.*) der Schotte; Einfaltspinsel, Tölpel.

sawyer, *see* [3]**saw.**

saxe [sæks], *s.* das Sächsischblau.

saxifrage ['sæksɪfreɪdʒ, -frɪdʒ], *s.* der Wiesensteinbrech, Körnersteinbrech (*Bot.*).

saxophon-e ['sæksəfoun], *s.* das Saxophon. **-ist,** *s.* der Saxophonbläser.

say [seɪ], 1. *ir.v.a.* sagen; äußern; aussagen, hersagen (*one's lesson*); erzählen, berichten; - *grace*, das Tischgebet lesen; *what have you to - for yourself?* was können Sie zu Ihrer Rechtfertigung sagen? *no sooner said than done*, gesagt, getan; *to - nothing of*, ganz zu schweigen von; *what do you - to it?* wie denkst du darüber? *what I - is*, ich meine; *sad to -*, bedauerlicherweise; *when all is said and done*, letzten Endes, schließlich und endlich; *he is said to be*, er soll sein; *that is -ing a great deal*, das besagt sehr viel, das will viel sagen; *never - die!* nur nicht verzagt! - *nay*, verweigern, abschlagen; - *the word!* schlag ein! 2. *v.n.* die Meinung äußern; gesagt werden; *I -!* hör mal! fürwahr!; *you don't - (so)!* was Sie nicht sagen!; *just as you -*, genau wie Sie sagen; *it -s here*, hier wird gesagt, hier heißt es; *that is to -*, das heißt, das will sagen; *that goes without -ing*, das versteht sich von selbst; *who -s so?* wer sagt das?; (*shall we*) - *20 years*, zum Beispiel *or* etwa 20 Jahre; *100 - one hundred*, 100 sage und schreibe ein Hundert; *they -, it is said*, man sagt, es heißt. 3. *s.* only in *final -*, letztes Wort, die Entscheidung; *have a (no) - in*, (nicht) mitzusprechen haben bei; *have one's -*, seine Meinung äußern *or* sagen (dürfen), sich aussprechen; *now it is his -*, jetzt kommt er daran. **-ing** [-ɪŋ], *s.* die Rede; Redensart; das Sprichwort; *as the -ing goes* or *is*, wie man zu sagen pflegt; *that goes without -ing*, das versteht sich von selbst; *there is no -ing*, man kann nicht wissen *or* sagen.

scab [skæb], *s.* der Grind, Schorf (*of wound*); die Krätze, Räude (*in sheep, etc.*); (*coll.*) der Streikbrecher; (*sl.*) Schuft. 2. *v.n.* (also - *over*) Schorf bilden. **-bed** [-d], *adj.* schorfig, Schorf-. **-by,** *adj.*, *see* **-bed;** räudig; (*coll.*) schäbig, erbärmlich.

scabbard ['skæbəd], 1. *s.* die (Degen)Scheide. 2. *v.a.* in die Scheide stecken.

scab-ies ['skeɪbɪz], *s.* die Krätze; Räude (*Vet.*). **-ious** [-bɪəs], 1. *adj.* krätzig, räudig. 2. *s.* die Skabiose (*Bot.*). **-rous** [-brəs], *adj.* rauh, holperig; heikel, schlüpfrig, anstößig.

scaffold ['skæfould], *s.* das Gerüst, Baugerüst, Schafott, Blutgerüst. **-ing,** *s.* das (Bau)Gerüst; Rüstzeug. **-(ing)-pole,** *s.* der Gerüstbaum.

scala-ble ['skeɪləbl], *adj.* ersteigbar. **-r** [-lə], 1. *adj.* skalar (*Math.*), leiterförmig (*Bot.*). 2. *s.* der Skalar (*Math.*).

scalawag, *see* **scallywag.**

[1]**scald** [skɔːld], 1. *s.* die Verbrühung, Brandwunde. 2. *v.a.* verbrennen, verbrühen; abkochen, heiß brühen, abbrühen (*Cook.*); - *out*, auskochen, sterilisieren. **-ing,** *adj.* brühend; *-ing hot*, brühheiß.

[2]**scald** [skɔːld], *s.* der Skalde, Barde. **-ic,** *adj.* skaldisch.

[1]**scal-e** [skeɪl], 1. *s.* die Schale, Hülse; das Blättchen, die Schuppe (*of fish, also Med.* & *fig.*); der Hammerschlag, Glühspan, Kesselstein (*Tech.*); *the -es fell from his eyes*, ihm fielen die Schuppen von den Augen. 2. *v.a.* abschuppen (*fish, etc.*); abschälen, abschaben, abkrusten; ausbrennen; Kesselstein entfernen, abklopfen *or* ausklopfen. 3. *v.n.* sich abschuppen *or* abschälen, abblättern. **-e-armour,** die Schuppenrüstung. **-ed,** *adj.* schuppig. **-eless,** *adj.* schuppenlos. **-iness,** *s.* schuppiger Charakter, das Schuppige. **-ing,** *s.* das Abschuppen. **-y,** *adj.* schuppig, geschuppt, Schuppen-, schuppenförmig.

[2]**scale,** 1. *s.* (*often pl.*) die Waagschale; Waage (*also Astr.*); *pair of -s*, eine Waage; *hold the -s evenly*, gerecht urteilen; *throw into the -(s)*, geltend machen, in die Waagschale werfen; *turn the -s*, den Ausschlag geben. 2. *v.a.* wiegen. 3. *v.n.* gewogen werden. **--beam,** *s.* der Waagebalken.

[3]**scal-e,** 1. *s.* die Stufenleiter, Abstufung, Gradeinteilung, Skala; Tonleiter (*Mus.*); der Maßstab, das Größenverhältnis; *according to -e*, maßstabgerecht; *descending -e*, absteigende Tonleiter; *on a large -e*, im großen Maße, im Großen; *reduced -e*, verjüngter Maßstab; *play* or *practice* (*one's*) *-es*, Tonleitern üben; *social -e*, soziale Abstufung; *to a -e of 1 : 10*, im Maßstab 1 : 10; *-e model*, verkleinertes Model; *wage -e*, die Lohnskala, Lohngruppe. 2. *v.a.* ersteigen, erklettern; erstürmen (*Mil.*); einen Maßstab festlegen für; *-e down*, nach einem Maßstab herabsetzen; herunterschrauben (*wages, etc.*); *-e up*, nach einem Maßstab hinaufsetzen; erhöhen (*wages*). **-e-paper,** *s.* das Millimeterpapier. **-ing,** *s.* das Erklettern, Erstürmen; die Festlegung nach einem Maßstab. **-ing-ladder,** *s.* die Sturmleiter.

scalene [skə'liːn], 1. *adj.* ungleichseitig (*Geom.*). 2. *s.* ungleichseitiges Dreieck.

scal-iness, -ing, *see* [1]**scale** & [3]**scale.**

scall [skɔːl], *s.* (*archaic*) der (Kopf)Grind.

scallawag, *see* **scallywag.**

scallion [skælɪən], *s.* die Schalotte (*Bot.*).

scallop ['skæləp], 1. *s.* die Kammuschel (*Zool.*); kleine Schüssel, die Muschelform (*Cook.*); der Kerbschnitt; die Ausbogung, Langette (*Dressm.*). 2. *v.a.* in der Schale zubereiten (*oysters, etc.*); bogenförmig ausschneiden, auszacken.

scallywag ['skælɪwæg], *s.* (*coll.*) der Nichtsnutz, Lump.

scalp [skælp], 1. *s.* die Kopfhaut, der Skalp; (*fig.*) die Siegestrophäe. 2. *v.a.* skalpieren.

scalpel ['skælpl], *s.* das Seziermesser.

scaly *see* [1]**scale.**

scammony ['skæmənɪ], *s.* die Purgierwurzel (*Bot.*), das Skammonium (*Pharm.*).

[1]**scamp** [skæmp], *s.* der Schurke, Spitzbube, Taugenichts, Lump.

[2]**scamp,** *v.a.* schluderig *or* schlampig ausführen, liederlich arbeiten; verpfuschen.

scamper, 1. *v.n.* (usually - *about*) herumtollen, herumjagen, hetzen, sich umhertummeln; - *off*, davonlaufen, dahinjagen. 2. *s.* der Lauf, Galopp.

scan [skæn], 1. *v.a.* skandieren (*verses*); (*fig.*) kritisch *or* genau prüfen, scharf *or* forschend ansehen; abtasten (*Television*); *-ning frequency*, die Rasterfrequenz (*Television*). 2. *v.n.* sich skandieren lassen (*Pros.*), flüchtig überblicken. **-sion** [-ʃən], *s.* das Skandieren.

scandal ['skændl], *s.* der Skandal, Anstoß, Aufsehen, öffentliches Ärgernis; die Schmach, Verleumdung, der Klatsch; *School for* –, die Lästerschule; *talk* –, klatschen, Skandalgeschichten verbreiten. **–ize** [–dəlaɪz], *v.a.* Ärgernis geben (*Dat.*), Anstoß erregen bei; *be –ized at*, empört sein über, Anstoß nehmen an; *–ize a sail*, das Baumnock hochschlagen (*Naut.*). **–monger,** *s.* das Lästermaul, die Klatschbase, Klatsche. **–ous** [–dələs], *adj.* Ärgernis *or* Anstoß erregend, anstößig, ärgerlich, skandalös; schimpflich, verleumderisch. **–ousness,** *s.* die Anstößigkeit.

scansion, *see* **scan.**

scansorial [skæn'sɔ:rɪəl], *adj.* Kletter– (*Orn.*).

scant [skænt], *adj.* knapp, spärlich, karg, kärglich, gering; ermangelnd (*of* (*Gen.*)); – *of breath*, kurzatmig. **–iness, –ness,** *s.* die Knappheit; Unzulänglichkeit. **–y,** *adj.* knapp, eng, beschränkt, karg, dürftig, unzulänglich.

scantling ['skæntlɪŋ], *s.* kleine Menge; kleiner Balken (*unter 13 cm. Querschnitt*); vorgeschriebene Größe (*of timber or stone*); Normalmessungen (*pl.*) (*Shipb.*); das Faßgestell (*for casks*); *pl.* Kanthölzer, Pfosten (*pl.*) (*Carp.*).

scant–ness, *see* **scant.**

scape [skeɪp], *s.* der Säulenschaft (*Arch.*), Blütenschaft (*Bot.*), Schaft (*of feather*).

scapegoat ['skeɪpgout], *s.* der Sündenbock.

scapegrace ['skeɪpgreɪs], *s.* der Taugenichts.

scaphoid ['skæfɔɪd], *adj.* Kahn– (*Anat.*).

scapula ['skæpjulə], *s.* das Schulterblatt (*Anat.*). **–r** [–lɑ], 1. *adj.* Schulter–, Schulterblatt–. 2. *s.*, **–ry** [–lərɪ], *s.* das Skapulier (*Eccl.*).

[1]**scar** [skɑ:], 1. *s.* die Narbe, Schramme; (*fig.*) der (Schand)Fleck, Makel; zurückgebliebene Spur. 2. *v.a.* schrammen, (*fig.*) entstellen. 3. *v.n.* (also – *over*) vernarben. **–red** [–d], *adj.* narbig, verschrammt.

[2]**scar,** *s.* steiler Abhang, die Klippe.

scarab ['skærəb], *s.* der Skarabäus; (also **–ee** [–ɪ]), der Mistkäfer.

scaramouch ['skærəmautʃ], *s.* der Aufschneider, Bramarbas; (*coll.*) Schuft.

scarc–e ['skɛ:əs], 1. *adj.* selten, rar; spärlich; (*coll.*) knapp; (*coll.*) *make o.s. –e*, sich rar machen, sich aus dem Staub machen. 2. *adv.*; **–ely,** *adv.* kaum; schwerlich, nur eben, nur mit Mühe; *–ely anything*, fast nichts; *–ely ever*, fast nie. **–eness,** *s.* die Seltenheit; Knappheit, der Mangel (*of*, an). **–ity** ['skɛ:sɪtɪ], *s.* die Seltenheit; Knappheit, der Mangel (*of*, an (*Dat.*)); Lebensmittelmangel, die Lebensmittelnot, Lebensmittelknappheit, Teuerung; *–ity value*, der Seltenheitswert.

scare ['skɛ:ə], 1. *v.a.* erschrecken, aufschrecken, in Schrecken jagen; (also – *away*) (ver)scheuchen, verjagen; (*coll.*) *–d stiff*, zu Tode erschrocken. 2. *s.* der Schreck, die Panik, blinder Alarm. **–crow,** *s.* die Vogelscheuche; (*fig.*) das Schreckbild, der Schreckschuß, Popanz. **–monger,** *s.* der Bangemacher, Miesmacher, Unruhestifter.

[1]**scarf** [skɑ:f], *s.* der Schal, das Halstuch, die Halsbinde; Schärpe (*Mil.*). **– –pin,** *s.* die Krawattennadel.

[2]**scarf,** 1. *s.* schräges Blatt (*Carp.*), abgekantetes Eisen; (also *– –joint*) die Laschung, Scherbe (*Naut.*). 2. *v.a.* zusammenblatten (*Carp.*); splissen (*Shipb.*).

scarif–ication [skɛ:rɪfɪ'keɪʃən], *s.* das Skarifizieren, Hauteinritzen (*Surg.*). **–ier** ['skɛ:rɪfaɪə], *s.* der Kultivator (*Agr.*). **–y** ['skɛ:rɪfaɪ], *v.a.* skarifizieren, einreißen, ritzen (*Surg.*); lockern (*the soil*) (*Agr.*); (*fig.*) scharf kritisieren, heruntermachen; tief verletzen (*feelings*).

scarlatina [skɑ:lə'tɪ:nə], *s.* das Scharlachfieber.

scarlet ['skɑ:lɪt], 1. *adj.* scharlachrot; *flush* or *turn* –, puterrot werden. 2. *s.* das Scharlachrot. – *fever*, das Scharlachfieber; – *hat*, der Kardinalshut; – *runner*, *s.* die Feuerbohne, türkische Bohne.

scarp [skɑ:p], 1. *s.* steile Böschung, die Eskarpe (*Mil.*). 2. *v.a.* abböschen, abdachen. **–ed,** *adj.* steil, abschüssig.

scarred *see* [1]**scar.**

scarus ['skɛ:rəs], *s.* der Seepapagei (*Ichth.*).

scary ['skɛ:rɪ], *adj.* (*coll.*) ängstlich, furchtsam; *see* **scare.**

scath–e [skeɪð], 1. *s.* (*archaic*) der Schaden, Nachteil. 2 *v.a.* (*archaic*) beschädigen, verletzen. **–eless,** *adj.* (*archaic*) unbeschädigt, unverletzt. **–ing,** *adj.* (*usually fig.*) verletzend, vernichtend, scharf, beißend (*as criticism*).

scatology [skə'tələdʒɪ], *s.* die Untersuchung von Koprolithen (*Geol.*); (*fig.*) Pornographie.

scatter ['skætə], 1. *v.a.* ausstreuen, verbreiten, verteilen, versprengen, zerstreuen; bestreuen (*a place*) (*with*, mit); (also – *about*) umherstreuen; *be –ed to the four winds*, in alle Winde zerstreut werden. 2. *v.n.* sich zerstreuen *or* verbreiten *or* zerteilen, auseinanderfliegen, streuen (*Gun.*). 3. *s.* die Streuung. **– –brain,** *s.* (*coll.*) der Wirrkopf; flatterhafter Mensch. **– –brained,** *adj.* flatterhaft, konfus. **–ed** [–d], *adj.* zerstreut liegend, vereinzelt (auftretend).

scaup [skɔ:p], *s.* (also *– –duck*) die Bergente (*Orn.*).

scaur [skɔ:], *see* [2]**scar.**

scaveng–e ['skævəndʒ], *v.a.* säubern, reinigen, kehren (*streets, etc.*). **–er,** *s.* der Straßenkehrer; Aasgeier, Aaskäfer. **–ing,** *s.* die Straßenreinigung; Spülung (*Tech.*).

scenario [sɪ:'nɛ:ərɪou], *s.* das Drehbuch (*Films*).

scene [sɪ:n], *s.* der Auftritt, die Szene (*of play*); der Schauplatz, Tatort (*of a crime*); das Bühnenbild, die Bühnenaustattung, Kulisse; *arrive on the* –, auftreten, erscheinen; *behind the –s*, hinter den Kulissen (*also fig.*); *change of* –, der Wechsel des Schauplatzes; *the – changes*, der Schauplatz wird verlegt; *the – closes*, der Vorhang fällt; *the – is laid* or *set in*, die Handlung *or* das Stück spielt in; *make a – with s.o.*, einem eine Szene machen; *the – opens with*, der Auftritt beginnt mit; *shift the –s*, Kulissen schieben; *quit the* –, von der Weltbühne abtreten; *sylvan* –, die Waldszene; *have an upsetting – with s.o.*, einen erregten Auftritt mit einem haben. **– –painter,** *s.* der Theatermaler. **–s-dock,** *s.* der Requisitenraum. **– –shifter,** *s.* der Kulissenschieber.

scen–ery ['sɪ:nərɪ], *s.* die Landschaft, das Landschaftsbild, die Szenerie, (Bühnen)Dekoration, Bühnenausstattung (*Theat.*). **–ic** ['sɪ:nɪk], *adj.* Bühnen–, Theater–, Ausstattungs–, szenisch; Landschafts–; *–ic railway*, die Liliputbahn. **–ically,** *adv.* in bühnentechnischer Hinsicht. **–ographic** [–ogræfɪk], *adj.* perspektivisch. **–ography** [–'nɔgrəfɪ], *s.* perspektivische Zeichnung, die Perspektivmalerei.

scent [sɛnt], 1. *s.* der (Wohl)Geruch, Duft, das Parfüm; Riechstoff; die Witterung, Fährte (*Hunt.*); (*fig.*) Spur; das Witterungsvermögen (*of dogs*); (*fig.*) die Nase; *on the* –, auf der Fährte; *on the false* or *wrong* –, auf falscher Fährte; *put* or *throw off the* –, einen von der Fährte abbringen. 2. *v.a.* riechen; durchduften, parfümieren; (also – *out*) wittern (*Hunt. & fig.*). **–ed** [–ɪd], *adj.* wohlriechend, parfümiert. **–less,** *adj.* geruchlos. **– –bottle,** *s.* das Riechfläschchen. **– –spray,** *s.* der Parfümzerstäuber.

scep–sis ['s(k)ɛpsɪs], *s.* die Skepsis. **–tic** [–tɪk], *s.* der Zweifler, Ungläubige(r), *m.*; Skeptiker. **–tical** [–tɪkl], *adj.* zweifelnd, mißtrauisch, skeptisch; *be –tical about*, bezweifeln. **–ticism** [–tɪsɪzm], *s.* der Skeptizismus, Zweifel.

sceptre ['sɛptə], *s.* das Zepter; (*fig.*) königliche Macht; *wield the* –, herrschen, das Zepter schwingen. **–d** [–d], *adj.* zeptertragend; (*fig.*) herrschend.

schedule ['ʃɛdju:l, (*Amer.*) 'skɛdju:l], 1. *s.* die Liste, Tabelle, das Verzeichnis; der Fahrplan, Stundenplan; *on* or (*according*) *to* –, fahrplanmäßig; *on* –, pünktlich; *behind* –, verspätet; *before* –, frühzeitig. 2. *v.a.* in eine Liste eintragen; tabellarisch zusammenstellen; festlegen, festsetzen; in einem Fahrplan anzeigen; *be –d to start*, fahrplanmäßig abfahren sollen; *–d time*, fahrplanmäßige Zeit.

schem–atic [skɪ'mætɪk], *adj.* schematisch, zusammenfassend, anschaulich, umrißhaft. **–atism** ['skɪ:mətɪzm], *s.* die Schematisierung, anschauliche *or* (übertrieben) schematische Anordnung. **–e** [skɪ:m], 1. *s.* das Schema; systematische Anordnung *or* Zusammenstellung; die Tabelle, Liste, Übersicht; Methode, der Plan, Entwurf; (*coll.*)

Anschlag, die Intrige; *colour –e*, die Farbenzusammenstellung; *work to a –e*, nach einem Plan arbeiten; *some –e is afoot*, etwas ist im Werke. 2. *v.a.* systematisch anordnen; planen, entwerfen; (*coll.*) anstiften. 3. *v.n.* Pläne machen, intrigieren, Ränke schmieden. **–er** [–ə], *s.* der Ränkeschmied, Intrigant, Projektenmacher. **–ing**, 1. *adj.* intrigierend, ränkevoll. 2. *s.* das Pläneschmieden; die Intrige, der Schlich, Schliche (*pl.*).

scherzo [ˈskɛːtsoʊ], *s.* das Scherzo (*Mus.*).

schipperke [ˈʃɪpəkə], *s.* holländischer Schoßhund.

schism [sɪzm], *s.* das Schisma; die Kirchenspaltung; (*fig.*) Spaltung, Trennung (*with*, von). **–atic** [–ˈmætɪk], 1. *adj.* schismatisch; ketzerisch, abtrünnig. 2. *s.* der Schismatiker, Abtrünnige(r), *m.* **–atical**, *adj. see* **–atic** 1.

schist [ʃɪst], *s* der Schiefer. **–ose** [–oʊs], **–ous** [–əs], *adj.* schiefrig, Schiefer–.

schizanthus [skɪːˈzænθəs], *s.* die Spaltblume.

schizo–genic [skɪːzoˈdʒɛnɪk], **–genous** [skɪˈzɔdʒənəs], *adj.* durch Spaltung entstanden. **–mycetes** [skɪːzomaɪˈsɪːtɪz], *pl.* Spaltpilze (*pl.*). **–phrenia** [–ˈfrɪːnɪə], *s.* die Schizophrenie. **–phrenic** [–ˈfrɪːnɪk], *adj.* schizophren.

schnap(p)s [ʃnæps], *s.* der Schnaps.

scholar [ˈskɔlə], *s.* der Schüler, Gelehrte(r), *m.*, der Stipendiat (*Univ.*); *a good German –*, im Deutschen gut beschlagen. **–ly**, *adj.* gelehrt, Gelehrten–. **–ship**, *s.* die Gelehrsamkeit; das Stipendium; *travelling –ship*, das Reisestipendium.

scholastic [skɔˈlæstɪk], 1. *adj.* schulmäßig, pädagogisch, scholastisch, Schul–; Lehr–; *– agency*, die Schulagentur; *– institution*, die Lehranstalt; *– learning*, die Schulgelehrsamkeit; *– philosophy*, die Scholastik; *– profession*, der Lehrstand, Lehrberuf, das Schulamt; 2. *s.* der Scholastiker. **–ism** [–tɪsɪzm], *s.* die Scholastik.

scholi–ast [ˈskoʊlɪəst], *s.* der Scholiast, Kommentator. **–um** [–lɪəm], *s.* die Scholie, gelehrte Anmerkung.

[1]**school** [skuːl], 1. *s.* die Schule (*also fig.*); das Schulgebäude; der (Schul)Unterricht; die Fakultät (*Univ.*); *pl.* Universitätsprüfungen (*pl.*). (*a*) (*with nouns*) *– of Art(s)*, die Kunstakademie; *– of theology*, theologisches Seminar; *– of thought*, die Ideenrichtung. (*b*) (*with attrib.*) *board –*, (*archaic*) die Volksschule; *boys' –*, die Knabenschule; *boarding –*, das Internat, Pensionat; *commercial –*, die Handelsschule; *continuation –*, die Fortbildungsschule; *day –*, das Externat; *elementary –*, die Volksschule; *endowed –*, die Stiftsschule; *girls' –*, die Mädchenschule; *grammar –*, höhere Schule, das Gymnasium; *high –*, höhere Schule (*Scotland & Amer.*); (*in England usually*) höhere Mädchenschule, das Lyzeum; *lower –*, die unteren Klassen, die Unterstufe; *medical –*, medizinische Fakultät; *primary –*, die Grundschule; *preparatory –*, die Vorschule; *public –*, vornehme höhere Schule, die Standesschule (*England*), Volksschule (*Scotland & Amer.*); *secondary –*, höhere Schule; *senior* or *upper –*, die oberen Klassen, die Oberstufe; *Sunday –*, die Bibelschule. (*c*) (*with prepositions*) *at –*, in *or* auf der Schule; *from –*, aus der Schule; *in –*, im Unterricht; *tell tales out of –*, aus der Schule schwatzen; *go to –*, zur *or* in die Schule gehen; *send to –*, in die Schule schicken. 2. *v.a.* (ein)schulen, unterrichten, unterweisen; dressieren (*horses*): (*fig.*) tadeln, verweisen; *– o.s. to*, sich durch Schulung gewöhnen an. **– age**, schulpflichtiges Alter; *of – age*, schulpflichtig. **– attendance**, der Schulbesuch. **– –board**, die Erziehungsrat für Volksschulen. **– –book**, *s.* das Schulbuch. **–boy**, *s.* der Schuljunge, Schüler. **– certificate** (= *etwa*) das Einjährige; *higher – certificate* (= *etwa*) das Abitur, die Matura (*Austria*), Reifeprüfung, das Abschlußzeugnis. **–days**, die Schulzeit, Schuljahre (*pl.*). **– edition**, *s.* die Schulausgabe. **– fees** *pl.*, das Schulgeld. **–fellow**, *s.* der Schulkamerad, Mitschüler. **–girl**, *s.* das Schulmädchen, die Schülerin; *–girl complexion*, jugendlich frisches Aussehen. **–house**, *s.* das Schulgebäude; Wohnhaus des Lehrers. **– –leaving age**, das Schulentlassungsalter. **– –leaving certificate**, *see* **– certificate.** **–ing**, *s.* der Schulunterricht; das Zureiten (*of horses*); (*fig.*) die Schulung. **–man** [–mən], *s.* der Scholastiker. **– –marm**, *s.* die Schulmeisterin (*ironic*). **–master**, *s.* der Lehrer, (*fig.*) Schulmeister. **–mate**, *s. see* **–fellow**. **–mistress**, *s.* die Lehrerin. **–room**, *s.* das Klassenzimmer. **– –story**, *s.* der Schulroman. **– –teacher**, *s.* der Schullehrer. **– –time**, *s.* die Schulzeit. **–work**, *s.* die Schularbeit.

[2]**school**, *s.* die Herde, Schar, der Schwarm, Zug (*of whales, etc.*).

schooner [ˈskuːnə], *s.* der Schoner.

schorl [ʃɔːl], *s.* der Schörl, schwarzer Turmalin.

schottische [ʃɔˈtɪːʃ], *s.* der Schottisch(e) (*dance*).

scia–gram [ˈsaɪəgræm], **–graph** [–græf], *s.* das Röntgenbild. **–graphy** [saɪˈægrəfɪ], *s.* der Schattenriß, die Schattenmalerei; Röntgenphotographie. **–machy** [saɪˈæməkɪ, skɪˈæməkɪ], *s.* das Scheingefecht, die Spiegelfechterei.

sciatic [saɪˈætɪk], *adj.* Ischias–. **–a** [–ɪkə], *s.* die Ischias.

scien–ce [ˈsaɪəns], *s.* die Wissenschaft; (also *natural –ce*) die Naturwissenschaft(en); (*archaic*) das Wissen, Kenntnisse (*pl.*); (*coll.*) das Geschick, Können (*Sport*); *Christian –ce*, der Szientismus; *man of –ce*, der (Natur)Wissenschaftler. **–tific** [–ˈtɪfɪk], *adj.* (natur)wissenschaftlich, exakt, systematisch. **–tist** [ˈsaɪəntɪst], *s.* der Naturwissenschaftler; Gelehrte(r), *m.*

scilicit [ˈsaɪlɪsɪt], *adv.* das heißt, nämlich.

scimitar [ˈsɪmɪtə], *s.* der Türkensäbel.

scintilla–nt [ˈsɪntɪlənt], *adj.* schillernd, funkelnd. **–te** [–leɪt], *v.n.* funkeln, schillern, Funken sprühen; (*fig.*) glänzen. **–tion** [–ˈleɪʃən], *s.* das Funkeln, Schillern.

sciolis–m [ˈsaɪəlɪzm], *s.* das Halbwissen. **–t** [–lɪst], *s.* Halbwisser.

scion [ˈsaɪən], *s.* der Ableger, das Pfropfreis (*Bot.*); (*fig.*) der Sprößling, Sproß.

scirrh–ous [ˈs(k)ɪrəs], *adj.* verhärtet. **–us** [–əs], *s.* die Krebsgeschwulst.

scissel [ˈsɪsl], *s.* Metallspäne (*pl.*), der Metallabfall.

scission [ˈsɪʃən], *s.* das Spalten, die Spaltung; (*fig.*) der Schnitt, Einschnitt.

scissor [ˈsɪzə], *v.a.* (*coll.*) mit der Schere (zer)schneiden. **–s** [–əs], *pl.* (also *pair of –s*) die Schere. **–(s)-case**, *s.* das Scherenfutteral. **–(s)-grinder**, *s.* der Scherenschleifer.

scissure [ˈsɪʃə], *s.* das Spalt, Riß, Einschnitt.

sciurine [sɪˈjuːərɪn], *adj.* Eichhörnchen–.

scler–iasis [sklɪːˈraɪəsɪs], **–oma** [–ˈroʊmə], *s.* harte Geschwülst. **–osis** [–ˈroʊsɪs], *s.* die Verhärtung, Sklerose, (Arterien)Verkalkung (*Med.*). **–otic** [–ˈrɔtɪk], 1. *adj.* hart, verhärtet. 2. *s.* die Lederhaut (*of eye*). **–ous** [–rəs], *see* **–otic.**

scoff [skɔf], 1. *s.* der Spott, Hohn. 2. *v.n.* spotten, höhnen; *– at*, spotten über, verspotten, verhöhnen. **–er** [–ə], *s.* der Spötter. **–ing**, *adj.* spöttisch, höhnisch.

scold [skoʊld], 1. *v.n.* schelten, zanken. 2. *v.a.* ausschelten, auszanken. 3. *s.* der Dragoner, zänkisches *or* böses Weib. **–ing**, *s.* das Schelten; die Schelte; *give a p. a good –ing*, einen tüchtig ausschelten.

scollop [ˈskɔləp], *see* **scallop.**

sconce [skɔns], 1. *s.* die Verschanzung, Schutzwehr; der Wandleuchter, Klavierleuchter, Lichthalter; (*sl.*) Schädel, Kopf. 2. *v.a.* verschanzen.

scone [skoʊn, skɔn], *s.* weicher Gersten– *or* Weizenmehlkuchen.

scoop [skuːp], 1. *s.* die Schippe, Schöpfkelle, Schaufel, der Löffel; Spatel (*Surg.*); (*coll.*) Schub; (*sl.*) journalistischer Treffer, die Erstmeldung, Alleinmeldung (*Press*), großer Gewinn, der Treffer; *at*, *in* or *with one –*, mit einem Schub. 2. *v.a.* schöpfen, schaufeln; (*sl.*) zuerst berichten *or* melden (*Press*), einheimsen; *– out*, aushöhlen, ausschaufeln, ausgraben; *– up*, aufschaufeln, zusammenschaufeln, zusammenscharren.

scoot [skuːt], *v.n.* (*sl.*) rasen, schießen, sausen; ausreißen. **–er** [–ə], *s.* der Roller.

scope [skoʊp], *s.* der Gesichtskreis, Wirkungskreis, Bereich, Rahmen, Umfang, das Ausmaß, Feld, Gebiet, die Reichweite, der Spielraum; *free –*, die Bewegungsfreiheit; *give full* or *free –*, freien Lauf lassen (*to* (*Dat.*)); *have more –*, mehr Spiel-

raum *or* bessere Möglichkeiten haben (*for*, für); *beyond* (*within*) *my* –, außerhalb (innerhalb) meines Bereiches.
scorbutic [skɔːˈbjuːtɪk], 1. *adj.* skorbutisch, Skorbut–. 2. *s.* Skorbutkranke(r), *m.*
scorch [skɔːtʃ], 1. *v.a.* versengen, ansengen, (ver)brennen; trocknen, dörren. 2. *v.n.* versengt werden; (aus)dörren; (*sl.*) dahinrasen, rücksichtlos fahren (*Motor.*, *Cycl.*); *–ed earth*, verbrannte Erde. **–er** [–ə], *s.* (*sl.*) etwas sehr Heißes, (*sl.*) sehr heißer Tag. **–ing**, *adj.* (*coll.*) glühend, brennend (*weather*).
scor–e [skɔː], 1. *s.* die Kerbe, der Einschnitt, Riß, Strich; die Rechnung, Zeche; das Spielergebnis, die Punktzahl, Leistung (*Sport*); Partitur (*Mus.*); (der Satz von) 20 Stück; *pl.* eine große Anzahl, große Mengen (*pl.*); *three –e years and ten*, siebzig Jahre. (*a*) (*with verbs*) *what's the –e?* wie steht die Partie or das Spiel? *run up a –e*, Schulden machen; *settle a –e with s.o.*, mit einem eine Rechnung begleichen. (*b*) (*with prepositions*) *on the –e of s.th.*, um einer S. willen, wegen einer S., in Hinsicht auf etwas; *on this –e*, was dies betrifft, diesetwegen; *upon what –e?* aus welchem Grunde? 2. *v.a.* (ein)kerben, einschneiden; zerkratzen; aufschreiben, anschreiben, festlegen, aufzeichnen, auf (die) Rechnung setzen, anrechnen; zählen, machen (*points*, *runs*) (*Sport*, *etc.*); in Partitur setzen, instrumentieren (*Mus.*); *–e a goal*, ein Tor machen *or* schießen; *–e a hit*, einen Treffer erzielen; (*fig.*) einen Riesenerfolg haben; *–e a success* or *victory*, einen Erfolg davontragen; *–e out*, ausstreichen; *–e up*, anschreiben, aufschreiben. 3. *v.n.* Punkte zählen, zählen, gezählt werden; Punkte machen, gewinnen (*at games*); Glück *or* Erfolg haben; *–e against* or *off a p.*, einen übertrumpfen *or* ausstechen; *that –es for me*, das zählt zu meinen Gunsten; *he –ed heavily*, er hat großen Erfolg gehabt; **–e-board**, *s.* die Anzeigetafel. **–er** [–ə], *s.* der Punktzähler, Punktrichter. **–ing**, *s* die Punktzählung.
scori–a [ˈskɔːrɪə], *s.* die Schlacke (*Metall.*), Gesteinschlacke (*Geol.*). **–aceous** [–rɪˈeɪʃəs], *adj.* schlackig, schlackenreich, Schlacken–. **–fication** [–rɪfɪˈkeɪʃən], *s.* die Schlackenbildung, Verschlackung. **–fy** [ˈskɔrɪfaɪ], *v.a.* verschlacken.
scorn [skɔːn], 1. *s.* die Verachtung, Geringschätzung, Verspottung, der Spott; *hold in* –, verachten; *laugh to* –, verlachen, auslachen, lächerlich machen; *treat with* –, verächtlich behandeln. 2. *v.a.* verachten, verschmähen; von sich weisen. **–ful**, *adj.* verächtlich, verachtend; *–ful of*, nicht achtend (*Acc.*), zum Trotz (*Dat.*).
Scorpio [ˈskɔːpɪoʊ], *s.* der Skorpion (*Astr.*). **–n** [–pɪən], *s.* der Skorpion (*Zool.*).
scot [skɔt], *s.* (*archaic*) die Steuer, Abgabe; *pay one's* –, seinen Beitrag leisten; *pay – and lot*, auf Heller und Pfennig bezahlen; *great –!* großer Gott! **– -free**, *adj.* (*fig.*) ungestraft.
Scot, *see Index of Names.*
[1]**scotch** [skɔtʃ], 1. *s.* der Einschnitt, Riß, die Ritze. 2. *v.n.* einritzen; unterdrücken, unschädlich machen, vernichten; – *one's chances*, seine Aussichten stark beeinträchtigen.
[2]**scotch**, 1. *v.a.* (durch Unterlage) hemmen (*a wheel*). 2. *s.* der Hemmkeil, Hemmklotz.
scotia [ˈskoʊʃə], *s.* die Kehlung (*Arch.*).
scoundrel [ˈskaʊndrəl], *s.* der Schuft, Schurke, Halunke. **–ism**, [–ɪzm], *s.* die Schurkerei. **–ly**, *adj.* schurkisch.
[1]**scour** [ˈskaʊə], *v.a.* scheuern, abreiben, schrubben, blank machen; putzen, reinigen, ausspülen, wegschwemmen, waschen; entschweißen (*wool*); (*fig.*) säubern. **–ings** (*pl.*), der Abschaum.
[2]**scour**, 1. *v.n.* schnell dahinfahren, eilen, jagen; – *about*, umherstreifen. 2. *v.a.* abstreifen, durchstreifen, durchsuchen (*an area*).
scourge [skɔːdʒ], 1. *v.a.* peitschen, geißeln; (*fig.*) quälen, bedrücken, züchtigen, plagen. 2. *s.* die Peitsche, Geißel (*also fig.*); (*fig.*) Plage.
[1]**scout** [skaʊt], 1. *s.* das Spähen, die Suche, Lauer; der Späher, Kundschafter (*Mil.*), das Aufklärungsflugzeug (*Av.*); der Diener, Aufwärter (*Univ. sl.*); (also *boy* –) Pfadfinder. 2. *v.n.* spähen, auskundschaften; rekognoszieren (*Mil.*); – *about*, erkunden, herumsuchen; *–ing party*, der Spähtrupp. **– -master**, *s.* der Pfadfinderführer.
[2]**scout**, *v.a.* verächtlich abweisen, zurückweisen *or* von sich weisen.
scow [skaʊ], *s.* das Fährboot, Lichterschiff, Leichterschiff, der Leichter, Prahm.
scowl [skaʊl], 1. *v.n.* finster blicken. – *at*, finster anblicken. 2. *s.* finsterer Blick. **–ing**, *adj.* finster; grollend.
scrabble [ˈskræbl], 1. *v.n.* (*coll.*) scharren, krabbeln; kritzeln. 2. *v.a.* bekritzeln.
scrag [skræg], 1. *s.* hagere Person; das Gerippe; etwas Dünnes; – (*end*) *of mutton*, das Hammelhalsstück. 2. *v.a.* (*sl.*) aufknüpfen, erdrosseln, erwürgen. **–giness**, *s.* die Magerkeit, Hagerkeit. **–gy**, *adj.* hager, dürr, mager; zottig, ungepflegt, verwahrlost.
scram [skræm], *v.a.* (*sl.*) verduften, sich aus dem Staube machen.
scramble [ˈskræmbl], 1. *s.* die Kletterei; Jagd (*for*, nach), Balgerei (*for*, um). 2. *v.n.* krabbeln, herumklettern; – *for*, grapsen nach, sich reißen *or* balgen um. – *to one's feet*, sich schnell auf die Beine bringen. 3. *v.a.* umherwerfen; verrühren (*eggs*); – *together*, rasch zusammenlesen; aufraffen; *–d eggs*, das Rührei.
scran [skræn], *s.* (*sl.*) Speisereste (*pl.*), schlechtes Essen; *bad – to*, zum Teufel mit.
scrap [skræp], 1. *s.* der Rest, Brocken (*pl.*), das Stückchen das *or* der Schnitzel, der Fetzen, (Zeitungs)Ausschnitt; Ausschuß, Abbruch, Abfall, Schrot, altes Eisen, das Altstoff; (*sl.*) die Rauferei, Schlägerei, der Streit, Zank, Boxkampf; *pl.* Überreste, Bruchstücke, Brocken (*pl.*); *pl.* (= *coloured cut-outs collected by children*), Oblaten (*pl.*); – *of paper*, der Fetzen Papier; *–s of paper*, Papierschnitzel (*pl.*); *not a* –, nicht ein bißchen; *I don't care a* –, es ist mir ganz einerlei. 2. *v.a.* verschrot(t)en, zum alten Eisen werfen, (*fig.*) über Bord werfen, wegwerfen, ausrangieren. 3. *v.n.* sich raufen, balgen *or* streiten. **– -book**, *s.* das Sammelbuch, Einklebebuch. **– -heap**, *s.* der Abfallhaufen. **– -iron**, *s.* das Alteisen, der Schrot(t); *see* **scrappy.**
scrap–e [skreɪp], 1. *s.* das Kratzen; der Kratzer, die Schramme; der Kratzfuß; (*coll.*) die Not, Klemme, Patsche; (*sl.*) *bread and –e*, dünn beschmiertes Brot. 2. *v.a.* schaben, kratzen; *–e acquaintance with*, sich anbändeln mit, sich anvettern bei; *–e one's feet*, mit den Füßen scharren; *–e a living*, sich mühsam durchschlagen; *–e off*, abschaben, abkratzen; *–e out*, auskratzen; *–e together*, *–e up*, zusammenscharren, zusammenkratzen. 3. *v.n.* sich reiben *or* schaben, scharren; (*coll.*) sparen, sparsam sein; kratzen (*on the violin*); *bow and –e*, buckeln und dienern, einen Kratzfuß machen; *–e along*, sich abquälen; *–e through*, sich durchwinden *or* durchschlagen; mit Ach und Krach durchkommen (*in an exam.*, bei einer Prüfung). **–er** [–ə], *s.* der (Fuß)Abstreicher, die Kratzbürste, das Kratzeisen, Schabeisen, (*fig.*) Knauser. **–ing**, *s.* das Kratzen, Scharren; Schabsel, Zusammengekratzte(s), *n.*; *pl.* Abfälle, Überbleibsel (*pl.*), (*fig.*) der Abschaum, Auswurf; mühsam Erspartes.
scrappy [ˈskræpɪ], *adj.* bruchstückartig, zusammengestoppelt, zusammengewürfelt; unzusammenhängend, sprunghaft.
scratch [skrætʃ], 1. *s.* das Kratzen; der Riß, Ritz; die Schramme, Kratzwunde; (*coll.*) leichte Verwundung; die Startlinie (*races*), Normalklasse (*Sport*); *pl.* die Mauke (*Vet.*); *come up to* (*the*) –, seinen Mann stehen, sich nicht drücken, sich einstellen; *keep s.o. up to* (*the*) –, einen bei der Stange halten; *start from* –, ohne Vorgabe starten (*Sport*), (*fig.*) von vorne *or* ohne Hilfe anfangen; *up to* –, auf der Höhe. 2. *v.a.* (zer)kratzen, ritzen; kritzeln; von der Liste streichen, zurückziehen (*a horse*, *etc.*); – *out*, (aus)streichen, auskratzen, ausradieren; – *a p.'s eyes out*, einem die Augen auskratzen; – *one's head*, sich den Kopf kratzen; – *the surface of*, flüchtig berühren; – *up*, zusammenkratzen. 3. *v.n.* kratzen; ausscheiden, die Anmeldung zurücknehmen (*Sport*). 4. *attrib. adj.* zusammengewürfelt, hastig zusammengestellt, improvisiert.

--race, *s.* das Rennen ohne Vorgabe. **-y,** *adj.* kratzend, kratzig, kritzlig (*writing*); unausgeglichen (*Sport*).
scrawl [skrɔ:l], 1. *v.n.* kritzeln, schmieren. *- over*, beschmieren. 2. *v.a.* hinschmieren. **-ed, -y,** *adj.* gekritzelt, hingeschmiert. 2. *s.* das Gekritzel, Geschmiere.
scrawny [ˈskrɔ:nɪ], *adj.* (*coll.*) hager, knochig.
scray [skreɪ], *s.* die Seeschwalbe (*Orn.*).
scream [skrɪ:m], *s.* der Schrei, das Gekreisch, Geschrei; (*sl.*) der Hauptspaß, das Mordsding; spaßiger Bursche; (*sl.*) *what a -!* wie komisch! 2. *v.n.* schreien; kreischen; heulen (*as wind*); *- out*, laut aufschreien; *- with laughter*, laut auflachen. 3. *v.a.* (usually *- out*), ausrufen. **-er** [-ə], *s.* das Straußhuhn (*Orn.*); (*sl.*) das Mordsding; der Mordsspaß; Mordskerl. **-ing,** *adj.* kreischend, schrill; (*sl.*) toll, ulkig; grell (*as headlines*); (*sl.*) *-ingly funny*, zum Totlachen.
scree [skrɪ:], *s.* das (Stein)Geröll, der Gehängeschutt.
screech [skrɪ:tʃ], 1. *v.n.* kreischen, schrillen. 2. *s.* das Gekreisch. **-ing,** *adj.* schrill. **--owl,** *s.* der Baumkauz, Waldkauz (*Orn.*).
screed [skrɪ:d], *s.* lange Liste *or* Reihe, langatmige Rede.
screen [skrɪ:n], 1. *s.* der Schirm, die Blende; der Ofenschirm, Windschutz; die Deckung, Schranke, Zwischenwand (*Arch.*); der Raster (*Phot.*), die Leinwand (*Films*), (Fernseh)Scheibe (*Television*), Windschutzscheibe (*Motor.*); grobes Sieb (*Min.*, *etc.*). (*fig.*) die Maskierung, Verschleierung (*Mil.*); der Film, das Kino; der Schutz, die Schutzwand; *folding -*, spanische Wand; *on the -*, im Film, *bring to the -*, verfilmen; *sight--*, weiße Bretterwand (*Crick.*); *smoke -*, künstliche Einnebelung. 2. *v.a.* (be)schirmen, (be)schützen (*from*, vor); (ver)decken; verschleiern, maskieren (*Mil.*), abblenden (*light*); (durch)sieben (*coal, etc.*); verfilmen; *-ed coal*, Würfelkohle (*pl.*). **--grid,** *s.* das Anodenschutznetz, Anodenschutzgitter (*Rad.*); *--grid valve*, die Schirmgitterröhre, Zweigitterröhre, Vierelektrodenröhre (*Rad.*). **-ing,** *s.* die Abschirmung (*also Rad.*), Verschleierung; das Durchsieben. **--wiper,** *s.* der Scheibenwischer.
screw [skru:], 1. *s.* die Schraube; das Effet (*Bill.*, *etc.*); die Schiffsschraube (*Naut.*), (also *air-*) Luftschraube (*Av.*); (*fig.*) der Druck; (*sl.*) der Lohn, das Gehalt; (*sl.*) der Gefängnisaufseher; (*coll.*) der Geizhals, Geizkragen; *apply the -* (*fig.*), Druck ausüben; *endless -*, die Schraube ohne Ende; *female -*, die Schraubenmutter; *give it a -*, zieh es fest an; (*coll.*) *he has a - loose*, bei ihm ist eine Schraube los; *male -*, die Schraubenspindel; *put the - on*, Druck ausüben auf; *put a - on a ball*, einem Ball Effet geben; *turn the -*, die Schraube anziehen. 2. *v.a.* schrauben; (*fig.*) drücken; (*vulg.*) vögeln, ficken; (*sl.*) *- a p.'s neck*, einem den Hals umdrehen; *- down*, zuschrauben, festschrauben; *- in*, einschrauben; *- on*, anschrauben, aufschrauben; (*coll.*) *have one's head -ed on the right way*, den Kopf an der rechten Stelle haben; *- out of s.o*, aus einem herauspressen, einem abbringen; *- up*, zuschrauben; (*fig.*) hochschrauben (*prices*); *- up one's courage*, Mut fassen; *- one's face up*, sein Gesicht verziehen. 3. *v.n.* sich schrauben lassen, sich drehen. **-ball,** *s.* (*sl.*) der Wirrkopf (*Amer.*). **--bolt,** *s.* der Schraubenbolzen. **--cap,** *s.* die Schraubkapsel, Überwurfmutter. **--clamp,** *s.* die Schraubzwinge, Festklemmschraube. **--compasses,** *pl.* der Schraubenzirkel. **--coupling,** *s.* die Schraubenkupplung. **--cutter,** *s.* der Gewindeschneider. **--cutting,** *s.* das Gewindeschneiden. **--die,** *s.* der Gewindeschneider, die Schneidbacke, das Schneideisen. **-driver,** *s.* der Schraubenzieher. **--jack,** *s.* die Schraubenwinde, der Wagenheber. **-nut,** *s.* die Schraubenmutter. **--propeller,** *s.* die Schiffsschraube. **- steamer,** *s.* der Schraubendampfer. **--stock,** *s.* die Schneidkluppe. **--tap,** *s.* der Gewindebohrer. **--vise,** *s.* der Schraubstock. **--wrench,** *s.* der Schraubenschlüssel, Engländer. **-y,** *adj.* (*sl.*) leicht betrunken, beschwipst; knauserig, geizig; verdreht, verrückt, närrisch.
scribbl-e [ˈskrɪbl], 1. *v.n.* kritzeln, schmieren. 2. *v.a.* (also *-e down*) hinkritzeln, hinschmieren, flüchtig hinschreiben; krempeln (*wool*). 3. *s.* das Gekritzel. **-er** [-lə], *s.* der Schmierer, Sudler; die Krempelmaschine. **-ing,** *s.* die Kritzelei, Schmiererei; das Krempeln; *-ing-pad*, der Notizblock; *-ing-paper*, das Konzeptpapier.
scribe [skraɪb], *s.* der Schreiber, Kopist; (*B.*) Schriftgelehrte(r), *m.*; (also **-r**) die Reißahle (*Mach.*).
scrim [skrɪm], *s.* das Polsterfutter.
scrimmage [ˈskrɪmɪdʒ], *s.* die Balgerei, das Getümmel, Handgemenge; Gedränge (*Footb.*).
scrimp [skrɪmp], 1. *v.a.* knapp halten (*a p.*), knapp bemessen, knausern mit (*a th.*). 2. *v.n.* knausern. 3. *adj.* knapp, kärglich. **-y,** *adj.* knapp, eng.
scrimshank [ˈskrɪmʃæŋk], *v.n.* (*sl.*) sich drücken, eine ruhige Kugel schieben. **-er,** *s.* (*sl.*) der Drückeberger.
scrimshaw [ˈskrɪmʃɔ:], *s.* die Muschel- *or* Elfenbeinschnitzerei.
[1]**scrip** [skrɪp], *s.* (*archaic*), das Ränzel, die Tasche.
[2]**scrip,** *s.* der Interimsschein, die Interimsaktie.
script [skrɪpt], 1. *s.* die Handschrift, Urschrift, das Manuskript, Original; schriftliche Prüfungsarbeit; Geschriebene(s), *n.*; die Schreibschrift (*Typ.*); Schrift, Schriftart; das Drehbuch (*Films*); *phonetic -*, die Lautschrift. **-orium** [-ˈtɔrɪəm], *s.* das Schreibzimmer (*of monastery*).
scriptur-al [ˈskrɪptʃərəl], *adj.* schriftmäßig, biblisch. **-e** [ˈskrɪptʃə], *s.* (also *the -es* (*pl.*)) die Bibel, Heilige Schrift; (also *-e class*, *-e lesson*), *s.* die Religionsstunde.
scrivener [ˈskrɪvənə], *s.* der Berufsschreiber (*Hist.*).
scroful-a [ˈskrɔfjulə], *s.* Skrofeln (*pl.*), die Skrofulose. **-ous** [-ləs], *adj.* skrofulös.
scroll [skroul], *s.* die (Pergament- *or* Papier)Rolle; Liste, Tabelle; der Schnörkel (*Arch.*). **--work,** *s.* die Laubsägearbeit, Schnörkelverzierung (*Arch.*).
scrotum [ˈskroutəm], *s.* der Hodensack.
scrounge [skraundʒ], *v.a.* (*sl.*) klauen, stibitzen, mausen, nassauern, schnorren, organisieren. **-r,** *s.* der Schnorrer, Nassauer, Schmarotzer.
[1]**scrub** [skrʌb], 1. *v.a.* scheuern, schrubben (*Naut.*), tüchtig reinigen; abreiben (*off*, von); auswaschen (*gas*) (*Chem.*); *- o.s.* sich abreiben. 2. *v.n.* scheuern. 3. *s.* das Scheuern; *give s.th. a -*, etwas (ab)scheuern. **-ber,** *s.* der Schrubber; die Scheuerbürste. **-bing-brush,** *s.* die Scheuerbürste.
[2]**scrub,** *s.* das Gestrüpp, Buschwerk, Unterholz. **-by,** *adj.* struppig; (*sl.*) schäbig, verkommen.
scruff [skrʌf], *s.* (also *- of the neck*) das Genick; *seize by the - of the neck*, beim Kragen packen. **-y,** *adj.* (*sl.*) schäbig, verkommen.
scrummage [ˈskrʌmɪdʒ], *s. see* **scrimmage.**
scrumptious [ˈskrʌmʃəs], *adj.* (*sl.*) köstlich, famos, fabelhaft.
scrunch [skrʌntʃ], 1. *v.a.* zerkauen, zermalmen. 2. *v.n.* krachen, knirschen. 3. *s.* das Krachen, Knirschen.
scrup-le [ˈskru:pl], 1. *s.* das Skrupel (= 1,3 g.) (*Pharm.*); der Skrupel, Zweifel, das Bedenken; *have (no) -les*, sich ein (kein) Gewissen machen (*about doing*, zu tun), *make no -le*, kein Bedenken tragen; *without -le*, skrupellos, gewissenlos. 2. *v.n.* (*usually neg.*) Bedenken tragen, sich (*Dat.*) ein Gewissen machen. **-ulosity** [-pjuˈlɔsɪtɪ], *s.* das Bedenken, die Bedenklichkeit, Gewissenhaftigkeit; Ängstlichkeit, Genauigkeit. **-ulous** [-pjuləs], *adj.* überbedenklich, ängstlich, gewissenhaft, genau, peinlich; *be -ulous*, sich (*Dat.*) ein Gewissen (daraus) machen. **-ulousness,** *see* **-ulosity.**
scrutin-eer [skru:tɪˈnɪ:ə], *s.* der (Wahl)Prüfer (*Parl.*). **-ize** [ˈskru:tɪnaɪz], *v.n.* untersuchen, genau prüfen. **-y** [-tɪnɪ], *s.* genaue Untersuchung *or* Prüfung, die Nachforschung; Wahlprüfung, Kontrolle; prüfender Blick.
scud [skʌd], 1. *s.* vom Wind gejagte Wolke, der Windbö. 2. *v.n.* eilen, fliehen, jagen; treiben, lenzen (*Naut.*).
scuffle [ˈskʌfl], 1. *s.* die Balgerei, das Handgemenge, Gewühl. 2. *v.n.* sich balgen, sich raufen, handgemein werden; scharren, schlurren.

scull [skʌl], 1. *s.* kurzes Ruder, das Skull. 2. *v.a.* & *n.* skullen (*with sculls*); wricken, wriggen (*with one oar*).
scullery [ˈskʌlərɪ], *s.* die Spülküche, Aufwaschküche. **--maid,** *s.* die Küchenmagd.
scullion [ˈskʌlɪən], *s.* (*Poet.*) der Küchenjunge.
sculpt-or [ˈskʌlptə], *s.* der Bildhauer. **-ress** [-trɪs], *s.* die Bildhauerin. **-ural** [-tʃərəl], *adj.* Bildhauer-, plastisch. **-ure** [-tʃə], 1. *s.* die Bildhauerkunst; Skulptur, Plastik, das Bildwerk. 2. *v.a.* modellieren, schnitzen, aushauen, meißeln. **-uresque** [-tʃəˈrɛsk], *adj.* plastisch.
scum [skʌm], 1. *s.* der Schaum, Schlacken (*pl.*) (*Metal.*); (*fig.*) der Abschaum, Auswurf; (*sl.*) Halunke. 2. *v.a.* abschäumen. **-my,** *adj.* schaumig, Schaum-.
scupper [ˈskʌpə], 1. *s.* das Speigatt (*Naut.*). 2. *v.a.* (*sl.*) vereiteln, zuschanden machen, einen Strich durch die Rechnung machen (*Dat.*).
scurf [skə:f], *s.* der Schorf, Grind. **-iness,** *s.* die Schorfigkeit. **-y,** *adj.* schorfig, grindig.
scurril-ity [skʌˈrɪlɪtɪ], *s.* die Gemeinheit; Zotigkeit. **-ous** [ˈskʌrɪləs], *adj.* gemein, zotig.
scurry [ˈskʌrɪ], 1. *v.n.* eilen, rennen, dahintrippeln. 2. *s.* das Hasten, Jagen; – *of rain*, der Regenschauer.
scurvy [ˈskə:vɪ], 1. *adj.* gemein, niederträchtig. 2. *s.* der Skorbut (*Med.*). **--grass,** *s.* das Löffelkraut (*Bot.*).
scut [skʌt], *s.* der Stutzschwanz.
scutage [ˈskju:tɪdʒ], *s.* die Lehnsdienstpflicht; Dienstpflichttaxe.
scutch [skʌtʃ], 1. *v.a.* schwingen (*flax*). 2. *s.* (also *-er*) die Flachsschwingmaschine.
scutcheon [ˈskʌtʃən], *s. see* **escutcheon;** das Schlüssellochschild; Namenschild.
scute [skju:t], *s.* die Schuppe (*Zool.*). **-llate(d)** [-əleɪt(ɪd)], *adj.* mit einem Schild bedeckt (*Zool.*, *Bot.*). **-lliform** [-ˈtɛlɪfɔ:m], *adj.* schildförmig. **-llum** [-ˈtɛləm], *s.* das Schildchen.
[1]**scuttle** [ˈskʌtl], *s.* (usually *coal--*) der Kohlenkasten, Kohleneimer.
[2]**scuttle,** 1. *v.a.* anbohren, selbst versenken, versenken (*ships*). 2. *s.* die Springluke, kleine Luke (*Naut.*).
[3]**scuttle,** 1. *v.n.*; – *away*, forteilen, sich drücken. 2. *s.* eilige Flucht, eiliger Schritt.
scythe [saɪð], *s.* die Sense. 2. *v.a.* (ab)mähen.
sea [sɪ:], *s.* die See, das Meer (*also fig.*), der Ozean; der Seegang, Wellen (*pl.*); (*fig.*) der Strom, die Flut. *at* –, auf dem Meer, auf See; zu See (*as a seaman*); (*fig.*) ratlos; *beyond the* –(*s*), über See, Übersee, übers Meer; *breaking* –, die Sturzsee; *by* –, auf dem Seeweg, zu Wasser; *by the* –, an der See; *freedom of the* –*s*, die Meeresfreiheit; (*sl.*) *half* –*s over*, benebelt, beschwipst; *heavy* –, hochgehende See, hoher Seegang; *a heavy* –, große Welle; *high* –*s fleet*, die Hochseeflotte; *on the high* –*s* or *open* –, auf hoher See; *go to* –, in See gehen; Seemann werden; *put* (*out*) *to* –, in See stechen. **– air,** *s.* die Seeluft, Meeresluft. **--anchor,** *s.* der Treibanker. **– bathing,** *s.* das Baden in der See. **– bird,** *s.* der Seevogel. **-board,** *s.* die Küstenlinie, Seeküste, das Seeufer, Meeresufer. **--born,** *adj.* (*Poet.*) meerentsprungen. **--borne,** *adj.* auf dem Seewege befördert; von der See getragen; *--borne aircraft*, das Trägerflugzeug; *--borne trade*, der Seehandel. **– bottom,** *s.* der Meeresgrund. **--bound,** *adj.* vom Meer umgeben. **-breeze,** *s.* der Seewind. **--calf,** *s.* der Seehund, die Robbe. **– captain,** *s.* der Schiffskapitän. **--chest,** *s.* die Seemannskiste. **– coast,** *s.* die Seeküste, Meeresküste. **--cock,** *s.* das Seeventil, der Seehahn. **--cow,** *s.* das Walroß, die Seekuh. **– cucumber,** *s.* die Seegurke. **– current,** *s.* die Meeresströmung. **--dog,** *s.* der Seehund; (*fig.*) alter Matrose, der Seebär. **-farer,** *s.* der Seefahrer. **-faring,** 1. *adj.* seemännisch, seefahrend; 2. *s.* die Seefahrt. **– forces,** *pl.* Seekräfte (*pl.*). **--fowl,** *s.* der Seevogel. **– front,** *s.* die Strandpromenade. **--girt,** *adj.* (*Poet.*) meerumschlungen. **--god,** *s.* der Meeresgott. **-going,** *adj.* seefahrend, See- (*ship, etc.*); *-going tug*, der Hochseeschlepper. **--green,** 1. *s.* das Meergrün; 2. *adj.* meergrün. **-gull,** *s.* die (See)Möwe. **--hog,** *s.* das Meerschwein. **--horse,** *s.* das Seepferdchen (*Ichth.*), Walroß (*Zool.*). **– kale,** *s.* Meerkohl. (*coll.*) **– lawyer,** *s.* der Besserwisser. **--legs,** *pl.* die Seetüchtigkeit; *find one's --legs*, seefest werden. **– level,** *s.* der Meeresspiegel, die Normalnull. **--line,** *s.* die Kimm. **– lion,** *s.* der Seelöwe. **– lord,** *s.* der Chef des Marinestabs. **-man** [-mən], *s.* (also *ordinary -man*), der Seemann, Matrose, Matrosengefreite(r), *m.*; *able -man*, der Vollmatrose, Matrosenobergefreite(r), *m.*; *leading-man*, Matrosenhauptgefreite(r), *m.* **-manlike,** *adj.* seemännisch. **-manship,** *s.* die Seemannskunst. **--mark(er),** *s.* das Seezeichen, die Markierungsboje. **--mew,** *s. see* **-gull.** **– mile,** *s.* die Seemeile. **– mud,** *s.* der Schlick. **--piece,** *s.* das Seestück (*Paint.*). **-plane,** *s.* das Wasserflugzeug, Seeflugzeug. **-port,** *s.* der Seehafen, die Hafenstadt. **– power,** *s.* die Seemacht. **--risk,** *s.* das Seerisiko, die Seegefahr. **--room,** *s.* die Seeräumte. **– route,** *s.* der Seeweg, Schiffahrtsweg. **– rover,** *s.* der Seeräuber. **--salt,** *s.* das Seesalz. **-scape,** *s.* die Seelandschaft; das Seestück (*Paint.*). **– serpent,** *s.* die Seeschlange. **-shore,** *s.* die Meeresküste, Seeküste. **-sick,** *adj.* seekrank. **-sickness,** *s.* die Seekrankheit. **-side,** 1. *s.* die (Meeres)Küste; *at the -side*, an der See, *to the -side*, an die See. 2. *adj.* Küsten-, Strand-; *-side resort*, das Seebad; *-side town*, die Küstenstadt. **--term,** *s.* seemännischer Ausdruck. **--tossed,** *adj.* von der See umhergeworfen. **– trade,** *s.* der Seehandel, Seeverkehr, die Schiffahrt. **– trout,** *s.* die Meerforelle. **--urchin,** *s.* der Seeigel. **– voyage,** *s.* die Seereise. **--wall,** *s.* der Damm, Deich. **-ward,** 1. *adj.* zum Meere hin, nach der See gerichtet. 2. *adv.* (*also* **-wards**) seewärts. **--water,** *s.* das Meer(es)wasser, Seewasser. **--way,** *s.* offene See; der Seegang. **-weed,** *s.* die Alge, der Seetang, das Seegras. **-worthiness,** *s.* die Seetüchtigkeit. **-worthy,** *adj.* seefest, seetüchtig.
[1]**seal** [sɪ:l], *s.* der Seehund, die Robbe. **-er,** *s.* der Robbenfänger. **-ery** 2. die Brutstätte der Robben. **--fishery, --fishing,** *s.* der Robbenfang. **-skin,** *s.* das Seehundsfell.
[2]**seal,** 1. *s.* das Siegel, Petschaft; der Siegelabdruck, Stempel, die Matrize; (*fig.*) Besiegelung, Bekräftigung, Bestätigung; wasserdichter *or* luftdichter Verschluß, die Abdichtung (*Tech.*); *Great* –, das Großsiegel; *Lord Keeper of the Great* –, der Großsiegelbewahrer (*Hist.*); *Privy* –, das Geheimsiegel; *Lord Privy* –, Königlicher Geheimsiegelbewahrer; *set one's* – *on*, besiegeln (*Acc.*), sein Siegel aufdrücken (*Dat.*); *set one's* – *to*, (*fig.*) bekräftigen; *under* –, besiegelt, versiegelt; *under my hand and* –, unter Brief und Siegel; *under the* – *of secrecy*, unter dem Siegel der Verschwiegenheit. 2. *v.a.* siegeln, besiegeln (*also fig.*), versiegeln, mit einem Siegel versehen, (*fig.*) bekräftigen, bestätigen; – *a p.'s lips*, einem Stillschweigen auferlegen; – *off*, abriegeln (*Mil.*); – *up*, versiegeln, fest verschließen, abdichten; – *with lead*, plombieren; *a -ed book*, ein Buch mit sieben Siegeln; *his fate is -ed*, sein Untergang ist bestimmt. **--engraver,** *s.* der Stempelschneider. **-ing-wax,** *s.* der Siegellack.
seam [sɪ:m], 1. *s.* der Saum, die Naht (*also Anat.*); das Lager, Flöz, die Nutzschicht (*Geol.*); Fuge, Spalte (*Tech.*); Narbe; *flat* –, die Kappnaht. 2. *v.a.* zusammennähen, einen Saum sticken; (*usually pass.*) furchen, schrammen, ritzen. **-ed** *adj.* gefurcht, vernarbt. **-less,** *adj.* ohne Naht, nahtlos, **-stress** [-strɪs], *s.* die Näherin. **-y,** *adj.* gesäumt; *-y side*, (*fig.*) unangenehme Seite, die Schattenseite.
seaman, *see* **sea.**
seance [ˈseɪəns], *s.* spiritistische Sitzung.
seaplane, seaport, *see* **sea.**
sear [sɪ:ə], 1. *adj.* (*Poet.*) verwelkt, welk. 2. *v.a.* austrocknen, ausdörren; versengen, brennen, ätzen, brandmarken; (*fig.*) verhärten.
search [sə:tʃ], 1. *v.a.* untersuchen, durchsuchen (*for*, nach); prüfen (*one's heart*), absuchen (*the horizon, etc.*), prüfend ansehen; – *out*, forschen nach, auskundschaften, ausfindig machen; – *me!* (*sl.*) keine Ahnung! was weiß ich! 2. *v.n.* eifrig suchen, nachsuchen; – *after*, streben nach, zu erlangen suchen; – *for*, suchen *or* forschen nach,

sich umsehen nach; – *into*, sich erkundigen nach, ergründen, sich versenken in. 3. *s.* das Suchen, Forschen, Streben (*for*, nach), die Suche, Durchsuchung, Untersuchung, Prüfung; *in – of*, auf der Suche nach; *go in – of*, suchen, auf die Suche gehen nach; *make a – for*, suchen; *right of –*, das Durchsuchungsrecht. **–ing,** *adj.* suchend, forschend; tiefgehend, eingehend, eindringend, durchdringend, gründlich; *–ing fire*, das Streufeuer (*Mil.*); *–ing look*, durchdringender *or* forschender Blick; *–ing test*, eingehende Prüfung; *–ing wind*, scharfer Wind. **–ingness,** *s.* die Schärfe, Eindringlichkeit, Genauigkeit. **–light,** *s.* der Scheinwerfer. **– -party,** *s.* die Rettungsmannschaft. **– -warrant,** *s.* der Haussuchungsbefehl.

seaside, *see* **sea.**

season [ˈsɪ:zən], 1. *s.* die Jahreszeit; (rechte) Zeit, die Geschäftszeit (*C.L.*), Reifezeit (*of fruit, etc.*), Badezeit, Kurzeit, Saison; (*coll.*) *see* **– -ticket;** *dead* or *dull –*, stille Geschäftszeit; *for a –*, für eine Weile; *in –*, zur rechten Zeit; *everything in its –*, alles zu seiner Zeit; *in (–) and out of –*, zu jeder Zeit, zu allen Zeiten; *compliments of the –*, beste Wünsche fürs Fest; *height of the –*, die Hochsaison; *out of –*, zur Unzeit, ungelegen; nicht zu haben, nicht saisongemäß. 2. *v.a.* würzen; reifen, zum Reifen bringen; ablagern, austrocknen (*wood*); (*fig.*) gewöhnen an, eingewöhnen, abhärten (*a p.*); *be* or *become –ed to*, sich gewöhnen an (*Acc.*); *– o.s. to*, sich abhärten gegen. 3. *v.n.* reifen, trocknen. **–able,** *adj.* zeitgemäß, angebracht, passend. **–ableness,** *s.* rechte Zeit, das Zeitgemäße. **–al,** *adj.* Saison–; *–al trade*, das Saisongewerbe; *–al worker*, der Saisonarbeiter. **–ed,** abgelagert, ausgetrocknet, abgehärtet; (*fig.*) erfahren, gewiegt. **–ing,** *s.* die Würze. **– -ticket,** *s.* die Wochenkarte, Monatskarte, Dauerkarte, Abonnementskarte.

seat [sɪ:t], 1. *s.* der Sitz (*also Parl., and of a chair*); Sessel, Stuhl, die Bank, der Sitzplatz (*Theat.*), Sitzort; Familiensitz, Wohnsitz, Landsitz, Platz, Ort, Schauplatz; die Sitzart, Haltung; das Sitzrecht, die Mitgliedschaft (*Parl.*); der Hosenboden, das Gesäß, Hinterteil (*of trousers*); der Boden (*of a chair*); das Lager (*Tech.*); *– of judgement*, der Richterstuhl; *– of war*, der Kriegsschauplatz; *– on the council*, der Sitz im Rat; *keep one's –*, sitzen bleiben; *take a –*, sich setzen, Platz nehmen; *take a back –*, sich in den Hintergrund zurückziehen; *take one's –*, den angewiesenen Platz einnehmen; *take your –s*, einsteigen (*Railw.*). 2. *v.a.* setzen; einen Sitz verschaffen (*Dat.*), (ein)setzen; mit Sitzplätzen versehen (*a church, etc.*); Hosenboden einsetzen in (*trousers*); den Sitz erneuern in (*a chair*); lagern, betten (*Tech.*); *– o.s.*, sich (hin)setzen; *be –ed*, sitzen; *– s.o. on the throne*, einen zum Thron erheben; *– 60 persons*, Sitzplätze für 60 Personen haben (*of a building*); *be –ed*, sitzen; wohnen, liegen, gelegen sein, seinen (Wohn)Sitz haben (*in*, in); *pray be –ed*, nehmen Sie Platz. **–ed,** *adj.* sitzend; (*also suff.*) –sitzig; *deep –ed*, tiefsitzend. **–er** [–ə], *s.* (*as suff.*) *four –er*, der Viersitzer. **–ing,** 1. *adj.*; *–ing accommodation*, Sitzgelegenheiten (*pl.*). 2. *s.* das Setzen; Stoff für Stuhlsitze; Fundament (*Tech.*).

seaward(s), seaweed, seaworthy, *see* **sea.**

sebac–eous [sɪˈbeɪʃəs], *adj.* Talg–, Fett– (*Physiol.*). **–ic** [–ˈbæsɪk], *adj.* Fett–, fettsauer (*Chem.*).

sec [sɛk], *adj.* trocken, ungesüßt (*wine*).

secant [ˈsɪ:kənt], 1. *adj.* schneidend. 2. *s.* die Sekante.

seccotine [ˈsɛkətɪ:n], *s.* der Klebestoff.

secede [sɪˈsɪ:d], *v.n.* abfallen, sich trennen *or* losmachen (*from*, von); übertreten, übergehen (*to*, zu). **–r** [–ə], *s.* der Separatist.

secernent [sɪˈsə:nənt], 1. *adj.* sekretierend, absondernd. 2. *s.* sekretierendes Organ (*Physiol.*).

secession [sɪˈsɛʃən], *s.* der Abfall, die Loslösung, Lossagung (*from*, von); der Übertritt (*to*, zu); kirchliche Spaltung; *War of –*, amerikanischer Bürgerkrieg. **–ist,** *s.* der Separatist, Sezessionist; Sonderbündler (*Pol.*).

seclu–de [sɪˈklu:d], *v.a.* abschließen, absondern (*from*, gegen *or* von); *–de o.s.*, sich abschließen *or* zurückziehen. **–ded,** *adj.* abgeschlossen, zurückgezogen, einsam. **–sion** [–ʒən], *s.* die Abschließung; Abgeschiedenheit, Abgeschlossenheit, Zurückgezogenheit.

second [ˈsɛkənd], 1. *adj.* zweite(–r, –s), andere(–r, –s), nächst, folgend; nachstehend, untergeordnet (*to* (*Dat.*)); *be* or *stand – (to a p.)*, (einem) nachstehen; *come –*, als zweite(r) *or* an zweiter Stelle kommen; *– Chamber*, das Oberhaus; *– channel interference*, das Wellenecho (*Rad.*); *– driver*, der Beifahrer; *– fermentation*, die Nachgärung; *play – fiddle*, die Nebenrolle *or* untergeordnete Rolle spielen; *– lieutenant*, der Leutnant; *at – hand*, aus zweiter Hand; *see* **– -hand;** *– line defences*, Auffangstellungen (*Mil.*); *– mate*, zweiter Steuermann; *come as* or *be – nature to a p.*, einem zur zweiten Natur werden; *– to none*, unerreicht, keinem nachstehend, hinter keinem zurückstehend; *in the – place*, zweitens, an zweiter Stelle; *– quality*, untergeordnete Qualität; *– sight*, das Hellsehen; *on – thoughts*, bei *or* nach näherer Überlegung; *a – time*, noch einmal, zum zweitenmale; *every – year*, alle zwei Jahre, ein Jahr ums andere. 2. *s.* der, das *or* die Zweite *or* Nächste; die Sekunde (*of time; also Mus.*); begleitende Stimme (*Mus.*); der Sekundant (*duels*), (*fig.*) Beistand; (*coll.*) Augenblick; (*coll.*) zweite Klasse in einer Universitätsprüfung; *pl.* Waren zweiter Güte (*pl.*) (*C.L.*); *– of exchange*, der Sekundawechsel; *– in command*, der Unterbefehlshaber; *act as a –*, sekundieren; *run s.o. a good –*, einem sehr nahekommen; *take the –*, die begleitende Stimme übernehmen (*Mus.*). 3. *v.a.* beistehen, beipflichten, helfen, (*Dat.*); sekundieren (*Dat.*) (*in a duel*); unterstützen, (*also a motion* (*Parl.*)); [*usually* sɪˈkənd], abkommandieren (*Mil.*) (*for* or *to*, zu). **–ariness,** *s.* das Sekundäre, Untergeordnete. **–ary,** 1. *adj.* in zweiter Linie stehend, in zweiter Hinsicht, nebensächlich, untergeordnet, abhängig, entlehnt, abgeleitet, Neben–, Hilfs–; sekundär (*Geol., Elec., & Phil.*), Sekundär– (*Elec.*); *–ary accent*, der Nebenton; *–ary cause*, die Nebenursache; *–ary colour*, die Mischfarbe, Mittelfarbe, Zwischenfarbe; *–ary current*, der Sekundärstrom; *–ary education*, höhere Schulbildung; *–ary fever*, das Fieber nach der Krise; *a matter of –ary importance*, eine Nebensache; *–ary objective*, das Ausweichziel (*Mil.*); *–ary proposition*, der Nebensatz; *–ary school*, höhere Schule, die Mittelschule (*Austria*). 2. *s.* der Stellvertreter, Untergeordnete(r), *m.*; die Mischfarbe, zusammengesetzte Farbe; hintere Schwungfeder (*Orn.*). **– -best,** 1. *s.* das Zweitbeste. 2. *adj.* zweitbest; *come off – -best*, unterliegen, den kürzeren ziehen. **– -class,** *adj.* zweiten Ranges *or* Grades, zweiter Klasse; zweitklassig; *– -class matter*, Postsachen zweiter Ordnung, die Drucksache. **– -cousin,** *s.* der Vetter zweiten Grades. **– -hand,** 1. *adj.* alt, gebraucht, antiquarisch; (*fig.*) nicht ursprünglich, entlehnt; *– -hand bookseller*, der Antiquar; 2. *adv.* aus zweiter Hand, antiquarisch. 3. *s.* (also *–s-hand*) der Sekundenzeiger (*Horol.*). **–ly,** *adv.* zweitens, an zweiter Stelle. **– -rate,** *adj.* (nur) zweiten Ranges, zweitklassig, zweitrangig, minderwertig, mittelmäßig. **– -rater,** *s.* (*coll.*) zweitklassige Person.

secre–cy [ˈsɪ:krɪsɪ], *s.* die Heimlichkeit, Verborgenheit, Verschlossenheit, Verschwiegenheit, Schweigepflicht, Geheimhaltung; *in –cy*, (ins)geheim, heimlich, im Geheimen; *observe –cy*, Verschwiegenheit bewahren; *be sworn to –cy*, zur Amtsverschwiegenheit verpflichtet werden. **–t** [–t], 1. *adj.* geheim, Geheim–, heimlich, verborgen, verschwiegen; *–t ballot*, geheime Wahl; *–t door*, die Geheimtür; *–t service*, der Geheimdienst; *–t society*, der Geheimbund; *–t treaty*, der Geheimvertrag; *keep –t*, geheimhalten, verheimlichen. 2. *s.* das Geheimnis (*from*, vor); *dead –t*, tiefes Geheimnis; *in –t*, insgeheim, heimlich, im Vertrauen; *be in the –t*, eingeweiht sein; *let a p. into the –t*, einen in das Geheimnis einweihen; *keep a –t*, ein Geheimnis bewahren; *let a –t out* or *let out a –t*, ein Geheimnis preisgeben; *make no –t of*, kein Geheimnis *or* Hehl machen aus; *open –t*, offenes Geheimnis.

secreta–ire [sɛkrəˈtɛ:ə], *s.* der Schreibschrank. **–rial** [–ˈtɛ:rɪəl], *adj.* Schreib–, Büro–, Sekretär–; **–riat** [–ˈtɛ:rɪət], *s.* das Sekretariat; die Kanzlei; Kanzleiangestellte (*pl.*). **–ry** [ˈsɛkrətərɪ], *s.* der

Sekretär (*to*, bei), Schriftführer, Schriftwart; (Kabinett)Minister; *see also* **-ire**; *-ry of State*, der Minister (*England*), Außenminister (*Amer.*); *-ry of State for Foreign Affairs* or *Foreign -ry*, der Außenminister (*England*); *-ry of State for Home Affairs* or *Home -ry*, der Innenminister (*England*); *-ry of State for War*, der Kriegsminister; *-ry of War*, der Kriegsminister (*Amer.*); *general -ry*, der Geschäftsführer; *private -ry*, der Privatsekretär. **-ryship,** *s.* das Schriftführeramt. **-ry-bird,** *s.* der Schlangenadler.

secret-e [sɪˈkrɪ:t], *v.a.* verbergen, verstecken (*from*, vor); absondern, ausscheiden, sekretieren (*Physiol.*); *-e o.s.*, sich verbergen. **-ion** [-ʃən], *s.* die Absonderung, Ausscheidung, Sekretion; das Sekret, der Ausfluß. **-ive** [ˈsɪ:krɪtɪv], *adj.* verschwiegen, verschlossen; geheim, verstohlen, verborgen; [sɪˈkrɪ:tɪv], Absonderungs- (*Physiol.*). **-iveness,** *s.* die Verschwiegenheit, *etc.*

sect [sɛkt], *s.* die Sekte, Partei. **-arian** [-ˈtɛ:ərɪən], 1. *adj.* sektiererisch, Sekten-; konfessionell. 2. *s.* der Sektierer. **-arianism,** *s.* die Sektiererei, das Sektentum.

section [ˈsɛkʃən], *s.* die Durchschneidung, Teilung; Öffnung, Sektion (*Surg.*); der Teil, das Stück; die (Bahn)Strecke, Teilstrecke (*Railw.*); der Abschnitt, Absatz, Paragraph; die Klasse, Gruppe, (Unter)-Abteilung; der Schnitt (*Math.*), Durchschnitt (*Geom.*); die Abteilung (*Mil.*). *conic -*, der Kegelschnitt; *cross -*, der Querschnitt. **-al,** *adj* Teil-, Abteilungs-, Durchschnitts-; zusammensetzbar, zusammenlegbar; Form-, Fasson- (*Tech.*); *-al interests*, lokale *or* partikularistische Interessen. **-alism,** *s.* der Partikularismus.

sector [ˈsɛktə], *s.* der Sektor, Kreisausschnitt (*Geom.*); Proportionalzirkel (*Draw.*); Kreissektor (*Surv.*); (Gelände)Abschnitt (*Mil.*).

secular [ˈsɛkjulə], 1. *adj.* weltlich, nicht kirchlich, Säkular-, diesseitig; hundertjährlich, hundertjährig; *- clergy*, die Weltgeistlichkeit; *- music*, weltliche Musik. 2. *s.* der Weltgeistliche (*R.C.*). **-ity** [-ˈlærɪtɪ], *s.* die Weltlichkeit, Diesseitigkeit, weltliche Interessen (*pl.*). **-ization** [-raɪˈzeɪʃən], *s.* die Verweltlichung, Säkularisation; Verstaatlichung. **-ize** [-raɪz], *v.a.* säkularisieren; einziehen, verstaatlichen (*church property*), (*fig.*) verweltlichen.

secund [sɪˈkʌnd], *adj.* einseitig (*Bot.*). **-ine** [ˈsɛkəndaɪn], *s.* (*pl.*) die Nachgeburt.

secur-able [sɪˈkjuərəbl], *adj.* erreichbar, zu erlangen(d). **-e** [sɪˈkjuə], 1. *adj.* sicher, gesichert (*against* or *from*, vor); sorglos, ruhig, gewiß, zuversichtlich. 2. *v.a.* sichern, schützen (*from* or *against*, vor); sicherstellen; befestigen (*also Mil.*), festmachen (*to*, an), fest zumachen (*as a door*), zurren (*Naut.*); festnehmen, einsperren (*a thief, etc.*), in Gewahrsam *or* Sicherheit bringen; Sicherheit geben (*Dat.*); sich (*Dat.*) sichern *or* beschaffen, erlangen; belegen (*a seat, etc.*). **-ity** [sɪˈkjuərɪtɪ], *s.* die Sicherheit, der Schutz (*from* or *against*, gegen); die Sorglosigkeit, Zuversicht, Gewißheit; Garantie, Bürgschaft, Kaution, Sicherheitsleistung, Deckung, das Unterpfand, der Bürge; *pl.* die Wertpapiere, Effekten (*pl.*); *bearer -ities*, Inhaberpapiere; *collateral -ity*, mittelbare Sicherheit, die Nebensicherheit; *collective -ity*, kollektive Sicherheit; *gilt-edged -ities*, mündelsichere Wertpapiere, *in -ity*, in Sicherheit; *in -ity for*, als Sicherheitsleistung für; *public -ities*, Staatspapiere; *furnish* or *give -ity*, Bürgschaft leisten; *with -ity*, mit Sicherheit; *-ity market*, die Effektenbörse; *-ity pact*, der Sicherheitspakt; *-ity police*, die Sicherheitspolizei.

sedan [sɪˈdæn], *s.* (also *--chair*) die Sänfte; Limousine (*Mot.*).

sedat-e [sɪˈdeɪt], *adj.* gesetzt, gelassen, ruhig, **-eness,** *s.* die Gesetztheit, Gelassenheit, Ruhe. **-ive** [ˈsɛdətɪv], 1. *adj.* beruhigend, besänftigend. 2. *s.* das Beruhigungsmittel.

sedentary [ˈsɛdəntərɪ], *adj.* sitzend; *- life*, sitzende Lebensweise.

sederunt [sɪˈdɛərənt], *s.* die Sitzung.

sedg-e [sɛdʒ], *s.* das Schilfgras, Riedgras. **-y,** *adj.* schilfig, Schilf-; mit Riedgras bewachsen.

sediment [ˈsɛdɪmənt], *s.* der (Boden)Satz, Niederschlag, Rückstand; die Hefe; Ablagerung, das Sediment (*Geol.*). **-ary** [-ˈmɛntərɪ], *adj.* Sediment-, sedimentär (*Geol.*).

seditio-n [sɪˈdɪʃən], *s.* der Aufruhr, Aufstand, die Meuterei, Empörung. **-us** [-ʃəs], *adj.* aufständisch, aufrührerisch.

seduc-e [sɪˈdju:s], *v.a.* verführen (*a girl, also fig.*), (*fig.*) verleiten. **-er** [-ə], *s.* der Verführer. **-ible,** *adj.* verführbar. **-tion** [-ˈdʌkʃən], *s.* die Verführung, Verleitung, Versuchung; verführerischer Reiz. **-tive** [-ˈdʌktɪv], *adj.* verführerisch; reizvoll, gewinnend.

sedul-ity [sɪˈdju:lɪtɪ], *see* **-ousness.** **-ous** [ˈsɛdjuləs], *adj.* emsig, fleißig. **-ousness,** *s.* die Emsigkeit, der Fleiß.

[1]**see** [sɪ:], **1.** *ir.v.n.* sehen, (*fig.*) einsehen, verstehen; nachsehen; *- fit*, es für angebracht *or* zweckmäßig halten *or* erachten; *I -*, ich verstehe (schon), ach so!; *let me -*, warte mal, einen Augenblick; *we'll - !* mal abwarten! *you - ?*, wohlgemerkt, nämlich; *wait and -*, abwarten; *- about*, besorgen, Sorge tragen für; *- after*, sich kümmern um, achten auf, achtgeben auf; *- into*, veranlassen, sich annehmen (*Gen.*), untersuchen; durchschauen; *- over*, besichtigen; *- through*, durchschauen; *- to*, besorgen, in die Hand nehmen; achten auf; *- to it that*, gib acht daß. **2.** *ir.v.a.* sehen; ansehen, nachsehen; einsehen, verstehen, gewahr werden, erkennen, erfahren, erleben; darauf achten, sorgen für; ersehen (*by*, aus); besuchen, aufsuchen, empfangen; befragen, konsultieren. (*a*) (*with nouns*) *- action*, mitkämpfen (*at*, bei); *- company*, Gesellschaften geben; in Gesellschaft gehen; *have -n better days*, bessere Tage gesehen *or* erlebt haben; *what the eye does not -, the heart does not grieve over*, was man nicht weiß, macht nicht heiß; *- a joke*, einen Spaß verstehen; *- justice done to a p.*, dafür sorgen, daß einem Gerechtigkeit widerfährt; *- a lawyer* (*doctor*, etc.), zu einem Anwalt (Arzt, *etc.*) gehen; *- life*, das Leben kennenlernen, Erfahrungen machen; *now I - (the) light*, jetzt geht mir ein Licht auf; *- a play*, ein Stück ansehen; *- fair play*, den Schiedsrichter machen; *- the point*, den Zweck der S. einsehen; *- his point*, seinen Standpunkt verstehen; (*sl.*) *- red*, die Fassung verlieren, wütend werden; *I cannot - my way*, ich sehe keine Möglichkeit; *you've not -n the worst of it yet*, das Schlimmste steht dir noch bevor. (*b*) (*with verbs*) *- s.o. come* or *coming*, einen kommen sehen; *go and -*, siehe nach; *go* or *come to* or *and - a p.*, einen besuchen *or* aufsuchen; *live to -*, erleben; *it remains to be -n*, es bleibt abzuwarten. (*c*) (*with adverbs*) *- a p. home* or *to the door*, einen nach Hause *or* an die Tür bringen *or* begleiten; *- a p. off*, einen an die Bahn (*etc.*) bringen; *- a th. out*, etwas bis zum Ende sehen *or* mitmachen; *- a p. out*, einen hinausbegleiten *or* zur Tür bringen; *- a p. through*, einem durchhelfen; *- a th. through*, etwas durchführen *or* zu Ende führen; etwas durchhalten, ausharren. **-ing** [-ɪŋ], 1. *adj.*; *worth -ing*, sehenswert. 2. *conj.* *-ing* (*that*), da nun mal, in Anbetracht daß; *-ing it is so*, da es nun mal so ist. 3. *prep.* in Anbetracht, angesichts (*Gen.*). 4. *s.* das Sehen; *-ing is believing*, was man sieht, das glaubt man.

[2]**see,** *s.* (erz)bischöflicher Stuhl, das (Erz)Bistum; *Holy -*, Päpstlicher Stuhl.

seed [sɪ:d], 1. *s.* die Saat, der Samen; (*B.*) die Nachkommenschaft; (*fig.*) der Keim, Ursprung; *sow the -s of discord*, Zwietracht säen *or* stiften; *run to -*, in Samen schießen, (*fig.*) an Leistung nachlassen. 2. *v.n.* Samen tragen, in Samen schießen. 3. *v.a.* besäen (*a field*); entkernen (*fruit*); setzen (*a competitor*) (*Sport*). **--bearing,** *adj.* samentragend. **--cake,** *s.* der Kümmelkuchen. **--drill,** *s.* die Reihensähmaschine. **-er** [-ə], *s. see* **--drill.** **-iness,** *s.* (*coll.*) die Unpäßlichkeit; Schäbigkeit. **--leaf,** *s.* das Keimblatt, Samenblatt. **-less,** *adj.* kernlos. **-ling,** *s.* der Sämling. **--pearls,** *pl.* Samenperlen, Staubperlen. **--plot,** *s.* die Pflanzschule; (*fig.*) Brutstätte, der Keimherd. **--potatoes** *pl.* Saatkartoffeln (*pl.*). **-sman** [-zmən], *s.* der Samenhändler. **--vessel,** *s.*, die Fruchthülle. **-y,** *adj.* voller Samen, in Samen

schießend; (*coll.*) schäbig, fadenscheinig; unwohl, unpäßlich, katzenjämmerlich.
seek [sɪːk], 1. *ir.v.a.* suchen; zu entdecken, erforschen *or* bekommen suchen; erstreben, streben *or* trachten nach; erbitten (*from*, von); – *a p.'s life*, einem nach dem Leben trachten; – *in marriage*, anhalten um; – *out*, aufsuchen. 2. *ir.v.n.* suchen (*for*, nach); – *after*, jagen nach, (*esp. pass.*) begehren, verlangen; *there is s.th. to* –, es läßt noch zu wünschen übrig; *not far to* –, leicht zu finden. **–er** [–ə], *s.* der Sucher; *–er after truth*, Wahrheitsuchende(r), *m.*
seel [sɪːl], *v.a.* (*archaic*) blenden (*a hawk, also fig.*), (*fig.*) täuschen, irreführen.
seem [sɪːm], *v.n.* scheinen, den Anschein haben; zu sein scheinen, erscheinen (*to* (*Dat.*)); *all –ed pleased*, allen schien es zu gefallen; *it –s*, es scheint, dem Anschein nach; *it –s to me*, es scheint mir *or* kommt mir vor, mich dünkt; *as –s possible*, wie es wahrscheinlich ist. **–ing,** *adj.* anscheinend, scheinbar; schicklich. **–liness,** *s.* die Schicklichkeit, der Anstand. **–ly,** *adv.* geziemend, schicklich.
seen [sɪːn], *see* **see.**
seep [sɪːp], *v.n.* (durch)sickern; – *away*, versickern; – *into*, einsickern in. **–age,** *s.* das Durchsickern; Durchsickerte(s), *n.*
seer [sɪːə], *s.* der Seher, Prophet.
seesaw [ˈsɪːsɔː], 1. *s.* die Wippe, Schaukelbank; das Wippen, Schaukeln, (*fig.*) Auf und Ab, Hin und Her. 2. *v.n.* wippen, (sich) schaukeln, (*fig.*) auf und ab gehen, hin und her schwanken, steigen und fallen. 3. *attrib. adj.* hin und her– *or* auf und abgehend, wechselnd, schwankend.
seethe [sɪːð], *v.n.* sieden, kochen; schäumen, aufwallen, gären.
segment [ˈsɛgmənt], *s.* der Abschnitt, das Segment; Glied, der Teil (*Biol.*). **–al** [–ˈmentl], *adj.* segmentär. **–ation** [–ˈteɪʃən], *s.* die Segmentation.
segregat–e [ˈsɛgrɪgeɪt], *v.a.* absondern, trennen, ausscheiden. 2. *v.n.* sich absondern. 3. [–ət], *adj.* getrennt, isoliert. **–ion** [–ˈgeɪʃən], *s.* die Absonderung, Aufspaltung (*Biol.*), Abtrennung, Segregation. **–ive** [ˈsɛgrəgətɪv], *adj.* sich absondernd.
seign–eur [seɪnˈjəː], **–ior** [ˈsɪːnjə], *s.* der Lehnsherr, Grundherr. **–iorage** [–rɪdʒ], *s.* königliche Münzgebühr. **–iorial** [–ˈjɔːrɪəl], *adj.* grundherrlich, feudal (*also fig.*).
seine [seɪn], *s.* das Schlagnetz, Schleppnetz.
seisin [ˈsɪːzɪn], *s. see* **seizin.**
seism–ic [ˈsɑɪzmɪk], *adj.* Erdbeben–, seismisch. **–ograph** [–məgrɑːf], *s.* der Erdbebenanzeiger. **–ologist** [–ˈmɔlədʒɪst], *s.* der Erdbebenforscher, Seismologe. **–ology** [–ˈmɔlədʒɪ], *s.* die Seismik, Erdbebenkunde. **–ometer** [–ˈmɔmɪtə], *s.* der Erdbebenmesser. **–oscope** [–məskoʊp], *s. see* **–ograph.**
seiz–able [ˈsɪːzəbl], *adj.* (er)greifbar. **–e** [sɪːz], 1. *v.a.* ergreifen, fassen, packen; sich bemächtigen (*Gen.*), sich (*Dat.*) aneignen, an sich reißen; beschlagnahmen, in Beschlag *or* Besitz nehmen, mit Beschlag belegen; in den Besitz setzen (*a p.*) (*of*, von) (*Law*), festnehmen (*a p.*); (*fig.*) begreifen, erfassen; festbinden, zurren, laschen, zeisen (*Naut.*); *–ed of*, im Besitz von (*Law*); *be –ed with*, ergriffen *or* befallen sein von. 2. *v.n.* (also *–e up*) festfahren, sich einfressen (*Tech.*); (*fig.*) sich festklemmen, stecken bleiben; *–e* (*up*)*on*, sich bemächtigen (*Gen.*), ergreifen, (*a p.*), aufgreifen (*an idea*). **–ing,** *s.* das Ergreifen, *etc.*; das Bändsel, der Zurring, Lasching, Zeising, die Zurrung, Laschung (*Naut.*). **–ure** [ˈsɪːʒə], *s.* die Ergreifung (*of power*), Besitznahme, Beschlagnahme (*Law*), Verhaftung, Festnahme; plötzlicher Anfall, der Schlaganfall (*Med.*).
sejant [ˈsɪːdʒənt], *adj.* sitzend (*Her.*).
selachian [sɪˈleɪkɪən], 1. *s.* der Haifisch. 2. *adj.* Haifisch–.
seldom [ˈsɛldəm], *adv.* selten.
select [sɪˈlɛkt], 1. *v.a.* auslesen, auswählen. 2. *adj.* (aus)erlesen, auserwählt, exklusiv, vornehm, wählerisch; – *committee*, der Sonderausschuß, engerer Ausschuß. **–ed** [–ɪd], *adj.* auserwählt. **–ion** [–ʃən], *s.* das Auswählen; die Auslese, Auswahl (*from*, aus); *for –ion*, zur Auswahl; *make a –ion*, eine Auswahl treffen; *make one's own –ion*, selbst die Auswahl treffen; *natural –ion*, natürliche Zuchtwahl *or* Auslese. **–ive** [–tɪv], *adj.* auswählend, Auswahl–; selektiv, trennscharf (*Rad.*). **–ivity** [–ˈtɪvɪtɪ], *s.* die Abstimmschärfe, Trennschärfe, Selektivität (*Rad.*). **–or** [–ˈlɛktə] *s.* der Auswähler; Wähler (*Rad.*).
selen–ate [ˈsɛlɪneɪt], *s.* selensaures Salz (*Chem.*). **–ic** [səˈlɛnɪk], *adj.* selensauer. **–ium** [sɪˈlɪːnɪəm], *s.* das Selen. **–ography** [sɛlɪːˈnɔgrəfɪ], *s.* die Mondbeschreibung. **–ology** [sɛlɪːˈnɔlədʒɪ], *s.* die Mondkunde.
self [sɛlf], 1. *s.* (pl. *selves* [sɛlvz]) das Selbst, Ich; *his better* –, sein besseres Ich; *love of* –, die Selbstliebe, Eigenliebe; *my other* –, mein zweites Ich; *one's own* –, das eigne Ich; *my poor* or *humble* –, meine Wenigkeit. 2. *pron.* (*only in comps.*) selbst; *he him*–, er selbst. 3. *pref.* (*emphatic*), Selbst–, Eigen–. **––abandonment,** *s.* die Selbstvergessenheit, Hingabe. **––abasement,** *s.* die Selbstbeschämung. **––absorbed,** *adj.* in sich selbst vertieft. **––abuse,** *s.* die Selbstbefleckung, Onanie. **––acting,** *adj.* selbsttätig, automatisch. **––adjusting,** *adj.* selbstregulierend. **––aggrandizement,** *s.* die Selbsterhebung. **––appointed,** *adj.* selbsternannt. **––assertion,** *s.* das Selbstbewußtsein, die Selbstbehauptung, die Anmaßung. **––assertive,** *adj.* selbstbewußt, anmaßend. **––assurance,** *s.* die Selbstsicherheit, das Selbstbewußtsein. **––assured,** *adj.* selbstbewußt, selbstsicher. **––awareness,** *s.* das Selbstbewußtsein. **––centred,** *adj.* egozentrisch, egoistisch. **––coloured,** *adj.* naturfarbig; einfarbig. **––complacent,** *adj.* selbstgefällig, selbstzufrieden. **––conceit,** *s.* der Eigendünkel. **––conceited,** *adj.* dünkelhaft; eingebildet. **––confidence,** *s.* das Selbstbewußtsein, Selbstvertrauen. **––conscious,** *adj.* verlegen, befangen, unfrei. **––consciousness,** *s.* die Verlegenheit, Befangenheit. **––contained,** *adj.* in sich abgeschlossen, vollständig; *––contained house*, das Einfamilienhaus, abgeschlossenes Haus. **––contempt,** *s.* die Selbstverachtung. **––contradiction,** *s.* der Selbstwiderspruch. **––contradictory,** *adj.* sich (*Dat.*) selbst widersprechend, widerspruchsvoll. **––control,** *s.* die Selbstbeherrschung. **––criticism,** *s.* die Selbstkritik. **––deception,** *s.* die Selbsttäuschung. **––defence,** *s.* die Selbstverteidigung, Notwehr; *in ––defence*, aus Notwehr. **––denial,** *s.* die Selbstverleugnung. **––denying,** *adj.* selbstverleugnend. **––depreciation,** *s.* die Selbstunterschätzung. **––determination,** *s.* die Selbstbestimmung. **––discipline,** *s.* die Selbstzucht. **––educated,** *adj.*; *––educated person*, der Autodidakt. **––evident,** *adj.* selbstverständlich, einleuchtend, augenscheinlich. **––feeder,** *s.* der Dauerbrandofen. **––feeding,** *adj.* sich selbst speisend, selbstregulierend. **––forgetful,** *adj.* sich selbst vergessend. **––glorification,** *s.* die Selbstverherrlichung. **––governing,** *adj.* sich selbst verwaltend, autonom. **––government,** *s.* die Selbstregierung, Selbstverwaltung, Autonomie. **––help,** *s.* die Selbsthilfe. **––ignition,** *s.* die Selbstentzündung. **––importance,** *s.* das Selbstgefühl, der Eigendünkel, die Selbstüberhebung, Wichtigtuerei. **––incrimination,** *s.* die Selbstanklage, Selbstbeschuldigung. **––induction,** *s.* die Selbstinduktion (*Elec.*). **––indulgence,** *s.* die Genußsucht. **––indulgent,** *adj.* bequem. **––inflation,** *s.* die Aufgeblasenheit. **––inflicted,** *adj.* selbstgeschlagen, selbstbeigebracht. **––interest,** *s.* der Eigennutz. **–ish,** *see* **selfish.** **––knowledge,** *s.* die Selbsterkenntnis. **–less,** *see* **selfless.** **––love,** *s.* die Eigenliebe. **––made,** *adj.* selbstgemacht; *––made man*, der Emporkömmling. **––mutilation,** *s.* die Selbstverstümmelung. **––opinionated,** *adj.* dünkelhaft, eigensinnig. **––portrait,** *s.* das Selbstbildnis. **––possessed,** *adj.* gefaßt, gelassen, (selbst)beherrscht. **––possession,** *s.* die Selbstbeherrschung; Fassung, Ruhe. **––praise,** *s.* das Eigenlob. **––preservation,** *s.* die Selbsterhaltung; *instinct of ––preservation*, der Selbsterhaltungstrieb. **––propelled,** *adj.* Selbstfahr–. **––protection,** *s.* der Selbstschutz; *in*

--*protection*, zum Selbstschutz. **--regard,** *s.* der Eigennutz, die Selbstachtung. **--regulating,** *adj.* sich selbst regulierend. **--reliance,** *s.* die Selbstsicherheit, das Selbstvertrauen, Selbstgefühl. **--reliant,** *adj.* selbstvertrauend, selbstsicher. **--reproach,** *s.* der Gewissensvorwurf. **--respect,** *s.* die Selbstachtung. **--restraint,** *s.* die Selbstbeschränkung, Selbstbeherrschung. **--righteous,** *adj.* selbstgerecht. **--righteousness,** *s.* die Selbstgerechtigkeit. **--sacrifice,** *s,* die Selbstaufopferung. **--sacrificing,** *adj.* sich selbst aufopfernd, aufopferungsvoll. **-same,** *adj.* ebenderselbe, ein und derselbe. **--satisfied,** *adj.* selbstzufrieden. **--sealing,** *adj.* selbstdichtend, schußsicher (*tank*). **--seeker,** *s.* der Egoist. **--seeking,** *adj.* egoistisch, eigennützig. **--starter,** *s.* der Anlasser. **--styled,** *adj.* selbstbenannt. **--sufficiency,** *s.* der Hochmut, die Selbstgenügsamkeit, Selbstüberhebung; Selbstversorgung, Autarkie. **--sufficient,** *adj.* selbstgenügsam. **--suggestion,** *s.* die Autosuggestion. **--supporting,** *adj.* Selbstversorger–. **--surrender,** *s.* die Selbstaufgabe, Selbstpreisgabe. **--taught,** *adj.*; --*taught person*, der Autodidakt. **--timer,** *s.* der Selbstauslöser (*Phot.*). **--will,** *s.* der Eigenwille. **--willed,** *adj.* eigenwillig, eigensinnig.

self-ish [ˈsɛlfɪʃ], *adj.* selbstsüchtig, egoistisch. **-ishness,** *s.* die Selbstsucht, der Egoismus. **-less,** *adj.* selbstlos. **-lessness,** *s.* die Selbstlosigkeit.

sell [sɛl], 1. *ir.v.a.* verkaufen *to*, an; *at*, zu), veräußern, absetzen; (*sl.*) den Vorteil herausstellen, anpreisen; (*sl.*) (usually pass. *be sold*) anschmieren, anführen, hereinlegen (*a p.*); – *one's country*, sein Vaterland verraten; – *one's life dearly*, sein Leben teuer verkaufen; – *the pass*, Verrat begehen, treulos sein; *to be sold*, zu verkaufen; – *by auction*, versteigern; – *off* or *out*, ausverkaufen, räumen; *be sold out*, ausverkauft *or* nicht mehr auf Lager sein; – *a p. up*, einen auspfänden. 2. *ir.v.n.* verkaufen, handeln; sich verkaufen (lassen), Absatz finden, abgeben (*as goods*); – *out*, ausverkaufen. 3. *s.* (*sl.*) der Kniff, Schwindel, Betrug, Reinfall. **-er** [-ə], *s.* der Verkäufer; (*of goods*) Verkaufsschlager; *best -er*, sehr erfolgreiches Buch, der Reißer, Bestseller.

seltzer [ˈsɛltsə], *s.* das Selterwasser.

selvage, selvedge [ˈsɛlvɪdʒ], *s.* das Salband, die Salleiste, Gewebeleiste, Borte, feste (Webe)Kante.

sema-ntics [sɪˈmæntɪks], *pl.* (*sing. constr.*), die Wortbedeutungslehre, Semantik. **-phore** [ˈsɛməfɔ:], 1. *s.* der Signalapparat, Signalarm, das Flügelsignal (*Railw.*), optischer Telegraph, das Flaggenwinken (*Naut.*). 2. *v.a.* durch Winkzeichen signalisieren, winken. **-siology** [sɪmeɪzɪˈɔlədzɪ], *s. see* **-ntics.**

semblance [ˈsɛmbləns], *s.* die Ähnlichkeit (*to*, mit), der Anschein, äußere Form *or* Gestalt, die Erscheinung.

semeio-logy, -tics, *see* **semiology.**

sem-en [ˈsɪ:mən], *s.* (tierischer) Same(n). **-inal** [ˈsɛmɪnəl], *adj.* Samen– (*Bot., Anat.*), Zeugungs– (*Anat.*), Keim– (*Bot.*); (*fig.*) ursprünglich; schöpferisch, fruchtbar. **-ination** [-ˈneɪʃən], *s.* die Samenbildung (*Bot.*).

semi– [ˈsɛmɪ], *prefix* (*usually stressed*) Halb–, halb–. **--annual,** *adj.* halbjährlich, halbjährig. **--automatic,** *adj.* halbselbsttätig. **-breve,** *s.* ganze Note (*Mus.*). **--cantilever,** *adj.* halbfreitragend (*Arch.*). **-circle** *s.* der Halbkreis. **--ˈcircular,** *adj.* halbkreisförmig, Halbkreis–. **-ˈcolon,** *s.* der Strichpunkt, das Semikolon. **--detached,** *adj.* an einer Seite angebaut; --*detached house*, die eine Hälfte eines alleinstehenden Doppelhauses. **--educated,** *adj.* halbgebildet. **--final,** *s.* die Vorschlußrunde (*Sport*). **--fluid, --liquid,** *adj.* halbflüssig. **--manufactured,** *adj.* halbfertig. **--official,** *adj.* halbamtlich. **--precious,** *adj.* Halbedel–. **-quaver,** *s.* die Sechszehntelnote (*Mus.*). **--rigid,** *adj.* halbstarr (*airships*). **--skilled,** *adj.* angelernt. **--solid,** *adj.* halbfest. **-tone,** *s.* der Halbton, halber Ton (*Mus.*). **--tracked,** *adj.* Halbketten– (*vehicle*). **--transparent,** *adj.* halbdurchsichtig. **--tropical,** *adj.* halbtropisch. **--vowel,** *s.* der Halbvokal.

seminar [ˈsɛmɪnɑ:], *s.* das Seminar (*Univ.*). **-y** [-ərɪ], *s.* die Bildungsanstalt, Akademie, das (Priester)Seminar (*R.C.*); (*fig.*) die Pflanzschule, Pflanzstätte.

semi-ology [sɪ:mɪˈɔlədʒɪ], *s.*, **-otics** [-ˈɔtɪks], *pl.* (*sing. constr.*) die Symptomatologie (*Med.*).

semolina [sɛməˈlɪ:nə], *s.* der (Weizen)Gries.

sempiternal [sɛmpɪˈtə:nəl], *adj.* immerwährend, ewig.

sempstress [ˈsɛmpstrɪs], *s. see* **seamstress.**

senat-e [ˈsɛnət], *s.* der Senat (*also Univ.*), das Oberhaus (*Amer.*); *-e-house*, das Senatsgebäude (*Univ.*). **-or** [-ə], *s.* der Senator. **-orial** [-ˈtɔ:rɪəl], *adj.* senatorisch, Senats–. **-us** [səˈneɪtəs], der Senat (*Scots Univ.*).

send [sɛnd], **1.** *ir.v.a.* senden, schicken; befördern, absenden, übersenden, zuschicken, zukommen lassen. (*a*) (*with nouns*) – *one's love*, herzlich grüßen lassen (*to* (*Acc.*)); – *a message*, Bescheid schicken (*to* (*Dat.*)); – *one's regards*, grüßen lassen (*to* (*Acc.*)); *God – him a speedy release!* Gott gebe ihm baldige Erlösung; – *word*, sagen lassen (*Dat.*), benachrichtigen. (*b*) (*with verbal complement*) – *flying*, hinschleudern; – *packing*, fortjagen (*a p.*); – *staggering*, ins Taumeln bringen. (*c*) (*with adverbs*) – *away*, fortschicken, wegschicken; entlassen; – *down*, (zeitweise) relegieren (*Univ.*); – *forth*, hinausschicken, aussenden (*light*), hervorbringen, ausstoßen, von sich geben (*a cry*), veröffentlichen, verbreiten; – *in*, hineinschicken; einschicken, einreichen; – *in one's name*, sich melden; – *in one's papers*, seinen Abschied einreichen; – *off*, abschicken (*a th.*), entlassen (*a p.*); – *on*, vorausschicken; nachsenden (*a letter*); – *out*, hinausschicken, aussenden, verbreiten, veröffentlichen; – *round*, herumreichen, umlaufen lassen; – *up*, hinaufschicken; von sich geben, ausstoßen (*a cry*), in die Höhe treiben (*prices*), (*sl.*) einsperren. (*d*) (*with prepositions*) – *s.o. on an errand*, einem einen Auftrag geben, einen einen (Boten)Gang tun lassen; – *s.o. out of his mind*, einen rasend machen; – *a stone through the window*, einen Stein durchs Fenster werfen; – *a th. to a p.*, einem etwas schicken; – *to school*, zur Schule schicken; – *a p. to prison*, einen einsperren. **2.** *v.n.* schicken; – *for*. holen lassen, bestellen (*a th.*), kommen lassen (*a p.*); – *for the doctor*, den Arzt holen *or* rufen. **-er** [-ə], *s.* der (Ab)Sender. (*coll.*) **--off,** *s.* der Abschied, die Abschiedsfeier.

senescen-ce [səˈnɛsəns], *s.* das Altwerden, Altern. **-t** [-sənt], *adj.* alternd.

seneschal [ˈsɛnəʃəl], *s.* der Hausmeier, Majordomus (*Hist.*).

senil-e [ˈsɪ:nɑɪl], *adj.* greisenhaft, altersschwach; *-e decay*, die Altersschwäche. **-ity** [-ˈnɪlɪtɪ], *s.* die Greisenhaftigkeit, Altersschwäche.

senior [ˈsɪ:nɪə], 1. *adj.* älter; dienstälter, Haupt–; Ober– (*Mil.*); – *common room*, das Dozentenzimmer; – *partner*, der Hauptinhaber. 2. *s.* Ältere(r), *m.*, der Senior, Dienstältere(r), Rangältere(r), Vorgesetzte(r) *m.*; *he is my – by five years* or *five years my –*, er ist fünf Jahre älter als ich; *he is my – in office*, er geht mir im Dienstalter vor. **-ity** [-nɪˈɔrɪtɪ], *s.* höheres (Dienst)Alter; *by -ity*, nach der Anciennität.

senna [ˈsɛnə], *s.* Sennesblätter (*pl.*) (*Pharm.*).

sennight [ˈsɛnɑɪt], *s.* (*archaic*) acht Tage, eine Woche; *this day –*, heute vor *or* in acht Tagen.

sens-ation [sɛnˈseɪʃən], *s.* die Sinnesempfindung, Sinneswahrnehmung, der Sinneseindruck, das Gefühl; (*coll.*) der Eindruck, das Aufsehen, die Sensation; *make* or *create a -ation*, Aufsehen erregen. **-ational,** *adj.* (*coll.*) aufsehenerregend, Sensations–, sensationell; Sinnes–, Gefühls–, Empfindungs– (*Psych.*). **-ationalism,** *s.* (*coll.*) die Effekthascherei, Sensationssucht; der Sensualismus (*Psych.*). **-e** [sɛns], **1.** *s.* der Sinn; Sinnesfunktion, das Sinnesvermögen, Sinnesorgan; das Gefühl, Verständnis, die Empfänglichkeit, Empfindung; Vernunft, der Verstand; die Bedeutung, der Sinn (*of a word, etc.*). (*a*) (*with nouns*) *-e of beauty*, das Verständnis für Schönheit; *-e of direction*, der Orientierungssinn, Ortssinn, das Ortsgedächtnis; *-e of dread*, das Gefühl der Furcht; *-e of duty*, das Pflichtbewußtsein; *-e of feeling*, der Tastsinn; *-e of honour*, das Ehrgefühl; *-e of humour*, der Sinn für Humor;

–*e of justice*, der Gerechtigkeitssinn; –*e of proportion*, das Gefühl fürs richtige Verhältnis; –*e of propriety*, das Gefühl für Anstand; –*e of security*, sicheres Gefühl. (*b*) (*with adjectives*) *common –e*, gesunder Menschenverstand; *figurative* **–e**, übertragener *or* bildlicher Sinn; *the five –es*, die fünf Sinne; *good –e*, richtiges Gefühl; *proper –e*, eigentliche Bedeutung; *strict –e*, engerer Sinn. (*c*) (*with prepositions*) *in a* or *one –e*, in gewissem Sinne *or* gewisser Hinsicht; *be in one's* (*right*) *–es*, bei Sinnen sein; *man of –e*, verständiger Mann; *devoid of all –e*, völlig sinnlos; *out of one's –es*, von *or* nicht bei Sinnen; *bring s.o. to his –es*, einen zur Vernunft *or* Besinnung bringen. (*d*) (*with verbs*) *have the –e to do it*, gescheit genug sein es zu tun; *make –e of*, Sinn hineinbringen in, klug werden aus; *make no –e*, keinen Sinn geben; *talk –e*, vernünftig reden. **2.** *v.a.* ahnen, fühlen, empfinden, spüren. **–eless,** *adj.* sinnlos, unvernünftig, unsinnig; gefühllos, empfindunglos; ohnmächtig. **–elessness,** *s.* die Sinnlosigkeit; Gefühllosigkeit. **–ibility** [–ɪˈbɪlɪtɪ], *s.* das Empfindungsvermögen; die Empfänglichkeit, Empfindlichkeit (*to*, für), Empfindung, das Gefühl; *pl.* das Feingefühl, Zartgefühl. **–ible** [ˈsɛnsɪbl], *adj.* fühlbar, empfindbar, bemerkbar, wahrnehmbar, erkennbar, spürbar, merklich; verständig, vernünftig, einsichtig; *be –ible of*, empfinden, fühlen, merken; einsehen, würdigen, sich (*Dat.*) bewußt sein (*Gen.*). **–ibleness,** *s.* die Klugheit, Einsicht, Vernünftigkeit, Verständigkeit. **–itive** [–ɪtɪv], *adj.* Empfindungs–; Sinnes–; empfindend, empfindsam, zartfühlend, feinfühlig, fein (*ear, etc.*), empfindlich (*to*, für *or* gegen) (*also Phys.*); reizbar; lichtempfindlich (*Phot.*); *be –itive to*, empfänglich sein für, lebhaft empfinden; *–itive plant*, die Sinnpflanze, Mimose. **–itiveness, –itivity** [–ɪˈtɪvɪtɪ], *s.* die Empfindungsfähigkeit; Empfindlichkeit(*also Phys.*); das Feingefühl. **–itization** [–ɪtaɪˈzeɪʃən], *s.* das Lichtempfindlichmachen (*Phot.*). **–itize** [ˈsɛnsɪtaɪz], *v.a.* sensibilisieren, (licht)empfindlich machen. **–itized,** *adj.* lichtempfindlich. **–itizer,** *s.* der Sensibilisator (*Phot.*). **–orial** [–ˈsɔːrɪəl], *adj. see* **–ory. –orium** [–ˈsɔːrɪəm], *s.* der Sitz der bewußten Sinneswahrnehmungen (im Gehirn) (*Anat.*). **–ory** [ˈsɛnsərɪ], *adj.* Sinnes–, Empfindungs–. **–ual** [ˈsɛnsjʊəl], *adj.* (*often derogatory*) sinnlich, fleischlich, körperlich, wollüstig; sensualistisch (*Phil.*). **–ualism** *s.* der Sensualismus (*Phil.*), die Sinnlichkeit. **–ualist** *s.* der Sensualist (*Phil.*); Sinnenmensch. **–uality** [–juˈælɪtɪ], *s.* die Sinnlichkeit. **–ualize** [ˈsɛnsjʊəlaɪz], *v.a.* sinnlich machen. **–uous** [ˈsɛnsjʊəs], *adj.* sinnlich, Sinnes–, Sinnen–, sinnfällig. **–uousness** *s.* die Sinnlichkeit, Sinnfälligkeit.

sent [sɛnt], *see* **send;** *heaven* –, vom Himmel gesandt.

sentence [ˈsɛntəns], 1. *s.* der Satz (*Gram.*); Rechtsspruch, das Urteil (*Law*); die Strafe; *pass* –, das Urteil fällen (*on*, über); (*fig.*) ein Urteil fällen; *serve one's* –, seine Strafe absitzen; – *of death*, das Todesurteil; *pass* – *of death* (*up*)*on*, zum Tode verurteilen; *under* – *of death*, zum Tode verurteilt; – *of imprisonment*, die Freiheitsstrafe; *life* –, lebenslängliche Zuchthausstrafe. 2. *v.a.* das Urteil fällen *or* sprechen über (*Acc.*), verurteilen.

sententious [sɛnˈtɛnʃəs], *adj.* spruchreich, sentenzenreich, kurz und bündig; (*fig.*) aufgeblasen, affektiert, salbungsvoll. **–ness,** *s.* die Kürze, Bündigkeit; Aufgeblasenheit, Affektiertheit.

sentien–ce [ˈsɛnʃəns], *s.* das Gefühl, die Empfindung. **–t** [–ənt], *adj.* empfindend, fühlend.

sentiment [ˈsɛntɪmənt], *s.* das Gefühl, die Gefühlsregung; Empfindung, Empfindsamkeit, Gefühlsduselei; (*often pl.*) Meinung, Gesinnung, Haltung, der Gedanke; *man of* –, zartfühlender Mensch. **–al** [–ˈmɛntl], *adj.* gefühlvoll, empfindsam, rührselig, sentimental; gefühlsmäßig, Gefühls–; *–al novel*, empfindsamer *or* kitschiger Roman. **–alism,** *s.*, **–ality** [–ˈtælɪtɪ], *s.* die Empfindsamkeit, Sentimentalität, Gefühlsduselei. **–alist** [–ˈmɛntəlɪst], *s.* gefühlsduseliger Mensch. **–alize,** 1. *v.n.* sentimental sein *or* werden *or* reden *or* schreiben (*over* or *about*, über). 2. *v.a.* sentimental gestalten.

sent–inel [ˈsɛntɪnəl], *s.* die Schildwache, der Posten; (*fig.*) die Wache; *stand –inel*, Wache stehen. **–ry** [ˈsɛntrɪ], *s.* die Schildwache; Wache, der Posten; *on –ry*, auf Posten *or* Wache; *keep –ry over*, bewachen, Wache halten über; *stand –ry*, Posten stehen. **–ry-box,** *s.* das Schilderhaus. **–ry-go,** *s.* der Wachdienst.

sepal [ˈsɛpl], *s.* das Kelchblatt (*Bot.*).

separa–bility [sɛpərəˈbɪlɪtɪ], *s.* die Trennbarkeit. **–ble** [ˈsɛpərəbl], *adj.* trennbar. **–bleness,** *s.* die Trennbarkeit. **–te** [ˈsɛpəreɪt], 1. *v.a.* (ab)trennen, absondern, (aus)scheiden, entfernen; unterscheiden, auseinanderhalten; (zer)teilen, trennen (*Chem.*). 2. *v.n.* sich trennen, sich lossagen, sich lösen, sich (zer)teilen, sich absondern. 3. [ˈsɛpərət], *adj.* getrennt, geschieden, abgesondert, isoliert; einzeln, besonder, Sonder–, Separat– (*C.L.*); verschieden, zu unterscheiden(d); *keep –te*, auseinanderhalten. **–tely,** *adv.* besonders, getrennt. **–teness,** *s.* die Abgeschiedenheit, Isoliertheit. **–tion** [–ˈreɪʃən], *s.* die Trennung; Scheidung (*Chem.*); Ehescheidung, Ehetrennung (*Law*); *–tion allowance*, die Familienunterstützung (*Mil.*). **–tism,** *s.* der Separatismus, das Loslösungsbestreben. **–tist,** *s.* der Separatist, Sonderbündler; Sektierer (*Eccl.*). **–tive,** *adj.* Trennungs–, trennend. **–tor** [–reɪtə], *s.* der Scheidekamm, Schlichtkamm (*Weav.*), die Zentrifuge, der Milchentrahmer (*for milk*).

sepia [ˈsɪːpɪə], *s.* der Kuttelfisch, die Tintenschnecke (*Ichth.*); die Sepia (*colour*).

sepoy [ˈsɪːpɔɪ], *s.* der Sepoy.

sepsis [ˈsɛpsɪs], *s.* die Sepsis, Blutvergiftung; *see* **septic.**

sept– [sɛpt], *prefix* sieben–. **–ˈangular,** *adj.* siebenwinklig, siebeneckig. **–ˈember,** *s.* der September; *in –ember*, im September. **–enary** [sɛpˈtɪːnərɪ], 1. *adj.* Sieben–; *see* **–ennial.** 2. *s.* der Satz von sieben Dingen. **–ennial** [sɛpˈtɛnɪəl], *adj.* siebenjährig, siebenjährlich, alle sieben Jahre. **–entrional** [sɛpˈtɛntrɪənl], *adj.* nördlich, Nord–. **–et** [sɛpˈtɛt], *s.* das Septett (*Mus.*). **–i** [ˈsɛptɪ], *prefix, see* **sept–. –uagenarian** [sɛptjʊədʒəˈnɛːərɪən], 1. *adj.* siebzigjährig. 2. *s.* Siebzigjährige(r), *m.* **–uagesima** [–ˈdʒɛsɪmə], *s.* der (Sonntag) Septuagesimä. **–uagint** [ˈsɛptjʊədʒɪnt], *s.* die Septuaginta. **–uple** [ˈsɛptjuːpl], *adj.* siebenfach.

sept–al [ˈsɛptl], *adj.* Septal– (*Bot.*). **–ate** [–teɪt], *adj.* durch eine Scheidewand getrennt (*Bot., Zool.*). **–um** [–əm], *s.* die Scheidewand.

septic [ˈsɛptɪk], *adj.* fäulniserregend, septisch. **–aemia** [–tɪˈsɪːmɪə], *s.* die Sepsis.

sepul–chral [sɛˈpʌlkrəl], *adj.* Grab–, Begräbnis–; (*fig.*) Grabes–, düster. **–chre** [ˈsɛpəlkə], *s.* das Grab, die Gruft, Grabstätte. **–ture** [ˈsɛpəltʃə], *s.* das Begräbnis, die Beerdigung, (Toten)Bestattung.

seque–l [ˈsɪkwəl], *s.* die Folge; Folgeerscheinung, Wirkung; Fortsetzung (*of a story*); *in the –l*, nachher, in der Folge, wie sich herausstellte. **–nce** [–kwəns], *s.* die Reihenfolge, Aufeinanderfolge, Reihe, (Stufen)Ordnung; Sequenz (*Cards, Mus.*); Szene(*films*); (*fig.*) Folgerichtigkeit, logische Folge, die Konsequenz; *–nce of tenses*, die Zeitenfolge (*Gram.*). **–nt** [–wənt], 1. *adj.* (aufeinander)folgend (*to* or *on*, auf). 2. *s.* zeitliche *or* logische Folge. **–ntial** [sɪˈkwenʃəl], *adj.* folgend (*to*, auf).

sequest–er [sɪˈkwɛstə], *v.a.* (*usually v.r.*), entfernen, zurückziehen; *see also* **–rate** (*Law*). **–ered** [–təd], *adj.* abgeschieden, zurückgezogen, einsam. **–rate** [–treɪt, ˈsɪːkwəstreɪt], *v.a.* sequestrieren, beschlagnahmen (*Law*). **–ration** [sɪːkwəsˈtreɪʃən], *s.* die Absonderung, Entfernung, Ausschließung; Beschlagnahme, Sequestration, Zwangsverwaltung, der Sequester. **–rator** [ˈsɪːkwəstreɪtə], *s.* der Zwangsverwalter.

sequestrum [sɪˈkwɛstrəm], *s.* das Sequester, abgestorbenes Knochenstück (*Med.*).

sequin [ˈsɪːkwɪn], *s.* die Zechine (*Hist.*); die Spange.

sequoia [sɪˈkwɔɪə], *s.* die Riesentanne, der Mammutbaum (*Bot.*).

seraglio [səˈrɑːljoʊ], *s.* das Serial; der Harem.

serai [səˈrɑɪ, səˈreɪ, səˈrɑːɪ], *s.* die Karawanserei.

seraph [ˈsɛrəf], *s.* (pl. *–s* or *–im*) der Seraph. **–ic** [səˈræfɪk], *adj.*, seraphisch, (*fig.*) ekstatisch.

sere [sɪ:ə], *adj. see* **sear.**

serenade [sɛrəˈneɪd], 1. *s.* das Ständchen, die Abendmusik, Nachtmusik, Serenade. 2. *v.a.* ein Ständchen bringen (*Dat.*).

seren–e [səˈrɪ:n], *adj.* klar, hell; heiter, gelassen, ruhig; *His –e Highness*, Seine Durchlaucht. **–ity** [səˈrɛnɪtɪ], *s.* die Heiterkeit; Gelassenheit, heitere Ruhe; Durchlaucht (*as title*).

serf [sə:f], *s.* Leibeigne(r), *m.* **–dom** [–dəm], *s.* die Leibeigenschaft.

serge [sə:dʒ], *s.* die Serge, Sersche, Sarsche.

sergeant [ˈsɑ:dʒənt], *s.* der Sergeant, Unteroffizier (*Mil.*); *colour-–*, der Feldwebel; *drill-–*, der Exerzierunteroffizier; *quartermaster-–*, der Furier; *staff-–*, der Unterfeldwebel (*infantry*), Unterwachtmeister (*cavalry, artillery*). **–-major,** *s.* der Feldwebel (*infantry*), Wachtmeister (*cavalry, artillery*).

seria–l [ˈsɪ:ərɪəl], 1. *adj.* periodisch, Reihen–, Serien–; *–l number*, die Seriennummer. 2. *s.* das Lieferungswerk, Serienwerk, Fortsetzungswerk. **–lly,** *adv.* in Lieferungen, reihenweise. **–te** [–rɪeɪt], *adj.* in Reihen geordnet, Reihen–. **–tim** [–rɪˈeɪtɪm], *adv.* der Reihe nach.

seric–eous [sɛˈrɪʃəs], *adj.* seidig, seidenartig, Seiden–. **–ulture** [ˈsɛrɪkʌltʃə], *s.* die Seidenzucht.

series [ˈsɪ:ərɪz], *s.* die Reihe (*also Math.*), (Reihen)-Folge, Serie, der Satz; die Abteilung, Gruppe; – *of books*, die Bücherfolge; – *connexion*, die Reihenschaltung (*Elec.*).

serif [ˈsɛrɪf], *s.* der Haarstrich (*Typ.*).

serin [ˈsɛrɪn], *s.* der Girlitz (*Orn.*).

seringa [səˈrɪŋgə], *s.* der Pfeifenstrauch (*Bot.*).

serio-comic [ˈsɪ:rɪoʊˈkɔmɪk], *adj.* ernst-komisch.

serious [ˈsɪərɪəs], *adj.* ernst, ernst gemeint, ernsthaft, ernstlich, ernstzunehmend, gefährlich; bedeutend, (ge)wichtig, seriös; gesetzt, feierlich; *be –*, es ernst meinen (*about*, mit); – *attempt*, ernsthafter Versuch; – *enemy*, ernstzunehmender Feind; – *illness*, gefährliche *or* schwere Krankheit; – *matter*, wichtige Sache. **–ly,** *adv.* ernst, im Ernst, ernstlich; *–ly now*, allen Ernstes, ernst gesprochen. **–ness,** *s.* die Ernsthaftigkeit, der Ernst; die Wichtigkeit.

serjeant [ˈsɑ:dʒənt], *s. see* **sergeant;** *–-at-arms*, der Stabträger, höchster Ordnungsbeamter (*Parl.*); *–-at-law*, (*archaic*) höherer Rechtsanwalt.

sermon [ˈsə:mən], *s.* die Predigt; (*coll.*) Gardinenpredigt, Strafpredigt; *preach a –*, eine Predigt halten; – *on the Mount*, die Bergpredigt. **–ize** [–naɪz], 1. *v.n.* im Predigerton sprechen; Moral predigen. 2. *v.a.* vorpredigen (*Dat.*), eine Moralpredigt halten (*Dat.*), abkanzeln.

sero–logy [sɪəˈrɔlədʒɪ], *s.* die Serumkunde. **–sity** [–sɪtɪ], *s*, seröser Zustand; seröse Flüssigkeit. **–us** [–əs], *adj.* (blut)wässerig; serös.

serpent [ˈsə:pənt], *s.* (große und giftige) Schlange (*also Astr. & fig.*). **–ine** [–ɑɪn], 1. *adj.* schlangenartig, schlangenförmig, Schlangen–; (*fig.*) sich schlängelnd *or* windend, geschlängelt. 2. *s.* die Serpentine, Schlangenlinie; der Serpentin (*Miner.*).

serpig–inous [səˈpɪdʒɪnəs], *adj.* flechtenartig. **–o** [–ˈpɑɪgoʊ], *s.* fressende Flechte (*Med.*).

serradilla [sɛrəˈdɪlə], *s.* die Serradella (*Bot.*).

serrat–e [ˈsɛrɛɪt], *adj.* **–ed** [səˈreɪtɪd], *adj.* gezähnt, gezackt, zackig. **–ion** [səˈreɪʃən], *s.* die Auszackung, Auszähnung.

serried [ˈsɛrɪd], *adj.* dicht(gedrängt), geschlossen (*ranks*).

serum [ˈsɪ:ərəm], *s.* das Blutwasser, Blutserum; Heilserum, Schutzserum.

serval [ˈsə:vəl], *s.* der Serval, die Buschkatze.

servant [ˈsə:vənt], *s.* der Diener (*also fig.*), Dienstbote, Knecht; (also *–-girl*) das Dienstmädchen, die Magd, Dienerin; *pl.* Dienstboten (*pl.*), das Gesinde; *civil –*, Staatsbeamte(r) *m.*; *domestic –*, Hausangestellte(r) *m.*; (*coll.*) *your humble –*, meine Wenigkeit; *your obedient –*, Ihr sehr ergebener (*in official letters*); *–-girl*, das Dienstmädchen, die Magd; – *problem*, die Dienstbotenfrage; *–'s hall*, die Gesindestube.

serve [sə:v], 1. *v.a.* dienen (*Dat.*); bedienen (*customers, guns*); servieren, reichen, vorlegen, auftragen (*food*); verwalten (*an office*); befriedigen, begnügen; bekleiden (*ropes*) (*Naut.*); belegen (*female animal*); – *an apprenticeship*, in die Lehre gehen; – *the ball*, den Ball angeben *or* anschlagen (*Tenn.*); – *his needs*, seine Bedürfnisse befriedigen; – *a notice* or *summons on a p.*, einen vorladen *or* vor Gericht zitieren. – *my purpose*, meinen Zwecken dienen; – *no purpose*, nichts nützen; – *one's sentence*, – *time*, seine Strafe abbußen *or* absitzen; – *one's time*, seine Zeit abdienen; *it –s his turn*, es paßt sich gerade für ihn, es erweist ihm einen Dienst; – *a warrant* or *writ on a p.*, – *a p. with a warrant* or *writ*, einem einen Gerichtsbefehl zustellen; *first come first –d*, wer zuerst kommt mahlt zuerst; *if my memory –s me right*, wenn mein Gedächtnis mich nicht im Stiche läßt; *it –s him for a handkerchief*, es dient ihm als Taschentuch *or* statt eines Taschentuchs; – *out*, austeilen (*supplies*); ausdienen (*time*); (*fig.*) sich rächen an (*Dat.*), vergelten (*a p.* (*Dat.*), *for a th.* (*Acc.*)), mit gleicher Münze bezahlen; – *up*, auftragen, servieren (*food*); (*fig., coll.*) auftischen. 2. *v.n.* dienen (*also Mil.*), nützen (*for*, zu); Dienst tun (*Mil.*) (*with*, bei); in Dienst sein *or* stehen, angestellt sein (*with*, bei); aufwarten, bedienen (*C.L.*), servieren (*at table*); passen, geeignet *or* günstig sein; sich bieten; genügen, reichen, hinlänglich sein; – *on a committee*, in einem Ausschuß tätig sein; angeben (*Tenn.*); *as occasion –s*, bei passender Gelegenheit; *it –s him right*, das geschieht ihm recht; – *s.o. shamefully*, einen schändlich behandeln; – *to convince*, dazu dienen zu überzeugen. 3. *s.* die Angabe (*Tenn.*). **–r** [–ə] *s.* der Gehilfe des Zelebranten (*Eccl.*); *pl.* das Besteck.

service [ˈsə:vɪs], **1.** *s.* der Dienst; die Dienstleistung, Hilfe, Gefälligkeit, der Beistand; Nutzen, Vorteil; die (Dienst)Stellung (*of servants*); öffentlicher Dienst, der (Heeres– *etc.*)Dienst; die Bedienung (*also Artil.*), das Aufwarten, Servieren; (also *divine –*) der Gottesdienst, kirchliche Handlung; das Service, Tafelgerät; der Verkehr, Verkehrsdienst, Transport; die Angabe (*Tenn.*); das (Tau)Bekleidungsmaterial (*Naut.*); die Zustellung (*of a writ*) (*Law*); *the –s*, die Wehrmacht; **(a)** (*with attrib.*) – *abroad*, der Auslandsdienst; *active –*, der Wehrdienst, Gefechtsdienst, aktiver Dienst; *civil –*, der Staatsdienst, die Beamtenschaft; *divine –*, der Gottesdienst; *foreign –*, see – *abroad*; *marriage –*, die Trauhandlung; *merchant –*, die Handelsmarine; *military –*, der Kriegsdienst, Waffendienst, Militärdienst; *universal military –*, die allgemeine Wehrpflicht; *news –*, der Nachrichtendienst; *night –*, der Nachtdienst (*Railw., etc.*); *passenger –*, der Personenverkehr; *postal –*, der Postdienst; *press –*, der Pressedienst; *public –*, öffentlicher Dienst; *senior –*, die Marine; *social –*, soziale Arbeit; *telephone –*, der Telephondienst; *train –*, die Bahnverbindung, der Bahnverkehr; **(b)** (*with verbs*) *attend –*, den Gottesdienst besuchen; *conduct* or *take the –*, den Gottesdienst abhalten; *do* or *render s.o. a –*, einem einen Gefallen erweisen *or* Dienst leisten; **(c)** (*with prepositions*) *be at a p.'s –*, einem zu Diensten stehen; *place s.th. at a p.'s –*, einem etwas zur Verfügung stellen; *in –*, in Dienst (*of a p.*), dienstbar sein (*to* (*Dat.*)) (*of a th.*); *in the –*, im Dienst; *go into –*, in Stellung gehen; *take s.o. into –*, einen in Stellung nehmen; *go into –*, dienstbar werden (*to* (*Dat.*)) (*of a th.*); *be of – to*, nützlich sein *or* nützen (*Dat.*), von Nutzen sein für; *on active –*, im aktiven Dienst; *on Her Majesty's –*, frei durch Ablösung (*on letters*); *out of –*, außer Betrieb; *go out to –*, in Stellung gehen. **2.** *v.a.* instandhalten, warten (*a vehicle, etc.*) (*Mil.*). **–able** [–əbl], *adj.* tauglich, dienlich, nützlich (*to*, für); brauchbar, verwendbar; haltbar, dauerhaft, strapazfähig (*as cloth*). **–ableness,** *s.* die Zweckdienlichkeit, Nützlichkeit, Brauchbarkeit. **–-corps,** *s.* Versorgungstruppen, Fahrtruppen (*pl.*) (*Mil.*). **–-court,** *s.* das Aufschlagsfeld (*Tenn.*). **–-dress,** *s.* der Dienstanzug (*Mil.*). **–-flat,** *s.* die Etagenwohnung mit Bedienung. **–-hatch,** *s.* die Serviertür. **–-line,** *s.* die Aufschlagslinie (*Tenn.*). **–-pipe,** *s.* das Zuleitungsrohr, Anschlußrohr.

--station, *s.* die Tankstelle, Reparaturwerkstätte (*Motor.*).
service-berry [–ˈbɛrɪ], *s.* die Elzbeere. **--tree,** *s.* der Sperberbaum.
serviette [sə:vɪˈɛt], *s.* die Serviette, das Mundtuch.
servil–e [ˈsə:vɑɪl], *adj.* sklavisch, knechtisch; unterwürfig; kriechend, Sklaven–. **–ity** [–ˈvɪlɪtɪ], *s.* sklavische Unterwürfigkeit, der Knechtsinn, die Kriecherei.
serving [ˈsə:vɪŋ], see **serve;** *s.* die Portion. **--girl,** *s.* (*archaic*) das Dienstmädchen. **--man,** *s.* (*archaic*) der Diener.
servit–or [ˈsə:vɪtə], *s.* (*Poet.*) der Diener; (*archaic*) Stipendiat. **–ude** [–tju:d], *s.* die Knechtschaft, Sklaverei; die Servitut (*Scots Law*); *in –ude to,* in einem Dienstverhältnis zu; *penal –ude,* die Zwangsarbeit, Zuchthausstrafe.
sesame [ˈsɛsəmɪ], *s.* der Sesam (*Bot.*); das Sesamöl; *open –!* Sesam, tu dich auf!
seseli [ˈsɪsɪlɪ], *s.* der Bergfenchel, Sesel (*Bot.*).
sesqui– [ˈsɛskwɪ], *prefix* anderthalb. **–alter,** *s. see* **–ocellus. –alteral,** *adj.* anderthalbmal soviel, im Verhältnis von 3:2. **–centennial,** *adj.* (& *s.*) hundertfünfzigjährig(e Feier). **–ocellus,** *s.* großer Tupfen mit eingeschlossenem kleinerem (*butterflies' wings*). **–pedalian,** *adj.* vielsilbig, schwerfällig, ungelenk (*of a word*). **–tertial,** *adj.* im Verhältnis von 4:3.
sessile [ˈsɛsɑɪl], *adj.* stiellos (*Bot.*).
session [ˈsɛʃən], *s.* die Sitzung, Sitzungsperiode; akademisches Jahr (*Univ.*); *pl.* Gerichtssitzungen (*pl.*); *petty –s,* summarisches Gericht; *quarter –s,* das vierteljährliche Grafschaftsgericht. **–al,** *adj.* Sitzungs–.
sest–et [sɛsˈtɛt], *s.* das Sextett (*Mus.*), zweite Hälfte eines Sonetts (*Metr.*). **–ina** [–ˈtɪ:nə], *s.* die Sestine (*Metr.*).
set [sɛt], **1.** *ir.v.a.* setzen (*also sails, type*), stellen (*also a watch, a problem*), legen; (ein)richten, einsetzen, festsetzen, bestimmen, niederlegen; angeben (*tempo*); zurechtsetzen, zurechtstellen, zurechtmachen, anlegen, anordnen; fassen (*precious stones*); decken (*the table*); in Musik setzen, vertonen; (ein)pflanzen (*trees, etc.*): gerinnen machen (*milk*); erstarren machen (*metals*); einrichten, einrenken (*broken limb*): schärfen, schleifen, abziehen (*knives*), richten (*files*), schränken (*saws*); richten (*one's mind on,* die Gedanken auf (*Acc.*)); (vor)stehen (*birds*) (*Sport*); **(a)** (*with nouns*) *– bounds to,* see *– limits to*; *– a dog on* or *at,* einen Hund hetzen auf; *– an examination paper,* Prüfungsfragen stellen, Prüfungsaufgaben stellen; *– an example,* ein Beispiel geben; *– eyes on,* zu Gesicht bekommen; *– one's face against,* eine ablehnende Haltung annehmen gegen; *– the fashion,* den Ton angeben, die Mode angeben *or* einführen; *– fire to,* Feuer legen an, in Brand stecken; *have one's hair –,* sich die Haare in Wellen legen lassen; *– one's hand to,* Hand legen an; unterschreiben; *– one's heart on,* see *– one's mind on*; *– a hen,* eine Henne setzen; *– one's hopes on,* Hoffnung setzen auf; *– limits to,* Grenzen setzen (*Dat.*); *– one's mind on,* versessen sein auf; *– one's mouth,* den Mund zusammenziehen; *– the pace,* den Schritt angeben; *– pen to paper,* die Feder ansetzen; *– a price on,* einen Preis setzen auf; *– s.o. a problem,* einem ein Problem zur Aufgabe stellen; *– sail,* in See gehen; *– sail for,* auslaufen *or* abreisen nach; *– store by,* Wert legen auf, hochschätzen, Wert beimessen (*Dat.*); *– s.o. a task,* einem eine Aufgabe stellen; *– one's teeth,* die Zähne zusammenbeißen; *– a trap,* eine Falle stellen; *– great value on,* hoch bewerten, hohen Wert legen auf; **(b)** (*with adverbs*) *– afoot,* see *– on foot*; *– apart,* beiseitelegen, auf die Seite legen; *– aside,* beiseitelegen, beiseitesetzen; verwerfen; aufheben, umstoßen; *– back,* zurücksetzen; *– by,* zurücklegen, sparen; *– down,* niedersetzen, hinsetzen (*a th.*); absetzen; aussteigen lassen (*a p.*); niederschreiben, aufschreiben (*in writing*); halten (*for,* für); zuschreiben (*to* (*Dat.*)); auslegen, erklären (*to,* als); *– forth,* darlegen, dartun, an den Tag legen, zeigen; erklären, auseinandersetzen; *– off,* schmücken, zieren; hervorheben, hervortreten lassen, zur Geltung bringen; anrechnen, ausgleichen, beheben (*deficiency, etc.*); veranlassen (*doing,* zu tun); *– on,* anstellen, antreiben (*a p.*), hetzen (*dogs, etc.*) (*to,* auf); *be – on,* erpicht *or* versessen sein auf; **(c)** (*with prepositions*) *– against,* entgegensetzen, gegenüberstellen (*Dat.*); *– a p. against a th.,* einen gegen etwas einnehmen; *– o.s. against,* sich auflehnen gegen, sich zur Wehr setzen gegen; *– at defiance,* Trotz bieten (*Dat.*); *– at ease,* beruhigen; *– s.o. at his ease,* einem die Befangenheit nehmen; *– at liberty,* befreien, in Freiheit setzen; *– at nought* or *naught,* in den Wind schlagen; *– at rest,* beruhigen; *– s.o.'s mind at rest,* einen beruhigen; *– at variance,* entzweien; *– before,* vorsetzen, vorlegen, darlegen, ausbreiten (*Dat.*); *in action,* in Gang *or* zum Funktionieren bringen; *– in order,* ordnen, in Ordnung bringen; *– one's house in order,* sein Haus bestellen; *– s.o. on doing s.th.,* einen veranlassen *or* bewegen etwas zu tun, einem aufgeben etwas zu tun; *– on edge,* hochkantig stellen; (*fig.*) *– s.o.'s teeth* or *nerves on edge,* einen nervös machen; *– on fire,* in Brand stecken; *he won't – the Thames on fire,* er ist keine Geistesgröße, er hat das Pulver nicht erfunden; *– on foot,* zustande bringen, in die Wege leiten, einleiten, beginnen; *– on high,* erheben; *– to music,* vertonen, in Musik setzen, komponieren; *– to rights,* in Ordnung bringen; *– to work,* beschäftigen, zur Arbeit anstellen; **(d)** (*with verbs*) *– s.o. to do,* einem aufgeben zu tun; *– o.s. to do,* sich vornehmen, sich angelegen sein lassen zu tun; *– going,* in Gang setzen; *– a p. laughing,* einen zum Lachen bringen; *– a p. thinking,* einem zu denken geben. **2.** *ir.v.n.* gerinnen, erstarren, fest werden, ansetzen, einen starren Ausdruck annehmen (*of face*); laufen (*of tide*), wehen, kommen (*of wind*); untergehen (*sun, etc.*); vorstehen (*as dogs*) (*Hunt.*); **(a)** (*with prepositions*) *– about,* anfangen, beginnen, sich anschicken (*doing,* zu tun) (*coll.*) herfallen über (*a p.*); *– to work,* sich daranmachen *or* darangehen; *– upon,* herfallen über (*a p.*); **(b)** (*with adverbs*) *– forth,* sich aufmachen, aufbrechen, ausziehen (*for,* nach); *– forth on a journey,* eine Reise antreten; *– forward,* sich aufmachen *or* auf den Weg machen; *– in,* eintreten, sich einstellen; einsetzen (*as weather*); *– off,* sich aufmachen; sich anschicken; *– on,* anfangen, einsetzen (*machines, etc.*); *– out,* aufbrechen, sich auf den Weg machen (*for,* nach); *– out on a journey,* eine Reise antreten; sich anschicken, damit beginnen (*by* or *with doing,* zu tun); (*fig.*) ausgehen (*from,* von); *– to,* ernstlich darangehen, sich machen an; zu kämpfen beginnen; *– up,* sich niederlassen *or* etablieren; *– up for o.s.,* sich selbstständig machen, sich einen eignen Hausstand gründen, (ein Geschäft) anfangen; *– up for,* sich ausgeben für, sich aufspielen als; sich anmaßen. **3.** *adj.* fest, unbeweglich, starr, festgesetzt, bestimmt, vorgeschrieben; versessen, erpicht (*on,* auf), entschlossen (*on,* zu); wohlgesetzt, wohldurchdacht, formell (*speech, etc.*); *be hard –,* in bedrängter Lage *or* großer Not; *– books,* vorgeschriebene Bücher; *at – distances,* in bestimmten Entfernungen; *– face,* starre Miene; *– purpose,* die Absicht, fester Vorsatz; *– speech,* wohldurchdachte Rede; *with – teeth,* mit zusammengebissenen Zähnen; *thick-–,* untersetzt; *well-–,* gut gebaut. **4.** *s.* (*of things*) der Satz (*also Tenn.*), die Garnitur, das Besteck (*of instruments*), Service (*of crockery*); die Menge (*Math.*), Reihe, Folge, Serie, Sammlung, Kollektion (*C.L.*); (*of persons*) der Kreis, die Gruppe, Gesellschaft, Clique, Sippschaft, Bande; Haltung, Lage (*of head, etc.*); der Sitz, Schnitt (*of dress*); Lauf, die Richtung (*of wind*); (*fig.*) Strömung; Neigung; die Dekoration, (Bühnen)Ausstattung, das Bühnenbild (*Theat., Film*); das Gerät, der Apparat (*Rad.*); die Tour (*Danc.*); der Ableger, Setzling (*Hort.*); die Partie (*Tenn., etc.*), das Festwerden, Hartwerden (*of liquids*); Stehen, Vorstehen (*of dogs*) (*Hunt.*); der Untergang (*of sun*) (*Poet.*); das Lager (*of a badger*); *– of teeth,* das Gebiß; (*coll.*) *a bad –,* schlechte Gesellschaft; (*sl.*) *make a dead – at,* heftig angreifen, nicht loslassen wollen; (*sl.*) *make a dead – at men,* nach Männern angeln (*of women*). **--back,** *s.* derbe Abfertigung, der Dämpfer. **--off,** *s.* der Kontrast, Gegensatz; Schmuck, die Zierde; die Gegenforderung, Gegenrechnung; Entschädigung,

der Ausgleich (*against*, für) (*C.L.*). **--screw,** *s.* die Klemmschraube, Stellschraube (*Tech.*). **--square,** *s.* das Zeichendreieck, Winkellineal. **--to,** *s.* (*coll.*) heftiger Streit, die Schlägerei, das Handgemenge. **--up,** *s.* (*coll.*) der Aufbau, die Anlage, Anordnung, Haltung; der Plan, Entwurf; *see* **setting.**

setaceous [sɪˈteɪʃəs], *adj.* borstig, Borsten–, borstenartig.

settee [sɛˈtɪ:], *s.* das Sofa, der Polsterbank, Polstersitz.

setter [ˈsɛtə], *s.* der Vorstehhund; (*often in comps.*) Setzer, e.g. *type--*, der Schriftsetzer. **–wort,** *s.* stinkende Nieswurz (*Bot.*).

setting [ˈsɛtɪŋ], *s.* das Setzen; Fassen, Einfassen (*of jewels*); die Fassung; Bettung (*Tech.*); (*fig.*) das Milieu, die Umgebung, der Hintergrund, Rahmen; Untergang (*of sun, etc.*); das Hartwerden, Festwerden, Erstarren, die Gerinnung (*of fluid body*); Einstellung, Einrichtung (*Tech.*), Vertonung (*Mus.*); Bühnenausstattung, Szenerie (*Theat.*); *claw--*, die Ajourfassung; *crown--*, die Kastenfassung. **--rule,** *s.* die Setzlinie (*Typ.*). **--stick,** *s.* der Winkelhaken (*Typ.*).

settl–e [ˈsɛtl], 1. *s.* der Ruhesitz, lange Holzbank. 2. *v.n.* sich setzen *or* niederschlagen (*as sediment*); sich festsetzen (*as a disease*); sich ansiedeln *or* niederlassen, ansässig werden (*in a place*); sich senken *or* sacken (*as walls*); anlagern, sich abklären (*as a liquid*); fest werden; (*fig.*) sich entscheiden *or* entschließen; sich einigen *or* abfinden, abrechnen, eins werden; sich aufklären, beständig werden (*as weather*); nachlassen, sich legen (*as fury*); *allow to –e*, absitzen lassen; (*with adverbs*) *–e down*, sinken, sich senken; sich setzen (*as sediment*); sich niederlassen, sich häuslich einrichten, sich ins tägliche Leben zurückfinden, sich zurechtfinden *or* hineinfinden; *not –e down*, nicht zur Ruhe kommen; *–e down to work*, Arbeit wieder aufnehmen; *–e in*, einziehen (*in a new house*); *it –ed for rain*, es wurde regnerisch; *–e into*, allmählich annehmen, übergehen in (*Acc.*); *–e up*, (*coll.*) eine Rechnung bezahlen *or* begleichen; *–e* (*up*) *on*, sich entschließen *or* entscheiden über; *–e out*, ausscheiden, ausfallen (*of sediment*). 3. *v.a* setzen, zurechtmachen, festigen, festsetzen, feststellen; entscheiden, bestimmen, abschließen, abmachen, ordnen, regeln (*a matter*); bezahlen, begleichen (*a debt*); schlichten, ausgleichen (*disputes, etc.*); ansiedeln (*population*), versorgen, sicherstellen, etablieren (*a p.*); aussetzen (*on a p.*, einem) (*sum of money*); sicher stellen, verschreiben, vermachen (*on a p.* (*Dat.*)), übertragen (*on*, auf) (*property*); (*coll.*) erledigen, abtun (*a p.*); *that –es it*, das hat noch gefehlt; *that is –ed*, das ist ausgemacht; *–e o.s.*, sich niederlassen, (*fig.*) sich in Ruhe anschicken (*to*, zu), sich heranmachen (*to*, an). **–ed** [–d], *adj.* fest, bestimmt; versorgt, verheiratet; entschieden, entschlossen; *be –ed*, ansässig sein; *–ed abode*, ständiger Wohnort; *–ed conviction*, feste Überzeugung; *–ed habit*, eingewurzelte Gewohnheit; *–ed life*, ruhiges Leben; *–ed weather*, beständiges Wetter. **–ement,** *s.* die Festsetzung, Beilegung, Schlichtung, Begleichung, der Ausgleich, das Abkommen, Übereinkommen; Liquidierung, Abrechnung, der Abschluß (*C.L.*); die Versorgung, Unterbringung, Etablierung (*of dependents*); Besiedelung, Ansiedelung, Niederlassung, Siedlung; Kolonie, soziale Arbeitsgemeinschaft (*in England*); die Aussetzung, (Eigentums)Übertragung, das Vermächtnis, die Rente (*Law*); *act of –ement*, das Gesetz zur Festsetzung der Thronfolge; *come to* or *reach a –ement*, ein Übereinkommen treffen, zu einem Vergleich gelangen; *compulsory –ement*, der Zwangsvergleich; *day of –ement*, (*fig.*) der Tag der Abrechnung; *make a –ement upon*, einem ein Vermächtnis aussetzen; *marriage –ement*, der Ehekontrakt; *University –ement*, das Universitätshilfswerk (im Armenviertel). **–er** [ˈsɛtlə], *s.* der Ansiedler, Kolonist; (*coll.*) das Ausschlaggebende *or* Entscheidende; (*sl.*) derbe Abfertigung *or* derber Schlag. **–ing,** *s.* die Ansiedelung (*of a country*); Beilegung (*of disputes*); Abrechnung (*C.L.*); Anlagerung, Ablagerung, das Ablagern, Absetzen (*Tech.*); *pl.* der Bodensatz (*Tech.*). **–ing-day,** *s.* **der Abrechnungstag.**

seven [ˈsɛvən], 1. *num. adj.* sieben; *–-league boots*, Siebenmeilenstiefel (*pl.*); *–-Years War*, Siebenjähriger Krieg. 2. *s.* die Sieben; *the – of clubs*, Treff sieben (*Cards*); *be at sixes and –s*, auf dem Kopf stehen, in Verwirrung sein; uneinig sein (*about*, über). **–fold,** *adj.* siebenfach. **–teen** [–ˈtɪ:n], *num. adj.* siebzehn; *sweet –teen*, blühende Jugendschönheit. **–teenth,** 1. *num. adj.* siebzehnt. 2. *s.* das Siebzehntel. **–th,** 1. *num. adj.* siebent. 2. *s.* das Siebentel; die Septime (*Mus.*). **–thly,** *adv.* siebentens. **–ties** [–tɪz], *pl.* die Siebziger, siebziger Jahre. **–tieth** [–tɪ:ɪθ], 1. *num. adj.* siebzigst. 2. *s.* das Siebzigstel. **–ty** [–tɪ], 1. *num. adj.* siebzig; *–ty-one*, einundsiebzig. 2. *s.* die Siebzig.

sever [ˈsɛvə], 1. *v.a.* trennen, abtrennen; teilen (*Law*); (*fig.*) lösen. 2. *v.n.* sich trennen, reißen (*as a rope*). **–ance,** *s.* die Trennung; *–ance of relations*, die Lösung *or* der Abbruch der Beziehungen.

several [ˈsɛvərəl], 1. *adj.* besonder, einzeln; Sonder– (*Law*); *pl.* mehrere, verschiedene; *three – armies*, drei verschiedene Heere; *joint and –*, Gesamt– (*Law*); *each – part*, jeder einzelne Teil; *– large ships*, mehrere große Schiffe; *– times*, mehrmals; *they went their – ways*, sie gingen jeder ihrer Wege. 2. *s.* mehrere, verschiedene. **–ly,** *adv.* besonders, einzeln; *jointly and –ly*, einzeln und gemeinsam.

severance *see* **sever.**

sever–e [sɪˈvɪ:ə], *adj.* streng ((*up*)*on*, gegen); heftig stark (*as pain*); ernst, schmucklos (*in style*); rauh (*as weather*), genau, gründlich, exakt (*as a test*); schlimm, schwer (*accident, etc.*); hart, schwierig, mühsam; *leave –ely alone*, überhaupt nichts zu tun haben wollen mit. **–ity** [–ˈvɛrɪtɪ], *s.* die Strenge, Schärfe (*on*, gegen); Genauigkeit; Härte, Heftigkeit, Rauheit.

sew [soʊ], 1. *v.a.* nähen; heften, broschieren (*a book*); *– on*, annähen; *– up*, zunähen, zusammennähen. 2. *v.n.* nähen. **–er,** *s.* der Näher, die Näherin. **–ing,** *s.* das Nähen, die Näharbeit, Näherei; *–ing-machine*, die Nähmaschine.

sew–age [ˈsjʊ:ɪdʒ], *s.* das Kloakenwasser, Sielwasser; *–age-farm*, das Rieselgut. **–er** [ˈsjʊ:ə], *s.* der Abzugskanal, Siel, die Kloake; *–er-gas*, das Faulschlammgas; *–er-rat*, die Wanderratte.

sewing *see* **sew.**

sex [sɛks], *s.* (natürliches) Geschlecht; Geschlechtliche(s), *n.*, geschlechtliche Eigenart; *– appeal*, erotische Anziehungskraft, der Sexappeal; *of both –es*, beiderlei Geschlechts; *the fair –*, das schöne Geschlecht; *the gentle –*, das zarte Geschlecht. **--crime,** *s.* das Sexualverbrechen. **--determination,** *s.* die Geschlechtsbestimmung. **--education,** *s.* die Sexualpädagogik. **--equality,** *s.* die Gleichheit der Geschlechter. **–less,** *adj.* geschlechtslos, asexuell. **–ual** [–jʊəl], *adj.* geschlechtlich, Geschlechts–, sexuell, Sexual–; *–ual desire*, der Geschlechtstrieb; *–ual intercourse*, geschlechtlicher Verkehr; *have –ual intercourse with*, geschlechtlich verkehren mit; *–ual pleasure*, der Geschlechtsgenuß. **–uality** [–jʊˈælɪtɪ], *s.* die Geschlechtlichkeit, Sexualität. **–ually,** *adv.* in geschlechtlicher Hinsicht. **–y,** *adj.* (*sl.*) geschlechtlich erregt *or* interessiert.

sexage–narian [sɛksədʒɪˈnɛ:ərɪən], 1. *s.* der *or* die Sechzigjährige. 2. *adj.* sechzigjährig. **–nary** [–ˈdʒɪ:nərɪ], *adj.* sechzigteilig; sechzigjährig. **–sima** [–ˈdʒɛsɪmə], *s.* der Sonntag Sexagesimä. **–simal** [–ˈdʒɛsɪməl], *adj.* sechzigst; Sexagesimal–, mit 60 als Grundzahl, sechzigfach untergeteilt.

sex–angle [ˈsɛksæŋgl], *s.* das Sechseck, Hexagon. **–angular** [–gjʊlə], *adj.* sechseckig, sechswinkelig, hexagonal. **–centenary** [–sɛnˈtɪ:nərɪ], 1. *s.* die Sechshundertjahrfeier. 2. *adj.* sechshundertjährig. **–digitate** [–ˈdɪdʒɪteɪt], *adj.* sechsfingerig. **–ennial** [–ˈɛ:nɪəl], *adj.* sechsjährig sechsjährlich. **–fid** [–fɪd], *adj.* sechsspaltig (*Bot.*). **–foil** [–fɔɪl], *s.* sechsblätterige Figur (*Arch.*). **–illion** [–ˈɪlɪən], *s. see* **–tillion.** **–partite** [–ˈpɑ:tɑɪt], *adj.* sechsteilig. **–tain** [ˈsɛksteɪn], *s.* sechszeilige Strophe, das Hexastichon. **–tant** [ˈsɛkstənt], *s.* der Sextant. **–tet(te)** [–ˈtɛt], *s.* das Sextett. **–tillion** [–ˈtɪlɪən], *s.* sechste Potenz einer Million (= 1 mit 36 Nullen); (*French & Amer.*) tausend zur siebten Potenz (= 1 mit 21 Nullen). **–to**

[ˈsɛkstou], *s.* das Sextoformat, Sextern. **–todecimo** [–ˈdɛsɪmou], *s.* das Sedez(format), die Sechzehntelbogengröße. **–tuple** [–ˈtjuːpl], 1. *adj.* sechsfach. 2. *v.a.* versechsfachen.
sexton [sɛkstən], *s.* der Küster; Totengräber. **– -beetle,** *s.* der Aaskäfer.
sexual, *see* **sex.**
shabb–ily [ˈʃæbɪlɪ], *adv. see* **–y.** **–iness** [–ɪnɪs], *s.* die Schäbigkeit. **–y** [ˈʃæbɪ], *adj.* schäbig (*also fig.*), abgetragen, abgenutzt, fadenscheinig; (*fig.*) niederträchtig, lumpig, gemein; (*coll.*) filzig, knickerig. **–y-genteel,** *adj.* schäbig-fein.
shabrack [ˈʃæbræk], die Schabracke (*Mil.*).
shack [ʃæk], *s.* die Hütte, Bude.
shackle [ˈʃækl], 1. *s.* das Kettenglied; die Schake, der Schäkel (*Naut.*); *pl.* (*fig.*) Fesseln, Ketten (*pl.*). 2. *v.a.* schäkeln (*Naut.*); (*fig.*) fesseln, hemmen.
shad [ʃæd], *s.* die Alse (*Ichth.*).
shaddock [ˈʃædək], *s.* (*archaic*) die Pampelmuse.
shad–e [ʃeɪd], 1. *s.* der Schatten; das Dunkel; schattiger *or* dunkler Ort; die Schattierung, Abstufung, Farbstufe, der Farbton (*Paint.*); (Lampen)-Schirm; (*coll.*) die Kleinigkeit, Spur; (*Poet.*) der Geist, das Gespenst; *the –es*, die Unterwelt, das Schattenland, Schattenreich; *leave in the –e*, weit hinter sich lassen; *light and –e*, Licht und Schatten, (*fig.*) die Kontrastwirkung; *put* or *throw into the –e*, in den Schatten stellen (*also fig.*) *eye- –e*, der Augenschirm; *sun–e*, der Sonnenschirm. 2. *v.a.* beschatten, überschatten; abhalten (*light*) (*from*, von); schützen (*the eyes*) (*from*, vor); verhüllen, verdecken (*from*, vor); verdunkeln, in den Schatten stellen; schattieren, abtönen (*Paint.*). 3. *v.n.* unmerklich übergehen (*into*, in (*Acc.*)); *–e away* or *off*, allmählich verschwinden. **–iness,** *s.* das Schattige; (*coll.*) die Anrüchigkeit. **–ow** [ˈʃædou], 1. *s.* der Schatten, das Dunkel; Schattenbild; (*fig.*) der Abglanz, Rest, leerer Schein; die Kleinigkeit, Spur; der Schutz; (*coll.*) ständiger Begleiter; der Detektiv; *cast a –ow*, einen Schatten werfen; *without a –ow of doubt*, ohne den geringsten Zweifel; *under the –ow of night*, unter dem Schutz der Dunkelheit; *may your –ow never grow less*, ich wünsche dir allen Erfolg; *land of –ows*, das Schattenreich. 2. *v.a.* beschatten, verdunkeln; (also *–ow forth*) dunkel andeuten, undeutlich darstellen, versinnbildlichen; (*coll.*) auf dem Ferse folgen (*Dat.*), unter Beobachtung halten. **–ow-factory,** *s.* das Schattenwerk. **–owless,** *adj.* schattenlos. **–owy,** *adj.* schattig, dunkel, düster, schattenhaft, dämmerig; verschwommen, wesenlos. **–y** [ˈʃeɪdɪ], *adj.* schattig, geschützt; zweifelhaft, anrüchig; *on the –y side of 40*, über die vierzig hinaus.
shaft [ʃɑːft], *s.* der Schaft (*of spear, etc.*), Stiel (*of axe*), die Deichsel (*of cart*), Welle, Spindel, Achse (*Mach.*); (*Poet.*) der Pfeil; (*fig. Poet.*) Lichtstrahl; der Schacht (*Min.*); *light-–*, der Lichtschacht; *– of light*, der Lichtstrahl; *–s of ridicule*, Pfeile des Spottes; *sink a –*, einen Schacht abteufen (*Min.*). **– -horse,** *s.* das Deichselpferd.
shag [ʃæg], *s.* (*rare*) zottiges Haar; (*archaic*) rauhes Tuch; der Plüsch (*Amer.*); Feinschnitt, der Shag (*tobacco*); die Krähenscharbe (*Orn.*). **–gy,** *adj.* zottig, struppig.
shagreen [ʃæˈgrɪːn], *s.* das Chagrinleder, Körnerleder.
shah [ʃɑː], *s.* der Schah.
shak–e [ʃeɪk], 1. *ir.v.a.* schütteln; rütteln, ausschütteln (*carpets, etc.*); (*fig.*) erschüttern; (*Amer.*) mischen (*cards*); *–e s.o. by the arm*, einen am Arm schütteln; *–e the dust off one's feet*, den Staub von den Füßen schütteln; *–e hands*, sich (*Dat.*) die Hand geben; *–e a p.'s hand* or *a p. by the hand*, einem die Hand geben *or* schütteln; *–e one's head*, den Kopf schütteln (*also fig.*) (*at* or *over*, über); (*coll.*) *–e a leg*, das Tanzbein schwingen; *–e one's sides with laughing*, sich vor Lachen schütteln; *be –en*, ergriffen *or* erschüttert sein; *badly –en*, arg mitgenommen; *to be –en before taken*, vor dem Gebrauch schütteln; *–e down*, herunterschütteln (*fruit, etc.*), ausbreiten (*straw*), bereiten (*a bed, etc.*); *–e off*, abschütteln; *–e out*, ausschütteln; *–e to pieces*, auseinanderrütteln; *–e up*, zusammenschütteln, zusammenschütten (*as components*); aufschütteln (*as a cushion*); (*fig.*) aufrütteln. 2. *ir.v.n.* zittern, beben (*with*, vor); sich schütteln, trillern (*Mus.*); (*coll.*) *–e down*, sich angewöhnen *or* eingewöhnen *or* einleben; sich ein Notlager bereiten; *–e in one's shoes*, vor Angst zittern; *–e with laughter*, sich vor Lachen schütteln. 3. *s.* das Schütteln, Rütteln; der Triller (*Mus.*); Sprung, Riß, Spalt (*in wood*); (*fig.*) die Erschütterung; *–e of the hand*, der Händedruck; *–e of the head*, das Kopfschütteln; (*sl.*) *no great –es*, nichts Besonderes; *in three –es of a duck's tail*, im Handumdrehen *or* Nu. (*coll.*) **–e-down,** *s.* das Notlager, Nachtlager. **–er,** *s.* der Mischbecher (*for cocktails*); *the –ers*, Zitterer (*pl.*) (*Rel.*). (*coll.*) **–e-up,** *s.* die Umwälzung, Umgruppierung, der Umschwung. (*coll.*) **–iness,** *s.* die Wackligkeit; Gebrechlichkeit. **–ing,** 1. *adj.* zitternd, schüttelnd; *–ing palsy*, die Schüttellähmung (*Path.*). 2. *s.* das Schütteln; die Erschütterung. **–y,** *adj.* zitternd, zittrig; wankend, unsicher, unzuverlässig; (*coll.*) wackelig, schwach, gebrechlich; rissig (*of wood*).
shako [ˈʃækou], *s.* der Tschako.
shale [ʃeɪl], *s.* der Schieferton, Bandschiefer. **– -oil,** *s.* das Schieferöl.
shall [ʃæl], *ir.aux.v.* (*only pres.*) (*see* **should**). 1. (*1st p. sing. & pl.*) werde(n) (*with inf. to form future*); *– not* ((*coll.*) *shan't*), werde(n) nicht. 2. (*2nd & 3rd p. sing. & pl.*) soll(st), sollt, *or* sollen; *– not*, soll(st), darf(st), sollen, *or* dürfen nicht. 3. (*in questions*) (*1st & 3rd p. sing. & pl.*) soll(en), darf, *or* dürfen; (*1st p. only*) werde(n); (*in 2nd p. sing. & pl. rare, usually* will) wirst *or* werdet. 4. (*in dependent clauses*) (*1st, 2nd, & 3rd p. sing. or pl.*) soll(en), sollst *or* sollt. *I – go*, ich werde gehen, (*coll.*) ich gehe; *he – go*, er soll gehen; *you – not go*, du sollst *or* darfst nicht gehen; *– I fetch it?* soll *or* darf ich es holen?
shalloon [ʃəˈluːn], *s.* der Chalon.
shallop [ˈʃæləp], *s.* die Schaluppe.
shal(l)ot [ʃəˈlɔt], *s.* die Schalotte.
shallow [ˈʃælou], 1. *adj.* flach, seicht (*also fig.*), nicht tief; (*fig.*) oberflächlich. 2. *s.* die Untiefe, seichte Stelle; *pl.* seichtes Gewasser. **– -brained,** *adj.* oberflächlich, seicht. **–ness,** *s.* die Seichtheit (*also fig.*), (*fig.*) Oberflächlichkeit.
shalt [ʃælt], *archaic 2nd p. sing. of* **shall.**
sham [ʃæm], 1. *v.a.* vortäuschen, vorspiegeln. 2. *v.n.* sich (ver)stellen, heucheln. 3. *s.* die Täuschung, der Schwindel, Trug; Schwindler, Heuchler, Scharlatan. 4. *adj.* unecht, nachgemacht, falsch; Schein–, fingiert. **–mer,** *s.* der Heuchler.
shamble [ˈʃæmbl], 1. *v.n.* schlenkern, watscheln. 2. *s.* der Watschelgang.
shambles [ˈʃæmbəlz], *pl.* (*sing. const.*) die Schlachtbank; das Schlachthaus; (*fig.*) Schlachtfeld; (*coll.*) die Verwirrung, Patsche, der Mischmasch, die Schweinerei.
shame [ʃeɪm], 1. *s.* die Scham, das Schamgefühl; die Schmach, Schande; *bring – upon*, Schande bereiten (*Dat.*); *cry – upon*, sich entrüsten über; *feel – at*, sich schämen über; *for –!* pfui!; *more's the –*, um so schlimmer; *– on you!* schäme dich!; *put to –*, beschämen (*a p.*), in den Schatten stellen (*a th.*); *what a –!* wie schade! 2. *v.a.* beschämen, schamrot machen; Schande machen (*Dat.*); *– s.o. into doing*, einen durch Beschämung dahin bringen zu tun. **–faced** [–feɪst], *adj.*, **–facedly** [–feɪsɪdlɪ], *adv.* verschämt, kleinlaut. **–facedness** [–feɪsɪdnɪs], *s.* die Verschämtheit. **–ful,** *adj.* schändlich, unanständig. **–fulness,** *s.* die Schändlichkeit, Unanständigkeit. **–less,** *adj.* schamlos, unverschämt; *see* **–ful.** **–lessness,** *s.* die Schamlosigkeit, Unverschämtheit; *see* **–fulness.**
shammy(-leather) [ˈʃæmɪ], *s.* (*coll.*) das Sämischleder.
shampoo [ʃæmˈpuː], 1. *s.* das Haarwaschmittel; Schampunieren; *dry –*, das Haarreinigungspulver. 2. *v.a.* schampunieren, waschen und massieren (*hair*); (*rare*) massieren, frottieren.
shamrock [ˈʃæmrək], *s.* (irischer) Klee.
shandy(gaff) [ˈʃændɪ(gæf)], *s.* Bier mit Sprudelwasser.
shanghai [ʃæŋˈhaɪ], *v.a.* schanghaien (*sailors*), gewaltsam verschleppen.

shank [ʃæŋk], 1. *s.* das Schienbein, der Unterschenkel (*Anat.*); Stiel (*Bot.*); Schaft (*Tech.*); (*coll.*) das Bein; (*coll.*) *on –'s pony*, auf Schusters Rappen. **–ed** [–t], *adj. suff.* –schenkelig. 2. *v.n.*; *– off*, abfallen (*Bot.*).
shanny ['ʃænɪ], *s.* grüner Schleimfisch.
shan't [ʃɑ:nt], *see* **shall.**
shantung [ʃæn'tʌŋg], *s.* der Schantung.
[1]**shanty** [ʃæntɪ], *s.* die Hütte, Baracke, der Schuppen.
[2]**shanty,** *s.* das Matrosenlied.
shape [ʃeɪp], 1. *s.* (äußere) Form, die Gestalt, der Umriß; die Form (*also Tech. & Cook.*), Figur, Fasson; das Modell (*for hats*); *in the – of*, in Gestalt von; (*coll.*) *lick into –*, zustutzen (*a th.*), gute Manieren beibringen (*a p.* (*Dat.*)); *out of –*, außer Fasson; *take* (*definite*) *–*, feste Form *or* Gestalt annehmen; *put into –*, formen, (*fig.*) ordnen. 2. *v.a.* formen, gestalten, bilden, einrichten, ordnen; *– a course for*, steuern auf *or* nach (*Naut. & fig.*). 3. *v.n.* sich formen lassen, Form annehmen; (*fig.*) sich gestalten *or* entwickeln. **–d** [–t], *adj. suff.* –gestaltet. **–less,** *adj.* formlos, ungestalt(et), unförmig. **–lessness,** *s.* die Formlosigkeit, Umförmigkeit. **–liness,** *s.* die Wohlgestalt, Formschönheit, das Ebenmaß. **–ly,** *adj.* wohlgestaltet, schöngeformt. **–n** (*archaic*) *see* **–d.**
shard [ʃɑ:d], *s.* (*archaic*) die Scherbe; Flügeldecke (*Ent.*).
[1]**share** [ʃɛ:ə], *s.* die Pflugschar. **--beam,** *s.* der Pflugbaum, Grindel.
[2]**share,** 1. *s.* der Anteil, Teil; die Beteiligung (*in*, an); der Beitrag (*towards*, zu); die Quote, das Kontingent; die Aktie, der Geschäftsanteil, Gewinnanteil (*C.L.*); *– and – alike*, zu gleichen Teilen; *bear one's –*, seinen Teil tragen von; *do one's –*, seinen Teil tun an; *fall to one's –*, einem zuteil werden, einem zufallen; *go –s*, teilen (*in a th.*, etwas; *with a p.*, mit einem); *hold –s*, Aktionär sein (*in* (*Gen.*)); *have a – in*, see *take a – in*; *mining –*, der Kux; *ordinary –*, die Stammaktie; *preference –*, die Vorzugsaktie; *take a – in*, Anteil haben an, beteiligt sein an, teilhaben *or* teilnehmen an. 2. *v.a.* teilen (*a th.*) (*with a p.*, mit einem; *among*, unter); teilhaben *or* teilnehmen an (*Dat.*); *they must both – the blame*, die beiden müssen sich in die Schuld teilen; *– an opinion*, eine Meinung teilen; *generally –d opinion*, allgemein geteilte Meinung; *– out*, verteilen, austeilen (*to*, an). 3. *v.n.*; *– in*, teilhaben *or* teilnehmen an (*Dat.*); *– and – alike*, gleich teilen, sich gleich daran beteiligen, gleiche Teile bekommen. **--certificate,** *s.* die Aktie, der Anteilschein. **--broker,** *s.* der Aktienmakler. **–holder,** *s.* der Aktionär, Aktieninhaber (*in* (*Gen.*)). **--pusher,** *s.* (*coll.*) der Winkelmakler.
shark [ʃɑ:k], *s.* der Hai(fisch); (*coll.*) Gauner, Schwindler, Hochstapler, Preller.
sharp [ʃɑ:p], 1. *adj.* scharf (*also fig.*), spitz; (*fig.*) herb, sauer (*as taste*), schneidend (*as cold*), schrill (*as sound*), heftig (*as contest & pain*), zu hoch, um einen halben Ton erhöht (*Mus.*); (*of persons*) scharfsinnig, aufgeweckt, aufmerksam, wachsam, (*coll.*) schlau, gerieben, gerissen; *C –*, Cis (*Mus.*); *– eyes*, scharfe *or* gute Augen; *look – !* mach schnell! hurtig!; *– practice*, skrupellose Praktiken, Ränke, Kniffe (*pl.*); *– tongue*, böse Zunge; *– words*, bittere Worte. 2. *adv.* plötzlich; pünktlich; *be – on a th.*, versessen auf etwas sein; *sing –*, zu hoch singen. 3. *s.* das Kreuz; durch ein Kreuz erhöhte Note (*Mus.*). **--edged,** *adj.* scharfkantig. **–en,** *v.a.* schärfen, (an)spitzen, wetzen, schleifen; (*fig.*) verschärfen, zuspitzen. **–ener,** *s.*; *pencil-–ener*, der Bleistiftspitzer. **–er,** *s.* der Gauner, Bauernfänger. **–ly,** *adv.* scharf; schrill; heftig, barsch. **–ness,** *s.* die Schärfe, Spitze; (*fig.*) Herbheit, Bitterkeit, Heftigkeit, Deutlichkeit; der Scharfsinn, die Schlauheit. **--pointed,** *adj.* spitz(ig). **–shooter,** *s.* der Scharfschütze, Freischärler (*Mil.*). **--witted,** *adj.* scharfsinnig.
shatter ['ʃætə], 1. *v.a.* zerschlagen, zerbrechen, zertrümmern, zerschmettern; (*fig.*) vernichten, zunichte machen (*hopes*), zerrütten (*nerves*). 2. *v.n.* zerbrechen, in Stücke gehen; (*coll.*) *I am –ed*, ich bin erschüttert. **–ing,** *adj.* (*fig.*) überwältigend, vernichtend.

shav–e [ʃeɪv], 1. *v.a.* abrasieren (*beard, etc.*), rasieren (*a p.*), abschaben (*skins, etc.*), falzen (*leather*); (*coll.*) streifen; *–e o.s.*, sich rasieren; *be or get –ed*, sich rasieren lassen. 2. *v.n.* sich rasieren. 3. *s.* das Rasieren; *he needs a –e*, er muß sich rasieren; (*coll.*) *have a close or narrow –e*, knapp *or* mit heiler Haut davonkommen; (*coll.*) *by a narrow –e*, um ein Haar. **–eling,** *s.* der Glatzkopf. **–en,** *adj.* rasiert; geschoren (*head*). **–er,** der Barbier; Rasierapparat; (*coll.*) *young –er*, der Grünschnabel, Milchbart. **–ing,** *s.* das Rasieren; der Span, Splitter; *pl.* Späne, Schnitzel, Abschabsel; *–ing brush*, der Rasierpinsel; *–ing kit*, das Rasierzeug; *–ing soap, –ing stick*, *s.* die Rasierseife.
shawl [ʃɔ:l], *s.* der Schal, das Umschlagetuch, Umhängetuch.
shawm [ʃɔ:m], *s.* (*archaic*) die Schalmei (*Mus.*).
she [ʃɪ:] 1. *pers. pron.* sie (*of females*); er, sie *or* es (*personified ships, countries, etc.*); *– who*, diejenige welche. 2. *s.* die Sie, das Weib(chen); *--bear*, die Bärin; *--devil*, das Teufelsweib; *--wolf*, die Wölfin.
shea [ʃɪ:ə], *s.* (also *--tree*) der (Schi)Butterbaum (*Bot.*); *– butter*, die Bambukbutter, Schibutter.
sheaf [ʃɪ:f], 1. *s.* die Garbe, das Bündel. 2. *v.a.* in Garben binden (*corn*).
shealing, *see* **shieling.**
shear [ʃɪ:ə] 1. *ir.v.a.* scheren (*sheep*), mähen; (usually *– off*) abschneiden; *see* **shorn.** 2. *v.n.* schneiden. 3. *s.* (*dial.*) die Schur (*of sheep*); der Schub, die Schiebung, Scherung (*Tech.*). **–er,** *s.* der Schafscherer; Schnitter (*Scots*). **–ing,** *s.* die Schur; das Mähen; *pl.* die Scherwolle; *wool of the second –ing*, zweischürige Wolle; *–ing force*, die Schubkraft; *–ing stress*, die Schubbeanspruchung, Scherbeanspruchung; *–ing time*, die Schurzeit. **--legs,** *pl.* der Scherenkran, Mastenkran (*Naut.*). **–ling,** *s.* das Schaf nach der ersten Schur. **–s,** *pl.* große Schere, die Gartenschere, Metallschere. **–water,** *s.* der Sturmtaucher (*Orn.*). **– zone,** *s.* das Gangsystem, der Gangzug (*Geol.*).
sheath [ʃɪ:θ], *s.* (pl. *–s* [–ðz]) die Scheide (*also Bot.*); Flügeldecke (*Ent.*); *– knife*, der Dolch. **–e** [–ð], *v.a.* in die Scheide (ein)stecken (*the sword*); einhüllen, umhüllen, überziehen, bekleiden. **–ing** [–ðɪŋ], *s.* das Verschalen, Beschlagen; die Verschalung, Beschlagung, Bekleidung, Haut, der Beschlag.
[1]**sheave** [ʃɪ:v], *s.* die Rolle, Scheibe (*Mech.*).
[2]**sheave,** *v.a. see* **sheaf. –s,** *pl. of* **sheaf.**
[1]**shed** [ʃɛd], *ir.v.a.* (*also imperf. & p.p.*) vergießen, ausschütten; abwerfen (*horns, leaves, etc.*); verlieren (*teeth*), abstreifen, ablegen (*clothes*); verbreiten, ausbreiten (*light, heat, etc.*), vergießen (*tears, blood*); *– light on*, (*fig.*) erhellen; *– one's skin*, sich häuten. **–der,** *s.* der Vergießer (*of blood, etc.*).
[2]**shed,** *s.* der Schuppen, die Hütte, das Wetterdach, Schirmdach.
sheen [ʃɪ:n], *s.* der Schein, Glanz. **–y,** *adj.* glänzend.
sheeny ['ʃɪ:nɪ], *s.* (*pej.*) der Jude, die Jüdin.
sheep [ʃɪ:p], *s.* (*also pl.*) das Schaf (*also fig.*); *black –*, (*fig.*) schwarzes Schaf; *a wolf in –'s clothing*, der Wolf im Schafspelz; *cast –'s eyes at*, verliebt *or* schmachtend ansehen. **–ish,** *adj.* einfältig, schüchtern, blöde. **–ishness,** *s.* die Einfalt, Blödheit, Blödigkeit. **--cot(e),** *s.* (*rare*), *see* **--pen. --dog,** *s.* der Schäferhund. **--farm** *s.* die Schäferei. **--farming,** *s.* die Schafzucht. **--fold,** *s.* (*archaic*) *see* **--pen. --hook,** *s.* der Hirtenstab. **--pen,** *s.* die Schafhürde. **--shearing,** *s.* die Schafschur. **–skin,** *s.* das Schaffell, Schafleder. **--run,** *s.*, **--walk,** *s.* die Schafweide, Schaftrift.
[1]**sheer** [ʃɪ:ə], 1. *adj.* lauter, rein, unvermischt, absolut, pur, völlig, bar; senkrecht, steil, jäh; dünn, durchsichtig (*of fabric*). 2. *adv.* direkt, kerzengerade.
[2]**sheer** 1. *v.n.* gieren (*Naut.*), ausweichen; *– off*, abscheren, abgieren (*Naut.*); (*coll.*) sich fortmachen. 2. *s.* das Abgieren, die Abweichung; die Erhöhung, der Sprung (*of deck*), die Linien (*pl.*) (*of a ship*); *pl.* (also *--legs*) *see* **shear-legs.**
sheet [ʃɪ:t], 1. *s.* das Bettuch, (Bett)Laken; Blatt (*of paper or metal*), der Bogen (*of paper*), die Platte (*of metal*), Tafel, Scheibe (*of glass*), Fläche (*of*

water); der Schot, die Schote, Segelleine (*Naut.*); *as white as a –*, kreideweiß; *blank –*, unbeschriebenes Blatt; *clean –*, (*fig.*) tadellose Führung, reine Weste; *in –s*, uneingebunden, ungefalzt (*Bookb.*); *come down in –s*, in Strömen regnen; (*sl.*) *three –s in the wind*, benebelt; *– of flame*, die Feuermasse, das Flammenmeer; *– of pins*, der Brief Stecknadeln. 2. *v.a.* (in Leintücher) einhüllen; falzen (*Bookb.*). **--anchor,** der Notanker, (*fig.*) die Stütze, letzte Rettung. **– copper,** das Kupferblech. **– glass,** das Tafelglas, Scheibenglas. **– ice,** das Glatteis. **–ing,** *s.* die Leinwand zu Bettüchern; der Beschlag (*of metal*). **– iron,** das Eisenblech. **– lead,** das Tafelblei. **– lightning,** der Flächenblitz, das Wetterleuchten. **– metal,** das Blech.

sheik(h) [ʃɪ:k], *s.* der Scheich, Scheik; (*sl.*) unwiderstehlicher Mann.

shekel [ˈʃɛkl] *s.* der Sekel; *pl.* (*sl.*) Pinke(pinke).

sheldrake [ˈʃɛldreɪk], *s.* die Brandente.

shelf [ʃɛlf], *s.* (pl. *shelves* [–vz], *q.v.*) das Brett, Bord, Regal, (Bücher)Gestell, der Sims, das Fach; Riff, die Sandbank; Felsenplatte; *put on the –*, beiseitelegen, beiseiteschieben, auf die lange Bank schieben; *on the –*, abgetan, ausrangiert; sitzengeblieben (*of women*).

shell [ʃɛl], 1. *s.* die Muschel; das (Schnecken)Haus (*of snails*), die Schale (*egg, nut, also fig.*), Hülse (*also fig.*); (*fig.*) Rinde; das Gerippe, Gerüst (*of a house, etc.*); die Granate, Bombe (*Mil.*); (*fig.*) äußere Form; die Mittelstufe (*at school*); (*fig.*) *come out of one's –*, aus seiner Zurückhaltung heraustreten. 2. *v.a.* schälen (*an egg*); aushülsen, enthülsen (*nuts, peas, etc.*); beschießen, bombardieren (*Mil.*); (*sl.*) *– out*, herausrücken (*money*). 3. *v.n.*; (*sl.*) *– out*, zahlen, mit dem Geld herausrücken. **--crater,** *s.* der Granattrichter. **–ed** [–d], *adj.* schalig. **--fire,** *s.* das Granatfeuer. **--fish,** *s.* das Schaltier. **–ing,** *s.* die Beschießung. **--proof,** *adj.* bombenfest, schußsicher. **–shock,** *s.* die Erschütterung durch Granatexplosion; *be –shocked*, im Krieg eine Nervenerschütterung erleiden. **--work,** *s.* das Muschelwerk.

shellac [ʃəˈlæk], *s.* der Schellack.

shelter [ˈʃɛltə], 1. *s.* das Obdach, die Unterkunft; der Schuppen, das Schutzdach; (*fig.*) der Schutz, Schirm; *air-raid –*, der Schutzraum, Bunker; *night-–*, das Obdachlosenheim; *take – from*, Schutz suchen vor *or* gegen; *give –*, *see –* 2; *fly for –*, Zuflucht suchen (*to*, bei); *under –*, unter Dach und Fach; *under the – of*, unter dem Schutz von. 2. *v.a.* (be)schützen, (be)schirmen (*from*, vor); aufnehmen, beherbergen (*a p.*), Zuflucht geben (*Dat.*); (*fig.*) sich verstecken *or* verbergen. 3. *v.n.* Obdach *or* Schutz suchen; sich unterstellen. **–less,** *adj.* obdachlos, schutzlos.

shelv–e [ʃɛlv], 1. *v.a.* auf ein Brett legen *or* stellen (*books*); mit Brettern, Fächern *or* Regalen versehen; (*fig.*) beiseitelegen, beiseiteschieben, nicht berücksichtigen, aufschieben; beilegen (*differences*). 2. *v.n.* sich neigen, schräg hinablaufen. **–es** [–z], *see* **shelf. –ing.** 1. *s.* Regale, Fächer (*pl.*); das Beiseiteschieben. 2. *adj.* schräg, abschüssig.

shepherd [ˈʃɛpəd], 1. *s.* der Schäfer, Hirt; *–'s crook*, der Schäferstab; *–'s dog*, der Schäferhund; *–'s pie*, der Kartoffelauflauf mit Fleisch; *–'s plaid*, schwarz und weiß gewürfelter Wollstoff; *–'s purse*, die Hirtentasche (*Bot.*); *–'s rod* or *staff*, die Karddistel (*Bot.*). 2. *v.a.* (wie ein Schäfer) hüten; (*usually fig.*) führen, geleiten. **--boy,** *s.* der Hirtenknabe. **–ess,** *s.* die Schäferin, Hirtin.

sherbet [ˈʃə:bət], *s.* der Sorbet(t), das Limonadenpulver.

sherd, *see* **shard.**

sherif [ʃəˈrɪ:f], *s.* arabischer Gouverneur *or* Fürst.

sheriff [ˈʃɛrɪf], *s.* der Sheriff; Bezirksrichter (*Amer.*); (also *--depute*) erster Grafschaftsbeamter (*Scots*); *high –*, erster Grafschaftsbeamter (*England*).

sherry [ˈʃɛrɪ], *s.* der Sherry, Jerezwein.

shew, *see* **show.**

shibboleth [ˈʃɪbəlɛθ], *s.* das Erkennungswort, Losungswort.

shield [ʃɪ:ld], 1. *s.* der Schild (*also fig.*), Wappenschild (*Her.*); (*fig.*) Schutz, Schirm, Schützer, Schirmer; die Schutzplatte; Schutzvorrichtung (*Tech.*), der Panzer, Rückenschild (*Zool.*). 2. *v.a.* (be)schirmen, bedecken, schützen (*from*, vor); verteidigen, beschützen (*from*, vor *or* gegen). **--bearer,** *s.* der Schildträger. **--fern,** *s.* der Schildfarn (*Bot.*). **--hand,** *s.* linke Hand. **–less,** *adj.* ohne Schild; (*fig.*) schutzlos.

shieling [ˈʃɪ:lɪŋ], *s.* die Schutzhütte (*Scots*).

shift [ʃɪft], 1. *v.a.* (ver)schieben, wegschieben, versetzen, verstellen, verändern, verlegen, wechseln (*scene, etc.*), schieben (*blame*) (*to* or *on*, auf); (*sl.*) loswerden, beseitigen; *– one's ground*, den Standpunkt ändern. 2. *v.n.* sich bewegen, die Lage ändern, sich verschieben, verschoben *or* verlegt werden; sich verlagern (*as cargo, etc.*); sich ändern *or* wenden, umspringen (*as wind*); *– for o.s.*, sich selbst helfen, auf sich selbst angewiesen werden. 3. *s.* die Veränderung, Verschiebung, Verstellung, Abwechslung, der Wechsel; die Schicht, Ablösung, Belegschaft (*of workmen*); das Hilfsmittel, der (Not)Behelf, Ausweg, die Ausflucht; List, der Kniff, das Übergreifen (*Mus.*); (*archaic*) Frauenhemd; *day –*, die Tagschicht; *make –*, sich behelfen. **–er,** *s.* die Rangiermaschine, Verstellvorrichtung, Schaltung; (*coll.*) unzuverlässiger Mensch; *scene-–er*, der Kulissenschieber. **–iness,** *s.* die Veränderlichkeit, Unzuverlässigkeit, Verschmitztheit. **–ing,** *adj.* sich bewegend *or* verschiebend, veränderlich, beweglich; *–ing sand*, der Treibsand. **--key,** *s.* die Umschalttaste (*typewriter*). **–less,** *adj.* hilflos, ungewandt, unfähig, nutzlos, ratlos, zwecklos. **–lessness,** *s.* die Ratlosigkeit, Hilflosigkeit. **–y,** *adj.* veränderlich, unzuverlässig, unstet; durchtrieben, gerissen, verschmitzt.

shillelagh [ʃɪˈleɪlə], *s.* eichener Knüttel (*Irish*).

shilling [ˈʃɪlɪŋ], *s.* der Schilling; *take the King's* or *Queen's –*, sich anwerben lassen, Rekrut werden; *a – in the pound*, 5 Prozent; *cut off with a –*, enterben. **--shocker,** *s.* der Schauerroman.

shilly-shally [ˈʃɪlɪˈʃælɪ], 1. *s.* die Unentschlossenheit, das Schwanken, Zögern. 2. *adj.* unschlüssig, schwankend. 3. *v.n.* schwanken, zögern, unentschlossen *or* unschlüssig sein.

shim [ʃɪm], *s.* der Ausfüllstreifen, das Einlegestück, Futterholz, Toleranzplättchen.

shimmer [ˈʃɪmə], 1. *v.n.* schimmern, flimmern. 2. *s.* der Schimmer, das Flimmern. **–y,** *adj.* schimmernd, flimmernd.

shimmy [ˈʃɪmɪ], *s.* (*coll.*) das (Frauen)Hemd; (*coll.*) ein Tanz mit Schüttelbewegungen.

shin [ʃɪn], 1. *s.* das Schienbein; *– of beef*, die Rindshachse. 2. *v.n.* (*coll.*) klettern; *– up*, hinaufklettern; *– down*, hinunterklettern; (*sl.*) *– round*, herumlaufen. **--bone,** *s.* der Schienbeinknochen. **--guard,** *s.* der Schienbeinschutz.

shindy [ˈʃɪndɪ], *s.* der Krach, Krawall, Spektakel.

shine [ʃaɪn], 1. *s.* der Schein, Glanz, (*coll.*) das Aufheben, der Krach; *in rain or –*, bei jedem Wetter; (*coll.*) *take the – out of*, ausstechen, in der Schatten stellen (*a p.*), den Glanz nehmen (*Dat.*) (*a th.*); *take a – to*, liebgewinnen (*a p.*) (*Amer.*); *make a – about*, Aufhebens machen über; *kick up a –*, Skandal machen. 2. *ir.v.n.* scheinen, leuchten, strahlen, glänzen (*also fig.*); (*fig.*) sich hervortun; *– forth* or *– out*, hervorleuchten, aufleuchten. 3. *ir.v.a.* (*coll.*) blank machen, putzen; (*shoes, etc.*). **–r,** *s.* (*sl.*) das Goldstück. *See* **shining, shiny.**

[1]**shingl–e** [ˈʃɪŋgl], 1. *s.* die (Dach)Schindel; der Herrenschnitt (*ladies hair*). 2. *v.a.* mit Schindeln decken; in Herrenschnitt *or* kurz schneiden; *–ed hair*, der Herrenschnitt. **–ing,** *s.* die Schindelbedachung.

[2]**shingl–e,** *s.* der Strandkies, steiniger Strand. **–y,** *adj.* kiesig, steinig.

shingles [ˈʃɪŋglz], *s.* die Gürtelrose (*Med.*).

shin–ing [ˈʃaɪnɪŋ], *adj.* leuchtend, glänzend (*also fig.*). **–y,** *adj.* hell, klar, glänzend, strahlend; blank (*of shoes, etc.*); fadenscheinig, abgetragen (*of clothes*).

ship [ʃɪp], 1. *s.* das Schiff; dreimastiges (Segel)-Schiff, das Vollschiff (*Naut.*); *aboard* (or *on board*) –, an Bord, auf dem Schiff; *by –*, mit dem *or* per Schiff; *when my – comes home*, wenn ich mein Glück mache, wenn das Geldschiff ankommt; *capital –*, das Großkampfschiff; – *of the desert*, das Wüstenschiff; – *of the line*, das Linienschiff; *take* –, an Bord gehen, sich einschiffen (*for*, nach); *–'s articles*, der Heuervertrag; *–'s company*, die Schiffsmannschaft; *–'s husband*, der Mitreeder, Schiffsbevollmächtigte(r) *m.*; *–'s manifest*, das Ladungsverzeichnis, Manifest; *–'s papers*, Schiffspapiere (*pl.*). 2. *v.a.* an Bord bringen *or* nehmen, verladen, einschiffen; (also – *off*) verschiffen, absenden; anmustern, dingen, heuern (*sailors*); – *the mast*, den Mast festmachen; – *the oars*, die Ruder einlegen *or* klarmachen; – *a sea*, eine Sturzwelle bekommen. 3. *v.n.* sich (als Matrose) verdingen; sich einschiffen. **–board,** *s.* (only in) *on –board*, auf dem Schiffe, an Bord. **--biscuit,** *s.* der Schiffszwieback. **--breaker,** *s.* der (Schiffs)Verschrotter, Schröter. **--broker,** *s.* der Schiffsmakler. **–builder,** *s.* der Schiffsbaumeister. **–building,** *s.* der Schiff(s)bau. **--chandler,** *s.* der Schiffslieferant. **– hoist,** *s.* das Schiff(s)hebewerk. **–load,** *s.* die Schiffsladung. **–mate,** *s.* der Schiffskamerad. **–ment,** *s.* die Verladung, Verschiffung, Schiffsladung, Sendung, der Versand. **--money,** *s.* die Kriegsschiffsteuer (*Hist.*). **–owner,** *s.* der Schiffseigentümer, Reeder. **–ping,** 1. *s.* die Verladung, Verschiffung, Spedition, Sendung, der Versand; die Schiffahrt, das Schiffswesen; (alle) Schiffe (*pl.*), die Flotte; *ready for –ping*, zur Verladung bereit; *the harbour is crowded with –ping*, es liegen sehr viele Schiffe im Hafen. 2. *attrib. adj.* Schiffs–, Schiffahrt–. **–ping-agent,** der Schiffsmakler, Schiffsagent. **–ping-articles,** see *ship's articles*. **–ping intelligence,** die Schiffahrtsberichte. **–ping-note,** der Schiffszettel. **–ping-office,** *s.* das Speditionsbüro. **--rigged,** *adj.* als Vollschiff getakelt. **–shape,** *adj.* (*fig.*) gehörig, richtig, ordentlich, in guter Ordnung. **–wreck,** 1. *s.* der Schiffbruch, schiffbrüchiges Schiff; (*fig.*) völliger Zusammenbruch, der Ruin, das Scheitern; *make a –wreck of a th.*, (*fig.*) etwas vernichten *or* zerstören. 2. *v.a.* scheitern lassen; zum Scheitern bringen; (*fig.*) zerstören, vernichten (*hopes, etc.*); *be –wrecked*, Schiffbruch erleiden, gestrandet, gescheitert *or* schiffbrüchig werden *or* sein. 3. *v.n.* scheitern, Schiffbruch erleiden; (*fig.*) vernichtet *or* zerstört werden. **–wright,** *s.* der Schiffsbaumeister, Schiffbauer; Zimmermann, Meister (*Naut.*). **–yard,** *s.* die Werft.

shippen [ˈʃɪpən], *s.* (*dial.*) der Kuhstall, Viehstall.

shire [*as suffix* ˈʃɪə *or* ʃə, *otherwise* (*Scots always*) ˈʃaɪə], die Grafschaft. **--horse,** *s.* schweres Zugpferd. **--mote,** *s.* angelsächsisches Grafschaftsgericht (*Hist.*).

shirk [ʃəːk], 1. *v.a.* ausweichen, sich entziehen (*Dat.*); umgehen. 2. *v.n.* (*coll.*) sich drücken. **–er,** *s.* (*coll.*) der Drückeberger.

shir(r) [ʃəː], 1. *s.* eingewebtes Gummiband, elastisches Gewebe (*Amer.*). 2. *v.a.* in Falten ziehen. **–ed** [–d], *adj.* mit Gummi durchwebt, gekräuselt.

shirt [ʃəːt], *s.* das Hemd; (*coll.*) *boiled* –, gestärktes Hemd; – *of mail*, das Panzerhemd; (*coll.*) *not have a – to one's back*, kein Hemd am *or* auf dem Leibe haben; (*sl.*) *keep one's – on*, ruhig bleiben, ruhig Blut behalten, sich nicht aufregen; (*sl.*) *put one's – on a horse*, alles auf ein Pferd setzen. **--cuffs,** *pl.* Manschetten. **--front,** *s.* das Vorhemd, der Oberhemdeinsatz. **–ing,** das Hemdentuch. **--sleeve,** *s.* der Hemd(s)ärmel; *in o.'s --sleeves*, in Hemd(s)ärmeln. (*sl.*) **–y,** *adj.* ärgerlich, verdrießlich, kurz angebunden.

shit [ʃɪt], **shite** [ʃaɪt], 1. *s.* (*vulg.*) die Scheiße. 2. *v.n.* (*vulg.*) scheißen.

¹shiver [ˈʃɪvə], 1. *v.a.* zertrümmern, zersplittern. 2. *v.n.* zersplittern, zerbrechen. 3. *s.* kleines Stück, das Bruchstück, der Splitter; der Schiefer (*Min.*).

²shiver, 1. *s.* der Schauer, das Schauern, Frösteln, Zittern, der Schüttelfrost, Fieberschauer; (*coll.*) *the –s*, *pl.* die Gänsehaut. 2. *v.n.* schauern, frösteln, zittern (*with*, vor); flattern, killen (*Naut.*). **–ing,** *s.* das Schauern, der Schauer; *–ing fit*, der Schüttelfrost, Fieberschauer. **–y,** *adj.* fröstelnd, fiebrig.

¹shoal [ʃoul], 1. *s.* der Schwarm, Zug (*of fish*); (*fig. coll.*) (*often pl.*) die Menge, Unmenge, Masse. 2. *v.n.* in Schwärmen auftreten, ziehen (*of fish*).

²shoal, 1. *s.* die Untiefe, Sandbank, flache Stelle. 2. *v.n.* an Tiefe abnehmen, flacher *or* seichter werden. 3. *adj.* flach, seicht, untief (*of water*). **–y,** *adj.* durch Untiefen gefährlich, voll an flachen Stellen.

¹shock [ʃɔk], 1. *s.* die Hocke, (Korn)Puppe, der Garbenhaufen, der *or* die Mandel. 2. *v.a.* in Hocken aufstellen (*corn*).

²shock, 1. *s.* der Stoß, Schlag (*also Elec. & fig.*), der Zusammenstoß (*also Mil.*), Anprall, die Erschütterung, (*fig.*) der Schicksalsschlag, Anstoß, das Ärgernis (*to*, für), Nervenschock (*Med.*); *get the – of one's life*, sein blaues Wunder erleben, wie vom Schlag getroffen werden; *give s.o. quite a* –, einen erschüttern. 2. *v.a.* erschrecken, entsetzen, empören, Anstoß erregen *or* geben, schokieren; Ärgernis geben, anstößig sein; *be –ed*, entsetzt, empört *or* schokiert sein, (*by*, durch; *at*, über); *I was –ed to see*, mit Entsetzen sah ich. **--absorber,** *s.* der Stoßdämpfer. **--absorption,** *s.* die Federung. **–er,** *s.* (*coll.*) etwas Aufregendes *or* Sensationelles; der Schauerroman. **–ing,** *adj.* empörend, unerhört, anstoßerregend, anstößig, ungehörig; schrecklich, furchtbar, ekelhaft, scheußlich. **--proof,** *adj.* stoßsicher. **--troops,** *pl.* Stoßtruppen.

³shock, *s.*; – *of hair*, der Haarschopf, zottiges Haar. **--headed,** *adj.* struppig, zottig, strubbelig, struw(w)elig.

shod [ʃɔd], 1. *see* **shoe.** 2. beschlagen (*of horse*).

shoddy [ˈʃɔdɪ], 1. *s.* die Kunstwolle, Lumpenwolle, das Shoddy, Shoddytuch; (*fig.*) der Schund; Protz (*Amer.*). 2. *adj.* Shoddy–; unecht, wertlos, erbärmlich, schlecht, kitschig, Schund–; protzig (*Amer.*).

shoe [ʃuː], 1. *s.* der (Halb)Schuh; das Hufeisen (*of horses*); eiserner Beschlag, der Hemmschuh, Bremsschuh; *another pair of –s* (*fig.*) etwas ganz anderes; *wait for dead men's –s*, auf jemandes Tod warten; *know where the – pinches*, wissen wo der Schuh drückt; *be* or *stand in his –s*, in seiner Haut stecken, an seiner Stelle sein; *now the – is on the other foot*, nun paßt es ihm (*etc.*) nicht mehr in den Kram; *shake in one's –s*, vor Angst zittern, Bammel haben; *step into his –s*, sein Amt übernehmen. 2. *ir.v.a.* beschuhen; beschlagen (*horses, wheels, sticks, etc.*). **–black,** *s.* der Schuhputzer. **--brush,** *s.* die Schuhbürste. **–horn,** *s.* der Schuhanzieher. **–ing,** *s.* das Beschlagen, Beschuhen. **–ing-smith,** *s.* der Hufschmied. **–lace,** *s.* das Schuhband, der Schuhriemen, Schnürsenkel. **--leather,** *s.* das Schuhleder; (*coll.*) *save --leather*, einen Gang sparen. **–less,** *adj.* ohne Schuhe, barfuß. **--lift,** *s.*, *see* **–horn.** **–maker,** *s.* der Schuhmacher, Schuster. **--thread,** der Pechdraht. **–making,** *s.* das Schuhmachen, Schustern; *–making trade*, das Schuhmachergewerbe, Schusterhandwerk. **--polish,** *s.* die Schuhwichse. **--scraper,** *s.* der Schuhkratzer, das Schuheisen. **--string,** *s.* (*archaic*) *see* **–lace.**

shone [ʃɔn], *see* **shine.**

shoo [ʃuː], 1. *v.a.* (also – *away*), (ver)scheuchen. 2. *int.* husch!

shook [ʃuk], *see* **shake.**

shoot [ʃuːt], 1. *ir.v.n.* schießen (*also fig.*), feuern (*at*, nach); (*fig.*) fliegen, flitzen, rasen, stürzen; keimen, sprossen, ausschlagen, Knospen treiben (*Bot.*); stechen (*pain*); filmen, eine Aufnahme machen (*Phot.*); ins Tor schießen (*Footb.*); *go –ing*, auf Jagd gehen; – *ahead*, voraneilen; – *ahead of*, überholen, hinter sich lassen; – *up*, aufschießen, hochschießen, in die Höhe schießen. 2. *ir.v.a.* schießen (*game, etc.*), erschießen, totschießen (*a p.*), abschießen, abfeuern (*bullets, arrows*); werfen, schleudern (*glance, etc.*), auswerfen (*anchor*), ausschütten, abladen, ausleeren (*rubbish, etc.*), aussenden (*rays*), vorschieben (*a bolt*); – *down*, niederschießen, niederknallen, abschießen (*aircraft*); – *out*, vorstrecken (*one's leg*), ausstrecken (*one's tongue*), ausstoßen (*words*); – *up*, zusammenschießen; – *a bridge*, unter einer Brücke durchfahren; – *rapids*, über Stromschnellen fahren; (*sl.*) – *the moon*, heimlich ausziehen (ohne die Miete zu zahlen). 3. *s.* der Sprößling (*Hort.*); die Jagd, Jagdgesellschaft; das Jagdrevier; (*sl.*) *the whole* –. der ganze Rummel. **–er,** *s.* der Schütze; *six--er*.

sechsschüssiger Revolver. **–ing,** 1. *s.* das Schießen, die Schießerei; das Erschießen (*of a p.*); die Jagd; *go –ing*, auf die Jagd gehen; *–ing of a film*, die Filmaufnahme. 2. *adj.* stechend (*as pain*). **–ing-boots,** *pl.* die Jagdstiefel. **–ing-box,** *s.* das Jagdhäuschen. **–ing-gallery,** *s.* die Schießbude. (*sl.*) **–ing-iron,** *s.* das Schießeisen. **–ing-licence,** *s.* der Jagdschein. **–ing-lodge,** *see* **–ing-box. –ing-match,** *s.* das Wettschießen, Preisschießen. **–ing-party,** *s.* die Jagdgesellschaft. **–ing-range,** *s.* der Schießstand. **–ing-season,** *s.* die Jagdzeit. **–ing star,** die Sternschnuppe.

shop [ʃɔp], 1. *s.* der Laden, das Geschäft, die Werkstatt; (*coll.*) *the –*, die Militärakademie zu Woolwich; (*sl.*) *all over the –*, überall verstreut, in großer Unordnung; *keep a –*, einen Laden halten; *set up –*, ein Geschäft aufmachen; *shut up –*, das Geschäft aufgeben; *talk –*, fachsimpeln; (*coll.*) *come to the wrong –*, an die falsche Adresse kommen. 2. *v.n.* einkaufen, Einkäufe *or* Besorgungen machen. **– -assistant,** *s.* der Ladengehilfe, (die) Verkäufer(in). **– -boy,** *s.* der Ladenbursche. **– -front,** *s.* das Schaufenster. **– -girl,** *s.* das Ladenmädchen, die Verkäuferin. **– -hours,** *pl.* Ladenstunden (*pl.*). **– -keeper,** *s.* der Ladenbesitzer, Krämer. **– -keeping,** *s.* der Kleinhandel, das Detailgeschäft. **–lifter,** *s.* der Ladendieb. **–lifting,** der Ladendiebstahl. **– -man** [-mən], *s.* der Ladengehilfe. **–per,** *s.* der Einkäufer. **–ping,** *s.* das Einkaufen; Besorgungen (*pl.*), Einkäufe (*pl.*); *do one's* or *go –ping*, Einkäufe machen; *–ping centre*, das Geschäftszentrum. **– -price,** *s.* der Ladenpreis. **– -soiled,** *adj.* beschädigt, angestaubt. *– -soiled goods*, die Ausschußware. **– -steward,** *s.* der Vertrauensmann (der Arbeiter). **–walker,** *s.* der Ladenaufseher. **– -window,** *s.* das Schaufenster. **– -woman,** *s.* die Verkäuferin, das Ladenfräulein.

[1]**shore** [ʃɔ:], *s.* das Ufer, Gestade, die Küste, der Strand; *on –*, an Land, ans Land *or* Ufer, auf dem Land, am Ufer. **– -battery,** *s.* die Küstenbatterie. **–less,** *adj.* uferlos (*also fig.*). **–ward,** *adj.* Küsten–. **–wards,** *adv.* nach der Küste zu.

[2]**shor–e,** 1. *s.* die Stütze, Strebe, Stützstrebe, der Strebebalken, die Schore (*Naut.*). 2. *v.a.* (usually *–e up*) stützen. **–ing,** *s.* das Stützen.

shorn [ʃɔ:n], *see* **shear;** *adj.*; *– of*, beraubt (*Gen.*).

short [ʃɔ:t], 1. *adj.* kurz (*time & space, also fig.*); klein (*stature*), brüchig, bröckelig, mürbe (*pastry, metal*), schwach, schlecht (*as memory*), kurzfristig (*C.L.*), kurzangebunden, barsch (*with*, gegen), knapp, fehlend, mangelhaft, unzureichend; (*a*) *– of*, knapp an; kurz vor; weniger als; *– of breath*, kurzatmig; *– of cash*, nicht bei Kasse; *little – of*, beinahe, kaum weniger als; *nothing – of*, nichts als, geradezu, überaus; *be – of*, Mangel haben an; *come* or *fall – of*, nicht entsprechen (*Dat.*), zurückbleiben hinter, nicht erreichen; *go – of*, Mangel leiden an; *run – of*, knapp werden an; *stop – of nothing*, vor nichts zurückschrecken; (*b*) *– bill*, ungedeckter Wechsel, der Blankowechsel, der Wechsel auf kurze Sicht; *– cut*, nächster Weg, der Kurzweg, Richtweg; *at – date*, auf kurze Sicht (*C.L.*); *– drink*, starkes *or* unvermischtes Getränk; *on the – list*, auf der Auswahlliste *or* engen Wahl; *– loan*, kurzfristige Anleihe; *a – 10 miles*, knappe 10 Meilen; *a – 10 minutes*, knappe 10 Minuten; *at – notice*, in kurzer Zeit, in kurzem; *– pastry*, der Mürbeteig; *– shrift*, die Galgenfrist; *give – shrift*, kurzen Prozeß machen mit; *he will get – shrift*, mit ihm wird kurzer Prozeß gemacht; *– sight*, die Kurzsichtigkeit; *– story*, die Novelle, Kurzgeschichte; *to cut a long story –*, um es kurz zu machen *or* fassen; *– temper*, die Reizbarkeit; *in a – time*, in kurzer Zeit, in kurzem; *– weight*, das Fehlgewicht; *make – work of*, kurzen Prozeß machen mit; (*c*) (*with adjectives*) *– and sweet*, kurz und gut *or* bündig; (*d*) (*with verbs*) *be –*, sich kurz fassen; *be – with*, kurz abfertigen; *make it –*, sich kurz fassen; (*e*) (*with prepositions*) *– for*, eine Abkürzung für. 2. *adv.* kurz, plötzlich; *cut –*, unterbrechen; *stop –*, plötzlich innehalten (*of*, vor); *sell –*, ohne Deckung verkaufen; (*coll.*) *be taken –*, Durchfall bekommen; *take s.o. up –*, einen plötzlich unterbrechen. 3. *s.* kurze Silbe (*Metr.*), kurzer Vokal; der Kurzschuß (*Artil.*); Kurzschluß (*Elec.*); Kurzfilm; *for –*, der Kürze halber, in Kürze, kurz; *the long and the – of it is*, die Sache ist in Kürze diese; *pl.*, *see* **–s. –age** [–ɪdʒ], *s.* der Mangel, die Knappheit (*of*, an (*Dat.*)); der Fehlbetrag. **–bread,** *s.* der Mürbekuchen. **– -circuit,** 1. *s.* der Kurzschluß (*Elec.*). 2. *v.a. & n.* kurzschließen (*Elec.*). **–coming,** *s.* (*usually pl.*) die Unzulänglichkeit, schwache Seite, der Fehler, Mangel. **– -dated,** *adj.* auf kurze Sicht. **–en,** 1. *v.a.* (ver)kürzen, abkürzen; stutzen, beschneiden (*Hort.*), vermindern, bergen, verkleinern (*sail*); *–en range*, zurückverlegen (*Artil.*). 2. *v.n.* kürzer werden, abnehmen, sich senken, fallen (*as price*). **–ening,** *s.* die Verkürzung, das Kürzen; das Fett (zum Backen). **–hand,** *s.* Kurzschrift, Stenographie; *–hand-typist*, der Stenotypist. *–hand-writer*, *s.* der Stenograph. **–horn,** *s.* kurzhörniges Rindvieh. **–ish,** *adj.* etwas *or* ziemlich kurz. **–lived,** *adj.* kurzlebig, von kurzer Dauer. **–ly,** *adv.* in kurzem, in kurzer Zeit, alsbald; kurz, bündig, schroff; *–ly after*, bald *or* kurze Zeit nachher, bald nachdem; *–ly before*, kurz vorher. **–ness,** *s.* die Kürze; Knappheit, der Mangel; die Schroffheit; *–ness of breath*, die Kurzatmigkeit. **– -range,** *attrib. adj.* Nahkampf–. **–s,** *pl.* die Kniehose, kurze Hose. **– -sighted,** *adj.* kurzsichtig. **– -sightedness,** *s.* die Kurzsichtigkeit (*also fig.*). **– -tempered,** *adj.* reizbar. **– -term,** *adj.* kurzfristig. **– -wave,** 1. *s.* die Kurzwelle. 2. *attrib. adj.* Kurzwellen–. **– -winded,** *adj.* kurzatmig.

[1]**shot** [ʃɔt], 1. *s.* der Schuß, das Geschoß, die Kugel; der Schütze; Stoß, Wurf, Schlag (*Sport*); die Aufnahme (*Films*); (*coll.*) der Versuch, (*coll.*) die Einspritzung, Spritze (*Med.*); (*a*) (*with adjectives*) *dead –*, unfehlbarer Schütze; *good –!* gut getroffen!; *long –*, der Schuß auf weites Ziel, (*fig.*) kühner Versuch; (*sl.*) *not by a long –*, i wo; *small –*, das Schrot(korn); *at the third –*, beim dritten Versuch; *like a –*, sofort, blitzschnell; (*b*) (*with verbs*) (*coll.*) *have a – at*, (zu bekommen) versuchen; *make a –*, ins Blaue hinein *or* aufs Geratewohl raten; *make a bad –*, fehlschießen, falsch raten, danebenschießen; *putting the –*, das Kugelstoßen; *take a – at*, schießen auf *or* nach; *take a pot-– at*, einen Schuß ins Blaue machen, aufs Geratewohl schießen. 2. *see* **shoot;** *– dead*, erschossen. 3. *adj.* gesprenkelt, schillernd; *– silk*, schillernde Seide; *–through with*, durchschossen *or* durchsetzt mit. **– -effect,** *s.* der Changeanteffekt (*Dye.*). **–gun,** *s.* die Schrotflinte. **–proof,** *adj.* kugelfest. **– -tower,** *s.* der Schrotturm. **– -wound,** *s.* die Schußwunde.

[2]**shot,** *s.* der Beitrag, die Zeche.

should [ʃʊd], *see* **shall;** 1. sollte(st), sollten. 2. (*for subjunctive*) (*1st pers. sing. & pl.*) würde(n) (*in princip. clause*). 3. (*indic. in subord. clause with* that) *it is unbelievable that he – be* (*have been*) *so stupid*, es ist unglaublich daß er so dumm (gewesen) ist (*as to*, zu); *I – like to*, ich möchte (gern); *he – have done it*, er hätte es tun sollen.

shoulder ['ʃouldə], 1. *s.* die Schulter (*also of a horse*), Achsel; der Bug, das Vorder-Schulterblatt (*of quadrupeds*); Schulterstück (*Butch.*); der Vorsprung, die Brüstung; *– to –*, Schulter an Schulter; *give a person the cold –*, einen ignorieren *or* geringschätzig behandeln, einen links liegen lassen; *put one's – to the wheel*, etwas fest anpacken, alle Anstrengungen machen; *– of mutton*, die Hammelkeule; *you cannot put old heads on young –s*, Jugend hat keine Tugend; (*coll.*) *rub –s with*, verkehren mit. 2. *v.a.* schultern, auf die Schulter nehmen, (*fig.*) auf sich nehmen; stoßen, schieben, drängen; *– one's way*, sich drängen; *– arms!* Gewehr über! **–ed,** *adj. suffix*, –schulterig. **– -belt,** *s.* das Schultergehenk, Wehrgehenk. **– -blade,** *s.* das Schulterblatt (*Anat.*). **– -strap,** *s.* das Achselband (*on underclothes*); die Achselklappe, das Achselstück (*Mil.*).

shout [ʃaʊt], 1. *s.* der Ruf, Schrei, das Geschrei; *give a –*, schreien. 2. *v.n.* schreien (*with*, vor; *for*, nach *or* um), rufen; *– for s.o.*, nach jemand rufen; *– for joy*, vor Freude jauchzen; *– at*, anschreien; *– out*, aufschreien; *– to*, zurufen (*Dat.*). 3. *v.a.* laut rufen *or* schreien; *– a p. down*, einen niederschreien; *– out*, ausrufen. **–ing,** *s.* das Geschrei, Schreien.

shove [ʃʌv], 1. *v.a.* schieben, stoßen, (*coll.*) stellen, legen, stecken; – *aside*, beiseiteschieben; – *away*, wegschieben; – *off*, abstoßen (*boat*). 2. *v.n.* sich drängen; – *by*, sich vorbeidrängen; – *off*, abstoßen (*Naut.*). (*sl.*) sich wegbegeben, verduften; (*sl.*) – *on*, weitergehen. 3. *s.* der Schub, Stoß.

shovel [ˈʃʌvl], 1. *s.* die Schaufel, die Schippe. 2. *v.a.* schaufeln, schippen. **--board,** *s.* das Beilkespiel; die Beilketafel. **-er,** die Löffelente (*Orn.*). **-ful,** *s.* die Schaufelvoll. **--hat,** breitkrempiger Hut (*Eccl.*).

show [ʃou], **1.** *ir.v.a.* zeigen (*a th. to a p.* or *a p. a th.*, einem etwas); ausstellen, zur Schau stellen; darstellen, darlegen, dartun, erkennen lassen, aufweisen, beweisen, aufzeigen; erzeigen, erweisen (*kindness, etc.*); führen, geleiten (*a p.*); *be –n to be*, sich erweisen als; – *dirt*, leicht schmutzen; – *a p. the door*, einen vor die Tür setzen; – *a p. to the door*, einen zur Tür geleiten; *not – one's face*, sich nicht sehen lassen; – *the white feather*, sich feige benehmen; – *fight*, sich kampflustig zeigen; – *one's hand*, seine Karten aufdecken, seine Absichten zu erkennen geben; – *a* (*clean*) *pair of heels*, ausreißen; – *o.s.*, sich zeigen, erscheinen; – *proof*, einen Beweis nachweisen *or* liefern; *as is –n by*, wie erwiesen wird durch; – *one's teeth*, fletschen, die Zähne zeigen; *have s.th. to – for*, ein Ergebnis aufzuweisen haben; – *forth*; aufzeigen, darlegen, dartun; – *in*, (her)einführen, eintreten lassen; – *off*, vorlegen, vorführen, hervorheben; prahlen mit, zur Schau tragen; – *over* or *round*, führen durch, herumführen, zeigen; – *a p. out*, einen an die Tür bringen; – *up*, heraufführen; darlegen, aufdecken, entlarven, bloßstellen. **2.** *ir.v.n.* sich zeigen, sichtbar *or* zu sehen sein, gesehen werden, erscheinen; *be –ing*, gezeigt *or* vorgeführt werden (*as films*); *time will –*, die Zeit wird es lehren; – *off*, sich brüsten, großtun, prahlen; – *up*, sich abheben (*against*, gegen); (*coll.*) erscheinen, sich ziegen, auftauchen. **3.** *s.* das Erscheinen, die Erscheinung, Schau, der Anschein, Anblick, (leerer) Schein, der Vorwand; das Schauspiel, die Ausstellung; (*coll.*) die Vorstellung, Vorführung, Aufführung; (*sl.*) das Unternehmen, die Sache, Angelegenheit, Einrichtung, der Kram ; (*a*) (*with nouns*) *make a – of anger*, sich zornig stellen; – *of hands*, das Hochheben der Hände; – *of teeth*, das Fletschen; (*b*) (*with adjectives*) (*sl.*) *oh, bad –!* wie schade!; *dumb –*, die Pantomime; *make a fine –*, prächtig aussehen; *put on a fine –*, eine prachtvolle Darbietung aufführen; *put up a fine –*, eine schöne Leistung vollbringen; (*c*) (*with verbs*) *give the – away*, das Geheimnis verraten; *make a – of*, zur Schau tragen, sehen lassen; *make a – of doing*, so tun *or* sich stellen als wenn man tun wollte; (*coll.*) *run the –*, die Sache leiten, dirigieren *or* schmeißen; (*d*) (*with prepositions*) *for –*, um zu renommieren; *on –*, zu besichtigen; *under a – of*, unter dem Schein *or* Vorwand von. **--bill,** *s.* der Theaterzettel. **--bread,** *s.* das Schaubrot, Opferbrot. **--card,** *s.* das Reklameplakat. **--case,** *s.* der Schaukasten, Ausstellungskasten, die Vitrine. (*coll.*) **--down,** *s.* der Entscheidungskampf, endgültige Auseinandersetzung. **-iness,** *s.* der Prunk, die Pracht, Prunkhaftigkeit, Auffälligkeit. **-ing,** *s.* die Darstellung, Vorführung; *on his own –ing*, nach seiner eigenen Aussage; *make a poor –ing*, sich als eine Niete *or* ein Versager ausweisen. **-man** [-mən], *s.* der Schausteller, Schaubudenbesitzer. **-manship,** *s.* effektvolle Darbietung. **--piece,** *s.* das Ausstellungsstück, Paradestück. **--pupil,** *s.* der Paradeschüler. **-room,** *s.* der Ausstellungsraum, Vorführungsraum. **-y,** *adj.* prunkhaft, auffallend, auffällig, prächtig.

shower [ˈʃauə], 1. *s.* der Guß, Schauer, Hagel (*of arrows or bullets*), (*fig.*) Erguß, die Fülle, Menge; *see also* **--bath;** – *of rain*, der Regenguß. 2. *v.a.* (also – *down*), regnen *or* herunterströmen lassen, herabschütten, (*fig.*) überschütten (*a p. with th.* or *th.* (*up*)*on a p.*, einen mit S.). **--bath,** *s.* die Brause, Dusche, das Brausebad. **-iness,** *s.* das Regnerische. **-y,** *adj.* regnerisch; *–y weather*, das Regenwetter.

shrank [ʃræŋk], *see* **shrink.**

shrapnel [ˈʃræpnəl], *s.* das Schrapnell.

shred [ʃrɛd], 1. *s.* der Fetzen, das & der Schnitzel; (*fig.*) das Stückchen, der Funken, die Spur; *tear to –s*, in Fetzen zerreißen; *not a – of*, keine Spur von. 2. *v.a.* zerfetzen, zerreißen, zerschneiden, schnitzeln (*vegetables*).

shrew [ʃru:], *s.* böses Weib, der Zankteufel; (also *--mouse, s.*) die Spitzmaus; *Taming of the –*, Der Widerspenstigen Zähmung. **-ish,** *adj.* zänkisch, boshaft.

shrewd [ʃru:d], *adj.* scharfsinnig, scharfsichtig, klug; schlau; *have a – guess*, gut raten. **-ness,** *s.* der Scharfsinn, die Klugheit, Schlauheit.

shriek [ʃri:k], 1. *s.* der Schrei, das Geschrei, Kreischen, Gekreisch; *–s of laughter*, lautes Gelächter. 2. *v.n.* schreien (*with*, vor), laut aufschreien, kreischen.

shrievalty [ˈʃri:vəltɪ], die Scheriffswürde, Scheriffsgerichtsbarkeit.

shrift [ʃrɪft], *s.* (*archaic*) die Beichte; (only in) *short –*, die Galgenfrist; *give a p. short –*, kurzen Prozeß mit einem machen; *he will get short –*, mit ihm wird kurzer Prozeß gemacht.

shrike [ʃraɪk], *s.* der Würger (*Orn.*).

shrill [ʃrɪl], 1. *adj.* gellend, grell, schrill, scharf, durchdringend. 2. *v.n.* schrillen, gellen. **-ness,** *s.* schrille Stimme. **--voiced,** *adj.* mit gellender Stimme.

shrimp [ʃrɪmp], 1. *s.* die Garnele, (*fig.*) der Knirps. 2. *v.n.* Garnelen fangen. **-er,** *s.* der Garnelen fischer.

shrine [ʃraɪn], *s.* der Heiligenschrein, Reliquienschrein; (*fig.*) der Altar, geweihter Platz, das Heiligtum.

shrink [ʃrɪŋk], 1. *ir.v.n.* (ein- *or* zusammen)schrumpfen, sich zusammenziehen (*into*, zu), einlaufen, eingehen (*of fabric*), sich werfen (*of wood*); (*fig.*) abnehmen, kleiner werden; zurückschrecken, zurückfahren (*from*, vor); – *from a th.*, sich scheuen vor einer S.; – *from doing*, widerwillig tun; – *away* or – *back*, zurückfahren, zurückschrecken (*from*, vor). 2. *ir.v.a.* einschrumpfen, zusammenschrumpfen *or* einlaufen lassen, krimpen, krumpen (*fabric*); (*fig.*) vermindern, verkürzen. **-age** [-ɪdʒ], *s.* das Einschrumpfen, Zusammenschrumpfen, Einlaufen; Schwindmaß, die Schrumpfung, (*fig.*) der Schwund, die Abnahme. **-ing,** *adj.* (*fig.*) ausweichend, widerwillig, scheu, verschüchtert.

shrive [ʃraɪv], *ir.v.a.* beichten lassen, die Beichte abnehmen (*Dat.*), Absolution erteilen (*Dat.*).

shrivel [ʃrɪvl], 1. *v.n.* (also – *up*), (ein)schrumpfen, zusammenschrumpfen, sich zusammenziehen, runz(e)lig werden; (*fig.*) verkümmern. 2. *v.a.* einschrumpfen lassen, runz(e)lig machen. **-led,** *adj.* runz(e)lig, welk.

¹**shroud** [ʃraud], 1. *s.* das Leichentuch; Grabtuch; (*fig.*) die Hülle, Decke, Bedeckung, Umhüllung. 2. *v.a.* in ein Leintuch einhüllen, (*usually*) (*fig.*) verbergen (ver)hüllen, bedecken.

²**shroud,** *s.* die Want, (usually *–s*, Wanten).

shrove [ʃrouv], *see* **shrive.** **--tide,** *s.* die Fastenzeit. **--Tuesday,** *s.* die Fastnacht.

¹**shrub** [ʃrʌb], *s.* die Staude, der Strauch, Busch. **-berry,** *s.* das Gebüsch, Gesträuch; Büsche, Sträuche (*pl.*). **-by,** *adj.* strauchig, buschig, dicht, Strauch-.

²**shrub,** *s.* eine Art Punsch.

shrug [ʃrʌg], 1. *s.* das Achselzucken; *give a –*, die Achseln zucken. 2. *v.n. & a.*; – (*one's shoulders*), die Achseln zucken.

shrunk [ʃrʌŋk], *see* **shrink.** **-en,** *adj.* eingeschrumpft, eingefallen, verkümmert, abgemagert.

shuck [ʃʌk], 1. *s.* die Hülse, Schale, Schote. 2. *v.a.* enthülsen, entschalen. **-s.** *int.* (*coll.*) Unsinn! Blech!

shudder [ˈʃʌdə], 1. *v.n.* schaudern, zittern, beben, besorgt sein, befürchten (*lest*, daß); – *at*, – *away from*, schaudern bei, zurückschaudern vor, Ekel empfinden über; *I – to think*, ich denke mit Schaudern, es schaudert mich bei dem Gedanken. 2. *s.* der Schauder, das Zittern, Schaudern; *it gives me the –s*, es macht mich schaudern.

shuffl-e [ˈʃʌfl], 1. *v.a.* hin und her schieben, mischen (*Cards*); *–e one's feet*, (mit den Füßen) scharren; *–e off*, von sich schieben, abschütteln, abstreifen.

2. *v.n.* (die Karten) mischen; schlürfen, nachlässig *or* schleppend gehen; abstreifen; mit den Füßen schlurren; (mit den Füßen) scharren; unruhig sitzen; (*fig.*) Ausflüchte machen, sich herauszuhelfen suchen; *–e off*, sich fortschleppen. 3. *s.* das (Karten)Mischen; Schlürfen, schlürfender Gang; die Ausflucht, der Kunstgriff, Schwindel. **–ing,** *adj.* schlürfend, schleppend, schlodderig, schlaksig (*gait*); (*fig.*) ausweichend, unredlich. 4. *s.* das Kartenmischen; schlürfender Gang; (*fig.*) Winkelzüge, Ausflüchte (*pl.*).

shun [ʃʌn], *v.a.* meiden; ausweichen (*Dat.*), sich fernhalten von.

shunt [ʃʌnt], 1. *v.a.* auf ein Nebengeleis *or* anderes Geleis fahren, verschieben (*Railw.*); parallel schalten (*Elec.*); (*fig.*) (also – *off*), abzweigen, ableiten, beiseiteschieben (*a th.*), kaltstellen (*a p.*). 2. *v.n.* auf ein Nebengeleis fahren, rangieren (*Railw.*). 3. *s.* der Neben(an)schluß, die Nebenleitung, Parallelschaltung (*Elec.*); das Nebengeleis, die Weiche (*Railw.*); (*fig.*) das Ausweichen. **–er,** *s.* der Rangierer, Weichensteller (*Railw.*). **–ing,** *s.* das Rangieren. **–ing-engine,** *s.* die Rangierlokomotive. **–ing-yard,** *s.* der Rangierbahnhof, Verschiebebahnhof.

shut [ʃʌt], 1. *ir.v.a.* (*also imperf. & p.p.*) (ver)schließen, zumachen, zuklappen (*a book, etc.*), zusammenklappen, zusammenfalten (*folding articles*); – *one's eyes to*, (*fig.*) die Augen verschließen vor, nicht sehen wollen; – *the door on*, (*fig.*) unmöglich machen; – *one's mouth*, den Mund schließen; – *a p.'s mouth*, einen zum Stillschweigen bringen *or* verpflichten, einem den Mund stopfen; – *o.s. away*, sich abschließen (*from*, von); – *down*, einstellen, stillegen (*a business, etc.*); – *in*, einschließen; die Aussicht versperren; – *off*, absperren, abdrehen, abstellen (*water, gas, etc.*); – *out*, ausschließen, aussperren, versperren (*the view*); – *to*, zuschließen; – *up*, verschließen, einschließen, abschließen; – *o.s. up*, sich einschließen; – *a p. up*, einen einsperren; (*sl.*) einen den Mund stopfen; (*coll.*) – *up shop*, (*fig.*) den Laden *or* die Bude zumachen. 2. *ir.v.n.* sich schließen, zugehen; – *down*, stillgelegt werden; – *to*, sich schließen; – *up!* halt's Maul! 3. *s.* **– -down,** die Stillegung, Betriebseinstellung. (*sl.*) **– -eye,** das Nickerchen.

shutter [ˈʃʌtə], der Fensterladen, die (Schließ)-Klappe, der Verschluß (*Phot.*); *put up the –s*, die Fensterläden schließen; (*fig.*) das Geschäft schließen. **–less,** *adj.* ohne Fensterläden.

shuttle [ˈʃʌtl], *s.* das Weberschiff, der Schützen (*Weav.*); das Schiffchen (*Sewing-mach.*); die Schleuse, Schütze, das Schütz. **–cock,** *s.* der Federball, (*fig.*) der Streitgegenstand, Fangball. **– -service,** *s.* der Pendelverkehr (*Railw., etc.*). **– -thread,** *s.* der Spulenfaden, Querfaden.

[1]**shy** [ʃaɪ], 1. *adj.* scheu (*of animals*), schüchtern, zurückhaltend (*of persons*); behutsam, vorsichtig; mißtrauisch, argwöhnisch; (*coll.*) *fight – of*, meiden; vorsichtig aus dem Wege gehen (*Dat.*); nicht angehen wollen, nicht heranwagen an; *fight – of doing*, sich scheuen zu tun. 2. *v.n.* scheuen (*of horses*) (*at*, vor); – *at* or *away from*, (*fig.*) zurückschrecken vor. **–ness,** *s.* die Scheu, Schüchternheit, Zurückhaltung, der Argwohn.

[2]**shy,** 1. *v.a.* (*coll.*) werfen, schleudern. 2. *s.* der Wurf, Hieb, Versuch; *have a – at*, werfen nach; es versuchen mit.

shyster [ˈʃaɪstə], *s.* (*sl.*) unsauberer Anwalt; der Lump, Halunke.

si [siː], *s.* siebenter Ton der Tonleiter, das H (*Mus.*).

sibila–nce [ˈsɪbɪləns], *s.* das Zischen (*Phonet.*). **–nt,** 1. *adj.* zischend, Zisch–. 2. *s.* der Zischlaut. **–te,** *v.a. & n.* zischen. **–tion** [–ˈleɪʃən], *s.* das Zischen.

sibyl [ˈsɪbɪl], *s.* die Sybille, Wahrsagerin. **–line** [–ˈbɪlɪːn], *adj.* sibyllinisch, prophetisch, dunkel.

siccative [ˈsɪkətɪv], 1. *adj.* trocknend. 2. *s.* das Sikkativ, Trockenmittel.

sick [sɪk], 1. *adj.* krank, unwohl, übel; zum Erbrechen geneigt; (*fig.*) angewidert, überdrüssig; *be –*, sich übergeben; *as – as a dog*, hundeelend; *fall –*, krank werden; *feel –*, sich übergeben müssen, Brechreiz fühlen; *I feel –*, mir ist schlecht; *go –*, sich krank melden (*Mil.*); *it makes me –*, es ekelt mich, mir wird übel dabei; – *of*, (*archaic*) krank an; – *to death*, (*archaic*) todkrank (*of*, von), (*coll.*) überdrüssig; (*coll.*) *be – and tired of it*, es gründlich satt haben, mehr als genug davon haben, es hängt (*with Dat.*) schon zum Halse heraus. 2. *s.* *the –*, die Kranken (*pl.*). **– -bed,** *s.* das Krankenbett. **– -benefit,** *s.* das Krankenkassengeld. **–en,** 1. *v.n.* erkranken, krank werden, kränkeln; müde *or* überdrüssig werden (*of* (*Gen.*)), sich ekeln, Ekel empfinden (*at*, vor); *be –ening for s.th.*, etwas in den Gliedern haben. 2. *v.a.* anekeln, *be –ened*, Ekel *or* Widerwillen empfinden; überdrüssig werden; *be –ening*, widerwärtig, ekelhaft *or* zum Überdruß sein. **– headache,** *s.* die Migräne. **–ish,** *adj.* kränklich, unpäßlich, unwohl. **– -leave,** *s.* der Erholungsurlaub; *on – -leave*, wegen Krankheit beurlaubt. **–liness,** *s.* die Kränklichkeit; Ungesundheit (*of climate*); Widerlichkeit. **– -list,** *s.* der Krankenstand. **–ly,** *adj.* kränklich; schwächlich, ungesund (*as climate*), krankhaft (aussehend), blaß, bleich; Ekel erregend, widerlich; *be –ly*, kränkeln. **–ness,** *s.* die Krankheit, Übelkeit, das Erbrechen, (*fig.*) der Überdruß; *–ness insurance*, die Krankenversicherung, Krankenkasse; *sleeping –ness*, die Schlafsucht (*morbus dormitivus*); *sleepy –ness*, die Gehirnentzündung (*Encephalitis lethargica*). **– -nurse,** *s.* die Krankenschwester. **– -report,** *s.* der Krankenschein (*Mil.*). **– -room,** *s.* das Krankenzimmer.

sickle [ˈsɪkl], *s.* die Sichel. **–man,** *s.* der Schnitter.

side [saɪd], 1. *s.* die Seite (*also Anat.*), Mannschaft (*Sport*); Partei (*Sport, etc.*), das Ufer(gelände) (*of river*), der Abhang, die (Seiten)Wand (*of hill*), der (Seiten)Rand (*of road, etc.*), die Abteilung (*at school*); das Effet (*Bill., etc.*); (*coll.*) die Batzigkeit. (*a*) (*with adjectives*) *blind –*, schwache Seite; *bright –*, die Lichtseite; *classical –*, die Gymnasialabteilung; *modern –*, die Realabteilung (*in schools*); *dark* or *shady –*, die Schattenseite; *near* (*off*) *–*, linke (rechte) Seite (*of vehicle*); *no –!* Spiel aus! fertig! (*Sport*); *there are two –s to every question*, alles hat (seine) zwei Seiten. (*b*) (*with verbs*) *change –s*, sich zu einer anderen Partei schlagen, Seiten wechseln (*games*); *choose –s*, die Parteien wählen; (*coll.*) *hold* or *split one's –s* (*with laughing*), sich (*Dat.*) (vor Lachen) den Bauch halten; (*coll.*) *put on –*, vornehm tun, protzen; *put – on a ball*, einem Ball Effet geben; *take a p.'s –*, *take –s with s.o.*, Partei für einen nehmen, sich einem anschließen; *take –s*, sich für eine Partei entscheiden. (*c*) (*with prepositions*) *at the –s*, an der (den) Seite(n); *at* or *by his –*, an seiner Seite, ihm zur Seite, neben ihm; *– by –*, nebeneinander; *– by – with*, neben; *by the – of*, neben, (*fig.*) im Vergleich mit; *stand by my –*, neben mir stehen, (*fig.*) mir zur Seite stehen, mir helfen; *by* or *on the female* or *mother's –*, mütterlicherseits; *from every –* or *all –s*, von allen Seiten; *off–*, abseits (*Footb.*); *on –*, nicht abseits (*Footb.*); *on all –s* or *every –*, auf *or* von allen Seiten; (*on*) *either – of*, auf beiden Seiten von; *on every –*, nach allen Seiten; (*coll.*) *on the –*, extra, außerdem, dazu; *on the hot –*, ziemlich heiß; *on my –*, meinerseits; *put on one –*, beiseitelegen; *the mistake was on the right –*, der Fehler wirkte sich gut aus; *on the right – of 40*, unter 40; *get on the right – of s.o.*, sich mit einem auf guten Fuß stellen; *keep on the right – of a p.*, mit einem in Güte auskommen; *be on the safe –*, vorsichtig sein *or* gehen; *on the shady* or *wrong – of 30*, über 30 Jahre alt; *err on the – of generosity*, zu freigebig sein; *be on the small –*, klein geraten sein; *turn over on one's –*, sich auf die Seite legen; *on the other – of*, jenseits (*Gen.*); *on this – of*, diesseits (*Gen.*); *get out of bed on the wrong –*, (*fig.*) mit dem linken Fuß aufstehen; *win over to one's –*, für sich gewinnen. 2. *v.n.*; *– with*, Partei nehmen *or* ergreifen für, es halten mit. **– -aisle,** *s.* das Seitenschiff. **– -arms,** *pl.* das Seitengewehr (*Mil.*). **– -band,** *s.* das Seitenband (*Rad.*). **–board,** *s.* der Anrichtetisch, das Büfett. **– -car,** *s.* der Beiwagen (*Motor.*). **–d,** *suffix* –seitig. **– -dish,** *s.* das Nebengericht. **– -door,** *s.* die Seitentür. **– -drum,** *s.* die (Wirbel)Trommel. **– -entrance,** der Seiteneingang. **– -face,** *s.* die Seitenansicht, das Profil.

--issue, *s.* die Nebenfrage, Nebensache, Frage von nebensächlicher Bedeutung; *be only a --issue,* erst in zweiter Linie in Betracht kommen. **-light,** *s.* das Seitenlicht, Seitenfenster, (*fig.*) Streiflicht. **--line,** *s.* der Nebenerwerb, Nebenberuf, Nebenbeschäftigung; die Seitenlinie (*Sport*), der Nebenartikel (*C.L.*). **-long,** 1. *adv.* seitwärts, zur Seite. 2. *adj.* Seiten-, seitwärts, schräg, indirekt. **--on,** *attrib. adj.* Seiten-. **--saddle,** *s.* der Damensattel. **--show,** *s.* die Jahrmarktsbude. **--slip,** *v.n.* schleudern (*Motor.*), abrutschen, abtrudeln. **-sman,** *s.* Kirchenratsmitglied (*Eccl.*). **--splitting,** *adj.* zwerchfellerschütternd (*laughter*). **--step,** 1. *v.n.* zur Seite treten, ausweichen, entgehen (*Dat.*). 2. *s.* das Seitwärtstreten, der Schritt seitwärts, Seitenschritt. **--stroke,** *s.* das Seitenschwimmen. **--table,** der Seitentisch. **--track,** 1. *s.* das Seiten- *or* Nebengeleise (*Railw.*), (*fig.*) die Sackgasse. 2. *v.a.* auf ein Nebengleis schieben, (*fig.*) ablenken, kaltstellen, beiseiteschieben. **--view,** *s.* die Seitenansicht. **-walk,** *s.* der Gehweg, Bürgersteig (*Amer.*). **-ward,** 1. *adj.* seitlich, Seiten-, seitwärts-. 2. *adv.* seitwärts. **-wards,** *adv.* seitwärts. **-ways, -wise,** 1. *adv.* seitwärts, von der Seite. 2. *adj.* seitlich.

sider-eal [sɪˈdɪːərɪəl], *adj.* siderisch, Sternen-, Stern-. **-ite** [ˈsɪdəraɪt], *s.* der Meteorstein. **-ography** [-əˈrɔgrəfɪ], *s.* die Stahlstecherkunst, der Stahlstich.

siding [ˈsaɪdɪŋ], *s.* das Neben- *or* Seitengleis, Rangiergleis, Ausweichegleis, Abstellgleis (*Railw.*); die Parteinahme.

sidle [ˈsaɪdl], *v.n.* sich seitwärts bewegen; *- up to,* sich heranschleichen, heranmachen *or* heranschlängeln an.

siege [sɪːdʒ], *s.* die Belagerung (*Mil.*), (*fig.*) Bestürmung; der Werktisch (*Tech.*); *state of -,* der Belagerungszustand; *lay - to,* belagern (*Mil.*); (*fig.*) bestürmen; *raise the -,* die Belagerung aufheben; *undergo a -,* belagert werden. **--train,** *s.* der Belagerungspark.

sienna [sɪːˈɛnə], *s.* die Sienaerde.

siesta [sɪːˈɛstə], *s.* die Mittagsruhe, Siesta.

sieve [sɪv], 1. *s.* das Sieb; *pass* or *put through a -,* durchsieben, durchseihen, durch ein Sieb passieren; 2. *v.a.* durchsieben, durchseihen, (*fig.*) sieben, sichten.

sift [sɪft], 1. *v.a.* (durch)sieben, beuteln, sichten, sortieren, sondern (*from,* von), (*fig.*) prüfen, untersuchen, erforschen; *- the chaff from the wheat,* die Spreu von dem Weizen sondern; *- to the bottom,* bis auf den Grund untersuchen. 2. *v.n.* (also *- through*) eindringen (*into,* in). **-er,** *s.* das Sieb. **-ing,** *s.* das Sieben; *pl.* Durchgesiebte(s), *n.*, Siebabfälle (*pl.*).

sigh [saɪ], 1. *s.* der Seufzer; *with a -,* seufzend; *heave* or *fetch a -,* seufzen, aufatmen; *heave a - of relief,* erleichtert aufatmen. 2. *v.n.* seufzen, (*fig.*) schmachten (*for,* nach); *- with relief,* erleichtert aufatmen (*with,* vor). 3. *v.a.* seufzend äußern, aushauchen.

sight [saɪt], 1. *s.* das Sehvermögen, Gesicht, Augenlicht, die Sehkraft, (*fig.*) das Auge; der Anblick, das Schauspiel, die Sehenswürdigkeit; (*coll.*) traurige *or* seltsame Erscheinung; (*sl.*) heidenmäßig, bannig, eine Stange; das Korn, Visier (*of gun*); die Sicht (*C.L.*); *the -s,* die Sehenswürdigkeiten (*of a town, etc.*); *line of -,* die Ziellinie (*Gun.*); *bomb--,* die Bombenzielvorrichtung (*Av.*). (*a*) (*with adjectives*) *at first -,* auf den ersten Blick, im ersten Augenblick; *have good -,* gute Augen haben; *long -,* die Weitsichtigkeit, Fernsichtigkeit; *near -,* see *short -*; *second -,* zweites Gesicht, das Hellsehen, seherische Gabe; *short -,* die Kurzsichtigkeit; *at short -,* auf kurze Sicht (*C.L.*). (*b*) (*with verbs*) *catch - of,* erblicken; *get a - of,* zu Gesicht bekommen; *hate the - of,* nicht ausstehen können; *lose - of,* aus den Augen verlieren, (*fig.*) übersehen; *lose one's -,* blind werden; *ruin one's -,* sich (*Dat.*) die Augen verderben; *take -,* visieren. (*c*) (*with prepositions*) *after -,* nach Sicht (*C.L.*); *at -,* beim (ersten) Anblick; vom Blatt (*Mus.*); nach Sicht (*C.L.*); *shoot at -,* sofort niederschießen; *by -,* von Ansehen; *play from -,* vom Blatt spielen; (*with*)*in -,* in Sicht *or* Sehweite, in der Nähe; *come in -,* sichtbar werden, zum Vorschein kommen; *in - of a th.,* (*fig.*) einer Sache nahe; *in - of completion,* kurz vor der Vollendung; *in the - of,* vor den Augen (*Gen.*); *in the - of God,* vor Gott; *keep in -,* im Auge behalten; *out of -,* außer Sicht; *out of - of a p.,* unsichtbar für einen; *get out of my - !* mir aus den Augen! *put out of -,* aus den Augen legen; *he watched it out of -,* er beobachtete es, bis er es nicht mehr sehen konnte; *out of -, out of mind,* aus den Augen, aus dem Sinn; *fire over open -s,* über Kimme und Korn schießen. (*d*) (*coll. & sl.*) *- for sore eyes,* die Augenweide, freudiger Anblick; *a - for the gods,* ein Anblick für Götter; *a dashed - harder,* verflucht schwieriger; *a long - better,* viel besser; *not by a long -,* noch lange *or* bei weitem nicht; *look a -,* toll aussehen; *a - to see,* prächtig anzusehen; *what a - he is,* wie sieht er nur aus! 2. *v.a.* erblicken, zu Gesicht bekommen, sichten; zielen auf, aufs Korn *or* Visier nehmen, anvisieren; akzeptieren, präsentieren (*a bill.*) (*C.L.*). **--bill, --draft,** *s.* die Sichttratte (*C.L.*). **-ed,** *adj., suffix* -sichtig. **-ing,** *s.* das Zielen, Visieren; *-ing shot,* der Probeschuß; *-ing telescope,* das Zielfernrohr. **-less,** *adj.* blind. **-lessness,** *s.* die Blindheit. **-liness,** *s.* stattliches Aussehen, die Schönheit, Wohlgestalt. **-ly,** *adj.* ansehnlich, gut aussehend, schön. **--reading,** *s.* das Spielen *or* Singen vom Blatt. **-seeing,** *s.* die Besichtigung der Sehenswürdigkeiten. *go -seeing,* die Sehenswürdigkeiten besichtigen. **-seer,** *s.* Schaulustige(r), *m.*

sigmoid(al) [ˈsɪgmɔɪd, sɪgˈmɔɪdl], *adj.* sigmaförmig, S-förmig.

sign [saɪn], 1. *s.* das Zeichen, Anzeichen, Symptom (*of,* von *or* für), Kennzeichen (*of,* von), Merkmal; der Wink, die Handbewegung, Gebärde; das (Aushänge)Schild; Vorzeichen (*Math., Mus.*); Himmelszeichen, Wunderzeichen; *conventional -,* das Kartenzeichen; *- of the cross,* das Zeichen des Kreuzes; *give a -,* einen Wink *or* ein Zeichen geben; *good -,* gute Vorbedeutung, gutes Zeichen; *- of life,* das Lebenszeichen; *make a -,* see *give a -*; *make no -,* sich nicht rühren. 2. *v.a.* (be)zeichnen, kennzeichnen; unterzeichnen, unterschreiben (*a document*), schreiben (*one's name*); *-ed (and) sealed and delivered,* unterschrieben, besiegelt und vollzogen (*Law*); *- away,* durch seine Unterschrift abtreten; *- on,* anstellen, anmustern, anwerben, verpflichten. 3. *v.n.* winken, ein Zeichen geben (*to* (*Dat.*)); unterzeichnen, zeichnen (*C.L.*); *- for,* quittieren; *- on,* sich anwerben lassen, sich verdingen; *- off,* eine Sendung beenden (*Rad.*). **-board,** *s.* das (Aushänge)Schild. **--manual,** *s.* (eigenhändige) Unterschrift. **--painter,** *s.* der Schildermaler. **-post,** *s.* der Wegweiser.

signal [sɪgnəl], 1. *s.* das Signal, Zeichen (*for,* für *or* zu) (*also fig.*); (*fig.*) die Losung, der Anlaß, die Veranlassung (*for,* zu); *all clear -,* die Entwarnung; *call -,* das Rufzeichen; *danger -, - of distress,* das Notsignal. 2. *adj.* bemerkenswert, außerordentlich, ungewöhnlich, hervorragend. 3. *v.n.* Signale geben, durch Signale anzeigen. 4. *v.a.* ein Zeichen geben, winken (*a p.* (*Dat.*)), signalisieren, durch Signale melden. **--box,** *s.* das Stellwerk (*Railw.*). **--gun,** der Signalschuß. **--halyards,** die Flaggleine (*Naut.*). **-ize,** *v.a.* auszeichnen, signalisieren, charakterisieren, an den Tag legen, zu erkennen geben, vermerken, buchen; *-ize o.s.,* sich auszeichnen *or* hervortun. **-ler,** *s.* der Melder, Blinker (*Mil.*), Signalgast (*Naut.*). **--lamp,** die Blinklampe. **-man,** *s.* der Bahnwärter (*Railw.*), Signalgast (*Naut.*). **--rocket,** die Leuchtrakete. **--strength,** die Lautstärke (*Rad.*).

signat-ory [ˈsɪgnətərɪ] 1. *adj.* unterzeichnend; *-ory power,* die Signatarmacht. 2. *s.* der Unterzeichner. **-ure** [-tʃə], *s.* (eigenhändige) Unterschrift, der Namenszug; charakteristisches Zeichen, das Kennzeichen, der Stempel, die Bezeichnung, Signatur (*Typ., Mus.*). **-ure tune,** die Kennmusik, Einleitungsmelodie (*Rad.*).

signet [ˈsɪgnɪt], *s.* das Siegel, Petschaft; *writer to the -,* der Rechtsanwalt (*Scots*). **--ring,** *s.* der Siegelring.

signif–icance [sɪgˈnɪfɪkəns], *s.* **–icancy,** *s.* die Bedeutung (*to*, für), der Sinn, die Wichtigkeit. **–icant,** *adj.* bedeutsam, wichtig (*for*, für); bezeichnend (*of*, für); *be –icant of*, bedeuten, beweisen. **–ication** [–ˈkeɪʃən], *s.* die Bedeutung, Bezeichnung. **–icative,** bezeichnend, kennzeichnend (*of*, für); bedeutsam, Bedeutungs–. **–y** [ˈsɪgnɪfaɪ], 1. *v.a.* bezeichnen, andeuten, bedeuten; bekanntmachen, ankündigen, kundtun; zu verstehen *or* erkennen geben. 2. *v.n.* von Bedeutung sein, zu bedeuten haben; *it doesn't –y*, es tut *or* macht nichts, es hat nichts auf sich, es ist von keiner Bedeutung.
signpost, *see under* **sign.**
silage [ˈsaɪlɪdʒ], *s.* konserviertes Grünfutter.
silen–ce [ˈsaɪləns], 1. *s.* das (Still)Schweigen; die Ruhe, Stille; Schweigsamkeit, Verschwiegenheit; *impose –ce*, Stillschweigen auferlegen (*on* (*Dat.*)); *keep* or *preserve –ce*, Stillschweigen beobachten; *pass over in –ce*, mit Stillschweigen übergehen; *–ce gives consent*, wer schweigt, gibt zu; *–ce is golden*, Schweigen ist Gold. 2. *int.* Ruhe!, (*Studs. sl.*) Silentium! 3. *v.a.* zum Schweigen bringen (*also Mil.*); (*fig.*) unterdrücken. **–cer,** *s.* der Schalldämpfer, der Auspufftopf (*Motor.*). **–t,** *adj.* schweigend, stumm, still, ruhig, geräuschlos; schweigsam, verschwiegen; *be –t*, schweigen; *be –t on*, sich ausschweigen über; *–t consent*, stillschweigende Zustimmung; *–t film*, stummer Film; *as –t as the grave*, stumm wie das Grab; *–t syllable*, stumme Silbe; *–t partner*, *s.* stiller Teilhaber; *–t prayer*, stilles Gebet.
silhouette [sɪluˈɛt], 1. *s.* der Schattenriß, das Schattenbild, die Silhouette. 2. *v.a.* (*usually pass.*) *be –d*, sich wie ein Schattenriß abheben.
silic–a [ˈsɪlɪkə], *s.* die Kieselerde, Kieselsäure. **–ate,** *s.* kieselsaures Salz, das Silikat. **–eous, –ious** [sɪˈlɪʃəs], kieselartig, kieselhaltig, kieselig, Kiesel–. **–ic** [sɪˈlɪsɪk], *adj.*; *–ic acid*, die Orthokieselsäure. **–iferous** [–ˈlɪfərəs], *adj.* kieselhaltig. **–ify** [sɪˈlɪsɪfaɪ], 1. *v.a.* verkieseln. 2. *v.n.* sich in Kiesel verwandeln. **–on** [ˈsɪlɪkən], *s.* das Silizium; **–osis** [–ˈkoʊsɪs], *s.* die Silikose (*Med.*).
silk [sɪlk], 1. *s.* die Seide, der Seidenstoff, das Seidengewebe; die Seidenfaser, der Seidenfaden; (*coll.*) *you cannot make a – purse out of a sow's ear*, aus nichts wird nichts; *in –s and satins*, in Samt und Seide; *tussore –*, die Rohseide; *take –*, höherer Anwalt werden; *watered –*, die Moiréseide. 2. *adj.* seiden. **–en,** *adj.* (*Poet.*) seiden; (*fig.*) seidenartig, weich, glänzend. **–iness,** *s.* das Seidenartige, Weiche. **– hat,** *s.* (*coll.*) der Zylinder(hut). **– -moth,** *s.* der Seidenspinner (*Ent.*). **– ribbon,** das Seidenband. **– stocking,** der Seidenstrumpf. **–worm,** *s.* die Seidenraupe. **–y,** *adj.* seiden(artig), (seiden)weich, glänzend, sanft, zart, lieblich, einschmeichelnd; *–y lustre*, der Seidenglanz.
sill [sɪl], *s.* die Schwelle (*of a door, etc.*), das Fensterbrett (*of a window*), das *or* der Süll, der Lagergang (*Min.*).
sillabub [ˈsɪləbʌb], *s.* süßer Trank aus Wein und Milch.
sill–iness, [ˈsɪlɪnɪs], *s.* die Albernheit, Dummheit **–y,** *adj.* albern, einfältig, töricht, dumm, blöd; leichtfertig, unklug; *–y season*, die Sauregurkenzeit.
silo [ˈsaɪloʊ], *s.* der Silo, Getreidespeicher, die Grünfuttergrube.
silt [sɪlt], *s.* der Schlamm, Triebsand (*Min., etc.*). 2. *v.n.* (also *– up*) verschlammen. 3. *v.a.* (usually *– up*), verschlammen, versanden.
silvan, *adj. see* **sylvan.**
silver [ˈsɪlvə], 1. *s.* das Silber; Silbergeld, Silberzeug, Silbergeschirr; *German –*, das Neusilber; *loose –*, einzelnes Silbergeld. 2. *adj.* silbern; *be born with a – spoon in one's mouth*, ein Glückskind sein. 3. *v.a.* versilbern, mit Silber überziehen, mit Folie belegen (*a mirror, etc.*). **– -coloured,** *adj.* silberfarbig. **– fir,** *s.* die Edeltanne, Weißtanne, Silbertanne. **– foil,** *s.* die Silberfolie. **– fox,** *s.* der Silberfuchs. **– gilt,** *s.* vergoldetes Silber. **– -glance,** *s.* das Schwefelsilber. **– -grey,** 1. *adj.* silbergrau. 2. *s.* silbergraue Farbe. **– -haired,** *adj.* silberhaarig. **– -lace,** die Silbertresse. **– leaf,** *s.* das Blattsilber. **– lining,** (*fig.*) die Lichtseite. **–nitrate,** *s.* der Höllenstein. **– paper,** das Silberpapier, Staniolpapier. **– plate,** *s.* das Silbergeschirr, Silberzeug. **–plated,** *adj.* silberplattiert. **–plating,** *s.* die Silberplattierung. **– poplar,** *s.* die Silberpappel (*Bot.*). **–smith,** *s.* der Silberschmied. **–ware,** *s. see* **– plate. – wedding,** *s.* silberne Hochzeit. **–y,** *adj.* silberweiß, silberfarben; (*fig.*) silberhell (*as voice*).
silviculture [ˈsɪlvɪkʌltʃə], *s.* die Baumkultur, Forstkultur.
simil–ar [ˈsɪmɪlə], *adj.* ähnlich, gleich, gleichartig, verwandt. **–arity** [–ˈlærɪtɪ], *s.* die Ähnlichkeit (*to*, mit), Gleichartigkeit, der Vergleich. **–e** [–lɪː], *s.* das Gleichnis, der Vergleich. **–itude** [–ˈmɪlɪtjuːd] *s.* die Ähnlichkeit.
simmer [ˈsɪmə], *v n.* leicht, schwach *or* langsam kochen, wallen, (*fig.*) kochen, aufwallen, gären; *– down*, sich abkühlen, (*usually fig.*) sich beruhigen, ruhig werden.
simony [ˈsɪmənɪ], *s.* die Simonie, der Ämterkauf, Pfründenschacher.
simoom [sɪˈmuːm], *s.* der Samum.
simper [ˈsɪmpə], 1. *s.* geziertes *or* albernes Lächeln. 2. *v.n.* geziert *or* albern lächeln.
simpl–e [ˈsɪmpl], 1. *adj.* einfach, nicht zusammengesetzt *or* verwickelt, klar, unkompliziert, gewöhnlich, schlicht, anspruchslos, ungekünstelt; dumm, einfältig, leichtgläubig (*of a p.*); *–e interest*, Kapitalzinsen (*pl.*) (*C.L.*), (*coll.*) *pure and –e*, schlechthin; *–e Simon*, der Dummerjan, Einfaltspinsel. 2. *s.* das Simplum; das Heilkraut; *pl.* einfache Arzneipflanzen, Heilkräuter. **–e-hearted,** *adj.* arglos, unschuldig. **–e -minded,** *adj.* arglos, leichtgläubig, einfältig. **–eton** [–tən], *s.* der Einfaltspinsel, Tropf. **–icity** [–ˈplɪsɪtɪ], *s.* die Einfachheit, Unkompliziertheit, Klarheit, Deutlichkeit, Schmucklosigkeit, Schlichheit; Einfalt, Arglosigkeit, Unschuld. **–ification** [–ˈkeɪʃən], *s.* die Vereinfachung. **–ify,** *v.a.* vereinfachen, erleichtern. **–y,** *adv.* einfach, klar, leicht; schlicht, schmucklos, unauffällig; geradezu, schlechthin; *–y and solely*, einzig und allein.
simulacrum [sɪmjuˈleɪkrəm], *s.* das Abbild, Scheinbild, leerer Schein, hohle Form.
simulat–e [ˈsɪmjuleɪt], *v.a.* vorgeben, vortäuschen, (er)heucheln, simulieren, nachahmen. **–ion** [–leɪʃən], *s.* die Verstellung, Vorspiegelung, Heuchelei, Nachahmung.
simultane–ity [sɪməltəˈnɪːɪtɪ], *s.* die Gleichzeitigkeit. **–ous** [–ˈteɪnɪəs], *adj.* gleichzeitig. **–ousness,** *s. see* **–ity.**
sin [sɪn], 1. *s.* die Sünde, das Vergehen, die Versündigung (*against*, gegen *or* an); *besetting –*, die Gewohnheitssünde; (*sl.*) *like –*, heftig; *live in –*, in unerlaubtem Umgang leben; *mortal –*, die Todsünde, *original –*, die Erbsünde; *– of omission*, die Unterlassungssünde. 2. *v.n.* sündigen, eine Sünde begehen; sich versündigen, verstoßen *or* vergehen (*against*, gegen). 3. *v.a.*; *– a –*, eine Sünde begehen. **– -offering,** *s.* das Sühnopfer; *see* **sinful, sinless, sinner.**
sinapism [ˈsɪnəpɪzm], *s.* das Senfpflaster.
since [sɪns], 1. *adv.* seitdem, seither, später; *ever –*, von jeher; *long –*, seit langem, vor langer Zeit, *how long – ?* seit wann? seit wie lange? vor wie langer Zeit? *how long is it – ?* wie lange ist es her? *a week –*, eine Woche her, vor einer Woche. 2. *prep.* seit. 3. *conj.* seit(dem); weil, da . . (ja); *how long is it – he was here?* wie lange ist es her, daß er hier war?; *– you are here, I can go*, da Sie (ja) hier sind, kann ich gehen.
sincer–e [sɪnˈsɪːə], *adj.* aufrichtig, offen, treu, echt, lauter, rein, im Ernst; *yours –ely*, Ihr ergebener (*in letters*). **–ity** [–ˈsɛrɪtɪ], *s.* die Aufrichtigkeit, Offenheit, Echtheit, Reinheit.
sinch [sɪntʃ], (*sl.*) *see* **cinch.**
sinciput [ˈsɪnsɪpʊt], *s.* das Vorderhaupt, Schädeldach.
[1]**sine** [saɪn], *s.* der Sinus (*Geom.*); *– of an angle*, der Sinuswinkel; *– wave*, die Sinuswelle, harmonische Schwingungswelle (*Rad.*).
[2]**sine** [ˈsaɪnɪ], *prep.* ohne (*Law*); *– die*, auf unbestimmte Zeit; *– qua non*, unerläßliche Bedingung.
sinecur–e [ˈsɪnəkjʊə], *s.* die Sinekure, der Ehren-

posten, einträgliches Ruheamt, fette Pfründe. **-ist,** *s.* der Inhaber einer Sinekure.
sinew ['sɪnjʊ], *s.* die Sehne, Flechse; (*fig.*) die Stärke, Hauptstütze, der Nerv; (*fig.*) *the -s of war,* das Geld, Moneten (*pl.*). **-less,** *adj.* kraftlos, schwach. **-y,** *adj.* sehnig, zäh (*as meat*); (*fig.*) nervig, kräftig, kraftvoll.
sinful ['sɪnfʊl], *adj.* sündhaft, sündig. **-ness,** *s.* die Sündhaftigkeit.
sing [sɪŋ], 1. *ir.v.n.* singen (*also of birds*), (*Poet.*) dichten, (*coll.*) summen (*as a kettle*); sausen, klingen (*as the ears*), heulen (*of the wind*); *- of,* singen von, besingen; *- out,* schreien, laut rufen; *- out of tune,* falsch singen; (*coll.*) *- small,* kleinlaut werden, klein beigeben; *- to a p.,* einem vorsingen; *- up,* lauter singen. 2. *ir.v.a.* singen, besingen, vorsingen (*to* (*Dat.*)); *- another tune,* (*fig.*) andere Saiten aufziehen; *- a child to sleep,* ein Kind in den Schlaf singen; *- a p.'s praise,* einen besingen, preisen *or* verherrlichen; *- the same song,* (*fig.*) in dasselbe Horn blasen; *- out,* ausrufen. **-able,** *adj.* singbar. **-er,** *s.* der Sänger. **-ing,** 1. *adj.* singend. 2. *s.* das Singen, der Gesang; das Sausen, Heulen, Summen, Klingen; *-ing in the ears,* das Ohrensausen. **-ing bird,** der Singvogel. **-ing-lesson,** die Gesangstunde. **-ing-master,** *s.* der Gesanglehrer. **-ing-voice,** *s.* die Singstimme. **-song,** 1. *s.* der Singsang, das Gesinge; Gemeinschaftssingen. 2. *adj.*; *in a -song voice,* eintönig, im Leierton.
singe [sɪndʒ], 1. *v.a.* (ver)sengen, absengen (*poultry*). 2. *v.n.* sengen. 3. *s.* (leichter) Brandschaden.
single [sɪŋgl], 1. *adj.* einzig, nur ein, alleinig, bloß; einzeln, Einzeln-, alleinstehend; ledig, unverheiratet; einmalig, einfach, *- bed,* das Einzelbett; *- bill,* der Solowechsel; *- blessedness,* (*hum.*) lediger Stand, der Ledigenstand; *- combat,* der Zweikampf; *book-keeping by - entry,* einfache Buchhaltung; *with the - exception,* mit der bloßen *or* alleinigen Ausnahme; *- file,* der Gänsemarsch; *- game,* das Einzelspiel; *- man,* der Junggeselle, Hagestolz; *with a - mind,* aufrichtig; *- payment,* einmalige Bezahlung; *- room,* das Einzelzimmer; *- ticket,* einfache Karte; *with a - voice,* mit vereinter Stimme; *not a - one,* kein(e) einzig(er es e); *- woman,* alleinstehende Frau. 2. *v.a.* (usually *- out*), auslesen, auswählen; hervorheben, herausheben, bestimmen (*for,* zu). 3. *s.* einzelnes Stück, einfache Fahrkarte; ein (1) Lauf (*Crick.*); (*often pl.*) das Einzelspiel (*Tenn.*). **--breasted,** *adj.* einreihig (*coat*). **--decker,** *s.* der Eindecker. **--eyed,** *adj.* zielbewußt, geradeheraus. **--handed,** *adj.* einhändig, (*fig.*) alleinig, ohne Hilfe, auf eigene Faust. 2. *adv.* allein, selbständig. **--hearted,** *adj.* aufrichtig, redlich, zielbewußt. **-ness,** *s.* die Vereinzelung; Aufrichtigkeit; Ehelosigkeit, der Ledigenstand; *-ness of purpose,* die Zielstrebigkeit. **--phase,** *adj.* einphasig, Einphasen- (*Elec.*). **--seater,** *s.* der Einsitzer. **-stick,** *s.* das Stockfechten; der Korbschläger.
singlet ['sɪŋglɪt], *s.* das Unterhemd.
singly ['sɪŋglɪ], *adv. see* **single.**
singsong, *see* **sing.**
singular ['sɪŋgjʊlə], 1. *adj.* einzeln, vereinzelt; einzigartig, ungewöhnlich, sonderbar, eigentümlich; ausgezeichnet, hervorragend; singularisch, Singular- (*Gram.*). 2. *s.* die Einzahl, der Singular (*Gram.*). **-ity** [-'lærɪtɪ], *s.* die Einzigartigkeit, Eigenheit, Besonderheit, Eigentümlichkeit, Seltsamkeit. **-ly,** *adv.* besonders, höchst.
sinist-er ['sɪnɪstə], *adj.* böse, schlimm, schlecht, unheimlich, unheilvoll, finster; link, zur Linken (*Her.*). **-ral** [-'nɪstrəl], *adj.* link, link(s)seitig, links gewunden.
sink [sɪŋk], 1. *ir.v.n.* sinken, versinken, niedersinken, untergehen, fallen, sich senken *or* neigen, (*fig.*) eindringen, sich einprägen (*into* (*Dat.*)); übergehen (*into,* in), verfallen, erliegen (*under,* unter), nachlassen, abnehmen, herabsinken; *his heart sank* (*within him*), ihm schwand der Mut; *he is -ing fast,* mit ihm geht es rasch zu Ende; *- or swim,* zugrunde gehen oder durchhalten; *- back,* zurücksinken; *- down,* niederfallen, sich niederlassen; *- in,* sich einprägen; *- into oblivion,* in Vergessenheit geraten; *- into sleep,* in Schlaf (ver)sinken. 2. *ir.v.a.* versenken (*a ship*), senken (*head, voice, etc.*), sinken lassen, fallen lassen; herabsetzen, herabdrücken, niederdrücken (*prices, etc.*); abteufen, ausgraben, bohren (*a hole*); (*fig.*) anlegen (*money*), tilgen, abtragen (*debt*); beilegen (*a difference*), aufgeben, übergehen; eingravieren, einsetzen, einlassen; schneiden (*a die*); *be sunk in thought,* in Gedanken versunken sein. 3. *s.* der Spülstein, Ausguß, das Ausgußbecken, der Ablaufkanal (*in kitchen*); die Versenkung (*of stage*); *- of iniquity,* der Sündenpfuhl. **-able,** *adj.* versenkbar. **-er,** *s.* das Senkblei; der Stempelschneider. **-ing,** *s.* das Sinken, Untergehen; die Senkung, Vertiefung, Aushöhlung; das Schwächegefühl; *-ing in the stomach,* die Beklommenheit, das Angstgefühl. **-ing-fund,** *s.* der Tilgungsfond.
sin-less ['sɪnlɪs], *adj.* sündenfrei, sündlos, unschuldig. **-lessness,** *s.* die Sündlosigkeit. **-ner,** *s.* der Sünder.
sinu-ate ['sɪnjʊət], *adj.* ausgebuchtet. **-osity** [-'ɔsɪtɪ], *s.* die Krümmung, Windung, Biegung, Gewundenheit. **-ous** [-əs], *adj.* gewunden, gekrümmt, sich windend, krumm; geschmeidig, eng anliegend.
sinus ['sɑɪnəs], *s.* die Krümmung, Kurve, Ausbuchtung, Höhlung (*Bot.*), Knochenhöhle (*Anat.*).
sip [sɪp], 1. *s.* das Schlückchen, Nippen. 2. *v.a.* nippen, schlürfen.
siphon ['sɑɪfən], *s.* der (Saug)Heber; die Druckflasche, Siphonflasche.
sippet ['sɪpɪt], *s.* geröstete Brotschnitte.
sir [sə:], *s.* Herr (*in addressing*); Sir (*as title*); *yes -,* ja mein Herr; *dear -,* sehr geehrter Herr.
sire [sɑɪə], 1. *s.* (*archaic*) (Euere) Majestät (*in addressing*); der Herr, Gebieter; (*Poet.*) Vater, Vorfahr; männliches Stammtier (*of horses, dogs, etc.*). 2. *v.a.* zeugen (*of horses*).
siren ['sɑɪərən], 1. *s.* die Sirene (*also Acoust., fig.*); das Heulsignal; der Armmolch (*Zool.*); (*fig.*) die Verführerin, weibliches Ungeheuer. 2. *attrib. adj.* Sirenen-, verführerisch. **-ion** [sɑɪ'rɪ:nɪən], *s.* die Seekuh, Sirene (*Zool.*).
sirloin ['sə:lɔɪn], *s.* das Lendenstück (*of beef*).
sirocco [sɪ'rɔkoʊ], *s.* der Schirokko.
sirup, *see* **syrup.**
sisal ['sɪsəl], *s.* (also *--grass* and *--hemp*), der Sisalhanf.
siskin ['sɪskɪn], *s.* der Zeisig (*Orn.*).
sissy, *see* **cissy.**
sister ['sɪstə], 1. die Schwester; Nonne (*Eccl.*), Oberschwester (*in hospitals*); *they are brother and -,* sie sind Geschwister; *my brothers and -s,* meine Geschwister; *foster--,* die Pflegeschwester; *half--,* die Halbschwester; *- language,* die Schwestersprache. **--in-law,** *s.* die Schwägerin. **- of Mercy,** barmherzige Schwester. **--ship,** *s.* das Schwesterschiff. **-hood** *s.* die Schwesternschaft (*also Eccl.*); schwesterliches Verhältnis; der Schwesternorden (*Eccl.*). **-less,** *adj.* ohne Schwester. **-liness,** *s.* die Schwesterlichkeit. **-ly,** *adj.* schwesterlich, Schwester-.
sistine ['sɪstɪn], *adj.* sixtinisch.
sisyphean [sɪ'sɪfɪən], *adj.* Sisyphus-.
sit [sɪt], 1. *ir.v.n.* sitzen (*also of hens and clothes*); sich setzen, einen Sitz haben, ruhen, liegen (*of things*); Sitzung halten, zur Sitzung zusammentreten, tagen; Mitglied sein (*on* (*Gen.*)), ein Amt innehaben; brüten (*as birds*); passen (*as clothes*); *- close,* eng sitzen *or* anliegen; *the wind -s fair,* der Wind sitzt gut; *- still,* ruhig *or* still sitzen; *- in judgement upon,* zu Gericht sitzen über (*Acc.*); (*a*) (*with adverbs*) *- back,* sich zurücklehnen; *- down,* sich niedersetzen, niederlassen, *or* (hin)setzen, Platz nehmen; *- down and do nothing,* die Hände in den Schoß legen; *- down under an insult,* eine Beleidigung einstecken *or* ruhig hinnehmen; *- out,* aussetzen (*a dance*), nicht mittanzen; nicht mitspielen (*Cards*); *- out* (*in the open*), draußen sitzen; *- up,* sich aufrichten, geradesitzen; aufbleiben, aufsitzen; wachen (*with,* bei); *- up!* mach schön (*to dog*); (*coll.*) *make a p. - up,* einen aufrütteln; einen in Staunen versetzen; (*coll.*) *- tight,* eine abwartende Haltung einnehmen, abwarten; (*b*) (*with prepositions*) *- by,* sich setzen zu, sitzen neben; *for a*

constituency, einen Wahlkreis vertreten; – *for an examination*, sich einer Prüfung unterziehen, eine Prüfung machen; – *for one's portrait*, sich malen lassen; – (*in judgement*) *on*, richten (über), beraten (über); – *on a committee*, einem Ausschuß angehören; – *on the bench*, Polizeirichter sein; – *on a jury*, Geschworener sein; – *on a case*, see – *in judgement on*; – *heavy on a p.*, (*fig.*) einen bedrücken, schwer lasten auf einem; (*sl.*) – *on a p.*, einen ducken, rüffeln *or* Mores lehren, einem die Flötentöne beibringen; – *through*, ganz anhören (*a lecture*), bis zum Ende (*Gen.*) bleiben; – *upon*, see – *on*. 2. *ir v.a.* setzen; – *a horse*, zu Pferde sitzen; – *o.s.*, sich setzen; – *a p. out*, länger bleiben *or* aushalten als einer; – *a piece out* or *through*, ein Stück zu Ende hören. **--down**, *adj.*; --*down strike*, der Sitzstreik; --*down supper*, das Abendessen zu Tische. **-ter**, *s.* Sitzende(r) *m.*; die Bruthenne; das Modell (*Art*); (*sl*) leichter Treffer *or* Fang. **-ting**, 1. *adj.* sitzend; -*ting member*, gegenwärtiger Abgeordneter. 2. *s.* das Sitzen, Brüten; die Sitzung (*of committee or for artist*); (*coll.*) *at one* or *a* -*ting*, ohne Unterbrechung; -*ting-room*, das Wohnzimmer.

site [saɪt], *s.* die Lage, der Platz, Sitz; (also *building* –) Bauplatz.

situat-e ['sɪtjʊeɪt], *adj.* (*archaic & Law*), **-ed** [-ɪd], *adj.* gelegen, liegend (*of things*); in einer Lage befindlich (*of persons*); -*ed as he is*, in seiner Lage; *be -ed on*, liegen an *or* auf; *be badly -ed*, sich in einer üblen Lage befinden (*of a p.*); *well -ed*, gut gestellt (*of a p.*). **-ion**[-ʃən], *s.* die Lage, Situation, der Zustand, Umstand; die Stelle, Stellung, der Posten.

six [sɪks], 1. *num. adj.* sechs; – *of one and half a dozen of the other*, das ist Jacke wie Hose. 2. *s.* die Sechs; *be at -es and sevens*, in völliger Verwirrung sein, auf dem Kopf stehen, uneinig sein (*with*, mit; *about*, über). **--cylinder**, *attrib. adj.* sechszylindrig (*Motor*). **-fold**, *adj.* sechsfach. (*coll.*) **--footer**, *s.* zwei Meter großer Mensch. **-pence**, *s.* das 6-Pence-Stück. **-penny**, *adj.* Sechspenny-; --*pennyworth of*, für sechs Pence. **--pounder**, *s.* der Sechspfünder. **--shooter**, *s.* sechsschüssiger Revolver. **--sided**, *adj.* sechsseitig. **-teen**, 1. *num. adj.* sechzehn. 2. *s.* die Sechzehn. **-teenth**, 1. *num. adj.* sechzehnt. 2. *s.* der, die, das Sechzehnte; das Sechzehntel. **-th**, 1 *num. adj.* sechst; -*th form*, die Prima; -*th form boy*, der Primaner; -*th of March*, der 6. März. 2. *s.* der, die, das Sechste; das Sechstel; die Sexte (*Mus.*). **-thly**, *adv.* sechstens. **-tieth**, 1. *num. adj.* sechzigst. 2. *s.* der, die, das Sechzigste; das Sechzigstel. **-ty**, 1. *num. adj.* sechzig. 2. *s.* die Sechzig; *the -ties*, die sechziger Jahre.

sizable ['saɪzəbl], *adj.* ziemlich *or* beträchtlich groß, ansehnlich.

sizar ['saɪzə], *s.* der Stipendiat (*Cambridge & Dublin Univ.*).

[1]**siz-e** [saɪz], 1. *s.* der Umfang, die Größe (*also of clothes*), Länge, Dicke, das Format (*of a book, also fig.*); die Nummer (*of clothes*); (*fig.*) die Bedeutung, das Ausmaß; *life--e*, die Lebensgröße; *what -e (do you take in) shoes?* welche Schuhgröße (haben Sie)?; *what -e is it?* wie groß ist es?; *they are of a -e*, sie sind von derselben Größe; *the -e of an elephant*, ebenso groß wie ein Elefant;(*coll.*) *that's about the -e of it*, da hast Du es gerade getroffen. 2. *v.a.* nach Größe ordnen (*or* aufstellen (*Mil.*)); (*coll.*) -*e up*, richtig einschätzen *or* abschätzen, sich ein Urteil bilden über. 3. *v.n.* gleichkommen (*with* (*Dat.*)). **-able**, *see* **sizable**. **-ed** [-d], *adj. suffix*; *fair--ed*, ziemlich groß; *middle--ed*, von mittlerer Größe, mittelgroß; *small--ed*, klein.

[2]**size**, 1. *s.* der Leim, Kleister; das Planierwasser (*Bookb.*). 2. *v.a.* leimen, planieren, grundieren (*Paint.*).

sjambok ['ʒæmbɔk], *s.* die Nilpferdpeitsche.

skald [skɔ:ld], *s.* der Skalde, Barde.

skat [skæt], *s.* der Skat (*Cards*).

[1]**skat-e** [skeɪt], 1. *s.* der Schlittschuh; *roller--e*, der Rollschuh. 2. *v.n.* Schlittschuh- *or* Rollschuhlaufen; (*fig.*) leicht dahingleiten; -*e on* or *over thin ice*, ein großes Risiko eingehen, nahe an die Grenze des Schlüpfrigen kommen. **-er**, *s.* der Schlittschuhläufer, Rollschuhläufer. **-ing**, *s.* das Schlittschuhlaufen, Rollschuhlaufen. **-ing-rink**, *s.* die Eisbahn, Rollschuhbahn.

[2]**skate**, *s.* der Glattrochen (*Ichth.*).

skean [skɪ:n], *s.*, **--dhu** [-dʊ], *s.* irischer *or* schottischer Dolch.

skedaddle [skɪ'dædl], 1. *v.n.* (*coll.*) ausreißen, sich aus dem Staube machen, verduften. 2. *s.* (*coll.*) das Ausreißen, hastige Flucht.

skein [skeɪn], *s.* der Strang, die Docke, Strähne (*wool, etc.*); die Schar, der Schwarm, Flug (*wild geese, etc.*).

skelet-al ['skɛlətəl], *adj.* Skelett-. **-on** [-ən], *s.* das Skelett, Gerippe (*also fig*); (*coll.*) Knochengerüst (*thin p.*); (*fig.*) Gerüst, Gestell, der Rahmen; Kader, Stamm(bestand) (*Mil., etc.*); der Umriß, Entwurf; -*on in the cupboard*, das Familiengeheimnis; *reduced to a -on*, zum Skelett abgemagert; -*on army*, das Rahmenheer; -*on bill*, unausgefülltes Formular; -*on construction*, der Skelettbau, Stahlbau; -*on crew*, die Stammbesatzung; -*on enemy*, markierter Feind (*Mil.*); -*on key*, der Dietrich. **-onize**, *v.a.* skelettieren (*animals*); (*fig.*) in großen Zügen darstellen, im Rohbau vorbereiten, skizzieren.

skelp [skɛlp], 1. *s.* (*Scots*) der Schlag. 2. *v.a.* (*Scot.*) schlagen.

skene, *see* **skean.**

skep [skɛp], *s.* (*dial.*) der Korb, Bienenkorb.

skerry [skɛrɪ], *s.* das Felsenriff.

sketch [skɛtʃ], 1. *s.* die Skizze, Studie, der Entwurf; Sketch (*Theat.*); *rough* –, die Faustzeichnung, (*fig.*) flüchtiger Entwurf. 2. *v.a.* skizzieren; (*fig.*) (also – *out*) entwerfen, in großen Zügen schildern. 3. *v.n.* Skizzen entwerfen, zeichnen. **--book**, *s.* das Skizzenbuch. **-er**, *s.* der Skizzenzeichner. **-iness**, *s.* das Skizzenhafte, Flüchtige, Oberflächliche. **-ing**, *s.* das Skizzieren. **-ing-block**, *s.* der Skizzenblock. **-y**, *adj.* skizzenhaft, leicht hingeworfen, oberflächlich, flüchtig, unzureichend.

skew [skjʊ:], *adj.*, schief, schräg, schiefwinkelig; – *bridge*, schräge Brücke. **-bald**, *adj.* scheckig (*horse*).

skewer ['skjʊ:ə], 1. *s.* der Speil, Speiler, Fleischspieß, die Spindel. 2. *v.a.* (auf)speile(r)n.

ski [ʃɪ:, skɪ.], 1. *s.* der Ski, Schi, Schneeschuh. 2. *v.n.* skilaufen. **-er**, *s.* der Skiläufer. **-ing**, *s.* das Skilaufen. **--jump**, *s.* die Sprungschanze.

skia-gram, -graph, *see* **sciagram**, *etc.*

skid [skɪd], 1. *s.* der Hemmschuh, Bremsschuh, die Hemmkette, Kufe, der Sporn; das Rutschen, Schleudern. 2. *v.a.* hemmen, bremsen (*a wheel*). 3. *v.n.* ins Rutschen kommen, ausrutschen, schleudern. **--mark**, *s.* die Bremsspur.

skies [skaɪz], see **sky.**

skiff [skɪf], *s.* kleines Boot, der Kahn; Renneiner.

skil-ful ['skɪlfʊl], *adj.* geschickt, gewandt. **-fulness, -l**, *s.* die Geschicklichkeit, Gewandtheit, Fertigkeit, Kenntnis. **-led** [skɪld], *adj.* gewandt, geschickt, geübt; erfahren, bewandert; -*led hands*, geschickte Hände; (*fig.*) gelernte Arbeiter (*pl.*); -*led work*, die Facharbeit; -*led workman* or *worker*, der Facharbeiter, gelernter Arbeiter.

skillet ['skɪlɪt], *s.* der Tiegel; (*Amer.*) die Bratpfanne.

skilly ['skɪlɪ], *s.* dünner Haferschleim.

skim [skɪm], 1. *v.a.* abschäumen, abschöpfen, abstreichen; abfeimen, entrahmen, abrahmen (*milk, etc.*); streifen, hinstreifen über, leicht berühren; flüchtig lesen, durchblättern, durchfliegen, rasch durchsehen (*a book*); – *the cream off*, den Rahm abschöpfen von (*also fig.*). 2. *v.n.* streifen, schnell gleiten. **-mer**, *s.* die Schaumkelle, Rahmkelle; der Scherenschnabel (*Orn.*). **-ming**, *s.* (*often pl.*) das Abgeschäumte; -*ming ladle*, *see* **-mer**. **--milk**, *s.* abgerahmte Milch, die Magermilch.

skimp, -y, *see* **scrimp.**

skin [skɪn], 1. *s.* die Haut; Hautschicht (*Anat.*); das Fell, der Pelz, Balg (*of beasts*); die Schale, Hülse, Rinde (*Bot.*); Oberfläche, Bekleidung, Außenhaut (*Tech.*); *have a thick* –, dickfellig sein, ein dickes Fell haben; *have a thin* –, feinfühlig sein; *jump out of one's* –, aus der Haut fahren; *nothing but* or *mere*

– *and bone(s)*, nichts als Haut und Knochen; *save one's* –, sich in Sicherheit bringen, mit heiler Haut davonkommen; *by* or *with the – of one's teeth*, mit knapper Not, mit Hängen und Würgen; *be in his* –, in seiner Haut stecken; *to the* –, bis auf die Haut; *next to one's* –, auf der bloßen Haut. 2. *v.a.* häuten, abbalgen (*animals*), abschälen (*fruit*), abrinden (*a tree*); (*sl*) ausrauben, ausplündern (*a p.*); – *one's finger*, den Finger abschaben; (*coll.*) – *a flint*, geizig sein; *keep one's eyes –ed*, auf der Hut sein. 3. *v.n.* abblättern, sich häuten; (also – *over*) neue Haut bekommen, vernarben, verharschen, zuheilen. **--deep,** *adj.* nicht tiefgehend, oberflächlich. **--disease,** *s.* die Hautkrankheit. **--dresser,** *s.* der Kürschner. (*coll.*) **–flint,** *s.* der Geizhals, Knicker. **--friction,** *s.* die Oberflächenreibung. (*vulg.*) **–ful,** *s.* der Bauchvoll. (*Amer., coll.*) **--game,** *s.* der Betrug. **--grafting,** *s.* die Hautübertragung. **–ned** [–d], *suffix* –häutig, –fellig. **–ner,** *s.* der Kürschner, Pelzwarenhändler, Rauchwarenhändler; Abdecker. **–ning,** *s.* das Abblättern; die Hautbildung. **–ny,** *adj.* häutig; (*fig.*) abgemagert, mager, (*sl.*) geizig. **--tight,** *adj.* eng anliegend.

[1]**skip** [skɪp], 1. *v.a.* (also – *over*), überspringen; (*fig.*) auslassen, übergehen, überschlagen. 2. *v.n.* seilspringen, springen, hüpfen; (*sl.*) – *it*, sich davonmachen. 3. *s.* der Hupf, Sprung. **–jack,** *s.* der Springer, Blaufisch (*Ichth.*), Schnellkäfer (*Ent.*), Springauf, Stehaufmännchen (*toy*). **–per,** *s.* der Hüpfer, Springer; Schnellkäfer, Dickkopf (*Ent.*). **–ping,** *s.* das (Seil)Springen. **--ping-rope,** *s.* das Springseil.

[2]**skip,** *s.* der Mannschaftsführer (*at bowls, curling, etc.*).

[3]**skip,** *s.* der Förderkorb, Eimer, Kübel (*Min.*).

skipper, *s.* der Schiffer, Schiffsherr, Kapitän; (*coll.*) Mannschaftsführer (*Sport*).

skippet [ˈskɪpɪt], *s.* die Siegelklausel (*Hist.*).

skirl [skəːl], *s.* die Musik des Dudelsacks.

skirmish [ˈskəːmɪʃ], 1. *s.* das Scharmützel, Geplänkel, (*fig.*) Wortgeplänkel. 2. *v.n.* plänkeln. **–er,** *s.* der Plänkler.

skirt [skəːt], 1. *s.* der (Frauen)Rock; Rockschoß (*of a coat*); der Saum, Rand, die Grenze (*of a wood, etc.*); (*sl.*) die Frau, das Mädchen. 2. *v.a.* grenzen; entlang gehen, kommen, *or* fahren an, sich am Rande hinziehen. 3. *v.n.* (– *along*) entlang gehen *or* fahren, sich am Rande hinziehen. **--dance,** *s.* der Serpentinentanz. **–ing,** *s.* der Rand; das Tuch für Damenröcke. **–ing-board,** *s.* die Wandleiste, Scheuerleiste.

skit [skɪt], *s.* sarkastische Bemerkung, die Stichelei; leichte Parodie *or* Satire (*on*, über *or* auf (*Acc.*)). **–tish,** *adj.* scheu, bockig (*as horses*), leichtfertig, flatterhaft, tändelnd, ausgelassen.

skitter [ˈskɪtə], *v.n.* an der Wasseroberfläche fliegen (*as ducks*). **–y,** *adj.* schipperig, schüpperig (*Dye.*).

skittle [ˈskɪtl], 1. *s.* der Kegel; *pl.* (*sing. constr.*), das Kegelspiel; *play at –s*, Kegel schieben; *life is not all beer and –s*, das Leben ist nicht eitel Freude. 2. *v.a.* – *out*, in rascher Folge abfertigen (*a team*) (*Crick.*). **--alley, --ground,** *s.* die Kegelbahn.

skive [skaɪv], 1. *s.* das Schleifrad (*for diamonds*). 2. *v.a.* abschleifen (*precious stones*); spalten (*leather*). **–r,** *s.* das Lederspaltmesser; Spaltleder.

skivvy [ˈskɪvɪ], *s.* (*sl.*) die Dienstspritze, der Besen.

skua [skjʊə], *s.* die Riesenraubmöwe (*Orn.*).

skulduggery [ˈskʌldʌgərɪ], *s.* (*coll.*) die Gaunerei.

skulk [skʌlk], *v.n.* lauern, sich verstecken, (umher)-schleichen; sich drücken; – *away*, sich fortschleichen. **–er,** *s.* der Schleicher, Drückeberger. **–ing,** *adj.* lauernd, hinterhältig, feige.

skull [skʌl], *s.* die Hirnschale, der Schädel; (*fig.*) Kopf; *fractured* –, der Schädelbruch; *thick* –, (*fig.*) harter Schädel. **--cap,** *s.* das Käppchen.

skunk [skʌŋk], *s.* der Skunk, das Stinktier; (*fig.*) der Schuft.

sky [skaɪ], 1. *s.* sichtbarer Himmel, der Wolkenhimmel, das Himmelsgewölbe, Firmament; (*often pl.*) die Gegend, der Himmelstrich; das Klima; *in the* –, am Himmel; *under the open* –, unter freiem Himmel; *praise (up) to the skies*, bis in den Himmel erheben. 2. *v.a.* (zu) hoch hängen (*a picture*); hoch schlagen (*a ball*); **--blue,** 1. *adj.* himmelblau. 2. *s.* das Himmelblau. **--high,** *adj. & adv.* himmelhoch. **–lark** 1. *s.* die Feldlerche (*Orn.*). 2. *v.n.* Possen *or* Ulk treiben. **–larking,** *s.* das Possenreißen, die Ulkerei; tolle Streiche (*pl.*). **–light,** *s.* das Oberlicht, Dachfenster. **--line,** *s.* der Horizont. **--marker,** *s.* der Zielbeleuchter (*Av.*). **--pilot,** *s.* (*sl.*) der Geistliche. **--rocket,** *s.* die Signalrakete. **--scraper,** *s.* das Hochhaus, der Wolkenkratzer. **--sign,** *s.* hohes Reklameschild. **–ward,** 1. *adv.* himmelwärts, himmelan. 2. *adj.* himmelwärts gerichtet. **–wards,** *adv., see* **–ward,** *adv.* **–way,** *s.* (*Amer.*) die Luftroute (*Av.*). **–writing,** *s.* die Himmelsschrift.

slab [slæb], 1 *s.* die (Stein- *or* Marmor)Platte; Tafel, das Schalholz, die Schwarte, das Schwartenbrett, Schalbrett, Schellstück (*of wood*); die Bramme, der Rohblock (*of metal*). 2. *v.a.* zurichten, behauen (*tree trunk*).

slabber [ˈslæbə], *see* **slobber.**

slack [slæk], 1. *adj.* schlaff (*also fig.*), locker, lose, (*fig.*) (nach)lässig, träge (*of a p.*); flau (*as trade*), geschäftslos (*season*), langsam, gemächlich (*pace*); – *vowel*, offener Vokal; – *water*, das Stillwasser, totes *or* stilles Wasser. 2. *s.* herabhängendes Ende, das *or* die Lose (*of rope or sail*); das Stillwasser (*of tide, etc.*); flaue *or* geschäftlose Zeit, die Flaute (*C.L.*); das Kohlenklein, der Kohlengrus. 3. *v.a.* (usually *–en, q.v.*). 4. *v.n.* (*coll.*) faulenzen, trödeln; – *off* (also *–en off, q.v.*). **–en,** 1. *v.n.* schlaff *or* locker werden, (*fig.*) erschlaffen, nachlassen; (usually *–en off*) sich verlangsamen, abnehmen (*as a current, etc.*); flau werden, stocken (*C.L.*). 2. *v.a.* (also *–en off*) lockern, loslassen, losmachen, lösen, lose geben, losgeben, fieren (*a rope*), losmachen; verlangsamen, vermindern, mäßigen (*speed, efforts, etc.*). **–er,** *s.* (*coll.*) der Faulenzer, Drückeberger. **–ness,** *s.* die Schlaffheit, Lockerheit, Flaute, Flauheit (*of business*); (*coll.*) (Nach)Lässigkeit, Trägheit, Langsamkeit. **–s,** *pl.* lange weite Hose.

slag [slæg], 1. *s.* die Schlacke (*of metals, etc.*). 2. *v.n. & a.* verschlacken. **–gy,** *adj.* schlackig. **--heap,** die Halde.

slain [sleɪn], *see* **slay.**

slake [sleɪk], *v.a.* löschen (*also lime*), stillen (*thirst*).

slalom [ˈslæləm], *s.* der Slalom, Schneehindernislauf (*Ski-ing*).

slam [slæm], 1. *v.a.* zuwerfen, zuschlagen (*a door, etc.*); (*coll.*) schlagen; einen Schlemm machen (*Cards*); – *the door to*, die Tür zuschlagen; – *the door in a p.'s face*, einem die Tür vor der Nase zuschlagen. 2. *v.n.* heftig zufallen, zugeschlagen werden. 3. *s.* das Zuwerfen; der Schlemm (*Cards*).

slander [ˈslɑːndə], 1. *s.* die Verleumdung, üble Nachrede; mündliche Ehrenkränkung (*Law*). 2. *v.a.* verleumden, verunglimpfen. **–er** [–rə], *s.* der Verleumder. **–ous** [–rəs], *adj.* verleumderisch, ehrenrührig.

slang [slæŋ], *s.* der *or* das Slang, niedere Umgangssprache, die Sondersprache besonderer Kreise, der Jargon; *thieves'* –, die Gaunersprache. 3. *v.a.* (*coll.*) tüchtig ausschimpfen, heruntermachen, herunterreißen (*a p.*). **–y,** *adj.* slangartig, Slang–, derb, unfein; slangsprechend (*a p.*).

slant [slɑːnt], 1. *v.a.* schräge Richtung geben (*Dat.*), schräg legen. 2. *v.n.* schräg liegen *or* sein, schräge Richtung haben, sich neigen, kippen. 3. *s.* die Schräge, schiefe Ebene, schräge Lage, die Neigung; *on the* –, schief, schräg. **–ing,** *adj.*, **–wise,** *adv.* schief, schräg, schräglaufend, schrägliegend.

slap [slæp], 1. *s.* der Klaps, Schlag; – *in* or *on the face*, die Ohrfeige; (*fig.*) Enttäuschung, Beleidigung. 2. *v.a.* klapsen, klopfen, schlagen, einen Klaps geben (*Dat.*); – *a p.'s face*, einen ohrfeigen. 3. *v.n.* schlagen. 4. *adv.* (*coll.*) stracks, plumps, gerade(s)-wegs. **--bang,** *adv.* (*coll.*) Hals über Kopf, spornstreichs, stracks, blindlings, plumps. **–dash,** 1. *adj.* hastig, ungestüm, sorglos, fahrig. 2. *adv. see* **--bang.** **–stick,** *s.* die Pritsche, der Narrenstock; (*usually fig.*) *–stick* (*comedy*), die Radaukomödie. (*sl.*) **--up,** *adj.* erstklassig, famos.

slash [slæʃ], 1. *v.a.* aufschlitzen, zerfetzen, zerschneiden; (*fig.*) peitschen, hauen; (*sl.*) erbarmungslos kritisieren, herunterreißen; *–ed sleeve*, der

Schlitzärmel. 2. *v.n.* hauen; – *out*, um sich hauen. 3. *s.* tiefe Schnittwunde, der Schnitt; Schlitz (*in a dress*); (Schwert)Streich, (Peitschen)Hieb. **–ing,** *adj.* (*fig.*) schneidend, beißend, vernichtend, scharf.

slat [slæt], *s.* dünner Streifen *or* Stab, die Leiste (*of blinds, etc.*).

slat–e [sleɪt], 1. *s.* der Schiefer (*Geol.*), Dachschiefer (*Build.*), die Schiefertafel (*for children*); *clean –e*, (*fig.*) reine Weste, reiner Tisch; *wipe the –e clean* (*fig.*), alles als ungeschehen betrachten. 2. *v.a.* mit Schiefer decken; (*coll.*) tadeln, ausschimpfen, heruntermachen, abkanzeln. **– -blue,** *see* **– -coloured. –e-club,** *s.* private Sparkasse. **–e-coloured,** *adj.* schiefergrau. **–e-pencil,** *s.* der Griffel, Schieferstift. **–e-quarry,** *s.* der Schieferbruch. **–er,** *s.* der Dachdecker, Schieferdecker; die Holzlaus (*Ent.*). **–ing,** *s.* das Schieferdecken; die Schieferbedachung, Schiefer (*pl.*); (*coll.*) scharfe Kritik, die Strafpredigt. **–y,** *adj.* schiefrig, schieferartig, schieferfarben.

slattern [ˈslætən], *s.* die Schlampe, Schlumpe. **–liness,** *s.* die Schlamperei. **–ly,** *adj.* schlampig, schlump(e)rig.

slaughter [ˈslɔːtə], 1. *s.* das Schlachten (*of animals*); Gemetzel, Blutbad; – *of the Innocents*, der Kindermord zu Bethlehem. 2. *v.a.* schlachten (*cattle*); niedermetzeln. **–er,** *s.* der Schlächter; Mörder. **– -house,** *s.* das Schlachthaus. **–ous,** *adj.* mörderisch.

slav–e [sleɪv], 1. *s.* der Sklave, die Sklavin, (*fig.*) der Knecht; *a –e to* or *the –e of a th.*, ein Sklave einer S. 2. *v.n.* wie ein Sklave arbeiten, schuften, sich plagen *or* abrackern *or* schindern *or* placken. **–e-born,** *adj.* als Sklave geboren. **–e-dealer,** *s.* der Sklavenhändler. **–e-driver,** *s.* der Sklavenaufseher; (*fig.*) Menschenschinder. **–e-trade,** *s.* der Sklavenhandel; *white –e-traffic*, der Mädchenhandel. **–er** [–ə], *s.* das Sklavenschiff; der Sklavenhändler. **–ery** [–ərɪ], *s.* die Sklaverei, (*fig.*) sklavische Abhängkeit (*to*, von); die Schinderei, Plackerei. **–ey** [–ɪ], *s.* (*sl.*) das Mädchen für alles, (*vulg.*) der Besen. **–ish,** *adj.* sklavisch, (*fig.*) knechtisch. **–ishness,** *s.* sklavisches Wesen.

slaver [ˈslævə], 1. *s.* der Geifer, (*fig.*) kriecherische Schmeichelei. 2. *v.a.* belecken, (*fig.*) schmeicheln. 3. *v.n.* geifern, sabbern. **–er,** *s.* der Geiferer, (*fig.*) Speichellecker.

slay [sleɪ], *ir.v.a.* (*Poet.*) erschlagen, töten; *the slain*, die Erschlagenen, Toten. **–er,** *s.* der Totschläger.

sled [slɛd], *s.* kleiner Schlitten.

[1]**sledg–e** [slɛdʒ], 1. *s.* der Schlitten. 2. *v.n.* Schlitten fahren. 2. *v.a.* auf einem Schlitten befördern.

[2]**sledge, – -hammer,** *s.* der Vorschlaghammer, Schmiedehammer; (*fig.*) kräftiger Angriff *or* Schlag.

sleek [slɪːk], 1. *adj.* glatt (*also fig.*), (*fig.*) ölig, schmeichlerisch, geschmeidig. 2. *v.a.* glatt machen, glätten; glatt kämmen (*hair*). **–ness,** *s.* die Glätte, (*fig.*) Geschmeidigkeit.

sleep [slɪːp], 1. *ir.v.n.* schlafen; entschlafen sein; *the bed has been slept in*, im Bett ist geschlafen worden; – *on a th.*, etwas überschlafen. – *like a top* or *log*, wie ein Dachs schlafen; – *in*, im *or* zu Hause schlafen (*of servants*); – *out*, auswärts schlafen. 2. *ir.v.a.* – *a* –, einen Schlaf tun; *not – a wink*, kein Auge zutun; – *one's last* –, seinen letzten Schlaf tun; (*coll.*) Schlafgelegenheit bieten (*Dat.*); – *away* or *off*, verschlafen (*the time, a headache*); (*coll.*) – *off the effects*, – *o.s. sober*, seinen Rausch ausschlafen. 3. *s.* der Schlaf; (*fig.*) die Ruhe, Untätigkeit; *beauty* –, erster erfrischender Schlaf; *broken* –, unruhiger Schlaf, *the – of the dead*, der Todesschlaf; *get* or *go to* –, einschlafen; *have one's – out*, sich ausschlafen; *put to* –, einschläfern; *walk in one's* –, nachtwandeln. **–er,** *s.* der Schläfer, Schlafende(r), *m.*; (*coll.*) der Schlafwagen (*Railw.*); die Schwelle (*Railw.*); *be a light –er*, unruhig schlafen; *be a sound –er*, fest schlafen. **–iness,** *s.* die Schläfrigkeit, (*fig.*) Trägheit. **–ing,** *adj.* schlafend; *let –ing dogs lie*, an Vergangenes soll man nicht rühren; *–ing partner*, stiller Teilhaber. **–ing-accommodation,** *s.* die Schlafgelegenheit. **–ing-bag,** *s.* der Schlafsack. **–ing-berth,** *s.* das Schlafwagenbett (*Railw.*), die Koje (*Naut.*). **–ing Beauty,** Dornröschen. **–ing car,** *s.*, **–ing-compartment,** *s.* der Schlafwagen (*Railw.*). **–ing-draught,** *s.* der Schlaftrunk. **–ing-sickness,** *s.* die Schlafsucht. **–ing-suit,** *s.* der Schlafanzug. **–less,** *adj.* schlaflos; (*fig.*) ruhelos, wachsam. **–lessness,** *s.* die Schlaflosigkeit. **– -walker,** *s.* der Nachtwandler. **– -walking,** *s.* das Nachtwandeln. **–y,** *adj.* schläfrig, (*fig.*) träge, träumerisch (*of a p.*), verschlafen (*of a place*). **–yhead,** *s.* die Schlafmütze, der Dussel. **–y sickness,** *s.* die Gehirnentzündung.

sleet [slɪːt], 1. *s.* die Schloße, Schloßen (*pl.*), der Graupelregen. 2. *v.n.* graupeln. **–y,** *adj.* Graupel–.

sleeve [slɪːv], 1. *s.* der Ärmel; die Muffe (*Tech.*); *laugh in one's* –, sich (*Dat.*) ins Fäustchen lachen; *wear one's heart on one's* –, seine Gefühle offen zur Schau tragen; *have s.th. up one's* –, etwas bereithalten, vorhaben, in Bereitschaft *or* in petto haben; *roll* or *turn up one's –s*, sich die Ärmel aufkrempeln. 2. *v.a.* mit Ärmeln versehen. **–d,** *suffix*, –ärmelig. **– -fish,** *s.* der Tintenfisch (*Ichth.*). **–less,** *adj.* ärmellos, ohne Ärmel. **– -link,** *s.* der Manschettenknopf. **– -valve,** *s.* das Muffenventil.

sleigh [sleɪ], 1. *s.* der Schlitten. 2. *v.n.* im Schlitten fahren.

sleight [slaɪt], *s.* der Kunstgriff, die Geschicklichkeit; *– -of-hand*, das Kunststück, der Taschenspielerstreich.

slender [ˈslɛndə], *adj.* schlank; dünn, (*fig.*) karg, spärlich, dürftig, unzulänglich (*as means*); schwach, gering (*as hopes*). **–ness,** *s.* die Schlankheit; (*fig.*) Kargheit, Unzulänglichkeit.

slept [slɛpt], *see* **sleep.**

sleuth [sl(j)uːθ], 1. *s.* (*coll.*) der Detektiv. 2. *v.a.* jemandes Spur verfolgen. 3. *v.n.* (*coll.*) den Detektiv spielen. **– -hound,** *s.* der Spürhund, Bluthund.

[1]**slew** [sluː], *see* **slay.**

[2]**slew** 1. *v.a.* (often – *round*), herumdrehen, herumwerfen. 2. *v.n.* sich herumdrehen.

slice [slaɪs], 1. *s.* die Schnitte, Scheibe, das Stück, der Schnitt; der Spatel (*Pharm.*); *fish-* –, die Fischkelle; – *of bread and butter*, das Butterbrot; – *of meat*, die Scheibe Fleisch; (*coll.*) – *of luck*, die Portion Glück. 2. *v.a.* in dünne Scheiben zerschneiden; – *a ball*, einen Ball nach der Seite schlagen (*Golf*); – *off*, abschneiden.

slick [slɪk], 1. *adj.* (*coll.*) glatt; flott. 2. *adv.* glattweg, schnell. **–er,** *s.* (*sl.*) der Gauner, Gaudieb, gewichster Kerl.

slid [slɪd], *see* **slide.**

slid–e [slaɪd], 1. *ir.v.n.* gleiten, schlüpfen, rutschen; schlittern, schurren (*on the ice*); ausgleiten, ausglitschen, ausrutschen; (*fig.*) übergehen, hineingleiten; *–e down s.th.*, an einer S. hinuntergleiten; *–e over a th.*, (*fig.*) etwas übergehen; *let things –e*, die Dinge laufen lassen, den Dingen ihren Lauf lassen. 2. *ir.v.a.* gleiten lassen; schieben. 3. *s.* das Gleiten, Rutschen; der Rutsch; die Schurrbahn, Schlittenbahn, Rodelbahn, Rutschbahn; die (Haar)-Spange; der Schieber (*Tech.*), Objektträger, Glasstreifen (*microscope*); das Lichtbild (*magic lantern*). **–er,** *s.* der Schieber (*Tech.*). **–e-rule,** *s.* der Rechenschieber. **–e-valve,** *s.* das Schieberventil, der Schieber. **–ing,** 1. *adj.* gleitend, verschiebbar; *–ing contact*, der Gleitkontakt; *–ing door*, die Schiebetür; *–ing scale*, der Schiebmaßstab; (*fig.*) bewegliche (Lohn- *or* Preis)Skala, der Staffeltarif; *–ing seat*, der Rollsitz (*of boat*); *–ing surface*, die Gleitfläche. 2. *s.* das Gleiten.

slight [slaɪt], 1. *adj.* schwach, leicht, mild, oberflächlich, gering, klein, unwichtig, unbedeutend; dünn, schmächtig (*of a p.*); – *cold*, leichte Erkältung; – *effort*, geringe Anstrengung. 2. *v.a.* geringschätzig behandeln, mißachten, vernachlässigen, nicht beachten, ignorieren. 3. *s.* geringe Achtung, die Geringschätzung, Mißachtung, Nichtachtung (*for*, vor); Zurücksetzung. **–ing,** *adj.* geringschätzig, nichtachtend. **–ness,** *s.* die Schlankheit, Schmächtigkeit, Schwäche; Geringfügigkeit.

slim [slɪm], 1. *adj.* schlank, (*fig.*) gering, dürftig. 2. *v.n.* eine Abnahmekur machen, abnehmen, schlank werden. **–ming,** *s.* die Abnahmekur. **–ness,** *s.* die Schlankheit, (*fig.*) Dürftigkeit.

slim-e [slaɪm], *s.* der Schleim, Schlamm, Schlick. **-iness,** *s.* das Schleimige, Schlammige. **-y,** *adj.* schleimig, schlammig, schlickig; (*fig.*) kriecherisch, schmeichlerisch.

sling [slɪŋ], 1. *s.* die Schlinge, Binde (*Surg., etc.*); Schleuder, Wurfmaschine (*Hist.*); (*coll.*) der Wurf, Schwung; Tragriemen, Schulterriemen (*of rifle, etc.*); Stropp (*Naut.*). 2. *ir.v.a.* schleudern, werfen, schwingen; schlingen, (auf)hängen; – *mud at*, (*fig*) mit Schmutz bewerfen; (*coll.*) – *out*, hinauswerfen; *be slung from*, hängen von.

[1]**slink** [slɪŋk], *ir.v.n.* schleichen; – *away* or *off*, (sich) wegschleichen *or* wegstehlen.

[2]**slink,** 1. *v.n.* fehlgebären, vor der Zeit gebären (*of animals*). 2. *v.a.* vor der Zeit werfen. 3. fehlgeborenes Tier.

slip [slɪp], **1.** *s.* das (Aus)Gleiten; der (Erd)Rutsch, Schlipf; die Schlüpfung (*of airscrew*) (*Av.*); Helling (*Naut.*); der Fehltritt (*also fig.*), Flüchtigkeitsfehler, Verstoß, das Versehen; der Streifen, Zettel, das Stückchen (*of paper, etc.*); der Fahnenabzug (*Typ.*); der Ableger, das Steckreis, der Sproß, Sprößling (*Hort.*); die (Hunde)Leine, Koppel (*for dogs*); der (Kissen)Überzug, Bezug; das Unterkleid, der Unterrock, Schlüpfer (*women's dress*), die Badehose; der Eckmann (*Crick.*); *pl.* (*archaic*) Kulissen (*pl.*) (*Theat.*). (*a*) (*with verbs*) (*coll.*) *give a p. the* –, einem ausweichen; (*Prov.*) *there is many a – 'twixt the cup and the lip*, es ist nicht aller Tag Abend; *make a* –, sich versehen, einen Fehltritt tun. (*b*) (*with prepositions*) *a – of a girl*, unscheinbares *or* schmächtiges junges Mädchen; – *of paper*, das Stück Papier, der Zettel, – *of the pen*, der Schreibfehler; *it was a – of the tongue*, ich habe mich versprochen. **2.** *v.a.* gleiten lassen, schieben, stecken, (unbemerkt) hineinschieben *or* hineinstecken; loslassen (*dogs*), schießen lassen, schlippen (*a cable*) (*Naut.*), (während der Fahrt) abhängen (*a coach*) (*Railw.*); abstreifen (*fetters*), überziehen (*Knitting*); – *s.th. to s.o.* (*or coll.*) – *s.o. s th.*, einem etwas zustecken; – *one's memory*, einem entfallen: (*with adverbs*) – *in*, einfließen lassen (*a word*); – *off*, ausziehen, abstreifen (*clothes*); – *on*, anziehen, überwerfen (*clothes*); – *over*, überziehen. **3.** *v.n.* gleiten, ausgleiten, rutschen, sich verschieben, aufgehen, losgehen (*as knots*), (*fig.*) sich irren, Fehler machen; schlüpfen, entschlüpfen; *his foot -ed*, er glitt aus; *let an opportunity* –, sich (*Dat*) eine Gelegenheit entgehen lassen. (*a*) (*with adverbs*) – *away*, entschlüpfen, entgehen (*from* (*Dat.*)), (sich) fortschleichen *or* wegstehlen, see also – *by*; – *by*, verstreichen (*time*); – *down*, hinfallen; – *in*, sich einschleichen; – *off*, see – *away*; – *out*, hinausschlüpfen; – *up*, sich hochschieben, stolpern; (*fig.*) sich irren, im Irrtum sein, auf dem Holzwege sein. (*b*) (*with prepositions*) – *down*, hinuntergleiten an (*a rope, etc.*); – *from one's hand*, aus der Hand gleiten, der Hand entgleiten; – *from one's mind*, dem Gedächtnis entfallen; – *into*, hineinschlüpfen in (*clothes*), sich einschleichen *or* (heimlich) hineinschieben in (*a room*), (unmerklich) geraten in (*difficulties*); – *off*, hinabgleiten von; – *out*, entschlüpfen (*Dat.*) (*as a remark*); einen Sprung hinausmachen; – *out of*, see – *from*. **--carriage,** *s.* der Abhängewagen (*Railw.*). **--knot,** *s.* der Schleifknoten, Ziehknoten. **--on,** *s.* (*coll.*) der Pullover, die Schlupfjacke. **--proof,** *s.* der Fahnenzug (*Print.*). **--rope,** *s.* das Schlipptau (*Naut.*). **-shod,** *adj.* (*fig.*) nachlässig, unordentlich, liederlich, schlampig. **-stream,** *s.* die Propellerbö, der Schraubenstrahl (*Av.*). **-way,** *s.* der Stapel, die Helling (*Shipb.*).

slipper [ˈslɪpə], *s.* der Pantoffel, Hausschuh; Hemmschuh (*for cart*). **-ed,** *adj.* Pantoffeln tragend.

slipp-eriness [ˈslɪpərɪnɪs], *s.* die Schlüpfrigkeit, (*fig.*) Unzuverlässigkeit. **-ery,** *adj.* schlüpfrig, glitschig, glatt; (*fig.*) unzuverlässig, unsicher, zweifelhaft. **-y,** *adj.* (*coll.*) schlüpfrig, glitschig; (*coll.*) fix, schnell; *look -y*, sich beeilen.

slit [slɪt], 1. *ir.v.a.* (*also imp. & p.p.*), (auf)schlitzen, aufschneiden, spalten, ritzen. 2. *v.n.* sich aufspalten. 3. *s.* der Schlitz, Spalt, die Spalte. **--eyed,** *adj.* schlitzäugig. **-ing,** *s.* das Aufschneiden. **-ting-mill,** *s.* das Schneidewerk. **--trench,** der Deckungsgraben (*Mil.*).

slither [ˈslɪðə], *v.n.* (*coll.*) rutschen, (aus)gleiten.

sliver [ˈslɪvə], 1. *s.* der Splitter, Span; Kammzug (*Weav*). 2. *v.a.* zerspalten, abspalten. 3. *v.n.* sich spalten.

slobber [ˈslɔbə], 1. *v.n.* geifern, sabbern; (*coll.*) – *over a p.*, einen abküssen. 2. *v.a.* begeifern. 3. *s.* der Geifer, Sabber. **-y,** *adj.* sabbernd; (*fig.*) salbadernd, gefühlsduselig.

sloe [slou], *s.* die Schlehe, der Schwarzdorn, Schlehdorn.

slog [slɔg], 1. *v.a.* (*coll*) heftig schlagen. 2. *v.n.* (often – *away* or *on*) (*sl.*) schuften, sich placken, mühsam vorwärts kommen. 3. *s.* wuchtiger Schlag, die Plackerei. **-ger,** *s.* tüchtiger Schläger *or* Boxer; anhaltender Arbeiter.

slogan [ˈslougən], *s.* das Schlagwort, der Wahlspruch, die Losung; das Kriegsgeschrei (*Scots*).

sloid [slɔɪd], *s.* der Handfertigkeitsunterricht.

sloop [slu:p], *s.* die Schaluppe; Korvette, das Geleitschiff.

[1]**slop** [slɔp], 1. *s.* (*often pl.*) das Spülicht, (*fig. sing. only*) der Kitsch; *make a* –, Flüssigkeit verschütten. 2. *v.a.* verschütten. 3. *v.n.* überfließen, überschwappen. **--basin,** *s.* der Spülnapf, die Schale zum Ausleeren der Teetassen. **--pail,** *s.* der Spüleimer. **-piness,** *s.* die Nässe, Matsche, der Matsch; (*coll.*) die Albernheit, Oberflächlichkeit, Gefühlsduselei, Rührseligkeit. **-py,** *adj.* naß, matschig, wässerig, lappig, schwabbelig; (*coll.*) unordentlich, liederlich, albern, rührselig, weichlich, kitschig. **-s.** *pl.* flüssige *or* breiige Krankenspeise; das Spülicht, (*sl.*) fertige Kleider (*pl.*), die Konfektionskleidung; das Bettzeug (*Naut.*); weite Hose; *empty the -s*, schmutziges Wasser ausgießen.

[2]**slop,** *s.* (*sl.*) der Polizist.

slop-e [sloup], 1. *s.* der Hang, Abhang das Gefälle, die Steigung, Neigung; Böschung (*Fort.*), Abdachung, Schräge, Gehre (*Tech.*); *on the -e*, schräg, schief; abschüssig (*as ground*); *at the -e*, übergenommen (*of rifle*); *steep -e*, der Steilhang; *windward -e*, die Luvseite. 2. *v.n.* sich neigen *or* senken, abfallen (*as ground*); schräg abgehen, (*sl.*) *-e off*, sich davonmachen *or* aus dem Staube machen. 3. *v.a.* abböschen (*Fort.*), neigen, senken; abdachen, abschrägen; *-e arms!* Gewehr über! (*Mil.*). **-ing,** *adj.* schräg, abgeschrägt, ansteigend, abfallend, abschüssig.

slosh [slɔʃ], 1. *s. see* **slush.** 2. *v.n.* (*coll.*) panschen. 3. *v.a.* verschütten, (*sl.*) schlagen.

[1]**slot** [slɔt], 1. *s.* der Schlitz(einwurf); schmale Öffnung, die Vertiefung, der Einschnitt, die Kerbe, Nut(e). 2. *v.a.* auskerben. **--machine,** *s.* der (Waren)Automat. **-ted wing,** *s.* der Schlitzflügel, Spaltflügel (*Av.*). **-ting-machine,** *s.* die Nutenstanzmaschine.

[2]**slot,** *s.* die Fährte (*of deer*).

[3]**slot,** *s.* (*dial.*), der Riegel, das Querholz.

sloth [slouθ], *s.* die Faulheit; das Faultier (*Zool.*). **-ful,** *adj.* träge, faul. **-fulness,** *s.* die Trägheit.

slouch [slautʃ], 1. *s.* latschiger *or* schleppender Gang, schlottrige *or* schlaffe Haltung; (*sl.*) der Schlendrian; – *hat*, der Schlapphut. 2. *v.n.* schlaff niederhängen (*of hat*); sich schlaff halten, latschen; – *about*, umherschlendern.

[1]**slough** [slau], *s.* die Pfütze, sumpfige Stelle, der Morast; – *of despond*, hoffnungslose Verzweiflung.

[2]**slough** [slʌf], 1. *s.* abgestreifte *or* abgeworfene Haut (*of animals*); der Schorf (*of a wound*). 2. *v.n.* sich häuten (*of animals*); – *off*, sich ablösen. 3. *v.a.* abwerfen (*skin*); (*fig.*) (also – *off*) aufgeben. **-y,** *adj.* schorfig.

sloven [ˈslʌvən], *s.* die Schlampe, Schlumpe, Schmutzliese; der Schmutzfink, Liederjahn. **-liness,** *s.* die Schlampigkeit, Unordentlichkeit, Schmutzigkeit, Liederlichkeit; Nachlässigkeit. **-ly,** *adj.* unordentlich, schlampig, liederlich, nachlässig.

slow [slou], 1. *adj.* langsam; spät, unpünktlich, säumig, (nach)lässig; langweilig, öde, langwierig; flau, träg(e), untätig; schleichend (*fever*), allmählich (*growth*), schwerfällig, dumm (*of a p.*); – *and* or *but sure*, langsam aber sicher; *my watch is* –, meine Uhr geht nach; – *in arriving*, unpünktlich ankommen; *be* – *in doing*, nur langsam tun; (*coll.*) – *in* or *on the uptake*, schwer von Begriff, eine lange Leitung haben; – *of apprehension*, schwach von Begriff, begriffsstutzig, begriffsstützig; – *of payment*, nachlässig im Bezahlen; – *of speech*, langsam im Sprechen; – *to take offence*, nicht leicht übelnehmen; *be* – *to do*, widerwillig tun; *not be* – *to do*, schnell tun, sich nicht zweimal sagen lassen; – *to wrath*, geduldig, langsam zum Zorn (*B.*). 2. *v.n.* (usually – *down*), langsamer fahren, sich verlangsamen, nachlassen. 3. *v.a.* (usually – *down*) verlangsamen, langsamer fahren lassen. (*coll.*) **–coach,** *s.* langsamer Mensch, der Trödelfritz. **– -combustion stove,** *s.* der Dauerbrandofen. **– -match,** *s.* die Lunte (*Artil.*). **– -motion,** *s.* die Zeitlupe (*Films*). **–ness,** *s.* die Langsamkeit, Trägheit, Schwerfälligkeit, Dummheit, Langwierigkeit, Öde; das Nachgehen (*of a watch, etc.*). **– train,** *s.* der Personenzug, (*sl.*) Bummelzug. **– -witted,** *adj.* schwer von Begriff, begriffsstutzig, begriffsstützig. **– -worm,** *s.* die Blindschleiche (*Zool.*).

sloyd, *see* **sloid.**

slub [slʌb], 1. *s.* das Vorgespinst. 2. *v.a.* grob verspinnen. **–ber,** *s.* die Vorspinnmaschine.

sludge [slʌdʒ], *s.* der Matsch, Schlamm (*also Geol.*), der Bodensatz, das Abfallprodukt (*Tech.*).

slue, *see* **slew.**

[1]**slug** [slʌg], 1. *s.* die Wegschnecke. 2. *v.n.* (*coll.*) faulenzen, träge sein. **– -abed,** *s.* (*coll.*) der Langschläfer. **–gard,** [–əd], 1. *s.* der Faulpelz. 2. *adj.* träge, faul. **–gish,** *adj.* träge, schwerfällig; langsam fließend; flau (*C.L.*); *–gish vat*, ermüdete Küpe (*Dye.*). **–gishness,** *s.* die Trägheit, Schwerfälligkeit, Langsamkeit.

[2]**slug,** *s.* der Metallklumpen, das Metallstück; der Posten, grober *or* grobes Schrot; die Flintenkugel; Reglette, der Zeilensatz, Zeilenguß (*Typ.*).

[3]**slug,** *v.a.* (*sl.*) in die Fresse hauen.

sluice [slu:s], 1. *s.* die Schleuse, das Siel, die Waschrinne (*Gold-mining*). 2. *v.a.* schleusen, durch eine Schleuse abfließen lassen (*water*), Wasser (*with Gen.*) ablassen (*a pond, etc.*); begießen überschwemmen; ausspülen.

slum [slʌm], 1. *s.* schmutziges Hintergäßchen *or* Haus; *pl.* das Elendsviertel, Armenviertel. 2. *v.n.* (*go –ming*) Sozialarbeit in Elendsvierteln tun. **– -clearance,** *s.* die Umsiedlung der Einwohner aus Elendsvierteln.

slumb–er [ˈslʌmbə], 1. *s.* (*often pl.*) ruhiger Schlaf, der Schlummer. 2. *v.n.* schlummern. 3. *v.a.*; *–er away*, verschlummern. **–erer** [–rə], *s.* der Schläfer. **–(e)rous** [–(ə)rəs], *adj.* schläfrig, einschläfernd.

slummock [ˈslʌmək], *v.n.* (*coll.*) sich schlaff *or* schlotterig halten *or* bewegen.

slump [slʌmp], 1. *v.n.* hinplumpsen, plötzlich fallen; plötzlich sinken, stürzen (*C.L.*). 2. *s.* der Preissturz, Tiefstand, die Baisse, Wirtschaftskrise, schlechte Konjunktur (*C.L.*).

slung [slʌŋ], *see* **sling.**

slunk [slʌŋk], *see* **slink.**

slur [slə:], 1. *s.* der Schandfleck, Vorwurf, Tadel; die Bindung, das Bindungszeichen (*Mus.*); unreiner Druck (*Typ.*); *cast a* – *on*, eine Schmach antun (*Dat.*), in ein schlechtes Licht bringen, verunglimpfen. 2. *v.a.* undeutlich sprechen, verschleifen (*words, etc.*); binden (*Mus.*); (*fig.*) verwischen, verschmelzen; – *over*, hastig übergehen, leicht hinweggehen über; – *one's words*, undeutlich sprechen.

slush [slʌʃ], *s.* der Schlamm, Matsch, Schmutz; die Schmiere (*Tech.*); (*fig.*) der Schund, Kitsch; gefühlsduseliges Geschwätz. **–y,** *adj.* schlammig, matschig; (*fig.*) wertlos, Schund–.

slut [slʌt], *s.* die Schlumpe, Schlampe; Range. **–tish,** *adj.* schlampig, schmutzig.

sly [slaɪ], *adj.* schlau, listig, verschlagen, hinterhältig; (*coll.*) schelmisch, schalkhaft; *on the* –, verstohlen, insgeheim, im Geheimen. **–boots,** *pl.* (*sing. constr.*) der Schlauberger, Pfiffikus. **–ness,** *s.* die Schlauheit., Verschlagenheit.

[1]**smack** [smæk], 1. *s.* (leichter) (Bei)Geschmack; ein bißchen; der Anstrich, Anflug, die Spur. 2. *v.n.* schmecken *or* riechen (*of*, nach); (*fig.*) einen Anstrich, Anflug *or* Beigeschmack haben von.

[2]**smack,** 1. *s.* der Schlag, Klatsch, Klaps, Schmatz; das Schmatzen, Klatschen; (*coll.*) – *in the eye*, der Schlag ins Gesicht *or* Kontor. 2. *v.a.* schlagen, klapsen; – *one's lips*, mit den Lippen schmatzen; – *the whip*, mit der Peitsche knallen. 3. *int.* patsch! klatsch! plauz! 4. *adv.* (*coll.*) direkt, bums. **–er,** *s.* (*coll.*) schmatzender Kuß; (*sl.*) der Dollar (*Amer.*). **–ing,** 1. *adj.* heftig, frisch (*of a breeze*). 2. *s.* die Tracht Prügel.

[3]**smack,** *s.* die Schmack(e) (*Naut.*).

small [smɔ:l], 1. *adj.* klein, noch jung; dünn, schmal, schwach, gering(fügig), unbedeutend, armselig, dürftig. (*a*) (*with nouns*) (*coll.*) – *beer*, unbedeutende P. *or* S.; *think no* – *beer of o.s.*, sich nicht wenig einbilden; – *blame to him*, er ist wenig zu tadeln, er hat ganz recht; – *change*, das Kleingeld; – *coal*, die Schmiedekohle; – *farmer*, der Kleinbauer; (*coll.*) – *fry*, kleines Volk, Kinder (*pl.*); – *hours*, frühe Morgenstunden; *a* – *matter*, eine Kleinigkeit, geringfügige Sache; *– -talk*, leichte Plauderei, das Geplauder; – *wares*, *pl.* Kurzwaren (*pl.*). *in a* – *way*, ärmlich; (*fig.*) im Kleinen, unbedeutend. (*b*) (*with verbs*) *feel* –, sich schämen; zerknirscht sein; *make a p. feel* –, einen beschämen; *look* –, beschämt aussehen, kleinlaut werden. 2. *adv.* (only in) *sing* –, kleinlaut sein, klein beigeben. 3. *s.* schmaler *or* dünner Teil; *pl.* (*coll.*) das Unterzeug; – *of the back*, das Kreuz. **– -arms,** *pl.* Handwaffen (*pl.*). **– -clothes,** *pl.* Beinkleider (*pl.*). **–holder,** *s.* der Kleinbauer. **–holding,** *s.* der Kleinlandbesitz. **–ish,** *adj.* ziemlich *or* etwas klein. **–ishness,** *s.* die Kleinheit, Dünnheit, Geringheit, Kleinlichkeit. **– -minded,** *adj.* engstirnig, borniert. **–pox,** *s.* die Pocken, Blattern (*pl.*). **– -scale map,** *s.* die Großraumkarte.

smalt [smɔ:lt], *s.* die Schmalte, Smalte, das Kobaltglas, Schmelzblau.

smaragd [sməˈrægd], *s.* der Smaragd.

smart [smɑ:t], 1. *adj.* schick, fesch, elegant, modisch; patent, schmuck, flott, schneidig; heftig, kräftig, tüchtig; schneidend, beißend, derb, witzig, naseweis; geschickt, gerissen; frisch, munter, lebhaft, rührig; – *blow*, derber Schlag; – *pain*, heftiger Schmerz; – *reply*, schlagfertige *or* spitzige Antwort; – *set*, elegante Welt. 2. *s.* der Schmerz. 3. *v.n.* schmerzen, wehe tun, brennen (*as a wound*); Schmerz empfinden, leiden (*under*, unter); – *for*, büßen. (*coll.*) **–aleck,** *s.* der Alleswisser, Besserwisser, Klugschnacker, Schlaumeier. **–en,** 1. *v.a.* (usually *–en up*) aufputzen, herausputzen. 2. *v.n.* *–en up*, sich aufputzen; sich sputen. **– -money,** *s.* das Reugeld, Schmerzensgeld. **–ness,** *s.* die Schärfe, Heftigkeit, Lebhaftigkeit; Klugheit, Aufgewecktheit; Schneidigkeit, Eleganz, der Schick.

smash [smæʃ], 1. *v.a.* (also – *up*) zerschmettern, zertrümmern, zerbrechen; vereiteln, vernichten (*opposition*); schmettern (*ball*) (*Tenn.*). 2. *v.n.* zusammenbrechen, zerschmettert werden; stürzen (*as a vehicle*), vernichtet werden; Bankerott machen. 3. *s.* das Zerschmettern, der Schlag, Krach (*also fig.*); (*fig.*) (also *– -up*) Zusammenbruch, Zusammenstoß; Bankerott; Schmetterball (*Tenn.*); (*coll.*) *all to* –, in tausend Stücken; (*coll.*) *go* –, Bankerott machen. **– -and-grab raid,** *s.* der Schaufenstereinbruch. **–er,** *s.* (*sl.*) hinreißendes Mädchen; ausgezeichnetes Beispiel. **–ing,** *adj.* heftig, vernichtend; (*sl.*) famos.

smattering [ˈsmætərɪŋ], *s.* seichte *or* oberflächliche Kenntnis (*of*, von).

smear [ˈsmɪ:ə], 1. *v.a.* beschmieren, einschmieren, einfetten, einreiben; beschmutzen (*a th.*) (*with*, mit); auftragen, schmieren (*grease, etc.*) (*on*, auf); verwischen, verschmieren (*as writing*). 2. *v.n.* schmieren, sich verwischen. 3. *s.* der Schmutzfleck, Fettfleck; – *of grease*, leichte *or* dünne Fettschicht. **–y,** *adj.* schmierig, beschmiert.

smell [smɛl], 1. *s.* der Geruchssinn; Geruch, Duft; *a* – *of gas*, der Gasgeruch. 2. *ir.v.a.* riechen; riechen an, beriechen; (*fig.*) – *out*, herausfinden, affiunden, aufspüren; (*coll.*) – *a rat*, Lunte riechen. 3. *ir.v.n.* riechen (*at*, an; *of*, nach) (*also fig.*), duften (*of*, nach); stinken, muffig riechen; – *of the lamp*, nach Gelehrsamkeit riechen. **–er,** *s.* (*sl.*) der Riecher, die Nase. **–ing,** *s.* das Riechen. **–ing-bottle,** *s.* das Riechfläschchen. **–ing-salts,** *pl.* das Riechsalz. **–y,** *adj.* übelriechend; muffig.

[1]**smelt** [smɛlt], *see* **smell.**

[2]**smelt,** *v.a.* schmelzen (*Tech.*); – *down*, einschmelzen. **–er,** *s.* der Schmelzarbeiter; die Schmelzhütte, Schmelzerei. **–ing-furnace,** *s.* der Schmelzofen.

[3]**smelt,** *s.* der Stint (*Ichth.*).

smilax [ˈsmaılæks], *s.* die Stechwinde (*Bot.*).

smil–e [smaıl], 1. *s.* das Lächeln; *give a –e*, lächeln; *–e of contempt*, verächtliches Lächeln; *with a –e*, lächelnd. 2. *v.n.* lächeln; (*coll.*) *come up –ing*, den Kopf nicht hängen lassen; *–e at*, anlächeln; zulächeln (*Dat.*) (*a p.*); lächeln über (*Acc.*) (*a p. or th.*); (*fig.*) belächeln (*a th.*); *–e on*, zulächeln (*Dat.*), gnädig *or* hold sein (*Dat.*) (*a p.*); *–e through one's tears*, unter Tränen lächeln. 3. *v.a.* durch Lächeln ausdrücken; *–e acknowledgement*, die Anerkennung durch Lächeln ausdrücken (*of*, für); *–e away* or *off*, durch Lächeln vertreiben. **–eless,** *adj.* ohne Lächeln. **–ing,** *adj.* lächelnd; (*fig.*) günstig, freundlich, heiter.

smirch [smə:tʃ], 1. *v.a.* (*usually fig.*) beschmutzen, beschmieren, besudeln. 2. *s.* der Fleck; die Beschmutzung.

smirk [smə:k], 1. *s.* das Schmunzeln, geziertes Lächeln. 2. *v.n.* schmunzeln, geziert lächeln.

smite [smaıt], 1. *ir.v.a.* (*Poet.*) schlagen; erschlagen, töten, hinstrecken; schlagen auf, treffen; (*fig.*) ergreifen, bewegen, rühren, quälen, peinigen; *his conscience –s him*, das Gewissen peinigt ihn, er fühlt Gewissensbisse; *be smitten with*, befallen, ergriffen *or* getroffen werden von; verzehrt werden von; verliebt sein in (*Acc.*). 2. *ir.v.n.* schlagen.

smith [smıθ], *s.* der Schmied. **–ery** [[–ərı], *s.* das Schmiedehandwerk, die Schmiedearbeit. **–y** [ˈsmıðı], *s.* die Schmiede.

smither–eens [smıðəˈrı:nz], **–s** *pl.* (*coll.*) kleine Stücke, Fetzen, Trümmer; Splitter (*pl.*); (*sl.*) *gone to –eens*, entzwei, kaput.

smitten [ˈsmıtən], *see* **smite.**

smock [smɔk], 1. *s.* (also *–-frock*) der Arbeitskittel, Spielkittel, Schmutzkittel. 2. *v.a.* fälteln (*Semp.*). **–ing,** *s.* der Faltenbesatz.

smok–able [ˈsmoukəbl], *adj.* rauchbar. **–e** [smouk], 1. *v.n.* rauchen; qualmen, blaken (*as a fire*); dampfen (*with*, von); (Pfeife, Zigarre *or* Zigarette) rauchen. 2. *v.a.* rauchen (*tobacco, pipe, etc.*); räuchern (*hams, etc.*), durch Rauch schwärzen; *be –ed*, Rauch annehmen (*as milk, etc.*); *–e out*, ausräuchern; *–e s.o. out of*, einen durch Rauch vertreiben aus. 3. *s.* der Rauch, Qualm, Dunst; *want a –e*, rauchen wollen; (*coll.*) *like –e*, sofort, schnell; (*Prov.*) *no –e without fire*, wo Rauch ist, muß auch Feuer sein; *end in –e*, zu Wasser werden, sich im Sand verlaufen. **–e-ball,** *s.*, **–e-bomb,** *s.* die Rauchbombe, Rauchgranate, Nebelgranate. **–e-black,** *s.* die Rußschwärze, der Kienruß. **–e-box,** *s.* der Rauchkasten. **–e-candle,** *s.* die Rauchkerze, Nebelkerze. **–e-consumer,** *s.* der Rauchverzehrer. **–ed,** *adj.* **–e-dried,** *adj.* geräuchert. **–eless,** *adj.* rauchlos. **–er,** *s.* der Raucher; der (Fleisch)-Räucherer; (*coll.*) das Raucherabteil (*Railw.*); *heavy –er*, starker Raucher. **–e-room,** *s. see* **–ing-room. –e-screen,** *s.* der Nebelschleier, die Nebelwand, Einnebelung (*Mil.*). **–e-stack,** *s.* der Schornstein, Rauchfang. **–e-stained,** *adj.* verräuchert. **–ing,** *s.* das Rauchen; Räuchern; *no –ing*, Rauchen verboten! **–ing-carriage,** *s.*, **–ing-compartment,** *s.* das Raucherabteil. **–ing concert,** *s.* das Konzert bei dem geraucht werden darf. **–ing-room,** *s.* das Rauchzimmer. **–y,** *adj.* rauchig, voll Rauch, verräuchert, **rauchfarbig**; *–y chimney*, rauchiger Kamin.

smooth [smu:ð], 1. *adj.* glatt, eben; ruhig (*as sea*), geglättet (*hair*); (*fig.*) weich, geschmeidig, reibungslos (*as movement*), fließend (*style, etc.*); sanft, schmeichelnd; glattzüngig (*of a p.*); – *crossing*, ruhige Überfahrt; *make –*, glätten, ebnen. 2. *v.a.* glätten, ebnen; ausglätten, glatt machen, plätten; – *the way for*, den Weg bahnen *or* ebnen (*Dat.*); – *away*, entfernen, wegräumen (*difficulties*); – *down*, glatt streichen; (*fig.*) beruhigen, schlichten; – *out*, ausplätten (*creases, etc.*), see also – *away*; – *over*, beschönigen, bemänteln. 3. *v.n.* (also – *down*) sich glätten; (*fig.*) sich beruhigen. **–-bore,** *attrib. adj.* mit glattem Lauf (*firearm*). **–faced,** *adj.* bartlos, glatt rasiert; (*fig.*) glattzüngig. **–-haired,** *adj.* glatthaarig. **–ing,** *s.* das Glätten. **–ing-iron,** *s.* das Plätteisen, Bügeleisen. **–ing-plane,** *s.* der Schlichthobel. **–ness,** *s.* die Glätte, Ebenheit, Weichheit, Geschmeidigkeit, Sanftheit. **–-tongued,** *adj.* glattzüngig, schmeichlerisch.

smother [ˈsmʌðə], 1. *v.a.* ersticken; (*fig.*) dämpfen; unterdrücken (*rage, etc.*); (*coll.*) verbergen, verdecken; bedecken, überhäufen; festhalten (*Footb.*). 2. *v.n.* ersticken.

smoulder [ˈsmouldə], *v.n.* schwelen; glimmen (*also fig.*); qualmen, rauchen.

smudg–e [smʌdʒ], 1. *s.* der Schmutzfleck. 2. *v.a.* beschmutzen, beschmieren, verschmieren. 3. *v.n.* schmieren, klecksen. **–ed,** *adj.*, **–y,** *adj.* verschmiert, beschmutzt, verwischt, klecksig, schmierig.

smug [smʌg], 1. *adj.* schmuck, geschniegelt; selbstgefällig, spießig. 2. *s.* (*Univ. sl.*) der Streber.

smuggl–e [ˈsmʌgl], 1. *v.a.* schmuggeln; *–e in*, einschmuggeln (*also fig.*). 2. *v.n.* schmuggeln. **–er,** *s.* der Schmuggler. **–ing,** *s.* das Schmuggeln, der Schmuggel, Schleichhandel.

smut [smʌt], 1. *s.* der Ruß, Rußfleck; der Schmutzfleck; Brand (*Bot.*); die Zote, Zoten (*pl.*), die Schlüpfrigkeit; *talk –*, zoten. 2. *v.a.* beschmutzen; brandig machen (*Bot.*). 3. *v.n.* brandig werden (*Bot.*). **–ch** [smʌtʃ], 1. *v.a.* beschmutzen, besudeln. 2. *s.* der Schmutzfleck; Ruß, die Rußflocke; der Getreidebrand (*Bot.*). **–tiness,** *s.* die Schmutzigkeit; Rußigkeit; Zotigkeit, das Zotige. **–ty,** *adj.* schmutzig, rußig; brandig; zotig, schlüpfrig.

snack [snæk], *s.* der Imbiß; (*coll.*) *go –s*, teilen. **–-bar,** *s.* die Imbißhalle.

snaffle [snæfl], 1. *s.* die Trense. 2. *v.a.* die Trense anlegen (*a horse*) (*Dat.*); (*sl.*) ergreifen, stibitzen, klauen.

snag [snæg], 1. *s.* der Aststumpf, Baumstumpf, Knorren, Knoten; im Fluß treibender Baumstamm; (*Amer.*) der Raffzahn; (*coll.*) unerwartetes Hindernis, der Haken; (*coll.*) *there is a –* (*in it*), da ist ein Haken dabei. 2. *v.a.* von treibenden Baumstämmen säubern (*a river*); gegen einen Baumstamm treiben (*a boat*); (*coll.*) zuschanden machen, durchkreuzen, zuvorkommen (*Dat.*).

snail [sneıl], *s.* die Schnecke; *at a –'s pace*, im Schneckentempo. **–-shell,** *s.* das Schneckenhaus. **–-wheel,** *s.* das Schneckenrad (*Horol.*).

snak–e [sneık], *s.* die Schlange; *–e in the grass*, geheimer Feind; verborgene Gefahr. **–e-bird,** *s.* der Wendehals (*Orn.*). **–e-bite,** *s.* der Schlangenbiß. **–e-charmer,** *s.* der Schlangenbändiger. **–e-stone,** der Ammonit, das Ammonshorn. **–y,** *adj.* schlangenartig, Schlangen–; (*fig.*) sich windend *or* schlängelnd; schlangengleich, hinterlistig.

snap [snæp], 1. *v.a.* haschen, erschnappen, ergreifen; zerbrechen, durchbrechen, entzweibrechen; knipsen (*Phot.*); – *one's finger at a p.*, einen verhöhnen, einem ein Schnippchen schlagen; – *off*, abbrechen; – *a p.'s head* or *nose off*, einen anfahren; – *to*, zuklappen; – *up*, aufschnappen, erhaschen; aufkaufen. 2. *v.n.* schnappen, beißen (*at*, nach); zuschnappen (*as a dog*); abbrechen, zerbrechen, zerspringen; knipsen, knacken; – *at a p.*, einen anfahren; – *at a th.*, etwas gierig erschnappen; – *to*, sich schließen, zuschnappen (*as a door*). 3. *s.* das Schnappen; der Biß; Knacks, Sprung, Bruch; Knall (*of a whip*); das Schnappschloß, der Schnapper (*of bracelets, etc.*); Schneid, Schwung, die Lebhaftigkeit; plötzlicher Kälteeinbruch; (*coll.*) der Schnappschuß, das Foto, die Momentaufnahme; *ginger–*, der Ingwerkeks; *make a – at*, schnappen nach; *not worth a –*, wertlos; – *division*, – *vote*, unerwartete Abstimmung. **–dragon,** *s.* das Löwenmaul (*Bot.*). **–-lock,** *s.* das Schnappschloß. **–pish,** *adj.* bissig (*as dogs*); (*fig.*) auffahrend, schnippisch, reizbar. **–pishness,** *s.* die Bissigkeit, schnippisches Wesen. **–py,** *adj.* (*coll.*) lebhaft, flott, schneidig, schick; (*sl.*)

make it –py, mach ein bißchen fix. **––shot,** *s.* der Schnellschuß. **–shot,** 1. *s.* der Schnappschuß, die Momentaufnahme (*Phot.*). 2. *v.a.* eine Momentaufnahme machen von, knipsen.

snare ['snεə], 1. *s.* die Schlinge (*also fig.*), der Fallstrick; (*fig.*) die Falle; Schnarrsaite, Sangsaite (*of a drum*); *lay* or *set a –*, eine Falle stellen (*for*, (*Dat.*)). 2. *v.a.* mit einer Schlinge fangen; (*fig.*) eine Falle stellen (*Dat.*), verstricken. **–r,** *s.* der Schlingenleger.

[1]**snarl** [snɑ:l], 1. *s.* das Knurren. 2. *v.n.* knurren (*as a dog*) (*also fig.*); (*fig*) brummen, murren; *– at* anknurren, bissig anfahren.

[2]**snarl,** 1. *s.* die Verwickelung, das Gewirr. 2. *v.a.* verwirren, verwickeln. 3. *v.n.* sich verwirren *or* verwickeln. **–ing-iron,** *s.* das Bossiereisen.

snatch [snætʃ], 1. *s.* das Haschen, Schnappen; der Griff; das Bruchstück; *by –es*, in Absätzen, ruckweise; *–es of a conversation*, (unzusammenhängende) Brocken eines Gespräches; *–es of sunshine*, sonnige Augenblicke. 2. *v.a.* hastig ergreifen, erschnappen, erhaschen, erwischen, an sich reißen; entreißen (*from* (*Dat.*)); *– away*, wegraffen, entreißen (*from* (*Dat.*)); *– a kiss*, einen Kuß stehlen *or* rauben; *– up*, aufraffen. 3. *v.n.* heftig schnappen, greifen *or* haschen (*at*, nach).

snead [snɪ:d], *s.* (*dial.*) der Sensengriff.

sneak [snɪ:k], 1. *s.* der Schleicher, Kriecher; Angeber, Petzer. 2. *v.n.* schleichen, kriechen; angeben, petzen; mausen; *– about*, herumschnüffeln; *– away* or *off*, sich fortschleichen. **–ing,** *adj.* kriechend, schleichend, gemein.

sneer [snɪ:ə], 1. *s.* das Hohnlächeln; der Spott, Hohn. 2. *v.n.* spötteln, höhnisch lächeln (*at*, über); *– at*, bespötteln, verhöhnen. **–ing,** *adj.* höhnisch, spöttisch.

sneez–e [snɪ:z], 1. *s.* das Niesen. 2. *v.n.* niesen; (*coll.*) *not to be –ed at*, nicht zu unterschätzen *or* verachten. **–wort,** *s.* die Sumpfgarbe (*Bot.*).

snib [snɪb], 1. *s.* der Riegel (*Scots*). 2. *v.a.* verriegeln; (*fig.*) fangen (*Scots*).

snick [snɪk], 1. *s.* der Einschnitt, die Kerbe; leichter Schlag (*Crick.*). 2. *v.a.* hacken, schneiden; nach oben parieren (*the ball*) (*Crick.*). **–ersnee** [–əsnɪ:], *s.* das Messer, Schwert.

snicker ['snɪkə], 1. *s.* das Kichern. 2. *v.n.* kickern; wiehern (*of horses*).

sniff [snɪf], 1. *s.* das Schnüffeln; schnüffelnder Atemzug; (*fig.*) das Naserümpfen. 2. *v.a.* (also *– in* or *– up*) durch die Nase einziehen; beriechen; wittern. 3. *v.n.* schnüffeln, schnuppern (*at*, an); *– at*, riechen an; (*fig.*) die Nase rümpfen über. **–y,** *adj.* (*coll.*) übelriechend, muffig; verächtlich, hochfahrend; schnüfflig (*as a cold*).

snigger ['snɪgə], 1. kichern (*at* or *over*, über). 2. *s.* das Kichern, Gekicher.

snip [snɪp], 1. *v.a.* schnippeln, schneiden; *– off*, abschneiden. 2. *s.* der Schnitt; das Stückchen, Schnitzel, (*coll.*) der Schneider; (*sl.*) leichte *or* sichere S. **–pet** [–ɪt], *s.* das Stückchen, Bruchstück, der *or* das Schnippel. **–ping,** *s.* (*usually pl.*) der *or* das Schnippel, das Schnitzel, der Schnipfel.

snipe [snɑɪp], 1. *s.* die Schnepfe (*Orn.*). 2. *v.n.* Schnepfen schießen; aus dem Hinterhalt schießen (*Mil.*). 3. *v.a.* aus großer Entfernung *or* aus dem Hinterhalt niederschießen (*Mil.*). **–r,** *s.* der Heckenschütze, Scharfschütze (*Mil.*).

snip–pet, –ping, *see* **snip.**

snitch [snɪtʃ], 1. *v.n.* (*sl.*) angeben, petzen (*Amer.*). 2. *s.* (*sl.*) der Riecher, Rüssel; (*sl.*) der Angeber (*Amer.*).

snivel ['snɪvl], 1. *v.n.* schnüffeln, aus der Nase triefen; (*fig.*) wimmern, schluchzen, heulen, wehleidig tun; scheinheilig tun, heucheln. 2. *s.* der Nasenschleim, Rotz; das Gewimmer. **–ling,** *adj.* triefnasig; heulend, weinerlich, wehleidig, wehklagend.

snob [snɔb], *s.* der Snob, Vornehmtuer; Philister (*Univ. sl.*). **–bery,** *s.* der Snobbismus, eitle Vornehmtuerei; schöngeistiges Protzentum. **–bish,** *adj.* vornehmtuend, protzend, aufgeblasen. **–bishness,** *s. see* **–bery.**

snood [snu:d], *s.* das Stirnband (*Scots*).

[1]**snook** [snu:k], *s.*; (*sl.*) *cock a –*, eine lange Nase machen (*at* (*Dat.*)).

[2]**snook,** *s.* der Seehecht (*Ichth.*).

snooker ['snu:kə], *s.* eine Art Billardspiel.

snoop [snu:p], (*sl.*) *v.n.* (also *– about*) herumschnüffeln. **–er,** *s.* der Schnüffler.

snoot [snu:t], (*sl.*) *s.* die Fresse, Fratze. **–y,** *adj.* (*sl.*) großkotzig, batzig, patzig, schnoddrig.

snooze [snu:z], 1 *s.* das Schläfchen. 2. *v.n.* nicken, ein Schläfchen *or* Nickerchen halten.

snore [snɔ:], 1. *s.* das Schnarchen. 2. *v.n.* schnarchen.

snort [snɔ:t], 1. *v.n.* schnauben, schnaufen. 2. *s.* das Schnauben, Schnaufen. **–er,** *s.* der Schnaufer; (*coll.*) grober Schlag; die Abfuhr; der Mordskerl; das Mordsding. **–ing,** *adj.* (*coll.*) heftig, ungeheuer.

snot [snɔt], *s.* (*vulg.*) der Rotz. **–ty,** 1. *adj.* (*vulg.*) rotzig; (*fig.*) gemein. 2. *s.* (*sl.*) der Seekadett.

snout [snɑut], *s.* die Schnauze, der Rüssel; (*sl.*) der Schnorchel, Riecher; (*fig.*) die Tülle, das Mundstück, der Schnabel.

snow [snou], 1. *s.* der Schnee; Schneefall; Schneeverhältnisse (*pl.*); (*sl.*) das Kokain. 2. *v. imp.* schneien; (*fig.*) fallen, hageln; *– in*, hereinschneien. 3. *v.a.* *– in* or *up*, einschneien, zuschneien; *– under*, in Schnee begraben; (*fig.*) begraben, überschütten, überhäufen (*with*, von), ersticken (*with*, in). **–ball,** 1. *s.* der Schneeball; *–ball system*, das Schneeballsystem, Hydrasystem. 2. *v.a.* (*& n.*) (sich) schneeballen. 3. *v.n.* (*fig.*) anwachsen, sich vervielfältigen. **––berry,** *s* die Schneebeere (*Bot.*). **––bird,** *s.* der Schneefink (*Orn.*). **––blind,** *adj.* schneeblind. **––bound,** *adj.* eingeschneit. **–bunting,** *s.* die Schneeammer (*Orn.*). **––capped,** *adj.* schneebedeckt. **–drift,** *s.* die Schneewehe, das Schneetreiben. **–drop,** *s.* das Schneeglöckchen (*Bot.*). **–fall,** *s.* der Schneefall, die Schneemenge. **–flake,** *s.* die Schneeflocke. **––goggles,** *pl.* die Schneebrille. **––line,** *s.* die Schneegrenze. **–man,** *s.* der Schneemann. **––plough,** *s.* der Schneepflug. **–shoe,** 1. *s.* der Schneeschuh. 2. *v.n.* Schneeschuh laufen. **––slip,** *s.* die (Schnee)Lawine. **–storm,** *s.* der Schneesturm. **––white,** *adj.* schneeweiß. **––wreath,** *see* **–drift.** **–y,** *adj.* schneebedeckt, Schnee–, schneeweiß; schneeig.

snub [snʌb], 1. *v.a.* kurz abweisen, derb zurückweisen, abfertigen, anfahren. 2. *s.* derbe Zurückweisung *or* Abfertigung, der Verweis; *meet with a –*, kurz abgefertigt werden. **––nose,** *s.* die Stumpfnase, Stupsnase. **––nosed,** *adj.* stumpfnasig, stupsnasig.

[1]**snuff** [snʌf], 1. *s.* der Schnupftabak; (*coll.*) *up to –*, gescheit, schlau, pfiffig; *take –*, schnupfen; *pinch of –*, die Prise Schnupftabak. 2. *v.n.* schnüffeln (*at*, an). 3. *v.a.* (also *– up*) (durch die Nase) einatmen *or* einziehen, beschnüffeln. **––box,** *s.* die Schnupftabakdose. **––coloured,** *adj.* bräunlich gelb. **––taker,** *s.* der Schnupfer. **––taking,** *s.* das Schnupfen. **–y,** *adj.* nach Schnupftabak riechend, mit Schnupftabak beschmutzt; (*coll.*) ärgerlich; verschnupft.

[2]**snuff,** 1. *s.* die Schnuppe (*of a candle*). 2. *v.a.* putzen (*a candle*); *– out*, auslöschen. 3. *v.n.* (*coll.*) *– it* or *– out*, sterben. **–ers,** *pl.* die Lichtschere.

snuffle ['snʌfl], 1. *v.n.* schnaufen, schnüffeln, schnuppern; durch die Nase sprechen, näseln. 2. *s.* das Schnaufen, Schnüffeln; Näseln. **–s,** *pl.* (*coll.*) chronischer Schnupfen.

snug [snʌg], 1. *adj.* dicht, eng; behaglich, gemütlich, traulich; gut eingerichtet, geschützt, geborgen, eingeschlossen, warm; verborgen, versteckt; seetüchtig (*Naut.*). 2. *v.n.*; *– down*, es sich behaglich machen. **–gery,** *s.* (*coll.*) behagliche *or* gemütliche Wohnung *or* Stube. **–gle,** 1. *v.n.* sich (an)schmiegen (*up to*, an (*Acc.*)); *–gle up*, sich einhüllen; *–gle down*, sich behaglich niederlegen. 2. *v.a.* herzen, an sich drücken. **–ness,** *s.* die Behaglichkeit.

so [sou], 1. *adv.* so, also, auf diese Art, dermaßen, in der Weise; *be – kind as to come*, sei so gut and komme; *– be it*, so sei es; *– am I*, ich auch; *– beautiful a day*, ein so schöner Tag; *– early as Monday*, schon am Montag; *even –*, selbst dann, selbst in dem Falle; *– far – good*, so weit sehr schön; *– far as I know*, soweit ich weiß; *– help me God*, so wahr mir Gott helfe; *and – forth*, see *and – on*; *just –*, ganz recht; (*coll.*) *just* – –, nichts Besonderes; – *long!* auf Wiedersehen! *not* –, nicht doch, nicht so; *not – rich as*, nicht so reich wie; – *it is true?* also ist es doch wahr? *and – on*, und so weiter; *quite* –, ganz recht; – *to speak*, sozusagen; *is that* –? wirklich? *she is – pretty*, sie ist sehr *or* überaus hübsch; (*coll.*) *I won't, – there*, ich will es nicht, nun weißt du's; *why* –? wieso? warum? 2. *pron. adv.* es; *I think* –, ich glaube (es); *I said* –, das sagte ich; – *saying*, bei diesen Worten; – *he is*, das ist er auch. 3. (*in stock phrases*) – *as* (*with inf.*) so daß, damit, um zu; – *long as*, wenn nur, vorausgesetzt daß; – *much*, lauter, (eben)soviel; *not – much as*, nicht einmal; – *much for that*, damit basta; – *much the better*, um so besser; (*coll.*) *ever – much*, sehr; – *that*, so daß; *if* –, wenn ja, wenn dies der Fall ist; *or* –, etwa; *the more – as*, um so mehr als. 4. *conj.* so (*often with inversion*); daher, deshalb; *as a man thinks, – will he act*, wie ein Mensch denkt, so handelt er; – *far from blaming him*, weit entfernt ihn zu tadeln; *I spoke and – did he*, ich sprach und er auch; – *we did it*, daher *or* so taten wir es. **– -and- –**, *s.* so und so; *Mr. – -and- –*, Herr Soundso. **– -called**, *adj.* sogenannt, vermeintlich.

soak [souk], 1. *v.a.* einweichen, durchtränken, durchfeuchten; (auf)quellen (*dried fruit, etc.*); durchweichen, durchnässen (*with rain*); – *up*, aufsaugen, einsaugen; *be –ed in*, (*fig.*) durchtränkt werden von; – *o.s. in*, (*fig.*) sich vertiefen in; (*sl.*) – *a p.* einen schröpfen. 2. *v.n.* wässern, weich werden, weichen; (*vulg.*) saufen; – *in*, einsickern in; (*fig.*) eingehen, eindringen, einsinken; – *through*, (durch)sickern durch. 3. *s.* das Einweichen, Durchweichen; die Weiche; (*sl.*) die Sauferei; der Säufer; *give a th. a* –, etwas einweichen; *lie in* –, in der Weiche sein; (*sl.*) *on the* –, beim Saufen. **–age**, *s.* das Durchsickern; durchgesickerte Flüssigkeit. **–er**, *s.* (*coll.*) der Regenguß; der Säufer. **–ing**, 1. *s.* das Durchnässen, Einweichen; *get a –ing*, durch und durch naß werden. 2. *adv.* (only in) *–ing wet*, durch und durch naß.

soap [soup], 1. *s.* die Seife; *soft* –, die Schmierseife; (*coll.*) die Schmeichelei; *cake of* –, das Stück Seife. 2. *v.a.* (ein)seifen. **– -boiler**, *s.* der Seifensieder. **– -boiling**, *s.* die Seifensiederei. **– -box**, *s.* (*coll.*) die Rednerbühne. **– -bubble**, *s.* die Seifenblase. **– -dish**, *s.* der Seifennapf. **– -flakes**, *pl.* Seifenflocken. **– -maker**, *see* **– -boiler**. **– -powder**, *s.* das Seifenpulver. **–stone**, *s.* der Speckstein, gemeiner Talk, Seifenstein. **– -suds**, *pl.* die Seifenlauge, das Seifenwasser. **– -works**, *pl.* die Seifenseiderei. **–wort**, *s.* das Seifenkraut (*Bot.*). **–y**, *adj.* seifig, Seifen–, seifenartig; schmeichlerisch, salbungsvoll.

soar [sɔ:], *v.n.* sich erheben, (auf)steigen; (*fig.*) sich aufschwingen *or* emporschwingen; schweben; hoch fliegen, in die Höhe gehen (*prices*); luftsegeln (*Av.*). **–ing**, 1. *adj.* (*often fig.*) hochfliegend, emporstrebend erhaben; *–ing flight*, der Segelflug. **2. s.** das Luftsegeln, Segelfliegen.

sob [sɔb], **1. *v.n.*** schluchzen. 2. *v.a.* (usually – *out*) schluchzend *or* unter Schluchzen äußern. 3. *s.* das Schluchzen; (*sl.*) – *stuff*, der Kitsch, rührselige Geschichte, die Geschichte mit 'Wein'-Zwang. **–bing**, 1. *adj.* schluchzend. 2. *s.* das Schluchzen.

sob–er ['soubə], 1. *adj.* nüchtern (*also fig.*); (*fig.*) mäßig, züchtig; ernsthaft, besonnen, gesetzt, ausgeglichen; ruhig, matt (*as colour*); *in –er earnest*, allen Ernstes, in vollem Ernste; *as –er as a judge*, vollkommen nüchtern; *sleep o.s. –er*, seinen Rausch ausschlafen. 2. *v.a.* nüchtern machen; (*fig.*) (also – *down*) ernüchtern, beruhigen, dämpfen. 3. *v.n.* *–er down*, nüchtern werden; (*fig.*) sich ernüchtern *or* beruhigen, besonnen werden. **–er-minded**, *adj.* besonnen, ruhig. **–er-mindedness**, *s.* die Besonnenheit. **–erness**, *s.* die Nüchternheit; Mäßigkeit, Besonnenheit; Schlichtheit; der Ernst. **–riety** [–'braɪətɪ], *s.* die Nüchternheit, Mäßigkeit.

sobriquet ['soubrɪkeɪ], *s.* der Spitzname.

soc [sɔk], *s.* (*archaic*) die Gerichtsbarkeit; der Gerichtsbezirk. **–(c)age** [–ɪdʒ], *s.* (*archaic*) der Frondienst(besitz), das Bauernlehen.

soccer ['sɔkə], *s.* (*coll.*) das Fußballspiel.

sociab–ility [souʃə'bɪlɪtɪ], *s.* die Geselligkeit. **–le** ['souʃəbl], 1. *adj.* gesellig, umgänglich; freundschaftlich, gemütlich, ungezwungen. 2. *s.* (*archaic*) der Phaeton; zweisitziges Dreirad; die Causeuse (*sofa*); (*Amer.*) gesellige Zusammenkunft. **–leness**, *see* **–ility**.

social ['souʃəl], 1. *adj.* gesellschaftlich, Gesellschafts–, sozial; gesellig lebend (*of animals*); gesellig, umgänglich; – *contract*, der Gesellschaftsvertrag; – *democrat*, der Sozialdemokrat; – *evening*, geselliger Abend; – *evil*, die Prostitution; – *gathering*, gesellige Zusammenkunft; – *intercourse*, gesellschaftlicher Verkehr; – *science*, die Sozialwissenschaft; – *service*, der Gemeinschaftdienst, die Wohlfahrt; – *services*, soziale Einrichtungen; – *work*, die Fürsorge; – *worker*, der Fürsorger. 2. *s.* (*coll.*) gesellige Zusammenkunft . **–ism**, *s.* der Sozialismus. **–ist**, 1. *s.* der Sozialist. 2. *adj.*, **–istic** [–'lɪstɪk], *adj.* sozialistisch. **–ization** [–aɪ'zeɪʃn], *s.* die Sozialisierung, Vergesellschaftung, Verstaatlichung. **–ize**, *v.a.* sozialisieren, vergesellschaften, verstaatlichen.

society [sə'saɪɪtɪ], *s.* die Gesellschaft (*also C.L.*), (Volks)Gemeinschaft; der Verkehr, Umgang (*with*, mit); Verein, Verband (*C.L.*); *co-operative* –, die Konsumgenossenschaft, der Konsumverein; *fashionable* –, die feine Welt; – *of Friends*, die Quäker (*pl.*); *in* –, in der guten Gesellschaft; *go into* –, in Gesellschaft gehen; – *of Jesus*, der Jesuitenorden.

sociolog–ical [souʃə'lɔdʒɪkl], *adj.* soziologisch. **–ist** [–ʃɪ'ɔlədʒɪst], *s.* der Soziologe. **–y** [–ʃɪ'ɔlədʒɪ], *s.* die Soziologie. Gesellschaftslehre.

[1]**sock** [sɔk], *s.* die Socke, (kurzer) Strumpf; die Einlegesohle; (*coll.*) *pull one's –s up*, sich zusammennehmen; (*sl.*) *put a – in it!* halt's Maul!

[2]**sock**, 1. *s.* (*sl.*) der Schlag; (*sl.*) *give s.o. –s*, einen verhauen *or* durchhauen; (*sl.*) *have a – at it*, es versuchen *or* probieren. 2. *v.a.* hauen, prügeln. **–dolager** [–'dɔlədʒə], *s.* (*sl.*) entscheidender Schlag; ausschlaggebende Antwort.

socket ['sɔkɪt], *s.* die (Steck)Hülse, Buchse, der Flansch, Rohransatz, Stutzen, Schuh; die Höhle (*of eyes*); Pfanne (*of bones*); *lamp-* –, die Fassung (*Elec.*); *wall-* –, die Steckdose, der Steckkontakt (*Elec.*). **– -joint**, *s.* das Kugelgelenk (*Anat.*).

socle ['sɔkl], *s.* der Sockel, Untersatz (*Arch.*).

[1]**sod** [sɔd], 1. *s.* der Rasen, die Rasendecke, das Rasenstück; *under the* –, im Grabe, unter dem grünen Rasen. 2. *v.a.* mit Rasen bedecken. **– -widow**, *s.* (*Amer. sl.*) die Witwe.

[2]**sod**, *s.* (*vulg.*) der Luder, Schurke.

soda ['soudə], *s.* das Natriumkarbonat, kohlensaures Natron, das *or* die Soda; *bicarbonate of* –, doppelkohlensaures Natron; *caustic* –, das Ätznatron. **– -fountain**, *s.* der Mineralwasserausschank. **– -lye**, *s.* die Sodalauge. **– -water**, *s.* das Sodawasser, Mineralwasser, Selters(wasser).

sodality [so'dælɪtɪ], *s.* karitative Bruderschaft (*R.C.*).

sodden ['sɔdən], *adj.* durchnäßt, durchweicht; nicht aufgegangen *or* ausgebacken, teigig, schleifig, streifig (*as bread*); (*fig.*) aufgedunsen, aufgeschwemmt; (*sl.*) versoffen.

sodium ['soudɪəm], *s.* das Natrium, Natron; – *carbonate*, kohlensaures Natron, das *or* die Soda; – *hydroxide*, das Ätznatron, Natriumhydrat; – *nitrate*, das Chilesalpeter, Natriumnitrat, salpetrigsaures Natron; – *sulphate*, das Glaubersalz, schwefelsaures Natron *or* Natrium; – *sulphide*, das Schwefelnatrium; – *sulphite*, das Natriumsulfit, schwefligsaures Natrium.

sodom–ite ['sɔdəmaɪt], *s.* der Sodomit, Päderast. **–y**, *s.* widernatürliche Unzucht, die Sodomie, Päderastie.

soever [sou'ɛvə], *adv. suff.* auch *or* nur immer

sofa ['soufə], *s.* das Sofa.

soffit ['sɔfɪt], *s.* die Gewölbedecke, Soffitte; Unterfläche (*of an arch*) (*Arch.*).

soft [sɔft], 1. *adj.* weich, geschmeidig, angenehm; leise, leicht, sacht, sanft, zart, milde, nachgiebig; zärtlich, liebenswürdig; (*coll.*) empfindsam, weich(lich); (*coll.*) einfältig; (*sl.*) verliebt (*on*, in, (*Acc.*)); – *answer*, milde Antwort; – *colour*, weiche Farbe; – *drink*, alkoholfreies Getränk; – *goods*, Tuchwaren, Webwaren, Textilwaren (*pl.*); – *hat*, schlapper Hut; – *note*, leiser Ton; – *pedal*, das Pianopedal (*Mus.*); (*fig.*) *apply the – pedal*, einen sanften Ton anschlagen; – *in the head*, blöde; – *iron*, das Weicheisen; – *roe*, die Milch (*Ichth.*); *have a – spot in one's heart for*, eine Schwäche *or* ein Herz haben für; *–er sex*, zartes Geschlecht; – *soap*, die Schmierseife; (*coll.*) Schmeichelei; – *solder*, das Weichlot, Zinnlot; – *water*, kalkfreies *or* weiches Wasser. **–en** ['sɔfn], 1. *v.a.* weich machen, erweichen (*also water*); rühren (*the heart*); lindern (*pain*), mildern (*pain, colour, etc.*); verschmelzen, abstufen, vertreiben (*colouring*); enthärten (*metal*); (ab)schwächen, entkräften, verweichlichen; *–en up*, aufweichen, sturmreif machen (*Mil.*). 2. *v.n.* weich(er) werden; sanft(er) werden; sich erweichen, sich mildern, sich verschmelzen (*as colours*), sich erwärmen (*to*, für) (*as a p.*). **–ener**, *s.* die Linderung; das Linderungsmittel (*of pain*); die Erweichung, Enthärtung; das Erweichungsmittel (*for water*). **–ening**, *s.* das Weichwerden, die Erweichung; Nachgiebigkeit, Rührung; *–ening of the brain*, die Gehirnerweichung. **– -eyed**, *adj.* sanftäugig. **– -headed**, *adj.* einfältig, schwachköpfig. **– -hearted**, *adj.* weichherzig. **– -heartedness**, *s.* die Weichherzigkeit. **–ly**, *adv.* weich, zart; leise, ruhig, sachte, sanft. **–ness**, *s.* die Weichheit; Sanftmut, Milde, Nachgiebigkeit, Weichlichkeit. **– -nosed**, *adj.* zersprengend (*bullet*). (*coll.*). **– -soap** (*a p.*) *v.a.* (einem) Honig um den Mund schmieren. **– -spoken**, *adj.* leise sprechend; (*fig.*) sanft, friedlich. **– -voiced**, *adj.* mit sanfter Stimme. **–y**, *s.* (*coll.*) der Schwachkopf, Einfaltspinsel.

soggy ['sɔgɪ], *adj.* feucht, naß, durchnäßt; sumpfig; schleifig, klitschig.

soho [so'hoʊ], *int.* hallo! (*Hunt.*).

soi-disant [swɑ'dɪ:zɑ̃], *adj.* angeblich, sogenannt.

[1]**soil** [sɔɪl], *s.* der Boden, die Erde; Bodenbeschaffenheit, Bodenart; (*fig.*) das Land; *native* –, das Heimatland; *racy* or *redolent of the* –, erdrüchig, bodenständig.

[2]**soil**, 1. *s.* der Fleck, Schmutz, Abfall, Dung; Pfuhl, die Suhle. 2. *v.a.* besudeln, beschmutzen, verunreinigen; düngen (*fields*); – *one's hands with*, (*fig.*) sich beschmutzen mit. 3. *v.a.* schmutzig *or* fleckig werden, schmutzen. **–ed** [–d], *adj.* schmutzig, beschmutzt, angeschmutzt; *–ed linen*, schmutzige Wäsche. **– -pipe**, das Abflußrohr (*of W.C.*).

[3]**soil**, *v.a.* mit Grünfutter füttern (*cattle*).

soirée[swɑ'reɪ], *s.* die Abendgesellschaft, Soiree.

sojourn ['sɔdʒə:n], 1. *s.* der Aufenthalt, das Verweilen; der Aufenthaltsort. 2. *v.n.* sich aufhalten, verweilen (*in* or *at*, an; *with*, bei). **–er**, *s.* der Gast, Besucher, Fremde(r), *m.*

soke [soʊk], *s.* die Gerichtsbarkeit, der Gerichtsbezirk (*Hist.*).

sol [sɔl], *s.* fünfter Ton der Tonleiter, das G (*Mus.*).

solace ['sɔləs], 1. *s.* der Trost (*to*, für), die Erleichterung (*from*, von). 2. *v.a.* trösten; – *o.s. with*, sich trösten mit, Trost suchen in. 3. *v.n.* trösten, Trost bieten.

solanum [so'leɪnəm], *s.* der Nachtschatten (*Bot.*).

solar ['soʊlə], *adj.* Sonnen–; – *eclipse*, die Sonnenfinsternis; – *plexus*, der Solarplexus, das Sonnengeflecht; – *system*, das Sonnensystem. **–ize**, *v.a.* überbelichten (*Phot.*).

solatium [so'leɪʃɪəm], *s.* die Entschädigung, Vergütung (*Law*).

sold [soʊld], *see* **sell.**

solder ['sɔldə], 1. *s.* das Lot, Lötmetal, Lötmittel, Lötblei, die Lötmasse; *hard* –, das Hartlot, Schlaglot; *soft* –, das Weichlot, Zinnlot. 2. *v.a.* löten. **–ing**, *s.* das Löten, die Lötung. **–ing-flux**, *s.* die Lötflüssigkeit. **–ing-iron**, *s.* der Lötkolben.

soldier ['soʊldʒə], 1. *s.* der Soldat, Krieger, Kämpfer. 2. *v.n.* als Soldat dienen, Soldat werden. **–like**, **–ly**, *adj.* soldatisch. **–y** [–rɪ], *s.* das Militär, Soldaten (*pl.*); der Soldatenhaufen. die Soldateska.

[1]**sole** [soʊl], *adj.* einzig, alleinig, Allein–; – *agent*, der Alleinvertreter; – *bill*, der Solawechsel (*C.L.*); *corporation* –, der Einzelne als Rechtsträger (*Law*); *feme* –, unverheiratete Frau (*Law*); – *heir*, der Universalerbe; – *owner*, der Alleininhaber (*C.L.*). **–ly**, *adj.* allein, ausschließlich; nur. **–ness**, *s.* das Alleinsein.

[2]**sole**, 1. *s.* die Sohle, Fußsohle, Schuhsohle. 2. *v.a.* besohlen. **– -leather**, *s.* das Sohlenleder. **– -plate**, *s.* die Grundplatte (*Mach.*).

[3]**sole**, *s.* die Seezunge (*Ichth.*).

solecis–m ['sɔləsɪzm], *s.* der Sprachfehler, Sprachverstoß, Sprachschnitzer; (*fig.*) Verstoß, die Ungehörigkeit, Ungeschicklichkeit. **–tic** [–'sɪstɪk], *adj.* fehlerhaft.

solemn ['sɔləm], *adj.* feierlich, weihevoll; formell; ernst, würdevoll, wichtigtuend. **–ity** [–'lɛmnɪtɪ], *s.* die Feierlichkeit; feierlicher Ernst, würdevolles Aussehen; die Steifheit. **–ization** [–nɑɪ'zeɪʃən], *s.* die Feier. **–ize** [–nɑɪz], *v.a.* feiern, feierlich begehen; weihen; *–ize a marriage*, eine Ehe schließen.

solenoid ['sɔlənɔɪd], *s.* das Solenoid, die Magnetspule (*Elec.*).

sol-fa ['sɔl'fɑ:], 1. *v.n.* solfeggieren. 2. *s.* die Solmisation (*Mus.*).

solfatara [sɔlfə'tɑ:rə], *s.* Schwefelwasserstoff ausströmendes Becken, Schwefeldampf aushauchender Krater (*Geol.*).

solfeggio [sɔl'fɛdʒjoʊ], *s.* das Solfeggio, die Gesangsübung ohne Text (*Mus.*).

solicit [sə'lɪsɪt], *v.a.* bitten, angehen, ersuchen (*a p.*) (*for*, um); ansprechen, anhalten (*a p.*); erbitten (*a th.*) (*of* or *from*, von); werben, sich bewerben *or* sich bemühen um (*a th.*). **–ation** [–'teɪʃən], *s.* das Ansuchen, die Bitte, Einladung, Bewerbung, Aufforderung. **–or** [–tə], *s.* der Anwalt, Sachwalter; *–or General*, zweiter Kronanwalt. **–ous** [–təs], *adj.* besorgt, bekümmert (*about, for* or *of*, um). **–ude** [–tju:d], *s.* die Sorge, Besorgtheit, Besorgnis (*about* or *for*, um).

solid ['sɔlɪd], 1. *adj.* fest (*also fig.*); dicht, starr, stark, haltbar, dauerhaft, kräftig, solid (*also fig., C.L.*), gediegen, massiv; Raum–, Kubik– (*Math.*); (*fig.*) gründlich, zuverlässig (*of a p.*), kreditfähig, reell (*of a p.*) (*C.L.*); (*fig.*) triftig, wahrhaft, stichhaltig (*of reasons, etc.*); (*coll.*) einmütig (*of persons*); *be – for*, sich einmütig entscheiden für; *be –ly behind a p.*, geschlossen hinter einem stehen; – *angle*, körperlicher Winkel; – *capacity*, der Raumgehalt, Kubikgehalt; – *content*, der Körpergehalt; – *food*, feste Nahrung; – *fuel*, der Festkraftstoff; – *geometry*, die Stereometrie; *two – hours*, zwei volle *or* geschlagene Stunden; – *lubricant*, die Starrschmiere; – *matter*, kompresser Satz (*Typ.*); – *meal*, nahrhafte Mahlzeit; – *measure*, das Raummaß, Kubikmaß; – *oak*, *adj.* massiveichen; – *silver*, gediegenes Silber; – *tyre*, der Vollreifen. 2. *s.* fester Körper (*Phys.*); der Körper (*Geom.*); (*usually pl.*) feste Speise (*Cook.*). 3. *adv.* (*coll.*) einmütig, einstimmig; *vote* –, einmütig stimmen. **–arity** [–'dærɪtɪ], *s.* die Solidarität, der Zusammenhalt, das Zusammengehörigkeitsgefühl. **– -drawn**, *adj.* nahtlos gezogen (*as tubes*). **– -hoofed**, *adj.* einhufig. **–ifiable** [–'lɪdɪfɑɪəbl], *adj.* verdichtbar. **–ification** [–fɪ'keɪʃən], *s.* die Verdichtung, das Festwerden. **–ify** [–'lɪdɪfɑɪ], 1. *v.a.* fest machen, verdichten. 2. *v.n.* sich verdichten, erstarren. **–ity** [–'lɪdɪtɪ], *s.* die Festigkeit, Dichtheit, Dichtigkeit; Gediegenheit; Gründlichkeit; Kreditfähigkeit, Zuverlässigkeit, Solidität (*C.L.*). **–ness**, *s.* die Wahrhaftigkeit, Gültigkeit, Echtheit. **–ungulate** [sɔlɪ'dʌŋgjʊleɪt], 1. *adj.* einhufig. 2. *s.* der Einhufer (*Zool.*).

soliloqu–ize [sə'lɪləkwɑɪz], *v.n.* ein Selbstgespräch führen. **–y** [–kwɪ], *s.* das Selbstgespräch, der Monolog.

soliped ['sɔlɪpɛd], *s.* *see* **solidungulate.**

solipsism ['sɔlɪpsɪzm], *s.* der Solipsismus (*Phil.*).

solitaire [sɔlɪ'tɛ:ə], *s.* der Solitär, einzeln gefaßter Edelstein (*Jewellery*); das Grillenspiel, die Patience (*Cards*).

solit–ariness ['sɔlɪtərɪnɪs], *s.* die Einsamkeit. **–ary** [–tərɪ], 1. *adj.* einsam; einzeln, Einzel–; einzig, alleinig (*exception, etc.*); alleinlebend, einsiedlerisch; einzeln lebend (*of animals*), abgelegen (*of places*); *–ary confinement*, die Einzelhaft. 2. *s.* der Einsiedler. **–ude** [–tju:d], *s.* die Einsamkeit; Öde, Einöde.

solmization [sɔlmɪˈzeɪʃən], *see* **sol-fa** 2.
solo [ˈsoulou], 1. *s.* (pl. *-s* [-z]) das Solo; (*coll.*) der Alleinflug (*Av.*); *– flight*, der Alleinflug. 2. *v.n.* allein fliegen (*Av.*). **–ist,** *s.* der Solist, Solospieler.
solsti–ce [ˈsɔlstɪs], *s.* die Sonnenwende. **–tial** [–ˈstɪʃəl], *adj.* Sonnenwend–.
solu–bility [sɔljuˈbɪlɪtɪ], *s.* die Löslichkeit; (*fig.*) Lösbarkeit. **–ble** [ˈsɔljubl], *adj.* löslich; (*fig.*) (auf)lösbar, erklärbar. **–tion** [səlˈ(j)u:ʃən], *s.* die Lösung (*also fig., to,* für), Auflösung (*Chem.*); (*fig.*) Erklärung (*of* or *to* (*Gen.*)); *rubber –tion*, die Gummilösung.
solv–able [ˈsɔlvəbl], *adj.* (auf)lösbar; (*fig.*) erklärbar. **–e** [sɔlv], *v.a.* (auf)lösen; lösen (*Chem.*); erklären, beseitigen (*a matter*); *be –ed*, eine Lösung *or* Erklärung finden. **–ency** [–ənsɪ], *s.* die Zahlungsfähigkeit. **–ent** [–ənt], 1. *adj.* (auf)lösend (*Chem.*); zahlungsfähig (*C.L.*). 2. *s.* das Lösungsmittel, (*fig.*) Auflösungsmittel.
somat–ic [soˈmætɪk], *adj.* körperlich, physisch, leiblich; *–ic cell*, die Somazelle. **–ology** [souməˈtɔlədʒɪ], *s.* die Körperkunde.
sombre [ˈsɔmbə], *adj.* düster, dunkel; (*fig.*) schwermütig, trüb, traurig. **–ness,** die Düsterkeit.
sombrero [sɔmˈbrɛ:ərou], *s.* breitkrempiger spanischer Hut.
some [sʌm, səm], 1. *adj.* (*before sing.*) irgendein, irgendwelch; etwas, ein wenig; beträchtlich; (*sl.*) (*emphatic*) groß, bedeutend; (*before pl.*) einige; (*emphatic*) etliche, manche; (*with num.*) etwa, ungefähr, gegen; *– ability*, beträchtliche Anlagen; *– bread*, etwas Brot; *– day*, see *at – time*; *to – extent*, einigermaßen; *– few*, einige wenige; *– more*, noch etwas; *at – time or other*, irgendeinmal, eines Tages; *for – time*, einige Zeit; *– such*, ein solches *or* derartiges; *– 7 persons*, etwa 7 Personen; *– 70 miles*, etwa, ungefähr *or* gegen 70 Meilen; *in – way or other*, irgendwie; *for – years*, schon manches Jahr. 2. *pron.* (*with sing.*) etwas, ein Teil von; (*with pl.*) einige. **–body** [–bədɪ], *s.* irgendeiner, jemand; (*coll. emphatic*) (*also pl.*) bedeutende Persönlichkeit. **–how,** *adv.* auf irgendeine Weise, irgendwie; *–how or other*, auf eine oder die andere Weise, so oder so; aus irgendeinem Grund. **–one,** *s.* jemand, irgendeiner; *–one or other*, irgendeiner. **–thing,** 1. *s.* das Etwas; etwas; *–thing of a*, so etwas wie, ein leidlicher; *a certain –thing*, ein gewisses Etwas; *–thing new*, etwas Neues; *or –thing*, oder so etwas, *there is –thing in that*, es ist etwas daran *or* hat etwas für sich. 2. *adv.* (*coll.*) *–thing like*, ungefähr, annähernd, so etwas wie; (*coll.*) *that is –thing like*, das läßt sich hören *or* sehen, das lasse ich mir gefallen. **–time,** 1. *adv.* einst, dereinst, ehemals, früher; eines Tages, irgendwann, irgendeinmal. 2. *adj.* ehemalig, weiland. **–times,** *adv.* manchmal, zuweilen, bisweilen, dann und wann, gelegentlich. **–what,** 1. *pron.* ziemlich, etwas. 2. *adv.* etwas, ein wenig, einigermaßen. **–where,** *adv.* irgendwo(hin); *–where else*, anderswo(hin); (*coll.*) *–where about*, etwa, annähernd.
somersault [ˈsʌməsɔ:lt], 1. *s.* der Purzelbaum, Salto, Luftsprung; *turn a –*, einen Purzelbaum schlagen, einen Salto machen. 2. *v.n.* einen Purzelbaum schlagen, einen Salto machen, sich überschlagen.
somnambul–ate [sɔmˈnæmbjuleɪt], *v.n.* (*rare*) nachtwandeln, schlafwandeln. **–ism** [–lɪzm], *s.* das Nachtwandeln. **–ist** [–lɪst], *s.* der Nachtwandler. **–istic** [–ˈlɪstɪk], *adj.* nachtwandlerisch, schlafwandlerisch.
somni–ferous [sɔmˈnɪfərəs], *adj.* schlafbringend, einschläfernd. **–loquence** [–ləkwəns], *s.* das Sprechen im Schlaf.
somnolen–ce [ˈsɔmnələns], *s.* die Schlafsucht, Schläfrigkeit. **–t** [–ənt], *adj.* schläfrig, schlafsüchtig.
son [sʌn], *s.* der Sohn; (*often pl.*) Nachkomme, Abkomme; *– and heir*, der Stammhalter; *every mother's –*, jedermann; *– of God*, der Sohn Gottes; *– of man*, der Menschensohn, Christus. **––in-law,** *s.* der Schwiegersohn. (*coll.*) **––of-a-gun,** *s.* der Teufelskerl.
sonan–cy [ˈsounənsɪ], *s.* die Stimmhaftigkeit. **–t** [–ənt], 1. *adj.* stimmhaft (*Phonet.*). 2. *s.* stimmhafter Laut.
sonat–a [səˈnɑ:tə], *s.* die Sonate. **–ina** [sonəˈtɪ:nə], *s.* die Sonatine.
song [sɔŋ], *s.* das Lied, der Gesang; (lyrisches) Gedicht; *be in (full) –*, (laut) singen (*of birds*); *burst into –*, zu singen anfangen; *drinking –*, das Trinklied; *give a –*, ein Lied singen *or* zum Besten geben; *for a mere* (or *an old*) *–*, um einen Pappenstiel, spottbillig; *– of joy*, der Freudengesang; (*coll.*) *nothing to make a – about*, gar nicht wichtig, nichts Wichtiges; *part-–*, mehrstimmiges Lied; (*coll.*) *plug a –*, ein Lied ewig wiederholen; *– of Solomon* or *of Songs*, das Hohelied (Salomonis). **––bird,** *s.* der Singvogel. **––book,** *s.* das Gesangbuch, Liederbuch. (*coll.*) **––hit,** *s.* der (Lied)Schlager. **–ster,** *s.* der Sänger; Singvogel; (*fig.*) Dichter. **–stress,** *s.* die Sängerin.
sonnet [ˈsɔnɪt], *s.* das Sonett. **–eer** [–ˈtɪ:ə], 1. *s.* (also *––writer*), der Sonettdichter. 2. *v.n.* Sonette dichten.
sonny [ˈsʌnɪ], (*only in address*) *s.* Junge, Kleiner.
sono–meter [səˈnɔmɪtə], *s.* der Schallmesser, Sonometer. **–rity** [–rɪtɪ], *s.* der Klang, die Klangfülle, Schallfülle, der Wohlklang. **–rous** [ˈsɔnərəs], *adj.* (voll)tönend, klingend, wohlklingend, klangvoll. **–rousness,** *s. see* **–ity.**
sonsy [ˈsɔnzɪ], *adj.* (*Scots*) drall, (*esp. in*) *– lass*, dralle Dirne.
soon [su:n], *adv.* bald; früh, frühzeitig; schnell, unverzüglich, gern; *– after(wards)*, bald darauf; *as – as*, so bald als, so früh wie; (*coll.*) ebenso gern *or* gut wie. **–er,** *comp. adv.* eher, früher; schneller; lieber; *–er or later*, früher oder später; *no –er . . . than*, kaum . . . als; *no –er said than done*, gesagt, getan; *I would –er . . . than . . .*, ich möchte lieber *or* eher . . . als . . .; *the –er the better*, je eher desto besser. **–est,** *sup. adv.* frühestens, schnellstens, nächstens.
soot [sut], 1. *s.* der Ruß, das Sott. 2. *v.a.* berußen. **–iness,** *s.* die Rußigkeit. **–y,** *adj.* rußig, berußt; rußartig.
sooth [su:θ], *s.* (*archaic*) die Wahrheit (*only in*) *in –, – to say*, um die Wahrheit zu sagen, wahrlich, fürwahr. **–fast,** *adj.* (*archaic*) wahrhaft, treu. **–say,** *v.n.* wahrsagen, weissagen, prophezeien. **–sayer,** *s.* der Wahrsager.
sooth–e [su:ð], *v.a.* besänftigen, beruhigen, beschwichtigen; mildern, lindern, stillen (*pain*). **–ing,** *adj.* besänftigend, lindernd, wohltuend.
soot–iness, –y, *see* **soot.**
sop [sɔp], 1. *s.* eingetunkter Bissen; (*fig.*) das Beruhigungsmittel (*to*, für); (*coll.*) *– to Cerberus*, die Bestechung, der Beschwichtigungsversuch; *throw a – to*, (zu) beschwichtigen (suchen). 2. *v.a.* eintunken, eintauchen; durchnässen; *see* **sopping.**
sophis–m [ˈsɔfɪzm], *s.* der Trugschluß, Sophismus, die Spitzfindigkeit, Tüftelei. **–t** [–fɪst], *s.* der Sophist; Klügler, Tüftler. **–ter,** *s.* der Student im zweiten (*or* dritten) Jahre (*Cambridge*). **–tic(al)** [səˈfɪstɪk(l)], *adj.* spitzfindig, tüftelnd, sophistisch. **–ticate** [–ˈfɪstɪkeɪt], *v.a.* sophistisch darstellen *or* verdrehen; (ver)fälschen. **–ticated** [–ˈfɪstɪkeɪtɪd], *adj.* verfälscht, unecht, unnatürlich hochentwickelt, kultiviert, aufgeklärt; anspruchsvoll; weltklug. **–tication** [–ˈkeɪʃən], *s.* die Sophisterei; Verfälschung, der Trugschluß; Intellektualismus, die Geistigkeit, Kultiviertheit. **–try** [ˈsɔfɪstrɪ], *s.* die Sophisterei, Spitzfindigkeit, der Trugschluß.
sophomore [ˈsɔfəmɔ:], *s.* der Student im zweiten Jahre (*Amer.*).
soporif–erous [sɔpəˈrɪfərəs], **–ic,** [–ˈrɪfɪk], 1. *adj.* einschläfernd. 2. *s.* das Schlafmittel, Narkotikum.
sopp–iness [ˈsɔpɪnɪs], *s.* (*coll.*) die Sentimentalität, Rührseligkeit. **–ing,** adj. durchnäßt, triefend; *–ing wet*, durchnäßt. **–y,** *adj.* durchweicht, durchnäßt; regnerisch; (*coll.*) rührselig, sentimental; (*sl.*) *–y on*, vernarrt in.
soprano [səˈprɑ:nou], *s.* der Sopran, die Sopranistin (*Mus.*).
sorb [sɔ:b], *s.* die Eberesche, der Sperberbaum (*Bot.*); die Vogelbeere.
sorbet [ˈsɔ:bət], *s.* der Sorbett.

sorbo ['sɔ:bou], *attrib.*; – *rubber*, der Schwammgummi.
sorcer–er ['sɔ:sərə], *s.* der Zauberer. **–ess** [–rɪs], *s.* die Zauberin, Hexe. **–y**, *s.* die Zauberei, Hexerei.
sordid ['sɔ:dɪd], *adj.* gemein, niedrig, schmutzig; geizig, eigennützig. **–ness**, *s.* die Gemeinheit, Schmutzigkeit; Filzigkeit.
sordine ['sɔ:dɪ:n], *s.* der Dämpfer (*Mus.*).
sore [sɔ:], 1. *adj.* wund, schmerzhaft, weh, empfindlich, entzündet; schlimm, schwer (*as a calamity*); (*coll.*) reizbar, ärgerlich, gekränkt (*about*, über); *my eyes are* –, meine Augen tun weh; – *feet*, wunde Füße; – *finger*, schlimmer Finger; (*coll.*) *like a bear with a* – *head*, mürrisch, verdrießlich; – *place*, empfindliche *or* wunde Stelle; – *point*, wunder *or* peinlicher *or* heikler Punkt; – *throat*, Halsschmerzen (*pl.*). 2. *s.* wunde Stelle; (*fig.*) *open* –, altes Übel, ständiges Ärgernis. 3. *adv.* (*Poet.*), **–ly**, *adv.* arg, schlimm, heftig, äußerst, sehr; *–ly grieved*, tief betrübt; *–ly tried*, schwer geprüft; *–ly vexed*, sehr verärgert. **–ness**, *s.* die Empfindlichkeit (*also fig.*); Schmerzhaftkeit; (*fig.*) Reizbarkeit. Entrüstung, der Groll (*at*, über).
sorites [sə'raɪtɪ:z], *s.* der Kettenschluß (*Log.*).
sorority [sə'rɔrɪtɪ], *s.* die Schwesternschaft.
sorosis [sə'rousɪs], *s.* die Sammelfrucht.
[1]**sorrel** ['sɔrəl], *s.* der Sauerampfer (*Bot.*).
[2]**sorrel**, 1. *adj.* rotbraun (*of horse*). 2. *s.* das Rotbraun, der Fuchs (*horse*).
sorr–iness ['sɔrɪnɪs], .. die Armseligkeit. **–ow** ['sɔrou], 1. *s.* der Kummer, Schmerz, Gram (*for*, um; *at*, über), das Bedauern, Klagen, Jammern (*for*, um), die Reue (*for*, wegen), Trauer, Betrübnis, Trübsal, das Leid; *to my –ow*, zu meinem Bedauern *or* Leidwesen. 2. *v.n.* trauern, sich grämen *or* härmen, klagen (*for a p.*, um einen; *over*, *at* or *for a th.*, über etwas). **–owful**, *adj* kummervoll, betrübt, traurig, düster; elend kläglich. **–owfulness**, *s.* die Traurigkeit, Betrübtheit, Betrübnis, der Kummer. **–y**, *adj.* (*only pred.*) bekümmert, betrübt, traurig (*for*, um); (*only attrib.*) elend, erbärmlich, kläglich, unglücklich, armselig; *I am –y!* Verzeihung! es tut mir leid; *I am –y for you*, ich bedaure Sie, Sie tun mir leid; *I am –y to say*, leider muß ich sagen; *–y excuse*, klägliche *or* jämmerliche Entschuldigung; *a –y sight*, trauriger Anblick.
sort [sɔ:t], 1. *s.* die Sorte, Art, Gattung, Klasse; Qualität; *pl.* einzelne Buchstaben eines Sortiments (*Typ.*); (*coll.*) *a good* –, anständiger *or* guter Kerl; (*before* of) *all –s of people*, allerlei Leute; *all –s of things*, alles Mögliche, alle möglichen *or* allerlei Dinge; *no – of*, durchaus kein; (*sl.*) – *of*, *adv.* gewissermaßen, gleichsam; *a strange – of man*, seltsamer Mensch; *that – of thing*, so etwas, etwas Derartiges; *and that – of thing*, und dergleichen; (*after* of) *s.th of the* –, etwas Ähnliches; *nothing of the* –, nichts dergleichen; *have looks of a* –, nicht gerade häßlich sein; *of all –s*, aller Arten; (*coll.*) *a painter of –s*, so etwas wie ein Maler; (*after other prepositions*) *after a* –, gewissermaßen, bis zu einem gewissen Grade; *in some – of way*, in gewisser Weise; (*coll.*) *out of –s*, unpäßlich; verstimmt. 2. *v.a.* auslesen, sortieren; einteilen; assortieren (*C.L.*); (*Scots*) reparieren, wiederherstellen, herrichten; – *out*, sortieren, aussuchen; aussondern, ausscheiden; trennen, unterscheiden. 3. *v.n.* (*archaic*) passen (*with*, zu), angemessen sein (*with* (*Dat.*)). **–er**, *s.* der Sortierer.
sortie ['sɔ:tɪ], *s.* der Ausfall (*Mil.*), Einsatz (*Av.*).
sortilege ['sɔ:tɪlɪdʒ], *s.* das Wahrsagen durch Lose.
so-so ['sousou], (*coll.*) 1. *pred. adj.* leidlich, mäßig. 2. *adv.* so lala.
sostenuto [sɔstə'nu:tou], *adv.* gehalten, getragen (*Mus.*).
sot [sɔt], 1. *s.* der Trunkenbold, Säufer. 2. *v.n.* saufen, sich betrinken. **–tish**, *adj.* versoffen trunksüchtig; blöde. **–tishness**, *s.* die Versoffenheit, Trunksucht.
sotto voce ['sɔtou'voutʃɪ], *adv.* mit gedämpfter Stimme.
soubrette [su:'brɛt], *s.* die Soubrette (*Theat.*).
souffle [su:fl], *s.* das Geräusch (*Med.*).
soufflé ['su:fleɪ], *s.* der Auflauf, Eiweißschnee (*Cook.*).
sough [sau, sʌf], 1. *s.* das Sausen, Heulen, Pfeifen. 2. *v.n.* sausen, heulen, pfeifen (*of the wind*).
sought [sɔ:t], *see* **seek**. **––after**, *adj.* begehrt, gesucht, umworben.
soul [soul], *s.* die Seele (*also fig.*), das Innenleben; (*fig.*) Herz, der Geist; das Sinnbild, die Verkörperung, das Wesen, der Kern; Leiter, Führer, das Haupt, die Triebkraft; der Sinn (*for*, für), die Neigung (*for*, zu); (*usually pl.*) der Mensch, Einwohner; *call one's – one's own*, über sich selbst verfügen können; *good* –, gute Seele; *the – of honour*, die Ehrenhaftigkeit selbst; *be kindred –s*, seelenverwandt sein; *the life and – of the party*, die Seele der Gesellschaft, *not a* –, keine Menschenseele; *poor* –, armes Ding, armer Kerl *or* Teufel *or* Wicht! *upon my* –, (bei) meiner Seele! *with heart and* –, von ganzem Herzen, mit Leib und Seele. **––bell**, *s.* die Totenglocke. **––destroying**, entmutigend, bedrückend, trostlos. **–ful**, *adj.* seelenvoll; (*fig.*) gefühlvoll. **–less**, *adj.* seelenlos; (*fig.*) gefühllos. **––stirring**, *adj.* herzergreifend.
[1]**sound** [saund], 1. *adj.* gesund (*in mind and body*; *also fig.*); unversehrt, unbeschädigt, tadellos, gut erhalten, ganz, fehlerfrei; unverdorben (*as fruit*); fest, ungestört (*as sleep*); kräftig, tüchtig, gehörig (*as a blow*); stichhaltig, gültig, begründet, rechtmäßig, vernünftig (*as arguments*); zuverlässig, einwandfrei (*of a p.*); solid, sicher (*C.L.*); (*as*) – *as a bell*, kerngesund; – *health*, gute Gesundheit; – *in mind and limb*, an Geist und Körper gesund; *safe and* –, gesund und munter. 2. *adv.*; – *asleep*, fest schlafend. **–ness**, *s.* die Gesundheit, Unversehrtheit, Unverletztheit; Richtigkeit, Echtheit, Rechtmäßigkeit, Rechtgläubigkeit; Gründlichkeit, Tiefe, Festigkeit (*of sleep*), Zuverlässigkeit, Sicherheit, Stabilität, Solidität (*C.L.*); *–ness of health*, gute Gesundheit; *–ness of judgement*, gesundes Urteil.
[2]**sound**, *s.* der Sund, die Meerenge.
[3]**sound**, *s.* die Schwimmblase (*Ichth.*).
[4]**sound**, 1. *v.n.* tönen, ertönen klingen (*also fig.*), erklingen, erschallen; (*fig.*) scheinen, sich anhören, den Eindruck machen (*as if*, als wenn). 2. *v.a.* ertönen *or* erklingen *or* erschallen lassen; – *abroad*, verkündigen, ausposaunen, – *a note*, einen Ton anschlagen; – *the retreat*, zum Rückzug blasen; – *a p.'s praises*, jemandes Lob singen; – *the trumpet*, die Trompete blasen. 3. *s.* der Ton, Schall, Laut, Klang; das Geräusch; – *and fury*, leerer Schall und Rauch; *velocity of* –, die Schallgeschwindigkeit; *to the – of*. unter dem Klang von; *within* –, in Hörweite; *without a* –, lautlos. **––board**, *s.* der Resonanzboden (*also fig.*), das Schallbrett. **––box**, *s.* die Schalldose. **––chart**, *s.* die Lauttafel. **––detector**, *s.* (Flug)Horchgerät (*Av.*). **––film**, *s.* der Tonfilm. **–ing**, 1. *adj.* klingend, schallend, tönend; hochklingend. **–ing-board**, *see* **––board**. **–less**, lautlos, klanglos. **––locator**, *s. see* **––detector**. **––post**, *s* der Stimmpfosten (*of violin, etc.*). **––proof**, *adj.* schalldicht. **––ranging**, *s.* das Schallmeßverfahren, die Schallmessung. **––shift**, *s.* die Lautverschiebung. **––wave**, *s.* die Schallwelle.
[5]**sound**, 1. *v.a.* loten, peilen, abmessen, pegeln (*Naut.*); sondieren (*Surg.*, *also fig.*), (*fig.*) erkunden, untersuchen, abhorchen, auf den Zahn fühlen (*Dat.*). 2. *v.n.* tauchen (*as a whale*). 3. *s.* die Sonde. **–ing**, *s.* das Loten, die Lotung (*Naut.*); *pl.* der Ankergrund, lotbare Wassertiefe (*pl.*); *take a –ing* or *–ings*, loten. **–ing-lead**, *s.* das Senkblei, Peillot. **–ing-line**, *s.* die Lotleine. **–ing-rod**, *s.* der Peilstock.
soup [su:p], *s.* die Suppe, Fleischbrühe; (*sl.*) dicker Nebel; (*coll.*) *in the* –, in der Klemme *or* Patsche *or* Tinte. **––kitchen**, *s.* die Volksküche. **––ladle**, *s.* der Suppenlöffel. **––tureen**, *s.* die Suppenschüssel, Suppenterrine.
soupçon ['su:psɔ̃], *s.* die Spur (*of*, von).
sour [sauə], 1. *adj.* sauer; herb, bitter, scharf; kalt und feucht (*as soil*); (*fig.*) verdrießlich, griesgrämlich, verbittert, sauertöpfisch, mürrisch (*of a p.*); – *gourd*, der Affenbrotbaum (*Bot.*); – *grapes*, (*fig.*) sauere Trauben; *grow* –, mürrisch *or* bitter werden; – *milk*, sauere Milch, die Sauermilch; *turn* –, sauer werden. 2. *v.a.* sauer machen; säuern, ansäuern,

absäuern. einsäuern; (*fig.*) verbittern. 3. *v.n.* sauer werden; (*fig.*) mürrisch *or* verdrießlich werden. **–ish,** *adj.* säuerlich. **–ness,** *s.* die Säure, Herbheit; (*fig.*) Bitterkeit, Verdrießlichkeit, das Verbittertsein.

source [sɔːs], *s.* die Quelle (*of*, von *or* für), der Ursprung; (*Poet.*) der Quell, Strom; *draw from a –*, einer Quelle entnehmen, aus einer Quelle schöpfen; *from a reliable –*, aus sicherer *or* zuverlässiger Quelle; *take its – from*, herstammen von, entspringen (*Dat.*); *have its – in*, seinen Ursprung haben in; *– of supply*, die Bezugsquelle.

sous–e [saʊs], 1. *s.* der Pökel, die Pökelbrühe, Salzbrühe, Lake; Gepökeltes, *n.*, das Pökelfleisch; *see also* **–ing.** 2. *v.a.* (ein)pökeln, einsalzen; ins Wasser werfen, eintauchen; durchnässen. **–ed** [–t], *adj.* (ein)gepökelt, Pökel–; (*sl.*) besoffen. **–ing,** *s.* der Sturz ins Wasser, das Durchnässen; *get a –ing*, durchnäßt werden.

soutane [suː'tɑːn], *s.* die Sutane (*R.C.*).

souteneur [suːtə'nəː], *s.* der Zuhälter.

south [saʊθ], 1. *s.* der Süden; (*Poet.*) Süd; die Südseite, südlicher Teil; *the – of France*, Südfrankreich; *from the –*, aus Süden (*wind*); aus dem Süden (*a p.*); *in the – of*, im Süden von; *to the – of*, südlich von; *towards the –*, nach Süden. 2. *attrib. adj.* südlich, Süd–; nach Süden gelegen; aus Süden kommend; *– sea*, die Südsee; *– wind*, der Südwind. 3. *adv.* südwärts, nach Süden; *– of*, südlich von. **– -east,** 1. *adj.* südöstlich, Südost–. 2. *adv.* nach Südosten; *–east of*, südöstlich von. 3. *s.* der Südost; *to the – -east of*, südöstlich von. **– -easter,** *s.* der Südostwind. **– -easterly,** 1. *adj.* südöstlich, Südost–. 2. *adv.* nach Südosten. **– -eastern,** *attrib. adj.* südöstlich, Südost–. **– -eastward.** 1. *adv.* südostwärts, südöstlich. 2. *s.* der Südosten; *to the – -eastward*, nach Südosten. **– -eastwards,** *adv.* südostwärts, südöstlich. **–erly** ['sʌðəlɪ], *adj.* südlich, Süd–. **–ern** ['sʌðən], *attrib. adj.* südlich; *–ern England*, Südengland; *–ern States*, die Südstaaten (*Amer.*). **–erner,** *s.* der Südländer, Südstaatler (*Amer.*). **–ing** ['saʊθɪŋ], *s.* die Südrichtung; Kulmination (*Astr.*); südliche Fahrt. **–(ern)most** ['saʊθmoʊst, 'sʌðənmoʊst], südlichst. **– – – -east,** *adv.* südsüdöstlich. **– – – -west,** *adv.* südsüdwestlich (*for forms as adj. & n. see under –*). **–wards(s),** *adv.* südwärts. **– -west,** 1. *adj.* südwestlich, Südwest–. 2. *adv.* südwestlich, nach Südwesten. 3. *s.* der Südwesten. **– -wester,** *s.* der Südwestwind; [saʊ'wɛstə], Südwester (*fisherman's hat*). **– -westerly, – -western, – -westward(s),** (*for forms see under* **– -easterly,** *etc.*).

souvenir ['suːvənɪə], *s.* das Andenken.

sovereign ['sɔvrɪn], 1. *adj.* oberst, allerhöchst, unumschränkt, souverän; unfehlbar, allerbest, wirksamst (*remedy*); *– contempt*, tiefste Verachtung; *– emblem*, das Hoheitszeichen; *– imagination*, allumfassende Einbildungskraft; *our – lady, Queen Elizabeth*, Ihre Majestät, die Königin E. 2. *s.* der Herrscher, Souverän, Landesherr; das Zwanzigschillingstück, der Sovereign. **–ty,** *s.* höchste Staatsgewalt; die Landeshoheit, Souveränität; Oberherrschaft, unumschränkte Gewalt.

soviet ['soʊvjət, 'sɔvjət], 1. *s.* der Sowjet. 2. *attrib adj.* Sowjet–, sowjetisch.

[1]**sow** [saʊ], *s.* die Sau (*Zool.*); Gießform, (Gieß)-Mulde (*Metal*), die Massel (*of pig-iron*). **– -bread,** *s.* das Saubrot, Alpenveilchen (*Bot.*). **– -bug,** *s.* die Kellerassel (*Ent.*). **– -thistle,** *s.* die Saudistel, Gänsedistel (*Bot.*).

[2]**sow** [soʊ], 1. *ir.v.a.* säen (*seed*), besäen (*field*); (*fig.*) ausstreuen, verbreiten; *– the seeds of hatred*, Haß säen; *– one's wild oats*, sich (*Dat.*) die Hörner ablaufen. 2. *ir.v.n.* säen. **–er,** *s.* der Sämann, Säer; die Sämaschine; (*fig.*) der Verbreiter, Anstifter. **–ing,** *s.* das Säen, die (Aus)Saat. **–ing-corn,** *s.* das Saatkorn. **–ing-machine,** *s.* die Sämaschine. **–n,** *adj.* (*often fig.*) besät, besetzt.

sowar [sə'wɑː], *s.* eingeborener Kavallerist (*in India*).

soya ['sɔɪə], *s.* (also *– -bean*) die Sojabohne.

spa [spɑː], *s.* die Mineralquelle, Heilquelle; der Kurort, Badeort, das Bad.

spac–e [speɪs], 1. *s.* der Raum; Zwischenraum, Abstand, die Lücke; Weite, Ausdehung, Fläche der Zeitraum, die Weile, Frist; das Spatium (*Typ.*); *disappear into –e*, in Nichts verschwinden; *leave (some) –e*, Platz lassen; *look into –e*, vor sich hinblicken; *save –e*, Raum sparen; *for a short –e*, ein Weilchen; *within the –e of*, innerhalb (*Gen.*). 2. *v.a.* (also *–e out*), spatiieren, spationieren (*Typ.*), sperren, in Zwischenräumen anordnen. **–ed,** *adj.* gesperrt, Sperr– (*Typ.*). **–e-bar,** *s.* **–er,** *s.* die Zwischenraumtaste (*typewriter*). **–ial,** *adj. see* **spatial. –ing,** *s.* das Sperren; der Zwischenraum (*Typ.*). **–ious** [–ʃəs], *adj.* geräumig, ausgedehnt; (*fig.*) weit, umfangreich, umfassend. **–iousness,** *s.* die Geräumigkeit; (*fig.*) Weite, der Umfang, Ausmaß.

[1]**spade** [speɪd], 1. *s.* der Spaten; *call a – a –*, das Ding beim rechten Namen nennen. 2. *v.a.* mit dem Spaten umgraben. **–ful,** *s.* der Spatenvoll. **– -work,** *s.* (*fig.*) die Pionierarbeit, Vorarbeit.

[2]**spade,** *s.* (*usually pl.*) das Pik, Schippen (*Cards*); *ace of –s*, das Pikas.

spadix ['speɪdɪks], *s.* (*pl.* –dices [–dɪsiːz]) der Kolben (*Bot.*).

spado ['speɪdoʊ], *s.* der Eunuch, Entmannte(r), *m.*

spaghetti [spə'gɛtɪ], *s.* Spaghetti, Fadennudeln (*pl.*).

spahi [spɑː'hɪː], *s.* algerischer Kavallerist (*Mil.*).

spall [spɔːl], 1. *v.a.* zerkleinern, zerstückeln. 2. *v.n.* sich abspalten.

spalpeen ['spælpɪːn], *s.* der Schurke (*Irish*).

[1]**span** [spæn], 1. *s.* die Spanne (*also as measure and fig.*); gespreizte Hand; (*fig.*) die (Zeit)Spanne (*of time*); Stützweite (*of a bridge*); Spannweite (*Arch., Av.*), Spannung (*Arch.*); der Hanger (*Naut.*); das Gespann (*Amer.*). 2. *v.a.* (um– *or* über)spannen; abmessen; zurren (*Naut.*). **– -roof,** *s.* das Satteldach.

[2]**span,** *see* **spin.**

spandrel ['spændrəl], *s.* die Spandrille (*Arch.*).

spangle ['spæŋgl], 1. *s.* der Flitter, Flimmer; die Spange. 2. *v.a.* beflittern; (*fig.*) schmücken, übersäen, besprenkeln; *–d heavens*, gestirnter Himmel.

spaniel ['spænjəl], *s.* der Wachtelhund.

spank [spæŋk], 1. *v.a.* schlagen, prügeln. 2. *v.n.* (also *– along*) dahineilen. 3. *s.* dcr Klaps, Schlag. **–er,** *s.* schneller Läufer (*horse*); (*sl.*) der Prachtkerl, das Prachtexemplar; der Besan (*Naut.*). **–ing,** *adj.* schnell laufend *or* dahinfahrend; (*sl.*) stark, kräftig, tüchtig, fein.

spanner ['spænə], *s.* der Schraubenschlüssel.

[1]**spar** [spɑː], *s.* der Spat (*Min.*); *heavy –*, der Schwerspat, das Barium; *light –*, das Lenzin.

[2]**spar,** *s.* die Spiere, der Sparren; das Rundholz (*Naut.*); der Tragholm (*Av.*). **– -deck,** *s.* das Spardeck.

[3]**spar,** 1. *v.n.* Scheinhiebe machen; boxen; (*fig.*) sich zanken *or* streiten. 2. *s.* der Boxkampf, Hahnenkampf; (*fig.*) Streit, Zank.

sparable ['spærəbl], *s.* die (Schuh)Zwecke, der Schuhnagel (*Shoem.*).

spar–e [spɛːə], 1. *adj.* spärlich, kärglich; mager, dürr; überflüssig, überschüssig, überzählig, übrig; Reserve–; *–e anchor*, der Notanker; *–e diet*, schmale Kost; *–e figure*, hagere Gestalt; *–e horse*, das Reservepferd; *–e lead*, das Füllblei (*for propelling pencil*); *–e moment*, freier Augenblick; *–e money*, überschüssiges Geld; *–e parts*, Ersatzteile; *–e room*, das Gastzimmer, Fremdenzimmer; *–e time*, die Mußezeit, Freizeit; *–e wheel*, das Reserverad. 2. *s.* der Ersatzteil (*Tech.*). 3. *v.a.* sparsam sein *or* umgeben mit, sparen; ersparen (*Dat.*); übrig haben *or* erübrigen für, ablassen (*Dat.*); (ver)schonen (*a p.*); entbehren, missen; *–e my blushes*, schonen Sie mein Zartgefühl; *can you –e me a cigarette?* haben Sie eine Zigarette für mich übrig? *–e no expense*, keine Kosten scheuen; *–e a person's life*, einem das Leben schenken; *if I am –ed*, wenn ich am Leben bleibe; *can you –e me a moment?* haben Sie einen Augenblick Zeit für mich? *–e no pains*, keine Mühe scheuen; *–e o.s.*, sich schonen; *–e s.o.* (or *o.s.*) *the trouble of coming*, einem (*or* sich) die Mühe (er)sparen zu kommen; *no time to –e*, keine Zeit übrig; *enough and to –e*, vollauf, reichlich. 4. *v.n.* sparen, sparsam sein; Nachsicht haben, nachsichtig sein, Gnade walten lassen. **–eness,** *s.* die Spärlichkeit, Magerkeit, Dürftigkeit. **–e-rib,**

s. das Schweinsrippchen, Rippenstückchen. **–ing,** *adj.* sparsam, karg (*of*, mit), dürftig, spärlich, knapp. **–ingness,** *s.* die Sparsamkeit, Kargheit (*of*, mit *or* an); Spärlichkeit; Seltenheit.

[1]**spark** [spɑ:k], 1. *s.* der Funke(n); (*fig.*) zündender Funke; der Zündfunke (*Motor.*); *pl.* (*used as sing.*) (*coll.*) der Funker (*Tele.*, *Rad.*); (*fig.*) *not a* –, nicht ein Funke; *vital* –, der Lebensfunke. 2. *v.n.* Funken sprühen; zünden (*Motor.*). **––gap,** *s.* die Funkstrecke (*Elec.*). **–ing,** *s.* die Funkenbildung (*Elec.*). **–ing-plug,** *s.* die Zündkerze (*Motor.*).

[2]**spark,** *s.* (*coll.*) flotter Bursche.

sparkl–e [spɑ:kl], 1. *s.* der Funke; das Funkeln, Strahlen; Schäumen (*wine*, *etc.*); der Glanz, Schimmer; die Lebhaftigkeit (*of a p.*). 2. *v.n.* fünkeln, blitzen, strahlen, glänzen (*also fig.*), glitzern, flimmern; perlen, schäumen, moussieren (*as wine*); (*fig.*) sprühen (*as wit*). **–er,** *s.* die Wunderkerze; (*sl.*) der Diamant. **–ing,** *adj.* funkelnd, glänzend, strahlend; perlend, schäumend, moussierend, Schaum– (*of wine*); (*fig.*) sprühend, geistsprühend.

sparrow [ˈspærou], *s.* der Sperling, Spatz. **––hawk,** *s.* der Sperber.

sparry [spɑ:rɪ], *adj.* spatartig; Spat–; – *gypsum*, das Marienglas; – *iron*, der Spateisenstein; *see* [1]**spar.**

sparse [spɑ:s], *adj.* dünn, spärlich, zerstreut, selten. **–ness,** *s.* die Zerstreutheit, Spärlichkeit, Seltenheit.

spasm [ˈspæzm], *s.* der Krampf, die Zuckung; (*fig.*) Anfall. **–odic** [–ˈmɔdɪk], *adj.* krampfhaft; (*fig.*) sprunghaft, unregelmäßig. **–odically,** *adv.* sprunghaft, stoßweise.

spastic [ˈspæstɪk], *adj.* Krampf– (*Med.*).

[1]**spat** [spæt], *s.* der Laich (*oysters*, *etc.*).

[2]**spat,** *see* **spit.**

[3]**spat,** *s.* (*usually pl.*) die Schuhgamasche.

spatchcock [ˈspætʃkɔk], 1. *s.* frisch geschlachtetes und zubereitetes Huhn (*Cook.*). 2. *v.a.* (*coll.*) einflicken, einfügen (*words*, *etc.*).

spate [speɪt], *s.* die Überschwemmung, das Hochwasser; (*fig.*) die Flut; – *of talk*, die Redeflut.

spath–e [speɪð], *s.* die Blütenscheide (*Bot.*). **–ose** [–θous], **–ous** [–θəs], *adj.* Blütenscheiden– (*Bot.*).

spathic [ˈspæθɪk], *adj.* spatartig, blätterig (*Geol.*).

spatial [ˈspeɪʃəl], *adj.* räumlich, Raum–.

spats, *see* [3]**spat.**

spatter [ˈspætə], 1. *v.a.* spritzen, sprenkeln (*on*, auf), bespritzen (*with*, mit); (*fig.*) besudeln. 2. *v.n.* spritzen, sprühen, sprudeln, abspritzen. **–dash,** *s.* die Gamasche.

spatula [ˈspætjulə], *s.* der Spachtel, Spatel. **–r** [–lɑ], *adj.* **–te** [–lət], *adj.* spatelförmig.

spavin [ˈspævɪn], *s.* der Spat (*Vet.*). **–ed,** *adj.* spatig (*Vet.*); (*fig.*) lahm.

spawn [spɔ:n], 1. *s.* der Laich (*of fishes and frogs*); der Rogen (*of fishes*); (*fig.*) die Brut, das Gezücht. 2. *v.n.* laichen; legen (*eggs*); (*vulg.*) gebären, erzeugen (*young*); (*fig.*) ausbrüten, aushecken, hervorbringen. **–er,** *s.* der Rog(e)ner. **–ing,** 1. *attrib. adj.* Laich–. 2. *s.* das Laichen.

speak [spi:k], 1. *ir.v.n.* sprechen, reden; *who is it –ing? Smith –ing*, wer ist am Apparat? Schmidt am Apparat (*Phone*); *generally* or *roughly –ing*, im allgemeinen, über dem Daumen gepeilt; *so to* –, sozusagen; *strictly –ing*, streng genommen. (*a*) (*with prepositions*) – *about*, sprechen über, besprechen; – *for*, sprechen für, ein gutes Wort *or* gute Worte einlegen für (*with*, bei); *it –s well for him*, es spricht für ihn; – *for o.s.*, selbst sprechen, nur die eigene Meinung äußern; *that –s for itself*, das spricht für sich selbst; – *of*, sprechen von; – *highly* or *well of*, loben, gut sprechen von; *not to – of*, geschweige, ganz zu schweigen von; *nothing to – of*, nichts Erwähnenswertes; – *of the devil and he appears*, wenn man den Teufel an die Wand malt, dann kommt er; – *on a subject*, über ein Thema sprechen *or* eine Rede halten; – *to*, sprechen zu *or* mit; anreden, ansprechen. (*b*) (*with adverbs*) – *on*, weiter reden; – *out*, frei heraus *or* weg sprechen *or* reden; laut *or* deutlich sprechen; sich aussprechen; – *up*, laut *or* deutlich sprechen; frei heraus *or* von der Leber weg sprechen, mit der Sprache herausrücken; – *up for a p.*, sich für einen verwenden, für einen eintreten. 2. *ir.v.a.* (aus)sprechen; äußern, sagen (*the truth*, *etc.*); – *English*, sich in Englisch ausdrücken, Englisch sprechen; – *a p. fair*, einem gute *or* schöne Worte geben; – *one's mind*, seine Meinung sagen; – *one's piece*, sich aussprechen; – *a ship*, ein Schiff anrufen, (an)preien (*Naut.*); *that –s volumes*, das spricht Bände. **–easy,** *s.* (*sl.*) verbotener Alkoholausschank, unkonzessionierte Kneipe. **–er,** *s.* der Sprecher; Redner; der Präsident *or* Vorsitzende(r) des Unterhauses; *previous –er*, der (Herr) Vorredner. **–ing,** *adj.* sprechend, beredt, ausdrucksvoll; sprechend ähnlich (*of likeness*); *–ing acquaintance*, flüchtige *or* oberflächliche Bekanntschaft; *–ing likeness*, sprechend ähnliches Bild; *on –ing terms*, flüchtig *or* oberflächlich bekannt; *not on –ing terms with*, nicht (mehr) sprechen mit; *–ing voice*, die Sprechstimme. **–ing-trumpet,** *s.* **–ing-tube,** *s.* das Sprachrohr.

spear [spɪ:ə], 1. *s.* der Speer, Spieß; die Lanze. 2. *v.a.* (auf)spießen, durchbohren, durchstechen. **––grass,** *s.* liegende Quecke (*Bot.*). **––head,** *s.* die Lanzenspitze. **–head,** *s.* (*fig.*) die Spitze, Spitzenlinie, Kampflinie; Stoßgruppe. **–man,** *s.* der Lanzenträger. **–mint,** *s.* grüne Minze (*Bot.*); (*coll.*) der Kaugummi. **––shaped,** *adj.* lanzenförmig. **––side,** *s.* (*archaic*) männliche Linie. **––thistle,** *s.* die Speerdistel, Heildistel (*Bot.*). **–wort,** *s.* das Egelkraut, der Hahnenfuß (*Bot.*).

spec [spɛk], *s. abbr. of* speculation.

special [ˈspɛʃəl], 1. *adj.* besonder, Sonder–, Separat–, speziell, Spezial–, außergewöhnlich, vorzüglich; eigen, individuell; bestimmt, ausdrücklich (*as orders*); – *areas*, Notstandsgebiete (*pl.*); – *bargain*, das Sonderangebot; – *constable*, der Hilfspolizist; – *correspondent*, der Sonderberichterstatter; – *edition*, die Sonderausgabe, das Extrablatt; – *knowledge*, die Fachkenntnis · – *line*, das Spezialfach; – *pass*, der Sonderausweis; – *pleading*, die Sophisterei; – *subject*, das Spezialgebiet; – *train*, der Sonderzug. 2. *s.* (*coll.*) der Sonderzug; das Extrablatt; der Hilfspolizist. **–ist,** *s.* der Spezialist, Fachmann; Spezialarzt, Facharzt. **–ity** [–ʃɪˈælɪtɪ], *s. see* **–ty. –ization** [–laɪˈzeɪʃən], *s.* die Spezialisierung. **–ize** [–laɪz], 1. *v.n.* sich spezialisieren (*in*, auf), sich besonders ausbilden (*in*, in); *–ize in*, als Spezialfach studieren. 2. *v.a.* einzeln erwähnen, gesondert anführen *or* aufführen, nach besonderer Richtung entwickeln (*Biol.*). **–ly,** *adv.* besonders, im besonderen, eigens, extra, ausdrücklich, in der besonderen Absicht. **–ty,** *s.* die Besonderheit, unterscheidendes Merkmal; die Spezialität (*also C.L.*); das Spezialfach, Spezialgebiet; der Sonderartikel, die Neuheit (*C.L.*); besiegelte Urkunde (*Law*).

specie [ˈspi:ʃɪ:], *s.* (pl. –) das Metallgeld, Hartgeld, Bargeld; *in* –, in bar.

species [ˈspi:ʃɪ:z], *s.* die Art (*also fig.*); Spezies (*Zool.*, *Bot.*); sichtbare Gestalt (*Theol.*); (*fig.*) die Sorte; *human* –, menschliche Gattung; *a – of*, eine Art von; *origin of* –, die Entstehung der Arten.

specif–ic [spəˈsɪfɪk], 1. *adj.* arteigen, spezifisch, Art–, Gattungs–; bestimmt, kennzeichnend, wesentlich; *–ic gravity*, spezifisches Gewicht, das Volumengewicht; *–ic heat*, spezifische Wärme, die Eigenwärme; *–ic name*, der Artname. 2. *s.* spezifisches Mittel. **–ication** [spɛsɪfɪˈkeɪʃən], *s.* die Spezifizierung; genaues Verzeichnis, ausführliche Beschreibung; die Angabe, Aufzählung; die Patentbeschreibung. **–y** [ˈspɛsɪfaɪ], *v.a.* spezifizieren, einzeln angeben *or* aufzählen *or* aufführen *or* bezeichnen.

specimen [ˈspɛsɪmən], *s.* das Muster, Beispiel (*of*, für); die Probe, das Exemplar (*of*, von) (*also fig.*); (*coll.*) der Kerl; *museum* –, das Museumstück; – *copy*, das Freiexemplar, Musterexemplar.

specious [ˈspi:ʃəs], *adj.* bestechend, blendend, trügerisch, Schein–, scheinbar einleuchtend. **–ness,** *s.* die Scheinbarkeit, trügerischer Schein, das Bestechende.

speck [spɛk], *s.* der Fleck, das Fleckchen; Stückchen, Bißchen. **–le,** 1. *s.* das Fleckchen, der Tupfen, Tüpfel, Punkt. 2. *v.a.* flecken, sprenkeln, tüpfeln; masern (*Pap.*). **–led,** *adj.* gefleckt, gesprenkelt, punktiert, meliert, bunt. **–less,** *adj.* fleckenlos, tadellos, untadelig, sauber.

spec–s [spɛks], *pl.* (*coll.*) die Brille. **–tacle** [ˈspɛktəkl], *s.* das Schauspiel, Schaustück, die Schaustellung, Aufmachung; der Anblick; *pl.* (also *pair of –tacles*) die Brille. **–tacle-case,** *s.* das Brillenfutteral. **–tacled,** *adj.* bebrillt, brillentragend. **–tacular** [spɛkˈtækjulə], *adj.* auffallend, in die Augen fallend; schauspielerisch, schauspielmäßig, Schau–. **–tator** [spɛkˈteɪtə], *s.* der Zuschauer.

spectr–al [ˈspɛktrəl], *adj.* geisterhaft, gespensterhaft, gespenstisch; Spektral– (*Opt.*). **–e** [–tə], *s.* die (Geister)Erscheinung, das Gespenst; (*fig.*) Phantom, Hirngespinst. **–ograph** [–trəgrɑ:f], *s.* der Spektrograph. **–oscope** [–trəskoʊp], *s.* das Spektroskop. **–oscopic** [–ˈskɔpɪk], *adj.* spektroskopisch, spektralanalytisch. **–um** [ˈspɛktrəm], *s.* das Spektrum, Farbenbild (*Phys.*); *solar –um*, das Sonnenspektrum; *–um analysis*, die Spektralanalyse.

specular [ˈspɛkjulə], *adj.* spiegelnd, Spiegel–; – *gypsum*, das Marienglas; – *iron*, der Roteisenstein, Eisenglanz, Hämatit (*Min.*).

speculat–e [ˈspɛkjuleɪt], *v.n.* nachdenken, nachsinnen, grübeln ((*up*)*on*, *about* or *as to*, über); spekulieren (*C.L.*). **–ion** [–ˈleɪʃən], *s.* das Nachdenken, Nachsinnen, Grübeln; die Grübelei, Betrachtung; Theorie, Vermutung; Spekulation (*C.L.*). **–ive** [–lətɪv], *adj.* nachdenklich, grübelnd (*of a p.*); theoretisch, erdacht, übersinnlich; spekulativ (*Phil.*, *C.L.*), Spekulations– (*C.L.*). **–or,** *s.* der Grübler, Theoretiker; Spekulant (*C.L.*).

speculum [ˈspɛkjuləm], *s.* der Spiegel, das Spekulum.

sped [spɛd], *see* **speed.**

speech [spɪ:tʃ], *s.* die Sprache, Sprechweise, Aussprache, das Sprechen, Sprachvermögen; die Rede, der Vortrag; *have – with*, sprechen mit, Rücksprache nehmen mit; *deliver* or *make a –*, eine Rede halten (*on*, über; *to*, an); *figure of –*, die Redensart; *freedom* or *liberty of –*, die Redefreiheit. **– -centre,** *s.* das Sprachzentrum. **– -day,** *s.* die Schulschlußfeier. **–ifier,** *s.* (*coll.*) der Vielredner. **–ify,** *v.n.* (*coll.*) viel(e) Worte machen, unermüdlich reden *or* sprechen. **–less,** *adj.* sprachlos (*with*, vor); wortkarg, stumm (*as a p.*); unsagbar (*grief, etc.*). **–lessness,** *s.* die Sprachlosigkeit.

speed [spɪ:d], 1. *ir* (*& reg.*) *v.n.* sich beeilen, eilen; (*only reg.*) (*coll.*) die Höchstgeschwindigkeit überschreiten, schnell fahren, rasen (*Motor.*); (*archaic*) gedeihen, vorwärtskommen, glücken; – *up*, sich beschleunigen. 2. *ir.* (*& reg.*) *v.a.* eilig fortschicken, schnell befördern, absenden, ausführen, abfertigen *or* erledigen; (*only reg.*) (also – *up*) beschleunigen; (*archaic*) fördern, Glück wünschen (*Dat.*), gedeihen lassen; (*archaic*) *God – you*, Gott geleite dich! – *the parting guest*, sich von dem scheidenden Gast verabschieden; – *up* (*only reg.*) die Geschwindigkeit vergrößern; (*fig.*) erhöhern (*output, etc.*). 3. *s.* die Eile, Schnelligkeit, (Fahr)Geschwindigkeit; der Gang (*Motor.*); (*archaic*) Erfolg; *air –*, die Eigengeschwindigkeit (*Av.*); *at a – of 60 m.p.h.*, in einer Geschwindigkeit von 100 km in der Stunde; *at full –*, mit voller *or* größter Geschwindigkeit; *gather –*, an Geschwindigkeit zunehmen; *ground –*, absolute Geschwindigkeit (*Av.*); *high* or *top –*, die Höchstgeschwindigkeit; *half –*, halbe Fahrt (*Naut.*); *slow –*, kleine Fahrt (*Naut.*); *three-quarter –*, große Fahrt (*Naut.*); *with all possible –*, mit möglichster Eile; (*Prov.*) *more haste, less –*, Eile mit Weile. **– -boat,** *s.* das Schnellboot. (*sl.*) **– -cop,** *s.* motorisierter Verkehrspolizist. **–er,** *s.* der Schnellfahrer. **– -gauge,** *s.* der Geschwindigkeitsmesser. **–iness,** *s.* die Eile, Eilfertigkeit, Geschwindigkeit. **–ing,** *s.* das Schnellfahren. **– -limit,** erlaubte Höchstgeschwindigkeit. (*coll.*) **– -merchant,** *s.* der Kilometerfresser (*Motor.*). **–ometer** [–ˈdɔmɪtə], *s.* der Geschwindigkeitsmesser. (*coll.*) **–ster,** *s.* der Kilometerfresser. **– -up,** *s.* die Beschleunigung. **–way,** *s.* die (Auto)Rennbahn. **–y,** *adj.* schnell, geschwind; unverzüglich.

speedwell [ˈspɪ:dwɛl], *s.* der Ehrenpreis (*Bot.*).

speiss [spɑɪs], *s.* die Speise (*Iron-founding*).

[1]**spell** [spɛl], *s.* bestimmte Arbeit *or* Arbeitsleistung; die Ablösung, Schicht, Arbeitszeit; kurze Zeit, Frist *or* Dauer, die Weile, Zeitlang, Zeitspanne, andauernde Periode; *for a –*, eine Weile; *hot –*, die Hitzewelle; *long – of fine weather*, andauernde Periode gutes Wetter; *take a – at*, eine Zeitlang arbeiten an.

[2]**spell,** *s.* der Zauber (*also fig.*); Zauberspruch, die Zauberformel; (*fig.*) der Bann, Reiz, die Anziehungskraft; *under a magic –*, verzaubert; *cast a – over*, verzaubern, behexen. (*coll.*) **–binder,** *s.* fesselnder Redner. **–binding,** *adj.* fesselnd. **–bound,** *adj.* bezaubert, verzaubert; festgebannt, im Banne.

[3]**spell,** 1. *ir.v.a.* (imperf. & pp. *spelt* or *–ed*) buchstabieren; richtig schreiben; (*fig.*) bedeuten, besagen (*to*, für); *how do you – this word?* wie schreibt man das Wort? *be spelt with*, sich schreiben mit; – *out*, buchstabieren. 2. *v.n.* orthographisch schreiben. **–er,** *s.* die Fibel; *be a good* (*bad*) *–er*, orthographisch (nicht) richtig schreiben. **–ing,** *s.* das Buchstabieren; die Rechtschreibung. **–ing-bee,** *s.* das Buchstabierspiel. **–ing-book,** *s.* die Fibel.

[1]**spelt** [spɛlt], *see* **spell.**

[2]**spelt,** *s.* der Spelz, Dinkel (*Bot.*).

spelter [ˈspɛltə], *s.* rohes *or* roher Zink.

[1]**spencer** [ˈspɛnsə], *s.* der Spenzer (*Dressm.*).

[2]**spencer,** *s.* das Gaffelsegel (*Naut.*).

spend [spɛnd], 1. *ir.v.a.* ausgeben (*money*) (*on*, für); aufwenden, verwenden, anlegen (*time*) (*on*, in *or* für); zubringen, verbringen (*time*); durchbringen, vergeuden, verausgaben (*in*, für) (*a fortune*); aufbrauchen, erschöpfen (*a supply, etc.*); – *o.s.*, sich verausgaben *or* erschöpfen. 2. *v.n.* Aufwand *or* Ausgaben machen, Geld ausgeben. **–thrift,** 1. *s.* der Verschwender. 2. *adj.* verschwenderisch.

spent [spɛnt], 1. *see* **spend.** 2. *adj.* erschöpft, entkräftet (*with*, von); kraftlos, verbraucht; matt (*as a bullet*); – *liquor*, das Abwasser, die Ablauge.

[1]**sperm** [spə:m], *s.* (männlicher) Same. **–ary,** *s.* männliche Samendrüse. **–atic** [–ˈmætɪk], *adj.* Samen–, samenhaltig.

[2]**sperm,** *s.* (also *– -whale*) der Pottwal, Potfisch. **–aceti** [–əˈsɛtɪ], *s.* der Walrat.

spermato–blast [ˈspə:mətəblæst], *s.* die Ursamenzelle. **–genesis** [–toˈdʒɛnɪsɪs], *s.* die Samenbildung. **–phore** [–fɔ:], *s.* der Samenträger. **–rrhoea** [–ˈrɪ:ə], *s.* der Samenfluß. **–zoon** [–ˈzoʊən] (*usually pl.* –*zoa* [–ˈzoʊə]), das Samenkörperchen, der Samenfaden, die Samenzelle.

spermo [ˈspə:moʊ], (*prefix*) Samen–.

spew [spju:], (*coll.*) 1. *v.a.* (also – *up* or *out*) ausspeien, ausspucken, auswerfen. 2. *v.n.* speien; sich erbrechen. 3. *s.* der Auswurf.

sphacelat–e [ˈsfæsəleɪt], *v.n.* brandig werden (*Path.*). **–ion** [–ˈleɪʃən], *s.* die Nekrose; Brandbildung.

sphagnum [ˈsfægnəm], *s.* das Torfmoos, Sumpfmoos (*Bot.*).

sphenoid–(al) [ˈsfɪ:nɔɪd, sfɪˈnɔɪdl], *adj.* keilförmig, keilartig, Keil–; – *bone*, das Keilbein.

spher–e [ˈsfɪ:ə], *s.* die Kugel (*Math.*); der Himmelskörper; die Erdkugel, das Himmelsgewölbe; (*Poet.*) der Himmel; (*fig.*) die Sphäre, der Kreis, Bereich; *celestial –e*, das Himmelsgewölbe; *–e of activity*, der Wirkungskreis, Wirkungsbereich; *–e of interest*, die Interessensphäre; *quite in his –e*, ganz auf seinem Gebiet; *music of the –es*, die Sphärenmusik; *out of* (or *beyond*) *his –e*, außerhalb seines Bereichs. **–ic** [ˈsfɛrɪk], *adj.* sphärisch (*also Poet.*); kugelförmig (*Math.*); (*Poet.*) himmlisch. **–ics,** *pl.* (*sing. constr.*) die Kugellehre, Sphärik (*Math.*). **–ical** [ˈsfɛrɪkl], *adj.* kugelförmig, kugelrund; sphärisch (*Math.*). **–icity** [–ˈrɪsɪtɪ], *s.* die Kugelgestalt, sphärische Gestalt. **–oid** [ˈsfɪ:ərɔɪd], *s.* das Sphäroid. **–oidal** [sfəˈrɔɪdl], *adj.* sphäroidisch. **–ule** [ˈsfɛrjul], *s.* das Kügelchen. **–ulite** [ˈsfɛrjulɑɪt], *s.* der Sphärolith (*Min.*).

sphincter [ˈsfɪnktə], *s.* der Schließmuskel (*Anat.*).

sphinx [ˈsfɪnks], *s.* die Sphinx (*Myth.*), der Sphinx (*in Egypt*). **– -like,** *adj.* sphinxartig, rätselhaft. **– -moth,** *s.* der Nachtfalter (*Ent.*).

sphragistics [sfræˈdʒɪstɪks], *pl.* (*sing. constr.*) die Siegelkunde.

sphygmo–gram [ˈsfɪgmogræm], *s.* die Pulskurve. **–graph** [–grɑ:f], *s.* der Pulskurvenmesser. **–manometer** [–məˈnɔmɪtə], *s.* der Blutdruckmesser.

spica ['spaɪkə], *s.* die Ähre. Granne (*Bot.*). **-te** [-keɪt], *adj.* ährenförmig

spic-e [spaɪs], 1. *s.* das Gewürz, die Würze; (*fig.*) der Anstrich, Beigeschmack. 2. *v.a.* würzen (*also fig.*). **-iness**, *s.* die Würzigkeit; das Pikante. **-y**, *adj.* würzig, gewürzt, pikant.

spick-and-span ['spɪkən'spæn], *adj.* geschniegelt, wie aus dem Ei gepellt; *make* –, auf Glanz herrichten.

spicul-ar ['spɪkjulə], *adj.* ährenförmig, nadelförmig. **-e** [-juːl], *s.* das Ährchen, die Nadel, nadelförmiger Fortsatz.

spicy ['spaɪsɪ], *see* **spice**.

spider ['spaɪdə], *s.* die Spinne; der Dreifuß (*Tech.*); *-'s web*, das Spinngewebe, die Spinnwebe. **--catcher**, *s.* der Mauerspecht (*Orn.*). **--like**, *adj.* spinnenartig. **-y**, *adj.* (*usually fig.*) spinnenartig, dünn.

spiff-ing ['spɪfɪŋ], *adj.* (*coll.*) glänzend. **-y**, *adj.* (*sl.*) schmuck.

spif(f)licat-e ['spɪflɪkeɪt], *v.a.* (*sl.*) vernichten, abtun. **-ion** [-'keɪʃən], *s.* die Vernichtung.

spigot ['spɪgət], *s.* der Zapfen, Hahn.

spik-e [spaɪk], 1. *s.* langer Nagel, der Bolzen, Spieker; Dorn, Stachel; die Ähre (*Bot.*). 2. *v.a.* mit eisernen Spitzen versehen; vernageln (*a gun, etc.*); *-e s.o.'s guns*, (*fig.*) seine Pläne vereiteln. **-elet** [-lɪt], *s.* kleine Ähre *or* Granne. **-enard** [-nɑːd], *s.* die Narde (*Bot.*); das Nardenöl. **-e-oil**, *s.* das Lavendelöl. **-y**, *adj.* spitzig, spitz, stach(e)lig.

spile [spaɪl], 1. *s.* der Spund, Zapfen, Pflock; Pfahl. 2. *v.a.* anzapfen, spünden (*a cask*).

[1]**spill** [spɪl], *s.* der Fidibus.

[2]**spill**, 1. *ir.v.a.* (imperf. & pp. *spilt* & *-ed*) verschütten; vergießen; werfen, schleudern; killen lassen (*a sail*); *it's no use crying over spilt milk*, geschehene Dinge sind nicht zu ändern; (*sl.*) – *the beans*, ein Geheimnis verraten. 2. *ir.v.n.* verschüttet werden, überlaufen. 3. *s.* (*coll.*) der Sturz, Fall. **-way**, *s.* der Abflußkanal, das Sturzbett.

spillikins ['spɪlɪkɪnz], *pl.* das Federspiel.

spilt, *see* [2]**spill**.

spin, 1. *ir.v.a.* spinnen, wirbeln, drehen (*a top*); trudeln lassen (*Av.*); – *a yarn*, eine Geschichte erzählen; – *out*, in die Länge ziehen, ausziehen. 2. *ir.v.n.* spinnen, wirbeln, sich drehen; trudeln (*Av.*); *my head is -ning*, mir schwindelt; *send s.o. -ning*, einen hinschleudern; – *along*, schnell dahinrollen; – *out*, sich ausspinnen *or* in die Länge ziehen; – *round*, sich drehen. 3. *s.* das Wirbeln, schnelle Drehung; rasche Fahrt, kurze Spazierfahrt; das Trudeln, die Sturzspirale (*Av.*). **-ner**, *s.* der Spinner, die Spinnmaschine; Spinne (*Ent.*); die Spinndrüse. **-neret**, *s.* die Spinndrüse. **-ning**, *s.* das Spinnen, die Spinnerei. **-ning-jenny**, *s.* die Feinspinnmaschine. **-ning-mill**, *s.* die Spinnerei. **-ning-wheel**, *s.* das Spinnrad.

spinach ['spɪnɪtʃ], *s.* der Spinat.

spinal ['spaɪnəl], *adj.* Rückgrat(s)–; – *column*, das Rückgrat, die Wirbelsäule; – *curvature*, die Rückgratsverkrümmung; – *cord* or *marrow*, das Rückenmark.

spindl-e ['spɪndl], *s.* die Spindel; Welle, Achse. **-e-shanks**, *pl.* (*coll.*) dünne Beine; (*sing. constr.*) dünnbeiniger Mensch. **-e-shaped**, *adj.* spindelförmig. **-e-side**, *s.* weibliche Linie. **-y**, *adj.* spindeldürr.

spindrift ['spɪndrɪft], *s.* der Gischt, (Wellen)-Schaum.

spin-e [spaɪn], *s.* das Rückgrat, die Wirbelsäule (*Anat.*); der Dorn, Stachel (*Bot.*); (Buch)Rücken (*Bookb.*); (Gebirgs)Grat. **-eless**, *adj.* rückgratlos; (*fig.*) haltlos. **-ose**, *adj. see* **-ous**. **-osity** [-'nɔsɪtɪ], *s.* das Dornige. **-ous**, *adj.* dornig, stach(e)lig; *-ous process*, der Dornfortsatz. **-y**, *adj.* see **-ous**.

spinel ['spɪnəl], *s.* der Spinell (*Min.*).

spinet [spɪ'nɛt], *s.* das Spinett (*Mus.*).

spinnaker ['spɪnəkə], *s.* das Dreiecksegel (*Naut.*).

spin-ner, -ning, *see* **spin**.

spinney ['spɪnɪ], *s.* das Gehölz, Gestrüpp, Gebüsch, Dickicht.

spinster ['spɪnstə], *s.* unverheiratete Frau, alte Jungfer; – *aunt*, unverheiratete Tante. **-hood**, *s.* das Altjungferntum.

spiny ['spaɪnɪ], *see* **spine**.

spiracle ['spaɪrəkl], *s.* das Luftloch, Atemloch, die Trachealöffnung; das Nasenloch, Spritzloch (*of a whale*).

spiraea [spaɪː'rɪːə], *s.* die Spiräe, Spierstaude, der Geißbart (*Bot.*).

spiral ['spaɪərəl], 1. *adj.* schraubenförmig, spiralförmig, schneckenförmig; Spiral–; gewunden; – *spring*, die Spiralfeder; – *staircase*, die Wendeltreppe. 2. *s.* die Spirale, Schneckenlinie, der Spiralgleitflug (*Av.*). 3. *v.n.* sich spiralförmig bewegen.

spirant ['spaɪərənt], 1. *s.* der Reibelaut, Spirant, die Spirans (*Phonet.*). 2. *adj.* spirantisch.

[1]**spir-e** ['spaɪə], *s.* die Turmspitze, spitzer Kirchturm; spitzer Körper. **-y**, *adj.* spitzzulaufend; vieltürmig.

[2]**spir-e**, *s.* die Windung, Spirale. **-y**, *adj.* spiralförmig.

spirit ['spɪrɪt], 1. *s.* der Geist, die Seele, der Odem; das Gespenst; Feuer, Leben, der Charakter, Mut, die Lebhaftigkeit; Bedeutung, der Inhalt, Sinn, die Gesinnung; der Alkohol, Spiritus (*Chem., etc.*); *pl.* geistige Getränke, Spirituosen; *pl.* (*only with attrib.*) die Stimmung. (*a*) (*with nouns*) – *of the age*, der Zeitgeist; – *of charity*, die Nächstenliebe; *-s of wine*, der Weingeist. (*b*) (*with adjectives*) *good* or *high -s*, die Heiterkeit, Munterkeit, der Frohsinn; gehobene Stimmung; *in good -s*, heiter, gut aufgelegt; *Holy* –, Heiliger Geist; *low -s*, die Niedergeschlagenheit; gedrückte Stimmung; *in low -s*, niedergeschlagen; *methylated -s*, denaturierter Spiritus, der Methylalkohol; *public* –, der Gemeinsinn. (*d*) (*with prepositions*) *in* (*the*) –, im Geist; *enter into the* –, mitmachen; *revive a p.'s -s*, einen aufheitern; *with* –, mit Feuer *or* Mut. 2. *v.a.* – *away*, hinwegzaubern, verschwinden lassen. **-ed**, *adj.* lebhaft, lebendig, mutig, feurig; (*in comps.*) -gesinnt, -gesonnen; *high--ed*, ausgelassen, feurig; *low--ed*, niedergeschlagen; *public--ed*, gemeinsinnig; *poor--ed* or *tame--ed*, verzagt, mutlos. **-edness**, *s.* das Feuer, der Mut, die Lebhaftigkeit. **-ism**, *s.* der Spiritismus. **-ist**, *s.* der Spiritist. **-istic** [-'tɪstɪk], *adj.* spiritistisch. **--lamp**, *s.* die Spirituslampe. **-less**, *adj.* niedergeschlagen; verzagt, mutlos, kleinlaut, kleinmütig, leblos, geistlos, temperamentlos, schlapp. **-lessness**, *s.* die Niedergeschlagenheit, Mutlosigkeit; Geistlosigkeit, Temperamentlosigkeit, der Kleinmut. **--level**, *s.* die Libelle, Nivellierwaage. **--like**, *adj.* geisterähnlich. **--rapping**, *s.* das Geisterklopfen. **--stain**, *s.* die Spritbeize. **--stove** *s.* der Spirituskocher. **-ual** [-juəl], 1. *adj.* geistig, seelisch; geistlich (*Eccl.*); *-ual life*, das Seelenleben; *Lords -ual*, die Bischöfe im Oberhaus. 2. *s.* das Negerlied. **-ualism**, *s.* der Spiritualismus, Spiritismus. **-ualist**, *s.* der Spiritualist, Spiritist. **-ualistic** [-juə'lɪstɪk], *adj.* spiritualistisch, spiritistisch. **-uality** [-ju'ælɪtɪ], *s.* die Geistigkeit, das Seelische; geistige Natur *or* Eigenschaft. **-ualization** [-juəlaɪ'zeɪʃən], *s.* die Vergeistigung. **-ualize** [-juəlaɪz], *v.a.* vergeistigen. **-uous** [-juəs], *adj.* geistig; weingeisthaltig, alkoholisch, Alkohol–; *-uous liquors*, Spirituosen (*pl.*). **--varnish**, *s.* der Spritlack.

spirketing ['spəːkətɪŋ], *s.* der Plankengang (*Naut.*).

spirt, *see* **spurt**.

[1]**spiry**, *see* [1]**spire**.

[2]**spiry**, *see* [2]**spire**.

[1]**spit** [spɪt], 1. *s.* der (Brat)Spieß; die Landzunge (*Geog.*). 2. *v.a.* auf den Bratspieß stecken; (*fig.*) aufspießen.

[2]**spit**, 1. *s.* der Speichel, die Spucke; das Fauchen (*of a cat*); (*coll.*) der Sprühregen; (*coll.*) *the very* or *dead* – *of his father*, genaues Ebenbild seines Vaters. 2. *ir.v.n.* speien, spucken; fauchen (*as a cat*); (*coll.*) sprühen (*as rain*); spritzen (*as boiling fat*); – *at* or *on*, anspucken, bespucken; (*fig.*) verächtlich behandeln; – *in s.o.'s face*, einem ins Gesicht spucken. 3. *v.a.* speien, spucken; – *out* or *forth* ausspucken; (*sl.*) – *it out!* heraus damit! **-fire**, *s.* der Hitzkopf, Brausekopf. **-tle** [-l], der Speichel, die Spucke. **-toon** [-'tuːn], *s.* der Spucknapf.

[3]**spit**, *s.* der Spatenstich.

spite [spaɪt], 1. *s.* die Boshaftigkeit, Bosheit, der Groll, Ärger; *have a – against a p.*, einem grollen; *in – of*, trotz (*Gen.*), ungeachtet (*Gen.*); *in – of that*, dessenungeachtet; *in – of you*, dir zum Trotz; *out of –*, aus Bosheit. 2. *v.a.* ärgern, kränken; *cut off one's nose to – one's face*, sich ins eigene Fleisch schneiden. **–ful,** *adj.* boshaft, gehässig. **–fulness,** *s.* die Bosheit, Gehässigkeit.

splanchnic [ˈsplæŋknɪk], *adj.* Eingeweide–.

splash [splæʃ], 1. *v.a.* bespritzen (*with*, mit), spritzen. 2. *v.n.* spritzen, aufspritzen, verspritzen, planschen, patschen, platschen, plätschern. 3. *s.* das Spritzen, Plätschern; plätscherndes Geräusch; der Klecks, Spritzfleck; (*coll.*) große Aufmachung; – *of colour*, der Farbfleck; (*coll.*) farbige Aufmachung; (*fig.*) *make a –*, Aufhebens machen, Aufsehen erregen, in großer Aufmachung bringen. **–er,** *s.* das Schutzblech (*Cycl., etc.*), der Kotflügel; Wandschoner. **– -board,** *s.* das Spritzbrett, Schutzbrett. **–y,** spritzend, platschend; bespritzt.

splatter [ˈsplætə], *v.n.* patschen, platschen, planschen, plätschern. **–dash,** *s.* der Lärm, das Getöse.

splay [spleɪ], 1. *adj.* auswärts gebogen (*as foot*), schief, schräg. 2. *s.* die Schräge, Ausschrägung (*Arch.*). 3. *v.a.* ausschrägen (*Arch.*); abschrägen; verrenken (*Vet.*). 4. *v.n.* ausgeschrägt sein, schräg liegen. **– -foot,** *s.* der Spreizfuß.

spleen [spliːn], *s.* die Milz (*Anat.*); (*fig.*) schlechte *or* üble Laune, der Ärger, Verdruß. **–ful, –ish, –y,** *adj.* griesgrämig, übelgelaunt, mürrisch.

splend–ent [ˈsplɛndənt], *adj.* glänzend, leuchtend. **–id** [–dɪd], *adj.* glänzend, prächtig, herrlich; (*coll.*) großartig, ausgezeichnet, famos. (*sl.*) **–iferous** [–ˈdɪfərəs], *adj.* prächtig, herrlich. **–our** [–də], *s.* der Glanz, die Pracht, Herrlichkeit.

splen–ectomy [spləˈnɛktəmɪ], *s.* die Splenotomie, Splenektomie (*Surg.*). **–etic** [–ˈnɛtɪk], 1. *adj.* Milz–, milzsüchtig; (*fig.*) verdrießlich, mürrisch. 2. *s.* der Hypochonder. **–ic** [ˈsplɛnɪk], *adj.* Milz–; *–ic fever*, der Milzbrand. **–itis** [spləˈnaɪtɪs], *s.* die Milzentzündung.

splice [splaɪs], 1. *s.* die Splissung (*Naut.*); das Falzen (*Carp.*). 2. *v.a.* spleißen, splissen (*ropes*) (*Naut.*); falzen (*Carp.*); zusammenfügen, verbinden; (*sl.*) ehelich verbinden, verheiraten; (*coll.*) – *the main brace*, die Rumration austeilen *or* ausgeteilt bekommen (*Naut.*); (*sl.*) *get –d*, sich verheiraten.

spline [splaɪn], *s.* die (Metall– *or* Holz)Feder (*Tech.*).

splint [splɪnt], 1. *s.* die Schiene (*Surg.*); *in –s*, geschient, in Schienen (*Surg.*). 2. *v.a.* anschienen, einschienen (*a broken limb*). **– -bone,** *s.* das Wadenbein. **– -coal,** *s.* die Splitterkohle.

splinter [ˈsplɪntə], 1. *s.* der Splitter, Span; *shell– –*, der Granatsplitter; *break* or *fly in(to) –s*, in Stücke gehen. 2. *v.a.* (zer)splittern. 3. *v.n.* sich splittern, in Stücke gehen. **– -bar,** *s.* der Schwengel, das Ortscheit. **– -bone,** *s.* das Wadenbein. **– -proof,** *adj.* splittersicher. **–y,** *adj.* splitt(e)rig, leichtsplitternd, Splitter–.

split [splɪt], 1. *s.* der Spalt, Riß, Sprung; (*fig.*) die Spaltung, Entzweiung, der Bruch; *pl.* die Grätsche, Grätschstellung (*Gymn.*). 2. *ir.v.a.* (*also imperfect. & pp.*) (zer)spalten, zerteilen; (*coll.*) unter sich teilen, aufteilen; – *the difference*, sich den Differenzbetrag teilen; – *hairs*, Haarspalterei treiben; – *off*, abspalten; – *one's sides* (*with laughing*), sich totlachen; – *up*, aufspalten, zerlegen. 3. *ir.v.n.* sich spalten, bersten, platzen, reißen; sich teilen; (*fig.*) sich entzweien *or* trennen; (*sl.*) aus der Schule schwatzen; *my head is –ting*, mir will der Kopf springen; (*sl.*) – *on a p.*, einen verraten *or* angeben; – *off*, sich spalten; – up, abbauen (*Chem.*). **–ting,** 1. *adj.* Spalt–; *–ting headache*, rasende Kopfschmerzen; *ear-–ting*, *adj.* ohrenzerreißend. 2. *s.* das Spalten; *hair-–ing*, die Haarspalterei.

splodg–e [splɔdʒ], *s.* **splotch,** *s.* der Klecks, Schmutzfleck. **–y,** *adj.* fleckig.

splurge [spləːdʒ], *s.* (*sl.*) offensichtliche Anstrengung, auffällige Bemühung, die Zurschaustellung.

splutter [ˈsplʌtə], 1. *s.* das Sprudeln. 2. *v.n.* hastig reden, plappern; sprudeln, spritzen; klecksen (*a pen*); kleckern (*a candle*); kotzen (*an engine*). 3. *v.a.*; – *out*, heraussprudeln, herausplappern.

spoil [spɔɪl], 1. *v.a.* (imperf. & pp. usually *–t*) verderben, vernichten, zerstören, beeinträchtigen; verziehen, verwöhnen (*child*); vereiteln (*plan*); (*archaic*) (imperf. & pp. usually *–ed*) berauben, ausrauben, verwüsten, plündern. 2. *v.n.* (imperf. & pp. usually *–t*) verderben, schlecht werden; *be –ing for*, sich heftig sehnen nach, sehnlichst wünschen; *–ing for a fight*, streitsüchtig, rauflustig. 3. *s.* (*usually pl.*) die Beute, der Raub; *–s of war*, die Kriegsbeute; (*fig.*) die Ausbeute, Errungenschaft, der Gewinn; (*sing. only*) ausgehobene Erde; der Abfall. **–age,** *s.*, die Makulatur (*Typ.*). **–er,** *s.* der Plünderer, Verderber, Verwüster. **–sman,** *s.* (*Amer.*) der Postenjäger, Schieber. **– -sport,** *s.* der Spielverderber. **–s-system,** *s.* das Futterkrippensystem (*Amer. Pol.*).

[1]**spoke** [spoʊk], *see* **speak.**

[2]**spoke,** *s.* die Speiche (*of a wheel*), Sprosse (*of a ladder*); Spake (*Naut.*); Bremse, der Hemmschuh; (*coll.*) *put a – in a p.'s wheel*, einem ein Bein stellen, einem den Knüppel zwischen die Beine werfen. **– -bone,** *s.* die Speiche (*Anat.*). **–shave,** *s.* der Schabhobel.

spoke–n [ˈspoʊkən], *see* **speak;** *adj.* mündlich; (*in comp.*) sprechend, redend. **–sman,** *s.* der Sprecher, Wortführer; Fürsprecher.

spoliat–e [ˈspoʊlɪeɪt], 1. *v.a.* (aus)plündern, berauben. 2. *v.n.* plündern. **–ion** [–ˈeɪʃən], *s.* die Plünderung, Beraubung.

spond–aic [spɔnˈdeɪɪk], *adj.* spondeisch. **–ee** [ˈspɔndɪ], *s.* der Spondeus (*Metr.*).

spondulic(k)s [spɔnˈdjuːlɪks], *pl.* (*sl.*) Moneten (*pl.*).

spondyl–(e) [ˈspɔndaɪl], *s.* der Wirbelknochen (*Anat.*). **–itis** [–ˈlaɪtɪs], *s.* die Wirbelentzündung.

spong–e [spʌndʒ], 1. *s.* der Schwamm; Wischer (*Artil.*); (*fig.*) Schmarotzer; *pass the –e over*, für erledigt erklären; auslöschen; *throw up the –e*, sich für besiegt erklären (*Boxing*); (*fig.*) die Flinte ins Korn werfen, es aufgeben. 2. *v.n.* sich vollsaugen; (*fig.*) schmarotzen (*upon*, bei). 3. *v.a.* (mit einem Schwamme) abwischen *or* abwaschen; auswischen (*Artil.*); *–e down*, abwaschen; *–e up*, aufsaugen. **–e-bag,** *s.* der Schwammbeutel. **–e-cake,** *s.* die Sandtorte. **–e-cloth,** *s.* loser Stoff. **–e-down** *s.* die Abwaschung; *have a –e-down*, sich abwaschen. **–er,** *s.* der Schwammfischer; (*fig.*) Schmarotzer. **–iness,** *s.* die Schwammigkeit. **–ing-house,** *s.* provisorisches Schuldgefängnis (*Hist.*). **–iole,** *s.* das Schwammgewebe (*Bot.*). **–ology** [–ˈgɔlədʒɪ], *s.* die Schwammkunde. **–y,** *adj.* schwammig; porös, locker; sumpfig (*as soil*); *–y platinum*, der Platinschwamm.

sponsal [ˈspɔnsəl], *adj.* bräutlich, Verlobungs–, hochzeitlich, Hochzeits–.

spons–ion [ˈspɔnʃən], *s.* die Bürgschaft. **–or** [–sə], 1. *s.* der Bürge; Pate, Taufzeuge (*to a child*); (*fig.*) Gönner, Förderer; *stand –or to*, Pate stehen bei. 2. *v.a.* unterstützen, fördern. **–orial** [–ˈsɔːrɪəl], *adj.* Paten–. **–orship,** *s.* die Patenschaft, Bürgschaft.

sponson [ˈspɔnsən], *s.* das Radgehäuse, der Radkasten (*paddle-steamers*).

spontane–ity [spɔntəˈniːɪtɪ], *s.* die Freiwilligkeit, eigener *or* freier Antrieb, die Ungezwungenheit, Natürlichkeit, Spontaneität. **–ous** [–ˈteɪnɪəs], *adj.* spontan, freiwillig, aus eignem *or* freiem Antrieb, von selbst, von innen heraus, unwillkürlich, unvorbereitet, Selbst–, natürlich; *–ous combustion*, die Selbstverbrennung; *–ous generation*, die Urzeugung; *–ous ignition*, die Selbstzündung. **–ousness,** *see* **–ity.**

spoof [spuːf], 1. *s.* (*sl.*) der Schwindel, Betrug, Humbug. 2. *v.a.* (*sl.*) beschwindeln.

spook [spuːk], 1. *s.* (*coll.*) das Gespenst, der Spuk. 2. *v.n.* (*coll.*) spuken. **–y,** *adj.* (*coll.*) spukhaft, gespenstisch.

spool [spuːl], 1. *s.* die Spule, Rolle (*of thread*). 2. *v.a.* (auf)spulen.

[1]**spoon** [spuːn], 1. *s.* der Löffel; *be born with a silver – in one's mouth*, ein Sonntagskind sein. 2. *v.a.* (auf)löffeln. **– -bait,** *s.* der Blinker (*fishing*). **–bill,** *s.*

der Löffler, die Löffelente (*Orn.*). **–drift,** *see* **spendrift.** **– -fed,** *adj.* (*fig.*) verhätschelt, aufgepäppelt. **– -feed,** *v.a.* (*fig.*) helfen (*Dat.*); unterstützen, hochzüchten. **–ful,** *s.* der Löffelvoll. **–wort,** *s.* das Löffelkraut (*Bot.*).

²**spoon,** 1. *s.* (*sl.*) der Einfaltspinsel, Tropf. 2. *v.n.* (*sl.*) poussieren. **–y,** *adj.* (*sl.*) verliebt; vernarrt, verschossen (*on*, in).

spoonerism ['spu:nərɪzm], *s.* der Schüttelreim.

spoor ['spu:ə], 1. *s.* die Spur, Fährte. 2. *v.a.* aufspüren, verfolgen. 3. *v.n.* einer Spur folgen.

sporadic(al) [spə'rædɪk(l)], *adj.* vereinzelt auftretend, zerstreut, sporadisch.

spor–ange ['spərənd3], *s.*, **–angium** [spə'rænd3ɪəm], *s.* der Sporenbehalter. **–e** [spɔ·], *s.* die Spore, das Keimkorn (*Bot.*, *Zool.*); (*fig.*) der Keim. **–iferous** [–'rɪfərəs], *adj.* sporenbildend. **–ogenesis** [spɔ:ro'd3ɛnɪsɪs], *s.* die Sporenbildung. **–ozoon** [spɔ:ro'zouən], *s.* (usually pl. *–zoa* [–zouə]) das Sporentierchen.

sporran ['spərən], *s.* (schottische) Ledertasche.

sport [spɔ:t], 1. *s.* der Sport, das Spiel; der Scherz, Spaß; die Belustigung, Kurzweil, der Zeitvertreib; (*fig.*) das Spielzeug, Opfer; die Abart, Spielart (*Biol.*); (*sl.*) anständiger Kerl; *pl.* der Sport, Bewegungsspiele (*pl.*), sportliche Veranstaltung, – *of every wind*, das Spielzeug der Winde; *capital* or *great* –, der Hauptspaß, das Hauptvergnügen; *make* – *of*, zum besten haben, seinen Spaß haben mit, Spaß treiben mit, sich belustigen über; *in* or *for* –, im *or* zum Scherz; *go in for* –, Sport treiben. 2. *v.n.* spielen, scherzen, sich belustigen, sich tummeln (*with*, mit). 3. *v.a.* zur Schau tragen, paradieren mit; – *one's oak*, die Tür seiner Bude schließen *or* verschlossen halten (*Univ. coll.*). **–ing,** *adj.* sporttreibend, sportliebend, sportlerisch, sportlich, Sport–; Jagd–; (*coll.*) ritterlich, anständig, (*coll.*) *–ing chance*, die Chance, gute Aussicht; *take a –ing chance*, es wagen; *–ing gun*, das Jagdgewehr; *–ing news*, der Sportbericht, Rennergebnisse, Nachrichten über (Pferde)Wettrennen (*pl.*); *–ing paper*, das Sportblatt. **–ive,** *adj.* scherzhaft, spaßhaft. **–iveness,** *s.* die Scherzhaftigkeit, Spaßhaftigkeit. **–s badge,** *s.* das Sportabzeichen. **–s car,** *s.* der Sportwagen. **–s clothes,** *pl.* die Sportkleidung. **–s day,** *s.* das Sportfest. **–s ground,** *s.* der Sportplatz. **–s jacket,** *s.* die (Herren)Tweedjacke. **–sman,** *s.* der Sportler, Sportsmann, Sportliebhaber; Jäger, Fischer, Pferderennenliebhaber; (*coll.*) anständiger Kerl. **–smanlike,** *adj.* sportlerisch, sportlich, sportsmännisch; weidmännisch. **–smanship,** *s.* die Sportlichkeit, sportliche Geschicklichkeit; (*coll.*) die Anständigkeit. **–s outfitter,** *s.* der Sportwarenhändler. **–swoman,** *s.* die Sportlerin.

sporul–ar ['spərju.lɑ], *adj.* Sporen–, sporenartig (*Biol.*). **–e** ['spərju:l], *s.* die Spore.

spot [spɔt], 1. *s.* der Fleck (*also fig.*), Klecks, Flecken (*also Med.*); Pickel, die Pustel, Eiterung (*Med.*); Stelle, der Platz, Ort; Tropfen, (*coll.*) das Bißchen, Stückchen; der Point (*Bill.*); (*fig.*) Schandfleck, Makel; *pl.* (also – *goods*) Lokowaren (*pl.*) (*C.L.*); – *cash*, die Zahlung bei Lieferung, Barzahlung; – *goods*, Lokowaren (*C.L.*); *on the* –, zur Stelle, an Ort und Stelle; (*coll.*) auf der Stelle, sogleich, sofort, unverzüglich; (*sl.*) *knock –s off s.o.*, einen nach Strich und Faden besiegen; – *price*, der Preis bei sofortiger Zahlung; *sore* –, wunde Stelle; – *transaction*, das Kassageschäft. 2. *v.a.* beflecken (*also fig.*), fleckig machen; sprenkeln, tüpfeln; (*fig.*) beschmutzen; (*coll.*) bemerken, erkennen, entdecken, herausfinden, ausfindig machen; auf den Point setzen (*the ball*) (*Bill.*). 3. *v.n.* flecken, fleckig werden. **–less,** *adj.* fleckenlos, unbefleckt, makellos. **–lessness,** *s.* die Fleckenlosigkeit, Unbeflecktheit, Makellosigkeit. **–light,** 1 *s.* das Scheinwerferlicht (*Theat.*); (*fig.*) das Rampenlicht der Öffentlichkeit. 2. *v.a.* mit Scheinwerferlicht beleuchten (*Theat.*); (*fig.*) in den Vordergrund (der Aufmerksamkeit) ziehen, die Aufmerksamkeit lenken auf. **–ted,** *adj.* gefleckt, getüpfelt, gesprenkelt; (*fig.*) befleckt, besudelt; (*coll.*) *–ted dog*, der Korinthenpudding; *–ted fever*, die Genickstarre. **–ter,** *s.* der Erkundungsflieger (*Av.*), Anzeiger (*rifle-shooting*), der Flugmelder, die Flugwache, das Mitglied des Fliegerwarndienstes (*anti-aircraft*). **–tiness,** *s.* die Fleckigkeit, Beflecktheit. **–ting,** *s.* die Erkundung, Aufklärung (*Av.*), der Fliegerwarndienst (*anti-aircraft*). **–ty,** *adj.* fleckig, gefleckt; befleckt; pickelig.

spous–al ['spɑuzl], 1. *s.* (*usually pl.*) (*archaic*) die Hochzeit. 2. *adj.* hochzeitlich, Hochzeits–, ehelich, bräutlich. **–e** [spɑus], *s.* der Gatte, die Gattin, der (die) Gemahl(in).

spout [spɑut], 1. *s.* die Tülle, Schneppe (*of a vessel*), das Abflußrohr, Speirohr, der Ausguß (*of a gutter*); (*coll.*) die Dachrinne, Traufe; die Wasserhose; (*sl.*) *up the* –, verpfändet, uneinkassierbar; dahin, fort, weg. 2. *v.a.* ausspeien, herauswerfen, spritzen, (*sl.*) deklamieren, hersagen (*verse, etc.*). 3. *v.n.* sprudeln, quellen, spritzen (*also of whales*); (*sl.*) deklamieren, ein gutes Mundwerk haben, schwatzen, schnattern. **–er,** *s.* (*sl.*) der Kannegießer.

sprag [spræg], *s.* der Hemmschuh, Bremskeil.

sprain [spreɪn], 1. *s.* die Verrenkung, Verstauchung. 2. *v.a.* verrenken, verstauchen.

sprang [spræŋ], *see* **spring.**

sprat [spræt], 1. *s.* die Sprotte; *throw a* – *to catch a mackerel* or *herring*, mit der Wurst nach der Speckseite werfen. 2. *v.n.* Sprotten fangen, nach Sprotten fischen.

sprawl [sprɔ:l], 1. *v.n.* sich rekeln; sich spreizen, ausgestreckt daliegen; sich ausbreiten, erstrecken *or* dehnen; wuchern (*Bot.*). 2. *s.* ausgestreckte Lage.

¹**spray** [spreɪ], 1. *s.* der Zweig, das Reis, Reisig; – *of flowers*, der Blumenzweig.

²**spray,** 1. *s.* der Sprühregen, Wasserstaub, das Sprühwasser, Spritzwasser; der Schaum, Wellenschaum, Gischt; die Dusche, Spritze, der Zerstäuber. 2. *v.a.* (be)spritzen, (mit Wasser) besprengen; zerstäuben. 3. *v.n.* spritzen, sprühen, zerstieben. **–er,** *s.* die Spritze, der Zerstäuber. **– -gun,** *s.* die Spritzpistole.

spread [sprɛd], 1. *ir.v.a.* (*also imp. & p.p.*) ausbreiten, ausdehnen; streichen (*bread*, *also butter on bread* (*on*, auf); bedecken, bestreichen, überziehen (*with*, mit), (*fig.*) verbreiten, ausstreuen; – *abroad*, aussprengen (*rumours*); – *the cloth*, den Tisch decken; *the peacock –s his tail*, der Pfau schlägt ein Rad; – *o.s.*, sich ausbreiten; (*fig.*) sich wichtig tun; – *out*, ausbreiten. 2. *ir v.n.* (also – *out*) sich ausbreiten *or* ausdehnen; sich strecken; (*fig.*) sich verbreiten; – *like wildfire*, sich wie ein Lauffeuer verbreiten. 3. *s.* die Verbreitung, Ausbreitung; Ausdehnung, der Umfang, die Spanne, Differenz; Spannweite; Stellage; der Brotaufstrich; (*coll.*) Schmaus; *lateral* –, die Seitenausdehnung, (*coll.*) *middle-age* –, die Behäbigkeit. 4. *adj.* verstreut; gespreizt. **– -eagle,** 1. *s.* die Stellage (*C.L.*) (*Amer.*) 2. *adj.* prahlerisch, anmaßend (*Amer*). 3. *v.a.* (*coll.*) ausbreiten, spreizen. **–er,** *s.* die Spannvorrichtung; der Verteiler; die Spreize, Raa. **–ing,** *adj.*, ausgebreitet, verbreitet, weit. **– -over,** *s.* die Verteilung, Austeilung.

spree [sprɛ:], *s.* (*coll*) das Zechgelage; lustiger Streich, der Spaß, Feez, *go on the* –, auf den Bummel gehen.

sprig [sprɪg], 1. *v.a.* mit kleinen Zweigen verzieren; mit Zwecken befestigen. 2. *s.* der Zweig, Sprößling, das Reis; der Stift, die Zwecke (*Naut.*, *Carp.*).

sprightl–iness ['sprɑɪtlɪnɪs], *s.* die Lebendigkeit, Lebhaftigkeit, Behendigkeit, Munterkeit. **–y,** *adj.* lebhaft, munter.

spring [sprɪŋ], 1. *ir.v.n.* springen, hüpfen; schnellen; entspringen, quellen, sprudeln (*from*, aus), herkommen, herstammen (*from*, von): sich werfen (*wood*). (*a*) (*with prepositions*) – *at*, losspringen auf (*Acc.*); – *at a p.'s throat*, einem an die Kehle springen; *into existence*, (plötzlich) entstehen; – *into fame*, plötzlich berühmt werden; – (*up*)*on*, springen auf (*Acc.*), anfallen; – *to arms*, zu den Waffen greifen; – *to attention* stramm stehen (*Mil.*); – *to one's feet*, aufspringen; – *to the eyes*, in die Augen springen. (*b*) (*with adverbs*) – *back*, zurückspringen, – *open*, aufspringen; – *to*, zuspringen; – *up*, aufspringen, aufkommen (*wind*); – *up like mushrooms*, wie Pilze aus der Erde schießen. 2. *ir.v.a.* sprengen, springen lassen, spielen lassen (*mines, etc.*)

aufjagen, aufscheuchen (*game, etc.*); unerwartet hervorbringen; (*coll.*) auftreiben, vorschießen (*money*); federn (*chairs, etc.*); – *a leak*, leck werden, ein Leck bekommen; – *a mine*, (*fig.*) mit der Tür ins Haus fallen; – *a rattle*, schnarren, eine Schnarre drehen; – *a surprise on a p.*, einen mit einer Überraschung überfallen. 3. *s.* die Quelle (*also fig.*), der Brunnen; (*fig.*) Quell, Ursprung; der Sprung, Satz, die Sprungkraft, Schnellkraft, Federkraft, Elastizität; (*fig.*) Spannkraft; (Sprung)Feder (*Mach.*), Triebfeder (*Mach. & fig.*); das Springtau (*Naut.*); der Frühling, das Frühjahr; *coil* –, die Bandfeder, Schraubenfeder; *compression* –, die Druckfeder; *impulse* –, die Antriebsfeder; *leaf* –, die Blattfeder; *main* –, die Hauptfeder, Schlagfeder; *retaining* –, die Sperrfeder; *spiral* –, die Spiralfeder; *early* –, der Vorfrühling; *hot* –, heiße Quelle. **--balance,** *s.* die Federwaage. **-board,** *s.* das Sprungbrett. **-bok,** *s.* der Springbock. **--bolt,** *s.* der Federriegel. **--bows,** *pl.* der Federzirkel. **--clean,** *v.a. & n.* gründlich reinmachen. **--cleaning,** *s.* das Gründlichreinmachen, Großreinmachen. **-er,** *s.* der (Gewölbe)Anfangstein, Tragstein (*Arch.*); Stöberhund. **--gun,** *s.* das Selbstgeschoß, der Selbstschuß. **-iness,** *s.* die Sprungkraft, Federkraft, Schnellkraft, Elastizität, Schwungkraft. **-ing,** *s.* die (Ab)Federung (*of vehicles, etc.*). **--lock,** *s.* das Federschloß, Schnappschloß. **--mattress,** *s.* die Sprungfedermatratze. **– tide,** die Springflut. **-tide** (*Poet.*), **-time,** *s.* der Frühling, die Frühlingszeit. **– water,** *s.* das Brunnenwasser. **– wheat,** *s.* der Sommerweizen. **-y,** *adj.* federnd, elastisch; (*fig.*) schwungvoll, leichtbeschwingt.

springe [sprɪndʒ], 1. *s.* die Schlinge, Falle, der Sprenkel. 2. *v.a.* in einer Schlinge fangen; (*fig.*) verstricken.

spring-iness, -y, *see* **spring.**

sprinkl-e [ˈsprɪŋkl], 1. *v.a.* streuen, sprengen (*on*, auf); bestreuen, sprenkeln, übersäen (*with*, mit); anfeuchten, befeuchten, benetzen, besprengen; *-e sand on the ice*, Sand auf das Eis streuen; *-e the ice with sand*, das Eis mit Sand bestreuen. 2. *v.n.* tröpfeln, sprühen. 3. *s.* leichter Regenschauer, der Sprühregen; *-e of rain*, der Spritzer; *-e of salt*, etwas Salz. **-er,** *s.* die Gießkanne, Sprengmaschine, der Sprengwagen, Rasensprenger; Weihwedel (*Eccl.*). **-ing,** *s.* das Sprengen, Spritzen; Gesprengsel; dünne Schicht; (*fig.*) *a -ing of*, ein bißchen, etwas, ein paar, einige; ein Anstrich *or* Anflug von; *-ing of rain*, der Spritzer.

sprint [sprɪnt], 1. *s.* der Kurzstreckenlauf, Sprint. 2. *v.n.* sprinten, schnell rennen. **-er,** *s.* der Kurzstreckenläufer, Sprinter.

sprit [sprɪt], *s.* das Spriet. **-sail,** s. das Sprietsegel.

sprite [sprɑɪt], *s.* der Geist; Kobold, Schrat.

sprocket [ˈsprɔkɪt], *s.* der Radzahn. **--wheel,** *s.* das Zahnrad, Kettenrad.

sprout [sprɑut], 1. *v.n.* keimen, sprießen, sprossen, aufschießen. 2. *v.a.* hervorbringen, entwickeln. 3. *s.* der Sproß, Sprößling; *pl.* (also *Brussels -s*) der Rosenkohl.

[1]**spruce** [spruːs], 1. *adj.* sauber, ordentlich, geputzt, geleckt, geschniegelt, schmuck. 2. *v.a.* (also – *up*), herausputzen. **-ness,** *s.* die Sauberkeit.

[2]**spruce,** *s.* die Fichte, Rottanne.

sprung [sprʌŋ], *see* **spring;** *adj.* gefedert; zersprungen.

spry [sprɑɪ], *adj.* flink, hurtig.

spud [spʌd], 1. *s.* kurzer Spaten; (*coll.*) die Kartoffel. 2. *v.a.* (– *out*) ausgraben, ausjäten.

spue, *see* **spew.**

spum-e [spjuːm], *s.* der Schaum, Gischt. **-ous, -y,** *adj.* schaumig, schäumend.

spun [spʌn], *see* **spin;** *adj.* – *glass*, Glasfasern (*pl.*); – *gold*, der Goldfaden; – *silk*, das Seidengarn; – *yarn*, das Schiemannsgarn (*Naut.*).

spunk [spʌŋk], *s.* die Lunte, der Zunder, Zündschwamm; (*coll.*) der Mut, das Feuer.

spur [spəː], 1. *s.* der Sporn (*Mil., Bot., Zool.*), Dorn, Stachel (*Bot.*); die Strebe, Stütze (*Arch.*); die Ramme, der Schiffsschnabel (*Naut.*); das Vorwerk (*Fort.*); der Vorsprung, Ausläufer (*of mountain*); (*fig.*) der Antrieb, Ansporn, Anreiz (*to*, für); *on the – of the moment*, ohne Überlegung, unter dem ersten Eindruck, spornstreichs, einer plötzlichen Eingebung folgend; *clap* or *put* or *set -s to one's horse*, seinem Pferde die Sporen geben; *win one's -s*, sich die Sporen verdienen. 2. *v.a.* mit Sporen versehen (*a boot*), die Sporen geben (*Dat.*) (*a horse*); (*fig.*) anspornen; *booted and -red*, gestiefelt und gespornt; – *on*, anspornen, antreiben, anstacheln, anfeuern. 3. *v.n.* die Sporen geben; schnell reiten, eilen, sich beeilen. **--gear,** das Stirnradgetriebe. **--wheel,** *s.* das Stirnrad.

spurge [spəːdʒ], *s.* die Wolfsmilch (*Bot.*). **--laurel,** *s.* der Lorbeerseidelbast.

spurious [ˈspjuːrɪəs], *adj.* unecht, falsch, gefälscht, nachgemacht, untergeschoben; unehelich. **-ness,** *s.* die Unechtheit, Falschheit; Unehelichkeit.

spurn [spəːn], *v.a.* mit Füßen stoßen *or* treten; (*fig.*) von sich weisen, abweisen, zurückstoßen (*a p.*); zurückweisen, verschmähen (*an offer, etc.*).

spurr-ey, -y [ˈspʌrɪ], *s.* der Knöterich, Spergel (*Bot.*).

[1]**spurt** [spəːt], 1. *v.n.* hervorspritzen, aufspritzen. 2. *v.a.* ausspritzen. 3. *s.* der (Wasser)Strahl.

[2]**spurt,** 1. *s.* plötzliche Anstrengung, der Spurt (*Sport*), plötzliches Anziehen *or* Steigen (*C.L.*); *put on a* –, *see* – 2. 2. *v.n.* eine kurze Anstrengung machen, alle seine Kräfte zusammennehmen, plötzlich aus sich herausgehen.

sputter [ˈspʌtə], 1. *v.n.* sprühen, sprudeln; spritzen, klecksen (*as a pen*). 2. *v.a.* heraussprudeln. 3. *s.* das Sprudeln, Gesprudel.

sputum [ˈspjuːtəm], *s.* der Speichel, der Auswurf.

spy [spɑɪ], 1. *s.* der Spion, Kundschafter, Späher. 2. *v.a.* gewahren, wahrnehmen; – *out*, erspähen, auskundschaften. 3. *v.n.* spionieren; – *into*, nachspüren, nachforschen (*Dat.*); – (*up*)*on*, nachspionieren (*Dat.*), herspionieren hinter, heimlich belauschen, nachspüren (*Dat.*). **--glass,** *s.* das Fernglas. **--hole,** *s.* das Guckloch. **-ing,** *s.* das Spionieren, die Spionage.

squab [skwɔb], 1. *s.* junge Taube, ungefiederter Vogel; (*fig.*) feiste Person; das Polstersofa, Polsterkissen, Sitzkissen. 2. *adj.* ungefiedert, noch nicht flügge (*of birds*); feist, plump, untersetzt (*of a p.*); **-by,** *adj.* feist, plump, untersetzt.

squabble [ˈskwɔbl], 1. *v.n.* (sich) zanken *or* streiten. 2. *v.a.* verrücken (*Typ.*). 3. *s.* der Streit, das Gezänk.

squad [skwɔd], *s.* die Korporalschaft, Abteilung, der Zug, Trupp (*Mil.*); die Gruppe, Riege (*Gymn.*); (*coll.*) *awkward* –, nicht ausgebildete Mannschaft (*Mil.*); *flying* –, das Überfallkommando. **--car,** *s.* der Streifenwagen.

squadron [ˈskwɔdrən], *s.* die Eskadron, Schwadron (*Mil.*); das Geschwader (*Naut.*); die Staffel (*Av.*). **--leader,** *s.* der Staffelführer, Major der Luftwaffe (*Av.*).

squal-id [ˈskwɔlɪd], *adj.* schmutzig, garstig, eklig, unsauber; (*fig.*) erbärmlich, armselig, ärmlich. **-idness, -or** [-ə], *s.* der Schmutz, die Unsauberkeit (*also fig.*).

[1]**squall** [skwɔːl], *s.* der Stoßwind, Windstoß, die Bö. **-y,** *adj.* böig, stürmisch.

[2]**squall,** 1. *v.n.* laut schreien, aufschreien. 2. *s.* lauter Schrei, der Aufschrei. **-er,** *s.* der Schreier, Schreihals.

squalor, *see under* **squalid.**

squam-a [ˈskweɪmə], *s.* (pl. *-ae* [-mɪː]) die Schuppe (*Bot. & Zool.*). **-iferous** [-ˈmɪfərəs], *adj.* schuppentragend. **-ose** [-mous], **-ous** [-əs], *adj.* schuppig, schuppenartig, Schuppen-.

squander [ˈskwɔndə], *v.a.* verschwenden, vergeuden. **-ing,** 1. *s.* die Verschwendung, Vergeudung. 2. *adj.* verschwenderisch. (*coll.*) **-mania,** [-ˈmeɪnɪə], *s.* die Verschwendungssucht.

square [skwɛːə], 1. *adj.* viereckig, vierkantig; rechtwinklig (*to*, zu), Quadrat-, aufrecht, gerade; (*fig. coll*) ehrlich, aufrichtig; reichlich (*as a meal*); quitt, ausgeglichen (*as accounts*); *all* –, in Ordnung; gleichstehend (*Golf*); – *deal*, reeller Handel, anständige Behandlung; – *mile*, die Quadratmeile; – *measure*, das Flächenmaß, Quadratmaß; – *neck*, viereckiger Ausschnitt; – *number*, die Quadratzahl; – *peg in a round hole*, einer der für etwas völlig ungeeignet ist; – *roof*, das Winkeldach – *root*, die Quadratwurzel; *extract the – root*, die Quadratwurzel ausziehen; *be – with*, quitt sein mit (*a p.*); *get – with*, sich abfinden *or* quitt werden mit (*a p.*). 2. *adv.* rechtwinklig, direkt gegenüber. 3. *s.* das Viereck, Quadrat (*also Math.*); die Quadratzahl; viereckiges Stück (*of material*), die Scheibe (*of glass*); der Platz (*in a city*); das Winkelmaß (*Draw.*); Karree (*Mil.*); Feld (*of chessboard*); *on the –*, im rechten Winkel, (*coll.*) ehrlich, in Ordnung; (*coll.*) *be on the –*, es ehrlich meinen; *out of –*, unregelmäßig; *T-–*, die Reißschiene. 4. *v.a.* viereckig machen; im rechten Winkel legen zu; auf den rechten Winkel prüfen; vierkantig behauen (*timber*); ausgleichen, begleichen (*an account*); ins Quadrat erheben, quadrieren (*a number, etc.*); einrichten, anordnen, regeln, regulieren, in Ordnung bringen; anpassen (*to*, an), in Einklang bringen (*with*, mit); (*sl.*) sich abfinden mit, befriedigen, bezahlen, bestechen (*a p.*); *– the circle*, den Kreis quadrieren; (*fig.*) Unmögliches leisten; *– one's conscience*, sein Gewissen beruhigen; *– one's shoulders*, sich in die Brust werfen; *– the yards*, die Rahen vierkant brassen (*Naut.*); *– up*, beilegen. 5. *v.n.* passen, stimmen (*with*, zu); übereinstimmen, im Einklang stehen (*with*, mit); *– up to*, (*fig.*) herausfordern. **–-built,** *adj.* viereckig gebaut; (*fig.*) vierschrötig, breitschulterig. **– dance,** *s.* der Kontertanz. **–head,** *s.* (*coll.*) deutscher *or* skandinavischer Einwanderer (*Amer.*). **–ness,** *s.* das Viereckige. **–-rigged,** *adj.* mit Rahsegeln getakelt. **–-rigger,** *s.* das Rahschiff. **– sail,** *s.* das Rahsegel. **–-shouldered,** *adj.* breitschulterig. **–-toed,** *adj.* vorne breit (*of shoes*); (*fig.*) altmodisch, formell, steif. (*coll.*) **–-toes,** *pl.* (*sing. const.*) der Pedant, Kleinigkeitskrämer.

squash [skwɔʃ], 1. *s.* der Matsch, Brei; das Patschen, der Platsch; der Fruchtsaft; (*coll.*) die Menge, das Gedränge; (also *– rackets*) eine Art Raketspiel. 2. *v.a.* (zer)quetschen, zerdrücken, zusammenpressen; (*coll.*) unterdrücken, mundtot machen. **–y,** *adj.* breiig, matschig.

squat [skwɔt], 1. *v.n.* kauern, hocken, (*coll.*) sitzen; sich ohne Rechtstitel niederlassen. 2. *adj.* gedrungen, untersetzt, vierschrötig, stämmig. **–ter** [–ə], *s.* der Ansiedler ohne Rechtstitel; Schafzüchter (*Australia*).

squaw [skwɔ:], *s.* das Indianerweib, die Indianerin.

squawk [skwɔ:k], 1. *v.n.* quietschen, kreischen, schreien, (*sl.*) protestieren. 2. *s.* greller Aufschrei, das Quietschen.

squeak [skwɪ:k], 1. *s.* das Gequiek, Gepiepe, Quietschen, Knarren; (*coll.*) *narrow –*, knappes Entkommen; *have a narrow –*, mit knapper Not davonkommen. 2. *v.n.* quieken, piep(s)en (*as mice*), quietschen (*as boots*), knirschen, knarren (*as a door*), (*sl.*) petzen. **–er,** *s.* der Schreier, Schreihals; junger Vogel; (*sl.*) Petzer, Angeber. **–y,** *adj.* quiekend, quietschend, knarrend.

squeal [skwɪ:l], 1. *s.* lautes Quieken, der Schrei. 2. *v.n.* quieken, schreien. **–er,** *s.* der Schreier, Schreihals; junger Vogel; (*sl.*) der Petzer, Angeber.

squeamish [ˈskwɪ:mɪʃ], *adj.* Ekel empfindend, sehr empfindlich, zimperlich (*about*, über); wählerisch, übergewissenhaft. **–ness,** *s.* der Ekel, die Übelkeit, übertriebene Empfindlichkeit, die Zimperlichkeit, Übergewissenhaftigkeit.

squeegee [ˈskwɪ:dʒɪ:], *s.* der Rollenquetscher (*Phot.*).

squeez-able [ˈskwɪ:zəbl], *adj.* zusammendrückbar, zerdrückbar. **–e** [skwɪ:z], 1. *s.* der Druck, die Quetschung, Pressung; der Händedruck; das Gedränge; innige Umarmung; (*coll.*) die Geldknappheit; Erpressung; (*coll.*) *be in a tight –e*, in der Klemme sitzen. 2. *v.a.* drücken, pressen, (aus)quetschen, ausdrücken (*juice, etc.*); (hinein- *or* hinaus)drängen *or* -zwängen; (*coll.*) bedrängen, schinden (*a p.*); erpressen (*a th.*) (*from* or *out of*, von); *–e s.o.'s hand*, einem die Hand drücken; *–e one's way*, sich drängen; *–e in*, hineinzwängen; *–e out*, auspressen, ausquetschen. 3. *v.n.* sich zwängen *or* drängen; *–e in*, sich hineinzwängen; *–e through*, sich durchdrängen. **–er,** *s.* die Preßmaschine, Quetsche; *lemon-–er*, die Zitronenpresse.

squelch [skweltʃ], 1. *v.a.* zerdrücken, zermalmen, zerquetschen. 2. *v.n.* platschen, glucksen. 3. *s.* das P(l)atschen, Glucksen.

squib [skwɪb], *s.* der Schwärmer; Frosch (*Firew.*); (*fig.*) die Stichelei, das Spottgedicht.

squid [skwɪd], 1. *s.* der Tintenfisch; künstlicher Köder. 2. *v.n.* mit künstlichem Köder angeln.

squiffy [ˈskwɪfɪ], *adj.* (*sl.*) beschwipst, angeheitert.

squill [skwɪl], *s.* die Meerzwiebel (*Bot.*); eine Garnelenart (*Zool.*).

squint [skwɪnt], 1. *adj.* schielend, schief, schräg. 2. *s.* das Schielen, schielender Blick; (*sl.*) der Blick; *have a –*, schielen; (*sl.*) *have a – at*, angucken. 3. *v.n.* schielen (*at*, nach); (*sl.*) *– at*, angucken. **–-eyed,** *adj.* schielend. **–ing,** 1. *adj.* schielend. 2. *s.* das Schielen.

squire [skwɑɪə], 1. *s.* der Junker, Rittergutsbesitzer, Landedelmann; Schildknappe (*Hist.*). 2. *v.a.* geleiten; Ritterdienste leisten; den Hof machen (*Dat.*) (*a lady*). **–archy** [–rɑ:kɪ], *s.* der Großgrundbesitz; die Junkerherrschaft, das Junkertum; Junker (*pl.*), die Junkerschaft. **–en** [–ˈrɪ:n], *s.* irischer Landjunker, kleiner Gutsbesitzer.

squirm [skwə:m], 1. *v.n.* sich krümmen *or* winden (*also fig.*). 2. *s.* die Krümmung; das Kink (*in a rope*) (*Naut.*).

squirrel [ˈskwɪrəl], *s.* das Eichhörnchen, Eichkätzchen (*Zool.*); das Feh (*fur*).

squirt [skwə:t], 1. *s.* die Spritze; der (Wasser)Strahl; (*sl.*) der Wichtigtuer. 2. *v.a.* & *n.* spritzen, sprudeln.

stab [stæb], 1. *s.* der Stich (*also fig.*), (Dolch)Stoß; (*sl.*) Versuch; (*sl.*) *have a – at*, versuchen, probieren, wagen; *– in the back*, (*fig.*) der Dolchstoß. 2. *v.a.* stechen; erstechen, erdolchen (*a p.*); durchstechen, durchbohren; bohren, jagen (*a weapon*) (*into*, in); mit Draht heften (*Bookb.*); (*fig.*) verwunden, angreifen; *– in the back*, hinterrücks anfallen; *– to the heart*, (*fig.*) einen Stich ins Herz geben (*Dat.*). 3. *v.n.* stechen.

stab-ility [stəˈbɪlɪtɪ], *s.* die Beständigkeit (*also fig.*), Festigkeit, Stetigkeit, Unveränderlichkeit, Dauerhaftigkeit, Stabilität (*Phys., etc.*); dynamisches Gleichgewicht (*Av.*); (*fig.*) die Standhaftigkeit; Zahlungsfähigkeit (*C.L.*). **–ilization** [steɪbɪlɑɪˈzeɪʃən], *s.* die Stabilisierung, Festigung. **–ilize** [ˈsteɪbɪlɑɪz], *v.a.* stabilisieren. **–ilizer,** *s.* die Dämpfungsflosse, Höhenflosse (*Av.*), das Stabilisierungsmittel, Antikoagulationsmittel, der Stabilisator (*Chem., etc.*). **–le** [ˈsteɪbl], *adj.* stabil, fest, unveränderlich; haltbar, dauerhaft, beständig (*also fig.*); (*fig.*) standhaft. **–leness,** *s. see* **–ility.**

stabl-e [steɪbl], 1. *s.* der Stall; *pl.* Stallungen (*pl.*); der Rennstall(bestand) (*Racing*); Stalldienst (*Mil.*). 2. *v.a.* (ein)stallen. 3. *v.n.* hausen. **–e-boy,** *s.* der Stalljunge. **–e-call,** *s.* der Stalldienstsignal (*Mil.*). **–e-door,** *s.* die Stalltür; *shut the –e door when the horse is stolen*, den Brunnen zudecken, wenn das Kind ertrunken ist. **–e-man** [–mən], *s.* der Stallknecht. **–e-yard,** *s.* der Stallhof, Viehhof. **–ing** [–blɪŋ], *s.* die Stallung, Ställe (*pl.*).

staccato [stəˈkɑ:toʊ], *adv.* stakkato (*Mus.*).

stack [stæk], 1. *s.* die Miete, der Schober, Feim (*of hay, etc.*); der Stoß, Stapel (*of wood, books, etc.*); ein Holzmaß (= *108 cu. ft.*); die Pyramide (*of rifles*); Bücherregale (*pl.*); (*coll.*) (*usually pl.*) große Menge, großer Haufen; (also *smoke-–*) der Schornstein. 2. *v.a.* aufschichten (*hay, etc.*); aufstapeln (*wood, etc.*); zusammenstellen (*arms, etc.*).

stadium [ˈsteɪdɪəm], *s.* das Stadion, die Kampfbahn (*Sport*); das Stadium, die Phase (*Med. & fig.*).

Stad(t)holder [ˈstædhoʊldə], *s.* der Statthalter.

staff [stɑ:f], 1. *s.* der Stab (*also fig. & Mil., etc.*), Stock, die Stange (*for flag*); Stütze; (pl. *staves* [steɪvz]) die Notenlinien (*pl.*), das Notensystem (*Mus.*); (*no pl.*) das Personal, der Betrieb, Angestellten (*pl.*) (*C.L.*), der Lehrkörper (*school, etc.*); die Unruhewelle (*Horol.*); *editorial –*, die Schriftleitung, Redaktion, der Redaktionsausschuß; *general –*, der Generalstab; *medical –*, das Ärztepersonal (*of a hospital*), Stabsärzte, Militärärzte (*pl.*) (*Mil.*); *pastoral –*, der Bischofsstab; *regimental –*, der Regimentsstab; *be on the –*, zum Stabe gehören (*Mil.*); fest angestellt sein, eine feste Anstellung haben (*C.L.*); zum Lehrkörper gehören. 2. *v.a.* mit Personal, Lehrern, *etc.* versehen *or* besetzen. **– college,** *s.* die Kriegsschule (*Mil.*). **– notation,** *s.* die Bezeichnung (*Mus.*). **– officer,** *s.* der Stabsoffizier. **– outing,** *s.* der Betriebsausflug. **– -room,** *s.* das Lehrerzimmer. **– -sergeant,** *s.* der Unterfeldwebel (*Infantry, etc.*), Unterwachtmeister (*Cav., Artil., etc.*). **– -surgeon,** *s.* der Oberstabsarzt (*Nav.*).

stag [stæg], 1. *s.* der Hirsch; das Männchen (*of various animals*); (*sl.*) der Aktenspekulant (*C.L.*); (*sl.*) Herr ohne Dame; (*sl.*) *go –*, ohne Dame gehen; *warrantable –*, fünfjähriger Hirsch. 2. *v.n.* (*sl.*) in Aktien spekulieren (*C.L.*); ohne Dame gehen. 3. *v.a.* (*sl.*) hochtreiben (*the market*) (*C.L.*). **– -beetle,** *s.* der Hirschkäfer. **– -evil,** *s.* die Maulsperre (*of horses*). **–gard,** *s.* vierjähriger Hirsch, der Sechsender. **– -horn,** *s.* das Hirschhorn; der Hirschfarn (*Bot.*). **– -hunt(ing),** *s.* die Hirschjagd. **–hound,** *s.* der Hetzhund. **– -party,** *s.* (*coll.*) die Herrengesellschaft.

stag–e [steɪdʒ], 1. *s.* das Gerüst, Gestell; die Bühne (*Theat.*); (*fig.*) das Theater, der Schauspielberuf; die (Post)Station, Haltestelle; Etappe, Teilstrecke; (*fig.*) der Abschnitt, die Periode, das Stadium, die Stufe (*also Geol.*), der Grad; Schauplatz; *–es of appeal*, der Instanzenweg (*Law*); *at this –e*, in diesem Stadium; *by* or *in –es*, etappenweise; *by* or *in easy –es*; in kurzen Absätzen; *have a clear –e*, freies Feld haben; *hold the –e*, sich auf der Bühne halten (*of plays*); *landing-–e*, die Landungsbrücke, Landungsstelle; *be on the –e*, Schauspieler *or* an der Bühne sein; *bring on* or *to the –e*, auf die Bühne bringen; *come on* (*to*) *the –e*, auftreten, eintreten (*of actors*); *go off* or *leave the –e*, abtreten; *go on the –e*, Schauspieler werden, zur Bühne gehen; *off –e*, hinter der Szene; *report –e*, die Erörterung vor der dritten Lesung (*Parl.*). 2. *v.a.* auf die Bühne bringen, inszenieren, in Szene setzen, (*fig.*) veranstalten. **–e-box,** *s.* die Proszeniumsloge. **–e-coach,** *s.* die Postkutsche. **–ecraft,** *s.* die Bühnentechnik, Bühnenerfahrung. **–e direction,** *s.* die Bühnenanweisung. **–e door,** *s.* der Bühneneingang. **–e effect,** *s.* die Bühnenwirkung. **–e fright,** *s.* das Lampenfieber. **–e hand,** *s.* der Bühnenarbeiter. **–e-manage,** *v.n.* (& *a.*) Regie führen (über). **–e management,** *s.* die Regie, Bühnenleitung. **–e manager,** *s.* der Regisseur, Bühnenleiter, Inspizient. **–e property,** *s.* Theaterrequisiten (*pl.*). **–er,** *s.*; *old –er*, (*coll.*) alter Praktikus. **–e rights,** *pl.* das Aufführungsrecht. **–e-struck,** *adj.* für das Theater begeistert. **–e whisper,** *s.* weit hörbares Geflüster. **–ey,** *see* **–y.** **–iness,** *s.* die Effekthascherei. **–ing,** *s.* das Gerüst; Postkutschenwesen; die Inszenierung (*Theat.*). **–y** [–dʒɪ], *adj.* theatralisch, effekthaschend, gespreizt.

staggard [ˈstægəd], *see under* **stag.**

stagger [ˈstægə], 1. *v.n.* schwanken (*also fig.*), wanken, taumeln (*with*, vor). 2. *v.a.* stutzig *or* wankend *or* schwankend *or* taumelig machen, ins Taumeln bringen; (*fig.*) verblüffen, erschüttern, stutzig machen; staffeln (*defences*); geteilt nehmen (*holidays*); abwechselnd anordnen (*Mech.*). **–ing,** *adj.* wankend, schwankend, taumelnd; (*coll.*) verblüffend, überwältigend, phantastisch, hoch (*price, etc.*), niederschmetternd (*blow*). **–s,** *pl.* (*sing. constr.*) die Drehkrankheit (*of sheep*), der Koller (*of horses & cattle*), (*coll.*) der Schwindel (*of a p.*).

staging, *see under* **stage.**

stagna–ncy [ˈstægnənsɪ], *s.* die Stockung, der Stillstand. **–nt** [–nənt], *adj.* (still)stehend, stockend, stagnierend, abgestanden; flau (*C.L.*), träge. **–te** [–neɪt], *v.a.* stillstehen, stocken; stagnieren; träge werden (*of a p.*); flau werden *or* sein (*C.L.*). **–tion** [–ˈneɪʃən], *see* **–ncy.**

stagy, *see under* **stage.**

staid [steɪd], *adj.* gesetzt, ruhig, nüchtern, gelassen. **–ness,** *s.* die Gesetztheit, Gelassenheit, Ruhe.

stain [steɪn], 1. *s.* der (Schmutz)Fleck; der Färbstoff, die Beize; (*fig.*) der Flecken, Makel, Schandfleck. 2. *v.a.* färben, beizen; beflecken (*also fig.*), beschmutzen; (*fig.*) besudeln; *–ed glass*, buntes Glas, das Buntglas. *–ed-glass windows*, bunte Fenster. 3. *v.n.* flecken. **–ing,** *s.* das Beizen, Färben; *–ing of glass*, die Glasmalerei. **–less,** *adj.* unbefleckt, ungefleckt; rostfrei, nichtrostend (*steel*); (*fig.*) fleckenlos, makellos.

stair [stɛ:ə], *s.* die (Treppen)Stufe, der (Treppen)-Tritt; (*usually pl.*) die Treppe, Stiege; *flight of –s*, die Treppe; *above –s*, bei der Herrschaft; *below –s*, bei dem Dienstpersonal; *see also* **down–s** *and* **up–s.** **– -carpet,** *s.* der Treppenläufer. **–case,** *s.* das Treppenhaus, der Treppenaufgang, die Treppe; *back –case*, die Hintertreppe; *main –case*, der Hauptaufgang; *moving –case*, die Rolltreppe; *spiral* or *winding –case*, die Wendeltreppe. **– -head,** *s.* oberster Treppenabsatz. **– -rail,** *s.* das Treppengeländer. **– -rod,** *s.* die (Treppen)Läuferstange. **–way,** *s.* (*Amer.*) die Treppe.

[1]**stake** [steɪk], 1. *s.* die Stange, der Pfahl; Brandpfahl, Scheiterhaufen; *die at the –*, auf dem Scheiterhaufen sterben. 2. *v.a.* einpfählen (*ground, etc.*); auf einem Pfahle aufspießen; *– off* or *out*, abpfählen, abstecken. **– -boat,** *s.* das Startboot. **– -net,** *s.* das Staknetz.

[2]**stake,** 1. *s.* der (Wett)Einsatz; *pl.* die Einlage, der Preis; das Preisrennen; *be at –*, auf dem Spiele stehen; *have at –*, auf dem Spiel stehen haben; *have a – in*, ein Interesse haben an; *sweep the –s*, den ganzen Gewinn einstreichen; *play for high –s*, (*fig.*) sich hohe Ziele setzen. 2. *v.a.* zum Pfande *or* aufs Spiel setzen; (als Einsatz) setzen (*money*) (*on*, auf); *– one's word*, sein Wort verpfänden (*on*, für). **– -holder,** *s.* der Verwahrer der Wetteinsätze.

stala–ctic(al) [stəˈlæktɪk(l)], **–ctiform** [–ˈlæktɪfɔ:m], *adj. see* **–ctitic.** **–ctite** [ˈstæləktaɪt], *s.* der Tropfstein, Stalaktit. **–ctitic** [stæləkˈtɪtɪk], *adj.* tropfsteinartig, stalaktitisch. **–gmite** [–əgmaɪt], *s.* der Säulentropfstein, Stalagmit. **–gmitic** [–əgˈmɪtɪk], stalagmitisch.

[1]**stale** [steɪl], *adj.* schal, abgestanden (*beer*), fade (*wine*); trocken, altbacken (*bread*); verbraucht, verdorben, schlecht, muffig (*air, etc.*); (*fig.*) abgenutzt, abgearbeitet, überanstrengt, stumpf (*of a p.*); alt, veraltet, alltäglich, abgegriffen, abgedroschen (*of things*); flau (*C.L.*); *– cheque*, verjährter Scheck. **–ness,** *s.* die Schalheit, Abgestandenheit, Abgenutztheit, Abgedroschenheit; Überarbeitung.

[2]**stale,** 1. *v.n.* stallen, harnen (*of horses, etc.*). 2. *s.* der Harn (*of horses, etc.*).

stalemate [ˈsteɪlmeɪt], 1. *s.* das Patt (*Chess*); (*fig.*) das Stocken, der Stillstand, die Sackgasse, Gleichgewichtslage. 2. *v.a.* patt setzen; (*fig.*) zum Stillstand bringen; matt setzen, in die Enge treiben.

[1]**stalk** [stɔ:k], *s.* der Stiel (*also of feather, glass, & Zool.*), Stengel (*of a flower*); Halm (*of corn*); der Träger (*Zool.*); *on the –*, auf dem Halm (*corn*). **–ed** [–t], *adj.* gestielt; (*as suffix*) –stielig. **–less,** *adj.* stiellos. **–y,** *adj.* stielartig, stengelartig, (*fig.*) langstielig, stakig.

[2]**stalk,** 1. *v.n.* pirschen, birschen (*game*); (*fig.*) schleichen; stolzieren, stolz einherschreiten. 2. *v.n.* sich heranpirschen an. 3. *s.* die Pirsch, Birsch; stolzer *or* stolzierender Schritt. **–er,** *s.* der Pirschjäger. **–ing,** *s.* das Pirschen, Birschen; Einherstolzieren. **–ing-horse,** *s.* das Versteckpferd; (*fig.*) der Vorwand, Deckmantel.

stall [stɔ:l], 1. *s.* der Stand, die Box (*in a stable*); der (Verkaufs)Stand, die Marktbude; der Kirchenstuhl, Chor(herren)stuhl (*Eccl.*); Sperrsitz, Parkettsitz (*Theat.*); Stillstand (*Motor.*), Sackflug, überzogener Flug (*Av.*); *book-–*, der Bücherstand; *finger-–*, Fingerling, Däumling. 2. *v.a.* einstallen, im Stalle halten (*cattle*); zum Stillstand bringen, abdrosseln (*an engine*); überziehen (*Av.*). 3. *v.n.* stehenbleiben (*Motor.*); durchsacken (*Av.*). **–age,** *s.* das Standgeld, Marktgeld. **– -feed,** *v.a.* im Stalle füttern. **– -feeding,** *s.* die Stallfütterung.

stallion [ˈstæljən], *s.* der (Zucht)Hengst.

stalwart [ˈstɔ:lwət], 1. *adj.* stark, kräftig, handfest; (*fig.*) fest, entschlossen, standhaft, unentwegt; treu. 2. *s.* standhafter Verfechter.

stamen [ˈsteɪmən], *s.* der Staubfaden, das Staubgefäß (*Bot.*).

stamin–a [ˈstæmɪnə], *s.* die Kraft, Stärke, Widerstandskraft, Ausdauer. **–al,** *adj.* [ˈstæmɪnəl],

Widerstands–; ['steɪmɪnəl], Staubgefäß– (*Bot.*). **-ate** ['steɪmɪneɪt], **-iferous** [–'nɪfərəs], *adj.* Staubgefäße tragend, staubfädentragend; *–iferous flower*, männliche Blüte.

stammer ['stæmə], 1. *v.n.* stammeln, stottern. 2. *s.* das Stammeln, Stottern. **-er,** *s.* der Stammler, Stotterer. **-ing,** 1. *adj.* stammelnd, stotternd. 2. *s.* das Stammeln, Stottern; Gestammel, Gestotter.

stamp [stæmp], 1. *s.* das Stampfen (*with the foot*); der Stempel; die Stampfe, der Pochstempel (*Tech.*); (Amts)Stempel, die Stempelmarke; (also *postage –*), die (Brief)Marke, das Postwertzeichen; (*fig.*) der Stempel, das Gepräge, der Schlag, Charakter; *of a different –*, anders veranlagt; *a man of that –*, ein Mann von diesem Schlag; *affix a –* or *put a – on* (*adv.*), eine Marke aufkleben; *give a – to a th.*, einer S. Gepräge verleihen; *put a – on* (*prep.*) eine Marke kleben auf; *set one's – on a th.*, (*fig.*) einer S. seinen Stempel aufdrücken. 2. *v.a.* stampfen; frankieren, freimachen (*letters, etc.*); stempeln (*with a rubber stamp*); pochen (*metal*); prägen (*coins*); drucken (*cloth*); (often *– out*) ausstanzen (*a design*); (*fig.*) stempeln, kennzeichen (*as*, als); einprägen, eingraben (*on* (*Dat.*)); *– down*, niedertreten; *– one's foot*, mit dem Fuße stampfen; *that –ed him in my eyes*, das charakterisierte ihn in meinen Augen; *– out*, austreten (*a fire*); ausstanzen (*Tech.*); (*fig.*) ausrotten, ausmerzen, unterdrücken; *– to the ground*, stampfen auf, zerstampfen, niedertreten. 3. *v.n.* stampfen, mit Füßen treten. **–Act,** *s.* das Stempelgesetz. **--album,** *s.* das Briefmarkenalbum. **--collection,** *s.* die Markensammlung. **--collector,** *s.* der Markensammler; **--duty,** *s.* die Stempelgebühr. **-er** [–ə], *s.* der Stampfer, die Ramme, Stampfe(*for paper*); der Briefstempler. **-ing,** *s.* das Stampfen; Stanzen (*Tech.*); *pl.* Stanzstücke (*pl.*). **-ing-die,** *s.* der Stempel. (*coll.*) **-ing-ground,** *s.* der Lieblingsaufenthalt. **-ing-press,** *s.* die Stempelpresse. **-ing-mill,** *s.* das Pochwerk, die Prägmaschine. **--mill,** *s.* die Stampfmühle (*Pap.*). **--office,** *s.* das Stempelamt. **--pad,** *s.* das Stempelkissen.

stampede [stæm'pɪ:d], 1. *s.* wilde Flucht, die Massenflucht, plötzlicher Schrecken, die Panik. 2. *v.n.* durchgehen; in wilder Flucht davonlaufen. 3. *v.a.* in wilder Flucht jagen *or* treiben.

stance [stɑ:ns], *s.* die Haltung, Stellung (*esp. golf*).

[1]**stanch** [stɔ:ntʃ], *see* [1]**staunch.**

[2]**stanch,** *see* [2]**staunch.**

stanchion ['stænʃn], 1. *s.* die Stütze, Strebe, der Pfosten, die Fensterstange, der Gitterstab; der Stieper, Steiper (*Naut.*). 2. *v.a.* an einen Pfosten binden.

stand [stænd], **1.** *ir.v.n.* stehen, aufstehen, aufrechtstehen, hochstehen; stehenbleiben, stillstehen, stocken; standhalten, Widerstand leisten; sich stellen, sich befinden, liegen, gelegen sein, dauern, sich halten, bestehen, beharren; gelten (*as*, als), gültig *or* in Kraft sein; steuern, segeln, Kurs haben (*for*, nach) (*Naut.*); *– and deliver!*, halt! das Geld her!; *– or fall*, siegen oder sterben; *leave –ing*, stehenlassen; *and so it –s*, und dabei bleibt es; *as things –*, wie die Dinge liegen. **(a)** (*with adjectives, nouns, or inf.*) *– aghast*, bestürzt sein; *– alone*, allein stehen, ohne Hilfe sein; unerreicht dastehen; *– condemned*, überführt sein; *– corrected*, sein Unrecht zugeben; *– fast*, feststehen, nicht weichen; *– first*, zuerst kommen, obenan stehen; *– godfather*, Gevatter stehen (*to*, zu); *– good*, gültig sein; *– high*, hohes Ansehen genießen; *let –*, abstehen lassen (*liquids*); (*coll.*) *– pat*, am alten feststehen (*Amer.*); *– security*, sich verbürgen, Sicherheit leisten; *– still*, stillstehen; *– to lose* (or *win*), sicherlich verlieren (*or* gewinnen), einen Verlust (*or* Gewinn) zu gewärtigen haben (*by*, durch *or* bei); *– well with*, gutstehen mit; *– well over 6 ft.*, gut über 6 Fuß hoch sein *or* Fuß messen. **(b)** (*with adverbs*) *– about*, umherstehen; *– aloof*, sich fernhalten; *– apart*, beiseite stehen; *– aside*, auf die Seite treten, aus dem Wege gehen; *– back*, zurücktreten; *– by*, dabeistehen, dabei sein, in Bereitschaft sein; klarstehen, bereitstehen (*Naut.*); *– down*, zurücktreten, abtreten (*Sport*), sich zurückhalten *or* fernhalten; *– easy!*, rührt euch! (*Mil.*); *– forth*, hervortreten; *– in*, landwärts segeln (*Naut.*); (*coll.*) einspringen, es übernehmen; *– in for*, lossteuern auf (*Naut.*); *– in with*, teilnehmen, teilhaben (*in*, an); *– off*, abseitsstehen, sich abseits halten, abstehen, sich fernhalten; *– off from the shore*, sich abseits von der Küste halten; *– out*, sich herausheben (*from*, aus), sich abheben, hervorragen (*from*, von; *against*, gegen); nicht teilnehmen, sich fernhalten; *– out against*, widerstehen, Stellung nehmen gegen, Verwahrung einlegen; *– out for*, eintreten für; bestehen auf; *– out to sea*, in See gehen; *– over*, liegen *or* unerledigt bleiben, aufgeschoben *or* zurückgestellt werden (*as a case, etc.*); *– to*, sich zum Angriff vorbereiten (*Mil.*), bereit stehen; *– up*, aufstehen (*from a seat*), aufrecht stehen, sich aufrecht halten, sich aufrichten; *– up against*, sich behaupten gegen, sich erheben wider; *– up for*, rechtfertigen, verteidigen, eintreten für; *– up to*, standhalten, sich gewachsen zeigen (*Dat.*); es aufnehmen mit, entgegentreten. **(c)** (*with prepositions*) *– against*, widerstehen, sich halten gegen; *– at attention*, stramm stehen (*Mil.*); *– by*, beistehen (*Dat.*) (*a p.*), festhalten *or* beharren bei, treubleiben (*Dat.*) (*a th.*); *– by one's word*, zu seinem Wort stehen; *– for*, stehen *or* gelten für, bedeuten, bezeichnen; vertreten; kandidieren für (*Parl.*); (*coll.*) hinnehmen, dulden; *– in awe of*, Ehrfurcht haben vor; *– in dread of*, Angst haben vor; *– in need of*, nötig haben; *– a p. in good stead*, einem nützlich sein *or* zustatten kommen; *– instead of*, dienen als; *– on*, bestehen *or* beharren auf, Wert legen auf; *– on ceremony*, Umstände machen; *– on end*, aufrechtstehen, zu Berge stehen (*as hair*); *– on one's guard*, auf der Hut sein; *– on record*, aufgezeichnet sein; *– on one's rights*, auf seinem Recht bestehen; *– to*, bleiben *or* verharren bei, sich halten an; *– to one's guns*, nicht zurückweichen, nicht nachgeben, seinen Ansichten treubleiben; *it –s to reason*, es ist selbstverständlich, es versteht sich (von selbst), es leuchtet ein; *– upon*, see *– on.* **2.** *ir.v.a.* stellen (*against*, an); standhalten (*Dat.*); leiden, dulden, aushalten, (er)tragen, vertragen, ausstehen; (*coll.*) spendieren, zum besten geben (*a p. a th.*, einem etwas); *– a chance*, Aussicht haben; (*coll.*) *– a p. a dinner*, einem ein Mittagessen spendieren; (*sl.*) *not – an earthly*, nicht die geringste Aussicht haben; *– one's ground*, sich behaupten, seinen Mann stehen; *I cannot – him*, ich kann ihn nicht ausstehen; *I cannot – it*, ich kann es nicht aushalten, es ist mir zuviel, das geht mir über die Hutschnur; (*coll.*) *– it out*, es stehend zum Ende aushalten; *– the loss*, den Verlust tragen; *– a lot*, viel vertragen, sich viel gefallen lassen; *– no nonsense*, nicht mit sich spaßen *or* spielen lassen; (*coll.*) *– the racket*, die Suppe auslöffeln; *– the test*, die Probe bestehen, sich bewähren; *– one's trial*, gerichtlich verhört werden, sich vor Gericht verantworten. **3.** *s.* der Stand, die (Auf)Stellung; das Stehen, der Stillstand; Widerstand; Stand(platz), (Halte)Platz, die Stelle; der Ständer, Untersatz, das Gestell, Stativ(*for camera, etc.*); die Bude, der (Verkaufs)Stand; (also *grand–*) die Tribüne; *band –*, der Musikkiosk; *– of arms*, vollständige (Waffen)Ausrüstung; *– of wheat*, stehendes Korn; *bring to a –*, zum Stehen bringen; *come to a –*, steckenbleiben; *make a –*, Widerstand leisten, sich widersetzen; standhalten (*against* (*Dat.*)); *make a last –*, einen letzten Verteidigungsversuch machen; *take a –*, eine Stellung einnehmen; *take one's –*, sich aufstellen. **-ard,** *see* **standard. --by,** 1. *s.* die Hilfe, der Beistand, Helfer. 2. *attrib.* Ersatz–, Reserve–. **--easy,** *s.* die Ruhepause. **--in,** *s.* das Double (*Films, etc.*). **-ing,** 1. *adj.* stehend; dauernd, beständig, fest; *all –ing*, unvorbereitet, so wie man ist; *–ing army*, stehendes Heer; *–ing bath*, die Flotte (*Dye.*); *–ing committee*, beständiger, bleibender *or* stehender Ausschuß; *–ing corn*, stehendes Korn; *–ing joke*, altbewährter Witz; *–ing jump*, der Sprung aus dem Stand; *–ing order*, fester *or* laufender Auftrag (*C.L.*); *–ing orders*, die Geschäftsordnung (*Parl.*), Dauerbefehle (*pl.*) (*Mil.*); *–ing rigging*, fester *or* stehendes Tauwerk (*Naut.*); *sold –ing*, auf dem Halm verkauft; *–ing stone*, der Steinblock, Monolith. 2. *s.* das Stehen; die Stellung, der Stand, Posten; die Dauer, der Bestand;

Rang, Ruf, das Ansehen; *of good –ing*, hochangesehen; *of long –ing*, alt, langjährig; *no –ing*, keine Stehplätze; *be of 10 years –ing*, zehnjährigen Bestand haben, schon 10 Jahre bestehen. **–ing-room,** *s.* der Stehplatz. **– -offish,** *adj.* abweisend, unnahbar, überheblich. **– -pipe,** *s.* das Standrohr. **–point,** *s.* der Standpunkt, Gesichtspunkt. **–still,** *s.* der Stillstand; *–still agreement*, das Stillhalteabkommen; *be at a –still*, stillstehen, stocken; *bring to a –still*, zum Stehen *or* Stocken bringen; *come to a –still*, ins Stocken *or* zum Stillstand kommen, stehenbleiben; *fight to a –still*, bis zur Erschöpfung kämpfen. **– -up,** *attrib.* (hoch)stehend, Steh–; *– -up collar*, der Stehkragen; *– -up fight*, regelrechter Kampf.

standard ['stændəd], 1. *s.* die Standarte, Fahne (*also fig.*), der Pfosten, Pfeiler, Ständer; freistehender (Baum)Stamm (*Hort.*); das Normalmaß, Eichmaß, Richtmaß (*also fig.*); der Normalpreis, Münzfuß, die Währung, Valuta; gesetzlicher Feingehalt (*metal*), der Titer (*liquids*); (*fig.*) Maßstab, Durchschnitt, die Regel, Norm, das Niveau; die Klasse, Stufe (*at school*); *above* (*below*) –, über (unter) dem Durchschnitt; *below* –, geringhaltig (*Metall.*); *according to* or *by a* –, nach einem Maßstab; *gold* –, die Goldwährung; *lamp* –, der Lampenständer; – *of life* or *living*, der Lebensstandard, die Lebenshaltung; *set a* –, vorbildlich *or* mustergültig sein; *set the – for*, den Maßstab abgeben für; *be up to* (*the*) –, den Anforderungen genügen; – *of value*, der Wertmesser. 2. *adj.* maßgebend, führend; mustergültig, Muster–, Standard–, Normal–; Einheits–; stehend, aufrecht, Steh–; hochstämmig (*Hort.*); – *author*, klassischer Schriftsteller; – *candle*, die Normalkerze; – *gauge*, die Normalspurweite (*Railw.*); – *English*, mustergültiges Englisch; – *German*, deutsche Bühnensprache *or* Schriftsprache, die Hochsprache, Gemeinsprache, Einheitssprache; – *gold*, das Münzgold; – *lamp*, die Stehlampe; – *measure*, das Normalmaß; *–work*, maßgebendes Werk. **– -bearer,** *s.* der Fahnenträger, Standartenträger. **–ization** [–aɪ'zeɪʃən], *s.* die Standardisierung, Normierung, Normung, Vereinheitlichung. **–ize** [–aɪz], *v.a.* standardisieren, normalisieren, normieren, normen, eichen, einstellen, vereinheitlichen, festlegen.

standpoint, *see under* **stand.**

standstill, *see under* **stand.**

stank [stæŋk], *see* **stink.**

stann–ary ['stænərɪ], *s.* das Zinn(berg)werk. **–ate** [–eɪt], 1. *adj.* zinnsauer. 2. *s.* zinnsaures Salz. **–ic,** *adj.* Zinn–, zinnsauer; *–ic acid*, die Zinnsäure; *–ic oxide*, das Stannioxyd, Zinndioxid. **–iferous** [–'nɪfərəs], *adj.* zinnhaltig. **–ous** [–əs], *adj.* zinnähnlich; *–ous oxide*, das Zinnmonoxyd, Zinnoxydul; *–ous salt*, das Stannosalz, Zinnoxydulsalz.

stanza ['stænzə], *s.* die Strophe, Stanze. **–ic,** *adj.* Stanzen–, strophenförmig.

[1]**staple** ['steɪpl], 1. *s.* das Haupterzeugnis, der Haupthandelsartikel (*of a country*); (*fig.*) Hauptgegenstand, Hauptinhalt; der Stapel, einzelne Fadenlänge *or* Faser (*of wool, etc.*); die Rohwolle; (*fig.*) der Rohstoff; der Stapelplatz, Markt (*Hist.*). 2. *attrib. adj.* Stapel–, Haupt–; – *fibre*, die Zellwolle; – *food*, das Hauptnahrungsmittel. 3. *v.a.* (nach der Faser) sortieren (*wool, etc.*). **–r** [–lə], *s.* der Sortierer (*of wool, etc.*); Wollgroßhändler.

[2]**stapl–e,** 1. *s.* die Krampe, Haspe, Kramme; Heftklammer, der Heftdraht (*Bookb.*). 2. *v.a.* mit einer Klammer *or* Krampe befestigen; mit Draht heften (*Bookb.*). **–ing-machine,** *s.*, **–er,** *s.* die Heftmaschine (*Bookb.*).

star [stɑː], 1. *s.* der Stern (*also fig.*); Ordensstern; das Sternchen (*Typ.*); (*fig.*) das Geschick, Schicksal; berühmter Künstler, Schauspieler *or* Sänger, die Größe; der (Bühnen)Stern, (Film)-Star, die Filmgröße; hervorragender Mensch; *my – is in the ascendent* or *ascendant*, mein Stern ist im Aufgehen; – *of Bethlehem*, der Milchstern (*Bot.*); *fixed* –, der Fixstern; (*coll.*) *I see –s*, es flimmert mir vor den Augen; *my – has set*, mein Stern ist erloschen; *shooting* –, die Sternschnuppe; *thank one's* (*lucky*) *–s*, seinem Schicksal verdanken; *unlucky* –, der Unstern. 2. *v.a.* besternen, mit einem Sternchen versehen (*Typ.*); eine Hauptrolle geben (*Dat.*) (*Theat.*). 3. *v.n.* glänzen, die Hauptrolle spielen, in der Hauptrolle gastieren (*Theat.*). **– Chamber,** *s.* die Sternkammer (*Hist.*). **– -crossed,** *adj.* nicht von den Sternen begünstigt. **–dom,** *s.* die Welt der Filmgrößen *or* Stars. **– -drift,** *s.* das Sterntreiben. **–finch,** *s.* das Rotschwänzchen (*Orn.*). **–fish,** *s.* der Seestern. **– -gazer,** *s.* der Sterngucker (*also fig.*). **– -gazing,** *s.* das Sterngucken. **–less,** *adj.* sternenlos. **–light,** 1. *s.* das Sternenlicht. 2. *adj.*, **–lit,** *adj.* sternhell. **–like,** *adj.* sterngleich, sternartig. **– performance,** *s.* die Elitevorstellung, *see* **– turn. –riness,** *s.* die Sternenhelle. **–ry,** *adj.* gestirnt (*sky*), stern(en)hell, strahlend (*eyes*); sternenförmig, Sternen–. **–shell,** *s.* die Leuchtkugel (*Mil.*). **– -spangled,** *adj.* sternbesät; *– -spangled banner*, das Sternenbanner (*Amer.*); amerikanisches Nationallied. **– -thistle,** *s.* die Flockenblume (*Bot.*); (*coll.*) **– turn,** *s.* die Hauptattraktion.

starblind ['stɑːblaɪnd], *adj.* halbblind.

starboard ['stɑːbəd], 1. *s.* das Steuerbord. 2. *adj.* Steuerbord–; – *side*, das Steuerbord. 3. *v.a.*; – *the helm!*, Ruder am Steuerbord!

starch [stɑːtʃ], 1. *s.* die (Pflanzen)Stärke; (Wäsche)-Stärke; (*fig.*) die Steifheit, Formalität; das Stärkemehl (*Chem.*). 2. *v.a.* stärken, stiefen. **–ed** [–t], *adj.* gestärkt; (*fig.*) steif, formell. **–iness,** *s.* die Stärkehaltigkeit; (*fig.*) Steifheit, Formalität. **–y,** *adj.* stärkehaltig (*food*); (*fig.*) steif, formell.

star–e [stɛːə], 1. *s.* das Starren, Stieren, starrer Blick. 2. *v.n.* starren, stieren, große Augen machen; *–e at*, anstarren; *–e into space*, vor sich hinstarren; *make a p. –e*, einen in Erstaunen setzen; *–e back at s.o.*, seinen starrenden Blick erwidern. 3. *v.a.*; *–e s.o. in the face*, einen anstarren (*a p.*); deutlich vor Augen stehen (*Dat.*) (*of things*); *–e out of countenance*, durch starre Blicke verblüffen. **–ing,** *adj.* starrend, stier; grell, auffallend (*colours*).

stark [stɑːk], *adj.* & *adv.* steif, starr; völlig, gänzlich, ganz; – *staring mad*, ganz und gar verrückt; – *naked*, splitternackt.

[1]**starling** ['stɑːlɪŋ], *s.* der Star (*Orn.*).

[2]**starling,** *s.* das Pfeilerhaupt, der Eisbrecher, Strombrecher (*of a bridge*).

starry, *see under* **star.**

start [stɑːt], **1.** *v.n.* anfangen, beginnen, seinen Anfang nehmen; (*fig.*) ausgehen (*from*, von); **auf**brechen, abreisen, sich auf den Weg machen; abgehen, abfahren (*as trains, etc.*), abfliegen (*Av.*), losgehen (*as an engine*), starten (*Sport*); zusammenfahren, auffahren, in die Höhe fahren, aufschrecken, aufspringen; sich werfen *or* krümmen (*as planks*); sich lockern (*as nails*); (*a*) (*with adverbs*) – *back*, die Rückreise antreten; zurückspringen, zurückschrecken; (*coll.*) – *in*, beginnen; – *off*, abfahren, aufbrechen, die Reise antreten; – *out*, die Reise antreten, aufbrechen; (*coll.*) sich vornehmen; – *up*, auffahren, aufschrecken, aufspringen, stutzen (*at*, bei); anspringen (*as a car*); (*coll.*) entstehen; (*b*) (*with prepositions*) *his eyes –ed from his head*, ihm traten die Augen aus dem Kopfe; – *in business*, ein Geschäft eröffnen *or* anfangen; – *on a th.*, etwas beginnen; (*coll.*) – *on a p.* Händel suchen mit einem; *to – with*, als erstes, erstens, zum Anfang. **2.** *v.a.* aufjagen, aufschrecken, aufscheuchen, auftreiben, aufstöbern (*game*); gründen, einrichten, aufmachen (*a business*); ins Leben rufen, in Gang bringen, in Gang *or* Betrieb setzen, anlassen (*an engine*), starten lassen (*Sport*); in die Welt setzen (*a theory, etc.*), anregen, aufbringen, aufwerfen (*a question*), verbreiten (*a rumour*), antreten (*a journey*), stürzen (*a cask*), lockern, losmachen (*nails, planks, etc.*); – *the ball rolling*, die S. ins Rollen bringen; – *a p. in business*, einen etablieren; – *another hare*, ein neues Thema anschneiden; – *up*, in Bewegung *or* Gang setzen. **3.** *s.* der Anfang, Beginn; Aufbruch, die Abfahrt, Abreise; der Ausgangsort, Start, Startlinie (*Sport*); der Abflug, Aufstieg (*Av.*); Vorsprung, die Vorgabe (*Sport*); der Ruck, das Auffahren, Stutzen; *at the* –, bei Beginn; *by (fits and) –s*, ruckweise, sprungweise; *from – to finish*, von Anfang bis zu Ende; *get the – of a p.*, einem zuvorkommen; *give a* –, erschrecken; *give a p. a* –, einen erschrecken;

have the – of or *a – over*, einen Vorsprung haben vor; *an hour's –*, eine Vorgabe von einer Stunde; *make a –*, anfangen, beginnen; *make an early –*, früh aufbrechen. **–er,** *s.* der Starter (*Racing*); das Rennpferd, der Teilnehmer (*in a race*); der Anlasser (*Motor.*); *–er-motor*, *s.* die Antriebsmachine. **–ing,** *s.* der Aufbruch; Starten (*Sport*); *order of –ing*, die Startordnung. **–ing-handle,** *s.* die Anlaßkurbel. **–ing-place,** *s.* der Ausgangsort, Aufbruchsplatz. **–ing-point,** *s.* der Ausgangspunkt (*of*, für). **–ing-post,** *s.* die Startlinie, das Startmal. **–ing-price,** *s.* der Startpreis (*racing*), Eröffnungspreis (*auction*).

startl–e [ˈstɑːtl], *v.a.* überraschen, aufschrecken, erschrecken, aufscheuchen. **–ing,** *adj.* erschreckend, bestürzend, überraschend, aufsehenerregend.

starv–ation [stɑːˈveɪʃən], *s.* das Verhungern, die Aushungerung, der Hungertod; *–ation wages*, der Hungerlohn. **–e** [stɑːv], 1. *v.n.* verhungern; hungern, Hunger leiden, fasten; (*coll.*) *be –ing*, vor Hunger fast umkommen, sehr hungrig sein; *be –ed*, ausgehungert sein; *–e for*, hungern *or* dürsten nach; *–e to death*, Hungers *or* vor Hunger sterben; *be –ed with cold*, frieren. 2. *v.a.* verhungern lassen, aushungern; hungern lassen; verkümmern lassen (*plants, etc.*); *–e to death*, Hungers sterben lassen; *–e into*, durch Hunger zwingen zu; *–e out*, aushungern. **–eling** [–lɪŋ], 1. *s.* ausgehungertes Tier, verkümmerte Pflanze, der Hungerleider. 2. *adj.* hungrig, ausgehungert, abgezehrt.

stasis [ˈsteɪsɪs], *s.* die Blutstockung.

[1]**state** [steɪt], 1. *s.* der Zustand, Stand, die Lage, Beschaffenheit; der Staat, die Regierung, politische Macht; die Pracht, der Staat, Glanz, Pomp; Stand, Rang, die Klasse; (*coll.*) schlechter *or* erregter Zustand; *pl.* Stände (*pl.*). (*a*) (*with nouns*) *– of affairs*, die Sachlage; *– of health*, der Gesundheitszustand; *– of mind*, der Geisteszustand; (*coll.*) *– of nature*, nackt; *– of siege*, der Belagerungszustand; *– of things*, see *– of affairs*. (*b*) (*with prepositions*) *run by the –*, staatlich, Staats–; (*coll.*) *in –*, mit großem Pomp; in Galauniform; (*coll.*) *be in a –*, sehr aufgeregt sein (*a p.*), toll aussehen (*a th.*); *lie in –*, auf dem Paradebette liegen; *live in great –*, großen Staat machen; *affairs of –*, Staatsgeschäfte (*pl.*); *Secretary of –*, der Staatssekretär, Minister. 2. *attrib. adj.* staatlich, Staats–; feierlich. **–-aided,** *adj.* staatlich unterstützt. **– apartments,** *pl.* Galaräume, Paraderäume. **– cabin,** *s.* die Luxuskabine. **– control,** *s.* staatliche Aufsicht. **–craft,** *s.* die Staatskunst, Staatsklugheit. **– Department,** *s.* das Außenministerium (*Amer.*). **– interference,** *s.* staatliche Einmischung. **–less,** *adj.* staatenlos. **–liness,** *s.* die Stattlichkeit, Würde, Pracht. **–ly,** *adj.* stattlich, majestätisch, imposant, erhaben, würdevoll, prunkvoll, prächtig. **– occasion,** *s.* der Staatsakt. **– papers,** *pl.* Staatsakten (*pl.*). **– prison,** *s.* das Staatsgefängnis. **– property,** *s.* der Staatsbesitz. **–-room,** *s.* der Prunksaal; die Luxuskabine. **–sman** [–smən], *s.* der Staatsmann, Diplomat. **–smanlike,** *adj.* staatsmännisch, diplomatisch. **–manship,** *s.* die Staatskunst, Regierungskunst, Diplomatie.

[2]**state,** *v.a.* angeben, klarlegen, darlegen, aussagen, erklären, anführen; behaupten, berichten, melden, erzählen; festsetzen, feststellen; aufstellen (*Math.*); *as –d*, wie erwähnt; *he was –d to have said*, er soll gesagt haben. **–d** [–ɪd], *adj.* bestimmt, festgesetzt, regelmäßig; *at –d intervals*, in regelmäßigen Zwischenräumen; *at the –d time*, zur festgesetzten Zeit. **–ment** [–mənt], *s.* die Feststellung, Behauptung, Angabe; Darstellung, Darlegung, Erklärung, der Bericht; die Aufstellung, der Auszug (*C.L.*), die Bilanz (*Banking*); *–ment of account*, der Rechnungsauszug; *as per –ment*, laut Angabe *or* Bericht (*C.L.*); *–ment of charges*, die Kostenrechnung; *–ment of claim*, die Klageschrift; *make a –ment*, eine Behauptung aufstellen; *–ment of prices*, die Preisliste; *prisoner's –ment*, die Gefangenenaussage.

static [ˈstætɪk], *adj.* statisch, bewegungslos; *– gain*, die Verstärkung pro Stufe (*Rad.*); *– warfare*, der Stellungskrieg; *– water-tank*, der Feuerlöschteich. **–s.** *pl.* (*sing. constr.*) die Statik; (*pl. constr.*) atmosphärische Störungen (*pl.*) (*Rad.*)

station [ˈsteɪʃən], 1. *s.* der Standort, die Lage; Stellung, (amtliche) Stelle; Station (*Mil., etc.*); Haltung, der Stand; hoher Rang; der Bahnhof (*Railw.*); die Haltestelle, der Aufenthalt(sort), der (scheinbare) Stillstand (*Astr.*); Standpunkt (*Surv.*); *pl.* Stationen (*R.C.*); *above one's –*, über seinem Stand; *at the –*, auf dem Bahnhof; *–s of the Cross*, der Kreuzweg; *duty –*, die Dienststelle; *filling –*, die Tankstelle; *fire –*, die Feuerwehrwache, das Feuerwehrdepot; *free –*, bahnfrei (*C.L.*); *– in life*, gesellschaftliche Stellung; *man of –*, der Mann von hohem Rang; *naval –*, die Marinestation; *police –*, die Polizeiwache; *radio –*, der Sender, die Radiostation; *take up one's –*, seinen Standort einnehmen. 2. *v.a.* stationieren, aufstellen, postieren. **–al** [–əl], *adj.* Standorts–. **–ary** [–ərɪ], *adj.* stillstehend; feststehend, sich gleichbleibend, bleibend, unverändert; unbeweglich, seßhaft, stationär (*Mach., etc.*); *remain –ary*, nicht weiterkommen *or* fortschreiten, stillstehen, sich gleichbleiben. **–-house,** *s.* die Polizeiwache (*Amer.*). **–-master,** *s.* der Bahnhofsvorsteher. **–-pointer,** *s.* die Meßrute (*Surv.*).

stationer [ˈsteɪʃənə], *s.* der Papierhändler, Schreibwarenhändler; *–s' Company*, Londoner Buchhändlergilde; *–s' Hall*, Londoner Buchhändlerbörse; *–'s shop*, das Papiergeschäft, die Schreibwarenhandlung. **–y** [–rɪ], *s.* Schreibwaren (*pl.*), das Briefpaper; (*H.M.*) *–y Office*, Königlicher Staatsverlag.

statist [ˈsteɪtɪst], *s.* (*archaic*) der Staatsmann; Statistiker. **–ic(al)** [stəˈtɪstɪk(l)], *adj.* statistisch. **–ician** [stætɪsˈtɪʃən], *s.* der Statistiker. **–ics** [stəˈtɪstɪks], *pl.* (*sing. constr.*) die Statistik (*the science*); (*pl. constr.*) die Statistik (*about*, über), statistische Angaben; *prove by –ics*, statistisch nachweisen.

stator [ˈsteɪtə], *s.* der Stator.

statu–ary [ˈstætjuərɪ], 1. *s.* Standbilder, Statuen, Bildhauerarbeiten (*pl.*); die Bildhauerkunst, Bildhauerarbeit. 2. *adj.* Bildhauer–; *–ary marble*, der Bildsäulenmarmor. **–e** [ˈstætjuː], *s.* das Standbild, die Bildsäule, Statue. **–esque** [–ˈɛsk], *adj.* statuenartig, bildsäulenartig; (*fig.*) würdevoll. **–ette** [–ˈɛt], *s.* kleine Statue, die Statuette.

stature [ˈstætʃə], *s.* die Gestalt, Statur, der Wuchs; (*fig.*) das Format, Kaliber.

status [ˈsteɪtəs], *s.* rechtliche Lage (*Law*), (soziale) Stellung, der Rang; Zustand (*Science*); Stand, die Lage (*of things*); *equality of –*, politische Gleichberechtigung; *national –*, die Staatsangehörigkeit; *– quo*, gegenwärtiger Zustand; *– quo ante*, voriger Zustand.

statut–e [ˈstætjuːt], *s.* (geschriebenes) Gesetz, die Parlamentsakte, Verordnung, Satzung, das Statut; *–e of limitations*, das Verjährungsgesetz. **–e-book,** *s.* das Reichsgesetzbuch, die Gesetzsammlung; *be put on the –e-book*, Gesetz werden. **–e-labour,** *s.* vorgeschriebener Frondienst. **–e-law,** *s.* vorgeschriebenes Recht, das Gesetzesrecht. **–ory** [–trɪ], *adj.* gesetzlich, Gesetz–; *–ory corporation*, die Körperschaft des öffentlichen Rechts; *–ory declaration*, eidesstattliche Erklärung; *–ory holidays*, staatliche Feiertage.

[1]**staunch** [stɔːntʃ, stɑːntʃ], treu, zuverlässig, unerschütterlich (*of a p.*); fest, stark (*of a th.*).

[2]**staunch,** *v.a.* stillen (*blood, also fig.*), hemmen (*flow of blood*).

stave [steɪv], 1. *s.* die (Faß)Daube; (Leiter)-Sprosse; Strophe (*Metr.*), Notenlinien (*pl.*) (*Mus.*). 2. *reg. & ir.v.a.* mit Dauben *or* Sprossen versehen; *– in*, einschlagen; *– off*, abhalten, abwenden, abwehren; aufschieben, aufhalten, verzögern.

[1]**stay** [steɪ], 1. *v.n.* stehenbleiben, (an)halten, bleiben, verweilen, sich aufhalten; (*Scots*) wohnen; zu Besuch sein (*with*, bei); aushalten, durchhalten (*Sport*); *– at home*, zu Hause bleiben; (*coll.*) *come to –*, festgesetzt, fest eingebürgert; (*coll.*) *– put*, an Ort und Stelle bleiben; (*a*) (*with prepositions*) *– for*, warten auf; *– to dinner*, zum Mittagessen bleiben; (*b*) (*with adverbs*) *– away*, wegbleiben; *– behind*, zurückbleiben; *– in*, zu Hause bleiben; *– on*, länger bleiben, den Aufenthalt verlängern; *– out*, draußenbleiben; *– up*, aufbleiben. 2. *v.a.* zurückhalten,

aufhalten, anhalten, hindern, hemmen; einstellen, verschieben (*Law*); zum Stehen bringen (*an advance*); stillen (*hunger*); befriedigen (*desire*); – *the course*, bis zum Ende durchhalten; (*coll.*) – (*for*) *lunch*, bis zum Mittagessen bleiben; (*coll.*) – *the night*, übernachten, über Nacht bleiben. 3. *s.* das Bleiben, Verweilen, der Aufenthalt; die Einstellung (*Law*); *make a* –, sich aufhalten; *put a* – *on*, hemmen. **--at-home,** 1. *s.* der Stubenhocker. 2. *adj.* häuslich, solid. **–er,** *s.* der Steher, durchhaltender Renner (*Sport*). **–ing,** *adj.* aushaltend; *–ing power*, die Widerstandskraft, Ausdauer.

[2]**stay,** 1. *s.* das Stag, Stütztau (*Naut.*); die Strebe, Stütze (*also fig.*); *pl.* das Korsett; *a pair of –s*, ein Korsett; *in –s*, im Wenden (*Naut.*); *miss –s*, das Wenden verfehlen (*Naut.*). 2. *v.a.* stagen (*a mast*); durch den Wind bringen (*a ship*). **–sail** [–səl], *s.* das Stagsegel, die Stagfock (*on a cutter*).

stead [stɛd], *s.* (*fig.*) die Stelle; *in his* –, an seiner Stelle; *stand s.o. in good* –, einem zustatten kommen *or* nützlich sein.

stead-fast [ˈstɛdfɑːst], *adj.* fest, unentwegt, standhaft, unerschütterlich (*of a p.*); unverwandt (*of a glance*), unbeweglich, unveränderlich. **–fastness,** *s.* die Festigkeit, Beständigkeit, Standhaftigkeit. **–iness** [–ɪnɪs], *s.* die Sicherheit, Festigkeit; Beständigkeit, Beharrlichkeit, Standhaftigkeit; Stetigkeit, Gleichmäßigkeit. **–y,** 1. *adj.* fest (*also fig.*), sicher; (*fig.*) unerschütterlich, standhaft, beständig, stetig, gleichbleibend, gleichmäßig, regelmäßig; zuverlässig, solid, gesetzt; stabil (*C.L.*); *–y!* langsam! vorsichtig! ruhig!; *–y hand*, sichere Hand; *remain –y*, sich halten (*as prices*); *–y toil*, anhaltende Mühe. 2. *v.a.* festmachen, festigen, sichern; zügeln, zurückhalten (*a horse, etc.*); verlangsamen (*the pace*); zur Vernunft bringen (*a person*); *–y o.s.*, sich stützen. 3. *v.n.* fest, ruhig *or* sicher werden.

steak [steɪk], *s.* das Steak, die (Fleisch)Schnitte.

steal [stiːl], 1. *ir.v.a.* stehlen (*from* (*Dat.*)); – *a march on a p.*, einem zuvorkommen; – *a glance*, einen verstohlenen Blick werfen (*at*, auf *or* nach); – *a p.'s thunder*, einem den Wind aus den Segeln nehmen. 2. *ir.v.n.* sich stehlen *or* schleichen; – *away*, sich fortstehlen; – *into*, sich einschleichen in; – *over*, beschleichen, sich einschleichen bei (*of feelings, etc.*); – *upon*, beschleichen, überfallen. **–th** [stɛlθ], *s.* die Heimlichkeit; *by –th*, verstohlen, verstohlenerweise, heimlich, hinterrücks. **–thiness** [ˈstɛlθɪnɪs], *s.* die Heimlichkeit. **–thy** [ˈstɛlθɪ], *adj.* verstohlen, heimlich.

steam [stiːm], 1. *s.* der (Wasser)Dampf, die Dampfkraft; der Dunst, die Feuchtigkeit; (*fig.*) Kraft, Energie; *exhaust* –, der Abdampf; *at full* –, mit Volldampf (*also fig.*); *full – ahead*, Volldampf voraus; *get – up*, heizen (*Tech.*); (*fig.*) alle Kraft zusammennehmen; *let off* –, Dampf ablassen (*Tech.*); (*fig.*) sich Luft machen, den Gefühlen freien Lauf lassen. 2. *v.n.* dampfen, dunsten; fahren, laufen (*of a steamer*). 3. *v.a.* dämpfen, mit Dampf behandeln; dünsten (*Cook.*); dekatieren (*cloth*). **–boat,** *s.* das Dampfschiff, der Dampfer. **--boiler,** *s.* der Dampfkessel. **--chest,** *s.* der Schieberkasten. **--coal,** *s.* die Kesselkohle. **--engine,** *s.* die Dampfmaschine. **–er,** *s.* der Dampfer, das Dampfschiff; der Dampfkochtopf; *by –er*, mit dem Dampfer *or* Dampfschiff. **--gauge,** *s.* das Manometer, der Dampfdruckmesser. **–hammer,** *s.* der Dampfhammer. **--jacket,** *s.* der Dampfmantel. **--navigation(-company),** *s.* die Dampfschiffahrt(sgesellschaft). **– navvy,** *s.* der Trockenbagger. **--pipe,** *s.* das Dampfrohr. **--power,** *s.* die Dampfkraft. **–roller,** *s.* die Dampfwalze, Straßenwalze. **–ship,** *s.* der Dampfer, das Dampfschiff. **--vessel,** *s. see* **–ship.** **–y,** *adj.* dampfig, dunstig, dampfend, Dampf–.

stea-rate [ˈstɪəreɪt], 1. *s.* das Stearat, stearinsaures Salz. 2. *adj.* stearinsauer. **–ric** [stɪˈærɪk], *adj.* Stearin–; *–ric acid*, die Stearinsäure, Talgsäure. **–rin** [ˈstɪərɪn], *s.* das Stearin; *–rin candle*, die Stearinkerze. **–tite** [ˈstɪətaɪt], *s.* der Speckstein.

steed [stiːd], *s.* (*Poet.*) das (Schlacht)Roß.

steel [stiːl], 1. *s.* der Stahl (*also fig.*); der Schleifstahl; die Stange (*in a corset*); (*Poet.*) das Schwert; (*fig.*) die Härte; *cast* –, der Gußstahl; *cold* –, Stahlwaffen (*pl.*); *forged* –, das Schmiedeeisen; *high-speed* –, der Schnellschnittstahl; *ingot* or *mild* –, der Flußstahl; *foe worthy of one's* –, ebenbürtiger Gegner 2. *adj.* stählern, Stahl–. 3. *v.a.* (ver)stahlen; (*fig.*) stählen, verhärten. **--clad,** *adj.* stahlgepanzert. **– engraving,** *s.* die Stahlstecherkunst; der Stahlstich. **– helmet,** *s.* der Stahlhelm; Stahlhelmer (*Pol.*). **–iness,** *s.* die Stahlhärte. **–pen,** *s.* die Stahlfeder. **--plated,** *adj.* stahlgepanzert. **–wool,** *s.* Stahlspäne (*pl.*). **–work,** *s.* die Stahlarbeit, Stahlteile (*pl.*). **--works,** *pl.*, (*sing. constr.*) das Stahlwerk. **–y,** *adj.* stählern, stahlhart (*also fig.*). **–yard,** *s.* die Laufgewichtswaage, Schnellwaage.

[1]**steep** [stiːp], 1. *adj.* steil, jäh, schroff, abschüssig; (*coll.*) unglaubhaft (*story*), gepfeffert (*prices*); – *coast*, die Steilküste; – *slope*, der Steilhang; – *turn*, die Steilkurve (*Av.*). 2. *s.* der Steilhang, steiler Abhang. **–en,** 1. *v.a.* steiler machen. 2. *v.n.* steiler werden. **–ness,** *s.* die Steilheit, Abschüssigkeit.

[2]**steep,** 1. *s.* das Einweichen, Eintauchen; Einweichwasser, die Lauge; *put the clothes in* –, die Wäsche einweichen. 2. *v.a.* einweichen, durchfeuchten, (ein)tauchen, (auf)quellen, wässern, sättigen, imprägnieren, tränken; (*fig.*) (*usually pass.*) *–ed in* versenkt, versunken, verstrickt *or* befangen in; *o.s. in*, sich versenken in.

steeple [ˈstiːpl], *s.* der Kirchturm, Spitzturm. **–chase,** *s.* **–chasing,** *s.* das Hindernisrennen. **--jack,** *s.* der Turmdecker, Schornsteinarbeiter.

[1]**steer** [stɪːə], *s.* junger Ochs.

[2]**steer,** 1. *v.a.* steuern; (*fig.*) lenken, leiten; – *a course*, einen Kurs einhalten. 2. *v.n.* steuern, gesteuert werden, sich steuern lassen; fahren, laufen, segeln, schiffen (*for*, nach); – *clear of*, (*usually fig.*) meiden, sich fernhalten von, aus dem Wege gehen (*Dat.*). **–able** [ˈstɪərəbl], *adj.* lenkbar. **–age** [–ɪdʒ], *s.* die Steuerung, Lenkung; das Zwischendeck, Heck. **–age-way,** *s.* die Steuerkraft, Fahrkraft (*Naut.*). **–ing** *s.* das Steuern. **–ing-gear,** *s.* die Steuerung, Lenkvorrichtung, das Lenkgetriebe. **–ing-play,** *s.* toter Gang (*Motor.*). **–ing-wheel,** *s.* das Steuerrad, Lenkrad. **–sman** [ˈstɪəzmən], *s.* der Rudergänger.

steeve [stiːv], *s.* der Erhöhungswinkel des Bugspriets (*Naut.*).

stele [ˈstiːlɪ], *s.* die Stele, freistehende Pfeilersäule.

stell-ar [ˈstɛlə], *adj.* sternförmig, Sternen–. **–ate** [–eɪt], *adj.* sternförmig; *–ate flower*, die Strahlenblume. **–ular** [–julə], *adj.* sternchenartig, Sternen–.

[1]**stem** [stɛm], 1. *s.* der Stamm (*of a tree, also Gram.*), Stiel (*also of wineglass*), Stengel (*of a plant, fruit*); die Röhre (*of a thermometer*); das Rohr (*of a pipe*); die (Aufzieh)Krone (*of a watch*); der Notenschwanz (*Mus.*); der Grundstrich (*Typ.*). 2. *v.a.* abstengeln, entstengeln, abstielen, von Stengeln befreien. 3. *v.n.*; – *from*, abstammen *or* herrühren von. **–less,** *adj.* ungestielt, stiellos, stengellos. **–med,** *suffix*, –stämmig. **--winder,** *s.* die Remontoiruhr.

[2]**stem,** 1. *s.* der Vordersteven, Schiffsschnabel (*Naut.*); *from – to stern*, von vorn bis hinten. 2. *v.a.* sich entgegenstemmen (*Dat.*), ankämpfen gegen (*as a ship*); dämmen, hemmen (*also fig.*), stillen (*blood*); (*fig.*) eindämmen, hindern, abhalten, abwehren; – *the tide*, gegen den Strom *or* die Flut ankämpfen (*also fig.*).

stench [stɛntʃ], *s.* der Gestank, übler Geruch. **--trap,** *s.* die Schließklappe.

stencil [ˈstɛnsl], 1. *s.* (also *--plate*) die Schablone, Patrone, Matrize; die Schablonenzeichnung; *make* or *type a* –, auf einer Matrize tippen *or* schreiben; *roll off a* –, eine Matrize abziehen. 2. *v.a.* schablonieren, mit Schablonen malen, auf Matrizen tippen *or* schreiben.

sten-gun [ˈstɛnˈgʌn], *s.* die Maschinenpistole.

steno-graph [ˈstɛnogrɑːf], 1. *v.a.* stenographieren. 2. *s.* das Stenogramm. **–grapher** [–ˈnɔgrəfə], *s.* der Stenograph. **–graphic** [–ˈgræfɪk], *adj.* stenographisch, in Kurzschrift. **–graphy** [–ˈnɔgrəfɪ], *s.* die Kurzschrift, Stenographie. **–tic** [–ˈnɔtɪk], *adj.*; *–tic murmur*, das Durchpreßgeräusch (*Med.*) **–typist** [–taɪpɪst], *s.* der Stenotypist.

stenter [ˈstɛntə], *s.* der Trockenrahmen.

stentorian [stɛnˈtɔːrɪən], *adj.* überlaut, Stentor–

[1]**step** [stɛp], 1. *s.* der Schritt (*also fig.*), Tritt, Tanzschritt; Fußstapfen; die Stufe (*also Mus.*), der (Leiter–, Treppen–, *or* Wagen)Tritt, die Sprosse (*of a ladder*); Spur (*of a mast*); das Intervall (*Mus.*); (*coll.*) kurze Strecke *or* Entfernung; *pl.* die Trittleiter; Schritte, Maßnahmen (*pl.*); *a pair of –s*, eine Trittleiter; *at every –*, bei jedem Schritt; *bend* or *direct one's –s to*, seine Schritte lenken nach; *– by –*, Schritt für Schritt, schrittweise; *by –s*, stufenweise; *false –*, der Fehltritt (*also fig.*); *fire –*, der Schützenauftritt, die Feuerstufe (*Mil.*); *hop, – and jump*, der Dreisprung (*Sport*); (*fig.*) kurze Strecke; *in – with*, im gleichen Schritt mit; *keep – with*, Schritt halten mit; *make* or *take a –*, einen Schritt tun; *mind the –!* Vorsicht, Stufe!; *out of –*, nicht im Schritt mit; *retrace one's –s*, denselben Weg zurückgehen; (*fig.*) eine S. rückgängig machen; *stone –s*, die Steintreppe; *walk in s.o.'s –s*, in seinen Fußstapfen folgen; (*fig.*) seinem Beispiel folgen; (*coll.*) *watch your –!* sei vorsichtig! paß auf!; (*coll.*) *within a – of*, nur eine kurze Entfernung von. 2. *v.n.* schreiten, gehen, treten; *– this way*, treten Sie näher; (*sl.*) *– on the gas*, Gas geben (*Motor.*), (also *– on it*) sich beeilen; *– into the breach*, einspringen; (*with adverbs*) *– aside*, beiseitetreten; *– back*, zurücktreten; *– down*, hinuntergehen; (*fig.*) einen Rückzieher machen, nachgeben; *– in*, eintreten; (*fig.*) eingreifen, sich ins Mittel legen; *– out*, hinaustreten, ausgehen; ausschreiten; (*coll.*) *– it out*, tüchtig ausschreiten; *– round* (*to*), auf einen Sprung besuchen; *– up to a p.*, auf einen zugehen *or* zutreten *or* zuschreiten. 3. *v.a.* ausführen, machen (*a pace*), abschreiten (*a distance*); einspuren, einsetzen (*a mast*); (*coll.*) *– up*, erhöhen, verstärken (*production, etc.*). **–-dance**, *s.* der Stepptanz. **–-ladder**, *s.* die Trittleiter. **–ped**, *adj.* gestaffelt, Stufen–. **–per**, *s.* guter Gänger (*of horse*). **–ping**, *s.* das Schreiten, Gehen. **–ping-stone**, *s.* der Schrittstein; (*fig.*) die Stufenleiter, das Sprungbrett, Mittel, die Stufe (*to*, zu). (*coll.*) **–-up**, *s.* die Beförderung; Verstärkung (*Rad.*).

[2]**step**, *prefix* Stief– (*mother, brother, etc.*).

steppe [stɛp], *s.* die Steppe.

stereo–graphy [stɛrɪˈɔgrəfɪ], *s.* die Stereographie, perspektivische Zeichnung, räumliche Abbildung. **–metry** [–ˈɔmɪtrɪ], *s.* die Stereometrie, Raumbildmessung. **–scope** [ˈstɛrɪəskoʊp], *s.* das Stereoskop. **–scopic** [–ˈskɔpɪk], *adj.* stereoskopisch. **–type** [–taɪp], 1. *s.* die Stereotypie, Stereotypplatte, der Plattendruck (*Typ.*). 2. *adj.* Stereotyp– (*Typ.*); (*fig.*) feststehend, unabänderlich, stereotyp, abgedroschen. 3. *v.a.* stereotypieren, von Platten drucken; (*fig.*) unverändert wiederholen, unveränderlich *or* ein für allemal festlegen. **–typed** [–taɪpt], *adj.* stets wiederkehrend, ständig gebraucht, abgedroschen, stereotyp. **–typography** [–taɪˈpɔgrəfɪ], *s.* der Stereotypdruck, das Stereotypdruckverfahren.

steril–e [ˈstɛraɪl], *adj.* unfruchtbar (*also fig.*), keimfrei, steril, (*fig.*) fruchtlos, öde, hohl, leer (*in* or *of*, an). **–ity** [–ˈrɪlɪtɪ], *s.* die Unfruchtbarkeit (*also fig.*), Sterilität, Keimfreiheit; (*fig.*) Hohlheit. **–ization** [–ɪlaɪˈzeɪʃən], *s.* die Sterilisation. **–ize** [ˈstɛrɪlaɪz], *v.a.* unfruchtbar machen (*animals, etc.*), entkeimen, sterilisieren (*milk, etc.*). **–izer**, *s.* das Sterilisationsmittel; Sterilisierapparat.

sterling [ˈstə:lɪŋ], 1. *s.* der Sterling (*engl. Währung*). 2. *adj.* dem engl. Münzfuße entsprechend; (*fig.*) echt, erprobt, bewährt, gediegen, gehaltvoll, vollwertig; *a pound –*, ein Pfund Sterling.

[1]**stern** [stə:n], *s.* das Heck, Hinterschiff, Schiffshinterteil; der Spiegel (*of an animal*); (*coll.*) das Hinterteil; *down by the –*, achterlastig (*Naut.*). **–-chaser**, *s.* das Heckgeschütz. **–-fast**, *s.* das Hecktau. **–-frame**, *s.* das Spiegelspant. **–most**, *adj.* achterst, hinterst. **–-port**, *s.* die Hinterpforte, Heckpforte. **–-post**, *s.* der Achtersteven. **–sheets**, *pl.* Achtersitze (*pl.*). **–-way**, *s.* die Bewegung achteraus, Rückwärtsbewegung; das Deinsen. **–-wheel**, *s.* das Heckrad. **–-wheeler**, *s.* der Heckraddampfer.

[2]**stern**, *adj.* hart, unerbittlich, unnachgiebig, streng, ernst (*with* or *towards*, gegen); *– glance*, düsterer Blick; *– necessity*, harte Notwendigkeit. **–ness**, *s.* die Härte, Strenge, der Ernst.

stern–al [ˈstə:nəl], *adj.* Brustbein–. **–um** [–nəm], *s.* das Brustbein.

sternutat–ion [stə:njuˈteɪʃən], *s.* das Niesen. **–ory** [–ˈteɪtərɪ], 1. *adj.* zum Niesen reizend, Nies–. 2. *s.* das Nies(reiz)mittel.

stertorous [ˈstə:tərəs], *adj.* schnarchend.

stet [stɛt], *imper.* es bleibe stehen (*Typ.*).

stethoscop–e [ˈstɛθəskoʊp], 1. *s.* das Hörrohr, Horchrohr, Stethoskop (*Med.*). 2. *v.a.* abhorchen. **–ic** [–ˈskɔpɪk], adj. Hörrohr–.

stevedore [ˈstɪ:vədɔ:], *s.* der Stauer, Hafenarbeiter, Schiffsbelader, Güterpacker.

stew [stju:], 1. *v.a.* dämpfen, schmoren, langsam kochen. 2. *v.n.* schmoren, gedämpft werden; (*coll.*) *let s.o.* or *leave s.o. to – in his own juice*, einen seinem eigenen Schicksal überlassen; *–ed apples*, das Apfelkompott; *–ed fruit*, das Kompott; *–ing apples*, Kochäpfel (*pl.*). 3. *s.* das Schmorfleisch, geschmortes Fleisch; (*fig.*) die Herzensangst, große Aufregung, die Verwirrung; (also *Irish –*) das Eintopfgericht; (*usually pl.*) (*archaic*) das Bordell. **–pan**, *s.* der Schmortopf.

steward [ˈstjuəd], *s.* der Verwalter (*of estates*); Haushofmeister, Majordomus (*in princely houses*); Proviantmeister, Steward, Aufwärter (*Naut.*); Aufseher, Festordner (*of races, etc.*); *Lord High –*, der Großhofmeister. **–ess**, *s.* die Aufwärterin; Wirtschafterin (*Naut., etc.*), Stewardeß, Flugzeugkellnerin (*Av.*). **–ing**, *s.* der Ordnerdienst. **–ship**, *s.* das Verwalteramt.

stibi–al [ˈstɪbɪəl], *adj.* Antimon–, Spießglanz–. **–um** [–ɪəm], *s.* das Antimon, der Spießglanz.

stich [stɪk], *s.* der Vers. **–ic**, *adj.* stichisch, (*Metr.*). **–omythia** [–oˈmɪθɪə], *s.* die Stychomythie, Wechselrede (*in drama*).

[1]**stick** [stɪk], 1. *s.* der Stock; (also *walking-–*) Spazierstock; Stab, Stecken, die Stange, das Holzstück, Scheit; der Taktstab (*Mus.*); Winkelhaken (*Typ.*); (*coll.*) Mast, Knüppel (*Naut.*); Steuerknüppel (*Av.*); (*sl.*) langweiliger Mensch; *pl.* das Brennholz, Reisig(holz); der Dreistab (*Crick.*); *broom–*, der Besenstiel; *drum–*, der Trommelstock; (*coll.*) *fiddle–*, der Geigenbogen; (*coll.*) *fiddle–s!* Unsinn!, Quatsch!; (*coll.*) *get the –*, eine Tracht Prügel bekommen; *get hold of the wrong end of the –*, die Lage völlig mißdeuten; (*coll.*) *give s.o. the –*, einem eine Tracht Prügel geben; *hockey-–*, der Hockeyschläger; *take the – to s.o.*, einen verprügeln; *walking-–*, der Spazierstock. 2. *v.a.* mit einem Stock stützen (*plants, etc.*); mit Stäben versehen; in den Winkelhaken nehmen (*Typ.*). **–-insect**, *s.* die Gespenstheuschrecke (*Ent.*).

[2]**stick**, 1. *ir.v.a.* stecken, stoßen, durchstecken, durchbohren, durchstoßen; abstechen, schlachten (*a pig, etc.*); befestigen, heften, kleben, zusammenkleben; (*sl.*) (*usually neg.*) aushalten, ausstehen, leiden, ertragen; *– no bills*, das Anschlagen von Plakaten ist verboten; (*coll.*) *be stuck*, festsitzen, nicht weiterkönnen; (*sl.*) *be stuck for*, in Verlegenheit sein um; (*sl.*) *be stuck on*, versessen sein auf, eingenommen sein für, verliebt sein in; (*with adverbs*) *– out*, herausstecken (*tongue*); herausdrücken (*chest*); *– together*, zusammenkleben; *– up*, ankleben, anschlagen (*bills*); aufstellen; (*sl.*) anhalten und überfallen (*a p.*). 2. *ir.v.n.* festkleben, haften bleiben, klebenbleiben; steckenbleiben, sich festfahren, (*fig.*) nicht weiterkönnen, stocken; (*coll.*) bleiben; festhaften, verbunden bleiben (*to*, mit *or* an); festsitzen (*as ideas*); (*a*) (*with prepositions*) *– at*, bleiben *or* beharren bei, aushalten; sich stoßen an, Anstoß *or* Anstand nehmen an, zurückschrecken vor; *– by*, treubleiben (*Dat.*); bleiben bei, nicht weichen von; *– in s.o.'s throat*, einen anwidern; *– to a p.*, einen treubleiben; *– to a th.*, festhalten, bei einer S. bleiben *or* beharren, sich an eine S. halten; *– to one's guns*, seiner S. treu bleiben; *– to the point*, bei der S. bleiben; (*b*) (*with adverbs*) *– out*, hervorstehen, abstehen (*from*, aus); (*sl.*) *– (it) out*, aushalten, durchhalten, standhalten, nicht nachgeben; (*sl.*) *– out for*, bestehen auf; (*coll.*) *it –s out a mile*, es ragt deutlich hervor, es ist klar zu sehen; *– together*, zusammenhalten (*people*); zusammenbacken, zusammenkleben (*pages, etc.*); *– up*,

aufrechtstehen, hervorragen, emporragen, aufragen; (*coll.*) – *up for*, eintreten *or* Partei nehmen für; (*coll.*) – *up to*, Widerstand leisten (*Dat.*); (*sl.*) *stuck up*, eingebildet. (*coll.*) **–er,** *s.* beharrlicher Arbeiter; der Ladenhüter (*C.L.*); (*sl.*) verwirrende Bemerkung, schwierige Frage; *bill-–er*, der Plakatankleber; *pig-–er*, der Schweineschlächter, (*sl.*) langes Messer. **–-fast,** *s.* die Klebepaste, der Kleister. **–iness,** *s.* die Klebrigkeit, Zähigkeit. **–ing-place,** *s.*, **–ing point,** *s.* der Haltepunkt, Höhepunkt, Wendepunkt. **–ing-plaster,** *s.* das Heftpflaster. (*coll.*) **–-in-the-mud,** *s.* der Schlendrian, Faulenzer, schwerfälliger Mensch. (*sl.*) **–-up,** *s.* der Überfall. **–y,** *adj.* klebrig, zäh, (*fig.*) heikel, kitzlig; *–y bomb*, die Haftmine.

stickle [ˈstɪkl], *v.n.* eifern, kämpfen, eintreten *or* Partei nehmen (*for*, für); zanken, streiten (*about*, um); – *for a th.*, eine S. verfechten. **–r,** *s.* der Eiferer, Kämpfer (*for*, für), eifriger Verfechter (*for* (*Gen.*)); *–r for detail*, der Kleinigkeitskrämer.

stickleback [ˈstɪklbæk], *s.* der Stichling (*Ichth.*).

stiff [stɪf], 1. *adj.* steif (*also fig.*); starr, dick(flüssig), zäh(e) (*as liquids*); (*fig.*) förmlich, formell (*of manners*); ungelenk (*as style*); fest entschlossen, hartnäckig, unbeugsam; stark (*as wind*); kräftig (*of drinks*); hoch, fest, steigend (*of prices*); schwierig, beschwerlich; *bore s.o.* –, einen tödlich langweilen; – *climb*, beschwerlicher Anstieg; – *collar*, steifer Kragen; – *examination*, schwere Prüfung; *keep a – face*, ernst bleiben; *my legs are* –, ich habe steife Beine; *keep a – upper lip*, sich nicht unterkriegen lassen; – *neck*, steifer Hals. 2. *s.* (*sl.*) der Kassiber; unangenehmer *or* unbelehrbarer Mensch; die Leiche. **–en,** 1. *v.a.* steif *or* starr machen, steifen (*cloth, etc.*); (*fig.*) ungelenk *or* unbeugsam machen. 2. *v.n.* steif(er), stärker *or* fester werden, erstarren, versteifen, (*fig.*) förmlich *or* fest entschlossen werden; anziehen (*of prices*) (*C.L.*). **–ener** [–ənə], *s.* steife Einlage; (*coll.*) das Stärkungsmittel, der Versteifer. **–ening,** *s.* das Steifen, Stärken (*of clothes, etc.*); steife Einlage, die Versteifung, das Steifmaterial, Steifleinen. **–-necked,** *adj.* steifnackig, halsstarrig, hartnäckig. **–ness,** *s.* die Steifheit, Steife, Starrheit, Unbiegsamkeit; Zäheit, Dickflüssigkeit; (*fig.*) Förmlichkeit.

[1]**stifl–e** [ˈstaɪfl], *v.a.* ersticken (*also fig.*); (*fig.*) zurückdrängen, unterdrücken; vernichten. **–ing,** *adj.* stickend; *–ing atmosphere*, die Stickluft.

[2]**stifle,** *s.* (also *–-joint*) das Kniegelenk (*of a horse*); die (Fluß)Galle (*Vet.*). **–-bone,** *s.* die Kniescheibe (*of a horse*).

stigma [ˈstɪgmə], *s.* (pl. *–ta* [–mətə]) Wundmale Christi (*Eccl.*); böses Symptom (*Med.*); die Atmungsöffnung (*Ent.*); das Stigma, die Narbe (*Bot.*); (pl. *–s*) (*fig.*) das Brandmal, der Schandfleck, Schimpf. **–tization** [–taɪˈzeɪʃən], *s.* die Stigmatisierung; Brandmarkung. **–tize** [–taɪz], *v.a.* brandmarken, stigmatisieren.

stile [staɪl], *s.* der Zauntritt.

stiletto [stɪˈlɛtoʊ], *s.* das Stilett, der Dolch; Pfriem, Stecher.

[1]**still** [stɪl], 1. *v.a.* beruhigen, stillen. 2. *adj.* still, ruhig; unbeweglich, bewegungslos, regungslos; nicht schäumend (*of drinks*); *sit* –, stillsitzen; *stand* –, stillstehen; – *life*, das Stilleben (*Paint.*); (*Prov.*) – *waters run deep*, stille Wasser sind tief. 3. *adv.* noch immer, immer noch; (*before compar.*) noch; – *more* or *more* –, noch mehr *or* mehr noch; – *more so because*, um so mehr als. 4. *conj.* doch, dennoch, jedoch, trotzdem, indessen. 5. *s.* (*Poet.*) die Stille, Ruhe; (*coll.*) das Stilleben (*Paint.*); Filmphoto, die Photographie. **–birth,** *s.* die Totgeburt. **–-born,** *adj.* totgeboren. **–ness,** *s.* die Stille, Ruhe, das Schweigen. **–y,** (*Poet.*) *adj.* still, ruhig, schweigend.

[2]**still,** 1. *s.* der Destillierapparat, Kolben, die Blase, Brennerei (*for spirits*). 2. *v.a.* (*archaic*) distillieren. **–-room,** 1. *s.* der Destillationsraum; die Hausbrennerei; Vorratskammer. **–age** [–ɪdʒ], 2. *s.* das Faßlager, Faßgestell; Abtropfbrett.

stilliform [ˈstɪlɪfɔ:m], *adj.* tropfenförmig.

stilt [stɪlt], *s.* (*usually pl.*) die Stelze. **–ed** [–ɪd], *adj.* gestelzt, erhöht (*Arch.*); Stelz– (*Orn.*); (*fig.*) geschraubt, gespreizt, hochtrabend. **–-bird,** *s.* der Stelzenläufer. **–edness,** *s.* die Geschraubtheit, Gespreiztheit.

stimul–ant [ˈstɪmjʊlənt], 1. *s.* das Reizmittel (*also fig.*), erregender *or* anregendes Mittel, das Stimulans; (*fig.*) der Antrieb (*to*, zu). 2. *adj.* anreizend, erregend; (*Med., etc.*). **–ate** [–eɪt], *v.a.* & *n.* reizen, anregen (*also fig.*), erregen (*also fig.*); (*fig.*) anspornen (*to*, zu), antreiben (*into*, zu). **–ation** [–ˈleɪʃən], *s.* der Reiz, die Reizung, Erregung, (*fig.*) Anregung, der Antrieb. **–ative** [–lətɪv], *adj.* Anreiz–, anspornend, antreibend. **–us** [–ləs] (pl. *–i* [–laɪ]), *s.* der Reiz, das Reizmittel (*Med.*); (*fig.*) der Ansporn, Antrieb, Anreiz (*to a th.*, zu; *to a p.*, für).

sting [stɪŋ], 1. *ir.v.a.* stechen (*also fig.*); (*fig.*) verwunden, verletzen, kränken, aufstacheln, antreiben (*to* or *into*, zu); (*sl.*) übervorteilen, überteuern; (*sl.*) *be stung*, geneppt werden; (*sl.*) – *s.o. for a pound*, ein Pfund bei einem anpumpen; *stung with remorse*, von Gewissensbissen gequält; – *s.o.'s tongue*, einem auf die Zunge beißen. 2. *ir.v.n.* stechen, brennen, schmerzen. 3. *s.* der Stachel (*Zool., also fig.*); das Brennhaar (*Bot.*); Stechen, der Stich; (*fig.*) der Anreiz, Antrieb; – *of conscience*, der Gewissensbiß. (*coll.*) **–er,** *s.* schmerzender Schlag· beißende Bemerkung. **–iness** [ˈstɪndʒɪnɪs], *s.* der Geiz. **–ing,** *adj.* stechend, schmerzend (*also fig.*), scharf. **–ing-nettle,** *s.* die Brennessel. **–y** [ˈstɪndʒɪ], *adj.* geizig; *be –y with*, knausern *or* geizen mit.

stink [stɪŋk], 1. *ir.v.n.* stinken, übel riechen; (*sl.*) anstößig sein, in üblem Rufe stehen; nichts wert *or* eine faule Sache sein; – *in a p.'s nostrils*, einem widerwärtig sein *or* zum Halse heraushängen. 2. *v.a.*; – *out*, durch Gestank austreiben, ausstänkern. 3. *s.* der Gestank, übler Geruch; (*sl.*) die Schererei, viel Aufhebens; *pl.* (*coll.*) die Chemie. **–ard** [–əd], *s.* das Stinktier (*Zool.*). **–-bomb,** *s.* die Stinkbombe. **–er,** *s.* (*sl.*) ausgesprochener Ekel, ekliger Kerl; billige Zigarette.

stint [stɪnt], 1. *v.a.* einschränken, verkürzen (*a th.*); (*fig.*) knausern mit, scheuen; einschränken, knapp halten (*a p.*) (*of*, mit); – *o.s.*, sich einschränken (*of*, mit), sich beschränken (*to*, auf); sich nichts vergönnen, sich vom Munde absparen. 2. *s.* die Einschränkung; das Maß; festgesetzter Betrag; *without* –, ohne Einschränkung, unbeschränkt; *work by* –, auf Schicht arbeiten. **–ed** [–ɪd], *adj.* knapp, karg, beschränkt.

stip–ate [ˈstaɪpeɪt], *adj.* gedrängt (*Bot.*). **–e** [staɪp], *s.* der Stengel, Stiel, Strunk (*Bot.*). **–ellate** [–əleɪt], *adj.* mit Nebenblättchen (*Bot.*); *see* **stipule.**

stipend [ˈstaɪpɛnd], *s.* die Besoldung, das Gehalt. **–iary** [–ˈpɛndjərɪ], 1. *adj.* besoldet. 2. *s.* der Gehaltsempfänger; (also *–iary magistrate*) der Polizeirichter.

stipple [ˈstɪpl], 1. *v.a.* & *n.* in Punktmanier malen *or* stechen, punktieren, tüpfeln. 2. *s.* die Punktiermanier.

stipul–ar [ˈstɪpjʊlə], *adj.* Nebenblatt–. **–e** [ˈstɪpu:l], *s.* das Nebenblättchen, der Blattansatz.

stipulat–e [ˈstɪpjʊleɪt], 1. *v.a.* ausmachen, ausbedingen, festsetzen, vereinbaren, verabreden; verlangen, sich ausbedingen. 2. *v.n.*; *–e for*, ausbedingen, zur Bedingung machen, übereinkommen über. **–ion** [–ˈleɪʃən], *s.* die Übereinkunft, Abmachung; Bedingung, Klausel. **–or** *s.* der Kontrahent.

stir [stə:], 1. *v.a.* rühren, bewegen, in Bewegung setzen: anrühren, durchrühren, umrühren, quirlen (*liquids*); (*fig.*) anregen, erregen, aufregen, aufrühren, aufrütteln, hervorrufen; – *up*, tüchtig umrühren, (*fig.*) aufrühren, aufrütteln, aufhetzen (*a p.*), erregen, hervorrufen (*a th.*), 2. *v.n.* sich regen *or* bewegen *or* rühren; *be –ring*, auf(gestanden) sein; im Gange *or* Umlauf sein; sich ereignen; – *abroad*, ausgehen; *not – from*, nicht verlassen. 3. *s.* die Bewegung; der Aufruhr; Lärm, das Treiben, Aufsehen, die Aufregung; *give a th. a* –, etwas umrühren; *not a* –, keine Bewegung. **–ring,** *adj.* aufregend, bewegt (*times, etc.*), geschäftig, tätig, rührig (*a p.*).

stirps [stə:ps], *s.* der Familienzweig, (Familien)-Stamm (*Law*); die Abart (*Zool.*).

stirrup [ˈstɪrəp], *s.* der Steigbügel; Bügel, die

Klampe (*Tech.*); *be firm in one's –s*, fest im Sattel sitzen. **––bone,** *s.* der Steigbügel (*in ear*) (*Anat.*). **––cup,** *s.* der Abschiedstrunk. **––iron,** *s.* das Steigbügeleisen. **––leather,** *s.* der Steigbügelriemen. **––pump,** *s.* die Handspritze.

stitch [stɪtʃ], 1. *s.* der Stich (*Sew.*); die Masche (*knitting*); der (Schmerz)Stich, das Stechen (*Med.*); *buttonhole –*, der Langettenstich; *chain –*, der Kettenstich; *without a – of clothing*, ohne jede Kleidung; *cross-–*, der Kreuzstich; *not do a –*, keinen Strich tun; *have not a dry – on*, keinen trockenen Faden am Leibe haben; *drop a –*, eine Masche fallen lassen; (*coll.*) *get the –*, Stiche bekommen; *every – of canvas*, alle Segel; *pick* or *take up a –*, eine Masche aufnehmen; *– in the side*, das Seitenstechen; *a – in time saves nine*, was du heute kannst besorgen, das verschiebe nicht auf morgen. 2. *v.a.* nähen; broschieren, heften (*Bookb.*); zusammennähen (*Surg.*); *– up*, zusammennähen, vernähen, zuflicken. 3. *v.n.* nähen, Stiche machen; heften. **–ing,** *s.* das Nähen, die Näherei; Stickerei; das Heften. **–wort,** *s.* die Sternmiere (*Bot.*).

stithy [ˈstɪðɪ], *s.* (*archaic*) die Schmiede.

stiver [ˈstaɪvə], *s.* der Stüber; (*coll.*) Heller, Deut, das Bißchen.

stoa [ˈstoʊə], *s.* die Stoa (*Arch.*).

stoat [stoʊt], *s.* das Hermelin.

stock [stɔk], **1.** *s.* der (Baum)Stamm; Stengel, Strunk; Block, Klotz; das Gerüst, die Stütze, der Grundstock (*Tech.*); Amboßklotz; Ankerstock (*Naut.*); Glockenstuhl; Schaft, Stiel, Griff (*of a gun*); die (Rad)Nabe; das Geschlecht, der Stamm, die Familie, Herkunft, Abkunft; Levkoje (*Bot.*); der Stehkragen, steife Halsbinde; der Vorrat, Bestand, das Lager; Stammkapital, Grundvermögen, der (Gesellschafts)Anteil; die Staatsanleihe; das Inventar; Vieh (*Agric.*); die (Suppen)Brühe (*Cook.*); Masse, Mischung, das Rohmaterial, der Rohstoff (*Tech.*); *pl.* der (Zwang)Stock (*Hist.*), Stapel (*Naut.*), Staatspapiere, Aktien (*pl.*) (*C.L.*); *dead –*, totes Inventar (*Agric.*); *live –*, lebendes Inventar (*Agric.*); *– in bank*, das Bankkapital; *– in trade*, der Betriebsvorrat; *in –*, vorrätig, auf Lager; *lock, – and barrel*, ganz und gar, als Ganzes; *– on hand*, der Warenbestand; *on the –s*, auf Stapel (*Naut.*); (*fig.*) in Vorbereitung; im Bau *or* Werden; *out of –*, nicht mehr vorrätig, ausverkauft; *rolling –*, das Betriebsmaterial (*Railw.*); *–s and shares*, Börsenpapiere (*pl.*) (*C.L.*); *over – and stone*, über Stock und Stein; *take –*, Inventur machen (*also fig.*); *take – of*, sich klar werden über, in Augenschein nehmen, in Betracht ziehen; (*coll.*) aufmerksam beobachten. **2.** *adj.* auf Lager, stets vorrätig (*C.L.*); Repertoir– (*Theat.*); (*fig.*) stehend, stereotyp, Normal–. **3.** *v.a.* versehen, versorgen, ausrüsten; schäften (*a gun*); stocken (*an anchor*); führen, vorrätig haben, auf Lager halten (*goods*). **––account,** *s.* das Kapitalkonto, Warenkonto, die Effektenberechnung (*C.L.*). **––book,** *s.* das Lagerbuch, Warenverzeichnis. **––breeder,** *s.* der Viehzüchter. **–broker,** *s.* der Börsenmakler, Effektenhändler. **–broking,** *s.* das Effektengeschäft. **–dove,** *s.* die Holztaube. **– exchange,** die (Effekten)Börse, Fondsbörse. **––farming,** *s.* die Viehzucht. **–fish,** *s.* der Stockfisch. **––gilliflower,** *s.* die Levkoje. **––holder,** *s.* der Aktionär, Effekteninhaber. **––in-trade,** *s.* das Arbeitsmaterial; (*fig.*) charakteristisches Merkmal, stereotype Züge (*pl.*). **––jobber,** *s.* der Agioteur, Börsenmakler. **––jobbing,** *s.* die Börsenspekulation. **––list,** *s.* der Kurszettel. **––market,** *s.* die Effektenbörse, Fondsbörse; der Viehmarkt. **––pot,** *s.* der Suppentopf. **––still,** *adj.* stockstill, mäuschenstill. **–taking,** *s.* die Inventur, Bestandsaufnahme; *–taking sale*, der Inventurausverkauf. **–y,** *see* **stocky.** **––yard,** *s.* der Viehhof.

stockade [stɔˈkeɪd], 1. *s.* die Einpfählung, Einfried(ig)ung, das Staket. 2. *v.a.* einfried(ig)en, mit einem Staket umgeben.

stockin–et [stɔkɪˈnɛt], *s.* das Trikot, Baumwollgewebe. **–g** [ˈstɔkɪŋ], *s.* der Strumpf; *elastic –g*, der Gummistrumpf; *in one's –g-feet*, ohne Schuhe. **–g-foot,** *s.* der Füßling. **–g-frame,** *s.* der Strumpfwirkerstuhl.

stocky [ˈstɔkɪ], *adj.* untersetzt.

stodg–e [stɔdʒ], 1. *v.a.* vollstopfen. 2. *v.n.* sich vollstopfen, sich vollfressen. 3. *s.* (*sl.*) der Brei, Matsch; das Gedränge. **–iness,** *s.* die Unverdaulichkeit, Schwerfälligkeit, Fadheit. **–y,** *adj.* breiig, klumpig; schwer verdaulich, unverdaulich; schwerfällig, fade.

stoic [ˈstoʊɪk], 1. *s.* der Stoiker. 2. *adj.*, **–al,** *adj.* stoisch, gelassen. **–ism** [–sɪsm], *s.* der Stoizismus, Gleichmut.

stoke [stoʊk], *v.a.* (also *– up*) schüren (*also fig.*), heizen. **––hold,** *s.* der Heizraum (*Naut.*). **––hole,** *s.* das Schürloch, der Heizraum. **–r,** *s.* der Heizer.

[1]**stole** [stoʊl], *s.* die Stola (*Eccl.*); der Pelzkragen, Umhang.

[2]**stole, –n,** *see* **steal;** *–n goods*, das Diebsgut; *receiver of –n goods*, der Hehler.

stolid [ˈstɔlɪd], *adj.* stumpf, schwerfällig, gleichgültig, gleichmütig. **–ity** [–ˈlɪdɪtɪ], *s.* die Schwerfälligkeit, Stumpfheit.

stolon [ˈstoʊlən], *s.* der Schößling, Ausläufer (*Bot.*).

stoma [ˈstoʊmə], *s.* (pl. *–ta* [stoˈmɑːtə]) die Öffnung, Mündung (*Zool.*, *Anat.*), Spaltöffnung (*Bot.*).

stomach [ˈstʌmək], 1. *s.* der Magen; (*coll.*) Bauch, Leib; (*fig.*) Hunger (*for*, nach); die Eßlust, Neigung, Lust (*for*, zu); *on an empty –*, auf leeren *or* mit leerem Magen, nüchtern; *go against one's –*, einem im Magen liegen; *lie heavy on one's –*, einem schwer im Magen liegen; *lining of the –*, die Magenwand; *turn a p.'s –*, einem Ekel *or* Erbrechen verursachen. 2. *v.a.* (*fig.*) sich (*Dat.*) gefallen *or* bieten lassen, hinnehmen, ertragen, einstecken (*an affront*). **––ache,** *s.* Magenschmerzen (*pl.*). **–er,** *s.* (*archaic*) das Mieder, der Latz. **–ic** [stoˈmækɪk], 1. *adj.* magenstärkend, Magen–. 2. *s.* das Magenmittel, die Magenstärkung. **––pump,** *s.* die Magenpumpe.

stomat–itis [stɔməˈtaɪtɪs], *s.* die Mundfäule, Mundschleimhautentzündung (*Med.*). **–ology** [–ˈtɔlədʒɪ], *s.* die Lehre von Mundkrankheiten.

ston–e [stoʊn], 1. *s.* der Stein (*also Med.*); Steinblock, Felsstein, Felsen; (Obst)Kern; (also *precious –e*) der Edelstein; (also *gall–e*) das Steinleiden (*Med.*); (also *grave–e*) der Grabstein; (*coll.*) (*usually pl.*) der *or* die Hode, der Hoden (*Anat.*); (*no pl.*) der Stein (*weight = 14 lb.*); *kill two birds with one –e*, zwei Fliegen mit einer Klappe schlagen; *break –es*, Steine klopfen; *heart of –e*, steinernes Herz; *leave no –e unturned*, nichts unversucht lassen; *philosopher's –e*, der Stein der Weisen; *rolling –e*, (*fig.*) unsteter Mensch; *a rolling –e gathers no moss*, ein rollender Stein setzt kein Moos an; *–e's throw*, die Steinwurfweite, kurze Entfernung; *throw –es at*, Steine werfen nach; (*fig.*) tadeln, angreifen; *people in glass houses shouldn't throw –es*, wer im Glashause sitzt, soll nicht mit Steinen werfen; *turned to –e*, (wie) versteinert. 2. *adj.* Stein–, steinern. 3. *v.a.* entsteinen (*fruit*); (also *–e to death*) steinigen. **–e Age,** *s.* die Steinzeit. **–e-blind,** *adj.* stockblind. **–ebreak,** *s.* der Steinbrech (*Bot.*). **–e-breaker,** *s.* der Steinklopfer; die Steinbrechmaschine (*Tech.*). **–echat,** *s.* das Schwarzkehlchen; Steinschmätzer (*Orn.*). **–e-coal,** *s.* die Steinkohle. **–e-cold,** *adj.* eiskalt. **–e-coloured,** *adj.* steinfarben. **–ecrop,** *s.* der Mauerpfeffer, die Fetthenne, das Steinkraut (*Bot.*). **–e-cutter,** *s.* der Steinmetz, Steinschleifer (*gems*). **–e-dead,** *adj.* mausetot. **–e-deaf,** *adj.* stocktaub. **–e-dresser,** *s.* *see* **–e-cutter.** **–e-fruit,** *s.* das Steinobst, Kernobst. **–eless,** *adj.* steinlos, kernlos (*fruit*). **–e-marten,** *s.* der Steinmarder (*Zool.*). **–emason,** *s.* der Steinmetz, Steinhauer. **–e-quarry,** *s.* der Steinbruch. **–ewall,** *v.n.* (*coll.*) Obstruktion treiben. **–e-walling,** *s.* die Obstruktion. **––ware,** *s.* das Steingut. **–e-work,** *s.* das Mauerwerk. **–iness,** *s.* das Steinige; (*fig.*) die Härte, Starrheit. **–ing,** *s.* die Steinigung. **–y,** *adj.* steinig, steinern, (stein)hart (*also fig.*); (*sl.*) *see* **–y-broke;** *–y ground*, der Steinboden. (*sl.*) **–y-broke,** *adj.* pleite, abgebrannt. **–y-hearted,** *adj.* hartherzig.

stood [stʊd], *see* **stand.**

stooge [stuːdʒ], *s.* (*sl.*) der Handlanger, willenloses Werkzeug, unterwürfige Kreatur; der Statist (*Theat.*).

stook [stʊk], 1. *s.* der Garbenhaufen, die Hocke. Puppe, die *or* der Mandel. 2. *v.a.* in Haufen zusammensetzen.
stool [stuːl], *s.* der Hocker, Bock; (also *foot*--) Schemel; (also *night*--, *close*--) Nachtstuhl; Stuhl(gang) (*Med.*); Baumstumpf, Wurzelstock; *go to* –, Stuhlgang haben; *office* –, der Kontorstuhl; *fall between two* –*s*, sich zwischen zwei Stühle setzen. **--pigeon,** *s.* (*sl.*) der Lockspitzel.
stoop [stuːp], 1. *v.n.* sich bücken, sich beugen; gebeugt gehen, sich krumm *or* gebeugt halten; (*fig.*) sich herablassen, erniedrigen *or* demütigen; niederschießen (*on*, auf) (*as a bird*). 2. *s.* gebeugte Haltung, krummer Rücken; das Niederschießen (*of a bird*); *have a* –, sich krumm halten; *walk with a* –, gebeugt *or* krumm gehen. **–ing,** *adj.* gebeugt, gebückt; *–ing shoulders*, hängende Schultern (*pl.*).
stop [stɔp], **1.** *v.a.* aufhalten, abhalten, stoppen, hemmen (*movement*); einstellen (*proceedings, payment, work, etc.*), sperren (*a cheque*), zurückhalten, festhalten (*money*), stillen (*blood*), anhalten, zum Stehen bringen (*machines, etc.*), abstellen (*steam, water, etc.*), parieren (*a blow*); ein Ende machen (*Dat.*), unterbinden, abbrechen, aufhören mit (*an activity*); versperren, absperren (*a way, etc.*); (also – *up*) verstopfen, zustopfen, ausfüllen, zumachen (*a hole*), füllen, plombieren (*a tooth*); (also – *short*) zurückhalten, unterbrechen, hindern (*a p.*); greifen (*strings*) (*Mus.*); *be –ped*, aufhören; (*coll.*) – *a bullet*, von einer Kugel getroffen werden; – *a gap*, eine Lücke ausfüllen; – *it!* hör auf damit! laß das! – *a p.'s mouth*, einem den Mund stopfen; – *writing*, hör auf zu schreiben *or* mit Schreiben; (*with adverbs*) – *down*, abblenden (*Phot.*); – *out*, abdecken (*etching*); – *up*, zustopfen, verstopfen. **2.** *v.n.* halten; stillstehen, stehenbleiben (*as clocks*); stoppen, stocken; (also – *short* or *dead*) aufhören, einhalten, anhalten, innehalten; bleiben, sich aufhalten, zu Besuch sein (*with*, bei); interpunktieren (*writing*); –*!* halt! stopp! – *at nothing*, vor nichts zurückschrecken; – *for*, warten auf (*Acc.*); (*with adverbs*) – *in*, zu Hause bleiben; – *out*, ausbleiben, nicht nach Hause kommen; (*coll.*) – *over*, Fahrt unterbrechen; (*coll.*) – *short of*, nicht erreichen; – *up*, aufbleiben. **3.** *s.* das Anhalten, Haltmachen; der Halt, Aufenthalt; Haltepunkt, die Haltestelle, Station; das Aufhalten, Aufhören, Ende, der Einhalt, Stillstand, die Pause; Aufhaltung, Hemmung, Sperrung, Sperre, das Hindernis; die Sperrvorrichtung, Hemmvorrichtung, der Bolzen, Pflock, das Bindsel (*Naut.*); die Blende (*Phot.*); der Zug, das Register, die Stimme (*Org.*); der Griff (*violin*); die Klappe, das Loch, Ventil (*wind instruments*); (*fig.*) der Ton, die Saite, das Stimmregister; Satzzeichen, Interpunktionszeichen (*Typ.*); (also *full* –) der Punkt; Verschlußlaut (*Phonet.*); *come to a* (*dead*) –, (plötzlich) anhalten *or* aufhören; *come to a full* –, zu Ende kommen, nicht weiter kommen; *glottal* –, der Knacklaut (*Phonet.*); *put a* – *on*, sperren, anhalten; *put a* – *to*, abstellen, einstellen, Einhalt tun (*Dat.*), ein Ende machen (*Dat.*). **–cock,** *s.* der Sperrhahn. **–gap,** *s.* der Lückenbüßer, Notbehelf. **--light,** *s.* das Stopplicht, Schlußlicht. **--over,** *s.* (*coll.*) die Fahrtunterbrechung. **–page** [–ɪdʒ], *s.* die Stockung (*traffic, etc.*); Sperrung (*supplies, etc.*); Hemmung (*activity*); Einstellung (*work, payment*); das Anhalten, der Stillstand; Aufenthalt; (Gehalts)-Abzug; die Verstopfung (*Med.*). **–per,** 1. *s.* der Stöpsel, Propf(en); Verschluß; Stopper (*Naut.*); (*coll.*) *put a –per on*, Einhalt tun (*Dat.*), zum Stillstand bringen. 2. *v.a.* verstopfen, zustöpseln. **–ping,** *s.* das Verschließen, die Schließung; Plombe, Zahnfüllung; der Griff (*Mus.*). **–ping-brush,** *s.* die Abdeckbürste (*etching*). **–ping distance,** der Bremsweg, die Bremsstrecke (*Motor.*). **–ping-place,** *s.* die Haltestelle. **–ping train,** der Bummelzug. **–ple,** 1. *s.* der Stöpsel, Pfropf, Spund. 2. *v.a.* zustöpseln **--press,** *s.* letzte Nachrichten. **--volley,** *s.* der Stoppflugball (*Tenn.*). **--watch,** *s.* die Stoppuhr.
stor–age [ˈstɔːrɪdʒ], *s.* das Lagern, Aufspeichern, die Aufbewahrung, Lagerung, (*of goods*); das Lagergeld; *–age battery* or *cell*, der Akkumulator; die Sammlerbatterie; *cold –age*, die Aufbewahrung im Kühlraum *or* auf Eis. **–e** [stɔː], 1. *s.* der Vorrat, das Lager; die Menge, Fülle (*of*, an); (*fig.*) der Schatz, Reichtum (*of*, an); das Lagerhaus, Magazin, der Speicher; Laden (*Amer.*), (*also pl.*) das Warenhaus, Kaufhaus; *pl.* Ausrüstungsgegenstände, Kriegsvorräte, Schiffsvorräte; *for –e*, zum Aufbewahren; *in –e*, vorrätig, auf Lager; *be in –e for a p.*, einem vorbehalten sein *or* bevorstehen; *have in –e for*, bereit *or* aufbewahrt haben für; *put into –e*, einlagern (*furniture, etc.*); *set great –e by*, großen Wert legen auf (*Acc.*); hochschätzen. 2. *v.a.* (also *–e up*) aufbewahren, aufspeichern, sammeln, (ein)lagern (*furniture, etc.*); versehen, versorgen (*with*, mit); verproviantieren (*a ship*); *–e furniture*, Möbel einlagern (*as the owner*); Lagerraum für Möbel bieten. **–ehouse,** *s.* das Lagerhaus, Magazin, der Speicher; (*fig.*) die Schatzkammer, Fundgrube. **–e-keeper, –eman,** *s.* der Lagermeister, Magazinverwalter; (*Amer.*) der Ladenbesitzer. **–e-room,** *s.* die Vorratskammer, Rumpelkammer. **–ey,** *see* ²**story.**
stork [stɔːk], *s.* der Storch (*Orn.*). **–'s-bill,** *s.* der Storchschnabel (*Bot.*).
storm [stɔːm], 1. *s.* der Sturm (*also Mil. & fig.*); das Unwetter; (also *thunder–*) Gewitter; – *of applause*, der Beifallssturm; *the calm after the* –, die Ruhe nach dem Sturm; *after the* – *comes a calm*, auf Regen folgt Sonnenschein; *hail*--, schwerer Hagelfall; *rain*--, der Platzregen; *raise a* –, Aufruhr erregen; *snow*--, der Schneesturm; – *and Stress Period*, die Sturm- und Drangperiode; *take by* –, im Sturm nehmen; *a* – *in a tea-cup*, ein Sturm im Wasserglas. 2. *v.a.* erstürmen, im Sturm nehmen, (*fig.*) bestürmen. 3. *v.n.* toben, wüten (*of wind, rain, etc., also fig.*) (*at*, gegen). **--beaten,** *adj.* vom Sturm gepeitscht. **--bird,** *s.* die Sturmschwalbe. **--bound,** *adj.* vom Sturm festgehalten. **--centre,** *s.* das Sturmzentrum; (*fig.*) der Mittelpunkt *or* Herd der Unruhe. **--cloud,** *s.* die Gewitterwolke. **–cock,** *s.* die Misteldrossel (*Orn.*). **--cone,** *s.* der Sturmkegel (*Naut.*). **–iness,** *s.* das Stürmische, Ungestüm. **–ing** 1. *s.* das Stürmen, Sturmlaufen, die Erstürmung (*Mil.*). 2. *attrib.* Sturm–; *–ing party*, die Sturmkolonne. **–proof,** *adj.* sturmfest. **--sail,** *s.* das Sturmsegel. **--signal,** *s.* das Sturmzeichen, Sturmsignal. **--tossed,** *adj.* vom Sturm umhergetrieben. **–troops,** *pl.* die Sturmtruppen. **–y,** *adj.* stürmisch, (*fig.*) ungestüm; *–y petrel*, die Sturmschwalbe; *--y weather*, das Sturmwetter, Unwetter (*also fig.*).
¹**story** [ˈstɔːrɪ], *s.* die Erzählung, Geschichte; der Bericht; (*coll.*) die Flunkerei, Finte; Handlung; *cock-and-bull* –, das Ammenmärchen; *fairy*--, das Märchen; *as the* – *goes*, wie man sagt, wie es heißt, wie verlautet; *quite another* or *a different* –, etwas völlig anderes; *the* (*same*) *old* –, das alte Lied; *cut* or *make a long* – *short*, um es kurz zu sagen, um zum Ende zu kommen; *short* –, die Novelle. **--book,** *s.* das Geschichtenbuch, Märchenbuch. **--teller,** *s.* der (Geschichten)Erzähler; (*coll.*) Flunkerer. **--telling,** *s.* das Erzählen; (*coll.*) Flunkern.
²**story,** *s.* das Stockwerk, Geschoß, der Stock; *third-- window*, das Fenster im 3. Stock; (*sl.*) *upper*--, der Kopf, das Oberstübchen.
stoup [stuːp], *s.* das Trinkgefäß; Weihwasserbecken.
stout [staʊt], 1. *adj.* stark, fest, kräftig, dauerhaft (*of a th.*); rüstig, tapfer, kühn, wacker, mannhaft, standhaft, standfest (*of p., qualities, resistance, etc.*); dick, beleibt (*of p.*). 2. *s.* starkes dunkles Bier. **–ish,** *adj.* ziemlich beleibt *or* kräftig. **–ness,** *s.* die Stärke, Festigkeit (*of th.*); Mannhaftigkeit, Standhaftigkeit, der Mut; die Beleibtheit. **--hearted,** *adj.* herzhaft, beherzt.
¹**stove** [stoʊv], 1. *s.* der Ofen; das Treibhaus (*Hort.*); *cooking*--, der Kochherd; *gas*--, der Gasherd; *slow-combustion* –, der Dauerofen. 2. *v.a.* trocknen; schwefeln, (mit Schwefelsäuregas) bleichen (*Tech.*); im Treibhaus ziehen (*Hort.*). **--pipe,** *s.* das Ofenrohr; (*coll.*) *--pipe hat*, der Zylinderhut, die Angströhre.
²**stove,** *see* **stave.**
stow [stoʊ], 1. *v.a.* (ver)stauen, (ver)packen, unterbringen, aufbewahren (*things*); vollpacken, füllen

(*a receptacle*) (*with*, mit), (*sl.*) aufhören mit; weglegen, wegschaffen, beiseitelegen, beiseiteschaffen, wegpacken; (*sl.*) – *it!* hör damit auf! 2. *v.n.*; – *away*, als blinder Passagier mitfahren. **-age** [-ɪdʒ], *s.* das Stauen, Packen; der Stauraum, Packraum (*Naut.*); der Stauerlohn (*Naut.*). **-away,** *s.* blinder Passagier.

strab-ismal [strəˈbɪzməl], **-ismic** [-ˈbɪzmɪk], *adj.* Schiel-, schielend. **-ismus** [-ˈbɪzməs], *s.* das Schielen. **-otomy** [-ˈbɔtəmɪ], *s.* die Schieloperation.

straddle [ˈstrædl], 1. *v.n.* die Beine spreizen, breitbeinig gehen *or* stehen, rittlings sitzen; (*fig.*) sich ausdehnen; wankelmütig sein; 2. *v.a.* spreizen (*legs*); breitbeinig stehen auf, rittlings sitzen auf; verdoppeln (*stake*) (*Cards*); eingabeln, decken (*Artil., etc.*). 3. *s.* das Spreizen, Rittlingssitzen; die Stellage, Arbitrage (*C.L.*). **--legged,** *adj.* breitbeinig.

strafe [strɑ:f], 1. *v.a.* strafen; (*coll.*) beschießen, bombardieren (*Mil.*). 2. *s.* (*coll.*) der Angriff, die Beschießung, Bombardierung.

straggl-e [ˈstrægl], *v.n.* umherstreifen, umherschweifen; sich hinziehen, zerstreut *or* abseits liegen *or* gehen; zurückbleiben, sich entfernen; wuchern (*as plants*); (*fig.*) abweichen, abschweifen. **-er,** *s.* der Herumstreicher; Nachzügler (*Mil.*); wilder Schößling (*Hort.*). **-ing,** *adj.*, (*coll.*) **-y,** *adj.* umherschweifend, zerstreut, sich zerstreuend *or* abseits halten; zurückgeblieben; widerspenstig (*hair*); wuchernd (*Hort.*).

straight [streɪt], 1. *adj.* gerade (*also fig.*); unmittelbar, direkt; (*coll.*) offen, redlich, anständig, rechtschaffen, verläßlich, zuverlässig; (*only pred.*) geordnet, in Ordnung; – *as an arrow* or *a poker*, kerzeng(e)rade; – *as a die*, (*fig.*) grundehrlich; *keep a – face*, ein ernstes Gesicht bewahren; (*sl.*) *get a p.* –, einen richtig verstehen; – *hair*, glattes Haar; *make* or *put* –, in Ordnung bringen; – *line*, die Gerade (*Math.*); (*coll.*) – *play*, das Drama; – *tip*, zuverlässiger Tip. 2. *adv.* gerade, geradewegs, in gerader Linie, stracks, direkt, unmittelbar; (also – *out*) geradezu, offen heraus; (*coll.*) *think* –, logisch denken; – *away*, sofort, sogleich; stracks, auf der Stelle; – *ahead*, – *on*, geradeaus; – *off*, see – *away*. **--edge,** *s.* das Richtscheit, Lineal. **-en** 1. *v.a.* (also *-en out*) gerade machen *or* richten, glatt ziehen; (usually *-en out*) in Ordnung bringen, entwirren. 2. *v.n.* gerade werden; sich aufrichten; *-en out*, sich fangen (*Av.*); *-en up*, sich aufrichten. **-forward,** *adj.* schlicht, einfach; (*fig.*) gerade, ehrlich, aufrichtig, offen, redlich. **-forwardness,** *s.* die Offenheit, Ehrlichkeit, Redlichkeit, Aufrichtigkeit. **-ness,** *s.* die Geradheit; (*coll.*) Offenheit, Ehrlichkeit. **-way,** *adv.* sofort, auf der Stelle.

[1]**strain** [streɪn], 1. *v.a.* straff anziehen *or* anspannen, strecken, spannen; (*fig.*) überanstrengen (*one's eyes, etc.*); Gewalt antun (*Dat.*), übertreiben, pressen (*meaning*); schädigen, beeinträchtigen; verstauchen, verrenken, zerren (*a muscle, etc.*); drücken, pressen (*to one's heart, etc.*); (durch)pressen, (durch)seihen, (durch)sieben, filtrieren, läutern (*a fluid*); – *one's eyes towards*, die Augen richten auf; – *every nerve*, sein Äußerstes tun, alles aufbieten; – *a point*, zu weit gehen. 2. *v.n.* fest ziehen, zerren (*at*, an); sich anstrengen *or* abmühen, streben, eifern (*for* or *after*, nach); beim Stuhlgang drücken; durchsickern; – *at a gnat*, bei Kleinigkeiten Umstände machen. 3. *s.* die Anstrengung, Anspannung; Überanstrengung; der Druck, die Spannung, Belastung, Beanspruchung, Inanspruchnahme; Verstauchung, Verrenkung, Zerrung (*Surg.*); (*often pl.*) Weise, Melodie, Tonfolge, Klänge (*pl.*); der Gesang, das Gedicht; (*fig.*) die (Ausdrucks)Weise, (Ton)Art, Manier; der Ton, Stil, Charakter; *at full* –, mit höchster Anstrengung; *be a – on one's nerves*, einem auf die Nerven gehen *or* fallen; – *on his pocket*, starke Inanspruchnahme seines Geldbeutels; *put a great – on*, große Anforderungen stellen an; *march to the – of*, unter den Klängen (*Gen.*) marschieren; *be under a* –, unter Druck stehen. **-ed,** *adj.* gespannt (*relations, etc.*); gezwungen, unnatürlich. **-er,** *s.* das Filtriertuch, der Filter; (Tee)Sieb.

[2]**strain,** *s.* die Linie, Abkunft, das Geschlecht; die Zucht, Art; Charaktereigenschaft; ererbter Charakter; die Neigung, der Hang (*of*, zu); die Beimischung, der Anflug.

strait [streɪt], 1. *adj.* (*archaic*) eng, schmal; hart, streng. 2. *s.* (*usually pl.*) die Meerenge, Straße; (*fig.*) Verlegenheit, Klemme, Patsche; *financial -s*, finanzielle Schwierigkeiten; *reduce to desperate -s*, in eine Zwangslage bringen. **-en,** *v.a.* (*archaic*) eng machen, verengen; begrenzen, beschränken, einengen; (*only pass.*) in Verlegenheit bringen, bedrängen; *-ened circumstances*, beschränkte *or* bedrängte Verhältnisse. **– jacket,** *s.* die Zwangsjacke. **--laced,** *adj.* (*fig.*) prüde, korrekt, pedantisch, engherzig, gestreng. **-ness,** *s.* die Enge, Strenge.

strake [streɪk], *s.* der Plankengang (*Naut.*).

stramineous [strəˈmɪnɪəs], *adj.* Stroh-, strohfarben.

[1]**strand** [strænd], 1. *s.* (*Poet.*) der Strand, das Ufer. 2. *v.a.* auf den Strand setzen *or* werfen; (*fig.*) zum Scheitern bringen, scheitern lassen; *be left -ed*, auf dem Trockenen sitzen. 3. *v.n.* stranden; *-ed property*, das Strandgut.

[2]**strand,** *s.* die Faser; Ducht, Litze (*of rope*); Strähne (*of hair*); – *of wire*, die Drahtlitze; *-ed wire*, der Litzdraht.

strange [streɪndʒ], *adj.* fremd, unbekannt, neu (*to* (*Dat.*)); fremdartig, wunderlich, seltsam, merkwürdig, sonderbar; ausländisch; nicht vertraut, unerfahren (*to*, mit) (*of a p.*); – *to say*, seltsamerweise. **-ness,** *s.* die Fremdartigkeit, Merkwürdigkeit, Seltsamkeit, Wunderlichkeit; Fremdheit. **-r,** *s.* Fremde(r) *m.*, der Fremdling; Unbekannte(r) *m.*, Unerfahrene(r) *m.*, der Neuling; Unbeteiligte(r) *m.* (*Law*); *be a -r to*, unbekannt sein mit, unerfahren sein in, nicht vertraut sein mit, fremd sein; (*coll.*) *you are quite a -r*, ich habe dich ewig nicht gesehen; (*coll.*) *little -r*, das Nesthäkchen; *be -rs to each other*, sich nicht kennen; *no -r to*, wohl vertraut mit; *spy -rs*, die Räumung der Galerie beantragen (*Parl.*).

strang-le [ˈstrængl], *v.a.* erwürgen, erdrosseln; einschnüren (*as a collar*); (*fig.*) unterdrücken, ersticken. **-lehold,** *s.* der Halsgriff (*wrestling*). (*fig.*) **-les,** *pl.* (*usually sing. constr.*) die Druse (*Vet.*). **-ulate,** *v.a.* abbinden, abschnüren (*Med., Bot.*); *-ulated hernia*, eingeklemmter Bruch. **-ulation** [-ˈleɪʃn], *s.* die Erwürgung, Erdrosselung; Abschnürung, Einklemmung (*Med.*). **-ury** [-jərɪ], *s.* der Harnzwang, Harndrang (*Med.*).

strap [ˈstræp], 1. *s.* der Riemen; Gurt, die Strippe, das Schnürband; der Treibriemen (*Tech.*); Metallbügel, das Metallband (*Tech.*); Blatthäutchen, die Ligula (*Bot.*); der Stropp (*Naut.*); der Tragriemen (*of a rucksack*); *shoulder--*, der (Achsel)Träger (*of underwear*); die Achselklappe (*Mil.*). 2. *v.a.* mit Riemen befestigen; festschnallen, anschirren; mit Heftpflaster befestigen (*Med.*); mit einem Riemen züchtigen. **--hanger,** *s.* stehender Fahrgast (*in a bus, etc.*). **-less,** *adj.* trägerlos (*dress*). **-pado** [strəˈpeɪdoʊ], 1. *s.* der Wippgalgen (*Hist.*). 2. *v.a.* wippen. **-per,** *s.* (*coll.*) strammer Bursche, strammes Mädchen. **-ping,** 1. *adj.* (*coll.*) stämmig, stramm; drall (*of a girl*). 2. *s.* Riemen, Bänder (*pl.*).

strat-agem [ˈstrætədʒəm], *s.* der Kriegsplan, die Kriegslist (*Mil.*); (*fig.*) die List, der Kunstgriff. **-egic(al)** [strəˈtɪ:dʒɪk(l)], *adj.* strategisch. **-egist** [ˈstrætədʒɪst], *s.* der Stratege. **-egy** [ˈstrætədʒɪ], *s.* die Feldherrnkunst, Kriegskunst; Strategie; (*fig.*) List, Taktik.

strathspey [stræθˈspeɪ], *s.* lebhafter schottischer Tanz.

strati-fication [strætɪfɪˈkeɪʃən], *s.* die Schichtung (*Geol.*). **-form** [ˈstrætɪfɔ:m], *adj.* schichtenförmig. **-fy** [ˈstrætɪfaɪ], *v.a.* schichten; *-fied rock*, das Schichtgestein. **-graphic(al)** [-ˈgræfɪk(l)], *adj.* Formations-, stratigraphisch. **-graphy** [-ˈtɪgrəfɪ], *s.* die Formationskunde (*Geol.*).

strato-cracy [strəˈtɔkrəsɪ], *s.* die Militärherrschaft, Militärregierung. **--cumulus** [ˈstreɪtoˈkju:mjʊləs], *s.* der Stratokumulus, (geschichtete) Haufenwolke. **-sphere** [ˈstrætəsfɪ:ə], *s.* die Stratosphäre.

strat-um ['streɪtəm] *s.* (pl. *-a* [-tə]) die Schicht (*also fig.*); Lage; *social -a*, die Gesellschaftsschichten. **-us** [-təs], *s.* niedrige Schichtwolke.

straw [strɔ:], 1. *s.* das Stroh; der Strohhalm (*also fig.*); (*fig.*) die Kleinigkeit; *not care a* –, sich nichts daraus machen; *clutch* or *grasp at a* –, sich an die letzte Hoffnung klammern, nach einem Strohhalm greifen; *last* –, letzter Schlag, der Rest; *that's the last* –, das fehlte (mir, *etc.*) gerade noch; das ging (mir, *etc.*) über die Hutschnur; *the* (*last*) – *that breaks the camel's back*, der Tropfen, der das Faß zum Überlaufen bringt; *not worth a* –, keinen Heller *or* Pfifferling wert; *man of* –, der Strohmann; (*fig.*) vorgeschobene Person. **– bid,** *s.* das Scheingebot (*Amer.*). **--board,** *s.* die Strohpappe. **--coloured,** *adj.* strohfarben, strohgelb. **-hat,** der Strohhut. **--thatched,** *adj.* strohgedeckt. **– vote,** *s.* die Probeabstimmung (*Pol.*). **-y** *adj.* strohartig.

strawberry ['strɔ:bərɪ], *s.* die Erdbeere; *– jam*, die Erdbeermarmelade. **--mark,** *s.* das (rote) Muttermal.

stray [streɪ], 1. *v.n.* sich verirren *or* verlaufen; herumirren; abgehen, abirren (*from*, von); weglaufen (*from*, von); umherstreifen, wandern (*as eyes*); (*fig.*) irren, vom Wege abweichen; abschweifen (*as the attention*). 2. *adj.* verirrt, verlaufen; einzeln, vereinzelt, zerstreut, gelegentlich, zufällig; – *thoughts*, Gedankensplitter. 3. *s.* verirrtes Tier; Heimatlose(r) *m.*, Herumirrende(r) *m.*; *pl.* atmosphärische Störungen (*Rad.*). **-ed,** *adj.* verirrt, verlaufen.

streak [strɪ:k], 1. *s.* der Streifen, Strich; die Schliere (*Geol.*); Ader, Maser (*in wood*); (*fig.*) der Anflug, Einschlag; – *of lightning*, der Blitz(strahl). 2. *v.a.* streifen. 3. *v.n.* rasen, flitzen, wie ein geölter Blitz sausen. **-y,** *adj.* streifig, gestreift; geädert, gemasert (*as wood*); durchwachsen (*as bacon*).

stream [strɪ:m], 1. *s.* der Bach, Fluß, Strom, (Wasser)Lauf, die Strömung (*also fig.*); das Fahrwasser; (*fig.*) die Richtung; Flut (*of light*); *against the* –, gegen *or* wider den Strom; *down*-–, stromabwärts; *up*-–, stromaufwärts; *with the* –, mit dem Strom; *drift with the* –, (*fig.*) mit dem Strom schwimmen; – *of words*, der Wortschwall. 2. *v.n.* strömen, fließen, fluten; überlaufen, triefen (*with*, von); flattern, wehen (*as a flag.*). 3. *v.a.* auswerfen, ausströmen. **--anchor,** *s.* der Stromanker, Warpanker. **-er,** *s.* der Wimpel, kleine Fahne, fliegendes Band; die Papierschlange; der Plakatstreifen, das Transparent; der Lichtstrahl, Lichtstrom. **-ing,** *adj.* strömend. **-let,** *s.* das Bächlein. **--line,** 1. *s.* die Stromlinie. 2. *adj.* (also *--lined*) stromlinienförmig, Stromlinien–; (*fig.*) zeitgemäß, fortschrittlich; schnittig, rassig. 3. *v.a.* Stromlinienform geben (*Dat.*); (*fig.*) modernisieren. **-y,** *adj.* fließend, strömend, flutend.

street [strɪ:t], 1. *s.* die Straße, (*Austr.*) Gasse; *in the*–, auf der Straße; *the man in the* –, (gewöhnlicher *or* einfacher) Mann aus dem Volke, die große Masse; *not in the same – with*, nicht zu vergleichen mit; *be on the -s*, auf den Strich gehen, Prostituierte sein; *walk the -s*, die Straßen ablaufen; see also *be on the -s*. **– arab,** der Straßenjunge, Gassenjunge. **--car,** *s.* die Straßenbahn (*Amer.*). **--corner,** *s.* die Straßenecke. **--door,** *s.* die Haustür. **--fighting,** *s.* der Straßenkampf. **--lamp,** *s.* die Straßenlaterne. **--lighting,** *s.* die Straßenbeleuchtung. **--sweeper,** *s.* der Straßenkehrer; die Straßenkehrmaschine. **-walker,** *s.* die Straßendirne, das Strichmädchen. **-walking,** *s.* die Prostitution.

strength [strɛŋθ], *s.* die Kraft, Stärke (*also Mil.*); Festigkeit, Härte (*of things*); Widerstandskraft (*of a fortress, etc.*); Stärke(wirkung) der Gehalt, Titer (*of liquids*); die Stammrolle, Etatstärke, der (Soll)-Bestand (*Mil.*); überzeugende Kraft (*of argument*); besondere Stärke (*of a p.*); *actual* –, die Iststärke (*Mil.*); *below* –, unter Normalstärke (*Mil.*), unvollzählig; *beyond a p.'s* –, über seine Kraft; *feat of* –, das Kraftstück; *at full* –, vollzählig; *gather* –, wieder zu Kräften kommen; *go from – to* –, von Erfolg zu Erfolg schreiten; *measure one's – with s.o.*, sich mit einem messen; *on the* –, in der Stammrolle (*Mil.*); *on the – of a th.*, auf Grund einer **S., auf eine S. hin, unter Berufung auf eine S.**; *on the – of it*, daraufhin; – *of purpose*, die Willensstärke, Charakterstärke; *squander one's* –, sich verzetteln. **-en,** 1. *v.a.* stärken, stark machen, kräftigen, neue Kraft geben (*Dat.*); verstärken, bekräftigen, vermehren. 2. *v.n.* erstarken, stark *or* stärker werden. **-ener,** *s.* die Stärkung (*to*, für); der Verstärker, das Stärkungsmittel (*Med.*). **-ening,** 1. *adj.* stärkend. 2. *s.* die Verstärkung. **-less,** *adj.* kraftlos.

strenuous ['strɛnjuəs], *adj.* tätig, eifrig, emsig, rastlos, betriebsam, unentwegt; anstrengend; tüchtig, energisch. **-ly,** *adv.* angestrengt. **-ness,** *s.* die Tätigkeit, Energie, Tüchtigkeit, der Eifer.

streptococcus [strɛptə'kɔkəs], *s.* der Streptokokkus.

stress [strɛs], 1. *s.* der Druck, die Kraft, das Gewicht (*also fig.*); (*fig.*) der Nachdruck, die Wichtigkeit; Anspannung, Anstrengung, Beanspruchung; Heftigkeit, das Ungestüm (*of weather, etc.*); die Betonung, der Ton, Akzent (*Metr.*); *lay* – (*up*)*on*, Gewicht *or* Nachdruck legen auf (*Acc.*); *Storm and* –, der Sturm und Drang; *times of* –, Zeiten der Not; *under the – of*, unter dem Druck von, gezwungen durch. 2. *v.a.* Nachdruck *or* Gewicht legen auf; betonen (*also Metr.*), unterstreichen, den Akzent legen auf (*Metr.*); – *the point*, betonen.

stretch [strɛtʃ], 1. *v.a.* strecken, spannen, ziehen, ausdehnen; (also *--out*) ausbreiten, ausstrecken; niederstrecken, zur Strecke bringen (*a p.*); (*fig.*) zu weit ausdehnen, übertreiben, pressen (*meaning*); überschreiten; anspannen (*credit*) (*C.L.*); – *one's legs*, die Beine ausstrecken; (*fig.*) sich Bewegung machen; – *o.s.*, sich (aus)strecken *or* recken *or* rekeln; – *forth* or *out one's hand*, die Hand ausstrecken *or* vorstrecken; – *a point*, ein Übriges tun, fünf gerade sein lassen, ein Auge zudrücken *or* zumachen, eine Ausnahme machen. 2. *v.n.* sich strecken recken *or* rekeln (*of a p.*); sich (aus)dehnen *or* erstrecken, reichen (*to*, bis); sich (aus)weiten (*clothes, etc.*); (*usually neg.*) sich dehnen *or* strecken lassen; (*coll.*) übertreiben, aufschneiden. 3. *s.* die (Aus)Dehnung, Ausweitung; das Strecken, Recken, Rekeln; die (An)Spannung, Anstrengung, Übertreibung, Überschreitung, Überspannung; (Raum- *or* Zeit)Strecke, Reihe; Spanne (*of time*); Fläche, Weite (*in space*); (*sl.*) Zuchthausstrafe; *at a* –, in einem Zuge, durchlaufend, hintereinander; *by any – of* (*the*) *imagination*, bei kühnster Phantasie, beim besten Willen; *give a* –, sich recken; *go for a* –, einen Spaziergang machen; (*coll.*) *go up for a* –, Zuchthausstrafe bekommen; *be on the* –, mit Anspannung aller Kräfte, (*fig.*) angespannt *or* in großer Spannung sein; *nerves on the* –, angespannte Nerven. **-er,** *s.* der (Handschuh)Strecker, Schuhleisten, das Streckwerkzeug; der Spannstab (*of an umbrella*); Fußlatte, das Stemmbrett (*in a boat*); die Tragbahre, Krankenbahre, Krankentrage, Pritsche (*for the sick, etc.*); der Läufer (*Build.*); (*coll.*) die Übertreibung, Flunkerei. **-er-bearer,** *s.* der Krankenträger. (*coll.*) **-y,** *adj.* dehnbar, elastisch; (*coll.*) *be -y*, sich rekeln wollen.

strew [stru:], *v.a.* (be)streuen (*an area*); (also – *about*) ausstreuen (*material*). **-n,** *adj.* bestreut.

stria ['straɪə], *s.* (pl. *striae* [straɪɪ:]) der Streifen, die Furche, Riefe (*on shells*); Riffel (*on pillars*); Schramme (*Geol.*). **-te,** 1. *adj.* ['straɪət], gestreift; gerieft, gefurcht. 2. *v.a.* [straɪ'eɪt], furchen, kritzen (*Geol.*). **-ted** [-'eɪtɪd], *adj. see* **-te,** 1. **-tion** [-'eɪʃən], *s.* die Riefung; Furchung, Riffelung. **-ture** [-'eɪtʃə], *s.* die Anordnung der Furchen.

stricken ['strɪkən], 1. *adj.* getroffen (*of things*); ergriffen, heimgesucht, schwer betroffen (*with*, von) (*of a p.*); (*fig.*) wund, krank (*with*, an); (*archaic*) verwundet; – *in years*, hochbetagt, hochbejahrt; *terror*-–, schreckerfüllt. 2. *pp. of* **strike** (*Amer.*).

strickle [strɪkl], *s.* das Streichholz (*for corn*), das Modelholz (*casting*), das Schleifbrett.

strict [strɪkt], *adj.* streng (*with*, mit *or* gegen); genau, exact, peinlich, strikt; *in – confidence*, streng vertraulich; *in the – sense* (*of the word*), *-ly speaking*, genau genommen. **-ness,** *s.* die Strenge, Genauigkeit.

stricture ['strɪktʃə], *s.* die Striktur, krankhafte Verengerung (*Med.*); (*usually pl.*) tadelnde Bemerkung (*on*, über), scharfe Kritik (*on*, an).

stridden [ˈstrɪdən], *see* **stride.**
stride [straɪd], 1. *s.* langer Schritt; die Schrittlänge; (*fig.*) der Fortschritt; *get into one's –*, richtig in Schwung kommen; *take long –s*, lange Schritte machen; (*fig.*) *make rapid –s*, schnelle Fortschritte machen; *take a th. in one's –*, etwas ohne Schwierigkeiten, so nebenbei *or* spielend bewältigen. 2. *ir.v.n.* schreiten, lange Schritte machen, mit langen Schritten gehen; – *across*, überschreiten, schreiten über; – *along*, dahinschreiten; – *out*, tüchtig ausschreiten. 3. *ir.v.a.* abschreiten, durchschreiten, überschreiten; rittlings sitzen auf (*a horse*).
strident [ˈstraɪdənt], *adj.* kreischend, grell, knarrend.
stridul–ate [ˈstrɪdjʊleɪt], *v.n.* zirpen, schwirren. **–ation** [–ˈleɪʃən], *s.* das Zirpen, Schwirren.
strife [straɪf], *s.* der Streit, Hader, Zank; Krieg, Kampf; *at –*, uneins.
strig–a [ˈstraɪgə], *s.* kleine Borste, steifes Haar. **–ose** [–oʊs], *adj.* borstig.
strik–e [straɪk], **1.** *ir.v.a.* schlagen (*a p. or th.*); ausführen, versetzen (*a blow*); treffen, stoßen an *or* auf, zusammenstoßen mit; einschlagen in (*as lightning*); aufschlagen (*Artil.*); prägen, münzen (*coin, etc.*); streichen (*a flag, sails, etc.*); abbrechen (*a tent*); anstreichen, anzünden (*matches*); einstellen (*work*); (*fig.*) auffallen (*Dat.*), in den Sinn kommen (*Dat.*), Eindruck machen auf; *–e an attitude*, eine (theatralische) Haltung annehmen; *–e an average*, den Durchschnitt nehmen; *–e a balance*, den Saldo ziehen; (*fig.*) einen Ausgleich finden; *–e a bargain*, einen Handel abschließen, handelseinig werden; *–e 8 bells*, 8 Glas glasen (*Naut.*); *–e a blow for*, eine Lanze brechen für; *–e camp*, das Lager abbrechen; *–e a p.'s fancy*, einem gefallen; *the clock has struck the hour*, die Uhr hat voll geschlagen; *–e one's head against*, mit dem Kopfe stoßen gegen; (*Prov.*) *–e while the iron is hot*, man muß das Eisen schmieden, solange es heiß ist; *–e oil*, Petroleum entdecken, (*fig.*) Glück haben, es gut treffen; *–e a rock*, auf einen Felsen auflaufen; *–e roots*, Wurzel schlagen, (*fig.*) fortpflanzen; *–e terror into s.o.*, einem Schrecken einflößen *or* einjagen; *the thought struck me*, mir kam der Gedanke; (*a*) (*with adjectives*) *–e blind*, blind machen, erblinden; *–e dead*, erschlagen; *–e dumb*, zum Schweigen bringen, betäuben; (*sl.*) *–e me pink!* Gott strafe mich!; *–e as strange*, sonderbar vorkommen (*Dat.*); (*b*) (*with adverbs*) *–e down*, niederstrecken, zu Boden schlagen, fällen; *–e off*, abschlagen, abhauen; abziehen, Probedruck machen (*Typ.*); *–e out*, ausstreichen, tilgen, (*fig.*) sich bahnen (*a path*); *–e up*, anstimmen (*a tune*), anknüpfen (*friendship*); (*c*) (*with preposition*) *–e off*, streichen von (*list, etc.*); *–e with*, erfüllen mit (*awe, etc.*); (*fig.*) *be struck with*, ergriffen werden von, eingenommen sein von. **2.** *ir.v.n.* schlagen (*also of clocks*), losschlagen, zustoßen; ausholen, (hin)zielen (*at*, nach); stoßen (*against*, gegen; *on*, an *or* auf), zusammenstoßen, auflaufen (*on a rock*); fallen (*on*, auf) (*of light*); einschlagen (*of lightning*); sich entzünden, angehen (*matches*); sich ergeben, die Flagge streichen; streiken, die Arbeit einstellen; (*fig.*) auffallen, in die Augen fallen; *–e at the root of a th.*, etwas an der Wurzel treffen; *–e back*, sich zur Wehr setzen; *–e home*, sicher treffen, sitzen (*of blows*), (*fig.*) Eindruck machen, wirken; *the hour has struck*, es hat voll geschlagen; *his hour has struck*, seine Stunde hat geschlagen; *–e inwards*, nach innen schlagen (*of disease*); *–e out*, ausschreiten; schwimmen (*for*, nach); einschlagen (*at*, auf); ausholen (*at*, nach); *–e out for o.s.*, sich selbst einen Weg bahnen; *–e up*, anstimmen (*as a singer*), aufspielen (*of an orchestra*). **3.** *s.* der Stoß, Schlag (*at*, nach); Glockenschlag (*Horol.*); Treffer, Aufschlag (*Artil.*); Streik (*Pol.*); das Streichen, die Richtung (*Geol.*); das Abstreichholz (*Tech.*); (*coll.*) der Erfolg, Fund; *on –e*, ausständig, streikend; *be on –e*, streiken; *call off a –e*, einen Streik abbrechen; *come out* or *go on –e*, in den Streik treten; (*coll.*) *make a –e with*, Erfolg haben mit. **–e-breaker,** *s.* der Streikbrecher. **–er,** *s.* der Schläger; Schlagbolzen (*of a gun*); Streikende(r) *m.* **–ing,** *adj.* schlagend (*also fig.*); Schlag– (*clock, etc.*); (*fig.*) auffallend, wirkungsvoll, eindrucksvoll, ausdrucksvoll, treffend; *–ing likeness*, auffallende *or* sprechende Ähnlichkeit. **–ing-distance,** *s.* die Schlagweite. **–ingness,** *s.* das Auffallende, Treffende. **–ing-velocity,** die Aufschlagsgeschwindigkeit (*of a shell*).
string [strɪŋ], 1. *s.* der Bindfaden, die Schnur, das Band; die Sehne (*of a bow*); Saite (*Mus.*); Schnur, Kette (*of pearls, etc.*); Fiber, Faser (*Bot.*); (*fig.*) das Gängelband; (*coll.*) die Reihe, Folge; *pl.* Streichinstrumente; *have* or *lead a p. on a –*, einen am Bande führen *or* gängeln; *hold all the –s*, alle Fäden in der Hand haben; *have two –s to one's bow*, zwei Eisen im Feuer haben; (*fig.*) *pull the –s*, der Drahtzieher sein; *be always harping on the same –*, immer auf der alten Leier spielen. 2. *ir.v.a.* (auf)reihen, aufziehen (*beads, etc.*); besaiten, mit Saiten beziehen (*Mus.*); spannen (*a bow*); abziehen (*beans*); bespannen (*rackets*); (also – *up*) binden, verschnüren; (*coll.*) hängen, schlingen; (*coll.*) (also – *out*) ausstrecken, ausdehnen, (*fig.*) anspannen; *highly strung*, erregbar, reizbar, feinbesaitet, nervös; (*coll.*) – *together*, aneinanderreihen; zusammenfügen; (*sl.*) – *up*, aufhängen. 3. *v.n.* Fäden ziehen (*fluids*). **– -band,** *s.* das Streichorchester. **– -beans** *pl.* grüne Bohnen (*pl.*). **– -course,** *s.* der Sims, Fries (*Arch.*). **–ed,** *adj.* Saiten–, besaitet (*Mus.*). **–er,** *s.* der Tragbalken, Streckbalken (*Bridgeb.*). **–iness,** *s.* die Faserigkeit, Zähigkeit. **– -quartet,** *s.* das Streichquartett. **–y,** *adj.* faserig, zäh; klebrig, Fäden ziehend.
stringen–cy [ˈstrɪndʒənsɪ], *s.* die Strenge, Schärfe, Bündigkeit, Knappheit (*money, etc.*). **–t,** *adj.* streng, scharf, hart; bindend, zwingend, kräftig, nachdrücklich, überzeugend; knapp (*C.L.*).
string–iness, –y, *see* **string.**
strip [strɪp], 1. *v.a.* abstreifen, abziehen; (ab)schälen, abrinden; entkleiden (*also fig.*), ausziehen (*a p.*); abtakeln (*ships*); abmontieren, demontieren (*Mach.*); – *a p. of a th.*, einem etwas entziehen, einen einer S. (*Gen.*) berauben *or* (*of a post*, des Amtes) entkleiden; – *naked* or *to the skin*, nackt *or* bis auf die Haut entkleiden *or* ausziehen. 2. *v.n.* sich ausziehen. 3. *s.* (schmaler) Streifen; – *cultivation*, die Dreifelderwirtschaft (*Agric.*); – *iron*, das Bandeisen. **–ped** [–t], *adj.* nackt, entkleidet. **–per,** *s.* die Schälmaschine. **–ping,** *s.* die Entfärbung (*of walls, etc.*); *–ping agent*, das Abziehmittel, Entfärbungsmittel; *–ping bath*, die Abziehflotte.
stripe [straɪp], 1. *s.* der Streifen, Strich; Striemen, die Strieme; der Hieb, Schlag; die Tresse, Litze, der Ärmelstreifen (*Mil.*); *get one's –s*, die Tressen bekommen, Unteroffizier werden; *stars and –s*, das Sternenbanner; *wound –*, das Verwundetenabzeichen (*Mil.*). 2. *v.a.* streifen. **–d** [–t], *adj.* gestreift, streifig.
stripling [ˈstrɪplɪŋ], *s.* junger Bursche, der Gelbschnabel.
stripy [ˈstraɪpɪ], *see* **striped.**
strive [straɪv], *ir.v.n.* streben (*after*, nach), sich bemühen (*for*, um); sich streiten, kämpfen, ringen, wetteifern (*for*, um).
strode [stroʊd], *see* **stride.**
[1]**stroke** [stroʊk], 1. *s.* der Strich (*of a brush or pen*), Zug (*of a pen*), Schlag (*also Med., Sport, Rowing, and of a clock*), Streich, Hieb (*of an axe, etc.*), Stoß (*Bill., Swimming*); die Schlagart (*Sport*), der (Schicksals)Schlag; Schlaganfall (*Med.*); Hub (*of a piston*), Takt (*of an engine*); (*fig.*) die Leistung; der Vormann, Schlagmann (*Rowing*); *at one –*, mit einem Schlage; – *of business*, ein gutes Geschäft; *down– –*, der Grundstrich; *four– –*, *attrib.* Viertakt– (*engine*); – *of genius*, geniale Leistung; *have a –*, einen Schlaganfall bekommen; – *of luck*, der Glücksfall; *masterly –*, das Meisterstück; *at* or *with a – of the pen*, mit einem Federstrich; *on the –*, pünktlich; *on the – of three*, Schlag drei; *row –*, als Vormann *or* Schlagmann rudern; *up– –*, der Haarstrich; *not do a – of work*, keinen Handschlag arbeiten. 2. *v.a.*; – *a boat*, als Schlagmann rudern. **– -oar,** *s.* **–s-man** [–smən], *s.* der Schlagmann.
[2]**stroke,** *v.a.* streichen, streicheln; – (*up*) *the wrong way*, ärgern, reizen.
stroll [stroʊl], 1. *s.* das Herumziehen, Herumschlendern; kleiner Spaziergang; *go for* or *take*

a –, einen Bummel machen. 2. *v.n.* spazierengehen, bummeln, schlendern, herumschlendern. **–er,** *s.* umherziehender Schauspieler; der Bummler. **–ing,** *adj.* umherziehend; *–ing players*, die Wandertruppe.

stroma [ˈstroumə], *s.* das Bindegewebe, Grundgewebe.

strong [strɔŋ], 1. *adj.* stark (*of a p. or a th., also Gram.*); kräftig (*of a p., voice, etc.*), gesund (*of a p.*); heftig (*as wind*); ranzig (*as a smell, taste, etc.*); laut (*as a voice*); hell, grell (*as light*); (*fig.*) eifrig (*of a p.*), zwingend, überzeugend (*as argument*), triftig, gewichtig, nachdrücklich (*as reasons*); – *candidate*, der Kandidat mit guten Aussichten; *of – character*, charakterfest, willensstark; – *constitution*, feste Gesundheit; – *conviction*, feste Überzeugung; *have – feelings about*, sich erregen über; *with a – hand*, mit Gewalt; – *impression*, tiefer Eindruck; – *language*, Kraftausdrücke (*pl.*); *use – language*, sich kraftvoll ausdrücken, fluchen; – *mind*, kluger Kopf; (*coll.*) *be – on*, Anteil nehmen an, Wert legen auf; *– –point*, *s.* der Stützpunkt (*Mil.*); *my – point*, meine starke Seite; *1000 –*, 1000 Mann stark; *– will*, die Willensstärke; – *on the wing*, schon gut flügge (*of young birds*). 2. *adv.* (*sl.*); *be going –*, sehr gut gehen, noch auf der Höhe sein; *come* or *go it –*, ins Geschirr gehen. (*coll.*) **– –arm methods,** Gewaltmaßnahmen (*pl.*). (*sl.*) **– –arm squad,** die Verbrecherbande. **– –bodied,** *adj.* stark, voll (*of wine*). **– –box,** *s.* die Geldkassette. **–hold,** *s.* die Festung, Feste; der Kampfstand; (*fig.*) das Bollwerk. **–ly,** *adv.* kräftig; *be –ly of the opinion*, der festen Meinung sein; *feel –ly about*, sich erregen über; *–ly recommend*, sehr empfehlen. **– –minded,** *adj.* willensstark, unerschütterlich. **– –room,** der Geldtresor, feuerfestes Gewölbe. **– –willed,** *adj.* eigenwillig, eigensinnig, rechthaberisch.

stronti–a(n) [ˈstrɔnʃɪə(n)], *s.* die Strontianerde, das Strontiumoxyd. **–um** [–ɪəm], *s.* das Strontium.

strop [strɔp], 1. *s.* der Streichriemen (*for razors*); Stropp (*Naut.*). 2. *v.a.* abziehen.

stroph–e [ˈstroufɪ], *s.* die Strophe. **–ic** [–fɪk], *adj.* strophisch.

strove [strouv], *see* **strive.**

strow [strou], (*archaic*) *see* **strew.**

struck [strʌk], *see* **strike;** getroffen, betroffen, bestürzt; ergriffen (*at*, über; *with*, von).

structur–al [ˈstrʌktʃərəl], *adj.* baulich, Bau–, Struktur–; organisch (*disease*); *–al parts*, Bauteile (*pl.*); *–al steelwork*, das Stahlfachwerk; *–al timber*, das Bauholz; *–al weight*, das Rüstgewicht (*Av.*); *–al works*, bauliche Anlagen (*pl.*). **–e** [–tʃə], *s.* das Gebäude, der Bau; Organismus (*Biol.*); Aufbau, die Bauart, Struktur, Anordnung, Gliederung, Zusammensetzung; das Gefüge; *sentence –e*, der Satzbau. **–ed,** *adj.* organisch gegliedert; (*in comps.*) –gebaut, –gefügt. **–eless,** *adj.* unorganisch, ohne Gliederung.

struggle [ˈstrʌgl], 1. *s.* das Ringen, Sträuben, die Anstrengung; der Kampf (*for*, um); *carry on a –*, einen Kampf durchführen; – *for existence*, der Daseinskampf, Kampf ums Dasein; *mental –*, der Seelenkampf. 2. *v.n.* sich anstrengen, sich abmühen, Anstrengungen machen; sich winden, sich sträuben, zappeln; ringen (*for*, um), kämpfen (*for*, für; *with*, mit); – *for breath*, nach Atem ringen; – *to one's feet*, mühsam hochkommen *or* auf die Beine kommen. **–r,** *s.* der Kämpfer.

strum [strʌm], 1. *v.n.* klimpern (*on*, auf). 2. *v.a.* klimpern auf. **–ming,** *s.* das Geklimper.

strum–a [ˈstruːmə], *s.* die Skrofel; der Kropf (*Med.*). **–ose** [–mous], **–ous** [–məs], *adj.* Kropf–, kropfartig; skrofulös.

strumpet [ˈstrʌmpɪt], *s.* die Dirne, Metze, Hure.

strung [strʌŋ], *see* **string;** *highly–*–, nervös.

¹strut [strʌt], 1. *v.n.* sich brüsten *or* spreizen, stolzieren. 2. *s.*, **–ting,** *s.* das Sichbrüsten, Stolzieren; die Geziertheit, Affektiertheit.

²strut, *s.* der Strebebalken, die Strebe, Stütze, Steife, Verstrebung (*Build.*). **–ting,** *s.* Strebebalken (*pl.*), die Versteifung, Verstrebung.

struthious [ˈstruːθɪəs], *adj.* Strauß– (*Orn.*).

strychnine [ˈstrɪknɪn], *s.* das Strychnin.

stub [stʌb], 1. *s.* der Stumpf, Stummel; (also *– –nail*) Kuppnagel; (*coll.*) die Kippe. 2. *v.a.* (usually – *up*) roden (*land*), ausroden, entwurzeln (*stumps*); (*coll.*) sich stoßen an; (*coll.*) – *out*, ausmachen (*cigarette*); – *one's toe*, mit dem Fuß stoßen (*against* or *on*, gegen *or* an). (*coll.*) **–by,** *adj.* untersetzt.

stubbl–e [ˈstʌbl], *s.* die Stoppel; das Stoppelfeld; (Bart)Stoppeln (*pl.*). **–y,** *adj.* Stoppel–, stopp(e)lig, spitz(ig).

stubborn [ˈstʌbən], *adj.* hartnäckig, widerspenstig, eigensinnig, starrköpfig, halsstarrig (*of a p.*); unbeugsam, beharrlich, starr, standhaft (*of things*); strengflüssig, spröde (*Metall.*). **–ness,** *s.* die Hartnäckigkeit, Halsstarrigkeit, der Eigensinn (*of a p.*); die Strengflüssigkeit.

stubby, *see* **stub.**

stucco [ˈstʌkou], 1. *s.* der Stuck, (also *– –work*) die Stuckatur, Stuckarbeit, Stuckverzierung. 2. *v.a.* mit Stuck überziehen.

stuck [stʌk], *see* **²stick;** (*coll.*) – *up*, *adj.* aufgeblasen, hochnäsig.

¹stud [stʌd], *s.* das Gestüt; Pferde eines Rennstalles (*pl.*). **– –book,** *s.* das Zuchtbuch, Stammbuch von Vollblutpferden. **– –farm,** *s.* das Gestüt. **– –groom,** *s.* der Stallknecht. **– –horse,** *s.* der Zuchthengst. **– –mare,** *s.* die Zuchtstute.

²stud, 1. *s.* der Knauf, Beschlagnagel, (Vorhemd– *or* Kragen)Knopf; (*Amer.*) Manschettenknopf; Steg, die Warze, Stiftschraube (*Tech.*); der Ständer, Pfosten, die (Wand)Säule (*Build.*). 2. *v.a.* beschlagen, verzieren (*with nails, etc.*); (*fig.*) besetzen, besäen. **– –bolt,** *s.* der Schraubenbolzen. **– –chain,** *s.* die Stegkette.

studding-sail [ˈstʌdɪŋseɪl], *s.* das Beisegel (*Naut.*).

stud–ent [ˈstjuːdənt], *s.* der Student, Studierende(r) *m.*, der Hörer (*Univ.*); Forscher, Gelehrte(r) *m.*; der Liebhaber; *pl.* die Studentenschaft (*Univ.*), Hörer (*pl.*) (*of a professor*); Schüler (*pl.*); *be a –ent of*, studieren; *–ent of law*, der Student der Rechte; *medical –ent*, der Student der Medizin; *–ents' hostel*, das Studentenheim; *–ents' union*, der Studentenausschuß. **–entship,** *s.* das Stipendium; die Studentenzeit; *travelling –entship*, das Reisestipendium. **–ied** [ˈstʌdɪd], *adj.* durchdacht, wohlüberlegt, gut einstudiert; vorbedacht, vorsätzlich, geflissentlich, gesucht; studiert, gelehrt. **–io** [ˈstjuːdɪou], *s.* das (Künstler)Atelier; Aufnahmeatelier (*Films*); der Senderaum, Aufnahmeraum (*Rad.*). **–ious** [–dɪəs], *adj.* fleißig, arbeitsam, wissensdurstig; gelehrtenhaft; bedacht (*of*, auf (*Acc.*)), beflissen, bemüht; geflissentlich, gesucht. **–iousness,** *s.* der Fleiß, Eifer. **–y** [ˈstʌdɪ], 1. *s.* das Studieren, Lernen, (wissenschaftliches) Studium; das Forschen, die Forschung, wissenschaftliche Untersuchung, die Studie (*in* or *of*, über *or* zu) (*also Arts*); Etüde (*Mus.*); der Fleiß, das Bestreben, Bemühen; (*coll.*) etwas Untersuchungswertes, das (Studien)Fach; das Arbeitszimmer, Herrenzimmer, Studierzimmer; *brown –y*, die Träumerei; *make a –y of*, eingehend studieren; *make a –y of doing*, es darauf absehen zu tun. 2. *v.a.* studieren, durchforschen, sorgsam untersuchen *or* lesen; (er)lernen, einstudieren (*a part, etc.*); sorgsam beobachten, bedacht sein auf; entgegenkommen, zu gefallen suchen (*Dat.*). 3. *v.n.* studieren (*at a univ.*); dem Studium obliegen; suchen, sich bemühen. **–y-group,** *s.* die Arbeitsgemeinschaft.

stuff [stʌf], 1. *s.* der Stoff (*also fig.*), das Material, der Rohstoff; Wollstoff, das Zeug, Gewebe; die Masse, der Ganzstoff, das Feinzeug (*Paperm.*); Baumaterial; (*fig.*) innerer Gehalt; (*coll.*) dummes Zeug, der Unsinn; (*coll.*) – *gown*, der Wolltalar (*Law*); (*sl.*) *good – !* ausgezeichnet! trefflich! bravo! *green –*, das Gemüse; – *and nonsense!* dummes Zeug! *the – that heroes are made of*, das Holz aus dem Helden geschnitzt sind; (*sl.*) *that's the – !* so ist's richtig! 2. *v.a.* vollstopfen, vollpacken; ausstopfen (*dead animals, etc.*); farcieren, füllen (*Cook.*); (*coll.*) stecken, schieben, packen, polstern (*chairs*); (*vulg.*) – *o.s.*, sich vollstopfen *or* überessen; – *up*, zustopfen, verstopfen, (*coll.*) zum besten haben, einseifen (*a p.*); (*sl.*) *–ed shirt*, vornehmer Wichtigtuer. 3. *v.n.* (*coll.*) sich vollstopfen, fressen. **–iness,** *s.* die Dumpfigkeit;

Muffigkeit, Schwüle (*air, etc.*); (*coll.*) Blasiertheit, Lang(e)weile (*of a p.*). **-ing,** *s.* das Stopfen, die Verstopfung; Füllung (*also Cook.*); das Polstermaterial; Füllsel, die Farce (*Cook.*); (*coll.*) *knock the -ing out of a p.*, einen klein kriegen *or* gefügig machen. **-y,** *adj.* stickig, dumpf, schwül, muffig; verstopft (*nose, etc.*); (*coll.*) langweilig, stumpf.

stultify ['stʌltɪfaɪ], *v.a.* dumm *or* lächerlich machen; nutzlos *or* wirkungslos machen, widerlegen; – *itself*, sich zum Narren halten.

stumbl-e ['stʌmbl], 1. *v.n.* stolpern (*also fig.*), straucheln; (*fig.*) fehlen, einen Fehltritt machen; in der Rede stocken; *-e into* unerwartet geraten in; *-e (up)on*, zufällig stoßen auf (*Acc.*), geraten auf (*Acc.*), unerwartet finden. 2. *s.* das Straucheln, Stolpern; (*fig.*) der Fehler, Fehltritt. **-ing,** *s.* das Stolpern, Gestolper. **-ing-block,** *s.* das Hindernis (*to*, für), der Stein des Anstoßes.

stumer ['stju:mə], *s.* (*sl.*) gefälschte Münze.

stump [stʌmp], 1. *s.* der Stumpf (*of a tree, a tooth, a limb*), Stummel (*of a cigar, etc.*), Strunk (*of a branch*); Stab (*Crick.*); der Wischer (*Draw.*); (*coll.*) das Bein; *buy on the* –, auf dem Stamm kaufen (*timber*); (*coll.*) *stir one's -s*, Beine machen, die Beine unter die Arme nehmen; *go on the –, take the –*, politische Propagandareise machen; *draw (the) -s*, das Spiel abbrechen (*Crick.*). 2. *v.a.* (*esp. pass.*) in Verlegenheit setzen, verblüffen; (also – *out*) den Dreistab eines außerhalb der Schlagmallinie stehenden Schlägers umwerfen (*Crick.*); abtönen (*Draw.*); – *the country*, als Wahlredner herumziehen; (*coll.*) – *up*, blechen, berappen (*money*). 3. *v.n.* schwerfällig gehen, stapfen, tappen; (*sl.*) – *up*, mit dem Gelde herausrücken, Kosten bestreiten, bluten, herhalten *or* aufkommen müssen (*for*, für). **-ed** [-t], *adj.* (*coll.*) verblüfft. (*coll.*) **-er,** *s.* verblüffende Frage; der Torhüter (*Crick.*). **--orator,** *s.* der Wahlredner, Volksredner. **-y,** *adj.* stämmig, untersetzt.

stun [stʌn], *v.a.* betäuben; niederschmettern, überwältigen; verblüffen; erschlagen. **-ner,** *s.* (*sl.*) der Prachtkerl, die Pfundsache, Bombensache. **-ning,** *adj.* betäubend, niederschmetternd; (*sl.*) fabelhaft, famos.

stung [stʌŋ], *see* **sting.**

stunk [stʌŋk], *see* **stink.**

[1]**stunt** [stʌnt], *v.a.* im Wachstum hindern, (*fig.*) verkümmern. **-ed,** *adj.* verkümmert, verkrüppelt. **-edness,** *s.* die Verkümmerung.

[2]**stunt,** 1. *s.* (*coll.*) die Kraftleistung, Kraftprobe, das Kunststück; der Kunstflug (*Av.*); Reklameschlager, das Reklamestück, Schaustück; sensationelle Überraschung *or* Aufmachung, großes Tamtam, der Jux; die Sache, das Geschäft; – *flying*, das Kunstfliegen; – *film*, der Trickfilm; – *press*, die Sensationspresse. 2. *v.n.* (*coll.*) Kunstflugstücke machen. **-er,** *s.* der Kunstflieger. **-ing,** *s.* das Kunstfliegen.

stupe [stju:p], 1. *s.* heißer Umschlag, die Bähung. 2. *v.a.* einen heißen Umschlag anlegen *or* auflegen (*Dat.*); bähen. **-faction** [stu:pə'fækʃən], *s.* die Betäubung, Abstumpfung; (*fig.*) Verblüffung, Bestürzung. **-fy** ['stju:pəfaɪ], *v.a.* betäuben, abstumpfen; verdummen; verblüffen, bestürzen, verdutzen.

stupendous [stjʊ'pɛndəs], *adj.* erstaunlich, riesig. **-ness,** *s.* das Ungeheure, Erstaunliche.

stupid ['stju:pɪd], *adj.* dumm; töricht, einfältig, albern, stumpfsinnig; (*archaic*) betäubt, benommen (*with*, von); – *fellow*, der Dummkopf. **-ity** [stjʊ'pɪdɪtɪ], *s.*, **-ness,** *s.* die Dummheit, Albernheit, Einfalt, der Stumpfsinn. **-ly,** *adv.* dummerweise.

stupor ['stju:pə], *s.* die Betäubung, Erstarrung; Stumpfheit, der Stumpfsinn.

sturd-iness ['stə:dɪnɪs], *s.* die Stärke, Kräftigkeit, Festigkeit. **-y,** *adj.* stark, kräftig, derb, fest, standhaft.

sturdy ['stə:dɪ], *s.* die Drehkrankheit (*of sheep*).

sturgeon ['stə:dʒən], *s.* der Stör (*Ichth.*).

stutter ['stʌtə], 1. *v.n.* stottern, stammeln. 2. *v.a.* (often – *out*) herausstammeln. 3. *s.* das Stottern, Stammeln; *have a* –, stottern. **-er,** *s.* der Stotterer, Stammler.

[1]**sty** [staɪ], 1. *s.* der (Schweine)Stall (*also fig.*). 2. *v.a.* in einen Schweinestall einsperren.

[2]**sty(e),** *s.* das Gerstenkorn (*in*, an) (*Med.*).

stygian ['stɪdʒɪən], *adj.* stygisch; höllisch, abscheulich.

styl-e [staɪl], 1. *s.* der Stil, die Ausdruckweise, Schreibweise; guter Stil; der (Bau)Stil, die Bauart, der (Kunst)Stil, die Manier, das Genre; die Lebensart, der Lebensstil, die Mode; Art, Art und Weise; Aufmachung, Machart, der Typ; die Anrede, Benennung, Bezeichnung, der Titel; die Zeitrechnung; der Griffel (*Hist.*, *also Bot.*); Zeiger (*of sun-dial*); (Grab)Stichel, die (Radier)-Nadel; Sonde (*Surg.*); *in -e*, stilvoll; (*coll.*) *in fine -e*, fein, nobel; *latest -e*, letzte *or* neueste Mode; *live in (grand or great) -e*, auf großem Fuße leben; *new -e*, neuer Stil, neue Zeitrechnung; *in the same -e*, in derselben Art; *that -e of thing*, derartiges; *under the -e of*, unter dem Namen *or* der Firma von. 2. *v.a.* benennen, betiteln, anreden. **-et** [-lɪt], *s.* das Stilett; die Sonde (*Surg.*). **-iform** [-ɪfɔ:m], *adj.* griffelförmig (*Bot.*). **-ish** [-ɪʃ], *adj.* stilvoll, modisch, elegant, fesch. **-ishness,** *s.* die Eleganz. **-ist,** *s.* der Stilist, Meister des Stils. **-istic** [-'lɪstɪk], *adj.* stilistisch, Stil–. **-istically,** *adv.* dem Stil nach, in stilistischer Hinsicht. **-ite** [-laɪt], *s.* der Säulenheilige(r) *m.*, der Stilit. **-ize** [-aɪz], *v.a.* stilisieren. **-o** [-loʊ], *s. see* **-ograph.** **-obate** [-ləbeɪt], *s.* abgestuftes Fußgestell (*Arch.*). **-ograph** [-ləgrɑ:f], *s.* die Füllfeder, der Kugelschreiber. **-oid** [-lɔɪd], *adj.* griffelförmig; *-oid process*, der Griffelfortsatz (*Anat.*).

stym-ie, -y ['staɪmɪ], 1. *s.* die Lage der Bälle in gerader Linie mit dem Loch (*Golf*); (*fig.*) Lahmlegung. 2. *v.a.* durch diese Lage das Spiel des Gegners hindern; (*fig.*) lahmlegen, hindern, durchkreuzen (*a plan, etc.*).

styptic ['stɪptɪk], 1. *adj.* blutstillend; – *pencil*, der Alaunstift. 2. *s.* blutstillendes Mittel.

suasi-on ['sweɪʒən], *s.* die Überredung; *moral -on*, gütliches Zureden. **-ve** [-sɪv], *adj.* überredend, überzeugend, zuredend (*of*, zu).

suav-e [sweɪv], *adj.* höflich, verbindlich, gewinnend, glatt; lieblich (*as wine*). **-ity,** *s.* die Höflichkeit, Anmut; Lieblichkeit, Annehmlichkeit.

sub [sʌb], 1. *prep.* unter; – *judice*, vor Gericht, noch nicht entschieden; – *rosa*, vertraulich, unter dem Siegel der Verschwiegenheit. 2. *s. coll. abbr. for* **subaltern, submarine, subordinate, substitute,** *or* **subscription,** *q.v.* 3. *v.n.* (*coll.*); – *for*, vertreten. 4. *prefix* Unter–, Grund–; Neben–, Hilfs–, Nach–; annähernd, kaum, teilweise. **-acetate,** *s.* basischessigsaures Salz. **-acid,** 1. *s.* säuerliche Substanz. 2. *adj.* säuerlich. **--acute,** *adj.* latent (*Med.*). **-alpine,** *adj.* subalpin. **-arctic,** *adj.* subarktisch. **--audible,** *adj.* kaum or nicht mehr hörbar. **--breed,** *s.* die Unterart (*Zool.*). **--calibre gun,** *s.* die Abkommkanone. **-caudal,** *adj.* unter dem Schwanz liegend. **-clavian,** *adj.* unter dem Schlüsselbein befindlich. **--committee,** *s.* der Unterausschuß. **-conscious,** 1. *s.* das Unterbewußtsein. 2. *adj.* unterbewußt. **-consciousness,** *s.* das Unterbewußtsein. **--continent,** *s.* der Landteil. **--contract,** *s.* der Nebenvertrag. **--contractor,** *s.* der Nebenlieferant. **-contrary,** *adj.* subkonträr (*Log.*). **-costal,** *adj.* unter den Rippen liegend. **-cutaneous,** *adj.* subkutan, unter der Haut befindlich. **--dean,** *s.* der Unterdechant. **--deity,** *s.* die Nebengottheit. **-divide,** 1. *v.a.* unterteilen, noch einmal teilen. 2. *v.n.* in Unterabteilungen zerfallen. **-division,** *s.* die Unterabteilung; Unterteilung. **--dominant,** *s.* die Unterdominante, Quarte (*Mus.*). **-duct,** *v.a.* abziehen. **--editor,** *s.* der Hilfsredakteur, zweiter Redakteur. **--equal,** *adj.* fast gleich. **--family,** *s.* die Unterfamilie. **-febrile,** *adj.* annähernd fiebernd. **--genus,** *s.* die Unterart. **-glacial,** *adj.* teilweise glazial; unter dem Gletscher befindlich. **-heading,** *s.* der Untertitel. **-human,** *adj.* annähernd menschlich; (*fig.*) minderwertig. **-jacent,** *adj.* darunter *or* tiefer liegend; (*fig.*) zugrundeliegend. **-join,** *v.a.* hinzufügen, hinzusetzen; beilegen, beifügen. **--kingdom,** *s.* die Unterabteilung (*Bot. & Zool.*). **-lease,** *s.* die

Afterverpachtung, Untervermietung. **–lessee,** *s.* der Untermieter, Unterpächter. **–let,** *v.a.* weitervermieten, untervermieten. **– -librarian,** *s.* der Bibliothekar. **– -lieutenant,** *s.* der Leutnant (*Nav.*). **–lingual,** *adj.* unter der Zunge liegend. **–lunar(y),** *adj.* unter dem Monde befindlich; (*fig.*) irdisch. **– -machine-gun,** *s.* die Maschinenpistole. **–marine,** 1. *adj.* unterseeisch, Untersee–. 2. *s.* das Unterseeboot. **–maxillary,** *adj.* unter dem Kinnbacken befindlich. **–multiple,** *s.* der in einer Zahl mehrere Male enthaltene Faktor. **–normal,** *adj.* unternormal. **– -order,** *s.* die Unterabteilung, Unterordnung (*Zool. & Bot.*). **–rogation,** *s.* die Subrogation, Unterschiebung (*Law*). **–section,** *s.* der Unterabschnitt, die Unterabteilung. **–soil,** *s.* der Untergrund (*Agric.*). **– -species,** *s.* die Unterart. **–stage,** die Unterstufe (*Geol.*); der Träger (*of a microscope*). **– -station,** *s.* die Nebenstelle. **–stratum,** *s.* die Unterschicht (*Geol.*); Unterlage, Grundlage, das Substrat (*Phil.*); der Nährboden, Keimboden (*Biol.*). **–struction,** *s.* **–structure,** *s.* der Unterbau, die Grundlage. **–tenancy,** *s.* die Untermiete. **–tenant,** *s.* der Untermieter, Unterpächter. **–title,** *s.* der Untertitel; *pl.* die Unterschrift, erklärende Worte (*Films*). **–tonic,** *s.* 7. Ton der Tonleiter (*Mus.*). **–tropic(al),** *adj.* subtropisch. **–tropics,** *pl.* subtropische Gegenden (*pl.*). **--variety,** *s.* die Unterart (*Bot.*).

subaltern [ˈsʌbəltən], 1. *s.* der Leutnant (*Mil.*); Unterbeamte(r), Untergebene(r) *m.* 2. *adj.* subaltern, untergeordnet, Unter–.

subdivide, *see under* **sub–.**

subdu-al [səbˈdjuːəl], *s.* die Unterwerfung. **–e** [–ˈdjuː], *v.a.* unterwerfen, unterjochen (*a p.*) (*to* (*Dat.*)); bezwingen, überwältigen (*a th.*); (*fig.*) bändigen, bezähmen (*feelings, etc.*); unterdrücken, mildern, dämpfen (*light, colours, etc.*). **–ed** [–ˈdjuːd], *adj.* matt, gebrochen, zart (*as colours*).

suber [ˈsjuːbə], *s.* der Kork. **–ic** [–ˈbɛrɪk], *adj.* Kork–. **–in** [–bərɪn], *s.* der Korkstoff. **–ose** [–bəroʊs], **–ous** [–bərəs], *adj.* Kork–, korkig.

subjacent, *see under* **sub–.**

subject [ˈsʌbdʒɛkt], 1. *adj.* untertan (*to* (*Dat.*)); ausgesetzt, unterworfen (*to* (*Dat.*)); (*coll.*) empfindlich (*to,* gegen), geneigt (*to,* zu); – *to* (*often adverbially*), abhängig von, vorbehaltlich, gemäß, nach; – *to this,* unter diesem Vorbehalt; *be – to,* unterliegen (*Dat.*), abhängig sein von; vorbehalten sein; – *to duty,* zollpflichtig; – *to reservations,* unter Vorbehalt. 2. *s.* der Untertan, Staatsangehörige(r), *m.*; das Thema (*also Mus.*), der Gegenstand, Stoff, Inhalt, die Veranlassung, Ursache (*for,* zu); das (Studien)Fach; Subjekt (*Log., Gram.*); Ich, die Substanz (*Phil.*); der (Versuchs)Gegenstand; die Leiche, der Kadaver (*Anat.*); die Person, Versuchsperson (*Med.*); *British –,* britischer Staatsangehöriger; *compulsory –s,* obligatorische Fächer; *on the –,* hinsichtlich (*of* (*Gen.*)); *optional –s,* wahlfreie *or* fakultative Fächer; – *catalogue,* der Realkatalog; – *index,* das Sachverzeichnis, Sachregister; – *matter,* der Gegenstand, (Gegenstands)Stoff; – *reference,* der Gegenstandsverweis. 3. *v.a.* [səbˈdʒɛkt], unterwerfen, unterziehen; (*to* (*Dat.*)); aussetzen (*Dat.*); *be –ed to,* unterzogen werden (*Dat.*). **–ion** [səbˈdʒɛkʃən], *s.* die Unterwerfung (*to,* unter), die Abhängigkeit (*to,* von); *be in –ion,* unterworfen sein, unterstehen (*to* (*Dat.*)); *bring under –ion,* unterwerfen. **–ive** [–ˈdʒɛktɪv], 1. *s.* der Nominativ. 2. *adj.* subjektiv, persönlich, einseitig; Subjekts– (*Gram.*). **–iveness,** *s.,* **–ivity** [sʌbdʒɛkˈtɪvɪtɪ], *s.* die Subjektivität. **–ivism** [–ˈdʒɛktɪvɪzm] *s.* der Subjektivismus.

subjoin, *see under* **sub–.**

subjugat-e [ˈsʌbdʒʊgeɪt], *v.a.* unterjochen, unterwerfen (*to* (*Dat.*)). **–ion** [–ˈgeɪʃən], *s.* die Unterjochung.

subjunctive [səbˈdʒʌŋktɪv], 1. *adj.* konjunktivisch. 2. *s.* der Konjunktiv.

sublet, *see under* **sub–.**

sublimat-e [ˈsʌblɪmət], 1. *s.* das Sublimat. 2. *adj.* sublimiert. 3. *v.a.* [–meɪt], sublimieren, verflüchtigen (*Chem.*); (*fig.*) veredeln, vergeistigen, erhöhen, erheben (*to,* zu *or* in). **–ion** [–ˈmeɪʃən], *s.* die Sublimation, Verflüchtigung (*Chem.*), (*fig.*) Veredelung, Vergeistigung, Erhebung.

sublim-e [səˈblaɪm], 1. *adj.* erhaben, hoch, hehr; (*coll.*) vollendet, hervorragend, hochgradig, kraß; *–e Porte,* die Hohe Pforte. 2. *s.* das Erhabene. **–inal** [–ˈlɪmɪnəl], *adj.* unterbewußt. **–ity** [–ˈlɪmɪtɪ], *s.* die Erhabenheit, Vornehmheit.

submarine, *see under* **sub–.**

submer-ge [səbˈməːdʒ], 1. *v.a.* unter Wasser setzen, überschwemmen (*land, etc.*), untertauchen; (*fig.*) übertönen, unterdrücken; *–ged tenth,* allerärmste Bevölkerungsschicht. 2. *v.n.* untersinken, untertauchen; tauchen (*as submarines*). **–gence,** *s.* das Untertauchen, Untersinken; die Überschwemmung; (*fig.*) das Versunkensein. **–sion** [–ˈməːʃən], *s.* das Untertauchen.

submissi-on [səbˈmɪʃən], *s.* die Unterwerfung (*to,* unter); Ergebenheit, Unterwürfigkeit, der Gehorsam. **–ve** [–ˈmɪsɪv], *adj.* unterwürfig, ergeben, gehorsam; *be –ve to,* gehorchen (*Dat.*). **–veness,** *s.* die Unterwürfigkeit, Ergebenheit.

submit [səbˈmɪt], 1. *v.a.* vorlegen, übergeben, beibringen (*to* (*Dat.*)) (*testimonial, etc.*); anheimstellen (*to* (*Dat.*)) (*suggestion, etc.*); unterwerfen, aussetzen (*to* (*Dat.*)) (*a p. or th.*); zu erwägen *or* bedenken geben; – *o.s.,* sich unterwerfen *or* unterziehen (*to* (*Dat.*)), sich fügen (*to,* in). 2. *v.n.* sich ergeben *or* fügen (*to,* in), sich unterwerfen (*to* (*Dat.*)), nachgeben; – *to treatment,* sich behandeln lassen.

subordinat-e [səˈbɔːdɪnət], 1. *adj.* untergeordnet, nachgeordnet, unterstellt (*to* (*Dat.*)); Unter–, nebensächlich, unwichtig; *be –e to a th.,* einer S. an Bedeutung nachstehen; *–e clause,* der Nebensatz. 2. *s.* Untergebene(r), *m.*; nebensächliche *or* untergeordnete S. 3. *v.a.* [–neɪt], unterordnen (*a th.*) (*Dat.*), zurückstellen (*a p.*) (*to,* hinter). **–ion** [–ˈneɪʃən], *s.* die Unterordnung, Unterwerfung (*to,* unter); Unterwürfigkeit. **–ive,** *adj.* unterordnend.

suborn [səˈbɔːn], *v.a.* anstiften, verleiten, bestechen. **–ation** [–ˈneɪʃən], *s.* die Anstiftung, Verleitung, Bestechung.

subpoena [səbˈpɪːnə], 1. *s.* (also *writ of –*) die Vorladung unter Strafandrohung. 2. *v.a.* unter Strafandrohung vorladen.

subreption [səbˈrɛpʃən], *s.* die Erschleichung (*Law*).

subrogation, *see under* **sub–.**

subscribe [səbˈskraɪb], 1. *v.a.* unterschreiben (*a document*), unterzeichnen (*one's name*); zeichnen, (*to,* zu; *for,* für), beitragen, beipflichten (*to* (*Dat.*)), anerkennen. 2. *v.n.*; *– for,* vorausbestellen (*a book*); zeichnen auf (*a loan*); – *to,* anerkennen, einwilligen in, zustimmen (*Dat.*), annehmen (*a proposal*), sich verschreiben (*Dat.*) (*a doctrine*), abonnieren auf (*a newspaper*). **–r** [–bə], *s.* der Unterzeichner; Abonnent, Subskribent (*to,* auf), Vorausbesteller (*for* (*Gen.*)) (*a book*), Zeichner (*to* or *for,* auf), der Fernsprechteilnehmer (*Phone*).

subscription [səbˈskrɪpʃən], *s.* die Unterzeichnung, Unterschrift, Einwilligung (*to,* zu *or* in), Zustimmung (*to,* zu); (Geld)Zeichnung, Subskription (*to,* auf), das Abonnement (*to,* auf) (*to newspapers, etc.*); gezeichnete Summe (*to a loan*), der (Mitglieds)-Beitrag (*club, etc.*); die Grundgebühr (*Phone*). **– -list,** *s.* die Subskriptionsliste, Zeichnungsliste. **– -price,** *s.* der Subskriptionspreis, Bezugspreis.

subsequen-ce [ˈsʌbsɪkwəns], *s.* späteres Eintreten. **–t,** *adj.* folgend, später, nachherig, Nach–; subsequent (*Geol.*); *–t to,* nach, später als, folgend auf; *–t upon,* infolge. **–tly,** *adv.* darauf, später, hernach, nachher, nachträglich.

subserv-e [səbˈsəːv], *v.a.* förderlich *or* dienlich sein (*Dat.*), fördern. **–ience** [–ɪəns], *s.,* **–iency,** *s.* die Dienlichkeit, der Nutzen (*to,* für); die Unterwürfigkeit (*to,* gegenüber); *in –ience to,* aus Willfährigkeit gegen. **–ient,** *adj.* dienlich, nützlich, förderlich (*to,* für), dienstbar, untergeordnet; unterwürfig, gehorsam (*to* (*Dat.*)).

subside [səbˈsaɪd], *v.n.* sich setzen, absetzen (*Chem.*), sich senken, sinken, absacken (*of a th.*), einsinken, zusammensinken (*as ground*), sich niederlassen (*of a p.*); (*fig.*) sich legen, nachlassen, abnehmen, abflauen, (ver)fallen. **–nce** [ˈsʌbsɪdəns], *s.* das Sinken, Sichsetzen; Zusammensinken; die

(Boden)Senkung; (*fig.*) Abnahme, das Nachlassen, Versinken.
subsidiary [səbˈsɪdɪərɪ], 1. *adj.* Hilfs–, Neben–, Subsidiar–, untergeordnet; behilflich, mitwirkend (*to*, bei); *be – to*, ergänzen, unterstützen, dienen (*Dat.*); – *company*, die Tochtergesellschaft; – *subject*, das Nebenfach; – *treaty*, der Subsidienvertrag. 2. *s.* (*usually pl.*) die Hilfe, Stütze; der Gehilfe, Helfer; die Filiale; *pl.* Hilfstruppen.
subsid–ize [ˈsʌbsɪdɑɪz], *v.a.* Subsidien zahlen für, mit Geld unterstützen, Zuschuß geben (*Dat.*), subventionieren. **–y,** *s.* (staatliche) Unterstützung, die Subvention, Geldbeihilfe; *pl.* Subsidien (*pl.*).
subsist [səbˈsɪst], 1. *v.n.* existieren, bestehen, in Gebrauch *or* Kraft sein; sich erhalten; – *on*, leben *or* sich ernähren von 2 *v.a.* erhalten, unterhalten **–ence,** *s.* das Dasein, die Existenz; der (Lebens)Unterhalt, das Auskommen; *–ence allowance*, der Unterhaltzuschuß (*Mil.*); *–ence minimum*, das Existenzminimum.
subsoil, *see under* **sub–.**
substan–ce [ˈsʌbstəns], *s.* die Substanz (*Phil. and Phys.*), Wesenheit (*Phil.*, *Theol.*), der Stoff (*Phys. and fig.*), Körper, die Masse; das Wesen, Wesentliche; die Hauptsache; (*fig.*) der Inhalt, Gehalt, Kern, Gegenstand; das Kapital, Vermögen, Mittel (*pl.*); *in –ce*, im Wesentlichen; *man of –ce*, vermögender Mann. **–tial** [səbˈstænʃəl], *adj.* wesenhaft, substantiell (*Phil.*), wesentlich, materiell, wirklich, echt, wahrhaft, beträchtlich, ansehnlich; nahrhaft, reichlich, gehaltvoll (*as food*); stark, fest, kräftig, solid(e), dauerhaft; wohlhabend, vermögend. **–tiality** [–stænʃɪˈælɪtɪ], *s.* die Wesenheit, Substantialität, Wirklichkeit; Stärke, Festigkeit, Gediegenheit. **–tially,** *adv.* in der Hauptsache, im Wesentlichen. **–tiate** [–ˈstænʃɪeɪt], *v.a.* bestätigen, erhärten; dartun, nachweisen, beweisen; stärken, kräftigen; Dasein *or* Wirklichkeit geben (*Dat.*). **–tiation** [–ˈeɪʃən], *s.* die Erhärtung, Bestätigung; der Beweis; die Verwirklichung.
substantiv–al [sʌbstənˈtɑɪvl], *adj.* substantivisch, Substantiv–. **–e** [ˈsʌbstəntɪv], 1. *adj.* wirklich, real, wesentlich, beträchtlich; unabhängig, selbständig; besoldet (*Mil.*); substantivisch (*Gram.*); *–e law*, materielles Recht. 2. *s.* das Hauptwort, Substantiv.
substitut–e [ˈsʌbstɪtjut], 1. *v.a.* ersetzen (*for*, durch), austauschen (*for*, für) (*a th.*); einsetzen (*in the place of*, an Stelle von), an die Stelle setzen (*for*, für) (*a p. or th.*). 2. *v.n.*; *–e for*, vertreten (*a p*). 3. *s.* der Ersatz; Ersatzstoff; Stellvertreter, Ersatzmann (*Mil.*); Ersatz, das Ersatzmittel, Surrogat; *act as a –e for*, vertreten (*a p.*), als Ersatz dienen für (*a th.*). **–ion** [–ˈtjuːʃən], *s.* der Ersatz, die Ersetzung (*also Biol.*), Substitution (*for*, durch), Einsetzung (*for*, für), Stellvertretung; Einsetzung eines Nacherben (*Law*). **–ive,** *adj.* Ersatz–.
substratum, *see under* **sub–.**
subsum–e [səbˈsjuːm], *v.a.* subsumieren, zusammenfassen (*under*, unter); einbegreifen, einschließen, einreihen (*in*, in); in sich schließen. **–ption** [–ˈsʌmpʃən], *s.* die Zusammenfassung, Einreihung (*under*, unter).
subtend [səbˈtɛnd], *v.a.* gegenüberliegen (*Dat.*); *–ed by*, einer Seite gegenüberliegend (*Geom.*).
subterfuge [ˈsʌbtəfjuːdʒ], *s* die Ausflucht, der Vorwand.
subterrane–an [sʌbtəˈreɪnɪən], *adj.*, **–ous** [–nɪəs], *adj.* unterirdisch; (*fig.*) heimtückisch, heimlich.
subtil–e [ˈsʌbtɪl], *adj.* (*archaic*) *see* **subtle. –ization** [–ɑɪˈzeɪʃən], *s.* die Verfeinerung (*also fig.*), Verdünnung; (*fig.*) Spitzfindigkeit. **–ize** [–ɑɪz], 1. *v.a.* verfeinern, verflüchtigen; (*fig.*) ausklügeln, spitzfindig erklären. 2. *v.n.* spitzfindig sein, sich in Spitzfindigkeiten ergehen.
subtl–e [ˈsʌtl], *adj.* fein (*also fig.*), zart, dünn; (*fig.*) kunstreich, sinnreich, scharfsinnig; spitzfindig; heimtückisch, hinterlistig. **–ety** [ˈsʌtəltɪ], *s.* die Feinheit, Zartheit (*also fig.*); (*fig.*) der Scharfsinn; Spitzfindigkeit, Hinterlist, Schlauheit.
subtra–ct [səbˈtrækt], *v.a.* abziehen, subtrahieren. **–ction** [–ˈtrækʃən], *s.* das Abziehen, die Subtraktion; (*fig.*) der Abzug, die Wegnahme **–hend** [ˈsʌbtrəhɛnd], *s.* der Subtrahend (*Arith.*).
suburb [ˈsʌbəːb], *s.* (*often pl.*) die Vorstadt, der Vorort. **–an** [səˈbəːbən], 1. *adj.* vorstädtisch, Vorstadt–, Vororts–, (*fig.*) spießig, kleinstädtisch. 2. *s.* der Vorstadtbewohner, Vorstädter. **–anite,** *s.* der Kleinstädter, Vorstädter. **–ia** [–ˈbəːbɪə], *s.* die Vorstadtswelt.
subvention [səbˈvɛnʃən], *s.* der Zuschuß, die Beisteuer, Subvention, Unterstützung. **–ed,** *adj.* subventioniert.
subver–sion [səbˈvəːʃən], *s.* der Umsturz, die Zerstörung, Vernichtung, gewaltsame Beseitigung. **–sive** [–sɪv], *adj.* umstürzlerisch, umstürzend, Umsturz–, Wühl–, zerstörend; *be –sive of* or *to*, untergraben, zerstören. **–t** [–ˈvəːt], *v.a.* umstürzen, unstoßen, gewaltsam beseitigen, zerstören; erschüttern, untergraben.
subway [ˈsʌbweɪ], *s.* die Unterführung; (*Amer.*) Untergrundbahn.
succeed [səkˈsiːd], 1. *v.n.* folgen (*to* (*Dat.*)) *or* auf (*Acc.*)) (*of things*); folgen (*to*, auf (*Acc.*)), nachfolgen (*to* (*Dat.*)) (*of a p.*); glücken (*with*, bei); gelingen (*of things*), Erfolg haben (*with*, bei) (*of a p.*); *I –ed in doing*, es gelang mir zu tun; *he –s in everything*, alles gelingt ihm *or* glückt bei ihm; *nothing –s like success*, ein Erfolg zieht den andern nach sich; – *to a p.*, einen beerben; – *to the throne*, auf den Thron folgen; – *to the title*, den Titel erben; – *with a p.*, sich bei einem durchsetzen. 2. *v.a.* folgen (*Dat. or* auf (*Acc.*) (*a p. or th.*), nachfolgen (*Dat.*) (*a p.*)); – *a p. in office*, sein Amt antreten; – *a p. to the throne*, einem auf den Thron folgen.
success [səkˈsɛs], *s.* der Erfolg, erfolgreicher Ausgang, das Gelingen, Glück, glückliches Ergebnis; erfolgreiche Person *or* Sache, die Glanzleistung, der Furore; *be a –*, ein Erfolg sein, Erfolg haben (*of a th.*), erfolgreich sein (*of a p.*), *make a – of*, Erfolg haben mit; *wish a p. – in*, einem Glück wünschen zu; *with –*, erfolgreich; *without –*, erfolglos. **–ful,** *adj.* erfolgreich, glücklich; *be –ful*, Erfolg haben. **–ion** [–ˈsɛʃən], *s.* das Folgen; die Folge, Reihe, Reihenfolge; Erbfolge, Nachfolge, Übernahme (*to* (*Gen.*)); das Erbfolgerecht; die Erbfolgeordnung; Erbschaft, das Erbe (*to* (*Gen.*)); die Nachkommenschaft; Fruchtfolge (*of crops*); *apostolical –ion*, apostolische Nachfolge *or* Sukzession; *in –ion*, aufeinander, nacheinander, hintereinander; *in quick –ion*, in rascher Folge; *in –ion to*, als Nachfolger von; *be next in –ion to*, als nächster auf einen folgen; *right of –ion*, das Erbfolgerecht; *–ion states*, Nachfolgestaaten (*pl.*); *–ion to the throne*, die Thronfolge; *war of –ion*, der Erbfolgekrieg. **–ive** [–ˈsɛsɪv], *adj.* aufeinanderfolgend. **–ively,** *adv.* nacheinander, hintereinander **–or** [–ˈsɛsə], *s.* der Nachfolger (*of* (*Gen.*); *to*, für *or* (*Gen.*) (*a p.*); *of* or *to*, auf *or* in (*a th.*)); *–or to the throne*, der Thronfolger.
succinct [səkˈsɪŋkt], *adj.* kurz, bündig. **–ness,** *s.* die Kürze, Bündigkeit.
succory [ˈsʌkərɪ], die Zichorie (*Bot.*).
succose [ˈsʌkous], *adj.* saftig.
succotash [ˈsʌkətæʃ], *s.* ein Gericht aus Bohnen, Mais, etc. (*Amer.*).
succour [ˈsʌkə], 1. *s.* die Hilfe, Unterstützung, der Beistand; das Hilfsmittel, der Entsatz (*Mil.*); *pl.* Hilfstruppen (*pl.*). 2 *v.a.* helfen, beistehen (*Dat.*).
succulen–ce [ˈsʌkjuləns], **–cy** [–ənsɪ], *s.* die Saftigkeit. **–t,** *adj.* saftig (*also fig.*).
succumb [səˈkʌm], *v.n.* unterliegen (*to* (*Dat.*)), weichen, nachgeben (*before*, vor) (*to a p.*), erliegen (*Dat.*), zusammenbrechen (*to*, unter) (*to a th.*); sterben.
succursal [səˈkəːsəl], 1. *adj.* Filial–, Tochter– (*Eccl.*) 2. *s.* die Zweigniederlassung (*of a sect*).
succuss [səˈkʌs], *v.a.* schütteln. **–ion,** *s.* das Schütteln, die Erschütterung.
such [sʌtʃ], 1. *adj.* solch, derartig, so groß, so (*before adjectives*); – *and* –, so einer, der und der; – *another*, eben ein solcher, auch so einer; – *as it is*, so wie es (*etc.*) ist, wenn man es (*etc.*) so nennen darf; *a thing – as this*, ein derartiges Ding; *be – as to . . .*, so groß sein daß . . .; – *as* (*after pl. noun*), wie zum Beispiel; – *a one*, ein solcher, eine solche, so eine; *I never heard – a thing*, ich habe so etwas nie gehört; *there is – a thing*, so etwas gibt es; *no* –

thing, nichts dergleichen; – *thoughts as those*, solche *or* derartige Gedanken wie diese; *at – a time*, zu solcher *or* einer solchen Zeit; *at – a time as suits you*, zu jeder Zeit die Ihnen paßt; – *is life*, so geht's in der Welt; – *a tone*, ein solcher Ton; – *was the noise*, der Lärm war dermaßen groß. 2. *pron.* ein solche (–r, –s), eine solche, solche (*pl.*); *and* –, und dergleichen; *another* –, ein anderer solcher, noch ein solcher; *cold as* –, Kälte als solche; – *as*, diejenigen *or* solche welche; alle die. **–like,** *adj.* (*coll.*) dergleichen.

suck [sʌk], 1. *v.a.* saugen, lutschen; saugen *or* lutschen an; einsaugen; (*fig.*) aufnehmen, holen, gewinnen (*from*, aus); – *the blood of s.o.*, (*fig.*) einem das Blut aussaugen; – *one's thumb*, an dem Daumen lutschen; – *a pipe*, eine Pfeife ziehen; – *in*, einsaugen, absorbieren, aufnehmen, (hin)-einziehen; – *out*, aussaugen; – *up*, aufsaugen. 2. *v.n.* saugen, lutschen (*at*, an), ziehen (*at*, an); einziehen (*as a pump*); (*vulg.*) – *up to a p.*, einen am Arsch lecken. 3. *s.* das Saugen; der Strudel, Wirbel; *give – to*, säugen, stillen; *take a – at*, saugen an. **–er,** *s.* der Sprößling (*Hort.*); das Saugorgan (*Zool.*); der Seehase, Lumpfisch (*Ichth.*); die Saugscheibe, das Saugrohr (*Mech.*); (*coll.*) der *or* das Lutschbonbon; (*sl.*) der Dummerjan, Dummkopf, Gefoppte(r), *m.* **–ing,** 1. *adj.* saugend. 2. *s.* das Saugen. **–ing-pig,** *s.* das Spanferkel. **–ing-pump,** *s.* die Saugpumpe. **–le,** *v.a.* säugen, stillen. **–ling,** *s.* das Säugen; der Säugling.

sucrose [ˈsuːkrous], *s.* der Rohrzucker.

suct–ion [ˈsʌkʃən], *s.* das Saugen (*also fig.*), Ansaugen, die Einsaugung, Zugkraft, der Sog. **–ion-pipe,** *s.* das Ansaugrohr, Einsaugrohr. **–ion-pump,** *s.* die Saugpumpe. **–orial** [sʌkˈtɔːriəl], *adj.* Saug– (*Bot.*, *Zool.*).

suda–rium [sjuˈdɛːərɪəm], *s.* (pl. *–ria* [–rɪə]), das Schweißtuch (der Heiligen Veronika). **–tion** [–ˈdeɪʃən], *s.* der Schweiß, das Schwitzen. **–torium** [–dəˈtɔːrɪəm], *s.* das Schwitzbad. **–tory** [ˈsjuː-dətərɪ], 1. *s.* schweißtreibendes Mittel; *see also* **–torium.** 2. *adj.* schweißtreibend, Schweiß–, Schwitz–.

sudden [ˈsʌdən], *adj.* plötzlich, unvorhergesehen, unerwartet; hastig, vorschnell (*as actions*); (*all*) *of a* –, (ganz) plötzlich. **–ness,** *s.* die Plötzlichkeit.

sudorif–erous [sjuːdəˈrɪfərəs], *adj.*, **–ic** [–ˈrɪfɪk], 1. *adj.* schweißtreibend, schweißabsondernd. 2. *s.* schweißtreibendes Mittel.

suds [sʌdz], *pl.* (usually *soap*-–) das Seifenwasser, die Seifenlauge.

sue [sjuː], 1. *v.a.* verklagen (*for*, wegen), belangen (*for*, um), anhalten (*for*, um). 2. *v.n.* klagen (*for*, auf), eine Klage einreichen (*for*, um; *to*, bei); flehen, bitten (*for*, um); – *for a th.*, etwas einklagen.

suède [sweɪd], *s.* das Wildleder.

suet [sjuɪt], *s.* das Nierenfett; der Talg; – *pudding*, der Pudding aus Mehl und Talg. **–y,** *adj.* talgig, Talg–.

suffer [ˈsʌfə], 1. *v.a.* ertragen, erdulden, (er)leiden; (*usually neg.*) leiden, dulden, ausstehen; (zu)-lassen, gestatten, erlauben. 2. *v.n.* leiden (*from*, an; (*fig.*) *from* or *under*, unter); Schaden erleiden; erleiden (*death, casualties, etc.*); bestraft werden, büßen (*for*, für). **–able** [–rəbl], *adj.* erträglich. **–ance** [–əns], *s.* die Duldung, Einwilligung; (*archaic*) das Leiden, Erdulden; *on –ance*, unter stillschweigender Duldung, nur geduldet. **–er,** *s.* Leidende(r) *m.* (*from*, an); der Dulder, Märtyrer; Geschädigte(r), *m.*; *fellow –er*, der Unglücksgefährte, *be a –er by*, leiden durch, verlieren bei; *be a –er from*, leiden an. **–ing,** 1. *adj.* leidend. 2. *s.* das Leiden, Dulden.

suffice [səˈfaɪs], *v.n.* genügen, ausreichen, hinreichen, hinreichend sein (*for*, für]; – *it to say*, es genüge zu sagen.

sufficien–cy [səˈfɪʃənsɪ], *s.* die Genüge Hinlänglichkeit, Zulänglichkeit, Angemessenheit; hinreichendes Auskommen; hinreichende Zahl *or* Menge; (*archaic*) hinreichende Fähigkeit. **–t,** *adj.* genügend, ausreichend, hinlänglich, hinreichend (*for*, für), genug; (*archaic*) tauglich, fähig (*for*, zu); *be –t*, genügen; *it is –t for me*, es genügt mir; *–t reason*, zureichender Grund; (*B.*) *–t unto the day is the evil thereof*, jeder Tag hat seine Plage. **–tly,** *adv.* genügend, zur Genüge.

suffix [ˈsʌfɪks], 1. *s.* die Nachsilbe, das Suffix. 2. *v.a.* [səˈfɪks], als Suffix anfügen (*to*, an) (*Gram.*); (*fig.*) anhängen, anfügen (*to*, an).

suffocat–e [ˈsʌfəkeɪt], 1. *v.a.* ersticken; *be –ed*, (*fig.*) erdrückt *or* benommen werden (*with*, von). 2. *v.n.* ersticken; (*fig.*) umkommen (*with*, vor). **–ing,** *adj.* erstickend; stickig (*air*). **–ion** [–ˈkeɪʃən], *s.* die Erstickung, das Ersticken; *death by –ion*, der Erstickungstod; (*fig.*) *to –ion*, bis zum Ersticken.

suffrag–an [ˈsʌfrədʒən], (also *–an bishop*), *s.* der Suffraganbischof. **–e** [ˈsʌfrɪdʒ], *s.* das Stimmrecht, Wahlrecht; die (Wahl)Stimme; die Abstimmung; *female –e*, das Frauenstimmrecht; *universal –e*, allgemeines Wahlrecht. **–ette** [–rəˈdʒɛt], *s.* die Frauenrechtlerin. **–ist,** *s.* der Stimmrechtler.

suffus–e [səˈfjuːz], *v.a.* übergießen, benetzen (*of liquids*); überziehen, bedecken (*of colours*), überfluten, überströmen, durchfluten (*of light*); (*fig.*) erfüllen; *–ed with blushes*, schamrot. **–ion** [–ˈfjuːʒən], *s.* die Übergießung, Überflutung; die Blutunterlaufung; Schamröte, Errötung.

sugar [ˈʃugə], 1. *s.* der Zucker; *beet* –, der Rübenzucker; *cane* –, der Rohrzucker; *castor* –, der Streuzucker; *lump* –, der Stückenzucker; *lump of* –, das Stück Zucker; – *of lead*, der Bleizucker; *maple* –, der Ahornzucker. 2. *v.a.* zuckern, (*fig.*) versüßen. **-–basin,** *s.* die Zuckerdose. **-–beet,** *s.* die Zuckerrübe. **– candy,** *s.* der Kandis(zucker). **-–cane,** das Zuckerrohr. **-–caster,** der Zuckerstreuer. **-–coated,** *adj.* verzuckert. (*coll.*) **-–daddy,** *s.* der Weihnachtsmann. **– icing,** *s.* der Zuckerguß. **–iness,** *s.* die Süße; (*fig.*) Süßlichkeit. **–less,** *adj.* ungezuckert. **-–loaf,** *s.* der Zuckerhut, (*fig.*) Bergkegel. **-–maple,** *s.* der Zuckerahorn. **-–mite,** *s.* die Zuckermilbe. **-–plantation,** *s.* die Zucker(rohr)pflanzung. **–plum,** *s.* das Zuckerplätzchen (*also fig.*). **-–refinery,** *s.* die Zuckerfabrik, Zuckerraffinerie. **-–tongs,** *pl.* die Zuckerzange. **–y,** *adj.* zuck(e)rig, zuckersüß; (*fig.*) süßlich.

suggest [səˈdʒɛst], *v.a.* vorschlagen; andeuten, nahelegen, empfehlen, hinweisen auf (*Acc.*), zu verstehen geben; suggerieren, eingeben, einflößen, anregen; – *itself*, sich aufdrängen (*as an idea*); – *itself to a p.*, einem in den Sinn kommen. **–ibility,** *s.* die Beeinflußbarkeit. **–ible,** *adj.* beeinflußbar, zu beeinflussen(d), suggerierbar, suggestibel (*of a p.*). **–ion** [–tʃən], *s.* der Vorschlag, Wink, die Andeutung, Idee, Spur; Anregung; Eingebung, Einflüsterung, Beeinflussung, Suggestion; *at the –ion of*, auf Anregung von; *make a –ion*, einen Vorschlag machen; *no –ion of*, keine Idee von. **–ive** [–tɪv], *adj.* andeutend, anregend; vielsagend; (*fig.*) zweideutig, schlüpfrig; *be –ive of*, deuten auf (*Acc.*), andeuten. **–iveness,** *s.* das Gedankenanregende, Vielsagende; (*fig.*) die Schlüpfrigkeit.

suicid–al [s(j)uːɪˈsaɪdl], *adj.* selbstmörderisch, Selbstmord–. **–e** [ˈs(j)uːɪsaɪd], *s.* der Selbstmord; der Selbstmörder; *commit –e*, Selbstmord begehen.

suint [swɪnt], *s.* das Schafwollfett, der Wollschweiß.

suit [sjuːt], 1. *s.* der Prozeß, die Klage, der Rechtshandel (*Law*); das Gesuch, die Bitte (*to*, an); die Werbung, der (Heirats)Antrag; Satz, die Garnitur; die Farbe (*Cards*); (also – *of clothes*) der Anzug (*of a man*), das Kostüm (*of a woman*); – *of armour*, vollständige Rüstung; *cut one's – according to one's cloth*, sich nach der Decke strecken; *follow* –, Farbe bekennen (*Cards*), (*fig.*) dasselbe tun; – *of harness*, die Geschirrgarnitur. 2. *v.a.* anpassen (*to* (*Dat.*)), einrichten (*to*, nach), sich anpassen an; passen, gefallen, recht sein (*Dat.*) (*a p.*); angemessen sein, entsprechen (*Dat.*), zutreffen auf, passen zu, anstehen (*Dat.*); passen, stehen (*Dat.*), kleiden (*Acc.*) (*as clothes*); bekommen, zusagen (*Dat.*) (*as climate*); – *the action to the word*, dem Worte die Tat folgen lassen; – *the occasion*, sich der Lage anpassen; (*coll.*) – *a p.'s book*, einem in den Kram passen; *the hat –s her* (Scots, *she –s the hat*), der Hut steht ihr; – *a p.'s purpose*, seinem Zwecke entsprechen; (*coll.*)

– *yourself*, tu wie dir beliebt; *are you –ed?* haben Sie etwas passendes gefunden? 3. *v.n.* passen (*Dat.*); übereinstimmen. **–ability** [–əˈbɪlɪtɪ], *s.* die Eignung, Angemessenheit, Schicklichkeit. **–able** [ˈsjuːtəbl], *adj.* passend, geeignet (*to* or *for*, zu *or* für), angemessen (*to* or *for* (*Dat.*)). **–ableness,** *s. see* **–ability. – –case,** *s.* der Handkoffer. **–ed,** *adj.* geeignet, passend (*to* or *for*, zu *or* für). **–ing,** *s.* der Herrenstoff. **–or,** *s.* Prozeßführende(r), *m.* (*Law*); der Freier; Bewerber (*for*, um), Bittsteller.

suite [swiːt], *s.* das Gefolge (*of a prince, etc.*); die Reihe, Folge (*of*, von); Zimmereinrichtung, (Möbel)Garnitur; Suite (*Mus.*); – *of rooms*, die Zimmerflucht.

sulc–ate(d) [ˈsʌlkeɪt, sʌlˈkeɪtɪd], gefurcht, furchig (*Bot.*, *Anat.*). **–us,** *s.* die Furche.

sulk [sʌlk], 1. *v.n.* schmollen, trotzen. 2. *s.* (*usually pl.*) das Schmollen, Trotzen; *have the –s*, schlechte Laune haben. **–iness,** *s.* das Schmollen, schlechte Laune. **–y** 1. *adj.* mürrisch, verdrießlich, schmollend, übelgelaunt. 2. *s.* (*archaic*) zweirädriger einsitziger Einspänner.

sullen [ˈsʌlən], *adj.* düster, finster, mürrisch, grämlich; trotzig, eigensinnig, widerspenstig. **–ness,** *s.* die Düsterkeit, Verdrießlichkeit; der Trotz, Eigensinn.

sully [ˈsʌlɪ], *v.a.* besudeln, beschmutzen (*usu. fig.*).

sulph–ate [ˈsʌlfeɪt], *s.* das Sulfat, schwefelsaures Salz; *–ate of copper*, das Blauvitriol; *–ate of soda*, schwefelsaures Natron, das Glaubersalz. **–ide** [–fɑɪd], *s.* das Sulfid; *hydrogen –ide*, der Schwefelwasserstoff. **–ite** [–fɑɪt], *s.* das Sulfit, schwefligsaures Salz. **–ur** [–fə], *s.* der Schwefel; *–ur dioxide*, das Schwefeldioxyd; *flowers of –ur*, die Schwefelblüte, Schwefelblumen (*pl.*); *milk of –ur*, die Schwefelmilch; *stick –ur*, der Stangenschwefel; *–ur spring*, die Schwefelquelle. **–urate** [–fjəreɪt], *v.a.* (ein)schwefeln. **–uration** [–fjəˈreɪʃən], *s.* das Schwefeln, die (Aus)Schwefelung. **–ureous** [–ˈfjuərɪəs], *adj.* schweff(e)lig, schwefelhaltig, Schwefel–. **–uret** [–fjurət], *s.* (*archaic*) die Schwefelverbindung. **–uretted,** *adj.* geschwefelt; *–uretted hydrogen*, der Schwefelwasserstoff. **–uric** [–ˈfjuərɪk], *adj.* Schwefel–; *–uric acid*, die Schwefelsäure. **–urize** [–fjərɑɪz], *v.a.* (aus)schwefeln, sulfieren, sulfonieren, sulfurieren, vulkanisieren. **–urous** [–fjərəs], *adj.* Schwefel–, schwefelig; *–urous acid*, schwef(e)lige Säure.

sultan [ˈsʌltən], *s.* der Sultan. **–a** [–ˈtɑːnə], *s.* die Sultanin; (also *–a raisin*) Sultanine. **–ate** [–tənət], *s.* das Sultanat.

sultr–iness [ˈsʌltrɪnɪs], *s.* die Schwüle. **–y,** *adj.* schwül, drückend.

sum [sʌm], 1. *s.* die Summe (*also fig.*), Geldsumme, der (Gesamt)Betrag, Endsumme (*Math.*); (*fig.*) das Ganze, Wesen, der Hauptinhalt, Inbegriff; Höhepunkt, Gipfel; (*coll.*) die Rechenaufgabe; *pl.* (*coll.*) das Rechnen; – *total*, die Gesamtsumme, der Gesamtbetrag; *do a –*, (eine Aufgabe) rechnen; *good at –s*, gut im Rechnen sein, gut rechnen können. 2. *v.a.* zusammenrechnen, zusammenzählen, summieren, addieren; (*fig.* usually – *up*) (kurz) zusammenfassen. 3. *v.n.* (*fig.*) – *up*, zusammenfassen, eine Übersicht geben, *see* **summary, summing-up.**

summa–riness [ˈsʌmərɪnɪs], *s.* die Kürze, summarisches Verfahren. **–rize** [–rɑɪz], *v.a.* zusammenfassen. **–ry** [–rɪ], 1. *adj.* (kurz) zusammenfassend, summarisch (*also Law*); *–ry court*, einfaches Militärgericht; *–ry jurisdiction*, das Schnellverfahren. 2. *s.* die Zusammenstellung, Zusammenfassung, Übersicht, der Auszug, Abriß, Hauptinhalt. **–tion** [sʌˈmeɪʃən], *s.* die Summierung (*Math.*); das Zusammenzählen; die Summe.

[1]**summer** [ˈsʌmə], *s.* der Trägerbalken, die Oberschwelle (*Arch.*).

[2]**summer,** 1. *s.* der Sommer; *Indian –*, der Spätsommer, Nachsommer, Altweibersommer; *of 18 –s*, von 18 Jahren. 2. *adj.* sommerlich, Sommer–; – *clothes*, Sommerkleider (*pl.*); *–('s) day*, der Sommertag. 3. *v.n.* den Sommer verbringen *or* zubringen, auf der (Sommer)Weide sein (*of cattle*). **– –house,** *s.* das Gartenhaus. **– lightning,** *s.* das Wetterleuchten. **–like, –ly,** *adj.* sommerlich. **– –resort,** *s.* die Sommerfrische. **– school,** der Sommerkurs, Sommerkursus. **– solstice,** *s.* die Sommersonnenwende. **– term,** *s.* das Sommersemester. **– –time,** *s.* die Sommerzeit. **–y,** *adj. see* **–like.** 4. *v.a.* auf (Sommer)Weide halten (*cattle*).

summing-up [ˈsʌmɪŋˈʌp], *s.* das Resümee, kurze Zusammenfassung; die Rechtsbelehrung (*Law*).

summit [ˈsʌmɪt], *s.* der Gipfel (*also fig.*), die (Berg)-Spitze; (*fig.*) der Höhepunkt; – *level*, höchste Erhebung.

summon [ˈsʌmən], *v.a.* (ein)berufen, zusammenrufen (*a meeting*); vorladen, vor Gericht laden, zitieren (*Law*); rufen, kommen lassen, auffordern; (*fig.*) (also – *up*) zusammennehmen, aufbieten (*strength*), fassen (*courage*). **–er,** *s.* der Gerichtsbote (*Hist.*). **–s** [–z], 1. *s.* die Aufforderung (*to*, an) Berufung, Zusammenrufung; Vorladung, Ladung (*Law*); *issue a –s*, eine Vorladung erlassen; *take out a –s*, eine Vorladung erwirken. 2. *v.a.* vor Gericht laden, vorladen, zitieren (*Law*).

sump [sʌmp], *s.* die Senkgrube, der Sumpf; der Sammelbehälter, die Ölwanne (*Motor.*).

sumpter [ˈsʌmptə], *s.* (*archaic*) (*usually attrib.*) das Saumtier, Packtier. **– –saddle,** *s.* der Packsattel.

sumption [ˈsʌmpʃən], *s.* der Obersatz (*Log.*).

sumptu–ary [ˈsʌmptʃuərɪ], *adj.* den Aufwand betreffend, Aufwand(s)–. **–ous** [–tʃuəs], *adj.* kostbar, kostspielig, herrlich, prächtig. **–ousness,** *s.* der (Pracht)Aufwand, die Pracht.

sun [sʌn], 1. *s.* die Sonne; der Sonnenschein, das Sonnenlicht, die Sonnenwärme; (*Poet.*) der Tag; *against the –*, gegen die Sonne *or* das Licht (*Phot.*); in der entgegengesetzten Richtung der Uhrzeiger; *have the – in one's eyes*, die Sonne im Gesicht haben; *in the –*, in der Sonne, im Sonnenschein; (*fig.*) *a place in the –*, ein Platz an der Sonne; *shoot* or *take the –*, durch Sonnenbeobachtung den Breitengrad feststellen (*Naut.*); *under the –*, unter der Sonne, auf Erden; *with the –*, in der Richtung der Uhrzeiger; mit Tagesanbruch. 2. *v.n.* sich sonnen, ein Sonnenbad nehmen. 3. *v.a.* sonnen, der Sonne aussetzen, in die Sonne stellen; – *o.s.*, sich sonnen. **– –and-planet gear,** *s.* das Planetengetriebe. **– –baked,** *adj.* an der Sonne ausgetrocknet. **– –bath,** *s.* das Sonnenbad. **– –bathe,** *v.n.* sich sonnen, ein Sonnenbad nehmen. **–beam,** *s.* der Sonnenstrahl. **– –blind,** *s.* die Markise. **–burn,** 1. *v.a.* bräunen. 2. *s.* der Sonnenbrand. **–burned, –burnt,** *adj.* sonnverbrannt. (*Poet.*). **–clad,** *adj.* sonnenhell. **–day,** *see* **Sunday. –dew,** *s.* das Sonnenkraut (*Bot.*). **–dial,** *s.* die Sonnenuhr. **–down,** *s.* der Sonnenuntergang. **–downer,** *s.* australischer Landstreicher. **– –dried,** *adj.* an der Sonne getrocknet. **–fish,** *s.* der Sonnenfisch, Mondfisch, Klumpfisch. **–flower,** *s.* die Sonnenblume. **– –god,** *s.* der Sonnengott. **– –helmet,** *s.* der Tropenhelm. **– –lamp,** *s.* künstliche Höhensonne. **–less,** *adj.* sonnenlos, ohne Licht. **–light,** *s.* das Sonnenlicht. **–like,** *adj.* sonnenähnlich, Sonnen–. **–lit,** *adj.* von der Sonne beleuchtet *or* beschienen. **– –myth,** *s.* der Sonnenmythus. **–niness,** *s.* die Sonnigkeit; (*fig.*) Heiterkeit. **–ny,** *adj.* sonnig (*also fig.*), sonnenhell, sonnenklar; (*fig.*) heiter; *the –ny side*, die Sonnenseite; (*fig.*) Lichtseite, heitere Seite. **– –parlour,** *s.* die Glasveranda (*Amer.*). **–proof,** *adj.* für Sonnenstrahlen undurchdringlich, lichtecht, sonnenbeständig. **– –ray,** *s.* der Sonnenstrahl. **–rise,** *s.* der Sonnenaufgang. **–set,** *s.* der Sonnenuntergang; *at –set*, bei Sonnenuntergang; *–set sky*, das Abendrot. **–shade,** *s.* der Sonnenschirm. **–shine,** *s.* der Sonnenschein, das Sonnenlicht, sonniges Wetter; (*fig.*) die Fröhlichkeit, Heiterkeit; das Glück, der Glanz. **–shiny,** *adj.* sonnig (*also fig.*); (*fig.*) heiter. **– –spot,** *s.* der Sonnenfleck. **–stroke,** *s.* der Hitzschlag, Sonnenstich. **– –up,** *s.* der Sonnenaufgang (*Amer.*). **–ward,** 1. *adj.* nach der Sonne gerichtet. 2. *adv.* (also *–wards*) nach der Sonne hin. **– –worship,** *s.* die Sonnenanbetung. **– –worshipper,** *s.* der Sonnenanbeter.

Sunday [ˈsʌndeɪ], 1. *s.* der Sonntag; *on –*, am Sonntag; *on –s*, sonntags; *a month of –s*, unendlich lange

Zeit, die Ewigkeit, sehr lange, ewig. 2. *attrib.* sonntäglich, Sonntags–; – *best*, – *clothes*, Sonntagskleider (*pl.*), der Sonntagsstaat; – *school*, die Sonntagsschule.

sunder [ˈsʌndə], 1. *v.a.* (*Poet.*) sondern, trennen; entzweien. 2. *v.n.* zerreißen, sich trennen. 3. *s.*; (*Poet.*) *in* –, entzwei, auseinander.

sundr–ies [ˈsʌndrɪz], *pl.* Verschiedenes; Extraspesen, Nebenkosten (*pl.*). **–y** [–drɪ], *adj.* verschiedene, mannigfaltige, allerlei, allerhand, mehrere; *all and –y*, all und jeder, alle miteinander.

sung [sʌŋ], *see* **sing.**

sunk [sʌŋk], *see* **sink;** *adj.* versenkt, vertieft (*Tech.*); – *fence*, das Aha. **–en** [–ən], *adj.* versunken, eingesunken; tief eingelassen, versenkt (*Tech.*); eingefallen, hohl (*cheeks, etc.*); *–en road*, der Hohlweg; *–en rock*, blinde Klippe.

sunn–iness, –y, *see under* **sun.**

sup [sʌp], 1. *s.* der Schluck, Mundvoll; *a bite and a* –, etwas zu essen und zu trinken; *neither bite nor* –, weder zu beißen noch zu nagen. 2. *v.a.* (*esp. Scots*) in kleinen Mengen essen *or* trinken; (*fig.*) auskosten, erleben. 3. *v.n.* zu Abend essen; nippen.

super [ˈsjuːpə], 1. *s.* (*coll.*) *abbr. for* **superintendent** *or* **supernumerary** (*Theat.*). 2. *adj.* (*sl.*) fabelhaft, erstklassig. 3. *prefix* über–, Über–, ober–. **–able** [–rəbl], *adj.* überwindbar, überwindlich. **–abound,** *v.n.* überreichlich vorhanden sein; Überfluß haben (*in* or *with*, an). **–abundance,** *s.* der Überfluß (*of*, an). **–abundant,** *adj.* überreichlich, im Überfluß vorhanden. **–add,** *v.a.* noch hinzufügen (*to*, zu). **–addition,** *s.* weitere Hinzufügung, der Zusatz (*to*, zu). **–annuate,** *v.a.* in den Ruhestand versetzen, pensionieren. **–annuated,** *adj.* pensioniert, in den Ruhestand versetzt, entpflichtet, ausgedient; (*coll.*) überaltert, verjährt, veraltet, unmodern. **–annuation,** *s.* die Pensionierung, Entpflichtung; die Pension, Altersrente, das Ruhegehalt. **–b,** *see* **superb. –cargo** [ˈsjuː-pəkɑːgoʊ], *s.* der Ladungsaufseher, Kargadeur. **–charged,** *adj.* vorverdichtend (*engine*). **–charger,** *s.* der Überverdichter, Vorverdichter; Lader, Kompressor (*Motor.*). **–ciliary,** *adj.* Augenbrauen–. **–cilious** [–ˈsɪlɪəs], *adj.* hochmütig, anmaßend, herablassend, geringschätzig. **–ciliousness,** *s.* der Hochmut, die Anmaßung, Geringschätzigkeit. **–ˈdominant,** *s.* die Oberdominante (*Mus.*). **–ˈeminence,** *s.* die Vorzüglichkeit, hoher Ruhm, hohe Stellung. **–ˈeminent,** *adj.* vorzüglich, vortrefflich, hervorragend (*for*, wegen). **–erogation** [–rɛrəˈgeɪʃən], *s.* die Mehrleistung, übergebührliche Leistung; *works of –erogation*, über Gebühr getane gute Werke (*R.C.*). **–erogatory** [–rəˈrɔgətərɪ], *adj.* übergebührlich, überflüssig. **–ˈexcellence,** *s.* höchste Vortrefflichkeit. **–ˈexcellent,** *adj.* höchst vortrefflich. **–fecunˈdation,** *s.*, **–foeˈtation,** *s.* die Überfruchtung, Überschwängerung (*Biol.*); (*fig.*) Überproduktion, der Überfluß (*of*, an). **–ˈficial,** *adj.* Oberflächen–; Flächen–, Quadrat– (*measure*); (*fig.*) oberflächlich, seicht **–ficiˈality,** *s.* die Flächenlage; (*fig.*) Oberflächlichkeit. **–ficies** [–ˈfɪʃɪiːz], *s.* die Oberfläche, Außenseite. **ˈ–fine,** *adj.* extrafein, hochfein, superfein. **–ˈfluity,** *s.* der Überfluß (*of*, an); die Überflüssigkeit. **–fluous** [sjuˈpəːfluəs], *adj.* überflüssig, überreichlich (*of*, an). **–ˈheated steam,** der Heißdampf. **ˈ–het** (*abbr. for* **–heterodyne**), *s.* der Überlagerungsempfänger (*Rad.*). **–ˈhuman,** *adj.* übermenschlich. **–imˈpose,** *v.a.* legen (*on*, auf *or* über), lagern (*on*, auf), auflegen; hinzufügen (*on*, zu). **–imposed,** *adj.* übereinanderliegend, darübergelegt, übereinandergeschichtet; überlagert (*with*, von). **–inˈcumbent,** *adj.* daraufliegend, darüberliegend. **–inˈduce,** *v.a.* noch hinzufügen (*on* (*Dat.*)), neu einführen *or* dazubringen. **–inˈtend,** *v.a.* überwachen, beaufsichtigen, verwalten. **–intendence,** *s.* die (Ober)Aufsicht (*over*, über), Verwaltung (*of* (*Gen.*)). **–intendent,** 1. *s.* der Oberaufseher, Inspektor; Superintendent (*Eccl.*); *–intendent of police*, der Polizeidirektor. 2. *adj.* Aufsichts–, aufsichtführend; höher (gelegen) (*in space*), vorgesetzt (*in rank*), größer, besser, vortrefflicher (*to*, als). **–ior,** *see* **superior. –lative** [sjuˈpəːlətɪv], 1. *adj.* höchst, hervorragend, unübertrefflich; superlativisch, Superlativ– (*Gram.*); *–lative degree*, der Superlativ (*Gram.*). 2. *s.* der Superlativ, die Meiststufe (*Gram.*); *speak in –latives*, übertreiben, in den höchsten Tönen sprechen. **–lativeness,** *s.* höchster Grad, die Vortrefflichkeit. **–man,** *s.* der Übermensch. **–ˈmundane,** *adj.* überweltlich. **–nal** [sjuˈpəːnəl], *adj.* (*Poet.*) erhaben, überirdisch, himmlisch. **–ˈnatural,** *adj.* übernatürlich, wunderbar. **–naturalism,** *s.* der Supernaturalismus, Wunderglaube, Offenbarungsglaube. **–naturalness,** *s.* die Übernatürlichkeit. **–ˈnormal,** *adj.* übernormal, ungewöhnlich. **–ˈnumerary,** 1. *adj.* außerplanmäßig, überzählig, extra. 2. *s.* Überzählige(r), *m.*; Hilfsbeamte(r), *m.*, der Statist (*Theat.*). **–ˈoxide,** *s.* das Superoxyd. **–ˈphosphate,** *s.* das Superphosphat, überphosphorsaures Salz. **–ˈpose,** *v.a.* legen, lagern *or* schichten (*on*, auf *or* über). **–position,** *s.* die Über(einander)lagerung, Schichtung (*Geol.*). **– royal,** *adj.* größer als 16·5 × 25 cm. (*paper*). **–ˈsaturate,** *v.a.* übersättigen. **–satuˈration,** *s.* die Übersättigung. **ˈ–scribe,** *v.a.* überschreiben, adressieren. **–ˈscription,** *s.* die Überschrift, Aufschrift. **–ˈsede,** *v.a.* beiseitesetzen, abschaffen, außer Gebrauch setzen, aufheben (*a th.*), ersetzen (*a th.* or *p.*), verdrängen, überflüssig machen, an (jemandes) Stelle treten, bei der Beförderung übergehen (*a p.*); *be –seded by*, abgelöst werden von. **–sedeas** [–ˈsɪːdɪəs], *s.* der Suspendierungsbefehl, Hemmungsbefehl (*Law*). **–sedence** [–ˈsɪːdəns], *s.*, **–sedure** [–ˈsɪːdjə], *s.* die Ersetzung, der Ersatz (*by*, durch); die Verdrängung, Abschaffung, Absetzung, Enthebung. **–ˈsensitive,** *adj.* überempfindlich. **–ˈsensual,** *adj.*, **–ˈsensuous,** *adj.* übersinnlich. **–session** [–ˈsɛʃən], *s. see* **–sedence.** –ˈ**sonic,** *adj.* über Schallgeschwindigkeit. **–stition** [–ˈstɪʃən], *s.* der Aberglaube. **–stitious** [–ˈstɪʃəs], *adj.* abergläubisch. **–stitiousness,** *s.* der Aberglaube. **–ˈstratum,** *s.* obere Schicht. **ˈ–structure,** *s.* der Oberbau, Überbau, Aufbauten (*pl.*). **–tax,** *s. see* **surtax. –ˈtemporal,** *adj.* überzeitlich. **–ˈvene,** *v.n.* dazukommen, hinzukommen, hinzutreten ((*up*)*on*, zu), unvermutet eintreten, sich plötzlich einstellen. **–ˈvention,** *s.* das Hinzukommen, unvermutetes Eintreten. **–vise** [ˈsjupəvaɪz], *v.a.* die Aufsicht haben über; beaufsichtigen, überwachen. **–ˈvision,** *s.* die Überwachung, Aufsicht, Leitung, Kontrolle. **ˈ–visor,** *s.* der Aufseher, Inspektor. **ˈ–visory,** *adj.* Aufsichts–.

superb [s(j)uːˈpəːb], *adj.* hervorragend, prächtig, stattlich, herrlich. **–ness,** *s.* die Herrlichkeit, Prächtigkeit.

supercargo, supercilious, supererogation, superficial, superfluous, superintend, *see under* **super–.**

superior [s(j)uˈpɪːərɪə], 1. *adj.* ober–, Ober–, höher (*in space or rank*); überlegen (*to* (*Dat.*)) (*in quality*); erhaben (*to*, über), ausgezeichnet (*C.L.*), Edel– (*as wine*); (*ironic*) überheblich, herablassend, vornehm; *be – to*, übertreffen (*in*, in *or* an); – *court*, das Obergericht; – *force*, die Übermacht; – *officer*, Vorgesetzte(r), *m.* 2. *s.* Überlegene(r), *m.* (*in*, in *or* an), Vorgesetzte(r), *m.* (*usually with poss. pron.*); der Superior, Oberer (*Eccl.*); *mother* –, die Oberin; *he is my* –, er übertrifft mich *or* ist mir überlegen (*in*, in *or* an). **–ity** [–pɪːrɪˈɔrɪtɪ], *s.* die Überlegenheit (*to*, *above* or *over*, über; *in*, in *or* an); Übermacht, das Übergewicht, der Vorzug, Vorrang; (*ironic*) die Überheblichkeit.

supin–ation [sjupɪˈneɪʃən], *s.* die Drehung (des Unterarms) nach innen. **–e** [ˈsjuːpaɪn], 1. *adj.* auf dem Rücken liegend, rückwärts gestreckt, zurückgelehnt; (*fig.*) untätig, träg, nachlässig. 2. *s.* das Supinum (*Gram.*). **–ness,** *s.* die Nachlässigkeit, Sorglosigkeit, Gleichgültigkeit, Untätigkeit, Trägheit.

supper [ˈsʌpə], *s.* das Abendessen, Abendbrot, Abendmahl (*also Eccl.*); *the Lord's* –, das Heilige Abendmahl. **–less,** *adj.* ohne Abendessen.

supplant [səˈplɑːnt], *v.a.* vom Platz *or* Amt verdrängen (*a p.*); ersetzen (*a th.*). **–er,** *s.* der Verdränger (*of a p.*), Ersatz (*of a th.*).

supple [ˈsʌpl], 1. *adj.* biegsam, geschmeidig (*also fig.*), nachgiebig, elastisch; (*fig.*) lenkbar, willfährig. 2. *v.a.* biegsam machen. **–ness** [–nɪs], *s.* die Biegsamkeit, Geschmeidigkeit, Nachgiebigkeit, Willfährigkeit.

supplement 1. *s.* [ˈsʌpləmənt], die Ergänzung, der Nachtrag, Anhang, Zusatz (*to*, zu); die Beilage (*to a newspaper*); der Ergänzungsband, Nachtragsband (*to a book*); das Supplement (*Geom.*). 2. *v.a.* [sʌplɪˈmɛnt], ergänzen, nachtragen; einen Nachtrag liefern zu, hinzufügen. **–al** [–ˈmɛntl], *adj.*, **–ary** [–ˈmɛntərɪ], *adj.* ergänzend, Ergänzungs–, Nachtrags–, Zusatz– (*to*, zu); Supplement– (*Geom.*); *be –al* or *–ary to*, ergänzen; *be –ary to*, einen Nachtrag bilden zu; *–ary order*, die Nachtragsbestellung; *–ary engine*, der Hilfsmotor, Ersatzmotor. **–ation** [–ˈteɪʃən], *s.* die Ergänzung, der Ersatz.

suppli–ant [ˈsʌplɪənt], 1. *adj.* demütig bittend, flehend. 2. *s.*, **–cant** [–plɪkənt], *s.* der Bittsteller. **–cate** [–keɪt], 1. *v.a.* demütig bitten, anflehen, ersuchen (*a p.*); erflehen, erbitten, bitten um (*a th.*). 2. *v.n.* demütig bitten, nachsuchen (*for*, um). **–cation** [–ˈkeɪʃən], *s.* demütige Bitte (*for*, um); das (Bitt)Gesuch, die Bittschrift; (Bitt)Gebet. **–catory** [–kətərɪ], *adj.* flehend, demütig bittend, Bitt–.

suppl–ier [səˈplaɪə], *s.* der Versorger, Lieferant (*C.L.*). **–y** [səˈplaɪ], 1. *v.a.* liefern, verschaffen, beschaffen, gewähren, beistellen (*a th.*); versehen (*a th.*) (*with*, mit); beliefern, versorgen (*a p.*) (*with*, mit); abhelfen (*Dat.*), ersetzen (*a lack*), decken (*a need*), ausfüllen, ergänzen (*the background*); *–y the place of*, vertreten. 2. *s.* die Lieferung (*to*, an); Versorgung, Belieferung, Zufuhr; das Lager, der Vorrat, Bedarf (*of*, an); die Ersetzung, Stellvertretung, Ergänzung; der Stellvertreter, Ersatzmann; das Angebot (*C.L.*); der Nachschub (*Mil.*); *pl.* **–ies,** Vorräte (*pl.*), der Proviant; Nachschub, Verstärkungen, Zufuhren (*pl.*) (*Mil.*); gesondert zu bewilligende Gelder (*pl.*) (*Parl.*); *–y and demand*, Angebot und Nachfrage; *on –y*, als Stellvertreter *or* Ersatz; *water –y*, die Wasserzufuhr, Wasserversorgung; *–y base*, der Stapelplatz (*Mil.*); *–y column*, die Fahrtruppe, Nachschubkolonne (*Mil.*); *–y lines*, Nachschubverbindungen (*pl.*) (*Mil.*); *–y pipe*, die Zuleitung, das Zuführungsrohr; *–y ship*, das Troßschiff, Versorgungsschiff.

support [səˈpɔ:t], 1. *v.a.* stützen, tragen, (aufrecht)-halten; ertragen, dulden; eintreten für, fördern, verteidigen (*a cause*); bestätigen, bekräftigen, begründen, rechtfertigen, (aufrecht)erhalten, behaupten (*an opinion, etc.*); unterhalten, ernähren (*on*, von) (*o.s., a family*); unterstützen (*Acc.*), Hilfe leisten, helfen, beistehen, den Rücken decken (*Dat.*) (*a p.*); *– arms!* Gewehr in Arm! *– o.s. on*, sich erhalten von. 2. *s.* die Unterstützung, Hilfe, der Beistand; die Bekräftigung, Verteidigung; der Rückhalt, die Rückendeckung; Stütze, der Halt (*for*, für); die Erhaltung, Unterhaltung; der (Lebens)Unterhalt; Untersatz, Ständer, das Gestell, Stativ, der Träger die Strebe, Unterlage, Absteifung (*Tech.*); die Einlage (*for shoes*); das Auskommen, Mittel; *give – to*, unterstützen; *in –*, in Reserve (*Mil.*); *in – of*, zur Stütze *or* Verteidigung von; *with the – of*, mit Hilfe von. **–able,** *adj.* erträglich, zu ertragen(d), leidlich; haltbar. **–er,** *s.* der Unterstützer, Helfer, Gönner; Verteidiger, Verfechter (*of an opinion, etc.*); Anhänger (*of a cause*); Träger, die Stütze (*Tech.*); Wappenhalter, Schildhalter (*Her.*). **–ing,** *adj.* Stütz–, Unterstützungs–; *–ing film*, zweiter Film; *–ing player*, der Spieler einer Nebenrolle (*Theat.*).

suppos–e [səˈpouz], *v.a.* (als möglich *or* gegeben) annehmen; vermuten, glauben, sich (*Dat.*) denken, meinen, halten für, voraussetzen; *I –e*, ich glaube es; *I –e you are aware . . .*, Sie wissen vermutlich . . .; *they are soldiers, I –e*, es werden wohl Soldaten sein; *–e he didn't do it*, angenommen *or* gesetzt, er täte es nicht; wenn er es nun nicht täte; *–e we go or went?* wie wäre es, wenn wir gingen? *she is –ed to be clever*, sie gilt *or* man hält sie für klug, sie soll klug sein; *he is –ed to know*, man glaubt *or* erwartet daß er im Bilde ist, er soll im Bilde sein. **–ed** [–d], *adj.* vermutlich, angeblich, mutmaßlich, vermeintlich. **–ition** [sʌpəˈzɪʃən], *s.* die Voraussetzung, Annahme, Vermutung, Mutmaßung; *on the –ition*, unter der Voraussetzung, in der Annahme. **–itional** [–ˈzɪʃənəl], *adj.* angenommen, hypothetisch. **–ititious** [səpɔzɪˈtɪʃəs], *adj.* untergeschoben, erdichtet, unecht, nur angenommen.

suppository [səˈpɔzɪtərɪ], *s.* das Darmzäpfchen, Stuhlzäpfchen; Scheidezäpfchen.

suppress [səˈprɛs], *v.a.* unterdrücken (*a rising, publication, feelings*); hemmen, stillen (*haemorrhage*), ersticken (*feelings*), tilgen, beseitigen (*a passage*); abschaffen, aufheben (*abuses, etc.*), verheimlichen, verschweigen, vertuschen (*the truth, etc.*). **–ible,** *adj.* unterdrückbar. **–ion** [–ˈprɛʃən], *s.* die Unterdrückung (*of a riot, rumour, book, the truth, etc.*). Aufhebung, Abschaffung; Zurückhaltung, Verheimlichung, Vertuschung; Auslassung, Weglassung (*of a word*); Hemmung, Verhaltung (*of the urine*). **–ive** [–sɪv], *adj.* unterdrückend, Unterdrückungs–. **–or grid,** *s.* das Fanggitter (*Rad.*).

suppurat–e [ˈsʌpjʊreɪt], *v.n.* eitern. **–ion** [–ˈreɪʃən], *s.* die Eiterung. **–ive** [–rətɪv], *adj.* Eiter–, eiternd.

supra [ˈsju:prə], *prefix* über–, ober–; *see* **super–.** **––axillary,** *adj.* oberwinkelständig (*Bot.*). **–lapsarian,** *adj.* dem Sündenfall vorhergehend. **–mundane,** *adj.* überweltlich, überirdisch.

suprem–acy [sjʊˈprɛməsɪ], *s.* die Obergewalt, das Supremat (*of the king*); höchste Gewalt, die Oberhoheit, Herrschaft (*over*, über); (*fig.*) Vorherrschaft, der Vorrang, die Überlegenheit, das Übergewicht (*over*, über); *oath of –acy*, der Suprematseid. **–e** [sjʊˈprɪ:m], *adj.* oberst, höchst (gelegen), größt, äußerst, letzt; *–e authority*, oberste Regierungsgewalt; *be –e*, herrschen (*over*, über); *–e Being*, das höchste Wesen; *–e command*, das Oberkommando (*Mil.*); *–e Court*, Oberstes Bundesgericht (*Amer.*); *–e Court of Judicature*, Oberster Gerichtshof (*Engl.*), das Reichsgericht (*Germany*); *the –e good*, das höchste Gut (*Phil.*); *–e moment*, kritischer Augenblick; *reign –e*, unumschränkte Herrschaft haben.

sural [ˈsju:rəl], *adj.* Waden–.

sur–base [ˈsə:beɪs], *s.* der Kragen *or* Kranz des Postaments (*Arch.*). **–ˈcease** (*archaic*) 1. *s.* das Aufhören, Nachlassen, die Unterbrechung. 2. *v.n.* aufhören, ablassen (*from*, von). **ˈ–charge,** 1. *v.a.* überlasten (*a p., also fig.*), überladen (*a p. or th.*), übersättigen (*a th.*); (*fig.*) überfordern, überteuern; niederdrücken; mit Strafgebühr *or* Zuschlagsporto belegen (*a p.*); überdrucken (*postage stamps*). 2. die Überbürdung, Überbesteuerung, Überforderung (*C.L.*); Zuschlagsgebühr, Strafgebühr, das Zuschlagsporto, Nachporto, Strafporto; der Überdruck, neuer Aufdruck (*postage stamps*). **ˈ–cingle,** *s.* der (Sattel)Gurt, Leibgurt (*Eccl.*). **ˈ–coat,** *s.* der Überrock (*Hist.*).

surd [sə:d], 1. *adj.* stimmlos (*Phonet.*); irrational (*Math.*). 2. *s.* stimmloser Konsonant (*Phonet.*), irrationale Größe (*Math.*).

sure [ʃuə] 1. *adj.* sicher (*of* (*Gen.*)), überzeugt (*of*, von); gewiß, bestimmt, zweifellos; zuverlässig, vertrauenswürdig; fest, unfehlbar, gesichert; (*coll.*) *as – as eggs is eggs*, totsicher; *as – as I live!* so wahr ich lebe! *be* or *feel – that*, überzeugt sein daß; *I am –*, allerdings, wirklich, sicherlich; *I am not –*, ich bin nicht sicher; *are you – ?* wirklich? *to be –*, freilich, sicherlich, in der Tat, natürlich; *be – to come*, sicher kommen; *be – and* or *to come!* Sie müssen ja *or* gewiß kommen; *you may be – that . . .*, du kannst dich darauf verlassen daß . . .; *– enough*, tatsächlich, in der Tat, allerdings, so gut wie sicher; *for –*, sicher, gewiß; *make –*, sich überzeugen (*of*, von), sich versichern *or* vergewissern (*of* (*Gen.*)), feststellen, sicherstellen (*of* (*Acc.*)) (*a th.*); sich bemächtigen (*of* (*Gen.*)) (*a fortress, throne, etc.*); (*sl.*) *– thing*, see *for –*; (*sl.*) *– !* sicherlich. 2. *adv.*, **–ly,** *adv.* sicher, sicherlich, wahrhaftig, zweifellos, unzweifelhaft, in der Tat, doch, doch wohl; *he –ly cannot mean it*, es kann doch (wohl) nicht sein Ernst sein; *slowly but –ly*, langsam aber sicher. **––footed,** *adj.* fest auf den Füßen. **–ness,** *s.* die Sicherheit, Gewißheit, Überzeugung, Zuverlässigkeit. **–ty** [–rɪtɪ], *s.* die Sicherheit, Gewißheit; Bürgschaft, Kaution; (*archaic*) der Bürge; *of a –ty*, wahrhaftig, ganz

gewiß, ohne Zweifel; *stand -ty*, Bürgschaft *or* Sicherheit leisten.
surf [sə:f], *s.* die Brandung. **--board,** *s.* der Wellenreiter. **--riding,** *s.* das Wellenreiten.
surface ['sə:fɪs], 1. *s.* die Oberfläche (*also fig.*), Außenseite, Äußere(s), *n.*; die Fläche (*Geom.*); tragende Fläche, die Tragfläche (*Av.*); der Tag (*Min.*); Spiegel (*of water*); *on the* –, oberflächlich, oberflächlich betrachtet, bei oberflächlicher Betrachtung; *bring to the* –, an die Oberfläche bringen; zutage fördern (*Min.*); *come to the* –, an die Oberfläche *or* nach oben kommen. 2. *adj.* Oberflächen–; (*fig.*) oberflächlich, äußerlich, Schein–. 3. *v.a.* spachteln. 4. *v.n.* auftauchen (*as submarines*). **--coat,** *s.* der Deckanstrich. **--crack,** *s.* der Anriß. **--craft,** *s.* das Überwasserfahrzeug. **--noise,** *s.* das Störgeräusch (*Gramophones*). **--printing,** *s.* der Reliefdruck, Hochdruck (*Typ.*); Reliefwalzendruck (*calico printing*). **--raider,** *s.* der Handelsstörer. **--tension,** *s.* die Oberflächenspannung. **--value,** *s.* der Augenschein, äußerer Eindruck.
surfeit ['sə:fɪt], 1. *v.a.* übersättigen (*also fig.*), überfüttern; (*fig.*) überfüllen, überladen. 2. *v.n.* übersättigt sein *or* werden, überreichlich essen, sich den Magen überladen. 3. *s.* die Übersättigung (*of*, an); (*fig.*) Überfüllung (*of*, mit), das Übermaß (*of*, an), der Überdruß, Ekel; *to (a)* –, bis zum Überdruß.
surg-e [sə:dʒ], 1. *s.* die Woge, Sturzsee; das Wogen, die Wellenbewegung, Brandung. 2. *v.n.* branden; (*fig.*) (often *-e up*) wogen, aufwallen, hochgehen; heftig schwingen (*Elec.*). 3. *s.* heftige Schwingung (*Elec.*). **-ing,** *adj.* brandend, hoch wogend, ungestüm.
surg-eon ['sə:dʒən], *s.* der Chirurg, Wundarzt, Schiffsarzt, Stabsarzt; *dental -eon*, der Zahnarzt. **-ery** [-dʒərɪ], *s.* die Chirurgie, chirurgische Behandlung; das Operationszimmer; Sprechzimmer; *-ery hours*, die Sprechstunde. **-ical** [-dʒɪkl], *adj.* chirurgisch.
surl-iness ['sə:lɪnɪs], *s.* die Verdrießlichkeit, Schroffheit, Grobheit. **-y** [-lɪ], *adj.* mürrisch, verdrießlich, schroff, grob.
surmise [sə:'maɪz], 1. *v.a.* vermuten, mutmaßen, sich einbilden; argwöhnen. 2. *s.* die Vermutung, Mutmaßung, Einbildung; der Argwohn.
surmount [sə:'maʊnt], *v.a.* übersteigen, überwinden (*difficulty*); (*fig.*) überragen. **-able,** *adj.* übersteigbar, überwindlich.
surname ['sə:neɪm], 1. *s.* der Familienname, Zuname; (*archaic*) Beiname. 2. *v.a.* einen Zunamen geben (*Dat.*), (be)nennen.
surpass [sə:'pɑ:s], *v.a.* übersteigen (*a th.*); übertreffen (*a p. or th.*); *- o.s.*, sich selbst übertreffen; *not to be -ed*, unübertrefflich. **-ing,** *adj.* hervorragend, vortrefflich, unübertrefflich, unerreicht, außerordentlich.
surplice ['sə:plɪs], *s.* das Chorhemd, die Stola (*Eccl.*).
surplus ['sə:pləs], 1. *s.* der Überschuß, Mehrbetrag, Rest. 2. *adj.* überschüssig, Überschuß–, Über–, Mehr–, Reserve–; – *brought forward*, der Gewinnvortrag (*C.L.*); – *fund*, die Rücklage, der Reservefond; – *population*, die Überbevölkerung; – *profit*, der Übergewinn; – *value*, der Mehrwert; – *weight*, das Mehrgewicht. **-age** [-ɪdʒ], *s.* der Überschuß; unwesentlicher Umstand (*Law*).
surpris-al [sə:'praɪzl], *s.* (*archaic*) die Überraschung. **-e** [sə:'praɪz], 1. *v.a.* überraschen; überrumpeln, überfallen, in Erstaunen setzen, befremden; *be -ed at*, sich wundern über (*Acc.*). 2. *s.* die Überraschung (*to*, für); der Überfall, die Überrumpelung (*Mil.*); das Erstaunen, Befremden, die Bestürzung, Verwunderung (*at*, über); *come as a -e*, als Überraschung *or* unerwartet kommen (*to* (*Dat.*)); *get the -e of one's life*, sein blaues Wunder erleben; *give a p. a -e*, *spring a -e on a p.*, einen überraschen; *stare in -e*, große Augen machen; *take by -e*, überraschen, überrumpeln; überfallen; *to my -e*, zu meiner Überraschung. **-ing,** *pr. p. & adj.* überraschend, erstaunlich.
surrealism [sə:'rɪ:əlɪzm], *s.* der Surrealismus.
sur-rebutter [sʌrə'bʌtə], *s.* die Quintuplik (*Law*). **-rejoinder** [-rɪ'dʒɔɪndə], *s.* die Triplik (*Law*).
surrender [sə'rɛndə], 1. *v.a.* übergeben, aushändigen, ausliefern (*to* (*Dat.*)); verzichten auf, (freiwillig) aufgeben; abtreten (*to*, an (*Acc.*)) (*Law*). 2. *v.n.* sich ergeben, die Waffen strecken, kapitulieren; sich stellen (*to* (*Dat.*)). 3. *s.* die Waffenstreckung, Kapitulation, Übergabe (*to*, an) (*Mil.*); Hingabe, Aufgabe; Herausgabe, Auslieferung, Überlieferung, Abtretung (*to*, an (*Acc.*)); – *value*, der Rückkaufswert (*insurance*).
surreptitious [sʌrɛp'tɪʃəs], *adj.* erschlichen, betrügerisch, unecht; heimlich, verstohlen; – *edition*, unerlaubter Nachdruck.
surrogate ['sʌrəgət], *s.* der Stellvertreter (*esp. of a bishop*); Ersatz, das Surrogat.
surround [sə'raʊnd], 1. *v.a.* umgeben (*also fig.*), einschließen (*a th. or p.*), einkreisen, umzingeln (*a p.*); herumstehen um. 2. *s.* die Einfassung, der Fußboden zwischen Teppich und Wand; (*Amer.*) die Treibjagd. **-ing,** *adj.* umgebend, umliegend; *-ing country*, die Umgebung, Umgegend. **-ings,** *pl.* die Umgegend, Umgebung.
surtax ['sə:tæks], *s.* der Steuerzuschlag, Steueraufschlag.
surtout ['sə:tu:], *s.* (*archaic*) der Überrock, Überzieher.
surveillance [sə:'veɪl(j)əns], *s.* die Kontrolle, Aufsicht, Bewachung, Überwachung.
survey 1. *v.a.* [sə:'veɪ], überblicken, überschauen (*a region*), prüfen, mustern, besichtigen (*a thing*), begutachten, (ab)schätzen (*a problem*), ausmessen, vermessen, aufnehmen (*land*). 2. *s.* ['sə:veɪ], der Überblick, die Übersicht (*of*, über), Prüfung, Besichtigung, Schätzung, Begutachtung; das Gutachten, der (Prüfungs)Bericht; die Ausmessung, Vermessung, Aufnahme (*Surv.*); der Plan, Riß; *make or take a – of*, übersehen, überblicken; prüfen; beschreiben; *Ordnance* –, amtliche Landesvermessung. **-ing,** *s.* das Vermessen; die Vermessungskunst, Feldmeßkunde. **-or** [-'veɪə], *s.* der Feldmesser, Landmesser (*Surv.*), Verwalter, Inspektor; Sachverständige(r), *m.* (*insurance*).
surviv-al [sə'vaɪvl], *s.* das Überleben, Lebenbleiben, Übrigbleiben, Weiterleben; der Überrest, das Überbleibsel; *-al of the fittest*, das Überbleiben der Lebenskräftigsten. **-e** [-'vaɪv], 1. *v.a.* überleben, überdauern (*a p. or th.*), überstehen, aushalten (*a th.*). 2. *v.n.* am Leben bleiben, sich erhalten (*into*, bis zu); noch erhalten *or* am Leben sein, noch leben, fortleben, noch bestehen, übriggeblieben sein. **-or** [-ə], *s.* der (die) Überlebende, Hinterbliebene.
suscept-ibility [səsɛptɪ'bɪlɪtɪ], *s.* die Empfänglichkeit (*to*, für), Empfindlichkeit; *pl.* empfindliche Stellen. **-ible** [-'sɛptɪbl], *attrib. & pred. adj.* empfänglich, zugänglich, aufnahmefähig (*to*, für), empfindlich (*to*, gegen); (*only pred.*) *be -ible of*, zulassen. **-ive** -tɪv], *adj.* aufnahmefähig, empfänglich (*of*, für). **-ivity** [-'tɪvɪtɪ], *s.* die Aufnahmefähigkeit, Empfänglichkeit.
suspect [səs'pɛkt], 1. *v.a.* beargwöhnen, bezweifeln, Mißtrauen hegen gegen (*a th.*), verdächtigen, im Verdacht haben (*of*, wegen; *o doing*, getan zu haben) (*a p*).; vermuten, mutmaßen, annehmen, für wahrscheinlich *or* möglich halten. 2. *v.n.* Argwohn *or* Verdacht hegen. 3. ['sʌspɛkt], *adj.* (*only pred.*) verdächtig (*of* (*Gen.*)); *be* –, irgendwie belastet sein. 4. ['sʌspɛkt], *s.* die Verdachtsperson, Verdächtigte(r), *m.* **-ed** [-'pɛktɪd], *adj.* verdächtig, verdächtigt.
suspen-d [səs'pɛnd], *v.a.* (auf)hängen, (*from*, an (*Acc.*)); aufschieben, verschieben, in der Schwebe lassen, aussetzen (*judgement*), einstellen (*payment, etc.*), zurückhalten mit; des Amtes entheben, suspendieren, entlassen (*a.p.*), (zeitweise) ausschließen (*a p., also Chem.*); aufschwemmen, anschlämmen (*Chem.*). **-ded,** *adj.* hängend, schwebend; *-ded animation*, der Scheintod; *be -ded*, hängen (*by*, an; *from*, von; *in*, in). **-der** [-ə], *s.* der Strumpfhalter; *pl.* (*Amer.*) Hosenträger (*pl.*). **-der-belt,** *s.* der Hüfthalter. **-se** [-pɛns], s. die Ungewißheit, Spannung; der Aufschub, die Aussetzung; *in -se*, in Spannung; in der Schwebe; *keep in -se*, in Ungewißheit lassen *or* halten; *tortured with -se*, in peinlicher Ungewißheit; *-se account*, das Interimskonto (*C.L.*). **-sion** [-ʃən], *s.*

das (Auf)Hängen; die Aufhängung, Federung (*Motor.*); Aussetzung, Aufhebung, der Aufschub (*of judgement*), Einstellung (*of payment*), Unterbrechung; die Amtsenthebung, Suspension (*from*, von); Ausstoßung, Ausschaltung (*of a p.*); der Ausschluß (*Sport*); Vorhalt (*Mus.*); die Aufschlämmung, Schwebe, Suspension (*Chem.*); *be held in –sion*, in der Schwebe erhalten werden; *front-wheel –sion*, die Vorderrad-Aufhängung (*Motor.*); *–sion of hostilities*, der Waffenstillstand; *–sion of payment*, die Zahlungseinstellung (*C.L.*); *points of –sion*, die Aufhängepunkte. **–sion-bridge,** *s.* die Hängebrücke, Kettenbrücke. **–sion-railway,** *s.* die Schwebebahn. **–sion-spring,** *s.* die Tragfeder (*Motor.*). **–sory** [–sərɪ], *adj.* hängend, Hänge–, schwebend, Schwebe–; Aufschub–, Aussetzungs–; *–sory bandage*, der Tragbeutel, das Tragband, Suspensorium (*Surg.*).

suspicio–n [səsˈpɪʃən], *s.* der Verdacht, Argwohn, das Mißtrauen (*of*, gegen), der Zweifel (*of*, an), die Verdächtigung; Vermutung; (*usually neg.*) Ahnung, Spur, Kleinigkeit, der Anflug, das Bißchen (*of*, von); *entertain* or *have a –n*, Verdacht *or* Zweifel hegen (*of*, an); *above –n*, über jeden Verdacht erhaben; *on –n*, unter dem Verdacht (*of* (*Gen.*)); *cast –n on*, Verdacht lenken auf (*Acc.*); *be under –n*, im Verdacht stehen, verdächtig werden. **–us** [–ʃəs], *adj.* argwöhnisch, mißtrauisch (*of* gegen); verdachterregend, verdächtig; *be –us of*, in Verdacht haben, mißtrauen (*Dat.*); befürchten. **–usness,** *s.* das Mißtrauen, der Argwohn (*of*, gegen); die Verdächtigkeit.

suspir–ation [sʌspɪˈreɪʃən], *s.* das Seufzen, der Seufzer. **–e** [səsˈpɑɪə], *v.n.* (*archaic*) seufzen; (*Poet.*) tief atmen; (*fig.*) schmachten, sich sehnen (*after* or *for*, nach).

sustain [səsˈteɪn], *v.a.* (aufrecht)halten, stützen (*also fig.*); (*fig.*) erhalten, unterhalten, unterstützen (*life, etc.*), stärken, Kraft geben (*Dat.*) (*a p.*), aushalten, (er)tragen, widerstehen (*attack, comparison, etc.*), aufrechterhalten (*a claim, charge, etc.*), wachhalten (*interest*), erleiden (*a loss*), davontragen (*an injury*), aushalten (*Mus.*); bestätigen, bekräftigen, als rechtsgültig anerkennen (*Law*). **–able,** *adj.* haltbar, tragbar, aufrechtzuerhalten(d). **–ed** [–d], *adj.* ununterbrochen, durchgeführt, aufrechterhalten; getragen (*Mus.*). **–ment,** *s.* die Stütze, Erhaltung, Nahrung.

susten–ance [ˈsʌstənəns], *s.* der (Lebens)Unterhalt, das Auskommen; *pl.* die Nahrung, Ernährung, Erhaltung, Lebensmittel (*pl.*). **–tation** [–ˈteɪʃən], *s.* die Unterstützung, (Aufrecht)Erhaltung, Ernährung, Versorgung, der Unterhalt.

sutler [ˈsʌtlə], *s.* der Heereslieferant, Marketender. **--woman,** *s.* die Marketenderin.

suttee [sʌˈtiː], *adj.* freiwilliger Feuertod einer indischen Witwe.

sutur–al [ˈsjuːtʃərəl], *adj.* Naht–. **–e** [–tʃə], 1. *s.* die Naht (*Anat., Bot., Ent., Surg.*), das Zusammennähen. 2. *v.a.* vernähen, zusammennähen (*Surg.*).

suzerain [ˈsjuːzəreɪn], 1. *s.* der Ober(lehns)herr, die Oberhoheit. 2. *attrib. adj.* oberherrlich, oberhoheitlich. **–ty,** *s.* die Oberlehnsherrlichkeit, Oberherrschaft, Obergewalt.

svelte [svɛlt], *adj.* schlank, graziös, anmutig.

swab [swɔb], 1. *s.* der Kehrwisch, Schrubber, Scheuerlappen; Schwabber (*Naut.*); Abstrich (*Med.*). 2. *v.a.* aufwischen, tupfen; schwabbern, schrubben (*Naut.*).

swaddl–e [ˈswɔdl], 1. *pl.* **–es** (*Amer.*) Windeln (*pl.*). 2. *v.a.* in Windeln legen, wickeln (*a child*); (*fig.*) (also *–e up*) einwickeln. **–ing-bands,** *pl.*, **–ing-clothes,** *pl.*, Windeln (*pl.*).

swag [swæg], *s.* (*sl.*) die Diebesbeute.

swagger [ˈswægə], 1. *v.n.* prahlen, großtun (*about*, mit), renommieren, einherstolzieren. 2. *s.* die Großtuerei, Prahlerei; das Stolzieren. 3. *adj.* (*coll.*) elegant, schick. **--coat,** *s.* loser Damenmantel, der Hänger. **--cane,** *s.* das Ausgehstöckchen (*Mil.*).

swain [sweɪn], *s.* der Bauernbursch; (*Poet.*) Schäfer, Liebhaber.

[1]**swallow** [ˈswɔlou], *s.* die Schwalbe (*Orn.*); (*Prov.*) *one – does not make a summer*, eine Schwalbe macht keinen Sommer. **--tail,** *s.* der Schwalbenschwanz (*Bot., Fort., Carp.*); *pl.* (*coll.*) der Frack. **--tailed,** *adj.* schwalbenschwanzartig, Schwalbenschwanz–; *--tailed coat*, der Frack.

[2]**swallow,** 1. *s.* der Schlund, die Kehle, Gurgel; der Schluck, das Schlucken. 2. *v.a.* (ver)schlucken, verschlingen; hinnehmen, herunterschlucken, einstecken (*an insult*); gierig aufnehmen, für bare Münze nehmen (*statements, opinion, etc.*); (also *– down*) unterdrücken (*anger, etc.*), zurücknehmen, widerrufen (*one's words*); *– the bait*, auf etwas hineinfallen; *– the bitter pill*, in den sauren Apfel beißen; *– down*, hinunterschlucken; *– up*, verschlucken, verschlingen; (*fig.*) überschlucken (*territory, etc.*). 3. *v.n.* schlucken; *– the wrong way*, sich verschlucken.

swam, *see* **swim.**

swamp [swɔmp], 1. *s.* der Sumpf, Morast, das Moor. 2. *v.a.* überschwemmen, versenken; (*fig.*) (*usually pass.*) unterdrücken, überwältigen; erdrücken; *be –ed*, (*also fig.*) überschwemmt werden mit. **–y,** *adj.* sumpfig, morastig, Sumpf–.

swan [swɔn], *s.* der Schwan; *– of Avon*, Shakespeare; (*Prov.*) *all his geese are –s*, er übertreibt alles *or* schlägt alles zu hoch an. **--like,** *adj.* schwanenhaft. **--maiden,** *s.* die Schwanenjungfrau; **--neck,** *s.* der Schwanenhals. **–nery** [–ərɪ], *s.* der Schwanenteich. **–'s-down,** *s.* die Schwanendaune. **–skin,** *s.* weicher Flanell. **--song,** *s.* der Schwanen(ge)sang. **--upping,** *s.* jährliches Zeichnen der Themseschwäne.

swank [swæŋk], 1. *s.* (*coll.*) die Großtuerei, Prahlerei, Aufschneiderei. 2. *v.n.* (*coll.*) großtun, renommieren, flunkern, aufschneiden. 3. *adj.* (*sl.*) protzig. (*coll.*) **--pot,** *s.* der Protz. (*coll.*). **–y,** *adj.* elegant, schick, fesch.

swap [swɔp], 1. *v.a.* (*sl.*) vertauschen, austauschen, wechseln (*things*); tauschen (*with*, mit); *– a th. for*, etwas eintauschen für *or* vertauschen mit. 2. *v.n.* tauschen. 3. *s.* das Tauschen; der Tausch, Tauschgegenstand.

sward [swɔːd], *s.* der Rasen, die Rasenfläche. **--cutter,** *s.* der Rasenstecher.

swarf [swɔːf], *s.* der Abdraht, Abdrehspäne (*pl.*).

[1]**swarm** [swɔːm], 1. *s.* der Schwarm (*of bees, etc., also fig.*); (*fig.*) das Gewimmel, der Haufe. 2. *v.n.* schwärmen (*as bees*); (*fig.*) strömen, wimmeln (*with*, von); sich drängen, zusammenströmen. **–ing time,** die Schwärmzeit. **--spore,** *s.* die Schwärmspore.

[2]**swarm,** 1. *v.a.* (also *– up*) hinaufklettern *or* hochklettern an, erklettern. 2. *v.n.* klettern.

swart [swɔːt], *adj.* (*Poet.*) *see* **–hy. –hiness** [ˈswɔːðɪnɪs], *s.* das Schwärzliche, Dunkelfarbige, dunkle Gesichtsfarbe. **–hy** [–ðɪ], *adj.* schwärzlich, dunkelfarbig, dunkelhäutig.

swash [swɔʃ], 1. *s.* das Schwappen, Plan(t)schen, Klatschen. 2. *v.a. & n.* schwappen, plan(t)schen, klatschen (*of liquids*). **–buckler,** *s.* der Säbelrassler, Schaumschläger, Prahlhans. **–buckling,** *adj.* säbelrasselnd, prahlerisch. **--letter,** *s.* der Zierbuchstabe.

swastika [ˈswɔstɪkə], *s.* das Hakenkreuz.

swat [swɔt], *v.a.* (*coll.*) schlagen, zerquetschen.

swath [swɔːθ], *s.* der Schwaden (*of cut grass*).

swathe [sweɪð], 1. *v.a.* einhüllen, einwickeln, umwickeln. 2. *s.* die Hülle, Binde, der Umschlag.

sway [sweɪ], 1. *v.a.* schwingen, schwenken, hin-und-her– *or* auf-und-abbewegen; (*fig.*) beeinflussen, bewegen, lenken, regieren; *– the audience*, das Publikum mit sich reißen; *– the sceptre*, das Zepter führen. 2. *v.n.* schwanken, sich schwingen; sich wiegen, sich hin-und-her– *or* auf-und-abbewegen; sich neigen; herrschen (*over*, über). 3. *s.* das Schwingen; der Schwung, die Wucht; (*fig.*) das Übergewicht (*over*, über); der Einfluß, Bann, die Herrschaft, Macht; *hold –*, herrschen (*over*, über); *fall under a p.'s –*, unter jemandes Einfluß geraten

swear [swɛːə], 1. *ir.v.a.* schwören, beteuern, geloben, eidlich aussagen; beschwören, durch Schwur bekräftigen; den Eid abnehmen (*Dat.*), vereidigen, eidlich verpflichten (*to*, zu) (*a p.*); *– an oath*, einen Eid leisten *or* ablegen; *– in*, vereidigen (*a p.*); (*coll.*)

– *off*, abschwören (*smoking, etc.*). 2. *ir.v.n.* einen Schwur leisten; fluchen; (*coll.*) fauchen; – *by* or *on the Bible*, auf die Bibel schwören; – *at*, fluchen auf, beschimpfen, ausschimpfen; – *by all that's holy*, Stein und Bein schwören; (*coll.*) – *by*, schwören auf, sich rückhaltslos verlassen auf; (*coll.*) – *to*, (die Wahrheit) beschwören; *see* **sworn**; – *like a trooper*, fluchen wie ein Landsknecht. **–ing**, *s.* das Schwören, Fluchen. **–ing-in**, *s.* die Vereidigung. **–-word**, *s.* das Schimpfwort, der Fluch.

sweat [swɛt], 1. *s.* der Schweiß; (*coll.*) *be in a* –, schwitzen; Angst schwitzen; *bloody* –, der Blutschweiß; *by the – of one's brow*, im Schweiße seines Angesichts; *cold* –, kalter Schweiß; (*sl.*) *old* –, der Zwölfender, alter Knochen. 2. *v.n.* schwitzen (*with*, vor), sich ausdünsten; (*coll.*) sich abschinden *or* abmühen (*at*, an); für Hungerlohn arbeiten. 3. *v.a.* schwitzen (*blood, etc.*); (*coll.*) schinden, ausbeuten, aussaugen; schweißen (*Tech.*); – *out*, ausschwitzen (*a cold, etc.*); schwitzen lassen (*a p.*). **–-duct**, *s.* der Schweißkanal. **–ed** [–ɪd], *adj.* für Hungerlohn hergestellt (*goods*); schlecht bezahlt (*labour*). **–er** [–ə], *s.* der Sweater, die Strickjacke, wollene Jacke; der (Leute)Schinder. **–-gland**, *s.* die Schweißdrüse. **–iness**, [–ɪnɪs], *s.* schweißiger Zustand, die Schweißigkeit. **–ing**, *s.* das Schwitzen. **–ing-bath**, *s.* das Schwitzbad. **–ing-shop**, *s.* der Ausbeutebetrieb. **–ing-sickness**, *s.* das Schweißfieber, Englischer Schweiß. **–ing-system**, *s.* das Ausbeutungssystem. **–y** [–ɪ], *adj.* schweißig, schwitzig, verschwitzt.

swede [swɪ:d], *s.* die Steckrübe.

sweeny [swɪ:nɪ], *s.* der Muskelschwund (*Vet.*).

sweep [swɪ:p], 1. *ir.v.a.* kehren, (aus)fegen (*a room*); überschwemmen, schlagen über (*as waves*); absuchen (*the horizon*); bestreichen (*as bullets*), fortjagen, forttreiben (*the enemy, etc.*); ausschlagen, berühren (*a harp, etc.*); ausbaggern (*a river, etc.*); – *aside*, abtun, beseitigen, beiseiteschieben; – *away*, wegfegen; (*fig.*) fortraffen, wegreißen, mit sich fortreißen; beseitigen, zerstören; – *before one*, vor sich her treiben; – *the board*, alles gewinnen; – *the dust*, den Staub mitnehmen (*as a skirt*); – *off*, dahinraffen; – *s.o. off his feet*, einen überrennen, (*fig.*) einen mitreißen; – *one's hand over*, mit der Hand streichen *or* gleiten über. 2. *ir.v.n.* fegen (*also fig.*); (*fig.*) schießen, sausen, stürmen, rauschen; peitschen; sich erstrecken; jagen (*as wind*), sich ergießen, fluten (*as feelings*); einherschreiten (*as a p.*); schweifen (*as the eyes*); – *across one's mind*, einem durch den Sinn fahren; – *by*, vorübersausen an; – *down*, sich stürzen (*on*, auf). 3. *s.* das Fegen, Kehren; das Schwingen, der Schwung, schwungvolle Bewegung; der Bereich, Spielraum, die Ausdehnung, das Ausmaß; die Streife (*Mil., etc.*); Kurve, Windung, Krümmung, der Bogen, fließende Linie (*of drapery*); langes Ruder (*Naut.*); (also *chimney-–*) der Schornsteinfeger; *make a clean – of*, reinen Tisch machen mit, ausräumen; *give the room a* –, das Zimmer ausfegen; – *of the hand*, schwungvolle Handbewegung; *a – of* or *with his sword*, ein Schwung mit seinem Schwert; – *of the tiller*, der Leuwagen des Ruders. **–er** [–ə], *s.* (also *road-–er* or *crossing-–er*) der (Straßen)Kehrer; (also *carpet-–er*) die Kehrmaschine. **–ing**, *adj.* gründlich, durchgreifend, weittragend, umfassend; mitreißend, fortreißend, schwungvoll, heftig; *–ing measures*, durchgreifende Maßnahmen; *–ing statement*, zu allgemeine Behauptung; *–ing victory*, der Sieg auf der ganzen Linie. **–ings**, *pl.* der Kehricht; (*fig.*) Auswurf, Abgang. **–-net**, *s.* das Schleppnetz. **–stake**, *s.* (*also pl.*) die Lotterie.

sweet [swɪ:t], 1. *adj.* süß (*also fig.*); süßlich, süß schmeckend; (*fig.*) duftig, wohlriechend, lieblich (*as smell*), melodisch, wohlklingend, angenehm (*as sound*), köstlich, wohltuend (*as sleep*), frisch (*as soil, butter, etc.*), lieb (*to*, zu), liebenswürdig, gütig (*to*, gegen) (*of a p.*); (*coll.*) reizend, entzückend; (*sl.*) *be – on*, verliebt sein in; – *herbs*, Küchengewächse; – *nature*, sanftes *or* liebliches Gemüt; – *seventeen*, noch unschuldig (*of a girl*), mädchenhaft; *have a – tooth*, ein Leckermäulchen sein; – *and twenty*, in strahlender Jugendblüte (*of a girl*); *at one's own – will*, wie es einem gefällt. 2. *s.* das Süße; die Süßigkeit, der *or* das Bonbon; (*sometimes pl.*) der Nachtisch, die Süßspeise; *my* –, mein Liebes; (*usually pl.*) die Freude, Annehmlichkeit; (*coll.*) der Liebling. **–bread**, *s.* das Bröschen, die Kalbsmilch. **–brier**, *s.* wilde Rose. – **chestnut**, *s.* die Eßkastanie. – **corn**, *s.* der Mais. **–en**, *v.a.* süßen, süß machen; (*fig.*) versüßen, angenehm *or* gefällig machen. **–ener**, *s.* das Versüßungsmittel, Beschwichtigungsmittel. **–heart**, 1. *s.* der Schatz, das Liebchen. 2. *v.n.* (*coll.*) poussieren. **–ie**, *s.* (*coll.*) (*usually pl.*) der *or* das Bonbon, die Süßigkeit; (*sl.*) der Schatz. **–ing**, *s.* der Johannisapfel. **–ish**, *adj.* süßlich. **–meat**, *s.* das Zuckerkonfekt, der *or* das Bonbon. **–-natured**, *adj.* sanft, lieblich. **–ness**, *s.* die Süßigkeit, Frische, der Wohlgeruch, die Lieblichkeit, Liebenswürdigkeit, Anmut, Annehmlichkeit. – **oil**, *s.* das Olivenöl. – **pea**, *s.* die Gartenwicke. – **potato**, *s.* die Batate. **–-shop**, *s.* das Schokoladengeschäft. **–-scented**, **–-smelling**, *adj.* wohlriechend, duftend. **–-tempered**, *adj.* sanftmütig. – **violet**, *s.* das Märzveilchen. **–-william**, *s.* die Bartnelke. **–y**, *s. see* **–ie**.

swell [swɛl], 1. *ir.v.n.* (also – *out* or *up*) (*also fig.*, *into*, zu) (an)schwellen, dick werden, sich weiten, sich bauschen *or* blähen; aufquellen, ansteigen (*water*); (*fig.*) zunehmen, (an)wachsen (*into* or *to*, zu), sich ausbauchen (*into*, zu) (*Arch.*), sich steigern (*as feelings*), sich aufblähen, schwellen (*with pride*), bersten (*with rage*). 2. *ir.v.a.* anschwellen lassen, dick werden lassen, zum Schwellen bringen; aufblasen, dehnen, ausweiten; steigen lassen, (an)schwellen (*rivers*); (*usually pass.*) aufblähen; (*fig.*) steigern, vergrößern, vermehren. 3. *s.* die Anschwellung, Schweifung, Ausbauchung (*Arch.*); Dünung, der Wellengang, Seegang (*of the sea*); die Steigung, Anhöhe (*of land*), das Anschwellen (*of sound*); der Schweller (*Org.*); (*sl.*) Stutzer, Modeherr, hoher Herr, großes Tier, die Kanone. 4. *adj.* (*sl.*) vornehm, hochelegant, aufgedonnert; prima, fein, fabelhaft. **–-box**, *s.* das Schwellergehäuse (*of an organ*). **–ed** [–d], *adj.* angeschwollen (*Med.*); (*sl.*) *–ed head*, die Aufgeblasenheit. **–ing**, 1. *adj.* (an)schwellend, ansteigend; geschwollen, schwülstig; *–ing heart*, überladenes Herz. 2. *s.* die Anschwellung, Aufschwellung, Aufblähung; Quellung, Bauchung, Wölbung, der Vorsprung; die Geschwulst (*Med.*). **–-fish**, *s.* der Kugelfisch. (*sl.*) **–-headed**, *adj.* aufgeblasen. **–mob(sman)**, *s.* der Hochstapler. **–-pedal**, *s.* der Rollschweller (*of an organ*).

swelt-er [ˈswɛltə], 1. *v.n.* vor Hitze umkommen *or* vergehen, in Schweiß gebadet sein. 2. *s.* drückende Hitze. **–ering**, *adj.* **–ry**, *adj.* drückend, schwül.

swept [swɛpt], *see* **sweep**.

swerve [swə:v], 1. *v.n.* eine Seitenbewegung machen; abschweifen (*from*, von); abweichen, das Ziel aus den Augen verlieren. 2. *v.a.* ablenken, zum Abweichen bringen; Effet geben (*Dat.*) (*a ball*). 3. *s.* die Abweichung, Seitenbewegung.

swift [swɪft], 1. *adj.* schnell, geschwind, rasch, eilig, hurtig, flink; flüchtig (*moment, etc.*); – *action*, sofortige Ausführung; – *reply*, umgehende Antwort; – *to do*, schnell bereit zu tun. 2. *s.* der Mauersegler, die Turmschwalbe (*Orn.*); der Molch (*Zool.*). **–ness**, *s.* die Schnelligkeit, Geschwindigkeit.

swig [swɪg], (*sl.*) 1. *v.a.* saufen, hinunterschlucken, austrinken. 2. *v.n.* einen tüchtigen Zug tun (*at*, aus *or* von). 3. *s.* der Zug, Schluck.

swill [swɪl], 1. *v.a.* (ab)spülen, abwaschen; (*sl.*) herunterspülen (*a drink*). 2. *v.n.* (*sl.*) saufen. 3. *s.* das Spülen; Spülwasser, Spülicht; der Spültrank (*for pigs*); Speisereste (*pl.*), der Abfall, die Schlempe; (*sl.*) das Gesöff.

swim [swɪm], 1. *ir.v.n.* schwimmen (*also fig.*); (*fig.*) überfließen; treiben, getragen *or* getrieben werden (*of things*); – *with the stream* or *tide*, mit dem Strome schwimmen; *my head –s*, es schwimmt mir vor den Augen, es schwindelt mir; – *in* or *with blood*, von Blut überschwemmt sein. 2. *ir.v.a.* durchschwimmen (*a distance*), schwimmen über (*a river*), schwimmen lassen (*horses, etc.*). 3. *s.* das Schwimmen; (*fig.*) schwindelndes Gefühl; (*coll.*) der Strom des Lebens; *have* or *take a* –, schwimmen, baden; *go for a* –, zum Schwimmen gehen; *be in the* –, auf dem Laufenden sein; mit dazu gehören; *be out of the* –, nicht mehr dazugehören. **–mer,** *s.* der Schwimmer; Schwimmvogel (*Orn.*). **–meret,** *s.* der Schwimmfuß. **–ming,** 1. *adj.* schwimmend; schwindelnd; *–ming eyes,* tränende Augen. 2. *s.* das Schwimmen; *go –ming,* (zum) Schwimmen gehen. **–ming-bath,** *s.* (*often pl.*) die Badeanstalt, das Schwimmbad. **–ming-bladder,** *s* die Schwimmblase. **–ming-lesson,** *s.* die Schwimmstunde; *take –ming-lessons,* Schwimmunterricht nehmen *or* haben. **–mingly,** *adv.* leicht, mühelos, glatt, von selbst, ohne Schwierigkeit; *get on –mingly,* glänzend auskommen *or* vorankommen; *go –mingly,* glatt vonstatten gehen. **–ming-pool,** *s.* das Freibad. **–ming-race,** das Wettschwimmen.

swindl–e ['swɪndl], 1. *v.a.* beschwindeln, betrügen (*out of,* um) (*a p.*); erschwindeln (*out of,* von) (*a thing*). 2. *v.n.* schwindeln, betrügen. 3. *s.* der Betrug, Schwindel. **–er** [–lə], *s.* der Schwindler, Betrüger, Gauner. **–ing,** 1. *adj.* schwindelhaft, betrügerisch, Schwindel–. 2. *s.* das Schwindeln, Betrügen.

swin–e [swɑɪn], *s.* (pl. *–e*) (*Poet.*) das Schwein (*also fig.*); (*pl.*) Schweine; (*fig.*) der Schweinehund; *cast pearls before –e,* Perlen vor die Säue werfen. **–e-bread,** *s.* die Trüffel. **–eherd,** *s.* der Schweinehirt. **–e-pox,** *s.* die Schweinepest. **–ish,** *adj.* Schweins–, Schweine–; (*fig.*) schweinisch. **–ishness,** *s.* die Schweinerei.

swing [swɪŋ] 1. *ir.v.n.* schwingen, pendeln, baumeln, schaukeln; sich schaukeln (*on a swing*); sich drehen *or* wenden; schwoien, schwojen (*Naut.*); (*sl.*) gehängt werden (*for,* wegen *or* für); sich hinziehen; – *along,* flott dahinziehen; – *into line,* einschwenken (*Mil.*); – *open,* auffliegen, sich auftun; – *past,* mit Schwung vorbeimarschieren; – *round,* sich umdrehen; – *to,* zuschlagen. 2. *ir.v.a.* schwingen, schwenken; schlenkern (*one's arms, etc.*); baumeln *or* hangen lassen, hängen (*from,* an); schaukeln; durchdrehen (*a propeller*); (*sl.*) beeinflussen; (*sl.*) – *it,* es erfolgreich durchführen, es schaffen; (*coll.*) *there's no room to – a cat in,* man kann sich kaum umdrehen; – *the lead,* peilen (*Naut.*); (*sl.*) sich krank stellen, sich drücken. 3. *s.* das Schwingen, Schaukeln; die Schwingung, Schwenkung; die Schaukel; (*fig.*) der Schwung, Rhythmus; das Schaukeln, Auf-und-Ab, Hin-und-Her, der Spielraum, die Schwungweite; *be on the* –, hin und her schaukeln; – *of the pendulum,* die Pendelschwingung; *in full* –, in Schuß *or* Fluß *or* vollem Gange, im Schwung, im Zuge; *go with a* –, leicht dahinfließen, glatt verlaufen; *get into the – of a th.,* sich an etwas gewöhnen; *give full – to a th.,* einer S. ihren freien Lauf lassen; *what you lose on the –s, you make up* or *gain on the roundabouts,* ein Verlust hier wird aufgewogen durch einen Gewinn dort, du hältst dich schadlos *or* machst deine Verluste wett. **– -away,** *s.* das Abschwenken. **– -back,** *s.* die Einstellscheibe (*Phot.*), (*fig.*) Wandlung, Umstellung; Umkehr; Rückkehr (*to,* zu). **–boat,** *s.* bootförmige Schaukel. **– -bridge,** *s.* die Drehbrücke. **– -door,** *s.* die Klapptür, Drehtür. **–ing,** *adj.* schwebend, wiegend, rhythmisch; schwunghaft, wuchtig (*blow, etc.*).

swinge [swɪndʒ], *v.a.* (*archaic*) peitschen, prügeln.

swingl–e [swɪŋgl], 1. *v.a.* schwingen (*flax, etc.*). 2. *s.* die Schwinge, Schwingmaschine, das Schwingbrett. **–etree,** *s.* der Schwengel. **–ing,** *s.* das (Flachs)Schwingen. **–ing-tow,** *s.* das Werg, die Hede.

swinish, *see* **swine.**

swipe [swɑɪp], 1. *v.n.* (*coll.*) kräftig schlagen (*at,* nach). 2. *v.a.* kräftig schlagen; (*sl.*) stibitzen. 3. *s.* kräftiger *or* derber Schlag; *pl.* das Dünnbier (*Amer.*).

swirl [swəːl], 1. *v.n.* einen Strudel bilden (*as water*), sich drehen, wirbeln. 2. *s.* der Wirbel, Strudel.

swish [swɪʃ], 1. (*coll.*) *v.n.* sausen, schwirren, zischen, flutschen; plätschern, rauschen; rascheln (*as a dress*). 2. *s.* das Sausen, Rauschen, Rascheln. 3. *adj.* (*sl.*) vornehm, elegant.

switch [swɪtʃ], 1. *s.* die Gerte, Rute; Weiche, das Stellwerk (*Railw.*); der (Um)Schalter (*Elec.*); falscher Zopf; *two-way* –, der Wechselschalter (*Elec.*). 2. *v.a.* peitschen; rangieren (*a train*); (um)schalten (*Elec.*); (*fig.*) umlenken, herüberführen (*a p.*); – *off,* abdrehen, ausschalten, ausknipsen (*light, etc.*), abstellen (*Rad.*); – *on,* andrehen, anknipsen, einschalten; – *over to,* umstellen, umschalten *or* übergehen auf. **– -back,** *s.* die Rutschbahn, Berg- und Talbahn. **–board,** *s.* die Schalttafel, das Schaltbrett; der Klappenschrank, die Vermittlung (*Tele.*). **–man,** *s.* der Weichensteller. **– -point,** .. die Zungenschiene (*Railw.*).

swivel [swɪvl], 1. *s.* der Drehring, Drehzapfen, Wirbel (*Tech.*); der Karabinerhaken; *butt- –,* der Klammerfuß (*of rifle*). **– -bridge,** *s.* die Drehbrücke. **– -chair,** *s.* der Drehstuhl. (*sl.*) **– -eyed,** *adj.* schieläugig. **– -gun,** *s.* die Drehbasse. **– -mounted,** *adj.* schwenkbar (*Artil.*). **– -mounting,** *s.* Drehgestell.

swollen ['swoulən], *see* **swell.**

swoon [swuːn], 1. *s.* die Ohnmacht, der Ohnmachtsanfall. 2. *v.n.* in Ohnmacht fallen, ohnmächtig werden.

swoop [swuːp], 1. *v.n.* (also – *down*) (herab)stoßen, (nieder)schießen, (sich) stürzen ((*up*)*on,* auf); (*fig.*) herfallen ((*up*)*on,* über). 2. *v.a.*; – *up,* wegschnappen, aufraffen. 3. *s.* der Sturz, Stoß, (*fig.*) Überfall; *at one* (*fell*) –, mit einem Stoß.

swop [swɔp], *see* **swap.**

sword [sɔːd], *s.* das Schwert, der Säbel, Degen; – *in hand,* mit dem Schwert in der Hand; *at the point of the* –, mit Gewalt; *draw* –, kämpfen; *draw one's* –, zum Schwert greifen; *fall to the* –, durch das Schwert fallen; *put to the* –, über die Klinge springen lassen. **– -arm,** *s.* rechter Arm. **– -bayonet,** *s.* das Säbelbajonett. **– -bearer,** *s.* der Schwertträger. **– -belt,** *s.* das Degengehenk. **– -cane,** *s.* der Stockdegen. **– -cut,** *s.* der Säbelhieb. **– -dance,** *s.* der Schwertertanz. **–fish,** *s.* der Schwertfisch. **– -guard,** *s.* das Stichblatt. **– -hilt,** *s.* der Degengriff. **– -knot,** *s.* die Degenquaste, der Faustriemen. **–lily,** *s.* die Schwertlilie, Siegwurz (*Bot.*). **– -play,** *s.* die Fechtkunst, das Säbelfechten. **–sman,** *s.* der Fechter. **–smanship,** *s.* die Fechtkunst. **– -stick,** *s. see* **– -cane.** **– -thrust,** *s.* der Schwertstoß.

swor–e [swɔː], *see* **swear.** **–n,** 1. *see* **swear;** 2. *adj.* durch Eid gebunden; Eid–; vereidigt, beeidigt; *–n enemy,* der Todfeind; *–n member,* vereidigtes Mitglied.

swot [swɔt], 1. *v.n.* (*sl.*) büffeln, ochsen, stucken, pauken; – *up,* (sich (*Dat.*)) einpauken. 2. *s.,* **–ter,** *s.* der Büffler, Ochser. **–ting,** *s* die Paukerei, Büffelei.

swum [swʌm], *see* **swim.**

swung [swʌŋ], *see* **swing.**

sybarit–e ['sɪbərɑɪt], *s.* der Sybarit, Genüßling, Schwelger, Schlemmer, Wollüstling. **–ic** [–'rɪtɪk], *adj.* sybaritisch, schwelgerisch, verweichlicht. **–ism** [–ɑtɪzm], *s.* die Genußsucht, Schwelgerei.

sycamore ['sɪkəmɔː], *s.* die Sykomore, der Bergahorn.

sycophan–cy ['sɪkəfənsɪ], *s.* die Kriecherei, Angeberei. **–t,** *s.* der Kriecher, Schmeichler, Angeber. **–tic** [–'fæntɪk], *adj.* kriecherisch, schmeichlerisch, angeberisch.

sycosis [sɑɪ'kousɪs], *s.* die Bartflechte.

syenite ['sɑɪənɑɪt], *s.* der Syenit (*Geol.*).

syllab–ary ['sɪləbərɪ], *s.* die Silbentabelle, Silbenliste. **–ic** [sɪ'læbɪk], *adj.* syllabisch, Silben–; silbenbildend, silbig. **–le** ['sɪləbl], 1. *s.* die Silbe; *one- -le word,* einsilbiges Wort; *not a –le,* nicht ein Wort. 2. *v.a.* in Silben bringen, syllabieren. **–led** [–bəld], *adj. suffix* –silbig. **–us** ['sɪləbʌs], *s.* (pl. *–i* [–bɑɪ]) das Verzeichnis, Programm, der Prospekt; Lehrplan; Syllabus (*R.C.*).

sylleps–is [sɪ'lɛpsɪs], *s.* (*pl. –es* [sɪːz]) die Syllepsis.

syllogi–sm ['sɪlədʒɪzm], *s.* der Syllogismus, Vernunftschluß. **–stic** [–'dʒɪstɪk], *adj.* syllogistisch. **–ze** [–dʒɑɪz], *v.n.* durch Syllogismus schließen.

syl–ph [sɪlf], *s.* die Sylphe, der Luftgeist; der Waldgott; (*fig.*) die Sylphe, zierliches Mädchen. **–phlike,** *adj.* sylphenartig. **–van** ['sɪlvən], *adj.* (*Poet.*) waldig, Wald–.

symbio–sis [sɪmbɪˈousɪs], *s.* die Symbiose. **–tic** [–ˈɔtɪk], *adj.* symbio(n)tisch.
symbol [ˈsɪmbəl], *s.* das Sinnbild, Symbol, Zeichen. **–ic(al)** [–ˈbɔlɪk(l)], *adj.* sinnbildlich, symbolisch (*of*, für); *be –ic of*, versinnbildlichen. **–ics**, *pl.* (*sing. constr.*) die Symbolik (*Eccl.*). **–ism** [–bəlɪzm], *s.* sinnbildliche Darstellung, die Symbolik; der Symbolismus (*Art*, *Liter.*). **–ist** [–bəlɪst], *s.* der Anhänger des Symbolismus. **–ization** [–laɪˈzeɪʃən], *s.* die Versinnbildlichung, Symbolisierung. **–ize** [–laɪz], *v.a.* versinnbildlichen, sinnbildlich darstellen, symbolisieren.
symmetr–ic(al) [sɪˈmɛtrɪk(l)], *adj.* gleichmäßig, ebenmäßig, symmetrisch (*also Math.*, usually *–ical*). **–ize** [ˈsɪmɪtraɪz], *v.a.* symmetrisch machen, in Symmetrie bringen. **–y** [ˈsɪmɪtrɪ], *s.* das Ebenmaß, die Symmetrie.
sympath–etic [sɪmpəˈθɛtɪk], *adj.* mitfühlend, teilnehmend, mitleidend, wohlwollend; gleichgestimmt, seelenverwandt, geistesverwandt, kongenial, sympathisch; (*archaic*) geheimwirkend, sympathetisch; *–etic cure*, die Heilung durch Besprechung; *–etic ink*, sympathetische Tinte, die Geheimtinte; *–etic nerve*, der Sympathikus, sympathisches Nervensystem; *–etic strike*, der Sympathiestreik. **–ize** [–θaɪz], *v.n.* mitfühlen, sympathisieren (*with a th.*, mit etwas, *with a p. in a th.*, mit einem in etwas), mitleiden, mitempfinden, sein Mitgefühl *or* Beileid ausdrücken (*with* (*Dat.*)), wohlwollend gegenüberstehen (*with* (*Dat.*)); übereinstimmen, gleichgestimmt sein. **–izer**, *s.* Mitfühlende(r), *m.*; der Anhänger (*with* (*Gen.*)). **–y** [ˈsɪmpəθɪ], *s.* die Sympathie, Zuneigung (*for*, für); Neigung, das Wohlwollen, Mitgefühl, die Mitempfindung (*in*, für); das Mitleid (*for* or *with*, mit), Beileid, die Anteilnahme; Mitleidenschaft, wechselseitige Wirkung (*Physiol.*); die Harmonie, Übereinstimmung, der Einklang; *feel –y for* or *with*, Mitleid haben mit (*a p.*), Anteil nehmen an (*a th.*), teilnehmen an (*Dat.*); *letter of –y*, das Beileidschreiben; *in* or *out of –y with*, aus Zuneigung zu.
sympetalous [sɪmˈpɛtələs], *adj.* mit verwachsener Blumenkrone (*Bot.*).
symphon–ic [sɪmˈfɔnɪk], *adj.* symphonisch, sinfonisch; Symphonie–, Sinfonie–. **–ious** [–ˈfounɪəs], *adj.* harmonisch (*to*, mit). **–ist** [ˈsɪmfənɪst], *s.* der Symphonie-Komponist, Symphoniker. **–y** [ˈsɪmfənɪ], *s.* die Symphonie, Sinfonie, (*also fig.*) harmonischer Zusammenklang.
symphysis [ˈsɪmfɪsɪs], *s.* die Symphyse, Knochenfügung (*Anat.*).
sympodium [sɪmˈpoudɪəm], *s.* die Scheinachse (*Bot.*).
symposi–um [sɪmˈpouzɪəm], *s.* (pl. *–a* [–zɪə]) das Gastmahl, Gelage (*Hist.*); die Sammlung von Beiträgen.
symptom [ˈsɪmptəm], *s.* das Symptom (*of*, für *or* von); Krankheitszeichen; (äußeres) Zeichen, das Anzeichen (*of*, von). **–atic** [–ˈmætɪk], *adj.* symptomatisch; charakteristisch, bezeichnend (*of*, für); *be –atic of*, kennzeichnen, andeuten. **–atology** [–məˈtɔlədʒɪ], *s.* die Symptomatik (*Med.*).
synagogue [ˈsɪnəgɔg], *s.* die Synagoge.
synalepha [sɪnəˈlɪ:fə], *s.* die Verschmelzung zweier Silben.
synantherous [sɪˈnænθərəs], *adj.* mit vereinigten Staubbeuteln (*Bot.*); *– plant*, die Komposite, der Korbblüter.
syncarp [ˈsɪnkɑ:p], *s.* zusammengewachsener Fruchtknoten (*Bot.*).
synchromesh [ˈsɪŋkromɛʃ], *adj.*; *– gear*, das Synchrongetriebe (*Motor.*).
synchron–ism [ˈsɪŋkrənɪzm], *s.* die Gleichzeitigkeit, der Gleichlauf, Synchronismus; synchronistische Zusammenstellung *or* Tabelle. **–ization** [–ˈzeɪʃən], *s.* die Synchronisierung, zeitliches Zusammenfallen; das Zusammenspiel (*Mus.*). **–ize** [–naɪz], 1. *v.n.* gleichzeitig sein, (zeitlich) zusammenfallen, Schritt halten; gleichgehen, synchron laufen (*as clocks*) (*with*, mit). 2. *v.a.* zusammenfallen lassen, zum Zusammenspiel bringen, (zeitlich) in Übereinstimmung bringen; gleichgehend machen (*clocks*); synchronisieren (*film*). **–ous** [–nəs], *adj.* gleichzeitig, gleichlaufend; synchron, gleichgehend (*as clocks*); *be –ous with*, zusammenfallen *or* (*as clocks*) gleichgehen mit.
synclin–al [sɪnˈklaɪnəl], *adj.* muldenförmig (*Geol.*). **–e** [ˈsɪŋklaɪn], *s.* die Mulde (*Geol.*).
syncop–al [ˈsɪŋkəpəl], *adj.* Ohnmachts–. **–ate** [–peɪt], *v.a.* kürzen, zusammenziehen (*words*); synkopieren (*Mus.*). **–ation** [–ˈpeɪʃən], *s.* die Synkope, Synkopierung (*Metr.*, *Mus.*). **–e** [ˈsɪŋkəpɪ], *s.* die Ohnmacht, Bewußtlosigkeit (*Med.*); Synkope (*Mus.*, *Metr.*). **–ic, –tic** [sɪnˈkɔp(t)ɪk], *adj.* Ohnmachts–.
syncret–ic [sɪnˈkrɛtɪk], *adj.* synkretistisch. **–ism** [ˈsɪnkrətɪzm], *s.* der Synkretismus. **–istic** [–ˈtɪstɪk], *adj.*, *see* **–ic.**
syndic [ˈsɪndɪk], *s.* der Syndikus, Vertreter, Bevollmächtigte(r), *m.* **–alism** [–əlɪzm], *s.* der Syndikalismus. **–ate** [–ət], 1. *s.* das Syndikat, Kartell, Konsortium, der Ring (*C.L.*). 2. *v.a.* [–eɪt], zu einem Syndikat zusammenschließen. **–ation** [–ˈkeɪʃən], *s.* die Bildung eines Syndikats.
syne [saɪn], *adv.* (*Scots*) seitdem, lange her; *auld lang –*, vor langer Zeit.
synecdoche [sɪˈnɛkdəkɪ], *s.* die Synekdoche (*Rhet.*).
synergic [sɪˈnə:dʒɪk], *adj.* synergetisch, synergistisch, zusammenwirkend.
synod [ˈsɪnəd], *s.* die Kirchenversammlung, Synode, das Konzil (*Eccl.*). **–al** [–əl], *adj.* **–ic(al)** [–ˈnɔdɪk(l)], *adj.* Synodal–; synodisch (*Astr.*).
synonym [ˈsɪnənɪm], *s.* sinnverwandtes Wort, das Synonym. **–ous** [–ˈnɔnɪməs], *adj.* sinnverwandt, synonym, gleichbedeutend.
synop–sis [sɪˈnɔpsɪs], *s.* (pl. *–ses* [sɪ:z]) die Übersicht, Zusammenfassung; Zusammenschau, der Abriß. **–tic** [–ˈnɔptɪk], 1. *adj.* synoptisch (*Eccl.*), übersichtlich. 2. *s.*, **–tist**, *s.* der Synoptiker.
synovi–a [sɪˈnouvɪə], *s.* die Gelenkschmiere (*Anat.*). **–al** [–vɪəl], *adj.* Gelenkschleim–. **–tis** [saɪnəˈvaɪtɪs], *s.* die Gelenkentzündung.
synta–ctic(al) [sɪnˈtæktɪk(l)], *adj.* syntaktisch **–x** [ˈsɪntæks], die Satzlehre, Syntax.
synthe–sis [ˈsɪnθəsɪs], *s.* (pl. *–ses* [–sɪ:z]) die Synthese, Zusammensetzung, Zusammenfügung, Verbindung; der Aufbau (*Chem.*). **–size**, *see* **–tize.** **–tic(al)** [sɪnˈθɛtɪk(l)], *adj.* synthetisch, zusammensetzend· künstlich hergestellt, Kunst–; *–tic rubber*, der Kunstgummi. **–tize** [ˈsɪnθətaɪz], aufbauen; künstlich herstellen (*from*, aus).
synton–ic [sɪnˈtɔnɪk], *adj.* auf derselben Wellenlänge abgestimmt (*Rad.*). **–ize** [ˈsɪntənaɪz], abstimmen, einstellen (*to*, auf) (*Rad.*). **–y** [ˈsɪntənɪ], *s.* die Resonanz, Abstimmung.
syphili–s [ˈsɪfɪlɪs], *s.* die Syphilis. **–tic** [–ˈlɪtɪk], *adj.* syphilitisch.
syphon, *see* **siphon.**
syringa [sɪˈrɪŋgə], *s.* der Flieder (*Bot.*).
syringe [ˈsɪrɪndʒ], 1. *s.* die Spritze. 2. *v.a.* ausspritzen (*ears, etc.*), bespritzen.
syrin–gitis [sɪrɪnˈdʒaɪtɪs], *s.* die Entzündung der Eustachischen Röhre (*Med.*). **–gotomy** [–ŋˈgɔtəmɪ], *s.* der Fistelschnitt (*Surg.*). **–x** [ˈsɪrɪŋks], *s.* (pl. *–ges* [–dʒɪ:z]) die Syrinx, Hirtenflöte (*Hist.*) Eustachische Röhre (*Anat.*), die Fistel (*Surg.*).
syrup [ˈsɪrʌp], *s.* der Sirup; (Frucht)Saft. **–y**, *adj.* sirupartig, dickflüssig.
system [ˈsɪstəm], *s.* das System, die Anordnung; der Plan, die Methode, Ordnung; Formation (*Geol.*); (*coll.*) der Organismus, Körper; *nervous –*, das Nervensystem; *on the – of*, nach dem Plan *or* System von; *– of pulleys*, der Flaschenzug; *railway –*, das Eisenbahnnetz. **–atic(al)** [–ˈmætɪk(l)], *adj.* planmäßig, methodisch, systematisch, planvoll, zielbewußt. **–atist** [–mətɪst], *s.* der Systematiker. **–atization** [–mətaɪˈzeɪʃən], *s.* die Systematisierung. **–atize** [–mətaɪz], *v.a.* systematisieren, planmäßig *or* methodisch ordnen, in ein System bringen.
systole [ˈsɪstəlɪ], *s.* die Zusammenziehung (des Herzens), das Herzspannen (*Med.*); die Silbenkürzung (vor der Hebung) (*Metr.*).
systyle [ˈsɪstaɪl], *adj.* dicht aneinanderstehend (*of pillars*) (*Arch.*).

T

T, t [tiː], *s.* das T, t; (*coll.*) *to a* –, aufs Haar genau. **– -girder,** *s.* der T-Träger. **– -square,** *s.* die Reißschiene. **– -shaped,** *adj.* T-förmig; *see list of abbreviations.*
ta [tɑː], *int.* (*nursery talk*) danke!
taal [tɑːl], *s.* das Afrikaans(ch).
tab [tæb], *s.* die Latsche, Litze, (Schuh)Strippe; der Zipfel; Kragenspiegel, das Abzeichen (*Mil.*); Schildchen, Etikett, die Etikette; der (Kartei)-Reiter; (*sl.*) die Rechnung; (*sl.*) *keep a – on,* kontrollieren, genau beobachten, registrieren.
tabard [ˈtæbəd], *s.* der Heroldsrock, Wappenrock.
tabby [ˈtæbɪ], 1. *s.* das *or* der Moiré; der Kalkmörtel; (also – *cat*), *s.* getigerte Katze; (*coll.*) alte Jungfer, die Klatschbase. 2. *adj.* gewässert, schillernd, Moiré-gestreift, scheckig. 3. *v.a.* moirieren (*fabric*).
tabernac–le [ˈtæbənækl], 1. *s.* das Zelt, die Hütte, Stiftshütte (*B.*), das Tabernakel (*R.C.*); die Nische mit Schutzdach (*R.C.*); das Bethaus (*of dissenters*); der Sockel (*Naut.*); *feast of –les,* das Laubhüttenfest. 2. *v.n.* wohnen, seine Zelt aufschlagen. 3. *v.a.* schützen, verwahren. **–ular** [–ˈnækjʊlə], *adj.* gegittert, Gitter– (*Arch.*).
tabe–s [ˈteɪbɪːz], *s.* die Auszehrung, Schwindsucht; *dorsal –s,* Rückenmarksschwindsucht. **–scence** [təˈbɛsəns], *s.* die Auszehrung. **–tic** [təˈbɛtɪk], 1. *adj.* schwindsüchtig. 2. *s.* Schwindsüchtige(r), *m.*
tablature [ˈtæblətjʊə], *s.* die Tabulatur (*Mus.*); die Deckenmalerei, Wandmalerei (*Paint.*); (*fig.*) das Phantasiebild.
table [ˈteɪbl], 1. *s.* der Tisch, die Tafel (*also Arch.*), (*fig.*) die Kost, Mahlzeit, das Essen, die Tischgesellschaft, Spielgesellschaft; die Tabelle, das Verzeichnis, Register; das Feld (*Arch.*); Plateau, die Landfläche (*Top.*); *bedside* –, der Nachttisch; *dining* –, der Eßtisch; *folding* –, der Klapptisch; *multiplication* –, das Einmaleins; *occasional* –, der Gartentisch; *Round* –, die Tafelrunde; *sliding* –, der Ausziehtisch; *time-* –, der Stundenplan; Fahrplan, das Kursbuch; (*a*) (*with nouns*) – *of contents,* das Inhaltsverzeichnis; (*B.*) *–s of the Law,* Gesetzestafeln, 10 Gebote (*pl.*); – *of logarithms,* die Logarithmentafel; (*b*) (*with verbs*) *clear the* –, (den Tisch) abdecken; *keep a good* –, eine gute Küche führen; *lay the* –, (den Tisch) decken; *learn one's –s,* rechnen lernen; *take the head of the* –, bei Tisch obenan sitzen; *turn the –s,* der Sache eine andre Wendung geben, den Spieß umdrehen ((*up*)*on,* gegen); *the –s are turned,* das Blatt hat sich gewendet; (*c*) (*with prepositions*) *at* –, bei Tisch, beim Essen; *sit at a* –, an einem Tisch sitzen; *rise from* –, die Tafel aufheben; *lay a th. on the* –, etwas zurückstellen *or* liegenlassen (*Parl.*); *lie on the* –, verschoben werden; *put on to the* –, vorbringen (*a proposal*); *sit down to a* –, sich zu Tisch setzen. 2. *v.a.* tabellarisch verzeichnen *or* eintragen; vorlegen, auf den Tisch legen (*a proposal*). **– -centre,** *s.* der Tischläufer. **–cloth,** *s.* das Tischtuch. **– d'hôte,** *s.* feste Speisefolge. **– -knife,** *s.* das Tischmesser. **– -lamp,** *s.* die Tischlampe. **–land,** *s.* die Hochebene. **– -linen,** *s.* das Tischzeug. **– -mat,** *s.* der Untersatz. **– -napkin,** *s.* die Serviette. **– -rapping,** *s.* das Tischklopfen. **– -salt,** *s.* das Tafelsalz. **– -spoon,** *s.* der Eßlöffel. **– -talk,** *s.* das Tischgespräch. **– -tennis,** *s.* das Tischtennis. **– -turning,** *s.* das Tischrücken. **– -top,** *s.* die Tischplatte. **–ware,** *s.* das Tischgeschirr. **– -water,** *s.* das Mineralwasser.
tableau [ˈtæbloʊ], *s.* (pl. *–s* or *–x*) das Gemälde, anschauliche Darstellung; das Gruppenbild; – *vivant,* lebendes Bild.
tabl–et [ˈtæblɪt], *s.* das Täfelchen, die Inschrifttafel, Gedenktafel; Schreibtafel, der Notizblock; die Tafel (*of chocolate*), das Stück (*of soap, etc.*); die Tablette (*Med.*). **–oid,** 1. *s.* die Pastille, Tablette, das Plätzchen (*Med.*). (*coll.*) die Volkszeitung mit kurzen Nachrichten und vielen Bildern. 2. *attrib.* konzentriert.
taboo [təˈbuː[, 1. *s.* der Bann, Verruf, das Verbot, der Tabu; *put under* –, für Tabu erklären. 2. *pred. adj.* unantastbar, tabu, verboten, verrufen, verpönt, in Verruf. 3. *v.a.* für Tabu *or* in Verruf erklären, in den Bann tun, meiden.
tabor [ˈteɪbə], *s.* die Handtrommel, das Tamburin.
tabouret [ˈtæbərɪt], *s.* der Hocker; der Strickrahmen.
tabula [ˈtæbjʊlə], *s.*; – *rasa,* unbeschriebenes Blatt; reiner Tisch; völlige Leere.
tabula–r [ˈtæbjʊlə], *adj.* tafelförmig; Tafel–, dünn, flach; blätterig; tabellarisch, Tabellen–. **–te** [–leɪt], 1. *adj.* tafelförmig. 2. *v.a.* in Tabellen bringen, tabellarisch ordnen. **–tion** [–leɪʃən], *s.* die Tabellarisierung, tabellarische Darstellung. **–tor,** *s.* der Tabulator, Spalten– *or* Kolonnensteller (*typewriters*).
tachometer [tæˈkɔmɪtə], *s.* der Tourenzähler, Umdrehszähler.
tacit [ˈtæsɪt], *adj.* stillschweigend. **–turn** [–təːn], *adj.* schweigsam, wortkarg. **–urnity** [–ˈtəːnɪtɪ], *s.* die Schweigsamkeit, Verschlossenheit, Wortkargheit.
tack [tæk], 1. *v.a.* heften (*sewing*); befestigen, anheften (*Carp., etc.*); (*fig.*) anschließen, anhängen ((*on*)*to,* an); – *together,* zusammenheften. 2. *v.n.* wenden, kreuzen, lavieren (*Naut.*). 3. *s.* kleiner Nagel, der Stift, die Zwecke, der Heftelstich (*sewing*); der Hals (*of a sail*); das Lavieren (*Naut.*); der Gang (beim Lavieren); (*coll.*) die Handlungsweise, Richtung, der Weg, Kurs, Plan; die Kost, Nahrung (*Naut.*); (*sl.*) der Bafel, das Brack; der Ausschuß, die Ausschußware; *change one's* –, eine neue Richtung einnehmen; *hard* –, der Schiffszwieback; *on the wrong* –, auf der falschen Fährte, auf dem Holzwege; *get down to brass –s,* zur Sache *or* zu der Tatsache kommen; *be on a new* –, (*fig.*) einen neuen Kurs einschlagen; *on the port* –, nach Backbord lavieren. (*Amer.*) *thumb-* –, die Reißzwecke.
tack–iness [ˈtækɪnɪs], *s.* die Klebrigkeit. **–y,** *adj.* klebrig.
tackle [ˈtækl], 1. *s.* die Talje (*Naut.*); das Takel, Takelwerk; (also *block and* –) der Flaschenzug; (*coll.*) das Gerät, Gerätschaften, Werkzeuge, die Ausrüstung; das Angreifen (*Footb.*); *fishing-* –, das Angelgerät; *ground-* –, das Ankertauwerk (*Naut.*); *hoisting-* –, der Flaschenzug, das Hebewerk; (*coll.*) *shaving-* –, das Rasierzeug. 2. *v.a.* (*coll.*) angreifen, (an)packen (*Footb.*); (*fig.*) angehen (*a p.*) (*on,* betreffs); in Angriff nehmen, anpacken (*a th.*).
tact [tækt], *s.* der Takt (*also Mus.*); das Taktgefühl, Feingefühl, Zartgefühl. **–ful,** *adj.* taktvoll. **–fulness,** *s. see* **–. –less,** *adj.* taktlos. **–lessness,** *s.* die Taktlosigkeit.
tactic–al [ˈtæktɪkl], *adj.* taktisch (*Mil.*); (*fig.*) klug, planvoll. **–ian** [–ˈtɪʃən], *s.* der Taktiker. **–s,** *pl.* (*sing. constr.*) die Taktik (*also fig. pl. constr.*).
tact–ile [ˈtæktaɪl], *adj.* fühlbar, greifbar; tastfähig, Tast–. **–ility** [–ˈtɪlɪtɪ], *s.* die Fühlbarkeit, Tastfähigkeit. **–ual** [–tjʊəl], *adj.* tastbar, Tast–.
tactless, *see* **tact.**
tadpole [ˈtædpoʊl], *s.* die Kaulquappe.
taedium vitae [ˈtiːdɪəmˈvaɪtɪ], *s.* die Lebensmüdigkeit.
taenia [ˈtiːnɪə], *s.* die Längsfaserschicht des Dickdarms (*Anat.*); der Bandwurm.
taffeta [ˈtæfɪtə], *s.* der Taft, Taffet.
taffrail [ˈtæfreɪl], *s.* das Heckbord, die Heckreling (*Naut.*).
[1]**tag** [tæg], 1. *s.* das Anhängsel, der Zipfel; die (Schuh)Strippe; der Stift eines Schnursenkels; die Etikette, das Etikett, Schildchen, angehängter Zettel; (*fig. coll.*) stehende Redensart, bekannter Ausspruch, feste Wendung; (*coll.*) (also – *end*) das Ende, der Rest; *rag, – and bobtail,* Krethi und Plethi; das Lumpenpack. 2. *v.a.* mit einem Stift versehen; (*sl.*) verfolgen (*a p.*). 3. *v.n.* (*coll.*) – *along after a p.*, einem überall nachlaufen.
[2]**tag,** 1. *s.* das Letztengeben, Kriegenspielen (*game*). 2. *v.a.* den Letzten geben (*Dat.*), kriegen, haschen.
[1]**tail** [teɪl], *s.* die Beschränkung der Erbfolge (*Law*); *in – male,* vererblich an die männlichen Erben.
[2]**tail,** 1. *s.* der Schwanz (*also of a letter*), (*Poet.*)

Schweif (*also of a comet*); Schoß (*of a coat, shirt, etc.*); die Schleppe (*of a dress*); der Hals (*of a note*) (*Mus.*); die Rückseite, Kehrseite (*of coins*); (*fig.*) der Schluß, das Ende; der Anhang; *pl.* (*coll.*) der Frack; *out of the – of one's eye*, mit einem Seitenblick; *turn –*, Fersengeld geben, ausreißen; (*coll.*) *– between the legs*, betreten, bedeppert; (*coll.*) *–sup*, in guter Stimmung. 2. *v.a.* mit einem Schwanz versehen (*as a kite*); stutzen; (*coll.*) dicht folgen (*Dat.*) (*a p.*); *– in*, in die Wand einlassen (*a beam, etc.*). 3. *v.n.*; *– after*, hergehen hinter (*a p.*); *– away*, abnehmen, sich verziehen *or* verlieren; *– off*, abfallen, abnehmen, kleiner werden. **--board,** *s.* das Rückbrett (*Motor.*). **--coat,** *s.* der Frack. **-ed,** *adj.* geschwingt; (*as suffix*) -schwänzig. **--end,** *s.* das Ende, der Schluß. **--gate,** *s.* unteres Tor (*of a lock*). **-ings,** *pl.* (Erz)Abfälle, Rückstände (*pl.*); das Ausschußmehl. **-less,** *adj.* schwanzlos, ohne Schwanz, ungeschwänzt; *-less airplane*, das Nurflügelflugzeug. **--light,** *s.* das Schlußlicht. **--piece,** *s.* die Schlußverzierung, Schlußvignette (*Typ.*); der Saitenhalter (*of a violin*). **--plane,** *s.* die Höhenflosse (*Av.*). **--race,** *s.* das Schußwasser. **--skid,** *s.* der (Schwanz)Sporn (*Av.*). **--spin,** *s.* das Trudeln (*Av.*). **--unit,** *s.* das Leitwerk (*Av.*). **--wind,** *s.* der Rückenwind.

tailor ['teɪlə], 1. *s.* der Schneider; *-'s dummy*, die Modellierpuppe. 2. *v.n.* & *a.* schneidern. **-ess,** *s.* die Schneiderin. **-ing,** *s.* die Schneiderarbeit. **--made,** 1. *adj.* nach Maß. 2. *s.* das Schneiderkleid, Schneiderkostüm.

taint [teɪnt], 1. *v.a.* vergiften, anstecken; verderben, beeinträchtigen; beflecken, besudeln. 2. *v.n.* verderben, schlecht werden. 3. *s.* die Ansteckung, der Fleck, Makel, die Verderbtheit; *hereditary –*, erbliche Belastung. **-less,** *adj.* unbefleckt, makellos, rein.

take [teɪk], **1.** *ir.v.a.* nehmen (*a p. or th.*); (*a p.*) annehmen (*also shape*), aufnehmen; bringen, führen, begleiten, ergreifen, (*also a th.* **or** *fig.*) fassen, packen, fangen, gefangennehmen, sich bemächtigen (*Gen.*), überfallen, ertappen, überraschen (*in*, bei); (*a th.*) in Besitz nehmen, kapern (*ship*), erobern (*town*), einnehmen (*place*), mieten (*a room*), beziehen (*a newspaper*), auf sich nehmen (*duty, etc.*), zu sich nehmen, einnehmen (*food*), wählen, einschlagen (*way*), sich zuziehen (*illness*); mitnehmen, bringen; erfordern, in Anspruch nehmen, kosten, bedürfen, brauchen (*time*); verstehen, begreifen, erfassen, aufnehmen, auffassen, auslegen, der Meinung sein, annehmen, hinnehmen, glauben; entnehmen, fortnehmen, wegnehmen (*from* (*Dat.*)). **(a)** (*with nouns, pronouns, or adjectives.*) *– account of*, beachten; *– action*, Schritte unternehmen; *– his advice*, seinem Rat folgen; *– aim at*, zielen auf *or* nach; *– the air*, frische Luft schöpfen; abfliegen, aufsteigen (*Av.*); *– alarm at*, in Angst geraten über; *– a bath*, ein Bad nehmen, sich baden; *– a breath*, aufatmen, Atem holen; *– a p.'s breath away*, einem den Atem nehmen; *– a breather*, Luft holen, Ruhepause machen; *– care*, sich in acht nehmen, sich hüten; *– care of*, acht geben auf, sorgen für (*a th.*), sich annehmen (*Gen.*) (*a p.*); *– care to do*, trachten *or* nicht vergessen zu tun; *– the chair*, den Vorsitz übernehmen; *– one's chance*, die Gelegenheit ausnützen, es darauf ankommen lassen; *– a chance*, auf gut Glück versuchen; *– chances*, die Gefahr auf sich nehmen, sich der Gefahr aussetzen; *– charge*, die Verantwortung übernehmen (*of*, für); *– a class*, Stunde *or* Unterricht geben; *– comfort*, sich trösten; *– compassion on*, Mitleid empfinden mit, sich erbarmen über; *– counsel*, sich beraten; *– the consequences*, die Konsequenzen ziehen, die Folgen tragen; *– courage*, Mut fassen; *let s. th. – its course*, einer S. freien Lauf lassen; *– cover*, Deckung nehmen; *– the curtain*, vor dem Vorhang erscheinen (*Theat.*); *– a drive*, eine Spazierfahrt machen; ausfahren; *– effect*, in Kraft treten; *– exercise*, sich (*Dat.*) Bewegung machen; *– a fancy to*, eine Neigung fassen zu; *– the field*, ins Feld rücken; *– fire*, Feuer fangen, aufflammen; *– flight*, fliehen; *– the floor*, das Wort ergreifen; *– heart*, sich (*Dat.*) ein Herz fassen, Mut fassen; *– a hedge*, über eine Hecke setzen; *– a hint*, einen Wink verstehen, es sich (*Dat.*) gesagt sein lassen; *– a hold of*, erfassen (*a th.*), sich bemächtigen (*Gen.*) (*a p.*); *– hold on*, Eindruck machen auf, beeindrucken (*Acc.*); *– a holiday*, Ferien machen, Urlaub nehmen; *– horse*, reiten, aufsitzen; *be –n ill*, krank werden; (*coll.*) *– it or leave it*, das ist mein alleräußerstes Angebot; *as I – it*, nach meiner Auffassung *or* Meinung, wie ich es verstehe; (*coll.*) *– it easy*, es sich (*Dat.*) bequem machen, sich nicht überanstrengen, sich schonen; (*coll.*) sich nicht aufregen; *I – it to be*, ich finde *or* denke *or* nehme an es ist; (*coll.*) *I can – it*, ich kann es ertragen; *– it from me*, glauben Sie mirs; *– a journey*, eine Reise machen; *– the lead*, die Führung übernehmen; (*fig.*) den Ton angeben; *– leave to do*, sich (*Dat.*) erlauben zu tun; *– one's leave*, fortgehen; *– one's leave of*, Abschied nehmen von; *– leave of one's senses*, nicht bei Sinnen sein; *– the liberty of doing*, sich (*Dat.*) die Freiheit nehmen zu tun; *– liberties*, sich (*Dat.*) Freiheiten herausnehmen *or* gestatten (*with*, gegenüber); *– measures*, Maßregeln ergreifen; *– one's life*, sich (*Dat.*) das Leben nehmen; *it will – me too long*, es wird mich zu weit führen; *how long will it –?* wie lange dauert es?; *– the minutes*, das Protokoll aufnehmen; *– note of*, berücksichtigen; *– a note* or *notes of*, aufschreiben, notieren; *– notice*, aufachten; *– notice of*, Kenntnis nehmen von (*a th.*), beachten, Notiz nehmen von (*a p.*); *– no notice of*, nicht beachten, ignorieren; *– an oath*, schwören, einen Eid ablegen; *– offence at*, Anstoß nehmen an, sich beleidigt fühlen über, übelnehmen; *– office*, ein Amt antreten; *– o.s.*, sich begeben (*to*, nach); *– pains*, sich Mühe geben; *– a part in*, teilnehmen an; *– a part*, eine Rolle übernehmen; *– a p.'s part*, seine Partei ergreifen; *– s.o.'s photograph*, einen aufnehmen; *– pity on*, Mitleid haben mit *or* über; *– place*, stattfinden, sich ereignen; *– the place of*, ersetzen (*a p. or th.*), die Stellung einnehmen (*Gen.*) (*a p.*); *– your places!* setzen Sie sich! *– pleasure in*, Vergnügen finden an; *– one's pleasure*, sich amüsieren; *– possession of*, Besitz ergreifen, sich bemächtigen; *– pot-luck*, vorlieb nehmen müssen; *– pride in*, stolz sein auf, seinen Stolz *or* Ehrgeiz setzen in; *– a rest*, sich ausruhen; *– one's rise*, entspringen (*in*, in; *from*, aus); (*coll.*) *– a rise out of*, in die Wolle bringen; *– a risk*, sich einer Gefahr aussetzen; *– a seat*, Platz nehmen, sich setzen; *– shelter*, sich unterstellen, Schutz suchen (*from*, vor); *– ship*, an Bord gehen, sich einschiffen; *what size does he – in shoes?* welche Schuhgröße hat er?; *– one's stand*, sich aufstellen; (*fig.*) eine Stellung einnehmen; *– steps*, Maßregeln ergreifen; *– a stick to*, verprügeln; *the word –s the stress on the first syllable.* das Wort hat den Ton auf der ersten Silbe; *taking one th. with another*, eins ins andere gerechnet; *that –s time*, das erfordert, bedarf, braucht *or* kostet Zeit; *– the time*, sich (*Dat.*) die Zeit nehmen; *– one's time*, sich Zeit lassen; *it will – me a long time*, ich brauche viel Zeit; *– trouble*, sich (*Dat.*) Mühe geben (*over*, bei); *– the trouble*, sich die Mühe nehmen *or* machen; *– a turn for the worse*, sich zum Schlechtern wenden; *– a turn*, einen Spaziergang machen; *– a turn at*, sich vorübergehend befassen mit, sich versuchen an; *– one's turn*, an die Reihe kommen; *– turns*, (sich) abwechseln; *– umbrage*, see *– offence*; *– a view of*, eine Auffassung haben von; *– a walk*, einen Spaziergang machen; *– warning*, sich warnen lassen (*by*, von); *– the water*, ins Wasser gehen, vom Stapel laufen (*as ship*); *– the waters*, Brunnen trinken; *– wing*, davonfliegen. **(b)** (*with prepositions*) *– s.o. at his word*, einen beim Worte nehmen; *– by surprise*, überraschen, überrumpeln; *– for*, nehmen *or* halten für; *– for granted*, als selbstverständlich *or* erwiesen annehmen, voraussetzen; *– too much for granted*, sich (*Dat.*) zu viel herausnehmen; *– s.o. for a walk*, einen auf einen Spaziergang mitnehmen; *– from*, wegnehmen, abziehen von; *you can – it from me*, du kannst es mir glauben; *– in hand*, unternehmen (*a th.*), sich annehmen (*Gen.*) (*a p.*); *– a woman in marriage*, jemand zur Frau nehmen; *– s.o. into one's confidence*, einen ins Vertrauen ziehen; *– into account* or *consideration*, in Betracht *or* in Erwägung ziehen, berücksichtigen; – *into one's own hands*, sich selbst annehmen (*Gen.*); – *into one's head*, sich in den Kopf setzen; – *the edge off*, abstumpfen (*a knife*); (*fig.*) die Spitze abbrechen (*Dat.*), stillen (*appetite*); – *s.o. off his feet*, einen umwerfen; – *a th. off s.o.'s hands*, einem etwas abnehmen; – *s.o.'s mind off a th.*, einen von einer S. ablenken; – *a load off his mind*, ihm einen Stein vom Herzen nehmen; – *the skin off*, die Haut abziehen (*Dat.*), enthäuten; – *out of*, herausnehmen, fortnehmen *or* entfernen aus, nehmen (*Dat.*); (*coll.*) – *it out of s.o.*, einen ermüden *or* erschöpfen *or* hernehmen; einem stark zusetzen, einen arg mitnehmen; seine Wut auslassen an einem, sich rächen an einem; *be –n out of o.s.*, sich selbst vergessen; – *a p. out of himself*, einen über sich selbst erheben; – *a p. out of his way*, einen einen Umweg machen lassen; – *to heart*, sich (*Dat.*) zu Herzen nehmen; – *to pieces*, auseinandernehmen, zerlegen; – *a woman to wife*, jemand zur Frau nehmen; – *upon o.s.*, auf sich (*Acc.*) nehmen; – *with one*, mitnehmen; (*coll.*) *be –n with*, entzückt *or* begeistert werden von. **(c)** (*with adverbs*) – *aback*, überraschen, verblüffen; – *along*, mitnehmen; – *amiss*, übelnehmen; – *away*, wegnehmen, fortnehmen; abziehen; – *away a p.'s breath*, einem den Atem rauben; – *back*, zurücknehmen, zurückbringen; widerrufen (*a statement*); zurückversetzen, zurückführen (*a p.*) (*in spirit*); – *down*, herunternehmen; fällen (*tree*), abreißen, abtragen (*building*); niederschreiben, zu Papier bringen; demütigen, einen Dämpfer aufsetzen (*Dat.*) (*a p.*); – *forward*, weiterbringen; – *in*, einnehmen; annehmen, übernehmen (*work, money, etc.*), ankaufen, einkaufen, einlegen (*goods*), einschließen (*expanse, etc.*), einlassen, einnähen, enger machen (*dress*), einziehen (*sail*), einführen, zu Tisch führen, beherbergen, aufnehmen (*a p.*), halten (*newspaper*); (*fig.*) in sich fassen, umfassen, erkennen, erfassen; überschauen; (*coll.*) anführen, übers Ohr hauen (*a p.*); – *in petrol*, tanken; – *off*, abnehmen (*hat, etc.*), ablegen, ausziehen (*coat, etc.*); einstellen (*train, etc.*); (*coll.*) nachahmen, aufziehen, karikieren (*a p.*); – *a day off*, sich (*Dat.*) einen Tag freinehmen; – *o.s. off*, sich fortmachen; – *on*, annehmen (*appearance*), anstellen, einstellen, engagieren (*a p.*), unternehmen (*a job*), eingehen (*a bet*); (*coll.*) es aufnehmen mit (*a p.*); – *out*, herausnehmen; entfernen (*a spot*), entleihen (*a book*), abheben (*money*), abschließen (*insurance*), lösen, erwerben (*a licence*), herausbringen, herausführen (*a p.*); – *over*, übernehmen; (*coll.*) *be –n short*, Durchfall bekommen; – *up*, aufnehmen (*loan, stitch*), aufreißen (*the street*), sich zuwenden, ergreifen (*career*), einnehmen (*a post*), antreten (*a place*), mitnehmen (*passengers*), anziehen, enger machen (*loose belt, etc.*), nehmen (*residence*), beziehen (*a position*), (*coll.*) (*fig.*) unterbrechen, zurechtsetzen (*a p.*); unternehmen, sich befassen mit *or* verlegen auf, sich widmen *or* annehmen (*Dat.*), anfangen mit (*activity*), antreten (*duties*); einnehmen (*space*), wegnehmen (*time*); – *up the cudgels for*, eintreten *or* Partei nehmen für; – *s.o. up short*, einen anfahren; *be –n up with*, vertieft sein in, beschäftigt sein mit. **2.** *ir.v.n.* wirken, Wirkung haben (*as medicine*), Eindruck machen, anschlagen, eindringen; Beifall, Gefallen *or* Anklang finden, einschlagen (*with*, bei); Wurzel fassen (*of plants*), anbeißen (*of fish*); Feuer fangen; sich photographieren lassen; (*with prepositions*) – *after*, nachgeraten, nachschlagen, ähneln (*Dat.*); – *from*, herabsetzen, schwächen, Abbruch tun (*Dat.*); – *off*, abfliegen (*Av.*); (*coll.*) – *on*, gerührt sein; sich aufregen; sich grämen; (*coll.*) gut aufgenommen werden; – *to*, sich begeben nach, Zuflucht nehmen zu, Zuflucht suchen in; liebgewinnen; sich beschäftigen mit, sich abgeben mit, sich legen auf (*Acc.*); sich widmen (*Dat.*); Gefallen finden an; – *to drinking*, sich das Trinken angewöhnen, zu trinken anfangen; – *to one's heels*, Fersengeld geben, sich aus dem Staube machen; – *to the water*, gern ins Wasser gehen (*as a dog*); sich ins Wasser flüchten; – *to the woods*, sich in den Wald schlagen; – *kindly to a p.*, einem freundlich begegnen, Sympathie fassen für einen; – *up with bad company*, sich mit schlechter Gesellschaft einlassen. **3.** *s.* der Fang (*of fish*), die Einnahme (*at box office*), Szenenaufnahme (*films*), die Schiebung (*Typ.*). **--in** *s.* (*sl.*) der Betrug. **-n,** *see* **–**. **--off,** *s.* (*coll.*) die Karikatur; der Start, Abflug (*Av.*), Absprung (*diving*); *--off run*, der Anlauf (*Av.*). **-r,** *s.* der Käufer, Abnehmer.

taking, 1. *adj.* einnehmend, anziehend, reizend, fesselnd. 2. *s.* das Nehmen, die Einnahme (*of a fortress, etc.*); (*usually pl.*) Einnahmen (*pl.*), der Gewinn.

talc [tælk], *s.*, **-um** [-əm] *s.* der Talk(um); *-um powder*, der Hautpuder.

tale [teɪl], *s.* die Erzählung, Geschichte, der Bericht; (also *fairy--*) das Märchen, (*archaic*) die Zahl, Aufzählung; *thereby hangs a –*, daran knüpft sich eine Geschichte; *old wives' –*, das Ammenmärchen; *dead men tell no –s*, tote Hunde beißen nicht; *tell –s* (*out of school*), aus der Schule schwatzen *or* plaudern, klatschen, angeben. **--bearer,** *s.* der Zwischenträger, Angeber, das Quatschmaul.

talent [ˈtælənt], *s.* die Gabe, Anlage, Begabung, Fähigkeit, das Talent (*also coin, Hist.*) *man of –*, talentvoller *or* begabter Mann. **-ed** [-ɪd], *adj.* begabt, talentiert, talentvoll. **-less,** *adj.* talentlos, unbegabt.

tales [teɪlz], *s.* die Liste der Ersatzgeschworenen (*Law*). **-man,** *s.* der Ersatzmann eines Schwurgerichts.

talion [ˈtælɪən], *s.* die Wiedervergeltung (*Law*).

talisman [ˈtælɪzmən], *s.* der Talisman, das Zaubermittel. **-ic** [-ˈmænɪk], *adj.* zauberisch, magisch.

talk [tɔ:k], **1.** *v.n.* reden; sich unterhalten (*to* or *with*, mit; *of*, von; *about* or *on*, über); klatschen; (*coll.*) *now you are –ing*, nun hat dein Reden Sinn, das läßt sich hören; (*coll.*) *you can –*, Sie haben gut reden; (*coll.*) – *big*, aufschneiden, großreden; (*a*) (*with preps.*) (*coll.*) – *about your roses, you should see mine*, wenn deine Rosen gut sein sollen, dann mußt du meine erst sehen; – *of*, sprechen von; – *of doing*, davon sprechen zu tun; *-ing of*, bezüglich, da wir gerade sprechen von; – *over the heads of one's audience*, über die Köpfe der Zuhörer hinwegreden; – *round a th.*, um etwas herumreden *or* herumsprechen; (*sl.*) – *through one's hat*, dummes Zeug reden; – *to*, sprechen mit; (*coll.*) tadeln, schelten; die Meinung sagen (*Dat.*); – *to o.s.*, vor sich hinreden; (*b*) (*with adverbs*) (*coll.*) – *back*, grob antworten. **2.** *v.a.* sprechen (*German, etc.*); – *nonsense*, Unsinn reden; – *sense*, vernünftig reden; – *shop*, fachsimpeln; (*sl.*) – *turkey*, offen *or* ohne Umschweife reden; – *a p. down*, einen zum Schweigen bringen *or* unter den Tisch reden; – *a p. into*, einen durch Reden bringen zu, überreden; – *o.s. into*, sich einreden; – *a p. out of*, einem ausreden, einen durch Reden abbringen von (*his plan*) *or* bringen um (*his money, etc.*); – *one's head off*, sich heiser reden; – *over*, besprechen; – *a p. over* or *round*, einen überreden. **3.** *s.* das Gespräch, die Unterhaltung; der Vortrag, die Ansprache; *it is all –*, es ist nur leeres Gerede; *it is all the –*, es geht das Gerücht; *idle –*, leeres Geschwätz; *small –*, das Geplauder, leichte Plauderei; – *of the town*, das Stadtgespräch. **-ative,** *adj.* gesprächig, redselig, geschwätzig. **-ativeness,** *s.* die Gesprächigkeit, Geschwätzigkeit, Redseligkeit. (*sl.*) **-ee--ee,** *s.* das Geschwätz, Gewäsch. **-er,** *s.* der Schwätzer. (*coll.*) **-ie,** *s.* der Tonfilm. **-ing,** 1. *s.* das Geplauder; *all the -ing was on his side*, er führte allein das Wort. 2. *attrib.*; *-ing-film* or *-picture*, *s.* der Tonfilm. (*coll.*) **-ing-to,** *s.* die Schelte, Standpauke; *give s.o. a -ing-to*, einem ins Gewissen reden, einen ins Gebet nehmen.

tall [tɔ:l], *adj.* groß, lang, schlank (*of stature*), hoch (*as trees, houses, etc.*); (*coll.*) – *order*, starke Zumutung, starkes Stück, harte Nuß; (*coll.*) – *story*, unglaubliche *or* übertriebene Geschichte, das Seemannsgarn; (*coll.*) – *talk*, großspuriges Reden. **-boy,** *s.* die Kommode. **-ish,** *adj.* ziemlich groß. **-ness,** *s.* die Länge, Höhe, Größe.

tallow [ˈtæloʊ], 1. *s.* der Talg, das Unschlitt. 2. *v.a.* mit Talg einschmieren; – *candle*, das Talglicht. **--chandler,** *s.* der Lichtzieher. **--faced,** *adj.* bleich. **-y,** *adj.* talgig.

tally ['tælɪ], 1. *s.* das Kerbholz; (*coll.*) die Rechnung; Etikette, das Etikett, die Marke, der Schein, Kupon; das Seitenstück, Gegenstück, Duplikat (*of*, zu). 2. *v.a.* anholen, einziehen (*Naut.*); buchen, registrieren, kontrollieren; bezeichnen. 3. *v.n.*; – *with*, passen zu, (überein)stimmen mit; entsprechen, gleichkommen (*Dat.*). **--sheet,** *s.* der Zählbogen, das Protokoll. **--system,** *s.* das Abzahlungssytem. **--trade,** *s.* das Abzahlungsgeschäft.
tally-ho ['tælɪ'hoʊ], 1. *int.* halali! (*Hunt.*). 2. *s.* der Weidruf, Jagdruf.
talmi-gold ['tælmɪ'goʊld], *s.* das Talmi.
talmud ['tælmʌd], *s.* der Talmud. **–ic** [–'mʌdɪk], *adj.* talmudisch.
talon ['tælən], *s.* die Klaue, Kralle; die Kehlleiste (*Arch.*), der Talon (*Cards*, *C.L.*), der Zinskupon, die Zinsleiste, der Erneuerungsschein (*C.L.*).
talus ['teɪləs], *s.* das Sprungbein (*Anat.*); die Böschung, Abdachung (*Fort.*); die Schutthalde, das Geröll (*Geol.*).
tamable, *see* **tameable.**
tamarack ['tæməræk], *s.* Amerikanische Lärche (*Bot.*).
tamarin ['tæmərɪn], *s.* der Tamarin, Seidenaffe (*Zool.*).
tamarind ['tæmərɪnd], *s.* die Tamarinde (*Bot.*).
tamarisk ['tæmərɪsk], *s.* die Tamariske (*Bot.*).
tambour ['tæmbəː], 1. *s.* die Trommel; runde Stickrahmen; die Säulentrommel, zylindrischer Unterbau einer Kuppel (*Arch.*). 2. *v.a.* tamburieren, sticken. **--frame,** *s.* der Stickrahmen. **–ine** [–bə'riːn], *s.* das Tamburin, die Handtrommel. **--stitch,** *s.* der Tamburierstich. **--work,** *s.* die Tamburierarbeit.
tame [teɪm], 1. *v.a.* zähmen, bändigen (*an animal*); (*fig.*) bezähmen, gefügig machen, unterwerfen, beugen. 2. *adj.* zahm; (*fig.*) mutlos, unterwürfig; gefügig; (*coll.*) geistlos, matt, schal, langweilig, eindruckslos. **–able,** *adj.* (be)zähmbar. **–ness,** *s.* die Zahmheit; Mutlosigkeit; Langweiligkeit, Geistlosigkeit. **–r,** *s.* der Bändiger (*of animals*).
tam-o'-shanter ['tæmə'ʃæntə], *s.* Baskenmütze.
tamp [tæmp], 1. *v.a.* abdämmen (*hole*); feststampfen (*the charge*). 2. *s.* die Handramme. **–ing,** *s.* die Stopfmasse, Stampfmasse.
tamper ['tæmpə], *v.n.* sich einmischen, hineinpfuschen; – *with*, sich (ein)mischen in, hineinpfuschen in, herumpfuschen an (*a th.*); verfälschen (*a document*); intrigieren *or* heimlich unterhandeln mit, zu bestechen suchen (*a p.*).
tampion ['tæmpɪən], *s.* der Mündungspfropfen (*of a gun*).
tampon ['tæmpən], 1. *s.* der Pfropfen; Mullbausch, Wattebausch, Gazestreifen (*Surg.*). 2. *v.a.* tamponieren (*a wound*).
tan [tæn], 1. *s.* die Lohe; die Lohfarbe, braune Farbe; der Sonnenbrand. 2. *v.a.* gerben; bräunen (*one's face*); (*sl.*) durchgerben, (durch)prügeln (*a p.*). 3. *v.n.* braun *or* sonnenverbrannt werden. 4. *adj.* lohfarben, (gelb)braun. **–ned,** *adj.* sonn(en)-verbrannt. **–ner,** *see* **tanner.** **--pit,** *s.* die Lohgrube. **--yard,** *s.* die Gerberei.
tandem ['tændəm], 1. *s.* das Tandem (*also Cycl.*); zwei hintereinander gespannte Pferde. 2. *adv.*; *drive* –, mit hintereinander gespannten Pferden fahren.
¹tang [tæŋ], 1. *s.* scharfer Ton *or* Klang, scharfer Geschmack *or* Geruch; (*fig.*) der Beigeschmack, Anflug (*of*, von). 2. *v.n.* laut ertönen. 3. *v.a.* anschlagen (*a bell*).
²tang, 1. *s.* der Griffzapfen, Heftzapfen (*of a knife*), Dorn, die Angelzunge (*of a buckle*). 2. *v.a.* mit einer Angel versehen.
³tang, *s.* der Seetang, die Braunalge (*Bot.*).
tangen–cy ['tændʒənsɪ], *s.* die Berührung. **–t** [–ənt], 1. *s.* die Tangente; *–t of an angle*, die Winkeltangente; *fly* or *go off at a –t*, vom Gegenstande abspringen; *–t elevation*, der Aufsatzwinkel (*Artil.*); *–t plane*, die Berührungsebene. 2. *adj.* **–tial** [–'dʒɛnʃəl], *adj.* Berührungs–, Tangential–, (*fig.*) flüchtig, sprunghaft, oberflächlich; *be –tial to*, berühren; *–tial coordinates*, Linienkoordinaten; *–tial force*, die Tangentialkraft, Zentrifugalkraft.
tangerine [tændʒə'riːn], *s.* die Mandarine.
tangib–ility [tændʒɪ'bɪlɪtɪ], *s.* die Greifbarkeit, Fühlbarkeit, Berührbarkeit. **–le** ['tændʒɪbl], *adj.* greifbar (*also fig.*), fühlbar; real, materiell (*Law*), (*fig.*) handgreiflich; *–le property*, das Sachvermögen (*Law*).
tangle ['tæŋgl], 1. *s.* das Gewirr (*also fig.*), Durcheinander, die Verwicklung (*also fig.*), der Knoten, (*fig.*) die Verwirrung; der Seetang (*Bot.*). 2. *v.a.* durcheinanderbringen, verwickeln, verstricken, verwirren. 3. *v.n.* sich verwickeln *or* verwirren, verstrickt werden.
tango ['tæŋgoʊ], *s.* der Tango.
tank [tæŋk], 1. *s.* der Behälter, das Bassin, Becken; die Zisterne; der Tank (*Tech. & Mil.*), Panzer (*Mil.*). (also *--engine*) die Tenderlokomotive (*Railw.*). 2. *v.n.* tanken. **–age,** *s.* der Fassungsraum eines Tanks. **--car,** *s.* der Tankwagen, Kesselwagen. **--carrier,** *s.* Panzertransportwagen. **–er, --ship,** *s.* das Tankschiff, der Tankdampfer.
tankard ['tæŋkəd], *s.* der Deckelkrug, die Kanne, das Seidel.
tann–ate ['tæneɪt], *s.* gerbsaures Salz. **–ed,** *see under* **tan.** **–er,** *s.* der (Loh)Gerber. **–ery,** *s.* die Gerberei. **–ic,** *adj.* Gerb–; *–ic acid*, die Gerbsäure. **–in,** *s.* see *–ic acid*. **–ing,** *s.* das Gerben.
tanner ['tænə], *s.* (*sl.*) das Sechspence(stück).
tansy ['tænzɪ], *s.* der Rainfarn, Gänserich (*Bot.*)
tantal–ization [tæntəlaɪ'zeɪʃən], *s.* die Tantalusqual. **–ize** ['tæntəlaɪz], *v.a.* quälen, peinigen; *be –ized*, Tantalusqualen leiden. **–izing,** *adj.* quälend, peinigend, schmerzlich.
tantalum ['tæntələm], *s.* das Tantal (*Chem.*).
tantamount ['tæntəmaʊnt], *adj.* gleichwertig gleichbedeutend (*to*, mit); *be – to*, gleichkommen (*Dat.*), hinauslaufen auf.
tantivy [tæn'tɪvɪ], 1. *s.* rasender Galopp; der Jagdruf. 2. *adv.* geradewegs, spornstreichs.
tantrum ['tæntrəm], *s.* (*usually pl.*) schlechte Laune, die Wut.
¹tap [tæp], 1. *v.a.* leicht schlagen, klopfen an, auf *or* gegen; besohlen (*shoes*). 2. *v.n.* schlagen, klopfen. 3. *s.* das Klopfen, leichter Schlag; das Stück Leder; *pl.* der Zapfenstreich (*Mil.*). **--dance,** *s.* der Stepptanz. **--dancing,** *s.* das Steppen.
²tap, 1. *v.a.* anzapfen (*also fig. a p.*), anstechen (*a cask*); mit Schraubengewinde versehen (*Tech.*); abzapfen (*Surg.*); (*fig.*) abfangen, abhören (*message, etc.*), angehen um (*a p.*), erschließen (*resources*); – *a telegraph wire*, Telegramme abfangen. 2. *s.* der Zapfen, Spund, (Faß)Hahn; Gashahn, Wasserhahn, die Wasserleitung; (also *screw--*) der Schraubenbohrer, Gewindebohrer (*Tech.*); *on* –, angestochen; (*fig.*) auf Lager, verfügbar. **--room,** *s.* die Schankstube. **--root,** *s.* die Hauptwurzel, Pfahlwurzel. **–ster,** *see* **tapster.** **--water,** das Leitungswasser.
tape [teɪp], 1. *s.* das (Zwirn)Band; der Papierstreifen (*Tele.*); das Zielband (*Sport*); *adhesive* –, das Leukoplast; *breast the* –, durchs Ziel gehen (*racing*); *insulating* –, das Isolierband; *red* –, der Bürokratismus, Amtsschimmel. 2. *v.a.* (*usually pass.*) (*sl.*) *have –d*, unter Kontrolle haben. **--measure,** *s.* das Bandmaß, Zentimetermaß, Zollmaß. **--machine,** *s.* automatischer Telegraphenapparat. **--recorder,** *s.* das Tonbandgerät, Magnetophon. **--worm,** *s.* der Bandwurm.
taper ['teɪpə], 1. *s.* die Wachskerze, der Fidibus. 2. *adj.* spitz (zulaufend); verjüngt (*Arch.*). 3. *v.a.* zuspitzen, spitz zulaufen lassen. 4. *v.n.* (also – *off* or *away*) spitz zulaufen; – *to a point*, in eine Spitze zulaufen. **–ing,** *adj. see* – 2.
tapestry ['tæpəstrɪ], 1. *s.* gewirkte Tapete, der Wandteppich, die Tapisserie. 2. *v.a.* mit Wandteppichen behängen.
tapioca [tæpɪ'oʊkə], *s.* die Tapioka.
tapir ['teɪpɪə], *s.* der Tapir (*Zool.*).
tapis [tæ'piː], *s.*; only in *be on the* –, erörtert werden, aufs Tapet gebracht werden; *come on the* –, aufs Tapet kommen.
tappet ['tæpɪt], *s.* der Stößel (*of a valve*), Nocken, Hebel, Daumen, die Steuerknagge (*Motor.*).
tapster ['tæpstə], *s.* der Schenkkellner, Schankkellner.

[1]**tar** [tɑː], 1. *s.* der Teer. 2. *v.a.* teeren, mit Teer beschmieren; *–red with the same brush,* die nämlichen Mängel aufweisen. **--board,** *s.* die Teerpappe. **--brush,** *s.* die Teerquaste; (*pej.*) *dash of the --brush,* der Negereinschlag. **-mac,** *s.* der Teerbeton; (*coll.*) die Rollbahn (*Av.*). **-ry,** *adj.* teerig.

[2]**tar,** *s.* (*coll.*) (also *Jack –*), die Teerjacke, der Matrose.

tar(r)adiddle [tærəˈdɪdl], *s.* (*coll.*) die Flunkerei, Flausen (*pl.*).

tarant-ella [tærənˈtɛlə], *s.* die Tarantella (*dance*). **-ula** [təˈræntjʊlə], *s.* die Tarantel (*Ent.*).

tarboosh [ˈtɑːbuʃ], *s.* der Tarbusch, Fes.

tard-igrade [ˈtɑːdɪgreɪd], 1. *adj.* langsam. 2. *s.* (–igrades *pl.*) Tardigraden (*pl.*) (*Ent.*). **-iness,** *s.* die Langsamkeit, Säumigkeit, Trägheit. **-y,** *adj.* langsam, säumig, träge; (*Amer.*) verspätet, spät.

[1]**tare** [tɛə], *s.* die Wicke (*Bot.*); (*fig.*) das Unkraut.

[2]**tare,** 1. *s.* die Tara (*C.L.*); *– and tret,* Tara und Gutgewicht; *– weight,* das Eigengewicht. 2. *v.a.* tarieren.

target [ˈtɑːgɪt], *s.* die (Schieß)Scheibe; (*fig.*) Zielscheibe; (*archaic*) Tartsche; *--practice,* das Scheibenschießen, die Schießübung.

tariff [ˈtærɪf], *s.* der Tarif; Zolltarif, das Preisverzeichnis (*C.L.*); *– reform,* die Schutzzollpolitik; *– reformer,* der Schutzzöllner; *– wall,* die Zollschranke.

tarlatan [ˈtɑːlətən], *s.* der Tarlatan.

tarn [tɑːn], *s.* kleiner Bergsee.

tarnish [ˈtɑːnɪʃ], 1. *v.a.* trüben, matt *or* trübe machen; mattieren; (*fig.*) beschmutzen, beflecken (*reputation*). 2. *v.n.* trübe *or* matt werden, sich trüben; anlaufen (*metal*). 3. *s.* der Belag; (*fig.*) Fleck.

taro [ˈtæroʊ], *s.* eßbare Zehrwurzel (*Bot.*).

tarpaulin [tɑːˈpɔːlɪn], *s.* die Persenning, Zeltbahn, geteertes Segeltuch; (*also pl.*) das Ölzeug, die Ölkleidung.

tarradiddle *see* **taradiddle.**

tarragon [ˈtærəgən], *s.* der Estragon (*Bot.*).

tarr-ed, -y, *see* **tar.**

tarry [ˈtærɪ], 1. *v.n.* zögern, säumen, zaudern, sich aufhalten. 2. *v.a.* abwarten.

tars-al [ˈtɑːsəl], *adj.* Fußgelenk–, Tarsal– (*Anat.*). **-us** [–səs], *s.* die Fußwurzel.

[1]**tart** [tɑːt], *adj.* scharf, sauer, herb; (*fig.*) schroff, beißend, bissig. **-ness,** *s.* die Säure, Herbheit; Schärfe, Schroffheit.

[2]**tart,** *s.* die (Obst)Torte. **-let,** *s.* das (Obst)-Törtchen.

[3]**tart,** *s.* (*sl.*) die Nutte, Fose.

tartan [ˈtɑːtən], *s.* der Tartan, buntkarieres Muster, das Schottentuch.

tartar [ˈtɑːtə], *s.* der Weinstein (*Chem.*); Zahnstein (*dentistry*); *cream of –,* gereinigter Weinstein, doppelweinsteinsaures Kali; *– emetic,* der Brechweinstein, das Antimonkaliumnitrat. **-ic** [–ˈtærɪk], *adj.*, Weinstein–; weinsauer; *–ic acid,* die Wein(stein)säure.

tartlet, *see* [2]**tart.**

tartness, *see* [1]**tart.**

tartrate [ˈtɑːtreɪt], *s.* wein(stein)saures Salz.

task [tɑːsk], 1. *s.* die Aufgabe; Schularbeit, aufgegebene Arbeit; *take to –,* zur Rede stellen, ins Gebet nehmen (*for,* wegen). 2. *v.a.* beschäftigen, in Anspruch nehmen, (*fig.*) anstrengen. **--force,** *s.* die (Sonder)Kampfgruppe (*Mil.*) **-master,** *s.* der Aufseher, strenger Zuchtmeister (*also fig.*). **--work,** *s.* die Akkordarbeit.

tassie [ˈtæsɪ], *s.* (*Scots*) kleiner Becher.

tassel [tæsl], 1. *s.* die Troddel, Quaste. 2. *v.a.* mit Quasten schmücken.

tast-e [teɪst], 1. *v.a.* schmecken, kosten, probieren; prüfen (*wine, tea, etc.*); (*fig.*) erfahren, erleben, genießen; versuchen, essen, trinken; *I had never –ed it before,* ich hatte es noch nie gegessen *or* getrunken; *I cannot –e anything,* ich habe keinen Geschmack. 2. *v.n.* schmecken (*of,* nach). 3. *s.* der Geschmack (*also fig.*); die (Kost)Probe, der Bissen, das Stückchen, Schlückchen, Tröpfchen; das Schmecken, der Geschmackssinn; die Geschmacksrichtung; der Appetit (*for,* auf), die Neigung (*for,* zu), Vorliebe, der Sinn (*for,* für); *in bad –e,* geschmacklos, unfein; *give s.o. a –e of,* einen schmecken lassen; *leave a bad –e in the mouth,* einen üblen Eindruck *or* Nachgeschmack zurücklassen; (*fig.*) *in good –e,* geschmackvoll; *man of –e,* der Mann von gutem Geschmack; *leave a nasty –e,* see *leave a bad –e; popular –e,* allgemeiner Geschmack; *there is no accounting for –es,* über den Geschmack läßt sich nicht streiten. **-eful,** *adj.* schmackhaft; (*fig.*) geschmackvoll. **-efulness,** *s.* (*fig.*) guter Geschmack. **-eless,** *adj.* unschmackhaft, fade; (*fig.*) geschmacklos. **-elessness,** *s.* die Geschmacklosigkeit. **-er,** *s.* der Koster, Schmecker (*tea, wine, etc.*), Probestecher (*for cheese, etc.*). **-iness,** *s.* die Schmackhaftigkeit. **-y,** *adj.* schmackhaft.

[1]**tat** [tæt], only in *tit for –,* mit gleicher Münze (bezahlt).

[2]**tat,** *v.a. & n.* Frivolitätenarbeit *or* Schiffchenarbeit machen. **-ting,** *s.* die Frivolitätenarbeit, Schiffchenarbeit, Occyarbeit; (*coll.*) Handarbeit.

tata [tæˈtɑː], 1. *s.* (*nursery talk*) der Spaziergang. 2. *interj.* (*nursery talk*) auf Wiedersehen.

tatter [ˈtætə], *s.* (*usually pl.*) der Lumpen, Fetzen; *in –s,* zerfetzt. **-demalion** [–dəˈmeɪlɪən], 1. *s.* zerlumpter Kerl. 2. *attr.* zerlumpt. **-ed,** *adj.* zerlumpt, zerfetzt.

tatting, *see* [2]**tat.**

tattle [tætl], (*coll.*) 1. *s.* das Geschwätz, Gewäsch, der Tratsch, Klatsch. 2. *v.n.* schwatzen, klatschen, plaudern. **-r,** *s.* der Schwätzer, Plauderer.

[1]**tattoo** [tæˈtuː], 1. *s.* der Zapfenstreich (*Mil.*), militärisches Schaustück, die Parade mit Vorführungen; *beat a devil's –,* ungeduldig mit den Fingern trommeln. 2. *v.n.* den Zapfenstreich schlagen *or* blasen.

[2]**tattoo,** 1. *v.a.* tätowieren, tatauieren (*the skin*), eintatauieren (*a design*). 2. *s.* die Tätowierung, Tatauierung.

taught, *see* **teach.**

taunt [tɔːnt], 1. *s.* der Spott, Hohn, die Stichelei. 2. *v.a.* (ver)höhnen, verspotten. *– a p. with a th.,* einem etwas vorwerfen. **-ing,** *adj.* höhnisch, spöttisch.

taur-ine [ˈtɔːraɪn], *adj.* Stier–, stierartig. **-us** [–rəs], *s.* das Stier (*Astr.*).

taut [tɔːt], *adj.* straff, stramm, angespannt; dicht (*Naut.*). **-en,** 1. *v.a.* straff ziehen. 2. *v.n.* sich straffen, straff werden. **-ness,** *s.* die Straffheit.

tautolog-ical [tɔːtəˈlɔdʒɪkl], **-ous** [–ˈtɔlədʒəs], *adj.* tautologisch; dasselbe besagend. **-y** [–ˈtɔlədʒɪ], *s.* die Tautologie.

tavern [ˈtævən], *s.* die Schenke, Kneipe, das Wirtshaus. **--keeper,** *s.* der Schenkwirt.

[1]**taw** [tɔː], *v.a.* weiß gerben. **-er** [–ə], *s.* der Weißgerber. **-ery,** *s.* die Weißgerberei.

[2]**taw,** *s.* die Murmel, das Murmelspiel.

tawdr-iness [ˈtɔːdrɪnɪs], *s.* das Flitterhafte, der Flitter, Flitterstaat, (*fig.*) die Wertlosigkeit. **-y,** *adj.* flitterhaft; (*fig.*) wertlos.

tawer, -y, *see* [1]**taw.**

tawn-iness, *s.* die Lohfarbe, das Gelbbraun. **-y,** *adj.* lohfarben, gelbbraun, braungelb; *–y owl,* der Waldkauz.

taws(e) [tɔːz], *s.* (*Scots*) die Peitsche, Gerte, Fuchtel, der Riemen.

tax [tæks], 1. *s.* die (Staats)Steuer, Abgabe; Besteuerung (*on* (*Gen.*)); Gebühr, Taxe; (*fig.*) Last, Bürde, Belastung, Inanspruchnahme; *income –,* die Einkommensteuer; *land –,* die Grundsteuer; *property –,* die Vermögensteuer; *purchase –,* die Warenumsatzsteuer; *rates and –es,* Kommunal- und Staatssteuern. 2. *v.a.* besteuern, eine Steuer auferlegen (*a p. or th.* (*Dat.*)); einschätzen, taxieren (*costs*) (*Law*); (*fig.*) belasten, in Anspruch nehmen, auf die Probe stellen; *– a p. with a th.,* einen einer S. beschuldigen, einem etwas vorwerfen. **-able,** *adj.* besteuerbar, steuerpflichtig, gebührenpflichtig (*costs*) (*Law*). **-ation** [–ˈeɪʃən], *s.* die Besteuerung; Abschätzung (*Law*); (*coll.*) Steuern (*pl.*). **– avoidance,** *s.* die Steuerhinterziehung. **– collector,** *s.* der Steuereinnehmer, Steuerbeamte. **--free,** *adj.* steuerfrei. **-payer,** *s.* der Steuerzahler. **--return,** *s.* die Steuererklärung.

taxi ['tæksɪ], 1. *s.* (also *--cab*) die Taxe, das (*or Swiss* der) Taxi, das Miet(s)auto. 2. *v.n.* in einem Taxi fahren (*Motor.*); (also – *along*) rollen, anrollen, abrollen (*Av.*). **--cab,** *s. see* – 1. **--driver, --man,** *s.* der Taxichauffeur. **–meter** [tæks'ɪmɪtə], *s.* der Taxameter, Fahrpreisanzeiger, Zähler.
taxiderm–al [tæksɪ'də:məl], **–ic** [–'də:mɪk], *adj.* Ausstopf–. **–ist** ['tæksɪdə:mɪst], *s.* der Tierausstopfer. **–y,** *s.* die Kunst des Tierausstopfens.
taxpayer, *see under* **tax.**
tea [tɪ:], *s.* der Tee; *after* –, nach dem Tee; *beef*–, die Kraftbrühe; *five o'clock* –, der Fünf-Uhr-Tee; *high* –, *meat* –, kaltes Abendessen; *blend* –, Teesorten mischen. **--caddy,** *s.* **--canister,** *s.* die Teedose, Teebüchse. **--cake,** *s.* einfaches Teegebäck. **--chest,** *s.* die Teekiste. **--cloth,** *s.* das Trockentuch, Geschirrtuch. **--cosy,** *s.* die Tee– *or* Kaffeemütze. **–cup,** *s.* die Teetasse; *storm in a –cup,* der Sturm im Wasserglas. **--gown,** *s.* das Hauskleid. **--grower,** *s.* der Teepflanzer. **--leaf,** *s.* das Teeblatt. **--leaves,** *pl.* der Teesatz. **--party,** *s.* die Teegesellschaft, der Kaffeeklatsch. **–pot,** *s.* die Teekanne. **--room,** *s.* das Kaffee(haus). **--rose,** *s.* die Teerose. **--service,** *s.,* **--set,** *s.* das Teeservice. **--shop,** *s. see* **--room. –spoon,** *s.* der Teelöffel. **–spoonful,** *s.* der Teelöffelvoll. **--table,** *s.* der Teetisch. **--taster,** *s.* der Teeprüfer. **--things,** *pl.* (*coll.*) das Teegeschirr. **--time,** *s.* die Teestunde. **--tray,** *s.* das Tablett, Servierbrett. **--urn,** *s.* die Teekochmaschine.
teach [tɪ:tʃ], *ir.v.a. & n.* lehren, unterrichten (*a p. or th.*), unterweisen, beibringen (*Dat.*) (*a p.*), Unterricht geben in (*a th.*), trainieren, abrichten (*animals*); – *a p. a th.* or *a th. to a p.*, einen etwas lehren, einem etwas beibringen, einem Unterricht in etwas geben; (*coll.*) *that will – you better,* das wird dich eines Besseren belehren; (*coll.*) *I will – you to laugh at me,* ich will dir das Lachen vertreiben; – *s.o. to read,* einen lesen lehren. **–able,** *adj.* gelehrig (*a p.*), lehrbar (*a th.*). **–ableness,** *s.* die Gelehrigkeit (*of a p.*), Lehrbarkeit (*of a th.*). **–er,** *s.* der Lehrer. **–ing,** 1. *s.* das Unterrichten, Lehren; der Lehrberuf; der Unterricht; die Lehre. 2. *attrib.*; *–ing profession,* der Lehrberuf; *–ing staff,* der Lehrkörper, die Dozentenschaft.
teak [tɪ:k], *s.* der Tiekbaum, Teakbaum; das Tiekholz, Teakholz.
teal [tɪ:l], *s.* die Krickente (*Orn.*).
team [tɪ:m], *s.* das Gespann, die Bespannung (*of horses, etc.*); der Zug, Flug (*of birds*), die Gruppe, Schicht (*of workmen, etc.*); die Mannschaft (*games*). **--spirit,** *s.* der Mannschaftsgeist; (*fig.*) Korpsgeist, das Gemeinschaftsgefühl. **–ster,** *s.* der Fuhrmann. **--work,** *s.* die Zusammenarbeit; das Ensemblespiel (*Theat.*).
[1]**tear** [tɛə], 1. *ir.v.a.* zerreißen; ausraufen (*one's hair*); ritzen, aufreißen, zerfleischen (*the skin*). herausreißen (*out of,* aus), fortreißen (*from,* von); entreißen (*from* (*Dat.*)); – *in* or *to pieces,* in Stücke reißen; – *in two,* entzweireißen; – *one's clothes,* sich (*Dat.*) die Kleider zerreißen; – *o.s. away,* sich fortreißen; (*fig.*) *torn between,* hin und her gerissen zwischen; (*sl.*) *that's torn it,* da ist nichts mehr zu machen; – *apart,* auseinanderreißen; – *down,* abreißen, niederreißen, herunterreißen; – *off,* abreißen, von sich reißen (*clothes*); – *out,* herausreißen; – *up,* zerreißen, ausreißen (*by the roots,* mit den Wurzeln). 2. *ir.v.n.* reißen, zerren (*at,* an (*Dat.*)); (zer)reißen; (*coll.*) jagen, stürzen, stürmen; wüten, rasen; – *about,* umherrennen; – *ahead,* vorausstürmen, voranstürmen; – *along,* angerannt kommen; – *off,* losrennen; (*coll.*) – *through,* fliegen durch (*a book, etc.*). 3. der Riß (*in clothes*); *wear and* –, die Abnutzung. (*coll.*) **–ing,** *adj.* wild, rasend, heftig. **--off,** *attrib.*; *--off calendar,* der Abreißkalender.
[2]**tear** [tɪ:ə], *s.* die Träne; (*fig.*) der Tropfen; *burst into –s,* in Tränen ausbrechen; *crocodile –s,* Krokodilstränen (*pl.*); *in –s,* weinend, in *or* unter Tränen; *reduce to –s,* zu Tränen bringen; *shed –s,* Tränen vergießen. **–drop,** *s.* der Tränentropfen. **--duct,** *s.* Tränenkanal. **–ful,** *adj.* tränenvoll, in Tränen, weinerlich, traurig; *be –ful,* Tränen vergießen. **–fulness,** *s.* die Weinerlichkeit. **--gas,** *s.* das Tränengas. **--gland,** *s.* die Tränendrüse. **–less,** *adj.* ohne Tränen, ohne zu weinen. **--stained,** *adj.* tränenbenetzt; verweint (*eyes*).
tease [tɪ:z], 1. *v.a.* kämmen, krempeln (*wool*); hecheln (*flax*), kardieren, rauhen (*cloth*); (*fig.*) necken, hänseln, aufziehen, foppen, zum Besten haben, ärgern, plagen. 2. *s.* (*coll.*) der Necker, Quälgeist, Plagegeist. **–r,** *s.* der Necker, Quälgeist, Plagegeist; (*coll.*) schwierige Frage, harte Nuß.
teasel, teazle [tɪ:zl], 1. *s.* die Kardedistel (*Bot.*); die Karde, Kardätsche, Krempel (*Tech.*). 2. *v.a.* rauhen, kardieren, krempeln (*cloth*).
teaspoon, *see under* **tea.**
teat [tɪ:t], *s.* die Zitze, Brustwarze; (also *rubber* –) der Lutscher.
tec [tɛk], *s.* (*coll.*) *abbr. for* detective.
techn–ic ['tɛknɪk], 1. *adj. see* **–ical.** 2. *pl.* (*sing. constr.*) technische Handhabung, die Handfertigkeit, Kunstfertigkeit; *see also* **–ique. –ical,** *adj.* technisch; kunstgerecht, fachgemäß, Fach–; (*fig.*) buchstäblich, regelrecht; *–ical college,* Technische Hochschule; *–ical language,* die Fachsprache; *–ical school,* die Gewerbeschule; *–ical term,* der Fachausdruck. **–ically,** *adv.* (*coll.*) eigentlich. **–icality** [–'kælɪtɪ], *s.* das Technische; technische Eigentümlichkeit, der Fachausdruck; *pl.* technische Einzelheiten (*pl.*). **–ician** [–'nɪʃən], *s.* der Techniker. **–icolour,** *s.* das Farbfilmverfahren; *film in –icolour,* der Farbfilm. **–ique** [–'nɪ:k], *s.* die Technik, Kunstfertigkeit, Methode *or* Art der technischen Ausführung. **–ocracy** [–nɔkrəsɪ], *s.* die Herrschaft der Maschine. **–ological** [–nə'lɔdʒɪkl], *adj.* technologisch, gewerblich, gewerbekundlich. **–ologist** [–'nɔlədʒɪst], *s.* der Technolog, Gewerbekundige(r) *m.* **–ology,** *s.* die Technologie, Gewerbekunde; *school of –ology,* Technische Hochschule.
tect–ology [tɛk'tɔlədʒɪ], *s.* die Strukturlehre (*Biol.*). **–onic** [–'tɔnɪk], *adj.* tektonisch, baulich, Bau–. **–onics,** *pl.* (*sing. constr.*) die Tektonik, Gliederung, der Aufbau. **–orial** [–'tɔ:rɪəl], *adj.* bedeckend, Deck– (*Anat.*). **–rices** [–trɪ:sɪ:z], *pl.* Deckfedern (*pl.*) (*Orn.*).
Te Deum ['tɪ:'dɪəm], *s.* der Dankgottesdienst, Lobgesang.
tedi–ous ['tɪ:dɪəs], *adj.* lästig, langweilig, weitschweifig, ermüdend. **–ousness,** *s.* die Langweiligkeit; Weitschweifigkeit. **–um,** *s.* die Langeweile, der Überdruß. *See also* **–ousness.**
tee [tɪ:], 1. *s.* das Ziel, Mal, der Erdhaufen, von dem aus der Ball geschlagen wird (*Golf*). 2. *v.a.* auf den Erdhaufen legen (*the ball*) (*Golf*). 3. *v.n.*; – *off,* den Ball abschlagen, starten (*Golf*).
teem [tɪ:m], *v.n.* wimmeln, strotzen, erfüllt sein (*with,* von); wuchern, überreichlich vorhanden sein; gießen (*rain*); (*archaic*) fruchtbar *or* schwanger sein. **–ing,** *adj.* wimmelnd, strotzend, gedrängt voll (*with,* von), fruchtbar; (*coll.*) *it is –ing down,* es gießt in Strömen.
teen--ager ['tɪ:neɪdʒə], *s.* (*coll.*) Jugendliche(r) *m.* or *f.* (*usually of a girl*). **–s,** *pl.* die Lebensjahre von 13 bis 19; *be in one's –s,* noch nicht 20 Jahre alt sein, noch in den Kinderschuhen stecken.
teeny ['tɪ:nɪ], *adj.* (also *--weeny*) (*nursery talk*) winzigklein.
teeth [tɪ:θ], *see* **tooth. –e** [tɪ:ð], *v.n.* zahnen. **–ing** [–ðɪŋ], *s.* das Zahnen; *–ing-ring,* der Zahnring.
teetotal [tɪ:'toutl], *adj.* abstinent, antialkoholisch. **–(l)er,** *s.* der Antialkoholiker, Abstinent, Abstinenzler. **–ism,** *s.* die Abstinenz(bewegung).
teetotum [tɪ:'toutəm], *s.* der Drehwürfel.
tegument ['tɛgjumənt], *s.* die Hülle, Decke; Membran (*Zool. Anat.*). **–al** [–'mɛntl], **–ary** [–'mɛntərɪ], *adj.* Decken–, Hüllen–, Haut–.
telamon ['tɛləmən], *s.* (*pl.* –es) die Tragsäule in Männergestalt.
tele– ['tɛlɪ], *prefix,* Tele–, Fern–. **–communication,** *s.* (*often pl.*) das Rundfunkwesen. **–gram,** *s.* das Telegramm, die Drahtnachricht, Drahtung; *by –gram,* telegraphisch. **–graph,** 1. *v.a. & n.* drahten, telegraphieren. 2. *s.* der Telegraph; die Anzeigetafel (*Sport*). **–graph boy,** der Telegraphenbote. **–graph code,** der Telegramm-

schlüssel. **–graphese** [–grəˈfɪ:z], *s.* der Telegrammstil. **–graph form,** das Telegrammformular. **–graphic,** *adj.* telegraphisch; Telegramm– (*as style*); *–graphic address*, die Drahtanschrift. **–graphist** [təˈlɛgrəfɪst], *s.* der Telegraphist. **–graph line,** *s.* die Telegraphenleitung. **–graph office,** *s.* das Telegraphenamt. **–graph pole,** *s.* die Telegraphenstange. **–graph wire,** der Telegraphendraht. **–graphy** [təˈlɛgrəfɪ], *s.* die Telegraphie; *wireless –graphy*, drahtlose Telegraphie. **–kinesis** [tɛlɪkɪˈnɪ:sɪs], *s.* die Telekinese. **–ological** [tɛlɪəˈlɔdʒɪkl], *adj.* teleologisch, zweckbestimmt. **–ology,** *s.* die Teleologie. **–pathic** [–ˈpæθɪk], *adj.* telepathisch. **–pathy** [təˈlɛpəθɪ], *s.* die Telepathie, Gedankenübertragung. **–phone,** 1. *s.* der Fernsprecher, das Telephon; *automatic –phone*, der Selbstanschluß(fernsprecher); *at the –phone*, am Telephon *or* Apparat; *enquiry by –phone*, telephonische Anfrage: *on the –phone*, am Telephon; telephonisch, durch Fernsprecher; *be on the –phone*, Telephon(anschluß) haben; am Apparat sein; *over the –phone*, durch (das) Telephon. 2. *v.n.* telephonieren. 3. *v.a.* telephonieren (*a th.*), antelephonieren, (telephonisch) anrufen (*a p.*). **–phone-box,** *s.* die Fernsprechzelle. **–phone-call,** *s.* der Telephonanruf, das Telephongespräch. **–phone connexion,** der Fernsprechanschluß. **–phone directory,** *s.* das Telephon-Adreßbuch. **–phone-exchange,** *s.* das Fernsprechamt, die Zentrale, Vermittlung. **–phone-message,** *s.* telephonische Bestellung, das Telephongespräch. **–phone-operator,** *s.* das Telephonfräulein. **–phone-receiver,** *s.* der Hörer. **–phonic** [tɛlɪˈfɔnɪk], *adj.* telephonisch, Fernsprech–. **–phonist** [təˈlɛfənɪst], *s.* der Telephonist. **–phony** [təˈlɛfənɪ], *s.* die Telephonie, das Fernsprechwesen. **–photo,** *abbr. for* **–photograph** *and* **–photographic**; *usually attrib.*; *–photo lens*, das Teleobjektiv. **–photograph,** *s.* die Fernaufnahme. **–photographic** [tɛlɪfoutəˈgræfɪk], *adj.* fernfotographisch. **–photography** [–fəˈtɔgrəfɪ], *s.* die Fernfotographie. **–printer,** *s.* der Fernschreiber, Fernschreibeapparat. **–scope,** 1. *s.* das Fernrohr, Teleskop. 2. *v.a.* (*& n.*) (sich) ineinanderschieben. **–scopic** [–ˈskɔpɪk], *adj.* teleskopisch; ineinanderschiebbar; Auszieh– (*as a table*); *–scopic sight*, der Fernrohraufsatz (*for rifle*). **–vise** [ˈtɛlɪvɑɪz], *v.a.* durch Fernsehen übertragen. **–vision,** 1. *s.* das Fernsehen, der Bildfunk. 2. *attrib.* Fernseh–.

tell [tɛl], 1. *ir.v.a.* erzählen, berichten, mitteilen, erklären, versichern; sagen, äußern, offenbaren, ausdrücken; angeben, anzeigen (*the time: as clocks*); heißen, befehlen; unterscheiden (*from*, von), erkennen (*by* or *from*, an); zählen; *all told*, alles in allem, im ganzen; *do as you're told!* tu wie dir geheißen!; *– one's beads*, den Rosenkranz beten (*Eccl.*); *– fortunes*, wahrsagen; *– lies*, lügen; *– me his name*, nennen Sie mir seinen Namen; *I told you so*, ich hab's dir gleich gesagt; *– tales*, flunkern, aus der Schule plaudern; *– its own tale*, für sich selbst sprechen, sich von selbst erklären; *– that to the marines!* mache das einem anderen weis!; *– the truth*, die Wahrheit sagen; *to – the truth* or *truth to –*, offen gesagt; *be able to – the time*, die Uhr lesen können; *can you – me the time?* können Sie mir sagen, wieviel Uhr es ist? *– off*, abzählen; abkommandieren (*a p.*); (*coll.*) anschnauzen (*a p.*). 2. *ir.v.n.* erzählen, berichten, sprechen (*about*, über; *of*, von); erkennen (*by*, an); hervortreten; Eindruck *or* sich bemerkbar *or* sich geltend machen; sich auswirken, wirksam sein; (*coll.*) petzen; *you never can –!* man kann (es) nie wissen!; *it –s against him*, es spricht gegen ihn; *every shot told*, jede Kugel traf; (*coll.*) *– on*, angeben, anzeigen. **–er,** *s.* der Zähler; Stimmenzähler (*Parl.*); Kassier(er) (*in banks*); (also *story –er*) Erzähler; *fortune-–er*, Wahrsager. **–ing,** 1. *adj.* wirkungsvoll, wirksam, eindrucksvoll, effektvoll, durchschlagend. 2. *s.* das Erzählen; *in the –ing*, beim Erzählen; *there is no –ing*, es läßt sich *or* man kann nicht wissen *or* sagen, es ist nicht zu sagen. **–-tale,** 1. *s.* der Angeber, Ohrenbläser, Zuträger, Zwischenträger. 2. *attr. adj.* sprechend, verräterisch; Warnungs–, Erkennungs–.

tellur–al [təˈluərəl], *adj.* irdisch, Erde–. **–ian** [–ɪən], 1. *adj. see* **–al.** 2. *s.* der Erdbewohner.

tellur–ate [ˈtɛləreɪt], *s.* tellursaures Salz. **–ic** [təˈlurɪk], *adj.* tellurisch, Tellur–. **–ium** [təˈluərɪəm], *s.* das Tellur.

telpher [ˈtɛlfə], *adj.* der elektrischen Beförderung dienend. **–age** [–rɪdʒ], *s.* elektrische Lastenbeförderung. **–-line,** *s.* elektrische Drahtseilbahn, die Elektrohängebahn.

temer–arious [tɛməˈrɛərɪəs], *adj.* verwegen, unbesonnen, tollkühn. **–ity** [təˈmɛrɪtɪ], *s.* die Verwegenheit, Unbesonnenheit, Tollkühnheit.

temper [ˈtɛmpə], 1. *v.a.* richtig mischen; abhärten (*metals*), glühfrischen, tempern (*steel*), anmachen (*colours*), anrühren (*clay, etc.*); (*fig.*) mäßigen, mildern, abschwächen; temperieren (*Mus.*); *– justice with mercy*, Gnade für Recht ergehen lassen; *God –s the wind to the shorn lamb*, Gott legt niemand mehr auf als er (v)ertragen kann. 2. *s.* richtige Mischung, gehörige Beschaffenheit; die Härte, der Härtegrad (*Metall.*), die Festigkeit (*of clay*); (*fig.*) natürliche Anlage, die Natur, das Naturell, Temperament, der Charakter; die Stimmung, Laune, das Gemüt; die Gereiztheit, Heftigkeit, Erregung, Wut; *have an evil –*, jähzornig sein; *have a quick –*, heftig sein; *keep one's –*, die Ruhe behalten; *lose one's –*, heftig *or* wütend werden; *be in a –*, wütend sein; *in a good –*, in guter Laune; *get into a –*, wütend werden; *out of –*, aufgeregt, aufgebracht, ungehalten; *put out of –*, erzürnen; die Laune verderben (*Dat.*); *try s.o.'s –*, einen reizen *or* aufbringen. **–ed** [–d], *adj.* gehärtet, gestählt, Temper–; (*in comps. fig.*) –gelaunt, –gestimmt; *even-–ed*, gleichmütig. **–ing,** *s.* das Härten.

tempera [ˈtɛmpərə], *s.* die Tempera(malerei).

temperament [ˈtɛmpərəmənt], *s.* das Temperament, die Gemütsart, Natur, Veranlagung; Temperatur (*Mus.*). **–al** [–ˈmɛntl], *adj.* launenhaft, reizbar. **–ally,** *adv.* von Natur.

tempera–nce [ˈtɛmpərəns], 1. *s.* die Mäßigkeit, Beherrschung, Enthaltsamkeit. 2. *attrib.*; *–nce hotel*, alkoholfreies Hotel; *–nce movement*, die Temperenzbewegung. **–te** [–rət], *adj.* mäßig, enthaltsam; maßvoll (*language, etc.*); gemäßigt (*climate*). **–teness,** *s.* die Mäßigung, Mäßigkeit, das Maß.

temperature [ˈtɛmprətʃuə], *s.* die Temperatur; *at a –*, bei einer Temperatur; (*coll.*) *have a –*, Fieber *or* Temperatur haben; *take the –*, Temperatur messen. **–-curve,** *s.* die Fieberkurve.

tempest [ˈtɛmpɪst], *s.* der Sturm, das Gewitter. **–-tossed,** *adj.* von Sturm getrieben. **–uous** [–ˈpɛstjuəs], *adj.* stürmisch, ungestüm. **–uousness,** *s.* das Ungestüm, die Heftigkeit.

templar [ˈtɛmplə], *s.* der Tempelritter, Tempelherr; Student der Rechte in London.

[1]**temple** [ˈtɛmpl], *s.* die Schläfe (*Anat.*); *see* [1]**temporal.**

[2]**temple,** *s.* der Tempel; eins der beiden Rechtsinstituten in London (*Inner –, Middle –*).

templet [ˈtɛmplɪt], *s.* die Schablone, Lehre (*Tech.*); Pfette (*Build.*).

tempo [ˈtɛmpou], *s.* das Tempo (*Mus.*); (*coll.*) die Geschwindigkeit; *see* [2]**temporal.**

[1]**temporal,** [ˈtɛmpərəl], *adj.* Schläfen–. *See* [1]**temple.**

[2]**tempor–al,** *adj.* zeitlich; weltlich, irdisch, diesseitig; temporal, Zeit– (*Gram.*); *–al power*, weltliche Macht; *spatial and –al*, räumlich und zeitlich; *spiritual and –al*, geistlich und weltlich. **–ality** [–ˈrælɪtɪ], *s.* die Weltlichkeit, Diesseitigkeit; *pl.* weltliche *or* irdische Güter. **–ariness** [–rərɪnɪs], *s.* die Zeitweiligkeit. **–ary** [–rərɪ], *adj.* zeitweise, einstweilig, zeitweilig, vorübergehend; vorläufig, provisorisch, Gelegenheits–, Aushilfs–. **–ization** [–rɑɪˈzeɪʃən], *s.* das Warten, Zögern, Zeitabwarten, die Zeitgewinnung. **–ize** [–rɑɪz], *v.n.* die Zeit abwarten, den Mantel nach dem Winde hängen, sich nicht binden, sich vorläufig anpassen *or* anbequemen, zögern, warten; *–ize with*, hinhalten, verhandeln mit. **–izer,** *s.* der Achselträger. **–izing,** *adj.* hinhaltend, abwartend, achselträgerisch; liebedienerisch.

tempt [tɛmpt], *v.a.* verführen, verlocken, in Versuchung führen; überreden, dazu bringen (*a p.*); reizen (*of things*); *be -ed*, gereizt sein; *– fate*, das Schicksal versuchen. **–ation** [–ˈteɪʃən], *s.* die Versuchung, Verlockung, Verführung, der Anreiz; *lead into –ation*, in Versuchung führen. **–er,** *s.* der Versucher, Verführer. **–ing,** *adj.* verführerisch, verlockend, reizvoll; appetitanregend (*of food*). **–ingness,** *s.* das Verführerische. **–ress** [–trɪs], *s.* die Verführerin.

ten [tɛn], 1. *num. adj.* zehn. 2. *s.* die Zehn; *–s of thousands*, Zehntausende (*pl.*); *nine out of –*, neun von zehnen; (*coll.*) *– to one*, zehn zu eins, todsicher. **–fold,** *adj.* zehnfach. **–th,** *see* **tenth.**

tena–ble [ˈtɛnəbl], *adj.* haltbar (*also fig.*), verteidigungsfähig (*Mil.*); (*fig.*) tragbar, überzeugend; *be –ble*, verliehen *or* vergeben werden (*as a scholarship*). **–cious** [təˈneɪʃəs], *adj.* zusammenhaltend, klebrig, zähe (*also fig.*), fest, festhaltend (*also fig.*); (*fig.*) beharrlich, hartnäckig (*as an enemy*); gut, treu (*of memory*); *be –cious of*, festhalten an, bestehen auf; *be –cious of life*, zähe am Leben festhalten. **–ciousness,** *s.* **–city** [təˈnæsɪtɪ], *s.* die Zähigkeit, Hartnäckigkeit, Treue, Stärke.

tenail [təˈneɪl], *s.* das Zangenwerk (*Fort.*).

tenan–cy [ˈtɛnənsɪ], *s.* der Pachtbesitz, Mietbesitz; das Pachtverhältnis, Mietverhältnis; die Pachtdauer, Mietdauer. **–t** [–ənt], 1. *s.* der Pächter, Mieter, Einwohner, Bewohner, Insasse; *–t at will*, der Pächter der nach Belieben kündigen kann. 2. *v.a.* (*usually pass.*) bewohnen. **–table,** *adj.* pachtbar, mietbar; wohnbar, **–tless,** *adj.* unvermietet, unbewohnt. **–t-farmer,** *s.* der Gutspächter. **–t-right,** *s.* das Recht des Pächters. **–try,** *s.* (*collect.*) (*pl.*) Pächter.

tench [tɛntʃ], *s.* die Schleie (*Ichth.*).

[1]**tend** [tɛnd], *v.a.* bedienen, hüten (*flocks*), pflegen (*invalid*), aufwarten (*machine*).

[2]**tend,** *v.n.* sich bewegen *or* richten, streben, gerichtet sein (*towards*, nach); (*fig.*) hinauslaufen, abzielen, gerichtet sein (*to*, auf), führen, neigen (*to*, zu); *it –s to distract attention*, es führt dazu, daß die Aufmerksamkeit abgelenkt wird. **–ency** [–ənsɪ], *s.* die Richtung, der Lauf, Gang; die Strömung, Absicht, Tendenz, der Zweck; Hang (*to*, zu), das Streben (*to*, nach); *have a -ency to do*, geneigt sein zu tun. **–entious** [–ˈdɛnʃəs], *adj.* tendenziös, Tendenz–.

[1]**tender** [ˈtɛndə], 1. *s.* das Anerbieten, Lieferungsangebot, Zahlungsangebot, die Offerte (*for*, auf), Kostenanschlag; *by –*, durch *or* in Submission; *legal –*, gesetzliches Zahlungsmittel. 2. *v.a.* anbieten, darbieten, darreichen, einreichen, beantragen; *– an oath*, einen Eid zuschieben (*to* (*Dat.*)); *– one's resignation*, seine Entlassung beantragen; *– one's thanks*, seinen Dank aussprechen.

[2]**tender,** *s.* der Wärter, der Tender (*Railw.*, *Naut.*); der Leichter, Lichter, das Beiboot, Begleitschiff.

[3]**tender,** *adj.* zart (*also fig.*), weich, mürbe (*as food*), zerbrechlich, schwach, schwächlich; (*fig.*) schonend, sorgsam, besorgt (*of*, um), gütig, zärtlich (*as love*); sanft, mitleidig (*heart*), empfindlich (*as a wound*); *at a – age*, im zarten Alter; *– conscience*, empfindliches Gewissen. **–foot,** *s.* der Neuling, Unerfahrene(r), *m.* **––hearted,** *adj.* weichherzig. **–ness,** *s.* die Zartheit; Weichheit; Zärtlichkeit (*to*, gegen); Empfindlichkeit (*of a wound, etc.*).

tend–inous [ˈtɛndɪnəs], *adj.* sehnig. **–on** [–dən], *s.* die Sehne, Flechse.

tendril [ˈtɛndrɪl], *s.* die Ranke.

tenebrous [ˈtɛnɪbrəs], *adj.* (*archaic*) dunkel, finster.

tenement [ˈtɛnəmənt], 1. *s.* das Wohnhaus, die (Miet(s))Wohnung, der Wohnsitz; ständiger Besitz (*Law*); (also *– house*) das Mietshaus, die Mietskaserne. **–al** [–ˈmɛntl], **–ary** [–ˈmɛntərɪ], *adj.* Pacht–, Miets–.

tenet [ˈtɛnət], *s.* der (Grund)Satz, Lehrsatz, die Lehre.

tenfold, *see* **ten.**

tenner [ˈtɛnə], *s.* (*coll.*) die Zehnpfundnote.

tennis [ˈtɛnɪs], *s.* das Tennis. **––ball,** *s.* der Tennisball. **––court,** der Tennisplatz. **––racket,** *s.* der (Tennis)Schläger.

tenon [ˈtɛnən], 1. *s.* der Zapfen. 2. *v.a.* verzapfen. **––saw,** *s.* der Fuchsschwanz.

[1]**tenor** [ˈtɛnə], *s.* der (Fort)Gang, (Ver)Lauf; Sinn, Inhalt, sachlicher Kern; *even –*, die Gleichförmigkeit.

[2]**tenor,** *s.* der Tenor, Tenorsänger, die Tenorstimme.

[1]**tense** [tɛns], *s.* die Zeitform, das Tempus.

[2]**tens–e,** *adj.* (an)gespannt, stramm, straff, (*fig.*) gespannt (*with*, vor). **–eness,** *s.* die Spannung (*also fig.*); Straffheit. **–ibility** [–ɪˈbɪlɪtɪ], *s.* die Dehnbarkeit. **–ible, –ile** [ˈtɛnsɑɪl], *adj.* dehnbar, Dehnungs–, Spannungs–; *–ile strength*, die Zugfestigkeit, (Zer)Reißfestigkeit. **–ion** [–ʃən], *s.* die Spannung (*also fig.*), Streckung, Spannkraft; (*fig.*) gespanntes Verhältnis; *high –ion*, die Hochspannung (*Elect.*). **–ion-rod,** *s.* die Spannstange. **–ion-roller,** *s.* die Spannrolle. **–or** [–sɔː], *s.* der Spannmuskel.

[1]**tent** [tɛnt], *s.* das Zelt; *pitch one's –*, sein Zelt aufschlagen; (*fig.*) sich häuslich niederlassen. **––cloth,** *s.* die Zeltbahn, Zeltleinwand. **–ed** [–ɪd], *adj.* Zelt–. **––peg,** *s.* der Zeltpflock, Hering. **––pole,** *s.* der Zeltstock.

[2]**tent,** 1. *s.* die Mullgaze (*Surg.*). 2. *v.a.* offen halten (*a wound*).

[3]**tent,** *s.* der Tintowein.

tent–acle [ˈtɛntəkl], *s.* der Fühler, Fühlarm, das Fühlhorn. **–acular** [–ˈtækjʊlə], *adj.* Fühler–. **–ative** [–tətɪv], 1. *adj.* versuchend, Versuchs–, probend, Probe–, Tast–. 2. *s.* der Versuch, die Probe. **–atively,** *adv.* versuchsweise.

tenter [ˈtɛntə], *s.* der Spannrahmen. **––hook,** *s.* der Spannhaken; (*fig.*) *be on ––hooks*, in größter Spannung *or* Ungewißheit sein, wie auf heißen Kohlen sitzen.

tenth [tɛnθ], 1. *num. adj.* zehnt. 2. *s.* der, die *or* das Zehnte; das Zehntel; die Dezime (*Mus.*). **–ly,** *adv.* zehntens.

tenu–is [ˈtɛnjʊɪs], *s.* die Tenuis, stimmloser Verschlußlaut. **–ity** [təˈnjuːɪtɪ], *s.* die Dünnheit; Zartheit, Feinheit; (*fig.*) Dürftigkeit, Spärlichkeit. **–ous** [ˈtɛnjuːəs], *adj.* dünn, fein, zart; (*fig.*) dürftig, spärlich.

tenure [ˈtɛnjə], *s.* der (Land)Besitz, das Lehen; die Besitzart; der Besitzanspruch, Besitztitel; die Bekleidung, das Innehaben; (*fig.*) der Genuß; *– of office*, die Amstdauer.

tepee [ˈtɪːpɪː], *s.* das Indianerzelt.

tep–efy [ˈtɛpɪfɑɪ], 1. *v.a.* lau machen. 2. *v.n.* lau werden. **–id** [–pɪd], *adj.* lau (*also fig.*), lauwarm. **–idity** [–ˈpɪdɪtɪ], **–idness,** *s.* die Lauheit (*also fig.*).

terce [təːs], *s.* dritte kanonische Stunde (*R.C.*).

tercel [ˈtəːsəl], *s.* männlicher Falke.

tercentenary [təːsənˈtɪːnərɪ], 1. *adj.* dreihundertjährig. 2. *s.* die Dreihundertjahrfeier.

tercet [ˈtəːsɪt], *s.* die Triole (*Mus.*), Terzine (*Metr.*).

terebinth [ˈtɛrəbɪnθ], *s.* die Terebinthe, Terpentinpistazie (*Bot.*).

teredo [təˈrɪːdoʊ], *s.* der Bohrwurm.

tergiversat–e [ˈtəːdʒɪvəːseɪt, ˈtəːgɪvəːseɪt], *v.n.* Ausflüchte *or* Winkelzüge machen, sich widersprechen, sich winden, sich wenden und drehen. **–ion** [–vəːˈseɪʃən], *s.* die Ausflucht, Finte; der Wankelmut, die Inkonsequenz, Unbeständigkeit.

term [təːm], 1. *s.* bestimmte Zeitdauer, die Frist; der Termin, die Zeitgrenze, das Ziel, die Laufzeit (*C.L.*); (*in space*) der Grenzpunkt, die Grenzlinie, (Raum)Grenze; der Grenzstein, Terme (*Arch.*); die Sitzungsperiode (*Law*); das Semester (*Univ., etc.*); der Jahresabschnitt, Quartalstag, das Quartal; der Begriff (*Log.*), (Fach)Ausdruck, Terminus, das Wort; das Glied (*Math.*); *pl.* Ausdrücke (*pl.*), die Ausdrucksweise, der Wortlaut; *pl.* Zahlungsforderungen (*pl.*), der Preis, das Honorar; *pl.* Bedingungen (*pl.*), Beziehungen (*pl.*); *–s of delivery*, Lieferungsbedingungen (*pl.*); *– of life*, die Lebensdauer; *– of office*, die Amtsdauer, Amtszeit; *– of payment*, der Zahlungstermin; *–s of payment*, Zahlungsbedingungen; *–s of reference*, die Leitsätze; *by the –s of the contract*, nach Wortlaut des Kontrakts; *exact –s*, genauer Wortlaut; *for a –*, eine Zeit lang; *in –*, im Semester; *contradiction in –s*, innerer Widerspruch; *in –s of*, in der Form *or* Sprache (*Gen.*); *in –s of approval*, beifällig; *in the following –s*, folgendermaßen; *in plain* or *round –s*, rund heraus (gesagt); *in set –s*, festgelegt; *inclusive –s*, der Pauschalpreis; *keep –s*, Jura studieren; *long-–, attrib.* langfristig; *end of the –*, der Schulschluß (*schools*), Semesterschluß (*universities*); *on –*, auf Zeit (*C.L.*); *on any –s*, unter jeder Bedingung; *on the best of –s*, auf bestem Fuße; *on easy –s*, unter günstigen Bedingungen; auf vertrautem Fuße (*with a p.*); *on equal –s*, unter gleichen Bedingungen; *on –s of equality*, auf gleichem Fuße (*with a p.*); *be on good –s with*, auf gutem Fuße stehen mit; *on reasonable –s*, zu billigem Preise; *on speaking –s*, im Sprechverhältnis; *on visiting –s*, auf Besuchsfuße; *set a –*, eine Grenze setzen (*to* (*Dat.*)); *bring a p. to –s*, einen zur Annahme der Bedingungen zwingen; *come to –s*, sich einigen *or* vergleichen (*with*, mit). 2. *v.a.* (be)nennen, bezeichnen.

termagant [ˈtəːməgənt], 1. *s.* zanksüchtige Frau, der Hausdrache. 2. *adj.* zänkisch, zanksüchtig.

terminab–ility [təːmɪnəˈbɪlɪtɪ], *s.* die Begrenztheit, Begrenzbarkeit, Befristung. **–le** [ˈtəːmɪnəbl], *adj.* zeitlich begrenzt, begrenzbar, befristet, auf begrenzter Zeit; lösbar, kündbar (*as contract, etc.*).

termin–al [ˈtəːmɪnəl], 1 *adj.* begrenzend, Grenz–, End– (*of place*); (Ab)Schluß–, Termin–, terminmäßig, letzt (*of time*), gipfelständig (*Bot.*); *–al examination*, die Semesterprüfung; *–al station*, die Endstation, Kopfstation; *–al velocity*, die Endgeschwindigkeit. 2. *s.* die Spitze, das Endstück, Ende; der Pol, die Klemme, Klemmschraube (*Elec.*); (*coll.*) die Endstation (*Railw.*), Semesterprüfung (*Univ.*). **–ate** [–neɪt], 1. *v.a.* (be)endigen; begrenzen. 2. *v.n.* enden, aufhören, ausgehen, auslaufen (*in*, in). 3. *adj.* begrenzt, endlich (*Math.*). **–ation** [–ˈneɪʃən], *s.* das Aufhören; der (Ab)Schluß, Ablauf, Ausgang, das Resultat, Ende; die Beendigung; Endung (*Gram.*). **–ative** [–nətɪv], *adj.* End–, Schluß–.

terminolog–ical [təːmɪnəˈlɔdʒɪkl], *adj.* terminologisch; *–ical inexactitude*, (*hum.*) die Unwahrheit. **–y** [–ˈnɔlədʒɪ], *s.* die Terminologie, Fachsprache; (*collect.*) Fachausdrücke (*pl.*).

terminus [ˈtəːmɪnəs], *s.* die Endstation (*Railw., etc.*); das Ende, Endziel, der Endpunkt.

termite [ˈtəːmaɪt], *s.* die Termite (*Ent.*).

tern [təːn], *s.* die Seeschwalbe, Meerschwalbe (*Orn.*).

tern–ary [ˈtəːnərɪ], 1. *adj.* dreifach, drei–, ternär; dreizählig (*Bot.*). 2. *s.* die Dreizahl. **–ate** [–neɪt], *adj.* dreiteilig; dreizählig (*Bot.*).

terra [ˈtɛrə], *s.* die Erde. **–cotta**, *s.* die Terrakotta(figur). **– firma**, festes Land. **– incognita**, unbekanntes Land; (*fig.*) unerforschtes Gebiet.

terrace [ˈtɛrəs], 1. *s.* die Terrasse; Erdstufe, Erderhöhung (*Geol.*); der Söller (*Arch.*); die Häuserreihe; abgelegene Straße. 2. *v.a.* in Terrassen anlegen. **–d** [–t], *adj.* flach (*as a roof*).

terrain [təˈreɪn], *s.* das Terrain, Gelände.

terr–aneous [təˈreɪnɪəs], *adj.* auf dem Land wachsend (*Bot.*). **–aqueous** [–ˈrækwɪəs], *adj.* aus Land und Wasser bestehend. **–ene** [–rɪːn], *adj.* irdisch, weltlich, diesseitig, Erd–. **–estrial** [–ˈrɛstrɪəl], *adj.* irdisch, weltlich; Erden–, Erd–; Land–, terrestrisch; *–estrial globe*, der Globus.

terrible [ˈtɛrɪbl], *adj.* schrecklich, entsetzlich, furchtbar, fürchterlich. **–ness**, *s.* die Schrecklichkeit, Furchtbarkeit.

[1]**terrier** [ˈtɛrɪə], *s.* der Terrier; (*sl.*) (*abbr. for* **territorial**) der Landwehrmann.

[2]**terrier**, *s.* das (Land)Grundbuch (*Law*).

terrif–ic [təˈrɪfɪk], *adj.* furchtbar, fürchterlich; (*sl.*) wuchtig, ungeheuer. **–y** [ˈtɛrɪfaɪ], *v.a.* erschrecken; *be –ied*, sich fürchten *or* erschrecken (*of*, vor).

territor–ial [tɛrɪˈtəːrɪəl], 1. *adj.* Grund–, Boden–, Gebiets–, Landes–, territorial; *–ial Army*, die Landwehr; *–ial waters*, Hoheitsgewässer (*pl.*). 2. *s.* der Landwehrmann. **–y** [ˈtɛrɪtərɪ], *s.* das (Staats)Gebiet, Landesgebiet, Territorium; das Land, die Landschaft, Gegend; (*fig.*) das Gebiet, der Bereich; *on British –y*, auf britischem Staatsgebiet.

terror [ˈtɛrə], *s.* der Schrecken, Terror; (*coll.*) lästige Person; *in – of*, besorgt *or* in Angst um; *reign of –*, die Schreckensherrschaft; *strike – into a p.*, einem Schrecken einflößen. **–ism** [–rɪzm], *s.* die Schreckensherrschaft, der Terrorismus. **–ist** [–rɪst], *s.* der Terrorist (*Hist.*). **–ize** [–raɪz], *v.a.* terrorisieren, einschüchtern. **–-stricken, –-struck,** *adj.* erschreckt, von Schrecken ergriffen.

terry [ˈtɛrɪ], *s.* ungeschnittener Samt.

terse [təːs], *adj.* kurz und bündig, markig (*of style*). **–ness,** *s.* die Kürze, Bündigkeit.

tertia–n [ˈtəːʃn], 1. *adj.* dreitägig, Tertian–. 2. *s.* das Tertianfieber. **–ry** [–ʃərɪ], 1. *adj.* an dritter Stelle, tertiär; Tertiär–. 2. *s.* das Tertiär, die Tertiärzeit (*Geol.*).

terz–a rima [ˈtɛːtsəˈrɪːmə], die Terzine mit Reimfolge aba, bcb, cdc, usw. **–etto** [tɛːˈtsɛtoʊ], *s.* dreistimmiges Gesangstück.

tessella–r [ˈtɛsələ], *adj.* würfelförmig. **–te** [–leɪt], *v.a.* mit Täfelchen auslegen; tesselieren; *–ted pavement*, der Mosaikfußboden. **–tion** [–ˈleɪʃn], *s.* die Mosaikarbeit.

test [tɛst], 1. *s.* die Probe (*also Chem., etc.*), der Versuch, die Untersuchung; die Stichprobe, der Prüfstein (*of*, für); die (Eignungs)Prüfung, der Test; Analyse, das Reagens (*Chem.*); der Versuchstiegel, die Kapelle (*Metall.*); der Testeid (*Hist.*); *blood –*, die Blutprobe; *acid* or *crucial –*, die Feuerprobe; *put to the –*, auf die Probe stellen; *stand the –*, die Probe bestehen, sich bewähren; *take the –*, den Testeid leisten (*Hist.*); *undergo a –*, eine Prüfung machen, sich einer Prüfung unterziehen. 2. *v.a.* (über)prüfen, erproben, (aus)probieren, auf die Probe stellen (*for*, in bezug auf); analysieren, untersuchen (*Chem.*). **– Act,** *s.* die Testakte (*Hist.*). **– case,** *s.* das Schulbeispiel; der Präzedenzfall (*Law*). **– cricketer,** *s.* der Nationalmannschaftspieler (*Crick.*). **–er,** *s.* der Prüfer; Prüfapparat. **– flight,** *s.* der Probeflug. **–-match,** *s.* internationales Kricketspiel. **–-paper,** *s.* das Reagenspapier, Reagenzpapier (*Chem.*). **– pilot,** *s.* der Einflieger (*Av.*). **–-tube,** *s.* das Reagensglas, Reagenzglas, die Probierröhre (*Chem.*).

testace–an [tɛsˈteɪʃn], 1. *adj.* schalentragend, Schaltier–. 2. *s.* das Schaltier (*Zool.*). **–ous** [–ʃəs], *adj.* hartschalig, Schal–.

testa–ment [ˈtɛstəmənt], *s.* das Testament (*B.*); (*only in*) *last will and –ment*, letzter Wille (*Law.*). **–mentary** [–ˈmɛntərɪ], *adj.* testamentarisch, Testaments–, letztwillig (*Law*). **–te** [–teɪt, –tət], *adj.* mit Hinterlassung eines Testaments. **–tor** [–ˈteɪtə], *s.* der Erblasser. **–trix** [–ˈteɪtrɪks], *s.* die Erblasserin.

tester [ˈtɛstə], *s.* der Himmel, Baldachin (*of a bed, etc.*). **–-bed,** *s.* das Himmelbett.

testicle [ˈtɛstɪkl], *s.* die Hode (*Anat.*).

testif–ication [ˈtɛstɪfɪˈkeɪʃən], *s.* der Beweis, das Zeugnis (*to*, für). **–y** [–faɪ], 1. *v.a.* eidlich bezeugen, zeugen von, bekunden, bescheinigen (*Law*). 2. *v.n.* Zeugnis ablegen, bezeugen, beweisen; *–y to*, erweisen, bezeugen.

testimon–ial [tɛstɪˈmoʊnɪəl], *s.* das Zeugnis, Attest; *give a –ial*, ein Zeugnis ausstellen (*to* (*Dat.*); *on* or *about*, über). **–y** [ˈtɛstɪmənɪ], *s.* das Zeugnis, der Beweis (*to*, für); die Zeugenaussage (*Law*), Offenbarung (*Eccl.*); *bear –y*, Zeugnis ablegen (*to* (*Dat.*)); *in –y whereof*, urkundlich dessen.

test–iness [ˈtɛstɪnɪs], *s.* die Verdrießlichkeit, Gereiztheit, Reizbarkeit. **–y** [ˈtɛstɪ], *adj.* reizbar, verdrießlich.

testis [ˈtɛstɪs], *s.* (*usually pl.* –es) *see* **testicle.**

testudo [tɛsˈtjuːdoʊ], *s.* die Schildkröte.

tetanus [ˈtɛtənəs], *s.* der Starrkrampf.

tetch–iness [ˈtɛtʃɪnɪs], *s.* die Verdrießlichkeit, Reizbarkeit, Empfindlichkeit. **–y** [ˈtɛtʃɪ], *adj.* verdrießlich, reizbar, empfindlich.

tête-à-tête [ˈteɪtəˈteɪt], 1. *s.* das Gespräch unter vier Augen. 2. *adv.* unter vier Augen, vertraulich.

tether [ˈtɛðə], 1. *s.* das Haltseil, Spannseil, Haltetau; (*fig.*) der Spielraum; *be at the end of one's –*, am Ende seiner Kraft sein, keine Geduld mehr haben; ratlos sein, sich nicht mehr zu helfen wissen. 2. *v.a.* anbinden (*to*, an); (*fig.*) binden (*to*, an).

tetra–chord [ˈtɛtrəkɔːd], *s.* der *or* das Tetrachord (*Mus.*). **–d** [ˈtɛtræd], *s.* die Vierzahl. **–gon** [ˈtɛtrəgən], *s.* das Viereck. **–gonal** [–ˈtrægənəl], *adj.* viereckig. **–gynous** [–ˈdʒɪnəs, –ˈgɪnəs], mit 4

Griffeln (*Bot.*). **–hedral** [–ˈhɪ:drəl], *adj.* vierflächig. **–hedron** [–ˈhɪ:drən], *s.* das Tetraeder. **–logy** [tɛˈtræləd͡ʒɪ], *s.* die Tetralogie. **–meter** [–ˈtræmɪtə], *s.* der Tetrameter. **–ndrous** [–ˈtrændrəs], *adj.* mit 4 Staubgefäßen (*Bot.*). **–pod** [ˈtɛtrəpɔd], *s.* der Vierfüßler (*Zool.*). **–rch** [ˈtɛtrɑ:k], *s.* der Vierfürst. **–rchy** [ˈtɛtrɑ:kɪ], *s.* das Vierfürstentum. **–syllabic** [–sɪˈlæbɪk], *adj.* viersilbig.

tetrode [ˈtɛtroud], *s.* die Vierelektrodenröhre (*Rad.*).

tetter [ˈtɛtə], *s.* die Hautflechte, der Hautausschlag (*Med.*).

teuton [ˈtju:tən], *s.* der Germane. **–ic** [–ˈtɔnɪk], *adj.* germanisch; *–ic Order*, der Deutschorden. **–ism** [–nɪzm], *s.* das Germanentum, germanische Eigenart; der Germanismus (*in language*).

text [tɛkst], *s.* der Text, Wortlaut; die Bibelstelle; (*coll.*) *stick to one's –*, bei der S. bleiben. **– –book,** *s.* das Lehrbuch, der Leitfaden. **– –hand,** *s.* große Schreibschrift (*Typ.*). **–ual** [–tjuəl], *adj.* textlich, Text–; wörtlich, wortgetreu.

text–ile [ˈtɛkstɑɪl], 1. *adj.* gewebt, Web–, Textil–; *–ile industry*, die Textilindustrie. 2. *s.* der Webstoff, das Gewebe; *pl.* Textilwaren. **–ure** [–tʃə], *s.* das Gewebe (*also Anat.*), die Struktur (*of minerals*); Maserung (*of wood*); (*fig.*) Beschaffenheit, das Gefüge.

thalamus [ˈθæləməs], *s.* der Hügel (*Anat.*).

thalli–c [ˈθælɪk], *adj.* Thallium– (*Chem.*). **–um** [–lɪəm], *s.* das Thallium.

than [ðæn], *conj.* (*after comparatives*) als; *a man – whom no one . . .*, ein Mann der wie kein anderer . . .

thane [θeɪn], *s.* der Lehnsmann; (*Scots*) Than.

thank [θæŋk], 1. *v.a.* danken (*Dat.*); *– you*, bitte (*affirm.*), danke (*neg.*); *yes, – you*, wenn ich bitten darf; *no, – you*, nein, danke; (*coll.*) *– goodness!*, *– heavens!* Gott sei Dank!; *you have yourself to – for it*, du hast es dir selbst zuzuschreiben; *I will – you*, ich möchte Sie bitten (*to do*, zu tun; *for*, um); *– you for nothing*, es geht dann auch ohne Sie. 2. *s.* (*only pl.*) der Dank, die Danksagung, Dankesbezeigung; (*coll.*) *–s!* danke!; *express –s*, Dank aussprechen *or* sagen; *in –s for*, zum Dank für; *letter of –s*, das Dankschreiben; *many –s*, vielen Dank; *return –s*, Dank sagen (*to* (*Dat.*)); *–s* (*be*) *to God*, Gott sei Dank *or* gedankt; *no* or *small –s to you!* ohne deine Hilfe *or* dein Zutun; *–s to*, dank (*Dat.*); *vote of –s*, die Dankadresse, Dankesworte (*pl.*); *with –s*, mit Dank, dankend. **–ful,** *adj.* dankbar (*to* (*Dat.*)), erkenntlich (*to*, gegen). **–fulness,** *s.* die Dankbarkeit, Erkenntlichkeit. **–less,** *adj.* undankbar (*of a p. or th.*), wenig erfreulich, unfruchtbar (*of a th.*). **–lessness,** *s.* die Undankbarkeit. **– –offering,** *s.* das Dankopfer. **–sgiving,** *s.* die Danksagung; das Dankfest.

that [ðæt], 1. *dem. pron.* (*a*) (*absolute, no pl.*) das; *and – was –*, das wäre erledigt; *so –'s –*, und damit basta; *and all –*, und allerlei anderes; *for all –*, trotz alledem; *– is so*, so ist es; (*is*) *– so?* ist das wirklich so?; *–'s what it is*, daran *or* so liegt es; *talk of this and –*, von allerlei Dingen reden; *– which*, das was; *– is* (*to say*), das heißt; *– is my child*, das ist mein Kind; *– is the children*, das sind die Kinder; das haben die Kinder getan; *– is my fault*, das ist meine Schuld; *– is my hat*, das ist mein Hut; *–'s it!* so ist es!, so ist's recht!; (*b*) (*with pl.* those) (*of things*) der, das, die; *of the two hats I like – better*, von den beiden Hüten habe ich den lieber; (*of persons, only with* to be) das; *– is his son*, das ist sein Sohn; (*coll.*) *–'s a good boy*, so bist du ein artiger Junge. 2. *dem. adj.* (*sing.*) der, das, die, jene(–r, –s), diese(–r, –s); (*vulg.*) *– there*, jene(–r, –s); (*pl.*) *see* **those.** 3. *rel. pron.* (*introd. defining clause, rarely used of a p.*) der, die, das, welche(–r, –s), was; *the best – I have*, das Beste was ich habe; *it was you – said so*, Sie waren es, der (*or* die) es sagte; *it was no one – I know*, es war niemand den ich kenne. 4. *conj.* daß; ob; damit, so daß; *it was here – he died*, hier starb er; *in –*, deshalb weil, insofern als; *in order –*, damit; *I do not know – I am right*, ich weiß nicht ob ich recht habe; *not –*, nicht daß, nicht weil; *now –*, nun da, jetzt da; *I'm not sure –*, ich bin nicht sicher ob; *seeing –*, see *in –*; *so –*, so daß. 5. *adv.* (*coll.*) so, derartig.

thatch [θætʃ], 1. *s.* das Strohdach; Dachstroh. 2. *v.a.* mit Stroh decken; *–ed roof*, das Strohdach. **–er,** *s.* der Strohdecker. **–ing,** *s.* das Dachstroh; Strohdecken.

thaumaturg–ic(al) [θɔ:məˈtə:d͡ʒɪk(l)], *adj.* wundertätig; Wunder–. **–ist,** *s.* der Wundertäter. **–y,** *s.* die Zauberei, Wundertätigkeit.

thaw [θɔ:], 1. *s.* das Tauen; Tauwetter. 2. *v.n.* tauen; (*fig.*) auftauen. 3. *v.a.* schmelzen, (*fig.*) zum Auftauen bringen, auftauen lassen.

the [ðɪ, ðə *acc. to emphasis*], *def. art.* der, die, das; *all – men*, alle Männer; *all – world*, die ganze Welt; *by – dozen*, dutzendweise; *sixpence – pound*, fünfzig Pfennig das Pfund; *– Smiths*, die Familie Schmidt. 2. *adv.* desto, um so mehr; *– fewer – better*, je weniger desto besser; *so much – worse*, um so schlimmer; *not any – worse*, keineswegs schlechter; *– more as*, um so mehr als.

theatr–e [ˈθɪ:ətə], *s.* das Theater, Schauspielhaus; (*fig.*) der Schauplatz (*of war*); die Bühne, das Theaterwesen; *lecture –e*, der Hörsaal; *operating –e*, der Operationssaal; *open-air –e*, die Freilichtbühne; *go to the –e*, ins Theater gehen; *the world of the –e*, die Bühnenwelt. **–e-goer,** *s.* der Theaterbesucher. **–e-going,** *s.* der Theaterbesuch. **–ical** [–ˈætrɪkl], 1. *adj.* bühnenmäßig, Bühnen–, Theater–, (*fig.*) theatralisch, prunkend. **–icality** [–ˈkælɪtɪ], *s.* theatralisches Wesen. **–icals** [–trɪkəlz], *pl.* Theateraufführungen (*pl.*); *amateur* or *private –icals*, Liebhaberaufführungen (*pl.*).

thee [ðɪ:], (*archaic, Poet. & B.*) dich (*Acc.*); dir (*Dat.*); *of –*, deiner.

theft [θɛft], *s.* der Diebstahl (*from a p.*, an einem; *from*, aus (*a place*)).

theine [ˈθɪ:ɪn], *s.* das Tein (*Chem.*).

their [ðɛə], *poss. adj.* ihr (*sing.*); ihre (*pl.*). **–s** [–z], *poss. pron.* der, die *or* das ihrige, ihr(–e, –es); *it is –s*, es gehört ihnen.

theis–m [ˈθɪ:ɪzm], *s.* der Theismus. **–t,** *s.* der Theist. **–tic(al)** [–ˈɪstɪk(l)], *adj.* theistisch.

them [ðɛm], 1. *pers. pron.* sie (*Acc.*); ihnen (*Dat.*); *of –*, ihrer; *to –*, ihnen. 2. *refl. pron.* sich. **–selves,** *pl. pron.* sie selbst; (*used reflexively*) sich (selbst); *they –selves*, sie selbst; *things in –selves innocent*, an und für sich unschuldige Dinge.

them–atic [θəˈmætɪk], *adj.* thematisch. **–e** [θɪ:m], *s.* das Thema (*also Mus.*), der Stoff, Gegenstand; der Aufsatz, die (Schul)Aufgabe; das Motiv (*Mus.*). **–e-song,** der Hauptschlager (*film, etc.*).

then [ðɛn], 1. *adv.* damals; dann, darauf; in dem Falle, denn, also; *long before –*, lange vorher; *now –*, aber bitte, nun also; *now and –*, dann und wann; *every now and –*, alle Augenblicke; *but –*, aber andererseits *or* freilich; *by –*, bis dahin, inzwischen, zu der Zeit; *from –*, von da ab; *all right –*, see *well –*; *– and there* or *there and –*, auf der Stelle, in demselben Augenblick, sofort; *till –*, bis dahin; *not till –*, erst dann; *well –*, nun gut denn; *what –?* was dann? was weiter? 2. *adj.* damalig. 3. *conj.* dann, ferner, außerdem; also, folglich.

thence [ðɛns], *adv.* von da *or* dort (*place*); von da an, seit jener Zeit (*time*). **–forth, –forward,** *adv.* von da ab, von der Zeit an, seitdem, hinfort.

theo–cracy [θɪ:ˈɔkrəsɪ], *s.* die Theokratie, Gottesherrschaft; Priesterherrschaft. **–cratic** [θɪ:əˈkrætɪk], *adj.* theokratisch. **–dicy** [θɪ:ˈɔdɪsɪ], *s.* die Theodizee. **–dolite** [θɪ:ˈɔdəlɑɪt], *s.* der Theodolit (*Surv.*). **–gony** [–ˈɔgənɪ], *s.* die Theogonie, Götterabstammungslehre. **–logian** [θɪ:əˈloud͡ʒən], *s.* der Theolog(e). **–logical** [–ˈlɔd͡ʒɪkl], *adj.* theologisch. **–logy** [–ˈɔləd͡ʒɪ], *s.* die Theologie, Gottesgelehrtheit. **–machy** [–ˈɔməkɪ], *s.* der Kampf unter den Göttern. **–morphic** [θɪ:əˈmɔ:fɪk], *adj.* gottähnlich, in göttlicher Gestalt. **–phany** [–ˈɔfənɪ], *s.* die Erscheinung Gottes in menschlicher Gestalt.

theor–em [ˈθɪ:ərəm], *s.* der Lehrsatz. **–etical** [–ˈrɛtɪkl], *adj.* theoretisch, spekulativ. **–ist** [ˈθɪ:ərɪst], *s.* der Theoretiker. **–ize** [ˈθɪ:ərɑɪz], *v.n.* theoretisieren, Theorien aufstellen, spekulieren. **–y** [ˈθɪ:ərɪ], *s.* die Theorie; *in –y*, theoretisch; (*coll.*) *have a –y*, sich einbilden.

theosoph–ic(al), [θɪ:əˈsɔfɪk(l)], *adj.* theosophisch.

–ist [θɪːˈɔsəfɪst], *s.* der Theosoph. **–y** [–ˈɔsəfɪ], *s.* die Theosophie.
therap–eutic(al) [θɛrəˈpjuːtɪk(l)], *adj.* therapeutische, Heil–. **–eutics** [–ˈpjuːtɪks], *pl.* (*sing. const.*) die Therapeutik. **–y** [ˈθɛrəpɪ], *s.* die Therapie, das Heilverfahren.
there [ðɛə], 1. *adv.* da, dort, daselbst; hin, dahin, dorthin; es (*before intr. verbs*); (*sl.*) *be all* –, aufgeweckt sein; *not all* –, übergeschnappt; – *and back*, hin und zurück; – *is*, es ist, es gibt; – *are*, es sind, es gibt; *will* – *be dancing?* wird getanzt (werden)?; – *is no saying* . . ., es läßt sich nicht sagen . . .; – *he is*, da ist er; – *it is*, so ist es, so steht es; –*'s a good boy*, das ist ein braver Junge, so ist es brav; –*'s a good chap*, sei so gut; *down* –, da unten; *in* –, da drinnen; *here and* –, da und dort; *out* –, da draußen; *over* –, da drüben; – *and then* or *then and* –, auf der Stelle, sofort; *up* –, da oben; – *you are!* hab' ich es nicht gesagt? da haben Sie es! 2. *int.* so! sieh! – –*!* sei ruhig!; – *now*, nun weißt du's; *now* –, da sieht man nun; *so* –, see – *now*; damit basta, Punktum! **–about(s)**, *adv.* da herum; ungefähr so(viel), etwa. **–after**, *adv.* danach, seither. (*archaic*) **–at**, *adv.* dabei, daselbst, bei der Gelegenheit. **–by**, *adv.* daneben; damit, dadurch. (*archaic*) **–for**, *adv.* dafür. **–fore**, *adv.* & *conj.* deswegen, deshalb, darum; daher, also, folglich. **–from**, *adv.* daher, daraus. **–in**, *adv.* darin, in dieser Hinsicht. **–inafter**, *adv.* später unten (*Law*). (*archaic*) **–of**, *adv.* daraus, davon; dessen, deren. (*archaic*) **–on**, *adv.* darauf. (*archaic*) **–to**, *adv.* dazu, dafür, daran; außerdem. (*archaic*) **–under**, *adv.* darunter. **–upon**, *adv.* darauf, hierauf; infolgedessen. **–with**, *adv.* damit, darauf. **–withal**, *adv.* damit; überdies, außerdem.
therm [θəːm], *s.* die Wärmeeinheit. **–ae** [–ɪː], *pl.* warme Quellen. **–al**, *adj.* Thermal–, Warm–; *–al springs*, Thermen *pl.*; *–al unit*, die Wärmeeinheit. **–ic**, *adj.* Hitze–, Wärme–, thermisch. **–ionic** [θəːmɪˈɔnɪk], *adj.* Kathoden–, Elektronen– (*Rad.*). **–ite**, *s.* das Thermit (*Chem.*). **–o**, *prefix*, Wärme–, Thermo–. **–o-chemistry**, *s.* die Thermochemie. **–o-couple**, *s.* das Thermoelement. **–odynamics**, *pl.* (*sing. constr.*) die Wärmekraftlehre, die Thermodynamik. **–o-electric(al)**, *adj.* thermoelektrisch. **–o-electricity**, *s.* die Thermoelektrizität. **–ometer** [θəˈmɔmɪtə], *s.* der *or* das Thermometer. **–ometric-(al)** [θəːməˈmɛtrɪk(l)], *adj.* thermometrisch. **–opile**, *s.* die Thermosäule. **–os-(flask)** [ˈθəːməs], *s.* die Thermosflasche. **–ostat**, *s.* der Thermostat, Wärmeregler.
thesaurus [θɪːˈsɔːrəs], *s.* der Wortschatz, das Lexikon.
these [ðiːz], (*pl. of* **this**) 1. *dem. adj.* diese; – *9 years*, schon 9 Jahre, seit 9 Jahren; *one of* – *days*, eines Tages. 2. *pron.* diese; (*with verb* to be) dies; – *are my children*, dies sind meine Kinder.
thesis [ˈθɪːsɪs], *s.* der Leitsatz, der (Streit)Satz; die These; Dissertation, Doktorarbeit.
thews [θjuz], *pl.* Muskeln, Sehnen; (*fig.*) die Kraft.
they [ðeɪ], *pers. pron.* sie; – *who*, die(jenigen) welche; – *say*, man sagt, es heißt.
thick [θɪk], 1. *adj.* dick, dicht besät (*with*, mit), voll, reich (*with*, von); trübe (*fluids*); dicht (*woods, fog, etc.*); heiser, belegt (*voice*); (*coll.*) intim, vertraut, (*coll.*) stumpf(sinnig); – *with dust*, mit Staub bedeckt; (*sl.*) – *ear*, geschwollenes Ohr; (*sl.*) *a bit* –, ein starkes Stück, zu arg, happig; – *soup*, legierte Suppe; (*coll.*) *as* – *as thieves*, dicke Freunde. 2. *adv.* dick, dicht; *come* or *fall* – *and fast*, dicht hintereinander kommen; *lay it on* –, dick auftragen. 3. *s.* schwierigster Teil; (*fig.*) der Brennpunkt; das Gewoge; *in the* – *of the fight*, im dichtesten Kampfgewühl; *be in the* – *of*, mitten stehen in; *be in the* – *of it*, mittendrin stehen; *through* – *and thin*, durch dick und dünn. **–en**, 1. *v.a.* dick(er) machen, verdicken, eindicken (*Cook.*); (*fig.*) verstärken. 2. *v.n.* dicker werden, sich verdichten; Fäden ziehen (*of fluids*), sich trüben; sich verstärken *or* vermehren; *the fight –ens*, der Kampf wird heftiger. **–ening**, *s.* die Verdickung, Ausschwellung; das Verdickungsmittel (*Cook.*). **–-headed**, *adj.* dickköpfig. **–-lipped**, *adj.* dicklippig. **–ness**, *s.* die Dicke, Stärke; Dichtheit; Trübheit; Lage, Schicht. **–-set**, 1. *adj.* untersezt (*a p.*); dicht bepflanzt (*plants*). **–-skinned**, *adj.* dickhäutig, dickschalig; (*fig.*) dickfellig. **–-skulled**, *adj.* dickköpfig.
thicket [ˈθɪkɪt], *s.* das Dickicht, Gebüsch.
thie–f [θɪːf], *s.* (*pl.* –ves [θɪːvz]), der Dieb, Räuber; (*Prov.*) *set a –f to catch a –f*, den Bock zum Gärtner machen. **–ve** [θɪːv], *v.n.* & *a.* stehlen. **–very**, *s.* die Dieberei. **–es**, *pl. see* **–f**; *–ves' Latin*, die Gaunersprache. **–vish**, *adj.* diebisch, Diebs–, spitzbübisch (*also fig.*). **–vishness**, *s.* der Hang zum Stehlen; das Diebische, Spitzbübische (*of a look, etc.*).
thigh [θaɪ], *s.* der (Ober)Schenkel. **–-bone**, *s.* das Schenkelbein.
thill [θɪl], *s.* die (Gabel)Deichsel. **–er**, **–-horse**, *s.* das Deichselpferd.
thimble [ˈθɪmbl], *s.* der Fingerhut (*Sew.*), Metallring (*Tech.*), die Kausche (*Naut.*). **–ful**, *s.* ein Fingerhutvoll; (*fig.*) bißchen, das Schlückchen. **–rig**, 1. *v.n.* Taschenspielerkunststücke vorführen; täuschen, betrügen. 2. *s.* das Kunststück; (*fig.*) die List.
thin [θɪn], 1. *adj.* dünn; leicht, zart, fein, schwach; mager, hager, dürr (*figure*); spärlich (*as hair*); wässerig, verdünnt; (*fig.*) ärmlich, kümmerlich, inhaltlos; *grow* –, dünn *or* mager werden; *a* – *crop*, eine spärliche Ernte; – *clothes*, leichte Kleidung; – *excuse*, fadenscheinige Entschuldigung; – *house*, schwach besuchte Vorstellung; *as* – *as a lath* or *rake*, spindeldürr; *have a* – *time of it*, übel dran sein; *wear* –, sich abnutzen *or* verbrauchen. 2. *v.a.* dünn machen, verdünnen; strecken; (also – *out*) lichten (*woods, etc.*); (also – *down*) vermindern. 3. *v.n.* sich verdünnen, dünn(er) *or* spärlich(er) werden; (also – *out*) sich vermindern, geringer werden, abnehmen; sich lichten (*as woods*), sich auskeilen (*Geol.*). **–-bodied**, *adj.* dünnflüssig (*oil, etc.*). **–-faced**, *adj.* schmalbackig. **–ness**, *s.* die Dünnheit, Magerheit, Spärlichkeit, *etc.*; (*fig.*) Seichtheit, Inhaltlosigkeit. **–-skinned**, *adj.* dünnhäutig; (*fig.*) empfindlich. **–-spun**, *adj.* dünngesponnen.
thine [ðaɪn], 1. *poss. pron.* (*archaic*) der, die, *or* das Deine *or* Deinige.
thing [θɪŋ], *s.* (*without pl.*) (beliebiges) Ding, die Sache, Angelegenheit, das Geschäft; (*with pl.*) (beliebiger) Gegenstand; lebendes Wesen, das Geschöpf, die Person; *pl.* Dinge, Sachen, Angelegenheiten, Verhältnisse, Einrichtungen (*pl.*), die Sachlage; (*coll.*) das Gegebene, Richtige, Passende, Schickliche; Wichtige, die Hauptsache; *pl.* (*coll.*) Sachen (*pl.*), die Kleidung, das Zeug, Zubehör, Eigentum, Geräte, Werkzeuge (*pl.*); *above all –s*, vor allen Dingen, vor allem; *in all –s*, in jeder Hinsicht; *of all –s*, vor allen Dingen; *for another* –, andererseits; *that's another* –, das ist (et)was anderes; *–s as they are*, die Wirklichkeit; *how are –s?* wie geht's?; *not an earthly* –, (gar)nichts; *first* –, zu allererst, als Erstes; *first* – *in the morning*, in aller Frühe; *as –s go*, wie es in der Welt geht; *make a good* – *of*, Nutzen *or* Gewinn ziehen aus; *the one good* – *was*, das eine Gute war; *do the handsome* –, sich großzügig *or* anständig verhalten (*by*, gegen); *just the* – *we need*, gerade das was wir nötig haben; *know a* – *or two*, Bescheid wissen (*about*, über), bewandert sein (*about*, in), einiges verstehen (*about*, von); *too much of a good* –, zuviel des Guten; *poor little* –, armes, kleines Ding *or* Wesen; *in the nature of –s*, in der Natur der Verhältnisse; *it was a near* –, es ging um Haaresbreite; *that's a nice* –, das ist eine schöne Geschichte; (*coll.*) *old* –, mein Lieber; *for one* –, erstens einmal, als erstes, einerseits, einesteils, überhaupt, an und für sich; *tell me one* –, sagen Sie mir eins; *one* – *or the other*, das eine oder das andere; *taking one* – *with another*, im großen ganzen; *poor* –*!* der *or* die Arme; *be out of –s*, abseits *or* ausgeschlossen bleiben; *that's the* –*!* so ist's richtig, das ist das Richtige; *that is not quite the* – (*to do*), es schickt sich nicht (zu tun), das tut man eigentlich nicht; *it comes to the same* –, es läuft auf dasselbe hinaus; *no small* –, keine Kleinigkeit; *as –s stand*, wie die Dinge liegen; *it's a strange* – *that*, es ist merkwürdig daß; *no such* –, nichts

dergleichen. **-amy, -umabob, -umajig, -ummy,** *s.* das Dings, der, die, *or* das Dingsda.

think [θɪŋk], 1. *ir.v.a.* denken, sich vorstellen; nachdenken über, ausdenken; meinen, der Meinung sein, glauben, annehmen, halten für, betrachten als, erachten, gedenken, beabsichtigen, im Sinn haben; – *o.s. clever*, sich für klug halten; – *it advisable*, es für angebracht halten; – *it best*, es für das beste halten; – *it fit*, – *it proper*, es für richtig halten; (*with adverbs*) – *out*, ausdenken; zu Ende denken, überlegen; – *over*, überlegen; (*coll.*) – *up*, ausdenken, aushecken. 2. *ir.v.n.* (sich) denken, sich vorstellen, nachdenken, überlegen; meinen, der Meinung sein, glauben, urteilen, halten (*of*, von); verfallen *or* sich besinnen auf; erwarten, gefaßt sein; – *about*, nachdenken über; – *of*, denken an; *I – so*, ich glaube (es); *I should – so*, das will ich meinen; *I should – not*, das fehlte noch; – *highly of*, eine hohe Meinung haben von; – *much of*, viel halten von; – *nothing of a th.*, sich nichts machen aus etwas; – *better of it*, sich eines Besseren besinnen; – *the world of*, Wunder was halten von. **-able,** *adj.* denkbar. **-er,** *s.* der Denker, Philosoph. **-ing,** *s.* das Denken, die Meinung; *way of -ing*, die Denkart; *to my -ing*, meiner Meinung (nach).

thinness, *see* **thin.**

third [θə:d], 1. *num. adj.* dritt; (*coll.*) – *degree*, scharfes Verhör mit Anwendung von Zwangsmethoden; – *party*, dritte Person (*Law*). 2. *s.* der, die, *or* das Dritte; das Drittel; die Terz (*Mus.*); (*coll.*) dritte Klasse (*Railw.*). **-ly,** *adv.* drittens. **--party insurance,** *s.* die Haftpflichtversicherung. **- rail,** *s.* die Stromschiene (*Railw.*). **--rate,** *adj.* dritten Ranges.

thirst [θə:st], 1. *s.* der Durst (*for*, nach) (*also fig.*). 2. *v.n.* dursten, dürsten (*for*, *after*, nach). **-iness,** *s.* die Durstigkeit, der Durst. **-y,** *adj.* durstig (*also fig.*); dürr, trocken (*as soil*); *I am -y*, ich habe Durst, mich durstet.

thirt-een [θə:ˈtɪ:n], 1. *num. adj.* dreizehn. 2. *s.* die Dreizehn. **-eenth,** 1. *num. adj.* dreizehnt. 2. *s.* der, die, *or* das Dreizehnte; das Dreizehntel. **-ieth** [ˈθə:tɪəθ], 1. *num. adj.* dreißigst. 2. *s.* der, die *or* das Dreißigste; das Dreißigstel. **-y** [ˈθə:tɪ], 1. *num. adj.* dreißig. 2. *s.* die Dreißig. *pl.* die dreißiger Jahre.

this [ðɪs], 1. *dem. pron.* (*with pl.* these); (*of things*) diese(-r, -s); (*of persons, only with verb* to be), dies; (*without pl.*) dies; *all* –, dies alles; *before* –, schon vorher; *by* –, inzwischen, indessen; *like* –, so, folgendermaßen; – *is my son*, dies ist mein Sohn; – *is what I said*, ich sagte Folgendes; – *happened some years ago*, dies geschah vor einigen Jahren. 2. *dem. adj.* (*pl.* these) diese(-r, -s); – *day week*, heute vor *or* in 8 Tagen; – *morning*, heute morgen; – *much*, so viel; – *once*, dieses eine Mal; – *one*, dieser; *by – time*, mittlerweile; – *year*, dieses *or* das laufende Jahr.

thistle [ˈθɪsl], *s.* die Distel. **-down,** *s.* die Distelwolle, Distelfrucht.

thither [ðɪðə], *adv.* dorthin, dahin; *hither and* –, hin und her.

thole [θoʊl], *s.* (also *--pin*) die Dolle, der Ruderpflock.

thong [θɔŋ], *s.* der Riemen, Gurt, die Peitschenschnur.

thora-cic [θəˈræsɪk], *adj.* Brust-. **-x** [ˈθɔ:ræks], *s.* der Brustkasten, Brustkorb (*Anat.*), das Bruststück (*Ent.*).

thorium [ˈθɔ:rɪəm], *s.* das Thorium.

thorn [θɔ:n], *s.* der Dorn, Stachel; *be a – in a p.'s side* or *flesh*, einem ein Dorn im Auge sein; *be* or *sit on -s*, wie auf heißen Kohlen sitzen. **--apple,** *s.* der Stechapfel. **--bush,** *s.* der Dornbusch, Hagedorn, Weißdorn. **--hedge,** *s.* die Dornenhecke. **-less,** *adj.* dornenlos. **-y,** *adj.* dornig, stach(e)lig; (*fig.*) dornenvoll, beschwerlich, mühselig.

thorough [ˈθʌrə], *adj.* gründlich, durchgreifend; völlig, gänzlich, vollständig, vollendet, vollkommen. **--bass,** *s.* der Generalbaß (*Mus.*). **-bred,** 1. *adj.* rasserein, reinrassig, Vollblut-; (*fig.*) gediegen, erstklassig; gründlich, richtiggehend. 2. *s.* das Vollblut, der Vollblüter. **-fare,** *s.* der Durchgang, die Durchfahrt; die (Haupt)Verkehrsstraße. **--going,** *adj.* richtiggehend, durchgreifend, gründlich, tatkräftig, energisch, extrem. **-ness,** *s.* die Vollständigkeit, Gründlichkeit, Gediegenheit. **--paced,** *adj.* gründlich, echt, gediegen, ausgemacht, ausgekocht, abgefeimt, durchtrieben, Erz- (*thief, scoundrel*).

those [ðoʊz], *dem. pron. & adj.* (*pl. of* **that**).

thou [ðaʊ], 1. *pers. pron.* (*archaic & B.*) du. 2. *v.a. & n.* (also – *and thee*) duzen.

though [ðoʊ], 1. *conj.* obgleich, obwohl, obschon, wenn auch, wenngleich; *as* –, als ob, als wenn; *as – he were ill*, als wenn er krank wäre; *even* –, selbst wenn; *important – it is*, so wichtig es auch ist; *what – it rains?* was macht es wenn es regnet? wenn es nun auch regnet?; – *I say it* (*myself*), ohne mich zu rühmen. 2. *adv.* (*coll.*) (*usually at end of sentence*) doch, immerhin, zwar, dennoch, indessen; *you will come* –, Sie kommen aber doch; *I wish you had told me* –, hätten Sie es mir doch gesagt!

thought [θɔ:t], 1. *v.a. & n. see* **think.** 2. *s.* (*sing. only*) das Denken, die Denkarbeit, der Denkprozeß; die Gedankenwelt; Sorge, Rücksicht; (*coll.*) *a* –, ein wenig, etwas (*with adjectives*); (*also pl.*) der Gedanke (*of*, an), Einfall; die Absicht; (*usually pl.*) die Meinung, Ansicht; *it never entered my -s*, es kam mir nie in den Sinn; *a penny for your -s*, woran denkst du nur? *give a – to*, denken an, Aufmerksamkeit schenken (*Dat.*); *happy* –, guter Einfall; *lost in* –, in Gedanken vertieft; *modern* –, moderne Gedankenwelt; *he has no – of going*, er hat nicht die Absicht zu gehen; *on second -s*, bei reiflicher Überlegung; *take* –, mit sich zu Rate gehen; *take – for*, Sorge tragen um; *without* –, ohne Gedanken. **-ful,** *adj.* gedankenvoll; gedankenreich (*as a book*); nachdenklich, beschaulich; rücksichtsvoll, zuvorkommend; bedacht (*of*, auf). **-fulness,** *s.* die Nachdenklichkeit, Beschaulichkeit; Rücksichtnahme; Zuvorkommenheit. **-less,** *adj.* gedankenlos; sorglos; unbekümmert (*of*, um); rücksichtslos; leichtsinnig, leichtfertig, unbesonnen. **-lessness,** *s.* die Gedankenlosigkeit, Unbesonnenheit, Sorglosigkeit, Rücksichtslosigkeit. **--reading,** *s.* das Gedankenlesen. **--transference,** *s.* die Gedankenübertragung.

thousand [ˈθaʊzənd], 1. *num. adj.* tausend; (*fig.*) – *and one*, zahllos, unzählig; – *times*, tausendmal. 2. *s.* das Tausend; *one in a* –, einer unter Tausenden; *ten* –, zehntausend; *in their -s*, zu Tausenden. **-fold,** *adj.* tausendfach. **-th,** 1. *num. adj.* tausendst. 2. *s.* der, die *or* das Tausendste; das Tausendstel.

thral-dom [ˈθrɔ:ldəm], *s.* die Knechtschaft, Hörigkeit. **-l** [θrɔ:l], *s.* Leibeigene(r) *m.*, der Knecht, Sklave (*also fig.*); (*fig.*) die Knechtschaft, Gefangenschaft.

thrash [θræʃ], 1. *v.a.* (durch)prügeln, durchhauen; (*fig.*) schlagen, besiegen; – *the life out of a p.*, einen tüchtig vermöbeln. 2. *v.n.* (also – *about*), hin und her schlagen, sich vorwärtsarbeiten (*Naut.*). **-er,** *s.* der Seefuchs (*Ichth.*). **-ing,** *s.* die Dresche, Tracht Prügel; *give s.o. a -ing*, einen tüchtig verprügeln. *See also* **thresh.**

thread [θrɛd], 1. *s.* der Faden (*also fig.*), Zwirn, das Garn; (Schrauben)Gewinde, der Schraubengang (*Tech.*); (*fig.*) Zusammenhang; *resume the – of one's discourse*, den Faden seiner Rede wieder aufnehmen; *hang by a* –, an einem Faden hängen. 2. *v.a.* einfädeln (*a needle*); aufreihen (*beads*); durchziehen (*with threads*); (*fig.*) sich winden *or* durchschlängeln durch; – *one's way*, sich hindurchschlängeln. **-bare,** *adj.* fadenscheinig, abgetragen; (*fig.*) abgedroschen. **-bareness,** *s.* die Fadenscheinigkeit, Abgedroschenheit.

threat [θrɛt], *s.* die Drohung (*to*, gegen; *of*, mit), Androhung, Bedrohung, Gefahr (*to*, für); – *to peace*, die Bedrohung des Friedens; *there is a – of snow*, es droht Schnee *or* zu schneien. **-en** 1. *v.a.* drohen (*Dat.*, *with*, mit), androhen (*Dat.*; *with* (*Acc.*)); (*fig.*) bedrohen (*Acc.*; *with*, mit); (*fig.*) gefährden. 2. *v.n.* drohen; (*fig.*) im Anzuge sein. **-ening,** *adj.* drohend; (*fig.*) bedrohlich; *-ing letter*, der Drohbrief.

three [θrɪ:], 1. *num. adj.* drei; (*coll.*) – *parts finished*, fast *or* beinahe fertig. 2. *s.* die Drei; *by* or *in -s*, zu dreien. **--colour process,** *s.* der Dreifarbendruck. **--cornered,** *adj.* dreieckig. **--decker,** *s.* der Dreidecker. **-fold,** *adj.* dreifach. **--foot,** *adj.* drei Fuß lang. **--halfpence,** *s.* anderthalb Penny. **--legged race,** *s.* das Dreibeinwettlaufen. **--master,** *s.* der Dreimaster (*Naut.*). **-pence** [ˈθrɛpɛns, ˈθrɪpəns], *s.* drei Pence. **-penny** [ˈθrɛpənɪ, ˈθrɪpənɪ], *adj.* für drei Pence; drei Pence wert; *-penny piece* or *bit*, das Dreipencestück. **-per cent,** *adj.* dreiprozentig. **--phase current,** *s.* dreiphasiger Wechselstrom, der Drehstrom. **--phase motor,** *s.* der Drehstrommotor. **--ply,** *adj.* dreischichtig (*wood*), dreifach (*thread*); *--ply wood*, das Sperrholz. **--quarter,** *adj.* dreiviertel; *--quarter backs, pl.* die Dreiviertel-Reihe (*Rugby Footb.*). **-score,** *adj.* sechzig. **--speed gear,** *s.* dreifache Übersetzung (*Cycl., etc.*). **--sided,** *adj.* dreiseitig. **-some,** *s.* das Dreierspiel. **--storied,** *adj.* dreistöckig. **--year-old,** *s.* Dreijährige(r), *m.* (*Racing*).

threnody [ˈθrɪːnədɪ], *s.* das Klagelied.

thresh [θrɛʃ], 1. *v.a.* dreschen; (*fig.*) – *out* (also *thrash* –) gründlich erörtern (*a problem*); – *straw*, leeres Stroh dreschen. 2. *v.n.* Korn dreschen. **-er,** *s.* der Drescher, die Dreschmaschine. **-ing,** *s.* das Dreschen; der Drusch; *-ing floor*, *s.* die Tenne. *See also* **thrash.**

threshold [ˈθrɛʃould], *s.* die Schwelle, (*fig.*) der Anfang, Eingang.

threw [θruː], *see* **throw.**

thrice [θraɪs], *adv.* dreimal; (*fig.*) überaus, höchst, sehr.

thrift [θrɪft], *s.* die Wirtschaftlichkeit, Sparsamkeit; Seenelke, Meernelke; Grasnelke (*Bot.*). **-iness,** *s.* die Wirtschaftlichkeit, Sparsamkeit. **-less,** *adj.* verschwenderisch. **-lessness,** *s.* die Verschwendung. **-y,** *adj.* haushälterisch, sparsam (*of* or *with*, mit); gedeihlich, gedeihend.

thrill [θrɪl], 1. *s.* der Schauer, das Zittern, Erbeben; seelische Erregung, die Freude, das Entzücken; die Sensation, spannendes Erlebnis. 2. *v.a.* durchdringen, durchschauern; erregen, erschüttern, packen. 3. *v.n.* erschauern, erbeben, ergriffen *or* erschüttert werden (*at*, über; *with*, vor). **-er,** *s.* der Sensationsroman, Schauerroman, Detektivroman. **-ing,** *adj.* aufregend, spannend, packend, sensationell.

thriv-e [θraɪv], *reg. & ir. v.n.* gedeihen (*also fig.*), fortkommen, geraten (*as plants*); vorwärtskommen, Glück *or* Erfolg haben; reich werden (*of a p.*); (*fig.*) blühen. **-ing,** *adj.* blühend, gedeihend, emporkommend, gedeihlich; *-ing town*, blühende Stadt; *-ing trade*, gut gehendes Geschäft.

throat [θrout], *s.* die Gurgel, Kehle, der Rachen, Schlund; der Hals; der Eingang, Durchgang, die Öffnung, Gicht, Ausladung (*Tech.*), Hohlkehle (*Arch.*), Klau (*Naut.*), Zahnlücke (*of a saw*); *be at one another's -s*, sich in den Haaren liegen; *clear one's* –, sich räuspern; *cut one's* (or *a p.'s*) –, sich (*or* einem) den Hals abschneiden; (*coll.*) *jump down a p.'s* –, einem an die Gurgel fahren; *lie in one's* –, unverschämt lügen; *sore* –, Halsschmerzen (*pl.*); *the words stuck in my* –, die Worte blieben mir im Halse stecken; *seize* or *take s.o. by the* –, einen an der Kehle packen; *thrust s. th. down a p.'s* –, einem etwas einrammen. **--plate,** *s.* die Stichplatte (*Sew.-mach.*). **-y,** *adj.* guttural, Kehl–; heiser.

throb [θrɔb], 1. *s.* das Schlagen, Klopfen, Pochen, Pulsieren; der Pulsschlag (*also fig.*). 2. *v.n.* schlagen, pochen, klopfen; pulsieren.

throe [θrou], *s.* (*usually pl.*) Schmerzen; (Geburts)-Wehen (*pl.*). (*fig.*) die Gärung; (*fig.*) *in the -s of*, im Kampfe mit.

thrombosis [θrɔmˈbousɪs], *s.* die Thrombose.

throne [θroun], 1. *s.* der Thron; (*fig.*) königliche Macht; *come to the* –, auf den Thron kommen; *succeed to the* –, auf den Thron folgen. 2. *v.a.* auf den Thron setzen. **-less,** *adj.* ohne Thron.

throng [θrɔŋ], 1. *s.* das Gedränge; der Andrang, Zulauf; die Menge, Schar. 2. *v.n.* sich drängen, scharen, herbeiströmen; – *upon*, bedrängen, sich aufdrängen (*Dat.*). 3. *v.a.* bedrängen, umdrängen; (an)füllen, überschwemmen (*a place*). **-ed,** gedrängt voll.

throstle [θrɔsl], *s.* die (Sing)Drossel, Zippe (*Orn.*); Spinnmaschine (*Tech.*).

throttle [θrɔtl], 1. *s.* (*coll.*) die Kehle, Luftröhre Drossel, Drosselklappe, das Drosselventil (*Tech.*); *open the* –, Gas geben (*Motor.*). 2. *v.a.* (er)-drosseln; (*fig.*) unterdrücken, niederhalten; (often – *down*) (ab)drosseln (*an engine*).

through [θruː], 1. *prep.* durch (*also fig.*), quer durch, durch . . . hindurch (*space*); während . . . hindurch (*time*); (*fig.*) aus, vor; mittels(t); *go* or *pass* –, durchmachen; *see* –, durchschauen. 2. *adv.* (mitten) durch; zu Ende; – *and* –, durch und durch, ganz und gar; *you are* –, hier ist Ihre Verbindung, der Teilnehmer meldet sich (*Phone*); (*coll.*) *be* –, fertig *or* erledigt sein; *carry* –, *go* – *with*, ausführen, durchführen, zu Ende bringen; (*coll.*) *fall* –, nicht zustande kommen, ins Wasser fallen; *go* –, angenommen *or* bewilligt werden; *the whole night* –, die ganze Nacht hindurch; *wet* –, durch und durch naß. 3. *attrib. adj.*; – *passenger*, Durchreisende(r) *m.*; – *ticket*, direkte *or* durchgehende Fahrkarte; – *traffic*, der Durchgangsverkehr; – *train*, durchgehender Zug. **-out,** 1. *prep.* ganz (hin)durch (*space*); während, hindurch (*time*). 2. *adv.* durchaus, in jeder Beziehung; ganz und gar, durch und durch; die ganze Zeit hindurch; überall.

throw [θrou], **1.** *ir.v.a.* werfen (*also fig. & wrestling*), schleudern, zuwerfen (*a p. a th.* or *a th. to a p.*, einem etwas); werfen mit (*stones, etc.*); abwerfen (*rider, skin*); aufwerfen (*defences, etc.*); zwirnen (*silk*); formen, drehen (*Pott.*); – *dice*, würfeln; (*coll.*) – *a party*, eine Gesellschaft geben; **(a)** (*with adverbs*) – *away*, fortwerfen, wegwerfen; (*fig.*) vergeuden, verschwenden (*time, etc.*) (*on*, an), verpassen (*opportunity*); *be -n away*, wertlos sein; – *back*, zurückwerfen (*also fig.*); *be -n back upon*, angewiesen sein auf, seine Zuflucht nehmen zu; – *down*, hinwerfen, niederwerfen; umwerfen, umstürzen; – *in*, hineinwerfen, (*fig.*) einwerfen, einschieben, einschalten; (hin)zufügen, dazugeben; *meals -n in*, Mahlzeiten einbegriffen; – *in one's hand* or *the towel*, den Kampf aufgeben; – *in one's lot with a p.*, jemandes Partei nehmen *or* Los teilen; mit einem gemeinsame Sache machen; – *off*, abwerfen; von sich werfen, loswerden; ablegen, abstreifen, ausziehen (*clothes*); abschütteln (*a p.*); (*fig.*) sich freimachen *or* befreien von; von der Spur ablenken (*Hunt.*); hervorbringen, von sich geben, produzieren; abziehen (*Typ.*); – *on*, schnell anziehen, überwerfen; – *open*, aufreißen (*door*), eröffnen (*meeting*), ausschreiben (*for competition*), zugängig machen (*to* (*Dat.*)); – *out*, (hin)auswerfen, hinausschleudern; von sich geben, ausbreiten, aussenden (*also troops*), ausstellen (*sentries*), äußern, fallen lassen, hinwerfen (*hint, etc.*); verwerfen, ablehnen, ausscheiden; – *out a feeler*, einen Fühler ausstrecken; – *out one's chest*, sich in die Brust werfen; – *over*, über den Haufen werfen; (*fig.*) im Stich lassen, verlassen, aufgeben; – *up*, in die Höhe werfen; aufwerfen (*defences*); aufgeben (*an office*), niederlegen (*a post*); – *up one's hands*, die Hände hochheben; **(b)** (*with prepositions*) – *at a p.'s head*, einem an den Kopf werfen; *be -n from one's horse*, vom Pferd abgeworfen werden; – *in a p.'s face*, einem ins Gesicht schleudern; – *into the bargain*, (beim Kauf) draufgeben, als Draufgabe hinzufügen; – *into confusion*, in Verwirrung bringen; – *into prison*, verhaften; – *into raptures*, in Entzücken versetzen; – *into the shade*, in den Schatten stellen; – *one's heart and soul into*, ganz aufgehen in; – *o.s. into*, sich versenken in; *be -n off the line*, entgleisen; – *the blame on s.o.*, einem die Schuld in die Schuhe schieben; – *out of gear* (*fig.*), aus dem Gleis bringen; – *out of work*, außer Arbeit stellen, arbeitslos machen; – *a bridge over*, eine Brücke schlagen über; *be -n* (*together*) *with*, zusammengebracht werden mit; – *o.s.* (*up*)*on a p.*, sich an einen wenden, an einen appellieren; – *o.s.* (*up*)*on a th.*, sich stürzen auf etwas; *be -n upon s.o.'s resources*, von einem abhängig sein; *be -n upon o.s.*, auf sich selbst angewiesen sein. **2.** *ir.v.n.* werfen; würfeln (*with dice*); – *back*, zurückkehren zu, Spuren aufweisen von, zurückgreifen auf. **3.** *s.* das Werfen (*also wrestling*), der Wurf; der

Hubspiel (*of a piston*); *stone's* –, ein Steinwurf weit. **--back,** *s.* die Rückkehr (*to*, zu), der Rückschlag, Atavismus, das Wiederauftreten (*to* (*Gen.*)). **--out,** *s.* Abgelegte(s), Beschädigte(s) *n.* **-er,** *s.* der Seidenzwirner; Former (*Pott.*). **-ing the hammer,** *s.* das Hammerwerfen (*Sport*). **-ing the javelin,** *s.* das Speerwerfen (*Sport*). **-n,** *adj.* gezwirnt (*Tech.*); *-n silk*, das Seidengarn. **-ster,** *s.* der Seidenspinner.

[1]**thrum** [θrʌm], 1. *s.* (*usually pl.*) die Webkante, Salkante, das Salband, der *or* das Trumm, der Saum, die Franse, grobes Garn; *pl.* Garnabfälle (*pl.*), (*fig.*) Bruchstücke (*pl.*). 2. *v.a.* befransen.

[2]**thrum,** 1. *v.n.* klimpern, mit den Fingern trommeln (*on*, auf). 2. *v.a.* klimpern *or* trommeln auf.

[1]**thrush** [θrʌʃ], *s.* die Drossel (*Orn.*).

[2]**thrush,** der Mundschwamm (*Med.*); der Hufgrind, die Strahlfäule (*Vet.*).

thrust [θrʌst], 1. *ir.v.a.* (*also imperf. & p.p.*) stoßen; stecken, schieben (*into*, in), drängen, treiben (*into*, zu); – *o.s. forward*, sich vordrängen; – *s. th. forward*, etwas vorwärts schieben; – *home*, angreifen, losschlagen; – *one's hands into one's pockets*, die Hände in die Taschen stecken; – *one's nose into*, die Nase stecken in; – *into prison*, ins Gefängnis werfen; – *o.s. into*, sich drängen in, eindringen in; – *out one's hand*, die Hand ausstrecken; – *a p. through*, einen durchstoßen, durchbohren; – *upon a p.*, einem aufdrängen. 2. *ir.v.n.* stoßen (*at*, nach); sich drängen. 3. *s.* der Stoß, Hieb; der Schub, Druck (*Mech.*, *Arch.*); der Vorstoß (*towards*, nach), Angriff (*at*, auf) (*Mil.*); *cut and* –, Hieb und Gegenhieb; (*fig.*) das Hin und Her; *home* –, sitzender Hieb. **--bearing,** *s.* das Drucklager (*Mech.*). **-er,** *s.* der Draufgänger, Streber.

thud [θʌd], 1. *v.n.* dumpf aufschlagen; dröhnen. 2. *s.* dumpfer Schlag *or* Ton, das Dröhnen (*of engines, hoofs, etc.*).

thug [θʌg], *s.* der Raubmörder; (*coll.*) Rowdy, Rohling.

thumb [θʌm], 1. *s.* der Daumen; *by rule of* –, erfahrungsmäßig, empirisch, auf praktischem Wege; *under her* –, unter ihrer Fuchtel, in ihrer Gewalt; (*coll.*) *his fingers are all -s*, er hat zwei linke Hände. 2. *v.a.* abgreifen, beschmutzen (*book, etc.*); (*sl.*) – *a lift*, per Anhalter fahren, sich mitnehmen lassen; – *a vehicle*, einen vorbeifahrenden Wagen anhalten. **--mark,** *s.* Schmutzfleck. **--nail,** *s.* der Daumennagel. **--nut,** *s.* (*Amer.*) die Flügelschraube. **--print,** *s.* der Daumenabdruck. **-screw,** *s.* die Daumenschraube (*Hist.*); die Flügelschraube. **--stall,** *s.* der Däumling. **--tack,** *s.* (*Amer.*) die Heftzwecke.

thump [θʌmp], 1. *s.* dumpfer Schlag, der Bums, Puff, Knuff. 2. *v.a.* schlagen, puffen, knuffen. 3. *v.n.* schlagen (*on*, auf; *against*, gegen) (*also of heart*); (laut) klopfen (*the heart*). (*coll.*) **-er,** *s.* etwas Erstaunliches, faustdicke Lüge. (*coll.*) **-ing,** *adj.* gewaltig, ungeheuer; *-ing great*, überaus groß, faustdick.

thunder [ˈθʌndə], 1. *s.* der Donner; *clap* or *peal of* –, der Donnerschlag; – *of applause*, tosender *or* brausender Beifall; (*coll.*) *steal a p.'s* –, einem den Wind aus den Segeln nehmen, einem die Trümpfe aus der Hand nehmen. 2. *v.n.* donnern (*also fig.*); (*fig.*) brausen, toben; wettern (*of a p.*). 3. *v.a.* (also – *forth*, – *out*) herausdonnern, brüllen. **-bolt,** *s.* der Donnerkeil (*Geol.*), Blitzstrahl, (*fig.*) Blitz, plötzlicher Schlag. **--clap,** *s.* der Donnerschlag. **--cloud,** *s.* die Gewitterwolke. **-ing,** *adj.* donnernd, tobend, brüllend; (*sl.*) riesig, ungeheuer. **-ous,** *adj.* donnernd; (*fig.*) donnerartig, brausend, tosend. **--shower,** *s.* der Gewitterregen. **-storm,** *s.* das Gewitter. **--struck,** *adj.* wie vom Donner gerührt; wie (vom Blitz) erschlagen. **-y,** *adj.* gewitterhaft, gewitterschwül.

thuri-ble [ˈθjuːrəbl], *s.* das Weihrauchfaß. **-fer** [-fə], *s.* der Rauchfaßträger. **-fication** [-fɪˈkeɪʃən] *s.* die Räucherung.

Thursday [ˈθəːzdeɪ], *s.* der Donnerstag; *Holy* –, der Himmelfahrtstag; *Maundy* –, der Gründonnerstag; *on* –, am Donnerstag; *on -s*, donnerstags.

thus [ðʌs], *adv.* so, auf die(se) Art *or* Weise, folgendermaßen, wie folgt; demgemäß, daher, folglich; – *far*, so weit; – *much*, so viel.

thwack [θwæk], 1. *v.a.* schlagen, prügeln, durchbleuen, durchwalken. 2. *s.* der Puff, Schlag.

thwart [θwɔːt], 1. *adj.* (*archaic*) quer, schräg. 2. *v.a. prep.* (*archaic*) quer durch, quer über. 3. *v.a.* durchkreuzen, vereiteln (*a plan, etc.*); einen Strich durch die Rechnung machen, in die Quere kommen, entgegenarbeiten (*a p.*, einem). 4. *s.* die Ducht (*Naut.*).

thy [ðaɪ], *poss. adj.* (*Poet. & B.*) dein(e). **-self,** *pron.* (*Nom.*) du (selbst); (*Dat.*) dir (selbst), (*Acc.*) dich (selbst).

thyme [taɪm], *s.* der Thymian (*Bot.*).

thymus [ˈθaɪməs], *s.* die Thymusdrüse (*Anat.*).

thyroid [ˈθaɪrɔɪd], *adj.* Schilddrüsen–; – *gland*, die Schilddrüse.

thyrsus [ˈθəːsəs], *s.* der Thyrsus(stab).

tiara [tɪˈɑːrə], *s.* die Tiara; der (Damen)Kopfschmuck; (*fig.*) päpstliche Würde.

tibia [ˈtɪbɪə], *s.* (*pl.* -e, -s) das Schienbein. **-l,** *adj.* Schienbein–.

tic [tɪk], *s.* krampfhaftes Zucken; nervöser Gesichtsschmerz, das Gesichtszucken.

[1]**tick** [tɪk], *s.* die Zecke, Milbe.

[2]**tick,** *s.* der Kissenbezug, Matratzenbezug, das (Daunen)Inlett. **-ing,** *s.* der Drell, Drillich.

[3]**tick,** *s.* (*sl.*) der Pump, Borg, Kredit; *on* –, auf Pump.

[4]**tick,** 1. *s.* das Ticken; (*coll.*) der Augenblick; das Häkchen, Vermerkzeichen; (*coll.*) *in two -s*, im Augenblick; (*coll.*) *on* or *to the* –, pünktlich, auf den Glockenschlag. 2. *v.n.* ticken (*as a clock*); – *over*, leer laufen (*of an engine*). 3. *v.a.* (also – *off*), anzeichnen, anstreichen; (*sl.*) tadeln, anschnauzen. **-er,** *s.* der Börsentelegraph (*Tele.*); (*coll.*) die Uhr. **--tack,** *s.* (*sl.*) der Buchmachergehilfe (*Racing*). **--tock,** *s.* das Ticktack (*of clock*); (*nursery talk*) die Ticketacke, Uhr.

ticket [ˈtɪkɪt], 1. *s.* der Zettel, Schein, das Etikett, die Etikette, Karte; Fahrkarte, der Fahrschein; die (Eintritts)Karte, das Billet (*Theat., etc.*); (*sl.*) das Richtige; (*coll.*) das Strafmandat; (*coll.*) der Führerschein (*Av.*); Wahlliste, das (Partei)Programm (*Pol., Amer.*); *be on* – *of leave*, unter Polizeiaufsicht stehen; bedingungsweise entlassen werden; *lottery* –, das (Lotterie)Los; *pawn*–, der Pfandschein; *price* –, der Preiszettel; *season* –, die Abonnements-Karte; (*sl.*) *work one's* –, sich drücken. 2. *v.a.* mit Etikett versehen, etikettieren (*goods*). **--clerk,** *s.* der Schalterbeamte. **--collector,** *s.* der (Bahnsteig)Schaffner. **--inspector,** *s.* der (Fahrkarten)Kontrolleur. **--office,** *s.* die Fahrkartenausgabe, der Schalter. **--window,** *s.* (*Amer.*) *see* **--office.**

ticking, *see* [2]**tick.**

tickl-e [ˈtɪkl], 1. *v.a.* kitzeln (*also fig.*); (*fig.*) reizen, schmeicheln; (*coll.*) amüsieren, belustigen; *-e s.o.'s nose*, einen an der Nase kitzeln; (*coll.*) *he was -ed to death*, er wollte sich totlachen. 2. *v.n.* kitzeln, jucken; *my nose -es*, es juckt mich an der Nase, die Nase juckt mich. 3. *s.* das Kitzeln, Jucken; der Kitzel, Reiz. **-er,** *s.* (*coll.*) kitzlige Frage. **-ish,** *adj.* kitz(e)lig (*also fig.*); heikel, schwierig. **-ishness,** *s.* die Kitz(e)ligkeit.

tid-al [ˈtaɪdl], *adj.* Flut–; Gezeiten–; *-al basin*, das Flutdock; *-al chart*, die Gezeitentabelle; *-al river*, von Ebbe und Flut abhängiger Fluß; *-al wave*, die Sturmflut, Flutwelle. **-e** [taɪd], 1. *s.* die Ebbe und Flut, Gezeiten (*pl.*); (*fig.*) der Lauf, Strom; die Zeit (*archaic, except in comps.*); *the -e is going out*, die Flut fällt; *Christmas-e*, die Weihnachtszeit; *the -e is coming in*, die Flut steigt; *ebb -e*, die Ebbe; *even-e*, die Abendzeit; *flood -e*, die Flut; *-e of events*, die Zeitströmung; *go* or *swim with the -e*, mit dem Strom schwimmen; *high -e*, die Flut; höchster Flutstand, das Hochwasser; (*fig.*) der Höhepunkt; *the -e is in*, es ist Flut; *low -e*, die Ebbe, niedrigster Flutstand, das Niedrigwasser; *neap -e*, die Nippflut; *the -e is out*, es ist Ebbe; *spring -e*, die Springflut; *turn of the -e*, der Flutenwechsel; (*fig.*) die Wendung, der Umschwung, Glückswechsel; *the -e turns*, (*fig.*) das Blatt *or* Glück wendet sich; 2. *v.n.* (mit dem Strom) treiben; (*fig.*) *–e over*, hinwegkommen über, überwinden. 3. *v.a.*; *–e over*, hinweghelfen über (*a p.*, einem), über Wasser halten. **–e gate,** *s.* das Fluttor, Flutgatter. **–eland,** *s.* das Flutland. **–eless,** *adj.* flutlos, ohne Ebbe und Flut. **–e-mark,** *s.* das Flutzeichen. **–e-tables,** *pl.* Fluttabellen. **–e-waiter,** *s.* der (Hafen)Zollbeamte. **–e-water,** *s.* das Gezeitenwasser, Flutwasser, Küstenwasser. **–eway,** *s.* der Flutkanal.

tiddler ['tɪdlə], *s.* (*coll.*) der Stichling (*Ichth.*).

tiddley ['tɪdlɪ], 1. *s.* (*sl.*) das Gesöff. 2. *adj.* (*sl.*) beschwipst, angeheitert, angesäuselt, im Tran.

tiddly-winks ['tɪdiɪ'wɪŋks], *s.* das Flohhupfspiel.

tid–iness ['taɪdɪnɪs], *s.* die Ordnung; Sauberkeit, Nettigkeit. **–y,** 1. *adj.* ordentlich, sauber, nett; (*coll.*) beträchtlich. 2. *s.* die Schutzdecke, der Schoner; Arbeitsbeutel. 3. *v.a.* (also *–y up*) sauber machen, zurechtmachen, in Ordnung bringen, aufräumen.

tie [taɪ], 1. *v.a.* binden (*also Mus.*), befestigen (*to*, an), zusammenbinden, verknüpfen; verankern (*Arch.*); (*fig.*) verpflichten; *– in a bow*, in eine Schleife binden; (*fig.*) *my hands were –d*, mir war die Freiheit beschnitten, mir waren die Hände gebunden; *– one's –*, den Schlips binden; *be –d for time*, sehr beschäftigt sein; *– down*, festbinden; (*fig.*) festlegen; binden, festhalten, fesseln (*to*, an); hindern; *– up*, zusammenbinden; verschnüren (*a parcel, etc.*); anbinden (*to a pole, etc.*); verbinden (*a wound*); (*fig.*) festlegen; *– up money*, unter Verfügungsbeschränkung vermachen; *get –d up in knots*, sich verwickeln. 2. *v.n.*; *– with*, gleichstehen mit, punktgleich sein mit; *– up*, festmachen (*Naut.*); *– up with*, sich verbinden mit. 3. *s.* der Schlips, die Krawatte, Schleife, Binde (*for the neck, etc.*); das Band (*also fig. & Arch.*); das Bindestück, die Klammer (*Tech.*), Bahnschwelle (*Railw.*), der Anker (*Arch.*), die Bindung (*Mus., also fig.*); Beschlagzeising (*Naut.*); (*fig.*) Verpflichtung, lästige Fessel, die Last; unentschiedenes Spiel, das Unentschieden, der Gleichstand (*Sport*); die Stimmengleichheit (*Parl.*); das Ausscheidungsspiel (*Sport*). **–-beam,** *s.* der Ankerbalken (*Arch.*). **–-bolt,** *s.* der Anker (*Arch.*). **–d,** *adj.* gebunden, gefesselt; *–d house*, das Wirtshaus im Besitz einer Brauerei. **–r,** *s.* der Binder; das Band; (*Amer.*) die Schürze. **–-on,** *attrib. adj.* zum Festmachen *or* Anbinden. **–-rod,** *s.* die Kuppelstange. **–-up,** *s.* das Kartell, die Vereinigung; (*Amer.*) Arbeitseinstellung, der Streik (*esp. Railw.*), die Verkehrseinstellung. **–-wig,** *s.* die Knotenperücke.

tier [tɪə], *s.* die Reihe, Lage, Linie, Schicht, die Sitzreihe, der Rang (*Theat.*); *in –s*, lagenweise.

tierce ['tɪəs], *s.* die Terz (*Mus., Fenc.*).

tiercel [tə:sl], *s.* das Falkenmännchen.

tiers état ['tɪ:ɛ:z'eta], der dritte Stand, das Bürgertum.

[1]**tiff** [tɪf], *s.* (*coll.*) die Kabbelei, das Theater, der Krach, Stank, Stunk.

[2]**tiff,** *s.* der Schluck.

tiffin ['tɪfɪn], *s.* das Gabelfrühstück (*in India*).

tig [tɪg], *s. see* [2]**tag.**

tige [tɪ:ʒ], *s.* der Schaft (*Arch.*); der Stamm, Stengel (*Bot.*).

tiger ['taɪgə], *s.* der Tiger; (*fig.*) grausamer Mensch, der Wüterich; (Livree)Bediente(r), *m.*; (*Amer. sl.*) letzter Hochruf, der Schlußtusch; *American –*, der Jaguar. **–-cat,** *s.* die Wildkatze. **–ish,** *adj.* tigerartig; grausam, blutdürstig.

tight [taɪt], *adj.* dicht, abgedichtet, undurchlässig; fest, gespannt, straff; knapp (*as money*); (zu) eng, dicht anliegend, fest anschließend, sitzend (*as clothes*); (*fig.*) schwierig, heikel, kritisch; (also *–-fisted*) knickerig, knauserig, geizig; (*sl.*) besoffen, (sternhagel)voll, blau; *– corner or squeeze*, die Klemme; *–fit*, enges Anliegen; *hold – !* festhalten!; *keep a – rein on*, straff halten; *sit –*, sitzen bleiben, sich nicht rühren. **–en,** 1. *v.a.* zusammenziehen, festmachen, festigen, fest, straff *or* enger machen, verengen; *–en one's belt*, den Gürtel enger schnallen; *make s.o. –en his belt*, einem den Brotkorb höher hängen. 2. *v.n.* sich zusammenziehen, straff *or* enger werden. **–-fisted,** *adj.* geizig, knauserig, knickerig. **–-fitting,** *adj.* fest anliegend. **–-laced,** *adj.* fest geschnürt, (*fig.*) engherzig, pedantisch. **–ness,** *s.* die Dichtheit, Dichtigkeit; Straffheit; Enge, Engheit; Knappheit; der Geiz. **–-rope,** *s.* gespanntes Seil, das Drahtseil. **–-rope-walker,** *s.* der Seiltänzer. **–s,** *pl.* der Trikotanzug.

tigress ['taɪgrəs], *s.* die Tigerin.

tike [taɪk], *s.* der Lümmel, Grobian.

tilbury ['tɪlbərɪ], *s.* zweirädriger Wagen.

tilde ['tɪldə], *s.* die Tilde, das Wiederholungszeichen.

tile [taɪl], 1. *s.* der (Dach)Ziegel; die Fliese; (Ofen)-Kachel; (*sl.*) der Zylinder(hut), die Angströhre; (*sl.*) *have a – loose*, einen Klaps *or* Fimmel *or* Rappel haben, bematscht *or* plemplem sein; (*sl.*) *be out on the –s*, sumpfen. 2. *v.a.* mit Ziegeln decken; mit Fliesen *or* Kacheln auslegen; *–(d) floor*, der Fliesenfußboden; *–(d) roof*, das Ziegeldach. **–r,** *s.* der Ziegeldecker; (also *tyler*) der Tempelhüter, Logenwächter (*Freem.*). **–-works,** *s.* die Ziegelbrennerei, Ziegelei.

tiliaceous [tɪlɪ'eɪʃəs], *adj.* Linden- (*Bot.*).

[1]**till** [tɪl], 1. *prep.* bis, bis in, bis zu; *not –*, erst; *– now*, bis jetzt, bisher; *– then*, bis dahin, bis nachher. 2. *conj.* bis; *not –*, erst wenn, erst als.

[2]**till,** *s.* die Ladentischkasse, Geldschublade.

[3]**till,** *v.a.* bebauen, bestellen, bearbeiten, pflügen, beackern; *– the soil*, Ackerbau treiben. **–age** ['tɪlɪdʒ], *s.* der Ackerbau, Feldbau; das Ackerland, bestelltes Land. **–er,** *s.* der Ackersmann, Pflüger; *–er of the soil*, der Ackerbauer.

[1]**tiller** ['tɪlə], *s.* die Ruderpinne. **–-rope,** *s.* das Steuerreep.

[2]**tiller,** *s.* der Schößling, Wurzelsproß (*Bot.*).

[1]**tilt** [tɪlt], 1. *s.* die Plane, (Wagen)Decke. 2. *v.a.* bedecken.

[2]**tilt,** 1. *s.* die Neigung, schiefe Lage; das Tournier, Lanzenstechen (*of knights*); *at* or *on a –*, in schiefer Lage; *run full – against*, anrennen gegen; *run full – at*, mit voller Wucht *or* in vollem Galopp rennen auf *or* gegen. 2. *v.a.* neigen, (um)kippen, schief *or* schräg stellen *or* legen; schmieden, hämmern (*steel, etc.*). 3. *v.n.* sich neigen, kippen, kentern; turnieren; *– at*, stechen *or* stoßen nach; (*fig.*) kämpfen gegen, ansturmen; *– over* or *up*, überkippen. **–-cart,** *s.* der Sturzkarren, Kippkarren. **–-hammer,** *s.* der Schwanzhammer. **–ing,** 1. *s.* das Turnier. 2. *attrib.* Turnier-. **–-yard,** *s.* der Turnierplatz.

tilth [tɪlθ], *s.* der Ackerbau; das Ackerland.

timbal ['tɪmbl], *s.* die (Kessel)Pauke (*Hist.*).

timber ['tɪmbə], 1. *s.* das Bauholz, Nutzholz; (also *standing –*) das Holz, Bäume *pl.*; der Spant, das Inholz (*Naut.*); *pl.* das Rippenwerk, Gerippe. 2. *attrib.* Holz-. **–ed** [–d], *adj.* bewaldet; bezimmert; (*fig.*) beschaffen, gebaut. **–ing,** *s.* die Zimmerung, Verschalung; das Bauholz, Zimmerholz. **–-line,** *s.* die Baumgrenze. **–-merchant,** *s.* der Holzhändler. **–-trade,** *s.* der Holzhandel. **–-work,** *s.* der Holzbau, das Zimmerwerk. **–-yard,** *s.* der Zimmerhof.

timbre ['tæmbə, tɛ̃br], *s.* die Klangfarbe.

timbrel ['tɪmbrəl], *s.* die Schellentrommel, das Tamburin.

time [taɪm], **1.** *s.* die Zeit, der Zeitpunkt, Zeitabschnitt, die Zeitdauer, das Intervall; Zeitalter, die Epoche, Ära; die Zeitrechnung; die Lebenszeit; Arbeitszeit; kurzeste Zeit (*Sport*); die Gelegenheit; der Takt, das Tempo, Zeitmaß (*Mus.*); das Mal; *pl.* Zeiten, (Zeit)Verhältnisse (*pl.*); **(a)** (*with nouns*) *bed–*, die Zeit des Schlafengehens; *dance –*, das Tanztempo; *day–*, am Tage; *– of day*, die Tageszeit; *– of delivery*, die Lieferzeit (*C.L.*), Briefbestellung (*post*); *– of departure*, die Abfahrtszeit; *dinner–*, die Zeit des Essens; *– of life*, das Alter; *– out of mind*, seit *or* vor unvordenklichen Zeiten; *–s without number*, unzählige Male; *a work of –*, zeitraubende Arbeit; **(b)** (*with adjectives & adverbs*) *all that –*, die ganze Zeit; *– and again*, *– after –*, wiederholt, immer wieder; fortwährend; *broken –*, der Verlust an Arbeitszeit und Stundenlohn; *each* or *every –*, jedesmal, zu jeder Zeit; *– enough*, früh *or* Zeit genug; *little –*, wenig Zeit; *a little –*, etwas *or* ein wenig Zeit; *a long – since*, seit langer Zeit; *take a long –*, lange (Zeit) brauchen; *many a –*, manches Mal; *many –s*, oft, häufig; *most of the –*, die meiste Zeit; *quick –*, der Geschwindschritt (*Mil.*); *the right –*, die genaue *or* richtige Zeit; *slow –*, langsames Tempo; *solar –*, wahre Sonnenzeit; *standard –*, die Ortszeit; *some – about*, etwa um; *some – longer*, noch einige Zeit; *this – yesterday*, gestern um diese Zeit; *this – twelve months*, heute übers Jahr; *12 –s as many* or *as much as*, 12mal soviel wie; *12 –s the size of*, 12mal so groß wie; *12 –s the number of*, 12mal so viele wie; *12 –s 12 is* or *are 144*, 12 mal 12 ist *or* macht 144. **(c)** (*with verbs*) *what is the – ? what – is it ?*, wieviel Uhr ist es? wie spät ist es?; *the – is* or *has come*, es ist an der Zeit; *the – is up*, die Zeit ist abgelaufen; *the –s are out of joint*, die Welt ist aus den Fugen; *there is a – for everything*, alles zu seiner *or* hat seine Zeit; *– was when*, es gab eine Zeit in der, die Zeit ist vorüber als; *beat –*, Takt schlagen; (*sl.*) *do –*, Knast schieben; *gain –*, vorgehen (*as a clock*); *as –s go*, bei den jetzigen Zeiten; *have a bad –*, schlimmes durchmachen; *have a good –* (*of it*), es gut haben, es sich (*Dat.*) gut gehen lassen, sich gut amüsieren; *have a good – !* viel Vergnügen!; *have – on one's hands*, viel Zeit *or* nichts zu tun haben; *have the – of one's life*, eine großartige Zeit haben, sich köstlich amüsieren; *have a lean* or *thin –*, schlechte Zeiten mitmachen; *have no – for*, nichts übrig haben für; *he did not know what the – was*, er wußte nicht, wie spät es war; *keep –*, Takt halten; *keep good –*, richtiggehen (*as clocks*); *kill –*, die Zeit totschlagen; *lose –*, nachgehen (*as a clock*); *no – to lose*, es eilt, es ist keine Zeit zu verlieren; *mark –*, auf der Stelle treten (*Mil.*); (*fig.*) abwarten; *be pressed for –*, es eilig haben; *serve one's –*, seine Zeit abdienen (*Mil.*); *– will show*, die Zeit wird's lehren; *take –*, sich (*Dat.*) Zeit nehmen *or* lassen; *take – by the forelock*, die Gelegenheit beim Schopfe fassen; *– will tell in our favour*, die Zeit arbeitet für uns; *watch one's –*, den günstigen Augenblick abpassen; *watch the –*, auf die Uhr achten; **(d)** (*with prep.*) *speak against –*, äußerst schnell sprechen; *at a –*, zusammen, auf einmal; *one at a –*, einzeln; *at –s*, zu Zeiten; *at any –* or *all –s*, stets, immer, zu jeder Zeit; *at no –*, nie(mals); *at one –*, seinerzeit, einst; *at the present –*, gegenwärtig; *at the same –*, zur selben Zeit, zu gleicher Zeit, gleichzeitig; zugleich, ebenfalls; *at some other –*, ein anderes Mal; *at some – or other*, irgendwann; *at such –s*, bei solchen Gelegenheiten; *at that –*, damals; *at the –*, zu der Zeit, damals, seinerzeit; *at this –*, zu der *or* dieser Zeit; *at this – of day*, so spät; *before one's –*, zu früh; *behind one's –*, zu spät; *be behind –*, Verspätung haben; *behind the –s*, rückständig; *between –s*, in der Zwischenzeit; *by that –*, unterdessen, inzwischen, bis dahin; *by this –*, unterdessen, jetzt; *for a* or *some –*, eine Zeitlang, einige Zeit; *for all –*, für alle Zeiten; *for that –*, für damals; *for the – being*, vorläufig, vorderhand, für den Augenblick, unter den Umständen; *for the first –*, zum ersten Male; *for this –*, für diesmal; *from – to –*, von Zeit zu Zeit; *from – immemorial*, seit un(vor)denklichen Zeiten; *in –*, zur rechten Zeit, zeitlich; mit der Zeit; *in – to come*, in Zukunft; *in good –*, rechtzeitig, gerade recht; *all in good –*, alles zu seiner Zeit; *in your own good –* wenn es dir paßt; *in the mean–*, mittlerweile, inzwischen; *in the nick of –*, im richtigen Augenblick; *in no –*, im Handumdrehen, sehr bald, sofort; *in the –*, zur Zeit (*of* (*Gen.*)); *in the – of Goethe*, zu Goethes Lebzeiten; *in –s of old, in olden –s*, in alten Zeiten; *near one's –*, der Entbindung nahe; *on –*, pünktlich, zur rechten Zeit; *out of –*, aus dem Takte; *be out of one's –*, ausgedient *or* ausgelernt haben; *till such – as*, so lange als, bis; *to –*, rechtzeitig, pünktlich; *up to –*, pünktlich; *up to the present* or *this –*, bis jetzt; *up to that –*, bis dann *or* dahin; *once upon a –*, vor Zeiten, einst(mals), einmal; *with –*, mit der Zeit. **2.** *v.a.* die Zeit einrichten, regeln *or* wählen für, zeitlich bestimmen *or* feststellen, zur richtigen Zeit tun; den Takt angeben *or* schlagen zu (*Mus.*); die Zeit ansetzen *or* festsetzen für; *– o.s.*, feststellen wie lange man braucht; *– one's words ill*, seine Worte zur Unzeit anbringen. 3. *v.n.* Takt halten (*to*, mit); übereinstimmen (*with*, mit). **– -bargain,** *s.* das Termingeschäft, Zeitgeschäft. **-base voltage,** *s.* die Kippspannung. **--bomb,** *s.* die Bombe mit Zeitzündung. **--expired,** *adj.* ausgedient (*of soldiers*). **--exposure,** *s.* die Zeitaufnahme (*Phot.*). **--honoured,** *adj.* altehrwürdig. **-ing,** *s.* die Regelung, Einstellung (*Motor.*). **--keeper,** *s.* das Chronometer; der Zeitmesser; Aufseher (*in factories, etc.*); Zeitnehmer (*Sport*). **--lag,** *s.* die Zwischenzeit, Zeitverzögerung. **-less,** *adj.* zeitlos, ewig. **--limit,** die Frist. **-liness,** *s.* die Rechtzeitigkeit. **-ly,** *adj.* (recht)zeitig; zeitgemäß, aktuell, angebracht. **-piece,** *s.* die Uhr. **--saving,** *adj.* zeit(er)sparend. **--server,** *s.* der Heuchler, Achselträger, Konjunkturritter. **--serving,** 1. *adj.* achselträgerisch. 2. *s.* die Achselträgerei. **--sheet,** *s.* die Stempelkarte, Kontrollkarte. **--signal,** *s.* das Zeitzeichen. **--table,** *s.* das Kursbuch, der Fahrplan (*Railw.*); Stundenplan, Lehrplan (*in schools, etc.*). **--work,** *s.* nach der Zeit bezahlte Arbeit. **-worn,** *adj.* abgenutzt.

timid [ˈtɪmɪd], *adj.* schüchtern, furchtsam, zaghaft, ängstlich (*of*, vor). **-ity** [tɪˈmɪdɪtɪ], *s.*, **-ness,** *s.* die Schüchternheit, Furchtsamkeit, Ängstlichkeit.

timorous [ˈtɪmərəs], *adj.*, **-ness,** *s. see* **timid.**

timpan-o [ˈtɪmpənou], *s.* (*usually pl.* -i) die Kesselpauke (*Mus.*).

tin [tɪn], 1. *s.* das Zinn; (Weiß)Blech; die (Blech)-Dose, (Konserven)Büchse; (*sl.*) der Kies, das Moos. 2. *adj.* zinnern, Zinn-, Blech-; *– can*, die Blechbüchse; (*sl.*) *– fish*, das Torpedo; der Aal; (*coll.*) *little – god*, eingebildeter aber unbedeutender Mensch; (*coll.*) *– hat*, der Stahlhelm. 3. *v.a.* verzinnen, in Büchsen *or* Dosen einmachen *or* packen; *–ned meat*, das Konservenfleisch, Büchsenfleisch. **-foil,** *s.* das Blattzinn, Stanniol. **-man,** *s.* der Blechschmied, Klempner. **-ny,** *adj.* zinnhaltig; blechern, metallen. **--opener,** *s.* der Büchsenöffner, Dosenöffner. **-plate,** *s.* das Weißblech. **-smith,** *s. see* **-man.** **--tack,** *s.* verzinnter Nagel. **-ware,** *s.* das Zinngeschirr, Blechwaren (*pl.*). **--works,** *pl.* (*sing. constr.*) die Zinnhütte, Zinngießerei.

tincal [tɪŋkl], *s.* roher Borax.

tincture [ˈtɪŋktʃə], 1. *s.* die Tinktur (*Chem.*); die Färbung, der Anstrich, Beigeschmack. 2. *v.a.* leicht färben, einen Anstrich geben (*Dat.*) (*with*, von).

tinder [ˈtɪndə], *s.* der Zunder. **--box,** *s.* das Feuerzeug.

tine [taɪn], *s.* die Zinke, Zacke.

ting [tɪŋ], 1. *v.a.* läuten. 2. *v.n.* (er)klingen. 3. *s.* das Klingen.

tinge [tɪndʒ], 1. *s.* die Farbe, Färbung, Tönung, Schattierung; (*fig.*) die Spur, der Anstrich, Anflug, Beigeschmack. 2. *v.a.* färben, schattieren; (*fig.*) (*usually pass.*) einen Anstrich *or* Geschmack geben (*Dat.*) (*with*, von).

tingle [ˈtɪŋgl], 1. *v.n.* prickeln, stechen (*as pain*); klingen, summen (*as a noise*); kribbeln; *my ears –*, mir klingen die Ohren; *my skin –s*, meine Haut prickelt. 2. *s.* das Klingen, Summen, Prickeln, Stechen.

tinker [[ˈtɪŋkə], 1. *s.* (reisender) Kesselflicker, Klempner, Spengler; (*coll.*) Schelm, Racker; *not worth a –'s cuss*, keinen roten Heller wert. 2. *v.n.* herumpfuschen (*at* or *with*, an), basteln.

tinkle [ˈtɪŋkl], 1. *v.n.* klingeln, (er)klingen. 2. *v.a.* klingeln, läuten. 3. *s.* das Geklingel, Klingen, Läuten.

tinman, *s. see* **tin.**

tinnitus [tɪˈnaɪtəs], *s.* ständiges Ohrenklingen (*Med.*).

tinny, *see* **tin.**

tinsel [ˈtɪnsl], 1. *s.* das Rauschgold, Flittergold, Flittersilber; (*fig.*) der Flitter(kram), täuschender Glanz. 2. *adj.* Schein-, flimmernd, flitterhaft. 3. *v.a.* mit Flitterwerk schmücken.

tinsmith, *s. see* **tin.**

tint [tɪnt], 1. *s.* zarte Farbe, die Färbung, Tönung, Schattierung, der Farbton; *autumn –s*, die Herbstfärbung; *have a reddish –*, einen Stich ins Rote *or* rötlichen Schimmer haben. 2. *v.a.* färben, (ab)-tönen, schattieren; *–ed paper*, das Tonpapier; *–ed spectacles*, farbige Brille.

tintinnabul–ary [tɪntɪˈnæbjʊlərɪ], *adj.* klingelnd. **–ation** [ˈtɪntɪnæbjəˈleɪʃən], *s.* das Klingeln, Klingen, Tönen.
tiny [ˈtaɪnɪ], *adj.* klein, winzig.
[1]**tip** [tɪp], 1. *s.* die Spitze, der Zipfel (*of ear*), die Zwinge (*of a stick, etc.*); das Mundstück (*of cigarettes*); (*coll.*) leichter Schlag *or* Stoß; (*coll.*) der Wink, Tip; (*coll.*) das Trinkgeld; *to the finger-–s*, bis an die Fingerspitzen; *have s. th. at the – of one's fingers* or *at one's finger-–s*, etwas aus dem Handgelenk schütteln; *on the –s of one's toes*, auf Zehenspitzen; *have it on the – of my tongue*, mir schwebt es auf der Zunge; (*coll.*) *take my –*, folge meinem Rat; *wing-–*, das Flügelende (*Av.*). 2. *v.a.* mit einer Spitze *or* Zwinge versehen; (*coll.*) Trinkgeld geben (*Dat.*); (*coll.*) tippen auf (*a winner*); (*sl.*) geben, reichen (*a p. a th.*, einem etwas); (*sl.*) – *a p. off* or *a p. the wink*, einem einen Wink geben, einen rechtzeitig warnen; *cork-–ped, adj.* mit Korkmundstück (*cigarettes*). (*sl.*) **–-off,** *s.* rechtzeitige Warnung, der Wink, Tip. **–-and-run raider,** *s.* der Einbruchsflieger (*Av.*). *See* **tipster.**
[2]**tip,** 1. *v.a.* (um)kippen, umwerfen, umstürzen; abladen (*rubbish*); – *out*, ausschütten, ausgießen; – *over*, umwerfen, umstürzen; – *to one side*, auf die Seite schieben *or* kippen. 2. *v.n.* sich neigen; – *out*, herausfallen; – *over* or *up*, umkippen. 3. *s.* die Neigung; der Abladeplatz. **–-cart,** *s.* der Kippkarren, Sturzkarren. **–-cat,** *s.* ein Knabenspiel mit gespitztem Holzklotz. **–-up seat,** *s.* der Klappsitz.
tippet [ˈtɪpɪt], *s.* der Pelzkragen, die Pelerine.
tipple [ˈtɪpl], *v.n.* picheln, saufen, zechen. **–r,** *s.* der Trinker, Säufer, Trunkenbold.
tipstaff [ˈtɪpstɑ:f], *s.* (*pl.* –staves) der Amtsstab; Gerichtsdiener.
tipster [ˈtɪpstə], *s.* der Tipgeber; Ratgeber, Auskunftgeber.
tipsy [ˈtɪpsɪ], *adj.* beschwipst, angeheitert. **–-cake,** *s.* eine Art Kuchen mit Weingeschmack.
tiptoe [ˈtɪptoʊ], 1. *adv.*; *on –*, auf Zehenspitzen, (*fig.*) neugierig, gespannt; *on – with expectation*, voller Erwartung. 2. *v.n.* auf Zehenspitzen gehen.
tiptop [tɪpˈtɔp], 1. *s.* (*coll.*) der Gipfel, höchster Grad, das Höchste *or* Beste. 2. *adj.* (*coll.*) erstklassig, vortrefflich, ausgezeichnet, tadellos.
tirade [tɪˈreɪd], *s.* die Tirade, der Wortschwall, Rede(er)guß.
tirailleur [tɪraɪˈjə:], *s.* der Tirailleur, Schütze.
[1]**tir–e** [ˈtaɪə], 1. *v.a.* (*archaic*) schmücken, putzen. 2. *s.* (*archaic*) der Kopfputz. (*archaic*) **–e-woman,** *s.* die Kammerjungfer. (*archaic*) **–ing-room,** *s.* das Ankleidezimmer, die Garderobe (*Theat.*).
[2]**tir–e,** 1. *v.a.* müde machen, ermüden (*also fig.*), erschöpfen; (*fig.*) langweilen; *–e to death* or *out*, gänzlich ermüden, totmüde machen. 2. *v.n.* ermüden, ermatte , müde werden (*with*, vor (*or fig. Gen.*)); (*fig.*) überdrüssig werden (*with* (*Gen.*)). **–ed,** *adj.* müde, ermüdet, erschöpft; verbraucht, abgenutzt; *be –ed of a th.*, einer S. (*Gen.*) satt *or* überdrüssig sein, eine S. satt haben; *make a p. –ed*, einen langweilen *or* ermüden. **–edness,** *s.* die Ermüdung, Müdigkeit; (*fig.*) der Überdruß. **–eless,** *adj.* unermüdlich. **–elessness,** *s.* die Unermüdlichkeit. **–esome,** *adj.* ermüdend, langweilig; lästig, verdrießlich. **–esomeness,** *s.* die Langweiligkeit. **–ing,** *adj.* ermüdend.
[3]**tire,** *s. see* **tyre.**
tiro, *see* **tyro.**
tissue [ˈtɪsju:, ˈtɪʃju:, ˈtɪʃu:], *s.* (feines) Gewebe (*also fig.*); *cellular –*, das Zellengewebe. **–-paper,** das Seidenpapier.
[1]**tit** [tɪt], *s.* kleines Pferd; *see* **titmouse.**
[2]**tit,** *s.* (*vulg.*) die Zitze.
[3]**tit,** *s.*; – *for tat*, wie du mir, so ich dir, eine Hand wäscht die andere, Wurst wider Wurst; *give s.o. – for tat*, einem Gleiches mit Gleichem vergelten.
titan [ˈtaɪtən], *s.* der Titan. **–ic** [–ˈtænɪk], *adj.* titanenhaft, riesengroß, gigantisch, Titan–. **–ium,** [–ˈteɪnɪəm], *s.* das Titan (*Chem.*).
titbit [ˈtɪtbɪt], *s.* der Leckerbissen.
tith–able [ˈtaɪðəbl], *adj.* zehnpflichtig. **–e** [taɪð], 1. *s.* das Zehntel; der Zehnte (*Eccl.*); (*fig.*) *not a –e of*, nicht der zehnte Teil von. 2. *v.a.* den Zehnten erheben *or* bezahlen von. **–ing,** *s.* die Zehntschaft (*Hist.*).
titillat–e [ˈtɪtɪleɪt], *v.a.* kitzeln, reizen, angenehm anregen. **–ion** [–ˈleɪʃən], *s.* das Kitzeln, (*fig.*) der Kitzel, das Wohlgefallen, die Lust.
titivate [ˈtɪtɪveɪt], 1. *v.a.* herausputzen, zurechtmachen. 2. *v.n.* sich herausputzen *or* fein machen.
titlark [ˈtɪtlɑ:k], *s.* die (Wiesen)Pieper (*Orn.*).
title [ˈtaɪtl], 1. *s.* der Titel; die Überschrift, Benennung, der Name; (Adels)Titel, Ehrentitel, Amtstitel; Rechtstitel, Rechtsanspruch (*to*, auf); (*fig.*) Anspruch (*to*, auf); – *of nobility*, der Adelsbrief, das Adelsprädikat. **–d,** betitelt, tituliert; adlig (*people*). **–-deed,** *s.* die Eigentumsurkunde. **–-holder,** *s.* der Titelinhaber, der Titelverteidiger (*Sport*). **–-page,** *s.* das Titelblatt. **–-role,** *s.* die Titelrolle.
titling [ˈtɪtlɪŋ], see **titlark.**
titmouse [ˈtɪtmaʊs], *s.* die Meise (*Orn.*).
titrat–e [ˈtɪtreɪt], *v.a.* titrieren. **–ion** [–ˈtreɪʃən], *s.* das Titrieren, die Maßanalyse, Titrieranalyse (*Chem.*).
titter [ˈtɪtə], 1. *v.n.* kichern. 2. *s.* das Kichern, Gekicher.
tittle [ˈtɪtl], *s.* der Tüttel, i-Punkt; (*fig.*) das Tüttelchen, Jota, bißchen; *not one jot or –*, nicht das geringste, nicht die Bohne; *to a –*, aufs Haar genau. **–-tattle,** a. *s.* das Geschwätz, Geklatsch. 2. *v.n.* schwatzen, klatschen.
titubation [tɪtjʊˈbeɪʃən], *s.* das Taumeln, Schwanken, Wanken.
titular [ˈtɪtjələ], 1. *adj.*, **–y** [–lərɪ], *adj.* Titel–, Titular–, nominell. 2. *s.* der Titular.
to [tu:, tʊ, tə *acc. to emphasis*], **1.** *part.* (*before inf.*) zu, um zu; – *be or not – be*, sein oder nicht sein; *he was the first – arrive*, er kam als erster an; *I want – come*, ich will *or* möchte kommen; *I expect him – come*, ich erwarte, daß er kommt; *he was seen – come*, man sah ihn kommen; *the best is yet – come*, das Beste kommt nach; *in years – come*, in zukünftigen Jahren; – *hear him talk*, wenn man ihm reden hört; *is there no one – help you?* ist niemand da der dir hilft?; *what is there – say?* was soll ich sagen? *what is – be said?* was ist zu sagen; (*with inf. omitted*) *I certainly meant –*, ich hatte gewiß die Absicht; *I was coming but I had no time –*, ich wollte kommen, hatte aber kein Zeit dazu; *I want –*, ich möchte es gern. **2.** *part.* (*forming Dat.*) (*coll. often omitted*) *I gave it* (–) *him*, ich gab es ihm; *I made it clear – him*, ich erklärte es ihm. **3.** *prep.* (*place*) (bis) zu, nach (. . . hin), bis nach, (bis) an, in, auf; (*time*) bis zu, vor; (*aim or effect*) zu, für, zwecks; (*degree or extent*) bis zu, bis auf; (*fig.*) für, gegen; *that's all there is – it*, das ist alles was drum und dran ist; – *all appearance*, allem Anscheine nach; *as –*, betreffs, was . . . anbetrifft; *back – back*, Rücken an Rücken; – *bursting point*, zum Platzen; *have you been – Cologne?* sind Sie in Köln gewesen?; *go – Cologne*, nach Köln fahren; – *the contrary*, im Gegenteil; – *his cost*, auf seine Kosten, zu seinem Schaden; – *his credit*, zu seinen Gunsten; – *a degree*, bis zu einem gewissen Grade; – *a high degree*, in hohem Grade; – *his delight*, zu seiner Freude; – *the end that*, damit, zu dem Zwecke daß; – *a p.'s face*, einem ins Gesicht; *face – face*, Auge in Auge, unter vier Augen; *spring – one's feet*, auf die Füße springen, aufspringen; – *and fro*, hin und her, auf und ab; – *the good*, zum Guten; *play – an empty house*, vor einem leeren Hause spielen (*Theat.*); *jump – the ground*, zur Erde *or* auf den Boden springen; *strike – the ground*, zu Boden schlagen, niederstrecken; – (*one's*) *hand*, zur Hand, bereit; erhalten (*C.L.*); *hand – hand*, Mann gegen Mann (*fighting*); *from hand – hand*, von Hand zu Hand; – *my knowledge*, meines Wissens, soviel ich weiß; – *a* or – *the last man*, bis auf den letzten Mann; – *the left*, links, auf der linken Seite; – *the life*, getreu nach dem Leben; – *my mind*, meiner Ansicht nach; *10 minutes – 6*, 10 Minuten vor 6; – *a nicety*, aufs Haar; – *the point*, zur Sache; *when it comes – the point*, wenn es soweit ist; *full – suffocation*, zum Ersticken voll; – *my taste*, nach meinem Geschmacke; *heir – the throne*, der Thronerbe; – *time*, pünktlich; – *a tune*, nach einer Melodie;

(*coll.*) *here's – you!* Prosit! auf dein Wohl!; (*after adjectives, verbs, etc.*) *what is that – you?* was bedeutet das für dich?; *admit* –, zulassen zu, gültig sein für; gestehen, zugeben, einräumen (*a p.*, einem gegenüber); *admit – doing*, gestehen getan zu haben; *agreeable* –, angenehm für *or* (*Dat.*); *alive* –, bewußt (*Dat.*), empfänglich für, aufmerksam auf; *the answer* –, die Antwort auf; *attend* –, hören, achten *or* achtgeben auf (*a p.*); besorgen, erledigen, sich befassen mit (*a th.*); *averse* –, abgeneigt gegen, abhold (*Dat.*); *aversion* –, die Abneigung gegen; *belong* –, gehören (*Dat.*) (*a p.*); angehören (*Dat.*) (*a group*); *complain* –, sich beschweren *or* beklagen bei; *deaf* –, taub gegen; *due* –, infolge von *or* (*Gen.*), veranlaßt durch; zukommen, gebühren (*Dat.*) (*a p.*); *be due – do*, tun müssen *or* sollen; (*coll.*) im Begriff sein zu tun; *be due* –, zurückzuführen sein auf; *duty* –, die Pflicht gegen; *enemy* –, der Feind (*Gen.*); *faithful* –, treu (*Dat.*); *familiar* –, bekannt (*Dat.*); *grateful* –, dankbar *or* erkenntlich (*Dat.*); *happen* –, zustoßen, passieren (*Dat.*); *what is going – happen – ?* wie wird es mit? *have – do*, tun müssen; *have – o.s.*, für sich haben; *the injury – one's head*, die Verletzung am Kopfe; *known* –, bekannt (*Dat.*); *keep – o.s.*, für sich behalten; *listen* –, horchen *or* lauschen auf (*a th.*); zuhören, Gehör schenken (*Dat.*) (*a p.*); befolgen (*Acc.*), gehorchen (*Dat.*); *listen – reason*, Vernunft annehmen; *loss* –, der Schaden *or* die Einbuße für *or* an; *lost* –, nicht mehr empfänglich für, bar (*Gen.*); *mean* –, zu bedeuten haben für (*a p.*); *nothing* –, nichts im Vergleich zu; *read* –, vorlesen (*Dat.*); *secretary* –, der Sekretär (*Gen.*); *speak* –, sprechen zu *or* mit; *a stranger* –, fremd (*Dat.*) (*to a p.*); *be a stranger – these parts*, sich in dieser Gegend nicht auskennen; *subscribe* –, zeichnen zu (*a fund*); zustimmen (*Dat.*), einwilligen in, anerkennen (*an idea*); *subscribe – a doctrine*, sich einer Lehre verschreiben; *subscribe – a proposal*, einen Vorschlag annehmen; *subscribe – a newspaper*, auf eine Zeitung abonnieren; *swear* –, beschwören; *10 is – 5 as 2 is – 1*, 10 verhält sich zu 5 wie 2 zu 1; *10 – 1*, 10 gegen *or* zu 1; *fall a victim* –, zum Opfer fallen (*Dat.*). **4.** *adv.* geschlossen, zu; *buckle* –, an die Arbeit gehen, anfangen; *bring a p.* –, einen zu sich bringen; *come* –, zu sich kommen, wieder zu Bewußtsein kommen; *fall* –, zulangen, zugreifen; – *and fro*, hin und her, auf und ab; *go* –, herangehen, losgehen.

toad [toud], *s.* die Kröte; – *in the hole*, Fleischstücke *or* Wurst in Kuchenteig gekocht. **--flax,** *s.* das Leinkraut (*Bot.*). **-stone,** *s.* der Krötenstein. **-stool,** *s.* der Giftpilz. **-y,** 1. *s.* der Speichellecker. 2. *v.a.* niedrig schmeicheln (*Dat.*). **-ying,** *s.*, **-yism,** *s.* die Speichelleckerei.

[1]**toast** [toust], 1. *s.* geröstetes Brot, der Toast; (*sl.*) *have a p. on* –, einen in seiner Gewalt haben; *make* –, Brot rösten. 2. *v.a.* rösten; (*fig.*) wärmen; – *one's toes*, sich die Füße wärmen. **-er,** *s.* der (Brot)Röster. **-ing-fork,** *s.* die Röstgabel. **--rack,** *s.* das Gestell für Röstbrot.

[2]**toast,** 1. *s.* der Trinkspruch, Toast; *loyal* –, der Trinkspruch auf Herrscher und Herrscherhaus; *propose the – of s.o.*, einen Trinkspruch auf einen ausbringen. 2. *v.a.* trinken auf. **--master,** *s.* der Toastmeister.

tobacco [tə'bækou], *s.* der Tabak; – *heart*, das Nikotinherz. **-nist** [–kənɪst], *s.* der Tabakhändler; *–nist's* (*shop*), der Tabakladen. **--pipe,** *s.* die Tabakspfeife. **--plant,** *s.* die Tabakpflanze. **--pouch,** *s.* der Tabaksbeutel.

toboggan [tə'bɔgən], 1. *s.* der Rodel(schlitten). 2. *v.a.* rodeln. **-er,** *s.* der Rodler. **-ing,** *s.* das Rodeln. **-ist,** *s. see* **-er.** **--slide,** *s.* die Rodelbahn.

toccata [tə'kɑ:tə], *s.* die Tokkata.

tocsin ['tɔksɪn], *s.* die Sturmglocke, Alarmglocke, das Alarmsignal.

today [tʊ'deɪ, tə'deɪ], 1. *adv.* heute; heutzutage, heutigentags; – *week*, heute vor (*or usually* in) 8 Tagen *or* über 8 Tage. 2. *s.* der heutige Tag, das Heute, die Gegenwart; –'*s*, heutig.

toddle ['tɔdl], *v.n.* watscheln; (*coll.*) (usually – *off* or *along*) abrücken, abschieben, sich trollen. **-r,** *s.* das Kleinkind.

toddy ['tɔdɪ], *s.* der Eisbrecher, Punsch, Grog.

to-do [tʊ'du:, tə'du:], *s.* (*coll.*) das Aufheben, der Lärm; *make a* –, Aufhebens machen (*about*, über *or* von).

toe [tou], 1. *s.* die Zehe, Spitze (*of stocking*), Kappe (*of shoe*); *from top to* –, von (*or* vom) Kopf bis zu(m) Fuß; (*fig.*) *tread on a p.'s –s*, einem auf die Füße *or* Hühneraugen treten; *turn one's –s in*, einwärts gehen; *turn one's –s out*, auswärts gehen; (*sl.*) *turn up one's –s*, krepieren. 2. *v.a.* mit neuen Spitzen versehen (*stockings*), vorschuhen (*shoes*), mit den Zehen berühren; (*sl.*) treten; – *the line*, in einer Linie antreten, zu einem Rennen antreten; (*fig.*) sich unterwerfen, einfügen *or* gleichschalten. **--cap,** *s.* die (Schuh)Kappe. **-d** [toud], *adj. suff.* (*in comps.*) –zehig. **--dancer,** *s.* der Zehentänzer. **--nail,** *s.* der Zehennagel.

toff [tɔf], *s.* (*sl.*) der (Patent)Fatzke.

toffee ['tɔfɪ:], *s.* der Rahmbonbon; (*coll.*) *he cannot sing for* –, vom Singen hat er keine Ahnung.

tog [tɔg], 1. *v.a.*; (*sl.*) – *up*, sich fein machen. **-s** [–z], (*sl.*) Klamotten (*pl.*).

toga ['tougə], *s.* die Toga.

together [tʊ'gɛðə, tə'gɛðə], *adv.* zusammen, miteinander, gemeinsam; aufeinander, ineinander (*of movement*); nacheinander, hintereinander (*of time*); zugleich, zu gleicher Zeit, gleichzeitig (*in time*); – *with*, zusammen mit, (mit)samt; *for days* –, tagelang (hintereinander); *fight* – gegeneinander kämpfen.

toggery ['tɔgərɪ], *s.* (*sl.*) *see* **togs.**

toggle ['tɔgl], 1. *s.* der Knebel (*Naut.*). 2. *v.a.* knebeln, mit einem Querholz verbinden *or* befestigen. **--joint,** *s.* das Kniegelenk, Knebelgelenk. **--switch,** *s.* der Kippschalter (*Elec.*).

[1]**toil** [tɔɪl], 1. *s.* schwere Arbeit, die Mühe, Plage, Plackerei, Schererei. 2. *v.n.* mühselig arbeiten (*at*, an), sich abmühen *or* placken, schuften. **-er,** *s.* Schwerarbeitende(r), *m.* **-some,** *adj.* mühsam, mühselig. **-someness,** *s.* die Mühsamkeit, Mühseligkeit. **--worn,** *adj.* abgearbeitet.

[2]**toil,** *s.* (*usually pl.*) das Netz, die Schlinge; *in the –s of*, verstrickt in.

toilet ['tɔɪlɪt], *s.* das Anziehen, Ankleiden; die Toilette, das Klosett, Abort; *make one's* –, sich anziehen. **--case,** *s.* das Reisenecessaire. **--paper** *s.* das Toilettenpapier, Klosettpapier. **--roll,** *s.* die Rolle Toilettenpapier. **--set,** *s.* die Toilettengarnitur. **--soap,** *s.* die Toilettenseife.

token [toukn], *s.* das Zeichen, Anzeichen, Merkmal (*of*, für), der Beweis (*of*, für *or* (*Gen.*)); das Andenken; *in – of*, zum Zeichen von *or* (*Gen.*), zum Andenken an; *by the same* –, ebenfalls, ferner, desgleichen; genau so gut, mit demselben Recht. **– money,** die Scheidemünze.

told [tould], *see* **tell**; *all* –, alles in allem.

tolera–ble ['tɔlərəbl], *adj.* erträglich (*to*, für), leidlich, mittelmäßig. **-bleness,** *s.* die Erträglichkeit, Leidlichkeit, Mittelmäßigkeit. **-bly,** *adv.* leidlich, ziemlich. **-nce** [–əns], *s.* die Duldung, Nachsicht (*of*, mit), Duldsamkeit, Toleranz; die Fehlergrenze, zugelassene Abweichung (*Tech.*), die Widerstandsfähigkeit (*Med.*). **-nt** [–ənt], *adj.* duldsam, tolerant (*of*, gegen); nachsichtig (*towards*, gegen); widerstandsfähig (*of*, gegen) (*Med.*). **-te** [–eɪt], *v.a.* dulden, duldsam sein gegen, ertragen, leiden, sich abfinden mit, sich gewöhnen an, gestatten, zulassen, vertragen (*Med.*). **-tion** [–'reɪʃən], *s.* die Duldung, Nachsicht, Duldsamkeit, Toleranz.

[1]**toll** [toul], *s.* der Zoll (*also fig.*), die Steuer, Abgabe, Maut; das Wegegeld, Brückengeld; *see also* **--call;** (*fig.*) der Tribut; – *of the road*, Verkehrsunfälle (*pl.*); *take – of*, (*fig*) (Tribut) fordern; *take a heavy – of their lives*, ihnen schwere Menschenverluste zufügen. **--bar,** *s.* der Schlagbaum, die Zollschranke. **--bridge,** *s.* die Zollbrücke. **--call,** *s.* Vorortsgespräch, Nahverkehrgespräch (*Phone*). **--gate,** *s. see* **--bar.** **--house,** *s.* das Zollhäuschen. **--keeper,** *s.* der Zolleinnehmer, Zöllner, Mautner.

[2]**toll,** 1. *v.a.* (in langsamen Zwischenräumen) läuten (*a bell*); (an)schlagen, erschallen lassen (*of a bell*). 2. *v.n.* (an)schlagen, läuten. 3. *s.* langsames feierliches Läuten, der Glockenschlag.

tolu-ene ['tɔlʊi:n], *s.* das Toluin (*Chem.*). **-ol** [-ʊəl], *s.* das Toluol (*Chem.*).
tom [tɔm], *s.* das Männchen (*of animals*); – *Dick and Harry*, Hinz und Kunz; – *Thumb*, der Däumling. **-boy,** *s.* die Range, der Wildfang. **--cat,** *s.* der Kater. **-fool** [-'fu:l], *s.* der Einfaltspinsel. **-foolery** [-'fu:lərɪ], *s.* der Unsinn, dummes Zeug, albernes Benehmen, die Narrheit, Narretei, Albernheit, *see* **tommy.**
tomahawk ['tɔməhɔ:k], 1. *s.* die Streitaxt (*of American Indians*). 2. *v.a.* mit der Streitaxt töten.
tomato [tə'mɑ:toʊ], *s.* (*pl.* -es) die Tomate.
tomb [tu:m], *s.* das Grab, die Grabstätte, das Grabgewölbe, Grabmal. **-stone,** *s.* der Grabstein, Leichenstein.
tombac ['tɔmbək], *s.* der Tombak.
tombola ['tɔmbələ], *s.* die Tombola, das Lottospiel.
tomboy ['tɔmbɔɪ], *see under* **tom.**
tome [toʊm], *s.* (*coll.*) dicker Band, der Wälzer, Schmöker.
tomfool, *see under* **tom.**
tommy ['tɔmɪ], *s.* (also – *Atkins*) (*sl.*) englischer Soldat; (*sl.*) das Brot, die Nahrung. **--gun,** *s.* die Maschinenpistole. **-rot,** *s.* (*sl.*) das Blech, der Quatsch, Blödsinn. **--system,** *s.* das Trucksystem.
tomorrow [tʊ'mɔroʊ, tə'mɔroʊ], 1. *adv.* morgen; – *morning*, morgen früh; *the day after* –, übermorgen. – *week*, morgen in 8 Tagen. 2. *s.* das Morgen, morgiger Tag; –'*s*, morgig.
tomtit ['tɔmtɪt], *s.* die Blaumeise (*Orn.*).
tom-tom ['tɔmtɔm], *s.* das Tamtam, der Gong, die Trommel.
[1]**ton** [tɔn], *s.* die Mode, Modenwelt.
[2]**ton** [tʌn], *s.* die Tonne (also *long* or *gross* –, = *2,240 lb.*; also *short* –, = *2,100 lb.*; *metric* –, = *2,205 lb.*; *displacement* –, = *35 cu. ft.*; *freight* –, = *40 cu. ft.*; *register* –, die Registertonne = *100 cu. ft.*); (*coll.*) *weigh a* –, sehr schwer wiegen; *pl.* (*sl.*) große Menge, die Unmenge; (*sl.*) –*s of*, sehr viel(e); *see* **tonnage.**
tonal ['toʊnl], *adj.* Ton–. **-ity** [-'nælɪtɪ], *s.* die Tonalität, der Toncharakter, die Klangfarbe (*Mus.*), der Farbton (*Paint.*).
tone [toʊn], 1. *s.* der Ton, Klang, Laut, die Tonhöhe, Klangart; der (Voll)Ton (*Mus.*); die Betonung, Intonation (*Phonet.*); der Farbton, die Tönung, Färbung, Schattierung (*Paint.*); (*fig.*) die Stimmung, Haltung, das Verhalten, der Stil; die (Spann)Kraft (*Med.*); *semi*–, halber Ton (*Mus.*); *set the* –, den Ton angeben. 2. *v.a.* Ton *or* Färbung geben, abtönen; tonen (*Phot.*); – *down*, herabstimmen, mildern; – *in with*, abstimmen auf; – *up*, kräftigen, stärken. 3. *v.n.*; – *down*, milder werden; – *in with*, stimmen zu, sich verschmelzen mit. **--control,** *s.* die Klangfarbenregelung (*Rad.*). **-less,** *adj.* tonlos. **--poem,** *s.* die Tondichtung.
tongs [tɔŋgz], *pl.* die Zange; *a pair of* –, eine Zange; *curling* –*s*, die Brennschere; (*coll.*) *hammer and* –, mit allen Kräften.
tongue [tʌŋ], *s.* die Zunge; (*fig.*) Sprache; (*fig.*) die (Land)Zunge; der Klöppel (*of a bell*); Zeiger (*of a balance*), Latsche (*of a shoe*), der Dorn (*of a buckle*); *find one's* –, die Sprache wiederfinden; *give* –, anschlagen, bellen (*as dogs*); *hold one's* –, den Mund halten; *malicious* –, böse Zunge; *mother* –, die Muttersprache; *put out one's* –, die Zunge herausstrecken; *slip of the* –, unvorsichtiges Wort; *it was a slip of the* –, ich habe mich versprochen; *I had the word on the tip of my* –, das Wort schwebte mir auf der Zunge; *with his* – *in his cheek*, ironisch. **-d,** *adj. suff.* (*in comps*) -züngig. **-less,** *adj.* ohne Zunge; (*fig.*) sprachlos. **--shaped,** *adj.* zungenförmig. **--tied,** *adj.* mundfaul, schweigsam, stumm, sprachlos. **--twister,** *s.* der Zungen(zer)brecher; *this is a* --*twister*, daran kann man sich die Zunge abbrechen.
tonic ['tɔnɪk], 1. *adj.* tonisch (*Mus.*, *Med.*); Ton–, Klang– (*Mus.*), stärkend, kräftigend (*Med.*); – *accent*, musikalischer Akzent; – *chord*, der Grundakkord; – *sol-fa*, eine Methode des Elementargesangsunterrichts; – *spasm*, der Starrkrampf. 2. *s.* stärkendes Mittel (*Med.*, *also fig.*); die Tonika, der Grundton (*Mus.*). **-ity** [-'nɪsɪtɪ], *s.* die Spannkraft, Elastizität (*Med.*), musikalischer Ton (*Mus.*).
tonight [tʊ'naɪt, tə'naɪt], 1. *adv.* heute abend, heute nacht. 2. *s.* heutiger Abend, diese Nacht.
tonn-age ['tʌnɪdʒ], *s.* die Tragfähigkeit, der Tonnengehalt, Frachtraum (*of a ship*); die Frachtgebühr, das Tonnengeld; (*fig.*) die Gesamttonnage, gesamte Handelsschiffe (*pl.*) (*of a country*). **-er** ['tʌnə], *s.* (*in comps.*) das Schiff von . . . Tonnen.
tonneau ['tɔnoʊ], *s.* der Wagenfond, hinterer Innenraum (*Motor.*).
tonometer [to'nɔmɪtə], *s.* der Tonmesser.
tonsil ['tɔnsɪl], *s.* die Mandel (*Anat.*). **-lar** [-ə], *adj.* Mandel–. **-litis** [-'lɑɪtɪs], *s.* die Mandelentzündung.
tons-orial [tɔn'sɔ:rɪəl], *adj.* Barbier–. **-ure** ['tɔnʃə], 1. *s.* die Tonsur; das Haarschneiden, die Haarschur. 2. *v.a.* eine Tonsur schneiden, die Haare scheren, tonsurieren.
too [tu:], *adv.* (*before adverbs or adjectives*) (all)zu; (*never at beginning*) auch, ebenfalls, außerdem, dazu, obendrein, überdies; (*coll.*) sehr, höchst, außergewöhnlich; *all* – *familiar*, nur zu vertraut; *none* – *good*, nicht allzu gut; *it is cold* –, obendrein *or* noch dazu ist es kalt; *you are* – *kind*, du bist sehr freundlich; – –, übertrieben, überschwenglich.
toodle-oo ['tu:dl'u:], *int.* (*coll.*) tjüs, auf Wiedersehen.
took [tʊk], *see* **take.**
tool [tu:l], 1. *s.* das Werkzeug (*also fig.*); das Instrument, Gerät; (*fig.*) die Kreatur, das Geschöpf; *pl.* Gerätschaften (*pl.*), das Handwerkzeug. 2. *v.a.* punzen (*Bookb.*). 3. *v.n.* mit einem Werkzeug arbeiten. **--bag,** *s.*, **--kit,** *s.* die Werkzeugtasche. **--chest,** *s.*, **--box,** *s.* der Werkzeugkasten. **-ing,** *s.* die Punzarbeit (*Bookb.*). **-maker,** *s.* der Werkzeugschlosser.
toot [tu:t], 1. *v.a.* & *n.* tuten, blasen. 2. *s.* das Tuten, der (Trompeten)Stoß.
tooth [tuθ], 1. *s.* (*pl.* teeth) der Zahn (*also Mach.*); die Zinke, Zacke (*Mach. etc.*); *brush* or *clean one's teeth*, sich die Zähne putzen; *cut one's teeth*, zahnen, die ersten Zähne bekommen; *draw s.o.'s teeth*, (*fig.*) einen unschädlich machen; *have a* – *drawn* or *extracted*, sich einen Zahn ziehen lassen; (*coll.*) *fed up to the teeth*, es mehr als satt haben; *get one's teeth into*, sich die Zähne ausbeißen an; *in the teeth of*, trotz (*Dat.* or *Gen.*), zum Trotz, direkt entgegen (*Dat.*); *cast a th. in s.o.'s teeth*, einem etwas vorwerfen; *long in the* –, alt; – *and nail*, mit aller Kraft *or* Wucht, unerbittlich; *pick one's teeth*, sich die Zähne (aus)stochern; *show one's teeth*, fletschen, die Zähne zeigen; *set one's teeth*, die Zähne zusammenbeißen; *set s.o.'s teeth on edge*, einen nervös machen; *by the skin of one's teeth*, mit Hängen und Würgen, mit knapper Not; *have a sweet* –, ein Leckermaul, genäschig *or* naschhaft sein; *have a* – *stopped*, sich einen Zahn plombieren lassen; *armed to the teeth*, bis an die Zähne bewaffnet. 2. *v.a.* verzahnen (*a wheel*). 3. *v.n.* ineinandergreifen (*wheels*). **-ache,** *s.* das Zahnweh, Zahnschmerzen (*pl.*). **--brush,** *s.* die Zahnbürste. **-ed** [tʊθt], *adj.* gezahnt, gezähnt, gezähnelt, gezackt (*Bot.*); -*ed wheel*, das Zahnrad. **-ing,** *s.* die Verzahnung (*of a wheel*), Zahnung (*of a saw*). **-less,** *adj.* zahnlos. **--paste,** *s.* die Zahnpaste. **-pick,** *s.* der Zahnstocher. **--powder,** *s.* das Zahnpulver. **-some,** *adj.* schmackhaft.
tootle ['tu:tl], 1. *v.a.* & *n.* leise tuten, blasen. 2. *s.* leises Tuten.
[1]**top** [tɔp], 1. *s.* oberes Ende, oberster Teil, der Oberteil, die Spitze, der Kopf (*of tree, page*), Wipfel, die Krone (*of tree*), der Gipfel (*of hill, also fig.*), Scheitel (*of head*), das Verdeck (*of vehicle*), der Topp, Mars, Mastkorb (*Naut.*), die Stulpe, das Oberleder (*of boot*), Kopfende (*of bed*), die Oberfläche, obere Fläche *or* Seite (*of objects or water*), die Blume (*of beer*), (*fig.*) die Höhe, höchste Stufe, höchster Punkt, Rang *or* Grad; *see also* **-knot**; *at the* –, an der Spitze; *be* (*at*) *the* – *of the class*, Primus sein; *at the* – *of one's form*, in allerbester Form; *at the* – *of the ladder* or *tree*, (*fig.*) auf höchster Stufe, an erster Stelle *or* oberster Spitze, in höchster Stellung; *page 1 at the* –, Seite 1 oben; *at the* – *of one's speed*, mit höchster Geschwindigkeit; *at the* – *of the table*, obenan; *at the* – *of one's*

voice, aus voller Kehle; (*sl.*) *blow one's* –, aus der Haut fahren; *from – to bottom*, von oben bis unten; *from – to toe*, von (*or* vom) Kopf bis zu(m) Fuß; *on* (*the*) – *of*, oben auf; *on – of everything else*, noch dazu, obendrein, zu allem anderen; *be on* – (*of the world*), obendrauf sein; *come out on* –, als Erster *or* Sieger hervorgehen; *come out* –, am besten abschneiden; *come to the* –, nach oben kommen, (*fig.*) sich durchsetzen, an die Spitze kommen; *go over the* –, einen Sturmangriff machen; *to the – of one's bent*, nach besten Kräften. 2. *adj.* oberst, höchst, Haupt–; – *boy*, der Primus; – *coat*, der Deckanstrich (*of paint*), *see* **– -coat**; (*sl.*) – *dog*, der Sieger, Erste(r), *m.*; – *drawer*, oberste Schublade; (*coll.*) *in the – flight*, unter den Ersten, an der Spitze; – *gear*, dritter Gang (*Motor.*); – *line*, die Kopfzeile, Titelzeile; – *score*, beste Leistung; – *speed*, größte Geschwindigkeit. 3. *v.a.* bedecken, bekränzen, krönen; (an Größe) übertreffen, überragen, überbieten, hinausgehen über; beschneiden, stutzen, kappen; die Spitze erreichen (*a hill*); – *up*, vollfüllen. **– -beam,** *s.* der Hahnbalken am Dachstuhl. **– -boots,** *pl.* Stulpenstiefel, Langschäfter (*pl.*). **– -coat,** *s.* der Überrock, Mantel; see – *coat*. **– -dressing,** *s.* die Bodenflächendüngung, Kopfdüngung. **–gallant,** 1. *adj.* Bram–. 2. *s.* das Bramsegel. **–hamper,** *s.* obere Takelung (*Naut.*), (*fig.*) die Belastung. **– -hat,** *s.* der Zylinder(hut). **– -heavy,** *adj.* toppslastig (*Naut.*); kopflastig, oberlastig. (*sl.*) **– -hole,** *adj.* erstklassig. **-knot,** *s.* der Haarbüschel, Haarknoten; Federbüschel (*of birds*). **–less,** *adj.* sehr hoch. **–light,** *s.* die Topplaterne. (*Naut.*). (*sl.*) **– -liner,** *s.* der Haupthahn, tonangebender Mann. **–mast,** *s.* die Marsstenge (*on square rigger*). **–most,** *adj.* höchst, oberst. (*sl.*) **– -notch,** *adj.* hochwertig. **–sail** ['tɔpsl], *s.* das Marssegel (*on square riggers*), Toppsegel (*on schooners*). **– -sergeant,** *s.* (*Amer.*) der Feldwebel. **–sides,** *pl.* oberer Teil der Schiffseite. **– -soil,** *s.* die Bodenfläche.

[2]**top,** *s.* der Kreisel; *spin a* –, den Kreisel schlagen; *sleep like a* –, wie ein Murmeltier schlafen.

topaz ['toupæz], *s.* der Topas.

tope [toup], *v.n.* (*sl.*) zechen, saufen. **–r,** *s.* der Säufer.

topee ['toupɪ:], *s.* der Tropenhelm.

topiary ['toupɪərɪ], *s.* die Kunst des Baumschneidens.

topic ['tɔpɪk], *s.* der Gegenstand, das Thema; die Topik (*Phil.*). **–al** [–l], 1. *adj.* aktuell; örtlich, lokal (*Med.*); *–al news*, die Tagesneuigkeiten. 2. *s.* (*coll.*) aktueller Film. **–ality** [–'kælɪtɪ], *s.* aktuelle Bedeutung.

topograph–ic(al) [tɔpə'græfɪk(l)], *adj.* topographisch; *–ical features*, die Bodengestaltung. **–y** [tə'pɔgrəfɪ], *s.* die Ortsbeschreibung, Topographie, Geländekunde.

topp–er ['tɔpə], *s.* oberer Stein (*Arch.*); (*sl.*) der Zylinder(hut), die Angströhre; (*sl.*) etwas Großartiges *or* Erstklassiges; der Mordskerl. **–ing,** *adj.* (*sl.*) fabelhaft, großartig, famos, erstklassig, tiptop, knorke.

topple ['tɔpl], 1. *v.n.* wackeln, kippen, stürzen; – *down* or *over*, umfallen, umkippen, niederstürzen. 2. *v.a.*; – *down* or *over*, umstürzen, niederwerfen.

topsy-turvy ['tɔpsɪ'tə:vɪ], 1. *adv.* das Oberste zuunterst, das Unterste zuoberst, kopfüber, durcheinander; auf den Kopf gestellt, drunter und drüber. 2. *adj.* durcheinanderliegend, verwirrt. 3. *s.* Durcheinander.

toque [touk], *s.* runder Frauenhut.

tor [tɔ:], *s.* (*dial.*) spitziger Felsen.

torch [tɔ:tʃ], *s.* die Fackel; *electric* –, die Taschenlampe. **– -bearer,** *s.* der Fackelträger. **–light,** *s.* die Fackelbeleuchtung, der Fackelschein; *–light procession*, der Fackelzug.

tore [tɔ:], *see* [1]**tear.**

toreador ['tɔrɪədɔ:], *s.* der Stierkämpfer.

torment ['tɔ:mənt], 1. *s.* die Pein, Qual, Marter, Folter; der Plagegeist, Quälgeist. 2. [tɔ:'mɛnt] *v.a.* foltern, martern, quälen, peinigen, belästigen. **–or** [–'mɛntə], *s.* der Quäler, Peiniger, Quälgeist.

tormina ['tɔ:mɪnə], *s.* das Bauchgrimmen, die Kolik, Leibschmerzen (*pl.*) (*Med.*).

torn [tɔ:n], *see* [1]**tear.**

tornado [tɔ:'neɪdou], *s.* (*pl.* –oes) der Wirbelsturm, Tornado; (*fig.*) Ausbruch, Sturm (*of abuse, etc.*).

tor–ose [tə'rous], **–ous** ['tɔrəs], *adj.* knorrig, wulstig.

torpedo [tɔ:'pɪ:dou], 1. *s.* der Torpedo (*Nav.*); (*sl.*) der Aal; (also *– -fish*) Zitterrochen (*Ichth.*). 2. *v.a.* torpedieren (*also fig.*); (*fig.*) vernichten, zunichte machen. **– -boat,** *s.* das Torpedoboot: –(*-boat*) *destroyer*, der Torpedobootzerstörer.

torp–id ['tɔ:pɪd], *adj.* starr, erstarrt, betäubt; (*fig.*) träge, schlaff, stumpf. **–idity** [–'pɪdɪtɪ], *s.*, **–idness,** *s.* die Erstarrung, Betäubung, Starrheit, Trägheit, Stumpfheit. **–or** ['tɔ:pə], *s.* die Gefühllosigkeit, Starrheit, Trägheit, Stumpfheit.

torque [tɔ:k], *s.* das Drehmoment; die Drehkraft, der Drall (*Tech.*).

torref–action [tɔrɪ'fækʃən], *s.* das Dörren, Rösten. **–y** ['tɔrɪfɑɪ], *v.a.* dörren, rösten.

torrent ['tɔrənt], *s.* der Gießbach, Gebirgsstrom, reißender Strom; (*coll.*) Regenguß; (*fig.*) Strom, Schwall, Ausbruch, die Flut; *rain in –s*, in Strömen gießen. **–ial** [–'rɛnʃl], *adj.* gießbachartig, wolkenbruchartig, strömend, reißend; (*fig.*) überwältigend, ungestüm; *–ial rain*, der Wolkenbruch.

torrid ['tɔrɪd], *adj.* brennend heiß, Glut–; dürr, ausgedörrt; – *heat*, brennende Hitze; – *zone*, heiße Zone, Tropen (*pl.*).

torsion ['tɔ:ʃn], *s.* die Drehung, Windung, Drillung, Torsion (*Phys.*), Abschnürung (*of an artery*) (*Med.*). **–al** [–ʃənl], *adj.* Drehungs–, Torsions–. **– -balance,** *s.* die Drehwaage, Torsionswaage.

torso ['tɔ:sou], *s.* der Torso (*also fig.*), Rumpf, (*fig.*) unvollendetes Werk.

tort [tɔ:t], *s.* das Unrecht, Delikt.

tortile ['tɔ:tɑɪl], *adj.* gedreht, gewunden.

tortoise ['tɔ:tɔɪz, 'tɔ:təs], *s.* die Schildkröte; (*as*) *slow as a* –, langsam wie eine Schnecke. **– -shell,** *s.* das Schildpatt; *– -shell butterfly*, Großer *or* Kleiner Fuchs (*Ent.*); *– -shell cat*, dreifarbige Katze.

tortuo-sity [tɔ:tju'ɔsɪtɪ], *s.* die Windung, Krümmung; Gewundenheit; (*fig.*) Unehrlichkeit. **–us** ['tɔ:tjuəs], *adj.* gewunden, (*fig.*) sich windend, unehrlich. **–usness,** *s. see* **–sity.**

torture ['tɔ:tʃə], 1. *s.* die Folter, Tortur (*also fig.*); (*fig.*) Marter, Qual, der Schmerz; *put to the* –, auf die Folter spannen. 2. *v.a.* auf die Folter spannen, foltern, (*fig.*) quälen, peinigen; pressen, verdrehen (*words, etc.*). **– -chamber,** *s.* die Folterkammer. **–r** [–rə], *s.* der Folterknecht, Henker; (*fig.*) Peiniger, Quäler.

torus ['tɔ:rəs], *s.* der Wulst (*Anat. & Arch.*).

tory ['tɔ:rɪ:], 1. *s.* der Tory, Konservative(r), *m.* 2. *adj.* Tory–, konservativ. **–ism,** *s.* der Konservatismus.

tosh [tɔʃ], *s.* (*coll.*) der Quatsch, das Blech.

toss [tɔs], 1. *v.a.* (hoch)werfen, (empor)schleudern; hin- und her- *or* auf- und niederwerfen (*as the sea*); zurückwerfen (*the head*); – *hay*, Heu wenden; – *oars*, die Riemen pieken (*Naut.*); – *a p. for*, mit einem losen um; – *about*, herumwerfen, herumschleudern; – *off*, hinunterstürzen (*a drink*). 2. *v.n.* (also – *about*) sich hin und her wälzen, sich herumwerfen (*in sleep*); hin und her geworfen *or* umhergeworfen werden; rollen, stoßen (*as ships*); auf und ab gehen (*as waves*); – *for*, (also – *up*) durch Münzwurf losen um. 3. *s.* das Werfen, Schleudern; Zurückwerfen, Hochwerfen (*of the head*); der Wurf (*of coin*); *take a* –, (vom Pferde) abgeworfen werden; *win the* –, beim Losen *or* Wurf gewinnen. **– -up,** *s.* der Wurf, das Losen; (*fig.*) reiner Zufall.

[1]**tot** [tɔt], 1. *v.a.*; (*coll.*) – *up*, zusammenzählen, addieren. 2. *v.n.*; (*coll.*) – *up to*, sich belaufen auf (*Acc.*).

[2]**tot,** *s.* (*coll.*) das Wurm; (*coll.*) das Gläschen, Schlückchen.

total ['toutl], 1. *adj.* ganz, gesamt, Gesamt–; gänzlich, völlig. 2. *s.* das Ganze, die Summe, (also *grand* or *sum* –) der Gesamtbetrag; die Gesamtsumme. 3. *v.a.* sich (im ganzen) belaufen auf; zusammenzählen. 4. *v.n.*; – *up to*, sich (im ganzen) belaufen auf (*Acc.*). **–itarian** [–tælɪ'tɛərɪən], *adj.* total, Total–. **–ity** [–'tælɪtɪ], *s.* das Ganze, die Gesamtheit, Vollständigkeit. **–izator** ['toutəlɑɪzeɪtə], **–izer** [–ɑɪzə], *s.* der Totalisator. **–ize** [–ɑɪz], *v.a.* zu einem Ganzen abrunden, zusammenzählen.

[1]**tote** [toʊt], 1. *v.a.* (*Amer.coll.*) tragen, schleppen. 2. *s.* (*sl.*) die Last.
[2]**tote,** *s.* (*coll.*) *abbr. of* **totalizator.**
totem [ˈtoʊtəm], *s.* das Totem, Stammwappen (*of Indians*). **–ism** [–ɪzm], *s.* der Totemismus.
totter [ˈtɔtə], *v.n.* wanken, torkeln (*of a p.*); wackeln, schwanken (*of a th.*); – *to one's grave*, nicht mehr lange mitmachen; – *to its fall*, zusammenbrechen, niederstürzen. **–ing,** *adj.* (sch)wankend, wack(e)lig.
toucan [ˈtuːkən], *s.* der Tukan, Toko, Pfefferfresser (*Orn.*).
touch [tʌtʃ], **1.** *v.a.* (*of persons*) berühren, angreifen, anfassen, antasten, anfühlen, betasten, befühlen; (*fig.*) (*usually neg.*) sich befassen mit, behändeln; anrühren, essen *or* trinken; anlegen an, anlaufen (*Naut.*); (*sl.*) anpumpen, anhauen (*for*, um); (*of things*) berühren, in Berührung kommen mit, grenzen *or* stoßen an, reichen an; betreffen, sich beziehen auf; (*fig. of persons or things*) beeindrucken, beeinflussen, erregen, reizen; bewegen, rühren; Verwandschaft haben mit, sich berühren mit; erreichen, heranreichen an, nahekommen, gleichkommen; – *the bell*, klingeln; – *bottom*, auf Grund geraten; – *glasses*, anstoßen; – *one's hat to a p.*, einen grüßen; (*coll.*) *no one can – him*, niemand reicht an ihn heran; – *s.o. on the raw*, einen schwer kränken; (*Prov.*) *they that – pitch will be defiled*, wer Pech angreift, besudelt sich; (*coll.*) *it –es my pocket*, das reißt in meinen Beutel; – *s.o. to the heart*, einen bis ins Innerste rühren; (*coll.*) – *wood*, unter den Tisch klopfen; – *wood!* unberufen!; – *off*, zum Explodieren bringen, (*fig.*) in Bewegung setzen; – *up*, aufbessern, auffrischen, retuchieren, restaurieren (*a picture, etc.*). **2.** *v.n.* sich berühren; aneinanderkommen; – *at*, berühren, landen, anlegen in; – *down*, landen (*Av.*), die Hand auflegen (*Footb.*); – (*up*)*on*, berühren, behandeln, zu sprechen kommen auf, zur Sprache bringen, kurz erwähnen. **3.** *s.* die Berührung, das Berühren, Anrühren, Anfühlen; leichte Berührung, leichter Druck, Schlag *or* Stoß; leichter Anfall (*of illness*); der Anschlag (*of pianist*), Strich (*of violinist*), (Pinsel)-Strich (*Draw. etc.*); der Tastsinn, das Tastgefühl, Tastempfinden; (*fig.*) die Fühlung; der Anflug, Hauch, Beigeschmack, Zug, die Note, Spur; *see also* **––line;** *at a –*, beim Anrühren; *fine –*, schöner Zug; *give* or *put the finishing* or *final –*(*es*) *to*, die letzte Feile *or* Hand legen an, den letzten Schliff geben (*Dat.*); *in – with*, in Fühlung mit; *get in – with*, Fühling suchen *or* nehmen mit, sich in Verbindung setzen mit; *keep in – with*, in Fühlung bleiben mit, *put in – with*, verbinden mit; *personal –*, persönliche Note; *put to the –*, auf die Probe stellen; *on the slightest –*, bei der leisesten Berührung; – *of red*, rötliche Färbung; – *of the sun*, der Sonnenstich; *be rough to the –*, sich rauh anfühlen; *sure –*, sichere Hand, sicherer Griff. **––and-go,** 1. *s.* gewagte Sache, brenzlige Lage. 2. *adj.* riskant, zweifelhaft; *it was* (*a matter of*) *––and-go whether*, es fehlte nicht viel daß, es stand auf des Messers Schneide ob; *it was ––and-go with him*, es stand sehr kritisch mit ihm. **––down,** *s.* das Handauf (*Footb.*). **–ed** [–t], *adj.* gerührt, ergriffen, bewegt (*by* or *with*, von), angegangen, angesteckt; (*coll.*) verdreht, klapsig, bekloppt. **––hole,** *s.* das Zündloch. **–iness,** *s.* die Empfindlichkeit, Reizbarkeit. **–ing,** 1. *adj.* rührend, ergreifend. 2. *prep.* betreffs, betreffend. **––judges,** *pl.* Linienrichter, Seitenrichter. **––line,** *s.* die (Seiten)-Grenzlinie, Seitengrenze, Mark (*Footb.*). **––me-not,** *s.* das Rührmichnichtan, Nolimetangere (*Bot.*). **––needle,** *s.* die Probiernadel. **––paper,** *s.* das Zündpapier. **–stone,** *s.* der Probierstein; (*fig.*) der Prüfstein, die Prüfung, das Kriterium. **–wood,** *s.* das Zunder(holz). **–y,** *adj.* empfindlich, reizbar (*on*, in bezug auf) (*of a p.*); heikel (*of a th.*).
tough [tʌf], 1. *adj.* zäh(e), hart, (bruch)fest; (*coll.*) zäh, kräftig, robust (*of a p.*); (*coll.*) schwierig, unangenehm (*usually of a th., but sl. of a p.*). 2. *s.* (*sl.*) der Raufbold, Halbstarke(r), *m.*, schwerer Junge; der Kraftmensch, Kraftmeier; (*coll.*) – *customer*, der Grobian, grober Kunde; (*coll.*) – *job*, schwierige Aufgabe; (*coll.*) – *luck*, das Pech. **–en,** 1. *v.a.* zäh(e) *or* fest machen, kräftigen. 2. *v.n.* zäh(e) werden. **–ness,** *s.* die Zähigkeit, Bruchfestigkeit, Stärke, Hartnäckigkeit.
toupee [ˈtuːpeɪ], 1. *s.* das Toupet, falscher Schopf.
tour [ˈtuːə], 1. *s.* die (Rund)Reise, Tour, der Ausflug; Rundgang, die Runde, Dienstzeit, der (Fuß)Dienst (*esp. Mil.*); die Gastspielreise, Tournée (*Theat.*); *circular –*, die Rundreise; *grand –*, die Europareise; *foreign –*, die Reise ins Ausland; – *of inspection*, der Besichtigungsrundgang; *walking –*, die (Fuß)-Wanderung, Fußreise; *on –*, auf Tournée (*Theat.*). 2. *v.n.* reisen. 3. *v.a.* bereisen, eine Rundreise machen durch; einen Rundgang machen um *or* durch (*Mil.*). **–er,** *s.* **–ing car,** der Tourenwagen. **–ism,** *s.* der Reiseverkehr, Fremdenverkehr. **–ist,** *s.* (Vergnügungs)Reisende(r), *m.*, der Tourist; *–ist agency*, das Reisebüro; *–ist season*, die Reisezeit; *–ist ticket*, das Rundreisebillet.
tourn–ament [ˈtuːənəmənt, ˈtɔːnəmənt], *s.* das Turnier (*also Sport*), der Wettkampf (*Sport*). **–ey** [ˈtuːənɪː, ˈtɔːnɪː], 1. *s.* das Tournier (*Hist.*). 2. *v.n.* tournieren.
tourniquet [ˈtuːənɪket], *s.* die Aderpresse (*Surg.*).
tousle [taʊzl], *v.a.* (zer)zausen (*hair, etc.*).
tout [taʊt], 1. *v.n.* Kunden werben; – *for custom*, nach Kundschaft suchen. 2. *s.* der Kundensucher; (also *racing –*) der Tipgeber.
[1]**tow** [toʊ], 1. *v.a.* (am Seil *or* Strick) schleppen, einschleppen, anschleppen, treideln, bugsieren (*Naut.*), abschleppen (*a car*). 2. *s.* das Schleppen; (also *––rope*, *––line*) das Schlepptau; der Schleppzug (*of boats*), geschleppter Wagen; *take in –*, ins Schlepptau nehmen, (*fig.*) unter seinen Schutz *or* seine Aufsicht nehmen; *have in –*, schleppen, (*fig.*) im Schlepptau haben, in der Gewalt haben. **–age,** *s.* das Schleppen, Bugsieren; der Schlepplohn, die Schleppgebühr. **––boat,** *s.* der Schlepper, das Bugsierboot. **–(ing)-path,** *s.* der Leinpfad, Treidelweg. **––line,** *s.*, **––rope,** *s.* das Schlepptau, Treidel.
[2]**tow,** *s.* das Werg, die Hede.
toward 1. [ˈtoʊəd], *adj.* (*only pred.*) (*archaic*) geneigt, (bereit)willig; im Gange, am Werk; nahe, bevorstehend. 2. [twɔːd, tɔːd] *prep.* (*rare or Poet.*) *see* **–s.** **–s** [twɔːdz, tɔːdz], *prep.* (*place*) zu . . . hin, nach . . . zu, auf . . . zu, gegen; (*time*) gegen, ungefähr um; (*purpose or relation*) zum Zwecke von *or* (*Gen.*), für; gegenüber, betreffend.
towel [ˈtaʊəl], 1. *s.* das Handtuch; *roller –*, das Rollhandtuch; (*coll.*) *throw in the –*, sich für besiegt erklären. 2. *v.a.* abtrocknen, abreiben. (*sl.*) (ver)-wichsen, verhauen. 3. *v.n.* sich abtrocknen. **–ling,** *s.* der Handtuchdrell; (*sl.*) die Tracht Prügel. **––rail,** *s.* der Handtuchhalter.
tower [ˈtaʊə], 1. *s.* der Turm, die Feste, Burg, der Zwinger, das Kastell; (*fig.*) der Hort, Schutz; – *of strength*, (*fig.*) starke Stütze. 2. *v.n.* sich emporragen, türmen *or* erheben (*to*, bis an); – *above*, ragen *or* sich erheben über; (*fig.*) hervorragen über. **–ed,** *adj.* mit Türmen; getürmt. **–ing,** *adj.* turmhoch, aufragend, sehr hoch; (*fig.*) gewaltig, heftig (*rage, etc.*).
town [taʊn], *s.* die Stadt; (*without art.*) Stadtinnere(s), *n.*; London; die Bürgerschaft (*Univ.*); – *and gown*, Bürgerschaft und Studentenschaft; *the – of Berlin*, die Stadt Berlin; *man about –*, der Lebemann; *in –*, in der Stadt, in London; *out of –*, verreist, auf dem Lande; *talk of the –*, der Gegenstand des Stadtgesprächs; *go up to –*, nach London reisen. **––bred,** *adj.* in der Stadt aufgewachsen. **––clerk,** *s.* der Stadtsyndikus. **––council,** *s.* der Stadtrat. **––councillor,** *s.* der Stadtrat, Stadtverordnete(r), *m.* **––crier,** *s.* der Ausrufer. **––hall,** *s.* das Rathaus. **– house,** das Stadthaus. **––major,** *s.* der Ortskommandant (*Mil.*). **––planning,** *s.* die Kunst des Städtebaus. **–ship,** *s.* die Stadtgemeinde, das Stadtgebiet; das Gemeinwesen; (*Amer.*) der Grafschaftsbezirk; (*Amer.*) das Gebiet von 6 Quadratmeilen; Dorf (*in Australia*). **––sfolk, –speople,** *pl.* Stadtleute. **–sman,** *s.* der Bürger, Städter, der Philister (*Univ.*); *fellow –sman*, der Mitbürger. **–ward,** *adj.* nach der Stadt zu. **–wards,** *adv.* stadtwärts.
tox–aemia [tɔkˈsɪːmɪə], *s.* die Blutvergiftung, Toxiämie. **–ic** [ˈtɔksɪk], *adj.* giftig, gifthaltig,

Gift–. **–icant**, 1. *s.* der Giftstoff, das Gift. 2. *adj.* toxisch, giftig. **–icological** [–kəˈlɔdʒɪkl], *adj.* toxikologisch. **–icology** [–ˈkɔlədʒɪ], *s.* die Toxikologie, Giftlehre. **–in** [ˈtɔksɪn], *s.* das Toxin, der Giftstoff.

toxophilite [tɔkˈsɔfɪlɑɪt], *s.* der Bogenschütze, Armbrustschütze.

toy [tɔɪ], 1. *s.* das Spielzeug (*also fig.*); (*fig.*) der Tand, die Lappalie; *pl.* Spielsachen, Spielwaren (*pl.*); – *dog*, der Schoßhund; – *soldiers*, Bleisoldaten. 2. *v.n.* spielen, tändeln, liebäugeln. **– -dealer**, *s.* der Spielwarenhändler. **– -railway**, *s.* die Kleinbahn. **–shop**, *s.* die Spielwarenhandlung.

[1]**trac–e** [treɪs], 1. *s.* die Spur (*also fig.*), die Fährte; (*fig.*) das (An)Zeichen; die Kleinigkeit; der Grundriß, die Skizze, Zeichnung (*Arch.*); *be on s.o.'s –es*, einem auf der Spur sein; *not a –e*, keine Spur. 2. *v.a.* durchzeichnen, durchpausen, abpausen, nachzeichnen; (also *–e out*) entwerfen, skizzieren, (auf)zeichnen; der Spur (*Dat.*) nachgehen (*a p. or th.* (*Gen.*)), aufspüren, nachspüren (*Dat.*); verfolgen, auffinden, ausfindig machen, feststellen, nachweisen, herleiten (*from*, von); *–e back*, zurückverfolgen (*to*, bis zu), zurückführen (*to*, auf); *–e down*, nachweisen, feststellen, ausfindig machen. **–eable**, *adj.* auffindbar, nachweisbar, nachweislich, zurückzuverfolgen(d). **–er**, *s.* (also *–er bullet*) das Lichtspurgeschoß, Rauchspurgeschoß. **–ing**, *s.* das (Durch)Zeichnen, Durchpausen; die Pauszeichnung; der Riß, die Zeichnung (*Build.*, *etc.*). **–ing-paper**, *s.* das Pauspapier.

[2]**trace**, *s.* der Strang, Zugriemen; *in the –s*, angespannt; (*fig.*) *kick over the –s*, über die Stränge schlagen.

tracery [ˈtreɪsərɪ], *s.* das Maßwerk, die Verzierung (*Arch.*), (*fig.*) das Flechtwerk.

trache–a [trəˈkɪːə, ˈtreɪkɪə], *s.* (*pl.* –ae) die Luftröhre (*Anat.*), Trachee (*Zool.*), das Spiralgefäß (*Bot.*). **–al** [ˈtreɪkɪəl], *adj.* Luftröhren–. **–itis** [trækɪˈɑɪtɪs], *s.* die Luftröhrenentzündung. **–otomy** [–ˈɔmətɪ], *s.* der Luftröhrenschnitt.

track [træk], 1. *s.* die Spur (*also fig.*), Fährte, Fußspur; das Fahrwasser (*of a ship*); der Pfad, Weg; die Bahn (*Racing*); Schiene, das Geleise (*Railw.*); die Raupenkette, Laufkette (*Tech.*); *beaten* –, der Trampelweg, (*fig.*) a tes *or* ausgetretenes Gleise; *caterpillar* –, die Gleiskette; *cover up one's –s*, seine Spuren verwischen; *keep – of*, verfolgen, sich auf dem Laufenden halten über; *lose – of*, aus dem Auge verlieren (*a p.*), nicht mehr verfolgen (*a th.*); (*sl.*) *make –s*, ausreißen, sich begeben (*for*, nach); *off the* –, auf falscher Fährte, auf dem Holzweg; *on the* –, auf der Spur (*of* (*Gen.*)); (*fig.*) *be on a p.'s –(s)*, einem auf der Spur sein. 2. *v.a.* aufspüren; nachspüren (*Dat.*), verfolgen; – *down*, aufspüren, ausfindig machen. 3. *v.n.* Spur verfolgen; in der Wagenspur *or* auf der Schiene bleiben (*of wheels*). **–age**, *s.* (*coll.*) der Schienenstrang, Schienen (*pl.*) (*Railw.*). **–ed vehicle**, *s.* das Kettenfahrzeug. **–er**, *s.* der Spürhund; Aufspürer, Fährtenfinder; Verfolger. **–less**, *adj.* spurlos, pfadlos.

[1]**tract** [trækt], *s.* die Strecke, Gegend, der Strich, das Gebiet, ausgedehnte Fläche; die Zeitspanne, der Zeitraum; *digestive* –, das Verdauungssystem.

[2]**tract**, *s.* die Abhandlung; der Traktat, das Traktätchen, (religiöse) Flugschrift. **–arian** [–ˈtɛərɪən], *s.* der Traktarianer. **–ate**, *s. see* [2]**–**.

tract–ability [træktəˈbɪlɪtɪ], *s.* die Lenksamkeit, Gefügigkeit. **–able** [–əbl], *adj.* lenksam, fügsam, folgsam (*of a p.*), leicht zu bearbeiten(d), handlich (*of material*).

tract–ile [ˈtræktɑɪl], *adj.* dehnbar, streckbar. **–ion** [ˈtrækʃən], *s.* das Ziehen, der Zug; das Dehnen; die Zugkraft, Zugleistung (*Tech.*); die Zusammenziehung (*Anat.*); der Transport, die Fortbewegung. **–ional** [–ʃənl], **–ive** [–tɪv], *adj.* Zug–. **–ion-engine**, *s.* die Zugmaschine, Straßenlokomotive, der Trecker, Traktor. **–or** [–tə], *s. see* **–ion-engine**; der Raupenschlepper (*Agr.*); die Zugschraube (*Av.*); *–or-plough*, der Motorpflug.

trad–e [treɪd], 1. *s.* der Handel, Verkehr; der Kleinhandel, das Geschäft, Gewerbe, Handwerk, der Beruf, die Beschäftigung; (*coll.*) *the –es*, *pl. see* **–e-winds**; *Board of –e*, das Handelsministerium (*Engl.*), die Handelskammer (*Amer.*); *be in –e*, Geschäftsmann sein; *carry on a –e*, ein Geschäft betreiben; *carrying –e*, die Spedition; *do –e with*, Handel treiben mit; *do a good –e*, gute Geschäfte machen; *Jack of all –es*, Hans Dampf in allen Gassen; *sell to the –e*, an Wiederverkäufer verkaufen. 2. *v.n.* handeln, Handel treiben (*in* (*a th.*), *with* (*a p.*), mit); *–e* (*up*)*on*, ausnutzen, mißbrauchen; spekulieren *or* reisen auf. **–e-allowance**, *s.* der Rabatt für Wiederverkäufer. **–e-balance**, *s.* die Handelsbilanz. **–e board**, *s.* die Arbeitgeber- und -nehmerbehörde. **–e-directory**, *s.* das Firmenverzeichnis. **–e-disputes**, *pl.* Streiks und Aussperrungen, Arbeitsstreitigkeiten (*pl.*). **–e-fair**, *s.* die Handelsmesse. **–emark**, *s.* die Schutzmarke, das Warenzeichen. **–e-name**, *s.* der Markenname (*article*); Firmenname. **–e-price**, *s.* der Großeinkaufspreis, Handelspreis, Engrospreis. **–er**, *s.* der Händler, Kaufmann; das Handelsschiff, Kauffahrteischiff, der Fahrer, Tourendampfer. **–e-route**, *s.* der Handelsweg, die Handelsstraße. **–e-school**, *s.* die Gewerbeschule. **–e-show**, *s.* die Vorführung eines Films für Abnehmer. **–esman**, *s.* der Geschäftsmann, (Klein)Händler, Gewerbetreibende(r), *m*; (*esp. Scots*) Handwerker; *–esmen's entrance*, der Eingang für Lieferanten. **–espeople**, *pl.* Geschäftsleute, Handelsleute, Gewerbetreibende (*pl.*). **–e-union**, die Gewerkschaft. **–e-unionism**, die Gewerkschaftsbewegung; das Gewerkschaftswesen. **–e-unionist**, *s.* der Gewerkschaftler. **–e-winds**, *pl.* Passatwinde. **–ing**, *s.* das Handeln, der Handel; *–ing capital*, das Betriebskapital; *–ing estate*, die Industriesiedlung; *–ing-port*, der Handelshafen; *–ing vessel*, das Handelsschiff.

tradition [trəˈdɪʃən], *s.* die Überlieferung, Tradition, alter Brauch, das Herkommen, Brauchtum; die Übergabe, Auslieferung (*Law*); (*coll.*) *be in the* –, sich im Rahmen der Tradition halten. **–al** [–əl], *adj.* traditionell, Traditions–, überliefert; herkömmlich, hergebracht, brauchtümlich, üblich. **–alism**, *s.* der Traditionalismus, das Festhalten an der Tradition.

traduce [trəˈdjuːs], *v.a.* verleumden. **–ment**, *s.* die Verleumdung. **–r**, *s.* der Verleumder.

traduction [trəˈdʌkʃən], *s.* die Übertragung, Fortpflanzung; *see also* **traducement**.

traffic [ˈtræfɪk], 1. *s.* der Handel (*in*, mit); (öffentlicher) Verkehr, Straßenverkehr; *freight* or *goods* –, der Güterverkehr; *heavy* –, der Andrang, starker Verkehr; *one-way* –, die Einbahnstraße; *passenger* –, der Personenverkehr; *white-slave* –, der Mädchenhandel. 2. *v.n.* handeln, Handel treiben (*in*, *with*, mit); schachern (*for*, um). 3. *v.a.* (also – *away*) verschachern. **– -jam**, *s.* die Verkehrsstockung. **–ker**, *s.* der Kaufmann, Geschäftsmann; Schacherer, Intrigant. **– -light**, *s.* das Verkehrssignal, die Verkehrsampel. **– -manager**, *s.* der Betriebsinspektor (*Railw.*). **– regulations**, *pl.* die Verkehrsordnung. **– policeman**, *s.* der Verkehrspolizist. **– -returns**, *pl.* die Betriebsstatistik. **– -sign**, *s.* das Verkehrszeichen, die Verkehrstafel.

tragacanth [ˈtrægəkənθ], *s.* der Tragant(gummi).

trag–edian [trəˈdʒɪːdɪən], *s.* der Tragödiendichter, Tragiker; tragischer Schauspieler, der Tragöde. **–edienne** [–ɪɛn] *s.* tragische Schauspielerin, die Tragödin. **–edy** [ˈtrædʒədɪ], *s.* das Trauerspiel, die Tragödie; (*fig.*) tragischer Vorfall, das Unglück; Tragische. **–ic** [ˈtrædʒɪk], *adj.* tragisch (*also fig.*); (*fig.*) unheilvoll, unselig. **–ical**, *adj.* (*rare*) *see* **–ic**. **–icalness**, *s.* die Tragik, das Tragische. **–i-comedy**, *s.* die Tragikomödie. **–i-comic**, *adj.* tragikomisch.

trail [treɪl], 1. *v.a.* (nach)schleppen, (nach)schleifen, hinter sich herziehen; aufspüren, auf der Spur verfolgen (*Sport*); – *arms!* Gewehr rechts! 2. *v.n.* sich (hin)schleppen *or* hinziehen; kriechen (*plants*); – *along*, sich weiterschleppen; – *off*, verklingen, verhallen. 3. *s.* die Witterung, Fährte, Spur; ausgetretener Weg *or* Pfad; der Schweif, Schwanz (*of meteor*), schmaler Streifen (*of smoke*, *etc.*); die Kondensfahne (*Av.*); der (Lafetten)-Schwanz (*Artil.*); *on the* –, auf der Fährte; *on a p.'s* –, einem auf der Spur. **–er**, *s.* der Anhänger;

Anhängewagen (*Motor.*); die Kriechpflanze (*Bot.*); der Spürhund; die Vorschau, Voranzeige, Vorankündigung (*Films*). **-ing,** *adj.* kriechend (*Bot.*); *-ing aerial*, freihängende Antenne (*Av.*); *-ing axle*, die Hinterachse (*Motor.*); *-ing edge*, die Hinterkante, hintere Flügelkante (*Av.*). **--net,** *s.* das Schleppnetz.

train [treɪn], 1. *v.a.* abrichten, dressieren (*animals*); trainieren (*athletes, horses*); erziehen, aufziehen, bilden, schulen (*children, etc.*), ausbilden, (ein)-exerzieren, drillen (*recruits*); ziehen (*plants*); zielen, richten (*a gun*). 2. *v.n.* (sich) üben, (sich) trainieren (*for*, für) (*Sport*), sich ausbilden (*for*, als *or* zu); (*sl.*) – (*it*), mit der Eisenbahn fahren; *well -ed*, durchgebildet. 3. *s.* die Schleppe (*of a dress*); die Reihe, Kette, Folge; der Zug, die Kolonne, der Train, Troß (*Mil.*); (also *railway* –) (Eisenbahn)Zug; das Gefolge, die Begleitung; der Schweif (*of a comet*); das Räderwerk (*Mech.*); die Zündlinie, das Leitfeuer (*Mil. etc.*); *bring in its* –, mit sich bringen; *by* –, mit dem Zuge, per Bahn; *change -s*, umsteigen; *in* –, in Gang, im Zuge, im Entstehen; *put in* –, in Gang setzen; *be on the* –, mitfahren, im Zuge sein; *slow* –, der Personenzug, Bummelzug; *special* –, der Sonderzug; – *of thought*, die Gedankenfolge, der Gedankengang. **– accident,** *s.* das Eisenbahnunglück, der Eisenbahnunfall. **--bearer,** *s.* der Schleppenträger. **-ee,** *s.* der Kursteilnehmer, Anlernling (*in industry*). **-er,** *s.* der Trainer, Sportlehrer; Lehrmeister, Exerziermeister; Abrichter, Zureiter (*of horses*); Dresseur (*of dogs, etc.*); das Schulflugzeug (*Av.*). **--ferry,** *s.* das Eisenbahntrajekt. **-ing,** *s.* die Erziehung, Ausbildung, Schulung, Schule, Übung; Trainierung, das Training (*Sport*); Einüben, Einexerzieren, Abrichten, Zureiten; *emergency -ing* (*for industry*), die Anlehre; *in good -ing*, gut im Training. **-ing-camp,** *s.* das Schulungslager. **-ing-college,** *s.* das Lehrerseminar. **-ing-film,** *s.* der Lehrfilm. **-ing-ground,** *s.* der Exerzierplatz. **-ing-ship,** *s.* das Schulschiff. **– journey,** *s.* die Bahnfahrt. **– service,** *s.* die Eisenbahnverbindung, der Eisenbahnverkehr. **--staff,** *s.* das Zugpersonal.

train-oil [ˈtreɪnˈɔɪl], *s.* der Tran, das Fischöl.

traipse. *see* **trapes.**

trait [treɪ(t)], *s.* der Charakterzug, Zug, das Merkmal.

trait-or [ˈtreɪtə], *s.* der Verräter (*to*, an). **-orous** [-ərəs], *adj.* verräterisch. **-ress,** *s.* die Verräterin.

traject 1. [trəˈdʒɛkt], *v.a.* (*rare*) übertragen (*thoughts, etc.*). 2. [ˈtrædʒɛkt], *s.* (*rare*) die Fähre, Überfahrt. **-ory** [ˈtrædʒəktrɪ], *s.* die Bahn (*Math.*), Wurfbahn, Flugbahn (*Artil., etc.*); *flat -ory fire*, das Flachfeuer.

tram [træm], *s.* der Laufkarren, Förderwagen, die Lore (*Min.*); (also *--road*) die Grubenschiene (*Min.*); (also *--car*), die Straßenbahn, der Straßenbahnwagen; *by* –, mit der Straßenbahn. **--car,** *s.* der Straßenbahnwagen. **--conductor,** *s.* der Straßenbahnschaffner. **--driver,** *s.* der Straßenbahnführer. **--line,** *s.* die Straßenbahnschiene. **--stop,** *s.* die Straßenbahnhaltestelle. **--ticket,** *s.* der Straßenbahnfahrschein. **-way,** *s.* die Straßenbahn, Elektrische.

trammel [ˈtræml], 1. *s.* der Spannriemen (*for horses*); das Schleppnetz; der Kesselhaken; (*fig.*) (*usually pl.*) die Fessel, das Hindernis. 2. *v.a.* hindern, hemmen, fesseln.

tramontane [trəˈmɔnteɪn], *adj.* jenseits der Alpen, transalpin(isch); (*fig.*) fremd.

tramp [træmp], 1. *v.n.* derb auftreten, trampeln; (zu Fuß) wandern. 2. *v.a.* durchstreifen, durchwandern; – *down*, niedertreten, niedertrampeln. 3. *s.* das Getrampel; Trampeln; der Landstreicher, Vagabund; die Fußwanderung, Fußreise; der Tramp(dampfer); *on the* –, auf der Wanderschaft. **-le** [-l], 1. *v.a.* (also *-le down*) niedertrampeln; niedertreten; *-le out*, austreten (*a fire*); (*fig.*) *-le under foot* or *down*, niedertreten, mit Füßen treten. 2. *v.n.* treten, trampeln; (*fig.*) *-le upon a p.*, einen mit Füßen treten. 3. *s.* das Getrampel, Trampeln.

trance [trɑːns], *s.* die Verzückung, Ekstase, hypnotischer Schlaf, der Entrückungszustand, die Trance.

tranquil [ˈtræŋkwɪl], *adj.* ruhig, friedlich, ungestört, unbewegt, gelassen. **-lity** [-ˈkwɪlɪtɪ], *s.* die Ruhe, Stille; Gelassenheit, Gemütsruhe. **-lization** [-leɪˈzeɪʃən], *s.* die Beruhigung. **-lize,** *v.a.* beruhigen.

transact [trænˈzækt], *v.a.* verrichten, abmachen, abschließen, zustande bringen, durchführen, erledigen; – *business*, Geschäft machen, ein Geschäft abmachen *or* abwickeln. **-ion** [-ˈzækʃən], *s.* die Verrichtung, Durchführung, Abwicklung; Verhandlung; Abmachung; der Vergleich (*Law*); das Geschäft, geschäftliches Unternehmen, geschäftliche Angelegenheit, die Transaktion (*C.L.*); *pl.* Verhandlungen, (Sitzungs)Berichte, Abhandlungen (*pl.*). **-or,** *s.* der Unterhändler.

trans-alpine [trænzˈælpɑɪn], *adj.* jenseits der Alpen, transalpin(isch). **-atlantic,** *adj.* transatlantisch, Übersee–; *-atlantic flight*, der Ozeanflug.

transceiver [trænˈsɪːvə], *s.* der Senderempfänger (*Rad.*).

transcend [trænˈsɛnd], *v.a.* übersteigen, überschreiten, übertreffen. **-ence, -ency,** *s.* die Überlegenheit, Vortrefflichkeit, Erhabenheit; Transzendenz (*Phil., Theol.*). **-ent** [-ənt], *adj.* vortrefflich, vorzüglich, überragend, hervorragend, höchst; transzendent; (*Phil., Theol.*). **-ental** [-sənˈdɛntl], *adj.* übernatürlich, außergewöhnlich, phantastisch, unklar, abstrus; transzendental (*Phil.*); transzendent (*Math.*). **-entalism** [-ˈdɛntəlɪzm], *s.* transzendentale Philosophie.

transcribe [trænˈskrɑɪb], *v.a.* abschreiben, kopieren; ausschreiben (*notes*); umschreiben; transkribieren, umsetzen (*Mus.*).

transcript [ˈtrænskrɪpt], *s.* die Abschrift, Kopie. **-ion** [-ˈskrɪpʃən], *s.* das Abschreiben, Umschreiben, die Übertragung, Abschrift, Umschrift; Transkription (*Mus.*).

transept [ˈtrænsɛpt], *s.* das Querschiff, Kreuzschiff (*Arch.*).

transfer [trænsˈfəː], 1. *v.a.* übertragen (*to*, auf) (*also Typ. & Law*), versetzen (*a p.*), verlegen (*to*, nach), überweisen (*money*) (*to*, auf), umbuchen (*C.L.*); hinübertragen, hinüberbringen (*to*, nach), abtreten, zedieren (*to* (*Dat.*)) (*Law*), umdrucken (*Typ.*). 2. *v.n.* verlegt werden (*to*, nach), übertreten (*to*, zu). 3. [ˈtrænsfəː], *s.* die Versetzung, Verlegung, Überführung (*to*, nach), Übertragung (*to*, auf), (Geld)Überweisung, (Geld)Anweisung, Abtretung, Zession (*to*, an) (*Law*); der Übertrag, die Umbuchung (*C.L.*); Abzug, Umdruck (*Typ.*); das Abziehbild; – *of balance*, der Saldoübertrag. **-ability** [-rəˈbɪlɪtɪ], *s.* die Übertragbarkeit. **-able** [-ˈfəːrəbl], *adj.* übertragbar (*to*, auf), abtretbar (*to*, an). **--book,** *s.* das Übertragungsbuch. **--deed,** *s.* die Übertragungsurkunde. **-ee** [-ˈrɪː], *s.* der Indossatar (*C.L.*), Zessionat (*Law*). **-ence** [ˈtrænsfərəns], *s.* die Übertragung, Verlegung. **-ential** [-fəˈrɛnʃəl], *adj.* Übertragungs–. **-or** [ˈtrænsfəːrə], *s.* der Zedent, Abtretende(r), *m.* (*Law.*); der Indossant, Übertrager (*C.L.*). **-rer** [-ˈfəːrə], *s.* der Übertrager. **--ink,** *s.* die Umdrucktinte. **--paper,** *s.* das Umdruckpapier. **--ticket,** *s.* Umsteigebillett (*Railw.*), der Verrechnungsscheck (*C.L.*).

transfigur-ation [trænsfɪgjʊˈreɪʃən], *s.* die Umgestaltung; Verklärung (*Eccl.*). **-e** [-ˈfɪgə], *v.a.* umgestalten, verwandeln; verklären.

transfix [trænsˈfɪks], *v.a.* durchstechen, durchbohren; (*fig.*) *be -ed with pain*, vor Schmerz starr sein. **-ion** [-kʃən], *s.* die Durchbohrung, (*fig.*) das Erstarrtsein.

transform [trænsˈfɔːm], *v.a.* umgestalten (*also Alg.*), umbilden, umformen, umlagern; verwandeln, umwandeln (*also Elec.*), transformieren (*Elec.*). **-able** [əbl], *adj.* umwandelbar, verwandelbar. **-ation** [-fəˈmeɪʃən], *s.* die Umbildung, Umformung, Umgestaltung, Umwandlung, Verwandlung, Transformation (*Elec.*), Metamorphose (*Zool., etc.*); (*fig.*) Wandlung; *-ation scene*, die Verwandlungsszene. **-ative** [-ˈfɔməːtɪv], *adj.* umgestaltend, umwandelnd. **-er** [-ˈfɔːmə], *s.* der Umformer, Transformator (*Elec.*).

transfus-e [trænsˈfjuːz], *v.a.* übergießen, umgießen; übertragen (*blood*); (*fig.*) durchtränken; einflößen (*into a p.*, einem). **-ion** [-ˈfjuːʒn], *s.* das Umgießen;

(*fig.*) die Übertragung; Blutübertragung, Transfusion (*Med.*).

transgress [træns'grɛs, trænz'grɛs], 1. *v.a.* überschreiten, übertreten, verletzen, verstoßen gegen, nicht innehalten. 2. *v.n.* sich vergehen, fehlen. **–ion** [–'grɛʃn], *s.* die Überschreitung, Übertretung, (Gesetz)Verletzung, das Vergehen; übergreifende Auflagerung (*Geol.*). **–ive** [–'grɛsɪv], *adj.* verstoßend (*of*, gegen). **–or** [–'grɛsə], *s.* der Übertreter, Missetäter.

tranship [træn'ʃɪp], *v.a.* umladen, umschiffen. **–ment,** *s.* die Umladung, der Umschlag; *–ment port*, der Umladehafen, Umschlag(e)platz.

transien–ce ['trænzɪəns], *s.*, **–cy,** *s.* die Flüchtigkeit, Vergänglichkeit, rasches Verfliegen. **–t,** *adj.* vorübergehend; vergänglich, flüchtig.

transilient [træn'sɪlɪənt], *adj.* überspringend, ineinander übergehend.

transire [træn'zɪərə], *s.* der Passierschein, Begleitschein.

transit ['trænzɪt], *s.* das Durchfahren, Durchschreiten; die Durchfuhr, der Durchgang (*also fig.*); Durchgangsverkehr, (*fig.*) Übergang (*to*, zu); *in –*, beim Transport, auf der Fahrt, unterwegs. **––camp,** das Durchgangslager. **––duty,** *s.* der Durchgangszoll. **––hotel,** das Passantenhotel. **––visa,** das Durchreisevisum. **–ion** [–'zɪʃn], *s.* der Übergang; *–ion period*, die Übergangsperiode; *–ion stage*, das Übergangsstadium. **–ional** [–'zɪʃənl], *adj.* Übergangs–. **–ive** ['trænzɪtɪv], *adj.* übergehend (*also fig.*); transitiv (*Gram.*). **–oriness** ['trænzɪtərɪnɪs], *s.* die Vergänglichkeit, Flüchtigkeit. **–ory** ['trænzɪtərɪ], *adj.* vergänglich, flüchtig.

translat–able [træns'leɪtəbl, trænz'leɪtəbl], *adj.* übersetzbar. **–e** [træns'leɪt, trænz'leɪt], *v.a.* übersetzen, übertragen (*also fig.*); (*fig.*) umsetzen; versetzen (*a bishop, etc.*); (*archaic*) entrücken, befördern; aufarbeiten, umarbeiten, ummodeln (*into*, in *or* zu) (*Tech.*). **–ion** [–'leɪʃn], *s.* die Übersetzung, Übertragung; (*archaic, esp. Eccl.*) Versetzung, Entrückung. **–or,** *s.* der Übersetzer, Dolmetscher.

transliterat–e [trænz'lɪtəreɪt], *v.a.* transkribieren. **–ion** [–'reɪʃn], *s.* die Transkription, Umschreibung.

translucen–ce [trænz'lu:səns], *s.*, **–cy,** *s.* das Durchscheinen, die Halbdurchsichtigkeit. **–t,** *adj.* durchscheinend; halbdurchsichtig; (*fig.*) hell.

transmarine [trænzmə'rɪ:n], *adj.* überseeisch, Übersee–.

transmigrat–e [trænzmaɪ'greɪt], *v.n.* auswandern, übersiedeln, wegziehen, wandern (*as souls*). **–ion** [–'greɪʃn], *s.* die Auswanderung, Übersiedelung; *–ion of souls*, die Seelenwanderung. **–ory** [–'maɪgrətərɪ], *adj.* wegziehend, wandernd, Wander–.

transmissi–bility [trænzmɪsɪ'bɪlɪtɪ], *s.* die Übertragbarkeit. **–ble** [–'mɪsɪbl], *adj.* übertragbar, übersendbar (*to*, auf). **–on** [–'mɪʃn], *s.* die Verschickung, Übersendung, Übermittlung, Mitteilung; der Versand, die Spedition (*C.L.*); Beförderung, Weitergabe; Überlassung, Übertragung (*also Rad. & Mech.*), Transmission, das Getriebe (*Mech.*), die Sendung (*Rad.*), Fortpflanzung (*Phys.*); Vererbung (*Biol.*), Überlieferung (*of texts, etc.*); *–on gear*, das Triebwerk, Vorgelege; *–on shaft*, die Triebwelle.

transmit [trænz'mɪt], *v.a.* überschicken, übersenden, übermitteln, überliefern (*to* (*Dat.*)); befördern, weitergeben (*telegrams, etc.*); überlassen, hinterlassen (*property*) (*to* (*Dat.*)), übertragen (*to*, auf); vermitteln, mitteilen (*impressions*) (*to* (*Dat.*)); weiterleiten, fortleiten, verbreiten (*waves, etc.*), durchlassen (*light, heat*), übertragen, senden (*Rad.*); vererben (*to* (*Dat.*)). **–ter** [–'mɪtə], *s.* der Übersender; Sender (*Rad.*). **–ting,** *adj.* Sende– (*Rad.*); *–ting station*, der Sender (*Rad.*).

transmut–ability [trænzmju:tə'bɪlɪtɪ], *s.* die Umwandelbarkeit. **–able** [–'mju:təbl], *adj.* umwandelbar. **–ation** [–'teɪʃn], *s.* die Verwandlung, Umwandlung; Umbildung, Transmutation (*Biol.*). **–e** [–'mju:t], *v.a.* verwandeln, umwandeln (*into*, in (*Acc.*)).

transoceanic [trænzoʊʃɪ'ænɪk], *adj.* überseeisch, Übersee–; *– flight*, der Ozeanflug.

transom ['trænsəm], *s.* das Querholz, der Querbalken das Oberlicht (*Amer.*).

transparen–ce [træns'pɛərəns, trænz'pɛərəns], **–cy,** *s.* die Durchsichtigkeit, Transparenz; das Transparent(bild), Leuchtbild. **–t,** *adj.* durchsichtig, (*also fig.*), transparent, lichtdurchlässig, durchscheinend, lasierend; klar (*also fig.*); (*fig.*) offenkundig, hell; offen, ehrlich; *–t colour*, die Lasurfarbe.

transpierce [trænz'pɪ:əs], *v.a.* durchbohren.

transpir–ation [trænspə'reɪʃn, trænzpə'reɪʃn], *s.* die Ausdünstung, der Schweiß. **–e** [–'paɪə], 1. *v.a.* ausdünsten, ausschwitzen. 2. *v.n.* ausgedünstet werden, ausdunsten; (*fig.*) durchsickern, bekannt *or* ruchbar werden, verlauten, verlautbaren; (*often, though incorrect*) sich ereignen.

transplant [træns'plɑ:nt trænz'plɑ:nt], 1. *v.a.* umpflanzen; (*fig.*) verpflanzen, versetzen. 2. *v.n.* sich umpflanzen lassen. **–ation** [–plən'teɪʃn], *s.* die Umpflanzung; (*fig.*) Verpflanzung, Versetzung.

transport, 1. [træns'pɔ:t], *v.a.* transportieren, befördern, versenden, fortschaffen, fortbringen; deportieren (*criminals, etc.*); (*fig.*) hinreißen, entzücken; *be –ed with*, außer sich, entzückt *or* hingerissen sein von; *– a p. back*, einen zurückversetzen. 2. ['trænspɔ:t], *s.* der Transport, die Beförderung, Überführung, Fortschaffung, Spedition, der Versand; Troß (*Mil.*); Truppentransporter, das Transportschiff, Truppenschiff; Transportflugzeug; (*fig.*) Entzücken, die Hitze, Leidenschaft; *go into –s* (*of joy*), vor Freude außer sich *or* in Entzücken geraten; *Minister of –*, der Verkehrsminister; *– of rage*, rasende Wut. **–ability** [–ə'bɪlɪtɪ], *s.* die Transportfähigkeit, Versandfähigkeit. **–able** [–'pɔ:təbl], *adj.* versendbar, transportierbar. **–ation** [–'teɪʃn], *s.* die Beförderung, Fortschaffung, Versendung, Verschickung, Überführung, der Transport; Deportierung, Landesverweisung (*of criminals*). **––charges,** *pl.* Speditionskosten, Transportkosten (*pl.*). **–er** [–'pɔ:tə], *s.* der Beförderer; die Transportvorrichtung. **––worker,** *s.* der Transportarbeiter.

transpos–al [træns'poʊzl, trænz'poʊzl], *s.* die Umstellung. **–e,** *v.a.* umstellen, umsetzen, umlagern, verstellen, versetzen (*also Typ.*); transponieren (*Mus.*). **–ition** [–pə'zɪʃn] *s.* das Umstellen; die Umstellung, Umlagerung, Versetzung; Transposition (*Mus.*).

trans-ship [trænz'ʃɪp], *see* **tranship.**

transubstantiat–e [trænsəb'stænʃɪeɪt], *v.a.* verwandeln (*also Eccl.*), umwandeln. **–ion** [–'eɪʃn], *s.* die (Substanz– *or* Stoff)Umwandlung, Transsubstantiation (*Eccl.*).

transud–ation [trænsju'deɪʃn], *s.* die Aussonderung, Absonderung. **–e** [–'sju:d], 1. *v.n.* durchsickern, dringen. 2. *v.a.* absondern.

transvers–al [trænz'və:sl], 1. *adj.* querhindurchgehend, Quer–. 2. *s.* die Transversale. **–e** [–'və:s, 'trænzvə:s], 1. *adj.* quer, querlaufend, Quer–, diagonal; *–e section*, der Querschnitt. 2. *s.* die Querachse.

[1]**trap** [træp], 1. *s.* die (Tier)Falle; (*fig.*) Falle, Schlinge, der Fallstrick; Hinterhalt (*Mil.*), Betrug, Kniff; Fänger, Ableiter, Gasverschluß, Wasserverschluß (*for drains, etc.*); die Lüftungstür; leichter zweirädiger Wagen; (also *––door*) die Falltür, Versenkung (*Theat.*); (*sl.*) die Klappe (*mouth*); *fall* or *walk into the –*, in die Falle gehen; *lay* or *set a –*, eine Falle stellen (*for a p.*, einem). 2. *v.a.* fangen; (*fig.*) ertappen; gegen Gase verschließen *or* abschließen (*a pipe, etc.*). 3. *v.n.* Fallen setzen. **––ball,** *s.* der Schlagball. **––door,** *s.* die Falltür. **–per,** *s.* der Fallensteller; Trapper, Pelztierjäger.

[2]**trap,** *s.* (*coll.*) (*usually pl.*) das Gepäck, die Habe, Siebensachen (*pl.*).

[3]**trap,** *s.* der Trapp (*Geol.*).

trapes [treɪps], *v.n.* (*coll.*) umherschlendern, umherziehen, bummeln.

trapez–e [trə'pɪ:z], *s.* das Trapez (*Circus*), Schwebereck (*Gymn.*). **–iform** [–'pɪ:zɪfɔ:m], *adj.* trapezförmig. **–ium** [–'pɪ:zɪəm], *s.* das Trapez (*Math.*); viereckiger Handwurzelknochen (*Anat.*). **–oid** ['træpəzɔɪd], *s.* das Trapezoid (*Math.*).

trapper, see [1]**trap.**

trappings ['træpɪŋz], *pl.* das Pferdegeschirr, der Pferdeschmuck, (*fig.*) der Putz, Schmuck, Staat.

trapse, *see* **trapes.**
trash [træʃ], 1. *s.* der Abfall, Auswurf, Ausschuß, Plunder, Schund (*also fig.*), Schofel; (*fig.*) Kitsch (*as books*); der Unsinn, das Blech. 2. *v.a.* beschneiden, entblättern. **–iness**, *s.* die Wertlosigkeit, Minderwertigkeit. **–y**, *adj.* wertlos, minderwertig, kitschig, Kitsch–, Schund–, schofel, schoflig.
trauma [ˈtrɔːmə], *s.* die Wunde, Verletzung (*Med.*), seelische Erschütterung, das Trauma. **–tic** [–ˈmætɪk], *adj.* traumatisch; *–tic neurosis*, durch Schreck entstandene nervöse Störung.
travail [ˈtræveɪl], 1. *v.n.* (*rare*) kreißen, in Wehen liegen; (*archaic*) sich mühen *or* plagen, schwer arbeiten. 2. *s.* (Geburts)Wehen (*pl.*), das Kreißen; (*archaic*) mühevolle Arbeit; (*usually fig.*) *be in – with*, schwer zu ringen haben mit.
travel [ˈtrævl], 1. *v.n.* reisen (*also C.L.*), eine Reise machen; fahren; (*fig.*) sich ausdehnen; bewegen, hin und her gehen, wandern (*Mech.*); (*coll.*) sich schnell bewegen, sausen. 2. *v.a.* bereisen, durchreisen, durchwandern; durchlaufen, zurücklegen (*a distance*). 3. *s.* das Reisen; die Bewegung, der Lauf, Hub (*Mech.*); *pl.* Reisen (*pl.*), Wanderungen (*pl.*); *be on one's –s*, auf Reisen sein; *book of –s*, die Reisbeschreibung. **– -agency**, *s.* das Reisebüro. **– -guide**, *s.* der Reiseführer. **–led**, *adj.* weit gereist; bewandert, erfahren. **–ler**, *s.* der Reisende(r), *m.*; die Laufkatze (*Mach.*); *commercial –ler*, Geschäftsreisende(r), *m.*, Handlungsreisende(r), *m.*; *fellow –ler*, (politischer) Mitläufer; *–ler's cheque*, der Reisescheck; *–ler's joy*, Deutsche Waldrebe (*Bot.*); *–ler's tale*, die Münchhausiade. **–ling**, 1. *adj.* Reise–, Wander–. 2. *s.* das Reisen; *–ling bag*, der Reisekoffer; *–ling clock*, die Reiseuhr; *–ling crane*, der Laufkran; *–ling companion*, der Reisegefährte, Mitfahrende(r), *m.*; *–ling expenses*, Reisekosten, Reisespesen; *–ling rug*, die Reisedecke; *–ling-scholarship*, das Reisestipendium.
travers–able [ˈtrævəsəbl], *adj.* Rechtseinwand zulassend; überschreitbar; durchkreuzbar, passierbar. **–e**, 1. *adj.* quer, querlaufend. 2. *s.* das Querstück, Querholz, der Querriegel, Querbalken, die Querschwelle; Galerie, der Quergang (*Arch.*); die Traverse (*also Tech. & Mount.*), Schulterwehr, der Querwall, Querdamm (*Fort.*); Zickzackkurs, die Querfahrt (*Naut.*); Leugnung, der Rechtseinwand (*Law*); (*fig.*) der Querstrich, das Hindernis, die Widerwärtigkeit. 3. *v.a.* durchgehen (*also fig.*), durchwandern, durchreiten, durchfahren, durchziehen, durchqueren, durchkreuzen (*also fig.*); (*fig.*) behandeln; bestreiten, widersprechen (*Dat.*); leugnen (*Law*); zurücklegen (*distance*); schwenken, seitwärts richten (*guns*). 4. *v.n.* traversieren (*of horse, also Mount.*), seitwärts ausfallen (*Fenc.*); eine Traverse machen (*Fort.*), sich drehen (*Mech.*). **–er**, *s.* der Leugner (*Law*); die Drehscheibe (*Railw.*). **–e-sailing**, *s.* der Koppelkurs, Zickzackkurs. **–e-table**, *s.* die Logtafel (*Naut.*).
travesty [ˈtrævəstɪ], 1. *s.* die Travestie. 2. *v.a.* travestieren, karikieren.
trawl [trɔːl], 1. *s.* (also *– -net*) das (Grund)Schleppnetz. 2. *v.n.* mit dem Schleppnetz fischen. 3. *v.a.* schleppen (*the net*), im Schleppnetz fangen (*fish*). **–er**, *s.* der Fischdampfer.
tray [treɪ], *s.* das Teebrett, Kaffeebrett, Servierbrett, Tablett; der Präsentierteller; der (Koffer)-Einsatz (*in a trunk*); *loading– –*, die Ladeschale (*of a gun*). **– -cloth**, *s.* die Tablettdecke.
treacher–ous [ˈtrɛtʃərəs], *adj.* verräterisch, treulos, falsch (*to*, gegen), trügerisch, unsicher (*as ice*), unzuverlässig (*as memory*), tückisch (*as a dog*). **–ness**, *s.* die Treulosigkeit. **–y**, *s.* der Verrat (*to*, an), die Falschheit, Tücke, Treulosigkeit.
treacl–e [ˈtrɪːkl], *s.* der Sirup, die Melasse. **–y**, *adj.* sirupartig, (*fig.*) süßlich, salbungsvoll.
tread [trɛd], 1. *ir.v.n.* treten, trampeln ((*up*)*on*, auf); schreiten; sich paaren (*of birds*); – (*up*)*on*, treten auf, zertreten; – *on air*, wie auf Wolken gehen; – *on s.o.'s corns* or *toes*, einem auf die Hühneraugen treten; – *in his footsteps*, in seinen Fußstapfen treten; – *on a p.'s heels*, einem auf den Fersen folgen. 2. *v.a.* betreten, beschreiten; treten, begatten (*a hen*); – *the boards*, als Schauspieler auftreten; – *grapes*, Trauben keltern; – *the ground*, gehen; – *a measure*, tanzen; – *a path*, einen Weg gehen; sich (*Dat.*) einen Weg bahnen; – *water*, Wasser treten; – *down*, niedertreten; zertreten; – *out*, austreten (*fire*); – *under foot*, niedertreten, zertreten; (*fig.*) vernichten. 3. *s.* der Tritt, Schritt, Gang, die Gangart; Schuhsohle (*of a shoe*); Lauffläche (*of a tyre*); Trittstufe, das Trittbrett, der Tritt (*of a step*); Hahnentritt (*in eggs*); die Begattung, das Treten (*of fowls*); Laufband (*Mach.*). **–le** [ˈtrɛdl], 1. *s.* das Trittbrett, der Fußhebel; das Pedal (*Cycl.*). 2. *v.a. & n.* treten. **–mill**, *s.* die Tretmühle.
treason [ˈtrɪːzn], *s.* der (Landes)Verrat (*against* or *to*, an *or* gegen); *high –*, der Hochverrat. **–able** [–zənəbl], *adj.* verräterisch, Hochverrats–. **–ableness**, *s.* die Verräterei.
treasur–e [ˈtrɛʒə], 1. *s.* der Schatz (*also fig.*), Schätze (*pl.*), Reichtümer (*pl.*), (*fig.*) die Kostbarkeit, Seltenheit; (*coll.*) *a perfect –e*, eine wahre Perle. 2. *v.a.* (hoch)schätzen, hegen, werthalten; (usually *–e up*) (auf)bewahren, sammeln, aufhäufen. **–e-house**, *s.* die Schatzkammer. **–er** [–rə], *s.* der Schatzmeister, Kassier(er), Kassenwart; (*Lord*) *High –er*, Lord Oberschatzmeister. **–ership**, *s.* das Schatzmeisteramt, Kassieramt. **–e-trove**, *s.* herrenloser Schatz. **–y** [–rɪ], *s.* die Schatzkammer, der Staatsschatz; das Schatzamt, Finanzministerium (*in England*); (*fig.*) die Anthologie, Blumenlese; *First Lord of the –y*, der Präsident des Schatzamtes. **–y bench**, *s.* die Ministerbank (*in House of Commons*). **–y bill**, *s.* kurzfristiger Schatzwechsel. **–y bond**, *s.* die Schatzanweisung. **–y Department**, *s.* das Finanzministerium (*Amer.*). **–y note**, *s.* der Schatzwechsel; Reichskassenschein.
treat [trɪːt], 1. *v.a.* behandeln, umgehen mit, (ärztlich) behandeln (*for*, wegen *or* auf) (*Med.*); bearbeiten (*with*, mit) (*Chem., etc.*); – *a p. to s.th.*, einen bewirten, freihalten *or* traktieren *or* einem aufwarten mit etwas, einem etwas spendieren; – *o.s. to s.th.*, sich etwas leisten. 2. *v.n.*; – *of*, handeln von, behandeln, erörtern; – *with*, verhandeln, unterhandeln mit. 3. *s.* die Bewirtung, der Schmaus, das Fest; der Ausflug; (*fig.*) Hochgenuß, die Freude; *it is my –*, es geht auf meine Rechnung; *stand* (*a*) –, zum besten geben, traktieren, bewirten. **–ise** [–ɪz], *s.* die Abhandlung, Monographie. **–ment**, *s.* (ärztliche) Behandlung, die Kur (*Med.*); das Verfahren, die Handhabung; Bearbeitung; *under –ment*, in Behandlung (*Med.*).
treaty [ˈtrɪːtɪ], *s.* der Vertrag, die Verhandlung, Unterhandlung; *be in – with s.o. for a th.*, in Unterhandlungen mit einem wegen einer S. stehen; *commercial –*, der Handelsvertrag; *peace –*, der Friedensvertrag. **– -port**, *s.* der Vertragshafen. **– powers**, *pl.* Vertragsmächte (*pl.*).
treble [ˈtrɛbl], 1. *adj.* dreifach; Diskant–, Sopran– (*Mus.*); hoch, schrill; – *clef*, der Violinschlüssel; – *figures*, dreistellige Zahlen. 2. *s.* das Dreifache; der Diskant, Sopran, die Sopranstimme. 3. *v.a.* (*& n.* sich) verdreifachen.
trecento [treɪˈtʃɛntou], *s.* das 14. Jahrhundert (*Art.*).
tree [trɪ], 1. *s.* der Baum; Stamm, Schaft (*Tech.*); *boot– –*, der Stiefelleisten; *fruit– –*, der Obstbaum; *as the – is, so is the fruit*, der Apfel fällt nicht weit vom Baum; *family* or *genealogical –*, der Stammbaum; (*B.*) – *of Knowledge*, der Baum der Erkenntnis; – *of life*, der Lebensbaum (*Bot.*); Baum des Lebens (*Eccl.*); (*coll.*) *at the top of the –*, in höchster Stellung, an oberster Spitze *or* erster Stelle; *not see the wood for the –s*, den Wald nicht vor Bäumen sehen; (*coll.*) *up a –*, in der Klemme *or* Patsche, schlimm dran. 2. *v.n.* aufbäumen. 3. *v.a.* auf einen Baum treiben (*an animal*), auf den Leisten schlagen (*shoes*); (*fig.*) in Verlegenheit bringen. **– -creeper**, *s.* der Baumläufer. **– -frog**, *s.* der Laubfrosch. **–less**, *adj.* baumlos. **– -line**, *s.* die Baumgrenze. **– -louse**, *s.* die Blattlaus. **– -nail**, *s.* der Döbel, Dübel, langer Holzstift. **– -pipit**, *s.* der Baumpieper. **– -top**, *s.* der Wipfel.
trefoil [ˈtrɛfɔɪl], *s.* der Klee (*Bot.*), das Dreiblatt, spitzes Kleeblatt (*Arch.*).
trek [trɛk], 1. *v.n.* (mit *or* im Ochsenwagen) ziehen, trekken, trecken, reisen, wandern. 2. *s.* der Auszug, Treck, die Wanderung. **– -ox**, *s.* der Zugochse.

trellis ['trɛlɪs], 1. *s.* das Gitter, Gatter; Spalier (*for plants*). 2. *v.a.* vergittern; am Spalier ziehen (*Hort.*); *-ed window*, das Gitterfenster. **--work,** *s.* das Gitterwerk, Lattenwerk.

trembl-e ['trɛmbl], 1. *v.n.* zittern (*also fig.*), zucken, beben (*also of the earth*) (*with*, vor); flattern (*as leaves*); (*fig.*) erschrecken, ängstlich werden (*at*, bei), fürchten, in Furcht sein (*for*, um *or* für); *-e all over*, am ganzen Leibe zittern; *-e in the balance*, in der Schwebe sein; *-e to think*, bei dem Gedanken zittern. 2. *s.* das Zittern; (*coll.*) *be all of a -e*, am ganzen Leibe zittern; *in a -e*, zitternd. **-er,** *s.* der Selbstunterbrecher, Schwingungshammer (*Elec.*). **-ing,** *adj.* zitternd; *-ing grass*, das Zittergras (*Bot.*); *-ing poplar*, die Zitterpappel, Espe, Aspe (*Bot.*).

tremendous [trɪ'mɛndəs], *adj.* furchtbar, fürchterlich, entsetzlich, schrecklich; (*usually coll.*) ungeheuer, riesig, kolossal.

trem-olo ['trɛməlou], *s.* das Tremolo (*Mus.*). **-or** ['trɛmə], *s.* das Zittern, Beben, Zucken; (*coll.*) die Furcht, Angst, Erregung. **-ulous** [-mjələs], *adj.* zitternd, bebend; nervös, furchtsam. **-ulousness,** *s.* das Zittern.

trenail, *s. see* **tree-nail.**

trench [trɛntʃ], 1. *v.a.* mit Gräben durchziehen, tief graben, umgraben, rigolen (*land*), durch Gräben befestigen, verschanzen (*Mil.*). 2. *v.n.* Gräben ziehen *or* ausheben; Schützengräben anlegen *or* ausheben; - (*up*)*on*, beeinträchtigen, übergreifen auf, eingreifen in. 3. *s.* der Graben, die Rinne, Furche; der Schützengraben, Laufgraben (*Mil.*); *cut -es*, Gräben ziehen *or* ausheben; *mount the -es*, die Schützengräben beziehen. **--coat,** *s.* der Regenmantel, Wettermantel, Trenchcoat. **--fever,** *s.* das (Schützen)Grabenfieber. **--feet** *or* **-foot,** *s.* der Fußbrand (*Med.*). **--mortar,** *s.* der Minenwerfer. **--warfare,** *s.* der Stellungskrieg.

trenchan-cy ['trɛntʃənsɪ], *s.* die Schärfe. **-t** [-ənt], *adj.* (ein)schneidend, scharf, entschieden, durchdringend, wirksam, schneidig.

trencher ['trɛntʃə], *s.* das Tranchierbrett, Schneidebrett; (*fig.*) die Tafel, Nahrung. **--cap,** *s.* viereckige Studentenmütze. **-man,** *s.* (starker) Esser.

trend [trɛnd], 1. *s.* (allgemeine) Neigung *or* Richtung, die Tendenz, der Gang, Lauf, das Streben. 2. *v.n.* sich neigen, streben (*towards*, in der Richtung nach), sich erstrecken, in eine bestimmte Richtung laufen *or* abgehen, eine bestimmte Richtung haben; streichen (*Geol.*).

[1]**trepan** [trɪ'pæn], *v.a.* in einer Falle fangen, bestricken, überlisten.

[2]**trepan,** 1. *s.* der Schädelbohrer (*Surg.*), die Bohrmaschine (*Min.*). 2. *v.a.* trepanieren.

trepidation [trɛpɪ'deɪʃn], *s.* das (Glieder)Zittern, Zucken (*Med.*); die Angst, Bestürzung, nervöse Unruhe.

trespass ['trɛspəs], 1. *v.n.* Land widerrechtlich betreten; sich vergehen, sündigen (*against*, wider *or* gegen); - *against*, übertreten, zuwiderhandeln; - *upon*, zu sehr *or* über Gebühr in Anspruch nehmen, mißbrauchen. 2. *s.* unbefugtes Betreten, der Übergriff, unbefugter Eingriff (*on*, in); der Mißbrauch (*on* (*Gen.*)); das Vergehen, die Übertretung, Sünde. **-er,** *s.* der Übertreter, Rechtsverletzer; *-ers will be prosecuted*, Durchgang, Eintritt *or* unbefugtes Betreten bei Strafe verboten.

tress [trɛs], 1. *s.* die (Haar)Flechte, Locke. 2. *v.a.* flechten, binden (*hair*). **-ure** [-ʊə], *s.* das Haarband.

trestle ['trɛsl] *s.* das (Bock)Gestell, der Bock, Schragen, das Gerüst.

tret [trɛt], *s.* die Gewichtsvergütung, Refaktie, das Gutgewicht (*C.L.*).

trews [tru:z], *pl.* (*Scots*) die Hose; *a pair of* -, eine Hose.

triable ['traɪəbl], *adj.* verhörbar, verhandlungsreif (*a case*), belangbar, verfolgbar (*a p.*) (*Law*).

triad ['traɪæd], *s.* die Dreiheit; die Dreieinigkeit; Dreiwertigkeit, dreiwertiges Element (*Chem.*); der Dreiklang (*Mus.*).

trial ['traɪl], *s.* der Versuch, die Probe (*of*, mit), Prüfung; das Verhör, die Anklage, der Prozeß, gerichtliche Untersuchung, das Gerichtsverfahren (*Law*); Probefahrt (*Motor.*), der Probeflug (*Av.*), die (Schicksals)Prüfung, Heimsuchung; Sorge, der Kummer; (*coll.*) die Plage, Belästigung; *commit for* -, dem Schwurgericht überweisen *or* übergeben; - *and error*, die Regula Falsi (*Math.*); *give s.o. a* -, einen Versuch machen mit einem; einen prüfen; *give a th. a* -, etwas ausprobieren *or* erproben; *make a* -, eine Probe anstellen; *make a - of*, erproben, ausprobieren, versuchen; - *by jury*, die Schwurgerichtsverhandlung; *he is a great - to us*, er ist unsere große Sorge; *by way of* -, versuchsweise; *on* -, zur Prüfung, auf Probe; *be on* or *stand* -, unter Anklage stehen (*for*, wegen); *put on* or *bring to* -, vor Gericht stellen; *under* -, vor Gericht *or* unter Anklage gestellt; - *flight*, der Probeflug; - *run*, die Probeaufführung (*Theat.*); - *trip*, die Probefahrt.

triang-le ['traɪæŋgl], *s.* das Dreieck (*Geom.*), der Triangel (*Mus.*). **-ular** [-'æŋgjʊlə], *adj.* dreieckig, dreiwinklig. **-ularity** [-'lærɪtɪ], *s.* dreieckige Form. **-ulate** [-'æŋgjʊleɪt], *v.a.* triangulieren, in Dreiecken vermessen (*land*). **-ulation** [-'leɪʃn], *s.* die Triangulation, Dreiecksaufnahme (*Surv.*).

trias ['traɪəs], *s.* die Trias(formation) (*Geol.*). **-sic** [-'æsɪk], *adj.* Trias-.

trib-al ['traɪbl], *adj.* Stammes-. **-alism** [-bəlɪzm], *s.* die Stammesorganisation, das Stammessystem; Stammesgefühl. **-e** [traɪb], *s.* der Stamm; das Geschlecht; die Klasse, Tribus (*Bot.*, *Zool.*); (*coll.*) Zunft, Clique, Sippe. **-esman** [-zmən], *s.* der Stammesgenosse.

tribulation [trɪbju'leɪʃn], *s.* die Trübsal, Drangsal, das Leiden.

tribun-al [traɪ'bju:nəl, trɪ'bju:nəl], *s.* der Richterstuhl (*also fig.*), Gerichtshof, das Gericht, (*fig.*) Tribunal. **-ate** ['trɪbjənət], *s.* das Tribunat (*Anc. Hist.*). **-e** ['trɪbju:n], *s.* der (Volks)Tribun (*Anc. Hist.*); (*fig.*) öffentlicher Verteidiger *or* Beschützer; die Rednerbühne, die Tribüne; Apsis, der Bischofsthron. **-eship,** *s.* das Tribunat.

tribut-ary ['trɪbjətərɪ], 1. *adj.* tributpflichtig, abgabepflichtig, zinspflichtig (*to* (*Dat.*)); beisteuernd (*to*, zu); Neben- (*as a river*); *be -ary to*, sich ergießen in (*of a river*). 2. *s.* Tributpflichtige(r), Zinspflichtige(r), *m.*; der Nebenfluß. **-e** ['trɪbju:t], *s.* der Tribut (*also fig.*); Zins, Zoll, die Abgabe, Steuer; (*fig.*) die Ehrung, Huldigung, Hochachtung; *hold s.o. to -e*, sich (*Dat.*) einen tributpflichtig halten; *lay s.o. under -e*, sich (*Dat.*) einen tributpflichtig machen; *pay one's* or *a -e*, seinen Tribut zollen (*to* (*Dat.*)); *-e of respect*, die Achtungsbezeigung. **-e-money,** *s.* der Zinsgroschen.

tricar ['traɪkɑ:], *s.* dreirädriger Kraftwagen.

trice [traɪs], *s.*; *in a* -, im Nu *or* Handumdrehen.

triceps ['traɪseps], *s.* dreiköpfiger Muskel (*Anat.*).

trichin-a ['trɪkɪnə], *s.* die Trichine. **-osis,** [-'nousɪs] *s.* die Trichinose, Trichinenkrankheit.

trichoma [trɪ'koumə], *s.* die Behaarung (*Bot.*).

trichord ['traɪkɔ:d], 1. *adj.* Dreisaiten-. 2. *s.* das Dreisaiteninstrument (*Mus.*).

trichotomy [trɪ'kɔtəmɪ], *s.* die Dreiteilung, Dreiheit.

trick [trɪk], 1. *s.* der Kniff, Trick, die List; Täuschung, Illusion; der Scherz, Spaß, dummer Streich, die Posse; der Kunstgriff, das Kunststück; die Eigenheit, Eigentümlichkeit, üble Angewohnheit; der Stich (*Cards*); der Dienst (am Steuer) (*Naut.*); *pl.* Schliche, Ränke, Winkelzüge (*pl.*); (*coll.*) *the whole bag of -s*, der ganze Kram; *be up to one's -s*, Unfug or dumme Streiche machen; *be up to a p.'s -s*, jemandes Schliche durchschauen; *dirty* or *mean* -, gemeiner Streich; (*coll.*) *do the* -, den Zweck erreichen; *know the* -, den Kniff kennen; *know a - worth two of that*, noch gerissener sein; *play s.o. a* - or *play a - on a p.*, einem einen Streich spielen; *play -s*, Unfug *or* Mätzchen machen; *-s of the trade*, besondere Kunstgriffe. 2. *v.a.* betrügen; prellen (*out of*, um), verführen, verleiten (*into doing*, zu tun); - *up* or *out*, (auf)putzen, schmücken; **-ery,** *s.* die Gaunerei, der Betrug. **-iness,** *s.* die Verschmitztheit, List (*of a p.*); Kompliziertheit, Schwierigkeit (*of a th.*). **-ish,** *adj.* (*rare*) *see* **-y.** **-ster,** *s.* der Schwindler, Gauner. **-sy,** *adj.* schalkhaft, schelmisch. **-y,** *adj.* schlau, listig,

verschmitzt, durchtrieben (*of a p.*); (*coll.*) schwierig, verwickelt, heikel, verflixt (*of a th.*).
trickle ['trɪkl], 1. *v.n.* sickern, rieseln, sintern, tröpfeln, träufeln; (*coll.*) langsam rollen (*of a ball*). 2. *s.* das Tröpfeln, Rieseln; der Tropfen. **--charger,** *s.* das Akkumulator-Ladegerät, der Trockengleichrichter (*Elec.*).
triclinic [traɪ'klɪnɪk], *adj.* triklin (*of crystals*).
tricolour ['trɪkʌlə], *s.* die Trikolore.
tricot ['trɪkoʊ], *s.* der & das Trikot, das Trikot-(kleidungsstück).
tricuspid [traɪ'kʌspɪd], *adj.* Dreikuspidal- (*Anat.*).
tricycl-e ['traɪsɪkl], 1. *s.* das Dreirad. 2. *v.n.* Dreirad fahren. **-ist** [-klɪst], *s.* der Dreiradfahrer.
trident ['traɪdənt], *s.* der Dreizack, dreizackiger Speer. **-al** [-əntl], *adj.* dreizackig.
trie-d [traɪd], *see* **try**; *adj.* erprobt, bewährt, zuverlässig. **-r** ['traɪə], *s.* (*coll.*) strebsamer Mensch.
triennial [traɪ'ɛnɪəl], *adj.* dreijährig, dreijährlich.
trierarchy ['traɪərɑːkɪ], *s.* die Dreiherrschaft, Trierarchie.
trifl-e ['traɪfl], 1. *s.* die Kleinigkeit, Lappalie; süßer Auflauf (*Cook.*); *mere -e*, bloße Kleinigkeit; *a -e odd*, etwas *or* ein wenig merkwürdig; *not stick at -es*, sich nicht mit Kleinigkeiten abgeben. 2. *v.n.* tändeln, spielen, scherzen; sein Spiel treiben; *he is not to be -ed with*, er läßt nicht mit sich spaßen, mit ihm ist nicht zu spaßen *or* fackeln. 3. *v.a.* (usually *-e away*) vertändeln, vertrödeln. **-er,** *s.* der Tändler, Müßiggänger. **-ing,** *adj.* tändelnd, spielend; geringfügig, unbedeutend, läppisch. **-ingness,** *s.* die Geringfügigkeit, Bedeutungslosigkeit.
trifoli-ate [traɪ'foʊlɪət], *adj.* dreiblätt(e)rig. **-um,** [-'foʊlɪəm], *s.* die Gattung der Kleegewächse (*Bot.*).
trifori-um [traɪ'fɔːrɪəm], *s.* die auf Säulen gestützte Gallerie (*Arch.*).
trifurcate ['traɪfəːkeɪt], 1. *adj.* dreizackig, dreigablig. 2. *v.a.* (*& n.*) (sich) in drei Teile gabeln.
¹**trig** [trɪg], 1. *v.a.* hemmen (*wheels*); *- up*, stützen. 2. *s.* der Hemmschuh, Hemmkeil, Hemmklotz.
²**trig,** *adj.* nett, schmuck.
³**trig,** *s.* (*coll.*) *abbr. for* **trigonometry.**
trigger, *s.* der Abzug, Drücker (*of a gun*), Auslöser (*Phot.*); *pull the -*, abdrücken.
triglyph ['trɪglɪf, 'traɪglɪf], *s.* der Triglyph, die Triglyphe, der Dreischlitz (*Arch.*).
trigonometr-ic(al) [trɪgənə'mɛtrɪk(l)], *adj.* trigonometrisch. **-y** [-'nɔmətrɪ], *s.* die Trigonometrie.
trihedral [traɪ'hiːdrəl], *adj.* dreiflächig, dreiseitig.
trilateral [[traɪ'lætərəl], *adj.* dreiseitig.
trilby ['trɪlbɪ], *s.* (also *- hat*) weicher (Filz)Hut.
trilinear [traɪ'lɪnɪə], *adj.* dreizeilig.
trilingual [traɪ'lɪŋgwəl], *adj.* dreisprachig.
trill [trɪl], 1. *s.* der Triller. 2. *v.a. & n.* trillern (*Mus.*); rollen (*Phonet.*); *-ed r*, das Zungen-r, gerolltes r.
trillion ['trɪlɪən], *s.* die Trillion (= 10^{18}), (*Amer.*) die Billion (= 10^{12}).
trilobate [traɪ'loʊbeɪt], *adj.* dreilappig (*Bot.*).
trilogy ['trɪlədʒɪ], *s.* die Trilogie.
trim [trɪm], 1. *adj.* ordnungsmäßig, ordentlich, gut in Ordnung; hübsch, nett, schmuck. 2. *s.* die Ordnung, Bereitschaft, richtiger *or* ausgerüsteter Zustand, richtige Verfassung; richtige Stellung (*of sails*), richtige Verstauung (*of cargo*), die Schwimmlage, Gleichgewichtslage, der Trimm (*Naut. & Av.*); der Putz, Staat; das Harrschneiden; *in fighting -*, gefechtsbereit; *in fine* or *good -*, in bester Verfassung; *in sailing -*, segelfertig. 3. *v.a.* ordnen, in Ordnung bringen, zurechtmachen; schmücken, putzen (*also a lamp*), garnieren, besetzen (*hats, etc.*); schneiden, pflegen, stutzen (*hair, etc.*); beschneiden, zurechtschneiden (*hedges, etc.*); behauen, zurichten (*stone*); schüren (*the fire*); stellen, setzen, brassen (*sails*), trimmen (*sails or boat*); vorteilhaft verstauen (*cargo*); *- one's sails to every wind*, (*fig.*) den Mantel nach dem Winde hängen; *- up*, aufputzen. 4. *v.n.* die Mitte halten; schwanken, sich anpassen; *- with the times*, Opportunistenpolitik treiben, mit den Zeiten gehen, sich den Zeiten anpassen. **-mer,** *s.* die Besatznäherin, Putzmacherin; der Wechselbalken (*Arch.*); Kohlentrimmer; (*fig.*) Opportunist, Achselträger. **-ming,** *s.* das Aufputzen; Beschneiden; der Besatz, die Garnitur, Einfassung, Borte; *pl.* Besatzartikel, Borten, Posamenten (*pl.*) (*for dress*); die Garnierung, Beilage, Zutaten (*pl.*) (*for food*); die Verteilung, Verstauung, das Trimmen; (*fig.*) die Achselträgerei; *-ming flap*, die Trimmklappe (*Av.*); *-ming tank*, die Trimmzelle (*submarine*). **-ness,** *s.* gute Ordnung; die Sauberkeit, Nettigkeit, Niedlichkeit, gutes Aussehen.
trimester [trɪ'mɛstə], *s.* das Trimester (*Univ.*).
trimeter ['trɪmɪtə], *s.* der Trimeter (*Metr.*).
trin-al ['traɪnl], *adj.* dreifach. **-e** [traɪn], 1. *adj.* *see* **-al.** 2. *s.* der Gedrittschein, Trigonalschein, Trigonalaspekt (*Astrol.*).
trinit-arian [trɪnɪ'tɛərɪən], 1. *adj.* Dreieinigkeits-. 2. *s.* der Trinitarier. **-arianism** [-ɪzm], *s.* die Dreieinigkeitslehre. **-y** ['trɪnɪtɪ], *s.* die Dreieinigkeit (*Eccl.*), (*fig.*) Dreiheit; *-y Sunday*, der Sonntag Trinitatis; *-y term*, das Sommersemester.
trinket ['trɪnkɪt], *s.* das Schmuckstück; *pl.* Schmucksachen (*pl.*), der Schmuck, das Geschmeide; der Tand, Flitterkram.
trinomial [traɪ'noʊmɪəl], 1. *adj.* dreigliedrig, dreinamig. 2. *s.* dreigliedrige Größe; das Trinom.
trio ['triːoʊ], *s.* das Trio (*Mus., also fig.*); (*fig.*) das Kleeblatt (*of persons, etc.*). **-de** ['traɪoʊd], *s.* die Dreielektrodenröhre (*Rad.*). **-let** ['triːəlɛt], *s.* das Triolett, achtzeiliges Ringelgedicht.
trip [trɪp], 1. *s.* der Ausflug, die Tour, (Vergnügungs)Reise, (See)Fahrt; das Straucheln, Stolpern; Vergehen, der Fehltritt; das Beinstellen; *go on, make* or *take a -*, einen Ausflug machen. 2. *v.a.* (also *- up*) ein Bein stellen (*Dat.*), zu Fall bringen, (*fig.*) ertappen, erwischen (*in*, bei) (*a p.*); vereiteln, zunichte machen (*a plan*); lichten (*an anchor*). 3. *v.n.* trippeln, tänzeln; (also *- up*) straucheln, stolpern, fehltreten, ausgleiten, (*fig.*) sich vergehen *or* irren, fehlgehen, einen Fehltritt tun. **--hammer,** *s.* der Schmiedehammer. **--lever,** *s.* der Auslösehebel. **--wire,** *s.* der Trampelfaden, Stolperdraht. **-per,** *s.* der Ausflügler, Tourist. **-ping,** 1. *adj.* trippelnd, hüpfend, leicht, schnell, flink, munter; stolpernd; *catch a p. -ping*, einen bei einem Irrtum ertappen. 2. *s.* das Hüpfen; Beinstellen (*Footb.*); *-ping device*, die Sperrvorrichtung, der Auslöser.
tripartite [traɪ'pɑːtaɪt], *adj.* dreiteilig, Dreier-.
tripe [traɪp], *s.* Kaldaunen (*pl.*); Flecke (*pl.*) (*Cook.*); (*sl.*) der Unsinn, Quatsch, Kitsch, Schund.
triphthong ['trɪfθɔŋ], 1. *s.* der Dreilaut, Triphthong (*Phonet.*).
triplane ['traɪpleɪn], *s.* der Dreidecker (*Av.*).
tripl-e ['trɪpl], 1. *adj.* dreifach; dreimal(ig), Drei-, Tripel-; dreiteilig (*Mus.*); *-e Alliance*, der Dreibund; *-e time*, der Tripeltakt. 2. *v.a.* verdreifachen. **-et** [-lət], *s.* der Satz von drei (Personen *or* Dingen), (*fig.*) das Kleeblatt, Trio; die Triole (*Mus.*), der Dreireim (*Metr.*); der Drilling; *pl.* Drillinge (*pl.*). **-ex** [-lɛks] 1. *adj.* dreifach. 2. *s.* (also *-ex glass*) splitterfreies Glas. **-icate** [-lɪkət], 1. *adj.* dreifach ausgefertigt. 2. *s.* dritte Ausfertigung, das Triplikat; *in -icate*, in dreifacher Ausfertigung *or* Ausführung. 3. [-lɪkeɪt], *v.a.* dreifach ausfertigen, verdreifachen. **-ication** [-'keɪʃn], *s.* die Verdreifachung.
tripod ['traɪpɔd], *s.* der Dreifuß, das Dreibein, Dreigestell; Stativ (*Phot.*).
tripoli ['trɪpəlɪ], *s.* der Trippel, Polierschiefer.
tripos ['traɪpɔs], *s.* höheres Schlußexamen (*Univ.*).
triptych ['trɪptɪk], *s.* das Triptychon.
trireme ['traɪərɪːm], *s.* die Trireme, Triere, der Dreiruderer.
trisect [traɪ'sɛkt], *v.a.* in drei gleiche Teile teilen. **-ion** [-'sɛkʃən], *s.* die Dreiteilung.
trisyllab-ic [traɪsɪ'læbɪk], *adj.* dreisilbig. **-le** [trɪ'sɪləbl], *s.* dreisilbiges Wort.
trite [traɪt], *adj.* abgedroschen, abgegriffen, abgenutzt, seicht, platt. **-ness,** *s.* die Abgedroschenheit, Seichtheit, das Alltägliche.
triton ['traɪtən], *s.* der Triton, Meergott.
triturat-e ['trɪtjureɪt], *v.a.* zerreiben, zermahlen, zerkleinern, zerquetschen, zerstoßen, pulverisieren, schlämmen. **-ion** [-'reɪʃn], *s.* die Zerreibung, Zerstoßung, Pulverisierung.
triumph ['traɪəmf], 1. *s.* der Triumph, Sieg (*over,*

über); die Siegesfreude (*at*, über), das Frohlocken; (*fig.*) glänzender Erfolg, die Errungenschaft; *in* –, triumphierend. 2. *v.n.* den Sieg davontragen, Sieger bleiben, siegen; frohlocken, jubeln, triumphieren (*over*, über); – *over*, besiegen, niederringen, überwinden, obsiegen über. **–al** [traɪˈʌmfəl], *adj.* Triumph–, Sieges–; *–al arch*, der Triumphbogen; *–al procession*, der Siegeszug. **–ant** [–ˈʌmfənt], *adj.* triumphierend; siegreich, glorreich, erfolgreich; jubelnd, frohlockend.
triumvir [traɪˈʌmvɪə], *s.* der Triumvir. **–ate** [–ˈʌmvɪrət], *s.* das Triumvirat, (*fig.*) das Dreigestirn.
triune [ˈtraɪuːn], *adj.* dreieinig.
trivet [ˈtrɪvɪt], *s.* der Dreifuß, (*coll.*) *as right as a* –, ganz in Ordnung, sauwohl.
trivial [ˈtrɪvɪəl], *adj.* gering(fügig), unbedeutend, nichtssagend, trivial, armselig, alltäglich, gewöhnlich, unerheblich. **–ity** [–ˈælɪtɪ], *s.* die Trivialität, Plattheit, Geringfügigkeit, Unerheblichkeit, Unbedeutendheit, Nebensächlichkeit.
troch–aic [troˈkeɪɪk], *adj.* trochäisch. **–ee** [ˈtroukɪː] *s.* der Trochäus.
trod [trɔd], **trodden** [trɔdn], *see* **tread.**
troglodyt–e [trɔgləˈdaɪt], *s.* der Höhlenbewohner, Troglodyt, (*fig.*) Einsiedler. **–ic** [–ˈdɪtɪk], *adj.* troglodytisch.
troika [ˈtrɔɪkə], *s.* die Troika, russisches Dreigespann.
[1]**troll** [troul], *s.* der Kobold, Troll, Unhold.
[2]**troll**, 1. *v.a.* (*archaic*) rollen, trudeln (*a ball, etc.*); trällern, im Rundgesang singen (*a song*); herumgehen lassen. 2. *v.n.* rollen, sich drehen, trudeln; trällern, einen Rundgesang anstimmen; mit der Schleppangel fischen (*for*, nach); 3. *s.* der Rundgesang; die Schleppangel.
trolley [ˈtrɔlɪ], *s.* der Karren; Förderkarren, Hund (*Min.*); die Draisine (*Railw.*); der Rolltisch, Teewagen; die Kontaktrolle (*of tramcar*); (*Amer.*) der Straßenbahnwagen. **––bus**, *s.* der Oberleitungsomnibus, O-Bus, Obus. **––car**, (*Amer.*) der Straßenbahnwagen. **––pole**, die Stromzuführungsstange.
trollop [ˈtrɔləp], 1. *v.n.* schlampen, schlumpen, schlunzen. 2. *s.* die Schlampe, Schlumpe, Schlunze.
trombon–e [ˈtrɔmboun], *s.* die Posaune. **–ist**, *s.* der Posaunenbläser.
troop [truːp], 1. *s.* der Trupp, Haufe, die Schar, der Beritt (*cavalry*); *pl.* Truppen (*pl.*); 2. *v.n.* sich scharen, sich sammeln; (*fig.*) (in Scharen) ziehen, strömen; – *away* or *off*, sich davonmachen, abziehen. 3. *v.a.*; – *the colours*, die Fahnenparade abnehmen; *–ing the colours*, die Fahnenparade. **––carrier**, *s.* das Truppentransportflugzeug. **–er**, *s.* der Reiter, Kavallerist; das Kavalleriepferd; *swear like a –er*, fluchen wie ein Türke. **––horse**, *s.* das Kavalleriepferd. **–ship**, *s.* das Truppentransportschiff.
trop–e [troup], *s.* bildlicher Ausdruck. **–ical** [–ɪkl], *adj.* figürlich, bildlich. **–ological** [–əˈlɔdʒɪkl], *adj.* metaphorisch, bildlich. **–ology** [–ˈpɔlədʒɪ], *s.* bildliche Ausdrucksweise.
troph–ied [ˈtroufɪd], *adj.* mit Trophäen geschmückt. **–y** [–fɪ], *s.* die Trophäe, Siegesbeute, das Siegeszeichen.
tropic [ˈtrɔpɪk], 1. *s.* der Wendekreis; *pl.* die Tropen. 2. *adj.*, **–al**, *adj.* tropisch, Tropen–; *–al disease*, die Tropenkrankheit; *–al fruit*, Südfrüchte (*pl.*); *–al heat*, tropische Hitze.
troposphere [ˈtroupəsfɪə], *s.* die Troposphäre.
trot [trɔt], 1. *s.* der Trott, Trab (*also fig.*); *at a* –, im Trabe. 2. *v.n.* trotten, traben (*of horses*), im Trab reiten (*of riders*); (*coll.*) – *along* or – *off*, davongehen, fortgehen, hingehen; (*coll.*) – *out*, vorführen, entfalten; anführen, vorbringen. 3. *v.a.* trotten *or* traben lassen. **–ter**, *s.* der Traber; *pigs' –ters*, Schweinsfüße, Schweinspfoten (*pl.*). **–ting**, *s.* das Trabrennen.
troth [trouθ], *s.* (*archaic*) die Treue, das Treuegelöbnis; *by* or *upon my* –, meiner Treu, wahrlich; *pledge one's* –, sein Wort geben (*to* (*Dat.*)), ewige Treue schwören; *plight one's* –, sich verloben; *plighted* –, die gelobte Treue.
troubadour [ˈtruːbədɔː], *s.* der Troubadour.
troubl–e [ˈtrʌbl], 1. *v.a.* stören, belästigen, behelligen, bemühen; Mühe machen, Unannehmlichkeiten, Kummer *or* Verdruß bereiten (*Dat.*); beunruhigen, verwirren, ängstigen, plagen, quälen, heimsuchen; anführen; trüben (*waters*); *be –ed about*, sich ängstigen über; *I will –e you to keep your mouth shut*, ich werde dich noch lange bitten, den Mund zu halten; *–e a p. for*, einen bemühen *or* bitten um; *–e one's head*, sich den Kopf zerbrechen (*about*, über); *be –ed in mind*, sich beunruhigen; (*fig.*) *–ed waters*, getrübte Verhältnisse; *pour oil on –ed waters*, Frieden stiften; *–ed with gout*, von der Gicht geplagt. 2. *v.n.* sich die Mühe machen, sich Umstände machen; sich beunruhigen *or* sorgen; *don't –e*, mach dir keine Umstände; *I shan't –e if*, ich werde beruhigt wenn. 3. *s.* die Sorge, der Kummer, Verdruß, das Unglück, Leid; die Bemühung, Mühe, Beschwerde, Unannehmlichkeit, Belästigung, Last, Schwierigkeit, Scherereі; der Fehler, Haken, Defekt, die Störung, Panne (*Tech.*); Unruhe, Aufruhr (*Pol.*); *ask* or *look for –e*, das Unglück herausfordern; *be a –e to s.o.*, einem zur Last fallen; *be in –e*, in Not *or* Verlegenheit *or* einer mißlichen Lage sein; *bring –e upon*, Unheil bringen über; *get into –e*, sich (*Dat.*) Unannehmlichkeit zuziehen, sich in die Nesseln setzen; *get a p. into –e*, einem Unannehmlichkeit bereiten; *give a p. –e*, einem Mühe verursachen; *make –e*, Schwierigkeiten machen; *put a p. to the –e*, einem die Mühe machen; *save o.s. the –e*, sich (*Dat.*) die Mühe ersparen; *take –e*, sich (*Dat.*) Mühe geben; *take the –e*, sich die Mühe nehmen *or* machen. **–er**, *s.* der Störenfried, Unruhestifter. **–esome**, *adj.* störend, beschwerlich, lästig; unbequem, unangenehm. **–esomeness**, *s.* die Lästigkeit, Beschwerlichkeit. **–ous**, *adj.* (*archaic*) unruhig, aufgeregt.
trough [trɔf], *s.* der Trog, Bottich, die Wanne; Mulde; Rinne, Vertiefung; der Tiefpunkt, das Tief (*Meteor.*); – *of the sea*, das Wellental.
trounce [trauns], *v.a.* prügeln, züchtigen, durchhauen, verwichsen.
troupe [truːp], *s.* die (Schauspieler)Truppe.
trouser–ing [ˈtrauzərɪŋ], *s.* der Hosenstoff. **–s** [–zəz], *pl.* (also *pair of –s*) die Hose, das Beinkleid. **––button**, *s.* der Hosenknopf. **––leg**, *s.* das Hosenbein. **––pocket**, *s.* die Hosentasche. **––press**, *s.* der Hosenstrecker.
trousseau [ˈtruːsou], *s.* die Aussteuer, (Braut)-Ausstattung.
trout [traut], *s.* die Forelle. **––fishing**, *s.* der Forellenfang. **––stream**, *s.* der Forellenbach.
trover [ˈtrouvə], *s.* rechtswidrige Inbesitznahme (*Law*); *action of* –, die Fundklage (*Law*).
trow [trau, trou], *v.n.* (*archaic*) glauben (*Dat.*), meinen.
trowel [ˈtrauəl], 1. *s.* die (Maurer)Kelle, der Ausheber (*Hort.*); (*coll.*) *lay it on with a* –, übertreiben, dick auftragen. 2. *v.a.* mit der Kelle glätten.
troy [trɔɪ], *s.* (also – *weight*) das Troygewicht (*1 lb. = 12 oz. = 372·25 gr.*).
truan–cy [ˈtruənsɪ], *s.* das Ausbleiben, Wegbleiben, (Schul)Schwänzen. **–t**, 1. *adj.* die Schule schwänzend, schulschwänzend, (*fig.*) zerstreut (*as thoughts*), müßig, träge. 2. *s.* der (Schul)Schwänzer; *play –t*, (die Schule) schwänzen.
truce [truːs], *s.* der Waffenstillstand, die (Waffen)-Ruhe; (*fig.*) das Ende, Aufhören. – *of God*, der Gottesfriede; *a – to . . . !* hör auf *or* Schluß mit . . . !
[1]**truck** [trʌk], 1. *v.n.* Tauschhandel treiben, handeln, schachern (*for*, um). 2. *v.a.* (aus)tauschen, vertauschen (*for*, gegen), eintauschen (*for*, für). 3. *s.* der Tausch(handel), (Tausch)Verkehr, Handel; Hausbedarf, Trödel, Plunder; das Gemüse (*Amer.*); *have no – with*, nichts zu tun haben mit. **–er**, **––farmer**, *s.* der Handelsgärtner, Gemüsegärtner (*Amer.*). **– system**, das Trucksystem, die Bezahlung der Arbeiter durch Waren.
[2]**truck**, *s.* der Blockwagen, Rollwagen, Handwagen, Handkarren; Förderwagen, Hund (*Min.*); die Lore, offener Güterwagen (*Railw.*); der Lastkraftwagen, das Lastauto; Untergestell, Radgestell, Drehgestell (*Railw.*); der Flaggenknopf (*Naut.*). **–age**, *s.* das Rollgeld, Wagengeld; der Wagentransport. **––driver**, *s.* der Wagenführer.

truckle, *v.n.* sich unterwerfen, fügen *or* demütigen, kriechen (*to*, vor). **--bed,** *s.* das Rollbett, Schiebebett.
truculen-ce [ˈtrʌkjələns], *s.* die Streitsucht, Händelsucht, Unversöhnlichkeit, Gehässigkeit. **-t,** *adj.* händelsüchtig, streitsüchtig, ausfällig, unversöhnlich, gehässig, bramarbasierend.
trudge [trʌdʒ], 1. *v.n.* mühsam zu Fuß gehen; – *along*, sich mühsam weiterschleppen. 2. *v.a.* mühsam durchwandern. 3. *s.* langer mühsamer *or* mühseliger Weg.
true [truː], 1. *adj.* (*of a p.*) wahr(haft), redlich, aufrichtig, zuverlässig; treu (*to* (*Dat.*)); (*of a th.*) echt, getreu; wahr, wirklich, richtig, genau, (regel)recht, rechtmäßig; – *as steel*, treu wie Gold; *it is – I did it*, ich habe es zwar, freilich *or* allerdings getan; – *bearing*, die Abweichung der Nordnadel; – *bill*, vom Schwurgericht bestätigte *or* für begründet erklärte Anklage; *come* –, sich bewahrheiten *or* bestätigen, sich erfüllen (*as dreams*); – *copy*, getreue Abschrift; – *course*, rechtweisender Kurs; – *friend*, treuer Freund; – *heir*, rechtmäßiger Erbe; *be – of*, zutreffen auf; *prove* (*to be*) –, sich bewahrheiten *or* als wahr erweisen; – *story*, wahre Geschichte; – *to*, in Einklang mit; – *to life*, lebenswahr; – *to myself*, mir selbst treu; – *to nature*, naturgetreu; – *to size*, maßgerecht; – *to type*, typisch, artgemäß; – *to one's word*, seinem Worte treu. – *weight*, richtiges *or* genaues Gewicht. 2. *adv.* wahrheitsgemäß, wahrhaftig; *breed* –. sich rasseecht vermehren. 3. *v.a.* (usually – *up*) zentrieren (*wheels*), ausrichten (*a bearing*). **--blue,** 1. *adj.* waschecht; standhaft, treu. 2. *s.* standhafter Anhänger. **--born,** *adj.* echt (von Geburt). **--bred,** *adj.* rasserein, rasseecht. **--hearted,** *adj.* treuherzig, treugesinnt. **--heartedness,** *s.* die Treuherzigkeit, treue Gesinnung. **--love,** *s.* das Lieb, Liebchen, Geliebte(r), *m. or f.*; *--lover('s) knot*, der Liebesknoten. **-ness,** *s.* die Wahrheit, Treue, Echtheit, Richtigkeit, Genauigkeit.
truffle [trʌfl], *s.* die Trüffel.
truism [ˈtruːɪzm], *s.* die Binsenwahrheit, der Gemeinplatz.
trull [trʌl], *s.* (*archaic*) die Dirne, Hure.
truly [ˈtruːlɪ], *adv.* aufrichtig, wahrheitsgemäß, wahrhaftig, offen (gesagt), wirklich, in der Tat; *yours* –, Ihr ergebener, hochachtungsvoll (*in letters*).
[1]**trump** [trʌmp], 1. *s.* der Trumpf (*Cards*; *also fig.*) *see also* **--card;** (*fig., coll.*) guter Kerl, der Prachtmensch; *no –s*, ohne Trümpfe; (*fig.*) *turn up –s*, sich als das beste erweisen (*a th.*), immer Glück haben (*a p.*). 2. *v.a.* (über)trumpfen (*also fig.*); (*fig.*) ausstechen, stechen. 3. *v.n.* Trumpf spielen, trumpfen. **--card,** *s.* die Trumpfkarte; *play one's --card*, den letzten Trumpf ausspielen.
[2]**trump,** *v.a.* (usually – *up*) erdichten, anzetteln, abkarten, zurechtschwindeln. **-ed-up,** *adj.* erfunden, erdichtet.
[3]**trump,** *s.* (*Poet.*) der Trompetenstoß; (*archaic*) die Trompete; – *of doom*, die Posaune des Jüngsten Gerichts.
trumpery [ˈtrʌmpərɪ], 1. *s.* der Trödel(kram), Plunder, Ramsch, die Ramschware, wertloses Zeug; das Geschwätz, der Quatsch. 2. *adj.* wertlos, belanglos, nichtssagend, Schund–.
trumpet [ˈtrʌmpɪt], 1. *s.* die Trompete; (*B.*) Posaune; der Schalltrichter; *blow one's own* –, sein eigenes Lob ausposaunen *or* singen; *ear-*–, das Hörrohr; *the last* –, die Posaune des Jüngsten Gerichts. 2. *v.a. & n.* trompeten (*also of elephants*), Trompete blasen; (also – *forth*) ausposaunen, laut verkünden. **--call,** *s.* das Trompetensignal. **--major,** *s.* der Stabstrompeter (*Mil.*). **-er,** *s.* der Trompeter; (*fig.*) Ausposauner; die Trompetentaube (*Orn.*). **--tongued,** *adj.* mit Posaunenstimme.
truncat-e [ˈtrʌnkeɪt], 1. *v.a.* stutzen, beschneiden, verstümmeln. 2. *adj.* abgestumpft, abgestutzt. **-ed,** *adj.* verstümmelt, abgekürzt, verkürzt; *-ed cone*, gestumpfter Kegel. **-ion** [–ˈkeɪʃn], *s.* die Stutzung, Verstümmelung.
truncheon [ˈtrʌnʃən], *s.* der (Polizei)Knüppel; (Feldherrn)Stab.
trundle [ˈtrʌndl], 1. *v.a.* rollen, wälzen, trudeln; schlagen (*a hoop*). 2. *v.n.* rollen, trudeln, sich wälzen. 3. *s.* die Rolle, Walze. **--bed,** *s.* das Rollbett.
trunk [trʌŋk], *s.* der (Baum)Stamm; Rumpf, Leib, Körper (*of men, etc.*); Torso (*Sculp.*); Schaft (*of a column*); Rüssel (*of an elephant*); Reisekoffer, die Kiste; *pl.* die Badehose; Kniehose (*Theat.*); *–s please!* Fernamt bitte! **--bending,** *s.* das Rumpfbeugen (*Gymn.*). **--call,** *s.* das Ferngespräch. **--exchange,** *s.* das Fernamt. **-fish,** *s.* der Kofferfisch. **--hose,** *pl.* die Kniehose (*Hist.*). **-less,** *adj.* rumpflos. **--line,** *s.* die Hauptstrecke, Hauptlinie (*Railw.*); die Fernleitung (*Phone*). **--road,** *s.* die Hauptstraße, Landesstraße, Autostraße.
trunnion [ˈtrʌnjən], *s.* der (Dreh)Zapfen; Schildzapfen (*Mil.*). **--hole,** *s.* das Schildzapfenlager. **--plate,** *s.* die Schildzapfenpfanne.
truss [trʌs], 1. *s.* das Bund, Bündel (= 60 *lb.*); Bruchband (*Surg.*); Rack (*Naut.*); Hängewerk, Gerüst (*Build.*) 2. *v.a.* zäumen (*poultry*); durch Hängewerk stützen (*Arch.*); (also – *up*) zusammenbinden, aufbündeln; festschnüren, (an)binden; (*archaic*) aufstecken, hochschürzen (*clothes*); aufhängen (*of a criminal*). **--beam,** *s.* der Eisenbalken. **--bridge,** *s.* die Gitterbrücke, Fachwerkbrücke. **--frame,** *s.* das Hängewerk.
trust [trʌst], 1. *s.* das Vertrauen, Zutrauen (*in*, auf), die Zuversicht, zuversichtliche Hoffnung *or* Erwartung, der Glaube; Trust, Ring, das Kartell (*C.L.*); der Kredit, Borg; anvertrautes Gut, die Treuhand, Pflegschaft (*Law*); Verwahrung, das Treuhandvermögen, der Treubesitz; *fulfil one's* –, seine Verpflichtung erfüllen; *in* –, zur Verwahrung, zu treuen Händen; *hold in* –, verwahren, verwalten; *breach of* –, der Treubruch, Vertrauensbruch; *position of* –, der Vertrauensposten; *on* –, auf Kredit *or* Borg; *take on* –, auf Treu und Glauben hinnehmen; *put one's – in*, sein Vertrauen setzen auf. 2. *v.a.* (ver)trauen, glauben (*Dat.*); sich verlassen auf (*Acc.*); anvertrauen ((*Dat.*); *with a th.*, etwas); zuversichtlich hoffen *or* erwarten, überzeugt sein; kreditieren, Kredit geben (*Dat.*); *I don't – him*, ich traue ihm nicht; – *me for that!* verlaß dich nur auf mich! – *him to lose his way*, es sieht ihm ähnlich, sich zu verirren; – *o.s. to s.o.*, sich einem anvertrauen. 3. *v.n.* Vertrauen haben, vertrauen *or* sich verlassen (*in* or *to*, auf), zuversichtlich hoffen *or* erwarten; – *in God*, sein Vertrauen auf Gott setzen. **--company,** *s.* die Treuhandgesellschaft. **--deed,** *s.* die Übertragungsurkunde eines Treuhandvermögens. **-ee,** *s.* der Treuhänder, Sachwalter, Verwalter, Kurator, Bevollmächtigte(r), Beauftragte(r), *m.*; *-ee in bankruptcy*, *official -ee*, der Konkursverwalter; *board of -ees*, das Kuratorium; *-ee stock*, mündelsichere Papiere (*pl.*). **-eeship,** *s.* die Treuhandverwaltung, Sachwalterschaft, das Kuratorium. **-ful,** *adj.* vertrauend, vertrauensvoll. **-fulness,** *s.* das Vertrauen. **--house,** *s.* von einem Trust verwaltetes Hotel. **-ification,** *s.* die Trustbildung, Vertrustung. **-iness,** *s.* die Treue, Zuverlässigkeit. **-ing,** *adj.* vertrauensvoll, vertrauenerwekkend; *too -ing*, vertrauensselig. **--money,** *s.* das Mündelgeld. **-worthiness,** *s.* die Zuverlässigkeit, Vertrauenswürdigkeit. **-worthy,** *adj.* zuverlässig, vertrauenswürdig. **-y,** *adj.* treu, zuverlässig.
truth [truːθ], *s.* die Wahrheit; Wirklichkeit, Echtheit, Treue, Genauigkeit, Richtigkeit; Wahrhaftigkeit, Aufrichtigkeit, Ehrlichkeit; *in* (*very*) –, (*archaic*) *of a* –, wahrhaftig; *home –s*, eindrückliche Wahrheiten; *tell s.o. some home –s*, einem gehörig die Meinung *or* Wahrheit sagen; *there is no – in it*, daran ist nichts Wahres; *that's the — of it*, das ist die volle Wahrheit; *out of* –, aus der richtigen Lage (*Tech.*); *tell the* –, die Wahrheit sagen; *to tell the* – or – *to tell*, um die Wahrheit zu sagen; – *to life*, die Lebenstreue. **-ful,** *adj.* wahrhaftig; ehrlich, wahrheitsliebend; wahrheitsgemäß, wahr, echt, getreu, genau. **-fulness,** *s.* die Wahrhaftigkeit, Wahrheitsliebe; Echtheit, Genauigkeit, Wahrheit. **--loving,** *adj.* wahrheitsliebend.

try [trɑɪ], 1. *ir.v.a.* es versuchen mit, einen Versuch machen mit, durch Versuch feststellen, ausprobieren, (durch)probieren; prüfen, erproben, auf die Probe stellen, auf eine harte Probe stellen; stark in Anspruch nehmen, anstrengen, angreifen (*eyes, etc.*), plagen, quälen, arg mitnehmen (*a p.*); versuchen, in Angriff nehmen; verhören, vor Gericht bringen *or* stellen (*a p.*) (*for*, wegen), untersuchen (*a case*) (*Law*); scheiden, reinigen, raffinieren (*metals*), rektifizieren (*spirit*), eichen (*standards*); – *one's best*, sein Bestes tun; – *the door*, die Tür zu öffnen suchen; – *one's hand*, seinen (ersten) Versuch machen (*at*, mit); – *one's hardest*, sich die größte Mühe geben, sein Äußerstes tun; – *one's luck*, sein Glück versuchen (*with*, bei); – *on*, anprobieren (*a coat, etc.*); (*sl.*) – *it on*, einen Versuch machen (*with*, bei); *don't – that on me*, machen Sie mir nichts vor; – *out*, ausprobieren, erproben; – *over*, durchprobieren, durchgehen (*music, etc.*). 2. *ir.v.n.* versuchen, einen Versuch machen, es versuchen; sich bemühen (*for*, um), trachten (*for*, nach). 3. *s.* der Versuch, die Probe; 3 Punkte (*Rugby Footb.*); *have a –*, versuchen, probieren (*at a th.*, etwas), einen Versuch machen (*at*, mit). **–ing,** *adj.* unangenehm, schwierig, belästigend, quälend (*a p.*); anstrengend (*to*, für), beschwerlich, mühsam (*a th.*); *be –ing*, auf die Nerven gehen (*to* (*Dat.*)). **– -on,** *s.* die Anprobe (*of clothes*); (*coll.*) der Versuch, Täuschungsversuch. **– -out,** *s.* die Erprobung, Probe, der Vorversuch. **–sail,** *s.* das Gaffelsegel. **– -square,** *s.* der Anschlagwinkel.

tryst [trɪst, trɑɪst], 1. *s.* die Verabredung, das Stelldichein; (*Scots*) der Viehmarkt. 2. *v.n.* sich verabreden. 3. *v.a.* hinbestellen (*a p.*), verabreden (*time*). **–ing,** *s.* die Verabredung. **–ing-place,** *s.* der Zusammenkunftsort, Treffpunkt, Ort des Stelldicheins.

tsar [zɑ:, tsɑ:], *s.* der Zar. **–evitch,** *s.* der Zarewitsch. **–ina,** *s.* die Zarin.

tsetse(-fly) [ˈtsetsɪ], *s.* die Tsetsefliege.

tub [tʌb], 1. *s.* das Faß, der Kübel, Zuber, Bottich, die Bütte, Balge, Kufe; der Förderkarren, Förderkorb (*Min.*); das Übungsboot (*Rowing*); (*coll.*) plumpes Schiff; (*coll.*) die Badewanne, das (Wannen)Bad; (*coll.*) *take a –*, baden. 2. *v.a.* in Kübel setzen (*plants*); (*coll.*) baden (*children*); (*sl.*) Ruderunterricht geben (*Dat.*). 3. *v.n.* baden; trainieren, rudern. **–by,** *adj.* tonnenartig; (*coll.*) dumpf *or* hohl klingend; (*coll.*) dickbäuchig, untersetzt. (*sl.*) **– -thumper,** *s.* der Hetzredner. (*sl.*) **– -thumping,** *adj.* eifernd, Hetz–.

tuba [ˈtjʊ:bə], *s.* die Baßtuba.

tube [tjʊ:b], *s.* die Röhre (*also, Bot., Anat.*), das Rohr; (usually *inner –*) der Schlauch (*Cycl., etc.*); die Tube (*of paint, etc.*); Londoner Untergrundbahn; (*Amer.*) die Radioröhre; *by –*, mit der Untergrundbahn; *glass –*, die Glasröhre; *rubber –*, der Gummischlauch; *speaking-–*, das Sprachrohr; *test-–*, das Probeglas (*Chem.*).

tuber [ˈtjʊ:bə], *s.* der Knollen, die Knolle (*Bot.*), der Knoten, die Schwellung (*Anat.*). **–cle** [ˈtjʊ:bəkl], *s.* kleine Knolle (*Bot.*); kleine Schwellung, kleiner Knoten (*Anat.*); der *or* die (Lungen)-Tuberkel (*on the lungs*). **–cular** [tjʊˈbə:kjʊlə], *adj.* warzig, höckerig, knotig (*Bot.*), tuberkulös, Tuberkel– (*Path.*). **–culosis** [–ˈloʊsɪs], *s.* die Tuberkulose. **–culous** [–ˈbə:kjʊləs], *adj.* tuberkulös, Tuberkel–. **–ose** [ˈtjʊ:bəroʊs], 1. *s.* die Tuberrose, Nachthyazinthe (*Bot.*). 2. *adj. see* **–ous. –osity** [–ˈrɔsɪtɪ], *s.* die Schwellung, der Knoten. **–ous** [ˈtjʊ:bərəs], *adj.* knotig, knollig, höckerig.

tub-ing [ˈtjʊ:bɪŋ], *s.* das Röhrenmaterial; Röhrenwerk, die Röhrenanlage, Rohrleitung; (*coll.*) das Stück Röhre; Röhren (*pl.*); *rubber –ing*, der Gummischlauch. **–ular** [–bjələ], *adj.* rohrförmig, röhrenförmig, Röhren–. **–ule** [–jʊ:l], *s.* das Röhrchen.

tuck [tʌk], 1. *s.* die (Quer)Falte, der Saum, Umschlag (*in dresses, etc.*); die Gillung (*Naut.*); (*sl.*) Süßigkeiten (*pl.*), gutes Essen; *make or take a – in*, eine Falte legen in. 2. *v.a.* in Falten legen (*material*), einschlagen (*a tuck*), umlegen, umnähen (*a hem*); (*fig.*) stecken, klemmen; – *away*, wegstecken; unterbringen, verstauen; verstecken; verbergen; – *in*, einschlagen, einnähen (*cloth, etc.*); – *up*, aufschürzen, aufschlagen, aufstecken; – *up one's sleeves*, die Ärmel aufkrempeln *or* hochstreifen; – *a p. up in bed*, einen im Bett fest einpacken *or* einwickeln. 3. *v.n.* (sich in) Falten legen, sich zusammenziehen; (*sl.*) – *in*, tüchtig zugreifen, schmausen. **–er,** 1. *s.* der Faltenleger (*sewing machine*); (*coll.*) *bib and –er*, der Sonntagsstaat. 2. *v.n.* (*sl.*) *be quite –ered out*, gänzlich erledigt sein (*Amer.*). (*sl.*) **– -in,** *s.* der Schmaus, die Schmauserei. (*sl.*) **– -shop,** *s.* die Konditorei, das Schokoladengeschäft.

Tuesday [ˈtjʊ:zdeɪ], *s.* der Dienstag; *on –*, am Dienstag; *on –s*, dienstags.

tuf-a [ˈtjʊ:fə], *s.* der (Kalk)Tuff, Tuffstein. **–aceous** [–ˈfeɪʃəs], *adj.* Tuff–, Tufa–. **–f** [tʌf], *s. see* **–a.**

tuft [tʌft], *s.* der Büschel, Busch, Schopf; die Quaste, Troddel; – *of hair*, der Haarbüschel, Haarschopf. **–ed** [–ɪd], *adj.* büschelig. (*coll.*) **– -hunter,** *s.* der Streber, Schmarotzer, Speichellecker. **–y,** *adj.* büschelig.

tug [tʌg], 1. *s.* heftiger Zug *or* Ruck, das Zerren, Ziehen; (*fig.*) die Anstrengung, erbitterter Kampf (*for*, um); (also *– -boat*) der Schlepper, Schleppdampfer, Bugsierdampfer (*Naut.*); *give a – at*, heftig ziehen an. 2. *v.a.* heftig ziehen, reißen, zerren; schleppen (*Naut.*). 3. *v.n.* heftig ziehen (*at*, an (*Dat.*)); (*fig.*) sich anstrengen *or* Mühe geben. **– -of-war,** *s.* das Seilziehen; (*fig.*) wogender Kampf (*for*, um).

tuition [tjʊ:ˈɪʃn], *s.* der Unterricht; die Belehrung; *private –*, der Privatunterricht, Privatstunden (*pl.*). **–al,** *adj.*, **–ary,** *adj.* Unterrichts–.

tula [tʊ:lə], *s.* das Tula, Niello.

tulip [ˈtjʊ:lɪp], *s.* die Tulpe. **– -tree,** *s.* der Tulpenbaum, die Magnolie.

tulle [tyl, tʊl], *s.* der Tüll.

tulwar [ˈtʊlwɑ:], *s.* indischer Säbel.

tumble [ˈtʌmbl], 1. *v.n.* (hin)fallen, stürzen, purzeln; sich wälzen *or* herumwerfen, Purzelbaum schlagen; – *down*, einstürzen, einfallen, hinunterstürzen, niederfallen; – *in*, einstürzen, (*coll.*) zu Bett gehen; – *on*, stoßen auf; – *out of bed*, aus dem Bett herausfallen; eilig aufstehen; – *over*, umfallen, hinfallen, niederfallen; – *over a th.*, über etwas fallen *or* stolpern; – *over each other*, sich überschlagen; – *to pieces*, in Stücke fallen; (*coll.*) – *to a th.*, etwas plötzlich begreifen *or* erfassen. 2. *v.a.* zu Fall bringen, umwerfen, niederwerfen, (um)-stürzen; in Unordnung bringen; – *a p. out of*, einen schleudern *or* (hinaus)werfen aus. 3. *s.* der Sturz, Fall; die Unordnung, das Durcheinander; der Purzelbaum; *rough and –*, die Rauferei. **– -down,** *adj.* baufällig.

tumbler [ˈtʌmblə], *s.* das (Trink)Glas, der Becher; Akrobat, Gaukler; der Tümmler, die Purzeltaube (*Orn.*); Nuß (*on guns*); Zuhaltung (*of locks*). **– -spring,** *s.* die Zuhaltungsfeder. **– -switch,** *s.* der Kippschalter.

tumbr-el, –il [ˈtʌmbrɪl], *s.* der Schuttkarren; Munitionswagen (*Artil.*).

tume-facient [tjʊ:mɪfeɪsɪənt], *adj.* aufschwellend, anschwellend. **–faction** [–ˈfækʃn], *s.* die Anschwellung; Geschwulst. **–fy** [tjʊ:mɪfɑɪ], 1. *v.a.* anschwellen lassen. 2. *v.n.* anschwellen, aufschwellen. **–scent** [–ˈmɛsənt], *adj.* angeschwollen, aufgeschwollen.

tumid [ˈtjʊ:mɪd], *adj.* geschwollen, schwellend; (*fig.*) schwülstig, hochtrabend. **–ity** [–ˈmɪdɪtɪ], *s.* die Geschwollenheit; (*fig.*) Schwülstigkeit.

tummy [ˈtʌmɪ], *s.* (*coll.*) der Magen. **– -ache** *s.* das Bauchweh.

tumour [ˈtjʊ:mə], *s.* die Geschwulst, der Tumor.

tumular [ˈtjʊ:mjʊlə], *adj.* hügelförmig, hügelig.

tumult [ˈtjʊ:mʌlt], *s.* der Lärm, Tumult; Auflauf, Aufruhr, (*fig.*) die Erregung. **–uary** [–ˈmʌltjʊərɪ], *adj.* undiszipliniert, unordentlich, verworren; aufrührerisch, tumultuarisch. **–uous** [–ˈmʌltjʊəs], *adj.* lärmend, ungestüm, stürmisch, heftig. **–uousness,** *s.* stürmisches *or* lärmendes Wesen *or* Treiben.

tumul-us [ˈtjʊ:mjələs], *s.* (pl. **–i**) der Grabhügel, das Hügelgrab.

tun [tʌn], *s.* die Tonne (*as measure = 252 gallons = 1,145 l.*); das Faß.

tun–e [tjuːn], 1. *s.* die Melodie, Weise; (richtige) Stimmung (*of a piano, etc.; also fig.*); (*fig.*) der Einklang; *call the –e*, den Ton angeben *or* anschlagen; *catchy –e*, einnehmende Melodie; *change one's –e*, einen anderen Ton anschlagen, andere Saiten aufziehen, ein anderes Lied singen; *give us a –e*, sing *or* spiel uns eine Melodie; *in –e*, richtig gestimmt; (*fig.*) *be in –e with*, im Einklang stehen mit; (*fig.*) *be in –e with one another*, auf einander abgestimmt sein; *not in –e*, see *out of –e*; *sing in –e*, richtig *or* rein singen; *out of –e*, verstimmt; (*fig.*) *be out of –e with*, nicht überstimmen mit, in einem Mißverhältnis stehen zu; *sing out of –e*, unrichtig *or* unrein singen; *sing another –e*, auf ein anderes Loch pfeifen; *to the –e of*, nach der Melodie von; (*fig.*) in der Höhe *or* im Ausmaß von, von sage und schreibe. 2. *v.a.* stimmen; abstimmen (*to*, auf) (*also Rad.*); einstellen (*to*, auf) (*Rad.*); (*fig.*) anpassen (*to*, an); *–e in*, einstellen, abstimmen (*Rad.*); *–e out*, ausschalten, abstellen (*Rad.*); *–e up*, höher stimmen (*an instrument*); startbereit machen (*Av.*); (*fig.*) hinaufschrauben (*expectations, etc.*); *–ed circuit*, abgestimmter Kreis (*Rad.*). 3. *v.n.* singen, klingen, tönen; zu singen anfangen, anstimmen. **–eful,** *adj.* melodisch, wohlklingend. **–efulness,** *s.* der Wohlklang. **–eless,** *adj.* unmelodisch, mißtönend; klanglos, stumm. **–er,** *s.* der (Klavier)Stimmer; die Abstimmspule; der Abstimmknopf (*Rad.*). **–ing,** *s.* das Stimmen; die Abstimmung (*also Rad.*); Abstimmschärfe (*Rad.*); *–ing circuit*, der Abstimmkreis (*Rad.*); *–ing coil*, die Abstimmspule (*Rad.*); *–ing condenser*, der Abstimmkondensator (*Rad.*); *–ing fork*, die Stimmgabel (*Mus.*).

tungst–ate [ˈtʌŋsteɪt], *s.* das Wolframsäuresalz, Wolframat, wolframsaures Salz; *–ate of*, wolframsauer. **–en** [–stən], *s.* der Wolfram. **–ic,** *adj.* Wolfram–. **–ite,** *s.* der Wolframocker.

tunic [ˈtjuːnɪk], *s.* die Tunika (*Anc. Hist.*), der Kittel; Waffenrock (*Mil.*); (also *–a*) die Haut, das Häutchen (*Anat., Bot.*). **–ate,** *adj.* häutig (*Bot.*), Mantel– (*Zool.*). **––shirt,** *s.* (rockähnliches) Sporthemd.

tunnel [ˈtʌnl], 1. *s.* der Tunnel, die Unterführung, der Stollen, Schachtgang, unterirdischer Gang (*Min.*); *wind––*, der Windkanal (*Av.*). 2. *v.n.* (& *a.*) einen Tunnel anlegen *or* bauen *or* stechen (durch). **–ling,** *s.* der Tunnelbau; die Tunnelanlage.

tunny [ˈtʌnɪ], *s.* (also *––fish*) der Thunfisch.

tup [tʌp], 1. *s.* der Widder; Rammklotz, Rammbär, Hammerkopf. 2. *v.a.* bespringen, belegen (*of rams*).

tuppence [ˈtʌpəns], *s.* (*sl.*) see **twopence.**

turban [ˈtəːbən], *s.* der Turban.

turbary [ˈtəːbərɪ], *s.* das Torfmoor; Recht, Torf zu stechen (*Law*).

turbid [ˈtəːbɪd], *adj.* trüb, getrübt, dick, schlämmig; (*fig.*) verworren, verschwommen, unklar. **–ity** [–ˈbɪdɪtɪ], *s.*, **–ness,** *s.* die Trübung, Trübheit, Schlämmigkeit; (*fig.*) Verworrenheit.

turb–ine [ˈtəːbaɪn], *s.* die (Dampf– *or* Wasser)-Turbine. **–ojet,** *s.* die Strahlvortriebturbine (*Av.*).

turbot [ˈtəːbət], *s.* der Steinbutt (*Ichth.*).

turbulen–ce [ˈtəːbjʊləns], *s.* die Unruhe, der Sturm, Aufruhr, das Ungestüm. **–t,** *adj.* unruhig, stürmisch, ungestüm.

turd [təːd], *s.* (*vulg.*) das Stück Kot.

tureen [tjʊˈrɪːn], *s.* die Terrine, Suppenschüssel.

turf [təːf], 1. *s.* der Rasen, Rasenplatz; das Rasenstück, der Torf; *a –*, ein Stück Torf; *the –*, die Rennbahn; (*fig.*) das Pferderennen, der Rennsport. 2. *v.a.* mit Rasen belegen; (*sl.*) *– out*, hinausschmeißen. **––cutter,** *s.* der Torfstecher. **–y,** *adj.* rasenreich; torfartig.

turg–escence [təːˈdʒɛsəns], *s.* die Anschwellung, Aufgedunsenheit; (*fig.*) Schwulst, Schwülstigkeit, der Bombast. **–escent** [–ənt], *adj.* (an)schwellend, (*fig.*) schwülstig. **–id** [ˈtəːdʒɪd], *adj.* (an)geschwollen; aufgedunsen; (*fig.*) schwülstig, pomphaft, aufgeblasen. **–idity** [–ˈdʒɪdɪtɪ], *s.*, **–idness,** *s.* die Geschwollenheit; (*fig.*) Schwülstigkeit, der Schwulst.

turion [ˈtjʊrɪən], *s.* die Überwinterungsknospe, der Sprößling.

Turk [təːk], *s.* see *Index of Proper Names*; (*coll.*) der Schelm, unbändiger Junge. **–ey,** *s.* see *Index of Proper Names*; (also *–ey-cock*) der Puter, Truthahn; *as red as a –ey-cock*, puterrot; (also *–ey-hen*), die Pute, Truthenne; *–ey carpet*, türkischer Teppich; *–ey red*, das Türkischrot; (*Amer. coll.*) *talk –ey*, gerade heraus reden, mit der Sprache herauskommen. **–ish,** *adj.* see *Index of Proper Names*; *–ish bath*, das Schwitzbad, Dampfbad, die Sauna; *–ish delight*, türkisches Konfekt; *–ish towel*, das Frottier(hand)tuch.

turmeric [ˈtəːmərɪk], *s.* die Gelbwurz, Gilbwurz (*Bot.*); Turmerikwurzel, Kurkuma; das Kurkumagelb (*Dye.*); *– paper*, das Kurkumapapier (*Chem.*).

turmoil [ˈtəːmɔɪl], *s.* der Aufruhr, Tumult, die Unruhe.

turn [təːn], **1.** *v.a.* (um eine Achse) drehen, (her)-umdrehen; drehen, wenden (*also a coat, etc.*), kehren, richten (*to*, auf); (ver)ändern, wechseln, verwandeln, unwandeln, umändern, umtauschen (*into*, in (*Acc.*)); abwenden, abwehren, abbringen (*from*, von); übersetzen, übertragen (*into*, in); drechseln (*on a lathe*); formen, runden (*a sentence*); **(a)** (*with nouns*) *– one's back*, sich umdrehen; *– one's back on*, den Rücken kehren (*Dat.*), (*fig.*) im Stich lassen; *– the balance*, den Ausschlag geben; *– the other cheek*, dem Frieden dienen, etwas einstecken; (*coll.*) *– one's coat*, abtrünnig werden; *– colour*, die Farbe wechseln; *– the conversation*, die Unterhaltung ändern *or* wechseln; *– a corner*, um eine Ecke (herum)gehen *or* fahren; (*fig.*) *– the corner*, über den Berg kommen, die Krise überstehen *or* überwinden; *– a deaf ear*, sich taub stellen (*to*, gegen); *– the edge of*, abstumpfen; *– one's face*, sein Gesicht wenden; *– the enemy('s flank)*, den Feind umgehen; *– a glance*, einen Blick richten (*on*, auf); *– the ground*, das Land umgraben; *not – a hair*, ganz gelassen bleiben, die Dinge ruhig hinnehmen; *– one's hand to*, beginnen, in Angriff nehmen; *be able to – one's hand to anything*, zu allem zu gebrauchen sein; *– a p.'s head*, einem den Kopf verdrehen; *– head over heels*, einen Purzelbaum schlagen; *– the key*, zuschließen; *– the page*, die Seite umdrehen; *– the pages*, umblättern; *– an honest penny*, sich ehrlich durchschlagen (*by*, mit); *– the points*, die Weichen stellen; *– the scale*, den Ausschlag geben; *– one's steps*, gehen, seine Schritte lenken (*towards*, nach); *– s.o.'s stomach*, einem den Appetit verderben; *– the tables*, den Spieß umdrehen (*on*, gegen), der S. eine andere Wendung geben; *– tail*, davonlaufen; Fersengeld geben; *– one's thoughts*, seine Gedanken lenken *or* richten (*to*, auf); *– turtle*, kentern (*Naut.*), sich überschlagen, umkippen; **(b)** (*with adjectives*) machen; *– loose*, freimachen, freigeben, freilassen, befreien; **(c)** (*with adverbs & prepositions*) *– about*, umdrehen; *– adrift*, dem Winde und den Wellen preisgeben (*Naut.*), seinem Schicksal überlassen, auf die Straße setzen, fortjagen; *– s.o. against*, einen aufbringen, hetzen *or* verstimmen gegen; *– aside*, abwenden; *– away*, wegwenden, abwenden (*o.s.*); abweisen, fortschicken (*others*); *be –ed away*, keinen Eintritt finden; *– away money*, die Türe schließen müssen (*Theat.*); *– back*, zurückschicken, zur Umkehr veranlassen (*others*); umkehren (*o.s.*); *– down*, umbiegen, umlegen, herunterklappen, einschlagen (*a page*), herunterschrauben, kleinstellen (*gas, etc.*), abschwächen (*light*), aufschlagen (*a bed*), (*coll.*) abweisen, ablehnen (*offer, etc.*), (*coll.*) im Stich lassen, einen Korb geben (*Dat.*) (*a p.*); *– in*, einschlagen, nach innen biegen; verdecken, eingraben (*weeds, etc.*); einwärts *or* nach innen setzen (*one's feet*); (*sl.*) aufgeben, zurücklegen; *– in one's mind*, überlegen; *– inside out*, das Innere nach außen kehren; *– into money*, zu Geld machen, *– into ridicule*, lächerlich machen; *– off*, abstellen (*water, radio, etc.*), ausmachen, ausschalten (*light*), zudrehen (*a tap*), ablenken, abhalten, abwenden (*a th.*), fortschicken, entlassen (*a p.*); *– off with a laugh*, mit einem Scherz hinweggehen über; *– on*, andrehen, aufdrehen (*a tap*), anstellen (*water, radio, etc.*), anmachen, einschalten (*light*); (*coll.*)

anknipsen (*light, radio, etc.*); – *out*, auswärts wenden *or* setzen (*one's feet*); hinauswerfen, vertreiben, fortjagen (*a p.*); herstellen, produzieren, liefern (*goods*); hinaustreiben, auf die Weide treiben (*cattle*); ausräumen, leeren, gründlich reinmachen (*a room*); umkehren (*one's pockets*); stürzen (*government*); ausmachen (*light*); ausstatten, ausrüsten; (*coll.*) *be well –ed out*, gut angezogen sein, eine gute Erscheinung sein; – *out into the world*, in die weite Welt schicken; – *over*, umwenden, umdrehen (*a page, etc.*); übertragen, übergehen, überweisen, ausliefern (*to* (*Dat.*)); umsetzen (*money*) (*C.L.*); *please – over*, bitte wenden; – *over a new leaf*, ein neues Leben anfangen, sich bessern; – *over the pages*, die Seiten umblättern *or* umschlagen; ein Buch durchblättern; – *over in one's mind*, sich (*Dat.*) überlegen, sich durch den Kopf gehen lassen; – *round*, umdrehen, umkehren; – *a p. round one's little finger*, einen um den Finger wickeln; – *to* (*good*) *account*, sich zunutze machen, vorteilhaft verwenden, Nutzen ziehen aus, mit Nutzen verwenden; – *up*, nach oben wenden, umschlagen, aufschlagen; aufstecken (*a dress, etc.*); aufdecken (*a card*); weiter aufdrehen (*gas*); ans Licht bringen, ausgraben; (*sl.*) aufgeben, niederlegen, hinschmeißen (*a job, etc.*); (*sl.*) Übelkeit bereiten (*Dat.*); – *up one's nose at*, die Nase rümpfen über; (*coll.*) – *up one's toes*, abkratzen, hops gehen; – *upside down*, auf den Kopf stellen. **2.** *v.n.* sich (um die Achse) drehen, sich herumdrehen, wenden *or* kehren; sich umdrehen *or* umwenden, (sich) umkehren; gehen, sich begeben, seinen Weg nehmen, sich richten; sich abwenden; umschlagen (*as weather*); sich (ver)ändern, sich verwandeln ((*in*)*to*, zu), werden; **(a)** (*with adjectives*); gerinnen, sauer werden (*as milk*); sich drechseln lassen (*on a lathe*); *not know where to* –, nicht wissen was zu tun; *her head is –ed*, ihr ist der Kopf verdreht (*with*, von); – *Christian*, zum Christentum übertreten, Christ werden; *be –ed fifty*, gerade fünfzig sein; – *grey*, grau werden; – *homewards*, nach Hause zurückkehren; – *left!* links abbiegen! *the milk has –ed* (*sour*), die Milch ist sauer geworden; – *nasty*, unangenehm werden; – *soldier*, Soldat werden; *my stomach –s*, mir wird übel; *the tide has –ed*, die Flut hat sich gewendet, (*fig.*) das Blatt hat sich gewendet; – *traitor*, zum Verräter werden; *even a worm will* –, selbst ein Wurm krümmt sich; **(b)** (*with adverbs*) – *about*, sich umwenden *or* umdrehen, (sich) umkehren; – *aside*, sich abwenden; – *away*, sich abwenden; – *back*, zurückgehen, zurückkehren, umkehren; – *down*, nach unten gebogen sein; – *in*, sich einwärts wenden; eintreten, einkehren, hineingehen (*at*, durch); (*coll.*) schlafen *or* zu Bett gehen; – *off*, abbiegen, abzweigen, sich seitwärts wenden; – *out*, hinausgehen, hinausziehen (*from*, aus); sich auswärts wenden, auswärts gerichtet sein; in Streik treten, die Arbeit einstellen; werden, sich gestalten zu, sich erweisen, sich herausstellen, ablaufen, ausfallen, antreten, ausrücken (*Mil.*); – *out well*, einen guten Ausgang nehmen; – *over*, sich umdrehen (*in bed*); umschlagen, umkippen; – *round*, sich umdrehen; (*fig.*) sich anders besinnen; (*coll.*) – *to*, sich befleißigen, fleißig werden; – *up*, sich nach oben wenden, nach oben gerichtet sein, sich aufrichten; (*coll.*) zum Vorschein *or* ans Licht kommen, erscheinen, auftreten, auftauchen; sich heraustellen als; kommen; *wait for s.th. to – up*, sich abwartend verhalten; **(c)** (*with prepositions*) – *against*, sich wenden gegen; – *from*, sich wenden von; – (*in*)*to*, werden *or* sich verändern *or* verwandeln zu; übergehen *or* umschlagen in; – *on*, see – *upon*; – *on one's heel*(*s*), sich kurz umdrehen; – *to*, sich befassen mit (*a th.*); sich anschicken (*doing*, zu tun); sich wenden *or* richten an, seine Zuflucht nehmen zu, sich (*Dat.*) Rat holen bei (*a p.*); see also – *into*; – *to the left*, sich nach links wenden; – (*up*)*on*, sich drehen um, abhängen von; handeln von, zum Gegenstand haben. **3.** *s.* die (Um)-Drehung, der Umschwung; die Wendung (*also Av. & fig.*); der Lauf, Weg; die Krümmung, Windung, Biegung, Kurve; der Wechsel, die Veränderung; (*fig.*) Wende, der Wendepunkt, die Krise, Krisis; der Doppelschlag (*Mus.*); Umschlag (*C.L., also fig.*); kurzer (Spazier)Gang; die Reihenfolge, der Turnus, die (Arbeits)Schicht, der Dienst, die Gelegenheit (*for*, zu *or* für), herrschende Richtung, die Neigung, Eignung, das Talent (*for*, zu *or* für); die Form, Art, Beschaffenheit, Gestalt, der Zuschnitt; die Nummer (*Theat.*); (*coll.*) der Schreck, Nervenschock. **(a)** (*with nouns*) – *of the century*, die Jahrhundertwende; – *of the market*, der Marktumschlag; – *of mind*, die Denkart, Denkweise, geistiger Zuschnitt; – *of the scale*, der Ausschlag; – *of the tide*, der Wechsel der Gezeiten, (*fig.*) der Umschlag, die Wendung der Lage; **(b)** (*with adjectives*) *give a certain* –, eine gewisse Wendung geben (*to* (*Dat.*)); *do a p. a good* –, einem einen Dienst *or* eine Gefälligkeit erweisen; (*Prov.*) *one good – deserves another*, eine Liebe ist der andern wert; eine Hand wäscht die andere; *right –!* rechtsum! *right about –!* rechtsum kehrt! **(c)** (*with verbs*) *await one's* –, warten, bis man an die Reihe kommt; *it is my* –, ich bin an der Reihe, die Reihe ist an mir; *give s.o. a* –, einen an die Reihe nehmen, einen darannehmen; einem einen Schrecken einjagen; *serve one's* –, seinem Zweck dienen; *take a* –, einen (Spazier)Gang machen; *take a – at*, sich versuchen an, sich vorübergehend beschäftigen mit; *take one's* –, an die Reihe kommen; *take –s* (*at*), mit einander *or* sich abwechseln; *take a – for the worse*, sich zum Schlechtern wenden; **(d)** (*with prepositions*) *at every* –, auf allen Seiten, bei jeder Gelegenheit, auf Schritt und Tritt; *by –s* or *by – and – about*, nacheinander, abwechselnd; *in –*(*s*), der Reihe nach; *he in his* –, er als seine Gelegenheit kam *or* als er an die Reihe kam; *be on the* –, sich umwenden, umschlagen; *the tide is on the* –, die Gezeit wechselt, (*fig.*) die Lage bessert sich; *to a* –, aufs Haar tadellos; *when it comes to my* –, wenn die Reihe an mich kommt, wenn ich daran *or* an die Reihe komme. **––buckle,** *s.* die Spannvorrichtung, der Wirbel, Spanner. **–coat,** *s.* der Überläufer, Abtrünnige(r), *m.* **––down,** *attrib. adj.* Umlege–. **–ed,** *adj.* gedreht, gedrechselt; *–ed-down, see* **––down**; *–ed-up nose*, die Stülpnase. **–er,** *s.* der Dreher, Drechsler. **–ery,** *s.* die Drechslerei. **–ing,** *s.* das Drehen, Drechseln; die Drehung, Wendung, Windung, Biegung, Krümmung; Querstrasse; *–ing-lathe*, die Drehbank; *–ing movement*, die Umgehung (*Mil.*); *–ing-point*, die Wendemarke (*in races, etc.*), (*fig.*) der Wendepunkt. **–key,** *s.* der Schließer, Gefangenenwärter. (*coll.*) **––out,** *s.* die Aufmachung, Ausstattung, Ausstaffierung, äußere Erscheinung; die Gesamtproduktion, Gesamtherstellung (*C.L.*); Versammlung, Zuschauer, Besucher (*pl.*); die Arbeitseinstellung, der Ausstand (*of workers*). **–over,** *s.* der Umsatz (*C.L.*); die Umgruppierung, Umänderung, Veränderung, Verschiebung; *apple –over*, der Apfel im Schlafrock, die Apfeltasche (*Cook.*). **–pike,** *s.* die Zollschranke; der Schlagbaum; *–pike-man*, der Chausseegeldeinnehmer; *–pike-road*, die Landstraße, Chaussee. **––round,** *s.* der Umschlag (*of ship in port*). **–screw,** *s.* der Schraubenzieher. **–spit,** *s.* der Bratenwender. **–stile,** *s.* das Drehkreuz. **–table,** *s.* die Drehscheibe. **––up,** *s.* der Umschlag (*on trousers, etc.*).

turnip ['tə:nɪp], *s.* (weiße) Rübe; (*sl.*) große Taschenuhr. **––tops,** *pl.* das Rübenkraut.

turp–entine ['təp:əntaɪn], *s.* das Terpentin; (also *oil of –entine*) das Terpentinöl. **–s** [tə:ps], *s.* (*coll.*) abbr. for *oil of –entine*.

turpitude ['tə:pɪtju:d], *s.* die Schlechtigkeit, Schändlichkeit, Verworfenheit.

turquoise ['tə:kwɔɪz, 'tə:kɔɪz], *s.* der Türkis; das Türkisblau.

turret ['tʌrɪt], *s.* das Türmchen; der Geschützturm, Panzerturm (*Mil.*), die Kanzel (*Av.*). **–ed** [–ɪd], *adj.* betürmt. **––gun,** *s.* das Turmgeschütz. **––lathe,** *s.* die Revolverdrehbank.

turtle ['tə:tl], *s.* die (Meer)Schildkröte; *turn* –, kentern (*Naut.*), umschlagen, umkippen. **––dove,** *s.* die Turteltaube. **––soup,** *s.* die Schildkrötensuppe.

tush [tʌʃ], *int.* pah!

tusk [tʌsk], *s.* der Fangzahn, Stoßzahn, Eckzahn,

Hauzahn, Hauer. **–ed** [–t], *adj.* mit Hauern. **–er,** *s.* der Elefant *or* das Wildschwein mit ausgebildeten Stoßzähnen. **–y,** *adj. see* **–ed.**

tussle [ˈtʌsl], 1. *s.* das Ringen, der Kampf, Streit, die Rauferei, Balgerei. 2. *v.n.* kämpfen, ringen, sich balgen *or* raufen (*with*, mit; *for*, um).

tussock [ˈtʌsək], *s.* der Büschel (*of grass, etc.*).

tussore [ˈtʌsə], *s.* (also – *silk*) die Rohseide, Tussahseide.

tut [tʌt], *int.* Unsinn! dummes Zeug! ach was!

tutela–ge [ˈtjuːtɪlɪdʒ], *s.* die Unmündigkeit; (*fig.*) der Schutz, die Leitung. **–r** [–lə], *adj.*, **–ry** [–lərɪ], *adj.* schützend, Schutz–, Vormunds–, Vormundschafts–.

tutor [ˈtjuːtə], 1. *s.* der (Haus)Lehrer; Hofmeister; Vormund (*Scots Law*); (*college*) –, Studienleiter (*Univ.*); *private* –, Hauslehrer, (*coll.*) Einpauker. 2. *v.a.* unterrichten; erziehen, schulen. **–ial** [–ˈtɔːrɪəl], 1. *adj.* Lehrer–; *–ial college*, die Presse. 2. *s.* (*coll.*) die Arbeitsgemeinschaft, Studiengruppe (*Univ.*).

tuxedo [tʌkˈsiːdou], *s.* der Smoking (*Amer.*).

twaddle [ˈtwɔdl], 1. *s.* albernes Geschwätz *or* Gewäsch, der Unsinn, Quatsch. 2. *v.n.* schwatzen, quatschen.

twain [tweɪn], *adj.* (*archaic*) zwei; *in* –, entzwei.

twang [twæŋ], 1. *s.* gellender *or* scharfer Ton, das Schwirren; (also *nasal* –) näselnde Aussprache. 2. *v.n.* gellend klingen, schwirren (*of an arrow, etc.*). 3. *v.a.* zupfen (*violin string, etc.*).

tweak [twiːk], *v.a.* zwicken, kneifen.

tweed [twiːd], *s.* der Tweed; das Tweedkostüm, der Tweedanzug.

tweeny [ˈtwiːnɪ], *s.* (*coll.*) (also *––maid*), das Aushilfsmädchen.

tweezers [ˈtwiːzəz], *pl.* die Pinzette, Haarzange, Federzange; *a pair of* –, eine Pinzette.

twel–fth [twɛlfθ], 1. *num. adj.* zwölft. 2. *s.* der, die, *or* das Zwölfte; das Zwölftel; *–fth-night*, der Dreikönigsabend, das Dreikönigsfest. **–ve** [–lv], 1. *num. adj.* zwölf. 2. *s.* die Zwölf. **–vemo** [–vɪmou], *s.* das Duodez(format). **–vemonth,** *s.* das Jahr, die Jahresfrist; *this day –month(s)*, heute in *or* vor einem Jahr.

twent–ieth [ˈtwentɪəθ], 1. *num. adj.* zwanzigst. 2. *s.* der, die, *or* das Zwanzigste; das Zwanzigstel. **–y,** 1. *num. adj.* zwanzig. 2. *s.* die Zwanzig; *pl.* die zwanziger Jahre (*of a century*), die zwanziger Zahlen (*21 to 29*); *in his –ies*, in den Zwanzigern. **–yfold,** *adj.* zwanzigfach.

twice [twaɪs], *adv.* zweimal; doppelt, zweifach; – *the amount*, doppelter Betrag; *think* –, sich zweimal überlegen; *not think – about*, nicht lange überlegen (*doing*, zu tun), ohne Bedenken (tun). **––told,** *adj.* alt, oft erzählt.

twiddle [ˈtwɪdl], *v.a.* müßig herumdrehen, spielen mit; – *one's thumbs* or *fingers*, Daumen drehen, (*fig.*) die Hände in den Schoß legen.

[1]**twig** [twɪg], *s.* der Zweig, die Rute; Wünschelrute; (*sl.*) *hop the* –, hops gehen, von der Bühne verschwinden.

[2]**twig,** *v.a.* & *n.* (*sl.*) kapieren.

twilight [ˈtwaɪlaɪt], 1. *s.* das Zwielicht, Halbdunkel, die Dämmerung; *by* –, in der Dämmerung; – *sleep*, der Dämmerschlaf; – *of the gods*, die Götterdämmerung. 2. *adj.* dämmernd, Dämmerungs–, schwach erleuchtet, schattenhaft.

twill [twɪl], 1. *s.* der Köper. 2. *v.a.* köpern.

twin [twɪn], 1. *s.* der Zwilling. 2. *adj.* Zwillings–, doppelt, Doppel–, gepaart (*Bot., etc.*); (*fig.*) eng verwandt; – *brother*, der Zwillingsbruder; – *souls*, verwandte Seelen; **––cylinder,** *s.* der Doppelzylinder. **––engined,** *adj.* Zweimotoren–, zweimotorig. **––screw,** *adj.* Doppelschrauben–.

twine [twaɪn], 1. *s.* starker Bindfaden, der Zwirn, Strick, die Schnur; die Windung, das Geflecht. 2. *v.a.* zwirnen, zusammendrehen (*threads, etc.*); (ver)flechten, binden (*a wreath*); umschlingen, umwinden; (*fig.*) verflechten, verschlingen, (*one's fingers, etc.*); – *o.s. round*, sich schlingen um. 3. *v.n.* sich verflechten; sich winden *or* schlingen (*as plants*); sich schlängeln. **–r,** *s.* die Schlingpflanze.

twinge [twɪndʒ], 1. *s.* der Stich (*also fig.*), stechender Schmerz, das Stechen; – *of conscience*, der Gewissensbiß. 2. *v.a.* & *n.* stechen, zwicken, kneifen.

twinkl–e [ˈtwɪŋkl], 1. *v.n.* funkeln, blitzeln, blitzen, blinken (*with*, von), flimmern, aufblitzen, zwinkern (*of the eyes*). 2. *s.* das Funkeln, Blinzeln, Blitzen, Blinken, Zwinkern; *merry –e*, lustiges Zwinkern (mit den Augen). **–ing,** *s. see* **– 2**; *in the –ing* (*of an eye*), *in a –ing*, im Augenblick, im Nu, im Handumdrehen.

twirl [twəːl], 1. *s.* schnelle Umdrehung, der Wirbel; Schnörkel. 2. *v.a.* drehen, wirbeln, zwirbeln (*the moustache, etc.*), schwingen (*a stick*). 3. *v.n.* wirbeln, sich schnell drehen. **–ing-stick,** *s.* der Quirl.

twist [twɪst], 1. *v.a.* drehen; flechten, zwirnen (*threads*), winden, wickeln, schlingen; biegen, krümmen; (*fig.*) verflechten, verwickeln; verzerren, verziehen (*features*), verdrehen, entstellen (*meaning*); – *one's ankle*, den Fuß verrenken *or* umknicken; – *a p. round one's little finger*, einen um den Finger wickeln; *–ed barrel*, gezogener Lauf (*of a gun*). 2. *v.n.* sich drehen; sich winden (*also fig.*) *or* schlängeln (*as roads, rivers*); – *round*, sich umdrehen. 3. *s.* die Drehung, Windung (*also fig.*), Biegung, Krümmung; der Drall (*of barrel and thread*); das Effet (*on a ball*); das Geflecht, die Spirale; der Twist, das Maschinengarn (*Spin.*); die Rolle (Kau)Tabak; (*fig.*) Wendung, der Dreh; die Verdrehung, Verzerrung; Schlinge, Verschlingung; (*coll.*) Unehrlichkeit, Schikane, Schliche, Prellerei, Büberei; *give a th. a* –, etwas (um)drehen. **–er,** *s.* der Seiler, Flechter, Zwirner, die Zwirnmaschine; der Schnittball (*Tenn., etc.*); (*coll.*) harte Nuß, schwierige Frage; (*coll.*) der Schurke, Gauner, Halunke; (*coll.*) die Wasserhose, der Tornado. **–ing,** *attrib. adj.* Zwirn–; *–ing-machine*, die Drehmaschine. **–y,** *adj.* sich windend.

twit [twɪt], *v.a.* (*coll.*) aufziehen; – *with*, vorwerfen (*Dat.*).

twitch [twɪtʃ], 1. *v.a.* zerren, zupfen, zucken mit. 2. *v.n.* zerren, zupfen (*at*, an); zucken (*with*, vor). 3. *s.* das Zerren, Zupfen; Zucken, die Zuckung, der Krampf; das Stechen, Zwicken, Kneifen (*of pain*).

twitter [ˈtwɪtə], 1. *s.* das Gezwitscher, Zwitschern, (*fig.*) Zittern, Beben, die Angst, Aufregung; *in a* –, zitternd, ängstlich, aufgeregt. 2. *v.n.* zwitschern (*of birds*); zirpen (*of insects*); piepsen (*of a p.*), (*fig.*) zittern, aufgeregt sein. 3. *v.a.* zwitschern.

two [tuː], 1. *num. adj.* zwei, beide; *one or* –, einige, ein paar; *in a day or* –, in ein paar *or* in einigen Tagen. 2. *s.* die Zwei; der Zweier; – *and* –, paarweise; *put – and – together*, seine Schlüsse ziehen aus, sich (*Dat.*) zusammenreimen; – *is company*, zwei machen ein Paar; *by* or *in –s*, zu zweien; *in* –, entzwei; – *can play at that game*, so grob kann ich auch sein, das kann ein anderer auch; *the* –, beide, die beiden; *the – of them*, sie beide. **––edged,** *adj.* zweischneidig. **––faced,** *adj.* falsch, doppelzüngig. **–fold,** *adj.* zweifach, doppelt. **––foot,** *attrib. adj.* zwei Fuß lang. **––handed,** *adj.* zweihändig. **––horse,** *attrib. adj.* zweispännig. **––legged,** *adj.* zweibeinig. **–pence** [ˈtʌpəns], *s.* zwei Pence; *I don't care –pence*, es ist mir ganz einerlei; *–pence halfpenny*, zwei(und)einhalb Pence. **–penny** [ˈtʌpnɪ], *adj.* zwei Pence wert *or* kostend, (*fig.*) wertlos, armselig; (*coll.*) *–penny-halfpenny* minderwertig, elend. **––phase,** *attrib. adj.* zweiphasig. **––piece,** *attrib. adj.* zweiteilig. **––ply,** *attrib. adj.* zweischäftig (*ropes*), zweisträhnig (*wool*). **––seater,** *s.* der Zweisitzer. **––sided,** *attrib. adj.* zweiseitig. **––speed gear,** *s.* doppelte Übersetzung. **––step,** *s.* der Twostep (*dance*). **––story,** *attrib. adj.* zweistöckig. **––way,** *attrib. adj.* Doppel–. **––year-old,** 1. *attrib. adj.* zweijährig. 2. *s.* zweijähriges Kind *or* Tier.

tyke [taɪk], *s.* der Lümmel, Grobian.

tylosis [taɪˈlousɪs], *s.* die Schwielenbildung, Gewebeverhärtung (*Med.*).

tympan [ˈtɪmpən], *s.* der Preßdeckel (*Print.*); *see* **–um. –ic** [tɪmˈpænɪk], *adj.* Mittelohr–, Trommelfell–; *–ic membrane*, das Trommelfell (*Anat.*). **–um** [ˈtɪmpənəm], *s.* das Trommelfell, Mittelohr (*Anat.*); das Giebelfeld (*Arch.*); *see also* **timpano.**

type [taɪp], 1. *s.* der Typ, Schlag, die Art, Kategorie, das Kaliber; der Typus, die Grundform, das Urbild, Vorbild, Muster, Baumuster; das Sinnbild, Symbol, Zeichen; die Type, (Druck)-Letter; (*collect.*) der Druckbuchstabe, Schrift, Lettern (*pl.*); *bold* –, der Fettdruck; *in* –, gedruckt, gesetzt; *set up in* –, setzen; *German* –, die Fraktur; *italic* –, der Kursivdruck; *roman* –, lateinischer Druck; *set of* –, der Satz Schrift; *spaced* –, der Sperrdruck; *specimen of* –, die Satzprobe, Schriftprobe. 2. *v.a.* & *n.* auf der Schreibmaschine schreiben, tippen. **--face,** *s.* das Schriftbild. **--founder,** *s.* der Schriftgießer. **--foundry,** *s.* die Schriftgießerei. **--metal,** *s.* das Schriftmetall. **-script,** *s.* die Maschinenschrift. **--setter,** *s.* der (Schrift)Setzer. **-write,** *v.a.* & *n.* auf der Maschine schreiben, tippen. **-writer,** *s.* die Schreibmaschine. **-writing,** *s.* das Maschineschreiben, Tippen; *-writing paper,* das Maschinenpapier; *-writing ribbon,* das Farbband. **-written,** *adj.* mit der Maschine geschrieben; *-written copy,* das Maschinenschriftexemplar.

typh-oid ['taɪfɔɪd], 1. *adj.* Typhus–. 2. *s.* (also *-oid fever*) der Unterleibstyphus. **-us** [–fəs], der Flecktyphus, das Fleckfieber.

typhoon [taɪ'fu:n], *s.* der Taifun, Orkan.

typi-cal ['tɪpɪkl], *adj.* typisch, bezeichnend, kennzeichnend, charakteristisch (*of,* für), regelrecht, vorbildlich; sinnbildlich, symbolisch; *be -cal of,* kennzeichnen, charakterisieren; verkörpern, sinnbildlich darstellen. **-calness,** *s.* das Typische, die Sinnbildlichkeit. **-fy** [–faɪ], *v.a.* (sinn)bildlich darstellen, verkörpern; typisch *or* ein typisches Beispiel sein für.

typ-ist ['taɪpɪst], *s.* der Maschinenschreiber, Typist; *shorthand -ist,* der Stenotypist. **-ographer** [–'pɒgrəfə], *s.* der Druckberater. **-ographic(al)** [–pə'græfɪk(l)], *adj.*, **-ographically,** *adv.* drucktechnisch, typographisch, Buchdrucker–; *-ographic error,* der Druckfehler. **-ography** [–'pɒgrəfɪ], *s.* die Buchdruckerkunst, Typographie. **-ological** [–pə'lɒdʒɪkl], *adj.* Typen–, typologisch. **-ology** [–'pɒlədʒɪ], *s.* die Typologie, Typik (*Theol.*); Typenlehre.

tyran-nical [tɪ'rænɪkl, taɪ'rænɪkl], *adj.* tyrannisch, despotisch. **-nicidal** [–'saɪdl], *adj.* Tyrannenmord–. **-nicide** [–'rænɪsaɪd], *s.* der Tyrannenmord; Tyrannenmörder. **-nize** ['tɪrənaɪz], 1. *v.n.* despotisch *or* tyrannisch herrschen; *-nize over,* tyrannisieren. 2. *v.a.* tyrannisieren. **-nous** ['tɪrənəs], *adj.* tyrannisch, despotisch; grausam, unerbittlich. **-ny** ['tɪrənɪ], *s.* die Tyrannei, Willkürherrschaft, der Despotismus. **-t** ['taɪrənt], *s.* der Tyrann, Despot.

tyre ['taɪə], *s.* der Reifen; *pl.* die Bereifung. **--lever,** *s.* der Montierhebel.

tyro ['taɪroʊ], *s.* der Anfänger, Neuling.

tzar, *see* **tsar.**

U

U, u [ju:], *s.* das U, u. *For abbreviations see end of English-German Vocabulary.*

uberous ['ju:bərəs], *adj.* viel Milch gebend; (*fig.*) voll, reichlich.

ubiquit-ous [ju:'bɪkwɪtəs], *adj.* überall zu finden(d), allgegenwärtig. **-y** [–tɪ], *s.* die Allgegenwart.

U-boat ['ju:boʊt], *s.* (deutsches) Unterseeboot.

udal ['ju:dəl], *s.* das Freigut (*in Orkney & Shetland*).

udder ['ʌdə], *s.* das Euter. **-less,** *adj.* (*fig.*) mutterlos (*of a lamb*).

udometer [ju:'dɒmɪtə], *s.* der Regenmesser.

ugh [ʊ:], *int.* hu!

ugl-iness ['ʌglɪnɪs], *s.* die Häßlichkeit, Garstigkeit; Widerwärtigkeit. **-y,** *adj.* häßlich, garstig, widerwärtig, abstoßend; bedrohlich, gefährlich (*as weather*), bösartig, unangenehm; (*coll.*) *-y customer,* gefährlicher Bursche.

ukase [ju:'keɪs], *s.* der Ukas.

ukelele [ju:kə'leɪlə], *s.* kleine vierseitige Gitarre.

ulcer ['ʌlsə], *s.* das Geschwür, (*fig.*) die Beule, der Schandfleck. **-ate** [–reɪt], *v.n.* schwären, eitern. **-ated** [–reɪtɪd], *adj.* vereitert, eitrig. **-ation** [–'reɪʃn], *s.* das Schwären, die Eiterung; das Geschwür. **-ous,** *adj.* geschwürig, eiternd, Eiter–, (*fig.*) schädlich, giftig.

ullage ['ʌlɪdʒ], *s.* die Leckage, das Flüssigkeitsmanko.

ulmic ['ʌlmɪk], *adj.*; *– acid,* die Humussäure, Ulminsäure.

ulna ['ʌlnə], *s.* (*pl.* –e) die Elle (*Anat.*). **-r** [–nɑ:], *adj.* Ellen–.

ulster ['ʌlstə], *s.* der Ulstermantel.

ulterior [ʌl'tɪərɪə], *adj.* jenseitig, darüber hinausliegend (*space*), weiter, später, ferner, (später)-folgend (*time*), (*fig.*) anderweitig, sonstig, verdeckt, verheimlicht; *– motives,* Hintergedanken (*pl.*).

ultim-ate ['ʌltɪmət], *adj.* (aller)letzt, endlich, schließlich (*time*), entferntest, äußerst (*space*), (*fig.*) elementar, Grund–. **-ately,** *adv.* schließlich, endlich, letzten Endes, im Grunde. **-atum** [–'meɪtəm], *s.* das Ultimatum (*to,* an), letzter Vorschlag, letztes Wort. **-o** ['ʌltɪmoʊ], *adv.* (abbr. *ult.*) vorigen *or* letzten Monats (*C.L.*).

ultra ['ʌltrə], 1. *attrib. adj.* extrem, Ultra–, Erz–. 2. *attrib.* & *pred. adj.* übertrieben, übermäßig. 3. *prep.* über, jenseits. 4. *pref.*; **--fashionable,** *adj.* übermodern. **-marine** [–mə'rɪ:n], 1. *adj.* ultramarin; überseeisch, Übersee–. 2. *s.* das Ultramarin. **--modern,** *adj.* übermodern. **-montane** [–'mɒnteɪn], 1. *adj.* jenseits der Berge liegend, (*fig.*) ultramontan, streng päpstlich gesinnt. 2. *s. see* **-montanist. -montanism** [–'mɒntənɪzm], *s.* der Ultramontanismus. **-montanist** [–'mɒntənɪst], *s.* Ultramontane(r), *m.*, der Erzkatholik. **--short wave,** die Ultrakurzwelle. **--violet,** *adj.* ultraviolett; *--violet light* or *rays,* das Uviollicht.

ululat-e ['ʌlju:leɪt], *v.n.* heulen. **-ion** [–'leɪʃn], *s.* das Heulen, Geheul.

umbel ['ʌmbl], *s.* die Dolde. **-late** [–bəleɪt], *adj.* doldenblütig, Dolden–. **-lifer** [–'bɛlɪfə], *s.* das Doldengewächs. **-liferous** [–bə'lɪfərəs], *adj.* doldentragend, Dolden–.

umber ['ʌmbə], *s.* die Umbra, Umber, Umbererde.

umbilic-al [ʌm'bɪlɪkl, ʌmbə'laɪkl], *adj.* Nabel–; *-al cord,* die Nabelschnur. **-ate** [–'bɪlɪkət], *adj.* nabelförmig. **-us** [–'laɪkəs], *s.* der Nabel.

umbo ['ʌmboʊ], *s.* der Buckel (*on a shield*); Vorsprung, die Wölbung (*Bot., Zool.*).

umbra ['ʌmbrə], *s.* der Erdschatten, Mondschatten (*Astr.*). **-ge** [–brɪdʒ], *s.* der Anstoß, Ärger; (*archaic*) Schatten (*of trees*); *give -ge to,* Anstoß erregen bei, beleidigen; *take -ge at,* Anstoß nehmen an, übelnehmen. **-geous** [–'breɪdʒəs], *adj.* (*archaic*) schattig, schattenreich. **-geousness,** *s.* der Schattenreichtum. **-l** [–brəl], *adj.* Schatten– (*Astr.*).

umbrella [ʌm'brɛlə], 1. *s.* der (Regen)Schirm; (*fig.*) die Deckung durch Jagdverbände (*Av.*). 2. *attrib. adj.* Dach– (*organization, etc.*). **--stand,** *s.* der Schirmständer.

umpire ['ʌmpaɪə], 1. *s.* der Schiedsrichter (*Sport*), Unparteiische(r), *m.* 2. *v.n.* Schiedsrichter sein. 3. *v.a.* als Schiedsrichter leiten (*a game*).

umpteen ['ʌmptɪ:n], *adj.* (*sl.*) x-beliebig.

un- [ʌn], *negating pref.* = Un–, un–, nicht (*with nouns, adjectives, & adverbs*); ver–, los–, ent–, auf– (*with verbs*); *the stress is variable; with nouns, adjs., & advs. usually stressed or with secondary stress, though with common adjs. often unstressed; with verbs usually there is double stress. For words not listed see the simple words.*

unabashed ['ʌnə'bæʃt], *adj.* unverschämt, unverfroren, schamlos; furchtlos.

unabat-ed ['ʌnə'beɪtɪd], *adj.* unvermindert, ungeschwächt. **-ing,** *adj.* anhaltend, nicht nachlassend.

unabbreviated ['ʌnə'brɪ:vɪeɪtɪd], *adj.* unverkürzt, ungekürzt.

unable [ʌnˈeɪbl], *adj.* unfähig; *be* –, nicht können; nicht imstande *or* in der Lage sein, außerstande sein; – *to pay*, zahlungsunfähig.
unabridged [ˈʌnəˈbrɪdʒd], *adj.* unverkürzt.
unaccented [ˈʌnəkˈsɛntɪd], *adj.* unbetont.
unacceptab–le [ˈʌnəkˈsɛptəbl], *adj.* unannehmbar (*to*, für), unwillkommen, unangenehm. **–ility** [–ˈbɪlɪtɪ], *s.* die Unannehmbarkeit.
unaccommodating [ˈʌnəˈkɔmədeɪtɪŋ], *adj.* ungefällig, unnachgiebig, unverträglich, unkulant.
unaccompanied [ˈʌnəˈkʌmpənɪd], *adj.* unbegleitet; ohne Begleitung (*Mus.*).
unaccomplished [ˈʌnəˈkɔmplɪʃt], *adj.* unvollendet; (*fig.*) ungebildet.
unaccountabl–e [ˈʌnəˈkauntəbl], *adj.* unerklärlich, unerklärbar, eigenartig, sonderbar; nicht verantwortlich. **–y,** *adv.* auf unerklärliche Weise.
unaccredited [ˈʌnəˈkrɛdɪtɪd], *adj.* nicht anerkannt, unbeglaubigt.
unaccustomed [ˈʌnəˈkʌstəmd], *adj.* ungewohnt, nicht gewöhnt (*to*, an); ungewöhnlich, fremd. **–ness,** *s.* die Ungewohntheit, Ungewöhnlichkeit.
unachievable [ˈʌnəˈtʃiːvəbl], *adj.* unausführbar, unerreichbar.
unacknowledged [ˈʌnəkˈnɔlɪdʒd], *adj.* nicht anerkannt; nicht eingestanden *or* zugegeben; nicht bestätigt, unbeantwortet (*letter*).
unacquainted [ˈʌnəˈkweɪntɪd], *adj.* unbekannt (*with*, mit), unkundig (*with* (*Gen.*)); *be – with*, nicht kennen.
unact–able [ʌnˈæktəbl], *adj.* nicht aufführbar. **–ed** [–tɪd], *adj.* nicht aufgeführt.
unadapted [ˈʌnəˈdæptɪd], *adj.* ungeeignet, nicht eingerichtet (*to*, für).
unaddressed [ˈʌnəˈdrɛst], *adj.* unadressiert.
unadorned [ˈʌnəˈdɔːnd], *adj.* ungeschmückt, einfach.
unadulterated [ˈʌnəˈdʌltəreɪtɪd], *adj.* unverfälscht, unvermischt, unverschnitten, rein; echt.
unadventurous [ˈʌnədˈvɛntʃərəs], *adj.* ereignislos (*as a journey*), ohne Abenteuergeist (*as a p.*).
unadvis–able [ˈʌnədˈvaɪzəbl], *adj.* unratsam, nicht ratsam, nicht zu empfehlen(d). **–ed** [–ˈvaɪzd], *adj.* unbedacht, unbesonnen, unklug, unvorsichtig, vorschnell; unberaten.
unaffected [ˈʌnəˈfɛktɪd], *adj.* unberührt, unbeeinflußt (*by*, von), unverändert (*by*, durch), unempfindlich (*by*, gegen); ungerührt; ungekünstelt, natürlich, schlicht, einfach; aufrichtig, echt (*pleasure*). **–ness,** *s.* die Natürlichkeit, Schlichtheit.
unafraid [ˈʌnəˈfreɪd], *adj.* unerschrocken; nicht bange (*of*, vor).
unaided [ʌnˈeɪdɪd], *adj.* ohne Hilfe (*by*, von *or* durch); unbewaffnet (*of eye*).
unalienable [ʌnˈeɪlɪənəbl], *adj.* unveräußerlich.
unallowable [ˈʌnəlauəbl], *adj.* unzulässig, nicht erlaubt.
unalloyed [ˈʌnəˈlɔɪd], *adj.* unvermischt, unlegiert (*metals*); ungemischt, echt, rein, lauter.
unalter–able [ʌnˈɔːltərəbl], *adj.* unabänderlich, unveränderlich. **–ableness,** *s.* die Unabänderlichkeit, Unveränderlichkeit. **–ed** [–təd], *adj.* unverändert.
unamazed [ˈʌnəˈmeɪzd], *adj.* nicht verwundert; *be – at*, sich nicht wundern über.
unambiguous [ˈʌnæmˈbɪgjuəs], *adj.* eindeutig, unzweideutig. **–ness,** *s.* die Unzweideutigkeit.
unambitious [ˈʌnæmbɪʃəs], *adj.* nicht ehrgeizig (*of a p.*); schlicht, anspruchslos (*of a th.*).
unamenable [ˈʌnəˈmɪːnəbl], *adj.* unzugänglich (*to*, für); unnahbar.
unamended [ˈʌnəˈmɛndɪd], *adj.* unabgeändert, unverbessert.
unamiable [ʌnˈeɪmjəbl], *adj.* unliebenswürdig.
unamusing [ˈʌnəˈmjuːzɪŋ], *adj.* nicht unterhaltend, langweilig.
unanim–ity [juːnəˈnɪmɪtɪ], *s.* die Einmütigkeit, Einstimmigkeit; *with –ity*, einmütig, einstimmig. **–ous** [–ˈnænɪməs], *adj.* einmütig, einstimmig; *be –ous*, sich einig sein (*on*, über).
unannounced [ˈʌnəˈnaunst], *adj.* unangemeldet.
unanswer–able [ʌnˈɑːnsərəbl], *adj.* nicht zu beantworten(d), unlösbar (*riddle*); unwiderlegbar (*charge*); nicht verantwortlich. **–ableness,** *s.* die Unwiderlegbarkeit. **–ed** [–səd], *adj.* unbeantwortet (*letter*), unwiderlegt (*charge*).
unapparent [ˈʌnəˈpærənt, ˈʌnəˈpɛərənt], *adj.* nicht sichtbar.
unappeasable [ˈʌnəˈpɪːzəbl], *adj.* unversöhnlich, nicht zu befriedigen(d) *or* besänftigen(d), unersättlich (*hunger*).
unapplied [ˈʌnəˈplaɪd], *adj.* nicht gebraucht *or* angewandt.
unappreciated [ˈʌnəˈprɪʃɪeɪtɪd], *adj.* nicht gehörig beachtet, geschätzt *or* gewürdigt.
unapproachable [ˈʌnəˈproutʃəbl], *adj.* unzugänglich, nicht betretbar (*places*), unnahbar (*of a p.*); unvergleichbar.
unappropriated [ˈʌnəˈprouprɪeɪtɪd], *adj.* nicht verbraucht *or* verwendet, herrenlos; – *funds*, tote Kapitalien.
unapproved [ˈʌnəˈpruːvd], *adj.* ungebilligt.
unapt [ʌnˈæpt], *adj.* ungeeignet, untauglich (*for*, zu), ungeschickt (*at*, in), nicht geneigt.
unarm [ʌnˈɑːm], *v.a.* entwaffnen. **–ed** [–d], *adj.* unbewaffnet, wehrlos; unbewehrt (*Zool. & Bot.*). **–oured** [–əd], ungepanzert.
unascertained [ʌnˈæsəteind], *adj.* unermittelt, unbekannt.
unashamed [ˈʌnəˈʃeɪmd], *adj.* nicht beschämt, schamlos, unerschrocken.
unasked [ʌnˈɑːskt], *adj.* ungefragt, ungebeten, unaufgefordert, unverlangt.
unaspiring [ˈʌnəˈspaɪərɪŋ], *adj.* anspruchslos, bescheiden.
unassailable [ˈʌnəˈseɪləbl], *adj.* unangreifbar, (*fig.*) unanfechtbar, unantastbar, unerschütterlich.
unassisted [ˈʌnəˈsɪstɪd], *adj.* ohne Unterstützung, Stütze *or* Hilfe, unbewaffnet (*as eye*).
unassuming [ˈʌnəˈsjuːmɪŋ], *adj.* bescheiden, anspruchslos.
unattached [ˈʌnəˈtætʃt], *adj.* nicht verbunden (*to*, mit) *or* befestigt (*to*, an); nicht gehörig (*to*, zu), zur Disposition gestellt (*Mil.*); zu keinem College gehörig, extern (*Univ.*); (*coll.*) ohne Anhang.
unattainable [ˈʌnəˈteɪnəbl], *adj.* unerreichbar, unerfüllbar.
unattempted [ˈʌnəˈtɛmptɪd], *adj.* unversucht.
unattended [ˈʌnəˈtɛndɪd], *adj.* unbegleitet, ohne Begleitung *or* Gefolge, (*fig.*) unbeaufsichtigt, vernachlässigt; unverbunden (*wounds*).
unattested [ˈʌnəˈtɛstɪd], *adj.* unbezeugt, unbewiesen.
unattractive [ˈʌnəˈtræktɪv], *adj.* reizlos, unansehnlich, nicht einnehmend *or* anziehend.
unauthorized [ʌnˈɔːθəraɪzd], *adj.* nicht bevollmächtigt, eigenmächtig, unberechtigt, vorschriftswidrig, unrechtmäßig, unbefugt, unerlaubt.
unavail–able [ˈʌnəˈveɪləbl], *adj.* nicht erreichbar, unbrauchbar. **–ing** [–lɪŋ], *adj.* vergeblich, unnütz, fruchtlos.
unavoidable [ʌnəˈvɔɪdəbl], *adj.* unvermeidlich, unabwendbar. **–ness,** *s.* die Unvermeidlichkeit.
unaware [ˈʌnəˈwɛə], *pred. adj.* unbewußt (*of* (*Gen.*)); *be* –, nicht ahnen; *be – of*, nicht wissen. **–s** [–z], *adv.* unversehens, aus Versehen, unbeabsichtigt; unerwartet, unvermutet; plötzlich; *catch* or *take –s*, überraschen.
unbalance [ʌnˈbæləns], *v.a.* aus dem Gleichgewicht bringen. **–d** [–t], *adj.* aus dem *or* nicht im Gleichgewicht, (*fig.*) unausgeglichen, unstet, ungefestigt; nicht ausgeglichen *or* saldiert (*C.L.*).
unbaptized [ˈʌnbæpˈtaɪzd], *adj.* ungetauft.
unbar [ˈʌnˈbɑː], *v.a.* aufriegeln, öffnen.
unbearable [ʌnˈbɛːrəbl], *adj.* unerträglich.
unbeaten [ʌnˈbɪːtn], *adj.* ungeschlagen; unbetreten (*path*); unbesiegt.
unbecoming [ˈʌnbɪˈkʌmɪŋ], *adj.* unkleidsam (*dress*); unschicklich, unziemlich, unpassend, unangebracht.
unbefitting [ˈʌnbɪˈfɪtɪŋ], *adj.* nicht geziemend, unpassend.
unbefriended [ˈʌnbɪˈfrɛndɪd], *adj.* freundlos, ohne Freunde.
unbeknown [ˈʌnbɪˈnoun], *pred. adj.* unbekannt (*to* (*Dat.*)).
unbelie–f [ˈʌnbɪˈlɪːf], *s.* der Unglaube; das Miß-

trauen, der Zweifel. **–vable** [–ˈlɪːvəbl], *adj.* unglaubhaft, unglaublich. **–ver** [–ˈlɪːvə], *s.* Ungläubige(r), *m.* **–ving,** *adj.* ungläubig.
unbend [ʌnˈbɛnd], 1. *ir.v.a.* entspannen, (*a bow*); abschlagen (*sails*); losmachen (*a rope*). 2. *ir.v.n.* sich herablassen, freundlich *or* mitteilsam werden, sich gehen lassen, auftauen; sich entspannen. **–ing,** *adj.* (*fig.*) unbeugsam, unnachgiebig, entschlossen.
unbias(s)ed [ʌnˈbaɪəst], *adj.* unvoreingenommen, ohne Vorurteil, vorurteilslos, unbefangen, unbeeinflußt, unparteiisch.
unbidden [ʌnˈbɪdn], *adj.* ungebeten, unaufgefordert; freiwillig.
unbind [ʌnˈbaɪnd], *ir.v.a.* losbinden; aufbinden; lösen.
unbleached [ʌnˈblɪːtʃt], *adj.* ungebleicht.
unblemished [ʌnˈblɛmɪʃt], *adj.* fleckenlos; (*fig.*) unbefleckt, makellos, rein.
unblushing [ʌnˈblʌʃɪŋ], *adj.* schamlos.
unbolt [ʌnˈboʊlt], *v.a.* aufriegeln, öffnen.
unborn [ʌnˈbɔːn], *adj.* (noch) ungeboren; zukünftig.
unbosom [ʌnˈbuzm], *v.r.* sein Herz ausschütten, sich eröffnen *or* offenbaren (*to* (*Dat.*)).
unbound [ʌnˈbaʊnd], *adj.* lose, ungebunden; geheftet, broschiert (*as books*); (*fig.*) nicht gebunden, frei. **–ed** [–ɪd], *adj.* unbegrenzt; (*fig.*) grenzenlos, schrankenlos, unbeschränkt.
unbreakable [ʌnˈbreɪkəbl], *adj.* unzerbrechlich.
unbreeched [ʌnˈbrɪtʃt], *adj.* noch kein Hosen tragend (*of a boy*).
unbribable [ʌnˈbraɪbəbl], *adj.* unbestechlich.
unbridgeable [ʌnˈbrɪdʒəbl], *adj.* unüberbrückbar.
unbridled [ʌnˈbraɪdld], *adj.* ungezäumt, (*usually fig.*) zügellos.
unbroken [ʌnˈbroʊkn], *adj.* ungebrochen, ganz, heil; ununterbrochen; nicht zugeritten (*of horses*); ungepflügt (*land*); unübertroffen (*record*), (*fig.*) unvermindert, ungeschwächt, unverletzt.
unbrotherly [ʌnˈbrʌðəlɪ], *adj.* unbrüderlich.
unbuckle [ʌnˈbʌkl], *v.a.* losschnallen, aufschnallen.
unburden [ʌnˈbəːdn], *v.a.* entlasten; entladen; – *one's mind of,* sein Herz befreien *or* erleichtern von; – *one's heart,* sein Herz ausschütten (*to* (*Dat.*)).
unburied [ʌnˈbɛrɪd], *adj.* unbegraben, unbeerdigt.
unburn–ed [ʌnˈbəːnt], **–t,** *adj.* nicht verbrannt; ungebrannt (*as bricks*).
unbusinesslike [ʌnˈbɪznɪslaɪk], *adj.* unkaufmännisch, nicht geschäftsmäßig; (*fig.*) nachlässig, unpünktlich.
unbutton [ʌnˈbʌtn], *v.a.* aufknöpfen, losknöpfen. **–ed** [–d], *adj.* frei, ungehemmt.
uncalled [ʌnˈkɔːld], *adj.* ungerufen, unaufgefordert; *– –for,* unaufgefordert, unerwünscht, nicht begehrt; unnötig, überflüssig, unangebracht; ungerechtfertigt.
uncanny [ʌnˈkænɪ], *adj.* unheimlich, nicht geheuer.
uncared-for [ʌnˈkɛədfɔː], *adj.* unbeachtet, unversorgt, vernachlässigt.
uncarpeted [ʌnˈkɑːpɪtɪd], *adj.* ohne Teppich.
unceasing [ʌnˈsɪːsɪŋ], *adj.* andauernd, unaufhörlich, unablässig.
unceremonious [ˈʌnsɛrɪˈmoʊnɪəs], *adj.* zwanglos, ungezwungen, schlicht, ohne Umstände, formlos, unzeremoniell.
uncertain [ʌnˈsəːtɪn], *adj.* unsicher, ungewiß, unbestimmt, zweifelhaft (*of a th.*); unzuverlässig, unstät, unberechenbar, veränderlich, schwankend, launenhaft (*of a p.*); unbeständig (*weather*); *be – of,* einer Sache nicht gewiß *or* sicher sein. **–ty** [–tɪ], *s.* die Unsicherheit, Ungewißheit; Unzuverlässigkeit, Unberechenbarkeit.
uncertifi–cated [ˈʌnsəˈtɪfɪkeɪtɪd], *adj.* ohne Zeugnis. **–ed** [ʌnˈsəːtɪfaɪd], *adj.* unbeglaubigt, unbezeugt, unbewiesen.
unchain [ʌnˈtʃeɪn], *v.a.* losketten.
unchallenge–able [ʌnˈtʃælənd ʒəbl], *adj.* unanfechtbar, nicht anzuzweifeln(d). **–d** [–əndʒd], *adj.* unangefochten, unbeanstandet, nicht angezweifelt.
unchang–eable [ʌnˈtʃeɪndʒəbl], *adj.* unveränderlich, unverwandelbar. **–eableness,** *s.* die Unveränderlichkeit. **–ed** [–ˈtʃeɪndʒd], *adj.* unverändert. **–ing,** *adj.* gleich bleibend, unveränderlich.
uncharitable [ʌnˈtʃærɪtəbl], *adj.* hartherzig, lieblos. **–ness,** *s.* die Hartherzigkeit, Lieblosigkeit.
unchart–ed [ʌnˈtʃɑːtɪd], *adj.* (auf Karten) nicht verzeichnet *or* angegeben; (*fig.*) unbekannt. **–ered** [–təd], *adj.* ohne Freibrief, nicht privilegiert.
unchast–e [ʌnˈtʃeɪst], *adj.* unkeusch. **–ity** [–ˈtʃæstɪtɪ], *s.* die Unkeuschheit.
unchecked [ʌnˈtʃɛkt], *adj.* ungehindert, ungehemmt; nicht kontrolliert *or* geprüft.
unchivalrous [ʌnˈʃɪvəlrəs], *adj.* unritterlich.
unchristened [ʌnˈkrɪsnd], *adj.* ungetauft.
unchristian [ʌnˈkrɪstʃn], *adj.* unchristlich.
uncial [ˈʌnʃl], 1. *adj.* Unzial–. 2. *s.* der Unzialbuchstabe.
unci–form [ˈʌnsɪfɔːm], *adj.* hakenförmig (*Anat.*). **–nate** [–neɪt], *adj.* hakenförmig; stacheltragend (*Bot., Zool.*).
uncircumcis–ed [ʌnˈsəːkəmsaɪzd], *adj.* unbeschnitten. **–ion** [–sɪʒn], *s.* die Unbeschnittenheit; *the –ion* (*B.*), Heiden (*pl.*).
uncivil [ʌnˈsɪvɪl], *adj.* unhöflich, grob, schroff, barsch (*to,* gegen). **–ized** [–laɪzd], *adj.* unzivilisiert, ungesittet.
unclaimed [ʌnˈkleɪmd], *adj.* nicht beansprucht *or* angesprochen; nicht abgenommen (*as goods*); nicht abgehoben (*as money*), unbestellbar (*as letters*).
unclasp [ʌnˈklɑːsp], *v.a.* loshaken, lösen, öffnen.
unclassified [ʌnˈklæsɪfaɪd], *adj.* nicht (nach Klassen) geordnet; nicht klassifiziert.
uncle [ʌnkl], *s.* der Onkel, Oheim; (*sl.*) Pfandverleiher.
unclean [ʌnˈklɪːn], *adj.*, **–ly** [–ˈklɛnlɪ], *adj.* unrein(lich), schmutzig; unkeusch. **–ness** [–ˈklɪːnnɪs], *s.*, **–liness** [–ˈklɛnlɪnɪs], *s.* die Unrein(lich)keit.
unclerical [ʌnˈklɛrɪkl], *adj.* ungeistlich, einem Geistlichen nicht geziemend.
uncloak [ʌnˈkloʊk], *v.a.* den Mantel abnehmen (*a p.,* einem); (*fig.*) enthüllen, entlarven.
unclothe [ʌnˈkloʊð], *v.a.* entkleiden, auskleiden, entblößen, enthüllen. **–d** [–d], *adj.* unbekleidet, nackt.
unclouded [ʌnˈklaʊdɪd], *adj.* wolkenlos, unbewölkt; (*fig.*) heiter, klar.
unco' [ˈʌnkə], 1. *adj.* (*Scots*) ungewöhnlich. 2. *adv.* äußerst, höchst; *the – guid,* die Selbstgerechten.
uncock [ʌnˈkɔk], *adj.* entspannen (*a gun*).
uncoil [ʌnˈkɔɪl], *v.a.* (*& n.* sich) abwickeln, abrollen, abspulen.
uncollected [ˈʌnkəˈlɛktɪd], *adj.* nicht eingesammelt *or* erhoben.
uncoloured [ʌnˈkʌləd], *adj.* ungefärbt; (*fig.*) ungeschminkt.
uncomel–iness [ʌnˈkʌmlɪnɪs], *s.* die Unschönheit. **–y** [–lɪ], *adj.* unschön, unansehnlich; ungeziemend.
uncomfortable [ʌnˈkʌmfətəbl], *adj.* unbequem, unbehaglich, ungemütlich, unangenehm; unerfreulich, beunruhigend.
uncommitted [ˈʌnkəˈmɪtɪd], nicht begangen; nicht gebunden (*to,* an).
uncommon [ʌnˈkɔmən], *adj.* ungewöhnlich, selten, außergewöhnlich, außerordentlich. (*coll.*) **–ly,** *adv.* ungemein, äußerst. **–ness,** *s.* die Ungewöhnlichkeit, Seltenheit, Außergewöhnlichkeit.
uncommunica–ble [ˈʌnkəˈmjuːnɪkəbl], *adj.* nicht mitteilbar. **–tive** [–kətɪv], *adj.* nicht mitteilsam, verschlossen. **–tiveness,** *s.* die Verschlossenheit.
uncompanionable [ˈʌnkəmˈpænjəbl], *adj.* ungesellig, nicht umgänglich.
uncomplaining [ˈʌnkəmˈpleɪnɪŋ], *adj.* nicht murrend *or* klagend, geduldig. **–ness,** *s.* die Geduld, Ergebung.
uncomplaisant [ˈʌnkəmˈpleɪsnt], *adj.* ungefällig.
uncompleted [ˈʌnkəmˈplɪːtɪd], *adj.* unvollendet, nicht vollendet.
uncomplicated [ʌnˈkɔmplɪkeɪtɪd], *adj.* nicht kompliziert, einfach.
uncomplimentary [ˈʌnkɔmplɪˈmɛntərɪ], *adj.* nicht schmeichelhaft, unhöflich.
uncompromising [ʌnˈkɔmprəmaɪzɪŋ], *adj.* zu keinem Vergleich geneigt, unbeugsam, unnachgiebig, unversöhnlich.
unconcern [ˈʌnkənˈsəːn], *s.* die Gleichgültigkeit, Sorglosigkeit. **–ed** [–d], *adj.* gleichgültig (*about,*

gegen), uninteressiert (*with*, an); sorglos, unbekümmert (*about*, über *or* um); unbeteiligt (*in*, an), nicht verwickelt (*in*, in). **–edness,** *s.* die Sorglosigkeit (*about*, um), Gleichgültigkeit, Uninteressiertheit.

uncondition–al [ˈʌnkənˈdɪʃənl], *adj.* unbedingt, bedingungslos, vorbehaltlos, uneingeschränkt. **–ed,** *adj.* bedingungslos, unbedingt, absolut.

unconfined [ˈʌnkənˈfɑɪnd], *adj.* unbeschränkt, unbegrenzt, unbehindert.

unconfirmed [ˈʌnkənfəːmd], *adj.* unbestätigt, unverbürgt; unkonfirmiert (*Eccl.*).

uncongenial [ˈʌnkənˈdʒɪːnɪəl], *adj.* ungleichartig, nicht kongenial; unsympathisch, unangenehm, nicht zusagend; nicht passend (*to*, zu).

unconnected [ˈʌnkəˈnɛktɪd], *adj.* nicht verbunden *or* zusammenhängend, isoliert; unzusammenhängend; unverbunden.

unconquer–able [ʌnˈkɔŋkərəbl], *adj.* unbesiegbar, unüberwindlich. **–ed** [–kəd], *adj.* unbesiegt.

unconsci–entious [ˈʌnkɔnʃɪˈɛnʃəs], *adj.* gewissenlos, skrupellos. **–onable** [ʌnˈkɔnʃənəbl], *adj.* gewissenlos, unverantwortlich; (*coll.*) unglaublich, enorm, ungeheuer. **–ous** [ʌnˈkɔnʃəs], 1. *adj.* unbewußt; unbeabsichtigt, unfreiwillig, unwillkürlich; bewußtlos, ohnmächtig (*Med.*); *be –ous of a th.*, sich einer S. nicht bewußt sein, etwas nicht ahnen. 2. *s.* das Unbewußte. **–ousness,** *s.* die Unbewußtheit, Unkenntnis; Bewußtlosigkeit (*Med.*).

unconsecrated [ʌnˈkɔnsɪkreɪtɪd], *adj.* ungeweiht.

unconsidered [ˈʌnkənˈsɪdəd], *adj.* unüberlegt, unbedacht; nicht beachtet.

unconstitutional [ˈʌnkɔnstɪˈtjuːʃənl], *adj.* verfassungswidrig.

unconstrain–ed [ˈʌnkənˈstreɪnd], *adj.* ungezwungen, frei. **–t** [–nt], *s.* die Ungezwungenheit.

uncontaminated [ˈʌnkənˈtæmɪneɪtɪd], *adj.* nicht angesteckt, unbefleckt, unberührt, rein.

uncontested [ˈʌnkənˈtɛstɪd], *adj.* unbestritten, unumstritten, unangefochten; – *election*, die Wahl ohne Gegenkandidat.

uncontradicted [ˈʌnkɔntrəˈdɪktɪd], *adj.* unbestritten, unwidersprochen.

uncontroll–able [ˈʌnkənˈtroʊləbl], *adj.* unbändig, unbeherrscht, zügellos, unkontrollierbar. **–ed** [–ˈtroʊld], *adj.* ohne Aufsicht, ungehindert, unbeherrscht, zügellos.

unconventional [ˈʌnkənˈvɛnʃənl], *adj.* unkonventionell, formlos, nicht förmlich; ungezwungen, zwanglos, natürlich. **–ity** [–ˈnælɪtɪ], *s.* die Zwanglosigkeit, Ungezwungenheit.

unconversant [ˈʌnkənˈvəːsənt], *adj.* unbewandert, nicht bekannt.

unconvert–ed [ˈʌnkənˈvəːtɪd], *adj.* unbekehrt (*Eccl.*); unverändert, unverwandelt; (*fig.*) nicht überzeugt. **–ible** [–tɪbl], *adj.* unverwandelbar; unkonvertierbar, nicht umsetzbar (*C.L.*).

unconvinc–ed [ˈʌnkənˈvɪnst], *adj.* nicht überzeugt. **–ing** [–sɪŋ], *adj.* nicht überzeugend.

uncooked [[ˈʌnˈkʊkt], *adj.* roh, ungekocht.

uncork [ˈʌnˈkɔːk], *v.a.* entkorken.

uncorrected [ˈʌnkəˈrɛktɪd], *adj.* unverbessert, nicht berichtigt.

uncorroborated [ˈʌnkəˈrɔbəreɪtɪd], *adj.* unbestätigt.

uncorrupted [ˈʌnkəˈrʌptɪd], *adj.* nicht verdorben, (*fig.*) unverdorben, unbestochen.

uncount–able [ʌnˈkaʊntəbl], *adj.* unzählbar, unzählig. **–ed** [–tɪd], *adj.* ungezählt, zahllos.

uncouple [ˈʌnˈkʌpl], *v.a.* loskoppeln; trennen, loslösen; abhängen, abkuppeln, auskuppeln, loskuppeln, ausrücken, ausschalten (*Tech.*).

uncouth [ʌnˈkuːθ], *adj.* unbeholfen, ungehobelt, ungeschlacht, linkisch; roh, ungebildet.

uncovenanted [ʌnˈkʌvənəntɪd], *adj.* nicht kontraktlich verpflichtet *or* gesichert.

uncover [ˈʌnˈkʌvə], 1. *v.a.* aufdecken (*also fig.*), bloßlegen, freilegen; entblößen (*one's head*); ohne Deckung lassen (*Mil.*); (*fig.*) enthüllen, offenbaren (*feelings, etc.*). 2. *v.n.* den Hut abnehmen. **–ed** [–d], *adj.* unbedeckt, unbekleidet, nackt; barhäuptig; ungedeckt, ungeschützt, ohne Deckung (*Mil.*).

uncritical [ʌnˈkrɪtɪkl], *adj.* unkritisch; kritiklos.

uncross [ˈʌnˈkrɔs], *v.a.* gerade legen. **–ed** [–t], *adj.* nicht gekreuzt; ungekreuzt (*cheque*); (*fig.*) nicht gehindert (*by*, von *or* durch).

uncrushable [ʌnˈkrʌʃəbl], *adj.* knitterfrei (*stuffs*); (*fig.*) nicht einzuschüchtern(d).

unct–ion [ˈʌŋkʃn], *s.* die Salbung (*also fig.*), Ölung (*Eccl.*), Einreibung (*Med.*); das Öl, die Salbe; (*fig.*) das Pathos, die Rührung, Wärme, Inbrunst; *extreme –ion*, letzte Ölung; *with –ion*, mit innerem Behagen. **–uous** [–ʃʊəs], *adj.* ölig, fettig; (*fig.*) salbungsvoll.

uncult–ivated [ʌnˈkʌltɪveɪtɪd], *adj.* unbebaut, unkultiviert (*also fig.*) (*as land*); ungebildet, roh, verwildert, vernachlässigt. **–ured** [–tʃəd], *adj.* nicht bebaut; ungebildet, ungesittet.

uncumbered [ʌnˈkʌmbəd], *adj.* unbeschwert, unbelastet.

uncurbed [ʌnˈkəːbd], *adj.* ohne Kinnkette (*horses*), (*fig.*) ungehemmt, ungezähmt, zügellos.

uncured [ʌnˈkjʊəd], *adj.* ungeheilt; ungesalzen, ungepökelt.

uncurl [ˈʌnˈkəːl], 1. *v.a.* entkräuseln. 2. *v.n.* glatt *or* gerade werden.

uncurtailed [ˈʌnkəːˈteɪld], *adj.* ungekürzt; unbeschnitten.

uncut [ʌnˈkʌt], *adj.* ungeschnitten; ungemäht (*as grass*); nicht aufgeschnitten (*as books*); (*fig.*) ungekürzt (*as a text*); unbeschnitten.

undamaged [ʌnˈdæmɪdʒd], *adj.* unbeschädigt, unversehrt.

undamped [ˈʌnˈdæmpt], *adj.* ungedämpft (*oscillations*), nicht entmutigt (*courage*).

undate(d) [ˈʌndeɪt(ɪd)], *adj.* wellenförmig, wellig (*Bot.*)

undated [ʌnˈdeɪtɪd], *adj.* undatiert, ohne Datum.

undaunted [ʌnˈdɔːntɪd], *adj.* unerschrocken, unverzagt, furchtlos.

undecaying [ˈʌndɪˈkeɪɪŋ], *adj.* unverwelklich, unvergänglich.

undeceive [ˈʌndɪˈsɪːv], *v.a.* über Irrtum aufklären; die Augen öffnen (*Dat.*), die Illusion zerstören (*Dat.*), eines Besseren belehren. **–d** [–d], *adj.* nicht getäuscht *or* irregeführt (*by*, durch).

undecided [ˈʌndɪˈsɑɪdɪd], *adj.* unentschieden, unbestimmt (*also fig.*), unbeständig (*of a th.*), unentschlossen, unschlüssig (*of a p.*), (*fig.*) unausgesprochen (*as appearance*).

undecipherable [ˈʌndɪˈsɑɪfərəbl], *adj.* nicht zu entziffern(d) *or* entzifferbar, unerklärlich.

undeclared [ˈʌndɪˈklɛəd], *adj.* nicht erklärt, nicht bekannt gemacht; nicht deklariert (*C.L.*).

undefended [ˈʌndɪfɛndɪd], *adj.* unverteidigt.

undefiled [ˈʌndɪˈfɑɪld], *adj.* unbefleckt, makellos.

undefined [ˈʌndɪfɑɪnd], *adj.* unbestimmt, unklar, vage.

undemonstrative [ˈʌndɪˈmɔnstrətɪv], *adj.* zurückhaltend, gemessen, unaufdringlich.

undeniabl–e [ˈʌndɪˈnɑɪəbl], *adj.* unleugbar; unbestreitbar, nicht abzuleugnen(d) . **–y,** *adv.* unleugbar, unstreitig, gewiß.

undenominational [ˈʌndɪnɔmɪˈneɪʃnl], *adj.* interkonfessionell; – *school*, die Simultanschule.

undependable [ˈʌndɪˈpɛndəbl], *adj.* unzuverlässig.

under [ˈʌndə], **1.** *adv.* unten; unterhalb; *as* –, wie unten *or* hierunter; *go* –, zugrundegehen, unterliegen, erliegen; *keep* –, niederhalten, im Zaume halten; *knuckle* –, nachgeben, klein beigeben, sich unterwerfen (*to* (*Dat.*)). **2.** *adj.* unter, Unter–, untergeordnet; ungenügend. **3.** *prep.* unter; unterhalb; (*fig.*) laut, auf Grund von; weniger, niedriger *or* geringer als; – *age*, minderjährig, unmündig; – *arms*, unter den Waffen; – *one's breath*, leise, flüsternd; – *the burden*, unter der Last; – *chloroform*, in der Narkose; – *these circumstances*, unter diesen Umständen; *be – a cloud*, übel beleumdet sein, unter dem Verdacht stehen; *be – consideration*, noch erwogen *or* erörtert werden; *I speak – correction*, nach meiner unmaßgeblichen Meinung; – *cover of*, unter dem Schutze von; – *this cover*, beiliegend (*C.L.*); – (*the*) *date*, unter dem Datum (*of* (*Gen.*)); – *the direction of*, unter Leitung von; *be – discussion*, zur Diskussion stehen; – *fire*, unter Feuer; – *foot*, unter dem Fuße, auf dem Boden; (*fig.*) unter die Füße; *from* –, unter . . . (*Dat.*) hervor. – *ground*, unter dem (Erd)Boden, unter der Erde; – *his hand and seal*, von ihm unterschrieben und gesiegelt; – *King George*, während der Zeit König Georgs; – *lock and key*, hinter Schloß und Riegel; – *2 miles*, weniger als 2 Meilen; *be* or *labour* – *a misapprehension*, sich in einem Irrtum befinden; *be* – *the necessity of*, genötigt sein zu; – *a p.'s nose*, einem vor der Nase; – *oath*, unter Eid; – *an obligation*, verpflichtet; – *pain of death*, bei Todesstrafe; – *protest*, unter Protest; – *repair*, in Reparatur; – *restraint*, in Gewahrsam (*as lunatics*), (*fig.*) im Zaume; – *the rose*, im Vertrauen; – *sail*, unter Segel; – *sentence of* . . ., zu . . . verurteilt; – *treatment*, in Behandlung; – *the treaty*, laut Vertrag; – *way*, in Fahrt, in vollem Lauf (*Naut.*, *also fig.*). **4.** *prefix*. Unter– (*before nouns*; *stressed*), unter– (*before verbs*; *secondary stress*); **–act** [–ˈækt], 1. *v.a.* ungenügend darstellen (*a play*), nicht gerecht werden (*a part*). 2. *v.n.* ungenügend spielen. **–arm** [ˈʌndəɑ:m], 1. *adv.* mit dem Unterarm. 2. *attrib.* von unten. **–bid** [–ˈbɪd], *v.a.* unterbieten. **–bred** [–ˈbrɛd], *adj.* unfein, ungebildet. **–carriage,** *s.* das Fahrgestell (*Av.*); *float –carriage*, das Schwimmergestell (*Av.*); *retractable –carriage*, das Verschwindfahrgestell (*Av.*). **–charge** [–ˈtʃɑ:dʒ], *v.a.* zu gering berechnen *or* belasten (*a p.*) (*for*, für); ungenügend laden (*a gun*, *etc.*). **–clothes,** *pl.*, **–clothing,** *s.* die Unterwäsche, Leibwäsche. **–coat,** *s.* der Untergrund (*Paint.*). **–croft,** *s.* unterirdisches Gewölbe, die Krypta (*Arch.*). **–current,** *s.* die Unterströmung, (*fig.*) untere *or* verborgene Strömung *or* Tendenz. **–cut,** 1. *v.a.* [–ˈkʌt], aushöhlen, unterhöhlen; unterbieten (*C.L.*). 2. *s.* [ˈʌndəkʌt], das Filet(stück). **––develop,** *v.a.* unterentwickeln (*Phot.*). **–do** [–ˈdu:], *v.a.* nicht genug kochen *or* braten (*Cook.*), unvollkommen tun. **– dog,** Benachteiligte(r), Unterlegene(r), Besiegte(r), *m.* **–done** [–dʌn], *adj.* nicht gar *or* durchgebraten (*Cook.*). **–estimate,** 1. [–ˈɛstɪmeɪt], *v.a.* unterschätzen. 2. [–ˈɛstɪmət] *s.*, **–estimation,** die Unterschätzung. **––expose,** *v.a.* unterbelichten (*Phot.*). **––exposure,** *s.* die Unterbelichtung (*Phot.*). **–fed** [–ˈfɛd], *adj.* unterernährt. **–feed** [–ˈfɪ:d], 1. *v.a.* unterernähren, nicht genügend ernähren *or* füttern. 2. *v.n.* sich ungenügend ernähren. **–feeding,** *s.* die Unterernährung. **–foot** [–fʊt], *adv.* unter den Füßen, unten, darunter, auf dem Boden, (*fig.*) in untergeordneter Stellung. **––frame,** *s.* das Untergestell (*Motor.*). **–garment,** *s.* das Unterkleid; *pl.* die Unterwäsche, Leibwäsche. **–go** [–ˈgoʊ], *ir.v.a.* durchmachen, erfahren, erleiden, erdulden; sich unterziehen (*an operation*, einer (*Gen.*) Operation). **–graduate** [–ˈgrædjʊət], *s.* der Student. **–ground,** 1. [–ˈgraʊnd], *adj.* & *adv.* unterirdisch (*also fig.*), Untergrund– (*Railw.*), Erd– (*cable*), Tiefbau– (*workings*), unter Tage (*Min.*), (*fig.*) geheim, Geheim–, verborgen; *–ground engineering*, der Tiefbau; *–ground mining*, der Untertagebau; *–ground movement*, die Untergrundbewegung (*Pol.*); *–ground railway*, die Untergrundbahn; *–ground water*, das Grundwasser. 2. [ˈʌndəgraʊnd], *s.* die Untergrundbahn. **–growth,** *s.* das Unterholz, Gebüsch, Gestrüpp. **–hand** [–ˈhænd], *adj.* & *adv.* heimlich; [ˈʌndəhænd], mit dem Handrücken nach unten (*Crick.*, *etc.*); (*fig.*) [–ˈhænd], unterderhand, hinter dem Rücken, unehrlich, hinterlistig, verstohlen. **–handed** [–ˈhændɪd], *adj.* unter der Hand, heimlich, hinterlistig. **––handedness,** *s.* die Hinterlist, Heimlichkeit, Unehrlichkeit. **–hung** [–ˈhʌŋ], *adj.* über den Oberkiefer vorstehend (*as a jaw*), mit vorstehendem Unterkiefer (*of a p.*). **–lay** [–ˈleɪ], 1. *v.a.* unterlegen, stützen. 2. *v.n.* sich neigen, einfallen (*Min.*). 3. [ˈʌndəleɪ], *s.* die Unterlage. **–lie** [–ˈlaɪ], *ir.v.n.* liegen *or* sich befinden unter; unterworfen sein, unterliegen (*Dat.*), (*fig.*) zugrunde liegen (*Dat.*). **–line** [–ˈlaɪn], *v.a.* unterstreichen (*also fig.*) (*fig.*) betonen, hervorheben. **–linen,** *s.* die Leibwäsche, Unterwäsche. **–ling** [ˈʌndəlɪŋ], *s.* der Gehilfe, Handlanger, Untergegebene(r), *m.* **––lip,** *s.* die Unterlippe. **–lying** [–ˈlaɪɪŋ], *adj.* zugrundeliegend; *–lying idea*, der Grundgedanke. **–manned** [–ˈmænd], *adj.* nicht genügend bemannt. **–mentioned** [–ˈmɛnʃənd], *adj.* unten erwähnt. **–mine** [–ˈmaɪn], *v.a.* unterminieren, (*fig.*) untergraben, aushölen, unterhöhlen; zerstören, schwächen. **–most** [ˈʌndəmoʊst], 1. *adv.* zuunterst. 2. *adj.* unterst. **–neath** [–ˈnɪ:θ], 1. *adv.* unten, unterhalb; unterwärts, darunter (liegend); *from –neath*, von unten her. 2. *prep.* unter, unterhalb; *from –neath*, von unter . . . her. **–nourished** [–ˈnʌrɪʃt], *adj.* unterernährt. **–paid** [–ˈpeɪd], *adj.* ungenügend *or* schlecht bezahlt. **–pin** [–ˈpɪn], *v.a.* unterbauen, untermauern (*also fig.*), stützen (*also fig.*). **–pinning,** *s.* die Untermauerung, der Unterbau. **––populated** [–ˈpɔpjʊleɪtɪd], *adj.* unterbevölkert. **––production** [–prəˈdʌkʃən], *s.* die Unterproduktion. **–rate** [–ˈreɪt], *v.a.* unterschätzen. **–score** [–ˈskɔ:], *v.a.* unterstreichen. **––secretary** [–ˈsɛkrətɛrɪ], *s.* Unterstaatssekretär. **–sell** [–ˈsɛl], *ir.v.a.* unterbieten, billiger verkaufen als (*another person*); unter dem Werte verkaufen, verschleudern (*goods*). **–shot** [ˈʌndəʃɔt], *adj.* unterschlächtig (*of water-wheels*); mit vorstehendem Unterkiefer. **–signed** [–ˈsaɪnd], *s.* Unterzeichnete(r), *m.* **–sized** [–ˈsaɪzd], *adj.* unter der normalen Größe. **–skirt** [ˈʌndəskə:t], *s.* der Unterrock. **––staffed** [–ˈstɑ:ft], *adj.* unterbesetzt.

understand [ʌndəˈstænd], 1. *ir.v.a.* verstehen; begreifen, einsehen, erkennen, erfahren, hören; meinen, annehmen, voraussetzen; schließen (*from*, aus), entnehmen (*from* (*Dat.*) *or* aus); sich verstehen auf (*Acc.*); *he –s horses*, er versteht sich auf Pferde; *as I – it*, wie ich es auffasse; *give a p. to –*, einem zu verstehen geben, einen erkennen lassen; – *by*, verstehen unter (*Dat.*); *be it understood*, wohlverstanden; *he was understood to say*, man nahm als sicher an, daß er sagte; dem Vernehmen nach soll er gesagt haben; *an understood thing*, eine selbstverständliche *or* ausgemachte S., das versteht sich von selbst; *make o.s. understood*, sich verständlich machen. 2. *ir.v.n.* begreifen; erfahren. **–able,** *adj.* verständlich; begreiflich. **–ing,** 1. *s.* der Verstand, die Intelligenz, der Intellekt, das Begriffsvermögen, das Verständnis (*of*, für), Einvernehmen; Übereinkommen, die Einigung, Vereinbarung, Verständigung, Abmachung (*on*, über); *come to* or *have an –ing with*, sich verständigen mit; *have a good –ing with*, in gutem Einvernehmen stehen mit; *on the –ing that*, unter der Voraussetzung *or* Bedingung daß. 2. *adj.* verständig, urteilsfähig, einsichtsvoll, verständnisvoll.

under-state [ʌndəˈsteɪt], *v.a.* zu gering angeben; mit Vorbehalt aussagen, bewußt mildern *or* abschwächen. **–statement,** *s.* ungenügende Angabe, die Unterschätzung, Unterbewertung; maßvolle Aussage *or* Darstellung. **–study** [ˈʌndəstʌdɪ], 1. *s.* der Ersatzschauspieler. 2. *v.a.* als Ersatzspieler einstudieren (*a part*), als Ersatzspieler *or* Vertreter stehen für (*an actor*). **–take** [–ˈteɪk], *ir.v.a.* auf sich nehmen, übernehmen (*a task*), unternehmen (*a journey*, *etc.*); sich verpflichten *or* verbürgen (*to do*, zu tun). **–taker** [ˈʌndəteɪkə], *s.* der Leichenbestatter. **–taking** [–ˈteɪkɪŋ], *s.* das Unternehmen, Unterfangen, die Unternehmung; Bedingung, bindendes Versprechen; *give an –taking*, sich verpflichten; *on the –taking*, mit der Zusicherung, unter der Bedingung. **–tone** [ˈʌndətoʊn], *s.* gedämpfte Stimme; der Unterton, die Unterströmung; *in an –tone* or *–tones*, mit gedämpfter Stimme. **–tow** [ˈʌndətoʊ], *s.* die Rückströmung, Unterströmung. **–value** [–ˈvæljʊ:], *v.a.* zu niedrig einschätzen, unterschätzen; geringschätzen. **–vest** [ˈʌndəvɛst], *s.* das Unterhemd. **–wear** [ˈʌndəwɛə], *s.* das Unterzeug, die Leibwäsche. **–weight** [ʌndəˈweɪt], *s.* das Untergewicht, Fehlgewicht, der Gewichtsausfall. **–went** [–ˈwɛnt], *see* **–go.** **–wood** [ˈʌndəwʊd], *s.* das Gestrüpp, Unterholz. **–world** [ˈʌndəwə:ld], *s.* die Unterwelt. **–write** [–ˈraɪt], *ir.v.a.* & *n.* versichern, assekurieren (*C.L.*). **–writer** [ˈʌndəraɪtə], *s.* der Versicherer, Garant, Assekurant. **–writing,** *s.* die (See)Versicherung, Assekuration; das Versicherungsgeschäft.

undeserv–ed [ˈʌndɪˈzə:vd], *adj.* unverdient. **–ing,** *adj.* unwert, unwürdig (*of* (*Gen.*)); *be –ing of*, nicht verdienen.

undesign-ed ['ʌndɪ'zaɪnd], *adj.* unbeabsichtigt, unvorsätzlich. **-ing,** *adj.* harmlos, ehrlich.
undesir-ability ['ʌndɪzaɪərə'bɪlɪtɪ], *s.* die Unerwünschtheit. **-able** [-'zaɪərəbl], 1. *adj.* unerwünscht, nicht wünschenswert, lästig. 2. *s.* lästige *or* unerwünschte Person; *pl.* unbequeme Elemente. **-ed** [-'zaɪəd], *adj.* ungewünscht, unerwünscht. **-ous** [-'zaɪərəs], *adj.* nicht begierig (*of,* nach); *be -ous of,* nicht wünschen.
undetected ['ʌndɪ'tɛktɪd], *adj.* nicht entdeckt; unbemerkt (*by,* von).
undetermined ['ʌndɪ'tə:mɪnd], *adj.* unbestimmt, unentschieden (*of a th.*), unentschlossen, schwankend (*of a p.*).
undeterred ['ʌndɪ'tə:d], *adj.* nicht abgeschreckt (*by,* durch).
undeveloped ['ʌndɪ'vɛləpt], *adj.* unentwickelt; unerschlossen (*land*).
undeviating [ʌn'dɪ:vɪeɪtɪŋ], *adj.* nicht abweichend, unbeirrbar, unwandelbar, unentwegt.
undid ['ʌn'dɪd], *see* **undo.**
undies ['ʌndɪz], *pl.* (*coll.*) die (Damen)Unterwäsche.
undifferentiated ['ʌndɪfə'rɛnʃɪeɪtɪd], *adj.* homogen.
undigested ['ʌndɪ'dʒɛstɪd], *adj.* unverdaut.
undignified [ʌn'dɪgnɪfaɪd], *adj.* würdelos, unedel.
undiluted ['ʌndɪl(j)ʊ:tɪd], *adj.* unverdünnt, unvermischt, unverschnitten, unverfälscht.
undiminished ['ʌndɪ'mɪnɪʃt], *adj.* unvermindert, ungeschmälert.
undiplomatic ['ʌndɪplə'mætɪk], *adj.* undiplomatisch.
undirected ['ʌndɪ'rɛktɪd], *adj.* ungeleitet, führungslos; ohne Adresse, unadressiert (*as letters*).
undiscern-ed ['ʌndɪsə:nd], *adj.* unbemerkt, nicht erkannt. **-ing,** *adj.* einsichtslos, urteilslos.
undisciplined [ʌn'dɪsɪplɪnd], *adj.* zuchtlos, undiszipliniert.
undisclosed ['ʌndɪs'klouzd], *adj.* nicht bekanntgegeben, geheimgehalten.
undiscouraged ['ʌndɪskʌrɪdʒd], *adj.* nicht entmutigt.
undiscover-able [ʌndɪ'skʌvərəbl], *adj.* unentdeckbar, nicht aufzufinden(d). **-ed** [-vəd], *adj.* unentdeckt, unenthüllt, unbemerkt.
undiscriminating ['ʌndɪskrɪmɪneitɪŋ], *adj.* unterschiedslos, unkritisch.
undisguised ['ʌndɪsgaɪzd], *adj.* unverhüllt, unverstellt, unverkleidet, (*fig.*) unverhohlen, offen.
undismayed ['ʌndɪsmeɪd], *adj.* unerschrocken, unverzagt.
undisposed ['ʌndɪspouzd], *adj.* nicht geneigt, unwillig; – *of,* nicht vergeben *or* verteilt, unverkauft.
undisputed ['ʌndɪspjʊ:tɪd], *adj.* unbestritten.
undistinguished ['ʌndɪs'tɪŋgwɪʃt], *adj.* unbekannt, nicht ausgezeichnet.
undisturbed ['ʌndɪstə:bd], *adj.* ungestört (*by,* durch), ruhig.
undivided ['ʌndɪ'vaɪdɪd], *adj.* ungeteilt; ganz, alleinig.
undo ['ʌn'dʊ:], *ir.v.a.* aufmachen, öffnen (*a parcel, etc.*), auflösen (*a knot*); aufknöpfen (*coat, etc.*), abnehmen, losbinden (*collar, etc.*); auftrennen (*a seam*); aufheben, ungeschehen *or* rückgängig machen (*s.th. done*); (*coll.*) vernichten, zerstören, zugrunde richten, unglücklich machen. **-ing** [ʌn'dʊ:ɪŋ], *s.* das Aufmachen, *etc.*; Rückgängigmachen: Verderben, der Untergang, Verderb, die Vernichtung, das Unglück. **-ne** ['ʌn'dʌn], *adj.* ungetan, unvollendet; aufgemacht, unbefestigt; (*coll.*) verloren, vernichtet, hin, aus; *I am -ne,* es ist aus mit mir; *come -ne,* aufgehen; *leave -ne,* ungetan lassen, nicht vollenden, unterlassen; *leave nothing -ne,* nichts unterlassen, alles tun.
undoubted [ʌn'daʊtɪd], *adj.* unbezweifelt, unbestritten, unzweifelhaft, zweifellos. **-ly,** *adv.* unstreitig, gewiß, zweifelsohne, ohne Zweifel.
undream-ed [ʌn'drɪ:md] *or* **-t** [-drɛmt]; *-ed* or *-t of,* völlig unerwartet, ungeahnt, unerhört.
undress [ʌn'drɛs], 1. *v.a.* ausziehen, auskleiden, entkleiden. 2. *v.r. & n.* sich ausziehen, sich entkleiden. 3. *s.* das Hauskleid, Negligé; die Interimsuniform (*Mil.*). **-ed** [-t], *adj.* unbekleidet, nackt; ungarniert, unzubereitet (*salad*); unverbunden (*wounds*), ungegerbt (*leather*).
undried ['ʌndraɪd], *adj.* ungetrocknet.
undrinkable [ʌn'drɪŋkəbl], *adj.* nicht trinkbar.
undue [ʌn'djʊ:], *adj.* unpassend, unangemessen, ungebührlich, ungehörig, übermäßig, übertrieben.
undulat-e ['ʌndjʊleɪt], *v.n.* sich wellenförmig bewegen, Wellen werfen, wallen, wogen. **-ing,** *adj.* wallend, wogend; wellenförmig, wellig, gewellt. **-ion** [-'leɪʃn], *s.* wellenförmige Bewegung, die Wellenbewegung, Wellenschwingung, Schwingungswelle, Undulation (*Geol.*). **-ory** ['ʌndjʊleɪtərɪ], *adj.* wellenförmig, Wellen-.
undutiful [ʌn'djʊ:tɪfəl], *adj.* pflichtvergessen, ungehorsam, unehrerbietig. **-ness,** *s.* die Pflichtwidrigkeit, Pflichtvergessenheit, der Ungehorsam.
undying [ʌn'daɪɪŋ], *adj.* unsterblich, unvergänglich, unaufhörlich.
unearned ['ʌnə:nd], *adj.* unverdient; – *income,* das Einkommen aus Kapitalvermögen. – *increment,* unverdienter Wertzuwachs *or* Mehrertrag.
unearth [ʌn'ə:θ], *v.a.* ausgraben (*beasts*), (*fig.*) ans Tageslicht bringen, ausstöbern. **-ly** [-lɪ], *adj.* überirdisch, übernatürlich, geisterhaft, unheimlich; (*coll.*) *at an -ly hour,* unmenschlich früh.
uneas-iness [ʌn'ɪ:zɪnɪs], *s.* innere Unruhe, die Besorgnis, Unbehaglichkeit, das Unbehagen. **-y,** *adj.* unbehaglich, unbequem; unruhig, besorgt, ängstlich (*about,* über *or* wegen), verlegen.
uneat-able [ʌn'ɪ:təbl], *adj.* ungenießbar. **-en** [-tn], *adj.* ungegessen.
uneconomical ['ʌnɪ:kə'nəmɪkl], *adj.* unwirtschaftlich.
unedifying [ʌn'ɛdɪfaɪɪŋ], *adj.* unerbaulich.
uneducated [ʌn'ɛdjʊkeɪtɪd], *adj.* ungebildet.
unembarrassed ['ʌnəm'bærəst], *adj.* ungeniert, nicht verlegen; von (Geld)Sorgen frei, schuldenfrei, unbelastet.
unemotional ['ʌnɪ'mouʃənl], *adj.* leidenschaftslos, teilnahmslos, passiv, nüchtern; nicht aufregend.
unemploy-able ['ʌnɪm'plɔɪəbl], *adj.* arbeitsunfähig (*of a p.*), verwendungsunfähig, nicht verwendbar (*of a th.*). **-ed** [-'plɔɪd], 1. *adj.* arbeitslos, erwerbslos, unbeschäftigt (*of a p.*), ungebraucht, unbenutzt (*of a th.*); *-ed capital,* totes Kapital. 2. *pl.* die Arbeitslosen (*pl.*). **-ment,** *s.* die Arbeitslosigkeit, Erwerbslosigkeit. **-ment-benefit** *or* **-relief,** *s.* die Arbeitslosenunterstützung. **-ment-insurance,** *s.* die Arbeitslosenversicherung.
unencumbered ['ʌnɪn'kʌmbəd], *adj.* unbelastet (*as an estate*), unbehindert (*by,* durch).
unending [ʌn'ɛndɪŋ], *adj.* endlos, nicht endend, unaufhörlich, ständig.
unendowed ['ʌnɪn'daʊd], *adj.* undotiert, nicht ausgestattet; unbegabt (*with,* mit).
unendurable [['ʌnɪn'djʊərəbl], *adj.* unerträglich.
unenlightened ['ʌnɪn'laɪtənd], *adj.* unaufgeklärt.
unenterprising [ʌn'ɛntəpraɪzɪŋ], *adj.* nicht unternehmend *or* unternehmungslustig, ohne Unternehmungsgeist.
unenviable [ʌn'ɛnvjəbl], *adj.* nicht beneidenswert *or* zu beneiden(d).
unequal [ʌn'ɪ:kwəl], *adj.* ungleich(artig); unverhältnismäßig; unangemessen; *be – to,* nicht gewachsen sein (*Dat.*). **-led** [-d], *adj.* unvergleichlich (*for,* wegen), unübertroffen, unerreicht (*by,* von); (*pred. only*) ohnegleichen.
unequivocal ['ʌnɪ'kwɪvəkl], *adj.* unzweideutig, eindeutig.
unerring [ʌn'ə:rɪŋ], *adj.* nicht irregehend, unfehlbar, sicher, untrüglich. **-ly,** *adv.* ohne irrezugehen.
unessential ['ʌnɪ'sɛnʃəl], 1. *adj.* unwesentlich, unwichtig, nebensächlich. 2. *s.* (*usually pl.*) die Nebensache, unwesentliches Ding.
unestablished ['ʌnɪ'stæblɪʃt], *adj.* nicht beamtet (*official*), nicht verstaatlicht (*church*).
uneven [ʌn'ɪ:vn], *adj.* uneben (*ground, etc.*), ungleich (*performance*), ungerade (*number*), ungleichmäßig. **-ness,** *s.* die Ungleichheit, Unebenheit.
uneventful ['ʌnɪ'vɛntfəl], *adj.* ereignislos, ereignisleer, ruhig, still.
unexampled ['ʌnɪgza:mpəld], *adj.* beispiellos,

unvergleichlich; (*pred. only*) ohnegleichen; *not* –, nicht ohne Beispiel.
unexceptiona-ble [ˈʌnɪkˈsɛpʃənəbl], *adj.* tadellos, einwandfrei, nicht zu beanstanden(d). **-l** [-ʃənl], *adj.* ausnahmslos.
unexciting [ˈʌnɪkˈsɑɪtɪŋ], *adj.* ruhig, reibungslos.
unexpected [ˈʌnɪkˈspɛktɪd], *adj.* unerwartet, unvermutet, unvorhergesehen. **-ness,** *s.* das Unerwartete; die Überraschung.
unexpired [ˈʌnɪkˈspɑɪəd], *adj.* noch nicht abgelaufen.
unexplain-able [ˈʌnɪksˈpleɪnəbl], *adj.* unerklärlich. **-ed** [-ˈpleɪnd], *adj.* unerklärt.
unexplored [ˈʌnɪksˈplɔ:d], *adj.* unerforscht, unerschlossen.
unexpressed [ˈʌnɪksˈprɛst], *adj.* unausgedrückt, unausgesprochen.
unexpurgated [ʌnˈɛkspə:geɪtɪd], *adj.* ungekürzt, unverstümmelt.
unfading [ʌnˈfeɪdɪŋ], *adj.* unverwelklich, nicht verblassend, (*fig.*) unvergänglich.
unfailing [ʌnˈfeɪlɪŋ], *adj.* unfehlbar, sicher; unversieglich, unerschöpflich, nie versagend.
unfair [ʌnˈfɛə], *adj.* ungerecht, unbillig, unfair (*to*, gegenüber), parteiisch, unehrlich; – *competition*, unlauterer Wettbewerb. **-ly,** *adv.* mit Unrecht. **-ness,** *s.* die Unbilligkeit, Unehrlichkeit.
unfaithful [ʌnˈfeɪθful], *adj.* un(ge)treu, treulos; nicht (wort)getreu, ungenau (*translation*). **-ness,** *s.* die Treulosigkeit, Untreue.
unfaltering [ʌnˈfɔ:ltərɪŋ], *adj.* nicht schwankend, ohne Zaudern; fest, entschlossen, mutig.
unfamiliar [ˈʌnfəˈmɪlɪə], *adj.* unbekannt, nicht vertraut (*to* (*Dat.*)), ungewohnt. **-ity** [-mɪlɪˈærɪtɪ], *s.* die Unbekanntheit, Unvertrautheit (*with*, mit).
unfashionable [ʌnˈfæʃənəbl], *adj.* altmodisch, unmodern, aus der Mode. **-ness,** *s.* das Unmoderne, Unmodische.
unfasten [ʌnˈfɑ:sn], 1. *v.a.* aufmachen, aufbinden, losbinden, lösen. 2. *v.n.* aufgehen, sich lösen. **-ed** [-sənd], *adj.* unbefestigt, lose.
unfatherly [ʌnˈfɑ:ðəlɪ], *adj.* unväterlich, lieblos.
unfathomable [ʌnˈfæðəməbl], *adj.* unergründlich (tief); (*fig.*) unermeßlich, unfaßbar, unerklärlich.
unfavourable [ʌnˈfeɪvərəbl], *adj.* ungünstig, unvorteilhaft (*to* or *for*, für), widrig. **-ness,** *s.* die Unvorteilhaftigkeit, Ungunst.
unfeasible [ʌnˈfɪ:zəbl], *adj.* unausführbar.
unfeeling [ʌnˈfɪ:lɪŋ], *adj.* gefühllos, unempfindlich. **-ness,** *s.* die Gefühllosigkeit.
unfeigned [ʌnˈfeɪnd], *adj.* unverstellt, nicht geheuchelt, echt, wahr.
unfeminine [ʌnˈfɛmɪnɪn], *adj.* unweiblich.
unfenced [ˈʌnˈfɛnst], *adj.* uneingehegt, unverschanzt, unbefestigt.
unfermented [ˈʌnfəˈmɛntɪd], *adj.* ungegoren.
unfettered [ʌnˈfɛtəd], *adj.* (*usually fig.*) entfesselt, ungezwungen, unbehindert.
unfilial [ʌnˈfɪlɪəl], *adj.* unkindlich.
unfilled [ˈʌnˈfɪld], *adj.* unausgefüllt; unbesetzt (*post*).
unfinished [ʌnˈfɪnɪʃt], *adj.* unvollendet, unfertig.
unfit [ʌnˈfɪt], 1. *adj.* untauglich (*also Mil.*), unfähig, ungeeignet (*for*, zu); *medically* –, dienstuntauglich (*Mil.*). 2. *v.a.* untauglich *or* unfähig machen. **-ness,** *s.* die Untauglichkeit, Unbrauchbarkeit (*for*, zu). **-ted** [-ɪd], *adj.* untauglich, ungeeignet, nicht ausgestattet *or* ausgerüstet (*with*, mit). **-ting,** *adj.* unpassend, ungeeignet; unschicklich.
unfix [ˈʌnfɪks], *v.a.* losmachen, lösen; – *bayonets!* Bajonett ab! **-ed** [-t], *adj.* lose, locker, unbefestigt, beweglich.
unflagging [ʌnˈflægɪŋ], *adj.* nicht erschlaffend, unermüdlich.
unflattering [ʌnˈflætərɪŋ], *adj.* nicht schmeichelnd *or* schmeichelhaft (*to*, für).
unfledged [ʌnˈflɛdʒd], *adj.* nicht flügge, (*fig.*) unreif, unentwickelt.
unfleshed [ʌnˈflɛʃt], *adj.* ungeatzt (*as hounds*), (*fig.*) unerprobt.
unflinching [ʌnˈflɪntʃɪŋ], *adj.* nicht wankend *or* zurückweichend, entschlossen, unentwegt, unnachgiebig.
unfold [ʌnˈfould], 1. *v.a.* entfalten, ausbreiten; (*fig.*) enthüllen, offenbaren; darlegen, klarlegen. 2. *v.n.* sich entfalten *or* öffnen.
unforced [ʌnˈfɔ:st], *adj.* ungezwungen, natürlich.
unforeseen [ˈʌnfɔ:ˈsɪ:n], *adj.* unvorhergesehen. unerwartet.
unforgettable [ˈʌnfəˈgɛtəbl], *adj.* unvergeßlich.
unforgiv-able [ˈʌnfəˈgɪvəbl], *adj.* unverzeihlich. **-en** [-gɪvn], *adj.* unverziehen. **-ing,** *adj.* unversöhnlich, nachtragend.
unforgotten [ˈʌnfəˈgɔtn], *adj.* unvergessen.
unformed [ˈʌnˈfɔ:md], *adj.* ungeformt, formlos, (*fig.*) unausgebildet, unentwickelt, unfertig.
unfortified [ʌnˈfɔ:tɪfɑɪd], *adj.* unbefestigt.
unfortunate [ʌnˈfɔ:tjunət], 1. *adj.* unglücklich, Unglücks–, verhängnisvoll; unglückselig, elend, bedauernswert. 2. *s.* Unglückliche(r), *m.* **-ly,** *adv.* unglücklicherweise, leider.
unfounded [ʌnˈfɑundɪd], *adj.* unbegründet, grundlos, gegenstandslos.
unframed [ʌnˈfreɪmd], *adj.* ungerahmt.
unfree [ˈʌnfrɪ:], *adj.* unfrei.
unfrequent [ʌnˈfrɪ:kwənt], *adj.* selten (*usually neg., otherwise* **infrequent**). **-ed** [ˈʌnfrɪˈkwɛntɪd], *adj.* nicht *or* wenig besucht, einsam.
unfriend-ed [ʌnˈfrɛndɪd], *adj.* freundlos. **-liness,** *s.* die Unfreundlichkeit. **-ly,** *adj.* unfreundlich (*to*(*wards*), gegen).
unfrock [ˈʌnˈfrɔk], *v.a.* ein geistliches Amt entziehen (*Dat.*).
unfruitful [ʌnˈfru:tful], *adj.* unfruchtbar, (*usually fig.*) fruchtlos, ergebnislos. **-ness,** *s.* die Unfruchtbarkeit, Fruchtlosigkeit
unfulfilled [ˈʌnfulfɪld], *adj.* unerfüllt, nicht verwirklicht.
unfunded [ʌnˈfʌndɪd], *adj.* nicht fundiert, schwebend.
unfurl [ʌnˈfə:l], 1. *v.a.* entfalten, ausbreiten, auseinanderbreiten; losmachen (*sails*); aufspannen (*a fan*). 2. *v.n.* sich ausbreiten *or* entfalten.
unfurnished [ʌnˈfə:nɪʃt], *adj.* nicht ausgerüstet; unmöbliert (*as houses*).
ungainl-iness [ʌnˈgeɪnlɪnɪs], *s.* die Plumpheit, Ungeschicktheit. **-y,** *adj.* plump, ungeschickt, linkisch.
ungallant [ʌnˈgælənt], *adj.* unhöflich, ungalant; nicht tapfer.
ungenerous [ʌnˈdʒɛnərəs], *adj.* nicht freigiebig; unedel(mütig).
ungenteel [ʌndʒɛnˈtɪ:l], *adj.* unfein, unhöflich, unartig.
ungentle [ʌnˈdʒɛntl], *adj.* unsanft, unhöflich, grob, rauh, hart. **-manlike** [ʌnˈdʒɛntlmənlɑɪk], *adj.* unfein, unvornehm, unedel. **-manliness** [ʌnˈdʒɛntlmənlɪnɪs], *s.* unedles, unvornehmes *or* unwürdiges Benehmen. **-manly,** *see* **-manlike.**
unget-at-able [ʌngɛtˈætəbl], *adj.* (*coll.*) unzugänglich, unnahbar, schwer erreichbar.
ungird [ʌnˈgə:d], *v.a.* losgürten, lockern. **-ed** [-ɪd], **ungirt** [-gə:t], *adj.* nicht gegürtet, gelockert.
unglazed [ʌnˈgleɪzd], *adj.* unglasiert; unverglast, glaslos; – *paper*, das Fließpapier.
ungodl-iness [ʌnˈgɔdlɪnɪs], *s.* die Gottlosigkeit. **-y,** *adj.* gottlos, verrucht; (*coll.*) anstößig.
ungovernable [ʌnˈgʌvənəbl], *adj.* unlenksam, zügellos, unbändig.
ungrac-eful [ʌnˈgreɪsful], *adj.* nicht graziös, ohne Anmut; plump, ungelenk. **-ious** [-ˈgreɪʃəs], *adj.* ungnädig, unliebenswürdig, unfreundlich.
ungrammatical [ʌngrəˈmætɪkl], *adj.* ungrammatisch.
ungrateful [ʌnˈgreɪtful], *adj.* undankbar (*to*, gegen) (*also fig.*). **-ness,** *s.* die Undankbarkeit.
ungratified [ʌnˈgrætɪfɑɪd], *adj.* unbefriedigt.
ungrounded [ʌnˈgrɑundɪd], *adj.* unbegründet.
ungrudging [ʌnˈgrʌdʒɪŋ], *adj.* (bereit)willig, ohne Murren; *be* – *in*, reichlich spenden.
ungual [ˈʌŋgwəl], *adj.* Huf–, Klauen–, Nagel–.
unguarded [ʌnˈgɑ:dɪd], *adj.* unbewacht (*also fig.*), ungeschützt, ungedeckt; (*fig.*) unvorsichtig, unbedacht, übereilt.
unguent [ˈʌŋgwənt], *s.* die Salbe.
ungulate [ˈʌŋgjulət], 1. *adj.* hufförmig, Huf–. 2. *s.* das Huftier.
unhallowed [ʌnˈhæloud], *adj.* ungeweiht, nicht geheiligt; unheilig, gottlos.

unhampered [ʌn'hæmpəd], *adj.* ungehindert, frei.
unhand ['ʌn'hænd], *v.a.* loslassen.
unhandiness [ʌn'hændɪnɪs], *s.* die Ungeschicklichkeit, das Ungeschick (*of a p.*), die Unhandlichkeit (*of a th.*).
unhandsome [ʌn'hænsəm], *adj.* unschön, unansehnlich; unedel, unfein (*behaviour*).
unhandy [ʌn'hændɪ], *adj.* unhandlich, unbequem (*of a th.*), ungeschickt, ungelenk (*of a p.*).
unhapp–ily [ʌn'hæpɪlɪ], *adv.* unglücklich(erweise), leider. **–iness** [–pɪnɪs], *s.* das Unglück; das Elend, die Unglückseligkeit. **–y,** *adj.* unglücklich, elend, un(glück)selig, unheilvoll.
unharmed [ʌn'hɑ:md], *adj.* unversehrt, unbeschädigt.
unharmonious [ʌn'hɑ:mounɪəs], *adj.* unharmonisch (*also fig.*), unmelodisch.
unharness [ʌn'hɑ:nɪs], *v.a.* abschirren, ausspannen.
unhealth–iness [ʌn'hɛlθɪnɪs], *s.* die Ungesundheit. **–y,** *adj.* ungesund (*also of things and places*), kränklich; gesundheitsschädlich; (*fig.*) krankhaft.
unheard [ʌn'hə:d], *adj.* ungehört. **––of,** *adj.* unerhört, beispiellos, noch nicht dagewesen.
unheed–ed [ʌn'hɪ:dɪd], *adj.* unbeachtet. **–ful** [–fʊl], *adj.* sorglos, unachtsam; nicht achtend (*of*, auf). **–ing,** *adj.* unachtsam, sorglos.
unhelpful [ʌn'hɛlpfʊl], *adj.* nicht hilfreich (*a p.*); (*pred. only*) nutzlos, ohne Nutzen (*to*, für).
unhesitating [ʌn'hɛzɪteɪtɪŋ], *adj.* nicht zögernd, unverzüglich; bereitfertig; unbedenklich, anstandslos. **–ly,** *adv.* ohne Zögern, ohne weiteres.
unhindered [ʌn'hɪndə:d], *adj.* ungehindert, ungehemmt.
unhinge [ʌn'hɪndʒ], *v.a.* aus den Angeln heben; (*fig.*) verwirren, zerrütten, aus der Fassung *or* dem Gleichgewicht bringen.
unhistorical [ʌnhɪs'tɔrɪkl], *adj.* unhistorisch.
unhitch ['ʌn'hɪtʃ], *v.a.* loshaken, losmachen; ausspannen (*horses*).
unholy [ʌn'houlɪ], *adj.* unheilig, ungeweiht, profan; gottlos, ruchlos; (*coll.*) gräßlich, schrecklich, abscheulich.
unhonoured [ʌn'ɔnə:d], *adj.* nicht verehrt *or* geehrt.
unhook ['ʌn'hʊk], *v.a.* aufhaken, loshaken.
unhoped-for [ʌn'houptfɔ:], *adj.* unerhofft, unverhofft, ungeahnt, unerwartet.
unhorse [ʌn'hɔ:s], *v.a.* aus dem Sattel heben, abwerfen.
unhung [ʌn'hʌŋ], *adj.* nicht gehenkt, noch nicht aufgehängt.
unhurt [ʌn'hə:t], *adj.* unbeschädigt, unverletzt.
unicellular ['ju:nɪ'sɛljulə], *adj.* einzellig (*Biol.*).
unicorn ['junɪkɔ:n], *s.* das Einhorn.
unification [ju:nɪfɪ'keɪʃn], *s.* die Vereinigung, Einigung, Vereinheitlichung.
uniform ['ju:nɪfɔ:m], 1. *adj.* gleichförmig, übereinstimmend, gleichmäßig, einheitlich, einförmig, Einheits–; eintönig. 2. *s.* die Uniform (*also Mil.*). **–ed** [–d], *adj.* uniformiert. **–ity** [–'fɔ:mɪtɪ], *s.* die Gleichförmigkeit, Übereinstimmung, Einheitlichkeit, Gleichmäßigkeit, Einförmigkeit; Eintönigkeit.
unify ['ju:nɪfɑɪ], *v.a.* einigen, verein(ig)en, vereinheitlichen.
unilateral ['ju:nɪ'lætərəl], *adj.* einseitig.
unimagin–able ['ʌnɪ'mædʒɪnəbl], *adj.* undenkbar, unvorstellbar. **–ative** [–'mædʒɪnətɪv], *adj.* phantasielos, phantasiearm.
unimpaired ['ʌnɪm'pɛəd], *adj.* unvermindert, ungeschwächt.
unimpassioned ['ʌnɪm'pæʃənd], *adj.* leidenschaftslos.
unimpeachable ['ʌnɪm'pɪ:tʃəbl], *adj.* unanfechtbar, unantastbar; vorwurfsfrei, untadelhaft.
unimpeded ['ʌnɪm'pɪ:dɪd], *adj.* unbehindert.
unimportant ['ʌnɪm'pɔ:tənt], *adj.* unwichtig, nebensächlich.
unimposing ['ʌnɪm'pouzɪŋ], *adj.* eindruckslos, nicht imponierend.
unimpress–ionable ['ʌnɪm'prɛʃənəbl], *adj.* (für Eindrücke) unempfänglich. **–ive** [–'prɛsɪv], *adj.* eindruckslos.
unimproved ['ʌnɪm'pru:vd], *adj.* unverbessert; unausgenutzt; nicht kultiviert, unbebaut (*land*).
uninflected ['ʌnɪn'flɛktɪd], *adj.* unflektiert, flexionslos (*Gram.*).
uninfluen–ced [ʌn'ɪnfluənst], *adj.* unbeeinflußt (*by*, durch). **–tial** ['ʌnɪnflu'ɛnʃəl], *adj.* einflußlos; *be –ial*, keinen Einfluß haben.
uninformed ['ʌnɪnfɔ:md], *adj.* nicht unterrichtet (*on* or *about*, über), uneingeweiht (*on* or *about*, in); unwissend, ungebildet.
uninhabit–able ['ʌnɪn'hæbɪtəbl], *adj.* unbewohnbar. **–ed** [–tɪd], *adj.* unbewohnt.
uninitiated ['ʌnɪ'nɪʃɪeɪtɪd], *adj.* uneingeweiht (*into*, in).
uninjured [ʌn'ɪndʒə:d], *adj.* unbeschädigt, unverletzt.
uninspir–ed ['ʌnɪn'spɑɪəd], *adj.* nicht begeistert, schwunglos. **–ing** [–'spɑɪərɪŋ], *adj.* nicht anregend.
uninstruct–ed ['ʌnɪn'strʌktɪd], *adj.* nicht unterrichtet; (*pred. only*) ohne Verhaltungsmaßregeln. **–ive** [–tɪv], *adj.* nicht belehrend.
unintellig–ent ['ʌnɪn'tɛlɪdʒənt], *adj.* nicht intelligent, geistlos, dumm, beschränkt. **–ibility** [–'bɪlɪtɪ], *s.* die Unverständlichkeit. **–ible** [–dʒɪbl], *adj.* unklar, unverständlich.
uninten–ded ['ʌnɪn'tɛndɪd], **–tional** [–'tɛnʃənl], *adj.* unbeabsichtigt, unabsichtlich.
uninterest–ed [ʌn'ɪnt(ə)rəstɪd], *adj.* uninteressiert, gleichgültig, unbeteiligt. **–ing,** *adj.* uninteressant, langweilig.
uninterrupted ['ʌnɪntə'rʌptɪd], *adj.* ununterbrochen, durchgehend, fortlaufend, anhaltend, andauernd.
uninvit–ed ['ʌnɪn'vɑɪtɪd], *adj.* ungebeten, uneingeladen. **–ing,** *adj.* nicht verlockend, anziehend *or* einladend, reizlos; unappetitlich (*food, etc.*).
union ['ju:nɪən], 1. *s.* das Vereinigen, Verbinden; die Vereinigung, Verbindung, der Anschluß (*with*, an); eheliche Verbindung, die Ehe; die Eintracht, Einheit, Harmonie, Übereinstimmung; der Verein; Staatenbund, die Union (*Pol., etc.*); der (Zweck)-Verband, (also *trade-–*) die Gewerkschaft; (*archaic*) der Kirchspielverband (*for the care of the poor*), das Armenhaus; (also *––joint*) die Röhrenkupplung, Schraubverbindung (*Tech.*); (also *– flannel*) ein Mischgewebe. **– jack,** *s.* Großbritannische Nationalflagge. **–ism** [–ɪzm], *s.* (*archaic*) konservative Politik; die Gewerkschaftspolitik. **–ist,** *s.* der Unionist, Konservative(r), *m.*; der Gewerkschaftler.
uniparous [ju:'nɪpərəs], *adj.* nur ein Junges bei einem Wurf gebärend.
unipartite ['ju:nɪ'pɑ:tɑɪt], *adj.* einteilig, aus einem Teil bestehend.
unipolar ['ju:nɪ'poulə], *adj.* einpolig.
unique [ju:'nɪ:k], 1. *adj.* einzig(artig), einmalig; ohnegleichen; (*coll.*) außerordentlich; *– of its kind*, einzig in seiner Art. 2. *s.* das Unikum, die Seltenheit. **–ness,** *s.* die Einzigartigkeit.
unisexual ['ju:nɪ'sɛksuəl], *adj.* eingeschlechtig.
unison ['ju:nɪsən], *s.* der Einklang (*also fig.*), Gleichklang; (*fig.*) die Übereinstimmung; *in –*, einstimmig, unisono (*Mus.*); (*fig.*) in Einklang. **–ous** [ju:'nɪsənəs], *adj.* einstimmig, gleichtönend, (*fig.*) übereinstimmend.
unit ['ju:nɪt], *s.* die Einheit, der Grundmaßstab; ganze Zahl, einzelne Größe (*Math.*), der Einer (*Math.*); das Einzelding; *military –*, der Truppenverband; *– of power*, die Leistungseinheit; *power –*, das Triebwerk (*Tech.*), Netzteil (*Rad.*). **–arian** [–'tɛərɪən], 1. *s.* der Unitarier. 2. *adj.* unitarisch. **–arianism** [–'tɛərɪənɪzm], *s.* die Lehre der Unitarier. **–ary** ['ju:nɪtərɪ], *adj.* Einheits–, einheitlich. **–e** [ju:'nɑɪt], 1. *v.a.* einen, (durch Ehe) verbinden; verheiraten (*to*, mit); vereinigen (*to*, mit) (*pieces*); verbinden (*Chem.*); in sich vereinigen (*qualities*). 2. *v.n.* sich vereinigen *or* zusammenschließen (*with*, mit) (*a p.*), sich verbinden (*Chem.*), sich verheiraten *or* ehelich verbinden (*with*, mit). **–ed** [–'nɑɪtɪd], *adj.* vereinigt, verbunden; vereint, gemeinsam, Einheits–; *–ed front*, die Einheitsfront; *–ed Kingdom*, Großbritannien und Nordirland; *–ed Nations*, Vereinte Nationen; *–ed Provinces*, die Vereinigten Niederlande; *–ed States* (*of America*), die Vereinigten Staaten (von

Amerika). **–y** ['ju:nɪtɪ], *s.* die Einheit (*also Math., etc.*); Einheitlichkeit; Einigkeit, Eintracht, Übereinstimmung; *be at –y with*, übereinstimmen mit; *give –y to a th.*, einer S. Einheitlichkeit verleihen; (*Prov.*) *–y is strength*, Einigkeit macht stark; *the three –ies*, die drei Einheiten (des Dramas).
univalent [ju:'nɪvələnt], *adj.* einwertig (*Chem.*).
univalve ['ju:nɪvælv], 1. *adj.* einschalig (*Zool.*). 2. *s.* das Einschaltier.
univers–al [ju:nɪ'və:sl], 1. *adj.* allgemein (bindend), universal, Universal–, universell; allumfassend, weltumfassend, Welt–; ganz, gesamt; *–al heir*, der Alleinerbe; *–al joint*, das Universalgelenk; *–al language*, die Weltsprache; *–al legacy*, das Universalvermächtnis; *–al mind*, allumfassender Geist; *–al Postal Union*, der Weltpostverein; *–al remedy*, das Universalmittel; *–al screw-wrench*, der Engländer; *–al suffrage*, allgemeines Wahlrecht. 2. *s.* das Allgemeine, allgemeiner Begriff; *pl.* Allgemeinbegriffe (*pl.*). **–alism** [–'və:səlɪzm], *s.* der Universalismus. **–ality** [–'sælɪtɪ], *s.* die Allgemeinheit, Universalität, Allgemeingültigkeit; Vielseitigkeit. **–alize** [–'və:səlaɪz], *v.a.* allgemein verbreiten, verwenden *or* bindend machen; allgemeinen Charakter verleihen (*Dat.*). **–e** [['ju:nɪvə:s], *s.* das Weltall, Universum, der Kosmos. **–ity** [–'və:sɪtɪ], *s.* die Hochschule, Universität; *go* (*up*) *to the –ity*, die Universität beziehen; *go down from the –ity*, die Universität verlassen; *at the –ity*, ən *or* auf der Universität; *the –ity of Berlin*, die Universität Berlin, Berliner Universität; *–ity chair*, der Lehrstuhl; *–ity education*, die Hochschulbildung; *–ity extension*, die Volkshochschule; *–ity lecturer*, der Universitätsdozent; *–ity man*, der Akademiker, akademisch Gebildete(r), *m.*; *–ity professor*, der Ordinarius, ordentlicher Professor; *-ity register*, die Universitätsmatrikel.
univocal [ju:'nɪvəkəl], *adj.* eindeutig, unzweideutig.
unjaundiced [ʌn'dʒɔ:ndɪst], *adj.* neidlos, nicht eifersüchtig.
unjust ['ʌn'dʒʌst], *adj.* ungerecht, unbillig (*to*, gegen). **–ifiable** [–ɪ'faɪəbl], *adj.* nicht zu rechtfertigen(d), unverantwortlich. **–ified** [–ɪfaɪd], *adj.* unberechtigt, ungerechtfertigt. **–ness,** *s.* die Ungerechtigkeit, Unbilligkeit.
unkempt [ʌn'kɛmpt], *adj.* ungekämmt, ungepflegt; unordentlich, vernachlässigt, schlampig, liederlich.
unkind [ʌn'kaɪnd], *adj.* unfreundlich, ungefällig, lieblos, rücksichtslos (*to*, gegen). **–liness,** *s.* die Unfreundlichkeit. **–ly,** 1. *adj.* unfreundlich (*as weather*), lieblos. 2. *adv.* unfreundlich. **–ness,** *s.* unfreundliche Behandlung, die Ungefälligkeit.
unknot ['ʌn'nɔt], *v.a.* aufknoten, aufmachen.
unknow–ing [ʌn'nouɪŋ], *adj.* unwissend; (*pred. only*) ohne zu wissen. **–ingly,** *adv.* ohne zu wissen, unwissentlich. **–n** [–'noun], 1. *adj.* unbekannt (*to* (*Dat.*)); *–n to him*, ohne sein Wissen. 2. *s.* das Unbekannte; die Unbekannte (*Math.*).
unlabelled [ʌn'leɪbəld], *adj.* nicht etikettiert, ohne Zettel.
unlaboured [ʌn'leɪbəd], *adj.* ungezwungen, leicht, fließend, natürlich (*of style*).
unlace ['ʌn'leɪs], *v.a.* aufschnüren.
unladen [ʌn'leɪdn], *adj.* unbeladen, (*fig.*) unbelastet.
unladylike [ʌn'leɪdɪlaɪk], *adj.* unfein, unvornehm, unschicklich.
unlamented ['ʌnlə'mɛntɪd], *adj.* unbeklagt, unbeweint.
unlatch ['ʌn'lætʃ], *v.a.* aufklinken.
unlawful [ʌn'lɔ:ful], *adj.* ungesetzlich, rechtswidrig, widerrechtlich, unerlaubt, unrechtmäßig. **–ness,** *s.* die Ungesetzlichkeit, *etc.*
unlay ['ʌn'leɪ], *v.a.* aufflechten (*a rope*).
unleash ['ʌn'lɪ:ʃ], *v.a.* loskoppeln (*hounds*), (*fig.*) loslassen, befreien.
unlearn ['ʌn'lə:n], *v.a.* verlernen, vergessen. **–ed** [–ɪd], *adj.* nicht gelernt; unwissend, ungelehrt.
unleavened [ʌn'lɛvənd], *adj.* ungesäuert.
unless [ʌn'lɛs], *conj.* wenn *or* wofern *or* falls nicht, vorausgesetzt daß nicht, außer *or* ausgenommen wenn, es sei denn daß.
unlettered [ʌn'lɛtəd], *adj.* ungelehrt, ungebildet.
unlicensed [ʌn'laɪsənst], *adj.* nicht konzessioniert, unerlaubt, unberechtigt.
unlicked ['ʌn'lɪkt], *adj.* (*usually fig.*) ungeleckt, unbeleckt, ungeformt, ungebildet, roh; *– cub*, ungeleckter Bär, grüner Junge.
unlike [ʌn'laɪk], 1. *adj.* unähnlich, ungleich (*Dat.*), verschieden. 2. *prep.* anders als, verschieden von; *it is quite – him*, das ist garnicht seine Art, das sieht ihm garnicht ähnlich. **–lihood** [–lɪhud], **–liness,** *s.* die Unwahrscheinlichkeit. **–ly,** *adj.* & *adv.* unwahrscheinlich.
unlimber [ʌn'lɪmbə], *v.a.* abprotzen (*Mil.*).
unlimited [ʌn'lɪmɪtɪd], *adj.* unbegrenzt, unbeschränkt, (*fig.*) grenzenlos, uferlos; *– liability*, unbeschränkte Haftung *or* Haftpflicht (*C.L.*).
unlined [ʌn'laɪnd], *adj.* ungefüttert, ohne Futter (*clothes*); unliniert, ohne Linien (*paper*).
unlinked ['ʌn'lɪŋkt], *adj.* ungebunden.
unliquidated [ʌn'lɪkwɪdeɪtɪd], *adj.* unbezahlt, unbeglichen; nicht festgestellt, offenstehend.
unload [ʌn'loud], *v.a.* entladen (*vehicle, gun*), abladen, ausladen (*goods*), löschen (*Naut.*); (*fig.*) entlasten, erleichtern, befreien; auf den Markt werfen, verkaufen, abstoßen, verschleudern (*C.L.*).
unlock [ʌn'lɔk], *v.a.* aufschließen, aufsperren, öffnen. **–ed** [–t], *adj.* unverschlossen.
unlooked-for [ʌn'luktfɔ:], *adj.* unerwartet, überraschend, unvorgesehen.
unloosen [ʌn'lu:sn], *v.a.* losmachen, aufmachen, (auf)lösen.
unlov–able [ʌn'lʌvəbl], *adj.* nicht liebenswert, unliebenswürdig. **–ed** [–d], *adj.* ungeliebt. **–ely,** *adj.* unschön, häßlich, unansehnlich; widerlich, eklig. **–ing,** *adj.* lieblos, unfreundlich.
unluck–ily [ʌn'lʌkɪlɪ], *adv.* unglücklicherweise. **–y,** *adj.* unglücklich, ungünstig, unheilbringend, unheilvoll; *be –y*, Unglück *or* Pech haben.
unmade ['ʌn'meɪd], *adj.* ungemacht, unfertig.
unmaidenly [ʌn'meɪdənlɪ], *adj.* nicht mädchenhaft, unschicklich.
unmake ['ʌn'meɪk], *ir.v.a.* aufheben, umstoßen, widerrufen, rückgängig machen (*decisions*); von Grund auf ändern, vernichten, zerstören; absetzen (*king*).
unman ['ʌn'mæn], *v.a.* entmannen, der Manneskraft berauben; entkräftigen, entmutigen; der Mannschaft berauben (*Naut.*).
unmanageable [ʌn'mænədʒəbl], *adj.* unlenksam, unkontrollierbar, widerspenstig; schwer zu bewältigen(d) *or* handhaben(d), schwierig, unhandlich.
unmanl–iness [ʌn'mænlɪnɪs], *s.* die Unmännlichkeit. **–y,** *adj.* unmännlich.
unmannerl–iness [ʌn'mænəlɪnɪs], *s.* die Ungezogenheit. **–y,** *adj.* ungezogen, unmanierlich.
unmarked [ʌn'mɑ:kt], *adj.* unbezeichnet, ungezeichnet, nicht gekennzeichnet (*by*, durch); unbemerkt, unbeobachtet.
unmarketable [ʌn'mɑ:kɪtəbl], *adj.* unverkäuflich, nicht marktfähig.
unmarri–ageable [ʌn'mærɪdʒəbl], *adj.* nicht heiratsfähig. **–ed** [–rɪd], *adj.* unverheiratet, ledig.
unmask [ʌn'mɑ:sk], 1. *v.a.* die Maske abnehmen (*Dat.*), demaskieren, (*fig.*) entlarven. 2. *v.n.* sich demaskieren, die Maske abnehmen; (*fig.*) seinen wahren Charakter zeigen. **–ing,** *s.* die Entlarvung.
unmatched [ʌn'mætʃt], *adj.* unvergleichlich, unübertroffen. unerreicht; *be –*, nicht seinesgleichen haben.
unmean–ing [ʌn'mɪ:nɪŋ], *adj.* nichtssagend, bedeutungslos, sinnlos. **–t** [–'mɛnt], *adj.* unbeabsichtigt, ungewollt.
unmeasured [ʌn'mɛʒəd], *adj.* unermeßlich, unbegrenzt, grenzenlos, übermäßig, unmäßig.
unmeet [ʌn'mɪ:t], *adj.* (*archaic*) ungeeignet, unpassend (*for*, für *or* zu), unziemlich, unschicklich.
unmelodious ['ʌnmə'loudɪəs], *adj.* unmelodisch, mißtönend.
unmention–able [ʌn'mɛnʃənəbl], *adj.* nicht zu erwähnen(d), unnennbar, unaussprechlich. **–ed** [–ənd], nicht erwähnt (*by*, von).
unmerciful [ʌn'mə:sɪful], *adj.* unbarmherzig. **–ness,** *s.* die Unbarmherzigkeit.
unmerited [ʌn'mɛrɪtɪd], *adj.* unverdient.
unmetalled [ʌn'mɛtəld], *adj.* nicht beschottert.

unmethodical ['ʌnmə'θɔdɪkl], *adj.* unmethodisch, planlos.
unmindful [ʌn'maɪndful], *adj.* uneingedenk (*of* (*Gen.*)), ohne Rücksicht (*of*, auf); *be – of*, vergessen, nicht beachten, nicht achten auf, nicht denken an, sich nicht abhalten lassen durch.
unmistakabl–e ['ʌnmɪs'teɪkəbl], *adj.* unverkennbar, deutlich.
unmitigated [ʌn'mɪtɪgeɪtɪd], *adj.* ungemildert, ungeschwächt; (*fig.*) unbedingt, völlig, ausgesprochen, Erz–.
unmixed ['ʌnmɪkst], *adj.* ungemischt (*also fig.*), nicht gemischt, unvermischt, (*fig.*) rein, ungetrübt.
unmodified [ʌn'mɔdɪfaɪd], *adj.* nicht abgeändert, unverändert.
unmolested ['ʌnmə'lɛstɪd], *adj.* unbelästigt, ungestört, in Frieden.
unmoor ['ʌn'muːə], 1. *v.a.* (von der Vertäuung) losmachen (*a ship*). 2. *v.n.* die Anker lichten, abankern.
unmoral ['ʌn'mɔrəl], *adj.* amoralisch.
unmortgaged ['ʌn'mɔːgɪdʒd], *adj.* unverpfändet; hypothekenfrei, nicht belastet.
unmounted [ʌn'maʊntɪd], *adj.* unberitten (*troops*), nicht montiert (*gun*), nicht aufgezogen (*print*), nicht eingefaßt (*gem*).
unmourned [ʌn'mɔːnd], *adj.* unbetrauert, unbeweint.
unmov–ed [ʌn'muːvd], *adj.* unbewegt, ungerührt, unerschüttert, unverändert, fest, standhaft, ruhig, gelassen. **–ing**, *adj.* bewegungslos, regungslos.
unmurmuring [ʌn'məːmərɪŋ], *adj.* ohne Murren.
unmusical [ʌn'mjuːzɪkl], *adj.* unmusikalisch (*a p.*), unmelodisch, mißtönend (*sounds*).
unmuzzle [ʌn'mʌzl], *v.a.* den Maulkorb abnehmen (*Dat.*), (*fig.*) freie Meinungsäußerung gewähren (*Dat.*).
unname–able [ʌn'neɪməbl], *adj.* unnennbar, unsagbar, unbeschreibbar. **–d** [–d], *adj.* ungenannt, unbenannt, namenlos.
unnatural [ʌn'nætʃərəl], *adj.* unnatürlich, widernatürlich, naturwidrig; übernatürlich, außergewöhnlich, ungewöhnlich; abscheulich, ungeheuerlich.
unnavigable [ʌn'nævɪgəbl], *adj.* nicht befahrbar, nicht schiffbar.
unnecessar–ily [ʌn'nɛsəsɛrəlɪ], unnötigerweise. **–y**, *adj.* unnötig, überflüssig.
unneed–ed [ʌn'niːdɪd], *adj.* nicht benötigt (*by*, von). **–ful**, *adj.* unnötig.
unneighbourly [ʌn'neɪbəlɪ], *adj.* nicht nachbarlich, unfreundlich.
unnerve ['ʌn'nəːv], *v.a.* entnerven, erschüttern, entkräften, schwächen; entmutigen, mürbe machen.
unnot–ed ['ʌn'noutɪd], *adj.* unbemerkt, unbeachtet, nicht bedacht. **–iced** [–'noutɪst], *adj. see* **–ed**; vernachlässigt.
unnumbered [ʌn'nʌmbəd], *adj.* ungezählt, zahllos, unnummeriert (*seats, etc.*), ohne Seitenzahlen (*as books*).
unobjectionable ['ʌnəb'dʒɛkʃənəbl], *adj.* untadelhaft, einwandfrei.
unobliging ['ʌnə'blaɪdʒɪŋ], *adj.* unzuvorkommend, ungefällig.
unobscured ['ʌnəb'skjuəd], *adj.* nicht verdeckt *or* verdunkelt (*by*, durch).
unobserv–ant ['ʌnəb'zəːvənt], *adj.* unachtsam, unaufmerksam (*of*, auf). **–ed** [–əːvd], *adj.* unbemerkt, unbeobachtet.
unobstructed ['ʌnəb'strʌktɪd], *adj.* ungehindert, unversperrt.
unobtainable ['ʌnəb'teɪnəbl], *adj.* unerreichbar, nicht erhältlich, nicht zu haben.
unobtrusive ['ʌnəb'truːsɪv], *adj.* unaufdringlich, zurückhaltend, bescheiden. **–ness**, *s.* die Zurückhaltung, Bescheidenheit.
unoccupied [ʌn'ɔkjupaɪd], *adj.* frei (*also fig.*), unbesetzt (*seat*), unbewohnt (*house*); (*fig.*) unbeschäftigt.
unoffending ['ʌnə'fɛndɪŋ], *adj.* unanstößig, harmlos.
unofficial ['ʌnə'fɪʃəl], *adj.* inoffiziell, nicht amtlich.
unopened [ʌn'oupənd], *adj.* ungeöffnet, verschlossen.
unopposed ['ʌnə'pouzd], *adj.* unbehindert (*by*, durch); – *by*, ohne Widerstand *or* Einspruch seitens (*Gen.*).
unorganized [ʌn'ɔːgənaɪzd], *adj.* nicht organisiert, ohne Organisation *or* organischen Aufbau.
unoriginal ['ʌnə'rɪdʒɪnl], *adj.* nicht originell, entlehnt.
unorthodox [ʌn'ɔːθədɔks], *adj.* unorthodox.
unostentatious ['ʌnɔstən'teɪʃəs], *adj.* nicht prunkend; nicht grell, schreiend *or* auffallend (*as colours*); anspruchslos, einfach, bescheiden.
unpack ['ʌn'pæk], *v.a.* auspacken.
unpaid ['ʌn'peɪd], *adj.* unbezahlt (*debt*), unbesoldet, ehrenamtlich (*a p.*), unfrankiert (*letter*), rückständig (*wages, etc.*).
unpalatable [ʌn'pælətəbl], *adj.* unschmackhaft, ungenießbar, unangenehm, widrig.
unparalleled [ʌn'pærəlɛld], *adj.* unvergleichlich, bespiellos.
unpardonable [ʌn'pɑːdənəbl], *adj.* unverzeihlich.
unparliamentary ['ʌnpɑːlɪə'mɛntərɪ], *adj.* unparlamentarisch.
unpatriotic ['ʌnpeɪtrɪ'ɔtɪk, 'ʌnpætrɪ'ɔtɪk], *adj.* unpatriotisch.
unpaved ['ʌn'peɪvd], *adj.* ungepflastert.
unpeg ['ʌn'pɛg], *v.a.* lospflöcken; (*coll.*) nicht (fest)-halten (*the market*), von Einschränkungen befreien, nicht mehr stützen (*currency*) (*C.L.*).
unperceived ['ʌnpə'siːvd], *adj.* unbemerkt, unbeachtet.
unperforated [ʌn'pəːfəreɪtɪd], *adj.* nicht perforiert (*stamps*).
unperformed ['ʌnpə'fɔːmd], *adj.* nicht ausgeführt, unverrichtet, ungetan.
unperplexed ['ʌnpə'plɛkst], *adj.* nicht verwirrt.
unperturbed ['ʌnpə'təːbd], *adj.* nicht beunruhigt, unbeirrt.
unperused ['ʌnpə'ruːzd], *adj.* ungelesen.
unphilosophical ['ʌnfɪlə'sɔfɪkl], *adj.* unphilosophisch.
unpick ['ʌn'pɪk], *v.a.* auftrennen (*a seam*). **–ed** [–t], *adj.* ungepflückt; unsortiert, nicht ausgelesen.
unpin ['ʌn'pɪn], *v.a.* losstecken, losheften, die Nadeln herausnehmen (aus).
unpit–ied ['ʌn'pɪtɪd], *adj.* unbemitleidet. **–ying** [–'pɪtɪɪŋ], *adj.* unbarmherzig, erbarmungslos.
unplaced [ʌn'pleɪst], *adj.* nicht untergebracht *or* angestellt, unversorgt, unplaciert (*Racing*).
unplait ['ʌn'plæt], *v.a.* aufflechten, glätten (*hair, etc.*).
unplayable ['ʌn'pleɪəbl], *adj.* nicht zu spielen(d) (*music*), schwierig (*ball*), zum Spielen untauglich (*pitch*).
unpleasant [ʌn'plɛsənt], *adj.* unangenehm, unerfreulich, mißfällig, widerlich, eklig. **–ness**, *s.* die Unannehmlichkeit, Widerlichkeit; Mißhelligkeit, Reibung, das Mißverständnis.
unplumbed ['ʌn'plʌmd], *adj.* unergründet, unergründlich.
unpoetical ['ʌnpou'ɛtɪkl], *adj.* unpoetisch, undichterisch.
unpolished [ʌn'pɔlɪʃt], *adj.* unpoliert, ungeschliffen, ungeglättet (*also fig.*); (*fig.*) unausgeglichen; unkultiviert, ungebildet, unvornehm.
unpolitical ['ʌnpə'lɪtɪkl], *adj.* nicht politisch, politisch unfähig.
unpolluted ['ʌnpə'l(j)uːtɪd], *adj.* unbefleckt.
unpopular [ʌn'pɔpjulə], *adj.* unbeliebt, unpopulär, unvolkstümlich. **–ity** ['ʌnpɔpjə'lærɪtɪ], *s.* die Unbeliebtheit, Unvolkstümlichkeit.
unposted [ʌn'poustɪd], *adj.* nicht zur Post gebracht; uninformiert.
unpract–ical [ʌn'præktɪkl], *adj.* unpraktisch. **–ised** [–tɪst], *adj.* ungeübt, unerfahren (*in*, in).
unprecedented [ʌn'prɛsɪdɛntɪd], *adj.* unerhört, beispiellos, noch nie dagewesen.
unprejudiced [ʌn'prɛdʒədɪst], *adj.* vorurteilslos, vorurteilsfrei, unbefangen, unvoreingenommen, unparteiisch.
unpremeditated ['ʌnprɪ'mɛdɪteɪtɪd], *adj.* unüberlegt, unvorbereitet, nicht vorbedacht; improvisiert, aus dem Stegreif.
unprepared ['ʌnprɪ'pɛəd], *adj.* unvorbereitet (*for* auf); nicht bereit.

unprepossessing [ˈʌnprɪ:pəˈzɛsɪŋ], *adj.* nicht einnehmend *or* anziehend, reizlos.
unpresentable [ˈʌnprɪˈzɛntəbl], *adj.* nicht präsentabel, nicht gesellschaftsfähig.
unpresum-ing [ˈʌnprɪˈzjuːmɪŋ], **-ptuous** [-ˈzʌmpʃəs], *adj.* bescheiden, anspruchslos.
unpreten-ding [ˈʌnprɪˈtɛndɪŋ], *adj.* nicht auffällig, schlicht. **-tious** [-ˈtɛnʃəs], *adj.* bescheiden, anspruchslos.
unprincipled [ʌnˈprɪnsɪpəld], *adj.* ohne feste Grundsätze, charakterlos, gewissenlos, pflichtvergessen.
unprinted [ʌnˈprɪntɪd], *adj.* ungedruckt (*writings*), unbedruckt (*fabric*).
unprivileged [ʌnˈprɪvɪlɪdʒd], *adj.* nicht bevorrechtet, bevorrechtigt *or* privilegiert.
unproclaimed [ˈʌnprəˈkleɪmd], *adj.* nicht verkündet *or* bekanntgegeben.
unprocurable [ˈʌnprəˈkjuərəbl], *adj.* nicht zu haben(d) *or* zu beschaffen(d).
unproductive [ˈʌnprəˈdʌktɪv], *adj.* unfruchtbar, unergiebig; nicht einträglich, nichts eintragend. **-ness,** *s.* die Unfruchtbarkeit, Unergiebigkeit, Unproduktivität.
unprofessional [ˈʌnprəˈfɛʃənl], *adj.* nicht berufsmäßig, unfachmännisch, laienhaft.
unprofitable [ʌnˈprɔfɪtəbl], *adj.* uneinträglich, nicht gewinnbringend, unvorteilhaft; nutzlos, unnütz. **-ness,** *s.* die Uneinträglichkeit, Nutzlosigkeit.
unprogressive [ˈʌnprəˈgrɛsɪv], *adj.* nicht fortschrittlich, rückständig, reaktionär.
umpromising [ʌnˈprɔmɪsɪŋ], *adj.* nicht vielversprechend; aussichtslos.
unprompted [ʌnˈprɔmptɪd], *adj.* nicht beeinflußt (*by*, von), aus eignem Antrieb, freiwillig.
unpronounceable [ˈʌnprəˈnaunsəbl], *adj.* unaussprechlich.
unpropitious [ˈʌnprəˈpɪʃəs], *adj.* ungünstig (*to* or *for*, für), ungnädig, unglücklich.
unprotected [ˈʌnprəˈtɛktɪd], *adj.* ungeschützt, ungedeckt, schutzlos, nicht geschützt.
unprovided [ˈʌnprəˈvaɪdɪd], *adj.* unversorgt, nicht versehen (*with*, mit); *– for*, nicht vorgesehen.
unprovoked [ˈʌnprəˈvoukt], *adj.* nicht herausgefordert *or* gereizt *or* veranlaßt, ohne Veranlassung *or* Grund.
unpublished [ʌnˈpʌblɪʃt], *adj.* unveröffentlicht.
unpunctual [ʌnˈpʌŋktjuəl], *adj.* unpünktlich. **-ity** [ˈʌnpʌŋktjuˈælɪtɪ], *s.* die Unpünktlichkeit.
unpunished [ʌnˈpʌnɪʃt], *adj.* unbestraft, straffrei; *go –*, straflos ausgehen.
unqualified [ʌnˈkwɔlɪfaɪd], *adj.* ungeeignet, unbefähigt, unberechtigt, unqualifiziert; uneingeschränkt, unbedingt, (*coll.*) regelrecht, handgreiflich.
unquenchable [ʌnˈkwɛntʃəbl], *adj.* unlöschbar, unstillbar; (*fig.*) unauslöschlich, unersättlich.
unquestion-able [ʌnˈkwɛstjənəbl], *adj.* unzweifelhaft, unbestritten, unbestreitbar. **-ably,** *adv.* unstreitig, zweifellos. **-ed** [-tʃənd], *adj.* ungefragt, unbefragt, unbestritten, unbezweifelt. **-ing,** 1. *attrib. adj.* blind, bedingungslos. 2. *pred. adj.* ohne zu fragen *or* zu zweifeln, ohne Neugier. **-ingly,** *adv.* ohne Zögern *or* zu fragen; bedingungslos.
unravel [ˈʌnˈrævl], 1. *v.a.* ausfasern, entwirren (*also fig.*); (*fig.*) enträtseln, lösen. 2. *v.n.* sich auffasern.
unread [ˈʌnˈrɛd], *adj.* ungelesen, unbelesen, unbewandert (*in*, in). **-able** [ʌnˈrɪːdəbl], *adj.* unleserlich, undeutlich (*handwriting*), unlesbar (*book*).
unread-iness [ʌnˈrɛdɪnɪs], *s.* die Unbereitschaft, das Nichtgerüstetsein, die Unbereitwilligkeit. **-y,** *adj.* nicht bereit (*for*, zu), nicht fertig, ungerüstet; langsam, zaudernd.
unreal [ʌnˈrɪːəl], *adj.* unwirklich, wesenlos, nur eingebildet. **-ity** [ˈʌnrɪˈælɪtɪ], *s.* die Unwirklichkeit, Wesenlosigkeit. **-izable** [-ˈrɪːəlaɪzəbl], *adj.* nicht realisierbar *or* zu verwirklichen(d), nicht verwertbar *or* verkäuflich. **-ized** [-laɪzd], *adj.* nicht verwirklicht *or* erfüllt, nicht begriffen *or* erkannt (*by*, von).
unreason [ʌnˈrɪːzn], *s.* die Unvernunft. **-able** [-zənəbl], *adj.* unvernünftig; unbillig, ungerechtfertigt; übertrieben, übermäßig, unmäßig. **-ableness,** *s.* die Unbilligkeit, Unmäßigkeit. **-ing,** *adj.* vernunftlos, vernunftwidrig, unlogisch.
unreceipted [ˈʌnrɪˈsɪːtɪd], *adj.* unquittiert.
unreceptive [ˈʌnrɪˈsɛptɪv], *adj.* unempfänglich, nicht aufnahmefähig.
unreciprocated [ˈʌnrɪˈsɪprəkeɪtɪd], *adj.* unerwidert.
unreclaimed [ˈʌnrɪˈkleɪmd], *adj.* nicht gebessert; ungezähmt (*as a hawk*); nicht kultiviert, unbebaut (*as land*).
unrecogniz-able [ʌnˈrɛkəgnaɪzəbl], *adj.* nicht wiederzuerkennen, unerkennbar. **-ed** [-naɪzd], *adj.* nicht erkannt, nicht anerkannt.
unrecompensed [ʌnˈrɛkəmpɛnst], *adj.* unbelohnt.
unreconciled [ʌnˈrɛkənsaɪld], *adj.* unversöhnt, unausgesöhnt (*to*, mit).
unrecorded [ˈʌnrɪˈkɔːdɪd], *adj.* nicht aufgezeichnet *or* eingetragen, unverzeichnet.
unrecovered [ˈʌnrɪˈkʌvəd], *adj.* nicht wiedererlangt; unwiederhergestellt (*from*, von).
unrectified [ʌnˈrɛktɪfaɪd], *adj.* unberichtigt, unverbessert; ungereinigt (*Chem.*).
unredeemed [ˈʌnrɪˈdɪːmd], *adj.* nicht erlöst (*Theol.*); nicht losgekauft *or* zurückgenommen, uneingelöst, ungetilgt (*as debts*), (*fig.*) nicht gemildert (*by*, durch).
unredressed [ˈʌnrɪˈdrɛst], *adj.* ungesühnt, nicht wieder gutgemacht.
unreel [ˈʌnˈrɪːl], 1. *v.a.* abhaspeln, abspulen, abrollen. 2. *v.n.* sich abwickeln *or* abspulen.
unrefined [ˈʌnrɪˈfaɪnd], *adj.* ungereinigt, ungeläutert, Roh–, (*fig.*) unfein, ungebildet.
unreflecting [ˈʌnrɪˈflɛktɪŋ], *adj.* nicht reflektierend (*Phys.*); unüberlegt, gedankenlos.
unregard-ed [ˈʌnrɪˈgɑːdɪd], *adj.* unberücksichtigt, unbeachtet, vernachlässigt. **-ful,** *adj.* unachtsam, rücksichtslos; *be -ful of*, nicht beachten.
unregenera-cy [ˈʌnrɪˈdʒɛnərəsɪ], *s.* die Sündhaftigkeit, Verderbtheit, Unverbesserlichkeit. **-te** [-rət], *adj.* sündhaft, sündig, verderbt, unverbesserlich; nicht wiedergeboren (*Theol.*).
unregistered [ʌnˈrɛdʒɪstəd], *adj.* nicht eingetragen *or* approbiert; nicht eingeschrieben (*letter*).
unregretted [ˈʌnrɪˈgrɛtɪd], *adj.* unbedauert, unbeklagt.
unregulated [ʌnˈrɛgjuleɪtɪd], *adj.* ungeregelt, ungeordnet.
unrehearsed [ˈʌnrɪˈhəːst], *adj.* ungeprobt.
unrelated [ˈʌnrɪˈleɪtɪd], *adj.* nicht verwandt, in keiner Beziehung stehend, ohne Beziehung; nicht erzählt.
unrelenting [ˈʌnrɪˈlɛntɪŋ], *adj.* unerbittlich, unnachgiebig, unbeugsam, hart.
unreliab-ility [ˈʌnrɪlaɪəˈbɪlɪtɪ], *s.* die Unzuverlässigkeit. **-le** [-ˈlaɪəbl], *adj.* unzuverlässig.
unrelieved [ˈʌnrɪlɪːvd], *adj.* unerleichtert, ungelindert, ungemildert (*by*, durch), ununterbrochen, nicht unterbrochen (*by*, von), ungeschwächt, unvermindert.
unremitting [ˈʌnrɪˈmɪtɪŋ], *adj.* unablässig, unermüdlich, unaufhörlich.
unremunerative [ˈʌnrɪˈmjuːnərətɪv], *adj.* nicht einträglich *or* lohnend.
unrepair [ˈʌnrɪˈpɛə], *s.* die Schadhaftigkeit.
unrepealed [ˈʌnrɪˈpɪːld], *adj.* nicht widerrufen *or* aufgehoben.
unrepent-ant [ˈʌnrɪˈpɛntənt], *adj.* unbußfertig, reuelos. **-ed** [-tɪd], *adj.* unbereut.
unrepining [ˈʌnrɪˈpaɪnɪŋ], *adj.* gelassen, nicht klagend; (*pred. only*) ohne Klage *or* Murren.
unrepresented [ˈʌnrɛprɪˈzɛntɪd], *adj.* nicht vertreten, ohne Vertreter.
unrequited [ˈʌnrɪˈkwaɪtɪd], *adj.* unerwidert (*love*) unbelohnt (*work*), unvergolten (*crime*).
unreserved [ˈʌnrɪˈzəːvd], *adj.* nicht reserviert (*seats*); offen, freimütig; vorbehaltlos, rückhaltlos, uneingeschränkt. **-ness,** *s.* die Offenheit, Rückhaltlosigkeit.
unresist-ed [ˈʌnrɪˈzɪstɪd], *adj.* ungehemmt; *be -ed*, keinen Widerstand finden. **-ing,** *adj.* widerstandslos.
unresolved [ˈʌnrɪˈzɔlvd], *adj.* ungelöst (*problem*);

unentschlossen, unentschieden (*as a p.*); unaufgelöst (*Chem. & Mus.*).
unresponsive [ˈʌnrɪsˈpɔnsɪv], *adj.* unempfänglich (*to*, für), teilnahm(s)los (*to*, gegen), nicht reagierend (*to*, auf).
unrest [ˈʌnˈrɛst]. *s.* die Unruhe. **–ful,** *adj.* rastlos, unruhig. **–ing,** *adj.* unermüdlich.
unrestrain–ed [ˈʌnrɪˈstreɪnd], *adj.* ungehemmt, uneingeschränkt, zügellos, unbeherrscht. **–t** [–nt], *s.* die Ungehemmtheit, Zwanglosigkeit, Ungezwungenheit.
unrestricted [ˈʌnrɪˈstrɪktɪd], *adj.* unbeschränkt, uneingeschränkt, schrankenlos.
unreturned [ˈʌnrɪˈtəːnd], *adj.* nicht zurückgegeben; unerwidert; nicht gewählt (*Parl.*).
unrevealed [ˈʌnrɪˈvɪːld], *adj.* unenthüllt, nicht (ge)offenbart *or* entdeckt.
unrevised [ˈʌnrɪˈvaɪzd], *adj.* nicht revidiert *or* durchgesehen.
unrewarded [ˈʌnrɪˈwɔːdɪd], *adj.* unbelohnt.
unrhymed [ʌnˈraɪmd], *adj.* ungereimt, reimlos.
unrighteous [ʌnˈraɪtʃəs], *adj.* ungerecht, sündhaft, gottlos (*Theol.*). **–ness,** *s.* die Ungerechtigkeit, Gottlosigkeit.
unrip [ˈʌnˈrɪp], *v.a.* auftrennen, aufreißen.
unripe [ʌnˈraɪp], *adj.* unreif. **–ness,** *s.* die Unreife.
unrivalled [ʌnˈraɪvəld], *adj.* ohne Nebenbuhler *or* Gleichen, unvergleichlich, unerreicht, beispiellos.
unroll [ʌnˈroʊl], 1. *v.a.* aufrollen, entrollen, abrollen; entfalten, ausbreiten. 2. *v.n.* sich auseinanderrollen *or* entfalten.
unromantic [ˈʌnroˈmæntɪk], *adj.* unromantisch, prosaisch.
unround [ˈʌnˈraʊnd], *v.a.* entrunden (*Phonet.*).
unruffled [ʌnˈrʌfəld], *adj.* ungekräuselt, glatt, (*fig.*) ruhig, unbewegt, gelassen.
unrul–ed [ʌnˈruːld], *adj.* unliniiert (*paper*); unregiert, unbeherrscht. **–iness,** *s.* die Unbändigkeit, Widerspenstigkeit. **–y,** *adj.* unbändig, ungestüm, widerspenstig.
unsaddle [ʌnˈsædl], *v.a.* absatteln (*horse*), aus dem Sattel werfen (*rider*).
unsafe [ʌnˈseɪf], *adj.* unsicher; gefährlich. **–ness,** *s.* die Unsicherheit.
unsaid [ʌnˈsɛd], *adj.* ungesagt.
unsalaried [ʌnˈsælərɪd], *adj.* unbesoldet, ehrenamtlich.
unsal(e)able [ʌnˈseɪləbl], *adj.* unverkäuflich.
unsalted [ʌnˈsɔːltɪd], *adj.* ungesalzen.
unsanctified [ʌnˈsæŋktɪfaɪd], *adj.* ungeheiligt, ungeweiht.
unsanctioned [ʌnˈsæŋkʃənd], *adj.* unbestätigt, unbekräftigt.
unsatisf–actoriness [ˈʌnsætɪsˈfæktərɪnɪs], *s.* das Unbefriedigende; die Unzulänglichkeit. **–actory** [–ˈfæktərɪ], *adj.* ungenügend,unbefriedigend, unzulänglich, unerfreulich. **–ied** [ʌnˈsætɪsfaɪd], *adj.* unzufrieden, unbefriedigt. **–ying** [–faɪɪŋ], *adj.* unbefriedigend.
unsavour–iness [ʌnˈseɪvərɪnɪs], *s.* die Unschmackhaftigkeit; Widerlichkeit. **–y,** *adj.* unschmackhaft; widerlich, anstößig.
unsay [ˈʌnˈseɪ], *ir.v.a.* zurücknehmen, widerrufen.
unscathed [ʌnˈskeɪðd], *adj.* unbeschädigt, unversehrt.
unscholarly [ʌnˈskɔləlɪ], *adj.* unwissenschaftlich, ungelehrt.
unschooled [ʌnˈskuːld], *adj.* ungeschult, ungeübt (*in*, in); ungelehrt, ungebildet.
unscientific [ˈʌnsaɪənˈtɪfɪk], *adj.* unwissenschaftlich.
unscreened [ʌnˈskrɪːnd], *adj.* nicht geschützt; ungesiebt.
unscrew [ʌnˈskruː], 1. *v.a.* aufschrauben, abschrauben, losschrauben. 2. *v.n.* sich abschrauben *or* aufschrauben (lassen).
unscriptural [ʌnˈskrɪptjərəl], *adj.* unbiblisch, schriftwidrig.
unscrupulous [ʌnˈskruːpjələs], *adj.* skrupellos, gewissenlos, bedenkenlos. **–ly,** *adv.* ohne Bedenken. **–ness,** *s.* die Skrupellosigkeit, Gewissenlosigkeit.
unseal [ʌnˈsɪːl], *v.a.* entsiegeln, das Siegel abnehmen; (*fig.*) öffnen (*s.o.'s lips*), enthüllen. **–ed** [–d], *adj.* unversiegelt.
unsearchable [ʌnˈsəːtʃəbl], *adj.* unerforschlich, unergründlich.
unseason–able [ʌnˈsɪːzənəbl], *adj.* unzeitgemäß, unzeitig; ungelegen, unangebracht, ungünstig. **–ableness,** *s.* die Ungelegenheit. **–ed** [–zənd], *adj.* nicht ausgetrocknet (*as wood*); (*fig.*) nicht abgehärtet; ungewürzt (*Cook.*).
unseat [ˈʌnˈsɪːt], *v.a.* aus dem Sattel heben, abwerfen; stürzen, absetzen (*as politicians*).
unseaworth–iness [ʌnˈsɪːwəːðɪnɪs], *s.* die Seeuntüchtigkeit. **–y,** *adj.* seeuntüchtig, nicht seefest.
unsectarian [ˈʌnsɛkˈtɛərɪən], *adj.* nicht sektiererisch, frei von Sektiererei.
unsecured [ˈʌnsɪˈkjuəd], *adj.* nicht gesichert *or* befestigt; nicht sichergestellt (*C.L.*).
unseeml–iness [ʌnˈsɪːmlɪnɪs], *s.* die Unziemlichkeit. **–y,** *adj.* unziemlich, unschicklich, unschön.
unseen [ˈʌnˈsɪːn], 1. *adj.* ungesehen, unbemerkt, unsichtbar; unvorbereitet (*translation*). 2. das Unsichtbare; die Klausur(arbeit).
unselfish [ʌnˈsɛlfɪʃ], *adj.* uneigennützig, selbstlos, altruistisch. **–ness,** *s.* die Uneigennützigkeit, Selbstlosigkeit.
unsentimental [ˈʌnsɛntɪˈmɛntl], *adj.* unsentimental, frei von Sentimentalität.
unserviceable [ʌnˈsəːvɪsəbl], *adj.* undienlich, unzweckmäßig, unnütz, unbrauchbar; untauglich (*Mil.*). **–ness,** *s.* die Unbrauchbarkeit, Untauglichkeit.
unsettle [ʌnˈsɛtl], *v.a.* aus der Lage bringen; wegrücken; (*fig.*) verwirren, in Verwirrung *or* Unordnung bringen; zum Wanken bringen, aus den Angeln heben, beunruhigen, aufregen. **–d** [–təld], *adj.* nicht festgesetzt, unbestimmt, unsicher, unstet, schwankend; unerledigt, unbezahlt, unbeglichen (*as an account*); unbeständig, veränderlich (*as weather*); unruhig, aufgeregt (*as times*); ungewiß, unentschlossen, unentschieden (*as a p.*); unbesiedelt (*as land*).
unsex [ˈʌnˈsɛks], *v.a.* der Eigenschaften als Frau berauben; (*coll.*) – *o.s.*, sich emanzipieren (*of women*).
unshackle [ʌnˈʃækl], *v.a.* die Fesseln abnehmen; ausschäkeln (*Naut.*); (*fig.*) entfesseln, befreien.
unshaded [ʌnˈʃeɪdɪd], *adj.* unbeschattet, nicht verdunkelt, schattenlos.
unshak–able [ʌnˈʃeɪkəbl], *adj.* unerschütterlich. **–en** [–ˈʃeɪkn], *adj.* unerschüttert, fest, beharrlich.
unshapely [ʌnˈʃeɪplɪ], *adj.* ungestalt, unförmig.
unshave–d [ʌnˈʃeɪvd], **–n** [–ˈʃeɪvn], *adj.* unrasiert.
unsheathe [ʌnˈʃɪːθ], *v.a.* aus der Scheide ziehen; (*fig.*) – *the sword*, den Krieg erklären *or* beginnen.
unshed [ˈʌnˈʃɛd], *adj.* unvergossen.
unsheltered [ʌnˈʃɛltəd], *adj.* ungeschützt.
unshielded [ʌnˈʃɪːldɪd], *adj.* unbeschirmt.
unship [ʌnˈʃɪp], *v.a.* ausschiffen (*passengers*), ausladen, löschen (*cargo*), herausheben (*mast*), losmachen (*oars*).
unshod [ˈʌnˈʃɔd], *adj.* unbeschuht, barfuß; unbeschlagen (*as horses*).
unshorn [ˈʌnˈʃɔːn], *adj.* ungeschoren.
unshortened [ʌnˈʃɔːtənd], *adj.* unverkürzt.
unshrink–able [ʌnˈʃrɪŋkəbl], *adj.* nicht einlaufend. **–ing,** *adj.* nicht zurückweichend, unverzagt.
unsifted [ʌnˈsɪftɪd], *adj.* ungesiebt, (*fig.*) ungeprüft.
unsightl–iness [ʌnˈsaɪtlɪnɪs], *s.* die Unansehnlichkeit, Häßlichkeit. **–y,** *adj.* unansehnlich, häßlich.
unskil–ful [ʌnˈskɪlful], *adj.* ungeschickt, unbeholfen. **–led** [–ˈskɪld], *adj.* unerfahren, unkundig, ungelernt; *–led labour*, mechanische Arbeit, die Handarbeit; die ungelernten Arbeiter.
unskimmed [ˈʌnˈskɪmd], *adj.* nicht abgerahmt; – *milk*, die Vollmilch.
unslackened [ʌnˈslækənd], *adv.* nicht nachgelassen *or* erschlafft, ungeschwächt.
unslaked [ˈʌnˈsleɪkt], *adj.* ungelöscht (*also fig.*); (*fig.*) ungestillt, unbefriedigt.
unsmoked [ˈʌnˈsmoʊkt], *adj.* ungeräuchert (*bacon*), nicht aufgeraucht (*cigarette*).
unsocia–bility [ˈʌnsoʊʃəˈbɪlɪtɪ], *s.* die Ungeselligkeit. **–ble** [–soʊʃəbl], *adj.* ungesellig, reserviert.

-l [–ˈsoʊʃl], *adj.* unsozial, asozial, ungesellschaftlich.
unsoiled [ˈʌnˈsɔɪld], *adj.* unbefleckt.
unsold [ˈʌnˈsoʊld], *adj.* unverkauft.
unsolder [ˈʌnˈsoʊldə], *v.a.* ablöten.
unsoldierly [ʌnˈsoʊldʒəlɪ], *adj.* unsoldatisch, unmilitärisch.
unsolicited [ˈʌnsəˈlɪsɪtɪd], *adj.* unverlangt, unaufgefordert, ungebeten; nicht begehrt, nicht erbeten, freiwillig.
unsolved [ˈʌnˈsɔlvd], *adj.* ungelöst.
unsophisticated [ˈʌnsəˈfɪstɪkeɪtɪd], *adj.* naturhaft, natürlich, einfach; ungekünstelt, nicht vergeistigt, unverfälscht, echt, rein, unverdorben, arglos.
unsought [ˈʌnˈsɔːt], *adj.* (*also coll.* – for) ungesucht, nicht erstrebt.
unsound [ˈʌnˈsɑʊnd], *adj.* ungesund (*also fig.*), angegangen, verdorben, verfault, wurmstichig; (*fig.*) nicht stichhaltig, unzuverlässig; – *argument*, nicht stichhaltiger Beweisgrund; – *doctrine*, die Irrlehre (*Theol.*); – *ice*, unzuverlässiges *or* unsicheres Eis; *of – mind*, geisteskrank. **-ness**, *s.* die Ungesundheit, Verdorbenheit; Unrichtigkeit, Fehlerhaftigkeit, Unzuverlässigkeit.
unsparing [ʌnˈspɛərɪŋ], *adj.* freigebig, verschwenderisch (*in*, mit); schonungslos (*to* or *with*, gegen); *be – in*, nicht kargen *or* zurückhalten mit.
unspeakable [ʌnˈspɪːkəbl], *adj.* unsagbar, unbeschreiblich, unaussprechlich, unsäglich, entsetzlich, scheußlich, greulich.
unspecified [ʌnˈspɛsɪfɑɪd], *adj.* nicht besonders *or* einzeln angegeben *or* vorgeschrieben, nicht spezifiziert.
unspent [ˈʌnˈspɛnt], *adj.* nicht verbraucht, erschöpft *or* ausgegeben.
unspiritual [ʌnˈspɪrɪtjʊəl], *adj.* nicht geistig, geistlos.
unspoil-ed [ʌnˈspɔɪld], **-t** [–spɔɪlt], *adj.* unverdorben.
unspoken [ʌnˈspoʊkn], *adj.* ungesagt, ungesprochen; – *of*, unerwähnt; – *to*, unangeredet.
unsport-ing [ʌnˈspɔːtɪŋ], **-smanlike** [–ˈspɔːtsmənlɑɪk], *adj.* unsportlich, unritterlich; nicht sportlerisch *or* sportmäßig; unweidmännisch (*Hunt.*).
unspotted [ʌnˈspɔtɪd], *adj.* ungefleckt, unbefleckt (*also fig.*), fleckenlos; (*coll.*) unentdeckt.
unstable [ʌnˈsteɪbl], *adj.* nicht fest, unsicher (*also fig.*), schwankend; labil (*also fig.*); (*fig.*) unbeständig.
unstained [ʌnˈsteɪnd], *adj.* ungefärbt, ungebeizt; unbefleckt (*also fig.*), fleckenlos.
unstatesmanlike [ʌnˈsteɪtsmənlɑɪk], *adj.* unstaatsmännisch.
unstead-fast [ʌnˈstɛdfɑːst], *adj.* schwankend, unbeständig. **-iness** [–ɪnɪs], *s.* das Schwanken, die Unsicherheit, Unfestigkeit, Unbeständigkeit. **-y**, *adj.* unsicher, schwankend, wack(e)lig; unregelmäßig, uneben; (*fig.*) unstet, unbeständig, unzuverlässig.
unstint-ed [ʌnˈstɪntɪd], *adj.* uneingeschränkt, unbeschränkt. **-ing**, *adj.* nicht geizend *or* kargend, freigebig, reichlich.
unstitch [ʌnˈstɪtʃ], *v.a.* auftrennen (*sewing*); *come -ed*, aufgehen, sich lostrennen.
unstrained [ʌnˈstreɪnd], *adj.* nicht angestrengt *or* angespannt; unfiltriert; (*fig.*) ungezwungen, zwanglos, natürlich.
unstrap [ˈʌnˈstræp], *v.a.* losschnallen.
unstressed [ˈʌnˈstrɛst], *adj.* unbetont.
unstrung [ˈʌnˈstrʌŋ], *adj.* ungespannt; abgereiht (*pearls*); (*fig.*) abgespannt, nervös.
unstudied [ʌnˈstʌdɪd], *adj.* ungekünstelt, zwanglos, ungezwungen, natürlich.
unsubdued [ʌnsəbˈdjʊːd], *adj.* unbesiegt, unbezwungen, nicht unterjocht.
unsubmissive [ˈʌnsəbˈmɪsɪv], *adj.* nicht unterwürfig, widerspenstig.
unsubstantial [ˈʌnsəbˈstænʃəl], *adj.* wesenlos, substanzlos, stofflos, unkörperlich; gehaltlos (*a meal, etc.*); (*fig.*) unwirklich, unwesentlich; unbegründet, haltlos.
unsuccessful [ˈʌnsəkˈsɛsfʊl], *adj.* erfolglos, fruchtlos; durchgefallen (*in an examination*); zurückgewiesen (*candidate*). **-ness**, *s.* die Erfolglosigkeit, das Mißlingen.
unsuit-ability [ˈʌnsjʊːtəˈbɪlɪtɪ], *s.* die Ungeeignetheit, Untauglichkeit, Unangemessenheit. **-able** [ʌnˈsjʊːtəbl], *adj.* ungeeignet, untauglich, unangemessen, unpassend (*to* or *for*, zu *or* für). **-ed** [–tɪd], *adj.* ungeeignet (*to*, zu).
unsullied [ʌnˈsʌlɪd], *adj.* (*usually fig.*) unbefleckt.
unsummoned [ʌnˈsʌmənd], *adj.* ungeladen, unaufgefordert.
unsung [ˈʌnˈsʌŋ], *adj.* ungesungen; nicht besungen.
unsupported [ˈʌnsəˈpɔːtɪd], *adj.* nicht gestützt *or* bestätigt.
unsure [ʌnˈʃʊə], *adj.* ungewiß, unsicher, zweifelhaft.
unsurpass-able [ˈʌnsəˈpɑːsəbl], *adj.* unübertrefflich. **-ed** [–ˈpɑːst], *adj.* unübertroffen.
unsusp-ected [ˈʌnsəsˈpɛktɪd], *adj.* nicht verdächtigt, unverdächtig; ungeahnt, nicht vermutet. **-ecting** [–ˈpɛktɪŋ], *adj.* arglos, nicht argwöhnisch *or* mißtrauisch. **-icious** [–ˈpɪʃəs], *adj.* unverdächtig; ohne Mißtrauen, nicht mißtrauisch, arglos.
unsweetened [ʌnˈswɪːtənd], *adj.* ungesüßt; (*fig.*) unversüßt.
unswerving [ʌnˈswəːvɪŋ], *adj.* nicht wankend, fest, standhaft, unentwegt, unerschütterlich, unwandelbar.
unsymmetrical [ˈʌnsɪˈmɛtrɪkl], *adj.* unsymmetrisch.
unsympathetic [ˈʌnsɪmpəˈθɛtɪk], *adj.* gefühllos, teilnahm(s)los, unbarmherzig, nicht mitempfindlich, unsympathisch.
unsystematic [ˈʌnsɪstəˈmætɪk], *adj.* unsystematisch, planlos.
untainted [ʌnˈteɪntɪd], *adj.* unverdorben, unbefleckt.
untam-able [ʌnˈteɪməbl], *adj.* unbezähmbar, unbezwingbar. **-ed**, *adj.* unbezähmt; ungebändigt, ungezügelt.
untangle [ʌnˈtæŋgl], *v.a.* entwirren.
untanned [ʌnˈtænd], *adj.* ungegerbt.
untarnished [ʌnˈtɑːnɪʃt], *adj.* blank, ungetrübt; unbefleckt.
untasted [ʌnˈteɪstɪd], *adj.* ungekostet, unberührt, unversucht.
untaught [ʌnˈtɔːt], *adj.* ungelehrt, unwissend, nicht unterrichtet.
untaxed [ʌnˈtækst], *adj.* unbesteuert, steuerfrei.
unteachable [ʌnˈtɪːtʃəbl], *adj.* unbelehrbar, unlehrig (*pupils*), nicht lehrbar (*doctrine*).
untempered [ʌnˈtɛmpəd], *adj.* ungehärtet (*Tech.*); (*fig.*) nicht gemildert *or* gemäßigt (*by* or *with*, durch).
untenable [ʌnˈtɛnəbl], *adj.* unhaltbar.
untenanted [ʌnˈtɛnəntɪd], *adj.* unbewohnt, unvermietet.
untended [ʌnˈtɛndɪd], *adj.* unbehütet, unbeaufsichtigt; ungepflegt, vernachlässigt.
unthink-able [ʌnˈθɪŋkəbl], *adj.* undenkbar, unvorstellbar, unbeschreiblich, höchst unwahrscheinlich. **-ing**, *adj.* gedankenlos; unbesonnen.
unthought [ʌnˈθɔːt], *adj.* ungedacht. **- -of**, *adj.* unvermutet, unerwartet, nicht geahnt.
unthread [ˈʌnˈθrɛd], *v.a.* ausfädeln (*a needle*), ausfasern, (*fig.*) auflösen, entwirren.
unthrifty [ʌnˈθrɪftɪ], *adj.* unsparsam, unwirtschaftlich, nicht haushälterisch, verschwenderisch.
unthrone [ˈʌnˈθroʊn], *v.a.* entthronen.
untid-iness [ʌnˈtɑɪdɪnɪs], *s.* die Unordnung. **-y**, *adj.* unordentlich.
untie [ʌnˈtɑɪ], *v.a.* aufbinden, losbinden, aufknoten, aufknüpfen; (*fig.*) lösen.
until [ʌnˈtɪl], 1. *prep.* bis; bis zu. 2. *conj.* bis; *not* –, erst als, erst wenn.
untilled [ʌnˈtɪld], *adj.* unbebaut.
untimel-iness [ʌnˈtɑɪmlɪnɪs], *s.* die Unzeitigkeit. **-y**, *adj.* unzeitig, frühzeitig, vorzeitig; unpassend, ungünstig, ungelegen.
untiring [ʌnˈtɑɪərɪŋ], *adj.* unermüdlich.
unto [ˈʌntʊ], *prep.* (*archaic*) *see* **to.**
untold [ʌnˈtoʊld], *adj.* unerzählt, nicht berichtet; ungezählt, zahllos (*before pl.*), unsäglich, unermeßlich, ungeheuer (*before sing.*).

untouch–able [ʌn'tʌtʃəbl], 1. *adj.* unberührbar, unantastbar, unnahbar, unerreichbar. 2. *s.* der Hindu der niedrigsten Kaste. **–ed** [–t], *adj.* unberührt, unangetastet; nicht zurechtgemacht *or* retuschiert; nicht gekostet (*food*); (*fig.*) ungerührt (*by*, durch), nicht beeinflußt (*by*, von); ungeschminkt, ungefärbt.
untoward [ʌn'touwəd], *adj.* widrig, widerwärtig, ungünstig, widerspenstig, widerhaarig, eigensinnig, steif, starr, schwer zu bearbeiten(d) *or* zu behandeln(d). **–ness,** *s.* die Widerwärtigkeit, Widerspenstigkeit, Ungunst, der Eigensinn.
untrained [ʌn'treɪnd], *adj.* ungeschult, unausgebildet, ungeübt; undressiert, unabgerichtet (*animals*), untrainiert (*Sport*).
untrammelled ['ʌntræməld], *adj.* ungehindert, unbehindert, ungebunden, ungefesselt.
untranslatable ['ʌntræns'leɪtəbl], *adj.* unübersetzbar.
untravelled [ʌn'trævəld], *adj.* ungereist (*as a p.*); unbereist (*as a land*).
untraversed [ʌn'trævə:st], *adj.* nicht durchschritten, nicht durchquert.
untried [ʌn'traɪd], *adj.* unversucht; unerprobt, unerfahren; unverhört, ununtersucht (*Law*).
untrimmed ['ʌntrɪmd], *adj.* unbesetzt, ungeputzt; unbeschnitten.
untrodden [ʌn'trɔdn], *adj.* unbetreten.
untroubled [ʌn'trʌbəld], *adj.* ungestört, unbelästigt; ungetrübt, ruhig, still.
untru–e [ʌn'tru:], *adj.* unwahr, falsch, irrig; treulos, untreu; *–e to*, nicht in Übereinstimmung mit. **–th** [–'tru:θ], *s.* die Unwahrheit, Falschheit; Lüge, Unaufrichtigkeit. **–thful,** *adj.* falsch, irrig (*of a th.*), unwahr (*of a p. or th.*), unaufrichtig (*of a p.*). **–thfulness,** *s.* die Unaufrichtigkeit, Unwahrheit, Falschheit.
untrustworth–iness [ʌn'trʌstwə:ðɪnɪs], *s.* die Unzuverlässigkeit. **–y,** *adj.* nicht vertrauenswürdig, unzuverlässig.
unturned [ʌn'tə:nd], *adj.* ungewendet, nicht umgewendet; *leave no stone –*, nichts unversucht lassen.
untutored [ʌn'tju:təd], *adj.* unerzogen, ungebildet, unbeaufsichtigt; naturhaft, roh (*as instincts*).
untwine [ʌn'twaɪn], **untwist** [–'twɪst], 1. *v.a.* aufflechten; losflechten, losmachen. 2. *v.n.* sich aufdrehen, losgehen, aufgehen.
unus–ed [ʌn'ju:zd], *adj.* unbenutzt, ungebraucht; nicht gewöhnt (*to*, an); *be –ed to*, nicht gewohnt sein (*an* (*Acc.*)). **–ual** [–'ju:zuəl], *adj.* ungewöhnlich, außergewöhnlich, ungebräuchlich, selten. **–ualness,** *s.* die Außergewöhnlichkeit, Ungewöhnlichkeit, Seltenheit.
unutter–able [ʌn'ʌtərəbl], *adj.* unaussprechlich, unbeschreibbar, unsagbar; ausgefeimt (*scoundrel, etc.*). **–ed** [–təd], *adj.* unausgesprochen.
unvalued [ʌn'vælju:d], *adj.* nicht geschätzt *or* geachtet, untaxiert, nicht abgeschätzt.
unvar–ied [ʌn'vɛərɪd], *adj.* unverändert, einförmig. **–ying,** *adj.* unveränderlich, unwandelbar, andauernd.
unvarnished [ʌn'vɑ:nɪʃt], *adj.* unlackiert, ungefirnißt; unpoliert (*nails*); (*fig.*) ungeschminkt, ungeschmückt, schmucklos, schlicht.
unveil [ʌn'veɪl], 1. *v.a.* entschleiern (*face*), enthüllen (*a statue, etc., also fig.*), (*fig.*) aufdecken. 2. *v.n.* sich entschleiern *or* enthüllen.
unverified [ʌn'vɛrɪfaɪd], *adj.* nicht bestätigt.
unversed [ʌn'və:st], *adj.* unerfahren, unbewandert (*in*, in).
unvisited [ʌn'vɪsɪtɪd], *adj.* unbesucht, nicht aufgesucht *or* heimgesucht.
unvoiced [ʌn'vɔɪst], *adj.* unausgesprochen, nicht geäußert; stimmlos (*Phonet.*).
unvouched [ʌn'vaʊtʃt], *adj.*; *– for*, unverbürgt, unbezeugt.
unwalled [ʌn'wɔ:ld], *adj.* unbefestigt, nicht ummauert.
unwanted [ʌn'wɔntɪd], *adj.* nicht begehrt, ungewünscht, unerwünscht.
unwar–iness [ʌn'wɛərɪnɪs], *s.* die Unbehutsamkeit, Unbedachtsamkeit. **–y,** *adj.* unachtsam, unvorsichtig, unbedacht(sam).
unwarlike [ʌn'wɔ:laɪk], *adj.* unkriegerisch.
unwarrant–able [ʌn'wɔrəntəbl], *adj.* ungerechtfertigt, unverantwortlich; ungebührlich, untragbar, unhaltbar. **–ableness,** *s.* die Unverantwortlichkeit, Unhaltbarkeit. **–ably,** *adv.* in unverantwortlicher Weise. **–ed,** *adj.* ungerechtfertigt, unberechtigt, unbefugt, unverbürgt.
unwashed [ʌn'wɔʃt], *adj.* ungewaschen, unbespült (*by sea, etc.*); (*coll.*) *the great –*, der Pöbel.
unwatched [ʌn'wɔtʃt], *adj.* unbewacht, unbeobachtet.
unwatered ['ʌn'wɔ:təd], *adj.* unbewässert, unbegossen, unbesprengt; unverdünnt, unverwässert.
unwavering [ʌn'weɪvərɪŋ], *adj.* nicht wankend, standhaft, beharrlich, fest.
unweaned [ʌn'wɪ:nd], *adj.* nicht entwöhnt.
unwearable [ʌn'wɛərəbl], *adj.* nicht zu tragen(d).
unwear–ied [ʌn'wɪ:ərɪd], *adj.* nicht ermüdend *or* ermüdet, unermüdlich. **–ying** [–rɪɪŋ], *adj.* unermüdlich, nicht ermüdend.
unwed(ded) [ʌn'wɛd(ɪd)], *adj.* unverheiratet, unvermählt, ledig.
unweighed [ʌn'weɪd], *adj.* ungewogen; (*fig.*) unbedacht.
unwelcome [ʌn'wɛlkəm], *adj.* unwillkommen (*to*, für).
unwell [ʌn'wɛl], *pred. adj.* unwohl, nicht wohl, unpäßlich, übel; *I am –*, ich fühle mich nicht wohl, mir ist übel.
unwept [ʌn'wɛpt], *adj.* unbeweint, unbeklagt.
unwholesome [ʌn'houlsəm], *adj.* ungesund; schädlich. **–ness,** *s.* die Ungesundheit, Schädlichkeit.
unwield–iness [ʌn'wɪ:ldɪnɪs], *s.* die Schwerfälligkeit, Unbeholfenheit; Unhandlichkeit. **–y,** *adj.* schwerfällig, unbeholfen (*persons*); unhandlich, schwer zu handhaben(d), massig, sperrig (*of things*).
unwilling [ʌn'wɪlɪŋ], *adj.* nicht gewillt, widerwillig, abgeneigt; *be –*, nicht wollen, keine Lust haben; *I am – to admit*, ich gebe ungern zu; *willing or –*, man mag wollen oder nicht. **–ly,** *adv.* ungern, widerwillig, wider Willen. **–ness,** *s.* die Abgeneigtheit, der Widerwille.
unwind [ʌn'waɪnd], 1. *ir.v.a.* loswickeln, abwickeln, abwinden, abrollen. 2. *ir.v.n.* sich abwickeln, loswickeln *or* abwinden.
unwise [ʌn'waɪz], *adj.* unklug, töricht.
unwished [ʌn'wɪʃt], *adj.* ungewünscht. **– –for,** *adj.* unerwünscht.
unwithered [ʌn'wɪθəd], *adj.* unverwelkt.
unwitting [ʌn'wɪtɪŋ], *adj.* unwissentlich, unbewußt, unbeabsichtigt.
unwomanl–iness [ʌn'wumənlɪnɪs], *s.* die Unweiblichkeit. **–y,** *adj.* unweiblich, unfraulich.
unwonted [ʌn'wountɪd], *adj.* (*Poet.*) ungewohnt, ungewöhnlich.
unwooded [ʌn'wudɪd], *adj.* unbewaldet.
unwork–able [ʌn'wə:kəbl], *adj.* unausführbar (*plan*), nicht zu handhaben(d) *or* behandeln(d) *or* bearbeiten(d) (*material*), nicht betriebsfähig *or* bauwürdig. **–ed** [–t], *adj.* unbearbeitet (*ground*), unverritzt (*Min.*); *–ed coal*, anstehende Kohle. **–manlike,** *adj.* nicht fachgemäß *or* unsauber ausgeführt, stümperhaft.
unworldl–iness [ʌn'wə:ldlɪnɪs], *s.* die Unweltlichkeit, Weltfremdheit, Geistigkeit, unweltliche Gesinnung, die Uneigennützigkeit. **–y,** *adj.* unweltlich, weltfremd, geistig, uneigennützig.
unworn [ʌn'wɔ:n], *adj.* nicht getragen (*clothes*).
unworth–iness [ʌn'wə:ðɪnɪs], *s.* die Unwürdigkeit. **–y,** 1. *attrib. adj.* unwürdig, verächtlich (*of a p.*), unverdient (*treatment*). 2. *pred. adj.*; *be –y of a th.*, etwas nicht verdienen, einer S. nicht wert *or* würdig sein; *he is –y of it*, er ist dessen unwürdig.
unwound [ʌn'waʊnd], *adj.* abgewickelt, losgewunden; nicht aufgezogen (*as a watch*); *come –*, sich loswinden.
unwounded [ʌn'wu:ndɪd], *adj.* unverwundet, unverletzt.
unwrap [ʌn'ræp], *v.a.* auswickeln, auspacken, aufwickeln, loswickeln.
unwrinkled [ʌn'rɪŋkəld], nicht gerunzelt.
unwritten [ʌn'rɪtn], *adj.* ungeschrieben, unbeschrieben; *– law*, das Gewohnheitsrecht.

unwrought [ʌn'rɔ:t], *adj.* unbearbeitet, unverarbeitet, roh, Roh–.
unyielding [ʌn'jɪ:ldɪŋ], *adj.* unbiegsam, steif, hart; (*fig.*) unnachgiebig, unbeugsam, hartnäckig; unzugänglich (*to*, für).
unyoke [ʌn'jouk], *v.a.* losspannen, ausspannen, (*fig.*) lösen, lostrennen.
up [ʌp], **1.** *adv.* auf, hoch, oben; aufrecht; in die *or* der Höhe, empor, aufwärts; herauf, hinauf, heran, hinan; auf(gestanden); aufgegangen (*sun, plants, etc.*); abgelaufen, vorüber, vorbei, aus (*time*); – *and* –, immer höher; – *and down*, auf und ab, hin und her; – *there*, dort oben; **(a)** (*before preps.*) *be – against*, gegenüberstehen (*Dat.*); *run – against*, anrennen gegen; (*fig.*) stoßen auf; *be – before the court*, verhört (*of a p.*) *or* verhandelt (*of a case*) werden; – *from the country*, vom Lande; *be – for discussion*, erörtert werden; (*coll.*) *be – in*, bewandert sein in; (*coll.*) *be well – in*, beherrschen; *be – in arms*, die Waffen ergriffen haben, unter Waffen stehen, (*coll.*) sich auf die Hinterbeine stellen; – *into the sky*, hinauf in den Himmel; (*coll.*) *be – on*, höher *or* mehr sein als; – *till*, bis; – *to*, hinauf zu, bis zu *or* an; – *to town*, nach London; – *to date*, bis heute; (*coll.*) – *to scratch*, auf der Höhe; – *to strength*, in voller Stärke; (*coll.*) *be – to*, gefaßt *or* vorbereitet sein auf, geeignet sein zu, gewachsen sein (*Dat.*); (*coll.*) *be – to his tricks*, seine Schliche wohl kennen; *come – to*, reichen bis an, entsprechen (*Dat.*); *draw – to*, vorfahren vor; (*coll.*) *be – to the mark*, auf der Höhe sein; (*coll.*) *feel – to doing*, in Stimmung *or* bereit sein zu tun; (*coll.*) *not – to much*, nicht viel wert; (*coll.*) *what are you – to?* was machen Sie da?; (*coll.*) *be – to mischief*, Unfug im Schilde führen; – *to now* or *the present*, bis auf den heutigen Tag; (*coll.*) *it is – to you*, es ist *or* liegt an dir, es hängt von dir ab, es ist deine Pflicht *or* Sache; *keep – with*, Schritt halten mit; (*coll.*) *it is all – with him*, es ist aus mit ihm; **(b)** (*with* to be) *his blood is* –, sein Blut ist in Wallung; *he is not – yet*, er ist noch nicht auf(gestanden); (*sl.*) *what's –?* was gibt's *or* ist los? *be – and about*, wieder auf den Beinen sein; (*coll.*) *be – and coming*, flink, aktiv *or* tüchtig sein; (*coll.*) *be – and doing*, rege *or* tätig sein; (*coll.*) *the game is* –, es ist aus, erledigt *or* verloren; (*coll.*) *be hard* –, in schlechten Umständen *or* in der Klemme *or* böse dran sein; *prices are* –, die Preise stehen hoch *or* sind im Steigen *or* gestiegen *or* in die Höhe gegangen; *the sun is* –, die Sonne ist aufgegangen; *be 10* –, 10 Punkte voraus sein; *be – a whole tone*, einen ganzen Ton zu hoch sein; **(c)** (*with verbs*) (*only a representative cross-section of the many usages; see under the separate verbs*): *add* –, addieren; *be – all night*, die ganze Nacht auf sein *or* aufbleiben; *bind* –, verbinden; *bound – with*, verbunden sein mit; *bring* –, aufziehen, erziehen; *burn* –, aufflammen; gänzlich verbrennen; *clean* –, gänzlich reinigen, (*sl.*) einheimsen; *coil* –, aufrollen, sich zusammenrollen; *come* –, herankommen; *crop* –, zum Vorschein kommen, (*coll.*) auftauchen; *dry* –, eintrocknen, vertrocknen; (*sl.*) zu reden aufhören; *finish* –, beendigen; *fold* –, zusammenlegen; *follow* –, (eifrig) verfolgen, ausnutzen; *gather* –, aufsammeln, zusammennehmen; *get* –, aufstehen; *give o.s.* –, sich stellen (*to* (*Dat.*)); sich widmen (*to* (*Dat.*)); *go* –, steigen, hochgehen; *grow* –, aufwachsen, groß werden; *hurry* –, sich beeilen; *jump* –, aufspringen; *lock* –, einsperren; *look* –, hinaufblicken; *make* – (*for many meanings see* **make**): *move – in the world*, in der Welt vorankommen; *own* –, offen gestehen; *pluck – courage*, Mut fassen; *polish* –, herausputzen; *set* – (*for many meanings see* **set**); *settle* –, abmachen, abschließen; *sit* –, sich aufrichten (see also *be* –), *speak* –, lauter sprechen; *spring* –, aufspringen, aufschießen; aufkommen (*wind*); (*fig.*) auftauchen; *stand* –, aufstehen, sich erheben; *stay* – (see *be* –); *take* – (*for many meanings see* **take**); *tear* –, zerreißen, ausreißen; *turn* – (*for many meanings see* **turn**); **(d)** (*absolute*) (*Poet.*) *then – and spake*, dann erhob sich und sprach; (*sl.*) *he –s and says*, er sagte plötzlich. **2.** *int.* (elliptical for *get –, hold –, put –, etc.*) auf!; – *and away!* auf und davon! *hands –!* Hände hoch! **3.** *prep.* hinauf, auf . . . hinauf; – *country*, in das Land hinein; – *the hill*, den Berg hinauf, bergan; (*sl.*) – *the pole*, in der Klemme; übergeschnappt; – *the river*, flußaufwärts; (*sl.*) – *the spout*, als Pfand gelassen; dahin; kaputt; – *five flights of stairs*, fünf Treppen hoch; – *the street*, die Straße *or* auf der Straße entlang; *further – the street*, weiter oben an der Straße. **4.** *s.*; *the –s and downs*, das Auf und Ab, die Wechselfälle (*pl.*). **5.** *attrib. adj.*; **--bow,** *s.* der Aufstrich (*violin*). **--country,** 1. *s.* das Binnenland, Landinnere. 2. *adj.* binnenländisch, Binnen–. **--current,** *s.* der Aufwind (*Av.*). **--grade,** 1. *s.* der Aufstieg, die Steigung; *on the --grade*, im Aufstieg *or* Steigen. 2. *v.a.* auf eine höhere Stufe befördern *or* heben. **--line,** *s.* die Bahnlinie nach der Stadt (nach London). **--platform,** *s.* der Bahnsteig für Züge nach London, Ankunftsbahnsteig. **--river,** *see* **--stream.** **--stream** *adv.* stromauf(wärts), gegen den Strom an. **--stroke,** *s.* der Hub, Kolbenaufgang; *see* **upstroke.** **--train,** *s.* nach London gehender Zug.
upas ['ju:pəs], *s.* (*also* **--tree**) der Giftbaum, Upasbaum.
upbraid [ʌp'breɪd], *v.a.* tadeln, schelten; vorwerfen, vorhalten, zur Last legen (*a p. with s.th.*, einem etwas). **–ing,** 1. *adj.* vorwurfsvoll. 2. *s.* der Tadel, Vorwurf.
upbringing ['ʌpbrɪŋgɪŋ], *s.* die Erziehung, das Aufziehen, Großziehen.
upcast ['ʌpkɑ:st], 1. *adj.* aufgeschlagen (*eyes*), emporgerichtet (*glance*). 2. *s.* (also – *shaft*) der Ausflußschacht, Luftschacht (*Min.*).
up-end [ʌp'ɛnd], *v.a.* (*coll.*) hochkant stellen *or* stehen, umstülpen.
upheav-al [ʌp'hɪ:vl], *s.* die Erhebung, Umwälzung, die Bodenerhebung (*Geol.*). **–e,** *v.a.* emporheben.
uphill, 1. ['ʌphɪl], *adj.* (an)steigend, bergauf; (*fig.*) mühsam, mühselig, beschwerlich. 2. [ʌp'hɪl], *adv.* bergauf(wärts), bergan, aufwärts.
uphold [ʌp'hould], *ir.v.a.* hochhalten, aufrechthalten, stützen, (*fig.*) aufrechterhalten, festhalten an, (unter)stützen. **–er,** *s.* der Erhalter, Verteidiger; die Stütze.
upholster [əp'houlstə], *v.a.* (aus)polstern, überziehen; ausstatten (*a room*). **–er,** *s.* der Tapezierer, Dekorateur. **–y,** *s.* die Polsterung, Möbelbezüge, Polsterwaren (*pl.*).
upkeep ['ʌpkɪ:p], *s.* die Instandhaltung; Unterhaltungskosten (*pl.*).
upland ['ʌplənd], 1. *s.* das Hochland, Oberland. 2. *adj.* Hochlands–.
uplift, 1. [ʌp'lɪft], *v.a.* hochheben, aufheben, emporheben (*voice*). 2. ['ʌplɪft], *s.* die Erhebung (*Geol.*); (*fig.*) der Aufschwung, die Besserung, Erbauung, Aufbauarbeit, soziale Reform. **–ing** [–'lɪftɪŋ], *adj.* erbauend.
up-line, *see under* **up.**
upmost ['ʌpmoust], 1. *adj.* oberst, höchst. 2. *adv.* zuoberst.
upon [ə'pɔn], *prep.* (= on, *which is generally commoner, esp. in coll. usage. – is used partic. fig. & in stock phrases, viz.*) – *inquiry*, nach Erkundigung; *my blood be – your head*, mein Blut komme über euer Haupt; *rush* –, sich werfen *or* stürzen auf (*Acc.*); – *this*, hierauf; *once – a time*, es war einmal; – *my word*, auf mein Wort.
upper ['ʌpə], 1. *adj.* ober, höher, Ober–; – *arm*, der Oberarm; – *beds*, das Hangende (*Min.*); – *case*, große Buchstaben (*pl.*) (*Typ.*); – *circle*, erster Rang (*Theat.*); *the – classes*, die oberen Klassen; – *deck* das Oberdeck; – *hand*, (*fig.*) die Oberhand, der Vorteil; *get* or *gain the – hand*, die Oberhand gewinnen; – *house*, das Oberhaus (*Parl.*); – *jaw*, der Oberkiefer; – *leather*, das Oberleder; – *lip*, die Oberlippe; – *story*, oberes Stockwerk, (*coll.*) das Oberstübchen; *the – ten* (*thousand*), die oberen Zehntausend, die Aristokratie, die Reichen (*pl.*), die vornehme Welt. 2. *s.* (*usually pl.*) ['ʌpəz], das Oberleder; (*down*) *on one's –s*, mit zerlumpten Schuhen, (*usually fig.*) herunterkommen, ganz auf dem Hund. **--cut,** *s.* der Kinnhaken (*Boxing*). **–most,** 1. *adj.* höchst, oberst. 2. *adv.* zuoberst; vorherrschend; *say whatever comes –most*, sagen, was einem auf die Zunge kommt.

uppish ['ʌpɪʃ], *adj.* (*coll.*) anmaßend, frech.
up-platform, *see under* **up.**
upraise [ʌp'reɪz], *v.a.* (*archaic*) erheben, erhöhen. **–d** [–d], *adj.* erhoben.
uprear [ʌp'rɪ:ə], *v.a.* aufrichten.
upright, 1. *adj.* [*pred.* 'ʌpraɪt, ʌp'raɪt, *attrib.* 'ʌpraɪt], aufrecht, gerade, stehend, aufgerichtet; aufrichtig, ehrlich, bieder, rechtschaffen; – *piano*, das Klavier, Pianino. 2. ['ʌpraɪt], *s.* der Ständer (*Carp.*, *etc.*), Stutzbalken, Pfeiler, Pfosten; *pl.* Torpfosten (*pl.*) (*Footb.*). **–ness** ['ʌpraɪtnɪs], *s.* die Gradheit; Aufrichtigkeit, Ehrlichkeit, Biederkeit, Rechtschaffenheit.
upris–e [ʌp'raɪz], *v.n.* (*Poet.*) sich erheben, aufheben. **–ing** [–'raɪzɪŋ], *s.* das Aufstehen; Aufgehen, der Aufgang (*of the sun*); (*fig.*) die Erhebung, der Aufstand, Aufruhr.
up-river, *see under* **up.**
uproar ['ʌprɔ:ə], *s.* das Geschrei, der Lärm, Tumult, Radau, Aufruhr. **–ious** [ʌp'rɔ:rɪəs] *adj.* lärmend, laut, tosend, tobend, stürmisch.
uproot [ʌp'ru:t], *v.a.* entwurzeln, ausreißen, (*fig.*) entreißen (*from* (*Dat.*)), herausreißen (*from*, aus) (*a p.*); ausrotten, ausmerzen (*a th.*).
upset [ʌp'set], 1. *v.a.* umwerfen, umstürzen, umstoßen, stürzen (*government*), über den Haufen werfen, vereiteln (*plans*); stauchen (*metals*); (*fig.*) aus der Fassung bringen, stören, beunruhigen, verwirren; (*coll.*) – *the apple-cart*, die Pläne zunichte machen; *his stomach is* –, er hat sich (*Dat.*) den Magen verdorben; *the sausage has* – *me*, die Wurst ist mir schlecht bekommen; *she is very* – *about it*, sie ist sehr bestürzt darüber. 2. *v.n.* umschlagen, umfallen, umkippen; kentern (*Naut.*). 3. *s.* das Umwerfen, Umstürzen, der Umsturz; das Umfallen, Umkippen, der Fall; (*fig.*) die Bestürzung, Verwirrung, Erregung; Unordnung. 4. ['ʌpset], *adj.*; – *price*, der Anschlagpreis, Einsatzpreis (*at auctions*).
upshot ['ʌpʃɔt], *s.* der Ausgang, das Ende, (End)-Resultat, Ergebnis, der Schlußeffekt; *in the* –, am Ende, schließlich, letzten Endes.
upside-down ['ʌpsaɪd'daʊn], *adv.* das Oberste zuunterst, mit dem Kopf nach unten; (*fig.*) drunter und drüber, vollkommen in Unordnung; *turn a th.* –, etwas auf den Kopf stellen (*also fig.*).
upstage [ʌp'steɪdʒ], *adj.* im Hintergrund der Bühne (befindlich); (*fig. coll.*) kühl, steif.
upstairs 1. [ʌp'stɛəz], *adv.* oben, nach oben, die Treppe hinauf. 2. ['ʌpstɛəz], *adj.* oben gelegen, im oberen Stockwerk.
upstanding [ʌp'stændɪŋ], *adj.* aufrecht, ehrlich.
upstart ['ʌpstɑ:t], 1. *s.* der Emporkömmling, Parvenü. 2. *attrib. adj.* emporgekommen.
upstroke ['ʌpstroʊk], *s.* der Aufstrich, Haarstrich (*in writing*); *see* **– -stroke** *under* **up.**
upsurge ['ʌpsə:dʒ], *s.* die Aufwallung, das Ansteigen.
upswing ['ʌpswɪŋ], *s.* der Aufschwung, Aufstieg.
uptake ['ʌpteɪk], *s.*; (*coll.*) *quick in* or *on the* –, rasch begreifen; *be slow in the* –, eine lange Leitung haben, begriffsstützig sein.
upthrow ['ʌpθroʊ], *s.* die Verwerfung (*Geol.*).
upthrust ['ʌpθrʌst], *s.* das Emporschleudern (*Geol.*).
up-to-date ['ʌptə'deɪt], *adj.* modern, neuzeitlich, der Neuzeit gemäß, zeitgemäß; modisch, auf der Höhe; see *up to date* under **up.**
upturn ['ʌp'tə:n], *v.a.* aufwerfen, hochwerfen; umstülpen. **–ed** [–d], *adj.* nach oben gebogen *or* gerichtet; umgeworfen, umgekippt; gekentert (*Naut.*); *–ed nose*, die Stupsnase.
upward ['ʌpwəd], 1. *adj.* nach oben *or* aufwärts gerichtet; (*fig.*) aufwärtssteigend; (an)steigend (*C.L.*). 2. *adv.* (*Poet.*), **–s,** *adv.* aufwärts, nach oben, in die Höhe, (*fig.*) darüber (hinaus); *–s of*, mehr als, über (*with numbers*).
uraemia [juə'rɪ:mɪə], *s.* die Urämie (*Med.*).
uran–ite ['juərənaɪt], *s.* der Uranpecherz, die Pechblende. **–ium** [juə'reɪnɪəm], *s.* das Uran. **–ography** [–'nɔgrəfɪ], *s.* die Himmelsbeschreibung. **–ous** [ju:ərənəs], *adj.* Uran–.
urban ['ə:bn], *adj.* Stadt–, städtisch; – *district*, der Stadtbezirk. **–ization** [–bənaɪ'zeɪʃn], *s.* die Verstädterung; Verfeinerung. **–ize** ['ə:bənaɪz], *v.a.* städtisch machen; verfeinern.
urchin ['ə:tʃɪn], *s.* der Schelm, Balg; (*rare*) Igel (*Zool.*); *sea*-–, der Seeigel.
ure–a ['juərɪə], *s.* der Harnstoff, das Karbamid. **–al** [–rɪəl], *adj.* Harnstoff–. **–ter** [juə'rɪ:tə], *s.* der Harnleiter. **–thra** [–'rɪ:θrə], *s.* die Harnröhre. **–tic** [juə'retɪk], *adj.* harntreibend.
urge [ə:dʒ], 1. *v.a.* (also – *on*) antreiben, drängen, nötigen, dringend auffordern, dringen in (*Acc.*); nahelegen (*Dat.*), zusetzen (*Dat.*), anspornen (*a p.*); betreiben, vor(wärts)treiben, antreiben, vorwärtsdrängen (*a th.*); vorbringen, vorstellen, nahelegen, einschärfen, bestehen auf, ans Herz legen, vor Augen führen, hervorheben, eindringlich betonen *or* empfehlen (*upon a p.*, einem) (*a point of view*). 2. *s.* der Drang, Antrieb, Impuls; das Feuer, die Inbrunst; *creative* –, der Schaffensdrang. **–ncy** [–ənsɪ], *s.* die Dringlichkeit, dringende Eile *or* Not, die Bedrückung; Eindringlichkeit. **–nt** [–ənt], *adj.* dringend, ernstlich; drängend, dringlich, eilig; *be –nt*, darauf drängen, drängend *or* begierig sein (*of a p.*); drängen, eilen (*of a th.*).
uri–c ['juərɪk], *adj.* Harn–, Harnsäure–; *–c acid*, die Harnsäure. **–nal** ['juərɪnl], *s.* die Bedürfnisanstalt, das Pissoir, der Nachttopf. **–nary** ['juərɪnərɪ], 1. *adj.* Harn–, Urin–. 2. *s.* das Pissoir. **–nate** ['ju:rɪneɪt], *v.n.* harnen, urinieren, Harn lassen. **–ne** ['juəraɪn], *s.* der Urin, Harn. **–nometer** [ju:rɪ'nɔmɪtə], *s.* der Urinmesser.
urn [ə:n], *s.* die Urne, der (Wasser)Krug; *funeral* –, die Graburne; *tea* –, die Teemaschine.
uroscopy [ju:'rɔskəpɪ], *s.* die Harnuntersuchung.
ursine ['ə:saɪn], *adj.* bärenartig, Bären–.
urtica ['ə:tɪkə], die Gattung der Nesselpflanzen.
urus ['juərəs], *s.* der Auerochse.
us [ʌs], *pers. pron.* uns; *to* –, (zu) uns; *all of* –, wir alle; *both of* –, wir beide.
us–able ['ju:zəbl], *adj.* brauchbar, gebräuchlich. **–age** ['ju:zɪdʒ], *s.* der Brauch, die Gewohnheit, Gepflogenheit, Sitte, das Herkommen; der Gebrauch, die Benutzung; Behandlung, Behandlungsweise, das Verfahren; der Sprachgebrauch; Geschäftsbrauch. **–ance** ['ju:zəns], *s.* der Gebrauch, die Gewohnheit; (*usually C.L.*) der Geschäftsbrauch, die Usance, der Uso; *at –ance*, nach Uso; *bill at –ance*, der Usowechsel. **–e,** **1.** [ju:s], *s.* der Gebrauch; die Benutzung, Verwendung; der Brauch, die Gewohnheit; Praxis; der Nutzen, die Nützlichkeit, Brauchbarkeit; der Zweck, Vorteil; Genuß, die Nutznießung (*Law*); *for –e*, zum Gebrauch; *for the –e of*, zum Nutzen von; *in –e*, gebräuchlich, im Gebrauch; *be of –e*, nützlich, dienlich *or* von Nutzen sein (*to*, für); *can I be of any –e?* kann ich helfen? *is it of any –e to you?* können Sie es gebrauchen? *of no –e*, nutzlos, ohne Nutzen; *it is* (*of*) *no –e*, es ist zwecklos *or* hilft nichts; *what –e is it? what is the –e of it?* was nützt *or* hilft es? was für Sinn *or* Zweck hat es? *out of –e*, ungebräuchlich, außer Gebrauch; *fall*, *go*, or *pass out of –e*, ungebräuchlich werden, außer Gebrauch kommen; *have no –e for*, nichts übrig haben für, nichts anfangen können mit, nicht brauchen können; *have the –e of*, benutzen können; *make* (*good*) *–e of*, (gut) anwenden *or* gebrauchen, (guten) Gebrauch machen von; *put to –e*, nutzbar *or* mit Nutzen anwenden, gebrauchen; *with –e*, beim, im, durch *or* nach Gebrauch. **2.** [ju:z], *v.a.* gebrauchen, benutzen, verwenden, anwenden, sich bedienen (*Gen.*), sich (*Dat.*) zunutze machen, zur Anwendung bringen, ausüben; behandeln, verfahren mit, begegnen (*Dat.*) (*a p.*); verbrauchen, verausgaben; handhaben (*a th.*); *–e discretion*, nach Gutdünken handeln; *–e strong language*, fluchen, schimpfen; *–e threatening language*, mündlich bedrohen; *–e up*, aufbrauchen; abnutzen; *–ed up*, abgenutzt, erschöpft, erledigt, verbraucht; *how has the world –ed you?* wie ist es dir ergangen? **3.** *v.n.* (*only past tense*) pflegte; *we –ed to live here*, wir wohnten früher hier; *he –ed to say*, er pflegte zu sagen. **–ed,** 1. [ju:zd] *p.p.* & *attrib. adj. see* **–e 2.** 2. *pred. adj.* [ju:st] gewöhnt (*to*, an); *get –ed to*, sich gewöhnen an. **–eful** ['ju:sful], *adj.* nützlich, brauchbar; dienlich; nutzbar, Nutz– (*esp. Tech.*); *make o.s. –eful*, sich nützlich machen; *–eful effect*, der Nutzeffekt; *–eful load*, das Zuladegewicht, die Nutzlast. **–eful-**

ness, *s.* die Nützlichkeit, Brauchbarkeit, Verwendungfähigkeit. **–eless** [ˈjuːslɪs], *adj.* nutzlos, unbrauchbar (*to*, für); unnütz, sinnlos, zwecklos, fruchtlos; vergeblich; *be –eless*, sich erübrigen. **–elessness,** *s.* die Nutzlosigkeit, Unbrauchbarkeit. **–er** [ˈjuːzə], *s.* der Benutzer, Gebraucher; der Genuß, die Nutznießung, das Benutzungsrecht (*Law*).

usher [ˈʌʃə], 1. *s.* der Gerichtsdiener; Platzanweiser, Pförtner, Türsteher; *Gentleman –*, Zeremonienmeister (*in Parliament, etc.*); (*archaic*) der Unterlehrer, Hilfslehrer. 2. *v.a.* (usually – *in*) (hin)einführen, anmelden; (*fig.*) ankündigen, einleiten.

usual [ˈjuːʒuəl], *adj.* gewöhnlich, gebräuchlich, üblich; Stamm–; *it is – for me to be here*, ich bin gewöhnlich hier; *the rudeness – with him*, die ihm eigene Grobheit; *as –*, wie gewöhnlich *or* üblich; *more than –*, mehr als gewöhnlich; *the – thing*, das Übliche. **–ly,** *adv.* gewöhnlich, meistens, in der Regel.

usu–capion [juːzjuˈkæpɪən], **–caption** [–ˈkæpʃən], *s.* die Ersitzung (*Law*). **–fruct** [ˈjuːzjufrʌkt], *s.* der Nießbrauch, die Nutznießung. **–fructuary** [juːzjəˈfrʌktjuərɪ], *s.* der Nutznießer.

usur–er [ˈjuːʒərə], *s.* der Wucherer. **–ious** [juːˈzjuərɪəs, ˈjuːʒjurɪəs], *adj.* wucherisch, wucherhaft, Wucher–. **–iousness,** *s.* das Wucherische, die Wucherei. **–y** [ˈjuːʒərɪ], *s.* der Wucher, Wucherzinsen (*pl.*); *lend at* or *on –y*, auf *or* zu Wucherzinsen ausleihen.

usurp [juːˈsəːp], *v.a.* an sich reißen, sich (*Dat.*) widerrechtlich aneignen, sich bemächtigen (*Gen.*). **–ation** [–ˈpeɪʃn], *s.* rechtswidrige *or* widerrechtliche Besitzergreifung, Besitznahme *or* Aneignung (*of* (*Gen.*)), unberechtigter Eingriff (*on*, in). **–er,** *s.* der Usurpator, unrechtmäßiger Besitzergreifer, rechtswidrige Throninhaber, der Thronräuber; (*fig.*) der Eindringling (*on*, in). **–ing,** *adj.* widerrechtlich (sich aneignend).

utensil [juːˈtensɪl], *s.* das Gerät, Geschirr, Gefäß, Handwerkszeug; *pl.* Utensilien (*pl.*), das Geschirr.

uter–ine [juːˈtərɪn], *adj.* Gebärmutter–; von derselben Mutter geboren (*Law*); *–ine brother*, der Halbbruder von der Mutterseite. **–o-gestation,** *s.* die Schwangerschaft (*Med.*). **–us,** *s.* die Gebärmutter.

utili–tarian [jutɪlɪˈtɛərɪən], 1. *adj.* utilitaristisch, Nützlichkeits–. 2. *s.* der Utilitarier, Anhänger des Nützlichkeitsprinzips; Nützlichkeitsmensch. **–tarianism,** *s.* die Nützlichkeitslehre, der Utilitarismus. **–ty** [juˈtɪlɪtɪ], *s.* die Nützlichkeit, der Nutzen (*to*, für); *public –ty*, öffentliche Einrichtung; *–ty actor* or *man*, der Schauspieler für kleine Rollen; *–ty goods*, Gebrauchswaren, Einheitswaren (*pl.*). **–zable** [juːtɪˈlɑɪzəbl], *adj.* benutzbar, verwertbar. **–zation** [–tɪlɑɪˈʒəɪʃn], *s.* die Nutzbarmachung, Verwertung, Ausnützung, (Nutz)Anwendung, Benutzung. **–ze** [ˈjuːtɪlɑɪz], *v.a.* benutzen, verwerten, ausnutzen, nutzbar *or* zunutze machen.

utmost [ˈʌtmoust], 1. *adj.* äußerst, fernst, weitest, entlegenst; (*fig.*) höchst, größt. 2. *s.* das Äußerste, Höchste; *do one's –*, sein möglichstes *or* äußerstes tun; *at the –*, höchstens; *to the –*, aufs äußerste; *to the – of my power*, nach besten Kräften.

utopia [juːˈtoupɪə], *s.* das Luftschloß, Idealland, der Idealzustand, Zukunftstraum, die Utopie. **–n** [–ɪən], 1. *adj.* utopisch, ideal, traumhaft, phantastisch; *–n ideas*, die Utopie. 2. *s.* der Utopist, Phantast, Schwärmer. **–nism,** *s.* der Utopismus, die Schwärmerei.

utric–le [ˈjuːtrɪkl], *s.* der Schlauch, kleines Bläschen (*Bot.*), blasenartiges Gefäß (*Anat.*). **–ular** [–ˈtrɪkjulə], *adj.* schlauchartig, blasenartig.

[1]**utter** [ˈʌtə], *adj.* äußerst, gänzlich, völlig; endgültig; regelrecht, ausgekocht, abgefeimt. **–ly,** *adv.* durchaus, gänzlich, völlig. **–most,** *see* **utmost.**

[2]**utter,** *v.a.* äußern, aussprechen, ausstoßen, hervorbringen, von sich geben (*sounds*), ausdrücken (*thoughts*); in Umlauf bringen *or* setzen (*coins, etc.*); **–ance** [–əns], *s.* das Äußern, die Äußerung, Aussprache, Ausdrucksweise; der Ausdruck, Ausspruch; die Ausgabe (*of coin, etc.*); *give –ance to*, Ausdruck geben (*Dat.*), äußern. **–er,** *s.* Äußernde(r), *m.*, der Verbreiter.

uvula [ˈjuːvjələ], *s.* das Zäpfchen. **–r,** *adj.* Zäpfchen–.

uxorious [ʌgˈzɔːərɪes], *adj.* dem Weibe völlig unterwürfig *or* ergeben, unter dem Pantoffel stehend. **–ness,** *s.* übertriebene Unterwürfigkeit (gegenüber seiner Frau).

V

V, v [viː], *s.* das V, v; *see Index of Abbreviations.* **–-shaped,** *adj.* V-förmig, keilförmig; *–-shaped neck*, spitzer Ausschnitt (am Kleid).

vac [væk], *abbr. for* **vacation.**

vacan–cy [ˈveɪkənsɪ], *s.* die Leere, leerer Raum; freie Stelle, die Vakanz; Lücke; geistige Leere, die Geistesabwesenheit, Leerheit; *stare into –cy*, ins Leere blicken. **–t,** *adj.* leer(geworden); frei, unbesetzt (*seat, post, etc.*), leerstehend, unbewohnt (*house*), offen, vakant (*post*); gedankenleer, geistlos, ausdruckslos (*appearance*); *–t look*, leerer Blick; *–t possession*, sofort zu beziehen; *fall –t*, frei *or* vakant werden.

vacat–e [vəˈkeɪt], *v.a.* leer machen, leeren, räumen (*place*), frei machen (*seat*), aufgeben, niederlegen (*post*). **–ion,** *s.* Ferien (*pl.*), der Urlaub; die Niederlegung, Aufgabe (*of a post*); Räumung (*of a house, etc.*); *long –ion*, große Ferien, Sommerferien (*pl.*).

vaccin–ate [ˈvæksɪneɪt], *v.a.* impfen. **–ation** [–ˈneɪʃən], *s.* die (Schutzpocken)Impfung. **–ator,** *s.* der Impfarzt. **–e** [ˈvæksɪn], 1. *adj.* Impf–, Kuhpocken–. 2. *s.* der Impfstoff, die Lymphe, das Vakzin. **–ia** [–ˈsɪnɪə], *pl.* Kuhpocken (*pl.*).

vacillat–e [ˈvæsɪleɪt], *v.n.* schwanken (*also fig.*), wackeln, unsicher sein; (*usually fig.*) unentschlossen *or* unschlüssig sein. **–ing,** *adj.* schwankend, unschlüssig. **–ion** [–ˈleɪʃn], *s.* das Schwanken; die Unentschlossenheit, der Wankelmut.

vacu–ity [væˈkjuɪtɪ], *s.* die Leere, (*usually fig.*) Gedankenlosigkeit. **–ous** [ˈvækjuəs], *adj.* leer; (*usually fig.*), gedankenlos, ausdruckslos, inhaltlos, nichtssagend. **–um** [ˈvækjuəm], *s.* leerer *or* luftleerer Raum, das Vakuum; (*fig.*) die Lücke, Leere. **–um-brake,** *s.* die Vakuumbremse. **–um-cleaner,** *s.* der Staubsauger. **–um flask,** *s.* die Thermosflasche.

vade-mecum [ˈveɪdɪˈmɪːkəm], *s.* das Handbuch, Vademecum.

vagabond [ˈvægəbɔnd], 1. *s.* der Landstreicher, Vagabund, (*coll.*) Halunke, Spitzbube. 2. *adj.* herumstreichend, vagabundierend; fahrend, herumwandernd. **–age** [–ɪdz], *s.*, **–ism** [–ɪzm], *s.* die Landstreicherei, das Vagabundieren, Vagabundenleben. **–ize** [–ɑɪz], *v.n.* vagabundieren, umherschweifen, umherstreichen.

vagary [vəˈgɛərɪ], *s.* (*usually pl.*) die Laune, Grille, Schrulle, Unberechenbarkeit; wunderlicher Einfall.

vagin–a [vəˈdʒɑɪnə], *s.* die Scheide (*Anat.*). **–al** [–əl], *adj.* scheidenförmig, Scheiden–. **–itis** [vædʒɪˈnɑɪtɪs], *s.* die Scheidenentzündung.

vagran–cy [ˈveɪgrənsɪ], *s.* die Landstreicherei, das Vagabundieren. **–t** [–ənt], 1. *adj.* wandernd, umherziehend, vagabundierend. 2. *s.* der Landstreicher, Vagabund.

vague [veɪg], *adj.* unbestimmt, undeutlich, unklar, verschwommen, nebelhaft, vag (*of a th.*); zerstreut (*of a p.*); *– answer*, zweideutige Antwort; *not the –st notion*, nicht die leiseste Ahnung; *– promise*, nichtssagendes Versprechen; *– rumour*, dunkles Gerücht; *– suspicion*, unklarer Verdacht. **–ness,** *s.* die Unbestimmtheit.

vain [veɪn], *adj.* eitel, eingebildet, großspurig (*of a p.*); vergeblich, fruchtlos, unnütz; leer, hohl, inhaltlos, wesenlos, nichtig, eitel (*of a th.*); *in* –, umsonst, vergebens; – *effort*, vergebliche Mühe; – *hope*, leere Hoffnung; – *pleasure*, nichtige Freude; – *show*, hohle Prahlerei; – *threat*, inhaltlose Drohung; – *wish*, eitler Wunsch. **-glorious** [veɪn'glɔ:rɪəs], *adj.* großsprecherisch, prahlerisch, aufgeblasen, großspurig, hoffärtig, ruhmredig. **-glory** [veɪn'glɔ:rɪ], *s.* die Großtuerei, Prahlerei, Aufgeblasenheit, Hoffart. **-ly,** *adv.* vergebens, umsonst. **-ness,** *s.* die Vergeblichkeit, Fruchtlosigkeit, Nichtigkeit.

valance ['væləns], *s.* der (Bett)Vorhang; Bettbehang.

[1]vale [veɪl], *s.* (*Poet.*) das Tal; – *of tears* or *woe*, das Jammertal.

[2]vale [veɪlɪ], 1. *int.* lebewohl! 2. *s.* das Lebewohl. **-diction** [vælɪ'dɪkʃn], *s.* der Abschied, Abschiedsworte (*pl.*); das Abschiednehmen, Lebewohl. **-dictory** [–'dɪktərɪ], 1. *adj.* Abschieds–. 2. *s.* die Abschiedsansprache, Abschiedsrede.

valenc–e, –y ['veɪləns(ɪ)], *s.* die Wertigkeit, Valenz (*Chem.*).

valentine ['væləntaɪn], *s.* der Valentingruß; Schatz.

valerian [və'lɪərɪən], *s.* der Baldrian (*Bot.*, *Pharm.*).

valet ['vælɛ, 'vælɪt], 1. *s.* der (Kammer)Diener. 2. *v.a.* Diener sein bei, bedienen, versorgen.

valetudinar–ian [vælɪtju:dɪ'nɛərɪən], 1. *adj.* kränkelnd, kränklich, schwächlich. 2. *s.* kränkliche Person, Kränkelnde(r), *m.* **-ianism** [–'nɛərɪənɪzm], *s.* die Kränklichkeit. **-y** [–'tju:dɪnərɪ], *adj.* *see* **-ian** 1 and 2.

valiant ['vælɪənt], *adj.* tapfer, mutig, heldenhaft, heldisch, Helden–, heroisch.

valid ['vælɪd], *adj.* rechtskräftig, (rechts)gültig (*Law*); bindend, zwingend, wohlbegründet, unbestreitbar, triftig, stichhaltig (*as arguments*); *be* –, gelten. **-ate** [–eɪt], *v.a.* rechtskräftig *or* gültig erklären, bestätigen. **-ation** [–'deɪʃn], *s.* die Gültigkeitserklärung, Inkraftsetzung. **-ity** [və'lɪdɪtɪ], *s.* die (Rechts)Gültigkeit; Triftigkeit, bindende *or* zwingende Kraft; die Gültigkeitsdauer (*of a ticket*).

valise [və'lɪ:s], *s.* der Handkoffer; der Mantelsack; das Gepäck (*Mil.*).

vall–ey ['vælɪ], *s.* das Tal, Flußgebiet; die Dachrinne, (Dach)Kehle (*Build.*); *-ey bottom*, die Talsohle. **-um,** [–əm], *s.* der Verteidigungswall.

valoriz–ation [vælərаɪ'zeɪʃn], *s.* die Aufwertung. **-e** ['vælərаɪz], *v.a.* aufwerten.

valo–rous ['vælərəs], *adj.* tapfer, mutig, kühn, heldenmütig, heldenhaft. **-ur** ['vælə], *s.* die Tapferkeit, der (Helden)Mut.

valu–able ['væljuəbl], 1. *adj.* wertvoll (*to* or *for*, für (*a p.*), zu (*a th.*)), kostbar, teuer; abzuschätzen(d), abschätzbar. 2. *s.* (*usually pl.*) Wertsachen, Kostbarkeiten (*pl.*). **-ation** [–ju'eɪʃn], *s.* die Abschätzung, Wertbestimmung, Veranschlagung; Bewertung, Taxe; der Schätzungswert, abgeschätzter Preis *or* Wert; (*fig.*) die Wertung, Wertschätzung; *take a p. at his own -ation*, einen so werten wie er gewertet sein will. **-ator** ['væljueɪtə], *s.* der Taxator, Abschätzer. **-e** ['vælju:], 1. *s.* der Wert (*also Maths.*, *Mus.*, & *fig.*), Nutzen (*to*, für); die Valuta, der Preis, Betrag, Tauschwert, Gegenwert (*C.L.*); (*fig.*) die Bewertung, Wertschätzung, Bedeutung, Geltung, der Gehalt. *at -e*, zum Tageskurs; *cash* (*or surrender*) *-e*, der Rückkaufwert; *estimated -e*, der Schätzungswert; *exchange -e*, der Marktpreis; *-e in exchange*, der Tauschwert; *get good -e for one's money*, reell bedient werden, preiswert kaufen; *give good -e*, reell bedienen; *of good -e*, vollwertig; *in -e*, an Wert; *intrinsic -e*, innerer Gehalt; *-e as per invoice*, Wert in Faktura; *-e received*, Gegenwert *or* Gegenleistung erhalten; *be of -e to*, wertvoll *or* nützlich sein (*to* (*Dat.*)); *place* or *set much*, *great* or *a high -e* (*up*)*on*, (großen *or* hohen) Wert legen auf, (hoch) bewerten; *standard of -e*, der Wertmesser; *to the -e of*, im Betrag von; im *or* bis zum Werte von. 2. *v.a.* (ab)schätzen, bewerten, (ver)anschlagen, taxieren (*at*, auf); (*fig.*) Wert legen auf, werten, (hoch)schätzen, (hoch)achten, werthalten; **-eless,** *adj.* wertlos. **-er** ['væljuə], *s.* der Abschätzer, Taxator. **-ta** [və'lju:tə], *s.* die Währung.

valv–e [vælv], *s.* die Klappe (*also Anat.*, *Bot.*); Röhre (*Rad.*); das Ventil (*Tech.*); *output -e*, die Endröhre (*Rad.*); *safety -e*, das Sicherheitsventil; *thermionic -e*, die Elektrodenröhre. **-e-gear,** *s.* das Ventilgetriebe, die Ventilsteuerung. **-e-set,** *s.* der Röhrenapparat. **-ular,** *adj.* klappig, klappenförmig, Klappen–. **-ule** [–ju:l], *s.* kleine Klappe. **-ulitis** [–ju'laɪtɪs], die Herzklappenentzündung (*Med.*).

vamo(o)se [və'mous, və'mu:s], *v.n.* (*sl.*) ausreißen, durchbrennen.

[1]vamp [væmp], 1. *s.* das Oberleder (*on shoes*), (*fig.*) das Flickwerk; (*coll.*) improvisierte Begleitung (*Mus.*). 2. *v.a.* vorschuhen; (*fig.*) ausbessern, flicken; aus dem Stegreif begleiten (*Mus.*). 3. *v.n.* Begleitung improvisieren (*Mus.*).

[2]vamp, 1. *s.* (*coll.*) der Vamp. 2. *v.a.* behexen, neppen.

vampir–e ['væmpaɪə], *s.* (*-e-bat*) der Vampir (*also fig.*); der Blutsauger. **-ism,** *s.* der Vampirglaube, die Blutsaugerei (*also fig.*).

[1]van [væn], *s.* die Vorhut (*also fig.*), der Vortrab (*Mil.*); (*fig.*) die Spitze; *see* **vanguard.**

[2]van, 1. *s.* die (Getreide)Schwinge; Schwingschaufel (*Min.*); Schwingprobe (*Min.*). 2. *v.a.* sieben, worfeln, schwingen, waschen (*ore*).

[3]van, *s.* der Planwagen, Lastwagen, Transportwagen; *delivery* –, Lieferwagen; *furniture* –, Möbelwagen; *luggage* –, Gepäckwagen. **--load,** *s.* die Wagenladung.

vanadi–c [və'nædɪk], *adj.* Vanadium–. **-um** [və'neɪdɪəm], *s.* das Vanadium, Vanadin.

vandalism ['vændəlɪzm], *s.* der Vandalismus, die Zerstörungswut, (Natur)Verschandelung.

vandyke [væn'daɪk], *s.* das Zackenmuster, die Zackenspitze; der Spitzenkragen; – *beard*, der Knebelbart; – *brown*, das Vandykbraun; – *collar*, ausgezackter Halskragen.

vane [veɪn], *s.* der Wetterhahn, die Wetterfahne; das Visier, der Diopter; der (Windmühlen)Flügel, das (Schrauben)Blatt.

vanguard ['væŋgɑ:d], *s.* der Vortrab, die Vorhut (*Mil.*); (*fig.*) Spitze, der Führer.

vanilla [və'nɪlə], *s.* die Vanille.

vanish ['vænɪʃ], *v.n.* (also – *away*) (ver– *or* ent)schwinden, dahinschwinden, weichen (*from*, von), zergehen, vergehen (*into*, in), Null werden (*Math.*); – *from* (*a p.'s*) *sight*, (einem) aus den Augen entschwinden; – *into air*, zu Wasser werden. **-ing,** *s.* das Verschwinden; *-ing cream*, die Hautcreme; *-ing fraction*, der Infinitesimalbruch; *-ing line*, die Fluchtlinie; *-ing point*, der Fluchtpunkt, (*fig.*) Nullpunkt.

vanity ['vænɪtɪ], *s.* die Eitelkeit, Selbstgefälligkeit (*of a p.*), die Nichtigkeit, Leerheit, Hohlheit, Nutzlosigkeit (*of a th.*); – *bag*, die Handtasche; – *fair*, der Jahrmarkt der Eitelkeit.

vanquish ['væŋkwɪʃ], 1. *v.a.* besiegen, überwältigen, überwinden. 2. *v.n.* Sieger sein, siegen. **-er,** *s.* der Eroberer, Sieger, Überwinder.

vantage ['vɑ:ntɪdʒ], *s.* günstige Gelegenheit; der Vorteil (*Tenn.*); – *set*, die Partie mit Spiel vor (*Tenn.*). **--ground, --point,** *s.* vorteilhafte Stellung, die Überlegenheit.

vapid ['væpɪd], *adj.* schal (*also fig.*), geschmacklos, abgestanden; (*fig.*) inhaltlos, geistlos, fade, flach, leer. **-ity** [və'pɪdɪtɪ], *s.*, **-ness,** *s.* die Schalheit, Flachheit, Leere, Geistlosigkeit, Fadheit.

vapo–rization [veɪpəraɪ'zeɪʃn], *s.* die Verdunstung, Abdunstung. **-rize** ['veɪpəraɪz], 1. *v.n.* verdunsten, abdunsten. 2. *v.a.* verdünsten, verdampfen (lassen). **-rizer** [–raɪzə], *s.* der Verdampf(ungs)apparat, Verdampfer, Zerstäuber. **-rous** [–rəs], *adj.* dampfig, dunstig; (*fig.*) nebelhaft, verschwommen, substanzlos; duftig, gazeartig (*of fabric*). **-ur** ['veɪpə], 1. *s.* der Dampf, Dunst (*also fig.*); (*fig.*) der Wahn, das Hirngespinst; *pl.* (*archaic*) die Hypochondrie, Melancholie; *water* –, der Wasserdampf; – *bath*, das Dampfbad. 2. *v.n.* (ver)dampfen, (*fig.*, *rare*) prahlen. **-ry** [–pərɪ], *adj.* dunstig, Dunst–, (*fig.*) verschwommen, nebelhaft.

variab–ility [vɛərɪə'bɪlɪtɪ], *s.* die Veränderlichkeit, das Schwanken; die Variabilität (*Biol.*); (*fig.*) Unbeständigkeit. **–le** ['vɛərɪəbl], 1. *adj.* veränderlich, schwankend; variabel (*Biol., Math.*), unbeständig, wandelbar; *–le pitch*, ungleicher Ton; *–le pitch propeller*, verstellbare Luftschraube (*Av.*). 2. *s.* veränderliche *or* variable Größe, die Variable, Veränderliche (*Math.*). **–leness,** *s. see* **–ility.**

varia–nce ['vɛərɪəns], *s.* die Veränderung, der Wechsel; die Abweichung, Verschiedenheit, Unvereinbarkeit, der Widerstreit; Widerspruch (*Law*); die Uneinigkeit, Entzweiung, der Streit, Zwist; *be at –nce*, uneinig sein, sich streiten (*of persons*), unvereinbar sein, sich widersprechen, in Widerspruch stehen (*with*, mit *or* zu); *set at –nce*, entzweien, uneinig machen. **–nt** [–ənt], 1. *adj.* abweichend. 2. *s.* die Variante, Spielart; Lesart. **–tion** [–'eɪʃn], *s.* die Veränderung, Abänderung, Abwechs(e)lung; der Wechsel, Unterschied, die Verschiedenheit, Schwankung, Abweichung; Mißweisung, Deklination (*of compass needle*), Variation (*Mus., Astr., Math., Biol.*).

varico–cele ['værɪkəsɪ:l], *s.* der Krampfaderbruch. **–se** ['værɪkous], *adj.* krampfadrig; Krampfader–; *–se vein*, die Krampfader.

varie–d ['vɛərɪd], *adj.* verschieden(artig), mannigfaltig, abwechselnd, abwechslungsreich, abwechslungsvoll, bunt. **–gate** [–rɪəgeɪt], *v.a.* farbig *or* bunt machen, (*fig.*) durch Abwechslung beleben, Abwechslung hineinbringen in. **–gated** [–'geɪtɪd], *adj.* bunt, vielfarbig; wechselvoll, wechselnd, gemischt. **–gation** [–'geɪʃn], *s.* die Vielfarbigkeit, Buntfarbigkeit, Buntheit. **–ty** [və'raɪətɪ], 1. *s.* die Mannigfaltigkeit, Verschiedenheit, Verschiedenartigkeit; Abwechs(e)lung, Buntheit, Vielseitigkeit; Art, Abart, Spielart, Varietät (*Nat. Hist.*); die Anzahl, Auswahl, Reihe, Menge (*of*, von); das Varieté (*Theat.*); *a –ty of things*, allerlei *or* verschiedenartige Dinge; *–ty show*, die Varietévorstellung.

variol–a [və'rɪələ], *s.* Blattern, Pocken (*pl.*). **–ar** [–lɑ], *adj.* Pocken–. **–ite** ['vɛərɪəlaɪt], *s.* der Blatterstein (*Geol.*).

variorum-edition [vɛərɪ'ɔ:rəm], die Ausgabe mit Anmerkungen verschiedener Ausleger.

various ['vɛərɪəs], *adj.* verschieden(artig); (*before pl.*) verschiedene, mehrere, viele.

vari–x ['vɛərɪks], *s.* (*pl.* –ces ['værɪsɪ:z]) die Krampfader.

varlet ['vɑ:lɪt], *s.* der Knappe (*Hist.*); (*archaic*) Schuft, Halunke.

varmint ['vɑ:mɪnt], *s.* (*sl.*) der Taugenichts, Racker.

varnish ['vɑ:nɪʃ], 1. *s.* der Firnis (*also fig.*), Lack; (*fig.*) die Politur, Glasur, der Anstrich. 2. *v.a.* firnissen, lackieren; polieren; glasieren; (*fig.*) (also – *over*) einen Anstrich geben (*Dat.*), übertünchen, beschönigen.

varsity ['vɑ:sɪtɪ], *abbr. for* **university.**

vary ['vɛərɪ], 1. *v.a.* wechseln, (ab)ändern, verändern, variieren. 2. *v.n.* (ab)wechseln, sich (ver)ändern, variieren; sich unterscheiden, voneinander verschieden sein, abweichen (*from*, von); veränderlich sein (*as wind*). **–ing,** *adj.* verschieden, abwechselnd, veränderlich.

vascular ['væskjulə], *adj.* Gefäß–, gefäßförmig (*Bot., Anat.*); – *system*, das Blut- und Lymphgefäßsystem (*Physiol.*).

vase [vɑ:z], *s.* die Vase.

vaseline ['væsəlɪ:n], *s.* das Vaselin, die Vaseline.

vassal ['væsl], *s.* der Lehnsmann, Vasall; (*fig.*) Sklave, Knecht, Untertan. **–age** [–səlɪdʒ], *s.* der Lehndienst, die Lehnspflicht, das Lehnsverhältnis, Vasallentum; (*fig.*) die Unterwerfung, Knechtschaft, Abhängigkeit.

vast [vɑ:st], *adj.* unermeßlich, weit ausgedehnt (*in extent*); (*fig.*) ungeheuer, gewaltig, groß, riesig; (*coll.*) bedeutend, beträchtlich; *a – crowd*, eine Unmenge; – *majority*, überwiegende Mehrzahl; – *quantities*, Unmengen. **–ly,** *adv.* in hohem Grade *or* Maße, weit. **–ness,** *s.* die Unermeßlichkeit, Weite; ungeheure Größe.

vat [væt], *s.* großes Faß, großer Kübel, der Bottich, Trog, die Bütte, Kufe; (Färber)Küpe (*Dye.*); (Loh)Grube (*Tan.*).

vaticina–l [və'tɪsɪnl], *adj.* prophetisch. **–te** [–neɪt], *v.a.* prophezeien, weissagen. **–tion** [–'neɪʃn], *s.* die Weissagung, Prophezeiung.

vaudeville ['voudvɪl], *s.* das Varieté.

[1]**vault** [vɔ:lt], 1. *s.* das Gewölbe; Grabgewölbe, die Gruft; die Stahlkammer, Schatzkammer, der Tresor (*of a bank, etc.*); die Wölbung, Höhlung (*also Anat.*); (*often pl.*) das Kellergewölbe, der Keller; – *of heaven*, das Himmelsgewölbe; *wine –s*, der Weinkeller. 2. *v.a.* überwölben. **–ed** [–ɪd], *adj.* gewölbt. **–ing,** *s.* das Gewölbe, der Gewölbebau, die Wölbung.

[2]**vault,** 1. *v.n.* springen, sich schwingen; Kunstsprünge machen. 2. *v.a.* springen *or* hinwegsetzen über, überspringen. 3. *s.* der Sprung, Satz; *flank –*, die Flanke (*Gymn.*); *front –*, die Wende (*Gymn.*); *pole –*, der Stabhochsprung (*Sport*); *rear –*, die Kehre (*Gymn.*). **–ing,** *s.* das Springen. **–ing-horse,** *s.* das Pferd (*Gymn.*).

vaunt [vɔ:nt], 1. *v.a.* rühmen, (an)preisen; protzen *or* sich brüsten mit. 2. *v.n.* prahlen (*of*, mit), sich rühmen (*of* (*Gen.*)). **–er,** *s.* der Prahler. **–ing,** *adj.* prahlerisch.

veal [vɪ:l], *s.* das Kalbfleisch; *roast –*, der Kalbsbraten; – *cutlet*, das Kalbskotelett.

vector ['vɛktə], *s.* der Vektor (*Math.*).

vedette [və'dɛt], *s.* die Vedette, der Kavalleriewachtposten.

veer [vɪ:ə], 1. *v.n.* sich drehen, lavieren (*as ship*), umspringen, fieren (*as wind*); (*fig.*) sich (um)drehen *or* wenden; – *about*, umspringen (*as wind*); – *round*, (*fig.*) umschwenken (*to*, nach), hinüberschwenken (*to*, zu), umschlagen (*as fortune, etc.*). 2. *v.a.* vor dem Winde wenden, halsen (*a ship*); (also – *away* or *out*) loslassen, laufen lassen, fieren (*a cable*).

vegeta–ble ['vɛdʒətəbl], 1. *s.* die Pflanze; das Gemüse (*for cooking*); *pl.* das Gemüse, Gemüsearten (*pl.*); *green –bles*, grünes Gemüse. 2. *attrib. adj.* vegetabilisch, pflanzlich, Pflanzen–, Gemüse–; *–ble diet*, die Pflanzenkost; *–ble dye*, der Pflanzenfarbstoff; *–ble garden*, der Gemüsegarten; *–ble kingdom*, das Pflanzenreich; *–ble marrow*, der Kürbis. **–l** ['vɛdʒɪtl], *adj.* pflanzlich, vegetativ, vegetabilisch, Pflanzen–. **–rian** [–ɪ'tɛərɪən], 1. *adj.* vegetarisch. 2. *s.* der Vegetarier. **–rianism** [–rɪənɪzm], *s.* der Vegetarismus. **–te** ['vɛdʒɪteɪt], *v.n.* wie eine Pflanze wachsen; (*usually fig.*) vegetieren, dahinleben, ein Pflanzenleben führen. **–tion** [–'teɪʃn], *s.* der Pflanzenwuchs, die Vegetation; Pflanzenwelt, Pflanzen (*pl.*); die Wucherung (*Med.*); (*fig.*) das Dahinvegetieren. **–tive** ['vɛdʒɪtətɪv], *adj.* pflanzlich,vegetativ, wie Pflanzen wachsend; dem Wachstum dienend, das Wachstum fördend, Wachstums–.

vehemen–ce, –cy (*rare*) ['vɪ:əməns(ɪ)], *s.* die Heftigkeit, das Ungestüm; Feuer, die Hitze, Leidenschaft. **–t** [–ənt], *adj.* heftig, ungestüm, heiß (*as desires*); hitzig, leidenschaftlich (*as a p.*).

vehic–le ['vɪ:əkl], *s.* das Fuhrwerk, Fahrzeug, Gefährt, Beförderungsmittel, (*fig.*) der Träger, Vermittler; die Vermittlung, das (Hilfs)Mittel, Werkzeug, Vehikel (*of*, für). **–ular** [vɪ:'ɪkjulə], *adj.* Wagen–, Fuhrwerk–.

veil [veɪl], 1. *s.* der Schleier (*also fig.*); die Umhüllung, das (Kelch)Velum (*Eccl.*); das Segel (*Bot., Anat., Zool.*); die Hülle, Maske, Verschleierung, der Deckmantel; *draw a – over*, verschleiern, verdecken; *take the –*, den Schleier nehmen, Nonne werden. 2. *v.a.* verschleiern (*one's face*), (*fig.*) verhüllen, verdecken, verbergen, bemänteln, tarnen. **–ing,** *s.* die Verschleierung; der Schleierstoff.

vein [veɪn], *s.* die Ader (*Anat., Bot.*); der Gang (*Min.*); die Rippe (*Bot.*); Maser, der Strich, Streifen (*in wood, marble, etc.*); (Wesens)Zug (*in a p.*), Beigeschmack (*in a th.*), Hang, die Neigung, Anlage; Art, der Stil; die Stimmung, Laune; *be in the – for*, aufgelegt sein zu; – *of ore*, der Erzgang. **–ed,** *adj.* geädert, äd(e)rig, gerippt, marmoriert, gemasert. **–ing,** *s.* die Äderung, Maserung.

velar ['vɪ:lə], 1. *adj.* Gaumen–, velar. 2. *s.* der Gaumenlaut, Velarlaut.

veld(t) [vɛlt, fɛlt], *s.* das Grasland, Weideland.

velleity [və'lɪ:ɪtɪ], *s.* (*archaic*) kraftloser Wille.

vellum [ˈvɛləm], *s.* das Schreibpergament, Velin. **--paper,** *s.* das Velin(papier).
velocipede [vəˈlɔsɪpɪ:d], *s.* (*archaic*) das Fahrrad.
velocity [vəˈlɔsɪtɪ], *s.* die Geschwindigkeit, Schnelligkeit; – *of sound*, die Schallgeschwindigkeit.
velour(s) [vəˈlu:ə], *s.* der Velours.
velum [ˈvɪ:ləm], *s.* weicher Gaumen, das Gaumensegel (*Anat.*), das Segel, die Membran (*Bot.*).
velvet [ˈvɛlvɪt], 1. *s.* der Samt, Sammet; Bast (*on antlers*); (*coll.*) *be on* –, glänzend dastehen. 2. *adj.* Samt–; samtweich, samtartig. **–een** [vɛlvəˈtɪ:n], *s.* der Baumwollsamt, Man(s)chester. **–y** [ˈvɛlvətɪ], *adj.* samtartig, samtweich; lieblich (*as wine*).
venal [ˈvɪ:nl], *adj.* käuflich, feil, bestechlich. **–ity** [vɪˈnælɪtɪ], *s.* die Käuflichkeit, Feilheit, Bestechlichkeit.
venation [vəˈneɪʃn], *s.* die Äderung, das Geäder (*Bot.*).
vend [vɛnd], *v.a.* verkaufen, feilbieten (*Law*). **–ee** [–ˈdɪ:], der Käufer (*Law*). **–er** [–ə], *s.* der Verkäufer, Händler. **–ibility** [–ɪbɪlɪtɪ], *s.* die Verkäuflichkeit. **–ible** [–ɪbl], *adj.* verkäuflich. **–ition** [–ˈdɪʃn], *s.* der Verkauf (*Law*). **–or** [–dɔ:], *s.* der Verkäufer (*Law*).
vendetta [vɛnˈdɛtə], *s.* die Blutrache.
veneer [vəˈnɪə], 1. *s.* das Furnier(holz), Furnierblatt; (*fig.*) äußerer Anstrich, der Schein, die Tünche. 2. *v.a.* furnieren, (*fig.*) einen äußeren Anstrich geben (*Dat.*), verdecken (*with*, durch), umkleiden (*with*, mit). **–ing** [–rɪŋ], *s.* das Furnieren, die Furnierarbeit.
venera–bility [vɛnərəˈbɪlɪtɪ], *see* **–bleness.** **–ble** [ˈvɛnərəbl], *adj.* ehrwürdig, verehrungswürdig; (*as title*) hochwürdig; *–ble Sir*, Hochwürden. **–bleness,** *s.* die Verehrungswürdigkeit, Ehrwürdigkeit. **–te** [ˈvɛnəreɪt], *v.a.* (ver)ehren. **–tion** [–ˈreɪʃn], *s.* die Verehrung, Ehrfurcht, Hochachtung (*for* or *of*, vor); *hold in –tion*, verehren. **–tor,** *s.* der Verehrer.
vener–eal [vəˈnɪərɪəl], *adj.* geschlechtlich, sexuell, Sexual–, Geschlechts–; geschlechtskrank, venerisch; *–eal disease*, die Geschlechtskrankheit. **–y** [ˈvɛnərɪ], *s.* (*archaic*) der Geschlechtsgenuß, Geschlechtsverkehr.
venery [ˈvɛnərɪ], *s.* (*archaic*) die Jagd, das Weidwerk.
venesection [vɛnɪˈsɛkʃn], *s.* der Aderlaß.
venge–ance [ˈvɛndʒəns], *s.* die Rache; *take –ance on*, sich rächen an (*Dat.*); (*coll.*) *with a –ance*, tüchtig, ganz gehörig, gewaltig, erst recht; und wie; daß es eine Art hat. **–ful,** *adj.* rachsüchtig.
venial [ˈvɪ:nɪəl], *adj.* verzeihlich, entschuldbar; läßlich (*Eccl.*); – *sin*, die Erlaßsünde (*R.C.*). **–ity** [–ˈælɪtɪ], *s.* die Verzeihlichkeit.
venison [ˈvɛnɪzn], *s.* das Wildbret.
venom [ˈvɛnəm], *s.* das Tiergift; (*less accurately*) Gift; (*fig.*) die Gehässigkeit, Bosheit, Tücke. **–ed** [–d], *adj.* (*usually fig.*) giftig, boshaft, gehässig. **–ous** [–əs], *adj.* giftig (*also fig.*), (*fig.*) boshaft. **–ousness,** *s.* die Giftigkeit, (*fig.*) Boshaftigkeit.
veno–se [ˈvɪ:nous], *adj.* geädert (*Bot.*). **–sity** [–ˈnɔsɪtɪ], *s.* venöse Beschaffenheit. **–us** [–nəs], *adj.* venös, Venen– (*Anat.*), geädert (*Bot.*).
vent [vɛnt], 1. *s.* die Öffnung; das Spundloch (*of a cask*); Zündloch (*of guns*); der After (*of birds and fishes*); Vulkanschlot; Ausfluß, Abfluß (*also fig,*); (*fig.*) Ausweg, Ausgang; *give* –, Luft machen, freien Lauf lassen (*to* (*Dat.*)). 2. *v.a.* (*usually fig.*) lüften, auslassen (*on*, an); äußern, von sich geben; Luft machen, freien Lauf lassen ((*Dat.*); *on*, gegenüber). **–age** [–ɪdʒ], *s.* das Fingerloch (*of wind instruments*). **--hole,** *s.* das Luftloch, Zugloch.
venter [ˈvɛntə], *s.* der Bauch, die Magenhöhle (*of insects*).
ventilat–e [ˈvɛntɪleɪt], *v.a.* ventilieren (*also fig.*), entlüften, auslüften, (durch)lüften (*a room, etc.*), Luftlöcher anbringen in (*a box, etc.*); schwingen (*corn*); (*fig.*) erörtern, erwägen, anschneiden (*a question*). **–ion** [–ˈleɪʃn], *s.* die Ventilation, Lüftung, der Luftzufuhr, Luftwechsel (*in a room*), die Wetterfuhrung (*Min.*); (*fig.*) freie Erörterung. **–or** [–leɪtə], *s.* der Ventilator, Entlüfter, die Lüftungsvorrichtung, Lüftungsanlage.
ventr–al [ˈvɛntrəl], *adj.* Bauch–. **–icle** [–trɪkl], *s.* die Höhlung, Höhle (*in brain*), Kammer (*in the heart*) (*Anat.*). **–icular** [–ˈtrɪkjulə], *adj.* Höhlen–, Kammer–. **–iloquial** [–trɪˈloukwɪəl], *adj.* Bauchrede–. **–iloquism** [–ˈtrɪləkwɪzm], *s.* die Bauchredekunst, das Bauchreden. **–iloquist** [–ˈtrɪləkwɪst], *s.* der Bauchredner. **–iloquize** [–ˈtrɪləkwaɪz] *v.n.* bauchreden. **–iloquous** [–ˈtrɪləkwəs], *adj.* bauchrednerisch.
venture [ˈvɛntʃə], 1. *s.* das Wagnis, Risiko; Unternehmen, die Spekulation (*C.L.*); das Geratewohl; *at a* –, aufs Geratewohl, auf gut Glück; *draw a bow at a* –, auf den Busch klopfen; *put to the* –, versuchen, riskieren, es versuchen mit. 2. *v.a.* wagen, riskieren, aufs Spiel setzen; zu äußern wagen (*an opinion*); (*Prov.*) *nothing* –, *nothing have*, frisch gewagt ist halb gewonnen. 3. *v.n.* sich erlauben *or* unterstehen, (sich) wagen; – *on a th.*, sich in eine S. einlassen, etwas wagen; *I – to ask*, ich erlaube *or* gestatte mir zu fragen. **–some** [–səm], *adj.* kühn, verwegen, waghalsig; riskant, gefährlich. **–someness,** *s.* die Verwegenheit, Unternehmungslust, Waghalsigkeit.
venue [ˈvɛnju:], *s.* zuständiger Gerichtsort (*Law*); (*coll.*) der Schauplatz, Zusammenkunftsort, Treffpunkt.
veraci–ous [vəˈreɪʃəs], *adj.* wahrhaft, wahrheitsliebend, vertrauenswürdig, glaubwürdig (*of a p.*), wahr (*of a statement*). **–ty** [–ˈræsɪtɪ], *s.* die Wahrhaftigkeit, Glaubwürdigkeit, Wahrheitsliebe (*of a p.*), Wahrheit (*of a statement*).
veranda [vəˈrændə], *s.* die Veranda.
verb [və:b], *s.* das Zeitwort, Verb(um). **–al** [–bəl], 1. *adj.* wörtlich, wortgetreu, wortwörtlich, Wort für Wort, buchstäblich; Verbal–, Wort–; mündlich; verbal (*Gram.*); *–al agreement*, mündliches Abkommen; *–al inspiration*, die Verbalinspiration (*Eccl.*); *–al memory*, das Wortgedächtnis; *–al note*, die Verbalnote (*diplomacy*). **–alism,** *s.* die Wortklauberei. **–alist,** *s.* der Wortklauber. **–alize** [–əlaɪz], 1. *v.a.* in ein Zeitwort verwandeln. 2. *v.n.* wortreich sein, viele Worte machen. **–atim** [–ˈbeɪtɪm], *adv.* wörtlich, wortgetreu, Wort für Wort. **–iage** [ˈvə:bɪədʒ], *s.* der Wortschwall. **–ose** [və:ˈbous], *adj.* wortreich, überladen (*of language*), weitschweifig (*of a p.*). **–osity** [–ˈbɔsɪtɪ], *s.* die Wortfülle, der Wortschwall; die Weitschweifigkeit.
verdan–cy [ˈvə:dənsɪ], *s.* das Grün(e), frisches Grün, grüne Frische; (*fig.*) die Unreife. **–t** [–ənt], *adj.* grün, grünend, frisch; (*fig.*) unerfahren, naiv.
verderer [ˈvə:dərə], *s.* königlicher Förster (*Hist.*).
verdict [ˈvə:dɪkt], *s.* der Urteilsspruch, Rechtsspruch, Wahrspruch, (*fig.*) das Urteil, die Entscheidung, Meinung, Ansicht; – *of not guilty*, der Freispruch; *pass a – upon*, ein Gutachten abgeben über; *return a – of murder*, auf Mord erkennen.
verdigris [ˈvə:dɪgrɪ:s], *s.* der Grünspan.
verdure [ˈvə:djə], *s.* das Grün, grüne Vegetation, frischer Pflanzenwuchs; (*fig.*) die Frische, Kraft, Blüte.
verge [və:dʒ], 1. *s.* der Rand, die Grenze; (Gras)-Einfassung; der Amtsstab (*Hist.*); die Spindel (*Horol.*); *on the* –, an der Grenze *or* am Rande (*of* (*Gen.*)); nahe daran, im Begriff (*of doing*, zu tun). 2. *v.n.* streifen, grenzen, liegen (*on*, an (*Acc.*)); (*fig.*) sich nähern (*on* (*Dat.*)); sich neigen (*towards*, nach . . . hin), übergehen (*into*, in). **–r** [–ə], *s.* der Stabträger (*Hist.*); Kirchendiener, Küster (*Eccl.*).
veriest [ˈvɛrɪɪst], *see* **very** 2.
verif–iable [ˈvɛrɪfaɪəbl], *adj.* erweislich, nachweislich, nachweisbar, beweisbar, nachprüfbar. **–ication** [–fɪˈkeɪʃn], *s.* der Wahrheitsnachweis, Beleg, die Bewahrheitung, Bestätigung, Beurkundung; *in –ication of which*, urkundlich dessen (*Law*). **–y** [ˈvɛrɪfaɪ], *v.a.* bestätigen, erweisen, beurkunden, belegen, beglaubigen, als wahr nachweisen *or* beweisen, auf die Wahrheit *or* Echtheit (nach)prüfen, die Richtigkeit feststellen; wahr machen, erfüllen.
veri–ly [ˈvɛrɪlɪ], *adv.* (*archaic*) wahrlich, wahrhaftig, fürwahr. **–similitude** [vɛrɪsɪˈmɪlɪtju:d], *s.* die Wahrscheinlichkeit. **–table** [ˈvɛrɪtəbl], *adj.* wahr, wahrhaftig, wirklich. **–ty** [–ɪtɪ], *s.* die Wahrheit, Wirklichkeit; (*also pl.*) wahre Tatsache, die Grundwahrheit; *of a –ty*, (*archaic*) wahrhaftig! wirklich!

verjuice [ˈvəːdʒuːs], *s.* unreifer Obstsaft, das Holzapfelessig, die Säure.
vermeil [ˈvəːmɪl], *adj.* (*Poet.*) purpurrot, scharlachrot, hochrot.
vermi-celli [vəːmɪˈsɛlɪ], *s.* Fadennudeln (*pl.*). **–cide** [ˈvəːmɪsaɪd], *s.* das Wurm(tötungs)mittel. **–cular** [–ˈmɪkjulə], *adj.* Wurm–; wurmartig, wurmförmig; gewunden. **–culate** [–ˈmɪkjulət], (*usually fig.*) wurmartig, wurmförmig. **–culated** [–ˈmɪkjuleɪtɪd], *adj.* wurmstichig; mit gewundenen Verzierungen. **–culation** [–ˈleɪʃn], *s.* die Wurmstichigkeit; wurmlinige Verzierung. **–form** [ˈvəːmɪfɔːm], *adj.* wurmförmig; *–form appendix*, der Wurmfortsatz (*Anat.*). **–fuge** [–fjuːdʒ], *s.* das Wurmmittel.
vermilion [vəːˈmɪlɪən], 1. *s.* das Zinnober, Mennig, das Zinnoberrot. 2. *adj.* zinnoberrot, scharlachrot.
vermin [ˈvəːmɪn], *s.* (*usually pl. constr.*) der Schädling, das Ungeziefer, Gewürm, (*fig.*) Gesindel, Geschmeiß, die Brut. **–ate** [–eɪt], *v.n.* Ungeziefer erzeugen. **– -killer**, *s.* das Insektenpulver. **–ous** [–əs], *adj.* verlaust; (*fig.*) gemein, parasitisch.
vermouth [ˈvəːmuːθ], *s.* der Wermut(wein).
vernacular [vəˈnækjulə], 1. *adj.* einheimisch, Landes–, Volks– (*of language*). 2. *s.* die Muttersprache, Landessprache, Volkssprache; der Dialekt, Jargon, die Lokalsprache, Fachsprache.
vernal [ˈvəːnl], *adj.* Frühlings–, frühlingsartig; (*fig.*) jugendlich, frisch; – *equinox*, die Frühlings-tag- und Nachtgleiche; – *grass*, das Ruchgras (*Bot.*).
vernier [ˈvəːnɪə], *s.* der Nonius, Vernier, Feinsteller.
veronal [ˈvɛrənəl], *s.* das Veronal.
veronica [vəˈrɔnɪkə], *s.* der Ehrenpreis (*Bot.*).
verruca [vəˈruːkə], *s.* die Warze.
versatil-e [ˈvəːsətaɪl], *adj.* wendig, geschmeidig, anpassungsfähig, beweglich, gewandt, vielseitig (begabt); wandelbar, wandlungsfähig, veränderlich, unbeständig; drehbar, sich drehend (*Bot.*, *Zool.*). **–ity** [–ˈtɪlɪtɪ], *s.* die Vielseitigkeit, Gewandtheit, Beweglichkeit, Wandelbarkeit, Veränderlichkeit, Unbeständigkeit.
vers-e [vəːs], *s.* der Vers (*also B.*), die Verszeile, die Strophe; (*coll.*) (*no art.*) Verse (*pl.*), die Poesie, Dichtkunst, Dichtung, metrische Form; *in –e*, in Versen. **–ed** [–t], *adj.* erfahren, bewandert (*in*, in). **–icle** [–ɪkl], *s.* der Bibelvers, Psalmvers. **–fication** [–ɪfɪˈkeɪʃn], *s.* das Versemachen, die Verskunst, der Versbau, das Metrum. **–ifier** [–faɪə], *s.* der Verseschmied, Dichterling. **–ify** [–faɪ], 1. *v.n.* Verse machen, reimen, dichten. 2. *v.a.* in Verse bringen, in Versen besingen.
version [ˈvəːʃn], *s.* die Übersetzung; Darstellung, Fassung, Lesart, Version.
verso [ˈvəːsou] (*pl.* –s [–z]), *s.* die Rückseite (*of a page or coin*).
verst [vəːst], *s.* die Werst.
versus [ˈvəːsəs], *prep.* gegen (*Law & Sport*).
vert [vəːt], 1. *v.n.* übertreten, den Glauben wechseln. 2. *s.* Übertretene(r), *m.*, der Konvertit.
vertebra [ˈvəːtɪbrə], *s.* (*pl.* –ae [–brɪː]) der Rückenwirbel; *pl.* die Wirbelsäule. **–l** [–əl], *adj.* Wirbel–; *–l column*, die Wirbelsäule. **–te** [–ət], 1. *adj.* mit Rückenwirbeln versehen, Wirbel–. 2. *s.* das Wirbeltier. **–ted** [–breɪtɪd], *adj. see* **–te** 1. **–tion** [–ˈbreɪʃn], *s.* die Wirbelbildung.
vert-ex [ˈvəːteks], *s.* (*pl.* –tices [–tɪsɪːz]) der Scheitel(punkt); die Spitze (*Geom. & fig.*), der Zenit, Scheitelpunkt (*Astr.*); (*fig.*) die Krone, der Gipfel. **–ical** [–tɪkl], 1. *adj.* senkrecht, lotrecht, vertikal (*to*, auf); Scheitel–, Höhen–, Vertikal–; *–ical angle*, der Scheitelwinkel; *–ical circle*, der Vertikalkreis; *–ical engine*, (senkrecht) stehende Maschine; *–ical ray*, senkrecht fallender Lichtstrahl. 2. *s.* senkrechte Linie, die Senkrechte.
verti-cil, -cel [ˈvəːtɪsɪl], *s.* der Quirl, Wirtel, quirlige Blattstellung (*Bot.*). **–cilate, –celate** [–ˈtɪsɪlət], *adj.* quirlig, quirlblätterig. **–ginous** [–ˈtɪdʒɪnəs], *adj.* wirbelnd, Wirbel–; schwindlig, Schwindel–; schwindelnd (*height*). **–igo** [–tɪgou, –ˈtɪːgou], *s.* der Schwindel(anfall), das Schwindelgefühl.
vertu, *see* **virtu**.
vervain [ˈvəːveɪn], *s.* das Eisenkraut.
verve [vəːv], *s.* der Schwung, die Begeisterung, das Feuer.
very [ˈvɛrɪ], 1. *adv.* sehr, in hohem Grade; – *good*, nun gut, einverstanden; – *well*, freilich, nun gut, bitte sehr; *not* –, nicht gerade; – *much fatigued*, sehr ermüdet; (*before superl.*) aller–; *to the – last piece*, bis auf das (aller)letzte Stück; *the – same*, genau derselbe; *for his – own*, für sich (allein). 2. *adj.* wahrhaftig, rein, wirklich, echt; (*after* the) allein, bloß, gerade, genau, derselbe; (*after* this *or* that) derselbe, *etc.*; (*after poss. pron.*) schon, allein; (*comp.*) *verier*, (*after indef. art.*) (*archaic*) reiner, echter; (*superl.*) *veriest*, (*after def. art.*) reinst, größt; *in the – act*, auf frischer Tat; *at the – beginning*, gleich am Anfang; *the – air you breathe*, selbst die Luft, die man einatmet; *to the – bone*, bis auf den Knochen; *the – day*, am selben Tage; *that – day*, noch derselbe Tag; *this – day*, noch *or* gerade heute; *the – devil*, das ist rein *or* direkt zum Totärgern; *the – idea*, der bloße Gedanke, schon der Gedanke; *the – opposite*, das gerade Gegenteil; *from the – outset*, schon von Anfang an; *the – thing*, gerade das Richtige; *the – thought*, schon der (bloße) Gedanke; *the – truth*, die reine *or* lautere Wahrheit.
vesic-a [vəˈsɪːkə], *s.* die Blase (*Anat.*, *Zool.*), das Säckchen (*Bot.*). **–al** [ˈvɛsɪkəl], *adj.* Blasen–. **–ant** [–ənt], 1. *adj.* blasenziehend. 2. *s.* blasenziehendes Mittel, das Zugmittel. **–ate** [–eɪt], 1. *v.a.* Bläschen ziehen auf. 2. *v.n.* Blasen ziehen. **–ation** [–ˈkeɪʃn], *s.* die Blasenbildung. **–atory** [–kətrɪ], *s. & adj. see* **–ant**. **–le** [ˈvɛsɪkl], *s.* das Bläschen. **–ular** [vəˈsɪkjulə], *adj.* blasenartig, blasenförmig, Bläschen–, vesikulär.
vesper [ˈvɛspə], *s.* (*Poet.*) der Abend; Abendstern; *pl.* die Vesper, der Abendgottesdienst (*Eccl.*). **–tine** [–taɪn, –tɪn], *adj.* abendlich, Abend–.
vessel [ˈvɛsl], *s.* das Gefäß (*also fig.*); das Fahrzeug, Schiff (*Naut.*); *blood-–*, das Blutgefäß.
vest [vɛst], 1. *s.* das Unterhemd (*for men*), Hemdchen (*for women*); die Weste, Unterjacke (*in the tailoring trade*). 2. *v.a.* bekleiden, ausstatten (*Poet. or Eccl., except when fig.*); verleihen, übertragen (*in a p.*, einem) (*Law*); (*usually pass.*) *be –ed in a p.*, in den Händen (*Gen.*) liegen. 3. *v.n.* sich ankleiden (*Eccl.*); (*fig.*) zufallen, anheimfallen, übertragen werden (*in a p.*, einem). **–ed** [–ɪd], *adj.* althergebracht (*interests*), erworben (*rights*).
vesta [ˈvɛstə], *s.* (also *wax* –) das Wachsstreichholz. **–l** [–əl], 1. *adj.* vestalisch (*Myth.*); (*fig.*) keusch, jungfräulich. 2. *s.* die Vestalin.
vestibule [ˈvɛstɪbjuːl], *s.* der Vorhof (*also Anat.*), Vorplatz, Vorsaal, das Vorzimmer, die Vorhalle, (*Amer.*) der Durchgang (*Railw.*). **– -train**, *s.* der D-Zug, Durchgangszug (*Amer.*).
vestig-e [ˈvɛstɪdʒ], *s.* die Spur (*also fig.*), sichtbares Merkmal; (*fig.*) der Rest, das Überbleibsel, bißchen; Rudiment, verkümmertes Glied (*Biol.*). **–ial** [–ˈtɪdʒɪəl], *adj.* rudimentär, verkümmert (*Biol.*).
vestment [ˈvɛstmənt], *s.* das Meßgewand (*Eccl.*); Gewand, die Amtskleidung, der Talar, Ornat.
vestry [ˈvɛstrɪ], *s.* die Sakristei; (also *common* –) der Kirchenvorstand, die Gemeindevertretung. **– -clerk**, *s.* der Kirchenbuchführer. **–man**, *s.* das Mitglied des Kirchenvorstands, der Gemeindevertreter.
vesture [ˈvɛstʃə], *s.* (*Poet.*) Kleider (*pl.*), die Kleidung, das Kleid, Gewand.
vet [vɛt], 1. *s. abbr. of* **veterinary surgeon.** 2. *v.a.* (*coll.*) genau prüfen, überholen.
vetch [vɛtʃ], *s.* die Wicke (*Bot.*). **–ling**, *s.* die Platterbse (*Bot.*).
veteran [ˈvɛtərən], 1. *adj.* altgedient, ausgedient; (*fig.*) erprobt, erfahren; – *troops*, kampferprobte Truppen. 2. *s.* ausgedienter Soldat, der Veteran, (*esp. Amer.*) Kriegsteilnehmer; (*fig.*) alter Haudegen.
veterinary [ˈvɛtərɪnrɪ], *adj.* tierärztlich; – *science*, die Tierarzneikunde; – *surgeon*, der Tierarzt, Veterinär.
veto [ˈvɪːtou], 1. *s.* das Einspruchsrecht, Veto (*also fig.*), (*fig.*) der Einspruch (*on*, gegen). 2. *v.a.* Veto

einlegen gegen, (*fig.*) Einspruch erheben gegen, untersagen, verbieten.
vex [vɛks], *v.a.* ärgern; plagen, quälen, belästigen, schikanieren; beunruhigen, ängstigen; *be –ed with*, sich ärgern über, böse sein auf. **–ation** [–ˈeɪʃn], *s.* die Plage, Belästigung, Schikane; der Verdruß, Ärger; die Beunruhigung, Sorge, der Kummer. **–atious** [–ˈeɪʃəs], *adj.* ärgerlich, verdrießlich, lästig; schikanös (*Law*). **–atiousness** [–ˈeɪʃəsnɪs], *s.* die Verdrießlichkeit, Ärgerlichkeit, Lästigkeit. **–ed** [–t], *adj.* ärgerlich, verärgert (*at* or *with*, über); umstritten, strittig; *–ed question*, viel umstrittene Frage. **–ing,** *adj.* ärgerlich, verdrießlich, lästig, quälend, beunruhigend.
via [ˈvaɪə], 1. *s.*; – *Lactea*, die Milchstraße (*Astr.*); – *media*, der Mittelweg. 2. *prep.* über (*place*), mit Hilfe von.
viable [ˈvaɪəbl], *adj.* lebensfähig.
viaduct [ˈvaɪədʌkt], *s.* der Viadukt, die Überführung, Überbrückung.
vial [ˈvaɪəl], *s.* die Phiole, das Fläschchen; *pour out the –s of one's wrath*, die Schale seines Zorns ausgießen.
viands [ˈvaɪəndz], *pl.* Lebensmittel (*pl.*).
viaticum [vaɪˈætɪkəm], *s.* das Reisegeld, die Wegzehrung, der Zehrpfennig; letztes Abendmahl (*Eccl.*).
vibr–ant [ˈvaɪbrənt], *adj.* vibrierend, schwingend, Schwingungs–; pulsierend, erregt (*with*, von), bebend, zitternd (*with*, vor). **–ate** [–ˈbreɪt], 1. *v.n.* vibrieren, schwingen, pulsieren, zittern, (*fig.*) nachschwingen, nachzittern; erschauern, erschüttert sein. 2. *v.a.* in Schwingung versetzen, schwingen lassen. **–ation** [–ˈbreɪʃn], *s.* das Schwingen, Vibrieren, Zittern; die Schwingung. **–ator** [–ˈbreɪtə], *s.* der Summer (*Tech.*). **–atory** [ˈvaɪbrətrɪ], *adj.* vibrierend, schwingend, zitternd; Schwingungs–.
vicar [ˈvɪkə], *s.* der Pfarrer (*C. of E.*); Vikar, stellvertretender Bischof, der Stellvertreter des Papstes (*R.C.*); – *of Christ*, der Stellvertreter Christi. **–age** [–rɪdʒ], *s.* das Pfarrhaus. **––general,** *s.* der Generalvikar. **–ious** [–ˈkɛərɪəs], *adj.* stellvertretend.
vice [vaɪs], *s.* das Laster; die Untugend, Verderbtheit; der Mangel, Irrtum, Fehler, das Gebrechen; die Unart (*in a horse*, eines Pferdes).
²**vice,** *s.* der Schraubstock; *hand––*, der Feilkloben.
³**vice–**, *prefix* Vize–, Unter–. **––admiral,** *s.* der Vizeadmiral. **––chairman,** *s.* stellvertretender Vorsitzender, der Vizepräsident. **––chancellor,** *s.* der Rektor (*Univ.*). **––consul,** *s.* der Vizekonsul. **–gerent** [–ˈdʒɛrənt, –ˈdʒɪərənt], *s.* der Statthalter, Verweser. **––president,** *s.* der Vizepräsident. **–regal,** *adj.* vizeköniglich, Vizekönigs–. **–roy** [ˈvaɪsrɔɪ], *s.* der Vizekönig. **–royal** [–ˈrɔɪəl], *adj.* vizeköniglich.
⁴**vice** [ˈvaɪsɪ], *prep.* an Stelle von, (an)statt; – *versa*, *adv.* umgekehrt.
vici–nage [ˈvɪsɪnɪdʒ], *s.* die Nachbarschaft, Nähe. **–nal** [–nəl], *adj.* benachbart, nahe. **–nity** [vɪˈsɪnɪtɪ] *s.* die Nähe, Umgebung, Nachbarschaft.
vicious [ˈvɪʃəs], *adj.* lasterhaft, verderbt, verwerflich, unmoralisch, böse, boshaft; bösartig (*as a horse*); – *circle*, der Zirkelschluß. **–ness,** *s.* die Lasterhaftigkeit, Verderbtheit, Bosheit, Bösartigkeit.
vicissitud–e [vɪˈsɪsɪtjuːd], *s.* der Wechsel, Wandel, die Veränderung; *pl.* Wechselfälle (*pl.*). **–inous** [–ˈtjuːdɪnəs], *adj.* wechselvoll.
victim [ˈvɪktɪm], *s.* das Opfer (*also fig.*); Schlachtopfer, Opfertier (*of a sacrifice*); *fall a –*, erliegen, zum Opfer fallen (*to* (*Dat.*)), überwältigt werden (*to*, von). **–ize** [–aɪz], *v.a.* opfern, preisgeben; prellen, peinigen, quälen, belästigen.
victor [ˈvɪktə], *s.* der Sieger.
victoria [vɪkˈtɔːrɪə], *s.* zweisitziger Einspänner. **–n** [–n], 1. *adj.* viktorianisch. 2. *s.* der Viktorianer.
victor–ious [vɪkˈtɔːrɪəs], *adj.* siegreich, Sieges–; *be –ious*, Sieger sein, den Sieg davon tragen, siegen. **–y** [ˈvɪktərɪ], *s.* der Sieg; Erfolg, Triumph.
victual [ˈvɪtl], 1. *v.a.* (*& n.*, sich) verproviantieren, (sich) mit Lebensmitteln versehen. 2. *s.* (*usually pl.*) Lebensmittel, Eßwaren (*pl.*), der Proviant. **–ler** [ˈvɪtələ], *s.* der Lebensmittellieferant; (also *–ling ship*) das Proviantschiff (*Naut.*); *licensed –ler* der Schankwirt, Schenkwirt. **–ling,** *s.* die Verproviantierung.
vide [ˈvaɪdɪ], *int.* siehe. **–licet** [vɪˈdɪːlɪkət], *adv.* (*abbr.* viz.; *read*: namely *or* that is) das heißt (*abbr.* d.h.).
vie [vaɪ], *v.n.* wetteifern (*with*, mit; *for*, um; *in*, an), es aufnehmen (*with*, mit; *in*, in).
view [vjuː], 1. *v.a.* besehen, besichtigen, überblicken, überschauen, ansehen; betrachten, beurteilen, auffassen; prüfen, mustern. 2. *s.* die Sicht, der Blick, Ausblick, die Aussicht (*of*, auf (*Acc.*)), der Anblick (*of*, von); das Bild, die Ansicht (*also fig.*); die Auffassung, der Gesichtspunkt, Standpunkt; das Ziel, der Plan, Zweck, die Absicht (*often pl.*); die Meinung, das Urteil; *aerial –*, die Luftaufnahme; *at first –*, auf den ersten Blick; *back –*, die Rückansicht; *dissolving –s*, Nebelbilder, Wandelbilder; *disappear from –*, verschwinden; *front –*, die Vorderansicht; *in –*, sichtbar, in Sicht; *the end in –*, beabsichtigter Zweck; *be in –*, in Sicht sein, vor Augen liegen; *have in –*, im Auge haben, beabsichtigen, bezwecken; *keep in –*, im Auge behalten, berücksichtigen; *in my –*, nach meiner Ansicht; *in* (*full*) *– of all the people*, (direkt) vor den Augen aller Menschen; *in – of*, angesichts, in Anbetracht (*Gen.*), im Hinblick auf, mit Rücksicht auf (*Acc.*); *come into –*, sichtbar werden; *– of life*, die Lebensanschauung; *point of –*, der Standpunkt, Gesichtspunkt; *form a – of*, sich eine Ansicht *or* Auffassung bilden über; *take a – of*, einen Standpunkt einnehmen, eine Auffassung haben von; *hold* or *take the –*, die Ansicht *or* den Standpunkt vertreten; *take a bright* or *rosy – of*, etwas in rosigem Licht betrachten; *take a grave – of*, etwas ernst beurteilen *or* auffassen; *take the long –*, auf weite Sicht denken; *on –*, ausgestellt, zu besichtigen, zur Besichtigung, zu sehen, zur Ansicht; *–s on a matter*, die Ansicht über eine S.; *on nearer –*, bei näherer Betrachtung; *private –*, private Vorführung (*of films*); *with that –*, in dieser Absicht; *lost to –*, aus dem Auge verloren; *to outward –*, dem äußeren Ansehen nach; *with a – to*, zum Zwecke (*Gen.*), in der Absicht (*doing*, zu tun). **–able,** *adj.* zu besichtigen(d). **–er,** *s.* der Beschauer. **––finder,** *s.* der Sucher (*Phot.*). **––hallo,** das Hallo, der Halloruf (*Hunt.*). **–point,** *s.* der Standpunkt, Gesichtspunkt.
vigil [ˈvɪdʒɪl], *s.* das Wachen, die Nachtwache; der Vorabend (*of a festival*); *pl.* Vigilien (*pl.*) (*R.C.*). **–ance** [–əns], *s.* die Wachsamkeit, Sorgfalt, Umsicht; Schlaflosigkeit (*Path.*); *–ance committee*, der Überwachungsausschuß, Sicherheitsausschuß. **–ant** [–ənt], *adj.* wachsam, aufmerksam, umsichtig. **–ante** [–ˈlæntɪ], *s.* (*Amer.*) das Mitglied eines Selbstschutzverbandes.
vignette [vɪːˈnjɛt], *s.* die Vignette; das Zierbild, Titelbildchen.
vigo–rous [ˈvɪgərəs], *adj.* stark, kräftig, energisch, lebhaft, tätig, tatkräftig (*of a p.*); nachdrücklich, eindringlich, kernig (*of a th.*). **–ur** [ˈvɪgə], *s.* die Kraft, Stärke, Energie, Lebhaftigkeit, Lebenskraft, Tatkraft (*of a p.*); der Nachdruck, die Wirksamkeit (*of a th.*).
viking [ˈvaɪkɪŋ], *s.* der Wiking.
vile [vaɪl], *adj.* gemein, niederträchtig, niedrig, schlecht, nichtswürdig; (*coll.*) abscheulich, ekelhaft, widerlich. **–ness,** *s.* die Gemeinheit, Niederträchtigkeit, Schlechtigkeit.
vilif–ication [vɪlɪfɪˈkeɪʃn], *s.* die Verleumdung, Schmähung, Herabsetzung. **–ier** [ˈvɪlɪfaɪə], *s.* der Verleumder, Schmäher. **–y** [ˈvɪlɪfaɪ], *v.a.* verleumden, schmähen, herabsetzen.
villa [ˈvɪlə], *s.* das Landhaus, die Villa.
village [ˈvɪlɪdʒ], 1. *s.* das Dorf, die Ortschaft, der Ort. 2. *attrib.* dörflich, Dorf–. **–r** [–ə], *s.* der Dorfbewohner.
villain [ˈvɪlən], *s.* der Schuft, Schurke (*also Theat.*), Bösewicht (*also coll.*), (*coll.*) Schelm. **–ous** [–əs], *adj.* schändlich, schurkisch, (*coll.*) scheußlich, abscheulich. **–y** [–ənɪ], *s.* die Schurkerei, Gemeinheit, Schändlichkeit; der Schurkenstreich.
villein [ˈvɪlən], *s.* Leibeigene(r), *m.*, der Hintersaß, Hintersasse (*Hist.*). **–age** [–ɪdʒ], *s.* die Leibeigenschaft, der Frondienst; das Hintersassengut.

vill–iform ['vɪlɪfɔ:m], *adj.* faserig (*Zool.*). **–ous** ['vɪləs], *adj.* rauh, haarig, behaart, zottig. **–us** ['vɪləs], *s.* (*pl.* –i ['vɪlɑɪ]) die Darmzotte (*Anat.*), das Härchen (*Bot.*).
vim [vɪm], *s.* (*coll.*) die Kraft, der Schwung.
vinaceous [vɪ'neɪʃəs], *adj.* Wein–, Trauben–, weinfarbig.
vinaigrette [vɪnɪ'grɛt], *s.* das Riechfläschen.
vincible ['vɪnsɪbl], *adj.* besiegbar, überwindlich.
vinculum ['vɪŋkjələm], *s.* der Verbindungsstrich (*Math.*), (*fig.*) das Band.
vindic–able ['vɪndɪkəbl], *adj.* zu verteidigen(d) *or* rechtfertigen(d). **–ate** [-keɪt], *v.a.* rechtfertigen, in Schutz nehmen, verteidigen (*from*, gegen); schützen, sichern, behaupten, aufrechterhalten, in Anspruch nehmen, beanspruchen. **–ation** [–'keɪʃn], *s.* die Rechtfertigung, Verteidigung, Behauptung. **–atory** [-kətrɪ], *adj.* verteidigend, rechtfertigend; rächend, ahndend.
vindictive [vɪn'dɪktɪv], *adj.* rachsüchtig, nachtragend. **–ness**, *s.* die Rachsucht.
vine [vɑɪn], *s.* der Weinstock, Rebstock, die Rebe. **--clad,** *adj.* rebenbekränzt. **--disease,** *s.* die Reblauskrankheit. **--dresser, --grower,** *s.* der Weinbauer, Winzer. **--growing,** *s.* der Weinbau. **--leaf,** *s.* das Weinblatt. **--louse, --pest,** *s.* die Reblaus. **–yard** ['vɪnjɑ:d], *s.* der Weinberg, Weingarten.
vinegar ['vɪnɪgə], 1. *s.* der (Wein)Essig; *mother of –*, die Essigmutter. 2. *v.a.* Essig tun an (*Acc.*), säuern, marinieren.
vin–ery ['vɑɪnərɪ], *s.* das Treibhaus für Weinstöcke. **–iculture** ['vɪnɪkʌltʃə], *s.* der Weinbau. **–ification** [–fɪ'keɪʃn], *s.* die Weinkelterung. **–osity** [–'nɔsɪtɪ], *s.* der Weingeistgehalt, die Weinartigkeit. **–ous** ['vɑɪnəs], *adj.* weinig, Wein–. **–tage** ['vɪntɪdʒ], *s.* die Weinlese, Traubenernte, Weinernte; der Weinertrag; (Wein)Jahrgang; (*fig.*) die Ernte, der Jahrgang; *–tage wine*, der Qualitätswein. **–tager,** *s.* der Winzer, Weinleser. **–tner** ['vɪntnə], *s.* der Weinhändler.
viol ['vɑɪəl], *s.* (*Hist.*), **–a** [vɪ'oulə], *s.* die Viola, Bratsche.
viola ['vɑɪələ], *s.* die Viole, das Veilchen (*Bot.*).
viol–able ['vɑɪələbl], *adj.* verletzbar. **–ate** [–leɪt], *v.a.* verletzen (*as oath*), entweihen (*a sacred place, etc.*), übertreten, brechen (*a law*), schänden, notzüchtigen (*a woman*). **–ation** [–'leɪʃn], *s.* die Verletzung, Übertretung, Zuwiderhandlung, der Bruch (*of an oath, etc.*), die Entweihung; Entehrung, Schändung; *in –ation of*, bei *or* unter Verletzung von. **–ator** ['vɑɪəleɪtə], *s.* der Verletzer, Übertreter; Schänder. **–ence** ['vɑɪələns], *s.* die Gewalt, Gewalttätigkeit, Gewaltsamkeit, Heftigkeit, das Ungestüm; *by –ence*, gewaltsam; *do –ence to*, Gewalt antun (*Dat.*); *offer –ence to*, gewalttätig behandeln; schänden, notzüchtigen (*a woman*); *with –ence*, mit Gewalt. **–ent** [–ənt], *adj.* gewaltig, heftig, stark, kräftig (*as a blow*); gewaltsam, gewalttätig (*as an action*); unnatürlich (*death*); ungestüm, hitzig, leidenschaftlich (*as a p.*); grell (*as colour*); *lay –ent hands on*, Gewalt antun (*Dat.*).
violet ['vɑɪələt], 1. *s.* das Veilchen (*Bot.*); Violett (*colour*). 2. *adj.* violett, veilchenblau.
viol–in [vɑɪə'lɪn], *s.* die Geige, Violine; *play the –in*, Geige spielen; *play first –in*, die erste Geige spielen. **–inist** [–'lɪnɪst], *s.* der Geiger. **–ist** ['vɑɪəlɪst], *s.* der Bratschenspieler. **–oncellist** [vɪələn'tʃɛlɪst], *s.* der Cellist. **–oncello** [–'tʃɛlou], *s.* das (Violon)-Cello.
viper ['vɑɪpə], *s.* die Viper, Natter, (Kreuz)Otter, (*fig.*) Schlange. **–ine** [–rɑɪn], *adj.*, **–ish** [–rɪʃ], *adj.* (*only fig.*) viperartig, Viper–. **–ous** [–rəs], *adj.* (*fig.*) schlangenähnlich, giftig.
virago [vɪ'reɪgou], *s.* das Mannweib; (*fig.*) der Zankteufel.
virgin ['və:dʒɪn], 1. *s.* die Jungfrau (*also Astr.*); *blessed – Mary*, die heilige Jungfrau. 2. *adj.* jungfräulich (*also fig.*), Jungfern–, unberührt; (*fig.*) rein, keusch, ungebraucht, unbebaut (*soil*), gediegen (*metal*); *– forest*, der Urwald; *– honey*, der Jungfernscheibenhonig; *– soil*, unbebauter Boden, (*fig.*) unerforschtes *or* noch nicht bearbeitetes Gebiet. **–al** [–əl], 1. *adj.* jungfräulich, Jungfrauen–, (*fig.*) keusch, rein, mädchenhaft; *–al membrane*, die Jungfernhaut. **–hood**, *s.* die Jungfräulichkeit. **–ity** [–'dʒɪnɪtɪ], *s.* die Jungfräulichkeit, Unberührtheit, (*fig.*) Reinheit, Unbeflecktheit.
virginal ['və:dʒɪnl], *s.* (*also pl.*) das Cembalo, Spinett (*Mus.*).
Virginia [və:'dʒɪnɪə], *s.* (also *– tobacco*) der Virginiatabak; *– creeper*, wilder Wein (*Bot.*).
virgo ['və:gou], *s.* die Jungfrau (*Astr.*).
virid–escence [vɪrɪ'dɛsəns], *s.* (frisches) Grün. **–escent** [–'dɛsənt], *adj.* grün(lich). **–ity** [vɪ'rɪdɪtɪ], *s.* (frisches) Grün, (*fig.*) die Frische.
viril–e ['vɪrɑɪl], *adj.* männlich, mannhaft, stark, kräftig, Mannes– (*courage*), Männer– (*voice*). **–ity** [vɪ'rɪlɪtɪ], *s.* die Männlichkeit; Manneskraft, (*fig.*) Stärke, Kraft.
virtu [və:'tu:], *s.* die Kunstliebhaberei, der Kunstgeschmack; der Kunstwert; (*coll.*) Kunstgegenstände (*pl.*); *article of –*, der Kunstgegenstand.
virtual ['və:tjuəl], *adj.* eigentlich, tatsächlich, dem Wesen *or* Inhalt nach. **–ly,** *adv.* im Grunde genommen, im wesentlichen.
virtue ['və:tju:], *s.* die Tugend, Unbescholtenheit (*of a p.*), Sittsamkeit, Keuschheit (*of women*); Wirksamkeit, wirksame Kraft; die Vorzüglichkeit, der Vorzug, Wert (*of a th.*); *make a – of necessity*, aus der Not eine Tugend machen; *by – of*, kraft, vermöge (*Gen.*); *in – of*, infolge, auf Grund von.
virtuos–ity [və:tju'ɔsɪtɪ], *s.* die Virtuosität, Kunstfertigkeit; (*rare*) der Kunstsinn. **–o** [–'ouzou], *s.* der Virtuose; (*rare*) der Kunstkenner.
virtuous ['və:tjuəs], *adj.* tugendhaft, tugendsam (*of a p.*), züchtig, sittsam, keusch (*of women*), (*rare*) vorzüglich, wirksam (*of a th.*).
virulen–ce ['vɪrjuləns, 'vɪruləns], *s.*, **–cy** [–ɪ], *s.* die Virulenz, Giftkraft, (*fig.*) Giftigkeit, Schärfe, Bosheit. **–t** [–ənt], *adj.* virulent, giftig (*also fig.*), (*fig.*) bösartig, boshaft.
virus ['vɑɪərəs], *s.* das Virus, Gift (*also fig.*), der Giftstoff.
vis [vɪs], *s.* die Kraft; *– inertiae*, das Beharrungsvermögen (*Phys.*), (*fig.*) die Trägheit. *– major*, höhere Gewalt.
visa ['vɪ:zə], *s.* das Visum; der Sichtvermerk.
visage ['vɪzɪdʒ], *s.* das Gesicht, Antlitz, Angesicht.
vis-a-vis ['vɪ:zə'vɪ:], 1. *adv.* gegenüber (*to* or *with*, von). 2. *s.* das Gegenüber.
viscera ['vɪsərə], *pl.* Eingeweide (*pl.*). **–l** [–l], *adj.* Eingeweide–.
visc–id ['vɪskɪd], *adj.* klebrig, viskos, Fäden ziehend, seimig, dickflüssig, zähflüssig. **–idity** [–'kɪdɪtɪ], *s.* die Klebrigkeit, Viskosität, Dickflüssigkeit, Zähflüssigkeit. **–ose** [–kous], *s.* die Zellwolle, Viskose, Zellulose. **–osity** [–'kɔsɪtɪ], *s.* *see* **–idity.** **–ous** [–kəs], *see* **–id.**
viscount ['vɑɪkaunt], *s.* der Vicomte. **–ess,** *s.* die Vicomtesse.
vise [vɑɪs], *s. see* [2]**vice.**
visé ['vɪ:ze], *s. see* **visa.**
visib–ility [vɪzɪ'bɪlɪtɪ], *s.* die Sichtbarkeit; Sicht, Sichtigkeit (*Meteor.*). **–le** [–ɪbl], *adj.* sichtbar, greifbar, offensichtlich, offenbar, augenscheinlich. **–ly,** *adv.* sichtlich, offenbar, merklich.
vision ['vɪʒən], *s.* das Sehen, Sehvermögen; der (An)Blick; die Vision, Erscheinung, das Phantasiebild, Traumbild, Gesicht; die Einbildungskraft, Einsicht; *– frequency*, die Bildfrequenz (*television*). **–ary,** 1. *adj.* eingebildet, unwirklich, geträumt, phantastisch; hellseherisch, verstiegen, überspannt; Geister–, geisterhaft. 2. *s.* der Geisterseher, Hellseher; Phantast, Träumer, Schwärmer, Idealist.
[1]**visit** ['vɪzɪt], 1. *v.a.* besuchen; besichtigen, visitieren, untersuchen, durchsuchen, in Augenschein nehmen; heimsuchen, befallen; *be –ed with*, heimgesucht werden von, bestraft *or* geahndet werden mit; *– one's indignation upon a p.*, seinen Zorn an einem auslassen; *– the sins of the parents on the children*, die Sünden der Eltern an den Kindern heimsuchen. 2. *v.n.* Besuche machen; *go (out) –ing*, Besuche machen; *we don't –*, wir verkehren nicht miteinander. 3. *s.* der Besuch; *pay a –*, einen Besuch abstatten *or* machen (*to*, bei) (*a p.*), besuchen (*a place*); *flying –*, kurzer Besuch; *– to the doctor*, die Konsultation bei einem Arzt; *on a –*, auf *or* zu Besuch

(*to*, bei). **-ant**, 1. *s.* (*Poet.*) der Besucher; der Strichvogel (*Orn.*). 2. *adj.* (*Poet.*) besuchend. **-ation** [-ˈteɪʃn], *s.* die Visitation, Besichtigung, Untersuchung, Durchsuchung (*of an official*), Heimsuchung (*Eccl.*), (*coll.*) langer Besuch. **-atorial** [-əˈtɔːrɪəl], *adj.* Visitations-, Untersuchungs-, Aufsichts-, Überwachungs-. **-ing**, *adj.* Besuchs-; *-ing card*, die Visitenkarte; *-ing officer*, visitierender Offizier; *be on -ing terms with*, auf Besuchsfuß stehen mit, verkehren mit. **-or** [-ə], *s.* der Besucher, Gast (*to*, bei); Kurgast; Inspektor, Visitator; *pl.* der Besuch; *I am a -or here*, ich bin hier zu Besuch; *-or's book*, das Fremdenbuch. **-orial**, *adj.*, *see* **-tatorial.**

visor [ˈvaɪzə], *s.* das (Helm)Visier; der (Mützen)-Schirm.

vista [ˈvɪstə], *s.* weite Aussicht, die Fernsicht, der Ausblick (*also fig.*); die (Baum)Allee; der Gang, Korridor (*Arch.*); (*fig.*) lange Reihe, weite Strecke, die Perspektive.

visual [ˈvɪʒuəl], *adj.* visuell, Seh-, Gesichts-, sichtbar, wahrnehmbar; – *acuity*, die Sehschärfe; – *angle*, der Gesichtswinkel; – *arts*, bildende Künste; – *field*, das Gesichtsfeld; – *memory*, visuelles Gedächtnis; – *nerve*, der Sehnerv; – *reconnaissance*, die Augenerkundung (*Mil.*); – *signal*, das Sichtzeichen. **-ization** [-aɪˈzeɪʃn], *s.* geistige Vergegenwärtigung. **-ize** [-aɪz], *v.a.* sich im Geiste vergegenwärtigen, sich ein Bild machen von.

vital [ˈvaɪtl], 1. *adj.* vital, Lebens-; lebenswichtig, lebensnotwendig; (*fig.*) wesentlich, notwendig, hochwichtig (*to*, für); (*Poet.*) lebenskräftig, lebensprühend, lebenspendend; – *energy*, die Lebenskraft; – *functions*, Lebensfunktionen (*pl.*); *of – importance*, lebenswichtig, höchst wichtig; – *interests*, Lebensinteressen (*pl.*); – *part*, edler Teil (*of the body*), (*fig.*) notwendiger Bestandteil; – *power*, die Lebenskraft; – *question*, die Lebensfrage; – *spark*, der Lebensfunken. 2. **-s** [-z], *pl.* lebensnotwendige Organe, edle Körperteile (*pl.*); (*fig.*) das Wesentliche, Wichtigste. **-ism** [-ɪzm], *s.* der Vitalismus. **-ity** [-ˈtælɪtɪ], *s.* die Lebenskraft, Lebensfähigkeit, Vitalität; Lebensdauer. **-ization** [-aɪˈzeɪʃn], *s.* die Belebung, Kräftigung, (*fig.*) Verlebendigung, lebendige Gestaltung. **-ize** [-aɪz], *v.a.* beleben, kräftigen, (*usually fig.*) verlebendigen, lebendig gestalten.

vitamin(e) [ˈvɪtəmɪn], *s.* das Vitamin, der Ergänzungsstoff; – *deficiency*, die Mangelkrankheit.

vitiat-e [ˈvɪʃɪeɪt], *v.a.* verderben, beeinträchtigen, ungültig *or* untauglich machen, umstoßen, aufheben, entkräften (*Law*), verunreinigen (*air, etc.*). **-ion**, *s.* die Verderbnis, Beeinträchtigung; das Ungültigmachen, die Umstoßung, Aufhebung.

viticulture [ˈvɪtɪkʌltʃə], *s.* der Weinbau.

vitr-eous [ˈvɪtrɪəs], *adj.* gläsern; glasartig; Glas-; glasig (*lustre*), vitrophyrisch (*Geol.*); *-eous electricity*, die Glaselektrizität, positive Elektrizität; *-eous body* or *humour*, der Glaskörper (*of the eye*). **-escence** [-ˈtrɛsəns], *s.* die Verglasung. **-escent** [-ˈtrɛsənt], *adj.* verglasend. **-escible** [-ˈtrɛsɪbl], *adj.* verglasbar. **-ifaction** [-ɪˈfækʃn], *s. see* **-escence.** **-ifiable** [-faɪəbl], *adj. see* **-escible.** **-ify** [-ɪfaɪ], *v.a.* (& *n.* sich) verglasen.

vitriol [ˈvɪtrɪəl], *s.* das *or* der Vitriol; – *of lead*, schwefelsaures Bleivitriol; *oil of –*, rauchende Schwefelsäure, das Vitriolöl. **-ic** [-ˈɔlɪk], *adj.* vitriolisch, Vitriol-, (*fig.*) bissig, sarkastisch.

vituperat-e [vɪˈtjuːpəreɪt], *v.a.* schmähen, tadeln, schelten. **-ion** [-ˈreɪʃn], *s.* die Schmähung, Beschimpfung, der Tadel. **-ive** [-prətɪv], *adj.* tadelnd, scheltend, schmähend, Schmäh-.

[1]**viva** [ˈviːvɑ], 1. *s.* der Hochruf, das Hoch. 2. *interj.* hoch!

[2]**viva** [ˈvaɪvə], *s.* (*coll.*) *see* **viva-voce** 2.

vivac-e [vɪˈvɑːtʃe], *adj.* lebhaft (*Mus.*). **-ious** [vaɪˈveɪʃəs], *adj.* lebhaft, munter. **-ity** [-ˈvæsɪtɪ], *s.* die Lebhaftigkeit, Munterkeit.

viva-voce [ˈvaɪvəˈvousɪ], 1. *adj.* & *adv.* mündlich. 2. *s.* mündliche Prüfung.

vivi-d [ˈvɪvɪd], *adj.* lebhaft; lebendig, anschaulich; hell, glänzend. **-dness**, *s.* die Lebhaftigkeit, Lebendigkeit, Anschaulichkeit, Helligkeit. **-fy** [-faɪ], *v.a.* beleben, Leben geben (*Dat.*), lebendig *or* lebensvoll machen, verlebendigen. **-parous** [vaɪˈvɪpərəs], *adj.* lebendgebärend, vivipar. **-sect** [ˈvɪvɪsɛkt], *v.a.* & *n.* vivisezieren. **-section** [-ˈsɛkʃn], *s.* die Vivisektion.

vixen [ˈvɪksn], *s.* die Füchsin (*Zool.*), (*fig.*) Zänkerin, Keiferin, böse Sieben. **-ish** [-sənɪʃ], *adj.* zänkisch, keifend.

vizier [vɪˈzɪːe], *s.* der Wesir.

vocab-le [ˈvoukəbl], *s.* das Wort, die Vokabel. **-ulary** [vəˈkæbjulərɪ], *s.* das Wortverzeichnis, Wörterbuch; der Wortschatz (*of a p.*).

vocal [ˈvoukl], 1. *adj.* Stimm- (*Anat.*); Vokal-, Gesang-, gesanglich, stimmlich (*Mus.*); tönend (*also fig.*), stimmhaft (*Phonet.*); vokalisch (*Gram.*); gesprochen; mündlich, Sprech-, (*fig.*) widerhallend, klingend (*with*, von), laut, vernehmbar; *become –*, sich hören lassen, sich äußern; – *c(h)ords*, Stimmbänder (*pl.*); – *music*, die Vokalmusik, der Gesang; – *part*, die Singstimme; – *power*, der Stimmaufwand; – *recital*, der Liederabend; – *sound*, der Vokal. **-ic** [voˈkælɪk], *adj.* vokalisch. **-ism** [ˈvoukəlɪzm], *s.* die Stimmgebung. **-ist** [-kəlɪst], *s.* der Sänger. **-ization** [-aɪˈzeɪʃn], *s.* Vokalaussprache, Vokalisation (*Phonet.*), Stimmgebung (*Mus.*). **-ize** [-aɪz], 1. *v.a.* (stimmhaft) aussprechen, vokalisieren (*Phonet.*), singen (*Mus.*). 2. *v.n.* sprechen, singen. **-ly**, *adv.* mit der Stimme; in gesanglicher Hinsicht.

vocation [voˈkeɪʃn], *s.* die Berufung (*Theol.*), die Anlage, Eignung (*for*, für), Neigung (*for*, zu), der Beruf. **-al** [-ʃənl], *adj.* beruflich, berufsmäßig, Berufs-; *-al guidance*, die Berufsberatung; *-al testing*, die Eignungsprüfung; *-al training*, die Berufsausbildung.

vocative [ˈvɔkətɪv], 1. *adj.* Anrede-; – *case*, der Vokativ, Anredefall. 2. *s.* der Vokativ.

vocifer-ate [voˈsɪfəreɪt], 1. *v.n.* schreien, laut rufen, brüllen. 2. *v.a.* schreien, laut (aus)rufen. **-ation** [-ˈreɪʃn], *s.* das Schreien, Geschrei. **-ous** [-ˈsɪfərəs], *adj.* schreiend, lärmend, laut.

vodka [ˈvɔdkə], *s.* der Wodka.

vogue [voug], *s.* die Beliebtheit, hohes Ansehen, guter Ruf; die Mode; *be in –*, im Schwange *or* sehr beliebt sein; sich großer Beliebtheit erfreuen, großen Zulauf haben (*as a play*); *be the –*, (die herrschende) Mode sein; *all the –*, die neueste Mode; *come into –*, in Aufnahme kommen, modern werden. **--word**, *s.* das Modewort.

voice [vɔɪs], 1. *s.* die Stimme (*also fig.*); Sprache, Meinung; Stimmhaftigkeit, der Stimmton (*Phonet.*); *active –*, die Tätigkeitsform, das Aktiv(um); *passive –*, die Leideform, das Passiv(um); *give – to*, Ausdruck verleihen *or* geben (*Dat.*); *have a – in*, mitzusprechen *or* ein Wort mitzureden haben, eine Stimme *or* einen Einfluß haben in *or* bei; *in –*, bei Stimme; *at the top of one's –*, aus vollem Halse; *with one –*, einstimmig. 2. *v.a.* äußern, aussprechen, ausdrücken, Ausdruck verleihen *or* geben (*Dat.*), zum Ausdruck bringen, in Worte fassen; regulieren (*organ pipes*); stimmhaft aussprechen. **-d** [-t], *adj.* (*in comps.*) mit . . . Stimme; stimmhaft (*Phonet.*); *loud--d*, mit lauter Stimme. **-less**, *adj.* ohne Stimme; sprachlos, stumm; nicht stimmberechtigt (*Parl.*); stimmlos (*Phonet.*). **--production**, *s.* die Stimmausbildung.

void [vɔɪd], 1. *adj.* leer, unbesetzt; zwecklos, unwirksam, nichtig, ungültig; – *of*, arm *or* leer an (*Dat.*), ohne, frei von, ermangelnd (*Gen.*); *be – of*, ermangeln (*Gen.*); *null and –*, null und nichtig. 2. *s.* leerer Raum, die Leere, Lücke (*also fig.*); *fill the –*, die Lücke ausfüllen. 3. *v.a.* aufheben, ungültig machen (*Law*); ausleeren (*bowels*); (*archaic*) räumen, verlassen. **-able** [-əbl], *adj.* anfechtbar, aufhebbar (*Law*). **-ance** [-əns], *s.* die Ausleerung (*of the bowels*); Aufhebung, das Freiwerden (*Eccl.*). **-ness**, *s.* die Leere; Ungültigkeit.

voile [vɔɪl], *s.* der Schleierstoff.

volant [ˈvoulənt], *adj.* fliegend, flüchtig.

volatil-e [ˈvɔlətaɪl], *adj.* flüchtig (*also fig.*), sich verflüchtigend, verfliegend, verdunstend, ätherisch (*Chem.*); (*fig.*) flatterhaft, leichtfertig, unbeständig, sprunghaft; *-e salt*, das Riechsalz. **-eness**, *s.*, **-ity** [-ˈtɪlɪtɪ], *s.* die Flüchtigkeit, Verdampfungsfähigkeit; Flatterhaftigkeit, Unbeständigkeit. **-iza-**

tion [–lætılɑı'zeıʃn], *s.* die Verflüchtigung, Verdunstung. **–ize** [–'lætılɑız], 1. *v.a.* abdampfen, verflüchtigen. 2. *v.n.* sich verflüchtigen, verfliegen, verdunsten, sich auflösen.

vol-au-vent ['vɔlovɑ̃], *s.* eine Fleischpastete aus Blätterteig.

volcan–ic [vɔl'kænık], *adj.* vulkanisch (*also fig.*), Vulkan–, (*fig.*) feurig, ungestüm; *–ic glass*, das Obsidian. **–o** [–'keınoʊ] (*pl.* –oes) der Vulkan; *sit on the top of a –o*, auf einem Pulverfaß sitzen.

[1]**vole** [voʊl], *s.* die Vola, der Gewinn aller Stiche (*Cards*).

[2]**vole,** *s.* die Wühlmaus.

volition [vɔ'lıʃn], *s.* der Wille, das Wollen, die Willensäußerung, der Willensentschluß; die Willenskraft. **–al,** *adj.* willensmäßig, Willens–.

volley ['vɔlı], *s.* die Salve; (*fig.*) der Hagel; Schwall, Strom, die Flut (*of words, etc.*); der Flugball, Flugschlag (*Tenn.*). 2. *v.a.* in einer Salve abschießen; als Flugball nehmen *or* spielen (*Tenn.*). (*fig.*) (usually – *out* or *off* or *forth*) ausstoßen. 3. *v.n.* eine Salve abschießen, abfeuern *or* abgeben; einen Flugball spielen *or* nehmen (*Tenn.*), (*fig.*) strömen, sich ergießen; toben, brüllen.

volplane ['vɔlpleın], 1. *v.n.* im Gleitflug niedergehen (*Av.*). 2. *s.* der Gleitflug.

[1]**volt** [vɔlt], 1. *s.* die Volte (*Fenc. & Horsemanship*), Wendung (*Fenc.*). 2. *v.n.* eine Volte machen. **–-face,** *s.* die Kehre, Umdrehung (*Fenc.*), (*fig.*) Wendung, der Frontwechsel.

[2]**volt** [voʊlt], *s.* das Volt (*Elec.*). **–age** [–ıdʒ], *s.* die (Strom)Spannung. **–aic** [–'teıık], *adj.* voltaisch, galvanisch, Volta–. **–meter,** *s.* der Spannungsmesser, Voltmesser.

volub–ility [vɔlju'bılıtı], *s.* der Redefluß, die Zungenfertigkeit; Beweglichkeit, Drehbarkeit. **–le** ['vɔljəbl], *adj.* zungenfertig, redegewandt, redselig (*of a p.*), fließend, geläufig (*of language*), sich windend *or* rankend (*Bot.*).

volum–e ['vɔljuːm], *s.* der Band (*of a book*); das Volumen, der Rauminhalt (*Phys., etc.*); große Menge, die Masse; (*fig.*) der Gehalt; Umfang, (Stimm)Umfang (*of the voice*), die Klangfülle (*Mus.*), Lautstärke (*Rad.*); *that speaks –es*, das ist höchst bezeichnend für, das spricht Bände für; *–e-control*, der Lautstärkenregler (*Rad.*). **–etric** [–'mɛtrık], *adj.* Raum–, Volumenmaß–; *–etric analysis*, die Maßanalyse; *–etric content*, der Raumgehalt. **–inous** [və'ljuːmınəs], *adj.* umfangreich, ausgedehnt; groß, dick, massig, gewaltig, massenhaft; bändereich (*works*), vielschreibend (*writer*).

voluntar–iness ['vɔləntrınıs], *s.* die Freiwilligkeit; Selbstbestimmung, Willensfreiheit. **–y** [–tərı], 1. *adj.* freiwillig, spontan, willentlich, vorsätzlich, absichtlich; voluntaristisch, willensmäßig (*Psych.*); willkürlich (*Anat.*); *–y hospital*, durch freiwillige Spenden unterhaltenes Krankenhaus; *do –y work*, unbezahlte Arbeit tun; als Volontär arbeiten. 2. *s.* das Orgelsolo.

volunteer [vɔlən'tıə], 1. *s.* Freiwillige(r), *m.*, der Volontär (*C.L.*); *pl.* das Freiwilligenkorps (*Mil.*). 2. *adj.* Freiwilligen–. 3. *v.n.* als Freiwilliger dienen, sich freiwillig melden (*for*, zu) (*Mil.*); freiwillig tätig sein. 4. *v.a.* freiwillig übernehmen *or* anbieten (*services*), unaufgefordert geben (*information*), aus freien Stücken tun.

voluptu–ary [və'lʌptjərı], *s.* der Wollüstling. **–ous** [–tjuəs], *adj.* wollüstig, geil, sinnlich, lüstern, üppig. **–ousness,** *s.* die Wollust, Sinnenlust, Sinnlichkeit, Geilheit, Lüsternheit, Üppigkeit.

volut–e [və'ljuːt], *s.* die Schnecke, Volute, der Schnörkel (*Arch.*); die Rollschnecke (*Mollusc.*). **–ed** [–ıd], *adj.* schneckenförmig, spiralförmig, gewunden. **–ion** [–ljuːʃn], *s.* die Windung (*Anat.*), Drehung (*Tech.*), das Gewinde (*of a shell*).

vomit ['vɔmıt], 1. *v.a.* (also – *up, out* or *forth*) ausbrechen, auswerfen, ausspeien, ausstoßen, speien; ausladen. 2. *v.n.* sich übergeben *or* erbrechen, (*vulg.*) kotzen. 3. *s.* das Gespiene, Ausgebrochene, der Auswurf; das Brechmittel. **–ory** [–ərı], 1. *s.* das Brechmittel; der Hauptausgang (*of Classical theatre*). 2. *adj.* Erbrechen erregend, Brech–.

voodoo ['vuːduː], *s.* (*coll.*) die Hexerei, Zauberei.

voraci–ous [və'reıʃəs], *adj.* gefräßig, gierig, (*fig.*) unersättlich. **–ty** [–'ræsıtı], *s.* die Gefräßigkeit, (*fig.*) Gier, Sucht.

vort–ex ['vɔːtɛks], *s.* (*pl.* –ices [–tısıːz]) der Wirbel, Strudel (*also fig.*). **–ical** [–tıkl], *adj.* wirbelnd, Wirbel–, strudelartig, sich drehend.

votary ['voʊtərı], *s.* Geweihte(r), *m.*, der Verehrer, Anbeter, Jünger, Anhänger, Verfechter.

vot–e [voʊt], 1. *s.* die (Wahl)Stimme; das Stimmrecht, Wahlrecht; die Abstimmung, Stimmabgabe; das Votum, Wahlergebnis, der Beschluß; *by –e*, durch Abstimmung; *cast one's –e*, seine Stimme abgeben; *casting –e*, ausschlaggebende Stimme; *–e of censure*, das Mißtrauensvotum; *–e of confidence*, das Vertrauensvotum; *–e of no confidence*, das Mißtrauensvotum; *give one's –e to*, seine Stimme geben (*Dat.*), stimmen für; *have the –e*, wahlberechtigt *or* stimmberechtigt sein, Stimmrecht haben; *–es polled*, abgegebene Stimmen, die Gesamtstimmenzahl; *put to the –e*, zur Abstimmung bringen; *take a –e*, abstimmen (*on*, über). 2. *v.n.* (ab)stimmen, seine Stimme abgeben. 3. *v.a.* stimmen für, wählen (*a p.*), annehmen, genehmigen, beschließen (*a measure*), bewilligen (*money, etc.*); (*coll.*) vorschlagen, halten für; *–e down*, ablehnen, überstimmen; *–e in*, durch Abstimmung wählen. **–er** [–ə], *s.* Stimmberechtigte(r), *m.*, der Wähler. **–ing,** 1. *adj.* Wahl–, Stimm–, 2. *s.* das (Ab)Stimmen, die Wahl, Abstimmung, Stimmabgabe. **–ing-paper,** *s.* der Stimmzettel.

votive ['voʊtıv], *adj.* geweiht, gelobt, Weih–, Votiv–.

vouch [vɑʊtʃ], 1. *v.n.* sich verbürgen, zeugen, einstehen (*for*, für). 2. *v.a.* beteuern, bezeugen, bestätigen, verbürgen, erklären für. **–er** [–ə], *s.* der Zeuge, Gewährsmann (*for* (*Gen.*)); das Zeugnis, der Beleg, Belegschein, Gutschein, Kassenzettel, die Unterlage, Quittung, das Zahlungsattest; der Bezugsschein, die Eintrittskarte.

vouchsafe [vɑʊtʃ'seıf], 1. *v.a.* gewähren, bewilligen (*a p. a th.* or *a th. to a p.*, einem etwas); *not – a word to a p.*, einen nicht eines Wortes würdigen. 2. *v.n.* geruhen, sich herablassen.

voussoir ['vuːswɑː], *s.* der Wölbstein, Schlußstein.

vow [vɑʊ], 1. *v.a.* geloben, feierlich versprechen (*to* (*Dat.*)), schwören, beteuern, versichern, widmen, weihen (*to* (*Dat.*)). 2. *s.* das Gelübde; Gelöbnis, der Schwur, feierliches Versprechen; *be under a –*, ein Gelübde abgelegt haben; *make* or *take a –*, ein Gelübde tun *or* ablegen; *take the –s*, das Ordensgelübde ablegen, Profeß tun (*of a monk*), den Schleier nehmen, Nonne werden (*of a nun*).

vowel ['vɑʊəl], 1. *s.* der Vokal, Selbstlaut. 2. *attrib.* Vokal–, vokalisch, silbenbildend. **–-gradation,** *s.* der Ablaut. **–-modification,** *s.*, **–-mutation,** *s.* der Umlaut.

voyage ['vɔııdʒ], 1. *s.* die Reise, Seereise; *homeward –* or *– home*, die Heimreise; *– out* or *outward –*, Ausreise, Hinreise; *return –*, die Rückreise; *– of discovery*, die Forschungsreise. 2. *v.n.* eine Seereise machen, zur See reisen. 3. *v.a.* bereisen, befahren. **–r** [–ə], *s.* (See)Reisende(r), *m.*

vulcan–ite ['vʌlkənɑıt], *s.* der Hartgummi, Ebonit, Vulkanit. **–ization** [–ɑı'zeıʃn], *s.* das Vulkanisieren. **–ize** [–ɑız], *v.a.* vulkanisieren, schwefeln, härten (*rubber*).

vulgar ['vʌlgə], 1. *adj.* gemein, niedrig, ungebildet, ungesittet, unfein, vulgär, pöbelhaft, rüpelhaft; allgemein, gewöhnlich, üblich, gebräuchlich, landesüblich, volkstümlich; *– era*, christliche Zeitrechnung; *– fraction*, gemeiner *or* gewöhnlicher Bruch; *– tongue*, die Volkssprache, Landessprache. 2. *s.*; *the –*, das gemeine Volk, der Pöbel. **–ian** [–'gɛərıən], *s.* der Plebejer, Protz, gemeiner Mensch. **–ism** ['vʌlgərızm], *s.* vulgärer *or* gemeiner Ausdruck. **–ity** [–'gærıtı], *s.* die Gewöhnlichkeit, Gemeinheit, Roheit, Pöbelhaftigkeit, Vulgarität. **–ization** [–rɑı'zeıʃn], *s.* die Erniedrigung, Herabwürdigung, Popularisierung, allgemeine Verbreitung. **–ize** [–ɑız], *v.a.* erniedrigen, herabwürdigen, popularisieren, allgemein verbreiten. **–ly,** *adv.* allgemein, gemeinhin; gemein, vulgär.

vulgate ['vʌlgət], *s.* die Vulgata.
vulner-ability [vʌlnərə'bɪlɪtɪ], *s.* die Verwundbarkeit, Anfechtbarkeit. **-able** ['vʌlnərəbl], *adj.* verwundbar, verletzbar; (*fig.*) angreifbar, anfechtbar; ungeschützt (*as places*). **-ableness,** *s. see* **-ability. -ary** [-rərɪ], 1. *adj.* Wunden heilend, Wund-, Heil-. 2. *s.* das Wundmittel.
vulpine ['vʌlpaɪn], *adj.* Fuchs-, fuchsartig, (*fig.*) fuchsig, schlau, listig.
vultur-e ['vʌltʃə], *s.* der Geier, (*fig.*) Blutsauger. **-ine** [-raɪn], **-ous** [-rəs], *adj.* geierartig, (*fig.*) raubgierig.
vulv-a ['vʌlvə], *s.* die Vulva, äußere weibliche Scham. **-al** [-əl], **-ar** [-ɑ], *adj.* Scham-, Schamlippen-. **-itis** [-'vaɪtɪs], *s.* die Entzündung der Schamteile.
vying ['vaɪɪŋ], *adj.* wetteifernd; *see* **vie.**

W

W, w ['dʌbljuː], *s.* das W, w. *See Index of Abbreviations.*
wabble ['wɔbl], *v.n. see* **wobble.**
wad [wɔd], 1. *s.* das Bündel, der Propf(en) (*of cotton wool, etc.*), Ladepropf (*Artil.*); (*coll.*) Stoß, die Rolle, das Päckchen (*of banknotes, etc.*). 2. *v.a.* (aus)stopfen; wattieren (*a coat, etc.*). **-ding,** *s.* die Füllung, Polsterung, Wattierung, Watte.
waddle ['wɔdl], *v.n.* watscheln, wackeln.
wade [weɪd], 1. *v.n.* waten; (*fig.*) sich mühsam durcharbeiten (*through*, durch); (*sl.*) – *in*, sich einmischen, dazwischentreten. 2. *v.a.* durchwaten. **-r** [-ə], *s.* der Stelzvogel (*Orn.*); *pl.* Wasserstiefel (*pl.*).
wafer ['weɪfə], *s.* die Waffel; die Siegelmarke, Oblate (*for letters, also Eccl.*); Hostie (*Eccl.*).
[1]**waffle** ['wɔfl], *s.* die Waffel. **--iron,** *s.* das Waffeleisen.
[2]**waffle,** *v.n.* (*sl.*) schwafeln.
waft [wɑːft, wæft], 1. *v.a.* (fort)wehen, hauchen, (heran)tragen. 2. *v.n.* wehen, schweben. 3. *s.* der Hauch, Luftzug; Duft; (*fig.*) Anflug; das Flaggensignal, Notsignal (*Naut.*).
[1]**wag** [wæg], 1. *v.n.* wedeln (*of the tail*), sich hin und her bewegen; (*coll.*) immer in Bewegung sein (*of the tongue*); *set tongues -ging*, ein Gerede aufbringen. 2. *v.a.* hin und her bewegen, wackeln mit; – *its tail*, mit dem Schwanz wedeln; – *one's head*, mit dem Kopfe wackeln, den Kopf schütteln, nicken; – *one's finger*, mit dem Finger drohen (*at* (*Dat.*)). 3. *s.*; *give a – of one's head*, see – *one's head*; *give a – of the tail*, see – *its tail. See* **wagtail.**
[2]**wag,** *s.* (*coll.*) der Spaßvogel, Possenreißer, Witzbold; *see* **waggery, waggish.**
[1]**wage** [weɪdʒ], *s.* (*also pl.*) der (Arbeits)Lohn; die Vergeltung (*Eccl.*); (*fig.*) Belohnung, der Lohn; *earn good -s*, gut verdienen; *living –*, das Existenzminimum. **--earner,** *s.* der Lohnempfänger. **-s-fund,** *s.* der Lohnfonds. **--sheet,** *s.* die Lohnliste.
[2]**wage,** *v.a.* unternehmen, führen (*war, etc.*) (*on*, gegen).
wager ['weɪdʒə], 1. *s.* die Wette; der Einsatz, Wettpreis; *lay a –*, eine Wette machen, wetten. 2. *v.a.* (als Einsatz) setzen (*on*, auf) (*money*); wetten mit (*a p.*); (*fig.*) aufs Spiel setzen (*one's reputation, etc.*). 3. *v.n.* wetten, eine Wette eingehen.
wagg-ery ['wægərɪ], *s.* der Spaß, die Schelmerei. **-ish,** *adj.* schelmisch, schalkhaft, spaßig. **-ishness,** *s.* die Schalkhaftigkeit.
waggle ['wægl], *v.n.* wackeln.
wag(g)on ['wægn], *s.* der Lastwagen, Gepäckwagen, Frachtwagen, Rollwagen; Güterwagen, Waggon (*Railw.*); *by –*, per Achse (*C.L.*); (*sl.*) *be on the –*, Abstinenzler sein. **-age,** *s.* Frachtgeld, der Fuhrlohn. **--ceiling,** *s.* die Tonnendecke. **-er,** *s.* der Fuhrmann (*also Astr.*). **-ette** [-gə'nɛt], *s.* der Break. **wagon-lit,** *s.* der Schlafwagen (*Railw.*). **--load,** *s.* die Fuhre, Wagenladung; (*coll.*) *by the --load*, waggonweise.
wagtail ['wægteɪl], *s.* die (Bach)Stelze (*Orn.*).
waif [weɪf], *s.* heimatloser Mensch; (*usually*) verwahrlostes Kind; verlaufenes Vieh; herrenloses Gut, das Strandgut (*Law*); *-s and strays*, verwahrloste Kinder.
wail [weɪl], 1. *s.* die Wehklage, das Wehklagen, Wehgeschrei. 2. *v.n.* jammern, wehklagen, sich beklagen. **-ing,** 1. *adj.* wehklagend, Klage-, Jammer-; *-ing wall*, die Klagemauer. 2. *s.* das Wehklagen, Jammern.
wain [weɪn], *s.* (*Poet.*) der (Ernte)Wagen; *Charles's –*, Großer Bär (*Astr.*).
wainscot ['weɪnskət], 1. *s.* die Täfelung, Holzverkleidung, das Getäfel, Tafelwerk. 2. *v.a.* täfeln, verschalen, verkleiden. **-ing,** *s.* Verkleidungsbretter (*pl.*).
waist [weɪst], *s.* die Taille; die Schweifung (*of bells*); die Kuhl (*of a ship*). **-band,** *s.* der Bund (*of skirt or trousers*). **-coat,** *s.* die Weste, das Wams. **--deep,** *adj. & adv.* bis an die Taille (reichend). **-ed** [-ɪd], *adj. suffix* mit ... Taille. **--line,** *s.* die Gürtellinie.
wait [weɪt], 1. *v.n.* warten; *keep s.o. -ing*, *make s.o. –*, einen warten lassen; – *and see*, abwarten; (*a*) (*with prepositions*) – *at table*, bei Tisch bedienen *or* aufwarten; – *for*, warten auf; – *for him to come*, warten bis *or* daß er kommt; – *for it*, wart's ab! – *for dead men's shoes*, auf eine Erbschaft lauern; – (*up*)*on*, bedienen, pflegen, warten; seine Aufwartung machen (*Dat.*); (*rare*) begleiten; (*b*) (*with adverbs*) – *up for him*, aufbleiben bis er kommt. 2. *v.a.* warten auf, erwarten; abwarten; – *his convenience*, warten bis es ihm paßt; – *dinner for s.o.*, mit dem Essen auf einen warten; – *one's opportunity*, die Gelegenheit abwarten. 3. *s.* das Warten, Lauern; die Wartezeit; *pl.* Straßenmusikanten, Weihnachtssänger; *lie in – for*, auflauern (*Dat.*). **-er** [-ə], *s.* der Kellner, (*when addressing him*) Ober; der Präsentierteller; *dumb -er*, stummer Diener, drehbares Präsentierbrett. **-ing,** *s.* das Warten, Aufwarten, die Bedienung, Aufwartung; der Dienst (*at court, etc.*); (*coll.*) *play a -ing game*, das Ergebnis abwarten; *lady-in--ing*, königliche Hofdame; *lord-in--ing*, diensttuender Kammerherr. **-ing-maid,** *s.* das Kammermädchen. **-ing-room,** *s.* der Wartesaal (*Railw.*), das Wartezimmer. **-ress** [-rɪs], *s.* die Kellnerin.
waive [weɪv], *v.a.* verzichten auf (*Acc.*), aufgeben, fahren lassen; – *an advantage*, sich eines Vorteils begeben. **-r** [-ə], *s.* der Verzicht, die Verzichtleistung (*of*, auf) (*Law*).
[1]**wake** [weɪk], *s.* das Kielwasser (*of ship*), der Luftwirbel (*Av.*), (*fig.*) die Spur; – *of a torpedo*, die Blasenbahn, Torpedolaufbahn; *in the – of*, im Kielwasser (*Gen.*), (*fig.*) in den Fußstapfen (*Gen.*), auf der Spur (*Gen.*), unmittelbar hinter (*Dat.*), in Nachahmung (*Gen.*); *bring in its –*, zur Folge haben, nach sich ziehen; *follow in the – of*, unmittelbar folgen hinter (*Dat.*), auf dem Fuße folgen (*Dat.*).
[2]**wak-e,** 1. *ir.v.n.* (*imperf. also* -ed [-t]) wachen, wach sein *or* bleiben; (also *-e up*) aufwachen, erwachen (*from* or *out of*, aus), wach werden; (*fig.*) sich bewußt werden (*to* (*Gen.*)). 2. *ir.v.a.* (also *-e up*) wecken (*also fig.*), aufwecken, erwecken (*also fig.*), auferwecken (*from the dead*); (*fig.*) wachrufen; *-e a corpse*, bei einer Leiche wachen, einen Leichenschmaus halten (*Irish*). 3. *s.* die Leichenfeier, Totenwache; das Kirchweihfest, Dorffest, die Kirmeß. **-eful,** *adj.* wachend; schlaflos, ruhelos, (*fig.*) wachsam. **-efulness,** *s.* die Schlaflosigkeit; (*fig.*) Wachsamkeit. **-en** ['weɪkn], 1. *v.n.* erwachen, aufwachen, wach werden (*also fig.*); (*fig.*) (usually *-en up*) sich bewußt werden (*to* (*Gen.*)). 2. *v.a.* (auf)wecken (*from* or *out of*, aus); (*fig.*) erwecken, erregen, wachrufen. **-ing,** 1. *adj.*; *-ing hours*, wache Stunden. 2. *s.* das Wachen, Erwachen.
wale [weɪl], *s.* die Strieme, Schwiele; Salleiste,

das Salband (*of cloth*); das Bergholz, Krummholz, Gurtholz, Dollbord (*Naut.*).

walk [wɔ:k], **1.** *v.n.* gehen; spazierengehen, zu Fuß gehen; umgehen, spuken (*as ghosts*); im Schritt gehen (*as a horse*); – *in one's sleep*, nachtwandeln, im Schlaf wandeln; – *on air*, im siebenten Himmel sein; – *about*, umhergehen; – *along*, weitergehen; – *away*, fortgehen; – *back*, (zu Fuß) zurückgehen; – *backwards*, rückwärtsgehen; – *by*, vorübergehen; – *down*, hinuntergehen; – *in*, hineingehen, hereinkommen; näher treten; – *off*, davongehen; (*coll.*) – *off with*, ausreißen *or* durchgehen mit; – *on*, als Statist auftreten (*Theat.*); – *out*, hinausgehen; (*coll.*) verkehren, ausgehen (*with one's sweetheart*); (*coll.*) – *out on*, sitzen *or* im Stich lassen; (*coll.*) – *over*, leicht gewinnen; – *up*, hinaufgehen, heraufkommen; – *up to*, zugehen auf (*Acc.*). **2.** *v.a.* im Schritt gehen lassen (*a horse*); spazierenführen (*a person*); zu Fuß gehen, zurücklegen (*distance or time*); durchschreiten, auf und ab gehen in (*a room*); – *the boards*, Schauspieler sein; – *the hospitals*, die klinischen Semester durchmachen; – *the rounds*, die Runde machen; – *the streets*, auf der Straße auf und ab gehen; auf den Strich gehen (*as prostitutes*); – *off*, durch Gehen vertreiben (*a headache*), abführen, fortführen (*a p.*); – *out*, ausführen (*a p.*). **3.** *s.* das Gehen; Schrittgehen (*of horse*); der Schritt, Gang, die Gangart; der Spaziergang; Spazierweg, die Promenade, Allee; (*fig.*) Laufbahn, Lebensstellung, der Lebensgang; die Weide (*for sheep, etc.*); – *of life*, der Beruf, das Lebensgebiet, die Lebensstellung; *higher –s of society*, höhere Kreise der Gesellschaft; *a good* or *quite a* –, ein gutes Stück zu gehen; *two-hours'* –, zweistündiger Spaziergang, der Weg von zwei Stunden; *go for* or *take a* –, einen Spaziergang machen, spazierengehen; *take s.o. for a* –, einen zu einem Spaziergang ausführen. **--away,** *s.* leichter Sieg. **--bill,** *s.* der Platzwechsel (*C.L.*). **-er** [-ə], *s.* der Fußgänger, Spaziergänger; Geher (*Sport*); *be a good -er*, gut zu Fuß sein. **-er-on,** *s.* der Statist (*Theat.*). **-ie-talkie,** *s.* (*sl.*) tragbares Sprechfunkgerät. **-ing,** 1. *adj.* gehend; *-ing corpse*, wandelnde Leiche; *-ing encyclopedia*, wandelndes Lexikon; *within -ing distance*, zu Fuß zu erreichen; *-ing gentleman*, der Statist (*Theat.*); *-ing lady*, die Statistin (*Theat.*); *-ing part*, die Statistenrolle. 2. *s.* das Gehen. **-ing-boots,** *pl.* Marschstiefel. **-ing-dress,** *s.* das Straßenkleid. **-ing-on part,** *s.* see *-ing part*. **-ing-stick,** *s.* der Spazierstock. **-ing-tour,** *s.* die Fußwanderung, Fußreise. **-over,** *s.* leichter Sieg.

wall [wɔ:l], 1. *s.* die Wand (*inside*); die Mauer (*outside*); der Wall (*Fort.*); *come up against a blank* or *dead* –, kein Verständnis *or* taube Ohren finden; *be up against a brick* –, nicht weiter können; *run one's head against a* –, mit dem Kopf gegen die Wand rennen; *partition* or *party* –, die Trennungswand; *retaining* –, die Stützmauer; *with one's back to the* –, in die Enge getrieben; *have one's back to the* –, verzweifelt Widerstand leisten, sich verzweifelt zur Wehr setzen; *go to the* –, unterliegen, untergehen, zugrundegehen, an die Wand *or* beiseite gedrückt werden, hintenan gesetzt werden, Konkurs machen; *within the -s*, innerhalb der Stadt *or* Festung. 2. *v.a.* (also – *in*) mit einer Mauer umgeben; umwallen, ummauern; (*fig.*) umschließen, einschließen; – *up*, zumauern, vermauern. **--bars,** *pl.* die Sprossenwand (*Gymn.*). **--creeper,** *s.* der Mauerläufer (*Orn.*). **--eyed,** *adj.* glasäugig (*of horses*). **--fern,** *s.* die Korallenwurzel (*Bot.*). **-flower,** *s.* der Goldlack (*Bot.*), (*fig.*) das Mauerblümchen. **--fruit,** *s.* das Spalierobst. **--map,** *s.* die Wandkarte. **--painting,** *s.* die Wandmalerei; das Wandgemälde. **-paper,** *s.* die Tapete. **--plug,** *s.* der Stecker. **--socket,** *s.* die Steckdose, der Steckkontakt.

wallaby [ˈwɔləbɪ], *s.* kleines Känguruh.

wallah [ˈwɔlə], *s.* (*sl.*) der Bursche; *base* –, das Etappenschwein (*Mil.*).

wallet [ˈwɔlɪt], *s.* die Brieftasche, Geldtasche; kleine Werkzeugtasche; (*archaic*) der Ranzen, das Felleisen.

wallop [ˈwɔləp], 1. *s.* (*coll.*) heftiger Schlag; die Wucht, Schlagkraft; (*sl.*) das Bier. **2.** *v.n.* (*coll.*) poltern; brodeln; wallen. 3. *v.a.* (*coll.*) verprügeln, durchhauen; kräftig schlagen. **-ing,** 1. *adj.* (*sl.*) plump, riesig, mächtig. 2. *s.* (*coll.*) die Tracht Prügel.

wallow [ˈwɔloʊ], 1. *v.n.* sich wälzen, (*fig.*) schwelgen; *be -ing in money*, in Geld schwimmen. 2. *s.* das Sich-Wälzen, Schwelgen; die Suhle, das Mistlager, der Schmutz.

walnut [ˈwɔ:lnʌt], *s.* die Walnuß; der Walnußbaum; das Nußbaumholz.

walrus [ˈwɔlrəs], *s.* das Walroß.

waltz [wɔ:ls], 1. *s.* der Walzer. 2. *v.n.* Walzer tanzen, walzen; (*sl.*) wälzen, rollen. **--time,** *s.* der Dreivierteltakt.

wampum [ˈwɔmpəm], *s.* das Muschelgeld, die Muschelschmuck (*of Indians*).

wan [wɔn], *adj.* bleich, blaß (*as face*), schwach, farblos, glanzlos (*light*), gezwungen (*smile*). **-ness,** *s.* die Blässe.

wand [wɔnd], *s.* die Rute, der (Amts)Stab, Feldherrnstab, Kommandostab (*Mil.*); Taktstock (*Mus.*); Zauberstab.

wander [ˈwɔndə], 1. *v.n.* wandern, wandeln, streifen; umherwandern, umherziehen, umherschweifen, umherstreifen, umherirren; schweifen (*of the eye*); abweichen, abirren, abschweifen (*from*, von); sich verirren, irregehen; *be -ing*, phantasieren, faseln, irre reden; zerstreut *or* geistesabwesend sein; – *from the subject*, vom Gegenstand abkommen; – *off course*, vom Kurs abkommen, (*sl.*) franzen. 2. *v.a.* durchwandern (*the streets, etc.*). **-er** [-rə], *s.* der Wanderer. **-ing,** 1. *adj.* wandernd, Wander–, Nomaden–, umherschweifend; Kriech–, Schling– (*Bot.*); (*fig.*) unstet, ruhelos; konfus, zerstreut (*thoughts*); *-ing bullet*, abirrende Kugel; *-ing cell*, die Wanderzelle (*Anat.*); *-ing Jew*, der ewige Jude. 2. *s.* das Wandern, Umherstreifen, Umherirren; (*usually pl.*) die Wanderschaft, weite Wanderung; (*usually pl.*) das Irrereden, Phantasieren, die Fieberwahn. **-lust,** *s.* die Wanderlust.

wan-e [weɪn], 1. *v.n.* abnehmen (*moon, also fig.*), erbleichen, schwächer werden; (*fig.*) sinken, verfallen, abflauen, schwinden, zu Ende gehen. 2. *s.* das Abnehmen; (*fig.*) die Abnahme, der Verfall, das Abflauen; *at the -e of the moon*, bei abnehmendem Mond; *be on the -e*, abnehmen (*of the moon*); (*fig.*) im Abnehmen sein, schwinden, verfallen. **-ing,** *adj.* abnehmend, abflauend, schwindend, zu Ende gehend.

wangle [ˈwæŋgl], 1. *v.a.* (*sl.*) sich unter der Hand *or* von hinten herum beschaffen, deichseln, organisieren; durch List zustandebringen, herausschlagen, drehen, frisieren (*accounts, etc.*); – *a th. out of a p.*, einem etwas ablotsen. 2. *v.n.* mogeln; – *out of*, sich durch List herausarbeiten aus. 3. *s.* der Kniff, die Machenschaft, Schiebung. **-r,** *s.* der Schieber.

wanness [ˈwɔnnɪs], *s. see* **wan.**

want [wɔnt], 1. *s.* der Mangel (*of*, an), das Fehlen (*of* (*Gen.*)); der Bedarf, das Bedürfnis; die Armut, Not, Bedürftigkeit; *for* – *of*, aus Mangel an (*Dat.*), mangels (*Gen.*), in Ermangelung von; *be in* – *of*, bedürfen (*Gen.*), benötigen, brauchen, nötig haben, Mangel haben an (*Dat.*); – *of money*, der Geldmangel; – *of spirit*, die Mutlosigkeit; *supply a long-felt* –, einem seit langem fühlbaren Bedürfnis abhelfen. 2. *v.a.* bedürfen (*Gen.*), benötigen, nötig haben, brauchen; fehlen *or* Mangel haben an, ermangeln (*Gen.*), entbehren (*Gen. or Acc.*); haben mögen, wollen, wünschen; (*before inf.*) wollen; (*coll.* (*before inf.*)) sollen; – *badly*, dringend benötigen; *the story -s confirmation*, die Geschichte bedarf der Bestätigung; *he -s a hat*, er braucht einen Hut *or* muß einen Hut haben; *it -s 10 minntes to 9*, es fehlen 10 Minuten an 9 Uhr; *the piano -s tuning*, das Klavier müßte *or* sollte gestimmt werden; (*coll.*) *you don't* – *to be in such a hurry*, du sollst es nicht so eilig haben; *what do you* –? was wünschen *or* wollen Sie? – *none of him*, nichts mit ihm zu tun haben wollen; – *nothing more of him*, nichts mehr von ihm wünschen; *what do you* – *with me?* was wollen Sie von mir?; *what does he* – *with three cars?* wozu braucht er drei Autos?; *I* – *to do*, ich möchte *or* will tun; *I* – *him to do*, ich wünsche daß er tut; *I – it done*, ich wünsche daß es geschieht *or* gemacht wird; *badly –ed*, dringend erforderlich *or* gesucht; *he is –ed*, er wird gewünscht, man sucht ihn; *she is not –ed here*, man kann sie hier nicht brauchen *or* will sie hier nicht haben; *–ed by the police*, von der Polizei gesucht; *situations –ed*, Stellungsgesuche (*pl.*). 3. *v.n.* (*archaic*) mangeln, Mangel haben, Not leiden; *–for*, ermangeln (*Gen.*), nicht haben; *be –ing*, fehlen, es fehlen lassen (*in*, an); (*coll.*) geistesschwach sein; *he is –ing in energy*, es fehlt ihm an Tatkraft; *be found –ing*, mangelhaft befunden werden. **–age,** *s.* (*Amer.*) das Defizit, Fehlende, der Fehlbetrag (*C.L.*).

wanton [ˈwɔntən], 1. *adj.* mutwillig, übermütig, ausgelassen, üppig, wild, schwelgerisch (*as growth*); lüstern, wollüstig, geil, liederlich, ausschweifend. 2. *s.* der Wollüstling, Wüstling (*a man*), die Trulle (*a woman*). 3. *v.n.* Mutwillen treiben, ausgelassen sein, umhertollen; buhlen; üppig wachsen, wuchern (*plants*). **–ness,** *s.* der Mutwille, Übermut, Leichtfertigkeit, Ausgelassenheit, Ausschweifung; Üppigkeit, Lüsternheit, Geilheit.

wapentake [ˈwɔpnteɪk], *s.* (*Hist.*) der Gau, die Hundertschaft.

war [wɔ:ə], 1. *s.* der Krieg; *be at –*, Krieg führen; (*fig.*) auf Kriegsfuß stehen; *carry the – into the enemy's camp*, den Krieg ins feindliche Land tragen, (*fig.*) zum Gegenangriff übergehen; *civil –*, der Bürgerkrieg; *declare –*, den Krieg erklären (*on* (*Dat.*)); *drift into –*, in den Krieg (hinein)gezogen *or* (hinein)getrieben werden; *fight a –*, einen Krieg führen, (*fig.*) einen Kampf ausfechten; *the Great –*, der 1. Weltkrieg; *holy –*, der Religionskrieg; *in the –*, im Kriege, während des Krieges; am Kriege beteiligt; (*coll.*) *have been in the –s*, arg mitgenommen sein; *council of –*, der Kriegsrat; *declaration of –*, die Kriegserklärung; *prisoner of –*, Kriegsgefangene(r), *m.*; *seat* or *theatre of –*, der Kriegsschauplatz; *state of –*, der Kriegszustand; *– of attrition*, der Zermürbungskrieg; *– of Liberation*, der Freiheitskrieg; *make – on*, Krieg führen *or* im Kriege sein gegen; *– to the knife*, der Krieg bis aufs Messer, Vernichtungskrieg; *go to –*, Krieg beginnen (*with*, mit), sich bekriegen; *go to the –s*, im Heere *or* als Soldat dienen; *wage – against*, see *make – on*. 2. *v.n.* Krieg führen, kämpfen (*also fig.*) (*against* or *on*, gegen); sich bekriegen; (*fig.*) streiten (*against*, gegen). **– -baby,** *s.* das Kriegskind. **– -blinded,** 1. *pl.* Kriegsblinde (*pl.*). 2. *adj.* kriegsblind. **– -bond,** *s.* die Kriegsschuldverschreibung. **– -cloud,** *s.* die Kriegswolke. **– -criminal,** *s.* der Kriegsverbrecher. **– -correspondent,** *s.* der Kriegsberichterstatter. **– -cry,** *s.* das Kriegsgeschrei, der Schlachtruf. **– -damage,** *s.* Kriegsschäden (*pl.*). **– -dance,** *s.* der Kriegstanz. **– -debt,** *s.* die Kriegsschuld. **– Department,** *s.* (*Amer.*) das Kriegsministerium. **–fare,** *s.* der Kampf (*also fig.*), Kriegszustand; die Kriegführung; (*fig.*) Fehde, der Streit; *economic –fare*, der Wirtschaftskrieg; *psychological –fare*, psychologische Kriegführung. **– footing,** *s.* der Kriegsstand, die Kriegsbereitschaft; *place on a – footing*, kriegsbereit machen; auf Kriegsfuß bringen. **– -god,** *s.* der Kriegsgott. **– grave,** *s.* das Kriegsgrab. **– guilt,** *s.* die Kriegsschuld. **–head,** *s.* der Sprengkopf, Gefechtskopf (*of torpedo*). **– -horse,** *s.* das Streitroß, (*fig.*) der Haudegen. **– -industry,** *s.* die Kriegsindustrie, Rüstungsindustrie. **–like,** *adj.* kriegerisch, Kriegs–. **– loan,** die Kriegsanleihe. **– -lord,** *s.* der Kriegsherr. **– -memorial,** *s.* das Kriegerdenkmal. **– -minded,** *adj.* kriegerisch gesinnt. **– -monger,** *s.* der Kriegshetzer. **– Office,** das Kriegsministerium. **– -paint,** *s.* die Kriegsbemalung, (*fig.*) der Staat, Putz. **– -path,** *s.* der Kriegspfad; *on the –path*, (*fig.*) kampflustig. **– -plane,** *s.* das Kampfflugzeug, Militärflugzeug. **– profiteer,** *s.* der Kriegsgewinnler. **–ring,** *adj.* sich bekriegend *or* bekämpfend *or* streitend, (*fig.*) widerstreitend, widerstrebend, entgegengesetzt. **–rior** [ˈwɔrɪə], *see* **warrior.** **–ship,** *s.* das Kriegsschiff. **– stations,** *pl.* die Flugbereitschaft (*Av.*). **– -strength,** *s.* die Kriegsstärke. **–time,** *s.* die Kriegszeit. **– -weary,** *adj.* kriegsmüde. **– -weariness,** *s.* die Kriegsmüdigkeit. **– -whoop,** *s.* (indianisches) Kriegsgeschrei. **– years,** Kriegsjahre (*pl.*).

warbl–e [ˈwɔ:bl], 1. *v.n.* trillern; singen, schmettern, schlagen (*as birds*). 2. *v.a.* trillern; singen. 3. *s.* das Trillern. **–er** [–lə], *s.* der Singvogel; die Grasmücke (*Orn.*). **–ing** [–lɪŋ], *s.* das Trillern; der Triller.

ward [wɔ:d], 1. *v.a.* (usually *– off*) abwehren, abwenden, parieren (*a blow, etc.*); (*archaic*) schützen, verteiden, bewahren (*from*, vor). 2. *s.* der *or* das Mündel, die Mündel (*of a girl*); (*fig.*) der Schützling; (*rare*) die Aufsicht, Vormundschaft, Verwahrung, der Schutz; (*archaic*) die Wache (only in *keep watch and –*, Wache halten); die Parade, Abwehr(stellung) (*Fenc.*); das Gewirr(e) (*of a lock*); der (Schlüssel)Bart (*of a key*); die Abteilung (*in a prison*); Station (*in a hospital*); der Bezirk, Wahlkreis, das Viertel (*of a town*); *casual –*, das Obdachlosenasyl; *in –*, unter Vormundschaft; *private –*, das Privatzimmer (*in a hospital*). **–en** [–n], *s.* der Gouverneur, Vorsteher; Rektor (*of a college*); Herbergsvater (*of a youth hostel*); (also *church –en*) Kirchenvorsteher; (*Poet.*) Wärter, Wächter, Aufseher; (*fig.*) Hüter; *air-raid –en*, der Luftschutzwart; *–en of the Mint*, der Münzwardein. **–enship,** *s.* das Amt eines Vorstehers, Aufsehers, Rektors, *etc.* **–er** [–ə], *s.* der Gefängniswärter; (*archaic*) Wärter, Wächter. **–ress** [–rɪs], *s.* die Gefängniswärterin. **–robe** [–roub], *s.* der Kleiderschrank; Kleiderbestand, die Garderobe (*of a p.*). **–robe-master,** *s.* der Gewandmeister (*Theat.*). **–robe-trunk,** *s.* der Schrankkoffer. **– -room,** *s.* die Offiziersmesse (*Naut.*). **–ship,** *s.* die Vormundschaft (*also fig.*), Minderjährigkeit; (*fig.*) der Schutz, die Aufsicht.

–ward(s) [wəd(z)], *adj. or adv. suffix* –wärts.

[1]**ware** [wɛə], *v.a.* (*coll.*) (*usually imper.*) Achtung! Vorsicht! *see* **wariness, wary.**

[2]**ware,** *s.* (*only sing., usually in comps.*) die Ware, Waren (*pl.*); *china–*, das Geschirr, Porzellan; *earthen–*, das Steingut, Töpfenwaren (*pl.*); (*only pl.* [wɛ:əz]) Waren (*pl.*); *praise one's own –s*, sich selbst loben. **–house,** 1. *s.* das Warenlager, Niederlage, der Speicher, das Lagerhaus; Engrosgeschäft. 2. *v.a.* auf Lager bringen *or* nehmen, einlagern, aufspeichern; zur Aufbewahrung geben *or* nehmen (*furniture, etc.*). **–house-account,** *s.* das Lagerkonto. **–houseman,** *s.* der Lageraufseher, Lagerverwalter, Lagerist; Speicherarbeiter, Lagerarbeiter; Lagerinhaber, Engroshändler.

warfare [ˈwɔ:əfɛə], *s. see under* **war.**

wariness [ˈwɛərɪnɪs], *s.* die Vorsicht, Behutsamkeit; *see* **wary.**

warlock [wɔ:lɔk], *s.* (*archaic*) der Zauberer.

warm [wɔ:m], 1. *adj.* warm (*also fig.*), heiß; (*fig.*) warmherzig (*as thanks*), herzlich, innig, eifrig, enthusiastisch, lebhaft, hitzig, erregt, leidenschaftlich (*of a p.*); frisch (*scent*) (*Hunt.*); (*coll.*) nahe (*to a goal*); *– front*, die Warmluftfront (*Meteor.*). 2. *v.a.* wärmen, warm machen, anwärmen; heizen (*a room*); (*fig.*) erwärmen; (*sl.*) verprügeln; *– up*, aufwärmen. 3. *v.n.* warm *or* wärmer werden; sich erwärmen (*also fig.*) (*to*, für); (*fig.* also *– up*) interessiert werden (*to*, an); *– up*, warmlaufen (*of an engine*). 4. *s.* das Warme, die Wärme; das Wärmen; *come into the –*, ins warme Haus, Zimmer, *etc.* eintreten; *have a –*, sich wärmen. **– -blooded,** *adj.* warmblütig; (*fig.*) hitzig; *– -blooded animals*, Warmblüter (*pl.*). **– -hearted,** *adj.* warmherzig. **– -heartedness,** *s.* die Warmherzigkeit. **–ing,** 1. *adj.* wärmend. 2. *s.* das Wärmen; (*coll.*) die Tracht Prügel. **–th** [–θ], *s.* die Wärme (*also fig.*), (*fig.*) Lebhaftigkeit (*of colour*), Herzlichkeit, Erregtheit, Hitze, der Ärger, Eifer.

warn [wɔ:n], *v.a.* warnen (*of* (*a th.*), *against* (*a p.*), vor (*Dat.*)); ermahnen (*of*, an), verwarnen (*of*, vor); ankündigen, vorher verständigen *or* benachrichtigen (*of*, von), frühzeitig aufmerksam machen (*of*, auf); *– off*, abhalten, abbringen (*from*, von); mit einer Mahnung fortschicken. **–ing,** *s.* die Warnung (*of*, vor; *to*, an *or* für), Mahnung; der Wink, die Benachrichtigung, Verständigung, Voranzeige, der Bescheid; die Kündigung; *give a p. –ing*, einen ankündigen; *give fair –ing*, rechtzeitig ankündigen *or* warnen (*of*, vor); *take –ing by*, sich warnen *or* belehren lassen durch; *at a minute's –ing*, sofort, fristlos; *a month's –ing*, die Kündigung nach Monatsfrist; *without –ing*, unerwartet. **–ing-bell,** *s.* die Signalglocke. **–ing-colours,** *pl.* Warnfarben, Trutzfarben (*of insects, etc.*). **–ing-notice,** *s.* die Warnungstafel. **–ing-order,** *s.* der Vorbefehl (*Mil.*).

warp [wɔ:p], 1. *s.* die Kette, der Aufzug, Zettel, Kettenfäden, Längsfäden (*pl.*) (*Weav.*); der *or* das Warp, die Warpleine, Trosse, das Verholtau (*Naut.*); das Werfen, Ziehen, die Verkrümmung, Verwerfung (*of wood*); der Schlamm, Schlick, das Schwemmland (*Topog.*); (*fig.*) die Entstellung, Verdrehung, Verzerrung; – *and woof*, Zettel und Einschlag. 2. *v.a.* krumm machen, krümmen, verziehen (*wood, etc.*); verschlammen (*land*); (an)scheren, schären, die Kettenfäden ausspannen (*Weav.*); bugsieren, verholen (*Naut.*); (*fig.*) entstellen, verdrehen, verzerren, nachteilig beeinflussen; verleiten, abbringen, ablenken. 3. *v.n.* sich werfen *or* ziehen, krümmen, krumm werden (*as wood*); werpen, warpen (*Naut.*); (*fig.*) entstellt *or* verdreht werden, abweichen.

warrant [ˈwɔrənt], 1. *s.* die Ermächtigung, Befugnis, Vollmacht (*for*, zu); der Vollziehungsbefehl, das Patent, die Bestallungsurkunde; der Lagerschein (*C.L.*); die Berechtigung; – *of apprehension*, der Steckbrief; – *of arrest*, der Haftbefehl; – *of attorney*, die Prozeßvollmacht; – *of distress*, der Zwangsvollstreckungsbefehl, Pfändungsbefehl (*Law*); *a – is out against him*, er wird steckbrieflich verfolgt; *not without –*, nicht unberechtigt. 2. *v.a.* verbürgen, einstehen für, garantieren, gewährleisten; (*coll.*) behaupten, versichern. **–able,** *adj.* zu rechtfertigen(d), berechtigt, gerechtfertigt; jagdbar (*of stags*). **–er, –or** [–ə], *s.* der Gewährsmann, Bürge. **––officer,** *s.* der Oberfeldwebel, Feldwebelleutnant (*Mil.*); Deckoffizier (*Naut.*). **–y** [–ɪ], *s.* die Garantie, Gewähr(leistung); Ermächtigung, Berechtigung (*for*, zu), der Bürgschaftsschein.

warren [ˈwɔrən], *s.* das (Kaninchen)Gehege, der Kaninchenbau.

warrior [ˈwɔrɪə], *s.* der Krieger, Kämpfer.

wart [wɔ:t], *s.* die Warze; Mauke (*Vet.*), der Auswuchs (*Bot.*). **––hog,** *s.* das Warzenschwein. **–y,** *adj.* warzig, warzenartig.

wary [ˈwɛərɪ], *adj.* vorsichtig, umsichtig, bedächtig, behutsam, achtsam, wachsam; *be – of*, sich hüten vor, auf der Hut sein vor.

was [wɔz], *see* **be.**

wash [wɔʃ], **1.** *v.a.* waschen (*also Min., Paint.*), abwaschen (*crockery*); (aus)spülen (*glasses, etc.*); abspülen (*a deck, etc.*); schlämmen (*ore*); bespülen (*the shore*); tuschen (*Paint.*); dünn überziehen, plattieren (*Metall.*); – *one's hands of*, die Hände lassen von, nichts zu tun *or* schaffen haben wollen mit, nicht verantwortlich sein für, keine Verantwortung übernehmen für, unschuldig sein an; – *ashore*, ans Land schwemmen *or* spülen; – *away*, wegwaschen, abwaschen; wegspülen, wegschwemmen; – *down*, gründlich abwaschen (*walls, etc.*), hinunterspülen (*food*); – *off*, abwaschen, wegwaschen; – *out*, auswaschen, ausspülen, (*coll.*) tilgen, ausmerzen; *be –ed out*, ausgewaschen sein, die Farbe verloren haben; (*fig.*) blaß sein; müde *or* abgespannt sein; – *over*, überwaschen, überstreichen, übertünchen; – *overboard*, über Bord spülen; – *up*, aufwaschen, abwaschen (*crockery, etc.*); anspülen, ans Ufer spülen; (*sl.*) *–ed up*, erledigt, ausgeschieden. **2.** *v.n.* sich waschen; sich waschen (lassen), gewaschen werden können, waschecht sein (*of fabrics*); fließen (*of water*) (*over*, über); (*sl.*) (*usually neg.*) standhalten, stichhaltig sein, Annahme finden; (*sl.*) *that won't – with me*, das verfängt *or* zählt bei mir nicht; – *off* or *out*, sich auswaschen lassen, sich durch Waschen entfernen lassen; – *up*, aufwaschen, abwaschen. **3.** *s.* das Waschen; die Wäsche; der Wellenschlag, die Brandung, das Fahrwasser, Kielwasser; das Schwemmland; (Gesichts– *or* Haar– *or* Mund– *or* Schönheits)Wasser; Spülwasser, Spülicht; Schweinefutter; leicht aufgetragene Farbe, Tusche, Tünche (*Paint.*); der Metallüberzug, die Plattierung; *be at the –*, auf der Wäscherei sein; *give a th. a –*, etwas waschen; (*coll.*) *have a –*, sich waschen; *send to the –*, in die Wäsche geben. **–able,** *adj.* waschbar; waschecht. **––basin,** *s.* das Waschbecken, die Waschschüssel. **–board,** *s.* das Setzbord (*Naut.*); das Waschbrett. **––bottle,** *s.* der Reinigungsapparat (*for gases*) (*Chem.*). **––day,** *s.* der Waschtag, Wäschetag. **–er,** *s.* die Waschmaschine; die Scheibe, Unterlagsscheibe, Dichtungsscheibe, der Dichtungsring (*Tech.*); *spring –er*, der Federring. **–erwoman,** *s.* die Waschfrau, Wäscherin. **––hand-basin,** *see* **––basin. ––hand-stand,** *see* **–stand. ––house,** *s.* der Waschraum, das Waschhaus, die Waschküche. **–iness,** *s.* die Wässerigkeit, (*fig.*) Verwässerung, Kraftlosigkeit, Saftlosigkeit (*of style*). **–ing,** *s.* das Waschen, Spülen, Reinigen, die Waschung; das Auswaschen, Schlämmen (*Min.*); Fließen, Branden, Strömen (*of water*); der (Farb)-Überzug (*Paint.*); die Wäsche (zum Waschen), (gewaschene) Wäsche; *pl.* das Waschwasser, Spülicht, Spülwasser. **–ing-day,** *s.* der Waschtag. **–ing-machine,** *s.* die Waschmaschine. **–ing-powder,** *s.* das Waschpulver. **––leather,** *s.* das Waschleder, Putzleder. **––out,** *s.* das Ausspülen; der Durchbruch (*of floods*); (*sl.*) der Mißgriff, Mißerfolg, Durchfall, Versager, Fehlschlag, die Pleite, Niete. **––stand,** *s.* der Waschtisch, Waschständer. **––tub,** *s.* das Waschfaß, der Waschkübel. **–y,** *adj.* wässerig, dünn, schwach, (*fig.*) verwässert, seicht, lappig, kraftlos.

wasp [wɔsp], *s.* die Wespe. **–ish,** *adj.* wespenartig, (*usually fig.*) reizbar, gehässig, bissig. **–ishness,** *s.* die Reizbarkeit, Gehässigkeit. **––waisted,** *adj.* mit einer schmalen Taille.

wassail [ˈwæsl, ˈwɔsl], *s.* (*Poet.*) süßes Getränk, das Würzbier; Trinkgelage. **––cup,** *s.* der Humpen. **–er,** *s.* der Zecher.

wast-age [ˈweɪstɪdʒ], *s.* der Verlust (im Gebrauch), Abgang, Abfall, Schwund; Verschleiß; die Verschwendung, Vergeudung, (*fig.*) der Leerlauf. **–e** [weɪst], 1. *v.a.* verwüsten, verheeren, zerstören, vernachlässigen, verfallen *or* verkommen lassen; abzehren, verzehren, zehren an (*as a fever*); verschwenden, vergeuden, vertrödeln (*on*, an); *–e one's breath*, tauben Ohren predigen, vergeblich reden; *be –ed*, ohne Wirkung *or* nutzlos sein, am falschen Platz stehen; *–ing disease*, die Abzehrung. 2. *v.n.* (also – *away*) abnehmen, verfallen; hinschwinden, vergehen, aufgebraucht *or* verschwendet werden; dahinsiechen (*of a p.*). 3. *adj.* wüst, öde, brach, unbebaut (*of land*); Ab–, Abfall–; überschüssig, überflüssig, unbrauchbar, unnütz; *lay –e*, verwüsten, verheeren; *lie –e*, brach liegen. 4. *s.* die Vergeudung, Verschwendung (*of money, etc.*); der Verfall, Verderb, Verlust, die Abnahme, das Hinschwinden (*of strength, etc.*); die Wertminderung (*Law*); Wüste, Einöde; der Abfall (*cotton, etc.*), Abgang (*coal*), Abraum, Schutt (*Min.*), Schrott (*metal*); *cotton –e*, das Putzwerg; *–e of time*, die Zeitverschwendung; *go* or *run to –e*, verwildern, umkommen, verlottern, zugrundegehen, ungenutzt daliegen, vergeudet werden. **–eful,** *adj.* verschwenderisch (*of*, mit); (*Poet.*) wüst, leer; *be –eful of*, verschwenden. **–efulness,** *s.* die Verschwendung(ssucht). **–e-paper,** *s.* die Makulatur. **–e-(paper) basket,** *s.* der Papierkorb. **–e-pipe,** *s.* das Abflußrohr, Abzugsrohr. **–e-product,** *s.* das Abfallprodukt. **–er,** *s.* der Verschwender; *see* **–rel**; der Fehlguß (*Casting*). **–e-steam,** *s.* der Abdampf. **–e-water,** *s.* das Kondenswasser, Schmutzwasser, das Abwasser. **–e-wool,** *s.* der Twist. **–rel,** *s.* der Tunichtgut; verwahrlostes Kind; der Straßenbengel; minderwertige Ware, der Ausschuß, fehlerhaftes Exemplar (*C.L.*).

watch [ˈwɔtʃ], 1. *v.n.* Wache haben, Posten stehen (*Mil.*); wach sein, wachen (*with*, bei), lauern, aufpassen, achthaben, achtgeben (*for*, auf (*Acc.*)); wachsam sein, auf der Hut sein; – *out*, achtgeben, aufpassen; – *over*, wachen über, bewachen. 2. *v.a.* bewachen, achthaben auf, hüten (*sheep, etc.*), (sorgsam) beobachten *or* betrachten, ein wachsames Auge haben auf (*Acc.*), zusehen (*s.o. working*, wie er arbeitet *or* ihn beim Arbeiten); (*fig.*) im Auge behalten; wahrnehmen, abpassen, achtgeben auf (*an opportunity*), verfolgen (*course of events*), im Interesse eines Klienten verfolgen (*a case*) (*Law*). 3. *s.* die Wache, Wachsamkeit, Achtsamkeit, Lauer; Schildwache, der Posten; die Schiffswache (*Naut.*), Wachmannschaft (*Naut.*); Taschenuhr, Armbanduhr; (*archaic*) (*usually pl.*) Nachtwache; *horizontal* –, die Zylinderuhr; *keep* –, Wache halten; *keep – on s.o.*, einen bewachen *or* sorgsam beobachten; *morning* –, die Morgenwache; *on the* –, auf der Hut *or* Lauer (*for*, nach); *be on the* –, aufpassen (*for*, auf); *put a – on* (*or back*), eine Uhr vorstellen (nachstellen); *set a* –, eine Uhr stellen. **--box,** *s.* das Schilderhaus. **--case,** *s.* das Uhrgehäuse. **--chain,** *s.* die Uhrkette. **–committee,** städtischer Ordnungsdienst. **--dog,** *s.* der Kettenhund, Hofhund. **–er,** *s.* der Wächter, Beobachter. **--fire,** *s.* das Signalfeuer, Wachtfeuer. **–ful,** *adj.* wachsam, achtsam, aufmerksam (*of*, auf), lauernd (*for*, auf); *be –ful for*, lauern auf; *be –ful of*, beobachten, bewachen. **–fulness,** *s.* die Wachsamkeit, Achtsamkeit, Aufmerksamkeit (*of*, auf), das Wachen (*over*, über). **--glass,** *s.* das Uhrglas. **--guard,** *s.* das Uhrband, die Uhrkette. **--house,** *s.* das Wachthaus, die Wache. **–maker,** *s.* der Uhrmacher. **–making,** *s.* die Uhrmacherei. **–man,** *s.* der Wächter, (also *night-–man*) Nachtwächter. **--pocket,** *s.* die Uhrtasche. **--spring,** *s.* die Uhrfeder. **--stand,** *s.* der Uhrständer. **--tower,** *s.* der Wachturm, die Warte. **–word,** *s.* die Losung, Parole; das Schlagwort, Erkennungswort.

water [ˈwɔːtə], **1.** *s.* das Wasser; die Wasserfläche; *pl.* Wasser, Gewässer (*pl.*) (*Topog.*); (*usually pl.*) das Wasser, der Brunnen (*at a spa*); *fresh* –, das Süßwasser; *salt* –, das Salzwasser; *tap* –, das Leitungswasser; *holy* –, das Weihwasser; *subsoil* –, das Grundwasser; *surface* –, das Tagwasser; *mineral –s*, das Mineralwasser; *– on the brain*, der Wasserkopf (*Med.*); **(a)** (*with adjectives*) *throw cold – on s.th.*, etwas herabsetzen; *in deep –*(*s*), in der Klemme, in Schwierigkeiten; *of the first* –, von reinstem Wasser (*as a diamond, etc.*), (*fig.*) bester Art, erster Qualität; *high* –, die Flut; *get into hot* –, sich in die Nesseln setzen, in Teufels Küche kommen (*for*, wegen); in Konflikt geraten (*with*, mit); *low* –, die Ebbe; *be in low* –, (*fig.*) auf dem trockenen sitzen; *smooth –s run deep*, stille Wasser sind tief; *fish in troubled –s*, im trüben fischen; *pour oil on troubled –s*, Frieden stiften; **(b)** (*with verbs*) *drink the –s*, Brunnen trinken; *much – has flowed under the bridge*, viel Wasser ist den Fluß hinabgelaufen; *hold* –, wasserdicht sein, (*fig.*) stichhaltig sein; *pass* or *make* –, Wasser abschlagen *or* lassen, harnen, urinieren; *take the* –, ins Wasser gehen, vom Stapel laufen; *take the –s*, Brunnen trinken; **(c)** (*with prepositions*) *keep one's head above* –, (*fig.*) sich eben über Wasser halten; *by* –, zu Wasser, auf dem Wasserwege; *take off from the* –, abwassern (*Av.*); *on the* –, auf dem Wasser, zur See; *alight* or *land on the* –, wassern (*Av.*); *through fire and* –, durchs Feuer; *take to the* –, ins Wasser gehen; das Wasser lieben; *under* –, unter Wasser; *cast one's bread upon the –s*, sich ohne Bedenken ausgeben. **2.** *v.a.* bewässern (*land*); begießen (*flowers*); tränken (*horses, etc.*); wassern, flammen, moirieren (*silk, etc.*); (also *– down*) verdünnen, panschen (*wine, etc.*); (*coll. fig.*) *– down*, verwässern, abschwächern, mildern, populär *or* mundgerecht machen. **3.** *v.n.* wässern; tränen (*as the eyes*); wässerig werden; *his mouth –s*, ihm wird der Mund wässerig; *make his mouth* –, ihm den Mund wässerig machen. **--bed,** *s.* das Wasserbett. **--beetle,** *s.* der Wasserkäfer. **--bird,** *s.* der Wasservogel. **--blister,** *s.* die Wasserblase. **--borne,** *adj.* zu Wasser befördert, auf dem Wasser schwimmend. **--bottle,** *s.* die Wasserflasche, Feldflasche (*Mil., etc.*); *hot-– bottle*, die Wärmflasche. **--bus,** *s.* der Flußdampfer. **--butt,** *s.* das Regenfaß. **--carriage,** *s.* der Wassertransport. **--cart,** *s.* der Sprengwagen. **--chute,** *s.* die Wasserrutschbahn. **--clock,** *s.* die Wasseruhr. **--closet,** *s.* das (Wasser)Klosett, die Toilette. **--colour,** *s.* das Aquarell; *pl.* Wasserfarben, Aquarellfarben; (*painting in*) *--colours*, die Aquarellmalerei. **--colourist,** *s.* der Aquarellmaler. **--cooled,** *adj.* wassergekühlt. **–course,** *s.* der Wasserlauf, das Flußbett, Strombett. **–cress,** *s.* die Brunnenkresse. **--cure,** *s.* die Wasserkur. **–fall,** *s.* der Wasserfall. **--finder,** *s.* der Rutengänger. **--flag,** *s.* die Wasserschwertlilie. **--flea,** *s.* der Wasserfloh. **–fowl,** *s.* Schwimmvögel, Wasservögel (*pl.*). **--gate,** *s.* die Schleuse, das Schott. **--gauge,** *s.* der Wasserstandsmesser, Pegel. **--glass,** *s.* das Wasserglas. **--gruel,** *s.* der Haferschleim. **–hen,** *s.* das Wasserhuhn. **--ice,** *s.* das Wassereis. **–iness,** *s.* die Wässerigkeit, Feuchtigkeit, (*fig.*) Verwässerung, Seichtheit. **–ing,** *s.* das Bewässern, Besprengen, Begießen; Wässern, Tränken; Flammen, die Moirierung; das Panschen, Verdünnen, Verwässern; *–ing can*, die Gießkanne; *–ing cart*, der Sprengwagen; *–ing place*, die Tränke, Schwemme (*for animals*), der Badeort, das (See)-Bad. **--jacket,** *s.* der Kühlwassermantel. **–less,** *adj.* wasserlos. **--level,** *s.* der Wasserstand, die Wasserstandslinie; die Wasserwaage (*Tech.*); der Grundwasserspiegel (*Geol.*). **--lily,** *s.* die Wasserlilie, Wasserrose. **--line,** *s.* die Wasser(stands)-linie, Wasserhöhe. **–logged,** *adj.* voll Wasser (*of ships*), voll Wasser gesogen (*of wood*). **--main,** *s.* das Wasserleitungshauptrohr. **–man,** *s.* der Jollenführer. **–manship,** *s.* die Wassertüchtigkeit, Riemenkunst. **–mark,** 1. *s.* das Wasserzeichen (*on paper*); (N.B. *high-– mark*, das Flutzeichen, Hochwasserstandszeichen, (*fig.*) der Hochstand, Höhepunkt; *low-– mark*, das Tiefwasserstandszeichen, (*fig.*) der Tiefstand). 2. *v.a.* mit einem Wasserzeichen versehen. **--melon,** *s.* die Wassermelone. **--meter,** *s.* der Wassermesser. **--mill,** *s.* die Wassermühle. **--nymph,** *s.* die Najade. **--pipe,** *s.* das Wasser(leitungs)rohr. **--plane,** *s.* das Wasserflugzeug. **--plant,** *s.* die Wasserpflanze. **--plate,** *s.* der Wärmteller. **--polo,** *s.* der Wasserball. **--pot,** *s.* der Wasserkrug. **--power,** *s.* die Wasserkraft. **–proof,** 1. *adj.* wasserdicht, imprägniert. 2. *s.* der Regenmantel, Gummimantel. 3. *v.a.* wasserdicht machen, imprägnieren. **--proofing,** *s.* die Imprägnierung; wasserdichter Stoff. **--rat,** *s.* die Wasserratte. **--rate,** *s.* das Wassergeld. **--ret, --rot,** *v.a.* rosten, faulen lassen (*flax*). **–shed,** *s.* die Wasserscheide. **--shoot,** *s.* die Traufe, Wasserrinne (*of a roof*). **--shortage,** *s.* der Wassermangel. **–side,** *s.* das Meeresufer, die Wasserkante, Küste. **--soluble,** *adj.* in Wasser löslich. **–spout,** *s.* die Wasserhose. **--sprite,** *s.* der Wassergeist, die Wassernixe. **--supply,** *s.* die Wasserversorgung. **--table,** *s.* der Grundwasserspiegel (*Geol.*), die Wasserabflußleiste (*Arch.*). **--tank,** *s.* der Wasserbehälter. **–tight,** *adj.* wasserdicht; (*fig.*) sicher, zuverlässig, unangreifbar; selbständig. **--tower,** *s.* der Wasserturm. **--vole,** *s.* die Wasserratte. **--wagtail,** *s.* die Bachstelze. **--wave,** *s.* die Wasserwelle. **–way,** *s.* die Wasserstraße, der Schiffahrtsweg; Wassergang (*Shipb.*). **--wheel,** *s.* das Wasserrad. **–works,** *pl.* (*often sing. constr.*) das Wasserwerk; (*coll.*) die Wasserleitung; (*coll.*) *turn on the –works*, Tränen vergießen. **–y,** *adj.* wässerig (*also fig.*); feucht, naß; tränend (*of eyes*); regnerisch, Regen– (*of the sky*); (*fig.*) verwässert, blaß, dünn (*as colour*); seicht, fade, lappig; (*Poet.*) Wasser–; *–y waste*, die Wasserwüste.

watt [wɔt], *s.* das Watt (*Elec.*).

wattl–e [ˈwɔtl], 1. *s.* das Geflecht, Flechtwerk, Gitterwerk, die Hürde, Umzäunung; (*pl.*) der Bart (*of fishes*), Kehllappen (*of a cock*); *–e and daub*, das Fachwerk. 2. *v.a.* mit Ruten zusammen binden *or* flechten; aus Flechtwerk herstellen; in Fachwerk bauen; *–e bark*, die Akazienrinde. **–ing,** *s.* das Flechtwerk.

wav–e [weɪv], 1. *s.* die Welle (*also Phys. & fig.*), Woge, See (*Naut.*); Flamme (*in fabric*), Guilloche (*on paintwork*); das Winken; *pl.* (*Poet.*) das Meer; *–e of the hand*, der Wink mit der Hand; *heat –e*, die Hitzewelle; *permanent –e*, die Dauerwelle (*in hair*). 2. *v.n.* wehen, flattern (*in the wind, etc.*); wogen, wallen; winken (*to a p.* (*Dat.*)); sich wellen, wellig sein (*hair*). 3. *v.a.* schwingen, schwenken; hin und her bewegen; wellen, wellig machen, ondulieren (*hair*), flammen, moirieren (*fabric*), guillochieren (*paintwork, etc.*); *–e one's arms*, mit den Armen fuchteln; *–e aside*, abweisen, abwinken; *–e good-bye*, ein Lebewohl zuwinken (*to* (*Dat.*)); *–e one's hand*, mit der Hand winken. **–e-band,** *s.* das Wellenband (*Rad.*). **–e-length,** *s.* die Wellenlänge (*Rad.*). **–eless,** *adj.* wellenlos, glatt. **–elet** [–lɪt], *s.* kleine Welle. **–e-like,** *adj.* wellenartig, wellenförmig. **–e-motion,** *s.* die Wellenbewegung. **–e-range,** *s.* der Wellenbereich (*Rad.*). **–e-trap,** *s.* der Sperrkreis (*Rad.*). **–er** [–ə], *v.n.* wanken, schwanken (*also fig.*); (*fig.*) unschlüssig sein; zittern, flimmern, flackern (*as light*); *–er from*, abweichen von. **–erer** [–ərə], *s.* unschlüssiger Mensch. **–ering,** 1. *adj.* wankend, schwankend, unentschlossen, unschlüssig, unstet; flatternd, wogend, schwebend. 2. *s.* das Schwanken, die Unschlüssigkeit. **–iness,** *s.* das Wogen, Wellige, die Welligkeit, Wellenbewegung. **–y,** *adj.* wallend, wogend, Wellen schlagend, Wellen–; wellenförmig, wellig, gewellt (*of hair*); *–y lines*, die Wellenlinien; (*sl.*) *–y navy*, die Flottenreserve.

[1]**wax** [wæks], *v.n.* (*archaic & Poet.*) wachsen (*also fig.*), zunehmen (*of the moon, also fig.*); (*with adjectives*) werden.

[2]**wax,** 1. *s.* das (Bienen)Wachs; (also *ear-–*) das Ohrenschmalz; *cobbler's* or *shoemaker's* –, das Schusterpech; *sealing* –, der Siegellack. 2. *v.a.* wachsen, mit Wachs überziehen, wichsen (*boots*), bohnern (*floors*); *–ed paper, see* **–-paper. – candle,** *s.* das Wachslicht, die Wachskerze. **–-chandler,** *s.* der Wachszieher. **–en** [–n], *adj.* Wachs–, (*fig.*) wachsähnlich, wachsfarbig; weich. **–-end,** *s.* der Pechdraht. **–-figure,** *s.* die Wachsfigur. **–-light,** *see* **–-candle. –-paper,** *s.* das Pergamentpapier. **– vestas,** *pl.* Wachsstreichhölzer (*pl*). **–wing,** *s.* der Seidenschwanz (*Orn.*). **–-work,** *s.* die Wachsfigur; (*pl.*) das Wachsfigurenkabinett, die Wachsfigurenausstellung. **–y,** *adj.* Wachs–, wächsern, wachsartig; wachsfarbig, bleich; weich; (*sl.*) ärgerlich, wütend.

way [weɪ], *s.* der Weg; Pfad, die Straße; Bahn; der Gang, Lauf, die Fahrt; Strecke, Entfernung; Richtung, Wegroute, der Kurs (*Naut.*); der Fortgang, Fortschritte; (*fig.*) die Art und Weise, Methode, das Mittel, Verfahren; die Art, Beschaffenheit; Möglichkeit, Gelegenheit, der Raum, Platz; Zustand, die Lage; *one-– street*, die Einbahnstraße; *– in* (*out*), der Eingang (Ausgang); **(a)** (*with adjectives*) *any* –, auf jede *or* irgendeine Art; *any – you please*, ganz wie Sie wollen; *in a bad* –, in schlimmer Lage; *both –s*, hin und zurück; *every* –, in jeder Hinsicht; *in the family* –, in anderen Umständen, schwanger; *in a fair* –, auf dem Wege (*to* or *of* (*Gen.*)); *a little* –, eine kleine Strecke; *a long* –, eine weite Strecke; *a long – from*, weit entfernt von; *a long – off*, weit entfernt; *go a long – round*, einen weiten Umweg machen; *a long – to*, weit nach; *a long – towards*, viel *or* wesentlich dazu beitragen; *go a long – with s.o.*, sehr bei einem wirken; *one – or the other* or *another*, so oder so; *neither one – nor the other*, weder so noch so; *the other – round*, in umgekehrter Richtung, umgekehrt; *have one's own* –, seinen Willen bekommen *or* durchsetzen *or* haben; *have it all one's own* –, nur seinen Willen kennen, nach Gutdünken verfahren; *permanent* –, das Geleise (*Railw.*); *round about* –, der Umweg; *feel the same – about a th. as*, genau so denken über etwas wie; *silly –s*, alberne Manieren (*of a p.*); *in a small* –, in kleinem Ausmaße, auf kleinem Fuße; *some – or* (*an*)*other*, auf irgend eine Weise, auf die eine oder andere Art; *this* –, hierher! hierdurch! *there are no two –s about it*, es verhält sich so und nicht anders; *which – did he go?* wohin ging er?; *I don't know which – to turn*, ich weiß nicht, wohin ich mich wenden soll; *which –?* in welcher Richtung?; *the wrong* –, falsch; *go down the wrong* –, in die falsche Kehle kommen; *you go the wrong – to work*, Sie greifen die Sache verkehrt an; *how is the weather your –?* wie ist das Wetter bei euch *or* in eurer Gegend? **(b)** (*with nouns*) *–s and means*, Mittel und Wege; *parting of the –s*, die Stelle wo sich die Wege scheiden; *right of* –, das Wegerecht; Vorfahrtrecht (*Motor.*); *the – of the world*, der Gang *or* Lauf der Welt; **(c)** (*with verbs*) *ask one's* –, sich nach dem Wege erkundigen; *ask a p. the* –, einen nach dem Weg fragen (*to*, nach); *that's the* –, so ist es richtig; *beg one's* –, sich durchbetteln; *that is always the – with her*, so macht sie es immer, so ist es immer mit ihr, so geht es ihr immer; *come s.o.'s* –, einem begegnen *or* in den Weg *or* unter die Augen kommen; *find one's* –, sich zurechtfindem; *force one's* –, sich einen Weg bahnen; *gather* –, Geschwindigkeit entfalten (*Naut.*); *give* –, weichen (*to* (*Dat.*)), nachlassen, nachgeben (*of a p.*), einbrechen, zusammenbrechen (*of a th.*); *go one's* –, seines Weges gehen; *go the – of all flesh*, sterben; *go one's different –s*, jeder einen anderen Weg gehen; *go one's* (*own*) –, in allen Stücken seinen Kopf durchsetzen, seinen eigenen Weg gehen; *have a – with*, glänzend umzugehen wissen mit; *if I had my* (*own*) –, wenn es nach mir ginge; *know one's – about*, den Weg kennen, (*fig.*) Bescheid wissen; *lead the* –, vorangehen; *lose* –, an Geschwindigkeit abnehmen (*Naut.*); *lose one's* –, vom Weg abkommen, sich verirren; *make* –, Platz schaffen (*for* (*Dat.*)), (*fig.*) Platz machen (*for* (*Dat.*)), zurücktreten (*for*, vor); *make one's* –, sich begeben (*to*, nach), (*fig.*) sich Bahn brechen, sich durchsetzen, vorankommen; *mend one's –s*, sich bessern; *pave the* –, den Weg ebnen (*for* (*Dat.*)); *pay one's* –, auf seine Kosten kommen (*of a p.*), sich rentieren (*of a th.*); *point out the* –, den Weg zeigen (*to* (*Dat.*)); *see one's –* (*clear*) *to do*, eine Möglichkeit vor sich sehen, sich in der Lage sehen, sich dazu verstehen können *or* sich berechtigt fühlen zu tun; *see a – out*, einen Ausweg wissen *or* sehen; *work one's* –, Werkstudent sein; *work one's – up*, sich hoch arbeiten; **(d)** (*with prepositions*) *across the* –, see *over the* –; *by the* –; im Vorbeigehen, auf dem *or* am Wege, unterwegs; (*fig.*) nebenbei, beiläufig, übrigens; *not by a long* –, noch lange nicht, bei weitem nicht; *by – of*, auf dem Wege über; (*fig.*) an Stelle von, anstatt; in der Absicht *or* um zu, zum Zwecke, zwecks, vermittels, durch; *he is by – of being an artist*, man spricht von ihm als einem Künstler; *by – of excuse*, als Entschuldigung; *by – of jest*, im Scherz; *in a* –, gewissermaßen, sozusagen; *in the – of*, an; *in the ordinary* –, normalerweise; *be in the* –, im Wege sein, stören; *in the – of business*, auf dem üblichen Geschäftswege; *in a – of business*, in einem Geschäftszweig; *in no* –, keineswegs, in keiner Hinsicht; *once in a* –, ausnahmsweise, ab und zu einmal; *in her own* –, in ihrer *or* auf ihre Art; *in some* –, irgendwie; *in some –s*, in mancher Hinsicht; *in this* –, auf diese Weise, in dieser Weise; *put s.o. in the – to*, einem verhelfen *or* die Möglichkeit geben *or* einen in die Lage versetzen zu; *put* or *throw a th. in a p.'s* –, einem etwas zukommen lassen; *stand* or *be in s.o.'s* –, einem im Wege stehen *or* hinderlich sein; *be of his – of thinking*, seine Ansichten *or* Meinung teilen; *make the best of one's* – (*to*), so schnell wie möglich gehen (nach); *on the* –, auf dem Wege, unterwegs; *on the – back*, auf dem Rückwege; *on the – home*, auf dem Heimwege; *on the – out*, auf der Hinreise; *on the – through*, auf der Durchreise; *bring a p. on his* –, einen eine Strecke Weges begleiten; *set out on one's* –, sich auf dem Wege machen; *be well on the* –, ziemlich weit gekommen sein, (*fig.*) im Gange sein; *out of the* –, abgelegen, entlegen, (*fig.*) abwegig, ungewöhnlich; *nothing out of the* –, nichts Besonderes; *be out of the* –, aus dem Weg sein; *get out of the* –, aus dem Wege gehen; Platz machen; sich davon machen; Platz da! *go out of one's* –, (*fig.*) ein Übriges tun, keine Mühe scheuen, sich (*Dat.*) besondere Mühe geben; *keep out of the* –, sich abseits *or* fern halten; *put out of the* –, um die Ecke bringen, abmurksen (*a p.*), aus dem Wege räumen, wegstellen (*a th.*); *take s.o. out of his* –, einem einen Umweg machen lassen; *over the* –, über die Straße; *to my – of thinking*, nach meiner Meinung; *under* –, in Vorbereitung, in *or* im Gang, in Fahrt (*Naut.*); *get under* –, in Fahrt gehen, abfahren (*Naut.*), (*fig.*) in *or* im Gang *or* in Bewegung kommen. **–-bill,** *s.* die Passagierliste; der Frachtbrief. **–farer,** *s.* der (Fuß)Wanderer. **–faring,** 1. *adj.* wandernd, reisend; *–faring man*, Reisende(r), *m.* 2. *s.* (*usually* *pl.*) die Reise. **–lay** [–ˈleɪ], *v.a.* auflauern (*Dat.*), abpassen; ansprechen, angehen. **– -leave,** *s.* das Wegerecht. **–side,** 1. *s.* der Straßenrand, die Straßenseite; *by the –side*, an der Straße. 2. *adj.* am Wege (stehend); *–side inn*, der Gasthof an der Straße. **–ward,** *adj.* launisch, eigensinnig, unberechenbar, widerspenstig. **–wardness,** *s.* der Eigensinn, die Launenhaftigkeit, Unberechenbarkeit, Widerspenstigkeit. **–worn,** *adj.* wegmüde, reisemüde.

we [wɪː], *pers. pron.* wir.

weak [wɪːk], *adj.* schwach (*also C.L., Gram., & fig.*); schwächlich, kränklich, gebrechlich (*of a p.*); schwankend, labil (*character*), (*fig.*) kraftlos, schlaff, matt; auf schwachen Füßen stehend (*argument*), flau (*C.L.*), dünn (*liquid*); – *point* or *side*, schwache Seite, die Blöße, Schwäche; *the –er sex*, das schwache Geschlecht. **–en,** 1. *v.a.* schwächen (*also fig.*), schwächer machen, (*fig.*) entkräften. 2. *v.n.* schwach *or* schwächer werden; nachlassen, nachgeben, erschlaffen. **– -kneed,** *adj.* schlapp, unentschlossen, nachgiebig (*of a p.*), auf schwachen Füßen stehend (*argument*). **–ling,** *s.* der Schwächling. **–ly,** *adj.* schwächlich, kränklich. **– -minded,** *adj.* schwachsinnig; charakterschwach. **–ness,** *s.* die Schwäche, Schwächlichkeit, Kränklichkeit, Gebrechlichkeit; Charakterschwäche, schwache Seite, schwacher Punkt; der Mangel, Nachteil, die Unvollkommenheit; (*coll.*) *have a –ness for*, eine Schwäche *or* Vorliebe haben für. **– -spirited,** *adj.* mutlos.

[1]**weal** [wɪːl], *s.* (*archaic*) das Wohl, die Wohlfahrt; (only in) *the general* or *public –*, das Gemeinwohl; *in – and woe*, auf Gedeih und Verderb, in Wohl und Wehe, in guten und bösen Tagen.

[2]**weal,** 1. *s.* die Schwiele, Strieme. 2. *v.a.* schwielig schlagen.

weald [wɪːld], *s.* die Hügellandschaft (*in S. England*).

wealth [wɛlθ], *s.* der Reichtum (*also fig.*), Wohlstand, (*coll.*) Reichtümer, das Geld und Gut; (*fig.*) die Fülle (*of*, an *or* von). **–y,** *adj.* reich, wohlhabend.

wean [wɪːn], *v.a.* entwöhnen (*a child*), (*fig.* also *– away*) entfremden (*from* (*Dat.*)), abbringen (*from*, von); – *him from a th.*, ihm etwas abgewöhnen.

weapon [ˈwɛpn], *s.* die Waffe (*also fig.*). **–less,** *adj.* wehrlos, unbewaffnet.

[1]**wear** [ˈwɛə], 1. *ir.v.a.* tragen, anhaben (*a dress, etc.*); aufhaben (*a hat*); zeigen, zur Schau tragen, annehmen (*a look, etc.*); abtragen, abnutzen; aushöhlen, eingraben (*a furrow, etc.*); (*fig.*) erschöpfen, ermüden, zermürben; *what shall I – ?* was soll ich anziehen?; – *one's clothes into holes*, die Kleider so lange tragen, bis sie abgenutzt sind; – *one's fingers to the bone*, sich abplacken; – *away*, abtragen, abnützen, abnutzen, aushöhlen, zerstören; – *down*, abnützen, abnutzen, ablaufen (*heels*), austreten (*a step*), (*fig.*) zermürben (*a p.*), brechen (*opposition*); – *off*, abnutzen, abnützen; – *out*, abtragen, abnutzen, abnützen, (*fig., usually pass.*) aufzehren, verzehren, zerrütten; erschöpfen (*a p.'s patience, etc.*); – *o.s. out*, müde werden. 2. *ir.v.n.* sich tragen, sich halten, haltbar sein; sich abtragen *or* verbrauchen, verbraucht werden; – *well*, strapazierfähig sein (*as clothes*); sich gut konservieren (*as people*), (*coll.*) der Kritik standhalten; – *away*, verbraucht werden, abnehmen, vergehen; – *off*, sich abtragen *or* abnutzen, (*fig.*) vergehen, vorübergehen, sich verlieren, erlöschen; – *on*, weiterschreiten, fortschreiten, sich entwickeln; – *on* (*prep.*) *a p.*, einen ermüden; – *out*, sich abnützen *or* abnutzen, sich abtragen; verschleißen. 3. *s.* das Tragen; die Kleidung, Tracht; die Dauerhaftigkeit, Haltbarkeit; der Gebrauch, die Benützung, Benutzung; Abnützung, Abnutzung, der Verschleiß; *for everyday –*, zum Tragen am Alltag; *for hard –*, strapazierfähig; *be in –*, Mode sein, getragen werden; *have in –*, tragen; *still have a good deal of – in it*, sich noch gut tragen lassen; *town –*, Stadtkleider (*pl.*); – *and tear*, natürliche Abnutzung *or* Abnützung, der Verschleiß; *the worse for –*, abgetragen, (*fig.*) mitgenommen. **–able,** *adj.* tragbar, zu tragen(d). **–ing,** 1. *adj.* ermüdend, aufreibend, lästig; Abschleifungs– (*Tech.*). 2. *s.* das Tragen; (also *–ing away, –ing out*) Abtragen, Abnutzen (*Tech.*). **–ing apparel,** *s.* Kleidungsstücke (*pl.*).

[2]**wear,** 1. *v.a.* halsen (*Naut.*). 2. *v.n.* sich drehen *or* vor dem Winde wenden (*Naut.*).

wear–iness [ˈwɪərɪnɪs], *s.* die Müdigkeit, Ermüdung; der Überdruß (*of*, an); die Last, Lästigkeit (*to*, für). **–isome,** *adj.* ermüdend; mühsam, lästig, langweilig; *be –isome*, ermüden. **–isomeness,** *s.* die Ermüdung, Mühsamkeit, Lästigkeit. **–y,** 1. *adj.* müde (*also fig.*), erschöpft (*with*, von); (*fig.*) überdrüssig (*of* (*Gen.*)); beschwerlich, ermüdend, lästig; (*coll.*) *–y Willie*, der Schwächling, Schwachmatikus. 2. *v.a.* ermüden, müde machen; langweilen (*with*, mit *or* durch), belästigen, aufreiben, Geduld erschöpfen. 3. *v.n.* müde werden (*also fig.*), (*fig.*) satt *or* überdrüssig werden (*of* (*Gen.*)).

weasel [ˈwɪːzl], *s.* das Wiesel.

weather [ˈwɛðə], 1. *s.* das Wetter; die Witterung; Luv(seite) (*Naut.*); *make good –*, auf gutes Wetter stoßen (*Naut.*); *make heavy –*, (*fig.*) viel Aufhebens machen (*about*, über); – *permitting*, bei günstigem *or* gutem Wetter, wenn es das Wetter erlaubt; *in all –s*, bei jedem Wetter; *under stress of –*, durch das Wetter gezwungen; (*coll.*) *under the –*, nicht wohl, unpäßlich; niedergedrückt. 2. *v.a.* überstehen (*a storm, also fig.*), trotzen (*Dat.*) (*a storm*), (*fig.*) glücklich überwinden; luvwärts umfahren (*a cape*), luvwärts vorüberfahren an (*a ship*); dem Wetter aussetzen, austrocknen. 3. *v.n.* verwittern (*Geol.*). **– -beams,** *pl.* die Luvseite (*Naut.*). **– -beaten,** *adj.* wetterhart, abgehärtet; mitgenommen. **– -board,** 1. *s.* die Windseite, Luv(seite) (*Naut.*); das Schutzbrett, Schindelbrett, Schalbrett (*Arch.*). 2. *v.a.* mit Schutzbretten versehen, verschalen (*a wall*). **– -boarding,** *s.* die Verschalung; Schutzbretter (*pl.*). **– -bound,** *adj.* vom Wetter zurückgehalten, durch schlechtes Wetter festgehalten. **– -bureau,** *s.* der Wetterdienst. **– -chart,** *s.* die Wetterkarte. **–cock,** *s.* die Wetterfahne, der Wetterhahn, (*fig.*) wetterwendischer Mensch. **–ed** [–d], *adj.* verwittert (*Geol.*). **– -eye,** *s.*; *keep one's – -eye open*, auf Wind und Wetter achten, (*fig.*) gut aufpassen. **– -forecast,** *s.* der Wetterbericht, die Wettermeldung, Wettervoraussage. **– -gauge,** *s.* die Luv(seite), Windseite, (*fig.*) der Vorteil. **– -glass,** *s.* das *or* der Barometer. **–ing,** *s.* die Verwitterung (*Geol.*). **–ly,** *adj.* luvgierig (*Naut.*). **–most,** *adj.* am weitesten luvwärts (*Naut.*). **– -proof,** *adj.* wetterfest, wetterdicht. **– -prophet,** *s.* der Wetterprophet. **– -side,** *s.* die Luv(seite), Windseite. **– -station,** *s.* die Wetterwarte. **– -tight,** *adj.* wetterdicht, wetterfest. **– -vane,** *s. see* **–cock.** **– -wise,** *adj.* wetterkundig. **– -worn,** *adj.* verwittert.

weav–e [wɪːv], 1. *ir.v.a.* weben; wirken (*fabric*), flechten (*a wreath, etc.*); (*fig.*) zusammenfügen, einflechten, verflechten, verweben (*into*, in); erfinden, erdichten, ersinnen; *–e in*, verweben (*with*, mit). 2. *ir.v.n.* weben; hin und her wenden, durchschlängeln (*through*, durch). 3. *s.* die Webart, das Gewebe. **–er,** *s.* der Weber, Wirker; (also *–er-bird*) der Webervogel. **–ing,** *s.* das Weben, Wirken, die Weberei; *–ing loom*, der Webstuhl; *–ing mill*, die Weberei.

web [wɛb], 1. *s.* das Gewebe (*also fig.*); die Schwimmhaut (*Zool.*); Fahne, der Bart (*of a feather*); (also *spider's –*), das Spinn(en)gewebe, die Spinnwebe; das Blatt (*of a saw*); der Stiel, Stag (*of a rail*); die Papierbahn, Papierrolle (*Print.*). 2. *v.a.* mit Netzwerk überziehen. **–bed** [–d], *adj.* mit Schwimmfüßen versehen. **–bing,** *s.* das Gurtband, der Gurt. **– -foot,** *s.* der Schwimmfuß. **– -footed,** *adj.* schwimmfüßig.

wed [wɛd], 1. *v.a.* (*Poet.*) heiraten (*a p.*), verheiraten, trauen (*a couple*), (*fig.*) verbinden, vereinigen; *be –ded to a th.*, einer S. sehr zugetan sein, an einer S. hängen, an eine S. gefesselt *or* gebunden sein. 2. *v.n.* (sich ver)heiraten. **–ded** [–ɪd], *adj.* verheiratet; Ehe–, ehelich. **–ding,** *s.* der Heirat, die Verheiratung (*of* (*Gen.*); *to*, mit); Hochzeit, Trauung. **–ding-breakfast,** *s.* das Hochzeitsessen, Hochzeitsmahl. **–ding-cake,** *s.* der Hochzeitskuchen. **–ding-day,** der Hochzeitstag. **–ding-dress,** *s.* das Brautkleid. **–ding-march,** *s.* der Hochzeitsmarsch. **–ding-night,** *s.* die Brautnacht. **–ding-present,** *s.* das Hochzeitsgeschenk. **–ding-ring,** *s.* der Trauring. **–ding-trip,** *s.* die Hochzeitsreise.

wedge [wɛdʒ], 1. *s.* der Keil; *the thin end of the –,* erster Anfang *or* Schritt. 2. *v.a.* (ver)keilen; einkeilen, eindrängen, einzwängen; *– o.s. in,* sich hineindrängen. **– -shaped,** *adj.* keilförmig.

wedlock [ˈwɛdlɔk], *s.* die Ehe; *in –,* ehelich; *out of –,* unehelich.

Wednesday [ˈwɛnsdeɪ], *s.* der Mittwoch; *on –s,* mittwochs.

wee [wɪ:], *adj.* (*Scots*) klein, winzig, –chen, –lein.

weed [wɪ:d], 1. *s.* das Unkraut (*also fig.*), (*Poet.*) Kraut, die Pflanze; (*coll.*) der Tabak, die Zigarre; (*sl.*) schmächtiger Mensch; (*Prov.*) *ill –s grow apace,* Unkraut verdirbt *or* vergeht nicht. 2. *v.a.* jäten; (*fig.*) säubern, reinigen (*of,* von); *– out,* (*fig.*) ausmerzen (*from,* aus *or* von). 3. *v.n.* Unkraut jäten. **–er,** *s.* der Jäter, die Jätmaschine. **– -grown,** *adj.* voll Unkraut. **–ing-fork,** *s.* die Jätharke. **– -killer,** *s.* das Unkrautvertilgungsmittel. **–y,** *adj.* voll Unkraut; (*coll.*) klapperdürr, schmächtig.

weeds [wɪ:dz], *pl.* (*archaic*) (only in) *widow's –,* die Witwenkleidung.

week [wɪ:k], *s.* die Woche; *Holy –,* die Karwoche; *last Monday –,* Montag vor 8 Tagen; *this day –,* heute in acht Tagen *or* über acht Tage; *a – or two,* einige Wochen; *twice a –,* zweimal wöchentlich; *by the –,* wochenweise; *– by –,* Woche für *or* um Woche; *for –s,* wochenlang; *– in, – out,* Woche für Woche. **– -day,** 1. *s.* der Wochentag, Alltag. 2. *attr.* Wochentags–, Alltags–. **– -end,** 1. *s.* das Wochenende. 2. *attr.* Wochenend–; *– -end ticket,* die Sonntags(fahr)karte. 3. *v.n.* das Wochenende verbringen. **– -ender,** *s.* der Wochenendausflügler. **–ly,** 1. *adj.* wöchentlich, Wochen–. 2. *adv.* wöchentlich. 3. *s.* das Wochenblatt, die Wochenschrift.

ween [wɪ:n], *v.n.* (*archaic*) wähnen, glauben; hoffen, vermuten.

weep [wɪ:p], 1. *v.n.* weinen (*at* or *over,* über; *for,* wegen) Tränen vergießen; (*fig.*) triefen, tröpfeln, träufeln; feucht sein, schwitzen; *– for a p.,* einen beweinen, um einen weinen; *– for pain,* vor Schmerz weinen. 2. *v.a.* weinen (*tears*). 3. *s.*; *have a good –,* sich ausweinen. **–er,** *s.* Weinende(r), Klagende(r), *m.*; der Trauerschleier, Trauerflor; *pl.* weiße Trauermanschetten (*of widows*). **–ing,** 1. *s.* das Weinen; *fall a-–ing,* in Tränen ausbrechen. 2. *adj.* weinend, trauernd; tränenvoll (*eyes*); triefend, tropfend, nässend (*Med.*); Trauer– (*Bot.*); *–ing willow,* die Trauerweide. **–y,** *adj.* (*coll.*) weinerlich, rührselig.

weevil [ˈwɪ:vl], *s.* der Kornwurm, Wiebel.

weft [wɛft], *s.* der Einschlag, (Ein)Schuß, Querfäden (*pl.*).

weigh [weɪ], 1. *v.a.* wiegen; (*fig.*) wägen, abwägen, erwägen, prüfen; *– the anchor,* den Anker lichten; ankerauf gehen (*navy only*); *– one's words,* seine Worte wägen; *– down,* niederdrücken, niederbeugen; *be –ed down,* niedergebeugt sein; *– in,* vor dem Kampf *or* Rennen wiegen (*boxers, jockeys*); *– out,* abwiegen, auswiegen (*to* or *for a p.,* einem); *– up,* (*coll.*) prüfen, abschätzen. 2. *v.n.* wiegen, schwer sein; (*fig.*) Gewicht haben, gelten, ausschlaggebend sein (*with,* bei); lasten, drücken (*on,* auf); *– in,* sich vor dem Rennen *or* Kampf wiegen lassen (*jockeys, boxers*); (*coll.*) *– in with,* energisch vorbringen. 3. *s.* das Wiegen; *under –,* see **way.** **–able,** *adj.* wägbar. **–age,** *s.* die Wägegebühr, das Wägegeld. **– -bridge,** *s.* die Brückenwaage. **–er,** *s.* der Wäger; der Waagemeister. **– -house,** *s.* öffentliche Waage. **–ing,** *s.* das Wiegen; (*fig.*) Abwägen, Erwägen, Prüfen. **–ing-machine,** *s.* die (Brücken)Waage. **–t** [–t], 1. *s.* das Gewicht (*also fig.*), die Schwere, Wucht; (*fig.*) das Ansehen, der Einfluß, Wert, die Wichtigkeit, Bedeutung, Geltung; Last, der Druck; *add –t to,* verstärken, erhöhen; *atomic –t,* das Atomgewicht; *by –t,* nach Gewicht; *carry –t with,* schwer wiegen *or* viel gelten bei, Einfluß *or* Wirkung haben mit, ins Gewicht fallen bei; *dead –t,* das Eigengewicht, (*fig.*) drückende Last; *give due –t to a th.,* etwas gebührend würdigen, einer S. volle Beachtung schenken; *full –t,* vollwichtig; *gross –t,* das Bruttogewicht; *2 lb. in –t,* 2 Pfd. schwer; *live –t,* das Lebendgewicht; *lose –t,* abnehmen; *net –t,* das Nettogewicht; *of –t,* gewichtig; *pull one's –t,* das Seinige tun; *put the –t,* Kugel stoßen; *putting the –t,* das Kugelstoßen; *put on –t,* Fett ansetzen; *throw one's –t about,* seinen Einfluß zur Geltung bringen, auf seinen Einfluß pochen; *what is your –t?* wieviel wiegen Sie?; *the –t of years,* die Last der Jahre. 2. *v.a.* belasten, beschweren; relative Bedeutung geben (*Dat.*) (*Statistics*); *–t the scales in favour of,* etwas in die Waagschale werfen für. **–t-lifting,** *s.* das Gewichtheben. **–tiness,** *s.* die Schwere; (*fig.*) das Gewicht, die Wichtigkeit, Bedeutung, Bedeutsamkeit. **–ty,** *adj.* schwer; (*fig.*) (ge)wichtig, erheblich, schwerwiegend, bedeutsam.

weir [wɪ:ə], *s.* das Wehr; die Reuse (*for fish*).

weird [wɪ:əd], 1. *adj.* geisterhaft, geheimnisvoll, unheimlich; (*coll.*) seltsam, eigenartig, merkwürdig; *the – sisters,* die Schicksalsschwestern. 2. *s.* (*archaic & Scots*) das Schicksal; die Hexe, Zauberin; (*Scots*) *dree one's –,* sein Schicksal ertragen. **–ness,** *s.* das Unheimliche.

welcome [ˈwɛlkəm], 1. *adj.* willkommen (*of a p. or th.*), erfreulich, angenehm (*of a th.*); (*pred. only*) herzlich eingeladen (*of a p.*), gern zugelassen (*of a th.*); *make a p. –,* einen willkommen heißen; (*coll.*) *take it and –,* nehmen Sie es gern; (*coll.*) *you're –,* nichts zu danken, gern geschehen, keine Ursache; *you are – to do,* es steht Ihnen frei zu tun; *you are – (to it),* es steht Ihnen zur Verfügung, bitte behalten Sie es; (*coll.*) *you're – to your own opinion,* meinetwegen kannst du dir denken was du willst. 2. *s.* der Willkomm, der *or* das Willkommen; der Willkomm(en)sgruß (*to,* an); die Bewillkommnung, freundliche Aufnahme; *bid a p. –,* einen willkommen heißen; *give a kind – to s.o.,* einen freundlich aufnehmen; *outstay one's –,* länger bleiben als man gern gesehen ist; *words of –,* Willkommensworte (*pl.*). 3. *v.a.* bewillkommnen (*also fig.*), willkommen heißen, (*fig.*) begrüßen, gern annehmen. 4. *int.* willkommen!; *– home!* willkommen in der Heimat!

weld [wɛld], 1. *v.a.* (zusammen)schweißen, anschweißen; (*fig.*) zusammenfügen, zusammenschmieden, vereinigen. 2. *v.n.* sich schweißen (lassen). 3. *s.* die Schweißstelle, Schweißnaht. **–able,** *adj.* schweißbar. **–ed** [–ɪd], *adj.* geschweißt, Schweiß–. **–ing,** *s.* die Schweißarbeit, Schweißung. **–less,** *adj.* nahtlos.

welfare [ˈwɛlfɛə], *s.* die Wohlfahrt, das Wohlergehen; die Fürsorge. **– -centre,** *s.* das Fürsorgeamt, die Betreuungsstelle. **– -work,** soziale Fürsorge. **– -worker,** *s.* der Fürsorger.

welkin [ˈwɛlkɪn], *s.* (*Poet.*) der Himmel, das Himmelszelt.

[1]**well** [wɛl], 1. *s.* der (Zieh)Brunnen, die Quelle (*also fig.*); der (Öl)Schacht, das Bohrloch; der Pumpensod (*in a ship*); das Treppenhaus (*of stairs*); der Luftschacht, Lichtschacht, Fahrstuhlschacht; Gepäckraum (*in cars*); das Tintenfaß; der Fischbehälter (*in fishing boats*); (*fig.*) der Urquell, Ursprung; *sink a –,* einen Brunnen bohren *or* graben. 2. *v.n.* (also *– out, – up, – forth*), hervorquellen (*also fig.*), hervorsprudeln, hervorströmen (*from,* aus); *– over,* überfließen. **– -head,** *s.* die Urquelle; Brunneneinfassung. **– -spring,** *s.* die Quelle, der Urquell. **– -water,** *s.* das Brunnenwasser, Quellwasser.

[2]**well,** 1. *adv.* gut, richtig, befriedigend; tüchtig, beträchtlich, in hohem Grade; gründlich, wohl, mit Recht, vielleicht; (*before adjectives*) wohl, durchaus; *– able,* wohl *or* durchaus imstande; *as –,* (*at end of clause*) ebenso, noch dazu, außerdem, desgleichen, ebensogut; *you may just as – come,* du kannst ebensogut kommen; *that is just as –,* das ist ebensogut so; *as – as,* so gut wie, sowohl als auch; *you as – as I,* sowohl du wie ich, du sowohl wie ich; *– and truly,* gründlich, einwandfrei; *do –,* Erfolg haben; *he is doing –,* es geht ihm gut; *do o.s. –,* sich gütlich tun; *– done,* durchgebraten, gar (*of food*);

– *done!* bravo!; *let – alone*, die Hände davon lassen, sich nicht einmischen; *– met!* du kommst wie gerufen! *I don't – know*, ich weiß nicht recht; *you may – ask*, du kannst wohl *or* mit Recht fragen; *you cannot very – ask*, du kannst wohl nicht *or* nicht gerade *or* nicht gut fragen; *speak – of*, Gutes reden von, loben; *stand – with s.o.*, gut stehen mit einem, gut angeschrieben sein bei einem; *wish a p. –*, einem Erfolg wünschen; *take a th. –*, etwas gut aufnehmen; (*with adverbs & prepositions*) *– away*, weit weg, (*coll.*) gut im Zuge *or* Schwung; *– on in years*, an Jahren vorgeschritten; *– into*, bis spät *or* mitten in (*Acc.*). 2. *pred. adj.* wohl, gesund; in Ordnung; richtig, ratsam; *be* or *feel –*, sich wohl fühlen; *he is not –*, ihm ist nicht wohl; (*Prov.*) *all's – that ends –*, Ende gut, alles gut; *all being –*, wenn alles gut geht; *– and good*, schön und gut; *– enough*, ziemlich gut, ganz leidlich; *it is – for us that*, es ist gut *or* günstig daß; *it would be –*, es würde sich empfehlen (*to do*, daß . . .); *that's all very – but . . .*, das ist alles ganz schön und gut, aber. . . . 3. *int.*; *!* nun! schön! nun wohl! unerhört!; *– ?* nun? na? und nachher?; *– then!* nun also!; *– then ?* nun also? **--a-day,** *int.* (*archaic*) wehe! leider! **--advised,** *adj.* wohl überlegt, ratsam. **--appointed,** *adj.* wohl ausgestattet *or* ausgerüstet. **--balanced,** *adj.* im Gleichgewicht, (*fig.*) ausgeglichen, gesetzt, ruhig (*a p.*), abgewogen (*reasons, etc.*). **--behaved,** *adj.* wohlerzogen, artig, manierlich. **--being,** *s.* das Wohlsein, Wohlergehen; Wohl, die Wohlfahrt; das Wohlgefühl, Wohlbehagen. **--beloved,** *adj.* vielgeliebt. **--born,** *adj.* aus guter Familie. **--bred,** *adj.* wohlerzogen. **--built,** *adj.* wohlgebaut. **--chosen,** *adj.* gut gewählt, passend. **--connected,** *adj.* mit guten Beziehungen. **--deserved,** *adj.* wohlverdient. **--deserving,** *adj.* verdienstvoll. **--directed,** *adj.* gut gezielt (*blow*). **--disposed,** *adj.* wohlgesinnt (*towards*, gegen; *to a p.* (*Dat.*)). **--doing,** *s.* gute Werke, das Wohltun. **--dressed,** *adj.* gut angezogen. **--earned,** *adj.* wohlverdient. **--educated,** *adj.* gebildet. **--favoured,** *adj.* hübsch, schön. **--fed,** *adj.* wohl genährt. **--founded, --grounded,** *adj.* wohlbegründet. **--groomed,** *adj.* gut angezogen. **--informed,** *adj.* wohlunterrichtet. **--intentioned,** *adj.* wohlgemeint, wohlmeinend (*as a rebuke, etc.*), wohlgesinnt. **--judged,** *adj.* wohlangebracht, passend. **--kept,** *adj.* wohlgepflegt. **--knit,** *adj.* kräftig gebaut. **--known,** *adj.* (wohl)bekannt. **--loved,** *adj.* vielgeliebt, teuer. **--made,** *adj.* kräftig gebaut (*as a man*), gut gemacht (*as clothes, etc.*). **--mannered,** *adj.* wohlerzogen, manierlich. **--matched,** *adj.* gut zusammenpassend. **--meaning,** *adj.* wohlwollend, wohlmeinend; *she is --meaning*, sie meint es gut. **--meant,** *adj.* wohlgemeint. **--nigh,** *adv.* fast, beinahe. (*coll.*) **--off,** *adj.* in guten Verhältnissen, gut situiert, wohlhabend; *--off for*, gut versehen mit. (*sl.*) **--oiled,** *adj.* beschwipst. (*coll.*) **--padded,** *adj.* dick, fett, wohlbeleibt (*of a p.*). **--pleasing,** *adj.* wohlgefällig. **--preserved,** *adj.* wohlerhalten. **--proportioned,** *adj.* wohlgebaut. **--read,** *adj.* belesen, bewandert (*in*, in). **--regulated,** *adj.* wohlgeordnet. **--rounded,** *adj.* wohlabgerundet, elegant (*style*). **--set,** *adj.* muskulös, sehnig. **--spoken,** *adj.* höflich im Ausdruck. **--thought-out,** *adj.* wohldurchdacht. **--thumbed,** *adj.* abgegriffen. **--timed,** *adj.* angebracht, rechtzeitig; zeitgemäß. **--to-do,** *adj.* wohlhabend. **--tried,** *adj.* erprobt. **--trodden,** *adj.* ausgetreten, (*fig.*) oft behandelt, abgedroschen. **--turned,** *adj.* wohlabgerundet, wohlgedrechselt, wohlgesetzt (*speech*). **--wisher,** *s.* der Gönner, Freund. **--worded,** *adj.* wohlgesetzt (*of speech, etc.*). **--worn,** *adj.* abgenutzt, abgetragen; ausgetreten (*shoes*), (*fig.*) abgedroschen, abgegriffen.

wellington ['wɛlɪŋtən]; *– boots*, Schaftstiefel, Stulpenstiefel; (*usually*) Gummistiefel, Wasserstiefel (*m.pl.*).

wels [wɛls], *s.* der Wels (*Ichth.*).

Welsh [wɛlʃ], *adj.* *see Index of Names*; *– rabbit*, geröstete Käseschnitte. 2. *v.a.* (um sein Geld) betrügen. (*sl.*) **-er,** *s.* betrügerischer Buchmacher.

welt [wɛlt], 1. *s.* der Rand, die Einfassung (*of a shoe*); (*sl.*) der Striemen, Schmiß, die Strieme, Schmarre; der Schlag. 2. *v.a.* einfassen, säumen (*soles*); (*sl.*) schlagen, durchprügeln.

[1]**welter** ['wɛltə], 1. *v.n.* sich wälzen, rollen. 2. *s.* der Wirrwarr, das Gewirr, Durcheinander, Chaos, wirre Masse.

[2]**welter,** 1. *s.* schwerer Reiter. 2. *adj.* (also *-weight*) Weltergewichts- (*boxer*). **--weight,** *s.* das Weltergewicht (*Boxing*) (= *bis 147 lb.*).

wen [wɛn], *s.* die Geschwulst.

wench [wɛnʃ], 1. *s.* (*archaic or vulg.*) das Frauenzimmer, Mädchen; (*archaic*) die (Straßen)Dirne. 2. *v.n.* (*vulg.*) huren.

wend [wɛnd], *v.a.* (only in) *– one's way*, sich begeben, seinen Weg nehmen, seine Schritte lenken (*to*, nach *or* zu).

went [wɛnt], *see* **go.**

wept [wɛpt], *see* **weep.**

were [wɛə], *see* **be.** (*2nd pers. imperf.*) warst, waren; (*1st, 2nd, or 3rd pers. pl. imperf.*) waren, waret; (*sing. & pl. imperf. subj.*) wäre(n); *there –*, es gab, es waren; *we – to do it*, wir sollten es tun; *as it –*, gleichsam, sozusagen; *as you – !* (Griff) zurück! (*Mil. & coll.*).

we're [wɪə], abbr. of *we are.*

werewolf ['wɪəwʊlf], *s.* der Werwolf.

west [wɛst], 1. *s.* der Westen; West (*Poet. & Naut.*); (*Poet.*) Westwind; *the –*, das Abendland; westliche Staaten (*Amer.*); *– by north*, West zum Nord; *in the – of*, im westlichen Teil von; *the wind is in the –*, der Wind kommt von Westen; *to the – of*, westlich von. 2. *adv.* nach Westen, westwärts; (*sl.*) *go –*, untergehen, verlorengehen; sterben; *– of*, westlich von. **--bound,** *adj.* nach Westen fahrend. **– country,** *s.* der (Süd)Westen Englands. **– End,** *s.* das Westend. **-er,** 1. *adj.* (*Scots*) westlich gelegen. 2. *v.n.* (*Poet.*) nach Westen ziehen *or* neigen. **-erly,** *adj.* im Westen gelegen; aus dem *or* vom Westen kommend (*wind*). **-ern,** 1. *attrib. adj.* westlich, West-, abendländisch; *-ern empire*, weströmisches Reich. 2. *s.* der Weststaatler (*Amer.*), Wildwestfilm, Wildwestroman. **-erner,** *s.* der Abendländer; Weststaatler (*Amer.*). **-ernize,** *v.a.* abendländischen Charakter geben (*Dat.*). **-ernmost,** *adj.* westlichst. **-ing,** *s.* die Entfernung nach Westen, westliche Richtung. **-ward,** 1. *adj.* westlich. 2. *adv.* im Westen, westwärts. 3. *s.* westliche Richtung; *to the -ward of*, westlich von. **-wards,** *adv.* westwärts, westlich.

wet [wɛt], 1. *adj.* naß, feucht (*with*, von); regnerisch (*as weather*); (*coll.*) nicht unter Akoholverbot stehend; *– blanket*, der Dämpfer, kalte Dusche; der Spielverderber; *– and cold*, naßkalt; *– dock*, der Dockhafen; *– paint!* frisch gestrichen!; *– pack* or *poultice*, feuchte Packung; *– through*, durchnäßt; *– to the skin*, bis auf die Haut naß; *– with tears*, tränenbenetzt; *– weather*, das Regenwetter. 2. *s.* die Nässe, Feuchtigkeit; das Regenwetter; *out in the –*, draußen im Regen. 3. *v.a.* naß machen, (durch)nässen, anfeuchten, benetzen; (*sl.*) begießen; (*sl.*) *– one's whistle*, die Kehle anfeuchten. **-ness,** *s.* die Nässe, Feuchtigkeit. **--nurse,** 1. *s.* die Amme. 2. *v.a.* (als Amme) säugen. **-ting,** *s.* die Durchnässung; *get a -ting*, durchnäßt *or* naß werden. **-tish,** *adj.* ziemlich *or* etwas naß.

wether ['wɛðə], *s.* der Hammel, Schöps.

we've [wɪːv], abbr. of *we have.*

wey [weɪ], *s.* (*archaic*) ein Trockengewicht (40 Scheffel (*salt*), 182 Pfund (*wool*), 48 Scheffel (*corn, coal, etc.*).

whack [wæk], 1. *s.* (*coll.*) derber Schlag *or* Hieb; (*sl.*) der Anteil; Versuch; *get one's –*, seinen Anteil bekommen; *have a – at*, sich wagen an, anpacken. 2. *v.a.* (*coll.*) schlagen (*also at games*), verhauen, durchprügeln. **-er,** *s.* (*sl.*) das Mordsding, etwas Großartiges; plumper Schwindel. **-ing,** 1. *s.* (*sl.*) Schläge (*pl.*), die Tracht Prügel. 2. *adj.* (*sl.*) gewaltig, enorm.

whal-e [(h)weɪl], 1. *s.* der Wal(fisch); (*sl.*) *a -e of a time*, der Mordsspaß; (*sl.*) *be a -e on*, versessen sein auf. 2. *v.n.* auf Walfischfang gehen. **-ebone,** *s.* das Walfischbein. **-e-fishery,** *s.* der Walfischfang. **-e-oil,** *s.* der Walfischtran. **-er,** *s.* das Walfischboot, der Walfänger. **-ing,** *s.* der Walfischfang.

wharf [wɔ:f], *s.* der Kai, Landungsplatz, Ladeplatz. **–age** [–ɪdʒ], *s.* die Ladegelegenheit, Löschgelegenheit; das Kaigeld. **–inger,** *s.* der Kaimeister, Kaiaufseher.

what [(h)wɔt], 1. *rel. pron.* was, das was; *nothing (compared) to – . . .*, nichts im Vergleich zu dem, was . . .; *being – it is*, wie es nun mal ist; *with – appeared (to be)* or *was apparently a serious attempt*, mit einem scheinbar ernsten Versuch; *my opinion for – it is worth*, meine unmaßgebliche Meinung; *he spent – he had*, er gab alles aus, was er bei sich hatte; – *is more*, außerdem, vor allem. 2. *inter. pron.* was? wie?; – *about?* wie steht es mit?; – *for?* warum? zu welchem Zweck? wofür? wozu?; – *if?* wie wenn? – *next?* was nun? sonst noch was? was denn noch? – *of it?* wenn schon?; – *of that?* was liegt daran? was tut's?; (*coll.*) *Mr. –'s his name*, *Mr. – -do-you-call-him*, Herr Dingsda; – *is his name?* wie heißt er?; *not know – to say*, nicht wissen was man sagen soll; (*coll.*) *I know –*, ich weiß schon; (*coll.*) *I'll tell you –*, ich will dir was sagen; *know –'s –*, im Bilde sein, wissen was los ist; *tell s.o. –'s –*, einem sagen was eine Harke ist; *and – not*, und was nicht alles, und was weiß ich noch alles. 3. *adj.* was für (eine(r, –s)), welche(r, –s); – *time is it?* wieviel Uhr ist es? wie spät ist es?; *he spent – money he had*, er gab aus was er an Geld hatte; *we took – things were left*, wir nahmen alles was geblieben war; *come – time you like*, kommen Sie, wann Sie wollen; (*as interjection*) – *a man!* was für ein Mann!; – *virtue!* welche Tugend!; – *haven't we suffered!* wie sehr haben wir gelitten! 4. *adv. or conj.* – *though*, was tut es wenn, und wenn auch; – *with . . .*, – *with . . .*, or – *with . . . and . . .*, teils durch . . . teils durch . . .; – *with one thing and another*, wenn eins zum andern kommt. **–ever** [–ˈɛvə], (*emphatic*) **–soever,** 1. *rel. pron.* was auch (immer), was nur; *–ever you do*, was Sie auch tun; (*coll.*) *inter. pron.* (= – *ever*), was . . . nur? was in aller Welt? 5. *adj.* einerlei welche(r, –s, –n), was für . . . auch immer; (*after noun, emphatic*) *any person –ever*, jede beliebige P.; *nothing –ever*, absolut nichts; *no sense –ever*, nicht der geringste Verstand; (*coll.*) (*as interrogative* = – *ever*), was nur für ein? **– -not** [–nɔt], *s.* der Nipptisch, die Etagere.

wheat [(h)wɪ:t], *s.* der Weizen. **–ear,** *s.* der Steinschmätzer (*Orn.*). **–en,** *adj.* Weizen–.

wheedle [ˈ(h)wɪ:dl], 1. *v.a.* beschmeicheln, beschwatzen; – *a p. into*, einen durch glatte Worte *or* Schmeichelei überreden *or* beschwatzen zu; – *a p. out of a th.*, einem etwas abschwatzen. 2. *v.a.* schmeicheln.

wheel [(h)wɪ:l], 1. *s.* das Rad; (*fig.*) die Umdrehung, Schwenkung (*Mil.*); *at the –*, am Steuer, (*fig.*) am Ruder; *break on the –*, aufs Rad flechten, rädern; *break a fly on the –*, offene Türen einrennen; *the – has come full circle*, das Rad hat sich einmal gedreht; *free –*, der Freilauf; *put a spoke in s.o.'s –*, einem ein Hindernis in den Weg legen; *put one's shoulder to the –*, sich ins Zeug legen, tüchtig ins Zeug gehen, sich anstrengen; *potter's –*, die Töpferscheibe; *spinning –*, das Spinnrad; *steering –*, das Steuerrad; (*fig.*) *–s within –s*, verwickelte Verhältnisse, Verwicklungen. 2. *v.n.* sich (im Kreise) drehen, schwenken (*Mil.*); *left –!* links schwenkt!; (also – *round*) sich umdrehen. 3. *v.a.* schieben; (herum– *or* um)drehen; (auf Rädern) befördern; schwenken lassen (*Mil.*). **–barrow,** *s.* der Schubkarren, der Schiebkarren. **– -base,** *s.* der Radstand. **– -chair,** *s.* der Rollstuhl. **–ed** [–d], *suffix*, –räderig; *–ed traffic*, der Wagenverkehr **–er,** 1. *s.* see **– -horse.** 2. *suffix* –rädriger Wagen. **– -horse,** *s.* das Stangenpferd, das Deichselpferd. **– -house,** das Steuerhaus (*Naut.*). **–man,** *s.* (*coll.*) der Radfahrer, Radler. **–wright,** *s.* der Stellmacher, der Wagner.

wheez–e [(h)wɪ:z], 1. *v.n.* keuchen, schnaufen. 2. *s.* keuchender Ton; (*sl.*) witzige Zwischenbemerkung, der Scherz, Ulk, Jux. **–y,** *adj.* keuchend, schnaufend.

[1]**whelk** [(h)wɛlk], *s.* die Wellhornschnecke.

[2]**whelk,** *s.* der Pickel, die Pustel, Finne.

whelm [hwɛlm], *v.a.* (*Poet.*) verschütten, versenken; (*fig.*) überschütten, überdecken.

whelp [(h)wɛlp], 1. *s.* junger Hund, das Junge; (*fig.*) junger Bursche. 2. *v.n.* Junge werfen.

when [(h)wɛn], 1. *adv.* (*inter.*) wann?; *since – ?* seit wann?; *till – ?* bis wann?; (*coll.*) *say – !* sag halt!; (*relat.*) *since –*, seit dieser Zeit; *the time –*, die Zeit zu der *or* in der; *times –*, Zeiten in denen. 2. *conj.* als, sobald als, zu der Zeit als, während, nachdem (*with past tense*); wenn, jedesmal wenn (*with present tense*); – *due*, bei Verfall, zur Verfallzeit; *even –*, selbst dann wenn; – *received*, nach Empfang; *just –*, gerade *or* eben als. **–(so)ever,** *conj.* wenn (auch) immer, einerlei wann, allemal wenn, so oft als; (*coll.*) (= – *ever*) wann? (*emphatic*).

whence [(h)wɛns], 1. (*archaic*) *adv.* woher (*also fig.*), woraus, von wo, (*fig.*) wie. 2. *conj.* und daher.

where [(h)wɛə], 1. *adv.* (*inter.*) wo? wohin?; (*relat.*) (dort *or* da) wo, (dahin) wo, den Ort wo, wohin; (*sl.*) *tell s.o. – to get off*, einem zeigen was eine Harke ist. 2. *pron.* (*inter.*) – . . . *from?* woher? von wo?; – . . . *to?* wohin?; (*relat.*) *from –*, wo, von daher; *near –*, nahe an der Stelle wo; *the place –*, der Ort wo *or* an dem; *to –*, dahin wo, wo; *before they know – they are*, ehe sie wissen woran sie sind. **–abouts,** 1. *adv.* wo ungefähr *or* etwa, ungefähr den Ort wo. 2. *s.* zeitweiliger Aufenthalt *or* Wohnort. **–as,** *conj.* wohingegen, während (doch *or* sonst), da nun; (all)dieweil, in Anbetracht dessen daß (*Law*). **–at,** *adv.* (*inter.*) worüber?; (*relat.*) wobei, und dabei; worüber, und darauf; worauf, und darauf. **–by** *adv.* (*inter.*) wodurch? wie?; (*relat.*) wodurch, womit. **–fore,** 1. *adv.* (*inter.*) weshalb? warum? wozu?; (*relat.*) weswegen, und deshalb. 2. *s.* das Warum. **–from,** *adv.* (*archaic*), von wo. **–in,** *adv.* (*inter.*) worin?; (*relat.*) worin, in dem *or* der *or* denen; und hierein, worin. **–of,** *adv.* (*relat.*) von dem *or* der *or* denen; und hierein, worin. **–on,** *adv.* (*inter.*) worauf ?; (*relat.*) worauf, auf der *or* dem *or* denen. **–soever,** *adv.* (*emphatic*) *see* **–ver.** **–to, –unto,** *adv.* wohin, wozu, woran, worauf, wonach, und danach. **–ver,** *adv.* wo(hin) auch nur, wo(hin) auch immer, überall wo. **–with,** *adv.* womit. **the –withal,** das Nötige, das (nötige) Geld, die (Geld)Mittel (*pl.*).

wherry [ˈ(h)wɛrɪ], *s.* die Fähre, Jolle. **–man,** *s.* der Fährmann.

whet [(h)wɛt], 1. *v.a.* wetzen, schärfen, schleifen, (*fig.*) reizen, anregen (*the appetite*). 2. *s.* das Wetzen, (*fig.*) Reizmittel. **–stone,** *s.* der Wetzstein, der Schleifstein.

whether [(h)wɛðə], *conj.* ob; – . . . *or not*, ob . . . oder nicht; – *or no*, so oder so, auf jeden Fall.

whew [hwʊ:], *int.* huh! hui!

whey [hweɪ], *s.* die Molke, der Molken, das Käsewasser. **–ey** [ˈ–ɪ], *adj.* molkenartig, molkig. **– -faced,** *adj.* blaß, bläßlich.

which [(h)wɪtʃ], 1. *rel. pron.* der, die, das, welche(–r, –s) (*referring to things*), was (*referring to preceding clause or indef. pron.*); *all of –*, die alle, von denen alle; (*B.*) *our Father, – art in Heaven*, unser Vater, der du bist im Himmel; *I told him to go, – he did*, ich sagte, er sollte gehen, und das tat er; *everything –*, alles was; *take – you will*, nehmen Sie welche(–n, –s,) Sie wollen; *the crime of – you accuse him*, das Verbrechen, dessen Sie ihn beschuldigen. 2. *inter. pron.* welcher(–e, –s) (*of p. or th.*); – *of you?* wer *or* welcher von Ihnen? *I don't know – is –*, ich kann sie nicht unterscheiden. 3. *inter. adj.* welche(–r, –s). 4. *rel. adj.*; – *things always happen*, Dinge die immer vorkommen. **–ever,** *rel. pron.* welcher, welche, welches *or* was auch (immer).

whiff [(h)wɪf], *s.* der Hauch (*also fig.*), (Luft)Zug, (*fig.*) Anflug; Zug (*of a pipe, etc.*); kleine Zigarre; *take a – at one's pipe*, einen Zug aus der Pfeife tun. **–le** [–l] *v.n.* böig wehen (*of the wind*).

whig [(h)wɪg], (englischer) Liberale.

whil–e [ˈ(h)waɪl], 1. *s.* die Weile, (Zeit)Spanne (inzwischen); *a little –e*, eine (kleine) Weile; *in a little –e*, bald; *a little –e ago* or *since*, vor kurzem, kürzlich, unlängst, (erst) kurze Zeit her; *a long –e*, eine lange *or* ganze Weile; *a long –e ago*, vor langer Zeit, (schon) lange her; *between –es*, dann und wann, **zuweilen**; *quite a –e*, eine ganze Weile; *for a –e*, eine zeitlang; *worth (one's) –e*, der Mühe wert; *be worth –e*, sich lohnen; *make it worth s.o.'s –e*, es einem vergelten, einen belohnen; *worth–e, attrib. adj.* lohnend; *once in a –e*, gelegentlich, dann und wann; *the –e*, derweil, so lange, während der Zeit; *all the –e*, die ganze Zeit über; 2. *v.a.* (*usually*) *–e away* (*time*), sich (die Zeit) vertreiben, verbringen (*with*, mit). 3. *conj.* während, solange (als *or* nur), indem; während (hingegen), wo(hin)gegen. **–om** [ˈhwɑɪləm], (*archaic*) 1. *adj.* vormalig, früher. 2. *adv.* vormals, weiland. **–st** [(h)wɑ́ɪlst], *conj.* see **while** 3.

[1]**whim** [(h)wɪm], *s.* wunderlicher Einfall, die Laune, Grille.

[2]**whim,** *s.* der Göpel (*Mach.*).

whimbrel [ˈhwɪmbrəl], *s.* der Regenbrachvogel.

whimper [ˈ(h)wɪmpə], 1. *v.n.* wimmern, winseln. 2. *s.* das Wimmern, Winseln. **–ing,** *s.* das Gewimmer, Gewinsel.

whims–ical [ˈ(h)wɪmsɪkl], *adj.* grillenhaft, launisch, seltsam, wunderlich. **–icality** [–ˈkælɪtɪ], die Grillenhaftigkeit, Wunderlichkeit. **–y,** 1. *s.* die Laune, Grille, wunderlicher Einfall. 2. *adj.* wunderlich.

[1]**whin** [(h)wɪn], *s.* der Stechginster (*Bot.*). **–berry,** *s.* die Heidelbeere. **–chat,** *s.* das Braunkehlchen (*Orn.*).

[2]**whin,** *s.* der Basalt, Dolerit, Trapp (*Geol.*).

whin–e [(h)wɑɪn], 1. *v.n.* winseln, wimmern, greinen, quengeln, klagen, jammern. 2. *s.* das Greinen, Quengeln. **–ing,** 1. *adj.* wimmernd, winselnd. 2. das Gewimmel, Gejammer.

whinny [ˈ(h)wɪnɪ], 1. *v.n.* wiehern. 2. *s.* das Wiehern.

whinstone [ˈ(h)wɪnstoun], *s. see* [2]**whin.**

whip [(h)wɪp], 1. *s.* die Peitsche, (*fig.*) Zuchtrute, Geißel; der Kutscher; Einpeitscher (*Parl.*), Pikör (*Hunt.*); *––and-top*, der Kreisel; *be a good –*, gut fahren. 2. *v.a.* peitschen, mit der Peitsche schlagen *or* antreiben; treiben (*tops*); überschlagen, übernähen (*a seam*); überwendlich nähen (*a garment, etc.*); umwickeln (*a rope*); schlagen (*eggs, cream*); strafen, züchtigen (*a p.*); (*coll.*) schlagen, besiegen, übertreffen (*a p.*); *–ped cream*, die Schlagsahne; *–ped seam*, überwendliche Naht; *– the stream*, durch widerholtes Werfen den Fluß abangeln; *–ped white of egg*, der Eiweißschnee; (*coll.*) *– away*, fortreißen, schnell wegnehmen; *– in*, zusammentreiben (*hounds*) (*Hunt.*), zusammenbringen, zusammentrommeln (*members*) (*Parl.*); (*coll.*) *– off*, schnell wegnehmen (*a th.*), fortreißen, mit sich nehmen (*a p.*); (*coll.*) *– on*, schnell überwerfen, anziehen (*a garment*); (*coll.*) *– out*, schnell (aus der Tasche) ziehen; *– up*, antreiben (*a horse*), (*coll.*) schnell aufnehmen, aufraffen (*a th.*), zusammentrommeln (*persons*), aufpeitschen (*enthusiasm, etc.*). 3. *v.n.* hüpfen, springen, schnellen. **–cord,** *s.* die Peitschenschnur, die Schmicke; der Kord (*fabric*). **––hand,** *s.* rechte Hand; (*fig.*) *have the ––hand of a p.*, die Oberhand über einen haben, einen in seiner Gewalt haben. **––lash,** *s.* der Peitschenriemen. (*coll.*) **––round,** *s.* die Geldsammlung. **–per,** *s.* Peitschende(r); *m.* **–er-in,** *s.* der Pikör (*Hunt.*) (*coll.*). **–per-snapper,** freches Bürschchen, der Naseweis, Gelbschnabel. **–ping,** *s.* das Peitschen, das Züchtigen, die Tracht Prügel, Hiebe (*pl.*); das Umwickeln, umwickeltes Garn (*Naut.*). **–ing-boy,** *s.* der Prügeljunge. **–ping-post,** *s.* der Schandpfahl. **–ping-top,** *s.* see *––and-top.* **–py,** *adj.* biegsam, federnd. **–saw,** 1. *s.* die Schrotsäge, der Fuchsschwanz. 2. *v.n.* (*sl.*) Bestechung von zwei Seiten annehmen (*Amer. Pol.*).

whippet [ˈ(h)wɪpɪt], *s.* die Kreuzung zwischen Windhund und Terrier; leichter schneller Tank (*Mil.*).

whippletree [ˈ(h)wɪpltrɪː], *s.* das Ortscheit, der Schwenzel.

whip-poor-will [ˈ(h)wɪpʊəwɪl], *s.* der Ziegenmelker (*Orn.*) (*Amer.*).

whir, *see* **whirr.**

whirl [(h)wəːl], 1. *v.n.* wirbeln (*also fig.*), (sich) drehen, (*fig.*) schwindeln, schwindlig werden (*of the head*); *– around*, sich plötzlich umdrehen; *my head –s*, mir schwindelt, es wirbelt mir im Kopf. 2. *v.a.* (herum)drehen, schwingen; *– off* or *away*, fortwirbeln, fortschleudern, forttragen. 2. *s.* der Wirbel, Strudel; (*fig.*) wirres Forttreiben, das Gewirre; *in a –*, in wilder Eile; *his head was in a –*, ihm schwindelte der Kopf. **–bone,** *s.* das Kugelgelenk (*Anat.*). **–igig,** *s.* das Karussel, (*fig.*) der Taumel, Strudel. **–pool,** der Strudel, Wirbel. **–wind,** *s.* der Wirbelwind, die Windhose, (*fig.*) der Wirbel, das Gewirre.

whirr [(h)wəː], 1. *v.n.* schwirren. 2. *s.* das Schwirren.

whisht [(h)wɪʃt], *see* [1]**whist.**

whisk [(h)wɪsk], 1. *s.* der (Staub)Wedel, (Stroh)-Wisch, Wischer; der Eierschläger (*for eggs*); plötzliche Bewegung (*of the tail, etc.*). 2. *v.a.* fegen, kehren, wischen; schlagen (*eggs*); *– away* or *off*, schnell wegtun (*a th.*), schnell fortnehmen (*a p.*). 3. *v.n.* flitzen, huschen.

whisker [ˈ(h)wɪskə], *s.* (*usually pl.*) der Backenbart; Bart; Schnauzhaare (*of cats etc.*). **–ed** [–d], *adj.* bärtig.

whisky [ˈ(h)wɪskɪ], *s.* der Whisky, Kornbrandwein.

whisper [ˈ(h)wɪspə], 1. *s.* das Flüstern, Raunen, Rascheln; (*usually pl.*) die Zuflüsterung, das Gemunkel; *in a –*, im Flüsterton. 2. *v.n.* flüstern, wispern; raunen, munkeln; wispeln, rauschen, rascheln (*as leaves*); 3. *v.a.* (ins Ohr) flüstern, zuflüstern (*a th. to a p.*, einem etwas); *it is –ed*, man munkelt. **–er,** *s.* Zuflüsterer, Zuträger, Ohrenbläser. **–ing,** 1. wispernd, flüsternd. 2. das Flüstern, das Geflüster; *–ing gallery*, das Flüstergewölbe.

[1]**whist** [(h)wɪst], *int.* still! pst!

[2]**whist** *s.* das Whist(spiel). **––drive,** *s.* das Whisttournier.

whistl–e [(h)wɪsl], 1. *v.n.* pfeifen (*also of birds and fig.*), flöten; (*fig.*) heulen (*of wind*), schwirren (*of bullets*); (*coll.*) *–e for*, vergeblich erwarten *or* trachten nach; (*coll.*) *he can –e for it*, darauf kann er lange warten; *–e for one's money*, das Geld in den Schornstein schreiben. 2. *v.a.* pfeifen, flöten (*a tune*). 3. *s.* das Pfeifen, der Pfiff; die Pfeife, Flöte; *blow a –e*, pfeifen, das Pfeifensignal geben; (*sl.*) *wet one's –e*, sich (*Dat.*) die Kehle anfeuchten. **–ing,** 1. *adj.* pfeifend; *–ing kettle*, der Flötenkessel. 2. *s.* das Pfeifen.

whit [(h)wɪt], *s.* das Jota, bißchen; *every – as bad*, in jeder Hinsicht ebenso schlecht; *not* or *never a –*, nicht im geringsten, keineswegs, durchaus nicht.

Whit [hwɪt], *adj.* Pfingst–; *– Monday*, der Pfingstmontag; *– Sunday*, der Pfingstsonntag; *– week*, die Pfingstwoche; *see* **Whitsun.**

whit–e [(h)wɑɪt], 1. *adj.* weiß; farblos, bleich, rein, harmlos; (*coll.*) anständig; *–e as a sheet*, kreideweiß; *–e as snow*, schneeweiß. 2. *s.* weiße Farbe, das Weiß; Weiße(r), *m.* (*member of white race*); *pl.* weißer Fluß, die Leukorrhöe (*Med.*); *dressed in –e*, in weiß gekleidet; *–e of egg*, das Eiweiß; *–e of the eye*, das Weiße des Auges; *–e ant*, die Termite; *–e bear*, der Eisbär; *–e bread*, das Weißbrot; *–e corpuscle*, weißes Blutkörperchen; *–e elephant*, (*fig.*) lästiger Besitz; *–e ensign*, englische Marineflagge; *–e feather*, das Symbol der Feigheit; *show the –e feather*, sich feige zeigen; *–e friar*, der Karmeliter; *–e heat*, die Weißglut, (*fig.*) höchste Erregung; *–e horse*, der Schimmel; *–e horses, pl. see* **–e-caps;** *–e lead*, das Bleiwiß; *–e lie*, die Notlüge; *–e magic*, gutartige Magie; *–e man*, weißer Mann; (*fig.*) anständiger *or* ehrlicher Mann; *–e metal*, das Weißmetall, Lagermetall; *–e wine*, der Weißwein. **–ebait,** *s.* der kleine Weißfisch, die Sprotte, der Breitling (*Ichth.*). **–eboy,** *s.* das Mitglied einer irischen Geheimverbindung. **–e-caps,** *pl.* Schaumwellen (*pl.*). **–e-collar,** *attrib.* Kopf–, geistig. **––faced,** *adj.* blaß; *–e-faced horse*, der Bleß; *–e-faced cow*, die Blesse. **–e-fish,** *s.* der Weißfisch. **–e-haired,** *adj.* weißhaarig. **–e-heart cherry,** *s.* helle Herzkirsche. **–e-hot,** weißglühend. **–e-lipped,** *adj.* weiß bis in die Lippen. **–e-livered,** *adj.* feige. **–en** [–ən], 1. *v.a.* weißen, weiß machen, bleichen; 2. *v.n.* weißwerden, bleichen (*of a th.*), bleich werden, erblassen; (*of a p.*). **–eness,** *s.* die Weiße, Blässe, weiße Farbe. **–ening,** *s.* das Weißen; die Schlämmkreide. **–e-paper,** *s.* das Weißbuch (*Parl.*). **–e-**

skinned, *adj.* weißhäutig. **–e-slave traffic,** *s.* der Mädchenhandel. **–esmith,** *s.* der Blechschmied. **–ethorn,** *s.* der Weißdorn (*Bot.*). **–ethroat,** *s.* die Dorngrasmücke (*Orn.*). **–ewash,** 1. *s.* die Tünche, (*fig.*) die Ehrenrettung. 2. *v.a.* tünchen, weißen, kalken, (*fig.*) rein waschen. **–ing,** *s.* der Weißfisch; die Schlämmkreide, das Putzpulver. **–ish,** *adj.* weißlich.

whither [ˈ(h)wɪðə], 1. *inter. adv.* wohin? 2. *rel. adv.* dahin wo; *the place* –, der Ort zu dem. **–soever,** *rel. adv.* wohin auch immer, einerlei wohin.

whitlow [ˈ(h)wɪtloʊ], *s.* das Nagelgeschwür. **––grass** *s.* dreifingeriger Steinbrech (*Bot.*).

Whitsun [ˈ(h)wɪtsən], *adj.* Pfingst–; pfingstlich. **–tide,** *s.* das Pfingstfest, Pfingsten; *–tide recess*, die Pfingstferien.

whittle [(h)wɪtl], 1. *s.* das Schnitzmesser. 2. *v.a.* schnitzen, abschneiden, abschaben; (*fig.*) – *away* or *down*, verkleinern, beschneiden.

whiz(z) [(h)wɪz], 1. *v.n.* zischen, schwirren, surren, sausen. 2. *s.* das Zischen, Sausen; (*sl.*) *it's a* –, abgemacht!; (*coll.*) *gee –!* oh je! **––bang,** *s.* das Tschingbum, Geknack. **–er,** *s.* die Zentrifugaltrockenmaschine.

who [huː], 1. *rel. pron.* der, die, das, welche(–r, –s), wer; *–'s* –, wer ist's? *he – lies would also steal*, wer lügt, der stiehlt auch. 2. *inter. pron.* wer?; – *goes there?* wer da?; – *the deuce?* wer zum Kuckuck? **–(so)ever,** *rel. pron.* wer auch (immer), jeder der.

whoa [(h)woʊ], *int.* brr! halt!

whole [hoʊl], 1. *adj.* ganz; heil, intakt, unverletzt; Voll–; (*fig.*) vollständig, ungeteilt, vollkommen; (*archaic*) gesund; (*sl.*) *go the – hog*, aufs Ganze gehen, alles dransetzen; – *number*, ganze Zahl; *with a – skin*, mit heiler Haut; *the* –, das Ganze (*as a unity*), die Gesamtheit (*collect.*); *a* –, ein Ganzes; *the – of*, ganz; *as a* –, als Ganzes; *in – or in part*, ganz oder teilweise; *on the* –, im ganzen, alles in allem. **––coloured,** einfarbig. **––hearted,** *adj.* aufrichtig, warmherzig, rückhaltlos. **––heartedly,** *adj.* aus vollem Herzen. (*sl.*) **––hogger,** *s.* eingefleischter Anhänger. **––length,** *adj.* in Lebensgröße. **––life,** *adj.* auf Lebenszeit (*insurance*). **–meal,** *s.* das Vollmehl; *–meal bread*, das Vollkornbrot. **–ness,** *s.* die Ganzheit, Vollständigkeit. **––time,** *adj.* voll beschäftigt (*worker*).

wholesale [ˈhoʊlseɪl], 1. *adj.* Engros–, Groß–, Großhandels– (*C.L.*); (*fig.*) unterschiedslos, unbegrenzt, Massen–; – *business*, das Großhandelsgeschäft, die Großhandlung; – *dealer* or *merchant*, der Großhändler, Grossist; – *firm*, die Engrosfirma; – *slaughter*, das Massenschlachten; – *trade*, der Großhandel, Großbetrieb; *in his – way*, auf seine überschwengliche Weise. 2. *adv.* en gros, im großen *or* ganzen (*C.L.*); (*fig.*) in Massen, unterschiedslos, in großem Umfang. 3. *s.* der Verkauf *or* Handel im großen.

wholesome [ˈhoʊlsəm], *adj.* zuträglich, bekömmlich, gesund; heilsam, wohltuend, förderlich, nützlich, dienlich. **–ness,** *s.* Heilsamkeit, Nützlichkeit; Dienlichkeit.

wholly [ˈhoʊlɪ], *adv.* ganz, gänzlich, völlig, durchaus, ausschließlich.

whom [ˈhuːm], 1. (*Acc. of* **who** 1) den, die, welche(n); *to* –, dem, welchem, welcher, (*pl.*) denen, welchen. 2. (*Acc. of* **who** 2) wen?; *to* –, wem? **–(so)ever,** *rel. pron.* wen auch (immer), jeden den (*Acc.*); wem auch (immer), jedem dem (*Dat.*).

whoop [huːp], 1. *s.* lauter Schrei; das Keuchen; Kriegsgeschrei. 2. *v.n.* laut aufschreien; keuchen. **–ee** [ˈwuːpɪ], *s.* (*sl.*) der Budenzauber; *make –ee*, gewaltigen Klimbim machen (*about*, über). **–er** (*also* –er swan) *s.* der Singschwan, wilder Schwan (*Orn.*). **–ing cough,** *s.* der Keuchhusten.

whop [(h)wɔp], *v.a.* (*sl.*) schlagen, durchprügeln. **–per,** *s.* (*sl.*) das Mordsding, die Pfundssache; faustdicke Lüge. **–ping,** *adj.* (*sl.*) ungeheuer, kolossal, gewaltig.

whore [hɔːə], 1. *s.* die Hure. 2. *v.n.* huren. **––monger,** *s.* der Dirnenjäger.

whorl [(h)wɔːəl], *s.* der Wirtel (*Tech.*); Quirl, Wirbel (*Bot.*); Windung (*of a snail*).

whortleberry [ˈwəːtlbɛrɪ], *s.* die Heidelbeere; *red* –, die Preißelbeere, Kronsbeere.

whose [huːz], 1. (*poss. of* **who** 1.) dessen, deren. 2. (*poss. of* **who** 2.) wessen? **–soever,** *rel. pron.* (*archaic*) wessen auch immer.

why [(h)waɪ], 1. *rel. adv.* warum, weshalb, weswegen; *the reason* –, der Grund weshalb; *that is* –, deshalb, das ist der Grund weshalb. 2. *inter. adv.* warum? weshalb? weswegen? – *so?* warum das? wieso? 3. *int.* nun, wahrhaftig; –, *to be sure*, ja freilich. 4. *s.* das Warum; *the – and the wherefore*, das Wie und Warum.

wick [wɪk], *s.* der Docht.

wicked [ˈwɪkɪd], *adj.* schlecht, böse, sündhaft, gottlos, verrucht; (*coll.*) boshaft, ungezogen, unartig; (*coll.*) *a – shame*, eine Gemeinheit. **–ness,** *s.* die Schlechtigkeit, Gottlosigkeit, Bosheit.

wicker [ˈwɪkə], *adj.* geflochten. Flecht–, Weiden–, Korb–; – *basket*, der Weidenkorb; – *chair*, der Korbstuhl, Rohrstuhl. **––work,** *s.* das Flechtwerk, die Korbflechtwaren (*pl.*).

wicket [ˈwɪkɪt] (also *––gate*), das Pförtchen; die Seitentür, Nebentür; das Tor, der Dreistab, die Bahn zwischen beiden Toren (*Crick.*); *keep* –, Torwart sein; *take a* –, den Schläger ausmachen; *by 3 –s* or *with 3 –s in hand*, ohne daß 3 Spieler geschlagen haben; *3 –s down*, 3 Schläger ausgemacht; *wet* –, naßes Spielfeld; *sticky* –, die Spielfläche die den Werfer bevorzugt; (*fig.*) heikle Lage. **––keeper,** *s.* der Torwart, Torhüter.

wide [waɪd], *adj.* 1. breit, weit(reichend), ausgedehnt; (*usually pred.*) weit entfernt *or* abirrend; (*fig.*) umfangreich, groß, reich (*experience*), großzügig (*views*); – *ball*, der Ball außerhalb der Reichweite des Schlägers (*Crick.*); *give s.o. a – berth*, einem weit aus dem Wege gehen; – *culture*, die Allgemeinbildung; – *difference*, großer Unterschied; – *of the mark*, weit vom Ziel; (*fig.*) irrig, verkehrt; – *public*, breiteres Publikum; – *skirt*, weiter Rock; – *street*, breite Straße; *3 inches* –, 3 Zoll breit; – *world*, weite Welt. 2. *adv.* weit; *far and* –, weit und breit; – *apart*, weit getrennt; – *awake*, ganz wach, (*fig.*) wachsam, aufmerksam; – *open*, weit offen; *open* –, weit öffnen; *have one's eyes – open*, die Augen weit aufhalten, auf der Hut sein. 2. *s.*; see – *ball*; (*sl.*) *be broke to the* –, auf dem Trockenen sitzen, völlig pleite sein. **–ly,** *adv.* weit; *differ –ly*, sehr unterschiedlich sein; *–ly known*, allgemein bekannt; *most –ly used*, am meisten benutzt. **–n,** 1. *v.a.* erweitern (*also fig.*), breiter machen; (*fig.*) ausdehnen. 2. *v.n.* sich erweitern. **–ness,** *s.* die Weite, Breite, Ausdehnung; *–ness of range*, die Reichweite. **–ning,** die Erweiterung. **–spread,** *adj*, weit verbreitet.

widgeon [ˈwɪdʒən], *s.* die Pfeifente.

widow [ˈwɪdoʊ], *s.* die Witwe; *grass* –, die Strohwitwe. *–'s weeds*, die Witwentracht (*Poet.*). **––bird,** *s.* der Witwenvogel. **–ed** [–d], *adj.* verwitwet; verwaist, beraubt (*of* (*Gen.*)), verlassen. **–er,** *s.* der Witwer. **–hood,** *s.* die Witwenschaft.

width [wɪdθ], *s.* die Weite, Breite.

wield [wiːld], *v.a.* handhaben, schwingen, führen; (*fig.*) ausüben (*influence, etc.*); – *the pen*, schreiben; – *the sceptre*, das Zepter führen, regieren, herrschen.

wife [waɪf], *s.* (*pl.* wives [–vz]) die (Ehe)Frau, Gattin, Gemahlin, (*archaic*) das Weib; *old wives' tale*, die Altweibergeschichte, das Ammenmärchen; *take to* –, zur Ehefrau nehmen. **–hood,** *s.* der Ehestand. **–like,** *adj.* frauenhaft, fraulich.

wig [wɪg], *s.* die Perücke. **–ging**, *s.* (*coll.*) die Schelte, Rüge; *give s.o. a good –ging*, einem gehörig den Kopf waschen, einen tüchtig abkanzeln.

wight [waɪt], *s.* (*archaic*) der Wicht, Kerl.

wigwam [ˈwɪgwæm], *s.* das Indianerzelt, der Wigwam.

wild [waɪld], 1. *adj.* wild (wachsend) (*of plants*), wild, ungezähmt (*of animals*), (*fig.*) ausgelassen, toll, wütend, rasend, wahnsinnig, verrückt; verstört, wirr, unordentlich, wüst, unbebaut (*of land*), ungestüm, abenteuerlich, phantastisch; – *beast*, wildes Tier; – *fancies*, tolle Einfälle; – *horses will not make me do it*, keine vier Pferde bringen mich dazu; – *man of the woods*, wilder Mann; *sow one's – oats*, sich austoben, sich die Hörner ablaufen; *run* –, wild wachsen, ins Kraut schießen (*of plants*), (*fig.*) verwildern, wild aufwachsen; *shoot* –, ins Blaue schießen, drauflosschießen; *talk* –, sinnlos reden. 2. *s.* (*also pl.*) die Wildnis, Wüste, Einöde. **--boar,** *s.* das Wildschwein. **–cat,** 1. *s.* die Wildkatze, (*fig.*) der Schwindelunternehmer, wilder Spekulant. 2. *attrib.* (*fig.*) unsolid, unreell, Schwindel–; abenteuerlich, phantastisch. **--duck,** *s.* die Wildente. **–ebeest** ['wɪ:ldəbeɪst], *s.* das Gnu (*Zool.*). **–fire** *s.* griechisches Feuer; verheerender Brand; *spread like –fire*, sich wie ein Lauffeuer verbreiten. **–fowl,** *s.* die Wildhühner (*pl.*). **--goose,** *s.* die Wildgans; (*fig.*) *--goose chase*, vergebliche Bemühung, fruchtloses Unternehmen. **–ing,** *s.* der Wildling, unveredelte Pflanze; der Holzapfel(baum), der Wildapfel(baum). **–erness** ['wɪldənɪs], *s.* die Wildnis, Wüste, Einöde; *go into the –erness*, außer Amt sein (*Parl.*). **–ness,** *s.* die Wildheit, Verwilderung, Ausgelassenheit, Zügellosigkeit.

wile [waɪl], 1. *s.* (*usually pl.*) Kniffe, Ränke, Tücken, Schliche. 2. *v.a.* anlocken, verlocken; – *away*, (*coll. but incorrect for* while) angenehm verbringen, vertändeln (*the time*).

wilful ['wɪlful], *adj.* absichtlich, willentlich, vorsätzlich; eigenwillig, eigensinnig, halsstarrig. **–ness,** *s.* der Eigensinn, Eigenwille, die Vorsätzlichkeit.

wiliness ['waɪlɪnɪs], *s.* die List, Arglist, Verschlagenheit; *see* **wily.**

will [wɪl], 1. *s.* der Wille; die Willenskraft, das Willensvermögen, der Entschluß, die Willensäußerung, der Wunsch, das Verlangen, Belieben; letzter Wille, das Testament, letztwillige Verfügung (*Law*); *against his* –, gegen seinen Wunsch; *at* –, nach Belieben *or* Willen; *by* –, letztwillig, testamentarisch (*Law*); *free* –, die Willensfreiheit; *of o's own free* –, freiwillig, aus freien Stücken; *good* –, das Wohlwollen; *ill* –, das Übelwollen, die Feindschaft; *bear s.o. ill* –, einem grollen; *last – and testament*, letztwillige Verfügung (*Law*); *make one's* –, sein Testament machen (*Law*); *what is your –?* was wollen Sie?; (*Prov.*) *where there's a –, there's a way*, wo ein Wille ist, ist auch ein Weg; *with a* –, energisch, mit Energie. 2. *ir.v.a.* (*aux., only pres. and imperf.*) (*1st and 2nd pres.*) will, willst, *etc.*; (*to form future*: *2nd and 3rd pers.*) wird, wirst, werdet, (*Scots also 1st pers.*) werde(n); durch Testament bestimmen, vermachen, hinterlassen; bestimmen, entscheiden; *I – do it*, ich will es tun; (*Scots*) ich werde es tun, *you – do it, – you?* Sie werden *or* wollen es tun, nicht wahr? *call it what you* –, man mag es nennen wie man will; *he – have it*, er wird es haben; (*emphatic*) *boys – be boys*, Jungens sind nun mal Jungens; *it – not burn*, (*emphatic*) es brennt nicht *or* will nicht brennen; – *o.s. to do*, sich zwingen zu tun. 3. *ir.v.n.* (es haben) wollen; *as you* –, wie Sie (es) wollen. **–ed** [-d], *adj. suffix*, willig. **–ing,** *adj.* willig, bereit(willig); (*pred. only*) gewillt, willens, geneigt, einverstanden; willfährig, hilfreich; gern geschehen *or* geleistet (*action*); *God –ing*, so Gott will. **–ingly,** *adv.* gern; mit Vergnügen. **–ingness,** *s.* die (Bereit)Willigkeit, das Entgegenkommen.

willies ['wɪlɪz] *pl.*, (*sl.*) *the* –, die Beklemmung, der Bammel.

will-o'-the-wisp ['wɪləðə'wɪsp], *s.* das Irrlicht.

[1]**willow** ['wɪlou], *s.* die Weide; (*coll.*) das Schlagholz (*Crick.*); *weeping* –, die Trauerweide, *wear the* –, um die (den) Geliebte(n) trauern. **--herb,** *s.* der Weiderich, das Antonskraut (*Bot.*). **--pattern,** *s.* blaues chinesisches Muster mit Weidelandschaft (*porcelain*). **--wren,** *s.* der Weidenzeisig. **–y,** *adj.* biegsam, schlank.

[2]**willow,** 1. *s.* die Krempel(maschine), der Krempelwolf, Reißwolf, die Karde (*Tech.*). 2. *v.a.* krempeln, wolfen.

willy-nilly ['wɪlɪ'nɪlɪ], *adv.* wohl oder übel, gezwungenermaßen.

[1]**wilt** [wɪlt], (*archaic*) *2nd pers. sing. pres. of* **be.**

[2]**wilt,** *v.n.* (ver)welken, verblühen; (*fig.*) dahinwelken, schlapp *or* schwach werden, erschlaffen.

wily ['waɪlɪ], *adj.* listig, schlau, verschlagen, verschmitzt.

wimple ['wɪmpl], 1. *s.* (*archaic*) das Kopftuch; (*B.*) der Schleier. 2. *v.a.* (den Kopf, *etc.*) verschleiern *or* verhüllen.

win [wɪn], 1. *ir.v.a.* gewinnen (*a battle, prize, s.o.'s hand, etc.*), erringen (*a victory*); (*fig.*) erhalten, erlangen; – *the day*, den Sieg davontragen; – *s.th. from s.o.*, einem etwas abgewinnen; – *a p. over to*, einen gewinnen für; *it will – him much praise*, es bringt ihm viel Lob ein, – *one's spurs*, die Sporen erlangen; (*fig.*) sich die Sporen verdienen; – *one's way into*, gelangen *or* seinen Weg machen in (*Acc.*). 2. *ir.v.n.* siegen, Sieger sein, den Sieg davontragen; gewinnen (*at play, etc.*); – *hands down*, spielend siegen; – *through*, sich durchkämpfen *or* durchsetzen *or* Eingang verschaffen, gewinnen, siegen. 3. *s.* (*coll.*) der Sieg, Erfolg; *see* **winner, winning.**

winc–e [wɪns], 1 *v.n.* zurückweichen, zurückfahren, zurückzucken; *without –ing*, ohne mit der Wimper zu zucken. 2. *s.* das Zusammenfahren, Zurückfahren, Zucken.

winch [wɪntʃ], *s.* der Haspel, die Winde; Kurbel (*of a wheel, etc.*).

[1]**wind** [wɪnd], **1.** *s.* der Wind (*also Hunt., Med., & fig.*), die Blähung (*Med.*), Witterung (*Hunt.*); (*fig.*) Lunge, der Atem; *the* –, die Blasinstrumente (*pl.*). *against the* –, gegen den Wind; *before the* –, vor *or* mit dem Winde; *between – and water*, zwischen Wind und Wasser (*Naut*), (*fig.*) an gefährlicher Stelle; *break* –, Wind lassen; *by the* –, an *or* beim Winde (*Naut.*); *the – has changed*, der Wind ist umgesprungen; *down* –, see *before the* –; *break a horse's* –, ein Pferd überreiten; *the four –s*, die vier Windrichtungen; *from the four –s*, aus allen Richtungen, *to the four –s*, nach allen Richtungen; (*fig.*) *be in the* –, in der Luft *or* im Gange *or* am Werke sein; (*Prov.*) *it's an ill – that blows nobody any good*, kein Unglück ist so groß, es trägt ein Glück im Schoß; (*fig.*) *get – of*, Wind bekommen von, hören von; *get* (or *have*) *the – of*, den Wind abgewinnen (*a ship* (*Dat.*)), (*fig.*) Vorteil abgewinnen (*a p.* (*Dat.*)); (*sl.*) *get the – up*, Angst *or* Dampf bekommen; (*fig.*) *know how the – blows* or *lies*, wissen, woher der Wind weht; *like the* –, windschnell; – *and weather permitting*, bei günstigem Wetter; (*sl.*) *put the – up s.o.*, einen ins Bockshorn jagen; (*sl.*) *raise the* –, Geld auftreiben; *the – is rising*, der Wind nimmt zu; *sail close to the* –, hoch an den Wind gehen (*Naut.*), (*fig.*) sich strafbar machen, Gefahr laufen; *second* –, das Wieder-zu-Atem-kommen; *get one's second* –, frischen Atem holen; *take the – out of a p.'s sails*, einem den Wind aus den Segeln nehmen, *in the –'s eye, in the teeth of the* –, dem Winde trotzend *or* entgegen, *throw* or *cast to the –s*, in den Wind schlagen, über den Haufen werfen; ablegen (*one's fears*); *under the* –, in Leeseite (*Naut.*). **2.** *v.a.* wittern, spüren, lüften, blasen; überreiten (*a horse*); (*usually pass.*) erschöpfen, außer Atem bringen. **–age** [–ɪdʒ] *s.* der Spielraum (*of gun barrel*); die Ablenkung durch den Wind (*of a shell*). **–bag,** *s.* der Windbeutel, Schwätzer. **--bound,** *adj.* von widrigem Wind aufgehalten. **--broken,** *adj.* kurzatmig (*of horses*). **--chest,** *s.* der Windkasten (*organ*). **–ed** [–ɪd], *adj.* außer Atem. **--egg,** *s.* das Windei. **–fall,** *s.* das Fallobst, (*fig.*) unerwarteter Glücksfall. **–fallen** *adj.*; *–fallen tree*, der Windwurf; *–fallen wood*, der Windbruch. **--flower,** *s.* das Windröschen. **–iness,** *s.* die Windigkeit, (*fig.*) Aufgeblasenheit. **--gauge,** *s.* der Windmesser, das Anemometer. **--instrument,** *s.* das Blasinstrument. **--jammer,** *s.* großes, schnelles Segelschiff. **–less,** *adj.* windlos, windstill, ohne Wind. **–mill,** *s.* die Windmühle; *throw one's cap over the –mill*, sich in Phantastereien einlassen. **–pipe,** *s.* die Luftröhre (*Anat.*). **–row,** *s.* der Schwaden (*of hay*). **–screen,** *s.* die Windschutzscheibe; *–screen wiper*, der Scheibenwischer. **--tunnel,** *s.* der Windkanal. **–ward,** 1. *adj.* Wind–. 2. *adj.* windwärts, in *or* zu Luv, luvwärts. 3. *s.* die Windseite, Luv(seite); *sail to –ward*, gegen den Wind segeln. **–y,** *adj.* windig, stürmisch; blähend (*Med.*), (*fig.*) geschwätzig, langatmig, eitel, leer, hohl; (*sl.*) bangbüxig, benaut.

[2]**wind** [waɪnd], 1. *ir.v.a.* winden. wickeln, schlagen; drehen, kurbeln, spulen; wenden, herumholen (*a*

ship); – *a p. round one's little finger*, einen um den kleinen Finger wickeln; – *one's way*, sich durchschlängeln; – *on to a reel*, (auf)spulen; – *o.s. into*, sich einschmeicheln in *or* bei; – *off*, abwickeln; – *up*, in die Höhe winden, aufwinden; aufwickeln, aufspulen (*thread, etc.*); aufziehen (*a clock*); (*fig.*) abwickeln, abschleißen, zu Ende bringen; liquidieren, auflösen (*C.L.*). 2. *ir.v.n.* sich winden, sich schlängeln; sich drehen *or* wenden (*Naut.*); – *up*, Geschäft auflösen *or* liquidieren (*C.L.*), (*fig.*) schließen, Schluß machen. **–er,** *s.* der Aufwinder, Haspler; der & die Haspel, die Winde, Kurbel. **–ing,** 1. *adj.* sich windend *or* schlängelnd, Schlangen-, schief, krumm; *–ing curve*, die Wellenlinie; *–ing stairs*, die Wendeltreppe. 2. *s.* das Winden, Spulen, Haspeln, Aufwickeln; die Windung, Biegung, Krümmung, Wickelung (*Elec.*). **–ing-engine,** *s.* die Förderwelle, Dampfwinde. **–ing-rope,** *s.* das Förderseil. **–ing-sheet,** *s.* das Grabtuch, Leichentuch. **–ing-tackle,** *s.* das Gien (*Naut.*). **–ing-up,** *s.* das Aufziehen, Aufwinden, (*fig.*) der Abschluß, die Abwicklung, Auflösung, Liquidierung (*C.L.*). **–lass** ['wındləs], *s.* der *or* die Haspel, die Winde, der Kran; das Spill (*Naut.*). **– -up,** *s.* die Auflösung, Liquidierung (*C.L.*).

winded, *adj. see under* [1]**wind.**

windage, *see under* [1]**wind.**

window ['wındoʊ], *s.* das Fenster; *at the* –, am Fenster; *bay-–*, das Erkerfenster; *casement* –, das Flügelfenster; *French* –, die Verandatür; *sash* –, das Schiebefenster; *shop-–*, das Schaufenster; *look out of the* –, zum Fenster hinaussehen. **– -blind** *s.* der Fenstervorhang. Rollvorhang, die Jalousie, das Rouleau. **– -box,** *s.* der Blumenkasten. **– -cleaner,** *s.* der Fensterputzer. **– -curtain,** *s.* die Fenstergardine. **– -display,** *s.* die Schaufensterauslage. **– -dressing,** *s.* die Schaufensterdekoration, (*fig.*) äußere Aufmachung, die Schönfärberei; das Frisieren, die Bilanzverschleierung. **–ed** [–d], *adj.* mit Fenstern versehen. **– -envelope,** *s.* die Fensterbriefhülle. **– -frame,** *s.* der Fensterrahmen. **– -ledge,** *s.* die Fensterbrüstung. **–less,** *adj.* fensterlos. **– -pane,** *s.* die Fensterscheibe. **– -sash,** *s.* verschiebbarer Rahmen, Rahmen an Schiebefenstern. **– -seat,** *s.* der Fenstersitz. **– -shutters,** *pl.* Fensterläden (*pl.*). **– -sill,** *s.* die Fensterbank, das Fensterbrett.

windward, windy, *see under* [1]**wind.**

wine [waın], 1. *s.* der Wein; (*Prov.*) *good – needs no bush*, das Gute empfiehlt sich selbst. 2. *v.a.* mit Wein traktieren (*a p.*). **– -bibber,** *s.* der Weinsäufer. **– -bin,** *s.* das Weinflaschengestell. **– -bottle,** *s.* die Weinflasche. **– -cask,** *s.* das Weinfaß. **– -cellar,** *s.* der Weinkeller. **– -cooler,** *s.* der Weinkühler. **–glass,** *s.* das Weinglas. **– -grower,** *s.* der Weinbauer. **– -list,** *s.* die Weinkarte. **– -merchant,** der Weinhändler. **– -press,** *s.* die Weinkelter. **– -skin,** *s.* der Weinschlauch. **– -stone,** *s.* der Weinstein. **– -taster,** *s.* der Weinprober. **– -trade,** *s.* der Weinhandel. **– -vault,** *s.* der Weinkeller; die Weinstube, Weinhandlung.

wing [wıŋ], 1. *s.* der Flügel (*also Arch., etc.*); (*Poet.*) Fittich, die Schwinge (*of a bird*); Fliegergruppe (*Av.*); (*coll.*) der Außenstürmer (*Footb., etc.*); Kotflügel (*Motor.*); die Tragfläche (*Av.*); (also *side-–*) (*usually pl.*) die Kulisse (*Theat.*); *pl.* das Fliegerabzeichen (*Air Force*); *clip a p.'s –s*, einem die Flügel beschneiden; *lend –s to a th.*, etwas beschleunigen *or* beflügeln; auffliegen; *on the* –, im Fluge, fliegend; *on the –s of love*, auf Fittichen der Liebe; *on the –s of the wind*, mit Windeseile; *take* –, davonfliegen. (*fig.*) *take a p. under one's* –, einen unter seine Fittiche *or* seinen Schutz nehmen. 2. *v.a.* mit Federn versehen (*an arrow*); durchfliegen, seinen Flug richten *or* nehmen (*one's way*); (*fig.*) beflügeln, beschwingen, beschleunigen; flügeln, flügellahm schießen; treffen (*a bird*); (*coll.*) verwunden. **– -beat,** *s.* der Flügelschlag. **– -case,** *s.* die Flügeldecke (*Ent.*). **– -chair,** *s.* der Ohrenstuhl. **– -collar,** *s.* der Eckenkragen. **– -commander,** *s.* der Oberstleutnant der Luftwaffe. **– -covert,** *s.* die Deckfeder (*Orn.*). **–ed** [–d], *adj.* geflügelt (*also Bot.*), gefiedert (*Bot.*); (*as suffix*) = -flügelig; (*fig.*) beflügelt, beschwingt, schnell; (*coll.*) verwundet; *broken-–ed*, *adj.* flügellahm; *–ed creatures*, das Geflügel; *–ed horse*, der Pegasus; *–ed words*, geflügelte Worte. **–feather,** *s.* die Schwungfeder (*Orn.*). **– -footed,** *adj.* (*Poet.*) beschwingt. **–let,** *s.* kleiner Flügel. **– -nut,** *s.* die Flügelmutter (*Tech.*). **– -sheath,** *s. see* **– -case. – -spread,** *s.* die Flügelspanne (*Orn.*). Flügel- *or* Spannweite (*Av.*). **– -stroke,** *s. see* **– -beat. – -tip,** *s.* das Flügelende.

wink [wıŋk], 1. *s.* das Zwinkern, Blinzeln; (*coll.*) der Wink; (*coll.*) (*usually pl.*) das Schläfchen; (*coll.*) kurzer Augenblick; (*coll.*) *not get a – of sleep*, kein Auge zutun; (*coll.*) *forty –s*, kurzes Schläfchen; (*coll.*) *in a* –, im Nu; (*sl.*) *tip s.o. a* –, einem einen Wink geben; 2. *v.n.* zwinkern, blinzeln; (*fig.*) blinken; blitzen, leuchten, flimmern (*of light*); – *at s.o.*, einem zuzwinkern; – *at a th.*, ein Auge zudrücken bei einer S.; es (einem) nicht nachsehen. **–ing,** *s.* das Zwinkern, Blinzeln; Blinken, Leuchten, Flimmern; *as easy as –ing*, spielend leicht.

winkle ['wıŋkl], *s.* die Uferschnecke.

win-ner ['wınə], *s.* der Sieger, Gewinner; *he is the –ner*, er hat gewonnen. **–ning,** 1. *adj.* gewinnend (*also fig.*), Sieger-, (*fig.*) einnehmend; *–ning move*, entscheidender Zug (*chess*) *or* (*fig.*) Schritt; *–ning name*, der Name des Siegers; *–ning way*, einnehmendes Wesen. 2. *s.* das Gewinnen, der Sieg Abbau, die Förderung, Ausbeute (*Min.*); *pl.* der (Wett)Gewinn. **–ning-post,** *s.* das Ziel.

winnow ['wınoʊ], 1. *v.a.* worfeln, schwingen, wannen, sieben; (*fig.*) (also – *out*) trennen, sondern (*the good from the bad*), aussondern, ausscheiden, ausmerzen (*the bad from the good*); reinigen, säubern; sichten. 2. *s.* die Getreideschwinge. **–er,** *s.* der Worfler, die Kornreinigungsmaschine. **–ing,** *s.* das Worfeln, Schwingen, Wannen. **–ing-fan,** *s.* die Worfschaufel. **–ing-machine,** *s.* die Kornreinigungsmachine.

winsome ['wınsəm], *adj.* anziehend, reizend, einnehmend, gefällig. **–ness,** *s.* der Reiz, die Lieblichkeit.

winter ['wıntə], 1. *s.* der Winter; *in* –, im Winter. 2. *attrib.* winterlich, Winter–; –(*'s*) *day*, der Wintertag; – *garden*, der Wintergarten; – *quarters*, das Winterquartier; – *sleep*, der Winterschlaf; – *sports*, der Wintersport. 3. *v.n.* überwintern, den Winter zubringen. 4. *v.a.* für den Winter unterbringen. **– -crop,** *s.* der Winterfrucht. **–green,** *s.* das Wintergrün (*Bot., Pharm.*).

wintr-iness ['wıntrınıs], *s.* die Kälte, Winterlichkeit. **–y,** *adj.* winterlich, kalt.

wipe [waıp], 1. *v.a.* (ab)wischen; abtrocknen; reinigen; (*sl.*) hauen; – *one's boots*, sich (*Dat.*) die Schuhe putzen; – *one's eyes*, sich (*Dat.*) die Tränen abwischen; (*sl.*) – *a p. in the eye*, einen ausstechen; (*sl.*) – *the floor with s.o.*, einen gehörig abführen; – *one's lips*, sich (*Dat.*) den Mund abwischen; – *one's nose*, sich (*Dat.*) die Nase putzen; – *away*, abwischen; (*fig.*) begleichen (*an account*), tilgen (*a debt*); – *off*, abwischen; – *out*, auswischen, verwischen, auslöschen; (*fig.*) beseitigen, tilgen (*an insult, etc.*), zerstören; vernichten (*an army*), ausrotten (*a race, etc.*). 2. *s.* das (Ab)Wischen, Reinigen; (*sl.*) – *in the eye*, der Ausputzer, Wischer; *give a* –, abwischen. **–r,** *s.* der Wischer, das Wischtuch; der Scheibenwischer (*Motor.*).

wir-e [waıə], 1. *s.* der Draht; Leitungsdraht (*Elec., Tele.*); (*coll.*) das Telegramm, die Drahtnachricht; *barbed –e*, *s.* der Stacheldraht, Drahtverhau (*Mil.*); *by –e*, telegraphisch; *live –e*, geladener Draht, der Hochspannungsdraht, (*fig.*) der Quirl (*of a p.*); (*fig.*) *pull the –es*, der Drahtzieher *or* Urheber sein. 2. *v.a.* mit Draht befestigen, heften, steifen *or* stützen; Leitung anlegen in (*a room, etc.*); (*coll.*) telegraphieren, drahten (*a message*; *a p.* (*Dat.*)). 3. *v.n.* (*coll.*) telegraphieren, drahten. **–e-cutter(s),** *s.* (*pl.*) die Drahtzange. **–edraw,** *v.a.* (zu) Draht ausziehen; (*fig.*) in die Länge ziehen, hinziehen. **–edrawer,** *s.* der Drahtzieher. **–e-edge,** *s.* der Grat (*of a blade*). **–e-entanglement,** *s.* der Drahtverhau, das Drahthindernis (*Mil.*). **–e-fence,** *s.* der Drahtzaun. **–e-gauge,** *s.* die Drahtlehre. **–e-gauze,** *s.* das Drahtgewebe, Drahtnetz.

–ehaired, *adj.* Drahthaar– (*dog*). **–eless,** 1. *adj.* drahtlos, Funken–, Funk–; *–eless listener, s.* der Rundfunkhörer; *–eless message,* der Funkspruch; *–eless operator,* der Funktelegraphist, Funker; *–eless pirate,* der Schwarzhörer; *–eless programme,* das Rundfunkprogramm; *–eless set,* der Radioapparat, Empfänger; *–eless station,* die Funkstation; *–eless telegraphy,* die Funktelegraphie, drahtlose Telegraphie; *–eless transmitter,* der Sender. 2. *s.* der Rundfunk, das Radio; (also *–eless telegraphy*) die Funkentelegraphie, drahtlose Telegraphie; *by –eless,* durch Rundfunk; drahtlos, funktelegraphisch; *on the –eless,* im Rundfunk *or* Radio. **–e-nail,** *s.* der Drahtstift. **–e-netting,** *s.* das Drahtgeflecht, der Maschendraht. **–epuller,** *s.* (*fig.*) der Drahtzieher. **–epulling,** *s.* (*fig.*) Manipulationen, Geschäftskniffe (*pl.*). **–e-rope,** *s.* das Drahtseil. **–e-walker,** *s.* der Drahtseilakrobat, Seiltänzer. **–e-worm,** *s.* der Drahtwurm. **–e-wove,** *adj.* Velin– (*paper*); *–e-wove(n) mattress,* die Sprungfedermatratze. **–ing,** *s.* die Drahtleitung, Drahtanlage; das Drahtnetz; die Schaltung (*Elec., Rad.*); Verspannung (*Av.*); *–ing diagram,* das Schaltschema. **–y,** *adj.* sehnig, zäh (*of a p.*); borstig (*as hair*).

wis-dom [ˈwɪzdəm], *s.* die Weisheit, Klugheit. **–dom-tooth,** *s.* der Weisheitszahn. **–e** [waɪz], *adj.* weise, klug, einsichtig, vernünftig, verständig, gelehrt; unterrichtet, wissend; (*coll.*) *be* or *get –e to,* informiert sein über; (*sl.*) *–e guy,* der Schlaumeier, Besserwisser; *as –e as before,* so klug wie vorher; *none the –er,* um nichts klüger *or* gescheiter (*for,* durch); (*coll.*) *put a p. –e to,* einen aufklären, unterrichten *or* benachrichtigen über; *–e man,* Weise(r), *m.*; (*archaic*) *–e woman,* die Hebamme, Hexe. **–eacre,** *s.,* Überkluge(r), *m.,* der Naseweis, der Klugtuer, Gescheittuer; Klugredner. **–ecrack,** *s.* witzige Bemerkung. **–ecracker,** der Witzbold, Spaßmacher.

wise [waɪz], *s.* (*archaic*) die Weise, Art; *in any –,* irgendwie; *in no –,* auf keine Weise, keineswegs; *in such – as,* derartig daß; *in this –,* auf diese Weise.

–wise, *suffix* (*forming adverbs*), –weise.

wish [wɪʃ], 1. *v.a.* wünschen, verlangen; *I – he would come,* ich wünschte er käme; *I – to speak with you,* ich möchte mit dir reden; *I – you to come,* ich wünsche daß du kommst; *I –ed him dead,* ich wollte er wäre tot; *– a p. luck,* einem Glück wünschen. 2. *v.n.* wünschen; *as heart could –,* nach Herzenswunsch; *– a p. well,* einem wohl gesinnt sein; *– for,* haben wollen, sich wünschen, sich sehnen nach. 3. *s.* der Wille, Wunsch, das Verlangen (*for,* nach), die Bitte (*for,* um); *pl.* Grüße, Glückwünsche (*pl.*); *he has got his –,* er hat seinen Willen, sein Wunsch ist erfüllt. **–ful,** *adj.* verlangend, begierig, sehnlich, sehnsüchtig. **–fulness,** *s.* die Sehnsucht, das Verlangen. **– -bone,** *s.* das Brustbein des Geflügels. **–ed-for,** *adj.* ersehnt, erwünscht. **–ing,** *s.* das Wünschen. **–ing-bone,** *see* **– -bone.** **–ing-cap,** *s.* die Zauberkappe, Zaubermütze.

wish-wash [ˈwɪʃwɔʃ], *s.* (*coll.*) wasseriges Getränk; (*fig.*) das Geschwätz. **wishy-washy** [ˈwɪʃɪˈwɔʃɪ], *adj.* (*coll.*) wässerig; (*fig.*) saft- und kraftlos, farblos, fade, seicht.

wisp [wɪsp], *s.* der Wisch; Büschel, das Bündel; die Strähne (*of hair*); das Rudel (*of snipe*); *– of smoke,* die Rauchfahne.

wistaria [wɪsˈtɛːərɪə], die Glyzine (*Bot.*).

wistful [ˈwɪstful], *adj.* sehnsuchtsvoll, sehnsüchtig, schmachtend, wehmütig; sinnend, nachdenklich, gedankenvoll. **–ness,** *s.* die Sehnsucht, Wehmut, Nachdenlichkeit.

[1]**wit** [wɪt], *s.* der Witz; Verstand; (*usually pl.*) Geist, das Denkvermögen, geistige Fähigkeiten (*pl.*); (*rare*) witziger Mensch; der Witzbold; (*archaic*) großer Geist, kluger Kopf; *mother –,* der Mutterwitz; *be at one's –s' end,* mit seinem Verstande am Ende sein, sich nicht mehr zu helfen wissen, weder aus noch ein wissen; *he hasn't the –(s) to see,* er hat nicht den Kopf um einzusehen; *be out of one's –s,* den Kopf *or* Verstand verloren haben; *drive s.o. out of his –s,* einen verrückt machen; *frighten a p. out of his –s,* einem einen Todesschreck einjagen; *have one's –s about one,* seinen Verstand *or* seine fünf Sinne beisammen haben; *keep one's –s about one,* auf der Hut sein; *live by one's –s,* von andrer Leute Dummheit leben.

[2]**wit,** *v.n.* (*archaic*) wissen; (only in) *to –,* nämlich, das heißt; *see* **wittingly.**

witch [wɪtʃ], 1. *s.* die Hexe. 2. *v.a.* behexen, bezaubern. **–craft,** *s.* die Hexerei; (*fig.*) der Zauber, die Zauberkraft; *–craft trial,* der Hexenprozeß. **– -doctor,** *s.* der Medizinmann, Zauberer. **–ery,** *s. see* **–craft.** **– -hazel,** *s. see* **wych-hazel.** **–ing,** *adj.* Hexen–, Gespenster–, (*fig.*) bezaubernd; *–ing hour,* die Gespenserstunde, Geisterstunde.

witenagemot [ˈwɪtənægəˈmout], *s.* der Rat der Weisen, die Ratsversammlung der Angelsachsen.

with [wɪð], *prep.* mit, nebst, samt, zusammen mit; durch, vermittels; an, von, vor; trotz; **(a)** (*with adjectives*) *angry –,* böse auf (*Acc.*); *blue – cold,* blau vor Kälte; *mad –,* toll vor; *pleased –,* zufrieden mit; *popular – children,* bei Kindern beliebt; *be successful –,* Erfolg haben bei; **(b)** (*with nouns and pronouns*) *– age,* durch Alter; *– one another,* miteinander; *one – another,* zusammengerechnet, eins ins andere gerechnet; *– child,* schwanger; *I have difficulty – it,* es macht mir Schwierigkeiten; *– everyone looking on,* während alle zuschauten; *– all his experience,* trotz aller seiner Erfahrung; *– a grin,* grinsend; *that is usual – him,* das ist die Regel bei ihm; *he has a way – him,* er hat etwas an sich; *be down – influenza,* an der Grippe daniederliegen; *his influence – the king,* sein Einfluß auf den König *or* bei dem Könige; *it is just so – me,* es geht mir genau so; *– pleasure,* mit Vergnügen, sehr gern; *– all speed,* in aller Eile; *– the stream,* mit dem Strom; *– that,* damit, darauf; *– these words,* bei diesen Worten; *– this,* hiermit, hierauf; *– time,* mit der Zeit; *he is one – us,* er ist mit uns einig; *you are either against us or – us,* entweder sind Sie gegen uns oder für uns; *I am – you there,* ich bin ganz Ihrer Meinung, ich mache mit; *– young,* trächtig (*of animals*); **(c)** (*with verbs*) *be attended –,* begleitet sein von; *she came – him,* sie kam mit ihm; *she took him – her,* sie nahm ihn mit; *be out of conceit –,* nicht mehr Gefallen finden an (*Dat.*); *be concerned –,* betreffen, behandeln, sich beschäftigen mit; *cure – fasting,* durch Fasten heilen; *deal –,* handeln von; *differ –,* anderer Meinung sein als; *fight –,* kämpfen mit *or* gegen; *have – one,* bei sich haben; *ingratiate o.s. –,* sich einschmeicheln bei; *part –,* sich trennen von; *resound – applause,* vom Beifall ertönen; *it rests – you,* es steht bei Ihnen; *stay – s.o.,* bei einem wohnen; *nothing succeeds – him,* nichts gelingt ihm; *trust a p. –,* einem anvertrauen; *what do you want – me?* was wollen Sie von mir? *weep – joy,* vor Freude weinen; **(d)** (*introd. subord. clause*) *– everyone against him, he had to withdraw,* da alle gegen ihn waren, mußte er sich zurückziehen.

withal [wɪðˈɔːl], *adv.* (*archaic*) außerdem, überdies, obendrein, übrigens, zugleich, daneben.

withdraw [wɪðˈdrɔː], 1. *ir.v.a.* zurückziehen (*also C.L., Mil.*), wegnehmen, entfernen (*from,* von *or* aus), entziehen (*from* (*Dat.*)), widerrufen, zurücknehmen (*statement*), abheben (*C.L.*); *– one's assistance from,* seine Hand abziehen von; *– o.s.,* sich zurückziehen (*from,* von); *– a child from school,* ein Kind von der Schule wegnehmen. 2. *ir.v.n.* sich zurückziehen (*also Mil. & fig.*), zurücktreten, zurückgehen, zurückweichen, sich entfernen (*from,* von); *– within o.s.,* sich in sich zurückziehen. **–al** [–əl], *s.* das Zurückziehen, Einziehen, die Zurückziehung, Entfernung (*from,* von); das Zurücknehmen, die Zurücknahme, Widerrufung; das Zurückgehen, Zurücktreten, der Rücktritt; die Abhebung (*C.L.*); *–al form,* das Abhebungsformular.

withe [ˈwɪðɪ], *s.* die Weidenrute.

wither [ˈwɪðə], 1. *v.a.* welk machen, austrocknen, ausdorren, (*fig.*) vernichten, lahmen. 2. *v.n.* (ver)welken, vertrocknen, (*fig.*) vergehen, eingehen, verfallen. **–ed** [–d], *adj.* welk, verwelkt; dürr, verdorrt, ausgetrocknet, (*fig.*) gelähmt, lahm, eingeschrumpft. **–ing,** *adj.* verwelkend, (*fig.*) lähmend, niederschmetternd, vernichtend (*as a glance*).

wither-s [wɪðəz], *pl.* der Widerrist (*of horse*); (*fig.*) *my -s are unwrung*, das läßt mich kalt, das trifft mich nicht. **--wrung,** *adj.* am Widerrist verletzt.
withershins ['wɪðəʃɪnz], *adv.* (*Scots*) gegen den scheinbaren Lauf der Sonne.
withhold [wɪð'hould], *ir.v.a.* abhalten, hindern (*a p.*), zurückhalten (*a p. or th.*), zurückhalten mit (*a th.*); *- o.s. from a th.*, sich einer Sache entziehen; *- a th. from a p.*, einem etwas versagen *or* vorenthalten; *- one's hand*, sich zurückhalten.
within [wɪð'ɪn], **1.** *adv.* im Innern, d(a)rinnen, innen, zu Hause; *from -*, von innen. **2.** *prep.* innerhalb (*also of time & distance*), im Innern (*Gen.*), binnen, nicht mehr als (*of time*), nicht weiter als (*of distance*); *- an ace of being killed*, nahe daran getötet zu werden; *agree - an inch*, bis auf einen Zoll übereinstimmen; *- call*, in Ruf(weite); *- three days*, binnen drei Tagen, innerhalb drei(er) Tage; *- doors*, im Hause; *- hearing*, in Hörweite; *keep* or *live - one's income*, in den Grenzen seines Einkommens leben; *- the meaning of the act*, innerhalb des Gesetzes; *- memory*, soweit man zurückdenken kann; *- my powers*, innerhalb meiner Machtbefugnis; *- reach*, in Reichweite; *- sight*, in Sehweite; *be - the statute*, unter die Bestimmung fallen; *- a few steps of him*, nur einige Schritte von ihm entfernt; *keep well - the time*, nicht über den Zeitpunkt hinausgehen.
without [wɪð'ɑut], **1.** *adv.* außen, draußen, äußerlich; *from -*, von außen; (*coll.*) *go -*, nicht(s) bekommen. **2.** *prep.* ohne (*doing*, zu tun); (*archaic*) außerhalb; *- more ado*, ohne weitere Umstände; *- change*, ohne Umsteigen (*Railw.*); *be - a th.*, etwas entbehren *or* vermissen; *- delay*, ohne Verzug; *do - a th.*, etwas entbehren, auskommen *or* fertigwerden ohne etwas; *- doubt*, ohne Zweifel, *- end*, endlos; *go - a th.*, etwas entbehren, sich ohne etwas behelfen; *- number*, zahllos; *- prejudice to*, unbeschadet (*Gen.*); *that goes - saying*, das versteht sich von selbst; *- their* (*or coll.*) *them seeing me*, ohne daß sie mich sehen *or* sahen.
withstand [wɪð'stænd], *ir.v.a.* widerstehen (*Dat.*), sich widersetzen (*Dat.*), Widerstand leisten (*Dat.*).
withy ['wɪðɪ], *s.* die Weidenrute; Korbweide.
witless ['wɪtlɪs], *adj.* ohne Verstand; unvernünftig, töricht, einfältig; *see* [1]**wit.**
witness, 1. *s.* der Zeuge, Augenzeuge, Gewährsmann; das Zeugnis, der Beweis (*of* or *to*, für *or* (*Gen.*)); die Bezeugung, Bekräftigung, Bestätigung; *bear -*, Zeugnis ablegen (*to*, von), beweisen, bezeugen, bestätigen; *call* or *take to -*, zum Zeugen aufrufen; *in - hereof* or *whereof*, zum Zeugnis *or* urkundlich dessen; *- for the defence*, der Entlastungszeuge; *- for the crown* or *prosecution*, der Belastungszeuge. **2.** *v.a.* bezeugen, beweisen; als Zeuge unterschreiben, beglaubigen (*a document, signature*); (Augen)Zeuge sein von; (*fig.*) erleben, sehen; *- his brother*, als Beweis dient sein Bruder. **3.** *v.n.* zeugen, Zeuge sein, Zeugnis ablegen (*to*, für); *- to a th.*, etwas bezeugen, Zeuge sein von einer S. **--box,** *s.* der Zeugenstand, die Zeugenbank.
witt-ed [wɪtɪd], *adj. suffix*; *half--*, blöde, blödsinnig, einfältig, albern; *quick--*, scharfsinnig, geistreich, geweckt. **-icism** [-ɪsɪzm], *s.* der Witz, Scherz, witzige *or* geistreiche Bemerkung. **-iness** [-ɪnɪs], *s.* der Witz, die Witzigkeit. **-ingly,** *adv.* absichtlich, wissentlich, geflissentlich, vorsätzlich; *see* [2]**wit. -y,** *adj.* witzig (*of a p. or story, etc.*); geistreich, witzelnd (*of a p.*).
wive [wɑɪv], (*archaic*) **1.** *v.n.* (sich ver)heiraten. **2.** *v.a.* heiraten.
wivern [wɑɪvən], *s.* fliegender Drache (*Her.*).
wives [wɑɪvz], *see* **wife.**
wizard [wɪzəd], **1.** *s.* der Zauberer, Magier, Hexenmeister. **2.** *adj.* (*sl.*) erstklassig.
wizen, (*usually*) **-ed** ['wɪzən(d)], *adj.* dürr (*also fig.*), verwelkt, (*fig.*) eingeschrumpft, zusammengeschrumpft, runzlig.
woad [woud], *s.* der (Färber)Waid.
wobbl-e [wɔbl], **1.** *v.n.* wackeln, wanken, torkeln, schwanken (*also fig.*), nicht fest sitzen (*Tech.*), schlottern (*as knees*), flattern (*Motor.*). **2.** *s.* das Wackeln, Wanken, (*fig.*) Schwanken. **-y,** *adj.* wackelig, wankend, unsicher; (*fig.*) schwankend, wankelmütig.
woe [wou], **1.** *s.* (*usually Poet.*) das Weh, Leid; der Kummer, Jammer; *pl.* Sorgen, Kümmernisse, Nöte, Leiden (*pl.*); *face of -*, kummervolles Antlitz; *the weal and -*, das Wohl und Wehe; (*coll.*) *tale of -*, die Leidensgeschichte. **2.** *int.* wehe, ach; *- is me!* wehe mir! ach, ich Unglückliche(r); *- betide* (*you*)*!* wehe dir! **-begone,** *adj.* niedergebeugt, betrübt, trauervoll, jammervoll, vergrämt. **-ful,** *adj.* traurig, elend, jammervoll, kummervoll, sorgenvoll; betrüblich, beklagenswert.
wog [wɔg], *s.* (*sl.*) der Nichteuropäer, Farbige(r), *m.*
wold [would], *s.* das Hügelland, Moorland, Heideland.
wolf [wulf], **1.** *s.* (*pl.* wolves [wulvz]) der Wolf; *she--*, die Wölfin; *- in sheep's clothing*, der Wolf im Schafskleid; *cry -*, blinden Lärm schlagen; *keep the - from the door*, sich vorm Verhungern bewahren, sich eben durchschlagen, gegen Not und Elend vorbeugen. **2.** *v.a.* (*coll.*) herunterschlingen. **--cub,** *s.* junger Wolf; der Jungpfadpfinder, Pimpf. **--dog, --hound,** *s.* der Wolfshund. **-ish,** *adj.* wölfisch, Wolfs-, (*fig.*) gefrässig, gierig; *-ish appetite*, der Wolfshunger.
wolfram ['wulfrəm], *s.* das Wolfram.
wolverine ['wulvəri:n], *s.* der Vielfraß (*Zool.*).
wolves, *see* **wolf.**
wom-an ['wumən], *s.* (*pl.* -en ['wɪmɪn]) die Frau, das Weib; (*contemptuous*) Weibsbild; *gentle-an*, die Edelfrau; *needle-an*, die Näherin; *play the -an*, sich weiblich benehmen; *-an of the world*, die Weltdame; *-an doctor*, die Ärztin; *police -an*, die Polizeifürsorgerin; *-an student*, die Studentin; *-en's diseases*, Frauenkrankheiten (*pl.*); *-en's rights*, Frauenrechte (*pl*); *-en's team*, die Damenmannschaft. **-an-hater,** *s.* der Weiberfeind. **-anhood,** *s.* das Frauentum, der Frauenstand, die Weiblichkeit, Frauenwelt; *grow to* or *reach -anhood*, Frau werden. **-anish,** *adj.* weibisch. **-anize,** *v.n.* (*vulg.*) hinter Frauen her sein. **-ankind,** *s.* weibliches Geschlecht, die Weiblichkeit, Frauenwelt, Frauen (*pl.*). **-anliness,** *s.* die Weiblichkeit, Fraulichkeit. **-anly,** *adj.* weiblich, frauenhaft, fraulich.
womb [wu:m], *s.* die Gebärmutter (*Anat.*), der (Mutter)Leib, Schoß (*also fig.*).
wombat ['wɔmbæt], *s.* der Wombat, die Beutelmaus.
women, *see* **woman. -folk,** *s.* Frauen (der Familie) (*pl.*).
won [wʌn], *see* **win.**
wond-er [wʌndə], **1.** *s.* das Wunder, Wunderwerk, die Wundertat; das Staunen, Erstaunen, die Verwunderung; *the -er is that*, man muß sich wundern daß; *he is a -er*, er ist ein wahres Wunder; *do* or *work -ers*, Wunder tun; *excite -er*, Staunen erregen; *for a -er*, wunderbarerweise; *in -er*, verwundert; *in the name of -er!* um (des) Himmels willen!; *a nine days' -er*, sensationelles Tagesgespräch; *no -er*, kein Wunder! *little* or *small -er that*, es kann einig wundernehmen daß; *promise -ers*, goldene Berge versprechen. **2.** *v.n.* sich wundern, erstaunt sein (*at*, über); *it is not to be -ered at*, es ist nicht erstaunlich *or* zu verwundern (*that*, wenn); *I -er he came*, ich bin erstaunt, daß er gekommen ist; *I -er!* das möchte ich wohl wissen! *I shouldn't -er that*, es sollte mich nicht wundern *or* überraschen wenn; *I was -ering whether*, ich überlegte mir ob. **-erful,** *adj.* wundervoll, wunderbar, bewundernswert, wunderschön, erstaunlich; (*coll.*) herrlich, glänzend, prächtig, großartig, außerordentlich. **-erfulness,** *s.* das Wunderbare, Erstaunliche, die Prächtigkeit. **-ering** *adj.* staunend, verwundert. **-erland,** *s.* das Wunderland. **-erment,** *s.* das Staunen, die Verwunderung. **-er-struck,** *adj.* von Staunen ergriffen, vor Staunen platt, erstaunt, verwundert, verblüfft. **-er-working,** *adj.* wunderwirkend, wundertuend, wundertätig. **-rous** [-rəs], **1.** *adj.* (*Poet.*) wunderbar, herrlich, erstaunlich. **2.** *adv.* außerordentlich, erstaunlich.
wonky ['wɔnkɪ], *adj.* (*sl.*) wacklig, locker; schwankend, unsicher, unzuverlässig, schief.
won't [wount] = **will not.**
wont [wount], **1.** *s die* Gewohnheit; *use and -*, fester Brauch. **2.** *pred. adj.* gewohnt; *be - to do,*

zu tun pflegen. **-ed** [-ɪd], *attrib. adj.* gewohnt; gewöhnlich, üblich.

woo [wu:], 1. *v.a.* den Hof machen (*Dat.*), freien *or* werben um; (*fig.*) trachten nach, buhlen um, zu erreichen suchen, locken; *see* **-er, -ing.**

wood [wud], *s.* der Wald, die Waldung, das Gehölz; Holz; das Faß; *dead* –, dürres Holz, (*fig.*) leeres Stroh; *be out of the* –, (*fig.*) über den Berg sein; *he cannot see the – for the trees*, er sieht den Wald vor lauter Bäumen nicht; *touch –!* unberufen! *touch* –, unter den Tisch klopfen; *wine in the* –, Wein im Faß; *wine from the* –, Wein direkt vom Faß. **--agate,** *s.* versteinertes Holz. **--anemone,** *s.* das Windröschen. **-bine,** *s.* das Geißblatt (*Bot.*); billige Zigarettenmarke. **--block,** *s.* der Holzstock, Druckstock (*Typ.*). **-carver,** *s.* der Holzschnitzer. **-carving,** *s.* die Holzschneidekunst; Holzschnitzerei. **-chat,** *s.* der Rotkopfwürger (*Orn.*). **-chuck,** *s.* (*Amer.*) das Murmeltier. **--coal,** *s.* die Braunkohle. **-cock,** *s.* die Waldschnepfe (*Orn.*). **-craft,** *s.* die Waidmannskunst. **-cut,** *s.* der Holzschnitt. **-cutter,** *s.* der Holzfäller; Holzhauer, Holzhacker. **-ed** [-ɪd], *adj.* waldig, bewaldet, Wald–. **-en** [-n], *adj.* hölzern (*also fig.*), Holz–, (*fig.*) ledern, steif, unbeholfen; ausdruckslos, langweilig (*expression*); *-en spoon*, der Holzlöffel; *-en shoes*, Holzschuhe; *-en walls*, (*fig.*) Schiffe (*pl.*). **-en-headed,** *adj.* dickköpfig, dumm. **--engraver,** *s.* der Holzschneider. **--engraving,** *s.* die Holzschneidekunst; der Holzschnitt, Holzstich. **-enness,** *s.* (*fig.*) die Steifheit, Ausdruckslosigkeit. **-iness,** *s.* der Waldreichtum, die Waldigkeit; Holzigkeit, holzige Beschaffenheit. **-land,** 1. *s.* das Waldland, die Waldung. 2. *attrib.* waldig, Wald–. **-lark,** *s.* die Heidelerche. **-less,** *adj.* holzarm. **--louse,** *s.* die Bohrassel (*Ent.*) **-man,** *s.* der Holzfäller, Förster, Forstaufseher. **--notes,** *pl.* (*fig.*) die Naturdichtung. **--nymph,** *s.* die Waldnymphe. **-pecker,** der Specht; *spotted -pecker*, der Buntspecht. **--pigeon,** *s.* die Holztaube, Ringeltaube. **--pile,** *s.* der Holzhaufen. **--pulp,** *s.* der Holzschliff; Holzzellstoff, die Holzfasermasse. **-ruff,** *s.* der Waldmeister (*Bot.*). **--shavings,** *pl.* Hobelspäne *pl.* **--sorrel,** *s.* der Sauerklee. **--spirit,** *s.* der Methylalkohol (*Chem.*). **--tar,** *s.* der Holzteer. **-wind,** *s.* Holzinstrumente *pl.* **--wool,** *s.* die Holzwolle, der Holzzellstoff. **-work,** *s.* das Holzwerk, der Holzbau; die Holzarbeit. **-y,** *adj.* holzig, Holz–; waldig, Wald–. **-yard,** *s.* der Holzplatz.

wooer ['wuə], *s.* der Freier, Bewerber; *see* **woo.**

woof [wu:f], *s.* der Einschlag, Einschluß; das Gewebe.

wooing ['wuɪŋ], *s.* das Freien, Werben, die Werbung (*of*, um); *go a* –, auf Freiersfüßen gehen; *see* **woo.**

wool [wul], *s.* die Wolle (*also Bot.*), das Wollgarn, der Wollfaden; das Wolltuch, der Wollstoff; Faserstoff, die Zellwolle, Pflanzenwolle; (*coll.*) wolliges Haar; *dyed in the* –, in der Wolle gefärbt, (*fig.*) ausgepicht, ausgekocht, (*sl.*) *lose one's* –, sich auskollern; *pull the – over s.o.'s eyes*, einem etwas vormachen, einen täuschen. **--card,** *s.* die Wollkrempel, Wollkratze. **--comb,** *s.* der Wollkamm. **--dyed,** in der Wolle gefärbt. **--gathering,** 1. *s.* die Zerstreutheit. 2. *adj.* zerstreut, *be --gathering*, nicht bei der Sache sein; Luftschlösser bauen, sich müßigen Träumen hingeben. **--grower,** *s.* der Schafzüchter. **--hall,** *s.* die Wollbörse. **-len** ['wulən], *adj.* wollen, Woll–; *-len cloth*, wollenes Tuch, das Wollzeug; der Wollstoff; *-len draper*, *s.* der Wollwarenhändler; *-len goods*, *pl.* Wollwaren (*pl.*). **-lens** [-lənz], *pl.* Wollwaren (*pl.*), Wollkleidung, wollene Unterwäsche. **-liness,** *s.* wollige *or* flaumige Eigenschaft; (*fig.*) die Unklarheit, Unbestimmtheit, Verschwommenheit. **-ly,** 1. *adj.* wollig, Woll–; wollartig, weich, flaumig; (*fig.*) unklar, unbestimmt, verschwommen; unscharf; (*coll.*) *-ly bear*, die Bärenraupe. 2. *s.* (*coll.*) der Sweater, die Wolljacke; *pl.* wollene Unterwäsche. **--pack,** *s.* der Wollballen. **-sack,** *s.* der Wollsack (*seat of the Lord Chancellor*). **--staple,** *s.* der Wollmarkt. **--stapler,** *s.* der Wollgroßhändler. **--work,** *s.* die Wollstickerei.

woozy ['wu:zɪ], *adj.* (*sl.*) benebelt, beduselt.

wop [wɔp], *s.* (*pej.*) Italiener (*m.*).

word [wə:d], **1.** *s.* das Wort; (*without art.*) die Nachricht, Meldung, Botschaft, Mitteilung; Losung, das Losungswort; Versprechen, die Zusage, der Befehl; die Anweisung; *the* –, das Wort (*Theol.*), Evangelium; *pl.* der Text; **(a)** (*with nouns*) – *of command*, das Kommandowort; – *of God*, das Wort Gottes; – *of honour*, das Ehrenwort; *a – in s.o.'s ear*, ein Wort im Vertrauen, *a – in season*, ein angebrachter Rat; **(b)** (*with verbs*) *money's the* –, Geld ist die Losung! (*coll.*) *mum's the* –, nicht ein Wort! nichts gesagt; *sharp's the* –, schnell gemacht, flugs!; *bandy -s with*, see *have -s with*; *break one's* –, sein Wort brechen, wortbrüchig werden; *bring* –, Nachricht bringen; *eat one's -s*, siene Worte zurücknehmen (müssen), zu Kreuze kriechen; *give the* –, das Zeichen geben; *give one's* –, sein Wort geben; *have* –, see *receive* –; *have a – with*; ein paar Worte reden mit; *have a – to say*, etwas Wichtiges mitzuteilen haben; *you have my – for it*, auf mein Wort, ich gebe mein Wort darauf; *have -s with*, sich zanken *or* streiten, Worte wechseln mit; *keep one's* –, Wort halten; *leave – with*, Bescheid hinterlassen bei; *receive* –, Nachricht erhalten; *say the* –, den Wunsch aussprechen; *send – to*, ausrichten *or* sagen lassen (*Dat.*), Nachricht geben (*Dat.*); *speak a – for*, ein Wort einlegen für; *I take your – for it*, ich glaube es dir; *waste -s*, unnütz reden; **(c)** (*with prepositions*) *at a – from*, auf Anweisung von; *at these -s*, bei diesen Worten, *take a p. at his* –, einen beim Worte nehmen; *by – of mouth*; mündlich; – *for* –, Wort für Wort, wörtlich; *too funny for -s*, unsagbar komisch; *in a* –, mit einem Worte, kurz und gut; *in the -s of*, mit den Worten von; *in other -s*, mit anderen Worten; *put into -s*, in Worte kleiden *or* fassen; *a man of his* –, ein Mann von Wort; *on the* –, bei dem Wort; *hang on a p's. -s*, einem aufmerksam zuhören; *lead to -s*, zu Streitigkeiten führen; *suit the action to the* –, die Tat dem Wort auf den Fuß folgen lassen; (*upon*) *my –!* bei Gott!; *play* (*up*)*on -s*, das Wortspiel; **(d)** (*with adjectives*) *big -s*, prahlerische Worte, große Töne; *fair -s*, schmeichelnde Worte; *a man of few -s*, ein Mann von wenig Worten; *be as good as one's* –, sein Wort halten, zu seinem Wort stehen; *hot -s*, zornige Worte; *have the last* –, das letzte Wort haben; *the last* –, (*fig.*) die letzte Neuheit; das Vollkommendste. **2.** *v.a.* in Worte fassen *or* kleiden, ausdrücken, abfassen. **--blindness,** die Wortblindheit. **--book,** *s.* das Wörterbuch. **--building, --formation,** *s.* die Wortbildung. **-iness,** *s.* der Wortreichtum, die Wortfülle; Weitschweifigkeit. **-ing,** *s.* die Fassung, Ausdrucksweise, Formulierung, der Wortlaut. **-less,** *adj.* wortlos, sprachlos. **-y,** *adj.* wortreich, weitschweifig; Wort–. **--painting,** *s.* die Wortmalerei; lebendige Schilderung. **--perfect,** *adj.*; *be --perfect*, eine Rolle beherrschen.

wore [wɔ:], *see* **wear.**

work [wə:k], **1.** *v.n.* (*of a p.*) arbeiten (*at*, an), sich bemühen; beschäftigt *or* tätig sein (*at*, mit); (*of a th.*) arbeiten; (usually *be -ing*) in Betrieb sein (*factory, etc.*); wirken, wirksam sein; Wirkung tun, sich auswirken; gehen, funktionieren, laufen (*of machine, etc.*); gären (*as wine*); sich krampfhaft bewegen, verziehen, zucken (*of the features*); herumfuchteln (*with the arms*); (*coll.*) glücken, klappen (*with*, bei); *this wood -s easily*, dieses Holz läßt sich leicht bearbeiten; (*coll.*) *it won't* –, es wird nicht gehen; – *loose*, sich lockern; *refuse to* –, versagen (*of an engine*); – *against time*, aus allen Kräften arbeiten, um zur rechten Zeit fertig zu werden; – *at*, arbeiten an (*Dat.*); – *away*, drauflos arbeiten (*at*, an (*Dat.*)); – *in*, eindringen; (*fig.*) zusammengehen, harmonieren (*with*, mit); – *on*, wirken auf; – *out*, herauskommen; zum Vorschein kommen, gelöst werden; (*fig.*) sich auswirken, kommen, ergeben, sich belaufen; sich stellen (*at*, auf (*Acc.*)); – *out one's own salvation*, selbst damit fertig werden; – *round*, sich hindurcharbeiten (*to* nach), sich wenden (*of wind*); – *to windward*, lavieren (*Naut.*); – *together*, ineinandergreifen (*as wheels*); – *through*, durcharbeiten (*a book, etc.*), sich durcharbeiten, durchkommen (*as through a hole*); – *up*, sich emporarbeiten. **2.** *v.a.* bearbeiten, formen, gestalten (*into*, zu), bebauen (*land*), bewirtschaften (*a farm*), zurichten (*timber*), hämmern, schmieden (*metal*), fördern, gewinnen (*ore*), ausbeuten (*mines*), kneten (*dough*), ausrechnen, lösen (*Math.*), sticken, nähen (*a pattern*), führen, lenken, leiten (*a train, etc.*); arbeiten lassen (*a p. etc.*); zur Arbeit verwenden (*an animal*); bedienen (*a machine*); geschäftlich bereisen (*a district*) (*C.L.*); (*coll.*) zustande *or* zuwege bringen, fertigbringen, bewirken, deichseln; (*archaic*) tun, verrichten; – *one's jaws*, mit den Kinnbacken arbeiten; – *one's passage*, die Überfahrt durch Arbeit an Bord bezahlen; – *one's way*, sich einen Weg bahnen, sich durcharbeiten; – *wonders*, Wunder tun; – *itself loose*, sich lockern *or* lösen; – *itself right*, in die richtige Bahn kommen; – *o.s.*, sich aufschwingen *or* begeistern (*into*, zu); – *o.s. to the bone, to death* or *to a shadow*, sich abarbeiten; – *in*, einschalten, einfügen, hineinarbeiten; – *a change*, eine Änderung hervorrufen *or* bewirken; – *off*, abziehen, abdrucken (*Typ.*); loswerden, verabreichen (*on* (*Dat.*)); erledigen (*a task*); abarbeiten (*a debt*); abreagieren, Luft machen (*Dat.*) (*feelings*); – *out*, herausfinden, errechnen, lösen; ausarbeiten, ausgestalten, entwickeln; zustande bringen, ausführen; abbauen, erschöpfen (*a mine*); – *itself out*, sich auswirken; – *up*, entwickeln, aufarbeiten, verarbeiten (*into*, zu); erweitern, ausarbeiten ((*in*)*to*, zu), aufpeitschen (*feelings*), bearbeiten, studieren (*a subject, etc.*); – *o.s. up to*, sich aufregen. **3.** *s.* die Arbeit (also *Phys.*), Beschäftigung, Tätigkeit; der Arbeitsprozeß, das Werk, Resultat, die Tat, Handlung; das Erzeugnis, Produkt; (*coll.*) die Handarbeit, Stickerei, Näherei; *pl.* Arbeiten, Bauten, Anlagen (*pl.*); *pl.* Verteidigungswerke, Festungswerke (*pl.*); *pl.* das Maschinenwerk, (Uhr)Werk, Getriebe; *pl.* die Fabrik, Betriebsanlage; (**a**) (*with adjectives*) *defensive –s*, Verteidigungswerke; *good – !* gute Leistung! *good –s*, gute Werke (*Theol.*); *public –s*, öffentliche Arbeiten, staatliche *or* städtische Werke; *make sad – of*, etwas Schönes anrichten (*ironic*), arg wirtschaften mit; *make short – of*, kurzen Prozeß machen mit; (**b**) (*with verbs*) *have one's – cut out* (*for one*), schwer arbeiten müssen, viel zu schaffen haben; *do –*, Arbeit leisten; *let a th. do its –*, etwas seiner Wirkung überlassen; *make –*, Arbeit *or* Mühe verursachen; *strike –*, die Arbeit einstellen; (**c**) (*with prepositions*) *at –*, bei der Arbeit, tätig (*of a p.*), im Gang (*of a machine*); *hard at –*, tüchtig bei der Arbeit; *be at – on*, arbeiten an, beschäftigt sein mit; *be out at –*, auf Arbeit sein; *be in –*, Arbeit haben; *out of –*, arbeitslos; *a good piece of –*, eine gute Arbeit; *fall* or *go* or *set to –*, an die Arbeit *or* ans Werk gehen, sich an die Arbeit machen; *set s.o. to –*, einen anstellen; (**d**) (with *of*) – *of art*, das Kunstwerk; – *of the devil*, das Werk des Teufels; – *of God*, Gottes Werke; *–s of a clock*, das Uhrwerk; *Office* (now *Ministry*) *of –s*, die Behörde (das Ministerium) für öffentliche Bauten; *the –s of Shakespeare*, die Werke Shakespeares (N.B. *a – by Sh.*, ein Werk von Sh.; *a – on Sh.*, ein Werk über Sh.). **–able,** *adj.* zu bearbeiten(d) (*as soil*), nützlich, brauchbar; durchführbar, ausführbar. **–aday,** *adj.* Werktags–, Alltags–, alltäglich. **–-bag,** *s.* der Arbeitsbeutel. **–-basket,** *s.* der Arbeitskorb. **–-camp,** *s.* das Arbeitslager. **–day,** *s.* der Werktag, Alltag, Wochentag. **–er,** *s.* der Arbeiter (also *–er-ant, –er-bee*), (*fig.*) Urheber; *pl.* die Arbeiterschaft; Proletarier (*pl.*); *hard –er*, tüchtiger Arbeiter; *heavy –er*, der Schwerarbeiter; *office –ers*, das Büropersonal; *skilled –er*, gelernter Arbeiter; (*B.*) *–ers of iniquity*, Übeltäter (*pl.*). **–house,** *s.* das Armenhaus. **–ing,** 1. *s.* das Arbeiten; (*fig.*) Schaffen, Wirken; Gären; der Betrieb (*of a business, etc.*); die Tätigkeit (*of mind*); der Gang, die Bewegung (*of machines*); Bearbeitung, Verarbeitung (*of materials*); Ausbeutung, der Abbau (*of mines, etc.*); die (Aus)Wirkung; Handlung, Tat; (*often pl.*) die Grubenanlage, Bergwerksanlage, Grube, der Bau (*mines*). 2. *adj.* arbeitend, Arbeits–; *–ing capacity*, die Arbeitsleistung; *–ing capital*, das Betriebskapital; *–ing-class, adj.* Arbeiter–; *–ing classes, pl.* arbeitende Klassen, die Arbeiterbevölkerung, der Arbeiterstand; *–ing committee*, der Arbeitsausschuß; *–ing day*, der Arbeitstag; *–ing drawing*, der Bauplan, die Werkstattzeichnung; *–ing expenses*, die Betriebskosten; *–ing hours*, die Arbeitsstunden (*pl.*); *–ing instructions*, Gebrauchsanweisungen; *–ing knowledge*, ausreichende Kenntnisse; *–ing load*, die Nutzlast; *–ing majority*, arbeitsfähige Mehrheit; *–ing method*, das Arbeitsverfahren; *–ing model*, das Versuchsmodell; *in –ing order*, in Ordnung, betriebsfähig, funktionierend; *–ing-out*, *s.* das Ausarbeiten; *–ing population*, werktätige Bevölkerung; *–ing theory*, eine Theorie mit der sich arbeiten läßt; *–ing vocabulary*, genügender Wortschatz; *–ing voltage*, die Betriebsspannung; *–ing woman*, die Arbeitsfrau. **–less,** *adj.* arbeitslos. **–man,** *s.* der Arbeiter (*espec.* Handarbeiter), Handwerker; *–man's compensation*, die Arbeiterunfallversicherung, Betriebsunfallversicherung. **–manlike,** *adj.* fachmännisch, kunstgerecht, geschickt. **–manship,** *s.* die Geschicklichkeit, Kunstfertigkeit; (Art der) Ausführung; Arbeit, das Werk. **–people,** *pl.* Arbeitsleute, Arbeiter (*pl.*). **–-room,** *s.* der Arbeitsraum. **–s council,** *s.* der Betriebsrat. **–-shaft,** *s.* die Treibwelle (*Mech.*). **–shop,** *s.* die Werkstatt, Werkstätte. **–-shy,** *adj.* arbeitsscheu. **–-table,** *s.* der Nähtisch, Arbeitstisch. **–woman,** *s.* die Arbeiterin.

world [wə:ld], *s.* die Welt. (*a*) (*with nouns*) – *champion*, der (die) Weltmeister(in); *a – of care*, eine Welt voll Sorgen; – *of letters*, gelehrte Welt; *a – of trouble*, eine Unmenge Kummer; (*b*) (*with adjectives*) *be all the – to him* (*her*), sein (ihr) ein und alles sein; *for all the – like*, genau gleich (*Dat.*); *for all the – as if*, genau als ob; *all the – over*, über die ganze *or* auf der ganzen Welt; *all the – and his wife*, jedermann; *fashionable –*, feine Welt; *the next –*, das Jenseits, zukünftige Welt; *scientific –*, wissenschaftliche Welt; *sporting –*, die Sportwelt; (*c*) (*with verbs*) *carry the – before one*, Erfolg haben in der Welt; *the – to come*, das Jenseits; *forsake the –*, der Welt entsagen; (*coll.*) *give the –*, wer weiß nicht was geben; *as the – goes*, wie es in der Welt geht; *see the –*, Land und Leute kennen lernen; *think the – of*, Wunder was *or* sehr viel halten von; (*d*) (*with prepositions*) *not for –s* or *all the –*, nicht um alles in der Welt, um keinen Preis (der Welt); *from all over the –*, aus aller Herren Ländern; *in the –*, auf der Welt; *nothing in the –*, absolut *or* überhaupt nichts; *what in the – ?* was in aller Welt? *bring into the –*, auf die *or* zur Welt bringen; *come into the –*, auf die Welt kommen; *knowledge of the –*, die Weltkenntnis, Welterfahrung; *man of the –*, der Weltmann; *woman of the –*, die Weltdame; *that* or *such is the way of the –*, so geht es in der Welt; *ways of the –*, der Weltlauf, Lauf der Welt; (*sl.*) *blind to the –*, hilflos betrunken; – *without end*, von Ewigkeit zu Ewigkeit; **–-famous,** *adj.* weltberühmt. **–-language,** *s.* die Weltsprache. **–liness,** *s.* die Weltlichkeit, der Weltsinn, weltlicher *or* materieller Sinn. **–ling,** *s.* das Weltkind, weltlicher Mensch. **–ly,** *adj.* weltlich, Welt–; zeitlich, irdisch; *–ly-minded*, weltlich gesinnt; *–ly-mindedness*, der Weltsinn, weltliche Gesinnung; *–ly wisdom*, die Weltklugheit; *–ly-wise*, weltklug, welterfahren. **–-politics,** *s.* die Weltpolitik. **–-power,** *s.* die Weltmacht. **–-renowned,** *adj.* weltberühmt (*for*, wegen). **–-view,** *s.* die Weltanschauung. **–-weary,** *adj.* weltmüde. **–-wide,** *adj.* weitverbreitet; allgemein anerkannt; *of –-wide fame*, weltberühmt; *–-wide reputation*, der Weltruf.

worm [wə:m], 1. *s.* der Wurm; die Raupe, Made, Larve; das Gewinde, die Schnecke (*Tech.*); die (Kühl)Schlange (*Chem.*); (*fig. coll.*) elender *or* elendes Wurm; *even a – will turn*, auch der Wurm krümmt sich, wenn er getreten wird; *–'s eye view*, die Froschperspektive. 2. *v.a.* von Würmern befreien (*animals*); putzen (*a gun*); – *o.s.* or *one's way*, sich winden, schlängeln *or* einschleichen; – *a secret out of a p.* einem ein Geheimnis entlocken, einem die Würmer aus der Nase ziehen. 3. *v.n.* sich winden, schlängeln *or* einschleichen. **–-cast,** *s.* von Regenwürmern aufgeworfene Erde. **–-drive,** *s.* der Schneckenantrieb. **–-eaten,** *adj.* wurmstichig. **--gear,** *s.* das Schneckengetriebe. **--hole,** *s.* der Wurmstich. **-iness,** *s.* die Wurmstichigkeit. **--like,** *adj.* wurmartig. **--seed,** *s.* Wurmsamen (*pl.*). **--wheel,** *s.* das Schneckenrad. **-wood,** *s.* der Wermut, (*fig.*) die Bitterkeit; *it is* (*gall and*) *-wood to him*, es wurmt ihn. **-y,** *adj.* wurmig, madig, wurmstichig.

worn [wɔːn], *see* **wear**; *adj.* getragen (*of clothes*): (also – *out*) abgenutzt, abgetragen (*clothes*); abgehärmt, verhärmt (*features*). **--out,** *adj.* (*fig.*) erschöpft, zermürbt, abgespannt (*of a p.*); veraltet, überlebt, abgedroschen (*of a th.*).

worry [ˈwʌrɪ], 1. *v.a.* würgen, zerreißen, zerren, zausen; (*fig.*) plagen, belästigen, zusetzen (*Dat.*), ängstigen, beunruhigen; – *a p. into*, einen durch ständiges Quälen treiben zu; – *s.th. out of s.o.*, einem etwas durch Quälereien abringen *or* abpressen; – *a problem out*, ein Problem nicht loslassen bis es gelöst wird; – *o.s.* or *be worried*, sich ärgern *or* ängstigen. 2. *v.n.* zerren (*at*, an); sich Gedanken *or* Sorgen machen, sich sorgen, ängstigen, beunruhigen *or* aufregen. 3. *s.* die Sorge, Besorgnis, der Ärger, Verdruß, Kummer. **-ing,** *adj.* beängstigend, beunruhigend.

worse [wəːs], 1. *adj.* schlechter, schlimmer, übler; (*fig.*) ärger; *to make it* –, um das Unglück vollzumachen; *be the – for*, Schaden erlitten haben durch, schlechter daran sein wegen; *be the – for drink*, einen (Affen) sitzen haben; – *luck*, unglücklicherweise, leider, um so schlimmer; *so much the* –, um so schlimmer; *no* –, nicht schlechter; *your hands would be none the – for a wash*, waschen würde deinen Händen wahrhaftig nicht schaden; *he is none the – for it*, es hat ihm nichts geschadet; *the – for wear*, abgetragen *or* abgenutzt sein, (*fig.*) arg mitgenommen sein; – *and* –, immer schlechter. 2. *adv.* schlimmer, schlechter; *none the* –, nicht schlechter; *think none the – of*, nicht geringer denken von; *be – off*, schlechter dran sein; *go farther and fare* –, aus dem Regen in die Traufe kommen. 3. *s.* Schlimmeres, *n.*; *for better, for* –, was auch kommen mag, wohl oder übel, wie man es auch nimmt; *from bad to* –, aus dem Regen in die Traufe; *change for the* –, die Wendung zum Schlechtern, die Verschlechterung; – *followed*, Schlimmeres folgte. **-n,** 1. *v.a.* verschlechtern, schlechter machen, verschlimmern; schädigen. 2. *v.n.* schlechter *or* schlimmer werden, sich verschlechtern *or* verschlimmern. **-ning,** *s.* die Verschlechterung.

worship [ˈwəːʃɪp], 1. *s.* die Verehrung, Anbetung, der Gottesdienst (*Rel.*); Ritus, Kult(us); *your* –, Eure Gnaden *or* Hochwürden; *place of* –, die Kirche, das Gotteshaus. 2. *v.a.* anbeten, verehren, (*fig.*) vergöttern. 3. *v.n.* seine Andacht verrichten. **-ful,** *adj.* (*in titles*) ehrwürdig, ehrenwert, wohlangesehen, wohllöblich; (*archaic*) angesehen, achtbar. **-per,** *s.* der Verehrer, Anbeter; *pl.* Kirchgänger, Andächtige (*pl.*); *-per of idols*, der Götzendiener.

worst [wəːst], 1. *adj.* schlimmst, schlechtest, ärgst. 2. *adv.* am Schlimmsten *or* Schlechtesten *or* Ärgsten. 3. *s.* das Schlimmste, Ärgste; *at* (*the*) –, im schlimmsten Falle; *at its* –, selbst da wo es am schlechtesten ist; *do one's* –, es so arg machen, wie man nur kann; *do your – !* mach' was du willst; *get the – of it*, den kürzeren ziehen; *the – of it*, das Schlimmste daran; *the – is yet to come*, das Schlimmste kommt noch; *if the* – or *if it comes to the* –, schlimmstenfalls, wenn es zum Schlimmsten kommt; *be prepared for the* –, aufs Schlimmste gefaßt sein. 4. *v.a.* (*coll.*) unterkriegen.

worsted [ˈwustɪd], *s.* das Kammgarn; der Kammgarnstoff; – *stockings*, wollene Strümpfe.

1**-wort** [wəːt], *s.*; (*in comps.*) die . . .-wurz, das . . . -kraut.

2**wort,** *s.* die Bierwürze.

worth [wəːθ], 1. *pred. adj.* wert (*to* (*Dat.*) *or* für) (*also fig. of a p. or th.*); (*fig.*) würdig (*of a p.*); *it is – little to him*, es ist ihm *or* für ihn wenig wert; *be – a great deal*, viel wert sein; *not – a penny*, keinen Pfifferling wert; (*coll.*) *he is – a million*, er besitzt eine Million, er ist seine Million wert; (*coll.*) *he is – £1,000 a year*, er hat ein jährliches Einkommen von *or* er verdient jährlich £1,000; *be not – the trouble*, nicht der Mühe wert sein, sich nicht lohnen; (*coll.*) *for all one is* –, so gut man kann, mit allen Kräften *for what it is* –, unter Vorbehalt; *not – powder and shot*, keinen Schuß Pulver wert; (*coll.*) *not – the candle*, die Mühe nicht lohnen; (*Prov.*) *a bird in the hand is – two in the bush*, ein Sperling in der Hand ist besser als eine Taube auf dem Dach; *it is – its weight in gold*, das kann nicht mit Gold aufgewogen werden; *not – bothering about*, nicht der Mühe wert; *it is – doing*, es lohnt sich, es zu tun; es ist wert getan zu werden; – *mentioning*, erwähnenswert; – *reading*, lesenswert; – *seeing*, sehenswert; – *speaking of*, der Rede wert; *a tale – telling*, erzählenswerte Geschichte; *be* – (*one's*) *while*, (*coll.*) *be – it*, sich lohnen, der Mühe wert sein; *make it – someone's while*, es einem belohnen *or* vergelten. 2. *s.* der Wert (*also fig.*), (*fig.*) die Bedeutung, das Ansehen; *a shilling's – of oranges*, für einen Schilling Apfelsinen, Apfelsinen im Wert von einem Schilling; *of great* –, teuer, sehr wertvoll; *get one's money's* –, für sein Geld entsprechendes erhalten. **-ily** [ˈwəːðɪlɪ], *adv.* würdig, mit Recht, nach Verdienst. **-iness** [-ðɪnɪs], *s.* die Würdigkeit, der Wert. **-less** [ˈwəːθlɪs], *adj.* wertlos, ohne Bedeutung; (*fig.*) nichtswürdig, unwürdig, verächtlich. **-lessness,** *s.* die Wertlosigkeit. Nichtswürdigkeit, Unwürdigkeit, Schlechtigkeit. **--while,** *attrib. adj.* lohnend. **-y** [ˈwəːðɪ], 1. *pred. adj.* würdig, wert; *-y of death*, todeswürdig; *he is not -y of her*, er ist ihrer nicht wert *or* würdig; *be -y of praise*, Lob verdienen; *-y to be done*, wert sein getan zu werden. 2. *attrib. adj.* würdig, angesehen, ehrenwert, schätzbar (*of a p.*), angemessen, ausreichend (*of a th.*). 3. *s.* verdienstvoller Mann, große Persönlichkeit, der Held, die Größe.

wot [wɔt], *see* 2**wit.**

would [wud], *see* **will**; wollte(st), wollten, *etc.*; pflegte(st), pflegten, *etc.*; (*in princip. clauses 1st pers. sing. & pl.*) möchte(n), wünschte(n); (*2nd pers. in questions*) möchtest, möchten; (*with cond. clauses*) *2nd or 3rd pers. imperf. subj. or* würde(st), würden, würdet *with inf.*; – *to God!* wollte Gott! *I – rather not*, ich möchte lieber nicht; *he – not come*, er wollte durchaus nicht kommen; *he – do it if time – permit*, er würde es tun *or* täte es wenn die Zeit es erlaubte; *he – walk for hours*, er pflegte stundenlang zu gehen; *do what I* –, was ich auch täte; *I – have you know*, ich muß Ihnen sagen, Sie sollen wissen; *it – be about a week ago*, es mochte wohl eine Woche her sein; *it – seem*, es scheint fast; *one – think he was ill*, man sollte denken er sei krank. **--be,** *attrib. adj.* vorgeblich, angeblich, Schein-; *--be assassin*, einer der sich als Attentäter ausgibt; *--be important person*, der Gernegroß; *--be painter*, der Farbenkleckser; *--be poet*, der Dichterling; *--be politician*, der Biertischpolitiker; *--be sportsman*, der Sonntagsjäger; *--be wit*, einer, der witzig sein möchte. **-n't** = – *not*.

1**wound** [wuːnd], 1. *s.* die Wunde (*also fig.*), Verwundung (*in*, an), (*fig.*) Kränkung, Verletzung. 2. *v.a.* verwunden (*in*, an), verletzen; kränken. **-ed** [-ɪd], *adj.* verwundet; *war--ed*, Kriegsversehrte, Kriegsbeschädigte (*pl.*). **--stripe,** *s.* das Verwundetenabzeichen.

2**wound** [waund], *see* 2**wind.**

wove [wouv], 1. *see* **weave.** 2. *adj.*; – *paper*, das Velinpapier. **-n,** *see* **weave**; *adj.*; *-n fabrics*, Wirkwaren, Webwaren (*pl.*).

wow [wau], *s.* (*sl.*) großer Erfolg, die Pfundsache, der Mordskerl, Prachtkerl. **-ser,** *s.* der Moralinonkel.

1**wrack** [ræk], *s.* angeschwemmte Algen.

2**wrack,** *s.* ziehendes Gewölk, windgetriebene Wolken.

3**wrack,** *s.* (*archaic*) der Untergang; (*only in*) *go to – and ruin*, zugrunde gehen.

wraith [reɪθ], *s.* geisterhafte Erscheinung, der Geist, das Gespenst.

wrangl-e [ˈræŋgl], 1. *v.n.* zanken, streiten, sich in den Haaren liegen, sich katzbalgen. 2. *s.* der Zank, Streit, die Katzbalgerei. **-r** [-lə], *s.* der Zänker; *senior -r*, der Student, der die mathematische Schlußprüfung am besten besteht (*Cambridge Univ.*).

wrap [ræp], 1. *v.a.* (also – *up*), einwickeln, einhüllen, einschlagen, einpacken; wickeln (*paper*), hüllen (*a cloak, etc.*); (*fig.*) (ver)hüllen, verdecken, bedecken; verwickeln, verstricken; (*fig.*) *be –ped up in*, gänzlich aufgehen in, versunken sein in, vollkommen in Anspruch *or* eingenommen werden von; – *o.s. up* (*warm*), sich warm anziehen; (*fig.*) *–ped in silence*, in Schweigen gehüllt. 2. *v.n.* sich wickeln (*round*, um), sich legen (*over*, über); – *up*, sich einhüllen. 3. *s.* die Hülle, der Überwurf, Schal. **–per,** *s.* der Umschlag, die Hülle, Decke, Verpackung; das Deckblatt (*of a cigar*); der (Buch)-Umschlag, Schutzdeckel; der Packer; (*postal*) *–per*, das Kreuzband, Streifband. **–ping,** *s.* das Einwickeln, die Umhüllung, Verpackung; Decke, Hülle, der Wickel; *–ping paper*, das Packpapier, Einschlagpapier.

wrath [rɔ:θ], *s.* der Zorn, Grimm, die Wut. **–ful,** *adj.* zornig, grimmig, wütig, wütend (*with*, auf (*Acc.*)), ergrimmt, wutentbrannt.

wreak [rɪ:k], *v.a.* (*Poet.*) ausüben, auslassen (*anger, vengeance, etc.*) (*on*, an).

wreath [rɪ:θ], *s.* der Kranz, das Gewinde, die Girlande; – *of flowers*, der Blumenkranz; – *of smoke*, das Rauchwölkchen; – *of snow*, die Schneewehe. **–e** [rɪ:ð], 1. *v.a.* winden, drehen, wickeln (*round*, um); einhüllen (*in*, in), umgeben (*with*, mit); flechten, binden (*a garland*), bekränzen, schmücken (*a p.*). 2. *v.n.* sich drehen *or* winden, sich kräuseln *or* ringeln.

wreck [rɛk], 1. *s.* das Wrack (*also fig*), der Schiffbruch; die Zerstörung, Verwüstung, der Ruin, Untergang; das Strandgut (*Law*); *nervous* –, das Nervenbündel. 2. *v.a.* zerschellen, zum Scheitern bringen (*a ship, also fig.*), zugrunde richten, zu Fall bringen, zerstören, vernichten (*plans, etc.*); – *a train*, einen Zug zum Entgleisen bringen, *be –ed*, scheitern, stranden, Schiffbruch erleiden, zerschellen (*a ship*); entgleisen (*a train*), zerstört *or* vernichtet werden. **–age,** *s.* (Schiffs)Trümmer (*pl.*); das Strandgut. **–ed** [–t], *adj.* gescheitert (*also fig.*), gestrandet (*ship*), schiffbrüchig (*sailors*), Strand– (*goods*), (*fig.*) zerstört, zerrüttet, vernichtet. **–er,** *s.* der Stranddieb, Strandräuber; Eisenbahnattentäter; Abbrucharbeiter; (*fig.*) Zerstörer.

wren [rɛn], *s.* der Zaunkönig (*Orn.*); (*sl.*) die Flottenhelferin.

wrench [rɛntʃ], 1. *s.* heftiger Ruck, heftige Drehung; die Verrenkung. Verstauchung; der Schraubenschlüssel; (*fig.*) (Trennungs)Schmerz; *it was a – to me*, es war für mich sehr schmerzlich. 2. *v.a.* mit Gewalt ziehen *or* reißen; entwinden, entreißen (*from s.o.*, einem); verrenken, verstauchen (*a limb*); verzerren, verdrehen (*meaning*); – *o.s. from*, sich losreißen von, – *open*, mit Gewalt öffnen, aufreißen.

wrest [rɛst], *v.a.* reißen, zerren; verdrehen, entstellen, pressen (*meanings*); – *from*, entreißen *or* entwinden (*Dat.*).

wrestl–e [ˈrɛstl], 1. *v.n.* ringen (*also fig.*), sich ringen; (*fig.*) kämpfen, sich abmühen (*for*, um). 2. *v.a.* ringen mit (*a p.*). 3. *s.* der Ringkampf, (*fig.*) das Ringen, schwerer Kampf (*for*, um). **–er,** *s.* der Ringer. **–ing,** *s.* (also *–ing match*) das Ringen, der Ringkampf.

wretch [rɛtʃ], *s.* der Lump, Schuft; armes Wesen, Elende(r), *m.*; *poor* –, armer Teufel. **–ed** [–ɪd], *adj.* elend, unglücklich, armselig, traurig (*of a p.*), jämmerlich, erbärmlich, kläglich, dürftig, ärmlich, lumpig; *feel –ed*, sich elend *or* schlecht fühlen. **–edness,** *s.* das Elend, Unglück, die Erbärmlichkeit, Armseligkeit.

wriggle [ˈrɪgl], 1. *v.n.* sich winden, ringeln, hin und her bewegen *or* schlängeln; – *out of*, sich herauswinden aus. 2. *v.a.*; – *one's way*, sich winden; – *o.s. out of*, sich herauswinden aus. 3. *s.* das Ringeln, die Windung, Krümmung, der Schlängelweg.

–wright [raɪt], *s.* (*in comps.* = der . . . –anfertiger, –macher, –bauer; *play–*, der Schauspieldichter, Dramatiker.

wring [rɪŋ], 1. *ir.v.a.* ringen (*one's hands*), abdrehen (*fowl's neck*); (also – *out*) auswinden, aus(w)ringen (*clothes*); (*fig.*) beklemmen, bedrücken, martern, quälen (*the heart*); – *from*, entreißen, entwinden (*Dat.*), abgewinnen, abringen (*Dat.*), erpressen von (*taxes etc.*); drücken (*a p.'s hand*); (*fig.*) – *a p.'s neck*, einem den Hals umdrehen; – *a p. by the hand*, einem die Hand drücken; *it –s my heart*, es schmerzt mich tief. 2. *s.*; *give a thing a* –, etwas auswringen, auspressen *or* ausdrücken; *give a p.'s hand a* –, einem die Hand drücken. **–er,** *s.* die Wringmaschine (*for clothes*). **–ing,** 1. *adj.*; *–ing wet*, zum Auswringen naß, triefend naß, klitschnaß. 2. *s.* das Auswringen, Auswinden. **–ing-machine,** *s. see* **–er.**

wrinkle [ˈrɪŋkl], 1. *s.* die Runzel, Falte; Unebenheit, Vertiefung; (*coll.*) der Kniff, Handgriff, Wink, Tip. 2. *v.a.* falten, kniffen; (also – *up*) runzeln (*one's brow*), zusammenziehen (*one's eyes*); – *one's nose*, die Nase rümpfen. 3. *v.n.* sich falten; Falten schlagen, Runzeln bekommen, sich runzeln. **–d,** *adj.* runzlig, faltig.

wrist [rɪst], *s.* das Handgelenk; (also *––pin*) der (Wellen)Zapfen (*Tech.*). **–band,** *s.* das Bündchen, die Prise (*of shirt sleeves*), Hemdmanschette. **––drop,** *s.* die Handgelenkslähmung. **–let,** *s.* der Pulswärmer; das Armband; (*sl.*) die Handschelle; *–let watch*, *see* **–watch.** **––pin,** *s. see* **–.** **–watch,** *s.* die Armbanduhr.

writ [rɪt], *s.* die Schrift (*Theol.*), behördlicher Erlaß, die Urkunde, das Schriftstück; schriftliche Aufforderung, die Vorladung (*Law*); *serve a – upon a p.*, einem eine Vorladung zustellen; *take out a – against*, eine Vorladung gegen einen erwirken; – *of execution*, der Vollstreckungsbefehl; *Holy* or *Sacred* –, die Heilige Schrift.

write [raɪt], 1. *ir.v.a.* schreiben, verfassen, schriftlich niederlegen; brieflich mitteilen (*to* (*Dat.*)) (*news, etc.*); – *a cheque*, einen Scheck ausstellen *or* ausschreiben; (*sl.*) *nothing to – home about*, nichts besonderes; – *music*, komponieren; – *shorthand*, stenographieren; – *against time*, in der größtmöglichen Eile schreiben; – *to a p.*, einem *or* an einen schreiben; – *one's will*, sein Testament aufsetzen; (*fig.*) *writ large*, deutlich erkennbar; – *down*, niederschreiben, aufschreiben, aufzeichnen, notieren; (*fig.*) herabsetzen, herunterreißen; darstellen *or* beschreiben *or* hinstellen als; – *in*, eintragen; – *off*, herunterschreiben, schnell abfassen; (*fig.*) abbuchen, abschreiben (*a debt*); – *out*, ausschreiben, abschreiben; – *o.s. out*, sich ausschreiben; – *up*, ausführlich darstellen; (*fig.*) anpreisen, herausstreichen, rühmen, lobend erwähnen; nachtragen (*C.L.*). 2. *ir.v.n.* schreiben (*about* or *on*, über; *to* (*Dat.*) *or* an (*Acc.*)); schriftstellern; Briefe schreiben; – *to ask*, schriftlich anfragen; – *back*, wiederschreiben, antworten; – *for*, schriftlich bestellen, kommen lassen; – *on*, weiterschreiben, fortschreiben. (*coll.*) **––off,** *s.* die Abschreibung. **–r,** *s.* der Schreiber (*of a letter*); Schriftsteller, Verfasser; *–r's cramp*, der Schreibkrampf; *–r to the signet*, (*Scots*) der Rechtsanwalt. (*coll.*) **––up,** *s.* der (Presse)Bericht.

writhe [raɪð], *v.n.* sich winden *or* krümmen (*with*, vor).

writ–ing [raɪtɪŋ], 1. *adj.* schreibend, schriftstellernd, Schriftsteller–. 2. *s.* das Schreiben, Schriftstellern, die Schriftstellerei; schriftliche Ausfertigung, die Abfassung; das Schriftstück, die Urkunde, Schrift, der Aufsatz, Artikel, das Buch, literarisches Werk; Geschriebenes, *n.*, die Inschrift; der Stil, die Schreibart, Handschrift; *in –ing*, schriftlich; *be in –ing*, schriftlich aufgezeichnet sein; *take down* or *put in*(*to*) *–ing*, schriftlich aufsetzen. **–ing-book,** *s.* das Schreibheft. **–ing-case,** *s.* die Schreibmappe. **–ing-desk,** *s.* das Schreibpult. **–ing-pad,** *s.* die Schreibunterlage, der Schreibblock. **–ing-paper,** *s.* das Schreibpapier. **–ing-table,** *s.* der Schreibtisch. **–ten** [ˈrɪtn], 1. *see* **write**; *it is –ten*, es steht geschrieben. 2. *adj.* schriftlich, beschrieben; *–ten document*, das Schriftstück; *–ten evidence*, der Urkundenbeweis; *–ten language*, die Schriftsprache; *–ten law*, geschriebenes Recht.

wrong [rɔŋ], 1. *adj.* verkehrt, falsch; unrichtig, irrig, nicht in Ordnung, unrecht, unbillig; *be* –, nicht in Ordnung sein, nicht stimmen (*of a th.*), unrecht haben, sich irren (*of a p.*); *the clock is* –, die Uhr geht falsch; *what is – with?* was ist los mit? (*a th.*), was fehlt? (*Dat.*) (*a p.*); *that was – of you*, das war unrecht von Ihnen; (*coll.*) *get hold of the – end of the stick*, etwas falsch auffassen *or* völlig mißverstehen; *hit upon the – person*, an den Unrechten kommen; *– side*, linke Seite (*of cloth*); *on the – side of 30*, über 30 Jahre alt; *– side out*, das Innere nach außen, verkehrt herum; (*coll.*) *have got out of bed on the – side*, mit dem linken Fuß (*or* Bein) zuerst *or* mit dem falschen Bein aufgestanden sein; *he will laugh on the – side of his face*, ihm wird das Lachen vergehen; (*coll.*) *on the – tack*, auf dem Holzwege; *take s.th. the – way*, etwas übelnehmen. **2.** *adv.* unrecht, unrichtig, falsch; *get it –*, es falsch anrechnen (*a sum*), (*fig. coll.*) es völlig mißverstehen *or* ganz falsch verstehen, sich irren; *go –*, fehlgehen (*of a th.*), vom rechten Wege abkommen, auf Abwege geraten, sich irren (*of a p.*). **3.** *v.a.* Unrecht *or* Schaden tun (*Dat.*), Schaden zufügen (*Dat.*), schaden (*Dat.*); ungerecht behandeln, benachteiligen; eine falsche Meinung haben von; *I am –ed*, mir ist Unrecht geschehen. **4.** *s.* das Unrecht (*to*, an (*Dat.*)), die Ungerechtigkeit, Unbill; Kränkung, Beleidigung (*to*, für), der Schaden, die Rechtsverletzung (*Law*); *be in the –*, im Unrecht sein, Unrecht haben; *do –*, Unrecht tun, sündigen; *get s.o. in –*, einen in Mißkredit bringen; *put o.s. in the –*, sich ins Unrecht setzen. **–doer,** *s.* der Missetäter, Übeltäter, Sünder. **–doing,** *s.* die Sünde, Missetat, das Vergehen, Verbrechen. **–ful,** *adj.* unrecht, unbillig; ungerecht; unrechtmäßig, widerrechtlich, ungesetzlich; beleidigend, kränkend, nachteilig. **–fully,** *adv.* ungerechterweise, irrtümlicherweise; widerrechtlich. **–fulness,** *s.* die Unrichtigkeit; Ungerechtigkeit; Unrechtmäßigkeit, Ungesetzlichkeit. **–ly,** *adv.* irrtümlich(erweise), unrichtig, falsch; mit Unrecht, ungerecht(erweise); ungehörig, ungeziemend; *rightly or –ly*, mit Recht oder Unrecht. **– -headed,** *adj.* querköpfig, verschroben. **– -headedness,** *s.* die Verschrobenheit. **–ness,** *s.* die Unrichtigkeit, Verkehrtheit, Fehlerhaftigkeit, Unrechtmäßigkeit.

wrote [rout], *see* **write.**

wroth [rɔːθ, rɔθ], *pred. adj.* (*Poet.*) ergrimmt, erzürnt, zornig (*with*, auf (*Acc.*)).

wrought [rɔːt], (*archaic*), *imperf.* & *p.p. of* **work;** (*still used in*) *imperf.* brachte hervor, bewirkte (*change, etc.*); *p.p. as adj.* bewirkt; bearbeitet, gearbeitet, verarbeitet; gehämmert, geschmiedet (*metal*); *– iron*, das Schmiedeeisen. (*coll.*) **– -up,** *adj.* aufgeregt, aufgebracht.

wrung [rʌŋ], *see* **wring.**

wry [raɪ], *adj.* schief, krumm, verdreht, verzerrt; *make or pull a – face*, eine Grimasse schneiden. **– -mouthed,** *adj.* schiefmäulig. **–neck,** *s.* der Wendehals (*Orn.*).

wych– -elm [ˈwɪtʃˈɛlm], *s.* die Bergrüster, Bergulme. **– -hazel,** *s.* virginischer Zauberstrauch.

wyvern [ˈwaɪvən], *see* **wivern.**

X

X, x, *s.* das X, x; (erste) unbekannte Größe (*Math.*); *see Index of Abbreviations.*

xebec [ˈzɪːbɛk], *s.* die Schebecke (*Naut.*).

xeni–um [ˈzɪːnɪəm], *s.* (*pl.* –a [–nɪə]) das Gastgeschenk, die Xenie.

xenon [ˈzɛnɔn], *s.* das Xenon (*Chem.*).

xeno–gamy [zɪˈnɔgəmɪ], die Xenogamie (*Bot.*). **–phobia** [zɛnoˈfoubɪə], *s.* der Haß gegen Fremde.

xer–ansis [zɪəˈrænsɪs], *s.* die Austrocknung. **–asia** [–ˈreɪzɪə], *s.* die Trockenheit des Haares. **–ophagy** [–ˈrɔfəgɪ], *s.* die trockene Kost. **–ophilous** [–ˈrɔfɪləs], *adj.* xerophil (*Bot.*); *–ophilous plants*, Xerophyten, Dürrpflanzen. **–ophyte** [ˈzɪərofaɪt], *s.* die Xerophyt, Dürrpflanze.

xiphoid [ˈzɪfɔɪd], *adj.* Schwert– (*Anat.*).

Xmas [ˈɛksməs], *s.* (*coll.*) *abbr. of* **Christmas.**

x-ray [ˈɛksreɪ], **1.** *s.* (*usually pl.*) der Röntgenstrahl, X-strahl; (*coll.*) die Röntgenaufnahme. **2.** *v.a.* röntgen.

xyl–ene [ˈzaɪlɪːn], *s.*, **–ol** [–loul], das Xylol.

xylo–graph [ˈzaɪləgræf], *s.* der Holzschnitt. **–grapher** [–ˈlɔgrəfə], *s.* der Xylograph, Holzschneider. **–graphic** [–ləˈgræfɪk], *adj.* xylographisch, Holzschneide–. **–graphy** [–ˈlɔgrəfɪ], *s.* die Holzschneidekunst. **–lith** [–lɪθ], *s.* das Steinholz. **–nite** [–lənaɪt], das Zelluloid. **–phone** [–ləfoun], *s.* das Xylophon. **–se** [ˈzaɪlous], *s.* der Holzzucker.

xyster [ˈzɪstə], *s.* das Schabemesser (*Med.*).

xystus [ˈzɪstəs], *s.* (*pl.* –i [–taɪ]) gedeckter Säulengang.

Y

Y, y [waɪ], *s.* das Y, y; (zweite) unbekannte Größe (*Math.*). **2.** *attrib.* Gabel–, gabelförmig; *Y-connexion*, die Dreieckschaltung (*Elec.*); *Y-level*, die Wasserwaage, Libelle. *See Index of Abbreviations.*

y– [ɪ], *pref.* (*archaic*), ge–, *see* **yclept.**

yacht [jɔt], *s.* **1.** die Jacht, das Segelboot. **2.** *v.n.* segeln; *– club*, der Jachtklub. **–ing,** *s.* der Segelsport, das Segeln. **– -racing,** *s.* das Wettsegeln. **–sman,** *s.* der Segler, Segelsportler. **–smanship,** *s.* die Segelkunst.

yahoo [jəˈhuː], *s.* der Rohling, Bestie, brutaler Mensch.

yak [jæk], *s.* der Jak, Grunzochs.

Yale lock [ˈjeɪlˈlɔk], *s.* das Patentschloß.

yam [jæm], *s.* die Jam(s)wurzel.

yammer [ˈjæmə], *v.n.* (*Scots*) jammern.

yank [jæŋk], **1.** *v.a.* (*sl.*) zerreißen, reißen, heftig ziehen. **2.** *v.n.* heftig ziehen (*at*, an). **3.** *s.* der Ruck.

Yank [jæŋk], *s.* (*sl.*) *abbr. of* **–ee,** *s.* (*sl.*) der Nordamerikaner; (*Amer.*) Nordstaatler, Neuengländer.

yap [jæp], **1.** *v.n.* kläffen; (*sl.*) schwätzen, schwatzen. **2.** das Kläffen, Gekläff.

[1]**yard** [jɑːd], *s.* das Yard (= 0·914 Meter), die Elle; die Rah(e) (*Naut.*). **– -arm,** *s.* das Rahnock. **– -stick,** *s.* das Yardmaß, der Yardstock.

[2]**yard,** *s.* der Hof; eingefriedeter Platz; *farm–*, der Gutshof; *poultry– –*, das Geflügelgehege; *railway– –*, der Verschiebebahnhof, Rangierbahnhof; *ship–*, die Schiffswerft. **–sman,** *s.* der Hofarbeiter, Stallarbeiter, Werftarbeiter. **–master,** *s.* der Rangiermeister.

yarn [jɑːn], **1.** *s.* das Garn; (*coll.*) die Geschichte; *spin a –*, eine Geschichte erzählen. **2.** *v.n.* Garn spinnen, (*fig.*) Geschichten erzählen.

yarrow [ˈjærou], *s.* die Schafgarbe (*Bot.*).

yashmak [ˈjæʃmæk], *s.* mohammedanischer Gesichtsschleier.

yataghan [ˈjætəgæn], *s.* der Yatagan, Jatagan, türkisches Krummschwert.

yaw [jɔː], *v.n.* gieren (*Naut.*); (*fig.*) schwanken, wanken.

yawl [jɔːl], *s.* die Yawl, der Ewer (*Naut.*).

yawn [jɔːn], **1.** *s.* das Gähnen; *give a –*, gähnen (*also fig.*); (*fig.*) klaffen, sich weit auftun *or* öffnen, weit offen stehen. **–ing,** *adj.* gähnend (*also fig.*). **2.** *s.* das Gähnen.

yclept [ɪˈklɛpt], (*archaic*) genannt.

[1]**ye** [jɪː], *def. art.* (*pseudo-archaic*) der, die, das.

[2]**ye,** *pers. pron.* (*archaic*) Ihr, Sie.

yea [jeɪ], *adj.* (*archaic*) ja; gewiß, fürwahr, wahrhaftig. **2.** *s.* das Ja; *pl.* die Ja-Stimmen (*Parl.*).

yean [jɪ:n], 1. *v.n.* lammen, werfen (*of sheep*). 2. *v.a.* werfen (*a lamb*). **-ling,** *s.* das Lämmchen.
year [jɪə], *s.* das Jahr, *pl.* das Alter; *a – and a day*, Jahr und Tag; *500 a –*, £500 jährlich *or* das Jahr; *a – ago*, vor einem Jahr; *by the –*, jahresweise, jährlich; *– by –*, Jahr für Jahr; *every –*, jedes Jahr, jährlich; *every other –*, alle zwei Jahre, ein Jahr ums andre; *for –s*, Jahre lang, auf Jahre hinaus, seit Jahren; *for his –s*, für sein Alter; *well on in –s*, hochbetagt; *– in – out*, jahrein jahraus; *in a –'s time*, in einem Jahr; *of late –s*, in den letzten Jahren; *many –s' experience*, langjährige Erfahrung; *New –*, das Neujahr, neues Jahr; *New –'s Eve*, der *or* das Silvester, der Silvesterabend, die Silvesternacht; *best wishes for the New –*, fröhliche Wünsche zum Jahreswechsel; *–s of discretion*, gesetztes *or* mündiges Alter; *the – of grace*, das Jahr des Heils; *three-– -old child*, drei Jahre altes Kind; *once a –*, einmal im Jahr; *of recent –s*, see *of late –s*; *at this time of –*, zu dieser Jahreszeit; *this –'s*, diesjährig; *a – or two*, einige Jahre. **--book,** *s.* das Jahrbuch. **-ling,** *s.* der Jährling, einjähriges Tier; *–ling heifer*, einjährige Färse. **--long,** *adj.* jahrelang. **-ly,** *adj. & adv.* jährlich.
yearn [jə:n], *v.n.* sich sehnen, schmachten, verlangen (*for*, nach), sich hingezogen fühlen (*after*, nach; *towards*, zu). **-ing,** 1. *adj.* schmachtend, sehnend, verlangend, sehnsüchtig. 2. *s.* das Verlangen, die Sehnsucht (*for* or *after*, nach).
yeast [jɪ:st], *s.* die Hefe, der Barm(en); (*fig.*) der Sauerteig. **--powder,** *s.* das Backpulver. **-y,** *adj.* hefig, Hefen–, (*fig.*) gärend, schäumend, gischtig.
yell [jɛl], 1. *s.* der Aufschrei, gellender Schrei. 2. *v.n.* gellen, gellend schreien, laut aufschreien (*with*, vor); (*coll.*) weinen, heulen. 3. *v.a.* schreiend ausstoßen.
yellow ['jɛloʊ], 1. *adj.* gelb; (*sl.*) feige. **-back,** *s.* der Schundroman, Hintertreppenroman, Schmöker. **- earth,** *s.* das Okergelb. **- fever,** *s.* gelbes Fieber. **--hammer,** *s.* der *or* die Goldammer (*Orn.*). **-ish,** *adj.* gelblich. **- Jack,** *s.* (*sl.*) see **- fever,** **-ness,** *s.* gelbe Farbe. **- ochre,** *s.* das Berggelb. **the - peril,** die gelbe Gefahr. **- press,** *s.* die Hetzpresse. 2. *s.* das Gelb, gelbe Farbe. 3. *v.a.* gelb färben. 4. *v.n.* gelb werden; vergilben (*with*, von).
yelp [jɛlp], 1. *v.n.* kläffen, kreischen, bellen. 2. *s.* das Gekläff.
yeoman ['joʊmən], *s.* (*pl.* yeomen) der Freibauer, Freisasse; berittener Freiwilliger (*Mil.*); *– of the guard*, der Leibgardist. **-ly,** *adj.* (*fig.*) schlicht, einfach, kräftig. **-ry,** *s.* Freisassen (*pl.*); berittene Miliz (*Mil.*). **- service,** (*fig.*) guter Dienst, kräftige Hilfe.
yes [jɛs], *adv.* ja, jawohl; *say – to*, bejahen, sein Jawort geben (*Dat.*). **--man,** *s.* (*coll.*) der Jasager.
yester- [jɛstə], *pref.* (*Poet.*) gestrig, vergangen, letzt. **-day,** 1. *s.* gestriger Tag, (*fig.*) das Gestern; *pl.* vergangene Zeiten *or* Tage (*pl.*); *–day's*, gestrig; 2. *adv.* gestern. **-eve,** *s.* (*Poet.*) gestriger Abend, gestern abend. **-year,** *s.* (*Poet.*) letztes Jahr.
yet [jɛt], 1. *adv.* (immer) noch; außerdem, noch dazu; schon (jetzt), bis jetzt. (der)einst, jedoch, trotzdem; (*before comparative*) noch, sogar; *– again*, nochmals; *as –*, bis jetzt, bisher; soweit; *not –*, noch nicht; *not just –*, noch nicht gleich, nicht gerade jetzt; *nothing –*, noch nichts; *he'll do it –*, er wird es doch noch tun; *strange* (*and* or *but*) *– true*, seltsam aber wahr. 2. *conj.* (je)doch, dennoch, gleichwohl, nichtsdestoweniger.
yew [ju:], *s.* (also *--tree*) die Eibe; das Eibenholz.
yield [jɪ:ld], 1. *v.a.* einbringen, eintragen, abwerfen (*profit*) (*to* (*Dat.*)), hervorbringen, als Ertrag geben, ergeben, liefern (*result*), tragen (*crops*); (also *– up*) aufgeben (*the ghost*), hergeben; verraten, aufdecken (*secret*); übergeben, ausliefern, abtreten, überlassen (*fortress, etc.*) (*to* (*Dat.*) *or* an (*Acc.*)); (*fig.*) zugestehen, gewähren, einräumen (*a th. to a p.*, einem etwas); *– the palm to a p.*, einem die Siegespalme zugestehen; *– place to a th.*, einer Sache Platz machen; *– precedence to a p.*, einem den Vorrang einräumen. 2. *v.n.* Ertrag geben *or* liefern (*as crops*); (*of a p.*) sich ergeben, sich unterwerfen, sich fügen (*to* (*Dat.*)), einwilligen (*to*, in), nachgeben, weichen (*before*, vor), erliegen, unterliegen (*to* (*Dat.*)); (*of a th.*) nachgeben, sinken, zusammenbrechen, sich lockern; *– to*, beeinflußt werden durch, reagieren *or* eingehen auf (*Acc.*). 3. *s.* der Ertrag; die Ernte; Ausbeute, der Gewinn. **-ing,** *adj.* willfährig, nachgiebig (*of a p.*), nachgebend, biegsam, dehnbar (*of a th.*).
yodel ['joʊdl], 1. *v.n. & a.* jodeln. 2. *s.* der Jodel, Jodler.
yog-a ['joʊgə], *s.* der Joga. **-i** [-ɪ], *s.* der Jogi.
yo-(heave-)ho ['joʊhɪ:v'hoʊ, joʊ'hoʊ], *int.* hauruck! (*Naut.*).
yoicks [jɔɪks], *int.* hussah! hallo! (*Hunt.*).
yoke [joʊk], 1. das Joch (*of oxen, also fig.*); die Trage, das Tragholz (*for buckets*), das Ruderjoch (*of a boat*), der Sattel (*on a skirt*), die Passe (*on a bodice*), das Schulterstück (*on a shirt*); (*fig.*) die Unterwerfung, Knechtschaft. 2. *v.a.* ins Joch spannen, anspannen; (*fig.*) paaren, verbinden (*to* or *with*, mit), binden (*to*, an), unterwerfen, unterjochen (*to* (*Dat.*)). **--bone,** *s.* das Jochbein. **--fellow,** *s.* der Arbeitsgenosse, Mitarbeiter; Gefährte(r), Lebensgefährte(r); Leidensgefährte(r), *m.* **--lines,** *pl.* Taue am Ruderjoch (*pl.*). **-mate,** *s.* *see* **--fellow.**
yokel ['joʊkl], *s.* der Bauernlümmel, Bauerntölpel.
yolk [joʊk], *s.* das (*or* der) (Ei)Dotter, das Eigelb.
yon [jɔn], *dem. adj.* (*archaic*) jene(r, –s), der, die *or* das da drüben. **-der** [-də], 1. *dem. adj. see –.* 2. *adv.* da *or* dort drüben.
yore [jɔ:], *adv.*; *of –*, ehemals, ehedem, einstmals: *in days of –*, einst, vor alters.
you [ju:, jʊ *according to emphasis*], *pers. pron.* (*Nom.. Acc.*) Sie, (*Dat.*) (also *to –*) Ihnen; (*Nom.*) du, (*Acc.*) dich, (*Dat.*) (also *to –*) dir; (*Nom.*) Ihr, (*Acc., Dat.*) (*Dat.* also *to –*) Euch; (*impers. Nom.*) man, (*impers. Acc.*) einen, (*impers. Dat.*) (also *to –*) einem; (*refl. after prep.*) dich, euch, sich; *is it – ?* bist du es?
young [jʌŋ], 1. *adj.* jung; Jugend–, jugendlich, unentwickelt; unerfahren, neu; *– hopeful*, hoffnungsvoller Sprößling; *– in years*, jung an Jahren; *– love*, junge Liebe; *her – man*, ihr Schatz; *– Men's Christian Association*, Christlicher Verein Junger Männer; *– one*, das Junge; *– people*, junge Leute, die Jugend; *– person*, Jugendliche, *f.*, junges Mädchen; *– shoot*, der Schößling; (*coll.*) *– 'un*, der Jüngling; *the day is still –*, der Tag hat eben begonnen. 2. *s.* Junge(n) (*pl.*) (*of animals*); *with –*, trächtig. **-er,** *comp. adj.* jünger, neuer, weniger fortgeschritten; *–er hand*, die Hinterhand (*cards*). **-est,** *sup. adj.* jüngste(r, –s). **-ish,** *adj.* etwas *or* ziemlich junge. **-ster,** *s.* der Jüngling, Knabe, Junge, das Kind.
your [jʊə, jɔ:, jə:, jə *according to emphasis*], *poss. adj.* Ihr, dein, euer. **-s** [jʊez, jɔ:z *according to emphasis*], *poss. pron.* der, die *or* das Ihrige, deinige *or* eurige, deine, eure *or* Ihre; Ihr Schreiben (*C.L.*); *a friend of –s*, ein Freund von dir, einer deiner Freunde; *to you and –s*, an die Deinen, an deine Angehörigen; *this is –s*, dies gehört Ihnen; *–s faithfully*, Ihr sehr ergebener; *–s sincerely*, mit herzlichen Grüssen; *–s truly*, hochachtungsvoll, mit vorzüglicher Hochachtung (*C.L.*); *give me –s*, gib mir das deine. **-self** [–'sɛlf], *pron.* (*pl.* –selves [–'sɛlvz]) (*emphatic*) Sie du, ihr, *etc.* selbst; *you are not –self*, Sie sind nicht auf der Höhe; *are you by –self ?* sind Sie allein? *do it by –self*, tu es ohne Hilfe; *get one for –self*, verschaff' dir eins; *what will you do with –self ?* was fangen Sie an?
youth [ju:θ], *s.* (*pl.* –s [–ðz]) die Jugend; das Jungsein, die Jugendlichkeit, jugendliche Frische; die Jugendzeit; (*fig.*) Frühzeit, Jugendperiode; der Jüngling, junger Mann; junge Leute, die junge Welt, Jugend; *in –*, in der Jugend. **-ful,** *adj.* jung, jugendlich, Jugend–; jugendfrisch. **-fulness,** *s.* die Jugend, Jugendlichkeit, Jugendfrische. **- hostel,** *s.* die Jugendherberge. **- movement,** *s.* die Jugendbewegung.
yo-yo ['joʊjoʊ], *s.* das Yo-Yospiel.
ytt-erbium [ɪ'tə:bɪəm], *s.* das Ytterbium (*Chem.*) **-ria** ['ɪtrɪə], *s.* die Yttererde (*Chem.*). **-ric** ['ɪtrɪk] *adj.* ytterhaltig, Yttrium–. **-rium** ['ɪtrɪəm], *s.* das Yttrium.

yule [juːl], *s.* das Julfest, Weihnachtsfest. **--log,** *s.* der Weihnachtsklotz, Weihnachtsscheit. **-tide,** *s.* die Weihnachtszeit.

Z

Z, z [zɛd], *s.* das Z, z.
zany [ˈzeɪnɪ], *s.* der Hanswurst, Possenreißer.
zareba, zariba [zæˈrɪːbə], *s.* befestigtes Lager (*im Sudan*).
zeal [zɪːl], *s.* der Eifer, Diensteifer; *full of* –, (dienst)eifrig; – *for truth*, die Begeisterung für die Wahrheit. **-ot** [ˈzɛlət], *s.* der (Glaubens)Eiferer, Zelot. **-otry,** *s.* blinder (Glaubens)Eifer. **-ous** [ˈzɛləs], *adj.* eifrig, eifernd (*for*, nach), eifrig bedacht (*for*, auf); diensteifrig, begeistert, innig, warm; hitzig. **-ousness,** *s.* der Eifer.
zebra [ˈzɪːbrə], *s.* das Zebra.
zebu [ˈzɪːbuː], *s.* indischer Buckelochs.
zedoary [ˈzɛdoʊərɪ], *s.* die Zitwerwurzel.
zenana [zəˈnɑːnə], *s.* das Frauengemach in Indien.
zenith [ˈzɛnɪθ], *s.* der Zenit, Scheitelpunkt (*Astr.*), (*fig.*) der Höhepunkt, Gipfel; – *distance*, der Zenitabstand.
zephyr [ˈzɛfə], *s.* der Westwind, milder Wind; leichter Baumwollstoff.
zepp [zɛp], *s. abbr. of* **-elin** [-əlɪn], *s.* der Zeppelin.
zero [ˈzɪəroʊ], *s.* die Null (*also fig.*), das Nichts; der Nullpunkt, Gefrierpunkt (*thermometer*); (*fig.*) tiefster Punkt, der Tiefstand. *at* –, auf Null; *below* –, unter Null; – *hour*, die Angriffszeit; festgelegter *or* festgesetzter Zeitpunkt; die Stunde des Tiefpunktes in der Arbeitsleistung (*C.L.*).
zest [zɛst], *s.* die Würze, würzender Zusatz; (*fig.*) die Lust, Freude, der Genuß, Gefallen (*for*, an), das Behagen; – *for life*, der Lebenshunger; *give a – to*, Würze verliehen (*Dat.*); *with* –, mit Eifer *or* Wohlbehagen.
zeugma [ˈzjuːgmə], *s.* das Zeugma.
zigzag [ˈzɪgzæg], 1. *s.* der Zickzack, die Zickzacklinie. 2. *adj.* zickzackförmig, zickzacklaufend, Zickzack-. 3. *adv.* im Zickzack. 4. *v.n.* (im) Zickzack laufen *or* fliegen, Zickzackkurs fahren.
zinc [zɪŋk], 1. *s.* der *or* das Zink. 2. *v.a.* (*imperf.* & *p.p.* -ked *or* zinked; *pres. p.* -king) zinken. **-ograph.** [-əgræf], *s.* die Zinkogravüre, der Zinkdruck. **-ography** [-ˈkɔgrəfɪ], *s.* die Zinkographie, Zinkätzkunst. **-ous** [-əs], *adj.* zinkartig; Zink-. **--white,** *s.* das Zinkoxyd, Zinkweiß.
zinnia [ˈzɪnɪə], *s.* die Zinnie (*Bot.*).
Zionis-m [ˈzɑɪənɪzm], *s.* der Zionismus. **-t,** 1. *s.* der Zionist. 2. *adj.* zionistisch.
zip [zɪp], *s.* das Surren, Schwirren. **--fastener,** *s.* der Reißverschluß. **-per,** *s.* (*coll.*) *see* **--fastener.**
zircon [ˈzəːkn], *s.* das Zirkon, Zirkoniumsilikat. **-ium** [-ˈkoʊnɪəm], *s.* das Zirkonium.
zither [ˈzɪθə], *s.* die Zither.
zodiac [ˈzoʊdɪæk], *s.* der Tierkreis, Zodiakus; *signs of the* –, die Zeichen des Tierkreises. **-al** [zoˈdɑɪəkl], *adj.* Tierkreis-, Zodiakal-.
zombie [ˈzɔmbɪ], *s.* (*sl.*) krasser Laie.
zon-al [ˈzoʊnl], *adj.* Zonen-, ringförmig, kreisförmig. **-e** [zoʊn], *s.* die Zone, der Erdgürtel (*Geog.*); Landstrich, Gebietsstreifen; (*fig.*) Bereich, das Gebiet, der Umkreis; *temperate* (*frigid*) (*torrid*) *-e*, gemäßigte (kalte) (heiße) Zone; (*Poet.*) *-e of chastity*, der Keuschheitsgürtel. **-ing,** *s.* die Zonenabgrenzung.
[1]**zoo** [zuː], *s.* abbr. for *-logical garden.*
[2]**zoo-** [zoʊə], *prefix*, tierisch, Tier-, Zoo-. **ˈ-blast,** *s.* tierische Zelle. **-ˈchemistry,** *s.* die Zoochemie. **-graphy** [zoʊˈɔgrəfɪ], *s.* beschreibende Zoologie. **-latry** [zoʊˈɔlətrɪ], *s.* die Tieranbetung. **ˈ-lite,** *s.* fossiles Tier. **-ˈlogical,** *adj.* zoologisch; *-logical garden*, zoologischer Garten. **-logist** [zoʊˈɔlədʒɪst], *s.* der Zoologe. **-logy** [zoʊˈɔlədʒɪ], *s.* die Zoologie, Tierkunde. **-ˈmorphic,** *adj.* tiersymbolisch. **ˈ-phyte,** *s.* das Pflanzentier, der *or* das Zoophyt. **ˈ-sperm,** *s.* die Samenzelle. **-tomy** [zoʊˈɔtəmɪ], *s.* die Zootomie, Anatomie der Tiere.
zoom [zuːm], 1. *v.n.* hochschnellen, in steilem Winkel fliegen (*Av.*), schnell (an)steigen. 2. *v.a.* hochziehen, hochreißen (*Av.*).
zouave [ˈzuːɑːv], *s.* der Zuave.
zounds [zɑʊndz], *int.* (*archaic*) potztausend! Sakerment!
zygo-ma [zɑɪˈgoʊmə], *s.* (*pl.* -mata [-ˈgɔmətə]) das Jochbein, Wangenbein (*Anat.*). **-matic** [-gəˈmætɪk], *adj.* Jochbein-. **-te** [ˈzɑɪgoʊt], *s.* die Zygospore.
zymo-sis [zɑɪˈmoʊsɪs], *s.* die Gärung; ansteckende Krankheit. **-tic** [-ˈmɔtɪk], *adj.* Gärungs-, gärend; ansteckend.

INDEX OF COMMON ENGLISH ABBREVIATIONS

A

a.	acre(s).
A.	alto (*Mus.*), ampere.
A 1	first class (*of ships, and fig.*).
A.A.	Automobile Association, Anti-Aircraft.
A.A.A.	Amateur Athletic Association, Anti-Aircraft Artillery, Agricultural Adjustment Administration (*Amer.*).
A.A.F.	Auxiliary Air Force, American Air Force.
A.A. of A.	Automobile Association of America.
a.a.r.	against all risks.
A.B.	able-bodied seaman.
A.B.A.	Amateur Boxing Association.
abbr.	abbreviation.
A.B.C.	Aerated Bread Company, American *or* Australian Broadcasting Company.
A.B.C.A.	Army Bureau of Current Affairs.
abl.	ablative.
Abp.	archbishop.
abr.	abridged.
abs.	absolute.
A.C.	alternating current (*Elec.*), Alpine Club, Appeal Court.
A/C	aircraftsman (*Av.*).
a/c	account (*C.L.*).
A.C.A.	Associate of the Institute of Chartered Accountants.
A.C.C.	Allied Control Council.
acc.	acceptance, accepted, account, accusative, accompanied, according.
acct.	account (*C.L.*).
A.C.P.	Associate of the College of Preceptors.
A.C.T.	Australian Capital Territory.
ad.	advertisement.
a.d.	after date (*C.L.*).
A.D.	Anno Domini.
A.D.A.	Atom Development Administration.
A.D.C.	aide-de-camp, Army Dental Corps.
adj.	adjective.
Adm.	Admiralty, admiral.
A.D.M.S.	Assistant Director of Medical Services (*Mil.*).
adv.	adverb, advocate.
ad val.	to the value of (*C.L.*).
advt.	advertisement.
A.E.C.	Army Education Corps, Atomic Energy Commission.
A.E.F.	American Expeditionary Force.
A.E.U.	Amalgamated Engineering Union.
A.F.	audio frequency (*Rad.*).
A.F.A.	Amateur Football Association.
A.F.C.	Air Force Cross.
A.F.L.	American Federation of Labor.
A.F.M.	Air Force Medal.
A.F.N.	American Forces Network (*Rad.*).
A.F.S.	Auxiliary Fire Service.
A.F.V.	armoured fighting vehicle.
A.G.	Attorney-General (*Law*), Adjutant-General (*Mil.*), air gunner (*Av.*).
agr.	agriculture.
agt.	agent (*C.L.*).
A.I.C.	Associate of the Institute of Chemistry.
A.I.C.E.	Associate of the Institute of Civil Engineers.
A.I.D.	Army Intelligence Department.
a.l.	autograph letter.
Ala.	Alabama.
A.L.A.	American Library Association.
Alas.	Alaska.
Ald.	alderman.
alg.	algebra.
alt.	altitude.
a.m.	in the morning.
A.M.	Air Ministry, Albert Medal, Master of Arts (*Amer.*).
Am.	America, American.
A.M.C.	Army Medical Corps.
A.M.D.G.	to the greater glory of God.
Amer.	America, American.
A.M.G.(O.T.)	Allied Military Government (of Occupied Territory).
A.M.I.C.E.	Associate Member of the Institute of Civil Engineers.
A.M.I.E.E.	Associate Member of the Institute of Electrical Engineers.
A.M.I.Mech.E.	Associate Member of the Institute of Mechanical Engineers.
ammo	(*coll.*) ammunition.
amt.	amount.
anal.	analogy, analogous.
anat.	anatomy, anatomical.
anc.	ancient.
angl.	in English.
ann.	annual.
anon.	anonymous.
ans.	answer.
Anzac	Australia and New Zealand Army Corps.
A.O.	Army Order.
a/o	to the account of (*C.L.*).
A.O.D.	Army Ordnance Department.
A. of F.	Admiral of the Fleet.
Ap.	apostle.
A.P.	Associated Press.
A/P	account purchase (*C.L.*)
A.P.D.	Army Pay Department.
A.P.O.	Army Post Office.
app.	appendix, apparently, appointed, apprentice.
appro.	approbation, approval.
approx.	approximate(ly)
A.P.T.C.	Army Physical Training Corps.
A.R.	annual return, in the year of the reign.
A.R.A.	Associate of the Royal Academy.
arch.	archaic, archipelago.

archit.	architecture.
A.R.C.	American Red Cross.
A.R.C.M.	Associate of the Royal College of Music.
A.R.I.B.A.	Associate of the Royal Institute of British Architects.
arith.	arithmetic.
Ariz.	Arizona.
Ark.	Arkansas.
A.R.P.	Air Raid Precautions.
arr.	arranged, arrival.
A.R.S.A.	Associate of the Royal Scottish Academy, Associate of the Royal Society of Arts.
art.	article, artificial, artillery.
A/S	account sales (*C.L.*).
A.-S.	Anglo-Saxon.
A.S.A.	Amateur Swimming Association.
asdic	Anti-Submarine Detection Investigation Committee (*used as name of a type of hydrophone equipment*).
A.S.E.	Amalgamated Society of Engineers.
A.S.L.E. & F.	Amalgamated Society of Locomotive Engineers and Firemen.
A.S.R.	air-sea rescue (*Mil.*).
A.S.R.S.	Amalgamated Society of Railway Servants.
Ass.	assistant.
assoc.	association.
asst.	assistant.
astr(on).	astronomy.
A.T.	anti-tank, air temperature.
A.T.C.	Air Training Corps.
atm.	atmospheres.
A.T.S.	Auxiliary Territorial Service (*Mil.*).
A.T.T.	American Telephone and Telegraph Company.
Att.-Gen.	Attorney-General.
at. wt.	atomic weight.
Å.U.	Ångström Unit (*Phys.*).
aux(il).	auxiliary.
A.V.	Authorized Version (*B.*).
a/v	ad valorem (*C.L.*).
av.	average.
avdp.	avoirdupois.
Ave.	avenue.
A.W.O.L.	absent without leave (*Mil.*).
A.W.V.S.	American Women's Voluntary Service (*Mil.*).

B

B	black (*on pencils*), bishop (*chess*).
b.	bowled (*Crick.*), born.
B.A.	Bachelor of Arts, British Association, British Academy.
bact.	bacteriology.
bal.	balance.
Bap(t).	Baptist.
bar.	barometer, barrister.
Bart.	Baronet.
Bart's	Saint Bartholomew's Hospital.
batt.	battalion, battery (*Mil.*).
BB	double black (*on pencils*).
B.B.C.	British Broadcasting Corporation
B.C.	before Christ, British Columbia.
B.Ch.	Bachelor of Surgery.
B.Com.	Bachelor of Commerce.
bd	bound.
B.D.	Bachelor of Divinity.
Bde	Brigade (*Mil.*).
bds	boards.
b.e.	bill of exchange (*C.L.*).
B.E.	Board of Education (*obs.*).
B/E.	bill of exchange (*C.L.*).
B.E.A.	British European Airways.
Beds.	Bedfordshire.
B.E.F.	British Expeditionary Force.
Benelux	Belgium, Netherlands, and Luxemburg.
Beng.	Bengal.
Berks.	Berkshire.
B.E.S.A.	British Engineering Standards Association.
b.f. or *B.F.*	bloody fool (*vulg.*).
b/f	brought forward (*C.L.*).
B.F.B.S.	British and Foreign Bible Society.
B.F.N.	British Forces Network (*Rad.*).
B'ham	Birmingham.
b.h.p.	brake horse power.
B.I.	British India (*obs.*).
Bib.	Bible.
bibliog.	bibliography.
B.I.F.	British Industries Fair.
biog.	biography.
biol.	biology.
B.I.S.	Bank for International Settlements.
B.I.S.N.C.	British India Steam Navigation Company.
bk.	book, bank.
bkg.	banking.
bkt.	basket.
bl.	bale, barrel.
B.L.	Bachelor of Law.
B/L	bill of lading (*C.L.*).
bldg.	building.
B.Litt.	Bachelor of Letters.
B.LL.	Bachelor of Laws.
B.M.	Bachelor of Medicine, British Museum, Brigade Major.
B.M.A.	British Medical Association.
B.Mus.	Bachelor of Music.
Bn.	battalion (*Mil.*).
B.N.C.	Brasenose College (Oxford).
b.o.	buyer's option (*C.L.*), (*coll.*) body odour.
B/O	branch office (*C.L.*).
B.O.A.	British Optical Association, British Olympic Association.
B.O.A.C.	British Overseas Airways Corporation.
B. of E.	Board of Education (*obs.*).
B.O.P.	Boys' Own Paper.
bor.	borough.
bos'n	boatswain.
bot.	botany.
B.O.T.	Board of Trade.
b.p.	bills payable (*C.L.*), boiling point, below par.
B.P.	British Pharmacopœia.
Bp.	bishop.
b.pl.	birthplace.
b.r.	bills receivable (*C.L.*).
B.R.	British Railways.
B.R.C.S.	British Red Cross Society.
b.rec.	see *b.r.*
brev.	brevet (*Mil.*).
Brig.	Brigadier (*Mil.*).
Brig.-Gen.	Brigadier-General (*Mil.*).
Brit.	Britain, British.
bro.	brother, *bros.*, brothers.
b.s.	balance-sheet, bill of sale (*C.L.*).

B/S bill of sale (*C.L.*).
B.S. Bachelor of Surgery, (*Amer.*) Bachelor of Science.
B.S.A. British South Africa, Birmingham Small Arms Company.
B.S.A.A. British South American Airways.
B.Sc. Bachelor of Science.
B.Sc. (*Econ.*) Bachelor of Science (in Economics).
B.S.G. British Standard Gauge.
bsh. bushel.
bt. bought (*C.L.*).
bt.fwd. brought forward (*C.L.*).
Bt. Baronet.
B.Th.U. British Thermal Unit.
B.T.U. Board of Trade Unit.
Bucks. Buckinghamshire.
B.U.P. British United Press.
Bur. St. Bureau of Standards (*Amer.*).
B.V.M. Blessed Virgin Mary (*R.C.*).
B.W. Black Watch (42nd Highland Regiment).
B.W.G. Birmingham Wire Gauge.
B.W.I. British West Indies.
B.W.T.A. British Women's Temperance Association.

C

c. cent, centime, cubic, caught (*Crick.*), *circa.*
C. Centigrade, Cape, Catholic, Conservative.
C. 3 unfit for military service.
C.A. Chartered Accountant, Chief Accountant, Confederate Army (*Amer.*), Central America.
C/A current account (*C.L.*).
Cal. California.
Cambs. Cambridgeshire.
Can. Canada, canon, canto.
c. & b. caught and bowled (*Crick.*).
Cant. Canticles, Canterbury.
Cantab. of Cambridge University.
Cantuar. of Canterbury (*signature of the Archbishop*).
cap. capital letter, chapter.
Capt. Captain.
Card. Cardinal.
Cards. Cardiganshire.
Carmarths Carmarthenshire.
carr. pd. carriage paid (*C.L.*).
cat. catalogue, catechism.
Cath. Cathedral, Catholic.
cav. cavalry.
C.B. Companion of the Order of the Bath, confined to barracks (*Mil.*), County Borough.
C.B.C. Canadian Broadcasting Corporation.
C.B.E. Commander *or* Companion of the Order of the British Empire.
C.B.S. Columbia Broadcasting System (*Amer.*).
c.c. cubic centimetre(s).
C.C. County Council, County Court, Cricket Club, Cycling Club, Caius College (Cambridge), continuous current (*Elec.*).
C.C.C. Central Criminal Court, Corpus Christi College (Oxford *or* Cambridge).
C.C.G. Control Commission for Germany.
C.C.I. International Chamber of Commerce.
C.C.P. Court of Common Pleas.
c.d. with dividend (*C.L.*).
C.D. Chancery Division, Civil Defence.
C.E. Church of England, Chief Engineer, Civil Engineer.
C.E.B. Central Electricity Board.
Cels. Celsius.
Celt. Celtic.
cent. hundred, century, central.
Cent. Centigrade.
cert. certificate, certified, (*coll.*) certainty.
Cestr. of Chester (*signature of the Bishop*).
C.F. Chaplain to the Forces.
cf. compare.
c.f.i. cost, freight, and insurance (*C.L.*).
C.G. coastguard, Consul-General, Commissary-General, Coldstream Guards.
C.G.H. Cape of Good Hope.
C.G.M. Conspicuous Gallantry Medal.
C.G.S. Chief of the General Staff, centimetre-gramme-second.
C.H. Companion of Honour, clearing house, custom house.
ch. chapter, chief, chain (*measure*).
Ch. Church, Chancery.
Chamb. Chamberlain.
chap. chapter.
Chap. Chaplain.
Ch.B. Bachelor of Surgery.
Ch.Ch. Christ Church (Oxford).
chem. chemistry, chemical.
Ches. Cheshire.
Ch.M. Master of Surgery.
Chron. Chronicles (*B.*).
C.I. Channel Islands, Imperial Order of the Crown of India, certificate of insurance (*C.L.*).
C.I.C. Counter-Intelligence Corps (*Amer.*).
Cicestr. of Chichester (*signature of the Bishop*).
C.I.D. Criminal Investigation Department.
C.I.E. Companion of the Order of the Indian Empire.
c.i.f.c. cost, insurance, freight, and commission (*C.L.*).
C.I.G.S. Chief of the Imperial General Staff.
C.I.Mech.E. Companion of the Institute of Mechanical Engineers.
C.-in-C. Commander-in-Chief.
C.I.O. Congress of Industrial Organizations (*Amer.*).
cit. citation, cited.
C.I.V. City Imperial Volunteers (*Mil.*).
civ. civil, civilian.
C.J. Chief Justice.
cl. clause, class.
Clar. Clarendon (*Typ.*).
C.L.B. Church Lads' Brigade.
c.m. by reason of death.
C.M. Corresponding Member, Certified Master (*Naut.*), Master of Surgery.
Cmd. Command Paper.
Cmdr. Commodore (*Nav.*).
C.M.G. Companion of the Order of Saint Michael and Saint George.

C.M.S.	Church Missionary Society.
C.O.	Colonial Office, commanding officer, conscientious objector.
c/o	care of.
Co.	company, County (*in Ireland, Amer.*)
C.O.D.	cash on delivery.
C. of E.	Church of England.
cogn.	cognate.
Col.	Colonel, Colossians (*B.*), colony, colonial, column, Colorado.
coll.	colloquial, collection, collective(ly).
Coll.	College.
collat.	collateral.
colloq.	colloquial(ly).
Colo.	Colorado.
Col.-Sergt.	Colour-Sergeant.
com.	common, commerce, commission, comedy.
Com.	Commander, Commissioner, Committee, Commodore (*Nav.*), Communist.
Comdr.	Commander.
comm.	commentary.
comp.	compare, comparative, compound.
compl.	complement.
con.	against, contra, conics.
Con.	Consul.
conch.	conchology.
Cong.	Congress, congregation.
conj.	conjugation, conjunction, conjunctive.
Conn.	Connecticut.
conn.	connected.
cons.	consonant.
Consols.	Consolidated Stock (*C.L.*).
Co-op.	(*coll.*) Co-operative (Stores).
Cor.	Corinthians (*B.*), Coroner.
Corn.	Cornwall, Cornish.
Corp.	Corporal (*Mil.*), Corporation.
C.O.S.	Charity Organization Society.
cos	cosine.
cosec	cosecant.
cosmog.	cosmogony, cosmography.
cot	cotangent.
cox	coxswain.
C.P.	(Court of) Common Pleas, Court of Probate, Clerk of the Peace, carriage paid (*C.L.*).
c. p.	candle-power.
cp.	compare.
C.P.C.	Clerk of the Privy Council.
Cpl.	Corporal (*Mil.*).
C.P.R.	Canadian Pacific Railway.
C.P.R.E.	Council for the Preservation of Rural England.
C.P.S.	Keeper of the Privy Seal.
Cr.	credit, creditor (*C.L.*), Crown.
cresc.	rising (*Mus.*).
crim. con.	criminal conversation (*Law*).
C.S.	Civil Service, Christian Science, Court of Session, Common Serjeant (*Law*), Chemical Society.
C.S.A.	Confederate States of America (*Hist.*).
C.S.C.	Conspicuous Service Cross.
C.S.I.	Companion of the Star of India.
C.S.M.	Company Sergeant Major.
ct	caught (*Crick.*), cent.
Ct	Count, Court.
C.T.	commercial traveller, certified teacher.
C.T.C.	Cyclists' Touring Club.
C.U.	Cambridge University.
cub.	cubic.
cum.	cumulative.
Cumb.	Cumberland.
cum div.	with dividend (*C.L.*).
Cum. Pref.	Cumulative Preference (Shares) (*C.L.*).
C.U.P.	Cambridge University Press.
cur.	current, currency.
C.V.	Common Version (*B.*).
C.V.O.	Commander of the Royal Victorian Order.
c.w.o.	cash with order (*C.L.*).
C.W.S.	Co-operative Wholesale Society.
cwt.	hundredweight.
cyl.	cylinder.
Cym.	Cymric.

D

d.	dead, died, penny, pence, departs, delete, daughter.
D.	Doctor, Duke, diameter.
D/A	deposit account (*C.L.*).
D.A.B.	Dictionary of American Biography.
D.A.G.	Deputy Adjutant General (*Mil.*).
Dak.	Dakota.
Dan.	Danish, Daniel (*B.*).
dat.	dative.
dau.	daughter.
d.b.	day-book (*C.L.*).
D.B.E.	Dame Commander of the Order of the British Empire.
D.C.	direct current (*Elec.*), from the beginning (*Mus.*), District of Columbia.
D.C.L.	Doctor of Civil Law.
D.C.L.I.	Duke of Cornwall's Light Infantry.
D.C.M.	Distinguished Conduct Medal.
D.D.	Doctor of Divinity.
d.d.	days after date (*C.L.*).
d...d or *d—d*	damned.
deb.	debenture (*C.L.*), (*coll.*) débutante.
Dec.	December.
def.	definite, definition.
Def.	defendant (*Law*).
deg.	degree.
Del.	Delaware.
dele.	delete.
dent.	dental, dentist, dentistry.
dep.	deputy, departs, departure.
dept.	department.
deriv.	derivation.
Deut.	Deuteronomy (*B.*).
D.F.	Dean of the Faculty, direction finding (*Rad.*).
D.F.C.	Distinguished Flying Cross.
D.F.M.	Distinguished Flying Medal
dft.	draft.
D.G.	by the grace of God.
dial.	dialect, dialogue.
diam.	diameter.
dict.	dictionary.
diff.	different, difference.
dim.	diminishing (*Mus.*).
dimin.	diminutive.
Dioc.	diocese.
Dir.	director.
dis(c).	discount (*C.L.*).
dist.	distance, district, distinguished.
div.	divide, dividend.

Div. Division (*Mil.*).
D.L. Deputy Lieutenant.
D.L.I. Durham Light Infantry.
D.Lit. Doctor of Letters.
D.L.O. dead-letter office.
D.M.O. Director of Military Operations.
d...n or *d—n* damn.
D.N.B. Dictionary of National Biography.
do. ditto.
doc. document, (*coll.*) doctor.
dom. domestic.
Dom. Dominus, Dominion.
Dor. Doric.
D.O.R.A. Defence of the Realm Act.
dow. dowager.
doz. dozen.
D.P. displaced person.
D.P.H. Department of *or* Diploma in Public Health.
Dpt. department.
dr. dram, drawer (*C.L.*).
Dr. Doctor.
dr. debtor.
d.S. or *d/s.* days after sight (*C.L.*).
D.Sc. Doctor of Science.
D.S.O. Distinguished Service Order.
d.s.p. died without issue.
D.S.T. Daylight Saving Time.
d.t. or *D.T.* delirium tremens.
Du. Dutch.
Dubl. Dublin.
Dunelm. of Durham (*signature of the Bishop*).
d.v. God willing.
D.V.S. Doctor of Veterinary Science.
dwt. pennyweight.
dyn. dynamics.

E

E. East.
E. & O.E. errors and omissions excepted (*C.L.*).
Ebor. of York (*signature of the Archbishop*).
E.C. Eastern Central (*London postal district*).
E.C.A. Economic Cooperation Administration.
Eccl(es). ecclesiastical, Ecclesiastes (*B.*).
Ecclus. Ecclesiasticus (*B.*).
econ. economics.
E.C.U. English Church Union.
ed. edition, editor, edited.
E.D.C. European Defence Community.
E.D.D. English Dialect Dictionary.
Edin. Edinburgh.
E.E. errors excepted (*C.L.*).
E.E.T.S. Early English Text Society.
e.g. for example.
E.H.P. effective horse-power.
E.I. East Indies.
E.I.C. East India Company.
elec(tr). electric(al).
ellipt. elliptical.
E.M.F. electromotive force.
E.M.U. electromagnetic unit(s).
E.N.E. east-north-east.
Eng. engineer.
Eng(l). England, English.
ent(om). entomology.
E.P. electroplate.
Ep. Epistle.
E.P.D. Excess Profits Duty.
Eph. Ephesians (*B.*).
Epiph. Epiphany.
episc. episcopal.
E.P.U. European Payment Union.
E.R.P. European Recovery Programme.
eq. equal.
equiv. equivalent.
E.R. King Edward, Queen Elizabeth.
eschat. eschatology.
E.S.E. east-south-east.
esp. especially.
Esq. Esquire.
est. established.
Esth. Esther (*B.*).
E.S.U. electrostatic unit(s).
et al. among others.
etc. and so on *or* so forth.
ethnol. ethnology.
etym. etymology, etymological.
Eucl. Euclid.
euphem. euphemism, euphemistic(ally
ex. example.
Ex. Exodus (*B.*).
exam. examination.
exc. except(ing).
Exc. Excellency.
Exch. Exchange, Exchequer.
excl. exclusive, excluding.
ex. div. without dividend (*C.L.*).
ex. int. without interest (*C.L.*).
Exod. Exodus (*B.*).
exp. export.
ext. external.
Ezek. Ezekiel (*B.*).

F

f. farthing, fathom, foot, feminine, following, loud (*Mus.*).
F. Fellow (*Univ., etc.*), Fahrenheit, focal length.
F.A. Football Association.
f.a.a. free of all average (*C.L.*).
fac. facsimile.
facet. facetious.
Fahr. Fahrenheit.
fam. familiar.
F.A.O. Food and Agriculture Organization.
f.a.s. free alongside ship (*C.L.*).
F.B. Fenian Brotherhood, Fire Brigade, Free Baptist.
F.B.A. Fellow of the British Academy.
F.B.I. Federal Bureau of Investigation (*Amer.*), Federation of British Industries.
F.C. Free Church (of Scotland), Football Club.
F.C.A. Fellow of the Institute of Chartered Accountants.
fcap. foolscap.
F.C.G.I. Fellow of the City and Guilds of London Institute.
F.C.P. Fellow of the College of Preceptors.
F.C.S. Fellow of the Chemical Society.
F.D. Defender of the Faith.
fem. feminine.
F.G. Foot Guards (*Mil.*).
F.G.S. Fellow of the Geological Society.
F.I.A. Fellow of the Institute of Actuaries.

F.I.A.A.	Fellow of the Incorporated Association of Architects and Surveyors.
F.I.C.	Fellow of the Institute of Chemists.
F.I.D.	Field Intelligence Division (*Mil.*).
fig.	figure, figurative(ly).
fl.	florin, guilder.
Fla.	Florida.
flor.	flourished.
F.M.	Field-Marshal.
fm.	fathom.
F.M.D.	foot-and-mouth disease.
F.O.	Foreign Office, field-officer (*Mil.*)
fo.	folio.
f.o.b.	free on board (*C.L.*).
f.o.r.	free on rail (*C.L.*).
F.P.	freezing point, fire point, field punishment (*Mil.*), former pupil (*Scots*).
f.p.	foot-pound.
F.Phys.S.	Fellow of the Physical Society.
F.P.S.	Fellow of the Philosophical Society.
Fr.	France, French.
fr.	franc(s).
F.R.A.M.	Fellow of the Royal Academy of Music.
F.R.C.M.	Fellow of the Royal College of Music.
F.R.C.P.	Fellow of the Royal College of Physicians.
F.R.C.S.	Fellow of the Royal College of Surgeons.
F.R.C.V.S.	Fellow of the Royal College of Veterinary Surgeons.
freq.	frequent.
F.R.G.S.	Fellow of the Royal Geographical Society.
Fri.	Friday.
F.R.Hist.S.	Fellow of the Royal Historical Society.
F.R.H.S.	Fellow of the Royal Horticultural Society.
F.R.I.B.A.	Fellow of the Royal Institute of British Architects.
Frisco	(*coll.*) San Francisco.
F.R.S.	Fellow of the Royal Society.
F.R.S.A.	Fellow of the Royal Society of Arts.
F.S.	foot-second.
F.S.A.	Fellow of the Society of Arts.
F.S.A.A.	Fellow of the Society of Incorporated Accountants and Actuaries.
F.S.I.	Fellow of the Surveyors' Institute.
F.S.R.	Field Service Regulations (*Mil.*).
ft.	foot, feet.
ft.	fort.
fur.	furlong.
fut.	future.
F.W.B.	four-wheel brakes.
F.W.D.	four-wheel drive.
fwd.	forward (*C.L.*).
F.Z.S.	Fellow of the Zoological Society.

G

g.	gramme(s), guinea, gauge.
Ga	Georgia.
G.A.	General Assembly.
Gael.	Gaelic.
gal.	gallon(s).
Gal.	Galatians (*B.*).
gaz.	gazette, gazetteer.
G.B.	Great Britain.
G.B.E.	Knight Grand Cross of the British Empire.
G.B.S.	George Bernard Shaw.
G.C.	George Cross.
G.C.B.	Knight Grand Cross of the Bath.
G.C.F.	greatest common factor (*Math.*).
G.C.I.E.	Knight Grand Commander of the Indian Empire.
G.C.M.	greatest common measure (*Math.*).
G.C.M.G.	Knight Grand Cross of Saint Michael and Saint George.
G.C.S.I.	Knight Grand Commander of the Star of India.
G.C.V.O.	Knight Grand Cross of the Royal Victorian Order.
Gdns	Gardens.
Gds	Guards (*Mil.*).
gen.	gender, genitive.
Gen.	General (*Mil.*), Genesis (*B.*).
gent.	(*coll.*) gentleman.
geog.	geography, geographical.
geol.	geology.
geom.	geometry.
Ger.	Germany, German.
G.F.S.	Girls' Friendly Society.
G.H.Q.	General Headquarters (*Mil.*).
G.I.	Government Issue (*Amer.*), (*coll.*) American soldier.
Gib.	Gibraltar.
Gk.	Greek.
G.L.	Grand Lodge.
Glam.	Glamorganshire.
Glos.	Gloucestershire.
gloss.	glossary.
G.M.	Grand Master.
G.M.T	Greenwich Mean Time.
gns.	guineas.
G.O.	general order (*Mil.*).
G.O.C.	General Officer Commanding (*Mil.*).
G.O.C. in C.	General Officer Commanding in Chief (*Mil.*).
G.O.M.	Grand Old Man (i.e. Gladstone).
G.O.P.	Grand Old Party (i.e. Republican) (*Amer.*).
Goth.	Gothic.
Gov.	Government, Governor.
Gov.-Gen.	Governor-General.
Govt.	Government.
G.P.	general practitioner (*Med.*).
G.P.I.	general paralysis of the insane (*Med.*).
G.P.O.	General Post Office.
G.R.	King George.
gr.	grain, gross.
Gr.	Greece, Greek.
gram.	grammar.
grm.	gramme(s).
G.R.T.	gross registered tonnage (*Naut.*).
gr. wt.	gross weight (*C.L.*).
gs.	guineas.
G.S.	gold standard, General Secretary, General Staff (*Mil.*).
G.S.N.C.	General Steam Navigation Company.
G.S.O.	General Staff Officer (*Mil.*).
Gt. Br.	Great Britain.
guar.	guaranteed.
G.W.R.	Great Western Railway (*obs.*).
gym.	gymnastics, gymnasium.

H

H	hard (*on pencils*).
H.	hydrant.
h.	hour(s).
H.A	Horse Artillery.
hab.	habitat.
Hab.	Habakkuk (*B.*).
H.A.C.	Honourable Artillery Company.
Hag.	Haggai (*B.*).
h. & c.	hot and cold (water).
Hants.	Hampshire.
Harl.	Harleian.
HB	hard black (*on pencils*).
H.B.C.	Hudson's Bay Company.
H.B.M.	His *or* Her Britannic Majesty.
H.C.	House of Commons.
h.c.	honorary.
hcap.	handicap.
H.C.F.	highest common factor.
H.C.J.	High Court of Justice.
hdbk.	handbook.
hdqrs.	headquarters.
H.E.	high explosive, horizontal equivalent, His Excellency (*not an English title*).
Heb.	Hebrew, Hebrews (*B.*).
her.	heraldry.
Herts	Hertfordshire.
H.F.	high frequency (*Rad.*).
hf.	half. *hf.-bd.*, half-bound. *hf.-cf.*, half-calf. *hf.-cl.*, half-cloth.
H.G.	His *or* Her Grace, Horse Guards.
HH	double hard (*on pencils*).
H.H.	His Holiness.
hhd.	hogshead.
HICO	High Commission(er) for Germany.
H.I.H.	His *or* Her Imperial Highness.
hist.	history, historical.
H.L.	House of Lords.
H.L.I.	Highland Light Infantry.
H.M.	His *or* Her Majesty.
H.M.A.	Headmasters' Association.
H.M.G.	His *or* Her Majesty's Government.
H.M.I.	His *or* Her Majesty's Inspector (*of schools*).
H.M.S.	His *or* Her Majesty's Ship.
H.M.S.O.	His *or* Her Majesty's Stationery Office.
H.O.	Home Office.
ho.	house.
Hon.	Honourable (*in titles*), Honorary.
Hon. Sec.	Honorary Secretary.
hor.	horizon.
horol.	horology.
hort.	horticulture.
Hos.	Hosea (*B.*).
h.p.	horse-power.
H.P.	hire-purchase, high pressure, horse-power, House Physician.
H.Q.	Headquarters.
H.R.	House of Representatives (*Amer.*), Home Rule.
H.R.H.	His *or* Her Royal Highness.
hr(s).	hour(s).
H.S.	House Surgeon.
H.S.H.	His *or* Her Serene Highness.
H.T.	high tension (*Elec.*).
Hunts.	Huntingdonshire.
h.w.	hit wicket (*Crick.*).
hydr.	hydraulics.

I

I(s).	Island(s).
I.A.	Indian Army, Incorporated Accountant.
ib.	in the same place.
i.b.	in bond (*C.L.*).
I.B.A.	Institute of British Architects.
ibid.	in the same place.
i/c	in charge of (*Mil.*).
icht(h).	ichthyology.
icon.	iconography.
I.C.S.	Indian Civil Service.
I.D.	Intelligence Department (*Mil.*).
id.	the same.
i.e.	that is (to say).
I.E.E.	Institute of Electrical Engineers.
I.F.S.	Irish Free State (*1921–37, now* Irish Republic).
I.H.P. or *i.h.p.*	indicated horse-power.
Ill.	Illinois.
ill.	illustrated, illustration.
I.L.O.	International Labour Organization.
I.L.P.	Independent Labour Party.
I.Mech.E.	Institute of Mechanical Engineers.
I.M.F.	International Monetary Fund.
Imp.	Imperial, Emperor *or* Empress.
imper.	imperative.
imperf.	imperfect.
impers.	impersonal.
I.M.S.	Indian Medical Service.
in.	inch(es).
Inc.	Incorporated.
incl.	including, inclusive.
incog.	incognito.
Ind.	India, Indiana.
ind.	independent.
indecl.	indeclinable.
indef.	indefinite.
indic.	indicative.
inf.	below, infantry, infinitive.
infra dig.	(*coll.*) beneath one's dignity.
in loc.	in the place of.
I.N.S.	ship of the Indian Navy.
ins.	insurance.
insc.	inscribed (*C.L.*).
Insp.	Inspector.
inst.	of the present month.
Inst.	Institute.
instr.	instrumental.
int.	interior, internal, international, interest (*C.L.*), interjection.
inter.	intermediate, interrogative.
interrog.	interrogative.
in trans.	on the way.
intran(s).	intransitive.
intro(d).	introduction.
inv.	invoice (*C.L.*), inventor.
I. of M.	Isle of Man.
I. of W.	Isle of Wight, Inspector of Works.
IOU	I owe you.
I.R.	Inland Revenue.
Ir.	Ireland, Irish.
I.R.A.	Irish Republican Army.
I.R.O.	International Refugee Organization.
iron.	ironical(ly).
irreg.	irregular.
Is.	Isaiah (*B.*).
I.S.S	International Student Service.
isth.	isthmus.

I.T. Inner Temple, Indian Territory (*Amer.*).
It. Italy, Italian.
I.T.A. Independent Television Authority.
ital. italics.
itin. itinerary.
I.W. Isle of Wight.

J

J. justice, judge, joule (*Elec.*).
J.A. Judge-Advocate.
J/A joint account (*C.L.*).
J.A.G. Judge Advocate General.
Jam. James (*B.*), Jamaica.
Jer. Jeremiah (*B.*).
Jn. junction.
jnr. junior.
Jo. Joel (*B.*).
joc. jocular, jocose.
Jos. Josiah (*B.*).
J.P. Justice of the Peace.
jr. junior.
Jud. Judith (*B.*).
Judg. Judges (*B.*).
jun. or *junr* junior.
junc. junction.

K

(N.B. With the change of sovereign, titles with 'King' change to 'Queen', except in the name of regiments and colleges.)
Kan. Kansas.
K.B. King's Bench, Knight Bachelor, Knight of the Bath.
K.B.E. Knight Commander of the British Empire.
K.C. King's Counsel, Knight Commander, King's College.
kc. kilocycle(s) (*Rad.*).
K.C.B. Knight Commander of the Bath.
K.C.I.E. Knight Commander of the Indian Empire.
K.C.M.G. Knight Commander of Saint Michael and Saint George.
K.C.S.I. Knight Commander of the Star of India.
K.C.V.O. Knight Commander of the Royal Victorian Order.
K.E. kinetic energy.
K.G. Knight of the (Order of the) Garter.
K.G.C. Knight of the Grand Cross.
K.G.C.B. Knight of the Grand Cross of the Bath.
K.H.B. (*coll.*) King's hard bargain (*i.e. a no-good sailor*).
K.H.C. Honorary Chaplain to the King
K.H.P. Honorary Physician to the King.
K.H.S. Honorary Surgeon to the King.
K.K.K. Ku-Klux-Klan (*Amer.*).
K.L.I. King's Light Infantry.
K.M. Knight of Malta.
Knt Knight.
k.o. knock-out.
K.O.S.B. King's Own Scottish Borderers.
K.O.Y.L.I. King's Own Yorkshire Ligh. Infantry.
K.R. King's Regulations (*Mil.*).
K.R.R. King's Royal Rifles.
K.S.I. Knight of the Star of India.
K.T. Knight of the Order of the Thistle.
Kt Knight.
kWh. Kilowat-hour (*Elec.*).
Ky. Kentucky.

L

l. line, left, litre, lire.
L. Lake, Latin, Lance (*Mil.*), Linnaeus (*Bot.*), Liberal (Party).
£ pound sterling, *£A*, Australian pound, *£E*, Egyptian pound. *I£*, Israeli pound, *£NZ*, New Zealand pound, *£T*, Turkish pound.
La Louisiana.
L.A. Legislative Assembly, Law Agent.
Lab. Labour (Party), Labrador.
Lam. Lamentations (*B.*).
Lancs. Lancashire.
lang. language.
lat. latitude.
Lat. Latin.
lb. pound (*weight*).
l.b.w. leg before wicket (*Crick.*).
l.c. lower case (*Typ.*), letter of credit (*C.L.*).
L.C. Lower Canada, Lord Chancellor, Lord Chamberlain, left centre (*of stage*) (*Theat.*).
L.C.C. London County Council.
L.C.J. Lord Chief Justice.
L.C.M. lowest common multiple.
L.C.P. Licentiate of the College of Preceptors.
L.-Cpl. Lance-Corporal.
Ldp. Lordship.
L.D.S. Licentiate in Dental Surgery.
Leics. Leicestershire.
Lev. Leviticus (*B.*).
L.F. low frequency (*Rad.*).
l.h. left hand.
lib. book.
Lib. Liberal (Party), library.
Lieut. lieutenant.
Lieut.-Col. Lieutenant-Colonel.
Lieut.-Gen. Lieutenant-General.
Lieut.-Gov. Lieutenant-Governor.
Lincs. Lincolnshire.
liq. liquid.
lit. literally.
liter. literature, literary.
Litt.D. Doctor of Letters.
L.L. Lord Lieutenant.
ll. lines.
LL.B. Bachelor of Laws.
LL.D. Doctor of Laws.
L.M.S.(R.) London Midland and Scottish (Railway) (*obs.*).
L.N.E.R. London and North Eastern Railway (*obs.*).
L.N.U. League of Nations Union (*obs.*).
loc. cit. in the place cited.
log. logarithm.
long. longitude.
L.P. Lord Provost (*Scots*), low pressure (*Meteor.*), long primer (*Typ.*).
L'pool Liverpool.
L.P.T.B. London Passenger Transport Board.

L.R.A.M. Licentiate of the Royal Academy of Music.
l.s. left side.
L.S. Linnaean Society.
L.S.D. Lightermen, Stevedores, and Dockers.
£. s. d. pounds, shillings, and pence.
L.T. low tension (*Elec.*).
Lt. Lieutenant.
L.T.A. Lawn Tennis Association.
Lt. Col. Lieutenant Colonel.
Lt. Comm. Lieutenant Commander (*Nav.*).
Ltd. limited.
Lt. Gen. Lieutenant-General.
L.W.L. load-water-line.

M

m. married, masculine, mile, minute(s).
M.A. Master of Arts.
Macc. Maccabees (*B.*).
mach. machinery.
mag. magazine.
magn. magnetism.
Maj. Major.
Maj. Gen. Major General.
Mal. Malachi (*B.*).
Mancun. of Manchester (*signature of the Bishop*).
Man(it). Manitoba.
mar. married.
Mar. March.
March. Marchioness.
marg. margin, (*coll.*) margarine.
Marq. Marquess (*Engl.*), Marquis (*foreign*).
masc. masculine.
Mass. Massachusetts.
math. mathematics.
matric. matriculation.
Matt. Matthew (*B.*).
M.B. Bachelor of Medicine.
M.B.E. Member of the (Order of the) British Empire.
M.C. Member of Congress (*Amer.*), master of ceremonies, Member of Council, Military Cross.
M.C.C. Marylebone Cricket Club.
M.D. Doctor of Medicine.
Md. Maryland.
Md(d)x. Middlesex.
ME Middle English.
Me. Maine.
meas. measure.
M.E.C. Member of the Executive Council.
mech. mechanical, mechanics.
med. medical, medicine, medieval.
mem(o). memorandum.
Met. Metropolitan.
metal(l). metallurgy.
meteor. meteorology.
Meth. Methodist.
mfd. manufactured.
mfg. manufacturing.
M.F.H Master of Foxhounds.
M.F.N. most favoured nation.
mfr(s). manufacturer(s).
M.G. Military Government, machine-gun.
MHG Middle High German.
M.H.R. Member of the House of Representatives (*Amer.*).
Mic. Micah (*B.*).
M.I.C.E. Member of the Institute of Civil Engineers.
Mich. Michigan.
M.I.E.E. Member of the Institute of Electrical Engineers.
mil. military.
Mil. Att. Military Attaché.
Mil. Gov. Military Government.
M.I.Mech.E. Member of the Institute of Mechanical Engineers.
Min. Ministry, minister.
min. mineralogy.
Minn. Minnesota.
misc. miscellaneous.
Miss. Mississippi.
mkt. market.
M.M. Military Medal.
M.O. money-order, Medical Officer (*Mil.*).
Mo. Missouri.
mo. month(s).
mod. modern, moderate.
Mods. Moderations (*Oxford University*).
M.O.H. Medical Officer of Health.
mol. wt molecular weight.
Mon. Monday, Monmouthshire.
Mont. Montana.
M.P. Member of Parliament, Military Police.
m.p. melting point.
m.p.h. miles per hour.
M.P.S. Member of the Pharmaceutical Society.
M.R. Master of the Rolls.
Mr. Mister.
M.R.C.P. Member of the Royal College of Physicians.
M.R.C.S. Member of the Royal College of Surgeons.
M.R.I. Member of the Royal Institute.
Mrs. Mistress.
M.S. Military Secretary.
m.s. months after sight (*C.L.*).
M.S.L. mean sea level.
MS(S). manuscript(s).
M.Sc. Master of Science.
m.s.l. mean sea-level.
M.T. mechanical transport (*Mil.*).
Mt. Mount. *Mts.*, Mountains.
M.T.B. motor torpedo-boat.
mth. month.
mus. music, museum.
Mus.B. Bachelor of Music.
Mus.D. Doctor of Music.
M.V.O. Member of the Royal Victorian Order.
M.W.B. Metropolitan Water Board.
Mx. Middlesex.

N

n. neuter, nominative, noon, noun.
N. North, northern.
N.A. North America, Nautical Almanack.
n/a no account (*C.L.*).
N.A.A.F.I. Navy, Army, and Air Force Institutes.
Nah. Nahum (*B.*).
Nat. national, nationalist, Natal, Nathaniel (*B.*).

nat. hist. natural history.
N.A.T.O. North Atlantic Treaty Organization.
nat. ord. natural order.
Natsopa National Union of Operative Printers and Assistants.
naut. nautical.
nav. naval, navigation.
N.B. note particularly, New Brunswick, North Britain, North Borneo.
n.b. no ball (*Crick.*).
N.B.C. National Broadcasting Corporation (*Amer.*).
N.C. North Carolina.
N.C.B. National Coal Board.
N.C.O. non-commissioned officer.
N.C.U National Cyclists' Union.
n.d. no date.
N. Dak. North Dakota.
N.E. north-east, New England.
Neb(r). Nebraska.
N.E.D. New English Dictionary.
neg. negative.
Neh. Nehemiah (*B.*).
nem. con. no one contradicting.
nem. dis. with no dissentient voice.
Neth. Netherlands.
neut. neuter.
Nev. Nevada.
N.F. Newfoundland.
N/F no funds (*C.L.*)
N.F.C. National Fitness Council.
Nfd(l). Newfoundland.
N.F.U. National Farmers Union.
N.G. no good.
N.H. New Hampshire.
N.I. Northern Ireland.
N.J. New Jersey.
N.L. Navy League.
N. lat. north latitude.
N.L.I. National Lifeboat Institution.
N. Mex. New Mexico.
N.N.E. north-north-east.
N.N.W. north-north-west.
No. or *N* number.
nom. nominative.
non-com. non-commissioned officer.
Noncon. Nonconformist.
non obst. notwithstanding.
non seq. false conclusion.
Norm. Norman.
Northants. Northamptonshire.
Northumb. Northumberland.
Norvic. of Norwich (*signature of the Bishop*).
Norw. Norway, Norwegian.
Nos. or *N* numbers.
Notts. Nottinghamshire.
n.p. new paragraph.
N.P. Notary Public.
N.P.F.A. National Playing Fields Association.
n.p. or d. no place or date.
N.R. North Riding (*of Yorkshire*).
nr. near.
n.s. not sufficient.
N.S. New Style (*in dates*), Nova Scotia.
N.S.C. National Sporting Club.
N.S.P.C.C. National Society for the Prevention of Cruelty to Children.
N.S.W. New South Wales.
N.T. New Testament.
n.u. name unknown.
Num. Numbers (*B.*).
N.U.R. National Union of Railwaymen.
N.U.T. National Union of Teachers.
N.V. New Version.
N.V.M. Nativity of the Virgin Mary.
N.W. north-west.
N.W.F.P. North-West Frontier Province (*of Pakistan*).
N.W.T. Northwest Territories (*of Canada*).
N.Y. New York (*state*).
N.Z. New Zealand.

O

o/a on account of.
O.A.S. Organization of American States.
ob. died.
Obad. Obadiah (*B.*).
obdt. obedient.
O.B.E. Order of the British Empire.
obj. object, objective.
obl. oblong, oblique.
obs. obsolete, observation.
ob. s.p. died without issue.
obstet. obstetrics.
O.C. Officer Commanding.
Oct. October.
o/d on demand (*C.L.*).
OE Old English.
O.E.D. Oxford English Dictionary.
O.E.E.C. Organization of European Economic Co-operation.
O.F. Odd Fellow.
off. official, officinal, offered.
offic. official.
OF(r) Old French.
OFris. Old Frisian.
O.F.S. Orange Free State.
OHG Old High German.
O.H.M.S. On His *or* Her Majesty's Service
O.K. (*coll.*) all correct.
Okla. Oklahoma.
O.M. Order of Merit.
ON Old Norse.
Ont. Ontario.
O.P. out of print.
o.p. over proof (*of spirits*), opposite the prompt side (*Theat.*).
op. cit. in the work cited.
opp. opposite, opposed.
opt. optics, optional.
o.r. owner's risk (*C.L.*).
ord. ordained, order, ordinary, ordinance.
Ore(g). Oregon.
orn(ith). ornithology.
O.S. Old Style (*of dates*), Ordnance Survey, ordinary seaman.
OS Old Saxon.
O.S.A. Order of Saint Augustine.
O.S.B. Order of Saint Benedict.
O.S.D. Order of Saint Dominic.
O.S.F. Order of Saint Francis.
OSlav. Old Slavonic.
O.T. Old Testament.
O.T.C. Officers' Training Corps.
O.U.P. Oxford University Press.
Oxon. Oxfordshire, of Oxford University, of Oxford (*signature of the Bishop*).
oz. ounce(s).

P

P.	pawn (*chess*).
p.	page, participle, person (*Gram.*), soft (*Mus.*).
P.A.	Press Association.
p.a.	each year.
Pa.	Pennsylvania.
P.A.A.	Pan American Airways.
paint.	painting.
palaeog.	palaeography.
palaeont.	palaeontology.
pam.	pamphlet.
P. & O.	Peninsular and Oriental (Steamship Line).
par.	paragraph, parallel, parish.
parl.	parliament(ary).
pars.	paragraphs.
part.	participle.
pass.	passive (*Gram.*).
path.	pathology.
Pat. Off.	Patent Office.
P.A.U.	Pan American Union.
payt.	payment.
P.B.	British Pharmacopœia.
P.B.I.	(*vulg.*) poor bloody infantry.
p.c.	postcard, per cent.
p/c	price current (*C.L.*).
P.C.	police constable, Privy Council(lor).
P.D.	potential difference (*Elec.*), printer's devil (*Typ.*).
pd.	paid.
P.D.A.D.	Probate, Divorce, and Admiralty Division (*Law*).
pdr.	pounder (*Artil.*).
P.E.I.	Prince Edward Island.
pen.	peninsula.
Penn.	Pennsylvania.
Pent.	Pentecost, Pentateuch.
P.E.P.	Political and Economic Planning.
PEPSU	Patiala and East Punjab States Union.
perf.	perfect (*Gram.*), perforated (*postage stamps*).
per pro.	by proxy.
pers.	person (*Gram.*), personal.
Pet.	Peter (*B.*).
P.G.	paying guest.
pharm.	pharmacy, pharmacology, pharmaceutical.
Ph.D.	Doctor of Philosophy.
phil.	philosophy.
Phil.	Philadelphia, Philippians (*B.*).
Philem.	Philemon (*B.*).
philol.	philology.
Phil. Trans.	Philosophical Transactions of the Royal Society.
phon(et).	phonetics.
phot.	photography.
phren.	phrenology.
phys.	physics, physical.
physiol.	physiology, physiological.
pinx.	painted by.
pk.	peck.
Pk.	Park.
pkg.	package.
P/L	profit and loss (*C.L.*).
pl.	place, plural.
P.L.A.	Port of London Authority.
plen.	plenipotentiary.
plup.	pluperfect.
plur.	plural.
p.m.	afternoon.
P.M.	Prime Minister, Past Master, post-mortem (examination).
pm	premium (*C.L.*).
P.M.G.	Postmaster-General.
P.M.L.A.	Publications of the Modern Language Association (of America).
p.n.	promissory note (*C.L.*).
pnxt.	painted by.
P.O.	post-office, postal order, Petty Officer (*Nav.*), Pilot Officer (*Av.*).
p.o.a.	pay on delivery (*C.L.*).
pol.	politics, political.
P.O.O.	post-office order.
P.O.P.	printing-out paper (*Phot.*).
pop.	population, popular.
pos.	positive, position.
P.O.S.B.	post-office savings bank.
poss.	possession.
P.O.W.	prisoner of war.
p.p.	by proxy, past participle
pp.	pages.
ppa.	by proxy.
P.P.S.	additional postscript.
P.R.	proportional representation.
pr.	present, pronoun, price.
pr.	pair.
P.R.A.	President of the Royal Academy.
Preb.	Prebendary.
prec.	preceding.
pred.	predicate, predicative.
Pref.	Preference (*C.L.*).
pref.	preface, prefix.
prelim.	preliminary.
prelims	preliminary matter (*Typ.*).
prem.	premium.
prep.	preparatory, preposition.
Pres.	President.
pres.	present (*Gram.*).
Presb.	Presbyter(ian).
pret.	preterite.
prev.	previous.
P.R.I.B.A.	President of the Royal Institute of British Architects.
P.R.O.	Public Record Office, Public Relations Officer.
pro.	professional.
prob.	probably.
Proc.	Proceedings.
Prom.	(*coll.*) Promenade Concert.
pron.	pronoun, pronounced, pronunciation.
prop.	proposition, property.
propr.	proprietor, proprietary.
props	(*coll.*) properties (*Theat.*).
pros.	prosody.
pro tem.	for the time being.
prov.	provincial, proverbial.
Prov.	Proverbs (*B.*), Provençal.
prox.	next month.
prox. acc.	next in order.
P.S.	postscript, Permanent Secretary.
p.s.	prompt side (*Theat.*).
Ps.	Psalms (*B.*).
pseud.	pseudonym(ous).
P.S.N.C.	Pacific Steam Navigation Company.
psych.	psychic(al).
psychol.	psychology, psychological.
P.T.	physical training.

pt.	pint(s), point, part, payment.
Pte	Private (*Mil.*).
P.T.O.	please turn over.
pub.	public, publication, published, (*coll.*) public house.
punct.	punctuation.
P.W.D.	Public Works Department.
P.X.	Post Exchange (*Amer. Mil.*).

Q

N.B. See also under K for titles in which 'Queen' was formerly 'King'.

q.	query, quasi.
Q.	Queen, question, coulomb (*Elec.*).
Q.A.B.	Queen Anne's Bounty.
Q.B.D.	Queen's Bench Division (*Law*).
Q.C.	Queen's Counsel (*Law*).
Q.E.D.	which was to be proved.
Q.F.	quick-firing.
Q.M.	Quartermaster.
Q.M.A.A.C.	Queen Mary's Army Auxiliary Corps.
Q.M.G.	Quartermaster General.
Q.M.S.	Quartermaster-Sergeant.
qr	quarter.
Q.S.	Quarter Sessions.
q.s.	as much as is sufficient.
qt.	quantity.
q.t.	(*sl.*) on the quiet.
qu.	question, query, quasi.
quad.	quadrant, quadruple, quadrangle.
quart.	quarterly.
Q.U.B.	Queen's University, Belfast.
Que.	Quebec.
Queensl.	Queensland.
quot.	quotation (*C.L.*).
quote	(*coll.*) quotation (*literary*).
quotes	(*coll.*) quotation marks.
q.v.	which see, as much as you wish.
qy.	query.

R

R.	King, Queen, river, resistance (*Elec.*), railway, Réaumur.
r.	right, radius, rood, runs (*Crick.*), rupee(s).
R.A.	Royal Academy, Royal Artillery.
R.A.C.	Royal Automobile Club.
R.A.F.	Royal Air Force.
R.A.M.	Royal Academy of Music.
R.A.M.C.	Royal Army Medical Corps.
R.A.N.	Royal Australian Navy.
R.A.O.C.	Royal Army Ordnance Corps.
R.A.P.C.	Royal Army Pay Corps.
R.A.S.C.	Royal Army Service Corps.
R.A.V.C.	Royal Army Veterinary Corps.
R.B.	Rifle Brigade.
R.B.A.	Royal Society of British Artists.
R.C.	Roman Catholic, Red Cross.
R.C.A.	Royal College of Art, Radio Corporation of America.
R.C.M.P.	Royal Canadian Mounted Police.
R.D.	Rural Dean, refer to drawer (*C.L.*).
Rd.	road.
R.D.C.	Rural District Council.
R.E.	Royal Engineers.
rec.	recipe.
recd.	received.
recogns.	recognizances (*Law*).
recpt.	receipt.
rect.	rectified.
redupl.	reduplicated.
ref.	reference, reformed, (*coll.*) referee.
refd	referred.
refl.	reflexive.
reg.	regular.
regd	registered.
Reg.-Gen.	Registrar-General.
Reg. Prof.	Regius Professor.
regt.	regiment.
rel.	religion, relative (*Gram.*).
R.E.M.E.	Royal Electrical and Mechanical Engineers.
Rep.	representative, republic, report.
repr.	reprinted.
res.	resigned, reserve, residence.
ret.	retired.
retd.	returned, retired.
retnr	retainer (*Law*).
rev.	revised, revision, reverse, revenue, revolution (*Mach.*).
Rev.	Revelations (*B.*), Reverend, review.
Rev. Ver.	Revised Version (*B.*).
R.F.A.	Royal Field Artillery.
R.G.S.	Royal Geographical Society.
r.h.	right hand.
R.H.	Royal Highness.
R.H.A.	Royal Horse Artillery.
rhet.	rhetoric.
R.H.S.	Royal Horticultural *or* Humane Society.
R.Hist.S.	Royal Historical Society.
R.I.	Rhode Island.
R.I.B.A.	Royal Institute of British Architects.
R.I.P.	(may he *or* she) rest in peace.
rit.	gradually slower (*Mus.*).
R.L.O.	returned letter office.
R.L.S.	Robert Louis Stevenson.
Rly	railway.
R.M.	Royal Mail, Royal Marines, Resident Magistrate.
R.M.A.	Royal Military Academy (*Woolwich*).
R.M.C.	Royal Military College (*Sandhurst*).
R.M.S.P.	Royal Mail Steam Packet Company.
R.N.	Royal Navy.
R.N.L.I.	Royal National Lifeboat Institution.
R.N.R.	Royal Naval Reserve.
R.N.V.R.	Royal Naval Volunteer Reserve.
R.N.V.S.R	Royal Naval Volunteer Supplementary Reserve.
Roffen.	of Rochester (*signature of the Bishop*).
Rom.	Romans (*B.*), Roman, Romance.
rom.	roman type.
Rom. Cath.	Roman Catholic.
R.P. or *r.p.*	reply paid.
r.p.m.	revolutions per minute.
r.p.s.	revolutions per second.
R.P.S.	Royal Photographic Society.
rpt.	report.
R.S.	Royal Society.
R.S.A.	Royal Society of Arts, Royal Scottish Academy.
R.S.M.	Regimental Sergeant-Major, Royal School of Mines.
R.S.P.C.A.	Royal Society for the Prevention of Cruelty to Animals.

R.S.V.P. please reply.
R.T. or *R/T* radio-telegraphy *or* telephony.
R.T.C. Royal Tank Corps.
Rt Hon. Right Honourable.
R.T.O. Railway Transport Officer (*Mil.*).
Rt Rev. Right Reverend.
R.T.S. Religious Tract Society.
R.U. Rugby Union.
R.V. Rifle Volunteers, Revised Version (*B.*).
R.V.C.I. Royal Veterinary College of Ireland.
R.V.O. Royal Victorian Order.
R.W. Right Worthy *or* Worshipful.
Ry. railway.
R.Y.S. Royal Yacht Squadron.

S

S. south, Saint, Society, Socialist, solo (*Mus.*), soprano (*Mus.*).
s. shilling, second(s), son, singular, see.
S.A. Salvation Army, South Africa, South America.
s.a. without date
Salop. Shropshire.
Sarum. of Salisbury (*signature of the Bishop*).
Sask. Saskatchewan.
Sat. Saturday.
S.B. simultaneous broadcast (*Rad.*).
Sc. Scotland, Scottish, Scots, Scotch.
S.C. South Carolina, Security Council.
sc. namely, scene (*Theat.*).
s.caps. small capitals (*Typ.*).
Scand. Scandinavian.
Sc.D. Doctor of Science.
sch. school, scholar, schooner.
sched. schedule.
sci. science, scientific.
S.C.M. Student Christian Movement.
Scot. Scotland, Scottish.
Script. Scripture.
sculp(t). sculpture, sculptor.
s.d. indefinitely, standard displacement (*Navy*).
S.D. State Department (*Amer.*), Senior Dean.
S. Dak. South Dakota.
S.E. south-east.
Sec. secretary.
sec. second, section.
sect. section.
secy secretary.
sel. selected, select.
Sem. Semitic, Seminary.
Sen. Senate, Senator.
sen. or *senr* senior.
Sept. September, Septuagint (*B.*)
seq. the following (*sing.*); *seqq.*, the following (*pl.*).
ser. series.
Sergt. sergeant (*Mil.*).
Serjt. Serjeant (*Law*).
S.G. screened grid (*Rad.*), Solicitor-General, specific gravity.
Sgt. Sergeant.
sh. shilling.
shd should.
sim. similar(ly).
sin. sine (*Math.*).
sing. singular.
S.J.C. Supreme Judicial Court (*Amer.*).
Skr. or *Skrt* Sanskrit.
S.L. Solicitor at Law.
S. lat. south latitude.
Slav. Slav(on)ic.
s.l.p. without lawful issue.
S.M.M. Holy Mother Mary (*R.C.*).
Smith. Inst. Smithsonian Institution (*Amer.*).
s.m.p. without male issue.
S.N. shipping note.
s.o. seller's option.
S.O. sub-office, Stationery Office.
Soc. society, Socialist.
sociol. sociology.
sol. solution, solicitor.
Som. Somersetshire.
Song of Sol. Song of Solomon (*B.*).
sop. soprano.
S.O.S. or *SOS* distress signal.
sov. sovereign.
s.p. without issue.
Sp. Spain, Spanish.
S.P. small pica (*Typ.*), starting price.
S.P.C.K. Society for the Promotion of Christian Knowledge.
spec. special(ly), specification.
specif. specifical(ly).
S.P.G. Society for the Propagation of the Gospel.
sp. gr. specific gravity.
spirit. spiritualism.
S.P.Q.R. (*coll.*) small profits and quick returns.
S.P.R. Society for Psychical Research.
s.p.s. without surviving issue.
S.P.V.D. Society for the Prevention of Venereal Disease.
sq. square.
Sqd. Ldr Squadron Leader (*Av.*).
S.R. Southern Railway (*obs.*).
S.S. steamship, Straits Settlements, Secretary of State.
S.S.A.F.A. Soldiers', Sailors' and Airmen's Families Association.
S.S.E. south-south-east.
S.S.U. Sunday-School Union.
S.S.W. south-south-west.
St. saint, street, strait.
st. stone(s), stanza, stumped (*Crick.*).
Staffs. Staffordshire.
stat. statics, statistics, statute, stationary.
stereo. stereotype.
St. Ex. Stock Exchange.
stg. sterling.
Stip. Stipendiary.
Stn Station.
str. stroke (oar).
sub. subaltern, subscription, substitute, suburb, submarine.
subj. subject, subjunctive.
subst. substantive.
suff. suffix, sufficient.
Suffr. Suffragan.
sugg. suggestion, suggested.
Sun. Sunday.
sup. superior, supine.
super. superfine, supernumerary, superintendent.
superl. superlative.
suppl. supplement.
supr. supreme.

Supt	superintendent.
surg.	surgery, surgeon.
surv.	surveying, surviving.
s.v.	under the title, surrender-value (*C.L.*).
S.W.	south-west, South Wales.
Sw.	Sweden, Swedish.
S.W.G.	Standard Wire Gauge.
syll.	syllable.
syn.	synonym(ous).
syst.	system.

T

t.	ton, transitive.
T.A.	telegraphic address, Territorial Army.
tan	tangent.
Tasm.	Tasmania.
T.B.	tuberculosis.
Tce	Terrace.
T.D.	Territorial Decoration (*Mil.*).
tech.	technical(ly).
technol.	technology.
tel.	telephone, telegraph(y).
temp.	temperature, temporary, in the time of.
Tenn.	Tennessee.
term.	terminology, termination.
Terr.	Territory, Terrace.
Teut.	Teutonic.
Tex.	Texas.
T.G.W.U.	Transport and General Workers' Union.
theat.	theatre, theatrical.
theol.	theology, theological.
theor.	theorem.
theos.	theosophy.
therap.	therapeutics.
therm.	thermometer.
Thess.	Thessalonians (*B.*).
Thurs.	Thursday.
T.H.W.M.	Trinity High-Water Mark.
Tim.	Timothy (*B.*).
tinct.	tincture.
tit.	title.
Tit.	Titus (*B.*).
T.L.C.	tank-landing craft.
T.M.O.	telegraph money-order.
tn.	ton(s).
TNT	trinitrotoluene.
T.O.	telegraph office, turn over.
Tob.	Tobit (*B.*).
tonn.	tonnage.
topog.	topography, topographical.
tp.	troop.
Tpr	trooper (*Mil.*).
tr.	transpose (*Typ.*), transport, translate.
Tr.	trustee (*C.L.*).
trans.	transitive, transactions, translation.
transf.	transferred.
transl.	translated, translator, translation.
Treas.	Treasurer.
trig.	trigonometry.
Trin.	Trinity.
trop.	tropical, tropic(s).
Trs.	trustees.
trs.	transpose.
T.T.	teetotal(er).
T.U.	trade union.
T.U.C.	Trade Union Congress.
Tues.	Tuesday.
TV	television.
T.V.A.	Tennessee Valley Authority.
typ.	typography, typographical.

U

U.	Unionist.
u.c.	upper case (*Typ.*).
U.D.C.	Urban District Council.
U.F.C.	United Free Church (of Scotland).
U.G.C.	University Grants Committee.
U.K.	United Kingdom.
ult.	of last month.
U.N.	United Nations.
UNESCO	United Nations Education, Scientific, and Cultural Organization.
UNICEF	United Nations International Children's Emergency Fund.
Unit.	Unitarian.
Univ.	university.
unm.	unmarried.
U.N.S.C.	United Nations Security Council.
U.P.	United Press, United Provinces (*now* Uttar Pradesh).
u/s	unserviceable.
U.S.	United Services.
U.S.(A.)	United States (of America).
U.S.N.	United States Navy.
U.S.S.	United States Ship.
U.S.S.R.	Union of Soviet Socialist Republics.
usu.	usual(ly).
ut inf.	as below.
ut sup.	as above.
ux.	wife.

V

v.	against, see, verb, verse.
Va	Virginia.
V.A.	Royal Order of Victoria and Albert, Vicar Apostolic, Vice-Admiral.
V.A.D.	Volunteer Aid Detachment (*Mil.*).
val.	value.
var.	variety, variant.
vb.	verb.
V.C.	Victoria Cross (*Mil.*), Vice-Chancellor (*Univ.*), Vice-Consul.
V.D.	venereal disease.
v.d.	various dates.
V.D.H.	valvular disease of the heart.
Ven.	Venerable.
verb. sap.	a word suffices to the wise.
Vert.	vertebrates.
vet.	(*coll.*) veterinary surgeon.
veter.	veterinary.
V.G.	Vicar-General.
v.g. or *V.G.*	very good.
V.H.F.	Very High Frequency.
v.i.	intransitive verb.
Vic.	Victoria (*Australia*).
vid.	see.
vil.	village.
v.imp.	impersonal verb.
V.I.P.	very important person.
v.ir.	irregular verb.
Vis.	Viscount.
viz.	namely.
Vo. or *v°*	on the left-hand page.
voc.	vocative.
vocab.	vocabulary.

Vol.	volunteer.
vol.	volume; *vols*, volumes.
V.O.A.	Voice of America (*Rad.*).
V.P.	Vice-President.
v.r.	reflexive verb.
V.R. (*et I.*)	Victoria Queen (and Empress).
v.s.	see above.
vs.	against.
V.S.	veterinary surgeon.
v.t.	transitive verb.
Vt.	Vermont.
vulg.	vulgar.
Vulg.	Vulgate.
v.v.	conversely.
vv.	verses.

W

w.	with, wicket (*Crick.*).
W.	west, Welsh.
W.A.	Western Australia.
W.A.A.F.	Women's Auxiliary Air Force.
Warw.	Warwickshire.
Wash.	Washington (*state*).
W.B.	way-bill (*C.L.*), Water Board.
W.C.	West-Central (*London postal district*), water-closet.
w.c.	with costs.
W.D.	War Department, Works Department.
wd	would.
W.E.A.	Workers' Education Association.
Wed.	Wednesday.
w.f.	wrong fount (*Typ.*).
W.F.T.U.	World Federation of Trade Unions.
wh.	which.
whf.	wharf.
W.H.O	World Health Organization.
W.I.	West Indies.
Wilts.	Wiltshire.
Winton.	of Winchester (*signature of the Bishop*).
Wis(*c*).	Wisconsin.
Wisd.	Wisdom of Solomon (*B.*).
wk.	week, weak.
W/L	wave-length (*Rad.*).
W.N.W.	west-north-west.
W.O.	War Office, Warrant Officer.
Worcs.	Worcestershire.
W.P.B. or *w.p.b.*	waste-paper basket.
W.R.	West Riding (*of Yorkshire*).
W.R.A.C.	Women's Royal Army Corps.
W.R.N.S.	Women's Royal Naval Service.
W.S.W.	west-south-west.
W.T. or *W/T*	wireless telegraphy.
wt.	weight.
Wyo.	Wyoming.

X

x-d.	without dividend.
x-i.	without interest.
Xmas	Christmas.
Xt	Christ.
Xtian	Christian.

Y

y.	year.
yd(*s*)	yard(s).
Y.M.C.A.	Young Men's Christian Association.
Yorks.	Yorkshire.
yr.	your, year, younger.
Y.W.C.A.	Young Women's Christian Association.

Z

Zech.	Zechariah (*B.*).
Zeph.	Zephaniah (*B.*).
Z.S.	Zoological Society.

INDEX OF NAMES

GEOGRAPHICAL AND PROPER NAMES

THE following classes of words have in general been omitted from this list:

1. Those in which the English and German forms correspond exactly: e.g. Alexander, *Alexander*; Alexandra, *Alexandra*; Alfred, *Alfred*; Europa, *Europa*, etc.
2. Those names of countries in which the English terminations –ia, –ica, correspond to the German *–ien*, *–ika*: e.g. Anatolia, *Anatolien*; Attica, *Attika*, etc.
3. Those derived words in which the English terminations –ic and –ism correspond to the German *–isch* and *–ismus*: e.g. Buddhistic, *buddhistisch*; Homeric, *homerisch*; Platonic, *platonisch*; Plutonism, *Plutonismus*, etc.

The article has been printed in full with those names of countries with which the article is used in German, e.g. *die Schweiz*.

Names of the more important rivers in which the English and German forms correspond exactly have been included in the following lists in order to show their German gender.

A

Aar R. [ɑː], Aar (*f.*).
Abderite [ˈæbdəraɪt], Abderit (*m.*).
Abraham [ˈeɪbrəhæm], **Abram** [ˈeɪbrəm] Abraham (*m.*); *–'s bosom*, Abrahams Schoß.
Abruzzi [əˈbrutsɪ], die Abruzzen (*pl.*).
Abyssinia [æbɪˈsɪnjə], Abessinien (*n.*). **–n,** Abessinier (*m.*); abessinisch (*adj.*).
Achæan [əˈkɪːən], **Achaian** [əˈkaɪən], Achäer (*m.*); achäisch (*adj.*).
Achilles [əˈkɪlɪːz], Achill(es) (*m.*); *tendon of –*, die Achillesferse.
Acre [ˈeɪkə], Akka (*n.*); Akko(n) (*n.*) (*Hist.*).
Adela [ˈædələ], **Adelaide** [ˈædəleɪd], Adele, Adelheid (*f.*).
Adige R. [ˈɑːdɪdʒɪ], Etsch (*f.*).
Adolf [ˈædɔlf], **Adolphus** [əˈdɔlfəs], Adolf (*m.*).
Adonijah [ædəˈnaɪdʒə], Adonai (*m.*).
Adrian [ˈeɪdrɪən], Hadrian (*m.*).
Adrianople [eɪdrɪəˈnoupl], Adrianopel (*n.*).
Adriatic Sea [eɪdrɪˈætɪk], die Adria, das Adriatische Meer.
Ægean Sea [ɪːˈdʒɪːən], das Ägäische Meer.
Æneid [ˈɪːnɪɪd], die Äneide.
Æoli–an [ɪːouljən], **–c** [ɪːˈɔlɪk], äolisch (*adj.*); *–an harp*, die Äolsharfe.
Æsculapius [ɪːskjuˈleɪpjəs], Äskulap (*m.*).
Afghan [ˈæfgæn], Afghane (*m.*); afghanisch (*adj.*).
Africa [ˈæfrɪkə], Afrika (*n.*). **–n,** Afrikaner (*m.*); afrikanisch (*adj.*).
Agatha [ˈægəθə], Agathe (*f.*).
Ahasuerus [əhæzjuˈɪərəs], Ahasver(us) (*m.*).
Aix-la-Chapelle [ˈeɪkslaʃæˈpɛl], Aachen (*n.*).
Aladdin [əˈlædɪn], Aladin (*m.*).
Alaric [ˈælərɪk], Alarich (*m.*).
Albanian [ælˈbeɪnɪən], Albaner, Albanier, Albanese (*m.*); albanisch (*adj.*).
Albert [ˈælbət], Albert, Albrecht (*m.*). **–a** [ælˈbəːtə], Albertine (*f.*).
Albigenses [ælbɪˈdʒɛnsɪːz], die Albigenser (*pl.*).
Albina [ælˈbɪːnə], Alwine (*f.*).
Alec [ˈælɪk] (*dim. of* **Alexander** [ælɪgˈzɑːndə]), Alex (*m.*).
Aleman(n) [ˈælɪmæn], Alemanne (*m.*).
Alexandrian [ælɪgˈzɑːndrɪən], Alexandriner (*m.*); alexandrinisch (*adj.*).
Alger–ian, Algierer (*m.*); algierisch (*adj.*). **–s** [ælˈdʒɪəz], Algier (*n.*).
Alice [ˈælɪs], Alice, Alexia (*f.*).
Alick [ˈælɪk], *see* **Alec.**
Aller R. [ˈælə], Aller (*f.*).
Aloysius [æˈlɔɪsɪəs], Alois (*m.*).
Alphonso [ælˈfɔnzou], Alfons (*m.*).
Alp–ine [ˈælpaɪn], alpinisch (*adj.*), Alpen–. **–s** [ælps], die Alpen (*pl.*).
Alsace [ˈælsæs], Elsaß (*n.*). **Alsatian** [ælˈseɪʃən], Elsässer (*m.*); (*dog*) der Wolfshund; elsässisch (*adj.*).
Amazon [ˈæməzən], Amazone (*f.*); der Amazonas, Amazonenstrom.
Ambros–e [ˈæmbrouz], Ambrosius (*m.*). *–ian hymn*, der ambrosianische Lobgesang.
Amelia [əˈmɪːljə], Amalia, Amalie (*f.*).
America [əˈmɛrɪkə], Amerika (*n.*). **–n,** Amerikaner (*m.*); amerikanisch (*adj.*); *–n Indian*, Indianer (*m*).
Amy [ˈeɪmɪ] (*dim. of* **Amelia**), Malchen (*n.*).
Anacreontic [ənækrɪˈɔntɪk], anakreontisch (*adj.*); *– writer*, der Anakreontiker.
Anak [ˈeɪnæk], Enak (*m.*).
Andalusian [ændəˈl(j)uːʒən], andalusisch (*adj.*).
Andes [ˈændɪːz], die Anden (*pl.*).
Andrew [ˈændruː], Andreas (*m.*).
Angevin [ˈændʒɪvɪn], Anjou (*n.*).
Angles [ˈæŋgəlz], (*pl.*) die Angeln.
Anglo [ˈæŋglou]; **--German,** deutsch-englisch (*adj.*); **–ˈmania,** die Anglomanie, **--Norman,** Anglo-Normanne (*m.*); anglo-normannisch (*adj.*). **–phile** [–faɪl], englandfreundlich, anglophil (*adj.*). **–ˈphobia** [–ˈfoubɪə], die Anglophobie. **--Saxon,** Angelsachse (*m.*); angelsächsisch (*adj.*).
Ann(a) [æn (ˈænə)], **Anne** [æn], Anna, Anne (*f.*).
Annamese [ænəˈmɪːz], Annamit (*m.*); annamitisch (*adj.*).
Annie [ˈænɪ] (*dim. of* **Anna**), Anni (*f.*), Ännchen (*n.*).
Anspach [ˈænspæk], Ansbach (*n.*).
Ant(h)ony [ˈæntənɪ (ˈænθənɪ)], Anton, Antonius (*m.*).
Antilles [ænˈtɪlɪːz], die Antillen (*pl.*).
Antioch [ˈæntɪək], Antiochia (*n.*). **–ian** [–ˈoukɪən] antiochenisch (*adj.*).
Antwerp [ˈæntwəːp], Antwerpen (*n.*).
Apennines [ˈæpɪnaɪnz], die Apenninen (*pl.*).
Apollonian [æpəˈlounɪən], apollinisch (*adj.*).
Appalachians [æpəˈleɪtʃɪənz], die Appalachen (*pl.*).
Appian Way [ˈæpɪən weɪ], die Appische Straße.
Apulian [æˈpjuːlɪən], apulisch (*adj.*).
Aquit–aine [ækwɪˈteɪn], Aquitanien (*n.*). **–anian,** Aquitanier (*m.*); aquitanisch (*adj.*).
Arab [ˈærəb], **–ian** [əˈreɪbɪən], Araber (*m.*); arabisch (*adj.*), *–ian Nights' Entertainment*, Tausendundeine Nacht.
Aragon [ˈærəgən], Aragonien (*n.*).
Aram–æan [ærəˈmɪːən], Aramäer (*m.*); aramäisch (*adj.*). **–aic** [–ˈmeɪɪk], (*language*) Aramäisch (*n.*) & (*adj.*).
Arcadia [ɑːˈkeɪdɪə], Arkadien (*n.*). **–n,** arkadisch (*adj.*); (*fig.*) idyllisch (*adj.*).
Archimedean [ɑːkɪˈmɪːdɪən], archimedisch (*adj.*).
Ardennes [ɑːˈdɛn], die Ardennen (*pl.*).
Argentin–a [ɑːdʒənˈtɪːnə], Argentinien (*n.*); argentinisch (*adj.*). **–ian** [–ˈtɪnɪən], Argentin(i)er (*m.*).
Argovia [ɑːˈgouvɪə], das Aargau. **–n,** Aargauer (*m.*).
Arian [ˈɛərɪən], Arianer (*m.*); arianisch (*adj.*) (*Rel.*).
Aristot–elian [ærɪstoˈtɪːlɪən], der Aristoteliker; aristotelisch (*adj.*). **–le** [ˈærɪstɔtl], Aristoteles (*m.*).
Armenian [ɑːˈmɪːnɪən], Armenier (*m.*); armenisch (*adj.*).

Arminian [ɑ:ˈmɪnɪən], Arminianer (*m.*); arminianisch (*adj.*).
Arno R. [ˈɑ:noʊ], Arno (*m.*).
Arthur [ˈɑ:θə], Artur (*m.*); *King* –, König Artus; **–ian** [ɑ:ˈθjʊərɪən], Artus–.
Aryan [ˈɛərɪən], Arier (*m.*); arisch (*adj.*); indogermanisch (*adj.*).
Ashanti [əˈʃæntɪ], Aschanti (*n.*) (*country*); (*m.*) (*inhabitant*).
Asia Minor [ˈeɪzjə, ˈeɪʃə], Kleinasien (*n.*). **–tic** [eɪzɪˈætɪk, eɪʃɪˈætɪk], Asiat (*m.*); asiatisch (*adj.*).
Asshur [ˈæʃə:], Assur (*n.*).
Assyrian [æˈsɪrɪən], Assyrier (*m.*); assyrisch (*adj.*).
Asturia–n [æsˈtjʊərɪən], Asturier (*m.*); asturisch (*adj.*). **–s** [æsˈtjʊərɪæs], Asturien (*n.*).
Athanasian [æθəˈneɪʒən], athanasianisch (*adj.*).
Athen–ian [əˈθɪ:nɪən], Athener (*m.*); athenisch (*adj.*). **–s** [ˈæθənz], Athen (*n.*).
Attila [ˈætɪlə], Attila (*m.*) (*Hist.*); Etzel (*m.*) (*legend*).
Augean [ɔ:ˈdʒɪ:ən], augeisch (*adj.*); *cleanse the – stable*, den Augiasstall reinigen.
Augusta [ɔ:ˈgʌstə], Augusta, Auguste (*f.*). **–n,** *adj.*; augusteisch.
Augustin–(e) [ɔ:ˈgʌstɪn (ˈɔ:gəstɪ:n)], Augustin(us) (*m.*); *–e friar, see* **–ian.** **–ian** [ɔ:gəsˈtɪnɪən], Augustiner (*m.*); augustinisch (*adj.*).
Augustus [ɔ:ˈgʌstəs], August (*m.*); (*Roman emperor*) Augustus (*m.*).
Australian [ɔ:sˈtreɪljən], Australier (*m.*); australisch (*adj.*).
Austria [ˈɔ:strɪə], Österreich (*n.*). **–n,** Österreicher (*m.*); österreichisch (*adj.*).
Austro-Hungarian [ɔ:strohʌŋˈgɛərɪən], österreichisch-ungarisch (*adj.*).
Avars [ˈævɑ:z], die Avaren (*pl.*).
Aventine [ˈævəntaɪn], der Aventin, aventinische Hügel.
Azores [əˈzɔ:z], die Azoren (*pl.*).
Azov [ˈɑ:zɔv]; *Sea of* –, das Asowsche Meer.
Aztec [ˈæztɛk], Azteke (*m.*).

B

Babylonian [bæbɪˈloʊnɪən], Babylonier (*m.*); babylonisch (*adj.*).
Balaam [ˈbeɪlæm], Bileam (*m.*).
Balder [ˈbɔ:ldə], Baldur (*m.*).
Baldwin [ˈbɔ:ldwɪn], Balduin (*m.*).
Balearic Islands [bælɪˈærɪk], die Balearen (*pl.*).
Balkans, the [ˈbɔ:lkənz], der Balkan.
Balthazar [bælˈθæzə], Balthasar (*m.*).
Baltic Sea [ˈbɔ:ltɪk], die Ostsee; – *Provinces*, das Baltikum, das Baltenland.
Baluchistan [bəˈlu:kɪstɑ:n], Belutschistan (*n.*).
Barbado(e)s [bɑ:ˈbeɪdoʊz], Barbados (*n.*).
Barbary [ˈbɑ:bərɪ], die Berberei; – *horse*, das Berberpferd; – *States*, die Barbareskenstaaten (*pl.*).
Barnaby [ˈbɑ:nəbɪ], Barnabas (*m.*).
Bartholomew [bɑ:ˈθɔləmju:], Bartholomäus (*m.*); *Massacre of St. –'s*, die Bartholomäusnacht, Pariser Bluthochzeit.
Bashkir [ˈbæʃkə], Baschkire (*m.*). **–ia** [bæʃˈkɪ:rɪə], Baschkirenland (*n.*).
Basil [ˈbæzl], Basilius (*m.*).
Basle [bɑ:l], Basel (*n.*).
Basque [bæsk], Baske (*m.*); baskisch (*adj.*).
Batavian [bəˈteɪvɪən], Bataver (*m.*); batavisch (*adj.*).
Bathsheba [ˈbæθʃɪbə], Bathseba (*f.*).
Bavaria [bəˈvɛərɪə], Bayern (*n.*). **–n,** Bayer (*m*); bayrisch (*adj.*).
Beattie [ˈbɪ:tɪ] (*dim. of* **Beatrice**), Beate.
Bechuanaland [bɛtʃʊˈɑ:nəlænd], Betschuanaland (*n.*).
Becky (*dim. of* **Rebecca**).
Bede [bɪ:d], Beda (*m.*).
Bedouin [ˈbɛdʊɪn], Beduine (*m.*).
Belgi–an [ˈbɛldʒən], Belgier (*m.*); belgisch (*adj.*). **–um** [ˈbɛldʒəm], Belgien (*n.*).
Belgrade [bɛlˈgreɪd], Belgrad (*n.*).
Belisarius [bɛlɪˈsɛərɪəs], Belisar (*m.*).
Belle [bɛl] (*dim. of* **Anabel, Arabella,** *or* **Isobel**).
Belshazzar [bɛlˈʃæzə], Belsazar (*m.*).
Benedick [ˈbɛnɪdɪk], **Benedict** [ˈbɛnɪdɪkt], Benedikt(us) (*m.*).
Benedictine [bɛnɪˈdɪktaɪn], der Benediktiner (*monk & liqueur*).
Bengal [bɛŋˈgɔ:l], Bengalen (*n.*); bengalisch (*adj.*). **–i** [–ɪ], Bengale (*m.*); Bengali(sch) (*n.*) (*language*).
Berber [ˈbə:bə], Berber (*m.*); berberisch (*adj.*).
Bermudas [bə:ˈmju:dəz], die Bermuda(s)inseln (*pl.*).
Bernard [ˈbə:nəd], Bernhard (*m.*); *St.* – *dog*, der Bernhardiner. **–ine** [–ɪn]; *–ine monk*, der Bernhardinermönch.
Bern–(e) [bə:n], Bern (*n.*). **–ese** [bə:ˈnɪ:z], Berner (*m.*); bernisch (*adj.*); *–ese Alps*, das Berner Oberland.
Bert(ie) [ˈbə:t(ɪ)] (*dim. of* **Albert, Herbert**).
Bess(ie) [ˈbɛs(ɪ)] (*dim. of* **Elizabeth**), Betti (*f.*) Lieschen, Babette (*f.*).
Bethany [ˈbɛθənɪ], Bethanien (*n.*).
Betsy [ˈbɛtsɪ], **Betty** [ˈbɛtɪ], *see* **Bess.**
Beyrout(h) [ˈbeɪru:t], Beirut (*n.*).
Bill(ie), –(y) [ˈbɪl(ɪ)] (*dim. of* **William**), Billi (*m.*).
Biscay, Bay of [ˈbɪskeɪ], Biskayischer Meerbusen.
Black [blæk]; – *Forest*, der Schwarzwald: – *Sea*, das Schwarze Meer.
Blaise [bleɪz], Blasius (*m.*).
Blanch(e) [blɑ:ntʃ], Blanka (*f.*).
Blenheim [ˈblɛnɪm], Blindheim (*n.*); *battle of* – die Schlacht bei Höchstädt (1704).
Blucher [ˈblu:tʃə], Blücher (*m.*).
Bluebeard [ˈblu:bɪəd], Blaubart (*m.*).
Bob(by) [ˈbɔb(ɪ)] (*dim. of* **Robert**).
Bœotia [bɪˈoʊʃə], Böotien (*n.*). **–n,** Böotier (*m.*); böotisch (*adj.*); (*fig.*) stumpfsinnig, unkultiviert.
Boer [ˈboʊə, bɔ:], Bur (*m.*); – *War*, der Burenkrieg.
Bohemia [boʊˈhɪ:mjə], Böhmen (*n.*); (*fig.*) Boheme (*f.*) (*artists, etc.*). **–n,** Böhme (*m.*); (*fig.*) Bohemien (*m.*); böhmisch (*adj.*); (*fig.*) bohemien (*adj.*); *–n Forest*, der Böhmerwald.
Bokhara [boˈkɑ:rə], Buchara(n) (*town*); die Bucharei (*province*).
Bolognese (*adj.*), *see* **Bononian.**
Bolshevi–k [ˈbɔlʃəvɪk], Bolschewist (*m.*); bolschewistisch (*adj.*). **–sm** [ˈbɔlʃəvɪzm], der Bolschewismus. **–st** *see* **–k.**
Boniface [ˈbɔnɪfeɪs], Bonifatius, Bonifaz (*m.*).
Bononian [bəˈnoʊnɪən], bolognesisch (*adj.*).
Bosnia–c [ˈbɔznɪæk], **–n** [–nɪən], Bosnier, Bosniake (*m.*); bosnisch (*adj.*).
Bosphorus [ˈbɔsfərəs], Bosporus (*m.*).
Bothnia [ˈbɔθnɪə], Botten (*n.*); *Gulf of* –, der Bottnische Meerbusen. **–n,** bottnisch (*adj.*).
Boyard [ˈbɔɪɑ:d], Bojar (*m.*).
Brahman [ˈbrɑ:mən], **Brahmin** [–mɪn], Brahmane, Brahmine (*m.*). **–ic** [brɑ:ˈmænɪk, –ˈmɪnɪk], brahmanisch, brahminisch (*adj.*). **–ism** [–ɪzm], der Brahma(n)ismus.
Brazil [brəˈzɪl], Brasilien (*n.*); – *nut*, die Paranuß; – *wood*, das rote Brasilienholz. **–ian,** Brasilianer, Brasilier (*m.*); brasilianisch, brasilisch (*adj.*).
Breton [ˈbrɛtən], Bretagner, Bretone (*m.*); bretonisch (*adj.*).
Bridget [ˈbrɪdʒɪt], Brigitte, Brigitta (*f.*).
Britain [ˈbrɪtən], Britannien (*n.*).
Britanni–a [brɪˈtænjə], Britannien (*n.*). **–c,** britannisch, britisch (*adj.*); *Her –c Majesty*, Ihre Majestät die Königin von Großbritannien.
Brit(t)any [ˈbrɪtənɪ], die Bretagne.
British [ˈbrɪtɪʃ], britisch (*adj.*); *the* –, die Briten (*pl.*). **–er** [–ə], Engländer (*m.*) (*Amer.*).
Briton [ˈbrɪtən], Brite (*m.*).
Bruges [bru:ʒ], Brügge (*n.*).
Bruin [ˈbru:ɪn], (Meister) Braun (*m.*).
Brunswick [ˈbrʌnzwɪk], Braunschweig (*n.*).
Brussels [ˈbrʌslz], Brüssel (*n.*); – *lace*, Brüsseler Spitzen (*pl.*); – *sprouts*, der Rosenkohl.
Bucharest [ˈbju:kərɛst], Bukarest (*n.*).
Buddhist [ˈbʌdɪst], buddhistisch (*adj.*).
Bulgar [ˈbʌlgɑ:], Bulgare (*m.*). **–ian** [bʌlˈgɛərɪən], bulgarisch (*adj.*).
Burgund–ian [bə:ˈgʌndɪən], Burgunder (*m.*); burgundisch (*adj.*). **–y** [ˈbə:gəndɪ], Burgund (*n.*); (*wine*) der Burgunder.

Burm-a(h) ['bə:mə], Birma (*n.*). **-an, -ese** [-'mɪ:z], Birmane (*m.*); birmanisch (*adj.*).
Byzant-ian [bɑɪ'zænʃɪən], **-ine** [-tɑɪn], Byzantiner (*m.*); byzantinisch (*adj.*). **-ium** [bɑɪ'zæntɪəm], Byzanz (*n.*).

C

(*Many names omitted where the only change is* C *to* K.)
Cæsar ['sɪ:zə], Cäsar (*m.*); *the -s*, die Cäsaren (*pl.*). **-ean** [sɪ'zɛərɪən], cäsarisch (*adj.*); *-ean operation* or *section*, der Kaiserschnitt.
Caiaphas ['kɑɪəfæs], Kaiphas (*m.*).
Cain [keɪn], Kain (*m.*).
Cairo ['kɑɪərou], Kairo (*n.*).
Calabria [kə'leɪbrɪə], Kalabrien (*n.*). **-n,** Kalabrese, Kalabrier (*m.*); kalabresisch, kalabrisch (*adj.*).
Caledonia (kælɪ'dounɪə], (*Poet.*) Kaledonien, Schottland (*n.*). **-n,** Kaledonier, Schotte (*m.*); kaledonisch, schottisch (*adj.*).
California [kælɪ'fɔ:nɪə], Kalifornien (*n.*). **-n,** Kalifornier (*m.*); kalifornisch (*adj.*).
Calliope [kə'lɑɪəpɪ], Kalliope (*f.*).
Calmuck ['kælmʌk], Kalmück (*m.*); kalmückisch (*adj.*).
Calvary ['kælvərɪ], Golgatha (*n.*), die Schädelstätte, der Kalvarienberg, (*fig.*) Leidensweg.
Calvinist ['kælvɪnɪst], *adj.* kalvin(ist)isch.
Cambodia [kæm'boudɪə], Kambodscha (*f.*).
Cameroons ['kæməru:nz] **(The)**, Kamerun (*n.*).
Canaan ['keɪn(j)ən], **-ite** [-ɑɪt], Kanaaniter (*m.*); kana(a)näisch, kanaanitisch.
Canad-a ['kænədə], Kanada (*n.*). **-ian** [kə'neɪdɪən] Kanadier (*m.*); kanadisch (*adj.*).
Canary Islands [kə'nɛərɪ], **Canaries,** die Kanarischen Inseln (*pl.*).
Cancer ['kænsə], Krebs (*m.*); *Tropic of -*, der Wendekreis des Krebses.
Candia ['kændɪə], Kandia (*n.*).
Canute [kə'nju:t], Knut (*m.*).
Cape [keɪp]; - *Colony*, die Kapkolonie, das Kapland; - *Dutch*, Kapholländer (*m.pl.*), Buren (*m.pl.*); - *Town*, Kapstadt (*f.*); - *Verde Islands*, die Kapverdischen Inseln (*pl.*).
Capetians [kə'pɪ:ʃənz], die Kapetinger (*pl.*).
Capricorn ['kæprɪkɔ:n], Steinbock (*m.*); *Tropic of -*, der Wendekreis des Steinbocks.
Carey ['kɛərɪ]; *Mother -'s chicken*, die Sturmschwalbe.
Carib ['kærɪb], Kar(a)ibe (*m.*). **-bean Sea** [-'bɪ:ən], das Kar(a)ibische Meer.
Carinthia [kə'rɪnθɪə], Kärnten (*n.*). **-n,** Kärntner (*m.*); kärntnerisch, kärntisch (*adj.*).
Carloman ['kɑ:lomæn], Karlmann (*m.*).
Carlovingian [kɑ:lo'vɪndʒɪən], Karolinger (*m.*); karolingisch (*adj.*).
Carmelite ['kɑ:mɪlɑɪt], der Karmeliter; - *nun*, die Karmelit(er)in.
Carniola [kɑ:nɪ'oulə], Krain (*n.*). **-n,** Krainer (*m.*); krainisch (*adj.*).
Caroline Islands ['kærəlɪn], die Karolinen (*pl.*).
Carolingian [kæro'lɪndʒɪən], *see* **Carlovingian.**
Carpathian Mts. [kɑ:'peɪθɪən], die Karpat(h)en (*pl.*).
Carrie ['kærɪ] (*dim. of* **Caroline**), Lina, Line (*f.*) Linchen (*n.*).
Carthag-e ['kɑ:θɪdʒ], Karthago (*n.*). **-inian** [-'dʒɪnɪən], Karthager (*m.*); karthagisch (*adj.*).
Carthusian [kɑ:'θju:ʒən], (*friar*) der Kartäuser(mönch); Kartäuser- (*adj.*); - *monastery*, Kartause (*f.*).
Cashmere [kæʃ'mɪə], Kaschmir (*n.*).
Caspian Sea ['kæspɪən], das Kaspische Meer, der Kaspisee.
Castil-e [kæs'tɪ:l], Kastilien (*n.*). **-ian** [kæs'tɪlɪən], Kastiler (*m.*); (*language*) Kastilisch (*n.*); kastilisch (*adj.*).
Catalaunian Fields [kætə'lɔ:nɪən], die Katalaunischen Felder (*pl.*) (*battle of* A.D. 451).
Catharine, Catherine ['kæθərɪn], Katharina, Katharine (*f.*).
Catiline ['kætɪlɑɪn], Katilina (*m.*); *conspiracy of -*, die katilinarische Verschwörung.
Catullus [kə'tʌləs], Katull (*m.*).
Caucas-ian [kɔ:'keɪʒən], Kaukasier (*m.*); kaukasisch (*adj.*). **-sus** ['kɔ:kəsəs], Kaukasus (*m.*), Kaukasien (*n.*).
Cecilia [sɪ'sɪljə], **Cecily** ['sɪsɪlɪ], Cäcilie (*f.*).
Celestine ['sɛlɪstɪn], Zölestin (*m.*); Zölestine (*f.*); (*friar*) der Zölestiner(mönch).
Celt [kɛlt, sɛlt], Kelte (*m.*). **-ic,** keltisch (*adj.*).
Cevennes Mts. [sɪ'vɛn], die Cevennen (*pl.*).
Chald-æa [kæl'dɪə], Chaldäa (*n.*). **-æan, -ee** [-'dɪ:], Chaldäer (*m.*); chaldäisch (*adj.*).
Champagne [ʃæm'peɪn], (*country*) die Champagne; (*wine*) der Champagner.
Channel ['tʃænl]; *the English -*, der (Ärmel-) kanal; - *Islands*, die Kanalinseln (*pl.*).
Chanticleer [ʃæntɪ'klɪə], Henning (*m.*).
Charlemagne ['ʃɑ:ləmeɪn], Karl der Große.
Charles [tʃɑ:lz], Karl (*m.*); *-'s Wain*, der große Bär.
Charlie ['tʃɑ:lɪ] (*dim. of* **Charles**), Karlchen (*n.*).
Cherethites and Pelethites [kɛrɪ'θɑɪtɪ:z ənd pɛlɪ'θɑɪtɪ:z], Krethi und Plethi (*pl.*).
Chersonese ['kə:sonɪ:z], Chersones (*m.*).
Cherusc-an [kɪ'rʌskən], Cherusker (*m.*); cheruskisch (*adj.*). **-i** [kɪ'rʌsɑɪ], die Cherusker (*pl.*).
Cheshire cheese ['tʃɛʃə], der Chesterkäse.
Chilian ['tʃɪlɪən], Chilene (*m.*); chilenisch (*adj.*).
Chin-a ['tʃɑɪnə], China (*n.*). **-aman** ['tʃɑɪnəmən], Chinese (*m.*). **-ese** [-'nɪ:z], chinesisch (*adj.*); *-ese lantern*, der Lampion; *-ese puzzle*, das Vexierspiel, Mosaikspiel.
Chris [krɪs] (*dim. of* **Christopher**), Töffel (*m.*).
Chrissie ['krɪsɪ] (*dim. of* **Christina**), Christel (*f.*), Stinchen, Tinchen (*n.*).
Christ [krɑɪst], Christus (*m.*).
Christopher ['krɪstəfə], Christoph (*m.*).
Cicely ['sɪsɪlɪ], *see* **Cecilia.**
Ciceronian [sɪsə'rounɪən], ciceronianisch, ciceronisch (*adj.*).
Cimbri ['sɪmbrɑɪ], die Zimbern (*pl.*).
Cinderella [sɪndə'rɛlə], Aschenbrödel, (*dial.*) Aschenputtel (*n.*).
Cingalese [sɪŋgə'lɪ:z], Sing(h)alese (*m.*); Sing(h)alesisch (*n.*) (*language*); sing(h)alesisch (*adj.*).
Circassia [sə:'kæʃə], Tscherkessien (*n.*). **-n,** Tscherkesse (*m.*); tscherkessisch (*adj.*).
Cisalpine [sɪs'ælpɑɪn], zisalpin(isch) (*adj.*).
Cissie, Cissy (*dim. of* **Cecily**), Zilli (*f.*).
Cistercian (monk) [sɪs'tə:ʃɪən], der Zisterzienser(mönch).
Clar-a ['klɛərə], **-e** [klɛə], Klara (*f.*).
Claus [klɔ:z], Klaus (*m.*); *Santa -*, Sankt Nikolaus, Knecht Ruprecht (*m.*).
Clement ['klɛmənt], Klemens (*m.*).
Cleopatra [klɪo'pɑ:trə], Kleopatra (*f.*).
Cleves [klɪ:vz], Kleve (*n.*).
Clio ['klɑɪou], Klio (*f.*).
Clovis ['klouvɪs], Chlodwig (*m.*).
Cluniac (monk) ['klu:nɪæk], der Kluniazenser(mönch).
Cochin-China ['kɔtʃɪn'tʃɑɪnə], Kotschinchina (*n.*).
Cockaigne [ko'keɪn]; *land of -*, das Schlaraffenland.
Cœur de Lion, Löwenherz (*n.*).
Cologne [kə'loun], Köln (*n.*); - *cathedral*, der Kölner Dom; *Eau de -*, das kölnische Wasser, Kölnischwasser.
Colosseum [kɔlə'sɪ:əm], das Kolosseum.
Colossians [kə'lɔʃənz], Kolosser (*pl.*); *Epistle to the -*, der Kolosserbrief.
Columbia [kə'lʌmbɪə], Kolumbia (*U.S.A.*), Kolumbien (*S. Amer.*) (*n.*).
Como ['koumou]; *Lake -*, der Comer See.
Confuci-an [kən'fju:ʃɪən], konfuzianisch (*adj.*), **-us** [kən'fju:ʃɪəs], Konfutse (*m.*).
Congo R. ['kɔŋgou], Kongo (*m.*).
Connie ['kɔnɪ] (*dim. of* **Constance**), Stanze (*f.*).
Conrad(e) ['kɔnræd], Konrad (*m.*).
Constance ['kɔnstəns], (*town*) Konstanz (*n.*); (*name*) Konstanze (*f.*); *Lake -*, der Bodensee.
Constan-ta, *n.* Konstantza (*Rumania*). **-tine** ['kɔnstəntɪ:n], Konstantin (*m.*). **-tinople** [kɔnstæntɪ'noupl], Konstantinopel (*n.*).
Copenhagen [koupn'heɪgən], Kopenhagen (*n.*).

Copernican [ko'pə:nɪkən], kopernikanisch (*adj.*).
Copt [kɔpt], Kopte (*m.*). **–ic,** koptisch (*adj.*).
Cordilleras [kɔ:dɪ'lɛərəz], die Kordilleren (*pl.*).
Cordova ['kɔ:dəvə], Kordova (*n.*). **– –n,** korduanisch (*adj.*).
Corfu [kɔ:'fju:], Korfu (*n.*).
Corinth ['kɔrɪnθ], Korinth (*n.*). **–ian** [kə'rɪnθɪən], Korinther (*m.*); korinthisch (*adj*); *–ian order,* die korinthische Säulenordnung; *Epistle to the –ians,* der Korintherbrief.
Coriolanus [kɔrɪo'leɪnəs], Koriolan(us) (*m.*).
Cornelia [kɔ:'nɪ:lɪə], Kornelie (*f.*).
Corsair ['kɔ:sɛə], Korsar (*m.*).
Corsica ['kɔ:sɪkə], Korsika (*n.*). **–n,** Korse (*m.*); kors(ikan)isch (*adj.*).
Cossack ['kɔsæk], Kosak (*m.*).
Courland ['kuələnd], Kurland (*n.*). **–er** [–ə], Kurländer (*m.*).
Cracovian [krə'kouvɪən], Krakauer (*m.*); krakauisch (*adj.*).
Cracow ['kra:kou], Krakau (*n.*).
Creole ['krɪ:oul], Kreole (*m.*); kreolisch (*adj.*).
Cret–an ['krɪ:tən], Kreter (*m.*); kretisch (*adj.*). **–e** [krɪ:t], Kreta (*n.*).
Crimea [kraɪ'mɪə], die Krim; *–n war,* der Krimkrieg.
Croatia [krou'eɪʃɪə], Kroatien (*n.*). **–n,** Kroat(e) (*m.*); kroatisch (*adj.*).
Crœsus ['krɪ:səs], Krösus (*m.*).
Cuba ['kju:bə], Kuba (*n.*). **–n,** Kubaner (*m.*); kubanisch (*adj.*).
Cupid ['kju:pɪd], Kupido (*m.*).
Cyclades ['sɪklədɪ:z], die Zykladen (*pl.*).
Cypr–ian ['sɪprɪən], zyprisch (*adj.*); *–ian wine,* der Zyperwein. **–iot(e)** [–out], Zypriot (*m.*). **–us** ['saɪprəs], Zypern (*m.*).
Cyril ['sɪrɪl], Zyrillus (*m.*).
Czech [tʃɛk], Tscheche (*m.*); tschechisch (*adj.*). **–oslovakia** ['tʃɛkoslo'va:kɪə], die Tschechoslowakei.

D

Dahomey [də'houmɪ], Dahome (*n.*).
Daisy (*dim. of* **Margaret**), Grete (*f.*).
Dalmatian [dæl'meɪʃən], Dalmatiner (*m.*); dalmatisch, dalmatinisch (*adj.*).
Damasc–ene ['dæməsɪ:n], Damaszener (*m.*); damaszenisch (*adj.*). **–us** [də'mæskəs], Damaskus (*n.*); *–us blade,* die Damaszener Klinge.
Dan (*dim. of* **Daniel**).
Danaï ['dæneɪaɪ], die Danaer (*pl.*).
Dan–e [deɪn], Däne (*m.*). **–e-geld,** die Dänensteuer. **–ish** ['deɪnɪʃ], dänisch (*adj.*).
Dantzig ['dæntsɪg], Danzig (*n.*).
Danube R. ['dænju:b], Donau (*f.*).
Dardanelles [da:də'nɛlz], die Dardanellen (*pl.*).
Darwinian [da:'wɪnɪən], darwinsch, darwinistisch (*adj.*); *– theory,* die Darwinsche Lehre, der Darwinismus.
Dav–(e)y ['deɪvɪ] (*dim. of* **David**); *–y Jones's locker,* (*fig.*) die See.
Dead Sea [dɛd], das Tote Meer.
Deborah ['dɛbərə], Debora (*f.*).
Delaware R. ['dɛləwɛə], Delaware (*m.*).
Delilah [dɪ'laɪlə], Delila (*f.*).
Delphian ['dɛlfɪən], **Delphic** ['dɛlfɪk], delphisch (*adj.*).
Denis, Dennis ['dɛnɪs], Dionysus (*m.*).
Denmark ['dɛnma:k], Dänemark (*n.*).
Derrick ['dɛrɪk] (*dim. of* **Theodoric**). Dietrich (*m.*).
Dervish ['də:vɪʃ], Derwisch (*m.*).
Dick(y) ['dɪk(ɪ)] (*dim. of* **Richard**).
Dinah ['daɪnə], Dina (*f.*).
Dixie(land) ['dɪksɪ(lænd)], die Südstaaten (*U.S.A.*).
Dnieper R. ['dnɪ:pə], Dnjepr (*m.*).
Dniester R. ['dnɪ:stə], Dnjestr (*m.*).
Doll(y) ['dɔl(ɪ)] (*dim. of* **Dorothy**), Dorette, Dörthe (*f.*), Dorchen, Dortchen (*n.*).
Dolomites ['dɔləmaɪts], die Dolomiten (*pl.*).
Dominic ['dɔmɪnɪk]; *St. –,* der heilige Dominikus. **–an** [do'mɪnɪkən], der Dominikaner.
Don R. [dɔn], Don (*m.*); *– Cossacks,* die Donkosaken (*pl.*).
Don Quixote [dɔn 'kwɪksət], Don Quichotte, Don Quijote (*m.*).
Dora ['dɔ:rə] (*dim.* of **Dorothy**), Dora (*f.*).
Dori–an ['dɔ:rɪən], *adj.* dorisch; *–an mode,* die dorische Tonart. **–c** ['dɔrɪk], **1.** *adj.* dorisch; *–c order,* der dorische (Bau)Stil (*Arch.*); *see* **–an. 2.** *s.* der dorische (breite) Dialekt.
Dorothea [dɔrə'θɪə], **Dorothy** ['dɔrəθɪ], Dorothea (*f.*).
Dorrit, Dot (*dim. of* **Dorothy**), *see* **Dolly.**
Drave R. [dreɪv], Drau (*f.*).
Dresden china ['drɛzdən], Meißner Porzellan.
Druid ['dru:ɪd], Druide (*m.*). **–ic,** *adj.* druidisch.
Dunkirk ['dʌnkə:k], Dünkirchen (*n.*).
Dutch [dʌtʃ]; *the –,* die Holländer (*pl.*); holländisch *adj.*); *– ware,* das Delfter Geschirr. **–man** [–mən], Holländer (*m.*).
Dwina ['dwɪ:nə]; *Northern – River,* Dwina (*f.*); *Southern – River,* Düna (*f.*).

E

East [ɪ:st], der Osten; *the –,* das Morgenland, der Orient; *the Far –,* der Ferne Osten *or* Orient, Ostasien (*n.*); *the Near –,* der Nahe Osten, *– Indies,* Ostindien (*n.*). **– -India Company,** die Ostindische Kompanie.
Ebro R. ['ɪ:brou], Ebro (*m.*).
Ecclesiastes [ɪklɪ:zɪ'æstɪ:z], der Prediger Salomo.
Eddie ['ɛdɪ] (*dim. of* **Edward**).
Edinburgh ['ɛdɪnbʌrə], Edinburg (*n.*).
Edith ['ɪ:dɪθ], Edith, Editha (*f.*).
Edward ['ɛdwəd], Eduard (*m.*). **–ian** [ɛd'wɔ:dɪən], (*cf.* Wilhelminisch).
Effie ['ɛfɪ] (*dim. of* **Euphemia**).
Egypt ['ɪ:dʒɪpt], Ägypten (*n.*); *Lower –,* Unterägypten (*n.*); *Upper –,* Oberägypten (*n.*). **–ian** [ɪ'dʒɪpʃən], Ägypter (*m.*); ägyptisch (*adj.*).
Elbe R. [ɛlb], Elbe (*f.*).
Eleanor ['ɛlɪnə], Eleonore, Le(o)nore (*f.*).
Eleusinian [ɛlju:'sɪnɪən], eleusinisch (*adj.*); *– mysteries,* die Eleusinischen Mysterien.
Elia ['ɪ:lɪə], **–s** [ɪ'laɪəs], Elias (*m.*).
Elijah [ɪ'laɪdʒə], Elias (*m.*).
Elinor, *see* **Eleanor.**
Eliza [ɪ'laɪzə], Elise, Elisa (*f.*).
Elizabeth [ɪ'lɪzəbəθ], Elisabeth (*f.*). **–an** [–'bɪ:θən], elisabethanisch.
Ell–a ['ɛlə], **–en** ['ɛlən] (*dim. of* **Helena** *or* **Eleanor**), Ella, Lene, Lena (*f.*), Lenchen (*n.*).
Elsa ['ɛlsə], **Elsie** ['ɛlsɪ] (*dim. of* **Elisabeth**), Elli, Elsa, Else, Elsbeth (*f.*), Elschen (*n.*), Liese (*f.*), Lieschen (*n.*).
Elsinore [ɛlsɪ'nɔ:], Helsingör (*n.*).
Emery ['ɛmərɪ], Emmerich (*m.*).
Emil–ia [ə'mɪ:lɪə], **–y** ['ɛmɪlɪ], Emilie, Emilia (*f.*).
Emmanuel [ɪ'mænjuel], Emanuel (*m.*).
Emmy ['ɛmɪ] (*dim. of* **Emma** ['ɛmə]), Emmi (*f.*).
Ems R. [ɛmz], Ems (*f.*).
England ['ɪŋglənd], England (*n.*); *Church of –,* die Anglikanische Kirche.
English ['ɪŋglɪʃ], englisch; *the –,* die Engländer (*pl.*); *she is –,* sie ist Engländerin; *– Channel,* der Ärmelkanal; *Old – type,* die Frakturschrift. **–man** [–mən], Engländer (*m.*).
Ephesian [ɪ'fɪ:ʒən], Epheser (*m.*); ephesisch (*adj.*); *Epistle to the –s,* der Epheserbrief.
Epicurus [ɛpɪ'kjuərəs], Epikur (*m.*).
Epsom salts ['ɛpsəm], das englische Salz, Bittersalz.
Eric ['ɛrɪk], Erich (*m.*).
Erin ['ɛrɪn] (*Poet. for* **Ireland**), Irland (*n.*).
Erinnys [ɛ'rɪnɪs], **Erinyes** [ɛ'rɪnɪɪ:z], die Erinnye, Furie.
Ernest ['ə:nɪst], Ernst (*m.*).
Ernie ['ə:nɪ] (*dim. of* **Ernest**).
Erse [ə:s], ersisch (*adj.*); die irische Sprache.
Estonia [ɛs'tounɪə], Estland (*n.*). **–n,** Este, Estländer (*m.*); estnisch, estländisch (*adj.*).
Ethelbert ['ɛθəlbə:t], Adalbert (*m.*).
Ethiopia [ɪ:θɪ'oupɪə], Äthiopien, Abessinien (*n.*). **–n,** Äthiopier (*m.*); äthiopisch (*adj.*).

Etna ['ɛtnə], Ätna (*m.*).
Eton ['ɪ:tn]; – *crop*, der Herrenschnitt.
Etrurian [ɪ'truərɪən], **Etruscan** [ɪ'trʌskən], Etrusker (*m.*); etruskisch (*adj.*).
Euclid ['ju:klɪd], Euklid (*m.*). **–ian** [ju:'klɪdɪən], euklidisch (*adj.*).
Eugene [ju:'dʒɪ:n], Eugen (*m.*).
Euphrates R. [ju:'freɪtɪ:z], Euphrat (*m.*).
Eurasian [juə'reɪʒən], halbeuropäisch, halbasiatisch (*adj.*); der Halbeuropäer, Halbasiat.
Europe ['juərəp], Europa (*n.*); *Central* –, Mitteleuropa (*n.*). **–an** [–'pɪ:ən], Europäer (*m.*); europäisch (*adj.*). **–anize, –anise** [–'pɪ:ənɑɪz], europäisieren (*v.a.*).
Eustace ['ju:stəs], Eustach(ius) (*m.*).
Eva ['ɪ:və], **Eve** [ɪ:v], Eva (*f.*).
Evan ['ɛvən], Johann, Hans (*m.*) (*Welsh*).
Eveline, Evelyn ['ɪ:vlɪn] (*dim. of* **Eva**), Eveline (*f.*), Evchen (*n.*). (**Evelyn** *also m.*)
Everard ['ɛvərɑ:d], Eberhard (*m.*).
Evy ['ɪ:vɪ] (*dim. of* **Eve**), Evchen (*n.*).
Ezekiel [ɪ'zɪ:kjəl], Ezechiel, Hesekiel (*m.*).
Ezra ['ɛzrə], Esra (*m.*).

F

Fabii ['feɪbɪɑɪ], Fabier (*pl.*).
Fan(n)y ['fænɪ] (*dim. of* **Frances**), Fanni (*f.*).
Faroe Islands ['fɛərou], die Färöer-Inseln (*pl.*).
Faroese [fɛərou'ɪ:z], Färöer, Färinger (*m.*); färöisch (*adj.*).
Faustus ['fɔ:stəs], Faust (*m.*).
Fiji Islands [fɪ:'dʒɪ:], die Fidschi-Inseln (*pl.*).
Finn [fɪn], Finne (*m.*); finnisch (*adj.*). **–ish,** finnisch (*adj.*).
Finland ['fɪnlənd], Finnland (*n.*); *Gulf of* –, der Finnische Meerbusen. **–er** [–ə], Finnländer (*m.*).
Flanders ['flɑ:ndəz], Flandern (*n.*).
Flem–ing ['flɛmɪŋ], Flame, Flamländer (*m.*). **–ish,** flämisch, flamländisch, flandrisch (*adj.*).
Flo [flou], **Flora** ['flɔ:rə] (*dim. of* **Florence**).
Floren–ce ['flɔrəns], (*city*) Florenz (*n.*); (*Christian name*) Florentine (*f.*). **–tine** ['flɔrəntɑɪn], Florentiner (*m.*); florentinisch (*adj.*).
Florrie ['flɔrɪ], **Flossie** ['flɔsɪ] (*dim. of* **Florence**).
Flushing ['flʌʃɪŋ], Vlissingen (*n.*).
Fortunatus [fɔ:tju'neɪtəs], Fortunat (*m.*); *–'s purse*, der Glückssäckel.
France [frɑ:ns], Frankreich (*n.*).
Frances ['frɑ:nsɪs], Franziska (*f.*).
Francis ['frɑ:nsɪs], Franz (*m.*); *St.* –, der heilige Franziskus *or* Franz von Assisi.
Franciscan (friar) [fræn'sɪskən], der Franziskaner(mönch).
Franco--German ['fræŋko'dʒə:mən], deutsch-französisch (*adj.*). **–phile** [–fɑɪl], der Franzosenfreund; franzosenfreundlich (*adj.*).
Franconia [fræŋ'kounɪə], Franken (*n.*); *Lower* –, Unterfranken (*n.*). **–n,** Franke (*m.*); fränkisch (*adj.*); *–n emperors*, fränkische *or* salische Kaiser (*Hist.*).
Frank [fræŋk] (*dim. of* **Francis**), Franz (*m.*); (= *Franconian*) Franke (*m.*). **–ish,** fränkisch (*adj.*).
Fred [frɛd], **Freddy** ['frɛdɪ] (*dim. of* **Frederic(k)**), Fritz (*m.*).
Freda ['frɪ:də] (*dim. of* **Frederica**), Rike (*f.*), Rikchen (*n.*).
Frederic(k) ['frɛdrɪk], Friedrich (*m.*).
Frederica [frɛdə'rɪ:kə], Friederike (*f.*).
French [frɛntʃ], französisch (*adj.*); *she is* –, sie ist Französin; *the* –, die Franzosen (*pl.*); – *bean*, die welsche Bohne; – *chalk*, die Schneiderkreide; – *horn*, das Waldhorn; – *polish*, die Schellackpolitur; – *roll*, Brötchen, Franzbrot (*n.*); – *window*, Flügelfenster (*n.*), Verandatür (*f.*); (*coll.*) *take – leave*, sich heimlich drücken. **–ify,** französieren. **–man** [–mən], Franzose (*m.*).
Friendly Islands ['frɛndlɪ], die Freundschaftsinseln (*pl.*).
Frieslander ['frɪ:zləndə], Friese, Friesländer (*m.*).
Frisian ['frɪ:zjən] (*see* **Frieslander**), friesisch, friesländisch (*adj.*).
Friuli [frɪ'u:lɪ], Friaul (*n.*).
Fuegian [fu:'ɪ:dʒɪən], Feuerländer (*m.*); feuerländisch (*adj.*).
Fulda R. ['fuldə], Fulda (*f.*).
Fyen ['fju:ən], Fünen (*n.*).

G

Gael [geɪl], Gäle (*m.*). **–ic** ['geɪlɪk, 'gælɪk], gälisch (*adj.*).
Galatians [gə'leɪʃənz], Galater (*pl.*); *Epistle to the* –, der Galaterbrief.
Galicia [gə'lɪʃɪə], Galizien (*n.*).
Galilee ['gælɪlɪ:], Galiläa (*n.*). **–n,** Galiläer (*m.*); galiläisch (*adj.*).
Gallo–mania [gælo'meɪnɪə], die Französelei. **–phile** [–fɑɪl], franzosenfreundlich (*adj.*). **–phobe** [–foub], der Franzosenfeind, (*coll.*) Franzosenfresser; franzosenfeindlich (*adj.*). **–phobia** [–'foubɪə], der Franzosenhaß.
Ganges R. ['gændʒɪ:z], Ganges (*m.*).
Ganymede ['gænɪmɪ:d], Ganymed (*m.*).
Garonne R. [gæ'rɔn], Garonne (*f.*).
Gascon ['gæskən], Gaskogner (*m.*). **–y** ['gæskənɪ], die Gaskogne.
Gaul [gɔ:l], (*country*) Gallien (*n.*); (*inhabitant*) Gallier (*m.*). **–ish,** gallisch (*adj.*).
Gauntgrim ['gɔ:ntgrɪm], Isegrim (*m.*).
Genev–a [dʒɪ'nɪ:və], Genf (*n.*). *Lake of –a*, der Genfer See. **–ese** [dʒɛnɪ'vɪ:z], Genfer (*m.*); genferisch (*adj.*).
Genevieve ['dʒɛnəvɪ:v], Genoveva (*f.*).
Geno–a ['dʒɛnouə], Genua (*n.*). **–ese** [dʒɛnou'ɪ:z], Genuese(r) (*m.*); genuesisch (*adj.*).
Geoffrey ['dʒɛfrɪ], Gottfried (*m.*).
Geordie ['dʒɔ:dɪ] (*dim. of* **George**).
Georg–e [dʒɔ:dʒ], Georg (*m.*). **–ian** [–ɪən], georgianisch (*adj.*).
Georgia ['dʒɔ:dʒə], Georgien (*U.S.S.R.*) (*n.*); Georgia (*U.S.A.*). **–n** [–n], Georgier (*m.*); georgisch (*adj.*).
Georgiana [dʒɔ:dʒɪ'ɑ:nə], **Georgina** [dʒɔ:'dʒɪ:nə], Georgine (*f.*).
Georgie ['dʒɔ:dʒɪ] (*dim. of* **George** *and* **Georgina**).
Gerald ['dʒɛrəld], **Gerard** [dʒɪ'rɑ:d], Gerold Gerhard.
German ['dʒə:mən], deutsch (*adj.*); Deutsche(r) (*m. & f.*); *the –s*, die Deutschen (*pl.*); *he speaks – well*, er spricht gut Deutsch; – *clock*, Schwarzwälderuhr (*f.*); – *Confederation*, der Deutsche Bund (1815–66); – *measles*, die Röteln (*pl.*); – *Ocean*, die Nordsee; – *silver*, das Neusilber; – *steel*, der Schmelzstahl; – *tinder*, der Zündschwamm – *toys*, Nürnberger Spielsachen (*pl.*); – *type*, die Frakturschrift. **–ic** [dʒə:'mænɪk], germanisch (*adj.*). **–ism** [–ɪzm], der Germanismus (*of language*). **–ophile** [dʒə:'mænofɑɪl], der Deutschfreund; deutschfreundlich (*adj.*). **–y** ['dʒə:mənɪ], Deutschland (*n.*).
Gerry ['dʒɛrɪ] (*dim. of* **Gerald**), Gerd (*m.*).
Gertie ['gə:tɪ] (*dim. of* **Gertrude**), Trude (*f.*), Trudchen (*n.*), Trudel (*f.*).
Gertrude ['gə:tru:d], Gertrud(e) (*f.*).
Gervase ['dʒə:vəs], Gervasius (*m.*).
Ghent [gent], Gent (*n.*).
Ghibelline ['gɪbɪlɑɪn], Ghibelline, Waiblinger (*m.*).
Giles [dʒɑɪlz], Julius, Ägidius (*m.*); *St.–'s* (*Church*), die Ägidienkirche.
Gill(ian) ['dʒɪl(ɪən)], Juliane (*f.*).
Goddard ['gɔdəd], Gotthard (*m.*).
Godfrey ['gɔdfrɪ], Gottfried (*m.*).
Good Hope [gud houp]; *Cape of* – –, das Kap der Guten Hoffnung.
Gordian ['gɔ:dɪən], gordisch (*adj.*).
Gorgon ['gɔ:gən], Gorgo(ne) (*f.*).
Goshen ['gouʃən], Gosen (*n.*).
Goth [gɔθ], Gote (*m.*). **–ic,** gotisch (*adj.*); *–ic architecture*, der gotische Stil, die Gotik; *–ic letters*, die gotische Schrift, Frakturschrift. **–land,** Gotland (*in Sweden*).
Gotham ['gɔtəm], Abdera, Krähwinkel (*n.*). **–ite**

or **Wise man of –**, Abderit, Krähwinkler (*m.*), der Schildbürger.
Gracchi ['grækaɪ], die Gracchen (*pl.*).
Graces ['greɪsɪz], Grazien (*pl.*).
Grecian ['grɪ:ʃən], *see* **Greek.**
Greece [grɪ:s], Griechenland (*n.*).
Greek [grɪ:k], Grieche (*m.*); griechisch (*adj.*); *ancient* –, altgriechisch (*adj.*); (*coll.*) *that is – to me*, das sind mir böhmische Dörfer.
Greenland ['grɪ:nlənd], Grönland (*n.*). **–er** [–ə], Grönländer (*m.*).
Gregorian [grɪ'gɔ:rɪən], gregorianisch (*adj.*).
Gregory ['grɛgərɪ], Gregor(ius) (*m.*).
Griselda [grɪ'zɛldə], Griseldis (*f.*).
Grison ['grɪ:zɔ̃], Graubündner (*m.*); graubündnerisch (*adj.*). **–s,** Graubünden.
Guadalquivir R. [gwɑ:dəl'kwɪvə], Guadalquivir (*m.*).
Gueldern ['gɛldən], **Guelderland** ['gɛldəlænd], Geldern (*n.*).
Guelph [gwɛlf], Welfe (*m.*). **–ic, welfisch, Welfen–** (*adj.*).
Gueux [gə:], Geusen (*pl.*).
Gulf Stream [gʌlf], der Golfstrom.
Gus(sie) ['gʌs(ɪ)] (*dim. of* **Augusta, Augustus**), Gustel (*m. & f.*), Gustchen (*n.*).
Gustavus [gʌ'stɑ:vəs], Gustav (*m.*).
Guy [gaɪ], Veit, Guido (*m.*).

H

Habakkuk ['hæbəkʌk], Habakuk (*m.*).
Hague [heɪg]; *The* –, Den Haag; *at The* –, im Haag.
Hainault [heɪ'nɔ:lt], der Hennegau
Hal [hæl] (*dim. of* **Henry**), Heinz, Heini (*m.*).
Hamelin ['hæmlɪn], Hameln (*n.*); *Pied Piper of* –, der Rattenfänger von Hameln.
Hanover ['hænovə], Hannover (*n.*). **–ian** [–'vɪərɪən], Hannoveraner (*m.*); hannöversch, hannoversch (*adj.*).
Hanse [hænzə], die Hanse, Hansa; – *towns*, Hansestädte (*pl.*). **–atic** [hænzɪ'ætɪk], hansisch, hanseatisch (*adj.*); *–atic League*, die Hanse.
Hapsburg ['hæpsbə:g], Habsburg (*m.*); *the –s*, die Habsburger (*pl.*).
Harriet ['hærɪət] (*dim. of* **Henrietta**), Jettchen (*n.*).
Harry ['hærɪ] (*dim. of* **Henry**), Heinz, Heini (*m.*); *Old* –, der Teufel.
Harz Mts. [hɑ:ts], der Harz.
Hatty ['hætɪ], *see* **Harriet.**
Havana [hə'vænə], (*city*) Havanna.
Havel R. ['hɑ:fəl], Havel (*f.*).
Heb–raic [hɪ'breɪɪk], hebräisch (*adj.*). **–rew** ['hɪ:brʊ:], Hebräer (*m.*); hebräisch (*adj.*); *–rew Jew*, der Stockjude, Erzjude; *Epistle to the –rews*, der Hebräerbrief.
Hebrid–ean, –ian [hɛbrɪ'dɪ:ən], hebridisch (*adj.*). **–es** ['hɛbrɪdɪ:z], die Hebriden (*pl.*).
Hector ['hɛktə], Hektor (*m.*).
Hedjaz ['hɛdʒæz], Hedschas (*n.*).
Hegelian [hɛ'gɪ:lɪən], Hegelianer (*m.*); hegelsch, hegelianisch (*adj.*).
Hegira ['hɛdʒɪrə], Hedschra (*f.*).
Helen–(a) ['hɛlɪn(ə)], Helena (*f.*); – *of Troy*, die schöne Helena.
Heligoland ['hɛlɪgolænd], Helgoland (*n.*).
Hellen–e ['hɛlɪ:n], Hellene (*m*). **–ic** [hɛ'lɪ:nɪk], hellenisch (*adj.*). **–ism** [–ɪzm], der Hellenismus. **–istic** [–'nɪstɪk], hellenistisch (*adj.*). **–ize, –ise** [–aɪz], hellenisieren (*v.a.*).
Hellespont ['hɛlɪspɔnt], Hellespont (*m.*).
Helveti–a [hɛl'vɪ:ʃɪə], Helvetien (*n.*), die Schweiz. **–c** [–'vɛtɪk], helvetisch, schweizerisch (*adj.*).
Henrietta [hɛnrɪ'ɛtə], Henriette (*f.*).
Henry ['hɛnrɪ], Heinrich (*m.*).
Heraclitus [hɛrə'klaɪtəs], Heraklit (*m.*).
Hercule–s ['hə:kjulɪ:z], Herkules (*m.*). **–an** [hə:kjʊ'lɪ:ən], herkulisch (*adj.*), (*also fig.*).
Herman ['hə:mən], Hermann (*m.*).
Hermione [hə:'maɪənɪ], Hermine (*f.*).
Herod ['hɛrəd], Herodes (*m.*); *out-herod* –, alles überbieten.
Herzegovina [hɛətsəgo'vɪ:nə], die Herzegowina.
Hesperus ['hɛspərəs], Hesperos (*m.*), der Abendstern. **–ides** [hɛs'pɛrɪdɪ:z], die Hesperiden (*pl.*).
Hess–e ['hɛsə], Hessen (*n.*). **–ian** ['heʃən], Hesse (*m.*); hessisch (*adj.*); *–ian boots*, Schaftstiefel (*pl.*).
Hester ['hɛstə] (*for* **Esther** ['ɛsθə]), Esther.
Hetty ['hɛtɪ] (*dim. of* **Esther, Henrietta**), Jettchen (*n.*).
Hezekiah [hɛzɪ'kaɪə], Hiskia(s) (*m.*).
Highland–er ['haɪləndə], Hochländer, Bergschotte (*m.*). **–s** ['haɪləndz], das Hochland, das Hochlandsgebiet, die Hochlande (*pl.*).
Hilary ['hɪlərɪ], Hilarius (*m.*).
Hilda ['hɪldə], Hilde (*f.*).
Hindu, Hindoo [hɪn'du], Hindu (*m., f.*).
Hindustan [hɪndʊs'tɑ:n], Hindostan, Hindustan (*n*). **–i,** Hindostanisprache (*f.*).
Hora–ce ['hɔrəs], Horaz (*m.*). **–tian** [–'reɪʃɪən], horazisch (*adj.*).
Hottentot ['hɔtntɔt], Hottentott(e) (*m.*); hottentottisch (*adj.*).
Howleglass ['aʊlglɑ:s], (Till) Eulenspiegel (*m.*).
Hugh [hjʊ:], **Hugo** ['hjʊ:goʊ], Hugo (*m.*).
Huguenot ['hjʊ:gənɔt], Hugenotte (*m.*); hugenottisch (*adj.*).
Hun [hʌn], Hunne (*m.*); (*also* **–nic**) hunnisch (*adj.*).
Hungar–ian [hʌŋ'gɛərɪən], Ungar (*m.*); ungarisch (*adj.*). **–y** ['hʌŋgərɪ], Ungarn (*n.*).
Huron ['hjʊərən], Hurone (*m.*). **–ian** [–'roʊnɪən], huronisch (*adj.*).
Hussite ['hʌsaɪt], Hussit (*m.*).
Hyades ['haɪədɪ:z], die Hyaden (*pl.*).

I

Iberian [aɪ'bɪ:ərɪən], Iberer (*m.*); iberisch (*adj.*).
Icarian [aɪ:kɛərɪən], ikarisch (*adj.*).
Iceland ['aɪslənd], Island (*n.*). **–er** [–ə], Isländer (*m.*). **–ic** [aɪs'lændɪk], isländisch (*adj.*).
Ignatius [ɪg'neɪʃɪəs], Ignatius, Ignaz (*m.*).
Iliad ['ɪlɪəd], die Ilias, Iliade.
Illyrian [ɪ'lɪrɪən], Illyrier (*m.*); illyrisch (*adj.*).
Inca ['ɪŋkə], Inka (*m*).
India ['ɪndjə], Indien (*n.*); *East-* – *Company*, die Ostindische Gesellschaft; *Further* –, Hinterindien (*n.*).
Indian ['ɪndjən], (*American* or *Red* –) Indianer (*m.*); indianisch (*adj.*); (*Asiatic*) Inder, Indier (*m.*); indisch (*adj.*); – *club*, (Gymnastik)Keule (*f.*); – *corn*, der Mais, türkische Weizen; – *file*, der Gänsemarsch; – *ink*, die chinesische Tusche; – *summer*, der Nachsommer, Spätsommer, Altweibersommer.
Indies ['ɪndɪz]; *East* –, Ostindien (*n.*); *West* –, Westindien (*n.*).
Indo--China ['ɪndo'tʃaɪnə], Hinterindien (*n.*). **--Chinese,** hinterindisch (*adj.*). **--European,** indoeuropäisch (*adj.*). **--Germanic,** indogermanisch (*adj.*).
Indus R. ['ɪndəs] Indus (*m.*).
Inn R. [ɪn], Inn (*m.*).
Innocent ['ɪnəsənt], Innozenz (*m.*).
Ioni–an [aɪ'oʊnɪən], Ionier (*m.*); (*also* **–c** [aɪ'ɔnɪk]) ionisch (*adj.*).
Iphigenia [aɪfɪdʒɪ'nɪ:ə], Iphigenie (*f.*).
Iraq, Irak [ɪ'rɑ:k], Irak (*n.*). **–i,** Iraker (*m.*); irakisch (*adj.*).
Ireland ['aɪələnd], Irland (*n.*).
Irish ['aɪərɪʃ]; irisch, ersisch (*adj.*); *the* –, Irländer, Iren (*pl.*); – *Free State*, der irische Freistaat; **–ism** [–ɪzm], die irländische Spracheigenheit. **–man** [–mən], Irländer, Ire (*m.*).
Iroquois ['ɪrəkwɔɪ], Irokese (*m.*); irokesisch (*adj.*).
Isaac ['aɪzək], Isaak (*m.*).
Isabel(la), Isobel ['ɪzəbəl (ɪzə'bɛlə)], Isabelle, Isabella (*f.*).
Isaiah [aɪ'zaɪə], Jesaia(s) (*m.*).
Isar R. ['ɪ:zɑ:], Isar (*f.*).
Iscariot [ɪs'kærɪət], Ischariot (*m.*).
Isengrim ['ɪzəngrɪm], Isegrim (*m.*)

Ishmael ['ɪʃmeɪəl], Ismael (*m.*). **–ite** [–aɪt], Ismaelit (*m.*).
Isidore ['ɪzɪdɔ:], Isidor (*m.*).
Islam ['ɪzlɑ:m], der Islam. **–ism** [–ɪzm], der Islamismus. **–ite** [–aɪt], Islamit (*m.*); islamisch, islamitisch (*adj.*).
Israelite ['ɪzrɪəlaɪt], Israelit (*m.*); israelitisch (*adj.*).
Ital–ian [ɪ'tæljən], Italiener (*m.*); italienisch (*adj.*). **–y** ['ɪtəlɪ], Italien (*n.*); *North –*, Oberitalien (*n.*).

J

Jack [dʒæk], Hans (*m.*); *– -in-the-box*, Schachtelmännchen (*n.*); *– Frost*, der Winter, Frost, Reif; *– and Jill*, Hans und Grete; *– Ketch*, der Henker; *– in office*, der Bürokrat; *– of all trades*, Hans Dampf in allen Gassen; *– o' lantern*, das Irrlicht; *before you could say – Robinson*, im Nu, im Handumdrehn; *– Sprat*, der Dreikäsehoch; *yellow –*, Gelbfieber; *– -tar*, die Teerjacke.
Jacob ['dʒeɪkəb], Jakob (*m.*). **–ean** [dʒæko'bɪ:ən], im frühen 17. Jahrhundert (*English Hist.*); dunkeleiche (*of furniture*) (*adj.*). **–in** ['dʒækəbɪn], Jakobiner (*m.*). **–ite** ['dzækəbaɪt], Jakobit (*m.*); jakobitisch (*adj.*).
Jamaica [dʒə'meɪkə], Jamaika (*n.*).
James [dʒeɪmz], Jakob (*m.*); (*B.*) Jakobus (*m.*).
Jane [dʒeɪn], Johanna (*f.*).
Janet ['dʒænɪt] (*dim.* of **Jane**), Hannchen (*n.*).
Japanese [dʒæpə'nɪ:z], Japaner (*m.*); japanisch (*adj.*).
Jasper ['dʒæspə], Kaspar, Kasper (*m.*).
Javanese [dʒɑ:və'nɪ:z], Javaner (*m.*); javanisch (*adj.*).
Jeff(ery) ['dʒɛf(rɪ)] (*m.*) (*dim. of* **Geoffrey**), Gottfried (*m.*).
Jehoshaphat [dʒɪ'hɔʃəfæt], Josaphat (*m.*).
Jehovah [dʒɪ'houvə], Jehova (*m.*).
Jem(my) ['dʒɛm(ɪ)] (*dim. of* **James**).
Jenny ['dʒɛnɪ] (*dim. of* **Jane**), Hannele, Hannchen (*n.*).
Jeremiah [dʒɛrɪ'maɪə], **Jeremy** ['dʒɛrəmɪ], Jeremias (*m.*).
Jeroboam [dʒɛrə'bouəm], Jerobeam (*m.*).
Jerome [dʒə'roum], Hieronymus (*m.*).
Jerry ['dʒɛrɪ] (*dim. of* **Jeremiah**).
Jess–ica ['dʒɛsɪkə] (*dim.* **–ie** ['dʒɛsɪ]), Jettchen (*n.*), Jette (*f.*).
Jesuit–ical [dʒɛzjʊ'ɪtɪkl], jesuitisch (*adj.*). **–ism** [–ɪzm], **–ry** [–rɪ], der Jesuitismus.
Jew [dʒʊ], Jude (*m.*); (*as term of abuse*) Jud, Jüd (*m.*); *–'s harp*, die Maultrommel; *Wandering –*, der Ewige Jude. **–ess**, Jüdin (*f.*). **–ish**, jüdisch (*adj.*); *–ish Christian*, der Judenchrist. **–ry**, das Judentum, die Judenschaft; (*archaic*) das Judenviertel. **– -baiting**, die Judenhetze.
Jezebel ['dʒɛzəbl] Isebel (*f.*).
Jill [dʒɪl] (*dim. of* **Juliana**), Julie (*f.*), Julchen (*n.*).
Jim(my) ['dʒɪm(ɪ)] (*dim. of* **James**).
Jinny ['dʒɪnɪ] (*dim. of* **Jane**), Hannele (*f.*), Hannchen (*n.*).
Joan [dʒoun], **–na** [dʒou'ænə], Johanna; *– of Arc*, die Jungfrau von Orleans; *Pope–*, die Päpstin Johanna.
Job [dʒoub], Hiob (*m.*); *–'s comforter*, schlechter Tröster; *–'s patience*, die Engelsgeduld; (*B.*) *the Book of –*, das Buch Hiob.
Jocelyn ['dʒɔslɪn], Jobst, Jost, Jodokus (*m.*).
Joe(y) ['dʒou(ɪ)] (*dim. of* **Joseph**), Seppi, Sepperl, Sepp (*m.*).
John [dʒɔn], Johann(es); St. –, der heilige Johannes; *– the Baptist*, Johannes der Täufer; *– Bull*, (*fig.*) England (*n.*); *St. –'s day*, das Johannisfest; *Knight of St. –*, der Johanniter(ritter).
Johnny ['dʒɔnɪ] (*dim. of* **John**), Hans (*m.*), Hänschen (*n.*), Hansel (*m.*).
Jonah ['dʒounə], **Jonas** ['dʒounəs], Jona(s) (*m.*).
Jordan ['dʒɔ:dn], Jordan (*m.*) (*river*); Jordanien (*n.*) (*country*).
Jos [dʒɔs] (*dim. of* **Josiah** *or* **Joshua**).
Joseph ['dʒouzɪf], Joseph, Josef (*m.*). **–ine** [–ɪ:n], Josephine, Josepha, Josefa (*f.*).
Josh–ua ['dʒɔʃʊə] (*dim.* **–**) Josua (*m.*).
Josiah [dʒou'saɪə], Josias (*m.*).
Josie ['dʒouzɪ], (*dim. of* **Josephine**) Phinchen (*n.*).
Jove [dʒouv], Jupiter, Zeus (*m.*).
Judæa, Judea [dʒʊ:'dɪə], Judäa (*n.*).
Judah ['dʒʊ:də], Juda (*m.*).
Judaic, *adj. see* **Jewish.**
Jud–ith ['dʒʊ:dɪθ], Judith (*f.*). **–y** ['dʒʊ:dɪ] (*dim. of* **–ith**).
Jugoslav ['jʊ:goslɑ:v], Jugoslawe (*m.*); jugoslawisch (*adj.*). **–ia** [jʊ:go'slɑ:vɪə], Jugoslawien (*n.*).
Juli–a(na) ['dʒʊ:ljə (dʒʊ:lɪ'ɑ:nə)], Julie, Julia, Juliane, Juliana (*f.*). **–et**, Julchen (*n.*), Jule (*f.*).
Julian ['dʒʊ:ljən], julianisch (*adj.*); *– Alps*, die Julischen Alpen (*pl.*).
Juno-like ['dʒʊ:nolaɪk], junonisch (*adj.*).
Jut–ish ['dʒʊ:tɪʃ], jütisch (*adj.*). **–land** ['dʒʌtlənd], Jütland (*n.*); *battle of –land*, die Skagerrakschlacht. **–lander** [–ə], Jute (*m.*).

K

Kaffir ['kæfə], Kaffer (*m.*).
Kamchatka [kæm'tʃætkə], Kamtschatka (*n.*). **–n,** Kamtschadale (*m.*); kamtschadalisch (*adj.*).
Kantian ['kæntɪən], Kantianer (*m.*), kantisch (*adj.*).
Kate(y) ['keɪt(ɪ)] (*dim. of* **Katharine**), Käthchen (*n.*), Käthe, Trine (*f.*).
Katharine, Katherine ['kæθərɪn], Katharine, Katharina (*f.*).
Kathleen ['kæθlɪ:n], **Kathy** ['kæθɪ], **Katie** ['keɪtɪ], *see* **Kate(y).**
Kelt, see **Celt.**
Khalifa [kə'lɪ:fə], *see* **Caliph.**
Kiev [kɪ:'ɛv], Kiew (*n.*).
Kirghiz, ['kə:gɪ:z], Kirgise (*m.*); kirgisisch (*adj.*).
Kit [kɪt] (*dim. of* **Christopher**), Töffel (*m.*).
Kitty ['kɪtɪ] (*dim. of* **Katherine**), Käthchen (*n.*), Kathi (*f.*).
Kremlin ['krɛmlɪn], Kreml (*m.*).
Kurd [kə:d], Kurde (*m.*).

L

Laced–æmon [læsɪ'dɪ:mən], Lazedämon (*n.*). **–emonia** [læsɪdɪ'mounɪə], Lazedämonien (*n.*). **–emonian,** Lazedämonier (*m.*); lazedämonisch (*adj.*).
Laconia [lə'kounɪə], Lakonien (*n.*). **–n,** Lakonier (*m.*).
Lahn R. [lɑ:n], Lahn (*f.*).
Lambert ['læmbət], Lambert, Lamprecht (*m.*).
Lammas ['læməs], (Petri) Kettenfeier (*f.*).
La(u)ncelot ['lɑ:nslət], Lanzelot (*m.*).
Langobard ['læŋgobɑ:d], Longobarde (*m.*).
Lap–land ['læplænd], Lappland (*n.*). **–lander** [–ə], Lappe, Lappländer (*m.*). **–landish,** lappländisch (*adj.*). **–p,** *m.* Lappe, Lappländer, *adj.* lappländisch. **–pish,** *n.* die lappländische Sprache.
Lares ['lɛərɪ:z], die Laren (*pl.*).
Larry ['lærɪ] (*dim. of* **Lawrence**).
Lateran ['lætərən], Lateran (*m.*); *– councils*, die lateranischen Konzilien.
Latin ['lætɪn], (*inhabitant of Roman Empire*) Lateiner (*m.*); (*inhabitant of Latium*) Latiner (*m.*); (*language*) Latein (*n.*); lateinisch (*adj.*); *dog- –*, das Küchenlatein.
Latvia ['lætvɪə], Lettland (*n.*). **–n,** Lette (*m.*); lettisch (*adj.*).
Laura [lɔ:rə] (*dim. of* **Leonora**), Lore.
Laurence, Lawrence ['lɔrəns], Lorenz, Laurentius (*m.*); *St. Lawrence R.*, der Lorenzstrom.
Leah ['lɪə], Lea (*f.*).
Lebanon ['lɛbənən], Libanon (*m.*).
Leeward Islands ['ljʊ:əd], die nördliche Gruppe der Kleinen Antillen.
Leghorn [lɛg'hɔ:n], Livorno (*n.*).
Leipsic ['laɪpsɪk], **Leipzig** ['laɪpzɪg], Leipzig (*n.*).
Leman Lake ['lɪ:mən], der Genfer See.
Leonard ['lɛnəd], Leonhard (*m.*).
Leonora [lɪə'nɔ:rə], Lenore (*f.*).
Letitia [lɪ'tɪ:ʃɪə], Lätitia (*f.*).
Lett [lɛt] Lette (*m.*), lettisch (*adj.*).

Lett-ice [ˈlɛtɪs], **-y** (*dim. of* **Letitia**).
Levant [lɪˈvænt], Levante (*f.*). **-ine** [-ɑɪn], Levantiner (*m.*); levant(in)isch (*adj.*).
Levit-e [ˈlɪ:vɑɪt], Levit (*m.*). **-ical** [lɪˈvɪtɪkl], levitisch (*adj.*).
Leviticus [lɪˈvɪtɪkəs], das dritte Buch Mosis.
Lewis [ˈlu:ɪs], Ludwig (*m.*).
Libya [ˈlɪbjə], Libyen (*n.*). **-n** [ˈlɪbɪən], Libyer (*m.*) libysch (*adj.*).
Liège [lɪˈeɪʒ], Lüttich (*n.*).
Ligurian Sea [lɪˈgjuərɪən], das Ligurische Meer.
Lilian [ˈlɪlɪən], **Lil(y)** [ˈlɪl(ɪ)], Lilli (*f.*).
Lilliputian [lɪlɪˈpju:ʃən], Liliputaner (*m.*); liliputanisch, zwerghaft (*adj.*).
Linnean [lɪˈnɪ:ən]; – *system*, das Linneische System.
Lipari Islands [ˈlɪpərɪ], die Liparischen Inseln (*pl.*).
Lisbon [ˈlɪzbən], Lissabon (*n.*).
Lithuania [lɪθjuˈəɪnɪə], Litauen (*n.*). **-n**, Litauer (*m.*); litauisch (*adj.*).
Livonia [lɪˈvounɪə], Livland (*n.*). **-n**, Livländer (*m.*); livländisch (*adj.*).
Livy [ˈlɪvɪ], Livius (*m.*).
Liz(zie) [ˈlɪz(ɪ)] (*dim. of* **Elizabeth**), Lieschen, Liesel (*n.*), Liese (*f.*).
Lofoden Islands [ləˈfoudən], die Lofoten (*pl.*).
Lollards [ˈlələdz], die Lollarden (*pl.*).
Lombard [ˈləmbəd], Lombarde (*m.*); (*also* **-ic** [-ˈbɑ:dɪk]), lombardisch (*adj.*). **-y** [ˈləmbədɪ], die Lombardei.
Lora [ˈlɔ:rə] (*dim. of* **Leonora**), Lore (*f.*).
Lorraine [loˈreɪn], Lothringen (*n.*); lothringisch (*adj.*), *men of* –, Lothringer (*pl.*).
Lothario [loˈθɛərɪou], Lothar (*m.*); *gay* –, der Schürzenjäger.
Lottie [ˈlətɪ] (*dim. of* **Charlotte**), Lottchen (*n.*), Lotte (*f.*).
Louis [ˈluɪ], Ludwig (*m.*).
Louisa [luˈɪ:zə] (*dim.* **Lou(ise)**), Luise (*f.*).
Low Countries [lou], die Niederlande (*pl.*).
Lucas [ˈlu:kəs], Lukas (*m.*).
Lucerne [lu:ˈsə:n], (*town*) Luzern (*n.*); *inhabitant of* –, Luzerner (*m.*); *lake of* –, der Vierwaldstättersee.
Lucifer [ˈlu:sɪfə], Luzifer, Satan (*m.*); der Morgenstern.
Lucrece [lu:ˈkrɪ:s], **Lucretia** [lu:ˈkrɪ:ʃə], Lukrezia (*f.*).
Lucretius [lu:ˈkrɪ:ʃəs], Lukrez (*m.*).
Lucy [ˈlu:sɪ], Luca, Luzie (*f.*).
Luke [lu:k], Lukas (*m.*); *St.* –, der heilige Lukas.
Lusatia [lu:ˈseɪʃə], die Lausitz. **-n**, Lausitzer (*m.*); lausitzisch (*adj.*).
Lutheran [ˈlu:θərən], Lutheraner (*m.*); lutherisch (*adj.*). **-ism** [-ɪzm], das Luthertum.
Luxembourg [ˈlʌksəmbə:g], Luxemburg (*n.*); luxemburgisch (*adj.*); *inhabitant of* –, Luxemburger (*m.*).
Lycurgus [lɑɪˈkə:gəs], Lykurg (*m.*).
Lydia [ˈlɪdɪə], (*country*) Lydien (*n.*); (*Christian name*) Lydia (*f.*). **-n**, Lyder, Lydier (*m.*); lydisch (*adj.*).
Lyons [ˈlɑɪənz], Lyon (*n.*).

M

Maccab-ee [ˈmækəbɪ:], Makkabäer (*m.*). **-ean**, (*adj.*) makkabäisch.
Macedonia [mæsɪˈdounɪə], Mazedonien (*n.*). **-n**, Mazedonier (*m.*); mazedonisch (*adj.*).
Machiavellian [mækɪəˈvelɪən], machiavellistisch (*adj.*).
Madagascan [mædəˈgæskən], *see* **Malagasy.**
Madelene [ˈmædəlɪ:n], *see* **Magdalene.**
Madge [ˈmædʒ] (*dim. of* **Magdalene**), Magda (*f.*); (*dim. of* **Margaret**), Gretchen (*n.*).
Mæcenas [mɪ:ˈsɪ:nəs], der Mäzen.
Maelstrom [ˈmeɪlstroum], der Mahlstrom.
Mag(gie) [ˈmæg(ɪ)] (*dim. of* **Margaret**), Gretchen (*n.*).
Magdalen (*at Oxford*) [ˈmɔ:dlən], **-e** (*at Cambridge*) [ˈmægdəlɪn (-lɪ:n)], Magdalene, Magdalena (*f.*); (*as Christian name also*) Magda (*f.*).
Magellan [məˈgɛlən]; *straits of* –, die Magalhãesstraße.
Magi [ˈmeɪdʒɑɪ], die Magier (*pl.*).
Magyar [ˈmægjɑ:], Madjar, Magyar (*m.*); madjarisch (*adj.*).
Mahomet [məˈhəmɪt], Mohammed (*m.*). **-an,** Mohammedaner (*m.*); mohammedanisch (*adj.*).
Main R. [meɪn], Main (*m.*).
Malacca [məˈlækə], Malakka (*n.*).
Malachi [ˈmæləkɪ], Maleachi (*m.*)
Malagasy [mæləˈgæsɪ], Madagasse (*m.*); madagassisch (*adj.*).
Malay [məˈleɪ], Malaie (*m.*); – *Archipelago*, der Malaiische Archipel; – *States*, Malaienstaaten (*pl.*). **-an,** malaiisch (*adj.*).
Maldive Islands [ˈmɔ:ldɑɪv], die Malediven (*pl.*).
Malines [mæˈlɪ:n], Mecheln (*n.*); *see* **Mechlin.**
Maltese [mɔ:lˈtɪ:z], Malteser (*m.*); maltesisch (*adj.*); – *Cross*, das Malteserkreuz.
Mameluke [ˈmæmɪlu:k], Mameluk, Mamluck (*m.*).
Manasseh [məˈnæsɪ], Manasse (*m.*).
Manchu [mænˈtʃu:], Mandschu (*m.*); (*language*) Mandschu (*n.*); mandschurisch (*adj.*). **-ria** [mænˈtjuərɪə], die Mandschurei. **-rian,** mandschurisch (*adj.*).
Manich-(a)ean [mænɪˈkɪ:ən], **Manich-ee** [mænɪˈkɪ:], Manichäer (*m.*); manichäisch (*adj.*). **-(a)eism,** [ˈmænɪkɪɪzm], der Manichäismus.
Margaret [ˈmɑ:gərɪt], Margarete, Margareta (*f.*).
Margery [ˈmɑ:dʒərɪ] (*dim. of* **Margaret**), Grete (*f.*), Gretel (*n.*), Gretchen (*n.*).
Maria [məˈrɑɪə], Marie (*f.*); – *Theresa*, Maria Theresia (*f.*).
Marian [ˈmɛərɪən], Marion, Marianne (*f.*).
Marjory [ˈmɑ:dʒərɪ], *see* **Margery.**
Mark [mɑ:k], Markus (*m.*).
Marmora [ˈmɑ:mərə]; *Sea of* –, das Marmarameer.
Marseilles [mɑ:ˈseɪlz], Marseille (*n.*).
Martian [ˈmɑ:ʃɪən], der Marsbewohner.
Martin [ˈmɑ:tɪn]; *St.* *–'s summer*, der Altweibersommer, Spätsommer. **-mas** [-məs], Martini (*m.*).
Mary [ˈmɛərɪ], Marie, Maria (*f.*); – *Ann*, Marianne (*f.*); *Virgin* –, die Jungfrau Maria, Unsre Liebe Frau; *St.* *–'s Church*, die Marienkirche, Frauenkirche.
Mastersingers [ˈmɑ:stəsɪŋəz], die Meistersinger, Meistersänger (*pl.*).
Masurian [mæˈzjuərɪən], Masure (*m.*); masurisch (*adj.*).
Mat(h)ilda [məˈtɪldə], Mathilde, Mechthild(e) (*f.*).
Matthew [ˈmæθju:], (*B.*) Matthäus (*m.*); Matthias (*m.*).
Matty [ˈmætɪ] (*dim. of* **Matthew, Matthias, Martha,** *or* **Mat(h)ilda**).
Maud [mɔ:d] (*dim. of* **Matilda**), Thilde, Tilde (*f.*).
Maurice [ˈmərɪs], Moritz (*m.*).
May [meɪ] (*dim. of* **Mary**), Mariechen (*n.*), Mieze (*f.*).
Meander R. [mɪˈændə], Mäander (*m.*).
Mecca [ˈmɛkə], Mekka (*n.*).
Mechlin [ˈmɛklɪn], Mecheln (*n.*); – *lace*, Mecheler Spitzen (*pl.*).
Mede [mɪ:d], Meder (*m.*).
Medici [ˈmɛdɪtʃɪ] Mediceer (*pl.*); *Venus of* –, die mediceische Venus.
Mediterranean [mɛdɪtəˈreɪnjən], **1.** *s.* (– *Sea*) das mittelländische Meer, Mittelmeer. **2.** *adj.* mittelländisch.
Meg(gy) [ˈmɛg(ɪ)] (*dim. of* **Margaret**), Grete (*f.*), Gretchen (*n.*).
Melanesian [mɛləˈnɪ:zɪən], Melanesier (*m.*); melanesisch (*adj.*).
Memel R. [ˈmeɪməl], Memel (*f.*).
Mercury [ˈmə:kjurɪ], Merkur (*m.*).
Merovingian [meroˈvɪndʒɪən], Merowinger (*m.*); merowingisch (*adj.*).
Messiah [mɪˈsɑɪə], der Messias; (*fig.*) der Erlöser, Heiland.
Methuselah [mɪˈθju:zələ], Methusalem (*m.*); *as old as* –, steinalt.
Meuse R. [mə:z], Maas (*f.*).

Mexic–an [ˈmɛksɪkən], Mexikaner (*m.*); mexikanisch (*adj.*). **–o** [ˈmɛksɪkou], Mexiko (*n.*).
Micah [ˈmaɪkə], Micha (*m.*).
Michael [ˈmaɪkl], Mich(a)el (*m.*).
Milan [mɪˈlæn], Mailand (*n.*). **–ese** [ˈmɪlənɪːz], Mailänder (*m.*); mailändisch (*adj.*).
Millicent [ˈmɪlɪsənt], Melisande (*f.*).
Milly [ˈmɪlɪ] (*dim. of* **Millicent** *or* **Mildred**).
Minnesingers [ˈmɪnɪsɪŋəz], die Minnesinger, Minnesänger (*pl.*).
Minnie [ˈmɪnɪ] (*dim. of* **Wilhelmina** *or* **Hermione**), Minna.
Moabit–e [ˈmouəbaɪt], Moabiter (*m.*). **–ish**, moabitisch (*adj.*).
Mocha [ˈmoukə], (*city*) Mokka (*n.*).
Mohammed [moˈhæmɛd], *see* **Mahomet.** **–an**, Mohammedaner (*m.*); mohammedanisch (*adj.*). **–anism** [–ənɪzm], der Mohammedanismus.
Mohican [mouˈhɪːkən], Mohikaner (*m.*).
Moldavia [məlˈdeɪvɪə], Moldau (*f.*). **–n**, Moldauer (*m.*); moldauisch (*adj.*).
Moll(y) [ˈməl(ɪ)] (*dim. of* **Mary**), Mariechen (*n.*).
Moluccas [moˈlʌkəz], die Molukken (*pl.*).
Mongolia [məŋˈgoulɪə], die Mongolei. **–n**, Mongole (*m.*); mongolisch (*adj.*).
Montenegrin [məntɪˈnɪːgrɪn], Montenegriner (*m.*); montenegrinisch (*adj.*).
Moor [muə], Maure, Berber; Mohr (*m.*). **–ish** [–rɪʃ], maurisch (*adj.*).
Moravia [moˈreɪvjə], Mähren (*n.*). **–n**, Mähre (*m.*); (*member of –n sect*) der Herrnhuter, mährische *or* Böhmische Bruder; mährisch (*adj.*); *–n Brethren*, die Herrnhuter (*pl.*). **–nism** [–nɪzm], das Herrnhutertum.
Moresque [moˈrɛsk], maurisch, arabeskisch (*adj.*).
Morisco [məˈrɪskou], Maure (*m.*); maurisch (*adj.*).
Mormon [ˈmɔːmən], Mormone (*m.*); mormonisch (*adj.*). **–ism** [–ɪzm], das Mormonentum.
Morocc–an [məˈrɔkən], Marokkaner (*m.*); marokkanisch (*adj.*). **–o** [məˈrɔkou], Marokko (*n.*).
Morris [ˈmɔrɪs], *see* **Maurice.**
Moscow [ˈmɔskou], Moskau (*n.*).
Moselle R. [moˈzɛl], Mosel (*f.*).
Moslem [ˈmɔzləm], *see* **Mussulman.**
Mosul [ˈmousəl], Mossul (*n.*).
Munich [ˈmjuːnɪk], München (*n.*); Münchener (*adj.*).
Muscov–ite [ˈmʌskəvaɪt], Moskowiter (*m.*); moskowitisch (*adj.*). **–y** [ˈmʌskəvɪ], (*obs.*) das Fürstentum Moskovier.; (*in a wider sense*) Rußland (*n.*).
Mussulman [ˈmʌslmən], Muselman, Muselmann (*m.*); muselmanisch, muselmännisch (*adj.*).
Mycenæ [maɪˈsɪːnɪː], Mykenä, Mykene (*n.*). **–an** [maɪsɪˈnɪːən], mykenisch (*adj.*).

N

Nan [næn], **Nancy** [ˈnænsɪ] (*dim. of* **Ann(a)**, **Anne**), Ännchen (*n.*), Anni (*f.*).
Naples [ˈneɪpəlz], Neapel (*n.*).
Nathaniel [nəˈθænjəl], Nathanael (*m.*).
Nawab [nəˈwɑːb], Nabob (*m.*).
Nazarene [næzəˈrɪːn], Nazaräer, Nazarener (*m.*); nazarenisch (*adj.*).
Nazarite [ˈnæzəraɪt], Nasiräer (*m.*).
Neapolitan [nɪəˈpɔlɪtən], Neapolitaner (*m.*); neapolitanisch (*adj.*).
Nebuchadnezzar [nɛbjukədˈnɛzə], Nebukadnezar (*m.*).
Neckar R. [ˈnɛkə], Neckar (*m.*).
Ned(dy) [ˈnɛd(ɪ)] (*dim. of* **Edward**); (*pet name for a donkey*) das Grauchen.
Nehemiah [nɪːɪˈmaɪə], Nehemia (*m.*).
Nell(ie) [ˈnɛl(ɪ)] (*dim. of* **Helen**), Lenchen (*n.*), Lena, Lene (*f.*).
Nemean [nɪˈmɪːən], nemeisch (*adj.*).
Neptun–e [ˈnɛptjuːn], Neptun (*m.*). **–ian** [nɛpˈtjuːnɪən], neptunisch (*adj.*).
Nervii [ˈnɔːvɪaɪ], die Nervier (*pl.*).
Netherlands [ˈnɛðələndz], die Niederlande (*pl.*).
Nettie, Netty [ˈnɛtɪ] (*dim. of* **Henrietta**).
Neuchâtel [nɔːʃaˈtɛl], Neuenburg (*n.*).
Newcastle [ˈnjuːkɑːsl]; *carry coals to* –, Eulen nach Athen tragen.
Newfoundland [ˈnjuːfəndlænd], Neufundland (*n.*); (*dog*) [njuːˈfaundlənd], der Neufundländer.
New South Wales [njuː sauθ weɪlz], Neusüdwales (*n.*).
New York [njuːˈjɔːk], Neuyork (*n.*).
New Zealand [njuːˈzɪːlənd], Neuseeland (*n.*).
Nicæa, *see* **Nicea.**
Nice [nɪːs], Nizza (*n.*).
Nice–a [naɪˈsɪːə], Nicäa, Nizäa (*n.*). **–ne** [naɪˈsɪːn], nizäisch (*adj.*); *–ne creed*, das Nizänische Glaubensbekenntnis, Nicaenum.
Nicholas [ˈnɪkələs], Nikola(u)s (*m.*).
Nick [nɪk] (*dim. of* **Nicholas**), Klaus (*m.*); *Old* –, der Teufel.
Niger R. [ˈnaɪdʒə], Niger (*m.*).
Nigeria [naɪˈdʒɪərɪə], Nigerien (*n.*).
Nile [naɪl], der Nil.
Nimeguen [ˈnɪmeɪgən], Nimwegen (*n.*).
Nineveh [ˈnɪnɪvə], Ninive (*n.*).
Nora [ˈnɔːrə] (*dim. of* **Leonora**), Nora, Lore (*f.*).
Norman [ˈnɔːmən], Normanne (*m.*); normannisch (*adj.*).
Normandy [ˈnɔːməndɪ], die Normandie.
Norn [nɔːn], die Norne.
Norse [nɔːs], nordisch (*adj.*). **–man** [–mən], Wiking (*m.*).
North [nɔːθ]; – *Cape*, das Nordkap; – *Sea*, die Nordsee. **–man** [–mən], Skandinavier (*m.*).
Norw–ay [ˈnɔːweɪ], Norwegen (*n.*). **–egian** [nɔːˈwɪːdʒən], Norweger (*m.*); norwegisch (*adj.*).
Nova [ˈnouvə]; **– Scotia** [ˈskouʃɪə], Neuschottland (*n.*). **– Zembla** [ˈzɛmblə], Nowaja Semlja.
Nubian [ˈnjuːbɪən], Nubier (*m.*); nubisch (*adj.*).
Numidian [njuːˈmɪdɪən], Numid(i)er (*m.*); numidisch (*adj.*).
Nuremberg [ˈnjuərəmbəːg], Nürnberg (*n.*).

O

Obadiah [oubəˈdaɪə], Obadja (*m.*).
Oceania [ouʃɪˈeɪnɪə], Ozeanien (*n.*).
Oder R. [ˈoudə], Oder (*f.*).
Odin [ˈoudɪn], Wodan (*m.*).
Odyssey [ˈɔdɪsɪ], die Odyssee.
Olive [ˈɔlɪv], Olivia (*f.*).
Olives [ˈɔlɪvz]; *Mt. of* –, der Ölberg.
Olymp–iad [oˈlɪmpɪæd], die Olympiade. **–ian** [–pɪən], Olympier (*m.*); (*also* **–ic**) olympisch (*adj.*). **–us** [oˈlɪmpəs], Olymp (*m.*).
Orange [ˈɔrɪndʒ], Oranien (*n.*); – *Free State*, der Oranjefreistaat; – *R.*, der Oranjefluß. **–man** [–mən], irischer Protestant.
Orestes [oˈrɛstɪːz], Orest (*m.*).
Orph–ean [ɔːˈfɪːən], **–ic** [ˈɔːfɪk], orphisch (*adj.*).
Oscar [ˈɔskə], Oskar (*m.*).
Ostend [ɔsˈtɛnd], Ostende (*n.*).
Ostrogoth [ˈɔstrogɔθ], Ostgote (*m.*); ostgotisch (*adj.*).
Ottoman [ˈɔtomən], Osmane, Ottomane (*m.*); osmanisch, ottomanisch (*adj.*).
Owlglass [ˈaulglɑːs], *see* **Howleglass.**
Oxonian [ɔkˈsounɪən], Oxforder (Student) (*m.*).

P

Pacific Ocean [pəˈsɪfɪk], der Stille *or* Große Ozean.
Paddy [ˈpædɪ] (*dim. of* **Patrick**).
Palatin–ate [pəˈlætɪnɪt], die Pfalz; *Upper* – die Oberpfalz; *Rhenish* –, die Rheinpfalz. **–e** [ˈpælətaɪn], pfälzisch (*adj.*); *Count* –, der Pfalzgraf; *Elector* –, der Kurfürst von der Pfalz.
Palestin–e [ˈpælɪstaɪn], Palästina (*n.*). **–ian** [pælɪsˈtɪnɪən], Palästiner (*m.*); palästinisch (*adj.*).
Pancras [ˈpæŋkrəs], Pankraz (*m.*).
Parcæ [ˈpɑːsɪː], die Parzen (*pl.*).
Parian [ˈpɛərɪən], parisch (*adj.*).
Paris [ˈpærɪs]; *plaster of* –, gebrannter Gips. **–ian** [pəˈrɪzjən], Pariser (*m.*); parisisch (*adj.*). **–ienne** [pærɪːzɪˈɛn], Pariserin (*f.*).

Parmesan [pɑːmɪˈzæn], Parmaer, Parmesaner (*m.*); parmaisch, parmesanisch (*adj.*); – *cheese*, der Parmesankäse.
Parnass–ian [pɑːˈnæsɪən], parnassisch (*adj.*). **–us** [pɑːˈnæsəs], Parnaß (*m.*).
Parsee [pɑːˈsɪː], Parse (*m.*); parsisch (*adj.*). **–ism** [–ɪzm], der Parsismus.
Parthian [ˈpɑːθɪən], Parther (*m.*); parthisch (*adj.*).
Partlet [ˈpɑːtlɪt]; *Dame* –, (Frau) Krakefuß (*f.*).
Pat [pæt] (*dim. of* **Patrick**).
Patagonian [pætəˈgounɪən], Patagonier (*m.*); patagonisch (*adj.*).
Patrick [ˈpætrɪk], Patrizius (*m.*).
Patsy [ˈpætsɪ] (*dim. of* **Patricia**).
Paul [pɔːl], Paul(us) (*m.*); – *Pry*, Hans Dampf in allen Gassen; *St.* –, der heilige Paulus. **–ina** [pɔːˈlɪːnə] Pauline, Paula (*f.*). **–ine** [–ɪːn], *see* **–ina**; paulinisch (*adj.*).
Peg(gy) [ˈpɛg(ɪ)] (*dim. of* **Margaret**), Grete (*f.*); Gretchen, Gretel (*n.*).
Pekin [pɪːˈkɪn], Peking (*n.*).
Pelagian [pəˈleɪdʒɪən], Pelagianer (*m.*); pelagianisch (*adj.*).
Pelasgi(ans) [pəˈlæzgaɪ (pəˈlæzdzɪənz)], die Pelasger (*pl.*).
Peloponnesus [pɛləpəˈnɪːsəs], Peloponnes (*m. or f.*).
Penates [pəˈneɪtɪːz], die Penaten (*pl.*).
Pepin [ˈpɛpɪn], Pippin (*m.*).
Perc–eval, –ival [ˈpəːsɪvəl], Parzival (*m.*). **–y** (*dim. of* **–eval**).
Pericles [ˈpɛrɪklɪːz], Perikles (*m.*).
Perkin [ˈpəːkɪn] (*dim. of* **Peter**), Peterchen, Peterle (*n.*).
Pernambuco [pəːnæmˈbuːkou], Pernambuko, Fernambuk (*n.*).
Persian [ˈpəːʃən], Perser (*m.*); persisch (*adj.*); – *wars*, die Perserkriege (*pl.*).
Peruvian [pəˈruːvɪən], Peruaner (*m.*); peruanisch (*adj.*).
Peter [ˈpɪːtə], Peter (*m.*); (*B.*) Petrus (*m.*); *–'s pence*, der Peterspfennig; *St.* –, der heilige Petrus; *St. –'s* (*Church*), die Peterskirche, Petrikirche; *rob – to pay Paul*, ein Loch aufreißen, um das andere zuzustopfen. **–kin,** Peterchen, Peterle (*n.*).
Petrarch [ˈpɪːtrɑːk], Petrarka (*m.*).
Phæacia [fɪˈeɪʃɪə], Phäakien, Phäakenland (*n.*). **–n,** Phäake (*m.*); phäakisch (*adj.*).
Pharaoh [ˈfɛərou], Pharao (*m.*).
Phil [fɪl] (*dim. of* **Philip**). **–ippine** (*adj.*), philippinisch. **–ip** [ˈfɪlɪp], Philipp. **–ippa** [fɪˈlɪpə], Philippine (*f.*). **–ippians** [fɪˈlɪpɪənz], die Philipper (*pl.*); *Epistle to the –ippians*, der Philipperbrief. **–ippine Islands** [ˈfɪlɪpɪːn], die Philippinen (*pl.*); **–ippino,** Philippiner (*m.*).
Philistine [ˈfɪlɪstaɪn], Philister (*m.*); (*fig.*) der Spießbürger.
Phoci–an [ˈfouʃɪən], Phokier (*m.*); phokisch (*adj.*). **–s** [ˈfousɪs], Phokis (*n.*).
Phœbe [ˈfɪːbɪ], Phöbe (*f.*); (*fig.*) Luna (*f.*).
Phoenicia [fɪˈnɪːʃɪə], Phönizien. **–n** [fɪˈnɪːʃən], Phönizier (*m.*); phönizisch (*adj.*).
Phrygian [ˈfrɪdʒɪən], Phrygier (*m.*); phrygisch (*adj.*).
Picardy [ˈpɪkədɪ], die Pikardie.
Pict [pɪkt], Pikte (*m.*). **–ish,** piktisch (*adj.*).
Piedmont [ˈpɪːdmənt], Piemont (*n.*). **–ese** [–ˈtɪːz], Piemontese (*m.*); piemontisch, piemontesisch (*adj.*).
Piers Plowman [pɪəz ˈplaumən], Peter der Pflüger.
Pilate [ˈpaɪlət], Pilatus (*m.*).
Pip (*dim. of* **Philip**).
Piræus [paɪˈrɪːəs], Piräus (*m.*).
Platæa [pləˈtɪːə], Platää (*n.*).
Plate R. [ˈpleɪt] (**La Plata, Rio Plata** [ˈplɑːtə]), der Plataﬂuß.
Platonist [ˈpleɪtənɪst], der Platoniker.
Pleiades [ˈplaɪədɪːz], die Pleiaden (*pl.*).
Pliny [ˈplɪnɪ], Plinius (*m.*).
Po R. [pou], Po (*m.*)
Pol–and [ˈpoulənd], Polen (*n.*). **–e** [poul], Pole (*m.*). **–ish,** polnisch (*adj.*).
Polar Sea [ˈpoulə], das Eismeer.
Poll(y) [ˈpɔl(ɪ)] (*dim. of* **Mary**), Molly (*f.*), Mariechen (*n.*), Mieze (*f.*).
Polycrates [pəˈlɪkrətɪːz], Polykrates (*m.*).
Polynesian [pɔlɪˈnɪːzɪən], Polynesier (*m.*); polynesisch (*adj.*).
Pomerania [pɔməˈreɪnɪə], Pommern (*n.*); *Further* –, Hinterpommern (*n.*). **–n,** Pommer (*m.*); pommer(i)sch (*adj.*); *–n dog*, der Spitz.
Pompeii [pɔmˈpeɪɪː, pɔmˈpɪːaɪ], Pompeji (*n.*)
Pompey [ˈpɔmpɪ], Pompejus (*m.*).
Pontine [ˈpɔntaɪn]; – *marshes*, die pontinischen Sümpfe (*pl.*); – *Sea*, Pontus Euxinus (*m.*), das Schwarze Meer.
Porte [pɔːt]; *the Sublime* –, die Hohe Pforte.
Portuguese [ˈpɔːtjugɪːz], Portugiese (*m.*); portugiesisch (*adj.*).
Posnania [pɔzˈneɪnɪə], Posen (*n.*).
Prague [prɑːg], Prag (*m.*).
Premonstrant friar [prɪˈmɔnstrənt], der Prämonstratenser(mönch).
Pre-Raphaelite [ˈprɪːˈræfəlaɪt], der Präraphaelit.
Priam [ˈpraɪəm], Priamus (*m.*).
Procopius [proˈkoupɪəs], Prokop (*m.*).
Promethean [proˈmɪːθɪən], prometheisch (*adj.*).
Propertius [proˈpəːʃɪəs], Properz (*m.*).
Provençal [prəvənˈsɑːl], Provenzale (*m.*); provenzalisch (*adj.*).
Prudence [ˈpruːdəns], Prudentia (*f.*).
Prussia [ˈprʌʃə], Preußen (*n.*). **–n,** Preuße (*m.*); preußisch (*adj.*); *–n blue*, das Berlinerblau. **–nism** [–nɪzm], das Preußentum.
Ptolem–aic [tɔləˈmeɪɪk], ptolemäisch (*adj.*). **–ies** [ˈtɔləmɪz], die Ptolemäer (*pl.*). **–y** [ˈtɔləmɪ], Ptolemäus (*m.*).
Puck [pʌk], Kobold (*m.*).
Punch [pʌntʃ], Kasperle (*n.* or *m.*), Hanswurst (*m.*); – *and Judy show*, Kasperletheater (*n.*).
Punic [ˈpjuːnɪk], punisch (*adj.*).
Punjab [pʌnˈdʒɑːb], Pandschab (*n.*).
Puritan [ˈpjuːrɪtən], Puritaner (*m.*), puritanisch (*adj.*).
Puss-in-Boots [pus-ɪn-ˈbuːts], der Gestiefelte Kater.
Pyrenees [pɪrəˈnɪːz], die Pyrenäen (*pl.*).
Pyrrhic [ˈpɪrɪk]; – *victory*, der Pyrrhussieg.
Pythagorean [paɪθægɔːˈrɪːən], Pythagoreer (*m.*); pythagorisch (*adj.*).
Pythian [ˈpɪθɪən], pythisch (*adj.*).

Q

Quaker [ˈkweɪkə], Quäker (*m.*).

R

Rachel [ˈreɪtʃəl], Rahel (*f.*).
Rajput [ˈrɑːdʒput], Radschpute (*m.*).
Ralph [rælf, reɪf], Rudolf (*m.*).
Rameses [ˈræmɪsɪːz], Ramses (*m.*).
Rangoon [ˈræŋguːn], Rangun (*n.*).
Ratisbon [ˈrætɪzbən], Regensburg (*n.*).
Raymond [ˈreɪmənd], Raimund (*m.*).
Rebecca [rɪˈbɛkə], Rebekka (*f.*).
Red-Riding-Hood [rɛdˈraɪdɪŋhud], Rotkäppchen (*n.*).
Red Sea [rɛd sɪː], das Rote Meer.
Redskins [ˈrɛdskɪnz], die Rothäute (*pl.*).
Reginald [ˈrɛdʒɪnəld], Reinhold (*m.*).
Rehoboam [rɪːəˈbouəm], Rehabeam (*m.*).
Reuben [ˈruːbɪn], Ruben (*m.*).
Reynard [ˈrɛnəd], Reinhard (*m.*); – *the Fox*, Reineke Fuchs (*m.*).
Reynold [ˈrɛnəld], *see* **Reginald.**
Rheims [rɪːmz], Reims (*n.*).
Rhenish [ˈrɛnɪʃ], rheinisch (*adj.*); – *Franconia*, Rheinfranken (*n.*); – *Franconian*, Rheinfranke (*m.*); rheinfränkisch (*adj.*); – *Palatinate*, die Rheinpfalz.
Rhine [raɪn], Rhein (*m.*); *Lower* –, Niederrhein (*m.*); *Upper* –, Oberrhein (*m.*); – *province*, die Rheinprovinz; *Confederation of the* –, der Rheinbund.

Rhodes [roʊdz], Rhodus, Rhodos (*n.*).
Ripuarian [rɪpjʊˈɛərɪən], ripuarisch (*adj.*).
Robin [ˈrɔbɪn] (*dim. of* **Robert**); – *Goodfellow*, der gute Hauskobold; – *Redbreast*, das Rotkehlchen. **–son** [–sən]; *before one could say Jack –son*, ehe man sich's versah.
Rocky Mts. [ˈrɔkɪ], das Felsengebirge.
Roderick [ˈrɔdrɪk], Roderich (*m.*).
Ro(d)ger [ˈrɔdʒə], Rüdiger (*m.*).
Roland [ˈroulənd], Roland (*m.*); *give a – for an Oliver*, mit gleicher Münze bezahlen.
Rolf [rɔlf] (*dim.* of **Rudolf**).
Romaic [roˈmeɪɪk], neugriechisch (*adj.*).
Roman [ˈroumən], Römer (*m.*); römisch (*adj.*); *Epistle to the –s*, der Römerbrief; – *candle*, die Leuchtkugel; – *Catholic*, Katholik (*m.*); (römisch-) katholisch (*adj.*); – *characters*, lateinische Buchstaben (*pl.*), die Antiquaschrift; – *nose*, die Adlernase; – *road*, die Römerstraße. **–ce** [roˈmæns], romantisch (*adj.*); *–ce nations*, die Romanen (*pl.*); *–ce philologist*, der Romanist. **–esque** [roumәˈnɛsk], romanisch (*adj.*) (*Arch.*). **–sh** [roˈmænʃ], (*dialect*) Rhätoromanisch, Romaunsch, Romontsch (*n.*).
Romany [ˈrɔmənɪ], Zigeuner (*m.*); Zigeunersprache (*f.*).
Rom–e [roum], Rom (*n.*); (*Prov.*) *do in –e as the Romans do*, mit den Wölfen muß man heulen. **–ish** [ˈroumɪʃ], römisch-katholisch, papistisch (*adj.*).
Rosa–lind [ˈrɔzəlɪnd], Rosalinde (*f.*). **–mond** [ˈrɔzəmənd], Rosamunde (*f.*).
Rose [ˈrouz], Rosa (*f.*).
Rosicrucian [rouzɪˈkruːʃən], Rosenkreuzer (*m.*).
Rosie, Rosy [ˈrouzɪ] (*dim. of* **Rose, Rosalind, Rosemary**), Röschen (*n.*).
Rowland [ˈroulənd], *see* **Roland.**
Rubicon R. [ˈruːbɪkən], Rubikon (*m.*).
Rudolph [ˈruːdɔlf], Rudolf (*m.*).
Ruhr R. [ruə], Ruhr (*f.*).
Rumania [ruːˈmeɪnɪə], Rumänien (*n.*). **–n,** Rumäne (*m.*); rumänisch (*adj.*).
Rumelia [ruːˈmɪːlɪə], Rumelien (*n.*). **–n,** Rumelier (*m.*), rumelisch (*adj.*).
Rupert [ˈruːpət], Ruprecht (*m.*).
Russia [ˈrʌʃə], Rußland (*n.*); *Little* –, Kleinrußland (*n.*); – *in Asia*, Russisch-Asien *Autocrat of all the –s*, der Selbstherrscher aller Russen; – *leather*, der Juchten, das Juchtenleder. **–n,** Russe (*m.*); russisch (*adj.*). **–nize** [–naɪz], russifizieren (*v.a.*).
Ruthen–e [ruˈθɪːn], Ruthene (*m.*). **–ian,** ruthenisch (*adj.*).

S

Saarland [ˈsɑːlənd], das Saargebiet.
Sabaoth [sæˈbeɪɔθ], Zebaoth (*m.*); *Lord God of* – der Herr Zebaoth.
Sabine [ˈsæbaɪn], Sabiner (*m.*); sabinisch (*adj.*); *rape of the –s*, der Raub der Sabinerinnen.
Sadducee [ˈsædjʊsɪː], Sadduzäer (*m.*).
Sadowa [ˈsɑːdovə]; *battle of* –, die Schlacht bei Königgrätz (*n.*).
St. Gall [sənt ˈgɔːl], (*place*) Sankt Gallen (*n.*); (*person*) der heilige Gallus.
Sali–an [ˈseɪlɪən], Salier (*m.*); (*also* **–c** [ˈsælɪk]) salisch (*adj.*).
Sal(ly) [ˈsæl(ɪ)] (*dim. of* **Sarah**).
Sam [sæm] (*dim. of* **Samuel**); *Uncle* –,die Personifizierung der Vereinigten Staaten.
Samaritan [səˈmærɪtn], Samariter (*m.*); samaritisch (*adj.*); *the good* –, der barmherzige Samariter.
Samnite [ˈsæmnaɪt], Samniter (*m.*); samnitisch (*adj.*).
Samoan [səˈmouən], Samoaner (*m.*); samoanisch (*adj.*); – *islands*, die Samoa-Inseln.
Samoyed [səˈmɔɪɛd], Samojede (*m.*); samojedisch (*adj.*).
Samson [ˈsæmsən], Simson (*m.*).
Sandy [ˈsændɪ] (*dim. of* **Alexander**).
Sangraal [ˈsæŋgreɪl], der heilige Gral.
Sanskrit [ˈsænskrit], Sanskrit (*n.*); sanskritisch (*adj.*).
Santa Claus [ˈsæntə klɔːz], der heilige Nikolaus, Knecht Ruprecht.
Saracen [ˈsærəsn], Sarazene (*m.*); sarazenisch (*adj.*).
Sarah [ˈsɛərə], Sara (*f.*).
Sardanapalus [sɑːdəˈnæpələs], Sardanapal (*m.*).
Sardinian [sɑːˈdɪnɪən], Sardinier, Sarde (*m.*); sardinisch, sardisch (*adj.*).
Sarmatian [sɑːmeɪʃən], Sarmate (*m.*); sarmatisch (*adj.*).
Sassanidæ [sæˈsænɪdɪː], die Sassaniden (*pl.*).
Sassenach [ˈsæsənæk], Engländer (*m.*) (*term used by Scots in disparagement*).
Savoy [səˈvɔɪ], Savoyen (*n.*). **–ard** [–əd], Savoyer, Savoyarde (*m.*); savoyisch, Savoyer– (*adj.*).
Saxe [sæks]; **– –Coburg** [–ˈkoubəːg], Sachsen-Koburg (*n.*). **– –Meiningen** [–ˈmaɪnɪŋgən], Sachsen-Meiningen (*n.*). **– –Weimar** [–ˈvaɪmɑː], Sachsen-Weimar (*n.*).
Saxon [ˈsæksən], Sachse (*m.*); sächsisch (*adj.*). **–y** [ˈsæksənɪ], Sachsen (*n.*); *Electorate of* –, Kursachsen (*n.*); *Kingdom of* –, das Königreich Sachsen.
Scandinavia [skændɪˈneɪvɪə], Skandinavien (*n.*). **–n,** Skandinavier (*m.*); skandinavisch (*adj.*).
Scania [ˈskeɪnɪə], Schonen (*n.*).
Scheldt R. [skɛlt], Schelde (*f.*).
Scot [skɔt], Schotte (*m.*); **–ch** [skɔtʃ], schottisch (*adj.*) (*properly used only of foods and similar everyday things, though the English who know no better use it in all contexts*); *–ch broth*, Graupensuppe (*f*); *–ch heather*, die Hochlandsheide; *–ch mist*, Staubregen (*m.*). *–ch woodcock*, Rührei mit Anschovis; *–ch terrier*, *–ch whisky*, *etc.* **–chman** [–tʃmən], *see* **–sman** **–land** [ˈskɔtlənd], Schottland (*n.*); *–land Yard*, das Hauptpolizeiamt in London. **–s** [skɔts], Schottisch (*n.*), der schottische Dialekt; schottisch (*adj.*) (*commonly used by the Scots themselves, but rare in England except in a few set phrases such as* –s law, –s language); *–s Greys*, ein schottisches Reiterregiment. **–sman** [–smən], Schotte (*m.*). **–ticism** [ˈskɔtɪsɪzm], schottische Spracheigenheit. **–tish** [ˈskɔtɪʃ], schottisch (*adj.*) (*normal in Scotland, but dignified and literary in English usage, e.g.* –tish history, –tish literature, *etc.*)
Scylla [ˈsɪlə], Szylla (*f.*).
Scythian [ˈsɪðɪən], Szythe (*m.*); szythisch (*adj.*).
Seine R. [seɪn], Seine, (*f.*).
Seljuk [ˈsɛldʒʊk], Seldschuke (*m.*).
Semit–e [ˈsɪːmaɪt], Semit(e) (*m.*). **–ic** [sɪˈmɪtɪk], semitisch (*adj.*).
Sennacherib [səˈnækərɪb], Sanherib (*m.*).
Seoul [sɪˈuːl], Söul (*n.*).
Serb [səːb], *see* **–ian.** **–ia** [ˈsəːbɪə], Serbien (*n.*). **–ian,** Serbe (*m.*); serbisch (*adj.*).
Severn R. [ˈsɛvən], Severn (*m.*).
Seville [sɛˈvɪl], Sevilla (*n.*).
Seychelles (Islands) [seɪˈʃɛlz], die Seschellen (*pl.*).
Shalmaneser [ʃælməˈnɪːzə], Salmanassar (*m.*).
Shanghai [ʃæŋˈhaɪ], Schanghai (*n.*).
Shavian [ˈʃeɪvɪən], Bernard Shaw betreffend, Shawsch (*adj.*).
Sheba [ˈʃɪːbə], Saba (*n.*).
Shem [ʃɛm], Sem (*m.*).
Siamese [saɪəˈmɪːz], Siamese (*m.*); siamesisch (*adj.*); – *twins*, siamesische Zwillinge (*pl.*).
Siberia [saɪˈbɪərɪə], Sibirien (*n.*). **–n,** Sibirier (*m.*); sibirisch (*adj.*).
Sibyl [ˈsɪbɪl], **–la** [sɪˈbɪlə], Sibylle, Sibylla (*f.*).
Sicil–ian [sɪˈsɪlɪən], Sizilier (*m.*); sizilisch (*adj.*). **–y** [ˈsɪsɪlɪ], Sizilien (*n.*).
Sigismund [ˈsɪgɪsmənd], Sigismund, Siegmund (*m.*).
Silesia [saɪˈlɪːzɪə], Schlesien (*n.*). **–n,** Schlesier (*m*); schlesisch (*adj.*).
Silurian [saɪˈljʊərɪən], Silurier (*m.*); Silur (*n.*) (*Geol.*); silurisch (*adj.*).
Simon [ˈsaɪmən], Simon (*m.*); – *the Canaanite*, Simon von Kana; *Simple* –, der Dummerjan, Einfaltspinsel. – *Pure* or *the real* –, der wahre Jacob.
Singapore [sɪŋgəˈpɔː], Singapur (*n.*).
Singhalese [sɪŋgəˈlɪːz] Singhalese (*m.*); singhalesisch (*adj.*).
Sinn Fein [ʃɪn feɪn], die revolutionäre irische Nationalpartei.
Sion [ˈsaɪən], Sitten (*Switzerland*) (*n.*); Zion (*B.*).

Sistine ['sɪstaɪn], sixtinisch (*adj.*).
Slav [slɑ:v], Slawe (*m.*); slawisch (*adj.*). **-onian** [slə'vounɪən], **-onic** [slə'vɔnɪk], slawisch (*adj.*).
Sleeping Beauty ['slɪ:pɪŋ 'bju:tɪ], Dornröschen (*n.*).
Sleswig ['slɛzwɪg], Schleswig (*n.*); Schleswiger, schleswig(i)sch (*adj.*).
Slovak ['slouvæk], Slowake (*m.*); slowakisch (*adj.*). **-ia** [slou'veɪkɪə], die Slowakei.
Sloven-e ['slouvɪ:n], Slowene (*m.*); slowenisch (*adj.*). **-ian** [-'vɪ:nɪən], slowenisch (*adj.*).
Snow-White [snou'waɪt], Schneewittchen (*n.*).
Society Islands [sə'saɪətɪ], die Gesellschaftsinseln (*pl.*).
Socinian [so'sɪnɪən], Sozinianer (*m.*); sozinianisch (*adj.*).
Socrat-es ['sɔkrətɪ:z], Sokrates (*m.*). **-ic** [so'kræṭɪk], sokratisch (*adj.*).
Solomon ['sɔləmən], Salomo(n) (*m.*); *Song of* –, das hohe Lied Salomonis. – *Islands*, Salomoninseln (*pl.*).
Sophia [so'faɪə], **Sophy** ['soufɪ], Sophie (*f.*).
Sound [saund]; *the* –, der Sund.
South Sea [sauθ], die Südsee; – – *Islands*, die Südseeinseln, Ozeanien (*n.*).
Soviet ['souvɪət], Sowjet (*m.*); – *Russia*, Sowjetrußland (*n.*).
Spain [speɪn], Spanien (*n.*).
Spani-ard ['spænjəd], Spanier (*m.*). **-sh**, spanisch (*adj.*); *-sh chestnut*, Eßkastanie (*f.*); *-sh leather*, Saffian (*m.*).
Spartan ['spɑ:tən], Spartaner (*m.*); spartanisch (*adj.*).
Spice Islands [spaɪs], die Gewürzinseln, Molukken (*pl.*).
Spree R. [sprɪ:], Spree (*f.*).
Stephen, Steven ['stɪ:vn], Stephan (*m.*).
Strasbourg ['stræzbə:g], Straßburg (*n.*).
Styria ['stɪrɪə], die Steiermark. **-n**, Steiermärker, Steirer (*m.*); steiermärkisch, steirisch (*adj.*).
Styx R. [stɪks], Styx (*m.*).
Suabia, *see* **Swabia**.
Sudanese [su:də'nɪ:z], Sudaner (*m.*); sudanisch (*adj.*).
Sudetic Mts. [su'dɛtɪk], die Sudeten (*pl.*).
Sue [su:] (*dim. of* **Susan**)
Suevi ['swɪ:vaɪ], die Sueven (*pl.*).
Sumerian [sju:'mɪərɪən], Sumer(i)er (*m.*); sumerisch (*adj.*).
Susan(nah) ['su:zən (su:'zænə)], Susanne, Susanna (*f.*).
Susie ['su:zɪ] (*dim. of* **Susan**), Suschen (*n.*), Suse, Susi (*f.*).
Swabia ['sweɪbɪə], Schwaben (*n.*). **-n**, Schwabe (*m.*); schwäbisch (*adj.*); *-n emperors*, die Hohenstaufenkaiser (*pl.*).
Swed-e [swɪ:d], Schwede (*m.*). **-en** ['swɪ:dn], Schweden (*n.*). **-ish**, schwedisch (*adj.*).
Swedenborgian [swɪ:dn'bɔ:dʒɪən], Swedenborgianer (*m.*); swedenborgianisch (*adj.*).
Swiss [swɪs], Schweizer (*m.*); Schweizer–, schweizerisch (*adj.*); – *German*, das Schweizerdeutsch.
Switzerland ['swɪtsələnd], die Schweiz; *in* –, in der Schweiz.
Syracus-e ['saɪərəkju:z], Syrakus (*n.*). **-an**, Syrakuser (*m.*); syrakusisch (*adj.*).
Syria ['sɪrɪə], Syrien (*n.*). **-c** ['sɪrɪæk], **-n** [-ɪən], Syr(i)er (*m.*); syrisch (*adj.*).
Syrtis ['sə:tɪs], Syrte (*f.*); – *Major* (*Minor*), die Große (Kleine) Syrte.

T

Taal [tɑ:l], die Burensprache.
Tabitha [tə'bɪ:θə], Tabea (*f.*).
Table Mountain ['teɪbl], der Tafelberg.
Taffy ['tæfɪ] (*for* **David**), (*Welshman*) Walliser (*m.*).
Tagus R. ['teɪgəs], Tajo, Tejo (*m.*).
Tamburlaine, Tamerlane ['tæmə:leɪn], Tamerlan (*m.*).
Tamil ['tæmɪl], Tamule (*m.*); tamulisch (*adj.*).
Tangier(s) [tæn'dʒɪə(z)], Tanger (*n.*).
Taranto [tə'ræntou], Tarent (*n.*).
Tarpeian [tɑ:'pɪ:ən], tarpejisch (*adj.*).
Tarsian ['tɑ:sɪən], Tarser (*m.*); tarsisch (*adj.*).
Tartar ['tɑ:tə], Tatar (*m.*); tatarisch (*adj.*); (*coll.*) *catch a* –, übel ankommen, an den Unrechten kommen. **-y** ['tɑ:tərɪ], die Tatarei.
Tasmanian [tæz'meɪnɪən], Tasmane (*m.*); tasmanisch (*adj.*).
Tauric Chersonese ['tɔ:rɪk'kə:sənɪ:z], die taurische Halbinsel, Tauris, Taurien (*n.*).
Ted(dy) ['tɛd(ɪ)] (*dim.* of **Edward**); – *bear*, der Teddybär.
Telemachus [tɪ'lɛməkəs], Telemach (*m.*).
Teneriffe [tɛnə'rɪ:f], Teneriffa (*n.*).
Terence ['tɛrəns], Terenz (*m.*).
Terry ['tɛrɪ] (*dim. of* **Terence**).
Tess (*dim. of* **T(h)eresa**).
Teuton ['tju:tən], Germane, Teutone (*m.*). **-ic** [-'tɔnɪk], germanisch, teutonisch (*adj.*); *-ic Order*, der Deutsche Orden, Deutschritterorden; *Knights of the -ic Order*, die Deutschherren, Deutschritter (*pl.*).
Thaddeus ['θædɪəs], Thaddäus (*m.*).
Thames R. [tɛmz], Themse (*f.*); *he will not set the – on fire*, er wird die Welt nicht aus den Angeln heben, er hat das Pulver nicht erfunden.
Thebaid [θɪ'beɪɪd], Thebais (*n.*) (*in Egypt*).
Theb-an ['θɪ:bən], Thebaner (*m.*); thebanisch (*adj.*). **-es** [θɪ:bz], Theben (*n.*).
Theo ['θɪ:ou] (*dim. of* **Theobald, Theodore, Theophilus**).
Theocritus [θɪ:'ɔkrɪtəs], Theokrit (*m.*).
Theodore ['θɪədɔ:], Theodor (*m.*).
Theodoric [θɪ:'ɔdərɪk], Theodorich, Theoderich; — *of Verona*, Dietrich von Bern (*in legend*); Theodorich der Große (*in history*).
Theophilus [θɪ'ɔfɪləs], Gottlieb (*m.*).
Theresa [tə'rɪ:zə], Therese, Theresia (*f.*).
Thermopylae [θə:'mɔpɪlɪ:], die Thermopylen (*pl.*).
Thessal-ian [θə'seɪlɪən], Thessalier (*m.*); thessalisch (*adj.*). **-onian** [θɛsə'lounɪən], Thessalonicher (*m.*). **-onica** [θɛsəlo'naɪkə, -'lɔnɪkə], Thessalonich, Thessaloniki (*n.*). **-y** ['θɛsəlɪ], Thessalien (*n.*).
Thrac-e [θreɪs], Thrazien (*n.*). **-ian** ['θreɪʃən], Thrazier (*m.*); thrazisch (*adj.*).
Thurgovia [θə:'gouvɪə], Thurgau (*m.*). **-n**, Thurgauer (*m.*), thurgauisch (*adj.*).
Thuringia [θjuə'rɪndʒɪə], Thüringen (*n.*). **-n**, Thüringer (*m.*); thüringisch (*adj.*).
Tiber R. ['taɪbə], Tiber (*m.*).
Ticino R. [tɪ'tʃɪ:nou], Tessin (*n.*).
Tierra del Fuego [tɪ'ɛrə dəl fu'eɪgou], Feuerland (*n.*).
Tigris R. ['taɪgrɪs], Tigris (*m.*).
Tilly ['tɪlɪ] (*dim. of* **Matilda**), Thilde (*f.*).
Timbuctoo [tɪmbʌk'tu:], Timbuktu (*m.*).
Timothy ['tɪməθɪ], Timotheus (*m.*).
Titian ['tɪʃən], Tizian (*m.*).
Tob-ias [to'baɪəs], **-it** (*dim.* **-y**), Tobias (*m.*); *Book of Tobit*, das Buch Tobiä.
Tokay (wine) [tou'keɪ], der Tokaier, Tokajer.
Tom-(my) ['tɔm(ɪ)] (*dim. of* **Thomas** ['tɔməs]); –, *Dick and Harry*, Hinz und Kunz; – *Fool*, Einfaltspinsel (*m.*); – *Thumb*, Däumling (*m.*); *-my Atkins*, der (englische) gemeine Soldat; *-my rot*, (*coll.*) Quatsch (*m.*).
Tony ['tounɪ] (*dim. of* **Anthony**), Toni (*m.*).
Trans-caspian, transkaspisch (*adj.*). **-caucasian**, transkaukasisch (*adj.*). **-jordan**, Transjordanien (*n.*). **--siberian**, transsibirisch (*adj.*).
Transylvania ['trænsɪl'veɪnɪə], Siebenbürgen (*n.*). **-n**, Siebenbürger (*m.*); siebenbürgisch (*adj.*).
Trebizond ['trɛbɪzɔnd], Trapezunt (*n.*).
[1]**Trent R.** [trɛnt], Trent (*m.*).
[2]**Trent**, Trient (*n.*); *Council of* –, das Tridentiner Konzil.
Trieste [trɪ'ɛst], Triest (*n.*).
Tripoli ['trɪpəlɪ], Tripolis (*n.*). **-tan** [-'pɔlɪtən], Tripolitaner (*m.*); tripolitanisch (*adj.*).
Tristram ['trɪstrəm], Tristan (*m.*).
Trixy (*dim. of* **Beatrice**), Beate (*f.*).
Troad ['trouæd], Troas (*n.*).
Trojan ['troudʒen], Trojaner (*m.*); trojanisch (*adj.*); *like a* –, wacker; – *war*, der Trojanerkrieg.

Troy [trɔɪ], Troja (*n.*); *Helen of –*, die schöne Helena.
Tully [ˈtʌlɪ], Tullius (*m.*).
Tunisia [tjuˈnɪzɪə], Tunis (*n.*). **-n** [tjuˈnɪzɪən], Tuneser, Tunisier (*m.*); tunesisch, tunisisch (*adj.*).
Turcoman [ˈtəːkəmən], Turkmene (*m.*).
Turk [təːk], Türke (*m.*). **-estan** [təːkɪˈstɑːn], Turkestan, Turkistan (*n.*). **-ey** [ˈtəːkɪ], die Türkei; *-ey in Asia*, die asiatische Türkei.
Tuscan [ˈtʌskən], Toskaner (*m.*); toskanisch (*adj.*) **-y** [ˈtʌskənɪ], Toskana (*n.*).
Tweed R. [twɪːd], Tweed (*m.*).
Tyne R. [tɑɪn], Tyne (*m.*).
Tyr-e [tɑɪə], Tyrus (*n.*). **-ian** [ˈtɪrɪən], Tyrier (*m.*); tyrisch (*adj.*).
Tyrol [ˈtɪrəl]; *the –*, Tirol (*n.*). **-ese** [–ˈlɪːz], Tiroler (*m.*); tirolisch, Tiroler– (*adj.*).
Tzigane [tsɪˈgɑːn], Zigeuner (*m.*); zigeunerhaft, zigeunerisch Zigeuner– (*adj.*).

U

Ukraine [juːˈkreɪn], die Ukraine.
Ulrica [ʌlˈrɪːkə], Ulrike (*f.*).
Umbrian [ˈʌmbrɪən], Umbrier (*m.*); umbrisch (*adj.*).
United States [juˈnɑɪtɪd ˈsteɪts], die Vereinigten Staaten.
Uriah [juˈrɑɪə], Uria(s) (*m.*).
Ursuline [ˈəːsjulɪːn] (*nun*), Ursulinerin (*f.*); ursulinisch, Ursulinen– (*adj.*).

V

Vaal R. [vɑːl], Waal (*f.*).
Valais [ˈvæleɪ], Wallis (*n.*). **-an** [væˈleɪzən], Walliser (*m.*); wallisisch (*adj.*).
Valentine [ˈvæləntɑɪn], Valentin (*m.*).
Valhalla [vælˈhælə], Walhall(a) (*f.*).
Valkyrie [ˈvælkɪrɪ], die Walküre.
Vandal [ˈvændəl], Wandale (*m.*). **-ic** [vænˈdælɪk], wandalisch (*adj.*).
Varangian [vəˈrændʒɪən], Waräger (*m.*).
Vatican [ˈvætɪkən], der Vatikan; vatikanisch (*adj.*).
Vaud [vou], Waadt(land) (*n.*). **-ois** [voˈdwɑ], Waadtländer (*m.*); waadtländisch (*adj.*).
Vehm-e [feɪm], die Feme; (*-ic court*) das Femgericht.
Venetia [vɪˈnɪːʃjə], Venetien (*n.*). **-n** [–ʃn], Venezianer, Venediger (*m.*); venetianisch, venedisch (*adj.*).
Venice [ˈvɛnɪs], Venedig (*n.*).
Verde [vəːd], **Cape**, das Grüne Vorgebirge.
Vesuvi-an [vɪˈsjuːvɪən], vesuvisch (*adj.*). **-us** [vɪˈsjuːvɪəs], Vesuv (*m.*).
Vic(ky) [ˈvɪk(ɪ)] (*dim. of* **Victoria**).
Victoria [vɪkˈtɔːrɪə], Viktoria (*f.*). **-n,** viktorianisch.
Vienn-a [vɪˈɛnə], Wien (*n.*). **-ese** [vɪəˈnɪːz], Wiener (*m.*); Wiener–, wienerisch (*adj.*).
Viking [ˈvɑɪkɪŋ], Wiking (*m.*).
Vincent [ˈvɪnsənt], Vinzenz (*m.*).
Virgil [ˈvəːdʒɪl], Vergil (*m.*).
Vishnu [ˈvɪʃnuː], Wischnu (*m.*).
Visigoth [ˈvɪzɪgɔθ], Westgote (*m.*). **-ic** [–ˈgɔθɪk], westgotisch (*adj.*).
Vistula R. [ˈvɪstjulə], Weichsel (*f.*).
Vitus [ˈvɑɪtəs], Veit (*m.*); *St. –'s dance*, der Veitstanz.
Volga R. [ˈvɔlgə], Wolga (*f.*).
Vosges [vouʒ], die Vogesen (*pl.*).

W

Wagnerite [ˈvɑːgnərɑɪt], Wagnerianer (*m.*).
Waldenses [wɔːlˈdɛnsɪːz], Waldenser (*pl.*).
Wallachia [ˈwɔleɪkɪə], die Walachei. **-n,** Walache (*m.*); walachisch (*adj.*).
Walloon [wɔˈluːn], Wallone (*m.*); wallonisch (*adj.*).
Wally [wɔːlɪ] (*dim. of* **Walter**), Wälti (*m.*).
Walter [ˈwɔːltə], Walter, Walther (*m.*).
Warsaw [ˈwɔːsɔː], Warschau (*n.*).
Wat(tie) [ˈwɔt(ɪ)] (*dim. of* **Walter**).
Wayland Smith [ˈweɪlənd], Wieland der Schmied.
Welsh [welʃ], walisisch, Waliser (*adj.*); *the –*, die Waliser (*pl.*). **-man** [–mən], Waliser (*m.*).
Wenceslas [ˈwɛnsɪsləs], Wenzel, Wenzeslaus (*m.*).
Wend [wɛnd], Wende (*m.*); wendisch (*adj.*).
Weser R. [ˈveɪzə], Weser (*f.*).
Wesleyan [ˈwɛslɪən], Wesleyaner, Methodist (*m.*); wesleyanisch, methodistisch (*adj.*).
West Indies [wɛst ˈɪndɪz], Westindien (*n.*).
Westphalia [wɛstˈfeɪlɪə], Westfalen (*n.*); *Peace of –*, der westfälische Friede. **-n,** Westfale (*m.*); westfälisch (*adj.*).
Wilfred, Wilfrid [ˈwɪlfrɪd], Wilfried (*m.*).
Wilhelmina [wɪlhelˈmɪːnə], Wilhelmine (*f.*).
Will [wɪl] (*dim. of* **-iam**), Willi (*m.*). **-iam** [ˈwɪlɪəm], Wilhelm (*m.*). **-ie, -y** [ˈwɪlɪ] (*dim., see* **–**).
Wilton [ˈwɪltən]; *– carpet*, der Plüschteppich.
Win-ifred [ˈwɪnɪfrɪd] (*dim.* **-nie** [ˈwɪnɪ]), Winfried (*f.*).
Woden [ˈwoudn], Wodan, Wotan (*m.*).
Wurtemberg [ˈwəːtəmbəːg], Württemberg (*n.*). **-ian** [–ˈbəːgɪən], Württemberger (*m.*); würtembergisch (*adj.*).

X

Xavier [ˈzævɪə], Xaver (*m.*).

Y

Yangtze-kiang R. [ˈjæŋtsɪːˈkjæŋ], Jangtsekiang (*m.*).
Yankee [ˈjæŋkɪ], Yankee, Neu-Engländer (*m.*); (*coll.*) (*British usage*) Nordamerikaner (*m.*); *– Doodle*, amerikanisches Nationallied; *– States*, die Nordstaaten. (*coll.*) **-fied**, amerikanisiert (*adj.*). **-ism** [–ɪzm], amerikanische Eigentümlichkeit, amerikanische Spracheigenheit.
Yemen [ˈjeɪmən], Jemen (*n.*).
Yenisei R. [jɛnɪˈseɪɪ], Jenissej (*m.*).
Yiddish [ˈjɪdɪʃ], Jiddisch (*n. & adj.*).
Ypres [ˈɪːpr], Ypern (*n.*).
Yugoslavia [ˈjuːgouˈslɑːvɪə], Jugoslavien (*n.*).

Z

Zaccheus [zæˈkɪːəs], Zachäus (*m.*).
Zachar-iah [zækəˈrɑɪə], **-y** [ˈzækərɪ], Zacharias, Sacharja (*m.*).
Zambezi R. [zæmˈbɪːzɪ], Sambesi (*m.*).
Zamiel [ˈzæmɪəl], Samiel (*m.*).
Zanzibar [zænzɪˈbɑː], Sansibar (*n.*).
Zealand [ˈzɪːlənd], Seeland (*n.*). **-er** [–ə], Seeländer (*m.*).
Zebedee [ˈzɛbɪdɪː], Zebedäus (*m.*).
Zechariah [zɛkəˈrɑɪə], Sacharja (*m.*).
Zend [zɛnd], die Zendsprache; *– Avesta*, Zendawesta (*n.*).
Zephaniah [zɛfəˈnɑɪə], Zephanja (*m.*).
Zion [ˈzɑɪən], Zion (*m.*).
Zouave [zuːˈɑːv], Zuave (*m.*).
Zuleikah [zuːˈlɑɪkə], Suleika (*f.*).
Zurich [ˈzjuərɪk], Zürich (*n.*); züricherisch, Zürich–; (*Swiss dial.*) zürcherisch, Zürcher (*adj.*); *Lake of –*, der Züricher See; (*Swiss dial.*) Zürcher See, Zürichsee.
Zuyder Zee [ˈzɑɪdə zɪː], die *or* der Zuidersee.

STRONG AND ANOMALOUS VERBS

* = archaic or poetic. *A = archaic or poetic except as attributive adjective. R = rare. S = slang.

Infinitive	Past Indicative	Past Participle
abide	abode (*sometimes* abided)	abode (*sometimes* abided)
arise	arose	arisen
awake	awoke	awoke *or* awaked
be (*Pres. Ind.* am, are, is)	was, were	been
bear	bore	borne (born[1])
beat	beat	beaten[2]
become	became	become
beget	begot	begotten
begin	began	begun
bend	bent	bent[3]
bereave	bereave *or* bereft	bereaved *or* bereft
beseech	besought	besought
bestride	bestrode	bestridden *or* bestrode *or* bestrid
bid	bade *or* bid	bidden *or* bid
bide	bided *or* bode	bided
bind	bound	bound (*A bounden)
bite	bit	bitten (*sometimes* bit)
bleed	bled	bled
blow	blew	blown (S blowed)
break	broke (*brake)	broken (*sometimes* broke)
breed	bred	bred
bring	brought	brought
build	built	built
burn	burnt (*sometimes* burned)	burnt (*sometimes* burned)
burst	burst	burst
buy	bought	bought
Pres. Ind. can[4]	could	——[5]
cast	cast	cast
catch	caught	caught
chide	chid	chidden *or* chid
choose	chose	chosen
cleave (*v.a.* = *split*)	cleft *or* clove	cleft *or* cloven[6]
cleave (*v.n.* = *cling*)	cleaved *or* clave	cleaved
cling	clung	clung
clothe	clothed *or* clad	clothed *or* clad
come	came	come
cost	cost	cost
creep	crept	crept
crow	crowed *or* crew	crowed
cut	cut	cut
dare[7]	dared (*sometimes*[8] durst)	dared
deal	dealt	dealt
dig	dug (*digged)	dug (*digged)
do[9]	did[10]	done
draw	drew	drawn
dream	dreamt *or* dreamed	dreamt *or* dreamed
drink	drank	drunk (*A drunken)

Infinitive	Past Indicative	Past Participle
drive	drove	driven
dwell	dwelt	dwelt
eat	ate[11]	eaten
fall	fell	fallen
feed	fed	fed
feel	felt	felt
fight	fought	fought
find	found	found
flee	fled	fled
fling	flung	flung
fly	flew	flown
forbear	forbore	forborne
forbid	forbade *or* forbad	forbidden
forget	forgot	forgotten (*forgot)
forgive	forgave	forgiven
forsake	forsook	forsaken
freeze	froze	frozen
get	got	got (*A *and Amer.* gotten[12])
gird	girded or girt	girden *or* girt
give	gave	given
go	went	gone
grind	ground	ground
grow	grew	grown
hang (*v.n.*[13])	hung	hung
have[14]	had	had
hear	heard	heard
heave	heaved *or* hove	heaved *or* hove
hew	hewed	hewn *or* hewed
hide	hid	hidden *or* hid
hit	hit	hit
hold	held	held (*holden)
hurt	hurt	hurt
keep	kept	kept
kneel	knelt	knelt
knit	knitted *or* knit	knitted *or* knit[15]
know	knew	known
lade	laded	laden
lay	laid	laid
lead	led	led
lean	leant *or* leaned	leant *or* leaned
leap	leaped *or* leapt	leaped *or* leapt
learn	learned *or* learnt	learned *or* learnt
leave	left	left
lend	lent	lent
let	let	let
lie (= *recline*[16])	lay	lain
light	lit *or* lighted	lit *or* lighted[17]
lose	lost	lost
make	made	made
Pres. Ind. may[18]	might	—
mean	meant	meant
meet	met	met
melt	melted	melted (*A molten)
mow	mowed	mown
Pres. Ind. must[19]	—	—
pay	paid	paid
put	put	put (*dial.* putten)
quit	quitted *or* quit	quitted *or* quit

[1] *Used passively of birth except with 'by' referring to the mother, and also as predic. adj.* [2] *but* dead-beat. [3] *but* on bended knees. [4] *negative* cannot *or* can't. [5] *defective parts supplied from* be able to. [6] *as attrib. adj.* cloven hoof, cleft stick. [7] *3rd pers. sing. usually* dare *when before infin.* (*expressed or implied*) *without* 'to'; *otherwise* dares. [8] *though only before infin. without* 'to'. [9] do not *is commonly* don't; does not *is commonly* doesn't (don't *is vulgar*). [10] did not *is commonly* didn't. [11] *pron.* [ɛt]; *or* [eɪt](*Amer.*). [12] ill-gotten gains. [13] *v.a.* = execute by hanging *is regular.* [14] *negative is commonly* haven't, hasn't. [15] well-knit. [16] = to tell a lie *the verb is regular.* [17] *the latter is usual as an attrib. adj.* [18] *when expressing permission the negative is* must not *or* cannot. [19] *when expressing* be obliged *the negative is* need not.

Infinitive	Past Indicative	Past Participle
—	quoth[1]	—
read	read[2]	read[2]
rend	rent	rent
rid	rid *or* ridded	rid (R ridded)
ride	rode (*rid)	ridden (*rid)
ring	rang (R rung)	rung
rise	rose	risen
rive	rived	riven (R rived)
run	ran	run
saw	sawed	sawn *or* sawed
say	said	said
see	saw	seen
seek	sought	sought
sell	sold	sold
send	sent	sent
set	set	set
shake	shook	shaken
Pres. Ind. shall[3]	should[4]	—
shape	shaped	shaped (*shapen)
shear	sheared (*shore)	shorn *or* sheared
shed	shed	shed
shine	shone	shone
shoe	shod	shod
shoot	shot	shot
show (shew)	showed (shewed)	shown (shewn) *or* showed (shewed)
shrink	shrank	shrunk (*A shrunken)
shut	shut	shut
sing	sang (R sung)	sung
sink	sank (R sunk)	sunk (*A sunken)
sit	sat	sat
slay	slew	slain
sleep	slept	slept
slide	slid	slid
sling	slung	slung
slink	slunk (R slank)	slunk
slit	slit	slit
smell	smelt *or* smelled	smelt *or* smelled
smite	smote (*smit)	smitten (*smit)
sow	sowed	sown *or* sowed
speak	spoke (*spake)	spoken
speed	sped[5] *or* speeded[6]	sped[5] *or* speeded[6]
spell	spelt *or* spelled	spelt *or* spelled
spend	spent	spent
spill	spilled *or* spilt	spilled *or* spilt
spin	spun *or* span	spun

Infinitive	Past Indicative	Past Participle
spit *v.n. & a.* (= *expectorate*[7])	spat (*spit)	spat (*spit)
split	split	split
spread	spread	spread
spring	sprang	sprung
stand	stood	stood
stave	staved *or* stove	staved *or* stove
steal	stole	stolen
stick	stuck	stuck
sting	stung	stung
stink	stank *or* stunk	stunk
strew	strewed	strewed *or* strewn
stride	strode	strided (R stridden *or* strid)
strike	struck	struck (*A stricken[8])
string	strung	strung
strive	strove	striven
*strow	*strowed	*strown *or* strowed
swear	swore (*sware)	sworn
sweep	swept	swept
swell	swelled	swollen *or* swelled
swim	swam	swum
swing	swung (R swang)	swung
take	took	taken
teach	taught	taught
tear	tore	torn
tell	told	told
think	thought	thought
thrive	thrived *or* throve	thrived *or* thriven
throw	threw	thrown
thrust	thrust	thrust
tread	trod (*trode)	trodden
wake	woke *or* waked	waked *or* woken *or* woke
wear	wore	worn
weave	wove	woven (*A wove[9])
weep	wept	wept
will[10]	would[11]	—
win	won	won
wind	wound	wound
work	worked (*wrought[12])	worked (*wrought[12])
wring	wrung	wrung
write	wrote (*writ)	written (*writ)

[1] *1st and 3rd pers. sing.* (*rarely pl.*). [2] *pron.* [rɛd]. [3] *negative* shall not *or* shan't. [4] *negative* should not *or* shouldn't. [5] = go *or* send fast. [6] = regulate the speed (*of engines, etc.*). [7] *v.a.* = put on a spit *is regular*. [8] stricken with fever. [9] *chiefly for trade-processes, e.g.* vellum-wove paper. [10] *negative* will not *or* won't. [11] *negative* would not *or* wouldn't. [12] *archaic except of the craftsman's work in some materials, e.g.* wrought in brass.

ENGLISH–GERMAN APPENDIX

The sign † against a word shows that it has already been given in the Dictionary, although not necessarily in the same grammatical form.

ablation [æ'bleɪʃən], *s.* das Abschmelzen (*of snow*), die Abtragung (*of rock*); Amputation, operative Entfernung (*Surg.*).

abomasum [æbo'meɪsəm], *s.* der Labmagen.

abortionist [ə'bɔːʃənɪst], *s.* der Abtreiber.

abreact [æbrɪ'ækt], *v.n.* abreagieren.

activation [æktɪ'veɪʃən], *s.* die Aktivierung, Erregung, Anregung.

activist ['æktɪvɪst], *s.* der Aktivist.

actualize ['æktjuəlɑɪz], *v.a.* verwirklichen; realistisch darstellen.

actuarial [æktju'ɛərɪəl], *adj.* versicherungsstatistisch; – *rate*, die Tafelziffer.

acupuncture ['ækjupʌŋktʃə], *s.* die Nadelpunktierung, Akupunktur.

additive ['ædɪtɪv], *adj.* vermehrend, steigernd, hinzufügend.

ad-lib, 1. *adv.* nach Belieben. 2. *v.n.* extemporieren, improvisieren.

ad-man, *s.* (*coll.*) der Werbefachmann.

ad-mass, *s.* (*coll.*) das Massenpublikum.

advice bureau, *s.* die Beratungsstelle.

aero-dynamicist, *s.* der Aerodynamiker.

aero-embolism, *s.* die Luftembolie, Höhenkrankheit.

aero-engine, *s.* der Flug(zeug)motor.

afterburning, *s.* das Nachbrennen, die Nachverbrennung.

agamic [ə'gæmɪk], **agamous** ['ægəməs], *adj.* geschlechtlos, ungeschlechtlich.

aide-memoire, *s.* die Denkschrift; Notiz, Gedächtnisstütze.

airarm, *s.* die Luftstreitkräfte (*pl.*).

air-attack, *s.* der Luftangriff, Fliegerangriff.

air-compressor, *s.* der Preßlufterzeuger, Luftverdichter.

air-corridor, *s.* die Einflugschneise.

air-drop, *s.* der Abwurf vom Flugzeug.

air-foil, *s.* die Tragfläche; – *section*, das Tragflächenprofil.

air-inlet, air-intake, *s.* der Lufteinlaß, Lufteintritt.

air-lift, *s.* die Luftbrücke.

air-pollution, *s.* die Luftverunreinigung.

air-pressure, *s.* der Luftdruck, Atmosphärendruck.

air-raid warning, *s.* der Fliegeralarm.

air-strip, *s.* die Landebahn, Rollbahn, der Behelfsflugplatz.

air-terminal, *s.* der Großflughafen.

all-clear, *s.* (*coll.*) das Entwarnungssignal, die Entwarnung.

allergic [ə'lɜːdʒɪk], *adj.* allergisch; – *to*, überempfindlich gegen.

all-purpose, *adj.* Allzweck—, Mehrzweck—.

all-time, *adj.* (*coll.*) beispiellos, noch nie dagewesen, bisher unerreicht.

ambience ['æmbɪəns], *s.* die Umwelt, Umgebung; das Ambiente (*Art*).

ambivalence, ambivalency [æm'bɪvələns(ɪ)], *s.* die Doppelwertigkeit, Ambivalenz.

ambivalent, *adj.* doppelwertig, ambivalent.

ammo ['æmou], *s.* (*sl.*) die Muni(tion); – *boots*, die Kommißstiefel.

amperage [æm'pɛərɪdʒ], *s.* die Amperezahl, Stromstärke.

amphetamine [æm'fɛtəmiːn], *s.* das Benzedrin (*Chem.*).

amphoric [æm'fɔrɪk], *adj.* hohlklingend (*breathing, etc.*) (*Med.*).

ampoule [æm'puːl], *s.* die Ampulle (*Med.*).

anabatic [ænə'bætɪk], *adj.* nach oben ziehend (*Meteor.*); zunehmend (*fever*) (*Med.*); – *wind*, der Aufwind (*Meteor.*).

anachronistic [ə'nækrənɪstɪk], *adj.* anachronistisch.

anacrusis [ænə'kruːsɪs], *s.* der Vorschlag, Auftakt (*Metr.*).

anodize ['ænədɑɪz], *v.a.* eloxieren, anodisieren.

anorak ['ænəræk], *s.* der Anorak, die Windjacke.

antibiotic [æntɪbɑɪ'ɔtɪk], *s.* das Antibiotikum.

anticline ['æntɪklɑɪn], *s.* der Sattel.

anti-corrosive, *adj.* korrosionsfrei.

anti-dazzle lamp, *s.* die Blendschutzlampe.

anti-fouling paint, *s.* die Unterwassergleitfarbe.

anti-glare, *adj.* blendsicher; – *goggles*, die Blendschutzbrille.

anti-personnel, *adj.* gegen Menschen gerichtet; – *bomb*, die Splitterbombe; – *mine*, die Tretmine.

anti-skid, *adj.* Gleitschutz—.

apartheid [ə'pɑːteɪt], *s.* der Apartheid, die Rassentrennung.

apologia [æpə'loudʒə], *s.* die Entschuldigung, Abbitte; Ehrenerklärung.

aqualung ['ækwəlʌŋ], *s.* die Taucherlunge.

arc welding, *s.* das Lichtbogenschweißen.

arrester gear, *s.* das Fangkabel, Gummiseil.

arrester hook, *s.* der Fanghaken.

arty ['ɑːtɪ], *adj.* künstlerartig; (*coll.*) *--crafty*, kunstgewerblich, 'handgewebt'.

asexual [eɪ'sɛksjuəl], *adj.* geschlechtlos.

astrodome ['æstrədoum], *s.* die Astro(navigations)-kuppel.

astronaut ['æstrənɔːt], *s.* der Astronaut, Weltraumfahrer.

astrophysics [æstrə'fɪzɪks], *s.* die Astrophysik.

atavistic [ætə'vɪstɪk], *adj.* atavistisch.

atomic energy, *s.* die Atomenergie.

atomic fall-out, *s.* radioaktiver Niederschlag.

atomic fuel, *s.* der Kernbrennstoff, Atombrennstoff.

atomic number, *s.* die Ordnungszahl, Kernladungszahl.

atomic pile, *s.* der Atommeiler, die Atombatterie.

atomic power-plant or **power-station**, *s.* das Atomkraftwerk.

atomic reactor, *s.* der Atomreaktor.

atomic structure, *s.* der Atomaufbau, das Atomgitter.

atomic war(fare), *s.* der Atomkrieg, die Atomkriegführung.

atomic warhead, *s.* der Atomsprengkopf.

attested [ə'tɛstɪd], *adj.* erwiesen, bezeugt, bescheinigt, beglaubigt, bestätigt.

audiometer [ɔːdɪ'ɔmɪtə], *s.* der Audiometer.

audiomonitor [ɔːdɪo'mɔnɪtə], *s.* der Tonüberwacher.

audio-visual aids, *s. pl.* das Anschauungsmaterial.

authoritarianism [ɔːθɔrɪ'tɛərɪənɪzm], *s.* das Führerprinzip.

autoclave ['ɔːtokleɪv], *s.* der Dampfkochtopf.

automat ['ɔːtəmæt], *s.* der (Nahrungsmittel)Automat, das Automatenbüfett.

automated ['ɔːtəmeɪtɪd], *adj.* automatisiert.

automatic control, *s.* die Selbststeuerung.

automatic drive, *s.* der Selbstantrieb.

automation [ɔːtə'meɪʃən], *s.* die Automation, Automatisierung.

auxiliary rocket, *s.* die Zusatzrakete.

B

babysitter, *s.* der (die) Kinderhüter(in), Babysitter.

babysitting, *s.* das Kinderhüten.

backlog, *s.* der (Arbeits)Rückstand.

back-seat driver, *s.* der Mitfahrer, der alles besser wissen will als der Fahrer; Besserwisser.
ball-point (pen), *s.* der Kugelschreiber.
bargain basement, *s.* die Abteilung mit verbilligten Artikeln.
barograph [ˈbærəgrɑ:f], *s.* der Höhenschreiber, Barograph.
battle fatigue, *s.* die Frontneurose, Kriegsneurose.
beach buggy, *s.* der Dünebuggy.
beat music, *s.* der Beatjazz.
beatnik [ˈbi:tnɪk], *s.* (*coll.*) der Gammler.
†**beef,** *v.n.* meckern, sich beklagen.
belt conveyor, *s.* das Förderband.
belt up, *v.n.* (*coll.*) die Klappe halten.
bifocals [ˈbaɪfoukl̩z], **bifocal spectacles,** *s. pl.* die Bifokalgläser (*pl.*).
bikini [bɪˈki:nɪ], *s.* der Bikini, zweiteiliger Badeanzug.
biogenesis [baɪoˈdʒɛnəsɪs], *s.* die Biogenesis.
biogenetic [baɪodʒəˈnɛtɪk], *adj.* biogenetisch.
biosynthesis [baɪoˈsɪnθəsɪs], *s.* die Biosynthese.
bipartisan [baɪˈpɑ:tɪzæn], *adj.* Zweiparteien—.
bird-bath, *s.* die Vogeltränke.
bird-sanctuary, *s.* das Vogelschutzgebiet.
bird-table, *s.* der Futtertisch.
bird-watching, *s.* die Vogelbeobachtung.
bituminize [bɪˈtju:mɪnaɪz], *v.a.* bituminieren, mit Erdpech bestreichen; asphaltieren.
bleep [bli:p], 1. *s.* das Sputnikfunksignal, der Sputnik. 2. *v.n.* funken.
blind spot, *s.* (*fig.*) wunder Punkt.
blip [blɪp], *s.* (*coll.*) das Echozeichen, der Leuchtfleck (*radar, etc.*).
blood-bank, *s.* die Blutbank.
blood clot, *s.* das Blutgerinnsel.
blood group, *s.* die Blutgruppe.
blood plasma, *s.* die Blutflüssigkeit.
blowback, *s.* der Rückstoß, Gasdruck.
blue-pencil, *v.a.* (*coll.*) ausstreichen, korrigieren; zensieren.
†**blues,** *s.* der Blues (*Mus.*).
body-work, *s.* die Karosserie.
boffin [ˈbɔfɪn], *s.* (*sl.*) (vom Kriegsministerium beauftragter) Technokrat.
boiler-suit, *s.* der Overall.
bolt-hole, *s.* (*fig.*) das Schlupfloch.
bonanza [bəˈnænzə], *s.* (*coll.*) das Glück, der Glücksfall.
bone-idle, *adj.* stinkfaul.
†**boomerang,** *v.n.* (*fig.*) zum eigenen Schaden gereichen.
†**boot,** *s.* (*of a car*) der Gepäckraum.
boss-eyed, *adj.* (*fig.*) schief, einseitig.
bottle-party, *s.* die Bottle-Party.
†**bouncer,** *s.* (*coll.*) der Rausschmeißer.
boxroom, *s.* die Rumpelkammer.
brain-child, *s.* (*coll.*) das Geistesprodukt.
brainwash, *v.a.* Gehirnwäsche vornehmen bei.
brainwashing, *s.* die Gehirnwäsche.
breathalyser [ˈbrɛθəlaɪzə], *s.* das Alkoholtest-röhrchen.
breathing apparatus, *s.* das Sauerstoffgerät.
breech presentation, *s.* die Steißlage (*Med.*).
†**briefs,** *s. pl.* der (Damen)Schlüpfer, Slip.
brightness control, *s.* die Helligkeitsregelung, Helligkeitssteuerung (*T.V.*).
brinkmanship [ˈbrɪŋkmənʃɪp], *s.* (politische) Seiltanzerei.
brisling [ˈbrɪzlɪŋ], *s.* der Brisling, die Sprotte.
broiler [ˈbrɔɪlə], *s.* das Brathuhn, Brathähnchen.
brunch [brʌntʃ], *s.* (*coll.*) spätes und erweitertes Frühstück, das Gabelfrühstück.
bubble-bath, *s.* das Schaumbad.
bubble-car, *s.* der Kleinstwagen.
bubble-gum, *s.* das Knall(kau)gummi.
bucket seat, *s.* der Schalensitz.
budgerigar [ˈbʌdʒərɪgɑ:], *s.* der Wellensittich.
built-in, *adj.* umbaut; eingebaut; Einbau—.
burn-out, *s.* der Brennschluß.
burp [bə:p], 1. *s.* (*coll.*) der Rülpser. 2. *v.n.* rülpsen.
businessman, *s.* der Geschäftsmann.
business reply card, *s.* die Werbeantwortkarte.
busker [ˈbʌskə], *s.* der Straßensänger.
by-pass burner, *s.* der Gasbrenner mit Dauerflamme.
by-pass condenser, *s.* der Ableitkondensator, Nebenschlußkondensator.

C

cabin class, *s.* zweite Klasse, die Kajütsklasse.
cabin cruiser, *s.* der Kabinenkreuzer.
cahoots [kəˈhu:ts], *s. pl.* (*coll.*) *to be in – with s.o.*, mit einem unter einer Decke stecken.
calibration [kælɪˈbreɪʃən], *s.* die Kalibrierung, Eichung.
call-girl, *s.* die Prostituierte, das Callgirl.
campanologist [kæmpəˈnɔlədʒɪst], *s.* der Glockenläuter.
campanology, *s.* die Glockenkunde.
†**candlewick,** *s.* (*material*) das Frottee, Frotté.
candy floss, *s.* die Zuckerwatte.
candy-striped, *adj.* buntgestreift.
cannabis [ˈkænəbɪs], *s.* der Hanf (*Bot.*); Haschisch (*Med.*).
capacitance [kəˈpæsɪtəns], *s.* die Kapazität, kapazitiver Widerstand (*Elec.*).
carborundum [kɑ:bəˈrʌndəm], *s.* das Karborundum, Siliziumkarbid.
carcinogenic [kɑ:sɪnoˈdʒɛnɪk], *adj.* karzinogen, krebserzeugend.
carcinoid [ˈkɑ:sɪnɔɪd], *adj.* karzinoid, krebsähnlich.
cardiogram [ˈkɑ:dɪogræm], *s.* das Kardiogramm.
cardiograph [ˈkɑ:dɪogrɑ:f], *s.* der Kardiograph.
cardiography [kɑ:dɪˈɔgrəfɪ], *s.* die Kardiographie.
cardiologist [kɑ:dɪˈɔlədʒɪst], *s.* der Kardiologe, Herzspezialist.
cardiology, *s.* die Kardiologie, Herzheilkunde.
careers guidance, *s.* die Berufsberatung.
carinal [kəˈrɑɪnl], **carinate** [ˈkærɪneɪt], *adj.* kielähnlich, kammähnlich, Kiel—, Kamm—.
carom [ˈkærəm], *s.* die Karambol(ag)e (*Amer. Bill.*).
case history, *s.* die Krankengeschichte, Personalakte; der Tatsachenbericht, Erfahrungsbericht.
case study, *s.* die Einzelfallstudie.
case work, *s.* die Fürsorge(tätigkeit).
cassette [kæˈsɛt], *s.* die Kassette.
cartology [kɑ:ˈtɔlədʒɪ], *s.* die Kartenkunde.
catabolism [kəˈtæbəlɪzm], *s.* der Katabolismus, Abbau, Zersetzungsvorgang, Stoffwechsel.
cataplexy [ˈkætəplɛksɪ], *s.* die Kataplexie, plötzliche Lähmung.
cauliflower ear, *s.* das Boxerohr.
cavitation [kævɪˈteɪʃən], *s.* die Kavitation, Hohlraumbildung; Kavernenbildung, Höhlenbildung (*Med.*).
cereous [ˈsɪ:ərɪəs], *adj.* wächsern, wachsartig
cerous [ˈsɪ:ərəs], *adj.* wachshautartig (*Zool.*).
cervix [ˈsə:vɪks], *s.* der Hals, Gebärmutterhals.
chain-gang, *s.* die Kettensträflinge (*pl.*).
chair-lift, *s.* der Sessellift.
check-point, *s.* die Kontrollstelle, (Verkehrs)-Überwachungsstelle.
chemical engineering, *s.* die Industriechemie.
child guidance, *s.* heilpädagogische Führung (des Kindes).
child welfare, *s.* die Jugendfürsorge.
child welfare-worker, *s.* der Jugendpfleger.
choir loft, *s.* die Chorgalerie.
choir master, *s.* der Chordirigent.
cholesterol [kɔˈlɛstərɔl], *s.* das Cholesterin, Gallenfett.
chromogenesis [kroumoˈdʒɛnəsɪs], *s.* die Farbstoffbildung, Pigmentbildung.
chromogenic, *adj.* chromogen.
chucker-out, *s.* (*coll.*) der Rausschmeißer.
circa [ˈsə:kə], 1. *adv.* zirka, etwa, ungefähr. 2. *prep.* um . . . herum.
circumambulation [sə:kəmæmbjuˈleɪʃən], *s.* das Herumgehen, der Umweg; (*fig.*) Umschweif.
circumstantiate [sə:kəmˈstænʃɪeɪt], *v.a.* genau belegen *or* beweisen; ausführlich beschreiben.

circumstantiation [sə:kəmstænʃɪˈeɪʃən], *s.* die Ausschmückung, Ausstattung mit Einzelheiten.
civic centre, *s.* das Behördenviertel.
clanger [ˈklæŋə], *s.* (*coll.*) *to drop a* –, ins Fettnäpfchen treten.
clearway, *s.* die Halteverbotsstraße.
climactic [klɑɪˈmæktɪk], *adj.* sich steigernd *or* zuspitzend; eine Steigerung bildend.
clobber [ˈklɔbə], 1. *s.* (*coll.*) der Plunder, die Dinger, Klamotten (*pl.*). 2. *v.a.* (*coll.*) eine herunterhauen (*Dat.*).
clutch lining, *s.* der Kupplungsbelag.
clutch plate or **disk,** *s.* die Kupplungsscheibe.
coal-miner, *s.* der Grubenarbeiter, Bergmann.
coat-hook, *s.* der Kleiderhaken.
co-author, *s.* der Mitautor.
cocainism [kɔˈkeɪnɪzm], *s.* der Kokainismus, die Kokainvergiftung.
codeine [ˈkoudɪ:n], *s.* das Kodein.
coil antenna, *s.* die Spiralantenne.
coil ignition, *s.* die Abreißzündung.
coin box, *s.* der Münzfernsprecher.
cold-drawn, *adj.* kaltgezogen.
collage [kɔˈlɑ:ʒ], *s.* die Collage.
colour filter, *s.* der Farbfilter.
†**commercial,** *s.* die Werbesendung, Reklamesendung.
commercialization [kəmə:ʃəlɑɪˈzeɪʃən], *s.* die Kommerzialisierung.
common decency, *s.* natürlicher Anstand.
common denominator, *s.* gemeinsamer Nenner.
common fraction, *s.* gemeiner Bruch (*Math.*).
common law marriage, *s.* wilde Ehe.
Common Market, *s.* Gemeinsamer Markt, Europäische Wirtschaftsgemeinschaft (EWG).
compère [ˈkɔmpɛə], 1. *v.a.* ansagen bei. 2. *s.* der Conférencier, Ansager, die Ansagerin.
compliable [kəmˈplɑɪəbl], *adj.* fügsam, nachgiebig, willfährig.
comprehensive school, *s.* die Einheitsschule, Sammelschule.
compulsive [kəmˈpʌlsɪv], *adj.* zwingend; Zwangs—.
†**con,** *v.a.* (*sl.*) beschwindeln.
concert goer, *s.* der Konzertbesucher.
concert grand, *s.* der Konzertflügel.
concièrge [kɔnsɪˈɛəʒ], *s.* der Pförtner, Portier.
concrescence [kənˈkrɛsəns], *s.* die Verwachsung von Organen *or* Zellen.
conductress [kənˈdʌktrɪs], *s.* die Schaffnerin.
cone bearing, *s.* das Kegellager.
cone clutch, *s.* die Konuskupplung, Kegelkupplung.
conicity [kəˈnɪsɪtɪ], *s.* die Konizität, Kegelform.
conjunctivitis [kəndʒʌŋktɪˈvɑɪtɪs], *s.* die Bindehautentzündung.
conman [ˈkɔnmæn], *s.* (*sl.*) der Schwindler.
consortium [kənˈsɔ:tɪəm], *s.* das Konsortium, Syndikat.
contact lenses, *s. pl.* die Haftgläser (*pl.*).
contactor [ˈkɔntæktə], *s.* der Kontaktgeber, Impulsgeber.
containment [kənˈteɪnmənt], *s.* das In-Schach-Halten (*Mil.*).
continental basin, *s.* binnenländisches Beckengebiet.
continental shelf, *s.* der Festlandsockel.
continuity girl, *s.* das Skriptgirl.
continuous performance, *s.* die Nonstopvorstellung, ununterbrochene Vorstellung.
continuous wave, *s.* ungedämpfte Welle.
conurbation [kɔnə:ˈbeɪʃən], *s.* ineinandergreifende Stadtgebiete (*pl.*), der Groß(siedlungs)raum, gesamtes Siedlungsgebiet einer Großstadt.
conveyancing [kənˈveɪənsɪŋ], *s.* das Grundeigentums(übertragungs)recht; die Ausfertigung von Abtretungs- und Auflassungsurkunden (*Law*).
coolant [ˈku:lənt], *s.* das Kühlmittel.
copywriter, *s.* der Texter.
corm [kɔ:m], *s.* der Kormus, beblätterter Sproß.
coronary [ˈkɔrənərɪ], 1. *adj.* koronar; Kranz—. 2. *s.* (*coll.*), **coronary thrombosis,** *s.* die Koronarthrombose.
correspondence course, *s.* das Fernstudium.
cosmonaut [ˈkɔzmənɔ:t], *s.* der Kosmonaut, (Welt)raumfahrer.
costume jewellery, *s.* der Modeschmuck.
cotangent [koˈtændʒənt], *s.* die Kotangente (*Math.*).
cottage cheese, *s.* der Landkäse, Quark.
count-down, *s.* der Countdown, die Startzählung (*rocketry*).
counter-charge, *s.* die Gegenbeschuldigung, Widerklage.
counter-jumper, *s.* der Heringsbändiger.
counter-plea, *s.* der Gegeneinspruch.
counter-plot, *s.* der Gegenanschlag.
counter-reformation, *s.* die Gegenreformation.
counter-revolution, *s.* die Gegenrevolution.
counter-sabotage, *s.* die Sabotageabwehr.
cover-charge, *s.* das Gedeck.
coyp(o)u [ˈkɔɪpu:], *s.* die Biberratte (*Zool.*).
crap [kræp], *s.* das Crapsspiel; (*sl.*) der Unsinn, Quatsch.
crash-land, *v.n.* bruchlanden, eine Bruchlandung machen.
creamcake, *s.* die Kremtorte.
creepage [ˈkrɪ:pɪdʒ], *s.* das Kriechen (*Elec.*).
crew-cut, *s.* die Meckifrisur.
crosscheck, *v.a.* doppelt kontrollieren.
cross-fertilization, *s.* die Kreuzbefruchtung.
cross-hatching, *s.* die Kreuzschraffierung.
cross-pollination, *s.* die Fremdbestäubung.
†**cuff,** *s.* (*coll.*) *off the* –, improvisiert, aus dem Stegreif.
crown bit, *s.* der Kronenbohrer.
curettage [kjuˈrɛtɪdʒ], *s.* die Kürettage, Auskratzung.
curette [kjuˈrɛt]. 1. *v.a.* auskratzen. 2. *s.* die Kürette, der Auskratzer.
curlers [ˈkə:ləz], *s. pl.* die Lockenwickel (*pl.*).
curtain-call, *s.* der Hervorruf.
†**cut-back,** *s.* das Zurückschneiden; der Rückschnitt; die Reduzierung, Verringerung.
cut-off, *s.* die (Ab)Sperrung, Abschaltung, Ausschaltung (*Elec.*).
cybernetics [sɑɪbəˈnɛtɪks], *s.* die Kybernetik.
cyrtosis [sə:ˈtousɪs], *s.* die Rückgratverkrümmung.
cystocele [ˈsɪstəsɪ:l], *s.* der (Harn)Blasenbruch.
cystoscope [ˈsɪstəskoup], *s.* der Blasenspiegel.
cystotomy [sɪsˈtɔtəmɪ], *s.* der Blasenschnitt.
cytoblast [ˈsɑɪtoblɑ:st], *s.* der Zellkern.
cytogenous [sɑɪˈtɔdʒɪnəs], *adj.* zytogen, zellbildend.
cytoid [ˈsɑɪtɔɪd], *adj.* zellähnlich.
cytolysis [sɑɪˈtɔlɪsɪs], *s.* die Zellauflösung, Zytolyse.

D

data processing, *s.* die Datenverarbeitung (*computers*).
†**date,** 1. *s.* (*coll.*) die Verabredung; der (die) Verabredungspartner(in). 2. *v.a.* (*coll.*) sich verabreden mit.
dawn chorus, *s.* der Frühgesang (*Orn.*).
deadpan, *adj.* (*coll.*) ausdruckslos, dämlich.
deaf-aid, *s.* (*coll.*) das Hörgerät.
decibel [ˈdɛsɪbɛl], *s.* das Dezibel, Phon.
declivous [dɪˈklɑɪvəs], *adj.* abfallend, abschüssig, (abwärts)geneigt.
decompress [dɪ:kəmˈprɛs], *v.a.* entspannen.
decompression-chamber, *s.* die Unterdruckkammer.
decontamination squad, *s.* der Entgiftungstrupp.
décor [ˈdeɪkɔ:], *s.* der Dekor, die Ausschmückung.
decrepitude [dɪˈkrɛpɪtju:d], *s.* die Entkräftung, (Alters)Schwäche.
decrial [dɪˈkrɑɪəl], *s.* das Heruntermachen, (laute) Verurteilung.
decussation [dɪkʌˈseɪʃən], *s.* die (Durch)Kreuzung.
deep-freeze, 1. *v.a.* tiefkühlen. 2. *s.* der Tiefkühlschrank.
deep-fry, *v.a.* im Fett schwimmend braten.
defrost [dɪ:ˈfrɔst], 1. *v.a.* enteisen, abtauen, auftauen. 2. *v.n.* von Eis freiwerden, auftauen.
defuse [dɪ:ˈfju:z], *v.a.* entschärfen.

delivery service, *s.* der Zustelldienst.
de luxe [dɪˈlʌks], *adj.* Luxus—, erstklassig, hochelegant.
démarche [deɪˈmɑːʃ], *s.* die Demarche, diplomatischer Schritt.
demographic(al) [dɛmoˈgræfɪk(l)], *adj.* demographisch.
demography [dɪˈmɔgrəfɪ], *s.* die Demographie, Bevölkerungsstatistik.
denazification [dɪːnɑːtsɪfɪˈkeɪʃən], *s.* die Entnazifizierung.
deoxygenate [dɪːˈɔksɪdʒəneɪt], *v.a.* des Sauerstoffs berauben.
deoxygenization [dɪːɔksɪdʒənɑɪˈzeɪʃən], *s.* die Entziehung des Sauerstoffs.
departmentalization [dɪːpɑːtmɛntəlɑɪˈzeɪʃən], *s.* die Aufteilung in Abteilungen.
departmentalize [dɪːpɑːtˈmɛntəlɑɪz], *v.a.* in Abteilungen einteilen.
derequisition [dɪːrɛkwɪˈzɪʃən], *v.a.* freigeben.
derequisitioning, *s.* die Freigabe.
derestriction [dɪːrəˈstrɪkʃən], *s.* die Lockerung von Einschränkungsmaßnahmen.
dermatologist [dəːməˈtɔlɔdʒɪst], *s.* der Dermatologe, Hautarzt.
dermatosis [dəːməˈtousɪs], *s.* die Dermatose, Hautkrankheit.
desegregate [dɪːˈsɛgrəgeɪt], *v.a.* die Rassentrennung aufheben in.
desensitize [dɪːˈsɛnsɪtɑɪz], *v.a.* desensitieren, unempfindlich *or* immun machen; desensibilisieren, lichtunempfindlich machen (*Phot.*).
devaluate [dɪːˈvæljueɪt], *v.a.* abwerten, entwerten.
devaluation [dɪːvæljuˈeɪʃən], *s.* die Abwertung.
deviationism [dɪːvɪˈeɪʃənɪsm], *s.* der Mangel an Linientreue.
deviationist, *s.* Abtrünnige(r), *m.*, der Spalter.
dhow [dɑu], *s.* die D(h)au.
diatomic [dɑɪəˈtɔmɪk], *adj.* zweiatomig; zweiwertig.
dichotomy [dɪˈkɔtɔmɪ], *s.* die Zweiteilung, Gabelung (*Bot. & Zool.*); (*fig.*) der Zwiespalt.
dietetician [dɑɪətəˈtɪʃən], *s.* der Diätetiker, Ernährungssachverständige(r), *m.*
differentiable [dɪfəˈrɛnʃəbl], *adj.* unterscheidbar; differenzierbar (*Math.*).
dimwit, *s.* der Depp, Dussel.
dimwitted, *adj.* doof, blöd(e).
dinette [dɪˈnɛt], *s.* die Eßnische, Eßecke (*Amer.*).
dipole [ˈdɑɪpoul], *s.* der Dipol.
disallowable [dɪsəˈlɑuəbl], *adj.* zu verwerfen(d), nicht zu billigen(d).
disappropriate [dɪsəˈprouprɪeɪt], *v.a.* enteignen.
disappropriation [dɪsəprouprɪˈeɪʃən], *s.* die Enteignung.
disarming [dɪsˈɑːmɪŋ], *adj.* (*fig.*) entwaffnend.
discredited [dɪsˈkrɛdɪtɪd], *adj.* angezweifelt, unglaubwürdig; verrufen, diskreditiert.
disembodied [dɪsɪmˈbɔdɪd], *adj.* entkörperlicht, entstofflicht, immateriell.
disembroil [dɪsɪmˈbrɔɪl], *v.a.* aus einer verwickelten Lage helfen.
disincentive [dɪsɪnˈsɛntɪv], *s.* arbeitshemmender Faktor, das Abschreckungsmittel.
disk brake, *s.* die Scheibenbremse.
disorientate [dɪsˈɔːrɪənteɪt], *v.a.* desorientieren, verwirren.
disorientated, *adj.* verwirrt, unsicher, ziellos.
disorientation [dɪsɔːrɪənˈteɪʃən], *s.* die Desorientiertheit (*Psych.*); Verwirrtheit, Unsicherheit.
dispatch box, *s.* die Meldetasche.
district heating, *s.* die Fernheizung.
diverting [dɑɪˈvəːtɪŋ], *adj.* unterhaltsam, amüsant.
dizygotic [dɪzɪˈgɔtɪk], *adj.* zweieiig.
domesticity [domɛsˈtɪsɪtɪ], *s.* (gemütliches) Familienleben.
double-talk, *s.* ausweichende *or* zweideutige Redeweise.
doodle [ˈduːdl], *v.n.* gedankenlos hinkritzeln.
door-stop, *s.* der Türpuffer.
donkey-work, *s.* (schwere) Routinearbeit.
dramatis personae [ˈdræmətɪs pəːˈsounɑɪ], *s.* das Personenverzeichnis.
dressage [drɛˈsɑːʒ], *s.* das Schulreiten.
drip-dry, *adj.* bügelfrei, no iron.
drip-feed, *s.* die Tropf(öl)schmierung.
drive-in, 1. *adj.* Auto—, Sitz-im-Auto— (*Amer.*). 2. *s.* das Autokino (*Amer.*).
drop annunciator, *s.* der Fallklappen-Signaltafen.
drop curtain, *s.* der Vorhang.
†**drop-out,** *s.* (*coll.*) Asoziale(r), *m.*, *f.*
†**dubbing,** *s.* (*film, etc.*) das Überspielen.
duffel bag, *s.* der Kleidersack.
duffel coat, *s.* der Düffelmantel.

E

†**edit,** *v.a.* schneiden (*film, tape, etc.*).
egg head, *s.* Intellektuelle(r), *m.*, *f.*
egocentricity [ɛgosɛnˈtrɪsɪtɪ], *s.* egozentrisches Wesen, die Egozentrik, Ichbezogenheit.
egoistic(al) [ɛgoˈɪstɪk(l)], *adj.* egoistisch, selbstsüchtig.
ejector seat, *s.* der Schleudersitz.
election campaign, *s.* der Wahlkampf.
election meeting, *s.* die Wahlversammlung.
election returns, *s. pl.* das Wahlergebnis.
electrocardiography [ɛlɛktrokɑːdɪˈɔgrəfɪ], *s.* die Elektrokardiographie.
electronics, *s.* die Elektronik.
emotionalize [ɪˈmouʃənəlɑɪz], *v.a.* zur Gefühlssache machen, mit Gefühl behandeln.
emotionless, *adj.* gefühllos, unbewegt, kalt.
encapsulate [ɪnˈkæpsjuleɪt], *v.a.* einkapseln, verkapseln.
encapsulation [ɪnkæpsjuˈleɪʃən], *s.* die Verkapselung.
endoblast [ˈɛndoblɑːst], *s.* das Entoblast.
engraftation [ɪngrɑːfˈteɪʃən], *s.* das Einprägen, Pfropfen.
en route [ɔ̃ˈruːt], *adv.* auf dem Wege, unterwegs.
entelechy [ɛnˈtɛləkɪ], *s.* die Entelechie.
entertainment allowance, *s.* die Aufwandsentschädigung.
entitlement [ɪnˈtɑɪtlmənt], *s.* die Betitelung; Betrag, auf den man Anspruch hat.
entomophagous [ɛntoˈmɔfəgəs], *adj.* insektenfressend.
entophytic [ɛntoˈfɪtɪk], *adj.* Innenschmarotzer—.
entrainment [ɛnˈtreɪnmənt], *s.* die Verladung, das Verladen.
entrecote [ˈɔ̃trəkɔt], *s.* das Rippenstück.
enucleator [ɪˈnjuːklɪeɪtə], *s.* die Knopfsonde.
enuresis [ɛnjuˈrɪːsɪs], *s.* die Enuresis, Blasenschwäche.
eophyte [ˈɪːəfɑɪt], *s.* versteinerte Pflanze.
epee [ˈɛpeɪ], *s.* der (Fecht)Degen.
epiblastic [ɛpɪˈblæstɪk], *adj.* ektoderm.
epicentre [ˈɛpɪsɛntə], *s.* das Epizentrum; (*fig.*) der Mittelpunkt.
epicyclic [ɛpɪˈsɑɪklɪk], *adj.* epizyklisch, Epizykel—.
erg [əːg], *s.* das Erg.
escalate [ˈɛskəleɪt], *v.n.* eskalieren.
escalation [ɛskəˈleɪʃən], *s.* die Eskalation.
escape literature, *s.* die Unterhaltungsliterature.
escape mechanism, *s.* der Ausfluchtmechanismus.
escapism [ɪsˈkeɪpɪzm], *s.* die Flucht aus der Wirklichkeit.
escapist, 1. *s.* Wirklichkeitsflüchtige(r), *m.* 2. *adj.* Unterhaltungs—.
escapologist [ɛskəˈpɔlɔdʒɪst], *s.* der Entfesselungskünstler.
escargot [ɛsˈkɑːgou], *s.* (eßbare) Schnecke.
espresso-bar, *s.* die Espressobar.
estate car, *s.* der Kombi(wagen).
†**estreat,** *s.* beglaubigte Abschrift (*Law*).
euphoria [juˈfɔːrɪə], *s.* das Wohlbefinden; die Euphorie (*Med.*).
eviction order, *s.* der Räumungsbefehl.
excorticate [ɪksˈkɔːtɪkeɪt], *v.a.* entrinden, abkorken.
exhibitionism [ɛksɪˈbɪʃənɪzm], *s.* der Exhibitionismus.
exhibitionist, *s.* der Exhibitionist.

exogamy [ɪkˈsɔgəmɪ], *s.* die Exogamie, Fremdheirat.
expertise [ɛkspəːˈtɪːz], *s.* die Expertise, Sachkenntnis.
explicate [ˈɛksplɪkeɪt], *v.a.* erklären, deutlich machen.
ex post facto, *adv.* rückwirkend, nachträglich.
†**exposure,** *s. indecent* –, die Erregung öffentlichen Ärgernisses (*Law*).
expressway, *s.* die Schnell(verkehrs)straße. (*Amer.*)
expulsion order, *s.* der Ausweisungsbefehl.
extra-curricular, *adj.* außerhalb des Lehrplans.
extra-sensory, *adj.* den Sinnen nicht zugänglich; – *perception*, anomale Fähigkeit der Sinneswahrnehmung.

F

factorization [fæktəraɪˈzeiʃən], *s.* die Faktorenzerlegung (*Math.*).
factorize [ˈfæktəraɪz], *v.a.* in Faktoren auflösen *or* zerlegen (*Math.*).
fall-out, *s.* der Ausfall; radioaktiver Niederschlag.
farad [ˈfærəd], *s.* das Farad.
feasance [ˈfɪːzəns], *s.* die Erfüllung.
feed belt, *s.* der Patronengurt.
feed current, *s.* der Speisestrom.
feed mechanism, *s.* die Munitionszuführung.
fibreboard, *s.* die Holzfaserplatte.
fibreglass, *s.* die Glaswolle, Glaswatte.
fibrositis [faɪbrəˈsaɪtɪs], *s.* die Bindegewebsentzündung, der Muskelrheumatismus.
film-speed, *s.* die Lichtempfindlichkeit.
finalize [ˈfaɪnəlaɪz], *v.a.* abschließen, endgültig machen, erledigen, festlegen.
†**flap,** *s.* (*coll.*) das Durcheinander, die Aufregung.
flashback, *s.* die Rückblendung.
flash bulb, *s.* das Blitzlicht, die Blitzlichtlampe.
flash-over, *s.* der Überschlag.
flick-knife, *s.* das Schnappmesser.
flight personnel, *s.* fliegendes Personal.
flight sergeant, *s.* der Oberfeldwebel (der Luftwaffe).
flip-side, *s.* die Rückseite (*of a record*).
floorage [ˈflɔːrɪdʒ], *s.* die Bodenfläche.
floor manager, *s.* der Abteilungsleiter (*Amer.*).
floor plan, *s.* der Stockwerkgrundriß.
floor show, *s.* das Nachtklubprogramm.
floor space, *s.* die Bodenfläche.
florescence [flɔˈrɛsəns], *s.* die Blütezeit.
florescent, *adj.* (auf)blühend.
fluoridate [ˈfluərɪdeɪt], *v.a.* mit einem Fluorid versetzen (*water*).
fluoridize [ˈfluərɪdaɪz], *v.a.* mit einem Fluorid behandeln (*teeth*).
fly-over, *s.* die Hochstraße, (Straßen)Überführung.
foam-rubber, *s.* das Schaumgummi.
foreseeable [fɔːˈsɪːəbl], *adj.* überschaubar (*future*); vorhersehbar, absehbar.
forestation [fɔrɪsˈteɪʃən], *s.* die Beforstung, das Aufforsten.
forming [ˈfɔːmɪŋ], *s.* die Verformung, Fassonierung (*Tech.*).
fouling [ˈfaulɪŋ], *s.* der Anwuchs, Bewuchs (*Nav.*).
freeway, *s.* die Autobahn (*Amer.*).
frenetic [frəˈnɛtɪk], *adj.* wild, stürmisch, frenetisch; rasend, tobend, toll.
frequency response, *s.* die Frequenzwiedergabe, Frequenztreue (*Rad.*).
fringe benefits, *s. pl.* zusätzliche Sozialaufwendungen *or* Sozialleistungen (*pl.*).
frogman, *s.* der Froschmann, Kampfschwimmer.
frogmarch, *v.a.* (mit dem Kopf nachunter) fortschleppen.
fruitcake, *s.* englischer Kuchen.
fruit cocktail, *s.* kleingeschnittenes, gemischtes Obst.
fruit machine, *s.* (*coll.*) der Spielautomat.
full-time, *adj.* hauptamtlich, vollberuflich; ganztägig.
fungicidal [fʌndʒɪˈsaɪdl], *adj.* pilztötend.

G

Gallup poll, *s.* die Meinungsbefragung.
gameness, *s.* die Tapferkeit, der Mut.
gamin [ˈgæmæ̃, –mɪn], *s.* der Gassenjunge, Straßenjunge.
gaming house, *s.* die Spielhölle.
garden produce, *s.* das Gemüse.
garden suburb, *s.* die Gartenstadt.
garden warbler, *s.* die Gartengrasmücke (*Orn.*).
gastroenteritis [gæstrouɛntəˈraɪtɪs], *s.* der Magendarmkatarrh.
gate-crash, *v.n.* (*coll.*) eindringen, ungebeten erscheinen.
gaucherie [ˈgouʃərɪː], *s.* die Plumpheit; Taktlosigkeit.
gear ratio, *s.* die Übersetzung, das Übersetzungsverhältnis.
gelignite [ˈdʒɛlɪgnaɪt], *s.* das Gelatinedynamit.
gen [dʒɛn], *s.* (allgemeine) Anweisungen *or* Nachrichten (*pl.*).
genocide [ˈdʒɛnəsaɪd], *s.* der Völkermord, Gruppenmord.
genotype [ˈdʒɛnətaɪp], *s.* der Genotyp, das Erbbild.
geochemistry [dʒɪːoˈkɛmɪstrɪ], *s.* die Geochemie.
geochronology [dʒɪːokrɔˈnɔlədʒɪ], *s.* geologische Chronologie.
geopolitics [dʒɪːoˈpɔlɪtɪks], *s.* die Geopolitik.
geriatrician [dʒɛrɪəˈtrɪʃən], *s.* der Facharzt für Alterskrankheiten.
geriatrics [dʒɛrɪˈætrɪks], *s.* die Geriatrie.
germ-plasm, *s.* das Protoplasma, Keimplasma.
germ warfare, *s.* (*coll.*) der Bakterienkrieg, biologische Kriegführung.
gerontocracy [dʒɛrɔnˈtɔkrəsɪ], *s.* die Gerontokratie, Greisenherrschaft.
gestate [dʒɛsˈteɪt], *v.a.* (im Mutterleib) tragen.
get-together, *s.* (*coll.*) (zwangloses) Treffen *or* Beisammensein.
ghost town, *s.* die Geisterstadt, entvölkerte Stadt.
ghost writer, *s.* der Ghostwriter.
gift-wrap, *v.a.* geschenkmäßig verpacken.
gimmick [ˈgɪmɪk], *s.* (*coll.*) der Trick, die Tour, Dreh; Sensationswerbung, der Knüller, das Dings(da); persönliche Eigenheit.
gippo [ˈdʒɪpou], *s.* (*coll.*) der (die) Zigeuner(in).
gluteal [ˈgluːtɪəl], *adj.* Glutäal—.
gonad [ˈgɔnæd], *s.* die Keimdrüse.
grant-in-aid, *s.* die Subvention, Beihilfe.
grass-roots, *adj.* volkstümlich, –verbunden.
grease-gun, *s.* die Fettpresse.
green belt, *s.* der Grüngürtel (*round town*).
green fingers, *s. pl.* (*fig.*) gärtnerisches Geschick.
green light, *s.* (*fig.*) grünes Licht.
gremlin [ˈgrɛmlɪn], *s.* böser Kobold *or* Geist.
grid reference, *s.* die Planquadratangabe.
grommet [ˈgrʌmɪt], *s.* die Öse (*Metall.*); der Taukranz (*Naut.*).
group captain, *s.* der Oberst der Luftwaffe.
guard-dog, *s.* der Wachhund.
guest-house, *s.* die (Privat)Pension.
gun-dog, *s.* der Jagdhund.
gymnocarpus [dʒɪmnoˈkɑːpəs], *adj.* nacktfrüchtig.
gyro-magnetic, *adj.* gyromagnetisch.
gyro-stabilizer, *s.* der (Stabilisier)Kreisel, die Kreiselstabilisierung.

H

habit-forming, *adj.* zur Gewöhnung fürhend.
haematuria [hɪːməˈtjuːrɪə], *s.* die Hämaturie, das Blutharnen.
haemoleucocyte [hɪːməˈljuːkəsaɪt], *s.* weißes Blutkörperchen.
hair-do, *s.* (*coll.*) die Frisur.
hand-out, *s.* die Verlautbarung, Pressenotiz; der Handzettel.
handpicked, *adj.* handgepflückt; erlesen, ausgesucht.

hand-spring, *s.* das Radschlagen.
hangfire, *s.* das Nachbrennen.
hang-nail, *s.* der Niednagel.
harassment [ˈhærəsmənt], *s.* die Belästigung.
hardboard, *s.* die Hartfaserplatte.
H-bomb, *s.* die Wasserstoffbombe.
headset, *s.* das Kopfstück, der Kopfhörer.
hearing-aid, *s.* das Hörgerät.
heart throb, *s.* (*fig.*) der Schwarm.
heart transplant(ation), *s.* die Herzverpflanzung.
heavy duty, *adj.* Hochleistungs—, Hochdruck—.
heliport [ˈhɛlipɔ:t], *s.* der Hubschrauberlandeplatz, Hubschrauberflughafen.
heterochthonous [hɛtəˈrɔkθənəs], *adj.* nicht ursprünglich, fremd.
heterologous [hɛtəˈrɔləgəs], *adj.* heterolog, abweichend.
heteromorphic [hɛtəroˈmɔ:fɪk], **heteromorphous** [–fəs], *adj.* heteromorph, verschiedengestaltig.
hi-fi [ˈhɑɪˈfɑɪ], *adj.* (*coll.*) Hifi—.
high command, *s.* das Oberkommando.
higher education, *s.* die Hochschulbildung.
high-necked, *adj.* hochgeschlossen.
high-octane, *adj.* klopffest, . . . mit hoher Oktanzahl.
high pressure area, *s.* das Hochdruckgebiet.
high pressure salesmanship, *s.* harte Verkaufstechnik.
high spot, *s.* (*fig.*) der Hauptpunkt.
hijack [ˈhɑɪdʒæk], *v.a.* rauben, entführen.
hijacker, *s.* der Entführer.
hijacking, *s.* die (Flugzeug)Entführung.
hindsight [ˈhɑɪndsɑɪt], *s.* späte Einsicht, die Nachsicht.
hipsters [ˈhɪpstəz], *s. pl.* die Hüfthose.
histogram [ˈhɪstəgræm], *s.* das Histogramm.
hit-and-run driver, *s.* flüchtiger Fahrer, der Fahrerflucht Schuldige(r), *m.*
hit parade, *s.* die Schlagerparade.
homicide squad, *s.* die Mordkommission.
homing device, *s.* das Zielfluggerät.
homomorphic [hɔməˈmɔ:fɪk], *adj.* homomorph(isch), gleichgestaltig.
honky-tonk [ˈhɔŋkɪtɔŋk], *s.* die Spelunke, Kaschemme, das Bumslokal (*Amer.*).
honorific [ɔnəˈrɪfɪk], *adj.* Ehren—, ehrend.
hooey [ˈhu:ɪ], *s.* (*sl.*) der Quatsch.
hoo-ha [ˈhu:hɑ:], *s.* (*sl.*) der Krach; Streit.
hooky [ˈhukɪ], *s.* *to play* –, die Schule schwänzen (*Amer.*).
hoopla [ˈhu:plɑ:], *s.* das Ringwerfen.
hospitalization [hɔspɪtəlɑɪˈzeɪʃən], *s.* die Einlieferung in ein Krankenhaus, Unterbringung in einem Krankenhaus.
hospitalize [ˈhɔspɪtəlɑɪz], *v.a.* in ein Krankenhaus einliefern, in einem Krankenhaus unterbringen.
house-coat, *s.* der Morgenrock.
house-hunting, *s.* die Wohnungssuche.
house-martin, *s.* die Mehlschwalbe (*Orn.*).
house-proud, *adj.* übertriebene Sorgfalt auf den Haushalt verwendend.
house-sparrow, *s.* der Haussperling (*Orn.*).
house-to-house collection, *s.* die Haussammlung.
housework, *s.* die Hausarbeit.
hovercraft [ˈhɔvəkrɑ:ft], *s.* das Schwebeschiff, Luftkissenfahrzeug.
hubris [ˈhju:brɪs], *s.* die Hybris.
humous [ˈhju:məs], *adj.* Humus—, humusreich.
hunkydory [hʌŋkɪˈdɔ:rɪ], *adj.* ausgezeichnet, prima (*Amer.*).
hydraulic brake, *s.* die Öldruckbremse.
hydraulic engineering, *s.* der Wasserbau.
hydrofoil [ˈhɑɪdrəfɔɪl], *s.* die Tragfläche, der Tragflügel.
hydrous [ˈhɑɪdrəs], *adj.* wässerig; wasserhaltig.
hypertension [hɑɪpəˈtɛnʃən], *s.* (zu) hoher Blutdruck.
hypnotheraphy [hɪpnəˈθɛrəpɪ], *s.* die Hypnosebehandlung.
hypodermis [hɑɪpəˈdə:mɪs], *s.* das Hypoderm.
hypotactic [hɑɪpəˈtæktɪk], *adj.* hypotaktisch, unterordnend.
hypotaxis [hɑɪpəˈtæksɪs], *s.* die Hypotaxe, Unterordnung.

I

ice-cap, *s.* die Eiskappe.
iced [ɑɪst], *adj.* eisgekühlt; glasiert.
identity parade, *s.* polizeiliche Gegenüberstellung.
idioplasm [ˈɪdɪoplæzm], *s.* das Idioplasma, Erbplasma.
illuminated capital, *s.* die Initiale (*Typ.*).
imbalance [ɪmˈbæləns], *s.* die Unausgewogenheit; mangelhafte Zusammenarbeit.
imitation stone, *s.* der Kunststein.
immobilization [ɪmoubɪləɪˈzeɪʃən], *s.* die Immobilisierung, Festlegung; Einziehung (*money*).
impartment [ɪmˈpɑ:tmənt], *s.* die Mitteilung, Weitergabe.
impermissible [ɪmpə:ˈmɪsɪbl], *adj.* unzulässig, unstatthaft.
implausible [ɪmˈplɔ:zɪbl], *adj.* unglaubhaft, unglaubwürdig, unwahrscheinlich.
impolitic [ɪmˈpɔlɪtɪk], *adj.* unpolitisch, undiplomatisch, unklug, unvorsichtig.
imponderable [ɪmˈpɔndərəbl], 1. *adj.* unwägbar, unmeßbar; nicht abzuschätzen. 2. *s.* etwas Unwägbares; (*pl.*) Imponderabilien.
incoercible [ɪnkoˈə:sɪbl], *adj.* unbezwingbar; permanent.
inductile [ɪnˈdʌktɑɪl], *adj.* un(aus)dehnbar; unbiegsam.
inductility [ɪndʌkˈtɪlɪtɪ], *s.* die Un(aus)dehnbarkeit.
in extenso, *adv.* vollständig, ausführlich.
in extremis, *adv.* in äußerster Not; im Sterben.
infarct [ˈɪnfɑ:kt], *s.* der Infarkt.
infarction [ɪnˈfɑ:kʃən], *s.* die Infarktbildung, Infarzierung.
informative [ɪnˈfɔ:mətɪv], *adj.* belehrend, unterrichtend, bildend, instruktiv.
infuriation [ɪnfjuərɪˈeɪʃən], *s.* die Wut, Verärgerung.
ingestion [ɪnˈdʒɛstʃən], *s.* die Nahrungsaufnahme (*Biol.*); Einnahme (*Med.*).
ingratiation [ɪngreɪʃɪˈeɪʃən], *s.* die Einschmeichelung, Liebedienerei.
inhalant [ɪnˈheɪlənt], *s.* der Inhalationsapparat; Einsaugende(r).
inhaul [ˈɪnhɔ:l], *s.* der Niederholer.
in-laws, *s. pl.* (*coll.*) Verschwägerte (*pl.*).
innards [ˈɪnədz], *s. pl.* (*coll.*) der Magen.
in-phase, *adj.* gleichphasig, von gleicher Phase.
inrush [ˈɪnrʌʃ], *s.* der Zustrom.
insectifuge [ɪnˈsɛktɪfju:dʒ], *s.* das Insektenvertreibungsmittel.
inseminate [ɪnˈsɛmɪneɪt], *v.a.* (die) Saat legen in; befruchten, schwängern; (*fig.*) einpflanzen in.
insemination [ɪnsɛmɪˈneɪʃən], *s.* *artificial* –, künstliche Befruchtung.
institutionalize [ɪnstɪˈtju:ʃənəlɑɪz], *v.a.* institutionell *or* institutionsartig machen; als Institution behandeln.
insurgence, insurgency [ɪnˈsə:dʒəns(ɪ)], *s.* der Aufruhr, Aufstand, die Erhebung, Rebellion.
intercom [ˈɪntəkɔm], *s.* (*coll.*) die Wechselsprechanlage; Bordverständigung, Bordsprechanlage (*Naut. & Av.*).
interface [ˈɪntəfeɪs], *s.* die Zwischenfläche, Grenzfläche.
interior decoration, *s.* die Innendekoration.
interplanetary [ɪntəˈplænətərɪ], *adj.* interplanetarisch.
in toto, *adv.* im ganzen *or* gesamten.
invigilator [ɪnˈvɪdʒɪleɪtə], *s.* Aufsichtsführende(r), *m.*
ipso facto, *adv.* gerade dadurch.
irrelievable [ɪrəˈlɪ:vəbl], *adj.* nicht anzuhelfen(d) *or* abzustellen(d).
irrepealable [ɪrəˈpɪ:ləbl], *adj.* unwiderruflich.

irretraceable [ɪrəˈtreɪsəbl], *adj.* nicht zurückzuverfolgen(d) (*path, etc.*), nicht rückgängig zu machen(d) (*steps*).
isochromatic [ɑɪsokroˈmætɪk], *adj.* gleichfarbig, isochrom(atisch); orthochromatisch.
isochron [ˈɑɪsokrɔn], 1. *adj.* isochron. 2. *s.* die Isochrone.
isogamous [ɑɪˈsɔgəməs], *adj.* isogam.
isogenous [ɑɪˈsɔdʒɪnəs], *adj.* isogen.
isolationism [ɑɪsəˈleiʃənɪzm], *s.* die Isolationspolitik, der Isolationismus.
isomorphic [ɑɪsoˈmɔ:fɪk], *adj.* isomorph, gleichgestaltig.
isomorphism, *s.* die Gleichgestaltigkeit, Strukturgleichheit.
isotone [ˈɑɪsətoʊn], *s.* das Isoton.
isotron [ˈɑɪsətrɔn], *s.* das Isotron.
isotype [ˈɑɪsətɑɪp], *s.* das Schaubild.

J

jackpot, *s.* der Jackpot.
jackscrew, *s.* die Hebeschraube, Hebespindel.
jalopy [dʒəˈlɔpɪ], *s.* die Klapperkiste (*Amer. coll.*).
jet-stream, *s.* die Strahlstromung (*Meteor.*).
jockstrap, *s.* das Suspensorium.
judder [ˈdʒʌdə], 1. *v.n.* vibrieren, ruckeln. 2. *s.* das Vibrieren.
juke-box, *s.* der Musikautomat, die Musikbox.
junkie [ˈdʒʌŋkɪ], *s.* (*sl.*) Rauschgiftsüchtige(r), *m., f.*

K

key signature, *s.* die (Tonart)Vorzeichnung.
kilocycle [ˈkɪlosɑɪkl], *s.* das Kilohertz.
kindred spirit, *s.* der Gesinnungsgenosse.
king-size(d), *adj.* (*coll.*) überdurchschnittlich groß.
kinky [ˈkɪŋkɪ], *adj.* (*sl.*) schrüllenhaft, überspannt.
kitchenware, *s.* das Küchengeschirr.
koala (bear) [koˈɑ:lə], *s.* der Beutelbär.
kope(c)k [ˈkoʊpɛk], *s.* die Kopeke.
kyle [kɑɪl], *s.* die Meerenge, der Sund (*Scottish*).

L

land-rover, *s.* (*trade name*) der Geländewagen, geländegängiger Wagen.
lap joint, 1. *v.a.* überlappen. 2. *s.* die Überlappungsverbindung.
laser [ˈleɪzə], *s.* der Laserstrahl.
launching pad or **platform,** *s.* die Abschußrampe (*rocketry*).
laundrette [lɔ:nˈdrɛt], *s.* der Mietwaschsalon, die Schnellwascherei.
lay-about, *s.* (*coll.*) der Faulenzer, Gammler, Lungerer.
lay by, *s.* die Ausweichstelle, Raststelle (*Motor.*).
leatherneck, *s.* der Marineinfanterist (*Amer.*).
left wing, 1. *s.* linker Flügel (*Pol. & Footb.*). 2. *adj.* Links—.
left winger, *s.* Linkstehende(r), *m.* (*Pol.*), der Linksaußen (*Footb.*).
leprechaun [ˈlɛprɪkɔ:n], *s.* der Kobold (*Irish*).
lesbian [ˈlɛzbɪən], 1. *adj.* lesbisch. 2. *s.* die Lesbierin, Tribade.
lesbianism [ˈlɛzbɪənɪzm], *s.* lesbische Liebe, weibliche Homosexualität, die Tribadie.
liaise [lɪˈeɪz], *v.n.* eine Verbindung herstellen *or* aufnehmen.
libertarian [lɪbəˈtɛərɪən], *adj.* indeterministisch (*Phil.*), individuelle Freiheit aufrechterhaltend, für Freiheit eintretend (*Pol.*).
lido [ˈlɪ:doʊ], *s.* das Strandband, Freibad.
lie-detector, *s.* der Lügendetektor.
life expectancy, *s.* mutmaßliche Lebensdauer.
life raft, *s.* das Rettungsfloß.
life span, *s.* die Lebensdauer.
liminal [ˈl(ɑ)ɪmɪnl], *adj.* Schwellen— (*Psych.*).
list-price, *s.* der Katalogpreis.
lithophyte [ˈlɪθəfɑɪt], *s.* die Steinpflanze.
lithotomy [lɪˈθɔtəmɪ], *s.* der (Blasen)Steinschnitt (*Surg.*).
live programme, *s.* die Direktübertragung, Originalsendung (*Rad. & T.V.*).
loco [ˈloʊkoʊ], 1. *s.* die Lok (*Railw. coll.*). 2. *adj.* (*sl.*) verrückt.
lolly [ˈlɔlɪ], *s.* der *or* das Lutschbonbon; (*sl.*) Moneten (*pl.*), die Pinke-Pinke, der Kies.
long-playing, *adj.* Langspiel— (*record*).
long-term, *adj.* (*coll.*) langfristig, auf lange Sicht.
loo [lʊ:], *s.* (*sl.*) die Klo.
lope [loʊp], 1. *v.n.* mit leichten springenden Schritten gehen. 2. *s.* leichtes Dahinspringen.
low-temperature, *adj.* Ur— (*Tech.*).
lumber-jacket, *s.* der Lumberjack.
lunatic fringe, *s.* Übereifrigen, Extremisten (*pl.*).
lymphocyte [ˈlɪmfəsɑɪt], *s.* das Lymphkörperchen.

M

machine-twist, *s.* die (Näh)Maschinenseide.
maculation [mækjʊˈleɪʃən], *s.* die Befleckung, Beschmutzung; Musterung, Zeichnung (*Bot. & Zool.*).
magma [ˈmægmə], *s.* das Magma, dünnflüssiger Brei (*Chem., etc.*); der Gesteinsschmelzfluß, Glutbrei (*Geol.*).
mailing [ˈmeɪlɪŋ], *s.* der Postversand, die Verschickung (mit der Post).
mailing list, *s.* die Adressenkartei.
mail-order, *s.* die Postbestellung.
maintenance-man, *s.* der Wartungsmonteur.
maladjusted [ˈmælədʒʌstɪd], *adj.* milieugestört, entfremdet (*Psych.*).
malocclusion [mæləˈklu:ʒən], *s.* die Gebißanomalie (*Dent.*).
man-hour, *s.* die Arbeitsstunde pro Mann.
marathon [ˈmærəθən], 1. *s.* der Langstreckenlauf (*Sport*), (*also fig.*) Dauerlauf, (*fig.*) Dauerwettkampf. 2. *adj.* Langstrecken—, Dauer—.
marina [məˈrɪ:nə], *s.* das Jachtbassin.
marital status, *s.* der Familienstand.
market-quotation, *s.* die Börsennotierung (*stock-exchange*).
market-report, *s.* der Handelsbericht, Börsenbericht.
market-value, *s.* der Verkehrswert, Kurswert.
mascara [mæsˈkɑ:rə], *s.* die Wimperntusche.
mass media, *s. pl.* Massenmedien (*pl.*).
matchstick, *s.* das Streichhölzchen.
materially [məˈtɪərɪəlɪ], *adv.* materiell (*Phil.*); physisch, körperlich, stofflich; (*coll.*) wesentlich, erheblich, beträchtlich.
maxi skirt, *s.* der Maxi.
megaton bomb, *s.* die Bombe mit der Sprengkraft von 1000 Kilotonnen.
meritocracy [mɛrɪˈtɔkrəsɪ], *s.* die Leistungsgesellschaft.
mescalin [ˈmɛskəlɪn], *s.* das Mescalin.
microbiology [mɑɪkrobɑɪˈɔlɔdʒɪ], *s.* die Mikrobiologie.
microfilm [ˈmɑɪkrofɪlm], *s.* der Mikrofilm.
microgroove [ˈmɑɪkrogrʊ:v], *s.* die Mikrorille.
middle-bracket, *adj.* zur mittleren Gruppe gehörend.
middlebrow, 1. *adj.* mit mittelmäßigen geistigen Interessen. 2. *s.* geistiger Normalverbraucher.
middle-of-the-road, *adj.* unabhängig, neutral.
midi skirt, *s.* der Midi.
mine-crater, *s.* der Sprengtrichter, Minentrichter.
minibus [ˈmɪnɪbʌs], *s.* der Kleinbus.
minicab [ˈmɪnɪkæb], *s.* kleineres Taxi.

minuscule, *adj.* Minuskel—; (*fig.*) sehr klein.
misalignment [mɪsə'laɪnmənt], *s.* der Flucht-(ungs)fehler (*Tech.*).
miscast [mɪs'kɑ:st], *v.a.* unpassend besetzen (*rôle*), eine unpassende Rolle zuteilen (*Dat.*) (*actor*).
miscasting, *s.* unpassende Besetzung, die Fehlbesetzung.
mise-en-scène, *s.* die Inszenierung, das Bühnenbild; (*fig.*) die Umgebung, Umwelt.
mistle-thrush, *s.* die Misteldrossel (*Orn.*).
mixed-up, *adj.* (*coll.*) konfus, verwirrt.
mobocracy [mɔ'bɔkrəsɪ], *s.* (*coll.*) die Pöbelherrschaft.
mock-up, *s.* das Modell in natürlicher Größe.
†**monitor,** *v.a.* abhören; überwachen.
monkey-nut, *s.* die Erdnuß.
moped ['moupɛd], *s.* das Moped.
mores ['mɔ:reɪz], *s. pl.* Sitten (*pl.*).
motel [mo'tɛl], *s.* das Kraftfahrerhotel, Motel.
mothball, *s.* die Mottenkugel.
motorcade ['moutəkeɪd], *s.* die Autokolonne, Wagenkolonne (*esp. Amer.*).
motorway, *s.* die Autobahn.
mud-slinger, *s.* (*coll.*) der Verleumder.
†**mules,** *s. pl.* Hausschuhe (*pl.*).
multilingual [mʌltɪ'lɪŋgwəl], *adj.* vielsprachig, mehrsprachig.
multistage ['mʌltɪsteɪdʒ], *adj.* Mehrstufen— (*rocket*).
multistory [mʌltɪ'stɔ:rɪ], *adj.* vielstöckig, mehrstöckig, Hochhaus—.
mutate [mjʊ'teɪt], 1. *v.a.* verändern; umlauten (*Gram.*). 2. *v.n.* sich ändern; umlauten (*Gram.*); mutieren (*Biol.*).
mystery-novel, *s.* der Detektivroman.
myxomatosis [mɪksəmə'tousɪs], *s.* die Myxomatose.

N

nancy-boy, *s.* (*coll.*) Schwule(r), Warme(r), Homosexuelle(r), *m.*; der Weichling.
narcotherapy [nɑ:ko'θɛrəpɪ], *s.* die Psychotherapie mit Hilfe von Beruhigungsmitteln.
narrow-gauge, *adj.* schmalspurig, Schmalspur—.
natural gas, *s.* das Erdgas.
negatron ['nɛgətrɔn], *s.* das Negatron.
neon lamp or **light,** *s.* die Neonlampe.
neon sign, *s.* die Neonreklame.
neoplasticism [nɪ:o'plæstɪsɪzm], *s.* der Neoplastizismus.
nester ['nɛstə], *s.* der Brutvogel.
nesting-box, *s.* der Nistkasten.
neutralism ['nju:trəlɪzm], *s.* der Neutralismus, die Neutralitätspolitik.
news (broad)cast, *s.* die Nachrichtensendung, Nachrichten (*pl.*).
newscaster or **news reader,** *s.* der Nachrichtensprecher.
newsflash, *s.* die Kurznachricht.
news item, *s.* die Zeitungsnotiz.
news summary, *s.* die Nachrichten in Kurzfassung (*pl.*).
news theatre, *s.* das Aktualitätenkino.
noise level, *s.* der Geräuschpegel.
non-creasing, *adj.* knitterfrei.
non-fiction (book), *s.* das Sachbuch.
non-malignant, *adj.* nicht bösartig, gutartig.
non-productive, *adj.* unproduktiv.
non-profit (making), *adj.* gemeinnützig.
non-U, *adj.* nicht fein *or* vornehm, plebejisch.
nuclear attack, *s.* atomarer Angriff.
nuclear charge, *s.* die Kernladung.
nuclear deterrent, *s.* atomare Abschreckung.
nuclear physicist, *s.* der Atomphysiker, Kernphysiker.
nuclear plant or **power station,** *s.* das Atomkraftwerk.
nuclear power, *s.* die Atomkraft.
nuclear reactor, *s.* der Kernreaktor.
nuclear test, *s.* der Atomwaffenversuch, Kernwaffenversuch.
nuclear war(fare), *s.* der Atomkrieg.
nuclear warhead, *s.* der Atomsprengkopf.
nuclear weapons, *s. pl.* atomare Waffen, Atomwaffen (*pl.*).
numerate ['njʊ:mərɪt], *adj.* rechenkundig.
nursery slopes, *s. pl.* der Anfängerhügel, (*coll.*) Idiotenhügel (*skiing*).
nutritionist [njʊ:'trɪʃənɪst], *s.* der Diätetiker, Ernährungssachverständige(r), *m.*
nylon ['naɪlɔn], *s.* das Nylon; (*pl.*) Nylonstrümpfe (*pl.*).

O

oceanographer [ouʃə'nɔgrəfə], *s.* der Ozeanograph, Meereskundler.
octane ['ɔkteɪn], *s.* das Oktan; *high – fuel,* der Superkraftstoff.
off-beat, *adj.* (*fig.*) ungewöhnlich, ausgefallen.
off-centre, *adj.* nicht ganz gerade, verrutscht.
officialese [əfɪʃə'lɪ:z], *s.* der Beamtenjargon, Amtsjargon.
off-peak tariff, *s.* der Nachtstromtarif (*Elec.*).
off-stage, *adj.* hinter der Bühne.
off-the-record, *adj.* nicht für die Öffentlichkeit bestimmt, inoffiziell, vertraulich.
oil feed, *s.* die Ölzufuhr.
oil-fired or **oil-burning,** *adj.* mit Ölfeuerung.
oil gauge, *s.* der Ölstandsmesser.
oil gland, *s.* die Bürzeldrüse (*Orn.*).
one-armed bandit, *s.* (*coll.*) der Spielautomat.
one-night stand, *s.* einmaliges Gastspiel (*Theat.*).
one-track, *adj.* eingleisig, einspurig; (*coll., fig.*) einseitig, beschränkt, verbohrt.
open access, *s.* die Freihand (*library*).
opt out, *v.n.* sich drücken.
oscilloscope ['ɔsɪloskoup], *s.* das Oszilloskop.
osteomyelitis [ɔstɪomaɪə'laɪtɪs], *s.* die Knochenmarksentzündung, Myelomatose.
osteosclerosis [ɔstɪosklɛ'rousɪs], *s.* die Knochenverhärtung.
osteotomy [ɔstɪ'ɔtəmɪ], *s.* die Knochenresektion, Osteotomie.
outback, *s.* der Busch (*Australia*).
out-dated, *adj.* altmodisch, unmodern; veraltet, überholt.
out-point, *v.a.* an Punktzahl übertreffen, nach Punkten schlagen.
outré [u:'treɪ], *adj.* extravagant, übertrieben, outriert.
out-sell, *v.a.* sich besser *or* teurer verkaufen als.
out-talk, *v.a.* an Zungenfertigkeit übertreffen, in Grund und Boden reden.
overpass, *s.* die (Straßen)Überführung.
oversteer [ouvə'stɪ:ə], *v.n.* zu wenig Spiel bei der Lenkung haben (*Motor.*).
oxygenator ['ɔksɪdʒəneɪtə], *s.* der Sauerstofferzeuger.

P

package deal, *s.* das Kopplungsgeschäft.
paediatrician [pɪ:dɪə'trɪʃən], *s.* der Kinderarzt.
paediatrics [pɪ:dɪ'ætrɪks], *s.* die Kinderheilkunde.
†**pan,** 1. *v.a.* schwenken (*Film*). 2. *v.n.* panoramieren (*Film*).
panel discussion, *s.* das Podiumgespräch.
panellist ['pænəlɪst], *s.* der (die) Diskussionsteilnehmer(in).
paperback, *s.* das Buch im Pappband, Paperback.
paper-work, *s.* die Schreibarbeit(en).

paradrop [ˈpærədrɔp], *v.a.* (mit dem Fallschirm) abwerfen (*goods*) *or* absetzen (*men*).

†**parking,** *s. no* –! Parken verboten! Parkverbot!

parking light, *s.* das Standlicht.

parking meter, *s.* die Parkuhr.

parking problem, *s.* das Parkproblem.

party politics, *s. pl.* die Parteipolitik.

passenger flight, *s.* der Passagierflug.

passenger transport, *s.* die Personenbeförderung.

pastel shades, *s. pl.* die Pastelltöne (*pl.*).

patch-pocket, *s.* aufgesetzte Tasche.

patrol boat, *s.* das (Küsten)Wachschiff.

patrol car, *s.* der Streifenwagen.

patrolman, *s.* der Streifenpolizist (*Amer.*).

pay-as-you-earn, *s.* der Lohnsteuerabzug.

pay clerk, *s.* der Rechnungsführer.

pay-off, *s.* (*coll.*) die Heimzahlung.

pay packet, *s.* die Lohntüte.

payroll, *s.* der Gesamtbetrag der Löhne; *be on the* –, beschäftigt *or* angestellt sein.

peace-loving, *adj.* friedliebend, friedfertig.

peace treaty, *s.* der Friedensvertrag.

pen-friend, *s.* der (die) Brieffreund(in).

penicillin [pɛnɪˈsɪlɪn], *s.* das Penizillin.

period furniture, *s.* Stilmöbel (*pl.*).

period novel, *s.* zeitgeschichtlicher Roman.

period piece, *s.* das Museumsstück.

period play, *s.* historisches (Theater)Stück.

perspex [ˈpəːspɛks], *s.* (*trade name*) das Plexiglas.

pesticide [ˈpɛstɪsɑɪd], *s.* das Schädlingsbekämpfungsmittel.

pharyngoscope [fæˈrɪŋgəskoʊp], *s.* der Schlundspiegel.

†**phase,** *v.a.* in Phasen einteilen; in Phase bringen, synchronisieren (*Elec.*); (*coll.*) – *out*, abwickeln.

phenobarbitone [fɪːnoˈbɑːbɪtoʊn], *s.* das Phenobarbital, Luminal.

photo-cell, *s.* photoelektrische Zelle, die Photozelle.

photo-copy, 1. *s.* die Photokopie, Lichtpause. 2. *v.a.* photokopieren.

physiotherapist [fɪzɪoˈθɛrəpɪst], *s.* der Fachmann für physikalische Heilkunde, physikalischer Therapeut.

physiotherapy, *s.* physikalische Heilkunde.

piece rate, *s.* der Akkordsatz.

piece wages, *s. pl.* der Akkordlohn, Stücklohn.

pilot jet or **light,** *s.* die Zündflamme, der Sparbrenner.

pilot scheme, *s.* das Versuchsprojekt.

pin-ball machine, *s.* der Spielautomat.

pinking scissors, *s. pl.* die Zackenschere.

pin-stripe, *s.* der Nadelstreifen.

pin-table, *s.* der Spielautomat.

†**pipeline,** *s.* (*fig.*) (geheimer) Informationsweg.

pivot arm, *s.* der Schwenkarm.

pivot industry, *s.* die Schlüsselindustrie.

placement service, *s.* die Stellenvermittlung.

placement test, *s.* die Eignungsprüfung, Einstufungsprüfung.

placing [ˈpleɪsɪŋ], *s.* die Lage, Stellung, Haltung; der Platz (*Sport*).

†**plastic (compound),** *s.* der Preßstoff, Kunststoff.

plastic effect, *s.* (*fig.*) die Tiefenwirkung, Raumwirkung.

plasticize [ˈplæstɪsɑɪz], *v.a.* & *v.n.* knetbar *or* formbar machen *or* werden.

plastic mac, *s.* (*coll.*), **plastic raincoat,** *s.* die Regenhaut.

playboy, *s.* der Lebemann, Luftikus.

playpen, *s.* das Laufgitter, der Laufstall, (*coll.*) das Ställchen.

plenum heating, *s.* die Umwälzheizung.

police dog, *s.* der Polizeihund.

police escort, *s.* die Polizeibedeckung.

police inquiry, *s.* polizeiliche Untersuchung.

police record, *s.* das Strafregister.

police state, *s.* der Polizeistaat.

police surgeon, *s.* der Gerichtsarzt.

police van, *s.* der Zellenwagen, (*coll.*) grüne Minna.

police-woman, *s.* die Polizistin.

polo neck, *s.* der Rollkragen.

pop music, *s.* volkstümliche (Tanz)Musik.

pop song, *s.* der Schlager, die Schnulze.

postal delivery, *s.* die Postzustellung.

postal rates, *s. pl.* der Posttarif.

postal reply coupon, *s.* der Antwortschein.

potted [ˈpɔtɪd], *adj.* (*coll.*) zur späteren Wiedergabe aufgenommen (*music*).

power amplifier, *s.* der Endverstärker, Leistungsverstärker.

power boat, *s.* (schnelles) Motorboot.

power consumption, *s.* der Energieverbrauch, Stromverbrauch.

power point or **socket,** *s.* die Starkstrom-Steckdose.

power(-assisted) steering, *s.* die Servosteuerung, Servolenkung.

prefabrication [prɪːfæbrɪˈkeɪʃən], *s.* die Vorfertigung, Fertigbauweise.

prelims [ˈprɪːlɪmz], *s. pl.* (*coll.*) die Vorprüfung, Aufnahmeprüfung.

premium bond, *s.* der Prämienschein.

pre-shrunk, *adj.* nicht einlaufend, sanforisiert, schrumpffest.

press agent, *s.* der Presseagent.

press conference, *s.* die Pressekonferenz.

press correspondent, *s.* der Pressekorrespondent.

press-up, *s.* der Liegestütz (*Gymn.*).

pressure group, *s.* die Interessengruppe, der Interessenverband.

pressure point, *s.* der Druckpunkt (*Med.*).

pressure suit, *s.* der (Über)Druckanzug.

pressurized [ˈprɛʃərɑɪzd], *adj.* druckfest gemacht, mit Druckausgleich; – *cabin*, die Druckkabine.

pre-stressed concrete, *s.* der Spannbeton.

pretzel [ˈprɛtsəl], *s.* die (Salz)Brezel.

preview [ˈprɪvjʊː], *s.* private Voraufführung, die (Film)Vorschau.

price fixing, *s.* die Preisfestsetzung.

price level, *s.* die Preishöhe, das Preisniveau.

price maintenance, *s.* die Preisbindung.

price margin, *s.* die Preisspanne.

price range, *s.* die Preislage.

price tag or **ticket,** *s.* das Preisschild, der Preiszettel.

pricy [ˈprɑɪsɪ], *adj.* (*coll.*) teuer, unerschwinglich.

printable [ˈprɪntəbl], *adj.* druckfertig; druckfähig.

prize-giving, *s.* die Preisverteilung.

problem child, *s.* schwieriges Kind.

process(ed) cheese, *s.* der Schmelzkäse.

process printing, *s.* der Mehrfarbendruck.

production car, *s.* der Serienwagen.

production manager, *s.* der Betriebsleiter, Produktionsleiter.

production process, *s.* das Herstellungsverfahren, der Herstellungsprozeß.

profit margin, *s.* die Gewinnspanne, Gewinnschere.

†**programme,** *v.a.* programmieren (*computer*).

programmer, *s.* der Programmierer.

promptly [ˈprɔmptlɪ], *adv.* sofort, unverzüglich, kurzweg.

propane [ˈproʊpeɪn], *s.* das Propan(gas).

propellor shaft, *s.* die Schraubenwelle.

propellor slipstream, *s.* der Luftschraubenstrahl.

proprietary sign, *s.* die Hausmarke.

psephologist [sɛˈfɔlədʒɪst], *s.* der Wahlstatistiker.

psephology, *s.* die Wahlstatistik.

psychedelic [sɑɪkəˈdɛlɪk], *adj.* psychedelisch.

psychopathologist [sɑɪkopæˈθɔlədʒɪst], *s.* der Psychopathologe.

psychopathology, *s.* die Psychopathologie.

psychosomatic [sɑɪkosoˈmætɪk], *adj.* psychosomatisch.

publicity campaign, *s.* der Werbefeldzug.

publicity man, *s.* der Werbefachmann, Werbeleiter.

punch cutter, *s.* der Stempelschneider.

punch drunk, *adj.* (*coll.*) (wie) von Faustschlägen betäubt.

punch(ed) card, *s.* die Lochkarte.

punch line, *s.* die Pointe, der Knalleffekt.

punctual [ˈpʌŋktʃəl], *adj.* pünktlich, rechtzeitig, prompt.

punctuality [pʌŋktjʊˈælɪtɪ], *s.* die Pünktlichkeit.

puppet government, *s.* die Marionettenregierung.

purpose built, *adj.* zweckdienlich *or* zu dem Zweck gebaut.

push-over, *s.* (*coll.*) (*task*) das Kinderspiel, leichte S., die Kleinigkeit; (*a p.*) der Gimpel, nicht ernst zu nehmender Gegner.
pyrex [ˈpɑɪərɛks], *s.* (*trade name*) hitzebeständiges Glas(geschirr), Jenaer Glas (*trade name*).

Q

quantity production, *s.* die Massenherstellung.
quantity surveyor, *s.* der Baukostenfachmann.
†queer, *s.* (*sl.*) Schwule(r), Warme(r), *m.*
quick-freeze, *v.a.* tiefkühlen.
quick-freezer, *s.* der Tiefkühlschrank.
quick-freezing, *s.* das Tiefkühlen.

R

rabble-rouser, *s.* (*coll.*) der Hetzredner, Aufrührer.
racism [ˈreɪsɪzm], *s.* der Rassenkult, Rassenhaß.
radar screen, *s.* der Radarschirm.
radar station, *s.* die Radarstation.
radio-advertising, *s.* die Funkwerbung.
radio-biology, *s.* die Strahlungsphysiologie.
radio-car, *s.* der Funkwagen.
radio-carbon dating, *s.* die Radiokarbonmethode (der Altersbestimmung).
radiogenetics [reɪdɪodʒəˈnɛtɪks], *s.* die Strahlengenetik.
radio signal, *s.* die Funkmeldung, der Funkspruch.
radio silence, *s.* die Funkstille.
rapist [ˈreɪpɪst], *s.* Vergewältige(r), *m.*, der (Frauen)-Schänder.
rapport [ræˈpɔː], *s.* (enge) Beziehung *or* Verbindung, (enges) Verhältnis, freundschaftliche Beziehungen.
ratability [reɪtəˈbɪlɪtɪ], *s.* die (Gemeinde)Steuerpflicht; Steuerbarkeit, Abschätzbarkeit.
rat-race, *s.* (*sl.*) die Postenjägerei, mörderische Konkurrenz.
reappraisal [rɪːəˈpreɪzl], *s.* die Neubewertung, Neubeurteilung.
rear(view) mirror, *s.* der Rück(blick)spiegel (*Motor.*).
recap [rɪːˈkæp], (*coll.*) 1. *v.a.* kurz zusammenfassen. 2. [ˈrɪːkæp], *s.* zusammenfassende Wiederholung.
reconversion [rɪːkənˈvəːʃən], *s.* die Rückumwandlung; Wiederbekehrung (*Rel.*).
reconvert, *v.a.* rückumwandeln, wieder umändern; wieder bekehren (*Rel.*).
record holder, *s.* der Rekordhalter (*Sport*).
record library, *s.* das Schallplattenarchiv.
record player, *s.* der Plattenspieler.
†reefer, *s.* (*sl.*) die Marihuana-Zigarette.
relay station, *s.* die Relaisstation, Zwischenstation, Hilfsstation.
relay transmitter, *s.* der Zwischensender.
repair service, *s.* der Kundendienst.
request programme, *s.* das Wunschkonzert.
request stop, *s.* die Bedarfshaltestelle.
research institute or **station,** *s.* die Forschungsstelle.
research professor, *s.* der Professor mit Forschungsauftrag.
retro-rocket, *s.* die Bremsrakete, Rückstoßrakete.
reunification [rɪːjuːnɪfɪˈkeɪʃən], *s.* die Wiedervereinigung.
rewind [rɪːˈwɑɪnd], *v.a.* zurückspulen, umspulen (*film, tape, etc.*), neu wickeln (*electric motor, etc.*).
rewire [rɪːˈwɑɪə], *v.a.* neu verkabeln, wiederverdrahten.
ribbing [ˈrɪbɪŋ], *s.* das Bordmuster (*knitting*).
river police, *s.* die Wasserpolizei.
road accident, *s.* der Verkehrsunfall.
road block, *s.* die Straßensperre.
road construction, *s.* der Straßenbau, Wegebau.
road-holding, *s.* die Straßenlage (*Motor.*).
road roller, *s.* die Straßenwalze.
road user, *s.* der Verkehrsteilnehmer.
rocket launching site, *s.* die Raketen(abschuß)-basis.
rocket motor or **propulsion,** *s.* der Raketenantrieb.
rocket range, *s.* das Raketenversuchsgelände.
rocketry [ˈrɔkɪtrɪ], *s.* die Raketentechnik.
roll-on, *s.* (*coll.*) der Gummischlüpfer.
rotogravure [routougræˈvjuə], *s.* der Kupfer(tief)-druck.
rozzer [ˈrɔzə], *s.* (*sl.*) der Schupo.
ruckus [ˈrʌkəs], *s.* der Krach, Krawall, Spektakel (*Amer.*).

S

safari [səˈfɑːrɪ], *s.* die Safari, Großwildjagd.
safari park, *s.* das Großwild-Schutzgebiet, der Tierpark.
sal(e)ability [seɪləˈbɪlɪtɪ], *s.* die Marktfähigkeit, Gangbarkeit, Verkäuflichkeit, Absatzfähigkeit.
sale-goods, *s. pl.* Ramschwaren (*pl.*).
sales commission, *s.* die Verkaufsprovision.
sales promotion, *s.* die Absatzförderung.
sales representative, *s.* der Handelsvertreter.
sales resistance, *s.* die Kaufunlust.
sales talk, *s.* (*fig.*) Überredungskünste (*pl.*).
sales tax, *s.* die Umsatzsteuer.
sand yacht, *s.* der Strandsegler.
sauna [ˈsɔːnə], *s.* die Sauna.
scanner [ˈskænə], *s.* die Radarantenne, Drehantenne.
scanning lines, *s. pl.* Rasterlinien (*pl.*) (*T.V.*).
schematize [ˈskɪːmətɑɪz], *v.a.* schematisch anordnen, schematisieren.
school of motoring, *s.* die Fahrschule.
science-fiction, *s.* der Zukunftsroman, Zukunftsromane (*pl.*).
score-card, *s.* das Anschreibeblatt.
†scramble, *v.a.* verwürfeln (*message*).
scrambler [ˈskræmblə], *s.* die Verwürfelungsvorrichtung.
screen adaptation, *s.* die Filmbearbeitung.
†screening, *s.* die Eignungsauslese, Zuverlässigkeitsprüfung (*Pol.*).
screen play, *s.* das Drehbuch.
screen test, *s.* die Probeaufnahme.
screen writer, *s.* der Drehbuchautor.
script writer, *s.* der Textverfasser, Drehbuchautor.
scuff [skʌf], *v.a.* abnützen, abscheuern.
security risk, *s.* (*a p.*) für den Staatsdienst Ungeeignete(r), *m.*
sedation [səˈdeɪʃən], *s.* die Beruhigung (*Med.*).
seersucker [ˈsɪːəsʌkə], *s.* gestreiftes kreppartiges Leinen.
segregationist [sɛgrəˈgeɪʃənɪst], *s.* der Verfechter der Rassentrennung(spolitik).
self-service, *s.* die Selbstbedienung.
self-winding, *adj.* automatisch, mit Selbstaufzug.
sellers' market, *s.* verkaufsgünstiger Markt, der Verkäufermarkt.
sellers' option, *s.* die Rückprämie.
selling cost, *s.* Vertriebskosten (*pl.*).
selling price, *s.* der Ladenpreis, Verkaufspreis.
sell-out, *s.* (*coll.*) ausverkauftes Theaterstück, großer Erfolg; (*sl.*) der Verrat.
semi-durable, *adj.* beschränkt haltbar.
semi-finalist, *s.* der (die) Teilnehmer(in) an der Vorschlußrunde.
separates, *s. pl.* zweiteiliges Kleid.
serialize [ˈsɪːərɪəlɑɪz], *v.a.* in Fortsetzungen veröffentlichen.
service area, *s.* der Sendebereich (*Rad., etc.*).
service charge, *s.* der Bedienungszuschlag.
service depot, *s.* die Reparaturstelle, Kundendienststelle.
servicing [ˈsəːvɪsɪŋ], *s.* die Instandsetzung (*Motor.*).
shock tactics, *s. pl.* die Durchbruchstaktik, Überraschungsstrategie.
shock therapy or **treatment,** *s.* die Schockbehandlung.

†**shop,** *v.a.* (*sl.*) verraten, petzen, verpfeifen.
shopping bag, *s.* die Einkaufstasche.
shopping expedition, *s.* der Einkaufsbummel.
shortcake, *s.* der Mürbekuchen.
short-change, *v.a.* (*sl.*) übers Ohr hauen.
short division, *s.* abgekürzte Division (*Math.*).
short-list, *v.a.* in die engere (Aus)Wahl ziehen.
short-time (work), *s.* die Kurzarbeit.
showgirl, *s.* das Revuegirl.
show-jumping, *s.* das Bahnreiten, Reitturnier.
show-off, *s.* (*coll.*) der Angeber, Wichtigtuer, Protz, Großmaul.
show-place, *s.* die Sehenswürdigkeit.
shrink-proof, *adj.* schrumpffest.
sick-bay, *s.* das (Kranken)Revier, (Schiffs)-Lazarett.
sick-pay, *s.* das Krankengeld.
side-burns, *s. pl.* (*coll.*) der Backenbart, Koteletten (*pl.*).
side-car passenger, *s.* der Beifahrer.
side-effect, *s.* die Begleiterscheinung, Nebenwirkung.
sight-read, *v.n.* vom Blatt spielen (*Mus.*).
sight-reading, *s.* das Blattspielen.
sign language, *s.* die Zeichensprache, Gebärdensprache.
sign writer, *s.* der Schildermaler, Plakatmaler, Schriftmaler.
single-minded, *adj.* zielbewußt, zielbestrebig.
sinter [ˈsɪntə], 1. *s.* der Sinter. 2. *v.a.* sintern, fritten.
sinusitis [sɑɪnəˈsɑɪtɪs], *s.* die Nebenhöhlenentzündung, Sinu(s)itis.
skid chain, *s.* die Schneekette.
skid-proof, *adj.* rutschfest, gleitsicher.
ski jumping, *s.* das Schispringen.
ski lift, *s.* der Schilift.
skin diving, *s.* das Sporttauchen.
skint [skɪnt], *adj.* (*sl.*) pleit.
skull and crossbones, *s.* die Piratenflagge, Totenkopfflagge (*Naut.*); (*as warning*) der Totenkopf.
slap-happy, *adj.* (*coll.*) übermütig, tolldreist; holterdiepolter, ungestüm.
slip-ring, *s.* das Schleifrad.
slip-road, *s.* die Umgehungsstraße.
slob [slɔb], *s.* (*coll.*) der Banause; *fat* –, der Fettwanst.
smarmy [ˈsmɑːmɪ], *adj.* (*sl.*) kriecherisch; gefühlsduselig.
smash hit, *s.* (*coll.*) der Bombenerfolg.
smog [smɔg], *s.* (*coll.*) der Rauchnebel, die Dunstglocke.
smooch [smuːtʃ], *v.n.* (*sl.*) sich abknutschen.
snap fastener, *s.* der Druckknopf.
snap hook, *s.* der Karabinerhaken.
sneakers [ˈsniːkəz], *s. pl.* Turnschuhe (*pl.*) (*Amer.*).
sneak-thief, *s.* der Gelegenheitsdieb.
snide [snɑɪd], *adj.* (*coll.*) schmälernd, herabwürdigend, nachteilig.
social climber, *s.* der Streber, Emporkömmling.
social environment, *s.* gesellschaftliche Umwelt, das Milieu.
social insurance or **security,** *s.* die Sozialversicherung.
social organization, *s.* die Gesellschaftsstruktur.
social problem, *s.* soziales Problem.
social studies, *s. pl.* die Gesellschaftskunde.
sofa-bed, *s.* die Bettcouch.
song-thrush, *s.* die Singdrossel, Zippe.
sonic [ˈsɔnɪk], *adj.* Schall—.
sonic boom, *s.* der Überschall-Knall.
sonic depth-finder, *s.* das Echolot.
sound amplifier, *s.* der Lautverstärker.
sound barrier, *s.* die Schallgrenze, Schallmauer.
sound effects, *s. pl.* die Geräuschkulisse.
sound-radio, *s.* der Hörfunk, Ton(rund)funk.
sound-recording, *s.* die Tonaufnahme.
sound-track, *s.* die Tonspur, der Tonstreifen.
sozzled [ˈsɔzld], *adj.* (*sl.*) berotzt.
space-age, *s.* das Weltraumzeitalter.
space-fiction, *s.* der Weltraumroman, Weltraumromane (*pl.*).
space-flight, *s.* der (Welt)Raumflug.
spaceman, *s.* der Astronaut, (Welt)Raumfahrer.
space-research, *s.* die Raumforschung.
space-ship, *s.* das Raumschiff.
space-station, *s.* die Weltraumstation.
spacesuit, *s.* der Raumanzug.
space-travel, *s.* die Raumfahrt.
spectacle frame, *s.* das Brillengestell.
speed trap, *s.* die Straßenfalle, Autofalle.
speleologist [spɪlɪˈɔlədʒɪst], *s.* der Höhlenforscher.
speleology, *s.* die Höhlenforschung.
†**spikes,** *s. pl.* Spikes (*pl.*) (*Sport*).
spin-dryer, *s.* die Wäscheschleuder.
splinter-party, *s.* die Splittergruppe.
split-level, *adj.* mit Zwischenstockwerken (versehen) (*house*).
split peas, *s. pl.* halbe Erbsen.
split personality, *s.* gespaltene Persönlichkeit.
split phase, *s.* die Hilfsphase (*Elec.*).
split-pin, *s.* der Splint.
split-ring, *s.* der Spaltring.
split second, *s.* (*coll.*) der Moment, Nu.
spongeable [ˈspʌndʒəbl], *adj.* wischfest (*as wallpaper*).
sponge-rubber, *s.* der Schaumgummi.
spot-check, *s.* die Stichprobe.
spot-weld, *v.a.* punktschweißen.
spot-welding, *s.* die Punktschweißung.
sputnik [ˈsputnɪk], *s.* der Sputnik, Erdsatellit.
spy-ring, *s.* der Spionagering, die Spionageorganisation.
stamping machine, *s.* die Stampfe, Stanze (*Tech.*); (*post*) Frankiermaschine.
stamp machine, *s.* der Briefmarkenautomat.
standing headroom, *s.* die Stehhöhe.
squeeze-box, *s.* (*sl.*) die Quetschkommode.
station wagon, *s.* der Kombi(wagen) (*Amer.*).
status symbol, *s.* das Standeskennzeichen, Statussymbol.
stereophonic [stɛrɪoˈfɔnɪk], *adj.* Stereoton—, stereophonisch.
stereotypy [stɛrɪoˈtɑɪpɪ], *s.* die Stereotypie, das Stereotypieverfahren (*Typ.*), die Reiteration (*Med.*).
stiletto heel, *s.* der Pfennigabsatz.
stock-car racing, *s.* das Serienwagenrennen.
stockist [ˈstɔkɪst], *s.* der Fachhändler, das Fachgeschäft.
stock-pile, 1. *s.* der Vorrat, das Lager, die Reserve. 2. *v.a.* lagern, aufstapeln, anhäufen.
stock-piling, *s.* die Einlagerung, Vorratswirtschaft.
stock-size, *s.* die Normalgröße.
stratocruiser [ˈstrætokruːzə], *s.* das Stratosphärenflugzeug.
strike-bound, *adj.* bestreikt.
†**stripper** [ˈstrɪpə], *s.* (*coll.*) die Nackttänzerin.
strip-tease, *s.* der Nackttanz, Entkleidungsakt.
studio couch, *s.* die Schlafcouch, Bettcouch.
stuffed shirt, *s.* (*sl.*) aufgeblasene Null.
stultification [stʌltɪfɪˈkeɪʃən], *s.* die Blamage, Veralberung, das Lächerlichmachen.
stuntman [ˈstʌntmæn], *s.* der Double (*Film*).
stylus [ˈstɑɪləs], *s.* der (Schreib)Griffel, Durchschreibstift; (*record manufacture*) die Schneidnadel, (*on gramophone pick-up*) Nadel.
subliminal perception, *s.* unterschwellige Wahrnehmung.
sun glasses, *s. pl.* die Sonnenbrille.
sunray lamp, *s.* die Höhensonne.
supermarket, *s.* der Supermarkt, großes Selbstbedienungsbeschäft.
suppressor [səˈprɛsə], *s.* der Entstörkondensator, das Entstörungselement; Sperrgerät (*Tech.*).
sweat-shirt, *s.* die Trainingsbluse.
sweepback, 1. *adj.* pfeilförmig (*Av.*). 2. *s.* die Pfeilform.
swizzle-stick, *s.* das Rührstäbchen, der Sektquirl.

T

take-over, *s.* die Übernahme.
take-over bid, *s.* das Übernahmeangebot.
talking-point, *s.* der Gesprächsstoff.

tape-deck, *s.* die Spulenanlage.
tape-recording, *s.* die Tonbandaufnahme.
target area, *s.* der Zielraum.
tax bracket, *s.* die Steuerklasse.
tax exemption, *s.* die Steuerfreiheit.
tear-jerker, *s.* (*sl.*) der Schmachtfetzen, die Schnulze.
technochemistry [tɛkno'kɛmɪstrɪ], *s.* die Industriechemie.
Teddy boy, *s.* Halbstarke(r), *m.*
tee-shirt, *s.* das Sporthemd.
tee-shot, *s.* der Abschlag (*Golf*).
teething troubles, *s. pl.* (*fig.*) die Kinderkrankheiten.
telecamera ['tɛlɪkæmərə], *s.* die Fernsehkamera; Kamera mit Teleobjektiv.
telecast ['tɛlɪkɑ:st], 1. *v.a.* im Fernsehen übertragen. 2. *s.* die Fernsehübertragung.
telecaster, *s.* der Fernsehsprecher.
teleprint ['tɛlɪprɪnt], *v.a.* fernschreiben, durch Fernschreiber übermitteln.
telerecording [tɛlɪrɪ'kɔ:dɪŋ], *s.* die Fernsehaufzeichnung.
teletype, *see* **teleprint.**
teletypesetter [tɛlɪ'tɑɪpsɛtə], *s.* die Fernsetzmaschine.
television screen, *s.* der Bildschirm, die Bildröhre.
tenderer ['tɛndərə], *s.* der Offertsteller, Submittent (*C.L.*).
tenderloin ['tɛndəlɔɪn], *s.* das Lendenstück.
terrapin ['tɛrəpɪn], *s.* die Dosenschildkröte.
test run, *s.* der Probelauf.
test-tube baby, *s.* durch künstliche Befruchtung erzeugtes Kind.
three-point turn, *s.* die Wendung mit Hilfe des Rückwärtsgangs (*Motor.*).
three-way switch, *s.* der Dreiwegeschalter.
throughway, thruway, *s.* die Durchgangsstraße (*Amer.*).
time-and-motion study, *s.* Zeitstudien (*pl.*).
time card, *s.* die (Arbeitszeit)Kontrollkarte.
time clock, *s.* die (Arbeitszeit)Kontrolluhr, Stechuhr.
time-consuming, *adj.* zeitraubend.
time-fuse, *s.* der Zeitzünder.
tin can, *s.* die Blechdose.
tinpot, *adj.* (*sl.*) schäbig, lumpig.
tin soldier, *s.* der Bleisoldat.
tizzy ['tɪzɪ], *s.* (*coll.*) tolle Aufregung.
token strike, *s.* der Warnstreik.
topless, *adj.* oben ohne (*of dress*).
top-level, *adj.* auf höchster Ebene.
touch-type, *v.n.* blindschreiben.
tourist class, *s.* die Touristenklasse.
tourist guide, *s.* der Fremdenführer.
tourist industry, *s.* der Fremdenverkehr.
tow plane, *s.* das Schleppflugzeug
tow take-off, *s.* der Schleppstart.
track events, *s. pl.* Laufdisziplinen (*pl.*) (*Sport*).
track layer, *s.* das Raupenfahrzeug; Schienenleger (*Railw.*).
track suit, *s.* der Trainingsanzug.
trade cycle, *s.* der Konjunkturzyklus.
trafficator ['træfɪkeɪtə], *s.* der Winker, Blinker.
traffic control, *s.* die Verkehrsregelung.
traffic offence, *s.* der Verstoß gegen die Verkehrsordnung.
trampoline ['træmpəlɪ:n], *s.* das Trampolin, die Trampoline.
tranquillizer ['træŋkwɪlɑɪzə], *s.* das Beruhigungsmittel, Sedativum.
transistorize [træn'zɪstərɑɪz], *v.a.* transistorisieren.
transmogrify [trænz'mɔgrɪfɑɪ], *v.a.* gänzlich umgestalten.
travelling allowance, *s.* der Reisekostenzuschuß.
travelling library, *s.* die Wanderbücherei.
travelling salesman, *s.* Geschäftsreisende(r), Handlungsreisende(r), *m.*
travelling wave, *s.* fortschreitende Welle (*Elec.*).
travelogue ['trævəlɔg], *s.* der Reisebericht, die Reisebeschreibung, der Reisefilm.
trend analysis, *s.* die Konjunkturanalyse (*C.L.*).
tripperish ['trɪpərɪʃ], *adj.* (*coll.*) auf Ausflügler eingestellt.
troubleshooter, *s.* (*coll.*) der Störungssucher.
tundra ['tʌndrə], *s.* die Tundra.
turtleneck, *s.* der Rollkragen.
twin beds, *s. pl.* zwei Einzelbetten.
twinset, *s.* der *or* das Twinset.
†two-piece, *s.* das Komplet.
twosome ['tu:səm], *s.* das (Liebes)Pärchen; der Spiel für zwei Spieler.
tycoon [tɑɪ'ku:n], *s.* der Industriemagnat, Schlotbaron, Bonze.
type-cast, *v.a.* auf bestimmte Rollen festlegen (*an actor*).
typecaster or **typefounder,** *s.* der Schriftgießer (*Typ.*).
type page, *s.* der Satzspiegel.
type-setting, 1. *s.* das Setzen. 2. *adj.* Setz—.
tyre gauge, *s.* der Reifendruckmesser.
tyre marks, *s. pl.* die Reifenspur(en), Bremsspur(en).

U

ultra-high frequency, *s.* die Ultrahochfrequenz, Dezimeterwelle.
ultra-red, *adj.* ultrarot, infrarot.
unceremoniously, *adv.* kurzweg.
uncommercial, *adj.* unkaufmännisch.
undercover [ʌndə'kʌvə], *adj.* Geheim—.
undercover agent or **man,** *s.* der Spitzel, Geheimagent.
under-developed country, *s.* das Entwickelungsland.
underpass, *s.* die Unterführung.
under-privileged, *adj.* benachteiligt; *the* – (*classes*), die (wirtschaftlich) Schlechtgestellten.
underquote [ʌndə'kwout], *v.a.* niedriger berechnen *or* notieren.
understocked [ʌndə'stɔkt], *adj.* ungenügend versorgt *or* beliefert.
under-valuation, *s.* die Unterschätzung, Unterbewertung; (*fig.*) Geringschätzung.
uninhibited, *adj.* ungehemmt, hemmungslos, zügellos, maßlos, unbändig, ungestüm, überstürzt.
union card, *s.* der Gewerkschaftsausweis.
union dues, *s. pl.* der Gewerkschaftsbeitrag.
unionize ['ju:nɪənɑɪz], *v.a.* gewerkschaftlich organisieren.
unit furniture, *s.* Anbaumöbel (*pl.*).
University of the Air, *s.* das Telekolleg.
unpredictable, *adj.* unvorsehbar, unberechenbar.
unratified, *adj.* nicht ratifiziert.
unscripted, *adj.* unvorbereitet, nicht einstudiert, improvisiert, aus dem Stegreif.
unsuppressed, *adj.* nicht unterdrückt.
untaxable, *adj.* (*a p.*) nicht besteuerungsfähig, (*earnings*) nicht steuerpflichtig.
unzip, *v.a.* den Reißverschluß öffnen *or* aufmachen von.
up beat, *s.* der Auftakt.
up-date, *v.a.* auf den neuesten Stand *or* aufs laufende bringen, modernisieren.
urbane [ə:'beɪn], *adj.* höflich, verbindlich; weltmännisch, weltgewandt.
urbanity [ə:'bænɪtɪ], *s.* die Höflichkeit, feine Umgangsformen (*pl.*), die Weltgewandtheit.
urban planning, *s.* die Städteplanung.
usherette [ʌʃə'rɛt], *s.* die Platzanweiserin.
U-turn, *s.* die Kehrtwendung, Umkehr (*Motor.*).

V

vapour trail, *s.* der Kondensstreifen (*Av.*).
vending machine, *s.* der Verkaufsautomat, Warenautomat.
vertical take-off, *s.* der Senkrechtstart (*Av.*); – *plane*, der Senkrechtstarter.

viability [vɑɪəˈbɪlɪtɪ], *s.* die Lebensfähigkeit, Entwicklungsfähigkeit, Wachstumsfähigkeit.
video [ˈvɪdɪoʊ], *pref.* Fernseh, Bild—.
video-frequency, *s.* die Bildfrequenz.
video-tape, *s.* das Magnetbildband.
virologist [vɪˈrɔlədʒɪst], *s.* der (die) Virusforscher(in), Virologe.
virology, *s.* die Virusforschung, Virologie.
visual aids, *s. pl.* das Anschauungsmaterial.
vital statistics, *s. pl.* die Bevölkerungsstatistik; (*coll.*) Körpermaße (*pl.*), die Büsten-, Hüft- und Taillenweite.
volley-ball, *s.* der Volleyball(spiel).

W

wage-freeze, *s.* der Lohnstopp.
wage-packet, *s.* die Lohntüte.
walk-out, *s.* der Streik, Ausstand.
washroom, *s.* der Waschraum, die Toilette (*esp. Amer.*).
water-diviner, *s.* der Rutengänger.
water-front, *s.* der Uferbezirk, die Ufergegend; das Hafenviertel.
water-heater, *s.* der Warmwasserbereiter.
water-repellent, *adj.* wasserabstoßend.
water-ski, 1. *s.* der Wasserschi. 2. *v.n.* Wasserschi fahren.
water-softener, *s.* die (Wasser)Enthärter.
water system, *s.* das Stromgebiet.
water-wings, *s. pl.* der Schwimmgürtel.
wattage [ˈwɔtɪdʒ], *s.* die Wattleistung, der Stromverbrauch.
weather-ship, *s.* das Schiff des Wetterdienstes.
weather-strip, *s.* die Wetterleiste, der Dichtungsstreifen.
weeny [ˈwɪ:nɪ], *adj.* (*coll.*) winzig.
welfare department, *s.* das Fürsorgeamt, die Sozialabteilung.
well-established, *adj.* wohlbegründet, gut fundiert; lange bestehend, feststehend.
well-heeled, *adj.* (*sl.*) wohlhabend, gut bei Kasse.
wheel rim, *s.* die Felge, der Radkranz.
whereupon [(h)wɛərəˈpɔn], *conj.* worauf, wonach; daraufhin.
wide-angle, *adj.* Weitwinkel—; – *screen,* Breitwand—.
wiggle [ˈwɪgl], *v.n.* (& *v.a.*) (*coll.*) wackeln (mit).
windcheater [ˈwɪndtʃɪ:tə], *s.* die Windjacke, der Anorak.
window dresser, *s.* der Schaufensterdekorateur.
window shopping, *s.* der Schaufensterbummel.
windswept [ˈwɪndswɛpt], *adj.* sturmgepeitscht.
winkle out, *v.a.* (*coll.*) (mit Mühe) herausholen.
witch-burning, *s.* die Hexenverbrennung.
witch-hunt, *s.* die Hexenjagd (*Pol.*).
wolf-whistle, *s.* beifälliger *or* bewundernder Pfiff.
work-force, *s.* die Belegschaft.
work-out, *s.* (*coll.*) das Training, die Übung, der Probelauf.
work study, *s.* Zeitstudien (*pl.*).
work-to-rule (campaign), *s.* der Dienst nach Vorschrift, Bummelstreik.

Z

zoom lens, *s.* die Variooptik, (*coll.*) Gummilinse.